AN ENGLISH-ARABIC LEXICON

AN

ENGLISH-ARABIC

LEXICON,

IN WHICH THE EQUIVALENTS FOR ENGLISH WORDS AND IDIOMATIC SENTENCES ARE RENDERED INTO LITERARY AND COLLOQUIAL ARABIC,

GEORGE PERCY BADGER, D. C. L.

GYAN

Published by

Gyan Publishing House
5, Ansari Road
Daryaganj, New Delhi-110002
Phone: 011-47034999, 9811692060
E-mail: books@gyanbooks.com

Distribution Network
gyanbooks.com
India, USA, Canada, UK, Australia

ISBN: 978-81-212-5581-3 (HB)
First Published, 1881

2nd Impression 2024

Printed at: Gyan Press, Delhi.

AN ENGLISH-ARABIC LEXICON
Author: GEORGE PERCY BADGER

ENGLISH-ARABIC LEXICON.

AN

ENGLISH-ARABIC

LEXICON,

IN WHICH THE EQUIVALENTS FOR ENGLISH WORDS AND IDIOMATIC SENTENCES ARE RENDERED INTO LITERARY AND COLLOQUIAL ARABIC,

BY

GEORGE PERCY BADGER, D.C.L.,

LATE CHAPLAIN, BOMBAY PRESIDENCY.

"وَمِنْ آيَاتِهِ خَلْقُ ٱلسَّمَوَاتِ وَٱلْأَرْضِ وَٱخْتِلَافُ أَلْسِنَتِكُمْ وَأَلْوَانِكُمْ"

صورة ٱلرُّوم آيــة ٢١

"AND AMONG HIS SIGNS ARE THE CREATION OF THE HEAVENS AND THE EARTH AND YOUR VARIETY OF TONGUES AND COLOUR."—*Kur-án*, XXX. 21.

LONDON:

C. KEGAN PAUL & CO., 1, PATERNOSTER SQUARE.

1881.

STEPHEN AUSTIN AND SONS,

PRINTERS, HERTFORD.

DEDICATED,

WITH BEST WISHES FOR THEIR SUCCESS,

TO

ORIENTAL STUDENTS OF ENGLISH

AND

ENGLISH STUDENTS OF ARABIC

IN THE EAST AND WEST,

BY

GEORGE PERCY BADGER.

PREFACE.

Oriental scholars have always recognized the great importance of the study of the Arabic, not only in respect of philological and antiquarian researches, but also as the best means of acquiring a correct knowledge of the bent and development of the Eastern mind. It is, undoubtedly, the most perfect of Oriental tongues, possessing a vast literature—albeit now somewhat antiquated—in almost every department of science. Arabic is, furthermore, the sacred language of the Muslims throughout the world, and since the early conquests of Islâm has formed an integral part of several of the living languages of the East. The modern Persian, Turkish, and Hindustâny are so permeated with it that a thorough mastery of those tongues can hardly be attained without a competent acquaintance with the Arabic.

Within the last century students of Arabic have been provided with the Arabic-Latin lexicons by Golius and Freytag,—most valuable aids of their kind. English students have had, in addition, Richardson's *Persian, Arabic, and English Dictionary*, first published in 1777, in folio, and reprinted by Dr. Charles Wilkins in 1806, in quarto. In 1829 Professor Francis Johnson published a revised edition of the same for the Honourable East India Company, and in 1852 another containing 30,000 additional words. This edition Mr. Johnson called by his own name. Such students are now being supplied with the *Arabic-English Lexicon* by the late Mr. Edward William Lane, compiled from the writings of upwards of one hundred Arabian lexicographers. This marvellous work in its fullness and richness, its deep research, correctness, and simplicity of arrangement, far transcends the lexicon of any language ever presented to the world. Its perfection in all these respects leaves nothing to be desired.

But while so much has been and is still being done to render Arabic into English, the only aid which students possess for acquiring the equivalents of English words and phrases is Richardson's *English, Persian, and Arabic Dictionary*, first printed in 1780, and reprinted, in 1810, "with numerous additions and improvements," by Dr. Wilkins, if we except Catafago's *Arabic-English Dictionary*, published by Mr. Quaritch, which at best is merely a compendious vocabulary, forming a useful hand-book for ordinary travellers in the East, but utterly inadequate as an aid to the English-speaking student or writer who seeks to convey his thoughts in Arabic.

Richardson was unquestionably a painstaking man, but his knowledge of Arabic was very limited, and his *English, Arabic, and Persian Dictionary*, compiled mainly by reference backwards to the Arabic from the Latin glossary of Golius, is a jumble of Arabic and Persian words, so confusedly thrown together that the English student in looking for an Arabic equivalent is puzzled at every step which to select. For all practical purposes, indeed, as regards Arabic, that *Dictionary* is useless, and the same may fairly be said of the later edition by Wilkins.

It is, undoubtedly, owing to this want that so few Englishmen—otherwise tolerable Arabic scholars—are able to translate English into Arabic. Many natives of the East, moreover, who are desirous of acquiring a knowledge of our language, experience the greatest difficulty in the attempt, owing to the same want. But nowhere, perhaps, is this lack more felt than among the educated Muslims of India. Thousands of this class are now well read in English, and it would be deemed a great boon by them to be supplied with an English-Arabic lexicon as the most ready and effectual medium of aiding them to learn the language of their sacred book, the al-Kur-ân.

The idea of supplying this want has long been entertained by the Author of the present work. His first essay to carry it out was made nearly forty years ago in conjunction with Áhmad Fâris, Efendi, the Proprietor and Editor of the Arabic newspaper, *the al-Jawâïb*, who besides being allowedly one of the most learned Arabic scholars living is perfectly familiar with English. It was resumed from time to time during the Author's protracted residence in different parts of the East, and the work of compilation was begun in the midsummer of 1872. Twelve hours a day were devoted to that task and to revisions of the manuscript and press-proofs from that time until now. Freytag, and especially Lane, as far as his admirable Lexicon has been published, are his principal authorities for what may be termed the classical portions of the work. To these are added, especially in the latter part, frequent appropriate quotations from the al-Kur-ân, by way of illustration. The *Muhîtu-'l-Muhît*, a voluminous Arabic Dictionary, by Bútros, al-Bustâny, printed at Bairût in 1869, comprising as it does the literary, vernacular, and vulgar forms of speech, as also a large number of post-classical words and phrases, called *Muwálladah*, borrowed from various sources, has been of the utmost use to the Compiler, who regrets not having become acquainted with it till a considerable part of his Lexicon had passed through the press. Mons. A. Caussin de Perceval's revised edition of Bocthor's *Dictionnaire Français-Arabe* has been of great service as regards the colloquial dialects of Egypt and Syria. Redhouse's admirable *English and Turkish Lexicon*, and the *Manual Terminologique Français-Ottoman*, by the Baron O. de Schlechta-Wssehrd, owing to the large number of Arabic terms relating to politics, law, jurisprudence, and diplomacy used in Turkish and more or less generally adopted throughout the East, have been frequently referred to. Further, the numerous publications of the Arabic press in Syria and Egypt, and more especially the newspapers, wherein modern modes of thought, modern inventions, and modern sciences are expressed in appropriate native nomenclature, have supplied the Author with a large stock of equivalents for English phraseology and scientific terminology. These he has utilized to the best of his ability, and the order generally observed in the compilation is this:—Wherever two or more Arabic equivalents are given, the first is the more recondite, the last the colloquial or vulgar. Albeit the doing so entailed considerable labour and added largely to the cost of printing he eventually acted upon the advice of a friend, well versed in Oriental lore, and has attached the Arabic vowel and other orthographical points throughout the entire work. It is not his fault if the Arabic nautical phraseology, beyond what relates to the small craft of the Arabs, is meagre and unsatisfactory. He has been obliged in most cases to adopt the terms used in the Turkish and Egyptian navies, which, as regards the Mediterranean, are generally derived from the Italian. In the Eastern seas they are sometimes Arabicized from the English and sometimes from the Hindustâny.

The Author acknowledges the great obligation he is under to his old friend the learned Shaikh Áhmad Fâris, whom he consulted on several occasions, and who kindly sent him a list of Arabic titles for the work, from which that adopted was selected. For the Arabic Eulogy he is indebted to the late Ŕizku-'llah-Hassûn, whose untimely death left a sad blank in the ranks of Oriental poets, literati, and caligraphists. He offers his best thanks also to the Rev. John Louis Sâbunjy, a Syrian ecclesiastic and Arabic journalist, whose acquaintance he made after the Lexicon was compiled, but whose assistance has been very useful in the revision of the manuscript and proof-sheets.

Messrs. Stephen Austin and Sons, the printers, deserve much praise, not only for the typography of the work, but for their enterprising readiness to adopt, at their own cost, many suggestions for the improvement of their Arabic fount of types. Arab caligraphists have frequently expressed, in writing, their admiration of specimens of the Lexicon which have fallen into their hands. More surprising to the Author has been the comparative freedom from compositors' mistakes, even in the first proofs submitted to him, which in most cases have not exceeded those in ordinary English composition.

The Author regrets the long list of *Errata*, mainly referable to the first part of the work, which is appended to this volume. *Il n'y a que le premier pas qui coûte* is the only apology which he ventures to adduce for the deformity, beyond the expression of a hope that the difficulty of the task undertaken will be adequately appreciated by his critics. An Arabic adage says: "Perfection belongs to God only." No one can be more sensible than the Author of the imperfections of his work; nevertheless he confidently believes that it far surpasses, in every way, any attempt of the kind hitherto made, and that it will be found eminently useful to those for whom it was primarily intended. With pardonable pride he quotes the following opinions of the merits of the work, as expressed on some specimen extracts of the same, before the last improvements were adopted by the Author. The late lamented Edward William Lane wrote as follows:—"Considering Dr. Badger's long and very extensive intercourse with Arabic-speaking peoples, and the well-known facility which he has acquired in writing their language as well as of conversing in it, I feel confident that his English-Arabic Dictionary will supply a great desideratum of travellers, official men, and students, in various Eastern countries." The *Athenæum* published this testimony:—"Dr. Badger's Lexicon, as far as we can judge from the specimen before us, is well worthy of his profound scholarship, and will be welcomed by all whom business or pleasure calls to the East. The Lexicon is not merely a bare series of Arabic equivalents for English words, but contains under each word all the idiomatic sentences into which it enters, with an equally idiomatic rendering of the same in Arabic, so that the work will form a complete repository of colloquial and literary Arabic." To these favourable notices may be added the following translation of an extract from the *al-Jawáïb*, on the completion of sheet 125 of this work: "We are delighted to know that the English-Arabic Lexicon, the compilation of which was undertaken by that eminent scholar Dr. Badger many years ago, will soon be published. It is a work which no student of the two languages can dispense with, and one which will perpetuate the memory of its author for ages to come."

The Author thankfully recognizes a grant of £500 from the Right Honourable the Secretary of State for India in Council, promised on the completion of this Lexicon, towards defraying the heavy cost of printing and publishing the same.

GEORGE PERCY BADGER.

London, 20th January, 1881,
21, *Leamington-Road Villas*,
Westbourne Park. W.

KEY

TO THE ORTHOGRAPHICAL SYMBOLS, LEXICOGRAPHICAL TERMS, ABBREVIATIONS, ETC., USED IN THE FOLLOWING WORK.

The different Arabic equivalents given of an English word or sentence are divided by a long dash (—), and the same symbol is used in lieu of repeating throughout a sentence the English word in its renderings into Arabic. A smaller dash, or hyphen, is placed after transitive verbs, when coupled with a particle, to indicate the place of the appropriate suffixed nouns or pronouns, singular, dual, or plural; *e.g.*, حَرَّضَ-عَلَى — حَرَفَ-عَن — كَتَبَ-إِلَى — أَنْقَذَ-مِن. In like manner, after the usage of Arab lexicographers, the words كَذَا and فُلَان or فُلَانَة, according to the gender of the person indicated, are sometimes adopted to denote the locality of the unexpressed subject of the verb; *e.g.*, حَرَّضَ-عَلَى كَذَا He incited (me, him, her, both, you, or them,) to such an action; هَيَّجَ-عَلَى فُلَانٍ He stirred (him, her, both, you, them) against such an one. In some cases, where these vocables would be inappropriate, a different expedient has been resorted to, and the word شَيْءٌ has been introduced to prevent any misconception of the gender of the noun, with which the verb must agree; *e.g.*, كَانَتْ رَائِحَةُ ٱلشَّيْءِ كَرَائِحَةِ ٱلْ... The thing smelled or had the smell of a or an . . . The particles suffixed to verbs defining the mode of their action, concomitance, or the instrument employed, such as مِن — ل — عَلَى — فِي — بِ — بَيْن are given in their absolute form to be filled in or modified as the case may require; *e.g.*, أَمْسَكَ بِزَيْدٍ — ضَرَبَهُ بِسَيْفٍ — غَرِقَ فِي ٱلْبَحْرِ — قَامَ عَلَى ٱلسُّلْطَانِ — وَهَبَهُ لَهُ — يَهَبُهُ لِمَنْ يَشَآءُ — خَرَجَ مِنَ ٱلْبَيْتِ — اِنْسَلَّ مِنْ بَيْنِهِمْ *etc.*

After the expedient adopted by Lane the changeable vowel of the aorist of the first form is expressed by the symbols ـُ ـِ ـَ attached to the preterite. Thus كَتَبَ ـُ stands for كَتَبَ *aor.* يَكْتُبُ — سَلَّ ـُ for سَلَّ *aor.* يَسُلُّ — رَكِبَ ـَ for رَكِبَ *aor.* يَرْكَبُ — قَلَّ ـِ for قَلَّ *aor.* يَقِلُّ — بَرَدَ ـُ for بَرَدَ *aor.* يَبْرُدُ. When the aorist has two or three moveable vowels they are indicated thus رَبَطَ ـِ ـُ — نَبَعَ ـَ ـِ ـُ. In cases where the preterite contains one of the weak letters, ا و ى, the aorist in some cases, especially where open to misconception, is given in full; *e.g.* دَأَى (or دَأَا) *aor.* يَدْأَى — رَأَى *aor.* يَرَى — سَأَلَ *aor.* يَسْأَلُ — بَرِئَ *aor.* يَبْرَى — سَآءَ *aor.* يَسُوءُ.

The reader will understand that the third person preterite of the Arabic is made in this Lexicon to represent the English infinitive, for which there is no true equivalent in the former language, albeit the Arabic *másdars*, or infinite nouns, frequently supply its place. Thus "To kill" is rendered by قَتَلَ which strictly means "he killed."

The vowel and other orthographical signs are attached to the Arabic throughout, with these few exceptions:— The *tanwinu-'dh-dhámmi* (ٌ), indicative of the nominative absolute, is generally omitted when the word stands alone; but in instances where mistakes are likely to arise, owing to the penultimate letter being a prolonged ى, the *jázmah* (ْ) is placed over it, thus, سَقِيْط for سَقِيطٌ — شَرِيْف for شَرِيفٌ — بَدِيْع for بَدِيعٌ. The *fát-hah* (َ) also is frequently omitted over the *álif* of prolongation, and wherever it is otherwise impossible to make a mistake; *e.g.*, كِتاب for كِتَابٌ — سابِع for سَابِعٌ — جانِب for جَانِبٌ. When in construct, however, the ٌ is always expressed; *e.g.*, رَجُلٌ هَشٌّ بَشٌّ — رَجُلٌ خَيِّرٌ — دَارٌ وَاسِعَةٌ — اِمْرَأَةٌ جَمِيلَةٌ. The plurals are given in most cases, and the broken plurals, namely, those of the substantives and adjectives called غَيْرُ مُنْصَرِفٍ are always specified and punctuated.

Except in quotations, the vernacular "you" and "yours" are generally adopted throughout in lieu of "thou," "thee," and "thine." The pronouns of the Arabic will show at once whether the second or third person, the singular or plural, is indicated.

The rendering of adverbial English phrases into Arabic has been a task of much difficulty. As Mr. William Wright, in his admirable translation of Caspari's Arabic Grammar, truly remarks, "the *accusative* is the adverbial case *κατ' ἐξοχήν* in Arabic," of which he gives several examples, such as أَبَدًا – جِدًّا – لَيْلًا – نَهَارًا – غَدًا – اليَوْمَ. But this simple form fails to meet the requirements of the English language into which adverbial idioms, constructed from adjectives and participles, enter so largely. Hence it was found necessary to have recourse to other expedients, sanctioned by Arab lexicography, to express them. Among these are the use of the particles بِ – عَلَى – فَوْقَ – نَحْوَ *etc.;* as, for example, بِسَلَامٍ safely, or with safety; عَلَى ٱلْفَوْرِ at once, incontinently; عَلَى حِينٍ in time, opportunely; فَوْقَ ٱلْعَادَةِ in an unusual manner, extraordinarily; نَحْوَ ٱلْغَرْبِ towards the west, westerly. Arabic equivalents may also be constructed from such abstract Arabic nouns as خَارِجٌ – دَاخِلٌ and from other verbal forms; but care should be taken in such cases not to transgress the grammatical rules of the language. خَارِجًا and دَاخِلًا, when used alone, do not correctly represent *without* and *within;* whereas they would be perfectly correct after a verb, as for instance كَانَ خَارِجًا – قَعَدَ خَارِجَ ٱلْبَيْتِ – دَخَلَ دَاخِلًا – دَخَلَ دَاخِلَ ٱلدَّارِ. So, likewise, مُتَبَرِّعًا – مُتَطَوِّعًا are adverbial forms signifying *gratuitously*, *supererogatorily*, only correct however in connexion with a verb, as فَعَلَهُ مُتَبَرِّعًا (*or* مُتَطَوِّعًا). The more correct way in instances like these, when the adverbial form, as an equivalent of the English, is given in the absolute case, is to write فِي ٱلْخَارِجِ – فِي ٱلدَّاخِلِ – تَبَرُّعًا *or* بِتَبَرُّعٍ – تَطَوُّعًا *or* بِتَطَوُّعٍ. But the Arabic is so rich in verbs which inherently convey many of the ideas which in English we are often obliged to express by an adverbial periphrasis, that a tolerable mastery of that language will enable one in a great number of cases to dispense with adverbs. Considerable attention has been paid to the subject in this Lexicon,—with what success it is not for the Author to say.

As regards the Abbreviations adopted they are mostly such as are common to all English Dictionaries. Thus *v.t.* stands for verb transitive; *v.i.* for verb intransitive; *aor.* for aorist; *part.* for participle; *part. pass.* for passive participle; *n.* for noun; *pl.* for plural; *coll.* for collective (noun); *masc.* for masculine; *fem.* for feminine; *a.* for adjective; *ad.* for adverb; *conj.* for conjunction; *prep.* for preposition; *int.* for interjection. *Kur.* is the contraction for al-Kur-ân; *vulg.* for vulgar; *colloq.* for colloquial; *prov.* for proverb.

ENGLISH-ARABIC LEXICON.

A.

A, *indef. art.* There is no indefinite article in Arabic, the noun alone sufficing generally to express it. The form, however, called إِسْمُ ٱلْمَرَّةِ, constructed by substituting a *fát-hah* for the final *tanwínu-'dh-dhámmi* of the *másdars*, or infinitive nouns, of triliteral and quadriliteral verbs, and by adding thereto a final ةٌ, serves to convey the idea of indefinite unity, the form فَعْلٌ being selected in the first or ground-form and the *másdars* generally of the other forms of the triliteral, and that of فِعْلَالٌ in the quadriliteral verb: *e.g.* ضَرْبٌ the act of striking, ضَرْبَةٌ a stroke; إِنْطِلَاقٌ the act of going, إِنْطِلَاقَةٌ a or one going; دِحْرَاجٌ the act of rolling, دِحْرَاجَةٌ a roll. But should the noun of action end in ةٌ, the word وَاحِدٌ or وَاحِدَةٌ, according to the gender of the noun, must be added with that object; *e.g.* إِقَامَةٌ setting up, إِقَامَةٌ وَاحِدَةٌ a one, or once setting up. Primitive nouns, also, called أَسْمَآءٌ جَامِدَةٌ, and derivatives therefrom, أَسْمَآءٌ مُشْتَقَّةٌ, not in accordance with fixed grammatical rules, such as أَسَدٌ lion, أَبٌ father, إِبْنٌ son, أُسْلُوبٌ manner, إِسْوَارٌ horseman, يَنْبُوعٌ spring, يَدٌ hand, كُرْسِيٌّ chair, require the addition of وَاحِدٌ or وَاحِدَةٌ in like manner to express the same idea. Individuality is also indicated by the change of the last vowel and the addition of the letter ةٌ to primitive nouns denoting species; *e.g.* تِبْنٌ straw, تِبْنَةٌ a whisp of straw; جُبْنٌ cheese, جُبْنَةٌ a single cheese. Examples in construct cases: إِبْنُ مَلِكٍ a son of a king, a king's son; or, more clearly, إِبْنٌ لِلْمَلِكِ, literally, a son to the king; خَادِمُ تَاجِرٍ the servant of a merchant.

A, as a contraction for *Anno, see* A.D., A.H., A.M.; for *Artium, see* B.A., M.A.

Aback, *ad.* Backward, لِلْخَلْفِ ـ لِوَرَآءٍ. To take —, to surprise, بَدَأَ ـ بَغَتَ ـ حَيَّرَ. To be taken —, بُهِتَ ـ تَحَيَّرَ.

Abaft, *ad.* Towards the stern of a ship, نَحْوَ مُؤَخَّرِ ٱلْمَرْكَبِ. The wind is —, ٱلرِّيحُ عَدَلَتْ مِنْ فَمِ ٱلدَّفَّةِ.

Abandon, *v.t.* To relinquish, تَرَكَ ² ـ تَخَلَّى عَنْ ـ خَلَّى عَنْ. To forsake, تَارَكَ ـ أَجْفَرَ ـ بَايَنَ ـ أَهْجَرَ ـ هَجَرَ ². To cast off, خَلَعَ ـ رَفَضَ ² ـ طَرَدَ ². To leave, go from, بَرِحَ مِنْ ـ زَالَ مِنْ ² ـ نَزَلَ عَنْ. To forego, فَاتَ ² ـ نَزَلَ عَنْ. To give up, as an employment, إِسْتَعْفَى ـ تَجَرَّدَ مِنْ. To — one's self to, سَلَّمَ نَفْسَهُ إِلَى ـ تَجَرَّدَ لِ. He abandoned him to his fate, تَرَكَ ² إِلَى سُوْءِ بَخْتِهِ ـ خَذَلَهُ ². He abandoned himself to pleasure, إِنْهَمَكَ فِي ٱللَّذَّاتِ. His family abandoned, cast him off, خَلَعَهُ أَهْلُهُ.

Abandoned, *part.* and *a.* Forsaken, مَتْرُوكٌ ـ مَهْجُورٌ. Corrupted, فَاسِقٌ ـ مَرْذُولٌ ـ خَلِيعٌ. An — house, مَسْكَنٌ مَهْجُورٌ ـ مَسْكَنٌ خَالٍ مِنَ ٱلسُّكَّانِ. An — wretch, فَاجِرٌ ـ نَذْلٌ ـ رَذِيلٌ ـ لَعِينٌ ـ فَحَّاشٌ.

Abandonment, *n.* The act of abandoning, هِجْرَانٌ ـ هَجْرٌ ـ خَلْعٌ ـ مُتَارَكَةٌ ـ تِرْكَانٌ ـ تَرْكٌ; the state of being abandoned, حَالَةُ ٱلْمَتْرُوكِ. *See also* Relinquishment, *n.*

Abarticulation, *n.* Of the joints, عُقْدَةُ ٱلْمَفَاصِلِ *pl.* عُقَدٌ.

Abase, *v.t.* To bring low, وَطَّأَ ـ حَطَّ ² ـ أَنْزَلَ. To cast down, أَوْقَعَ ـ أَهْبَطَ. To humble, أَوْضَعَ ـ وَضَّعَ. To degrade, أَذَلَّ ـ أَخْزَى ـ أَهَانَ ـ أَرْذَلَ ـ أَحْقَرَ. To —, humble, one's self, يَضَعُ وَضَعَ نَفْسَهُ *aor.* ـ إِتَّضَعَ ـ تَخَشَّعَ ـ إِخْتَضَعَ ـ تَضَعْضَعَ. To —, degrade, one's self, تَذَلَّلَ.

Abased, *part.* Humiliated, مُخْضَعٌ ـ مَقْمُوعٌ ـ مُتَضَعْضِعٌ. Depressed, as in mind, مُنْكَسِرُ ٱلْقَلْبِ ـ مَهْبُوطٌ. Degraded, مُرْذُولٌ ـ ذَلِيلٌ.

Abasement, *n.* State of humiliation, خُشُوعٌ ـ ضَعَةٌ ـ ضَعْضَعَةٌ ـ تَوَاضُعٌ; of degradation, سَفَالَةٌ ـ حَقَارَةٌ ـ ذِلَّةٌ ـ ذُلٌّ.

Abash, *v.t.* أَخْجَلَ ـ أَحْشَمَ ـ حَشَمَ ². To be or to become abashed, إِسْتَحَى ـ حَشِمَ ـ خَجِلَ.

Abashed, *part.* خَجِلٌ ـ مَخْجُولٌ ـ مَحْشُومٌ.

Abate, *v.t.* To lessen, قَلَّلَ ـ أَنْقَصَ ـ نَقَّصَ. To assuage, of heat or discord, أَبَاخَ. To —, of a price, حَطَّ مِنَ ² ـ أَسْقَطَ ٱلثَّمَنَ ـ ٱلثَّمَنِ. I abated somewhat of the debt, حَطَطْتُ مِنَ ٱلدَّيْنِ.

Abate, *v.i.* To become less, إِنْتَقَصَ ـ تَنَقَّصَ ـ نَقَصَ ـ قَلَّ. To become assuaged, of heat, anger, a fever, *etc.*, بَاخَ *aor.* يَبُوخُ ـ إِرْتَخَى ـ خَمِدَ. To —, as in price, إِنْحَطَّ ـ هَبَطَ ـ حَطَّ. The waters abated, نَقَصَتِ ٱلْمِيَاهُ. Their anger abated, بَاخَ ـ خَمِدَ غَيْظُهُمْ ـ غَضَبُهُمْ. The wind abated, سَكَنَتِ ٱلرِّيحُ. The fever abated, خَمِدَتِ ٱلْحُمَّى.

Abatement, *n.* The act of lessening, تَقْلِيل ـ تَنْقِيص ـ نَقْص. The quantity taken away by —, هِبَة ـ سَمَاح ـ ٱلْمَحْسُومُ مِنْ كَذَا. Abatement, as of price, إِسْقَاط ـ هَبْط; of wind, هُدُوّ; of anger or fire, بُؤُوخ; of courage or of a fever, خُمُود. He made him an — of so much, سَمَحَ لَهُ بِكَذَا.

Abattis, *n.* حَسِيكَة ـ *vulg.* شَكْ فَلَكْ.

Abbacy, *n.* Condition of an abbot, رِئَاسَةُ دَيْرٍ. The income of an abbot, إِيرَادُ رَئِيسِ دَيْرٍ.

Abbess, *n.* رَئِيسَةُ دَيْرٍ.

Abbey, *n.* دَيْر *pl.* دُيُورَة *and* أَدْيَار.

Abbot, *n.* رَئِيسُ دَيْرٍ *pl.* رُؤَسَاءُ دُيُورَةٍ ـ رَئِيسُ رُهْبَانٍ.

Abbreviate, *v.t.* إِخْتَصَرَ ـ قَصَّرَ ـ أَوْجَزَ.

Abbreviated, *part.* مُخْتَصَر ـ مُوجَز.

Abbreviation, *n.* The act of, إِخْتِصَار ـ تَقْصِير ـ إِيجَاز; by omission of letters in a word, تَرْخِيم. The means used to abbreviate, إِخْتِصَار; *e.g.* س for سُؤَال Question; ج for جَوَاب Answer; إلخ for إِلَى آخِرِهِ And so forth.

Abdicate, *v.t.* خَلَعَ نَفْسَهُ مِنْ ـ تَخَلَّى ـ تَنَازَلَ عَنْ.

Abdication, *n.* خَلْعٌ مِنْ كَذَا ـ تَنَازُلٌ عَنْ كَذَا.

Abdomen, *n.* بَطْن ـ مَأْنَة ـ جَوْف ـ أُرْبِيَّة.

Abdominal, *a.* مَأْنِيّ.

Abduce, *v.t.* صَرَفَ عَنْ ـ حَرَّفَ عَنْ.

Abduct, *v.t.* سَلَبَ ـ خَطِفَ ـ مَضَى بِ ـ إِنْطَلَقَ بِ ـ إِخْتَلَسَ.

Abduction, *n.* The act of, إِخْتِلَاس ـ سَلْب ـ خَطْف.

Abed, *ad.* فِي ٱلْفِرَاشِ ـ نَائِم.

Aberrant, *a.* ضَالّ ـ زَائِغ ـ عَمِهٌ.

Aberration, *n.* ضَلَالَة ـ غُرُور ـ غَوَايَة; of the mind, هُتْر ـ هَتْرَة ـ طَيَشَان.

Abet, *v.t.* To aid, عَاضَدَ ـ ظَاهَرَ ـ عَاوَنَ. To move, incite, حَرَّضَ ـ إِسْتَفَزَّ ـ حَرَّكَ ـ هَيَّجَ.

Abetment, *n.* Aid, مُظَاهَرَة ـ مُحَالَفَة ـ مُسَاعَدَة ـ مُعَاضَدَة. Incitement, إِسْتِفْزَاز ـ تَحْرِيك ـ تَهْيِيج ـ تَحْرِيض.

Abettor, *n.* Helper, مُعَاضِد ـ مُسَاعِد. Instigator, مُحَرِّض ـ دَاعٍ لِلْعَصَبِيَّةِ.

Abeyance, *n.* حَالَةُ ٱلتَّعْطِيلِ ـ تَعَطُّل ـ إِلْغَاءٌ. In —, مُعَطَّل ـ مَحْذُوفٌ إِلَى غَيْرِ وَقْتٍ. To be in —, أُلْغِيَ.

Abhor, *v.t.* إِشْمَأَزَّ ـ قَلَا ـ إِسْتَفْظَعَ ـ تَقَفَّعَ ـ إِعْتَنَفَ ـ قَانَعَ ـ كَرِهَ ـ شَنَأَ ـ مِن.

Abhorrence, *n.* كَرَاهَة ـ إِسْتِكْرَاه ـ إِشْمِئْزَاز ـ شَنَاعَة.

Abhorrent, *a.* Hateful, بَغِيض ـ كَرِيه ـ شَنِيع ـ فَظِيع. Abhorrent to, inconsistent with, مُخَالِفٌ لِ ـ مُغَايِرٌ لِ ـ مُبَايِنٌ لِ.

Abide, *v.i.* and *t.* To continue in the same state or place, بَقِيَ ـ دَامَ ـ دَاوَمَ ـ وَاظَبَ ـ إِسْتَقَامَ. Not to cease doing, *etc.*, إِسْتَمَرَّ عَلَى. To endure, تَحَمَّلَ ـ أَطَاقَ. To —, as in a place, أَقَامَ فِي ـ ثَوَى ـ أَلَثَّ بِ ـ مَكَثَ ـ لَبَدَ بِ ـ قَطَنَ بِ ـ بَلَدَ بِ ـ سَكَنَ. To take up one's residence in, to sojourn in, أَحَالَ بِ ـ عَدَنَ بِ. I — by my opinion, أَتَمَسَّكُ بِرَأْيِي ـ أَسْتَبِدُّ بِرَأْيِي. I will — by him till he conquers or dies, أَدْرَأُ عَنْهُ حَتَّى يَغْلِبَ أَوْ يَمُوتَ. I — by his testimony, أَعْتَمِدُ عَلَى شَهَادَتِهِ ـ أَثِقُ بِشَهَادَتِهِ. I cannot — him, مَا أَقْدِرُ عَلَى أَنْ أَحْتَمِلَهُ. To — by one's word, قَامَ بِوَعْدِهِ ـ أَنْجَزَ وَعْدَهُ. To —, to wait for, إِنْتَظَرَ ـ تَوَقَّعَ ـ تَرَبَّصَ بِ.

Abiding, *n.* لَا زَوَالَ لَهُ ـ دَائِم ـ قَوَّام ـ ثَابِت.

Abigail, *n.* A female servant, خَادِمَة *pl.* خَادِمَات ـ جَارِيَة *pl.* جَوَارٍ.

Abject, *a.* سَفِيل ـ دَنِيّ ـ وَغْد ـ شَقِيّ ـ ذَلِيل ـ حَقِير.

Abjectness, *n.* ذِلَّة ـ ذُلّ ـ دَنَاءَة ـ حَقَارَة.

Abjectly, *ad.* بِدَنَاءَةٍ ـ بِذِلَّةٍ ـ بِحَقَارَةٍ.

Ability, *n.* Power, قُوَّة ـ مَقْدِرَة ـ ذَرْع ـ سَعَة ـ طَاقَة ـ طَوْل ـ قُدْرَة ـ إِسْتِطَاعَة. Capacity, cleverness, شَطَارَة ـ حِذْق ـ مَهَارَة. Abilities, capabilities, إِدْرَاك ـ شَمَائِل ـ تَعَلُّقَات ـ مَنَاقِب ـ فَرَاسَة. He exerted his —, بَلَغَ جُهْدَهُ ـ بَذَلَ جُهْدَهُ. I have not the — to do that, لَا أَسَعُ ذٰلِكَ. Each one according to his —, كُلٌّ وَاحِدٍ عَلَى قَدْرِ طَاقَتِهِ ـ حَسْبَمَا تَيَسَّرَ لِكُلٍّ مِنْهُمْ.

Abjuration, *n.* إِرْتِدَادٌ عَنْ ـ إِنْكَار ـ جَحْد. Abjuration, as of a creed, إِرْتِدَادٌ عَنْ.

Abjure, *v.t.* إِرْتَدَّ عَنْ ـ رَفَضَ ـ أَنْكَرَ ـ نَكِرَ ـ جَحَدَ.

Ablactate, *v.t.* To wean, فَطَمَ. To graft, لَقَّحَ.

Ablactation, *n.* Act of weaning, فِطَام; of grafting, تَلْقِيح.

Ablative, *n.* The ablative case, جَارٌّ وَمَجْرُورٌ.

Ablaze, *ad.* إِلْتِهَابًا ـ إِشْتِعَالًا. To be —, لَظِيَ ـ إِلْتَهَبَ.

Able, *a.* Capable, as of doing, قَدِير ـ قَادِرٌ عَلَى ـ مُعِيدٌ لِ ـ مُسْتَطِيع. Strong, able-bodied, ضَلِيع ـ قَوِيّ ـ أَبْتَعُ. Skilful, مَاهِر ـ حَاذِق ـ خَبِير ـ نِحْرِير ـ أَرِب. To be — to . . . , إِسْتَطَاعَ عَلَى ـ عَلَا بِ *aor.* يَعْلُو ـ أَطَاقَ عَلَى ـ قَدَرَ عَلَى. To have the authority, إِقْتَدَرَ – إِسْتَمْكَنَ. He is not — to rise, لا يُمْكِنُهُ النُّهُوض. Are you — to . . . ? هَلْ لَكَ أَنْ. They were not —, did not find the means, to . . . , لَمْ يَتَيَسَّرْ لَهُمْ أَن. To make — to, يَسَّرَ لِ – أَقْدَرَ عَلَى.

Ablution, *n.* The act of cleansing, washing, تَغْسِيل – تَنْظِيف. The — before prayers, تَوَضُّؤ – وُضُوء. To perform an —, with water, تَوَضَّأَ – تَطَهَّرَ بِالْمَاء; with sand, تَيَمَّمَ. The water used in —, مِطْهَرَة – وَضُوء. A place of —, مِيضَأَة.

Ably, *ad.* بِشَطَارَة – بِمَعْرِفَة – بِمَهْنَة – *vulg.* بِفِطْنَة.

Abnegation, *n.* *See* Abjuration, *n.*; *also under* Denial, *n.*

Abnormal, *a.* Out of the regular order, خَارِج – شَاذّ *pl.* شُذَّان. Strange, غَرِيب. خِلَاف الأُصُول – عَنِ القَانُون.

Abnormity, *n.* خِلَاف – شَيْء خَارِج عَنِ القِيَاس – أَمْر شَاذّ.

Aboard, *ad.* On board ship, فِي الْمَرْكَب – عَلَى ظَهْرِ السَّفِينَة. He went —, نَزَلَ فِي الْمَرْكَب.

Abode, *n.* Habitation, مَقَرّ – مَوْطِن – مَنْزِل – مَقَام – مَثْوَى – مَسْكَن – دَار. Continuance, إِقَامَة – مَكْث – لَبْث – ظَلَّة.

Abolish, *v.t.* To annul, أَبْطَلَ – أَسْقَطَ – نَسَخَ. To put an end to, أَزَالَ – نَقَضَ – هَدَمَ – عَدِمَ – مَحَا *aor.* يَمْحُو. To be abolished, annulled, أُبْطِلَ – نُسِخَ.

Abolishable, *a.* نَسْخُهُ – مِمَّا يُمْحَى – مِمَّا يُبْطَلُ – مِمَّا يُنْسَخُ – مُمْكِن.

Abolisher, *n.* مُبْطِل – مَاحٍ – نَاسِخ.

Abolition, *n.* إِسْقَاط – إِبْطَال – نَسْخ – بُطْلَان.

Abolitionist, *n.* Of slavery, قَائِم بِتَبْطِيل الرِّقّ – قَائِم بِتَبْطِيل العُبُودِيَّة.

Abominable, *a.* بَغِيض – كَرِيه – نَجِس – شَنِيع – فَظِيع. An — action, فِعْل مَكْرُوه – فَاحِشَة *pl.* فَوَاحِش – خَبَاثَة. Abominable conduct, دَعَارَة – دَعَر.

Abominate, *v.t.* أَبْغَضَ – إِشْمَأَزَّ مِن – إِسْتَفْظَعَ – شَنِعَ بِ – ذَرِي.

Abomination, *n.* Hatred, object of hatred, قِلَاء – شُنْعَة – بَغِيض. Pollution, دَنَس – خَبَاثَة – نَجَاسَة – قَذَر. Abominations, نَجَاسَات – رَجَاسَات – بِدْعَة.

Aboriginal, *a.* أَوَّل *fem.* أُولَى; *pl. masc.* أَوَّلُون – أَوَائِل; *pl. fem.* أُوَل.

Abortion, *n.* An untimely birth, سِقْط – سُقْط – سَقْط. The act of bringing forth untimely, إِسْقَاط الْجَنِين. She had an abortion, أَسْقَطَت. A failure, خَيْبَة – قُصُور.

Abortive, *a.* Brought forth untimely, سَاقِط. Unsuccessful, خَائِب – خَاسِر – غَيْر مُفْلِح – غَيْر نَاجِح – عَقِيم.

Abortively, *ad.* بِعَدَم نَجَاح – بِلَا فَائِدَة – بَاطِلًا – خَيْبَة.

Abound, *v.i.* To be in plenty, غَزُرَ – وَفُرَ *aor.* يَفِرُ – تَوَافَرَ – تَكَاثَرَ – كَثُرَ – إِزْدَادَ – أَخْصَبَ. To possess in abundance, إِزْدَادَ فِي – إِسْتَفْضَلَ. To be many, جَمَّ.

About, *prep.* Around, حَوَالَى – مَدَار – حَوْل: About him, حَوَالَيْهِ. Near to, close by, مُجَاوِر لِ – بِالْقُرْب مِن – عِنْدَ – نَحْوَ. Concerning, بِخُصُوص – مِنْ جِهَة – مِنْ نَحْو – مِنْ قِبَل – عَن – فِي شَأْنِ. About me, عَنِّي; about thee, عَنْكَ *fem.* عَنْكِ; about us, عَنَّا; about which, عَمَّا. Appendant to, مَع – بِمَعِيَّة كَذَا. To be —, engaged in, خَاضَ فِي – تَعَاطَى – تَشَاغَلَ فِي. What are you —? مَا ذَا تَفْعَلُ – فِي مَا ذَا تَخُوض. Have you a pen — you? أَمَعَكَ قَلَم.

About, *ad.* Circularly, حَوْم – دَوَرَان. In (its) compass, فِي دَائِرَتِهِ – فِي اسْتِدَارَتِهِ. About, near, around, حَوْل: We sat — him, قَعَدْنَا حَوْلَهُ. Nearly, نَحْو – تَقْرِيبًا. Here and there, هُنَا وَهُنَاك. About the end of the year, عِنْدَ أَوَاخِر السَّنَة. To-morrow — this time, غَدًا مِثْل الآن. About ten thousand, نَحْو عَشَرَة آلَاف. To be — to do, هَمَّ بِ – كَادَ – وَشُكَ أَن *aor.* يَوْشُكُ. Zaid was — to do it, كَادَ زَيْد يَفْعَلُهُ. He was — to write, كَانَ يَهُمّ بِالْكِتَابَة. He was — to weep, أَرَادَ الْبُكَاء. You are not — to do any such thing, مَا فِي قَصْدِكَ أَنْ تَفْعَلَ مِثْلَ هٰذَا الأَمْر. To bring —, cause, سَبَّبَ. To go —, دَارَ – جَالَ – طَافَ. To go — seeking for, طَلَبَ – جَعَلَ يَدُورُ عَلَى. Go — your business, أَبْعِدْ مِنْ هُنَا – إِذْهَبْ إِلَى شُغْلِكَ. To send — one's business, سَحَتَ.

Above, *prep.* Higher than, أَعْلَى مِن – فَوْق. More in quantity or number, إِنَافَة عَلَى – زِيَادَة – أَكْثَر. In a superior rank or degree, أَشْرَف – أَسْمَى – أَعْلَى – فَوْق. Beyond, more than, يَجِلُّ عَن – يَكْبُرُ عَن. Too high for, يَفُوق – يَجُوز. In excess of, يَنُوفُ عَلَى. Above all, especially, لَا سِيَّمَا – خَاصَّة – بِالأَخَصّ. Above measure, بِلَا حَدّ – بِفَرْط – جِدًّا – إِلَى الْغَايَة. From —, from heaven, مِنَ السَّمَاء – مِنَ الْعُلَى. Above, before, آنِفًا – قَبْل – قِدَمًا – سَبْقًا. From —, overhead, مِنْ فَوْق – مِنْ عَلٍ *or* عَالٍ. To be — (doing), تَرَفَّعَ عَن – تَعَظَّمَ عَن – تَجَالَّ عَن: He is — doing so vile an action, حَاشَى لَهُ مِنْ أَنْ يَأْتِيَ بِهٰذَا الْفِعْل الذَّمِيم.

Above-board, *ad.* بِلَا حِيلَة – جَهْرًا – عَلَانِيَة.

Above-cited,
Above-mentioned, *a.*
Above-named,
} مَذْكُور أَعْلَاهُ – مَذْكُور آنِفًا – مُشَار إِلَيْهِ – سَالِف الذِّكْر – مَذْكُور قَبْلًا.

Abrade, *v.t.* To rub, حَكَّ – جَرَشَ – سَحَجَ – سَحَجَ. To —, as an axle its socket, مَحَرَ. Abraded, مَحْكُوك – مَنْحُوت.

Abrasion, *n.* Act of abrading, سَحْج ـ جَرْش ـ حَكَاك.

Abreast, *ad.* صَفًّا ـ فِي صَفٍّ وَاحِدٍ ـ عَلَى سِمَاطٍ ـ سَطْرًا ـ سَوَآءً.

Abridge, *v.t.* To shorten, قَصَّرَ ـ قَلَّلَ ـ إِقْتَصَرَ. To summarize, أَوْجَزَ ـ إِخْتَصَرَ. To deprive of, خَلَعَ ـ أَسْقَطَ مِنْ ـ كَذَا ـ أَحْرَمَهُ. To restrain, حَصَرَ ـ مَنَعَ مِنْ كَذَا.

Abridgment, *n.* The act of, إِيجَاز ـ تَصْغِير ـ إِخْتِصَار ـ قَطْع. A compend, إِخْتِصَار ـ مُجْمَل ـ إِجْمَال. Restraint, ضَبْط ـ حَصْر ـ مَنْع ـ إِخْتِصَار.

Abroach, *ad.* Flowing out, diffused, فَيْضًا ـ إِنْتِشَارًا. In tap, إِبْتِزَالًا. Wine in tap, خَمْر بَزِيل.

Abroad, *ad.* At large, سَيَبَانًا ـ سَرْحًا ـ إِنْطِلَاقًا. Out of the house, فِي خَارِجِ ٱلْبَيْتِ ـ فِي ٱلْخَارِجِ ـ بَرًّا. In another country, فِي ٱلْغُرْبَةِ ـ فِي بِلَادٍ غَرِيبَةٍ ـ فِي ٱلْخَارِجِ. Far distant, عَلَى بُعْدٍ. In all directions, شَتَاتًا ـ فِي كُلِّ مَكَانٍ ـ هُنَا وَهُنَاكَ. To go —, as to a foreign country, تَغَرَّبَ ـ سَافَرَ إِلَى ٱلْغُرْبَةِ. To go —, as out of the house, خَرَجَ مِنَ ٱلْبَيْتِ. To go —, as for a walk, خَرَجَ يَتَمَشَّى. The news is spread —, شَاعَ ٱلْخَبَرُ ـ إِنْتَشَرَ ٱلْخَبَرُ ـ فَاضَ ٱلْخَبَرُ.

Abrogate, *v.t.* To annul, أَسْقَطَ ـ نَقَضَ ـ أَبْطَلَ ـ نَسَخَ ـ فَسَخَ.

Abrogation, *n.* نَسْخ ـ فَسْخ ـ نَقْض ـ إِبْطَال.

Abrupt, *a.* Craggy, حَزْن ـ حَرِيز ـ وَعِر ـ وَعْر. Sudden, بَاغِت ـ مُقْتَضَب ـ مَبْتُور. Rude, بَادِه ـ فَظّ ـ خَشِن. Unconnected, مُقْتَضَب ـ مَبْتُور. An — ascent, مُرْتَقَى نَاهِد ـ مَطْلَع نَاشِز ـ جُرُف *pl.* أَجْرَاف. He gave me an — answer, بَادَهَنِي بِٱلْجَوَابِ.

Abruptly, *ad.* Suddenly, بَدِيهَةً ـ بِدَارًا ـ بَدِيهَةً ـ بَغْتَةً. To come upon one —, بَدَهَ ـ بَادَهَ ـ بَغَتَ ـ بَاغَتَ ـ بَغَّتَ.

Abruptness, *n.* Suddenness, بَغْت ـ بَغْتَة ـ مُبَادَهَة ـ بَدَاهَة. Rudeness, فَظَاظَة. Cragginess, تَحَزُّز ـ تَخَر ـ تَثَلُّم ـ وُعُور. Abruptness of temper, بَدْرَة.

Abscess, *n.* دُمَّلَة *pl.* دَمَامِل *and* دَمَامِيل ـ دُمَّل.

Abscond, *v.i.* To hide one's self, تَوَارَى ـ تَسَتَّرَ ـ تَخَفَّى ـ إِكْتَمَنَ. To run away, هَرَبَ ـ وَلَّى هَارِبًا.

Absconder, *n.* مُتَوَارٍ ـ هَارِب.

Absence, *n.* The being absent, غِيَاب ـ غَيْبَة ـ بُعَاد. Want of, نُقْصَان ـ عَدَم. Inattention, تَغَافُل ـ إِهْمَال ـ قِلَّة ٱلْإِنْتِبَاهِ. Absence of mind, سَهْو ـ تَغَفُّل ـ شَتَاتُ ٱلْعَقْلِ. Absence from one's country, هَجْر ـ هِجْرَة ـ تَغَرُّب. Absence makes the heart grow fonder, ٱلْغِيَابُ يَزِيدُ ٱلْحِبَاب; an analogous idea is expressed by the Arab couplet: وَإِذَا ٱلْقُلُوبُ تَمَكَّنَتْ مِنْ حُبِّهَا فَٱلْهَجْرُ وَصْلٌ وَٱلْبِعَادُ تَدَانِي.

Absent, *a.* Not present, غَائِب *pl.* غُيَّاب *and* غَائِبُونَ ـ غَائِبُونَ ـ مُغْتَرِب. Abroad, هَجِير ـ مُتَغَرِّب. Absent in mind, سَاهٍ لَاهٍ ـ غَائِبُ ٱلْعَقْلِ. To be —, غَابَ ـ إِغْتَرَبَ ـ تَغَيَّبَ عَنْ. To be —, abroad, هَجَرَ ـ تَغَرَّبَ; in mind, غَابَ عَقْلُهُ. To — one's self from, غَابَ عَنْ ـ فَصَلَ مِنْ ـ مَا حَضَرَ. To speak ill of the —, إِغْتَابَ ـ غَيَّبَ ـ إِغْتَرَبَ. He absented himself from his country, فَصَلَ مِنْ بَلَدِهِ ـ عَنْ بَلَدِهِ. Whether we be present (in the country) or —, مُسْتَوْطِنِينَ كُنَّا أَوْ مُتَغَرِّبِينَ. He was — (called away) by the death of his mother, غَيَّبَهُ مَوْتُ أُمِّهِ. He who is — is always blamed, (prov.) مَنْ غَابَ خَابَ ـ ٱلْغَائِبُ مَا لَهُ نَائِبٌ. The present and the —, ٱلشَّاهِدُ وَٱلْغَائِبُ.

Absentee, *n.* غَائِب *pl.* غُيَّاب ـ مُغْتَرِب; from his property, غَائِبٌ عَنْ مُلْكِهِ.

Absenteeism, *n.* ٱلْغِيَابُ عَنِ ٱلْأَمْلَاكِ.

Absinthe, *n.* The liquor, رُوحُ ٱلْإِفْسَنْتِينِ.

Absolute, *adj.* Complete, تَامّ ـ وَافٍ ـ كَامِل ـ بَالِغ ـ كُلِّيّ. Unconditional, مُطْلَق ـ دُونَ شَرْطٍ. Not relative, غَيْرُ ذِي عَلَاقَةٍ. Not limited, غَيْرُ ذِي حَدٍّ ـ مُطْلَق ـ غَيْرُ مُقَيَّدٍ. Positive, بَتّ ـ أَكِيد ـ مُثْبَت ـ لَا مَحَالَةَ. Absolute power, إِسْتِقْلَال ـ قُوَّة مُطْلَقَة. An — decision, حُكْمٌ مُطْلَقٌ ـ فَصْلٌ بَتٌّ.

Absolutely, *ad.* Completely, إِتْمَامًا ـ بِٱلْإِسْتِيفَآءِ ـ رَأْسًا ـ أَصْلًا ـ بِٱلْكُلِّيَّةِ ـ بِٱلْمَرَّةِ ـ بَتَّةً. Without relation, بِدُونِ عَلَاقَةٍ ـ لِذَاتِهِ. Without limits, إِطْلَاقًا ـ عَلَى ٱلْإِطْلَاقِ. Without condition, بِدُونِ شَرْطٍ. Positively, حَتْمًا ـ جَزْمًا ـ بَتَّةً.

Absoluteness, *n.* Completeness, تَمَامَة ـ كُلِّيَّة. Arbitrary power, قُوَّة مُطْلَقَة ـ إِطْلَاقُ ٱلْقُوَّةِ.

Absolution, *n.* Acquittal, إِقَالَة ـ تَبْرِئَة ـ إِعْفَآء ـ عَفْو. Remission, as of sins, مُسَامَحَة ـ تَحْلِيل ـ مَغْفِرَة.

Absolutism, *n.* حُكْمٌ ٱخْتِيَارِيٌّ ـ يَدٌ قَوِيَّةٌ ـ حُكُومَة مُطْلَقَة.

Absolutist, *n.* مُتَمَسِّكٌ بِأُصُولِ ٱلْحُكُومَةِ ٱلْمُطْلَقَةِ.

Absolve, *v.t.* To free, as from an engagement, أَقَالَ ـ أَعْفَى. To acquit, as of a crime, عَفَا عَنْ ـ حَلَّلَ مِنْ ـ أَبْرَأَ مِنْ ـ صَفَحَ لِ عَنْ ـ غَفَرَ لِ. He is absolved from his sins, إِنْحَلَّ مِنْ خَطَايَاهُ.

Absolved, *part.* مَعْفُوّ ـ مُعْفًى ـ مَغْفُورٌ لَهُ.

Absorb, *v.t.* To swallow up, بَلِعَ ـ إِسْتَرَطَ ـ إِزْدَرَدَ ـ إِلْتَهَمَ. To suck up, إِلْتَقَمَ ـ قَدِمَ ـ تَشَرَّبَ ـ نَشَّفَ ـ تَنَشَّفَ ـ نَشِفَ. To annex, أَدْمَجَ. To be absorbed, engrossed, in, إِسْتَغْرَقَ بِ ـ كَلِفَ بِ ـ إِنْغَمَسَ فِي.

Absorbent, *a.* مُنَشِّف ـ شَارِب.

Absorbent, *n.* An absorbent drug, دَوَآءٌ مُنَشِّف ـ دَوَآءٌ شَارِب.

Absorption, *n.* State of being swallowed up, إِبْتِلَاع ـ إِلْتِهَام ; of being sucked up, تَشَرُّب ـ تَنَشُّف . Engrossment in, إِسْتِغْرَاق فِي ـ ; as in divine contemplation, mysticism, غَيْبَة ـ شِدَّةُ ٱلإِغْرَاق فِي تَصَوُّف ـ فَنَآء .

Abstain, *v.i.* To refrain from, كَفَّ عَن ـ إِحْتَمَى مِن ـ تَنَزَّهَ عَن ـ إِمْتَنَعَ عَن ـ إِجْتَنَبَ مِن . To —, as from what is illicit, إِسْتَعْفَفَ عَن ـ عَفَّ عَن ـ إِعْتَفَّ عَن ـ تَعَفَّفَ عَن ; from food, صَامَ ـ إِحْتَمَى مِنَ ٱلطَّعَام . To be temperate in, زَهِدَ فِي . To shun, تَوَقَّفَ عَن ـ وَقَفَ عَن aor. يَقِفُ . To cause to —, أَوْقَفَ عَن ـ مَنَعَ عَن ـ كَفَّ عَن .

Abstemious, *a.* نَزِيه ـ زَهِيد ـ ظَلِيفُ ٱلنَّفْسِ ـ قَتِين ـ عَفِيف . An — diet, مَا يَتَبَلَّغُ بِهِ مِنَ ٱلْعَيْشِ ـ طَعَامُ بُلْغَة .

Abstinence, *n.* Forbearance from, إِحْتِرَازٌ مِن ـ إِمْتِنَاعٌ عَن ـ إِجْتِنَابٌ مِن ـ كَفٌّ عَن ـ إِنْقِطَاعٌ عَن ; from food, صَوْم ; especially from flesh, صِيَام ـ قُطَاعَة . Moderation, زَهَادَة ـ قَنَاعَة . Abstinence, as from what is illicit, عِفَّة ـ رِعَة ـ وَرَع . A day of —, يَوْمُ قُطَاعَة . Are you in — (fasting from meat) or not? أَأَنْتَ قَاطِعٌ أَوْ مُرْتَز .

Abstinent, *a.* *See* Abstemious, *a.*

Abstract, *v.t.* To take one thing from another, حَذَفَ مِن ـ جَرَّدَ ـ أَزَالَ مِن . To separate, as ideas, *etc.*, إِعْتَبَرَ كُلًّا بِمُفْرَدِهِ . To separate by distillation, إِسْتَقْطَرَ . To epitomize, إِخْتَصَرَ ـ أَوْجَزَ ـ أَجْمَلَ ـ فَذْلَكَ . To distract, إِشْتَغَلَ ـ أَلْهَى ـ شَيَّبَ . To steal, سَرَقَ ـ أَسَلَّ ـ إِخْتَلَسَ . He became abstracted by it, شُغِلَ بِهِ ـ إِشْتَغَلَ بِهِ ـ تَلَهَّى بِهِ .

Abstract, *a.* Separated from something else, of mental perceptions, مُجَرَّد ـ مَعْنَوِيّ . An — term, إِسْمُ مَعْنًى . *See also* Abstruse, *a.*

Abstracted, *part.* Separated, مُنْفَرِد ـ مُعْتَزِل ـ مُفْتَرِق . Absent, of the mind, غَائِبٌ عَنْ نَفْسِهِ ـ مُسْتَغْرِقٌ فِي ٱلأَفْكَار ـ مُغَفَّل . Stolen, مَسْرُوق .

Abstractedly, *ad.* / Abstractly, إِنْفِرَادًا ـ مُنْفَرِدًا ـ بِٱعْتِزَالٍ ـ بِتَجَرُّدٍ .

Abstractedness, *n.* / Abstractness, إِنْفِرَاد ـ إِعْتِزَال ـ تَجَرُّد .

Abstraction, *n.* The act of abstracting, حَذْف ـ رَفْعٌ عَن . What is abstracted, pilfered, إِخْتِلَاس . Absence of mind, تَغَفُّل ـ سَهْو ـ شَتَاتُ ٱلْفِكْر . An abstract idea, رَأْيٌ مُجَرَّدٌ pl. آرَآءٌ مُجَرَّدَة ـ إِسْمٌ بِلَا مُسَمًّى .

Abstruse, *a.* Hidden, خَفِيّ ـ مُحْتَجِب ـ مُسْتَتِر . Difficult, عَوِيص ـ غَلِق ـ عَسِر ـ مُبْهَم ـ مُعَقَّد ـ مُغْلَق ـ مُسْتَعْجِم . Subtle, دَقِيق ـ دِقّ . To speak abstrusely, جَآءَ بِكَلَامٍ دِقٍّ aor. يَجِيءُ .

Abstrusely, *ad.* بِإِبْهَام ـ بِعَوَص ـ بِٱسْتِعْجَام .

Abstruseness, *n.* عُسْر ـ إِبْهَام ـ إِسْتِعْجَام ـ عَوَص . Subtlety, دِقَّة .

Absurd, *a.* Nonsensical, سَفْسَاف ـ هَذِر ـ غَبِيّ ـ عَبَث . Out of the question, مُسْتَحِيل ـ مُحَالٌ ب ـ مُحَال .

Absurdity, *n.* / Absurdness, تُرَّهَة pl. تُرَّهَات ـ سَخَافَة ـ تَفَاهَة ـ عَبَث ـ حَمَاقَة ـ غَبَاوَة . An impossibility, أَمْرٌ مُسْتَحِيل ـ عِزٌّ ـ عِزَّة ـ شَيْءٌ لَا يُسْتَطَاع . Absurdities, ٱلتُّرَّهَات ـ ٱلتُّرَّهَاتُ ٱلصَّحَاصِحُ ـ ٱلْبَسَابِسُ .

Absurdly, *ad.* عَنْ غَبَاوَةٍ ـ بِسَخَافَةٍ ـ عَبَثًا . To talk —, تَرَّهَ ـ لَحِيَ .

Abundance, *n.* غَزْر ـ تَزَايُد ـ وُفُور ـ فَرْط ـ فَيْض ـ جُمُوم ـ كَثْرَة ـ تَكَاثُر ـ عِزّ . Abundance, as of the produce of the earth, خِصْب ـ غَلَّة ـ بَرَكَة ـ وَفْرَة .

Abundant, *a.* وَافٍ ـ نَهِير ـ غَزِير ـ وَافِر ـ وَفْر ـ فَائِض ـ جَمّ ـ مُتَكَاثِر ـ كَثِير ـ غَفِير . Fertile, خَصِيب ـ مُثْمِر . To be abundant, تَكَاثَرَ ـ تَكَثَّرَ ـ جَمَّ ـ عَثِلَ . To make abundant, كَثَّرَ ـ وَفَّرَ .

Abundantly, *ad.* كَثِيرًا ـ بِكَثْرَةٍ ـ بِزِيَادَةٍ ـ بِوُفُورٍ .

Abuse, *v.t.* To make an ill use of, فَرَّطَ فِي ـ أَسَآءَ ـ إِنْتَهَكَ . To violate, خَلَبَ ـ أَضَلَّ ـ أَغْوَى ـ فَضَحَ ـ هَتَكَ . To deceive, أَبْذَى ـ عَيَّرَ ـ لَقَسَ ـ شَتَّرَ ـ غَشَّ . To vilify, عَرْبَدَ ـ سَبَّ ـ شَتَمَ ـ ذَمَّ ـ عَلَى . He abused his kindness, كَفَرَ إِحْسَانَهُ ـ كَنَدَ نِعْمَتَهُ . He abused his authority, طَغَا فِي ـ أَفْرَطَ (or تَجَاوَزَ or تَفَجَّسَ or تَغَطْرَسَ or تَعَدَّى) فِي حُكْمِهِ ـ حُكُومِهِ .

Abuse, *n.* Ill use, تَفْرِيط ـ إِسَآءَة ـ إِنْتِهَاك . Reproach, بَذْء ـ بَذَآءَة ـ بَذَآء ـ شَتْم ـ سَبّ ـ ذَمّ ـ عَرْبَدَة . Foul language, بَذَآء . A corrupt practice, فَسَاد ـ زَلَل ـ شَطَط ـ إِنْتِهَاك . The — of wealth, إِسْرَافُ ٱلْمَالِ ـ بَعْزَقَة ـ بَذْرَقَة . The —, as of authority, ظُلْم ـ تَعَدّ ـ جَوْر ـ جَنَف ـ غَطْرَسَة ـ حَيْف . The — of confidence, عَدَمُ وَفَآءٍ ـ خِيَانَة ـ غِشّ .

Abuser, *n.* One who makes an ill use of a thing, مُنْتَهِك ـ مُفْرِط ـ مُسِيء . A deceiver, غَشَّاش ـ غَاشّ ـ مُخَادِع . A reproacher, مُعَرْبِد ـ مُنَاقِر ـ سَابّ ـ بَاذِيء . One who uses foul language, مُبْذٍ ـ بَذِيء . A ravisher, فَاضِح ـ هَاتِك .

Abusive, *a.* سَفِيه ـ وَقِح ـ هَاجٍ ـ ذَامّ ـ قَادِح ـ ثَالِب . Contrary to rules, خِلَافُ ٱلأُصُولِ . To use — language, أَبْذَأَ .

Abusively, *ad.* Improperly, بِإِسَآءَةٍ ـ خَطَآءً ـ بِٱنْتِهَاكٍ . Reproachfully, بِعَارٍ ـ بِهَوَانٍ ـ بِتَشْتِيرٍ ـ شَتْمًا ـ تَعْيِيرًا .

Abut, *v.i.* لَحِقَ ب ـ إِتَّصَلَ مَعَ .

Abutment, *n.* A support, قَاعِدَة ـ مُسْنَد ـ عِمَاد ـ عُمْدَة ـ إِيَاد . Junction or joining with, إِلْحَاق ب ـ إِتِّصَال مَع .

Abyss, *n.* لُجَّة ـ غَمْر ـ عُمْق ـ هَاوِيَة ـ هُوَّة ـ جَوّ . The abyss, hell, جَهَنَّم ـ الهَاوِيَة .

Acacia, *n.* The tree, زَنْزَلَخْت ـ شَجَرَة ٱلْفِتْنَة ـ سَنْط . The fruit of the —, قَرَظ ; its juice, عُصَارَة ٱلْقَرَظ ـ أَقَاقِيَا . *Acacia gummifera,* طَلْح ; *the pods of which are called* عُلَّف .

Academial, *a.* } مَا نِيطَ بِمَدْرَسَةِ ٱلْعُلُومِ ٱلْجَلِيلَةِ (*or* بِجَمْعِيَّاتِ
Academical, } ٱلْمَعَارِف) .

Academic, *n.* } A Platonic philosopher, تِلْمِيذُ أَفْلَاطُون . A
Academician, } scholar at an academy, تِلْمِيذٌ فِي مَدْرَسَةِ ٱلْعُلُوم ; of a learned body, عُضْوٌ مِنْ أَعْضَاءِ مَجْمَعِ ٱلْعُلَمَاء .

Academy, *n.* A scientific association, مَجْمَع ـ دِيوَانُ ٱلْعُلَمَاء . A school, مَدْرَسَة *pl.* مَدَارِس .

Acanthus, *n.* The plant, شَوْكَةُ ٱلْيَهُود ـ طَابَةُ ٱلشَّوْك .

Accede, *v.i.* To assent to, ـَ قَبِلَ ـ أَجَابَ إِلَى ـ ـَ رَضِيَ ب . To give adherence to, ـَ لَحِقَ ب . He acceded to the throne, ـِ جَلَسَ عَلَى ٱلْكُرْسِيّ .

Accelerate, *v.t.* أَعْجَلَ ـ أَسْرَعَ ـ سَبَّقَ ـ أَنْكَظَ ـ أَوْفَزَ . An accelerated train, قِطَارٌ مُسْتَعْجِل .

Acceleration, *n.* إِعْجَال ـ إِسْرَاع ـ إِيفَاز ـ إِنْكَاظ .

Accelerative, *a.* سَرِيع ـ مُعْجِل ـ مُسْرِع .

Accent, *n.* Manner of speaking, لَفْظ ـ لُغَة . The sound of a syllable pronounced, نَبْرَة ـ هَمْزَة ـ تَفْخِيمُ ٱلْحَرْف . Mark made upon letters or syllables, عَلَامَةٌ تُوضَعُ عَلَى ٱلْحُرُوفِ دَلَالَةً عَلَى وَجْهِ ٱلتَّلَفُّظِ بِهَا . Modification of the voice, صَوْت ـ حِسّ ـ عِبَارَة . Pronunciation peculiar to a town, لَغْو ـ لِسَان ـ لَهْجَة ـ لُغَة .

Accent, *v.t.* To pronounce with the proper emphasis, ـِ نَبَرَ ـ أَعْجَمَ ـ أَشْكَلَ ـ ـَ فَخَّمَ ٱلْحَرْف . To write the accents to, ـِ هَمَزَ ـ ـِ ضَبَطَ ـ يَضَعُ *aor.* وَضَعَ ٱلْحَرَكَاتِ عَلَى .

Accentuate, *v.t.* *See to* Accent, *v.t.*

Accentuation, *n.* *See* Accent, *n.*

Accept, *v.t.* To admit with approbation, تَقَبَّلَ ـ زَكَّى ـ ـِ بَرَّرَ ـ أَجَابَ إِلَى ـ ـَ رَضِيَ ب ـ قَبِلَ ب ـ تَلَقَّى ـ ـَ قَبِلَ . To assent to, ـُ أَخَذَ بِٱلْوُجُوهِ ـ حَابَى ـ آثَرَ . To accept persons,

Acceptable, *a.* Regarded with pleasure, مَقْبُول ـ مَرْضِيّ . Opportune, وَاقِعٌ مَوْقِعَهُ ـ حَالٌّ مَحَلَّهُ . Receivable, قَرِينُ ٱلْقُبُولِ . Acceptable with God, نَفْلٌ عِنْدَ ٱللّٰهِ .

Acceptableness, *n.* } تَقَبُّل ـ قُبُول ـ حُسْن .
Acceptability, }

Acceptably, *ad.* بِرِضَاء ـ بِقُبُولٍ ـ بِتَقَبُّلٍ .

Acceptance, *n.* Reception, قُبُول . Good reception, تَقَبُّل ـ قُبُول . Acceptance of a draft, قُبُولُ ٱلْحَوَالَةِ ـ رِضَاء ـ رِضًى ب .

Acceptation, *n.* Meaning, مَعْنًى *pl.* مَعَانٍ . Ordinary —, مَعْنًى عُرْفِيّ ; technical —, مَعْنًى ٱصْطِلَاحِيّ ; original —, مَعْنًى أَصْلِيّ ; figurative —, مَعْنًى مَجَازِيّ . *See also* Acceptance, *n.*

Accepted, *part.* مَقْبُول . Approved, مَرْضِيّ ـ مُسْتَحْسَن .

Accepter, *n.* مُتَقَبِّل ـ قَابِل .

Access, *n.* Way of approach, وُصُول ـ مَنْفَذ ـ مَوْرِد ـ وِرْد ـ بَابٌ إِلَى ـ دُخُول . Liberty of approach, تَقَرُّب ـ دَالَّة . Increase, زِيَادَة ـ نُمُوّ ـ زَكَاء . The return, as of a fit, *etc.*, عُرَوَاء ـ نَوْر ـ وُرُود ـ مُعَاوَدَة . Means of —, سَبِيل *pl.* سُبُل . He has — unto the king, لَهُ دَالَّةٌ عِنْدَ ٱلْمَلِكِ . To find a way of — to, تَطَرَّقَ إِلَى كَذَا .

Accessary, *n.* Accomplice in a crime, مُعَاوِن ـ رَفِيقٌ فِي ٱلذَّنْبِ فِي ٱلْإِثْم .

Accessary, *a.* Acceding to, مُتَقَبِّل ـ قَابِل . "Do not be — to your own destruction," لَا تُلْقُوا بِأَيْدِيكُمْ إِلَى ٱلتَّهْلُكَةِ (Kur. ii. 191).

Accessibility, *n.* سُهُولَةُ ٱلْوُصُولِ إِلَى كَذَا .

Accessible, *a.* Easy of approach, هَيِّن ـ مَوْصُول ـ مَبْلُوغ ـ سَهْلُ ٱلْوُصُولِ إِلَيْهِ ـ ٱلْإِقْتِرَاب . Affable, خَيِّر ـ مُلَائِم ـ أَنِيس .

Accession, *n.* Increase, زِيَادَة ـ إِزْدِيَاد ـ نُمُوّ . The act of joining one's self to, إِشْتِرَاكٌ فِي ـ إِنْضِمَامٌ إِلَى ; of arriving at, وُصُولٌ إِلَى ـ بُلُوغ . Accession, as to a throne, جُلُوسٌ عَلَى .

Accessorily, *ad.* تَبَعًا ـ بِنَوْعِ ٱلْإِشْتِرَاكِ ـ عَلَى وَجْهِ ٱلْمُعَاوَنَةِ ـ إِنْضِمَامًا ـ إِلْحَاقًا ـ ضَمًّا .

Accessory, *a.* Additional, دَخِيل ـ مُلْحَق ـ إِضَافِيّ ـ ضَامّ .

Accidence, *n.* A book of rudiments, كِتَابُ مَبَادِئ .

Accident, *n.* Opposed to substance, عَارِض *pl.* عَوَارِض . An unforeseen circumstance, عَارِض ـ أَعْرَاض *pl.* عَرَض ـ فُجَاءَة ـ مُصِيبَة ـ حَوَادِث *pl.* حَادِث . A misfortune, صِدْفَة ـ إِتِّفَاق *pl.* مَصَائِب *pl.* آفَة آفَات . A serious accident, مُعْظَمَة .

Accidental, *a.* Happening by chance, إِتِّفَاقِيّ ـ عَرَضِيّ ـ فُجَائِيّ . Adventitious, مُلْحَق .

Accidentally, *ad.* صِدْفَةً ـ إِتِّفَاقًا ـ عَرَضًا ـ فُجَاءَةً .

Accipient, *n.* قَابِض ـ قَابِل .

Acclaim, *n.* } تَصْفِيق ـ تَهْلِيل . By —, with general
Acclamation, } consent, بِٱتِّفَاقٍ عَامٍّ .

Acclimate, *v.t.* } عَوَّدَ عَلَى ٱلْهَوَاءِ . To be or become acclima-
Acclimatize, } tized, تَعَوَّدَ عَلَى ٱلْهَوَاءِ .

Acclivity, *n.* تُلُول .*pl* تَلّ — طَلْعَة — طُلُوع — سَنَد — صُعُود — فَارِعَة.

Acclivous, *a.* Of land, elevated ground, صَعِيد.

Accolade, *n.* مُعَانَقَة أَوْ صَفْع كَفّ مِنَ ٱلْمَلِكِ عِنْدَ مُتَجَوِّرِيَّة ٱلْفَوَارِس إِلَى أَحَد.

Accommodate, *v.t.* To adapt to, طَبَّقَ-ل — أَصْلَحَ-ل — وَفَّقَ-ل. To settle, as of a difference, وَفَّقَ بَيْنَ — ـ لَأَمَ — أَصْلَحَ. To supply with conveniences, هَيَّأَ ل-(قَدَّمَ ل- *or*) ٱللَّوَازِمَ — جَهَّزَ. To — one's self to another, وَافَقَ — طَابَقَ. To — with money, أَسْلَفَ. This house will —, suit, me, هٰذَا ٱلْمَنْزِلُ يُوَافِقُنِي. These rooms will not — us, هٰذِهِ ٱلْبُيُوتُ لَمْ تَسَعْنَا. Will this — you? هَلْ يَصْلُحُ لَكَ هٰذَا.

Accommodating, *a.* Obliging, صَاحِبُ مَعْرُوف — لَطِيف — كَرِيم.

Accommodation, *n.* Adaptation, مُوَافَقَة — وَفْق. Adjustment of differences, مُصَالَحَة — مُوَافَقَة — إِصْلَاح. Provision of convenience, مَحَلّ كَافٍ — وَسْع — سَعَة. Room, space, مُنَاسَبَات — لَوَازِم — جِهَاز. Assistance, إِمْدَاد — مُعَاوَنَة. Accommodation, with money, سَلَف. Want of accommodation, عَدَمُ سَعَة — ضِيق — مَضِيق.

Accompaniment, *n.* Something joined with another, صُحْبَة — إِضَافَة — لَفَّة. The — to a song or instrument, مُرَافَقَة. The letter and its accompaniments arrived, وَصَلَ ٱلْمَكْتُوبُ وَكُلُّمَا إِحْتَوَى.

Accompany, *v.t.* To be with as a companion, رَافَقَ — ـ صَحِبَ. To join with, وَصَّلَ-ب — أَضَافَ-إِلَى. To join in with a song or musical instrument, ـ تَبِعَ-ب — رَافَقَ-ب. To — to, إِسْتَصْحَبَ-إِلَى — أَوْصَلَ-إِلَى. He accompanied him on the occasion of his departure, شَيَّعَهُ عِنْدَ رَحِيلِهِ. I will sing, and do you — me on the guitar, أَنَا أُغَنِّي وَأَنْتَ تَتْبَعُنِي بِٱلْقِيثَارَة.

Accomplice, *n.* As in crime, رَفِيقٌ فِي ٱلذَّنْبِ .*pl* رُفَقَاء — شَرِيكٌ فِي ٱلذَّنْبِ .*pl* شُرَكَاء.

Accomplish, *v.t.* To complete, أَنْفَذَ — تَمَّمَ — أَتَمَّ — أَنْهَى — أَدْرَكَ — ـ ـ نَالَ [2] فَرَغَ مِن — ـ قَضَى — كَمَّلَ — أَنْجَزَ — حَقَّقَ — أَكْمَلَ. To obtain, حَصَّلَ عَلَى — [2] بَلَغَ إِلَى. To fulfil, as a prophecy, أَنْجَزَ مَا قَصَدَهُ. To be able to —, تَمَكَّنَ مِن — يَعْلُو .*aor* عَلَا ب.

He accomplished what he had designed, أَنْجَزَ مَا قَصَدَهُ.

Accomplished, *part.* and *a.* Fulfilled, مُنْتَهٍ — مُتَمَّم — مُكَمَّل. Accomplished, in mind, مُوَشَّحٌ بِٱلْفَضَائِلِ — فَضِيل — بَارِع; in person, ظَرِيف — لَطِيف — جَمِيل. Learned, عَالِم — لَوْذَعِيّ .*pl* عُلَمَاء. To be —, as in an art, إِفْتَنَّ فِي; in a general sense, [2] بَرَعَ.

Accomplishment, *n.* Completion, إِنْهَاء — تَكْمِيل — إِتْمَام — بُلُوغ — نَوَال — فُرُوغ مِن — تَنْجِيز — قَضَاء. The act of obtaining, تَكْمِيل — تَحْقِيق — تَوْكِيد. Fulfilment, as of a prophecy, An — of mind, فَضْل — بَرَاعَة — فَضِيلَة .*pl* فَضَائِل. Accomplishments, مَحَاسِنُ ذَاتِيَّة. Personal accomplishments, شَمَائِل — فَضَائِل.

Accord, *v.t.* To make to agree, أَصْلَحَ — وَفَّقَ. *See also to* Grant, *v.t.*

Accord, *v.i.* *See to* Agree, *v.i.*

Accord, *n.* A compact, مُعَاهَدَة — قَوْل — شَرْط — عَهْد. Concurrence, إِجْمَاع — وِفَاق — رِضَاء — إِتِّفَاق — مُوَافَقَة. Symmetry, حُسْنُ نِظَام — مُتَابَعَة — مُطَابَقَة — هِنْدَام. Harmony, أَنْغَام — أُلْفَةُ ٱلْأَصْوَات. Of his own —, بِحُسْنِ إِرَادَتِهِ — مِنْ تِلْقَاءِ نَفْسِهِ. Of one —, بِنَفْسٍ وَاحِدَةٍ — إِتِّفَاقًا — بِخَاطِرِهِ. The door opened of its own —, ٱنْفَتَحَ ٱلْبَابُ مِنْ ذَاتِهِ.

Accordance, *n.* مُرَافَقَة — إِتِّحَاد — مُطَابَقَة — مُوَافَقَة. In — with, عَلَى مُقْتَضَى — عَلَى مُوجِبِ — بِحَسَبِ.

Accordant, *a.* Consenting, قَابِل — مُسَلِّم — رَاضٍ. Corresponding, مُوَافِق — مُطَابِق.

According, *a.* According to, عَلَى مَا — عَلَى — بِحَسَبِ — حَسَبَ — بِمُوجِبِ — حَسْبَمَا — عَلَى مُقْتَضَى. With regard to, نَظَرًا ل. According as you say, عَلَى قَوْلِكَ; according to your orders, حَسَبَ أَوَامِرِكَ; according to custom, حَسَبَ ٱلْعَادَة; according to my idea, عَلَى ظَنِّي; according, as befits, his rank, كَمَا يَلِيقُ بِمَرْتَبَتِهِ; according as circumstances may require, حَسَبَ ٱلْإِحْتِيَاجِ — ٱلْإِقْتِضَاء; according to what he says it ought to have taken place, نَظَرًا لِقَوْلِهِ كَانَ يَنْبَغِي أَنْ يَصِيرَ. *See also* Accordant, *a.*

Accordingly, *ad.* Conformably, مُنَاسَبَةً — مُوَافَقَةً. In consequence, بِنَاءً عَلَى ذٰلِكَ — مِنْ ثَمَّ — فَإِذًا. He ordered me, and I — took him away, أَمَرَنِي فَذَهَبْتُ بِهِ — ذَهَبْتُ بِهِ بِحَسَبِ أَمْرِهِ.

Accost, *v.t.* To approach, أَقْبَلَ عَلَى — دَنَا مِن .*aor* يَدْنُو; to address, salute, سَلَّمَ عَلَى — كَلَّمَ — خَاطَبَ.

Accoster, *n.* One who approaches, مُدْنٍ; a speaker, مُخَاطِب.

Accouchment, *n.* وِلَادَة.

Accoucheur, *n.* مُوَلِّد — طَبِيب — قَبِيل. Accoucheuse, قَابِلَة.

Account, *v.t.* To hold in opinion, ـ ـ حَسِبَ — [2] ظَنَّ — إِعْتَبَرَ — [2] زَعَمَ. To compute, أَحْصَى — [2] حَسَبَ — ـ عَدَّ. To — for, assign causes, عَبَّرَ — فَسَّرَ — أَوْضَحَ — ـ شَرَحَ; to explain, عَلَّلَ-ب — بَيَّنَ. To reckon with, تَحَاسَبَ مَعَ — حَاسَبَ. To hold in esteem, أَكْرَمَ — إِحْتَرَمَ — أَعَزَّ. He accounted for it by such a cause, عَلَّلَهُ بِكَذَا. If it is lost you must — for it, إِنْ ضَاعَ فَٱلْمَطْلُوبُ مِنْكَ. We must — for it, لَا بُدَّ أَنْ نُعْطِيَ — لَا بُدَّ أَنْ نُحَاسَبَ بِهِ جَوَابًا عَنْهُ. It was accounted against him, أُحْتُسِبَ عَلَيْهِ. It was accounted to him for righteousness, حُسِبَ لَهُ بِرًّا. To be accounted vile, إِسْتُحْقِرَ.

Account, *n.* Computation, إعْدَاد ـ عَدَد ـ حِسَاب. The result of a computation, مَبْلَغ ـ المَعْدُود ـ عَدَد ـ حِسَاب. A bill of accounts, جِسَاب ـ رَقْمُ حِسَاب ـ عِلْمُ حِسَاب. Estimation, إعْتِبَار ـ إكْرَام ـ مُرَاعَاة. A narrative, حَدِيثَة ـ قِصَّة ـ رِوَايَة ـ خَبَر ـ حِكَايَة ـ ذِكْر. Examination of an affair, فَحْص ـ بَحْث. The relations and reasons of a transaction, مُبَاحَثَة ـ تَقْرِير. Explanation, إيضَاح ـ بَيَان ـ عِبَارَة. To call to —, حَاسَبَ. To settle accounts, سَدَّ ٱلحِسَابَات. To settle an — with, حَاسَبَ مَع. To turn to —, إسْتَفَادَ مِن ـ إنْتَفَعَ بِ. To take, as of money, on — from, إسْتَسْلَفَ مِن ـ تَسَلَّفَ مِن. To keep the accounts, مَسَكَ ٱلحِسَابَات. To be of no —, بَطَلَ. No — is made of it, it is not considered of importance, لا يُعْتَدُّ بِهِ. The balance of an —, بَاقِي ٱلحِسَاب. To the — of, at the expense of, عَلَى كِيسِ فُلَانٍ ـ عَلَى حِسَابِ فُلَانٍ. His accounts were not correct, لَمْ تَكُنْ حِسَابَاتُهُ صَحِيحَة. He gave them an — of his adventures, قَصَّ عَلَيْهِم قِصَّتَهُ ـ حَدَّثَهُم بِمَا جَرَى لَهُ. They presented him with an — of their transactions, قَدَّمُوا لَهُ بَيَانَ مُعَامَلَاتِهِم. He gave them an — of what had transpired, أَخْبَرَهُم بِمَا قَدْ جَرَى. A thing of no —, أَمْرٌ وَجِيزٌ ـ شَيْءٌ زَهِيدٌ ـ تَفَاهَة. They do not hold him of any —, لا يَعْتَبِرُونَهُ. To take on one's own —, be responsible for, تَكَفَّلَ بِ. That will not turn to your —, مَا يَنْتِجُ لَكَ مِنْ ذٰلِكَ نَفْعٌ. On —, in part payment, جَانِبٌ مِنَ ٱلمَبْلَغ (or ٱلحِسَاب). On — of, in consequence of, لِأَجْلِ كَذَا ـ بِسَبَبِ كَذَا. On — of his being of their party, لِكَوْنِهِ مِنْ حِزْبِهِم. On your —, behalf, مِنْ جَرَاكَ ـ مِنْ شَأْنِكَ ـ مِنْ أَجْلِكَ ـ إعْتِبَارًا لَكَ ـ إكْرَامًا لَكَ. On what —? لِمَاذَا ـ لِأَيِّ سَبَب ـ لِمَا. On no —, ٱلبَتَّة. I will not speak to him on any —, لا أُخَاطِبُهُ ٱلبَتَّة. It does not appear in the —, or statement, لَمْ يُوجَدْ لَهُ تَقْيِيدٌ فِي ٱلمَضْبَطَة. On that —, لِأَجْلِ ذٰلِكَ ـ مِنْ ثَمَّ. The day of final —, يَوْمُ ٱلحِسَاب.

Accountable, *a.* Of whom an account may be required, عَلَيْهِ أَنْ مُطَالَبٌ بِ ـ مُعَرَّضٌ لِلْمُحَاسَبَة ـ يَعْطِي حِسَابًا. Responsible, كَفِيل ـ ضَامِن. You will be — should anything happen to him, المَطْلُوبُ مِنْكَ إنْ جَرَى لَهُ شَيْءٌ. You will be — for it with God, تَكُونُ أَنْتَ ٱلمُطَالَبَ بِهِ عِنْدَ ٱللّٰهِ.

Accountant, *n.* One skilled in accounts, عَارِفٌ بِعِلْمِ ٱلحِسَاب ـ حِسَابِيّ. A book-keeper, دَفْتَرْدَار ـ مُحَاسِب.

Accountantship, *n.* دَفْتَرْدَارِيَّة ـ مُحَاسَبَة.

Account-book, *n.* دَفْتَرُ حِسَاب ـ جَرِيدَةُ حِسَاب.

Accoutre, *v.t.* لَبَّسَ ٱلسِّلَاح ـ جَهَّزَ ـ سَلَّحَ ـ أَهَّبَ. To — one's self, تَسَلَّحَ ـ تَأَهَّبَ.

Accoutrement, *n.* The act of furnishing, تَجْهِيز; of arming, تَسْلِيح. Arms, آلَاتُ ٱلحَرْب ـ أَسْلِحَة ـ سِلَاحَات. A complete — for man and horse, تِجْفَاف *pl.* تَجَافِيف.

Accredit, *v.t.* To delegate to, فَوَّضَ إلَى ـ وَكَّلَ إلَى *aor.* يَكِلُ ـ عَيَّنَ لِ.

Accredited, *part.* مَأْمُور ـ مُوَكَّل ـ مُفَوَّض. Respected, مُعْتَبَر. An — ambassador, سَفِيرٌ مُفَوَّضٌ وَمُرَخَّص.

Accretion, *n.* زِيَادَة ـ إزْدِيَاد ـ نُمُوّ ـ إنْضِمَام ـ إلْتِحَاق.

Accrue, *v.i.* To grow, نَمَى ـ إلْتَمَّ ـ زَادَ. To arise out of, نَتَجَ مِن ـ حَصَلَ مِن ـ صَدَرَ عَن. To be added, as a profit, نَفَعَ: No profit accrued to me therefrom, مَا حَصَلَتْ مِنْهُ ذٰلِكَ مَا نَفَعَنِي أَصْلًا ـ مَنْفَعَة. Such a thing accrued therefrom, تَرَتَّبَ عَلَيْهِ كَذَا.

Accumulate, *v.t.* To heap together, جَمَعَ ـ لَمَّ ـ رَكَمَ ـ كَوَّمَ. To hoard, كَدَّسَ ـ قَشَّ.

Accumulate, *v.i.* تَرَاكَمَ ـ إجْتَمَعَ ـ إرْتَكَمَ ـ إلْتَمَّ.

Accumulated, *part.* مَجْمُوع ـ مَكْمُوم ـ مُتَرَاكِم ـ رُكَام.

Accumulation, *n.* Act of heaping up, رَكْم ـ تَكْوِيم ـ تَكْدِيس ـ جُمْلَة ـ إجْتِمَاع ـ مَجْمَعَة ـ جَمَاعَة ـ كُدَاسَة. A collection, جَمْع.

Accumulative, *a.* That which accumulates, مُكَوِّم ـ مُكَدِّس ـ مُجَمِّع. The state of being accumulated, مَجْمُوع ـ مُكَوَّم.

Accumulator, *n.* مُجَمِّع ـ مُكَدِّس ـ جَامِع.

Accuracy, *n.* / Accurateness, } Exactness, دِقَّة ـ ضَبْط ـ تَحْكِيم ـ هِنْدَام ـ صِحَّة ـ تَحْرِير ـ إتْقَان. Care, إعْتِنَاء.

Accurate, *a.* Exact, مَضْبُوط ـ صَحِيح ـ مُدَقِّق ـ مُثَقَّف ـ مُحَرَّر. Careful, مُعْتَنٍ. He was — in his speech, دَقَّ فِي كَلَامِهِ *aor.* يَدِقُّ.

Accurately, *ad.* Exactly, عَلَى عَيْنٍ ـ بِتَدْقِيقٍ ـ بِضَبْطٍ ـ بِٱلتَّحْرِير. With care, بِٱعْتِنَاء.

Accurse, *v.t.* لَعَنَ.

Accursed, *a.* Doomed, مَلْعُون ـ مَدْعُوٌّ عَلَيْهِ ـ مَبْهُول. Hateful, بَغِيض ـ كَرِيه ـ شَنِيع. Unholy, impure, نَجِس ـ دَنِس ـ قَذِر.

Accusant, *n.* *See* Accuser, *n.*

Accusable, *a.* Censurable, يُتَّهَمُ ـ تَهِيم ـ مَلِيم. Culpable, مَلُوم ـ مُجْرِم ـ جَانٍ ـ ذَمِيم ـ مُخْطِئ.

Accusation, *n.* شِكَايَة ـ ذَمّ ـ تُهْمَة ـ إتِّهَام ـ لَوْمَة ـ لَوْم ـ تَأْثِيم. A false —, شِكَايَةٌ كَاذِبَة ـ لَوْمُ ٱفْتِرَاء ـ عِضَة.

Accusative, *a.* or *n.* النَّصْب ـ المَفْعُولُ بِهِ. A noun in the — case إسْمٌ مَنْصُوب.

Accuse, *v.t.* To charge, as with a crime, إتَّهَمَ بِ ـ أَتْهَمَ ـ قَرَفَ عَلَى ـ طَعَنَ بِ or فِي ـ تَجَنَّى عَلَى ـ أَقْرَفَ بِ; to prefer a complaint against, إشْتَكَى عَلَى ـ شَكَا. To blame, لَامَ ـ ذَمَّ. To

— falsely, to calumniate, عَضَهَ ـ وَشَى بِ aor. يَشِي. He is accused of such a thing, هُوَ يُشْكَى بِكَذَا. He accused, complained of him, told him of his faults, شَكَاهُ — شَاكَاهُ ².

Accused, *part.* — مُشْتَكَى عَلَيْهِ — مُدَّعَى عَلَيْهِ — مُتَّهَم — تَهِيم مَشْكِيّ — مَشْنُوّ.

Accuser, *n.* شَاكٍ — مُشْتَكٍ — تَاهِم — لَائِم.

Accustom, *v.t.* — دَرَّبَ - فِي or عَلَى or بِ — مَرَّنَ - عَلَى — آلَفَ — عَوَّدَ عَلَى — طَبَّعَ عَلَى — دَرَّجَ - إِلَى - عَوَّدَ. To — one's self to, تَعَوَّدَ عَلَى — تَدَرَّجَ إِلَى — تَعَوَّدَ عَلَى — إِعْتَادَ بِ — تَدَرَّبَ عَلَى — طَابَقَ عَلَى. He accustomed him to it, دَرَّبَهُ بِهِ. He is accustomed to it, هُوَ إِسْتِعَادَةٌ — تَعَوُّدُهُ — دَارِبٌ بِهِ. He became accustomed to the work, طَابَقَ عَلَى ٱلْعَمَلِ. *See also under to* Addict, *v.t.*

Accustomed, *part.* and *a.* Habituated to, مُدْمِنٌ عَلَى — مُتَعَوِّدٌ عَلَى. Usual, مُعْتَاد — اعْتِيَادِيّ — جَارٍ. Trained, دَرِب — مَارِن. Capable of, مُعِيدٌ لِ.

Accustomarily, *ad.* مِرَارًا — إِعْتِيَادِيًّا.

Ace, *n.* Of cards, أَسّ — بَكّ. A small quantity, نُتْفَة — جُزَيْئَة. The — of diamonds, أَسُّ ٱلدِّينَارِي. Within an — of, فِي حَالِ ...أَنْ.

Acephalous, *a.* بِغَيْرِ رَأْسٍ.

Acerbity, *n.* Sourness of taste, حُمُوضَة — عُفُوصَة; as of temper, شَكَاسَة — خُشُونَة — حَمْز — حِدَّة.

Acescency, *n.* حَمَازَة — حَمْز — حُمُوضَة.

Acescent, *a.* حَامِز — حَامِضٌ نَوْعًا — يَضْرِبُ إِلَى ٱلْحُمُوضَةِ. To be —, حَمِزَ — حَمُضَ ².

Acetate, *n.* مِلْحٌ حُمُوضِيّ.

Acetic acid, *n.* حُمْضُ ٱلْخَلِّ — حُمُوضَةٌ خَالِصَةٌ.

Ache, *v.i.* أَلِمَ — وَجِعَ aor. يَيْجَعُ — تَفَجَّعَ — تَأَلَّمَ. To be in pain, تَوَجَّعَ. His head ached, صُدِّعَ — أَلِمَ رَأْسُهُ.

Ache, *n.* وَجَع *pl.* أَوْجَاع — أَلَم *pl.* آلَام. Head-ache, صُدَاع.

Achievable, *a.* سَهْلُ ٱلْمُنَاوَلَةِ — فِعْلُهُ مُمْكِنٌ — يُقْضَى — يُفْعَلُ — يُعْمَلُ.

Achieve, *v.t.* To perform, عَمِلَ — فَعَلَ — قَضَى — أَنْهَى — فَرَغَ مِن — تَمَّمَ — تَمَّنَ ² — بَلَغَ ٱلْمَقْصُودَ. To gain, نَالَ — حَصَّلَ — أَدْرَكَ.

Achievement, *n.* فِعْل *pl.* أَفْعَال — عَمَل *pl.* أَعْمَال — قَضِيَّة *pl.* قَضَايَا. An heroic action, صَنِيعَة *pl.* صَنَائِع — فِعْلَة *pl.* فِعَال.

Aching, *a.* مُوجِع — مُؤْلِم.

Achromatic, *a.* نَقِيّ صَافٍ مَجْلُوّ — بِغَيْرِ لَوْنٍ.

Acid, *a.* ثَقِيف — قَارِص — حَامِض; of milk, قَاطِع — مَاضِر — مَضِير. Acid and sweet, مِزّ — لَفَّان — مَزُوز. To be or become —, حَمُضَ — إِخْتَلَّ ².

Acid, }
Acidity, *n.* } حُمُوضَة — حُتُومَة.
Acidness, }

Acidify, *v.t.* } حَمَّضَ - قَلِيلًا — حَمَّضَ. To become acid, إِخْتَلَّ — حَمُضَ ².
Acidulate, }

Acknowledge, *v.t.* To own to the knowledge of, قَبِلَ — عَرَفَ — إِعْتَرَفَ بِ — أَقَرَّ بِ — سَلَّمَ بِ — أَقَرَّ بِ. To confess, as of a fault, To own, as of a benefit, شَكَرَ — عَرَفَ — رَاعَى ². To be obedient to, أَذْعَنَ لِ. To make to —, إِسْتَقَرَّ - بِ or عَلَى — قَرَّرَ - بِ or عَلَى. He acknowledged all the benefits which he had received from him, رَاعَى كُلَّ ٱلْأَفْضَالِ ٱلَّتِي نَالَهَا مِنْهُ. They acknowledged him as their rightful lord, أَذْعَنُوا لَهُ بِأَنَّهُ مَوْلَاهُمُ ٱلْأَحَقُّ. To — to one the receipt of a letter, عَرَّفَ - بِوُصُولِ ٱلْمَكْتُوبِ.

Acknowledgment, *n.* Admission of a position, تَسْلِيمٌ بِ — إِقْرَار; as of a fault, إِعْتِرَاف — إِقْرَار — بَوْء; of a benefit, رِضًى — مَمْنُونِيَّة — عُرْفَانُ ٱلْجَمِيلِ — مُرَاعَاةُ ٱلْجَمِيلِ — شُكْرَانُ ٱلْمَعْرُوفِ; of the authority of, تَسْلِيم — قُبُول — إِذْعَان.

Acme, *n.* Top, رَأْس — قُلَّة — قِمَّة. Crisis, as of a disease, بُحْرَان. Apogee, أَوْج.

Acolyte, *n.* A servitor in a church, قِنْدَلَفْت — شَمْعَدَانِيّ. One of the lowest order of deacons, شَمَّاسٌ فِي ٱلدَّرَجَةِ ٱلرَّابِعَةِ.

Aconite, *n.* خَانِقُ ٱلنَّمِرِ — خَانِقُ ٱلذِّئْبِ.

Acorn, *n.* بَلُّوط.

Acoustics, *n.* فَنُّ تَسْمِيعِ ٱلْأَصْوَاتِ — عِلْمُ ٱلْأَصْوَاتِ — عِلْمُ ٱلسَّمْعِ.

Acquaint, *v.t.* To inform, أَطْلَعَ - عَلَى — أَدْرَى - بِ — أَشْعَرَ - بِ — أَخْبَرَ - بِ — أَوْقَفَ - عَلَى — عَرَّفَ - عَن — أَكْشَفَ - عَلَى. To make one familiar with, عَرَّفَ — دَرَّى — مَرَّنَ — دَرَّبَ. To make one's self acquainted with, تَعَلَّمَ — تَعَرَّفَ. To be acquainted with, to know, عَرَفَ — إِطَّلَعَ عَلَى — شَعَرَ بِ ². He is acquainted with, of a person, لَهُ مَعْرِفَةٌ بِهِ. Before a man speaks on a subject he ought to be acquainted with it, يَنْبَغِي لِلْإِنْسَانِ قَبْلَ أَنْ يَتَكَلَّمَ عَلَى مَوْضُوعٍ مَا أَنْ يَكُونَ لَهُ وُقُوفٌ عَلَيْهِ. Is he well acquainted with the roads? هَلْ لَهُ خِبْرَةٌ بِٱلدُّرُوبِ.

Acquaintance, *n.* Knowledge, إِطِّلَاع — خِبْرَة — دِرَايَة — إِلْفَة — عِلْم — مَعْرِفَة — تَعَارُف. A slight knowledge, short of friendship, مَعْرِفَة — عَهْد. A person known, مِنَ ٱلْمَعَارِفِ. A practical — with, مَعْرِفَةٌ عَمَلِيَّةٌ بِ. To form an —, تَعَارَفَ — تَعَرَّفَ. I have no — with that family, لَيْسَ لِي بِتِلْكَ ٱلْعَايِلَةِ مَعْرِفَةٌ.

Acquainted, *part.* and *a.* Informed, عارِفٌ بِ ـ مُطَّلِعٌ عَلَى ـ مُتَفَنِّنٌ ـ ماهِرٌ بِ ـ مُفْتَنٌّ فِي. Versed in, خَبِيرٌ بِ.

Acquiesce, *v.i.* To yield assent, إِمْتَثَلَ ـ إِسْتَرْسَلَ ـ إِسْتَسْلَمَ ـ قَبِلَ ـ رَضِيَ بِ. To be contented with, قَنِعَ بِ.

Acquiescence, *n.* Consent, تَسْلِيم ـ إِنْقِياد ـ إِمْتِثال ـ رِضًى. Contentment, قَناعَة ـ قُنُوع. Submission, إِنْقِياد ـ خُضُوع ـ طاعَة ـ إِسْتِسْلام ـ إِذْعان.

Acquirable, *a.* مِمَّا يُحَصَّلُ ـ أَهْلٌ لِلإِكْتِساب ـ جَدِيرٌ بِالإِهْتِبالِ.

Acquire, *v.t.* To gain, إِحْتَظَى بِ ـ إِقْتَنَى ـ أَحْرَزَ ـ إِهْتَبَلَ ـ إِكْتَسَبَ ـ حَصَّلَ. To attain, نالَ ـ أَدْرَكَ ـ فازَ بِ ـ بَلَغَ ـ إِمْتَلَكَ ـ ظَفِرَ بِ. To —, as of knowledge, أَدْرَكَ; of strength, إِقْتَوَى ـ تَقَوَّى.

Acquired, *part.* مُهْتَبَل ـ مُحَصَّل ـ مَكْسُوب ـ مُكْتَسَب ـ مُقْتَبَس.

Acquirement, *n.* } Something acquired, إِقْتِباس ـ قِنًى *pl.* قِنْيَة
Acquisition, } إِكْتِساب. Attainment, إِحْراز ـ بُلُوغ ـ تَحْصِيل. That which is gained by labour, مُحْتَرَف ـ مُقْتَرَف ـ إِكْتِساب ـ مُجْتَنًى. A grace, زِينَة *pl.* زِيَن. *See also under* Accomplishment, *n.*

Acquisitiveness, *n.* رَغْبَةٌ فِي ٱلإِدْراكِ ـ إِهْتِمامٌ بِٱلْكَسْبِ.

Acquit, *v.t.* To set free, خَلَّصَ ـ أَعْتَقَ ـ حَرَّرَ ـ مَلَّسَ ـ أَنْقَذَ ـ أَطْلَقَ. To clear, as from a charge, بَيَّضَ ـ أَبْرَأَ ذِمَّتَهُ ـ أَبْرَأَ مِن ـ وَجْهَهُ. To forgive, سامَحَ بِ ـ عَفا عَن. To clear, as from an obligation, حَلَّلَ ـ أَعْفَى مِن. To — one's self, as of an obligation, وَفَى بِ *aor.* يَفِي ـ تَبَرَّأَ مِن. I acquitted him of the debt, أَبْرَأْتُهُ مِنَ ٱلدَّيْنِ ما عَلَيْهِ. To — one's self well, قَضَى ـ أَجادَ ـ أَحْسَنَ.

Acquittal, *n.* }
Acquitment, } تَخْلِيص ـ إِطْلاق ـ إِعْفاء.

Acquittance, *n.* A writing of, وَرَقَةُ خَلاصٍ ـ صَكُّ ٱلْوَفاءِ ـ رِجْعَة. Payment of a debt, وَفاءُ دَيْنٍ.

Acre, *n.* نَدْحَةٌ مِنَ ٱلأَرْضِ ـ فَدادِينُ *pl.* فَدّان ـ أَجْرِبَة *pl.* جَرِيب. God's Acre, المَقْبَرَة.

Acrid, *a.* حادٌّ ـ حامِز ـ حَرِيف.

Acridness, *n.* حَرافَة ـ حَمْز.

Acrimonious, *a.* Sour, of temper, عَزِق ـ شَكِس ـ شَرِس. *See also* Acrid, *a.*

Acrimony, *n.* Sourness, of temper, حِدَّة ـ شَكاسَة ـ شَراسَة ـ خُشُونَة ـ عُفُوصَة ـ مَرارَة. *See also* Acridness, *n.*

Acrobat, *n.* بَلْهَوان بَهْلَوان *vulg.* ـ مُهاجِم ـ خَلْبُوص ـ نَطّاط.

Acropolis, *n.* قَلْعَة *pl.* قِلاع.

Across, *ad.* Athwart, مُصَلَّبًا ـ مُعْتَرِضًا ـ عارِضًا. Over, عُبْرَ ـ عَبَّرَ ـ جَوَّبَ ـ عَبَرَ. To go —, عَبَرَ. I went — the river, عَبَرْتُ ٱلنَّهْرَ. To convey —, عَبَّرَ. Lay the two beams —, إِجْعَلِ ٱللَّوْحَيْنِ مُصَلَّبَيْنِ. Across the back, عَلَى عَرْضِ ٱلظَّهْرِ. The thing lay —, إِعْتَرَضَ ٱلشَّيْءُ. To place —, عَرَضَ.

Acrostic *n.* تَوْشِيح.

Act, *v.i.* To be in action, تَحَرَّكَ ـ سَلَكَ ـ سَعَى. To perform the proper functions, إِشْتَغَلَ. To practice, زاوَلَ ـ قَضَى ـ تَشَخَّصَ بِ ـ عَمِلَ ـ فَعَلَ ـ صَنَعَ ـ أَجْرَى. To personate, تَمَثَّلَ بِ. To — upon, فَعَلَ فِي ـ عَمِلَ فِي. To — up to, سَلَكَ بِحَسَبِ ـ عَمِلَ بِ. To — upon, to incite, أَنْهَضَ. To — well towards, أَحْسَنَ بِ *or* إِلَى.

Act, *v.a.* To perform, قَضَى ـ فَعَلَ. To counterfeit, as in a play, شَخَّصَ ـ لَعِبَ تَقْلِيدًا ـ حاكَى ـ أَوْهَمَ ـ قَلَّدَ.

Act, *n.* A deed, فِعْل *pl.* أَفْعال ـ عَمَل *pl.* أَعْمال ـ قَضِيَّة *pl.* قَضايا. A document, سَنَد *pl.* سَنَدات; an official —, سَنَدٌ رَسْمِيٌّ. Agency, operation, عَمَلِيَّة. State of reality, حَقِيقَة ـ فِعْلًا. Incipient agency, الهَمُّ بِ ـ الأَخْذُ بِ. Part of a play, قِسْمٌ مِنَ ٱلْكُومِيدِيَةِ أَوْ لَعِبِ ٱلتِّياتْرو. A decree, as of a court of legislature, حُكْم *pl.* أَحْكام ـ خُلاصَة; of a court of justice, حُكْم ـ فَتْوَى. A record of judicial proceedings, حُجَّة *pl.* حُجَج. An — of benevolence, إِحْسان ـ كَرَم ـ حَسَنَة. A course of action, قِدْيَة. An — of disobedience, إِثْم *pl.* آثام ـ ذَنْب *pl.* ذُنُوب. He was caught in the — of stealing, أُمْسِكَ وَهُوَ يَسْرِقُ. I was in the — of sending when . . . , كُنْتُ آخِذًا فِي ٱلإِرْسالِ حِينَ. The book of the Acts of the Apostles, الأَبْرَكْسِيس ـ سِفْرُ أَعْمالِ ٱلرُّسُلِ ـ قِصَصُ ٱلرُّسُلِ.

Acting, *part.* فاعِل ـ عامِل. Acting a part, pretending, صِناعِيٌّ.

Action, *n.* A process against, دَعْوَى ـ نِزاع ـ خُصُومَة *pl.* دَعاوٍ *and* دَعاوَى. A combat, قِتال ـ وَقْعَة ـ مَعْرَكَة. *See also* Act, *n.*

Actionable, *a.* القَوْلُ بِهِ مُمْكِنٌ ـ الحُكْمُ بِهِ مُمْكِنٌ ـ مِمَّا يُقْضَى بِهِ.

Active, *a.* Having the power of action, عامِل ـ فاعِل. Busy, فَعُول ـ عَمّال ـ عَمُول ـ عَمِل ـ كادِح ـ ذُو كَدٍّ ـ دائِب ـ كَدُود ـ طِرْفُ ٱلْعِنانِ ـ شَغّال. Nimble, خَفِيف ـ حَرِك ـ أَرْوَن ـ نَشِيط ـ نَدْب ـ سَرِيع ـ فَعّال. Strong, as of medicine, شَدِيد. An — verb, فِعْلٌ مُجاوِزٌ ـ فِعْلٌ واقِعٌ ـ فِعْلٌ مُتَعَدٍّ. The — voice, صِيغَةُ ٱلْمَعْلُومِ. To be — in, كَدَّ فِي.

Actively, *ad.* بِرَشاقَةٍ ـ بِخِفَّةٍ ـ بِرَشاقَةٍ ـ بِنَشاطٍ. *See also* Perseveringly, *ad.*

Activeness, *n.* } Quality of being active, قُوَّةٌ فاعِلِيَّةٌ ـ فاعِلِيَّةٌ.
Activity, } Diligence, as in business, مُرُوَّةٌ ـ نَشاط ـ كَدٌّ ـ حَرَكَة ـ هِمَّة.

Actor, *n.* An agent, شَرِيكٌ فِي ٱلْعَمَلِ ـ فاعِل. A comedian, مُقَلِّد ـ لَعِيبٌ فِي ٱلتِّياتِرو ـ لَعِيب ـ ...

Actress, *n.* A female agent, شَرِيكَةٌ فِي ٱلْعَمَلِ ـ عَمِيلَة. A female comedian, لَعِيبَةٌ فِي ٱلتِّياتِرو ـ لَعِبَة ـ مُقَلِّدَة.

Actual, *a.* بِعَيْنِهِ ـ يَقِين ـ ذاتِيٌّ ـ حَقِيقِيٌّ. The — state of affairs, ٱلْأَحْوالُ ٱلْحاضِرَةُ.

Actuality, *n.* عَيْن ـ حَقِيقَة ـ صِحَّة.

Actually, *ad.* Really, فِي ٱلْواقِعِ ـ فِعْلًا ـ يَقِينًا ـ حَقًّا. Presently, حالًا.

Actuary, *n.* مُحاسِب ـ كاتِب ـ صَكّاك.

Actuate, *v.t.* حَرَّكَ ـ حَرَّضَ ـ نَبَّهَ ـ حَمَّى ـ أَغْرَى.

Acumen, *n.* Sharpness, ذَرابَة ـ حِدَّة. Penetration of mind, وَهْنَة ـ فِطْنَة ـ نَباهَة ـ ذَكاء ـ بَراعَة.

Acuminate, *a.* صُلْبِيٌّ.

Acupuncture, *n.* شَكَّةُ إِبْرَةٍ ـ غَرْزٌ بِإِبْرَةٍ.

Acute, *a.* Opposed to blunt, بَتّار ـ باضِك ـ صارِم ـ ذَرِب ـ حادّ ـ قاطِع. Ingenious, ذَهِين ـ فَطِن ـ لَبِيب ـ فَهِيم ـ شَهْم ـ ماهِر ـ ذَكِيٌّ ـ حاذِق. An — disease, مَرَضٌ شَدِيدٌ. An — sound, صَوْتٌ عالٍ ـ حِسٌّ جَهْوَرٌ. An — angle, زاوِيَةٌ حادَّةٌ. An — triangle, مُثَلَّثٌ حادُّ ٱلزَّوايا.

Acutely, *ad.* Keenly, greatly, شَدِيدًا ـ بِحِدَّةٍ ـ كَثِيرًا ـ جِدًّا. With ingenuity, بِمَهارَةٍ ـ بِشَطارَةٍ ـ بِبَراعَةٍ.

Acuteness, *n.* Sharpness, حِدَّة ـ ذَرابَة. Power of intellect, مَهارَة ـ حِذْقُ ٱلْعَقْلِ ـ فِطْنَة ـ ذَكاء ـ نَباهَة ـ وَهْنَة. Acuteness of sight, حِدَّةُ ٱلْبَصَرِ ـ دِقَّةُ ٱلْبَصَرِ; of touch, دِقَّةُ (*or* لَطافَةُ) ٱللَّمْسِ; of a disease, شِدَّةُ ٱلْمَرَضِ.

A.D. (*Anno Domini*), فِي ٱلسَّنَةِ ٱلْمَسِيحِيَّةِ *or* ٱلْمِيلادِيَّةِ.

Adage, *n.* مَقالَة ـ أَمْثال *pl.* مَثَل.

Adam, *n.* آدَمُ ـ إِبْنُ ٱلطِّينِ.

Adam's apple, *n.* جَوْزَةُ ٱلْحَلْقُومِ ـ عُقْدَةُ ٱلْحَنْجُورِ ـ حَرْقَدَة.

Adamant, *n.* أَلْماس ـ سامُور.

Adamantine, *a.* ذُو أَلْماسٍ. Extremely hard, صُلْب ـ لا يَنْفَسِخُ.

Adapt, *v.t.* أَلَّفَ ـ عَلَى ـ وَفَّقَ ـ مَعَ ـ طَبَّقَ ـ عَلَى ـ ناسَبَ ـ جَعَلَ ـ صالِحًا ل ـ أَوْزَنَ ـ عَنِيَ ـ أَهَّلَ.

Adaptation, *n.* لِياقَة ـ تَلْبِيق ـ تَوْفِيق ـ مُطابَقَة ـ مُناسَبَة.

Adapted, *a.* Adapted to, قَمِينٌ ل *or* خَلِيقٌ ل ـ مُناسِبٌ ل ـ جَدِيرٌ ل *or* ب ـ ب *or* أَنْ. You are — for such a thing as this, أَنْتَ جَدِيرٌ بِأَنْ تَفْعَلَ شَيْئًا كَهٰذا.

Adaptedness, *n.* لِياقَةٌ ب ـ مَجْدَرَةٌ ل ـ مَخْلَقَةٌ ل.

Add, *v.t.* To join to, وَصَّلَ ـ ب ـ ضَمَّ ـ إِلَى ـ أَلْحَقَ ـ ب ـ زادَ ـ فِي. To — itself to, إِنْضَمَّ إِلَى. To be added to, إِنْضَمَّ إِنْضافَ إِلَى ـ إِلَى. To — up, جَمَعَ ـ أَجْمَلَ. To — something to one's words, أَعْقَبَ كَلامَهُ ب.

Addendum, *n.* إِضافَة ـ ضَمِيمَة.

Adder, *n.* The reptile, أَفْعَى *pl.* أَفاعِي ـ حَيَّة *pl.* حَيّات.

Addict, *v.t.* عَوَّدَ ـ عَلَى ـ دَرَّبَ ـ عَلَى ـ مَرَّنَ ـ عَلَى. To — one's self to, إِنْصَبَّ عَلَى ـ تَعَلَّقَ ب ـ غَرِيَ ب ـ تَدَرَّبَ ب ـ تَعَوَّدَ عَلَى ـ تَعاطَى. He addicted himself to study, تَوَلَّعَ بِٱلدَّرْسِ.

Addicted, *part.* Addicted to, مُدْمِن ـ مُصِرٌّ عَلَى. Addicted to wine, مُدْمِنٌ عَلَى ٱلْخَمْرِ ـ مُدْمِنُ ٱلْخَمْرِ.

Addictedness, *n.* } تَدَرُّب ـ وُلُوع ـ تَقْيِيدٌ فِي ـ تَدْرِيب
Addiction, } عادَة.

Additament, *n.* إِضافَة.

Addition, *n.* The thing added, إِنْضِمام ـ ضَمِيمَة ـ إِلْقاء ـ إِلْحاق ـ زِيادَة ـ إِضافَة. The rule in arithmetic, ٱلْجَمِيعَة ـ ٱلْجَمْعُ ـ ٱلْجُمْلَةُ. Additions, ضَمائِمُ ـ مُلْحَقات ـ إِضافات. In — to, besides, أَيْضًا ـ فَضْلًا عَنْ ـ ما عَدا. In — to what we said, فَضْلًا عَمّا قُلْناهُ. Do that in —, إِفْعَلْ ذٰلِكَ زِيادَةً.

Additional, *a.* غَيْر ـ مَزِيد ـ مُضاف ـ إِضافِيٌّ. Fresh, new, أَجْنَبِيٌّ ـ جَدِيد.

Additionally, *ad.* أَيْضًا ـ زِيادَةً.

Addle, *v.t.* أَمْذَرَ. To be addled, تَمَذَّرَ ـ مَذِرَ. To — the wits of, هَتَرَ.

Addle-headed, *a.* جاهِل ـ غَشِيم ـ أَحْمَق ـ بَلِيد.

Address, *v.t.* To apply to with words, خاطَبَ ـ كَلَّمَ ـ كالَمَ ـ أَقْبَلَ عَلَى ـ بِٱلْكَلامِ. To send to, أَرْسَلَ ـ إِلَى ـ بَعَثَ ـ إِلَى. To put the —, as on a letter, عَنْوَنَ. To — a petition, قَدَّمَ عَرْضَ حالٍ. To — one's self to, prepare for, تَحَضَّرَ ل ـ تَأَهَّبَ ل ـ تَهَيَّأَ ل. To apply to, وَقَعَ عَلَى ـ قَصَدَ إِلَى ـ تَعَرَّضَ ل aor. يَقَعُ. You must — yourself to such an one, ٱلْمَرْجِعُ إِلَى فُلانٍ. Your letter addressed to ..., كِتابُكَ ٱلْمُعَنْوَنُ إِلَى.

Address, *n.* Verbal application, إِلْتِماس ـ خِطاب ـ خُطْبَة ـ طَلَبَة ـ قَوْل. Petition, إِلْتِماس ـ رَجاء. A written petition, عَرْض ـ عَرْضُ حالٍ. Dexterity, خِفَّة ـ مَهارَة ـ حِذْق. Address, as of a letter, عُنْوان. To pay one's addresses to, to court, تَوَدَّدَ إِلَى. This is the — which was read over to ... by ..., هٰذا

ٱلخِطَابُ ٱلَّذِى قالَهُ ل. They presented him with an — signed by . . . , قَدَّمُوا لَهُ خِطَابًا مُمْضِيًا مِن.

Adduce, *v.t.* قَدَّمَ ـ جَآءَ بِ ـ أَوْرَدَ *aor.* يَجِيءُ. To —, as an argument, إِحْتَجَّ بِ. He adduced an instance to him, ضَرَبَ لَهُ مَثَلًا.

Adducent, *a.* مُورِد.

Adducible, *a.* مِمَّا يُقَدَّمُ ـ مِمَّا يُورَدُ ـ يُورَدُ.

Adept, *n.* أُسْتَاذ ـ شَاطِر ـ حَاذِق ـ مَاهِر ـ عَالِم.

Adequacy, *n.* / Adequateness, } أَهْلِيَّة ـ مُوَازَاة ـ كِفَايَة.

Adequate, *a.* مُوَافِق ـ مُنَاسِب ـ كَافٍ. Adequate to, capable of, قَادِرٌ عَلَى ـ قَابِلٌ ل.

Adequately, *ad.* مُوَافِقًا ـ لَائِقًا ـ كَافِيًا.

Adhere, *v.i.* To stick to, لَصِقَ بِ ـ إِلْتَصَقَ بِ ـ لَزِجَ بِ ـ دَبِقَ بِ; in a figurative sense, إِلْتَصَقَ بِ ـ إِلْتَحَمَ بِ ـ وَاصَلَ ـ إِتَّحَدَ مَعَ ـ تَعَلَّقَ بِ. He adhered to his opinions, تَبِعَ رَأْيَهُ ـ تَمَسَّكَ بِرَأْيِهِ ـ أَدْمَنَ عَلَى رَأْيِهِ. To cause to —, stick, لَزَّقَ ـ أَلْزَقَ ـ أَلْصَقَ. They adhered to one another, تَلَاتَبُوا.

Adherence, *n.* Tenacity, دَبَقِيَّة ـ لُزُوجَة; in a figurative sense. مُبَارَكَةٌ عَلَى ـ مُوَاصَلَة ـ اِلْتِحَام ـ اِلْتِصَاق ـ إِتِّحَاد. Persistence, لُزُوم ـ إِدْمَان.

Adherent, *a.* Stuck to, لَاصِقٌ بِ ـ مُلْصَقٌ بِ ـ مُلْتَزِقٌ بِ; figuratively, لَاتِب ـ لَازِم ـ مُتَعَلِّقٌ بِ ـ مُتَّحِدٌ مَعَ.

Adherent, *n.* مُلَازِم ـ لَاحِق ـ مِنْ حِزْبٍ ـ مُتَعَصِّب ـ مُضَاف ـ مِنْ جَمَاعَةٍ ـ تَابِع *pl.* تَابِعُون ـ حَلِيف.

Adhesion, *n.* (*See* Adherence, *n.*) He gave in his — to, وَافَقَ ـ أَوْقَعَ عَلَى. An act, document, of —, سَنَدُ ٱلْمُوَافَقَةِ ـ صَكُّ ٱلْإِتِّفَاقِ.

Adhesive, *a.* دَابِق ـ لَاصِق ـ لَازِج.

Adhesiveness, *n.* لُزُوجَة.

Adieu, *n.* وِدَاع. To bid — to, وَدَّعَ ـ وَادَعَ. Adieu! as uttered by a person who takes leave of another, تَمَّ فِي ـ كُنْ فِي أَمَانٍ ـ تَمَّ عَلَى خَيْرٍ ـ حِرَاسَةِ ٱللّٰهِ. As an equivalent for Good morning to you! صَبَّحْنَاكَ; for Good evening to you! مَسَّيْنَاكَ. Adieu! in reply to the preceding compliments, فِي أَمَانٍ ـ مَعَ ٱلسَّلَامَةِ ـ بِٱلْأَمَانِ ـ ٱللّٰهِ. The person visited generally says after these replies, شَرَّفْتَنَا ـ آنَسْتَنَا, *i.e.* You have delighted us; you have honoured us. To which the visitor subjoins, ٱللّٰهُ يُؤَنِّسُكَ ـ أَنْتَ ٱلْمُشَرِّفُ, *i.e.* May God give you joy! You are the honourer. Adieu! as an exclamation of despair, وَعَلَى ٱلدُّنْيَا ٱلسَّلَامُ, *i.e.* Farewell to the world! The same idea is expressed by the verb رَاحَ [2], to pass away, as in the proverb, مَاتَتِ ٱلْحِمَارَةُ رَاحَتِ ٱلزِّيَارَةُ, The she-ass is dead, Adieu to the Pilgrimage!

Ad infinitum, ad. إِلَى مَا لَا نِهَايَةَ لَهُ ـ إِلَى ٱلنِّهَايَةِ.

Ad interim, ad. زَمَنِيًّا ـ مُوَقَّتًا.

Adipose, *a.* سَمِين ـ دَهِن ـ دَسِم.

Adit, *n.* As to a mine, مَنْفَذٌ إِلَى مَعْدِنٍ *or* نَاقُورٌ *or* (دِهْلِيز).

Adjacency, *n.* قُرْب ـ إِتِّصَال ـ جِوَار ـ مُجَاوَرَة ـ وَلْيٌ ـ وِلَآء.

Adjacent, *a.* قَرِيبٌ ـ مُجَاوِر ـ مُتَاخِم ـ مُمَاسٌّ ـ مَا يَلِي ـ وَلِيٌّ مِن. To be — to, وَاصَلَ ـ قَارَبَ. His house is — to mine, دَارُهُ وَلِيُّ دَارِي.

Adjective, *n.* نَعْت *pl.* نُعُوت ـ صِفَة *pl.* صِفَات. An active participial —, إِسْمُ فِعْلٍ; a passive ditto, إِسْمُ مَفْعُولٍ.

Adjoin, *v.i.* إِتَّصَلَ بِ ـ وَلِيَ *aor.* يَلِي. Our land adjoins yours, أَرْضُنَا مُحَاذٌ أَرْضَكُمْ. To make to —, أَلْحَقَ بِ.

Adjoining, *a.* مُتَّصِل ـ وَلِيٌّ ـ مُلَاصِق. An — house, دَارٌ وَلِيَّةٌ.

Adjourn, *v.t.* حَذَفَ إِلَى غَيْرِ وَقْتٍ ـ سَوَّفَ ـ أَخَّرَ ـ أَبْقَى. The conference was adjourned, تَأَخَّرَ ٱلْمُؤْتَمَرُ.

Adjournment, *n.* تَوْقِيف ـ إِبْقَآء ـ تَأْخِير ـ تَأَخُّر.

Adjudge, *v.t.* / Adjudicate, } To decide for, حَكَمَ ل [2]. To decide against, حَكَمَ عَلَى [2]. To sentence, دَانَ ـ قَضَى عَلَى. The Kâdhi adjudged the mare to him, القَاضِي حَكَمَ لَهُ بِٱلْفَرَسِ.

Adjudication, *n.* قَضَآء ـ حُكُومَة ـ حُكْم. To refer to for —, حَاكَمَ ـ تَحَاكَمَ.

Adjunct, *n.* Something added, زِيَادَة ـ إِضَافَة ـ ضَمِيمَة ـ إِلْحَاق. An adherent, مُضَاف.

Adjunctive, *a.* مُضَافٌ إِلَى. An — particle, حَرْفٌ عَاطِفٌ ـ حَرْفُ عَطْفٍ.

Adjuration, *n.* إِسْتِحْلَاف ـ قَسَامَة ـ قَسَم.

Adjure, *v.t.* إِسْتَحْلَفَ ـ حَلَّفَ ـ نَاشَدَ ـ أَقْسَمَ عَلَى. I — you by the faithfulness of God, نَشَدْتُكَ أَمَانَةَ ٱللّٰهِ.

Adjust, *v.t.* To put in order, دَبَّرَ ـ عَدَّلَ ـ رَتَّبَ ـ نَظَّمَ. To make accurate, هَذَّبَ ـ أَصْلَحَ ـ عَدَّلَ ـ دَقَّقَ ـ صَحَّحَ ـ ضَبَّطَ. To make conformable to, طَبَّقَ ل ـ أَوْزَنَ عَلَى ـ وَزَنَ عَلَى ـ وَفَّقَ ل ـ نَاسَبَ. To — one's person, تَنَظَّمَ ـ تَزَيَّنَ. He adjusted the difference between them, صَالَحَهُمْ ـ سَوَّى بَيْنَهُمْ. To — a measure, ضَبَطَ ٱلْكَيْلَ [2].

Adjustment *n.* نِظَام ـ تَصْلِيح ـ تَضْبِيط ـ تَعْدِيل ـ ضَبْط ـ إِنْتِظَام; of one's person, زِينَة ـ تَزْيِين; of a difference, مُصَالَحَة.

Adjutancy, *n.* قُولْ أَغَاسِي (Turkish).

Adjutant, *n.* قُول آغاسِي مُفَوَّض بِتَعْلِيمِ ٱلعَسْكَرِ (Turkish) — تَعْلِيمْجِي — مُعِين.

Adjutant-General, *n.* سَرْ عَسْكَر وَظِيفَتُهُ إِجْرَآء كُلَّمَا يَتَعَلَّق بِٱلعَسْكَرِ فِي حَالَتَيْ مُرُورِهِمْ وَتَسْكِينِهِ. Deputy Adjutant-General, مُعَاوِن لِلْمَذْكُور.

Ad libitum, ad. حَسَبَ ٱلإِرَادَةِ — إِخْتِيَارًا.

Administer, *v.t.* To supply, أَغَاثَ — أَمَدَّ — مَنَحَ — أَعْطَى. To direct, بَاشَرَ — أَجْرَى — دَبَّرَ — تَوَلَّى عَلَى — حَكَمَ — تَدَّمَ لِ. To dispense the affairs of another, تَوَكَّلَ عَنْ — نَابَ. To — an oath, إِسْتَحْلَفَ — أَقْسَمَ عَلَى. To — the sacraments, خَدَمَ — مَنَحَ ٱلأَسْرَارَ ٱلأَسْرَار. To —, as of medicine, سَقَى — أَعْطَى.

Administration, *n.* Direction of any business, تَدْبِير — إِجْرَآء — حُكْم — إِيَالَة — تَوَلٍّ — خِدْمَة — مُبَاشَرَة — إِدَارَة. Government, حُكُومَة. Executorship, وَكَالَة — وَصِيَّة. Administration of the sacraments, مَنْحُ ٱلأَسْرَارِ. The public —, تَدْبِيرُ أُمُورِ ٱلجُمْهُورِ — ٱلحُكُومَة. Letters of —, حُجَّةٌ شَرْعِيَّةٌ بِإِجْرَآءِ وَصِيَّةٍ.

Administration of criminal judicature, إِدَارَةُ مَجْلِسِ ٱلجِنَايَاتِ — إِدَارَةُ ٱلأُمُورِ ٱلجِزَائِيَّةِ.

Civil —, إِدَارَةٌ مَدَنِيَّةٌ.

Financial —, إِدَارَةُ ٱلمَالِيَّةِ.

Military —, إِدَارَةُ أُمُورِ ٱلعَسْكَرِيَّةِ.

Political —, إِدَارَةٌ مَلَكِيَّةٌ *or* سِيَاسِيَّةٌ.

A regular —, إِدَارَةٌ مَضْبُوطَةٌ *or* مُنْتَظِمَةٌ.

A separate —, إِدَارَةٌ مُفْرَدَةٌ.

Administrative, *a.* مُتَعَلِّقٌ بِٱلحُكُومَةِ — تَدْبِيرِيٌّ. Administrative power, حُكُومَةٌ إِدَارِيَّةٌ مَلَكِيَّةٌ.

Administrator, *n.* مُبَاشِر — مُتَصَرِّف — مُدَبِّر — عَوَامِل *pl.* عَامِل — حَاكِم. Executor, نُوَّاب *pl.* نَائِب — وُكَلَآء *pl.* وَكِيل. Administrators, أَوْلِيَآء ٱلأُمُور.

Administratorship, *n.* مُتَصَرِّفِيَّة — وَكَالَة — مُبَاشَرَة — تَدْبِير.

Administratrix, *n.* إِمْرَأَةٌ وَصِيٌّ.

Admirable, *a.* غَرِيب — زَهِيّ — نَادِر — بَاهِر — مُعْجِب — عَجِيب — حَسِين — حَمِيد — بَدِيع — رَائِع. An — thing, عَجَائِب *pl.* عَجِيبَة. Admirable qualities, مَحَاسِن. Most — aims, حَبَّذَا — عَجَائِبُ عَلَى أَبْهَم. Admirable! لِلّٰهِ دَرُّهُ — أَعْجَبَ بِهِ.

Admirably, *ad.* حَسَنًا — نَادِرًا — بَاهِرًا — عَجِيبًا.

Admiral, *n.* قَبْطَان بَاشَا — أَمِيرُ ٱلبَحْرِ.

Admiralty, *n.* دِيوَانُ مُدَبِّرِي أُمُورِ ٱلبَحْرِ. The First Lord of the —, صَدْرُ مُدَبِّرِي أُمُورِ ٱلبَحْرِ. The Admiralty Court, مَحْكَمَةُ مُدَبِّرِي أُمُورِ ٱلبَحْرِ.

Admiration, *n.* إِعْتِبَار — تَعَجُّب — عَجَب — هَكَر. Self —, عُجْب. Note of —, عَلَامَةُ ٱلتَّعَجُّبِ. It excited my —, رَاقَنِي. It excited his —, أَعْجَبَهُ.

Admire, *v.i.* To wonder at, رَاعَ *aor.* يَرُوعُ — تَعَجَّبَ مِن — إِسْتَعْجَبَ مِن — إِسْتَعْظَمَ — إِسْتَصْوَبَ — إِسْتَصْلَحَ. To approve of, إِسْتَحْسَنَ. To love, وَدَّ — عَشِقَ — أَحَبَّ. To — one's self, أَعْجِبَ بِنَفْسِهِ. He admired it, أَعْجِبَ بِهِ.

Admirer, *n.* One who regards with admiration, مُسْتَعْجِب — مُعْتَبِر لِ. A lover, عَاشِق — مُحِبّ. One who has a great taste for a thing, رَاغِبٌ فِي — طَالِب. A self-admirer, مُعْجَبٌ بِنَفْسِهِ.

Admiringly, *ad.* بِٱعْتِبَار — بِٱسْتِعْجَاب — بِهَكَر. Lovingly, بِعِشْقٍ.

Admissibility, *n.* مَقْبُولِيَّة — قُبُولِيَّة.

Admissible, *a.* مُسَلَّم — يُسَلَّم — يُرْضَى بِ — مَقْبُول — يُقْبَلُ. An — excuse, عُذْرٌ مَقْبُولٌ.

Admission, *n.* } Access, دَخْلَة — دُخُول. Right of entrance,
Admittance, } حَقُّ ٱلدُّخُولِ — إِذْنٌ بِٱلدُّخُولِ. Concession, as of a position, إِجَابَة — تَسَلُّم — رِضَآء — قُبُول.

Admit, *v.t.* To give entrance to, دَخَّلَ — عَبَّرَ — أَوْلَجَ — طَرَّقَ لِ — أَدْخَلَ. To concede, رَضِيَ بِ — سَلَّمَ بِ — أَقَرَّ بِ — قَبِلَ. To make to —, إِسْتَقَرَّ بِ — عَلَى *or* قَرَّرَ عَلَى — أَجَابَ إِلَى.

Admittance, *n.* *See* Admission, *n.*

Admixture, *n.* مَزْجَة — أَدَمَة.

Admonish, *v.t.* نَبَّهَ — حَذَّرَ — أَنْذَرَ بِ — نَاصَحَ — نَصَحَ. To — against, وَعَظَ عَلَى — نَبَّهَ عَلَى *aor.* يَعِظُ. To be admonished by, إِتَّعَظَ بِ.

Admonisher, *n.* نَاصِح — وَاعِظ — مُنَبِّه — مُنْذِر.

Admonition, *n.* نَصِيحَة — تَحْذِير — عِظَة — تَنْبِيه — نَصَاحَة — إِنْذَار — ذِكْر — عِبْرَة. To deliver an —, خَطَبَ.

Admonitory, *a.* مُنَبِّه — إِنْذَارِيّ.

Ado, *n.* غَوْش — غَلْغَلَة — غَلَبَة — شَقْشَقَة — ضَجّ — إِضْطِرَاب. To make much ado, غَوَّشَ — ضَجَّ. Why make you this ado? لِمَاذَا تَضِجُّونَ.

Adolescence, *n.* غُلُومِيَّة — شُبُوبِيَّة — شَبِيبَة — سِنُّ ٱلنُّمُوِّ.

Adolescent, *a.* شَابّ — جُذْعَان *pl.* جَذَع — غِلْمَان *pl.* غُلَام.

Adopt, *v.t.* To take, as of a child, by choice, تَبَنَّى — تَبَنَّى بِ; of a boy, إِتَّخَذَهُ ٱبْنًا; of a girl, إِتَّخَذَهَا بِنْتًا. To choose in preference, إِخْتَارَ ـ آثَرَ ـ عَلَى ـ عَمِلَ بِ ـ إِسْتَصْوَبَ ـ إِسْتَحْسَنَ.

An adopted son, وَلَدُ ٱلتَّبَنِّي ـ مُتَبَنًّى.

Adoption, *n.* As of a child, تَبْنِيَة ـ تَبَنٍّ. Choice, إِخْتِيَار ـ عَمَلٌ بِ ـ إِتِّخَاذ ـ إِسْتِحْسَان.

Adoptive, *a.* Additional, إِضَافِيٌّ.

Adorable, *a.* Worthy of worship, وَاجِبُ ٱلسُّجُودِ لَهُ ـ مَعْبُود. Charming, بَدِيع.

Adorableness, *n.* وِمَّا يَسْتَوْجِبُ ٱلسُّجُودَ.

Adorably, *ad.* تَعَبُّدًا ـ بِٱلسُّجُودِ.

Adoration, *n.* Worship, سُجُود ـ تَعَبُّد ـ عِبَادَة. Admiration, عِزٌّ ـ عِشْق.

Adore, *v.t.* To worship, أَلَّهَ ـ عَبَدَ ـ سَجَدَ ـ خَرَّ لِ. To love, أَعَزَّ ـ عَشِقَ ـ أَحَبَّ.

Adorer, *n.* *See* Admirer, Worshipper, *n.*

Adorn, *v.t.* نَمْنَمَ ـ حَلَّى ـ حَسَّنَ ـ جَمَّلَ ـ زَيَّنَ ـ وَشَّمَ ـ حَبَّرَ ـ حَبَرَ. To — one's self, تَصَنَّعَ ـ تَزَيَّنَ ـ تَزَخْرَفَ. To —, as of language, حَبَّرَ ـ زَخْرَفَ. She adorned herself with ornaments, تَحَلَّتْ.

Adorning, *n.* } زِينَة ـ تَجْمِيل ـ حِلْيَة ـ تَزْيِين ـ زَخْرَفَة; of lan-
Adornment, } guage, زُخْرُفُ ٱلْقَوْلِ.

Adorned, *part.* مُزَخْرَف ـ مُتَزَيِّن ـ مُزَيَّن.

Adrift, *ad.* On the water, يَطُوفُ عَلَى وَجْهِ ٱلْمَآءِ ـ طَوَّاف. Wandering, طَائِح ـ تَائِه. To cast —, abandon, تَرَكَ ـ دَشَّرَ. To dismiss, طَرَدَ ـ دَشَّرَ. To turn —, as to pasture, أَسْرَحَ ـ سَرَّحَ.

Adroit, *a.* شَاطِر ـ نَشِيط ـ ذُو خِفَّةٍ ـ مَاهِر.

Adroitly, *ad.* بِشَطَارَةٍ ـ بِمَهَارَةٍ ـ بِخِفَّةٍ.

Adroitness, *n.* شَطَارَة ـ نَشَاط ـ خِفَّة ـ وَهْنَة.

Adscititious, *a.* عَرَضِيٌّ ـ زَائِد ـ مُلْحَق ـ مُلَسَّق.

Adulation, *n.* تَبَصْبُص ـ تَمْلِيق ـ تَمَلُّق ـ مَلَق ـ إِطْرَآء. *See also* Flattery, *n.*

Adulator, *n.* دَائِمُ ٱلْمَشْطِ ـ مُمَلِّق ـ مَلَّاق ـ دَحُول ـ مُطَرٍّ.

Adulatory, *a.* مَادِح ـ مُمَلِّق ـ مُطَرٍّ.

Adult, *n.* and *a.* بَالِغ ـ نَوَاشِئُ *pl.* نَاشِئٌ *pl.* نَشَأٌ, *fem.* نَاشِئَة ـ كَامِلُ ٱلسِّنِّ ـ بَالِغُ أَشُدِّهِ. An — man, رَجُل *pl.* رِجَال; woman, إِمْرَأَة *pl.* نِسَآء.

Adulterate, *v.t.* To corrupt, فَسَخَ ـ أَفْسَدَ ـ غَشَّ; of coin, زَغَلَ ـ شَقْشَقَ. To —, as the meaning of words, عَكَّسَ ـ حَرَّفَ ٱلْكَلَامَ ـ ٱلْمَعْنَى. To falsify, مَوَّهَ.

Adulteration, *n.* Corruption, تَزْوِير ـ تَمْوِيه ـ غِشّ ـ إِفْسَاد; as of coin, زَغَل ـ شَقْشَقَة ـ غِشّ; of meaning, تَعْكِيس ـ تَحْرِيف.

Adulterer, *n.* A fornicator, زَانٍ *pl.* زُنَاة ـ عَاهِر *pl.* عُهَّار ـ فَاجِر *pl.* فُجَّار ـ فَاسِق *pl.* فَسَقَة; of coin, زَغَلِيٌّ.

Adulteress, *n.* زَانِيَة *pl.* زَوَانٍ ـ قَرْتَا ـ فَاجِرَة.

Adulterous, *a.* زَانٍ ـ فَاجِر ـ فَاسِق.

Adultery, *n.* عِهْر ـ زِنًى ـ فِسْق. To commit —, عَنِتَ ـ زَنَى *aor.* يَزْنِي.

Adumbrate, *v.t.* To betoken, دَلَّ عَلَى ـ كَنَا عَنْ.

Adumbration, *n.* عِبَارَة ـ دَلِيل ـ كِنَايَة.

Ad valorem, ad. بِحَسْبِ ٱلسِّعْرِ.

Advance, *n.* Progression, مَشْيٌ ـ قُدُوم ـ تَقَدُّم. Preferment, تَشْرِيف ـ تَرْقِيَة ـ إِرْتِفَاع ـ تَرْفِيع ـ نَجَاح ـ تَرَقٍّ. Improvement, إِتْقَان ـ إِسْتِدْرَاج ـ إِرْتِقَآء ـ نَمِيَّة. Increase, زِيَادَة ـ إِزْدِيَاد. Distance in —, سَبْقَة. In —, as of a money payment, سَلَم ـ سَلَف ـ لِقُدَّامٍ. In — of, مُتَقَدِّمًا مِنْ. To make advances to one towards a reconciliation, بَادَى ـ بِطَلَبِ ٱلْمُصَالَحَةِ. She made advances towards him, عَرَضَتْ نَفْسَهَا لَهُ. To be in — of, in qualifications, بَرَعَ. He is in — of his companion, بَرَعَ صَاحِبَهُ.

Advance, *v.t.* To bring forward, in a local sense, قَرَّبَ ـ قَدَّمَ. To raise to preferment, عَظَّمَ ـ فَخَّمَ ـ رَقَّى ـ رَفَّعَ. To improve, أَصْلَحَ ـ حَسَّنَ ـ رَقَّى. To propose to, أَعْرَضَ ـ لِ. To — money to, أَسْلَفَ ـ فُلُوسًا. To — one over another, فَضَّلَ ـ عَلَى.

Advance, *v.i.* To come forward, تَقَدَّمَ ـ تَرَقَّى ـ تَدَرَّجَ ـ دَرَجَ. To improve, تَرَقَّى ـ أَتْقَنَ ـ إِزْدَادَ فِي ٱلنَّجَاحِ. To — in years, طَعَنَ فِي ٱلسِّنِّ. To — by degrees towards, تَدَرَّجَ إِلَى. The day advanced, زَالَ ٱلنَّهَارُ ـ يَعْلُو *aor.* عَلَا ٱلنَّهَارُ. He advanced towards him with an arrow, إِعْتَرَضَ لَهُ بِسَهْمٍ.

Advancement, *n.* *See* Advance, *n.*

Advance-guard, *n.* نَظِيرَة ـ سُلَّافُ ٱلْعَسْكَرِ ـ رَسِيلُ ٱلْعَسْكَرِ ـ مُقَدِّمَةُ ٱلْجُيُوشِ.

Advantage, *n.* Superiority, إِرْتِفَاع ـ إِسْتِعْلَآء ـ تَقَدُّم ـ فَضْل. Profit, مَكْسَب ـ مَنْفَعَة ـ خَيْر ـ فَائِدَة ـ نَفْع ـ حَاصِل. Victory over, ظَفَر ـ غَلَبَة ـ غُلْبَة ـ نَصْر. Opportunity, فُرْصَة ـ وَقْت. To derive — from, إِنْتَفَعَ مِنْ ـ إِسْتَفَادَ مِنْ. To give one the — over another, فَضَّلَ ـ عَلَى ـ رَفَعَ ـ عَلَى ـ قَدَّمَ ـ عَلَى. To procure — for, نَفَعَ ـ أَفَادَ. To gain the — over, إِنْتَصَرَ عَلَى ـ قَوِيَ عَلَى ـ غَلَبَ. To set off to —, جَمَّلَ ـ حَسَّنَ ـ زَيَّنَ. To take — of, to cheat, غَشَّ ـ خَانَ ـ غَدَرَ بِ.

Advantage, *v.t.* أَفَادَ ـ ءِ نَفَعَ ـ قَدَّمَ ـ فَضَّلَ .

Advantageous, *a.* Profitable, مُفِيد ـ نَافِع ـ خَيِّر . Convenient, مُوَافِق ـ مُنَاسِب . I hired the house upon the most — terms, إِسْتَكْرَيْتُ ٱلْبَيْتَ بِأَوْفَقِ كِرَاءٍ ـ . This is more — to me, هٰذَا أَنْفَعُ لِي ـ هٰذَا أَحْسَنُ لِي .

Advantageously, *ad.* Profitably, بِنَفْعٍ ـ بِفَائِدَةٍ . Conveniently, بِتَيَسُّرٍ ـ بِمُنَاسَبَةٍ . The house is — situated, مَوْضِعُ ٱلْبَيْتِ مُوَافِقٌ .

Advent, *n.* Arrival, مَقْدَم ـ وُفُود ـ وُصُول . The feast of —, عِيدُ ٱلْبِشَارَةِ . The fast of —, صَوْمُ ٱلْمِيلَادِ (the Copts style it صِيام كِيهك).

Adventitious, *a.* مُلْحَق ـ أَجْنَبِيٌّ ـ إِضَافِيٌّ ـ عَرَضِيٌّ .

Adventure, *n.* A hazard, قِصَّة ـ حَادِثَة ـ عَارِض . An enterprise, قَضِيَّة ـ مُبَاشَرَة ـ عَزِيمَة . A perilous —, مُخَاطَرَة . A mercantile —, مُضَارَبَة مَتْجَر ـ بِضَاعَة . The story of an —, قِصَّة . He met with an —, حَكَمَهُ عَارِضٌ ـ ءِ عَرَضَ عَلَيْهِ عَارِضٌ .

Adventure, *v.i.* To hazard, جَسَرَ عَلَى ـ ٤ تَجَاسَرَ ـ تَجَرَّأَ عَلَى . To — one's self, إِسْتَجْرَأَ ـ عَرَضَ نَفْسَهُ لِـ ـ ءِ عَرَّضَ نَفْسَهُ لِلنَّصِيبِ ـ خَاطَرَ بِنَفْسِهِ .

Adventurer, *n.* A traveller, سَيَّاح ـ وَسَفَر ـ مُسَافِر . A speculator, فَلَاتِيٌّ ـ ضَرَّابُ مَخَاوِين . A vagabond, هَامِل ـ ضَائِعٌ سَائِحٌ ـ هَائِش ـ دَائِش .

Adventurous, *a.* } Daring, جَسُور ـ هُمَامِيٌّ ـ هُمَام ـ نَدْب ـ
Adventuresome, } جَرِيٌّ ـ بَطَل . Full of hazard, مَهِيل ـ خَطِر ـ خَطِير ـ مَخُوف .

Adventurously, *ad.* بِجَرَاءَةٍ ـ بِشَجَاعَةٍ ـ بِجَسَارَةٍ .

Adverb, *n.* إِسْم ـ ظُرُوف *pl.* ظَرْف *pl.* حُرُوف ـ حَرْف . An affirmative —, حَرْفُ إِيجَابٍ ; a negative —, حَرْفُ نَهْيٍ ; an — of time, ظَرْفُ زَمَانٍ ; of place, ظَرْفُ مَكَانٍ . An —, in the form of an indeclinable noun, إِسْمٌ مَبْنِيٌّ ; *e.g.* أَمْسِ yesterday, إِذًا then.

Adverbial, *a.* ظَرْفِيٌّ . An — noun or expression, ظَرْف ـ كَلِمَةٌ ـ . An — phrase, جُمْلَةٌ فِي مَوْضِعِ ٱلنَّصْبِ ـ مَنْصُوبَةٌ عَلَى أَنَّهُ ظَرْف ـ جُمْلَةٌ عَلَى ٱلظَّرْفِيَّةِ .

Adverbially, *ad.* بِمَقَامِ ٱلظَّرْفِ ـ ظَرْفِيًا ـ ظَرْفًا . The quality of denoting place or time —, ظَرْفِيَّة .

Adversary, *n.* خَصْم *pl.* خِصَام ـ خَصِيم *pl.* خُصُوم ـ عَدُوٌّ *pl.* أَعْدَاء ـ ضِدٌّ ـ مُخَالِف ـ مُقَاوِم ـ خَائِن . To be an — to, خَاصَمَ ـ قَاوَمَ .

Adversitive, *a.* An — particle, حَرْفُ مُبَايَنَةٍ .

Adverse, *a.* Contrary, نَقِيض ـ مُضَادّ ـ مُخَاصِم ـ مُخَالِف . Calamitous, سُوء ـ نَحِس ـ حَزِين ـ مُؤْلِم ـ مُغِمٌّ . Adverse fortune, ٱلدَّهْرُ ٱلْمُخَالِفُ . An — party, خَصِيم ـ خَصْم . An — wind, عَسْرُ ٱلزَّمَانِ . The time, or fortune, was — to us, نُكْب *pl.* نَكْبَاء ـ عَلَيْنَا .

Adverseness, *n.* مُضَادَّة ـ مُخَالَفَة .

Adversity, *n.* نَكْبَة ـ شَقَاوَة ـ شَقَاء ـ شِدَّة ـ ضِيقَة ـ ضَنْك ـ بَلَاء ـ مُصِيبَة ـ نَكْب . In prosperity and in —, فِي حَالَتَيِ ٱلْيُسْرِ وَٱلْعُسْرِ ـ فِي ٱلشِّدَّةِ وَفِي ٱلرَّخَاءِ . Adverse circumstances, عَوَائِق ـ نَوَائِب ـ شَدَائِد .

Adversely, *ad.* بِٱلْعَكْسِ ـ بِٱلضِّدِّ ـ مُنَاقَضَةً . Unfortunately, بِشَقَاوَةٍ ـ بِشِدَّةٍ .

Advert, *v.i.* To hint at, أَشَارَ إِلَى ـ ءِ لَحَظَ إِلَى . To regard, attend to, تَنَبَّهَ عَلَى ـ اعْتَبَرَ ـ لَاحَظَ .

Advertence, *n.* } تَقَيُّد ـ إِعْتِبَار ـ إِنْتِبَاه ـ تَأَمُّل ـ مُلَاحَظَة
Advertency, } دَوَرَانُ بَالٍ .

Advertise, *v.t.* To inform of, عَرَّفَ ـ أَطْلَعَ ـ عَلَى ـ أَخْبَرَ ـ بِ ـ أَعْلَمَ ـ بِ ـ بِ . To give notice publicly, أَعْلَنَ بِ ـ نَادَى بِ ـ أَشْهَرَ .

Advertisement, *n.* Information, بِشَارَة ـ عِلْم ـ خَبَر . Admonition, نَصِيحَة ـ تَنْبِيه ـ إِنْذَار . Public notice, إِعْلَان ـ مُنَادَاة ـ إِشْهَار .

Advertiser, *n.* A proclaimer, مُنَادٍ ـ مُبَاشِر . An — through the press, مُنَادٍ بِأَغْرَاضِهِ فِي ٱلصَّحَائِفِ ٱلْمَطْبُوعَةِ .

Advice, *n.* Counsel, رَأْي ـ نَصِيحَة ـ مَشُورَة . Reflection, إِتْقَان ـ تَفَكُّر ـ تَأَمُّل . Intelligence, بِشَارَة ـ عِلْم ـ خَبَر . To give — to, أَشَارَ عَلَى ـ بِ . To ask — of, إِسْتَشَارَ ـ إِسْتَشَارَ ـ مِن ـ فِي . To give good — to, ءِ مَحَضَ ـ نُصْحًا ـ نَصَحَ . To take one's —, أَصْغَى إِلَى ـ أَنْصَتَ إِلَى . They took — of each other (of two), تَشَاوَرَا . A letter of —, خبر نامه ـ مَكْتُوبُ خَبَرٍ . They were tired of giving him —, كَلُّوا مِنَ ٱلنَّصِيحَةِ لَهُ .

Advisable, *adj.* أَخْيَر ـ أَوْفَق ـ وَمِمَّا يَلِيقُ ـ مُنَاسِب . To deem —, إِسْتَحْسَنَ ـ ءِ لَاقَ عِنْدَ .

Advisableness, *n.* مُوَافَقَة ـ مُلَاءَمَة ـ مُنَاسَبَة .

Advise, *v.t.* To counsel, نَبَّهَ عَلَى ـ ٤ نَصَحَ ـ أَشَارَ عَلَى ـ بِ ـ وَعَظَ ـ بِ *aor.* يَعِظُ . To inform of, أَخْبَرَ ـ بِ ـ أَعْلَمَ ـ بِ ـ أَفَادَ ـ عَرَّفَ ـ بِ .

Advise, *v.i.* To consult with, تَشَاوَرَ مَعَ ـ شَاوَرَ ; to deliberate, إِعْتَبَرَ ـ تَأَمَّلَ .

Advised, *a.* Well —, prudent, فَطِين ـ لَبِيب ـ مُنْتَبِهٌ . Ill —, imprudent, غافِل ـ غَبِيٌّ . Be — by me, أَنْصِتْ إِلَيَّ ـ إِسْمَعْ ـ كَلامِي .

Advisedly, *ad.* Prudently, بِعَقْلٍ ـ بِتَعَقُّلٍ ـ بِمَشُورَةٍ . Designedly, بِٱلْقَصْدِ ـ قَصْدًا ـ عَمْدًا .

Advocacy, *n.* مُباشَرَة ـ بَيان ـ مُحاجَجَة ـ مُحاماة .

Advocate, *n.* In a court of law, وَكِيل *pl.* وُكَلآء ـ مُحامٍ ـ المُتَكَلِّمُ عَنْ صاحِبِ ٱلدَّعْوَى أَمامَ ٱلقاضِي ـ وَكِيلُ ٱلدَّعْوَى . A defender in general, مُجْتَهِدٌ فِي ـ مُجِدٌّ ـ حامٍ . The —, Christ, الشَّفِيعُ . Judge —, أَحَدُ مَأْمُورِي دِيوانِ ٱلحَرْبِ .

Advowson, *n.* الخِيرَةُ بِقَسٍّ وَإِقامَتُهُ فِي أَبْرَشِيَّةٍ .

Adytum, *n.* A secret chamber in a temple, حَرَمُ هَيْكَلٍ .

Adze, *n.* قَدُوم ـ سَفَن .

Aegis, *n.* Protection, حِمايَة ـ سِحْن .

Aërate, *v.t.* هاوَى ـ هَوَّى ـ شَرَّبَ بِهَوآء . Aërated, مُشَرَّب مُهَوَّآء ـ مُهَوًّى ـ بِٱلْهَوآء .

Aerial, *a.* فِي ٱلْهَوآءِ ـ جَوِّيٌّ ـ مِنَ ٱلْهَوآءِ ـ هَوائِيٌّ . Lofty, شامِخٌ ـ مُرْتَفِعٌ ـ عالٍ .

Aerie, *n.* *See* Eyry, *n.*

Aerolite, *n.* نَيازِك ـ حَجَرٌ ساقِطٌ مِنَ ٱلجَوِّ .

Aerology, *n.* عِلْمُ طَبَقاتِ ٱلْهَوآءِ ـ عِلْمُ ٱلْهَوآءِ .

Aereometer, *n.* مِيزانُ ٱلْهَوآءِ .

Aereometry, *n.* مَعْرِفَةُ (*or* صِناعَةُ) وَزْنِ ٱلْهَوآءِ .

Aeronaut, *n.* مُسافِرٌ فِي ٱلْهَوآءِ بِقُبَّةٍ غازِيَّةٍ ـ مُسافِرٌ فِي ٱلْهَوآءِ ـ مُسافِرٌ فِي مَرْكَبَةٍ هَوآئِيَّةٍ .

Aeronautics, *n.* عِلْمُ ٱلسَّفَرِ فِي ٱلْهَوآءِ .

Aerostat, *n.* An air balloon, مَرْكَبَةٌ هَوآئِيَّةٌ ـ قُبَّةٌ هَوآئِيَّةٌ .

Aesthetic, *a.* مِمَّا يَتَعَلَّقُ بِإِدْراكِ ٱلجَمِيلِ وَٱلحَسِينِ .

Aesthetics, *n.* عِلْمُ ٱلمَلاحَةِ وَٱلجَمالِ ـ عِلْمُ ٱلجَمِيلِ وَٱلحَسِينِ .

Afar, *ad.* بَعِيدًا ـ عَلَى بُعْدٍ . From afar, عَنْ بُعْدٍ ـ مِنْ بَعِيدٍ .

Affability, *n.* لُطْف ـ لَطافَة ـ حِلْم ـ رَأْفَة ـ مُلائَمَة ـ وَداعَة ـ بَشاشَة .

Affable, *a.* لَطِيف *pl.* لِطاف *and* لُطَفآء ـ خَيِّر ـ مُلائِم ـ حَلِيمٌ ـ أَنِيسُ ٱلطَّبْعِ ـ أَنِيس *fem.* آنِسَة *or* أَنِيسَة ـ بَشُوش ـ كَيِّس . To be — to, تَلَطَّفَ لِ .

Affably, *ad.* بِلُطْفٍ ـ بِمُلاءَمَةٍ ـ بِأُنْسٍ ـ أَنِيسًا ـ بِرِقَّةٍ .

Affair, *n.* أَمْر *pl.* أُمُور ـ مَصْلَحَة *pl.* مَصالِح ـ شُغْل *pl.* أَشْغال ـ مَشْغَلَة *pl.* مَشاغِل ـ قَضِيَّة *pl.* قَضايا ـ قِصَّة *pl.* قِصَص ـ باب *pl.* أَبْواب ـ حاجَة *pl.* حاجات . A battle, يَوْم *pl.* أَيّام ـ مُحارَبَة ـ وَقْعَة ـ قِتال . The public affairs, أُمُور ـ أُمُورُ ٱلدَّوْلَةِ ـ ٱلجُمْهُورِ . Your — is settled, قُضِيَ قَضاآؤُكَ ـ حاجَتُكَ مَقْضِيَّةٌ ـ قُضِيَتْ حاجَتُكَ . The — reached that state until . . . ., إِنْقَضَى ٱلحالُ إِلَى أَنْ . Secretary for Foreign Affairs, مُدَبِّرُ أُمُورِ ٱلخارِجِيَّةِ ـ كاتِمُ أَسْرارِ ٱلخارِجِيَّةِ . To be at the head of affairs, تَصَدَّرَ . As affairs stand, نَظَرًا لِلْحالِ ـ حَسَبَ ٱلحالِ .

Affect, *v.t.* To act upon, أَثَّرَ فِي ـ فَعَلَ فِي ـ عَمِلَ فِي ـ أَخَذَ فِي . To move, as the passions, هَيَّجَ ـ نَجَعَ فِي ـ حَرَّكَ . To aspire to, إِدَّعَى ـ بَغَى ـ إِبْتَغَى ـ نافَسَ فِي ـ تَرَشَّمَ لِ . To imitate, قَلَّدَ . To love, بَغَى ـ إِبْتَغَى ـ تَبَغَّى ـ وَدَّ ـ أَحَبَّ . To pretend, أَظْهَرَ ـ صَوَّرَ ـ تَصَنَّعَ فِي ـ أَوْهَمَ بِ ـ عَلَى نَفْسِهِ ـ حَذْلَقَ . To strive after, رَغِبَ فِي . To infect, خالَطَ ـ خامَرَ . To go to annul, أَلْغَى ـ جَرَّحَ . To —, attack, as a pain, نَصَبَ ـ أَنْصَبَ ـ أَصابَ . To — eloquence, تَبالَغَ ; anger, تَغاضَبَ ـ تَغَضَّبَ ـ أَظْهَرَ ٱلْغَضَبَ ; ignorance, تَجاهَلَ ; sickness, تَمارَضَ . To — with grief, غَمَّ ـ أَلَّمَ ; with joy, أَفْرَحَ ـ فَرَّحَ ـ سَرَّ .

Affectation, *n.* } Artificial show, تَكَلُّف ـ تَصَنُّع ـ تَخَيُّل ـ
Affectedness, } تَظاهُر ـ مُباهاة ـ حِيلَة ـ تَحَذْلُق ـ حَذْلَقَة .

Affectation in speech, تَفَصُّح ; of superior etiquette, تَظَرُّف ـ تَكَيُّس ; of high parentage, تَفاخُر بِنَسَبِ ٱلجُدُودِ . Conceit, عُجْب . Cant, حَمِيَّة .

Affected, *part.* and *a.* Moved, مُحَرَّك . Pretended, مُمَوَّه . Studied with overmuch care, مُتَباهٍ ـ مُصَنَّع ـ مُبالِغ . Conceited, مُتَشَبِّع ـ مُتَكَبِّر ـ زاخِف ـ زَخِيف ـ مُعْجَب (*or* مُعْتَدّ) بِنَفْسِهِ . To be —, of affectation, تَصَلَّفَ ; as by a disease, أُصِيبَ بِ . To be well — towards, عَطَفَ عَلَى ـ تَعَطَّفَ عَلَى . To be — with grief or pain, تَأَلَّمَ ـ إِنْغَمَّ ; with joy, فَرِحَ ـ سُرَّ . To walk with an — gait, أَبْزَى ـ تَمَطَّطَ ـ تَبَخْتَرَ . Affected, as with illness, مُصابٌ بِ . An — woman, إِمْرَأَةٌ مُتَكَيِّسَةٌ ـ إِمْرَأَةٌ مُتَحَذْلِقَةٌ . *See also* Finical, *a.*

Affectedly, *ad.* بِمُباهاةٍ ـ بِتَصَنُّعٍ ـ بِتَخَيُّلٍ ـ بِتَحَذْلُقٍ .

Affecting, *a.* Touching the feelings, مُحَنِّن ـ مُرِقٌّ (*or* مُحَرِّكٌ) لِلْقَلْبِ .

Affectingly, *ad.* بِتَحَنُّنٍ .

Affection, *n.* Passion for anything, عاطِفَة ـ شَهْوَة ـ مَيْل ـ هَوًى ـ إِنْجِذاب ـ رَغْبَة ـ عَلاقَة ـ شَوْق . Love, مَوَدَّة ـ إِلْفَة ـ عِشْق ـ مَحَبَّة ـ مَيْل ـ خُلَّة . Tenderness, حُنُوّ ـ حَنان ـ حِنَّة . State of the body, مِزاج ـ طَبْع . A disease, دآء ـ عِلَّة ـ مَرَض .

The affections, اَلْأَشْوَاقُ . Mutual —, مُحَبَّةٌ مُتَشَارِكَةٌ ـ مُحَابَّةٌ . . To manifest — for, تَوَدَّدَ إِلَى ـ تَحَبَّبَ إِلَى . To gain the affections of, تَوَدَّدَ .

Affectionate, *a.* مُحِبٌّ ـ حَنُون ـ رَقِيق ـ وَدُود ـ مُودٌّ .

Affectionately, *ad.* بِمُحَبَّةٍ ـ بِودادٍ .

Affectionated, *a.* Inclined to, رَاغِبٌ فِي ـ مَائِلٌ إِلَى . Well — towards, حَانٌّ إِلَى ـ رَاغِبٌ فِي ـ مُرْتَاحٌ إِلَى . Ill — towards, رَاغِبٌ عَنْ .

Affiance, *n.* Marriage contract, شَبْكَةُ ٱلزَّوَاجِ ـ خِطْبَةٌ . Trust, إِعْتِقَاد ـ إِعْتِمَاد ـ إِتِّكَال ـ عِوَل ـ تَعْوِيل . To have — in God, تَوَكَّلَ عَلَى ٱللّٰهِ .

Affiance, *v.t.* شَبَكَ ـ بِٱلزِّيجَةِ ـ [2] خَطَبَ . Affianced, مَخْطُوب *fem.* مَخْطُوبَة .

Affiancer, *n.* خَاطِب ـ خَطَّاب .

Affidavit, *n.* تَصْرِيحٌ بِٱلْحَلْفِ ـ قَسَم . To make an — to, أَقْسَمَ ـ عَلَى . To require an — from, أَكَّدَ ـ بِٱلْحَلْفِ ـ أَنْ ـ ب .

Affiliate, *v.t.* To receive into a society, أَشْرَكَ ـ أَرْفَقَ . *See also to* Adopt, *v.t.*

Affiliated, *a.* مُقْتَرِنٌ بِ ـ مُشْتَرِكٌ مَعَ . *See also* Adopted, *a.*

Affiliation, *n.* The act of, تَشْرِيك ; the being affiliated, شِرْكَة ـ إِقْتِرَان ـ تَعَلُّق . *See also* Adoption, *n.*

Affinity, *n.* Relationship, أَهْلِيَّة ـ مُصَاهَرَة ـ نَسَابَة ـ قَرَابَة . Connection, as between things, إِضَافَة ـ مُجَانَسَة ـ مُقَارَبَة ـ مُنَاسَبَة .

Affirm, *v.t.* حَقَّقَ ـ ثَبَّتَ ـ قَرَّرَ ـ أَكَّدَ .

Affirm, *v.i.* شَهِدَ ـ جَزَمَ بِ ـ صَرَّحَ بِ ـ أَوْجَبَ ـ إِسْتَقَرَّ .

Affirmable, *a.* مِمَّا يُؤَكَّدُ ـ يَثْبُتُ فِي ـ يُقَالُ عَنْ .

Affirmation, *n.* The act of declaring, تَصْرِيح ـ تَعْرِيف ـ إِقْرَار ـ تَأْكِيد ـ قَوْل ـ إِيضَاح ـ إِشْهَار ـ إِيجَاب . Confirmation, إِثْبَات .

Affirmative, *a.* تَحْقِيقِيٌّ ـ تَعْرِيفِيٌّ ـ تَصْدِيقِيٌّ ـ إِيجَابِيٌّ . An — proposition, قَضِيَّةٌ مُوجِبَةٌ ـ كَلَامٌ مُوجَبٌ ـ كَلَامٌ مُثْبَتٌ . An — particle, حَرْفُ إِيجَابٍ . To answer in the —, نَعَمَ بِ . They replied in the —, أَجَابُوا بِٱلْإِيجَابِ .

Affirmatively, *ad.* بِٱلتَّأْكِيدِ ـ إِيجَابًا . Affirmatively and negatively, إِيجَابًا وَسَلْبًا .

Affirmer, *n.* مُحَقِّق ـ مُثْبِت .

Affix, *v.t.* To subjoin, أَلْزَمَ ـ بِ ـ وَصَلَ ـ بِ ـ أَضَافَ ـ إِلَى . To — a meaning to, شَرَحَ ـ فَسَّرَ . To be affixed to, إِنْضَافَ إِلَى .

Affix, *n.* مَوْصُول ـ وَصْلَة .

Afflation, *n.* نَفْخ .

Afflatus, *n.* Inspiration, إِلْهَام ـ وَحْي ـ رُوح .

Afflict, *v.t.* To cause grief to, أَكْرَبَ ـ أَحْزَنَ ـ [2] غَمَّ ـ أَهَمَّ . To torment, عَذَّبَ ـ أَبْلَى ـ أَضَرَّ ـ آذَى . God afflicted him with . . . , رَمَاهُ ٱللّٰهُ بِ . To — with pain, أَوْجَعَ .

Afflicted, *a.* مُضْطَرِب ـ مَحْزُون ـ مَكْرُوب . To be — with, as with a disease, أُصِيبَ بِ . To be —, agitated, كَدِرَ ـ إِضْطَرَبَ . Afflicted with, as with a disease, مُصَابٌ بِ . To be —, in pain, تَوَجَّعَ .

Afflictedness, *n.* } Grief, بَلَاءٌ ـ كَآبَة ـ شِدَّة ـ غَمّ ـ حُزْن . An
Affliction, } —, مُصِيبَة *pl.* مَصَائِبُ ـ بَلِيَّة *pl.* بَلَايَا ـ مَشَقَّة ـ شَقَاوَة ـ ضِيقَة . Pain, وَجَع *pl.* أَوْجَاع . Torment, أَذَاة ـ بَلْوَة ـ ضَرَّة . She had much —, كَانَ بِهَا هَمٌّ زَائِدٌ .

Afflictive, *a.* مُوحِش ـ مُؤْذٍ ـ مُعَذِّب ـ مُحْزِن ـ مُغِمّ ـ مُؤْلِم .

Affluence, *n.* Flow of water, سَيَلَان ـ سَيْل . Concourse, إِجْتِمَاع . Wealth, دَوْلَة ـ مَال ـ غَنَاء . Abundance, جِدّ ـ نِعْمَة ـ غَضَر ـ غَضَارَة ـ ثَرْوَة ـ كَثْرَة . Easy circumstances, سَعَةُ ٱلْعَيْشِ . To live in —, تَنَعَّمَ .

Affluent, *a.* Flowing to, يَصُبُّ فِي ـ جَارٍ إِلَى . Wealthy, صَاحِبُ مَالٍ وَافِرٍ ـ مُتَمَوِّل ـ ذُو مَالٍ ـ غَنِيّ . Abundant, وَافِر ـ كَثِير ـ فَائِض ـ مَغْضُور ـ نَهِير .

Affluent, *n.* A stream flowing into a river, رَافِد *pl.* رَوَافِدُ . A river with two affluents, نَهْرٌ لَهُ رَافِدَانِ .

Afford, *v.t.* To yield, as of produce, أَغَلَّ ـ أَثْمَرَ . To produce, generally, أَصْدَرَ ـ أَخْرَجَ ـ وَلَّدَ ـ أَنْتَجَ . To give, وَهَبَ *aor.* يَهَبُ ـ أَعْطَى ـ أَدَّى . To be able to bear, as of expense, قَدَرَ عَلَى ـ [2] قَدَرَ عَلَى نَفَقَةٍ .

Affranchise, *v.t.* أَعْتَقَ ـ أَطْلَقَ ـ خَلَّصَ ـ نَجَّى ـ مِنْ .

Affray, *n.* غَوْغَاءٌ ـ ضَجَّة ـ لَغَط ـ غَاغَة ـ رَجَّة ـ إِرْتِجَاج ـ هَوْشَة .

Affreight, *n.* *See* Freight, *n.*

Affright, *v.t.* فَزَّعَ ـ خَوَّفَ ـ أَرْعَبَ ـ رَعَّبَ . *See also to* Frighten, *v.t.*

Affright, *n.* رُعْب ـ خَضَّة ـ رَجْفَة .

Affront, *v.t.* To insult, سَخِرَ بِ ـ هَزَأَ مِنْ ـ بِ ـ [2] هَجَا ـ أَجْبَهَ ـ عَيَّبَ ـ [2] شَتَمَ ـ بَغَى عَلَى ـ أَسَاءَ إِلَى .

Affront, *n.* إِهَانَة ـ فَضِيحَة ـ مَلَامَة ـ هَتْك ـ أَسَاءَة ـ هَجْو ـ طَعْنَة ـ عَيْب .

Affronter, *n.* } هَاتِك ـ شَتَّام ـ ذَامّ ـ مُفْضِح .
Affronting, *a.* }

Affuse, *v.t.* To pour, سَكَبَ 2 ـ صَبَّ 2 ـ كَبَّ 2. To sprinkle, رَشَّ 2.

Affusion, *n.* صَبٌّ ـ إِنْصِبابٌ ـ إِنْسِكابٌ. Sprinkling, رَشٌّ ـ تَرْشاشٌ.

Afield, *ad.* فِي ٱلْخَلَاءِ ـ فِي ٱلْفَضاءِ.

Afire, *ad.* مُتَّقِدٌ ـ مُحْتَرِقٌ ـ مُضْطَرِمٌ ـ مُشْتَعِلٌ.

Afloat, *ad.* On the surface of the water, عَلَى وَجْهِ ٱلْمَاءِ. At sea, فِي ٱلْبَحْرِ. Current, شائِعٌ ـ رائِجٌ ـ دارِجٌ. To get —, to become known, ذاعَ ـ شاعَ.

Afoot, *ad.* On foot, ماشٍ ـ رَجْلًا. Current, شائِعٌ ـ دارِجٌ. To set —, to initiate, إِبْتَدَأَ بِ ـ باشَرَ ـ أَنْشَأَ ـ إِخْتَرَعَ ـ شَرَعَ فِي. To be set —, شُرِعَ فِي. To go —, مَشَى. They ran —, جَرَوا (*or* تَراكَضُوا) مُشاةً.

Afore, *ad.* قِدْمًا ـ سَبْقًا ـ قُدّامٌ ـ قَبْلُ.

Aforegoing, *a.* سابِقٌ ـ سالِفٌ ـ مُتَقَدِّمٌ.

Aforementioned,
Aforenamed, *a.*
Aforesaid,
} سالِفُ ٱلذِّكْرِ ـ مَذْكُورٌ آنِفًا ـ مَذْكُورٌ أَعْلاهُ ـ مُومَا إِلَيْهِ ـ مُشارٌ إِلَيْهِ. As aforesaid, كَما قَدْ ذُكِرَ.

Aforetime, *ad.* مُقَدَّمًا ـ سَبْقًا ـ فِي قَدِيمِ ٱلزَّمانِ.

A fortiori, *ad.* بِٱلْحَرِى ـ بِٱلْأَجْدَرِ ـ بِٱلْأَحْرَى ـ بِٱلْأَوْلَى.

Afraid, *a.* خائِفٌ ـ فَزْعانُ ـ رَعُوبٌ ـ مَرْعُوبٌ ـ مُشْفِقٌ ـ زَعِيقٌ ـ خِيفٌ. To be —, أَشْفَقَ ـ خافَ ـ وَخِفَ ـ فَزِعَ ـ إِرْتَعَبَ. To make —, أَفْزَعَ ـ أَرْعَبَ ـ رَعَّبَ. Do not ye be —, لا تَجْزَعُوا ـ لا خَوْفَ عَلَيْكُمْ.

Afresh, *ad.* ثانِي مَرَّةٍ ـ أَيْضًا ـ تَكْرارًا ـ ثانِيًا ـ مِنْ جَدِيدٍ.

Aft, *ad.* إِلَى مُؤَخَّرِ ٱلْمَرْكَبِ.

After, *prep.* and *ad.* Position in time, مِنْ بَعْدِ ـ بَعْدَ ـ غِبَّ ـ عُقْبَ. According to, تَبَعَ ـ حَسْبَما ـ بِحَسَبِ ـ عَلَى مُقْتَضَى. Behind, خَلْفَ ـ وَرَاءَ. After that, then, مِنْ بَعْدِ ـ بَعْدَ ذٰلِكَ ـ وَمَعَ ذٰلِكَ ـ أَمَّا بَعْدُ ـ مِنْ ثُمَّ ـ ثُمَّ ـ ذٰلِكَ. After all, أَخِيرًا ـ بَعْدَ هٰذا كُلِّهِ. To do —, to imitate, إِمْتَثَلَ بِ. To go —, لَحِقَ. To be —, to design, تَعَزَّمَ ـ تَعَمَّدَ. He remained — him, لَبِثَ خَلْفَهُ. He came — him, جاءَ خَلْفَهُ. The people came one — another, جاءَ ٱلْقَوْمُ عُرْفًا عُرْفًا. I came to him — his arrival, جِئْتُهُ عُقْبَ قُدُومِهِ. Call — to-morrow, إِرْجِعْ بَعْدَ غَدًا.

After-ages, *n.* المُسْتَقْبِلُ ـ الزَّمانُ ٱلْآتِى ـ الدُّهُورُ ٱلْآتِيَةُ.

Afterbirth, *n.* حَصِيرَةٌ ـ غِرْسٌ ـ هِتْكٌ ـ مَشِيمَةٌ ـ عَذَبٌ.

Afternoon, *n.* Just after noon, بَعْدَ ٱلظُّهْرِ. Somewhat later in the —, العَصْرُ ـ الرَّواحُ ـ الرَّياحُ. Good — to you! نَهارُكَ سَعِيدٌ. He should return this —, عَلَيْهِ أَنْ يَعُودَ بَعْدَ ٱلظُّهْرِ.

After-pains, *n.* مَغْصٌ بَعْدَ ٱلْوِلادَةِ.

After-piece, *n.* عُقْبَ ـ لُعْبَةٌ فِي ٱلتِّياتْرُو عُقْبَ ٱللُّعْبَةِ ٱلْكَبِيرَةِ ـ فُصُولُ ٱلْمَلْهَى.

Afterwards, *ad.* ثُمَّ ـ بَعْدُ. *See* After, *ad.*

Again, *ad.* A second time, مَرَّةً ثانِيَةً ـ أَيْضًا ـ مِنْ جَدِيدٍ ـ تَكْرارًا ـ كَمانْ. On the other hand, بِخِلافِ ذٰلِكَ ـ أَيْضًا ـ ثانِيًا. Besides, وَأَعْظَمُ مِنْ ذٰلِكَ ـ ما عَدا ذٰلِكَ. Again and —, مِرارًا كَثِيرَةً ـ جُمْلَةَ مِرارٍ ـ مِرارًا ـ مَرَّةً عَنْ مَرَّةٍ ـ تَكْرارًا. It may happen —, رُبَّما يَحْدُثُ مَرَّةً أُخْرَى ـ كَثِيرًا ما. To give back —, رَدَّ 2. To answer —, رَدَّ جَوابًا 2. To do anything —, كَرَّرَ ـ أَعادَ ـ ثَنَّى.

Against, *prep.* In opposition to, خِلافًا لِ ـ مُعارَضَةً ـ مُقاوَمَةً ـ عَلَى ـ ضِدَّ. Opposite, مُقابِلُ. Against the wall, فِي ٱلْحائِطِ. For and — me, مَعِى وَعَلَيَّ. They revolted — him, قامُوا عَلَيْهِ ـ عَصَوْهُ. Against his opinion, ضِدَّ رَأْيِهِ ـ بِخِلافِ رَأْيِهِ. Against the grain, عَلَى ٱلْقَلَمِ ـ كُرْهًا ـ بِٱلْعَكْسِ.

Agape, *adv.* فاتِحُ ٱلْحَنَكِ.

Agaric, *n.* الغارِيقُونُ ـ الأَغارِيقُونُ.

Agate, *n.* عَقِيقٌ يَمانِيٌّ ـ حَجَرٌ يَمانِيٌّ.

Age, *n.* Duration of life, حَيٰوةٌ ـ حَياةٌ ـ سِنٌّ ـ عُمْرٌ. The time in which a particular generation lived, عَصْرٌ ـ زَمانٌ ـ أَوانٌ ـ عَهْدٌ ـ دَوْرٌ ـ دَهْرٌ ـ قَرْنٌ. Oldness, عِتْقٌ. Tender —, سِنٌّ حَدَثٌ ـ صُغْرٌ ـ نُعُومَةُ أَظْفارٍ ـ حَداثَةٌ ـ الطُّفُولِيَّةُ. Age, as of a lad, البُلُوغُ. Age, as of a youth, شُبُوبِيَّةٌ ـ الشَّبابُ. Mature —, الكُبْرُ ـ الشَّيْخُوخِيَّةُ ـ الشَّيْخُوخَةُ ـ الكُهُولِيَّةُ ـ كَمالُ ٱلسِّنِّ. Old —, الكُهُولِيَّةُ. Of the same —, born at the same time, قِرْنٌ ـ اتْرابٌ تِرْبٌ *pl.* قِرانٌ أَقْرانٌ *pl.* A succession or generation of men, جِيلٌ *pl.* أَجْيالٌ. An iron —, أَيّامُ نَحْسٍ ـ أَيّامُ ظَلامٍ ـ أَيّامُ جَهالَةٍ. A golden —, أَيّامُ تَرَقٍّ ـ أَيّامُ عِزٍّ. He died about fifty years of —, ماتَ وَعُمْرُهُ نَحْوَ خَمْسِينَ سَنَةً. An — passed over him, مَضَى عَلَيْهِ دَهْرٌ. He is of my —, هُوَ عَلَى قَرْنِى. The man of the —, فَرِيدُ ـ واحِدُ دَهْرِهِ ـ نادِرَةُ ٱلزَّمانِ ـ عَصْرِهِ. Throughout all ages, إِلَى دَهْرِ ٱلدّاهِرِينَ ـ إِلَى أَبَدِ ٱلْآبِدِينَ. The Middle Ages, القُرُونُ ـ الأَجْيالُ ٱلْمُتَوَسِّطَةُ ٱلْمُتَوَسِّطَةُ.

Age, *v.i.* عَجَزَ ـ هَرِمَ ـ أَسَنَّ ـ شاخَ ـ بَدَّنَ.

Aged, *a.* Of age, طاعِنُ ٱلسِّنِّ ـ مُطْعِنٌ فِي ٱلسِّنِّ ـ شَيْخٌ ـ كَبِيرٌ فِي ٱلْعُمْرِ. Old, of articles, عَتِيقٌ. A middle-aged woman,

مُسْلِف. To grow —, طَعَنَ فِى ٱلسِّنِّ — أَسَنَّ — إِسْتَنَّ — كَبِرَ — تَشَيَّخَ.

Agency, *n.* Action, فاعِلِيَّة — عَمَل — فِعْل. The office of an agent, نِيابَة — وَكالَة.

Agenda, *n.* أَعْمال — تَعَلُّقات.

Agent, *n.* An actor, فاعِل — شَرِيكٌ فِى ٱلْعَمَلِ *pl.* شُرَكاءُ. A deputy, وَكِيل *pl.* وُكَلاءُ — نائِب. A factor, عامِل *pl.* عُمَّال — عَمِيل *pl.* عُمَلاءُ — مُجِيز. That which aids in producing, فاعِلٌ مَع — مُساعِدٌ فِى. A commercial —, وَكِيلُ تِجارَةٍ. A political —, مَأْمُور سِياسِىّ. A consular —, أَجَنْت. An — of the police, مَأْمُور ٱلضَّبْطِيَّة.

Agglomerate, *v.t.* *See to* Conglomerate, *v.t.*

Agglutinate, *v.t.* *See to* Glue, *v.t.*

Aggrandize, *v.t.* To exalt, شَرَّفَ — فَخَّمَ — عَظَّمَ. To enlarge, وَسَّعَ — كَبَّرَ.

Aggrandizement, *n.* The act of —, تَشْرِيف — تَفْخِيم — تَعْظِيم; state of, شَرَف — تَشَرُّف — تَعَظُّم. Enlargement, تَكْبِير — تَوْسِيع — زِيادَة.

Aggravate, *v.t.* To make heavy, ثَقَّلَ — شَدَّدَ — زادَ فِى. To make worse, أَضَرَّ — أَذَى. To vex, أَغاظَ — أَغْضَبَ. Aggravating circumstances, ظُرُوف مُثَقِّلَة — أَسْبابٌ مُشَدِّدَة.

Aggravation, *n.* A load, weight, بَهْظ — تَثْقِيل — تَشَدُّد. Vexation, ضُجْرَة — ضَجَر — تَصْدِيع.

Aggregate, *v.t.* ضَمَّ — جَمَّعَ — لَمَّ — كَوَّمَ — كَرْدَسَ.

Aggregate, *a.* مُجْمَل — مَضْمُوم — مَجْمُوع. An — sum, بَدْرَة — بَدْرَة مُبَدْرَة.

Aggregate, *n.* جُمْلَة — ضَمِيمَة — مَجْمُوع — جَمْع — مُعْظَم. In the —, جِمارًا — كَرْدَسَةً.

Aggregation, *n.* The act of collecting, جَمْع — ضَمّ — تَجْمِيع; the mass collected, جُمْلَة — مَجْمُوع — ضَمِيمَة.

Aggression, *n.* هُجُوم — إِقْدام — مُباداةٌ بِٱلشَّرِّ — تَجاوُز — تَعَدّ.

Aggressive, *a.* هَجُوم — قَدُوم — مُتَجاوِز — مُتَعَدّ.

Aggressor, *n.* مُتَجاوِز — مِيناف — البادِئُ بِٱلشَّرِّ — مُعْتَدٍ — البادِئ. This for that, but the — is most to blame (*prov.*), هَذِهِ بِتِلْكَ وَٱلْبادِئُ أَظْلَمُ.

Aggrieve, *v.t.* To grieve, أَحْزَنَ — أَغَمَّ. To injure, ظَلَمَ — تَعَدَّى عَلَى — قاهَرَ — أَذَى.

Agha, *n.* A lord, a chief, أَغا *pl.* أَغاوات.

Aghast, *ad.* حَيْران — مُتَحَيِّر — مَدْهُوش. To stand —, تَحَيَّرَ — إِنْدَهَشَ.

Agile, *a.* نَشِيط — نَدْب — سَرِيع *pl.* سُرْعان; *fem.* سَرِيعَة *pl.* سِراع — خَفِيف — شَوِل — حَرِك — شَمْلُول — خَفِيفُ ٱلْحَرَكَةِ.

Agileness, *n.* / Agility, مُرُوَّة — شَمْلَلَة — نَشاط — خِفَّة — سُرْعَة — شَوْل — شَهامَة.

Agio, *n.* صَرَّافَة — بِشْتَخْتَة — صَرّافِيَّة.

Agitate, *v.t.* To shake, قَلْقَلَ — زَعْزَعَ — حَرَّكَ — هَزَّزَ — رَجَّ. To disquiet, أَهَمَّ — أَحَمَّ — قَلْقَلَ — أَقْلَقَ — إِسْتَخَفَّ — تَرْتَرَ. To shake, as of water, خَضْخَضَ — خَضَّ. To discuss, بَحَثَ — فَحَصَ فِى. To stir up, as of a people, قَوَّمَ — هَيَّجَ. To — one's self, هاجَ — تَقَلْقَلَ — إِضْطَرَبَ. To be agitated, flurried, خَفَّ.

Agitated, *a.* Shaken, مُحَرَّك — مُرْتَجّ. Disquieted, مُضْطَرِب — تَقَلْقَلَ — مُقَلْقَل — مُهْتَمّ. To be —, disquieted, أَحِمَّ — إِهْتَمَّ — تَقَلْقَلَ — إِضْطَرَبَ — تَخَبَّطَ. A question that is being —, أَمْرٌ مَبْحُوثٌ عَنْهُ.

Agitation, *n.* The act of moving, زَعْزَعَة — هَزَّة — تَحْرِيك; of liquids, خَضّ. The state of being moved, حَرَكَة — رَجَّة — إِهْتِزاز. Disquietude, حَيْرَة — رَجْفَة — قَلْقَلَة — قَلَق — كَرْب — هَمّ — إِضْطِراب. Discussion, مُباحَثَة — فَحْص — مُفاحَصَة. Under —, inquiry, تَحْتَ ٱلْفَحْصِ — مَبْحُوثٌ عَنْهُ.

Agitator, *n.* A mover, مُحَرِّك. A stirrer up of the people, مُهَيِّج — زارِعُ ٱلْفَسادِ — رامِى ٱلْفِتَنِ — مُفَتِّن — مُقْلِق — فاتِن — مُفْسِد — ضَرّابُ فِتَنٍ. An — of a question, مُفاحِص — مُباحِث.

Agnail, *n.* داحُوس.

Agnate, *n.* نَسَبٌ بِٱلطُّولِ أَى مِنْ صُلْبِ ٱلْأَبِ.

Agnation, *n.* صَلِيبِيَّة — نَسَبِيَّةٌ أَبَوِيَّة — قَرابَةٌ مِنْ ناحِيَةِ ٱلْأَبِ.

Agnomen, *n.* لَقَب *pl.* أَلْقاب.

Agnus Castus, *n.* حَبُّ ٱلْفَقْدِ — كَفُّ مَرْيَمَ — بَنْجَكُسْت.

Ago, *ad.* سَلَفَ — مُدَّ زَمانٍ. Long ago, مُنْذُ زَمَنٍ طَوِيلٍ. Two days ago, مُنْذُ يَوْمَيْنِ. A year ago, مُنْذُ سَنَةٍ. A short time ago, مِنْ مُدَّةٍ يَسِيرَةٍ.

Agog, *ad.* مُشْتاق — مُتَرَقِّب — مُشْتَهٍ. To set — for or about, حَرَّضَ عَلَى — حَضَّ عَلَى — أَغْرَى بِ.

Agoing, *ad.* ماشٍ — سائِر — رائِح.

Agone, *ad.* *See* Ago, *ad.*

Agonize, *v.i.* نَزَعَ — ساقَ — كانَ فِى ٱلنَّزْعِ — إِحْتَمَلَ ٱلْآلامَ ٱلشَّدِيدَةَ.

Agonize, *v.t.* عَذَّبَ.

Agonizing, *a.* أَلِيم — مُعَذِّب — مُنازِع.

Agony, *n.* The pains of death, نَزْع — نَزْعُ ٱلْمَوْتِ — سِياق — الرَّوْق — سَكْرَةُ ٱلْمَوْتِ. Violent pain, أَلَمٌ شَدِيدٌ.

Agrarian, *a.* مُتَعَلِّقٌ بِتَقْسِيمِ ٱلْأَمْلَاكِ بَيْنَ ٱلْجُمْهُورِ عَلَى سَوِيَّةٍ ـ حَقْلِيٌّ.

Agree, *v.i.* To be in accord, إِجْتَمَعَ عَلَى ـ إِتَّحَدَ ـ إِتَّفَقَ ـ أَجْمَعَ عَلَى. To — to, to admit, أَقَرَّ بِ ـ سَلَّمَ بِ ـ قَبِلَ. To settle with by stipulation, رَبَطَ ـ شَارَطَ-عَلَى ـ رَضِيَ بِ. To suit with, صَلَحَ لِ ـ لَبِقَ لِ ـ لَاقَ بِ ـ وَافَقَ ـ مَعَ-أَنْ. Not to injure, لَا يَضُرُّ. To make to —, suit, وَفَّقَ ـ أَصْلَحَ. They agreed upon, أَجْمَعُوا عَلَى ـ إِتَّفَقُوا عَلَى. This food does not — with me, هٰذَا ٱلطَّعَامُ لَا يُلَائِمُنِي.

Agreeable, *a.* Suitable to, مُوَافِقٌ لِ ـ لَائِقٌ بِ ـ مُنَاسِبٌ لِ ـ مُلَائِمٌ. Acceptable, حَسَنٌ ـ مَقْبُولٌ. An — man, رَجُلٌ لَطِيفٌ ـ رَجُلٌ بَشُوشٌ ـ رَجُلٌ أَنِيسٌ. An — place, مَكَانٌ نَزِيهٌ ـ مُنْتَزَهَةٌ ـ مَكَانٌ مَأْنُوسٌ ـ مَوْضِعٌ شَرِحٌ. To be — towards, تَلَطَّفَ لِ. I am —, willing, أَنَا رَاضٍ. My mind was — to it, طَابَتْ نَفْسِي ـ إِرْتَاحَتْ لَهُ ـ عَلَيْهِ.

Agreeableness, *n.* Conformity, مُشَاكَلَةٌ ـ مُوَافَقَةٌ ـ مُطَابَقَةٌ. Quality of pleasing, بَشَاشَةٌ ـ ظَرَافَةٌ ـ لُطْفٌ ـ لَطَافَةٌ.

Agreeably, *ad.* Consistently with, عَلَى مُوجَبِ ـ مُنَاسَبَةً لِ ـ بِمُوجَبِ ـ بِمُقْتَضَى ـ نَحْوَ. Pleasingly, حَسَنًا ـ لِيَاقَةً ـ عَلَى طَيِّبَةٍ ـ بِلُطْفٍ ـ بِسُرُورٍ ـ بِظَرَافَةٍ. Agreeably with your orders, عَلَى مُوجَبِ أَوَامِرِكَ. Agreeably to or with, بِنَاءً عَلَى.

Agreed, *a.* Settled upon, مَعْهُودٌ ـ مُتَّفَقٌ عَلَيْهِ.

Agreement, *n.* Concord, وُدٌّ ـ إِتِّحَادٌ ـ مُوَافَقَةٌ ـ وِفَاقٌ ـ وَفْقٌ ـ أُلْفَةٌ. Resemblance, مُنَاسَبَةٌ ـ مُطَابَقَةٌ ـ مُشَابَهَةٌ. A compact, قَوْلٌ ـ مِيثَاقٌ ـ عَهْدٌ *pl.* عُهُودٌ ـ عَقْدٌ ـ شَرْطٌ *pl.* شُرُوطٌ. To enter into an — with, وَاثَقَ-بِ ـ عَاهَدَ ـ تَعَاهَدَ مَعَ. He broke the —, نَكَثَ ٱلْعَهْدَ ـ خَانَ ٱلْعَهْدَ. They entered into a mutual —, تَرَاضَوْا. If they wished to come to an — about..., لَوْ رَادُوا أَنْ يَتَوَاطَأُوا عَلَى.

Agricultural, *a.* مُتَعَلِّقٌ بِٱلْفَلَاحَةِ. Agricultural products, مَحْصُولَاتٌ زِرَاعِيَّةٌ.

Agriculture, *n.* فَلَاحَةٌ ـ حِرَاثَةُ ٱلْأَرْضِ ـ عِلْمُ ٱلْفَلَاحَةِ.

Agriculturist, *n.* فَلَّاحٌ *pl.* فَلَّاحُونَ ـ حَرَّاثٌ *pl.* حُرَّاثٌ ـ خَبِيرٌ بِٱلْفَلَاحَةِ.

Agrimony, *n.* غَافِثٌ ـ حَافِلٌ ـ نَبَاتٌ طِبِّيٌّ.

Aground, *ad.* Stranded, مُشَطَّطٌ ـ مَصْدُومٌ ـ مَلْطُومٌ. Hindered, مَوْقُوفٌ ـ مَمْنُوعٌ. The ship ran —, جَانَحَتِ ٱلسَّفِينَةُ. They ran the ship —, شَطَّطُوا ٱلسَّفِينَةَ ـ بَلَّطُوا ٱلسَّفِينَةَ.

Ague, *n.* بَرْدَاءُ ـ بُرَدِيَّةٌ ـ حُمَّى ـ سُخُونَةٌ.

Ah! *int.* Exclamation of compassion, آخ ـ آه ـ آح ـ آحو ـ آوه ـ أَنَّ ـ أَيَا ـ أَيْهَا.

Aha! *int.* Exclamation of contempt, أَفًّا ـ أُفٍّ ـ أُفٌّ ـ أَقًّا وَتُفًّا.

Ahead, *ad.* قُدَّام ـ سَبْقًا. To get — of, سَبَقَ. To be —, in excellence, *etc.* نَبَغَ ـ بَرَعَ.

Aid, *n.* مَدَدٌ ـ نُصْرَةٌ ـ إِعَانَةٌ ـ عَوْنٌ ـ مُعَاوَنَةٌ ـ مُسَاعَدَةٌ ـ أَيْدٌ ـ نَجْدَةٌ ـ مُعَاضَدَةٌ ـ إِغَاثَةٌ ـ غِيَاثٌ. To ask — of, إِسْتَعَانَ بِ. To ask — of one against, إِسْتَنْصَرَ-عَلَى ـ إِسْتَمَدَّ-عَلَى. By the — of God and His good providence, بِعَوْنِ ٱللّٰهِ وَحُسْنِ تَوْفِيقِهِ.

Aid, *v.t.* عَضَدَ ـ سَاعَدَ ـ أَغَاثَ ـ نَصَرَ ـ أَعَانَ. To be kind to, أَحْسَنَ إِلَى ـ أَفْضَلَ عَلَى. To — one against, أَعَانَ-عَلَى ـ نَصَرَ-عَلَى. To — one with, أَغَاثَ-بِ. To support, سَانَدَ ـ أَخَذَ بِيَدِ. They aided one another, تَنَاصَرُوا ـ تَعَاضَدُوا ـ تَعَاوَنُوا. To ask — of, إِسْتَعَانَ ـ إِسْتَعَانَ بِ.

Aid, *n.* } **Aider,** } عَضُدٌ ـ عَوْنٌ *pl.* أَعْوَانٌ ـ نَاصِرٌ *pl.* أَنْصَارٌ ـ مُغِيثٌ ـ مُعِينٌ.

Aide-de-Camp, *n.* أَهْلُ أَرْكَانِ ٱلْعَسْكَرِ ـ يَاوِرُ حَرْبٍ (Turkish).

Aigrette, *n.* رِيشَةٌ *coll.* رِيشٌ.

Aigulet, *n.* مَاصُورَةٌ.

Ail, *v.i.* To feel pain, to be ill, إِعْتَلَّ ـ مَرِضَ. To come upon, as of an illness or trouble, أُصِيبَ بِ. What ails you? مَا أَصَابَكَ ـ مَا عَرَضَ لَكَ ـ مَا لَكَ. What ails your eye? مَا لِعَيْنِكَ. Something ails me, بِي شَيْءٌ مَا.

Ail, *n.* } **Ailment,** } دَاءٌ *pl.* أَدْوَاءٌ ـ أَلَمٌ *pl.* آلَامٌ ـ وَجَعٌ *pl.* أَوْجَاعٌ ـ مَرَضٌ *pl.* أَمْرَاضٌ ـ غَمٌّ ـ تَشْوِيشٌ ـ إِنْحِرَافُ مِزَاجٍ.

Ailing, *a.* بِهِ دَاءٌ ـ مَرِيضٌ ـ عَلِيلٌ ـ مَعْلُولٌ ـ وِسْقَامٌ ـ مُشَوَّشٌ ـ كَيْفُهُ مَنْزُوعٌ ـ مَا لَهُ كَيْفٌ ـ مُنْحَرِفُ ٱلْمِزَاجِ.

Aim, *v.i.* To — at, to endeavour to hit, أَشْرَعَ ـ تَأَتَّى لِ ـ حَرَّرَ عَلَى ـ أَقْصَدَ ـ عَيَّنَ عَلَى ـ نَاشَنَ ـ أَخَذَ نِشَانًا. To aspire after, تَنَوَّى ـ عَمَدَ إِلَى ـ هَمَّ بِ ـ نَوَى ـ تَقَصَّدَ ـ طَلَبَ ـ قَصَدَ ـ عَزَمَ ـ رَغِبَ فِي ـ عَمَدَ إِلَى ـ جَدَّ فِي ـ أَرَادَ. He aimed at his head with the stick, أَهْوَى إِلَى ـ عَمَدَ لِرَأْسِهِ بِٱلْعَصَا ـ رَأْسِهِ.

Aim, *n.* The act of directing the eye to a certain point, طَلْعَةٌ ـ رَمْيَةٌ. A thing aimed at, رَمِيَّةٌ. The point at which a thing is aimed, هَدَفٌ ـ غَرَضٌ ـ عَلَامَةٌ ـ نِشَانٌ. Design, قَصْدٌ ـ أَمَدٌ ـ مُرَادٌ ـ أَغْرَاضٌ *pl.* غَرَضٌ ـ عَزِيمَةٌ ـ مَطْلُوبٌ ـ مَقْصُودٌ ـ غَايَةٌ. To attain one's —, نَالَ ٱلْمَقْصُودَ ـ حَصَّلَ ٱلْمَطْلُوبَ.

Air, *n.* Atmosphere, سَمَاءٌ ـ هَوَاءٌ *pl.* أَهْوِيَةٌ ـ جَوٌّ ـ أَجْوَاءٌ.

Climate, مُناخ ـ هَوآء. A gentle wind, نَسِيم *pl.* نِسام. Mien, وَجْه ـ مَنْظَر ـ سِيمآء ـ مَرْآة ـ رُؤْيَة ـ طَلْعَة ـ هَيْئَة. A tune, هَوآء ـ أَلْحان *pl.* لَحْن ـ نَغْمَة ـ قُدُود *pl.* قَدّ ـ مَقامات ـ مَقام ـ أَغانِي *pl.* أُغْنِيَّة ـ غِناء. The birds of the —, طُيُورُ ٱلسَّمآء. To take the —, شَمّ ٱلْهَوآء ـ تَفَسَّحَ ـ تَفَرَّجَ ـ تَنَزَّهَ. To assume the airs of, أَظْهَرَ ـ أَوْهَمَ بِ. To give one's self airs, تَعَظَّمَ ـ تَصَلَّفَ. Airs, affected importance, تَعَظُّم ـ تَصَلُّف. Castles in the —, هَوَس ـ غُرُور.

Air, *v.t.* To expose to the —, نَشَرَ. To — in the sun, شَمَّسَ.

Air-bladder, *n.* بَقْبُوقَة ـ بَقْبِيقَة ـ فَقاقِيعُ *pl.* فُقّاعَة.

Air-built, *a.* Visionary, وَهْمِيّ ـ خَيالِيّ.

Air-cell, *n.* حُجَيْرَة لِلْهَوآء.

Air-drawn, *a.* *See* Air-built, *a.*

Air-gun, *n.* بُنْدُقِيَّة تُطْلَقُ بِقُوَّةِ ٱلْهَوآء.

Air-hole, *n.* مَنْفَس ـ مَنْوَر ـ كُوآء *pl.* كُوَّة.

Airiness, *n.* Openness to the air, هَوآء. Delightfulness of situation, نُزْهَة ـ نَضارَة ـ نَضْرَة. Gaiety, طَرَب ـ بَهْجَة ـ لَطافَة. Levity, خِفَّة عَقْلٍ ـ بُطْل ـ هَزْل.

Airing, *n.* شَمُّ ٱلْهَوآء ـ تَفَرُّج ـ سَيْرَة. To take an —; *See under* Air, *n.*

Air-tight, *a.* مُحْكَمُ ٱلسَّدّ ـ لا يَنْفُذُ فِيهِ ٱلْهَوآء.

Air-vessel, *n.* عُرُوق *pl.* عِرْقٌ يَحْتَبِسُ فِيهِ ٱلْهَوآء.

Airy, *a.* Of the air, هَوائِيّ. Lofty, مُرْتَفِع ـ عالٍ ـ مُنِيع. Open to the air, pleasant, مُفَرِّح ـ نَضِر ـ نَزِه ـ شَرِح. Sprightly, بَطْران ـ حَرِك ـ لَطِيف. Frivolous, خَفِيفُ ٱلْعَقْلِ ـ هَزَلِيّ.

Aisle, *n.* جَناحٌ مِنْ أَجْنِحَةِ كَنِيسَة.

Ajar, *ad.* مَفْتُوحٌ بِٱلنِّصْفِ ـ مَفْتُوحٌ نِصْفَ فَتْحَةٍ ـ مَفْتُوحٌ قَلِيلًا ـ مُنْفَرِج.

Akimbo, *a.* Crooked, مُلْتَوٍ ـ مُنْحَنٍ ـ حانٍ ـ مُعَوَّج. With arms —, مُكَتَّفُ ٱلْيَدَيْن.

Akin, *a.* Related to by blood, مُقَرَّب ـ أَنْسِبآء *pl.* نَسِيب ـ بِٱلنَّسَب. Resembling, شَبِيه ـ مُماثِل ـ نَظِير ـ مُقَرَّب.

Alabaster, *n.* مَرْمَر ـ بَهآء ـ رُخام طَرِيّ. A slab of —, رُخامَة.

Alabaster, *a.* مِنْ رُخام.

Alack! *int.* }
Alack-a-day! } وَه ـ أَخ ـ أَح ـ آه.

Alacrity, *n.* Liveliness, خِفَّة ـ نَشاط ـ حَرارَة; joy, فَرَح.

A-la-mode, ad. عَلَى ٱلزِّيِّ ـ كَٱلزِّيّ. *See also under* Fashion, *n.*

Alarm, *n.* A cry to arms, تَنْبِيه ـ عِياطُ تَنْبِيهٍ لِلْقِتالِ ـ هُتاف. Notice, as of impending danger, تَنْبِيه ـ تَحْذِير. Sudden fear, رُعْبَة ـ فَزْعَة ـ غَمّ. Tumult, ضَجَّة ـ إِنْزِعاج ـ رَجْفَة. Inquietude, قَلَق ـ إِضْطِراب. To sound an —, ضَرَبَ هُتافًا; of war, نَبَّهَ ـ دَعَى إِلَى ٱلْقِتالِ ـ رَمَى ٱلصَّوْتَ ـ نادَى بِٱلْقِتالِ ـ بِٱلْقِتال.

Alarm, *v.t.* To frighten, خَوَّفَ ـ أَرْعَبَ ـ رَعَّبَ ـ أَفْزَعَ. To disquiet, شَوَّشَ ـ أَهَمَّ ـ قَلْقَلَ ـ أَقْلَقَ ـ قَلَّقَ. To call to arms, نَبَّهَ لِلْقِتال. To — one's self, تَخَشَّى. To be alarmed for, إِخْتَشَى ـ خافَ عَلَى.

Alarm-bell, *n.* جَرَسٌ مُنَبِّهٌ ـ جَرَسُ ٱلتَّنْبِيه.

Alarm-gun, *n.* مِدْفَعُ ٱلتَّنْبِيهِ ـ ضَرْبُ مِدْفَعٍ لِلتَّنْبِيه.

Alarming, *a.* مُرْجِف ـ مُزْعِج ـ مُخِيف ـ راجِف ـ مُفْزِع ـ مُنْذِرٌ بِٱلْخَطَرِ ـ مُذْعِر ـ مُرْعِب. Alarming reports, تَواتُرات مُوحِشَة; the like, unfounded, أَراجِيف.

Alarmingly, *ad.* بِنَوْعٍ مُخِيف.

Alarmist, *n.* One who is easily alarmed, مُخَوَّف ـ أَخْوَف ـ مُشَوَّش ـ مُخَوَّف ـ خِيف ـ رَجُوف ـ خَوّار. One who alarms, مُشَوِّش ـ مُخَوِّف.

Alarum, *n.* An — clock, ساعَةٌ تَدُقُّ بِجَرَسٍ لِلتَّنْبِيهِ ـ ساعَة مُنَبِّه ـ مُنَبِّهَة.

Alas! *int.* آه ـ آح ـ وای ـ وآه. Alas, for me! يا وَيْلَتِي. Alas, for Zaid! وا زَيْدَ.

Alb, *n.* كِيتُونَة ـ كِتُونَة ـ تُون *pl.* تُونِيَّة.

Albatross, *n.* نَوْعٌ مِنْ طُيُورِ ٱلْبَحْر.

Albeit, *conj.* and *ad.* وَلَوْ أَنَّ ـ وَأَنْ ـ وَلَوْ ـ مَعَ أَنْ.

Albino, *n.* مَوْلُودٌ بِجِلْدٍ وَشَعْرٍ فِي غايَةِ ٱلْبَياضِ وَعُيُونٍ حُمْر.

Albion, *n.* إِسْمُ بِلادِ ٱلْإِنْكِلِيزِ ٱلْعَتِيق.

Albugo, *n.* بَياضٌ عَلَى ٱلْعَيْنِ ـ بَياضَةٌ عَلَى ٱلْعَيْنِ ـ أَرْغامُن.

Album, *n.* مُجَلَّدٌ مُجَمَّع ـ مُجَلَّدٌ تُجْتَمَعُ فِيهِ ٱلتَّصاوِيرُ وَغَيْرُها.

Albumen, *n.* The white of egg, بَياضُ ٱلْبَيْض. A substance resembling the same, مادَّةٌ فِي ٱلْأَجْسامِ تُشابِهُ بَياضَ ٱلْبَيْض.

Albuminous, *a.* شَبِيهٌ بِبَياضِ ٱلْبَيْضِ ـ مُشابِهٌ بِبَياضِ ٱلْبَيْض.

Alcaid, *n.* القائِد. The star, القائِد.

Alcali, *n.* *See* Alkali, *n.*

Alchemical, *a.* كِيماوِيّ.

Alchemically, *ad.* عَلَى مُقْتَضَى ٱلْكِيمِيا.

Alchemist, *n.* أَهْلُ ٱلْكِيمِيآء ـ صانِعُ كِيمِيا.

Alchemy, *n.* الكِيمِيا ـ عِلْمُ ٱلْكِيمِيا.

Alcohol, *n.* الكُحُولُ ـ رُوحُ ٱلْعَرَق.

Alcoholization, *n.* إِسْتِقْطار ـ تَقْطِير ـ تَكْرِير.

Alcoholize, *v.t.* كَرَّرَ.

Alcoran, *n.* القُرْقانُ ـ ٱلْمُصْحَفُ ـ القُرْآنُ. To recite the —, ذَكَرَ ٱلْقُرْآنَ ـ يَتْلُو aor. تَلَا (or) قَرَأَ ٱلْقُرْآنَ. *See also* Kurân, *n.*

Alcove, *n.* A recess, رَفٌّ *pl.* رُفُوف ـ قُبَّة *pl.* قُبَب ـ سِدِلّي. A place to recline in, إِيْوان (*vulg.* لِيوان) ـ طَاق *pl.* طَواق مَضْجَع.

Alder, *n.* حَوْرَةٌ رُومِيَّةٌ.

Alderman, *n.* شَيْخُ ٱلْبَلَدِ *pl.* شُيُوخ.

Ale, *n.* بِيرَة ـ نَوْعٌ مِنَ ٱلْبُوزَةِ.

Alembic, *n.* أَنْبِيق ـ أَنْبَكٌ.

Alength, *ad.* بِٱلطُّولِ ـ عَلَى طُولِ.

Alert, *a.* On the —, صاحٍ ـ فائِق ـ ساهِر ـ مُتَيَقِّظ ـ مُتَنَبِّه. Brisk, نَشِط ـ ذُو جِدٍّ وَكَدٍّ ـ ذُو سَعْيٍ.

Alertness, *n.* Watchfulness, إِنْتِباه. Promptitude, سُرْعَة ـ نَشاط ـ مُرُوَّة ـ شَهامَة.

Alexander, *n.* إِسْكَنْدَر. Alexander the Great, إِسْكَنْدَرُ ذُو ٱلْقَرْنَيْنِ.

Alexandria, *n.* إِسْكَنْدَرِيَّة.

Alexipharmic, *n.* تِرْياق ـ إِكْسِير.

Algebra, *n.* عِلْمُ ٱلْجَبْرِ ـ عِلْمُ ٱلْجَبْرِ وَٱلْمُقابَلَةِ.

Algebraic, *a.* / **Algebraical,** } جَبْرِيٌّ ـ جَبْرِيَّة ـ مُخْتَصٌّ بِٱلْجَبْرِ.

Algebraist, *n.* عارِفٌ بِعِلْمِ ٱلْجَبْرِ وَٱلْمُقابَلَةِ ـ خارِقٌ فِي رِياضِيٌّ ـ ٱلرِّياضِيَّاتِ.

Algerine, *a.* مَغْرِبِيٌّ ـ مِنْ جَزِيرَةِ ٱلْغَرْبِ *pl.* مَغارِبَة.

Alguazil, *n.* الوَزِيرُ.

Alias, *ad.* بِنَوْعٍ آخَرَ ـ وَإِلَّا ـ أَوْ.

Alibi, *n.* عَدَمُ حُضُورٍ ـ حالُ غَيْبَةٍ ـ عَدَمُ وُجُودٍ ـ غِيابَة. He proved an —, ثَبَّتَ غِيابَةً.

Alien, *n.* غَرِيب ـ أَجْنَبُ ـ أَجْنَبِيٌّ ـ بَرّانِيٌّ ـ نَقِيل.

Alien, *a.* Foreign, أَعْجَمِيٌّ ـ غَرِيب ـ أَجْنَبِيٌّ ـ بَرّانِيٌّ. Opposed to, مُضادٌّ لِ ـ مُخالِفٌ لِ. Estranged from, مُمالٌ عَن ـ مُرَغَّبٌ عَن.

Alienable, *a.* قابِلُ ٱلتَّصَرُّفِ بِهِ ـ يُنْقَلُ ـ مُنْتَقِل.

Alienage, *n.* أَجْنَبِيَّة ـ تَغَرُّب ـ غُرْبَتْلِيَّة.

Alienate, *v.t.* To transfer, as of property, to, نَقَلَ-إِلَى. To estrange, آنَى ـ جَنَّبَ ـ أَبْعَدَ ـ إِخْتَزَعَ ـ حَوَّلَ-عَن. To withdraw, as the affections of one from, شَجَّرَ-عَن ـ نَحَا-عَن. To withdraw one's affections from, هَجَرَ ـ إِغْتَرَبَ مِن ـ أَمالَ ـ قَلَبَهُ عَن ـ صَدَّ عَن ـ أَبْعَدَ عَن ـ تَنَحَّى عَن ـ تَجَنَّبَ عَن ـ إِحْتَبَسَ عَن. They were alienated from one another, تَهاجَرُوا ـ إِهْتَجَرُوا.

Alienation, *n.* As of property, نَقْل ـ حَوالَة ـ مُبايَعَة; as of the affections, مُفارَقَة ـ تَنَفُّر ـ بُرُودَةُ ٱلْمُصاحَبَةِ ـ فُتُورٌ فِي ٱلرِّفْقِ; as of friends, إِنْقِطاعُ ٱلْمَوَدَّةِ ـ إِنْصِرام ـ صَرْم; of the mind, هَتْر ـ هَتْرَة ـ جُنُون ـ خَلَلٌ فِي ٱلْعَقْلِ.

Alight, *ad.* مُشْتَعِل ـ مَوْقُود.

Alight, *v.i.* To come down and stop, نَزَلَ ـ هَبَطَ ـ حَلَّ ـ حَطَّ. To —, as a bird on a tree, وَقَعَ عَلَى aor. يَقَعُ. To dismount, تَرَجَّلَ ـ حَوَّلَ عَن ـ أَعْلَى عَن ـ نَزَلَ عَن. To — upon, to attack, غارَ عَلَى ـ هَجَمَ عَلَى ـ نازَلَ ـ حَمَلَ عَلَى. To — upon, to find, لَقِيَ ـ وَجَدَ aor. يَجِدُ ـ أَصابَ. A place of alighting, مَرْحَلَة *pl.* مَراحِلُ ـ مَحَطٌّ ـ مَحَطَّة ـ قُناق.

Alike, *a.* نِدٌّ *pl.* أَنْداد ـ نَدِيد *pl.* نُدَداءُ, *fem.* نَدِيدَة *pl.* نَدائِدُ ـ مُتَساوٍ ـ نَظِير ـ مُتَماثِل ـ سَوِيٌّ ـ سَوَى ـ عَلَى حَدٍّ سَوَى ـ سِيّانِ. They are —, هُمْ عَلَى سَوِيَّةٍ. They are — in this matter, هُمْ فِي هٰذا ٱلْأَمْرِ سَوَآءٌ. They are not —, of one shape, ما هُمْ عَلَى شَكْلٍ واحِدٍ ـ بَيْنَهُمْ خَلْفَةٌ. To be —, ناسَبَ ـ ناظَرَ. *See also under* Like, *a.*

Aliment, *n.* Food, قُوت ـ مَعاش ـ طَعام ـ غِذاءٌ. Fuel, وَقُود ـ وَقِيد.

Alimental, *a.* / **Alimentary,** } قُوتِيٌّ ـ مَأْكُول ـ مَعاشِيٌّ. The — canal, مَجْرَى ٱلطَّعامِ فِي ٱلْبَدَنِ ـ أَقْنِيَةُ ٱلطَّعامِ.

Alimentation, *n.* تَغْذِيَة ـ إِغْتِذاءٌ ـ غِذاءٌ.

Alimony, *n.* مَعِيشَةٌ مُعَيَّنَةٌ لِلْمَرْأَةِ عِنْدَ ٱفْتِراقِها مِنْ زَوْجِها ـ مَعاش.

Alive, *ad.* Not dead, حَيٌّ *pl.* أَحْياءٌ ـ عائِش; of a tree, نَضْر ـ نَدْر. Sprightly, حَرِك ـ بَطْران. In full force, acting, فاعِل ـ مُشْتَغِل ـ رائِج. To be preserved —, عِيشَ ـ حُفِظَ حَيًّا. To make —, أَحْيَى. He is not —, لَيْسَ بِحَيٍّ. While he was yet —, وَهُوَ حَيٌّ. He is — to his duty, يَعْرِفُ بِما ـ دَرِيٌّ بِواجِباتِهِ ـ يَجِبُ عَلَيْهِ. May God preserve thee alive! حَيّاكَ ٱللّٰهُ. He is still —, or living, هُوَ فِي قَيْدِ ٱلْحَياةِ.

Alkali, *n.* القِلْيُ ـ مِلْحُ ٱلْقِلْيِ ـ حُرُض ـ خِتْم. Burnt glasswort, أُشْنان ـ حُرُض. A burner of —, حَرّاض. A place for burning it, حَرَضَة.

Alkaline, *a.* ذُو حُرُضٍ ـ ذُو خَصائِصَ قَلَوِيَّةٍ ـ قَلَوِيٌّ.

Alkanet, *n.* حِنّاءُ ٱلْغُولِ ـ شِنْجار.

Alkermes, *n.* مَعْجُونُ ٱلْقِرْمِزِ.

Al-Kuran, *n.* ٱلْقُرْقَانُ ـ ٱلْمُصْحَفُ ـ ٱلْقُرْآنُ. To read the —, ذَكَرَ ٱلْقُرْآنَ.

All, *a.* كُلٌّ ـ كُلِّيٌّ ـ جَمِيعٌ ـ جَمِيعُ ـ أَجْمَعُ ـ كَافَّةٌ ـ سَائِرٌ ـ قَاطِبَةٌ.

All men, جَمِيعُ ٱلنَّاسِ ـ ٱلنَّاسُ كُلُّهُمْ ـ ٱلنَّاسُ طُرًّا. All of them, them all, قَاطِبَةً ـ جَمِيعُهُمْ ـ بِأَسْرِهِمْ. He loves them with all his heart, يُحِبُّهُمْ بِكُلِّ قَلْبِهِ. I took all my right, أَخَذْتُ حَقِّي أَجْمَعَ. All the people came, جَآءَ ٱلنَّاسُ كَافَّةً. It is all over, إِنْقَضَى بِتَمَامِهِ.

All, *ad.* كُلِّيًّا ـ تَمَامًا. All on a sudden, حَالًا ـ بَغْتَةً ـ فُجَآءَةً ـ فَوْرًا ـ وَرَأْسًا ـ عَلَى ٱلْفَوْرِ. All on a sudden I saw men approaching me, مَا أَشْعَرْتُ وَإِذَا بِنَاسٍ مُقْبِلِينَ عَلَيَّ. All together, entirely, كُلِّيًّا ـ بِٱلْمَرَّةِ ـ عَلَى جِدَتِهِ ـ عَلَى وَحْدَهُ. All alone, by himself, وَحْدَهُ ـ عَلَى حِدَتِهِ. He came all alone, جَآءَ بِرَأْسِهِ. All at once, مَعًا ـ دَفْعَةً ـ سَوَآءً ـ حَقَّةً وَاحِدَةً. Nothing at all, لَا شَيْءَ أَصْلًا ـ لَا شَيْءَ. After all, وَمَعَ ذٰلِكَ ـ بَعْدَ هٰذَا كُلِّهِ. Above all, especially, خَاصَّةً ـ خُصُوصًا. In all, of the sum total, بِٱلْكُلِّيَّةِ ـ فِي ٱلْجُمْلَةِ ـ جُمْلَةً. Never at all, قَطُّ ـ أَبَدًا ـ أَصْلًا. No, not at all, كَلَّا. All along, by the length, عَلَى طُولٍ ـ بِطُولِ. All along, always, دَائِمًا. At all events, عَلَى كُلِّ حَالٍ. All that which, whatever, مَهْمَا. All the while, طَالَمَا ـ مَا دَامَ. I made myself all things to all men, إِسْتَعْبَدْتُ نَفْسِي لِلْجَمِيعِ. All but, إِلَّا. One and all, كَافَّةً. To walk on all fours, مَشَى كَذَوَاتِ ٱلْأَرْبَعِ.

Allay, *v.t.* To mitigate, أَخْمَدَ ـ لَطَّفَ ـ سَكَّنَ ـ رَقَّقَ ـ نَوَّمَ. To —, as of passion, سَكَّنَ ـ أَطْفَأَ ـ بَرَّدَ; as of pain, هَدَّأَ ـ خَفَّفَ; of a fever or a blazing fire, أَخْمَدَ.

Allegation, *n.* A declaration, دَعْوَةٌ ـ تَقْرِيرٌ ـ إِقْرَارٌ ـ تَعْرِيفٌ. A plea, إِفَادَةٌ ـ قَوْلٌ ـ إِدِّعَآءٌ ـ خُطْبَةٌ ـ حُجَّةٌ *pl.* حُجَجٌ. To adduce an —, plea, إِحْتَجَّ بِ.

Allege, *v.t.* To declare, قَرَّرَ ـ أَكَّدَ ـ بَيَّنَ ـ صَرَّحَ بِ. To plead in excuse, إِحْتَجَّ بِ ـ قَدَّمَ حُجَجًا. To cite as an authority, ذَكَرَ. *See also to* Cite, *v.t.*

Allegiance, *n.* Loyalty, إِسْتِقَامَةٌ ـ صَدَاقَةٌ ـ إِطَاعَةٌ. To give — to, بَايَعَ. They gave their — to the prince, عَقَدُوا لِلْأَمِيرِ ـ بَايَعُوا ٱلْأَمِيرَ. To seduce from —, أَفْتَنَ ـ أَضَلَّ. The act of giving — to, مُبَايَعَةٌ.

Allegoric, *a.*
Allegorical, رَمْزِيٌّ ـ مَجَازِيٌّ ـ حَاوِي ٱلْكِنَايَةِ.

Allegorically, *ad.* بِٱلْكِنَايَةِ ـ بِٱلرَّمْزِ ـ مَجَازًا ـ عَنِ ٱلْمَجَازِ ـ بِٱلْإِسْتِعَارَةِ ـ وَمِنْ بَابِ ٱلْإِسْتِعَارَةِ.

Allegorist, *n.* مُدَرِّسٌ بِأُسْلُوبِ ٱلْكِنَايَةِ.

Allegorize, *v.t.* فَسَّرَ بِمَعْنَى ٱلرَّمْزِ ـ جَعَلَ عَلَى أُسْلُوبِ ٱلْكِنَايَةِ. To use allegory, كَنَّا ـ كَنَى ـ رَمَزَ ـ وَٱلْكِنَايَةِ.

Allegory, *n* رَمْزٌ *pl.* رُمُوزٌ ـ كِنَايَةٌ ـ مِثَالٌ *pl.* أَمْثِلَةٌ ـ تَوْرِيَةٌ.

Allegro, ad. بِٱنْتِعَاشٍ.

Alleluiah! *int.* هَلِّلُويَا ـ ٱلْحَمْدُ لِلّٰهِ ـ سُبْحَانَ ٱللّٰهِ.

Alleviate, *v.t.* أَخْمَدَ ـ بَرَّدَ ـ لَطَّفَ ـ خَفَّفَ. *See also to* Allay, *v.t.*

Alleviation, *n.* تَلْطِيفٌ ـ تَسْكِينٌ ـ تَخْفِيفٌ; the being alleviated, رَاحَةٌ ـ سُكُونٌ ـ سَكْنَةٌ ـ تَخَفُّفٌ.

Alley, *n.* An avenue in a garden, شَجَرِيَّةٌ. A narrow street, زُقَاقٌ *pl.* أَزِقَّةٌ ـ زُقَاقٌ. A blind —, زُقَاقٌ سَدٌّ ـ خَانِقٌ ـ زُقَاقٌ ـ عَطْفَةٌ غَيْرُ نَافِذٍ.

All-hail! *int.* ٱلسَّلَامُ.

All-Hallows, *n.* All Saints' Day, عِيدُ جَمِيعِ ٱلْقِدِّيسِينَ.

Alliaceous, *a.* فِيهِ صِنَّةُ ثُومٍ ـ ثُومِيٌّ.

Alliance, *n.* League, union, مُعَاهَدَةٌ ـ عَهْدٌ ـ إِتِّفَاقٌ ـ إِتِّحَادٌ ـ وَثِيقَةٌ ـ مُحَالَفَةٌ ـ مِيثَاقٌ. Alliance, as by marriage, مُصَاهَرَةٌ ـ أَهْلِيَّةٌ ـ مُنَاسَبَةٌ. Consanguinity, مُقَارَبَةٌ ـ قَرَابَةٌ. To enter into an — with, عَاهَدَ عَلَى ـ تَعَاهَدَ ـ عَقَدَ مُعَاهَدَةً مَعَ. To seek an —, as by marriage, رَغِبَ فِي ٱلْمُصَاهَرَةِ.

Defensive alliance, تَعَاهُدٌ دِفَاعِيٌّ.

Offensive alliance, مُحَالَفَةٌ هُجُومِيَّةٌ.

Perpetual alliance, إِتِّفَاقٌ دَائِمٌ.

Temporary alliance, مُحَالَفَةٌ مُوَقَّتَةٌ ـ إِتِّفَاقٌ مُوَقَّتٌ.

Allied, *ad.* As by treaty, مُتَعَاهِدٌ ـ مُتَّحِدٌ; by marriage, مُقْتَرِنٌ. Like, مُشَابِهٌ ـ مُمَاثِلٌ ـ نَظِيرٌ. The — powers, ٱلدُّوَلُ ٱلْمُتَّحِدَةُ.

Alligator, *n.* تِمْسَاحٌ أُمِيرِيكَانِيٌّ *pl.* تَمَاسِيحُ.

Alliteration, *n.* جِنَاسٌ ـ تَجْنِيسٌ. Identical —, تَجْنِيسٌ عَيْنِيٌّ. Proximate —, جِنَاسٌ لَاحِقٌ (or مُقَارِبٌ).

Alliterative, *a.* تَجْنِيسِيٌّ ـ مُجَنَّسٌ.

Allocation, *n.* Location, وَضْعٌ ـ حَطٌّ. Passing an article into an account, تَقْيِيدٌ فِي ٱلْحِسَابِ.

Allocution, *n.* خُطْبَةٌ ـ خِطَابٌ ـ مُخَاطَبَةٌ.

Allodial, *a.* مُلْكٌ.

Allodium, *n.* أَرْضٌ مُلْكٌ ـ طُعْمَةٌ.

Allopathist, *n.* طَبِيبٌ يَصِفُ أَدْوِيَةً مُضَادَّةً لِلدَّآءِ.

Allopathy, *n.* فَنٌّ مِنَ ٱلطِّبِّ بِأَدْوِيَةٍ مُضَادَّةٍ لِلْمَرَضِ.

Allot, *v.t.* To distribute by share, قَسَّمَ. To grant, وَهَبَ لِ

aor. يَهَبُ – أَكْرَمَ عَلَى-بِ. To distribute among, قَسَّمَ-عَلَى – وَزَّعَ-عَلَى – فَرَّقَ-عَلَى. To give to by decision, حَكَمَ لِ-بِ – جَزَمَ لِ-بِ.

Allotment, *n.* The act of, تَقْسِيم – تَوْزِيع. A share, قِسْمَة – نَصِيب – حِصَّة.

Allow, *v.t.* To admit, قَبِلَ – سَلَّمَ – رَضِيَ بِ. To permit, جَوَّزَ – رَخَّصَ – فِي – رَخَّصَ-لِ – سَمَحَ لِ-بِ – أَذِنَ لِ-بِ. To pay to, to —, أَنْعَمَ – يَهَبُ وَهَبَ لِ *aor.* – أَعْطَى – سَوَّغَ. To take off from, عَيَّنَ-عَلَى-بِ – رَفَعَ مِن – أَسْقَطَ مِن. To force to — or admit, قَرَّرَ بِ (or) إِسْتَقَرَّ-. Allow me to . . ., دَعْنِي أَن. I must — (in an indefinite sense), الحَقُّ يُقَالُ. He should not — such conduct, لا يَسَعُهُ أَنْ يُرَخِّصَ فِي مِثْلِ هٰذِهِ ٱلسِّيرَةِ.

Allowable, *a.* Admissible, مَقْبُول – يُقْبَلُ. Lawful, جَائِز – مُبَاح – طِلْق – حَقّ – شَرْعِيّ – حَلال. To pronounce —, حَلَّلَ. To make —, أَبَاحَ. To consider —, جَوَّزَ – إِسْتَحَلَّ. The thing was —, حَلَّ ٱلشَّيْءُ – جَازَ ٱلشَّيْءُ. It is — for you, هُوَ حِلٌّ لَكَ. To make — to, أَطْلَقَ لِ. An — form of expression, لُغَةٌ عَابِرَةٌ.

Allowably, *ad.* بِجَوَازٍ – بِتَحْلِيلٍ – طِلْقًا.

Allowance, *n.* Admission, تَسْلِيم بِ – قُبُول – رِضَاءٌ. A pension, جَامْكِيَّة – مَعْلُوم – عُلُوفَة – رَاتِب – مُرَتَّبَات *pl.* مُرَتَّب. Abatement, سَمَاح – عَفْوٌ. He made him an —, abatement of, سَمَحَ لِ-بِ. To make allowances for, to excuse, عَذَرَ. A permanent —, جِرَايَة. He made him an —, gave him a pension, عَيَّنَ لَهُ رَاتِبًا (or مَعَاشًا).

Allowance, *v.t.* عَيَّنَ لِ-رَاتِبًا مَعْلُومًا.

Alloy, *n.* تَضْعِيف – غِشّ – خُمْلان.

Alloy, *v.t.* To mix with, خَلَطَ-بِ.

All-Saints' Day, *n.* عِيدُ جَمِيعِ ٱلْقِدِّيسِينَ.

Allspice, *n.* بَهَار.

Allude, *v.i.* To — to, لَمَحَ بِ – كَنَا عَن – أَشَارَ إِلَى – أَعْنَى – أَوْمَأَ إِلَى – عَبَّرَ بِ – أَوْمَأَ إِلَى – عَرَّضَ بِ. To insinuate, دَسَّ – لَمَحَ بِ.

Allure, *v.t.* To entice, جَذَبَ – أَطْمَعَ-فِي. To seduce, وَقَّعَ – أَغْوَى – خَدَعَ – تَمَلَّقَ. *See also to* Entice, *v.t.*

Allurement, *n.* جَذْب – تَطْمِيعَة – جَاذِبِيَّة. The allurements of the world, غُرُورُ ٱلعَالَمِ – رِبَاطُ ٱلدُّنْيَا – لَذَّاتُ ٱلعَالَمِ. The — of gain seduced him, أَغْوَاهُ حُبُّ ٱلْكَسْبِ.

Allurer, *n.* }
Alluring, *a.* } خَدَّاع – غَرَّار – مُوَارٍ – صَاحِبُ حِيَلٍ – غَاوٍ. *See also* Enticer, *n., and* Attractive, *a.*

Alluringly, *ad.* بِتَمَلُّقٍ – بِنَوْعٍ يَسْلُبُ ٱلْعَقْلَ – تَمَلُّقًا.

Allusion, *n.* تَعْرِيض – تَلْمِيح – عِبَارَة – إِشَارَة – رَمْز – كِنَايَة. An — in speech to an absent person, غِيبَة. An insinuation, دَسِيسَة – لِغَاط – لَغْط.

Allusive, *a.* تَلْمِيحِيّ – مُشِيرٌ إِلَى – رَمْزِيّ.

Allusively, *ad.* تَلْمِيحًا – بِإِشَارَةٍ – بِكِنَايَةٍ.

Alluvium, *n.* تَرَاكُمُ ٱلرَّمْلِ وَٱلطِّينِ – جُرُف – غِرْيَن – غِرْيَل – جُفَاءٌ – فِي قَرَارِ ٱلْأَنْهَارِ وَغَيْرِهَا.

Ally, *v.t.* يَصِلُ *aor.* وَصَلَ-بِ – أَخَذَ-مَعَ – قَرَنَ-بِ – وَفَّقَ-لِ. To —, as by marriage, عَقَدَ بَيْنَهُمُ ٱلزَّوَاجَ – زَوَّجَ. To — one's self with, إِرْتَبَطَ مَعَ – إِنْعَقَدَ مَعَ; by marriage, تَزَوَّجَ مَعَ.

Ally, *n.* A confederate, حَلِيف *pl.* حُلَفَاءُ – مُعَاهِد – مُتَّحِد. A companion, رَفِيق – أَرْفَاق *pl.* صَاحِب – أَصْحَاب.

Almagest, *n.* أَلْمَجَسْطِي.

Alma Mater, *n.* إِسْمٌ إِصْطِلَاحِيٌّ يَدُلُّ عَلَى ٱلْمَدْرَسَةِ ٱلْعَامَّةِ حَيْثُ دَرَسَ طَالِبُ ٱلْعِلْمِ – أُمُّ ٱلْعِلْمِ.

Almanac, *n.* رُزْنَامَة – تَقْوِيم. An astronomical —, زِيج *pl.* زِيجَة.

Almightiness, *n.* جَبَرُوت – قُدْرَةٌ مُطْلَقَةٌ – قُدْرَةٌ كُلِّيَّةٌ.

Almighty, *a.* قَهَّار – ضَابِطُ ٱلْكُلِّ – قَادِرٌ عَلَى كُلِّ شَيْءٍ. The —, القَهَّار.

Almond, *n.* لَوْزَة *coll.* لَوْز *pl.* لَوْزَات. A green —, عُقَّابِيَة. An — tree, لَوْزَة – شَجَرَةُ ٱللَّوْزِ. The almonds, or glands of the throat, اللَّوْزَتَانِ – لَوْزُ ٱلحَلْقِ. Stuffed with almonds, مُلَوَّز. An — cake, بَقْلاوَة.

Almoner, *n.* وَكِيلُ ٱلصَّدَقَاتِ.

Almonry, *n.* مَنْزِلٌ لِلْفُقَرَاءِ. *See also* Alms-house, *n.*

Almost, *ad.* نَحْوَ – غَالِبًا – عَنْ قَرِيبٍ – تَقْرِيبًا. Almost thou persuadest me to be a Christian, بِقَلِيلٍ تُقْنِعُنِي أَنْ أَصِيرَ مَسِيحِيًّا. Almost all the towns-people, تَقْرِيبًا كُلُّ أَهْلِ ٱلْمَدِينَةِ.

Alms, *n.* }
Alms-deed, } حَسَنَة – صَدَقَة – زَكَاة. To give — to, أَحْسَنَ إِلَى – تَصَدَّقَ عَلَى. To ask —, تَسَوَّلَ – سَأَلَ صَدَقَةً.

Alms-giver, *n.* مُتَصَدِّق.

Alms-house, *n.* مَثْوًى لِلْفُقَرَاءِ – مَثَاب *pl.* مَثَابَةٌ لِلْفُقَرَاءِ – مَأْوَى ٱلْفُقَرَاءِ – مَنْزِلٌ لِلْفُقَرَاءِ.

Alms-man, *n.* مُصَدَّق.

Almucanter, *n.* المُقَنْطَر.

Aloe, Aloes, *n.* The lign —, عُود – قُطْر – عُودُ ٱلطِّيبِ – العُودُ.

شَجَرَةُ عُودٍ. The tree of the —, عُودٌ قُمارِيٌّ ـ عُودُ ٱلنَّدِّ ـ ٱلْغَالُونِيُّ. The drug, صَبِرٌ. To perfume with —, قَطَّرَ. To perfume one's self with —, تَقَطَّرَ.

Aloft, *ad.* إِلَى فَوْقُ ـ فَوْقٌ. To go —, صَعِدَ إِلَى فَوْقُ.

Alone, *ad.* and *a.* مُنْجَرِدٌ ـ مُنْفَرِدٌ ـ فَرِيدٌ ـ فَضًّا ـ وَحِيدٌ ـ شَاذٌّ ـ مُتَوَحِّدٌ. To act — in, تَفَرَّدَ بِ. To be —, إِسْتَفْرَدَ ـ إِنْفَرَدَ. To wish to be —, إِسْتَفْرَدَ. To keep one's self —, أَفْرَدَ نَفْسَهُ. To leave —, to forsake, تَارَكَ. To let one —, to let him do as he likes, سَيَّبَ. He came —, جَآءَ تَوًّا. I remained —, بَقَيْتُ فَضًّا. He did it —, فَعَلَهُ مِنْ ذَاتِ جِدَتِهِ. They sat —, apart, جَلَسُوا عَلَى جِدَةٍ. Let it —, say nothing about it, دَعْ. Let it —, in its place, دَعْهُ فِي مَحَلِّهِ. Let it —, and be off, سِرْ عَنْكَ. Let me —, دَعْنِي. In London —, فِي لَنْدَنَ وَحْدِهَا.

Along, *ad.* فِي ـ حَوْلَ ـ عَلَى ٱلدَّائِرِ ـ مَعَ طُولِ ـ طُولَ. Along with, جَنْبَ ـ عَلَى ـ بِ ـ مَعًا ـ مَعَ. Along the river, عَلَى حَافَّةِ ٱلنَّهْرِ ـ ٱلنَّهْرِ. Along the road, فِي ٱلطَّرِيقِ. All —, always, دَائِمًا ـ فِي كُلِّ حِينٍ. Come along! تَعَالَ ـ هَلُمَّ. Come — with me, تَعَالَ مَعِي.

Aloof, *ad.* مِنْ بَعِيدٍ ـ بَعِيدًا ـ بَعِيد. To keep one's self — from, إِجْتَنَبَ عَنْ ـ جَانَبَ ـ تَمَنَّعَ مِنْ ـ تَبَاعَدَ ـ تَجَافَى عَنْ. He keeps — from us, from our company, يَتَبَاعَدُ عَنْ مُعَاشَرَتِنَا. To stand —, وَقَفَ *aor.* يَقِفُ.

Aloud, *ad.* بِأَعْلَى صَوْتٍ ـ بِصَوْتٍ عَالٍ. Speak aloud! إِرْفَعْ صَوْتَكَ.

Alpaca, *s.* The — sheep, نَوْعٌ مِنَ ٱلْغَنَمِ مَوْجُودٌ فِي بِلَادِ أَمِيرِيكَا; wool of the same, صُوفُ ٱلْغَنَمِ ٱلْمَذْكُورِ; cloth of the same, قُمَاشٌ مَنْسُوجٌ مِنَ ٱلصُّوفِ ٱلْمَذْكُورِ.

Alpha, *n.* أَوَّلُ حَرْفِ ٱلْهِجَآءِ فِي ٱللُّغَةِ ٱلْيُونَانِيَّةِ.

Alphabet, *n.* حُرُوفُ أَلِف بَا ـ ٱلتَّهَجِّي ـ حُرُوفُ ٱلْهِجَآءِ ـ حُرُوفُ ٱلْأَبْجَدِيَّةِ ـ حُرُوفُ ٱلْمُعْجَمِ.

Alphabetical, *a.* }
Alphabetically, *ad.* } عَلَى ٱلْحُرُوفِ ـ هِجَآءً ـ عَلَى ٱلتَّهَجِّي ـ مُرَتَّبٌ عَلَى ٱلْأَبْجَدِيَّةِ ـ ٱلْمُعْجَمَةِ. To arrange —, رَتَّبَ ـ عَلَى تَرْتِيبِ ٱلْحُرُوفِ ٱلْمُعْجَمَةِ.

Alpine, *a.* Very high, شَاهِقٌ ـ سَمِيٌّ ـ شَامِخٌ.

Already, *ad.* Before this time, إِلَى ٱلْآنَ ـ قَبْلَ ٱلْآنَ. Now, ٱلسَّاعَةَ. Already, as expressing a past sense joined with a verb, لَقَدْ ـ قَدْ. Much time has — passed, لَقَدْ بَرِحَ زَمَانٌ. He has — come, قَدْ جَآءَ. I have come twice —, قَدْ جِئْتُ مَرَّتَيْنِ قَبْلَ هٰذِهِ ٱلْمَرَّةِ.

Also, *ad.* and *conj.* كَمَانًا ـ كَمَان ـ كَذٰلِكَ ـ أَيْضًا.

Altar, *n.* مَذْبَحٌ *pl.* مَذَابِحُ. A communion-table, مَائِدَةُ ٱلشَّرِكَةِ ـ مَائِدَةُ ٱلرَّبِّ ـ ٱلْمُقَدَّسَةِ. The niche in a mosque corresponding in position with that of the communion-table in a church, مِحْرَاب *pl.* مَحَارِيبُ.

Altar-cloth, *n.* غِطَآءُ ٱلْمَذْبَحِ.

Altar-piece, *n.* نَقْشٌ أَوْ تَصْوِيرٌ مَصْمُودٌ عَلَى ٱلْمَذْبَحِ.

Alter, *v.t.* To change, قَلَّبَ ـ بَدَّلَ ـ غَيَّرَ ـ حَوَّلَ. To —, as the signification of words, غَيَّرَ ـ عَكَّسَ ـ حَرَّفَ. To —, as from one thing to another, حَرَّفَ. To — one's course, to cease from, أَحَالَ ـ أَضْرَبَ عَنْ ـ كَفَّ عَنْ. He altered his opinions of . . ., رَأْيَهُ فِي.

Alter, *v.i.* To change, تَبَدَّلَ ـ تَغَيَّرَ ـ إِنْحَالَ ـ تَحَوَّلَ. To — for the worse, تَغَيَّرَ وَفَسَدَ ـ [2] خَلَفَ. To — from . . . to . . ., تَغَيَّرَ مِنْ ـ إِلَى. To be altered, of a meaning, إِنْحَرَفَ.

Alter ego, *n.* Agent, plenipotentiary for one, وَكِيلٌ مُطْلَقٌ.

Alterable, *a.* قَابِلُ ٱلتَّغْيِيرِ ـ يُصْرَفُ.

Alteration, *n.* قَلْبٌ ـ تَحْوِيلٌ ـ تَغْيِيرٌ ـ تَبْدِيلٌ; of a meaning, تَحْرِيفٌ; for the worse, فَسَادٌ ـ خُلُوفٌ.

Alterative, *a.* مُبَدِّلٌ ـ مُغَيِّرٌ.

Alterative, *a.* Of a medicine, دَوَآءٌ مُغَيِّرٌ وَمُقَوٍّ.

Altercate, *v.i.* To quarrel, as with another, تَنَازَعَ ـ [2] لَدَّ ـ تَعَالَجَ ـ تَجَادَلَ.

Altercation, *n.* لَدَدٌ ـ مُجَادَلَةٌ ـ مُنَافَسَةٌ ـ مُشَاجَرَةٌ ـ مُنَازَعَةٌ ـ خُصُومَةٌ.

Alternate, *a.* بِٱلدَّوْرِ ـ مُتَعَاوِضٌ ـ مُتَعَقِّبٌ ـ دَوْرِيٌّ ـ عُقْبِيٌّ.

Alternate, *n.* مُتَوَالٍ ـ مُعَاقِبٌ ـ مُتَوَاتِرٌ ـ مُرَاسِلٌ.

Alternate, *v.i.* To act in turns with, إِعْتَقَبَ ـ أَعْقَبَ ـ عَاقَبَ. To act (they acted) by turns, سَعَوْا مُعَاوِضًا ـ عَوَّرُوا ـ تَعَاقَبُوا ـ سَعَوْا بِٱلدَّوْرِ. He is the person who alternates with him in singing, هُوَ رَسِيلُهُ فِي ٱلْغِنَآءِ. To cause to be done by turns, جَعَلَ ـ مُتَعَاقِبًا ـ جَعَلَ ـ بِٱلدَّوْرِ.

Alternately, *ad.* }
Alternatively, } بِٱلْمُعَاقَبَةِ ـ عَلَى ٱلتَّعَاقُبِ ـ عَلَى ٱلتَّنَاوُبِ ـ بِٱلدَّوْرِ ـ مُوَاتَرَةً ـ مُعَاقَبَةً. They acted —, فَعَلُوا بِٱلدَّوْرِ ـ سَعَوْا بِٱلنَّوْبَةِ ـ إِنْتَابُوا ـ تَعَاوَرُوا ـ تَعَاقَبُوا ـ تَوَاتَرُوا.

Alternation, *n.* }
Alternativeness, } تَعْوِيرٌ ـ تَعَاقُبٌ ـ مُعَاقَبَةٌ ـ مُوَاتَرَةٌ ـ وِتَارٌ ـ تَنَاوُبٌ.

Alternative, *n.* Another way, manner, بَابٌ آخَرُ ـ طَرِيقٌ آخَرُ ـ وَجْهٌ آخَرُ. Choice, إِخْتِيَارٌ ـ إِنْتِخَابٌ ـ خِيرَةٌ بَيْنَ شَيْئَيْنِ. To give one the —, خَيَّرَ بَيْنَ شَيْئَيْنِ . I offer you the —, أَنْتَ ٱلْمُخَيَّرُ بَيْنَ هٰذا وَهٰذاكَ . Your only — is to do this, قَصْرُكَ أَنْ تَفْعَلَ هٰذا .

Although, *conj.* وَلَوْ — وَأَنْ — مَعَ أَنْ — مَهْمَا — عَلَى أَنْ — وَٱلْحالُ أَنْ . The land is too narrow for you — it is so large, ضَاقَتْ عَلَيْكُمُ ٱلْأَرْضُ بِمَا رَحُبَتْ . Although it is not proper, yet ..., وَإِنْ كَانَ ذٰلِكَ غَيْرَ مُناسِبٍ إِلَّا أَنْ . Although it is the most difficult of all, مَعَ أَنَّهُ أَصْعَبُ ٱلْكُلِّ . Although I have seen him ten times, مَعَ أَنِّي رَأَيْتُهُ عَشَرَ مَرَّاتٍ . Although all should doubt yet will not I, وَإِنْ شَكَّ ٱلْجَمِيعُ فَأَنا لا أَشُكُّ .

Altitude, *n.* إِرْتِفاع — تَشامُخ — سُمُوّ — عَلاء — عُلُوّ . The — of a star, مَنْزِلَةُ كَوْكَبٍ — إِرْتِفاعُ كَوْكَبٍ . Altitude above the level of the sea, فَوْقَ مُساواةِ ٱلْبَحْرِ — فَوْقَ دَرَجَةِ ٱرْتِفاعِ ٱلْبَحْرِ ٱلْمالِحِ — إِرْتِفاعُ ٱلْأَراضِي عَنْ مُساواةِ ٱلْبَحْرِ . To take an —, إِصْطَنَعَ مَنْزِلَةً — [2] أَخَذَ ٱرْتِفاعًا فَلَكِيًّا .

Altogether, *ad.* At once, سَوآءً — بِٱلْمَرَّةِ — كُلًّا — جُمْلَةً — مَعًا . Entirely, بِأَسْرِهِ — بِٱلْكُلِّيَّةِ — كُلِّيًّا — بَتَّةً — أَجْمَعَ — جَمِيعًا . Take it —, خُذْهُ بِأَسْرِهِ . He did it — for our sakes, فَعَلَهُ مِنْ أَجْلِنَا عَلَى ٱلْإِطْلاقِ . I wish it to be not nearly, but — like this, أُرِيدُ أَنْ يَكُونَ لَيْسَ تَقْرِيبًا فَقَطْ بَلْ طِبْقَ هٰذا .

Alto-relievo, *n.* تَجْسِيم . In —, مُجَسَّم — بارِز .

Alum, *n.* شَبّ — حَجَرُ ٱلشَّبِّ .

Alumine, *n.* نَوْعٌ مِنَ ٱلصَّلْصالِ مَخْلُوطٌ بِجِنْسٍ مِنَ ٱلْمَعْدِنِ — ٱلْيُومِين .

Aluminium, *n.* المَعْدِنُ ٱلْخالِصُ ٱلْمَوْجُودُ فِي ٱلطِّينِ ٱلْمُسَمَّى ٱلْيُومِين .

Aluminous, *a.* شَبِّيّ — مِنَ ٱلشَّبِّ .

Alumnus, *n.* تِلْمِيذٌ فِي مَدْرَسَةٍ .

Alveolar, *a.* ذُو بُيُوتٍ — ذُو ثُغُورٍ . The — process, of the teeth, المَنْصَبُ — الدُّرْدُر .

Alvine, *a.* مُخْتَصٌّ بِٱلْأَمْعاءِ . Alvine secretion, بَرازُ ٱلْبَدَنِ .

Alway, *ad.* }
Always, } Continually, فِي كُلِّ — عَلَى ٱلدَّوامِ — بِتَواتُرٍ — أَمَدًا — مِرارًا مُتَوالِيَةً — دائِمًا — حِينٍ . For ever, أَبَدًا — إِلَى ٱلْأَبَدِ . I shall not live —, لا أَحْيا إِلَى ٱلْأَبَدِ . I — do what pleases him, إِنِّي فِي كُلِّ حِينٍ أَفْعَلُ ما يُرْضِيهِ . To be — with, لازَمَ .

Am; First person of the verb To Be. I am the man, أَنا ٱلرَّجُلُ . I — not, لَسْتُ أَنا . Am I not his brother? أَلَسْتُ بِأَخِيهِ . I — very glad, أَنا مَسْرُورٌ جِدًّا . Here I —, Sir, هٰذا يا سَيِّدِي .

Amain, *ad.* بِشِدَّةٍ — بِعَزْمٍ شَدِيدٍ — بِحَيْلٍ .

Amalgam, *n.* Mixture of metals by quicksilver, إِخْتِلاطُ ٱلْمَعادِنِ بِواسِطَةِ ٱلزِّئْبَقِ . A mixture, خَلِيط — إِمْتِزاج — إِخْتِلاط .

Amalgamate, *v.t.* Of metals, خَلَطَ ٱلْمَعادِنَ بِواسِطَةِ ٱلزِّئْبَقِ . To mix, جَمَّعَ بَيْنَ-وَبَيْنَ — مَزَجَ-بِ — خَلَّطَ .

Amalgamate, *v.i.* To blend, إِخْتَلَطَ — إِنْخَلَطَ .

Amalgamation, *n.* Of metals, مَزْجُ ٱلْمَعادِنِ بِواسِطَةِ ٱلزِّئْبَقِ . Mixture, إِخْتِلاط — إِتِّحاد — إِمْتِزاج .

Amanuensis, *n.* ناسِخ — كاتِب .

Amaranth, *n.* The plant, سالِفُ ٱلْعَرُوسِ — لَعَل — دَيْسَم — قَلَبَقُ ٱلْهُودِيَّةِ — طِنْطُورُ ٱلْجِنْدِيِّ .

Amaranthine, *a.* Unfading, لا يَذْبُلُ .

Amass, *v.t.* كَرْدَسَ — [2] قَشَّ — [2] ضَمَّ-إِلَى — [2] لَمَّ — كَوَّمَ — جَمَّعَ .

Amassment, *n.* إِجْتِماع — كُداسَة — رَكْم — أَكْوام *pl.* كُومَة .

Amateur, *n.* A comedian, لاعِب . One who has a great taste for anything, راغِبٌ فِي — طُلَّاب *pl.* طالِب .

Amativeness, *n.* عِشْق — مَعْشَق .

Amatory, *a.* هُيامِيّ — غَرامِيّ — عَشِيق — عِشْقِيّ .

Amaurosis, *n.* كُمْنَة .

Amaze, *v.t.* عَجَّبَ — حَيَّرَ — أَدْهَشَ — أَذْهَلَ . All who heard him were amazed, بُهِتَ جَمِيعُ ٱلَّذِينَ سَمِعُوهُ .

Amazed, *part.* مُتَعَجِّب — مَدْهُوش — مُتَحَيِّر .

Amazement, *n.* تَعَجُّب — تَحَيُّر — حَيْرَة — دَهْشَة . He was filled with —, إِمْتَلأَ دَهْشَةً وَحَيْرَةً .

Amazing, *a.* بَدِيع — غَرِيب — مُعْجِب — عَجِيب — مُدْهِش — رائِق .

Amazingly, *ad.* بِنَوْعٍ عَجِيبٍ — بِحَيْرَةٍ — تَعْجِيبًا .

Amazon, *n.* A masculine woman, إِمْرَأَةٌ — إِمْرَأَةٌ فَحْلَةٌ — مُذَكَّرَة — مُسْتَرْجِلَة .

Amazons, *n.* مَحْسُومَةُ ٱلثَّدْيِ وَهُوَ ٱسْمٌ لِنِسْوَةٍ كُنَّ يُحارِبْنَ فِي ٱلزَّمانِ ٱلْقَدِيمِ .

Ambassador, *n.* إِيلْچِيَّة — إِيلْچِي — سُفَرآءُ *pl.* سَفِير . A messenger, قاصِد *pl.* قُصَّاد — رَسُول *pl.* رُسُل .

Ambassadorial, *a.* مُتَعَلِّقٌ بِٱلسِّفارَةِ .

Ambassadress, *n.* إِمْرَأَةُ إِيلْچِي — إِمْرَأَةُ سَفِيرٍ .

Amber, *n.* كَهْرَبا . An — mouth-piece, بُزٌّ كَهْرَبا .

Ambergris, *n.* عَنْبَرٌ خامٌ — عَنْبَر — نَدٌّ .

Ambidexter, *n.* and *a.* ذُو ٱلْيَدَيْنِ — أَزْدَلُ — أَضْبَطُ — أَعْسَرُ يَسَرُ .

Ambient, *a.* مُحِيط .

Ambiguity, *n.* / Ambiguousness, } إِلْتِبَاس ــ شُبْهَة *pl.* شُبَه ــ إِشْتِبَاه ــ تَوْجِيه ــ وِرْيَة ــ تَعْقِيد .

Ambiguous, *a.* مُلْتَبِس ــ مُشْبَه ــ مُشْتَبِه ــ مُعَمًّى ــ مُعَقَّد ــ مُبْهَم . An — matter, شَكْل *pl.* أَشْكَال . An — speech, تَوْرِيَة ــ مِعْرَاض . To be — to, إِشْتَبَهَ عَلَى .

Ambiguously, *ad.* بِٱلْتِبَاسٍ ــ بِتَوْجِيهٍ ــ شُبْهَةً ــ إِلْتِبَاسًا .

Ambit, *n.* دَائِرَة *pl.* دَوَائِر ــ إِسْتِدَارَة .

Ambition, *n.* إِسْتِكْبَار ــ إِسْتِعْظَام ــ غَرَآء ــ طَلَبُ ٱلرِّفْعَةِ ــ رَغْبَةٌ فِي . Zeal, earnestness, هِمَّة ــ شَهَامَة ــ بُغَآء ــ طَمَع .

Ambitious, *a.* مُسْتَكْبِر ــ مُسْتَعْظِم ــ طَمَّاع ــ بَاغٍ *pl.* بُغَاة . Zealous, غَيُور ــ رَاغِبٌ فِي .

Ambitiously, *ad.* مُتَعَظِّمًا ــ مُتَكَبِّرًا ــ بِطَمَعٍ .

Amble, *v.i.* خَبَّ *aor.* يَخُبُّ ــ إِخْتَبَّ ــ هَرْوَلَ ــ مَشَى مِثْلَ ــ مَشَى رَهْوًا ــ رَهْوَن ــ ٱلرَّهْوَانِ ــ رَهَا *aor.* يَرْهُو . To make to —, أَخَبَّ .

Ambler, *n.* رَهْوَان .

Amblingly, *ad.* مِثْلَ ٱلرَّهْوَانِ .

Ambulance, *n.* مَحْمَلٌ أَوْ عَرَبِيَّةٌ لِنَقْلِ ــ مِنْقَلَةٌ لِمَرْضَى ٱلْعَسْكَرِ ــ مَرْضَى ٱلْعَسْكَرِ .

Ambulate, *v.i.* سَارَ ــ جَالَ ــ دَارَ .

Ambulation, *n.* سِيرَة ــ جَوَلَان ــ دَوْر ــ دَوَرَان .

Ambuscade, *n.* / Ambush, } رَصَد *pl.* أَرْصَاد ــ كَمِين ــ كَيْد ــ كَمْنَة . To lay in — for, رَصَدَ ــ رَاصَدَ ــ تَرَصَّدَ لِ . To place in — for, أَرْصَدَ عَلَى . Men in —, كَمِين *pl.* كُمَنَآء . A place of —, مَرْصَد ــ مُرْتَصَد .

Ameliorate, *v.t.* To correct, صَحَّحَ ــ أَصْلَحَ ــ صَلَّحَ ــ عَدَّلَ . To reform, هَذَّبَ ــ أَدَّبَ . To make better, in health, أَعْلَجَ .

Ameliorate, *v.i.* To grow better, in health, طَابَ ــ رَاقَ ــ مِزَاجُهُ ــ حَصَلَ عَلَى ٱلشِّفَآءِ ــ إِتَّجَهَ إِلَى ٱلْعَافِيَةِ . He began to —, in health, أَخَذَ فِي ٱلْعَافِيَةِ .

Amelioration, *n.* Correction, إِصْلَاح ــ تَصْلِيح ــ تَصْحِيح . Reformation, تَهْذِيب ــ تَقْوِيم ــ تَعْدِيل . Improvement, in health, شِفَآء ــ تَعْدِيلُ ٱلْمِزَاجِ ــ إِتِّجَاهٌ إِلَى ٱلصِّحَّةِ .

Amen, *n.* آمِين . To say —, هَيْمَنَ .

Amenable, *a.* تَحْتَ حُكْمٍ ــ مُسْتَلْزَمٌ لِ ــ مُحَاسَبٌ بِ ــ مُطَالَبٌ بِ .

Amend, *v.t.* *See to* Ameliorate, *v.t.*

Amendable, *a.* يُصْلَحُ ــ أَهْلٌ لِلْإِصْلَاحِ .

Amends, *n.* مُجَازَاة ــ مُكَافَاة ــ تَعْوِيض ــ خَسَارَة . To make — to for, كَافَى ــ جَازَى ــ أَفَاضَ .

Amenity, *n.* Of disposition, لَطَافَة ــ لُطْف ــ حَلَاوَةُ طَبْعٍ ; of situation, نُزْهَة .

Amerce, *v.t.* *See to* Fine, *v.t.*

Amethyst, *n.* جَمَسْت ــ كركهان ــ مَرْطِيس .

Amiability, *n.* / Amiableness, } لَطَافَة ــ وُدّ ــ ظَرَافَة ــ شَلَبْنَة . To treat with —, تَلَطَّفَ بِ .

Amiable, *a.* أَنِيس ــ لَطِيف ــ وَدُود ــ لَذِيذ ــ حَسَن .

Amicable, *a.* حُبِّيّ ــ أَنِيس . An — settlement, مُصَالَحَة .

Amicably, *ad.* بِٱلْمُصَاحَبَةِ ــ عَلَى سَبِيلِ ٱلْوِدَادِ . To settle an affair —, صَالَحَ .

Amid, Amidst, *prep.* *See* Among, *prep.*

Amiss, *ad.* خَطَأً ــ رَدَآءَةً ــ فَسَادًا ــ بَشَاعَةً ــ بِٱلسُّوءِ . We have done —, أَخْطَأْنَا . He has done nothing —, لَمْ يَفْعَلْ شَيْئًا لَيْسَ فِي مَحَلِّهِ . To take —, إِسْتَصْعَبَ ٱلشَّيْءَ عَلَى سُوءٍ .

Amity, *n.* مَوَدَّة ــ مَحَبَّة ــ صَدَاقَة ــ مُوَالَاة ــ صُحْبَة ــ أُلْفَة .

Ammoniac, *n* Sal —, نُشَادِر ــ مِلْحُ ٱلنُّشَادِرِ . Gum —, أُشَّق ــ وُشَّق ــ قَنَاوُشَق .

Ammunition, *n.* Military stores, ذَخِيرَة *pl.* ذَخَائِر ــ زَوَادَةُ ٱلْحَرْبِ . Gunpowder, بَارُود .

Amnesty, *v.t.* عَفْوٌ عَامّ ــ أَمَان . To proclaim a general —, أَعْلَنَ بِعَفْوٍ عَامٍّ .

Amnesty, *v.t.* عَفَا عَنْ .

Among, *ad.* / Amongst, } بَيْنَ ــ فِي ــ مَعَ ــ مَا بَيْنَ ــ عِنْدَ . Among the people, وَسْطَ ٱلْقَوْمِ . Among men, فِي ٱلنَّاسِ . What is that — so many? مَا هٰذَا لِمِثْلِ هٰؤُلَآءِ .

Amorous, *a.* عَاشِق *pl.* عُشَّاق . An — poem, غَزَل . Amorous behaviour, coquettishness, شِكْل ــ دَلّ ــ غُنْج .

Amorously, *ad.* عِشْقًا ــ بِتِلْقَآءِ ٱلْعِشْقِ . To behave —, تَغَنَّجَ .

Amorousness, *n.* عِشْق ــ مَحَبَّة ــ وُدّ ــ حُبّ ــ غُنْج .

Amorphous, *a.* غَيْرُ مُقَرَّرِ ٱلشَّكْلِ .

Amount, *v.i.* To — to, بَلَغَ إِلَى ــ حَصَلَ ــ صَارَ مَبْلَغَ . To result from, نَتَجَ مِنْ ــ حَصَلَ مِنْ . The expense amounted to about . . . , بَلَغَ ٱلْمَصْرُوفُ نَحْوَ . It amounts, therefore, to this, فَٱلْحَاصِلُ إِذًا .

Amount, *n.* Total, مَبْلَغ ــ جُمْلَة . Conclusion, نَتِيجَة ــ إِيجَاز ــ الحَاصِل . Price, ثَمَن ــ قِيمَة ــ سِعْر .

Amour, *n.* عِشْق ــ مُحَرَّمَة أُلْفَة .

Amphibious, *a.* يَعِيشُ فِي ٱلْمَآءِ وَعَلَى ٱلْبَرِّ ــ بَرِّيّ بَحْرِيّ .

Amphibology, *n.* إِشْتِبَاهُ ٱلْكَلَامِ .

Amphitheatre, *n.* مُدَرَّجَة ــ مَطْلَعَة مُدَرَّج ــ مَقْعَد ــ مَنْظَرَة .

Ample, *a.* Roomy, عَرِيض ـ مُتَّسِع ـ رَحِيب ـ وَاسِع ـ فَضْفَاض ـ بَسِيط ـ فَسِيح . Abundant, زَائِد ـ كَثِير . Full, of a garment, سَابِغ . Sufficient, كَافٍ . To be —, roomy, تَمَدَّحَ ـ 2 رَحُبَ . To make —, of a garment, أَسْبَغَ . Of — fortune, غَنِيٌّ ـ كَثِيرُ ٱلْمَالِ ـ ذُو مَالٍ ـ مُوسِر ـ مُتَمَوِّل .

Ampleness, *n.* } Roominess, إِتِّسَاع ـ سَعَة ـ بُسْطَة ـ رَحْبَة . Amplitude, } Size, كُبْر . Abundance, كَثْرَة . Sufficiency, كِفَايَة .

Amplification, *n.* إِتِّسَاع ـ تَوْسِيع .

Amplify, *v.t.* To enlarge, زَادَ فِي ـ عَظَّمَ ـ كَبَّرَ ـ وَسَّعَ ـ شَرَحَ . To exaggerate, بَالَغَ فِي .

Amply, *ad.* بِسَخَاءٍ ـ بِٱلْكَثْرَةِ ـ بِسَعَةٍ . Liberally, بِكَرَمٍ .

Ampulla, *n.* قَارُورَة ـ قَرَّان .

Amputate, *v.t.* قَطَعَ ـ بَضَكَ ـ 2 جَدَّ ـ حَسَمَ ـ 2 بَتَكَ . To — the arm, إِقْتَضَبَ ـ قَبَّ . An amputated limb, فَصِيل *pl.* فِصَال ـ قِطَاع ـ صَرِيم . An amputated arm, يَدٌ جَذَّآءُ .

Amputation, *n.* حَسْم ـ قَطْع .

Amulet, *n.* عُوذَة *pl.* عُوَذ ـ حِجَاب ـ تَعْوِيذ ـ حِرْز *pl.* أَحْرَاز ـ تَمِيمَة . An — suspended round the neck, حَمَائِلُ . An — bound round the upper arm, مِعْضَاد ـ مِعْضَد . Case for an —, بَيْتُ ٱلْحِجَاب .

Amuse, *v.t.* فَرَّجَ ـ شَرَحَ خَاطِرَ ـ فَرَّحَ ـ أَطْرَبَ ـ سَلَّى . To deceive, غَشَّ ـ 2 خَانَ . To — one's self, تَنَفَّسَ ـ تَفَرَّجَ ـ إِنْشَرَحَ ـ تَنَزَّهَ ـ إِنْبَسَطَ . To — one's self, in doing trifles, عَبِثَ . I — myself in reading, أَتَسَلَّى فِي ٱلْقِرَآءَةِ . To — with promises, تَضَاحَكَ بِ . To —, as of a child, with something to divert its attention, عَلَّلَ بِ . To be diverted, amused, with, إِعْتَلَّ بِ ـ تَعَلَّلَ بِ .

Amusement, *n.* تَفَرُّج ـ تَسْلِيَة ـ تَسَلٍّ ـ تَنَزُّه ـ لَهْو . A game, لُعْبَة *pl.* لُعَبَات . Anything to divert children and keep them quiet, عُلَالَة ـ تَعِلَّة . A place of —, مَكَانُ فَرَجٍ .

Amusing, *a.* مُفَرِّج ـ يَبْسُطُ ـ مُفْرِح ـ مُطْرِب ـ مُبْهِج ـ مُسَلٍّ .

Amusingly, *ad.* بِتَنَزُّهٍ ـ بِتَسَلٍّ ـ بِطَرَبٍ .

Amygdalate, *a.* مُلَوَّز .

An, *art.* *See notes under* A.

Anabaptist, *n.* نِسْبَةٌ لِطَائِفَةٍ مِنَ ٱلنَّصَارَى لَا يَسْتَحِلُّونَ ٱلْعِمَادَ إِلَّا لِلْبَالِغِينَ مِنَ ٱلرَّشَادِ .

Anachronism, *n.* غَلَطٌ فِي ٱلتَّوَارِيخِ .

Anacreontic, *a.* Jovial, فِكِهٌ ـ مُفْرِح ـ نِدَام .

Anæsthetic, *a.* مُخَمِّدُ ٱلْوَجَعِ . An —, سُلْوَان .

Anagram, *n.* قَلْبُ حُرُوفِ ٱلْكَلِمَةِ لِمَعَانٍ ـ تَحْرِيف ـ مَقْلُوب . شَتَّى كَقَلْبِ حَامَ إِلَى مَحَا وَسَلِمَ إِلَى لَمَسَ .

Anal, *a.* دُبُرِيٌّ ـ إِسْتِيٌّ ـ مُخْتَصٌّ بِٱلْإِسْتِ .

Analectics, *n.* مَجْمَعُ مُنْتَخَبَاتٍ .

Analogical, *a.* } According to analogy, مُقَيَّس ـ قِيَاسِيٌّ . Analogous, } Correspondent, مُطَابِق ـ مُوَافِق ـ تَمَاثُلِيٌّ ـ مُتَنَاسِب .

Analogically, *ad.* بِٱلتَّشَابُهِ ـ بِٱلتَّنَاسُبِ ـ بِٱلْمُقَارَنَةِ .

Analogue, *n.* قَرِينَة .

Analogy, *n.* قِيَاس . Correspondence, مُوَافَقَة ـ مُمَاثَلَة ـ مُقَارَنَة ـ مُشَابَهَة . To reason by —, تَكَلَّمَ بِٱلْقِيَاسِ .

Analysis, *n.* إِرْجَاعُ ٱلشَّيْءِ إِلَى أُصُولِهِ ـ تَحْلِيل ـ حَلّ ـ تَلْخِيص . A grammatical —, إِعْرَابُ ٱلْكَلِمَاتِ وَبَيَانُ سَائِرِ أَحْوَالِهَا ـ إِعْرَاب . A compendium, إِجْمَال ـ فِهْرِس .

Analyst, *n.* } مُسْتَخْرِجُ ٱلْأُصُولِ .
Analyzer, }

Analytically, *ad.* تَشْرِيحًا ـ عَلَى طَرِيقِ ٱلْإِيضَاحِ .

Analytics, *n.* عِلْمُ ٱلْبَيَانِ ـ عِلْمُ ٱلتَّحْلِيلِ .

Analyze, *v.t.* إِسْتَخْرَجَ ٱلْأُصُولَ ـ حَلَّلَ ـ 2 حَلَّ . To — a discourse, لَخَّصَ ـ شَرَحَ ـ إِسْتَخْرَجَ زُبْدَةَ ٱلْكَلَامِ وَأَصْلَ مَعَانِيهِ .

Anarchic, *a.* } بَاغٍ ـ عَدِيمُ ٱلنِّظَامِ ـ عَدِيمُ ٱلْحُكْمِ . Anarchical opinions, Anarchical, } نِيَّاتٌ إِخْتِلَالِيَّةٌ ـ أَفْكَارٌ بَاغِيَةٌ .

Anarchist, *n.* مُحَرِّكُ فَسَادٍ ـ بَاغٍ *pl.* بُغَاة ـ مُشَوِّش ـ مُفْسِد .

Anarchy, *n.* هَرْجٌ وَمَرْجٌ ـ تَشْوِيش ـ شَوَاش ـ عَدَمُ ٱلْحُكْمِ ـ إِخْتِلَالٌ كُلِّيٌّ .

Anasarsa, *n.* نَوْعٌ مِنَ ٱلْإِسْتِسْقَآءِ .

Anathema, *n.* حِرْم ـ لَعْنَة .

Anathematize, *v.t.* حَرَمَ ـ لَعَنَ ـ حَرَّمَ .

Anatomical, *a.* تَشْرِيحِيٌّ .

Anatomically, *ad.* حَسَبَ قَوَانِينِ عِلْمِ ٱلتَّشْرِيحِ ـ تَشْرِيحًا .

Anatomist, *n.* عَالِمٌ فِي ٱلتَّشْرِيحِ ـ شَرَّاح ـ مُشَرِّح .

Anatomatize, *v.t.* شَرَّحَ .

Anatomy, *n.* عِلْمُ ٱلتَّشْرِيحِ . The structure of animal bodies, تَرْكِيبُ جِبِلَّةِ ٱلْحَيَوَانَاتِ . A skeleton, هَيْكَلُ ٱلْبَدَنِ عَلَى ٱلتَّرْكِيبِ ٱلطَّبِيعِيِّ .

Ancestor, *n.* سَلَف *pl.* أَسْلَاف ـ جَدٌّ *pl.* جُدُود *and* أَجْدَاد .

Ancestorial, *a.* } مُتَعَلِّقٌ بِٱلْأَجْدَادِ .
Ancestral, }

Ancestress, *n.* جِدَّة *pl.* جِدَّات.

Ancestry, *n.* آل ـ نَسْل ـ نَسَب ـ ذُرِّيَّة ـ سِلْسِلَة ـ أَجْداد. Of noble —, شَرِيفُ ٱلأَصْلِ. Of Jewish —, مِنْ نَسْلِ ٱليَهُودِ.

Anchor, *n.* مِرْساة *pl.* مَراسِي ـ هِلِب *pl.* هُلُوب ـ أَنْجَر. The — stock, المَعابِيرُ. The buoy of an —, عَوَّامَة ـ شَمَنْدُورَة. To cast —, رَسا *aor.* يَرْسُو ـ أَلْقَى ٱلمِرْساةَ ـ رَبَطَ ². To weigh —, حَلَّ ٱلمِرْساةَ ² ـ قَلَعَ ٱلمِرْساةَ ². To — a ship, أَرْسَى ٱلسَّفِينَةَ. The ship anchored, رَسَتِ ٱلسَّفِينَةُ. At —, راسِيَة *pl.* رَواسِي.

Anchor, *v.t.* *See under* Anchor, *n.*

Anchorage, *n.* مَرْسًى *pl.* مَراسٍ ـ مَرْفَأ ـ فُرْضَة.

Anchoret, *n.*, Anchorite, } مُتَوَحِّد ـ زاهِد *pl.* زُهَّاد.

Anchovy, *n.* نَوْعٌ مِنْ صِغارِ سَمَكِ ٱلبَحْرِ ـ سَنامُورَة.

Ancient, *a.* سابِق ـ مُقَدَّم ـ عَتِيق ـ قَدِيم *pl.* قُدَماءُ ـ عادِيٌّ. From — times, مِنْ سالِفِ ٱلدَّهْرِ. The ancients, القُدَماءُ ـ السَّلَفُ ـ الأَوائِلُ. The — and moderns, المُتَقَدِّمُونَ وَٱلمُتَأَخِّرُونَ. In — times, فِيمَا مَضَى ـ فِي قَدِيمِ ٱلزَّمانِ وَسالِفِ ٱلعَصْرِ وَٱلأَوانِ ـ وَتَقَدُّمٍ مِنَ ٱلزَّمانِ.

Anciently, *ad.* قَبْلًا ـ سالِفًا ـ فِي ٱلقَدِيمِ ـ قَدِيمًا.

Ancientness, *n.* عِتْق ـ سَلَف ـ قِدَم.

And, *conj.* و ـ ف ـ ثُمَّ. And so forth, هَلُمَّ جَرًّا ـ وَما شابَهَ ـ وَقِسْ عَلَيْهِ ـ وَقِسْ عَلَيْهِ ـ ذٰلِكَ.

Andiron, *n.* أُثْفِيَّة *pl.* أَثافِيّ ـ مَنْصَبٌ لِلْحَطَبِ فِي ٱلكانُونِ.

Anear, *ad.* عِنْدَ ـ قَرِيبٌ مِنْ ـ قَرِيب.

Anecdote, *n.* نادِرَة *pl.* نَوادِرُ ـ حِكايَة *pl.* حِكايات ـ قِصَّة *pl.* قِصَص.

Anemometer, *n.* مِيزانُ ٱلهَواءِ.

Anemone, *n.* دِيْسَم ـ سَكَب ـ شَقِيق ـ شَقِيقٌ نُعْمانِيٌّ ـ شَقائِقُ ٱلنُّعْمانِ.

Anent, *prep.* عَنْ ـ فِي.

Aneurism, *n.* وَرَمٌ صادِرٌ مِنْ تَسْلِيعِ عِرْقٍ.

Anew, *ad.* أَيْضًا ـ مِنْ جَدِيدٍ ـ ثانِي مَرَّةٍ.

Angel, *n.* مَلَك ـ مَلاك *pl.* مَلائِكَة. A recording —, سِجِلّ *pl.* سِجِلَّات. The — of death, مَلاكُ ٱلمَوْتِ ـ عَزْرائِيل. The two angels believed by Muslims to question the departed in their graves, نَكِير وَمُنْكَر. Guardian angels, مَلائِكَةٌ حافِظَةٌ ـ المَلائِكَةُ ٱلحُرَّاسُ ـ مَلائِكَةٌ مُعَقِّبَة.

Angelic, *a.*, Angelical, } مَلائِكِيٌّ ـ مَلَكِيٌّ.

Angelically, *ad.* كَٱلمَلاكِ.

Anger, *n.* غَيْظ ـ غِياظ ـ غَضَب ـ سُخْطَة ـ حَنَق. The vehemence or an outburst of —, حُمَيًّا. His — was roused, ثارَ ثائِرُهُ ² ـ قامَ عِرْقُ ٱلغَضَبِ بَيْنَ عَيْنَيْهِ ². To appease —, سَكَّنَ ٱلغَضَبَ ـ بَرَّدَ ٱلحَلْقَ.

Anger, *v.t.* غاظَ ـ أَغاظَ ـ غاضَبَ ـ أَغْضَبَ ـ أَسْخَطَ ـ أَثارَ ـ غَضَّبَ.

Angered, *part.* *See* Angry, *a.*

Angina pectoris, *n.* أَلَمُ ضِيقِ ٱلصَّدْرِ ـ قُطْع ـ ضِيقَةُ نَفَسٍ.

Angle, *n.* زاوِيَة *pl.* زَوايا. A corner, رُكْن *pl.* أَرْكان ـ قُرْنَة *pl.* قَرانِي. A right —, زاوِيَةٌ قائِمَةٌ; an acute —, زاوِيَةٌ حادَّةٌ; a plane —, زاوِيَةٌ مُسْتَوِيَةٌ; an obtuse —, زاوِيَةٌ مُنْفَرِجَةٌ; a solid —, زاوِيَةٌ مُجَسَّمَةٌ. The interior —, as of the eye, مُؤْق ـ مَأْق ـ أُمْق; the exterior —, لِحاظ.

Angle, *v.i.* تَصَيَّدَ سَمَكًا.

Angler, *n.* صَيَّادُ سَمَكٍ.

Anglican, *a.* أَنْكِلِيزِيٌّ.

Anglicism, *n.* لَهْجَةٌ أَنْكِلِيزِيَّةٌ.

Anglicize, *v.t.* صَيَّرَ كَٱلأَنْكِلِيزِيِّ.

Anglo-Indian, *n.* أَنْكِلِيزِيٌّ فِي خِدْمَةِ حُكُومَةِ ٱلهِنْدِ أَوْ مُسْتَوْطِنٌ فِي ٱلهِنْدِ.

Angrily, *ad.* بِغَضَبٍ ـ بِٱلغَضَبِ ـ بِغَيْظٍ ـ بِسُخْطٍ.

Angry, *a.* سَخِط ـ ثائِر ـ غَضُوب ـ غَضْبانُ. Very —, حَنِق. Soon made —, سَرِيعُ ٱلغَضَبِ. To be or become —, إِغْتاظَ ـ إِنْغاظَ ـ إِسْتَشاطَ غَيْظًا ـ إِحْتَمَى غَضَبًا ـ غَضِبَ ـ إِسْتَغْضَبَ. To become very —, حَمِيَ أَنْفُهُ. To be — with, غَضِبَ عَلَى ـ سَخِطَ عَلَى. Making —, مُغْضِب. Don't be —, لا تَغْضَبْ.

Anguish, *n.* غُصَّة ـ كَرْب ـ غَمّ ـ أَلَم ـ إِضْطِراب. To suffer — from, غَصَّ بِ ـ إِغْتَصَّ ـ إِغْتَمَّ مِنْ ـ أَغَصَّ. To cause —, غَمَّ ² ـ أَغَمَّ.

Angular, *a.* ذُو زَوايا.

Angularly, *ad.* بِزَوايا.

Anil, *a.* خَرِف.

Anility, *n.* خَرَف.

Animadversion, *n.* تَعَقُّب ـ ذَمّ ـ مَذَمَّة ـ تَعْزِير ـ تَنْبِيه ـ لَوْم.

Animadvert, *v.i.* To censure, تَعَقَّبَ ـ ذَمَّ ² ـ أَذَمَّ بِ ـ عَزَّرَ ـ طَعَنَ فِي *or* بِ ².

Animal, *n.* حَيَوان *pl.* حَيَوانات. An irrational —, بَهِيم *pl.* بَهائِمُ. A wild —, وَحْش *pl.* وُحُوش ـ سَبُع *pl.* سِباع. A rational —, حَيَوانٌ ناطِقٌ ـ حَيَوانٌ عَقْلِيٌّ. A tame —, وَدِيع *pl.* وُدَعاءُ ـ

ـ بَقَر ـ فَسْفاس ـ طَنْبَل ـ بَهِيم ,A stupid fellow. دَبْشَة ـ إِنْسِيٌّ ثَوْر.

Animal, *a.* حَيَوانِيٌّ. Sensual, شَهْوانِيٌّ ـ نَفْسانِيٌّ.

Animalcule, *n.* دُوَيْبَّة ـ حُوَيْنات *pl.* حُوَيِّن ـ حُكَل.

Animalism, *n.* بَهِيمِيَّة ـ هِواس.

Animality, *n.* حَيَوانِيَّة.

Animate, *a.* حَيٌّ *pl.* أَحْيآء ـ عائِش. Animate nature, الخَلِيقَةُ ٱلحَيَوانِيَّةُ ـ الحَيَواناتُ.

Animate, *v.t.* To give life to, أَحْيَى. To inspirit, ـ حَضَّض ـ رَوَّج ـ حَمَّى ـ حَرَّك ـ شَوَّق ـ حَرَّض ـ أَنْهَض ـ أَنْفَس حَثَّ ب.

Animated, *a.* Having life, حَيٌّ *pl.* أَحْيآء ـ عائِش. Lively, cheerful, فَرْحانُ ـ مَبْسُوط. An — countenance, وَجْهٌ بَشُوشٌ. An — discourse, كَلامٌ حادٌّ. To become —, of the countenance, إِنْبَسَطَ وَجْهُهُ.

Animating, *a.* Enlivening, ـ مُفَكِّه ـ مُهَيِّج ـ مُنَشِّط ـ مُفَرِّح مُنْعِش.

Animation, *n.* Life, حَياة ـ حَيَوة. Energy, ـ شَهامَة ـ مُرُوَّة نارِيَّة ـ قُوَّة. Cheerfulness, غِبْطَة ـ طَرَب ـ بَشاشَة ـ نَشاط.

Animosity, *n.* ـ دِمْنَة ـ بُغْض ـ حِقْد ـ مُخاصَمَة ـ سَخَس ـ غِلٌّ ـ تَحَقُّد ـ عَداوَة ـ حَمِيَّة. To bear — against, حَقَدَ عَلَى إِحْتَقَدَ.

Animus, *n.* مُراد ـ مَرام ـ نِيَّة.

Anise, *n.* الحَبَّةُ ٱلحُلْوَةُ ـ كَمُّونٌ حُلْو ـ يانِيسُون.

Anisette, *n.* عَرَقُ يانِيسُونٍ ـ أَبُو يانِيسُونٍ.

Ankle, *n.* كَعْب *pl.* كِعاب *and* كُعُوب ـ عَقِب *pl.* ـ أَعْقاب عُرْقُوب *pl.* عَراقِيب. The water rose to the ankles, لَحِقَ ٱلْمآء ٱلْكَعْبَيْنِ.

Anklet, *n.* خَلْخال ـ حَجْل ـ مَجْوَل. She put on the —, تَخَلْخَلَت.

Annalist, *n.* مُوَرِّخ ـ راوٍ.

Annals, *n.* أَخْبار ـ تَوارِيخ *pl.* تارِيخ.

Anneal, *v.t.* To temper, أَعْدَلَ ـ لَطَّف. To fix colours by heat, رَسَّخَ ـ أَرْسَخَ صَبْغَ ٱلأَلْوانِ بِالنّارِ.

Annex, *v.t.* To — to, وَصَلَ ـ بِ ـ أَضافَ ـ إِلَى ـ أَلْحَقَ ـ بِ *aor.* يَصِلُ ـ ضَمَّ ـ إِلَى ـ زادَ ـ فِي. To seize upon, as a territory, حازَ. To be annexed to, إِنْضَمَّ إِلَى ـ إِنْضافَ إِلَى ـ واصَلَ.

Annex, *n.* Something annexed; *see next article.*

Annexation, *n.* Annexment, The act of —, إِلحاق ـ تَضْمِيم ـ إِضافَة ـ وَصْل. The thing annexed, مَوْصُول ـ مُضاف ـ إِنْضِمام; as of territory, حَوْز.

Annihilate, *v.t.* مَحا ـ أَعادَ ـ لِلعَدَم ـ أَفْنَى ـ أَعْدَمَ ـ أَبادَ ـ أَلْوَحَ وُجُودَ ـ دَرَس.

Annihilated, *part.* مُتَلاشٍ ـ مُنْعَدِم ـ مَعْدُوم.

Annihilation, *n.* The act of, إِزالَة ـ إِفْنآء ـ تَدْمِير ـ إِبادَة ـ تَبْطِيل ـ إِتْلاف ـ إِضْمِحْلال.

Anniversary, *a.* سَنَوِيٌّ.

Anniversary, *n.* عِيدٌ سَنَوِيٌّ. Anniversary of birth, مِيلاد ـ عِيدُ ٱلوِلادَةِ.

Anno Domini, فِي ٱلسَّنَةِ ٱلمَسِيحِيَّةِ.

Anno Hejiræ, فِي سَنَةِ ٱلهِجْرَةِ.

Anno Mundi, لِسَنَةِ ٱلخَلِيقَةِ.

Annotate, *v.t.* أَوَّلَ ـ عَبَّرَ ـ فَسَّرَ ـ شَرَحَ.

Annotation, *n.* حاشِيَة ـ تَعْلِيقَة ـ بَيان ـ شَرْح ـ تَفْسِير ـ تَعْبِير *pl.* حَواشٍ ـ تَذْيِيل.

Annotator, *n.* مُعَبِّر ـ مُفَسِّر ـ شارِح.

Announce, *v.t.* أَشْهَرَ ـ أَذاعَ ـ أَشاعَ بِ ـ نَبَّأَ بِ ـ بَشَّرَ. To — something to, بَشَّرَ ـ بِ ـ أَخْبَرَ ـ بِ ـ أَنْبَأَ ـ نَبَّأَ ـ بِ عَرَّفَ ـ بِ.

Announcement, *n.* تَبْشِير ـ إِعْلان ـ إِخْبار ـ بِشارَة ـ خَبَر.

Annoy, *v.t.* أَتْعَبَ ـ صَدَّعَ ـ آذَى ـ أَضْجَرَ ـ شَقَّ عَلَى ـ أَزْعَجَ ـ شَوَّشَ ـ كَدَّرَ. To be annoyed, تَضَجَّرَ. To be annoyed at, ضَجِرَ بِ *or* مِن.

Annoyance, *n.* مَشَقَّة ـ صَداعَة ـ تَكَلُّف ـ أَذِيَّة ـ شِقَّة ـ ضَجَر.

Annoyed, *part.* مُعْجَز ـ ضَجُور.

Annoyer, *n.* Annoying, *a.* مُكَدِّر ـ مُعْجِز ـ مُضْجِر.

Annual, *a.* سَنَوِيٌّ ـ حَوْلِيٌّ ـ عامِيٌّ.

Annual, *n.* An annual plant, نَباتٌ يَسْتَقِيمُ مُدَّةَ سَنَةٍ فَقَطْ. A book published annually, كِتابٌ يُطْبَعُ وَيُنْشَرُ مَرَّةً فِي ٱلسَّنَةِ.

Annually, *ad.* بِٱلسَّنَةِ ـ سَنَةً بِسَنَةٍ ـ فِي كُلِّ سَنَةٍ ـ فِي ٱلسَّنَةِ.

Annuitant, *s.* One who receives a yearly payment, صاحِبُ صاحِبُ مَجْعُولٍ سَنَوِيٍّ ـ مَعاشٍ سَنَوِيٍّ.

Annuity, *n.* A yearly allowance, مَعاش (*or* مُرَتَّب) سَنَوِيٌّ ـ فَرْضٌ سَنَوِيٌّ.

Contingent annuity, مَعاشٌ سَنَوِيٌّ تَحْتَ ٱلشُّرُوطِ.

Government annuity, سَهْمُ ٱلدَّوْلَةِ *pl.* أَسْهام.

Interminable annuity, مَعَاشٌ سَنَوِيٌّ بِلا تَعْيِينِ مُدَّتِهِ.
Life annuity, مَعَاشٌ سَنَوِيٌّ مُدَّةَ قَيْدِ ٱلْحَيَاةِ.
Long annuity, مَعَاشٌ سَنَوِيٌّ إِلَى مُدَّةٍ طَوِيلَةٍ.
Terminable annuity, مَعَاشٌ سَنَوِيٌّ إِلَى مُدَّةٍ مُعَيَّنَةٍ.
To buy a government annuity, إِشْتَرَى سَهْمًا مِنْ أَسْهَامِ ٱلدَّوْلَةِ.
To settle an annuity upon, خَصَّصَ ل-مَعَاشًا سَنَوِيًّا.

Annul, *v.t.* نَقَضَ ــ أَبْطَلَ ــ أَزَالَ ــ نَسَخَ.

Annular, *a.* بِشَكْلِ ٱلْحَلْقَةِ ــ مُدَوَّر ــ دَوَّارِيّ.

Annulment, *n.* نَسْخ ــ إِزَالَة ــ إِبْطَال.

Annulose, *a.* ذو زَرَدٍ ــ مُزَرَّد ــ ذو حَلَقٍ.

Annum, *n.* سَنَة. Per —, سَنَوِيًّا.

Annumerate, *v.t.* أَلْحَقَ-ب ــ أَضَافَ-إِلَى.

Annumeration, *n.* إِضَافَة ــ إِلْحَاق.

Annunciate, *v.t.* *See to* Announce, *v.t.*

Annunciation, *n.* *See* Announcement, *n.*

Annunciation-Day, *n.* عِيدُ ٱلْبِشَارَةِ.

Anodyne, *n.* مُلَوِّن ــ دَوَآءٌ مُسَكِّنٌ لِلْأَوْجَاعِ ــ دَوَآءٌ مُرَقِّدٌ ــ دَوَآءٌ مُخَمِّدٌ.

Anodyne, *a.* مُلَيِّن ــ مُرَقِّد ــ مُسَكِّن.

Anoint, *v.t.* دَلَكَ ــ مَسَحَ ــ دَهَنَ ــ طَلَّى ــ طَلَى-ب.
To be anointed with, إِطَّلَى ب ــ إِنْطَلَى ب. He anointed him king, مَسَحَهُ مَلِكًا.

Anointed, *pp.* مَدْهُون ــ مَمْسُوح. The Anointed, Christ, المَسِيحُ.

Anointer, *n.* مُدَهِّن ــ مَاسِح.

Anointing, *n.* / Anointment, تَدْهِين ــ مَسْح.

Anomalous, *a.* شَاذّ ــ غَيْرُ قِيَاسِيّ ــ بِغَيْرِ قِيَاسٍ ــ غَيْرُ سَالِمٍ ــ مُخَالِفُ ٱلْقَاعِدَةِ.

Anomaly, *n.* شُذُوذ ــ خِلَاف ــ خِلَافُ ٱلْقَاعِدَةِ ــ خِلَافُ ٱلْعَادَةِ.

Anon, *ad.* تَوًّا ــ حَالًا ــ فِي ٱلْحَالِ ــ ذَا ٱلْوَقْتَ. Ever and —, حِينًا فَحِينًا.

Anonymous, *a.* غُفْل *pl.* أَغْفَال ــ خَفِيُّ ٱلِاسْمِ ــ مَكْتُومُ ٱلِاسْمِ ــ مِنْ غَيْرِ ٱسْمِ ٱلْمُؤَلِّفِ (أَوِ ٱلْكَاتِبِ).

Anonymously, *ad.* بِكَتْمِ ٱلِاسْمِ.

Another, *a.* آخَر *fem.* أُخْرَى *pl.* أُخَر *and* آخَرُونَ ــ غَيْر ــ ثَانٍ ــ ثَانِي. One —, بَعْضُهُمْ بَعْضًا. Do not disclose the secret of —, لا تُبِحْ بِسِرِّ غَيْرِكَ. Wait for one —, إِنْتَظِرُوا بَعْضُكُمْ بَعْضًا. Pray for one —, صَلُّوا بَعْضُكُمْ لِأَجْلِ بَعْضٍ ــ صَلُّوا عَلَى بَعْضِكُمْ بَعْضٍ.

Ansated, *a.* ذُو عُرًى ــ ذُو مِقْبَضٍ.

Answer, *v.t.* To reply to a question, أَجَابَ ــ إِسْتَجَابَ ــ رَدَّ عَلَى ــ رَدَّ جَوَابًا. To — a letter, رَدَّ جَوَابَ ٱلْمَكْتُوبِ. He answered his letter, رَدَّ إِلَيْهِ جَوَابًا. To correspond to, وَافَقَ ــ سَاوَى ــ نَاسَبَ. To refute, نَاقَضَ ــ رَدَّ عَلَى. To be responsible for, ضَمِنَ ب ــ كَفَلَ ب. To act reciprocally, وَافَقَ-عَلَى. To hear, acquiesce in, قَبِلَ ــ إِسْتَجَابَ ــ سَمِعَ إِلَى ــ رَضِيَ ب. The Christian year which answers to the year of the al-Hijrah, السَّنَةُ ٱلْمَسِيحِيَّةُ ٱلْمُوافِقَةُ لِلسَّنَةِ ٱلْهِجْرِيَّةِ. I will — for you, أَنَا لَكَ ضَامِنٌ ــ أَنَا لَكَ كَفِيلٌ. He has not answered, responded to, my friendship, مَا وَافَقَنِي عَلَى ٱلصَّدَاقَةِ. To — indirectly, لَاتَ ــ مَسِكَ. Not to answer, سَكَتَ عَنِ ٱلْجَوَابِ ــ تَحَبَّسَ عَنْ رَدِّ ٱلْجَوَابِ ــ عَنِ ٱلْجَوَابِ.

Answer, *n.* جَوَاب *pl.* جَوَابَات *and* أَجْوِبَة ــ مُجَاوَبَة ــ رَدّ ــ جَوَاب. Refutation, مُنَاقَضَة. An — to a letter, رَجْعَةُ كِتَابٍ. A definitive —, جَوَابٌ قَاطِعٌ. A doubtful —, جَوَابٌ مُشْكِلٌ. Has the — to your letter arrived? هَلْ جَاءَتْ رَجْعَةُ كِتَابِكَ.

Answerable, *a.* That may be answered, ذُو جَوَابٍ ــ يُجَاوَبُ ــ أَهْلٌ لِلْجَوَابِ ــ مُمْكِنٌ ــ الجَوَابُ ل. Equivalent to, مُسَاوٍ ل ــ مُعَادِلٌ ل ــ مُقَاوِمٌ ل. Accountable, ضَامِن ــ كَفِيل ــ زَعِيم. I am — for, فِي ذِمَّتِي ــ فِي ضَمَانِي. If it is lost you will be — for it, إِنْ ضَاعَ فَٱلْمَطْلُوبُ مِنْكَ. Answerable to his merits, لَائِقٌ بِٱسْتِحْقَاقِهِ. To become — for, تَحَمَّلَ ب. To make —, أَكْفَلَ ــ كَفَّلَ.

Answerably, *ad.* مُطَابَقَةً ــ لِيَاقَةً ــ بِلِيَاقَةٍ.

Answerer, *n.* مُجَاوِب. The — of prayer, God, المُجِيبُ.

Ant, *n.* نَمْلَة *coll.* نَمْل *pl.* نِمَال. A red —, سُمْسُمَة *pl.* سَمَاسِمُ. An — hive, بَيْتُ نَمْلٍ ــ عِشُّ نَمْلٍ. Land abounding in ants, أَرْضٌ نَمِلَةٌ (*or* مُنْمِلَةٌ). Bitten by —, مَنْمُول.

Antacid, *n.* دَافِعُ ٱلْحُمُوضَةِ.

Antagonism, *n.* مُقَاوَمَة ــ عَدَاوَة ــ خُصُومَة ــ مُضَادَّة.

Antagonist, *n.* مُقَاوِم ــ خَصْم *pl.* خِصَام ــ خَصِيم *pl.* خُصَمَاء ــ عَدُوّ *pl.* أَعْدَاء.

Antagonistic, *a.* مُضَادّ ــ مُقَاوِمٌ ل ــ خَصْم ــ ضِدّ. To be —, inimical, to, قَاوَمَ. To be —, opposed, contrary, to, ضَادَّ.

Antarctic, *a.* جُنُوبِيّ.

Antecede, *v.i.* سَبَقَ ــ سَلَفَ ــ تَقَدَّمَ. To make to —, سَلَّفَ.

Antecedence, *n.* أَوَّلِيَّة ــ تَقَدُّم ــ سَبْق.

Antecedent, *a.* سَابِق *pl.* سُبَّاق ــ أَوَّل ــ سَالِف ــ مُقَدَّم. An —

people, قَوْمٌ سُلَّافٌ . Antecedent and consequent, مُقَدَّمٌ وَتَالٍ — سَابِقٌ وَلَاحِقٌ .

Antecedent, *n.* A prior event, سَابِقَةٌ *pl.* سَوَابِقُ — مُقَدَّمَةٌ *pl.* مُقَدَّمَاتٌ . The noun to which the relative is subjoined, المُضَافُ . Good antecedents, حُسْنُ سَابِقَةٍ ; bad antecedents, سُوءُ سَابِقَةٍ .

Antecedently, *ad.* سَبْقًا — أَوَّلًا — سَابِقًا .

Antechamber, *n.* مَابَيْن — مُتَّكَأٌ يُفْضِي إِلَى ٱلْقَاعَةِ .

Antedate, *v.t.* سَلَّفَ — قَدَّمَ ٱلتَّارِيخَ — أَرَّخَ بِتَارِيخٍ أَقْدَمَ .

Antedate, *n.* تَارِيخٌ مُقَدَّمٌ . Antedated, مُقَدَّمُ ٱلتَّارِيخِ .

Antediluvian, *a.* قَبْلَ ٱلطُّوفَانِ .

Antediluvian, *n.* نِسْبَةٌ لِمَا قَبْلَ — مَنْ عَاشَ قَبْلَ ٱلطُّوفَانِ ٱلطُّوفَانِ .

Antelope, *n.* ظَبْيٌ *fem.* ظَبْيَةٌ *pl. masc.* أَظْبٍ — أَرْآم رِئْم *pl.* *pl. fem.* ظَبَيَاتٌ — رَشَأٌ *pl.* أَرْشَاءٌ .

Antemeridian, *a.* قَبْلَ ٱلْقَائِلَةِ — قَبْلَ ٱلظُّهْرِ .

Antemundane, *a.* قَبْلَ ٱلدُّنْيَا — قَبْلَ ٱلْخَلِيقَةِ .

Ante-Nicene, *a.* قَبْلَ ٱلْمَجْمَعِ ٱلنِّيقَاوِيِّ — قَبْلَ مَجْمَعَةٍ نِيقِيَّةٍ .

Antenna, *n.* قَرْن *pl.* قُرُون .

Antepast, *n.* *See* Foretaste, *n.*

Antepenult, *n.* An — syllable, ٱلْهِجَاءُ ٱلْوَاقِعُ قَبْلَ آخِرِ ٱلْكَلِمَةِ بِهِجَائَيْنِ .

Antepenultimate, *a.* مَا قَبْلَ ٱلْآخِرِ .

Anteposition, *n.* تَقَدُّم — تَقْدِيم .

Anterior, *a.* سَالِف — أَوَّلُ — سَابِق — مُتَقَدِّم .

Anteriority, *n.* تَقَدُّم — سُلُوف — أَوَّلِيَّة .

Anthelmintic, *n.* دَوَاءٌ قَاطِعُ ٱلدِّيدَانِ .

Anthem, *n.* تَسْبِيح *pl.* تَسَابِيحُ — مَزْمُور *pl.* مَزَامِيرُ — تَسْبِحَة .
To sing an —, رَتَّلَ تَسْبِحَةً .

Anthony's (Saint) fire, *n.* حُمْرَة — رَشْكِين .

Anthracite, *n.* صِنْفٌ مِنَ ٱلْفَحْمِ ٱلْحَجَرِيِّ .

Anthropology, *n.* عِلْمٌ يَبْحَثُ فِي ٱلْبَشَرِيَّةِ .

Anthropomorphism, *n.* ٱلتَّشْبِيهُ .

Anthropomorphite, *n.* مُشَبِّهٌ *pl.* مُشَبِّهُون .

Anthropophagi, *n.* أَكَّالَةُ لَحْمِ ٱلْبَشَرِ .

Anthropophagy, *n.* أَكْلُ لَحْمِ ٱلْبَشَرِ .

Anti, لَفْظَةٌ يُونَانِيَّةٌ تَسْبِقُ جُمْلَةَ أَلْفَاظٍ فِي ٱللُّغَةِ ٱلْإِنْكِلِيزِيَّةِ وَتَتَرَكَّبُ مَعَهَا مَعْنَاهَا ٱلضِّدِّيَّةُ أَوِ ٱلدَّفْعُ مِثَالُ ذٰلِكَ febrile حُمِّيٌّ ; anti-febrile دَافِعُ ٱلْحُمَّى .

Antic, *a.* A buffoon, خَلْبُوص — قَشْمَر . A caper, نَطَّة — زَفْنَة — مَسْخَرَة — قَشْمَرَة — تَهْرِيج . *See also under* Caper, *n.*

Anti-chamber, *n.* *See* Antechamber, *also under* Chamber, Lobby, *n.*

Antichrist, *n.* المَسِيحُ ٱلْكَذَّابُ — ٱلدَّجَّالُ .

Antichristian, *a.* مُخَالِفٌ لِلدِّيَانَةِ ٱلْمَسِيحِيَّةِ .

Anticipate, *v.t.* To do before another, بَسَرَ [2] أَبْسَرَ — [2] سَبَقَ — بَادَرَ — إِلَى — أَسْبَقَ - إِلَى — قَدَّمَ — بَدَرَ - إِلَى . To expect, إِنْتَظَرَ — إِسْتَنْظَرَ — تَوَقَّفَ . To have a foretaste or impression of, قَبْلًا - حَسَّ بِ - قَبْلًا . To — something as impending, تَرَبَّصَ — شَعَرَ بِ - قَبْلًا .

Anticipation, *n.* The being before, بَسْر — سَبْق — تَقْدِيم — مُبَادَرَة . Previous opinion, رَأْيٌ سَابِقٌ — حِسٌّ مُتَقَدِّمٌ . Expectation, تَوَقُّع — تَوَقُّف — إِنْتِظَار — تَرَبُّص .

Antick, *n.* *See* Antic, *n.*

Anti-constitutional, مُغَايِرٌ (*or* مُخَالِفٌ) لِلْأَحْكَامِ .

Antidote, *n.* دَافِعُ ٱلسَّمِّ — بَادْزَهْر — قَرَابَاذِين — تِرْيَاق .

Antifebrile, *a.* دَافِعُ ٱلْحُمَّى . An — remedy, دَوَاءٌ لِلْحُمَّى .

Antimonarchical, *a.* مُخَالِفٌ لِلْحُكْمِ ٱلسُّلْطَانِيِّ .

Antimonial, *a.* كُحْلِيٌّ — مِنَ ٱلْكُحْلِ — إِثْمِدِيٌّ .

Antimony, *n.* حَجَرٌ — حَجَرُ ٱلْكُحْلِ — كِحَال — كُحْل — إِثْمِد — أَنْتِيمُون — ٱلرَّاسُخْت . To paint, as the eyes, with —, كَحَّلَ . The style for applying —, مِكْحَال — مِكْحَل . The vase for —, مُكْحُلَة . Having, as the eyes, painted with —, مَكْحُول .

Antipathy, *n.* كَرَاهَةٌ خِلْقِيَّةٌ — إِنْتِنَاف — نُفُور — كَرَاهَة . To have an — for, كَرِهَ — جَبَأَ — إِسْتَكْرَهَ — إِعْتَنَفَ — أَنِفَ .

Antiphone, *n.* تَسْبِيحٌ بِٱلدَّوْرِ .

Antipodes, *n.* مُقَابِلُوا ٱلْأَرْجُلِ وَهُمُ ٱلنَّاسُ ٱلَّذِينَ يَسْكُنُونَ فِي ٱلْجِهَةِ ٱلْأُخْرَى مِنَ ٱلْكُرَةِ أَرْجُلُهُمْ مُقَابِلَةٌ لِأَرْجُلِنَا .

Antiquarian, *a.* مُخْتَصٌّ بِعِلْمِ ٱلْآثَارِ ٱلْقَدِيمَةِ .

Antiquarian, *n.* } رَاغِبٌ فِي ٱلْآثَارِ — عَالِمٌ فِي ٱلْآثَارِ ٱلْقَدِيمَةِ
Antiquary, } ٱلْقَدِيمَةِ .

Antiquated, *a.* } عَتِيق — مُعَتَّق — قَدِيم . Obsolete, هَامِد —
Antique, } مَهْجُور — غَيْرُ مُسْتَعْمَلٍ .

Antique, *n.* أَثَرٌ قَدِيمٌ *pl.* آثَارٌ قَدِيمَةٌ — شَيْءٌ عَتِيقٌ *pl.* أَشْيَاءٌ عَتِيقَةٌ .

Antiquity, *n.* قِدَم — تَقَادُم . A vestige of —, أَثَرٌ قَدِيمٌ . Past ages, ٱلْأَجْيَالُ ٱلْمَاضِيَةُ . The ancients, ٱلْأَقْدَمُون — ٱلْأَوَائِلُ — ٱلْقُدَمَاءُ — ٱلسَّلَفَاءُ .

Antithesis, n. }
Antithetical, a. } نَقِيض .

Antitype, n. المَدْلُولُ عَلَيْهِ بِٱلرَّمْزِ — كَمالُ ٱلرَّمْزِ — الشَّيْءُ ٱلَّذِى تَدُلُّ عَلَيْهِ ٱلإِشارَةُ .

Antler, n. قَرْن pl. قُرُون .

Anus, n. جُحْر — إِسْت — دُبُر — مَجْعَر — خاتِم — مَقْعَدَة . The sphincter of the —, حَلْقَةُ ٱلدُّبُرِ — حِتارُ ٱلدُّبُرِ .

Anvil, n. زُبْرَة — عَلاة pl. عَلاوات — سِنْدان .

Anxiety, n. كَرْب pl. كُرُوب — حَوْبَة — إِهْتِمام — عَناء — قَلَق — هَمّ — حَصْرَةُ قَلْبٍ . Anxiety befell him, ضاقَهُ ٱلْهَمُّ . The — that arose in the public mind, القَلَقُ ٱلَّذِى قامَ فِى خَواطِرِ ٱلنّاسِ .

Anxious, a. Strongly desirous, مُشْتاق — رَغُوب — مُتَوَلِّع — مُتَلَهِّف إِلَى . Solicitous, كَرِيب — عانٍ — مُهْتَمّ — مُضْطَرِب — مَكْرُوب — قَلِق — مَشْغُولُ ٱلْفِكْرِ . To be —, desirous, for, إِشْتاقَ إِلَى . To be —, solicitous, إِهْتَمَّ — إِكْتَرَبَ — شَجِنَ ع — ضَجِرَ ب . To make —, solicitous, أَشْجَنَ — أَضْجَرَ — أَكْرَبَ . An — matter, هَمِيمَة .

Anxiously, ad. بِرَغْبَةٍ — بِٱشْتِياقٍ — بِتَحَسُّرٍ — بِحَرارَةٍ .

Any, a. ما . Any one, أَيُّ مَنْ كانَ — كُلُّ مَنْ كانَ . Any thing, مَهْما كانَ . Not —, لا أَحَدَ — وَلا واحِدٌ — أَصْلًا — قَطُّ . Any how, كَيْفَما كانَ . Any where, حَيْثُما كانَ — فِى كُلِّ مَكانٍ . Any wise, عَلَى كُلِّ حالٍ — كَيْفَما كانَ . Above — thing, فَوْقَ ٱلْكُلِّ . Without — expense, بِلا مَصْرُوفٍ أَصْلًا . Do not tell — one, لا تُخَبِّرْ أَحَدًا . If — of you have — thing against — one, إِنْ كانَ لَكُمْ عَلَى أَحَدٍ شَيْءٌ . Will you not take — thing? أَلا تَأْخُذُ شَيْئًا . Any thing else? هَلْ شَيْءٌ غَيْرُهُ — وَغَيْرُهُ . I did not find that he had — bread, ما وَجَدْتُ عِنْدَهُ خُبْزًا . I will not have —, لا أُرِيدُ شَيْئًا . Any reasonable person, كُلُّ ذِى عَقْلٍ .

Aorist, n. The — tense, المُضارِعُ . The indicative —, المُضارِعُ ٱلْمَرْفُوعُ . Apocopate —, المُضارِعُ ٱلْمَجْزُومُ .

Aorta, n. أَبْهَر — أَوْرِيطِى — وَتِين — عَمُودُ ٱلسَّحْرِ .

Apace, ad. بِسُرْعَةٍ — بِٱلْعَجَلِ — بِشِدَّةٍ .

Apart, ad. عَلَى جانِبٍ — عَلَى ناحِيَةٍ — بِٱنْفِرادٍ — عَلَى حِدَةٍ . They sat —, جَلَسُوا عَلَى وَحْدِهِم . To retire —, صَدَفَ ـِ — تَصَدَّفَ عَنْ . To set —, save, تَقَنَّى . To lay, cast, —, طَرَحَ ـَ .

Apartment, n. A room, قاعَة — مُتَّكَأ — أُوضَة pl. أُوضات — بَيْت pl. بُيُوت — مَحَلّ pl. مَحَلّات — حُجْرَة pl. حُجَر — مَطْرَح pl. مَطارِح . A suite, as of —, دائِرَة . The women's —, الحَرِيمُ — مَنْزِلُ ٱلنِّساءِ — الحَرَمُ .

Apathetic, a. فاتِر — جامِدُ ٱلنَّفْسِ — عَدِيمُ ٱلرَّغْبَةِ .

Apathy, n. فُتُور — عَدَمُ ٱلرَّغْبَةِ — بَلادَة — عَدَمُ ٱلْمُرُوَّةِ .

Ape, v.t. قَلَّدَ — مَثَّلَ بِ — شَخَّصَ بِ — حاكَى .

Ape, n. قِرْدَة coll. قِرْد pl. قُرُود and أَقْراد — سَعْدان . A keeper of apes, قَرّاد .

Aperient, a. مُفَتِّح — مُسْهِل .

Aperient, n. An aperient, medicine, مُسْهِلٌ — دَواءٌ — شَرْبَة .

Aperture, n. شَقّ pl. شُقُوق — فَتْحَة — نَقْب . An — for light, طاق — رَوْشَن pl. رَواشِن — سِهاء pl. سَهْوَة — طاقات — كُوَّة .

Apex, n. قُلَّة pl. قُلَل — قِمَّة pl. قِمَم — رَأْس pl. رُؤُوس .

Aphorism, n. مَثَل — ضَرْبُ مَثَلٍ — قاعِدَة pl. قَواعِد — قَوْل pl. أَقْوال .

Aphrodisiac, n. The medicine, عِلاجٌ باهِيٌّ .

Apiary, n. جِزْع — مَعْسَلَة — خَلِيَّة — كَوارَى — خَلايَةُ نَحْلٍ .

Apiece, ad. لِكُلِّ أَحَدٍ — لِكُلِّ واحِدٍ — عَلَى رَأْسِ كُلِّ واحِدٍ . They hold so much —, يَسَعُ كُلُّ واحِدٍ مِقْدارَ .

Apish, a. مِثْلَ ٱلْقِرْدِ .

Apishness, n. حَماقَة — جَهْل — تَصَلُّف — قِرْدَنَة .

Apocalypse, n. The —, كِتابُ ٱلْكَشْفِ لِمارِ يُوحَنّا — رُؤْيا مارِ يُوحَنّا — كِتابُ ٱلأَبُوكالِبْسِيس — سِفْرُ ٱلْجِلْيانِ .

Apocopate, v.t. حَذَفَ ـِ — رَخَّمَ .

Apocopated, a. مَحْذُوفٌ مِنْهُ — مُرَخَّم — مَجْزُوّ .

Apocope, n. حَذْف — حَذْفُ شَيْءٍ مِنْ آخِرِ كَلِمَةٍ — تَرْخِيم .

Apocrypha, n. The —, الكُتُبُ ٱلْغَيْرُ قانُونِيَّةٍ — الأَسْفارُ ٱلْمُحَرَّفَةُ .

Apocryphal, a. غَيْرُ قانُونِيٍّ — مُرِيب — ذُو رِيبَةٍ — مُحَرَّف .

Apodosis, جَوابُ شَرْطٍ — نَتِيجَةُ ٱلْكَلامِ .

Apogee, n. أَوْج — أَقْرَبُ مَسافَةٍ بَيْنَ ٱلْقَمَرِ وَٱلأَرْضِ .

Apologetic, n. }
Apologetical, } Excusatory, إِعْتِذارِيٌّ .

Apologetically, ad. إِعْتِذارًا — بِٱعْتِذارٍ .

Apologist, n. A defender, حامٍ pl. حُماة and حامِيَة — عَذِير — مُناجِد — مُدافِع . An excuser, مُتَعَذِّر .

Apologize, v.i. To make apologies, excuses, تَعَذَّرَ — إِعْتَذَرَ — إِسْتَعْذَرَ . To — to, إِعْتَذَرَ إِلَى .

Apology, n. Defence, مُحاماة — مُناجَدَة — بَرآءَة — جَواب . Excuse, تَعَذُّر — عُذْر pl. أَعْذار — إِعْتِذار . To receive an —, إِسْتَعْذَرَ . To offer an — excuse, for, عَذَرَ ـِ — أَعْذَرَ .

Apophthegm, n. مَثَل — ضَرْبُ مَثَلٍ — قَوْل pl. أَقْوال — كَلِمَة pl. كَلِمات .

Apoplectic, a. سَكْتِيّ .

Apoplexy, *n.* هَمْدَة ـ سَكْتَة ـ نُقْطَة.

Apostacy, *n.* إرْتِدادٌ عَنِ ٱلدِّينِ ـ إنْكارُ ٱلدِّينِ ـ رِدَّة ـ كُفْران ـ جَحْد.

Apostate, *n.* مُرْتَدٌّ ـ رافِضِيٌّ *pl.* رُفَّاض ـ تارِكُ ٱلدِّينِ ـ كافِر *pl.* كُفَّار ـ جاحِد.

Apostatize, *v.i.* إرْتَدَّ عَنِ ٱلدِّينِ ـ 2 تَرَكَ ٱلدِّينَ ـ = نَكِرَ ٱلدِّينَ ـ = كَفَرَ. He apostatized from Islâm, إرْتَدَّ عَنِ ٱلْإسْلامِ.

A-posteriori, *ad.* مُسْتَنْتَجٌ بَعْدَ ٱلْواقِعَةِ ـ مُسْتَنْتَجٌ مِنَ ٱلْمَفْعُولِ.

Apostle, *n.* رَسُول *pl.* رُسَلاءُ *and* رُسُل ـ حَوارِيٌّ. The holy Apostles, ٱلرُّسُلُ ٱلْأَطْهارُ ـ ٱلْحَوارِيُّونَ. The Apostles' Creed, قانُونُ إيمانِ ٱلرُّسُلِ

Apostleship, *n.* / **Apostolate,** } وَظِيفَةُ ٱلرُّسُلِ ـ رِسالَة ـ رَسُولِيَّة.

Apostolic, *a.* / **Apostolical,** } رَسُولِيٌّ.

Apostolically, *ad.* كَٱلرُّسُلِ ـ بِنَوْعٍ رَسُولِيٍّ

Apostrophe, *n.* An address, خِطاب ـ مُناداة. A mark of elision, عَلامَةُ ٱلْحَذْفِ.

Apostrophize, *v.t.* To address, خاطَبَ ـ كَلَّمَ. To mark with apostrophes, عَلَّمَ بِعَلاماتِ ٱلْحَذْفِ.

Apothecary, *n.* صَيْدَلانِيٌّ *pl.* صَيادِلَةُ ـ عَطَّار ـ بَيَّاعُ ٱلْأَدْوِيَةِ ـ أَجْزاجِي. An apothecary's shop, أَجْزاخانه. The business of an —, صَيْدَلَة.

Apotheosis, *n.* تَأْلِيه.

Appal, *v.t.* رَعَّبَ ـ هَوَّلَ ـ أَرْعَدَ ـ خَوَّفَ ـ جَفَّلَ. To be appalled, تَهَوَّلَ ـ إرْتَعَبَ ـ إرْتَعَدَ ـ إهْتالَ ـ تَخَوَّفَ.

Appalling, *a.* مُرْعِب ـ مَهُول ـ مُخِيف ـ فَظِيع. How — he is! ما أَهْوَلَهُ. An — thing, هِيلَة.

Appanage, *n.* أَقْطاعٌ لِمَعِيشَةِ أَوْلادِ ٱلْمَلِكِ. Lands in —, أَقْطاع.

Apparatus, *n.* عَتاد ـ آلات ـ عُدَّة ـ أَداة ـ مَتاع *pl.* أَمْتِعَة ـ أَسْباب ـ أُهْبَة ـ لَوازِمُ. Warlike —, آلاتُ ٱلْحَرْبِ ـ جِهاز. A cooking —, عُدَّةُ ٱلطَّبْخِ. Building —, حَضْرَة. Household —, مَتاعُ ٱلْبَيْتِ.

Apparel, *n.* كِساء ـ لِباس ـ ثِياب.

Apparel, *v.t.* أَلْبَسَ ـ لَبَّسَ ـ = كَسَى بِ.

Apparent, *a.* Plain, ظاهِر ـ بائِن ـ بارِز ـ بَيِّن ـ جَلِيّ ـ واضِح. Not real, put on, constrained, مُرْهَق ـ دَغِل ـ مُنَبِّس ـ غَيْرُ حَقِيقِيٍّ. As seen, حَسَبَ ٱلرُّؤْيَةِ. To be —, تَبَدَّى ـ إتَّضَحَ ـ 2 بَرَزَ ـ تَعَيَّنَ. To become —, to be divulged, باحَ *aor.* يَبُوحُ. To make —, 2 باحَ بِ ـ بَرَّزَ ـ بَيَّنَ ـ أَوْضَحَ. The heir —, وَلِيُّ ٱلْعَهْدِ.

Apparently, *ad.* فِي ٱلظَّاهِرِ ـ ظاهِرًا ـ فِي ٱلْبائِنِ.

Apparition, *n.* Appearance, ظُهُور ـ صُورَة ـ بَيان. A spectre, زَوْل *pl.* أَزْوال ـ خَيالَة ـ خَيال *pl.* أَخْيِلَة ـ طَيْف ـ عِفْرِيت.

Appeal, *n.* As from a judgment, إسْتِئْناف; to the same, مُرافَعَة; to a witness, إسْتِشْهاد; as for assistance, إسْتِغاثَة. Recourse to, إلْتِجاءٌ إلَى ـ طَلِبَةٌ مِن ـ تَعَرُّضٌ إلَى. A court of —, مَحْكَمَةُ ٱلْمُرافَعاتِ ـ مَحْكَمَةٌ إسْتِئْنافِيَّةٌ ـ دِيوانُ ٱلْإسْتِئْنافِ. Municipal and commercial appeals, مُرافَعاتٌ مَدَنِيَّةٌ وَتِجارِيَّةٌ. To lodge an —, أَعْلَنَ بِٱلْمُرافَعَةِ. Without further —, مَمْنُوعُ ٱلْإسْتِئْنافِ.

Appeal, *v.t.* and *i.* To refer to another as judge, = رَفَعَ ٱلدَّعْوَى إلَى. To call as a witness, إسْتَشْهَدَ. To ask assistance of, إسْتَغاثَ بِ. To have recourse to, إلْتَجَأَ إلَى. To — to God against any evil, 2 عاذَ بِٱللّٰهِ مِن ـ تَعَوَّذَ بِٱللّٰهِ مِن.

Appear, *v.i.* To be in sight, = ظَهَرَ ـ إسْتَبانَ ـ تَبَيَّنَ. To —, as of the sun, 2 لاحَ ـ أَلاحَ. To stand in the presence of, 2 حَضَرَ ـ 2 قامَ بَيْنَ يَدَيْهِ ـ إحْتَضَرَ. To seem, = بانَ. To be witnessed, شُوهِدَ. To make to —, be present, أَحْضَرَ. To make to —, to show, أَظْهَرَ. To —, to arrive, وَصَلَ *aor.* يَصِلُ ـ أَقْبَلَ عَلَى. To — for, in the cause of, حامَى عَن ـ ساعَدَ. To — for, in the place of, 2 حَضَرَ عِوَضَ ـ 2 قامَ بِمَقامِ. To — against, to oppose, ضادَدَ ـ قاوَمَ ـ قابَلَ. It appeared to him, تَخَيَّلَ لَهُ ـ تَشَبَّهَ لَهُ. It appears that…, البائِنُ أَنْ. *See also to* Seem, *v.i.*

Appearance, *n.* The being in sight, ظُهُور ـ بَيان. Form, صُورَة ـ مَرْآة ـ مَنْظَر ـ هَيْئَة *pl.* هَيْآت. Mien, طَلْعَة ـ سَمامَة. Probability, إحْتِمال ـ وَجْه. Similitude, مُناظَرَة ـ تَمْثِيل ـ مُشابَهَة. Presence, حُضُور. Arrival, قُدُوم ـ وُصُول. A spectre, خَيال. He has a fine appearance, هُوَ حَسَنُ ٱلسَّمامَةِ. In — but not in heart, بِٱلظَّاهِرِ لا بِٱلْقَلْبِ. Avoid all — of evil, إمْتَنِعُوا عَنْ كُلِّ شِبْهِ شَرٍّ. For appearance' sake, عَلَى عُيُونِ ٱلنَّاسِ ـ لِأَجْلِ ٱلصُّورَةِ. To save appearances, احْتِفاظًا بِٱلنَّامُوسِ ٱلظَّاهِرِ.

Appease, *v.t.* سَكَّنَ ـ هَدَّأَ ـ أَهْدَأَ. To —, as with words, = فَثَأَ بِ. To — an irritated person, طَيَّبَ خاطِرَ ـ أَخَذَ بِخاطِرِ.

Appeasement, *n.* تَسْكِين ـ إهْداء.

Appellant, *n.* رافِعُ دَعْواهُ ـ مُسْتَأْنِف.

Appellation, *n.* إسْم *pl.* أَسْماء *and* أَسامِي ـ لَقَب *pl.* أَلْقاب ـ تَسْمِيَة.

Appellative, *n.* إِسْمُ جِنْسٍ.

Append, *v.t.* إِسْتَدْرَكَ ـ أَضَافَ-إِلَى ـ عَلَّقَ-عَلَى ـ عَلَّقَ-فِي ـ أَلْزَقَ-فِي ـ عَلَى ـ إِلْتَزَقَ فِي ـ إِنْضَافَ إِلَى. To be appended to, إِنْضَافَ إِلَى ـ إِلْتَزَقَ فِي. To —, as notes, in the margin of a book, عَلَّقَ فِي حَاشِيَةِ كِتَابٍ.

Appendage, *n.* إِضَافَة ـ إِنْتِسَاب ـ ضَمِيمَة ـ تَابِعَة ـ تَعْلِقَة.

Appendant, *a.* مُتَعَلِّق بِ ـ مُضَاف إِلَى ـ مُسْتَدْرَك ـ تَذْيِيلِيّ ـ مَوْقُوف عَلَى ـ تَابِع *pl.* تُبَّاع.

Appendix, *n.* An — to a book, ضَمِيمَة ـ مُلْحَقَة ـ تَعْلِيقَة ـ ذَيْل *pl.* أَذْيَال ـ خَاتِمَة كِتَابَة. I added an — to his book, ذَيَّلْتُ.

Appertain, *v.i.* To belong to, إِنْتَسَبَ ـ ² خَصَّ ـ إِخْتَصَّ بِ ـ تَبِعَ ـ تَعَلَّقَ بِ ـ إِلَى. It appertains to you, you ought, يَلِيقُ بِكَ. And all that appertained to them, وَكُلُّ مَا لَهُمْ. One half of it appertains to me, يَخُصُّنِي مِنْهُ ٱلنِّصْفُ. It appertains to him to ..., it is proper for him to ..., يَحِقُّ عَلَيْهِ أَن ـ عَلَيْهِ أَن ـ مِن شَأْنِهِ أَن ـ يَصْلُحُ لَهُ أَن. It appertains to him, it is his, تَبَعُهُ (this is colloquial).

Appetence, *n.* / Appetency, } لَذَّة ـ نَفْس ـ مَيْل ـ رَغْبَة ـ شَوْق.

Appetite, *n.* قَابِلِيَّة لِلْأَكْلِ ـ إِشْتِهَاء ـ نَفْس ـ شَهْوَة ـ وَحَم. Loss of —, خُلْفَة. To have an — for, إِشْتَهَى ـ تَشَهَّى عَلَى. To sharpen, as of the —, ² سَنَّ ـ ² شَحَذَ ـ أَحَدَّ. To have no — for, ² فَهِمَ عَن. I have no —, مَا لِي ـ مَا لِي نَفْسٌ لِلْأَكْلِ ـ إِشْتِهَاء لِلْأَكْلِ.

Appetizer, *n.* مُزّ ـ مُحَرِّكُ ٱلْإِشْتِهَاء ـ لُهْنَة ـ لُمْجَة (*vulg.* مُزّ).

Applaud, *v.t.* To praise, ² حَمِدَ ـ إِسْتَحْسَنَ ـ ² مَدَحَ ـ أَثْنَى عَلَى. To — loudly, ² صَاحَ بِ ـ صَوَّتَ عَلَى. To — by clapping the hands, صَفَّقَ عَلَى يَدِهِ بِ ـ صَفَّقَ لِ.

Applause, *n.* Praise, تَلَقٍّ بِٱلْقَبُولِ ـ ثَنَاء ـ إِسْتِحْسَان ـ مَدْح ; with the hands, تَصْفِيق.

Apple, *n.* تُفَّاحَة *coll.* تُفَّاح *pl.* تَفَافِيحُ *and* تُفَّاحَات. The — of the eye, حَدَقَة ـ إِنْسَانُ ٱلْعَيْنِ ـ ذُبَابُ ٱلْعَيْنِ ـ بُؤْبُؤُ ٱلْعَيْنِ ـ حَبَّةُ ٱلْعَيْنِ ـ ٱلْعَيْن. Love —, the tomato, بَاذِنْجَان فِرَنْجِيّ. Custard —, سَفَرْجَل هِنْدِيّ. An — orchard, مَتْفَحَة.

Appliance, *n.* A thing applied, مَنْصُوب ـ مَوْضُوع. Appliances, تَسْهِيلَات ـ وَسَائِل ـ أَسْبَاب.

Applicable, *a.* Suitable, in its place, مُطَابِق ـ مُوَافِق لِ ـ فِي مَحَلِّهِ ـ أَلْيَق بِ. That may be applied, carried out, قَابِل ـ صَلَحَ لِ ². الإِجْرَاء بِهِ مُمْكِن ـ ٱلْإِجْرَاء. To be —, useful, to, صَلَحَ لِ ². To make —, أَصْلَحَ.

Applicableness, *n.* / Applicability, } مَصْلَحَة ـ لِيَاقَة ـ مُطَابَقَة ـ مُنَاسَبَة.

Applicant, *n.* طَالِب *pl.* طَلَبَة *or* طُلَّاب.

Application, *n.* The act of applying any thing to another, جَعْل ـ إِسْتِعْمَال ـ وَضْع. Application, by way of addition, إِضَافَة ـ إِلْسَاق ـ إِتِّصَال. Continued attention, مُرَابَطَة ـ جِدّ ـ تَقْيِيد ـ إِجْتِهَاد ـ جَهْد ـ مُلَازَمَة. Recourse, as to another, إِلْتِجَاء إِلَى. A petition, عَرْض ـ سُؤَال ـ طَلَبَة. Application may be made for these books at ..., هٰذِهِ ٱلْكُتُبُ يُسْأَلُ عَنْهَا مِن.

Apply, *v.t.* To put one thing to another, وَضَعَ-عَلَى *aor.* يَضَعُ ـ جَعَلَ ـ ² حَطَّ. To use, إِسْتَعْمَلَ. To —, as by addition, ² طَبَّقَ-بِ ـ ² ضَمَّ-إِلَى ـ يَصِلُ *aor.* وَصَلَ-بِ. To fix the mind upon, ² حَرَصَ ـ وَاظَبَ عَلَى ـ حَافَظَ عَلَى ـ إِلْتَبَطَ فِي ـ ² شَبَّكَ عَقْلَ-فِي ـ تَغَرَّسَ فِي ـ عَلَى. To have recourse to, إِلْتَجَأَ إِلَى ـ يَقَعُ *aor.* وَقَعَ عَلَى ـ إِلْتَبَطَ إِلَى ـ قَصَدَ إِلَى ـ ² قَصَدَ. To — to one's self, مَيَّزَ-لِنَفْسِهِ ـ إِخْتَصَّ-لِنَفْسِهِ ـ إِتَّخَذَ-لِنَفْسِهِ ـ خَاصَّةً. He applied himself to the task, رَابَطَ ٱلْأَمْرَ. To inquire, ² سَأَلَ عَن ـ تَعَرَّفَ. It (as a rule) applies to so and so, يَصْدُقُ عَلَى كَذَا وَكَذَا ـ يَنْطَبِقُ عَلَى كَذَا وَكَذَا.

Appoint, *v.t.* To fix, ² رَسَمَ ـ ² عَيَّنَ ـ جَعَلَ ـ ² كَرَّرَ ـ مَكَّنَ. To decree, ² حَكَمَ بِ ـ ² حَتَمَ عَلَى ـ رَتَّبَ. To name, as to an office, أَقَامَ ـ قَلَّدَ ـ عَيَّنَ ـ وَجَّهَ-إِلَى ـ ² كَتَبَ لِ. To —, as to a command, أَمَّرَ-عَلَى ـ عَمَّلَ-عَلَى. To —, as over a province, وَلَّى. To — a time, حَيَّنَ. To —, as a stipend, to, ² رَسَمَ لِ. To — a place of meeting, وَاعَدَ To —, as of a regular maintenance, أَجْرَى عَلَى To be appointed to a command, تَعَيَّنَ إِلَى ـ تَأَمَّرَ عَلَى. He appointed him to a command, كَتَبَ لَهُ وِلَايَةً. Exact no more than is appointed you, لَا تَسْتَوْفُوا أَكْثَرَ مِمَّا رُسِمَ لَكُمْ.

Appointed, *a.* مُرَتَّب ـ مَرْسُوم ـ مُعَيَّن ; as to an office, مُتَوَلٍّ ـ مَنْصُوب ـ مَأْمُور. Well —, مُجَهَّز ـ مُتَاح. An — time, a space of time, أَجَل. An — time, as agreed upon, مَوْعِد ـ مِيعَاد. He hath ordered the — times, ² فَرَزَ ٱلْأَزْمِنَةَ ٱلْمُعَيَّنَةَ. And there was — in his place, وَنُصِبَ فِي مَحَلِّهِ.

Appointment, *n.* A mandate, أَمْر *pl.* أَوَامِرُ ـ رَسْم *pl.* رُسُوم ـ حُكْم ـ قَضَاء *pl.* أَقْضِيَة ـ شَرِيعَة *pl.* شَرَائِع ـ تَرْتِيب. A salary, مَعَاش. A stipulation, شَرْط ـ عَهْد ـ مِيعَاد. An office, مَنْصِب ـ

تَقْلِيد – إِقامَة. Assignation, as to an office, وَظِيفَة pl. وَظائِف. Assignation, تَعْيِين. Appointments, تَسْمِيَة – تَوْجِيه pl. تَوْجِيهات. equipments, أُهْبَة – عُدَّة – سِلاح – آلات.

Apportion, *v.t.* قَسَّمَ – فَرَّقَ-بَيْنَ – فَرَّقَ-عَلَى. To —, as a task, ≤ قَطَعَ عَلَى.

Apportionment *n.* تَقْسِيم – تَخْصِيص.

Apposite, *a.* مُناسِب – مُوافِق – لائِق – فِي مَحَلِّهِ; of speech, سَدِيد. To be — to, ≤ [2] صَلَحَ ل. To make —, أَصْلَحَ.

Appositely, *ad.* بِمُناسَبَةٍ – بِمُوافَقَةٍ – إِحْكامًا – فِي مَحَلِّهِ – فِي وَقْتِهِ.

Appositeness, *n.* مُناسَبَة – مَصْلَحَة – مُوافَقَة; of speech, سُدُود.

Appraise, *v.t.* ثَمَّنَ – قَدَّرَ ٱلثَّمَنَ.

Appraisement, *n.* تَثْمِين – تَقْدِيرُ ٱلْقِيمَةِ.

Appraiser, *n.* مُثَمِّن – مُسَعِّر.

Appreciable, *a.* يُثَمَّنُ – يُقَدَّرُ.

Appreciate, *v.t.* To place a value upon, ثَمَّنَ – [2] حَطَّ عَلَى-قِيمَةً. To value, esteem, إِعْتَبَرَ – أَعَزَّ. To understand, [2] فَطَنَ بِ. To approve, إِسْتَصْوَبَ – إِسْتَصْلَحَ. He is among them like an incomparable pearl whose value they do not appreciate, هُوَ بَيْنَهُمْ مِثْلَ ٱلدُّرَّةِ ٱلْيَتِيمَةِ ٱلَّتِي لا يُعْرَفُ لَها قَدْرٌ وَلَا قِيمَةٌ.

Appreciation, *n.* Knowledge of value, عِرْفانٌ بِقِيمَةٍ. Respect, إِعْتِبار – عِزّ – قِيمَة.

Apprehend, *v.t. and i.* To lay hold of, ≠ قَبَضَ بِ – ≠ مَسَكَ – كَمَشَ. To understand, وَقَفَ عَلَى aor. يَقِفُ – [2] فَطَنَ بِ – أَدْرَكَ – أَحاطَ بِ-عِلْمًا – إِكْتَنَهَ. To conceive, إِفْتَكَرَ – [2] ظَنَّ – تَصَوَّرَ. To fear, خَشِيَ aor. يَخْشَى – ≤ فَزِعَ – أَشْفَقَ مِن. There is no cause to — the rupture of peace, لَيْسَ مِنْ سَبَبٍ يُخْشَى مِنْهُ نَقْضُ ٱلسِّلْمِ.

Apprehensible, *ad.* يُدْرَكُ.

Apprehension, *n.* Seizure, مَساكَة – قَبْض – قَبْضٌ عَلَى. Contemplation, تَأَمُّل – تَصَوُّر – ظَنّ. Opinion, فِكْر pl. أَفْكار – ظَنّ pl. ظُنُون – رَأْي pl. آراء. The faculty of conceiving, فَهْم – إِدْراك – عَقْل. Perspicacity, فِطْنَة; knowledge of, وُقُوفٌ عَلَى. Fear, خَوْف – فِزْع – خِشْيَة. Something feared, مَحْذُور. Apprehensions, مَحْذُورات. Giving rise to apprehensions, مُوجِبُ ٱلْوَهْمِ – مُوجِبُ ٱلْمَحْذُوراتِ.

Apprehensive, *a.* Fearful, خائِف – فَزِع – مَفْزُوع.

Apprehensiveness, *n.* Fear, خَوْف – فَزَع – وَحْشَة.

Apprentice, *n.* تِلْمِيذ pl. تَلامِيذُ and تَلامِذَة – تِلْمِيذٌ فِي صِناعَةٍ – صَبِيٌّ مُتَعَلِّمٌ صَنْعَةٍ. An operative, صانِع pl. صُنّاع.

Apprentice, *v.t.* [2] حَطَّ-عِنْدَ أُسْتاذٍ لِيَتَعَلَّمَ صَنْعَةً.

Apprenticeship, *n.* مُدَّةُ ٱلتَّعَلُّمِ عِنْدَ أُسْتاذٍ.

Apprise, *v.t.* أَشْعَرَ-بِ – عَلَّمَ-بِ – خَبَّرَ – بَشَّرَ. To be apprised of, [2] شَعَرَ بِ – وَقَفَ عَلَى aor. يَقِفُ.

Apprised, *part.* واقِفٌ عَلَى – مُطَّلِعٌ عَلَى – خَبِيرٌ بِ – دَرِيٌّ – ذُو دِرايَةٍ.

Approach, *v.i.* To draw near, locally, [2] قَرُبَ مِن – إِقْتَرَبَ – [2] دَنا مِن – ≤ قَدِمَ عَلَى – تَقَدَّمَ إِلَى. To be near arriving at a place, وَرَدَ إِلَى aor. يَرِدُ. To —, meet, a person, إِلْتَقَى مَع. To resemble, قارَبَ – شابَهَ. To cause to —, قَرَّبَ – أَدْنَى – قَدَّمَ. They approached one another, of many, تَدانُوا.

Approach, *n.* The act of drawing near, دُنُوّ – إِقْتِراب – تَقَدُّم; as from a journey, وُرُود. A passage to, مَنْفَذٌ إِلَى – قُدُومٌ عَلَى – مَدْخَل. Approaches (in fortification), خَنادِقُ وَمَتارِيسُ مُسْتَحْكَمَةٌ عَلَى مَحَلٍّ.

Approbation, *n.* Consent, رِضاء. The act of approving, إِسْتِصْواب – تَحْسِين – إِسْتِحْسان. Support, مُساعَدَة – ظَهْر.

Appropriate, *a.* Fit, مُوافِق – مُناسِب – لائِق. Belonging to peculiarly, مُخْتَصٌّ بِ. Appropriate, as of speech, سَدِيد – كَلامٌ سَدِيدٌ.

Appropriate, *v.t.* To assign to, خَصَّصَ-ل – عَيَّنَ-ل. To take, [2] أَخَذَ – ≠ مَلَكَ – ≠ [2] ضَبَطَ. To claim, إِدَّعَى بِ. To allot, قَسَّمَ – وَهَبَ aor. يَهَبُ. To — to one's self, إِتَّخَذَ-لِنَفْسِهِ – [2] خَصَّ-لِنَفْسِهِ – إِقْتَفَى بِ – إِحْتَفَظَ-لِنَفْسِهِ – إِنْتَحَلَ – إِحْتَفَظَ بِ – إِدَّعَى-لِنَفْسِهِ.

Appropriately, *ad.* مُناسَبَةً – بِحَسَبِ ما يَقْتَضِيهِ ٱلْحالُ.

Appropriateness, *n.* مُناسَبَة – مُوافَقَة – مُطابَقَة.

Appropriation, *n.* The act of placing to a particular use, تَخْصِيص; of taking, ضَبْط – أَخْذ – إِسْتِمْلاك – إِتِّخاذ.

Approvable, *a.* جَيِّد – حَمِيد – مِمّا يُسْتَحْسَنُ – لائِقٌ – بِٱلْإِسْتِصْوابِ – مُسْتَصْوَب.

Approval, *n.* إِسْتِحْسان – تَصْوِيب – رِضاء. On —, trial, لِأَجْلِ ٱلتَّجْرِبَةِ – لِأَجْلِ ٱلْإِمْتِحانِ. Mutual —, تَراضٍ. It excited his —, أَعْجَبَهُ.

Approve, *v.t.* إِسْتَطابَ ل – إِسْتَجادَ – إِسْتَصْلَحَ – إِسْتَحَبَّ – إِسْتَمْلَحَ – رَضِيَ عَن ≤. To praise, أَحْمَدَ. To —, or prove one self to be, أُخْتُبِرَ. To prove, show, بَرْهَنَ – ثَبَّتَ. To — or praise one for, ≤ حَمِدَ-عَلَى. I approved of it, رَضِيتُ بِهِ – رَضِيتُهُ – إِرْتَضَيْتُهُ.

Approved, *part.* صَائِب ـ مُسْتَحْسَن . Praiseworthy, حَمِيد . This is less — than that, هٰذا أَقَلُّ ٱسْتِحْسانًا مِنْ ذٰلِكَ .

Approver, *n.* One who confesses his crime and indicates his accomplices, مُعْتَرِف بِٱلذَّنْب وَوَاشٍ بِأَرْفَاقِهِ فِيهِ .

Approximate, *v.i.* *See to* Approach, *v.i.*

Approximate, *a.* تَقْرِيبًا ـ قَرِيبٌ مِن ـ قَرِيب .

Approximation, *n.* تَقْرِيب ـ قُرْب ـ مُقَارَبَة . By —, تَقْرِيبًا ـ تَخْمِينًا .

Appui, n. مُظَاهَرَة ـ مُعاوَنَة . *Point d'appui,* مُسْنَد ـ مَرْكَز .

Appurtenance, *n.* مُتَعَلِّقَة *pl.* مُتَعَلِّقات ـ تابِعَة *pl.* تَوابِعُ .

Apricot, *n.* مِشْمِشَة *coll.* مِشْمِش . Apricots with a sweet kernel, مِشْمِش لَوْزِيّ ; with a bitter kernel, مِشْمِش كَلابِيّ . Dried apricots, مِشْمِش نُقُوع .

April, *n.* نِيْسان ـ شَهْرُ نيسان ـ شَهْرُ أَبْرِيل .

April-fool, *n.* مَلْعُوب . To make an — of, لَعِبَ عَلَيْهِ مَلْعُوبًا فِي رَأْسِ شَهْرِ نِيسان .

A priori, ad. and *a.* Apparently, مِنَ ٱلظَّاهِرِ . Inferentially from what went before, إِسْتِنْتاجًا مِمّا سَبَقَ فَقَط .

Apron, *n.* مِيدَعَة *pl.* مَوادِعُ ـ مِئْزَرَة *pl.* مَآزِرُ ـ سِتْرُ ٱلْحِضْنِ . A child's —, نُفَاضَة ـ نِفاض . A covering, غِطاء *pl.* ذُبَيْبَة ـ أَغْطِيَة .

Àpropos, *ad.* and *a.* By the way, بِناءً عَلَى ما نَحْنُ بِصَدَدِهِ ـ فِي مَحَلِّهِ ـ فِي وَقْتِهِ ـ مُنَاسَبَةً . Conveniently, حَقًّا ـ وَأَمّا .

Apsis, *n.* As of a church, قُبَّةُ ٱلْهَيْكَلِ .

Apt, *a.* Fit, لائِق ـ مُوافِق ـ أَهْلٌ لِ . Clever, فَطِين ـ فاطِن . Inclined to, مائِلٌ إِلَى ـ مُبادِرٌ إِلَى . Capable of, جَدِيرٌ لِ *or* بِ . Apt to teach, صالِحٌ لِلتَّعْلِيم . He is very — to ..., خَلِيقٌ بِ مِنْ عادَتِهِ أَن . To be — in anything, إِفْتَنَّ فِي . To make —, أَصْلَحَ .

Aptitude, *n.* } Fitness, مَصْلَحَة ـ مُناسَبَة ـ مُوافَقَة ـ أَهْلِيَّة .
Aptness, } Cleverness, فِطْنَة ـ فَنّ ـ مَهارَة , Tendency, عِمْلَة ـ مُبادَرَة ـ قَرِيحَة ـ مَيْلٌ إِلَى .

Aptly, *ad.* Fitly, كَما يَجِبُ ـ لِيَاقَةً . Readily, بِٱلْخِفَّةِ ـ سَرِيعًا . Cleverly, بِفِطْنَةٍ ـ بِشَطارَةٍ .

Aptote, *n.* إِسْمٌ غَيْرُ مُنْصَرِف ـ إِسْمٌ لا يُعْرَبُ .

Aqua, n. ماء *pl.* مِياه .

Aquafortis, *n.* تِيزاب ـ ٱلْماءُ ٱلْغالِبُ ـ ماءُ ٱلْفِضَّةِ ـ ٱلْماءُ ٱلْكَذَّابُ .

Aquarium, *n.* حَوْضٌ لِتَرْبِيَةِ ٱلسَّمَكِ وَحَشائِشِ ٱلْماءِ .

Aquarius, *n.* The celestial sign, الدَّلْو ,

Aquatic, *a.* Living in water, مَوْطِنُهُ ٱلْماءُ ـ مُوطِنٌ بِٱلْماءِ ـ مائِيّ .

Aquavita, *n.* عَرَق ـ عَرَقِيّ .

Aqueduct, *n.* سِقايات ـ قَرِيّ *pl.* أَقْرِيَة ـ مِيزاب ـ قَناة *pl.* قُنِيّ ـ ساقِيَة ـ كَهْرِيز .

Aqueous, *a.* مائِيّ ـ ماءِيّ .

Aquila, *n.* The celestial sign, النَّسْرُ ٱلطَّائِرُ .

Aquiline, *a.* Like an eagle, مِثْلَ ٱلنَّسْرِ ـ نَسْرِيّ . An — nose, أَنْفٌ أَشْرَفُ .

Arab, *n.* عَرَبِيّ ـ اِبْنُ عَرَب . Arabs, عُرْب ـ عَرَب *pl.* عُرْب . The pure Arabs, العَرَبُ ٱلْعَرِبَةُ ـ العَرَبُ ٱلْعَرِباتُ ـ العَرَبُ ٱلْعارِبَةُ . The mixed Arabs, العَرَبُ ٱلْمُسْتَعْرِبَةُ ـ العَرَبُ ٱلْمُتَعَرِّبَةُ . The offspring of an Arab mother and foreign father, مُوَلَّد . The quality of being an —, عُرُوبَة ـ عُرُوبِيَّة .

Arabesque, *a.* مَنْقُوش عَلَى نَقْشِ ٱلْعَرَبِ ـ نُقُوش عَرَبِيَّة .

Arabia, *n.* بِلادُ ٱلْعَرَب ـ جَزِيرَةُ ٱلْعَرَبِ . Arabia Felix, اليَمَنُ . Arabia Petræa, الحِجازُ . Central —, النَّجْدُ .

Arabian, *n.* *See* Arab, *n.*

Arabic, *a.* عَرَبِيّ . The — language, اللِّسانُ ٱلْعَرَبِيُّ ـ العَرَبِيَّةُ ـ اللُّغَةُ ٱلْعَرَبِيَّةُ . He spoke pure —, عَرَّبَ مَنْطِقَهُ .

Arabicized, *a.* An — noun, إِسْمٌ مُعَرَّبٌ .

Arabism, *n.* A pure Arabism, عُرُوبَة ـ عُرُوبِيَّة ـ عَرَبٌ عُرُوبِيَّةٌ .

Arable, *a.* يُحْرَثُ ـ قابِلُ ٱلْحِراثَةِ ـ صالِحٌ لِلْحَرْثِ وَٱلزَّرْعِ .

Arbiter, *n.* فَيْصَل ـ فَيْصَلِيّ ـ مُمَيِّز ـ وَكِيلٌ عُرْفِيّ . A mediator, وَسِيط . A judge, حاكِم ـ قاضٍ . An absolute —, مُمَيِّزٌ مُسْتَقِلٌّ . To appoint an —, عَيَّنَ فَيْصَلًا ـ حاكِمًا . They two made the governor — in ..., حَكَّما فِي ٱلْوالِي .

Arbitrament, *n.* Will, إِرادَة ـ إِخْتِيار . Award, حُكْم ـ قَرار ـ حُكْمٌ عُرْفِيّ .

Arbitrarily, *ad.* By will only, إِخْتِيارًا . Forcibly, قَهْرًا ـ عَنْوَةً ـ خِلافَ ٱلْوَجْهِ ٱلشَّرْعِيِّ ـ بِٱلْيَدِ ٱلْقَوِيَّةِ ـ جَبْرًا ـ قَسْرًا . Any how, كَيْفَما ٱتَّفَقَ ـ عَلَى بابِ ٱللّٰهِ .

Arbitrariness, *n.* جَوْر ـ ظُلْم ـ عَنْف .

Arbitrary, *a.* Despotic, جائِر ـ مُطْلَق . Depending on the will, إِخْتِيارِيّ . Against law, مُغايِرٌ لِلْقَوانِينِ وَٱلْإِنْصافِ ـ بِخِلافِ ٱلْقَواعِدِ . An — act, ظُلْم ـ مَظْلِمَة *pl.* مَظالِمُ ـ تَعَدٍّ .

An — government, حكومة مطلقة. Arbitrary acts, معاملات عرفيّة.

Arbitrate, v.t. and int. ميّز بين ـ نظر بين ² ـ فتح بين ² ـ حكم عرفيًّا في ² ـ قضى ².

Arbitration, n. فيصل ـ فتاحة ـ فتح pl. فتوح ـ حكم عرفيّ.

Arbitrator, n. فتّاح ـ وكيل عرفيّ. See also Arbiter, n.

Arboreous, a. شجريّ ـ مشجر ـ كثير الأجام.

Arborist, n. عالم بالأشجار.

Arbour, n. مشجرة ـ عريشة. A thicket, عيكة ـ غابة ـ أجمة pl. آجام.

Arc, n. قطعة دائرة ـ قوس الدائرة.

Arcade, n. عقد pl. عقود ـ رواق ـ رواق.

Arcanum, n. سرّ pl. أسرار.

Arch, لفظة يونانية تسبق جملة ألفاظ في اللغة الأنكليزية وتتركّب معها معناها الرأس أو الرئيس أو المتقدّم مثال ذلك شمّاس Deacon, رئيس الشمامسة Archdeacon.

Arch, n. طاق pl. طاقات ـ قوس pl. قياس and أقواس ـ حنيّ pl. حنايا ـ قوصرة pl. قواصر. An — in a wall or a vault, عقد pl. عقود. A dome, قبّة pl. قبب and قباب. A triumphal —, باب انتصار ـ باب نصر. A bridge of one —, قنطرة ذات قوس ـ جسر ذو قنطرة.

Arch, v.t. To curve, قوّس ـ حجّن ـ حنا ². To build with an —, عقّد ـ قنطر; with a dome, قبّب.

Arch, a. Roguish, شاطر ـ خرّاج ـ شيطان.

Archæologist, n. عالم بالآثار القديمة ـ آثاريّ.

Archæology, n. علم الآثار القديمة ـ الأثريّة.

Archaic, a. عتيق ـ قديم. Obsolete, مهجور الإستعمال ـ ملغى.

Archangel, n. رئيس الملائكة pl. رؤساء الملائكة.

Archbishop, n. رئيس الأساقفة.

Archbishopric, n. أبرشيّة رئيس أساقفة.

Archdeacon, n. رئيس الشمامسة.

Archdeaconry, n. رياسة شمامسة ـ وظيفة رئيس الشمامسة.

Archduchess, n. زوجة رئيس أمراء ـ زوجة أرشيدوك ـ أرشيدوكسة.

Archduke, n. رئيس أمراء ـ أرشيدوك.

Arched, a. مقوّس. Domed, مقبّب. An — gateway or doorway, طاق.

Archer, n. نبّال pl. نبّالة ـ نابل pl. نبل ـ قوّاس ـ ضرّاب نشّاب. A body of archers, قوم نشّابون ـ قوم نشّابة.

Archery, n. علم القوس ـ ضرب نشّاب.

Arches-court, n. محكمة دينيّة يتولّى أمرها رئيس أساقفة كنتربري في بلاد الأنكليز.

Archetype, n. نموذج أصليّ ـ أصل.

Archimandrite, n. أرشيمندريت.

Archimedean, a. نسبة إلى أرشميديس. A — screw, ضرب من اللولب على مبادئ هندسة أرشميديس.

Archipelago, n. موضع في البحر كثير الجزائر. The Grecian —, بحر جزائر الروم. The islands of the Grecian —, جزائر الروم.

Architect, n. بنّاء pl. بنّاؤون ـ معمار ـ مهندس ـ معماريّ.

Architectural, a. متعلّق بصناعة البناء.

Architecture, n. The science of, علم البناء ـ علم العمارة. Style of building, بناء pl. أبنية ـ بنية.

Architrave, n. العارضة المركّبة على العمد.

Archives, n. Records, سجلّات ـ دفاتر ـ سفر أخبار. A depository for —, خزانة دفاتر ـ دفترخانه.

Archivist, n. أمين على الدفترخانه.

Archly, ad. بلطافة ـ بملاحة ـ بشطارة.

Archway, n. A passage under an arch, سكّة تحت قنطرة. See also Arch, n.

Arctic, a. شماليّ. The — pole, القطب الشماليّ. The — circle, الدائرة الشماليّة بينها وبين نقطة الأرض الشماليّة ثلاث وعشرون درجة ونصف درجة.

Arcturus, n. السماك المرزم ـ السماك الرامح.

Ardeb, n. A measure equivalent to five English bushels, إردبّ pl. أراديب.

Ardency, n. See Ardour, n.

Ardent, a. Hot, fiery, حامّ ـ حارّ ـ ملتهب. Vehement, غيران pl. غيارى ـ حريص على ـ كثير الرغبة ـ شديد الحرارة. Ardent in dispute, حامٍ في المشاجرة; in study, مجتهد في الدرس. Ardent spirits, liquors, مشروبات كحوليّة ـ أرواح مستقطرة.

Ardently, ad. بحرارة ـ بحرقة ـ برغبة ـ بلوعة ـ بشدّة ـ بالتياع ـ باشتياق كلّي.

Ardour, n. Heat, حرارة ـ حمّة. Fervour, ألب ـ غيرة ـ حرارة ـ رغبة ـ حرص على ـ شدّة الاشتياق. To lose one's — in, فتر عن ². The — of love, صبابة ـ هيام ـ غرام ـ ولع.

Arduous, a. عسر ـ عسير ـ صعب ـ مشكل ـ متعب. Most —, أعسر ـ أصعب.

Arduousness, *n.* صُعُوبَة ـ عُسْر ـ عُسْرَة.

Area, *n.* Space, مِقْدَار ـ وُسْعَة ـ سَعَة. An open space, سَاحَة ـ بَدْحَة ـ رَحْبَة ـ مِيدَان ـ صَاعَة. The — or court of a house, حَوْش ـ عَقَاة ـ عُقْر. An —, as before a temple, فَضَآء.

Areca, *n.* جَوْز بُوَّا.

Arena, *n.* مِيدَان ـ مَصْرَع.

Areola, *n.* The discoloration round the nipple, سَعْدَانَةُ ٱلثَّدْيِ.

Argand-lamp, *n.* نَوْعٌ مِنَ ٱلْقَنَادِيلِ.

Argent, *a.* بَيْضَآء ـ فِضِّيّ.

Argentiferous, *a.* كُلّ مَعْدِنٍ خَالَطَتْهُ فِضَّةٌ.

Argil, *n.* طُفَال.

Argillaceous, *a.* طُفَالِيّ.

Argosy, *n.* سَفِينَة ـ مَرْكَب.

Argue, *v.t.* and *i.* To reason about, بَرْهَنَ عَن ـ إِحْتَجَّ عَن ـ أَقَامَ ٱلْبُرْهَانَ عَلَى ـ بَاحَثَ عَن. To debate, تَكَلَّمَ فِي. To dispute with, جَادَلَ ـ تَقَاوَلَ مَع ـ تَشَاجَرَ مَع ـ تَقَاتَلَ مَع. To lead to an inference, دَلَّ عَلَى ـ نَتَجَ مِن. He argued against his opponent, إِحْتَجَّ عَلَى خَصْمِهِ.

Arguer, *n.* مُجَادِل ـ مُبَاحِث ـ جَدِل ـ مِجْدَال.

Argument, *n.* A reason, حُجَّة *pl.* حُجَج ـ دَلِيل *pl.* أَدِلَّآء ـ دِلِّيلَى. A subject, مَوْضُوع ـ مَادَّة *pl.* مَوَادّ. Contents, مَضْمُون ـ مُحَصَّلُ ٱلْكَلَامِ ـ إِجْمَال ـ مُجْمَل ـ مُوجَز. The —, as of a speech, عُرُوض. Controversy, مُبَاحَثَة ـ مُجَادَلَة ـ مُنَاظَرَة. A conclusive —, دَلِيلٌ قَاطِعٌ. To adduce, as of arguments, إِحْتَجَّ ـ إِسْتَدَلَّ.

Argumentation, *n.* مُبَاحَثَة ـ تَحَجُّج ـ تَبَرْهُن ـ إِسْتِدْلَال ـ إِيرَادُ دَلَائِل.

Argumentative, *a.* مُحْكَم ـ قِيَاسِيّ ـ إِسْتِدْلَالِيّ.

Argumentum ad hominem, دَلِيلٌ مَأْخُوذٌ مِنْ أَدِلَّآءِ ٱلْخَصْمِ وَٱلْمُحْتَجِّ عَلَيْهِ بِهِ.

Arian, *n.* تَابِعُ أَرْيُوس.

Arid, *a.* نَاشِف ـ ضَامِل ـ يَابِس. Arid land, أَرْضٌ قَاحِلَةٌ ـ أَرْضٌ يَابِسَةٌ.

Aridity, *n.* يُبُوسَة ـ جُفُوف ـ يُبْس ـ قُحُولَة.

Aries, *n.* The sign of, بُرْجُ ٱلْحَمَلِ ـ ٱلْحَمَلُ.

Aright, *ad.* جَيِّدًا ـ سَدَدًا ـ حَسَنًا ـ بِٱلصَّوَابِ ـ بِٱسْتِقَامَةٍ. To set —, أَصْلَحَ ـ صَلَّحَ ـ عَدَّلَ. To say or do —, أَسَدَّ.

Arise, *v.i.* As of the moon, طَلَعَ ـ أَشْرَقَ; as from a seat, قَامَ ـ نَهَضَ ـ إِنْتَهَضَ ـ إِنْتَصَبَ; as from sleep, إِنْتَبَهَ ـ فَاقَ ـ قَامَ مِنَ ٱلنَّوْمِ ـ إِسْتَيْقَظَ مِنَ ٱلنَّوْمِ; as from the dead, قَامَ مِنْ بَيْنِ ٱلْأَمْوَاتِ ـ إِنْبَعَثَ ـ بُعِثَ. To proceed from, جَآءَ مِن ـ نَتَجَ مِن ـ صَدَرَ عَن ـ إِنْبَثَقَ مِن. All these misfortunes arise from the fact that . . . , وَسَبَبُ هٰذِهِ ٱلْمَصَائِبِ كُلِّهَا هُوَ أَن.

Aristocracy, *n.* The —, ٱلْأَشْرَاف ـ ٱلْعِلْيَة ـ ٱلْعِلِّيَّة. Government by an —, حُكُومَةُ أَشْرَافٍ ـ مَشْيَخَة. They are the —, هُمْ عِلْيَةُ ٱلنَّاسِ.

Aristocrat, *n.* عَلِيّ *pl.* عِلْيَة.

Aristocratical, *a.* مُتَعَلِّقٌ بِٱلْأَشْرَافِ. An — government, حُكْمُ أَشْرَافٍ.

Aristocratically, *ad.* مُتَعَلِّقٌ بِٱلْأَشْرَافِ ـ عَلَى مِنْوَالِ ٱلشُّرَفَآءِ.

Aristotelian, *a.* أَرِسْطُوطَالِيّ ـ مَنْسُوبٌ لِأَرِسْطُطَالِيس.

Arithmetic, *n.* عِلْمُ ٱلرَّقْمِ ـ عِلْمُ ٱلْحِسَابِ.

Arithmetical, *a.* حِسَابِيّ ـ حَسَبَ قَوَانِينِ ٱلْحِسَابِ.

Arithmetically, *ad.* حَسَبَ قَوَانِينِ ٱلْحِسَابِ.

Arithmetician, *n.* عَارِفٌ بِعِلْمِ ٱلْحِسَابِ ـ مُعَلِّمُ حِسَابٍ ـ رَقْمِجِي.

Ark, *n.* A chest, صُنْدُوق ـ صُوَّنَة ـ تَابُوت. A boat, سَفِينَة. Noah's —, سَفِينَةُ نُوحٍ ـ فُلْكُ نُوحٍ. The — of the Covenant, تَابُوتُ ٱلْعَهْدِ. An — of bulrushes, سَفَطٌ مِنَ ٱلْبَرْدِيّ.

Arm, *n.* An — of the body, سَاعِد *pl.* سَوَاعِد; from shoulder to elbow, عَضُد *pl.* أَعْضَاد ـ عَظَمَة; from elbow to wrist, أَسَلَة; from elbow to tip of fingers, ذِرَاع *pl.* أَذْرِعَة *and* أَذْرُع. The inner side of the —, مَأْبِض. Arm, as of a river, شُعْبَة; of the sea, خَوْر *pl.* خُوُور ـ خَلِيج *pl.* خُلْجَان ـ بُوغَاز; of a chair, يَدُ كُرْسِيّ. To take in the arms, إِحْتَضَنَ ـ أَخَذَ فِي ٱلْحِضْنِ. To receive with open arms, أَقْبَلَ عَلَى ـ رَحَّبَ بِ. He took them up in his arms, إِحْتَضَنَهُمْ. To keep one at arm's length, بَاعَدَ ـ جَانَبَ ـ إِجْتَنَبَ عَن.

Arm, Arms, *n.* A weapon, سِلَاح *pl.* أَسْلِحَة *and* سِلَح ـ آلَةُ ٱلْحَرْبِ *pl.* آلَات ـ أَدَاةُ ٱلْحَرْبِ. Fire arms, أَسْلِحَةٌ نَارِيَّةٌ. Coat of —, عَلَامَةُ نَسَبٍ ـ آرْمَا. To bear —, حَمَلَ ٱلسِّلَاحَ. To lay down —, to submit, إِسْتَسْلَمَ ـ أَسْلَمَ. To beat to —, دَقَّ ٱلطَّبْلَ لِلْقِتَالِ. To present arms, سَلَّمَ. To arms! خُذُوا سِلَاحَكُمْ. Bearing —, شَاكِي ٱلسِّلَاحِ.

Arm, *v.t.* سَلَّحَ ـ جَهَّزَ بِأَسْلِحَةٍ ـ أَلْبَسَ عُدَّةَ ٱلْحَرْبِ. To — one's self, تَسَلَّحَ ـ تَقَلَّدَ بِٱلسِّلَاحِ; with a sword, تَقَلَّدَ بِسَيْفٍ; with patience, تَجَلَّدَ ـ لَازَمَ ٱلصَّبْرَ; with courage, تَشَجَّعَ. To arm, to fortify, حَصَّنَ. Completely armed, شَاكُ ٱلسِّلَاحِ ـ شَوِكُ ٱلسِّلَاحِ. A party fully armed in steel, قَوْمٌ شُكَّاكٌ فِي ٱلحَدِيدِ.

Armada, *n.* شُوَنٌ ـ أَسَاطِيلُ ـ دُونَنْمَا.

Armament, *n.* A war —, تَجْهِيزٌ لِلْحَرْبِ; of soldiers, تَجْهِيزُ عَسَاكِرَ ـ عَسَاكِرُ; of cannon, أَطْوَابٌ ـ مَدَافِعُ; of ships, تَجْهِيزُ دُونَنْمَا ـ عِمَارَةٍ.

Armchair, *n.* كُرْسِيٌّ ذُو يَدَيْنِ.

Armed, *a.* مُجَهَّزٌ بِسِلَاحٍ ـ مُسَلَّحٌ. Self-armed, مُتَسَلِّحٌ. Having, being provided with, ذُو ـ مُمَدَّدٌ بِ ـ مُوَشَّحٌ بِ *fem.* ذَاتُ *pl. masc.* ذَوُو *pl. fem.* ذَوَاتُ. Armed with a horn, of an animal, ذُو قَرْنٍ. Armed to the teeth, مُتَسَلِّحٌ بِكَثْرَةِ سِلَاحٍ. An armed body, جَمَاعَةٌ مُسَلَّحَةٌ.

Armenian, *a.* and *n.* أَرْمَنِيٌّ *coll.* أَرْمَن. Armenian, bole, طِينٌ أَرْمَنِيٌّ.

Armful, *n.* حِضْنَةٌ ـ حِضْنٌ.

Armhole, *n.* بَاطٌ ـ أَبَاطٌ *pl.* إِبْطٌ ـ أَوْصَالُ ٱلأَيْدِي *pl.* وَصْلُ ٱليَدِ *pl.* بَاطَاتٌ.

Armistice, *n.* رَفْعُ ٱلحَرْبِ بَيْنَ ـ مُتَارَكَةٌ ـ عَهْدٌ ـ هُدْنَةٌ ـ مُهْلَةُ تَوَقُّفِ ٱلحَرْبِ ـ مُحَارِبِينَ.

Armlet, *n.* دُمْلُجٌ *pl.* دَمَالِجُ ـ مِعْضَدٌ ـ مِعْضَادٌ.

Armorial, *a.* مُتَعَلِّقٌ بِٱلسِّلَاحِ. Armorial bearings, عَلَامَةُ نَسَبٍ ـ مَنَازِلُ عَلَامَةِ ٱلنَّسَبِ.

Armour, *n.* Arms, أَسْلِحَةٌ ـ سِلَاحٌ. Dress —, زُرُودٌ *pl.* زَرْدٌ ـ دُرُوعٌ *pl.* دِرْعٌ. Horse armour, تَجْفَافٌ. Armour-plated, مُدَرَّعٌ. An — man-of-war, بَارِجَةٌ مُدَرَّعَةٌ.

Armour-bearer, حَامِلُ سِلَاحٍ ـ حَامِلُ عُدَّةٍ.

Armourer, *n.* صَانِعُ سِلَاحٍ ـ غُنْدَقْلِي ـ غُنْدَقْجِي ـ صَنَّاعُ أَسْلِحَةٍ.

Armoury, سِلَاحْخَانَه ـ خِزَانَةُ سِلَاحٍ ـ بَيْتُ أَسْلِحَةٍ.

Armpit, *n.* بَاطِنُ ٱلإِبْطِ ـ أَبَاطٌ *pl.* إِبْطٌ ـ أَعْطَافٌ *pl.* عِطْفٌ.

Army, *n.* جُنْدٌ ـ فَيَالِقُ *pl.* فَيْلَقٌ ـ جُيُوشٌ *pl.* جَيْشٌ ـ جُنُودٌ *pl.* عَسْكَرٌ *pl.* عَسَاكِرُ. A regular —, عَسَاكِرُ نِظَامِيَّةٌ. A standing —, عَسْكَرٌ مُرَتَّبٌ مُوَظَّفٌ. A besieging —, عَسَاكِرُ مُحَاصِرُونَ. A relieving —, عَسَاكِرُ إِمْدَادِيَّةٌ ـ نَجْدَةٌ. To enter the —, تَجَنَّدَ ـ صَارَ عَسْكَرِيًّا.

Aroma, *n.* رَائِحَةٌ ـ عَصْفَةٌ ـ فَغْمَةٌ ـ عِطْرٌ.

Aromatic, *a.* }
Aromatical, } مُعَطَّرٌ ـ عِطْرِيٌّ ـ طِيبِيٌّ ـ مُطَرٌّ.

Aromatic, *n.* بُهَارٌ ـ أَطْيَابٌ *pl.* طِيبٌ ـ خَلُوقٌ.

Aromatize, *v.t.* طَيَّبَ ـ طَرَّى ـ خَلَّقَ.

Arose, *pret. of to* Arise, *q.v.*

Around, *ad.* دَائِرَ مَا دَارَ ـ حَوَالَ ـ فِي حَوْلِ ـ حَوْلَ. Around him, حَوَالَيْهِ. They sat — him, قَعَدُوا حَوْلَهُ. To make a trench — him, أَحَاطَ بِخَنْدَقٍ. He looked — him, نَظَرَ حَوْلَهُ.

Arouse, *v.t.* As from sleep, صَحَّى ـ نَبَّهَ ـ فَيَّقَ ـ بَعَثَ. To stir up, حَرَّكَ ـ حَضَّ ـ حَرَّضَ ـ أَنْهَضَ. To —, bestir, one's self, إِنْتَهَضَ ـ هَاجَ بِهِ ـ إِنْبَعَثَ.

Arquebuse, *n.* نَوْعٌ مِنَ ٱلمَكَاحِلِ مُسْتَعْمَلٌ قَدِيمًا.

Arrack, *n.* عَرَقِيٌّ ـ عَرَقٌ.

Arraign, *v.t.* To cite, دَعَا إِلَى ـ دَعَا إِلَى ٱلمَحْكَمَةِ ـ رَافَعَ ـ قَرَفَ بِ. To accuse, إِشْتَكَى عَلَى بِ ـ أَتْهَمَ بِ ـ ٱلشَّرْعِ عَلَى بِ. He arraigned him before the governor, رَافَعَهُ إِلَى ٱلحَاكِمِ.

Arraignment, *n.* A citation, مُرَافَعَةٌ ـ دَعْوَى عَلَى. A charge, شَكْوَى ـ مُشَاكَاةٌ ـ شَكَاوَةٌ ـ تُهْمَةٌ.

Arraigns, *n.* Clerk of the —, مُقَيِّدٌ فِي ٱلمَحْكَمَةِ.

Arrange, *v.t.* To put in order, دَبَّرَ ـ رَتَّبَ ـ نَظَّمَ ـ أَحْكَمَ ـ طَبَّقَ. To —, as of the hair, سَوَّى; as of a speech, نَسَّقَ ـ نَسَقَ. To — a difference between, جَمَعَ بَيْنَ ـ صَالَحَ ـ سَدَّدَ ـ سَاوَى بَيْنَ ـ صَرَفَ بَيْنَ. To promise, وَعَدَ بِ *aor.* يَعِدُ ـ أَوْعَدَ. They arranged to meet at, تَوَاعَدُوا إِلَى. To be or to become arranged, إِنْتَظَمَ ـ تَنَظَّمَ ـ تَرَتَّبَ. *See also to* Order, *v.t.*

Arrangement, *n.* Order, إِنْتِظَامٌ ـ نَظْمٌ ـ تَرْتِيبٌ ـ نَسَقٌ ـ تَصْفِيفٌ ـ تَدْبِيرٌ ـ نِظَامٌ. Mode of payment, صُورَةُ تَأْدِيَةٍ ـ خَلَاصَةٌ. Settlement, تَسَاوٍ ـ قَوْلٌ ـ قَرَارٌ ـ تَسْدِيدٌ ـ مُخَالَصَةٌ. Conciliation, صُلْحٌ ـ مُسَاوَاةٌ ـ تَسْوِيَةٌ. To make an — with, إِتَّصَلَ مَعَ.

Arrant, *a.* قَرَارِيٌّ ـ فَاحِشٌ ـ قَبِيحٌ. An — knave, حَرَامِيٌّ قَرَارِيٌّ.

Arras, *n.* طَنْفَسَةٌ.

Array, *v.t.* To dress, زَيَّنَ ـ كَسَا ـ لَبَّسَ ـ أَلْبَسَ. To put in order, to equip, أَعَدَّ ـ جَهَّزَ ـ رَتَّبَ. To be arrayed, dressed, لَبِسَ. He was arrayed in royal apparel, لَبِسَ ٱلحُلَّةَ ٱلمُلُوكِيَّةَ.

Array, *n.* Dress, زِيٌّ ـ ثِيَابٌ ـ كِسْوَةٌ ـ لِبْسٌ. Order, تَرْتِيبٌ ـ نِظَامٌ. To set an army in battle array, صَفَّ ٱلعَسْكَرَ لِلْقِتَالِ. They were arrayed against, إِصْطَفُّوا عَلَى.

Arrear, *n.* }
Arrears, } بَقَايَا ـ بَاقِيَاتٌ ـ تَأْخِيرَاتٌ. To be in arrear, of payment, تَأَخَّرَ عَنِ ٱلدَّفْعِ.

Arrest, *v.t.* To stop, أَوْقَفَ ـ وَقَّفَ. To seize, قَبَضَ عَلَى ـ مَسَكَ. To withhold, حَاشَ ـ حَجَزَ عَن. To imprison, حَبَسَ. To be arrested, withheld, إِحْتَبَسَ عَن. To be imprisoned, إِنْحَبَسَ ـ إِحْتَبَسَ.

Arrest, *n.* Seizure, مَسْكٌ ـ قَبْضٌ. Delay, تَأَخُّر. An order, أَمْر ـ حُكْم ـ حُكُومَة. An arrest of judgment, تَمْهِيلُ إِجْرَآءِ ٱلْحُكْمِ ـ مُهْلَة. Arrest, imprisonment, سَجْن ـ حَبْس. To place under —, جَعَلَ تَحْتَ ٱلتَّرْسِيمِ.

Arrière pensée, *n.* غَرَض ـ غَرَضٌ خَفِيٌّ.

Arrival, *n.* وُرُود ـ وُصُول ـ مَقْدَم ـ قُدُوم ـ آتِيَان ; as of an event, وُقُوع ـ حُدُوث. A person arriving, وَارِد *pl.* وُرَّاد *and* وَارِدُون ـ وَافِد *pl.* وُفَّاد *and* وَافِدُون.

Arrive, *v.i.* To reach, أَقْبَلَ عَلَى ـ لَحِقَ ـ أَلْحَقَ ـ وَفَدَ إِلَى ـ وَصَلَ إِلَى *aor.* يَصِلُ ـ أَوْفَى إِلَى ـ أَقْصَى إِلَى ـ وَفَدَ *aor.* يَفِدُ. To happen, حَدَثَ ـ جَرَى ـ صَارَ ـ وَقَعَ *aor.* يَقَعُ. To —, of time, حَانَ. To —, as of a letter, وَرَدَ إِلَى *aor.* يَرِدُ. The time of prayer has arrived, حَانَ وَقْتُ ٱلصَّلٰوةِ ـ حَانَتِ ٱلصَّلَاةُ.

Arriving, *n.* *See* Arrival, *n.*

Arrogance, *n.* غَطْرَفَة ـ غُرُور ـ رَهْدَلَة ـ نَفْخ ـ تَجَبُّر ـ غَطْرَسَة ـ تَكَبُّر. *See also* Presumption, *n.*

Arrogant, *a.* فَيَّاش ـ مُتَغَطْرِف ـ مُتَنَفِّخ ـ مَغْرُور ـ مُتَجَبِّر ـ مُتَغَطْرِس ـ مُتَكَبِّر. *See also* Presumptuous, *a.*

Arrogantly, *ad.* مُتَنَفِّخًا ـ بِغُرُورٍ. To act —, تَكَبَّرَ ـ غَطْرَفَ ـ تَغَطْرَفَ.

Arrogate, *v.t.* إِنْتَحَلَ ـ إِدَّعَى ـ إِدَّعَى ب. He arrogated to himself, إِنْتَحَلَ لِنَفْسِهِ. To — to one's self excellence over, تَفَضَّلَ عَلَى ـ تَطَاوَلَ عَلَى. He arrogated the thing falsely, تَفَيَّشَ ٱلشَّيْءَ.

Arrow, *n.* سَهْم *pl.* سِهَام ـ نُشَّابَة *pl.* نُشَّاب ـ نَبْلَة *pl.* أَنْبَال. The feathers of an —, رِيشُ ٱلسَّهْمِ ـ آذَانُ ٱلسَّهْمِ. A maker of arrows, نَشَّاب ـ سَهَّام.

Arrow-root, *n.* أَرُورُوت ـ جِنْسٌ مِنَ ٱلنَّشَآءِ مَصْنُوعٌ مِنْ جُذُورٍ.

Arse, *n.* إِسْت ـ خُوخَة ـ سُرْم.

Arsenal, *n.* تَرْسْخَانَه ـ خِزَانَةُ سِلَاحٍ.

Arsenic, *n.* سَمُّ ٱلْفَارِ ـ زَرْنِيخ ـ رَهْجٌ أَبْيَضُ ـ ٱلتُّرَابُ ٱلْهَالِكُ.

Arsenical, *a.* زَرْنِيخِيٌّ.

Art, *n.* Science, فَنّ *pl.* فُنُون. A trade, صَنْعَة *pl.* صَنَائِعُ ـ حِرْفَة ـ صِنَاعَة ـ كَار. Mode of doing any thing, صِنَاعَة ـ فَنّ. Address, صَنْعَة ـ حُسْنُ مَعْرِفَةٍ. Cunning, حِيلَة *pl.* حِيَل ـ شَطَارَة. The black art, ٱلسِّحْرُ ـ سِحْر. The fine arts, ٱلْآدَابُ. The mechanical —, ٱلصَّنَائِعُ. The military —, فَنُّ ٱلْحَرْبِ. Graven by —, مَنْقُوشٌ بِصِنَاعَةٍ.

Artemisia, *n.* شِيح.

Arterial, *a.* شِرْيَانِيٌّ ـ عِرْقِيٌّ.

Artery, *n.* شِرْيَان *pl.* شَرَايِينُ ـ عِرْق *pl.* عُرُوق ـ رَافِز *pl.* رَوَافِزُ ـ ضَارِب *pl.* ضَوَارِبُ.

Artesian, *n.* An artesian well, بِئْرٌ مَحْفُورَةٌ.

Artful, *a.* Cunning, حَوَالِيٌّ ـ شَدِيدُ ٱلإِحْتِيَالِ ـ عَذِق ـ غَدَّار ـ شَاطِر ـ شَيْطَان ـ ذُو كَيْدٍ ـ خَبِيث.

Artfully, *ad.* بِحِيلَةٍ ـ بِشَيْطَنَةٍ ـ حِيلَةً.

Artfulness, *n.* Cunning, فَنّ ـ حِيلَة ـ غَدْر.

Arthritic, *a.* Pertaining to the joints, مُتَعَلِّقٌ بِٱلْمَفَاصِلِ.

Arthritis, *n.* Gout, نِقْرِس.

Artichoke, *n.* أَرْضِي شَوْكِي ـ جِنَارَة ; called in Egypt, خُرْشُوف ; in Barbary, قِنَارِيَة. A Jerusalem —, صِنْفٌ مِنَ ٱلْكَمْأَةِ.

Article, *n.* The part of speech, or a definite —, لَامُ ٱلتَّعْرِيفِ ـ أَدَاةُ ٱلتَّعْرِيفِ ; an indefinite —, أَدَاةُ (*or* حَرْفُ) تَنْكِيرٍ. A thing, شَيْءٌ *pl.* أَشْيَآءُ ـ مَادَّة *pl.* مَوَادُّ ـ حَاجَة *pl.* حَاجَات. An article, as in a newspaper, مَقَالَة ـ عِبَارَة. An — of merchandise, بِضَاعَة *pl.* بَضَائِعُ ـ مَتَاع *pl.* أَمْتِعَة ـ أَسْبَاب. A clause, as in an agreement, شَرْط *pl.* شُرُوط ـ بَنْد *pl.* بُنُود ـ بَاب *pl.* أَبْوَاب ـ فَصْل *pl.* فُصُول. An — of furniture, مَاعُون *pl.* مَوَاعِينُ ـ مَتَاع *pl.* أَمْتِعَة. Articles of faith, مَذْهَب ـ عَقِيدَةُ ٱلدِّينِ *pl.* عَقَائِدُ. Articles of war, قَوَانِينُ عَسْكَرِيَّةٌ. Articles of apprenticeship, مُشَارَطَةٌ بَيْنَ أُسْتَاذٍ وَتِلْمِيذٍ. In the — of death, عِنْدَ ٱلْمَوْتِ ـ عِنْدَ ٱلْمَمَاتِ ـ عِنْدَ ٱلسِّيَاقِ. Article, clause, by article, بَنْد بَنْد.

Article, *v.i.* To stipulate with, شَارَطَ.

Articled, *a.* مَرْبُوطٌ بِشُرُوطٍ.

Articular, *a.* مُتَعَلِّقٌ بِٱلْمَفَاصِلِ.

Articulate, *a.* Having joints, ذُو مَفَاصِلَ. Distinct, مُمْتَاز ـ مُمَيَّز.

Articulate, *v.t.* To pronounce, بَيَّنَ ٱللَّفْظَ ـ تَلَفَّظَ. To joint, فَصَّلَ ـ عَضَا.

Articulation, *n.* Junction, place of junction, مَوْصِل ـ أَوْصَال. A joint, مَفْصِل *pl.* مَفَاصِلُ ـ مَعْقِد *pl.* مَعَاقِدُ. Formation of words by speech, تَلَفُّظ.

Artifice, *n.* Fraud, إِرْب ـ حِيلَة *pl.* حِيَل ـ كَيْد *pl.* كِيَاد ـ مَكْر ـ دُولَاب *pl.* دَوَالِيبُ ـ خِدْعَة ـ مَكِيدَة *pl.* مَكَائِدُ. To practise —, إِحْتَالَ. To use — to induce, حَاوَلَ. To use — against, إِحْتَالَ عَلَى.

Artificer, *n.* صَانِع *pl.* صُنَّاع ـ أَهْلُ حِرْفَةٍ.

Artificial, *a.* Made by art, عَمَلِيٌّ ـ صِنَاعِيٌّ ـ مَصْنُوع ـ عَمَّالَة. Counterfeit, مُزَوَّر ـ قَلْب. Is this thing — or natural? أَهٰذَا صَنْعَةٌ أَمْ خِلْقَةٌ.

Artificially, *ad.* صِنَاعَةً ـ إِصْطِنَاعًا.

Artillerist, *n.* طُوبْجِي ـ مَاهِرٌ فِي فَنِّ ٱلْأَطْوَابِ.

Artillery, *n.* أَطْوَابٌ ـ مَدَافِعُ. An — man, طُوبْجِي *pl.* طُوبْجِيَّة.

Artisan. *See* Artificer, Workman, *n.*

Artist, *n.* أَهْلُ فَنٍّ ـ أَهْلُ مَعْرِفَةٍ. A painter, مُصَوِّر ـ رَسَّام. A sculptor, نَقَّاش.

Artiste, *n.* A female dancer, رَقَّاصَة *pl.* رَقَّاصَات.

Artistic, *a.* } Conformed to art, عَلَى قَوَاعِدِ ٱلْفَنِّ. Belonging
Artistical, } to art, مُتَعَلِّقٌ بِٱلْفُنُونِ.

Artless, *a.* خَالِصُ ٱلْقَلْبِ ـ بَسِيط ـ سَلِيم ـ نَصُوح ـ سَاذِج.

Artlessly, *ad.* بِقَلْبٍ خَالِصٍ ـ بِبَسَاطَةٍ ـ بِنُصُوحٍ.

Artlessness, *n.* إِخْلَاص ـ بَسَاطَة ـ نُصُوح.

As, *ad.* and *conj.* In the same manner, كَ ـ مِثْلُ ـ مِثْلِ ـ كَمِثْلِ ـ زَيّ. Of time, when, لَمَّا ـ حِينَ ـ عِنْدَ مَا ـ وَقْتَ مَا ـ إِذَا ـ وَقْتَ ٱلَّذِي ـ مَحَلَّ ٱلَّذِي ـ حَيْثُمَا. Seeing that..., لَمَّا كَانَ ـ حَيْثُ أَن ـ بِحَيْثُ أَن ـ مَا دَامَ أَن. As if, كَأَنَّ ـ حَسْبَمَا أَن ـ بِحَسَبِ ـ وِمِثْلَمَا ـ كَمَا ـ عَلَى مَا. According to what, كَنَحْوِ ـ عَلَى مُقْتَضَى ـ حَسَبَ ـ تَبَعَ ـ وَمِنْ خُصُوصِ. As to..., أَمَّا. As, in fact, وَٱلْحَالُ ـ صَحِيح. As well as, also, أَيْضًا ـ كَمَان. As much as, عَلَى قَدْرِ مَا ـ بِمِقْدَارِ مَا ـ قَدْ مَا. As soon as, كَمَا أَنَّ ـ حَالَمَا ـ عِنْدَمَا ـ حِينَمَا ـ أَوَّلَ مَا ـ سَاعَةَ أَن. So as to..., حَتَّى ـ كَيْ. They did as he told them, عَمِلُوا عَلَى قَوْلِهِ. Few as they are, عَلَى قِلَّتِهِمْ. As long as I live, مَا دُمْتُ حَيًّا. As they say, وِمِثْلَمَا يَقُولُونَ. As I entered he arrived, لَمَّا دَخَلْتُ وَصَلَ. As justice is the basis of laws, لَمَّا كَانَ ٱلْعَدْلُ أَسَاسَ ٱلشَّرَائِعِ. But as the neighbouring nations opposed their designs, وَلٰكِنْ مِنْ حَيْثُ أَنَّ ٱلْأُمَمَ ٱلْمُجَاوِرَةَ تَعَارَضَتْ لَهُمْ فِي مَقْصُودِهِمْ. You behold him, priding himself as if he were above all, تَرَاهُ مُتَكَبِّرًا كَأَنَّهُ وَحِيدُ عَصْرِهِ. If he is a good man, as in fact he is, إِنْ كَانَ رَجُلٌ صَالِحٌ وَٱلْحَالُ هُوَ كَذٰلِكَ. As to this affair, وَبِخُصُوصِ هٰذِهِ ٱلْمَادَّةِ. He has not arrived as yet, إِلَى ٱلْآنَ مَا لِسَّا مَا أَجَى ـ وَصَلَ. As much as I can, عَلَى قَدْرِ طَاقَتِي ـ قَدْرَ مَا لِي طَاقَةٌ ـ عَلَى قَدْرِ ٱلْإِمْكَانِ. As above stated, كَمَا ذُكِرَ آنِفًا. As often as I tell him, كُلَّمَا أُخْبِرُهُ. It may have cost him as much as he says, لَعَلَّهُ سَاوَى كَمَا يَقُولُ. Call on me as you go by, زُرْنِي عِنْدَ مُرُورِكَ.

Asafœtida, *n.* حَنْتِيت ـ حَلْتِيتٌ مُنْتِن ـ حَلْتِيت.

Asbestos, *n.* كَتَّانٌ حَجَرِيٌّ.

Ascarides, *n.* دُودٌ قَرْعِيٌّ.

Ascend, *v.t.* and *i.* To rise, طَلَعَ ع ـ صَعِدَ ـ إِرْتَفَعَ ـ تَصَاعَدَ; as on a ladder, صَعِدَ فِي; as towards heaven, إِسْتَوَى إِلَى; as a mountain, عَلَا عَلَى ـ أَسْنَدَ فِي ـ سَنَدَ فِي ع ـ صَعَّدَ فِي or عَلَى *aor.* يَعْلُو ـ عَلَا بِ ـ إِسْتَعْلَى. To — by degrees, تَعَلَّى. To make to —, طَلَّعَ ـ صَعَّدَ. A rope whereby to ascend trees, مِصْعَاد. *See also to* Climb, Rise, *v.i.*

Ascendant, *a.* Superior, أَعْلَى *fem.* عُلْيَا *pl.* عُلًا ـ بَارِع ـ مُتَسَلِّط ـ غَالِب. Ascendant, in astronomy, طَالِع.

Ascendant, *n.* Of astronomy, طَالِع *pl.* طَوَالِعُ. The degrees of kindred reckoned upwards, ٱلْآبَاءُ وَٱلْأَجْدَادُ. His star is in the —, طَالِعُهُ سَعِيدٌ. To be in the —, أَنْجَمَ ـ غَلَبَ ـ ع.

Ascendency, *n.* نُفُوذ ـ حُكْم ـ طَمّ ـ طُمُوم ـ غَلَبَة ـ إِعْتِبَار. To gain the — over, غَلَا بِ *aor.* يَغْلُو ـ قَوِيَ عَلَى ـ ع ـ إِسْتَعْلَى عَلَى. The affair had —, طَمَّ ٱلْأَمْرُ ع.

Ascension, *n.* صُعُود ـ طُلُوع ـ إِرْتِفَاع. Ascension Day, عِيدُ ٱلصُّعُودِ ـ عِيدُ ٱلسُّلَّاقِ. Right —, مَطْلَعٌ إِسْتِوَائِيٌّ ـ ٱلصُّعُودُ ٱلْمُسْتَقِيمُ. Oblique —, مَطْلَعٌ مَائِلٌ ـ ٱلصُّعُودُ ٱلْمُتَوَارِبُ.

Ascent, *n.* Act of rising, صُعُود ـ طُلُوع. An acclivity, مِعْرَاج *pl.* مَعَارِيجُ ـ رُقِيَّة ـ عُلْوَة ـ طَلْعَة ـ طُلُوع ـ تَلَّة. A difficult —, صَعُودَاءُ ـ صَعُود. A place of —, مَظْهَر ـ مَرْقًى ـ مَطْلَع ـ مَصْعَد.

Ascertain, *v.t.* أَيْقَنَ بِ ـ إِسْتَيْقَنَ بِ ـ حَقَّقَ ـ تَحَقَّقَ ـ أَحَقَّ ـ ثَبَّتَ. To be ascertained, تَحَقَّقَ.

Ascertainment, *n.* إِيقَان ـ إِتْقَان ـ إِسْتِقْرَار ـ تَحْقِيق.

Ascetic, *a.* صُوفِيٌّ ـ زِهِّيد.

Ascetic, *n.* زَاهِد *pl.* زُهَّاد ـ زِهِّيد ـ صُوفِيٌّ.

Asceticism, *n.* تَزَهُّد.

Ascitis, *n.* إِسْتِسْقَاءٌ بَطْنِيٌّ.

Ascititious, *a.* *See* Adscititious, *a.*

Ascribable, *a.* يُنْسَبُ إِلَى ـ يُلْقَى عَلَى.

Ascribe, *v.t.* أَلْقَى عَلَى ـ نَسَبَ إِلَى ع ـ حَسَبَ لِ ع ـ خَصَّصَ بِ ـ جَعَلَ لِ ـ أَتْهَمَ بِ. To — to, as of a crime, إِشْتَكَى عَلَى بِ. Ascribed to, مَوْضُوعٌ لِ ـ مَنْسُوبٌ إِلَى.

Ascription, *n.* إِلْقَاءٌ عَلَى ـ إِنْتِسَابٌ إِلَى. Accusation, تُهْمَة ـ شِكَايَة. Ascription of praise, تَسْبِيح ـ ثَنَاءٌ.

Ash, *n.* The tree, شَجَرَةُ لِسَانِ ٱلْعَصَافِيرِ — بُودَاق — دَيْش .

Ashes, رَمَاد .

Ashamed, *a.* خَجِل — مُخْجِل — مَحْشُوم — حَيِيٌّ *fem.* حَيِيَّة — مُسْتَحٍ. Ashamed of, as of a bad action, خَزْيَان *pl.* خَزَايَا . To be —, خَجِل ـ — إِسْتَحَى — إِحْتَشَمَ . To make —, خَجَّلَ — أَخْجَلَ . To make one — of himself, أَخْزَى . Are you not —? أَمَا تَسْتَحِي .

Ash-coloured, *a.* أَرْمَدُ — أَشْهَبُ — رَمَادِيٌّ — أَغْبَسُ — أَطْحَلُ .

An ash colour, شُهْبَة — طُحْلَة — رُمْدَة .

Ashen, *a.* مَصْنُوعٌ مِنْ شَجَرَةِ ٱلْبُودَاقِ .

Ashes, *n.* رَمَاد . A dead body, جِنَازَة — مَيْتَة . The — of dead bodies, تُرَابُ ٱلْأَمْوَاتِ . To reduce to —, صَيَّرَ رَمَادًا . To lay in —, to burn, أَحْرَقَ . To rise from its —, تَجَبَّرَ — عَمِرَ ثَانِيَةً .

Ashore, *ad.* بِٱلْبَرِّ — فِي ٱلْبَرِّ . To go —, نَزَلَ إِلَى ٱلْبَرِّ . The ship ran —, جَنَحَتِ ٱلسَّفِينَةُ — بَلَّطَ ٱلْمَرْكَبُ — حَرَنَتِ ٱلْمَرْكَبُ .

Ash-Wednesday, *n.* أَرْبَعَاءُ ٱلرَّمَادِ .

Ashy, *a.* رَمَادِيٌّ — سِنْجَابِيٌّ . Ashy pale, أَصْفَرُ ٱللَّوْنِ .

Asia, *n.* آسِيَا — ٱلشَّرْقُ — بِلَادُ ٱلشَّرْقِ . Central Asia, أَوَاسِطُ آسِيَا . Asia Minor, أَنَاطُول .

Asiatic, *a.* and *n.* مِنْ آسِيَا — شَرْقِيٌّ *pl.* شَرْقِيُّون .

Aside, *ad.* فِي نَاحِيَةٍ — عَلَى جَانِبٍ — فِي جَانِبٍ — جَانِبًا — نَاحِيَةً . To go —, تَنَحَّى — إِجْتَنَبَ — إِنْحَرَفَ . To lay —, turn from, أَمَاطَ عَنْ — ضَرَبَ عَنْ — صَدَفَ عَنْ — أَلْقَى عَنْ . To take one —, as from a company, إِخْتَلَى مَعَ — عَنِ ٱلْجَمَاعَةِ — أَخَذَ — مِنْ بَيْنِ ٱلْجَمْعِ مُنْفَرِدًا . To incline —, *v.i.*, إِنْتَحَى . To turn one's self — towards, تَنَحَّى لِ . To turn one — from, ضَرَبَ — عَنْ . *See also under to* Turn, *v.t.*

Asinine, *a.* حِمَارِيٌّ — مِثْلُ ٱلْحِمَارِ .

Ask, *v.t.* and *i.* سَأَلَ *aor.* يَسْأَلُ — طَلَبَ إِلَى . To solicit, طَلَبَ مِنْ — إِلْتَمَسَ مِنْ — إِسْتَفْهَمَ مِنْ . To inquire of, سَأَلَ عَنْ — نَشَدَ — أَنْشَدَ — إِسْتَخْبَرَ عَنْ . To ask one for news of, To ask one for his name, إِسْتَسْمَى . To wish, أَرَادَ — طَلَبَ . To ask, as of a price, طَلَبَ . How much do you ask for it? كَمْ تَسُومُ بِهِ — كَمْ تَطْلُبُ فِيهِ . You ask too much, أَفْرَطْتَ فِي ٱلطَّلَبِ . To ask one, courteously, to do any thing, إِلْتَمَسَ مِنْ — أَنْ يَتَفَضَّلَ بِ . One asks for you, أَحَدٌ يَدْعُوكَ . He asks for nothing better than that . . ., يَتَمَنَّى أَنْ . The governor was asked about this question and he replied respecting it, هٰذَا سُؤَالٌ سُئِلَ عَنْهُ ٱلْحَاكِمُ فَأَجَابَ عَنْهُ . To be asked, سُئِلَ — قِيلَ لَهُ .

Askance, / Askew, *ad.* / Aslant, } عَنْ عُرْضٍ — إِنْحِرَافًا — خَزْرًا . To look —, تَخَازَرَ — نَظَرَ إِلَيْهِ عَنْ عُرْضٍ . He looked at him —, لَحَظَ إِلَى — لَاحَظَ . One who looks —, كَافِحَةُ — أَخْزَرُ ٱلْعَيْنِ .

Asleep, *a.* رَاقِد — نَائِم *pl.* نِيَام and نُوَّام . To be or fall —, رَقَدَ — نَامَ — نَعَسَ — نَوَّمَ — نَيَّمَ . To lull —, أَرْقَدَ . To be —, torpid, of any member of the body, أَمْذَلَ — نَمِلَ .

Aslope, *ad.* مَيَلَانًا — إِنْحِدَارًا .

Asp, *n.* صِلٌّ *pl.* أَصْلَال — أَفْعَى *pl.* أَفَاعِي .

Asp, Aspen, *n.* The tree, ٱلْحَوْرُ ٱلرَّجْرَاجُ .

Asparagus, *n.* هِلْيَوْن — يَرَامِيع — إِسْفَرَاج .

Aspect, *n.* Appearance, مَنْظَر — مَرْآة — وَجْه *pl.* وُجُوه — سَمَامَة — صُورَة — وَجْه . Countenance, هَيْئَة *pl.* هَيْئَات — طَلْعَة . Position, مَقَام . Colour, لَوْن *pl.* أَلْوَان . A woman of a beautiful —, حَسَنَةُ ٱلْمَنْظَرِ — رُؤْيَة — مَنْظَر . The — of affairs, صُورَةُ ٱلْأَحْوَالِ . How beautiful is the — of the earth! مَا أَحْسَنَ مَشْرَةَ ٱلْأَرْضِ . Under one aspect, بِوَجْهٍ — بِوَجْهٍ مِنَ ٱلْوُجُوهِ .

Asperity, *n.* Of disposition, عُرَام — مَظَاظَة — حُرْشَة — مَسَاحَة — خُشُونَة .

Asperse, *v.t.* To sprinkle, رَشَّ . To slander, نَمَّ — إِسْتَقَلَّ — هَتَكَ — فَضَحَ — إِفْتَرَى عَلَى — وَشَى بِ *aor.* يَشِي — مَزَّقَ — عِرْضَهُ — فِي عِرْضِهِ — طَعَنَ .

Aspersion, *n.* The act of, sprinkling, رَشّ — رُشُوش . Calumny, نَمِيمَة *pl.* نَمَائِمُ — هَتْك — إِفْتِرَاء — قَذْف — بُهْتَان .

Asphalt, *n.* / Asphaltum, } حُمَر — قِفْرُ ٱلْيَهُودِ .

Asphaltic, *a.* حُمَرِيٌّ . The — Lake, the Dead Sea, بَحْرُ لُوط — بُحَيْرَةُ لُوط .

Asphodel, *n.* بَرْوَاق — خُنْثَى — سِيرَاس .

Asphyxia, *n.* مَوْتَة — غَشْيٌ .

Aspirant, *n.* طَالِب *pl.* طُلَّاب — مُرِيد — رَاغِبٌ فِي *pl.* رَاغِبُون .

Aspirate, *v.t.* لَفَظَ مِنَ ٱلْحَلْقِ — لَفَظَ بِمِلْءِ نَفَسٍ .

Aspirate, *n.* An aspirated letter, حَرْفٌ يُلْفَظُ بِهِ مِنَ ٱلْحَلْقِ — حُرُوفُ ٱلْحَنْجَرَةِ .

Aspiration, *n.* Aspirated pronunciation, لَفْظٌ تَمَامٌ — تَلَفُّظٌ مِنَ ٱلْحَلْقِ . An ardent wish, نَفَس — رَغْبَة — شَوْق *pl.* أَشْوَاق — حُمَّة .

Aspire, *v.i.* To aim at, طَلَبَ – نَافَسَ فِي – إِدَّعَى – قَصَدَ. To long for, إِشْتَاقَ إِلَى – إِشْتَهَى.

Aspirer, *n.* *See* Aspirant, *n.*

Asquint, *ad.* بِٱحْوِلَالٍ – بِحَوَلٍ. To look at —, تَخَازَرَ. *See also under* Askance, *a.*

Ass, *n.* عَيْر *pl.* أَعْيَار – حِمَار *fem.* حِمَارَة *pl.* حَمِير. A young —, colt, جَحْش *pl.* أَجْحَاش. A little —, جُحَيْش. A wild —, عُفُوّ – حِمَارٌ وَحْشِيٌّ – يَحْمُور. A wild ass's colt, عُفُوّ. A blockhead, بَلِيد – أَحْمَق – حِمَار – بَقَر. An ass-driver, حَمَّار *pl.* حَمَّارَة. To grin as an ass when it smells urine, تَشَاخَسَ – شَخَسَ.

Assafœtida, *n.* *See* Asafœtida, *n.*

Assail, *v.t.* To assault, هَجَمَ عَلَى – حَمَلَ عَلَى – كَبَسَ – هَاجَ بِ – وَثَبَ عَلَى *aor.* يَثِبُ. To befall, نَزَلَ بِ – أَدْرَكَ. They were the first to — you, هُمْ بَدَؤُوكُمْ. We were assailed by a tempest, حَكَمَنَا نَوْءٌ. *See also to* Attack, *v.t.*

Assailable, *a.* مُمْكِنُ ٱلْهُجُومِ عَلَى.

Assailant, *n.* مُقَاتِل. The first to assail, مُتَعَدٍّ – عَادٍ – بَادِئٌ بِٱلشَّرِّ.

Assassin, *n.* قَاتِل *pl.* قُتَّال – فَاتِك *pl.* فُتَّاك. *See also* Murderer, *n.*

Assassinate, *v.t.* قَتَلَ – مَوَّتَ – فَتَكَ بِ – إِغْتَالَ. He assassinated him, قَتَلَهُ ظَهْرًا. To be assassinated, فُتِكَ – قُتِلَ ظَهْرًا.

Assassination, *n.* غِيلَة – قَتْل – تَقْتِيل – فَتَاكَة – فُتُوك – فَتْك – ٱلْقَتْلُ ظَهْرًا.

Assassinator, *n.* *See* Assassin, *n.*

Assault, *n.* An attack, هُجُوم – هَجْمَة – حَمْلَة. A blow, لَطْمَة – ضَرْبَة – بَطْش – بَطْشَة. A threat, تَهَدُّد.

Assault, *v.t.* هَجَمَ عَلَى – حَمَلَ عَلَى. To strike or attempt to strike, بَطَشَ بِ – هَدَّدَ – ضَرَبَ.

Assay, *n.* Trial, تَجْرِبَة – خِبْرَة – تَجْرِيب; as of metals, فَتْن – حَكّ – مُعَايَرَة. An — balance, طَيَّار.

Assay, *v.t.* To — metals, فَتَنَ – حَكَّ – عَايَرَ. To attempt, سَعَى فِي. To try, جَرَّبَ – إِخْتَبَرَ. An assaying stone, فَتَانَة – فَتَّانِيَّة – مِحَكّ.

Assayer, *n.* An — of metals, فَتَّان – حَكَّاكُ ٱلْمَعَادِنِ.

Assemblage, *n.* *See* Assembly, *n.*

Assemble, *v.t.* To bring together, جَمَعَ – حَشَرَ – حَشَدَ – جَمَّعَ – لَمَّ. To — an army, جَيَّشَ. To — in parties, حَزَّبَ.

Assemble, *v.i.* إِلْتَمَّ – إِنْتَدَى – إِجْتَمَعَ. They assembled together in parties, تَحَزَّبُوا – إِنْتَدَوا.

Assembly, *n.* مَجْمَع *pl.* مَجَامِع – مَجْمَعَة – مَحْشَر – مَحْضَر – جَمْعِيَّة – مَحْفِل. A council or body of councillors, أَهْلُ مَجْلِس – مَجْلِس. A deliberative —, مَجْلِسُ ٱلشُّورَى. A national —, جَمْعِيَّةٌ مِلِّيَّةٌ. An electoral —, جَمْعِيَّةٌ إِنْتِخَابِيَّةٌ. A place of —, مَجْمَع – مَجْلِس. The — broke up, إِنْفَضَّ ٱلْمَجْلِسُ. The — was confounded, كَانَ ٱلْمَحْفِلُ مُضْطَرِبًا – تَحَيَّرَ ٱلْمَجْلِسُ.

Assent, *n.* رِضَاءٌ – قُبُول – إِمْتِثَالٌ بِ. With the — of both parties, بِرِضَاءِ ٱلطَّرَفَيْنِ.

Assent, *v.i.* To consent to, رَضِيَ بِ – قَبِلَ – إِرْتَضَى. To —, as to a request, أَجَابَ إِلَى. He assented to his request, أَجَابَهُ إِلَى مَا طَلَبَ. *See also to* Grant, *v.t.*

Assenting, *a.* قَابِل *pl.* قَابِلُون – رَاضٍ بِ.

Assert, *v.t.* وَكَّدَ – زَعَمَ – جَزَمَ بِ – أَكَّدَ – ثَبَّتَ. He asserted his rights, إِدَّعَى بِحُقُوقِهِ. It is asserted that ..., قِيلَ أَنْ. To —, as against another, إِدَّعَى عَلَى. To maintain, حَكَمَ – تَحَكَّمَ.

Assertion, *n.* An affirmation, إِفَادَة – تَقْرِير – إِثْبَات. A declaration, زَعْم – زَعْمَة. A claim, إِدِّعَاءٌ – دَعْوَى *pl.* دَعَاوَى. An untrustworthy assertion, مَزْعَم *pl.* مَزَاعِم.

Assess, *v.t.* To tax, وَضَعَ عَلَى *aor.* يَضَعُ – فَلَجَ عَلَى – أَفْرَدَ فَرْدَةً عَلَى. To rate, حَسَبَ – قَوَّمَ – قَدَّرَ. *See also under to* Tax, *v.t.*

Assessment, *n.* A tax, وَضِيعَة – فَرْدَة – جِزْيَة. Valuation, تَقْدِير – تَقْوِيم – تَفْرِيد.

Assessor, *n.* An —, as of taxes, مُقَدِّر – مُقَرِّر. An assistant, وَكِيل *pl.* وُكَلَاء – مُعَاوِن *pl.* مُعَاوِنَة *and* مُعَاوِنُون.

Assets, *n.* مَالٌ بَاقٍ لِوَفَاءِ ٱلدُّيُونِ – مَال – أَمْوَال – طَابِق.

Asseverate, *v.t.* To swear, جَزَمَ – حَلَفَ. He asseverated that it was so, حَلَفَ أَنَّهُ كَذَا.

Asseveration, *n.* حَلْف – تَأْكِيد – جَزْم.

Assiduity, *n.* مُمَارَسَة – وُكُوبٌ عَلَى – إِدْمَانٌ عَلَى – كَدّ – جَهْد – مُلَازَمَة – مُوَاظَبَة – مُرَابَطَة – مُدَاوَمَة.

Assiduous, *a.* Active, عَمُول – كَدُود – فَعُول. Constant in application, مُوَاظِبٌ عَلَى – مُلَازِم – عَاقِرِفِي – مُبْتَرِك – لَاتِب.

To be — in, إِعْتَكَفَ عَلَى ـ لَزِمَ بِ ـ لَازَمَ ـ مَارَسَ ـ أَدْمَنَ ـ عَلَى ـ لَبَّ عَلَى ـ تَعَشَّقَ بِ ـ أَغْبَرَ فِي ـ وَاظَبَ عَلَى .

Assiduously, *ad.* بِالْمُدَاوَمَةِ ـ بِالْمُوَاظَبَةِ .

Assign, *v.t.* To appoint, give, جَعَلَ ـ عَيَّنَ لِ ـ رَسَمَ عَلَى ـ رَتَّبَ لِ ـ أَعْطَى ـ وَهَبَ *aor.* يَهَبُ . To — personally to, خَصَّصَ لِ . To attribute to, نَسَبَ إِلَى . To constitute, جَعَلَ ـ أَقَامَ . To —, as a stipend to, فَرَضَ لِ . I assigned him wages, جَعَلْتُ لَهُ جُعْلًا .

Assignable, *a.* That may be assigned, قَابِلُ التَّعْيِينِ وَالتَّخْصِيصِ ; that may be accounted for, قَابِلُ الْبَيَانِ وَالتَّحْدِيدِ .

Assignation, *n.* مُلْتَقًى ـ مَعْهَدَةٌ ـ مَوْعِدٌ ـ مِيعَادٌ . They made an — to meet at ..., تَوَاعَدُوا إِلَى .

Assignee, *n.* One to whom any thing is made over, مُسْتَوْدَعٌ ـ وَكِيلٌ . A representative, وَكِيلٌ *pl.* وُكَلَاءُ . An official —, مُتَسَلِّمٌ شَرْعِيٌّ .

Assigner, *n.* مُرَتِّبٌ ـ مُعَيِّنٌ ـ مُفَوِّضٌ ـ مُسَلِّمٌ .

Assignment, *n.* Act of appointing, جَعْلٌ ـ رَسْمٌ ـ تَعْيِينٌ . Assignment of a reason, شَرْحُ السَّبَبِ . The act of placing to account, تَقْيِيدٌ فِي الْحِسَابِ . A transfer, نَقْلٌ . An — in bankruptcy, تَسْلِيمُ مَالِ الْمُفْلِسِ إِلَى وُكَلَاءِ الْغُرَمَاءِ .

Assimilate, *v.t.* جَعَلَ بِمِثْلِ ـ مَثَّلَ بِ ـ نَاظَرَ بِ ـ شَبَّهَ بِ . To be or become assimilated to, تَشَبَّهَ بِ ـ إِقْتَرَنَ .

Assimilation, *n.* Act of —, تَسْوِيَةٌ ـ تَشْبِيهٌ ـ تَمْثِيلٌ , the thing assimilated, مُنَاظَرَةٌ ـ مُشَابَهَةٌ ـ مُسَاوَاةٌ .

Assinine, *a.* حِمَارِيٌّ .

Assinineness, *n.* حِمَارِيَّةٌ .

Assist, *v.t.* To help, سَاعَدَ ـ ظَاهَرَ ـ أَخَذَ بِيَدِ ـ عَاضَدَ ـ عَاوَنَ ـ أَعَانَ . To relieve, أَسْعَفَ ـ أَغَاثَ . To be present at, حَضَرَ . To — the needy, تَصَدَّقَ عَلَى ـ أَحْسَنَ إِلَى الْفُقَرَاءِ الْفُقَرَاءَ . This assists digestion, هٰذَا هَضَّامٌ ـ هٰذَا مُفِيدٌ لِلْهَضْمِ (مُهْضِمٌ or). *See also to* Aid, *v.t.*

Assistance, *n.* Help, إِسْعَافٌ ـ إِغَاثَةٌ ـ مُظَاهَرَةٌ ـ مَدَدٌ ـ حَسَنَةٌ ـ إِحْسَانٌ ـ مُسَاعَدَةٌ ـ مُعَاوَنَةٌ ـ عَوْنٌ . Benevolence, صَدَقَةٌ . Presence, حُضُورٌ . To ask — for, إِسْتَعْضَدَ بِ . To ask — against, إِسْتَمَدَّ عَلَى ـ إِسْتَنْجَدَ عَلَى . He went to his —, قَامَ لِمُعَاوَنَتِهِ . The Divine —, تَوْفِيقُ اللّٰهِ . To ask — of, إِسْتَغَاثَ ـ إِسْتَعَانَ ـ إِسْتَعَانَ بِ .

Assistant, *n.* ظَهِيرٌ ـ أَعْضَادٌ *pl.* عَضُدٌ ـ مُسَاعِدٌ ـ مُعَاوِنٌ ـ مُعِينٌ . Second in an office, ثَانٍ ـ وَكِيلٌ ـ نَائِبٌ .

Assize, *n.* A meeting of judges, مَجْلِسُ قُضَاةٍ . Assizes, جُلُوسُ الْمَحْكَمَةِ فِي الْوِلَايَاتِ عِنْدَ أَوْقَاتٍ مَوْقُوفَةٍ .

Assize, *v.t.* Of rates and measures, عَيَّنَ الْعِيَارَ وَالْقِيَاسَ .

Associate, *v.t.* and *i.* To connect one thing with another, أَضَافَ إِلَى . To join to, أَصْحَبَ بِ ـ أَرْفَقَ بِ . To keep company with, قَارَنَ ـ صَحِبَ ـ إِسْتَصْحَبَ ـ عَاشَرَ ـ صَادَقَ ـ رَافَقَ . To be associated with another, as in trade, شَارَكَ . To take as an —, أَشْرَكَ . He associated him with another, أَرْفَقَهُ بِغَيْرِهِ . شَارَكَ

Associate, *a.*
Associated, } مُشْتَرِكٌ ـ مَقْرُونٌ ـ مُقْتَرِنٌ .

Associate, *n.* A companion, رَفِيقٌ *pl.* رُفَقَاءُ ـ عَشِيرٌ *pl.* عُشَرَاءُ ـ أَصْحَابٌ *pl.* صَاحِبٌ ـ قُرَنَاءُ *pl.* قَرِينٌ . A partner, شَرِيكٌ *pl.* شُرَكَاءُ .

Association, *n.* The act of associating, تَشْرِيكٌ . A confederacy, جَمْعِيَّةٌ ـ رُفْقَةٌ ـ مَعْشَرٌ ـ صُحْبَةٌ . Connection between objects, إِقْتِرَانٌ ـ مُقَارَنَةٌ . Partnership, شَرِكَةٌ ـ شِرْكٌ . A literary —, جَمْعِيَّةٌ فُنُونِيَّةٌ ـ جَمْعِيَّةُ الْمَعَارِفِ . A commercial —, شِرْكَةٌ تِجَارِيَّةٌ . A federal —, إِجْتِمَاعُ دُوَلٍ . A trade —, شِرْكَةُ أَهْلِ أَصْنَافٍ . An — of ideas, تَسَلْسُلُ الْأَفْكَارِ .

Assonance, *n.* سَجْعٌ ـ قَافِيَةٌ ـ مُوَافَقَةُ الْأَصْوَاتِ .

Assort, *v.t.* To arrange into sorts, نَسَّقَ ـ صَنَّفَ . To arrange together, نَظَّمَ ـ وَفَّقَ .

Assortment, *n.* Distribution into sort, تَصْنِيفٌ . Things assorted, جُمْلَةٌ بَضَائِعَ ـ جُمْلَةٌ أَشْيَاءَ ـ نُخْبَةٌ . A set, عُدَّةٌ ـ طَقْمٌ .

Assuage, *v.t.* خَفَّفَ ـ أَهْدَأَ ـ لَيَّنَ ـ أَبَاخَ ـ فَتَّرَ . To be or become assuaged, تَهَدَّأَ ـ بَاخَ ـ فَتَرَ .

Assuagement, *n.* تَلْيِينٌ ـ تَلْيِيمٌ ـ تَخْفِيفٌ ـ تَسْكِينٌ .

Assuasive, *a.* مُخَفِّفٌ ـ مُسَكِّنٌ ـ مُلَيِّنٌ .

Assuetude, *n.* *See* Custom, *n.*

Assume, *v.t.* and *i.* To take, أَخَذَ ـ حَازَ ـ مَسَكَ . To become liable for, كَفَلَ بِ . To claim, إِدَّعَى بِ . To suppose, ظَنَّ ـ تَخَيَّلَ ـ تَصَوَّرَ ـ خَمَّنَ . To — superiority over, تَفَضَّلَ عَلَى . To — the form of, صَارَ . It assumed a form to my eye, تَجَسَّمَ فِي عَيْنِي . It assumed different shapes, تَغَوَّلَ . They assumed the command, تَقَلَّدُوا زِمَامَ الْحُكْمِ ـ إِتَّخَذُوا الرِّئَاسَةَ . An assumed name, إِسْمٌ إِخْتِيَارِيٌّ غَيْرُ الْإِسْمِ ـ إِسْمٌ مُسْتَعَارٌ ـ إِسْمٌ عَارِيَةٌ ـ الْحَقِيقِيِّ .

Assuming, *a.* Claiming, مُدَّعٍ . Arrogant, مُتَكَبِّرٌ ـ مُتَجَبِّرٌ . Meddlesome, فُضُولِيٌّ ـ مِعَنٌّ ـ مُتَرَهْدِلٌ .

Assumption, *n.* The taking to one's self, حَوْز ـ إِتِّخَاذ ـ إِخْتِيَار. Arrogance, تَجَبُّر ـ تَكَبُّر. Interference, فُضُول. Supposition, حَدْس ـ وَهْم ـ ظَنّ. The Assumption of the Virgin Mary, عِيدُ ٱنْتِقَالِ ٱلْعَذْرَآءِ ـ عِيدُ ٱلْعَذْرَآءِ.

Assumptive, *a.* مُتَصَوَّر ـ مُتَخَيَّل ـ مُتَخَمَّن.

Assurance, *n.* Certainty, تَحْقِيق ـ تَأْكِيد. Confidence, وَثِيقَة ـ ثَبَات ـ تَوَكُّل ـ إِتِّكَال ـ إِعْتِمَاد ـ إِعْتِقَاد. Firmness of heart, قُوَّةُ قَلْب ـ قَلْب. Impudence, وَقَاحَة ـ سَفَاهَة. Security, أَمْنِيَّة ـ أَمْن ـ أَمَانَة ـ أَمَان. A promise, إِقْرَار ـ وَعْد ـ تَعَهُّد. An — company, شَرَاكَةُ سِكُورْتَا. Assurance against loss, ضَمَانُ ٱلْخَسَارَةِ.

Assure, *v.t.* To tell positively about, أَصْدَقَ ـ عَن. To promise, تَعَهَّدَ إِلَى ـ أَمَّنَ ـ أَوْعَدَ ـ يَعِدُ *aor.* وَعَدَ ـ بِ. To make secure, ضَمَّنَ ـ فِي سِكُورْتَا. To — in an insurance office, ثَبَّتَ ـ مَكَّنَ. To be assured of, تَيَقَّنَ ـ أَيْقَنَ بِ. I — you, وَحَيَاتِكَ ـ صَدِّقْنِي. He was assured of it, إِئْتَمَنَ عَلَيْهِ. He was assured, guided, قَرَّ بِهِ عَيْنًا. Let every man be assured in his own mind, فَلْيَتَيَقَّنْ كُلُّ وَاحِدٍ فِي عَقْلِهِ. *See also to* Insure, *v.t.*

Assuredly, *ad.* Certainly, تَحْقِيقًا ـ عَلَى كُلِّ حَالٍ ـ يَقِينًا.

Assurer, *n.* An — in an assurance, مُسْكُورِيَّة *pl.* مُسْكُور ـ مُسُوكَر *pl.* مُسُوكَرُون.

Assuring, *a.* مُؤَكِّد ـ مُؤْمِن.

Aster, *n.* The flower, عَنْصِيف.

Asterisk, *n.* The mark, عَلَامَةٌ مِثْلَ ٱلنَّجْمَةِ لِإِشَارَةٍ مَّا.

Astern, *ad.* Towards the stern, فِي مُؤَخَّرِ ٱلْمَرْكَبِ. Backward, وَرَآءَ ـ إِلَى وَرَآءَ. Astern of the ship, خَلْفَ ٱلْمَرْكَبِ. To tow —, جَرَّ ـ خَلْفَ ٱلْمَرْكَبِ [2]. To go —, تَخَلَّفَ.

Asteroid, *n.* نُجَيْمَةٌ سَيَّارَةٌ ـ نُجَيْمَة.

Asthenic, *a.* مَنْهُوك ـ نَهِيك ـ ضَعِيف.

Asthma, *n.* رَبْو ـ قَصَبَة ـ ضِيقَةُ نَفَسٍ ـ ضِيقُ نَفَسٍ ـ نَهَج ـ بُهْر.

Asthmatic, *a.* بِهِ ٱلرَّبْو ـ مُبْتَلٍ بِضِيقِ ٱلنَّفَسِ.

Astonish, *v.t.* أَدْهَشَ ـ حَيَّرَ ـ عَجَّبَ ـ أَعْقَرَ. To be astonished, تَعَجَّبَ ـ تَحَيَّرَ ـ إِنْدَهَشَ ـ عَقِرَ [2].

Astonishing, *a.* عَجِيب ـ مُحَيِّر ـ مُدْهِش. How — it is! يا لِلْعَجَبِ.

Astonishingly, *ad.* بِنَوْعٍ عَجِيبٍ ـ بِتَحَيُّرٍ ـ بِمُعْجِزَةٍ ـ عَجِيبًا.

Astonishment, *n.* تَعَجُّب ـ عَجَب ـ تَحَيُّر ـ ذُهُول. They were filled with wonder and —, إِمْتَلَأُوا تَعَجُّبًا وَتَحَيُّرًا.

Astound, *v.t.* *See to* Astonish, *v.t.*

Astounding, *a.* *See* Astonishing, *a.*

Astraddle, *ad.* مُفَشِّخ ـ مُفَرْشِخ ـ فَجّ.

Astral, *a.* نُجُومِيّ.

Astray, *ad.* and *a.* ضَالّ ـ ضَائِع *pl.* ضُيَّاع ـ غَاوٍ ـ غَوِيّ ـ تَائِه. To go —, تَاهَ *aor.* يَتِيهُ ـ غَوَى [2] ـ ضَلَّ [2]. To lead —, تَوَّهَ ـ طَوَّحَ ـ ضَلَّلَ ـ غَوَّى ـ أَغْوَى. To suffer to go —, أَضَلَّ. To be led —, إِنْغَرَّ ـ إِنْغَوَى.

Astride, *ad.* Astride a horse, رَاكِبٌ عَلَى حِصَانٍ. *See also* Astraddle, *ad.*

Astringency, *n.* عُفُوصَة ـ قَبْض ـ قُبُوضَة.

Astringent, *a.* عَفِص ـ عَفْص ـ قَابِض. An — medicine, دَوَآءٌ قَابِضٌ ـ عَقُول.

Astrolabe, *n.* أَسْطُرْلَاب ـ أُصْطُرْلَاب.

Astrologer, *n.* صَاحِبُ عِلْمِ ٱلْفَلَكِ ـ مُتَنَاجِم ـ مُنَجِّم ـ مُفَلِّك ـ أَهْلُ أَحْكَامِ ٱلنُّجُومِ. The astrologers, الْفَلَكِيَّةُ ـ الْمُنَجِّمُونَ.

Astrological, *a.* نُجُومِيّ ـ تَنْجِيمِيّ.

Astrologically, *ad.* حَسَبَ قَوَانِينِ عِلْمِ ٱلتَّنْجِيمِ.

Astrologize, *v.i.* تَنَجَّمَ.

Astrology, *n.* عِلْمُ ٱلنُّجُومِ ـ عِلْمُ ٱلتَّنْجِيمِ. Judiciary —, عِلْمُ ٱلْأَحْكَامِ.

Astronomer, *n.* عَارِفٌ بِعِلْمِ ٱلْفَلَكِ ـ مُنَجِّم ـ أَهْلُ عِلْمِ ٱلْهَيْئَةِ.

Astronomical, *a.* مُطَابِقٌ لِعِلْمِ ٱلْهَيْئَةِ ـ فَلَكِيّ.

Astronomically, *ad.* حَسَبَ قَوَانِينِ عِلْمِ ٱلْهَيْئَةِ.

Astronomy, *n.* عِلْمُ ٱلْهَيْئَةِ ـ عِلْمُ ٱلْفَلَكِ.

Astute, *a.* شَاطِر ـ دَاهٍ ـ أَرِب ـ فَطِين ـ فَاطِن ـ سَعْتَرِيّ.

Astuteness, *n.* حِيلَة ـ فِطْنَة ـ هَبْل ـ إِرْب.

Asunder, *ad.* إِنْفِرَادًا. To cleave —, *v.t.* شَقَّ [2]; *v.i.* إِنْفَلَقَ ـ إِنْشَقَّ. To put —, فَرَّقَ. To cut — in the middle, شَقَّ [2] ـ شَطْرَيْنِ.

Asylum, *n.* مَلْجَأ ـ أَحْرَاز *pl.* حِرْز ـ مَأْوًى ـ مَخْلَص ـ مَنْجًا ـ مَلَاذ. A resource, such as prayer, فَلَاح. A place like home, كِنّ *pl.* أَكْنَان ـ مَأْوًى. To give an — to, آوَى. To flee to as to an —, إِلْتَجَأَ إِلَى. A lunatic —, بِيمَارِسْتَان.

At, *prep.* عِنْدَ ـ فِي ـ عَلَى ـ مِنْ قُرْبٍ ـ دُونَ. At sea, abroad, مُسَافِر. At hand, قَرِيب ـ حَاضِر. At leisure, unoccupied, عَلَى خَلَاءٍ ـ فَاضٍ; gently, عَلَى مَهْلٍ ـ رُوَيْدًا ـ عَلَى رَوْقَةٍ. At present, هٰذَا ٱلْوَقْتَ ـ حَالًا ـ الْآنَ. At that time, حِينَئِذٍ ـ يَوْمَهَا ـ وَقْتَهَا ـ عِنْدَ ذٰلِكَ ـ وَقْتَئِذٍ ـ ثُمَّ ـ إِذْ ذَاكَ. At some time, حِينًا ـ فِى بَعْضِ أَوْقَاتٍ. At no time, قَطُّ ـ أَصْلًا ـ أَبَدًا. At first, أَوَّلًا ـ فِى ٱلْبَدْءِ ـ فِى أَوَّلِ ٱلْأَمْرِ. At once, directly, حَالًا ـ عَلَى ٱلْفَوْرِ. At daybreak, عِنْدَ ٱلصُّبْحِ. At last, at length, أَخِيرًا ـ وَٱلْحَاصِلُ ـ غَايَةً. Not at all, لَا ـ كَلَّا ـ قَطُّ ـ أَبَدًا ـ أَصْلًا. At least, بِٱلْأَقَلِّ. He is at dinner, هُوَ عَلَى ٱلْغَدَآءِ. I rise at five in the morning, أَقُومُ صَبَاحًا فِى ٱلْخَامِسَةِ. To be at one, to importune, لَثْلَثَ عَلَى ـ لَجَّ عَلَى. To be at one, to agree, إِصْطَلَحُوا. At rest, مُرْتَاحٌ. At peace, فِى ٱلسَّلَامَةِ. To set, as a question, at rest, جَزَمَ ـ فَصَلَ.

Ate, *pret. of to* Eat, *q.v.*

Athanasius, *n.* Saint —, مَارُ أَثَانَاسِيُوسُ. The creed of —, قَانُونُ ٱلْإِيمَانِ ٱلْمَنْسُوبِ لِمَارِ أَثَانَاسِيُوسَ.

Atheism, *n.* زَنْدَقَةٌ ـ إِلْحَادٌ ـ إِنْكَارُ وُجُودِ ٱللّٰهِ.

Atheist, *n.* زِنْدِيقٌ *pl.* زَنَادِقَةٌ ـ مُلْحِدٌ ـ مُنَافِقٌ ـ نَاكِرُ وُجُودِ ٱللّٰهِ.

Atheistical, *a.* زِنْدِيقِيٌّ ـ نَاكِرُ وُجُودِ ٱللّٰهِ.

Athirst, *ad.* عَطْشَانُ *pl.* عَطْشَى *and* عِطَاشٌ.

Athlete, *n.* مُصَارِعٌ ـ مَغِثٌ ـ عَرِكٌ ـ بَطَلٌ. An acrobat, بَهْلَوَانِيٌّ.

Athletic, *a.* عَرِكٌ ـ بَطَلٌ ـ شُجَاعٌ. Robust, ضَلِيعٌ *pl.* ضُلْعٌ ـ قَوِيٌّ *pl.* أَقْوِيَآءُ. Athletic sports, لَعِبُ مُصَارَعَةٍ.

Athwart, *ad.* and *prep.* Across, بِٱلْعَرْضِ. Through, بَيْنَ ـ فِى ـ مِنْ وَسْطِ. The thing lay —, عَرَضَ ٱلشَّىْءُ ـ إِعْتَرَضَ ٱلشَّىْءُ. To place —, عَرَّضَ.

Atilt, *ad.* مُمَالًا ـ إِنْحِرَافًا.

Atlantic, *a.* The — ocean, بَحْرُ ٱلظُّلُمَاتِ ـ ٱلْبَحْرُ ٱلْمُحِيطُ ٱلْغَرْبِيُّ.

Atlas, *n.* A collection of maps, مَجْمُوعُ رُسُومِ ٱلْبُلْدَانِ ـ خَارِطَةٌ. Mount Atlas, جَبَلُ ٱلدَّرَنِ.

Atmosphere, *n.* هَوَآءٌ *pl.* أَهْوِيَةٌ ـ جَوٌّ *pl.* أَجْوَآءٌ.

Atmospheric, *a.* / Atmospherical, } مُخْتَصٌّ بِٱلْجَوِّ ـ هَوَائِيٌّ.

Atom, *n.* ذَرَّةٌ *pl.* ذَرَّاتٌ. A floating atom, هَبَآءٌ *pl.* أَهْبَآءٌ.

Atomic, *a.* / Atomical, } مُخْتَصٌّ بِٱلذَّرَّاتِ ـ ذَرِّيٌّ.

Atone, *v.t.* and *i.* To suffer for, عُوقِبَ عَنْ. To render satisfaction to for, جَزَى عَنْ. To expiate, كَفَّرَ عَنْ ـ جَزَى عَنْ. One soul shall not — for another, لَا تَجْزِى نَفْسٌ عَنْ نَفْسٍ شَيْئًا. He atoned for what he had done, effaced the evil, عَفَّى عَلَى مَا كَانَ مِنْهُ.

Atonement, *n.* Punishment, عُقُوبَةٌ ـ عِقَابٌ. Satisfaction, جَزَآءٌ. Expiation, كَفَّارَةٌ ـ فِدًى. To make — for, كَفَّرَ عَنْ. The day of —, يَوْمُ ٱلْكَفَّارَةِ.

Atonic, *a.* ضَعِيفٌ ـ مَنْهُوكٌ ـ رَكِيكٌ.

Atony, *n.* ضَعْفٌ.

Atop, *ad.* فَوْقَ ـ فِى رَأْسِ.

Atrocious, *a.* Flagitious, of a person, شِرِّيرٌ ـ فَاجِرٌ *pl.* فُجَّارٌ ـ فَاحِشٌ ـ شَقِيٌّ *pl.* أَشْقِيَآءُ; or of a thing, فَاسِدٌ ـ فَاحِشٌ ـ أَفْسَدُ ـ شَنِيعٌ ـ فَظِيعٌ. Great, كَبِيرٌ ـ عَظِيمٌ ـ لِلْغَايَةِ. To be —, of a thing, شَنُعَ ـ فَحُشَ; of a person, فَجَرَ ـ فَاجَرَ.

Atrociously, *ad.* بِفَحَاشَةٍ ـ فَحَاشَةً ـ بِأَشَدِّ شَنَاعَةٍ.

Atrociousness, *n.* فَظَاعَةٌ ـ فُحْشٌ ـ فُجُورٌ ـ فَحَاشَةٌ ـ شَقَاوَةٌ ـ شَنَاعَةٌ. Greatness, شِدَّةٌ ـ عِظَمٌ ـ عَظَامَةٌ.

Atrocity, *n.* فَاحِشَةٌ *pl.* فَوَاحِشُ ـ شَرَارَةٌ ـ كَبِيرَةٌ *pl.* كَبَائِرُ ـ فِعْلٌ فَظِيعٌ *pl.* أَفْعَالٌ فَظِيعَةٌ.

Atrophy, *n.* خَسْفٌ ـ هُزَالٌ.

Attach, *v.t.* and *i.* To join to, أَلْحَقَ بِ ـ عَلَّقَ فِى ـ أَلْزَقَ بِ ـ رَبَطَ إِلَى. To bind one, as by something pleasing, رَغَّبَ ـ أَرْغَبَ ـ أَغْرَمَ. To be or to become attached, joined, تَعَلَّقَ بِ ـ تَقَيَّدَ فِى ـ إِلْتَزَقَ بِ; as to a person, أَحَبَّ ـ وَدَّ ـ تَعَلَّقَ بِمَحَبَّةٍ. To be attached to, attendant upon, لَزِمَ. To be attached, addicted to, تَعَلَّقَ بِ. To seize, قَبَضَ عَلَى ـ مَسَكَ. He became attached to her, loved her, تَعَلَّقَ بِهَا.

Attaché, *n.* كَاتِبُ مَعِيَّةٍ *pl.* كُتَّابٌ ـ مَأْمُورُ مَعِيَّةٍ *pl.* مَأْمُورِيَّةٌ.

Attachment, *n.* Affection, عَلَقٌ ـ عِلَاقَةٌ ـ وُدٌّ ـ مَحَبَّةٌ ـ حُبٌّ. Application to, عِنَايَةٌ بِ ـ تَقَيُّدٌ فِى ـ رَغْبَةٌ فِى. Seizure, قَبْضٌ عَلَى ـ إِمْسَاكٌ بِ. To show — to, تَوَدَّدَ إِلَى. To gain the — of, تَوَدَّدَ.

Attack, *v.t.* To fall upon, هَجَمَ عَلَى ـ سَطَا بِ *aor.* يَسْطُو ـ دَخَلَ عَلَى ـ غَزَا ـ حَمَلَ عَلَى. To seize upon, as of a disease, أَصَابَ ـ وَرَدَ عَلَى *aor.* يَرِدُ. To be —, as by a disease, أُصَابَ. Attacked, as by a disease, affliction, *etc.*, مُصَابٌ بِ. He was — by a disease, بُلِىَ بِمَرَضٍ ـ إِعْتَرَاهُ مَرَضٌ. *See also to* Assault, Assail, *v.t.*

Attack, *n.* سَطْوَةٌ ـ هُجُومٌ ـ هَجْمَةٌ ـ حَمْلَةٌ ـ دُخُولٌ عَلَى; as of a disease, إِصَابَةٌ ـ مُصَابَةٌ.

Attain, *v.t.* To reach, وَصَلَ إِلَى *aor.* يَصِلُ ـ بَلَغَ إِلَى ـ وَرَدَ إِلَى *aor.* يَرِدُ. To gain, أَدْرَكَ ـ فَازَ بِ ـ حَصَّلَ ـ نَالَ ـ كَسَبَ ـ حَظِىَ بِ. To overtake, to equal, لَحِقَ بِ ـ أَلْحَقَ ـ أَدْرَكَ. He has attained full maturity, بَلَغَ أَشُدَّهُ ـ

إِسْتَوَى ٱلرَّجُلُ. To attain, as a point, object, نَجَحَ بِ . I lived till I attained his time, عِشْتُ حَتَّى أَدْرَكْتُ زَمَانَهُ. He attained his fiftieth year, بَلَغَ مِنَ ٱلْعُمْرِ خَمْسِينَ سَنَةً.

Attainable, *a.* تَحْصِيلُهُ ـ مِمَّا يُكْسَبُ ـ ٱلْبُلُوغُ إِلَى ـ مُمْكِنٌ إِدْرَاكُهُ مُمْكِنٌ ـ مُمْكِنٌ.

Attainableness, *n.* إِمْكَانُ ٱلْإِدْرَاكِ ـ إِمْكَانُ ٱلْبُلُوغِ إِلَى.

Attainder, *n.* حُكُومَةٌ شَرْعِيَّةٌ تَحْكُمُ بِضَبْطِ أَمْوَالِ ٱلْمَتْهُومِ وَتَعْزِيلِهِ عَنْ مَرَاتِبِهِ.

Attaint, *v.t.* To — a noble, حَكَمَ عَلَى أَحَدٍ مِنَ ٱلْأَشْرَافِ بِضَبْطِ أَمْوَالِهِ وَنَزْعِهِ عَنْ شَرَافَتِهِ.

Attainment, *n.* Acquirement, وُصُولٌ ـ بُلُوغٌ ـ إِدْرَاكٌ ـ لَحَاقٌ إِقْتِبَاسٌ ـ نَوَالٌ ـ إِصَابَةٌ ـ إِلَى. Attainments, knowledge, accomplishments, فَضَائِلُ ـ شَمَائِلُ ـ مَعَارِفُ ـ عِلْمٌ.

Attemper, *v.t.* To soften, لَيَّنَ. To regulate, طَابَقَ ـ وَافَقَ.

Attempt, *v.t.* To begin, حَاوَلَ ـ جَرَّبَ ـ شَرَعَ فِي ـ سَعَى فِي. To try, to endeavour, قَصَدَ ـ جَدَّ فِي ـ إِجْتَهَدَ فِي. To venture, risk, تَجَرَّأَ ـ إِجْتَرَأَ عَلَى ـ جَسَرَ عَلَى. To address one's self to, تَعَرَّضَ لِ. They conspired together to — the life of . . ., تَعَاوَوْا عَلَى قَتْلِ. Did they not — his life? أَلَمْ يَسْعَوْا فِي هَلَاكِهِ.

Attempt, *n.* Beginning, شُرُوعٌ ـ سَعْيٌ. Effort, جِدٌّ ـ إِجْتِهَادٌ عَزْمٌ ـ جَهْدٌ. A venture, إِجْتِرَاءٌ عَلَى. To give up an —, as through inability, تَرَكَ ـ مِنَ ٱلْفَشَلِ ـ إِنْفَشَّ عَنْ ـ تَفَيَّشَ عَنْ. He used every — in the matter, جَهَدَ فِي ٱلْأَمْرِ.

Attend, *v.t.* and *i.* To be present, لَازَمَ ـ حَضَرَ. To wait upon, to serve, خَدَمَ ـ لَازَمَ. To accompany, أَوْصَلَ ـ صَحِبَ. To assist, تَقَيَّدَ عَلَى ـ إِعْتَنَى بِ ـ عَاوَنَ ـ سَاعَدَ ـ رَافَقَ. To —, as upon a guest, رَحَّبَ ـ خَدَمَ ـ تَوَكَّفَ لِ. To — to, to listen to, أَصْغَى ـ إِكْتَنَتَ إِلَى ـ أَصَاخَ لِ ـ إِلْتَفَتَ إِلَى ـ أَنْصَتَ إِلَى إِلَى. To obey, سَمِعَ لِ ـ أَطَاعَ لِ ـ إِمْتَثَلَ. To be diligent in, to keep to, وَاظَبَ عَلَى ـ لَاحَظَ ـ بَاشَرَ ـ حَافَظَ عَلَى. To — to study, رَسَخَ فِي ٱلْعِلْمِ ـ إِسْتَفْطَنَ فِي ٱلدَّرْسِ. To — to one's self, تَقَيَّدَ عَلَى نَفْسِهِ. I attended their prayers, حَضَرْتُ صَلَوَاتِهِمْ. He attended before the judge, حَضَرَ مَجْلِسَ ٱلْقَاضِي. See that our baggage is properly attended to, أُنْظُرْ أَثْقَالَنَا هَلْ أَحْسَنَ ٱلنَّظَرَ إِلَيْهَا. Your commands shall be attended to immediately, أَمْرُكَ يُقْضَى حَالًا عَلَى ٱلرَّأْسِ وَٱلْعَيْنِ. *See also under* Present, *a.*

Attendance, *n.* Presence, presence at, حَضْرَةٌ ـ حُضُورٌ. Service, خِدْمَةٌ. Train, equipage, وَكْبَةٌ ـ خَدَمٌ وَحَشَمٌ ـ تَبَعٌ. Medical —; *see under* Medical, *a.* *See also* Attention, *n.*

Attendant, *n.* A servant, خَادِمٌ *pl.* خَدَمٌ ـ خُدَّامٌ *pl.* خُدَّامَةٌ ـ تَابِعٌ *pl.* تَبَعٌ *and* تَوَابِعُ. Consequence, عَاقِبَةٌ *pl.* عَوَاقِبُ ـ نَتِيجَةٌ *pl.* نَتَائِجُ. A medical —, حَكِيمٌ ـ طَبِيبٌ.

Attendant, *a.* مُعَقِّبٌ ـ مُسْتَعْقِبٌ ـ مُلَازِمٌ ـ تَابِعٌ. An — or guardian angel, مَلَاكٌ حَارِسٌ ـ مَلَاكٌ حَافِظٌ ـ مَلَاكٌ مُعَقِّبٌ.

Attention, *n.* Heed, نَظَرٌ ـ إِمْعَانٌ ـ حِرْصٌ ـ بَالٌ ـ وَعْيٌ. مُلَاحَظَةٌ. Endeavour, كَدٌّ ـ إِجْتِهَادٌ ـ جَهْدٌ ـ تَقَيُّدٌ. Observation, مُلَاحَظَةٌ. Obedience to, إِمْتِثَالٌ بِ ـ إِصْغَاءٌ إِلَى. Civility, as to a guest, تَرَحُّبٌ ـ تَوَكُّفٌ. Regard, civility, مَعْرُوفٌ ـ تَوَجُّهٌ. Attention, as to a business, مُبَاشَرَةٌ. To pay — to, listen to, إِكْتَنَتَ إِلَى أَصْغَى إِلَى. To show — to, أَقْبَلَ عَلَى. Give me thy —, إِعْطِنِي بَالَكَ. I do not pay any — to him, لَا أُلْقِي إِلَيْهِ بَالًا. To draw off the — of one from, شَاغَلَ ـ عَنْ. He paid me every —, عَمِلَ مَعِي كُلَّ مَعْرُوفٍ.

Attentive, *a.* Careful, مُعْتَنٍ بِ ـ لَبِيبٌ ـ نَظُورٌ ـ مُنْتَبِهٌ صَاحِبٌ ـ مُتَوَجِّهٌ ـ جِشِّيعٌ ـ حَرِيصٌ ـ مُتَقَيِّدٌ فِي. Courteous, مَعْرُوفٌ. To be — to, to heed, إِنْتَبَهَ إِلَى ـ تَقَيَّدَ بِ; to honour, تَعَرَّضَ لِلشَّيْءِ. To direct one's (own) — to a thing, أَوْجَهَ ـ وَجَّهَ.

Attentively, *ad.* بِدَوَرَانِ بَالٍ ـ بِتَدْقِيقٍ ـ بِتَقَيُّدٍ ـ بِٱنْتِبَاهٍ. To regard —, أَحَدَّ ٱلنَّظَرَ فِي ـ أَمْعَنَ ٱلنَّظَرَ فِي.

Attenuate, *v.t.* To make thinner, finer, لَطَّفَ ـ رَقَّقَ. To make less heavy, grave, خَفَّفَ. To be or become attenuated, رَقَّ ـ إِسْتَرَقَّ.

Attenuation, *n.* تَخْفِيفٌ ـ تَلْطِيفٌ ـ تَرْقِيقٌ.

Attest, *v.t.* To witness شَهِدَ بِ. To call to witness, أَشْهَدَ ـ إِسْتَشْهَدَ ـ عَلَى. To certify, حَقَّقَ ـ نَعَمَ بِ. To swear, إِسْتَحْلَفَ ـ أَقْسَمَ ـ أَحْلَفَ. *See also under to* Witness, *v.t.*

Attestation, *n.* Certification, إِقْرَارٌ ـ شَهَادَةٌ. An oath, حَلْفَةٌ ـ أُحْلُوفَةٌ ـ مَحْلُوفَةٌ. The causing another to make oath, إِسْتِحْلَافٌ.

Attester, *n.* شَاهِدٌ ـ شَهِيدٌ.

Attic, *n.* عُلِّيَّةٌ *pl.* عَلَالِيُّ.

Attire, *v.t.* زَيَّنَ ـ كَسَّى ـ بِ ـ لَبَّسَ.

Attire, *n.* كِسْوَةٌ ـ زِينَةٌ ـ كِسَاءٌ ـ ثِيَابٌ ـ لِبْسٌ.

Attitude, *n.* Position, وِضْعَةٌ ـ هِيئَةٌ ـ حَالَةٌ ـ قِعْدَةٌ. Disposition, bearing, طَوْرٌ وَحَرَكَةٌ ـ طَوْرٌ وَمِشْوَارٌ.

Attorney, *n.* مُبَاشِرٌ ـ وَكِيلٌ. An — at law, وَكِيلُ ٱلدَّعْوَى. Attorney General, وَكِيلُ ٱلدَّوْلَةِ فِي ٱلدَّعَاوَى بِأَسْرِهَا. Power of —, سِجِلُّ وَكَالَةٍ.

Attorneyship, *n.* وَكَالَةٌ.

Attract, *v.t.* To draw, جَذَبَ ـ ² جَلَبَ ـ ² جَرَّ-إِلَى. To allure, أَغْرَى ـ أَغْرَمَ أَغْرَمَ بِ. To be attracted, allured, by, To — the love of one, تَوَدَّدَ. He attracted the hearts of the people, إِجْتَذَبَ قُلُوبَ ٱلنَّاسِ.

Attraction, *n.* جَاذِبِيَّة ـ جَلْب ـ جَذْب. Attractions, beauty, مَحَاسِن ـ حُسْن وَجَمَال. The power of —, القُوَّةُ ٱلجَاذِبَةُ. Attraction of gravitation, جَاذِبِيَّة. Magnetic —, الجَاذِبِيَّةُ ٱلمَغْنَطِيسِيَّةُ. Electric —, الجَاذِبِيَّةُ ـ الجَاذِبِيَّةُ ٱلإِيلِكْتْرِيكِيَّةُ ٱلكَهْرَبَائِيَّةُ. Attraction of aggregation, جَاذِبِيَّةُ تَجَمُّعِ ٱلأَجْزَاءِ. Attraction of cohesion, جَاذِبِيَّةُ ٱللُّصُوقِ. Chemical —, جَاذِبِيَّةٌ كِيمَاوِيَّةٌ.

Attractive, *a.* Drawing, جَالِب ـ جَاذِب. Engaging, جَاذِبُ ٱلقَلْبِ ـ يَسْلُبُ ٱلعَقْلَ ـ مُشْحِط ـ حَبَّذَا. Of a place, كَثِيرُ ٱلمَنَازِلِ. *See also* Engaging, *a.*

Attractively, *ad.* With the power of attracting, جَذْبًا ـ جَلْبًا.

Attractiveness, *n.* Loveliness, بَهْجَة ـ جَمَال ـ رَوْنَق ـ لَطَافَة.

Attributable, *a.* يُلْقَى عَلَى ـ يُنْسَبُ إِلَى.

Attribute, *v.t.* To ascribe to, أَلْقَى-عَلَى ـ ² نَسَبَ-إِلَى ـ أَوْصَفَ-إِلَى ـ حَكَمَ-لِ ـ ² خَصَّصَ-بِ. To charge with, حَمَلَ-عَلَى ـ تَهَمَ-بِ ـ ² نَسَبَ-لِنَفْسِهِ. To — to one's self, إِخْتَصَّ بِ ـ إِدَّعَى بِ. To — error to, غَلَّطَ. He attributed what was false to us in his speech, ² شَنَّعَ فِي ٱلقَوْلِ عَلَيْنَا.

Attribute, *n.* A peculiar property, خَاصَّة *pl.* خَوَاصّ ـ خَاصِّيَّة ـ صِفَة *pl.* صِفَات. What may be affirmed or denied of a subject, مَلْزُوم ؛ صِفَة ـ مَحْمُول ـ مَحْكُومٌ بِ ـ مُسْنَد ـ خَبَر; *in rhetoric*, المُسْنَدُ وَٱلمُسْنَدُ إِلَيْهِ ـ المُبْتَدَأُ وَٱلخَبَرُ. The subject and the —, أَسْمَاءُ ٱللّٰهِ ٱلحُسْنَى ـ صِفَاتُ ٱللّٰهِ تَعَالَى. The attributes of God, صِفَاتُ ٱلإِيجَابِ. Positive attributes,

Attribution, *n.* The act of ascribing, تَخْصِيص ـ نِسْبَة ـ نَسَب; a quality ascribed, خَاصَّة ـ مَنْسُوب.

Attributive, *a.* إِخْتِصَاصِيّ ـ مُخَصِّص.

Attrition, *n.* Abrasion, حِكَاك ـ حَكّ ـ جَرْش. Sorrow for sin arising from dread of punishment, إِنْسِحَاقُ ٱلقَلْبِ عَلَى ٱلخَطَايَا مَخَافَةَ ٱلعَذَابِ.

Attune, *v.t.* أَصْلَحَ ـ عَدَّلَ. To — the strings of a musical instrument, وَفَّقَ ٱلأَنْغَامَ ـ ² شَدَّ ٱلأَوْتَارَ.

Auburn, *a.* أَسْمَرُ ـ مُوَر ـ لَوْنُ ٱلشَّاهْبَلُوطِ.

A. U. C. تَارِيخُ بِنَاءِ رُومِيَّةَ ٱلقَدِيمَةِ.

Auction, *n.* حَرَاج ـ مَزَاد ـ بَيْعَة. To sell anything by —, بَاعَ-بِٱلمَزَادِ ـ بَاعَ-بِٱلحَرَاجِ.

Auctioneer, *n.* حَرَّاج ـ دَلَّال *pl.* دَلَّالُونَ.

Audacious, *a.* Bold, جَرِيء ـ مُكَبِّس ـ جَسُور. Impudent, وَقِيح ـ جَبِيرِيّ ـ مَارِد.

Audaciously, *ad.* بِجَسَارَةٍ ـ بِجَرَاءَةٍ. Insolently, بِوَقَاحَةٍ ـ بِغَطْرَسَةٍ.

Audaciousness, *n.* } Boldness, جَسَارَة ـ جَرَاءَة ـ إِقْدَام. Im-
Audacity, } pudence, غَطْرَفَة ـ غَطْرَسَة ـ وَقَاحَة.

Audible, *a.* مَسْمُوع ـ سِمَاعِيّ. An — voice, صَوْتٌ مَسْمُوعٌ.

Audibleness, *n.* مَسْمُوعِيَّة.

Audience, *n.* Hearing, سَمَاعَة ـ إِسْتِمَاع. The power of hearing, القُوَّةُ ٱلسَّامِعَةُ. A congregation, مَحْضَر ـ جَمَاعَة ـ الحُضَّار. Time for receiving, مُلَاقَاة ـ مُوَاجَهَة ـ مُقَابَلَة. An official reception, دِيوَان ـ مُوَاجَهَةٌ رَسْمِيَّةٌ. To ask an — of, إِسْتَأْذَنَ-بِٱلمُوَاجَهَةِ ـ إِسْتَأْذَنَ-بِٱلدُّخُولِ إِلَى. To have an — of, تَلَاقَى مَعَ. Give me a moment's —, عَنْ إِذْنِكَ ـ بَالَكَ ـ أَعْطِنِي سَمْعَكَ. Can an — be had of the minister to-day, هَلِ ٱلمُلَاقَاةُ مَعَ ٱلوَزِيرِ مُمْكِنَةٌ اليَوْمَ.

Audience-chamber, *n.* دِيوَان.

Audit, *n.* Of accounts, مُحَاسَبَة ـ بَحْثٌ فِي ٱلحِسَابَاتِ وَتَصْحِيحُهَا. Audit-office, قَلَمُ أَمِينِ ٱلحِسَابَاتِ.

Auditor, *n.* سَامِع ـ مُسْتَمِع ـ سَمِيع ـ حَاضِر *pl.* حُضَّار. An — of accounts, مُحَاسِب ـ أَمِينُ ٱلحِسَابَاتِ.

Auditorship, *n.* وَظِيفَةُ أَمِينِ ٱلحِسَابَاتِ.

Auditory, *n.* مَسْمَع ـ مَحْضَر ـ السَّامِعُونَ ـ الحَاضِرُونَ ـ أَهْلُ ٱلمَجْلِسِ.

Auger, *n.* بَرِيمَة ـ مِثْقَب ـ عَتَلَة ـ بِيرَم.

Aught, *n.* شَيْء ـ مَهْمَا كَانَ ـ أَيْمَا كَانَ ـ أَيْش مَا كَانَ. For — I care, نَظَرًا إِلَى مَا أُبَالِي. I do not care — for it, مَا أُبَالِيهِ ـ مَا أُبَالِي بِهِ.

Augment, *v.t.* To increase in size, كَبَّرَ ـ عَظَّمَ ـ زَوَّدَ ـ زَادَ فِي ; in length, طَوَّلَ ; in width, عَرَّضَ ; in numbers, كَثَّرَ.

Augment, *v.i.* To increase in size, زَادَ ـ ² كَبُرَ جِرْمًا ـ ² عَظُمَ ; in price, إِرْتَفَعَ سِعْرًا ; in length, ² طَالَ ; in produce, نَمَى ; in numbers, تَكَثَّرَ.

Augment, *n.* } The act of, إِضَافَة ـ زِيَادَةٌ فِي ـ تَكْثِير ـ تَكْبِير ;
Augmentation, } the being augmented, كَثْرَة ـ إِزْدِيَاد ـ نَمِيَّة ـ نَمَاء.

Augmentative, *a.* مَزِيدٌ فِي. Augmentative particles, حُرُوفُ ٱلمُبَالَغَةِ. Augmentative power, قُوَّةٌ نَامِيَةٌ.

Augur, *v.t.* and *i.* To take an omen, عَافَ ـ تَفَاءَلَ ـ تَفَأَّلَ ـ

فَتَحَ ٱلْفَأْلَ ـَ. To take a favourable omen for or of, فَأَّلَ ـ ب; to be well augured of, تَفَآءَلَ ب. To take an evil omen for or of, تَشَأَّمَ ب ـ تَطَيَّرَ ب or مِن. To predict, تَنَبَّأَ ـ وَعَدَ aor. يَعِدُ. He augured from the birds, عَافَ ٱلطَّيْرَ. *See also to* Predict, *v.t.*

Augur, *n.* عَائِف ـ مُتَعَيِّف ـ عَرَّاف ـ رَمَّال ـ فَاتِحُ ٱلْفَأْلِ.

Auguration, *n.* عِيَافَة ـ تَفْئِيل ـ فَتْحُ ٱلْفَأْلِ ـ عِلْمُ ٱلتَّخْزِيرِ.

Augury, *n.* An omen, فَأْل ـ طَيْر ـ طَائِر ـ طِيَرَة. A sign, عَلَامَة. A good —, فَأْلٌ مُبَارَكٌ ـ بَشَارَةُ خَيْرٍ; a bad —, طَيْرٌ نَحْسٌ ـ فَأْلٌ نَحْسٌ.

August, *a.* جَلِيل ـ أَجَلّ ـ مُعَظَّم ـ مُفَخَّم. The august, المَنْصُورُ.

August, *n.* شَهْرُ آب ـ شَهْرُ أُغُسْت.

Augustness, *n.* جَلَالَة ـ عَظَمَة ـ مَهَابَة.

Aulic, *a.* دِيوَانِيّ.

Aunt, *n.* A father's sister, عَمَّة *pl.* عَمَّات; mother's sister, خَالَة *pl.* خَالَات.

Aureola, *n.* هَالَة ـ أَكْلِيلُ شُعَاعٍ مُصَوَّرٌ فِي تَصَاوِيرِ ٱلْقِدِّيسِينَ حَوْلَ رُؤُوسِهِم.

Auricle, *n.* An — of the ear, نُقْطَة; of the heart, أُذُنُ ٱلْقَلْبِ; the two auricles of the heart, أُذُنَا ٱلْقَلْبِ.

Auricular, *a.* أُذُنِيّ ـ مُخْتَصّ بِٱلْأُذُنِ. Auricular confession, إِعْتِرَافٌ لِلْقِسِّيسِ ـ إِعْتِرَافٌ سِرِّيّ.

Auriferous, *a.* بِهِ شُذُورٌ مِنَ ٱلذَّهَبِ ـ ذَهَبِيُّ ٱلتِّبْرِ.

Aurist, *n.* عَارِفٌ بِأَوْجَاعِ ٱلْآذَانِ ـ حَكِيمُ ٱلْآذَانِ.

Aurora, *n.* فَتَق ـ فَجْر ـ شَفَق.

Aurora-Borealis, *n.* أَنْوَارٌ شَمَالِيَّةٌ ـ الشَّفَقُ ٱلشَّمَالِيُّ.

Auroral, *a.* فَتَقِيّ ـ فَجْرِيّ.

Auscultation, *n.* البَحْثُ عَنْ دَآءِ ٱلصَّدْرِ بِبُوقٍ (or بِبُوقِ ٱلْأَطِبَّآءِ).

Auspice, *n.* / Auspices, حِمَايَة ـ نَظَر ـ عِنَايَة ـ حُسْنُ تَوَجُّهٍ. Under your —, بِنَظَرِكَ ـ عَلَى يَدِكَ ـ بِعِنَايَتِكَ.

Auspicious, *a.* فَرِح ـ مُفْرِح ـ مُوَافِق ـ سَعِيد ـ مُبَارَك. At the most — moment, فِي أَشْرَفِ سَاعَةٍ ـ فِي أَسْعَدِ وَقْتٍ.

Auspiciously, *ad.* مُوَافَقَةً ـ بِسَعْدٍ ـ بِخَيْرٍ.

Auspiciousness, *n.* سَعَادَة ـ هَنَآء ـ سَعْد ـ سُرُور.

Austere, *a.* Rough, stern, قَاسٍ ـ صَارِم ـ صَعْب ـ عَنِيف ـ فَظّ ـ عَدِيمُ ٱللُّطْفِ. Of an — countenance, كَاشِفُ ٱلْوَجْهِ ـ بَاسِر ـ مُتَقَلِّبُ ٱلْوَجْهِ ـ عَبُوس ـ عَبَّاس. Of an — mode of life, زَاهِد. To lead an — life, تَزَهَّدَ.

Austerely, *ad.* Harshly, قَسَاوَةً ـ بِقَسَاوَةٍ ـ بِعُنْفٍ. With mortification, بِزُهْدٍ. To look at —, جَهَمَ ـَ. To look —, كَلَحَ ـَ ـ تَعَبَّسَ ـ تَقَطَّبَ. He looked —, كَبَا وَجْهُهُ ـُ.

Austereness, *n.* / Austerity, Harshness, صُعُوبَة ـ قَسَاوَة ـ عُنْف ـ فَظَاظَة ـ كُهْر. Mortification, زُهْد ـ زَهَادَة. Austerity of countenance, كُلَاح ـ تَجَهُّم ـ كُلُوحُ ٱلْوَجْهِ. To treat with —, كَهَرَ ـ عَنَفَ عَلَى or ب ـ ـُ ـ أَعْنَفَ.

Austral, *a.* جُنُوبِيّ.

Australia, *n.* أُوسْتَرَالِيَا.

Australian, *a.* مِنْ أُوسْتَرَالِيَا ـ أُوسْتَرَالِيَانِيّ.

Austria, *n.* أُوسْتَرِيَا ـ دَوْلَةُ أُوسْتَرِيَا. Austria and Hungary, أُوسْتَرِيَا وَٱلْمَجَرُ.

Austrian, *a.* نَمْسَاوِيّ ـ أُوسْتَرِيَانِيّ. The Austrian-Hungarian monarchy, دَوْلَةُ أُوسْتَرِيَا وَمَجَارِسْتَان.

Authentic, *a.* True, approved, حَقِيقِيّ ـ مُحَقَّق صَحِيح ـ مُشْتَمِلٌ عَلَى شُرُوطِ ٱلصِّحَّةِ وَٱللُّزُومِ ـ وَثِيق ـ مُبَرْهَن. Genuine, أَصِيل ـ أَصْلِيّ. Trustworthy, مُعْتَقَد ـ يُعْتَمَدُ عَلَيْهِ. Official, رَسْمِيّ. Canonical, قَانُونِيّ. To be —, حَقَّ ـِ. Authentic news, خَبَرٌ وَاثِقٌ ـ مَعْلُومَاتٌ وَاثِقَةٌ.

Authentically, *ad.* بِإِثْبَاتٍ ـ بِصِحَّةٍ ـ حَقِيقَةً.

Authenticalness, *n.* / Authenticity, صِحَّة ـ حَقِيقَة ـ حَقّ ـ صِدْق ـ مَوْثُوقِيَّة.

Authenticate, *v.t.* حَقَّقَ. To —, as of a document, by signature, وَقَّعَ عَلَى ـ وَضَعَ ٱلْخَطَّ عَلَى aor. يَضَعُ.

Authentication, *n.* The act of, تَحْقِيق. Testimony by writing or seal, شَهَادَةُ خَطٍّ أَوْ خَتْمٍ.

Author, *n.* Cause of any thing, أَصْل ـ بَاعِث ـ بَارٍ ـ دَاعٍ ـ صَانِع ـ سَبَب ـ بَادٍ ب. An inventor, مُبْدِع ـ مُخْتَرِع ـ مُحْدِث ـ مُوَرِّث. The —, as of a crime, مُرْتَكِب ـ فَاعِل. Author, as of a book, مُؤَلِّف ـ مُصَنِّف. Abu-'l-Fáraj, author of the Book of Songs, أَبُو ٱلْفَرَجِ صَاحِبُ كِتَابِ ٱلْأَغَانِي.

Authoress, *n.* إِمْرَأَةٌ مُؤَلِّفَةٌ.

Authoritative, *a.* فَاصِل ـ أَمْرِيّ ـ شَافٍ ـ مَسْنُودٌ إِلَى أَمْرٍ ـ ذُو أَمْرٍ. An — decision, فَيْصَلٌ.

Authoritatively, *ad.* بِأَمْرٍ ـ بِسُلْطَانٍ ـ بِسَعَةٍ.

Authoritativeness, *n.* / Authority, Power, jurisdiction, سَعَة ـ مُعَامَلَة ـ حُكْم ـ حُكُومَة ـ مَكِينَة ـ سِيَادَة ـ إِقْتِدَار ـ إِمْرَة ـ قُوَّة ـ وِلَايَة ـ زَعَامَة. Credit, إِعْتِبَار. Testimony, نَصّ ـ شَهَادَة ـ إِسْنَاد ـ إِسْتِشْهَاد. Opinion cited for confirmation, إِسْنَاد ـ إِسْتِشْهَاد.

Absolute —, حُكُومَةٌ مُطْلَقَةٌ ـ قُوَّةٌ مُطْلَقَةٌ ـ حُكْمٌ مُطْلَقٌ. Competent —, شَهَادَةٌ ـ نَصُّ ٱللّٰهِ. The Divine —, مَحْكَمَةٌ مَرْجُوعِيَّةٌ ـ إِيجَابِيَّةٌ قَوْلُ ٱللّٰهِ ـ ٱللّٰهُ. The authorities, المَأْمُورِيَّةُ. The civil and military authorities, المَأْمُورِيَّةُ ٱلْمَلَكِيَّةُ وَٱلْعَسْكَرِيَّةُ. The organs of the authorities, وَسَائِطُ ٱلْمَأْمُورِيَّةِ. On the — of, بِأَمْرِ ـ حَسَبَ (عَلَى or) قَوْلِ. To exercise — over, تَحَكَّمَ عَلَى ـ تَسَلَّطَ عَلَى. To obtain — over, تَسَلَّطَ عَلَى. To place in —, قَدَّمَ ـ لِ. To quote as an — for, أَسْنَدَ ـ إِلَى. By what —? بِأَيِّ سُلْطَانٍ. To give —; *see to* Authorize, *v.t.*

Authorization, *n.* The act of, تَفْوِيضُ أَمْرٍ لِ ـ تَمْكِينٌ. Permission, إِذْنٌ ـ رُخْصَةٌ ـ إِجَازَةٌ. A paper giving —, a warrant, بَرَآءَةٌ. Legal —, مَسَاغٌ قَانُونِيٌّ ـ مَسَاغٌ شَرْعِيٌّ.

Authorize, *v.t.* To give power to, صَرَّفَ ـ فِي ـ مَكَّنَ ـ أَمْكَنَ ـ سَوَّغَ ـ جَوَّزَ ـ أَذِنَ ـ بِ. To permit, فِي or أَذِنَ ـ بِ ـ قَدَّرَ ـ عَلَى ـ فَوَّضَ إِلَى ـ أَوْسَعَ لِ. To — with full powers, قَلَّدَ ـ بِٱلْأَمْرِ وَٱلنَّهْيِ. To give authority over, سَلَّطَ ـ عَلَى. It is authorized by custom, سَنَّتْهُ ٱلْعَادَةُ.

Authorship, *n.* As of books, صَنْعَةُ تَأْلِيفِ ٱلْكُتُبِ ـ تَأْلِيفٌ.

Autobiography, *n.* تَرْجَمَةُ ٱلْمُؤَلِّفِ.

Autocracy, *n.* حُكُومَةٌ مُطْلَقَةٌ ـ إِسْتِبْدَادٌ ـ إِسْتِقْلَالٌ.

Autocrat, *n.* حَاكِمٌ مُطْلَقٌ ـ سُلْطَانٌ مُسْتَبِدٌّ ـ حَاكِمٌ إِسْتِقْلَالِيٌّ.

Autocratical, *a.* إِسْتِبْدَادِيٌّ ـ إِسْتِقْلَالِيٌّ.

Autograph, *n.* دَسْتَخَطٌّ ـ خَطُّ ٱلْمُؤَلِّفِ.

Autography, *n.* Of lithography, نَقْلُ ٱلْخَطِّ إِلَى حَجَرٍ لِلطَّبْعِ عَلَيْهِ.

Automaton, *n.* صُورَةُ إِنْسَانٍ أَوْ غَيْرِهِ مِنَ ٱلْحَيَوَانَاتِ تَتَحَرَّكُ مِنْ ذَاتِهَا أَوْ بِوَاسِطَةِ آلَةٍ.

Autonomous, *a.* مُمْتَازٌ. An — province, إِيَالَةٌ مُمْتَازَةٌ. Autonomous administration, إِدَارَةٌ مُمْتَازَةٌ ـ إِدَارَةٌ مُفْرَزَةٌ.

Autonomy, *n.* إِدَارَةٌ مُفْرَزَةٌ ـ إِدَارَةٌ مُمْتَازَةٌ ـ حُكُومَةٌ إِخْتِيَارِيَّةٌ.

Autopsy, *n.* مُشَاهَدَةٌ بِٱلْعَيْنِ ـ مُعَايَنَةٌ ـ عِيَانٌ.

Autumn, *n.* الرَّبِيعُ ٱلْآخِرُ ـ الْخَرِيفُ.

Autumnal, *a.* خَرَفِيٌّ ـ خَرْفِيٌّ ـ خَرِيفِيٌّ.

Auxiliar, *a.* } مُعَاوِنٌ ـ مُسَاعِدٌ ـ مُنَاصِرٌ. Auxiliary verbs,
Auxiliary, } أَفْعَالٌ مُسَاعِدَةٌ لِصَرْفِ غَيْرِهَا. An — force, فِرْقَةٌ إِمْدَادِيَّةٌ ـ نَجْدَةٌ. An — corps, مُسَاعِدٌ ـ عَسَاكِرُ إِمْدَادِيَّةٌ.

Avail, *v.t.* and *i.* To be useful to, صَلَحَ ـ لِ ـ سَاعَدَ ـ نَفَعَ ـ يَسَّرَ. To — one's self of, إِسْتَفَادَ مِنْ ـ إِنْتَهَزَ ـ إِغْتَنَمَ. This will not — you, مَا يُغْنِي عَنْكَ هٰذَا. It shall not — against the flame, لَا يُغْنِي عَنِ ٱللَّهَبِ (Kurân, lxxvii. 31).

Avail, *n.* خَيْرٌ ـ مَنْفَعَةٌ ـ نَفْعٌ ـ مَصْلَحَةٌ ـ طَائِلٌ ـ جَدَآءٌ. Of no —, بَطَّالٌ ـ بَاطِلٌ ـ غَيْرُ طَائِلٍ ـ عَبَثٌ. It is of no —, لَا طَائِلَ تَحْتَهُ ـ مَا هُوَ بِطَائِلٍ ـ هُوَ غَيْرُ طَائِلٍ.

Available, *a.* Profitable, مُفِيدٌ ـ طَائِلٌ. At hand, مِمَّا يُحَصَّلُ ـ تَحْتَ ٱلْيَدِ ـ مَوْجُودٌ ـ حَاضِرٌ.

Availability, *n.* } إِفَادَةٌ ـ مَصْلَحَةٌ ـ مَنْفَعَةٌ ـ جَدَآءٌ ـ طَائِلٌ
Availableness, } قُدْرَةٌ.

Availably, *ad.* بِإِفَادَةٍ ـ بِٱلْإِنْجَازِ ـ بِقُدْرَةٍ.

Avalanche, *n.* جُرُفٌ مِنَ ٱلثَّلْجِ سَاقِطٌ مِنَ ٱلْجِبَالِ.

Avant-guard, *n.* رَسِيلُ ٱلْعَسْكَرِ ـ سُلَافُ ٱلْعَسْكَرِ ـ مُجَنِّبَةٌ.

Avarice, *n.* إِمْسَاكٌ ـ مَسَاكَةٌ ـ بُخْلٌ ـ طَمَعٌ ـ شُحٌّ ـ مَلَامَةٌ ـ جُمُودُ ٱلْكَفِّ ـ خَسَاسَةٌ.

Avaricious, *a.* طَمَّاعٌ ـ طَامِعٌ ـ مَسَّاكٌ ـ شَحَّاحٌ ـ ضَنِينٌ ـ بَخِيلٌ ـ لَئِيمٌ ـ فَاشٍ ـ يَدُهُ مَاسِكَةٌ. To be —, بَخِلَ ـ لَؤُمَ. To be — towards, شَحَّ ـ بِ or عَلَى.

Avariciously, *ad.* بِخَسَاسَةٍ ـ بِبُخْلٍ.

Avariciousness, *n.* *See* Avarice, *n.*

Avaunt, *int.* الْأَبْعَدُ ـ الْبَعِيدُ ـ تُفٌّ عَلَيْكَ ـ تُفًّا.

Ave-Maria, *n.* السَّلَامُ عَلَيْكِ يَا مَرْيَمُ.

Avenge, *v.t.* أَخَذَ ٱلثَّأْرَ مِنْ ـ ثَأَرَ بِ ـ ثَأَرَ ـ إِنْتَقَمَ. To avenge one's self upon one for, إِنْتَقَمَ مِنْ ـ عَلَى ـ نَقَمَ مِنْ ـ عَلَى. To be avenged of, أَثْأَرَ مِنْ. He avenged himself of him, إِقْتَصَّ مِنْهُ ـ أَخَذَ مِنْهُ ٱلْقِصَاصَ. Avenge me of my adversary, إِنْتَقِمْ لِي مِنْ خَصْمِي. Mighty to —, ذُو ٱنْتِقَامٍ.

Avenger, *n.* المُنْتَقِمُ مِنْ ـ مُنْتَقِمٌ.

Avenue, *n.* Access, way, دَرْبٌ ـ مَدْخَلٌ ـ مَنْفَذٌ ـ طَرِيقٌ ـ زُقَاقٌ ـ مَمَرٌّ. An — of trees, مُشَجَّرَةٌ.

Aver, *v.t.* أَكَّدَ ـ ثَبَّتَ ـ أَثْبَتَ ـ جَزَمَ.

Average, *n.* Mean proportion, وَسَطٌ ـ بَيْنَ وَبَيْنَ ـ بَيْنَ بَيْنَ ـ مُعَدَّلُ ٱلْحِسَابِ ـ حِسَابٌ مُتَوَسِّطٌ.

Average, *v.t.* قَدَّرَ ـ وَسَّطَ.

Average, *v.i.* تَوَسَّطَ. It averages, عَلَى حِسَابِ بَيْنَ وَبَيْنَ ـ ضَرَبَ مُعَدَّلَ ٱلشَّيْءِ.

Averment, *n.* Statement, إِيضَاحٌ ـ إِفَادَةٌ. Affirmation, إِثْبَاتٌ ـ قَوْلٌ.

Averse, *a.* مُخَالِفٌ ـ مُضَادِدٌ لِ ـ ضِدٌّ. To be — from, disgusted with, نَفَرَ قَلْبُهُ ـ إِعْتَنَفَ ـ جَفَا عَنْ ـ نَفَرَ ـ كَرِهَ مِنْ. To be opposed to, خَالَفَ ـ ضَادَدَ. I am — from, إِنِّي أَجْفُو عَنْ.

Averseness, n. مُمَانَعَة — مُخَالَفَة — عَدَمُ ٱلرَّغْبَةِ — تَأَخُّر.

Aversion, n. — نَفْرَة — إِسْتِكْرَاه — إِعْتِنَاف — جَفَاء — عَوَاذ — عَوْن
بِغْضَة. To have an — for, إِسْتَكْرَهَ — ² كَرِهَ. To hold in —, تَطَهَّم
عَن. I gave him up only out of — to him, مَا تَرَكْتُهُ إِلَّا عَوَذًا مِنْهُ.

Avert, v.t. — أَنْحَى عَن — ² رَدَّ عَن — ² حَدَّ عَن — ² صَدَعَ عَن
رَجَّعَ عَن — صَرَّفَ عَن — بَعَّدَ عَن — ² دَفَعَ عَن. May God —
from thee! دَفَعَ ٱللّٰهُ عَنْكَ. There is no averting the decree of
God, أَمْرُ ٱللّٰهِ لَا مَرَدَّ لَهُ.

Aviary, n. قَفَصُ طُيُورٍ — مَحَلُّ طُيُورٍ — بَيْتُ طُيُورٍ.

Avidity, n. Greed, gluttony, شَرَاهَة. Strong desire, — حِرْص
— رَغْبَة — طَمَع. To eat with —, ² شَرِهَ — ² شَرِسَ — أَتْأَتَ —
² هَرَسَ — ² أَكَلَ بِٱلْعَجَلِ — أَكَلَ بِٱشْتِهَاء.

Avocation, n. حِرْفَة — وَظِيفَة — مَشْغَلَة — حَاجَة — صَنْعَة.

Avoid, v.t. — تَوَقَّفَ عَن — إِنْتَهَى عَن — ² حَادَ عَن — تَجَافَى عَن
² هَرَبَ — إِجْتَنَبَ — أَقْنَبَ — أَعْرَضَ — أَعْرَضَ عَن — أَحْبَطَ عَن
لَا بُدَّ — لَا مَحَالَةَ مِنْهُ. There is no avoiding it, إِحْتَرَزَ عَن — عَن
مِنْهُ. He avoided vice and acquired virtue, إِجْتَنَبَ ٱلرَّذَائِلَ
وَٱقْتَنَى ٱلْفَضَائِلَ. He avoided the blow, ² زَاغَ عَنِ ٱلضَّرْبَةِ. To
nullify, أَفْسَخَ — بَطَّلَ — أَبْطَلَ. He avoided all causes that might
lead to differences between . . . . جَانَبَ جَمِيعَ ٱلْأَسْبَابِ ٱلْمُؤَدِّيَةِ
إِلَى ٱلنِّزَاعِ بَيْنَ — قَطَعَ أَسْبَابَ ٱلنِّزَاعِ.

Avoidable, a. التَّحَرُّسُ مِنْهُ مُمْكِنٌ — الإِجْتِنَابُ مِنْهُ مُمْكِنٌ.

Avoidance, n. Act of avoiding, — تَوَقُّفٌ عَن — إِعْرَاضٌ عَن
إِجْتِنَابٌ مِن. Nullification, فَسْخ — تَبْطِيل — إِبْطَال.

Avoirdupois, n. and a. عِبَارَةٌ عَنْ وَزْنٍ جَارٍ عِنْدَ ٱلْإِنْكِلِيز.

Avouch, v.t. ² شَهِدَ بِ — أَكَّدَ — جَزَمَ.

Avow, v.t. To declare, أَظْهَرَ — أَشْهَرَ. To own, — ² قَبِلَ
أَقَرَّ بِ — إِعْتَرَفَ بِ. To make to —, قَرَّرَ.

Avowal, n. إِعْلَان — إِعْتِرَاف — تَعْرِيف — إِقْرَار.

Avowedly, ad. عَلَانِيَةً — بِإِقْرَارٍ.

Await, v.t. To wait for, — ² صَبَرَ ل — إِسْتَنْظَرَ — إِنْتَظَرَ — تَرَبَّصَ
رَاقَبَ — تَرَقَّبَ — إِرْتَقَبَ — ² رَقَبَ. To expect, ² رَصَدَ — نَظَرَ.
He sat awaiting his companion, قَعَدَ يَرْقُبُ صَاحِبَهُ. I — you
here, أَنَا نَاظِرُكَ هُنَا.

Awake, a. يَقْظَان — يَقُظ — مُسْتَيْقِظ — مُنْتَبِه fem. يَقْظَى pl. يَقَاظَى.
Wide —, on one's guard, careful, حَذِر — مُنْتَبِه.

Awake, v.t. As from sleep, — أَيْقَظَ — يَقَّظَ — أَهَبَّ مِنَ ٱلنَّوْمِ
صَحَّى — فَتَّقَ — نَهَّضَ مِنَ ٱلنَّوْمِ — أَنْبَهَ مِنَ ٱلنَّوْمِ. To rouse,
حَرَّضَ — أَنْهَضَ — أَنْفَسَ.

Awake, v.i. ² يَقِظَ — تَيَقَّظَ — إِسْتَيْقَظَ — إِنْتَبَهَ مِنَ ٱلنَّوْمِ —
² هَبَّ مِنَ ٱلنَّوْمِ — ² صَحَا مِنَ ٱلنَّوْمِ — أَفَاقَ مِنَ ٱلنَّوْمِ.

Award, v.t. ² قَضَى بِ — ² حَكَمَ. To — in favour of, ² حَكَمَ ل;
award against, ² حَكَمَ عَلَى.

Award, n. قَضَاء or قَضًا pl. أَقْضِيَة — إِنْفِصَال — شَرْع — حُكْم.

Aware, a. Foreseeing, حَرِيص — سَاهِر — وَاعٍ — مُنْتَبِه. Having
knowledge of, وَاقِفٌ عَلَى — عَارِفٌ بِ — خَبِيرٌ بِ. To be —
of, ² وَقَفَ عَلَى aor. يَقِفُ — ² عَرَفَ بِ — ² شَعَرَ بِ — ² نَذِرَ بِ.
To make —, عَرَّفَ — عَلَّمَ — أَشْعَرَ بِ. To be — of, on one's
guard, كَانَ عَلَى حِذْرٍ — إِحْتَذَرَ. You are —, you know,
عِنْدِي عِلْمُ ذٰلِكَ. I am — of it, لَا يَخْفَى عَلَيْكُمْ.

Away, ad. and int. Absent, مُغْتَرِب — غَائِب. Far from,
بَعِيد — بَعِيدٌ عَن. Let us away! هَلُمَّ مِنَّا. Away from me!
إِلَيْكَ عَنِّي — أَعْلِ عَنِّي — عَالِ عَنِّي. Away with such an idea!
هَيْهَاتَ. Away with him! carry him off! خُذُوهُ — إِذْهَبُوا بِهِ —
إِرْفَعُوهُ.

To carry away, off, ² مَضَى بِ.

To do away with, أَلْغَى — أَبْطَلَ.

To drive away, ² طَرَدَ.

To eat away, consume, ² لَحَسَ — ² سَرَفَ.

To fetch away, ² رَفَعَ — جَاءَ وَأَخَذَ.

To fly away, ² طَارَ.

To go away, إِنْطَلَقَ — ² مَضَى — ² ذَهَبَ.

To give away to, وَهَبَ ل aor. يَهَبُ.

To make away with, أَذْهَبَ بِ — أَذْهَبَ — أَتْلَفَ.

To send or drive away, سَوَّقَ — ² طَرَدَ — ² دَفَعَ — شَلْشَلَ.

To snatch away, تَخَطَّفَ — ² خَطِفَ.

To take away, ² رَفَعَ — ² مَضَى بِ.

Awe, n. Dread, خَوْف — هَيْبَة — خَشْيَان — خَشْيَة. Respect,
رِعَايَة — إِكْرَام — إِعْتِبَار.

Awe, v.t. أَدْهَشَ — خَوَّفَ — خَشَّى — هَيَّبَ. To be awed
with, stand in awe of, ² خَافَ مِن — إِنْدَهَشَ مِن — ² خَشِيَ مِن.

Aweary, ad. مُتْعَب — تَعْبَان — تَعِب.

Aweigh, ad. مُسَيَّب — مَقْلُوع. The anchor's —, إِنْقَلَعَتِ
ٱلْمِرْسَاةُ — إِرْتَفَعَتِ ٱلْمِرْسَاةُ.

Awful, a. Striking awe, مَهِيب — مَهُول — هَائِل — ذَرِيع;
of a place, مَخُوف — مَهَاب. Terrible, فَظِيع — مُخِيف. An —
thing, أَمْرٌ مُفْظِعٌ. *See also under* Solemn, a.

Awfully, ad. Dreadfully, بِهَوْلٍ — بِرَوْعٍ. Solemnly, بِهَيْبَةٍ —
بِرَزَانَةٍ.

Awfulness, *n.* مَهَابَة ـ مَهُولَة ـ وَقَار ـ رَزَانَة. Solemnity, وَقَار ـ رَزَانَة.

Awhile, *ad.* إِلَى مُدَّةٍ مِنَ ٱلزَّمَانِ ـ بُرْهَة ـ حِينًا ـ مُدَّةً.

Awkward, *a.* Clumsy, غَلِيظ ـ ثَقِيل ـ مُغَفَّل ـ أَخْرَق ـ عَدِيمُ ٱللَّطَافَةِ. Untoward, مَيْشُوم ـ نَحِس. Perverse, صَعْب *pl.* صِعَاب ـ رَدِيّ. To be — in, خَرِقَ فِي ـ خَرُقَ فِي ².

Awkwardly, *ad.* Clumsily, بِغَلَاظَةٍ ـ بِقِلَّةِ مَعْرِفَةٍ ـ بِخُرْقٍ. Untowardly, بِنَحْسٍ ـ بِٱلْإِعْتِسَافِ. Inopportunely, عَلَى غَيْرِ مُوَافَقَةٍ ـ فِي غَيْرِ وَقْتِهِ.

Awkwardness, *n.* Clumsiness, خُرْق ـ غَلَاظَة ـ خُشُونَة ـ ضِيق ـ بَلَادَة ـ عَدَمُ شَطَارَةٍ. Untowardness, عَدَمُ ٱللُّطْفِ ـ عَسْف. Inopportuneness, قِلَّةُ مُوَافَقَةٍ ـ ٱلْوُقُوعُ فِي غَيْرِ وَقْتِهِ.

Awl, *n.* مِخْصَف *pl.* مَخَاصِف ـ مِخْرَز *pl.* مَخَارِز ـ مِخْرَاز. To sew any thing with an —, خَرَزَ ² ـ.

Awning, *n.* ظُلَّة *pl.* ظُلَل ـ سُرَادِق *pl.* سُرَادِقَات ـ جَنْفَاصَة ـ جِلّ ـ خَيْمَة. (The following terms are in use on the Nile boats: Awning, تَنْدَة. Ropes of an —, مَشَّاشَة ـ وَرْدَوِيلَة; a side —, وَرْدَنُول; projecting part of —, رَفْرَف.) To put up an —, نَصَبَ خَيْمَة ² ـ نَصَبَ ٱلتَّنْدَة ². To cover with an —, سَرْدَقَ.

Awoke, *pret. of to* Awake, *q.v.*

Awork, *ad.* مَشْغُول. To set —, شَغَّلَ.

Awry, *ad.* بِٱلْتِوَاءٍ ـ مُلْتَوٍ ـ مُعَوَّج.

Axe, *n.* فَأْس ـ سَفَن *pl.* فُؤُوس ـ قَدُوم *pl.* قُدُم ـ مِخْرَط *pl.* مَخَارِط ـ فَرَّاعَة. An — for lopping trees, مِعْضَد *pl.* مَعَاضِد. A battle —, بَلْطَة. A double edged —, سِنَّة *pl.* سِنَن. To hit with an —, فَأَسَ ².

Axillary, *a.* Belonging to the armpit, إِبْطِيّ ـ مُتَعَلِّق بِٱلْإِبِطِ.

Axiom, *n.* قَاعِدَة *pl.* قَوَاعِد ـ مَوْضُوعَة. *See also* Adage, *n.*

Axiomatic, *a.* أُصُولِيّ ـ مِنْ قَبِيلِ ٱلْقَاعِدَةِ.

Axis, *n.* مِحْوَر *pl.* مَحَاوِر ـ مَدَار. The — of the earth, مَدَارُ ٱلدُّنْيَا ـ مِحْوَرُ ٱلْأَرْضِ.

Axle, *n.* } As of a carriage, عَمُود *pl.* عُمُد ـ لَوْلَب ـ دُولَاب.
Axle-tree, } The — of a hand-mill, قُطْب ـ قُطْبَة. The — hole of a pulley, خُطَّاف *pl.* خَطَاطِيف ـ قَبّ. An — hole, generally, وَقْب *pl.* أَوْقَاب.

Ay, Aye, *ad.* Yes, إِيْ ـ نَعَمْ ـ إِيْ نَعَمْ ـ إِيْوَا ـ بَلَى. Aye, aye, here I am (to obey), لَبَّيْكَ.

Aye, *ad.* Ever, أَبَدًا ـ دَائِمًا ـ لِلْأَبَدِ.

Azimuth, *n.* ٱلسَّمْتُ.

Azoic, *a.* عَدِيمُ ٱلْحَيَاةِ.

Azote, *n.* عِبَارَةٌ عَنْ نَوْعٍ مِنَ ٱلْغَازِ ٱلْمُهْلِكِ ـ عُنْصُرٌ غَازِيٌّ قَتَّالٌ.

Azotic, *a.* مُهْلِك.

Azure, *a.* لَازَوَرْدِيّ ـ لَازَوَرْد ـ سَمَاوِيّ. The — vault of heaven, ٱلْكُحْلُ.

Azymous, *a.* فَطِير.

B.

B.A. مُخْتَصَرُ لَفْظَةِ Bachelor of Arts وَهُوَ صَاحِبُ ٱلرُّتْبَةِ ٱلثَّانِيَةِ فِي ٱلْعُلُومِ وَٱلْفُنُونِ.

Baa, *v.t.* يَعِرَ *aor.* يَيْعَرُ — ثَغَا. To cause to —, أَثْغَى.

Baa, *n.* ثُغَآءٌ — نُعَاق.

Baal, *n.* بَعْل.

Babble, *v.i.* بَقَّ ² — بَقْبَقَ — لَغَطَ — ثَرْثَرَ — لَخِيَ = — فَشَرَ — تَشَدَّقَ — كَثَّرَ ٱلْكَلَامَ — أَكْثَرَ ٱلْقَوْلَ.

Babble, *n.* ثَرْثَرَةٌ — لَخًى — هَذَر — قِيلٌ وَقَالٌ — كَثْرَةُ كَلَامٍ — أَقَاوِيلُ بَاطِلَةٌ.

Babbler, *n.* مِهْذَار — بَقَّاق — قَوَّال — ثَرْثَار — شَذِر — لَقَّاش — فَشَّار.

Babe, *n.* طِفْل *fem.* طِفْلَة *pl.* أَطْفَال. A — at the breast, وَلَدٌ عَلَى ٱلْبِزِّ — رَضِيع.

Babel, *n.* بَابِل. The tower of —, بُرْجُ بَابِلَ.

Babish, *a.* طِفْلِيٌّ — مِثْلُ ٱلطِّفْلِ.

Babishly, *ad.* كَٱلطِّفْلِ. To act —, غَرَّ ² — صَبَى — تَصَابَى.

Babishness, *n.* طُفُولِيَّة — صَبْوَة — وَلَدَنَة.

Baboon, *n.* قِرْدَة *coll.* قِرْد *pl.* قُرُود — مَيْمُون.

Baby, *n.* *See* Babe, *n.*

Babyhood, *n.* طُفُولِيَّة — وَلَدَنَة.

Babyish, *a.* *See* Babish, *a.*

Babylon, *n.* بَابِل.

Babylonian, *a.* بَابِلِيٌّ — مِنْ بَابِلَ.

Bacchanalian, *n.* A toper, شَرَّاب — سُكَرِيٌّ — شِرِّيب.

Bachelor, *n.* An unmarried man, عَزَب *pl.* عُزَّاب — عَازِب *pl.* أَعْزَاب. To be a —, عَزَبَ ² — تَعَزَّبَ. Bachelor, as of a university, صَاحِبُ ٱلرُّتْبَةِ ٱلثَّانِيَةِ فِي ٱلْعُلُومِ وَٱلْفُنُونِ.

Bachelor of Arts, مُجَازٌ ثَانٍ فِي ٱلْعُلُومِ ٱلْأَدَبِيَّةِ.

Bachelor of Divinity, مُجَازٌ ثَانٍ فِي عِلْمِ ٱللَّاهُوتِ.

Bachelor of Laws, مُجَازٌ ثَانٍ فِي عِلْمِ ٱلْفِقْهِ.

Bachelor of Medicine, مُجَازٌ ثَانٍ فِي عِلْمِ ٱلطِّبِّ.

Bachelorship, *n.* Singleness, عُزْبَة — عُزُوبَة. The degree of a Bachelor, رُتْبَةُ ٱلْمُجَازِ ٱلثَّانِي فِي ٱلْعُلُومِ وَٱلْفُنُونِ.

Back, *n.* The hinder part of the body, دُبُر *pl.* أَدْبَار — ظَهْر *pl.* ظُهُور. The — of the hand, ظَهْرُ ٱلْكَفِّ — قَفَا ٱلْيَدِ. The —, as of a camel, غَارِب — مَتْن. The —, as of a horse or ass, سَمَآء. The — of a letter, ظَاهِرُ ٱلْكِتَابِ. The —, as of a sword or knife, كَلٌّ. That which is behind, وَرَآء — مُؤَخَّر — ٱلْخَلْف — خَلْف. At the — of the house, مِنْ وَرَآءِ ٱلْبَيْتِ. A back-tooth, ضِرْس *pl.* أَضْرَاس. That which is at the — of it, مَا عَلَى وَرَآئِهِ.

To lean one's back upon, إِتَّكَى عَلَى.

To lie on the back, إِسْتَلْقَى عَلَى ظَهْرِهِ — نَامَ عَلَى قَفَاهُ =.

To throw one on his back, سَدَحَ ².

To turn the back, to retreat, أَدْبَرَ — تَقَهْقَرَ. To flee, هَرَبَ ² — وَلَّى هَارِبًا.

To turn the back upon, دَابَرَ. They turned their backs on one another, تَدَابَرُوا.

Back, *ad.* Again, أَيْضًا — ثَانِيَةً — بَعْدُ. Behind, وَرَآء — إِلَى وَرَآء — خَلْف. A few days —, مُنْذُ بَعْضِ أَيَّامٍ — مِنْ أَيَّامٍ.

To bring back, رَجَّعَ — أَعَادَ — عَادَ ² جَآءَ بِ.

To draw back, go backward, to backslide, إِرْتَدَّ. To fall short of, قَصَّرَ عَنْ — تَقَصَّرَ فِي.

To expect back, تَرَقَّبَ رُجُوعَهُ.

To fall back, to retire, تَرَادَّ — تَرَاجَعَ — قَهْقَرَ — تَقَهْقَرَ.

To fall back upon, to have recourse to, إِلْتَجَأَ إِلَى — إِسْتَنَدَ إِلَى.

To give back, رَدَّ ².

To hang back, تَأَخَّرَ — تَقَاعَسَ عَنْ.

To hold back, to restrain one from, قَدَعَ عَنْ — أَمْسَكَ عَنْ.

To hold one's self back from, تَمَاسَكَ عَنْ — إِسْتَمْسَكَ عَنْ.

To keep back, not to give all, إِسْتَبْقَى; not to tell all, كَتَمَ ². To keep back something from, not to tell all to, كَتَمَ عَنْ.

To look back, نَظَرَ إِلَى وَرَآءٍ =.

To roll back, دَحْرَجَ.

To send back, رَجَّعَ — أَعَادَ — أَرْسَلَ ثَانِيَةً.

To write back, in reply, جَاوَبَ — أَجَابَ — رَدَّ جَوَابًا ².

Back, *v.t.* To support, شَدَّ ² — وَثَّقَ — سَاعَدَ — سَانَدَ — ظَاهَرَ — ظَهَرَ عَلَى =. To mount, as on a horse, رَكِبَ = — رَكِبَ عَلَى. To lay, as stones, *etc.*, on the back of any thing, أَعْقَبَ.

Back, *v.i.* To go —, رَجَعَ = — تَأَخَّرَ. To — out of, to fail to perform, أَخْلَفَ. He backed out of his promises to him, أَخْلَفَهُ مَا وَعَدَهُ.

Backbite, *v.t.* عَقَبَ ـ ثَلَبَ ـ إِغْتَابَ ـ نَمَّ عَلَى ـ لَمَزَ فِي إِثْرِ ٱلرَّجُلِ بِمَا يَكْرَهُ.

Backbiter, *n.* بَلَّاغ ـ مُغْتَاب ـ لَمَّاز ـ نَمَّامُونَ *pl.* نَمَّام ـ طَعَّان.

Backbiting, *n.* غَمْز ـ نَمِيمَة ـ نَمّ ـ لَمْز.

Backbone, *n.* سِلْسِلَةُ ٱلظَّهْرِ. The vertebræ of the —, خَرَزُ ٱلظَّهْرِ.

True to the —, دَائِمُ ٱلتَّصْدِيقِ ـ صِدِّيق ـ مُخْلِصٌ لِلْغَايَةِ.

Back-door, *n.* بَابٌ وَرَّانِيّ ـ بَابٌ سِرِّيّ. An excuse, حُجَّة.

Backed, *a.* Supported, مُسْنُود. Thrown on one's back, مُسْتَلْقٍ عَلَى ظَهْرِهِ.

Backer, *n.* مُسَانِد ـ مُظَاهِر.

Backgammon, *n.* لَعْبُ ٱلطَّاوِلَةِ ـ طَاوِلَةُ ٱلنَّرْدِ ـ نَرْد.

Background, *n.* Of a house, بَاعَةٌ خَلْفَ ٱلْبَيْتِ; of a picture, أَرْضِيَّة. To keep one in the —, أَبْعَدَ ـ جَنَّبَ. To keep one's self in the —, as from a thing, أَضْرَبَ عَنْ ـ عَتَّمَ عَنْ ـ عَتَمَ عَنْ ـ أَعْتَمَ عَنْ.

Backhanded, *a.* With the back of the hand, بِظَهْرِ ٱلْكَفِّ. Unfair, خَائِن.

Backing, *n.* Support, مُظَاهَرَة. Pasteboard or any similar support, مُقَوًّى.

Backside, *n.* The rear, وَرَآء ـ خَلْف. The podex, دُبُر *pl.* أَدْبَار ـ سُرْم *pl.* أَسْرَام ـ كَفَل ـ مَقْعَد. To kick on the —, كَسَعَ ـ كَعَبَ. To turn anything — before, عَكَسَ.

Backslide, *v.i.* To depart from, إِرْتَدَّ عَنْ ـ مَالَ عَنْ. To apostatize, كَفَرَ.

Backslider, *n.* An apostate, مُرْتَدّ ـ تَارِكُ ٱلدِّينِ ـ كَافِر *pl.* كُفَّار.

Backsliding, *n.* إِرْتِدَاد ـ تَرْكُ ٱلدِّينِ ـ رِدَّة ـ كُفْرَان.

Backstairs, *n.* سُلَّمٌ وَرَّانِيّ. An indirect way, طَرِيقَةٌ عَوْجَآء.

Backstairs influence, نُفُوذٌ خَفِيّ.

Backstays, *n.* (The following terms are used on board the Nile boats, جِلِيَّة ـ عَايَايِير ـ فَايَة ـ مَعَايِين); in Turkish, پتريجه.

Backward, *a.* Averse from, مُتَعَرِّضٌ لِ ـ مُتَنَفِّرٌ عَنْ ـ مُضَادِدٌ لِ. Dilatory, بَطِيّ ـ مُتَرَاخٍ ـ وَقَّاف ـ مُهْمِل ـ غَافِل. Negligent, غَافِل. Not advanced, مُتَأَخِّر. Stupid, بَلِيد ـ ثَخِينُ ٱلْعَقْلِ ـ ثَخِين.

Backward, *ad.* | Backwards, إِلَى خَلْفٍ ـ إِلَى وَرَآءٍ ـ لِوَرَآءٍ. To go —, رَجَعَ ـ ذَهَبَ إِلَى خَلْفٍ ـ أَدْبَرَ ـ وَلَّى إِلَى وَرَآءٍ. To be —, to hang back in a matter, تَقَاعَسَ عَنْ. To turn any thing —, backside before, عَكَسَ. To walk —, مَشَى ٱلْقَهْقَرَى ـ تَقَهْقَرَ. Walking —, مُنْكَع.

Backwardly, *ad.* Unwillingly, بِقِلَّةِ رِضَآءٍ ـ بِعَدَمِ رِضَآءٍ ـ كَرْهًا.

Backwardness, *n.* The being behind, تَأَخُّر ـ تَأْخِير. Dullness, عَدَمُ رِضَآءٍ. Aversion, إِعْرَاض ـ تَنَفُّر. بَلَادَة ـ تَوَانٍ. Unwillingness, تَقَاعُس.

Bacon, *n.* شَحْمُ ٱلْخِنْزِيرِ. To save one's —, نَجَا مِنْ.

Bad, *a.* Not good, عَاطِل ـ بَطَّال ـ رَدِيّ. Hurtful, مُضِرّ ـ ضَارّ ـ خَبِيث ـ أَشْرَار *pl.* شِرِّير ـ أَرْدِلَآء *pl.* رَذِيل. Vicious, مَرِيض ـ ذَمِيم ـ شَقِيّ ـ دَنِيّ ـ خِسَاس *pl.* خَسِيس. Sick, عَلِيل ـ ضَعِيف ـ مُشَوَّش. Counterfeit, of money, زَيْف. A — man, رَجُلُ سُوءٍ ـ بُغَاة *pl.* بَاغٍ ـ ظَالِم *pl.* ظُلَّام. A — action, فَاحِشَة ـ فِعْلُ سُوءٍ ـ خَسَائِس *pl.* خَسَاسَة ـ ظُلْم. To go to the —, هَلَكَ. To become —, to change for the worse, أَسَآءَ ـ أَرْدَأَ. To make —, to deprave, خَلَفَ ـ أَخْلَفَ. To be —, corrupt, vicious, رَدُؤَ ـ فَجَرَ ـ فَحُشَ ـ تَفَاحَشَ.

Bade, *pret. of to* Bid, *q.v.*

Badge, *n.* نِيشَان ـ إِشَارَة ـ عَلَامَة ـ سِمَة.

Badger, *n.* عُنُوق *pl.* عَنَاقُ ٱلْأَرْضِ ـ تُفَّة. A badger's hole, عَانِقَآء.

Badger, *v.t.* To worry, أَضْجَرَ ـ أَغْرَضَ.

Badly, *ad.* Not well, بَشِعًا ـ عَطِلًا ـ فَسَادًا ـ بِرَدَآءَةٍ. Viciously, بِخَبَاثَةٍ ـ شَرًّا. Sickly, ضَعِيف ـ مَعْلُول ـ مَرِيض. To act —, أَسَآءَ ـ أَقْبَحَ ـ أَذَمَّ. To treat —, أَسَآءَ إِلَى. I thought — of him, أَسَأْتُ بِهِ ظَنًّا.

Badness, *n.* In a general sense, فَسَاد ـ رَدَآءَة ـ خَرِبَة ـ خُرْبَة ـ خَسَاسَة ـ دَنَآءَة ـ خُرْبَة. Viciousness, خَلَاقَة ـ خُلْقَة ـ عَيْب ـ فَحَاشَة ـ قَبَاحَة ـ خُبْث ـ شَرّ ـ شَنَاعَة.

Baffle, *v.t.* To make ineffectual, أَفْسَدَ ـ فَسَخَ عَلَى ـ عَكَسَ ـ غَادَرَ ـ أَخْجَلَ ـ أَدْهَشَ ـ خَيَّبَ. To confound, أَبْطَلَ ـ بَطَّلَ. To defeat, غَلَبَ عَلَى ـ غَلَبَ ـ كَسَرَ. Baffling winds, أَرْيَاحٌ قَلَّابَة. The affair baffled him, غَلَبَهُ ٱلْأَمْرُ.

Bag, *n.* كِيس *pl.* أَكْيَاس. A travelling —, وِعَآء *pl.* أَوْعِيَة ـ مَزَاوِد *pl.* مِزْوَد. A — for provisions, جِرَاب *pl.* جُرُب; for an animal's provender, مِعْلَف. A large — for corn, *etc.* عِدْل *pl.* أَعْدَال ـ عَدِيلَة *pl.* أَعْدَال and عُدُول ـ زَكِيبَة *pl.* زَكَائِب ـ شَكَارَة *pl.* شَكَائِر ـ جُوَالِق *pl.* جَوَالِق ـ غِرَارَة *pl.* غَرَائِر ـ تِلِّيس *pl.* تَلَالِيس. A — of rice, فَرْدَة رُزّ *pl.* أَفْرَاد; of coffee, طَرْدُ بُنٍّ *pl.* أَطْرَاد. A nose-bag, مِخْلَاة ـ مِخْلَايَة. Saddle-bags, خُرْج *pl.* أَخْرَاج. A — of game, صَيْد.

Bag, *v.t.* To acquire, حَصَّلَ ـ إِقْتَنَى ـ قَنَى. To take, of game, إِصْطَادَ.

Bag, *v.i.* To become inflated, إِنْتَفَخَ. To become wrinkled, تَكَمَّشَ ـ تَغَضَّنَ.

Bagatelle, *n.* A trifle, شَيْءٌ وَجِيزٌ ـ عَبَثَةٌ ـ لا شَيْءَ ـ تَفَاهَةٌ ـ مَسْخَرَةٌ. The game of —, لَعِبٌ عَلَى طَاوِلَةٍ صَغِيرَةٍ بِطَابَاتٍ مِنْ عَاجٍ. *See also under* Trifle, *n.*

Baggage, *n.* عَفْشٌ ـ لَبِشَاتٌ ـ لَبْشٌ ـ أَسْبَابٌ. Loads, حُمُولٌ ـ أَحْمَالٌ. Heavy —, كَرْكَبَةٌ ـ أَثْقَالٌ. To pack up —, عَزَّلَ ـ لَبَّشَ ـ عَبَّى. To pack up loads of —, شَدَّ ٱلْأَحْمَالَ ². A worthless woman, كَلْبَةٌ ـ عَاهِرَةٌ ـ فَاجِرَةٌ.

Bagnio, *n.* A bath, حَمَّامٌ. A brothel, مرخانه ـ بَيْتُ قِحَابٍ ـ مَاخُور. A prison, حَبْسٌ.

Bagpipe, *n.* قِرْبَةٌ ـ زَمَّارَةٌ.

Bagpiper, *n.* قِرَابِيٌّ ـ زَمَّار.

Bah, *int.* *See* Pish, *int.*

Bail, *n.* Surety, كَفِيلٌ ـ ضَامِنٌ ـ قَبِيلٌ. Suretyship, ضَمَانَةٌ ـ كَفَالَةٌ. To become — for, تَكَفَّلَ بِ ـ كَفَلَ بِ ² ـ قَبِلَ بِ ـ ضَمِنَ ـ ضَمِنَ بِ. To give as —, أَكْفَلَ ـ كَفَّلَ.

Bail, *v.t.* To free from water, نَزَحَ. *See also preceding article.*

Bailable, *a.* الكَفَالَةُ عَنْ ـ جَائِزَةٌ ـ يُتَكَفَّلُ.

Bailiff, *n.* Of a court, قَوَّاسٌ مَحْكَمَةٍ ـ حَوَالَةٌ ـ قَوَّاسَةٌ *pl.* قَوَّاسَةٌ. A factor, عَامِلٌ *pl.* عُمَّالٌ ـ جَرِيٌّ *pl.* أَجْرِيَاءُ.

Bailiwick, *n.* An agency, وَكَالَةٌ ـ عَامِلِيَّةٌ.

Bairn, *n.* وَلَدٌ *pl.* أَوْلَادٌ.

Bait, *n.* A temptation, غِوَايَةٌ ـ إِغْوَاءٌ ـ تَطْمِيعَةٌ. A lure for animals, مَطْمَعٌ ـ طُعْمٌ. Provender, عَلِيقٌ.

Bait, *v.t.* To put on a —, طَعَّمَ. To feed animals, عَلَفَ ـ عَلَّقَ لِ ـ أَعْلَفَ. To allure, خَدَعَ ـ غَرَّ ² ـ أَغْوَى ـ طَمَّعَ. To set dogs upon, أَطْلَقَ ٱلْكِلَابَ عَلَى.

Baize, *n.* نَوْعٌ مِنَ ٱلْجُوخِ ٱلْخَشِنِ.

Bake, *v.t.* طَبَخَ فِي ٱلْفُرْنِ ² ـ شَوَى ـ طَهَا ². To — bread, خَبَزَ. To —, as of meat, bricks, *etc.*, طَبَخَ ².

Bakehouse, *n.* مَخْبَزٌ ـ فُرْنٌ *pl.* أَفْرَانٌ.

Baker, *n.* طَاهٍ *pl.* طُهَاةٌ *and* طُهِيٌّ ـ شَوَّاءٌ ـ فَرَّانٌ; of bread, خَبَّازٌ.

Bakery, *n.* *See* Bakehouse, *n.*

Balance, *n.* Scales, مِيزَانٌ; a large —, قَبَّانٌ ـ قَبَّانَةٌ. The — of a watch, رَقَّاصُ ٱلسَّاعَةِ. Equipose, مُعَادَلَةٌ ـ مُوَازَنَةٌ. Overplus, فَاضِلٌ ـ زَائِدٌ ـ بَقِيَّةٌ ـ بَاقٍ. The — of a debt, ضَمَادٌ. The constellation Libra, بُرْجُ ٱلْمِيزَانِ. Balance of political power, مُوَازَنَةٌ پُولِيتِيقِيَّةٌ ـ مِيزَانِيَّةٌ سِيَاسِيَّةٌ. The tongue of a —, مِيلٌ ٱلْمِيزَانِ. To hold up a —, scales, عَالَ ². To strike a —, فَصَلَ ـ رَجَحَ ٱلْمِيزَانُ ـ ٱلطَّابَقَ. To turn a —, the — or scales turned, تَرَجَّحَ ٱلْمِيزَانُ. The — of income and expenditure, ٱلْمُتَبَقِّى مِنَ ٱلْإِيرَادَاتِ وَٱلْمَصْرُوفَاتِ.

Balance, *v.t.* To weigh, وَزَنَ *aor.* يَزِنُ. To counterpoise, قَابَلَ ـ وَازَنَ. To keep in just proportion, عَادَلَ. To make up one thing by another, وَازَى ـ بِ. To — an account, نَضَّ ٱلْحِسَابَ ² ـ غَلَقَ ٱلْحِسَابَ ـ صَفَّى ٱلْحِسَابَ. The scales were balanced, رَكَدَ ٱلْمِيزَانُ ².

Balance-sheet, *n.* رُقْعَةُ ٱلْمُحَاسَبَةِ ـ حِسَابُ مَا لَهُ وَعَلَيْهِ.

Balcony, *n.* شُرْفَةٌ ـ دَرَابَزِين ـ شَهْنَشِين ـ قَيْسَارِيَّةٌ.

Bald, *a.* Hairless on the head, أَقْرَعُ ـ أَصْلَعُ ـ أَطْلَسُ *fem.* قَرْعَاءُ *pl.* قُرْعٌ *and* قُرْعَانٌ; on the body generally, أَجْرَدُ. Bald on the forepart of the head, أَصْلَعُ ـ أَجْلَحُ. Bare, مُجَرَّدٌ. Insipid, meagre, حَقِيرٌ ـ رَثٌّ ـ تَافِهٌ. A — patch, صُلْعَةٌ. To be —, قَرِعَ.

Balderdash, *n.* لَغْوٌ ـ هُجْرٌ ـ هَذَرٌ ـ عَبَثٌ. To talk —, أَهْجَرَ ـ هَذَرَ.

Baldly, *ad.* Meagrely, بِرَثَّةٍ ـ بِرَكَاكَةٍ.

Baldness, *n.* قَرْعَةٌ ـ قَرَعٌ ـ صَلَعٌ; on the two sides of the head, جَلَحٌ. Plainness, سَذَاجَةٌ ـ تَجَرُّدٌ. Meagreness, رِثَّةٌ ـ رَكَاكَةٌ ـ مَسْكَنَةٌ ـ حَقَارَةٌ.

Baldrick, *n.* مِنْطَقَةٌ لِحَمْلِ ٱلسَّيْفِ ـ مَحْمَلُ ٱلسَّيْفِ ـ مِحْمَلٌ.

Bale, *n.* شَدَّةٌ *pl.* شَدَّاتٌ ـ فَرْدَةٌ *pl.* فَرْدَاتٌ ـ طَرْدٌ *pl.* أَطْرَادٌ ـ بَالَةٌ ـ شَوَالٌ *vulg.* شَائِلٌ. A — of cotton, شَائِلُ قُطْنٍ; of cloth, بَالَةُ جُوخٍ; of paper, رِزْمَةُ وَرَقٍ *pl.* رِزَمٌ.

Bale, *v.t.* حَزَمَ بِضَاعَةً ـ حَزَّمَ.

Baleful, *a.* Sad, مُغِمٌّ ـ شَقِيٌّ ـ مُحْزِنٌ ـ كَرِيبٌ. Harmful, مَلْعُونٌ ـ مُضِرٌّ ـ نَحِسٌ.

Balefully, *ad.* Calamitously, نَحْسًا ـ حُزْنًا. Harmfully, بِمَضَرَّةٍ ـ بِضَرَرٍ.

Balefulness, *n.* ضَرَرٌ ـ نُحُوسَةٌ ـ مَضَرَّةٌ.

Balista, *n.* مَنْجَنِيقٌ. Stones for the —, جُنَقٌ.

Balk, *v.t.* To frustrate, حَاشَ ـ عَنْ ² ـ خَيَّبَ ـ أَعَاقَ ـ أَعْدَمَ ـ جَوَّنَ. To be balked, خَابَ ـ تَعَوَّقَ.

Ball, *n.* Any thing round, كُرَةٌ *pl.* كُرَاتٌ *and* كُرًى *and* كُرَيَاتٌ. A round mass, كُمْزَةٌ. A — to play with, طَابَةٌ *pl.* طَابَاتٌ. A —, as of thread or minced meat, كُبَّةٌ *pl.* كُبَبٌ. A bullet, رَصَاصَةٌ *coll.* رَصَاصٌ *pl.* رَصَاصَاتٌ. A cannon —, كُلَّةٌ *pl.* كُلَلٌ. An entertainment, عَزِيمَةٌ ـ مَأْدُبَةٌ. A dance,

زِفَاف — رَقْصَة — رَقْص. The — of dung rolled by beetles, جُعَل — دُحْرُوجَة pl. دَحَارِيج. To play at —, لَعِبَ (or) كَرَا ٤ بِالطَّابَةِ. To roll, as thread, into a —, كَبَّ ٤. To make into a —, or round mass, كَمَزَ ٤ — كَبَّبَ.

Ballad, n. غِنَاء — غِنْيَة pl. أَغَانِي — غِنْوَة. A — singer, مُغَنٍّ fem. مُغَنِّيَة.

Ballast, n. Of a ship, صُبْرَة — صَبُورَة — تَصْبِيرَة. Firmness, رُسُوخ — ثُبُوت — إِحْكَام. Being without —, unsteady, قَلَّاع — طَائِش — مُتَلَوِّن.

Ballast, v.t. To — a ship, صَبَّرَ.

Ballet, n. A dance, رَقْص.

Ballista, n. مَنْجَنِيق. *See also* Balista, n.

Balloon, n. طَابَةُ هَوَآءٍ — بَالُون — مَرْكَبَةٌ هَوَآئِيَّةٌ.

Ballot, n. مُقَارَعَةٌ بِكُرَيَّاتٍ مُخْتَلِفَةِ ٱللَّوْنِ أَوْ بِوُرَيْقَاتٍ يَكْتُبُ عَلَيْهَا ٱلْمُقْتَرِعُ ٱسْمَ مَنْ يَنْتَخِبُهُ.

Ballot, v.t. To — for, رَمَى ٱلْكُرَةَ أَوْ وُرَيْقَةَ ٱلْقُرْعَةِ ٱنْتِخَابًا لِ. To — against, رَمَى ٱلْكُرَةَ أَوْ وُرَيْقَةَ ٱلْقُرْعَةِ نَفْيًا لِ.

Balm, n. An odoriferous herb, رَيْحَان. The juice of certain trees, بَلَسَان — دُهْنُ ٱلْبَلَسَانِ. An unguent, مَرْهَم. Consolation, تَسْلِيَة — تَعْزِيَة. Balm-mint, or balm-gentle, ٱلْبَاذْرَنْجَبُويَةُ — ٱلْبَقْلَةُ ٱلْأُتْرُجِيَّةُ — حَبَقٌ تُرُنْجَانِ. Balm of Makkah, بَلَسَانٌ مَكِّيٌّ. Balm of Peru, بَلَسَانٌ هِنْدِيٌّ. Balm of Gilead, بَلَسَانُ إِسْرَائِيلَ.

Balmy, a. بَلَسَمِيٌّ. Sweet-scented, ذَكِيُّ ٱلرَّائِحَةِ. Soft, لَيِّن — لَطِيف — مُلَائِم. A — breeze, نَسِيم pl. نِسَام.

Balsam, n. *See* Balm, n.

Balsamic, a. *See* Balmy, a.

Baltic, a. ٱلْبَالْطِيقِيُّ. The Baltic Sea, بَحْرٌ — بَحْرُ ٱلْبَالْطِيقِ ٱلْبَلْطِيقِ.

Baluster, n. قُضْبَان pl. قَضِيبُ دَرَابْزِينٍ.

Balustrade, n. دَرَابْزُون. The gallery round a minaret, شُرْفَة.

Bamboo, n. نَوْعٌ مِنَ ٱلْخَيْزُرَانِ.

Bamboozle, v.t. مَكْرَبَ ٤ — مَسَّخَ — أَخْدَعَ — ضَحِكَ عَلَى.

Ban, n. An edict, حُكْم — أَمْر — تَنْبِيه. An interdiction, مَنْع — نَهْيَة. A malediction, حَرْم — لَعْنَة. Bans of marriage, مُنَادَاةُ زَوَاجٍ — خِطْبَةُ زَوَاجٍ. The Ban of Croatia, بَانُ ٱلْخَرْوَاتِ.

Banana, n. The fruit, مَوْزَة coll. مَوْز. A — tree, مَوْزَة — شَجَرَةُ ٱلْمَوْزِ.

Band, n. A bandage, رِبَاط — حِفَاظ — عِصَابَة pl. قُيُود قَيْد — عَصَائِب pl. A party, عُصْبَة — جَوْقَة — جَمَاعَة — فِرْقَة ; a small party, شِرْذِمَة pl. شَرَاذِمُ. A party of musicians, جَوْقُ ٱلنَّوْبَةِ. A regimental —, مُوسِيقَةُ ٱلْعَسْكَرِ. The — played airs during the dinner, ٱلْمُوسِيقَةُ طَرَّبَتِ ٱلْأَسْمَاعَ مُدَّةَ ٱلطَّعَامِ. The military — played English tunes, عَزَفَ أَصْحَابُ آلَاتِ ٱلطَّرَبِ ٱلْعَسْكَرِيَّةِ بِأَغَانِي أَنْكِلِيزِيَّةٍ. To loose the bands, حَلَّ ٱلْقُيُودَ ٤.

Band, v.t. To tie together, عَصَّبَ — شَدَّ ٤ — رَبَطَ ٤. To — together, جَوَّقَ — لَمَّ ٤ — جَمَعَ.

Band, v.i. To unite together, of many, تَعَاهَدُوا. To — together in favour of, تَعَصَّبُوا لِ ; against, تَعَصَّبُوا عَلَى.

Bandage, n. عِصَابَة — خَبِيبَة — رِبَاط — ضِمَاد — ضِمَادَة. He used it as a —, تَعَصَّبَ بِ — تَضَمَّدَ بِ.

Bandage, v.t. عَصَّبَ — ضَمَدَ ٤. To be bandaged, إِنْضَمَدَ.

Bandbox, n. عُلْبَة pl. عُلَب — عُلْبَةُ وَرَقٍ.

Bandit, n. قَاطِعُ ٱلطَّرِيقِ pl. قُطَّاع — لِصّ pl. لُصُوص — حَرَامِيٌّ pl. حَرَامِيَّة — زَالَّة pl. زَالِل — أَزْبَنْطُوط.

Bandrol, n. رَايَةٌ صَغِيرَةٌ.

Bandy, v.i. To exchange words with, عَاوَدَ — جَاوَبَ — حَاوَرَ — رَاجَعَ — رَادَّ ٱلْقَوْلَ — رَاجَعَ ٱلْكَلَامَ. The bandying of words, مُطَارَحَةُ ٱلْكَلَامِ — مُعَاوَدَة.

Bandy-legged, a. أَكْفَس — مُعَوَّجُ ٱلسَّاقَيْنِ. To be —, كَفِسَ.

Bane, n. Poison, سِمّ. A pest, جَائِحَة. Ruin, آفَة — هَلَاك — إِنْهِدَام — أَذًى. Cause of mischief, عَرَض — عَارِض.

Baneful, a. Poisonous, سَامّ — مُسِمّ. Noxious, مُضِرّ — ضَارّ — مُهْلِك.

Banefulness, n. أَذًى — آفَة — مَضَرَّة — تَهْلُكَة.

Banewort, n. عِنَبُ ٱلثَّعْلَبِ — عِنَبُ ٱلذِّئْبِ — حُمَّاط — ٱلْكَاكَنْج — أَفَانِيَة.

Bang, v.t. To push, صَدَعَ — دَفَعَ. To thump, ضَرَبَ — لَطَشَ ٤.

Bang, v.i. To clang, صَوَّتَ — صَرَّ — عَمِلَ حِسًّا.

Bang, n. A push, صَدْع — دَفْعَة. A blow, ضَرْبَة — كَبْسَة — لَطْشَة. Sound, as of a gun, ضَرْب — طَلَق — حِسّ.

Bangle, n. خَلْخَال pl. خَلَاخِيلُ. She put on bangles, تَخَلْخَلَتْ.

Banian, n. One of a caste in India, بَانِيَان. The Banians, طَائِفَةُ ٱلْبَانِيَانِ.

Banish, v.t. To expel, غَرَّبَ — نَفَا ٤ — نَفَى — طَرَدَ ٤ — طَرَّدَ. To drive away, as from the mind, سَرْكَلَ — جَرَّدَ — أَذْهَبَ — أَقْصَى. To be banished, إِطَّرَدَ — إِنْطَرَدَ — إِنْتَفَى. To order to be banished, أَطْرَدَ — أَخْرَجَ. To — one's self, to emigrate, جَلَا aor. يَجْلُو — أَجْلَى.

Banishment, *n.* The act of, إِخْرَاج ـ نَفْي ـ طَرْد. Emigration, جَلَاء.

Banister, *n.* *See* Baluster, *n.*

Bank, *n.* As of the sea or of a river, شَطّ ـ جُدَد *pl.* جُدَّة *pl.* سَاحِلُ ٱلْبَحْرِ ـ حَافَات *pl.* حَافَة ـ بَرّ ـ شَوَاطِئ *pl.* شَاطِئ ـ شُطُوط *pl.* سَوَاحِل. A heap of earth, كُومَة ـ أَسْدَاد *pl.* سَدّ ـ كُوفَة *pl.* أَكْوَام. An abrupt —, أَجْرَاف *pl.* جُرُف. A — of masonry, رَصَف. A reef, شُعَب *pl.* شُعْبَة (called on the Nile جِسْر). A banker's chest, صَنْدُوقُ ٱلصَّيَارِفَةِ. A place to receive deposits of money, بَنْك. A — of deposit, بَنْكُ أَمَانَةٍ. Bank notes, أَوْرَاقُ بَنْكٍ. To walk along a —, شَطَّأَ. On the opposite — of the river, عَلَى قَاطِعِ ٱلنَّهْرِ ـ عِبْرَ ٱلنَّهْرِ.

Bank, *v.t.* To raise a bank, كَوَّمَ كُومَةً. To inclose with a —, سَدَّ. To —, as of a fire, طَبَنَ ـ كَبَا ـ خَبَّأَ ٱلنَّارَ. To put, as money, in a —, وَضَعَ ـ فِي ٱلْبَنْكِ *aor.* يَضَعُ. I — with him, هُوَ صَرَّافِي.

Banker, *n.* صَرَّاف *pl.* صَيَارِف ـ صَيْرَف *and* صَيْرَفِيّ *pl.* صَيَارِفَة. An association of bankers, جَمْعِيَّةُ ٱلصَّرَّافَةِ.

Banking, *n.* The business of, صَرَّافِيَّة.

Bank-note, *n.* قَائِمَة *pl.* قَائِمَات. A treasury —, قَائِمَةُ ٱلْخَزْنَةِ. A banker's —, قَائِمَةُ صَرَّافٍ.

Bankrupt, *n.* مُفْلِس *pl.* مَفَالِيس ـ مَكْسُور. To become a —, إِنْكَسَرَ ـ أَفْلَسَ. To declare —, فَلَّسَ. Declared a —, مُفَلَّس.

Bankruptcy, *n.* إِنْكِسَار ـ فَلْس. On the verge of —, مُفَيْلِس. Court of —, مَحْكَمَةُ ٱلْبَحْثِ فِي حِسَابَاتِ ـ مَجْلِسُ ٱلْأَفْلَاسِ ٱلْمَفَالِيسِ. General —, تَعْمِيمُ ٱلْإِفْلَاسِ عَلَى ٱلنَّاسِ. Fraudulent —, فَلْسُ حِيلَةٍ ـ إِنْكِسَارٌ كَاذِبٌ.

Banner, *n.* عَلَم *pl.* أَعْلَام ـ لِوَآء *pl.* أَلْوِيَة ـ رَايَة *pl.* رَايَات ـ بَيْرَق *pl.* بَيَارِق. To hoist, as of a —, نَصَبَ ـ أَلْوَى.

Bannerol, *n.* رَايَةٌ صَغِيرَةٌ.

Bannock, *n.* رُقَاقَة *coll.* رُقَاق. Bannocks, رُقَاق ـ سَبَائِك.

Banns, *n.* To publish the —, أَشْهَرَ خِطْبَةَ ٱلزَّوَاجِ فِي ٱلْكَنِيسَةِ. *See also under* Ban, *n.*

Banquet, *n.* وَلِيمَة *pl.* وَلَائِم ـ ضِيَافَة ـ مَأْدُبَة ـ مُنَادَمَة ـ عَزُومَة. To give a —, إِتَّخَذَ مَأْدُبَةً ـ أَوْلَمَ.

Banquetting-hall, *n.* قَاعَةُ ٱلْوَلِيمَةِ ـ مَضْيَفَة ـ قَاعَة.

Banquette, *n.* دَكَّة *pl.* دِكَك ـ مَسْطَبَة *pl.* مَسَاطِب.

Banshee, *n.* *See* Apparition, Ghost, *n.*

Bantam, *n.* نَوْعٌ مِنَ ٱلدَّجَاجِ مُحَجَّلٌ أَيْ مَرِيشُ ٱلسِّيقَانِ.

Banter, *v.t.* إِسْتَهْزَأَ بِ ـ مَزَحَ ـ مَزَّة ـ تَمَسْخَرَ بِ ـ تَضَاحَكَ عَلَى.

Banter, *n.* مَزْح ـ مَزَّة ـ إِسْتِهْزَآء ـ تَهْرِيجَة ـ مُمَازَحَة ـ مَسْخَرَة.

Banterer, *n.* مُهَرِّج ـ مَازِح ـ هَذِل ـ ضَحَّاك ـ سُخْرَة ـ مَسْخَرَة.

Bantling, *n.* *See* Babe, *n.*

Banyan, *n.* The tree, شَجَرَةٌ مَشْهُورَةٌ تَنْبُتُ فِي ٱلْهِنْدِ.

Baptism, *n.* صِبْغَة ـ تَعْمِيد ـ عِمَاد ـ مَعْمُودِيَّة. Infant —, مَعْمُودِيَّةُ ٱلْأَطْفَالِ. Adult —, مَعْمُودِيَّةُ ٱلْبَالِغِينَ. Private —, المَعْمُودِيَّةُ فِي ٱلْبُيُوتِ.

Baptismal, *n.* عِمَادِيّ. A — font, جُرْنُ ٱلْمَعْمُودِيَّةِ.

Baptist, *n.* One of the sect of Baptists, أَحَدُ طَائِفَةٍ مِنَ ٱلنَّصَارَى لَا تَسْتَحِلُّ تَعْمِيدَ ٱلْأَطْفَالِ وَتُنْكِرُ ٱلْعِمَادَ بِٱلنَّضْحِ وَتَفْرِضُ ٱلْغَطْسَ عَلَى ٱلْبَالِغِينَ. St. John the Baptist, لَقَبُ مَارِ ـ حَضْرَةُ يَحْيَى يُوحَنَّا ٱلْمَعْمَدَانِيّ.

Baptistry, *n.* } بَيْتُ ٱلْمَعْمُودِيَّةِ. (Among the Syrians it is
Baptistery, } called خِنْكِي.)

Baptize, *v.t.* صَبَغَ ـ عَمَّدَ. To be baptized, إِعْتَمَدَ ـ تَعَمَّدَ. Baptized, مُعَمَّد.

Bar, *n.* A bolt for a door, مِتْرَس ـ شِجَار ـ لِزَاز ـ مِزْلَاج ـ مِغْلَاق *pl.* مَغَالِيق ـ دِرْبَاس *pl.* دَرَابِيس ـ دَقَل *pl.* دُقُول. An iron — for a door, كَتِيفَة *pl.* كَتَائِف. A — of iron, عَمُودٌ مِنْ حَدِيدٍ *pl.* أَعْمِدَة ـ حَدِيدَة ـ قَضِيبٌ مِنْ حَدِيدٍ *pl.* قُضْبَان. A — of wood, خَشَبَة. A —, as of gold or silver, سَبِيكَة *pl.* سَبَائِك. A — to secure a passage, سَدّ ـ حَاجِز. Any obstacle, حِجَاب ـ عَائِق ـ مَانِع ـ تَعَرُّض. A — of sand, جِسْرُ رَمْلٍ ـ شِعْبُ رَمْلٍ. The — of a court, مَوْضِعٌ مُخْتَصٌّ بِٱلْمُحَامِينَ فِي ٱلْمَحَاكِمِ. A court for trials, دِيوَان ـ مَحْكَمَة. Bar sinister, عَلَامَةٌ فِي رَسْمِ ٱلْأَرْمَا تَدُلُّ عَلَى ٱلنُّغُولَةِ. To be called to the —, صَارَ مِنْ أَهْلِ ٱلشَّرْعِ.

Bar, *v.t.* To fasten with a bar, دَرْبَسَ ـ غَلَّقَ ـ بِمِغْلَاقٍ. To stop up, سَدَّ. To hinder, مَنَعَ. To shut out from, حَرَّمَ ـ مِن ـ نَهَى ـ عَن.

Barb, *n.* The head of an arrow, نَصْل *pl.* نِصَال ـ نُصْلَان. A beard, لِحْيَة. A prickle of a plant, شَوْكَة *pl.* شَوْكَات ـ أَسَل. A Barbary horse, حِصَانٌ مَغْرِبِيّ *pl.* حُصُنٌ مَغْرِبِيَّةٌ.

Barb, *v.t.* نَصَّلَ.

Barbacan, *n.* عَنْبُور ـ خَارِجَ حُصُونِ ٱلْبَلَدِ (*or* مِتْرَاس) حِصْن.

Barbarian, *n.* A savage, وَحْشِيّ ـ مُوَحَّش. A foreigner (not an Arab), أَعْجَم *pl.* أَعَاجِم ـ عَجَمِيّ ـ رِقَابُ ٱلْمَزَاوِدِ. A cruel

...an, رَجُلٌ قَاسٍ — عَنِيفٌ — جَانِفٌ . A stupid, uncultivated ...an, رِجَالٌ هَمَجٌ pl. رَجُلٌ هَمَجَةٌ .

Barbarian, *a.* Savage, مُتَوَحِّشٌ — وَحْشِيٌّ . Foreign, عَجَمِيٌّ — غَرِيبٌ . Stupid, uncultivated, هَمَجَةٌ — هَمَجٌ .

Barbaric, *a.* غَلِيظٌ — غَرِيبٌ .

Barbarism, *n.* Savageness, تَوَحُّشٌ . Ignorance, جَهْلٌ — جَهَالَةٌ — خُشُونَةٌ . Cruelty, جَلَافَةٌ — قَسَاوَةٌ . Uncouth speech, غُتْمَةٌ — كَلَامٌ رَكِيكٌ — غَلَطٌ فِي ٱلْكَلَامِ — لَكَنٌ — لَحْنٌ — عُجْمَةٌ .

Barbarity, *n.* Cruelty, جَوْرٌ — صَرَامَةٌ — عَنْفٌ — قَسَاوَةٌ .

Barbarize, *v.t.* خَشَّنَ — صَيَّرَ وَحْشِيًّا .

Barbarous, *a.* Savage, wild, مُوَحِّشٌ — وَحْشِيٌّ . Cruel, قَاسٍ *pl.* قُسَاةٌ — عَنِيفٌ — ظَالِمٌ — مُتَفَرْعِنٌ — مُتَغَشْمِرٌ . Barbarous in speech, أَعْجَمُ .

Barbarously, *ad.* بِفَرْعَنَةٍ — بِجَفَاءٍ — بِعَنْفٍ — بِقَسَاوَةٍ .

Barbarousness, *n.* *See* Barbarity, *n.*

Barbary, *n.* بِلَادُ ٱلْمَغَارِبَةِ .

Barbated, *a.* Having a beard, ذُو لِحْيَةٍ ; having prickles, شَائِكٌ — ذُو كَلَالِيبَ — ذُو شَوْكٍ — ذُو أَسَلٍ .

Barbecue, *n.* An animal roasted whole, خَرُوفٌ أَوْ غَيْرُهُ مَشْوِيٌّ .

Barbed, *a.* أَبُو نَصْلٍ .

Barber, *n.* حَفَّافٌ — مُزَيِّنٌ — حَلَّاقٌ — حَجَّامٌ .

Barberry, *n.* أَمِيرُ بَارِيسَ — بَرْبَارِيسُ .

Barbican, *n.* A loop-hole, دَرْخُوشٌ لِلرَّمْيِ . *See also* Barbacan, *n.*

Bard, *n.* A poet, شَاعِرٌ *pl.* شُعَرَاءُ .

Bardic, *a.* مُخْتَصٌّ بِٱلشُّعَرَاءِ — شِعْرِيٌّ .

Bare, *a.* Naked, عَارٍ *pl.* عُرَاةٌ *fem.* عَارِيَةٌ *pl.* عَارِيَاتٌ — عُرْيَانٌ . Unadorned, سَاذَجٌ . Mere, لَا غَيْرُ — مُجَرَّدٌ — فَقَطْ . Bald, أَطْلَسُ . Unfurnished, غَيْرُ مَفْرُوشٍ . Worn —, رَثِيثٌ . Laid —, exposed, مَكْشُوفٌ . Under — poles, بِلَا شِرَاعٍ . To make —; *see under the following.*

Bare, *v.t.* جَرَّدَ — عَرَّى . To strip, as a tree of its leaves, مَرَّدَ . To strip the clothes off any part of the body, شَمَّرَ عَنْ . To — or strip one's self, إِنْجَرَدَ — تَجَرَّدَ — تَعَرَّى . To be —, naked, عَرِيَ *aor.* يَعْرَى — تَعَرَّى . *See also to* Strip, *v.t.*

Barefaced, *a.* فَاجِرٌ — قَلِيلُ ٱلْحَيَاءِ — سَفِيهٌ — وَقِحٌ .

Barefacedly, *ad.* بِلَا حَيَاءٍ — بِوَقَاحَةٍ — وَقَاحَةً .

Barefacedness, *n.* فَاجِرَةٌ — قِلَّةُ حَيَاءٍ — سَفَاهَةٌ — وَقَاحَةٌ .

Barefoot, *a.* حَافٍ *pl.* حُفَاةٌ — حُفْيَانٌ . To walk —, حَفِيَ ءَ . The being —, حِفَايَةٌ .

Bareheaded, *a.* مَكْشُوفُ ٱلرَّأْسِ — فَصْعَانٌ .

Barelegged, *a.* عُرْيَانُ ٱلسَّيْقَانِ — مَكْشُوفُ ٱلسَّيْقَانِ .

Barely, *ad.* Merely, فَقَطْ . Scarcely, تَقْرِيبًا فَقَطْ . He — entered, بِٱلْجَهْدِ دَخَلَ . And not — that, وَلَيْسَ ذٰلِكَ فَقَطْ . *See also* Hardly, Only, Scarcely, *ad.*

Bareness, *n.* Nudity, عَرَاءٌ — عُرْيَةٌ — عُرْيٌ . Poverty, فَاقَةٌ — فَقْرٌ . Leanness, عَجَفٌ . The being unfurnished, خُلُوٌّ — عَدَمُ فَرْشٍ مِنَ ٱلْفَرْشِ .

Bargain, *n.* An agreement, شَرْطٌ *pl.* شُرُوطٌ — عَهْدٌ — إِتِّفَاقٌ . A thing bought, شِرًى — مُشْتَرًى . A thing sold, مُبَاعٌ — بَيْعَةٌ . A — made by clasping the hand, صَفْقَةٌ . A chaffering in bargaining, مُسَاوَمَةٌ . It was a cheap —, كَانَ شِرًى رَخِيصًا .

Bargain, *v.i.* To fix a price, قَطَعَ ٱلثَّمَنَ ءَ . To make a condition with, شَارَطَ — شَرَطَ عَلَى - كَذَا — إِشْتَرَطَ عَلَى - كَذَا ; in buying, شَارَى ; in selling, بَايَعَ .

Bargainer, *n.* In selling, بَيِّعٌ ; in buying, مُشْتَرٍ — شَارٍ .

Barge, *n.* A boat, زَوْرَقٌ *pl.* زَوَارِقُ — قَائِقٌ — فَلُوكَةٌ ; for merchandize, شَخْتُورَةٌ — خَيَاسَةٌ — مَاعُونٌ ; for passengers, ذَهَبِيَّةٌ ; a small ditto, فَنْجَةٌ .

Barger, *n.* }
Bargeman, } مَاعُونْجِي — مَلَّاحٌ *pl.* مَلَّاحُونَ — نَوَاتِيُّ *pl.* نُوتِيٌّ .

Barilla, *n.* خِيمٌ .

Barium, *n.* نَوْعٌ مِنَ ٱلْمَعَادِنِ .

Bark, *n.* The rind of a tree, قِشْرٌ *pl.* قُشُورٌ — قِشْرَةٌ — نَجَبٌ — لِحَاءَةٌ — لِحَادَةٌ ; the inner —, هُبَايَةٌ . Bark, as of a dog, عُوَاءٌ — نَبْحٌ — نَبِيحٌ — تَنْبَاحٌ — عَوِيَّةٌ . Peruvian —, قِينَا قِينَا . Bark, a ship, سَفِينَةٌ *pl.* سَفَائِنُ — مَرْكَبٌ ذُو ثَلَاثَةِ سَوَارٍ .

Bark, *v.t.* To strip of the —, شَذَبَ ءَ — قَلَفَ — نَجَبَ ءَ — قَشَرَ — عَرَمَ ٢ .

Bark, *v.i.* As a dog, نَبَحَ ءَ — عَوَى . To — at, نَبَحَ عَلَى ءَ . To make to —, أَنْبَحَ — إِسْتَنْبَحَ .

Barley, *n.* The grain, شَعِيرٌ . Green — for fodder, خَصِيلٌ — قَصِيلٌ ; husked —, شَعِيرٌ مُقَشَّرٌ ; ground —, شَعِيرٌ مُقَشَّرٌ مَدْقُوقٌ . Fodder, عَلِيقٌ .

Barley-corn, *n.* شَعِيرَةٌ . (Seventy-two barley-corns or twenty Kirâts (قِيرَاط) make a Mithkâl مِثْقَال).

Barley-meal, دَقِيقُ ٱلشَّعِيرِ .

Barley-sugar, *n.* سُكَّرُ نَبَاتٍ .

Barley-water, *n.* مَاءُ ٱلشَّعِيرِ — كَشْكٌ — فُقَّاعٌ .

Barm, *n.* رَيْمَةُ ٱلْبُوزَةِ تُسْتَعْمَلُ لِتَخْمِيرِ ٱلْعَجِينِ.

Barn, *n.* هُرِّيٌّ *pl.* أَهْرَآءٌ ـ أَنْبَار ـ شُونَة *pl.* شُوَن ـ مَخْزَن *pl.* مَخَازِنُ.

Barnacle, *n.* نَوْعٌ مِنَ ٱلْمَحَارَةِ تَلْصَقُ بِقَعْرِ ٱلْمَرَاكِبِ.

Barnacles, *n.* A farrier's —, زِيَار ـ كُلَّابَة ـ مِشْخَس. *See also* Spectacles, *n.*

Barometer, *n.* مِيزَانُ ٱلْهَوَآءِ وَٱلطَّقْسِ.

Barometrical, *a.* مُخْتَصٌّ بِمِيزَانِ ٱلْهَوَآءِ وَٱلطَّقْسِ.

Baron, *n.* أَمِير ـ بَيْك ـ بَارُون.

Baronage, *n.* إِمَارَة ـ رُتْبَةُ ٱلْبَارُونِ. The body of Barons, ٱلْأُمَرَآءُ ـ ٱلْبَارُونَاتُ أَجْمَعُ ـ مَعْشَرُ ٱلْبَارُونَاتِ.

Baroness, *n.* إِمْرَأَةُ بَارُونٍ.

Baronet, *n.* بَارُونَتْ أَيْ صَاحِبُ رُتْبَةٍ دُونَ ٱلْبَارُونِ.

Baronetage, *n.* ٱلْبَارُونَاتُ أَجْمَعُ.

Baronetcy, *n.* مَنْزِلَةُ ٱلْبَارُونَتِ.

Baronial, *a.* مُخْتَصٌّ بِٱلْبَارُونِ أَوْ بِمُلْكِهِ.

Barony, *n.* أَمْلَاكُ ٱلْبَارُونِ.

Barouche, *n.* بَارُوش ـ نَوْعٌ مِنَ ٱلْعَرَبَانَاتِ.

Barque, *n.* A ship. *See* Bark, *n.*

Barrack, *n.* قَاعَةُ ٱلْعَسْكَرِ ـ قِشْلَة ـ قِشْلَا.

Barracoon, *n.* حُجْرَة *pl.* حُجَر *and* حُجُرَات.

Barratry, *n.* Fraud of a shipmaster, خِيَانَةٌ يَرْتَكِبُهَا رَئِيسُ مَرْكَبٍ.

Barred, *a.* Fastened, مَغْلُوق ـ مُدَرْبَس. Hindered, مَمْنُوع. Excluded from, مَحْرُومٌ مِن ـ مَنْهِيٌّ عَن. Striped, مُشَطَّب ـ مُقَلَّم.

Barrel, *n.* A cask, بَرْمِيل *pl.* بَرَامِيل. Barrel, as of a gun, مَاصُورَة *pl.* مَوَاصِيرُ ـ رُوح *pl.* أَرْوَاح. Any thing long and hollow, قَصَبَة *pl.* قَصَبَات ـ أُنْبُوب *pl.* أَنَابِيبُ. A cylinder, عَمُود *pl.* عُمُد ـ أُسْطُوَانَة *pl.* أَسَاطِينُ. A twisted —, مَاصُورَةٌ مَبْرُومَةٌ. A double —, of a musket, تَفْنَكَةٌ جِفْت ـ بَارُودَةٌ مُزْدَوِجَة.

Barrel, *v.t.* صَبَّ ـ فِي ٱلْبَرَامِيلِ ـ ² مَلَأَ ٱلْبَرَامِيلَ مِن.

Barrelled, *a* In barrels, فِي ٱلْبَرَامِيلِ. Having tubes, ذُو قَصَبَاتٍ ـ ذُو أَنَابِيبَ. A six-barrelled pistol, طَبَنْجَةٌ بِسِتَّةِ أَرْوَاحٍ.

Barren, *a.* Unfruitful, جَارِز ـ جَرِد ـ بَائِر ـ عَاقِر ـ عَقِيم; of a woman, عَقِيم *pl.* عَقَائِمُ *and* عُقُم ـ عَاقِر *and* عَاقِرَة *pl.* عُقَّر *and* عَاقِرَات. Unprofitable, عَقِيم ـ غَيْرُ مُثْمِرٍ. Barren ground, أَرْضٌ أَسِيفَةٌ ـ أَرْضٌ جَارِزَةٌ. A — year, عَامُ قَحْطٍ. A — woman, إِمْرَأَةٌ عَقِيم ـ رَحِمٌ عَقِيمَةٌ. To be —, unfruitful, جَرِدَ ـ ; of a woman, عُقِمَتْ. To make —, أَعْقَمَ. To be —, of man or beast, عَقُرَ ـ عَقِرَ ـ. To be —, of results, عَقَّرَ ²; to make so —, أَعْقَرَ.

Barren, *n.* أَرْضٌ أَسِيفَةٌ ـ بَادِيَة ـ مُسْتَوْحِشَة.

Barrenly, *ad.* بِلَا فَائِدَةٍ ـ بِلَا ثَمَرٍ.

Barrenness, *n.* قِلَّةُ ثَمَرَةٍ ـ عَقْرَة ـ عُقْم ـ جَدْب; of a woman, عُقْم ـ عَقْرَة ـ عَقْر ـ عُقْر; of results, عُقْر.

Barricade, *n.* سَدّ *pl.* أَسْدَاد ـ مِتْرَاس *pl.* مَتَارِيس. An obstruction, سِدَاد ـ مَوَانِعُ *pl.* مَانِع.

Barricade, *v.t.* سَدَّ ² ـ دَرْبَسَ ـ تَرْبَسَ ـ حَجَزَ ².

Barrier, *n.* An obstruction, حَاجِز ـ حِجَاب ـ سِدَاد. A boundary, حَدّ *pl.* حُدُود ـ تَخْم *pl.* تُخُوم. *See also* Bar and Barricade, *n.*

Barrister, *n.* مُحَام ـ وَكِيلٌ شَرْعِيٌّ ـ وَكِيلُ ٱلدَّعْوَى ـ ٱلْمُتَكَلِّمُ عَنْ صَاحِبِ ٱلدَّعْوَى قُدَّامَ ٱلْقَاضِي.

Bar-room, *n.* حُجْرَةٌ لِلْجُلُوسِ تَلِي ٱلْحَانُوتَ.

Barrow, *n.* A hand-carriage, نَقَّالَة ـ نَقَّالَةٌ بِعَجَلَاتٍ. A swine, خِنْزِير *pl.* خَنَازِيرُ. A tumulus, تَلُّ تُرْبَةٍ *pl.* تُلُول.

Barter, *v.t.* To buy in exchange for, إِشْتَرَى ـ بِ ـ بَادَلَ ـ بِ ـ بَايَعَ ـ بِ.

Barter, *v.i.* عَارَضَ ـ غَايَرَ ـ قَاوَضَ ـ بَادَلَ ـ دَاكَشَ.

Barter, *n.* تَعْرِيض ـ مُقَاوَضَة ـ مُعَارَضَة ـ مُشَارَاة ـ غِيَار ـ مُغَايَرَة ـ مُبَايَعَة ـ مُقَايَضَة ـ دَاكِش.

Barterer, *n.* مُبَادِل ـ مُقِيض ـ صَرَّاب.

Bartram, *n.* The plant pellitory, عَاقِرْقَرْحَا.

Basalt, *n.* بَاصَلْط وَهُوَ صِنْفٌ مِنَ ٱلرُّخَامِ ٱلْأَسْوَدِ.

Basaltic, *a.* مِنَ ٱلرُّخَامِ ٱلْمُسَمَّى بَاصَلْط.

Base, *n.* The pedestal of a pillar, عُمْدَة ـ عِمَاد *pl.* عُمُد ـ قَاعِدَة *pl.* قَوَاعِدُ. The bottom of any thing, أَسْفَل ـ سَفْح ـ قَعْر ـ تَحْت. A foundation, أَسَاس ـ وَطَائِدُ. A support, مَسْنَد. A source, أَصْل. The grave tone in music, بَمّ ـ دُوكَاه ـ دُوكَة. Centre, as of operations, مَرْكَز ـ مَرْجِع ـ مَسْنَدٌ وَمَرْجِعٌ. Base, as of any substance, أُسّ *pl.* آسَاس.

Base, *v.t.* To found, أَسَّسَ. To —, ground, upon, أَسْنَدَ ـ إِلَى ـ بَنَى ـ عَلَى.

Base, *a.* Vile, ذَلِيل ـ رَذِيل ـ قَبِيح ـ خَبِيث ـ شَقِيّ *pl.* أَشْقِيَآء ـ فَاجِر *pl.* فُجَّار. Mean, low, خَسِيس ـ دَنِيّ ـ سُفْلِيّ. Of little value, بَخْس ـ رَخِيص. Despicable, خَسِيس ـ حَقِير ـ مَسْكِين. A — action, رَذِيلَة *pl.* رَذَائِلُ ـ قَبَاحَة *pl.* قَبَائِحُ. Base, of money, قَلْب. To make or pronounce —, أَرْذَلَ.

Base-born, *a.* Bastard, نَغِل ـ مَوْلُودٌ مِنَ ٱلزِّنَآءِ ـ اِبْنُ زِنَآءٍ.

Baseless, *a.* مِنْ غَيْرِ ٱسْتِنَادٍ ـ بِدُونِ أَسَاسٍ ـ لا وَجْهَ لَهُ. Chimerical, وَهْمِيٌّ ـ خَيَالِيٌّ.

Basely, *ad.* بِدَنَآءَةٍ ـ بِرَذَالَةٍ ـ قَبَاحَةً. To act —, أَقْبَحَ.

Basement, *n.* A foundation, أَسَاس. A — floor, الطَّبَقَةُ ٱلتَّحْتَانِيَّةُ مِنْ بَيْتٍ. A room on the —, سَهْوَة *pl.* سِهَآءٌ ـ مَنْظَرٌ.

Baseness, *n.* Vileness, رَذَالَة ـ قَبَاحَة ـ خَبَاثَة ـ ذِلَّة ـ دَنَآءَة. Meanness, سَفْلَة ـ دَنَآءَة ـ خَسَاسَة. Low birth, bastardy, نُغُولَة.

Baseness, of metals, قَلْب.

Bashful, *a.* خَفِير ـ حَيِيٌّ *fem.* حَيِيَّة ـ خَجِل. To be —, إِسْتَحَى مِنْهُ ـ رَجَبَ [2]. He was — of him, إِحْتَشَمَ ـ إِسْتَحَى.

Bashfully, *ad.* بِحِشْمَةٍ ـ بِعَارٍ ـ بِحَيَآءٍ ـ بِخَفَرٍ.

Bashfulness, *n.* حِشْمَة ـ خَفَر ـ عَار ـ حَيَآء.

Báshi-Búzúk, *n.* بَاشِي بُوزُوق.

Basil, *n.* The plant, رَيْحَان ـ الحَبَقُ ٱلصَّعْتَرِيُّ ـ الحَبَقُ ٱلكِرْمَانِيُّ ـ الحَبَقُ ٱلقُرُنْفُلِيُّ. Wild —, الشَّاهِسْفَرَم ـ الرَّيْحَانُ ٱلمُطْلَقُ. Garden —, الحَبَقُ ٱلنَّبَطِيُّ ـ رَيْحَانُ ٱلحَمَاحِمِ.

Basilica, *n.* The vein of the arm, عِرْقُ ٱلبَاسِلِيقِ ـ حَبْلُ ٱلذِّرَاعِ ـ العِرْقُ ٱلإِبْطِيُّ. A large church, كَنِيسَةٌ كَبِيرَةٌ.

Basilisk, *n.* رَئِيسُ ٱلثَّعَابِينِ.

Basin, *n.* A bowl, قَصْعَة *pl.* قِصَاع ـ طَاس *pl.* طَاسَات ـ مَاجُور ـ طُسُوت *pl.* طَسْت ـ طَشْت ـ فَسَاقِيُّ *pl.* فَسْقِيَّة. A washing —, لَكَن ـ جُرْن ـ جِبَاب *pl.* جُبّ ـ حِيَاض *pl.* حَوْض. A trough, A piece of water, مُسْتَنْقَعُ مَآءٍ ـ بِرَك *pl.* بِرْكَة ـ حَوْض ـ بِرَك. A — with a jet d'eau, فَسَاقِيُّ *pl.* فَسْقِيَّة. The trough in which the plunging water is kept in a bath, مَغْطَس بِرْكَة. A small bay, خَوْر ـ بَنْط ـ بُنُط. The — or scale of a balance, كِفَف *pl.* كِفَّة *and* كِفَاف. The — and ewer, المِرْجَفَانِ ـ الطَّسْتُ وَٱلإِبْرِيقُ.

Basis, *n.* A foundation, أَسَاس ـ مَسْنَد. That on which anything is raised, مَغْرِز ـ قَاعِدَة *pl.* قَوَاعِدُ. A source, أَصْل. A pedestal, مَقْعَدَة *pl.* مَقَاعِدُ. On a firm —, عَلَى أَصْلٍ مَتِينٍ. See also Base, *n.*

Bask, *v.i.* As in the sun, تَشَمَّسَ ـ تَدَفَّى فِي ٱلشَّمْسِ. To enjoy, تَنَعَّمَ ـ تَمَتَّعَ بِ.

Basket, *n.* سَلَّة *pl.* سِلَال ـ قُفَف *pl.* قُفَّة ـ زَنَابِيلُ *pl.* زَنْبِيل ـ قِرْطَلَّة ـ مِقْطَف ـ مَشَانٌّ *pl.* مِشَنَّة. A — without handles, A — made of date-palm branches, قَفَص. A — for holding perfumes, جُونَة ـ حُنْجُور. A small —, سُلَيْلَة. Two baskets placed on an animal to carry one person each, مَحَايِرُ ـ شِبْرِيَّات. A basket-maker, سَلَّال ـ صَانِعُ مَذَارِعَ وَسِلَالٍ.

Basket-hilt, *n.* مِقْبَضُ سَيْفٍ عَلَيْهِ قَفَصٌ لِوِقَايَةِ ٱليَدِ.

Bass, *n.* In music, بَمّ ـ دُوكَاه ـ دُوكَة. A kind of fish, نَوْعٌ مِنَ ٱلسَّمَكِ. A mat, حَصِيرَة.

Bassoon, *n.* بَاسُون وَهُوَ صِنْفٌ مِنْ آلَاتِ ٱلمُوسِيقَةِ.

Basso-relievo, *n.* }
Bass-relief, } نَقْش *pl.* نُقُوش.

Bastard, *n.* اِبْنُ مُعَارَضَةٍ ـ غِيَّة ـ وَلَدُ غَيَّةٍ ـ اِبْنُ ٱلغَيِّ ـ نَغُول ـ اِبْنُ زِنَآءٍ ـ اِبْنُ حَرَامٍ ـ بَنْدُوق.

Bastard, *a.* Illegitimate, نَغِيل ـ نَغُول. Not genuine, مُصَنَّع ـ عَمَلِيٌّ ـ مَغْشُوش ـ كَذَّاب ـ غَيْرُ حَقِيقِيٍّ.

Bastardize, *v.t.* نَغُولاً ـ صَيَّرَ ـ أَنْغَلَ.

Bastardy, *n.* نُغُولَة.

Baste, *v.t.* To beat, ضَرَّبَ ـ ضَرَبَ بِعَصًا ـ ضَرَبَ بِٱلعَصَا ـ نَزَلَ عَلَى [2] ـ حَطَّ تَحْتَ ٱلضَّرْبِ [2] ـ مَلَّ [2] ـ كَفَّ [2] ـ حَاصَ [2]. To sew lightly, شَصَرَ [2] ـ شَلَّلَ. To drop fat upon meat while cooking, سَقَّى قَطْرَ ٱلسَّمْنِ عَلَى ٱلمَشْوِيِّ ـ ٱلطَّبِيخَ بِٱلدُّهْنِ.

Bastinade, *v.t.* ضَرَبَ عَصًا ـ ضَرَبَ عَلْقَةً ـ شَمَّطَ عَلْقَةً [2].

Bastinade, *n.* } ضَرْبُ عَصًا ـ عَلْق ـ عَلْقَة. To receive the —,
Bastinado, } أَكَلَ عَلْقَةً [2].

Basting, *n.* A beating, ضَرْب. A slight sewing, شَصْر ـ مَلَّة ـ تَشْلِيل. Moistening with fat, تَدْهِين.

Bastion, *n.* In fortification, مَتْن *pl.* مِتَان ـ بُرْج *pl.* أَبْرَاج ـ طَابِيَة *pl.* طَوَابِي. A wall, سُور *pl.* أَسْوَار.

Bat, *n.* The animal, وَطْوَاط *pl.* وَطَاوِطُ ـ خُفَّاش *pl.* خَفَافِيش ـ طَيْرُ ٱللَّيْلِ ـ طَوَّارُ ٱللَّيْلِ. A stick to strike a ball with, جُوكَان ـ صَوْلَجَان ـ صَوَالِجَة. A club, نَبُّوت. Bats' dung, طِبْطَابَة ـ عَدَسِيَّة.

Batch, *n.* A — of bread, خَبْزَة. A quantity, جُمْلَة ـ مِقْدَار *pl.* جُمَل.

Bate; *see to* Abate, *v.t.* and *i.*

Bath, *n.* حَمَّام *pl.* حَمَّامَات. To take a —, إِسْتَحَمَّ ـ تَحَمَّمَ. In order to take the baths, لِلْإِسْتِحْمَامِ. The undressing place in a —, مَصْطَبَةُ ٱلحَمَّامِ. The person who takes charge of the bathers' clothes, الثِّيَابِيُّ. The — attendant who washes the bathers, البَلَّانُ. The attendant who shampoos the bathers, الدَّلَّاكُ. The foot rasp used in a —, حَجَرُ ٱلحَمَّامِ. The rubber in a —, المُكَيِّس. The fibre for soaping used in a —, لِيف. The owner of a —, صَاحِبُ ٱلْحَمَّامِ ـ حَمَّامِيٌّ. The compliment usually addressed to a person after bathing, نَعِيمًا. The reply: ٱللّٰهُ يَنْعَمُ عَلَيْكَ.

The Order of the Bath, نِيشَانُ ٱلْبَاث.

Companion of the Bath, حَائِزُ ٱلدَّرَجَةِ ٱلثَّالِثَةِ مِنْ نِيشَانِ ٱلْبَاث.

Knight Commander of the Bath, حَائِزُ ٱلدَّرَجَةِ ٱلثَّانِيَةِ مِنْ نِيشَانِ ٱلْبَاث.

Knight Grand Cross of the Bath, حَائِزُ ٱلدَّرَجَةِ ٱلْأُولَى مِنْ نِيشَانِ ٱلْبَاث.

Bath-brick, *n.* نَوْعٌ مِنَ ٱلطُّوبِ لِصَقْلِ ٱلسَّكَاكِينِ.

Bath-chair, *n.* كُرْسِيٌّ نَقَّالَةٌ ـ نَوْعُ عَرَبَانَةٍ صَغِيرَةٍ لِلْمَرْضَى وَٱلْعَجَازِ.

Bathe, *v.t.* To wash, غَسَّلَ. To moisten with, بَلَّ ـ ب. To give a bath to, أَنْزَلَ ـ إِلَى ٱلْحَوْضِ ـ حَمَّمَ.

Bathe, *v.i.* To take a bath, تَحَمَّمَ ـ إِسْتَحَمَّ ـ إِغْتَسَلَ. To run close by, جَرَى حَوْلَ ـ جَرَى عِنْدَ. To swim, سَبَحَ.

Bather, *n.* A swimmer, سَابِح.

Bathing, *n.* Taking a bath, تَحَمُّم ـ إِسْتِحْمَام. Swimming, سَبْح. Laving, بَلّ. A — establishment, حَمَّام.

Bathing-tub, *n.* حَوْض *pl.* حِيَاض.

Bathos, *n.* لَغْو.

Bating, *prep.* Excepting, خِلَافَ ـ سِوَى ـ غَيْرَ أَنْ ـ غَيْرَ ـ إِلَّا.

Baton, *n.* A club, نَبُّوت. A staff of office, عَصًا مَأْمُورِيَّةٍ.

Battalion, *n.* كَتِيبَة *pl.* كَتَائِب ـ فَوْج *pl.* أَفْوَاج ـ طَابُور *pl.* طَوَابِير ـ طَابُورٌ عَسْكَرِيّ. In Egypt it is called أُرْطَة *pl.* أُرَط; and the commander a بِينْبَاشِي.

Battalioned, *a.* مَصْفُوفٌ طَابُورًا طَابُورًا ـ مُرَتَّبٌ عَلَى أَفْوَاجٍ.

Batten, *v.t.* To fatten, سَمَّنَ. To be battened, fattened, تَسَمَّنَ. To — down, stop up, سَدَّ. To cover, غَطَّا.

Batten, *n.* A scantling, قَضِيب *pl.* قُضْبَان ـ لَوْح *pl.* أَلْوَاح ـ دَفَّة.

Batter, *v.t.* خَرَّبَ ـ كَسَّرَ ـ دَقَّ ـ سَحَقَ.

Batter, *n.* عَجِينٌ بِحَلِيبٍ وَبَيْضٍ ـ عَجِين.

Battering-ram, *n.* مَنْجَنِيق.

Battery, *n.* The act of, تَكْسِير ـ دَقّ ـ سَحْق. The fortification, مِتْرَاس *pl.* مَتَارِيس ـ طَابِيَة *pl.* طَوَابِي. A number of guns, بَطَارِيَّة ـ بَطَارِيَات *pl.* بَطَارِيَةُ مَدَافِع ـ صَفٌّ مِنَ ٱلْمَدَافِعِ *pl.* بَطَرِيَّات. A personal assault, بَطْشَة ـ بَطْش.

A — *en barbette,* صَفٌّ مِنَ ٱلْمَدَافِعِ عَلَى سُورِ ٱلْإِسْتِحْكَامَاتِ.

A breaching —, بَطَارِيَةُ مَدَافِعِ كَبِيرَةٍ لِلْمُحَاصَرَةِ.

A casemated —, مَدَافِعُ فِي قُبَبٍ مِنَ ٱلطَّابِيَةِ.

An electric —, بَطَارِيَّةٌ أَيْلَكْتْرِيكِيَّةٌ وَهِيَ وَجْبَةٌ مِنَ ٱلْآنِيَةِ ٱلْخَزَفِيَّةِ لِإِسْتِحْضَارِ ٱلْكَهْرَبَائِيَّةِ.

A field —, طَابُور (or بَطَارِيَةٌ) مَدَافِعَ عَلَى عَجَلَاتٍ.

A mountain —, بَطَارِيَةُ مَدَافِعِ لِلْجِبَالِ.

Battle, *n.* مُحَارَبَة ـ وَقْعَة ـ وَاقِعَة *pl.* وَقَائِع ـ يَوْم *pl.* أَيَّام ـ حَرْب *pl.* حُرُوب ـ قِتَال ـ عَرَكَة. A field of —, سُوقُ ٱلْحَرْبِ ـ مُقْتَتَل ـ مُلْتَقَى ـ مَعْرَكَة. The thick of the —, رَحَى ٱلْحَرْبِ.

In — array, مُصْطَفُّونَ لِلْقِتَالِ. To gain a — over, غَلَبَ عَلَى.

To lose a —, إِنْكَسَرَ ـ إِنْغَلَبَ. A drawn —, قِتَالٌ غَيْرُ قَاطِعٍ ـ مُقَاتَلَةٌ مِنْ غَيْرِ نَصْرِ أَحَدِ ٱلطَّرَفَيْنِ. Prepared for —, مُعَدٌّ لِلْقِتَالِ.

A dispute, مُنَازَعَة ـ مُجَادَلَة. The — waxed hot, قَامَتِ ٱلْحَرْبُ عَلَى سَاقٍ.

Battle, *v.t.* and *i.* To fight, قَاتَلَ ـ ضَارَبَ ـ حَارَبَ. To dispute, نَازَعَ ـ جَادَلَ.

Battle-axe, *n.* بَلْطَة ـ بَلْط.

Battledoor, *n.* طَبْطَابَة ـ صَوْلَجَانَة ـ لُعْبَةُ ٱلْأَوْلَادِ.

Battlement, *n.* A gallery, parapet, شُرْفَة *pl.* شُرَف and شُرُفَات ـ شَرَّافَة. A wall, سُور *pl.* أَسْوَار ـ حَائِط *pl.* حِيطَان. A house with a —, شَرْفَاء *pl.* شُرُف.

Battue, *n.* الإِسْتِقْصَاءُ فِي طَلَبِ ٱلصَّيْدِ ـ نَجَاشَة. To beat in a —, نَجَشَ. A beater in a —, نَاجِش.

Bauble, *n.* A child's toy, لُعْبَة *pl.* لُعَب ـ شَخْشِيخَة ـ خَشْخُوشَة. A trifle, عَبْثَة ـ عَبَث.

Bavaria, *n.* بَافَارِيَا.

Bavarian, *a.* مِنْ بَافَارِيَا.

Bawble, *n.* *See* Bauble, *n.*

Bawd, *n.* تمرساق ـ طَنَّار ـ مُعَرِّس ـ قَوَّاد ـ دَلَّال.

Bawd, *v.i.* تَعَرَّسَ ـ عَرَّسَ ل.

Bawdiness, *n.* فُحَاشَة ـ عَهَارَة ـ فِسْقٌ وَفَسَادٌ ـ فُجُور.

Bawdy, *a.* فَاجِر *pl.* فُجَّار ـ فَاسِق ـ عَاهِر ـ فَاحِش.

Bawdy-house, *n.* مَاخُورُ ٱلزِّنَاءِ ـ بَيْتُ قِحَابٍ ـ بَيْتُ فَسَادٍ.

Bawl, *v.i.* زَعَقَ ـ صَرَخَ ـ عَيَّطَ ـ صَوَّتَ ـ صَيَّحَ ـ صَاحَ ـ فَدَّ.

Bawl, *v.t.* To proclaim, نَادَى ب ـ أَشْهَرَ ـ صَرَخَ ب.

Bawling, *a.* زَاعِق ـ صَيِّت ـ صَارِخ ـ فَدَّاد.

Bawling, *n.* صُرَاخ ـ عَوَّة ـ عِيَاط ـ فَدِيد.

Bay, *v.i.* To bark, نَبَحَ. *See also to* Howl, *v.i.*

Bay, *v.t.* To bark at, نَبَحَ عَلَى. To surround, أَحَاطَ ب.

To — the moon, of a dog, هَرَّ إِلَى ٱلْقَمَرِ.

Bay, *a.* Of the colour, كُمَيْت *pl.* كُمْت *and* كُمَاتِيّ — أَحْوَى — أَحْمَرُ أَدْرَم — أَزْرَق — أَحْ... A — horse, حِصَانٌ أَغْبَس.

Bay, *n.* The tree, رَنْد — شَجَرَةُ ٱلْغَار. A small gulf, شَرْم *pl.* شُرُوم — خَوْر *pl.* خُؤُور — خَلِيج *pl.* خُلْجَان — جُونَة. At —, at bay, فِي عِزّ — فِي شِدَّةٍ; in a predicament, ...distance, عَنْ بُعْدٍ — مِنْ بَعِيدٍ. To keep one at —, أَوْقَفَ — كَفّ عَن. To stand at —, تَحَفَّظَ — قَاوَمَ. A sick —, مُسْتَشْفَى (or خَسْتَه خَانَه) فِي ٱلضَّيْف... A — window, طَاقَةٌ مُقَوَّسَةٌ مَرْكَب.

Bayonet, *n.* حَرْبَة *pl.* حِرَاب — زَغَايَة.

Bayonet, *v.t.* طَعَن بِٱلْحَرْبَةِ.

Bay-salt, *n.* مِلْحُ ٱلْبَحْرِ ٱلْمَالِح.

Bazaar, *n.* سُوق *pl.* أَسْوَاق — مَحَلّ مَبَاع.

B.D. (Bachelor of Divinity), عِبَارَةٌ عَنْ مُجَازٍ ثَانٍ فِي عِلْمِ ٱللَّاهُوت.

Bd. (bound), عِبَارَةٌ عَنْ كِتَابٍ مُجَلَّدٍ.

Bdellium, *n.* مُقْل.

Bds. (boards), عِبَارَةٌ عَنْ كِتَابٍ مَعْرُومٍ بِلَا جِلْدٍ.

Be, *v.i.* كَانَ — صَارَ — بَانَ. To cause to be, كَوَّنَ — صَيَّرَ. To begin to be, أَخَذَ فِي. To let be, تَرَكَ — رَفَعَ ٱلْيَدَ عَن. To be at, about, up to, after, عَمِلَ — تَعَمَّدَ — هَمَّ بِ — خَلَّى. It is I, أَنَا هُوَ. There is, يُوجَدُ — فِي — أَكُو. How can this thing be? كَيْفَ يُمْكِنُ أَنْ يَكُونَ هٰذَا. Say, whose shall it be? قُلْ لِمَنْ يَصِيرُ. How long shall I be with you? إِلَى مَتَى أَكُونُ مَعَكُمْ — إِلَى مَتَى أَسْتَمِرُّ مَعَكُمْ. Let it be, let it alone, دَعْهُ — خَلِّ عَنْهُ. There are not any of them to be had, لَمْ يُوجَدْ مِنْهَا. He began to be in want, أَخَذَ فِي ٱلْعَوَزِ. Be it far from thee! حَاشَا لَكَ. It may be sufficient, لِعَلَّهُ كَافٍ. It may be so, رُبَّمَا يَكُونُ كَذَا. It was to be so, إِقْتَضَى أَنْ يَكُونَ كَذَا. It is well known what the town was in former times, لَا يَخْفَى مَا كَانَتْ عَلَيْهِ ٱلْمَدِينَةُ فِي ٱلزَّمَنِ ٱلْقَدِيمِ.

Beach, *n.* شَطّ *pl.* شُطُوط — بَرّ — سَاحِل. The sea —, سَاحِلُ ٱلْبَحْرِ.

Beach, *v.t.* بَلَّط — شَطَّطَ.

Beacon, *n.* A signal, عَلَامَة *pl.* عَلَامَات — إِشَارَة. A lighthouse, مَنَارَة *pl.* مَنَائِر — فَانُوس. A — of stones, صُوَّة *pl.* صُوًى.

Bead, *n.* خَرَزَة *coll.* خَرَز *pl.* خَرَزَات — حَبّ *pl.* حُبُوب. A silver —, جُمَانَة *coll.* جُمَان *pl.* جُمَانَات — حَبَّة *pl.* حَبَّات. A string of beads, a rosary, مِسْبَحَة — سُبْحَة. A Christian rosary, وَرْدِيَّة. To tell the beads, as in prayer, سَبَّحَ; of the Christian rosary, صَلَّى ٱلْوَرْدِيَّةَ.

Beadle, *n.* قَوَّاس *pl.* قَوَّاسَة; a church —, قَوَّاسٌ كَنَائِسِيٌّ.

Beak, *n.* Of a bird, حَنَك *pl.* أَحْنَاك — مِنْقَار *pl.* مَنَاقِير — مِنْقَاد *pl.* مَنَاقِيد. A point, head, رَأْس — أَنْف — سِنَان. *See also* Magistrate, *n.*

Beaked, *a.* Having a beak, ذُو مِنْقَارٍ. Pointed, مُؤَنَّف.

Beaker, *n.* قَدَح *pl.* أَقْدَاح.

Beam, *n.* Of a roof, جَائِز *pl.* أَجْوِزَة — جِذْع *pl.* جُذُوع — خَشَبَة — شُوحِيَّة. A transverse —, عَارِضَة *pl.* عَوَارِض. The beams, roofing, of a house, سَقْفُ ٱلْبَيْتِ — ٱلرَّوَافِدُ. A weaver's —, نَوْل *pl.* أَنْوَال — مِنْوَل. The — of a balance, قَبَّةُ ٱلْمِيزَانِ — عَمُودُ ٱلْمِيزَانِ. A ray of light, شُعَّة *coll.* شُعَاع *pl.* أَشِعَّة — لَمْعَة — سَاعُورَة. A — coming through a crevice, شِرْق. To be on her beam-ends, of a ship, نَامَتِ ٱلسَّفِينَةُ عَلَى جَنْبِهَا.

Beam, *v.i.* سَطَعَ — لَمَحَ — تَنَوَّرَ — إِسْتَنَارَ — أَضَاءَ — شَعْشَعَ — لَمَعَ.

Beaming, *a.* لَمُوح — لَمَّاح — مُنِير — نَيِّر. Cheerful, مَسْرُور — طَرِب.

Beaming, *n.* شَعْشَعَة — لَمَحَان — نُور — لَمَعَان — سَاطِع.

Beamy, *a.* *See* Beaming, *a.*

Bean, *n.* A horse —, فُولَة *coll.* فُول; a French —, بَاقِلَّى — فَاصُولِيَة — لُوبِيَة.

Bear, *n.* The animal, دُبّ *pl.* دِبَبَة — دُبَّة; a she —, دُبَّة *pl.* دُبَّات. The Great Bear, the constellation, ٱلدُّبُّ ٱلْأَكْبَرُ — بَنَاتُ ٱلنَّعْشِ ٱلْكُبْرَى. The Lesser Bear, ٱلدُّبُّ ٱلْأَصْغَرُ. A — on the Stock Exchange, مُتَشَبِّثٌ بِأَسْبَابٍ لِبَخْسِ ٱلسَّنَدَاتِ.

Bear, *v.t.* and *i.* To carry, حَمَلَ — شَالَ. To convey, نَقَلَ — حَمَلَ — جَلَبَ — رَفَعَ — أَخَذَ مِنْ مَوْضِعٍ إِلَى مَوْضِعٍ. To —, as an attack, تَلَقَّى — لَقِيَ — قَاوَمَ. To —, to bring forth, a child, حَمَلَتْ — وَلَدَتْ *aor.* تَلِدُ. To bear fruit, أَثْمَرَ — ثَمَرَ. To endure, إِحْتَمَلَ. To waft, سَارَ بِ. To bear, to be situated with respect to other places, حَكَمَ — صَارَ — كَانَ مِنْ جِهَةٍ — كَانَ.

To bear a price, to be worth, سَاوَى.

To bear a child to, أَوْلَدَتْ لِ — خَلَّفَتْهُ.

To bear a resemblance to, أَشْبَهَ — شَابَهَ.

To bear arms, تَسَلَّحَ — حَمَلَ ٱلسِّلَاحَ.

To bear away, carry off, ذَهَبَ بِ — حَمَلَ.

To bear away, sail from, تَغَرَّبَ — إِرْتَخَى — إِنْقَلَعَ.

To bear away the palm, غَلَبَ — ظَفِرَ.

To bear back, to come back, ضَرَبَ إِلَى ـ عَادَ إِلَى ـ رَجَعَ ـ اَلرُّجُوعِ.

To bear date, كَانَ تَارِيخُهُ ـ تَارِيخُهُ.

To bear down, to overcome, قَوِيَ عَلَى ـ تَغَلَّبَ عَلَى ـ غَلَبَ.

To bear down upon, to approach, تَقَرَّبَ إِلَى ـ نَزَلَ عَلَى ـ دَنَا مِن.

To bear envy to, بَغَى عَلَى ـ حَسَدَ عَلَى.

To bear esteem for, أَكْرَمَ ـ وَقَّرَ ـ إِحْتَرَمَ.

To bear hard upon, شَدَّ عَلَى ـ عَسَّرَ عَلَى.

To bear in mind, تَنَبَّهَ عَلَى ـ تَذَكَّرَ.

To bear love for, وَدَّ ـ أَحَبَّ ـ أَعَزَّ.

To bear off, to carry away, مَضَى بِ ـ ذَهَبَ بِ.

To bear one company, صَاحَبَ ـ رَافَقَ.

To bear one's self, to behave, عَاشَ ـ مَشَى ـ سَلَكَ سُلُوكًا.

To bear out, confirm, أَكَّدَ ـ أَثْبَتَ.

To bear rule, تَسَلَّطَ ـ حَكَمَ.

To bear the expense of, أَنْفَقَ عَلَى ـ تَكَلَّفَ عَلَى.

To bear through, sustain, أَنْجَى ـ أَسْنَدَ ـ مَكَّنَ.

To bear with, صَبَرَ عَلَى ـ طَالَ عَلَى ـ تَطَوَّلَ عَلَى.

To bear up against, صَبَرَ عَلَى ـ إِحْتَمَلَ.

To bear up for, or toward, a place, ضَرَبَ إِلَى.

To bear witness against, شَهِدَ عَلَى.

To bear witness for, شَهِدَ لِ.

To bring to bear, adduce arguments for, إِحْتَجَّ بِ.

Bearable, *a.* مِمَّا يُحْتَمَلُ ـ يُحْتَمَلُ.

Bear-baiting, *n.* إِطْلَاقُ ٱلْكِلَابِ عَلَى دُبٍّ.

Beard, *n.* لِحْيَة *pl.* لِحَى ـ ذَقَن *pl.* ذُقُون. A — of corn, شَوْكُ ٱلسُّنْبُلِ ـ أَمْرَاق *pl.* مُرُوق. The best beards are those a hand grasp in length, خَيْرُ ٱلذُّقُونِ قَبْضَةٌ تَكُونُ (*prov.*). *See also* Barb, *n.*

Beard, *v.t.* To pull by the —, أَخَذَ مِن لِحْيَتِهِ. *See also to* Defy, *v.t.*

Bearded, *a.* Having a beard, مُذَقَّن ـ بِذَقَنٍ ـ ذُو لِحْيَةٍ. Barbed, ذُو نَصْلٍ.

Beardless, *a.* أَمْرَدُ ـ سُنُط *pl.* سُنُوط ـ سُنُوطِيٌّ.

Bearer, *n.* A supporter, حَامِل *pl.* حَمَلَة. A porter, حَمَّال *pl.* حَمَّالَة *and* حَمَّالُون ـ شَيَّال *pl.* شَيَّالَة. The — of the letter, حَامِلُ ٱلْوَرَقَةِ. A messenger, قَاصِد *pl.* قُصَّاد.

Bearing, *n.* Position, مَوْضِع ـ مَقَام. Relation, عَلَاقَة ـ تَعَلُّق ـ مُنَاسَبَة. Aspect, مَنْظَر ـ هَيْئَة ـ ظَاهِر. Behaviour, سُلُوك ـ عَمَل ـ سِيرَة. Direction, جِهَة ـ سَمْت. Mode of placement, site, وَضْع *pl.* أَوْضَاع. Movements, حَرَكَات. Armorial bearings, آرْمَا. What a fine — he has, مَا أَحْسَنَ سَمْتَهُ.

Bearing-rein, *n.* عِنَانٌ ثَابِتٌ.

Bearish, *a.* فَظٌّ ـ غَلِيظ ـ كَٱلدُّبِّ.

Beast, *n.* An irrational animal, دَابَّة *pl.* دَوَابّ ـ حَوْبَة ـ بَهِيمَة *pl.* بَهَائِم ـ حَيَوَان *pl.* حَيَوَانَات. A savage animal, وَحْش *pl.* وُحُوش ـ سَبُع *pl.* سِبَاع. A brutal man, فَجَّار ـ رَذِيل ـ عَنِيف ـ جَانِف. Any — that is ridden, دَابَّة *pl.* دَوَابّ ـ رَكُوب *pl.* رُكُب.

Beastliness, *n.* نَجَاسَة ـ فَحْشَاء ـ فَظَاظَة ـ دَنَاءَة ـ رَذَالَة.

Beastly, *a.* Having the nature of beasts, بَهِيمِيّ ـ وَحْشِيّ ـ مُوَحَّش. Debased, فَاسِق ـ فَاحِش ـ فَظّ ـ نَجِس ـ جَانِف; in speech, obscene, بَذِئُ ٱللِّسَانِ.

Beat, *v.t.* To strike, ضَرَبَ. To — with the open hand, لَطَمَ. To punish with blows, طَعَمَ قَتْلَةً ـ ضَرَّبَ. To — with a stick, ضَرَبَ عَصًا ـ فَحَزَ. To overcome, قَوِيَ عَلَى ـ غَلَبَ. To surpass, as in learning, *etc.*, فَاقَ ـ بَهَرَ ـ بَرَعَ ـ بَرَزَ عَلَى *aor.* يَفُوقُ. To — cotton, نَدَفَ ٱلْقُطْنَ ـ نَجَّدَ ٱلْقُطْنَ. To — a drum, دَقَّ ٱلطَّبْلَ. To — with a hammer, مَطَلَ.

To beat against, لَطَمَ. The waves — against the ship, لَطَمَتِ ٱلْأَمْوَاجُ ٱلسَّفِينَةَ.

To beat back, cause to retreat, دَفَعَ ـ رَدَّ ـ أَهْرَبَ ـ هَزَمَ ـ طَرَدَ.

To beat or knock down, خَبَطَ. To destroy, هَدَمَ ـ خَرَّبَ.

To — down, as in price, شَارَى ـ بَخَّسَ ـ رَخَّصَ ـ أَهْبَطَ.

To beat off. *See* To — back, *suprà.*

To beat out, as of iron, فَطَسَ ـ مَطَلَ. To — out, as of corn, دَرَسَ.

To beat time, in music, وَطِئَ بِحِفْظِ ٱلْوَزْنِ *aor.* يَطَأُ.

To beat to death, قَتَلَ تَحْتَ ٱلضَّرْبِ.

To beat together, to mix, خَلَطَ.

To beat to pieces, نَشَّ ـ كَسَّرَ ـ رَضَّ ـ حَطَمَ.

To beat up, as eggs, *etc.*, شَمَطَ ـ سَاطَ *aor.* يَسُوطُ.

Beat, *v.i.* To palpitate, خَفَقَ ـ رَجَفَ. To —, as the pulse, عَثَرَ ـ دَرَّ ـ دَقَّ. To —, as the wind, ثَارَ ـ هَبَّ.

To beat, to veer, of a ship, عَمِلَ وُلْتَة ـ حَوَّلَ ٱلْقَرِيَة.

To beat about the bush, تَضَرَّبَ ـ تَعَيَّا ـ تَحَوَّلَ.

To beat to arms, دَقَّ بِأَخْذِ ٱلسِّلَاحِ.

To beat to quarters, دَقَّ لِلتَّعْلِيمِ.

To beat up for, طَلَبَ ². To — up for game, حَاشَ ٱلصَّيْدَ *aor.* إِحْتَاشَ ٱلصَّيْدَ ـ يَحُوشُ .

Beat, *n.* A stroke, ضَرْبَة ـ دَقَّة ـ لَطْمَة ; of the pulse, نَبْضَة . A round, دَائِرَة ـ حَدّ *pl.* حُدُود . A place of resort, مَعْهَد ـ مَأْلَف .

Beaten, *a.* Struck, مَضْرُوب . Beaten out, as with a hammer, مُطوَل ـ مُذَلَّل . Overcome, مَغْلُوب . Trodden, of a road, مُعَبَّد . A — path, دَرْبٌ مَطْرُوق .

Beater, *n.* A striker, ضَرَّاب ـ ضَارِب . An instrument to strike with, مِدَقّ ـ مِطْرَقَة *pl.* مَطَارِق .

Beatific, *a.} Beatifical, } مَسْعُود ـ سَعِيد ـ طُوبَاوِيّ .

Beatifically, *ad.* فِي ٱلنَّعِيمِ ـ بِكَمَالِ ٱلسَّعَادَةِ .

Beatification, *n.* تَطْوِيبُ ٱلْأَمْوَاتِ .

Beatify, *v.t.* أَسْعَدَ ـ ٢ جَعَلَ مِنَ ٱلطُّوبَاوِيِّينَ .

Beating, *n.* A drubbing, قَتْل ـ ضَرْب .

Beatitude, *n.* سَعَادَةٌ أَبَدِيَّةٌ ـ نَعِيم ـ طُوبَى .

Beau, *n.* A gallant, غَنْدُور ـ أَغْلَال *pl.* غَلّ ٱلنِّسَاءِ . A lover, عَاشِق ; one beloved, مَحْبُوب ـ مَعْشُوق .

Beau ideal, *n.* أُنْمُوذَج ـ قُدْوَة .

Beau monde, *n.* مَعْشَرُ ٱلْأَغْنِيَاءِ وَٱلْكُبَرَاءِ .

Beauteous, *a.* } Beautiful, } حَسِين ـ صَبِيح ـ نَاضِر ـ بَهِيّ ـ رَائِق ـ فَارِه ـ حُلْو ـ قَسِيم *pl.* قُسَّم ـ جَمِيل ـ ظَرِيف *fem.* كُوَيِّس ـ بَهِيج ـ لَطِيف ـ حُلْوَات *pl. fem.* حُلْوِين *pl. masc.* حُلْوَة .

To be —, بَهُجَ ² ـ حَسُنَ ² ـ حَلَا ² . To make —, حَلَّى ـ حَسَّنَ . To consider —, إِسْتَحْلَى ـ إِسْتَحْسَنَ . How — it is! مَا أَحْلَاهُ . God is — and loves that which is —, اَللّٰهُ جَمِيلٌ يُحِبُّ ٱلْجَمَالَ .

Beauteously, *ad.* } Beautifully, } بِجَمَالٍ ـ بِلَطَافَةٍ ـ بِظَرَافَةٍ ـ حَسَنًا .

Beauteousness, *n.* } Beautifulness, } قَسَامَة ـ جَهَارَة ـ بَهْجَة ـ نَضر ـ رَوْنَق ـ مَلَاحَة ـ جَمَال ـ حُسْن ـ بَهَاء ـ صَبَاحَة ـ كِيَاسَة ـ لَطَافَة ـ ظَرَافَة .

Beautifier, *n.* وَاشٍ ـ مُجَمِّل ـ مُزَخْرِف ـ مُنَمِّق ـ مُحَسِّن .

Beautify, *v.t.* حَلَّى ـ زَخْرَفَ ـ جَمَّلَ ـ أَبْهَجَ ـ حَسَّنَ . To — one's self, تَزَخْرَفَ ـ تَجَمَّلَ ـ تَحَسَّنَ ـ تَبَرَّقَ . To adorn, as with fine clothes, زَيَّنَ ـ وَشَّى .

Beauty, *n.* Any thing fine, لَطَائِف ـ لَطِيفَة *pl.* تُحْفَة ـ نَادِرَة ـ مَلَاحَة . A beautiful woman, إِمْرَأَة جَمِيلَة ـ إِمْرَأَةٌ ظَرِيفَةٌ ; called in Egypt, سَتُّوتَة . A lovely and accomplished —, woman, إِمْرَأَةٌ ذَاتُ بَهَاءٍ وَكَمَالٍ وَقَدٍّ وَٱعْتِدَالٍ . *See also* Beautifulness, *n.*

Beauty-spot, *n.* A mole, شَامَة *pl.* شَامَات .

Beaux, *n. pl.* of Beau, *q.v.*

Beaver, *n.* The animal, سِكْلَابِيّ ـ جُنْدُبَادَسْتَر ـ بِيدَسْتَر ـ كَلْبُ ٱلْمَاءِ ـ قُنْدُس . The — of a helmet, بُرْقُعُ ٱلْخُوذَةِ . A hat, شَبْقَة ـ بَرْنِيطَة .

Becalm, *v.t.* To quiet, هَدَّأَ ـ أَهْدَأَ ـ سَكَّنَ . We were becalmed, as at sea, حَكَمَنَا هُدُوّ .

Became, *pret. of to* Become, *q.v.*

Because, *conj.* مِنْ حَيْثُ ـ بِسَبَبِ أَنْ ـ كَوْنَ أَنْ ـ لِأَنَّ ـ بِسَبَبِ ـ لِأَجْلِ ذٰلِكَ ـ لِذٰلِكَ .

Bechance, *v.i.* عَرَضَ ² ـ حَصَلَ ² ـ وَقَعَ *aor.* يَقَعُ . *See also to* Befall, *v.i.*

Becharm, *v.t.* أَغْرَمَ ـ ٢ سَبَى ـ إِحْتَبَلَ .

Beck, *n.* } Beckon, } غَمْزَة ـ رَمْز ـ لَمْز ـ إِشَارَة ـ وَمَأ . At his beck and call, تَحْتَ أَمْرِهِ .

Beck, *v.i.* } Beckon, } لَمَزَ ² ـ غَمَزَ ² ـ أَشَارَ ـ رَمَزَ ² ـ أَوْمَأَ . He beckoned with his hand, أَشَارَ بِيَدِهِ . He beckoned to him, أَوْمَأَ إِلَيْهِ .

Becloud, *v.t.* أَغْتَمَ ـ غَيَّمَ .

Become, *v.t.* To suit, لَاقَ بِ ـ ² لَبِقَ بِ ـ ² صَلَحَ لِ ـ لَاءَمَ . It becomes thee, it behoves thee, وَاجِبٌ عَلَيْكَ ـ يَحِقُّ عَلَيْكَ . It does not — his dignity, لَا يَلِيقُ بِشَرَفِهِ . It does not — his position, لَا يَلِيقُ بِمَقَامِهِ .

Become, *v.i.* صَارَ ² ـ عَادَ إِلَى ² ـ خَرَجَ ² ـ أَصْبَحَ ـ حَصَلَ ² . To become of, to result from, حَدَثَ مِن ² ـ حَصَلَ مِن ² . The building became firm, صَارَ مِن ² ـ جَاءَ ٱلْبِنَاءُ مُحْكَمًا ـ صَارَ ٱلْبِنَاءُ مَتِينًا .

Becoming, *a.* Suitable, لَائِم ـ مُنَاسِب لَائِق ـ قَرِيف لِ ـ قَرِيب . Pretty, كُوَيِّس ـ لَطِيف ـ ظَرِيف . It is more — for thee, أَلْيَقُ لَكَ ـ أَشْبَهُ بِكَ .

Becomingly, *ad.* حَسَنًا ـ بِلَطَافَةٍ ـ بِمُنَاسَبَةٍ ـ بِلِيَاقَةٍ .

Becomingness, *n.* حُسْن ـ مُنَاسَبَة ـ لِيَاقَة .

Bed, *n.* A bed to sleep upon, مَضْجَع *pl.* مَضَاجِعُ ـ فَرْش *pl.* مَنَام ـ مَهْد *pl.* مِهَاد ـ فُرُوش *pl.* فِرَاش ـ فُرُوش . The bed of a river, مَجْرًى *pl.* مَجَارٍ ـ وَادٍ *pl.* أَوْدِيَة . Bed, a layer, طَبَقَة *pl.* طَبَقَات . A division, as in a garden, *etc.*, بُقْعَة *pl.* بِقَاع ـ مُرَبَّع . To go to bed, رَقَدَ ² ـ نَامَ ² . To make, as of a bed,

مَهَدَ ـ فَرَشَ. To make, put a bed in order, صَلَّحَ ٱلْفِرَاشَ. To keep to one's bed, لَزِمَ ٱلْفِرَاشَ. To bring to bed, to confine, وَلَّدَ. To be brought to bed, وَضَعَتْ aor. تَضَعُ. Bed, marriage, زَوَاج ـ نِكَاح. He is still confined to the house though he has left his bed, لَمْ يَزَلْ مُلَازِماً لِدَارِهِ وَإِنْ يَكُنْ قَدْ فَارَقَ فِرَاشَهُ.

Bed, v.t. To put into bed, نَوَّمَ ـ نَيَّمَ. To plant in beds, غَرَسَ بِقَاعًا بِقَاعًا. To fix firmly, ضَبَطَ ـ مَكَّنَ ـ قَرَّرَ ـ أَحْكَمَ.

Bedabble, v.t. بَلَّ ـ خَضَّلَ.

Bedaggle, v.t. وَعَّرَ ـ طَبَّعَ.

Bedaub, v.t. To smear with, طَلَى ـ دَمْدَمَ ـ دَمَّ. To soil, سَخَّمَطَ ـ لَوَّثَ ـ وَسَّخَ.

Bedawy, pl. Bedawin, n. A wandering Arab, بَدَوِيٌّ pl. بَدَاوَى vulg. بِدْوَان.

Bedazzle, v.t. خَطِفَ ٱلْبَصَرَ ـ أَخَذَ ٱلْبَصَرَ ـ غَطْمَشَ ـ نَغْشَشَ.

Bed-chamber, n. خَلْوَةُ ٱلرُّقَادِ ـ بَيْتُ ٱلنَّوْمِ ـ مَنَامَة.

Bed-clothes, n. } مِلْحَفَة ـ أَفْرَاش ـ مَفَارِش ـ مِفْرَش pl.
Bedding, } شَرَاشِف ـ شِرْشَف pl. مَلَاحِف.

Bedded, a. Laid in a bed, مُضْجَع. Stratified, ذُو طَبَقَاتٍ. Planted, مَغْرُوس. A single — room, خَلْوَةٌ بِفِرَاشٍ وَاحِدٍ.

Bedeck, v.t. زَخْرَفَ ـ جَمَّلَ ـ حَسَّنَ ـ زَيَّنَ. *See also to* Adorn, v.t.

Bedevil, v.t. To abuse, عَيَّرَ بِ ـ بَهْدَلَ ـ شَتَمَ.

Bedew, v.t. رَطَّبَ ـ ثَرَّى ـ أَنْدَى ـ طَلَّلَ.

Bed-fellow, n. ضَجِيع ـ كِمْع ـ كَمِيع. To sleep with a —, ضَاجَعَ ـ كَامَعَ. Hunger is a sorry —, بِئْسَ ٱلضَّجِيعُ ٱلْجُوعُ.

Bed-hangings, n. Curtains, سَجْفُ ٱلْمَنَامِ ـ سَجْف ـ كِلَّة.

Bedim, v.t. أَظْلَمَ عَلَى ـ عَتَّمَ عَلَى.

Bedizen, v.t. *See to* Bedeck, v.t.

Bedlam, n. A madhouse, بَيْتُ ٱلْمَجَانِينِ ـ مُسْتَشْفَى ٱلْمَجَانِينِ ـ بِيمَارِسْتَان.

Bedlamite, n. مَجْنُون pl. مَجَانِينُ.

Bed-post, n. عَمُودُ ٱلسَّرِيرِ pl. عُمُد.

Bed-quilt, n. لِحَاف pl. لُحُف.

Bedraggle, v.t. To dirty, لَوَّثَ ـ وَعَّرَ ـ وَسَّخَ.

Bedrench, v.t. غَمَّسَ ـ بَلَّ. To be bedrenched, إِغْتَمَسَ ـ إِبْتَلَّ.

Bed-ridden, a. طَرِيحُ ٱلْفِرَاشِ ـ مُلْقًى عَلَى ٱلْفِرَاشِ fem. مُلْقَاة.

Bed-room, n. *See* Bed-chamber, n.

Bedrop, v.t. نَقَّطَ عَلَى ـ قَطَّرَ عَلَى.

Bedside, n. عِنْدَ ٱلْفِرَاشِ ـ جَنْبَ ٱلْفِرَاشِ. By his —, جَنْبَ فِرَاشِهِ.

Bedstead, n. مَنَام ـ سُرُر and أَسِرَّة pl. سَرِير ـ تُخُوت pl. تَخْت.

Bed-tick, n. غِلَافُ ٱلْمَرْتَبَةِ.

Bed-time, n. وَقْتُ ٱلنَّوْمِ.

Bedwarf, v.t. قَصَّرَ ـ صَغَّرَ.

Bedye, v.t. صَبَغَ.

Bee, n. نَحْلَة coll. نَحْل. Queen bee, يَعْسُوب ـ مُلَيْكُ ـ أَمِيرُ ٱلنَّحْلِ ـ ٱلنَّحْلِ. Young bees, طِرْزُ ٱلنَّحْلِ ـ أَبْكَارُ ٱلنَّحْلِ. A swarm of bees, سِرْبُ نَحْلٍ ـ ثَوْل. He has a bee in his bonnet, فِي عَقْلِهِ هَبْتَةٌ.

Beech, n. The tree, زَان ـ شَجَرَةُ عَيْشِ ٱلسَّيَّاحِ.

Beechen, a. مِنْ زَانٍ.

Beech-mast, n. } ثَمَرَةُ شَجَرَةِ ٱلزَّانِ.
Beech-nut, }

Bee-eater, n. The bird, ٱلْوَرْوَارُ.

Beef, n. لَحْمُ بَقَرٍ.

Beef-steak, n. شَرِيحُ لَحْمِ ٱلْبَقَرِ ـ شَرِيحَةٌ مِنْ لَحْمِ ٱلْبَقَرِ.

Bee-hive, n. خَلِيَّة pl. خَلَايَا ـ خَلَايَةُ نَحْلٍ ـ مَعْسَالَة ـ عَسَّالَة ـ كُوَارَة pl. كَوَائِرُ ـ شُورَة.

Beelzebub, n. The god, بَعْلَزَبُول. The devil, إِبْلِيسُ ـ ٱلشَّيْطَانُ.

Beer, n. بُوزَة ـ فُقَّاع ـ بِيرَة. Ginger-beer, شَرْبَةُ ٱلزَّنْجَبِيلِ. Small —, بِيرَةٌ خَفِيفَةٌ. A seller of —, فُقَّاعِيٌّ.

Beeswax, n. شَمْعُ عَسَلٍ.

Beet, n. سِلْق ـ شَوَنْدَر ـ شَمَنْدُور.

Beetle, n. The insect, especially the black —, خُنْفُسَة pl. خَنَافِسُ ـ جُعَل pl. جِعْلَان ـ أَبُو زِبْلٍ. The roller —, ٱلْمُدَحْرِجُ. A beetle's ball, قُرْمُوط ـ قُعْمُوطَة ـ صُعْرُورَة: to make that ball, صَعْرَرَ. A mallet, دُقْمَاق ـ مِطْرَقَة ـ مِرْزَبَّة ـ مِدَقَّة ـ مِدَقّ ـ مِعْفَاج ـ خَشَب. A washerman's —, مِدَقٌّ. A fuller's —, شَوْكَةُ ٱلْكَتَّانِ ـ مِقْصَرَة. He is more persevering than the —, هُوَ أَلَحُّ مِنَ ٱلْخُنْفُسَاءِ.

Beetle-browed, a. نَاشِعُ ٱلْحَوَاجِبِ.

Beetling, a. مُشْرِف ـ كَابِس ـ نَاشِع.

Beeves, n. مَوَاشِي ـ بَقَر.

Befall, v.t. and i. To happen, حَصَلَ ـ حَدَثَ ـ صَارَ ـ جَرَى ـ إِعْتَرَضَ لِ. To happen to, نَابَ ـ نَجَمَ عَلَى. To happen to, as an evil, مَسَّ ـ حَصَلَ لِ ـ نَزَلَ بِ. To —

one suddenly, فَجَأَ ـ إِفْتَجَأَ ـ ². Difficulty befell me, أَدْرَكَنِي ٱلْجَهْدُ ـ حَاقَتْ بِي شِدَّةٌ ². No evil shall — you, لَا يُصِيبُكَ سُوءٌ. I know not what will — me, لَا أَدْرِي مَا يُصَادِفُنِي. He told me what befell the man and the dog, أَخْبَرَنِي كَيْفَ كَانَ أَمْرُ ٱلرَّجُلِ وَٱلْكَلْبِ. An accident has befallen me, حَدَثَ ـ حَكَمَنِي عَارِضٌ لِي عَارِضٌ.

Befit, *v.t.* *See to* Become, *v.t.*

Befitting, *a.* *See* Becoming, *a.*

Befool, *v.t.* ضَحِكَ عَلَى ـ ² مَكَرَ بِ ـ مَسَّخَ.

Before, *prep.* and *ad.* Farther on, إِلَى قُدَّامٍ ـ لِقُدَّامٍ ـ قُدَّامَ. In the presence of, بَيْنَ يَدَي ـ بِحَضْرَةِ ـ أَمَامَ ـ قُدَّامَ ـ قَبْلًا ـ عِنْدَ. Preceding in time, أَوَّلًا ـ قَبْلًا. Up to this time, إِلَى ٱلْآنَ. In preference to, أَخْيَرَ ـ خَيْرٌ. In time past, أَوَّلًا ـ مُقَدَّمًا ـ فِي مَا مَضَى وَتَقَدَّمَ مِنَ ٱلزَّمَانِ ـ سَابِقًا. Rather than, قَبْلَ أَنْ. Opposite to, قُبَالَةَ. That which is — one, صَدْرٌ. To get — to, تَقَدَّمَ-إِلَى ـ ² سَبَقَ-إِلَى. I came to you —, أَتَيْتُكَ قَبْلًا. Before dawn, قَبْلَ ٱلْفَجْرِ ـ غَلَسًا. An hour — the time, قَبْلَ ٱلْوَقْتِ بِسَاعَةٍ. Before his death, قَبْلَ مَوْتِهِ. Before that you . . ., مِنْ قَبْلِ أَنَّكَ.

Beforehand, *ad.* قَبْلًا ـ مُقَدَّمًا ـ سَابِقًا ـ مِنْ قَبْلُ ـ نَاجِزًا. To be — with, قَدَّمَ ـ تَفَارَطَ ـ ² عَجِلَ بِ ـ ² فَرَطَ. Money paid —, فُلُوسٌ لِقُدَّامٍ ـ سَلَفٌ ـ سَلَمٌ.

Beforetime, *ad.* سَابِقًا. *See* Before, *prep.* and *ad.*

Befoul, *v.t.* وَسَّخَ ـ لَوَّثَ ـ دَنَّسَ. To be befouled, تَوَسَّخَ. To — one's self, تَصَوَّكَ.

Befriend, *v.t.* ² شَدَّ ظَهْرَ ـ سَاعَدَ ـ أَعَانَ ـ صَادَقَ.

Befringe, *v.t.* كَنَّفَ ـ نَيَّرَ.

Beg, *v.t.* To ask, solicit, طَلَبَ مِنْ ـ ² طَلَبَ ـ إِلْتَمَسَ مِنْ ـ ² سَأَلَ. To implore, لَجَّ عَلَى ـ أَلَحَّ عَلَى ـ تَضَرَّعَ إِلَى. To ask alms of, ² سَأَلَ-حَسَنَةً ـ تَسَوَّلَ مِنْ.

Beg, *v.i.* To ask alms, ² شَحَذَ ـ تَسَوَّلَ.

Beget, *v.t.* وَلَدَ *aor.* يَلِدُ ـ وَلَّدَ ـ أَنْسَلَ ـ ² نَسَلَ ـ أَنْشَأَ. To be the cause of, سَبَّبَ. To be begotten of, تَوَلَّدَ مِنْ ـ وُلِدَ مِنْ. He neither begets nor is he begotten, لَمْ يَلِدْ وَلَمْ يُولَدْ.

Begetter, *n.* وَالِدٌ *fem.* وَالِدَةٌ ـ مُوَلِّدٌ.

Beggar, *n.* سَائِلٌ *pl.* سَأَلَةٌ ـ سَوَّالٌ ـ مُتَسَوِّلٌ ـ فَقِيرٌ *pl.* فُقَرَاءُ ـ شَحَّاذٌ *pl.* شَحَّاذَةٌ ـ صَعْلُوكٌ ـ مَسَاكِينُ ـ مِسْكِينٌ ـ طَالِبٌ *pl.* طُلَّابٌ.

Beggar, *v.t.* أَفْلَسَ ـ أَهْلَكَ ـ ضَيَّعَ.

Beggarliness, *n.* Poverty, فَقْرٌ ـ مَسْكَنَةٌ. Meanness, حَقَارَةٌ ـ سَفَلَةٌ.

Beggarly, *a.* Poor, فَقِيرٌ ـ مِسْكِينٌ. Mean, حَقِيرٌ ـ خَسِيسٌ ـ أَذِلَّةٌ *pl.* ذَلِيلٌ ـ دَنِيٌّ ـ حَقِيرٌ نَقِيرٌ.

Beggary, *n.* فَقْرٌ ـ فَاقَةٌ ـ مَسْكَنَةٌ ـ عَالَةٌ.

Begging, *n.* تَكَفُّفٌ.

Begin, *v.t.* and *i.* بَدَأَ بِ ـ ² بَدَأَ ـ ² بَدَأَ ـ إِبْتَدَأَ ـ إِبْتَدَأَ فِي ـ ² شَرَعَ فِي ـ أَنْشَأَ بِ. To put one's hand to, أَلْقَى يَدَهُ فِي. To set about, ² جَعَلَ ـ ² شَرَعَ فِي ـ ² أَخَذَ فِي ـ ² دَخَلَ فِي ـ ² هَبَّ. To take rise from, ² نَبَعَ مِنْ ـ ² خَرَجَ مِنْ ـ ² صَدَرَ مِنْ. To — something before another person, ² سَبَقَ-إِلَى. To —, as of a discourse, إِسْتَفْتَحَ بِ ـ إِفْتَتَحَ بِ. To — again, بَدَأَ أَيْضًا ـ بَدَأَ مِنْ جَدِيدٍ. The woman began to sob, قَامَتِ ٱلْمَرْأَةُ تَنُوحُ. Beginning to sink he cried out, إِبْتَدَأَ يَغْرَقُ فَصَرَخَ. It is for you to —, لَكَ ٱلْبَدْءُ. He was about to —, هَمَّ بِٱلشُّرُوعِ فِيهِ. I was about to — it, هَمَمْتُ بِأَنْ أَبْدَأَ بِهِ.

Beginner, *n.* مُبْتَدِئٌ ـ شَارِعٌ. A scholar, تِلْمِيذٌ *pl.* تَلَامِيذُ.

Beginning, *n.* بَدْءٌ ـ إِبْتِدَاءٌ ـ بَدْأَةٌ ـ بَدَاءَةٌ ـ بِدَايَةٌ. The first, أَوَّلٌ ـ رَأْسٌ. Opening, as of a discourse, فَاتِحَةٌ ـ إِفْتِتَاحٌ. The commencing of anything, بَدْءٌ ـ شُرُوعٌ ـ إِقَامَةٌ. A happy —, إِفْتِتَاحٌ (or إِسْتِفْتَاحٌ) مُبَارَكٌ. The — of the month, رَأْسُ ٱلشَّهْرِ. The — of the year, رَأْسُ ٱلسَّنَةِ. The — of the affair, مَبَادِئُ ٱلْأَمْرِ. To make a —, أَنْشَأَ بِ. I have read the book from the — to the end, قَرَأْتُ ٱلْكِتَابَ مِنْ أَوَّلِهِ إِلَى آخِرِهِ. Repeat your words from the —, أَعِدْ كَلَامَكَ مِنْ رَأْسٍ. Rudiments, مَبَادِئُ ـ أُصُولٌ. The — of the end, or the resurrection, أَوَّلُ أَشْرَاطِ ٱلسَّاعَةِ.

Begird, *v.t.* } To bind with a girdle, حَزَمَ ـ زَنَّرَ. To surround,
Begirt, } أَحَاطَ بِ. Begirt with a sword, by one's self, مُتَقَلِّدٌ بِسَيْفٍ; by another, مُقَلَّدٌ بِسَيْفٍ.

Begone, *int.* إِنْقَلِعْ. Begone from me! بَعِيدٌ عَنِّي ـ عَالِ عَنِّي ـ أَعْلِ عَنِّي. Far be it! هَيْهَاتَ.

Begrime, *v.t.* لَوَّثَ ـ وَسَّخَ ـ نَجَّسَ.

Begrudge, *v.t.* *See to* Grudge, *v.t.*

Beguile, *v.t.* To deceive, أَرَبَ ـ غَشَّ ـ ² خَدَعَ ـ ² أَغْوَى ـ ² غَرَّ ـ رَاوَغَ ـ أَوْقَعَ. To amuse, سَلَّى ـ شَرَحَ خَاطِرَ. To — one's time, enjoy one's self, تَسَلَّى. To fascinate, ² سَحَرَ. To be beguiled, deceived, by, إِغْتَرَّ بِ. Beguiled, deceived, غَرِيرٌ ـ مَغْرُورٌ. Beguiling, deceiving, غَرُورٌ.

Behalf, *n.* حَقّ ـ خاطِر ـ أَجْل. On your —, لِأَجْلِكُمْ ـ مِنْ شأْنِكُمْ. On this —, لِهٰذا ٱلسَّبَبِ. I am glad on your —, أَنَا مَسْرُورٌ بِمَا فِيكُمْ. On — of, as representing, بِٱلنِّيَابَةِ عَن.

Behave, *v.i.* تَصَرَّفَ ـ مَشَى ـ عَمِلَ ـ سَلَكَ سُلُوكًا. To — towards, صَنَعَ بِ. To — badly, سَآءَ ـ أَقْبَحَ فِي ٱلسِّيرَةِ ـ قَبُحَ ـ أَسَآءَ ٱلْعَمَلَ. He behaved well, تَحَسَّنَ فِي ٱلسُّلُوكِ. To — insolently towards, فَرَطَ عَلَى or بِ ـ تَعَدَّى فِي أَدَبِهِ. How he behaved among you, كَيْفَ سَلَكَ عِنْدَكُمْ ـ كَيْفَ صَارَ عِنْدَكُمْ. He behaved valiantly, تَشَدَّدَ ـ تَجَلَّدَ.

Behaviour, *n.* مُعَامَلَة ـ عَمَل ـ تَصَرُّف ـ سُلُوك ـ سِيرَة ـ أَدَب ـ مُرُوَّة. Good —, سِيرَةٌ حَسَنَةٌ. Bad —, سِيرَةٌ رَدِيئَةٌ ـ سُوءُ ٱلْأَدَبِ ـ وِشْيَة.

Behead, *v.t.* رَمَى رَقَبَةً ـ ضَيَّعَ رَأْسًا ـ قَطَعَ رَأْسًا ـ ضَرَبَ عُنُقًا.

Beheld, *pret. of to* Behold, *q.v.*

Behemoth, *n.* بَهِيمُوتُ وَهُوَ حَيَوَانٌ مَجْهُولٌ.

Behest, *n.* إِرَادَة ـ وَصِيَّة ـ حُكْم ـ أَمْر.

Behind, *ad.* and *prep.* In the rear, مِنْ وَرَآءِ ـ خَلْفَ ـ وَرَآء ـ غِبَّ ـ مِنْ خَلْفِ. From —, مِنْ وَرَآءِ ـ مِنْ دُبُرٍ. After, مِنْ بَعْدُ ـ بَعْدَ. To leave —, خَلَّفَ ـ وَرَآءَ ـ خَلَّفَ. To come —, after, عَقَبَ. To remain —, some one, تَأَخَّرَ خَلْفَ. To be —, late, أَنَى *aor.* يَأْنِي ـ تَعَوَّقَ. To stay —, to remain, تَخَلَّفَ عَن ـ إِسْتَمَرَّ ـ بَقِيَ. To come —, be wanting in, قَصَّرَ عَن ـ تَأَخَّرَ عَن. To fill up what is —, كَمَّلَ مَا نَقَصَ. He remained — us, خَلْفَنَا. I found him —, لَقِيتُهُ مِنْ وَرَآءٍ. He was — me, كَانَ خَلْفِي. That which is — it, مَا وَرَآءَهُ.

Behindhand, *ad.* To be —, wanting, قَصَّرَ ـ تَأَخَّرَ ـ تَخَلَّفَ. To be —, late, بَطُؤَ ـ تَعَوَّقَ ـ أَبْطَأَ. To be — with the world, in bad circumstances, أَعَازَ ـ إِفْتَقَرَ.

Behold, *v.t.* To see, شَافَ ـ رَأَى ـ شَهِدَ. To look at, طَالَعَ ـ تَطَلَّعَ إِلَى ـ نَظَرَ إِلَى. To contemplate, تَأَمَّلَ.

Behold, *int.* إِذَا بِ ـ إِذَا ـ هَا هُوَذَا ـ هَا. Behold the man! هُوَذَا ٱلرَّجُلُ. I looked, and — a man was ascending, نَظَرْتُ وَإِذَا بِرَجُلٍ طَالِعٍ.

Beholden, *a.* مَجْبُور ـ مَمْنُونٌ لِ ـ مَمْنُون. He is — to him for his advancement, مِنْ فَضْلِهِ أَنَّهُ ـ هُوَ كَانَ سَبَبَ ٱرْتِفَاعِ شَأْنِهِ. I do not wish to be — to him, لَمْ أُرِدْ أَنْ ـ مَا أُرِيدُ مِنَّتَهُ ـ تَقَدَّمَ يُحَمِّلُنِي مِنَّتَهُ.

Beholder, *n.* نَاظِر *pl.* نَظَّارَة ـ شَاهِد *pl.* شُهُود ـ مُتَشَاهِد. *See also* Spectator, *n.*

Behoof, *n.* *See* Behalf, *n.*

Behoove, *v.t.* To befit, لَزِمَ عَلَى ـ وَجَبَ عَلَى *aor.* يَجِبُ. It behooves thee, يَنْبَغِي لَكَ ـ يَحِقُّ عَلَيْكَ.

Being, *n.* Existence, كَوْن *pl.* أَكْوَان ـ وُجُود ـ حُدُوث. A creature, كَائِنَة *pl.* كَائِنَات ـ خَلِيقَة *pl.* خَلَائِق. A person, شَخْص *pl.* أَشْخَاص. In being, مَوْجُود ـ كَائِن. To call into —, خَلَقَ ـ أَوْجَدَ ـ كَوَّنَ. The Supreme Being, الْكَائِنُ ٱلْمُطْلَقُ ـ اللّٰهُ سُبْحَانَهُ وَتَعَالَى.

Belabour, *v.t.* ضَرَبَ ـ وَكَزَ *aor.* يَكِزُ ـ نَزَلَ عَلَى.

Belated, *a.* Late, بَطِيء. He was —, benighted, حَكَمَهُ ٱللَّيْلُ.

Belaud, *v.t.* حَمِدَ ـ حَمِدَ عَلَى ـ مَدَحَ ـ أَثْنَى عَلَى ـ أَطْرَأَ.

Belay, *v.t.* To waylay, رَصَدَ ـ رَاصَدَ ـ تَرَصَّدَ لِ. To fasten, رَبَطَ ـ شَدَّ. To cover, غَمَّ ـ كَمَّ. *See also to* Overlay, *v.t.*

Belch, *v.i.* تَجَشَّأَ ـ تَكَرَّعَ ـ تَدَشَّى. To — out, to emit, جَشَأَ بِ.

Belch, *n.* تَجَشُّوء ـ جُشَاءَة ـ تَكَرُّع ـ تَدَشِّي.

Beldam, *n.* عَاجِزَة ـ سَلِيطَة ـ فَاجِرَة.

Beleaguer. *See to* Besiege, *v.t.*

Belfry, *n.* بُرْجُ نَاقُوسٍ ـ مَنَارَةٌ لِلنَّوَاقِيسِ.

Belgian, *a.* مِنَ ٱلْبَلْجِيكْ.

Belgium, *n.* الْبَلْجِيكْ.

Belial, *n.* بِلِيعَال. Sons of —, wicked persons, أَشْرَار ـ بَنُو لَئِيمٍ.

Belie, *v.t.* To slander, إِفْتَرَى عَلَى ـ نَمَّ عَلَى ـ بَهَتَ ـ وَشَى بِ *aor.* يَشِي. To counterfeit, قَلَّدَ ـ زَوَّرَ. To give the lie to, كَذَّبَ ـ أَكْذَبَ. To give a false representation of to, وَشَى بِ ـ إِلَى *aor.* يَشِي ـ رَكَا عَلَى ـ إِلَى ـ وَصَفَ ـ تَزْوِيرًا لِ ـ شَهِدَ بِ ـ زُورًا إِلَى ـ يَصِفُ *aor.* To — the conscience, خَالَفَ ٱلضَّمِيرَ.

Belief, *n.* Credit given to any thing, إِعْتِبَار ـ إِعْتِمَاد ـ إِرْتِكَان. Religious faith, إِيمَان ـ إِعْتِقَاد *pl.* إِعْتِقَادَات ـ دِين. A sect, مِلَّة *pl.* مِلَل ـ شِيعَة *pl.* شِيَع and أَشْيَاع ـ مَذْهَب *pl.* مَذَاهِب ـ طَرِيقَة ـ دِين *pl.* أَدْيَان ـ إِيمَان. Opinion, ظَنّ ـ رَأْي. An article of —, عَقِيدَةٌ دِينِيَّةٌ *pl.* عَقَائِد. A Creed, شَهَادَة ـ صُورَةُ إِيمَانٍ ـ قَانُونُ إِيمَانٍ. Slow of —, ثَقِيلٌ عَنِ ٱلْإِيمَانِ بِ ـ قَلِيلُ ٱلتَّصْدِيقِ. Light of —, simple, مُصَدِّق ـ سَاذِج ـ غَشِيم. He holds the — of such an one, تَمَذْهَبَ ـ يَذْهَبُ عَلَى قَوْلِ فُلَانٍ. To hold a —, ذَهَبَ إِلَى مَذْهَبٍ ـ بِمَذْهَبِ فُلَانٍ.

Believable, *a.* مِمَّا يُصَدَّقُ ـ مُمْكِنُ ٱلْإِعْتِقَادِ بِهِ.

Believe, *v.t.* To credit, صَدَّقَ ـ آمَنَ بِ ـ إِعْتَقَدَ بِ. To

— تَوَهَّمَ — ²ظَنَّ. To imagine, إِتَّكَلَ عَلَى — إِعْتَمَدَ عَلَى trust, ²حَسِبَ — خَمَّنَ. To — in God, آمَنَ بِاللّٰهِ. What we —, صَدِّقْنِي. Believe me, ما نَحْنُ عَلَيْهِ من الإِيمَانِ.

Believer, *n.* / Believing, *a.* } One who credits another, مُصَدِّق. A — in religious matters, مُؤْمِن *pl.* مُؤْمِنُون.

Believing, *n.* *See* Belief, *n.*

Belike, *ad.* لَعَلَّ — تَخْمِينًا.

Bell, *n.* جَرَس *pl.* أَجْرَاس. A gong of wood made to serve as a bell, نَاقُوس *pl.* نَوَاقِيس: the mallet for the same, وَبِيلَة. A small bell hung round the necks of cattle, جُلْجُل *pl.* جَلَاجِل. A chime of bells, سِنْطِير — دَقُّ ٱلْأَجْرَاسِ. To bell the cat, أَخْطَرَ بِنَفْسِهِ أَوَّلًا.

Belladonna, *n.* The plant, حَشِيشَةُ ٱلْحُمْرَةِ.

Belle, *n.* إِمْرَأَةٌ حَسَنَةٌ. *See also* Beauty, *n.*

Belles lettres, *n.* العُلُومُ ٱلْأَدَبِيَّةُ — العُلُومُ.

Bell-fashioned, *n.* بِصُورَةِ جَرَسٍ.

Bell-founder, *n.* سَبَّاكُ ٱلْأَجْرَاسِ.

Bell-foundery, *n.* / Bell-foundry, } مَسْبَكُ ٱلْأَجْرَاسِ.

Bell-hanger, *n.* مُرَكِّبُ ٱلْأَجْرَاسِ.

Bell-man, *n.* بَرَّاح — مُنَادٍ.

Bell-ringer, *n.* دَقَّاقُ ٱلْأَجْرَاسِ.

Bell-shaped, *n.* *See* Bell-fashioned, *a.*

Bell-wether, *n.* الكَبْشُ ٱلْمُجَلْجَلُ ٱلَّذِي يَمْشِي قُدَّامَ ٱلْغَنَمِ.

Bellicose, *a.* Warlike, مُحِبُّ ٱلْحَرْبِ — حَرْبِيٌّ. Contentious, لَجُوج — خَصِيم.

Belligerent, *a.* and *n.* مُتَحَارِب — مُحَارِب. To recognize as a —, إِعْتَرَفَ مُحَارِبًا. The government does not regard them as belligerents, but as rebels, الدَّوْلَةُ لَمْ تَعْتَرِفْهُمْ بِصِفَةِ ٱلْمُحَارِبِينَ بَلْ بِصِفَةِ ٱلْعُصَاةِ.

Bellow, *v.i.* As of a bull, ²خَارَ — ²عَرَّ — ²عَجَّ — هَدَرَ — قَرْقَرَ. To cry out, صَيَّحَ — ²صَرَخَ — زَعَقَ. To —, as a camel, ²رَجَسَ.

Bellow, *n.* / Bellowing, } خُوَار — صَرِيخ — خُور — صِيَاح — عَجِيج. He has a voice like the — of a bull, لَهُ صَوْتٌ كَخُوَارِ ٱلثَّوْرِ.

Bellows, *n.* مِنْفَاخ — مِنْفَخ *pl.* مَنَافِخُ. A smith's —, كِير *pl.* أَكْيَار. To blow the —, نَفَخَ بِٱلْمِنْفَاخِ.

Belly, *n.* بَطْن *pl.* بُطُون and أَبْطُن — جَوْف *pl.* أَجْوَاف — كَبِد. The lower —, المَأْنَةُ. Having a large —, مِبْطَان — أَكْبَدُ — بَطِين — أَكْثَمُ. Lank in the —, مُبَطَّن.

Belly, *v.i.* To swell out, إِنْتَفَخَ — نَتَأَ — إِنْدَلَعَ.

Belly-ache, *n.* قُولَنْج — مَغْص — وَجَعُ ٱلْبَطْنِ — مَغَاص. Having the —, مَمْغُوص.

Belly-band, *n.* زُنَّار *pl.* زَنَانِير.

Belly-full, *n.* شَبْع — شِبَع — مِلَاءُ ٱلْبَطْنِ.

Belly-god, *n.* بَطِينِيٌّ — جُرَاف — أَكُول.

Belong, *v.i.* To be the property of, ²خَصَّ بِ — إِخْتَصَّ بِ — تَعَلَّقَ بِ — نُسِبَ لِ — تَبِعَ — مَالَ — or لِ. To be referred to, صَلَحَ لِ — حَقَّ لِ. To be proper to, This belongs to me, هٰذَا تَبَعِي — هٰذَا مَالِي — هٰذَا لِي. This belongs to you, هٰذَا تَبَعَكَ — هٰذَا لَكَ. The things which — to him, الأَشْيَاءُ ٱلْمُخْتَصَّةُ بِهِ. When he knew that he belonged to al-Yémen, لَمَّا عَلِمَ أَنَّهُ مِنَ ٱلْيَمَنِ. Where do you — to? مِنْ أَيْنَ أَنْتَ.

Belonging, *part.* Appertaining to, مَال — لِ — لَاحِق بِ; as of a duty, مَلْزُوم بِ; referring to, رَاجِعٌ إِلَى — مَنْسُوبٌ لِ — مُتَعَلِّق بِ.

Beloved, *a.* حَبِيب — عَزِيز — مَحْبُوب — حَبَّذَا; as by a woman, مَعْشُوق. Beloved friends, أَعِزَّاءُ — أَحِبَّاءُ.

Below, *ad.* and *prep.* Under, in place, أَسْفَلَ — تَحْتَ; a little —, تُحَيْتَ. Inferior to, تَحْتَ — أَوْطَى مِن — أَسْفَلُ مِن — دُونَ. Relating to what is —, تَحْتَانِيٌّ. This is —, beneath you, هٰذَا مِنْ دُونِكَ. He sat — him, جَلَسَ دُونَهُ. Below your rank, دُونَ مَقَامِكَ. To go —, into the hold of a ship, نَزَلَ فِي ٱلْأَنْبَارِ. To go —, down stairs, نَزَلَ تَحْتَ. Rivers run — it, تَجْرِي مِنْ تَحْتِهَا ٱلْأَنْهَارُ.

Belt, *n.* A girdle, حِزَام — مِنْطَقَة — زُنَّار — مِحْمَل — حِمَالَة. A zone, مِنْطَق *pl.* مَنَاطِق. A woman's waist —, نِطَاق — سَفِيفَة: the same, ornamented, حِيَاصَة. A sword —, مِحْمَلُ سَيْفٍ — عِلَاقَة — حِمَالَة. A soldier's cross-belts, حَمَائِل.

Belt, *v.t.* زَنَّرَ — حَزَّمَ. To surround with, أَحَاطَ بِ.

Belted, *a.* As with a sword, مُقَلَّد بِسَيْفٍ.

Belvedere, *n.* عُلِّيَّة — مَطَلّ — جَوْسَق *pl.* جَوَاسِق.

Bemaze, *v.t.* حَيَّرَ — أَضَلَّ — وَعَّرَ. To be bemazed, تَحَيَّرَ — تَوَعَّرَ.

Bemire, *v.t.* لَوَّثَ — وَسَّخَ — طَبَّعَ.

Bemoan, *v.t.* and *i.* To be sorry, تَحَسَّرَ — إِكْتَرَبَ. To be sorry for, تَأَسَّفَ عَلَى — حَزِنَ عَلَى — شَفَقَ عَلَى — تَحَسَّرَ عَلَى — بَكَى عَلَى.

Bemock, *v.t.* تَسَخَّرَ مِن — سَخِرَ مِن.

Ben, *n.* The tree, البَانُ. Nuts of the —, حَبُّ ٱلْبَانِ — فُسْتُقُ ٱلْبَانِ — جَوْزُ ٱلْبَانِ.

Bench, *n.* A long seat, صُفَّة *pl.* صُفَّات — مَرْتَبَة *pl.* مَرَاتِبُ — تَخْت *pl.* تُخُوت. A stone — before a door, مَصْطَبَة *pl.* مَصَاطِبُ — سَهْوَة — سَقِيفَة. A — to recline upon, دَكَّة *pl.* دِكَك. A court of justice, مَحْكَمَة — مَجْلِسُ ٱلشَّرْعِ. The justices, أَرْبَابُ ٱلشَّرْعِ. The King or Queen's Bench, حَبْسٌ مَخْصُوصٌ بِمَدِينَةِ لَنْدَن.

Bencher, *n.* مِنْ مُقَدَّمِي ٱلْوُكَلَاءِ ٱلشَّرْعِيِّينَ فِي مَدِينَةِ لَنْدَن.

Bend, *v.t.* To make curved or crooked, حَنَا — حَنَّثَ — حَجَّنَ — عَوَّجَ — ثَنَى — لَوَى — قَوَّسَ. To incline, حَنَا — عَطَفَ. To fold or double, عَطَّفَ. To make submissive, أَطَاعَ — أَخْضَعَ — أَذَلَّ رِقَابَ. To — the brow, قَطَّبَ ٱلْوَجْهَ — عَبَّسَ ٱلْوَجْهَ. To — the knee, جَثَا — ثَنَى ٱلرُّكْبَةَ — جَثَا عَلَى ٱلرُّكْبَةِ. To — a bow, أَطَرَ ٱلْقَوْسَ — شَدَّ ٱلْقَوْسَ — نَبَضَ ٱلْقَوْسَ. To —, as of a cable, to fasten, رَبَطَ. To — sails, حَلَّ ٱلشِّرَاعَ. He bent his steps towards, سَعَى إِلَى — ضَرَبَ إِلَى. He bent his steps towards the town, قَصَدَ ٱلْمَدِينَةَ.

Bend, *v.i.* As a bough, تَغَيَّفَ — نَاعَ. To —, as in prayer, رَكَعَ. To —, as a bow, تَأَطَّرَ. To be or to become bent, incurvated, تَحَجَّنَ — إِنْثَنَى — تَثَنَّى — إِنْعَطَفَ — تَحَنَّثَ — تَقَوَّسَ — تَعَوَّجَ. To — with age, تَحَنَّبَ. To —, of itself, إِعْوَجَّ. To — or stoop over, جَنَأَ عَلَى — أَكَبَّ عَلَى — إِنْحَنَى عَلَى.

Bend, *n.* A curvature, حِنْوٌ — إِنْحِنَاءٌ — عَطْف — إِنْعِطَاف — عَوَج — إِنْعِوَاج — إِعْوِجَاج — حَنِيَّة. A turn, لَفَّة. The — of a river or valley, مَحْنِيَة — ثِنْيٌ *pl.* أَثْنَاءٌ — جِزْع *pl.* أَجْزَاع — مُنْعَطَف — عَطْفَة. Having a —, winding, حَانٍ — مُنْحَنٍ. A bending of the back in prayer, حَنْوَة. A — or genuflexion in prayer, رُكُوع. One bending or posture in prayer, رَكْعَة *pl.* رَكَعَات.

Beneath, *prep.* and *ad.* *See* Below, *prep.* and *ad.*

Benedict, *n.* A newly married man, مُزَوَّجٌ حَدِيثًا.

Benedictine, *n.* A — monk, رَاهِبٌ مِنْ رَهْبَنَةِ بَنَادِكْتُس.

Benediction, *n.* بَرَكَة — مُبَارَكَة — تَبَرُّك — دُعَاءُ خَيْرٍ.

Benefaction, *n.* خَيْر — فَضْل — نِعْمَة *pl.* نِعَمَات — كَرَم — جَمِيل — مَعْرُوف — إِحْسَان — فَاضِلَة *pl.* فَوَاضِلُ.

Benefactor, *n.* مُنْعِم — وَلِيُّ ٱلنِّعَمِ — مُحْسِن — فَاعِلُ خَيْرٍ — مُتَفَضِّل. Our benefactors, ٱلْمُحْسِنُونَ إِلَيْنَا.

Benefactress, *n.* وَلِيَّةُ ٱلنِّعَمِ.

Benefice, *n.* أَبْرَشِيَّة — مَعِيشَةُ ٱلْقِسِّيسِ.

Beneficed, *a.* ذُو أَبْرَشِيَّةٍ — ذُو مَعَاشٍ كَنَائِسِيٍّ.

Beneficence, *n.* فِعْلُ ٱلْخَيْرِ — جُود — كَرَم — خَيْر — مَعْرُوف.

Beneficent, *a.* كَرِيم *pl.* كُرَمَاءُ — مُنْعِم — مِنْعَام — مُحْسِن — مَنَّان and كِرَام — خَيِّر — فَاعِلُ ٱلْخَيْرِ.

Beneficently, *ad.* إِنْعَامًا — كَرَامَةً — إِحْسَانًا.

Beneficial, *a.* طَائِل — مُفِيد — نَافِع — خَيِّر — طَيِّب — مَلِيح.

Beneficially, *ad.* إِفَادَةً — مَنْفَعَةً — خِيرَةً.

Beneficiary, *n.* One who holds a benefice, صَاحِبُ أَبْرَشِيَّةٍ; one who receives benefits, مُفَاض.

Benefit, *n.* A favour conferred, نِعْمَة *pl.* نِعَم and أَنْعُم — فَضْل — جَمِيل — فَاضِلَة *pl.* فَوَاضِلُ — مَعْرُوف — خَيْر — إِحْسَان. Profit, advantage, مَنْفَعَة — فَائِدَة — طَائِل — خَيْر — رِبْح. You will derive no — from it, لَا يَحْصُلُ لَكَ مِنْهُ مَنْفَعَةٌ. To confer a — upon, أَوْلَى مَعْرُوفًا — مَنَّ عَلَى — إِمْتَنَّ عَلَى — تَفَضَّلَ عَلَى. To ask a — of, إِسْتَمَنَّ فِي. He derived no — from it, لَمْ يَحُلْ مِنْهُ بِطَائِلٍ. A theatrical — night, لَيْلَةُ لَعِبٍ فِي ٱلتِّيَاتْرُو مَحْصُولُهَا لِأَحَدِ ٱللَّاعِبِينَ.

Benefit, *v.t.* To do good to, أَصْلَحَ إِلَى — أَفَادَ — أَحْسَنَ بِ — تَفَضَّلَ عَلَى or إِلَى — أَسْدَى إِلَى — أَكْرَمَ عَلَى — أَنْعَمَ عَلَى — نَفَعَ — نَفَعَ بِ. To derive advantage from, إِسْتَفَادَ مِن — إِنْتَفَعَ بِ. To profit, gain, كَسَبَ — رَبِحَ.

Benevolence, *n.* كَرَم — شَفَقَة — خَيْر — جُود — خُلَّة — خِلَالَة — مُرُوَّة — حُسْنُ ٱلْإِلْتِفَاتِ.

Benevolent, *a.* خَيِّر — خَائِر — مِنْعَام — كَرِيم — ذُو خُلَّةٍ — لَطِيف. To be — to, تَفَضَّلَ عَلَى.

Benevolently, *ad.* خُلَّةً — بِجُودٍ — خِيرَةً — كَرَمًا — بِمُرُوَّةٍ.

Benight, *v.t.* To darken, أَظْلَمَ عَلَى — عَتَمَ عَلَى. To be benighted, caught in the dark, هَجَمَ عَلَى ٱللَّيْلِ. To be in a state of ignorance, جَهِلَ — غَبِيَ — كَانَ فِي ٱلْجَهَالَةِ — كَانَ مِنَ ٱلْهَمَجِ.

Benign, *a.* } Kindly, رَؤُوف — لَطِيف — حَلِيمُ ٱلطَّبْعِ — لَيِّن
Benignant, } كَرِيمُ ٱلْقَلْبِ. Of a — countenance, طَلِيقُ ٱلْوَجْهِ. Happy, fortunate, سَعِيد.

Benignity, *n.* حِلْم — كَرَم — رَأْفَة — رِفْق — لَطَافَة — إِنْسَانِيَّة.

Benignly, *ad.* بِحِلْمٍ — بِرَأْفَةٍ — بِلَطَافَةٍ.

Benison, *n.* A reward, مَثُوبَة — ثَوَاب. *See also* Benediction, *n.*

Benjamin, *n.* The gum —, جَاوِيّ — بَخُورٌ جَاوِيٌّ — بَخُورٌ جَوِيّ.

Bennet, *n.* The herb, ٱلْحَشِيشَةُ ٱلْمُبَارَكَةُ.

Bent, n. Propensity, هَوِيَّة — هَوًى — مَيْل — مُمَال — مَشْرَب — خَاطِر. To be — upon, قَصَدَ — تَعَزَّمَ — أَزْمَعَ عَلَى.

Benumb, v.t. To make torpid, أَخْدَرَ — خَدَّرَ — سَبَّتَ — أَسْبَتَ. To — with cold, أَكَزَّ. To be benumbed, torpid, خَدِرَ; with cold, إِكْتَزَّ.

Benzoin, n. *See* Benjamin, n.

Bepraise, v.t. أَفْرَطَ فِي حَمْدِهِ — فَضَّلَ — أَطْرَأَ.

Bequeath, v.t. وَصَّى لِأَحَدٍ بِ — وَصَّى إِلَى — تَرَكَ بِوَصِيَّةٍ إِلَى — عَهِدَ إِلَى.

Bequest, n. وَصِيَّة pl. وَصِيٌّ — بِوَصِيَّةٍ (or تَرِكَةٌ) تِرْكَةٌ pl. تَرِكَات. A pious —, وَقْف pl. أَوْقَاف. An inalienable —, حَبِيسَة pl. حَبَائِس.

Berate, v.t. سَخِطَ عَلَى — وَنَزَلَ- صَعِدَ بِ.

Bereave, v.t. To deprive of, رَفَعَ عَن — أَعْدَمَ — حَرَمَ — أَفْقَدَ — عَرَّى-عَن. To — of children, أَثْكَلَ — أَعْدَمَ-الْأَوْلَادَ — صَيَّرَ-بِلَا أَوْلَادٍ. To —, as of a dignity, عَزَلَ. To — of reason, جَنَّنَ. To be bereft of a child, friend, *etc.*, ثَكِلَ; of reason, جُنَّ — ذَهَبَ عَقْلُهُ.

Bereavement, n. Deprivation, جِرْم — تَعَرٍّ — حِرْمَان; of children, ثُكْل — عَدَمُ الْأَوْلَادِ; of a dignity, عَزْل.

Bereft, *part. of to* Bereave, *q.v.*

Bergamot, n. A species of orange, نَوْعٌ مِنَ الْبُرْتُقَانِ; of pear, نَوْعٌ مِنَ الْكُمَّثْرَى; of a perfume, نَوْعٌ مِنَ الْعُطُورِ.

Berry, n. حَبَّة *coll.* حَبٌّ *pl.* حُبُوب.

Berth, n. An appointment, مَنْصَب *pl.* مَنَاصِب — خِدْمَة — مَأْمُورِيَّة. A room, as in a cabin, مَقْعَد — أُوضَة. A station, مَحَطّ — مَحَلّ — مَقَام. To give a wide — to, to avoid, اِجْتَنَبَ — اِبْتَعَدَ مِن.

Beryl, n. بَزَادِقٌ — الْحَجَرُ الْأَزْرَقُ.

Bescribble, v.t. سَوَّدَ.

Beseech, v.t. To ask, سَأَلَ — طَلَبَ. To entreat, قَنَعَ — طَلَبَ إِلَى — تَرَجَّى — تَضَرَّعَ إِلَى — اِلْتَمَسَ مِن — اِبْتَهَلَ إِلَى — تَدَخَّلَ عَلَى. I — you, أَطْلُبُ إِلَيْكَ — دَخِيلُكَ — أَنَا فِي عِرْضَكَ — أَنَا قُرْبَانُكَ.

Beseem, v.t. *See to* Become, v.t.

Beset, v.t. To hem in, أَحَاطَ بِ — حَاصَرَ — حَاوَطَ — اِشْتَمَلَ عَلَى. To —, of evil, حَاقَ بِ. To harass, ضَيَّقَ عَلَى — أَكَدَّ. To be — by, حُفَّ. Want — him, حَفَّتْهُ الْحَاجَةُ. They are — by ..., هُمْ مَحْفُوفُونَ بِ.

Besetting, *part.* Surrounding, مُحَاصِر — مُحِيطٌ بِ. Attending, pressing, مُلَازِم — مُشَدِّدٌ عَلَى — مُهَيِّج.

Beside, *prep.* and *ad.* / Besides, } Near, by the side of, فِي جَانِبِ — عَلَى جَانِبِ — قَرِيبٌ مِن — عِنْدَ — دُونَ — جَنْبَ. Over and above, سِوَى — دُونَ — غَيْر — غَيْرُ ذَلِكَ — فَضْلًا عَن — زِيَادَةً عَلَى ذَلِكَ. More than that, إِلَّا أَن — أَيْضًا — مَا عَدَا ذَلِكَ — مِنْ دُونِ ذَلِكَ. Besides all this, وَمَعَ هَذَا كُلِّهِ — زِدْ عَلَى ذَلِكَ — وَأَعْظَمُ مِنْ هَذَا كُلِّهِ. Thou owest me as much as that and more —, غَرِمْتَ لِي مَا سِوَى ذَلِكَ حَتَّى وَأَكْثَرَ مِنْهُ أَيْضًا. Besides his being, فَضْلًا عَنْ كَوْنِهِ. To be — one's self, هَذَى — جُنَّ. He is — himself, هُوَ مَعْتُوهٌ — تَحَوَّلَ إِلَى الْهَذَيَانِ.

Besiege, v.t. To lay siege to, حَاصَرَ — حَصَرَ — أَحَاطَ بِ. To put to straits, ضَيَّقَ عَلَى.

Besieger, n. مُحَاصِر *pl.* مُحَاصِرُونَ.

Besieging, n. *See* Siege, n.

Beslaver, v.t. To defile with slaver, تَفَلَ عَلَى. To — with praise, أَفْرَطَ فِي حَمْدِهِ — أَطْرَأَ.

Beslime, v.t. وَسَّخَ — لَوَّثَ.

Besmear, v.t. To smear with, طَلَى-بِ — دَهَنَ-بِ — دَلَكَ-بِ. To sully, stain, عَيَّبَ — لَوَّثَ. To be besmeared with, اِنْطَلَى بِ.

Besmoke, v.t. دَخَّنَ.

Besmut, v.t. سَوَّدَ — سَخَّمَ.

Besom, n. مِخْسَرَة — مِكْنَسَة *pl.* مَكَانِس — مِقَشَّة. A — maker, مُكَنِّس.

Besort, v.t. *See to* Fit, v.t.

Besot, v.t. To stupefy, أَدْهَشَ — حَامَقَ — اِسْتَجْهَلَ. To —, as with wine, أَسْكَرَ. Besotted with wine, سَكْرَانُ مِنَ الْمُدَامِ.

Besottedness, n. حَمَاقَة — جَهَالَة — سُكْر.

Besought, *pret. of to* Beseech, *q.v.*

Bespangle, v.t. زَيَّنَ-بِالصَّفَائِحِ — زَيَّنَ-بِالْبُرُوقِ.

Bespatter, v.t. To soil, لَوَّثَ — وَحَّلَ — طَرْطَشَ. To calumniate, عَرَّضَ بِ — هَتَكَ — نَمَّ عَلَى.

Bespeak, v.t. To order a thing beforehand, أَمَرَ بِ — وَصَّى عَلَى. To address, كَلَّمَ — خَاطَبَ. To forebode, دَلَّ عَلَى. To show, بَيَّنَ — أَظْهَرَ.

Bespot, v.t. بَقَّعَ — نَقَّطَ. To be bespotted, تَنَقَّطَ.

Bespread, v.t. فَرَشَ — غَمَرَ — غَشَّى عَلَى.

Besprinkle, *v.t.* رَشَّ ² ـ رَشَّحَ ـ. To — with praise, أَطْرَأَ ـ أَثْنَى عَلَى.

Bessarabia, *n.* بِيسَارَابِيَا.

Best, *a.* and *n.* The most good, ٱلْأَحْسَنُ ـ ٱلْأَفْضَلُ ـ ٱلْأَخْيَرُ ـ ٱلْأَفْخَرُ ـ ٱلْأَطْيَبُ. The best of any thing, صَفْوَة ـ صُفْوَة ـ زَكَاة ـ زُبْدَة ـ عِيبَة ـ صَمِيم. The best gifts, أَحْسَنُ ٱلْمَوَاهِبِ. He is the best of men, هُوَ خَيْرُ ٱلنَّاسِ. The best of all, بِلَا نَظِيرٍ ـ أَعْلَى ٱلْكُلِّ. To do one's best, جَدَّ ² ـ بَذَلَ جُهْدَهُ ². To have the best of, to overcome, بَهَرَ ـ غَلَبَ.

Bestain, *v.t.* نَقَّطَ ـ عَيَّبَ.

Bestead, *v.t.* To aid, to profit, أَفَادَ ـ نَفَعَ ـ أَعَانَ. To derive advantage from, إِسْتَفَادَ مِن.

Bestial, *a.* Like a beast, وَحْشِيٌّ ـ بَهِيمِيٌّ. Filthy, فَاحِش. Sodomitical, لُوطِيٌّ.

Bestiality, *n.* Brutishness, بَهِيمِيَّة. Sodomy, لَوْط.

Bestialize, *v.t.* صَيَّرَ مِثْلَ ٱلْبَهَائِمِ.

Bestially, *ad.* مِثْلَ ٱلْبَهَائِمِ.

Bestick, *v.t.* شَوَّكَ.

Bestir, *v.t.* To stimulate, حَرَّضَ ـ هَيَّجَ ـ أَنْهَضَ. To — one's self, هَاجَ ـ تَرَعْرَعَ ـ تَحَرَّكَ ـ أَتْعَبَ جُهْدَهُ ـ بَذَلَ هِمَّتَهُ ².

Bestow, *v.t.* مَنَحَ ـ وَهَبَ ل *aor.* يَهَبُ ـ أَنْعَمَ عَلَى ـ ب ـ بَخْشَشَ ـ أَعْطَى ـ مَنَّ عَلَى ² ـ أَكْرَمَ عَلَى ـ ب. To disburse, تَكَلَّفَ ـ أَنْفَقَ ـ بَذَلَ ² ـ صَرَفَ. To — attention upon, to endeavour, إِشْتَغَلَ فِي ـ تَقَيَّدَ فِي ـ سَعَى فِي ـ جَدَّ فِي ². To give one's attention to the affairs of another, تَمَنَّحَ. To — in marriage, زَوَّجَ.

Bestowal, *n.* دَفْع ـ مَنْح ـ وَهْب.

Bestower, *n.* وَاهِب ـ مَنَّاح ـ مَانِح.

Bestowment, *n.* A gift, عَطِيَّة ـ مَوْهَبَة ـ مِنْحَة *pl.* مِنَح.

Bestrew, *v.t.* بَذَرَ ² ـ فَرَشَ ².

Bestride, *v.t.* فَرْشَحَ ـ رَكِبَ.

Bestud, *v.t.* رَصَّعَ.

Bet, *n.* A wager, مُرَاهَنَة ـ مُسَاهَمَة ـ خَطَر *pl.* أَخْطَار ـ تَغَالُب. *See also* Wager, *n.*

Bet, *v.t.* To wager with, رَاهَنَ ـ تَرَاهَنَ مَع ـ عَلَى ـ تَغَالَبَ ـ شَارَطَ. To bet upon, إِقْتَرَعَ عَلَى. To bet with on, خَاطَرَ ـ عَلَى. They laid a bet, وَضَعُوا خَطَرًا. Such an one won the bet, فُلَانٌ أَحْرَزَ ٱلْخَطَرَ. Will you bet me? هَلْ تَتَرَاهَنُ مَعِي ـ أَتُشَارِطُنِي. What will you bet? عَلَى أَيْشٍ ـ بِأَيْشٍ. *See also to* Wager, *v.t.*

Betake, *v. refl.* To — one's self to, to set to, أَخَذَ فِي ² ـ صَمَدَ ² ـ وَاظَبَ عَلَى ـ تَوَلَّعَ ب ـ جَعَلَ ـ لَزِمَ. To be absorbed in, إِنْشَبَكَ ب. To have recourse to, إِعْتَمَدَ ـ تَعَمَّدَ ـ أَوَى إِلَى *aor.* يَأْوِي ـ إِلْتَجَأَ إِلَى ـ قَصَدَ ².

Betel, *n.* The nut, فَوْفَل; the leaf, تَنْبُول.

Bethink, *v t.* To — one's self of, إِفْتَكَرَ فِي ـ تَذَكَّرَ.

Betide, *v.t.* and *i.* To happen, جَآءَ ² *aor.* يَجِيءُ ² ـ حَصَلَ ² ـ حَدَثَ ـ جَرَى ـ صَارَ. To — one, تَاحَ ل *aor.* يَتِيحُ; *also the other verbs with* ل *suffixed.* Woe — thee! ٱلْوَيْلُ لَكَ. May good — thee, طُوبَى لَكَ.

Betime, *ad.* } **Betimes**, } Early, بَاكِرًا ـ بِدَارًا ـ بَدْرِي ـ بَكِير. Seasonably, عَلَى وَقْتٍ ـ لِلْوَقْتِ ـ لِوَقْتِهِ. You went to bed —, بَكَّرْتَ إِلَى ٱلرُّقَادِ.

Betoken, *v.t.* دَلَّ عَلَى ² ـ أَشَارَ إِلَى ـ عَلَّمَ ب ² ـ آلَ إِلَى *aor.* يَؤُولُ.

Betook, *pret. of to* Betake, *q.v.*

Betray, *v.t.* To give into the hands of, أَسْلَمَ ـ سَلَّمَ. To act treacherously towards, خَانَ *aor.* يَخُونُ. To reveal, كَشَفَ ـ أَفْشَى ب. To injure by deceit, غَدَرَ ² ـ غَدَرَ ب ـ خَانَ ب ². To expose, شَهَرَ. To — one's self, in a bad sense, فَضَحَ ـ إِفْتَضَحَ ـ نَفْسَهُ. Thy speech betrayeth thee, لَهْجَتُكَ تُشَهِّرُكَ. The liar betrays himself with his own mouth, بِذَاتِ فَمِهِ يَفْتَضِحُ ٱلْكَذَّابُ.

Betrayal, *n.* } **Betrayment**, } تَسْلِيم. A breach of trust, خِيَانَة ـ غَدْر. Divulging, إِفْشَآء.

Betrayer, *n.* خَوَّان ـ غَادِر ـ خَائِن.

Betroth, *v.t.* خَطَبَ ² ـ شَبَكَ ـ بِٱلزِّيجَةِ.

Betrothment, *n.* خَطْب ـ خِطْبَة.

Better, *a.* and *ad.* أَفْضَلُ ـ أَحْسَنُ ـ أَخْيَرُ ـ أَطْيَبُ ـ أَصْلَحُ ـ أَصْوَبُ. Better in health, أَصَحُّ مِزَاجًا ـ أَشْفَعُ. Better adapted, أَوْلَى ـ أَوْفَقُ. He is — than you, هُوَ أَخْيَرُ مِنْكَ. She is the — of the two women, هِيَ ٱلْخَيْرَةُ مِنَ ٱلْمَرْأَتَيْنِ. This is — than this, هٰذَا خَيْرٌ مِنْ هٰذَا. We are — than you, نَحْنُ لَكُمْ أَفْضَلُ. You had — ..., ٱلْأَوْلَى أَنَّكَ. It is — for you, خَيْرٌ لَكَ. Better than I thought, أَحْسَنُ مِمَّا حَسِبْتُ. He who marries does well, but he who abstains from marriage does —, مَنْ يَتَزَوَّجْ يَفْعَلْ حَسَنًا وَمَنْ لَا يَتَزَوَّجْ يَفْعَلْ خَيْرًا. To get the — of, to overcome, ظَفِرَ عَلَى ـ غَلَبَ. For — for worse, فِي حَالَتَيِ ٱلصَّلَاحِ وَعَدَمِ ٱلصَّلَاحِ ـ فِي ٱلسَّرَّآءِ وَٱلضَّرَّآءِ. It is — that ..., فَٱلْأَوْلَى أَنْ. It is — for you to ..., خَيْرٌ لَكَ أَنْ.

We might have known —, كَانَ مِنَ ٱلْمُمْكِنِ أَنْ نَعْرِفَ أَفْضَلَ مِنْ ذٰلِكَ.

Better, *n.* A superior, أَعْلَى قِيَامًا مِن ـ أَرْفَعُ قَدْرًا مِن.

Better, *v.t.* To improve, حَسَّنَ ـ أَعْدَلَ ـ صَحَّحَ ـ أَصْلَحَ. To promote, رَقَّى ـ قَدَّمَ ـ أَنْجَحَ ـ نَجَّحَ.

Betterment, *n.* تَحْسِين ـ تَعْدِيل ـ تَصْحِيح ـ إِصْلَاح.

Betting, *n.* *See* Bet, *n.* A — book, دَفْتَرٌ لِتَقْيِيدِ ٱلْأَخْطَارِ.

Bettor, *n.* مُخَاطِر ـ مُرَاهِن ـ مُسَاهِم.

Between, *prep.* } فِي ـ مَا بَيْنَ ـ بَيْنَ. He is — me and them,
Betwixt, } هُوَ بَيْنِي وَبَيْنَهُمْ. Betwixt themselves, مَعَ بَعْضِهِمْ. To mediate —, تَوَسَّطَ بَيْنَ. A go-between, وَسِيط. Betwixt and —, بَيْنَ بَيْنَ ـ مُتَوَسِّط. I am in a strait — two, أَنَا مَحْصُورٌ بَيْنَ ٱثْنَيْنِ.

Bevel, *n.* A slant, إِنْحِرَاف ـ حَرْف *pl.* حُرُوف. A mason's rule, مِضْمَار.

Bevel, *v.t.* To slant, حَرَّفَ.

Beverage, *n.* شَرْبَة *pl.* أَشْرِبَة ـ بَلُوع ـ شَرَاب.

Bevy, *n.* A bevy of birds, حَوْمَةٌ مِنَ ٱلطَّيْرِ ـ سِرْبَةٌ مِنَ ٱلطُّيُورِ. A bevy, a crowd, as of people, *etc.*, فَوْج *pl.* أَفْوَاج ـ جَمَاعَة ـ لَبِيكَة ـ جَوْنَة.

Bewail, *v.t.* تَأَسَّفَ عَلَى ـ ² عَجَّ عَلَى ـ ² نَدَبَ ـ ² نَاحَ عَلَى ـ ² بَكَى ـ ² نَحَبَ ـ ² شَفَقَ عَلَى. To — the dead, ² نَدَبَ ـ ² رَثَى ٱلْمَيْتَ ـ ٱلْمَيْتَ. The woman bewailed her (dead) husband, رَثَتِ ٱلْمَرْأَةُ زَوْجَهَا.

Bewailing, *n.* بُكَاء ـ حُزْن ـ تَأَسُّف عَلَى ـ نَحِيب.

Beware, *v.i.* To be cautious of, تَنَبَّهَ عَلَى ـ ² نَذِرَ بِ ـ يَعِي وَعَى *aor.* ـ تَحَفَّظَ مِن ـ إِحْتَرَزَ ـ إِحْتَذَرَ ـ إِحْتَذَرَ مِن. Beware thou! إِيَّاكَ. Beware of the lion, إِيَّاكَ وَٱلْأَسَدَ ـ دُونَكَ وَٱلْأَسَدَ.

Bewilder, *v.t.* To perplex, أَدْهَشَ ـ ² غَرَّ ـ حَيَّرَ ـ ² بَهَتَ ـ وَعَّرَ. To mislead, أَضَلَّ ـ ضَلَّلَ. To be bewildered, تَحَيَّرَ ـ تَوَعَّرَ.

Bewilderment, *n.* دَهْش ـ تَحَيُّر ـ حَيْرَة.

Bewitch, *v.t.* As by sorcery, ² رَقَى ـ ² سَحَرَ. To fascinate, ² نَفَثَ ـ ² فَتَنَ ـ خَبَّرَ ـ ² فَتَنَ.

Bewitching, *a.* Charming, يَسْلُبُ ـ حُلْو ـ بَدِيع ـ حَبَّذَا ـ أَعْجَب.

Bewitchingly, *ad.* Charmingly, بِلَطَافَةٍ ـ بِحَلَاوَةٍ.

Bewitchment, *n.* The act of, أَخْذَة ـ سِحْر; the being charmed, رِبَاط ـ تَحَيُّر.

Bewray, *v.t.* To expose, أَفْشَى بِ ـ ² كَشَفَ ـ ² شَهْرَبَ ـ ² شَهَرَ.

Bey, *n.* بَيْك *pl.* بَيْكَوَات ـ بَيْه *pl.* بَيْهَات.

Beyond, *ad.* and *prep.* Farther off, أَبْعَدُ ـ أَبْعَدُ مِن ـ فَوْقَ ـ هٰذَاكَ ـ وَرَاءَ ـ وَرَاء. On the other side, دُونَ ـ عِبْرَ ـ وَرَاءَ ـ مِنْ وَرَاءِ. Superior to, أَعْلَى مِن ـ فَائِق ـ فَوْقَ. Beyond measure, أَلصَّوْبَ ـ لِلْغَايَةِ. Beyond their power, فَوْقَ طَاقَتِهِمْ. Beyond the Tigris, عِبْرُ ٱلدِّجْلَةِ. Beyond hope, فَوْقَ ٱلْأَمَلِ. To go —, to defraud, ² غَشَّ ـ تَطَاوَلَ عَلَى.

Bezel, *n.* فَصّ *pl.* فُصُوص.

Bezoar, *n.* The stone, فَادْزَهْر ـ مَسُوس ـ تِرْيَاق.

Bias, *n.* Tendency, مَيْل ـ مَمَالَة ـ هَوًى ـ عِطْف ـ تَرْجِيح ـ عَاطِفَة.

Bias, *v.t.* أَمَالَ ـ مَيَّلَ ـ ² حَنَا ـ ² عَطَفَ. To — in favour of, ² عَطَفَ عَلَى ـ ² حَنَا عَلَى. To — against, ² لَفَتَ عَن.

Biassed, *a.* *See* Prejudiced, *a.*

Bib, *n.* نِفَاض.

Bibacious, *a.* شَرَّاب ـ شِرِّيب.

Bibber, *n.* مُحِبُّ ٱلدَّمْعَةِ ـ شِرِّيب.

Bible, *n.* ٱلْكُتُبُ ٱلْمُقَدَّسَةُ ـ ٱلْكُتُبُ ٱلْمُقَدَّسَةُ ـ كِتَابُ ٱلْعَهْدِ ٱلْعَتِيقِ وَٱلْجَدِيدِ ـ ٱلْكُتُبُ ٱلْعَتِيقَةُ وَٱلْجَدِيدَةُ.

Biblical, *a.* مُخْتَصٌّ بِٱلْكُتُبِ ٱلْمُقَدَّسَةِ.

Bibliographer, *n.* نَاسِخ ـ عَارِفٌ بِأَسْمَاءِ ٱلْكُتُبِ وَقِيمَتِهَا.

Bibliographic, *a.* }
Bibliographical, } مُخْتَصٌّ بِمَعْرِفَةِ ٱلْكُتُبِ.

Bibliography, *n.* مَعْرِفَةُ ٱلْكُتُبِ.

Bibliophile, *n.* مُحِبُّ ٱلْكُتُبِ.

Bibliopolist, *n.* كُتُبِيّ *pl.* كُتُبَة ـ صَحَّاف ـ سَفَّار.

Bibliotheke, *n.* قِمَطْرَة ـ خِزَانَةُ كُتُبٍ.

Biblist, *n.* عَالِمٌ بِٱلْكُتُبِ ٱلْمُقَدَّسَةِ.

Bibulous, *a.* شَارِب ـ مُسْتَسْقٍ ـ قَدِم.

Bi-capsular, *a.* ذُو خَرِيطَتَيْنِ.

Bicker, *v.i.* ² شَكِسَ. To — with, سَاهَمَ ـ تَقَاتَلَ مَعَ ـ عَالَجَ ـ نَاقَدَ.

Bickerer, *n.* شَرِس ـ شَرِيس ـ شُكُلِيّ.

Bickering, *n.* نِزَاع ـ مُنَاقَدَة ـ مُشَاجَرَة ـ شَرَاسَة ـ مُعَالَجَة.

Bi-coloured, *a.* ذُو لَوْنَيْنِ.

Bi-corned, *a.* }
Bi-cornous, } ذُو قَرْنَيْنِ.

Bi-corporal, *a.* ذُو جِسْمَيْنِ.

Bi-crural, *a.* ذُو رِجْلَيْنِ.

Bi-cuspid, *a.* ذُو نَصْلَيْنِ.

Bid, *v.t.* To order, أَمَرَ-بِ ـ فَرَضَ عَلَى ـ رَسَمَ عَلَى ـ حَكَمَ عَلَى ـ أَوْعَزَ إِلَى. To ask, to invite, سَأَلَ ـ دَعَا ـ أَعْرَضَ ـ كَلَّفَ ـ عَزَمَ عَلَى. To offer or propose to, عَرَضَ عَلَى ـ عَرَّضَ. To bargain with, شَارَى. To bid adieu to, وَدَّى. To bid up, زَادَ ـ زَيَّدَ. To bid defiance to, to dare, جَسَرَ عَلَى ـ تَجَاسَرَ عَلَى; to disobey, عَصَى عَلَى ـ عَانَدَ; to threaten, هَدَّدَ. To bid fair, وَعَدَ-بِ *aor.* يَعِدُ. You did not do as I bade you, لَمْ تَفْعَلْ كَمَا أَوْعَزْتُ إِلَيْكَ. We bade him to sit down, أَوْعَزْنَا إِلَيْهِ أَنْ يَجْلِسَ.

Bid, *n.* Offer of a price, إِعْرَاضُ سِعْرٍ.

Bidder, *n.* One who bids a higher price, مُزَيِّد.

Bidding, *n.* Direction, order, أَمْرٌ ـ قَوْلٌ ـ وَعْزٌ ـ أَوْعَازٌ ـ حُكْمٌ ـ وَصِيَّةٌ. To do one's —, قَامَ بِأَمْرٍ ـ إِمْتَثَلَ أَمْرًا.

Bide, *v.t.* and *i.* *See to* Abide.

Bidet, *n.* The utensil, طِشْت ـ طَسْت.

Biennial, *a.* Lasting two years, دَائِمٌ مُدَّةَ سَنَتَيْنِ; happening once in two years, وَاقِعٌ كُلَّ غِبِّ عَامَيْنِ ـ وَاقِعٌ مَرَّةً فِي سَنَتَيْنِ.

Bier, *n.* عَرْش ـ نَعْش ـ سَرِير *pl.* سُرُر *and* أَسِرَّة ـ تَابُوت ـ خَشَبَة. A bier with a corpse upon it, جَنَازَة ـ جِنَازَة *pl.* جَنَائِز ـ رَبْع.

Biestings, *n.* لِبَأٌ.

Bifurcated, *a.* ذُو شُعْبَتَيْنِ.

Big, *a.* Great in bulk, جَسِيم ـ عَظِيم ـ ضَخِين ـ كَبِير ـ مَدِيد. Burly, coarse, غَلِيظ. Big with, full of, مَمْلُوءٌ ـ مَمْلُوٌّ ـ فَائِض ـ مَلْآن *fem.* مَلْأَى *and* مَلْآنَة *pl.* مِلَاءٌ. Swollen, وَارِم ـ مَنْفُوخ. Big with child, حُبْلَى *pl.* حَبَالَى ـ حَامِلَة. Big with pride, مُتَكَبِّر. As big as, بِقَدْرِ ـ كُبْرُ. To grow big, كَبُرَ ـ عَظُمَ.

Bigamist, *n.* مُتَزَوِّجٌ بِآمْرَأَتَيْنِ.

Bigamy, *n.* الزِّيجَةُ بِآمْرَأَتَيْنِ.

Biggin, *n.* A cup, قَدَح *pl.* أَقْدَاح.

Bight, *n.* A small bay, خَوْر *pl.* خُؤُور. The bend, as of a rope, حَاوِيَة ـ ثِنْيٌ ـ طِيٌّ *pl.* أَطْوَاءٌ.

Bigness, *n.* كُبْر ـ كِبَر ـ جَسَامَة ـ فُسْحَة. Of the — of a walnut, بِقَدْرِ ٱلْجَوْزَةِ ـ قَدْرُ ٱلْجَوْزَةِ. Bulkiness, coarseness, غِلَاظَة.

Bigot, *n.* }
Bigoted, *a.* } مُتَعَصِّب ـ مُتَنَسِّك ـ مُعَانِد ـ مُتَوَسْوِس.

Bigotry, *n.* تَعَصُّب ـ تَنَسُّك ـ وَسْوَسَة ـ عَصَبِيَّة.

Bijou, *n.* A jewel, جَوْهَرَة *pl.* جَوَاهِرُ. A pretty object, as of art, *etc.*, تُحْفَة *pl.* تُحَف.

Bijoutry, *n.* جَوَاهِرُ ـ صِيغَة.

Bi-lateral, *a.* [illegible]

Bilboes, *n.* Stocks, مِقْطَرَة.

Bile, *n.* The secretion, مِرَّة. The yellow —, الصَّفَار ـ الصَّفْرَاءُ. The black —, السَّوْدَاءُ. The black and the yellow —, المِرَّتَانِ. He has the —, مُرِرَ بِهِ. *See also* Anger, *n.*

Bilge, *n.* The — of a ship, عَرْضُ خُنِّ ٱلْمَرْكَبِ; of a barrel, عَرْضُ بَرْمِيلٍ.

Bilge, *v.i.* إِخْتَلَّ فِي ٱلْقَعْرِ.

Bilge-water, *n.* مَاءُ ٱلْجَمَّةِ ـ مَاءٌ مُسْتَنْقَعٌ فِي خُنِّ ٱلْمَرْكَبِ. The place in a ship where — collects, جَمَّة ـ فِنْطَاس.

Biliary, *a.* مُتَعَلِّقٌ بِٱلصَّفْرَاءِ. The — ducts, مَجَارِي ٱلصَّفْرَاءِ.

Bilingual, *a.* فِي لِسَانَيْنِ ـ ذُو لِسَانَيْنِ.

Bilious, *a.* مَمْرُور ـ مُوَلِّدُ ٱلصَّفْرَاءِ ـ مَصْفُور ـ صَفْرَاوِيٌّ. He is —, مُرِرَ بِهِ.

Bilk, *v.t.* To frustrate, خَيَّبَ. To cheat, مَكَرَ-بِ ـ ضَامَ.

Bill, *n.* The beak of a bird, مِنْقَار *pl.* مَنَاقِيرُ. A hatchet, مِنْجَل *pl.* مَنَاجِلُ ـ عَتَلَة *coll.* عَتَل. An account, حِسَاب ـ قَائِمَةُ حِسَابٍ. An advertisement, إِعْلَان ـ وَرَقَةُ إِعْلَانٍ. A — of exchange, حَوَالَة *pl.* حَوَالَات ـ وَرَقَةُ حَوَالَةٍ ـ بُولِيصَة. A —, project of law, لَائِحَة *pl.* لَوَائِحُ. The government intends to present to parliament a — to ..., الدَّوْلَةُ عَازِمَةٌ عَلَى أَنْ تُقَدِّمَ إِلَى ٱلْمَشُورَةِ لَائِحَةً مَضْمُونُهَا. The bank gives bills on ..., البَنْكُ يُعْطِي حَوَالَاتٍ عَلَى. The bank buys bills on ..., البَنْكُ يَشْتَرِي حَوَالَاتٍ عَلَى.

Bill of divorce, صَكُّ ٱلطَّلَاقِ ـ كِتَابُ طَلَاقٍ.

Bill of fare, تَقْوِيمُ أَشْكَالِ ٱلطَّعَامِ وَأَلْوَانِهَا.

Bill of health, تَذْكِرَةٌ صِحِّيَّةٌ ـ تَذْكِرَةُ قُرَنْتِينَا ـ بَاتَنْتَة. A clean —, بَاتَنْتَةٌ نَظِيفَةٌ. A foul —, بَاتَنْتَةٌ وَسِخَةٌ.

Bill of lading, صَكُّ شَحْنَةٍ *pl.* صُكُوك.

Bill of mortality, دَفْتَرُ ٱلْوَفَاتِ.

Bill of sale, تَقْوِيمُ بَيْعٍ ـ سَنَدُ بَيْعٍ.

Private bill, in parliament, لَائِحَةٌ فَرْدِيَّةٌ.

Public bill, لَائِحَةٌ جُمْهُورِيَّةٌ.

True bill, مَضْبَطَةٌ مُثْبَتَةٌ.

Bill, of exchange, at sight, حَوَالَةٌ تُدْفَعُ عِنْدَ ٱلتَّقْدِيمِ.

Bill, of exchange, on demand, حَوَالَةٌ تُدْفَعُ عِنْدَ ٱلْمُطَالَبَةِ.

Exchequer bill, حَوَالَةُ ٱلْخَزِينَةِ.

To accept a bill, قَبِلَ ٱلْحَوَالَةَ.

To bring in a bill, as in parliament, قَدَّمَ لَائِحَةً.

To cash a bill, صَرَفَ ٱلْحَوَالَةَ.

To discount a bill, أَسْقَطَ ٱلْحَوَالَةَ.

To dishonour a bill, ع = رفَضَ ٱلحَوَالَةَ ـ ما قَبِلَ ٱلتَّحوِيلَ.

To draw a bill upon, حَوَّلَ عَلَى.

To honour a bill, = قَبِلَ ٱلحَوَالَةَ.

To indorse a bill, وَقَّعَ فِي ظَهْرِ ٱلحَوَالَةِ.

To throw out a bill, as in parliament, ع = رفَضَ ٱللَّائحَةَ.

Bill, v.i. To fondle, تَعَانَقَ ـ تَلَاطَفَ ـ تَدَلَّلَ. They billed, of two birds, تَطَاعَمَا ـ طَاعَمَا.

Bill-broker, n. سِمْسَارُ ٱلحَوَالَاتِ.

Billet, n. A note, تَذْكِرَةٌ ـ رُقْعَةٌ ـ كِتَابٌ. A log of wood, قَرْمَةٌ pl. قُرَمٌ ـ حَطَبَةٌ ـ زَنْدُ حَطَبٍ pl. أَزْنَادٌ. An order for lodging, تَذْكِرَةُ سُكْنَى.

Billet, v.t. To lodge soldiers, نَزَّلَ ـ بَوَّأَ (or مَكَّنَ) ٱلعَسَاكِرَ ٱلعَسْكَرَ.

Billet-doux, n. كِتَابٌ مِنْ عَاشِقٍ أَوْ عَاشِقَةٍ.

Billiards, n. طَاوِلَةٌ كَبِيرَةٌ يَلْعَبُونَ عَلَيْهَا بِطَابَاتٍ مِنْ سِنِّ ٱلفِيلِ ـ بِيلَاردُو.

Billing, n. Of birds, تَطَاعُمٌ ـ مُطَاعَمَةٌ. Caressing, مُعَانَقَةٌ ـ تَلَاطُفٌ ـ تَدَلُّلٌ.

Billion, n. بِلْيُونٌ ـ أَلْفُ أَلْفِ أَلْفٍ.

Billman, n. بَلْطَجِي ـ حَامِلُ بَلْطَةٍ.

Billow, n. مَوْجَةٌ coll. مَوْجٌ pl. أَمْوَاجٌ. The dashing of the billows, تَلَاطُمُ ٱلأَمْوَاجِ.

Billowy, a. عَاصِفٌ ـ مَوَّاجٌ.

Bill-sticker, مُلْزِقُ ٱلإِعْلَانَاتِ.

Bimanous, a. ذُو يَدَيْنِ.

Bimensal, a. طَالِعٌ (or وَاقِعٌ) مَرَّةً فِي شَهْرَيْنِ.

Bin, n. أَنْبَارٌ ـ مَاجُورٌ.

Binacle, n. بَيْتُ ٱلإِبْرَةِ ـ خِزَانَةُ ٱلبُوصْلَةِ.

Binary, a. مُضَاعَفٌ.

Bind, v.t. and i. To confine, to tie, = حَزَمَ = حَزَقَ ـ أَوْثَقَ ـ = رَبَطَ ـ ع أَسَرَ ـ أَرْبَطَ ـ ع شَدَّ. To tie on, ع = عَقَدَ ـ عَلَى. To oblige, أَلْزَمَ ـ أَوْجَبَ عَلَى ـ أَلْزَقَ ـ إِلَى ـ عَلَّقَ ـ فِي. To fasten to, أَلْزَقَ ـ إِلَى ـ عَلَّقَ ـ فِي. To dress a wound, دَاوَى ـ أَسَا ٱلجُرْحَ aor. يَأْسُو ـ ضَمَّدَ ٱلجُرْحَ.

To — books, ع = حَبَكَ ٱلكُتُبَ ـ ع شَدَّ ٱلكُتُبَ ـ جَلَّدَ ٱلكُتُبَ.

To —, to fetter, قَيَّدَ. To — the hands behind the back, = كَتَفَ.

To — the hands or feet, ع غَلَّ. To — in bundles, أَحْزَمَ ـ حَزَّمَ.

To prevent, = مَنَعَ ـ أَمْسَكَ. To — on, as clothes, أَلْبَسَ.

To — up the hair, جَمَّرَ ٱلشَّعْرَ. To —, as an apprentice to a master, ع حَطَّ عِنْدَ أُسْتَاذٍ. To —, to make costive, = قَبَضَ ٱلبَطْنَ ـ يَبَّسَ ٱلمِعْدَةَ ـ يَبَّسَ ٱلجَوْفَ. To — over to appear, أَلْزَمَ ـ بِٱلحُضُورِ.

To be bound for, going to, = قَصَدَ ـ = نَوَى. We are bound to thank God always, يَحِقُّ عَلَيْنَا أَنْ نَشْكُرَ ٱللّٰهَ دَائِمًا. To — one's self to, إِلْتَزَمَ بِ.

Binder, n. Of books, مُجَلِّدُ كُتُبٍ ـ حَبَّاكٌ. A bandage, عِصَابَةٌ ـ حُفَاظٌ.

Binding, n. Of a book, تَجْلِيدٌ ـ حَبْكَةٌ ـ شَدَّةٌ.

Bindweed, n. زَمْرُ ٱلسُّلْطَانِ ـ لَفْلَافَةٌ ـ غِيَارَةٌ ـ أَنْسِيسٌ ـ عُلَّيْقٌ.

Binding, a. Obligatory on, مُلْزِمٌ بِ. Legal, valid, شَرْعِيٌّ ـ صَحِيحٌ. To be — on, = حَقَّ عَلَى ـ ع وَجَبَ عَلَى aor. يَجِبُ ـ فَرْضٌ. To make — on, = أَثْبَتَ عَلَى ـ = جَزَمَ عَلَى. Binding, making costive, مُيَبِّسٌ ـ مُقَبِّضٌ.

Binnacle, n. *See* Binacle *n.*

Binocular, a. ذُو عَيْنَيْنِ ـ ذُو مِنْظَرَتَيْنِ. A — telescope, نَظَّارَةٌ ذَاتُ مِنْظَرَتَيْنِ.

Biographer, n. كَاتِبُ سِيَرٍ ـ مُتَرْجِمٌ ـ حَاكٍ ـ نَاقِلٌ pl. نَقَلَةٌ.

Biographic, a. }
Biographical, } نَقْلِيٌّ ـ مُتَعَلِّقٌ بِٱلسِّيَرِ.

Biography, n. تَرْجَمَةٌ pl. تَرَاجِمُ ـ نَقْلٌ ـ سِيرَةٌ pl. سِيَرٌ. A memoir, تَذْكِرَةٌ.

Biology, n. عِلْمُ ٱلحَيَاةِ ـ عِلْمُ أَسْبَابِ ٱلحَيَاةِ وَأَحْوَالِهَا.

Biparous, a. مُتْئِمَةٌ.

Bipartite, a. مُنَصَّفٌ.

Biped, n. ذُو رِجْلَيْنِ ـ ذُو سَاقَيْنِ.

Bipedal, a. *See the preceding.*

Bipennate, a. ذُو جَنَاحَيْنِ.

Bipetalous, a. ذُو وَرَقَتَيْنِ مِنَ ٱلزَّهْرِ.

Bipinnate, a. ذُو وُرَيْقَاتٍ عَلَى جَانِبَيِ ٱلشِّمْرَاخِ.

Birch, n. The tree, بَتُولَا. A rod, عَصًا ـ مِقْرَعَةٌ pl. مَقَارِعُ.

Bird, n. طَيْرٌ pl. طُيُورٌ. A small —, عُصْفُورٌ pl. عَصَافِيرُ. A — of prey, جَارِحَةٌ pl. جَوَارِحُ ـ طَيْرٌ جَارِحٌ. A night —, هَامَةٌ pl. هَامَاتٌ. A — of ill omen, طَيْرُ ٱلعَرَاقِيبِ. A — set up to be shot at, مُجَثَّمَةٌ. A bevy, as of birds, سِرْبَةٌ ـ حَوْمَةٌ. Birds of passage, قَوَاطِعُ. A resort of birds, مَطَارٌ. A land abounding in birds, أَرْضٌ مَطَارَةٌ. A dealer in birds, طُيُورِيٌّ. An early —, one who does his work early, غَاضِرٌ. Birds of a feather flock together, (*prov.*) شَبِيهُ ٱلشَّكْلِ مُنْجَذِبٌ إِلَيْهِ. To kill two birds with one stone, = قَرَنَ بَيْنَ.

Bird-cage, n. قَفَصٌ pl. أَقْفَاصٌ.

Bird-catcher, صَيَّادُ عَصَافِيرَ.

Birdlime, *n.* دِبْق . To catch with —, دَبَقَ ـ ع دَبِق . To be caught with —, تَدَبَّقَ .

Bird's-eye, *a.* A — view, مَنْظَرَةٌ مِنْ صُعُدٍ ـ مَنْظَرَةُ ٱلطَّيْرِ .

Bird's-nest, *n.* عُشٌّ *pl.* عِشَاش ; in a wall, وَكْرَة ; in the ground, أُفْحُوص .

Birdswort, *n.* لعية .

Birth, *n.* Coming into life, وِلَادَة ـ مِيلَاد ـ تَوَلُّد ـ طُلُوع . Lineage, نَسْل ـ جِنْس ـ نَسَب ـ أَصْل ـ بَيْت ـ قَبِيلَة . The beginning of any thing, مَبْدأ ـ إِبْتِدَآء ـ مَطْلَع ـ ظُهُور . Of noble —, شَرِيفُ ٱلْأَصْلِ ـ مِنْ بَيْتٍ أَكَابِر . Of ignoble —, دَنِيُّ ٱلْأَصْلِ . Blind from his —, أَكْمَهُ ـ أَعْمَى مُنْذُ وُلِدَ . To give — to, أَوْلَدَ . To travail in —, ع مَخَضَ .

Birth-day, *n.* مَوْلِد ـ مِيلَاد .

Birth-place, *n.* مَوْلِد ـ وَطَن *pl.* أَوْطَان .

Birthright, *n.* بَكُورِيَّة ـ حُقُوقُ ٱلْوَلَدِ ٱلْأَكْبَرِ فِي ٱلْعُمْرِ ـ حَقُّ ٱلْبَكُورِيَّةِ .

Biscuit, *n.* بَقْسَماط ; sweet —, كَعْك ـ مَعْمُول ـ قَرْقُوشَةٌ بِسُكَّرٍ ـ غُرَيْبَة .

Bisect, *v.t.* نَصَّفَ .

Bisection, *n.* تَنْصِيف .

Bisexual, *a.* ذُو جِنْسَيْنِ مُذَكَّرٌ وَمُؤَنَّثٌ .

Bishop, *n.* أُسْقُف *pl.* أَسَاقِفَة . To be made —, سُقِّفَ ـ تَسَقَّفَ .

Bishopric, *n.* أُسْقُفِيَّة ـ أَسْقَفِ ـ أَبْرَشِيَّةُ .

Bishopsweed, *n.* نانخواه ـ نانخَة ـ أُمُّ ٱلْحَلَالِ .

Bismuth, *n.* مَرْقَشِيطَةُ ٱلْقَصْدِيرِ ـ بِسْمُوت .

Bison, *n.* بَقَرٌ وَحْشِيٌّ مَوْجُودٌ فِي بِلَادِ أَمِيرِكا .

Bissextile, *a.* A — year, سَنَةٌ كَبِيسَةٌ .

Bistoury, *n.* مِشْرَاط ـ مِشْرَطَة *pl.* مَشَارِطُ .

Bisulcous, *a.* ذُو ظُلُوفٍ .

Bit, *n.* Of a bridle, فَكٌّ ـ لِجام . A small piece, حِتَّة *pl.* حِتَت ـ قِطْعَة *pl.* قِطَع ـ قَلِيل ـ جُزْء *pl.* أَجْزَآء . A bit of bread, a mouthful, لُقْمَة *pl.* لُقَم . A bit of cloth, a rag, رُقْعَة *pl.* رِقَاع ـ خِرْقَة *pl.* خِرَق . Not a bit, ولَا نُتْفَةٌ ـ قَطْعًا ـ لا شَيْءَ . He did not get a bit better, لَمْ يَسْتَفِدْ شَيْئًا . A borer, مِثْقَب . Bit by bit, شَيْئًا فَشَيْئًا .

Bit, *v.t.* To put the bit into an animal's mouth, صَفَرَ ٱلدَّابَّةَ .

Bitch, *n.* كَلْبَة *pl.* كَلْبَات . A vile woman, إِمْرَأَةٌ كَلْبَةٌ ـ عَاهِرَة .

Bite, *v.t.* As with the teeth, ع ضَرَسَ ـ ع لَعَسَ ـ ع عَضَّ بِ . To bite, as a horse, ع عَذَمَ ـ ع عَضَّ ; as insects, ع بَعَضَ ; as reptiles, [illegible] ; as a flea, ع قَرَصَ ; as frost, ع ضَرَبَ ـ أَصَابَ ; as fish at a bait, ع طَعِمَ . To hold, ع مَسَكَ بِ ـ ع ضَبَطَ . To reproach, عَيَّرَ عَلَى ـ ع قَذَفَ بِ . To bite one another, they bit one another, عَاضُّوا . To hold out something for one to bite, أَعَضَّ . To bite the dust, ع مَاتَ ـ عَضَّ ٱلثَّرَيَآءَ . To bite the fingers with regret, ع أَكَلَ كَفَّيْهِ نَدَمًا . To bite, for testing the hardness of any thing, ع عَجَمَ .

Bite, *n.* عَضَّ ـ لَعْسَة ـ عَضِيض ; of an insect, بَعْض ; of a flea, قَرْصَة ; of a reptile, نَهْسَة ـ نَهْشَة ; of a fish at a bait, طَعْم . A trick, غِشّ ـ خِدْعَة ـ حِيلَة .

Biter, *n.* لَعَّاس . A sharper, مَكَّار ـ حُوَّلٌ قُلَّبٌ .

Biting, *a.* عَذُوم . Pungent, حَرِيف ـ حَاذِق . Sarcastic, سَلِيط ـ نَقِر . Sharp, severe, حَاذِق ـ شَدِيد . A — horse, فَرَسٌ عَضُوض .

Biting, *n.* The act or fault of —, عَضَاض .

Bitingly, *ad.* Sarcastically, بِنَقْرٍ ـ بِسَلَاطَةٍ .

Bittacle, *n.* *See* Binacle, *n.*

Bitter, *a.* مُرٌّ *pl.* أَمْرَار ـ عَلْقَم . Pungent, حَاذِق ـ حَادّ . Bitter, of water, عُقّ ـ عُقَاق ـ زُعَاق . Saddening, مُؤْلِم ـ مُغِمّ ـ مُحْزِن . Sad, صَعْب ـ كَرِيب . Severe, قَاسٍ ـ صَارِم ـ عَنِيف . To be or make —, أَمَرَّ . To be — to, ع مَرَّ عَلَى . Made —, مُمَرّ . To be — to bear, ع صَعُبَ . The matter was — to him, إِسْتَصْعَبَ ٱلْأَمْرُ عَلَيْهِ .

Bitterish, *a.* مُرٌّ بَعْضَ ٱلْمَرَارَةِ ـ يَضْرِبُ إِلَى ٱلْمَرَارَةِ .

Bitterly, *ad.* Severely, عَنْفًا ـ قَسَاوَةً . To act — towards, ع مَرَّ عَلَى .

Bittern, *n.* نَوْعٌ مِنْ طَيْرِ ٱلْمَآءِ .

Bitterness, *n.* مَرَارَة . Malice, بُغْض ـ حِقْد . Severity, عُنْف ـ شِدَّة ـ قَسَاوَة ـ قَهْر . Sorrow, كَرْب ـ حُزْن ـ غَمّ . Keenness, حِدَّة .

Bitters, *n.* نَقُوعٌ مِنْ بَعْضِ ٱلنَّبَاتَاتِ ٱلْمُرَّةِ . An appetizer drink, مُرِّيٌّ (*vulg.* مُرِّي).

Bittervetch, *n.* كرسنة ـ كشني .

Bitterwort, *n.* جانصيان ـ جنسيانة .

Bitumen, *n.* قار ـ قَفْر ـ قِير . The — of Judea, حُمَر . To plaster with —, قَيَّرَ . A seller or collector of —, قَيَّار .

Bituminous, *a.* قَارِيّ ـ قِيرِيّ .

Bivalve, *a.* Having two valves, as a shell, صَدَفٌ مُزَوَّج .

Bivalvular, *a.* مُزَوَّجُ ٱلصَّدَفِ .

Bivouac, *n.* An open encampment of an army, مُعَسْكَرٌ بِلَا خِيَمٍ .

Bivouac, *v.t.* Of an army; they bivouacked, تَعَسْكَرُوا مِنْ غَيْرِ خِيَمٍ .

Bizarre, *a.* Fantastic, عَجِيب ـ غَرِيب . Whimsical, مُلْتَوٍ ـ مُتَلَوِّن ـ مُتَخَيِّل .

Blab, *v.t.* and *i.* To divulge, شَهَّرَ — أَشْهَرَ — أَفْشَى بِ — أَشَاعَ بِ. To babble, لَغَطَ — بَقَّ — أَكْثَرَ ٱلْقَوْلَ.

Blab, *n.* Tattle, قَالٌ وَقِيلٌ — بَقٌّ. A tell-tale, نَقَّالٌ — فِتَنِيٌّ.

Blabber, *n.* Babbler, بَقَّاقٌ — قَوَّالٌ. *See also* Blab, *n.*

Black, *a.* In colour, فَحِيمٌ — سَاحِمٌ — أَسْحَمُ — يَحْمُومٌ — حَالِكٌ — أَسْوَدُ *fem.* سَوْدَآءُ *pl.* سُودٌ; of animals, أَدْهَمُ *fem.* دَهْمَآءُ *pl.* دُهْمٌ. Very black, أَسْوَدُ قَاتِمٌ — أَسْوَدُ فَاحِمٌ. Dark, وَعِقٌ — مُعْتِمٌ — مُظْلِمٌ. Wicked, رَدِيٌّ — شِرِّيرٌ — شَنِيعٌ. Sullen, عَنِيفٌ — نَحِسٌ. Gloomy, doleful, كَرِيبٌ. To look — upon, نَظَرَ إِلَى- بِعَيْنِ ٱلْبُغْضِ. The — art, ٱلسِّحْرُ. Black weather, طَقْسٌ مُعَبِّسٌ — دُنْيَا مُغَيِّمَةٌ. To be —, فَحُمَ — إِسْوَدَّ.

Black, *n.* A negro, أَسْوَدُ *pl.* سُودٌ — أَسْوَدُ *pl.* سُودَانٌ. Black clothes, سَوَادٌ. The — of the eye, حَدَقَةُ ٱلْعَيْنِ.

Black, *v.t.* }
Blacken, } To make —, سَخَّمَ — فَحَّمَ — سَوَّدَ; as with charcoal, حَمَّمَ. To darken, عَتَّمَ. To —, as of boots, دَهَنَ — مَسَحَ. To defame, نَقَرَ — هَتَكَ — نَمَّ عَلَى — سَوَّدَ عِرْضَ. To become —, سَخِمَ — فَحُمَ — إِسْوَادَّ — إِسْوَدَّ.

Blackamoor, *n.* أَسْوَدُ *pl.* سُودَانٌ.

Blackball, *n.* A negative ball in voting, كُرَيَّةٌ سَوْدَآءُ تَدُلُّ عَلَى ٱلرَّفْضِ فِي ٱلْإِنْتِخَابِ. *See also* Ballot, *n.*

Blackball, *v.t.* رَفَضَ- فِي ٱلْإِنْتِخَابِ بِدَفْعِ ٱلْكُرَيَّةِ ٱلسَّوْدَآءِ. *See also to* Ballot, *v.t.*

Blackberry, *n.* عُلَّيْقٌ — تُوتٌ بَرِّيٌّ.

Blackbird, *n.* شُحْرُورٌ *pl.* شَحَارِيرُ.

Blackboard, *n.* لَوْحَةٌ — تَخْتَةُ ٱلدَّرْسِ.

Black-cattle, *n.* بَقَرٌ — مَوَاشِي.

Black-cock, *n.* دِيكٌ بَرِّيٌّ *pl.* دُيُوكٌ بَرِّيَّةٌ.

Blacken, *v.t.* and *i.* *See under to* Black, *v.t.*

Blackguard, *n.* رَذِيلٌ *pl.* أَرْذَالٌ — خَبِيثٌ — مَعْكُوسٌ — فَلَاتِيٌّ. *See also* Scoundrel, *n.*

Blackguardism, *n.* رَذَالَةٌ — دَعَرٌ — دِعَارَةٌ — قِلَّةُ أَدَبٍ — خُبْثٌ.

Blacking, *n.* For shoes, دِهَانٌ لِلْمَدَاسِ.

Blackish, *a.* سُوَيْدٌ — فَاحِمٌ — مُسْوَدٌّ — مَائِلٌ إِلَى ٱلسَّوَادِ — يَضْرِبُ إِلَى ٱلسَّوَادِ.

Blacklead, *n.* For blacking grates, دِهَانٌ لِلْكَوَانِينِ. Plumbago, أُسْرُبٌ. A — pencil, قَلَمُ رَصَاصٍ *pl.* أَقْلَامٌ.

Black-livered, *a.* (A term applied to an enemy), أَسْوَدُ ٱلْكَبِدِ *pl.* سُودُ ٱلْأَكْبَادِ.

Blackleg, *n.* لَعَّابٌ — لَعِيبٌ — قِمَرَانِيٌّ — قِمَارْبَازٌ,

Blackly, *ad.* Darkly, ظُلْمَةً — ظَلَامًا — عَتْمًا. Atrociously, تَسَخُّمًا — بِفَحَاشَةٍ — فَحَاشَةً.

Blackmail, *n.* غَفَرٌ — خَرَاجٌ زُورٌ.

Blackness, *n.* حَلَكٌ — حُلْكَةٌ — سُخَامٌ — سُخْمَةٌ — سَوَادٌ; of animals, دُهْمَةٌ. Darkness, ظَلَامٌ — ظُلْمَةٌ — عَتَمَةٌ. Atrociousness, رَدَآءَةٌ — خُبْثٌ — شِدَّةٌ.

Black-pudding, *n.* مُسَوَّدٌ.

Black-rod, *n.* حَامِلُ ٱلْعَصَا فِي دِيوَانِ ٱلْمَشُورَةِ.

Blacksmith, *n.* قَيْنٌ — حَدَّادٌ *pl.* حَدَّادُونَ. The art of the —, حِدَادَةٌ.

Blackwood, *n.* سَاجٌ.

Bladder, *n.* Of the body, مَثَانَةٌ — مَبْوَلَةٌ. An ox —, قُوفٌ. A gall —, مَرَارَةٌ. A pustule, بُقَيْبِقَةٌ. Having a pain in the —, مَثِنٌ — أَمْثَنُ.

Blade, *n.* As of grass, نَبْتٌ *coll.* نَبَاتٌ — وَرَقَةُ حَشِيشٍ *pl.* أَوْرَاقٌ; as of a sword, نَصْلٌ *pl.* نِصَالٌ — شَمْشِيرٌ. A gay fellow, صَغْمٌ — بَطِرٌ — خَلِيعُ ٱلْعِذَارِ — غَنْدُورٌ. The broad part of an oar, عَنْفَةُ ٱلْمِقْذَافِ. A — of corn, عَصْفٌ *or* عُصُوفٌ *pl.* عَصْفَةٌ.

Blade-bone, *n.* كِتْفٌ *pl.* أَكْتَافٌ.

Bladed, *a.* Having blades, ذُو نِصَالٍ.

Blain, *n.* بُقَيْبِقَةٌ — حَبَّةٌ *coll.* حَبٌّ — دُمَّلٌ *pl.* دَمَامِلُ — بَثْرَةٌ *pl.* بَثَرَاتٌ.

Blamable, *a.* يُلَامُ — عَلَيْهِ مَلَامٌ — مُسْتَحِقُّ ٱلْمَلَامِ — مُلِيمٌ.

Blamableness, *n.* مُلَامٌ — ذَمٌّ — لَوْمَةٌ — مَلَامَةٌ.

Blamably, *ad.* بِمَلَامَةٍ — بِوَجْهٍ يَسْتَحِقُّ ٱللَّوْمَ.

Blame, *n.* Fault, ثَلْبٌ — خَطَآءٌ — لَوْمَةٌ — لَامَةٌ — ذَنْبٌ. Censure, عَذْلٌ — لَوْمٌ — مَلَامَةٌ — مَلَامٌ — ذَمٌّ. A cause of blame, مَذَمَّةٌ.

Blame, *v.t.* عَذَلَ — ثَلَبَ — ذَأَمَ — ذَمَّ — طَعَنَ بِ — لَامَ- عَلَى — أَلْقَى ٱللَّوْمَ عَلَى. To lay one's self open to — to, إِسْتَلَامَ إِلَى. To reproach one with or for, عَيَّبَ عَلَى- بِ — عَيَّرَ- بِ.

Blamed, *part.* ثَلِبٌ — مَذْؤُومٌ — مَلُومٌ — ذَمِيمٌ. He was to be —, was blame-worthy, كَانَ مَلُومًا. To blame one's self, إِعْتَذَلَ — تَعَذَّلَ.

Blameful, *a.* لَامٌ — مُلِيمٌ.

Blameless, *a.* مُوَرَّكٌ — بَرِيٌّ *fem.* بَرِيَّةٌ *pl. masc.* بَرِيئُونَ *pl. fem.* بَرِيَّاتٌ — لَا إِثْمَ عَلَى — بِغَيْرِ لَوْمٍ — بِغَيْرِ عَيْبٍ — لَا يُلَامُ — بِلَا لَوْمٍ.

Blamelessly, *ad.* مِنْ غَيْرِ عَيْبٍ — بِلَا لَوْمٍ — بِبَرَآءَةٍ.

Blamelessness, *n.* بَرَآءَةٌ — بُرُوٌّ — عِصْمَةٌ.

Blameworthiness, *n.* لَامَةٌ — لَوْمَةٌ.

Blameworthy, *a.* يُلَامُ — عَلَيْهِ مَلَامٌ — مُسْتَحِقُّ ٱلْمَلَامِ — مُلِيمٌ.

Blanch, *v.t.* To whiten, بَيَّضَ — قَصَرَ ². To — almonds, قَشَّرَ اللَّوزَ. To obliterate, نَسَخَ ² — مَحَى — مَحَا ².

Blanched, *a.* مَقْصُور — مُبَيَّض.

Bland, *a.* مَلِق — لَيِّن — لَطِيف — حَلِيم — أَنِيس — وَدِيع — شَلَبِيّ.

Blandish, *v.t.* دَاجَنَ — دَارَى — مَسَّحَ — مَالَقَ — تَلَيَّنَ لِ — طَبْطَبَ لِ — لَاطَفَ — دَلَّلَ — حَايَلَ ; of a woman, هَنَّدَ. To be blandished, تَمَلَّقَ.

Blandisher, *n.* مَلَّاق.

Blandishment, *n.* مَلَق — تَمَلُّق — مُلَاطَفَة — تَدَلُّل ; of a woman, تَهْنِيد. To use —, to cajole, حَاوَلَ.

Blandness, *n.* لِيَنَة — لَيَان — مُدَارَاة — مُدَاجَنَة — لَطَافَة — حِلْم — شَلَبَنَة.

Blank, *a.* White, أَبْيَض. Void, خَالٍ — فَارِغ. Not written upon, عَلَى بَيَاضٍ. Pale, أَصْفَر. To look —, be taken aback, خَجِلَ — تَخَبَّلَ — تَحَيَّرَ. They fired guns with — cartridge, أَطْلَقُوا ٱلْمَدَافِعَ مِنْ دُونِ كُلَلٍ.

Blank, *n.* A void space, فَرَاغ. An unwritten paper, بَيَاض ². A lot by which nothing is gained, خُسْرَان. Disappointment, عَنَاقَة — خَيْبَة. To sign in —, (or) وَقَّعَ — خَتَمَ — عَلَى بَيَاضٍ.

Blanket, *n.* حِرَام *pl.* أَحْرَام — لِحَاف *pl.* لُحُف.

Blankly, *ad.* With astonishment, مُتَحَيِّرًا — بِتَحَيُّرٍ.

Blankness, *n.* Paleness, إِصْفِرَار — سَوَاد. Astonishment, تَحَيُّر.

Blarney, *n.* *See* Blandishment, *n.*

Blaspheme, *v.t.* أَكْفَرَ — جَدَّفَ عَلَى — إِفْتَرَى عَلَى — كَفَرَ بِ ². To swear, سَبَّ ². To curse, شَتَمَ ² ².

Blasphemer, *n.* مُجَدِّف — كَافِر — مُفْتَرٍ. A swearer, سِبّ — حَلَّاف — وَسَبّ.

Blasphemous, *a.* يَتَضَمَّنُ ٱلتَّجْدِيفَ. Blasphemous speech, كَلَامٌ تَجْدِيفٌ.

Blasphemously, *ad.* بِٱفْتِرَآءٍ — تَجْدِيفًا — بِتَجْدِيفٍ.

Blasphemy, *n.* تَجْدِيف — كُفْر — إِفْتِرَآء. Swearing, حَلْف — سَبّ.

Blast, *n.* Of wind, عَصْفَة — رِيحَة — نَفْحَة — هَبَّة — هَبْوَة. Sound, as of an instrument, صَوْت — حِسّ. A blight, حَرِيق — يَرَقَان — صِرّ — صِرَّة. An explosion, نَوْرَة — طَلْقَة.

Blast, *v.t.* To destroy, أَهْلَكَ. To blight, wither, جَفَّ ² — أَحْرَقَ — ضَرَبَ ² — نَشَّفَ — أَذْبَلَ. To injure, ضَرَّ ² — أَضَرَّ. To be blasted, blighted, إِحْتَرَقَ. To be struck by, ضُرِبَ بِ. To — one's character, عَكَسَ ² — لَلَّمَ صِيتَهُ — وَشَى بِ *aor.* يَشِي — عَكَسَ مَقْصُودَ ². To — one's projects, خَيَّبَ — جَرَّسَ بِ. To — rocks, فَقَأَ ٱلْحِجَارَةَ ² — فَزَرَ ٱلصُّخُورَ — خَرَّبَ شُغَلَ — كَسَّرَ ٱلصُّخُورَ.

Blasting, *n.* *See* Blast, *n.*

Blatant, *a.* Noisy, صَيِّت — صَائِت.

Blaze, *v.i.* and *t.* إِحْتَدَمَ — جَحَمَ ² — تَلَظَّى — أَلْظَى — أَجَّ ² — أَشْهَرَ — إِلْتَهَبَ — إِضْطَرَمَ. To — abroad, to publish, أَشَاعَ بِ — نَادَى بِ — شَهَرَ بِ ². A blazing fire, نَارٌ مُشْتَعِلَةٌ. The fire blazed, جَحَمَتِ ٱلنَّارُ.

Blaze, *n.* As of fire, إِشْتِعَال — شُعْلَة — لَهَبَان — لَهَاب جَحْمَة. Publication, خَبَر — إِعْلَان — إِشَاعَة — إِشْهَار — إِضْطِرَام. A white spot on a horse's forehead, غُرَّة *pl.* غُرَر — شَادِخَة — مُبَرْقِعَة. In a —, لَهَبَان. A horse with a —, فَرَسٌ أَغَرٌّ مُبَرْقَعٌ.

Blazing-star, *n.* نَجْمَةٌ بِذَنَبٍ. *See also* Comet, *n.*

Blazon, *v.t.* To explain the terms on armorial bearings, فَسَّرَ مَضْمُونَ ٱلْإِصْطِلَاحَاتِ ٱلْمُسْتَعْمَلَةِ فِي عِلْمِ بَيَانِ ٱلْآرْمَا. To adorn, زَيَّنَ — وَشَّحَ. To display, جَلَا ² — أَظْهَرَ. To publish, أَشَاعَ بِ — أَشْهَرَ. *See also under* Arms, *n.*

Blazonry, *n.* The art of describing coats of arms, عِلْمُ بَيَانِ ٱلصُّوَرِ وَٱلْإِصْطِلَاحَاتِ ٱلْمُسْتَعْمَلَةِ فِي تَرْقِيمِ ٱلْآرْمَا.

Bleach, *v.t.* and *i.* To whiten, make white, قَصَرَ ² — بَيَّضَ. To grow white, إِبْيَضَّ.

Bleacher, *n.* مُبَيِّض — قَصَّار — غَسَّال — حَوَارِيّ.

Bleachery, *n.* مَغْسَلَة — قِصَارَة.

Bleak, *a.* Cold, مُصَقِّع — قَارِس — صِرّ — بَارِد. To be —, إِزْمَهَرَّ.

Bleakly, *ad.* بِزَمْهَرِيرٍ — بِصِرَّةٍ — صِرَّةً.

Bleakness, *n.* صِرَّة — قَرْس — بَرْد — زَمْهَرِير.

Blear-eyed, *a.* أَرْمَدُ — أَغْمَصُ. To be —, رَمِدَ ².

Bleat, *n.* }
Bleating, } نُغَاء — نَغْوَة — يُعَار — نُعَاق — نَعِيق — نَعَقَان — نُوَاج — مَعْمَعَة.

Bleat, *v. int.* مَعْمَعَ — نَغَى ² — يَيْعَرُ *aor.* يَعِرَ. To make to —, أَنْغَى.

Bled, *a.* A person —, فَصِيد — مَفْصُود.

Bleed, *v.t.* and *i.* To make to —, as by a blow, دَمَّى. To open a vein, فَصَدَ ² — إِفْتَصَدَ — أَخَذَ دَمًا مِن ². To lose blood, نَفَحَ ² — غَذَى — فَاحَ بِ ² — دَمِيَ ² : it bled, (*fem.*) دَمِيَت. To drop, as of blood, نَقَطَ — دَمَعَ ². To drop, to distil, as gum from a tree, دَمَعَ ² — قَطَرَ ².

Bleeder, *n.* مَلَّاق — حَجَّام — فَصَّاد.

Bleeding, *n.* The act of opening a vein, فِصَادَة ــ فِصَاد ــ فَصْد. A flow of blood, تَغْذِيَة.

Blemish, *v.t.* To tarnish, بَقَّعَ ــ طَبَّعَ ــ عَيَّبَ. To defame, أَعَارَ ــ عَوَّرَ ــ ثَلَمَ صِيتَ ــ فَضَحَ ــ هَتَكَ ــ عَيَّبَ. To mar, عَوَّرَ.

Blemish, *n.* A stain, defect, عَيْب *pl.* عُيُوب ــ عَيْبَة ــ طَبْعَة ــ عَوْرَة ــ بُقْعَة ــ نَقْص ــ عَوَر ــ عَوَار. A disgrace, عَيْب ــ عار ــ جِنَايَة ــ مَسَبَّة ــ مَعَرَّة ــ ذَنْب.

Blench, *v.i.* To shrink from, فَلَطَ عَن ــ جَبَأَ عَن. *See also under to* Shrink, *v.i.*

Blend, *v.t.* To mix, خَلَطَ ــ خَلَّطَ ــ مَزَجَ ــ عَرْقَلَ. To be blended, إِخْتَلَطَ ــ إِخْتَلَطَ. To —, of a sound, إِنْحَشَى. A sound became blended in a sound, إِنْحَشَى صَوْتٌ فِي صَوْتٍ.

Bless, *v.t.* To make happy, بَارَكَ ــ هَنَّأَ ــ أَسْعَدَ ــ دَعَا لِ. To consecrate, قَدَّسَ ــ كَرَّسَ. To glorify, حَمِدَ ــ شَكَرَ لِ. To make to prosper, أَسْعَدَ ــ وَفَّقَ ــ أَنْجَحَ. God — thee, بَارَكَ اللّٰهُ عَلَيْكَ *or* فِيكَ.

Blessed, *a.* Happy, مُبَارَك ــ سَعِيد ــ طُوبَى. Said of one who is departed and to whom it is hoped mercy has been shown, المَرْحُوم. The —, the happy departed, الخَالِدُونَ. Blessed be God! تَبَارَكَ اللّٰهُ. It is more — to give than to receive, العِطَآءُ أَبْرَكُ مِنَ الأَخْذِ.

Blessedness, *n.* سَعَادَة ــ سَعْد ــ طُوبَى ــ حَظّ ــ عِزّ ــ نَعِيم ــ بَرَكَة. Eternal —, سَعَادَة أَبَدِيَّة ــ خُلْد ــ خُلُود.

Blessing, *n.* Invocation of happiness, دُعَآء ــ بَرَكَة. Blessings, benefits, بَرَكَة ــ نِعَم ــ خَيْرَات. Consecration, تَكْرِيس ــ تَقْدِيس. To ask a — over food, بَرَّكَ عَلَى الطَّعَام. That was due to God's —, كَانَ ذٰلِكَ خَيْرَة مِنَ اللّٰهِ.

Blight, *n.* آفَة ــ يَرَقَان.

Blight, *v.t.* *See to* Blast, *v.t.*

Blighted, *a.* Blasted, مَأْرُوق ــ مَيْرُوق. Frustrated, مَخْذُول ــ مُخَيَّب.

Blind, *a.* Without sight, ضَرِير *pl.* أَضِرَّآءُ ــ أَكْمَه ــ أَعْمَى *pl.* عُمْي *fem.* عَمْيَآءُ. Nearly —, أَمْلَح. Blind of an eye, أَعْوَر *fem.* عَوْرَآءُ *pl.* عُور *and* عُورَان *and* عِيرَان ــ أَبُو فَرْدِ عَيْنٍ. Ignorant, جَاهِل *pl.* جُهَّال ــ غَبِيّ ــ مُعَمًّى. Obscure, خَفِيّ ــ غَلِق. A — alley, زُقَاق سَدّ ــ سِكَّة رِبْح ــ غَيْر مُنْفِذٍ. He was — to his rights, عَمِيَ عَنْ حَقِّهِ *aor.* يَعْمَى. How — his mind is, مَا أَعْمَى قَلْبَهُ. To be —, عَمِيَ ــ تَعَمَّى *aor.* يَعْمَى. His two eyes became —, عَمِيَتَا عَيْنَاهُ. To be — in one eye, أَعْوَرَ ــ أَعْوَارَّ. He is — in one eye, عَوِرَتْ عَيْنُهُ. To make — in one eye, أَعْوَرَ ــ عَوَّرَ. To feign to be —, تَعَامَى.

Blind, *v.t.* To deprive of sight, عَمَّى ــ أَعْمَى. To dazzle, أَخَذَ بَصَرَ ــ خَطَفَ بَصَرَ ــ غَبَّسَ العَيْنَ. To deceive, مَكَرَ بِ ــ غَشَّ. Not to perceive, عَمِيَ عَن. To — a man's heart, خَتَمَ عَلَى قَلْبِ. To darken the understanding, أَبْهَلَ ــ غَرَّ.

Blind, *n.* Something to hinder the sight, سِتْر ــ غِطَآء. A pretext, حِيلَة ــ صُورَة ــ حُجَّة ــ مَكْر. A window —, سِتْر *pl.* سُتُور ــ شَمْسِيَّة.

Blindfold, *v.t.* عَصَبَ عَيْنَيْهِ ــ رَبَطَ عَيْنَيْهِ.

Blindly, *ad.* عَلَى العَمَى ــ عَمًا ــ مِثْلَ العُمْيَانِ. Thoughtlessly, مِنْ غَيْرِ مُبَالَاةٍ. He embarked in an affair —, رَكِبَ أَمْرًا عَلَى العَمَى.

Blindman's-buff, *n.* The game, طَقْطَقْ شَعِيرَكْ يَا دَبُّور.

Blindness, *n.* Deprivation of sight, عَمَى البَصَرِ ــ عَمًى. Ignorance, جَهْل ــ جَهَالَة ــ عَدَمُ إِدْرَاكٍ ــ غَبَاوَة. God cast a — over his sight, غَشَّى اللّٰهُ عَلَى بَصَرِهِ. To feign — or ignorance, تَعَامَى.

Blindside, *n.* Weakness, رَكْرَكَة ــ رُكُوكَة ــ رَكَاكَة ــ لِينُ جَانِبٍ ــ رِقَّةُ جَانِبٍ. To get on the — of one, قَوِيَ عَلَى رِقَّةِ جَانِبِهِ.

Blink, *v.i.* and *t.* To wink with the eyes, خَزَّرَ عَيْنَيْهِ ــ تَحَاوَصَ ــ بَرْقَقَ عَيْنَيْهِ ــ غَمَّضَ عَيْنَيْهِ ــ حَشَّفَ عَيْنَهُ. To — at, إِنْتَهَى عَن ــ إِلَى. To be blind to, عَمِيَ عَن. To shun, تَجَافَى عَن.

Blink, *n.* تَحْشِيف. A glance, لَحْظَة.

Blinkard, *n.* أَعْمَش *fem.* عَمْشَآءُ ــ أَعْشَى *fem.* عَشْوَآءُ ــ أَجْهَر *fem.* جَهْرَآءُ ــ أَغْمَص *fem.* غَمْصَآءُ.

Blinkers, *n.* غِمَامَة *pl.* غَمَائِم ــ رَفْرُوف *pl.* رَفَارِيف.

Bliss, *n.* *See* Blessedness, *n.*

Blissful, *a.* طُوبَانِيّ ــ نَعِيم ــ سَعِيد. *See also* Blessed, *a.*

Blister, *n.* A watery rising of the skin, مَجْلَة ــ مَجَل *pl.* مِجَال ــ بَقْبِيقَة. A pustule, بَثْر *pl.* بُثُور ــ دُمَّل *pl.* دَمَامِل. A blistering plaster, لَزْقَة *or* لَزِقَة ــ حَرَّاقَة.

Blister, *v.t.* and *i.* To raise in blisters, بَثَّرَ ــ طَلَّعَ دَمَامِل ــ بَقْبَقَ. To affix a — on, حَطَّ لَزْقَةً عَلَى ــ وَضَعَ حَرَّاقَةً عَلَى. To rise in blisters, بَثَرَ ــ مَجَلَ ــ أَمْجَلَ ــ تَبَقْبَقَ.

Blite, *n.* The plant, البَقْلَةُ اليَمَانِيَّةُ.

Blithe, *a.} Blithesome, } بَشُوش ــ بَجْبُوح ــ بَطِر ــ مَسْرُور ــ هَشّ بَشّ ــ خَلِيع *pl.* خُلَعَآءُ ــ مَبْسُوط.

Blithely, *ad.* بِهَشٍّ وَبَشٍّ ــ بِانْشِرَاحِ الصَّدْرِ ــ بِسُرُورٍ ــ بِفَرَحٍ.

Blithesomeness, *n.* إِنْشِرَاحٌ ـ كَيْف ـ بَشَاشَة ـ بَسْط ـ سُرُور ٱلصَّدْرِ.

Bloat, *v.t.* and *i.* To inflate, نَفَخَ ـ وَرَّمَ. To grow turgid, إِنْتَفَخَ ـ تَوَرَّمَ.

Bloated, *a.* Swollen, مُنْتَفِخ ـ مَنْفُوخ. Haughty, مُتَنَفِّخ ـ شَامِخ ـ غِطْرِس.

Blobber-lipped, *a.* حُشَارِمٌ.

Block, *n.* Of wood, عَلَاة *coll.* عَلًا ـ قِرْمَة *pl.* قَرَامِي ـ زَنْد *pl.* أَزْنَاد *and* زُنُود. A — to chop upon, وَضَم *pl.* أَوْضَام. A mass, كُتْلَة ـ قِطْعَة ـ جُمْلَة. A large — of stone, حَامِيَة *pl.* حَوَام ـ صَمْدَة. A pulley, بَكَرَة *pl.* بَكَر *and* بَكَرَات. (The following are used for a — on board the Nile boats: مُخَمَّس ـ قَرَادِيَّة ـ تَلَّة). A form, mould, قَالِب *pl.* قَوَالِب. An obstruction, سَدّ *pl.* أَسْدَاد ـ مَانِع ـ عُقْدَة. An ink —, مَحْبَرَة. A —, as of buildings, عَقْد *pl.* عُقُود. A crush, as of people, إِزْدِحَام. *See also* Blockhead, *n.*

Block, *v.t.* To stop us, سَدَّ عَلَى. To hinder, صَدَّ عَن ـ أَمْسَكَ. To throng, زَحَمَ ـ زَاحَمَ. To be blocked, stopped up, إِنْسَدَّ ـ إِسْتَدَّ.

Blockade, *v.t.* أَحَاطَ بِ ـ حَاصَرَ ـ ضَرَبَ حِلَاقًا عَلَى ـ أَجْرَى أَبْلُوقَة عَلَى.

Blockade, *n.* حِصَار ـ مُحَاصَرَة ـ ضَرْبُ حِلَاقٍ عَلَى ـ أَبْلُوقَة.
To break a —, نَقَضَ ٱلْأَبْلُوقَة.
To declare a —, أَعْلَنَ بِأَبْلُوقَةٍ.
To maintain a —, أَبْقَى ٱلْأَبْلُوقَة.
To raise a —, رَفَعَ ٱلْأَبْلُوقَة.
Under —, تَحْتَ ٱلْأَبْلُوقَةِ.

Blockhead, *n.* عَرِيضُ ٱلْقَفَا ـ أَحْمَق ـ أَبْلَه ـ بَهِيمَة ـ ثَوْر ـ جِمَار ـ قَسْقَاس ـ صَنْدَل.

Blockhouse, *n.* حُجْرَة *pl.* حُجَر *and* حُجُرَات ـ مَعْقِل *pl.* مَعَاقِل.

Blonde, *n.* أَبْيَضُ ٱلْوَجْهِ أَزْهَرُ ٱلشَّعْرِ وَأَزْرَقُ ٱلْعَيْنَيْنِ.

Blond-lace, *n.* تَخْرِيم مِنْ حَرِير.

Blood, *n.* دَم *pl.* دِمَاء. Kindred, lineage, قَرَابَة ـ نَسْل ـ ذُرِّيَّة ـ آل. Thick or clotted —, عَلَق. Child, progeny, وَلَد *pl.* أَوْلَاد ـ نَسْل. A violent death, قَتْل ـ حِمَاة. Death, مَوْت. Temperament, طَبْع ـ خُلْق ـ مِزَاج. The carnal part of man, جِسْدَانِيَّة. The juice of any thing, مَاء ـ عَصِير ـ نُقُوط. Blood relations, أُولُوا ٱلْأَرْحَام. Of noble —, شَرِيفُ ٱلْأَصْلِ. A blood-horse, حِصَان أَصْلِيّ. To shed —, سَفَكَ دِمَاء. To stir up one's —, to anger, أَوْغَرَ ـ أَغَاظَ.

Blood, *v.t.* To smear with —, رَمَّلَ ـ ضَرَّجَ بِٱلدَّمِ ـ شَحَّطَ بِٱلدَّمِ. To be smeared with —, تَشَحَّطَ بِٱلدَّمِ ـ دَمِيَ.

Blood-guiltiness, *n.* قَتْل ـ سَفْكُ دِمَاء ـ دِمَاء.

Blood-hound, *n.* سَلُوقِيّ يَصِيدُ ٱلرِّجَال.

Bloodily, *ad.* بِسَفْكِ ٱلدِّمَاء. Cruelly, بِعُنْف ـ فَظًّا ـ بِصَرَامَةٍ.

Bloodiness, *n.* Cruelty, صَرَامَة ـ جَوْر ـ عُنْف.

Bloodless, *a.* Having no blood, عَدِيمُ ٱلدَّمِ. Without shedding of blood, بِلَا سَفْكِ ٱلدِّمَاء. Innocent, بَرِيء.

Blood-letter, *n.* *See* Bleeder, *n.*

Blood-money, *n.* غِوَر *pl.* أَغْيَار ـ شَنَق ـ مَعَرَّة ـ عَقْل ـ مَعْقُلَة ـ دِيَة *pl.* دِيَات. To pay — for, عَقَلَ عَن. To satisfy with —, عَقَلَ لِ. To accept — for, from, إِعْتَقَلَ مِن. They agreed together about —, تَعَاقَلُوا.

Bloodshed, *n.* قَتْل ـ سَفْكُ دِمَاء ـ ذَبْح; of one person, مَقْتَلَة.

Blood-stained, *a.* مُشَحَّط بِٱلدَّمِ ـ دَمِ ـ دَامٍ.

Blood-stone, *n.* سَادَنْج ـ حَجَرُ ٱلدَّمِ.

Blood-sucker, *n.* A leech, عَلَقَة *coll.* عَلَق. An oppressor, بَاغٍ ـ سَفَّاك ـ فِرْعَوْن.

Bloodthirstiness, *n.* طَمَعٌ فِي سَفْكِ ٱلدِّمَاء.

Bloodthirsty, *a.* أَهْلُ ٱلدِّمَاء.

Blood-vessel, *n.* مَجْرَى ٱلدَّمِ *pl.* مَجَارِي ـ وِعَاء ٱلدَّمِ *pl.* أَوْعِيَة.

Bloody, *a.* Relating to blood, دَمَوِيّ. Murderous, قَتُول ـ قُتُل. A — man, رَجُلُ ٱلدِّمَاء ـ رَجُلٌ ذُو دَم. Bloody statutes, أَحْكَامُ ٱلدَّمِ. A — city, مَدِينَةُ ٱلدِّمَاء. *See also* Blood-stained, *a.*

Bloody-flux, *n.* إِسْهَالُ ٱلدَّمِ ـ سَحْج.

Bloody-minded, *a.* *See* Bloodthirsty, *a.*

Bloom, *n.* A blossom, فَاغِيَة ـ نَوْرَة ـ نَوْر ـ نُوَّار *pl.* نَوَاوِير ـ كِمّ *pl.* كِمَام ـ زَهْرَة *pl.* زُهُور *and* أَزْهَار. The time when the powers are strongest, عُنْفُوَان ـ أَشُدّ ـ عِزّ ـ رَعْرَعَة. Freshness, نَضْرَة. Beauty, زِينَة ـ جَمَال. He is in the — of his youth, هُوَ فِي عُنْفُوَانِ شَبَابِهِ.

Bloom, *v.i.* To blossom, أَزْهَرَ ـ وَرَّدَ ـ نَوَّرَ ـ عَيَّنَ ـ أَفْغَى. To flourish, نَبَغَ ـ إِبْتَهَى. To — with, إِزْدَهَرَ بِ. To prosper, إِسْتَفْلَحَ ـ أَفْلَحَ.

Blooming, *a.* } **Bloomy,** } Blossoming, مُنَوِّر. Prospering, مُيَسَّر ـ مُفْلِح ـ نَاجِح. Cheerful, سَارّ ـ طَرِب ـ فَارِح. Beauteous, جَمِيل.

Blossom, *n.* *See* Bloom, *n.*

Blossom, *v.i.* *See to* Bloom, *v.i.*

Blot, *v.t.* To spot with ink, طَبَّعَ - بَحْبَرَ . To stain, طَبَّعَ - كَحَّصَ - ≈ طَمَسَ ² - سَخَّمَطَ - وَسَّخَ - بَقَّعَ - عَيَّبَ . To obliterate, طَمَسَ ² - ≈ شَطَبَ - ≈ شَالَ - ≈ مَحَا ² - أَزَالَ . To dishonour, عَيَّبَ - ≈ هَتَكَ - ≈ فَضَحَ .

Blot, *v.i.* تَطَبَّعَ .

Blot, *n.* A stain, spot, طَبْعَة - نُقْطَة *pl.* نُقَط - عَيْب *pl.* عُيُوب - مَحْوٌ - طَلْس - نَسْخ - دَنَس *pl.* أَدْنَاس . An erasure, بُقْعَة - تَرْمِسَة . A spot in reputation, مَعِيبَة - عَيْبَة - عَار - عَوْرَة . A defect, قُصُور .

Blotch, *n.* In the skin, لُمْعَة *pl.* لُمَع *and* لِمَاع - طَبْعَة .

Blotting-paper, *n.* وَرَقٌ مُنَشِّف - وَرَقُ ٱلتَّنْشِيف .

Blouse, *n.* قَمِيصٌ مَشْلَح .

Blow, *n.* A stroke, ضَرْبَة - لَطْمَة - دَقَّة . A sudden event, calamity, دَاهِيَة - مُصِيبَة . An action, صَنِيعَة *pl.* صَنَائِعُ . A gale of wind, رِيحٌ سَاهِجَة . The egg of a fly, دُقْطَة *pl.* دُقْطَات - بَيْضَةُ ذُبَابٍ . A — out, a feast, ضِيَافَة . A — up, a row, هَوْشَة - غَلْغَلَة - بَلْبَلَة - نِزَاع . To strike one a —, ضَرَبَ - ≈ لَطَمَ - ≈ . To strike a — for, حَامَى عَن - قَاتَلَ عَن . To strike a —, to act, صَنَعَ ≈ . They came to blows among themselves, تَقَاتَلُوا . *See also* Bloom, *n.*

Blow, *v.t.* and *i.* To make a current of air, as with the mouth, نَفَخَ ≈ - نَفَخَ . To —, as of the wind, هَبَّ ≈ ; to — strongly, عَصَفَ ≈ - قَصَفَ ≈ - أَعْصَفَ ; to — softly, نَسَمَ ≈ . To pant, نَهَجَ ≈ - لَهَثَ ≈ - نَفَخَ . To open, as flowers, أَزْهَرَ - فَتَحَ . To —, as on an instrument, دَقَّ ² - رَنَّ ² . The wind blew violently, عَصَفَتِ ٱلرِّيحُ .

To blow away, to scatter, شَتَّتَ - بَثَّ ² - مَذَّرَ .

To blow off steam, فَرَّغَ ٱلْبُخَار .

To blow out, extinguish, أَخْمَدَ - أَطْفَأَ .

To blow over, pass away, ذَهَبَ ≈ - زَالَ ² .

To blow the nose, مَخَطَ ² ≈ - تَمَخَّطَ - مَخَطَ أَنْفَهُ .

To blow up, to be angry with, سَخِطَ عَلَى ≈ - إِغْتَاظَ عَلَى - عَتَبَ ² ≈ .

To blow up, as with gunpowder, طَيَّرَ - أَطَارَ .

To blow upon, injure in reputation, هَتَكَ ≈ - فَضَحَ ≈ .

Blower, *n.* نَفَّاخ - مِنْفَاخ .

Blowpipe, *n.* بُورِي .

Blubber, *n.* Of a whale, شَحْمُ سَمَكِ يُونُس - دُهْنُ ٱلْحُوتِ .

Blubber, *v.i.* بَكَى ≈ - نَاحَ ² .

Blubbering, *a.* Crying, عَيِين .

Bludgeon, *n.* تَقْصِيرَة - عُكَّاز - دَبُّوس .

Blue, *a.* أَزْرَقِيٌّ - أَزْرَق - كُحْلِيٌّ - أَزْرَقُ سَمَاوِيٌّ . Of a deep — colour, زُرْقُم . Blue or grey eyed, أَزْرَقُ ٱلْعُيُونِ *fem.* زَرْقَاءُ *pl.* زُرْق .

Blue, *n.* The colour, زُرْقَة - زَرَق .

Blue, *v.t.* أَزْرَق - بِلَوْنِ صَبْغ - بِٱلنِّيلِ صَبْغ .

Blue-bottle, *n.* The plant, ترنشان . The fly, ذُبَابَةٌ زَرْقَاءُ .

Blue-devils, *n.* }
Blues, } سَوْدَاءُ - طَفْطَفَة . *See also* Melancholy, *n.*

Blue-light, *n.* إِشَارَةٌ نَارِيَّةٌ .

Blueness, *n.* زُرْقَة - زَرَق ; of the eyes, زَرْقَمَة .

Blue-peter, *n.* إِشَارَةُ ٱلسَّفَرِ - عَلَمُ ٱلسَّفَرِ .

Bluff, *a.* Surly, rude, جَافٍ - فَظٌّ - غَلِيظ .

Bluff, *n.* A steep bank, شِنَاخ - طَنَف - عَقَبَة - جُرُف *pl.* أَجْرَاف .

Bluffness, *n.* Rudeness, جَفَاءٌ - فَظَاظَة - غِلَظ . Steepness, وُعُور - حُدُور .

Bluish, *a.* مُزْرَاقٌّ - مَائِلٌ إِلَى ٱلزُّرْقَةِ - أَزْرَقُ بَعْضَ ٱلزُّرْقَةِ .

Blunder, *v.i.* غَلِطَ فِي ≈ - خَطِئَ ≈ - أَخْطَأَ ≈ - سَقَطَ فِي ≈ ² - تَخَبَّصَ . To —, as in speech, لَغَا فِي ² . To attribute a — to, غَلَّطَ . To cause to —, أَغْلَطَ - أَسْقَطَ .

Blunder, *n.* غَلْطَة - سَقْط *pl.* أَسْقَاط - خَطَأ - خَطِيئَة *pl.* خَطَايَا - زَلَّة - قُصُور - ضَلَل - ضَلَال - هَفْوَة *pl.* هَفَوَات . He made a gross —, زَلَّ زَلَّةً قَبِيحَةً *aor.* يَزِلُّ .

Blunderbuss, *n.* قَرَابِينَة *coll.* قَرَابِينَات .

Blunderer, *n.* }
Blunderhead, *n.* } غَبِين - مِغْلَاط - ضِلِّيل . *See also under* Awkward, *a.*
Blundering, *a.* }

Blunderingly, *ad.* بِغَبَاوَةٍ - بِضَلَالٍ .

Blunt, *a.* Not sharp, فَسْفَاس - بَارِد - جَبِل - كَلِيل - كَهَام . Broken in the edge, فَلِيل - أَفَلّ . Dull, as of understanding, غَشِيم - أَبْلَهُ *fem.* بَلْهَاءُ *pl.* بُلْه - ثَقِيل - غَلِيظ - بَلِيد . Rude, خَشِن - خُشْنِيٌّ - إِنْفَلّ ≈ - كَلَّ ≈ - نَلِمَ . To be —, not sharp, كَلَّلَ . *See also* Candid, *a.*

Blunt, *v.t.* To take off the edge, ثَلَمَ ≈ - ثَلَّمَ - غَلَّظَ ٱلْحَدَّ - أَعْدَمَ ٱلْحَدَّ - كَلَّلَ - جَعَلَ ≈ - كَسَرَ حَدَّهُ - خَفَّفَ - لَيَّنَ . To soften, ضَبَطَ ≈ - خَفَضَ ≈ - أَوْقَفَ . To repress, To — vigour or courage, فَلَّ ² - فَلَّلَ - إِنْفَلَّ - إِفْتَلَّ . To be so blunted,

Bluntly, *ad.* Rudely, بِفَظَاظَةٍ ـ بِلَا لَطَافَةٍ ـ بِخُشُونَةٍ.

Bluntness, *n.* Want of edge, غِلَاظَةُ ٱلْحَدِّ ـ كَلٌّ. Rudeness, عَدَمُ لَطَافَةٍ ـ خُشُونَة. Candour, صِدْقٌ.

Blur, *n.* سَخْمَطَة ـ سُخْمَة ـ عَيْب ـ بُقْعَة.

Blur, *v.t.* سَخْمَطَ ـ طَبَعَ ـ بَقَّعَ.

Blurt, *v.t.* and *i.* To speak unadvisedly, تَغَفَّلَ فِي ـ فَرَطَ بِٱلْكَلَامِ ٱلْكَلَامَ. To talk profusely, بَقَّ. To — out, أَفْشَى بِ.

Blush, *v.i.* To be shy, إِسْتَحَى ـ إِسْتَحْيَى ـ خَجِلَ. To turn red, as in the face, إِحْمَرَّ ـ فَارَ وَجْهُهُ. To cause to —, خَجَّلَ ـ حَشَّمَ ـ أَخْجَلَ.

Blush, *n.* خَجْلَة ـ خَجَل ـ حَيَآء. Redness, إِحْمِرَار ـ حُمْرَة. Sudden appearance, طُلُوع ـ سُطُوع. The — of morn, شَقُّ ٱلْفَجْرِ.

Blushing, *a.* خَجْلَانُ ـ خَجِل. Rosy, أَحْمَرُ *fem.* حَمْرَآءُ *pl.* حُمْر ـ وَرْدِيٌّ ـ فَقِيع ـ فُقَاع ـ أَشْقَرُ.

Blushingly, *ad.* بِحَيَآءٍ ـ بِخَجَلٍ.

Blushless, *a.* Impudent, صَفِيقُ ٱلْوَجْهِ ـ صَفِيق ـ وَقِيح.

Bluster, *v.i.* To roar, as a storm, عَجَّ ـ تَهَيَّجَ ـ هَاجَ. To make a fuss, تَهَوَّرَ ـ عَوَّشَ ـ قَرْقَعَ ـ تَغَلْغَلَ ـ هَوَّشَ.

Bluster, *n.* حَتَات ـ عَوَّة ـ عَجَّة ـ غَاغَة ـ غَلْغَلَة ـ رَجَّة ـ كَرْكَبَة ـ تَهَوُّر.

Blusterer, *n.* وِهْيَاص ـ فَشَّار ـ سَلِيقِيٌّ.

Blustering, *a.* Noisy, صَيِّت. Braggart, بَاذِخ ـ فَيَّاش.

Boa, *n.* The serpent, نَوْعٌ مِنَ ٱلْحَيَّاتِ. A fur tippet, فَرْوَةٌ لِلرَّقَبَةِ.

Boar, *n.* خِنْزِيرٌ فَحْلٌ ـ خِنْزِير *pl.* خَنَازِيرُ. A wild —, هَلُوف ـ خِنْزِيرُ ٱلْغَابِ.

Board, *n.* A plank, دَفَّة ـ لَوْحَة *pl.* أَلْوَاح ـ تَخْتَة *pl.* تَخْتَات. A table, طَاوِلَة ـ سِمَاط ـ مَائِدَة ـ سُفْرَة ـ خِوَان. Food, أَكْل ـ مَأْكَل. A council, مَجْلِس إِدَارَةٍ ـ مَجْلِس *pl.* مَجَالِسُ. A meeting, لَجْنَة. A chess —, رُقْعَةُ (or طَاوِلَةُ) ٱلشِّطْرَنْجِ. The two boards of a book, ضِمَامَتَا كِتَابٍ ـ دَفَّتَا مُصْحَفٍ. On — of a ship, فِي مَرْكَبٍ. A — of health, مَجْلِسُ ٱلصِّحَّةِ ـ مَجْلِس صِحِّيٌّ.

Bed and board, } أَكْل وَسُكْنَى.
Board and lodging, }

Board wages, أُجْرَةٌ بِدُونِ أَكْلٍ.

Above board, openly, بِٱلْمَفْتُوحِ ـ عَلَانِيَةً ـ جَهْرًا.

In boards, of a book, مُجَلَّدٌ بِمُقَوًّى فَقَط.

To go by the board, إِنْكَسَرَ مِنَ ٱلْقَعْرِ.

To go on board, of a ship, نَزَلَ فِي ٱلْمَرْكَبِ. To be put on board, أُنْزِلَ (or صُعِّدَ) فِي ٱلْمَرْكَبِ.

To place out at board, حَطَّ فِي مَحَلٍّ لِلْأَكْلِ وَٱلسُّكْنَى.

Board, *v.t.* To floor with boards, فَرَشَ بِأَلْوَاحٍ. To roof or line with boards, تَخَّتَ. To enter a ship by force, هَجَمَ عَلَى مَرْكَبٍ ـ طَلَعَ إِلَى مَرْكَبٍ بِقُوَّةٍ. To give food and lodgings to, on payment, أَمَدَّ بِٱلْأَكْلِ وَٱلسُّكْنَى بِثَمَنٍ. To — with, as a boarder, عَاشَ مَعَ ـ سَكَنَ وَأَكَلَ مَعَ.

Boarded, *a.* Covered with boards, مُتَخَّت. Provided with food and lodgings, on payment, مُمَدٌّ بِٱلْأَكْلِ وَٱلسُّكْنَى بِثَمَنٍ.

Boarder, *n.* One who is provided with food and lodgings for payment, آكِلٌ وَسَاكِنٌ عِنْدَ أَحَدٍ بِثَمَنٍ. A — of a ship, هَاجِمٌ عَلَى مَرْكَبٍ.

Day boarder, of a school, آكِلٌ عِنْدَ صَاحِبِ ٱلْمَكْتَبِ فِي ٱلنَّهَارِ فَقَط.

Parlour boarder, of a school, تِلْمِيذٌ آكِلٌ مَعَ صَاحِبِ ٱلْمَكْتَبِ *pl.* تَلَامِيذُ.

Weekly boarder, آكِلٌ وَسَاكِنٌ عِنْدَ أَحَدٍ بِٱلْأُسْبُوعِ.

Boarding, *n.* Providing board, diet, for pay, إِمْدَادٌ بِٱلْأَكْلِ وَٱلسُّكْنَى بِثَمَنٍ. The — with for pay, أَكْلٌ وَسُكْنَى عِنْدَ أَحَدٍ بِثَمَنٍ. The act of entering by force, هُجُومٌ بِقُوَّةٍ.

Boarding-house, *n.* مَنْزِلٌ لِلْأَكْلِ وَٱلسُّكْنَى بِثَمَنٍ.

Boarding-pike, *n.* حَرْبَة *pl.* حِرَاب.

Boarding-school, *n.* مَدْرَسَةٌ تَسْكُنُ ٱلتَّلَامِيذُ فِيهَا وَتَقْتَاتُ بِثَمَنٍ.

Boarish, *a.* Rude, غَلِيظ ـ خُشْنِيٌّ ـ وَحْشِيٌّ.

Boast, *v.i.* فَشَّ ـ فَاشَ ـ فَايَشَ ـ فَخْفَخَ ـ طَرْمَذَ ـ بَذَخَ ـ إِعْتَزَّ بِ ـ تَفَاخَرَ بِ ـ إِفْتَخَرَ ـ تَفَاخَرَ. To — of, إِفْتَخَرَ بِ. A thing of which one boasts, مَفْخَرَة ـ مَفْخُرَة. He boasted of what he possessed, تَفَاخَرَ بِمَا عِنْدَهُ.

Boast, *n.* } خَرْطَة ـ مُبَاهَاة ـ مُفَاخَرَة ـ تَفَاخُر ـ طَرْمَذَة.
Boasting, } Mode of —, فِخْرَة. He boasted with a good —, in a good manner, فَخَرَ فِخْرَةً حَسَنَةً.

Boaster, *n.* } مُتَفَخِّر ـ فَشْفَاش ـ فِخِّير ـ فَيَّاش ـ مُفْتَخِر ـ فَشَّار ـ خَرَّاط ـ طِرْمَاذ ـ فَيَّاش.
Boastful, *a.* }

Boastingly, *ad.* } تَكَبُّرًا ـ بِٱلتَّفَاخُرِ ـ إِفْتِخَارًا ـ بِٱلْمُبَاهَاةِ.
Boastfully, }

Boat, *n.* زَوْرَق *pl.* زَوَارِقُ ـ قَارِب *pl.* قَوَارِبُ ـ نُقَيْرَة ـ مَاشُوَة ـ شَخْتُور *pl.* شَخَاتِيرُ. A small or ferry —, مِعْبَر ـ مِعْدِيَة. A small and swift —, طَرَّاد. (The following are the names of different boats used on the Nile: A large passenger — is called

ذُهَبِيَّة ; one smaller a كَنْجَة ; one smaller still with a single cabin a قَارِب . A large goods' — is called a مَرْكَب ; one of the largest size a خَيَاسَة . A — for merchandise is termed a صَنْدَل , and a jolly — a فَلُوكَة). بَغْلَة ; Baggala (!)

Boat-hooks, *n.* قَانْجَة .

Boating, *n.* مِشْوَار فِي زَوْرَق — سَيْرَة فِي قَارِب .

Boatman, *n.* / Boatsman, } قَايِقْجِي — مَلَّاح . (The following are used on the Nile: طَيْفِيّ — مَرَاكِبِيّ — نُوتِيّ).

Boatswain, *n.* بُورْصُون — مَرِيْنَل بَاشِي .

Bob, *n.* A motion, حَرَكَة ; as of a pendulum, تَنَوُّح . A bob up and down, طَلْعَة وَنَزْلَة . A fluttering, خَفَقَان . A shilling; *q v.* A bait for fishing, مَطْمَع . *See also* Nod, *n.*

Bob, *v.t.* and *i.* To move, as a pendulum, تَنَوَّح . To flutter, خَفَق ². To fish for eels, إِصْطَاد ٱلْأَنْقَلِيس . To jerk, shake, هَزّ — خَضّ ².

Bobbin, *n.* A spool, فِلْكَة — مِكَبّ — مِغْزَل . A kind of cord, قِيطَان .

Bobstay, *n.* رِبَاط ٱلسَّارِي ٱلَّذِي عَلَى مُقَدَّم ٱلْمَرْكَب .

Bobtail, *n.* A shortened tail, ذَنَب مُقَصَّر . The rabble, ٱلْحَرَافِيش — ٱلْجُعَيْدِيَّة — أَسَافِلُ ٱلنَّاسِ .

Bode, *v.t.* To presage, point to, دَلّ عَلَى ² — وَعَد بِ *aor.* يَعِدُ — تَنَبَّأ بِ .

Bodice, *n.* صُدَيْرِيَات *pl.* صُدَيْرِي — أَزْبِنَة *pl.* زَبُون .

Bodied, *a.* Having a body, ذُو جَسَدٍ .

Bodiless, *a.* لَا جَسَدَ لَهُ .

Bodily, *a.* جِسْمَانِيّ — بَدَنِيّ — جِسْمِيّ — جَسَدِيّ . Bodily presence, حُضُورُ ٱلْجَسَدِ — حُضُورٌ بِٱلْجِسْمِ . Bodily exercise, رِيَاضَةٌ جَسَدِيَّةٌ .

Bodily, *ad.* In the body, فِي ٱلْجَسَدِ — بِٱلْجَسَدِ . In a body, together, completely, بِٱلْمَرَّةِ — بَتَّةً — مَعًا .

Boding, *a.* يَؤُولُ إِلَى — مُسْتَدِلٌّ عَلَى .

Bodkin, *n.* An instrument to run in a string with, مِتَكّ ; a piercer, مِخْرَاز — مِخْرَز ; a — for applying collyrium to the eyes, مِيل — مِرْوَد . To insert, as a string, with a —, إِسْتَتَكّ .

Body, *n.* The material substance of an animal, جِرْن *pl.* أَجْرَان — أَجْسَام *pl.* جِسْم — أَجْسَاد *pl.* جَسَد — أَبْدَان *pl.* بَدَن — جِبَال . A person, نَفَر *pl.* أَنْفَار — ظَلْم *pl.* ظُلُوم — شَخْص *pl.* أَشْخَاص . A dead —, جُثَّة *pl.* جُثَث and أَجْثَاث — جِيفَة — مَيِّت . A society, جَمْعِيَّة — جَمَاعَة — صِرْم *pl.* أَصْرَام — فِرْقَة *pl.* فِرَق .

A — of soldiers, جُنْد *pl.* جُنُود — فَوْج *pl.* أَفْوَاج — فِرْقَةُ عَسْكَرٍ . A — politic, دَوْلَة — مِلَّة — جُمْهُور . A corporate —, صِنْف *pl.* أَصْنَاف . Outward condition, size, جُرْم — كِبَر — مِقْدَار . The main part of an animal, جُثَّة — بَدَن . Strength, قُوَّة ; as of wine, جِدَّة — سَوْرَة . The — of the clergy, ٱلْإِكْلِيرُوس — ٱلْقُسُوس . The — of a church, صَحْنُ ٱلْكَنِيسَةِ . The —, the larger part, أَكْثَر — أَغْلَب . They went in a body —, إِنْطَلَقُوا جَمِيعًا . Any body, كُلّ ٱلنَّاسِ — أَيًّا مَنْ كَانَ . Every body, كُلّ أَحَدٍ . To assume a —, تَجَسَّدَ . The heavenly bodies, ٱلْأَجْرَامُ ٱلْفَلَكِيَّةُ .

Body-guard, *n.* حُرَّاس — حَرَس ; one of the —, حَرَسِيّ — عَسَاكِرُ خَاصَّةٌ لِمُحَافَظَةِ ٱلنَّفْسِ .

Bog, *n.* A morass, غَيْضَة *pl.* غِيَاض — مَغِيض — أَجَمَة .

Boggle, *v.i.* and *t.* To hesitate, تَغَفَّل — تَصَرَّب — تَوَقَّف . To perplex, قَلَّق — دَهَّش — شَوَّش — تَشَوَّش . To — in speech, تَغَمْغَم .

Boggler, *n.* مُتَغَفِّل — غَشِيم — شَلُوش . A — in speech, مُتَغَمْغِم .

Boggy, *a.* مَكَانٌ سَبِخٌ — أَجَمِيّ . Boggy ground, أَرْضٌ سَبِخَةٌ .

Bogle, *n.* / Boggle, } A spectre, غُول — خَيَال *pl.* أَخْيِلَة — عِفْرِيت .

Bog-trotter, *n.* سَاكِنُ ٱلْغِيَاضِ *pl.* سُكَّان .

Bohemia, *n.* The province, بُوهِيمِيَا .

Boil, *n.* A tumour, جِبْنَة — جِبْن *pl.* جُبُون — دُمَّل *pl.* دَمَامِيل and دَمَامِل — حَبَّة .

Boil, *v.i.* and *t.* To be in a boiling state, فَاح — كَتّ — غَلَى . To —, of the sea, غَطْغَطَ ٱلْبَحْرُ . To — over, نَقَت — فَار ² . To make to —, أَغْلَى — غَلَّى — نَقَّت — أَفَاح . To make to — over, أَفَار . To —, of the blood, ثَار ². To — with rage, ثَار غَضَبُهُ ². To — to rags, هَرَأ — هَرَّأ . To cook by boiling, سَلَق ². *See also to* Cook, *v.t.*

Boiled, *a.* As of food cooked by boiling, سَلِيقَة — مَسْلُوق . A — egg, بَيْضَة مَسْلُوقَة .

Boiler, *n.* مَاعُون *pl.* مَوَاعِين — حَلَّة *pl.* حِلَل — قِدْر *pl.* قُدُور — قَزَان *pl.* قَزَانَات .

Boiling, *a.* Gurgling, مُبَقْبِق . Boiling, as of water, غَالٍ — فَائِر ; of the sea, مُغَطْغِط . The — point, دَرَجَةُ غَلَيَانٍ — دَرَجَةُ ٱلْغَلَيَانِ ٱلْمَاءِ .

Boisterous, *a.* Stormy, عَجَّاج — قَاصِف — عَاصِف . Noisy, مُتَهَوِّر — ضَجُوج — عَجَّاج .

Boisterously, *ad.* بِضَجِيجٍ — مُتَهَوِّرًا — عَصْفًا .

Boisterousness, *n.* Of wind, قَصْف ـ عُصُوف. Turbulence, عَجِيج ـ عَجّ ـ تَهَوُّر ـ ضِجَاج.

Bold, *a.* Daring, ذُو ـ مُجْدَآءُ *pl.* مَجِيد ـ سَنَدْرِيٌّ ـ مُكَبِّس. شُجَاع ـ بَطَل ـ جَسُور ـ جَرِيءٌ ـ غَطُوس ـ فَلَتَان ـ عَارِضَة. Impudent, forward, قَلِيلُ ٱلْحَيَآءِ ـ وَقِح ـ سَفِيه ـ مُتَجَهِّم. Prominent, بَارِز ـ مُشْرِف ـ شَادِخ. A — hand-writing, قَلَمٌ مَضْبُوطٌ. To be —, brave, جَرُؤَ ² جَشُرَ ² . To be —, to dare, تَجَاسَرَ ـ تَجَرَّأَ عَلَى ـ إِجْتَرَأَ عَلَى. To make —, to encourage, شَجَّعَ.

Boldly, *ad.* Courageously, بِجَسَارَةٍ ـ بِشَجَاعَةٍ. Impudently, وَقَاحَةً ـ بِوَقَاحَةٍ.

Boldness, *n.* Courage, إِقْدَام ـ مَجْدَة ـ جُرْأَة ـ عَارِضَة ـ سَفَاهَة ـ وَقَاحَة ـ مُجَازَفَة. شَجَاعَة ـ جَسَارَة. Impudence, قِلَّةُ حَيَآء. Relief, بُرُوز ـ نُتُوّ. Venturesomeness, تَجَاسُر ـ إِجْتِسَار.

Bole, *n.* Clay, طِين ـ تُرَاب. Armenian —, تُرَابٌ أَرْمَنِيٌّ ـ الطِّينُ ٱلْأَرْمَنِيُّ.

Boll, *n.* A seed-vessel, خَرِيطَة *pl.* خَرَائِط.

Boll, *v.i.* تَحَبَّبَ ـ ² بَرَزَ ـ إِسْتَفْرَكَ ـ أَفْرَكَ. The grain bolled, إِسْتَفْرَكَ ٱلْحَبُّ.

Bolster, *n.* A pillow, وِسَادَة *pl.* وُسُد ـ مِخَدَّة *pl.* مَخَادُّ. A support, عُمْدَة ـ مِسْنَد.

Bolster, *v.t.* To support with a pillow, وَسَّدَ. To support, سَنَّدَ ـ أَعْمَدَ.

Bolt, *n.* A bar of a door, شِجَار ـ قُفْل *pl.* قُفُول *and* أَقْفَال ـ لِسَانٌ ـ فَرَاشَة ـ دَرْبَاس ـ مَتَارِس *pl.* مِتْرَس. A — of a lock, ٱلْقُفْلِ. A sliding —, مِغْلَاق *pl.* مَغَالِيق. A dart, نَبْل *pl.* نِبَال ـ سَهْم *pl.* سِهَام ـ نُشَّابَة. A fetter, قَيْد *pl.* قُيُود. A pin to fasten any thing with, خِلَال *pl.* أَخِلَّة. A thunderbolt, صَاعِقَة. A measure of 28 ells, مِقْدَار ٢٨ ذِرَاع. Bolt upright, مُنْتَصِب.

Bolt, *v.t.* and *i.* To fasten, as with a —, أَفْرَسَ ـ غَلَّقَ ـ أَزْلَجَ ـ غَرْبَلَ ـ دَرْبَسَ ـ ² سَكَّ ـ ² قَفَلَ ـ سَكَّرَ. To sift, غَرْبَلَ ـ كَرْبَلَ. ² نَخَلَ. To run away quickly, وَلَّى ـ إِنْسَلَّ ـ إِنْفَلَتَ ـ فَرَّ. ² هَرَبَ ـ تَوَلَّى. To swallow quickly, سَلِجَ ـ تَلَهَّمَ ـ لَهِمَ.

Bolter, *n.* A sieve, غِرْبَال *pl.* غَرَابِيل ـ مُنْخُل.

Bolus, *n.* بَلُوع ـ حَبَّة ـ لُقْمَة *pl.* لُقَم.

Bomb, *n.* قُنْبُرَة *pl.* قَنَابِر.

Bombard, *v.t.* ضَرَبَ بِقَنَابِرَ.

Bombardier, ضَرَّابُ ٱلْقُنْبُرِ ـ قُنْبُرْجِي. *See also* Artilleryman, *n.*

Bombardment, *n.* ضَرْبُ ٱلْقُنْبُرِ.

Bombast, *n.* طَرْمَذَة ـ مُبَالَغَة ـ العَظَائِمُ.

Bombastic, *a.* طِرْمَاذ ـ مُبَالِغ ـ وَفِنٌّ. To be —, طَرْمَذَ.

Bombastically, *ad.* بِٱلْمُبَالَغَةِ ـ بِطَرْمَذَةٍ ـ بَاطِلًا.

Bombazine, *n.* قُمَاش بَابَازِيٌّ.

Bomb-proof, *a.* مُسْتَحْكَمٌ لا تُؤَثِّرُ فِيهِ ٱلْقَنَابِرُ.

Bona-fide, *a.* حَقِيقِيٌّ ـ صَحِيحٌ.

Bona-fide, *ad.* بِلَا رَيْبٍ ـ بِصِدْقٍ ـ حَقِيقَةً.

Bonbon, *n.* حَلَاوَة ـ مُلَبَّس *coll.* مُلَبَّسَة *pl.* مُلَبَّسَات.

Bond, *n.* A tie, عَلَاقَة ـ قَيْد ـ مِرْبَط ـ رِبَاط ـ رَبْطَة. A writing of obligation, تَمَسُّك ـ خَطّ ـ صُكُوك ـ صَكّ *pl.* صِكَاك *and* صُكُوك. Union, وَحْدَة ـ إِتِّفَاق ـ إِتِّحَاد ـ سَنَدَات *pl.* سَنَد. A fetter, قَيْد *pl.* قُيُود. A treasury —, حَوَالَةٌ عَلَى ٱلْخَزْنَةِ *pl.* حَوَالَات. In bonds, imprisonment, مَحْبُوس ـ بِٱلْوَثَاقِ. *See also* Bonded, *a.*

Bond, *v.t.* To become security for, ضَمِنَ ـ كَفَلَ.

Bondage, *n.* Slavery, عُبُودِيَّة ـ إِسْر.

Bonded, *a.* In bond, goods in bond, أَمْتِعَةٌ تِجَارِيَّةٌ مَوْضُوعَةٌ فِي ٱلْكُمْرُكِ يَتَكَفَّلُ صَاحِبُهَا بِدَفْعِ ٱلْمَفْرُوضِ عَلَيْهَا.

Bondmaid, *n.* أَمَة *pl.* آم ـ جَارِيَة *pl.* جَوَارٍ ـ رَقِيقَة.

Bondman, *n.* عَبْد *pl.* عَبِيد ـ مَمْلُوك *pl.* مَمَالِيك ـ رَقِيق *pl.* أَرِقَّاء ـ أَسِير *pl.* أَسْرَى *and* أُسَرَاء.

Bonds, *n.* قُيُود.

Bondservant, *n.* *See* Bondman, *n.*

Bondservice, *n.* أَسْر ـ عُبُودِيَّة.

Bondsman, *n.* ضَامِن ـ كَفِيل.

Bondwoman, *n.* *See* Bondmaid, *n.*

Bone, *n.* عَظْمَة ـ عَظْم *pl.* عِظَامَة *and* عِظَام. The jaw-bone, فَكّ *pl.* فُكُوك ـ لِهْزِمَة. The shoulder —, لَوْحُ ٱلْكَتِفِ. The hip —, وَرْك. The shin —, القَصَبَةُ ٱلصُّغْرَى. The collar —, تَرْقُوَة. To strip a — of its flesh, تَعَرَّمَ ـ ² عَرَمَ. A — with no meat on it, عُرَاق ـ عَرْق. To set, as of a —, جَبَرَ. The bones with which the Arabs play as with dice, كَعْبَة *pl.* كَعَبَات.

Bone, *v.t.* To take out bones, جَرَّدَ مِنَ ٱلْعِظَامِ. To furnish with whalebone, بَطَّنَ بِرِيشِ ٱلْحُوتِ.

Boneless, *a.* مِنْ غَيْرِ عَظْم.

Bonfire, *n.* نَارٌ مُشْعَلَةٌ ـ نَار ـ شُعْلَة.

Bon-mot, *n.* طَرِيفَة *pl.* طَرَائِف ـ لَطِيفَة ـ مَلَاحَة ـ نَادِرَة *pl.* نَوَادِر.

Bonnet, *n.* For the head, قَلَنْسُوَة ـ قَلُوسَة. A woman's —, عِصَابَةُ ٱلنِّسَآءِ ٱلْفِرَنْج.

Bonnie, *a.* *See* Bonny, *a.*

Bonnily, *ad.* حَبَّذا ـ بِلُطْفٍ ـ فَكاهَةً ـ جَيِّدًا .

Bonny, *a.* جَمِيل ـ نَادِر ـ فَكِه ـ جَيِّد ـ لَطِيف .

Bony-clabber, *n.* نَمِيرٌ حَامِضٌ .

Bonus, A premium in addition to interest, إِنْعَامٌ يُمْنَحُ عِلاوَةً عَلَى ٱلْقِيمَةِ وَٱلْفَائِدَةِ .

Bon vivant, *n.* صَاحِبُ عَيْشٍ ـ بَحْبُوح *pl.* بَحَابِحُ ـ عَيَّاش وَعِشْرَة .

Bony, *a.* Full of bones, كَثِيرُ ٱلْعِظَامِ ـ عَظْمِيٌّ . Robust, ضَلِيع ـ صُلْب ـ قَوِيّ . *See also* Scraggy, *a.*

Booby, *n.* تَيْس ـ ثَوْر ـ بَلِيد ـ أَهْبَل ـ غَشِيم . A large bird like the pelican, طَيْرٌ كَبِيرٌ يُشَابِهُ جَمَلَ ٱلْبَحْرِ .

Book, *n.* جَالَة ـ سِفْر *pl.* أَسْفَار ـ مُصْحَف *pl.* مَصَاحِفُ ـ كِتَاب *pl.* كُتُب . نُسْخَة ـ مُجَلَّد ـ مُصَنَّف *pl.* مُصَنَّفَات . The division, as of a work, جُزْء *pl.* أَجْزَآء ـ قِسْم *pl.* أَقْسَام ـ فَصْل *pl.* فُصُول ـ سِفْر *pl.* أَسْفَار . An account —, دَفْتَر *pl.* دَفَاتِرُ ـ كِتَاب ٱلْحِسَاب . A day —, كِتَابُ ٱلْمَدْخُولِ . The books of the Prophets, صُحُفُ ٱلْأَنْبِيَآء . The books of Moses, ٱلتَّوْرَاةُ ـ تَوْرَاةُ مُوسَى . The — of Psalms, ٱلزَّبُورُ ـ زَبُورُ دَاوُدَ ـ ٱلْمَزَامِيرُ . A — in folio, كِتَابٌ فِي قَطْعِ ٱلْكَامِلِ ; in quarto, كِتَابٌ فِي قَطْعِ ٱلرُّبْعِ . Without —, by memory, غَيْبًا ـ عَلَى ظَهْرِ قَلْبِهِ . To bring to —, حَاسَبَ ـ سَأَلَ عَنْ ـ حَظِيَ عِنْدَ . To be in one's good books, حَظِيَ عِنْدَ . To be in one's black books, كُرِهَ عِنْدَ .

Book, *v.t.* قَيَّدَ فِي ٱلدَّفْتَرِ ـ سَجَّلَ ـ ضَبَطَ .

Book-binder, *n.* مُجَلِّد ـ حَبَّاك .

Book-binding, *n.* تَجْلِيدُ ٱلْكُتُبِ .

Book-case, *n.* صَنْدُوقُ كُتُبٍ ـ خِزَانَةُ كُتُبٍ ـ قِمَطْرَة *pl.* قَمَاطِرُ .

Bookish, *a.* مُحِبُّ ٱلْكُتُبِ ـ مُدَرِّس .

Bookishness, *n.* حُبُّ ٱلْكُتُبِ ـ مُدَارَسَة .

Book-keeper, *n.* كَاتِب ـ دَفْتَرْجِي ـ دَفْتَرْدَار . Office of a —, دَفْتَرْدَارِيَّة .

Book-keeping, *n.* حِفْظُ ٱلْحِسَابَاتِ ـ دَفْتَرْجِيَّة .

Book-muslin, *n.* شَاشٌ نَاعِمٌ .

Book-oath, *n.* يَمِينٌ عَلَى ٱلْكُتُبِ ٱلْمُقَدَّسَةِ .

Bookseller, *n.* صَحَّاف ـ كُتُبِيٌّ ـ بَائِعُ كُتُبٍ .

Bookselling, *n.* بَيْعُ ٱلْكُتُبِ ـ صَحَّافَة .

Book-shop, *n.* دُكَّانُ صَحَّافٍ .

Book-stall, *n.* فَرْشُ كُتُبٍ .

Book-worm, *n.* A lover of books, مُحِبُّ ٱلْكُتُبِ ـ مُدَرِّس . A worm that eats books, عُثَّةٌ تَلْحَسُ ٱلْكُتُبَ .

Boom, *n.* Of a ship, بَاشْتُون ـ جَارِيَة . A chain or spar laid across a river, سِلْسِلَة ـ خَشَبَةٌ عَلَى نَهْرٍ لِمَنْعِ ٱلْعُبُورِ ـ زِنْجِيرٌ أَوْ. Noise, echo, حِسّ ـ صَدَى ; as of the waves, لَجَب ; as of the wind, قَصْف ـ عَصْفَة .

Boom, *v.i.* To sail quickly, as of a ship, شَمَّرَ . To swell and roar, as of the sea, مَاجَ وَلَجِبَ . To cry, as of the bittern, أَعْوَلَ ـ صَرَّ . The ship boomed through the water, تَشَمَّرَتِ ٱلسَّفِينَةُ مَعَ ٱلْمِيَاهِ .

Booming, *a.* Roaring, لَجِب ـ وَمْنَهَت ـ صَيِّت .

Boon, *n.* فَضْل ـ نِعَم ـ هَدِيَّة *pl.* هَدَايَا ـ إِحْسَان . A boon companion, نَدِيم *pl.* نُدَمَآء .

Boor, *n.*
Boorish, *a.* } أَمَّان ـ أُمِّيّ ـ جَافٍ ـ غَلِيظ ـ فَلَّاح . To be —, جَفَا .

Boorishness, *n.* جَفَآء .

Boosy, *a.* Tipsy, مُلْتَكّ ـ سَكْرَان *pl.* سُكَارَى . He was —, مَسَّهُ سُكْرٌ .

Boot, *v.t.* To profit, نَفَعَ ـ أَفَادَ . To put on the boots for, أَلْبَسَ ٱلْحِذَآءَ . It boots not to inquire, لا يَحْتَاجُ إِلَى ٱلسُّؤَالِ .

Boot, *n.* Profit, فَائِدَة ـ مَنْفَعَة ـ رِبْح ـ كَسْب . A boot for the feet, حِذَآء *pl.* أَحْذِيَة ـ نَعْل *pl.* نِعَال ـ جَزْمَة *pl.* جَزْمَات . To boot, besides, زِيَادَةً ـ أَيْضًا . Boot, as of a carriage, دُولاب .

Booth, *n.* خَيْمَة *pl.* خِيَم ـ كُوخ *pl.* أَكْوَاخ ـ خُصّ *pl.* أَخْصَاص ـ مِظَلَّة ـ عَرِيش *pl.* عُرُش ـ عَرِيشَة . To erect a —, عَرَّشَ ـ أَعْرَشَ ـ إِعْتَرَشَ .

Boot-jack, *n.* آلَةٌ لِخَلْعِ ٱلنَّعْلِ عَنِ ٱلرِّجْلِ .

Bootless, *a.* غَيْرُ طَائِلٍ ـ بَاطِل ـ غَيْرُ مُفِيدٍ ـ بِلا فَائِدَةٍ .

Bootlessly, *ad.* بِعَدَمِ طَائِلٍ ـ مِنْ غَيْرِ إِفَادَةٍ ـ بَاطِلًا .

Bootlessness, *n.* عَدَمُ مَنْفَعَةٍ .

Boot-maker, *n.* جَزْمَاتِي ـ سَكَّاف ـ حَذَّآء .

Boot-rack, *n.* رَفٌّ لِلنِّعَالِ .

Boots, *n.* A shoeblack at an hotel, مُنَظِّفُ ٱلْجَزْمَاتِ فِي لُوكَنْدَة ـ مَسَّاحُ ٱلنِّعَالِ .

Boot-tree, *n.* قَالِبٌ لِتَوْسِيعِ ٱلنِّعَالِ .

Booty, *n.* خُلْسَة ـ خَلِيسَة ـ نُهْبَة ـ نَهْب *pl.* نِهَاب ـ مَغْنَم *pl.* مَغَانِمُ ـ سَلَب ـ غَنِيمَة *pl.* غَنَائِمُ . To take as —, إِغْتَنَمَ ـ غَنِمَ . One who takes —, غَانِم . He who wins takes the —, مَنْ عَزَّ بَزَّ .

Borax, *n.* لِزَاقُ ٱلذَّهَبِ ـ مِلْحُ ٱلصَّاغَةِ ـ بَوْرَق ـ بُورَاق . Baker's borax, بَوْرَقُ ٱلْخَبَّازِينَ .

Border, *n.* The outer edge of any thing, كَنَف *pl.* أَكْنَاف — طَرَف *pl.* أَطْرَاف — حَافَة *pl.* حَافَات — شُفْر *pl.* أَشْفَار. The — of cloth, of a veil, *etc.*, عَلَم — صِنْفَة — طُرَّة — عِذْقَة — نِير *pl.* أَنْيَار. A fringe round a garment, ذَيْل — سِجَاف. The — of a river, حَافَةُ نَهْر — شَطُّ نَهْر. The confines of a country, تَخْم *pl.* تُخُوم — نَاحِيَة *pl.* نَوَاحِي — حَدّ *pl.* حُدُود. A row, صَفّ *pl.* صُفُوف.

Border, *v.t.* and *i.* To surround with a border, نَيَّرَ — أَنَارَ — أَعْلَمَ — كَنَّفَ. To — upon, to be adjacent to, تَاخَمَ — إِتَّصَلَ بِ — قَارَبَ. To reach, وَصَلَ إِلَى *aor.* يَصِلُ — لَحِقَ ـَ.

Borderer, *n.* سَاكِنٌ عَلَى ٱلْحُدُودِ *pl.* سُكَّان.

Bore, *v.t.* To pierce, جَابَ ـُ — خَرَقَ ـِ — ثَقَبَ ـُ — نَقَبَ ـُ — بَخَشَ ـُ. To weary, أَمَلَّ — كَدَّ ـُ — أَكَدَّ — أَعْجَزَ — كَلَّفَ — زَعَّلَ. To — a hole in the ground, حَفَرَ حُفْرَةً ـِ. To be bored, pierced, تَخَرَّقَ — إِنْثَقَبَ. To be bored, wearied, تَكَلَّفَ — زَعِلَ ـَ.

Bore, *n.* A hole made by boring, ثُقْب — نَقْب — خَرْق — بَخْش. An instrument for boring, مِبْزَل — مِنْقَب — مِثْقَب — بَرِّيمَة. The size, as of a hole, عِيَار. A strong tide, مَدٌّ شَدِيدٌ. A troublesome person, مُضْجِر — مُعْجِز — شَاقّ — مُزَعِّل.

Boreal, *a.* شَمَالِيٌّ.

Boreas, *n.* رِيحٌ شَمَالِيَّةٌ.

Borer, *n.* An insect that destroys wood, سُرْفَة. *See also* Bore, *n.*

Born, *part.* مَوْلُود. Stillborn, وُلِدَ مَيِّتًا — وَلَدٌ مَيِّتٌ. First-born, بِكْر *pl.* أَبْكَار. To be —, وُلِدَ. To be — of, تَوَلَّدَ مِن.

Borne, *part. of to* Bear, *q.v.*

Borough, *n.* بَلْدَة — قَصَبَة *pl.* قَصَبَات.

Borrow, *v.t.* تَعَوَّرَ — إِقْتَرَضَ مِن — إِسْتَعَارَ مِن — تَسَلَّفَ مِن — تَدَيَّنَ مِن — إِسْتَسْلَفَ مِن. To seek to — from, إِسْتَقْرَضَ مِن — إِسْتَسْلَفَ مِن. To take as a loan, أَخَذَ دَيْنًا ـُ. He borrows but he does not pay, يَسْتَقْرِضُ وَلَا يَفِي. They borrowed of one another, of many, إِعْتَوَرُوا. Borrowed, مُسْتَعَار.

Borrower, *n.* مُسْتَقْرِض.

Borrowing, *n.* إِسْتِقْرَاض — إِسْتِسْلَاف.

Bosh, *n.* Nonsense, هَذَر — عَبَث.

Bosnia, *n.* The province, البُشْنَاق — البُوسْنَة.

Bosom, *n.* حِجْر — حِضْن. The breast, جَوْش — صَدْر. The breast of a woman, نَهْد. The tender affections, the breast, فُؤَاد — مَحَبَّة — وُدّ — قَلْب. The — of the sea, جَوُّ ٱلْبَحْرِ. The — of the earth, أَحْشَاءُ ٱلْأَرْضِ. The — of the Church, حِضْنُ ٱلْكَنِيسَةِ. A — friend, جِلّ — خِدْن — خَلِيل. To carry in the —, حَضَنَ ـُ — إِحْتَضَنَ.

Boss, *n.* تَعْبِئَة — كُعْبُرَة *pl.* كَعَابِرُ — حَيْدَة *pl.* أَحْيَاد — مِسْمَار *pl.* مَسَامِير.

Botanic, *a.* | **Botanical**, — مُخْتَصٌّ بِعِلْمِ ٱلنَّبَاتِ. A — garden, بُسْتَانُ ٱلنَّبَاتَاتِ.

Botanist, *n.* عَشَّاب — عَارِفٌ بِٱلنَّبَاتَاتِ.

Botanize, *v.i.* جَمَعَ ٱلنَّبَاتَاتِ وَٱلْأَعْشَابَ ـَ.

Botany, *n.* عِلْمُ ٱلْأَعْشَابِ — عِلْمُ ٱلنَّبَاتَاتِ.

Botch, *n.* An eruption on the skin, قَرْح *pl.* قُرُوح — قَرْحَة — كُبَّة *pl.* كُبَب — غُدَّة *pl.* غُدَد. A patch, رُقْعَة *pl.* رِقَاع. A bungle, شَمْرَجَة.

Botch, *v.t.* To patch, رَقَّعَ. To bungle, شَمْرَجَ — خَرْبَطَ — عَطَّلَ.

Botcher, *n.* A patcher, مُرَقِّع. A bungler, مُخَرْبِط — غَشِيم.

Both, *a.* كِلَا *fem.* كِلْتَا — كِلْتَانِ — الِاثْنَانِ — كِلَاهُمَا — إِثْنَاهُمَا — الوَاحِدُ وَٱلْآخَرُ. Both the men came to me, جَاءَنِي كِلَا ٱلرَّجُلَيْنِ. I saw both the men, رَأَيْتُ كِلَا ٱلرَّجُلَيْنِ — رَأَيْتُ كِلَيْهِمَا. Both by sea and land, بَحْرًا وَبَرًّا. On both sides, مِنَ ٱلطَّرَفَيْنِ — مِنَ ٱلنَّاحِيَتَيْنِ. He forgave them both, غَفَرَ لَهُمَا كِلَيْهِمَا ـِ. He made both into one, جَعَلَ ٱلِاثْنَيْنِ وَاحِدًا ـَ.

Both, *conj.* وَ — مَعَ — أَيْضًا.

Bother, *v.t.* أَغْرَضَ — كَدَّ ـُ — أَكَدَّ — شَقَّ عَلَى ـُ — أَعْجَزَ.

Bottell, *n.* شِرْذِمَة *pl.* شَرَاذِمُ.

Bottle, *n.* قِنِّينَة *pl.* قَنَانِيُّ — قَارُورَة *pl.* قَوَارِيرُ — قِزَازَة *pl.* قَزَائِزُ — سَلَاحِيَّة. A small —, خِنْصَر *pl.* خَنَاصِر — فَتِيلَة. A liquor or spirit —, عَنْبَرِيَّة. A black —, سَوْدَايَة — مُسَوَّدَة. A bundle, as of hay, حُزْمَة *pl.* حُزَم — جُرْزَة *pl.* جُرَز — بَاقَة.

Bottle, *v.t.* To put into bottles, حَطَّ بِٱلْمُسَوَّدَاتِ ـُ — مَلَأَ ٱلْقَنَانِيَّ بِ. To — up, to retain, حَفِظَ ـَ.

Bottle-flower, *n.* ترنسان.

Bottom, *n.* The lowest part, عُمْق — قَعْر — قَرَار — وَطَأ — أَسْفَل. The lowest deep, غَوْر — غَوْرَى. The groundwork, foundation, أَسَاس — قَاعِدَة — أَصْل — مَبْنَى. The —, as of a vase, *etc.*, عَقِب. Sediment, عَكَر — رُسُوب. The — of the heart, صَمِيمُ ٱلْقَلْبِ. The — of a street, آخِرُ ٱلطَّرِيقِ — نِهَايَةُ ٱلزُّقَاقِ. The — of the sea, عُوطُبٌ — قَعْرُ ٱلْبَحْرِ — عُمْقُ ٱلْبَحْرِ. The — of the mountain, أَسْفَلُ ٱلْجَبَلِ. The —, or ground, as of a pattern, أَرْضِيَّة. To the —, completely, تَمَامًا — بِٱلْكَمَالِ وَٱلتَّمَام. Bottom, a ship, مَرْكَب. From top to —, مِنْ فَوْقُ إِلَى أَسْفَل. At —, inwardly, فِي ٱلْبَاطِنِ — فِي ٱلدَّاخِلِ — دَاخِلًا. To go to the —, to drown, غَرِقَ ـَ. To go to the — of a thing, to examine narrowly, أَغَارَ فِي . To get at the — of, find out, إِطَّلَعَ عَلَى — كَشَفَ ـ . To drink to the —, قَعَّرَ ـ . *See also* Buttocks, *n.*

Bottom, *v.t.* and *i.* To build upon, أَسَّسَ-عَلَى — بَنَى-عَلَى ـ . To rest upon, إِسْتَنَدَ عَلَى — إِتَّكَلَ عَلَى .

Bottomless, *a.* لا قَعْرَ لَهُ . The — pit, بِئْرُ ٱلْهَاوِيَةِ .

Bottomry, *n.* رَهِينَةُ مَرْكَبٍ — رَهْنُ مَرْكَبٍ .

Boudoir, *n.* خَاصَّةٌ — عِلِّيَّةٌ *pl.* عَلَالِيُّ — خَلْوَةٌ .

Bough, *n.* غَذَبَةٌ *pl.* عَذَبَاتٌ — غَارِزٌ *pl.* غُرَّازٌ — شُعْبَةٌ *pl.* شِعَابٌ — فَرْعٌ *pl.* فُرُوعٌ — غُصْنٌ *pl.* غُصُونٌ — شَغْنُونٌ .

Bought, *pret.* of *to* Buy, *q.v.*

Bougie, *n.* A wax candle, شَمْعٌ *pl.* شُمُوعٌ . A surgical instrument, لَوْلَبٌ .

Boulder, *n.* بُهْمَةٌ *pl.* بُهَمٌ — جَلْهَةٌ *pl.* جِلَاهٌ — قُلَّاعَةٌ — قُلَاعَةٌ .

Bounce, *v.i.* To spring, قَفَزَ ـ — نَطَّ ² — قَزَّ ـ — قَحَزَ ـ . To make a noise, قَرْقَعَ — فَوَّشَ . To — upon, وَثَبَ عَلَى *aor.* يَثِبُ — هَجَمَ عَلَى ـ — غَارَ عَلَى ² . To boast, فَخَرَ ـ — تَفَوَّشَ . To tell incredible stories, أَطْنَبَ فِي ٱلْحَدِيثِ — هَلَجَ ـ — فَشَرَ ـ .

Bounce, *n.* A jump, قَفْزَةٌ — نَطَّةٌ . A lie, كِذْبٌ — بُهْتَانٌ . An incredible story, إِطْنَابٌ — هَلْجٌ — فَشَارٌ .

Bouncer, *n.* A boaster, طِرْمَاذٌ — فَيَّاشٌ — فَشَّارٌ .

Bouncing, *a.* Lusty, ضَلِيعٌ . Great, جَسِيمٌ — كَبِيرٌ .

Bound, *n.* A limit, حَدٌّ *pl.* حُدُودٌ — خَطٌّ *pl.* خُطُوطٌ — تَخْمٌ *pl.* تُخُومٌ — حُدُودٌ . A leap, قَفْزَةٌ — نَطَّةٌ — وَثْبَةٌ — قَزَّةٌ — نَقْزَةٌ — نَفْزَةٌ . To go beyond bounds, جَازَ ٱلْحَدَّ ²; to exceed, أَفْرَطَ . To keep one within bounds, أَضْبَطَ . To keep one's self within bounds, إِنْضَبَطَ — تَحَفَّظَ . To go beyond bounds, in wickedness, طَغَا ² .

Bound, *v.t.* and *i.* To limit, حَدَّدَ . To confine, حَصَرَ ² — قَيَّدَ . To spring, وَثَبَ *aor.* يَثِبُ — نَقَزَ ² — قَزَّ ـ ² — قَزَّ ² . To cause to —, leap, نَفَّزَ — نَقَّزَ — أَقَزَّ . His heart bounded, رَقَصَ فُؤَادُهُ ² . To be — to ..., compelled to, حَلَّ عَلَى ² — أُلْزِمَ بِ — أُضْطُرَّ إِلَى . To be — for, going to, ضَارِبٌ إِلَى — رَادَ ² — مُسَافِرٌ إِلَى . To be —, confined, إِنْحَبَسَ — إِنْحَصَرَ . I'll be —, أَنَا كَفِيلٌ .

Boundary, *n.* تَخْمٌ *pl.* تُخُومٌ — حَدٌّ *pl.* حُدُودٌ . A — between two fields, أُرْثَةٌ . A — mark, تُخُومٌ .

Bounden, *a.* Necessary, وَاجِبٌ — ضَرُورِيٌّ — لَازِمٌ .

Boundless, *a.* غَيْرُ مُتَنَاهٍ — بِلَا حَدٍّ — بِلَا نِهَايَةٍ . Boundless love, مَحَبَّةٌ فَائِقَةٌ ٱلْحَدَّ . A — sea, بَحْرٌ لَا يَنْزِفُ .

Boundlessness, *n.* عَدَمُ ٱلْحَدِّ — عَدَمُ نِهَايَةٍ .

Bounteous, *a.* فَيَّاضٌ — جَحْجَاحٌ — مَنَّانٌ — كَرِيمٌ — جَائِدٌ — خَيِّرٌ — مُحْسِنٌ — سَخِيٌّ — فَضَّالٌ — مِفْضَالٌ — مُنْعِمٌ — مَفْتُوحُ ٱلْكَفِّ .

To be —, مَنَّ عَلَى ـ — وَسَّعَ عَلَى — أَنْعَمَ عَلَى — تَفَضَّلَ عَلَى — أَفْضَلَ عَلَى . The Bounteous One, God, ٱلْمَنَّانُ .

Bounteously, *ad.* بِكَرَمٍ — بِسَخَاوَةٍ — كَرَمًا — تَكَرُّمًا .

Bounteousness, *n.* فَيْضٌ — جُودٌ — فَضْلٌ — كَرَمٌ — سَخَاءٌ — سَخَاوَةٌ — خَيْرٌ — مَعْرُوفٌ . God's —, نَعِيمُ ٱللّٰهِ .

Bountiful, *a.* *See* Bounteous, *a.*

Bountifully, *ad.* *See* Bounteously, *ad.*

Bounty, *n.* A premium, إِنْعَامٌ . *See also* Bounteousness, *n.*

Bouquet, *n.* A nosegay, بَاقَةُ زَهْرٍ — رَبْطَةُ زَهْرٍ — ضُمَّةُ زَهْرٍ . Scent, aroma, رَائِحَةٌ — عَصْفَةٌ .

Bourn, *n.* A limit, حَدٌّ . An end, غَايَةٌ . A place of return, مَعَادٌ . A brook, جَدْوَلٌ — فَلَجٌ *pl.* فُلُوجٌ .

Bourse, *n.* Exchange, بُورْسٌ .

Bouse, *v. int.* تَعَاطَى ٱلْمُدَامَ — سَقَى ٱلْحَبَقَةَ ـ .

Bout, *n.* A turn, خَطْرَةٌ — دَوْرٌ — دَقَّةٌ — مَرَّةٌ . An attempt, سَعْيٌ — إِجْتِرَاءٌ عَلَى .

Bovine, *a.* بَقَرِيٌّ — مِنْ بَقَرٍ .

Bow, *v.t.* and *i.* To make to bend, ثَنَى ـ — حَنَى ـ — عَوَّجَ . To subdue, أَخْضَعَ — قَهَرَ ـ . To bow to, to salute, سَلَّمَ عَلَى . To bow the back, حَنَى ظَهْرَهُ ـ . To bow the knee, جَثَا ـ ² — جَثَا عَلَى ٱلرُّكْبَةِ . To bow the head, نَكَّسَ رَأْسَهُ ² . To bend one's self or to be bowed, إِنْحَنَى — إِنْثَنَى — تَعَوَّجَ . To stoop, أَكَبَّ — إِنْحَنَى . To sink under pressure, خَضَعَ ـ . To bow, as in prayer, رَكَعَ ـ . To bow before, to worship, سَجَدَ لِ ² — عَبَدَ ² . To bow one's self to the ground, خَرَّ إِلَى ٱلْأَرْضِ ² ـ . A bowing wall, حَائِطٌ مَائِلٌ .

Bow, *n.* An instrument of war, قَوْسٌ *pl.* أَقْوَاسٌ *and* قِسِيٌّ *and* قِيَاسٌ . The bow of a violin, قَوْسُ ٱلْعُودِ . The bow of a saddle, قَرَبُوسُ سَرْجٍ . The bow of a ship, مُقَدَّمُ ٱلْمَرْكَبِ — رَأْسُ ٱلْمَرْكَبِ . (The bow of a Nile boat, شَنَش . The top of the bow, أَبْسَةٌ). The bow used in cleaning cotton, مِنْدَفٌ — قَوْسُ ٱلنَّدَّافَةِ *pl.* مَنَادِفُ — قَوْسُ ٱلنَّدَّافِ . A noose, عُقْدَةٌ *pl.* عُقَدٌ . An inclination of the body, سَلَامٌ — خُضُوعٌ . To bend a bow, نَبَضَ ٱلْقَوْسَ ـ — أَوْتَرَ ٱلْقَوْسَ . To make a bow to, سَلَّمَ عَلَى — تَمَنَّ — ضَرَبَ لِ ـ — طَابُونَا — ضَرَبَ لِ ـ . A bow or bowing in prayer, رَكْعَةٌ *pl.* رَكَعَاتٌ — رُكُوعٌ . To draw a longbow, to exaggerate in speech, أَطْنَبَ فِي ٱلْكَلَامِ .

Bowels, *n.* Intestines, أَمْعَاءٌ — أَمْصِرَةٌ — مُصْرَانٌ — مَصَارِينُ .

فُؤَاد ـ أَحْشَآء . The inner part, أَحْشَآء ـ دَاخِل ـ بَاطِن . Tenderness, رِقَّةُ قَلْب ـ شَفَقَة ـ رَحْمَة ـ حَنَان ـ حِنَّة .

Bower, *n.* An arbour, عُرَيْشَة ـ عَرِيش ـ مُشَجَّرَة . An anchor, بُورٌ أَنْجَر ـ أَنْجَر ـ مِرْسَاة .

Bowery, *a.* ظَلِيل ـ كَثِيرُ ٱلْعَرِيش ـ مُشَجَّر .

Bowie-knife, *n.* خَنَاجِرُ *pl.* خَنْجَر .

Bowl, *n.* A cup, قَدَح *pl.* أَقْدَاح ـ كَأْس *pl.* كُؤُوس *and* كَأْسَات ـ قَصْعَة *pl.* قِصَاع ـ فِنْجَان *pl.* فَنَاجِين . A large bowl, طَاس *pl.* طَاسَات ـ قَصْعَة *pl.* قِصَع *and* قَصَاعات ـ جَفْنَة *pl.* جِفْنَات ـ مَجْوَل . A ball, كُرَة *pl.* كُرَات *and* كُرَيَات ـ طَابَة *pl.* طَابَات . The bowl, as of a pipe, حَجَرَة *pl.* أَحْجَار .

Bowl, *v.i.* and *t.* To play at bowls, ـَ لَعِبَ ٱلْكُرَة . To roll, زَحْرَف ـ دَحْرَج .

Bow-legged, *a.* أَطْرَق *fem.* طَرْقَآء ـ مُعَوَّجُ ٱلسَّاقَيْنِ ـ حَيْكَانَة . The being —, طَرَق .

Bowler, *n.* لَاعِبُ بِٱلْكُرَة *pl.* لَاعِبُون .

Bowline, *n.* حَبْلُ شُغُول ـ شُغُول .

Bowling-green, *n.* مَلْعَبُ ٱلْكُرَة .

Bow-man, *n.* رَامِي نُشَّاب ـ ضَارِبُ نُشَّاب ـ قَوَّاس .

Bow-shot, *n.* ضَرْبُ نُشَّاب .

Bowsprit, *n.* السَّارِي ٱلَّذِي عَلَى مُقَدَّمِ ـ جَبُّوم ـ جَوَادِرَة ٱلْمَرْكَب .

Bowstring, *n.* Of a bow, وَتَر ـ شِرْع *pl.* شِرَاع ـ شِرْعَة *pl.* شِرَع *pl.* أَوْتَار . A — used in strangulation, خِنَاق . To —, خَنَق .

Box, *n.* The tree, شِمْشَار ـ بَقْش ـ بَقْس . A case, صُنْدُوق *pl.* صَنَادِيق . A small —, عُلْبَة *pl.* عُلَب ـ حُقَّة *pl.* حُقَق . A small box for perfumes, حُقَّة . A money box, سَحَّارَة *pl.* سَحَاحِير ـ صُنْدُوقُ ٱلْمَالِ . A poor box, حَصَّالَة . A Christmas box, عِيدِيَّة ـ بَسْتِرِينَة . A (sentry) box, مَنْظَرَة . A snuff box, عُلْبَةُ نُشُوق . A blow, لَطْمَة ـ ضَرْبَة . A small house, سَهْوَة *pl.* سِهَآء . A box of a theatre, خَلْوَة فِي تِيَاترو .

Box, *v.t.* To put into a box, وَضَعَ ـ فِي صُنْدُوق *aor.* يَضَعُ ـ عَلَّبَ . To strike one with the fist, ـِ لَكَمَ ـ ـُ لَطَمَ ـ قَلَم ل ـ ـُ صَفَق ـ كَفَّا . They boxed, تَضَارَبُوا بِٱلْكَفّ . To box the compass, ذَكَرَ أَسَامِي ٱلدَّرَجَاتِ ٱلْمَرْقُومَة فِي ٱلْبُوصْلَةِ (or بَيْتِ ٱلْإِبْرَة) غَيْبًا .

Boxer, *n.* ضَارِبُ كَفّ .

Box-thorn, *n.* عَوْسَج .

Boy, *n.* صَبِيّ *pl.* صِبْيَان ـ طِفْل *pl.* أَطْفَال ـ فَتًى *pl.* فِتْيَان ـ وَلَد *pl.* أَوْلَاد . A son, ٱبْن *pl.* بَنُون ـ وَلَد . A servant boy, غُلَام *pl.* غِلْمَان ـ خَادِم . A school boy, تِلْمِيذ ـ وَلَدُ ٱلْكُتَّاب . A cabin boy, صَبِيُّ ٱلْمَعَاش .

Boyhood, *n.* طُفُولِيَّة ـ غُلُومَة .

Boyish, *a.* صَاحِبُ صَبْوَة ـ لِلطِّفْل ـ صُغَارِيّ ـ طِفْلِيّ .

Boyishly, *ad.* مِثْلَ ٱلصِّغَار ـ مِثْلَ ٱلطِّفْل . To act —, إِسْتَصْبَى .

Boyishness, *n.* وَلْدَنَة ـ صَبْوَة ـ صُغَارِيَّة ـ طُفُولِيَّة ـ صِبًا .

Brace, *n.* A pair, زَوْج *pl.* أَزْوَاج *vulg.* جَوْز *pl.* أَجْوَاز . A bandage, حِزَام ـ رِبَاط ـ رِبْطَة . A crooked mark used in printing, كُلَّاب ـ عُقَّافَة . A — of pistols, زَوْجُ طَبَنْجَات . The braces of a carriage, حَمَّالَاتُ عَرَبِيَّة . Suspenders, شِمَار ـ شِنَاط .

Brace, *v.t.* ـِ رَبَطَ ـ ـُ شَدَّ ـ ـِ حَزَمَ . To brace one's self to, تَجَلَّدَ ل .

Bracelet, *n.* رَسْوَة *pl.* رَسَوَات ـ سِوَار *pl.* أَسَاوِير *and* أَسَاوِرَة ـ دُمْلُج *pl.* دَمَالِج .

Brachial, *a.* ذِرَاعِيّ .

Bracket, *n.* A support, مِسْنَد ـ سَنَد ; for a light, شَمْعَدَان . In printing or writing, عَلَامَاتٌ كَذَا [ ] تَفْصِلُ ٱلْجُمَلَ ٱلْمُعْتَرِضَة فِي ٱلْإِنْشَآء .

Brackish, *a.* قَيْصُونِيّ ـ مَلِح ـ مَلِيح ـ مَسُوس ـ مَآج .

Brackishness, *n.* قَيْصُونِيَّة ـ مَلِيحَة .

Brad, *n.* مِسْمَارٌ بِلَا رَأْسٍ ـ مَسَامِيرُ صَغِيرَة *pl.* مِسْمَارٌ صَغِير .

Brag, *v.i.* فَشَّرَ ـ ـِ خَرَطَ ـ إِفْتَخَرَ ـ إِعْتَزَّ . *See also to* Boast, *v.i.*

Braggadocio, *n.*, Braggart, Bragger, } فَشَّار ـ وَهَّاص ـ فَيَّاش ـ مُفْتَخِر ـ فَشُوش ـ أَنْفُهُ فِي ٱلسَّمَاء وَٱسْتُهُ فِي ٱلْمَآء ـ طِرْمَان (*i.e.* one whose nose is in the sky and his rump in the water).

Brahmin, *n.* بَرْهَمِيّ *pl.* بَرَاهِمَة .

Brahminical, *a.* بَرَاهِمِيّ .

Brahminism, *n.* مَذْهَبُ ٱلْبَرَاهِمَة .

Braid, *v.t.* Of the hair, ـِ جَدَلَ ـ ـِ ضَفَرَ ـ ضَفَّرَ . To work with braid, زَيَّنَ ـ بِقَيْطَانٍ ـ قَيْطَنَ .

Braid, *n.* Of hair, دَمْج ـ جَدِيلَة *pl.* جَدَائِل . The hair twisted into fine braids with silken cords and left to hang down the back, جَدِيلَة ـ ضَفِيرَة *pl.* ضَفَائِر . A similar braiding without the silk cords, عَبِيدِيَّة . A fine cord, قَيْطَان ـ خَيْبَة ـ أَخْيِيَة .

Brail, *n.* Ropes to furl sails, رَانْدَه ـ أَعَاوِيل .

Brain, *n.* مُخّ *pl.* مِخَاخ ـ أَدْمِغَة *pl.* الدِّمَاغ ـ أُمُّ ٱلرَّأْس . The understanding, عَقْل ـ ذِهْن . The membranes of the —, أُمُّ ٱلدِّمَاغ . A wound affecting the —, دَامِغَة . To turn the —, ـِ هَتَرَ .

Brain, *v.t.* مَخَّخَ ـ دَمَغَ ـ ².

Brainless, *a.* مُعْتَلُّ ٱلدِّمَاغِ ـ مَلْطُوش ـ هَاجِر ـ غَبِين ـ مَجْنُون.

Brain-pan, *n.* قِحْف *pl.* أَقْحَاف ـ جُمْجُمَة *pl.* جَمَاجِم.

Brain-sick, *a.* بِهِ دَآءُ ٱلسِّرْسَام ـ مُسَرْسَم.

Brake, *n.* A thicket, عَيْكَة ـ أَيْك ـ غَرِيف ـ دَغْلَة. An instrument for thrashing hemp, مِدَقَّة; for arresting a wheel, *etc.*, ضَابِطَة.

Brakeman, *n.* ضَبَّاط ـ مَاسِكُ ٱلضَّابِطَةِ.

Braky, *a.* Thorny, ذُو شَوْك. Rough, وَعْر. Full of thickets, ذُو دَغَل.

Bramble, *n.* The shrub, عُلَّيْق ـ عَوْسَج. Any prickly shrub, حَسَك ـ عَاقُول.

Bramin, *n.* *See* Brahmin, *n.*

Bran, *n.* نُخَالَة ـ رِدَّة ـ نُخَال. To clear of bran, نَخَلَ ².

Branch, *n.* Of a tree, شُعْبَة *pl.* شِعَاب ـ فَرْع *pl.* فُرُوع ـ غُصْن *pl.* أَغْصَان *and* غُصُون. Any part shooting out from the rest, فَرْع ـ شُعْبَة. Branch, as of a river, ضَوْج *pl.* أَضْوَاج ـ شُعْبَة; of a family, شُعْبَة ـ فَرْع. Offspring, نَسْل ـ ذُرِّيَّة. A vine —, زَرَجُون *pl.* زَرَاجِين ـ شَعْشَاع ـ فَرْعُ دَالِيَةٍ. The river divides itself into three branches, ٱلنَّهْرُ يَتَشَعَّبُ ثَلَاثَ شِعَابٍ. While the branches are yet tender, إِذَا لَانَتِ ٱلْأَغْصَانُ. A — line, شُعْبَةٌ مِنْ خَطٍّ.

Branch, *v.i.* and *t.* To spread out in branches, شَعَّبَ ـ تَفَرَّعَ ـ إِنْشَعَبَ. To divide, as into branches, قَسَّمَ شِعَابًا ـ فَرَّعَ. To put forth branches, أَغْصَنَ ـ غَصَّنَ.

Branchless, *a.* لَا أَغْصَانَ لَهُ ـ بِلَا فُرُوع.

Branchlet, *n.* غُصَيْنَة.

Branchy, *a.* كَثِيرُ ٱلْفُرُوعِ ـ كَثِيرُ ٱلْأَغْصَانِ.

Brand, *v.t.* To mark with a —, وَسَمَ *aor.* يَسِمُ ـ عَلَّمَ بِجِذْوَةٍ ـ ² ـ كَوَى ـ جَرَسَ بِ. To — with infamy, فَضَحَ ـ عَرَّبَ ـ.

Brand, *n.* A lighted stick, جِذْوَة ـ جِذْمَة ـ مَشْعَلَة. The mark made by burning, وِسَام ـ نَار. A stigma, فَضَاحَة ـ عَيْب ـ عَار.

Branding-iron, *n.* لُوَيَا ـ مِكْوَاة ـ مِيسَم.

Brandish, *v.t.* To wave, shake, رَجَّ ² ـ هَزَّ ² ـ أَرْعَدَ. To flourish, as of a sword, أَجَالَ ـ أَهَبَّ; of a spear, خَطَرَ ².

Brand-new, *a.* جَدِيدٌ خَالِص.

Brandy, *n.* عَرَق فَرَنْسَاوِيّ ـ قُونْيَاق ـ بَرَانْدِي.

Brangle, *n.* مُنَازَعَة ـ مُشَاجَرَة ـ نِزَاع.

Brangle, *v.i.* نَازَعَ ـ شَاجَرَ.

Brasier, *n.* A worker in brass, نَحَّاس ـ صَفَّار. A pan for coals, مِنْقَل *pl.* مَنَاقِل.

Brass, *n.* صُفْر ـ نُحَاسٌ أَصْفَرُ. Impudence, وَقَاحَة. Brass wire, سِلْكٌ مِنَ ٱلنُّحَاسِ ٱلْأَصْفَرِ.

Brassiness, *n.* The colour of brass, لَوْنُ ٱلنُّحَاسِ ٱلْأَصْفَرِ.

Brassy, *a.* صُفْرِيّ ـ نُحَاسِيّ ـ مِنَ ٱلنُّحَاسِ.

Brat, *n.* طِفْل *pl.* أَطْفَال *fem.* طِفْلَة ـ وَلَد *pl.* أَوْلَاد *fem.* بِنْت *pl.* بَنَات.

Bravado, *n.* A boast, طَرْمَذَة ـ إِفْتِخَار ـ إِطْنَاب. A boaster, طِرْمَاذ ـ فَيَّاش ـ فَشَّار. To do a thing out of —, فَعَلَ مُجَازَفَةً ـ. To use — in speech, أَطْنَبَ فِي ٱلْكَلَامِ.

Brave, *a.* Courageous, بَطَل *pl.* أَبْطَال ـ شَجِيع *pl.* شُجْعَان ـ رَجَّال ـ مِقْدَام ـ فَتَّاك ـ فَاتِك *pl.* جَرِيء *pl.* أَجْرِآء ـ شُجَاع ـ جَذَع *pl.* جُذْعَان. Noble, نَبِيل ـ ذُو عِزٍّ. Showy, مُزَخْرَف. To be —, شَجُعَ ²; to make —, شَجَّعَ; to pretend to be —, تَشَجَّعَ.

Brave, *n.* An Indian warrior, إِبْنُ حَرْبٍ مِنَ ٱلْعَشَائِرِ ٱلْأَمِيرِيكَانِيَّةِ. A — man, بَطَل *pl.* أَبْطَال.

Brave, *v.t.* To defy, فَتَكَ ². To encounter with firmness, قَحَمَ فِي ² ـ عَنْتَرَ ـ تَغَرَّرَ. To — dangers, They braved great dangers, رَكِبُوا ٱلْأَخْطَارَ.

Bravely, *ad.* عَنْتَرَةً ـ بِشَجَاعَةٍ ـ بِجَرَآءَةٍ.

Bravery, *n.* Courageousness, عَنْتَرَة ـ جُرْأَة ـ جَرَآءَة ـ شَجَاعَة ـ جَذْعَنَة. Finery, زِينَة ـ تَزَخْرُف.

Bravo, *n.* An assassin, قَاتِل *pl.* قُتَّال ـ فَاتِك *pl.* فُتَّاك. *See also* Villain, *n.*

Bravo, *int.* حَبَّذَا. Well done! (to thee), أَحْسَنْتَ ـ عَافِيَة. Bravo! (well said, to thee), سَلِمَ فَمُكَ ـ عَافَاكَ ـ عَلَيْكَ.

Brawl, *v.i.* صَوَّتَ ـ عَجَّ ـ كَثُرَ ٱلْعِيَاطُ ـ غَوَّشَ.

Brawl, *n.* نِزَاع ـ هَوْشَة ـ لِجَاج وَصَخَب ـ غَيْشَرَة ـ غَوْشَة.

Brawler, *n.* / Brawling, *a.* } صَخَّاب ـ عَجَّاج ـ لَجُوج.

Brawn, *n.* Boar's flesh, لَحْمُ خِنْزِيرٍ. The muscular part of the arm, حَبْلُ ٱلذِّرَاعِ.

Brawniness, *n.* صَلَاعَة ـ عَضَل ـ قُوَّة.

Brawny, *a.* فَعْم ـ عَضِل ـ قَوِيّ ـ عَفِيّ ـ ضَلِيع.

Bray, *v.t.* To pound, سَحَقَ ـ دَقَّ ² ـ دَقَّقَ ـ دَكَّ ² ـ بَسَّ ² ـ هَرَسَ ² ـ جَرَشَ ـ أَجَشَّ ـ جَشَّ ² ـ سَحَنَ. To — coarsely, رَضَّ ². To be brayed, إِنْسَحَقَ; coarsely, إِرْتَضَّ.

Bray, *v.i.* As an ass, نَهَقَ ـ شَحَرَ ـ شَهَقَ ـ شَهْنَقَ.

Bray, *n.* }
Braying, } Of an ass, شَخِير ـ نَهِيق ـ نُهَاق.

Brayer, *n.* One who brays, as of an ass, جَعْجَاع ـ نَاهِق ـ صَرْصَاع ـ صَلْصَال. An instrument to bray with, مِسْحَنَة ـ مِسْحَل ـ صَلَايَات .pl صَلَاءَة ـ يَدُ ٱلسَّحْقِ.

Braze, *v.t.* To solder with brass, أَلْحَمَ ـ بِٱلنُّحَاسِ.

Brazen, *a.* Of brass, نُحَاسِيٌّ ـ صُفْرِيٌّ ـ مِنَ ٱلنُّحَاسِ. Impudent, سَفِيه ـ وَقِح.

Brazen, *v.i.* To be impudent, وَقُحَ *aor.* يَقِحُ. To be — towards, تَوَاقَحَ عَلَى. To — it out, ثَبَتَ عَلَى ـ بِوَقَاحَةٍ.

Brazen-faced, *a.* سَفِيه ـ قَلِيلُ ٱلْحَيَاءِ.

Brazenly, *ad.* بِوَقَاحَةٍ ـ وَقَاحَةً.

Brazenness, *n.* وَقَاحَة ـ سَفَاهَة.

Brazier, *n.* *See* Brasier, *n.*

Brazil-wood, *n.* بَقَّم ـ عَنْدَم.

Brazing, *n.* إِلْحَامٌ بِٱلنُّحَاسِ.

Breach, *n.* An aperture, خُرْق ـ فَاتِحَة ـ فُرْجَة ـ ثُغْرَة ـ ثَغْر ـ نُقْبَة ـ شَقّ. A gap, chink, خَلَل *pl.* خِلَال ـ خَلَّة. A difference, quarrel, نَقْض ـ مُنَازَعَة ـ خِلَاف ـ شِقَاق ـ صُرْم. Any rupture, كَسْر ـ فَسْخ. Violation, تَعْدِيَة. A —, as of faith, خُلْف ـ عَدَمُ وَفَاءٍ ـ نَقْض ـ إِخْلَاف. Breach of promise of marriage, نَقْضُ عَهْدِ ٱلزِّيجَةِ. A — of the peace, مُقَاتَلَة. He healed the — between them, رَتَقَ فَتْقَهُمْ.

Breach, *v.t.* ثَغَرَ ـ خَرَقَ ـ نَقَبَ ـ جَعَلَ شَقًّا فِي.

Bread, *n.* عَيْش ـ خُبْز. Bread made of any grain, خَبِيز. A loaf or roll of —, رَغِيف ـ قُرْصَة ـ خُبْزَة *pl.* رُغْف *and* رُغْفَان. Food in general, طَعَام ـ قُوت ـ غِذَاء ـ أُكُل. Unleavened —, خُبْزٌ فَطِير. New —, خُبْزٌ طَرِيٌّ. Stale —, خُبْزٌ بَائِتٌ. Bread with other food, خُبْزٌ بِإِدَامٍ. A piece of dry —, without anything to make it savoury, جِلْف *pl.* جِلْفَة. A sweet-bread, pancreas of a calf, لَوْزَةُ ٱلْعِجْلِ. To make —, خَبَزَ خُبْزًا. To break —, كَسَرَ ٱلْخُبْزَ. To beg —, to beg, تَسَوَّلَ ـ شَحَذَ. A maker of —, خَبَّاز. The trade of making bread, خِبَازَة.

Bread-corn, *n.* }
Bread-stuff, } حَبُّ خَبِيزٍ.

Bread-fruit, *n.* نَوْعٌ مِنَ ٱلثَّمَرِ.

Breadth, *n.* عَرْض ـ سَعَة. An oblong piece, سَبِيبَة مُسْتَطِيلَة ـ شُقَّة *pl.* شُقَق.

Breadthwise, *ad.* إِعْتِرَاضًا ـ بِٱلْعَرْضِ. The thing lay —, athwart, إِعْتَرَضَ ٱلشَّيْءُ ـ عَرَضَ ٱلشَّيْءُ. To place —, عَرَّضَ.

Break, *v.t.* قَضَّ ـ كَسَرَ ـ صَرَمَ ـ حَطَمَ ـ رَضَّ. To burst, صَدَعَ ـ قَطَعَ. To open, as of a seal, فَضَّ ـ فَكَّ. To overcome, surmount, غَلَبَ عَلَى ـ فَاقَ. To subdue, قَهَرَ ـ أَخْضَعَ. To batter, هَدَمَ ـ فَضَّ ـ ثَغَرَ ـ هَدَّ ـ كَسَرَ. To crush, سَحَقَ ـ هَشَمَ. To tear, شَقَّ ـ مَزَّقَ ـ خَرَقَ. To —, as of a seal, فَضَّ. To weaken, as the mind, with trouble, فَقَعَ. To —, as age does, حَطَمَ. To tame, رَاضَ ـ دَرَّسَ ـ طَبَّعَ ـ دَعَكَ. To make bankrupt, كَسَّرَ ـ فَلَّسَ. To reform, أَصْلَحَ ـ هَذَّبَ. To dismiss from office, عَزَلَ ـ وَضَعَ ـ عَن. To transgress, نَقَضَ ـ خَالَفَ ـ تَعَدَّى. To destroy, أَهْلَكَ ـ أَخْرَبَ ـ هَدَّ. To destroy, cut off, as of an army, قَرَضَ ـ مَحَقَ. To —, as of a rope, جَزَعَ.

To break asunder, قَطَعَ ـ مَزَّقَ.

To break bulk, فَرَّغَ وَسْقَ ٱلْمَرْكَبِ.

To break cover, خَرَجَ مِنَ ٱلْمَخْبَإِ.

To break down, هَدَمَ ـ هَدَّ.

To break faith, of a promise, *etc.* فَسَخَ ـ نَقَضَ ـ فَتَقَ ـ نَكَثَ.

To break ground, to commence, شَرَعَ فِي ـ أَنْشَأَ بِ.

To break in, as of an animal, خَزَا ٱلدَّابَّةَ ـ رَاضَ ـ دَرَّسَ.

To break in upon, attack, هَجَمَ عَلَى ـ حَمَلَ عَلَى; to come in upon suddenly, إِطَّلَعَ عَلَى ـ نَزَلَ عَلَى ـ دَخَلَ عَلَى. *See also to* Surprise, *v.t.*

To break on the wheel, to torture, عَذَّبَ.

To break one's heart, كَسَرَ قَلْبَهُ ـ كَسَرَ خَاطِرَهُ.

To break one off from, as from a habit, كَفَّ ـ عَن ـ أَضْرَبَ ـ عَن.

To break silence, نَطَقَ ـ حَكَى ـ تَكَلَّمَ.

To break the neck, to put an end to, أَنْهَى; to prevent, سَدَّ ـ مَنَعَ.

To break through, as of a wall, ثَغَرَ ـ نَقَبَ; to overcome, قَوِيَ عَلَى ـ أَفْلَجَ عَلَى.

To break up, as of an assembly, فَرَّقَ ـ فَضَّ ـ نَقَضَ. To — up, of soil, عَدَّنَ.

To break wind, ضَرَطَ ـ وَبَّعَ.

To break with, to be at variance with, خَالَفَ ـ شَذَّ عَن.

Break, *v.n.* To — of itself, be broken, إِنْكَسَرَ ـ إِنْقَطَعَ ـ إِنْفَضَّ ـ تَكَسَّرَ. To burst, إِنْفَقَعَ ـ تَصَدَّعَ ـ إِنْشَقَّ, of any thing hollow, فَقَعَ ; to be so broken, إِنْفَضَخَ. To —, as of a skin, إِنْشَقَّ ـ إِنْفَتَحَ ـ فَقَأَ. To —, as a boil, إِنْشَقَّ ـ تَخَرَّقَ. To —, as waves on a rock, لَطَمَ. To —, as the morning, أَصْبَحَ ـ شَقَّ ٱلْفَجْرِ ـ طَلَعَ ٱلْفَجْرُ. To —, become bankrupt, إِنْكَسَرَ ـ أَفْلَسَ. To —, as a rope, staff, *etc.* إِنْجَزَعَ. To —, decline in health, ضَعُفَ ـ ضَعُفَ ـ فَنِيَ.

To break down, to come to nothing, تَلَاشَى ـ خَابَ.

To break forth, to begin, صَارَ ـ أَشْرَعَ فِي ـ بَدَأَ. *See also to* Begin, *v.i.*

To break from, separate from, إِنْفَصَلَ عَنْ ـ إِنْفَرَقَ مِنْ.

To break in upon, to appear to, خَطَرَ ـ بَانَ لِ ـ ظَهَرَ لِ عَلَى بَالٍ.

To break loose, إِنْسَلَّ ـ إِنْفَلَتَ ـ جَفَلَ.

To break out, discover itself, إِشْتَهَرَ ـ شَاعَ ـ ظَهَرَ. To be witnessed, become visible, شُوهِدَ.

To break out, as an eruption, نَبَتَ ـ طَلَعَ ـ ثَارَ.

To break out into anger, ثَارَ غَضَبًا ـ إِنْحَمَقَ ـ غَضِبَ.

To break out into laughter, إِنْبَعَجَ مِنَ ـ تَضَحَّكَ ـ إِنْبَاقَ ٱلضَّحِكُ.

To break up, as an assembly, تَفَرَّقَ ـ إِنْفَضَّ.

To break up, to cease, إِنْتَهَى ـ إِفْتَرَّ مِنْ ـ إِنْقَطَعَ.

To break out into tears, بَكَى ـ تَدَمَّعَ ـ أَجْرَى دُمُوعًا.

To break out, become dissolute, إِنْفَرَطَ ـ غَمَطَ ـ فَسَدَ.

To break with, to separate from, إِنْقَطَعَ عَنْ ـ إِنْفَصَلَ عَنْ ـ إِعْتَزَلَ عَنْ.

Break, *n.* A rupture, كَسْرَةٌ. A chink, خَلَلٌ *pl.* خِلَالٌ. An interruption, رَكْزَةٌ ـ حَطَّةٌ ـ وَقْفٌ ـ قَطْعٌ. A pause, وَقْفَةٌ. A failure, قُصُورٌ ـ خَيْبَةٌ ـ فَشَلٌ. The — of day, شَقُّ ٱلْفَجْرِ ـ طُلُوعُ ٱلنَّهَارِ. To make a —, to pause, وَقَفَ *aor.* يَقِفُ ـ إِسْتَرَاحَ. An instrument to stop vehicles; *see* Brake, *n.*

Breakage, *n.* كَسْرَةٌ ـ كَسْرٌ.

Breaker, *n.* A transgressor, مُتَعَدٍّ ـ نَاكِثٌ. A rock, صَخْرَةٌ *pl.* صُخُورٌ. A wave, مَوْجَةٌ *coll.* مَوْجٌ *pl.* أَمْوَاجٌ. A —, as of horses, رَائِضٌ *pl.* رُوَّاضٌ. *See also* Tamer, *n.*

Breakfast, *n.* غَدَاءٌ *pl.* أَغْدِيَةٌ ـ تَرْوِيقَةٌ ـ كَسْرُ ٱلصَّفْرَاءِ ـ فُطُورٌ. It is time for —, حَانَ ٱلْفُطُورُ ـ ٱلْفُطُورُ حَاضِرٌ.

Breakfast, *v.i.* To take —, فَطَرَ ـ غَدِيَ ـ أَفْطَرَ. To give breakfast to another, فَطَّرَ ـ أَفْطَرَ.

Breakman, *n.* *See* Brakeman, *n.*

Breakneck, *a.* Dangerous, مُخْطِرٌ. A — place, مَهْلَكَةٌ *pl.* مَهَالِكُ.

Breakwater, *n.* سَدٌّ ـ بَنْدٌ ـ شَذَبٌ.

Breast, *n.* صَدْرٌ *pl.* صُدُورٌ. The — of a woman, نَهْدٌ *pl.* نُهُودٌ ـ صَدْرٌ ـ قَلْبٌ. ثَدْيٌ *dual* ثَدْيَانِ *pl.* ثُدِيٌّ *and* ثِدِيٌّ. The heart, صَدْرٌ ـ قَلْبٌ.

Breast, as of a fowl, with the flesh upon it, جُؤْجُؤٌ *pl.* جَآجِئُ ـ صَدْرٌ. A protuberant —, of a woman, ثَدْيٌ مُعَقَّدٌ. The breasts of a woman when small and round, رُمَّانَتَانِ. Having full breasts, نَاهِدٌ ـ ضَرِيعٌ ـ مُنَهِّدٌ. Having no breasts, أَمْسَحُ *fem.* مَسْحَاءُ. Large breasted, مُصَدَّرٌ ـ أَصْدَرُ. To smite upon the —, قَرَعَ ٱلصَّدْرَ ـ ضَرَبَ ٱلصَّدْرَ. To lean on the — of, إِتَّكَى عَلَى صَدْرٍ. He sucked the — of his mother, رَضَعَ ثَدْيَ أُمِّهِ. Breast-preserver, قَلْعٌ *pl.* قِلَاعٌ. To lie on the —, جَثَمَ.

Breast, *v.t.* تَصَدَّرَ.

Breast-bone, *n.* جُؤْجُؤٌ *pl.* جَآجِئُ ـ قَصٌّ ـ زَوْرٌ.

Breast-high, *a.* لَاحِقٌ إِلَى ٱلصَّدْرِ ـ عَلَى عُلُوِّ ٱلصَّدْرِ.

Breast-pin, *n.* حَلْيُ ٱلصَّدْرِ *pl.* حُلِيٌّ ـ حِلْيَةٌ لِلصَّدْرِ *pl.* حُلًى.

Breast-plate, *n.* صَفِيحَةٌ لِلصَّدْرِ ـ دِرْعٌ.

Breast-work, *n.* سِتَارَةٌ ـ مِتْرَسَةٌ.

Breath, *n.* تَنَفُّسٌ ـ نَسَمَةٌ ـ نَفَسٌ. Life, حَيَوةٌ ـ رُوحٌ ـ حَيَاةٌ. A breeze, نَسَمَةٌ ـ نَسِيمٌ. Respite, مُهْلَةٌ ـ وَقْتٌ ـ نَفَسٌ. Sweet —, نَغْمَةٌ. Fetid —, بَخَرٌ. Shortness of —, قِطْعٌ ـ قُطْعٌ. Out of —, مُبْتَهِرٌ ـ مَبْهُورٌ ـ بَهِيرٌ. A — of air, نَفْحَةٌ. In a —, instant, حَالًا ـ فِي لَحْظَةٍ. In the same —, مَعًا ـ فِي نَفَسٍ وَاحِدٍ. The last —, رَمَقٌ ـ آخِرُ نَفَسٍ ـ عِنْدَ ٱلْمَمَاتِ.

To be out of breath, إِبْتَهَرَ ـ إِنْبَهَرَ ـ بُهِرَ.

To take breath, تَنَفَّسَ ـ أَخَذَ نَفَسًا.

To put out of breath, بَهَرَ ـ قَطَعَ نَفَسًا.

Breathe, *v.t.* and *i.* To take breath, تَنَسَّمَ ـ تَنَفَّسَ ـ أَخَذَ نَفَسًا. To take breath, to rest, أَخَذَ نَفَسًا ـ إِسْتَرَاحَ ـ بَلَعَ رِيقَهُ. To live, عَاشَ. To — into, نَفَخَ فِي *or* بِ. To — out threatenings, تَهَدَّدَ ـ نَفَثَ. To — to, to inform, teach, لَقَّنَ. To — or whisper to, وَسْوَسَ ـ أَكَّ. To — hard, heavily, أَنَحَ ـ قَبَعَ ـ نَهَجَ ـ زَحَرَ ـ فَحَّ ; in sleep, فَحَّ.

Breathing, *n.* Prayer, صَلَاةٌ ـ تَضَرُّعٌ. Hard —, زَحِيرٌ ـ زُحُورٌ ـ زُحَارَةٌ ; in sleep, فَحِيحٌ ـ فَحٌّ. *See also* Breath, *n.*

Breathing-time, *n.* تَأَنٍّ ـ نَفَسٌ ـ وَقْتٌ ـ مُهْلَةٌ.

Breathless, *a.* Out of breath, مَبْهُورٌ ـ بَهِيرٌ ـ حَشٍ ـ حَشْيَانٌ. Dead, مَيِّتٌ. Breathless silence, سُكُوتٌ تَامٌّ ـ مَقْطُوعُ ٱلنَّفَسِ.

Breathlessness, *n.* حَشَى ـ بُهْر.

Breccia, *n.* نَوْعٌ مِنَ ٱلْحِجَارَةِ.

Bred, *part.* and *a.* Brought up, مُرَبًّى. Well-bred, صَاحِبُ حَسَنِ ٱلتَّرْبِيَةِ ـ أَوَادِمُ *pl.* آدَمِيٌّ ـ أَدَب. Ill-bred, بِلَا تَرْبِيَةٍ ـ جَافٍ ـ نِكْس ـ دَنِيّ. Half-bred, مُوَلَّد. Thorough-bred, أَصِيل.

Breech, *n.* The hinder part, مُؤَخَّر ـ وَرَآء. The buttock, دُبُر. The — of a gun, بُورُمَة.

Breech, *v.t.* To put in breeches, سَرْوَلَ ـ لَبَّسَ لِبَاسًا.

Breeches, *n.* لِبَاس ـ سِرْوَال *pl.* سَرَاوِيل. Small —, تُبَّان; those worn by females, شِنْتِيَان. The band to fasten the —, تِكَّة. The woman wears the —, سَادَتِ ٱلْمَرْأَةُ عَلَى زَوْجِهَا.

Breech-loader, *n.* تَفَنْكٌ (*or*) مِدْفَعٌ تَعْمِيرُهُ مِنَ ٱلْبُورُمَةِ.

Breed, *v.t.* To procreate, وَلَدَ *aor.* يَلِدُ ـ نَسَلَ [2]. To occasion, أَنْشَأَ ـ كَانَ سَبَبَ ـ سَبَّبَ ـ أَبْدَأَ. To educate, رَبَّى ـ أَدَّبَ. To contrive, إِخْتَرَعَ ـ دَبَّرَ. To stir up, هَيَّجَ.

Breed, *v.i.* To increase, multiply, إِزْدَادَ ـ تَكَاثَرَ ـ أَنْمَى ـ نَمَى [2]. To be produced, born, تَوَلَّدَ ـ وُلِدَ. To raise a breed, رَبَّى. They — in and in, يَتَنَاسَلُونَ مِنْ بَعْضِهِمْ بَعْض. The disease was bred among them, تَفَشَّى ٱلْمَرَضُ بَيْنَهُمْ.

Breed, *n.* Progeny, سِلْسِلَة ـ آل ـ نَسْل ـ ذُرِّيَّة. Kind, جِنْس *pl.* أَجْنَاس ـ نَوْع *pl.* أَنْوَاع ـ صِنْف *pl.* أَصْنَاف. A hatch, بَطْن ـ حَضْنَة. Origin, أَصْل. A horse of good —, فَرَسٌ أَصِيلِيٌّ.

Breeder, *n.* Of a woman, كَثِيرَةُ ٱلْبَرَكَةِ ـ وَالِدَة. One who raises a breed, مُرَبٍّ. A fomenter, مُفْتِن ـ مُهَيِّج ـ مُغْرٍ.

Breeding, *n.* Education, bringing up, تَرْبِيَة. Good —, أَدَب ـ شَلَبْنَة ـ ظَرَافَة ـ حُشْمَة ـ حُسْنُ تَرْبِيَةٍ.

Breeding, *a.* وَالِد ـ مُوَلِّد. A — sheep, شَاةٌ وَالِدٌ ـ شَاةٌ وَالِدَةٌ.

Breeze, *n.* A gentle wind, نَسِيم ـ نَسَمَة. Wind, رِيح *pl.* رِيَاح.

Breezy, *a.* نَسِيمِيّ ـ هَوَائِيّ.

Brethren, *n.* إِخْوَة ـ إِخْوَان.

Breve, *n.* In music, عِبَارَةٌ عَنْ عَلَامَةٍ فِي ٱلْمُوسِيقَةِ.

Brevet, *n.* The rank in the army, رُتْبَةٌ عَسْكَرِيَّةٌ بِدُونِ ٱلرَّاتِبَةِ ٱلْمُتَعَلِّقَةِ بِهَا. *See also* Patent, *n.*

Breviary, *n.* صَلَوَاتُ ٱلْفَرْضِ لِلْقُسُوسِ ـ كِتَابُ صَلَوَاتِ ٱلْفَرْضِ.

Brevity, *n.* قِصَر ـ إِخْتِصَار; in speech, إِيجَازٌ فِي ٱلْكَلَامِ.

Brew, *v.t.* and *i.* To mingle, مَازَجَ ـ خَلَطَ. To contrive, إِخْتَرَعَ. To make beer, صَنَعَ ٱلْبُوزَةَ [2]. To do the business of a brewer, إِسْتَعْمَلَ مِهْنَةَ ٱلْفُقَاعِيِّ. To — mischief, مَكَرَ [2] ـ إِخْتَرَعَ ٱلشَّرَّ ـ لَهِجَ بِٱلْإِغْتِصَابِ [2]. To be forming, وَاقِع ـ صَائِر ـ حَادِث.

Brewer, *n.* صَانِعُ ٱلْبِيرَةِ (*or*) ٱلْبُوزَةِ ـ فُقَاعِيّ.

Brewery, *n.* مَعْمَلُ ٱلْبِيرَةِ (*or*) ٱلْبُوزَةِ ـ مَعْمَلُ ٱلْفُقَاعِ.

Briar, *n.* *See* Brier, *n.*

Bribe, *n.* بَرْطِيل *pl.* بَرَاطِيل ـ رُشًا *pl.* رُشْوَة ـ جُعْل ـ جَعَالَة. To tip one a —, أَلْقَمَهُ ٱلْبَرْطِيلَ. I gave him a —, حَلَوْتُهُ. One who asks for a —, مُسْتَرْشٍ. The receiver of a —, مُرْتَشٍ. Bribes render victorious false allegations, (*prov.*) ٱلْبَرَاطِيلُ تَنْصُرُ ٱلْأَبَاطِيلَ.

Bribe, *v.t.* بَرْطَلَ ـ رَاشَى ـ صَانَعَ. To be bribed, تَبَرْطَلَ. To take a — from, إِرْتَشَى مِنْ.

Briber, *n.* مُبَرْطِل ـ رَاشٍ.

Bribery, *n.* بَرْطَلَة ـ مُرَاشَاة ـ رِشْوَة ـ غَوَايَة.

Brick, *n.* A burnt —, آجُرّ *pl.* آجُور ـ طُوبَة *coll.* طُوب. A sun-dried —, لِبْنَة *coll.* لِبْن ـ قِرْمِيد *pl.* قَرَامِيدُ. A brick-mould, مِلْبَن. To make bricks, لَبَّنَ. A baker of bricks, طَوَّاب.

Brick, *v.t.* فَرَشَ بِٱللِّبْنِ [2].

Brickbat, *n.* شِقْف *pl.* شِقْفَةُ طُوبَةٍ ـ فِلَاق (*or*) فِلْقَةُ آجُرٍّ.

Brickdust, *n.* تُرَابُ ٱلْآجُورِ.

Brick-kiln, *n.* طَوَّابَة.

Bricklayer, *n.* بَنَّآء *pl.* بَنَّاؤُونَ.

Brickmaker, *n.* طَوَّاب ـ لَبَّان.

Brickwork, *n.* شُغْلُ ٱللِّبْنِ ـ لِبْن.

Bridal, *n.* The nuptial festival, عُرْس *pl.* أَعْرَاس ـ فَرَح.

Bridal, *a.* مُخْتَصٌّ بِٱلْعُرْسِ ـ عُرْسِيّ ـ زِيجِيّ. A — procession, زِفَاف. A — night, لَيْلَةُ ٱلزِّفَافِ.

Bride, *n.* عَرُوس *pl.* أَعْرَاس ـ إِمْرَأَةٌ عَرُوسٌ ـ عَرُوسَة *pl.* عَرَائِس. A wife, زَوْجَة ـ قَرِينَة ـ حُرْمَة ـ حَلِيلَة.

Bride-cake, *n.* قُرْقُوشَةُ ٱلْعُرْسِ.

Bride-chamber, *n.* قَصُورَة ـ مَقْصُورَة.

Bridegroom, *n.* عَرُوس *pl.* أَعْرَاس ـ رَجُلٌ عَرُوسٌ ـ عَرِيس.

Bridemaid, *n.* عُجَاهِنَة ـ شَبِينَةُ ٱلْعَرُوسِ.

Brideman, *n.* شَبِينُ ٱلْعَرُوسِ.

Bridewell, *n.* بَيْتُ تَأْدِيب ـ حَبْس.

Bridge, *n.* جِسْر *pl.* جُسُور ـ قَنْطَرَة *pl.* قَنَاطِرُ. The — of the nose, حَائِلُ ٱلْمَنَاخِيرِ ـ قَصَبَةُ ٱلْأَنْفِ ـ وَتَرَةُ ٱلْأَنْفِ ـ ٱلْعِرْنِينُ. The — of a violin, غَزَالُ ٱلْكَمَنْجَةِ ـ حِمَارُ (*or*) مُشْطُ ٱلْكَمَنْجَةِ. To throw a — over, عَقَدَ جِسْرًا عَلَى.

Bridle, *n.* The bit with the reins, عِنَان — لِجَام *pl.* لُجُم and أَلْجِمَة. A — for a camel, زِمَام.

Bridle, *v.t.* لَجَّمَ — أَلْجَمَ. To restrain, أَلْجَمَ — قَمَعَ — أَخْضَعَ — قَهَرَ — …

Bridle-path, *n.* مَسْلَكٌ (or مَجَازٌ) لِلرَّجَّالَةِ وَٱلرُّكَّابِ فَقَطْ.

Brief, *a.* مُوجَز — قَصِير — مُقْتَصَر. To make —, أَوْجَزَ. To be — in speech, أَوْجَزَ فِي ٱلْكَلَامِ *aor.* يُوجِزُ. In —, to sum up, وَٱلْحَاصِلُ.

Brief, *n.* An epitome, مُخْتَصَر — إِيجَاز — مُوجَز — تَلْخِيص. Letters patent, بَرَآءَة *pl.* بَرَاآت — تَقْرِير *pl.* تَقَارِير — خَطّ. A lawyer's —, أَوْرَاقٌ مُخْتَصَّةٌ بِدَعْوَى فِي يَدِ ٱلْمُحَامِي عَنْ مُدَّعٍ — حُجَجُ مُدَّعٍ فِي يَدِ ٱلْمُحَامِي عَنْهُ. To explain in —, بَيَّنَ إِجْمَالًا.

Briefless, *a.* A lawyer without briefs, مُحَامٍ شَرْعِيٌّ بِدُونِ دَعَاوَى.

Briefly, *ad.* إِقْتِصَارًا — بِٱلِاقْتِصَارِ — بِٱلْإِيجَازِ — بِٱلْجُمْلَةِ.

Briefness, *n.* قِصَر — قَصْر — إِيجَاز — إِقْتِصَار.

Brier, *n.* شَوْك — عُلَّيْق. Sweet —, عَبَال — عُلَّيْقُ ٱلْكَلْبِ — وَرْدٌ جَبَلِيٌّ. Briers, حَسَك.

Brig, *n.* غُرَاب *pl.* أَغْرِبَة — إِبْرِيق *pl.* أَبَارِيق and أَبَارِقَة.

Brigade, *n.* فِرْقَةُ عَسْكَرٍ — لِوَآء. General of Brigade, أَمِيرُ لِوَآءٍ.

Brigade Major, مُعَاوِنُ أَمِيرِ لِوَآءٍ.

Brigade, *v.t.* صَفَّ ٱلْعَسْكَرَ لِوَآءً لِوَآءً.

Brigadier, *n.* / **Brigadier General**, قَائِمُ مَقَامِ أَمِيرِ ٱللِّوَآءِ.

Brigand, *n.* حَرَامِيّ *pl.* حَرَامِيَّة — قَاطِعُ ٱلطَّرِيقِ.

Brigandage, *n.* نَهْب — قَطْعُ ٱلطَّرِيقِ.

Brigandine, *n.* زَرَّادَة — زَرْد — دِرْع.

Brigantine, *n.* غُرَاب *pl.* أَغْرِبَة.

Bright, *a.* Shining, مُنِير — لَامِع — مُضِيء — زَاهِر — بَرَّاق — نَيِّر.

Bright, of a colour, نَضِر — نَاضِر; of a day, أَنْهَر; of coin, مَشُوف; of polished iron, أَزْرَق. Serene, صَافٍ. Illustrious, جَلِيّ — بَهِيّ — مُعَزَّز — بَا… Clever, حَاذِق — مَاهِر — ثَاقِبٌ فِي ٱلْعِلْمِ — لَوْذَعِيّ. Transparent, شَفَّاف. Evident, بَائِن — وَاضِح — مَعْلُوم — مَفْهُوم. Having a — countenance, طَلِيقُ ٱلْوَجْهِ. A — genius, ذَكِيُّ ٱلْعَقْلِ. As the — shining of a lamp, كَمَا يَضُوءُ ٱلسِّرَاجُ بِشُعَاعِهِ. A — cloud, سَحَابَةٌ نَيِّرَةٌ. The — morning star, كَوْكَبُ ٱلصُّبْحِ ٱلْمُضِيء. To be —, beautiful, نَضَرَ — أَنْضَرَ. To grow —, light, أَنَارَ — لَمَحَ — تَنَوَّرَ. How — it is! مَا أَضْوَأَهُ.

Brighten, *v.t.* and *i.* To make to shine, رَوَّقَ — جَلَا — صَقَلَ — لَمَّعَ — صَفَّى. To — a colour, كَشَفَ ٱللَّوْنَ. To render acute, حَذَّقَ — أَشْحَذَ — فَطَّنَ. To make illustrious, شَرَّفَ. To grow light, clear, تَنَوَّرَ — لَمَحَ — صَفَا — أَضَآءَ.

Brightly, *ad.* With shining, إِضَآءَةً — بِٱسْتِنَارَةٍ — بِبَهَآءٍ; with lustre, بِفَخْرَةٍ.

Brightness, *n.* Of a light, سَنًا — لَمَح — لَمَعَان — نُور — ضِيَآء; of a colour, نَضَر; of weather, صَفَآء. Lustre, بَهْجَة — رَوْنَق. Acuteness, ذَكَآء — نَبَاهَة — فِطْنَة. Polish, جَلَآء — جَلَال — فَخْر — صَقْل. The flowers vie in — with the sun, اَلنُّورُ يُضَاحِكُ ٱلشَّمْسَ.

Brilliancy, *n.* *See* Brightness, *n.*

Brilliant, *a.* *See* Bright, *a.*

Brilliant, *n.* أَلْمَاس — أَلْمَاسٌ بَرْلَانْت.

Brim, *n.* The edge of any thing, سَبَلَة — كَنَف *pl.* أَكْنَاف — طَرَف — حَافَة. To fill to the —, أَفَاضَ — مَلَأَ إِلَى فَوْقُ. He filled the cup to the —, مَلَأَ ٱلْكَأْسَ إِلَى أَسْبَالِهَا.

Brimful, *a.* / **Brimming**, مَلْآن *fem.* مَلْأَى *pl.* مِلَآء — مَمْلُوّ — مَوْفُور.

Brimmer, *n.* كَأْسٌ مَوْفُورَةٌ — كَأْسٌ مَلْآنَةٌ.

Brimstone, *n.* كِبْرِيت — كُبْرِيت.

Brinded, *a.* / **Brindled**, مُرَقَّط — أَرْقَط — مُنَقَّش — مُبَرْقَش.

Brindle, *n.* رُقْطَة — بَرْقَشَة — نَقْش.

Brine, *n.* Water impregnated with salt, سَلَامُول — سَلَامُورَة — شَرْش. The sea, ٱلْبَحْرُ. Tears, دُمُوع.

Brine-pan, *n.* مَمْلَحَة.

Bring, *v.t.* and *i.* To fetch, as from one place to another, جَلَبَ — أَقْصَى إِلَى — جَآءَ بِ *aor.* يَجِيءُ — أَتَى إِلَى بِ — نَقَلَ — أَحْضَرَ إِلَى. To cause to be present, أَحْضَرَ. To procure, حَصَلَ عَلَى — وَجَدَ *aor.* يَجِدُ. To induce, أَلْزَمَ — جَعَلَ. To attract, جَذَبَ — جَرَّ — أَمَالَ إِلَى. I brought him, جِئْتُ بِهِ. Bring the thing, هَلُمَّ ٱلشَّيْءَ. Bring him to me! عَلَيَّ بِهِ. Bring a light, هَاتِ ٱلنُّورَ. Bring the dinner, رُصَّ ٱلْغَدَآءَ. Bring me a pen, نَاوِلْنِي قَلَمًا. Bring me the ink, إِئْتِنِي بِٱلْحِبْرِ. I have brought you a doctor, أَتَيْتُكَ بِطَبِيبٍ. Let lights be brought in directly, حَيَّ بِٱلنُّورِ إِلَيْنَا سَرِيعًا. To be brought from a place, as of merchandise, إِنْجَلَبَ.

To bring about, to accomplish, قَضَى — أَنْفَذَ — تَمَّمَ — عَمِلَ — أَنْجَزَ. To occasion, سَبَّبَ — أَوْجَبَ.

To bring away, to take away, رَفَعَ — أَخَذَ — شَالَ بِ.

To bring back or again, رَدَّ — أَعَادَ.

To bring back, as to a former state, أَوَّلَ-إِلَى.

To bring close to, قَدَّمَ-إِلَى ـ قَرَّبَ-إِلَى.

To bring down, to lower, نَزَّلَ ـ أَنْزَلَ; of stocks, بَخَسَ ـَ. To debase, أَهَانَ ـ أَذَلَّ.

To bring down one's pride, كَسَرَ نَفْسَ ـِ.

To bring forth, to beget, وَلَدَ aor. يَلِدُ ـ خَلَّفَ; of a woman, to be confined, وَضَعَت aor. تَضَعُ. To produce, حَمَلَ ـ أَثْمَرَ ـِ.

To bring forward, to propose, عَرَضَ ـ قَدَّمَ ـِ.

To bring glad tidings to, بَشَّرَ-بِ.

To bring in, cause to submit, أَخْضَعَ. To gain from, حَصَّلَ مِن ـ قَرَّشَ مِن ـ كَسَبَ مِن ـِ.

To bring into or to a place, أَدْخَلَ بِ-إِلَى ـ أَوْصَلَ-إِلَى ـ دَخَلَ ـُ وَصَّلَ-إِلَى ـ أَدْخَلَ.

To bring in guilty, حَكَمَ عَلَى ـ سَجَّلَ عَلَى ـُ.

To bring in not guilty, أَبْرَأَ ـ بَرَّأَ ـ بَرَّرَ.

To bring into debt, أَرْكَبَ-الدَّيْنَ ـ شَبَكَ-فِي الدُّيُونِ ـِ.

To bring into question, to examine, بَحَثَ عَن ـ فَحَصَ عَن ـَ. To raise doubts of, رَمَى الشَّكَّ فِي ـِ.

To bring off, to get one acquitted, فَكَّ ـ خَلَّصَ ـُ.

To bring on, to occasion, أَوْجَبَ ـ عَلَّلَ ـ سَبَّبَ.

To bring one to reason, أَحْتَاجَ-إِلَى الطَّرِيقَةِ ـ ضَبَطَ ـُ ـِ.

To bring one's self to do a thing, أَلْزَمَ نَفْسَهُ بِ ـ أَضْطَرَّ إِلَى.

To bring over, as to a party, أَمَالَ-إِلَى ـ جَذَبَ-إِلَى ـِ.

To bring out, to exhibit, أَرْوَى ـ رَأَّى ـ أَرَأَى ـ أَظْهَرَ ـ بَيَّنَ.

To bring round, to convince, أَقْنَعَ ـ قَنَّعَ. To revive, بَعَثَ ـَ ـ أَحْيَى.

To bring to, to cause to reach, أَقْضَى بِ-إِلَى. The road brought him to . . . , أَقْضَى بِهِ الطَّرِيقُ إِلَى.

To bring to, of a ship, ضَبَطَ ـ وَقَّفَ ـ أَوْقَفَ ـِ ـُ.

To bring to bed, وَلَّدَ.

To bring together, as after a separation, جَمَعَ بَيْنَ ـَ. To cause to like (one another), أَلَّفَ بَيْنَ. To collect, حَشَدَ ـُ ـ لَمَّ ـُ ـ جَمَّعَ ـ جَمَّرَ.

To bring to life again, أَقَامَ-مِنَ الْمَوْتِ ـ أَحْيَى.

To bring under, to subject, قَمَعَ ـ سَخَّرَ ـ ضَبَطَ ـُ ـِ ـ أَخْضَعَ. To arrest, مَنَعَ ـ أَوْقَفَ ـَ.

To bring up, to educate, وَلَّدَ ـ نَشَّأَ ـ أَنْشَأَ ـ رَبَّى. To nourish, حَضَنَ ـُ. To — into use, أَوْجَدَ ـ إِخْتَرَعَ. To — up, as before a judge, etc., حَاكَمَ-إِلَى ـ أَحْضَرَ-أَمَامَ.

To bring upon the carpet, تَكَلَّمَ فِي ـ فَتَحَ سِيرَةً.

Brinish, a. Briny, } شَرِشِيٌّ ـ مَالِحٌ ـ مُمَلَّحٌ.

Brink, n. شَفِيرٌ ـ حَرْفٌ ـ حَاجِزٌ ـ شَفَةٌ ـ طَرَفٌ ـ شُفْرٌ ـ حَافَةٌ. The — of the river, شَفْرُ النَّهْرِ. The — of destruction, شَفْرُ عَلَى ـ التَّلَافُ ـ خَطَرُ الْهَلَاكِ. To draw near to the —, شَفْرُ عَلَى.

Brisk, ad. Lively, سَرِيعٌ ـ خَفِيفٌ ـ وَجْزٌ ـ نَاشِطٌ ـ نَشِيطٌ ـ قَوِيٌّ ـ شَدِيدٌ. Powerful, نَارِيٌّ ـ فَائِقٌ ـ نَبِيهٌ ـ فَلْتَانٌ ـ حَادٌّ. Cheerful, مَبْسُوطٌ ـ بَحْبُوحٌ ـ بَطْرَانٌ ـ مَسْرُورٌ ـ فَرِهٌ ـ طَيَّابٌ. To be —, lively, نَشِطَ ـ تَنَشَّطَ ـ فَرَهَ ـُ ـَ. To make —, نَشَّطَ. To be —, of a market, etc., رَاجَ ـُ ـ دَرَّ ـُ ـِ. The market was —, دَرَّتِ السُّوقُ.

Brisket, n. صَدْرٌ.

Briskly, ad. بِحَمِيَّةٍ ـ بِنَشَاطٍ ـ بِخِفَّةٍ.

Briskness, n. Gaiety, بَهْجَةٌ ـ سُرُورٌ ـ فَرْحَةٌ. Vigour, alacrity, مُرُوَّةٌ ـ حَرَارَةٌ ـ نَشَاطٌ ـ سُرْعَةٌ ـ خِفَّةٌ ـ رَوَاجٌ ـ جِدَّةٌ ـ فُرُوهَةٌ. Strength, شِدَّةٌ ـ قُوَّةٌ ـ جِدَّةٌ. As of a market, رَوَجٌ ـ دِرَّةٌ ـ رَوَاجٌ.

Bristle, n. شَعْرُ خِنْزِيرٍ ـ هُلْبٌ.

Bristle, v.i. and t. As a bird its feathers, تَنَفَّشَ. As a cat its hair, إِنْتَفَشَ ـ تَنَفَّشَ; of a dog or horse, إِزْبَارَّ. To make to —, صَيَّرَ-مُنَفَّشًا ـ زَابَرَ. To grow bristly hair, شَوَّكَ. Bristled up, رَجُلٌ ـ رَجُلٌ شَوِكُ السِّلَاحِ ـ مُنَفَّشٌ. A man bristling with arms, شَاكِي السِّلَاحِ.

Bristly, a. ذُو شَعْرٍ ـ أَهْلَبُ ـ هُلْبِيٌّ.

Britain, n. Britannia, } Great —, سَلْطَنَةُ الْأَنْكْلِيزِ ـ بَرِيطَانِيَا الْعُظْمَى.

Britannia, n. The metal, صِنْفٌ مِنَ الْمَعَادِنِ.

Britannic, a. أَنْكْلِيزِيٌّ. Her — Majesty, جَلَالَةُ سَعَادَةِ مَلِكَةِ الْأَنْكْلِيزِ.

British, a. Briton, n. } أَنْكْلِيزِيٌّ. The British, الأَنْكْلِيزُ.

Brittle, a. مُسْتَرْخٍ ـ رَخْوٌ ـ هَشٌّ ـ هَشَاشٌ ـ ذُو تَحَتُّمٍ ـ سَهْلُ الْكَسْرِ ـ سَرِيعُ الْعَطَبِ ـ مُنْكَسِرٌ ـ وَاهٍ ـ هَشِيمٌ. To be —, تَحَتَّمَ ـ رَخِيَ aor. يَرْخَى ـ إِسْتَرْخَى ـ هَشَّ ـُ ـِ. To make —, أَرْخَى.

Brittleness, n. سُرْعَةُ الْعَطَبِ ـ هَشِيمِيَّةٌ ـ هُشُوشَةٌ ـ تَحَتُّمٌ.

Broach, n. A spit, سِيخٌ pl. أَسْيَاخٌ.

Broach, v.t. To spit, شَكَّ-فِي سِيخٍ ـُ. To tap, بَزَلَ ـ بَزَّلَ ـُ ـ ثَقَبَ ـ أَنْفَذَ ـ نَقَبَ ـُ. To open a subject, فَتَحَ سِيرَةً ـَ ـ فَتَحَ ـَ.

I . شَرَحَ ـ أَشْهَرَ ب . To let out, utter, فَتَحَ ٱلْبَحْثَ فِي broached the wine for myself, إِبْتَزَلْتُ ٱلشَّرَابَ لِنَفْسِي .

Broad, *a.* Wide, وَسِيعٌ ـ وَاسِعٌ ـ عَرِيضٌ . Clear, open, as a space, فَضَآءٌ . Broad, of a road, نَهْرَجٌ . Coarse, غَلِيظٌ ـ خَشِنٌ . Indelicate, رَفَثٌ ـ فَاحِشٌ . In — daylight, بِٱلنَّهَارِ . To be or become —, wide, إِتَّسَعَ ـ أَعْرَضَ ـ ² عَرُضَ ـ إِمْتَدَّ ـ تَمَدَّدَ . To be —, indelicate, in speech, ² رَفَثَ فِي كَلَامِهِ . Broad and long, in breadth and length, عَرْضًا وَطُولًا . To make —, عَرَّضَ .

Broadcast, *ad.* Widely, إِنْتِشَارًا ـ تَشْرِيدًا . To sow broadcast, أَشَاعَ ب ـ ² نَشَرَ ـ ² ذَرَّ ب .

Broadcloth, *n.* جُوخٌ عَرِيضٌ ـ جُوخٌ .

Broadly, *ad.* بِٱلْعَرْضِ ـ إِعْتِرَاضًا . He put the question —, أَعْرَضَ ٱلْمَسْأَلَةَ .

Broadness, *n.* Indelicacy, رَفَثٌ ـ غِلَظٌ ـ خُشُونَةٌ ـ قَذَعٌ ـ فُحْشٌ . Width, عَرْضٌ ـ سَعَةٌ .

Broad-seal, *n.* طَابِعُ ٱلْمُلْكِ ـ وِهْرُ ٱلدَّوْلَةِ .

Broadside, *n.* The widest part, عُرْضٌ . It presented its —, إِعْتَرَضَ ـ تَعَرَّضَ . Discharge of the guns on one side of a ship, إِطْلَاقُ جَمِيعِ ٱلْمَدَافِعِ مِنْ جَنْبِ مَرْكَبٍ حَرْبِيٍّ .

Broadsword, *n.* سَيْفٌ *pl.* سُيُوفٌ ـ سَيْفٌ عَرِيضٌ .

Broadwise, *ad.* عَرْضًا ـ عَلَى ٱلْعَرْضِ .

Brocade, *n.* قُمَاشٌ مُقَصَّبٌ ـ دِيبَاجٌ ـ سُنْدُسٌ ـ إِسْتَبْرَقٌ .

Brocaded, *a.* مُقَصَّبٌ ـ مُسَنْدَسٌ .

Broccoli, *n.* زَنْبُوطٌ ـ قَلِيبَاتٌ .

Brochure, *n.* رِسَالَةٌ *pl.* رَسَائِلُ *and* رِسَالَاتٌ .

Brock, *n.* *See* Badger, *n.*

Brogue, *n.* A kind of shoe, نَوْعٌ مِنَ ٱلْمَرْكُوبِ ـ مَدَاسٌ . A corrupt dialect, لَغْوٌ ـ لَغْوَةٌ .

Broider, *v.t.* *See to* Embroider, *v.t.*

Broil, *n.* A tumult, خُصُومَةٌ ـ خِنَاقٌ ـ غَاغَةٌ ـ إِرْتِجَاجٌ ـ رَجَّةٌ ـ لَجَّةٌ ـ هَوْشَةٌ ـ ضَجَّةٌ .

Broil, *v.t.* ـ شَوَى ـ ⁷ شَوَى . To — on the gridiron, شَوَى عَلَى ٱلْمِصْبَعِ ; on the coals, شَوَى عَلَى ٱلْجَمْرِ . To be broiled, إِنْشَوَى ـ إِشْتَوَى . Any thing broiled, مَشْوِيٌّ ـ شَوِيٌّ ـ شِوَآءٌ .

Broke, *pret. of to* Break, *q.v.*

Broken, *a.* Rent, مَشْقُوقٌ ـ مَكْسُورٌ ـ مَفْضُوضٌ ـ فَضِيضٌ . Contrite, مُنْسَحِقٌ ـ مَوْطِيٌّ . Bankrupt, مُفْلِسٌ ـ مَكْسُورٌ . Infirm, ضَعِيفٌ ـ كَسِيحٌ ـ مَوْهُونٌ . Put to flight, مُنْكَسِرٌ . Broken meat, كِسَرُ ٱلطَّعَامِ .

Broken-headed, *a.* Having the head broken, مَدْمُوغٌ ـ دَمِيغٌ .

Broken-hearted, *a.* مُنْكَسِرُ ٱلْقَلْبِ ـ حَزِينٌ ـ مَكْسُورُ ٱلْخَاطِرِ .

Broken-winded, *n.* Of a horse, حِصَانٌ خَامٌّ ـ حِصَانٌ رَبِيطٌ .

Broker, *n.* An agent, دَلَّالٌ ـ سِمْسَارٌ *pl.* سَمَاسِرَةٌ . A dealer in old goods, مُضَارِبٌ ـ سَقَطِيٌّ ـ عُتَقِيٌّ . A pimp, قَوَّادٌ ـ مُعَرِّصٌ . To act as —, agent, سَمْسَرَ .

Brokerage, *n.* سَمْسَرَةٌ ـ دَلَالَةٌ .

Bromine, *n.* عُنْصُرٌ يُخَالِطُ مَآءَ ـ مَاهِيَّةٌ مَوْجُودَةٌ فِي مَآءِ ٱلْبَحْرِ ٱلْبَحْرِ .

Bronchi, *n.* / Bronchia, } مَجَارِي ٱلرِّيَآءِ .

Bronchial, *a.* مُخْتَصٌّ بِمَجَارِي ٱلرِّيَآءِ .

Bronchitis, *n.* عِلَّةٌ فِي ٱلرِّيَآءِ ـ إِلْتِهَابٌ فِي مَجَارِي ٱلرِّيَآءِ .

Bronchotemy, *n.* شَقُّ (*or* قَطْعُ) ٱلْحُلْقُومِ .

Bronchus, *n.* حُنْجُورٌ ـ حَنْجَرَةٌ ـ حُلْقُومٌ .

Bronze, *n.* نُحَاسٌ ـ تُوجٌ ـ خِلْطُ ثَلَاثَةِ مَعَادِنَ .

Bronze, *v.t.* ² صَبَغَ ـ لَوْنَ ٱلنُّحَاسِ . To brown, لَوَّحَ ـ صَيَّرَ أَسْمَرَ . To become bronzed, brown, إِسْمَرَّ . To —, of the sun, ² سَقَرَ ـ ² صَقَرَ . The sun bronzed him, سَقَرَتْهُ ٱلشَّمْسُ . Bronzed by the sun, مَسْقُورٌ مِنَ ٱلشَّمْسِ .

Brooch, *n.* حُلِيٌّ *pl.* حِلْيَةٌ لِلصَّدْرِ ـ جَوْهَرَةٌ لِلصَّدْرِ .

Brood, *n.* Offspring, نَسْلٌ ـ آلٌ ـ ذُرِّيَّةٌ . A hatch, حَضْنَةٌ ـ قَرْقَةٌ ـ بَطْنٌ . A brood-hen, حَاضِنَةٌ ـ مُرْخِمَةٌ . A nest of the brood, مَحْضَنٌ .

Brood, *v.i.* As a hen on its eggs, ² رَخِمَتْ عَلَى بَيْضِهَا ـ ² رَقَدَتْ عَلَى ٱلْبَيْضِ ـ ² حَضَنَ ـ أَرْخَمَتْ عَلَى ٱلْبَيْضِ . To make a hen to —, أَحْضَنَ . To flutter, hover over, رَفْرَفَ ـ ² رَفَّ . To mature by care, (*v.t.*) أَنْضَجَ ـ نَضَّجَ . To reflect upon, تَفَكَّرَ فِي ـ تَأَمَّلَ فِي .

Brook, *n.* فَلَجٌ *pl.* أَفْلَاجٌ *and* فُلُوجٌ ـ جَدْوَلٌ *pl.* جَدَاوِلُ ـ جَعْفَرٌ ـ سَاقِيَةٌ *pl.* سَوَاقِي ـ سَيْلٌ *pl.* سُيُولٌ ـ مَجْرَى مَآءٍ .

Brook, *v.i.* ⁷ صَبَرَ عَلَى ـ إِسْتَحْمَلَ ـ إِحْتَمَلَ .

Brooklet, *n.* فَلَجٌ صَغِيرٌ .

Broom, *n.* The plant, رَتَمَةٌ ـ وَزَالٌ ـ رَتَمٌ . A besom, مِكْنَسَةٌ ـ مِقَشَّةٌ *pl.* مَكَانِسُ ـ مُكَنِّسٌ . A maker of brooms, مُكَنِّسٌ . A new — sweeps clean, ٱلْمِكْنَسَةُ ٱلْجَدِيدَةُ تُجِيدُ ٱلتَّكْنِيسَ .

Broom-rape, *n.* خَانِقُ ٱلْكِرْسَنَّةِ .

Broomstick, *n.* نِصَابُ ٱلْمِكْنَسَةِ .

Broth, *n.* زُومٌ ـ مَسْلُوقَةٌ ـ مَرَقٌ ـ مَرَقَةٌ ـ حَسَآءٌ . Bread —, ثَرِيدٌ .

Brothel, *n.* مرخانة ـ مَاخُور ـ بَيْتُ قِحَاب .

Brother, *n.* أَخٌ *pl.* إِخْوَة *and* إِخْوَان *dual* أَخَوَانِ . A — by the same father and mother, شَقِيق ـ صِنْو *pl.* صِنْيَان *and* صِنْوَان *pl.* أَشِقَّاء ; *in the plural only,* أَعْيَان . A foster —, رَضِيع *pl.* رُضَعَاء ـ أَخٌ بِٱلرِّضَاع . A half —, أَخٌ مِنَ ٱلْأَبِ أَوْ مِنَ ٱلْأُمِّ فَقَط . A twin —, تَوْءَم *pl.* تَوَائِم *and* تُؤَام *dual* تَوْءَمَانِ . Brother-in-law : Wife's brother, صِهْر *pl.* أَصْهَار .

Wife's sister's husband, سِلْف *pl.* أَسْلَاف .

Sister's husband, صِهْر *pl.* أَصْهَار ـ زَوْجُ ٱلْأُخْتِ .

Husband's brother, صِهْر *pl.* أَصْهَار ـ أَخُ ٱلزَّوْجِ .

Brotherhood, *n.* خُوَّة ـ تَآخٍ ـ إِخَاء ـ أُخُوَّة . A company, رُفْقَة *pl.* رِفَاق *and* أَرْفَاق ـ أَخَوِيَّة . A sect, طائِفَة . A set of opinions, مَذْهَب ـ طَرِيقَة .

Brotherly, *a.* أَخَوِيّ .

Brought, *pret. of to* Bring, *q.v.*

Brow, *n.* The forehead, جَبِين *pl.* جُبُن ـ جَبْهَة *pl.* جِبَاه . The — of a hill, رَأْسُ جَبَلٍ ـ فَرْعَةُ جَبَلٍ ـ حَرْفُ جَبَل . To knit the brows, عَرْقَص ـ قَطَّبَ وَجْهَهُ ـ عَبَّسَ (*or* أَكْبَى) وَجْهَهُ حَوَاجِبَهُ .

Browbeat, *v.t.* عَزَّرَ ـ عَتَبَ عَلَى ـ عَنَفَ عَلَى .

Brown, *a.* أَسْمَر *fem.* سَمْرَاء *pl.* سُمْر ـ أَغْبَس ـ أَحْوَى .

Brown, *n.* سُمْرَة ـ حُوَّة .

Brown, *v.t.* سَمَّرَ ـ صَيَّرَ أَسْمَر . To colour as the sun does the skin, لَوَّحَ . *See also under to* Bronze, *v.t.*

Brownish, *n.* أَسْمَرُ بَعْضَ ٱلسُّمْرَةِ ـ سُمَيْر ـ يَضْرِبُ إِلَى ٱلسُّمْرَةِ .

Brown-study, *n.* إِفْتِكَار ـ خَيَال . In a —, غَارِقٌ فِي بَحْرِ ٱلْأَفْكَارِ .

Browse, *v.t.* قَرَضَ ٱلْخَصَل ـ رَتَعَ ـ حَشَّ .

Browse, *n.* Tender twigs, خَصْلَة *pl.* خُصَل ـ خُرْعُوب .

Bruin, *n.* دُبّ *fem.* دُبَّة *pl.* دِبَب .

Bruise, *v.t.* To hurt with blows, قَصَمَ ـ أَفْرَشَ ـ سَحَقَ ـ رَضْرَضَ ـ دَشْدَشَ ـ فَنَخَ ـ عَزَقَ ـ أَجَشَّ . To pound, جَشَّ ـ جَرَشَ ـ جَشَّرَ ـ دَقَّ . To be bruised, pounded, إِنْفَصَمَ ـ إِنْسَحَقَ ـ تَفَصَّمَ . To —, as stones, bones, *etc.,* رَضَخَ ـ رَضَحَ .

Bruise, *n.* دَشَّة ـ خَبْطَة ـ دَقَّة ـ رَضّ ـ فَنْخ ـ فَارِشَة .

Bruiser, *n.* A boxer, ضَرَّاب . A bruising-stone, مِرْضَاح ـ مِرْضَخَة ـ مِرْضَاخ .

Bruit, *n.* خَبَر ـ صَوْت ـ صِيت . To — abroad, أَشْهَرَ ـ أَشَاعَ بِ .

Brumal, *a.* شَتَوِيّ .

Brunette, *n.* إِمْرَأَةٌ سُمَيْرَةٌ ـ إِمْرَأَةٌ سَمْرَاء .

Brunt, *n.* ضَرْبَة ـ حَمْلَة ـ لَطْمَة ـ صَدْمَة . To bear the —, قَاوَمَ ـ إِحْتَمَلَ .

Brush, *n.* An instrument for brushing, بَرْشِيمَة ـ مِمْسَحَة ـ فُرْشَة . A tail, ذَيْل ـ ذَنَب . A — for painting, قَلَمُ شَعْرٍ ـ قَلَم . An assault, صَدْمَة ـ هُجُوم ـ حَمْلَة . Brushwood, عَقُول . A — for sweeping cobwebs, زَحَّافَة . To have a — with, عَارَكَ ـ قَاتَلَ .

Brush, *v.t.* and *i.* To clean with a —, نَظَّفَ بِٱلْبَرْشِيمَةِ ـ مَسَحَ ـ مَسَحَ بِٱلْفُرْشَةِ . To sweep, كَنَسَ . To — off, to remove, رَفَعَ ـ قَشَطَ ـ شَالَ . To — up, polish, جَلَا ـ صَقَلَ ; to make more elegant, لَطَّفَ ـ ظَرَّفَ ; to embellish speech, أَدْمَجَ ٱلْكَلَامَ ـ ضَرَّجَ ٱلْكَلَامَ ; to stir up, to rouse, أَنْهَضَ . To move lightly, *v.i.* خَفَّ ـ هَفَّ . To — off, to run away, فَرَّ ـ جَفَلَ ـ إِنْفَلَّ .

Brushwood, *n.* حَسَكَ ـ عَقُول ـ رَتَم .

Brushy, *a.* أَزَبّ ـ مُشْعِر .

Brusque, *a.* خَلِيف ـ عَنِيف . *See also* Rude, *a.*

Brussels-carpet, *n.* بِسَاطٌ مِنْ شُغْلِ ٱلْأَنْكِلِيزِ .

Brussels-sprouts, *n.* كُرُنْبِيَاتٌ فَلَمَنْك .

Brutal, *a.* Like a brute, بَهِيمِيّ ـ مُوَحَّش ـ وَحْشِيّ . Cruel, عَنِيف ـ قَاسٍ ـ فَظّ ـ جَائِر .

Brutality, *n.* Stupidity, بَهِيمِيَّة ـ حَمَاقَة . Cruelty, عُنْف ـ فَظَاظَة ـ قَسَاوَة ـ جَلَافَة .

Brutalize, *v.t.* and *i.* To make brutal, وَحَّشَ ـ بَلَّمَ . To grow brutal, تَوَحَّشَ ـ صَارَ مِثْلَ ٱلْوَحْشِ ـ صَارَ مِثْلَ ٱلدُّبِّ .

Brutally, *ad.* Like a brute, بِتَوَحُّشٍ ـ مِثْلَ ٱلْوَحْشِ . Savagely, عَنْفًا ـ بِقَسَاوَةٍ .

Brute, *n.* An irrational animal, بَهِيمَة *pl.* بَهَائِم . A blockhead, بَهِيمَة ـ دُبّ ـ ثَوْر . A cruel man, رَجُلٌ قَاسٍ ـ جَائِر ـ فَظّ .

Brutify, *v.t.* *See to* Brutalize, *v.t.*

Brutish, *a.* Like a brute, بَهِيمِيّ . Sensual, شَهْوَانِيّ ـ رَفَث ـ فَاسِق .

Brutishly, *ad.* Sensually, فُجُورًا ـ سِفَادًا . *See also* Brutally, *a.*

Brutishness, *n.* *See* Brutality, Beastliness, *n.*

Brutum fulmen, *n.* صَوْتٌ فَارِغٌ ـ خَبَرٌ بَاطِلٌ .

Bryony, *n.* كَرْمَةٌ بَيْضَاء ـ قَاشِر ـ قَاشِرِى ـ هَزَارْجَشَان .

Bubble, *n.* A bladder of water, حَبَب *pl.* حَبَاب ـ حُجَاة ـ حَبَبًا ـ نُفَّاخَة ـ فُقَّاعَة *pl.* فَقَاقِيع *coll.* Bubbles on wine, فَرَاش ;

— شَيْءٌ زَهِيدٌ — عَبَثَة. A trifle, بَقْبَقَة. A gurgle, نَقّ. on water, تَفَاهَة — شَيْءٌ بَاطِلٌ — تَنْتِيش. A fraud, مَكْر — غَدْر — غَبْن.

Bubble, *v.i.* To boil in bubbles, بَقْبَق — غَلَى — فَارَ ع. To gurgle, خَرَّ ـِ. To flow with a gentle noise, خَرَّ ـِ — نَضَخَ ـَ.

Bubo, *n.* كُبَّة *pl.* كُبَب — غُدَّة *pl.* غُدَد.

Buccaneer, *n.* } Bucanier, } لِصُّ ٱلْبَحْرِ *pl.* لُصُوص — ضَرَّابُ مَرَاكِبَ.

Buck, *n.* The male deer, ظَبْيٌ *pl.* ظِبَاءٌ *and* ظَبْيَات. A male, ذَكَر *pl.* ذُكُور. A gay fellow, غَنْدُور.

Buckbean, *n.* The plant, إِطْرِيفَل.

Bucket, *n.* جَوْب *pl.* أَجْوَاب — عُلْبَة *pl.* عُلَب; of brass or iron, سَطْل *pl.* سُطُول; of leather, دَلْو *pl.* دِلَاءٌ; a large ditto, غَرْب *pl.* غُرُوب — غُرُوف. He drew up the —, full of water, from the well, دَلَا ٱلدَّلْوَ ع. I let down the — (into the well), أَدْلَيْتُ ٱلدَّلْوَ.

Buckle, *n.* بَكْلَة — أَبَازِيمُ *pl.* إِبْزِيم — قُلَيْب. The — which fastens the crupper, عَقْرَب *pl.* عَقَارِبُ. The tongue of a —, شَوْكَةُ ٱلْإِبْزِيمِ.

Buckle, *v.t.* To fasten with a —, شَبَكَ ٱلْإِبْزِيمَ ـِ. To fasten, حَزَمَ — رَبَطَ ـِ ع — شَدَّ ع ـُ. To — on one, to invest, لَبَّسَ — تَلَدَ. To — to, to strive, جَدَّ فِي ـِ — كَدَّ ع. To — to a thing, to take up promptly, شَمَّرَ فِي ٱلْأَمْرِ. To — or cope with, قَاتَلَ — تَشَبَّثَ بِ.

Buckler, *n.* دَرَقَة *pl.* دَرَق — تُرْس *pl.* تِرَاس.

Buckmast, *n.* ثَمَرَةُ شَجَرَةِ ٱلزَّانِ.

Buckram, *n.* مُقَوِّيَات. (That used for stiff lining, called in Egypt فُرْتِزَة, from the Italian *fortezza*.)

Buckskin, *n.* جِلْدُ ظَبْيٍ.

Buckwheat, *n.* حِنْطَةٌ سَوْدَاءُ.

Bucolic, *a.* مُخْتَصٌّ بِٱلرُّعَاةِ.

Bud, *n.* Of a plant, بَاقِل — بُرْعُوم *pl.* بَرَاعِيم — لَبْلُوب — عُقْدَة *pl.* عُقَد — زِرّ *pl.* أَزْرَار — عَيْن *pl.* عُيُون.

Bud, *v.i.* أَبْقَلَ — بَرْعَمَ — تَزَرْزَرَ — بَزَّ ع. To bud, of trees, نَشَرَ ع.

Bud, *v.t.* To graft, طَعَّمَ — أَطْعَمَ.

Budding, *a.* Protuberant, نَاتِئٌ; of the breasts, مُعْقَد.

Budge, *v.i.* To move, تَحَرَّكَ; to move off, تَقَلَّعَ — إِجْتَنَبَ — إِنْصَرَفَ.

Budget, *n.* A bag, كِيس — جَيْب. A stock, ذَخِيرَة — مُؤْنَة. A portfolio, ضَمَامَة. Statement of the national finances, حِسَابُ التَّقْوِيمَاتِ — مِيزَانِيَّة — مَضْبَطَةٌ مَالِيَّةٌ — إِيرَادُ ٱلْبِلَادِ وَمَصَارِيفُهَا ٱلْمَالِيَّةُ.

Buff, *n.* The leather, جِلْدٌ نَاعِمٌ — جِلْدُ جَامُوسٍ. A — colour, صُفْرَة — لَوْنٌ أَصْفَرُ.

Buffalo, *n.* جَامُوس *pl.* جَوَامِيسُ.

Buffer, *n.* فَرَامِيلَة.

Buffet, *v.t.* To strike, لَطَمَ ـِ — لَطَّمَ — لَكَمَ ع — ضَرَبَ كَفًّا ـِ. To struggle against, صَارَعَ. To contend with, جَادَلَ. They were buffeted, as of waves, إِلْتَطَمُوا — تَلَاطَمُوا.

Buffet, *n.* A blow, لَطْمَة — لَكْمَة — كَفّ — مَشْط. A cupboard, خِرِسْتَانَات *pl.* خِرِسْتَان — دَوَالِيبُ *pl.* دُولَاب.

Buffoon, *n.* مُضْحِك — مَسْخَرَة — مُهَرِّج — خَلْبُوص — قَشْمَر.

Buffoonery, *n.* تَهْرِيج — قَشْمَرِيَّة — خَلْبَصَة.

Buffoonish, *a.* مَسْخَرَاتِيّ — مُهَرِّج.

Bug, *n.* The bed-bug, كَتَّان — بَقٌّ مُنْتِن — فَسْفَسَة *coll.* فَسْفَس *pl.* فَسَافِسُ. A wall bug, بَقُّ ٱلْحِيطَانِ. Mat bugs, بَنَاتُ ٱلْحَصِيرِ. Wood bugs, بَقُّ ٱلْخَشَبِ. A generic term for such insects, بَقّ.

Buggery, *n.* *See* Sodomy, *n.*

Bugbear, *n.* خَيَال — طَيْفُ خَيَالٍ — تَخْوِيفَة.

Buggy, *a.* مُفَسْفَس.

Buggy, *n.* The vehicle, عَرَبَانَةٌ خَفِيفَةٌ يَجُرُّهَا حِصَانٌ.

Bugle, *n.* A horn, نَفِير — بُوق *pl.* أَبْوَاق. A long bead, خَرَزَةٌ طَوِيلَةٌ. To blow a —, نَفَخَ فِي ٱلْبُوقِ ـُ.

Bugle, *n.* The plant, سنفيتون — جَمَاجُم — أُذُنُ ٱلْحِمَارِ.

Bugloss, *n.* The plant, لِسَانُ ٱلثَّوْرِ.

Buhl, *n.* عُودٌ أَوْ ذَبْلٌ مُرَصَّعٌ بِنَقْشٍ مِنْ ذَهَبٍ.

Build, *v.t.* عَمَرَ ع — عَمَّرَ — شَيَّدَ — بَنَى ـِ. To lay stones together, رَصَفَ ـُ ع. To — a nest, عَشَّشَ. To — a ship, أَنْشَأَ مَرْكَبًا — عَمَّرَ مَرْكَبًا — مَدَّ مَرْكَبًا ع. To — upon, to rely upon, تَوَكَّلَ عَلَى — إِعْتَمَدَ عَلَى — إِتَّكَلَ عَلَى.

Build, *n.* Make, هَيْئَة *pl.* هَيْآت — صُورَة *pl.* صُوَر — بِنْيَة.

Builder, *n.* بَانٍ *pl.* أَبْنَاءٌ — بَنَّاءٌ — مُهَنْدِس — مِعْمَار — مِعْمَارِيّ.

Building, *n.* بِنَاءٌ *pl.* أَبْنِيَة *and* بُنْيَان — عِمَارَة *pl.* عَمَائِرُ — بِنَايَة. A lofty —, عِمَادَة *pl.* عِمَاد. A —, construction of stones, whether artificial or not, رَصَف.

Bulb, *n.* بَصَل — رَأْس *pl.* رُؤُوس.

Bulbous, *a.* ذُو عُرُوقٍ مُبَصَّلَةٍ — بَصَلِيّ.

Bulgaria, *n.* بُلْغَارِيَا.

Bulge, *v.i.* To — out, ع بَرَزَ ـ ءِ نَتَأَ.

Bulk, *n.* Magnitude, ضُخْم ـ كِبَر ـ عُظْمَة ـ كَمِّيَّة ـ قَدْر. Size, of the body, قَامَة ـ قَدّ. A mass, هِدْفَة ـ كُومَة ـ جُمْلَة. The greater part, أَكْثَر ـ أَغْلَب ـ جُمْهُور ـ جُلّ ـ كُبْر ـ أَعْظَم. The bulk, as of an army, أَوْرَم. To sell in —, ءِ بَاعَ بِٱلْجُمْلَةِ. To break —, فَرَّغ وَسْق ٱلْمَرْكَبِ.

Bulk-head, *n.* حَاجِز ـ حَاجِز فِي مَرْكَب.

Bulkiness, *n.* Bigness, كِبَر ـ ضُخْم ـ جَسَامَة. Corpulence, ضَخَامَة ـ جُسْمَانِيَّة.

Bulky, *a.* Big, غَلِيظ ـ ثَقِيل ـ ثَخِين ـ جَسِيم. Corpulent, جُسْمَانِيّ ـ ضَخْم ـ خَدَلَّج ـ مَحْبُول ـ بَادِن. To be —, corpulent, ع ضَخُمَ.

Bull, *n.* The male of a cow, ثَوْر *pl.* ثِيرَان. A blunder, غَلْطَة ـ خَطَأ مِنَ ٱلْبَابَا ـ بَرَاءَة مِنَ ٱلْبَابَا. A Pope's letter, طُغْيَان ـ زَلَّة. The constellation, بُرْجُ ٱلثَّوْرِ. A — on the Stock Exchange, مُتَسَبِّب بِأَسْبَاب لِرَفْع أَسْعَارِ ٱلسَّنَدَاتِ.

Bull-baiting, *n.* إِطْلَاقُ ٱلْكِلَابِ عَلَى ٱلثِّيرَانِ.

Bull-dog, *n.* كَلْب يُقَاتِلُ ٱلثِّيرَان.

Bullet, *n.* Of iron, كُلَّة *pl.* كُلَل; of lead, رَصَاصَة *coll.* رَصَاص *pl.* رَصَاصَات.

Bulletin, *n.* فَذْلَكَة ـ خَبَر مُؤْذِن ـ تَقْرِير ـ إِخْبَار ـ إِعْلَام. They publish a — every day, يَنْشُرُونَ فِي كُلِّ يَوْمٍ خَبَرًا مُؤْذِنًا.

Bull-fight, *n.* قِتَال مَعَ ثِيرَانٍ.

Bullfinch, *n.* نَوْع مِنَ ٱلْعَصَافِيرِ ٱلصَّفَّارَةِ.

Bull-frog, *n.* ضَفْدَع كَبِير.

Bullhead, *n.* بَلِيد ـ أَحْمَق.

Bullion, *n.* Of gold —, سَبِيكَة مِنْ ذَهَب; of silver —, سَبِيكَة مِنْ فِضَّةٍ.

Bullock, *n.* ثَوْر جَذَع *pl.* ثِيرَان جِذْعَان ـ ثَوْر صَغِير.

Bull's-eye, *n.* A round window, طَاقَة مُدَوَّرَة ـ رَوْزَنَة مُدَوَّرَة. The centre of a butt, عَيْنُ ٱلنِّيشَانِ ـ قَلْبُ ٱلْهَدَفِ. A thick glass convex cover, طَبَق مُحَدَّب مِنْ بِلَّوْر ثَخِين.

Bully, *n.* فَشَّار ـ شَتَّام ـ عَتَّاب ـ وَهْيَاص.

Bully, *v.t.* ءِ هَزَأَ ب ـ تَجَهْرَمَ عَلَى ـ هَدَّدَ ـ ءِ هَاصَ.

Bully, *v.i.* ءِ عَمِلَ زَوَابِعَ ـ تَهَوَّرَ ـ ءِ حَنِقَ.

Bulrush, *n.* بَرْدِيَّة ـ فَشّ ـ دَيْس ـ أَسَل ـ حَلْف ـ حَلْفَاء *coll.* بَرْدِيّ. An ark of bulrushes, سَفَط مِنَ ٱلْبَرْدِيِّ.

Bulwark, *n.* A fortification, أَسْوَار *pl.* سُور ـ مِتْرَاس ـ كَانِفَة ـ حَفَارَة ـ صِيَانَة ـ كَنَف. Security, إِسْتِحْكَام. Rails round a ship's deck, حَاجِز مَدَار سَطْحِ ٱلْمَرْكَبِ.

Bulwark, *v.t.* إِسْتَحْكَمَ ـ حَصَّنَ.

Bum-bailiff, *n.* مُسْتَخْدَم فِي ٱلْمَحَاكِمِ.

Bumble-bee, *n.* دَبُّور ـ نَحْلَة كَبِيرَة.

Bumboat, *n.* صَنْدَلُ ٱلْمَأْكُولَاتِ ـ صَنْدَلُ ٱلْمُؤْنَةِ.

Bump, *n.* A swelling, نَفْخ ـ بَقْبِيقَة ـ وَرَم. A blow, shock, صَدْمَة ـ إِصَابَة ـ لَطْمَة ـ ضَرْبَة ـ كَبْسَة.

Bump, *v.t.* To thump, ع لَكَمَ ـ ضَرَبَ ـ ءِ لَطَمَ. To — against, أَصَابَ ـ تَصَادَمَ ـ تَلَاطَمَ. A protuberance on the skull, تَمْحُدُوَة *pl.* تَمَادِيح; on the hinder part of the same, قَذَال *pl.* قُذُل and أَقْذِلَة.

Bumper, *n.* كَأْس مَلْآنَة.

Bumpkin, *n.* خِشْنِيّ ـ فَلَّاح ـ غَشِيم. *See also* Greenhorn, *n.*

Bun, *n.* قُرْصَة *pl.* قُرَص ـ قُرَيْصَة.

Bunch, *n.* A mass, دُبْلَة ـ بَضْعَة. A swelling, وَرَم. A number of things tied together, حُزْمَة ـ رَبْطَة ـ شَدَّة. A — of sticks, firewood, حَطُوبَة ـ حُزْمَةُ حَطَب. A — of grapes, قِطْف ـ رِبَاطَةُ تَمْرٍ عَنَاقِيدُ *pl.* عُنْقُودُ عِنَبٍ ـ عِنَب. A — of dates, رِبَاطَةُ تَمْرٍ ـ عُرْجُونُ تَمْرٍ. A — of hair, شُوشَة. A — of flowers, بَاقَةُ زَهْرٍ ـ رَبْطَةُ زَهْرٍ ـ صُحْبَةُ زَهْرٍ. A — of feathers, هِلَال مِنْ رِيشٍ. The — on a camel's back, سَنَام *pl.* أَسْنِمَة.

Bunch, *v.t.* To grow in knobs, تَعَقَّدَ ـ إِنْعَقَدَ. To bulge out, ءِ نَتَأَ.

Bunchy, *a.* أَحْدَب ـ مُعَقَّد.

Bundle, *n.* حُزْمَة ـ أَرْبِطَة *pl.* رَبِيط ـ أَضَامِيم *pl.* إِضْمَامَة *pl.* حُزَم ـ رِزْمَة *pl.* رِزَم ـ كَارَة ـ صُرَّة *pl.* صُرَر ـ عُقْدَة. A small number, شَرَاذِم *pl.* شِرْذِمَة. One who ties up in bundles, a packer, حَزَّام. A — of wheat, صُبْرَة حِنْطَةٍ. A — of books, إِضْمَامَة مِنَ ٱلْكُتُبِ.

Bundle, *v.t.* To tie in a —, ع حَزَمَ ـ رَزَمَ ـ صَرَّ. To — off, send away, دَشَّرَ ـ ءِ طَرَدَ. To go away, وَلَّى ـ ءِ فَرَّ ـ إِنْطَلَقَ.

Bung, *n.* سِدَادُ بَرْمِيلٍ ـ سِدَاد.

Bung, *v.t.* ع سَدَّ.

Bungalow, *n.* مَسَاكِن *pl.* مَسْكَن ـ بُيُوت *pl.* بَيْت.

Bung-hole, *n.* بُخْش ٱلْبَرْمِيل ـ مَنْفَس ٱلْبَرْمِيل ـ سُرَّة.

Bungle, *v.t.* To manage clumsily, خَرْبَطَ ـ شَوَّشَ ـ لَبَّكَ ـ أَتْلَفَ ـ عَطَّلَ ـ خَبَّصَ.

Bungle, *v.i.* شَابَ *aor.* يَشُوبُ. To — in speech, شَمْرَجَ ـ

أَعْتَقِلَ لِسَانُهُ ; in a narrative, ضَغَثَ ٱلْحَدِيثَ ـ. *See also to* Muddle, *v.i.*

Bungler, *n.* } غَشِيم ـ مُلَخْبِط ـ مُخَبِّص ـ أَخْرَق ; in speech,
Bungling, *a.* } مُشَمْرِج. *See also under* Awkward, *a.*

Bunglingly, *ad.* تَلْبِيكًا ـ عَلَى غَشْم ـ بِلَا مِهْنَة ـ بِخُرْق. *See also* Awkwardly, *ad.*

Bunion, *n.* ثُؤْلُول *pl.* ثَآلِيل ـ عُضَّةُ أَرْض.

Bunting, *n.* Cloth of which flags are made, نَوْعٌ مِنَ ٱلْقُمَاشِ تُصْنَعُ مِنْهُ البَيَارِق. A flag, بَيْرَق. A lark, قُنْبَر ـ قُبَّر.

Buoy, *n.* بُوِيَة ـ گَاوِي ـ كُوبَار. An anchor buoy, عَوَّامَة.

Buoy, *v.t.* To mark with buoys, عَلَّمَ ـ بِبُوِيَاتٍ ². To keep afloat, عَوَّمَ ـ حَمَلَ ـ عَلَى وَجْهِ ٱلْمَاءِ ـ. To — with hopes, sustain, أَمَّنَ ـ ² شَدَّ ظَهْر.

Buoyancy, *n.* Quality of floating, سَابِحَة. Lightness, خِفَّة. Animation, cheerfulness, خِفَّة ـ نَشَاط ـ بَهْجَة ـ سُرُور.

Buoyant, *a.* That will not sink, يَطُوفُ عَلَى وَجْهِ ٱلْمَاءِ ـ عَوَّام. Light, خَفِيف. Cheerful, فَلْتَان ـ أَلُوب ـ مَسْرُور.

Buoyantly, *ad.* Cheerfully, بِسُرُور ـ بِنَشَاط ـ بِخِفَّة.

Bur, *n.* سُنْبُلَة *pl.* سَنَابِل.

Burden, *n.* A load, وِقْر *pl.* أَوْقَار ـ حِمْل *and* حَمْلَة *pl.* حِمَال *and* حُمُول *and* حُمُولَة *and* أَحْمَال ـ ثِقْل *pl.* أَثْقَال. As much as a man can carry, شَيْلَةُ ٱلرَّجُل ـ. A ship's —, وَسْقُ مَرْكَب ـ حُمُولَةُ ٱلْمَرْكَب. The —, as of a song or tale, زُبْدَة ـ مَوْضُوع ـ مَادَّة ـ بَاب. One who has to be supported by another, حَمِيلَة. An affliction, ضِيقَة ـ غَمّ ـ ثِقْل ـ صُعُوبَة ـ حُمُولَة. A beast of —, دَابَّة *pl.* دَوَابّ. The — of its proof rests with you, عُهْدَتُهُ عَلَيْكَ. Every man shall bear his own —, سَيَحْمِلُ كُلُّ إِنْسَانٍ حِمْلَ نَفْسِهِ. Cast thy — upon the Lord and He will sustain thee, أَلْقِ عَلَى ٱلرَّبِّ هَمَّكَ فَيَعُولَكَ.

Burden, *v.t.* To load, حَمَّلَ. To weigh upon, ثَقَّلَ عَلَى ـ كَلَّفَ. To — the mind, ضَيَّقَ عَلَى ـ أَضَاقَ.

Burdensome, *a.* Heavy, ثَقِيل. Oppressive, مُكَدِّر ـ مُتْعِب ـ مُثْقِل عَلَى.

Bureau, *n.* A chest of drawers, صَنْدُوقٌ بِدِرَاج. A writing table, طَاوِلَةٌ لِلْكِتَابَة. A public office, قَلَم *pl.* أَقْلَام ـ دِيوَان ـ دَائِرَة.

Bureaucracy, *n.* Centralization of government through its offices, حُكْمٌ مُسْتَقِلٌّ بِوَاسِطَةِ دَوَاوِينِ ٱلدَّوْلَة. Excessive influence of the authorities, شَطَطُ ٱلْوُلَاةِ فِي نَفَاذِ ـ إِفْرَاطٌ فِي نُفُوذِ أَرْبَابِ ٱلْحُكُومَةِ أَوَامِرِهِمْ.

Burgh, *n.* See Borough, *n.*

Burgamot, *n.* A kind of pear, نَوْعٌ مِنَ ٱلْكُمَّثْرَى ; of perfume, نَوْعٌ مِنَ ٱلْعُطُورِ.

Burgess, *n.* Citizen of a borough, أَهْلُ قَصَبَةٍ. A notable of a borough, مِنْ أَعْيَانِ قَصَبَةٍ.

Burgher, *n.* اِبْنُ بَلَدٍ ـ سَاكِنٌ فِي قَصَبَةٍ.

Burglar, *n.* لِصّ (or حَرَامِيّ) مُنَقِّبُ ٱلْبُيُوتِ.

Burglary, *n.* كَسْرُ بَابٍ أَوْ نَقْبُ حَائِطٍ مِنَ ٱللُّصُوصِ لِنَهْبِ ٱلْبُيُوتِ.

Burgomaster, *n.* مِنْ أَهْلِ ضُبَّاطِ ٱلْمَمْلَكَةِ ـ حَاكِمُ بَلَدٍ.

Burgundy, *n.* The wine, نَبِيذُ بُورْغُونِيا.

Burial, *n.* Act of, دَفْن. Rites of, carrying to —, تَقْبِير ـ جِنَازَة ـ جِنَاز. To prepare a corpse for — with perfumes, to embalm, حَنَّطَ. To be embalmed for —, تَحَنَّطَ. The perfumes used in —, حِنَاط ـ حُنُوط. To perform the — rites, أَدْفَنَ. *See also* Funeral, *n.*

Buried, *n.* As a corpse, مَدْفُون. Concealed in the earth, دَفِين ـ مَدْفُون. A — treasure, دَفِينَة.

Burin, *n.* An engraver's tool, قَلَم *pl.* أَقْلَام ـ مِنْقَاش.

Burke, *v.t.* ² قَتَلَ ـ حَتَّى يَبِيعَ جُثَّتَهُ لِلشَّرَّاحِينَ لِكَيْ يَسْتَفِيدُوا عِلْمًا مِنْ تَشْرِيحِهَا.

Burlesque, *a.* ضُحْكَة ـ سُخْرَة ـ مُضْحِك ـ هَزْلِيّ.

Burlesque, *n.* ضُحْكَة ـ سُخْرِيَّة ـ مَسْخَرَة.

Burlesque, *v.t.* تَسَخْرَبَ ـ تَهَزَّأَ بِ.

Burliness, *n.* جَسَامَة ـ ضَخَامَة.

Burly, *a.* Big, corpulent, جَسِيم ـ ضَخْم ـ غَضَنْفَر ـ خَدَلَّج. Boisterous, فَشَّار ـ صَيِّت. Coarse, غَلِيظ. To be —, corpulent, ضَخُمَ ².

Burn, *v.t.* To consume with fire, أَحْرَقَ. To — something with, حَرَقَ ـ بِ ـ. To make fire of, أَوْقَدَ ـ شَعَلَ ². To — or bronze, as the sun, صَقَرَ ² ـ سَقَرَ ². To — with an iron, كَوَى ـ. To — coffee, حَمَّصَ ٱلْبُنَّ. To — to ashes, صَيَّرَ ـ رَمَادًا. To — bricks, طَبَخَ ٱلطُّوبَ ². To — down, to melt, أَذَابَ.

Burn, *v.i.* To be on fire, إِحْتَدَمَ ـ إِتَّقَدَ ـ تَوَقَّدَ ـ وَهَجَ *aor.* يَهِجُ ـ تَوَهَّجَ ـ إِلْتَظَى. To be burnt, إِحْتَرَقَ ـ إِحْتَدَمَ. To make to —, to kindle, of a fire, لَظَّى. To — down, to melt, ذَابَ ². To — low, جَمَدَ ². To — with desire, إِحْتَرَقَ مِنَ ٱلشَّوْقِ. Did not our hearts — within us, أَلَمْ يَكُنْ قَلْبُنَا مُلْتَهِبًا فِينَا. His heart burned with the secret, فَاضَ صَدْرُهُ بِٱلسِّرِّ ـ. His bosom burned with rage, فَاضَ صَدْرُهُ مِنَ ٱلْغَيْظِ ـ.

Burn, *n.* حَرْقَة ـ حَرَق ; with an iron, كَيّ.

Burner, *n.* A light bearer, مَشْعَل *pl.* مَشَاعِل ـ قِنْدِيل *pl.* قَنَادِيل.

Burning, *n.* The act of, حَرَق ـ إِحْرَاق. The being burnt, إِحْتِرَاق. Heat, حَرَارَة. Pungency, جِدَّة ـ حَرَافَة.

Burning, *a.* That burns, مُحْرِق ـ حَامٍ ـ حَارّ ـ حِرَاق ـ حُرَاق. A — light, مَوْقُود. A — coal, جَمْرَة. A — fever, حُمَّة حَارَّة. Pungent, حَرِيف ـ أَجَاج ـ حَادّ. A — shame, عَارٌ عَظِيم. *See also* Scorching, *n.*

Burning-glass, *n.* بِلَّوْرَة مُحْرِقَة ـ قَزَازَة حَرَّاقَة.

Burnish, *v.t.* بَيَّض ـ جَلَا ـ صَقَل.

Burnisher, *n.* One who burnishes, صَقَّال ; a tool for burnishing, مِصْقَلَة ـ مِسْحَل.

Burnt, *a.* مَحْرُوق. To be burnt, as butter in the cooking, شَاطَ. A — child dreads the fire, مَنْ قَرَصَتْهُ ٱلْحَيَّةُ مِنْ جَرِّ ٱلْحَبْلِ يُخَافُ (*prov.*).

Burnt-offering, *n.* مُحْرَقَة.

Burr, *n.* The guttural sound of the letter *r*, تَلَفُّظ بِحَرْفِ ٱلرَّاء. A lobe of the ear, شَحْمَة ـ لُغْد.

Burrow, *n.* سَرَب *pl.* أَسْرَاب ـ وَكْر *pl.* وُكُور ـ جُحْرَة *pl.* جِحَار ـ وَجَار ـ بُيُوت *pl.* بَيْت ـ نُقُوب *pl.* نَقْب.

Burrow, *v.i.* To make a burrow, نَقَرَ وَجَارًا ـ سَرَّبَ سَرَبًا ـ تَجَحَّرَ ـ جَحَرَ. To enter, betake itself to its —, جَحَرَ ـ حَفَرَ جُحْرَة ـ إِنْجَحَرَ.

Burr-stone, *n.* نَوْعٌ مِنَ ٱلْحَجَرِ تُصْنَعُ مِنْهُ ٱلْأَرْحَاء.

Bursa-faucium, *n.* Of a camel, شِقْشِقَة.

Bursar, *n.* وَكِيل خَرْج.

Bursary, *n.* خِزَانَة ـ خَزِينَة.

Burse, *n.* } بُورْص ـ مَجْمَعُ ٱلتُّجَّارِ.
Bourse, }

Burst, *v.t.* To break, break open, كَسَرَ ـ فَقَأَ ـ صَدَعَ ـ بَعَجَ ـ فَرْقَع ـ أَفْرَزَ ـ شَقَّ. To burst open, of stitching, فَتَقَ. To break open, to hatch, فَقَسَ ـ فَقَصَ. To open, فَتَحَ.

Burst, *v.i.* To fly or break asunder, إِنْصَدَعَ ـ تَصَدَّعَ ـ تَشَقَّقَ ـ إِنْبَعَجَ ـ تَبَزَّلَ ـ فَقَأَ ـ فَقَعَ ـ إِنْفَرَزَ ـ إِنْفَلَقَ ـ إِنْبَاقَ. To —, as of skins, تَخَرَّقَ ; of seed pods, تَفَقَّأَ ; of a boil, فَقَأَ ـ إِنْفَقَأَ ـ تَفَقَّأَ ; of stitching, تَفَتَّقَ ـ إِنْفَتَقَ. To — forth, as of water, إِنْبَجَسَ ـ إِنْفَجَرَ ; of blood, ثَجَّ. To — out, as from its proper place, إِنْدَلَقَ. To — into tears, تَدَمَّعَ. To — into laughter, إِنْبَعَجَ مِنَ ٱلضَّحِكِ ـ فَقَعَ مِنَ ٱلضَّحِكِ.

Burthen, *n.* *See* Burden, *n.*

Bury, *v.t.* To inter, دَفَنَ ـ قَبَرَ. To place upon a bier and carry to burial, جَنَّزَ. To hide, as in the ground, طَمَرَ ـ دَسَّ فِي. To conceal, سَتَرَ ـ أَخْفَى.

Burying-ground, *n.* } تُرْبَة *pl.* تُرَب ـ مَدْفَن ـ مَقْبَرَة *pl.*
Burying-place, } مَقَابِر.

Bush, *n.* A shrub, دُغَيْلَة *pl.* دَغَل ـ دِغَال *pl.* أَدْغَال ـ عُلَّيْقَة *coll.* عُلَّيْق ـ عَوْسَجَة *pl.* عَوَاسِج ـ عَوْسَج. A metal lining to make a hole smaller, نُحَاسَة ـ لِكَاز ; one of wood, شِكَّة. A bush-lining of cloth, لِهَاز. The open country, ٱلصَّحْرَاء.

Bush, *v.t.* and *i.* To furnish with a metal lining, نَحَّسَ. To grow bushy, كَثَّ.

Bushel, *n.* مِكْيَال ـ مِدَاد *pl.* مُدّ ـ نَوْعٌ مِنَ ٱلْأَكْيَالِ. He measures other people's corn with his own bushel, قَاسَ ٱلنَّاسَ عَلَى نَفْسِهِ.

Bushiness, *n.* كَثَانَة ـ كُثُونَة.

Bushman, *n.* Of Africa, مِنْ أَهْلِ طَائِفَةٍ مُتَوَحِّشَةٍ سَاكِنَةٍ فِي ٱلْجِهَةِ ٱلْجَنُوبِيَّةِ مِنْ بَرِّ أَفْرِيقِيَّةَ.

Bushy, *a.* Full of bushes, مُدْغِل ـ جَثْل ـ مَمْلُوٌّ مِنَ ٱلْعُلَّيْقِ ـ مَلْآنٌ مِنَ ٱلْعَوْسَجِ. Thick, كَثِيث ـ كَثّ ـ مُكَلَّل. A — beard, لِحْيَة كَثِيثَة ـ لِحْيَة جَثْلَة.

Busied, *a.* مَشْغُول. The — is not like the free from business, مَا ٱلْمَشْغُولُ مِثْلَ ٱلْأَفْرَغِ.

Busily, *ad.* جِهَادًا ـ بِحِرْصٍ ـ بِهِمَّةٍ ـ بِحَرَارَةٍ ـ بِجِدٍّ وَجُهْدٍ.

Business, *n.* Employment, office, شُغْل *pl.* أَشْغَال ـ شُغْلَة ـ مَنْصَب *pl.* مَنَاصِب ـ وَظِيفَة *pl.* وَظَائِف. Trade, كَار ـ حِرْفَة ـ صَنْعَة. An affair in general, أَمْر *pl.* أُمُور ـ حَاجَة *pl.* حَاجَات ـ مَادَّة *pl.* مَوَادّ ـ دَعْوَى *pl.* دَعَاوَى ـ قَضِيَّة *pl.* قَضَايَا. Business engagements, تَعَلُّقَات. Right of action, حَقّ ـ تَفْوِيض ـ رُخْصَة ـ سُلْطَان. A matter of question, مَسْأَلَة ـ دَعْوَى ـ شَبَكَة. The subject of an action, غَرَض ـ شُغْل. A troublesome —, دَعْوَى مُشْكِلَة. An important —, أَمْرٌ مُهِمّ ـ دَعْوَى ـ مُهِمَّة. The public —, أُمُورُ ٱلدَّوْلَةِ ـ أُمُورُ ٱلْجُمْهُورِ. Pressing —, شُغْلٌ شَاغِل. I have — with you, لِي شُغْلٌ مَعَكَ ـ لِي كَلَام مَعَكَ. To do — for, بَاشَرَ أَشْغَالَ ـ قَضَى أُمُور. Let every one mind his own —, لِيُبَاشِرْ كُلُّ وَاحِدٍ مَا هُوَ لَهُ. Assist him in whatever — he may require of you, سَاعِدْهُ فِي كُلِّ مَا يَحْتَاجُ إِلَيْهِ مِنْكَ. What — have you here? مَا لَكَ وَٱلدُّخُولُ هُنَا. Go about your —, ٱلْزَمْ شُغْلَكَ. Mind your —, don't interfere, لَا تَتَعَرَّضْ. To retire from —, تَقَاعَدَ عَنِ ٱلْأَشْغَالِ. To send one about his —, سَخِطَ عَلَى — سَخَتَ — أَسْحَتَ. To do one's —, to ruin, أَهْلَكَ — خَرَّبَ بَيْتَ; to kill, قَضَى عَلَى — قَتَلَ ². To do one's —, to ease nature, قَضَى حَاجَتَهُ — دَخَلَ ٱلْغَائِطَ ².

Business-like, *a.* مِثْلَ أَهْلِ ٱلشُّغْلِ.

Busk, *n.* مُقَوِّيَةٌ لِلصُّدَيْرِي مِنْ حَدِيدٍ أَوْ رِيشِ ٱلْحُوتِ — مُقَوِّيَةٌ.

Buskin, *n.* بُلْغَةٌ *pl.* بُلَغ — خُفٌّ *pl.* أَخْفَاف.

Busky, *a.* Woody, حَطِيب — مُشَجَّر.

Buss, *n.* A kiss, بَوْسَة — بَوْس. An omnibus, عَرَبَانَةٌ لِلْجُمْهُورِ — أُمْنِيبُوس.

Buss, *v.t.* بَاسَ ².

Bust, *n.* The upper part of the body, ٱلنِّصْفُ ٱلْأَعْلَى مِنَ ٱلْبَدَنِ. A picture of the —, صُورَةُ إِنْسَانٍ إِلَى ٱلْوَسَطِ.

Bustard, *n.* حُبَارَى *pl.* حُبَارَات — خَرَب *pl.* خِرْبَان.

Bustle, *v.i.* تَبَغْدَدَ — تَبَاهَى — غَوَّشَ — نَفَشَ رُوحَهُ ² — نَشِطَ — إِنْتَهَضَ. To — about any thing, بَادَرَ بِ — إِهْتَمَّ بِ — إِضْطَرَبَ بِ.

Bustle, *n.* Commotion, غَاغَة — دَوْشَة — ضَجَاج — ضَجِيج — غَوْشَة — تَخْبِيط — هَرْجٌ وَمَرْجٌ — كَرْكَبَة. A woman's hind pad, غِلَالَة — حَشِيَّة — وِرْفَد — رِفَاعَة — إِعْجَازَة — عِظَامَة — عُظْمَة. She will wear no — but such as is real (*i e.* she does not require one), لَا تَحْتَشِي إِلَّا ٱلصَّمِيمَ ٱلصَّادِقَ. *See also* Fuss, *n.*

Bustler *n.* } *See* Busy, Fussy, *a.*
Bustling, *a.* }

Busy, *a.* Employed with earnestness, شَغِل — مَشْغُول — نَشِيط — مُقَيَّد — شَغَّال. Active, مَعْجُوق — غَارِقٌ فِي ٱلْأَشْغَالِ — مُتَعَرِّضٌ لِأُمُورِ غَيْرِهِ. Meddling, مَعِنٌ فِي ٱلْفُضُولِ — صَاحِبُ دِمَّةٍ.

Busy, *v.t.* To employ in, شَغَلَ بِ ² — أَشْغَلَ بِ. To be busied in, إِشْتَغَلَ بِ — تَصَرَّفَ بِ.

Busy body, *n.* تَيْحَان — تَيَّاح — مِتْيَاح — عِرِّيض — فُضُولِيّ — مُتَعَرِّضٌ لِأُمُورِ غَيْرِهِ — تَيَّاح — مَعِنَّة *fem.* مَعِنّ — فُضُولِيُّون *pl.* — مِتْعَم — مُتَكَلِّف.

But, *conj.* Except, إِلَّا — غَيْر — سِوَى — خِلَافَ. You have no other god but Him, مَا لَكُمْ مِنْ إِلٰهٍ غَيْرُهُ. None but boys, لَا أَحَدَ سِوَى ٱلْأَبْنَاءِ. Yet, nevertheless, بَلْ أَنَّمَا — بَلْ وَأَيْضًا — مَعَ ذٰلِكَ — غَيْرَ أَنَّ:—He was about to speak, but he kept silence, كَادَ يَتَكَلَّمُ بَلْ أَنَّمَا سَكَتَ. Many desired to see him, but did not see him, إِنَّ كَثِيرِينَ ٱشْتَهُوا أَنْ يَنْظُرُوهُ غَيْرَ أَنَّهُمْ مَا أَدْرَكُوهُ بَصَرًا. Now, بَقِيَ — وَ — فَ:—But (now) I say that . . ., فَأَقُولُ أَنَّ. Howbeit, لٰكِنْ — وَلٰكِنْ:—But I, لٰكِنِّي; but he, لٰكِنَّهُ. But for this cause I obtained mercy, لٰكِنْ لِأَجْلِ هٰذَا رُحِمْتُ. But for that I would not have spoken, لَوْلَا ذٰلِكَ مَا تَكَلَّمْتُ. Not but that I would have helped you had I known your circumstances, لَيْسَ أَنِّي مَا كُنْتُ مُسَاعِدًا لَكَ لَوْ عَرَفْتُ مَا أَنْتَ فِيهِ. But, in fact, وَٱلْحَالُ. But, for, and, وَ:—He said, I go, but went not, قَالَ أَنَا أَذْهَبُ وَلَمْ يَذْهَبْ. They have mouths to speak but speak not, eyes to see and see not, لَهُمْ أَفْوَاهٌ وَلَا تَتَكَلَّمُ وَلَهُمْ أَعْيُنٌ وَلَا تُبْصِرُ. He has grieved me but a little, لَمْ يَغُمَّنِي إِلَّا قَلِيلًا — قَلَّ مَا يَغُمُّنِي. The last but one, مَا قَبْلَ ٱلْآخِرِ.

But, *n.* The end, طَرَف — آخِر — حَدّ. The but-end, ٱلطَّرَفُ ٱلْأَكْبَرُ. The but, as of a musket, كرنيفة — قُنْدَق.

But, *v.i.* *See to* Abut, *v.i.*

Butcher, *n.* ذَابِح — قَصَّاب — جَزَّار. A butcher's knife, سَاطُور.

Butcher, *v.t.* ذَبَحَ — قَتَلَ ².

Butchery, *n.* A slaughter-house, مَجْزَرَة. Carnage, سَفْكُ دِمَاءٍ — ذَبْح — قَتْل.

Butler, *n.* رَئِيسُ ٱلسُّقَاةِ — سُفْرَجِي بَاشِي.

Butlership, *n.* مَقَامُ رَئِيسِ ٱلسُّقَاةِ — مَنْصَبُ سُفْرَجِي بَاشِي.

Butment, *n.* Of a bridge, إِسْنَادُ قَنْطَرَةٍ — تَمْكِينُ قَنْطَرَةٍ. *See also* Buttress, *n.*

Butt, *n.* A mark to shoot at, هَدَف — غَرَض *pl.* أَغْرَاض — نِيشَان. A blow with the head, نَطْحَة. A mark for ridicule, مَسْخَرَة — هُزْأَة — أُضْحُوكَة. A barrel, بَرْمِيل *pl.* بَرَامِيل. To make a — of, to ridicule, هَزَأَ بِ — تَسَخَّرَ بِ. Men are the butts of destiny, ٱلنَّاسُ أَغْرَاضُ ٱلْمَنِيَّةِ.

Butt, *v.t.* To strike with the horns, شَصَرَ ² — نَطَحَ — نَاطَحَ. They butted one another, of many, تَنَاطَحُوا. Butted, مَنْطُوح — نَطِيح.

Butter, *n.* سَمْن *pl.* سُمْنَان; a piece of —, سَمْنَة. Fresh —, زُبْد; a piece of fresh —, زُبْدَة. Liquid —, ghee, سِلَاءٌ — سَمْن. Camel's —, جُبَاب. A seller of —, سَمَّان.

Butter, *v.t.* To smear with —, سَمَّنَ — بِسَمْنٍ دَهَنَ ². To flatter, دَهَنَ ² — مَلَّقَ. To use flattery to, أَدْهَنَ — تَمَلَّقَ لِ.

Buttercup, *n.* زُبَيْعِيَّة.

Butterfly, *n.* فَرَاشَة *coll.* فَرَاش — فَرْفُور — بَشَّارَة — أَبُو دَقِيق.

Butteris, *n.* كَفَّة — آلَةٌ لِبَيْطَارٍ حَوَافِرِ ٱلدَّوَابِّ.

Butterman, *n.* سَمَّان.

Buttermilk, *n.* مَصْل — مَخِيض.

Butterprint, *n.* قَالِبٌ لِلزُّبْدَةِ.

Butterwort, *n.* The plant, حَشِيشَةُ ٱلدُّهْنِ ـ بَقْلَةُ ٱلْكَرْمِ.

Buttery, *n.* بَيْتُ ٱلْمُؤْنَةِ ـ دُولَاب.

Buttery, *a.* كَٱلزُّبْدِ ـ زُبْدِيٌّ.

Buttock, *n.* The rump, دُبُر ـ إِسْت ـ أَرْدَاف ـ عَجُز ـ قَطَاة ـ تَأْكِيم ـ أَبُو ٱلْأَسْتَاهِ ـ مَأْكَمَة ـ أَدْبَار *pl.* Having large buttocks, رَاجِح ـ رَجَاح. To kick on the —, سَتَهَ. To be large in the —, أَسْتِهَ.

Button, *n.* زِرّ *pl.* زُرُور ـ زِرَّة *pl.* أَزْرَار. The Aleppo —, the boil so called, شِيرِيَّة ـ بَثْرَة ـ حَبَّةُ سَنَةٍ ـ حَبَّةُ حَلَب.

Button, *v.t.* زَرَّ *aor.* يَزُرُّ ـ زَرَّرَ ـ كَلَّبَ ٱلْأَزْرَارَ. To stud with buttons, زَرَّرَ.

Button-hole, *n.* بَنِيقَة *pl.* بَنَائِقُ ـ عُرْوَة *pl.* عُرًى *or* عَرَاوِي. To put button-holes to, عَرَّى.

Button-maker, *n.* صَانِعُ ٱلْأَزْرَارِ.

Buttress, *n.* كَبْشَة *pl.* كِبَاش ـ عِمْدَة ـ سَنَد *pl.* أَسْنَاد ـ مِسْنَد *pl.* مَسَانِدُ. The — of a bridge, عَمُودُ قَنْطَرَةٍ; of a wall, بَغْلَةُ حَائِطٍ.

Buttress, *v.t.* عَمَدَ ـ أَسْنَدَ ـ سَنَّدَ.

Butts, *n.* مَيْدَانُ ٱلنُّشَّابَةِ ـ مَجْمَعُ ٱلنُّشَّابَةِ.

Butyraceous, *a.* زُبْدِيٌّ.

Buxom, *a.* Gay, مَبْسُوط ـ بَشُوش ـ فَرِح ـ بَطِر ـ بَحْبُوح.

Buxomly, *ad.* بِبَطَرَنَةٍ ـ بِٱنْبِسَاطٍ ـ بِبَشَاشَةٍ ـ فَرِحًا.

Buxomness, *n.* إِنْبِسَاط ـ بَطَرَنَة ـ سُرُور ـ بَشَاشَة.

Buy, *v.t.* إِشْتَرَى ـ شَرَى ـ إِبْتَاعَ. Is nothing like this to be bought? أَفَلَا يُوجَدُ مِثْلَ هٰذَا لِلْمَبِيعِ. A thing bought, a purchase, شِرًى *pl.* أَشْرِيَاءُ. Buying and selling, تَبَايُع ـ بَيْعٌ وَشِرَاءٌ.

Buyer, *n.* مُشْتَرٍ ـ شَارٍ *pl.* شُرَاة ـ مُتَبَايِع ـ بَائِع *pl.* بَاعَة.

Buzz, *n.* ⎫ طَنِين ـ رَنِين ـ رَنٌّ ـ دَنْدَنَة ـ غُنَان ـ عَنْتَرَة ـ
Buzzing, ⎭ وَظٌّ. A — in the ears, دَوِيٌّ. The flies made a —, طَنْطَنَ ٱلذُّبَابُ. The valley resounded with the buzzing, أَغَنَّ ٱلْوَادِي.

Buzz, *v.i.* As of insects, عَنْتَرَ ـ طَنْطَنَ ـ دَنْدَنَ ـ صَوَّتَ ـ وَزْوَزَ ـ أَغَنَّ ـ غَنَّ. To — abroad, to publish, أَشَاعَ بِ. To be buzzed about, شَاعَ.

Buzzard, *n.* The bird, صِنْفٌ مِنَ ٱلطُّيُورِ ٱلْجَوَارِحِ. A blockhead, ثَوْر ـ بَلِيد ـ أَحْمَق ـ بَهِيم.

By, *prep.* and *ad.* As expressing the cause of an action, مِن. The instrument or manner of an action, بِ. By this means, بِهٰذِهِ ٱلطَّرِيقَةِ. By force, قَهْرًا ـ بِٱلْغَصْبِ ـ غَصْبًا. He seized him by the foot, أَخَذَهُ مِنْ رِجْلِهِ. By land and by sea, بِٱلْبَحْرِ وَبِٱلْبَرِّ ـ بَحْرًا وَبَرًّا. To come by land, جَاءَ عَلَى ٱلْبَرِّ. To come by sea, جَاءَ فِي ٱلْبَحْرِ. Day by day, يَوْمًا بِيَوْمٍ ـ يَوْمًا فَيَوْمًا ـ مِنْ يَوْمٍ إِلَى يَوْمٍ. One by one, وَاحِدًا فَوَاحِدًا ـ وَاحِدًا وَاحِدًا ـ وَاحِدٌ بَعْدَ وَاحِدٍ. By turns, دَوْرٌ وَدَوْرٌ ـ بِٱلنَّوْبَةِ ـ بِٱلدَّوْرِ. Hard by, قَرِيبٌ مِن ـ قَرِيبٌ. By all means, عَلَى كُلِّ حَالٍ ـ مِنْ كُلِّ بُدٍّ. By no means, حَاشَى ـ أَصْلًا ـ قَطُّ ـ أَبَدًا ـ كَلَّا. By the by, فِي ٱلْحَالِ ـ مِنْ جِدٍّ ـ إِلَّا أَن ـ إِلَّا. By and by, then, لِسَاعَتِهِ ـ فِي سَاعَتِهِ ـ حَالًا. By and by, some time hence, بَعْدَ ـ بَعْدَهَا. She is by herself, هِيَ عَلَى وَحْدِهَا. He went out by himself, خَرَجَ مُنْفَرِدًا. To say good-by to, وَدَّعَ ـ وَادَعَ. A good-by, وَدَاع.

By, by the hands, of, through, صُحْبَةَ ـ عَلَى يَدِ. The letter came by a messenger, وَصَلَ ٱلْمَكْتُوبُ ـ جَاءَ ٱلْمَكْتُوبُ عَلَى يَدِ سَاعٍ صُحْبَةَ سَاعٍ.

By, near to, قَرِيبٌ مِن ـ عِنْدَ ـ جَنْبَ. By the fire, عَلَى ٱلنَّارِ ـ جَنْبَ ٱلنَّارِ. The judge stood by the king, وَقَفَ ٱلْقَاضِي جَنْبَ ٱلْمَلِكِ. He stood by the door, وَقَفَ عِنْدَ ٱلْبَابِ.

By, as a formula of swearing, بِ ـ تَ ـ وَ ـ لَحَقٌّ ـ حَقًّا ـ لَ. By God! بِٱللّٰهِ ـ وَٱللّٰهِ. By thy life, لَعَمْرُكَ ـ وَحَيَوٰةِ ـ وَحَيَاتِكَ. By the life of Pharaoh, وَحَيَوٰةِ فِرْعَوْنَ.

By, according to, تَبَعَ ـ بِحَسَبِ ـ بِمُوجَبِ ـ عَلَى. By your orders, عَلَى أَوَامِرِكَ.

By, in multiplication, فِي. Three by five, ثَلَاثَةٌ فِي خَمْسَةٍ. Fifty ells long by three wide, طُولُهُ خَمْسُونَ ذِرَاعًا فِي ثَلَاثَةِ أَذْرُعٍ عَرْضًا.

By-end, *n.* غَرَضٌ مَخْصُوصٌ.

Bygone, *a.* سَالِف. In — days, فِي ٱلْأَيَّامِ ٱلسَّالِفَةِ.

By-law, *n.* قَانُونٌ مَخْصُوصٌ *pl.* قَوَانِينُ مَخْصُوصَةٌ.

By-name, *n.* لَقَب *pl.* أَلْقَاب.

By-path, *n.* عَوْجَة ـ لَقَّة.

By-room, *n.* خَلْوَة.

Bystander, *n.* نَاظِر *pl.* نَاظِرُونَ ـ وَاقِف *pl.* وَاقِفُونَ ـ شَاهِد *pl.* شُهُود *and* أَشْهَاد ـ مُتَفَرِّج.

By-the-bye, *ad.* وَأَمَّا ـ مِنْ جِدٍّ.

By-way, *n.* مَسْلَك ـ عَطْفَة.

By-word, *n.* عِبْرَة ـ نُقْط ـ قَوْل ـ مَثَل *pl.* أَمْثَال. I will make him a — by way of example to others, أَجْعَلُهُ عِبْرَةً لِمَنْ يَعْتَبِرُ. Thou hast made us a — among the people, صَيَّرْتَنَا مَثَلًا فِي ٱلنَّاسِ.

Byzantian, *a.* مُتَعَلِّقٌ بِمَدِينَةِ إِسْتَانْبُولَ ٱلْعَتِيقَةِ ـ مِنْ بُوزَنْتِيَّة.

C.

Cab, *n.* The vehicle, عَرَبَانَةٌ بِرَأْسِ خَيلٍ ـ عَرَبَانَةٌ تَجُرُّهَا دَابَّةٌ.

Cabal, *n.* A private confederacy, عُصْبَةٌ ـ تَعَصُّب ـ عَصَبِيَّةٌ. A consultation, مُؤَامَرَةٌ. An intrigue, دُولَاب *pl.* دَوَالِيبُ ـ دَسِيسَةٌ. مُتَعَاهِدُونَ.

Cabal, *v.i. pl.* تَعَاهَدُوا ـ تَعَصَّبُوا. To — in favour of, تَعَصَّبُوا فِي. To — against, تَعَصَّبُوا عَلَى.

Cabala, *n.* القَبَلَةُ.

Cabalistic, *a.* مُخْتَصٌّ بِٱلْقَبَلَةِ. Occult, خَفِيٌّ.

Caballer, *n.* مُتَعَصِّب ـ مُتَعَاهِد ـ فَاتِن *pl.* فُتَّان.

Cabbage, *n.* بَقْلَةُ ٱلْأَنْصَارِ ـ كُرُنْبَة *coll.* كُرُنْب ـ مَلْفُوف; (called in Barbary مُكَوَّر). Cloth embezzled by a tailor, لِحَانَة ـ مَا يَسْرِقُهُ ٱلْخَيَّاطُ مِنَ ٱلْجُوخِ وَقْتَ ٱلتَّفْصِيلِ.

Cabbage, *v.t.* To embezzle cloth, of a tailor, بَخَسَ مِنَ ٱلْجُوخِ ـ ٤. To pilfer, تَسَرَّقَ ـ أَسَلَّ.

Cabin, *n.* A small room, حُجْرَةٌ. A hut, كُوخ *pl.* أَكْوَاخ ـ خُصّ *pl.* أَخْصَاص. The —, as of a ship, الطَّارِمَةُ ـ المَقْعَدُ. A —, as in a ship, خَزْنَةٌ ـ أُوضَةٌ *pl.* أُوضَات ـ كَمَرَةٌ.

Cabin-boy, *n.* صَبِيُّ ٱلْمَعَاشِ ـ غُلَامُ ٱلطَّارِمَةِ.

Cabinet, *n.* A small room, حُجْرَةٌ ـ خَلْوَةٌ ـ عُلِّيَّةٌ *pl.* عَلَالِيُّ. A case for any thing valuable, خَزْنَةٌ. The national executive, مُدَبِّرُوا ٱلْمَمْلَكَةِ. A — council, مَجْلِسُ مُدَبِّرِي ٱلْمَمْلَكَةِ.

Cabinet-maker, *n.* حُقَّاق ـ نَجَّارُ شُغْلٍ رَفِيعٍ ـ نَجَّارُ أَثَاثٍ فَاخِرَةٍ.

Cabinet-work, *n.* مَنْجُورَاتٌ فَاخِرَةٌ.

Cable, *n.* قَلْس *pl.* قُلُوس ـ جُمَالَة *pl.* جُمَالَات ـ لَبَان ـ گُومَنَةٌ. A chain —, زِنْجِير. They dragged the ship with the —, جَرُّوا ٱلسَّفِينَةَ بِٱلْقَلْسِ. To slip one's —, to run away, هَرَبَ ٢ ـ وَلَّى ـ إِنْسَلَّ ـ نَزَّ.

Cabman, *n.* قَائِدُ ٱلْعَرَبَانَةِ ـ عَرَبَجِي *pl.* عَرَبَجِيَّة.

Caboose, *n.* مَطْبَخُ ٱلْمَرْكَبِ; (that for the sailors is called فُجَيْر on the Nile boats).

Cabriolet, *n.* *See* Cab, *n.*

Cacao, *n.* The berry, لَوْزٌ هِنْدِيٌّ ـ لَوْزُ ٱلشُّوكُولَاتَه.

Cachetic, *a.* مَفْسُودُ ٱلدَّمِ وَٱلْمِزَاجِ ـ مَمْرُوض ـ مِمْرَاض.

Cachet, *n.* أَمْرٌ بِتَحْبِيسٍ.

Cachexy, *n.* فَسَادُ ٱلدَّمِ وَٱلْمِزَاجِ.

Cachinnation, *n.* قَهْقَهَةٌ. To break out into a —, قَهْقَهَ.

Cacique, *n.* أَمِير *pl.* أُمَرَآءُ ـ رَئِيس *pl.* رُؤَسَآءُ.

Cackle, *v.i.* Like a hen, قَاقَ ـ نَقْنَقَ ـ قَوْقَأَ. To giggle, قَهْقَهَ ـ ضَحِكَ ـ كَتْكَتَ ـ هَأْهَأَ.

Cackle, *n.* Of a hen, قَاقَةٌ ـ نَقْنَقَةٌ ـ قَيْق. A giggle, كَتْكَتَةٌ ـ قَهْقَهَةٌ ـ هَأْهَأَ.

Cackler, *n.* Of a hen, مُقَوْقِئٌ ـ مُنَقْنِق. A prattler, مُقَهْقِه ـ ضَحَّاك ـ قَوَّال ـ غَلْبَاوِيٌّ ـ فَشَّار.

Cacoethes, *n.* A bad habit of body, مَرَض ـ فَسَادُ ٱلْمِزَاجِ.

Cacoethes scribendi, هَوَسٌ بِٱلْكِتَابَةِ.

Cacophonous, *a.* مُبَلْبَل ـ مُهَأْهَأٌ.

Cacophony, *n.* هَأْهَأٌ ـ تَنَافُرُ (*or* شُذُوذُ) أَصْوَاتٍ ـ بَلْبَلَةٌ.

Cactus, *n.* نَبَاتٌ مِثْلَ ٱلتِّينِ ٱلْفِرَنْجِيِّ وَهُوَ ٱلصَّبِّيرُ.

Cadaverous, *a.* In look, شَبِيهُ ٱلْمَيِّتِ; in smell, جَائِف ـ جِيفِيٌّ.

Caddy, *n.* عُلْبَةٌ لِلشَّاي.

Cadence, *n.* } Measurement of sounds, وَزْن ـ مِيزَان. A flow
Cadency, } of verses, مَحَطٌّ ـ إِيقَاع ـ سَجْع. Tone, تَرْنِيم ـ نِظَام ـ مَقَام.

Cadet, *n.* A pupil in a military college, تِلْمِيذٌ فِي مَدْرَسَةٍ عَسْكَرِيَّةٍ. A younger brother, أَخٌ أَصْغَرُ. A volunteer, مُتَخَيِّر ـ مُتَطَوِّع.

Cadetship, *n.* مَنْصَبُ ٱلْمُبْتَدِئِ.

Cadi, *n.* *See* Kâdhi, *n.*

Cadre, *n.* جَرِيدَةٌ.

Caduceus, *n.* إِسْمُ قَضِيبٍ فِي يَدِ هِرْمِس أَحَدِ إِلٰهَةِ عَبَدَةِ ٱلْأَوْثَانِ.

Caducity, *n.* سُرْعَةُ ٱلْإِنْتِثَارِ.

Caducous, *a.* سَرِيعُ ٱلْإِنْتِثَارِ.

Cæsar, *n.* قَيْصَر *pl.* قَيَاصِرَةٌ.

Cæsarism, *n.* حُكُومَةٌ مُنْفَرِدَةٌ.

Café, *n.* A coffee shop, قَهْوَة *pl.* قَهَاوِي.

Caffeine, *n.* مَادَّةُ ٱلْقَهْوَةِ ٱلطَّبِيعِيَّةُ ـ أُسُّ ٱلْقَهْوَةِ.

Caftan, *n.* قُفْطَان *pl.* قَفَاطِين.

Cage, *n.* A bird's —, قَفَص *pl.* أَقْفَاص. A hen-coop, خُمّ *pl.* خِمَمَة ـ خُنّ. A prison, حَبْس.

Cage, *v.t.* حَطَّ-فِي قَفَصٍ ².

Caic, *n.* / Caique, } قَائِق *pl.* قَوَائِق *and* قَائِقَات.

Cairn, *n.* رُجْمَة ـ أَرْجَام *pl.* رَجْم ـ أَكَمَات *pl.* أَكَمَة ـ نُوِيَّة *pl.* رِجَام *and* رُجُم.

Caisson, *n.* A chest of bombs, صَنْدُوقٌ مَحْشِيٌّ بِبَارُودٍ وَكُلَلٍ. A — to serve as a support, صَنْدُوقٌ رُكْنِيٌّ. A provision waggon, عَرَبَانَةُ ذَخِيرَةٍ.

Caitiff, *n.* خَاسِر *pl.* خُسَّر ـ خَبِيث *pl.* خُبَثَاء *and* خِبَاث ـ اِبْنُ حَرَامٍ.

Cajeput, *n.* The seed, حَبُّ ٱلسَّلَاطِينِ.

Cajole, *v.t.* دَاهَنَ ـ دَارَى ـ مَلَّقَ ـ حَاوَلَ ـ مَشَّحَ ـ صَانَعَ ـ دَاجَنَ ـ لَاطَفَ. To be cajoled, تَمَلَّقَ.

Cajoler, *n.* كَثِيرُ ٱلتَّمْلِيقِ ـ حِيَلِيٌّ ـ مَلَّاق ـ مُدَاهِن ـ مُدَاجِن.

Cajolery, *n.* مُلَاطَفَة ـ مُحَاوَلَة ـ مُدَارَاة ـ مُدَاهَنَة ـ مُدَاجَنَة ـ تَمْلِيق.

Cake, *n.* A delicate kind of bread, قُرْص *pl.* أَقْرَاص. Cake made with honey and almonds, زَلَابِيَة ـ بَقْلَاوَة. A — of bread, رُقَاق ـ قُرْصَة ـ أَقْرَاص *pl.* قُرْص ـ رُغُف *pl.* رَغِيف ـ خُبْزٌ رُقَاقٌ ـ رِقَاقَة *pl.* قُرَص.

Cake, *v.t.* To make into cakes, قَرَّصَ. To form into a mass, جَمَعَ ـ رَغَفَ ـ كَمَزَ. *See also under to* Mat, *v.t.*

Cake, *v.i.* To become hard, dry, يَبِسَ *aor.* يَيْبَسُ ـ نَشِفَ ـ تَرَوَّبَ. *See also to* Mat, *v.i.*

Calabash, *n.* قَرْعَة *coll.* قَرْع.

Calamine, *n.* حَجَرُ ٱلتُّوتِيَةِ ـ حَجَرٌ سُلَيْمَانِيٌّ.

Calamint, *n.* The plant, حَبَقَةُ ٱلتِّمْسَاحِ ـ مَوْتَج ـ صرمران ـ كلمنتون ـ بَقْلَةُ ٱلْعَدَسِ.

Calamus aromaticus, *n.* The plant, قَصَب ـ قَصَبُ ٱلطِّيبِ ـ ٱلذَّرِيرَة.

Calamitous, *a.* مَنْحُوس ـ نَحِس ـ فَاجِع ـ مَشُوم ـ مَشْؤُوم ـ سُوء.

Calamity, *n.* رُزْء *pl.* أَرْزَاء ـ رَزِيَّة *or* رَزِيئَة *pl.* رَزَايَا ـ طَامَّة ـ بُؤْس ـ بَوَائِق *pl.* بَائِقَة ـ دَوَاهٍ *pl.* دَاهِيَة ـ خُطُوب *pl.* خَطْب ـ خُبُول ـ جَوَائِح *pl.* جَوْحَة ـ كَرَائِب *pl.* كَرِيبَة ـ فَاجِعَة ـ مَصَائِب *pl.* مُصِيبَة ـ آفَات *pl.* آفَة ـ بَلَايَا *pl.* بَلِيَّة ـ حَادِثَة. A sudden —, غَوْل *pl.* أَغْوَال ـ غَائِلَة *pl.* غَوَائِل ـ مَغَالَة. Suffering, as from a —, مُصَابٌ بِ. Calamities poured upon them, اِنْهَمَرَتْ عَلَيْهِمِ ٱلدَّوَاهِي.

Calamus, *n.* قَصَب; for writing, قَلَم *pl.* أَقْلَام.

Calash, *n.* عَرَبَانَةٌ خَفِيفَةٌ.

Calcareous, *a.* مَا تَقْلِبُهُ ٱلنَّارُ كِلْسًا. Calcareous stone, حَجَرُ ٱلْجِيرِ.

Calcedony, *n.* عَقِيقٌ أَبْيَضُ.

Calciferous, *a.* مُوَلِّدُ ٱلْكِلْسِ.

Calcinable, *a.* تَكْلِيسُهُ مُمْكِنٌ.

Calcination, *n.* تَكْلِيس.

Calcine, *v.t.* كَلَّسَ.

Calculable, *a.* مِمَّا يُحْصَى ـ مِمَّا يُحْسَبُ.

Calculate, *v.t.* and *i.* To reckon, عَدَّ ـ حَسَبَ ² ـ أَحْصَى. To intend, اِعْتَمَدَ ـ قَصَدَ ـ نَوَى إِلَى. It is calculated that…, اَلْمَحْسُوبُ أَنْ. To adjust to an end, طَبَّقَ-عَلَى ـ وَلَّفَ-عَلَى. To — upon, اِعْتَمَدَ عَلَى.

Calculation, *n.* تَخْمِين ـ حُسْبَان ـ إِحْصَاء ـ حِسَاب. To take into —, اِحْتَسَبَ.

Calculator, *n.* رَقَمْجِي ـ حَسِيب ـ حَاسِب.

Calculous, *n.* حَصَوِيّ.

Calculus, *n.* حَصَاة *pl.* حَصَوَات.

Caldron, *n.* طِنْجِير *pl.* طَنَاجِير ـ قُدُور *pl.* قِدْر ـ مَرَاجِل *pl.* مِرْجَل ـ حَلَّة ـ قَزَانَات *pl.* قَزَان ـ طَنْجَرَة *vulg.* طَنَاجِير.

Calefaction, *n.* تَسْخِين.

Calefactive, *a.* مُسَخِّن.

Calefy, *v.t.* أَسْخَنَ ـ سَخَّنَ.

Calendar, *n.* An almanac, تَقْوِيم ـ حِسَابُ أَيَّامِ ٱلسَّنَةِ ـ رُوزْنَامَة. A — month, مُدَّةُ شَهْرٍ حَسَبَ تَقْوِيمِ ٱلْفِرَنْجِ.

Calender, *n.* A smoothing instrument, آلَةٌ لِصَقْلِ ـ مِصْقَلَة ٱلْقُمَاشِ. A Muslim fakir, قَلَنْدَر *pl.* قَلَنْدَرِيَّة.

Calender, *v.t.* صَقَلَ ٱلْقُمَاشَ ².

Calends, *n.* عِبَارَةٌ عَنْ رَأْسِ ٱلشَّهْرِ عِنْدَ ٱلرُّومَانِيِّينَ ٱلْأَوَّلِينَ. The Greek —, عِبَارَةٌ عَنْ قَطُّ أَوْ أَصْلًا.

Calenture, *n.* حُمَّى.

Calf, *n.* The young of a cow, عِجْل *fem.* عِجْلَة *pl.* عِجَال *and* عُجُول. The — of the leg, حَمَاة *pl.* حَمَوَات ـ لَحْمُ ٱلسَّاقِ. A blockhead, بَلِيد ـ أَحْمَق ـ ثَوْر.

Caliber, *n.* / Calibre, } Diameter, عِيَار. Mental capacity, اَلْمُدْرِكَة ـ قُوَّةٌ مُدْرِكَةٌ ـ عَقْل.

Calico, *n.* بَزّ *pl.* بُزُوز ـ شِيت. Printed —, شِيتٌ هِنْدِيٌّ ـ شِيتٌ يَمَنِيٌّ.

Calid, *a.* Hot, حَارّ ـ حَام.

Calidity, *n.* حَرّ ـ حَرَارَة.

Calif, *n.* *See* Khalifah, *n.*

Caligraphic, *a.* مُتَعَلِّقٌ بِٱلْخَطِّ ٱلْحَسَنِ.

Caligraphist, *n.* خَطَّاط.

Caligraphy, *n.* خَطٌّ حَسَنٌ ـ كِتَابُ ٱلْخَاسِينِ ; *in the Persian style,* خَطٌّ تَعْلِيق.

Calisthenics, *n.* رِيَاضَةٌ لِإِنْمَاءِ قُوَّةِ ٱلْمَفَاصِلِ وَحُسْنِ حَرَكَاتِ ٱلْبَدَنِ ـ رِيَاضَةٌ جَسَدِيَّةٌ.

Calix, *n.* *See* Calyx, *n.*

Calk, *v.t.* قَلْفَطَ ـ قَلَّفَ ـ قَلَفَ.

Calker, *n.* مُقَلْفِط ـ مُقَلِّف.

Calking, *n.* تَقْلِيف.

Call, *v.t.* and *i.* To summon, نَادَى ـ دَعَا ـ صَيَّحَ ـ نَدَا. To name, قَالَ لِ ـ لَقَّبَ بِ ـ دَعَا بِ ـ سَمَّى بِ ـ سَمَّى. To demand, to call to appear, طَلَبَ ـ بَعَثَ طَلَبَهُ ـ بَعَثَ. To proclaim, نَادَى بِ ـ أَشْهَرَ. He sent to the town and called for all the elders, أَرْسَلَ إِلَى ٱلْمَدِينَةِ وَٱسْتَدْعَى بِجَمِيعِ ٱلْمَشَائِخِ. He called to prayer, from the mosque, أَذَّنَ بِٱلصَّلَاةِ.

To call aside, أَخْلَى بِ ـ عَن ـ دَعَا مُنْفَرِدًا.

To call at, to turn out of one's way to go to, عَاجَ عَلَى *aor.* يَعُوجُ.

To call back, by summons, دَعَا ثَانِيَةً ـ رَدَّ ـ رَجَّعَ ـ أَعَادَ.

To call back, to revoke, أَبْطَلَ ـ نَقَضَ.

To call for, as for a thing, إِسْتَدْعَى بِ ـ طَلَبَ.

To call forth or out, دَعَا خَارِجًا ـ إِسْتَخْرَجَ ـ أَخْرَجَ. To elicit, إِسْتَوْجَبَ.

To call in, to cause to come in, دَعَا دَاخِلًا ـ فَوَّتَ ـ أَدْخَلَ.

To call in question, مَارَى ـ شَكَّ فِي. To be called in question for, حُوكِمَ عَلَى ـ أُسْتُدْعِيَ عَلَى *aor.* يُحَاكَمُ.

To call in, to collect, حَشَدَ ـ جَمَعَ ـ لَمَّ.

To call names, to revile, سَبَّ ـ شَتَمَ ـ لَقَّشَ ـ نَبَزَ.

To call on, to require of, أَمَرَ بِ ـ طَلَبَ مِن ـ أَلْزَمَ.

To call out, to challenge, دَعَا لِلْقِتَالِ.

To call out to, إِسْتَدْعَى ـ دَعَا بِ.

To call over, as names, قَرَأَ. To call over, as a list, قَرَأَ ٱلْقَائِمَةَ.

To call to account, حَاسَبَ.

To call to memory, تَنَبَّهَ عَلَى ـ تَذَكَّرَ.

To call together, to convoke, نَادَى بِ ـ جَمَعَ ـ دَعَا ـ حَشَدَ.

To call to one another, تَنَادَى.

To call up, to make to appear, إِسْتَدْعَى ـ أَحْضَرَ.

To call up, to waken, نَبَّهَ ـ فَيَّقَ ـ صَحَّى ـ أَيْقَظَ.

To call upon, for aid, إِسْتَعَانَ بِ ـ إِسْتَغَاثَ بِ.

To call upon, to implore, دَعَا ـ إِبْتَهَلَ إِلَى ـ طَلَبَ ـ تَضَرَّعَ إِلَى.

To call upon, to visit, زَارَ ـ مَرَّ بِ or عَلَى.

Call, *n.* A vocal address, دَعْوَة ـ دُعَاء ـ نِدَاء. A claim, requisition, طَلَب ـ طَلَبَة. An inward —, or impulse, as from God, إِلْهَام ـ هِدَايَة. Authority, قُوَّة ـ أَمْر. The — of a drum, دَقُّ ٱلطَّبْلِ. A bird's —, صَفَّارَة. A — to prayer from the mosque أَذَان. Calls, engagements, تَعَلُّقَات.

Calling, *n.* A trade, حِرْفَة *pl.* حِرَف ـ صِنَاعَة *pl.* صَنَائِع ـ كَار ـ صَنْعَة. An office, شُغْل ـ مَنْصَب ـ وَظِيفَة. A trade corporation, حِرْفَة ـ جَمَاعَة ـ صِنْف *pl.* أَصْنَاف.

Callosity, *n.* Corneous hardness, كُبُوب ـ جُسْأَة ـ ثَفَن ـ دَمَان ـ دُحَاس.

Callous, *a.* Indurated, مُقَشَّب ـ مُدَمَّن ـ جَاسِئٌ. Unfeeling, عَدِيمُ ٱلْحِسِّ ـ جَافٍ عَن ـ قَاسِي ٱلْقَلْبِ. To become —, horned, جَسَأَ ـ أَثْفَنَ ـ ثَفِنَ ـ كَنِبَ. His hand became —, أَثْفَنَ يَدَهُ ; he or it made his hand —, ثَفِنَتْ يَدُهُ. A — hand, يَدٌ جَسْأَةٌ. To be —, unfeeling, قَسَا ; to make one's self —, أَقْسَى.

Callousness, *n.* Hardness of heart, عَدَمُ ٱلْحَاسِّيَّةِ ـ قَسَاوَةُ قَلْبٍ. *See also* Callosity, *n.*

Callow, *a.* مَنْتُوف ـ أَقَدُّ ـ أَمْلَطُ.

Callus, *n.* لَحْمٌ مُعَظَّمٌ.

Calm, *a.* Quiet, مُسْتَرِيح ـ مُرْتَاح ـ هَادٍ ـ سَاكِن. Sedate, مُطْمَئِنٌّ ـ سَاكِن. Unruffled, رَزِين ـ رَكِين ـ رَصِين. Calm, of the sea, رَاكِن. Calm, not stormy, سَاجٍ. To be —, of the sea, سَجَا. The sea is —, ٱلْبَحْرُ رَاكِنٌ. Be —, without anxiety, كُنْ بِلَا هَمٍّ ـ ثِقْ قَلْبًا ـ كُنْ مُطْمَئِنًّا.

Calm, *n.} Calmness, *n.* Quiet, هُدُوٌّ ـ رَاحَة ـ سُكُون. Sedateness, رَزَانَة ـ وَقَار. Of the sea, غَلِينَة ـ سُجُوٌّ. Composure of mind, رَاحَةُ بَالٍ ـ أَمَنَة ـ إِطْمِئْنَان. He rebuked the winds and the sea and there was a great —, إِنْتَهَرَ ٱلرِّيَاحَ وَٱلْبَحْرَ فَصَارَ هُدُوٌّ عَظِيمٌ. To be —, سَكَنَ ـ حَلُمَ ـ تَهَدَّأَ ـ هَدَأَ. The wind calmed, أَهْمَدَتِ ٱلرِّيحُ.

Calm, *v.t.* حَلَّمَ ـ رَيَّحَ ـ أَهْدَأَ ـ هَدَّأَ ـ سَكَّنَ ـ هَدَنَ. He calms the storm and the waves are still, يُهْدِئُ ٱلْأَنْوَاءَ فَتَسْكُنُ ٱلْأَمْوَاجُ.

Calmly, *ad.* بِهُدُوٍّ ـ بِرَاحَةٍ ـ إِطْمِئْنَانًا. Mildly, حِلْمًا.

Calomel, *n.* زِيبَقٌ حُلْوٌ.

Caloric, *n.* أَصْلُ (*or*) أُسُّ ٱلْحَرَارَةِ.

Calorific, *a.* حارٌّ – حامٍ.

Calotype, *n.* The art of —, ٱلرَّسْمُ بِوَاسِطَةِ ٱلضِّيَاءِ عَلَى أَوْرَاقٍ مُعَدَّةٍ لِذٰلِكَ.

Calthrop, *n.* آلَةٌ ذَاتُ أَسْنَانٍ لِمَنْعِ مُرُورِ ٱلْخَيَّالَةِ.

Calumet, *n.* إِسْمُ ٱلْغَلْيُونِ عِنْدَ ٱلْأَمِيرِيكَانِيِّينَ ٱلْبَدْوِ. They smoked the — of peace, تَصَالَحُوا.

Calumniate, *v.t.* غَمَصَ – حَطَبَ بِ – نَمَلَ – أَنْمَلَ – نَمَّ عَلَى – أَقْرَشَ بِ – قَذَفَ بِ – هَتَكَ – عَرَضَ بِ – غَمَزَ بِ – أَغْمَزَ فِي – إِغْتَمَزَ – لَمَزَ – هَجَلَ بِ – إِفْتَرَشَ – قَذَفَ فِي حَقِّهِ.

Calumniation, *n.* *See* Calumny, *n.*

Calumniator, *n.* لَمَّاز – هَمَّاز – نَمَّاس – نَمَّال – نَمٌّ *fem.* نَمَّةٌ *pl.* أَنِمَّاءُ – فَضَّاح – مُفْتَرٍ – تَاهِم.

Calumnious, *a.* نَمِيمِيٌّ – قَذْفِيٌّ – مُفْتَرٍ. *See also* Calumniator, *n.*

Calumny, *n.* إِقْرَاش – نَمِيمَةٌ *pl.* نَمَائِمُ – إِتِّهَام – غَمْز – تَغْمِيز – بَجَل – غِرَاة – إِنْمَال – بُهْتَان – قَذْف – تَجَنٍّ.

Calvary, *n.* The place of Christ's crucifixion, ٱلْجُمْجُمَةُ. A chapel in a graveyard, مُصَلًّى فِي مَقْبَرَةٍ.

Calve, *v.i.* The cow calved, وَضَعَتِ ٱلْبَقَرَةُ (from وَضَعَ *aor.* يَضَعُ).

Calvinism, *n.* مَذْهَبٌ مِنْ مَذَاهِبِ ٱلنَّصَارَى.

Calx, *n.* كِلْس – جِيْر.

Calyx, *n.* بُرْعُومَةٌ – بُرْعُوم *pl.* بَرَاعِيمُ – قُبْعَة – قُنُوب – كِمَامَةٌ – غُلُف *pl.* غِلَاف.

Cambist, *n.* صَرَّاف.

Cambric, *n.* قُمَاشٌ رَفِيعٌ – بَاتِسْتَة.

Came, *pret. of to* Come, *q.v.*

Camel, *n.* جَمَلٌ *and* جَمْلٌ *pl.* جِمَال *and* أَجْمَال *and* جِمَالَةٌ – بَعِير *pl.* بُعْرَان *and* أَبْعِرَة. A she —, نَاقَةٌ *pl.* نُوق *and* نَاقَات. A herd of camels, إِبِلٌ *pl.* آبَال. A — with two humps, بُخْتِيٌّ *pl.* بَخَاتِيُّ – قِرْعَوْش. A young —, بَكْر – قَاعُون – حُوَار *pl.* حُوْرَان *and* حِيرَان. A strong — for travelling, جَمَلٌ رَحِيلٌ. A riding —, رَحُول *pl.* رَحُولَة – رِكَاب. To cry as a male —, أَطَّ – عَرَّ – عَارَ. The cry of a —, عِرَار – رُغَاء – حَنَّة – أَطِيط. To moan as a —, ضَجَّ. The moan of a —, ضَجِيج. To kneel as a — to be laden, نَاخَ. To make a — to kneel, نَوَّخَ. A camel's saddle, رَحْل. A camel's girth, بِطَان – حَقَب; its under saddle, cloth, حِلْس; the rope by which it is led, رَسَن. Each of these two camels is a she —, كِلَا هٰذَيْنِ ٱلْبَعِيرَيْنِ نَاقَةٌ.

Cameleer, *n.* جَمَّال *pl.* جَمَّالَة.

Cameleon, *n.* حِرْبَاء *pl.* حَرَابِيُّ – حِرْبَايَة – بَرْبَخْتِيٌّ. Called in Syria, حِرْذَوْن *pl.* حَرَاذِينُ; in Barbary, تَاتَا.

Camelopard, *n.* زَرَافَةٌ *pl.* زَرَافَى.

Camel's-hair, *n.* وَبَر. A — pencil, قَلَمُ وَبَرٍ.

Cameo, *n.* قَامْيُو – جَوْهَرَةٌ أَوْ صَدَفَةٌ مَنْقُوشَةٌ.

Camera lucida, *n.* آلَةٌ لِلرَّسْمِ بِوَاسِطَةِ ٱلنُّورِ – بَيْتٌ مُضِيءٌ.

Camera obscura, *n.* بَيْتٌ مُظْلِمٌ – آلَةٌ بِهَا يَرْتَسِمُ خَيَالُ ٱلصُّوَرِ عَلَى حِجَابٍ فِي حُجْرَةٍ مُظْلِمَةٍ.

Camlet, *n.* مُخَيَّر – صُوف – شَال – بِشْت.

Camomile, *n.* قُحْوَان – نُقْد – بَابُونَج – أُقْحُوَان – حُرَّة – حَبَقُ ٱلْبَقَرِ.

Camp, *n.* A place where tents are pitched, مَضْرَبُ خِيَمٍ – مَحَطَّةُ خِيَمٍ. A — of soldiers, جَزْءُ عَسْكَرٍ – مُعَسْكَر – أُرْدِي. A —, army, عَسْكَر – عَسَاكِر. To break up a —, إِنْقَعَشَ.

Camp, *v.t.* To pitch tents, ضَرَبَ (*or*) نَصَبَ – تَخَيَّمَ – خَيَّمَ. To —, of soldiers, عَسْكَرَ – عَسْكَرَ فِي خِيَمٍ – ٱلْخِيَمَ.

Camp, *v.i.* حَوَّلَ – حَطَّ – تَخَيَّمَ – خَيَّمَ.

Campaign, *n.* سَفَرُ عَسْكَرٍ – سَرْحَةُ عَسْكَرٍ – سِيَر *pl.* سِيرَةُ عَسْكَرٍ – غَزَاة *pl.* غَزَوَات. An open country, دَشْت – صَحْرَاء. To plan a —, غَزَا. To send on a —, أَغْزَى – غَزَّى.

Campaigner, *n.* إِبْنُ حُرُوبٍ.

Campanology, *n.* فَنُّ ضَرْبِ ٱلنَّوَاقِيسِ.

Campestral, *a.* بَرِّيٌّ – دَشْتِيٌّ – صَحْرَاوِيٌّ.

Camphene, *n.* ٱلنَّفْطُ ٱلْخَالِصُ.

Camphor, *n.* كَافُور.

Camphorated, *a.* كَافُورِيٌّ – مُرَوَّجٌ بِٱلْكَافُورِ.

Campion, *n.* حَشِيشَةُ ٱلْقِبَالِ.

Can, *v.i.* To be able, قَدَرَ – إِسْتَطَاعَ – طَاقَ – أَطَاقَ – عَرَفَ – حَسَنَ – طَلَعَ مِنْ يَدِهِ – أَمْكَنَ – فِيهِ. Can you....? هَلْ لَكَ أَنْ. I can do nothing with him, لَا طَاقَةَ لِي بِهِ. I cannot walk, مَا أَقْدِرُ أَمْشِي – مَا يُمْكِنُنِي أَمْشِي. She hath done what she could, عَمِلَتْ مَا عِنْدَهَا. As much as he can, عَلَى قَدْرِ طَاقَتِهِ. You cannot do as I can, مَا فِيكَ أَنْ تَفْعَلَ مِثْلِي. I can do all things, أَسْتَطِيعُ كُلَّ شَيْءٍ. He can do nothing, مَا يَقْدِرُ عَلَى شَيْءٍ. He can read and write, يَعْرِفُ ٱلْقِرَاءَةَ وَٱلْكِتَابَةَ. Make it as safe as you can, أَحْكِمُوهُ كَمَا تَعْرِفُونَ.

Who can bear to hear it? مَنْ يُطِيقُ ٱسْتِمَاعَهُ. How can these things be? كَيْفَ يُمْكِنُ أَنْ يَكُونَ هٰذَا. How can I unless some one guide me? كَيْفَ يُمْكِنُنِي إِنْ لَمْ يُرْشِدْنِي أَحَدٌ.

Can, n. طَاس pl. طَاسَات — قَدَح pl. أَقْدَاح — كَأْس pl. كُؤُوس — مِشْرَبَةٌ مِنْ آنُكٍ — تَنَكَة pl. تَنَكَات — مِشْرَبَة.

Canaille, n. السُّفْلَةُ — ٱلْأَرَاذِلُ — ٱلْجَعِيدِيَّةُ — ٱلْحَرَافِيشُ.

Canal, n. نَهْر pl. أَنْهَار — نَاصِفَة pl. نَوَاصِف — خَلِيج pl. خُلْجَان ; for irrigation, تُرْعَة pl. تُرَع — قَنَاة pl. قَنَوَات — قَرِيّ pl. أَقْرِيَة and قُرْيَان — قَنَايَة — مِرْزَاب — مِيزَاب. A passage in the body, مَجْرًى pl. مَجَارٍ. A basin of water, بِرْكَة. The — of Suez, خَلِيجُ ٱلسُّوَيْسِ.

Canary, n. The bird, حَزَار — تَرَنْجِيّ.

Cancel, v.t. To obliterate, طَمَسَ ² — نَسَخَ — طَلَّسَ — مَحَا ². To make void, أَبْطَلَ.

Cancelier, n. قَانْشِلِير — قَاشْلِير.

Cancelleria, n. Office of the cancelier, مَكْتَبُ قَلَمِ ٱلْقَاشْلِيرِ — قَاشْلِرِيَّة.

Cancellated, a. Striped, مُقَلَّم — مُشَطَّب ; latticed, مُشَبَّك.

Cancellation, n. The act of defacing, طَلْس — تَطْلِيس — نَسْخ.

Cancer, n. A crab, سَرَطَانٌ بَحْرِيٌّ pl. سَرَطَانَات — زَلْعَطَان. The celestial sign, بُرْجُ ٱلسَّرَطَانِ — السَّرَطَانُ. A malignant sore, أَكِلَة — آكِلَة — سَرَطَان.

Canceration, n. تَقْرِيح — طُلُوعُ ٱلْآكِلَةِ.

Cancerous, a. تَأْكُّلِيّ — مِنْ جِنْسِ ٱلْآكِلَةِ — سَرَطَانِيّ.

Candelabrum, n. مَنَارَة pl. مَنَائِر — ثُرَيَّا pl. ثُرَيَّات.

Candent, a. Hot, حَارّ — حَامٍ. Bright, مُضِيءٌ — لَامِع.

Candid, a. White, أَبْيَض fem. بَيْضَاءُ. Frank, sincere, نَصُوح — صَرِيح pl. صُرَحَاءُ — صَادِق — صَدِيق pl. أَصْدِقَاءُ and صُدَقَاءُ — سَلِيم — سَلِيمُ ٱلْقَلْبِ — بَسِيط. To be —, صَدَقَ — صَفَا ².

Candidate, n. مُرِيد — طَالِب pl. طُلَّاب and طَلَبَة. To be a — for, طَلَبَ ².

Candidly, ad. بِنُصُوحٍ — بِٱسْتِقَامَةٍ — بِمُصَافَاةٍ — بِإِخْلَاصٍ.

Candidness, n. See Candour, n.

Candied, a. Preserved with sugar, مُقَنَّد — مُرَبًّى.

Candle, n. شَمْعَة coll. شَمْع pl. شُمُوع. A tallow —, شَمْعَةٌ شَحْمِيَّةٌ — شَمْعَةٌ مِنْ دُهْنٍ. A wax —, شَمْعٌ عَسَلِيٌّ. A light, سِرَاج. To give light, as a —, أَشْمَعَ.

Candle-holder, n. See Accomplice, n.

Candlemas, n. عِيدُ دُخُولِ ٱلْمَسِيحِ إِلَى ٱلْهَيْكَلِ وَتَطْهِيرِ ٱلْعَذْرَاءِ.

Candlestick, n. قِنْدِيل pl. قَنَادِيلُ — مَسْرَجَة — مَنَارَة — مِشْمَعَة pl. مَشَامِعُ — شَمْعَدَان pl. شَمْعَدَانَات.

Candour, n. صَرَاحَة — نُصُوح — صَدَاقَة — مُصَافَاة — سَلَامَةُ قَلْبٍ — ٱسْتِقَامَة — حَقِيقَة — بَيَاضُ ٱلْقَلْبِ — سَذَاجَة.

Candy, v.t. and i. To preserve with sugar, قَنَّدَ — عَمِلَ مُرَبًّى ² — رَبَّى. To congeal, as sugar, تَقَنَّدَ — سَكَّرَ — جَمَدَ ².

Candy, n. Sugar-candy, سُكَّرُ نَبَاتٍ — قَنْدَة — طَبَرْزَد — أَبْلُوجُ ٱلسُّكَّرِ.

Cane, n. A reed, قَصَب pl. قَصَبَات coll. قَصَبَة — أَسَل coll. أَسَلَة. A Malacca —, خَيْزُور — خَيْزُرَان — قَيْزُرَان. A walking stick, قَصَبُ مَصٍّ — قَصَبُ ٱلسُّكَّرِ. Sugarcane, عُصِيّ pl. عَصًا — عُصَايَة. A reed of the sugarcane, عُودُ قَصَبٍ pl. عِيدَان.

Cane, v.t. ضَرَبَ بِٱلْعَصَا — نَزَلَ عَلَى بِٱلْعَصَا — ضَرَبَ عَصًا. To be caned, أَكَلَ ضَرْبَ عَصًا ².

Canine, a. كَلْبِيّ. A — tooth, نَاب pl. أَنْيَاب.

Caning, n. ضَرْبُ عَصًا.

Canister, n. A small box, حُقَّة pl. حُقَق — عُلْبَة pl. عُلَب.

Canister-shot, مِسْكَة — عُلْبَةٌ مِنْ آنُكٍ مَحْشِيَّةٌ بِرَصَاصَاتٍ.

Canker, n. A blight in plants, يَرَقَان — آفَة. See also Cancer, n.

Canker, v.t. To corrode, corrupt, لَحَسَ — خَرَّبَ — سَرَفَ ² — فَسَّدَ.

Canker, v.i. To grow corrupt, إِنْفَسَدَ — خَسِرَ — صَدِئَ. To be or to become eaten by worms, قَرِدَ. To become a cancer, صَارَ آكِلَةً. Your gold and your silver is cankered, ذَهَبُكُمْ وَفِضَّتُكُمْ قَدْ صَدِئَا. Their words eat as doth a —, كَلِمَتُهُمْ تَرْعَى كَٱلْآكِلَةِ.

Canker-worm, n. أُسْرُوع — يُسْرُوع — خِمَاط.

Cannel-coal, n. }
Candle-coal, } فَحْمُ حَجَرٍ صُلْبٌ.

Cannibal, n. آكِلُ لَحْمِ ٱلْبَشَرِ pl. أَكَلَة.

Cannibalism, n. أَكْلُ لَحْمِ ٱلْبَشَرِ.

Cannon, n. مِدْفَع pl. مَدَافِعُ — طُوب pl. أَطْوَاب. To fire a —, ضَرَبَ مِدْفَعًا — أَطْلَقَ مِدْفَعًا.

Cannonade, n. ضَرْبُ مَدَافِعَ — إِطْلَاقُ مَدَافِعَ.

Cannonade, v.t. ضَرَبَ بِمَدَافِعَ — أَطْلَقَ ٱلْمَدَافِعَ عَلَى.

Cannon-ball, n. كُلَّة pl. كُلَل.

Cannonier, n. }
Cannoneer, } طُوبْجِي or طُبْجِي pl. طُبْجِيَّة.

Cannon-proof, a. مُسْتَحْكَمٌ لَا تُؤَثِّرُ فِيهِ ٱلْكُلَلُ.

Cannon-shot, n. Range of a —, مَسَافَةُ ضَرْبِ مِدْفَعٍ. See also Cannon-ball, n.

Cannot, *v. aux.* *See under* Can, *v.i.*

Canoe, *n.* بَلَم *pl.* أَبْلام ـ قارِب *pl.* قَوارِبُ ـ قاتِق *pl.* قَواتِقُ.

Canon, *n.* A rule, law, قانُون *pl.* قَوانِينُ ـ فَرْض *pl.* فِراض ـ قاعِدَة *pl.* قَواعِدُ. رَسْم *pl.* رُسوم ـ شَرِيعَة *pl.* شَرائِعُ. A dignitary of the Church, قِسِّيس فِي بِيعَةٍ أُسْقُفِيَّةٍ. Canons of the Church, قَوانِينُ ٱلْكَنِيسَةِ. The Canon law, ٱلشَّرِيعَةُ ٱلدِّينِيَّةُ. The — of Holy Scriptures, جَدْوَلُ ٱلْكُتُبِ ٱلْمُلْهَمَةِ.

Canon, *n.* A valley, عَقِيق *pl.* أَعِقَّة ـ وادٍ *pl.* أَوْدِيَة.

Canonical, *a.* شَرْعِيٌّ ـ قانُونِيٌّ. Canonical obedience, ٱلإِطاعَةُ إِلَى قَوانِينِ ٱلْكَنِيسَةِ. Canonical epistles, رَسائِلُ مُعْتَبَرَةٌ بِإِلْهامٍ ـ رَسائِلُ قانُونِيَّةٌ. Canonical hours, ساعاتُ ٱلْفَرْضِ.

Canonically, *ad.* حَسَبَ ٱلشَّرِيعَةِ ـ بِمُوجَبِ ٱلْقَوانِينِ.

Canonicals, *n.* حُلَّةُ ٱلْكَهَنَةِ ـ حُلَّةُ ٱلْإِكْلِيرُوسِ.

Canonicate, Canonry, *n.* Canonship, } مَنْصَبُ قِسِّيسٍ وَما لَهُ مِنَ ٱلرَّواتِبِ فِي بِيعَةٍ أُسْقُفِيَّةٍ.

Canonist, *n.* فَقِيه *pl.* فُقَهاءُ ـ عالِمٌ بِٱلْقَوانِينِ ٱلْكَنائِسِيَّةِ.

Canonization, *n.* تَقْدِيسُ ٱلْأَمْواتِ.

Canonize, *v.t.* قَدَّسَ ٱلْأَمْواتَ ـ صَيَّرَ ٱلْمَيِّتَ قِدِّيسًا.

Canopus, *n.* ٱلسُّهَيْلُ ـ ٱلْفَحْلُ ـ ٱلْفَحِيلُ.

Canopy, *n.* مِظَلَّة ـ خَيْمَة ـ قُبَّة ـ بَشْخانَة. The — of heaven, ٱلسَّماءُ.

Canopy, *v.t.* ظَلَّلَ عَلَى ـ نَصَبَ خَيْمَةً عَلَى ـ بَسَطَ لِ-غِطاءً.

Can't, Cannot; *see under* Can, *v.i.*

Cant, *v.t.* To incline, مَيَّلَ ـ أَمالَ. To — round, دَوَّرَ.

Cant, *v.i.* To talk as a hypocrite, تَكَلَّمَ ـ راءَى فِي ٱلْكَلامِ ـ تَظاهَرَ بِٱلتَّقْوَى فِي ٱلْحَدِيثِ ـ كَٱلْمُتَدَيِّنِ.

Cant, *n.* Inclination, مَيَلان. Hypocrisy, حَمِيَّةٌ كاذِبَةٌ ـ رِئاءٌ ـ مُراياة ـ تَصَنُّع ـ مَكْر. Slang, لُغَوَة ـ رِطانَة.

Cantankerous, *a.* *See* Perverse, *a.*

Cantata, *n.* مَقامَة.

Canteen, *n.* A case of travelling utensils, صَنْدُوقُ جِهازِ ٱلسَّفَرِ ـ بِشْتَخْتَة. A —, or shop for soldiers, خَمّارَةُ عَسْكَرٍ.

Canter, *v.t.* and *i.* To move in a moderate gallop, قَمَصَ ـ رَمَحَ ـ كَرْبَجَ. To ride upon a canter, رَكَضَ.

Canter, *n.* A moderate gallop, قِماص ـ كَرْبَجَة ـ رَمْح ـ رَمْحَة. A hypocrite, مُراءٍ. A simulator, مُتَصَنِّع.

Cantharides, *n.* ذُراح *pl.* ذَراريحُ ـ ذُرُوح ـ أَبُو ذُراحٍ ـ ٱلْأَخْيَدَرُ ـ ذُبابٌ هِنْدِيٌّ. To rub with —, ذَرَّحَ.

Canticle, *n.* A song of praise, تَسْبِحَة *pl.* تَسابِيحُ ـ تَسْبِيح ـ نَشِيد *pl.* أَناشِيدُ ـ مَدِيحَة *pl.* مَدائِحُ. The Canticles of Solomon, نَشِيدُ ٱلْأَنْشادِ لِسُلَيْمانَ بْنِ داوُدَ.

Canting, *n.* Hypocrisy; *see under* Cant, *n.*

Canting, *a.* Hypocritical, simulating; *see* Hypocrite, a simulator, *under* Canter, *n.*

Canto, *n.* A song, poem, قَصِيدَة *pl.* قَصائِدُ. The division of a poem, فَصْلُ قَصِيدَةٍ ـ بابُ قَصِيدَةٍ.

Canton, *n.* قِسْمُ بِلادٍ *pl.* أَقْسام ـ وِلايَة *pl.* وِلايات.

Canton, *v.t.* To divide into cantons, قَسَمَ-فِي وِلاياتٍ. To allot quarters to troops, نَزَّلَ ٱلْعَساكِرَ ـ بَوَّأَ ٱلْعَسْكَرَ.

Cantonal, *a.* مُتَعَلِّقٌ بِوِلايَةٍ.

Cantonment, *n.* Of soldiers, مَحَطُّ عَسْكَرٍ ـ مَنازِلُ ٱلْعَساكِرِ.

Canvas, *n.* A coarse cloth, جُنْفاص ـ خَيْش. Sails, قُلُوع ـ شِراع. Picture —, قُماشُ ٱلتَّصْوِيرِ. A picture, صُورَة *pl.* صُوَر ـ تَصْوِير *pl.* تَصاوِيرُ.

Canvass, *v.t.* To scrutinize, تَجَسَّسَ ـ بَحَثَ ـ فَحَصَ عَن ـ فَتَّشَ عَن. To solicit, أَلَحَّ عَلَى ـ أَبْرَمَ عَلَى-بِ ـ طَلَبَ إِلَى. To solicit interest in behalf of, إِسْتَعْطَفَ-عَلَى.

Canvass, *n.* Inquiry, تَفَحُّص ـ إِمْتِحان ـ بَحْث ـ تَفْتِيش. Solicitation, إِلْحاح ـ إِبْرام ـ طَلَب.

Canvasser, *n.* One who solicits, مُلْتَمِس ـ مُسْتَدْعٍ; one who acts for another, نائِب *pl.* نُوّاب ـ وَكِيل.

Cany, *a.* مِقْصاب. Cany ground, abounding in canes, أَرْضٌ مَقْصَبَةٌ.

Canzonet, *n.* قُصَيْدَة.

Caoutchouc, *n.* صَمْغٌ لَزِجٌ كَثِيرُ ٱلْمُرُونَةِ ـ قُومْلاسْتِيق ـ غُوم ـ ٱلْاسْتِيق, *called in Africa* مَبِيرَة.

Cap, *n.* A garment for the head, قَلَنْسُوَة. A night —, قَلَنْسُوَة ـ خَفِيفَةُ ٱلرَّأْسِ. A hairy — of a conical shape, قَلْبَق ـ قَلْباق. A similar —, without hair, with a lower border of twisted muslin, قاوُق *pl.* قَواوِيقُ. A — lined with cotton, تَنْبَقِيَّة ـ قاوُق. The red skull — or *tarbûsh*, طَرْبُوش *pl.* طَرابِيشُ ـ كَلْبُوس. A longer red —, such as is worn by the people of the Lebanon, طَرْبُوش مَشْمُوط. A small white cloth —, worn under the *tarbûsh*, طاقِيَّة *pl.* طَواقِي ـ عَرَقِيَّة *pl.* عَراقِي. A darwish's —, صَوْمَعَة. Cap, the top of anything, رَأْس. The — of the knee, ٱلدّاغِصَة. A percussion —, قَبْسُول.

Cap, *v.t.* To cover, as with a —, لَبَّسَ ـ غَطَّى-بِ. To match, حاذَى ـ بارَى ـ أَلْحَقَ ـ سَدَّ مَسَدَّ.

Capability, *n.* The power of containing, سَعَة ـ إتِّساع ـ فُسْحَة ـ Power, قُدْرَة ـ طاقَة ـ مَقْدِرَة. Force of mind, تَوْمِية ـ عَرْض. Fitness, حَذاقَة ـ مَهارَة ـ فَراسَة ـ قُدْرَة عَقْلٍ ـ فَهْم ـ إدْراك. مُناسَبَة ـ لِياقَة. *See also* Sensibility, *n.*

Capable, *a.* Competent for, كَفُو ل ـ قابِل ـ كافٍ ل ـ أَهْلٌ ل ـ عالِم ـ عارِف. Intelligent, مُعِيدٌ ل. Ready for, قادِرٌ عَلَى. صاحِب تَدْبِيرٍ ـ صاحِبُ مَعْرِفَةٍ ـ حاذِق ـ فَطِين. Able to contain, يَسَعُ ـ حاوٍ. To be — of, able to, قَدَرَ عَلَى ـ ع ـ You are not — of committing such an action, لَيْسَ طَلَعَ مِنْ يَدِهِ. I am not — of doing it alone, حاشاكَ أَنْ تَفْعَلَ ذٰلِكَ. To render — of, أَنا بِكِفايَةٍ لِذٰلِكَ مِنْ نَفْسِي ـ قَدَّرَ عَلَى ـ مَكَّنَ مِنْ ـ أَمْكَنَ عَلَى.

Capableness, *n.* *See* Capability, *n.*

Capacious, *a.* مَجْوُف ـ أَجْوَف ـ فَسِيح ـ وَسِيع ـ واسِع ـ حاوٍ ـ رَحِيب ـ عَرِيض.

Capaciousness, *n.* *See* Capacity, *n.*

Capacitate, *v.t.* قَدَّرَ ـ قَدَّرَ عَلَى ـ أَمْكَنَ ل ـ صَيَّرَ كَفُوًا ل.

Capacity, *n.* State, condition, حالَة ـ حال ـ صِفَة. He went with him in the — of interpreter, سافَرَ مَعَهُ تَرْجُمانًا. An official —, صِفَة رَسْمِيَّة. Measures of —, مَكائِيلُ *pl.* مِكْيال. Power of containing, ability; *see* Capability, *n.*

Cap-a-pie, *ad.* مِنَ الرَّأْسِ إلَى القَدَم. A man armed —, رَجُلٌ شاكُ السِّلاحِ ـ رَجُلٌ شَوِكُ السِّلاح.

Caparison, *n.* رُخُوت *pl.* رَخْت ـ كُوبانٌ لِلْخَيْلِ.

Caparison, *v.t.* وَضَعَ الرَّخْتَ عَلَى ـ رَخَّتَ *aor.* يَضَعُ.

Cape, *n.* A headland, شِناخ ـ طَنْف *pl.* طُنُوف ـ رَأْس *pl.* رُؤُوس. The — of a dress, بُرْنُس ـ طَيْلَسان.

Caper, *n.* The fruit, كُبَر ـ كُبّار ـ قَبّار; a — plant, شَجَرَة الكُبّار. A skip, قَفْزَة ـ نَطَّة ـ زَفْنَة ـ عَنْطَرَة.

Caper, *v.t.* نَطَّ ع ـ نَطْنَطَ ـ جَلَبَ ـ عَنْطَرَ.

Caperer, *n.* قَفّاز ـ بَهْلَوان.

Capillaceous, *ad.* شَعْرِيّ ـ مُشْعِر.

Capillary, *a.* رَفِيعٌ مِثْلَ الشَّعْرِ ـ شَعْرِيّ. Capillary attraction, جاذِبِيَّة شَعْرِيَّة ـ قُوَّة جاذِبِيَّة مُنْشَفة.

Capillary, *n.* عُرُوق *pl.* عِرْق رَفِيعٌ فِي النَّباتاتِ وَالحَيَوانات. The capillaries, العُرُوق الشَّعْرِيَّة.

Capital, *n.* A chief city, كُرْسِيُّ المَمْلَكَة ـ تَخْتُ مُلْكٍ ـ دارُ المُلْك ـ أَمْصار *pl.* مِصْر ـ قَواعِدُ *pl.* قاعِدَة. The chief town of a number of villages, قَصَبَة. The principal stock, رَأْسُ المال ـ أَصْلُ المال. The upper part of a pillar, تاجُ عَمُودٍ ـ رَأْسُ عَمُودٍ ـ تِيجان *pl.*

Capital, *a.* Chief, رَئِيسِيّ ـ أَصْلِيّ ـ أَفْضَل ـ مُطْلَق ـ خُصُوصِيّ. Excellent, فائِق ـ فاضِل ـ نَفِيس ـ جَيِّد ـ خَيْر. A — crime, ذَنْبٌ يَسْتَحِقُّ القَتْلَ ـ خَطِيئَة رُؤُوسِيَّة. Capital punishment, قِصاصُ المَوْتِ ـ قَلَمُ طُومارٍ. A — letter, حَرْفٌ ثُلُثِيّ ـ حَرْفٌ كَبِيرٌ فِي بَدْءِ الكَلِماتِ.

Capitalist, *n.* صاحِبُ مالٍ ـ صاحِبُ سَرْمايَة.

Capitally, *ad.* Excellently, حَسَنًا ـ جَيِّدًا ـ خَيْرًا ـ حَبَّذا.

Capitation, *n.* Numeration by the head, تَعْدِيدُ الأَنْفُسِ. Poll-tax, جالَة ـ جالِيَة ـ خَراج ـ جِزْيَة.

Capitol, *n.* The — of the United States, دارُ مَجْلِسِ النُّوّابِ فِي البِلادِ المُتَّحِدَةِ مِنْ أَمِيرِيكا.

Capitular, *n.* } The statutes of a chapter council, قَوانِينُ مَجْلِسِ
Capitulary, } الإكْلِيرُوسِ المُتَعَلِّقِينَ بِكَنِيسَةِ كُرْسِيِّ الأُسْقُفِ.

Capitular, *a.* ما نِيطَ بِمَجْلِسِ الإكْلِيرُوسِ المَذْكُورِينَ.

Capitulate, *v.i.* To surrender, إِسْتَسْلَمَ; to — on terms, إِتَّفَقَ عَلَى التَّسْلِيمِ ـ عَقَدَ شُرُوطًا لِلتَّسْلِيمِ ـ ع. To ask to —, طَلَبَ ع الأَمانَ.

Capitulation, *n.* تَسْلِيمٌ بِشُرُوطٍ ـ رَأْيٌ ـ شُرُوطُ تَسْلِيمٍ. By —, إِسْتِسْلامًا وَذٰلِكَ بِشُرُوطٍ.

Capitulations, *n.* The — with Turkey, عهدنامه هُمايُون.

Capivi, *n.* *See* Copaiba, *n.*

Capoch, *n.* قَلَنْسُوَة *pl.* قَلانِس *and* قَلانِيس.

Capon, *n.* دِيكٌ خَصِيّ *pl.* دُيُوكٌ خِصْيان; called in Barbary دِيكٌ مَبْغُوج.

Capote, *n.* بُرْنُس *pl.* بَرانِيس ـ مَشْلَح *pl.* مَشالِح.

Caprice, *n.* هَوًى *pl.* أَهْواء ـ هَوِيَّة ـ تَخَيُّل ـ زَنْطَرَة ـ وَعْقَة.

Capricious, *a.* وَعِق ـ مُلْتَوٍ ـ هَوائِيّ ـ مُتَقَلِّب ـ مُخَبَّل ـ وَعُق ـ تَلَوَّى. A — man, غَمْلَج ـ غُمْلُوج. To be —, مُزَنْطَر *aor.* يَعِقُ.

Capriciously, *ad.* عَلَى هَوَى نَفْسِهِ ـ بِالْهَواءِ وَاللَّواءِ ـ بِزَنْطَرَة. He treated him —, عامَلَهُ بِالْهَواءِ وَاللَّواءِ.

Capriciousness, *n.* *See* Caprice, *n.*

Capricorn, *n.* The sign of the —, الجَدْي ـ بُرْجُ الجَدْيِ.

Capsicum, *n.* فُلَيْفِلَة ـ فِلْفِلٌ أَحْمَرُ.

Capsize, *v.t.* أَوْقَعَ ـ قَلَبَ ـ كَبَّ ع.

Capstan, *n.* مِلْوَة ـ مِلْوَى ـ بوجورغات.

Capsular, *a.* فارِغ ـ مَجْوُف.

Capsulate, *a.* مُضَمَّنٌ فِي خَرِيطَةٍ.

Capsule, *n.* Of a plant, خَرِيطَةٌ *pl.* خَرَائِطُ ; of a bottle, شِدَادٌ — صِمَادٌ — عِفَاصٌ. To cover with a —, عَفَصَ ـِ — صَمَدَ ـُ.

Captain, *n.* A head, chief, رَئِيسٌ *pl.* رُؤَسَآءُ — ضَابِطٌ *pl.* ضُبَّاطٌ — قَائِدٌ *pl.* قُوَّادٌ — كَبِيرٌ *pl.* كُبَرَآءُ. Captain of a company, يُوزْ بَاشِي. Captain of a ship, قُبْطَانُ مَرْكَبٍ *pl.* قَبَاطِينُ — رَئِيسُ مَرْكَبٍ. Captain-general, سَرْعَسْكَرٌ. Flag —, أَمِيرَالٌ سُوَارٍ. Captain of a gun, قُبْطَانُ كُلِّ مِدْفَعٍ. Captain of the main-top, رَقِيبُ ٱلْغَابِيَةِ.

Captaincy, *n.* مَنْصِبُ ٱلْقُبْطَانِ — مَنْصِبُ ٱلْيُوزْ بَاشِي.

Captious, *a.* Given to cavil, شَرِسٌ — مُضَادِدٌ — مُمَارٌّ — مُتَعَرِّضٌ — مُلْتَوٍ. Quarrelsome, خَصِيمٌ — خَصُومٌ — خَصِمٌ. To be —, cavilling, تَلَوَّى. To be contentious, خَصِمَ ـَ.

Captiously, *ad.* بِشَرَاسَةٍ — مُتَعَرِّضًا — مُمَارَّةً.

Captiousness, *n.* خُصُمَانِيَّةٌ — خُصُومَةٌ — شَرَاسَةٌ — مُمَارَّةٌ.

Captivate, *v.t.* To charm, أَغْرَمَ — إِسْتَهْوَى — فَتَنَ ـِ — أَفْتَنَ — إِسْتَمْلَكَ عَقْلَهُ — أَسَرَ ـِ — إِسْتَبَى قَلْبَهُ — إِخْتَبَلَ — سَبَى ـِ. To be captivated, as by a woman, أُغْرِمَ بِ — تَوَجَّدَ بِ — عَلِقَ. She captivated my heart, فَلَجَتْ بِقَلْبِي.

Captivating, *a.* يَسْلُبُ ٱلْعَقْلَ — ذُو لَذَّةٍ — بَدِيعٌ — خَيِّرٌ — حَبَّذَا.

Captivation, *n.* سَبْيٌ — سِبَآءٌ — تَخَبُّلٌ.

Captive, *n.* أَسِيرٌ — أَخِيذٌ — سَبِيٌّ *pl.* سَبَايَا *fem.* سَبِيَّةٌ *pl.* سَبْيٌ — مَسْبِيٌّ — أُسَرَآءُ *pl.* To take captive, إِسْتَبَى — سَبَى ـِ.

Captivity, *n.* يَسْرٌ — أَسْرٌ — سِبَآءٌ — سَبْيٌ. Slavery, عُبُودِيَّةٌ.

Captor, *n.* مَاسِكٌ — ضَابِطٌ — قَابِضٌ.

Capture, *n.* غَارَةٌ — غَنِيمَةٌ — خَلِيسَةٌ — خُلْسَةٌ.

Capture, *v.t.* Of booty, غَنِمَ ـَ ; of prisoners, أَسَرَ ـِ. *See also to* Seize, Take, *v.t.*

Capuchin, *n.* رَاهِبٌ كُبُوشِيٌّ.

Car, *n.* عَجَلَةٌ — نَقَّالَةٌ — عَرَبَانَةٌ — عَرَبَةٌ *pl.* عَرَبَاتٌ.

Caracole, *n.* Of a horse, حَلَقَةٌ — نَوْرَةٌ. To —, دَارَ حَلْقَةً ـُ.

Carat, *n.* قِيرَاطٌ *pl.* قَرَارِيطُ. A term showing the fineness of gold, عِيَارٌ. Gold of 18 carats fine, ذَهَبٌ عِيَارُهُ ١٨ قِيرَاطًا عَلَى حِسَابِ ٢٤ قِيرَاطًا مِنَ ٱلذَّهَبِ ٱلنَّقِيِّ.

Caravan, *n.* قَافِلَةٌ *pl.* قَوَافِلُ — قَفَلٌ *pl.* قُفُولٌ — كَرْوَانٌ *pl.* كَرَاوِينُ. The yearly — of pilgrims to al-Makkah, ٱلْحَجُّ *or* ٱلْحَجِّ.

Caravansera, *n.* خَانٌ *pl.* خَانَاتٌ.

Caraway, *n.* The seed, تِقْدَةٌ — كَمُّونٌ أَرْمَنِيٌّ — كَرَوْيَا — كَرَاوِيَا — ٱلْمُبَارَكَةُ.

Carbine, *n.* / **Carabine,** } قَرَابِينَةٌ — قَرَبَانَةٌ *coll.* قَرَبَانٌ.

Carabinier, *n.* حَامِلُ قَرَابِينَةٍ.

Carbon, *n.* فَحْمٌ *or* فَحَمٌ — مَادَّةُ (أُسُّ *or*) ٱلْفَحْمِ.

Carbonaceous, *a.* فَحْمِيٌّ.

Carbonate, *n.* مُفَحَّمٌ — مُكَلَّسٌ.

Carbonic, *a.* فَحْمِيٌّ. Carbonic acid, حُمُوضَةُ ٱلْفَحْمِ.

Carbonization, *n.* The act of, تَفْحِيمٌ — إِحَالَةُ ٱلشَّيْءِ إِلَى فَحْمٍ ; the being carbonized, مُفَحَّمٌ.

Carbonize, *v.t.* فَحَّمَ — صَيَّرَ فَحْمًا.

Carbonize, *v.i.* صَارَ فَحْمًا.

Carboy, *n.* بَطَّةٌ *pl.* بُطَطٌ — دَبَّةٌ *pl.* دِبَابٌ.

Carbuncle, *n.* A tumour, دُمَّلَةٌ — جَمْرٌ — فَرْخُ جَمْرٍ — زَنْطَارِيَّةٌ — شَلْغُوطَةٌ. The jewel, عَقِيقٌ أَحْمَرُ — يَاقُوتٌ — جَمْرِيٌّ — بَهْرَمَانٌ.

Carcanet, *n.* A collar of jewels, عِقْدٌ *pl.* عُقُودٌ — قِلَادَةٌ *pl.* قَلَائِدُ — مُرْسَلَةٌ.

Carcass, *n.* A dead body, جِيفَةٌ *pl.* جِيَفٌ — جُثَّةٌ *pl.* جُثَثٌ — مَيْتٌ — نَبِيلَةٌ. A bundle of bones, رِمَّةٌ. A skeleton, هَيْكَلٌ — ٱلْبَدَنِ ; a very thin person, قَفَصُ عِظَامٍ — كَرْكُوبَةٌ — كَرْنِيبَةٌ. A body flayed of its skin, or the whole body of a slaughtered animal, جَلَمَةٌ. A warlike missile, آلَةٌ نَارِيَّةٌ فِي صُورَةِ عُلْبَةٍ مُشَقَّبَةٍ لِإِحْرَاقِ ٱلْمُدُنِ وَغَيْرِهَا. The — of an unfinished building, جِدَارُ بَيْتٍ غَيْرِ مُكَمَّلٍ.

Card, *n.* For playing, وَرَقُ ٱللَّعِبِ *pl.* أَوْرَاقٌ. A pack or game of cards, شَدَّةُ وَرَقٍ. Stiff paper, وَرَقٌ رَقٌّ. A visiting —, وَرَقَةُ زِيَارَةٍ. An instrument to — wool with, مِنْدَفٌ — مِنْدَفَةٌ — مُشْطٌ لِتَسْرِيحِ ٱلصُّوفِ. Mode of action, تِدْبِيَةٌ. An advertisement, إِعْلَانٌ. A compass-card, وَرَقَةُ ٱلْبُوصْلَةِ. It is upon the cards, possibly, لَعَلَّ — مُمْكِنٌ — مِنَ ٱلْمُحْتَمَلِ. He played his cards well, أَسَدَّ فِي ٱلْعَمَلِ.

Card, *v.t.* To comb, of wool or cotton, مَشَعَ ـَ — نَدَفَ ـِ — فَدَّكَ — قَرْدَشَ — مَشَّقَ — سَرَّحَ — نَدَفَ ـِ.

Cardamum, *n.* قَاقُلَّةٌ — هَالٌ — هَالُ بُوَا — هَيْلُ بُوَا — خَيْرُ بُوَا.

Cardboard, *n.* وَرَقٌ رَقٌّ — مُقَوًّى خَفِيفٌ.

Card-case, *n.* غِلَافُ أَوْرَاقِ ٱلزِّيَارَةِ.

Carder, *n.* One who cards, مُقَرْدِشٌ — نَدَّافٌ — مُمَشِّقٌ. A bow for carding, مِنْدَفٌ — مِنْدَفَةٌ.

Cardiac, *a.* / **Cardiacal,** } مُتَعَلِّقٌ بِٱلْقَلْبِ — قَلْبِيٌّ.

Cardialgia, *n.* أَلَمٌ فِي ٱلْقَلْبِ — قُلَابٌ.

Cardinal, *a.* Principal, أَصْلِيٌّ — أَكْبَرُ — أَعْظَمُ. The — points of the compass, الجِهَاتُ الأَرْبَعُ ـ الخَوَافِقُ. The — virtues, الفَضَائِلُ المُتَقَدِّمَةُ. The — numbers, أَسْمَاءُ العَدَدِ.

Cardinal, *n.* The dignitary, كَرْدِينَال *pl.* كَرْدِينَالِيَّة. A woman's cloak, فَرَاجَة.

Cardinalate, *n.* مَنْصِبُ الكَرْدِينَالِ.

Carding, *n.* تَشْيِيت ـ تَسْرِيح ـ نَدْف.

Carding-machine, *n.* آلَةُ التَّشْيِيتِ ـ دُولابُ النَّدْفِ.

Cardiology, *n.* عِلْمٌ يَبْحَثُ فِي أَحْوَالِ القَلْبِ.

Care, *n.* Attention, thought, إِهْتِمَام ـ عِنَايَة ـ جِدّ ـ فِكْر ـ تَقَيُّد. An object of care, هِمَّة *pl.* هِمَم. Caution, وَقَاء ـ حِذْر ـ إِنْتِبَاه ـ إِحْتِرَاز ـ إِحْتِيَاط ـ تَحَفُّظ. Management, مُدَارَاة ـ مُبَاشَرَة. Custody, وَاقِيَة ـ حِرَاسَة ـ حَرْس ـ حِيَاطَة ـ مُحَافَظَة. Regard, in order to preservation, إِعْتِصَام ـ إِهْتِمَام ـ إِعْتِنَاء ـ رَوْم. Anxiety, هَمّ ـ غَمّ ـ إِضْطِرَاب ـ عِنَايَة ـ فِكْر ـ إِنْقِبَاض. Free from —, فَرِج ـ فَارِغُ البَالِ ـ مُرْتَاحُ الخَاطِرِ ـ الخَاطِرِ. With scrupulous —, بِغَايَةِ الإِعْتِنَاءِ ـ بِأَوْفَرِ اعْتِنَاءٍ. The cares of the world, هُمُومُ العَالَمِ ـ هُمُومُ الحَيَاةِ. To be affected with —, إِهْتَمَّ.

To commit to the care of, فَوَّضَ إِلَى عِنَايَتِهِ.

To have the care or management of, تَوَلَّى فِي ـ إِعْتَنَى بِ ـ بَاشَرَ ـ أَجْرَى ـ تَصَرَّفَ بِ.

To take care, to be cautious, حَذِرَ ـ إِحْتَذَرَ.

To take care of, as of a child, دَارَى الوَلَدَ. To take care of, to attend to, إِسْتَفْقَدَ ـ تَقَيَّدَ فِي ـ دَارَ بَالُهُ عَلَى. To preserve, حَرَسَ ـ حَفِظَ ـ نَفِسَ بِ. To use sparingly, إِقْتَصَدَ فِي ـ وَفَّرَ.

To take care to do, إِهْتَمَّ بِ.

Care, *v.i.* To heed, to regard, إِهْتَمَّ فِي ـ بَالَى بِ ـ هَمَّ بِ ـ إِعْتَبَرَ مِن ـ عَلَى بَالِهِ. To be cautious, حَذِرَ ـ إِحْتَذَرَ. To pay attention to, أَلْقَى بَالَهُ عَلَى. To — for, to take — of, to guard, preserve, حَرَسَ ـ حَفِظَ ـ إِحْتَفَظَ بِ ـ حَاطَ بِ ـ لَوَى عَلَى ـ تَقَيَّدَ بِ. He cared for the thing, بَالَى بِالشَّيْءِ.

No one cares for me, لَيْسَ مَنْ يُبَالِي بِي. I don't —, it is no concern of mine, مَا عَلَيَّ ـ مَا عَلَى بَالِي ـ مَا يَخُصُّنِي. I do not —, do not pay any attention, to him or it, لَا أُلْقِي إِلَيْهِ بَالًا.

I do not — whether you sit or stand, لَا أُبَالِي أَقُمْتَ أَوْ قَعَدْتَ.

Careen, *v.t.* To heave on one side, أَمَالَ. To clean a ship's bottom, قَلْفَطَ أَسْفَلَ المَرْكَبِ. To repair, رَمَّمَ.

Careen, *v.i.* To incline on one side, مَالَ ـ إِسْتَمَالَ.

Career, *n.* A race, ضَمَّة ـ مُحَاضَرَة ـ رَكْض ـ شَوْط. Course of action, life, سِيرَة ـ عِيشَة ـ مَنَاقِب. *See also under* Course, *n.*

Career, *v.i.* To move rapidly, رَكَضَ ـ أَفَجَّ.

Careful, *a.* Anxious, مُهْتَمّ ـ عَنٍ ـ عَانٍ ـ مُعْنٍ ـ مُضْطَرِب ـ قَلِق ـ قَلْقَان ـ مَشْغُولُ الفِكْرِ. Cautious, مُعْتَنٍ ـ حَرِيص ـ مُتَحَذِّر ـ مُحْتَرِز ـ مُتَحَفِّظ ـ مُتَوَقٍّ. Diligent, مُجِدّ ـ مُجْتَهِد ـ ذُو هِمَّةٍ. Frugal, مُقْتَصِد ـ مُوَفِّر. They need to be —, يَلْزَمُهُمْ أَنْ يَكُونُوا مُتَحَفِّظِينَ. To be — about, إِعْتَنَى بِ ـ إِهْتَمَّ بِ ـ عَلَى.

Carefully, *ad.* بِعَقْلٍ ـ بِاعْتِنَاءٍ ـ بِالإِحْتِرَازِ ـ إِحْتِيَاطًا ـ عَلَى ـ عَنِيّ.

Carefulness, *n.* Vigilance, diligence, إِعْتِنَاء ـ إِهْتِمَام ـ هِمَّة ـ نَبَاهَة ـ إِنْتِبَاه ـ حَرْس ـ جَهْد ـ دَوَرَانُ بَالٍ. Anxiety, هَمّ ـ فِكْر ـ عِنَايَة. Frugality, تَوْفِير ـ إِقْتِصَاد.

Careless, *a.* غَارّ ـ سَهْوَانُ ـ غَبِيّ ـ سَاهٍ ـ مُتَغَفِّل ـ مُتَهَامِل ـ مُتَكَاسِل ـ تَارِك ـ مُتَوَانٍ ـ قَلِيلُ المُرُوَّةِ ـ قَلِيلُ الإِنْتِبَاهِ ـ قَلِيلُ الإِعْتِنَاءِ.

Carelessly, *ad.* بِتَهَامُلٍ ـ مِنْ غَيْرِ اعْتِنَاءٍ ـ بِتَغَافُلٍ.

Carelessness, *n.* سَهْو ـ غَبَاوَة ـ غَبْوَة ـ غِرَار ـ غِرَّة ـ قُصُور ـ فُتُور ـ تَغَافُل ـ تَهَامُل ـ قِلَّةُ انْتِبَاهٍ ـ تَوَانٍ ـ غَفْلَة ـ قِلَّةُ اعْتِنَاءٍ.

Caress, *v.t.* لاطَفَ ـ لَطَفَ بِ ـ دَلَّلَ ـ عَانَقَ.

Caress, *n.* مُلاطَفَة ـ تَدْلِيل ـ مُعَانَقَة.

Caret, *n.* عَلامَة كَذَا (٨) تَدُلُّ عَلَى مَا حُذِفَ مِنْ سَطْرٍ وَعَلَى مَا سُطِّرَ فَوْقَهُ.

Careworn, *a.* مُتَهَوِّش.

Cargo, *n.* وَسْق مَرْكَب ـ وَسْقَةُ مَرْكَب ـ تَعْبِيَة.

Caricature, *n.* صُورَة سُخْرَة ـ صُورَة ضُحْكَة ـ هُزْأَة ـ صُورَة هَزْلِيَّة.

Caricature, *v.t.* هَزَأَ بِ ـ صَيَّرَ مُضْحِكَةً ـ صَوَّرَ سُخْرَةً.

Caricaturist, *n.* مُسْتَهْزِئ ـ مُصَوِّرُ صُوَرٍ مُضْحِكَةٍ.

Caries, *n.* / Cariosity, } As of the bones, نَخِيرَة ـ رِمّ ـ عُفُونَة.

Carious, *a.* Of the bones, رَمِيم ـ رُمَام ـ نَخِر ـ نَاخِر; of the teeth, كَفُوف; of wood, مُسَوَّس. To become —, of the bones, رَمَّ *aor.* يَرِمُّ ـ بَلِيَ. Having — teeth, أَلَطُّ ـ فَطّ.

Carl, *n.* A rude man, خَشِن ـ غَلِيظ ـ فَظّ.

Carman, *n.* عَرَبْجِي ـ عَجَّال ـ تَرَّاس ـ (مُدَبِّرُ) العَرَبَانَةِ *or* سَائِقُ.

Carminative, *n.* دَوَاء لِلنَّفْخَةِ ـ عِلاج لِتَصْرِيفِ الأَرْيَاحِ.

Carminative, *a.* مُعَالِجُ النَّفْخَةِ ـ مُخْرِجُ الأَرْيَاحِ.

Carmine, *n.* لَعْل. Of a — colour, لَعْلِيّ.

Carnage, *n.* ذَبْح ـ قَتْل ـ سَفْكُ دِمَاءٍ. A place of —, رِبْضَة.

Carnal, *a.* Fleshly, جَسَدِيٌّ ـ جَسَدَانِيٌّ ـ جِسْمَانِيٌّ. Lewd, مُتَلَذِّذ ـ تَطَاوِيٌّ ـ شَهْوَانِيٌّ ـ وَمُغْلِيم ـ غَلِم ـ رَفِث. Carnal knowledge, جِمَاع.

Carnality, *n.* Sensuality, حُبّ ـ غُلْمَة ـ قَطِم ـ شَهْوَانِيَّة. اَللَّذَّاتِ وَالشَّهَوَاتِ.

Carnalize, *v.t.* أَخْبَثَ ـ فَسَّقَ ـ فَسَّدَ ـ أَفْسَدَ.

Carnally, *ad.* حَسَبَ شَهَوَاتِ الْجَسَدِ ـ بِتَلَذُّذٍ ـ بِشَهْوَانِيَّةٍ. To lie with —, ضَاجَعَ ـ جَامَعَ. Carnally minded, مُهْتَمٌّ بِمَا يَخْتَصُّ بِالْجَسَدِ.

Carnation, *n.* The colour, لَوْنٌ ـ لَوْنٌ قِرْمِزِيٌّ ـ لَوْنٌ أَحْمَرُ عُنَّابِيٌّ. A pink, مُخْمَلِيَّة ـ قَرَنْفُل.

Carneous, *a.* كَالْلَحْمِ ـ لَحْمِيٌّ.

Carnify, *v.i.* صَارَ لَحْمًا ـ إِلْتَحَمَ.

Carnival, *n.* The season between the Epiphany and Lent, الكَرِيزَة ـ الرِّفَاع ـ المَرْفَع. The feast or revelry of —, عِيدُ الْمَسْخَرَةِ.

Carnivorous, *a.* كَوَاسِرُ .pl كَاسِر ـ جَوَارِحُ .pl جَارِح. Carnivorous animals, الوُحُوشُ الْجَوَارِحُ ـ الجَوَارِحُ.

Carob, *n.* The fruit, خَرُّوب ـ خُرْنُوب. A — pod, خَرُّوبَة ـ خُرْنُوبَة ـ شَجَرَةُ الْخُرْنُوبِ. The — tree, قَرْنُ خَرُّوبٍ.

Carol, *n.* A song, غُنِيَّة .pl أَغَانِي ـ نَشِيد .pl أَنْشَاد. A Christmas —, مَدَائِحُ .pl مَدِيحٌ يَوْمِ الْمِيلَادِ ـ تَرْتِيلُ الْمِيلَادِ.

Carol, *v.i.* To sing, غَنَّى. To warble, تَرَنَّمَ ـ تَغَرَّدَ ـ غَرَّدَ.

Carol, *v.t.* رَتَّلَ ـ تَغَنَّى.

Carotid, *n.* The — artery, الوَرِيدُ. The two — arteries, the *aorta ascendens* and *aorta descendens*, which issue from the heart, أَبْهَتَا الدِّمَاغِ.

Carousal, *n.* مَشْرَبَة ـ مُنَادَمَة ـ بَطَر ـ إِدْمَانُ الْخَمْرِ. The songs of carousers, غَيَاطِلُ.

Carouse, *v.i.* سَقَى الْحَبَقَةَ ـ تَعَاطَى الْمُدَامَ ـ شَرِبَ ـ نَادَمَ ـ شَرِبَ نَبِيذًا.

Carouser, *n.* نَدِيم .pl نُدَمَاءُ ـ نَدْمَان .pl نَدَامَى ـ شِرِّيب ـ مَعْكُوس ـ عَيَّاش.

Carp, *v.i.* To — at, نَقَرَ ـ قَرَصَ بِ ـ نَاقَدَ.

Carp, *n.* The fish, لَبَتَة .coll لَبَت ـ بُنِّي ـ شَبُّوط .pl شَبَابِيطُ.

Carpal, *a.* Pertaining to the wrist, رُسْغِيٌّ ـ مُخْتَصٌّ بِالرُّسْغِ.

Carpenter, *n.* نَجَّار ـ فَيْتَق .pl نَجَّارُونَ and نَجَّارَة. A master —, نَجَّار بَاشِي ـ نَجَّار أُسْتَاذ.

Carpentry, *n.* نِجَارَة ـ كَارُ النَّجَّارِ.

Carper, *n.* A caviller, شَتِيم ـ مُنَاقِر ـ مُنَاقِد.

Carpet, *n.* بِسَاط .pl بُسُط and بُسْط and أَبْسِطَة and بِسَاطَات ـ كُبَايَة ـ حُمُول .pl حَمْل ـ طَنَافِس .pl طِنْفِسَة ـ أَكَالِيم .pl أَكْلِيم. A — with coarse pile, طَنْبَسَة. An under — to save the upper, جِلْس. A praying —, سَجَّادَة. A seller of carpets, بُسُطِيٌّ. To be on the —, to be talked about, إِنْفَتَحَتِ السِّيرَةُ ـ يُحَدَّثُ عَنْهُ عَلَيْهِ. A — knight, زِيرُ نِسَاءٍ ـ حَلُّ النِّسَاءِ .pl أَعْلَال.

Carpet, *v.t.* فَرَشَ ـ بِبِسَاطَاتٍ.

Carpeting, *n.* بِسَاط ـ طَنَافِس.

Carriage, *n.* The act of carrying, حُمُولَة ـ حُمْلَان ـ حَمْل ـ نَقْل ـ تَحْوِيل. Price of porterage, حَقُّ الْحَامِلِ ـ أُجْرَةُ الْحُمُولَةِ; as of a letter to a messenger, حَقُّ سَاعٍ. Animals, *etc.*, for the road, رَاحِلَة. A vehicle, عَجَلَة .pl عَجَل and عِجَال ـ عَرَبَة ـ عَرَبَانَة ـ قَرُوسَة .pl قَرُوسَات. A gun-carriage, جَرَّارُ مِدْفَعٍ ـ خَشَبَةُ الْمِدْفَعِ. Demeanour, وَضْع ـ هَيْئَة ـ سُلُوك ـ سَمْت. Carriage paid, خَالِصُ أُجْرَةِ الْحُمُولَةِ.

Carrier, *n.* A porter, شَيَّال ـ حَمَّال. A carman, عَرَبَجِي. A messenger, سَاعٍ .pl سُعَاة.

Carrier-pigeon, *n.* The —, الطَّائِرُ. Carrier-pigeons, المَنَاسِيبُ.

Carrion, *n.* مَيْت ـ جِيفَة ـ رِمَّة.

Carrion, *a.* Feeding on —, آكِلُ الْجِيَفِ.

Carronade, *n.* مِدْفَعٌ صَغِيرٌ.

Carrot, *n.* جَزَرَة .coll جَزَر.

Carroty, *a.* أَحْمَرَانِيٌّ ـ مُحْمَارٌّ.

Carry, *v.t.* and *i.* To convey, as from a place, حَمَلَ ـ رَفَعَ ـ نَقَلَ ـ أَخَذَ ـ مِن ـ إِلَى ـ أَخَذَ ـ إِلَى. To bear, حَمَلَ ـ شَالَ. To —, to have about one, حَمَلَ ـ مَعَهُ ـ حَمَلَ ـ سَحِبَ ـ مَعَهُ. To gain in competition, to effect, نَالَ ـ غَلَبَ ـ قَارَبَ ـ ظَفِرَ بِ. To urge, to excite to, حَمَلَ ـ عَلَى ـ حَرَّضَ ـ عَلَى ـ حَرَّكَ ـ إِلَى. To imply, to contain, تَضَمَّنَ ـ إِحْتَوَى عَلَى ـ إِشْتَمَلَ عَلَى. To convey, as in a vehicle, نَقَلَ ـ حَوَّلَ. To carry one's self, to behave, سَلَكَ سُلُوكًا ـ عَمِلَ. To manage, بَاشَرَ ـ دَبَّرَ. To endure, إِسْتَحْمَلَ. To —, as of arms, تَقَلَّدَ بِ ـ حَمَلَ ـ إِسْتَصْحَبَ. To aid, support, سَاعَدَ ـ أَسْنَدَ ـ مَكَّنَ. To —, to convey, as a gun a shot, *etc.*, رَمَى ـ مَسَافَةً. To be carried, communicated, extended, to, as a disease, *etc.*, سَرَى إِلَى .aor يَسْرِي. We brought nothing into this world and it is certain we shall — nothing out, لَمْ نَأْتِ إِلَى هٰذَا الْعَالَمِ بِشَيْءٍ وَلَا شَكَّ أَنَّنَا لَا نَقْدِرُ أَنْ نَأْخُذَ مِنْهُ شَيْئًا.

Clouds without water carried about of winds, غُيُومٌ بِلَا مَآءٍ تَسُوقُهَا ٱلرِّيَاحُ.

To carry all before one, أَنْجَحَ — ءَ غَلَبَ عَلَى ٱلْكُلِّ.

To carry away or off, remove, ءَ ذَهَبَ بِ — إِنْطَلَقَ بِ — أَنْقَلَ — ءَ مَضَى بِ — ءَ خَطِفَ.

To carry away, to influence to, ءَ نَحَزَ — ءَ سَاقَ-إِلَى.

To carry away, as a torrent, ءَ جَرَفَ.

To carry away, as the wind, ذَرَّى — ءَ ذَرَى; as the winds the clouds, ءَ جَفَلَ.

To carry away captive, ءَ سَبَى.

To carry off, to kill, ءَ قَتَلَ — أَمَاتَ. To carry by force, إِخْتَطَفَ — ءَ خَطِفَ.

To carry on, to continue, وَاظَبَ عَلَى — دَاوَمَ عَلَى — أَدْمَنَ عَلَى — لَمْ يَزَلْ عَامِلًا — إِسْتَمَرَّ عَلَى.

To carry on, as business, إِشْتَغَلَ بِ — بَاشَرَ. To prosecute, سَاقَ *aor.* يَسُوقُ. This work is carried on by machinery, هٰذَا ٱلشُّغْلُ يَتَعَاطَاهُ ٱلدَّوَالِيبُ.

To carry one through, to make successful, ظَفَّرَ — وَفَّقَ — أَنْجَحَ.

To carry out, to perfect, أَتَمَّ — ءَ قَضَى بِ — أَنْجَزَ.

To carry out, as an order, ءَ عَمِلَ بِ — ءَ قَامَ بِأَمْرٍ — أَمْضَى — أَجْرَى. It was not carried out in practice, لَمْ يَجْرِ فِعْلًا.

To carry the day, ءَ ظَفِرَ — ءَ غَلَبَ.

To carry to account, ءَ ضَمَّ إِلَى ٱلْحِسَابِ — ءَ حَسَبَ.

To carry up, ءَ نَقَلَ-إِلَى فَوْقُ.

To carry with a high hand, ءَ بَطِرَ فِي — تَكَبَّرَ فِي.

Cart, *n.* نَقَّالَة — عَرَبَانَة *pl.* عَرَبَانَات — عَجَلَة *pl.* عَجَلَات.

Cart, *v.t.* To carry away in a cart, ءَ نَقَلَ-فِي عَرَبَانَةٍ.

Cartage, *n.* The act of carting, نَقْلٌ فِي عَرَبَانَةٍ. Price of carting, أُجْرَةُ ٱلنَّقْلِ فِي عَرَبَانَةٍ.

Carte-blanche, *n.* رُخْصَةٌ مُطْلَقَةٌ — تَصْرِيفٌ كُلِّيٌّ.

Cartel, *n.* An agreement for the exchange of prisoners, إِتِّفَاقٌ عَلَى مُبَادَلَةِ ٱلْأَسْرَى. A challenge, إِسْتِدْعَآءٌ لِلْقِتَالِ.

Carter, *n.* سَائِقُ ٱلْعَرَبَانَةِ — تَرَّاس — مُدَبِّرُ ٱلْعَرَبَانَةِ — عَجَّال.

Cartilage, *n.* غُضْرُوف *pl.* غَضَارِيف (*vulg.* قُرْقُوش). The — of the nose, قَصَبَةُ ٱلْأَنْفِ; of the ribs, شُرْسُوف; of the ear, قُوف; of the shoulder blade, نُغْض. The ensiform —, ٱلْعَلْعَلُ.

Cartilaginous, *a.* غُضْرُوفِيٌّ.

Cartographer, *n.* خَرْطَجِي — رَسَّامُ ٱلْخَارِطَاتِ.

Cartographical, *a.* مُتَعَلِّقٌ بِرَسْمِ ٱلْخَارِطَاتِ.

Cartography, *n.* فَنُّ رَسْمِ ٱلْخَارِطَاتِ.

Cartoon, *n.* صُورَةٌ كَبِيرَةٌ عَلَى صَحِيفَةٍ كَبِيرَةٍ.

Cartouch, *n.* For cartridges, بَيْتُ ٱلْفِشَكِ — بَيْتُ ٱلْبَارُودِ. An Egyptian —, حَلْقَةٌ تَتَضَمَّنُ ٱسْمَ مَلِكٍ مِنْ مُلُوكِ مِصْرَ ٱلْقَدِيمَةِ.

Cartridge, *n.* عَمَارُ بَارُودٍ — فَشَكَة *pl.* فِشَك — فَوْشِيك *pl.* فَوَاشِك — قِرْطَاسُ بَارُودٍ *pl.* قَرَاطِيس. A blank —, of a gun, عَمَارُ بَارُودٍ مِنْ دُونِ كُلَّةٍ.

Cartridge-box, *n.* *See* Cartouch, *n.*

Cartridge-paper, *n.* وَرَقٌ خَشِنٌ.

Cartwright, *n.* نَجَّارُ ٱلْعَرَبَانَاتِ.

Caruncle, *n.* فُضُولَةُ ٱللَّحْمِ.

Carve, *v.t.* To cut wood or stone into forms, ءَ نَحَتَ — ءَ نَقَرَ — نَقَّشَ — ءَ نَقَشَ. To cut, as of meat, قَطَّعَ — شَرَّحَ. To — or choose for one's self, إِنْتَقَشَ — إِخْتَارَ. To engrave, ءَ نَقَشَ.

Carve, *v.i.* To cut up meat, قَطَّعَ ٱللَّحْمَ. To practise as a sculptor, إِسْتَعْمَلَ ٱلنَّقَاشَةَ.

Carver, *n.* One who carves, a sculptor, نَقَّار — نَقَّاش. A large knife, سِكِّينٌ كَبِيرٌ. The — at a table, قَطَّاعُ ٱلطَّعَامِ عَلَى ٱلسُّفْرَةِ. A tool to carve with, مِنْقَش.

Carving, *n.* A carved work, مَنْقُوش — نَقْش. Art of —, نِقَاشَة.

Cascade, *n.* دَرْبَكَةُ مَآءٍ — سَلْسَل. To fall in a —, تَسَلْسَلَ.

Case, *n.* A small box or receptacle, عُلْبَة *pl.* عُلَب — حُقَّة *pl.* حُقَق. A small box for perfumes, or a dressing-case, عَتِيدَة *pl.* عَتَائِد. A box, chest, صَنْدُوق *pl.* صَنَادِيق. A case of cloth, a covering, غِطَآء — كِيس — بَيْت. A sheath, غِلَاف *pl.* غُلُف — وِعَآء *pl.* أَوْعِيَة. A needle-case, ظَرْف *pl.* ظُرُوف — قِرَاب — إِبَارَة. A pen-case, قَلَمْدَان. A book-case, صَنْدُوق كُتُب — قِمَطْرَة *pl.* قَمَاطِر.

Case, *n.* State of things, حَالَة — حَال. A matter, مَادَّة *pl.* مَوَادّ — قِصَّة — أَمْر — وَارِد *pl.* أُمُور — قَضِيَّة *pl.* قَضَايَا. A contingence, عَارِض *pl.* عَوَارِض — حَادِث *pl.* حَوَادِث. A question, problem, مَسْأَلَة *pl.* مَسَائِل. The variation of declinable nouns, حَدّ — تَغْيِيرُ أَوَاخِرِ ٱلْأَسْمَآءِ ٱلْمُعْرَبَةِ: In the nominative —, فِي حَدِّ ٱلرَّفْعِ. Description, شَرْحُ حَالٍ — شَرْح. State of health, حَال — مِزَاج. A — of sickness, one attacked, مُصَاب. A — in point, مَثَل. A — of fever, مُصَابٌ بِٱلْحُمَّى. A — of distress, مَشَقَّة — مُصَابٌ بِبَلِيَّةٍ. In bad —, plight, فِي حَالٍ يُرْثَى لَهُ. All that you need know in this —, كُلُّ مَا يَقْتَضِي لَكَ أَنْ تَعْرِفَ فِي هٰذَا

ٱلْوَارِدِ. It is the general custom in such a —, جَرَتِ ٱلْعَادَةُ فِي مِثْلِ هٰذَا ٱلْأَمْرِ.

According to the exigency of the case, بِحَسَبِ ٱقْتِضَاءِ ٱلْحَالِ.

As the case stands, حَسَبَ وَضْعِ ٱلْحَالِ ـ حَسَبَ ٱلْحَالِ.

If the case be so, إِنْ كَانَ ٱلْأَمْرُ هٰكَذَا.

In any case, in all cases, فِي كُلِّ حَالٍ. By all means, لَا بُدَّ ـ عَلَى كُلِّ حَالٍ.

In case of, should (there be), إِنْ كَانَ ـ إِذْ ـ إِن ـ إِنْ حَدَثَ.

In no case, in no wise, كَلَّا ـ لَا ـ أَلْبَتَّةَ.

In such a case, فِي أَمْرٍ مِثْلِ هٰذَا ـ فِي مِثْلِ هٰذِهِ ٱلْأُمُورِ.

In that case, such being the case, كَوْنَ ٱلْأَمْرِ كَذَا ـ وَٱلْحَالَةُ هٰذِهِ.

Such being the case, وَٱلْحَالَةُ هٰذِهِ.

Supposing the case to be that . . . , فَرَضْنَا أَنْ.

That is not the case, ٱلْأَمْرُ لَيْسَ كَذَا.

That is not the case with me, أَمْرِي خِلَافُ ـ أَمْرِي لَيْسَ كَذَا ذٰلِكَ.

To make out, draw up, a case, وَصَفَ دَعْوَى aor. يَصِفُ. To establish a case, أَثْبَتَ ٱلدَّعْوَى. To make out a case against, أَثْبَتَ-عَلَى.

To put a case to one, to ask of one, سَأَلَ ـ إِسْتَفْتَى.

To state or set forth a case, عَرَضَ كَيْفِيَّةَ ٱلْحَالِ.

Case, *v.t.* To cover, غَلَّفَ ـ أَغْلَفَ. To lay over, لَبَّسَ ـ غَطَّى. To put into a —, عَبَّأَ ـ (وَضَعَ- aor. يَضَعُ or) عَلَّبَ فِي صَنْدُوقٍ. To line, بَطَّنَ. A well cased with brick or stone, or lime, طَوَى ـ طَيٌّ.

Caseharden, *v.t.* سَقَى ـ سَقَى وَجْهَ ٱلْحَدِيدِ.

Caseknife, *n.* سَاطُور pl. سَوَاطِيرُ.

Casemate, *n.* مَزْغَلٌ مُقَبَّبٌ ـ قُبَّةٌ ـ حَنِيرَةٌ.

Casemated, *a.* مُقَبَّبُ ٱلْمَزَاغِلِ.

Casement, *n.* بَرْوَاز ـ فِرْوَاز vulg. شُبَّاكٌ.

Caseous, *a.* جُبْنِيٌّ.

Casern, *n.* حُجْرَةُ عَسْكَرٍ ـ حُجْرَةٌ.

Case-shot, *n.* وِعَاءٌ مِنَ ٱلتَّنَكِ مَحْشِيٌّ بِكُلَلٍ.

Cash, *n.* مِصْرِيَّاتٌ ـ مُعَامَلَةٌ ـ فُلُوس ـ دَرَاهِمُ. Ready —, نَقْدٌ.

Cash, *v.t.* صَرَفَ-فُلُوسًا.

Cash-book, *n.* دَفْتَرُ حِسَابٍ ـ دَفْتَر ـ قُنْدَاق.

Cashew-nut, *n.* جَوْزٌ قَابُلِيٌّ.

Cashier, *n.* أَمِينُ ٱلصَّنْدُوقِ ـ نَقَّاد ـ خَزْنَدَار.

Cashier, *v.t.* عَزَلَ-مِن or عَن ـ عَزَلَ ـ خَلَعَ.

Cashmere, *n.* The stuff, شَال. A — shawl, شَالٌ كَشْمِيرِيٌّ pl. شَالَات.

Casing, *n.* The act of, تَطْبِيق. A covering, غِلَاف. A casing with stone, تَطْبِيقٌ بِحَجَرٍ.

Casino, *n.* كَازِينُو ـ قِمَارْخَانَه ـ مَلْعَبَة ـ مَلْعَب.

Cask, *n.* A barrel, بَرْمِيل pl. بَرَامِيلُ.

Cask, *n.*
Casque, } A helmet, خُوذَةٌ pl. خُوَذٌ.

Casket, *n.* A box for jewels, عُلْبَةٌ لِلْجَوَاهِرِ; for perfumes, عَتِيدَةٌ pl. عَتَائِدُ ـ صُوَّنَة.

Cassava, *n.* نَوْعٌ مِنَ ٱلنَّشَا يُسْتَخْرَجُ مِنَ ٱلشَّجَرَةِ ٱلْمُسَمَّاةِ مَانِيُوق. *See* Manioc, *n.*

Cassia, *n.* خِيَارُ شَنْبَرٍ. Aromatic —, قِرْفَةٌ حَطَبِيَّةٌ ـ سَلِيخَة.

Cassiopea, *n.* The sign of the zodiac, ذَاتُ ٱلْكُرْسِيِّ.

Cassock, *n.* A priest's garment, رِسْتَامِيَّةٌ ـ تُونِيَة.

Cassowary, *n.* نَوْعٌ مِنَ ٱلطَّيْرِ.

Cast, *v.t.* and *i.* To throw, رَمَى aor. يَرْمِي ـ طَرَحَ ـ أَلْقَى ـ نَبَذَ ـ لَقَّحَ ـ رَشَقَ. To — dice, لَعِبَ ٱلزَّاقَةَ. To — from a high place, أَهْبَطَ ـ أَسْقَطَ ـ هَبَطَ بِ ـ رَمَى-إِلَى أَسْفَلَ. To —, as in a mould, سَبَكَ. To — in wrestling, غَلَبَ عَلَى ـ وَقَّعَ ـ كَبَّ. To condemn in a trial, غَلَبَ عَلَى ـ قَضَى عَلَى ـ أَوْقَعَ بِ. To defeat, غَلَبَ. To leave behind in a race, سَبَقَ. To model, عَمِلَ صُورَةً ـ صَوَّرَ. To overweigh, رَجَحَ ـ فَاقَ. To contrive, دَبَّرَ ـ صَوَّرَ. To —, as a beast its skin or a bird its feathers, أَنْسَلَ ـ نَسَلَ; of a skin, specially, سَلَخَ جِلْدَهُ ـ إِنْسَلَخَ ـ غَيَّرَ جِلْدَهُ. To have abortions, to abort, أَسْقَطَ ـ طَرَحَ. To — in the mind, تَفَكَّرَ فِي ـ فَكَّرَ فِي ـ تَأَمَّلَ فِي. To be —, to be the loser, كَانَ خَاسِرًا ـ خَسِرَ. To —, as a tree its fruit, أَسْقَطَ ثَمَرَهَا.

To cast anchor, رَمَى ٱلْمِرْسَاةَ ـ أَلْقَى ٱلْمِرْسَاةَ ـ رَبَطَ ـ أَرْخَى ٱلْهَلَبَ.

To cast aside, as fit to be worn no longer, رَفَعَ.

To cast away, as useless, طَرَحَ ـ رَمَى بِ aor. يَرْمِي.

To cast away, to reject, طَرَحَ ـ قَطَعَ-عَن ـ رَفَضَ ـ طَرَحَ بِ.

To cast away, to ruin, أَتْلَفَ ـ أَفْنَى ـ أَهْلَكَ. To be —, as a ship, غَرِقَ ـ إِنْكَسَرَ ـ أَلْقَى بِ.

To cast away care, إِخْتَلَى عَنِ ٱلْهُمُومِ.

To cast down, to deject, شَجَّنَ ـ حَزَّنَ ـ هَابَطَ .

To cast down, to break, ruin, أَهْلَكَ ـ أَبْطَلَ ـ سَخَّطَ .

To cast down at one's feet, أَلْقَى عِنْدَ قَدَمَى .

To cast eyes at, to look at attentively, أَمْعَنَ ٱلنَّظَرَ فِي ـ ~ نَظَرَ إِلَى .

To cast in one's teeth, سَابَّ ـ عَيَّرَ .

To cast into, أَهْبَطَ فِي ـ أَرْمَى فِي ـ أَسْقَطَ فِي .

To cast into a sleep, نَوَّمَ ـ نَيَّمَ ـ رَقَّدَ .

To cast into prison, ~ حَبَسَ ـ أَلْقَى فِي ٱلسِّجْنِ .

To cast lots, ~ ضَرَبَ ٱلْقُرْعَةَ ـ إِقْتَرَعَ .

To cast off, to discard, دَشَّرَ ـ أَصْرَفَ ـ 2 طَرَدَ .

To cast one's horoscope, ~ كَشَفَ لَهُ ٱلنَّجْمَ .

To cast one's self on, إِرْتَمَى عَلَى ـ أَلْقَى نَفْسَهُ عَلَى .

To cast out, to turn out of doors, 2 طَرَدَ ـ أَخْرَجَ .

To cast out, to give vent to words, تَفَوَّهَ بِ ـ ~ نَطَقَ بِ ـ ~ فَتَحَ فَاهُ ـ تَكَلَّمَ .

To cast out one's name as evil, to defame, ~ فَضَحَ ـ ~ هَتَكَ .

To cast reproaches at, عَيَّرَ ـ عَتَبَ عَلَى ـ 2 عَتَبَ .

To cast stones at, ~ رَمَى بِحِجَارَةٍ ـ 2 رَجَمَ .

To cast up, to compute, 2 عَدَّ ـ 2 حَسَبَ .

To cast up, to vomit, ~ طَرَشَ ـ 2 نَتَقَ ـ تَقَيَّأَ ـ إِسْتَفْرَغَ .

To cast up, as the sea does pebbles, *etc.* ~ 2 جَفَلَ ـ ~ بَعَثَ بِ ـ 2 نَسَرَ .

Cast, *n.* A throw, رَمْيَة *pl.* رَمَيَات ـ نَبْذ ـ نَبْذَة ـ طَرْحَة . A — or glance of the eye, رَمْزَة ـ نَظْرَة . A mould, قَالِب *pl.* قَوَالِب . Something cast in a mould, سَبِيكَة *pl.* سَبَائِك . Exterior appearance, عِقْبَة ـ هَيْئَة ـ سِمَة ـ وَجْه ـ ظَاهِر . Cast, arrangement, تَرْتِيب ـ تَنْسِيق ـ تَنْظِيم . A tinge, تَشَرُّب ـ إِسْتِشْرَاب . A — in the eye, جُهْرَة . Having a —, squint, in the eye, أَحْوَل . A stone's —, رَمْيَةُ حَجَرٍ . It has a — of red in it, يَضْرِبُ إِلَى ٱلْحُمْرَةِ .

Cast, *a.* Useless, discarded, سَقَط ـ مَرْفُوض .

Castanets, *n.* صَنْج ـ سَاجَات ـ قُقَيْشَات ـ صَغَانَة ـ جَلَبَارَة . A player upon the —, صَنَّاج .

Castaway, *n.* ضَالّ *pl.* ضَالُّون and ضَالَّة ـ مَرْذُول ـ هَالِك .

Caste, *n.* قَوْم ـ فِرْقَة ـ طَائِفَة . Half-caste, مُوَلَّد .

Castellan, *n.* مُحَافِظُ ٱلْقَلْعَةِ ـ صَاحِبُ ٱلْحِصَارِ .

Castellated, *a.* Fortified, مُحَصَّن ـ حَصِين . *See also* Battlement, *n.*

Caster, *n.* A founder, سَاكِب ـ سَكَّاب . A — of fortunes, رَمَّال ـ كَاهِن *pl.* كَهَنَة . A reckoner, حَاسِب ـ مُحَاسِب ـ مُحَاسِبْجِي . A cruet-stand, آلَةُ ٱلْأَبَازِيرِ . A small wheel, بَكَرَة *pl.* بَكَرَات .

Castigate, *v.t.* عَاقَبَ ـ قَاصَصَ ـ أَدَّبَ .

Castigation, *n.* تَأْدِيب ـ عِقَاب ـ قِصَاص .

Castigator, *n.* مُؤَدِّب ـ مُعَاقِب ـ مُقَاصِص .

Casting, *n.* What is cast in a mould, سَبِيكَة .

Casting-net, *n.* شَبَكَة .

Casting-vote, *n.* فَصْلُ قَضِيَّةٍ بِقَوْلِ صَدْرِ ٱلْقَوْمِ مَتَى كَانَ عَدَدُ أَعْضَاءِ ٱلْمَجْلِسِ مُتَسَاوٍ أَيْ إِذَا رَضِيَ ٱلنِّصْفُ مِنْهُمْ بِمَا عُرِضَ عَلَيْهِمْ وَرَفَضَهُ ٱلْبَاقُونَ .

Castle, *n.* قَلْعَة *pl.* قُلُوع and قِلَاع ـ قَصْر *pl.* قُصُور ـ مَعْقَل *pl.* مَعَاقِل ـ حِصَار ـ بُرْج *pl.* بُرُوج ـ قِشْلَة *pl.* قِشَل . Castles in the air, هَوَس ـ هَتْرَة ـ تَوَهُّم . To build castles in the air, تَوَهَّمَ ـ تَخَيَّلَ .

Castle-builder, *n.* A visionary, خَيَالِيّ ـ صَاحِبُ خَيَالٍ .

Castor, *n.* The animal, كَلْبُ ٱلْمَاءِ ـ قُنْدُس ـ سَكَلَابِي ـ بِيدَسْتَر ـ حَيَوَانُ جُنْدْ بَادَسْتَر .

Castoreum, *n.* جُنْدْ بَادَسْتَر ـ خُصْيَةُ ٱلْجَرْدِ .

Castor-oil, *n.* زَيْتُ ٱلْخِرْوَعِ .

Castrametation, *n.* فَنُّ تَرْتِيبِ ٱلْأُرْدِي ـ فَنُّ ٱلْمُسْتَحْكَمَاتِ .

Castrate, *v.t.* 2 جَبَّ خُصَاهُ . To cut off the private parts, ~ خَصَى ـ طَوَّشَ ـ مَلَسَ ; of an ass, ~ مَعَلَ ; of a ram, ~ شَظَفَ .

Castrated, *a.* مَخْصِيّ ـ خَصُور ـ خَصِيّ . A — boy having his private parts excised, مَمْلُوس .

Castration, *n.* جَبُّ ٱلْخُصْيَتَيْنِ ـ خِصَاء ـ تَطْوِيش ; of a ram, شَظْف .

Cast-steel, *n.* صَبّ (or بُولَاد) فُولَاد .

Casual, *a.* Fortuitous, عَرَضِيّ ـ عَارِضِيّ ـ إِتِّفَاقِيّ ـ تَصَادُفِيّ . Sudden, فُجَائِيّ . A — visit, زِيَارَةٌ مُجَرَّدَةٌ .

Casually, *ad.* إِتِّفَاقًا ـ مِنْ غَيْرِ قَصْدٍ ـ عَرَضًا .

Casualty, *n.* A fortuitous occurrence, حَادِثَة *pl.* حَوَادِث ـ فُجَاءَة ـ عَارِض *pl.* عَوَارِض ـ وَاقِعَة ـ قَضَاء . A death, مَوْت *pl.* أَمْوَات ـ وَفَاة *pl.* وَفَايَات ـ مَمَات .

Casuist, *n.* فَقِيه *pl.* فُقَهَاء ـ حَلَّالُ ٱلْمُشْكِلَاتِ .

Casuistry, *n.* عِلْمُ ٱلْفِقْهِ ـ عِلْمُ حَلِّ ٱلْمُشْكِلَاتِ .

Cat, *n.* The animal, ٱلْمَائِيَة ـ هِرّ ـ سِنَّوْر *pl.* سَنَانِير ـ بَزُّونَة *pl.* بَزَازِين ـ قِطّ *pl.* قِطَاط ـ هِرّ *pl.* هِرَر ـ هِرَّة *fem.* *pl.* هِرَرَة .

A wild cat, سَبَنْسَب ـ شُنَارَى. A whip, سَوْط ـ فِرْقِلَة ـ دِرَّة. Tackle to draw up the anchor, قَابُون.

Cataclysm, *n.* طُوفَان.

Catacomb, *n.* An underground excavation, نَقِيرٌ تَحْتَ ٱلْأَرْضِ. Subterranean graves, قُبُورٌ تَحْتَ ٱلْأَرْضِ.

Catafalque, *n.* *See* Bier, *n.*

Catagraph, *n.* مُسْوَدَّةُ صُورَةٍ.

Catalepsy, *n.* نُقْطَة ـ دَآءُ ٱلسُّبَاتِ. To be seized with —, أُصِيبَ بِدَآءِ ٱلسُّبَاتِ.

Catalogue, *n.* A list of names, جَدْوَل (or) دَفْتَرُ ٱلْأَسْمَآءِ. An index, فِهْرِسْت ـ فِهْرِس. A — raisonné, فِهْرِسٌ مَشْرُوحٌ.

Catalogue, *v.t.* فَهْرَسَ.

Catamaran, *n.* A raft, رَمَث *pl.* أَرْمَاث.

Catamenia, *n.* حَيْض ـ حَيْضَة ـ طِمْث.

Catamite, *n.* مُخَنَّث ـ مَأْبُون ـ مِثْفَار ـ عُجْن *pl.* عُجْيَن ـ مَلُوط. To act the —, تَخَنَّثَ.

Cataphract, *n.* Horse armour, تِجْفَاف.

Cataplasm, *n.* لَبْخَة ـ لَبِيخَة ـ ضِمَاد.

Catapult, *n.* مَنْجَنِيق. A small —, عَرَّادَة. A child's —, مِخْذَفَة.

Cataract, *n.* A large waterfall, شَلَّال *pl.* شَلَّالَات. A disorder in the eye, بَيَاضٌ فِي ٱلْعَيْنِ ـ ظَفَرَة ـ سُدَّة *pl.* سُدَد.

Catarrh, *n.* نَزْلَة ـ لَبْطَة ـ غُمَام ـ طُشَاة ـ زُكَام. To have a —, نُزِلَ ـ زُكِمَ ـ لُبِطَ. Having a —, مَزْكُوم ـ مَلْبُوط.

Catarrhal, *a.* }
Catarrhous, } نُزُولِيّ ـ زُكَامِيّ.

Catastrophe, *n.* مُصِيبَة *pl.* مَصَائِب ـ بَلِيَّة *pl.* بَلَايَا ـ عَاقِبَةُ سُوءٍ ـ آخِرَةُ سُوءٍ ـ دَاهِيَة.

Catcall, *n.* صَفَّارَةُ ٱلْإِسْتِهْزَآءِ ـ صَفَّارَةُ مَهْزَأَةٍ.

Catch, *v.t.* and *i.* To seize, lay hold of, قَبَضَ بِ ـ مَسَكَ بِ. To overtake, لَحِقَ ـ أَلْحَقَ. To —, as of birds, fish, *etc.*, أَصَادَ ـ تَصَيَّدَ ـ إِصْطَادَ. To entrap, to deceive, غَشَّ ـ أَوْقَعَ. To — in falling, تَلَقَّى ـ تَلَقَّفَ. To — suddenly, to snatch, خَطِفَ ـ إِخْتَطَفَ. To —, as of the affections, to captivate, سَبَى ـ سَلَبَ. To —, to befall one suddenly, عَرَضَ لِ ـ دَقَّ فِي. To — or seize with craft, خَطِفَ بِٱلْحِيلَةِ. To —, as of a disease, عَرَضَ لِ ـ أَقْرَفَ ـ أَصَابَ بِ ـ إِعْتَرَى. To —, to cling to, to become caught in, تَعَلَّقَ بِ ـ إِعْتَلَقَ بِ ـ عَلِقَ بِ. He has caught a fever, مَسَكَتْهُ ٱلسُّخُونَةُ ـ سَخَنَ ـ حُمَّ. I have caught a cold, تَرَشَّحَتْ. My nail caught the thing, إِعْتَلَقَ ظُفْرِي بِٱلشَّيْءِ. The thorns caught, clung to, the garment, تَعَلَّقَ ٱلشَّوْكُ بِٱلثَّوْبِ. The animal was caught in the snare, تَعَلَّقَ ٱلْوَحْشُ بِٱلْحِبَالَةِ. Catch (thou), hold! عَلَيْكَ. Catch the child! عَلَيْكَ بِٱلْوَلَدِ. To catch an opportunity, إِسْتَفَادَ مِنَ ٱلْفُرْصَةِ ـ إِفْتَرَصَ فُرْصَةً. To catch a scolding, أَكَلَ مُعَاتَبَةً ـ عُتِبَ. To catch a thrashing, أَكَلَ قَتْلَةً. To catch fire, إِشْتَعَلَ ـ تَشَعَّلَ. To catch the eye of one, جَلَبَ نَظَرَهُ إِلَيْهِ.

Catch, *n.* The act of seizing, أَخْذ ـ مَسْك ـ قَبْض. A song sung in succession, غُنْيَةٌ مُتَرَاسِلَةٌ ـ نَشْدَة. A hook, عَقْرَب ـ تَوْقَة ـ عَقْفَآء ـ كُلَّاب. Profit, مَكْسَب ـ فَائِدَة. What is taken in fishing, hunting, *etc.*, صَيْدَة ـ صَيْد. A touch of any thing, لَوْنٌ مِن ـ وِن. A trick, خِدْعَة ـ حِيلَة.

Catcher, *n.* Of fish, *etc.*, صَيَّاد.

Catchfly, *n.* The plant, سِرَاجُ ٱلْقُطْرُبِ.

Catching, *a.* Infectious, مُعْتَدٍ ـ مُعْدٍ ـ عَادٍ. A — disease, سُعْر ـ عَدْوَى. More — than yawning, أَعْدَى مِنَ ٱلثُّوَبَآءِ.

Catch-penny, *n.* مَتَاعٌ صِنَاعِيٌّ.

Catchup, *n.* }
Catsup, } مَرَقٌ مُتَوَبَّلٌ ـ نَوْعٌ مِنَ ٱلتَّوَابِلِ.

Catchword, *n.* تَعْقِيبَة.

Catechetic, *a.* }
Catechetical, } عَلَى نَسَقِ ٱلسُّؤَالِ وَٱلْجَوَابِ.

Catechise, *v.t.* To instruct, عَلَّمَ عَلَى طَرِيقِ ٱلسُّؤَالِ وَٱلْجَوَابِ ـ دَرَّسَ ـ عَلَّمَ. To question of, سَأَلَ *aor.* يَسْأَلُ ـ نَصَّ ـ إِسْتَفْهَمَ ـ فَحَصَ عَن ـ وِن.

Catechiser, *n.* A teacher, مُدَرِّس ـ مُعَلِّم.

Catechism, *n.* تَعْلِيمٌ بِمُوجَبِ سُؤَالٍ وَجَوَابٍ. A Christian —, تَعْلِيمٌ مَسِيحِيٌّ.

Catechist, *n.* *See* Catechiser, *n.*

Catechu, *n.* فُوفَل ـ فَوْفَل.

Catechumen, *n.* One preparing himself for baptism, مُتَرَشِّح لِلْعِمَادِ ـ تِلْمِيذٌ لِلْعِمَادِ ـ طَالِبُ ٱلْعِمَادِ *pl.* طَلَبَة ـ طَالِبُ ٱلْمَعْمُودِيَّةِ.

Categorical, *a.* Positive, express, شَافٍ ـ قَاطِع. To the purpose, فِي مَحَلِّهِ ـ حَسَبَ ٱقْتِضَآءِ ٱلْأَمْرِ ـ مُسَدَّد ـ مُنَاسِب.

Categorically, *ad.* إِيجَابًا ـ قَطْعًا ـ بَتَّةً. To the purpose, مِنْ بَابِهِ ـ سَدَدًا ـ سَدَادًا ـ مُنَاسَبَةً.

Category, *n.* Class, طَبَقَة ـ أَبْوَاب *pl.* بَاب ـ نَسَق ـ قَبِيل ـ أَجْنَاس *pl.* جِنْس ـ طَرْز ـ مَقَام ـ شَأْن. Predicament, condition, حَال ـ. In grammar, حَدٌّ, as when a verb is said to be مِنْ حَدِّ ضَرَبَ, that is, in the category of ضَرَبَ.

Catenate, *v.t.* سَلْسَلَ.

Catenation, *n.* سِلْسِلَة ـ تَسَلْسُل.

Cater, *v.i.* تَمَوَّنَ.

Caterer, *n.* كِلَارْجِيّ ـ مُتَسَوِّق ـ مُوَّان.

Cateress, *n.* مُوَّانَة.

Caterpillar, *n.* دُودَة ـ طَرَاطِيرُ *pl.* طُرْطُر ـ اليَرَقَانَ ـ غَوْغَاء ـ *coll.* دُود.

Caterwaul, *v.i.* As a cat at particular seasons, صَرْوَقَتِ ٱلتَّعْشِير. To scream, إِعْتَوَلَ ـ أَعْوَلَ. To make a noise like a cat, أَمْوَأَ.

Cates, *n.* مَأْكُولَات ـ ضِيَافَة.

Cat-fish, *n.* ذِئَاب *pl.* ذِئْبُ ٱلْبَحْرِ.

Catgut, *n.* Strings for bows, *etc.*, أَوْتَار *pl.* وَتَر; for fishing, حَرِير. The sinews from which — is made, عَقَب.

Cathartic, *a.* } Cathartical, } مُنَقٍّ ـ مُلَيِّن ـ مُسْهِل.

Cathartic, *n.* A — medicine, شَرْبَة ـ دَوَاء مُسْهِل.

Cathead, *n.* Of an anchor, غُرَيْوَة.

Cathedra, *n.* كُرْسِيّ ـ مَقَام رَئِيس.

Cathedral, *n.* الكَنِيسَةُ ٱلْمَطْرَانِيَّةُ ـ أَوَّلُ كَنِيسَةٍ فِي أَبْرَشِيَّةٍ.

Cathedral, *a.* مُتَعَلِّقٌ بِٱلْكَنِيسَةِ ٱلْمَطْرَانِيَّةِ.

Catheter, *n.* قَاطَاتِر ـ آلَةٌ لِٱسْتِخْرَاجِ ٱلْبَوْلِ.

Catholic, *a.* Universal, جَامِع ـ عُمُومِيّ ـ عَمّ. Of the — religion, كَاثُولِيكِيّ.

Catholic, *n.* مُؤْمِنٌ بِٱلْإِيمَانِ ٱلْكَاثُولِيكِيِّ ـ كَاثُولِيكِيّ. A Roman —, بَابَاوِيّ.

Catholicism, *n.* الإِيمَانُ ٱلْكَاثُولِيكِيُّ.

Catholicity, *n.* Universality, جَامِعَة ـ عُمُومِيَّة; of the Catholic religion, كَاثُولِيكِيَّة.

Catholicon, *n.* عِلَاجٌ لِجَمِيعِ ٱلْأَمْرَاضِ.

Catholicos, *n.* جَثَالِقَة *pl.* جَاثَلِيق.

Catlap, *n.* سَخِينَة.

Cat-o'-nine-tails, *n.* فِرَقِلَّة ـ سَوْطٌ قَطِيعٌ ـ سَوْط.

Cat's-eye, *n.* The stone, عَيْنُ ٱلْهِرِّ.

Cat's-foot, *n.* The plant, خَمَا قِسُوس.

Catspaw, *n.* A dupe, زَبُون *pl.* زَبَائِنُ ـ غَرِير *pl.* أَغِرَّاء. A ripple on the water, تَرَج ـ حُبُك ـ حَبَبُ ٱلْمَاءِ ـ حَبَابُ ٱلْمَاءِ ـ نَسْج.

Catsup, *n.* *See* Catchup, *n.*

Cattle, *n.* Bovine —, أَبْقَار ـ بَقَر; generally, حَيَوَانَات ـ مَوَاشِي ـ بَهَائِم. A disease was observable in the cattle, شُوهِدَ دَاءٌ فِي ٱلْمَوَاشِي.

Caucasian, *a.* قَافِيّ.

Caucus, *n.* إِجْتِمَاعٌ مَخْصُوصٌ ـ عَصَبِيَّة.

Caudal, *a.* Pertaining to the tail, مُخْتَصٌّ بِٱلذَّنَبِ. The — bone, عُصْعُص ـ عَصْعَص.

Caudate, *a.* مُذَنَّب ـ أَبُو ذَنَب ـ ذُو ذَيْل ـ ذَائِل.

Caudle, *n.* A drink for the sick, شَرْبَةٌ لِلْمَرْضَى. A scolding, مَعْتِبَة ـ عِتَاب.

Caught, *pret. of to* Catch, *q.v.*

Caul, *n.* A membrane of the bowels, نَسِيجُ ٱلْمَصَارِينِ. The — of a head-dress, مِقْنَعَة ـ ضَفِيرَة. The membrane over the face of a new-born infant, لُقَاءَة ـ نَقَأ ـ قُصَاة ـ مَسَك.

Cauliflower, *n.* قَرْنَبِيط.

Causal, *a.* مُسَبِّب ـ سَبَبِيّ.

Causality, *n.* تَعْلِيلِيَّة ـ سَبَبِيَّة.

Causation, *n.* تَعْلِيل ـ إِحْدَاث ـ سَبَبِيَّة.

Causative, *a.* سَبَبِيّ ـ مُعَلِّل ـ مُسَبِّب.

Causatively, *ad.* بِٱعْتِلَالٍ ـ تَسَبُّبًا.

Cause, *n.* That which causes any thing, أَسْبَاب *pl.* سَبَب ـ دَاعٍ ـ سَبَب ـ بَاعِث ـ عِلَل *pl.* عِلَّة. Reason, motive, مُوجِب. A medium, وَاسِطَة ـ وَسَائِل *pl.* وَسِيلَة. A subject of litigation, خُصُومَة ـ دَعَاوَى *pl.* دَعْوَى ـ مُخَاصَمَة. A side, party, طَرَف ـ فِرْقَة ـ حِزْب. Cause and effect, عِلَّةٌ وَمَعْلُولٌ. The Causer of causes, or the first Great —, مُسَبِّبُ ٱلْأَسْبَابِ. God is the first — and the Causer of causes, ٱللّٰهُ هُوَ ٱلْعِلَّةُ ٱلْأُولَى وَعِلَّةُ ٱلْعِلَلِ. The — of God and religion, سَبِيلُ ٱللّٰهِ. A — deserving of death, عِلَّةٌ لِلْمَوْتِ.

For a certain cause, لِعِلَّةٍ مَا ـ لِعِلَّةٍ مِنَ ٱلْعِلَلِ.

For the cause of, for, بِسَبَبِ ـ لِأَجْلِ; out of love for, حُبَّةً فِي ـ حُبًّا بِ.

For this cause, بِسَبَبِ هٰذَا ـ مِنْ أَجْلِ ذٰلِكَ ـ لِهٰذَا.

Without cause, بَاطِلًا ـ بِغَيْرِ سَبَب.

A first cause, سَبَبٌ أَصْلِيّ ـ عِلَّةٌ أَصْلِيَّة.

A latent cause, سَبَبٌ خَفِيّ ـ سَبَبٌ مَجْهُول.

A material cause, عِلَّةٌ مادِّيَّةٌ.

A proximate cause, عِلَّةٌ قَرِيبَةٌ ـ سَبَبٌ قَرِيبٌ ـ وَاسِطَةٌ.

A secondary cause, عِلَّةٌ ثانِيَةٌ.

A secret cause, سَبَبٌ مَكْتُومٌ.

An efficient cause, عِلَّةٌ ـ سَبَبٌ مُوجِبٌ ـ بَاعِثٌ حَقِيقِيٌّ.

The apparent cause, السَّبَبُ ٱلظَّاهِرُ.

The principal cause, السَّبَبُ ٱلْأَخَصُّ.

The ultimate cause, المُوجِبُ ٱلْأَصْلِيُّ ـ العِلَّةُ ٱلْأَصْلِيَّةُ.

To assign a cause for, عَلَّلَ-بِ.

To espouse one's cause, حَامَى عَن ـ مَسَكَ طَرَفَهُ ـ.

To fight in the cause of God, جَاهَدَ فِي سَبِيلِ ٱللّٰهِ.

To gain one's (own) cause, نَجَحَ فِي دَعْوَاهُ ـ.

To investigate the cause of, فَتَّشَ عَنْ سَبَبِ.

To plead one's own cause, قَامَ بِدَعْوَاهُ ـ خَاصَمَ عَنْ دَعْوَاهُ.

To plead the cause of one, حَاجَجَ عَن ـ قَامَ بِدَعْوَى.

To show cause, بَيَّنَ ٱلسَّبَبَ.

Cause, *v.t.* To occasion, أَوْجَبَ ـ سَبَّبَ. To make to exist, كَوَّنَ ـ أَوْجَدَ. To — to rebel, أَفْتَنَ ـ حَرَّضَ-عَلَى فِتْنَةٍ. To — to sleep, رَقَّدَ ـ نَيَّمَ ـ نَوَّمَ. To — divisions, أَحْدَثَ ٱلشِّقَاقَ. To — sorrow to, أَغَمَّ. To — to be put to death, أَمَاتَ. To be caused, تَسَبَّبَ ـ تَعَلَّلَ.

Causeless, *a.* Original to itself, غَيْرُ مَعْلُولٍ ـ قَائِمٌ بِذَاتِهِ. Without cause, مِنْ غَيْرِ سَبَبٍ ـ بِدُونِ عِلَّةٍ.

Causelessly, *ad.* مِنْ غَيْرِ سَبَبٍ ـ بِلا مُوجِبٍ.

Causelessness, *n.* عَدَمُ ٱلسَّبَبِ.

Causer, *n.* مُسَبِّب ـ مُعَلِّل ـ سَبَب.

Causeway, *n.* جِسْر *pl.* جُسُور.

Caustic, *a.* Burning, مُحْرِق. Corrosive, أَكَّال. Pungent, أَجَاج ـ حَاذِق. Sarcastic, سَلِيط ـ طَاعِن.

Caustic, *n.* Nitrate of silver, حَجَرُ جَهَنَّمَ.

Causticity, *n.* Pungency, حَرَارَة ـ حُرَافَة. Sarcasm, سَلَاطَة ـ قَارِصَة.

Cauter, *n.* مِكْوَاة *pl.* مَكَاوِي ـ مِيْسَم.

Cauterism, *n.* وِسَام ـ كَيّ ـ تَنْوِير.

Cauterize, *v.t.* نَارَ ـ نَوَّرَ ـ وَسَمَ *aor.* يَسِمُ ـ قَلَّى ـ حَسَمَ ـ كَوَى. To be cauterized, إِكْتَوَى. To ask to be cauterized, إِسْتَكْوَى. To — one's self, إِتَّسَمَ.

Cautery, *n.* حَسْم ـ نَار ـ وِسَام ـ كَيّ. The place cauterized, كَيَّة.

Caution, *n.* Wariness, حِذْر ـ إِحْتِرَاس ـ إِحْتِيَاط ـ تَحَفُّظ ـ حَزْم ـ تَحَرُّس ـ تَحَذُّر. Warning, تَنْبِيه ـ نَصِيحَة ـ إِنْذَار. Security given, تَضْمِين ـ ضَمَانَة ـ كَفَالَة. Deliberation, تَعَنٍّ. He used — in the affair, تَأَنَّى فِي ٱلْأَمْرِ.

Caution, *v.t.* To warn against, نَبَّهَ-عَلَى ـ حَذَّرَ ـ حَذَّرَ-مِن ـ أَنْذَرَ-أَنْ لَا. To forewarn, عَرَّفَ-بِ ـ عَرَّفَ-عَن. To advise, نَبَّهَ ـ نَصَحَ.

Cautionary, *a.* Containing caution, نُصْحِيّ ـ تَنْبِيهِيّ. Given as a pledge, ضَمَانِيّ.

Cautious, *a.* مُنْتَبِه ـ حَذِر ـ مُتَحَفِّظ ـ مُحْتَذِر ـ حَرِيس ـ حَازِم ـ صَاحِبُ ٱحْتِيَاطٍ ـ صَاحِبُ رَأْيٍ وَتَدْبِيرٍ. I was rather — in the matter, أَخَذْتُ بِٱلْحَزْمِ فِي ٱلْمَادَّةِ. To be —, not precipitate, تَأَنَّى ـ إِسْتَأْنَى. To be —, wary, حَذِرَ ـ إِحْتَذَرَ ـ تَقَيَّدَ.

Cautiously, *ad.* بِٱحْتِرَاسٍ ـ بِحَذَرٍ ـ بِتَأَمُّلٍ ـ بِعَقْلٍ.

Cautiousness, *n.* *See* Caution, *n.*

Cavalcade, *n.* رَكْبَة ـ رُكَّاب ـ مَوْكِب.

Cavalier, *n.* A horseman, إِسْوَار *pl.* أَسَاوِرَة *and* أَسَاوِر ـ فَارِس ـ فُرْسَان *pl.* خَيَّال *pl.* خَيَّالَة. A knight, أَمِير *pl.* أُمَرَاء ـ بَكٌ. In fortification, كَاوَالِيرِ ـ طَابِيَة.

Cavalier, *a.* Haughty, غِطْرِيس *pl.* غَطَارِيس ـ مُتَكَبِّر.

Cavalierly, *ad.* Haughtily, مُتَكَبِّرًا ـ بِغَطْرَسَةٍ.

Cavalry, *n.* أَسَاوِرَة ـ فُرْسَان ـ خَيَّالَة ـ سَوَارِي. The enemy's — attacked us, غَارَتْ عَلَيْنَا خَيَّالَةُ ٱلْعَدُوِّ.

Cavass, *n.* *See* Kawwâs, *n.*

Cavatina, *n.* نَغْمَة.

Cave, *n.* غَار *pl.* غِيرَان *and* أَغْوَار ـ مَغَار ـ مَغَارَة; a small —, كَهْف *pl.* كُهُوف. A — in a mountain, قَعْبَة ـ قَعْب *pl.* قِعَاب.

Cave, *v.t.* To make hollow, حَفَرَ ـ نَقَّرَ فِي ـ جَوَّفَ. To — in, to form a hollow, تَجَوَّفَ. To give in, to submit, إِنْقَادَ ـ أَسْلَمَ ـ إِسْتَسْلَمَ ـ إِخْتَضَعَ.

Caveat, *n.* تَنْبِيه ـ مُمَانَعَة.

Cavern, *n.* *See* Cave, *n.*

Caverned, *a.* } كَثِيرُ ٱلْغِيرَانِ ـ مَمْلُوٌّ مَغَارَاتٍ ـ مُتَكَهِّف.
Cavernous, }

Caviar, *n.* } خَبْيَارِي.
Caviare, }

Cavil, *v.i.* كَابَرَ ـ نَاقَدَ ـ لَجَّ ـ. To — with, نَاقَدَ-فِي ـ نَاقَرَ ـ لَجَّ عَلَى-فِي ـ عَاتَلَ. They cavilled among themselves, تَعَالَجُوا.

Caviller, *n.* مُكَابِر ـ لَجُوج ـ مُنَاقِر ـ مُنَاقِد.

Cavity, *n.* حُفْنَة *pl.* حُفَن ـ حُفْرَة *pl.* حُفَر ـ قَعْر *pl.* قُعُور ـ وَقْبَة ـ فَرَاغَة ـ نُقْرَة. The —, as of the ear, مَحَارَة ـ صَدَفَة; as of the eye, نُقْرَة *pl.* نُقَر; in any part of the face, قَلْت *pl.* قِلَات. The small — on a date-stone, نُقْرَة ـ نَقِير.

Caw, *v.i.* نَعَقَ ـ نَعَبَ.

Cawing, *n.* نُعَاب ـ نَعْب ـ نُعَاق ـ نَعْق.

Cayenne, *n.* فِلْفِل ٱلْفُلَيْفِلَة.

Cayman, *n.* تِمْسَاح أَمِيرِكَانِيّ.

Cazique, *n.* شَيْخ ٱلْبَدَاوَى فِي أَمِيرِكَا.

C.B. (Companion of the Bath), عِبَارَة عَنِ ٱلدَّرَجَةِ ٱلثَّالِثَةِ مِنْ نِيشَانِ ٱلْبَاث.

Cease, *v.i.* To leave off, إِنْقَطَعَ عَن ـ كَفَّ عَن ـ قَعَدَ عَن ـ إِنْتَهَى عَن ـ أَزَال ـ بَطَلَ ـ خَلَّى عَن ـ إِنْتَزَعَ. To desist from, To — to be, زَالَ *aor.* يَزُول. To be at an end, إِنْقَطَعَ ـ تَمَّ ـ خَلَصَ. Not to —, مَا زَال ـ مَا إِنْفَكَّ ـ مَا بَرِحَ. I will not — until, لَا أَبْرَحُ حَتَّى. I ceased not to do it, مَا زِلْتُ أَفْعَلُهُ ـ مَا بَرِحْتُ أَفْعَلُهُ. He did not — to remember him, مَا إِنْفَكَّ ـ مَا فَتَأَ يَذْكُرُهُ ـ يَذْكُرُهُ. The wind ceased, سَكَنَتِ ٱلرِّيحُ ـ سَكَتَتِ ٱلرِّيحُ. He ceased speaking, إِنْقَطَعَ عَنِ ٱلْكَلَامِ. I — not to ..., لَا أَكُفُّ عَن ـ لَا أَزَال. Without ceasing, دَائِمًا ـ إِسْتِمْرَارًا ـ بِلَا إِنْقِطَاع. To cause to —, أَبْطَلَ ـ أَنْهَى.

Ceaseless, *a.* دَائِم ـ بِلَا ٱنْقِطَاع ـ بِلَا فُتُور.

Ceaselessly, *ad.* دَائِمًا ـ بِلَا ٱنْقِطَاع ـ إِسْتِمْرَارًا.

Cecity, *n.* عَمًى.

Cedar, *n.* شَارْبِين ـ شَرْبِين. A — of Lebanon, أَرْزَة لُبْنَان ـ *coll.* أَرْز.

Cede, *v.t.* To give up, سَلَّمَ بِ ـ سَيَّبَ ـ تَرَكَ. To yield, as to an argument, قَنَعَ إِلَى ـ إِنْقَادَ إِلَى ـ قَبِلَ. To make an abatement to, فَاتَ لِ ـ تَنَازَلَ لِ-عَن ـ سَمَحَ لِ-بِ ـ تَخَلَّى لِ-عَن.

Cedrine, *a.* شَارْبِينِيّ ـ أَرْزِيّ.

Ceil, *v.t.* سَقَّفَ ـ جَعَلَ لِ-سَمْكًا.

Ceiling, *n.* سَقْف ـ سَمَاء ـ سَمْك. (The last word properly means a roof, but is also used to express a ceiling.)

Celandine, *n.* The plant, بَقْلَة ٱلْخَطَاطِيف ـ ٱلْعُرُوق ٱلصُّفْر.

Celebrant, *n.* At mass, ٱلْقِسّ ٱلْمُقَدِّس. One who officiates at a service, خَادِم.

Celebrate, *v.t.* To praise, مَدَحَ ـ عَظَّمَ ـ مَجَّدَ. To praise (God), ذَكَرَ. To distinguish by solemn rites, عَيَّدَ ـ بَجَّلَ. To — mass, قَدَّسَ.

Celebrated, *a.* Renowned, شَهِير ـ مَشْهُور ـ مَذْكُور ـ مَمْدُوح ـ مَوْصُوف. A — man, إِبْنُ جَلَاء. To be — for, إِشْتَهَرَ بِ.

Celebration, *n.* تَعْيِيد ـ إِجْرَاء ـ ذِكْر ـ ذُكْرَان. The — of mass, إِجْرَاء ٱلْقُدَّاس; of marriage, تَكْلِيل; of a festival, إِقَامَة عِيد.

Celebrity, *n.* Fame, ذِكْر ـ صِيتَة ـ صِيت ـ شُهْرَة ـ سُمْعَة. A celebrated man, رَجُل مَشْهُور ـ رَجُل مَمْدُوح ـ إِبْنُ جَلَاء.

Celerity, *n.* سُرْعَة ـ رَوْجَة ـ خِفَّة ـ عَجَلَة.

Celery, *n.* كَرَفْس بُسْتَانِيّ; wild —, بطرساليون ـ كَرَفْس بَرِّيّ.

Celestial, *a.* Pertaining to the heavens, فَلَكِيّ ـ سَمَاوِيّ. Exalted, عَلَوِيّ. *See also* Heavenly, *a.*

Celibacy, *n.* عُزْبَة ـ عُزُوبَة ـ عُزُوبِيَّة.

Celibate, *n.* An unmarried person, عَزَب *pl.* أَعْزَاب, *fem.* عَزَبَة *pl.* عَزَبَات.

Cell, *n.* A small room, حُجْرَة *pl.* حُجَر ـ خَلْوَة ـ قِلَّيَّة *pl.* قَلَالِي ـ قِلِّيَّة ـ أَكْرَاح *pl.* كِرْح. A monk's —, صَوْمَعَة *pl.* صَوَامِع. A hermit's —, كِرْح *pl.* أَكْرَاح ـ صَوْمَعَة. A — made by insects in trees, مَخْرُوب *pl.* مَخَارِيب. Cells, as of a honey-comb, خَلَايَا. The — of a prison, مَحْبَس; prison cells, حَوَاصِل. A small cavity, بُيُوت ـ بُقَيْبِقَة. A vesicle, بَيْت *pl.* بُيُوت ـ نُقْرَة ـ كَهْف *pl.* كُهُوف. *See also* Cyst, *n.*

Cellar, *n.* An underground room, سِرْدَاب *pl.* سَرَادِيب. A — for provisions, مَطْمُورَة ـ قَبْو ـ زِرْزَمِيَّة; for wine, مَقْصُورَة. A salt-cellar, وِعَاء ٱلْمِلْح.

Cellarage, *n.* Cellars, مَخَازِن ـ سَرَادِيب. Charge for storage in a cellar, أُجْرَة سَرَادِيب ـ كِرْوَة مَخَازِن.

Cellular, *a.* جِلَالِيّ ـ خَلَلِيّ ـ ذُو بُيُوت. Cellular tissue, نَسِيجَة خَلَلِيَّة. *See also* Cystose, *a.*

Cellule, *n.* *See* Cell, *n.*

Celtic, *a.* مُتَعَلِّق بِمَغَارِبَةِ أُورُبَّا ٱلْأَقْدَمِين.

Cement, *n.* An adhesive substance, غِرَاء ـ لَاقُونَة. A kind of mortar, خَافِقِيّ ـ خُرَاسَانِيّ. A bond of union, قَيْد ـ رِبَاط.

Cement, *v.t.* To join with —, أَلْزَقَ-بِغِرَاء ـ أَلْحَمَ-بِلَاقُونَة. To — with mortar-cement, جَبَّرَ ـ ضَبَطَ-بِٱلْخُرَاسَانِيّ. To repair, لَأَمَ ـ وَفَّقَ. To unite, وَصَّلَ ـ أَحَّدَ. He cemented the building with gypsum, عَقَدَ ٱلْبِنَاءَ بِٱلْجِصّ.

Cement, *v.i.* To cohere, إِلْتَحَمَ ـ إِلْتَزَقَ.

Cementation, *n.* As with cement, مُلاحَمَة ـ إلحام. The act of uniting, تأكِيد ـ عَقْد.

Cementer, *n.* One who cements, مُلْحِم.

Cemetery, *n.* مَقْبَرَة ـ مَدافِن *pl.* مَدْفَن ـ تُرَب *pl.* تُرْبَة.

Cenobite, *n.* A monk, راهِب *pl.* رُهْبان.

Cenobitical, *a.* راهِبِيّ ـ رُهْبانِيّ.

Cenotaph, *n.* مَزار خالٍ ـ قَبْر خالٍ.

Cense, *v.t.* بَخَّر ـ طَرَّى ـ أطْرَى.

Censer, *n.* مَباخِر *pl.* مِبْخَرَة ـ مِقْطَرَة ـ مَجامِر *pl.* مِجْمَرَة ـ مِجْمَر; such as is used in churches, شُورِيَة.

Censor, *n.* An examiner, critic, باحِث ـ فاحِص ـ مُفَتِّش ـ مُدَقِّق. A reprover, corrector, مُؤَدِّب. An official — of the press, مُمَيِّز المَطْبُوعات ـ مأمُور (or) ناظِر المَطْبُوعات. *See also* Censurer, *n.*

Censorial, *a.* تَفَحُّصِيّ ـ مُفاحِص ـ فَحِيص.

Censorious, *a.* قادِح ـ عائِب ـ عَذُول ـ عاذِل ـ جادِب ـ هاجٍ.

Censoriously, *ad.* بِقَدْح ـ بِهَجْو ـ عَذْلاً ـ بِعَذْل.

Censoriousness, *n.* مَلامَة ـ هِجاء ـ هَجْو ـ عَذْل.

Censorship, *n.* وَظِيفَة الفاحِص ـ تَحْرِيج. Censorship of the press, نَظارَة المَطْبُوعات. The press is under a strict — by the Government, المَطْبُوعات عَلَيها تَحْرِيج شَدِيد مِن الحُكْم.

Censurable, *a.* مُسْتَحِقّ التَّوْبِيخ ـ يُلام. A — action, مَذَمَّة. To do what is —, أذَمّ. *See also* Blamable, *a.*

Censurably, *ad.* بِنَوْع مُسْتَحِقّ اللَّوْم.

Censure, *n.* Blame, شَتْم ـ مَلامَة ـ لَوْم ـ ذَمّ ـ عَذْل. Reprehension, تَوْبِيخ. Condemnation, حُكْم عَلَى ـ فَتْوَى ـ قَضاء عَلَى. Ecclesiastical —, تأدِيب البِيعَة ـ مَنْع الكاهِن ـ رَبْط الكاهِن. A vote of —, رأي وَقَرار عَلَى عَدَم اعْتِقاد.

Censure, *v.t.* To blame, ذَمّ ² ـ عَزَّر ـ ثَلَبَ ـ عَذَلَ ² ـ وَبَّخ ـ عَتَبَ عَلَى ² ـ لامَ ² ـ ذَمَّم ـ طَعَنَ ². To reprove, وَبَّخ ـ بَكَّت. To condemn, حَكَمَ عَلَى ² ـ قَضَى عَلَى.

Censurer, *n.* ذَمّام ـ مُعَيِّب ـ مُشَتِّم ـ لائِم *pl.* لُوَّم *and* لُوَّام ـ لَوّام.

Census, *n.* إحْصاء ـ تَعْداد النُّفُوس. A general — of a kingdom, إحْصاء نُفُوس سائِر المَمْلَكَة.

Cent, *n.* مِئَة ـ مِيَة *pl.* مِيات. Fifty per —, خَمْسُون فِي المِئَة. That is more than fifty per — above the prime cost, هٰذا أكْثَر مِن خَمْسِين فِي المِائَة زِيادَة عَلَى رأس المال.

Centage, *n.* حِساب المِائَة.

Centaur, *n.* The constellation, القَنْطُورُس.

Centaury, *n.* The plant, حَشِيشَة القَنْطَرِيَّة ـ قَنْطُورِيُون.

Centenary, *a.* and *n.* / Centennial, } Happening once in a hundred years, واقِع مَرَّة فِي مِائَة سَنَة ـ جِيلِيّ. A hundred, مِائَة. A — festival, عِيد جِيلِيّ.

Centesimal, *n.* جُزْء مِن مِائَة أجْزاء.

Centigrade, *a.* مُرَتَّب عَلَى مِائَة دَرَجَة. A — thermometer, مِيزان الحَرّ مُرَتَّب عَلَى مِائَة دَرَجَة ما بَيْن حَدَّى الانْجِماد والغَلَيان.

Centiped, *n.* أُمّ أرْبَع وَأرْبَعِين.

Central, *a.* Belonging to the middle point, راجِع إلَى مَرْكَزِيّ ـ مُخْتَصّ بِالمَرْكَز ـ المَرْكَز. Middle, مُتَوَسِّط. A — point, مَرْكَز ـ نُقْطَة مُتَوَسِّطَة. Central administration, إدارَة مَرْكَزِيَّة. Central Asia, أواسِط آسِيا ـ آسِيا الوُسْطَى.

Centrality, *n.* مَرْكَزِيَّة ـ رَكْزَة ـ تَوَسُّط.

Centralization, *n.* تَرْجِيع وَتَجْمِيع إلَى مَرْكَز واحِد.

Centralize, *v.t.* رَجَّع ـ وَجَمَّع ـ إلَى مَرْكَز واحِد.

Centrally, *ad.* فِي المَرْكَز ـ فِي الوَسَط.

Centre, *n.* As of a circle, مَرْكَز ـ وَسَط. The middle or heart of any thing, كَبِد. The point to which things tend, مَرْجِع. The —, as of a town or army, وَسَط ـ قَلْب. A place of gathering, a rendezvous, مَعْهَد.

Centre, *v.t.* To place in the —, وَسَّط. To be placed in the —, أُقِيمَ فِي الوَسَط ـ رُكِّب فِي المَرْكَز ـ تَوَسَّطَ. To repose on, confide in, إتَّكَى عَلَى ـ إتَّكَل عَلَى. All her love is centered on her child, مَحَبَّتها مُشْتَمِلَة عَلَى وَلَدها.

Centre-bit, *n.* مِثْقَب ـ مِبْزَل.

Centrifugal, *a.* مُتَباعِد مِن المَرْكَز ـ مُتَباعِد مِن الوَسَط.

Centripetal, *a.* مائِل إلَى الوَسَط ـ مائِل إلَى المَرْكَز.

Centuple, *a.* مِائَة ضِعْف.

Centuple, *v.t.* ضاعَف الواحِد مِائَة.

Centurion, *n.* قائِد مِائَة.

Century, *n.* قَرْن *pl.* قُرُون ـ مِائَة سَنَة. The last —, العَصْر السابِق.

Cephalalgia, *n.* وَجَع الرَّأس ـ غَوْل ـ صُداع.

Cephalic, *a.* Connected with the head, مُخْتَصّ بِالرأس ـ رأسِيّ. A — vein, قِيفال.

Cephalic, *n.* A medicine for the head, عِلاج لِلصُّداع.

Cephalotribe, *n.* A surgical instrument, used in midwifery, مِفْدَغ.

Ceraceous, *a.* مِثْلَ ٱلشَّمْعِ ـ شَمْعِيٌّ.

Cerastes, *n.* حَيَّةٌ قَرْنَآءُ.

Cerate, *n.* مَرْهَمٌ مُرَكَّبٌ مِنْ شَمْعٍ وَزَيْتٍ.

Cerberus, *n.* كَلْبُ جَهَنَّمَ.

Cere, *v.t.* شَمَّعَ.

Cereals, *n.* Edible grain, غِلَال ـ حُبُوب ـ بِذَار ـ مُغَلَّات ـ غَلَّات.

Cerebellum, *n.* مُخَيْخ ـ مُؤَخَّرُ ٱلْمُخِّ.

Cerebral, *a.* دِمَاغِيٌّ ـ مُخِّيٌّ ـ مُخْتَصٌّ بِٱلْمُخِّ.

Cerebrum, *n.* مُقَدَّمُ ٱلْمُخِّ.

Cerecloth, *n.* مُشَمَّع.

Cerement, *n.* قِمَاطُ ٱلتَّحْنِيطِ.

Ceremonial, *a.* Relating to external forms of courtesy and respect, مُتَعَلِّقٌ بِٱلتَّشْرِيفَاتِ ـ مُتَعَلِّقٌ بِٱلتَّبْجِيلِ ـ رَسْمِيٌّ ـ إِحْتِفَالِيٌّ. Pertaining to ritual, طُقُوسِيٌّ ـ مُخْتَصٌّ بِٱلطُّقُوسِ.

Ceremonial, *n.* Prescriptive formality, تَبْجِيل ـ تَشْرِيف ـ لِاتِّفَات ـ أُصُول ـ قَوَاعِد ـ إِحْتِفَال. An external rite, قَانُون *pl.* قَوَانِين ـ طَقْس *pl.* طُقُوس. The — of the Church, طَقْس ٱلْكَنِيسَةِ ـ مَنْسِك *pl.* مَنَاسِك.

Ceremonious, *a.* Full of ceremony, كَثِيرُ ـ صَاحِبُ تَكْلِيفٍ ـ مُتَكَلِّفٌ بِٱلتَّشْرِيفَاتِ ـ ٱلتَّكَالِيف.

Ceremoniously, *ad.* بِٱحْتِفَالٍ ـ بِٱلتَّكْلِيفِ.

Ceremoniousness, *n.* *See* Ceremony, *n.*

Ceremony, *n.* An external form generally, رَسْم *pl.* رُسُوم; in religion, شِعَارَة ـ طُقُوس *pl.* طَقْس ـ مَنَاسِك *pl.* مَنْسِك ـ تَشْرِيف ـ تَبْجِيل ـ إِكْرَام ـ إِحْتِفَال. Forms of civility, شَعَائِر ـ وَاجِبَات. Pomp, وَكَبْكَبَة ـ زِينَة ـ آئين. Importunate civility, كُلْفَة ـ تَكْلِيف ـ تَنَبُّه. Religious duties not obligatory, سُنَن ـ ٱلزَّوَائِد. There is no — between friends, لا تَكْلِيفَ بَيْنَ ٱلْمُحِبِّينَ. Where friendship exists — ceases, إِذَا حَصَلَتِ ٱلْأُلْفَةُ سَقَطَتِ ٱلْكُلْفَةُ. Without —, مِنْ غَيْرِ ـ بِلَا تَكْلِيفٍ ـ مِنْ غَيْرِ تَكْلِيفٍ ـ أَدَقّ. Ceremonies (generally), رُسُوم. To stand on —, تَكَلَّفَ ـ تَكَلَّفَ ـ فِي ٱلتَّشْرِيفَاتِ. *See also under* Formality, *n.*

Cereous, *a.* *See* Ceraceous, *a.*

Certain, *a.* Sure, indubitable, حَقِيقِيّ ـ مُؤَكَّد ـ وَكِيد ـ يَقِين ـ عَيْنُ ٱلْيَقِينِ ـ لَا رَيْبَ فِيهِ ـ مُحَقَّق. Fixed, settled, وَكِيد ـ مُقَرَّر ـ مُحَدَّد ـ مُعَيَّن ـ مَعْلُوم ـ ثَابِت. True, صَحِيح. Inevitable, لَا بُدَّ مِنْهُ ـ مُؤَكَّد. Some, some one, بَعْض ـ مَا. Fixed, as an abode, مُسْتَقِيم ـ مُسْتَقَرّ. A — king, مَلِكٌ مَا. He entered a — village, دَخَلَ قَرْيَةً مَا. Certain persons, بَعْض ـ قَوْم ـ بَعْض ـ أَشْخَاص. Certain things, بَعْضُ أَشْيَاءَ. A — night, فِي بَعْضِ ٱللَّيَالِي ـ ذَاتَ لَيْلَةٍ. For a — thing, لِأَمْرٍ مَا. For a — time, عَلَى مَمَرِّ ٱلزَّمَانِ ـ لِمُدَّةٍ مَا. Certain of your poets, بَعْضُ شُعَرَآئِكُمْ. He was cast into prison for a — rebellion, أُلْقِيَ فِي ٱلسِّجْنِ لِفِتْنَةٍ مَا. A — man, رَجُلٌ مِنَ ٱلرِّجَالِ ـ رَجُلٌ مَا. We have no — dwelling, مَا لَنَا مَوْضِعُ إِقَامَةٍ. It is certain, لَا شَكَّ ـ لَا مُحَالَ ـ لَا بُدَّ مِنْهُ. For certain, يَقِينًا. Certainly (in reply to a question), إِلَّا ـ ٱلْبَتَّةَ.

Certainly, *ad.* Indubitably, عَلَى ٱلتَّحْقِيقِ ـ تَحْقِيقًا ـ يَقِينًا ـ حَقًّا ـ عَلَى ٱلْيَقِينِ ـ تَوْكِيدًا. Without fail, عَلَى كُلِّ حَالٍ ـ مِنْ كُلِّ بُدٍّ.

Certainness, *n.* } Exemption from doubt, ٱلعِلْمُ ٱلْيَقِينُ ـ يَقِين ـ صِحَّة ـ حَقّ. Stability, ثَبَات ـ إِثْبَات ـ دَوَام ـ قَرَار.
Certainty, *n.* } The real state of the case, حَقِيقَةُ ـ ٱلْحَقِيقَةُ ٱلْأَمْرِ. I know this for a —, هٰذَا عِنْدِي مُؤَكَّدٌ وَمُحَقَّقٌ. There is no — in worldly matters, أُمُورُ ٱلدُّنْيَا مَا لَهَا قَرَارٌ. He could not know the — of the matter on account of the uproar, مَا قَدَرَ أَنْ يَعْلَمَ حَقِيقَةَ ٱلْأَمْرِ مِنَ ٱلضَّجَّةِ.

Certes, *ad.* ٱلْبَتَّةَ ـ حَقًّا.

Certificate, *n.* A testimonial in writing, وَرَقَةُ شَهَادَةٍ ـ تَقَارِير ـ شَهَادَةٌ نَامَه. A ship's —, بَرَآءَةُ مَرْكَبٍ. A — from a court of law, صَكّ ـ حُجَّة *pl.* حُجَج. A certified document generally, تَذْكَرَة ـ وَرَقَة ـ حُجَّة ـ صِكَاك *and* صُكُوك. A — of baptism, شَهَادَةُ ٱلْعِمَادِ ـ وَرَقَةُ ٱلْمَعْمُودِيَّةِ ـ وَرَقَةُ ٱلتَّنْصِيرِ. A — of death, سَنَدُ ٱلْوَفَاةِ.

Certify, *v.t.* To confirm, حَقَّقَ ـ ثَبَّتَ ـ نَعَمَ بِ. To give information of to, عَرَّفَ ـ بِ ـ أَعْلَمَ ـ بِ.

Certiorari, *n.* أَمْرٌ مِنَ ٱلْمَحْكَمَةِ ٱلْعَالِيَةِ إِلَى مَحْكَمَةٍ دُونَهَا بِإِحْضَارِ سِجِلَّاتِهَا.

Certitude, *n.* *See* Certainty, *n.*

Cerulean, *a.* } أَزْرَق ـ سَمَاوِيّ ـ لَازَوَرْدِيّ.
Ceruleous, }

Cerumen, *n.* أُفّ.

Ceruse, *n.* إِسْفِيدَاج.

Cervical, *a.* عُنُقِيّ.

Cervine, *a.* مِنَ ٱلظِّبَآءِ.

Cesarean, *a.* The — operation, إِخْرَاجُ ٱلْجَنِينِ مِنَ ٱلرَّحِمِ بِٱلْآلَاتِ.

Cess, *n.* وَضِيعَة *pl.* وَضَايِع ـ مَكْس ـ مِيرِيٌّ ـ رَسْم *pl.* رُسُوم.

Cess, *v.t.* *See to* Assess, *v.t.*

Cessation, *n.* تَوَقُّف ـ وُقُوف ـ زَوَال ـ إِنْقِطَاع ـ قَطْع. A — of hostilities, رَفْعُ ٱلسِّلَاحِ ـ ٱلْمُقَاتَلَةِ (or هُدْنَةٌ) مُتَارَكَةٌ.

Cession, *n.* Surrender, تَرْك ـ تَسْلِيم ـ تَخَلٍّ عَن. A making over to, a grant, تَفْوِيض ـ إِعْطَآء.

Cessionary, *n.* One who receives over, مُتَسَلِّم; one who makes over, مُسَلِّم.

Cessment, *n.* *See* Cess, *n.*

Cess-pool, *n.* إِرْدَبَّة ـ بَالُوعَة *pl.* بَوَالِيعُ ـ بَلَّاعَة *pl.* بَلَالِيعُ.

Cesura, *n.* مَقْطَع.

Cetaceous, *a.* }
Cetic, } مِنْ جِنْسِ ٱلْحُوتِ ـ مُخْتَصٌّ بِٱلْحُوتِ ـ حُوتِيٌّ.

Chafe, *v.t.* To warm, دَفَّى ـ سَخَّنَ. To rub, دَلَكَ ـ عَرَكَ ـ مَعَكَ ـ دَعَكَ. To gall, جَرَشَ ـ عَقَرَ. To irritate, أَكْرَبَ ـ أَغَاظَ ـ أَكَانَ ـ أَوْغَرَ. To incense, perfume, طَيَّبَ ـ عَطَّرَ ـ بَخَّرَ. To be chafed, galled, صَرِدَ ـ إِنْعَقَرَ. Chafed between the legs, أَمْذَحُ. To be chafed between the legs, مَذِحَ.

Chafe, *v.i.* To be vexed, حَمِيَ ـ ضَجِرَ ـ إِزْدَعَجَ ـ إِنْزَعَجَ ـ شَاطَ ـ فِي ٱلْغَضَبِ.

Chafe, *n.* Passion, حُمَيًّا ـ فَجْع ـ كَدَر ـ ضَجَر ـ زَعَج ـ حُمُوُّ ٱلْغَضَبِ.

Chafer, *n.* A species of beetle, نَوْعٌ مِنَ ٱلْخَنَافِسِ.

Chaff, *n.* Straw, تِبْن ـ حُتٌّ ـ قَشٌّ. Nonsense, هَجْر ـ هَذَر ـ عَبَث.

Chaffer, *v.i.* شَارَى *See also to* Bargain, *v.i.*

Chafferer, *n.* بَيِّع.

Chaffinch, *n.* The bird, دُجٌّ ـ شَرْشُور.

Chaffy, *a.* تِبْنِيٌّ ـ كَثِيرُ ٱلتِّبْنِ.

Chafing-dish, كَانُون *pl.* كَوَانِينُ ـ مِنْقَل.

Chagrin, *n.* كَرْب ـ ضَجَر ـ زَعَج ـ غَمٌّ ـ إِضْطِرَاب ـ كَسْرُ ٱلْخَاطِرِ.

Chagrin, *v.t.* أَضْجَرَ ـ فَجَّعَ ـ عَنَّى ـ أَزْعَجَ ـ قَلَّقَ ـ أَغَمَّ ـ حَفَا. To be chagrined, إِنْزَعَجَ ـ ضَجِرَ ـ إِضْطَرَبَ ـ تَقَلَّقَ ـ إِغْتَمَّ ـ إِنْغَمَّ.

Chain, *n.* سِلْسِلَة *pl.* سَلَاسِلُ ـ زِنْجِير *pl.* زَنَاجِيرُ. A bond, fetter, قَيْد *pl.* قُيُود. Concatenation, series, مُتَتَابِعَةٌ ـ سَلْسَلَةٌ ـ سِمَاط ـ تَتَابُع ـ نَسَق. Chains, slavery, أَغْلَال ـ عُبُودِيَّة. A — of ideas, أَفْكَارٌ مُتَتَابِعَةٌ.

Chain, *v.t.* To bind with chains, رَبَطَ بِسَلَاسِلَ ـ زَنْجَرَ. To enslave, عَبَّدَ ـ إِسْتَعْبَدَ. To fetter, رَبَطَ ـ قَيَّدَ. To bring into slavery, سَبَى.

Chain-pump, *n.* طُلُومْبَةٌ ذَاتُ لَوَالِبَ.

Chain-shot, *n.* كُلَّةٌ ذَاتُ زِنْجِيرٍ.

Chain-work, *n.* تَسَلْسُل ـ مُسَلْسَلَة.

Chair, *v.t.* طَافَ بِ ـ بِٱبْتِهَاجٍ وَمُبَاهَاةٍ *aor.* يَطُوفُ.

Chair, *n.* كُرْسِيٌّ *pl.* كَرَاسِيُّ. Seat of authority, مِنْبَر. Chair of state, تَخْت ـ مَسْنَد. Professorship, وَظِيفَةُ مُدَرِّسٍ. The — of philosophy, مَدْرَسَةُ ٱلْفَلْسَفَةِ. To take the —, presidency, تَصَدَّرَ. Pray take a —, تَفَضَّلِ ٱجْلِسْ.

Chairman, *n.* President, مُسَيْطِر ـ صَدْرُ ٱلْقَوْمِ ـ رَئِيسُ مَجْلِسٍ. To make one —, صَدَّرَ.

Chaise, *n.* نَوْعٌ مِنَ ٱلْعَجَلَاتِ ٱلْخَفِيفَةِ.

Chalcedony, *n.* أَخْلِيدُونِيَّة ـ عَقِيقٌ أَبْيَضُ.

Chalcography, *n.* ٱلنَّقْشُ فِي ٱلنُّحَاسِ.

Chaldaic, *n.* مُخْتَصٌّ بِٱلْكَلْدَانِ ٱلْقُدَمَآء ـ كَلْدَانِيٌّ عَتِيقٌ.

Chaldean, *n.* كَلْدَانِيٌّ.

Chaldee, *n.* لِسَانُ ٱلْكَلْدَانِ ٱلْقُدَمَآء.

Chaldron, *n.* نَوْعٌ مِنَ ٱلْأَكْيَالِ.

Chalice, *n.* كَأْس *pl.* كَأْسَات *and* كُؤُوس.

Chalk, *n.* طَبَاشِير ـ حَوَّارَة.

Chalk-stone, *n.* Of gout, حَصَاةُ ٱلنِّقْرِسِ.

Chalk, *v.t.* To mark with —, عَلَّمَ بِطَبَاشِيرٍ. To trace out, صَوَّرَ ـ رَسَمَ.

Chalky, *a.* طَبَاشِيرِيٌّ ـ حَوَّارِيٌّ.

Challenge, *v.t.* To call to combat, دَعَا لِلْقِتَالِ ـ إِسْتَدْعَى لِلْمِيدَانِ ـ لِشَرٍّ ـ طَلَبَ. To object to, إِعْتَرَضَ عَلَى ـ رَفَضَ ـ مَا قَبِلَ بِ. To call upon to perform the conditions, طَالَبَ بِٱلْوَعْدِ ـ بِإِنْجَازِ ٱلْمَوْعُودِ ـ أَمَرَ. To arrogate, إِدَّعَى بِ. To accuse, إِتَّهَمَ بِ ـ أَتْهَمَ. He challenged the whole world to make one like it, إِدَّعَى بِأَنَّ مَا يَسْتَطِيعُ أَحَدٌ عَلَى أَنْ يَعْمَلَ مِثْلَهُ.

Challenge, *n.* Summons to combat, إِسْتِدْعَآءٌ لِلْمِيدَانِ ـ طَلَبٌ لِلْمِيدَانِ ـ إِغْرَآءٌ بِٱلْمُبَارَزَةِ. Demand of something due, طَلَب ـ إِدِّعَآء ـ دَعْوَى. Exception against, إِعْتِرَاضٌ عَلَى ـ عَدَمُ قُبُولٍ بِ ـ عَدَمُ ٱلرِّضَآءِ بِ.

Challengeable, *a.* وممّا يُعترَضُ عليهِ.

Challenger, *n.* One who challenges, عادٍ ـ بادٍ ـ مُدَّعٍ. A claimant, طالِب ـ مُدَّعٍ.

Chalybeate, *a.* مَشْرُوبٌ بِحَدِيدٍ ـ ما حَلَّ فِيهِ الحَدِيدُ.

Chalybeate, *n.* Chalybeate water, مَاءٌ حُلَّ فِيهِ الحَدِيدُ.

Chamber, *n.* An apartment in a house, بَيْت ـ قَلَالِ *pl.* قِلِّيَّة *pl.* أُوضَة ـ بُيُوت *pl.* أُوَض *and* أُوضات. A small —, عُلِّيَّة *pl.* عَلالِيّ. A small side —, خِزانَة. An upper —, حُجْرَة *pl.* حُجَر *and* حُجَرات ـ غُرْفَة. A student's — in a mosque, رِواق *pl.* أَرْوِقَة. The — of a gun, الخِزانَة. The — of a mine, نَقْب ـ لَغْم. A court, as of justice, مَحْكَمَة ـ مَجْلِس. Any court or office, دِيوان. Chambers, special apartments of students, رِواق.

Chamberer, *n.* A wanton person, نَيَّاك ـ فاسِق ـ هَوّاس.

Chambering, *n.* Wantonness, فِسْق ـ عَهَر ـ شَبَق ـ هِواس ـ دِعارَة.

Chamberlain, *n.* حاجِب *pl.* حُجّاب. Lord High —, حاجِبُ الحُجّاب.

Chamberlainship, *n.* مَقامُ الحاجِبِ ـ حِجابَة.

Chamber-maid, *n.* ماشِطَة *pl.* مَواشِطُ ـ فَرّاشَة.

Chamber-pot, *n.* قَصْرِيَّة *pl.* قَصارِي ـ أَرْضِيَّة ـ مِسْتَعْمَلَة.

Chameleon, *n.* See Cameleon, *n.*

Chamfer, *v.t.* To cut grooves in, خَطَّطَ. To wrinkle, غَضَّنَ.

Chamfer, *n.* خَطّ *pl.* خُطُوط ـ خَطِيط.

Chamfering, *n.* تَخْطِيط.

Chamois, *n.* أَرْوِيَّة *pl.* أَراوِيّ ـ بَدَن ـ بُدُون ـ تَيْتَل *vulg.* تَيْتَل.

Chamomile, *n.* See Camomile, *n.*

Champ, *v.t.* As a horse the bit, غَضِبَ عَلَى اللِّجامِ ـ صَكَمَ ـ أَلَكَ ـ عَلَكَ ـ لاكَ ـ مَضَغَ ـ قَرْقَرَ. To chew, The horse champed his bit, عَضَّ الفَرَسُ عَلَى لِجامِهِ.

Champagne, *n.* The wine, نَبِيذٌ شامْبانِيا. Still —, شامْبانِيا غَيْرُ فائِرٍ.

Champaign, *n.* دَشْت ـ صَحْراء.

Champion, *n.* A defender, حامٍ *pl.* حُماة ـ مُناجِد. A combatant, غازٍ *pl.* غُزاة ـ مُبارِز ـ خَصْم *pl.* خِصام. A warrior, بَطَل *pl.* أَبْطال ـ ابْنُ حَرْبٍ.

Chance, *n.* Cause of fortuitous events, بَخْت ـ طالِع ـ الدَّهْر ـ الأَيّام ـ قِسْمَة ـ نَصِيب. An act of fortune, بَخْت ـ عارِض *pl.* عَوارِض. A fortuitous occurrence, قَضاء ـ نَصِيب ـ مُصادَفَة ـ اتِّفاق. A lucky —, بَرَكَة ـ حَظّ. An unlucky —, مُصِيبَة ـ حادِث. An opportunity, فُرْصَة. The chances of the times, صُرُوفُ الدَّهْرِ. The changes and chances of this life, تَقَلُّباتُ هٰذا العالَمِ المُخْتَلِفَة. By —, *à propos*, اتِّفاقًا. By —, possibly, لَعَلَّ. By — a man came down that way, اتَّفَقَ أَنَّ رَجُلًا كانَ نازِلًا فِي ذٰلِكَ الطَّرِيقِ. By —, accidentally, عَرَضًا ـ بِالمُصادَفَةِ ـ مِنْ غَيْرِ قَصْدٍ. To take one's —, رَكِبَ رَأْسَهُ ـ تَعَرَّضَ لِلنَّصِيبِ. How many chances they had! ما أَكْثَرَهُمْ مِنَ الفُرَصِ.

Chance, *a.* تَصادُفِيّ ـ اتِّفاقِيّ ـ عَرَضِيّ.

Chance, *v.i.* To happen, حَصَلَ ـ صارَ ـ حَدَثَ ـ جَرَى. To risk, خاطَرَ بِ. It may — to be to-day or to-morrow, رُبَّما يَكُونُ اليَوْمَ أَوْ غَدًا.

Chancel, *n.* Of a church, بَيْتُ المَقْدِسِ ـ مَذْبَح; of a mosque, مِحْراب.

Chancellor, *n.* Chief officer of justice, قاضِي قُضاة. Chancellor of the Exchequer, رَئِيسُ مَحْكَمَةِ مالِ الخِزانَةِ. One who holds the sovereign's seal, حامِلُ طابَعِ المَلِكِ. Chancellor of a university, ناظِرُ دارِ الفُنُونِ. Chancellor of a cathedral, مُدِيرُ الكَنِيسَةِ المَطْرانِيَّةِ.

Chancellorship, *n.* إِدارَة ـ نِظارَة.

Chancery, *n.* مَجْلِسُ العَدْلِيَّةِ ـ دِيوانُ مَحْكَمَةِ العَدالَةِ.

Chancre, *n.* تَأْكُولَة ـ آكِلَة ـ أَكِلَة.

Chancrous, تَأْكُولِيّ.

Chandelier, *n.* ثُرَيّا ـ مَنارَةٌ بِجُمْلَةِ قَنادِيلَ ـ شَمْعَدانٌ كَبِيرٌ.

Chandler, *n.* A seller of candles, شَمّاع. A small shopkeeper, بَقّال ـ سُوقِيّ ـ بَيِّع.

Chandlery, *n.* أَمْتِعَةُ بَقّالٍ ـ أَمْتِعَة.

Change, *v.t.* To put one thing in the place of another, بَدَّلَ ـ غَيَّرَ. To — for, to exchange, بَدَلَ ـ بِ ـ غَيَّرَ ـ بِ. To —, or exchange something with one, قاوَضَ ـ فِي ـ بادَلَ ـ فِي. To — coin for other money, صَرَفَ ـ بِ. To bring back to a former state, to convert, أَعادَ. To — into, حَوَّلَ ـ إِلَى ـ قَلَبَ. To — one's residence, تَحَوَّلَ ـ حالَ مِنْ مَكانِهِ. To — one's clothes, غَيَّرَ ثِيابَهُ. To — into a viler shape, as into that of a brute, مَسَخَ. To — the disposition, غَيَّرَ الطَّبْعَ. To — one's views, عَدَلَ عَنْ ـ أَحالَ رَأْيَهُ. To — for the worse, أَخْلَفَ. They changed the glory of God into an idol, إِسْتَبْدَلُوا مَجْدَ اللّٰهِ بِصَنَمٍ.

Change, *v.i.* To undergo a —, تَغَيَّرَ ـ تَبَدَّلَ ـ تَقالَبَ ـ إِسْتَحالَ. To —, to repent, تابَ. His colour changed,

لَوْنُهُ (حَالَ *or*) إِسْتَحَالَ. To — for the worse, خَلِفَ ع. He has not changed from what he was, لَمْ يَتَغَيَّرْ عَمَّا كَانَ سَابِقًا.

Change, *n.* Alteration of state, تَغَيُّر ـ تَقَلُّب ـ تَغْيِير ـ إِنْقِلَاب ـ تَحْوِيل ـ تَبْدِيل. Conversion, رَدّ ـ عِيَاد. Conversion into, إِسْتِحَالَة ـ إِحَالَة ـ قَلْب. Exchange, مُبَادَلَة. Change of money, صَرْف. Small money, فُرَاطَة ـ فُلُوس ـ خُرْدَة. Succession, خِلَافَة ـ تَعَاقُب. A — in one's estate, صَرْف. The changes of fortune, طَوَارِحُ ٱلزَّمَنِ ـ حَالَاتُ ٱلدَّهْرِ ـ تَقَلُّبَاتُ ٱلْأَحْوَالِ. The changes of the moon, أَدْوَارُ ٱلْقَمَرِ. A — of apparel, بَدْلَةٌ مِنَ ٱلثِّيَابِ *pl.* بَدْلَات ـ بَدْلَةٌ مِنَ ٱلثِّيَابِ.

Changeable, *a.* Subject to alteration, مُغَيَّر ـ مُتَغَيِّر. Inconstant, مُتَلَوِّن ـ فَرَّار ـ مُتَقَلْقِل ـ طَائِش. That may be changed, يُصْرَفُ ـ مُمْكِنٌ تَحْوِيلُهُ. Changeable in opinions, ذُو بَدَوَاتٍ.

Changeableness, *n.* تَلَوُّن ـ قِلَّةُ ثَبَاتٍ ـ عَدَمُ قَرَارٍ ـ إِنْقِلَاب ـ تَغْيِير.

Changeful, *a.* *See* Changeable, *a.*

Changeless, *a.* ثَابِت ـ مُقَرَّر ـ بِلَا تَغَيُّرٍ.

Changeling, *n.* A supposititious child, وَضِيعَة. A waverer, مُتَرَدِّد ـ مُتَلَوِّن ـ مُتَحَيِّر ـ شَقْلَبَانِيّ.

Changer, *n.* Of money, صَرَّاف *pl.* صَيَارِفُ *and* صَيَارِفَة.

Channel, *n.* The bed of a stream, مَجْرًى *pl.* مَجَارٍ. Road, passage, مَعْبَر ـ مَمَرّ ـ طَرِيقَة ـ مَجَاز. A gutter for running water, مَجْرًى ـ قَنَاة *pl.* قُنِيّ. A narrow sea, خَلِيج *pl.* خُلْجَان ـ بُوغَاز. Means to an end, طَرِيقَة ـ وَاسِطَة ـ وَصِيلَة. A — for tears, مَدْمَع *pl.* مَدَامِعُ.

Chant, *v.t.* رَتَّلَ. To — in a quick quavering manner, دَرَجَ ع ـ أَدْرَجَ. To celebrate, مَدَحَ ـ مَدَّحَ ـ غَنَّى بِ.

Chant, *v.i.* أَرْسَلَ ٱلتَّرْتِيلَ ـ أَرْسَلَ ٱلْغِنَاءَ. He chanted the preface, أَرْسَلَ ٱلْإِقَامَةَ.

Chant, *n.* تَرْتِيل ـ غِنَاء ـ دَرْج.

Chanter, *n.* Of a church, مُرَتِّل ـ أَرْشِيّ *pl.* أَرْشِيَة. Chantress, مُرَتِّلَة.

Chanticleer, *n.* دِيك ـ أَبُو يَقْظَانٍ.

Chanting, *n.* إِرْسَالُ ٱلْغِنَاءِ ـ تَرْتِيل.

Chantry, *n.* مَعْبَدٌ (*or* كَنِيسَةٌ صَغِيرَةٌ) يُقَدِّمُونَ فِيهَا ٱلدُّعَاءَ عَنْ أَرْوَاحِ ٱلْأَمْوَاتِ.

Chaos, *n.* Voidness, هَوَاء ـ خَوَاء. Confusion, إِخْتِلَالٌ كُلِّيّ ـ خِلْط ـ إِخْلَاط ـ تَشْوِيش ـ خَبْصَة ـ لَخْبَطَة ـ هَرْجٌ مَرْج.

Chaotic, *a.* Void, خَوَائِيّ ـ خَاوٍ ـ خَالٍ. Confused, مَرِيج ـ مُتَشَوِّش ـ مُتَبَلْبِل ـ مُلَخْبَط.

Chap, *n.* A fissure, وَقْرَة *pl.* وُقُور ـ شَقّ *pl.* شُقُوق ـ فَلَق *pl.* أَفْلَاق. A — in the lip, ثَرْد; in the feet, سَلَع *pl.* سُلُوع. A jaw, فَكّ *pl.* أَفْكَاك. A youth, جَذَع *pl.* جُذْعَان ـ غُلَام *pl.* غِلْمَان.

Chap, *v.t.* To crack, وَقَرَ ـ شَقَّ ع ـ شَقَّقَ ـ فَلَجَ ع.

Chap, *v.t.* To open, crack, تَفَلَّجَ ـ إِنْفَلَعَ ـ تَفَلَّعَ ـ إِنْشَقَّ. To have chaps on the feet, سَلِعَ. His foot became chapped, تَفَلَّجَتْ قَدَمُهُ.

Chapel, *n.* A small church, كَنِيسَةٌ صَغِيرَةٌ ـ مَعْبَد. A small mosque, زَاوِيَة ـ مَعْبَد. Any place of devotion, مَسْجِد *pl.* مَسَاجِدُ.

Chapelet, *n.* } A garland, إِكْلِيل *pl.* أَكَالِيلُ ـ إِكْلِيلُ زَهْرٍ. A
Chaplet, } rosary, سُبْحَة ـ مِسْبَحَة *pl.* مَسَابِحُ.

Chapelry, *n.* مَقَامُ ٱلْمَسْجِدِ ـ مَقَامُ ٱلْمَعْبَدِ.

Chaperon, *v.t.* رَافَقَ إِلَى مَحَافِلِ ٱلْإِجْتِمَاعَاتِ لِأَجْلِ ٱلتَّدْرِيبِ فِي عِلْمِ ٱلسُّلُوكِ وَٱلْمُرَاقَبَةِ.

Chaperon, *n.* مَنْ يُرَافِقُ ٱلشَّابَّاتِ إِلَى مَحَافِلِ ٱلْإِجْتِمَاعَاتِ لِأَجْلِ ٱلتَّدْرِيبِ فِي عِلْمِ ٱلسُّلُوكِ وَٱلْمُرَاقَبَةِ ـ دَيْدَبَان.

Chapfallen, *a.* مُنْقَطِعُ ٱلْقَلْبِ ـ مُخْتَبِط ـ مَبْهُوتٌ وَمَدْهُوش ـ مَعْيُوب ـ مَفْشُول.

Chapiter, *n.* رَأْسُ عَمُودٍ ـ عَمُودٍ (*or* إِكْلِيلُ) تَاجُ *pl.* تِيجَان.

Chaplain, *n.* قَسّ *pl.* قُسُوس ـ قِسِّيس. The — of a mosque, إِمَام *pl.* أَيِمَّة.

Chaplaincy, *n.* وَظِيفَةُ ٱلْقَسِّ.

Chaplet, *n.* *See* Chapelet, *n.*

Chapman, *n.* شَارٍ ـ مُشْتَرٍ ـ مُتَسَبِّب ـ زَبُون ـ مُعَامِل.

Chaps, *n.* The mouth or jaws, فَم ـ خَشْم ـ فُكُوك.

Chapter, *n.* Division of a book, بَاب *pl.* أَبْوَاب ـ فَصْل *pl.* فُصُول. A —, as of the Kurân, سُورَة *pl.* سُوَر. A — of the clergy, مَجْمَعُ ٱلْإِكْلِيرُوسِ. An association, جَمْعِيَّة.

Char, *v.t.* أَحْرَقَ ـ صَيَّرَ فَحْمًا.

Char, *n.* Work done by the day, شُغْلٌ يَوْمِيّ.

Charwoman, *n.* مُسْتَأْجَرَةٌ بِٱلْيَوْمِيَّةِ.

Character, *n.* Mark, stamp, رَسْم ـ رَقْم ـ عَلَامَة ـ إِشَارَة. A figure used in writing, حَرْف ـ قَلَم ـ كِتَابَة. Handwriting, قَلَم ـ خَطّ. Description of any thing good or bad, وَصْف ـ نَعْت ـ صِفَة. Disposition, أَوْصَاف ـ خِلْقَة ـ سَجِيَّة ـ خَلِيقَة ـ طَبْع ـ طَبِيعَة ـ خَصْلَة. Reputation, إِسْم ـ صِيت ـ شُهْرَة. Kind, quality,

مادية – جنس – نوع – صنف. A certificate of —, ورقة شهادة. A —, oddity, رجل غريب. In —, مطابق. Out of —, غير مطابق. What is their general national —? ما هي سجاياهم. He has the — of being very liberal, هو مشهور بالسخاوة. The — given of him is bad, صيته ردئ. His — is praised everywhere, إسمه ممدوح عند الكل. The — of the soil is clayey, جنس الأرض طيني. A public or official —, صاحب منصب. Written in small characters, منمل.

To clear the character of one, بيض وجهه.

To clear one's own character, برأ ذمته.

To injure the character of one, بهت – طعن بصيته.

To take away the character of one, أتلف صيت – خرب صيت.

Character, *v.t.* To mark, inscribe, علم – عين على – كتب على. To describe, وصف *aor.* يصف.

Characteristic, *a.* / Characteristical, } خاص – مميز – تعريفي – بياني – مخصوص. It was quite — of him, ما يميز الشيء عن غيره. هذا من عين أوصافه. It is — of, points to, يدل على.

Characteristic, *n.* سجية *pl.* سجايا – ضريبة – وصف *pl.* أوصاف – نعت – صفة *pl.* صفات. Characteristics (good), مرجوحة – فضائل – محاسن – شمائل; bad —, رذائل.

Characterize, *v.t.* وصف *aor.* يصف – إختص-ب – خص-ب – توصف ب – إتصف ب. To be characterized by, — To be deemed, حسب.

Charade, *n.* لغز *or* لغز *or* لغز *pl.* ألغاز.

Charcoal, *n.* فحم – فحم. A piece of coal or —, فحمة *pl.* فحمات. A seller of —, فحام.

Charge, *v.t.* To entrust with, إستأمن-على – آمن-على – وكل-على – أمر-ب – أوصى-ب – عهد إلى. To command, وصى. To — with a commission, وكل – وصى. To —, as with a commission to do anything, عهد إلى-ب. To — or impute to, نسب-إلى. To —, as with a crime, to accuse, إشتكى على-ب – إتهم-ب – أتهم-ب – قرف على. To — with, to censure for, لام – عير-ب. To admonish, نصح. To —, as a gun, دك – عمر. To load, as a burden on, حمل. To ask, as of a price, طلب. To fall on, to attack, حمل – زحف على – أغار على – شد على – هجم على – على. To — with, to throw upon, حمل-على. To — with errors, غلط. How much do you — for this? كم – كم تطلب بهذا. Nothing worthy of death was charged against him, تشكى بهذا لم يشك بشيء يوجب الموت. Charge it to the government, ضمه إلى حسابي. Charge it to my account, إحسبه على الميري. I will not be charged, saddled, with it, لم أتكلف به. He is charged, entrusted, with its execution, هو منوط بعهدته.

Charge, *n.* Custody, care, إعتناء – حفظ – حياطة – حراسة – عهدة. The thing entrusted, عهدة – وضيعة – أمانة. Injunction, عهد – حكم – وصية – أمر – خدمة. Commission, وكالة. Accusation, شكوى – شكاية – ذم – تهمة. Expense, كلفة – حملة – خرج – مصروف. Cost, ثمن – سعر. Attack, وقعة – إقتحام – غارة – كبة – شدة – هجوم. A — of ammunition, عمار بارود. Office, وظيفة – منصب. Price asked, طلب. Your —, is high, ثمنك غال. Lay not this sin to my —, لا تقم لي هذه الخطيئة. Without —, gratis, مجانا – بلا نفقة. At one's own —, على كيسه – بمعونة نفسه. He gave him in — to the police, سلمه إلى الضبطية. To take in —, to receive, تسلم. They brought it to his —, أقاموا الحجة عليه. Each division of it is under the — of an official, كل قسم منه يناط بعهدة مأمور. Unfounded charges, شكايات فارغة. *See also under* Cartridge, *n.*

Chargeable, *a.* Imputable to, مما يشكى على-ب – يتهم ب – نقل على – كلف. To be — to, at the expense of, يحسب ل. That we might not be — to any one, حتى لا نكلف أحدا.

Chargeableness, *n.* Expensiveness, ثمن – غلاء.

Chargé d'Affaires, *n.* مصلحتكذار – وكيل مصالح.

Charger, *n.* A dish, تبسي – صحن – طبق. A horse, حصان الهجوم *pl.* حصن – حصان.

Charily, *ad.* Warily, إحتياطا – على عين. Frugally, متقشفا – بتوفير – بتقتير.

Chariness, *n.* Wariness, إحتياط – حذر. Frugality, تقشف – توفير.

Chariot, *n.* عجلة – عربانة – مركبة.

Charioteer, *n.* ماسك العنان – سائق العربانة.

Charitable, *a.* Kind in giving alms, محسن للفقراء – متصدق. Benevolent, محب – كريم – ذو فضل – محسن – خير.

Charitableness, *n.* *See* Charity, *n.*

Charitably, *ad.* إحسانا – متصدقا – بكرم.

Charity, *n.* Love, ود – حب. Liberality to the poor, حسنة – حسن – كرم – ذكاة – صدقة. Compassion, ترحم. Benevolence, معروف – فضل. To bestow — upon, تصدق على.

Charlatan, *n.* حول قلب – خراط – فشار – بهلوان – عيار – مزور.

Charlatanry, *n.* مَكْر ـ خَرَاطَة ـ فَشْر.

Charles's-wain, *n.* اَلدُّبُّ ٱلْأَكْبَرُ.

Charm, *n.* An amulet, عُوذَة *pl.* عُوَذ ـ مَعَاذَة *pl.* مَعَاذَات ـ طَلْسَم ـ حُرْز ـ حِجَاب ـ تَعَاوِيذ *pl.* تَعْوِيذ. Enchantment, سِحْر. Something attracting the affections, مَا فِيهِ مَلَاحَة ـ طَلَاوَة. Beauty, مَلَاحَة ـ حَلَاوَة ـ جَمَال ـ لَطَافَة ـ حُسْن. Charms, spells, عَزَائِم. A written — against disease, رُقْيَة ـ عُوذَة. Charms for ornament attached to the girdle, تَعْلِيقَات ـ نَعَانِعُ.

Charm, *v.t.* To enchant, سَحَرَ ـ سَحَّرَ ـ رَقَى. To subdue by secret power, سَلَبَ ـ سَبَى ٱلْعَقْلَ ـ أَفْتَنَ ـ رَقَى ـ عَوَّذَ ٱلْقَلْبَ. To subdue into admiration, أَذْهَلَ ـ حَيَّرَ. To —, as of a serpent, رَقَى ـ صَدَّ. *See also to* Delight, Enrapture, *v.t.*

Charm, *v.i.* To be delighted with, تَأَنَّقَ فِي ـ إِنْحَظَّ بِ ـ حَلَا لِ ـ تَغَبَّطَ بِ ـ عَاجَ بِ.

Charmed, *a.* Bewitched, مَسْحُور. Delighted, مَسْرُور ـ مَحْظُوظ.

Charmer, *n.* An enchanter, سَحَّار ـ سَاحِر ـ مُعَزِّم. A serpent —, حَاوٍ ـ حَوَّآء. A beloved woman, مَحْبُوبَة.

Charming, *a.* Bewitching, مُسْحِر ـ مُعَزِّم. Highly pleasing, حَيِّر ـ جَمِيلٌ لِلْغَايَة ـ حُلْو ـ بَدِيع ـ حَبَّذَا. How — he, she, or it is to me! مَا أَحَبَّهُ إِلَيَّ. A perfectly — woman, إِمْرَأَةٌ كَامِلَةُ ٱلْأَوْصَافِ بَدِيعَةُ ٱلْحُسْنِ مَلِيحَةُ ٱلْأَطْرَافِ. A — prospect, مَنْظَرٌ بَهِيج ـ مَنْظَرٌ يَسْحَرُ. The woman was — to me, حَلِيَتِ ٱلْمَرْأَةُ بِعَيْنِي.

Charmingly, *ad.* حَسَنًا ـ بِحَلَاوَة ـ بِحَظٍّ.

Charnel-house, *n.* مَقْبَرَة ـ مَطْمُورَةُ عِظَامِ ٱلْمَوْتَى.

Charred, *a.* مَحْرُوق.

Charry, *a.* مِثْلُ ٱلْفَحْمِ.

Chart, *n.* خَارِطَة *pl.* خَارِطَات ـ وَرَقَةُ رَسْمِ ٱلْبِلَادِ.

Charter, *n.* A writing bestowing privileges, بَرَآءَة *pl.* بَرَآآت ـ فِرْمَان *pl.* فَرَامِين ـ عَهْدَنَامَه ـ خَطٌّ شَرِيف. A royal —, فِرْمَان. Immunity, إِعْفَآء ـ مُعَافَاة ـ بَرَآءَة.

Charter, *v.t.* To — a vessel, إِسْتَأْجَرَ (*or* إِسْتَكْرَى) مَرْكَبًا.

Charter-party, *n.* سَنَدٌ ـ حُجَّةٌ بَيْنَ رَئِيسِ ٱلْمَرْكَبِ وَٱلْمُسْتَأْجِرِ. مُقَاوَلَة.

Chary, *a.* Careful, wary, مُتَحَذِّر ـ مُنْتَبِه. Frugal, مُوَفِّر ـ مُقْتَصِد.

Chase, *v.t.* To hunt, as of game, صَادَ ـ تَصَيَّدَ ـ إِصْطَادَ ـ قَنَصَ. To pursue, as an enemy, طَرَدَ ـ طَارَدَ ـ إِقْتَفَى ـ لَاحَقَ ـ تَبِعَ. To follow after with desire, جَدَّ فِي طَلَبِ ـ سَعَى فِي طَلَبِ ـ عَقَّبَ فِي. To — away, صَرَفَ ـ شَرَّدَ. To — away, as of flies, كَشَّ ـ كَشْكَشَ. To — a vessel, طَرَدَ مَرْكَبًا ـ تَبِعَ مَرْكَبًا. To — from, أَذْهَبَ عَنْ. To emboss, نَقَشَ ـ قَلَّمَ.

Chase, *n.* Hunting, صَيْدَة ـ صَيْد ـ قَنْص. What is taken in hunting, قَنَص ـ مَصِيد. Pursuit, as of a person, طِرَاد ـ مُطَارَدَة ـ مُكَارَدَة ـ تَعْقِيب. Endeavour, مَسْعَاة ـ سَعْيٌ. Pursuit of something desirable, طَلَب ـ جِدٌّ فِي ـ إِرَادَةٌ إِلَى ـ رَغْبَةٌ فِي. Hunting-ground, مُصْطَاد ـ مَصَاد. A printer's —, قَرْوَاز *vulg.* بَرْوَاز.

Chaser, *n.* A hunter, قَنَّاص ـ صَيَّاد. A driver, طَارِد.

Chasm, *n.* سِلْع *pl.* سُلُوع ـ فَتْحَة ـ شَقّ ـ قَاع ـ قَعْر *pl.* ثُغُور ـ خَلَل *pl.* خِلَال. A void, فَرَاغ ـ جَوْف.

Chassepot, *n.* بُنْدُقِيَّةٌ مِنَ ٱلْبَنَادِقِ ٱلْمُسَمَّاةِ بِٱلشَّاسْبُو.

Chaste, *a.* Abstinent from illicit pleasures, عَفِيف ـ وَرِع. Pure, صَافٍ ـ خَالِص ـ صَرِيح ـ طَاهِرُ ٱلنَّفْسِ. Neat, ظَرِيف ـ لَطِيف. Chaste, as in style of writing, مُحَبَّر ـ مَضْبُوط; in speech, فَصِيح ـ فَتِيقُ ٱللِّسَانِ.

Chastely, *ad.* With abstinence, بِعِفَّة. Purely, بِصَفَاوَة ـ بِخُلُوص. Neatly, بِلَطَافَة ـ ظَرَافَة; of style, بِتَحْبِير ـ بِضَبْط ـ بِفَصَاحَة.

Chasten, *v.t.* To punish, عَذَّبَ ـ عَاقَبَ ـ قَاصَصَ. To correct, عَزَّرَ ـ وَبَّخَ ـ أَدَّبَ ـ نَبَّهَ.

Chasteness, *n.* Purity, صَفَاوَة ـ نَقَاوَة. Neatness, لَطَافَة ـ ظَرَافَة; of style, تَحْبِير ـ ضَبْط ـ فَصَاحَة. To speak with —, أَفْصَحَ فِي ٱلْكَلَامِ. To affect — of style, تَفَصَّحَ.

Chastening, *n.* *See* Chastisement, *n.*

Chastise, *v.t.* *See to* Chasten, *v.t.*

Chastisement, *n.* Punishment, تَعْذِيب ـ عَذَاب ـ عِقَاب ـ عُقُوبَة ـ قِصَاص. Correction, تَعْزِير ـ تَوْبِيخ ـ تَأْدِيب.

Chastiser, *n.* مُقَاصِص ـ مُؤَدِّب.

Chastity, *n.* Purity from the illicit, عِصْمَة ـ عِفَّة ـ وَرَع ـ رِعَة ـ إِمْتِنَاعٌ عَنِ ٱلشَّهَوَاتِ. *See also* Chasteness, *n.*

Chasuble, *n.* نَوْعٌ مِنَ ٱلْحُلَلِ لِلْقُسُوسِ.

Chat, *v.i.* تَكَلَّمَ ـ هَذْرَبَ ـ لَهْوَقَ ـ سَايَرَ ـ لَقْشَ. To — with, حَاوَرَ ـ فَاوَهَ. To — in the evening, سَامَرَ. They chatted together, تَفَاوَهُوا.

Chat, *n.* هَذْرَبَة ـ لَهْوَقَة ـ مُحَاوَرَة ـ قِيلٌ وَقَالٌ. An evening —, مُسَامَرَة.

Chateau, *n.* قَصْر *pl.* قُصُور ـ بَيْت ـ مَسْكَن *pl.* مَسَاكِن.

Chatelaine, *n.* *See* Chain, *n.*

Chattels, *n.* هَمّ ـ مَتَاع ـ أَثَاث ـ أَشْيَاء ـ مَنْقُولَات.

Chatter, *v.i.* To prate, زَحْلَفَ فِي ٱلْكَلَامِ ـ أَكْثَرَ ٱلْقَوْلَ ـ ² بَقَّ ـ هَذْرَمَ. To —, as birds, عَقْعَقَ بِصَوْتِهِ ـ صَاحَ ـ ² زَقَعَ ـ طَرْطَقَ. To —, as of the teeth, قَفْقَفَ ـ ² صَرَّ ـ ² نَقَّ ـ كَأْكَأَ. His teeth chattered, قُرْقِفَتْ أَسْنَانُهُ ـ إِصْطَكَّتْ أَسْنَانُهُ. *See also to* Prate, *v.i.*

Chatter, *n.* Prattle, بَقّ ـ قِيل وَقَال ـ هَذْرَمَة ـ لَقْش. Noise of birds, عَقْعَقَة ـ صِيَاحُ ٱلطُّيُورِ ـ نَعْق ـ نَعْب ـ تَكَأْكُؤ. Chattering of the teeth, قَفْقَفَةُ ٱلْأَسْنَانِ ـ طَرْطَقَةُ ٱلْأَسْنَانِ ـ إِصْطِكَاكُ ٱلْأَسْنَانِ.

Chatter-box, *n.* / Chatterer, } بَقَّاق ـ بَقَّاق ـ فَرْفَار ـ لِسَان طَلِق ـ قَوَّال ـ فَشَّار.

Chattering, *n.* *See* Chatter, *n.*

Chatty, *a.* مُحَدِّث ـ أَنِيس.

Chaw, *v.t.* *See to* Chew, *v.t.*

Cheap, *a.* Low in price, رَخِيص. Low, common, حَقِير ـ دُون. It was a — bargain, كَانَتْ شَرْيَةً رَخِيصَةً. To be or become —, ² رَخُصَ. To reckon —, إِسْتَرْخَصَ.

Cheapen, *v.t.* To lessen the value of, أَرْخَصَ ـ رَخَّصَ ـ وَطَّى. To bargain with, شَارَعَ ـ شَارَطَ ـ فَصَلَ ٱلثَّمَنَ مَع ـ ٱلثَّمَن.

Cheapener, *n.* بَيِّع.

Cheaply, *ad.* رُخْصًا ـ بِرُخْصٍ.

Cheapness, *n.* رُخْص.

Cheat, *n.* A fraud, غَبْن ـ غَبِينَة ـ غَدْر ـ خِيَانَة ـ خَوْن ـ مَكْر ـ غِشّ ـ خِدَاع. One guilty of fraud, غَدَّار ـ غَابِن ـ خَدَّاع ـ مَكَّار ـ خَائِن ـ غَشَّاش. A petty —, fraud, غَبْن يَسِير; an exorbitant —, غَبْن فَاحِش.

Cheat, *v.t.* ضَامَ ـ إِسْتَضَامَ ـ غَبَنَ-فِي ـ فَلَحَ ـ غَدَرَ ـ ² خَدَعَ ـ جَوَّنَ ـ غَشَّ ². To — in trading, مَكَسَ. To —, to ask too high a price, غَلَبَ فِي ٱلثَّمَنِ. They cheated one another, of many, تَغَابَنُوا. To be cheated, غُبِنَ.

Cheating, *n.* *See* Cheat, *n.*

Check, *v.t.* To repress, ضَبَطَ ـ وَقَّفَ ـ أَوْقَفَ ـ قَمَعَ ـ كَبَحَ ـ ² حَاشَ ـ إِزْدَجَرَ-عَن ـ ² زَجَرَ-عَن. To keep from, مَنَعَ-عَن ـ قَيَّدَ ٱلرُّجُوعَ. To control by a counter-reckoning, شَطَبَ ٱلْحِسَاب ². To reprove, أَدَّبَ ـ وَبَّخَ ـ لَامَ ². To be checked, kept from, إِنْزَجَرَ-عَن. To —, in chess, جَكَّمَتْ.

Check, *n.* A restraint, مَنْع ـ ضَبْط ـ تَحْدِيد ـ رَبْط ـ وَهَق ـ حَاجِز. A reproof, تَوْبِيخ ـ خُطْبَة ـ عِتَاب. An obstacle, عَائِق ـ مَانِع ـ حَاجِز ـ دِفَاع ـ دَفْع ـ تَرْدِيد ـ رَدّ. A repulse, دَفْعَة. A money —, وَرَقَةُ حَوَالَةٍ ـ تَحْوِيل ـ بُولِيصَة. A — in an account, سُؤَال عَنْ شَيْءٍ مَرْقُوم فِي حِسَاب ـ تَقْيِيد فِي ٱلْحِسَاب. A mark, إِشَارَة ـ عَلَامَة. A note, ticket, تَذْكِرَة *pl.* تَذَاكِر. Checkered cloth, قُمَاش مُخَطَّط (*or* مُقَلَّم). A check-book, كِتَاب حَوَالَات. To receive a —, to be repressed, رُدَّ ـ إِنْدَفَعَ. To give a — upon, حَوَّلَ-عَلَى.

Checker, *n.* / Checker-work, } تَخْطِيط ـ نَقْش ـ بَرْقَشَة ـ تَشْكِيل ـ تَصْلِيب.

Checker, *v.t.* عَيَّنَ ـ دَبَّجَ ـ رَقَّمَ ـ بَرْقَشَ ـ شَكَّلَ.

Checker-board, *n.* رُقْعَةُ ٱلشِّطْرَنْج ـ طَاوِلَةُ ٱلشِّطْرَنْج.

Checkered, *n.* مُعَيَّن ـ مُصَلَّب ـ مُخَطَّط ـ مُقَلَّم.

Checkers, *n.* دَامَة ـ لَعِبُ ٱلدَّامَةِ.

Checkmate, *n.* ٱلشَّاه مَات.

Checkmate, *v.t.* At chess, مَوَّتَ ٱلشَّاهَ. To defeat, كَسَرَ ² ـ خَيَّبَ. To frustrate, عَنَقَ ² ـ أَعْدَمَ ـ أَخْجَمَ ب.

Cheek, *n.* خَدّ *dual* خَدَّان *pl.* خُدُود; the upper part or ball of the —, أَجْنَة ـ وَجْنَة. The side of the —, عَارِضَة; the two sides of the —, ٱلْعَارِضَان. Impudence, وَقَاحَة. Cheek by jowl, جَنْب بَعْضِهِمْ.

Cheek-bone, *n.* فَكّ *pl.* فُكُوك ـ عَظْمُ ٱلْوَجْنَةِ.

Cheek-tooth, *n.* ضِرْس *pl.* أَضْرَاس.

Cheep, *v.i.* *See to* Chirp, *v.i.*

Cheer, *n.* Provisions, food, طَعَام ـ شُرْب ـ أَكْل وَشُرْب. Good —, dainties, أَفْخَرُ ٱلطَّعَامِ ـ أَلْوَانُ ٱلْمَأْكُولَاتِ ٱلْفَاخِرَةِ. An entertainment, وَلِيمَة ـ مَأْدُبَة ـ ضِيَافَة. Gaiety, enjoyment, طَرَب ـ إِنْبِسَاط ـ بَحْبَحَة ـ بَهْجَة ـ كَيْفِيَّة ـ فَكَاهَة. Courage, عَزْم ـ مُرُوَّة. A shout of joy, هَيْلُولَة ـ تَهْلِيل ـ هَنْهُونَة ـ هُتَاف. Be (thou) of good —, ثِقْ ـ تَشَجَّعْ ـ تَجَلَّدْ ـ قَوِّ قَلْبَكَ.

Cheer, *v.t.* To encourage, شَجَّعَ ـ رَغَّبَ ـ وَثَّقَ ـ شَدَّ عَزْمَ ² ـ سَرَّ ² ـ سَلَّى ـ آنَسَ ب ـ أَنِسَ ب. To comfort, قَوَّى قَلْبَ ـ جَبَرَ قَلْبَ ². To gladden, أَبْسَطَ ـ سَرَّ ² ـ أَبْهَجَ ـ عَزَّى ـ وَاسَى ـ شَرَحَ خَاطِرَ ². To welcome with a —, هَلَّلَ ل ـ هَنْهَنَ ل. The soldiers cheered him, حَيَّاهُ ٱلْعَسْكَرُ. All present cheered, تَهَلَّلَ ٱلْحَاضِرُونَ فَرَحًا وَسُرُورًا.

Cheer, *v.i.* To — up, become cheerful, سُرَّ ـ تَسَلَّى ـ تَفَرَّجَ ـ تَفَسَّحَ ـ إِبْتَهَجَ. To shout with cheers, هَلَّلَ ـ هَتَفَ ² ـ هَتَّفَ.

Cheerful, *a.* سارٌّ ــ مَسْرُور ــ أَنِيس ــ طَرِب ــ فَرِح ــ بَجْبُوح ــ بَشُوش ــ بَطْرَان ــ بَهِيج ــ فَكِه ــ طَيِّبُ ٱلنَّفْسِ ــ يَحْبُور ــ فَرْحَان. A — prospect, مَنْظَرٌ بَهِيجٌ. A — spot, مَنْزَهَة. To be —, فَكِهَ ــ تَفَرَّجَ ــ طَابَ قَلْبُهُ. His mind was —, طَابَتْ نَفْسُهُ. Not — news, خَبَرٌ غَيْرُ سارٍّ. Cheerful news, أَخْبَارٌ سَارَّةٌ.

Cheerfully, *ad.* Gaily, gladly, بِٱنْبِسَاطٍ ــ بِسُرُورٍ ــ بِفَرَحٍ. Readily, عَلَى ٱلرَّأْسِ وَٱلْعَيْنِ.

Cheerfulness, *n.* فَكَاهَة ــ أُنْس ــ طَرَب ــ سُرُور ــ حُبُور ــ بَشَاشَة ــ تَفَرُّج ــ إِبْتِهَاج ــ مَحْظُوظِيَّة ــ فَرَح ــ إِنْبِسَاط ــ كَيْف ــ بَهْجَة.

Cheerily, *ad.* *See* Cheerfully, *ad.*

Cheering, *a.* *See* Enlivening.

Cheerless, *a.* Comfortless, حَزِين ــ مُغْتَمّ ــ مِنْ غَيْرِ ٱنْبِسَاطٍ ــ وَحِش ــ كَرِيب ــ ظَلْمَانِيّ. Dreary, gloomy, مَغْمُوم ــ سَوْدَاوِيّ.

Cheerlessness, *n.* وَحْشَة ــ خَوْبَة ــ عُدْم ــ عَدَم ــ حُزْن.

Cheerly, Cheery, *a.* *See* Cheerful, *a.*

Cheese, *n.* جُبْن ــ جُبْنَة. A trundle of —, جُبْنَة ــ قَالِبُ جُبْنٍ *pl.* قَوَالِب. New —, أَقِط. To lay out fresh — to dry, شَرَّرَ. The cane-work on which — is dried, إِشْرَار. A cheese-market, سُوقُ ٱلْجُبْنِ.

Cheesemonger, *n.* جُبْنِيّ ــ بَيَّاعُ ٱلْجُبْنِ.

Cheese-vat, *n.* قَالِبٌ لِلْجُبْنِ.

Chef d'œuvre, *n.* صِنَاعَةُ أُسْتَاذٍ ــ خَلِيقَة ــ مُخَلَّقَة ــ مُلْحَة *pl.* مُلَح ــ مُعَلِّمِيَّة.

Chemical, *a.* مِنَ ٱلْكِيمِيَاءِ ــ كِيمَاوِيّ ــ مُخْتَصّ بِعِلْمِ ٱلْحَلِّ (ٱلتَّحْلِيلِ *or*).

Chemically, *ad.* عَلَى قَوَانِينِ ٱلْكِيمِيَاءِ ــ كِيمَاوِيًّا.

Chemicals, *n.* مُرَكَّبَاتٌ كِيمَاوِيَّةٌ.

Chemise, *n.* قَمِيص *pl.* قُمْصَان. *See also under* Shirt, *n.*

Chemisette, *n.* تَخْرِيمَةٌ لِلرَّقَبَةِ.

Chemist, *n.* كِيمَاوِيّ ــ عَارِفٌ بِٱلْحَلِّ ٱلْكِيمَاوِيِّ. An apothecary, أَجْزَاجِي. A chemist's shop, أَجْزَا خَانَه.

Chemistry, *n.* الكِيمِيَاءُ ــ ٱلْكِيمَاوِيّ ــ عِلْمُ ٱلْحَلِّ (ٱلتَّحْلِيلِ *or*).

Chequer; *see* Checker.

Cherish, *v.t.* To hold as dear, أَعَزَّ ــ عَزَّزَ. To support, مَانَ ــ أَمَدَّ بِ ــ كَلِفَ بِ ــ تَكَلَّفَ عَلَى ــ قَامَ بِمَعَاشٍ. To preserve, حَفِظَ ــ رَاعَى ــ رَعَى ــ كَفَى. To warm, دَفَّى. To caress, لَاطَفَ. To bring up, رَبَّى.

Cherisher, *n.* مُعَزِّز ــ مُحَافِظ ــ حَامٍ ــ مُحَامٍ ــ ظَهِير.

Cheroot, *n.* سِيغَارَة ــ نَوْعٌ مِنَ ٱلسِّغَارَةِ.

Cherry, *n.* قَرَاسِيَا ــ كَرَز. A wild —, مَحْلَب. Kernels of wild cherries, حَبُّ ٱلْمَحْلَبِ. A — tree, شَجَرَةُ كَرَزٍ. A — orchard, شَجَرِيَّةُ كَرَزٍ.

Cherry, *a.* كَرَزِيّ. Red, ruddy, أَحْمَر ــ فَقِيع ــ أَحْمَرُ قَرَّاسٍ ــ أَشْقَر *fem.* شَقْرَاءُ *pl.* شُقْر.

Chersonese, *n.* جَزِيرَة ــ شِبْهُ جَزِيرَةٍ.

Cherub, *n.* The cherubim, الكَارُوبِيم ــ الكَارُوبُون. A beautiful child, وَلَدٌ ظَرِيفٌ. An angel, مَلَك ــ مَلَاك *pl.* مَلَائِكَة.

Cherubic, *a.* / **Cherubical,** } مَلَكِيّ ــ مَلَائِكِيّ.

Cherup, *v.t.* and *i.* صَفَّرَ.

Chervil, *n.* The plant, مَقْدُونَس ــ كُزْبَرَةٌ خَضْرَاءُ ــ رِجْلُ ٱلْغُرَابِ ــ اطريلال.

Chess, *n.* شِطْرَنْج ــ سِطْرَنْج.

Chess-board, *n.* رُقْعَةُ ٱلشِّطْرَنْجِ ــ طَاوِلَةُ ٱلشِّطْرَنْجِ.

Chessman, *n.* بَيْدَق *pl.* بَيَادِق.

Chess-player, *n.* لَعَّابُ ٱلشِّطْرَنْجِ.

Chest, *n.* A box, صَنْدُوق *pl.* صَنَادِيق. A wardrobe, صِوَان *pl.* أَصْوِنَة. A — of drawers, دُولَاب ــ خُرِسْتَان. The breast, صَدْر *pl.* صُدُور ــ صُدْرَة. The thorax, الجَوْف. Having a large —, أَصْدَر ــ فُشْحُم ــ فُشَّح ــ مُصَدَّر. Affected in the —, مَصْدُور.

Chestnut, *n.* شَاه بَلُّوط ــ عَيْنُ ٱلْجَمَلِ ــ كَسْتَنَة ــ أَبُو فَرْوَة.

Chestnut, *a.* Of the colour, كُمَيْت *pl.* كُمْت ــ كُمَانِيّ ــ أَكْلَف *fem.* كَلْفَاءُ *pl.* كُلْف ــ مَوْر ــ لَوْنُ ٱلشَّاه بَلُّوطِ. A — colour, كُمْتَة. Chestnut-coloured horses, خَيْلٌ كُمَاتِيّ.

Chevalier, *n.* *See* Cavalier, *n.*

Chevalier d'industrie, *n.* نَصَّاب.

Chevaux-de-frise, *n.* جرخ فلك.

Chevron, *n.* The military badge, نِيشَانٌ عَلَى كُمِّ سُتْرَةِ ٱلْعَسْكَرِ.

Chew, *v.t.* and *i.* To masticate, عَلَكَ ــ مَضَغَ ــ لَاكَ. To — the cud, ruminate, أَفَاضَ ــ نَشَرَ ــ إِجْتَرَّ (*vulg.* إِشْتَرَّ). To meditate upon, تَأَمَّلَ فِي ــ تَفَكَّرَ فِي.

Chew, *n.* One act of chewing, عَلْكَة. A thing that is chewed, عُلَاك ــ عَلَاك ــ عَلُوك. The cud, قَرِيض.

Chibouque, *n.* عُود *pl.* عِيدَان ــ قَصَبَة ــ غَلْيُون ــ شُبُك *pl.* شُبُكَات.

Chicane, *n.* } Evasion, تَوْجِيه ـ غَدْر. Sophistry, سَفْسَطَة.
Chicanery, } Deceit, غَدْر ـ غَبْن ـ حِيلَة. To practice —, إِحْتَالَ ـ تَلَوَّى.

Chick, *n.* } The young of fowls, فَرُّوج *pl.* فَرَارِيجُ ـ فَرْخ *pl.*
Chicken, } أَفْرَاخ ـ فَلُّوس *pl.* فَلَالِيس. A newly hatched —, كَتْكُوت *pl.* كَتَاكِيتُ. A child, صِيصَان ـ صُوصَانَة ـ صُوص *pl.* وَلَد *pl.* أَوْلَاد. A hen with chickens, فَرُّوجَة.

Chicken-hearted, *a.* قَصِف ـ خَوَّار ـ رَعِيب ـ إِجْفِيل ـ خَوَّاف ـ جَفِيل ـ جَبَان.

Chicken-pox, *n.* جُدَرِيٌّ فَرُّوجِيٌّ ـ نَوْعٌ مِنَ ٱلْجُدَرِيِّ.

Chick-pea, *n.* حِمِّص ـ حُمُّص. One —, حِمِّصَة ـ حُمُّصَة.

Chicory, *n.* هِنْدَبَة.

Chide, *v.t.* To reprove, عَتَبَ عَلَى ـ عَاتَبَ ـ وَبَّخَ ـ عَيَّرَ ـ بِ ـ ذَمَّ ـ لَامَ عَلَى. To blame, زَجَرَ ـ زَمَّرَ فِي ـ عَيَّبَ عَلَى ـ بِ.

Chide, *v.i.* To quarrel, scold, تَشَاجَرَ ـ تَخَانَقَ.

Chider, *n.* A reprover, مُعَاتِب ـ مُوَبِّخ ـ عَتَّاب.

Chiding, *n.* عَتْب ـ سُخْط ـ عِتَاب ـ مُعَاتَبَة ـ تَوْبِيخ.

Chief, *a.* رَأْس ـ رَئِيس *pl.* رُؤَسَآء ـ أَخَصّ ـ أَهَمّ ـ كَبِير ـ أَكْبَر ـ أَوْلَى *fem.* وُلْيَا *pl.* وُلَى *and* وُلْيَيَات ـ أَشْرَف ـ أَصْلِيّ ـ مُتَقَدِّم ـ زَعِيم. The — seat, صَدْرُ ٱلْمَجْلِسِ. The — speaker, ٱلْخُطَبَآء ـ ٱلْمُتَكَلِّم. The — women, women of rank, نِسَآء ٱلْأَعْيَانِ. The — men of a town, أَعْيَانُ ٱلْبَلَدِ ـ رُؤَسَآء ٱلْمَدِينَةِ. The — reason, ٱلسَّبَبُ ٱلْأَكْبَرُ ـ أَكْبَرُ سَبَبٍ. Who is — among you? مَنْ هُوَ فِيكُمُ ٱلْأَعْظَمُ ـ مَنْ هُوَ فِيكُمُ ٱلْمُتَقَدِّمُ. He made a feast for his officers and — men, صَنَعَ وَلِيمَةً لِأُمَرَائِهِ وَرُؤَسَائِهِ. The — moral qualities, أَخَصُّ ٱلْفَضَائِلِ ٱلْأَدَبِيَّةِ. The — or greater part of it, أَغْلَبُهُ ـ أَكْثَرُهُ. A Chief Justice, صَدْرُ قُضَاةٍ. Commander-in-Chief, سَرْعَسْكَر.

Chief, *n.* A principal, زَعِيم *pl.* زُعَمَآء ـ رَئِيس *pl.* رُؤَسَآء ـ مُتَقَدِّم ـ كَبِير *pl.* كُبَرَآء. Chief of a tribe, a Shaikh, شَيْخ *pl.* شُيُوخ. Chief of a department, ضَابِطُ قَلَمٍ *pl.* ضُبَّاطُ أَقْلَامٍ. A — of higher dignity than a Shaikh, أَمِير *pl.* أُمَرَآء. The chiefs, nobles, ٱلْأَعْيَان. The chiefs of the rebels, زُعَمَآء ٱلْعُصَاةِ. To make — over, رَأَّسَ عَلَى. To be made — over, تَرَأَّسَ عَلَى.

Chiefly, *ad.* Principally, خُصُوصًا ـ بِٱلْأَخَصِّ ـ خَاصَّةً. Mostly, غَالِبًا ـ فِي ٱلْغَالِبِ ـ فِي ٱلْأَكْثَرِ. Salute all, and — those of my brother's family, سَلِّمْ عَلَى ٱلْجَمِيعِ وَلَا سِيَّمَا ٱلَّذِينَ هُمْ مِنْ أَهْلِ بَيْتِ أَخِي.

Chieftain, *n.* *See* Chief, *n.*

Chieftancy, *n.* } إِمَارَة ـ رِئَاسَة.
Chieftainship, }

Chignon, *n.* False hair, قُرْزُل ـ وَاصِلَة. A woman who wears a —, مُسْتَوْصِلَة. The natural hair plaited and ornamented and hanging down the back, ضَفَائِر.

Chilblain, *n.* حُرْقَةٌ مِنَ ٱلسَّقْعَةِ ـ دَاحُوسٌ مِنَ ٱلْبَرْدِ ـ قمطلص.

Child, *n.* طِفْل *fem.* طِفْلَة *pl.* أَطْفَال ـ وَلَد *pl.* أَوْلَاد. A little —, بُنَيٌّ. A male —, صَبِيٌّ *pl.* صِبْيَان. A female —, صَبِيَّة *pl.* صَبَايَا ـ بِنْت *pl.* بَنَات ـ بُنَيَّة. Any thing born, produced, حَاصِل ـ تَوْلِيد ـ نَشَآءَة ـ مَوْلُود. A supposititious —, وَضِيعَة. A sucking —, رَضِيع. An only —, وَلَدٌ وَحِيدٌ. A foster —, وَلَدُ ٱلتَّبَنِّي. A —, مُرَبَّى ـ رَبِيب ـ مَرْبُوب. An adopted —, إِحْتَبَلَتْ ـ (woman) with —, حُبْلَى ـ حَامِلَة. To be with —, حَبِلَت. To get with —, حَبَّلَ ـ صَيَّرَ حُبْلَى. To play with children, صَبَى. *See also* Daughter, Son, *n.*

Child-bearing, *n.* حَبَل ـ وِلَادَة.

Child-bed, *n.* وِلَاد ـ نِفَاس.

Child-birth, *n.* Travail, طَلْق ـ مَخَاض ـ وِلَادَة ـ تَوْلِيد.

Childermas-Day, *n.* عِيدُ قَتْلِ ٱلْأَطْفَالِ.

Childhood, *n.* صَبَآء ـ طُفُولِيَّة.

Childish, *a.* غِرّ ـ صُغَارِيّ ـ طِفْلِيّ. Trifling, جُزْئِيّ ـ جَاهِل ـ بَاطِل ـ عِبِيث. Foolish, جَاهِل.

Childishly, *ad.* مِثْلَ ٱلْأَطْفَالِ ـ مِثْلَ ٱلصِّغَارِ. To act —, غَرَّ ـ صَبَا *aor.* يَصْبُو ـ تَصَبَّى ـ تَصَابَى.

Childishness, *n.* صَبْوَة ـ صَغْرَنَة ـ وَلْدَنَة ـ جَهَالَة.

Childless, *a.* مِنْ غَيْرِ أَوْلَادٍ. Bereaved of children, ثَاكِل ـ ثَكُول. Barren, عَقِيم *pl.* عُقَمَآء ـ عَاقِر *pl.* عُقَّر *and* عَوَاقِرُ *and* عَاقِرَات. He died —, مَاتَ عَنْ غَيْرِ وَلَدٍ. Should he die —, إِذَا تُوُفِّيَ عَنْ غَيْرِ وَلَدٍ.

Childlike, *a.* Like a child, طِفْلِيّ. Adapted to a child, مُوَافِقٌ لِلْوَلَدِ. Gentle, حَلِيم.

Children, *n.* Descendants, آل ـ نَسَب ـ نَسْل ـ زَرْع ـ أَوْلَاد. The — of Israel, بَنِي إِسْرَائِيلَ. *See also* Child, *n.*

Chill, *a.* *See* Chilly, *a.*

Chill, } Of cold, بَرْد ـ قَرْس ـ قَرَس ـ بُرُودَة. De-
Chillness, *n.* } pression, خَفْض ـ إِنْخِفَاض ـ تَبْرِيدُ ٱلْهِمَّةِ.
Chilliness, }

Chill, *v.t.* To affect with cold, بَرَّدَ ـ بَرَدَ ـ أَبْرَدَ ـ قَرَّسَ. To blast, as with cold, أَذْبَلَ. To depress, discourage, بَرَّدَ هِمَّةً — خَفَّضَ ².

Chilly, *a.* Cold, بَرَّاد — بَارِد — قَارِس — قَرِيس. Feeling —, بَرْدَان. Frigid in disposition, وَعْق — بِلَا مُرُوَّةٍ. To feel —, بَرَدَ ². The night felt — to us, بَرَدَ عَلَيْنَا ٱللَّيْلُ. *See also* Frigid, Reserved, *a.*

Chime, *v.i.* To accord with, إِتَّفَقَ مَعَ — نَاسَبَ — وَافَقَ. To sound in harmony, صَحَّ ٱلْأَلْحَانُ ² — تَآلَفَتِ ٱلْأَصْوَاتُ. To — in, of speech, تَكَلَّمَ.

Chime, *v.t.* To strike in harmony, دَقَّ عَلَى ٱلْأَلْحَانِ ².

Chime, *n.* Harmony, أُلْفَةُ ٱلْأَصْوَاتِ — نَغَم — إِلْحَان. A — of bells, سِنْطِير — مَقَامُ ٱلْأَجْرَاسِ. Correspondence, as of proportions, هَنْدَام — إِتِّفَاق — مُوَافَقَة.

Chimera, *n.* An idle fancy, وَهْم — ضِغْث *pl.* أَضْغَاث — وَهْمِيَّة *pl.* وَهْمِيَّات — خَيَالٌ بَاطِلٌ — خَيَال.

Chimerical, *a.* مَا لَهُ أَصْلٌ — بَاطِل — وَهْمِيّ — خَيَالِيّ.

Chimerically, *ad.* بِٱلتَّخْيِيلِ — تَخَيُّلًا — بِٱلْوَهْمِ.

Chimney, *n.* مَدْخَنَة — قُمْنَاء *pl.* قَمِين — دَوَاخِنُ *pl.* دَاخِنَة *pl.* مَدَاخِنُ.

Chimney-piece, *n.* عَمُودُ ٱلْمَوْقِدِ — زِينَةُ ٱلْأَرَّةِ.

Chimney-sweeper, *n.* مُنَظِّفُ ٱلْمَدَاخِنِ.

Chimpanzee, *n.* نَوْعٌ مِنَ ٱلْقِرْدِ.

Chin, *n.* ذَقَن *pl.* أَذْقَان *and* ذُقُون — قَرْبُوسُ ٱلذَّقَنِ. Having a long —, أَذْقَنُ *fem.* ذَقْنَاءُ. He leant his — on his hand, ذَقَّنَ عَلَى يَدِهِ. A double —, غَبَب.

China, *n.* The country, ٱلصِّينُ — بِلَادُ ٱلصِّينِ.

China, *n.* Porcelain, فَرْفُورِيّ — صِينِيّ — فَغْفُورِيّ. Vessels of —, صَوَانِيّ — أَوَانٍ صِينِيَّةٌ. Dresden —, فَرْفُورِيّ سَكْسُونِيَا.

China-root, *n.* شِبْشِينَا — أَصْلُ ٱلْقِينَا.

Chincough, *n.* سُعَالٌ قَلْبِيّ.

Chine, *n.* The backbone, سِلْسِلَةُ ٱلظَّهْرِ. A piece of the back of an animal, فِلْذَةٌ مِنَ ٱلظَّهْرِ.

Chink, *n.* A cleft, فَتّ — وَقْرَة *pl.* وَقَرَات — خِلَال *pl.* خَلَل — شَقّ *pl.* شُقُوق — فَلَق *pl.* أَفْلَاق — فَاقُوش. The sound of money, خَشْخَشَة — طَنْطَنَة — صَرِيرَة. Chinking coin, دَرَاهِمُ صَرِيرَةٌ.

Chink, *v.t.* To jingle, أَطَنَّ — طَنَّنَ — خَشْخَشَ.

Chink, *v.i.* صَرَّ ² — تَخَشْخَشَ — طَنَّ ² — طَنْطَنَ. To crack, تَشَقَّقَ — تَفَلَّجَ — إِنْفَقَعَ.

Chinky, *a.* Full of cracks, فَاقُوشِيّ — مَفْرُوج — مَفْقُوع — مُشَقَّق.

Chintz, *n.* شِيتٌ مُلَوَّنٌ — مَقْصُورٌ بِرَنْجِيّ — شِيت.

Chip, *n.* A paring, بَرْوَة — بَرَايَة. A splinter, شِقَّة *pl.* شِقَق — شَظِيَّة *pl.* شَظَايَا. A — in a vessel, ثُلْمَة *pl.* ثُلَم. A shaving, نُجَارَة. Chips, parings, بُرَايَة. A — of the old block, شَبَّةٌ مِنْ أَبِيهِ.

Chip, *v.t.* قَطَعَ — ² فَلَجَ — ثَلَمَ — شَظَّى.

Chip, *v.i.* تَثَلَّمَ — إِنْثَلَمَ.

Chirographer, Chirographist, *n.* Chiromancer, } مَاهِرٌ بِعِلْمِ ٱلْأَسَارِيرِ — ضَرَّابُ ٱلسِّيمِيَاءِ — قَائِف.

Chirography, *n.* عِلْمُ ٱلْخَطِّ.

Chirology, *n.* عِلْمُ ٱلتَّكَلُّمِ — عِلْمُ ٱلتَّفْهِيمِ بِوَاسِطَةِ ٱلْأَصَابِيعِ بِٱلْإِشَارَاتِ.

Chiromancy, *n.* عِلْمُ ٱلْقِيَافَةِ — عِلْمُ ٱلْأَسَارِيرِ — عِلْمُ ٱلْكَفِّ.

Chironomy, *n.* عِلْمُ ٱلْإِيمَاءِ.

Chiropodist, *n.* طَبِيبُ ٱلثَّآلِيلِ فِي ٱلْأَقْدَامِ.

Chirp, *n.* زَقْزَقَة — مُنَاغَاةُ ٱلطُّيُورِ — تَغْرِيد — تَرْنِيم — تَرَنُّم ٱلْعَصَافِيرِ; as of a cricket, *etc.*, قَصِيص.

Chirp, *v.i.* تَرَنَّمَ — نَاغَى — غَرَّدَ — زَقْزَقَ — صَاحَ ²; as a cricket, *etc.*, قَصَّ ².

Chirping, *n.* *See* Chirp, *n.*

Chirrup, *v.t.* رَغَّبَ — سَوَّقَ — كَدَسَ ² — كَدْكَدَ.

Chirurgeon, *n.* جَرَائِحِيّ — جَرَّاح.

Chirurgery, *n.* عِلْمُ ٱلْجِرَاحَةِ.

Chirurgical, *a.* جِرَاحِيّ.

Chisel, *n.* A tool to pare with, مِنْحَت — مِنْقَار *pl.* مَنَاقِيرُ — مِنْقَاش. A carpenter's —, إِزْمِيل.

Chisel, *v.t.* نَحَتَ ² — نَقَرَ ² — نَقَشَ ². To — into shape, هَنْدَمَ — شَكَّلَ. A thing chiselled, مَنْحُوت. Scraps from chiselling, نُحَاتَة.

Chit, *n.* A sprout, نَبْت — شَجَرَة (*or* فَرْخ) فَرْع. A babe, طِفْل *fem.* طِفْلَة.

Chit, *v.i.* To sprout, قَصَعَ — فَرَّخَ — طَرَّ ².

Chit-Chat, *n.* *See* Chat, *n.*

Chitterlings, *n.* The small intestines, أَعْفَاج.

Chivalric, *a.* Chivalrous, } Noble, نَبِيل — شَرِيف. Gallant, بَطَل — شُجَاع — رَحِيبُ ٱلصَّدْرِ. Warlike, حَرْبِيّ — مُحَارِب — فِدَاوِيّ.

Chivalry, *n.* Knighthood, ٱلْإِمَارَةُ. The characteristics of —, مَحَاسِنُ ٱلْإِمَارَةِ وَمَحَامِدُهَا.

Chive, *n.* A small onion, صُغَار ـ نَوْعٌ رَفِيعٌ مِنَ ٱلْكُرَّاثِ ـ ٱلْكُرَّاثِ.

Chives, *n.* Filaments of flowers, عَسَالِيجُ ٱلزَّهْرِ.

Chlorate, *n.* ثَانِي مِلْحِ ٱلْكُلُورُورِ.

Chloric, *a.* The acid, حَمْضُ ٱلْكُلُورُورِ.

Chloride, *n.* مِلْحُ ٱلْكُلُورُورِ ـ مِلْحُ كُلُورُورِ.

Chlorine, *n.* مُوَلِّدُ ٱلْخُضْرَةِ ـ أُمُّ ٱلْخُضْرَةِ ـ كُلُورُور.

Chloroform, *n.* قُلُورُوفُرْم.

Chlorosis, *n.* رُطُوبَةُ ٱلنِّسَاءِ. *See also* Whites, *n.*

Chock, *n.* A wedge, سَفَن *pl.* أَسَافِينُ ـ شَرْخ *pl.* شُرُوخ. Chock or choke full, مَشْحُون ـ شَاحِن.

Chocolate, *n.* شُوكُولَاتَة. The — berry, لَوْزُ ٱلشُّوكُولَاتَةِ ـ لَوْزٌ هِنْدِيٌّ.

Choice, *n.* The act of choosing, إِتِّخَاذ ـ إِخْتِيَار ـ خِيرَة ـ تَنْقِيَة ـ نَقَاوَة ـ خِيَار ـ إِقْتِرَاح ـ خِيرَة. What is chosen, خِيرَة. The best of anything, أَحْسَن ـ أَفْخَر ـ زُبْدَة ـ صَمِيم ـ عِينَة ـ أَجْمَل ـ نَقَاوَة ـ سُلَاف ـ عَيْن ـ أَخْيَر. The — of returning a purchase within a given time, خِيَارُ ٱلشَّرْطِ. The — is yours, أَنْتَ بِٱلْخِيَارِ. To make — of, إِخْتَارَ ـ إِسْتَخَارَ ـ إِتَّخَذَ.

Choice, *a.* Of high value, ثَمِين ـ فَاخِر ـ نَفَائِس *pl.* نَفِيس ـ عَظِيم. Select, خَاصّ ـ خِيَار ـ مُخْتَار ـ مُنْتَخَب. Chary, مُعْتَنٍ ـ حَرِيص. Choice or picked soldiers, سُلَافُ ٱلْعَسَاكِرِ. The choicest persons, ٱلْحَمَائِمُ. A — collection of books, عِدَّةُ كُتُبٍ مُنْتَخَبَةٍ.

Choicely, *ad.* إِخْتِيَارًا ـ بِٱعْتِنَاءٍ ـ بِٱلتَّدْقِيقِ.

Choiceness, *n.* Valuableness, قِيمَة ـ عِزّ. Fineness, رِقَّة ـ رِفَاعَة.

Choir, *n.* A body of singers, جَمَاعَةٌ مِنَ ٱلْمُغَنِّينَ. The place of the — in a church, ٱلْخُورُوسُ.

Choke, *v.t.* To suffocate, خَنَقَ ـ ² خَنَّقَ; as with food or anger, أَغَصَّ. To stop up, ² سَدَّ. To fill up, ٢ كَبَسَ ـ ² طَمَّ. To suppress, ٢ مَنَعَ. To be choked, suffocated, إِخْتَنَقَ ـ ٱنْخَنَقَ; to be stopped up, إِنْسَدَّ. To be choked with spittle, ٤ جَرِضَ ـ ; as with food, ² غَصَّ ـ إِغْتَصَّ; ٤ جَرِضَ بِرِيقِهِ. He was choked with anger, ² غَصَّ بِٱلْغَيْظِ. It was choked up by the sands, طَمَّتْ عَلَيْهِ ٱلرِّمَالُ.

Choke-damp, *n.* غَازٌ مُسِمٌّ يَتَوَلَّدُ فِي ٱلْمَعَادِنِ.

Choler, *n.* Bile, سَوْدَاءُ ـ صَفْرَاءُ. Anger, غَضَب ـ شَكَاسَة ـ خُلُق ـ غَيْظ.

Cholera, *n.* }
Cholera-morbus, } التَّشْوِيطَة ـ ٱلْهَوَاءُ ٱلْأَصْفَرُ ـ هَيْضَة.

Choleric, *a.* Passionate, خُلُقَانِيٌّ ـ غَضُوب ـ شَكِس.

Choose, *v.t.* To elect, إِخْتَارَ ـ إِنْتَخَبَ ـ إِقْتَرَحَ ـ إِنْتَقَشَ ـ أَوْثَرَ ـ نَقَّى ـ تَنَقَّى ـ إِصْطَفَى. To — in preference, to prefer, إِخْتَارَ بِٱلتَّحَرِّي ـ تَحَرَّى ـ فَضَّلَ عَلَى ـ إِسْتَحْسَنَ ـ إِسْتَفْضَلَ.

Choose, *v.i.* To will, أَرَادَ ـ بَغَى ـ إِشْتَهَى ـ شَاءَ *aor.* يَشَاءُ. I chose to do so, أَوَدُّ أَنْ أَفْعَلَ كَذَا ـ بِوُدِّي أَنْ أَفْعَلَ كَذَا. What God hath chosen, مَا شَاءَ ٱللّٰهُ.

Chooser, *n.* مُنْتَخِب. You are the —, أَنْتَ بِٱلْخِيَارِ.

Chop, *n.* A piece chopped off, قِطْعَة ـ شِقَّة ـ فِلْذَة *pl.* فِلَذ ـ قَلِيذ. A rib, ضِلْع *pl.* ضُلُوع. A chop or slice, as of meat, شَرِيحٌ *pl.* شَرِيحَة ـ شَرْحَة ـ شَرَائِحُ ـ شَرْحَةٌ. A piece of grilled meat, لَحْمٌ مَشْوِيٌّ.

Chop, *v.t.* To cut into small pieces, قَطَّعَ ـ فَلَذَ ـ هَشَمَ ـ ٢. To mince, as of meat, كَبَّبَ ـ ² فَرَمَ. To break into chinks, شَقَّقَ. To — logic with, خَاصَمَ ـ جَادَلَ ـ نَازَعَ. To — off; *see under to* Amputate, *v.t.*

Chop, *v.i.* To truck, قَاوَضَ ـ بَادَلَ ـ دَاكَشَ. To turn, to change, suddenly, تَحَوَّلَ ـ إِنْقَلَبَ ـ إِلْتَفَّ.

Chop-fallen, *a.* مَدْهُوش ـ أَبْلَس ـ مُنْقَطِعُ ٱلْقَلْبِ ـ مَبْهُوت.

Chop-house, *n.* دُكَّانُ طَبَّاخٍ.

Chopper, *n.* سَاطُور *pl.* سَوَاطِيرُ.

Chopping, *a.* Plump, lusty, فَعْم ـ خَدْل ـ كِنَاز ـ ضَلِيع. A — sea, بَحْرٌ مُتَقَلِّبٌ.

Chopping-block, *n.* *See* Block, *n.*

Chopping-knife, *n.* *See* Chopper, *n.*

Chops, *n.* The mouth, jaws, فَمّ ـ بُقْبَاق ـ حَنَك ـ تُمّ *vulg.*

Chopsticks, *n.* شُوكَاتٌ لِلسُّفْرَةِ مُسْتَعْمَلَةٌ عِنْدَ أَهْلِ ٱلصِّينِ.

Choral, *a.* Belonging to the choir of a church, مُخْتَصٌّ بِٱلْخُورُوسِ. A — service, خِدْمَةٌ بِتَرْتِيلِ ٱلْخُورُوسِ.

Chorally, *ad.* بِتَرْتِيلِ ٱلْخُورُوس ـ بِٱلْغِنَاءِ ـ بِٱلتَّرْتِيلِ.

Chord, *n.* Of a musical instrument, وَتَر *pl.* أَوْتَار. Harmony, نَغَم.

Chord, *v.t.* وَتَّرَ ـ أَوْتَرَ.

Chore, *n.* *See* Char, *n.*

Chorist, *n.* }
Chorister, } A singer in a church, مُرَتِّل ـ أَرْشِيّ *pl.* أَرْشِيَة.

Chorographer, *n.* رَسَّامُ بِلَادٍ ـ عَالِمٌ بِتَخْطِيطِ ٱلْبِلَادِ ـ أَهْلُ ٱلْجُغْرَافِيَةِ.

Chorographical, *a.* مُتَعَلِّقٌ بِوَصْفِ ٱلْبِلَادِ.

Chorography, *n.* وَصْفُ بِلَادٍ ـ رَسْمُ بِلَادٍ ـ عِلْمُ آثَارِ ٱلْبِلَادِ ـ فَنُّ رَسْمِ ٱلْبِلَادِ.

Chorus, *n.* A company of singers, جَمَاعَةٌ مِنَ ٱلْمُغَنِّينَ . What is repeated of a song, لازِمَة .

Chose, *pret. of to* Choose, *q.v.*

Chough, *n.* نَوْعٌ مِنَ ٱلْقَاقِ .

Chouse, *v.t.* *See to* Cheat, *v.t.*

Chrestomathy, *n.* كِتَابُ مُنْتَخَبَاتٍ وَمُسْتَخْرَجَاتٍ .

Chrism, *n.* مَيْرُون ; the holy —, المَيْرُونُ ٱلْمُقَدَّسُ .

Christ, *n.* المَسِيحُ ـ حَضْرَةُ ٱلْمَسِيحِ . Antichrist, المَسِيحُ ٱلدَّجَّالُ .

Christen, *v.t.* نَصَّرَ ـ ² صَبَغَ ـ عَمَّدَ .

Christendom, *n.* البِلَادُ ٱلنَّصْرَانِيَّةُ ـ النَّصَارَى ـ النَّصْرَانِيَّةُ .

Christening, *n.* مَعْمُودِيَّة ـ عِمَاد ـ تَنْصِير ـ صَبْغَة .

Christian, *n.* and *a.* نَصْرَانِيٌّ *pl.* نَصَارَى ـ مَسِيحِيٌّ *pl.* مَسِيحِيُّونَ . To make a —, نَصَّرَ ; to become a —, تَنَصَّرَ .

Christianity, *n.* النَّصْرَانِيَّةُ ـ الدِّينُ ٱلْمَسِيحِيُّ .

Christianization, *n.* تَنْصِير .

Christianize, *v.t.* نَصَّرَ . They were christianized by . . . , دُعُوا إِلَى ٱلنَّصْرَانِيَّةِ عَلَى يَدِ .

Christianly, *ad.* كَمَا يَلِيقُ بِٱلنَّصْرَانِيَّةِ ـ بِطَرِيقَةٍ مَسِيحِيَّةٍ .

Christian-name, *n.* إِسْمُ ٱلْمَعْمُودِيَّةِ .

Christless, *a.* بِدُونِ مَسِيحٍ . Irreligious, فَاجِر ـ مُنَافِق .

Christmas, *n.* عِيدُ ٱلْمِيلَادِ ـ عِيدُ مِيلَادِ سَيِّدِنَا ٱلْمَسِيحِ .

Christmas-box, *n.* A box for festival presents, عُلْبَةٌ لِلْعِيدِيَّاتِ ـ بِسْتِرِينَة . A festival present, عِيدِيَّة .

Christmas-tree, *n.* شَجَرَةٌ تُعَلَّقُ عَلَيْهَا ٱلْعِيدِيَّاتُ فِي أَيَّامِ ٱلْمِيلَادِ .

Chromatic, *a.* Relating to colours, لَوْنِيٌّ ـ مُخْتَصٌّ بِٱلْأَلْوَانِ ـ مُلَوَّن .

Chromatics, *n.* عِلْمُ ٱلْأَلْوَانِ .

Chromium, *n.* مَعْدِنُ ٱلْقُرُوم ـ قُرُوم .

Chronic, *a.* / **Chronical**, } Of long continuance, مُزْمِنٌ . A — disease, دَنَف ـ مَرَضٌ مُزْمِنٌ ـ زَمَانَة ; a — cough, سُعَالٌ مُزْمِنٌ .

Chronicle, *n.* تَارِيخٌ *pl.* تَوَارِيخُ ـ سِفْرُ تَذْكَارٍ ـ تَارِيخٌ سَنَوِيٌّ . The Book of Chronicles, سِفْرُ ٱلْأَيَّامِ .

Chronicle, *v.t.* قَيَّدَ فِي ٱلتَّارِيخِ ـ سَجَّلَ .

Chronicler, *n.* مُؤَرِّخ .

Chronogram, *n.* تَارِيخُ حَادِثَةٍ .

Chronologer, *n.* / **Chronologist**, } مُؤَرِّخ ـ عَالِمٌ بِٱلتَّوَارِيخِ ـ مُعَلِّمُ تَوَارِيخَ .

Chronologic, *a.* / **Chronological**, } مُتَعَلِّقٌ بِٱلتَّوَارِيخِ .

Chronologically, *ad.* عَلَى سِلْسِلَةِ ـ مُرَتَّبٌ حَسَبَ ٱلتَّوَارِيخِ ٱلتَّوَارِيخِ .

Chronology, *n.* عِلْمُ تَقْوِيمِ ٱلتَّوَارِيخِ ـ عِلْمُ ٱلتَّوَارِيخِ .

Chronometer, *n.* سَاعَةٌ تَامَّةٌ ـ مِقْيَاسُ ٱلزَّمَانِ ـ مِيزَانُ ٱلزَّمَانِ .

Chronometric, *a.* / **Chronometrical**, } Measured by a chronometer, مَوْزُونٌ عَلَى مِقْيَاسِ ٱلزَّمَانِ .

Chrysalis, *n.* شَرْنَقَةٌ *pl.* شَرَانِقُ .

Chrysolite, *n.* زَبَرْجَد ـ نَوْعٌ مِنَ ٱلزَّبَرْجَدِ .

Chub, *n.* The fish, شَال *pl.* شِيلَان . A dunce, أَحْمَقُ ـ ثَوْر ـ بَلِيد .

Chubby, *a.* شَخِيص ـ كِنَاز ـ خَدْل . Chubby-faced, مُكَلْثَم ـ مُكَبْتَلُ ٱلْوَجْهِ . To be chubby-faced, كَلْثَمَ .

Chuck, *v.i.* and *t.* To make a noise as a hen, نَقْنَقَ ـ قَوْقَأَ ـ كَأْكَأَ . To throw, رَمَى . To hand to . . . , نَاوَلَ .

Chuck, *n.* Of a hen, تَكَأْكُؤٌ ـ قَرْق . A throw, رَمْيَة ـ رَمْيٌ ـ طَرْح . The — of a lathe, قَيْدُ ٱلْمِخْرَطِ .

Chuck-farthing, *n.* لُعْبَةٌ بِدَرَاهِمَ يَتَّخِذُهَا ٱلصِّبْيَانُ .

Chuckle, *v.i.* ضَحِكَ ـ قَهْقَهَ ـ قَرْقَرَ .

Chuckling, *n.* قَرْقَرَة ـ قَرْق ـ قَهْقَهَة ـ ضِحْك .

Chuff, **Chuffy**, *n.* and *a.* فَظٌّ ـ فَلْح ـ خَشِنِيٌّ ـ خَشِن ـ شَرِس .

Chum, *n.* رَفِيق *pl.* رُفَقَاءُ and رِفَاق ـ زَمِيل *pl.* زُمَلَاءُ ـ شَرِيك *pl.* شُرَكَاءُ ـ صَاحِب *pl.* أَصْحَاب ـ نَدِيم *pl.* نُدَمَاءُ ـ قَعِيد . *See also* Bedfellow, *n.*

Chump, *n.* / **Chunk**, } Of wood, زَنْدُ حَطَبٍ *pl.* أَزَانِدُ ـ قُرْمَةُ حَطَبٍ *pl.* قُرَم .

Church, *n.* The body of Christians, الكَنِيسَةُ ـ البِيعَةُ . A Christian place of worship, بِيعَة *pl.* بِيَع or بِيْع ـ كَنِيسَة *pl.* كَنَائِس . A particular body, as of Christians, *etc.*, مِلَّة ـ جَمَاعَة ـ طَائِفَة *pl.* طَوَائِف ـ مَذْهَب . To enter the —, to be ordained, اِرْتَسَمَ .

The Church of England, الكَنِيسَةُ ٱلْأَنْكَلِيزِيَّةُ ٱلرَّسْمِيَّةُ .

The Oriental Churches, الكَنَائِسُ ٱلشَّرْقِيَّةُ .

The Roman-Catholic Church, الكَنِيسَةُ ٱلبَابَاوِيَّةُ .

Church, *v.t.* أَجْرَى ٱلشُّكْرَ فِي ٱلْكَنِيسَةِ مِنْ أَجْلِ خُرُوجِ ٱلْمَرْأَةِ مِنَ ٱلنِّفَاسِ .

Churching, *n.* إِجْرَاءُ شُكْرِ ٱلنِّسَاءِ فِي ٱلْكَنِيسَةِ بَعْدَ ٱلْوِلَادَةِ .

Churchman, *n.* An ecclesiastic, قَسٌّ *pl.* قُسُوس ـ مِنْ أَهْلِ ٱلْإِكْلِيرُوسِ . An adherent of the Church of England, تَابِعُ ٱلْكَنِيسَةِ ٱلْأَنْكَلِيزِيَّةِ .

Churchmanship, *n.* شِرْكَةٌ فِي ٱلْكَنِيسَةِ.

Church-rate, *n.* ضَرِيبَةٌ لِأَجْلِ صِيَانَةِ تَعْمِيرَاتِ ٱلْكَنِيسَةِ.

Churchwarden, *n.* حَارِسُ ٱلْأَقْلُومِيَّةِ — وَكِيلُ ٱلْكَنِيسَةِ.

Churchyard, *n.* The yard of a church, حَوْشُ بِيْعَةٍ. A burial-place, مَقْبَرَةٌ.

Churl, *n.* A clown, فَلَّاحٌ — خَشِنِيٌّ. An ill-bred man, فَظٌّ — خَسِيسٌ — بَخِيلٌ. أَحْمَقُ — شَرِسٌ — عَدِيمُ ٱلْأَدَبِ. A miser, بَخِيلٌ.

Churlish, *a.* Rude, غَلِيظٌ — خَشِنِيٌّ — وَحْشِيٌّ. Morose, فَظٌّ — مُكَشِّرٌ — وَقِحٌ — عَنِيفٌ — مُعَفِّرٌ — جَافٍ. Avaricious, بَخِيلٌ.

To be —, فَظَّ — جَفَا ع.

Churlishly, *ad.* بِغِلَاظَةٍ — بِفَظَاظَةٍ — بِجَفَآءٍ.

Churlishness, *n.* Rudeness, فَظَاظَةٌ — جَفَآءٌ — غِلَاظَةٌ — خُشُونَةٌ. Moroseness, وَعَقَةٌ — عَنَفٌ. Niggardliness, بُخْلٌ.

Churn, *n.* آلَةٌ لِمَخْضٍ — ضِنِّيٌّ — مِمْخَضٌ — مِمْخَضَةٌ — إِبْرِيجُ ٱلْحَلِيبِ (generally a skin among the Arabs).

Churn, *v.t.* مَخَضَ ٱللَّبَنَ — ع ر مَخَضَ. To be churned, تَمَخَّضَ.

Chyle, *n.* كِيلُوسٌ.

Chylification, *n.* تَكْوِينُ ٱلْكِيلُوسِ.

Chyme, *n.* كِيمُوسٌ.

Chymical, *a.* *See* Chemical, *a.*

Chymist, *n.* *See* Chemist, *n.*

Chymistry, *n.* *See* Chemistry, *n.*

Cicatrix, *n.* أَثَرُ ٱلْجُرْحِ — نُدُوبٌ *pl.* نَدَبٌ.

Cicatrization, *n.* تَضْمِيمُ ٱلْجُرْحِ — إِنْدَابٌ.

Cicatrize, *v.t.* قَطَّبَ — خَتَمَ — ضَمَّمَ.

Cicatrize, *v.i.* قُطِبَ ٱلْجُرْحُ — ع نَدِبَ.

Cicerone, *n.* تَرْجُمَانٌ — أَدِلَّآءُ *pl.* دَلِيلٌ.

Cicisbee, *n.* A dangler about ladies, عَلُّ ٱلنِّسَآءِ — زِيرُ نِسَآءٍ.

Cider, *n.* خَمْرُ عَصِيرِ ٱلتُّفَّاحِ — شَرَابُ ٱلتُّفَّاحِ.

Cigar, *n.* سِيكَارَاتٌ *pl.* سِيكَارَةٌ — سِغَارَةٌ.

Cigarette, *n.* وَرَقُ دُخَانٍ.

Ciliary, *a.* مُخْتَصٌّ بِٱلْأَجْفَانِ — جَفْنِيٌّ.

Cilicious, *a.* أَزَبُّ — أَشْعَرُ — شَعْرِيٌّ.

Cimeter, *n.* سُيُوفٌ *pl.* سَيْفٌ — شَمْشِيرٌ.

Cimmerian, *a.* Dark, gloomy, ظُلْمَانِيٌّ — مُكْفَهِرٌّ — مُظْلِمٌ.

Cinchona, *n.* قِينَا قِينَا.

Cincture, *n.* A girdle, سِبْتَةٌ — زُنَّارٌ — حِزَامٌ — مِنْطَقَةٌ. An inclosure, حَدِيقَةٌ — إِحَاطَةٌ — طَوْقٌ — إِسْتِدَارَةٌ — سِيَاجٌ.

Cinder, Cinders, *n.* جَمَرَاتٌ *pl.* جَمْرَةٌ مُطْفِيَّةٌ.

Cinerary, *a.* مُخْتَصٌّ بِٱلرَّمَادِ — رَمَادِيٌّ.

Cineration, *n.* إِصَارَةٌ إِلَى رَمَادٍ.

Cinereous, *a.* Of colour, أَشْهَبُ — أَرْمَدُ — رَمَادِيُّ ٱللَّوْنِ.

Cingalese, *a.* مِنْ جَزِيرَةِ سِيلَانَ — سِيلَانِيٌّ.

Cinnabar, *n.* سُنْجُفْرٌ — زُنْجُفْرٌ.

Cinnamon, *n.* دَارُ صِينِيٌّ — ٱلْقِرْفَةُ ٱلْحُلْوَةُ — قِرْفَةٌ.

Cinque, *n.* خَمْسَةٌ.

Cion, *n.* A shoot, فُرُوعٌ *pl.* فَرْعٌ. An ingrafted shoot, طُعْمٌ — فَرْعٌ مُطَعَّمٌ.

Cipher, *n.* An arithmetical number, أَرْقَامٌ *pl.* رَقْمٌ. The sign denoting nothing, أَصْفَارٌ *pl.* صِفْرٌ. An interlacing of letters, رَقْمُ إِشَارَةٍ — خَطٌّ جَفْرٍ — خَطٌّ مُوَصَّلٌ. An occult manner of writing, كَلَامٌ خَفِيٌّ. To be a mere —, كَانَ كَلَا شَيْءٍ ع. The Sultan's —, طُغْرَةُ ٱلسُّلْطَانِ.

Cipher, *v.i.* To write figures, كَتَبَ ٱلْأَرْقَامَ ع — خَطَّ ٱلْعَدَدَ — حَاسَبَ.

Cipher, *v.t.* To write in cipher, كَتَبَ بِرَقْمِ ٱلْإِشَارَةِ ع — كَتَبَ بِٱلْجَفْرِ.

Ciphering, *n.* كِتَابَةُ ٱلْحِسَابِ — رَقْمٌ.

Circle, *n.* A circuit, دَوَائِرُ *pl.* دَائِرَةٌ — دَوْرٌ — إِسْتِدَارَةٌ. An orb, كُرَةٌ. A company, جَمَاعَةٌ — عِشْرَةٌ — حِلْقَةٌ — رِفْقَةٌ. A circumlocution, دَوْرٌ. A hoop or ring, أَطْوَاقٌ *pl.* طَوْقٌ — حَلْقَةٌ *pl.* حَلَقٌ. An inclosure, إِحَاطَةٌ — دَائِرٌ — إِسْتِدَارَةٌ. The — of the eye, ٱلْمَحْجِرُ — مَحْجِرُ ٱلْعَيْنِ. Circles parallel with the horizon, دَائِرَاتٌ أُفُقِيَّةٌ — مُقَنْطَرَاتٌ. An enchanted —, مَنْدَلٌ. To reason in a —, دَارَ ع. The question formed a —, دَارَتِ ٱلْمَسْأَلَةُ.

Circle, *v.t.* and *i.* To move or go round anything, إِسْتَدَارَ — دَارَ ع. To surround, أَحَاطَ بِ — أَحْدَقَ بِ. To comprehend, comprise, إِحْتَوَى عَلَى — حَصَرَ ع. To —, as for protection, حَاطَ بِ ع — تَحَوَّطَ.

Circlet, *n.* دَائِرَةٌ صَغِيرَةٌ.

Circling, *a.* Going round, دَوَّارِيٌّ — دَوَّارٌ. Encircling, مُحِيطٌ.

Circuit, *n.* The act of going round, دَوَرَانٌ — إِسْتِدَارَةٌ — دَائِرٌ. A district, خَطٌّ — تُخْمٌ — أَطْرَافٌ. To make a — round, حَافَ عَلَى ع — أَحَاطَ بِ — حَفَّ بِ ع — طَافَ حَوْلَ ع.

Circuit, *v.t.* and *i.* *See to* Circle, *v.t.* and *i.*

Circuitous, *a.* مُلْتَوٍ — مُوَرَّبٌ — دَوَّارِيٌّ.

Circuitously, *ad.* بِٱلْتِوَآءٍ.

Circular, *a.* Round, مُدَوَّر ـ مُسْتَدِير. Turning round, دَوَّار ـ دَوَّارِيّ. Circular motions, حَرَكَاتٌ مُسْتَدِيرَةٌ.

Circular, *n.* A circular letter, كِتَابٌ فِي تَعْرِيفِ شَيْءٍ تُبْعَثُ مِنْهُ صُورَةٌ إِلَى جُمْلَةِ أُنَاسٍ ـ مَنْشُور ـ نَشْرَة. Circulars, تَحْرِيرَاتٌ عُمُومِيَّةٌ.

Circularly, *ad.* إِسْتِدَارَةً ـ دَوْرًا.

Circulate, *v.i.* To move in a circle, دَارَ ـ دَالَ ـ جَالَ. To flow, جَرَى ـ سَرَى. To go from one to another, سَارَ ـ دَارَ. The poison circulated in his blood, سَرَى ٱلسُّمُّ فِيهِ. It circulated among them, دَارَ بَيْنَهُمْ. To become public, إِتَّضَحَ ـ إِشْتَهَرَ.

Circulate, *v.t.* To take one round, أَجَالَ ـ أَجَالَ بِ ـ دَوَّرَ. To disseminate, بَثَّ ـ بَذَرَ. To publish, شَاعَ بِ ـ أَشَاعَ بِ ـ أَشْهَرَ. A circulating bank, بَنْكُ ٱلتَّدَاوُلِ. A circulating library, كُتُبٌ تَتَدَاوَلُهَا ٱلنَّاسُ بِأُجْرَةٍ. A circulating medium, coin, سِكَّة ـ نَقْد.

Circulation, *n.* The act of going round, دَوَرَان ـ جَوَلَان ـ تَدَاوُل ـ إِسْتِدَارَة; of flowing, سَرَى ـ جَرْي ـ جَرَيَان. Distribution, currency, إِشَاعَة ـ إِذَاعَة ـ إِنْتِشَار. Currency, as of coin, رَوَاج.

Circumadjacent, *a.* مُتَّصِل ـ مُجَاوِر.

Circumambiency, *n.* إِحَاطَة.

Circumambient, *a.* مُحِيط ـ مُكْتَنِف.

Circumambulate, *v.t.* حَفَّ بِ ـ طَافَ حَوْلَ ـ حَاطَ ـ مَشَى حَوْلَ ـ دَارَ عَلَى *or* بِ.

Circumcise, *v.t.* أَعْذَرَ ـ عَذَرَ ـ قَلَفَ ـ خَتَنَ ـ طَهَّرَ. To — a girl, خَفَضَ. To be circumcised, إِخْتَتَنَ ـ تَطَهَّرَ; of a girl, إِخْتَفَضَتْ. A circumcised male, مَخْتُون ـ خَتِين; female, مَخْتُونَة ـ مَخْفُوضَة.

Circumciser, *n.* خَاتِن; a female — of girls, خَافِضَة.

Circumcision, *n.* قَلْف ـ عُذْرَة ـ خِتَان ـ خِتَانَة ـ تَطْهِير; of girls, خَفْض. The act of —, خِتَانَة. To give a feast on the occasion of a —, عَذَّرَ. To invite one to such a feast, أَعْذَرَ لِ; *the feast is called,* عَذِيرَة *or* خِتَان.

Circumference, *n.* دَوْر ـ دَائِرَة ـ مَدَار ـ إِسْتِدَارَة.

Circumflex, *n.* عَلَامَةٌ (~) تُوضَعُ عَلَى بَعْضِ ٱلْأَحْرُفِ لِأَجْلِ مَدِّ ٱلصَّوْتِ بِهَا.

Circumfluent, *a.* }
Circumfluous, } مُحِيط ـ جَارٍ حَوْلَ.

Circumforaneous, *a.* سَيَّاح ـ إِبْنُ ٱلسَّبِيلِ ـ عَابِرُ ٱلسَّبِيلِ.

Circumfuse, *v.t.* سَيَّحَ ـ سَيَّلَ ـ أَجْرَى.

Circumgyration, *n.* دَوَرَان ـ إِسْتِدَارَة.

Circumjacent, *a.* مُجَاوِر ـ مُتَّصِل ـ قَرِيب ـ حَوَالَى.

Circumlocution, *n.* تَسَلْسُل ـ دَوْرَةٌ فِي ٱلْكَلَامِ. Ambiguity, إِلْتِبَاسُ ٱلْمَعْنَى ـ تَعْقِيدَة.

Circumlocutory, *a.* مُتَسَلْسِل ـ دَوَّارِيّ. Ambiguous, مُلْتَبِس ـ مُشْتَبِه.

Circumnavigable, *a.* مَا يُسَافَرُ حَوْلَهُ بَحْرًا.

Circumnavigate, *v.t.* سَافَرَ فِي مَرْكَبٍ حَوْلَ بَحْرٍ. He circumnavigated the lake, أَقْلَعَ حَوْلَ ٱلْبُحَيْرَةِ.

Circumnavigation, *n.* سَفَرُ ٱلْبَحْرِ حَوْلَ بَحْرٍ. The — of a lake, إِقْلَاعٌ حَوْلَ بُحَيْرَةٍ.

Circumnavigator, *n.* مُسَافِرٌ فِي مَرْكَبٍ حَوْلَ بَحْرٍ.

Circumscribable, *a.* مِمَّا يُحَدَّدُ ـ ٱلْإِحَاطَةُ بِهِ مُمْكِنَةٌ ـ حَصْرُهُ مُمْكِنٌ.

Circumscribe, *v.t.* حَدَّ ـ حَدَّدَ ـ حَصَرَ ـ أَحَاطَ بِ.

Circumscribed, *a.* مَحْصُور ـ مَحْدُود ـ مُحَاط.

Circumscription, *n.* Limitation, تَحْدِيد ـ حَصْر. An inscription round, كِتَابَةٌ حَوْلَ شَيْءٍ.

Circumscriptive, *a.* مُحَدِّد.

Circumspect, *a.* حَرِيص ـ مُتَحَذِّر ـ بَصِير ـ مُحْتَرِز ـ رَزِين ـ عَاقِل. To be —, إِحْتَرَسَ ـ تَحَذَّرَ ـ إِحْتَرَزَ ـ إِحْتَرَصَ.

Circumspection, *n.* حِرْص ـ تَحَذُّر ـ إِحْتِرَاز ـ رَزَانَة ـ حَزْم ـ تَبَصُّر ـ إِعْتِصَام.

Circumspective, *a.* *See* Circumspect, *a.*

Circumspectly, *ad.* بِتَحَذُّرٍ ـ بِٱلتَّدْقِيقِ ـ بِحَزْمٍ ـ بِبَصِيرَةٍ ـ إِحْتِرَازًا.

Circumspectness, *n.* *See* Circumspection, *n.*

Circumstance, *n.* Having some relation to a fact, حَال *pl.* أَحْوَال ـ حَالَة ـ مُتَعَلِّقَة ـ كَيْفِيَّة. An event, قَضِيَّة *pl.* قَضَايَا ـ حَادِثَة *pl.* حَوَادِث ـ كَائِنَة *pl.* كَائِنَات ـ أَمْر *pl.* أُمُور ـ قِصَّة. Circumstances, matters, أَحْوَال ـ أَعْرَاض ـ حَوَادِث. Condition, شَأْن *pl.* شُؤُون ـ حَال ـ مَقَام ـ مَنْزِلَة. In easy —, فِي نِعْمَةٍ ـ فِي سَعَةِ ٱلْعَيْشِ ـ صَاحِبُ خَيْرٍ ـ حَالُهُ طَيِّبٌ. In poor —, خَفِيفُ ٱلْحَالِ. Circumstances, as of a case, تَعَلُّقَات ـ مُتَعَلِّقَات. The circumstances of the time, ظُرُوفُ ٱلْأَحْوَالِ. Under those circumstances ..., وَٱلْحَالَةُ هٰذِهِ ـ كَوْنُ ٱلْأَمْرِ كَذٰلِكَ. All the — of the case, لَوَاحِقُ ٱلْأَمْرِ وَمُتَعَلِّقَاتُهُ. He is not in — to ..., it is not in his power to ..., لَيْسَ فِي قُدْرَتِهِ أَنْ ـ لَيْسَ

I was guided by —, كُنْتُ مَا هُوَ تَحْتَ يَدِهِ أَن ـ فِيهِ أَن. أَنْقَادُ لِلْأَحْوَالِ. Under all circumstances, فِي جَمِيعِ ٱلْأَحْوَالِ. According to the circumstances of the case, عَلَى مُقْتَضَى ظُرُوفِ ٱلْحَالِ. They were in the most happy circumstances, كَانُوا فِي عَيْشٍ رَغِيدٍ وَحَالٍ سَعِيدٍ.

Circumstantial, *a.* Incidental, عَارِضِيٌّ ـ عَرَضِيٌّ. Particular, مُبَيِّنٌ لَوَاحِقَ ٱلْأَمْرِ وَمُتَعَلِّقَاتِهِ ـ مُبَيِّنٌ كُلَّ ٱلْأَحْوَالِ ـ مُفَصَّلٌ وَاضِحٌ ـ مُفَصِّلٌ جَمِيعَ ٱلْأَحْوَالِ وَمُتَعَلِّقَاتِهَا.

Circumstantially, *ad.* بِدِقَّةٍ ـ تَشْرِيحًا ـ بِشَرْحٍ ـ بِتَفْصِيلٍ.

Circumstantials, *n.* عَوَارِضُ ٱلْأَمْرِ ـ عَوَارِضُ.

Circumstantiate, *v.t.* To detail in full, بَيَّنَ جَمِيعَ ٱلْأَحْوَالِ ـ ² شَرَحَ ـ شَرْحًا مُفَصَّلًا.

Circumvallate, *v.t.* أَحَاطَ ـ بِخَنْدَقٍ ـ أَحَاطَ ـ بِمِتْرَاسٍ.

Circumvallation, *n.* A fortification round, مِتْرَاسٌ حَوْلَ مَحَلٍّ. A ditch, خَنْدَقٌ. A siege, مُحَاصَرَةٌ.

Circumvent, *v.t.* آرَبَ ب ـ آرَبَ ـ ² خَتَلَ ـ رَاوَغَ ـ خَدَّعَ ـ ² مَكَرَ ب ـ ² خَدَعَ ـ ² حَرَشَ ـ حَاوَطَ ـ حَاوَشَ ـ ² غَشَّ ـ إِخْتَدَعَ.

Circumvention, *n.* خَدِيعَةٌ ـ خَدْعٌ ـ مُرَاوَغَةٌ ـ مُوَارَبَةٌ ـ مَكْرٌ ـ غَدْرٌ ـ مُحَاوَلَةٌ ـ مُزَاوَغَةٌ.

Circumventive, *a.* | Circumventor, *n.* } خَادِعٌ ـ خَتَّالٌ ـ مُرَاوِغٌ ـ مُوَارِبٌ ـ خَدَّاعٌ.

Circumvolution, *n.* The act of turning round, دَوَرَانٌ; of becoming folded up, إِنْدِرَاجٌ.

Circumvolve, *v.t.* To cause to revolve, أَدَارَ ـ دَوَّرَ. To roll round, ² لَفَّ ـ (or أَدْرَجَ ـ) حَوْلَ ٱلشَّيْءِ.

Circus, *n.* A place for games, مِيدَانٌ ـ مَلْعَبٌ ـ مِضْمَارٌ; for horses, مَجَالٌ ـ مِضْمَارٌ. A round space, ring, دَائِرَةٌ.

Cirrus, *n.* Cirri (of the clouds), عِفَاءٌ ـ سَمَاحِيقُ ٱلسَّمَاءِ ـ ٱلسَّحَابِ.

Cis-alpine, *a.* جَنُوبُ جَبَلِ ٱلْأَلْبِ أَعْنِي مِنْ طَرَفِ إِيطَالِيَا.

Cis-atlantic, *a.* غَرْبُ ٱلْبَحْرِ ٱلْمُحِيطِ.

Cist, *n.* *See* Cyst, *n.*

Cistern, *n.* مَصْنَعَةٌ *pl.* مَصَانِعُ ـ بِرْكَةٌ *pl.* بِرَكٌ ـ صِهْرِيجٌ *pl.* صَهَارِيجُ.

Cit, *n.* *See* Citizen, *n.*

Citadel, *n.* قَلْعَةٌ *pl.* قِلَاعٌ *and* قُلُوعٌ.

Citation, *n.* A legal summons, ٱلطَّلَبُ ـ ٱلْإِسْتِدْعَاءُ لِلشَّرْعِ ـ لِلْمَحْكَمَةِ ـ طَلَبٌ إِلَى ٱلْقَاضِي ـ مُرَافَعَةٌ. A quotation, إِقْتِبَاسٌ ـ عَدٌّ ـ ذِكْرٌ ـ ذِكْرُ قَوْلٍ ـ إِيرَادُ شَاهِدٍ ـ تَضْمِينٌ. Enumeration, تَعْدَادٌ.

Citatory, *a.* طَلَبِيٌّ.

Cite, *v.t.* To summon before a judge, ² دَعَا ـ إِلَى ٱلْمَحْكَمَةِ ـ إِسْتَحْضَرَ ـ رَافَعَ ـ عِنْدَ ٱلْقَاضِي. To quote from, إِقْتَبَسَ ـ مِنْ ـ ² ذَكَرَ ـ قَالَ رَوَى عَنْ ـ سَمَّى ـ ² رَفَعَ ـ إِلَى ـ ² نَقَلَ ـ مِنْ. *See also to* Quote, *v.t.*

Citizen, *n.* مَدَنِيٌّ ـ مَدِينِيٌّ ـ بَلَدِيٌّ ـ إِبْنُ بَلَدٍ *pl.* أَوْلَادُ بَلَدٍ. An inhabitant, سَاكِنٌ *pl.* سُكَّانٌ ـ قَاطِنٌ ـ مُقِيمٌ. Rustics and citizens, أَهْلُ ٱلْوَبَرِ وَٱلْمَدَرِ.

Citizenship, *n.* صِفَةُ ٱلْمَدَنِيِّ. Rights of —, حُقُوقُ ٱبْنِ ٱلْبَلَدِ.

Citrate, *n.* مِلْحُ ٱللَّيْمُونِ.

Citric, *a.* حَامِضٌ لَيْمُونِيٌّ ـ مِنَ ٱلْحَامِضِ ٱللَّيْمُونِيِّ.

Citric acid, *n.* حَامِضٌ لَيْمُونِيٌّ ـ حَامِضُ ٱللَّيْمُونِ.

Citrine, *a.* The colour, لَوْنُ ٱللَّيْمُونِ.

Citron, *n.* The fruit, أُتْرُجٌّ ـ تُرُنْجٌ. A single —, أُتْرُجَّةٌ ـ تُرُنْجَةٌ.

City, *n.* فُسْطَاطٌ *pl.* فَسَاطِيطُ ـ مَدَرَةٌ *pl.* مَدَرٌ ـ مِصْرٌ *pl.* أَمْصَارٌ ـ بَلْدَةٌ *pl.* بُلْدَانٌ *and* بِلَادٌ ـ بَلَدٌ ـ مَدِينَةٌ *pl.* مُدُنٌ. Outside of the —, خَارِجُ (or ظَاهِرُ) ٱلْمَدِينَةِ. The most remarkable cities, أَشْهَرُ مُدُنٍ. The population of a —, their number, أَهْلُ ٱلْبَلَدِ وَعَدَدُهُمْ. To build or found a —, مَدَّنَ ـ إِخْتَطَّ مَدِينَةً. *See also* Capital, *n.*

Civic, *a.* بَلَدِيٌّ ـ مَدِينِيٌّ ـ مَدَنِيٌّ.

Civet, *n.* The — cat, قِطُّ ٱلزَّبَادِ ـ سِنَّوْرُ ٱلزَّبَادِ. The perfume, زَبَادٌ. A perfume compounded of — and other articles, *Galia moschata*, غَالِيَةٌ.

Civil, *a.* Relating to the community, شَعْبِيٌّ ـ مُتَعَلِّقٌ بِأَهْلِ ٱلْبِلَادِ ـ مُدُنِيٌّ ـ سِيَاسِيٌّ. Not connected with the government or the military and naval services, عَامِّيٌّ ـ غَيْرُ مُتَعَلِّقٍ بِٱلْحُكُومَةِ. In the — employ of the State, فِي خِدْمَةِ ٱلْحُكُومَةِ ٱلسِّيَاسِيَّةِ (or ٱلْقَلَمِيَّةِ). Civil, not criminal, حُقُوقِيٌّ ـ مُخْتَصٌّ بِقَضَايَا ٱلنَّاسِ مَعَ بَعْضِهِمْ. Well-bred, رَفِيقٌ ـ لَطِيفٌ ـ أَدُوبٌ ـ أَدِيبٌ ـ كَيِّسٌ ـ شَلَبِيٌّ ـ آدَمِيٌّ. Not barbarous, مُتَمَدِّنٌ. Civil rights, حُقُوقٌ مُدُنِيَّةٌ ـ حُقُوقٌ قَانُونِيَّةٌ ـ حُقُوقٌ عَادِيَّةٌ. A — tribunal, مَحْكَمَةٌ عَادِيَّةٌ (or نِظَامِيَّةٌ). Civil uniform, لِبَاسٌ عَادِيٌّ ـ أَلْبِسَةٌ عَادِيَّةٌ (or إِعْتِيَادِيَّةٌ). Civil employ or employments, ٱلْوَظَائِفُ ٱلْعُمُومِيَّةُ. Deprivation of — rights, إِسْقَاطُ ٱلْحُقُوقِ ٱلْعَادِيَّةِ. A — suit, دَعْوَةُ حُقُوقٍ. The Civil Service, خِدْمَةُ ٱلدَّوْلَةِ ٱلسِّيَاسِيَّةِ وَٱلْقَلَمِيَّةِ. The Civil List, مَاهِيَّةُ ٱلْمَلِكِ ـ مَدْخُولُ ٱلسُّلْطَانِ.

Civil war, حَرْبٌ أَهْلِيَّةٌ — فِتْنَةٌ — قَوْمَةُ أَهْلِ ٱلْبِلَادِ عَلَى بَعْضِهِمْ — مُحَارَبَةٌ دَاخِلِيَّةٌ. To be — to, رَفَقَ ² — تَلَطَّفَ ل — عَلَى or ب تَلَاطَفَ ل.

Civil engineer, *n.* مُهَنْدِسُ ٱلْأَبْنِيَةِ — مُهَنْدِس.

Civil engineering, *n.* هَنْدَسَةُ ٱلْأَبْنِيَةِ — هَنْدَسَة.

Civilian, *n.* One engaged in civil pursuits, مَنْ يَتَفَرَّغُ إِلَى ٱلْمَصَالِحِ ٱلْمَدَنِيَّةِ — عَامِّيٌّ — غَيْرُ مُتَعَلِّقٍ بِٱلْحُكُومَةِ. One in the civil service of the Government, صَاحِبُ وَظِيفَةٍ قَلَمِيَّةٍ أَوْ سِيَاسِيَّةٍ فِي خِدْمَةِ ٱلدَّوْلَةِ.

Civility, *n.* Politeness, رِفْق — لُطْف — تَظَرُّف — أَدَب — إِنْسِيَّة — شَلَبَنَة. A kindness, مَعْرُوف.

Civilization, *n.* The act of civilizing, تَهْذِيبُ ٱلْأَخْلَاقِ وَتَرْوِيجُ ٱلْعُلُومِ وَٱلْفُنُونِ — تَأْنِيس — تَأْدِيب — تَمْدِين; the state of being civilized, إِنْسَة — تَمَدُّن — عُمْرَان. Colonization, تَعْمِير.

Civilize, *v.t.* أَنَّسَ — أَدَّبَ — لَطَّفَ — ظَرَّفَ — طَبَّعَ — مَدَّنَ.

These people are civilized, هٰؤُلَاءِ ٱلنَّاسُ مُتَمَدِّنُونَ. The civilized nations, المِلَلُ ٱلْمُتَمَدِّنَةُ.

Civilizer, *n.* مُؤَنِّس — مُؤَدِّب — مُلَطِّف — مُطَبِّع — مُرَقٍّ.

Civil-law, *n.* The laws of a country, شَرَائِعُ ٱلْبِلَادِ. The Roman law, شَرَائِعُ رُومِيَّةَ ٱلْعَتِيقَةِ.

Civilly, *ad.* Relating to government, فِيمَا يَخُصُّ — سِيَاسَةَ ٱلدَّوْلَةِ. Politely, بِأَدَبٍ — بِلُطْفٍ — تَظَرُّفًا. Kindly, بِمَعْرُوفٍ. To behave politely, kindly, to, إِقْتَفَى ب.

Civism, *n.* See Citizenship, *n.*

Clabber, *n.* See Bonny-clabber, *n.*

Clack, *v.i.* To make a sudden sharp noise, زَمْزَمَ — طَرْطَقَ — لَقْلَقَ. See also to Chatter, Clapper, *v.i.*

Clack, *n.* } Noise, جِسّ — لَقْلَقَة; as of a mill, زَمْزَمَة — طَرْطَقَة.
Clacking, } See also Chatter, Clapper, *n.*

Clad, *part.* Clothed, مَلْبُوس. Clad in, لَابِس.

Claim, *v.t.* To demand, طَلَبَ ². To assert as a right, إِدَّعَى — إِدَّعَى ب or إِلَى. To — as against another, إِدَّعَى ب-عَلَى. He claims it as his own, يَدَّعِي بِأَنَّهُ لَهُ (or مَالَهُ). We have not claimed more than our due, لَمْ نَدَّعِ أَكْثَرَ (or بِأَكْثَرَ) مِنْ حَقِّنَا. They each claimed the thing for himself, إِدَّعَوا ٱلشَّيْءَ (or بِٱلشَّيْءِ) — تَدَاعَوا ٱلشَّيْءَ.

Claim, *n.* A demand, طَلَب — مُطَالَبَة. The thing demanded, المَطْلُوب. Title, حَقّ *pl.* حُقُوق. A demand of something in the possession of another, إِدِّعَاء ب — دَعْوَى *pl.* دَعَاوٍ and دَعَاوَى — دَعَاوَة — دِعْوَة. To have a — to, to deserve, إِسْتَحَقَّ.

I have a — in respect of this matter, لِي فِي هٰذَا ٱلْأَمْرِ دَعْوَى.

If men were given according to their claims, demands, لَوْ أُعْطِيَ ٱلنَّاسُ بِدَعَاوِيهِمْ. He denied the — of France to protect the Christians in the East, أَنْكَرَ عَلَى فَرَانْسَا تَعَرُّضَهَا لِحِمَايَةِ ٱلنَّصَارَى فِي ٱلشَّرْقِ. You have no — against me, لَيْسَ لَكَ دَعْوَةٌ وَلَا طَلَبَةٌ مَعِي. A false —, إِنْتِحَال.

Claimable, *a.* مِمَّا يُدَّعَى بِهِ — مِمَّا يُطْلَبُ.

Claimant, *n.* مُدَّعٍ — طَالِب.

Claimed, *a.* As of property, مُدَّعًى ب.

Clairvoyance, *n.* إِدِّعَاءٌ بِكَشْفِ ٱلْأَسْرَارِ وَٱلْعِلْمِ بِٱلْغَيْبِ.

Clairvoyant, *n.* مُدَّعٍ بِكَشْفِ ٱلْأَسْرَارِ وَعِلْمِ ٱلْغَيْبِ.

Clam, *n.* A kind of shell-fish, نَوْعٌ مِنَ ٱلْوَدَعِ — مَحَارَة — قَوْقَع.

Clam, *v.t.* أَلْزَقَ-ب — دَبَّقَ — لَزَّجَ.

Clam, *v.i.* إِلْتَزَقَ — تَدَبَّقَ.

Clamber, *v.i.* To — over, تَسَلَّقَ.

Clamminess, *n.* Stickiness, تَدَبُّق — لُزُوجَة. Moistness, عَرَق — رُطُوبَة.

Clammy, *a.* Sticky, لَزِج — دَبِق. Moist, عَرِق — رَطِيب — رَشِح — عَرْقَان fem. عَرْقَى.

Clamorous, *a.* Noisy, صَرِيخ — ضَجَّاج — صَيِّت — فَجُوج — وَشْشَر — وِلْطَاظ — مُفَرْقِع — زَائِط — عَجَّاج — صَارِخ. Importunate, لَجُوج — مُحَاجِج.

Clamour, *n.* حَتَات — صَرَّة — لَجَّة — صُرَاخ — عَوَّة — غَلْغَلَة — صَرِير — تَهْوِيت — ضَجَّة — صَوْت — عِيَاط.

Clamour, *v.i.* To be noisy, صَوَّتَ — أَضَجَّ — ضَجَّ ² — صَرَّ ² — هَوَّتَ — زَوَّطَ — عَيَّطَ. To — for, to be importunate for, لَجَّ ب ² — أَلَظَّ ب.

Clamp, *n.* Of iron, ضَبَّة *pl.* ضَبَّات — كُلَّاب — عَقْفَاء — مِشْبَك. A heap, عَرَمَة — كَوْمَة — جُمْلَة مِنْ حَدِيدٍ.

Clamp, *v.t.* شَدَّ-بِكَلَالِيبَ ² — ضَبَّبَ — سَكَّ ². He clamped the door, ضَبَّبَ ٱلْبَابَ.

Clan, *n.* A tribe, family, قَبِيلَة *pl.* قَبَائِل — عَشِيرَة *pl.* عَشَائِر — آل — أَهْل. A division, as of people, فِرْقَة *pl.* فِرَق — طَائِفَة *pl.* طَوَائِف.

Clandestine, *a.* Secret, سِرّ — مَسْتُور — خَفِيّ — كَاتِم — مُكَتَّم — مَحْظُور — سِرِّيّ. Fraudulent, غَدِير — غَادِر — خَائِن.

Clandestinely, *ad.* Secretly, سِرًّا — خِفْيَةً — عَلَى خَفَاءٍ. Fraudulently, بِغَدْرٍ — بِخِيَانَةٍ.

Clang, *v.t.* أَطَنَّ.

Clang, *v.i.* نَقَضَ ² — طَنَّ ² — صَرَّ ²; of arms, قَعْقَعَ.

Clang, *n.* } Noise, sound, طَنِين ـ دَوِيّ ـ قَرْقَعَة ـ نَقْض
Clangour, } ـ قَعْقَع ـ حِسّ . The —, as of arms, خَشْخَشَة ـ قَعْقَعَة ; as of a trumpet, صَفِير ـ نَعِيق .

Clank, *n.* As of chains, طَنِين ـ رَنّ ـ صَرَّة ; of money, صَرِيرَة ـ خَشْخَش .

Clank, *v.i.* صَرّ ² ـ طَنَّن ـ دَوَى ـ رَنّ ; of arms, تَخَشْخَش . To make to —, أَطَنّ ـ أَصَات .

Clannish, *a.* مِثْل عَشِيرَة ـ عَشَائِرِيّ ـ رَفِيقِيّ ـ أَهْلِيّ .

Clannishness, *n.* أُلْفَة ـ مُعَاشَرَة ـ أَهْلِيَّة .

Clanship, *n.* *See* Clan, *n.*

Clap, *v.t.* To strike together, صَفَق ـ صَدَم ـ صَدَع ـ نَقَس ² ـ لَطَع ـ صَكّ ². To —, of the wings, صَفَق . To —, as on the back, to pat, لَطَح . To — on the back in token of approbation, صَوَّب ـ صَفَح ـ صَفَح . To —, of the hands, صَفَق ـ صَوَّت . To — hands for one in applause, صَفَق ل ـ صَفَق ب . To — or put something to, وَضَع ل *aor.* يَضَع ـ حَطّ ل ² ـ عَلَى . To — in, to insert, رَتَّب ل ـ رَكَّب ل ـ جَعَل ل ـ غَلّ فِي ² ـ أَدْخَل ـ حَشَر فِي .

Clap, *n.* A blow, دَقَّة ـ ضَرْبَة ـ تَلَاطُم ـ تَصَادُم . A noise, حِسّ ـ نَقْر ـ نَقْض . A clapping of the hands, صَفْقَة ـ صَفْق ـ تَصْفِيق الْأَيَادِي . A — of thunder, قَصْفَة رَعْد ـ رَعْدَة . A venereal —, سَيَلَان فِرَنْجِيّ ـ نُزُول الْمَنَى .

Clapboard, *n.* لَوْحَة *pl.* أَلْوَاح .

Clapper, *n.* Of a bell, مِدَقّ الْجَرَس . The mallet with which a gong is struck, وَبِيلَة . The — of a door, حَلْقَة ـ مِدَقّ الْبَاب ـ مِقْرَعَة الْبَاب . The — of a mill, طَرْطَقَة طَاحُون .

Clapperclaw, *v.t.* نَقَر ² ـ سَخِط عَلَى .

Claptrap, *n.* Pretence, حِيلَة ـ رِيَاء ـ تَعَلُّل . Display, تَصَنُّع ـ تَكَبُّر . *See also* Nonsense, *n.*

Claret, *n.* نَوْع مِن الْخَمْر الْفَرَنْسَاوِيّ .

Claret-colour, *n.* لَوْن كُرْزِيّ ـ لَوْن الْقِرَامِيَا .

Clarification, *n.* تَرْوِيق ـ تَصْفِيَة .

Clarified *a.* مُصَفًّى . Clarified butter, سَمْن .

Clarify, *v.t.* رَوَّق ـ صَفَّى ـ أَصْفَى ـ خَلَّص ـ أَخْلَص . To — by transfusion, صَفَّق ـ أَصْفَق .

Clarify, *v.i.* صَفَا ² ـ تَرَوَّق .

Clarion, *n.* A trumpet, بُوق *pl.* أَبْوَاق . The — of trumpets, صَوْت الْبُوقَات .

Clarinet, *n.* } قَلَارِينِيتَة ـ نَوْع مِن الزَّمَّارَة .
Clarionet, }

Clary, *n.* The plant, كُلُّه طَيِّب .

Clash, *v.t.* and *i.* To dash against, صَادَم ـ صَدَم . To come into collision, تَلَاطَم ـ تَصَادَم . To oppose, تَعَرَّض ل ـ خَالَف ـ ضَادّ . To — with one another, as in opinion, تَخَالَف ـ تَعَارَض .

Clash, *n.* } A collision, صَدْم ـ صَدْمَة ـ لَطْم ـ مُصَادَمَة . A
Clashing, } conflict, كَبَّة ـ وَقْعَة . Opposition, مُعَارَضَة ـ مُخَالَفَة .

Clashing, *a.* مُتَعَارِض ـ مُخَالِف .

Clasp, *n.* A hook or buckle, عِلَاقَة *pl.* عَلَائِق ـ عُقَّافَة ـ مِشْبَك *pl.* مَشَابِك ـ بَكْلَة . An embrace, حَضْنَة ـ مُعَانَقَة .

Clasp, *v.t.* To shut with a —, شَبَّك ـ قَفَل ـ شَدّ ² . To embrace, عَانَق ـ إِحْتَضَن ـ إِلَى صَدْرِه ـ ضَمّ ² .

Clasper, *n.* One who embraces, عَنِيق . *See also* Tendril, *n.*

Class, *n.* A rank of persons or things, نَسَق ـ مَرْتَبَة *pl.* مَرَاتِب ـ بَاب *pl.* أَبْوَاب ـ طِبَاق *and* طَبَقَات *pl.* طَبَقَة ـ دَرَجَات *pl.* دَرَجَة ـ نَوْع *pl.* أَنْوَاع . A kind, صِنْف *pl.* أَصْنَاف ـ جِنْس *pl.* أَجْنَاس . A number in the same line, a series, صَفّ *pl.* صُفُوف . The higher classes, الْأَكَابِر ـ الْخَوَاصّ ـ الْأَغْنِيَاء . The lower classes, أَسَافِل النَّاس . The privileged classes, الصُّنُوف الْمُمْتَازَة .

Class, *v.t.* To arrange in a class or classes, صَفّ ² ـ صَفَّف ـ قَسَّم ـ رَتَّب ـ فِي طَبَقَات ـ نَسَّق ـ بَوَّب . To be classed, arranged in a series, إِصْطَفّ ـ تَرَتَّب ـ إِنْتَسَق . To be classed, reckoned, in degree, حُسِب ـ إِنْدَرَج .

Class-book, *n.* كِتَاب الدَّرْس .

Classic, *a.* } Relating to ancient authors, مُخْتَصّ بِالْعُلُوم
Classical, } وَالْمَعَارِف الْقَدِيمَة ـ مُعْتَبَر قَدِيمًا . Held in repute, مُعْتَبَر . A — author, مُؤَلِّف مُعْتَبَر ـ مُصَنِّف مُعْتَبَر .

Classically, *ad.* عَلَى أُصُول الْمُؤَلِّفِين الْمُعْتَبَرِين .

Classification, *n.* تَقْسِيم فِي مَرَاتِب ـ تَصْفِيف ـ تَرْتِيب ـ تَنْسِيق .

Classify, *v.t.* صَفَّف ـ رَتَّب ـ فِي طَبَقَات ـ قَسَّم ـ فِي مَرَاتِب ـ بَوَّب . To systematize, نَسَّق .

Clatter, *n.* } Noise, كَرْكَبَة ـ شَمَاتَة ـ غَاغَة ـ رَجَّة ـ نَقْض .
Clattering, } Prattle, غَلْغَلَة (or شَقْشَقَة) لِسَان ـ بَرْبَرَة ـ بَلْبَلَة .

Clatter, as of arms, خَشْخَشَة .

Clatter, *v.i.* Of speech, بَلْبَل ـ بَرْبَر . To —, as arms, تَخَشْخَش . To make a noise, نَقَض ² ـ قَرْقَع ـ غَلْغَل ـ غَوَّش .

Clause, *n.* A sentence, جُمْلَة *pl.* جُمَل ـ فَصْل *pl.* فُصُول ـ عِبَارَة *pl.* عِبَارَات . An article in an agreement, شَرْط *pl.* شُرُوط ـ بَاب *pl.* أَبْوَاب ـ مَادَّة *pl.* مَوَادّ ـ فَصْل *pl.* فُصُول ـ بَنْد *pl.* بُنُود .

Clavicle, *n.* The collar-bone, تَرْقُوَة *pl.* تَرَاقٍ *and* تَرَائِق.

Claw, *n.* Of a bird or animal, ظُفْر ـ كُلَّاب *pl.* كَلَالِيب *pl.* أَظَافِير *and* أَظْفَار; of birds and beasts of prey, مِخْلَب *pl.* مَخَالِب; of solid hoofed animals, حَافِر *pl.* حَوَافِر; of cloven-footed animals, ظِلْف *pl.* ظُلُوف *and* أَظْلَاف. The toes or nails of an animal, بُرْثُن *pl.* بَرَاثِين. The claws, as of wild beasts, خَطَاطِيف.

Claw, *v.t.* To seize with the claws, ظَفَّرَ ـ ظَفَرَ ـ كَدَشَ. To scratch, خَدَشَ ـ شَرَطَ ـ خَرْمَشَ ـ خَرْبَشَ ـ خَلَبَ.

Clawed, *a.* Having claws, ذُو مَخَالِب.

Clawless, *a.* بِدُونِ مَخَالِب.

Clay, *n.* طِين ـ طُفَال ـ طَفْل. Hard or baked —, سِجِّيل. Soft or liquid —, عَرِين. Stiff —, غَضُور. A lump of —, طِينَة. Dry —, صِلْصَال. Soap —, بَيْلُون. Pipe-clay, طِين يُشْبِهُ ٱلطَّبَاشِير. Plastic —, طِينُ ٱلْإِبْلِيز. To daub over, as with —, مَدَرَ ـ مَلَطَ ـ طَيَّنَ ـ طَفَّلَ ـ لَبَّسَ.

Clay-cold, *a.* Dead, مَيِّت.

Clayey, *a.* طِينِيّ ـ طَفْلِيّ.

Claymore, *n.* سَيْف *pl.* سُيُوف.

Clay-pit, *n.* مَمْدَرَة.

Clay-stone, *n.* سِجِّيل.

Clean, *a.* Free from dirt, نَقِيّ ـ نَظِيف. Neat, كَيِّس ـ مَضْبُوط ـ ظَرِيف. Free from defilement, نَقِيّ ـ طَاهِر. Free, as from guilt, بَرِيء *pl.* بَرِيئُون *and* بُرَآء *and* بُرَآء ـ نَقِيّ. Clear, as of water, *etc.*, صَافٍ. Empty, فَارِغ. To be —, free from dirt, نَظُفَ ـ تَنَظَّفَ. To be —, pure, نَقِيَ. Having — hands and a pure heart, طَاهِرُ ٱلْيَدَيْنِ نَقِيُّ ٱلْقَلْب.

Clean, *v.t.* To free from dirt, نَظَّفَ. To — a house, put it in order, نَظَّمَ ٱلْبَيْت ـ عَسَّفَ ٱلْبَيْت. To —, as for eating, نَقَّى. To wipe, مَسَحَ ـ مَسَّحَ. To polish, جَلَا ـ صَقَلَ. To — the teeth, بَيَّضَ ـ سَوَّكَ أَسْنَانَهُ ـ تَسَوَّكَ ـ خَلَّلَ أَسْنَانَهُ. To — out the ears, نَكَشَ آذَانَهُ. To — out, as a well, نَزَحَ ـ نَكَشَ. To empty, فَرَّغَ. To — one's self, تَنَظَّفَ.

Clean, *ad.* Entirely, بَتَّة ـ بِٱلْمَرَّة ـ أَلْبَتَّة. He has — gone, رَاحَ بِٱلْكُلِّيَّة ـ رَاحَ أَلْبَتَّة.

Cleanliness, *n.* Freedom from dirt, نَظَافَة ـ نَقَاوَة ـ صَفَاوَة. Neatness, ظَرَافَة ـ هِنْدَام.

Cleanly, *ad.* See Clean, Neat, *a.*

Cleanly, *ad.* In a clean manner, بِنَظَافَة. Nicely, neatly, بِظَرَافَة ـ بِهِنْدَام.

Cleanness, *n.* Purity, نَقَاوَة ـ إِسْتِقَامَة ـ طَهَارَة.

Cleanse, *v.t.* See to Clean, *v.t.*

Cleansing, *n.* تَنْظِيف ـ تَنْقِيَة.

Clear, *a.* Bright, transparent, رَوْق ـ جَلِيّ ـ زَاهِر ـ خَالِص ـ نَيِّر ـ مُضِيء ـ لَامِع ـ نُور ـ شَفَّاف. Clear, of a day, صَافٍ ـ يَوْم صَافٍ ـ يَوْمٌ أَنْهَر. Pure, without mixture, صَافٍ ـ خَالِص ـ صَرِيح. Evident, صَرِيح ـ بَيِّن ـ مُبَيَّن ـ بَاهِر ـ مَعْلُوم. Perspicuous, وَاضِح ـ مَفْهُوم ـ مَحْسُوس. Not dark, of a colour, فَاتِح ـ مَفْتُوحُ ٱللَّوْن. Innocent, بَرِيء ـ طَاهِر ـ نَقِيّ ـ مَا عَلَيْهِ عِتَاب. Unobstructed, سَالِك ـ مَفْتُوح. Vacant, فَارِغ ـ فَاضٍ ـ خَالٍ. Sounding distinctly, جَهْوَر. Impartial, عَدِيمُ ٱلْغَرَض ـ خَالٍ مِنَ ٱلتَّعَصُّب. Clear in speech, فَصِيح. Quick, acute, حَادّ ـ قَاطِع ـ زَكِيّ ـ مُسْتَبْصِر ـ شَهْم. Free from, خَالِصٌ مِن ـ سَالِمٌ مِن ـ يَخْلُو عَن. Safe, أَمِين. Clear evidence, حُجَّة بَيِّنَة. As — as crystal, صَافٍ كَٱلْبِلَّوْر. You are —, innocent, in this matter, أَنْتُمْ أَبْرِيَاء مِنْ هٰذَا ٱلْأَمْر. It is — that ..., هُوَ مِنَ ٱلْمَعْلُوم أَن ـ لَا رَيْبَ أَن. A — proof, بُرْهَانٌ قَاطِع. Clear information, جَلِيَّة. To be —, bright, رَاقَ ـ تَرَوَّقَ ـ زَرِقَ ـ خَلَصَ ـ نَقِيَ. To become —, as of news, تَجَلَّى. To get — of, نَجَا مِن ـ بَرِئَ مِنَ ـ تَبَرَّأَ مِنَ. To get — of debts, بَرِئَ مِنَ ٱلدَّيْن. To be —, manifest, بَانَ ـ تَبَيَّنَ ـ إِسْتَبَانَ. To be —, as of blame, بَرِئَ مِن. To be —, in speech, أَفْصَحَ. To be —, as of clouds, *etc.*, صَرَحَ ـ إِنْصَرَحَ. To keep — of, تَمَنَّعَ مِن. To — one's self, as of a charge, إِنْتَصَفَ مِن. To declare one's self free, as of a charge, تَبَرَّأَ مِن.

Clear, *v.t.* To free, as from the imputation of guilt, أَبْرَأَ ـ بَرَّرَ ـ بَرَّأَ ـ بَيَّضَ وَجْهَهُ. To cleanse, نَظَّفَ. To free from impurities, خَلَّصَ ـ أَخْلَصَ ـ نَقَّى. To clarify, as liquors, رَوَّقَ ـ صَفَّى ـ خَلَّصَ. To —, to free from obscurity, أَصْرَحَ ـ صَرَّحَ بِ ـ فَسَّرَ. To —, to explain, جَلَا *aor.* يَجْلُو ـ جَلَّى. To make manifest, صَفَّى ـ أَوْضَحَ ـ جَلَّى. To —, or — off, to remove any obstruction, فَرَّغَ ـ رَفَعَ ـ شَالَ بِ ـ قَضَى. To make vacant, عَطَّلَ ـ فَرَّغَ. To — or clean out a pipe, tube, *etc.*, سَلَكَ. To — a table of food, رَفَعَ ٱلطَّعَام ـ شَالَ ٱلطَّعَام. To —, as of a vessel for departure, رَخَّصَ لِ ـ فِي ٱلسَّفَر. To — out, as a well, *etc.*, نَكَشَ. To — up a doubt from ..., ثَبَّتَ ـ رَفَعَ ٱلشَّكَّ عَن ـ أَزَالَ ٱلشَّكَّ عَن. To — away, of grief, *etc.*, فَرَّجَ.

Clear, *v.i.* To become light, of the weather, رَاقَ ـ تَرَوَّقَ ـ

صَحَتِ ٱلدُّنْيَا ـ إِنْجَلَى. The sky cleared up after midday, إِنْجَلَى ٱلْجَوُّ بَعْدَ ٱلظُّهْرِ. *See also under* Clear, *a.*

Clear, *ad.* Entirely, ٱلْبَتَّةَ ـ أَجْمَعَ ـ بَتَّةً. Plainly, جِهَارًا ـ عَلَانِيَةً.

Clearance, *n.* Clearing, } A place made clear of trees, *etc.*, for cultivation, قَرَاحٌ *pl.* قَوَارِحُ *and* قَرَاح. Clearance, as of a ship, تَذْكِرَةُ إِجَازَةٍ لِلسَّفَرِ ـ إِجَازَةٌ لِلسَّفَرِ. Justification, تَبْيِيضُ ٱلْوَجْهِ ـ تَبْرِيرٌ ـ تَبْرِئَةٌ. Removal, as of obstructions, تَصْفِيَةٌ ـ تَسْلِيكٌ ـ تَفْرِيغٌ ـ رَفْعٌ.

Clearing-house, *n.* دَارٌ لِلصَّيَارِفَةِ تَجْرِي فِيهَا تَصْفِيَةُ حِسَابَاتِهِمْ.

Clearly, *ad.* Brightly, إِضَاءَةً. Evidently, جِهَارًا ـ بَيَانًا ـ تَمَامًا ـ بِصَرَاحَةٍ ـ إِيضَاحًا ـ عَلَانِيَةً. Entirely, ٱلْبَتَّةَ ـ بَتَّةً ـ بِٱلْمَرَّةِ ـ أَجْمَعَ. Honestly, بِصَلَاحٍ ـ كَٱلْوَاجِبِ. He saw them all —, رَأَى ٱلْجَمِيعَ جِهَارًا. To see —, تَبَصَّرَ. How — it shines! مَا أَضْوَأَهُ.

Clearness, *n.* Brightness, نُورٌ ـ ضِيَاءٌ ـ ضَوْءٌ. Splendour, جَلَالٌ ـ إِسْتِبْصَارٌ ـ ضِيَاءٌ ـ رَوْنَقٌ ـ بَهْجَةٌ. Clearness of intellect, فِطْنَةٌ ـ ذَكَاءٌ. Pureness, خُلَاصَةٌ ـ نَقَاوَةٌ. Clearness of sight, حَدُّ ٱلْبَصَرِ. Perspicuity in speech or writing, بَيَانٌ ـ وُضُوحٌ ـ تَصْرِيحٌ ـ إِيضَاحٌ ـ تَبْيِينٌ ـ بَيَانٌ ـ إِمْتِيَازٌ ـ وُضُوحٌ. Distinctness, فَصَاحَةٌ ـ بَلَاغَةٌ. Sincerity, مُصَافَاةٌ ـ صِدْقٌ ـ صَفَاوَةٌ. Clearness, as of the atmosphere, صَفْوٌ ـ صَحْوٌ. Plainness of speech, بَسْطٌ فِي ٱلْكَلَامِ. Purity, innocence, طَهَارَةٌ ـ نَقَاوَةٌ.

Clear-sighted, *a.* فَطِنٌ *pl.* فُطْنٌ ـ نَبِيهٌ ـ خَارِقٌ ـ بَصِيرٌ ـ ذَكِيٌّ ـ صَاحِبُ نَظَرٍ. To be —, ذَكِيَ *aor.* يَذْكَى ـ فَطِنَ ².

Clear-starch, *v.t.* رَوَّى بِٱلنَّشَاءِ ـ نَشَّى.

Clear-story, *n.* Clerestory, } طَبَقَةُ بِنَاءٍ فَوْقَانِيَّةٌ ذَاتُ كُوًى.

Clear-toned, *a.* جَهْوَرِيُّ ٱلصَّوْتِ ـ جَهْوَرٌ.

Cleavage, *n.* فَلْعٌ ـ تَشْقِيقٌ.

Cleave, *v.t.* To split, شَقَّ ² ـ بَزَلَ ـ شَبَحَ ـ فَلَعَ ² ـ فَجَرَ ² ـ فَلَقَ ². To divide into parts, قَسَّمَ ـ جَزَّأَ ـ جَزَأَ ². To —, as a ship the water, دَسَرَ ² ـ شَبَحَ. The ship clave the water with its prow, دَسَرَتِ ٱلسَّفِينَةُ ٱلْمَاءَ بِصَدْرِهَا. To — wood, فَلَجَ (*or* فَلَعَ) ٱلْحَطَبَ ².

Cleave, *v.i.* To part asunder, إِنْشَقَّ ـ إِنْفَلَجَ ـ إِنْفَلَقَ ـ إِنْبَعَجَ ـ إِنْفَتَحَ. To — or adhere to, إِرْتَصَعَ بِ ـ أَصَبَّ عَلَى ـ لَزِقَ بِ ² ـ لَزِجَ بِ ² ـ عَمِدَ بِ ² ـ رَصِعَ بِ ². To persevere in, أَدْمَنَ عَلَى. To unite, إِنْضَمَّ.

Cleaver, *n.* A chopper, سَاطُورٌ *pl.* سَوَاطِيرُ.

Cleff, *n.* In music, عَلَامَةٌ فِي ٱلْمُوسِيقَةِ تَدُلُّ عَلَى ٱلْمَقَامَةِ.

Cleft, *n.* A crack, fissure, شَقٌّ ـ شُقُوقٌ ـ فَلْجٌ ـ فَلْحٌ ـ فَلْقٌ ـ فُلُوقٌ *pl.* فَلْعٌ ـ فُلُوعٌ *pl.* نُقْبَةٌ. A hole, نَقْبٌ ـ نُقْبَةٌ *pl.* نُقَبٌ. The clefts of the rocks, نُقَبُ ٱلصُّخُورِ ـ شُقُوقُ ٱلْمَعَاقِلِ. A — in a mountain, فُجَّةٌ.

Cleft, *a.* مَشْقُوقٌ ـ مَفْلُوجٌ.

Clematis, *n.* The plant, دَالِيَةٌ شَوْكَاءُ.

Clemency, *n.* Mercy, رَحْمَةٌ ـ رَأْفَةٌ. Mildness, كَرَمٌ ـ حِلْمٌ ـ مُسَامَحَةٌ ـ جَمِيلٌ. To treat with, تَحَلَّمَ عَنْ ـ حَلُمَ عَنْ ².

Clement, *a.* Merciful, forgiving, رَؤُوفٌ ـ رَحِيمٌ ـ غَفُورٌ ـ غَفَّارٌ ـ رَفِيقٌ ـ مُسَامِحٌ. Forbearing, gentle, حَلِيمٌ ـ حَمُولٌ.

Clench. *See* Clinch.

Clergy, *n.* جَمْعِيَّةُ ٱلْكَهَنَةِ ـ ٱلْأَكْلِيرُوسُ.

Clergyman, *n.* قَسٌّ *pl.* قُسُوسٌ ـ مِنْ أَهْلِ ٱلْأَكْلِيرُوسِ.

Clerical, *n.* Pertaining to the clergy, أَكْلِيرِيكِيٌّ ـ كَنَائِسِيٌّ. Appertaining to writing, مُخْتَصٌّ بِٱلْكِتَابَةِ. A — error, غَلَطٌ فِي ٱلْكِتَابَةِ.

Clerk, *n.* A writer, كَاتِبٌ *pl.* كَتَبَةٌ. A — in orders, a priest, قَسٌّ *pl.* قُسُوسٌ ـ قِسِّيسٌ. A church —, سَاعُورٌ. A scholar, مُعَلِّمٌ ـ عَالِمٌ. A writer in an office, قَلَمٌ *pl.* أَقْلَامٌ. A chief —, رَئِيسُ كَتَبَةِ ٱلْمَحْكَمَةِ. Chief — of the court, قَلَمُ أَقْلَامٍ.

Clerkship, *n.* Office of a writer, شُغْلُ ٱلْكَاتِبِ ـ مَكْتُوبْجِيَّةٌ ـ وَظِيفَةُ ٱلْكَاتِبِ. Scholarship, عِلْمٌ. The — of the public works, قَلَمُ إِدَارَةِ ٱلنَّافِعَةِ ـ مَكْتُوبْجِيَّةُ (*or* قَلَمُ) إِدَارَةِ ٱلْإِنْشَاآتِ ٱلْمِيرِيَّةِ.

Clever, *a.* Skilful, مَاهِرٌ ـ تَقِنٌ ـ فَطِينٌ ـ خَارِقٌ ـ أَرِيبٌ ـ حَيَّالٌ ـ شَاطِرٌ ـ حَاذِقٌ. Amusing, مُسَلٍّ. Cunning, crafty, تَمَهَّرَ فِي ـ إِفْتَنَّ فِي ـ أَرِبَ بِ ². To be — in any work, شَيْطَانٌ.

Cleverly, *ad.* بِشَطَارَةٍ ـ بِمَعْرِفَةٍ ـ بِصِنَاعَةٍ ـ بِفَنٍّ.

Cleverness, مِهْنَةٌ ـ مَعْرِفَةٌ ـ نَبَاهَةٌ ـ فَنٌّ ـ صِنَاعَةٌ ـ حَذَاقَةٌ ـ شَطَارَةٌ.

Clew, *n.* Of thread, a hank, وَشِيعَةٌ ـ مُسَفَّرَةٌ. A ball, as of thread, كُبْكُوبٌ ـ سُلَالَةٌ ـ كُبَّابَةٌ ـ طَابَةٌ. A guide, indication, هِدَايَةٌ ـ دِلَالَةٌ ـ إِرْشَادٌ ـ دَلِيلٌ. The lower corner of a sail, بَرْدَوِيلٌ. To give one a — to, دَلَّ عَلَى ².

Clew, *v.t.* Of a sail, لَمَّ ٱلْبَرْدَوِيلَ ².

Click, *v.i.* تَكْتَكَ.

Click, *n.* تَكْتَكَةٌ.

Client, *n.* The employer of a lawyer, زَبُونُ وَكِيلِ ٱلدَّعْوَى *pl.*

تحت حكم ـ تحت يد غيره ـ تابع. A dependent, زبائن. أحد.

Clientship, *n.* زبانة ـ زبونات ـ زبائن.

Cliff, *n.* هضبة *pl.* هضب *and* هضبات ـ جرف *pl.* أجراف ـ إهب *pl.* ألهاب.

Climacteric, *a.* / Climacterical, } Denoting a particular period of life, ما دل على درجة مخصوصة من درجات حيوة الإنسان. Every seventh year of life, سبوعي. A — or fatal year, سنة قطوعية.

Climate, *n.* A division of the earth, إقليم *pl.* أقاليم ـ قطر *pl.* أقطار. Temperature, of the air, هوآء ـ مناخ.

Climatic, *a.* متعلق بالهوآء ـ أقليمي.

Climatology, *n.* علم يبحث عن كيفية الهوآء.

Climax, *n.* Gradation, تدريج ـ مدارجة. Highest gradation, درجة الإنتهاء ـ نهاية ـ آخر درجة.

Climb, *v.t.* and *i.* To ascend, mount, صعد في ـ صعد في ـ طلع إلى ـ تصاعد. To — up or over, as a tree or wall, تشعبط ـ تشعلق ـ تسور ـ تسلق.

Climber, *n.* متشعلق ـ متسور ـ متسلق. A climbing plant; *see under* Runner, *n.*

Clime, *n.* *See* Climate, *n.*

Clinch, *v.t.* To gripe, hold fast, ضبط. To — the fist, طبق يده. To — a nail, لوى (ثنى *or*) رأس المسمار ـ برشم. To —, as of an argument, حقق ـ ثبت ـ أكد. He overcame him with a clinching argument, رماه بسكاتة. To hold fast upon, تماسك ب ـ أمسك ب.

Clinch, *n.* A grasp, مسكة ـ ضباطة. A twist of meaning, تصحيف ـ تعسف. A pun, نكتة.

Clincher, *n.* A cramp, طوقة ـ عقفاء ـ كلاليب *pl.* كلاب. A clinching argument, صمات ـ سكات ـ سكاتة.

Cling, *v.i.* To hang upon, تعلق في *or* ب. To stick to, إلتزق ب ـ إلتصق ب. To adhere to, as of a friend or follower, تمسك مع ـ حالف ـ تعلق في ـ أعصم ب ـ إلتصق ب ـ شبك ب ـ عزق ب. To grapple with, تشبث ب. To —, as to a place or thing, أصب على. To — to, to hold fast by, إعتصم ب ـ أعصم ب. He clung to his companion, أعصم بصاحبه. He clung to the horse, أعصم بالفرس. They clung together, of many, تحالفوا.

Clingy, *a.* Adhesive, دبق ـ لزج.

Clinic, *a.* / Clinical, } متعلق بملازمي ـ مختص بالسريرات الطبية الفراش.

Clinics, *n.* أصول السريرات الطبية.

Clinic, *n.* One confined to bed through sickness, ملازم الفراش ـ ملقى *fem.* ملقاة.

Clink, *v.t.* أطن ـ طنن.

Clink, *v.i.* طن ـ طنطن.

Clink, *n.* طنطنة ـ طنين.

Clinker, *n.* رغوة المعادن ـ توبال.

Clip, *v.t.* To cut with shears, قص. To shear, جز. To shorten by cutting, قرطم ـ قرض ـ قصر. To — the hair, أخذ من الشعر ـ جلم من الشعر ـ حف من الشعر ـ حذف من الشعر. To confine, حصر. To —, of money, قرط ـ زيف. To diminish, قلل ـ غض من.

Clip, *n.* A blow, لطمة ـ ضربة. A shearing, جزة. An embrace, حضنة. A —, as for holding papers, محفظة.

Clipped, *a.* As of the wings, مقصوص; of money, مقرط ـ مزيف.

Clipper, *n.* Of money, قراط ـ زياف ـ زائف. A fast ship, مركب طيار.

Clippings, *n.* قلامة ـ قطاعة ـ قصاصة ـ حذاقة.

Clique, *n.* كتة *pl.* كتات ـ شمل ـ عصبة *pl.* عصب ـ حزب *pl.* أحزاب. A political —, فرقة سياسية.

Clitoris, *n.* بظر.

Cloak, *n.* / Cloke, } An outer garment, مشلح *pl.* مشالح. A hooded —, برنس *pl.* برانس. A — with short sleeves, بنيش ـ جبة ـ عباية ـ عباآت *and* عباآة *pl.* عباء. A pretext, تعلل ـ علة ـ صورة ـ ستور *pl.* ستر ـ حيلة ـ حجة.

Cloak, *v.t.* To conceal, حجب ـ خبأ ـ خبأ. To disguise, نكر. To use a false pretence, تحيل ـ تعلل.

Cloak-bag, *n.* جراب *pl.* جرب ـ عيبة *pl.* عياب *and* عيبات ـ جمدان.

Clock, *n.* ساعة دقاقة كبيرة *pl.* ساعات. What o'clock is it? ما الساعة. It is four o'clock, الساعة في الأربعة ـ الساعة أربعة. The — has struck, دقت الساعة.

Clock-maker, *n.* ساعاتي *pl.* ساعاتية.

Clock-making, *n.* حرفة الساعاتية.

Clock-work, *n.* The machinery of a clock, دواليب الساعة. Well adjusted work, شغل منظوم.

Clod, *n.* Of earth, عتلة ـ كدية ـ مدرة *pl.* مدر ـ سحيل ـ

دَبْشَة. An instrument for breaking clods, مِقَضَّة ـ مِقْضَاض. *See also* Clodpate.

Clod, *v.i.* إِنْعَقَدَ ـ تَرَوَّبَ ـ جَمَدَ ².

Cloddy, *a.* وَاعِر ـ خَشْبَاء ـ مَمْلُوٌّ مَدَرًا.

Clodhopper, *n.* A clown, فَلَّاح. *See also* Clodpate, *n.*

Clodpate, *n.* } Clodpoll, } أَحْمَق *pl.* حُمُق *and* جِلْف ـ جُلَيْف ـ ضَوْطَر ـ غَلِيظ ـ حَمَاقِي.

Clog, *v.t.* To encumber, لَبَّكَ ـ عَوَّقَ ـ أَعَاقَ ـ زَخَمَ ـ. To hinder from, مَنَعَ ـ عَن ـ عَاقَ ـ عَن ² ـ ثَقَّلَ عَلَى ـ أَثْقَلَ ـ حَاشَ ـ عَن ². *See also* to Stuff, *v.t.*

Clog, *v.i.* To be stuck, impeded, تَعَلَّقَ فِي ـ إِلْتَزَقَ. To be encumbered, تَعَوَّقَ ـ تَوَرَّطَ ـ تَوَحَّلَ.

Clog, *n.* An encumbrance, حِمْل ـ مَانِع ـ ثِقْل; of a person, عَائِق ـ عَوْق. A wooden shoe, قَبْقَاب *pl.* قَبَاقِيب.

Cloggy, *a.* مُثَقِّل ـ ثَقِيل ـ مُلَبِّك ـ مُعَوِّق.

Cloister, *n.* A monastery, دَيْر *pl.* دُيُورَة. A Muslim —, تَكِيَّة. صَوْمَعَة ـ دَسْكَرَة. A piazza, رِوَاق *pl.* أَرْوِقَة. A Christian cell,

Cloister, *v.t.* To shut up in a monastery, حَبَسَ ـ فِي دَيْر.

Cloistered, *a.* Confined in a monastery, مَحْبُوس فِي دَيْر. Built with piazzas, ذُو أَرْوِقَة (*or* سُدَدٍ). Solitary, وَحِيد ـ مُتَوَحِّد.

Close, *v.t.* To shut, lock, سَكَّرَ ـ غَلَقَ ـ أَغْلَقَ ـ أَرْتَجَ ـ طَبَقَ. To —, as of a door, أَرْتَجَ ـ ٱلْبَابَ (*or* أَغْلَقَ *or* أَطْبَقَ *or* رَدَّ ² *or* تَرَعَ). To — a book, أَطْبَقَ ٱلْكِتَابَ. To conclude, تَمَّمَ ـ كَمَّلَ ـ خَتَمَ ـ قَضَى ـ خَلَصَ ـ غَلَقَ ـ أَنْهَى. To inclose, أَحَاطَ ـ زَرَّبَ ـ حَصَرَ ². To — up, سَدَّ ². To —, as of the eyes, غَمَّضَ. To unite, as of fractures, وَصَّلَ ـ أَطْبَقَ; of a wound, لَأَمَ. To —, as of a door, *etc.*, against, أَغْلَقَ ـ عَلَى.

Close, *v.i.* To join its own parts together, إِنْطَبَقَ ـ إِجْتَبَرَ. To shut, تَسَكَّرَ ـ إِنْغَلَقَ. To —, as a flower, طَبَّقَ ـ قَبَعَ; of a wound, طَابَ ـ إِنْجَبَرَ ـ ضَمَّ ² ـ إِلْتَأَمَ. To terminate, as the time for redeeming a pledge, *etc.*, غَلِقَ. To — or grapple with, تَشَبَّثَ بِ. To — or agree with, إِتَّفَقَ مَعَ ـ رَضِيَ بِ. To —, to be closed or stopped up, إِسْتَدَّ ـ إِنْسَدَّ. To come to an end, إِنْتَهَى ـ تَمَّ.

Close, *n.* An inclosed field, غَيْط مُزَرَّب ـ حِكْر ـ حَاكُورَة ـ حُنْفَة. A pause, cessation, إِنْقِطَاع. A conclusion, خِتَام ـ آخِر ـ خَاتِمَة ـ إِنْتِهَاء. To come to a —, إِنْتَهَى ـ تَمَّ. To draw to a —, إِقْتَرَبَ إِلَى ٱلْإِنْتِهَاء.

Close, *a.* Shut, مُغْلُوق ـ مُسَكَّر ـ مَطْبُوق. Private, مَسْتُور ـ مَحْصُور ـ ضَيِّق ـ سِرِّيّ ـ خَفِيّ ـ مَكْنُون. Confined, narrow, غَيْر شَرِح. Sultry, عَكّ ـ عَكِيك ـ غَامّ ـ مُغِمّ ـ غَتْم. Solid, dense, كَثِيف ـ مَتِين ـ مُكْتَنِز. Concise, مُخْتَصَر ـ مُوجَز. Narrow, قَصِير ـ حَرِج ـ ضَيِّق ـ مُضِيق. Cloudy, not clear, مُغَيِّم. Close, closed up, مَسْدُود. Avaricious, شَحَّاح ـ شَحِيح ـ بَخِيل ـ يَدُهُ مَاسِكَة. Compact, سَفِيق ـ مُكْتَنِز. Close, of the flesh, وَثِيج. Trusty, أَمِين *pl.* أُمَنَاء ². Retired, solitary, مُتَوَحِّد ـ مُنْفَرِد ـ مُبْتَعِد. Without intervening space, مُلْتَصِق ـ مُتَّصِل ـ مُقْتَرِن ـ مَوْصُول بِ ـ مُتَّصِل بِ. Near to, joined to, مُلْتَصِق بِ ـ قَرِيب مِن. A — or narrow place, مَضِيق. Close study, attention, مُلَازَمَة ـ تَقَيُّد ـ جِهْد. Close connexion between persons, أُلْفَة ـ صُحْبَة أَكِيدَة; between things, إِقْتِرَان كُلِّيّ. Close cloth, قُمَاش مُطَبَّق. To keep a matter —, سَكَتَ عَن ². To be —, sultry, عَكَّ ـ غَمَّ ² ـ أَغَمَّ.

Close-fisted, *n.* يَدُهُ مَاسِكَة ـ بَخِيل.

Close, *ad.* } Closely, } Without much intervening space, قَرِيب مِن ـ تَقْرِيبًا. Attentively, بِٱنْتِبَاهٍ ـ بِٱلتَّدْقِيق ـ بِتَقَيُّد ـ بِٱجْتِهَاد. Secretly, سِرًّا ـ فِي ٱلسِّرّ ـ عَلَى خَفَاء ـ فِي خُفْيَة. Without deviation, إِلْتِزَامًا. To stick — to, عَلِقَ ـ إِلْتَصَقَ مَعَ ـ بِ. His house was — to the mosque, كَانَ بَيْتُهُ مُتَّصِلًا بِٱلْجَامِع.

Closeness, *n.* Narrowness, حَرَج ـ ضَيْق *or* ضِيق. Want of air, عَكَّة ـ عِكَاك ـ حَصَر ـ غَتْم. Compactness, إِكْتِنَاز ـ سَفَاقَة ـ كَثَافَة. Stinginess, بُخْل ـ خِسَّة ـ لَامَة ـ إِمْسَاك. Secrecy, سِرّ ـ وَحْدَة ـ خَلْوَة. Connexion, مُقَارَنَة ـ إِقْتِرَان. Retirement, إِنْفِرَاد. Application, إِنْتِبَاه ـ مُلَازَمَة ـ مُوَاظَبَة.

Close-quarters, *n.* Nearness, قُرْبَة. The being side by side, مُجَانَبَة. To come to — with, to grapple with, تَشَبَّثَ بِ.

Close-stool, *n.* كُرْسِيّ فِيهِ غَائِط.

Closet, *n.* A small room, مُخْدَع *pl.* مَخَادِع ـ خَادِعَة ـ حُجَيْرَة ـ حُجْرَة *pl.* حُجَر. A repository, خِزَانَة ـ مَقْصُورَة. A water —, كَنِيف ـ مُسْتَرَاح.

Closet, *v.i.* To be closeted with for consultation, تَشَاوَرَ مَعَهُ سِرًّا ـ أَخْلَى بِ (*or* إِسْتَخْلَى بِ) لِلْمُشَاوَرَة.

Closing, *a.* Last, آخِر ـ أَخِير. The — interview, ٱلْمُوَاجَهَة ٱلْأَخِيرَة.

Closing, *n.* End, خِتَام ـ إِنْتِهَاء ـ آخِر.

Closure, *n.* A seam, وَصْل *pl.* أَوْصَال ـ وُصْلَة. An inclosure; *see* Close, *n.*

Clot, *n.* A congelation, جَمَد ـ تَجْمِيدَة. A lump, جلْفَة. A — of blood, رُوبَة دَم ـ دَمَة ـ عَلَقَة.

Clot, *v.i.* تَحَبَّبَ ـ إِنْعَقَدَ ـ رَابَ *aor.* يَرُوبُ. Clotted blood, دَم مَرُوب.

Cloth, *n.* Any material woven for dress, قُمَاش *pl.* أَقْمِشَة. Woollen or broadcloth, جُوخ. Cloth woven of wool and silk, خَزّ. Open —, cloth badly woven, قُمَاش مُتَسَلْسَل. A table —, سُفْرَة ـ غِطَاء ٱلْمَائِدَة. A horse —, رَخْد ـ طَرَّاحَة. A bathing —, فُوطَة *pl.* فُوط. A floor —, فَرْش. The — worn round the loins by the Bedawin, بُرْدَة. A piece of —, a rag, رُقْعَة. A drying —, نَشَّافَة. Cut your coat according to your —, عَلَى قَدْرِ ٱلْكِسَاء مُدَّ رِجْلَيْكَ. *Literally,* Stretch your legs according to the length of your coverlid.

Clothe, *v.t.* سَرْبَلَ ـ وَشَّحَ ـ لَبَّسَ ـ كَسَّى ب. To — or dress one's self in, تَسَرْبَلَ ب ـ تَكَسَّى ب ـ إِتَّشَحَ ب ـ لَبِسَ ـ ؛ إِرْتَدَى ب ـ تَرَدَّى ب. One clothed in, لَابِس ـ مُتَرَدّ ب.

Clothes, *n.* } Clothing, } كِسْوَة ـ كِسَاء ـ كَسَاوِي ـ لِبْس ـ لِبَاس ـ مَلَابِس ـ ثِيَاب. Clothes generally, حَوَائِج. Clothes for the wash, غَسِيل. Cast —, ثِيَاب بَالِيَة ـ ثِيَاب مَخْلُوقَة. To rend one's —, مَزَّقَ ثِيَابَهُ. Gay clothing, ثِيَاب بَهِيَّة. Bed-clothes, شَرَاشِف ـ مَلَاحِف ـ مَنَامَات. His best —, أَفْخَر ثِيَابِهِ.

Clothes-basket, *n.* سَلَّة لِلثِّيَاب.

Clothes-brush, *n.* فُرْشَة ٱلثِّيَاب.

Clothes-horse, *n.* شِجَاب ـ مِشْجَب ـ مِشْجَر.

Clothes-line, *n.* حَبْلُ ٱلنَّشْرِ.

Clothes-peg, *n.* عِيَار *pl.* عَيْر لِلثِّيَاب.

Clothier, *n.* One who sells cloth, جُوخِيّ *pl.* جُوخِيَّة ـ بَيَّاع ٱلْجُوخ.

Clotted-cream, *n.* حَالُوم ـ أَقِط.

Clotty, *a.* مُعَقَّد ـ مُجَمَّد ـ مَرُوب.

Cloud, *n.* غَيْم *pl.* غُيُوم ـ سَحَابَة *coll.* سَحَاب *pl.* سَحَائِب ـ ضَبَابَة *coll.* ضَبَاب. A mass of clouds, حَبِيّ ـ حَبًا. Clouds covering the sky, غَمَامَة ـ غَمَام. A morning —, غَادِيَة ـ غَدِيَّة. A thunder —, مُجَلْجِل. A rain —, مَطِير. Mackerel clouds, سَمَاحِيقُ ٱلسَّمَاء. Redness of the clouds at sunset or sunrise, نَدِيّ. A — of dust, عَجَاج ـ عَجَاجَة ـ غُبَار ـ غُبْرَة. A —, as of people, غَزَارَة ـ جَوْق ـ زَحْم. To be under a —, in trouble, كَانَ فِي ضِيقَةٍ ـ كَانَ فِي شِدَّةٍ. He spread the clouds for a covering, بَسَطَ ٱلسَّحَابَ غِطَاءً. The clouds were broken up, تَفَتَّقَ ٱلسَّحَابُ. The clouds covered or concealed the stars, طَمَسَ ٱلْغَيْمُ ٱلنُّجُومَ.

Cloud, *v.t.* and *i.* To make dark, abstruse, عَتَمَ عَلَى ـ أَظْلَمَ ـ عَلَى ـ أَبْهَمَ عَلَى ـ حَجَبَ ـ غَلَّقَ. To become dark, عَتَمَ ـ أَظْلَمَ.

Cloud-capt, *a.* مُكَلَّل بِسَحَاب ـ مُعَمَّم بِسَحَاب.

Cloudily, *ad.* Darkly, عَتَمًا ـ ظَلْمًا ـ بِعَمَشٍ.

Cloudiness, *n.* Of the clouds, غَمَى ـ غَمًا ـ غَمَامَة ـ غَمَام. Darkness, عَتَمَة ـ ظَلَام. Dubiousness, إِبْهَام ـ غِمَّة.

Cloudless, *a.* مِنْ غَيْرِ سَحَاب ـ صَاحٍ ـ رَائِق ـ صَافٍ. The night became —, صَحِيَتِ ٱللَّيْلَةُ.

Cloudy, *a.* With clouds, dark, مُغَيَّم ـ كَدِر ـ مُغْتِم ـ عَتِم ـ مُظْلِم. Gloomy of aspect, عَابِس ـ عَبِس. Sad, كَئِيب ـ سَوْدَاوِيّ. Unintelligible, مُغْلَق ـ مُبْهَم ـ مُلْتَبِس ـ لَا يُفْهَم. To be —, of the sky, ٱلسَّمَاء (*or* تَغَيَّمَتِ) غَامَتِ ـ كَدِرَ ـ أَغْمَى. The sky begins to get —, أَخَذَ ٱلْجَوُّ فِي ٱلتَّغْيِيمِ. A — sky, سَمَاء جَلْوَاء. A — day, يَوْم غَيُوم. A — night, لَيْلَة جَلْوَاء. The moon became —, غُمَّ عَلَى ٱلْقَمَرِ. Covered with clouds, أَغَمّ ـ مُعَمَّم بِسَحَاب.

Clout, *n.* a rag for any mean use, جِرْدَة ـ مِمْسَحَة *pl.* مَمَاسِح ـ خُلْقَة *pl.* خُلَق ـ خِرْقَة ـ شَرْطُوطَة. A patch, رُقْعَة *pl.* رِقَاع ـ خِرْقَة ـ قِطْعَة. A dish-clout, نَشَّافَة. A nail, مِسْمَار. *See also* Clamp, *n.*

Clout, *v.t.* To patch, رَقَّعَ ـ رَدَمَ. To mend, رَفَا ـ صَلَّحَ.

Clouted, *a.* Patched, مُرَقَّع.

Clove, *n.* The spice, قَرَنْفُل ـ كَبْش قَرَنْفُل ـ قِرْفَة. A division of a fruit, *etc.*, فَصّ *pl.* فُصُوص ـ سِنَّة *pl.* أَسْنَان ـ شِرْذِمَة *pl.* شَرَاذِم. A — of garlick, فَصُّ ٱلثُّوم.

Cloven, *n.* *See* Cleft, *a.* A — foot, ظِلْف *pl.* ظُلُوف.

Cloven-footed, *a.* } Cloven-hoofed, } مَفْلُوق ـ مَفْرُوجُ ٱلظِّلْفِ ـ مَشْقُوقُ ٱلظِّلْفِ.

Clover, *n.* بِرْسِيم ـ دُرَق.

Clown, *n.* A peasant, فَلَّاح *pl.* فَلَّاحُون. A buffoon, بُهْلُول *pl.* بَهَالِيل ـ بَهْلَوَان. A boor, غَلِيظ ـ أُمَّان ـ صَوْطَر ـ فَظّ ـ جَافٍ.

Clownish, *a.* غَلِيظ ـ صَوْطَرِيّ ـ أُمِّيّ ـ فَظّ ـ فَلَّاح.

Clownishly, *ad.* بِغَلَاظَةٍ ـ بِخُشُونَةٍ ـ بِقِلَّةِ أَدَب.

Clownishness, *n.* خُرْق ـ غِلَاظَة ـ خُشُونَة ـ غِلْظَة ـ قِلَّة أَدَب.

Cloy, *v.t.* أَنْصَحَ ـ شَبَّعَ ـ أَشْبَعَ.

Club, *n.* A heavy stick, نَبُّوت *pl.* نَبَابِيتُ ـ نَبُّود ـ دَبُّوس ـ نَبْرِكْ. An assembly, نَدْوَة ـ نَادٍ ـ صُحْبَة ـ مَعْشَر ـ عُشْرَة. The place of meeting, نَدْوَة *pl.* نَدَوَات ـ نَادٍ ـ مَحَلُّ ٱلْعُشْرَةِ ـ دَارُ ٱلصُّحْبَةِ. The suit at cards, صَلِيب.

Club, *v.t.* To join together for a common purpose, of many, تَعَاقَدُوا عَلَى ـ سَعُوا فِي-جُمْلَةٍ ـ إِتَّحَدُوا مَعًا فِي ـ إِتَّفَقُوا عَلَى.

Club-fist, *n.* }
Club-hand, } فَدَع.

Club-foot, *n.* حَنَف.

Club-footed, *a.* أَحْنَفُ. Club-footed or club-handed, أَفْدَعُ. To be —, حَنِفَ [2].

Club-law, *n.* حُكُومَةُ بُغَاةٍ ـ ظُلْم ـ حَيْف.

Club-room, *n.* *See under* Club, *n.*

Club-shaped, *a.* فِي هَيْئَةِ ٱلدَّبُّوسِ.

Cluck, *v.i.* As a hen, تَكَأْكَأَ ـ نَقْنَقَ ـ نَقَّ.

Cluck, *n.* }
Clucking, } تَكَأْكُؤ ـ قَرْق ـ نَقِيق.

Clue. *See under* Clew, *n.*

Clump, *n.* A shapeless piece, بَضْعَة *pl.* بِضَاع. A — of trees, سِرْبُ شَجَرٍ ـ مَشَاجِرُ *pl.* مَشْجَر ـ غِيَاض *pl.* غَيْضَة.

Clump, *v.t.* To mass together, ضَمَّنَ.

Clumsily, *ad.* بِغَشْمٍ ـ بِقِلَّةِ مَعْرِفَةٍ ـ بِقِلَّةِ صَنْعَةٍ ـ بِخُرْقٍ. *See also* Awkwardly, *ad.*

Clumsiness, *n.* عَدَمُ ٱسْتِعْدَادٍ ـ غِلَاظَة ـ عَدَمُ صِنَاعَةٍ ـ خُرْق ـ عَدَمُ شَطَارَةٍ. *See also* Awkwardness, *n.*

Clumsy, *a.* Of a person, غَشِيم ـ قَلِيلُ ٱلصِّنَاعَةِ ـ أَخْرَقُ ـ شَلُوش ـ شَنِش; of a thing only, سَمِج ـ غَيْرُ طَائِلٍ. *See also* Fumbling, Awkward, *a.*

Clung, *pret. and part. of to* Cling, *q.v.*

Cluster, *n.* An assemblage of things, لَمَّة ـ كُوم ـ كُومَة ـ جَمْع ـ لَفِيفَة *pl.* لَفَائِف ـ كَبْشَة ـ جَمْعُ نَاسٍ ـ ثَوْل. A — of people, جَمْعٌ غَفِير ـ جَوْقَة. A — of bees, ثَوْل ـ نَحْلٍ (or) طَرْدُ ـ سِرْبَة. A —, as of grapes, عُنْقُود *pl.* عَنَاقِيدُ. A —, as of dates, عُرْجُون *pl.* عَرَاجِينُ ـ عِذْق *pl.* أَعْذَاق ـ عُنْقُودُ تَمْرٍ.

Cluster, *v.i.* To grow or unite in clusters, تَعَقَّدَ. To crowd, إِزْدَحَمَ. To collect, إِلْتَمَّ. To — round, إِلْتَمَّ-حَوْلَ.

Cluster, *v.t.* لَمَّ ـ حَشَدَ [2].

Clustering, *a.* Growing in clusters, ذُو عَنَاقِيدَ ـ مُتَعَقِّد. Clustering in parties, مُتَحَزِّب.

Clutch, *n.* A grasp, قَبْضَة ـ ضَبَاطَة ـ تَمْسِيك. Clutches, claws, أَظْفَار ـ مَخَالِيبُ. Power, سُلْطَة ـ يَد ـ تَسَلُّط. To free from the — of, فَصَّى-مِنْ. To be freed from the — of, إِنْفَصَى (or تَفَصَّى) مِنْ.

Clutch, *v.t.* ضَبَطَ ـ قَبَضَ ـ مَسَكَ بِ ـ قَمَطَ عَلَى [2]. To — or clench the fist, طَبَقَ ٱلْيَدَ.

Clutter, *n.* *See* Clatter, *n.*

Clutter, *v.i.* *See to* Bustle, *v.i.*

Clyster, *n.* An injection, حُقْنَة *pl.* حُقَن; the instrument for giving an injection, مِحْقَنَة. To give a — to, حَقَنَ [2]; to receive a —, إِحْتَقَنَ.

Co., *n.* تَرْخِيمُ لَفْظَةِ كُومْبَنِي يَعْنِي بِهَا شِرْكَة. Hanson and Co., بَيْتُ هَنْسَنَ ـ هَنْسَنُ وَشُرَكَاؤُهُ.

Coach, *n.* عَرَبِيَّة ـ عَرَبَانَة بِأَرْبَعِ عَجَلَاتٍ ـ كَرُّوصَة *pl.* كَرُّوصَات.

Coach, *v.t.* To convey in a coach, سَارَ بِهِ فِي عَرَبَانَةٍ ـ وَصَّلَ-فِي. He coached it, سَارَ فِي كَرُّوصَةٍ. To —, to teach, direct, عَلَّمَ ـ دَلَّ.

Coach-box, *n.* مَقْعَدُ سَوَّاقِ ٱلْعَرَبِيَّةِ.

Coach-house, *n.* إِصْطَبْل ـ مَحَطُّ ٱلْكَرُّوصَاتِ.

Coachmaker, *n.* صَانِعُ كَرُّوصَاتٍ.

Coachman, *n.* مَاسِكُ ٱلْعِنَانِ ـ سَوَّاقُ ٱلْعَرَبِيَّةِ.

Coachmanship, *n.* مَهَارَةٌ فِي سِيَاقَةِ ٱلْكَرُّوصَاتِ.

Coaction, *n.* Compulsion, جَبْر ـ إِلْزَام ـ غَصْب ـ قَهْر.

Coactive, *a.* Compelling, غَصْبِيّ ـ قَهْرِيّ ـ جَبْرِيّ. Acting in concurrence, مُتَّفِق.

Coadjutant, *a.* }
Coadjutor, *n.* } رَفِيق ـ شَرِيك ـ مُسَاعِد ـ مُعَاوِن.

Coagent, *n.* شَرِيك *pl.* شُرَكَاءُ ـ شَرِيكٌ فِي ٱلْوَكَالَةِ.

Coagulable *a.* تَجْمِيدُهُ مُمْكِنٌ ـ يَنْعَقِدُ ـ يَجْمُدُ.

Coagulate, *v.t.* رَوَّبَ ـ أَعْقَدَ ـ عَقَّدَ ـ جَمَّدَ.

Coagulate, *v.i.* تَرَوَّبَ ـ إِنْعَقَدَ ـ جَمَدَ [2] ـ رَابَ [2].

Coagulation, *n.* The act of, تَجْمِيد ـ تَرْوِيب; the result of —, إِنْجِمَاد ـ رَوْب ـ جَمْد.

Coagulative, *a.* مُعَقِّد ـ مُجَمِّد ـ مُرَوِّب.

Coagulum, *n.* Rennet, إِنْفَحَة ـ مَصْل ـ مِنْفَحَة. A coagulated mass, جَمَد.

Coal, *n.* Fossil, فَحْمٌ حَجَرِيّ ـ فَحْمٌ مَعْدِنِيّ. Charcoal, فَحْم. A live —, جَمْرَة ـ جَذْوَةٌ مِنَ ٱلنَّارِ ـ جُذًا *pl.* جَذْوَة ـ حُمَيْمَة ـ جَمَرَات *pl.* A small live —, نَارَة ـ بَصَّةُ نَارٍ ـ بَصُّ نَارٍ. To call over the coals, to call to account for, to reprove, حَاسَبَ-عَلَى ـ عَاتَبَ.

Coal, *v.t.* To supply or load with —, شَحَنَ - فَحْمًا ‎ ِ. To take in a supply of —, أَخَذَ فَحْمًا ‎ ُ.

Coal-agent, *n.* سِمْسَارُ ٱلْفَحْمِ.

Coal-bed, *n.* طَبَقَةُ فَحْمٍ حَجَرٍ.

Coal-cellar, *n.* مَطْمُورَةُ فَحْمٍ حَجَرٍ.

Coal-deposit, مُطَامِيرُ فَحْمٍ حَجَرٍ.

Coalesce, *v.i.* To unite with, إِتَّحَدَ مَعَ - إِنْعَقَدَ مَعَ - إِنْضَمَّ إِلَى - إِلْتَزَقَ بِ - إِتَّفَقَ مَعَ - إِجْتَمَعَ بِ. To — of itself to, إِنْضَمَّ إِلَى. To — in favour of, تَعَصَّبَ لِ; against, تَعَصَّبَ عَلَى.

Coalescence, *n.* Union, إِجْتِمَاع - إِنْضِمَام - إِتِّفَاق; of liquids, إِمْتِزَاج - إِخْتِلَاط.

Coalescent, *a.* مُتَّفِق - مُتَّحِد - مُنْضَمّ.

Coal-factor, *n.* *See* Coal-agent, *n.*

Coal-field, *n.* طَبَقَةٌ مِنْ طَبَقَاتِ مَعْدِنِ ٱلْفَحْمِ.

Coal-heaver, *n.* شَيَّالَة *pl.* شَيَّالُ ٱلْفَحْمِ - حَمَّالُ فَحْمٍ.

Coaling, *n.* شَحْنُ فَحْمٍ.

Coalition, *n.* A confederacy, حِزْب - عُصْبَة - تَعَصُّب. To form a — in favour of, تَعَصَّبَ لِ; against, تَعَصَّبَ عَلَى. *See also* Coalescence, *n.*

Coal-measure, *n.* *See* Coal-field, *n.*

Coal-mine, *n.* مَعْدِنُ فَحْمٍ حَجَرٍ.

Coal-miner, *n.* مُعَدِّنَة *pl.* مُعَدِّنُ ٱلْفَحْمِ - حَفَّارٌ فِي مَعْدِنِ ٱلْفَحْمِ.

Coal-owner, *n.* صَاحِبُ مَعَادِنِ فَحْمٍ.

Coal-pit, *n.* نَاقُورٌ فِي مَعْدِنِ فَحْمٍ حَجَرٍ.

Coal-scuttle, *n.* سُطُول *pl.* سَطْلٌ لِلْفَحْمِ.

Coal-seam, *n.* *See* Coal-bed, *n.*

Coal-wharf, *n.* إِسْكَلَةُ ٱلْفَحْمِ.

Coal-whipper, *n.* *See* Coal-heaver, *n.*

Coaly, *a.* فَحْمِيّ.

Coarse, *a.* Not fine, عُبُل *pl.* عَبْل - جِلّ - جَافٍ - خَشِب - عِبَال - أَخْشَب - غَلِيظ - خَشِن - مُخَيَّن; of cloth, سَفِيق. Not of first quality, دُون. Rude, غَلِيظ - جَافٍ - فَظّ - قَلِيلُ ٱلْأَدَب. Not polished, بِلَا صَقْل. Coarse flour, خُشْكَار - السَّمْرَآء. Coarse bread, خُبْزُ ٱلسَّمْرَآء. To be —, rough, stubborn, rude, فَظَّ ‎ ِ - غَلُظَ ‎ ُ - خَشُنَ ‎ ُ. To judge to be —, إِسْتَغْلَظَ - إِسْتَخْشَنَ. To make —, خَشَّنَ - غَلَّظَ.

Coarsely, *ad.* Rudely, بِلَا ظَرَافَةٍ - بِقِلَّةِ مَعْرِفَةٍ; uncivilly, بِقِلَّةِ أَدَبٍ - بِغِلَاظَةٍ - بِفَظَاظَةٍ. Not finely, خَشِنًا. To grind or pound —, جَرَشَ ‎ ُ ‎ ِ.

Coarseness, *n.* Want of fineness, خُشُونَة - خَشَانَة - خُشْن - غِلْظَة. Rudeness of manner, جَفَآء - فَظَاظَة - سَفَاهَة - غِلْظَة - قِلَّةُ أَدَبٍ.

Co-assessor, *n.* رَفِيقٌ فِي مَأْمُورِيَّةٍ.

Coast, *n.* The sea-coast, شُطُوط *pl.* شَطُّ ٱلْبَحْرِ - عَيْقَة - بَرّ - شَاطِئُ ٱلْبَحْرِ - حَافَةُ ٱلْبَحْرِ - سَوَاحِل *pl.* سَاحِلُ ٱلْبَحْرِ. Border, country, أَطْرَاف - بِلَاد - نَوَاحِي. The — is clear, there is no impediment, الدَّرْبُ سَالِكٌ - الدَّرْبُ مَفْتُوحٌ.

Coast, *v.i.* To go along the coast, شَطَأَ ‎ ِ - سَافَرَ بِٱلْقُرْبِ مِنَ ٱلسَّوَاحِلِ.

Coaster, *n.* } Sailing along the coast, مُسَافِرٌ بِٱلْقُرْبِ مِنَ
Coasting, *a.* } ٱلسَّوَاحِلِ. A coasting vessel, سُفُن *pl.* سَفِينَةٌ تَمُرُّ بِٱلسَّوَاحِلِ.

Coasting, *n.* The act of sailing along the coast, شُطُوء - شَطْء - سَفَرٌ بِٱلْقُرْبِ مِنَ ٱلسَّوَاحِلِ.

Coat, *n.* An upper garment, overcoat, ثَوْب - جُبَب *pl.* جُبَّة - عَبَآءَة *pl.* عَبَآءَات *and* عَبَآء. A frock or dress —, سُتَر *pl.* سُتْرَة. The — or fur of an animal, جِزَّة - فَرْوَة - صُوف - وَبَر. A covering, غِطَآء. A besmearing, مَسْحَة - دَهْنَة - صَبْغَة. That on which anything is portrayed, أَرْضِيَّة. A — of mail, زَرَدِيَّة - دِرْع - جُبَّة. Having a —, like an onion, مُتَبَصِّل. Having more coats than the onion, أَكْسَى مِنَ ٱلْبَصَلِ. Cut your — according to your cloth, عَلَى قَدْرِ بِسَاطِكَ ٱمْدُدْ رِجْلَيْكَ (*prov.*). To clad one's self in a — of mail, تَدَرَّعَ. A — of arms; *see under* Arms.

Coat, *v.t.* To cover, indue, لَبَّسَ. To besmear, paint, طَلَى ‎ ِ - صَبَغَ ‎ ُ - دَهَنَ ‎ ُ.

Coating, *n.* Cloth, جُوخ. A priming, as of paint, *etc.*, طَلْيَة - مَسْحَة - صَبْغَة - دَهْنَة - تَلْبِيس.

Coax, *v.t.* دَاجَنَ - دَلَّ ‎ ُ - دَارَى - جَامَلَ - رَاوَضَ - أَخَذَ بِخَاطِرِهِ - جَوَّنَ - تَلَطَّفَ بِ - تَلَيَّنَ لِ - مَاسَحَ - بِٱلْجَمِيلِ.

Coaxer, *n.* مَلَّاق - مُدَارٍ - مُرَاوِض.

Coaxing, *n.* تَأَلُّف - مُدَاجَنَة - مُدَارَاة - تَدْلِيَة.

Coaxingly, *ad.* بِمُدَاجَنَةٍ - بِمُدَارَاةٍ.

Cob, *n.* A rounded stone, كُبَب *pl.* كُبَّة - بُهَم *pl.* بُهْمَة. A spike, as of a plant, رَأْس. A pony, حُصُنٌ صِغَار *pl.* حِصَانٌ صَغِير.

Cobalt, *n.* حَجَرٌ مَعْدِنِيٌّ يَخْرُجُونَ مِنْهُ صِباغًا أَزْرَقَ.

Cobble, *n.* A small boat, قارِب *pl.* قَوارِبُ ــ فَلُوكَةٌ. *See also* Botch, *n.*

Cobble, Cobble-stone, *n.* *See under* Cob, *n.*

Cobble, *v.t.* *See to* Botch, Clout, *v.t.*

Cobbler, *n.* A mender of old shoes, (النِّعالِ *or*) مُرَقِّعُ الْأَصارِمِ ــ إِسْكاف ــ خَصَّاف. *See also* Botcher, Bungler, *n.*

Cobweb, *n.* عُشُّ الْعَنْكَبُوتِ ــ قُدْس ــ نَسْجُ الْعَنْكَبُوتِ. A — brush, زَحَّافَةٌ ــ هَلُوس.

Cobwebbed, *a.* أَقْدَس.

Cocciferous, *a.* حامِلُ حُبُوب ــ ذُو حُبُوب.

Coccyx, *n.* عُصْعُص ــ عَجْب.

Cochineal, *n.* The insect, دُودَةُ الْقِرْمِزِ. The material, قِرْمِز. Colour of —, قِرْمِزِيٌّ.

Cochleary, *a.* / Cochleate, } Spiral, لَوْلَبِيٌّ.

Cock, *v.t.* To set erect, نَصَبَ ــ شَمَّرَ ــ نَقَّفَ ــ قَوَّمَ. To gather into heaps, عَرَمَ ــ حَزَمَ ــ حَزْمًا. To — hay, عَرَمَ الْحَشِيشَ. To — a gun, شَدَّ دِيكَةَ الْبارُودَةِ.

Cock, *n.* Male of the hen, أَبُو يَقْظانَ ــ صَرْصَر ــ جِنْزاب ــ دِيك *pl.* دُيُوك *and* دِيَكَة *and* أَدْياك. The male of any small bird, ذَكَر *pl.* ذُكُور. A spout, حَنَفِيَّةٌ ــ لَوْلَب *pl.* لَوالِبُ. A weather-cock, دَوَّارَةُ هَواءٍ. The needle of a balance, لِسانُ الْمِيزانِ. The style of a sun dial, مِيل. A heap, sheaf, عَرَمَة *pl.* عُرَم ــ حُزْمَة *pl.* حُزَم. The —, as of a gun, جِقْمَق ــ دِيك. Cock of the walk, وَلِيُّ الْحالِ. To be at full —, of fire-arms, مَشْدُودُ الدِّيكِ.

Cockade, *n.* وَرْدَةٌ مِنْ حَرِيرٍ ــ إِشارَةٌ.

Cockatoo, *n.* نَوْعٌ مِنَ الْبَبْغانِ.

Cockatrice, *n.* صِلّ *pl.* أَصْلال.

Cockboat, *n.* قارِب *pl.* قَوارِبُ ــ فَلُوكَةٌ.

Cockchafer, *n.* نَوْعٌ مِنَ الْخُنْفُسِ.

Cock-crowing *n.* صِياحُ الدِّيكِ. Dawn, شَقُّ الْفَجْرِ ــ غَلَس ــ طُلُوعُ النَّهارِ.

Cocker, *v.t.* *See to* Caress, *v.t.*

Cockering, *n.* Indulgence, مُداراة ــ تَدَلُّل.

Cocket, *n.* تَذْكَرَةُ الْكُمْرُكِ.

Cock-eye, *n.* *See* Squint, *n.*

Cock-fight, *n.* / Cock-fighting, } مُعارَكَةُ الدُّيُوكِ.

Cockhorse, *a.* On horseback, راكِب. Triumphing, boasting, بَاذِخ ــ مُفْتَخِر ــ فَيَّاش.

Cockle, *n.* A kind of shell-fish, نَوْعٌ مِنَ الْمَحارَةِ. The flower, خَشْخاش بَرِّيٌّ ــ شُقَّيْق.

Cockle, *v.i.* To wrinkle, shrink, تَقَلَّصَ ــ تَغَضَّنَ.

Cockloft, *n.* عُلِّيَّةٌ فِي الطَّبَقَةِ الْعُلْيا.

Cockney, *n.* مَوْلُودٌ فِي مَدِينَةِ لَنْدَنَ.

Cockneyism, *n.* The dialect of cockneys, لَغْوُ أَهْلِ لَنْدَنَ.

Cockpit, *n.* A place where cocks fight, مَيْدانٌ ــ مَصْرَعُ الدُّيُوكِ لِأَجْلِ مُقاتَلَةِ الدُّيُوكِ. A hospital on board of ships of war, مُسْتَشْفًى فِي بارِجَةٍ ــ بَيْتُ الْمَرْضَى عَلَى ظَهْرِ بارِجَةٍ.

Cockroach, *n.* خُنْفُس ــ قَرْنَبَى ــ اِبْنُ الْفاسِياءِ ــ الْفاسِياءُ *pl.* خُنْفُسُ الْحَمَّامِ ــ خَنافِسُ.

Cock's-comb, *n.* The crest of a cock, عُرْفُ الدِّيكِ ــ ذال. The plant, طَنْطُورُ الْجُنْدِيِّ. *See also under* Comb, *n.*

Cockswain, *n.* مُسْتَعْمِلُ فَلُوكَةٍ.

Cocoa, *n.* *See* Chocolate, *n.*

Cocoa-nut, *n.* رانِج *pl.* رَوانِجُ ــ نارَجِيل ــ جَوْزُ الْهِنْدِ. The — tree, شَجَرَةُ جَوْزِ الْهِنْدِ ــ شَجَرَةُ النَّارَجِيلِ. The milk of the —, أَطْواق.

Cocoon, *n.* فَيْلَج *or* فَيْلَق ــ جَوْزَةُ الْقَزِّ *coll.* جَوْز ــ قَزّ ــ شُرْنُقَة *pl.* شَرانِقُ.

Coction, *n.* The act of boiling, سَلْق. Digestion, هَضْم ــ هُضُوم.

Cod, *n.* The codfish, بَقَلْيُو ــ سَمَكُ الْبَقَلَةِ. A pod, خَرِيطَة ــ غِمْد.

Coddle, *v.t.* To make much of, دَلَّلَ ــ هانَغَ ــ فَنَّقَ.

Code, *n.* A book of laws, دُسْتُورُ شَرائِعَ ــ كِتابُ شَرائِعَ ــ قانُونُ (*or* دُسْتُورُ) الْحُقُوقِ ــ قانُون نامه ــ مَجْمَعُ قَوانِينَ. A civil —, قانُونُ (*or* دُسْتُورُ) الْمَدَنِيَّةِ. A commercial —, قانُونُ (*or* دُسْتُورُ) التِّجارَةِ. A penal —, دُسْتُورُ (*or* قانُونُ) الْجَزاءِ. A military —, أُصُولٌ عَسْكَرِيَّةٌ. Those rules will form a — to be acted upon, تَصِيرُ تِلْكَ الْأَحْكامُ دُسْتُورًا لِلْعَمَلِ.

Codex, *n.* نُسْخَة ــ كِتاب ــ مُصْحَف ــ دُسْتُور. *See also* Code, *n.*

Codfish, *n.* *See* Cod, *n.*

Codger, *n.* *See* Clown, Rustic, *n.*

Codicil, *n.* مُلْحَقٌ أَوْ تَغْيِيرٌ فِي وَصِيَّةِ مَيِّتٍ.

Codification, *n.* The act of, جَمْعُ الشَّرائِعِ فِي دُسْتُورٍ ــ تَنْسِيقُ الشَّرائِعِ.

Codify, *v.t.* جَمَعَ الشَّرائِعَ وَالْقَوانِينَ فِي دُسْتُورٍ ــ نَسَّقَ الشَّرائِعَ.

Codling, *n.* An unripe apple, تُفَّاحَةٌ غَيْرُ نَاضِجَةٍ. A young codfish, بَقْلِيُو صَغِيرٌ.

Coefficiency, *n.* إِتِّفَاق ـ مُسَاعَدَة.

Coefficient, *a.* مُسَاعِد ـ مُعِين.

Cœliac, Celiac, *a.* أَمْعَائِيٌّ ـ بَطْنِيٌّ.

Coemption, *n.* الإِشْتِرَآءُ بِالْجُمْلَةِ.

Coequal, *a.* كُفْؤٌ *pl.* كِفَآءٌ ـ مُسَاوٍ ـ مُتَسَاوٍ ـ مُعَادِل ـ نَظِير ـ قَرِين ـ سَوَآءٌ ـ وَاحِدٌ ـ شَيْءٌ. *See also under* Equal, *a.*

Coequality, *n.* تَسْوِيَة ـ مُسَاوَاة ـ سَوِيَّة.

Coequally, *ad.* عَلَى سَوِيَّةٍ ـ بِالسَّوِيَّةِ.

Coerce, *v.t.* إِضْطَرَّ ـ غَصَبَ ـ أَلْزَمَ ـ قَهَرَ ـ حَتَمَ عَلَى ـ ضَبَطَ.

Coercible, *a.* يُضْطَرُّ ـ يُقْهَرُ ـ يُضْبَطُ ـ إِضْطِرَارُهُ مُمْكِن.

Coercion, *n.* إِضْطِرَار ـ قَهْر ـ غَصْب ـ حَتْم ـ إِلْزَام ـ ضَبْط ـ زَجْر.

Coercive, *a.* قَهْرِيٌّ ـ حَتْمِيٌّ ـ ضَبْطِيٌّ ـ إِضْطِرَارِيٌّ ـ زَجْرِيٌّ.

Coerciveness, *n.* قُوَّةٌ جَبْرِيَّةٌ.

Coessential, *a.* مُسَاوٍ فِي الْجَوْهَرِ ـ مُسَاوٍ ذَاتًا.

Coessentially, *ad.* مُسَاوَاةً فِي الْجَوْهَرِ.

Coetaneous, *a.* قَرِين ـ مُعَاصِر ـ مِنْ عَصْرِهِ ـ مِنْ ذَاتِ عَصْرٍ.

Coeternal, *a.* أَزَلِيٌّ مَعَ ـ مُشْتَرِكٌ فِي الْأَزَلِيَّةِ.

Coeternity, *n.* أَزَلِيَّةٌ مَعَ ـ إِشْتِرَاكٌ فِي الْأَزَلِيَّةِ.

Coeval, *n.* مُشْتَرِكُ الْقِدَمِ ـ مُشْتَرِكُ الْحُدُوثِ.

Co-executor, *n.* شَرِيكٌ وَكِيلٍ عَلَى وَصِيَّةِ مَيِّتٍ *pl.* شُرَكَآءُ.

Co-exist, *v.i.* وُجِدَ مَعًا ـ عَاشَ مَعًا ـ كَانَ مَعًا.

Co-existence, *n.* وُجُودٌ مَعًا.

Co-existent, *a.* مَوْجُودٌ مَعًا.

Co-extend, *v.i.* تَمَدَّدَ (*or*) إِمْتَدَّ بِالسَّوَآءِ ـ إِتَّسَعَ بِالسَّوَآءِ.

Co-extension, *n.*
Co-extensiveness, } مُسَاوَاةٌ فِي الْإِمْتِدَادِ ـ مُسَاوَاةٌ فِي الْإِتِّسَاعِ.

Co-extensive, *a.* مُتَسَاوٍ فِي الْإِمْتِدَادِ ـ مُتَسَاوٍ فِي الْإِتِّسَاعِ.

Coffee, *n.* The berry, بُنٌّ; the liquor, قَهْوَة; the husk, قِشْر.

Coffee-cup, *n.* فِلْجَان *pl.* فَلَاجِينُ ـ فِنْجَان *pl.* فَنَاجِينُ ـ فِنْجَانٌ لِلْقَهْوَةِ.

Coffee-house, *n.* قَهْوَة *pl.* قَهَوَات. Keeper of a —, قَهْوَجِي *pl.* قَهْوَجِيَّة ـ قَهْوَاتِيٌّ.

Coffee-mill, *n.* مِطْحَنَةُ الْبُنِّ ـ طَاحُونُ الْبُنِّ.

Coffee-pot, *n.* إِبْرِيقُ الْقَهْوَةِ *pl.* أَبَارِيقُ. {دلال D 223}

Coffer, *n.* A chest, safe-chest, صَنْدُوق *pl.* صَنَادِيقُ ـ صِوَان *pl.* أَصْوِنَة. A treasure-chest, سَحَّارَة *pl.* سَحَاحِيرُ ـ صَنْدُوقُ الْمَالِ.

Coffer-dam, *n.* صَنْدُوقٌ يُوضَعُ فِي قَعْرِ الْمَآءِ لِلْأَسَاسِ ـ صَنْدُوقُ الْأَسَاسِ.

Coffin, *n.* For the dead, تَابُوت *pl.* تَوَابِيتُ ـ صَنْدُوقُ الْمَيِّتِ. A shroud, كَفَن.

Coffin, *v.t.* تَوَبَّتَ ـ كَفَّنَ.

Cog, *v.t.* *See to* Cajole, *v.t.*

Cog, *n.* The tooth of a wheel, سِنُّ دُولَابٍ *pl.* أَسْنَان.

Cogency, *n.* Force, قُوَّة ـ شِدَّة ـ بَأْس ـ فَعَلِيَّة ـ إِضْطِرَار.

Cogent, *a.* Powerful, قَوِيٌّ ـ دَافِع ـ شَدِيد. Convincing, قَاطِع ـ مُلْزِم ـ مُقْنِع ـ مُبْرِم.

Cogently, *ad.* بِقُوَّةٍ ـ قُوَّةً ـ بِشِدَّةٍ ـ دَفَاعًا.

Cogged, *a.* Having cogs, مُسَنَّن.

Cogitate, *v.i.* To think, إِفْتَكَرَ ـ تَأَمَّلَ. To — about, إِفْتَكَرَ فِي ـ طَالَعَ ـ إِطَّلَعَ عَلَى ـ تَأَمَّلَ فِي. To purpose, intend, نَوَى ـ قَصَدَ.

Cogitation, *n.* فِكْر ـ تَأَمُّل ـ هَمٌّ ـ إِمْعَانُ الْفِكْرِ.

Cogitative, *a.* ظَنُون ـ فَكُور ـ مُفَكِّر ـ صَاحِبُ فِكْرٍ.

Cognate, *a.* Of the same stock, صِنْو ـ مُنَاسِب ـ مِنْ أَصْلٍ وَاحِدٍ. Like, مُشَابِه ـ مُمَاثِل ـ قِرْن *pl.* أَقْرَان.

Cognation, *n.* صِنْوِيَّة ـ قَرَابَة ـ مُنَاسَبَة ـ مَقْرِبَة.

Cogniac, *n.* *See* Brandy, *n.*

Cognition, *n.* مَعْرِفَة ـ عِلْم ـ إِطِّلَاعٌ عَلَى ـ وُقُوفٌ عَلَى ـ بَصَارَة ـ خَبَر.

Cognizable, *n.* That may be known, مِمَّا يُعْرَفُ ـ الإِطِّلَاعُ عَلَيْهِ مُمْكِنٌ. That may be inquired of, مِمَّا يُطَالَبُ بِ.

Cognizance, *n.* Knowledge, نَوْطُ النَّظَرِ (*or*) نِيَاطُ ـ إِطِّلَاع ـ شِعْر ـ شُعُور ـ عِلْم. Jurisdiction, حُكُومَة ـ أَمْر. Surety, قَبَالَة ـ ذِمَّة ـ ضَمَان. A badge, عَلَامَة ـ إِشَارَة.

Cognizant, *a.* مُطَّلِعٌ عَلَى ـ عَارِفٌ بِ ـ وَاقِفٌ عَلَى ـ خَبِيرٌ بِ.

Cognomen, *n.* قِنْزَك ـ نَسَب *pl.* أَنْسَاب ـ كُنْيَة *pl.* كُنًى ـ لَقَب *pl.* أَلْقَاب. Cognomens, عَلَاقِي ـ عِلَاوَات.

Cognominal, *a.* لَقَبِيٌّ. Having the same name, ذُو آسْمٍ وَاحِدٍ.

Cognoscence, *n.* *See* Cognition, *n.*

Cog-wheel, *n.* دُولَابٌ ذُو أَسْنَانٍ ـ دُولَابٌ مُسَنَّنٌ.

Cohabit, *v.i.* عَاشَ مَعَ ـ عَاشَ مَعًا. To — as husband and wife, عَاشَ عِيشَةَ الْمُتَزَوِّجِينَ.

Cohabitation, *n.* مُسَاكَنَةٌ ـ اَلسُّكْنَى مَعَ أَحَدٍ ; of husband and wife, عِيشَةُ ٱلْمُتَزَوِّجِينَ.

Co-heir, *n.* شَرِيكٌ فِي ٱلْإِرْثِ *pl.* شُرَكَآءُ ـ شَرِيكٌ مَعَ.

Co-heiress, *n.* شَرِيكَةٌ فِي ٱلْإِرْثِ *pl.* شَرَائِكُ ـ شَرِيكَةٌ مَعَ.

Cohere, *v.i.* To stick together, تَلَزَّجَ ـ إِلْتَزَقَ. To suit together, إِتَّفَقَ ـ نَاسَبَ ـ وَافَقَ.

Coherence, *n.* } A sticking together, لُزُوق ـ إِلْتِصَاق ـ مُلَاصَقَة.
Coherency, } Connexion, مُقَارَنَة ـ رِبَاط ـ مُلَازَمَة ـ إِلْحَاق.
Agreement, مُوَافَقَة ـ مُطَابَقَة ـ مُنَاسَبَة ـ تَنَاسُب.

Coherent, *a.* Sticking together, مُلْتَصِق ـ مُلْتَزِم. Connected, مُقْتَرِن ـ مُلْحَق ـ مَرْبُوط. Consistent with, مُوَافِقٌ لِ ـ مُطَابِقٌ بِ. Orderly, مُتَنَسِّق ـ مَنْظُوم. Coherent, of a speech, مُتَنَاسِق ـ مُنْسَجِم. Coherent in speech, سَدِيدُ ٱلْكَلَامِ. To be —, of a speech, تَنَاسَقَ ـ تَنَسَّقَ ـ إِنْسَجَمَ.

Coherently, *ad.* بِٱتِّصَالٍ ـ إِلْحَاقًا ـ مُطَابَقَةً ـ بِنِظَامٍ ; of a speech, بِٱنْسِجَامٍ ـ بِتَنَسُّقٍ ـ بِنَسَقٍ.

Cohesion, *n.* *See* Coherence, *n.*

Cohesive, *a.* مُلْتَصِق ـ مُلْتَحِم ـ مُتَلَازِق.

Cohesiveness, *n.* لُصُوق ـ لُزُوق ـ تَلَاصُق.

Cohort, *n.* جَيْش *pl.* جُيُوش ـ كَتِيبَة *pl.* كَتَائِبُ.

Coif, *n.* عَمْرَة ـ عَصَبَة ; a woman's —, مِقْنَعَة ـ كِسْوَةُ رَأْسِ ٱلنِّسَاءِ.

Coil, *v.t.* كَوَّرَ ـ كَفَّ ـ أَرَمَ ـ وَشَّعَ ـ كَوَّفَ ـ جَمَعَ. To coil itself, تَعَطَّفَ ; as of a serpent, تَطَوَّى ـ تَقَوَّرَ ـ إِسْتَكَفَّ ـ تَحَوَّى. The serpent coiled itself, رَحَتِ ٱلْحَيَّةُ *aor.* تَرْحُو ـ تَطَوَّتِ ٱلْحَيَّةُ.

Coil, *n.* ثِنْيٌ *pl.* أَثْنَآءُ ـ مَطْوًى. A — of rope, مِكْوَرَةُ حِبَالٍ ـ ثِنْيُ حِبَالٍ. The — of a serpent, of a gut, *etc.*, لِوَآءٌ *pl.* أَلْوِيَةٌ ـ حَوِيَّةٌ ـ حَاوِيَةٌ. Tumult, شَغْب ـ فِتْنَة ـ غَاغَا.

Coin, *n.* Stamped money, سِكَّة *pl.* سِكَك ـ مُعَامَلَة ـ دَرَاهِمُ. Money in general, عُمْلَة ـ دَرَاهِمُ ـ فُلُوس ـ مِصْرِيَّات. False —, مُعَامَلَةٌ زَغَلٌ. Good —, مُعَامَلَةٌ صَاغٌ ـ مُعَامَلَةٌ صَحِيحَةٌ. Coin with the impression erased, دَرَاهِمُ مُسَيَّفَةٌ. The principal — in all monetary dealings, مِحْوَرُ ٱلْمُعَامَلَةِ. To select good — from bad, تَنَقَّدَ ـ إِنْتَقَدَ ـ نَقَدَ. To weigh and test —, عَيَّرَ ٱلدَّنَانِيرَ. *See also* Quoin, *n.*

Coin, *v.t.* To stamp money, طَبَعَ سِكَّةً ـ ضَرَبَ ٱلسِّكَّةَ ـ دَقَّ مُعَامَلَةً. To invent, أَبْدَعَ ـ إِخْتَرَعَ ـ أَوْجَدَ. To forge, قَلَّدَ ـ زَوَّرَ.

Coinage, *n.* Money, سِكَّة. Stamping of money, دَقُّ مُعَامَلَةٍ ـ ضَرْبُ سِكَّةٍ. Invention, إِيجَاد ـ إِبْدَاع ـ إِخْتِرَاع. Standard of —, عِيَارُ ٱلسِّكَّةِ.

Coincide, *v.i.* إِتَّفَقَ ـ وَافَقَ ـ طَابَقَ.

Coincidence, *n.* Agreement, مُطَابَقَة ـ مُوَافَقَة ـ إِتِّفَاق. Concurrence, إِلْتِقَآء ـ مُجَايَاة.

Coincident, *a.* Agreeing, مُطَابِق ـ مُوَافِق. Concurrent, مُلْتَقٍ ـ مُتَصَادِف.

Coiner, *n.* Of money, ضَرَّابُ مُعَامَلَةٍ. A false —, ضَرَّابُ مُعَامَلَةٍ زَغَلٍ ـ كِيمَاوِيّ. An inventor, بَادِع ـ مُبْدِع ـ مُخْتَرِع ـ مُوجِد.

Coinheritance, *n.* إِشْتِرَاكٌ بِٱلْمِيرَاثِ.

Coinheritor, *n.* شَرِيكٌ فِي ٱلْمِيرَاثِ.

Coining, *n.* *See under* Coinage, *n.*

Coir, *n.* لِيفُ جَوْزِ ٱلْهِنْدِ.

Coition, *n.* بَاهٌ ـ بَآءَة ـ جِمَاع ـ مُجَامَعَة ـ هِوَاس ـ نِكَاح.

Coix lachryma, *n.* دَمْعُ أَيُّوبَ.

Cojoin, *v.t.* وَصَّلَ ـ وَاصَلَ ـ قَرَنَ بِ.

Coke, *n.* فَحْمُ حَجَرٍ مُسْتَخْرَجٌ مِنْهُ ٱلْغَازُ وَٱلْقَارُ.

Colander, *n.* مِنْطَب ـ نَاطِب ـ مِصْفَاة *pl.* مَصَافٍ. A dyer's —, مِمْصَل.

Colchicum, *n.* خَانِقُ ٱلْكَلْبِ.

Cold, *a.* قَرٌّ ـ ثَلِجٌ ـ مَقْرُور ـ قَارِس ـ بَارِد. Having the sensation of —, بَرْدَان. Without passion, بَارِدُ ٱلطَّبْعِ. Not hasty, رَزِين ـ صَاحِبُ فِكْرٍ. Unaffectionate, بِلَا وُدٍّ ـ لَا حُنُوَّ لَهُ. Unwelcome, غَيْرُ مَقْبُولٍ ـ مَكْرُوه. Cold water, مَآءٌ بَارِدٌ. Cold and limpid, of water, سَهْو. A — damp wind, بَلِيل ـ بَلِيلَة. To be or become —; also, as in death, بَرَدَ. You are neither — nor hot, إِنَّكَ لَسْتَ بِبَارِدٍ وَلَا حَارٍّ. To be bitterly —, إِزْمَهَرَّ.

Cold, *n.* The sensation of —, قُرٌّ ـ بَرْد ـ بُرُود. Excessive —, صِرَّة ـ صِرٌّ ـ زَمْهَرِير. A rheum, غُمَام ـ رَشْح ـ زُكَام. To catch —, تَرَشَّحَ ـ إِسْتَهْوَى. The — stage of a fever, بَرْدِيَّة. The — of the night affected us, بَرَدَ عَلَيْنَا ٱللَّيْلُ ـ بَرَدَنَا ٱللَّيْلُ. Left out in the —, isolated, فِي حَالِ ٱلْإِنْفِرَادِ.

Coldblooded, *a.* Without passion; *see under* Cold, *a.*

Coldhearted, *a.* عَدِيمُ ٱلشَّفَقَةِ ـ قَاسِي ٱلْقَلْبِ.

Coldheartedness, *n.* عَدَمُ ٱلشَّفَقَةِ ـ قَسَاوَةُ قَلْبٍ.

Coldly, *ad.* Without affection, بِعَدَمِ مَحَبَّةٍ ـ بِلَا وُدٍّ. Without zeal, بِعَدَمِ غَيْرَةٍ. Without passion, بِبُرُودَةٍ.

Coldness, *n.* Want of heat, بَرْد ـ بُرُود. Want of passion, بُرُودُ ٱلطَّبْعِ. Want of affection, قِلَّةُ وِدَادٍ ـ عَدَمُ ٱلْمَحَبَّةِ. Want of energy, عَدَمُ ٱلْمُرُوَّةِ ـ قِلَّةُ ٱلرَّغْبَةِ.

Colewort, *n.* نَوْعٌ مِنَ ٱلْكُرُنْبِ.

Colic, *n.* عِلَوْز ـ مَغْص ـ قُولَنْج ـ مُغِص. To have the —, مُغِصَ. Having the —, مَمْغُوص.

Collaborator, *n.* مُعَاوِن ـ رَفِيق ـ شَرِيكٌ فِي ٱلْعَمَلِ.

Collapse, *v.i.* To close so that one side touches the other, تَمَاسَّا. To shrink, shrivel, كَرِشَ ـ شَنِجَ ـ ذَبَلَ ـ إِنْشَنَّ ـ تَكَرْبَشَ. To come to an end, to fail, خَابَ ـ قَصُرَ ـ سَقَطَ.

Collapse, *n.* Prostration of strength, خَبْطَة ـ ضَعْف ـ دَمَار ـ ٱلْقُوَّةِ. Failure, خَيْبَة ـ سَقْط ـ قُصُور. To be in a state of —, إِضْمَحَلَّ.

Collar, *n.* A metal ring for the neck, طَوْق *pl.* أَطْوَاق. The part of the dress round the neck, يَاقَة ـ جَيْب ـ طَوْق. Harness round a horse's neck, زِنَاق. A dog's —, زُمَّارَة ـ سَاجُور ـ إِرْبَة ـ عِقْد ـ زِنَاق. An ornament for the neck, عُصْمَة ـ مِعْنَقَة ـ طَوْق. The — with which a captive's neck is bound, حِنَاك. The — bones, العَرَاقِي. To put a — on a dog, أَعْنَقَ. To slip the —, to run away, إِنْسَلَّ ـ وَلَّى هَارِبًا.

Collar, *v.t.* To invest with a collar, أَعْنَقَ ـ لَبَّسَ طَوْقًا. To seize by the —, عَنَقَ ـ دَقَّ فِي حِنَاقِهِ.

Collate, *v.t.* To compare with another of the same kind, قَارَنَ ـ بِ ـ قَابَلَ ـ بِ ـ عَارَضَ ـ بِ ـ ثَنَّى. To put in order, نَظَمَ. To bestow upon, جَمَعَ ـ إِلَى. To place in a benefice, أَقَامَ ـ فِي أَبْرَشِيَّةٍ.

Collateral, *a.* By the side, side by side, مُصَاقِب ـ مُجَانِب ـ مُسَاوٍ ـ مُتَوَازٍ. Not direct, زَائِغ ـ حَائِد. Concurrent, مُقَارِن. In equal relation to some ancestor, مُسَاوٍ فِي ٱلْقَرَابَةِ ـ فِي دَرَجَةٍ وَاحِدَةٍ مِنَ ٱلْقَرَابَةِ. Collateral relations, أَقْرِبَاء. Collateral security, كَفَالَةٌ مُلْحَقَة ـ شَهَادَةٌ مُصَدِّقَة. Collateral testimony, مِصْدَاق.

Collateral, *n.* مِنْ أَقْرِبَاء.

Collaterally, *ad.* Side by side, جَانِبًا إِلَى جَانِبٍ ـ تَجَانُبًا. Indirectly, تَعْرِيضًا ـ إِنْحِرَافًا. In collateral relation, فِي قَرَابَةٍ وَاحِدَةٍ.

Collation, *n.* Comparison, مُعَارَضَة ـ مُقَابَلَة ـ مُقَارَنَة. A gift, هِبَة ـ وَهْبَة ـ إِنْعَام. A repast, تَعْوِيذَة; a morning —, فُطُور. Collation to a benefice, إِقَامَةٌ فِي أَبْرَشِيَّةٍ.

Collative, *a.* مِنْ مَوْهِبَةِ ٱلْأَسْقُفِ.

Collator, *n.* Of books, مُقَابِلُ ٱلْكُتُبِ.

Colleague, *n.* شَرِيك *pl.* شُرَكَاء ـ رَفِيق ـ مُعَاوِن *pl.* مُعَاوِنَة.

Collect, *v.t.* To amass, حَشَرَ ـ حَشَدَ ـ جَلَبَ ـ جَمَّرَ ـ جَمَعَ ـ أَجْمَعَ ـ لَمَّ ـ هَمَشَ ـ أَجْمَلَ ـ جَمَلَ ـ حَبَّشَ ـ إِلْتَقَطَ. To infer as a consequence from, أَنْتَجَ مِنْ. To sum up, جَمَّعَ. To — into parties, حَزَّبَ. To — an army, جَيَّشَ. To — provisions, ذَخَرَ. To —, as of information, from one, respecting . . . , إِسْتَدَلَّ مِن ـ عَلَى. To acquire, حَصَّلَ ـ أَدْرَكَ. To — one's senses, رَجَعَ إِلَى نَفْسِهِ ـ جَمَعَ حَوَاسَّهُ.

Collect, *v.i.* إِجْتَمَعَ ـ تَحَبَّشَ ـ تَحَشَّدَ ـ تَجَمَّرَ.

Collect, *n.* A short prayer, صُلَيَّة ـ دُعَاء ـ إِبْتِهَال.

Collected, *a.* Gathered together, مَلْمُوم ـ شَامِل ـ مَعْكُوش ـ مُرْتَاحُ ٱلْبَالِ ـ مُطْمَئِنُّ ٱلْخَاطِرِ ـ رَزِين. Composed, calm, مَجْمُوع.

Collectedly, *ad.* Together, جُمْلَةً. Composedly, بِرَزَانَةٍ ـ بِٱطْمِئْنَانٍ.

Collectedness, *n.* Composure, رِفَاء ـ إِطْمِئْنَانُ ٱلْخَاطِرِ ـ رَاحَةُ بَالٍ.

Collection, *n.* The act of collecting, شَمْل ـ حَشْد ـ إِجْتِمَاع ـ تَحْصِيل ـ تَكْوِيم. Things collected, لَمَّة ـ كُومَة ـ جُمْلَة ـ مَجْمُوعَة. A deduction, نَتِيجَة ـ إِسْتِنْتَاج. A miscellany, مَجْمُوع. Collections, things brought together, مُشْتَمِلَات.

Collective, *a.* Gathered into a mass, مَلْقُوط ـ مَلْمُوم ـ مَشْمُول ـ مَجْمُوع. A — noun, إِسْمُ جَمْعٍ ـ إِسْمُ كَثْرَةٍ. A — body, حَضِيرَة. A place in which things are collected, مُجْتَمَع. A — note, تَحْرِيرَاتٌ مُشْتَرَكَةٌ. Collective proceedings, تَبْلِيغَاتٌ مُشْتَرَكَةٌ.

Collectively, *ad.* جِمَارًا ـ بِٱلْجُمْلَةِ ـ مَعًا ـ جَمْعًا.

Collector, *n.* A gatherer, حَاشِد ـ حَاشِر ـ جَمَّاع ـ جَامِع. A — of taxes, عَامِل *pl.* عَوَامِلُ ـ جَابِي ٱلْخَرَاجِ *pl.* جُبَاة ـ مُحَصِّل ـ خَرَّاج. A — of revenue, جَامِعُ ٱلْخَرَاجِ ـ تَحْصِيلْدَار. A — of port dues, شَاهُ بَنْدَرٍ ـ كُمْرُكْجِي. A compiler, جَامِع. The Collector, one of the names of God, الجَامِعُ.

Collectorate, *n.* }
Collectorship, *n.* } The office, وَظِيفَةُ ٱلْمُحَصِّلِ; the district, دَائِرَةُ ٱلْمُحَصِّلِ.

College, *n.* A society of learned men, مَجْمَعُ عُلَمَاء. The abode of collegians, مَدْرَسَة ـ مَدْرَسَةٌ جَامِعَةٌ ـ دَارُ ٱلْفُنُونِ. To attend —, جَاوَرَ.

Collegial, *a.* مُتَعَلِّق بِمَدْرَسَةٍ ـ مُخْتَصّ بِدَارِ ٱلْفُنُونِ.

Collegian, *n.* مُجَاوِر *pl.* مُجَاوِرُونَ ـ تِلْمِيذُ مَدْرَسَةٍ *pl.* تَلَامِيذُ.

Collegiate, *a.* Pertaining to a college, مُتَعَلِّق بِمَدْرَسَةٍ. Instituted like a college, مُرَتَّب عَلَى تَرْتِيبِ مَدْرَسَةٍ جَامِعَةٍ.

Collier, *n.* A dealer in coals, فَحَّام *pl.* فَحَّامُونَ. A digger of coal, مُعَدِّنُ ٱلْفَحْم. A coal ship, مَرْكَبٌ لِتَحْمِيلِ ٱلْفَحْم.

Colliery, *n.* مَعْدِنُ فَحْمٍ حَجَرٍ ـ فَحَّامَة.

Colligate, *v.t.* رَبَطَ ـ جَمَّعَ ـ جَمَلَ.

Collingual, *a.* مُشْتَرِكُ ٱللِّسَانِ.

Colliquate, *v.t.* ذَوَّبَ ; *v.i.* ذَابَ.

Colliquation, *n.* ذَوَبَان ـ ذَوْب.

Colliquative, *a.* مُتْلِف ـ مُضَيِّع.

Colliquefaction, *n.* ذَوَبَان ـ تَلَف.

Collision, *n.* صَدْع ـ كَبْسَة ـ كَبَّة ـ إِصَابَة ـ لَطْمَة ـ مُصَادَمَة ـ مُضَادَّة ـ إِصْطِدَام ـ تَلَاطُم. Opposition, مُعَارَضَة ـ عِنَاد. To come into — with, to clash against, صَادَمَ ـ أَصَابَ ـ صَدَعَ. To oppose, عَارَضَ ـ ضَادَّ.

Collocate, *v.t.* To place, وَضَعَ *aor.* يَضَعُ ـ جَعَلَ ـ فِي ـ حَطَّ ـ أَقَامَ. To set in order, نَظَّمَ ـ رَتَّبَ ـ نَسَّقَ.

Collocation, *n.* The act of placing, وَضْع ـ وَضْعَان ـ تَنْزِيل ـ إِقَامَة. Arrangement, نِظَام ـ تَنْظِيم ـ تَرْتِيب ـ تَنْسِيق.

Collocutor, *n.* مُتَكَلِّم ـ كَلِيم.

Collop, *n.* A slice, قِطْعَة ـ سَائِفَة ـ شَرِيحَة ـ حِتَّة *pl.* حِتَت ـ شُقَق *pl.* شُقَّة. A lump of fat, شَحْمَة. He had collops of fat on his face, شَحُمَ وَجْهُهُ.

Colloquial, *a.* مُتَعَلِّق بِٱلْمُحَاوَرَةِ ـ مُتَعَلِّق بِٱلْمُكَالَمَةِ. Dialectical, لُغَوِيّ. The — dialect, اللِّسَانُ ٱللُّغَوِيُّ ـ اللِّسَانُ ٱلسَّمَاعِيُّ ـ اللِّسَانُ ٱلْمُتَدَاوَل ـ اللِّسَانُ ٱلدَّارِجُ.

Colloquialism, *n.* لَغْوَة ـ لَغْو.

Colloquist, *n.* مُتَكَلِّم ـ كَلِيم.

Colloquy, *n.* مُرَاجَعَة ـ مُحَاوَرَة ـ مُجَاوَبَة ـ مُخَاطَبَة ـ خِطَاب ـ مُذَاكَرَة ـ مُعَاوَدَة ـ مُحَاوَرَة ـ مُكَالَمَة. To hold a — with, عَاوَدَ ـ رَاجَعَ ـ قَاوَلَ ـ خَاطَبَ. They held a —, of many, حَاوَرُوا ـ تَحَاوَرُوا ـ تَجَاوَبُوا.

Collude, *v.i.* تَعَصَّبَ عَلَى ـ شَرٍّ ـ تَحَالَفَ ـ تَخَاوَدَ عَلَى ـ تَخَامَرَ عَلَى.

Collusion, *n.* إِتِّفَاق فِي شَرٍّ ـ مُخَاوَدَة ـ مُخَامَرَة ـ إِرْتِكَاب ـ بَاب.

Collusive, *a.* خَادِع ـ خَائِن ـ غَادِر.

Collusively, *ad.* بِمُخَاوَدَةٍ.

Collusory, *a.* مَفْعُولٌ بِمُخَاوَدَةٍ ـ بِخَوْنٍ.

Collyrium, *n.* حَلَاءَة ـ حَلُوءَة ـ دِمَام. Collyrium-stone, إِثْمِد. *See also* Antimony, *n.*

Colocynth, *n.* *See* Coloquintida, *n.*

Colon, *n.* In punctuation, (:) عَلَامَةُ وَقْفٍ وَهِيَ. The large intestine, عُنُقُ ٱلْبَوَّابِ ـ قُولُون.

Colonel, *n.* بُلُوكْ بَاشِي ـ أَمِير آلاي.

Colonelcy, *n.* رُتْبَةُ ٱلْأَمِير آلاي ـ مَقَامُ ٱلْبُلُوكْ بَاشِي.

Colonial, *a.* مُتَعَلِّق ـ مُخْتَصٌّ بِٱلْمُسْتَوطِنِينَ ـ مُخْتَصٌّ بِٱلتَّعْمِيرِ. Colonial produce, produce of the colonies, مَحْصُولَاتٌ بِٱلْمِعْمَارِيَّةِ. Colonial Office, دَارُ نَظَارَةِ ٱلْمَمَالِكِ ٱلتَّابِعَةِ. Colonial Secretary, نَاظِرُ ٱلْمَمَالِكِ ٱلتَّابِعَةِ.

Colonist, *n.* مُسْتَوْطِنٌ فِي بِلَادٍ مُسْتَعْمَرَةٍ. Colonists, عُمَارَة ـ عَمَائِر.

Colonization, *n.* عِمَارَةُ بِلَادٍ ـ تَعْمِيرُ بِلَادٍ.

Colonize, *v.t.* إِسْتَوْطَنَ ـ أَهَّلَ ٱلْبِلَادَ ـ أَعْمَرَ بِلَادًا ـ عَمَّرَ بِلَادًا. To make to —, إِسْتَعْمَرَ ـ فِي ـ أَعْمَرَ.

Colonnade, *n.* صَفُّ أَعْمِدَةٍ.

Colony, *n.* بِلَادٌ مُسْتَعْمَرَةٌ ـ تَعْمِير ـ عِمَارَة. The English Colonies, مُسْتَعْمَرَاتُ ٱلْإِنْكِلِيزِ ـ البُلْدَانُ ٱلْمُسْتَعْمَرَةُ مِنَ ٱلْإِنْكِلِيزِ.

Coloquintida, *n.* عَلْقَم ـ حَنْظَل ـ شَرْي ـ هَنْدَل ـ الشَّجَرَةُ ٱلْخَبِيثَةُ. Unripe —, حَدَج.

Colour, *n.* A tint, رَنْك ـ صِبَاغ ـ لَوْن ـ وِشَاء *pl.* وَشْي. A dye, صِبْغ ـ أَلْوَان *pl.* لَوْن. A pretext, حِيلَة ـ عِلَّة ـ حُجَّة. A kind, species, هَيْئَة ـ شَكْل ـ وَجْه ـ صُورَة. Appearance, نَوْع ـ جِنْس. A light —, زَاهِي ٱللَّوْنِ. Of a bright —, لَوْنٌ فَاتِحٌ ـ لَوْنٌ زَاهٍ. A dark —, لَوْنٌ كَامِدٌ ـ لَوْنٌ غَامِقٌ. Of one —, مُصْمَت. Under —, as if, بِدَعْوَى أَنْ ـ كَأَنَّ. A man of —, أَسْمَرُ ٱللَّوْنِ *pl.* سُمْر ـ أَسْوَدُ *pl.* سُود *and* سُودَان. I fear its — will fade, أَخَافُ فَسْخَ لَوْنِهِ. To change or lose —, خُطِفَ ـ فَسَخَ لَوْنُهُ. To heighten the —, as of the face, تَغَيَّرَ لَوْنُهُ ـ لَوْنُهُ ـ شَبَّ.

Colours, *n.* A flag, بَيْرَق *pl.* بَيَارِق ـ لِوَاء *pl.* أَلْوِيَة ـ رَايَة *pl.* رَايَات. A stand of —, عَدَدُ بَيَارِقَ. To hoist —, أَلْوَى ـ نَصَبَ ٱلْبَيْرَقَ. To come off with flying —, غَلَبَ ـ أَنْجَحَ.

Colour, *v.t.* وَضَعَ ٱلْأَلْوَانَ عَلَى ـ زَوَّقَ ـ صَبَغَ ـ وَشَّى *aor.* يَضَعُ ـ صَوَّرَ ـ عَلَى ـ وَشَّى ـ بِٱلطَّيِّبِ ـ زَيَّنَ. To make plausible, صُورَةٍ حَسَنَةٍ. To give a bad colouring to an action, نَمَّ. To palliate, دَارَى عَن ـ سَتَرَ ـ أَعْذَرَ. To — with lies, وَشَّى *aor.* يَشِي. To give a false — to, صَحَّفَ ـ وَشَى *aor.* يَشِي. To —, as of the effects of the sun, a journey, لَوَّحَ ـ لَاعَ ². *See also to* Bronze, *v.t.*

Colour, *v.i.* To blush, خَجِلَ ـ إِحْمَرَّ ـ . To change —, from the effects of the sun, إِلْتَمَعَ.

Colourable, *a.* Specious, مُشْكِل ـ يَغُرّ ـ مُغِرّ ـ صِنَاعِيّ.

Colourably, *ad.* إِغْرَارًا ـ غُرُورًا ـ تَصَنُّعًا.

Colouring, *n.* وَضْعُ ٱلْأَلْوَانِ ـ أَلْوَان ـ لَوْن. A false —, تَصْحِيف. *See also* Colour, *n.*

Colourist, *n.* مُصَوِّرٌ مَاهِرٌ فِي ٱلْأَلْوَانِ ـ رَسَّام ـ مُلَوِّن.

Colourless, *a.* سَادَه ـ مِنْ غَيْرِ لَوْنٍ. Transparent, شَفَّاف.

Colourman, *n.* A seller of colours, بَيَّاعُ ٱلْأَلْوَانِ.

Colporteur, *n.* بَسَاطِيّ ـ خُرْدَجِيّ ـ مُتَسَبِّب ـ دَوَّار. A — of books, دَلَّالُ ٱلْكُتُبِ *pl.* دَلَّالَة.

Colt, *n.* مُهْر *pl.* مُهْرَة ـ أَمْهَار *pl.* مُهْر ـ أَجْحَاش *pl.* جَحْش ـ فِلْوٌ *pl.* أَفْلَاءٌ. Having a —, مُفْلٍ ـ مُمْهِر.

Colter, *n.* *See* Coulter, *n.*

Coltish, *a.* Frisky, فِلْتَان ـ نَقَّاز ـ قَفَّاز.

Columbary, *n.* بُرُوج *pl.* بُرْجُ حَمَامٍ.

Columbine, *n.* The plant, جُلْنِسْرِين. The heroine of a pantomime, المَلِكَةُ فِي لَعِبِ ٱلْمَسْخَرَةِ.

Column, *n.* A pillar, عِمَاد ـ نُصْبَة ـ أَسَاطِين *pl.* أُسْطُوَان ـ عَمُود *pl. pauc.* أَعْمِدَة, *pl. mult.* عُمُد (*vulg.* عَوَامِيد). A body of troops, كَتِيبَة *pl.* كَتَائِب ـ عَسْكَر ـ بَيْرَق *pl.* بَيَارِق ـ طَابُور ـ فِرْقَةُ عَسَاكِرَ ـ لِوَآء. A — of a book, جَدْوَلُ كِتَابٍ *pl.* جَدَاوِلُ. Two columns to the page, عَلَى عَمُودَيِ ٱلصَّفْحَةِ.

Columnar, *a.* فِي شَكْلِ ٱلْعَمُودِ ـ فِي هَيْئَةِ ٱلْأَعْمِدَةِ.

Colure, *n.* دَائِرَةُ ٱلسَّمَوَاتِ. The solstitial —, سَمْتُ ٱلْإِنْقِلَابِ; the equinoctial —, سَمْتُ ٱلْإِعْتِدَالِ.

Coma, *n.* Propensity to sleep, ثِقْل ـ خَفَقَان ـ دَآءُ ٱلسُّبَاتِ. The tail of a comet, ذُؤَابَة.

Comate, *a.* شَعْرَانِيّ ـ مُشْعِر ـ ذُو ذُؤَابَةٍ.

Comatose, *a.* رَقُود ـ خَافِق ـ مَسْبُوت.

Comb, *n.* مُشْط ـ مِشْط ـ مِمْشَط *pl.* أَمْشَاط. A tooth, of a —, سِنُّ مِشْطٍ *pl.* أَسْنَان. The crest of a cock, عُرْف ـ فُرْق ـ ذَال ـ جِدْرِيَة ـ عِفْرِيَة ـ فَلْفَلَةُ ٱلْبَرْبُوكِ ـ نَوَّارَةُ ٱلدِّيكِ ـ أَعْرَاف *pl.* The crest, as of birds, شُوشَة. Honey-comb, قُرْصُ عَسَلٍ.

Comb, *v.t.* مَشَطَ ² ـ خَلَّلَ ٱلشَّعْرَ بِٱلْمِشْطِ ـ سَرَّحَ ـ شَفَا ـ مَشَّطَ. To —, of wool, قَرْنَشَ ـ مَشَقَ ² ـ سَرَّحَ. To thrash, ضَرَبَ. To — one's self, تَمَشَّطَ ـ إِمْتَشَطَ.

Combat, *n.* مُعَارَضَة ـ وَقْعَة ـ عَرْكَة ـ مُقَاتَلَة ـ مُضَارَبَة ـ قِتَال. Single —, مُبَارَزَة ـ بِرَاز.

Combat, *v.t.* To oppose, خَالَفَ ـ رَدَّ عَلَى ² ـ عَارَضَ ـ ضَادَّ.

Combat, *v.i.* تَعَارَضَ ـ تَجَادَلَ ـ تَقَاتَلَ مَعَ ـ قَاتَلَ.

Combatant, *n.* مُحَارِب ـ مُبَارِز ـ مُجَادِل ـ مُقَاتِل. A — for the faith, مُجَاهِد.

Combative, *a.* Disposed to combat, جَدِيرٌ بِٱلْقِتَالِ. Disposed to quarrel, شُكُلِيّ ـ شَرِس ـ شِرِّيس.

Combativeness, *n.* Disposition to fight, غَرِيزَةٌ لِلْقِتَالِ. Disposition to quarrel, شَرَاسَة.

Combinable, *a.* الإِتِّصَالُ بَيْنَ مُمْكِنٌ ـ الإِمْتِزَاجُ بَيْنَ مُمْكِنٌ.

Combination, *n.* Union, league, تَحَالُف ـ شِرْكَة ـ عُصْبَة ـ إِتِّحَاد ـ مُوَافَقَة ـ إِتِّصَال. Union of bodies or qualities, حِلْفَة. Arrangement for a plan, تَدْبِير ـ تَرْتِيب ـ تَوْفِيق. تَرْكِيب ـ A concatenation, تَسَلْسُل ـ سِلْسِلَة. A compound body, تَرْكِيب ـ جِسْمٌ مُرَكَّبٌ.

Combine, *v.t.* To join together, جَمَعَ ـ ضَمَّ ² ـ وَصَّلَ. To mix, خَلَطَ ـ مَزَجَ ـ. To arrange, رَتَّبَ ـ دَبَّرَ ـ قَابَلَ ـ وَفَّقَ.

Combine, *v.i.* To unite with each other, إِتَّحَدَ ـ إِجْتَمَعَ مَعَ ـ إِخْتَلَطَ ـ أَمْتَزَجَ. To mingle, إِقْتَرَنَ مَعَ ـ إِتَّفَقَ مَعَ ـ مَعَ. To — in favour of, تَعَصَّبَ لِ; against, تَعَصَّبَ عَلَى.

Combings, *n.* مُشَاقَة.

Combustibility, *n.* قَابِلِيَّةُ ٱلْإِحْتِرَاقِ.

Combustible, *a.* يَحْتَرِق ـ يُوقَد.

Combustible, *n.* حُرَاق ـ رِبَة ـ مَأْكُولُ ٱلنَّارِ ـ وَمَّا يَحْتَرِق.

Combustion, *n.* Conflagration, حَرِيق ـ حَرِيقَة ـ إِحْتِرَاق ـ إِلْتِهَاب. Bustle, رَجَّة ـ غَاغَا.

Come, *v.i.* جَآءَ *aor.* يَجِيءُ ـ أَتَى *aor.* يَأْتِي ـ وَافَى إِلَى ـ قَدِمَ ـ. To — and go, تَرَدَّدَ ـ رَادَ ². To advance towards, إِشْتَقَّ ـ تَقَدَّمَ ـ تَقَرَّبَ إِلَى ـ دَنَا مِنْ ². To proceed, issue from, إِنْتَسَبَ إِلَى ـ خَرَجَ مِنْ ² ـ مِنْ. To attain any condition, يَفِدُ *aor.* وَفَدَ إِلَى ـ لَحِقَ ـ يَصِلُ *aor.* وَصَلَ إِلَى ـ بَلَغَ ² ـ يَعُودُ *aor.* يَصِيرُ ـ صَارَ ـ أَدْرَكَ ـ قَدِمَ إِلَى. To become, عَادَ *aor.* يَعُودُ ـ جَرَى لِ ـ. *aor.* يَصِيرُ. To happen to, حَدَثَ لِ ² ـ صَارَ ـ يَصِيرُ *aor.* صَارَ لِ ـ حَصَلَ لِ ² ـ حَكَمَ لِ ². To follow, as a consequence, طَلَعَ ـ نَتَجَ ـ صَدَرَ ² ـ تَبِعَ ². To be present, not absent, كَانَ حَاضِرًا ـ حَضِرَ; to be present, not future, كَانَ *aor.* يَكُونُ ـ صَارَ *aor.* يَصِيرُ. To — or happen one after another, تَوَالَى ـ تَتَابَعَ. Come! come along! تَعَالَ ـ هَلُمَّ ـ حَيَّ. Come thou quickly to us, حَيَّ بِكَ; come ye quickly to us, حَيَّ بِكُمْ.

Come to prayer! حَيَّ عَلَى ٱلصَّلَاةِ. To —, the time to —, المُسْتَقْبَلُ. It appears that the war is not coming to an end, الظَّاهِرُ أَنَّ ٱلْحَرْبَ لَمْ تُقَارِبِ ٱلْخِتَامَ وَٱلْإِنْتِهَاءَ.

To come about, to happen, حَدَثَ – جَرَى – عَرَضَ – إِتَّفَقَ – تَغَيَّرَ – يَدُورُ aor. دَارَ – قَلَبَ. To change, وَقَعَ aor. يَقَعُ.

To surround, أَحَاطَ بِ.

To come across, to meet, لَاقَى – صَادَفَ. To cross over, عَبَرَ – قَطَعَ.

To come after, to follow, تَبِعَ – تَلَا – أَتَى بَعْدَ.

To come again, to return, عَادَ aor. يَعُودُ – رَجَعَ. I will not come to you again, لَا آتِيكُمْ أَيْضًا. I will repay you when I come again, أُوفِيكَ فِي إِيَابِي. If I come to you again, إِذَا قَدِمْتُ إِلَيْكُمْ مَرَّةً أُخْرَى. His spirit came to him again, رَجَعَتْ إِلَيْهِ رُوحُهُ.

To come at or by, to get, to attain, أَدْرَكَ – نَالَ aor. يَنَالُ – حَظِيَ بِ – بَلَغَ – حَصَّلَ. To acquire, كَسَبَ – إِكْتَسَبَ – تَمَلَّكَ بِ. To reach, لَحِقَ – وَصَلَ إِلَى aor. يَصِلُ.

To come down, to descend, هَبَطَ – نَزَلَ. To — in one's price, أَسْقَطَ ٱلثَّمَنَ – حَطَّ مِنَ ٱلثَّمَنِ – بَخَسَ. To abase one's self, إِخْتَضَعَ – تَخَشَّعَ.

To come forth or out, خَرَجَ – طَلَعَ. To proceed from, خَرَجَ مِن – إِنْتَسَبَ إِلَى – إِشْتَقَّ مِن – صَدَرَ عَن. Come forth! هَلُمَّ خَارِجًا.

To come forward, in advance, تَقَدَّمَ. To be ready for, عَتَدَ لِ – تَهَيَّأَ لِ.

To come in, to enter, دَخَلَ – فَاتَ إِلَى دَاخِلٍ aor. يَفُوتُ – عَبَرَ إِلَى جُوًّا. To comply with, to yield to, رَضِيَ بِ aor. يَرْضَى – سَلَّمَ. To be an ingredient in any thing, دَخَلَ فِي. They came in among us privately, دَخَلُوا بَيْنَنَا خُفْيَةً.

To come in for, to be early enough to obtain, كَانَ لَهُ أَنْ يَأْخُذَ – حَصَّلَ – أَدْرَكَ. To obtain, وَصَلَ عَلَى وَقْتٍ لِيَنَالَ aor. يَصِلُ.

To come in to, to join with, to aid, نَصَرَ – عَاوَنَ – سَاعَدَ. To comply with, قَبِلَ – طَاوَعَ – إِرْتَضَى بِ – رَضِيَ بِ.

To come into fashion, صَارَ عَادَةً. To come into use, أُسْتُعْمِلَ.

To come near to, to approach, دَنَا مِن – قَرُبَ إِلَى. To —, as in excellence, *etc.*, قَارَبَ – شَابَهَ – ضَاهَى.

To come of, to be a descendant of, إِنْتَسَبَ إِلَى – كَانَ مِن ذُرِّيَّةِ.

To proceed, as effects from a cause, صَدَرَ – نَتَجَ – طَلَعَ – صَارَ.

To come off, to escape, خَلَصَ – إِنْعَتَقَ مِن – نَجَا مِن. To end, come to an end, تَمَّ – إِنْتَهَى – إِنْقَضَى. To take place, حَدَثَ. To be, كَانَ – صَارَ.

To come off from, to leave, تَرَكَ – خَلَّى – طَلَعَ عَن.

To come on, to make progress, قَدِمَ – تَقَدَّمَ – نَمَا – نَجَحَ.

To advance to combat with, ثَارَ إِلَى – هَجَمَ عَلَى.

To come out, to be made public, ظَهَرَ – إِشْتَهَرَ – عَلَنَ – بَانَ – صَارَ مَشْهُورًا – صَارَ مَعْلُومًا. To be discovered, إِنْكَشَفَ.

To leave, خَرَجَ مِن – طَلَعَ مِن – تَرَكَ.

To come out with, to give utterance to, أَبَاحَ بِ – نَطَقَ بِ – لَفَظَ بِ.

To come over, to cross, عَبَرَ – قَطَعَ. To come over to a party, to combine with, إِتَّفَقَ مَعَ – تَعَصَّبَ مَعَ. To overspread, cover, غَطَّى – غَطَّى عَلَى. To happen to, حَدَثَ لِ. To be seized with, عَرَضَ لِ – إِعْتَرَى.

To come round, as from anger, *etc.*, تَلَيَّنَ. To get better, شُفِيَ – إِشْتَفَى – إِنْجَبَرَ.

To come short, to fail, خَسِرَ – قَصَّرَ عَن – قَصَرَ عَن. His work came short, failed, حَبِطَ عَمَلُهُ.

To come together, to assemble, إِجْتَمَعَ. To come with one another, أَتَوْا مَعًا – جَاءُوا مَعًا – حَضَرُوا مَعًا.

To come to nothing, خَابَ – ٱلشَّيْ – مَا طَلَعَ شَيْءٌ مِنْهُ.

To come to one's self, إِسْتَفَاقَ – رَجَعَ إِلَى نَفْسِهِ – أَفَاقَ – صَحَا – وَعَى عَلَى نَفْسِهِ aor. يَعِي.

To come to one's senses, رَجَعَ إِلَى نَفْسِهِ – رَجَعَ إِلَى عَقْلِهِ.

To come to pass, to happen, حَدَثَ – جَرَى – عَرَضَ – إِتَّفَقَ. To be accomplished, تَمَّ – كَمَلَ – نَجَزَ – صَارَ – إِنْتَهَى.

To come to, to consent, to yield, إِرْتَضَى – رَضِيَ بِ – سَلَّمَ – قَبِلَ – أَطَاعَ. To amount to, بَلَغَ – لَحِقَ – صَارَ مَبْلَغَ. To revive, إِسْتَفَاقَ – عَاشَتْ رُوحُهُ – أَفَاقَ. To become, آلَ إِلَى. It is well known what the town has come to in these days, لَا يَخْفَى مَا آلَتْ إِلَيْهِ ٱلْبَلَدُ فِي هٰذِهِ ٱلْأَيَّامِ. The affair came to, reached, him, أَفْضَى إِلَيْهِ ٱلْأَمْرُ. To reach, أَفْضَى إِلَى.

To come upon, to attack, إِقْتَحَمَ – هَجَمَ عَلَى – حَمَلَ عَلَى. To befall, أَصَابَ – جَرَى لِ – أَتَى إِلَى. To befall, as a misfortune, نَزَلَ بِ; as a disease, أُصِيبَ بِ.

To come up, to grow, نَبَتَ – نَمَا – طَلَعَ. To make an appearance, ظَهَرَ – بَانَ – لَاحَ – بَدَا. To come into use, أُسْتُعْمِلَ – صَارَ عَادَةً.

To come up to, to amount to, بَلَغَ ـ طَلَعَ ـ لَحِقَ. To overtake, لَحِقَ ـ وَصَلَ إِلَى aor. يَصِلُ ـ أَدْرَكَ. To be equal with, قَارَبَ ـ سَاوَى ـ أَقْرَنَ ل.

To come up with, to overtake, لَحِقَ ـ إِقْتَرَبَ مِن.

Comedian, *n.* مِنْ أَهْلِ ٱلتِّيَاتْرُو ـ مِنْ أَهْلِ لَعِبِ ٱلتَّقْلِيدِ ـ مَرْسَحِيٌّ.

Comedy, *n.* لَعِبٌ يُقَلِّدُونَ فِيهِ زَلَّاتٍ ـ أُلْعُوبَة ـ لَعِبُ تَقْلِيدٍ ـ لَعِبُ ٱلتِّيَاتْرُو ـ ٱلنَّاسِ وَغَشْمَهُمْ.

Comeliness, *n.* كِيَاسَة ـ بَهَآءٌ وَكَمَال ـ مَلَاحَة ـ حُسْن ـ جَمَال.

Comely, *a.* لَائِق ـ ظَرِيف ـ حُلْو ـ حَسَن ـ جَمِيل ـ فَارِه ـ زَيْن ـ صَبِير.

Comely, *ad.* بِظَرَافَةٍ ـ بِأَدَبٍ ـ كَمَا يَلِيقُ.

Comer, *n.* آتٍ ـ وَارِد *pl.* وُرَّاد ـ وَافِد *pl.* وُفَّاد.

Comet, *n.* نَجْمٌ بِذَنَبٍ ـ ذُو ذُؤَابَةٍ.

Cometary, *a.* مَا نِيطَ بِٱلنُّجُومِ ـ مُخْتَصٌّ بِٱلنَّجْمِ ٱلذَّنَبِيَّاتِ ـ ذَوَاتِ ٱلذَّنَبِ.

Comfit, *n.* } Comfiture, } حَلَاوَة ـ حَلْوَى ـ مُرَبَّيَات ـ مُرَبًّى ـ مُلَبَّس.

Comfort, *v.t.* شَرَحَ ـ سَرَّ ـ عَزَّى ـ سَلَّى ـ أَسْلَى عَن ـ تَعَزَّى ـ أَخَذَ بِخَاطِرِهِ ـ خَفَّفَ عَن ـ خَاطِرَهُ. To be comforted, تَعَزَّى ـ تَسَلَّى ـ عَزِيَ.

Comfort, *n.* Consolation, جُبْرَان ـ مُوَاسَاة ـ تَعْزِيَة ـ تَسْلِيَة ـ ٱلْخَاطِرِ. Assistance, عَوْن ـ إِسْعَاف ـ مُعَاوَنَة ـ مُسَاعَدَة. Affluence, نِعْمَة ـ نَعِيم ـ هِينَة. Commodiousness, فُسْحَة ـ حُظْوَة ـ بَحْبَحَة ـ رَاحَة. You have given me —, سَقَيْتَنِي مِنْكَ سَلْوَة.

Comfortable, *a.* Consoling, سَارٌّ ـ مُعَزٍّ ـ مُسَلٍّ ـ مُرِيح ـ هَنِيءٌ. Commodious, وَاسِع ـ ذُو حُظْوَةٍ ـ ذُو هِينَةٍ ـ مُتَبَحْبِح ـ فَسِيح ـ فُسَاح ـ مَنْظُوم. Comfortable, of a life, مُتَرَفَّه ـ نَعِيم. To make (things) —, مَهَّدَ. In — circumstances, فِي عَيْشٍ رَغِيدٍ وَحَالٍ سَعِيدٍ.

Comfortable, *n.* A warm covering, لِحَاف.

Comfortably, *ad.* Consolingly, بِتَعْزِيَةٍ ـ بِتَسْلِيَةٍ. In ease and pleasure, مُتَرَفِّهًا ـ بِرَاحَةٍ ـ بِسُهُولَةٍ ـ عَلَى هِينَةٍ وَسَعَةٍ ـ حَسَنًا. In ease and plenty, فِي خَفْضٍ مِنَ ٱلْعَيْشِ.

Comforter, *n.* مُعَزٍّ ـ مُسَلٍّ ـ جَابِرُ ٱلْقَلْبِ. The Paraclete, ٱلْفَارَقْلِيط ـ ٱلرُّوحُ ٱلْقُدُسُ.

Comfortless, *a.* Without consolation, بِلَا تَسْلِيَةٍ ـ بِدُونِ تَعْزِيَةٍ ـ كَرِيب. Cheerless, بِلَا هَنَآءٍ ـ مُضِيف ـ يَتِيم.

Comic, *a.* } Comical, } مُضْحِك ـ سُخْرَة ـ هَزْلِيّ ـ مُهَرِّج ـ مُتَعَلِّق بِلَعِبِ ٱلتَّقْلِيدِ.

Comically, *ad.* مَسْخَرَةً ـ بِتَنْكِيتٍ ـ ضِحْكًا.

Coming, *n.* Approach, قُرْب ـ إِقْتِرَاب ـ تَقَدُّم. Arrival, جِيئَة ـ وُصُول ـ قُدُوم ـ وُرُود ـ مَجِيءٌ. Happening, حُدُوث ـ وُقُوع.

Coming, *a.* قَابِل ـ مُقْبِل ـ قَادِم.

Comity, *n.* حُسْنُ ٱلْمُعَاشَرَةِ ـ مُجَامَلَة. The — of nations, مُعَاشَرَةُ ٱلْمِلَلِ.

Comma, *n.* شَرْطَة ـ (،) عَلَامَةٌ تَدُلُّ عَلَى ٱلْوُقُوفِ فِي ٱلْقِرَآءَةِ وَهِيَ.

Command, *v.t.* To give orders, أَمَرَ ـ أَمَرَ بِ. To direct to be done, أَوْصَى بِ ـ وَصَّى. To —, to lay down precepts to ..., (of God), فَرَضَ عَلَى ـ أَفْرَضَ ل. To have the — of, حَكَمَ ـ مَلَكَ عَلَى ـ تَسَلَّطَ عَلَى. To have in power, قَادَ ـ عَلَى. To — not to do, to forbid, نَهَى. To overlook, شَرَفَ عَلَى ـ أَشْرَفَ عَلَى ـ إِشْتَرَفَ عَلَى ـ رَمَى عَلَى. My house commands the square, بَيْتِي يَشْرُفُ عَلَى ٱلْمَيْدَانِ. To — silence, سَكَّتَ ـ أَمَرَ بِٱلسُّكُوتِ.

Command, *v.i.* To have the — of, حَكَمَ عَلَى ـ تَسَلَّطَ عَلَى ـ رَأَسَ عَلَى.

Command, *n.* An order, أَمْر *pl.* أَوَامِرُ ـ حُكْم *pl.* أَحْكَام ـ مَرْسُوم ـ وَصِيَّة *pl.* وَصَايَا. A precept from God, فَرِيضَة *pl.* فَرَائِض ـ مَرَاسِمُ *pl.* Authority, حُكْم ـ أَمْر ـ سُلْطَان ـ رِئَاسَة ـ يَد. Power to order or forbid, أَمْرٌ وَنَهْيٌ. Power to direct anything, تَصَرُّفٌ بِ. The —, as of a province, إِمْرَة ـ حُكْم ـ وِلَايَة. The — over soldiers, حُكْمُ ٱلْعَسْكَرِ ـ قِيَادَةُ ٱلْجَيْشِ. To give the — to, رَأَّسَ عَلَى ـ وَلَّى بِ.

Commandant, *n.* } Commander, } حَاكِم *pl.* حُكَّام ـ وَالٍ *pl.* وُلَاة; of troops, قَائِد *pl.* قُوَّاد ـ حَاكِم ـ قُومَنْدَان; as of a ship, رَئِيس ـ قُبْطَان *pl.* قَبَاطِينُ; of a small craft, نَاخُوذَاة *pl.* نَوَاخِذَة ـ نَوْخَذَة. Commanders of ships generally, أَرْبَابُ ٱلسُّفُنِ. Commander-in-Chief, سَرْعَسْكَر. Commander of the Faithful, أَمِيرُ ٱلْمُؤْمِنِينَ. The —, as of a garrison, ضَابِط ـ مُحَافِظ. To be or become —, to have authority over, رَأَسَ ـ رَأُسَ عَلَى. To make — over, رَأَّسَ عَلَى. To be made — over, تَرَأَّسَ عَلَى.

Commandery, *n.* إِمَارَة.

Commanding, *a.* Overlooking, مُشْرِفٌ عَلَى. High, مُرْتَفِع. Holding command, آمِر ـ ضَابِط.

Commandment, *n.* أَمْر ـ حُكْم ـ وَصِيَّة ـ قَاعِدَة. The Ten Commandments, ٱلْعَشْرُ وَصَايَا ـ ٱلْعَشْرُ كَلِمَاتٍ. *See also* Command, *n.*

Commemorable, *a.* يُذْكَرُ ـ مُسْتَحِقُّ ٱلذِّكْرِ.

Commemorate, *v.t.* عَيَّدَ ل ـ عَيَّدَ لِذِكْرِ ـ ذَكَرَ.

Commemoration, *n.* عِيد ـ تَذْكَار.

Commemorative, *a.* مُذَكِّر ـ يُذَكِّر.

Commence, *v.t.* بَاشَرَ ـ شَرَعَ فِي ـ إِبْتَدَأَ ـ بَدَأَ. To make a commencement, أَنْشَأَ ب ـ إِفْتَتَحَ ب. To set about, جَعَلَ. To enter upon, دَخَلَ فِي ـ هَبَّ.

Commencement, *n.* إِفْتِتَاح ـ شُرُوع ـ رَأْس ـ إِبْتِدَآء ـ بَدْء ـ بِدَايَة.

Commend, *v.t.* To praise, أَثْنَى عَلَى ـ ذَكَرَ بِٱلْجَمِيلِ ـ حَمَدَ ـ مَدَحَ ـ أَطْرَى. To recommend to, وَصَّى فِي ـ أَوْصَى إِلَى ب ـ وَصَّى عَلَى. To deliver up to with confidence, أَوْدَعَ إِلَى. To approve, إِسْتَصْوَبَ ـ فَضَّلَ. To show, manifest, أَظْهَرَ. To — or commit to, إِسْتَسْلَمَ ـ إِسْتَوْدَعَ. I — my brother to you, أُوصِي إِلَيْكُمْ بِأَخِي ـ أَسْتَوْدِعُكُمْ أَخِي. To say "Well done!" to, حَبَّذَ ـ صَوَّبَ.

Commendable, *a.* مَدِيح ـ حَمِيد.

Commendably, *ad.* بِحَمْدٍ ـ حَسَنًا ـ جَيِّدًا.

Commendation, *n.* Praise, حَمْد ـ تَمْجِيد ـ مَدْح ـ ثَنَآء ـ إِثْنَآء. Recommendation, وَصِيَّة ـ تَوْصِيَة. Approbation, تَفْضِيل ـ إِسْتِصْوَاب ـ إِسْتِحْسَان.

Commendatory, *a.* مُثْنٍ عَلَى ـ مَدْحِيٌّ.

Commensurability, *n.* / Commensurableness, } مُنَاسَبَة ـ مُنَاسَبَةُ ٱلْعَدَدِ وَٱلْقِيَاسِ ـ مُقَايَسَة ـ قِيَاس.

Commensurable, *a.* / Commensurate, } مُنَاسِبٌ فِي ٱلْعَدَدِ وَٱلْقِيَاسِ ـ مُتَسَاوٍ ـ عَدِيل ـ عَلَى ذَاتِ قِيَاسٍ ـ مُتَنَاسِب ـ عَلَى قِيَاسٍ ـ مُتَعَادِل ـ مُعَادِل ـ *pl.* أَعْدَال. Proportionable, مُطَابِق ـ مُوَافِق ـ بِمِقْدَارٍ.

Commensurate, *v.t.* سَوَّى ـ طَابَقَ ـ جَعَلَ عَلَى قِيَاسٍ وَاحِدٍ. To be commensurated to, نَاسَبَ ـ عَادَلَ ـ سَاوَى.

Commensurately, *ad.* بِٱسْتِوَآءٍ ـ عَلَى ذَاتِ قِيَاسٍ ـ عَلَى قِيَاسٍ.

Commensuration, *n.* Reduction to a common measure, جُعْل عَلَى قِيَاسٍ وَاحِدٍ. Proportion, قِيَاس ـ مُوَافَقَة.

Comment upon, *v.t.* أَوَّلَ ـ فَسَّرَ ـ شَرَحَ ـ عَبَّرَ.

Comment, *n.* / Commentary, } An exposition, بَيَان ـ تَأْوِيل ـ تَفْسِير ـ شَرْح ـ تَعْبِير. A note, عِبَارَة. A — on the margin of a book, حَاشِيَة *pl.* حَوَاشٍ. To write such notes on the margin, حَشَّى.

Commentator, *n.* مُعَبِّر ـ مُفَسِّر ـ شَارِح.

Commerce, *n.* Trade, بَيْع وَشِرَآء ـ تِجَارَة ـ مَتْجَر ـ مُتَاجَرَة. Intercourse, أَخْذ وَعَطَآء ـ مُصَاحَبَة ـ مُخَالَطَة ـ مُبَاشَرَة. Sexual intercourse, مُجَامَعَة ـ هِوَاس. Extensive —, مَتْجَر وَاسِع. *See also* Trade, *n.*

Commerce, *v.i.* To trade, تَاجَرَ ـ بَاعَ وَٱشْتَرَى.

Commercial, *a.* مُتَعَلِّق بِٱلتِّجَارَةِ ـ تِجَارِيّ ـ مَتْجَرِيّ.

Commercially, *ad.* فِيمَا يَتَعَلَّق بِٱلْمَتْجَرِ ـ بِطَرِيقَةِ ٱلتِّجَارَةِ.

Commination, *n.* تَرْهِيب ـ تَهْدِيد. The — service, طَقْس إِجْرَآء ٱلتَّهْدِيدِ. A similar service in the Syrian churches is called, ٱلشَّبْقُونُو.

Comminatory, *a.* مُرَهِّب ـ تَهْدِيدِيّ.

Commingle, *v.t.* جَمَعَ ـ شَمَّطَ ـ خَلَطَ ـ مَازَجَ ـ مَزَجَ ب.

Commingle, *v.i.* إِمْتَزَجَ ـ إِخْتَلَطَ.

Comminute, *v.t.* جَرَشَ ـ سَحَقَ ـ دَكَّ ـ دَقَّقَ.

Comminution, *n.* جَرْش ـ سَحْق ـ دَكّ ـ تَدْقِيق.

Commiserable, *a.* يُرْثَى لَهُ ـ مُسْتَحِقّ ٱلشَّفَقَةِ.

Commiserate, *v.t.* شَفَقَ عَلَى ـ أَشْفَقَ عَلَى ـ رَثَى ل ـ رَقَّ ل ـ قَلْبُهُ ـ رَحِمَ ـ تَحَنَّنَ عَلَى ـ حَنَّ عَلَى. Commiserated, مُرْثًى ل ـ مَرْحُوم.

Commiseration, *n.* حَنَان ـ تَحَنُّن ـ شَفَقَة ـ شَفَق ـ مَرْثَاة ـ رِقَّة قَلْب ـ حِنَّةُ ٱلْقَلْبِ ـ رَأْفَة.

Commissarial, *a.* مُتَعَلِّق بِمَأْمُورِيَّةٍ.

Commissary, *n.* A deputy, نَائِب ـ وَكِيل. A — for a special purpose, مُبَاشِر ـ حَوَالَة ـ مُوَكَّل. A —, of troops, أَمِينُ ٱلنُّزُلِ. Commissary General, كَبِيرُ أُمَنَآءِ ٱلنُّزُلِ. Deputy Commissary General, مُعَاوِنُ كَبِيرِ أُمَنَآءِ ٱلنُّزُلِ. Assistant Commissary General, مُدِيرُ ٱلنُّزُلِ. Deputy Assistant Commissary General, مُعَاوِنُ مُدِيرِ ٱلنُّزُلِ.

Commission, *n.* A warrant, سَنَد ـ فِرْمَان ـ بَرَآءَة. Authority, place of authority, appointment, مَأْمُورِيَّة. Perpetration, صُنْع ـ مُبَاشَرَة ـ جُعْل ـ إِرْتِكَاب. Direction of anything, عَمَل ـ تَفْوِيض ـ تَوَكُّل ـ وَكَالَة. Agency, وَكَالَة. Duty, tax, حَقّ ـ حَقّ سَعْيٍ ـ رُسُوم ـ حَوَالَة ـ مَعْلُوم. A number of persons joined in a trust, *etc.*, مُبَاشَرَة ـ وُكَلَآء ـ وَكَالَة ـ لَجْنَة ـ قُومِيسِيُون ـ مَجْلِس. An order given to or by a tradesman, وَصِيَّة. Charge for —, أُجْرَة وَكَالَةٍ. On —, بِٱلْأُجْرَةِ ـ وَكَالَةً. The Commission of the Peace, مَأْمُورِيَّة ضَبْطِ أُمُورِ ٱلْبَلَدِ.

An administrative commission, لَجْنَة مَلَكِيَّة.

An executive commission, لَجْنَة ٱلْإِجْرَآءِ.

A mixed commission, لَجْنَة مُخْتَلِطَة.

Member of a commission, عُضْوُ لَجْنَةٍ.

Report of a commission, تَقْرِيرُ لَجْنَةٍ.

To charge a commission, ع طَلَبَ ـ ع طَلَبَ أُجْرَةً (or عُمُولَةً) قُومِيسِيُون.

To execute a commission, أَجْرَى مَا أُوصِيَ بِهِ ـ قَضَى ٱلْوَصِيَّةَ.

To obtain a commission, as in the army, ع حَازَ (or حَصَّلَ) بَرَآءَةَ ضَابِطٍ.

To put into commission, of ships, جَهَّزَ وَأَعَدَّ ٱلْبَوَارِجَ لِأَمْرٍ مَخْصُوصٍ.

To put out of commission, as of ships, *etc.*, وَزَّعَ.

To throw up a commission, as in the army, إِسْتَعْفَى وَرَدَّ ٱلْبَرَآءَةَ.

Commission, *v.t.* To empower in or with, أَجْرَى-فِي ـ صَرَّفَ-فِي ـ أَقَامَ ـ فَوَّضَ-إِلَى ـ عَهِدَ إِلَى-بِ ـ وَكَّلَ-بِ ـ وَكَّلَ ـ جَرَّى. To be commissioned, تَوَكَّلَ ـ تَصَرَّفَ فِي. To order, as from a tradesman, وَصَّى-عَلَى. *See also under* Commission, *n.*

Commissioner, *n.* جَرِيٌّ *pl.* أَجْرِيَآءُ ـ مُتَصَرِّفٌ ـ مُبَاشِرٌ ـ أَمِينٌ ـ حَوَالَةٌ. A — of customs, أَمِينُ ٱلْكُمْرُكِ. The Lords Commissioners of the Admiralty, مَأْمُورُوا إِجْرَآءِ ٱلْأُمُورِ ٱلْبَحْرِيَّةِ.

Commit, *v.t.* As in trust to, فَوَّضَ-إِلَى ـ وَكَلَ-إِلَى *aor.* يَكِلُ ـ إِيتَمَنَ-عَلَى ـ وَكَّلَ-بِ ـ وَضَعَ-عِنْدَ *aor.* يَضَعُ ـ إِسْتَوْدَعَ ـ أَسْلَمَ-إِلَى ـ سَلَّمَ-إِلَى. To — an office to, وَلَّى-ٱلْمَنْصِبَ ـ أَوْلَى-ٱلْمَنْصِبَ. To place, جَعَلَ ـ ع حَطَّ ـ أَقَامَ ـ وَضَعَ. To imprison, ع سَجَنَ ـ حَبَسَ. To do, صَنَعَ. To do something against another, جَنَى عَلَى. To — a crime, رَكِبَ ـ إِقْتَرَفَ ـ إِرْتَكَبَ ذَنْبًا ـ ذَنْبًا. To — one's self to, to be absorbed in, غَرِيَ بِ *aor.* يَغْرَى ـ إِنْهَمَكَ فِي. To — to memory, حَفِظَ ـ حَفِظَ-غَيْبًا. To — fornication, زَنَا. To — sacrilege, ع رَدَّ ـ إِخْتَلَسَ مَا هُوَ قُدُسٌ. He committed the affair to him, فَوَّضَهُ ٱلْأَمْرَ ـ ٱلْأَمْرَ إِلَيْهِ. They committed themselves to the sea, سَلَّمُوا أَنْفُسَهُمْ إِلَى ٱلْبَحْرِ ـ إِسْتَوْدَعُوا أَنْفُسَهُمْ إِلَى ٱلْبَحْرِ. A trust is committed to me, إِنِّي مُؤْتَمَنٌ عَلَى وَكَالَةٍ. Those who — such things are worthy of death, ٱلَّذِينَ يَفْعَلُونَ نَظَائِرَ هٰذِهِ يَسْتَوْجِبُونَ ٱلْمَوْتَ. If I have committed anything worthy of death, إِنْ كُنْتُ مُسِيئًا أَوْ مُرْتَكِبًا شَيْئًا يَسْتَحِقُّ ٱلْمَوْتَ. They committed great atrocities, إِرْتَكَبُوا فَوَاحِشَ ـ إِرْتَكَبُوا أَفْعَالًا قَبِيحَةً.

Commitment, *n.* The sending to prison, حَبْسٌ ـ تَحْبِيسٌ ـ تَسْلِيمٌ إِلَى ٱلْحَبْسِ.

Committal, *n.* Perpetration; *see* Commission, *n.* *See also* Commitment, *n.*

Committee, *n.* لَجْنَةٌ ـ مَشْوَرَةٌ ـ مَجْمَعٌ ـ مَجْلِسٌ. A — was formed, إِنْعَقَدَتْ لَجْنَةٌ.

Commix. *See to* Commingle.

Commixtion, *n.* مَزْجٌ ـ إِمْتِزَاجٌ ـ تَرْكِيبٌ.

Commixture, *n.* مُرَكَّبٌ ـ تَرْكِيبٌ ـ تَقْنِينٌ.

Commode, *n.* A bedside utensil, كُرْسِيٌّ فِيهِ مِسْتَعْمَلَةٌ.

Commodious, *a.* Suitable, مُنَاسِبٌ ـ مُوَافِقٌ. Useful, مُفِيدٌ ـ نَافِعٌ. Furnished with conveniences, مُتَجَهِّزٌ ـ فِيهِ جَمِيعُ ٱلْمُنَاسَبَاتِ ـ وَسِيعٌ ـ مَلِيحٌ. A — house, بَيْتٌ مَنْظُومٌ. Open, airy, ذُو نَفَسٍ.

Commodiously, *ad.* عَلَى هِينَةٍ وَسَعَةٍ ـ بِرَاحَةٍ ـ بِسُهُولَةٍ ـ عَلَى وَفْقٍ.

Commodiousness, *n.* نَفَسٌ ـ هِينَةٌ ـ رَاحَةٌ ـ سَعَةٌ ـ لِيَاقَةٌ ـ نِظَامٌ ـ فُسْحَةٌ ـ مَلَاحَةٌ.

Commodity, *n.* A ware, سِلْعَةٌ *pl.* سِلَعٌ ـ بِضَاعَةٌ *pl.* بَضَائِعُ ـ مَتَاعٌ *pl.* أَمْتِعَةٌ ـ سَبَبٌ *pl.* أَسْبَابٌ ـ تِجَارَةٌ. *See also* Commodiousness, *n.*

Commodore, *n.* Commander of a squadron, قُبْطَانُ عِمَارَةٍ ـ بَاشْبُوغ.

Common, *a.* General, عَامٌّ ـ عُمُومِيٌّ. Belonging to more than one, مُشْتَرَكٌ ـ مُشَاعٌ ـ لِلْعَامِّ. Having no particular owner, عُمُومِيٌّ. Easy to be procured, عَمِيمٌ ـ وَافِرٌ ـ كَثِيرُ ٱلْوُجُودِ. In ordinary use, مُعْتَادٌ. Mean, رَذِيلٌ ـ وَاطِئٌ. Not fine, عَبْلٌ ـ خَشِنٌ ـ مُسَكَّجٌ. Ordinary in quality, دُونٌ. Of no value, بَهْرَجٌ ـ عَادِيٌّ ـ دَارِجٌ. Common, vulgar, as of a dialect, حَقِيرٌ ـ بَطَّالٌ. Common to man, befalling all alike, شَامِلٌ ـ بَشَرِيٌّ. Common, unclean, نَجِسٌ. Generally known, broadspread, شَائِعٌ ـ شَيِّعٌ. To be —, general, عَمَّ ع. This house is — to them, هٰذَا ٱلْبَيْتُ شَيِّعٌ بَيْنَهُمْ. They had all things —, كُلُّ شَيْءٍ لَهُمْ كَانَ مُشْتَرَكًا. The — term used is..., ٱلْمُصْطَلَحُ عَلَيْهِ أَنْ يُقَالَ. Out of the —, خَارِجٌ عَنِ ٱلْعَادَةِ.

Common carrier, حَمَّالٌ; with a mule or horse, قَاطِرْجِي.

Common crier, دَلَّالٌ ـ صَارِخٌ ـ بَرَّاحٌ ـ مُنَادٍ.

Common divisor, مُشْتَرَكٌ فِيهِ.

Common faith, ٱلْإِيمَانُ ٱلْعَامُّ.

Common gender, لَيْسَ بِمُذَكَّرٍ وَلَا بِمُؤَنَّثٍ.

Common interest, مَنَافِعُ مُشْتَرَكَةٌ ـ مَنَافِعُ عُمُومِيَّةٌ.

Common man, مِنَ ٱلْعَوَامِّ ـ عُطُلٌ.

Common multiple, مُضَعَّفٌ مُشْتَرَكٌ.

Common noun, إِسْمُ جَمْعٍ ـ إِسْمُ جِنْسٍ.

Common people, the, العَوَامُّ ـ جَعْدُ ٱلْقَفَا ـ الجَعْدِيَّةُ ـ السُّفْلَةُ.

The distinguished and the — people, الخَاصَّةُ ـ الخَاصُّ وَٱلْعَامُّ وَٱلْعَامَّةُ.

Common prison, حَبْسٌ لِلْعَامِّ ـ الحَبْسُ ٱلْعَامُّ.

Common rate, السِّعْرُ ٱلْجَارِي ـ السِّعْرُ ٱلْمُعْتَادُ.

Common report, تَوَاتُرٌ ـ أَمْرٌ شَتَاتٌ ـ أَمْرٌ شَتٌّ.

Common saying, مَثَلٌ مَشْهُورٌ ـ مَثَلٌ سَائِرٌ ـ مَثَلٌ جَارٍ.

Common sense, عَقْلٌ سَلِيمٌ ـ وِهْنَةٌ.

Common sewer, بَلُّوعَةٌ ـ بَلَّاعَةٌ.

Common soldier, نَفَرٌ *pl.* أَنْفَارٌ ـ عَسْكَرِيٌّ *pl.* عَسَاكِرُ.

Common verb, neutral, فِعْلٌ لَازِمٌ.

Common woman, a prostitute, قَحْبَةٌ *pl.* قِحَابٌ.

Common, *n.* An open ground, مَحْجَرٌ *pl.* مَحَاجِرُ ـ فَضَآءٌ ـ أَرْضٌ مُشْتَرَكَةٌ. Ground common to all, خَلَآءٌ ـ سَاعَةٌ ـ صَاعٌ مَكَانٌ بَهْرَجٌ.

Common, *ad.* In common, equally, سَوَآءً ـ مُسَاوِلٌ ـ شِرْكَةً إِشْتِرَاكًا ـ بِمُسَاوَاةٍ.

Commonalty, *n.* The people generally, العَامَّةُ ـ العَوَامُّ ـ الأَوْبَاشُ ـ الغَثْرُ. The baser class, الأَسَافِلُ ـ الخَلْقُ ـ الشَّعْبُ الجَعْدِيَّةُ. One of the —, أَحَدُ ٱلْأَوْبَاشِ.

Common Council, *n.* مَجْلِسُ مَشَائِخِ ٱلْبَلَدِ.

Commoner, *n.* One of the people, عَامِّيٌّ ـ مِنْ أَهْلِ ٱلْعَوَامِّ. A gentleman —, مُتَقَدِّمٌ بَيْنَ ٱلْعَوَامِّ. A member of the House of Commons, مِنْ أَهْلِ مَجْلِسِ وُكَلَاءِ ٱلشَّعْبِ فِي مَمْلَكَةِ بَرِيتَانِيَا. A — at a college, تِلْمِيذٌ فِي مَدْرَسَةٍ عَامَّةٍ يُصْرَفُ عَلَيْهِ مِنْ أَوْقَافِ ٱلْمَدْرَسَةِ.

Common-law, *n.* أُصُولٌ شَرْعِيَّةٌ مُسْتَنِدَةٌ إِلَى ٱلْمَنْقُولِ وَٱلْعَوَائِدِ ٱلْجَارِيَةِ قَدِيمًا.

Commonly, *ad.* Generally, عُمُومًا ـ غَالِبًا ـ فِي ٱلْغَالِبِ. Frequently, كَثِيرًا مَا ـ تَارَةً. It was — reported, شَاعَ هٰذَا ٱلْقَوْلُ. *See also* Generally, *ad.*

Commonness, *n.* Equal participation, إِشْتِرَاكٌ ـ شِرْكَةٌ. Frequency, كَثْرَةٌ ـ وَفْرَةٌ. Ordinary quality, إِدَانَةٌ ـ دُونٌ ـ خُشُونَةٌ. Triteness, as being generally known, مَشَاعٌ ـ شُيُوعَةٌ.

Common-place, *n.* A common saying, مَثَلٌ جَارٍ ـ مَثَلٌ سَائِرٌ.

Common-place, *a.* Ordinary, دُونٌ; trite, مَشْهُورٌ ـ مُعْتَادٌ.

Common-place book, *n.* دُسْتُورٌ ـ سَفِينَةٌ ـ دَفْتَرٌ مُبَوَّبٌ ـ كِتَابُ تَذْكِرَةٍ.

Common Pleas, *n.* Court of, مَحْكَمَةُ ٱلدَّعَاوَى وَٱلْحُقُوقِ.

Common-prayer, *n.* صَلَوَاتٌ عَامَّةٌ. The Book of —, كِتَابُ ٱلصَّلَوَاتِ ٱلْعَامَّةِ.

Commons, *n.* The people, العَامَّةُ ـ العَوَامُّ ـ الشَّعْبُ. The House of Commons, دِيوَانُ وُكَلَاءِ ٱلشَّعْبِ فِي مَمْلَكَةِ بَرِيتَانِيَا. The Lords and Commons, الأَشْرَافُ وَوُكَلَاءُ ٱلشَّعْبِ. Food at a common table, سُفْرَةٌ لِلْجُمْهُورِ. Food, غِذَآءٌ ـ طَعَامٌ ـ أَكْلٌ ـ قُوتٌ. Short —, قِلٌّ مِنَ ٱلطَّعَامِ. Doctors Commons, دِيوَانُ آمْتِحَانِ وَصِيِّ ٱلْمَوْتَى وَإِقَامَةِ وُكَلَاءَ لِإِجْرَاءِ ٱلتَّرِكَاتِ.

Common-weal, *n.* خَيْرُ ٱلْجُمْهُورِ ـ إِفَادَةُ ٱلشَّعْبِ.

Common-wealth, *n.* Polity, حُكْمٌ ـ حُكُومَةٌ ـ دَوْلَةٌ. The public, الجُمْهُورُ ـ الرَّعِيَّةُ ـ الشَّعْبُ. A community, مَعْشَرٌ. A republic, مَشْيَخَةٌ ـ حُكُومَةُ ٱلشَّعْبِ ـ جُمْهُورِيَّةٌ.

Commotion, *n.* Tumult, خَنْخَنَةٌ ـ هَوْشَةٌ ـ هَيْشَةٌ ـ رَجْفَةٌ ـ إِرْتِجَاجٌ ـ هَرْجٌ وَمَرْجٌ ـ تَذَبْذُبٌ ـ هِزَّةٌ ـ فِتْنَةٌ ـ قَوْمَةٌ ـ إِخْتِبَاطٌ ـ ضَجَرٌ. Perturbation of mind, حَيْرَةٌ ـ هَيَجَانٌ ـ قَلَقٌ ـ إِضْطِرَابٌ ـ ضَجَرٌ. To be in a state of —, رَجَفَ ـ [2] تَذَبْذَبَ ـ إِضْطَرَبَ ـ تَضَرَّبَ ـ ذَبْذَبَ ـ رَجَّ [2] ـ أَزَّ ـ [2]. To put into —, إِرْتَجَّ ـ إِرْتَجَفَ. To be disturbed in mind, إِضْطَرَبَ ـ تَخَبَّطَ. To be in —, of a people, هَاشَ ـ ـ. In the greatest —, فِي غَايَةٍ. It has caused great —, كَدَّرَ ٱلْخَوَاطِرَ وَأَثَارَ ٱلْإِضْطِرَابَ وَٱلْقَلَقَ ٱلْهَوَاجِسَ.

Commune, *v.i.* To converse with, قَاوَلَ ـ رَاجَعَ ـ تَكَلَّمَ مَعَ ـ حَادَثَ مَعَ ـ حَاكَى ـ تَشَاوَرَ. They communed together, of many, تَنَاجَوْا ـ تَحَاوَرُوا.

Communicability, *n.* } That may be expressed, told,
Communicableness, } قَابِلِيَّةٌ مِمَّا يُبَلَّغُ ـ مِمَّا يُتَلَفَّظُ بِهِ ـ التَّبْلِيغُ. That may be imparted, of a disease, قَابِلِيَّةُ ٱلسِّرَايَةِ ـ مِمَّا يُعْدَى.

Communicable, *a.* That may become the possession of more than one, إِشْرَاكُ ٱلْغَيْرِ فِيهِ مُمْكِنٌ. That may be made known, said, يُلْفَظُ بِهِ ـ يُقَالُ ـ يُطْلَعُ عَلَيْهِ. That may be imparted, as of a disease, مُعْدٍ ـ مُعْتَدٍ ـ سَارٍ ـ ذُو عَدْوَةٍ.

Communicant, *n.* A —, as of the Lord's Supper, مُتَنَاوِلٌ ـ مُقْتَرِبٌ.

Communicate, *v.t.* To reveal to, أَلْقَى-عَلَى ـ أَفْضَى إِلَى-بِ ـ أَطْلَعَ-عَلَى ـ أَكْشَفَ-عَلَى ـ أَشْهَرَ-بِ ـ خَبَّرَ-بِ ـ عَرَّفَ بَيْنَهُمْ أَخْذٌ وَعَطَآءٌ. To have intercourse with, عَاشَرَ ـ خَالَطَ ـ. To correspond by letter or message, رَاسَلَ ـ كَاتَبَ. To give to of, أَعْطَى-مِنْ ـ أَشْرَكَ-فِي. To impart a disease, أَعْدَى-مِنْ

مَرَضٍ. To be communicated to, as a disease, *etc.*, سَرَى إِلَى *aor.* يَسْرِى. He does not — his thoughts to his greatest friend, لا يَبِيحُ بِأَفْكَارِهِ لِأَعْظَمِ أَحِبَّآئِهِ.

Communicate, *v.i.* To partake of the Lord's Supper, تَقَرَّبَ — تَنَاوَلَ ٱلْقُرْبَانَ. To have an outlet to, نَفَذَ إِلَى [2]. To —, as one room with another, *etc.*, إِتَّصَلَ مَعَ — ٢ نَفَذَ إِلَى بَعْضٍ.

Communication, *n.* The act of imparting information, إِعْلَامٌ بِ — إِخْبَارٌ — إِطْلَاعٌ عَلَى — تَبْلِيغٌ — إِفَادَةٌ. Information given, تَبْلِيغَاتٌ — إِفَادَةٌ — مَعْرُوضٌ — خَبَرٌ. The — of a secret, إِطْلَاعٌ عَلَى سِرٍّ — مُسَارَّةٌ — إِفْشَآءُ سِرٍّ. Bestowal upon, مَنْحٌ — إِجْدَآءٌ — إِعْطَآءٌ. A passage, طَرِيقٌ — مَنْفِذٌ. A conference, intercourse, أَخْذٌ وَعَطَآءٌ — مُخَالَطَةٌ — مُعَاشَرَةٌ — صُحْبَةٌ. Intercourse by letter, مُكَاتَبَةٌ — مُرَاسَلَةٌ. A — by letter, تَحْرِيرَاتٌ — رِسَالَةٌ. Participation, مُشَارَكَةٌ — شِرْكَةٌ — إِشْتِرَاكٌ. Official communications, تَبْلِيغَاتٌ رَسْمِيَّةٌ. Means of —, roads, *etc.*, طُرُقٌ وَمَعَابِرُ. Communication, as of disease, عَدْوَى — سِرَايَةٌ. To stop the —, سَدَّ ٱلْمَنَافِذَ إِلَى — ٢ سَدَّ ٱلطَّرِيقَ. In his secret — with him, فِي مُنَاجَاتِهِ إِيَّاهُ. They have cut off all the communications between ...., قَطَعُوا جَمِيعَ ٱلْمُوَاصَلَاتِ بَيْنَ. The best means of securing the English communications with India, أَقْوَمُ وَسِيلَةٍ لِإِدَامَةِ مُوَاصَلَاتِ ٱلْأَنْكِلِيزِ مَعَ ٱلْهِنْدِ. For facilitating the communications between ...., لِتَسْهِيلِ ٱلْمُوَاصَلَاتِ بَيْنَ.

Communicative, *a.* غَيْرُ كَتُومٍ — فَيَّاضٌ — مُفَتَّحٌ فِي ٱلْكَلَامِ. Unreserved, genial, صَاحِبُ عِشْرَةٍ — أَلِفٌ.

Communicativeness, *n.* إِبَاحَةٌ فِي ٱلْكَلَامِ — تَفَتُّحٌ فِي ٱلْكَلَامِ. Geniality, أُلْفَةٌ — عِشْرَةٌ.

Communicatory, *n.* Making clear, مُبَيِّنٌ. Useful, مُفِيدٌ.

Communion, *n.* Intercourse, مُعَاشَرَةٌ — صُحْبَةٌ — أُلْفَةٌ — مُخَالَطَةٌ. A body united in faith, جَمَاعَةٌ — طَائِفَةٌ *pl.* طَوَائِفُ — مَذْهَبٌ *pl.* مَذَاهِبُ — مِلَّةٌ *pl.* مِلَلٌ. The Lord's Supper, القُدَّاسُ — القُرْبَانُ ٱلْمُقَدَّسُ — الشِّرْكَةُ ٱلْمُقَدَّسَةُ — العَشَآءُ ٱلرَّبَّانِيُّ. Partaking of the —, تَقَرُّبٌ — تَنَاوُلُ ٱلْقُرْبَانِ. To enter the — of, as of a religion, دَخَلَ فِي [2]. The — Service, رُتْبَةُ مُنَاوَلَةِ عَشَآءِ — طَقْسُ ٱلْقُدَّاسِ — ٱلرَّبِّ.

Communiqué, *n.* An official intimation, وَرَقَةٌ — إِشْعَارٌ رَسْمِيٌّ — رَسْمِيَّةٌ.

Communism, *n.* الإِشْتِرَاكُ فِي مَالِ ٱلْجُمْهُورِ.

Communist, *n.* مِنْ أَهْلِ ٱلْمُدَّعِينَ بِحَقِّ ٱلْإِشْتِرَاكِ فِي مَالِ ٱلْجُمْهُورِ — كُومُونِسْت.

Community, *n.* The people generally, الشَّعْبُ — الرَّعِيَّةُ — الخَلْقُ — الجُمْهُورُ — الجَمْعِيَّةُ. Common possession, شِرْكَةٌ — إِشْتِرَاكٌ. A body, طَائِفَةٌ *pl.* طَوَائِفُ — مِلَّةٌ *pl.* مِلَلٌ — مَعْشَرٌ — عَشِيرَةٌ — جَمَاعَةٌ. Community in partnership, شِرْكَةٌ.

Commutability, *n.* Capacity of being interchanged, مِمَّا يُبْدَلُ — قَابِلِيَّةُ ٱلتَّبْدِيلِ; of being mitigated, قَابِلِيَّةُ ٱلتَّخْفِيفِ.

Commutable, *a.* Interchangeable, يُبْدَلُ — قَابِلُ ٱلتَّبْدِيلِ. That may be mitigated, قَابِلُ ٱلتَّخْفِيفِ.

Commutation, *n.* تَبْدِيلٌ — تَغْيِيرٌ — بَدَالٌ. A — of punishment, تَبْدِيلُ قِصَاصٍ وَمُلَاطَفَتُهُ. A ransom, فِدْيَةٌ — فِدًا.

Commutative, *a.* مُتَضَمِّنُ ٱلتَّبَادُلِ.

Commute, *v.t.* بَدَّلَ — قَاوَضَ. To — a punishment, بَدَّلَ ٱلْقِصَاصَ وَخَفَّفَهُ. To ransom, ٢ فَدَى. To fix at a lower rate, ٢ بَخَسَ — أَسْقَطَ ٱلثَّمَنَ.

Commutual, *a.* مُشْتَرَكٌ. *See also* Mutual, *a.*

Comose, *a.* ذُو شُوشَةٍ.

Compact, *a.* Firm, مُحْكَمٌ — صَمِيمٌ — رَصِينٌ — جَدِيلٌ — مَاكِنٌ — صَمْعَرٌ — وَثِيجٌ — مُكْتَنِزٌ — مَفْتُولٌ — مُحْصَفٌ — حَصِيفٌ. Thick, dense, جِلٌّ — كَثِيفٌ. Close in texture, سَفِيقٌ. Concise, قَصِيرٌ — مُخْتَصَرٌ — مُوجَزٌ. Matted together, مُتَلَبِّدٌ. To be —, of texture, سَفُقَ [2].

Compact, *n.* An agreement, ذِمَامٌ — ذِمَّةٌ *pl.* — عَقْدٌ — مُعَاقَدَةٌ — مِيثَاقٌ — قَوْلٌ — كِتَابٌ — شَرْطٌ — عَهْدٌ *pl.* عُهُودٌ — مُشَارَطَةٌ. To enter into a — with, عَاقَدَ — شَارَطَ. The people with whom a — is made, أَهْلُ ٱلذِّمَّةِ.

Compact, *v.t.* To make close, رَصَّصَ — أَرْصَنَ — ٢ جَدَلَ [2]. To be compacted, pressed together, إِكْتَنَزَ. Compacted together, كَنِيزٌ.

Compactedly, *ad.* } Compactly, } Closely, firmly, تَرْصِيصًا — بِٱكْتِنَازٍ — بِصَلَابَةٍ.

Compactedness, *n.* } Compactness, } Closeness of parts, إِكْتِنَازٌ — رَصَانَةٌ — جَدْلٌ — صَلَابَةٌ — وَثَاجَةٌ. Density, كَثَافَةٌ. Closeness of texture, سَفَاقَةٌ.

Companion, *n.* عَشِيرٌ *pl.* عُشَرَآءُ — رَفِيقٌ *pl.* رُفَقَآءُ and رِفَاقَةٌ and أَرْفَاقٌ — صَدِيقٌ — دَخِيلٌ — صَاحِبٌ *pl.* أَصْحَابٌ. A partner, شَرِيكٌ *pl.* شُرَكَآءُ. A helper, مُعَاوِنٌ. A pot —, نَدِيمٌ *pl.* نُدَمَآءُ. A crony, a familiar visitor, جَلِيسٌ *fem.* جَلِيسَةٌ. A female —, مُصَاحِبَةٌ. A companion, or one who had seen and been associated with Muhammad, صَحَابِيٌّ *pl.* الصَّحَابَةُ. To be a — of, ٢ صَحِبَ — إِسْتَصْحَبَ. To be joined as a — to, إِصْطَحَبَ. To offer one's self as a — to, صَاحَبَ. To ascribe a —, (as to God,)

أَشْرَكَ بِ-شَرِيكًا. One who does so, a polytheist, مُشْرِكٌ.
They were companions in travel, of many, تَرَافَقُوا فِي ٱلسَّفَرِ. A — ladder, سُلَّمُ ٱلكَمَرَةِ.

Companionable, *a.* صَاحِبُ عِشْرَةٍ ـ أَلِيف ـ أَنِيس ـ مُؤْنِس.

Companionless, *a.* بِدُونِ رَفِيقٍ ـ وَحِيد ـ فَرِيد.

Companionship, *n.* أُلْفَة ـ أُنْس ـ صُحْبَة ـ مُرَافَقَة.

Company, *n.* An assembly of persons, جَمَاعَة ـ جَمْع ـ جُقَّة ـ رُفْقَة ـ مُصَاحَبَة ـ مُعَاشَرَة. A society, مَحْفَل ـ شِرْذِمَة ـ صُحْبَة ـ مُرَافَقَة. An assembly met for conversation, *etc.*, مَجْلِس. A pleasant —, مُؤَانَسَة. Partnership, a firm, شِرْكَة ـ إِشْتِرَاك. A — of soldiers, فِرْقَةُ عَسْكَرٍ ـ بُلُوك. A ship's —, أَهْلُ (*or* نُوَاتِيُّ *or* بَحْرِيَّةُ) ٱلسَّفِينَةِ. A party, league, حِزْب *pl.* أَحْزَاب. A mercantile —, شِرْكَةُ تُجَّارٍ. A railway —, شِرْكَةُ سِكَّةِ حَدِيدٍ. An industrial —, شِرْكَةُ صَنَائِعَ. Let us shun their —, لِنَبْتَعِدْ عَنْ صُحْبَتِهِمْ. We did not expect — to-day, لَمْ نَتَوَقَّعِ ٱلْيَوْمَ أَغْتِنَامَ ٱلْعِشْرَةِ ٱلْمُؤْنِسَةِ. To bear or keep —, to associate with, عَاشَرَ ـ إِسْتَصْحَبَ. To go with in — to a place, رَافَقَ-إِلَى ـ أَوْصَلَ-إِلَى. To part —, فَارَقَ ـ إِفْتَرَقَ عَنْ.
Companions, travelling together, رُفْقَة ـ رِفْقَة.

Company, *v.t.* and *i.* *See to* Accompany, *and under* Companion, *n.*

Comparable, *a.* يُمَاثِلُ ـ يَتَشَبَّهُ بِ ـ مُشَابِه ـ شَبِيه ـ مُقَابِل ـ يُقَاسُ عَلَى.

Comparably, *ad.* قِيَاسًا.

Comparative, *a.* تَمْثِيلِيّ ـ مُشَابِه ـ تَشْبِيهِيّ. A — noun, إِسْمُ تَفْضِيلٍ. The — degree, صِيغَةُ ٱلتَّفْضِيلِ. Comparative Anatomy, عِلْمُ ٱلْمُقَابَلَةِ وَٱلتَّطْبِيقِ مَا بَيْنَ أَعْضَاءِ ٱلْحَيَوَانَاتِ وَٱلنَّبَاتَاتِ بِأَسْرِهَا ـ عِلْمُ تَشْرِيحٍ تَطْبِيقِيّ.

Comparatively, *ad.* نَظَرًا إِلَى بَعْضِهِمْ ـ بِٱلنِّسْبَةِ إِلَى بَعْضِهِمْ ـ بِٱلْمُمَاثَلَةِ ـ نِسْبَةً.

Compare, *v.t.* قَايَسَ بَيْنَ ـ شَبَّهَ-بِ ـ نَاظَرَ-بِ ـ قَابَلَ-بِ ـ قَابَلَ-عَلَى ـ طَابَقَ بَيْنَ ـ عَارَضَ-بِ ـ إِقْتَاسَ. To —, as of weights and measures, one with another, عَايَرَ ٱلْمَكَايِيلَ. To be compared, إِنْقَاسَ. To be likened to, تَشَبَّهَ بِ. These things are not worthy to be compared to ..., هٰذِهِ ٱلْأَشْيَاءُ غَيْرُ جَدِيرَةٍ بِأَنْ تُقَاسَ بِ. They — themselves with themselves, يُقَابِلُونَ أَنْفُسَهُمْ بِأَنْفُسِهِمْ. There is none to be compared to him, لَا كِفَا لَهُ. His state when compared with ..., حَالُهُ إِذَا قِيسَتْ بِ. Not to be compared, بَعِيدًا عَنِ ٱلْمُقَابَلَةِ.

Compare, *n.* / Comparison, } The state of being compared, مُشَابَهَة ـ تَشْبِيه. The act of comparing, قِيَاس ـ مُقَابَلَة ـ مُعَادَلَة ـ مُطَابَقَة. The object with which any thing is compared, مُشَبَّهٌ بِهِ. In — with, بِٱلنِّسْبَةِ إِلَى ـ فِي جَنْبِ. Without compare, مَا لَهُ شَبِيهٌ ـ مَا لَهُ نَظِيرٌ ـ مَا لَهُ مَثِيلٌ. A comparative estimate, مُقَارَنَة. Comparison, in grammar, ٱلتَّفْضِيل. With what — shall we compare it? بِأَيِّ مَثَلٍ نُمَثِّلُهُ. What is your age in — with that of Noah! أَيْنَ عُمْرُكَ وَعُمْرُ نُوحٍ. In — with, in relation to, بِٱلنِّسْبَةِ إِلَى ـ بِٱلْإِضَافَةِ إِلَى.

Compart, *v.t.* قَسَّمَ ـ بَوَّبَ.

Compartition, *n.* تَبْوِيب ـ تَقْسِيم. A division, قِسْم ـ بَاب *pl.* أَبْوَاب.

Compartment, *n.* قِسْم *pl.* أَقْسَام ـ جُزْء *pl.* أَجْزَاء ـ بَيْت *pl.* بُيُوت ـ بَاب *pl.* أَبْوَاب ـ عَيْن *pl.* عُيُون.

Compass, *v.t.* To surround with, أَحَاطَ-بِ ـ جَفَّ-بِ ². To walk round, إِكْتَنَفَ ـ تَكَنَّفَ ـ كَنَّفَ ـ حَوَّطَ-بِ ـ طَافَ ² ـ مَشَى حَوْلَ ². To besiege, حَاصَرَ. To obtain, نَالَ ² ـ بَلَغَ ² ـ حَصَّلَ ² ـ وَصَلَ إِلَى *aor.* يَصِلُ. To take measures towards, دَبَّرَ ² ـ عَمِلَ عَلَى ـ أَرَادَ ـ رَامَ *aor.* يَرُومُ ـ إِحْتَالَ عَلَى. To embrace, inclose, شَمَلَ ² ـ تَضَمَّنَ عَلَى.

Compass, *n.* Circuit, دَائِر ـ دَائِرَة ـ إِسْتِدَارَة. Extent, سَعَة ـ مَكَان ـ مَحَلّ. Room, مِقْدَار ـ إِمْتِدَاد. Space of time, مُدَّة. Moderation, قَانُون ـ عَقْل ـ إِعْتِدَال. The — of the voice, سَعَة ـ مَوْضِع ـ قُوَّةُ ٱلصَّوْتِ. The mariner's —, إِبْرَةُ ٱلْمَلَّاحِينَ ـ كُومْبَاس ـ بُوصْلَة. To fetch a —, to turn, دَارَ ². In the — of two days, فِي مُدَّةِ يَوْمَيْنِ. That is beyond my —, هٰذَا يَفُوقُ طَاقَتِي. To bring into a small —, صَغَّرَ ـ قَصَّرَ ـ أَوْجَزَ. To keep one within —, أَضْبَطَ ـ قَمَعَ ². To make the — of, to go round, أَحَاطَ بِ ـ جَفَّ بِ ².

Compasses, *n.* A pair of, فِرْجَار ـ دَوَّارَة ـ بِيكَار.

Compassion, *n.* حِنَّة ـ تَرَحُّم ـ حَنَان ـ رَأْفَة ـ رِقَّةُ قَلْبٍ ـ رَحْمَة ـ شَفَقَة. To have — on, رَحِمَ ² ـ تَرَحَّمَ عَلَى. To ask one's —, إِسْتَرْحَمَ.

Compassionate, *a.* مُشْفِق ـ رَحِيم ـ رَحْمٰن ـ رَؤُوف ـ رَأْف ـ حَنُون ـ رَقِيقُ ٱلْقَلْبِ ـ شَفِيق. The compassionate One, God, ٱلرَّحْمٰنُ. To make — towards, حَنَّنَ-عَلَى.

Compassionate, *v.t.* حَنَّ عَلَى ² ـ تَحَنَّنَ عَلَى ـ رَقَّ لِ ² ـ شَفِقَ عَلَى ² ـ تَرَحَّمَ عَلَى ـ رَثَى لِ ² ـ رَأَفَ بِ ² ـ تَرَفَّقَ لِ ـ تَوَجَّعَ لِ ـ أَشْفَقَ عَلَى.

Compassionately, *ad.* تَرَحُّمًا ـ شَفَقَةً ـ بِحِنُوٍّ ـ بِرَحْمَةٍ.

Compatibility, *n.* مُلَاءَمَة ـ مُنَاسَبَة ـ مُوَافَقَة.

Compatible, *a.* لائق ـ مُنَاسِب ـ مُوَافِق.

Compatibly, *ad.* بِلِيَاقَةٍ ـ مُنَاسَبَةً ـ مُوَافَقَةً.

Compatriot, *n.* هَمْشَهْرِيٌّ ـ اِبْنُ بَلَدٍ. He is my —, هُوَ ٱبْنُ بَلَدِي.

Compeer, *n.* Companion, comrade, زَمِيل ـ مُصَاحِب ـ رَفِيق. Equal, كُفْو. He has no —, لَا كُفْؤَ لَهُ.

Compel, *v.t.* ـ أَكْرَهَ-عَلَى ـ اِسْتَكْرَهَ ـ أَلْزَمَ-بِ ـ ² جَبَرَ ـ سَخَّرَ ـ ; غَصَبَ-عَلَى ـ أَلْحَصَ-إِلَى ـ اِضْطَرَّ-إِلَى. To be compelled, أُلْزِمَ بِ ـ اُضْطُرَّ إِلَى. I am compelled to ..., أَنَا مَجْبُورٌ إِلَى. Compel them to come in, أَلْزِمْهُمْ بِٱلدُّخُولِ. Can he — them? هَلْ يَقْدِرُ عَلَى إِجْبَارِهِمْ. Unless I am compelled by stress of weather, إِنْ لَمْ تُجْبِرْنِي شِدَّةُ ٱلطَّقْسِ.

Compellable, *a.* جَبْرَهُ مُمْكِنٌ ـ يُجْبَر ـ يُلْزَم.

Compellatory, *a.* ضَرُورِيٌّ ـ قَهْرِيٌّ ـ مُلْتَزِم.

Compend, *n.* } مُوجَز ـ إِجْمَال ـ إِيجَاز ـ مُخْتَصَر ـ مُقْتَصَر.
Compendium, } To make a —, أَوْجَزَ.

Compendious, *a.* مُخْتَصَر ـ مُجْمَل ـ مُوجَز. A — speech, كَلَامٌ مُوجَزٌ. To make —, of speech, أَدْمَجَ.

Compendiously, *ad.* بِٱخْتِصَارٍ ـ اِخْتِصَارًا ـ بِإِيجَازٍ.

Compendiousness, *n.* اِخْتِصَار ـ قُصْر ـ إِيجَاز.

Compensable, *a.* مِمَّا يُكَافَى ـ وِمِمَّا يُجَازَى.

Compensate, *v.t.* To recompense with or by, ـ كَافَى-بِ ـ كَافَى-عَلَى ـ عَوَّضَ-عَلَى ـ أَعَاضَ ـ عَوَّضَ ـ سَانَدَ-عَلَى. To — for, كَافَى-عَلَى ـ عَوَّضَ-عَلَى. To make amends to, ـ قَابَلَ-بِ ـ أَثَابَ ـ ثَوَّبَ ـ ; جَزَى. To counterbalance, تَقَابَلَ-بِ ـ ² سَدَّ ـ وَازَنَ ـ قَابَلَ. This year's gain compensates the loss of the last, مَكْسَبُ هٰذِهِ ٱلسَّنَةِ يُوَازِنُ (or يُقَابِلُ or يَسُدُّ) خَسَارَةَ ٱلْمَاضِيَةِ.

Compensation, *n.* Recompense, مُكَافَاة ـ جَزَآء ـ مُجَازَاة. An equivalent, ـ عِوَض ـ عِيَاض ـ عَوْض ـ مُعَاوَضَة ـ تَثْوِيب ـ خَسَارَة ـ مُعَاوَضَة ـ مُقَابَلَة ـ خَلَاص.

Compensative, *a.* } Remunerative, مُكَافِئ ـ جَازٍ. Counter-
Compensatory, } balancing, مُقَابِل ـ مُوَازِن.

Compete, *v.i.* To strive with, فَاخَرَ ـ جَارَى ـ بَارَى. He competed with him and surpassed him, فَاخَرَهُ فَفَخَرَهُ.

Competence, *n.* } Sufficiency, ـ حَسْب ـ طَوْل ـ غِنًى ـ غَنَآء
Competency, } مَا يَحْتَاجُ إِلَيْهِ ـ وَفِيٌّ ـ كِفَايَة. Fitness, أَهْلِيَّة ـ جَدَارَة. Authority to take cognizance of an affair, ـ حَقٌّ ـ دَائِرَة ـ مَأْمُورِيَّة ـ اِقْتِدَار ـ زَعَامَة. A — of fortune, ـ غُضَّة ـ سَعَةُ عَيْشٍ ـ حُظْوَة ـ حَظٌّ ـ سِدَاد ـ بُلْغَة ـ طَوْل ـ غِنًى ـ غِنًى ـ رَفَاهِيَة ـ رَفَاهَة ـ طَائِلَة ـ حَسْب. Having a —, ـ غَنِيٌّ ـ غَانٍ. To give a — to, أَغْنَى ـ غَنَّى ـ ; ² رَفَّ. To enjoy a —, اِسْتَغْنَى ـ تَغَنَّى ـ ; غَنِيَ ـ ; رَفَهَ.

Competent, *a.* Suitable, لائق ـ مُنَاسِب ـ مُوَافِق. Sufficient, ـ كَافٍ ـ وَافٍ ـ كَافٍ. Fit for, أَهْلٌ لِ ـ خَلِيقٌ لِ. Able to, ـ كَافٍ لِ ـ جَدِيرٌ لِ or بِ. Having the power of, قَادِرٌ عَلَى. Moderate, مُتَوَسِّط ـ مُعْتَدِل. Having a competency, of living, ـ غَانٍ ـ رَافِه ـ طَائِل. A — tribunal, مَحْكَمَةٌ إِيجَابِيَّةٌ. A — age, سِنُّ ٱلْبُلُوغِ ـ سِنُّ ٱلْإِيجَابِ. They are — to enjoy civil rights, لَهُمْ أَهْلِيَّةٌ وَجَدَارَةُ ٱلتَّمَتُّعِ بِٱلْحُقُوقِ ٱلْمَدَنِيَّةِ.

Competently, *ad.* عَلَى قَدْرِ ٱلْكِفَايَةِ ـ مُنَاسَبَةً ـ بِحَسْبٍ.

Competition, *n.* ـ مُغَارَة ـ مُجَارَاة ـ مُبَارَاة ـ اِسْتِبَاق ـ سَبْق ـ مُعَارَضَة. To enter into — with, ـ عَارَضَ ـ جَارَى ـ بَارَى ـ اِعْتَرَضَ-فِي.

Competitive, *a.* بِمُجَارَاةٍ ـ بِمُبَارَاةٍ. Competitive examination, اِمْتِحَانُ ٱلطُّلَّابِ ٱلْمُتَبَارِينَ.

Competitor, *n.* A rival, candidate, رَقِيب ـ طَالِب *pl.* طُلَّاب *pl.* ² رُقَبَآء ـ مُعَارِض. An opponent, خَصْم *pl.* أَخْصَام ـ مُقَابِل.

Compilation, *n.* The act of compiling, ـ تَجْمِيع ـ جَمْع ـ تَنْسِيق ـ تَصْنِيف ـ تَلْمِيم. A collection, مَجْمُوع ـ جُمْلَة.

Compile, *v.t.* To collect, arrange, ـ جَمَعَ ـ رَكَّبَ ـ ² ; نَسَجَ ـ نَسَّقَ. To compose, صَنَّفَ ـ أَلَّفَ.

Compiler, *n.* One who compiles, جَامِع. An author, ـ كَاتِب ـ مُصَنِّف ـ مُنْشِئ ـ مُؤَلِّف.

Complacence, *n.* } Gratification, ـ اِنْبِسَاط ـ لَذَّة ـ سُرُور ـ حَظّ
Complacency, } تَلَطُّف ـ كِيف ـ مَحْظُوظِيَّة. Self —, عُجْب.

Complacent, *a.* ـ بَشُوش ـ أَدِيب ـ لَطِيف ـ مُتَلَاطِف ـ جَامِعُ ٱلْخَوَاطِرِ ـ آدَمِيٌّ ـ شَلَبِيٌّ ـ صَاحِبُ مُرُوَّةٍ.

Complacently, *ad.* بِٱطْمِئْنَانِ ٱلْخَاطِرِ ـ بِسُرُورٍ ـ بِلَطَافَةٍ.

Complain, *v.i.* To lament, ـ تَأَلَّمَ ـ نَاجَى نَفْسَهُ ـ ; أَنَّ ـ تَحَسَّرَ ـ اِشْتَكَى ـ ² شَكَا ـ ² نَاحَ عَلَى ـ اِكْتَرَبَ. To — against, شَكَا-مِنْ ـ تَظَلَّمَ ـ اِشْتَكَى عَلَى ـ ² شَكَا. To —, as of a pain, تَشَكَّى مِنْ ـ تَوَجَّعَ ـ تَفَجَّعَ. To cause to —, أَشْكَى. He complained of his case to God, ² شَكَا أَمْرَهُ إِلَى ٱللّٰهِ.

Complainant, *n.* مُدَّعٍ ـ مُتَشَكٍّ ـ شَكِيٌّ ـ شَاكٍ.

Complaining, *a.* As of trouble or disease, مُتَشَكٍّ ـ شَكِيٌّ. Querulous, murmuring, مُتَذَمِّر ـ مُدَمْدِم.

Complaint, *n.* Expression of grief, شَكَاة ـ شَكِيَّة ـ شِكَايَة . Lamentation, شِكَايَة ـ أَنِين ـ كُرْبَة ـ كُرَب . A remonstrance against, دَعْوَى ـ تُهْمَة ـ شَكْوَة ـ شَكِيَّة ـ شَكَآءٌ . A malady, تَشْوِيش ـ دَآءٌ ـ عِلَّة ـ مَرَض ـ شَكْوَى . They laid many complaints against him, رَمَوهُ بِشَكَاوَى كَثِيرَةٍ . If any one has a — against another, إِنْ تَكُنْ لِأَحَدٍ خُصُومَةٌ مَعَ آخَرَ .

Complaisance, *n.* Civility, أَخْلَاق ـ مُهَاوَدَة ـ مُلَاطَفَة ـ لُطْف . An act of —, تَفَضُّل ـ مَعْرُوف . مُرَاعَاةُ ٱلْخَاطِرِ .

Complaisant, *a.* مُرَاعِي خَاطِرِ ٱلنَّاسِ ـ لَطِيف ـ مُلَاطِف . To be — towards, مُبَادِرٌ إِلَى مَا يُرْضِي بِهِ ٱلنَّاسَ ـ صَاحِبُ مَعْرُوفٍ . هَاوَدَ .

Complaisantly, *ad.* بِأَدَبٍ ـ بِإِخْلَاقٍ ـ بِمُلَاطَفَةٍ ـ بِمُهَاوَدَةٍ ـ بِلُطْفٍ .

Complement, *n.* Completion, كُمَالَة ـ تَمَامَة ـ تَمَام ـ تَتِمَّة . Full quantity, كُلِّيَّة ـ الكُلّ ـ كُمَالَة ـ تَمَّة . إِخْتِتَام ـ غَلَاقَة . An appendage, ذَيْل ـ مُلْحَقَة ـ ضَمِيمَة . جُمْلَة .

Complemental, *a.* تَضْمِيمِيّ ـ مُلْحَق . Adjunct, مُتَمِّم ـ مُكَمِّل .

Complete, *a.* Perfect, مُكَمَّل ـ كَامِل ـ تَامّ . Finished, مُكَمَّل ـ مُنْتَهٍ ـ مُنْقَضٍ . In the most — manner, مُكَمَّل ـ كَامِل . عَلَى أَكْمَلِ وَجْهٍ .

Complete, *v.t.* تَمَّمَ ـ كَمَّلَ ـ أَنْهَى ـ أَتَمَّ ـ أَنْفَذَ ـ أَمْضَى ـ فَرَغَ مِن ـ غَلَقَ .

Completely, *ad.* Fully, بِٱلْكُلِّيَّةِ ـ تَمَامًا ـ بَتَّةً . Perfectly well, عَلَى ٱلتَّمَامِ وَٱلْكَمَالِ ـ حَبَّذَا ـ حَسَنًا ـ عَلَى وَجْهِ ٱلْكَمَالِ . At once, بِٱلْمَرَّةِ .

Completement, *n.* تَكْمِيل ـ تَتْمِيم .

Completeness, *n.* عَدَمُ نُقْصَانٍ ـ تَمَامَة ـ كَمَال .

Completion, *n.* كُمَالَة ـ غَلَاقَة ـ تَكْمِيل ـ إِتْمَام .

Completive, *a.* *See* Complemental, *a.*

Complex, *a.* Compound, غَيْرُ مُفْرَدٍ ـ مُقْتَرِن ـ مُدَرَّج ـ مُرَكَّب .

Complicated, مُشَبَّك ـ لَبِك . A — argument, قِيَاس إِقْتِرَانِيّ .

Complexedness, Complexity, *n.* Complexness, } Compound state, إِرْتِبَاط ـ إِخْتِلَاط ـ تَرْكِيب . Complicateness, شُبُوك ـ إِلْتِبَاك ـ لَبَك .

Complexion, *n.* Colour, لَوْنُ ٱلْوَجْهِ ـ لَوْن . Temper, طَبْع ـ خِلْقَة ـ مِزَاج . Aspect, صُورَة ـ حَال ـ هَيْئَة ـ رُؤْيَة . Aggregate of form, *etc.*, حِلْيَة .

Complexional, *a.* مُتَعَلِّق بِٱلْمِزَاجِ .

Complexly, *ad.* بِٱرْتِبَاطٍ ـ إِخْتِلَاطًا ـ بِٱقْتِرَانٍ .

Complexure, *n.* Involution, إِمْتِزَاج ـ تَلْبِيك ـ تَشْبِيك ـ إِقْتِرَان .

Compliable, *a.* مُسْتَجِيب ـ مُلَائِم .

Compliance, *n.* تَنَازُل ـ مُرَاعَاة ـ مُهَاوَدَة ـ إِيجَاب ـ إِسْتِجَابَة ـ رِضَآءٌ ـ قُبُول ـ مُطَاوَعَة ـ مُلَاءَمَة ـ تَنَزُّل ـ إِطَاعَة .

Compliant, *a.* Obedient, مُطِيع ـ مَلِق ـ خَافِضُ ٱلْجَنَاحِ ـ حَلِيم ـ لَيِّنُ ٱلْجَانِبِ ـ خَاضِع ـ مُنْقَاد ـ مُطَاوِع . Civil, مُتَحَلِّم ـ لَانَ ـ صَاحِبُ مَعْرُوفٍ ـ مُتَلَاطِف . To be or become —, لَانَ ـ حَلُمَ . To be — towards, جَامَلَ . To make —, طَوَّعَ .

Compliantly, *ad.* Obediently, مُرَاعَاةً ـ بِمُطَاوَعَةٍ . Civilly, بِمُجَامَلَةٍ ـ بِلِينَةِ ٱلْجَانِبِ ـ بِحِلْمٍ .

Complicate, *v.t.* To perplex matters, شَبَّكَ ـ لَبَّكَ ـ لَبِكَ . To unite, involve, قَرَنَ ـ خَبَصَ ـ خَلَطَ ـ دَرَّجَ ـ عَكَسَ . To obscure, لَبَسَ ـ شَبَّهَ ـ جَمَعَ ـ نَسَجَ . To be —, confused, إِلْتَبَكَ ـ تَلَبَّكَ ـ إِشْتَجَرَ ـ شَجَرَ ـ إِرْتَبَكَ . To be obscure to, عَمِيَ عَلَى ـ إِشْتَبَهَ عَلَى . The condition became more complicated, إِزْدَادَتِ ٱلْأَحْوَالُ ٱرْتِبَاكًا .

Complicate, *a.* Complicated, } Confused, intricate, مُدَرَّج ـ مُشَبَّك ـ مُشْتَجِر ـ مُرْتَبِك ـ مُلْتَبِك ـ مُشْتَبِك ـ غَامِض ـ مُلْتَبِس ـ مُشْكِل ـ غَلِق ـ مُشْتَبِه ـ مُخْتَلِط . Not plain, A — affair, شَجْر *pl.* شُجُور *and* شِجَار ـ وَرْطَة . Complicated affairs, مُغَمَّضَات .

Complicateness, *n.* Complication, } تَعْكِيس ـ تَشْبِيك ـ إِلْتِبَاك ـ لَبَك ـ إِرْتِبَاك ـ تَعْقِيد ـ شَجْر ـ عُقَد ـ غُمُوض ـ إِلْتِبَاس ـ نَسْج ـ إِلْتِبَاك . Obscurity of meaning, Political complications, إِرْتِبَاكَاتٌ سِيَاسِيَّةٌ ـ مُشْكِلَاتٌ سِيَاسِيَّةٌ . He threw himself into a —, إِسْتَوْرَطَ فِي وَرْطَةٍ . Great complications, عَرَاقِيلُ عَظِيمَةٌ .

Complicative, *a.* مُلَبِّك ـ مُشْكِل ـ مُشَبِّك .

Complicity, *n.* رُفْقَة ـ رُفَاقَة ـ إِشْتِرَاك . Their —, or guilt, was proved, ثَبَتَ ٱرْتِكَابُهُمْ . *See also* Accomplice, *n.*

Compliment, *n.* A civility, تَحِيَّةٌ وَسَلَامٌ ـ تَحِيَّة . A favour bestowed, مَعْرُوف ـ تَكْلِيف . Praise, مَدْح ـ ثَنَآءٌ . Present my compliments to …. سَلِّمْ لِي عَلَى ـ أَهْدِ تَحِيَّاتِي إِلَى ; (*The ordinary replies are*: وَصَلَ سَلَّمَكَ ٱللّٰهُ ; خُصَّ بِٱلْإِكْرَامِ مِنِّي *or* بَارَكَ ٱللّٰهُ فِيكَ ; *or* لَا أَقْصُرُ ; *or* حُبًّا وَكَرَامَةً .) To pay one a —, وَصَفَ ـ بِ *aor.* يَصِفُ . أَثْنَى عَلَى . Compliments, formulæ of civility, الإِحْتِشَام ـ الحِشْمَة .

Compliment, *v.t.* To congratulate, حَيَّى ـ هَنَّأَ ـ بِ . To praise, وَصَفَ ـ بِ *aor.* يَصِفُ . أَثْنَى عَلَى . To flatter, مَلَّقَ ـ صَانَعَ .

Complimental, *a.* } Congratulatory, مُهَنِّئٌ – مُحَيِّئٌ. Adulatory, مَدِيحِيٌّ – مُثْنٍ عَلَى.
Complimentary, }

Compline, *n.* الدُّعَآءُ قَبْلَ ٱلنَّوْمِ.

Complot, *n.* *See* Plot, *n.*

Comply, *v.i.* To yield to, قَبِلَ – أَطَاعَ – طَاوَعَ – رَاضَى. To — with one's request, هَاوَدَ – إِسْتَجَابَ ل – طَابَقَ – رَاعَى خَاطِرَ-فِي – تَنَزَّلَ ل-فِي – طَاوَعَ-عَلَى.

Component, *a.* مُؤَلِّف – مُرَكِّب.

Component, *n.* جُزْءٌ مِنْ أَجْزَآءٍ.

Comport, *v.i.* To agree with, وَافَقَ – لَبِقَ ب – نَاسَبَ – إِتَّفَقَ مَعَ – لَاقَ ب. To — one's self; *see under to* Behave, *v.i.*

Comportable, *a.* لائِق – مُوَافِق – مُنَاسِب.

Comportment, *n.* *See* Behaviour, *n.*

Compose, *v.t.* To form a mass from different things, رَكَّبَ. To arrange, دَبَّرَ – رَتَّبَ – نَظَمَ – أَصْلَحَ – نَسَّقَ. To — a difference, سَاوَى بَيْنَ – صَالَحَ بَيْنَ – صَالَحَ – صَحَنَ بَيْنَ – لَثَّمَ – صَرَفَ ٱلْمَادَّةَ – صَرَفَ بَيْنَ. To make ready for any purpose, حَضَّرَ – هَيَّأَ – أَعَدَّ. To write, as an author, صَنَّفَ – سَطَّرَ – أَلَّفَ – يَضَعُ *aor.* وَضَعَ كِتَابًا. To — verses, نَسَجَ. To quiet, رَيَّحَ – سَكَّنَ – سَلَّى – أَهْدَأَ – هَدَّأَ. To — or set up types, as a printer, رَكَّبَ ٱلْأَحْرُفَ – صَفَّ ٱلْأَحْرُفَ. The meeting was composed of ..., كَانَتِ ٱللَّجْنَةُ مُؤَلَّفَةً مِن.

Composed, *a.* Tranquil, رَزِين – سَاكِن – سَلِيٌّ – مُطْمَئِنٌّ – رَكِين.

Composedly, *ad.* بِرَزَانَةٍ – إِطْمِئْنَانًا – بِهُدُوءٍ.

Composedness, *n.* } رِفَآء – رَاحَةُ بَالٍ – إِطْمِئْنَانُ ٱلْخَاطِرِ – عَدَمُ ٱضْطِرَابٍ – هُدُوء.
Composure, }

Composer, *n.* An author, مُؤَلِّف – مُصَنِّف – مُسَطِّر. A — of music, مُؤَلِّفُ ٱلْمُوسِيقَةِ – صَاحِبُ إِلْحَانٍ.

Composing, *a.* Quieting, مُرَيِّح – مُسَكِّن. A — draught, دَوَآءٌ مُسَدِّدٌ – سُلْوَان.

Composing-stick, *n.* جَدْوَلٌ لِصَفِّ ٱلْأَحْرُفِ.

Composite, *a.* مُتَرَكِّب – مُرَكَّب.

Composition, *n.* The act of putting together, تَرْكِيب. A mass formed by compounding, مَعْجُون – مُتَرَكِّب – مُرَكَّب. A written work, تَأْلِيف – تَصَانِيف *pl.* تَصْنِيف – إِنْشَآء. Arrangement, نِظَام – تَرْتِيب. An agreement, شَرْط – عَهْد – إِتِّفَاق. Regulation of anything, تَعْدِيل – إِصْلَاح. Congruity, إِتِّفَاق – مُوَافَقَة – تَنَاسُب. An arrangement of differences, مُصَالَحَة – مُسَاوَاة.

Compositor, *n.* Of types, مُرَتِّب (*or* مُرَكِّب) ٱلْأَحْرُفِ لِلطَّبْعِ.

Compost, *n.* Of manure, سَبْخ – سِرْجِين – سِرْقِين – سَمَاد – زِبْل.

Compost, *v.t.* سَبَّخَ – زَبَّلَ.

Compound, *n.* The open space round a house, وَصِيد – أَصِيد. *See also* Composition, *n.*

Compound, *a.* تَرْكِيبِيّ – مُرَكَّب. A — word, لَفْظٌ مُرَكَّب. Compound interest, فَائِدَةٌ عَلَى فَائِدَةٍ. A — quantity, جُمْلَةٌ مُرَكَّبَةٌ. A — fracture, كَسْرٌ مُتَفَلِّق.

Compound, *v.i.* To come to terms of agreement with, تَسَاوَى – إِصْطَلَحَ مَعَ – مَعَ. To bargain with, شَارَى – بَايَعَ – شَارَطَ – إِشْتَرَطَ مَعَ-عَلَى.

Compound, *v.t.* To mingle, جَبَلَ – خَلَطَ – مَزَجَ – رَكَّبَ. *See also to* Compose, *v.t.*

Compounder, *n.* A mingler, مُجَبِّل – مَازِج. A — of differences, وَسِيط – عَامِلُ ٱلسِّلْمِ – مُوَفِّق – مُصْلِح. A — of drugs, أَجْزَاجِيّ – صَيْدَلَانِيّ.

Comprehend, *v.t.* To include, إِضْطَمَّ – إِشْتَمَلَ عَلَى – شَمَلَ – وَسِعَ – تَضَمَّنَ – جَمَعَ – إِحْتَوَى عَلَى – إِحْتَوَى – عَلَى. To understand, أَحَاطَ ب – أَدْرَكَ – إِكْتَنَهَ – إِفْتَهَمَ – فَهِمَ – فَطَنَ – عِلْمًا. To make to —, include, أَشْمَلَ-ب – شَمَّلَ-ب. To make to understand, فَهَّمَ – أَفْهَمَ – فَطَّنَ. The sentence comprehended such a thing, تَضَمَّنَ ٱلْكَلَامُ كَذَا.

Comprehensible, *a.* That may be understood, يُدْرَكُ – يُفْهَمُ – يُدْرِكُهُ ٱلْعَقْلُ – مُدْرَك.

Comprehension, *n.* Quality of containing, إِتِّسَاع – سَعَة. A sum, compendium, مَضْمُون – مَجْمُول – شُمُول – إِحْتِوَآء. Understanding, عَقْل – إِدْرَاك – فِطْنَة – ذِهْن – فَهْم.

Comprehensive, *a.* Having the power of understanding, مُدْرِك – ذَهِين – صَاحِبُ فَهْمٍ – فَهِيم. Containing much, وَاسِع – مُتَّسِع. Signifying much, كَثِيرُ ٱلْمَعْنَى – مَعْنَوِيّ. Collective, شَامِل – جَامِع – مُشْتَمِل. Compendious, مُوجَز – مُخْتَصَر.

Comprehensively, *ad.* Collectively, تَضْمِينًا – بِٱلْإِجْمَاعِ – إِجْمَالًا. Clearly, عَلَانِيَةً – بَيَانًا – بِوُضُوحٍ.

Comprehensiveness, *n.* Quality of comprehending, containing, إِتِّسَاع – سَعَة. Intelligibility, بَيَان – إِيضَاح – وُضُوح. Compendiousness, تَحْكِيم – ضَبْط – إِيجَاز.

Compress, *v.t.* To put into a narrower compass, كَبَسَ – شَدَّ عَلَى – أَطْبَقَ – ضَيَّقَ – حَصَرَ – حَزَقَ. To shorten, قَصَّرَ – إِخْتَصَرَ.

Compress, *n.* A bandage, رِفَادَة ـ لِفَافَة *pl.* لَفَائِف.

Compressibility, *n.* / Compressibleness, } قَابِلِيَّةُ ٱلضَّغْطِ ـ لَيَان ـ قَابِلِيَّةُ ٱلْإِنْحِصَارِ ـ قَابِلِيَّةُ ٱلتَّضْيِيقِ.

Compressible, *a.* قَابِلٌ ـ يُخْتَصَرُ ـ قَابِلُ ٱلْإِنْضِمَامِ ـ يَنْحَصِرُ ٱلْإِكْتِنَازِ.

Compression, *n.* / Compressure, } The act of, ضَغْط ـ حَصْر ـ تَكْبِيس; the being compressed, إِكْتِنَاز ـ إِنْضِغَاط ـ إِنْحِصَار.

Compressive, *a.* مُضَيِّق ـ مُكَبِّس.

Comprisal, *n.* إِحْتِوَآء ـ إِشْتِمَال ـ إِحَاطَة.

Comprise, *v.t.* تَضَمَّنَ ـ جَمَعَ ـ إِحْتَوَى ـ إِحْتَوَى عَلَى ـ إِنْضَمَّ عَلَى.

Compromise, *n.* Submission to arbitration, إِقَامَةُ وُكَلَآء ـ تَوْكِيل. A bargain, arrangement, مُشَارَطَة ـ مُصَالَحَة ـ إِصْطِلَاح ـ شَرْط ـ تَرْتِيب ـ عَهْد.

Compromise, *v.t.* and *i.* To adjust, settle, سَاوَى ـ صَرَفَ; to settle between, صَرَفَ بَيْنَ. To subject to, عَرَّضَ-عَلَى. To subject one's self to, خَاطَرَ بِنَفْسِهِ ـ عَرَّضَ نَفْسَهُ ل. They compromised the matter, إِصْطَلَحُوا عَلَى ٱلْمَادَّةِ.

Compulsative, / Compulsive, *a.* / Compulsory, } قَهْرِيّ ـ مُلْزِم ـ جَبْرِيّ ـ جَابِر ـ غَصْبِيّ ـ ضَرُورِيّ ـ لا بُدَّ مِنَ ٱلْخُضُوعِ ل. Compulsory education, التَّعْلِيمُ بِٱلْإِكْرَاهِ. Compulsory military service, خِدْمَةٌ عَسْكَرِيَّةٌ جَبْرِيَّة.

Compulsion, *n.* إِكْرَاه ـ إِلْجَآء ـ إِلْزَام ـ غَصْب ـ إِغْتِصَاب ـ إِلْتِجَاء ـ قَهْر ـ إِجْبَار ـ عَسْف ـ لُزُوم ـ جَبْر.

Compulsively, *ad.* كَرْهًا ـ غَصْبًا ـ قَهْرًا ـ جَبْرًا.

Compunction, *n.* نَخْزُ ٱلضَّمِيرِ ـ لَسْعُ ٱلذِّمَّةِ ـ أَكْلُ ٱلسَّرِيرَةِ ـ تَأَسُّف ـ حُزْن ـ نَدَامَة ـ تَوْبَة.

Computable, *a.* يُحْسَبُ ـ يُحْصَى.

Computation, *n.* حَصَاة ـ عَدّ ـ عَدَد ـ جَمْع ـ حِسَاب.

Computation by conjecture, خَرْص.

Compute, *v.t.* حَسَبَ ـ أَحْصَى ـ عَدَّدَ ـ عَدَّ. To — a cost, to price, ثَمَّنَ. To — by conjecture, خَرَصَ ـ قَدَّرَ ـ حَزَرَ ـ حَزَّرَ. To be computed, إِنْعَدَّ.

Computer, *n.* مُحَاسِب ـ حَسِيب ـ مُقَدِّر.

Comrade, *n.* زَمِيل *pl.* زُمَلَآء ـ رَفِيق *pl.* رُفَقَآء ـ مُصَاحِب ـ صَاحِب *pl.* أَصْحَاب ـ إِلْف *pl.* آلَاف ـ أَلِيف *pl.* أُلَفَآء.

Con, *ad.* Against, عَلَى. Pro and con, ل-وَعَلَى.

Con, *v.t.* To know, عَلِمَ ـ عَرَفَ. To study, دَرَسَ ـ تَأَمَّلَ فِي.

Concamerate, *v.t.* قَبَّى ـ عَمِلَ-قُبَّة.

Concatenate, *v.t.* سَلْسَلَ ـ رَبَطَ. To — with, سَلْسَلَ-بِ.

Concatenation, *n.* سَلْسَلَة ـ تَسَلْسُل ـ رِبَاط.

Concave, *a.* مُجَوَّف ـ أَجْوَف ـ مُقَعَّر.

Concave, *n.* / Concavity, } صَحْن ـ قَعْرَة ـ تَجْوِيف.

Concavo-convex, *a.* مُقَعَّرٌ وَمُحَدَّبٌ.

Conceal, *v.t.* To hide, أَخْفَى ـ خَبَّأَ ـ حَجَبَ ـ دَسَّ ـ غَمَّى ـ كَتَمَ ـ كَتَّمَ ـ سَتَرَ. Not to reveal, سَكَتَ عَنْ. To — one's self or to be concealed, إِحْتَجَبَ ـ إِخْتَبَأَ ـ إِخْتَفَى ـ إِسْتَخْفَى ـ إِنْدَسَّ ـ تَغَشَّى ـ تَكَمَّنَ ـ إِنْكَتَمَ. To — in the ground, طَمَرَ.

Concealable, *a.* يُكْتَمُ ـ يُخْتَفَى.

Concealed, *a.* مُسْتَتِر ـ كَاتِم ـ خَفِيّ ـ مَحْجُوب ـ مُغَشًّى ـ مُكْتَتِم ـ مَسْتُور. Concealed in the ground, مَطْمُور ـ مَدْفُون. Concealed, as in the heart, مَكْنُون. A — secret, سِرٌّ كَاتِمٌ. A — thing, خَبِيئَة *pl.* خَبَايَا.

Concealer, *n.* مُخَبِّئ ـ كَاتِم. A — of a secret, كَاتِمُ ٱلسِّرِّ.

Concealment, *n.* The act of concealing, كِتْمَان ـ إِخْفَآء ـ مَخْبَأَة ـ تَسَتُّر. A place of —, مَخْبَأ ـ مَأْوًى ـ مَلْجَأ. Self —, إِخْتِفَآء.

Concede, *v.t.* To admit, قَنَعَ إِلَى ـ قَبِلَ ـ طَاوَعَ ـ سَلَّمَ ـ أَذْعَنَ ل. To grant, سَمَحَ ل-بِ ـ أَكْرَمَ عَلَى-بِ ـ وَهَبَ *aor.* يَهَبُ ـ أَعْطَى.

Conceit, *n.* A conception, إِدْرَاك ـ فِكْر ـ رَأْي. Thought, fancy, وَهْم ـ خَيَال ـ ظَنّ ـ تَصَوُّر ـ تَوَهُّم. Understanding, فَهْم ـ تَفَهُّم ـ ذِهْن. Opiniative pride, زَخْف ـ عُجْب ـ زَهْو ـ تَظَنُّن ـ كِبْرِيَآء ـ عِنَاد. To be out of — with, مَلَّ بِ ـ قَرِفَ ـ إِسْتَحْقَرَ ـ كَرِهَ ـ مَلَّ مِنْ. To put one out of — of, أَكْرَهَ-عَلَى ـ أَقْرَفَ-عَلَى ـ جَعَلَ-يَسْتَقِلّ.

Conceit, *v.t.* إِفْتَكَرَ ـ ظَنَّ ـ حَسَبَ ـ تَخَمَّنَ ـ رَأَى ـ تَخَيَّلَ.

Conceited, *a.* Vain, زَاخِف ـ مُفْتَخِر ـ مُتَكَبِّر ـ مُتَعَظِّم ـ مُعْجَب. Self —, حَكِيمٌ عِنْدَ نَفْسِهِ. To be —, تَعَجَّبَ ـ تَعَظَّمَ ـ أُعْجِبَ بِنَفْسِهِ.

Conceitedly, *ad.* زَخْفًا ـ مُتَكَبِّرًا ـ مُتَعَظِّمًا ـ مُتَفَخِّرًا ـ بِعُجْبٍ. To act —; *see* To be conceited, *under* Conceited, *a.*

Conceitedness, *n.* *See* Conceit, *n.*

Conceivable, *a.* يَتَخَيَّلُ ـ يُدْرَكُ ـ يُعْتَقَلُ ـ يَنْفَهِمُ ـ يَتَصَوَّرُ فِي ٱلْعَقْلِ. This is a thing that is not —, هٰذَا شَيْءٌ لَا يُعْتَقَلُ.

Conceivableness, *n.* تَوَهُّم ـ تَشَبُّه ـ تَخَيُّل.

Conceivably, *ad.* بِوَجْهِ ٱلْإِدْرَاكِ ـ بِوَجْهِ ٱلتَّصَوُّرِ ـ تَصَوُّرًا ـ تَخَيُّلًا.

Conceive, *v.t.* To form in the womb, عَلِقَتِ ٱلْمَرْأَةُ ـ حَمَلَتْ بِ ـ حَمَلَتِ ٱلنَّسْلَ. To understand, فَهِمَ ـ أَدْرَكَ ـ إِكْتَنَهَ ـ شَعَرَ بِ. To imagine, تَخَيَّلَ ـ تَعَقَّلَ ـ تَصَوَّرَ ـ تَوَهَّمَ ـ عَقَلَ ـ أَضْمَرَ. To be of opinion, ظَنَّ ـ حَسَبَ ـ تَوَهَّمَ ـ خَمَّنَ ـ شَافَ. To — fear, إِشْتَعَرَ خَوْفًا. She conceived by him, عَلِقَتْ مِنْهُ.

Concentrate, *v.t.* To join, جَمَّعَ ـ ضَمَّ. To reduce to a narrower compass, as of a salt, كَرَّرَ. To — the sight upon, أَمْعَنَ ٱلنَّظَرَ فِي. To — one's energies upon, بَذَلَ جَهْدَهُ فِي. To — troops, جَمَّعَ ٱلْعَسَاكِرَ. To —, to fix, رَكَزَ. To be wholly absorbed in, إِنْهَمَكَ فِي ـ إِسْتَغْرَقَ فِي. To — one's affections upon, حَطَّ كُلَّ مَحَبَّتِهِ فِي.

Concentration, *n.* Collection, تَجَمُّع ـ إِنْضِمَام. Concentration, as of a salt, تَكْرِير. Concentration of the sight, إِمْعَانُ ٱلنَّظَرِ. The being absorbed in, إِنْهِمَاكٌ فِي ـ إِسْتِغْرَاقٌ فِي. Concentration of energy, كَدٌّ ـ بَذْلُ ٱلْجَهْدِ.

Concentric, *a.* ذُو مَرْكَزٍ وَاحِدٍ. Concentric circles, دَوَائِرُ لَهَا مَرْكَزٌ وَاحِدٌ.

Conceptible, *a.* *See* Conceivable, *a.*

Conception, *n.* Pregnancy, حِبَالَة ـ حَبَل ـ حَمْل ـ عُلُوق. A notion, ظَنّ *pl.* ظُنُون ـ تَصَوُّر ـ تَوَهُّم ـ وَهْم *pl.* أَوْهَام ـ رَأْي *pl.* آرَاء ـ خَيَال. The faculty of comprehending, فَهْم ـ ضَمِير ـ إِدْرَاك. A purpose, مَقْصُود ـ غَايَة ـ قَصْد ـ نِيَّة.

Concern, *v.t.* To relate to, تَعَلَّقَ بِ ـ خَصَّ ـ إِخْتَصَّ بِ ـ نَسَبَ إِلَى. To make uneasy, نَكَّدَ عَلَى ـ أَزْعَجَ ـ عَنَّى ـ أَهَمَّ. To be concerned, disquieted, إِضْطَرَبَ ـ إِهْتَمَّ ـ تَعَنَّى. To interest, إِسْتَمَالَ ـ حَرَّكَ ـ رَغَّبَ ـ آلَ إِلَى *aor.* يَؤُولُ ـ عَطَفَ-عَلَى. To — one's self about other people's affairs, حَشَرَ ـ تَفَوْضَلَ ـ هُوَ فِي ٱلْفُضُولِ ـ تَدَاخَلَ فِي أُمُورِ غَيْرِهِ ـ حَالَهُ فِيمَا لَا يَعْنِيهِ. The agreements which — the interests of Europe, ٱلشُّرُوطُ ٱلَّتِي تَؤُولُ إِلَى مَصَالِحِ أُورُبَا. That does not — me, مَا لِي فِي ذٰلِكَ عَلَاقَةٌ ـ ذٰلِكَ مَا يَخُصُّنِي ـ لَا يَعْنِينِي. It concerns me, يَخُصُّنِي ـ يَعْنِينِي. It concerned him, تَعَلَّقَ بِهِ.

Concern, *n.* A business, thing, أَمْر *pl.* أُمُور ـ مَادَّة *pl.* مَوَادّ ـ غَرَض *pl.* أَغْرَاض ـ مَصْلَحَة *pl.* مَصَالِح ـ مُعَامَلَة ـ دَعْوَى *pl.* دَعَاوَى ـ شُغْل *pl.* أَشْغَال. Connexion, تَعَلُّق ـ عَلَاقَة ـ أَخْذٌ وَعَطَاءٌ. Importance, عِظَم ـ عَظَامَة ـ ضَرُورِيَّة ـ مُهِمَّة. Affection, مَوَدَّة ـ مَحَبَّة ـ مَيْل. Grief, حُزْن ـ غَمّ ـ كَرْب ـ مِحْنَة. Interest, غَيْرَة ـ رَغْبَة ـ عَطْف. A — of importance, أَمْرٌ مُهِمٌّ. The matter caused him much —, عَانَاهُ ٱلْأَمْرُ ـ تَعَنَّى مِنَ ٱلْأَمْرِ.

Concernedly, *ad.* With interest, بِعَطْفٍ ـ بِرَغْبَةٍ ـ بِٱعْتِنَاءٍ ـ بِٱهْتِمَامٍ ـ بِغَيْرَةٍ.

Concerning, *ad.* عَنْ ـ نَحْوَ ـ مِنْ نَحْوِ ـ فِي ـ بِخُصُوصِ ـ فِيمَا يَخُصُّ. Concerning which, عَمَّا ـ مِنْ قِبَلِ. Concerning me, فِيَّ; — thee, فِيكَ.

Concernment, *n.* *See* Concern, *n.*

Concert, *v.t.* To settle, contrive, إِخْتَرَعَ ـ رَتَّبَ ـ فَصَّلَ. To — or unite together for, إِتَّفَقُوا فِي ـ تَعَصَّبُوا بِ ـ إِرْتَبَطُوا فِي. He concerted the matter with ..., تَدَاوَلَ ٱلْأَمْرَ مَعَ ـ رَبَطَ ٱلْأَمْرَ مَعَ.

Concert, *n.* A compact, إِتِّفَاق ـ إِتِّحَاد ـ مُدَاوَلَة. Harmony, سَمَاع ـ نَوْبَة ـ أَصْوَاتٌ وَآلَاتٌ مُتَّفِقَةٌ. A company of singers and musicians, مَعْشَرُ مُغَنِّينَ وَمُزَمِّرِينَ ـ نَوْبَة.

Concession, *n.* The act of yielding, تَسْلِيم ـ قُبُول ـ قُبُولٌ بِ ـ قُبُولٌ وَٱعْتِرَاف ـ رِضَاء ـ إِسْتِرْضَاء. Permission, إِجَازَة ـ رُخْصَة. A grant, إِلْتِزَام ـ إِمْتِيَاز ـ إِحَالَة ـ عَطِيَّة *pl.* عَطَايَا ـ مِنْحَة. Aid, grace, إِحْسَان ـ إِنْعَام.

Concessionnaire, *n.* مُلْتَزِم ـ صَاحِبُ ٱلْإِمْتِيَازِ ـ مُعَاهِد.

Conch, *n.* نَوْعٌ كَبِيرٌ مِنَ ٱلْوَدَعَاتِ ـ صَدَف *pl.* أَصْدَاف.

Conchologist, *n.* عَالِمٌ بِٱلْأَصْدَافِ ـ مَاهِرٌ بِمَا يَتَعَلَّقُ بِٱلْأَصْدَافِ.

Conchology, *n.* عِلْمُ ٱلْأَصْدَافِ.

Conciliate, *v.t.* To reconcile, لَأَمَ بَيْنَ ـ جَمَعَ بَيْنَ ـ صَالَحَ ـ أَصْلَحَ ـ وَفَّقَ ـ سَاوَى ـ صَرَفَ بَيْنَ. To pacify, لَسَّمَ ـ أَهْدَأَ. To gain, win, إِكْتَسَبَ ـ إِسْتَمْلَكَ ـ جَذَبَ. To — the friendship of, for, إِسْتَعْطَفَ-عَلَى ـ أَمَالَ-إِلَى.

Conciliating, *a.* } Tending to conciliate, مُحِثٌّ عَلَى ٱلْمُصَالَحَةِ ـ مُصَالِح ـ مُتَضَمِّنُ ٱلْمُصَالَحَةِ.
Conciliatory, } Winning, engaging, مُعَطِّف ـ مُسْتَعْطِف.

Conciliation, *n.* Reconciliation, مُصَالَحَة ـ صُلْح ـ مُوَافَقَة. Act of gaining, winning over, إِسْتِعْطَاف ـ إِسْتِمْلَاك ـ إِكْتِسَاب ـ جَذْب.

Conciliator, *n.* مُصْلِح ـ مُصَالِح ـ شَفِيع ـ مُوَفِّق.

Concio, *n.* مَوْعِظَة ـ وَعْظ.

Concise, *a.* مُوجَز ـ وَجِيز ـ مُخْتَصَر ـ مُجْمَل. To be — in speech, حَذَفَ فِي قَوْلِهِ. To make —, of speech, أَدْمَجَ. A man — in speech, رَجُلٌ مُحَذَّفُ ٱلْكَلَامِ.

Concisely, *ad.* بإيجازٍ ـ بالإيجازِ ـ إقتصارًا ـ إختصارًا ـ بإدماجٍ.

Conciseness, *n.* إدماج ـ إختصار ـ إقتصار ـ قصر ـ إيجاز.

Concision, *n.* قطع.

Conclave, *n.* An assembly, ديوان ـ مجمع. An assembly of cardinals to elect a pope, ديوانُ الكارديناليّةِ لأجلِ انتخابِ بابا.

Conclude, *v.t.* To end, ختم ـ أنجز ـ أنهى ـ أنفذ ـ فرغ من ـ كمّل ـ أتمّ. To determine, خزم ب ـ فصل ـ قضى على ـ حكم ب. To infer, إستنتج ـ إستدلّ. To be concluded, ended, إنتهى ـ إنقضى. To — a discourse, ختم الكلامَ. To — a treaty, عقد شرطًا ـ عقد عهدًا. To conclude, (adverbially), نهايةُ الأمرِ ـ آخرُ الأمرِ ـ وبعدُ ـ النهايةُ ـ الحاصلُ ـ خاتمةُ الكلامِ.

Concluding, *a.* Ending, تالٍ ـ آخِر.

Conclusion, *n.* An end, إختتام ـ ختم ـ عاقبة ـ مجاز ـ خاتمة ـ ختام ـ إنتهاء ـ نهاية ـ إنقطاع. A last result, نهاية. A decision, عزم ـ حكم ـ حزم ـ فصل ـ جزم. A consequence, نتيجة ـ حاصل. To draw a —, إستنتج. They came to the —, resolved, أفادوا. He did not come to any —, لم يبتّ على رأيٍ. It began to come to a —, أخذ في الإشرافِ على النهايةِ.

Conclusive, *a.* Decisive, شافٍ ـ فارز ـ قاطع ـ مقنع ـ قطعيّ ـ منفصل. Consequential, مستنتج ـ متوالٍ.

Conclusively, *ad.* حزمًا ـ جزمًا ـ حتمًا ـ بتّةً.

Conclusiveness, *n.* قطعيّة ـ بتّة ـ جزم.

Concoct, *v.t.* To digest, هضم. To cook, طبخ. To mature, أنضج. To plan, رتّب ـ رسم ـ إرتأى ـ إخترع.

Concoction, *n.* Digestion, إنهضام ـ هضم. Maturation, طبخ ـ إنضاج. Planning, إختراع ـ ترتيب ـ إيجاد.

Concomitance, *n.* } The being in connexion with, مصاحبة ـ إتّحاد ـ إتّفاق ـ إلتحاق ـ ملازمة. Aid, معاونة.
Concomitancy, }

Concomitant, *a.* لاحق ـ منضمّ ـ ملازم ـ ملحق ـ مصاحب.

Concomitant, *n.* رفيق ـ إضافة ـ ملحقة ـ ألحاق *pl.* لحق ـ إتّصال.

Concomitantly, *ad.* سواءً ـ معًا ـ بالإضافةِ.

Concord, *n.* Agreement, موافقة ـ وفق ـ رفاهية ـ مرافاة ـ إتّحاد. Friendship, ألفة ـ صحبة ـ صلح ـ ودّ. An agreement, شرط ـ معاهدة ـ عهد. Harmony, ألحان ـ ألفةُ الأصواتِ. In grammar, ربط ـ إلتئام ـ مطابقة.

Concordance, *n.* An index to words, فهرسُ كلماتٍ. A Bible —, فهرسُ كلماتِ الكتبِ المقدّسةِ. A — to the Kurân (the title given to his Concordance by Flügel is), نجومُ الفرقانِ في أطرافِ القرآنِ. *See also* Concord, *n.*

Concordant, *a.* ملائم ـ موافق ـ مطابق.

Concordantly, *ad.* موافقةً ـ باتّفاقٍ ـ ألفةً ـ مطابقةً.

Concordat, *n.* A compact respecting religion, إتّفاق كنائسيّ ـ معاهدة على أمورٍ كنائسيّةٍ.

Concourse, *n.* A crowd, جمّة ـ إجتماع ـ إزدحام ـ زحام ـ كثرة ـ حشر. A place of meeting, ملتقى ـ مضمّ. A meeting together, إلتقاء.

Concrete, *v.i.* إستحجر ـ تحجّر ـ إنعقد ـ جمد ـ حثر.

Concrete, *v.t.* عقد ـ جمّد.

Concrete, *a.* Formed by concretion, مركّب ـ جامد ـ معقود. A — noun, إسمُ صفةٍ. A — number, عددٌ عينيّ. A — expression, تعبيرٌ تصديقيّ.

Concrete, *n.* A mass of lime, *etc.*, cemented together, أرضيّة ـ حجريّة.

Concretely, *ad.* *In grammar*, بصفةٍ ـ وصفًا. Not abstractly, إسنادًا ـ تقييدًا.

Concreteness, *n.* إستحجار ـ تحجّر ـ جمود.

Concretion, *n.* The act of concreting, تجميد. A mass formed by that process, إنجماد ـ إنعقاد. A stone, حجرة ـ حصاة *pl.* حصيات.

Concretive, *a.* إنعقاديّ ـ إنجماديّ ـ مجمّد.

Concubinage, *a.* إلفةُ رجلٍ ـ زناء ـ تسرّ ـ إستسرار ـ تسرّر مع امرأةٍ من غيرِ زيجةٍ.

Concubine, *n.* محظيّة ـ حظيّة *pl.* محظيّات *or* محاظي. A — slave, سرّيّة *pl.* سراريّ.

Concupiscence, *n.* Desire, هوى النفسِ ـ شهوة. Evil —, lust, غرام ـ شهوةٌ خبيثةٌ ـ قطم ـ إغتلام ـ غلمة.

Concupiscent, *a.* Lustful, شهوان ـ مغليم ـ قطاميّ ـ قطم ـ شهوانيّ.

Concur, *v.i.* To meet in one point, تصادف ـ تلاقى ـ تقابل. To agree, أجمع ـ إجتمع في *or* على ـ إتّفق ـ إلتقى بعضه. To contribute, as to an event, شارك على ـ ساعد على ـ على. إتّفق مع ـ في ـ أعان ـ إتّحد مع ـ في. They all concurred that . . . , إتّفقوا بأن ـ أجمعوا على أن. He did not —, had no hand, in the affair, ما كان له يدٌ في المادّةِ.

Concurrence, *n.* Union, إتّفاق ـ إجتماع ـ إتّحاد ـ إتّصال.

Consent, agreement, إِئْتِلافٌ وَٱتِّفَاقٌ ـ مُوَافَقَة ـ وَفْق ـ رِضَآءٌ ـ. A combination, تَوْفِيق ـ تَرْتِيب ـ تَدْبِير. Assistance, مُسَاعَدَة ـ عَوْن ـ تَأْيِيد. A — of events, مُجَامَعَةُ ٱلْأُمُورِ. In —, مَعًا ـ سَوَآءٌ. With the — of the government, بِٱتِّفَاقِ ٱلدَّوْلَةِ.

Concurrent, *a.* Coming together, مُلْحِق ـ مُصَادِف ـ مُلَازِم. In union, مُتَّحِد ـ مُتَّفِق. Aiding, مُسَاعِد ـ مُعَاوِن. Happening at the same time, حَادِثٌ فِي زَمَانٍ وَاحِدٍ ـ مُتَصَادِف.

Concurrently, *ad.* إِجْتِمَاعًا ـ إِتِّفَاقًا ـ مَعًا ـ سَوَآءً ـ بِٱئْتِلَافٍ وَٱتِّفَاقٍ.

Concussion, *n.* مُصَادَمَة ـ هَزَّة ـ تَزَعْزُع ـ حَرَكَة ـ خَضَّة ـ إِخْتِبَاط ـ كَبَّة.

Concussive, *a.* مُهَزِّز ـ مُزَعْزِع ـ مُحَرِّك ـ مُخِضّ.

Condemn, *v.t.* To sentence, قَضَى عَلَى ـ حَكَمَ عَلَى ـ دَانَ ـ. To blame, لَامَ ـ قَضَى بِ ـ عَابَ ـ ذَمَّ. أَوْقَعَ عَلَى ـ بِ. To declare unlawful, حَرَّمَ. To — in a fine, قَاصَصَ ـ بِمَعَرَّةٍ. To — to death, شَجَبَ ـ حَكَمَ عَلَى ـ بِٱلْمَوْتِ ـ قَضَى عَلَيْهِ بِجَرِيمَةٍ. They condemned him though they found no cause of death against him, قَضَوْا عَلَيْهِ مَعَ أَنَّهُمْ لَمْ يَجِدُوا عَلَيْهِ عِلَّةً لِلْمَوْتِ. To — one's self, to acknowledge one's error, أَقَرَّ بِذَنْبِهِ ـ إِعْتَرَفَ بِخَطِيَّتِهِ.

Condemnable, *a.* يُلَامُ ـ عَلَيْهِ مَلَامٌ ـ مُسْتَحِقُّ ٱللَّوْمِ ـ يُقْضَى ـ يُدَانُ ـ عَلَيْهِ.

Condemnation, *a.* Sentence, شَجْب ـ حُكْمٌ عَلَى ـ قَضَآءٌ عَلَى ـ. Punishment, قَضَآء. Judgment, دَيْنُونَة. قِصَاص ـ عِقَاب. Censure, ذَمّ ـ لَوْم ـ تَعْيِيب. Prohibition, حِرْم ـ حِرْمَان.

Condemnatory, *a.* حُكُومِيّ ـ مُحَرِّم ـ مُقَبِّح.

Condensable, *a.* Which may be made dense, يَتَجَمَّدُ ـ تَكْثِيفُهُ ـ مُمْكِنٌ ـ قَابِلُ ٱلتَّثْخِينِ. Which may be distilled, يُقَطَّرُ مِنْهُ ـ. That may be abbreviated, قَابِلُ ٱلتَّقْطِيرِ ـ قَابِلُ ٱلْإِقْتِصَارِ ـ يُوجَزُ.

Condensate, *v.t.* and *i.* *See to* Condense, *v.t.* and *i.*

Condensation, *n.* The act of making dense, تَجْمِيد ـ تَكْثِيف ـ تَثْخِين. The state of density, جُمُود ـ كَثَافَة. Distillation, إِخْرَاج ـ تَقْطِير ـ إِقْتِصَار ـ إِخْتِصَار. Abbreviation, إِيجَاز.

Condense, *v.t.* To make dense, قَبَّضَ ـ كَثَّفَ ـ ثَخَّنَ. To shorten, أَوْجَزَ ـ قَصَّرَ ـ إِخْتَصَرَ. To distil, قَطَّرَ ـ أَخْرَجَ.

Condense, *v.i.* To become dense, ثَخُنَ ـ تَكَثَّفَ.

Condenser, *n.* An alembic, أَنْبِيق ـ أَنْبَك. A distiller, خَرَّاج. An air —, طُلُومْبَةُ هَوَآءٍ.

Condescend, *v.i.* To depart from the privileges of superiority towards, تَوَاضَعَ لِ ـ خَضَعَ لِ ـ تَنَازَلَ لِ ـ فِي ـ صَارَ خَاضِعًا لِ. To yield to one more than justice requires, to consent to, سَمَحَ لِ ـ بِ ـ هَاوَدَ ـ رَاعَى خَاطِرَهُ فِي ـ طَاوَعَ ـ عَلَى ـ أَطَاعَ ـ قَبِلَ ـ إِرْتَضَى. I did not think that he had condescended to act so shamefully, مَا ظَنَنْتُ أَنَّهُ قَدْ رَذِلَ فِي ٱلْعَمَلِ بِهٰذَا ٱلْمِقْدَارِ.

Condescendence, *n.* } تَوَاضُع ـ تَنَازُل ـ مُهَاوَدَة ـ مُطَاوَعَة.
Condescension, } Civility, لَطَافَة ـ أَهْلِيَّة ـ إِنْسَانِيَّة ـ تَفَضُّل.

Condescending, *a.* Yielding to inferiors, مُتَوَاضِع. Obliging, لَطِيف ـ صَاحِبُ مَعْرُوفٍ ـ بَشُوش.

Condign, *a.* مُسْتَحِقٌّ ـ مُسْتَأْهِل ـ أَهْلٌ لِ ـ مُسْتَوْجِب.

Condignly, *ad.* كَمَا يَجِبُ ـ كَمَا يَلِيقُ ـ بِٱسْتِحْقَاقٍ ـ لِيَاقَةً.

Condignness, *n.* إِسْتِحْقَاق ـ لِيَاقَة.

Condiment, *n.* تَابِل *pl.* تَوَابِلُ ـ تَتْبِيل ـ بَهَار.

Condition, *n.* A quality, صِفَة ـ كَيْفِيَّة ـ شَأْن ـ مَاهِيَّة ـ نَوْع. An attribute, خَاصَّة ـ خَاصِّيَّة. A state, حَال ـ حَالَة ـ أَحْوَال. Rank, مَنْزِلَة ـ شَأْن ـ رُتْبَة ـ مَرْتَبَة ـ دَرَجَة ـ وَضْع ـ صُورَة. مَقَام. An agreement, شَرْط *pl.* شُرُوط. A good —, حَالَةٌ حَسَنَةٌ. In good —, fat, سَمِين. In bad —, lean, weak, نَحِيف ـ ضَعِيف. Conditions of peace, أَسْبَابُ ٱلصُّلْحِ. On —, عَلَى أَنْ ـ بِشَرْطٍ. He agreed to their proposition on — that they should aid him with arms, أَجَابَهُمْ عَلَى ذٰلِكَ عَلَى أَنْ يُمِدُّوهُ بِٱلسِّلَاحِ. He made a compromise with him on — of his doing such a thing, صَالَحَهُ عَلَى أَنْ يَفْعَلَ كَذَا.

Condition, *v.i.* To make conditions, تَشَارَطَ ـ إِشْتَرَطَ.

Condition, *v.t.* To stipulate for, إِشْتَرَطَ عَلَى ـ شَرَطَ عَلَى.

Conditional, *a.* مَشْرُوط ـ شَرْطِيّ ـ تَحْتَ شَرْطٍ. Conditional surrender, تَسْلِيمٌ تَحْتَ شَرْطٍ. The — mood, ٱلصِّيغَةُ ٱلشَّرْطِيَّةُ.

Conditionality, *n.* شَرْطِيَّة ـ إِشْتِرَاط.

Conditionally, *ad.* بِٱلشَّرْطِ ـ تَحْتَ ٱلشَّرْطِ ـ بِشُرُوطٍ.

Conditionary, *a.* مُشْتَرَط.

Conditioned, *a.* Stipulated, مَشْرُوط ـ مُشْتَرَط. Well —, fat, سَمِينُ ٱللَّحْمِ. Well —, in order, perfect, مُحْكَم ـ مَنْظُوم ـ مَضْبُوط ـ صَاغ. Badly —, defective, سَقَط ـ فِيهِ نَقْصٌ; lean, مَهْزُول ـ ضَعِيف. Ill-conditioned, unmannerly, عَدِيمُ ٱلْأَدَبِ.

Condole, *v.i.* To bewail, بَكَى عَلَى ـ حَزِنَ عَلَى ـ تَأَسَّفَ عَلَى. To — with, شَفَقَ عَلَى ـ أَشْفَقَ عَلَى. To console for, عَزَّى ـ فِي ـ سَلَّى ـ أَسْلَى ـ عَنْ.

Condolence, *n.* Grief, sympathy, حُزْن ـ إشْفاق ـ شَفَقَة.

Comfort, تَسْلِيَة ـ تَعْزِيَة. A letter of —, مَكْتُوبُ تَعْزِيَةٍ.

Condonation, *n.* عَفْوٌ وَسَمْحٌ ـ عَفْوٌ ـ تَجَاوُزٌ عَن.

Condone, *v.t.* ـَ صَفَحَ عَن ـ سَامَحَ ـ ـَ سَمُحَ-فِي.

Condoner, *n.* صَفُوح.

Condor, *n.* نَوْعٌ كَبِيرٌ مِنَ ٱلطُّيُورِ.

Conduce, *v.i.* To lead or tend to, آلَ إِلَى *aor.* يَؤُولُ. To occasion, سَبَّبَ ـ أَوْجَبَ ـ ـِ نَتَجَ. To be useful to, ـَ نَفَعَ ل. To aid, promote, ـَ صَلَحَ ل ـ قَدَّمَ ـ سَاعَدَ.

Conducive, *a.* Being a means to, مُفْضٍ إِلَى ـ وَسِيلَة. Useful towards, نَافِع ـ مُفِيدٌ ل ـ مُعَاوِنٌ ل. Occasioning, مُسَبِّب ـ مُورِث ـ مُوجِب ـ مُنْتِج.

Conduciveness, *n.* Utility, aid towards, مَصْلَحَة ـ فائدة ـ طائل ـ مُعاوَنَة.

Conduct, *n.* Management, القِيَامُ بِ ـ إِدَارَة ـ مُبَاشَرَة ـ تَدْبِير. Guidance, دِلالَة ـ هِدَايَة ـ إِرْشَاد. Leading, as troops, مُرَافَقَة ـ بَذْرَقَة ـ غَفَر. A convoy, ضَبْط ـ رِئَاسَة ـ قِيَادَة. Behaviour, مِشْيَة ـ مُعَامَلَة ـ سِيرَة ـ سُلُوك ـ سَمْت. A safe —, وَرَقَةُ أَمَانٍ ـ أَمَان. Good —, سِيرَةٌ حَسَنَةٌ ـ تَسْدِيد. Bad —, سِيرَةٌ بَشِعَةٌ. The — of public affairs, إِدَارَةُ ـ إِجْرَاءُ أُمُورِ ٱلدَّوْلَةِ ٱلْحُكُومَةِ. He knows your —, what you are about, يَعْلَمُ ما أَنْتُمْ عَمَلَه.

Conduct, *v.t.* To lead, direct, ـِ هَدَى ـ أَرْشَدَ ـ [2] دَلَّ. To accompany, بَاشَرَ ـ دَبَّرَ. To manage, [2] أَخَذَ-إِلَى ـ رَافَقَ ـ أَوْصَلَ. To head, as an army, [2] قَادَ. To — one's self, [2] سَلَكَ-سُلُوكًا ـ ـَ عَمِلَ ـ ـِ مَشَى. (*See also under to* Behave, *v.i.*) To — an affair, بَاشَرَ. To — well, سَدَّدَ. To —, as water, أَجْرَى. *See also to* Conduce, *v.i.*

Conductive, *a.* مُدِلٌّ إِلَى ـ مُرْشِد ـ هَادٍ.

Conductor, *n.* A guide, هَادٍ ـ دَلِيل ـ مُرْشِد. A chief, وَازِع ـ قَائِد. A manager, مُبَاشِر ـ مُدِير ـ مُدَبِّر ـ مُرَتِّب ـ قَيِّم. The — of a vehicle, بَوَّابٌ (or سَائِقُ) عَرَبَانَةٍ. A lightning —, سِيخٌ (or زِنْجِيرٌ) صِيَانَةً عَنِ ٱلصَّاعِقَةِ.

Conduit, *n.* مَجْرًى *pl.* مَجَارٍ ـ قَنَاة *pl.* قَنًا *and* قُنِيّ ـ مَثْعَب *pl.* مَثَاعِب. Conduits, مَسَالِكُ ٱلْمِيَاهِ.

Cone, *n.* مَخْرُوطَة *pl.* مَخْرُوطَات. A pine —, جَوْزُ صَنَوْبَرٍ.

Coney, *n.* *See* Cony, *n.*

Confabulate, *v.i.* فَاوَهَ ـ تَكَلَّمَ ـ قَاوَلَ ـ خَاطَبَ ـ تَحَدَّثَ.

Confabulation, *n.* مُنَادَمَة ـ مُحَاوَرَة ـ مُخَاطَبَة ـ حَدِيث.

Confect, *n.* } A sweetmeat, preserve, مُرَبًّى *pl.* مُرَبَّيَات ـ حَلْوًى.
Confection, } A composition, مَعْجُون.

Confectioner, *n.* حَلَاوَاتِيّ ـ حَلْوَانِيّ ـ حَلَّاء ـ مُرَبٍّ.

Confectionery, *n.* A shop for sale of —, دُكَّانُ حَلْوَاتِيّ.

Confederacy, *n.* A league, حِلْفَة ـ عَقْد ـ حِزْب ـ مُعَاهَدَة ـ مُحَالَفَة ـ إِتِّفَاق. A — against, conspiracy, عُصْبَةٌ عَلَى ـ فِتْنَة ـ إِتِّفَاقٌ عَلَى.

Confederate, *v.i.* تَعَاهَدَ ـ تَحَالَفَ ـ تَشَارَطَ ـ إِجْتَمَعَ. To join with in a confederacy, حَالَفَ. They confederated against him, تَعَاهَدُوا عَلَيْهِ عَهْدًا.

Confederate, *n.* عَقِيد ـ مُعَاقِد ـ حَلِيف ـ قَعِيد ـ رَبِيب *pl.* أَرِبَّاء ـ مُلْصِق ـ عَهِيد ـ جَار *pl.* جِوَار ـ شَرِيك *pl.* شُرَكَاء.

Confederate, *a.* مُتَعَاهِد ـ مُتَّحِد ـ مُشْتَرِك. Confederate States, دُوَلٌ مُجْتَمِعَةٌ.

Confederation, *n.* The act of confederating, تَعْقِيد ـ تَحْزِيب ـ إِجْتِمَاع. The — of the United States of America, جَمَاهِيرُ أَمِيرِيكا ٱلْمُتَّحِدَةُ. The Swiss —, جُمْهُورِيَّةُ ٱلسُّوِيسِ. *See also* Confederacy, *n.*

Confer, *v.i.* To consult upon, تَشَاوَرَ فِي ـ تَسَارَّ فِي ـ تَدَاوَلَ عَن ـ تَنَاجَى ـ تَحَاكَى عَن. They conferred together, إِئْتَمَرُوا ـ تَفَاوَضُوا ـ تَذَاكَرُوا. When he had conferred with the council, لَمَّا فَاوَضَ أَهْلَ ٱلْمَشْوَرَةِ.

Confer, *v.t.* To grant, ـَ مَنَحَ ـ وَهَبَ *aor.* يَهَبُ ـ أَنْعَمَ ـ عَلَى بِ ـ أَعْطَى ـ خَوَّلَ. To —, as an appointment, upon, وَجَّهَ ـ قَلَّدَ-بِ ـ وَظَّفَ ـ وَلَّى ـ أَقَامَ-فِي. To contribute to, ـَ نَفَعَ ل ـ أَصْلَحَ ل. To be conferred upon, as an honour, وُجِّهَ إِلَى.

Conference, *n.* مُؤْتَمَر ـ مَشْوَرَة ـ مُحَادَثَة ـ مُحَاوَرَة ـ مُدَاوَلَة ـ مُطَارَحَة ـ مُفَاوَضَة ـ مُذَاكَرَة ـ كُنْفَرَانْس. A private —, مُذَاكَرَةٌ فِي خَلْوَةٍ. A — was held, إِنْعَقَدَ مُؤْتَمَرٌ. The — still continues between ..., لَمْ تَزَلِ ٱلْمُذَاكَرَةُ جَارِيَةً بَيْنَ. Long conferences have taken place between ..., جَرَتْ مُفَاوَضَاتٌ طَوِيلَةٌ بَيْنَ.

Confess, *v.t.* To acknowledge, أَقَرَّ بِ ـ ـِ عَرَفَ ـ إِعْتَرَفَ بِ. To hear confessions, عَرَّفَ ـ ـَ سَمِعَ ٱلْإِعْتِرَافَ. To yield, grant, سَلَّمَ بِ ـ ـَ قَبِلَ ـ أَذْعَنَ ل. To attest, ـَ شَهِدَ بِ. To make to —, قَرَّرَ-بِ *or* عَلَى ـ إِسْتَقَرَّ-بِ *or* عَلَى. Confess your faults one to another, إِعْتَرِفُوا بَعْضُكُمْ لِبَعْضٍ بِسَيِّئَاتِكُمْ. To — the truth, I was in fault, أَقُولُ ٱلْحَقَّ أَنا كُنْتُ فِي غَلَطٍ.

Confessedly, *ad.* Avowedly, إِقْرَارًا ـ بَيَانًا ـ قَصْدًا ـ إِعْلَانًا.

Confession, *n.* Acknowledgment, إِقْرَار ـ إِعْتِرَاف. Avowal, إِعْلَان ـ تَعْرِيف ـ إِقْرَار بِ. A — of faith, صُورَةُ إِيمَانٍ ـ إِيمَان. Auricular —, إِعْتِرَاف سِرِّيّ ـ إِعْتِرَاف عِنْدَ ٱلْقَسّ. قَانُونُ إِيمَانٍ.

Confessional, *n.* كُرْسِيُّ ٱلْإِعْتِرَافِ.

Confessor, *n.* One who makes profession of the faith, مُعْتَرِف ـ مُقِرّ. A — in the face of danger, شَهِيد *pl.* شُهَدَآءُ. One who hears confessions, مُعَلِّمُ ٱلْإِعْتِرَافِ ـ مُعَرِّف.

Confidant, *n.* صَاحِبُ ٱلسِّرِّ ـ أَمِينُ ٱلسِّرِّ ـ نَجِيّ *pl.* أَنْجِيَة. He is the — of my secret, هُوَ مَوْضِعُ سِرِّي.

Confidante, *n.* أَمِينَةُ ٱلسِّرِّ ـ نَجِيَّة *pl.* نَجِيَّات.

Confide, *v.t.* and *i.* To intrust, إِسْتَوْدَعَ ـ إِسْتَأْمَنَ ـ آمَنَ. To trust in or upon, إِتَّكَلَ ـ تَوَكَّلَ عَلَى ـ عَوَّلَ عَلَى ـ إِسْتَكْفَى بِ ـ إِسْتَنَدَ إِلَى ـ إِعْتَمَدَ عَلَى ـ يَثِقُ *aor.* وَثِقَ بِ ـ عَلَى. To believe, credit, صَدَّقَ ـ بِ *or* فِي *or* عَلَى.

Confidence, *n.* Reliance, تَوَكُّل ـ إِتِّكَال ـ إِعْتِمَاد ـ ثِقَة ـ أَمَان ـ إِسْتِنَاد ـ عِوَل ـ وُثُوق ـ وَثِيقَة. Quiet assurance, إِعْتِمَاد ـ ثِقَة ـ أُمْنِيَّة ـ طُمَأْنِينَة. Confidence in one's self, قِلَّةُ حَيَآءٍ ـ زَهْو ـ وَقَاحَة. Effrontery, ـ جُرْأَة ـ غَيْرَة. Consciousness of innocence, ثَبَاتُ ٱلْقَلْبِ ـ جَسَارَة ـ بَرَآءَة. Boldness, شَجَاعَة. Perfect —, أُمْنِيَّةٌ كُلِّيَّةٌ. He began his business with —, أَخَذَ فِي أَمْرِهِ بِٱلْوَثِيقَةِ. To have — in one's self, وَثِقَ *aor.* يَثِقُ ـ تَوَثَّقَ. To have — about another, إِسْتَوْثَقَ مِن. We have — in him as regards you, لَنَا ثِقَةٌ بِهِ مِنْ قِبَلِكُمْ (*or* جِهَتِكُمْ). Want of — in, عَدَمُ وُثُوقٍ بِ. One in whom I have —, مَنْ أَثِقُ بِهِ. On account of his — in and his reliance on them, لِثِقَتِهِ بِهِمْ وَرُكُونِهِ إِلَيْهِمْ. Confidence, or tranquillity, was restored, عَادَتِ ٱلطُّمَأْنِينَةُ. Owing to the loss of — on the part of the merchants, بِسَبَبِ ٱلْأُمْنِيَّةِ ٱلَّتِي فَقَدَتْهَا ٱلتُّجَّارُ. It is not calculated to give us —, لَيْسَ مِمَّا تَرْتَاحُ إِلَيْهِ نُفُوسُنَا.

Confident, *a.* Assured, عَلَى ثِقَةٍ ـ مُتَأَكِّد ـ مُتَحَقِّق ـ مُتَيَقِّن ـ مُسْتَأْمِن ـ مُتَوَكِّل ـ وَاثِق ـ مُحَقِّق عَن. Void of suspicion, مُطْمَئِنّ. Bold, جَسُور. Impudent, سَفِيه ـ وَقِح. I am always — of his safety, إِنِّي عَلَى ثِقَةٍ دَائِمًا بِأَمْنِهِ. I am — in this matter, إِنِّي لَوَاثِقٌ بِهٰذَا ٱلْأَمْرِ.

Confidential, *a.* Private, secret, مَكْتُوم ـ سِرِّيّ. *See also under* Private, *a.*

Confidentially, *ad.* فِي ٱلسِّرِّ ـ سِرًّا.

Confidently, *ad.* Positively, بَتَّةً ـ بِلَا تَرَدُّدٍ ـ قَطْعًا. With confidence, بِٱعْتِمَادٍ ـ إِعْتِمَادًا ـ عَلَى ثِقَةٍ. Without fear, بِقَلْبٍ قَوِيٍّ ـ إِطْمِئْنَانًا ـ إِسْتِئْمَانًا. To affirm —, أَكَّدَ.

Configuration, *n.* جِبْلَة ـ تَرْتِيب ـ شَكْل ـ صُورَة.

Confine, *n.* A limit, حَدّ *pl.* حُدُود ـ تَخْم *pl.* تُخُوم. An end, أَوَاخِر *pl.* آخِرَة ـ إِنْتِهَآء.

Confine, *v.i.* To border upon, قَارَبَ ـ إِتَّصَلَ بِ ـ تَاخَمَ.

Confine, *v.t.* To limit, حَدَّدَ. To restrict to, أَلْزَمَ ـ بِ. To imprison, قَفَلَ عَلَى ـ حَبَسَ ـ سَجَنَ ـ قَيَّدَ. To restrain, مَنَعَ ـ حَصَرَ ـ ضَيَّقَ عَلَى ـ حَبَسَ. To bring to bed, وَلَّدَ. To — one's self, to shut one's self up, تَقَصَّرَ. To —, as the bowels, قَبَضَ. To — one's self to doing so much and no more, إِقْتَصَّ عَلَى. He confined the property to him, حَبَسَ ٱلْمِلْكَ عَلَيْهِ. I confined myself wholly to this matter, قَصَرْتُ نَفْسِي عَلَى هٰذَا ٱلْأَمْرِ. In this circular he confined himself to ..., إِقْتَصَرَ فِي هٰذِهِ ٱلنَّشْرَةِ عَلَى. That they should — themselves to their own special offices, أَنْ يَقْتَصِرُوا عَلَى وَظَائِفِهِمِ ٱلْخَاصَّةِ. She was confined, delivered of a child, وَضَعَتْ ـ وَلَدَتْ; of a male child, ذَكَّرَتْ. He was confined to his bed, أَلْزَمَ ٱلْفِرَاشَ.

Confined, *a.* Imprisoned, حَبِيس ـ مَحْبُوس. Narrow, حَصِر ـ ضَيِّق. Confined in the bowels, مُنْقَبِض ـ مُعْتَقَلُ ٱلْبَطْنِ. Is education — to the higher classes? هَلِ ٱلْمَعَارِفُ مَقْصُورَةٌ عَلَى ٱلْخَاصَّةِ. Confined to these limits, مَقْصُورٌ عَلَى هٰذِهِ ٱلْحُدُودِ.

Confinement, *n.* Imprisonment, تَقْيِيد ـ إِحْتِبَاس ـ حَبْس. Restraint, إِمْتِنَاع ـ تَضْيِيق ـ ضِيق ـ إِقْتِصَار ـ حَبْس. Confinement of the bowels, حُصْر. Parturition, وِلَادَة ـ مَوْلِد. She had a difficult —, أَعْسَرَتْ فِي ٱلْوِلَادَةِ. She had an easy —, أَيْسَرَتْ فِي ٱلْوِلَادَةِ.

Confirm, *v.t.* To render more stable, ثَبَّتَ ـ أَكَّدَ ـ قَرَّرَ ـ وَثَّقَ ـ حَقَّقَ. To strengthen by proofs, شَيَّدَ ـ أَثْبَتَ ـ شَدَّدَ. To ratify, عَقَدَ ـ عَقَّدَ. To — by the imposition of hands, مَنَحَ ـ نِعْمَةَ ٱلتَّثْبِيتِ ـ ثَبَّتَ. To — one in an office, إِسْتَمَرَّ ـ بِ *or* عَلَى *or* فِي. The supremacy was confirmed to him, إِسْتَوْثَقَتْ لَهُ ٱلرِّئَاسَةُ. Nothing has yet been received to — the news, لَمْ يَرِدْ بَعْدُ مَا يُؤَكِّدُ ٱلْخَبَرَ. If it be confirmed no man can annul it, إِنْ ثَبَتَ فَلَيْسَ لِأَحَدٍ أَنْ يُبْطِلَهُ. It was confirmed to us by those who heard it, تَحَقَّقَ لَنَا مِمَّنْ سَمِعُوهُ. To be confirmed, proved, تَوَكَّدَ. To be confirmed, ratified, إِنْعَقَدَ. All the items of information tend to confirm ..., جَمِيعُ ٱلْأَخْبَارِ مُتَّفِقَةٌ عَلَى تَأْكِيدِ.

Confirmable, *a.* قَابِلُ ٱلتَّحْقِيقِ ـ إِقْرَارُهُ مُمْكِنٌ ـ يُثْبَتُ.

Confirmation, *n.* The act of establishing any thing, تَأْكِيد ـ إِثْبَات ـ تَقْرِير ـ تَعْقِيد ـ إِقْرَار; of continuing in an office,

إِبْقَآء — إِقْرار ; of strengthening, — إِسْتِحْكام — تَشْدِيد — تَشْيِيد تَقْوِيَة. Additional proof, تَأْكِيد — إِثْبات — تَحْقِيق. This is a — of what the wazir said, هٰذا مِصْداقٌ عَلَى ما قالَهُ ٱلْوَزِيرُ. The rite of —, رُتْبَةُ ٱلتَّثْبِيتِ. In — of, — فِي صَدْرِ — إِثْباتًا عَلَى تَأْكِيدًا لِ.

Confirmative, *a.* } مُؤَكِّد — مُحَقِّق — مُقَرِّر — مُثَبِّت.
Confirmatory, }

Confiscable, *a.* يُقْبَضُ عَلَيْهِ — مِمَّا يُضْبَطُ — مُسْتَباح.

Confiscate, *v.t.* قَبَضَ لِلْمِيرِي — ضَبَطَ لِلْمِيرِي — إِسْتَباحَ.

Confiscation, *n.* قَبْضٌ لِلْمِيرِي — ضَبْطُ ٱلْأَمْوالِ — إِسْتِباحَة.

Confiture, *n.* مُلَبَّسٌ بِسُكَّرٍ — حَلْوٌ — مُرَبًّى.

Conflagration, *n.* — أَجِيج — إِحْتِراق — حَرِيقَة — ضِرام شِهاب — نار.

Conflict, *v.i.* To contend with, — قاوَمَ — صارَعَ — تَصارَعَ مَعَ تَنافَرَ. To — with, in meaning, ضادَّ — عاكَسَ.

Conflict, *n.* Collision, إِصْطِدام — لَطْمَة — صَدْمَة. A combat between two, مُبارَزَة — بِراز. A battle, — مُحارَبَة — عَرَكَة — وَاقِعَة حَرْب. A contest, مُقاتَلَة — قِتال. A debate, strife, — مُنازَعَة مُباحَثَة — مُعالَجَة — مُجادَلَة. Trouble, struggle, — شِدَّة — قَلَق كَرْب. There is a — in the testimony, الشَّهادَةُ غَيْرُ مُتَّفِقَةٍ.

Conflicting, *a.* غَيْرُ مُتَّفِقٍ — مُغايِر — مُخالِف — مُتَناقِض. Conflicting news, أَخْبارٌ مُتَناقِضَة.

Confluence, *n.* } Junction, as of streams, مَجْمَع pl. مَجامِع — مَصَبٌّ pl. مَصابٌّ — مُلْتَقًى — مُجْتَمَع. A
Conflux, }
crowd, جَمْع — جَمَّة — حَشْر — إِزْدِحام — مُزاحَمَة. A collection, لَمَّة — إِتِّحاد — إِلْتِقَآء — إِجْتِماع.

Confluent, *a.* مُلْتَقٍ.

Confluent, *n.* A stream flowing into another, رافِد pl. رُفَّد. A river with two confluents, نَهْرٌ لَهُ رافِدانِ.

Conform, *v.t.* طابَقَ-مَعَ *or* عَلَى — وَفَّقَ-مَعَ *or* لِ — مَثَّلَ. Be not conformed to this world, لا تَكُونُوا مُشاكِلِينَ لِهٰذا ٱلدَّهْرِ.

Conform, *v.i.* To comply with, — إِتَّفَقَ بِ — إِمْتَثَلَ — وافَقَ عَمِلَ بِمُوجَبِ — تَبِعَ. He conformed himself to his order, إِمْتَثَلَ قَوْلَهُ — إِهْتَدَى بِأَمْرِهِ — إِئْتَمَرَ أَمْرَهُ. He conformed to the creed of the ..., ذَهَبَ مَذْهَبَ آل.

Conformable, *a.* Suitable, like, مُناسِب — مُطابِق — مُوافِق. Compliant, حَلِيم — مُتَلاطِف — مُطاوِع. Consimilar, مُتَشابِهٌ. A thing — to itself, شَيْءٌ مُشابِهٌ ذاتَهُ. Conformable things, مُتَشابِهات. To be — to, like, شاكَلَ — جانَسَ — شابَهَ. To make — to, جَنَّسَ-بِ — وَفَّقَ-بِ.

Conformably, *ad.* — مُوافَقَة — حَسَبَ — بِمُوجَبِ — إِطْباقًا — بِمُقْتَضَى — عَلَى وَجْهِ ٱلْقَصْدِ — تَصْدِيقًا لِ — عَلَى — مُلاءَمَة عَلَى مُوجَبِ. Make it — to this pattern, إِضْرِبْهُ عَلَى طَبْعِ هٰذا.

Conformation, *n.* Form of things, هِيئَة pl. هِيئات — شَكْل — صُورَة — تَرْكِيب — جِبِلّ — تَشْكِيل. Congruity, — مُشابَهَة — إِتِّفاق مُطابَقَة.

Conformist, *n.* A — to the Church of England, تابِعُ كَنِيسَةِ ٱلدَّوْلَةِ ٱلْأَنْكْلِيزِيَّةِ وَمُمْتَثِلٌ قَوانِينَها.

Conformity, *n.* — مُناسَبَة — مُوافَقَة — مُطابَقَة — إِمْتِثال مُضارَعَة — مُلاءَمَة. In — with, بِمُقْتَضَى — بِمُوجَبِ — إِقْتِضاءَ بِ. Following the belief of the ..., التَّمَذْهُبُ بِمَذْهَبِ آل.

Confound, *v.t.* To mix things together, مَزَجَ — خَلَطَ. To jumble, خَبَّصَ — لَخْبَطَ — شَوَّشَ — لَبَّكَ. To surprise, astonish, حَيَّرَ — أَذْهَلَ — خَبَّلَ — بَهَتَ. To disturb, أَزْعَجَ — أَقْلَقَ. To put to shame, خَزَى — خَجَّلَ. To terrify, — أَدْهَشَ — دَهَّشَ هَوَّلَ — رَعَّبَ. To destroy, لاشَى — أَفْنَى — أَتْلَفَ. Not to distinguish between, لا يُفَرِّقُ بَيْنَ — خَلَطَ. To be confounded, perplexed, إِسْتَحارَ — تَحَيَّرَ — بُهِتَ ; through shame, خَجِلَ. To be —, jumbled together, تَلَخْبَطَ — تَلَبَّكَ — إِلْتَبَكَ. To be —, distracted, amazed, دَهِشَ — بُهِتَ — تَبَلْبَلَ.

Confounded, *a.* Wicked, abominable, — يُكْرَه — شَنِيع — لَعِين مَلْعُون — كَرِيه. In disorder, مُرْتَبِك. The existing confusion was worse —, إِزْدادَتِ ٱلْأَحْوالُ ٱرْتِباكًا.

Confoundedly, *ad.* بَشاعَة — بِكَراهَةٍ — شَناعَة.

Confraternity, *n.* أُخُوِيَّة — رُفْقَة — جَماعَة.

Confront, *v.t.* To stand face to face, واجَهَ — قابَلَ. To compare, قابَلَ. To — with, قابَلَ-عَلَى — قابَلَ-مَعَ *or* بِ — واجَهَ-مَعَ. To withstand, شاجَرَ — قاوَمَ.

Confrontation, *n.* مُقابَلَة — مُواجَهَة.

Confuse, *v.t.* As in speech, وَعَّرَ — أَعْجَمَ. To perplex, lead astray, تَوَّهَ. To make dubious, أَبْهَمَ. To be confused, perplexed, إِضْطَرَبَ — دَهِشَ — دَجِرَ — تَبَلْبَلَ — تاهَ — تَشَوَّشَ. His mind was confused, إِضْطَرَبَ رَأْيُهُ. To be confused, in speech, تَوَعَّرَ. *See also to* Confound, *v.t. passim.*

Confused, *a.* *See* Dubious, *a.*

Confusedly, *ad.* بِغَيْرِ نِظامٍ — خَلْطًا — إِلْتِباكًا وَٱرْتِباكًا. Tumultuously, هَوْشًا — شَذَرَ مَذَرَ — بِٱضْطِرابٍ — بِٱرْتِجاجٍ — إِضْطِرابًا وَبَوْشًا.

Confusedness *n.* } A medley, — وَشْوَشَة — شَواش — إِرْتِباك
Confusion, } — خَلَل — إِشْكالٌ وَٱلْتِباسٌ — بَلْبَلَة — إِخْلاط

— خَبَال . Embarrassment of mind, هَمْزَجَة — رُجْعَة — إِلْتِبَاك . Astonishment, إِضْطِرَاب — تَوَه — تَحَيُّر — حَيْرَة — خَبْلَة — دَجَر . Dubiousness, غِمَّة — شُبْهَة — رُعْب — حَيْرَة — دَهَش . The being put to shame, خَجَل — خِزْي . Destruction, إِبَادَة — هَلَاك — هَدْم — تَلَاشٍ . Tumult, شَغَب . A — of voices, رَجَّة . In a state of utter —, مُكَدَّرُ ٱلْبَالِ وَمُضْطَرِبُ ٱلْحَالِ . To throw into —, disorder, خَلَطَ — بَلْبَلَ — شَوَّشَ — لَبَّكَ . To be thrown into —, إِرْتَبَكَ — إِخْتَلَّ — تَشَوَّشَ . They were in a state of —, تَشَاوَشُوا . Where there is strife there is —, حَيْثُ ٱلْخِصَامُ فَهُنَاكَ ٱلْإِخْتِلَالُ . In —, فِي حَيْرَةٍ وَبَلْبَالٍ .

Confutable, *a.* يُرَدُّ عَلَيْهِ — مُحْتَجٌّ — قَابِلُ ٱلْإِنْتِقَاضِ — يَنْتَقِضُ .

Confutation, *n.* مُحَاجَّة — رَدٌّ عَلَى — إِنْتِقَاض — نَقْض .

Confute, *v.t.* غَلَّطَ — خَطَّأَ — رَدَّ عَلَى [2] — نَاقَضَ . He confuted him with an argument, دَفَعَهُ بِحُجَّةٍ .

Congé, *n.* A bow, سَلَام — تَسْلِيم . Leave, إِجَازَة — رُخْصَة . A farewell, وَدَاع . To take one's —, إِسْتَوْدَعَ — تَرَخَّصَ . To give —, وَدَّعَ — رَخَّصَ . A — d'élire, رُخْصَةٌ بِٱنْتِخَابِ أُسْقُفٍ .

Congeal, *v.t.* جَمَّدَ — قَرَّسَ — أَقْرَسَ — جَلَّدَ .

Congeal, *v.i.* تَقَرَّسَ — تَجَلَّدَ — جَمَدَ [2] — عَقَدَ [2] — قَرِسَ [2] . The water congealed, قَامَ ٱلْمَآءُ [2] .

Congealable, *a.* تَجْلِيدُهُ مُمْكِنٌ — يَنْعَقِدُ — يَتَجَلَّدُ .

Congealment, *n.*
Congelation, } تَجْلِيد — جُمُود — تَجْمِيد .

Congener, *n.*
Congeneric, *a.* } مُتَجَانِس — مِنْ جِنْسٍ وَاحِدٍ — جَنِيس .

Congenial, *a.* مُوَافِق — مِنْ طَبْعٍ وَاحِدٍ — مِنْ جِنْسٍ وَاحِدٍ — مُجَانِس — مُوَافِق — طَبْعًا . To be —, جَانَسَ . To make — with, جَنَّسَ بِ . *See also* Genial, *a.*

Congeniality, *n.*
Congenialness, } مُوَافَقَةٌ فِي ٱلطَّبْعِ — مُوَافَقَة — مُجَانَسَة — مُشَاكَلَة .

Congenital, *a.*
Congenite, } Equal in age, سَنِينَة — سَنِين . Natural, طَبِيعِيٌّ — خِلْقِيٌّ .

Congeries, *n.* جَمْع — تَرَاكُم — كُوْمَة .

Congest, *v.t.* جَمَّعَ — كَوَّمَ .

Congestion, *n.* تَرَاكُمُ أَخْلَاطٍ — نُزْل .

Conglobate, *v.t.* كَبَّبَ — كَوَّبَ .

Conglobe, *v.i.* تَكَبَّبَ — تَكَوَّبَ .

Conglobate, *a.*
Conglomerate, } مُجَمَّع — مُكَوَّب — مُكَبَّب .

Conglomerate, *n.* حَجَرٌ مُتَرَكِّبٌ .

Conglutinate, *v.t.* To glue, لَصَّقَ — لَزَّقَ . To unite, جَمَّعَ — جَمَعَ [2] — لَاحَمَ بِ . To be conglutinated, healed, إِلْتَحَمَ .

Conglutination, *n.* Of wounds, إِلْتِحَامُ ٱلْجُرْحِ .

Congou, *n.* Tea, نَوْعٌ مِنَ ٱلشَّايِ .

Congratulate, *v.t.* فَارَحَ — بَارَكَ — هَنَّأَ — هَنَأَ بِ [2] . To — one's self, فَرِحَ بِ [2] — سُرَّ بِ . I congratulated him on his safety, هَنَّأْتُهُ بِسَلَامَتِهِ . He congratulated him on his accession to the throne, هَنَّأَهُ بِجُلُوسِهِ عَلَى كُرْسِيِّ ٱلْمَمْلَكَةِ .

Congratulation, *n.* تَهْنِئَة — هَنَآء [2] . A form of salutation, سَلَام — تَحِيَّة . A — on the new year, تَبْرِيكٌ بِٱلْعَامِ . To convey his congratulations to ..., لِإِبْلَاغِ ٱلتَّهَانِي مِنْ طَرَفِهِ إِلَى . To convey the formal congratulations to ..., لِإِبْلَاغِ مَرَاسِمِ ٱلتَّهْنِئَةِ إِلَى .

Congratulatory, *a.* مُهَنِّئٌ . A — letter, رِسَالَةُ — تَهْنِئَةٍ — تَهْنِئَة .

Congregate, *v.t.* حَشَرَ [2] — أَحْضَرَ [2] — أَخْضَرَ — كَوَّمَ — لَمَّ [2] — أَمَرَ [2] — حَشَدَ [2] — جَمَّعَ — جَمَعَ [2] — بِٱلْإِجْتِمَاعِ .

Congregate, *v.i.* إِلْتَمَّ — تَقَصَّفَ — تَكَوَّمَ — تَرَاكَمَ — تَجَمَّعَ — إِجْتَمَعَ .

Congregation, *n.* An assembly, إِجْتِمَاع — مَحْضَر — جُمْلَة — مَجْلِس — مَحْفَل . The act of congregating, جَمْع — حَشْر . A religious body, sect, مَذْهَب *pl.* مَذَاهِب — فِرْقَة *pl.* تَلَامِيم — مِلَّة *pl.* مِلَل — طَرِيقَة — فِرَق . The day of —, the Day of Judgment, يَوْمُ ٱلْحَشْرِ .

Congregational, *a.* شَعْبِيٌّ — عُمُومِيٌّ — جَمْعِيٌّ .

Congregationalist, *n.* مِنْ أَهْلِ طَائِفَةٍ مِنَ ٱلنَّصَارَى تَدَّعِي بِأَنَّ لِكُلِّ جَمَاعَةٍ تَسَلُّطًا مُطْلَقًا فِي تَدْبِيرِ أُمُورِهَا ٱلرُّوحِيَّةِ .

Congress, *n.* A meeting of the representatives of sovereigns, مَجْمَعُ وُكَلَاءِ ٱلْمُلُوكِ وَٱلْحُكَّامِ . The — of the United States, دِيوَانُ نُوَّابِ جَمَاهِيرِ أَمِيرِيكَا ٱلشَّمَالِيَّةِ ٱلْمُتَّحِدَةِ . Congress, a meeting for discussion, مُؤْتَمَر . A — of war, *i.e.* to deliberate on the usages of war, مُؤْتَمَرُ ٱلْحَرْبِ . A — to be convened next month, مُؤْتَمَرٌ يَنْعَقِدُ ٱلشَّهْرَ ٱلْقَادِمَ .

Congruence,
Congruency, *n.*
Congruity, } لِيَاقَة — مُوَافَقَة — مُطَابَقَة — مُنَاسَبَة — مُجَانَسَة — مُشَابَهَة .

Congruent, *a.*
Congruous, } مُجَانِس — مُنَاسِب — مُطَابِق — مُوَافِق — نَظِير — مُتَشَابِه .

Congruously, *ad.* مُوَافَقَةً — كَٱلْوَاجِبِ — مُنَاسَبَةً .

Conic, *a.* } فِي شَكْلِ مَخْرُوطَةٍ ـ مَخْرُوطِيٌّ . Conic sections,
Conical, } قُطُوعٌ مَخْرُوطَةٌ . The science of — sections, عِلْمُ ٱلْمَخْرُوطَاتِ .

Conically, *ad.* فِي شَكْلِ جَوْزِ ٱلصَّنَوْبَرِ ـ فِي شَكْلٍ مَخْرُوطِيٍّ .

Coniferous, *a.* صَنَوْبَرِيٌّ ـ حَامِلُ ثَمَرٍ فِي شَكْلِ جَوْزِ ٱلصَّنَوْبَرِ .

Coniform, *a.* فِي شَكْلِ جَوْزِ ٱلصَّنَوْبَرِ .

Conjecturable, *ad.* يُتَخَمَّنُ ـ تَخْمِينُهُ مُمْكِنٌ ـ مِمَّا يُتَوَهَّمُ .

Conjectural, *a.* تَخْمِينِيٌّ ـ قِيَاسِيٌّ ـ حَدْسِيٌّ ـ وَهْمِيٌّ .

Conjecturally, *ad.* تَخْمِينًا ـ بِٱلْفَرْضِيَّةِ ـ بِٱلْقِيَاسِ ـ بِٱلْحَدْسِ .

Conjecture, *n.* ظَنٌّ ـ تَخْمِينٌ ـ خَمْنٌ ـ أَوْهَامٌ *pl.* وَهْمٌ ـ حَدْسٌ ـ قِيَاسٌ ـ تَصَوُّرٌ . If my — is correct, إِنْ صَدَقَنِي حَزْرِي . Most conjectures are false, أَكْثَرُ ٱلظُّنُونِ مُيُونٌ . The — of a wise man is more to be relied on than the assurance of a fool, ظَنُّ ٱلْعَاقِلِ خَيْرٌ مِنْ يَقِينِ ٱلْجَاهِلِ . To compute by —, طَمَسَ ـ ع . Computation by —, طَمَاسَةٌ .

Conjecture, *v.t.* تَوَهَّمَ ـ ظَنَّ [2] ـ أَزْهَدَ ـ تَصَوَّرَ ـ حَدَسَ ع [2] ـ قَطَعَ عَقْلُهُ أَنْ ـ خَمَنَ ع .

Conjecturer, *n.* مُتَوَهِّمٌ .

Conjoin, *v.t.* To unite to, أَضَافَ ـ إِلَى ـ أَلْزَقَ ـ بِ ـ قَرَنَ ـ بِ ع ـ جَمَعَ ع ـ لَاحَمَ ـ أَلَّفَ ـ يَصِلُ *aor.* وَصَلَ ـ بِ [2] ـ ضَمَّ ـ إِلَى . To associate, صَاحَبَ ـ ضَمَّ [2] ـ إِلَى ـ أَشْرَكَ . To — in marriage, زَوَّجَ .

Conjoin, *v.i.* إِلْتَحَمَ ـ إِقْتَرَنَ بِ ـ إِنْضَافَ إِلَى ـ إِنْضَمَّ إِلَى ـ إِتَّحَدَ ـ إِتَّفَقَ ـ إِتَّصَلَ .

Conjointly, *ad.* مَعًا ـ إِجْتِمَاعًا ـ جَمْعًا ـ جُمْلَةً ـ إِتِّصَالًا ـ سَوَآءً .

Conjugal, *a.* تَزْوِيجِيٌّ ـ زِيجِيٌّ . To violate the — vow, خَانَ [2] عَهْدَ ٱلزِّيجَةِ .

Conjugally, *ad.* بِمُوجَبِ ٱلزِّيجَةِ .

Conjugate, *v.t.* To — verbs, ذَكَرَ [2] تَصْرِيفَ ـ صَرَّفَ ٱلْفِعْلَ ٱلْفِعْلِ .

Conjugation, *n.* The act of uniting, جَمْعٌ ـ ضَمَامَةٌ ـ تَأْلِيفٌ . An assemblage, إِقْتِرَانٌ ـ إِنْضِمَامُ جَمَاعَةٍ . The form of inflecting verbs, تَصْرِيفُ ٱلْفِعْلِ .

Conjunct, *a.* مُجْتَمِعٌ ـ مُلْتَحِمٌ ـ مَقْرُونٌ ـ مُقْتَرِنٌ ـ مُتَّصِلٌ .

Conjunction, *n.* Union, إِلْتِزَاقٌ ـ ضَمٌّ ـ إِلْتِحَامٌ ـ إِقْتِرَانٌ ـ تَزَوُّجٌ ـ إِتِّحَادٌ . The part of speech, حَرْفُ عَطْفٍ ـ مَوْصُولٌ ـ حَرْفِيٌّ . Conjunction, as of the planets, especially a happy —, إِجْتِمَاعٌ ـ قِرَانٌ . The conjunctions of the planets on which astrologers say the fate of men depends, ٱلْقِرَانَاتُ . To find out the — of the planets by..., إِسْتَخْرَجَ ٱلْإِجْتِمَاعَاتِ بِ .

Conjunctive, *a.* مُتَّصِلٌ ـ مَوْصُولٌ . The — mood, ٱلْفِعْلُ ٱلْمَجْزُومُ . A — particle, مَوْصُولٌ حَرْفِيٌّ . A — noun, مَوْصُولٌ إِسْمِيٌّ . A — preposition, قَضِيَّةٌ مُتَّصِلَةٌ ـ صِلَةٌ .

Conjunctively, *ad.* *See* Conjointly, *ad.*

Conjuncture, *n.* A joining together, تَلْحِيمٌ ـ تَوْصِيلٌ . An occasion, وَقْتٌ ـ نَوْبَةٌ ـ مَحَلٌّ ـ فُرْصَةٌ ـ خَطْرَةٌ ـ حَالٌ . At that —, عِنْدَ ذَلِكَ . A critical —, حَالٌ خَطِرٌ .

Conjuration, *n.* Incantation, تَسْحِيرٌ ـ سِحْرٌ ـ عَزِيمَةٌ ـ تَعْزِيمٌ . The summoning in a solemn manner, مُنَاشَدَةٌ ـ قَسَامَةٌ .

Conjure, *v.t.* To call upon to swear, إِسْتَحْلَفَ . To — in the name of God, نَاشَدَهُ ٱللّٰهَ ـ أَقْسَمَ عَلَى ـ بِٱللّٰهِ . To entreat earnestly, إِبْتَهَلَ إِلَى ـ تَشَفَّعَ بِ *or* لِ ـ تَضَرَّعَ إِلَى ـ عَزَمَ عَلَى ع . He conjured the man, عَزَمَ عَلَى ٱلرَّجُلِ ع .

Conjure, *v.i.* To practice enchantments, إِسْتَعْمَلَ ـ عَزَمَ ٱلرَّاقِي ع ـ أَجْرَى ٱلرُّقْيَةَ ـ ٱلسِّحْرَ .

Conjurement, *n.* Earnest solicitation, إِبْتِهَالٌ ـ تَضَرُّعٌ .

Conjurer, *n.* سَحَّارٌ ـ فَتَّانٌ ـ رَاقٍ ـ سَاحِرٌ .

Connate, *a.* مَوْلُودٌ فِي زَمَانٍ وَاحِدٍ ـ صِنْوٌ .

Connatural, *a.* مِنْ ذَاتِ طَبْعٍ ـ طَبِيعِيٌّ ـ غَرِيزِيٌّ .

Connect, *v.t.* To join with, وَصَلَ ـ بِ ـ أَوْصَلَ ـ بِ ـ قَرَنَ ـ بِ ع ـ جَمَعَ ـ رَبَطَ ع [2] . To unite, as with a cement, *etc.*, لَحَمَ [2] ـ أَلْزَقَ . To bind, عَقَدَ ع ـ رَبَطَ [2] ع ـ شَدَّ [2] ع . To mingle, مَزَجَ ع ـ خَلَطَ ع . Connected with him, مُرْتَبِطٌ بِهِ .

Connect, *v.i.* إِرْتَبَطَ ـ إِتَّصَلَ ـ إِلْتَحَقَ .

Connectedly, *ad.* مَعًا ـ جُمْلَةً ـ إِتِّفَاقًا ـ عَلَى ٱلْإِتِّصَالِ ـ سَوَآءً ـ بِٱتِّفَاقٍ .

Connection, *n.* Union, عَطْفٌ ـ إِتِّحَادٌ ـ إِتِّصَالٌ ـ وَاشِجَةٌ ـ وُصْلَةٌ ـ عُلْقَةٌ ـ رَابِطَةٌ ـ سِلْسِلَةٌ ـ إِرْتِبَاطٌ ـ عَقْدٌ . A link, bond, مُنَاسَبَةٌ ـ إِقْتِرَانٌ ـ مُقَارَنَةٌ . Just relation, عَلَاقَةٌ . Attachment, أُلْفَةٌ ـ عِشْرَةٌ ـ صُحْبَةٌ . Relationship, نِسْبَةٌ ـ قَرَابَةٌ . A relation, نَسِيبٌ ـ قَرِيبٌ *pl.* أَقْرِبَآءُ [*] . Partnership, مُشَارَكَةٌ ـ إِشْتِرَاكٌ .

Connective, *a.* مُسَلْسِلٌ ـ رَابِطٌ ـ مُوَصِّلٌ .

Connective, *n.* عَلَاقَةٌ ـ وُصْلَةٌ ـ عُلْقَةٌ ـ رَابِطَةٌ .

Connexion, *n.* *See* Connection, *n.*

Connivance, *n.* تَغْمِيضٌ ـ مُمَاشَاةٌ ـ مُحَابَاةٌ ـ إِغْضَآءٌ عَنْ ـ تَجَاهُلٌ ـ مُوَالَسَةٌ .

Connive, *v.i.* To — at, وَالَسَ بِ ـ أَبْهَمَ ـ حَابَى ـ أَغْضَى عَنْ ـ غَمَّضَ عَنْ ـ أَغْمَضَ عَنْ ـ إِغْتَمَضَ عَنْ .

Connoisseur, *n.* مَاهِرٌ ـ أَهْلُ خِبْرَةٍ ـ خَبِيرٌ بِ ـ عَارِفٌ بِ .

Connubial, *a.* نِكَاحِيٌّ ـ زِيجِيٌّ .

Conoidal, *a.* شَبِيهُ ٱلْمَخْرُوطِ.

Conquer, *v.t.* To overcome, إِنْتَصَرَ ـ ظَفِرَ عَلَى ـ أَنْجَحَ ب ـ أَفْلَجَ عَلَى ـ غَلَبَ عَلَى ـ غَلَبَ ـ عَلَى. To take, as a town, فَتَحَ ـ سَخَّرَ ـ إِسْتَوْلَى عَلَى ـ طَوَّعَ ـ أَخْضَعَ ـ قَهَرَ. To subdue, كَسَرَ ـ تَغَلَّبَ عَلَى ـ ضَبَطَ ـ قَمَعَ. To — one's passions, قَمَعَ نَفْسَهُ ـ قَهَرَ شَهَوَاتِهِ. To — one's anger, كَظَمَ ٱلْغَضَبَ.

Conquerable, *a.* ٱلظَّفَرُ بِهِ مُمْكِنٌ ـ يُغْلَبُ. Tameable, يُطَبَّعُ.

Conqueror, *n.* قَاهِرٌ ـ مُظَفَّرٌ ـ مَنْصُورٌ ـ غَالِبٌ. A frequent —, أَبُو ٱلْفُتُوحَاتِ ـ فَاتِحُ ٱلْفُتُوحِ ـ فَتَّاحٌ. Who is the — ? لِمَنِ ٱلْفَلْجُ.

Conquest, *n.* The act of conquering, نَصْرٌ ـ فَتْحٌ ـ ظَفَرٌ ـ غَلَبَةٌ ـ إِنْتِصَارٌ. An acquisition by victory, (عَلَيْهِ *or*) مُلْكٌ ـ مَظْفُورٌ بِهِ. Subjection, the act of, ضَبْطٌ ـ قَمْعٌ ـ تَسْخِيرٌ.

Consanguineous, *a.* مُشْتَرِكُ ٱلنَّسَبِ ـ مِنْ دَمٍ وَاحِدٍ ـ قَرِيبٌ.

Consanguinity, *n.* إِشْتِرَاكُ ٱلنَّسَبِ ـ دَنَاوَةٌ ـ مُنَاسَبَةٌ ـ قَرَابَةٌ.

Conscience, *n.* ضَمِيرٌ *pl.* ضَمَائِرُ ـ قَلْبٌ ـ نِيَّةٌ ـ سَرِيرَةٌ ـ ذِمَّةٌ ـ طَوِيَّةٌ. Knowledge, as of one's own actions, عِلْمٌ ـ مَعْرِفَةٌ ـ نِيَّةٌ صَالِحَةٌ ـ إِخْلَاصُ ٱلنِّيَّةِ ـ حِسٌّ. A good —, نِيَّةٌ ـ بَصِيرَةٌ ـ ذِمَّةٌ مُعَابَةٌ ـ نِيَّةٌ رَدِيَّةٌ. An evil —, صَفَاءُ ٱلضَّمِيرِ ـ ضَمِيرٌ صَافٍ. A troubled —, ذِمَّةٌ مُتَقَلْقِلَةٌ. Remorse of —, نَخْزُ ٱلضَّمِيرِ ـ أَكْلُ ٱلسَّرِيرَةِ ـ لَسْعُ ٱلذِّمَّةِ. The public —, أَرَآءُ ٱلْعَامَّةِ. Examination of the —, فَحْصُ ٱلضَّمِيرِ. A scruple, تَشَكُّكٌ ـ شَكٌّ. I have lived in all good — unto this day, تَصَرَّفْتُ بِكُلِّ نِيَّةٍ صَالِحَةٍ إِلَى هٰذَا ٱلْيَوْمِ. They were convicted by their own —, تُبَكِّتُهُمْ ضَمَائِرُهُمْ. A — void of offence, نِيَّةٌ خَالِيَةٌ مِنْ عَثْرَةٍ. Their consciences bearing them witness, نِيَّاتُهُمْ شَاهِدَةٌ. For conscience' sake, مِنْ أَجْلِ ٱلنِّيَّةِ. According to the dictates of his own —, حَسْبَ مَا يُلْهِمُهُ ضَمِيرُهُ. The duties binding on our —, ٱلْفُرُوضُ ٱلْوَاجِبَةُ عَلَى ذِمَّتِنَا. Liberty of —, إِبَاحَةُ ٱلنِّيَّةِ ـ حُرِّيَّةُ ٱلنِّيَّةِ. Liberty of —, of worship, حُرِّيَّةُ ٱلْمَذَاهِبِ ـ حُرِّيَّةٌ دِينِيَّةٌ.

Conscientious, *a.* مُقَرِّطٌ ـ مُدَقِّقٌ ـ أَنْصَفُ ـ صَاحِبُ ذِمَّةٍ ـ عَادِلٌ.

Conscientiously, *ad.* بِصَفَاءِ ٱلنِّيَّةِ ـ بِإِنْصَافٍ ـ بِتَدْقِيقٍ ـ بِذِمَّةٍ.

Conscientiousness, *n.* دِقَّةٌ ـ دِيَانَةٌ ـ إِسْتِقَامَةٌ ـ إِنْصَافٌ ـ تَدْقِيقٌ ـ تَقْيِيدٌ ـ عَدْلٌ.

Conscionable, *a.* حَقٌّ ـ عَادِلٌ ـ مُنْصِفٌ ـ مَعْقُولٌ.

Conscionably, *ad.* حَقًّا ـ بِعَدَالَةٍ ـ بِإِنْصَافٍ.

Conscious, *a.* وَاقِفٌ عَلَى ـ خَبِيرٌ ب ـ عَالِمٌ ب ـ مُسْتَبْصِرٌ ـ دَارٍ. To be — of, عَرِفَ ب ـ أَحَسَّ ب ـ حَسَّ ب ـ دَرَى ب.

Consciously, *ad.* بِمَعْرِفَةٍ ـ عِلْمًا ـ إِسْتِبْصَارًا.

Consciousness, *n.* إِطِّلَاعٌ عَلَى ـ عِلْمٌ ـ حِسٌّ ـ إِسْتِبْصَارٌ ـ وُقُوفٌ عَلَى.

Conscript, *n.* A soldier by lot, مَجْبُورٌ عَلَى ٱلْعَسْكَرِيَّةِ بِٱلْقُرْعَةِ. One forced into the service, سُخْرَةٌ ـ سُخْرِيٌّ *coll.* سُخْرَةٌ. These are the Sultan's conscripts, هٰؤُلَاءِ سُخْرَةٌ لِلسُّلْطَانِ.

Conscription, *n.* As of soldiers by lot, جَمْعُ ٱلْعَسَاكِرِ بِٱلْقُرْعَةِ ـ فَرْضُ ٱلْخِدْمَةِ ٱلْعَسْكَرِيَّةِ. Forced services, تَسْخِيرٌ. To levy by forced —, سَخَّرَ.

Consecrate, *v.t.* To devote to some special purpose, نَذَرَ ـ ل ـ قَدَّمَ ـ ل ـ خَصَّصَ ـ ل ـ أَوْقَفَ ـ ل. To make sacred, قَدَّسَ ـ كَرَّسَ. To — the elements in the Holy Communion, قَدَّسَ ٱلْقُرْبَانَ. To — a church, كَرَّسَ كَنِيسَةً. To —, to ordain, قَلَّدَ ـ رَسَمَ. To —, to anoint, مَسَحَ. To —, or devote one's self to, قَدَّمَ نَفْسَهُ ل. To — one's self to God, تَعَبَّدَ لِلّٰهِ.

Consecrate, *a.* } Made sacred, مُكَرَّسٌ ـ مُقَدَّسٌ. Devoted, set
Consecrated, } apart, مُخَصَّصٌ ـ مَوْقُوفٌ ـ مَنْذُورٌ. Devout, مُتَنَسِّكٌ. The — elements, ٱلْقُرْبَانُ ٱلْمُقَدَّسُ.

Consecration, *n.* As of a church, تَكْرِيسٌ; as of a priest, رَسْمٌ ـ إِرْتِسَامٌ ـ رِسَامَةٌ; of the eucharistic elements, تَقْدِيسُ ٱلْقُرْبَانِ.

Consecrator, *n.* مُكَرِّسٌ ـ رَاسِمٌ.

Consecutive, *a.* مُتَوَاتِرٌ ـ مُتَوَالٍ ـ مُتَتَابِعٌ ـ مُتَّصِلٌ ـ حَاشِكٌ ـ مُتَرَادِفٌ ـ مُتَعَاقِبٌ ـ مُتَلَاحِقٌ ـ مُتَدَارِكٌ. To be —, تَرَادَفَ ـ تَتَابَعَ ـ تَوَالَى ـ تَدَارَكَ. The language was —, إِطَّرَدَ ٱلْكَلَامُ.

Consecutively, *ad.* عَلَى ـ بِتَدَارُكٍ ـ بِتَوَالٍ ـ بِتَتَالٍ ـ بِٱطِّرَادٍ ـ عَلَى ٱلْإِتِّصَالِ ـ ٱلدَّوَامِ. The events followed —, تَتَالَتِ ٱلْأُمُورُ.

Consent, *n.* The act of consenting, رِضَآءٌ ـ رِضْوَانٌ ـ قُبُولٌ ـ إِجَابَةٌ. Concord, *n.* مُوَافَقَةٌ ـ إِتِّفَاقٌ ـ وِفَاقٌ. Permission, إِجَازَةٌ. To obtain the — of another to, أَقْبَلَ ـ عَلَى. With the — of both parties, بِرِضَاءِ ٱلطَّرَفَيْنِ. Mutual —, تَرَاضٍ.

Consent, *v.i.* أَجَابَ إِلَى ـ إِرْتَضَى ـ رَضِيَ عَنْ ـ رَضِيَ ب ـ قَبِلَ. I —, قَبِلْتُ ـ رَضِيتُ. To —, as to the proposal of another, أَجَابَ ـ إِلَى ـ وَافَقَ ـ عَلَى ـ أَطْبَقَ عَلَى ـ طَاوَعَ ـ أَطَاعَ ـ قَبِلَ سُؤَالَهُ ـ مَا طَلَبَ.

Consentaneous, *a.* مُتَوَافِقٌ ـ لَائِقٌ ب ـ مُوَافِقٌ ل ـ مُنَاسِبٌ ب.

Consentaneously, *ad.* بِٱتِّفَاقٍ ـ إِتِّفَاقًا ـ مُنَاسَبَةً ـ مُوَافَقَةً.

Consentaneousness, *n.* تَوَافُقٌ ـ مُوَافَقَةٌ.

Consentient, *a.* مُوَافِقٌ ـ مُتَّفِقٌ.

Consequence, *n.* Conclusion of a proposition, نَتِيجَةٌ *pl.* نَتَائِجُ ـ

حاصل الكلام. Effect of a cause, عُقَيْب — عَاقِبَة pl. عَوَاقِب — مُلحَقَة — إطْبَاع — أَثَر pl. آثار — ثَمَرَة. Influence, أَثَر — تأثِير — حُكْم. Importance, ثِقَل — عِظَم — عَظَامَة — ضَرُورَة. An end, نِهَايَة — إنجام — آخِرَة. A man of —, رَجُل — صَاحِب مَقَام — مُعْتَبَر. An affair of —, أَمْرٌ مُهِمٌّ — أَمْرٌ ضَرُورِيٌّ — رَجُل عَظِيمٌ — مُهِمَّة. An affair of little —, تَفَاهَة — أَمْرٌ وَجِيزٌ — أَمْرٌ يَسِيرٌ — أَمْرٌ زَهِيدٌ. Serious consequences, نَتَائِج وَخِيمَة. Eventual consequences, نَتَائِج عَرَضِيَّة. What is the — thereof? ما عَاقِبَة ذَلِكَ. He who is regardless of consequences will not have a friend in the world, مَنْ لَمْ يَحْسِبِ ٱلعَوَاقِبَ ما لَهُ فِي ٱلدَّهْرِ صَاحِبٌ. To make one's self of —, تَعَظَّمَ. What is the — of all that? ما عَاقِبَةُ هٰذَا كُلِّهِ. It is of no —, لا عِبْرَةَ بِهِ — لا طَائِلَ تَحْتَهُ. To follow as a —, أَعْقَبَ. To look to the — of anything, تَعَقَّبَ.

Consequent, *a.* مُتَتَالٍ — مُتَعَاقِب — مُتَتَابِع — مُنْتَج — تَالٍ — مُلْحَق.

Consequent, *n.* *See* Consequence, *n.*

Consequential, *a.* Assuming importance, مُتَكَبِّر — مُتَعَظِّم — مُنْتَفِخ. *See also* Consequent, *a.*

Consequentially, *ad.* With assumed importance, تَكَبُّرًا — تَعَظُّمًا — بِٱنْتِفَاخٍ. *See also* Consequently, *ad.*

Consequently, *ad.* By consequence, بِٱلتَّبَعِيَّةِ — عَاقِبَةً — بِتَتَالٍ — مُلَازَمَةً. Therefore, لِذٰلِكَ — بِنَاءً عَلَى ذٰلِكَ — فَإِذًا — وَمِنْ ثَمَّ — عَلَى ذٰلِكَ.

Conservable, *a.* مِمَّا يُصَانُ.

Conservation, *n.* وِقَايَة — صِيَانَة — حِرَاسَة — حِفْظ — صَوْن.

Conservatism, *n.* الإجْتِهَادُ فِي حِفْظِ ٱلأُصُولِ وَٱلقَوَانِينِ ٱلعَتِيقَةِ.

Conservative, *n.* مُجْتَهِدٌ فِي حِفْظِ ٱلأُصُولِ وَٱلقَوَانِينِ ٱلعَتِيقَةِ.

Conservator, *n.* نَاظِر — حَامٍ — مُحَافِظ — حَافِظ.

Conservatory, *n.* A place for preserving things, صُوَان — صِوَان — مَخْزَن. A — of plants, صِوَانُ ٱلنَّبَاتَاتِ.

Conserve, *n.* Sweetmeat, رِيْصَال — مُرَبَّى.

Conserve, *v.t.* As of fruits, رَبَّى — عَمِلَ مُرَبًّا — بِسُكَّرٍ — لَبَّسَ. To guard, keep, حَفِظَ — ٢ ٱسْتَحْفَظَ عَلَى — تَقَيَّدَ فِي — حَرَسَ ٢.

Consider, *v.t.* To examine, أَضْمَرَ عَلَى — هَمَّ بِ ٢ — طَالَعَ — نَظَرَ فِي ٢ — أَطْلَعَ عَلَى — تَأَمَّلَ — إعْتَبَرَ — تَبَصَّرَ. To think upon, إسْتَشْعَرَ — تَعَقَّلَ — تَفَرَّسَ — تَأَمَّلَ — حَسِبَ ٢. To have regard to, إعْتَبَرَ — نَظَرَ إلَى ٢. To deem, جَعَلَ — عَدَّ ٢ — إعْتَبَرَ — أَنْزَلَ مَنْزِلَةَ — أَقَامَ مَقَامَ — حَسِبَ ٢. To requite, قَابَلَ — كَافَى — جَازَى — عَاقَبَ. I — the boy to be superior to his father, عِنْدِي ٱلوَلَدُ أَفْضَلُ مِنْ أَبِيهِ. He considered it more expedient for him, تَفَكَّرَ فِي أَنَّهُ أَوْفَقُ لَهُ. Blessed is he who considers the poor, طُوبَى لِمَنْ يُرَاعِي ٱلمَسَاكِينَ. To — the result, تَعَقَّبَ.

Consider, *v.i.* To ponder, عَقَلَ ٢ — تَأَمَّلَ — إفْتَكَرَ — تَشَاوَرَ.

Considerable, *a.* Worthy of consideration, مُعْتَبَر — وَاجِبُ ٱلإعْتِبَارِ. Important, مُهِمٌّ. More than little, عَظِيم — جَسِيم — كَبِير — وَافِر — كَثِير. Many, A — sum, مَبْلَغٌ عَظِيمٌ.

Considerableness, *n.* Greatness, عَظَامَة — عِظَم — جَسَامَة; of weight, ثِقَل; of numbers, وَفْرَة — كَثْرَة; of price, ثَمَن. Importance, مُهِمَّة.

Considerably, *ad.* كَثِيرًا — بِزِيَادَةٍ — بِكَثْرَةٍ. He was — more polite to-day than he was yesterday, كَانَ ٱليَوْمَ ذَا أَدَبٍ أَكْثَرَ جِدًّا مِمَّا كَانَ بِٱلأَمْسِ.

Considerate, *a.* Prudent, نَظُور — رَزِين — مُحْتَرِز — صَاحِب — تَمْيِيز — مُتَفَكِّر — حَرِيص — عَاقِل. Moderate, مُعْتَدِل — مُنْصِف. Having thought for others, مُشْفِق — مُرَاعٍ — إعْتِبَارِيٌّ — صَاحِب — آعْتِبَارٍ — صَاحِبُ حِلْمٍ.

Considerateness, *n.* Prudence, تَفَكُّر — رَزَانَة — إحْتِرَاز — حَرْس. Thought for others, مُرَاعَاة — مُلَاءَمَة — فِكْرٌ فِي — فِكْرٌ لِ — شَفَقَة.

Considerately, *ad.* Coolly, رَزَانَةً — بِعَقْلٍ — بِتَأَمُّلٍ. With thought for others, بِمُرَاعَاةٍ — بِحِلْمٍ — بِشَفَقَةٍ.

Consideration, *n.* Mature thought, إعْتِبَار — مُلَاحَظَة — تَفَرُّس — مُطَالَعَة — إنْتِبَاه — تَبَصُّر — نَظَرٌ فِي — تَفَكُّر. Claim to notice, إعْتِبَار — مَعَزَّة — إحْتِرَام. Compensation, تَعْدِيل — بَدَل — مُكَافَاة — عِوَض. Price, ثَمَن. A motive, سَبَب pl. أَسْبَاب — دَاعِيَة — دَاعٍ — بَاعِث. In — of, with respect to, إعْتِبَارًا لِ — نَظَرًا إلَى. That deserves —, ذٰلِكَ مُسْتَحِقٌّ بِٱلمُلَاحَظَةِ. To act in any matter without —, تَعَسَّفَ فِي ٱلأَمْرِ. The acting without —, إعْتِسَاف.

Considering, *prep.* بِنَاءً عَلَى — نَظَرًا إلَى — كَوْن — لِأَجْلِ.

Consign, *v.t.* To transfer, make over, وَدَعَ *aor.* يَدَعُ — أَوْدَعَ. To appropriate, قَدَّمَ لِ — خَصَّصَ — سَلَّمَ. To intrust to, إسْتَأْمَنَ عَلَى — آمَنَ عَلَى — وَدَّعَ إلَى — فَوَّضَ إلَى. To send to, أَرْسَلَ ٱلبِضَاعَةَ إلَى. To — goods to,

Consignee, *n.* مُرْسَلٌ إلَيْهِ.

Consigner, *n.* مُرْسِلٌ إلَيْهِ.

Consignment, *n.* The act of consigning, تَوْدِيع — وَدْع — تَفْوِيض —

تَسْلِيم. What is consigned, أَمَانَة ـ وَدِيعَة. A — of goods, وَدِيعَة بِضَاعَة.

Consist, *v.i.* To exist, وُجِدَ ـ كَانَ ² *aor.* يُوجَدُ. To continue fixed, تَقَرَّرَ ـ ثَبَتَ ². To be comprised, إِشْتَمَلَ ـ أَشْمَلَ عَلَى تَرَكَّبَ مِن ـ تَضَمَّنَ عَلَى ـ إِحْتَوَى عَلَى ـ عَلَى. To co-exist, وُجِدَ مَعًا. To — or agree with, وَافَقَ ـ نَاسَبَ. The regiment consists of a thousand men, الآلاى يَشْتَمِلُ عَلَى أَلْفِ نَفَرٍ. Courage consists in . . . , الشَّجَاعَةُ هِيَ أَن. This does not — with what you said before, هٰذا لا يُوَافِقُ مَا قُلْتَ سَابِقًا. Man's life does not — in the abundance of his possessions, حَيَاةُ ٱلْإِنْسَانِ لَيْسَتْ بِكَثْرَةِ أَمْوَالِهِ.

Consistence, *n.* } Degree of density, جُمُود ـ قَوَام ـ كَثَافَة
Consistency, } جَمَاد. State with respect to material existence, تَرْكِيب ـ تَقْوِيم ـ ذَات. Form, kind, شَكْل ـ وَصْف ـ نَوْع. Stability, ثَبَات ـ قَرَار ـ مُدَاوَمَة. Congruity, مُنَاسَبَة ـ مُوَافَقَة ـ مُطَابَقَة ـ مُلَاءَمَة. Consistency, as of behaviour, إِسْتِقَامَة. To acquire —, to become established, كَسَبَ ثَبَاتًا ².

Consistent, *a.* Not opposed, مُنَاسِب ـ مُطَابِق ـ مُوَافِق. Firm, مُقَرَّر ـ ثَابِت. Not fluid, جَامِد ـ صُلْب.

Consistently, *ad.* مُطَابَقَةً ـ مُنَاسَبَةً. Agreeably with, بِمُوجَبِ ـ بِمُقْتَضَى ـ بِحَسَبِ ـ حَسَبَ ـ عَلَى مُوجَبِ.

Consistorial, *a.* مُخْتَصّ بِمَجْمَعِ ٱلْأَكْلِيرُوسِ.

Consistory, *n.* An ecclesiastical court, مَجْمَعُ ٱلْأَكْلِيرُوسِ.

Consociate, *n.* رَفِيق ـ شَرِيك *pl.* شُرَكَاء.

Consociate, *v.t.* جَمَعَ بَيْنَ ـ أَشْرَكَ ـ فِي ـ ضَمَّ ـ إِلَى ² ـ قَرَنَ ـ بِ ².

Consociate, *v.i.* إِقْتَرَنَ ـ إِصْطَحَبَ ـ إِشْتَرَكَ ـ إِلْتَمَّ.

Consociation, *n.* تَقْرِين ـ مُرَافَاة ـ رِفَاء.

Consolable, *a.* قَابِلُ ٱلتَّسْلِيَةِ ـ يُسَلَّى ـ يُعَزَّى.

Consolation, *n.* جَبْرَانُ ٱلْخَاطِرِ ـ مُوَاسَاة ـ تَعْزِيَة ـ تَسْلِيَة. Escape from trouble, فَرَج. For we have great joy and — in your prosperity, لِأَنَّ لَنَا فَرَحًا عَظِيمًا وَتَعْزِيَةً فِي نَجَاحِكُمْ.

Consolatory, *a.* مُعَزٍّ ـ بَاعِثٌ عَلَى ٱلتَّسْلِيَةِ ـ يُسَلِّي ـ يُعَزِّي ـ مُسَلٍّ.

Console, *v.t.* أَخَذَ خَاطِرَ ـ وَاسَى ـ عَزَّى ـ أَسْلَى ـ عَن ـ سَلَّى ـ جَبَرَ قَلْبَ ². To be consoled, تَسَلَّى ـ تَعَزَّى ـ تَأَسَّى.

Console, *n.* A pedestal, قَاعِدَة *pl.* قَوَاعِدُ ـ مَقَام.

Consoler, *n.* مُسَلٍّ ـ مُعَزٍّ. A — of the afflicted, مُفَرِّجٌ عَنْ كُلِّ مَحْزُونٍ ـ جَابِرُ ٱلْقُلُوبِ ٱلْمُنْكَسِرَةِ ـ مُفَرِّجُ ٱلْكُرُبَاتِ.

Consolidate, *v.t.* To make firm, compact, حَكَمَ ـ قَرَّرَ ـ جَمَّدَ ² ـ لَحَمَ ـ جَبَرَ ـ لَأَمَ بَيْنَ ² ـ أَحْكَمَ. To bring together, to join, لَأَمَ بَيْنَ. To — a debt, أَمَّنَ دَيْنًا وَنَظَّمَهُ. A consolidated debt, دُيُونٌ مُنْتَظِمَةٌ.

Consolidate, *v.i.* To become hard, جَمَدَ ² ـ تَقَرَّرَ ـ إِسْتَحْكَمَ.

Consolidate, *a.* مُسْتَحْكَم ـ مُحْكَم ـ مُقَرَّر ـ مُتَجَمِّد.

Consolidation, *n.* The act of consolidating, إِقْرَار ـ تَجْمِيد ـ جَبْر ـ جَمْد ـ تَحْكِيم ـ تَقْرِير. The result of consolidating, إِسْتِحْكَام. Union, جَمْعِيَّة ـ إِقْتِرَان ـ جَمْع. Consolidation of the public debt, تَنْظِيمُ ٱلدُّيُونِ ٱلْمِيرِيَّةِ. Consolidation of a floating debt, تَنْظِيمُ ٱلدُّيُونِ ٱلْغَيْرِ مُنْتَظِمَةِ.

Consoling, *a.* *See* Consoler.

Consols, *n.* Consolidated bonds, أَوْرَاقُ ٱلْكُونْسُولِيد ـ كُونْسُولِيد ـ أَسْهَامٌ عُمُومِيَّةٌ. The consolidated debt of a country, الدُّيُونُ ٱلْمِيرِيَّةُ ٱلْمُنْتَظِمَةُ.

Consonance, *n.* Of sounds, أُلْفَةُ أَصْوَاتٍ ـ مُوَافَقَةُ أَصْوَاتٍ ـ نَغَم. Agreement, مُنَاسَبَة ـ إِتِّحَاد ـ إِتِّفَاق ـ مُوَافَقَة.

Consonant, *a.* مُنَاسِب ـ مُطَابِق ـ مُوَافِق.

Consonant, *n.* حَرْف سَالِم ـ حَرْف صَحِيح.

Consonantly, *ad.* بِٱتِّفَاقٍ ـ مُوَافَقَةً ـ مُطَابَقَةً.

Consonous, *a.* مُتَّفِقٌ فِي ٱلْأَصْوَاتِ.

Consort, *n.* A companion, صَاحِب ـ شَرِيك ـ رَفِيق ـ وَصِيلَة ـ مُصَاحِب. A husband or wife, عِرْس *pl.* أَعْرَاس. A wife, حُرْمَة ـ قَرِينَة ـ زَوْجَة ـ صَاحِبَة ـ حَلِيلَة. A husband, زَوْج. Queen Consort, تَاجْدَارْ زَوْجَةُ مَلِكٍ. Prince Consort, تَاجْدَارْ زَوْجُ مَلِكَةٍ.

Consort, *v.t.* To join, جَمَعَ بَيْنَ ـ أَشْرَكَ ². To marry, زَوَّجَ.

Consort, *v.i.* To — with, عَاشَرَ ـ آلَفَ ـ أَلِفَ ² ـ لَصِقَ بِ ² ـ إِتَّحَدَ مَعَ ـ رَافَقَ ـ شَارَكَ ـ أَشْرَكَ. They consorted together, تَعَاشَرُوا. They consorted with my brother, صَاحَبُوا أَخِي.

Conspectus, *n.* إِيجَاز ـ وَجْز.

Conspicuous, *a.* Open to view, مَجْهُورٌ بِهِ ـ مُسْتَبْصَر ـ جَلِيّ ـ مَعْلُوم ـ جَاهِر ـ بَائِن ـ وَاضِح ـ مَرْئِيّ ـ يُرَى ـ ظَاهِر ـ عَيَان. Eminent, مَجِيد ـ شَهِير ـ جَلِيل ـ مَشْهُور. Conspicuous for power and dignity, ذُو قَدْرٍ وَٱحْتِرَامٍ ـ مُمْتَاز; in estimation, مُوَجَّه; in situation, جَاهِر ـ بَارِز. Clear, manifest, جَلِيّ. To be or become —, known, clear, إِتَّضَحَ ـ تَجَلَّى ـ إِجْتَهَرَ ـ جَهَرَ ². To make —, clear, أَوْضَحَ.

Conspicuously, *ad.* Obviously to the sight, بِوُضُوحٍ ـ بَيَانًا ـ عِيَانًا ـ عَلَانِيَةً ـ جَهْرًا ـ جَهْرَةً. Eminently, إِشْتِهَارًا ـ شُهْرَةً ـ بِشُهْرَةٍ.

Conspicuousness, *n.* Exposure to the view, جَهْرَة ـ ظُهُور ـ

بَيَا. Clearness, إِيضَاح – وُضُوح – جَلَآء – جَلِيَّة. Eminence, سُمُ – إِشْتِهَار – شَرَف.

Conspiracy, n. / Conspiration, } A plot, مُعَاهَدَة – مُحَالَفَة – مُرَابَطَة – إِتِّفَاق خَفِيٌّ – مُؤَامَرَةُ أُنَاسٍ بِشَرٍّ. Concurrence, إِتِّفَا – إِتِّحَاد.

Conspirator, n. / Conspirer, } مُؤَامِرٌ بِشَرٍّ – مُتَعَصِّب – مُتَعَاهِد – مُتَوَامِر – مِنَ ٱلْعُصْبَةِ – مُتَّفِقٌ مَعَ غَيْرِهِ عَلَى شَرٍّ.

Conspire, v.t. To unite in some evil design, plot, تَرَابَطَ عَلَى فَسَادٍ مَعَ – عَلَى شَرٍّ – إِتَّفَقَ (or تَعَاهَدَ or تَحَالَفَ or تَعَصَّبَ) مَعَ. To — together, to help towards, سَاعَدَ – عَاوَنَ – وَفَّقَ – عَمِلَ = مَعًا. All things — together for our good, ٱلْأَشْيَآءُ كُلُّهَا تَعْمَلُ مَعًا لِخَيْرِنَا.

Constable, n. ضَابِطٌ مَأْمُورٌ بِحِفْظِ نِظَامِ ٱلْبَلَدِ وَسَلَامَتِهِ pl. ضُبَّاط or ضَبْطِيَّة. High —, مُدِيرُ ٱلضَّبْطِيَّةِ. Lord High —, رَئِيسُ مُدِيرِي ٱلضَّبْطِيَّةِ. A petty —, قَوَّاس – تُفَكْجِي.

Constabulary, n. مَأْمُورِيَّةُ ٱلْقَوَّاسَةِ – جُمْلَةُ ٱلْقَوَّاسَةِ.

Constancy, n. Fixedness, إِسْتِمْرَار – ثَبَات – قَرَار – رُسُوخ – مَتَانَة. Resolution, عِصْمَة – جَلَد – صَبْر – عَزِيمَة – وَقَار – عَزْم – وَثَاقَة. Perseverance, مُدَاوَمَة – عَزْم – حَزْم – عَقْد. Lasting affection, قَرَارٌ فِي ٱلْمَحَبَّةِ – وَفَآء. Constancy and perseverance, ٱلْعَزِيمَةُ وَٱلْمُوَاظَبَةُ.

Constant, a. Firm, unchangeable, ثَابِت – رَاتِب – رَاسِخ – مَتِين – لَا يَتَغَيَّرُ. Resolute, مُدَاوِم – مُسْتَمِرّ – مُسْتَقِرّ. Certain, مُحَقَّق – مُؤَكَّد – مَثْبُوت. Persevering, مُوَاظِبٌ عَلَى – مُدَاوِم. Constant in one's designs, صَاحِبُ عَزْمٍ – صَاحِبُ حَزْمٍ. Patient, صَبِير. Constant in friendship, صَاحِبُ وَفَآءٍ – وَفِيّ – أَمِين – ثَبِيت – قَائِمٌ فِي ٱلْمَحَبَّةِ. To be — in, أَقَامَ. He was — in prayers, أَقَامَ ٱلصَّلَاةَ.

Constantinople, n. قُسْطَنْطِينِيَّة – إِسْتَانْبُول – ٱلْإِسْتَانَة.

Constantinopolitan, a. إِسْتَانْبُولِيّ.

Constantly, ad. Steadily, بِثَبَاتٍ – بِمُدَاوَمَةٍ – عَلَى ٱلدَّوَامِ – بِدُونِ تَغْيِيرٍ. Always, عَلَى ٱلدَّوَامِ – بِلَا ٱنْقِطَاعٍ – دَائِمًا. He — affirmed, ظَلَّ يُؤَكِّدُ 2.

Constellation, n. بُرْج pl. بُرُوج.

Consternation, n. ذَهْلَة – دَهْشَة – حَيْرَة – تَحَيُّر – خَوْف. They were filled with wonder and —, إِمْتَلَأُوا تَعَجُّبًا وَتَحَيُّرًا. He created a —, حَيَّرَ ٱلْأَفْهَامَ وَشَوَّشَ ٱلْأَذْهَانَ.

Constipate, v.t. To crowd, كَنَتَ = – حَصَرَ 2. To stop up, سَدَّ 2. To make costive, قَبَضَ ٱلْبَطْنَ = – حَبَّسَ = (or يَبَّسَ) ٱلْمِعْدَةَ – قَبَضَ ٱلْمِعْدَةَ =. To be constipated, costive, حَصِرَ – إِنْقَبَضَ – تَقَبَّضَ.

Constipation, n. The act of crowding, إِكْنَاب – حَصْر; of thickening, تَكْثِيف; of stopping up, تَسْدِيد. Constipation of the bowels, حَصْر – قَبْض – إِنْقِبَاضُ ٱلْبَطْنِ – إِعْتِقَالُ ٱلْبَطْنِ – يَبْسُ ٱلْبَطْنِ – إِحْتِبَاس.

Constituency, n. The body of electors, مَعْشَرُ ٱلْمُنْتَخِبِينَ. Customers, زَبَائِنُ.

Constituent, a. Elemental, أَصْلِيّ – جَوْهَرِيّ. Of which anything consists, يَدْخُلُ (or دَاخِلٌ) فِي ٱلتَّرْكِيبِ. Having the power of constituting, مُقِيم – مُفَوِّض – مُحْكِم – وَاضِع. A — assembly, مَجْلِسُ تَنْظِيمَاتٍ.

Constituent, n. A part of a thing, جُزْء pl. أَجْزَآء. A radical —, ذَات pl. ذَوَات – جَوْهَر pl. جَوَاهِر – مَاهِيَّة pl. مَاهِيَّات. One who deputes another, مُفَوِّض – مُوَكِّل – مُنِيب. One deputed to settle any matter, نَائِب pl. نُوَّاب – مُبَاشِر. A customer, زَبُون pl. زَبَائِنُ.

Constitute, v.t. To form, establish, أَقَامَ – جَعَلَ = – عَيَّنَ – قَرَّرَ – نَصَبَ 2 – سَامَ 2. To give an appointment to, أَقَامَ بِمَقَامٍ – وَكَّلَ – أَقَامَ وَكِيلًا – قَلَّدَ بِ. To depute, وَفَّدَ – وَجَّهَ إِلَى – جَعَلَ = وَكِيلًا. To arrange, رَتَّبَ – أَحْكَمَ. The constituted authorities, ٱلْمَحَاكِمُ ٱلْمَوْضُوعَةُ – ٱلْحُكَّامُ ٱلنِّظَامِيَّةُ.

Constitution, n. The act of constituting, تَقْوِيم – إِقَامَة – جَعْل – وَضْع – تَعْيِين – نِظَام. State of being, حَال – كَوْن – وُجُود. Temper of mind or body, خُلْق – مِزَاج – طَبْع – بِنْيَة – خِلْقَة – تَرْكِيب. Essence, substance, مَاهِيَّة – جَوْهَر. System of laws, نِظَامَاتٌ أَسَاسِيَّةٌ – دُسْتُور – قَانُونٌ أَسَاسِيٌّ – قَاعِدَةُ ٱلشَّرَائِعِ – قَوَانِينُ ٱلْمَمْلَكَةِ. A particular law, usage, شَرِيعَة – نِظَام – أَمْر pl. أَوَامِر – قَانُون pl. قَوَانِين – عَادَة. It agrees with my —, يُوَافِقُ مِزَاجِي. The —, formation, of Bulgaria into an independent province, صَيْرُورَةُ ٱلْبُلْغَارِ إِمَارَةً مُسْتَقِلَّةً.

Constitutional, a. Radical, أَصْلِيّ – جِبِلِّيّ – طَبِيعِيّ. Legal, شَرْعِيّ – مُوَافِقٌ لِقَوَانِينِ ٱلْمَمْلَكَةِ. On a — basis, مُرَتَّبٌ عَلَى أُصُولٍ شُورِيَّةٍ وَقَوَاعِدَ دَوْلِيَّةٍ. A — defect, عَيْبٌ خِلْقِيٌّ. A — fault, عَيْبٌ ذَاتِيٌّ.

Constitutionalism, n. أُصُولُ حُكُومَةٍ مَشْرُوطَةٍ – اصول حُكُومَةٍ مُقَيَّدَةٍ.

Constitutionally, ad. بِمُوجَبِ أُصُولِ ٱلْحُكُومَةِ ٱلْمُقَيَّدَةِ – حَسَبَ قَوَانِينِ ٱلْمَمْلَكَةِ – حَسَبَ ٱلدُّسْتُورِ – شَرْعًا. Naturally, طَبْعًا – فِطْرَةً – خِلْقَةً.

Constitutive, *a.* That constitutes, orders, مُنَظِّم ـ مُرَتِّب ـ مُحْكِم ـ مُرَكِّب.

Constrain, *v.t.* To compel, أَكْرَهَ ـ أَلْجَأَ ـ جَبَرَ ـ أَلْزَمَ. To confine, restrain, حَصَرَ ـ ضَيَّقَ عَلَى ـ غَصَبَ ـ أَضْطَرَّ. To importune, لَجَّ عَلَى ـ مَنَعَ. To ravish, قَهَرَ ٱلْمَرْأَةَ ـ إِفْتَعَلَ فِيهَا غَصْبًا. I was constrained to appeal to the governor, أُضْطُرِرْتُ إِلَى أَنِ ٱسْتَغِيثَ بِٱلْحَاكِمِ. He constrained his companions to go into the boat, أَلْزَمَ أَرْفَاقَهُ بِٱلطُّلُوعِ إِلَى ٱلسَّفِينَةِ. They constrained him to do it, غَصَبُوهُ عَلَى ـ أَكْرَهُوهُ عَلَى ذٰلِكَ. To be constrained, أُلْزِمَ ـ أُضْطُرَّ. I am constrained to..., أَنَا مُضْطَرٌّ إِلَى ـ أَنَا مُدْفَعٌ إِلَى.

Constrainable, *a.* يُكْرَهُ ـ يُلْزَمُ ـ يُجْبَرُ.

Constrainedly, *ad.* عَنِ ٱضْطِرَارٍ.

Constraint, *n.* Force, إِلْجَاءٌ ـ إِلْزَام ـ إِكْرَاه ـ جَبْر ـ ضَغْط ـ زَوْر ـ إِغْتِصَاب ـ غَصْب ـ إِضْطِرَار. Restraint, ضِيق ـ إِقْتِصَار. Confinement, حَبْس ـ قَيْد. Not by —, but willingly, لا عَنِ ٱضْطِرَارٍ بَلْ عَنِ ٱخْتِيَارٍ. By —, بِٱلزُّورِ ـ جَبْرًا ـ عَنْ كَرَاهِيَةٍ.

Constrict, *v.t.* To narrow, draw together, ضَيَّقَ ـ حَصَرَ ـ قَبَضَ. To control, أَحْكَمَ.

Constriction, *n.* إِنْقِبَاض ـ قَبْض ـ تَضْمِيم ـ تَضْيِيق ـ حَصْر.

Constrictor, *n.* قَابِض. A — muscle, عَضَلَةٌ قَابِضَةٌ. A boa —, نَوْعٌ مِنَ ٱلثُّعْبَانِ.

Constringe, *v.t.* See to Constrict, *v.t.*

Constringent, *a.* ضَامّ ـ قَابِض مُمْسِك.

Construct, *v.t.* To build, بَنَى ـ عَمَّرَ. To join stones together, رَصَفَ. To form, arrange, نَظَّمَ ـ أَحْكَمَ ـ رَكَّبَ ـ رَتَّبَ. To —, of a ship, مَدَّ ـ عَمَّرَ ـ أَنْشَأَ ـ صَوَّرَ. To — words, رَكَّبَ ٱلْكَلَامَ.

Constructer, *n.* بَنَّآء ـ بَانٍ ـ مِعْمَار ـ مِعْمَارِيّ coll. مِعْمَارِيَّة.

Construction, *n.* The act of building, تَعْمِير ـ بِنَآء ـ تَرْصِيف; of drawing up, إِبْرام. A building, عِمَارَة ـ بِنَايَة. Stones joined together, artificially or not, رَصَف. Arrangement, تَرْكِيب ـ تَرْتِيب ـ بَرْمَة ـ نِظَام. Mode, form, صُورَة ـ بِنْيَة. Interpretation, تَأْوِيل ـ تَفْسِير ـ مَعْنًى ـ مَضْمُون. Judgment or opinion passed, ظَنّ ـ قَضَآء ـ حُكْم. Connecting words well, تَرْصِيفُ ٱلْكَلَامِ. The — of one noun with another, إِضَافَة. A false —, تَصْحِيف. To put a false — upon, صَحَّفَ ـ تَصَحَّفَ عَلَى. He put a wrong — on my words, ظَنَّ ـ عَكَسَ مَضْمُونَ كَلَامِي ـ ٱلسُّوءَ فِي كَلَامِي. He put the best — upon it, حَمَلَهُ أَحْسَنَ مَحْمَلٍ.

The governments are conferring about the — of a new treaty, ٱلدُّوَلُ مُتَذَاكِرَةٌ فِي إِبْرَامِ مُعَاهَدَةٍ جَدِيدَةٍ.

Constructional, *a.* Appertaining to construction, building, مُتَعَلِّق بِٱلتَّعْمِيرِ; to interpretation, تَفْسِيرِيّ ـ مَعْنَوِيّ.

Constructive, *a.* Inferential, مُسْتَدَلّ بِهِ ـ إِسْتِدْلَالِيّ.

Constructively, *ad.* مَعْنًى ـ ضِمْنًا. It is — in his words, هُوَ فِي مَطَاوِيهِ ـ هُوَ فِي ضِمْنِ كَلَامِهِ.

Constructure, *n.* عِمَارَة ـ صُورَة ـ بِنْيَة.

Construe, *v.t.* To parse, أَعْرَبَ. To explain, أَوَّلَ ـ فَسَّرَ ـ عَبَّرَ. To think that..., ظَنَّ أَنْ ـ تَوَهَّمَ أَنْ. *See also to* Parse, *v.t.*

Constuprate, *v.t.* He constuprated her, غَصَبَهَا (or) إِغْتَصَبَهَا نَفْسَهَا.

Consubstantial, *a.* لَهُ جَوْهَرٌ وَاحِدٌ مَعَ ـ مُتَّحِدُ ٱلْجَوْهَرِ مَعَ ـ مُتَّحِدٌ بِٱلذَّاتِ.

Consubstantially, *ad.* بِمُوجَبِ ٱتِّحَادِ ٱلْجَوْهَرِ.

Consubstantiation, *n.* إِتِّحَادُ ٱلْجَوْهَرِ.

Consul, *n.* بَالْيُوس ـ قُنْصُل *pl.* قَنَاصِلُ. A consul-general, قُنْصُلٌ جِنِرَال *pl.* قَنَاصِلُ جِنِرَالِيَّةٌ.

Consular, *a.* مُخْتَصّ بِٱلْقُنْصُلِ ـ قُنْصُلِيّ. Consular functions, مَأْمُورِيَّةُ ٱلْقُنْصُلِ.

Consulate, *n.* قُنْصُلِيَّة ـ قُنْصُلَات.

Consulship, *n.* قُنْصُلِيَّة ـ وَظِيفَةُ ٱلْقُنْصُلِ.

Consult, *v.t.* To ask advice from, رَاجَعَ ـ إِسْتَنْصَحَ ـ شَاوَرَ ـ إِسْتَشَارَ مِن. To act with respect to, حَسَبَ حِسَابَ ـ إِعْتَبَرَ. He consulted the dictionary, طَالَعَ فِي ـ رَاجَعَ فِي ٱلْقَامُوسِ ـ ٱلْقَامُوسَ. To — one's own interest, طَلَبَ ٱلْمَنَافِعَ ٱلذَّاتِيَّةَ ـ طَلَبَ مَا هُوَ لِنَفْسِهِ. He consulted his own judgment, إِئْتَمَرَ رَأْيَهُ. The right of the governments to be consulted in the matter, حَقُّ ٱلدُّوَلِ فِي أَنْ تَكُونَ مُسْتَشَارَةً فِي ٱلْأَمْرِ.

Consult, *v.i.* تَوَازَرَ فِي ـ تَشَاوَرَ ـ شَاوَرَ. To — together against, تَشَاوَرُوا عَلَى. They consulted, debated, together, إِيْتَمَرُوا.

Consultation, *n.* The act of asking advice, مُشَاوَرَة ـ إِسْتِنْصَاح ـ إِسْتِشَار; of consulting together, مُذَاكَرَة ـ مَشْوَرَة ـ إِئْتِمَار. A council, دِيوَان ـ مُؤْتَمَر ـ مَجْلِس ـ مَشْوَرَة. A determination, شَوْر. The person consulted, ٱلْمُسْتَشَارُ. The heads of the town held a —, تَشَاوَرَ رُؤَسَآءُ ٱلْبَلَدِ.

Consultative, *a.* إِسْتِشَارِيّ ـ إِئْتِمَارِيّ ـ شُورَوِيّ. Having a — voice, صَاحِبُ رَأْيٍ شُورَوِيٍّ.

Consumable, *a.* يُفْنَى ـ عَدَمُهُ مُمْكِن ـ يُصْرَفُ ـ يُخْرَبُ. That may be burnt, مِمَّا يَحْتَرِقُ.

Consume, *v.t.* To destroy, أَتْلَفَ ـ أَذْهَبَ ـ أَفْنَى ـ أَعْدَمَ. To scatter, شَتَّتَ ـ بَدَّدَ ـ فَرَّقَ. To spend, waste, ضَيَّعَ ـ أَتْلَفَ ـ أَنْفَقَ. To — by fire, حَرَقَ ـ أَحْرَقَ. To — by disease, أَضْنَى. To eat, أَقَاتَ ـ أَكَلَ. He consumed all his wealth in riotous living, بَذَّرَ أَمْوَالَهُ فِي عَيْشٍ مُسْرِفٍ. The fire consumed their dwellings, أَكَلَتِ ٱلنَّارُ مَسَاكِنَهُمْ. My eyes are consumed through sorrow, تَعَكَّرَتْ عَيْنِي مِنَ ٱلْغَمِّ. To — one's time in ..., ضَيَّعَ أَوْقَاتَهُ فِي (or عَلَى). Sickness and trouble have consumed him, أَضْنَاهُ ٱلْمَرَضُ وَٱلْهَمُّ.

Consume, *v.i.* To waste away, ذَهَبَ ـ تَلِفَ ـ تَدَمَّرَ ـ بَادَ ـ تَخَرَّبَ ـ ضَنِيَ.

Consumer, *n.* A waster, عُثُّ مَالٍ ـ مُبَذِّرٌ ـ مُسْرِفٌ ـ قِطَّاعٌ ـ مُتْلِفٌ. Consumers and producers, ٱلْمُسْتَهْلِكُونَ وَٱلْمُحَصِّلُونَ.

Consummate, *v.t.* أَتَمَّ ـ تَمَّمَ ـ كَمَّلَ ـ نَجَزَ ـ أَجْرَى فِعْلًا.

Consummate, *a.* Perfect, بَالِغٌ ـ كَامِلٌ ـ تَامٌّ ـ تَمَامٌ ـ مُكَمَّلٌ. Real, أَصْلٌ ـ أَصْلِيٌّ.

Consummately, *ad.* تَمَامًا ـ بِكَمَالٍ ـ تَكْمِيلًا ـ بَتَّةً.

Consummation, *n.* Completion, كَمَالٌ ـ تَكْمِيلٌ ـ تَمَامٌ ـ إِنْجَازٌ. An end, آخِرٌ ـ نِهَايَةٌ. The — of the world, إِنْقِضَآءُ ٱلدَّهْرِ. The — of marriage, تَكْمِيلُ ٱلنِّكَاحِ ـ نِكَاحٌ.

Consumption, *n.* The act of wasting, إِفْنَآءٌ ـ إِتْلَافٌ ـ إِسْرَافٌ ـ تَبْدِيدٌ ـ أَكْلٌ. The being wasted, دَمَارٌ ـ تَلَفٌ ـ تَبَدُّدٌ; as by disease, ضَنًى; as by burning, إِحْتِرَاقٌ. The disease, سُحَافٌ ـ سِلٌّ ـ سُلَالٌ ـ سَلَّةٌ ـ هُلَاسٌ ـ وَرًى ـ وَارِيَةٌ ـ نَفْشَانٌ ـ دَآءُ ٱلسِّلِّ. To be struck with —, أُسِلَّ.

Consumptive, *a.* Wasting, هَادِمٌ ـ مُتْلِفٌ ـ هَالِكٌ ـ مُفْنٍ. Having the consumption, مَهْلُوسٌ ـ مَسْحُوفٌ ـ مَسْلُولٌ ـ بِهِ دَآءُ ٱلسِّلِّ. To be —, سُلَّ. A — fever, حُمَّى ٱلدِّقِّ.

Contact, *n.* إِصَابَةٌ ـ مُمَاسَّةٌ ـ مَسٌّ ـ لَمْسٌ ـ إِتِّصَالٌ ـ مِسَاسٌ. To be in — with another, مَاسَّ. To come in — with, أَصَابَ. It came in — with my foot, لَطَمَتْ رِجْلِي ـ صَدَمَتْ رِجْلِي. I came in — with him, met him, لَاقَيْتُهُ ـ تَلَاقَيْتُ مَعَهُ.

Contagion, *n.* Communication of a disease, عَدْوَى ـ تَعَدٍّ ـ إِصَابَةٌ. A plague, وَبَآءٌ ـ طَاعُونٌ. The people were affected by the —, تَعَادَى ٱلْقَوْمُ. To communicate —, أَعْدَى. He communicated the — of his disease to such an one, أَعْدَى فُلَانٌ فُلَانًا مِنْ عِلَّتِهِ بِهِ.

Contagionist, *n.* مُصَدِّقٌ بِٱلْعَدْوَى.

Contagious, *a.* مُتَعَدٍّ ـ مُعْدٍ. A — disease, عَدْوَى.

Contagiousness, *n.* عَدْوَى ـ سِرَايَةٌ.

Contain, *v.t.* To hold, إِضْطَمَّ إِلَى ـ جَمَعَ ـ إِحْتَوَى عَلَى ـ إِحْتَوَى ـ شَمَلَ ـ إِشْتَمَلَ عَلَى ـ تَضَمَّنَ ـ وَسِعَ *aor.* يَسَعُ ـ أَخَذَ. To restrain, قَمَعَ ـ حَاشَ ـ ضَبَطَ. It contains an index and a preface, يَشْتَمِلُ عَلَى فِهْرِسٍ وَخُطْبَةٍ. This box contains a rotolo of raisins, هٰذِهِ ٱلْعُلْبَةُ تَحْتَوِي عَلَى رَطْلِ زَبِيبٍ ـ هٰذِهِ ٱلْعُلْبَةُ فِيهَا رَطْلُ زَبِيبٍ. If a man cannot — himself let him marry, إِنْ لَمْ يَقْدِرِ ٱلرَّجُلُ عَلَى ٱلتَّعَفُّفِ فَلْيَتَزَوَّجْ. Contained, or written, in ..., ٱلْمَسْطُورُ فِي.

Contain, *v.i.* To live in continence, عَاشَ عَفِيفًا ـ كَفَّ عَنِ ٱللَّذَّاتِ (or عَفَّ عَنِ or إِسْتَعَفَّ عَنِ).

Containable, *a.* ٱلْإِحْتِوَآءُ عَلَيْهِ مُمْكِنٌ ـ يُتَضَمَّنُ.

Contaminate, *v.t.* قَشَّبَ ـ قَشَبَ ـ لَطَخَ بِ ـ نَجَّسَ ـ دَنَّسَ ـ أَفْسَدَ. To be contaminated, تَلَطَّخَ ـ لَطِسَ ـ تَنَجَّسَ.

Contamination, *n.* لُطُوخٌ ـ تَنْجِيسٌ ـ نَجَاسَةٌ ـ دَرَنٌ ـ دَنَسٌ.

Contemn, *v.t.* أَهَانَ ـ سَافَهَ ـ قَانَحَ ـ قَرَّدَ ـ إِسْتَخَفَّ ـ إِسْتَقَلَّ ـ إِحْتَقَرَ ـ زَرَى (or أَزْرَى) عَلَى ـ جَاوَنَ ـ بَهْدَلَ. He who is contemned is debarred (from what is good), مَنْ حُقِرَ حُرِمَ.

Contemner, *n.* مُهِينٌ ـ مُحْتَقِرٌ ـ مُبَهْدِلٌ.

Contemplate, *v.t.* or *i.* As with the sight, نَظَرَ إِلَى ـ رَامَقَ ـ أَعْيَنَ ـ شَاهَدَ ـ أَبْصَرَ بِ; with the mind, تَفَرَّسَ فِي ـ تَأَمَّلَ فِي ـ إِطَّلَعَ عَلَى ـ تَصَوَّفَ ـ تَبَصَّرَ ـ إِفْتَكَرَ فِي. To design, عَمَدَ ـ تَنَوَّى ـ عَزَمَ عَلَى.

Contemplation, *n.* Thought, نَظَرَانٌ ـ تَأَمُّلٌ ـ تَصَوُّفٌ ـ تِلَاوَةٌ ـ مُلَاحَظَةٌ ـ تَفَكُّرٌ. Looking, مُشَاهَدَةٌ ـ نَظَرٌ. Lost in — of God, فَانٍ فِي ٱللّٰهِ. To have in —, to design, عَمَدَ إِلَى ـ عَمَدَ ـ عَزَمَ عَلَى.

Contemplative, *a.* مُتَصَوِّفٌ ـ مُتَأَمِّلٌ ـ نَظَرِيٌّ.

Contemplatively, *ad.* مُتَأَمِّلًا ـ مُتَفَكِّرًا ـ بِتَأَمُّلٍ ـ بِمُطَالَعَةٍ.

Contemplator, *n.* *See* Contemplative, *a.*

Contemporaneous, *a.*
Contemporary, } قَرِينٌ *pl.* قُرَنَآءُ ـ قَرِينُ ٱلزَّمَانِ ـ مُعَاصِرٌ ـ مِنْ عَصْرٍ وَاحِدٍ ـ مِنْ عَصْرِهِ ـ صَائِرٌ فِي زَمَانٍ وَاحِدٍ. To be — with, عَاصَرَ.

Contemporaneousness, *n.*
Contemporariness, } مُعَاصَرَةٌ ـ وُجُودٌ فِي عَصْرٍ وَاحِدٍ ـ وُقُوعٌ (or إِتِّفَاقٌ) فِي زَمَانٍ وَاحِدٍ.

Contemporary, *n.* *See* Contemporaneous, *a.*

Contempt, *n.* The act of contemning, حَقْرٌ ـ تَحْقِيرٌ ـ إِهَانَةٌ ـ إِسْتِحْقَارٌ ـ تَذْلِيلٌ ـ تَرْذِيلٌ. The being held in —, vileness, حَقْرٌ ـ إِحْتِقَارٌ ـ هُونٌ ـ هَوَانٌ ـ خَسَاسَةٌ ـ ذَلَالَةٌ ـ رَذَالَةٌ. To hold in —, إِحْتَقَرَ ـ إِسْتَخَفَّ بِ ـ أَهَانَ. He spoke of him with —, قَصَّرَ بِهِ بِٱلْقَوْلِ.

Contemptible, *a.* أَهْوَنُ ـ حَقِيرٌ ـ شَقِيٌّ ـ خَسِيسٌ ـ ذَمِيمٌ ـ

ذَلِيلٌ ـ أَذِلَّاءُ .pl دَنِيٌّ ـ أَدْنِيَاءُ ـ قَبِيحٌ ـ تَافِهٌ ـ رَذِيلٌ. To make —, أَزْرَى عَلَى ـ زَرَى عَلَى ـ أَهَانَ ـ أَذَلَّ ـ رَذَّلَ ـ حَقَّرَ. To be or to become —, حَقُرَ ـ تَحَاقَرَ ـ أُهِينَ. His speech is —, كَلَامُهُ حَقِيرٌ. He was — in his own eyes, هَانَتْ نَفْسُهُ عَلَيْهِ ـ تَحَاقَرَتْ نَفْسُهُ. A — abode, مَسْكَنٌ حَقِيرٌ. A — thing, شَيْءٌ تَفِهٌ.

Contemptibleness, *n.* نَكْبَةٌ ـ دَنَاءَةٌ ـ إِحْتِقَارٌ ـ ذِلَّةٌ ـ حَقَارَةٌ.

Contemptibly, *ad.* بِدَنَاءَةٍ ـ إِحْتِقَارًا فِي ـ بِٱحْتِقَارٍ ـ حَقَارَةً.

Contemptuous, *a.* مُتَكَبِّرٌ ـ مَغْرُورٌ ـ وَقِحٌ ـ مُسْتَحْقِرٌ ـ مُزْدَرٍ.

Contemptuously, *ad.* بِٱلْكِبْرِيَاءِ ـ إِسْتِحْقَارًا ـ بِٱلْإِزْدِرَاءِ. To behave —, تَكَبَّرَ.

Contemptuousness, *n.* إِهَانَةٌ ـ إِسْتِحْقَارٌ. *See also* Contempt, *n.*

Contend, *v.i.* To struggle in opposition to, نَازَعَ ـ شَاجَرَ ـ قَاتَلَ ـ عَانَدَ ـ إِعْتَرَضَ ـ نَاظَرَ ـ نَاكَدَ ـ خَاصَمَ ـ جَالَحَ ـ خَالَجَ. To vie with, نَافَسَ ـ خَايَرَ ـ بَارَى. To — with, as in argument, تَخَاصَمَ مَعَ ـ تَقَاوَلَ مَعَ ـ نَاكَدَ. To wage war with, حَارَبَ. To — for, in defence of, قَاتَلَ عَنْ. To —, strive, against, لَجَّ عَلَى. To —, to wrestle, عَارَكَ. They contended, quarrelled, together, تَنَاجَزُوا. They contended, struggled, together, إِخْتَصَمُوا ـ تَدَافَعُوا. To — earnestly for the faith, جَاهَدَ بِجِدٍّ فِي ٱلْإِيمَانِ. He contended against labours, تَعَنَّى ٱلْأَتْعَابَ.

Contender, *n.* An adversary, خَصْمٌ .pl أَخْصَامٌ. A disputer, مُعَارِضٌ. A candidate, طَالِبٌ .pl طُلَّابٌ. A — for the faith, مُجَاهِدٌ.

Content, *n.* *See* Contentment, *n.*

Content, *v.t.* To satisfy, أَقَرَّ ـ أَرْضَى ـ كَافَى ـ صَيَّرَ مَبْسُوطًا. To —, by remuneration, أَجْزَأَ; by proof, أَقْنَعَ ـ قَنَّعَ. To quiet with, إِسْتَقَرَّ بِ or عَلَى. To endeavour to —, رَاضَى. Does not this —, satisfy thee? أَمَا يَكْفِيكَ هٰذَا. *See also under* Content, *a.*

Content, *a.* Contented,	رَضِيٌّ ـ رُضَاةٌ .pl رَاضٍ ـ قَنِيعٌ ـ قَنُوعٌ ـ قَانِعٌ ـ مَبْسُوطٌ ـ سَلِيٌّ ـ طَيِّبُ ٱلنَّفْسِ ـ مُسْتَغْنٍ.

To be — with, جَزَأَ بِ ـ إِكْتَفَى بِ ـ إِقْتَنَعَ بِ ـ قَنِعَ بِ ـ إِغْتَنَى بِ ـ إِغْتَصَبَ بِ ـ تَعَصَّبَ بِ ـ غَنِيَ بِ. To be — with one, رَضِيَ عَنْ .aor يَرْضَى. To show one's self contented, إِقْتَنَعَ. Be — with what you possess, كُونُوا مُكْتَفِينَ بِأَرْزَاقِكُمْ. He was not — with that, but ..., مَا ٱكْتَفَى بِذٰلِكَ بَلْ. He was — with what I gave him, إِرْتَضَى بِمَا أَعْطَيْتُهُ. He was — therewith, طَابَ بِذٰلِكَ نَفْسًا. He is not one of us who is not — with ..., لَيْسَ هُوَ مِنَّا مَنْ لَمْ يَتَغَنَّ بِ.

Contentedly, *ad.* بِٱنْبِسَاطٍ ـ بِرَاحَةِ بَالٍ ـ بِرِضَاءٍ ـ بِقَنَاعَةٍ.

Contention, *n.* Dispute, نِزَاعٌ ـ مُنَازَعَةٌ ـ مُخَاصَمَةٌ ـ مُشَاجَرَةٌ ـ مُنَاظَرَةٌ ـ مُنَاقَدَةٌ ـ مُغَاضَبَةٌ ـ مُنَاقَشَةٌ ـ ضِجَاجٌ ـ مُجَالَحَةٌ ـ مُخَالَفَةٌ ـ مُدَافَعَةٌ. Ardour, رَغْبَةٌ ـ سَعْيٌ ـ هَمٌّ ـ جَهْدٌ ـ جِهَادٌ. A — arose between the two so that ..., فَصَارَ بَيْنَهُمَا مُغَاضَبَةٌ حَتَّى. Under —, in dispute, فِيهِ مُنَازِعٌ. *See also* Strife, *n.*

Contentious, *a.* مُنَازِعٌ ـ خَصِمٌ ـ خَصُومٌ ـ ذُو مِغْلَاقٍ ـ مِغْلَاقٌ ـ مُخَاصِمٌ ـ يُحِبُّ ٱلْخِصَامَ ـ مِنْ أَهْلِ ٱلتَّحَزُّبِ ـ مُعَارِضٌ ـ مُعَانِدٌ.

Contentiously, *ad.* مُتَمَرِّدًا ـ مُخَالَفَةً ـ مُخَاصَمَةً ـ بِمُنَازَعَةٍ.

Contentiousness, *n.* تَمَرُّدٌ ـ شَكَاسَةٌ ـ شَرَاسَةٌ.

Contentment, *n.* إِنْبِسَاطٌ ـ رَاحَةُ بَالٍ ـ إِكْتِفَاءٌ ـ رِضَاءٌ ـ قَنَاعَةٌ ـ قُنُوعٌ. Godliness with — is great gain, ٱلتَّقْوَى مَعَ ٱلْقَنَاعَةِ فَهِيَ تِجَارَةٌ عَظِيمَةٌ. Contentment is the key to repose, ٱلْقَنَاعَةُ مِفْتَاحُ ٱلرَّاحَةِ.

Contents, *n.* That which is contained, مَضْمُونٌ. Power of containing, مُتَضَمَّنٌ ـ إِمْتِدَادٌ ـ سَعَةٌ. The —, table, of a book, فِهْرِسٌ. The — of a letter, its substance, مَضْمُونُ ٱلْكِتَابِ ـ فَحْوَى ٱلْمَكْتُوبِ ـ ٱلْمُحَرَّرُ.

Conterminate, *a.* Conterminous,	مُتَلَاقٍ ـ مُتَّصِلٌ ـ مُجَاوِرٌ ـ مُحَاذٍ. Our land is — with yours, أَرْضُنَا مُحَاذٍ أَرْضَكُمْ.

Contest, *n.* *See* Contention, *n.*

Contest, *v.t.* To controvert, نَازَعَ ـ نَكِرَ ـ نَاكَدَ ـ شَاجَرَ ـ إِعْتَرَضَ. *See also to* Contend, *v.t.*

Contestable, *a.* إِنْكَارُهُ مُحْتَمَلٌ ـ تَحْتَ ٱلْجِدَالِ ـ فِيهِ جِدَالٌ ـ فِيهِ خِلَافٌ ـ ٱلْإِنْكَارُ بِهِ مُمْكِنٌ.

Contestant, *n.* *See* Contender, *n.*

Contestation, *n.* إِعْتِرَاضٌ ـ مُعَارَضَةٌ ـ مُنَازَعَةٌ ـ نِزَاعٌ ـ مُنَاقَدَةٌ.

Context, *n.* سِيَاقٌ وَسِبَاقٌ ـ مَقَامٌ ـ عَلَاقَةٌ ـ قَرِينَةٌ ـ مَتْنٌ ـ سِيَاقُ ٱلْكَلَامِ وَسِيَاقُهُ.

Contexture, *n.* جَمْعٌ ـ وَصْدٌ ـ نَسِيجٌ ـ تَرْكِيبٌ.

Contiguity, *n.* Contiguousness,	Contact, مُلَاصَقَةٌ ـ لُصُوقٌ ـ إِلْتِصَاقٌ ـ إِتِّصَالٌ ـ مُمَاسَّةٌ. Nearness, جِوَارٌ ـ إِقْتِرَابٌ ـ قُرْبٌ.

Contiguous, *a.* In contact, مُلْتَصِقٌ بِ ـ مُتَّصِلٌ بِ. Near, بِجِوَارٍ ـ قَرِيبٌ مِنْ. To be — to, وَاصَلَ. A — house, دَارٌ وَلِيَّةٌ.

Contiguously, *ad.* In contact, إِتِّصَالًا. Near, بِٱلْقُرْبِ مِنْ ـ قَرِيبٌ مِنْ.

Continence, *n.* Continency,	Chastity, إِجْتِنَابٌ ـ عِفَّةٌ ـ عِصْمَةٌ ـ وَرَعٌ ـ رِعَةٌ (or) إِمْتِنَاعٌ عَنِ ٱلشَّهَوَاتِ. Moderation, إِقْتِصَادٌ.

Continent, *a.* Chaste, مُسْتَمْسِكٌ ـ عَفِيفٌ ـ وَرِيعٌ. Moderate, تَعَفُّفٌ ـ يَرِعُ ـ مُعْتَدِلٌ ـ مُقْتَصِدٌ. To be —, وَرِعَ .aor يَرِعُ.

Continent, *n.* Land not disjoined by sea, قُطْر ـ بَرّ ـ أَصْلُ ٱلْبَرِّ. The — of Europe, بَرُّ أُورُبَّا. The four continents, ٱلْأَقْطَارُ ٱلْأَرْبَعَةُ.

Continental, *a.* مُتَعَلِّقٌ بِقُطْرٍ مِنَ ٱلْأَقْطَارِ ٱلْأَرْبَعَةِ ـ مُتَعَلِّقٌ بِٱلْبَرِّ.

Continently, *ad.* بِعِفَّةٍ ـ عِصْمَةً ـ وَرَعًا ـ رِعَةً.

Contingence, Contingency, *n.* Contingent, } Something happening, حَوَادِثُ. *pl.* حَادِثَة ـ عَوَارِضُ *pl.* عَارِضَة ـ حُصُول ـ حُدُوث ـ إِتِّفَاق.

Contingent, *a.* Accidental, إِتِّفَاقِيّ ـ حَادِث ـ غَيْبِيّ ـ عَارِضِيّ ـ مُحْدَثُ ٱلْوُقُوعِ. Contingent upon, connected with, مَوْقُوف عَلَى ـ مُتَعَلِّق بِ.

Contingently, *ad.* By chance, مُصَادَفَةً ـ عَرَضًا. In dependence upon, بِٱلْوُقُوفِ عَلَى ـ إِتِّفَاقًا.

Continual, *a.* Constant, مُلَازِم ـ مُسْتَمِرّ ـ مُسْتَدِيم ـ دَائِم. Steady, رَاتِب. Unbroken, continuous, مُتَوَاصِل ـ سَرْد ـ مُتَّصِل ـ مُتَوَالٍ ـ مُتَتَابِع. Continual going to, تَرَدُّد ـ وُرُود. He wearies me with his — coming, يُزْعِجُنِي بِتَرَدُّدِهِ إِلَيَّ. I have — sorrow in my heart, فِي قَلْبِي غَمٌّ غَيْرُ زَائِلٍ. *See also* Continually, *ad.*

Continually, *ad.* عَلَى ٱلِٱسْتِمْرَارِ ـ سَرْمَدًا ـ عَلَى ٱلدَّوَامِ ـ فِي ٱلْمُدَاوَمَةِ ـ بِلَا فُتُورٍ ـ مِنْ غَيْرِ ٱنْقِطَاعٍ ـ بِٱطِّرَادٍ ـ بِٱلِٱسْتِدَامَةِ ـ دَائِمًا. They are — talking, مَا يَنْقَطِعُونَ عَنِ ـ أَبَدًا يَتَكَلَّمُونَ ٱلْكَلَامَ. One of the soldiers who waited on him —, وَاحِدٌ مِنَ ٱلْجُنْدِ مِمَّنْ كَانُوا يُلَازِمُونَهُ. They were — in the house, كَانُوا كُلَّ حِينٍ فِي ٱلْبَيْتِ. They used to do it year by year —, كَانُوا يَعْمَلُونَهُ مِنْ سَنَةٍ إِلَى سَنَةٍ دَائِمًا. The sky rained —, أَغْبَطَتِ ٱلسَّمَاءُ.

Continuance, *n.* Permanence, مُدَاوَمَة ـ دَوَام ـ مُوَالَاة ـ بَقَاء ـ عَدَمُ ٱنْقِطَاعٍ ـ إِسْتِبْقَاء ـ إِسْتِمْرَار ـ ظُلُول ـ ثُبُوت ـ ثَبَات. Abode, residence, إِقَامَة ـ ظَلَّة. Perseverance, إِدْمَان ـ مُلَازَمَة ـ مُوَاظَبَة ـ إِلْحَاح. Succession, إِلْحَاق ـ تَتَالٍ ـ تَوَالٍ ـ تَتَابُع ـ مُوَاصَلَة ـ إِتِّصَال. Of long —, مُزْمِن ـ زَمِن. By patient — in..., بِٱلصَّبْرِ عَلَى.

Continuation, *n.* Succession, إِتِّصَال ـ تَتَابُع. An adjunct, إِلْحَاق ـ ذَيْل. To do in — of, وَاصَلَ فِي. This is a — of that, هٰذَا لَاحِقٌ بِذٰلِكَ. *See also* Continuance, *n.*

Continuate, *a.* United, مُلْحَق بِ ـ مُلَازِم ـ مُتَّصِل. Unbroken, مُسْتَمِرّ ـ دَائِم ـ سَرْد.

Continue, *v.t.* To protract, extend, مَدَّ ـ طَوَّلَ. To — one, as in the possession of, أَبْقَى لِ ـ أَدَامَ لِ ـ إِسْتَمَرَّ عَلَى فِي *or*. To unite, join, تَابَعَ ـ وَاصَلَ. To — to do, لَمْ يَزَلْ عَامِلًا ـ لَا بَرِحَ يَفْعَلُ ـ إِسْتَمَرَّ عَلَى ـ وَاظَبَ عَلَى ـ دَاوَمَ عَلَى ـ أَدْمَنَ عَلَى ـ أَزْمَنَ. To — to do a long time, ظَلَّ عَلَى ـ ظَلَّ يَفْعَلُ. I continued it, that is, to do it, مَا زِلْتُ أَفْعَلُهُ. "To be continued," سَتَأْتِي تَتِمَّتُهُ.

Continue, *v.i.* To remain, وَالَى ـ إِسْتَدَامَ ـ دَامَ ـ ثَبَتَ ـ بَقِيَ ـ إِسْتَمَرَّ ـ ظَلَّ ـ قَعَدَ ـ أَقَامَ ـ مَكَثَ. To persevere, وَاظَبَ فِي ـ دَاوَمَ عَلَى ـ أَدْمَنَ عَلَى. To stick to, to be in action continually, أَغْبَطَ عَلَى. His name shall — as long as the sun, يَدُومُ ٱسْمُهُ مَا دَامَتِ ٱلشَّمْسُ. He continued knocking, ظَلَّ قَارِعًا. He continued speaking till midnight, أَطَالَ ٱلْكَلَامَ حَتَّى إِلَى نِصْفِ ٱللَّيْلِ. The rain continued upon us incessantly, أَغْبَطَ عَلَيْنَا ٱلْمَطَرُ. The fever continued upon him persistently, أَغْصَنَ عَلَيْهِ ٱلْحُمَّى. It shall — to be executed, carried out, يَبْقَى مَعْمُولًا بِهِ.

Continuity, *n.* عَدَمُ ٱنْقِطَاعٍ ـ تَسَلْسُل ـ إِتِّصَال ـ مُوَاصَلَة ـ عَدَمُ ٱنْفِصَالٍ.

Continuous, *a.* جَارٍ ـ بِلَا ٱنْقِطَاعٍ ـ مُتَوَاصِل ـ سَرْد.

Continuously, *ad.* دَائِمًا ـ إِسْتِمْرَارًا ـ بِلَا ٱنْقِطَاعٍ ـ بِلَا ٱنْفِصَالٍ.

Contort, *v.t.* To twist, شَنَّجَ ـ فَتَلَ ـ أَبْرَمَ ـ لَوَى ـ طَوَى. To — the face, عَبَسَ ٱلْوَجْهَ ـ قَبَّسَ ٱلْوَجْهَ ـ نَسَجَ.

Contortion, *n.* A twisting, فَتْلَان ـ تَبْرِيم ـ لَيَّة ـ لَوِيّ. A — of the face, عُبُوسُ ٱلْوَجْهِ ـ تَقْبِيحُ ٱلْوَجْهِ. A — of the bowels, مَغْص.

Contour, *n.* شَكْل ـ حُدُود ـ مُحِيط.

Contraband, *a.* Prohibited, مُحَرَّج ـ خِلَافُ ٱلشَّرْعِ ـ مَمْنُوع ـ بِضَاعَةٌ مَمْنُوعَةٌ ـ بِضَاعَةٌ مُحَرَّجَةٌ ـ نَفَاذ. Contraband trade, يَسَق. By —, مِنْ وَرَاءِ ٱلْكُمْرُكِ ـ بِٱلتَّهْرِيبِ ـ شَيْءٌ يَسَق.

Contract, *v.t.* To draw together, ضَمَّ ـ قَبَضَ ـ كَمَّشَ ـ طَبَّقَ ـ ضَيَّقَ ـ قَصَّرَ ـ جَمَعَ ـ عَقَدَ. To make less ample, To epitomise, إِخْتَصَرَ ـ أَوْجَزَ. To get, attain, بَلَغَ ـ أَدْرَكَ ـ حَصَّلَ. To —, as of the nerves, قَبَضَ ـ شَنَّجَ ـ قَلَّصَ; of the eyes, أَغَضَّ ـ غَضَّ. To — marriage, عَقَدَ ٱلنِّكَاحَ ـ صَاهَرَ. To — the countenance, غَاضَنَ ـ إِنْشَبَكَ بِٱلزِّيجَةِ ـ خَطَبَ بِنْتًا. To — acquaintances, إِسْتَأْنَسَ مَعَ ـ صَاحَبَ ـ عَاشَرَ ـ ٱلْوَجْهَ. To — a habit, تَعَوَّدَ عَلَى ـ طُبِعَ عَلَى ـ إِنْشَبَكَ مَعَ. To — a disease, إِعْتَرَى ٱلْمَرَضُ ـ إِنْعَدَى مِنَ ٱلْمَرَضِ. To — rust, صَدِئَ. It is contracted thus in writing, يُكْتَبُ بِٱلْإِيجَازِ كَذَا.

Contract, *v.i.* To shrink up, تَكَمَّشَ ـ تَقَبَّضَ ـ إِنْقَبَضَ ـ إِنْضَمَّ. To grow short, شَنِجَ ـ تَقَلَّصَ ـ إِنْطَبَقَ ـ ضَاقَ ـ قَصُرَ. To — or bargain with, عَاقَدَ ـ تَشَارَطَ مَعَ ـ تَكَتَّعَ ـ طَرْمَسَ.

فَاصَلَ ـ تَعَاهَدَ عَلَى ـ عَامَلَ ـ وَاطَى عَلَى. The two contracting parties, الطَّرَفَانِ ٱلْمُتَعَاهِدَانِ.

Contract, *n.* A bargain, عَقْد ـ إِقْرَار ـ عَهْد ـ إِتِّفَاق ـ إِرْتِبَاط ـ ذِمَّة ـ مُوَاطَاة ـ شَرْط ـ قَوْل ـ قُونْطَرَاطُو. A — of marriage, عَقْدُ نِكَاحٍ. A written marriage —, كِتَابُ نِكَاحٍ. A written —, حُجَّة *pl.* حُجَج ـ صَكّ ـ تَمَسُّك ـ كِتَاب.

Contracted, *a.* A — mind, صَدْرٌ ضَيِّقٌ.

Contractedness, *n.* قِلَّة ـ إِخْتِصَار ـ ضَيْق.

Contractibility, *n.* }
Contractibleness, } قَابِلِيَّةُ ٱلتَّشَنُّجِ ـ قَابِلِيَّةُ ٱلتَّقَبُّضِ.

Contractible, *a.* يُخْتَصَرُ ـ يَنْضَمُّ ـ يَتَقَبَّضُ ـ يُشَنَّجُ.

Contractile, *a.* مُشَنِّج ـ قَابِض ـ مُخْتَصِر ـ ضَامٌّ.

Contracting, *a.* مُعَاهِد ـ مُتَعَاهِد. The two high — parties, الطَّرَفَانِ ٱلْمُتَعَاهِدَانِ ٱلْفَخِيمَانِ.

Contraction, *n.* The act of shortening, تَقْصِير ـ إِخْتِصَار ; of shrinking, تَقَلُّص ـ قَبْض ـ طَرْمَسَة ـ كَشّ ـ كَشَاسَة. Abbreviation, as of letters, إِدْغَام ـ حَذْفُ بَعْضِ ٱلْأَحْرُفِ لِٱخْتِصَارِ ٱلْكَلِمَةِ. A — of the eyebrows, a frown, قَطْبَة ـ غَضَن. A spasm, specially of a tendon of the feet, تَعَص ـ مَعَص ; to have such a spasm, تَعِصَ ـ.

Contractor, *n.* One who enters into a contract, مُتَعَاهِد ـ مُتَشَارِط. A supplier, مُوَّان *pl.* مُوَّانَة ـ مُبَاشِر.

Contradict, *v.t.* To deny, gainsay, نَاقَدَ ـ خَالَفَ ـ كَذَّبَ ـ مَارَى ـ نَكَثَ [2] ـ إِعْتَرَضَ ـ طَلَعَ ل ـ مِنْ خِلَافِ ما يَقُولُ [2] ـ. To be contrary to, خَالَفَ ـ عَانَدَ ـ ضَادَدَ. I contradicted his statement, رَدَدْتُ قَوْلَهُ. They spoke against what I said, contradicting, قَالُوا ضِدَّ ما قُلْتُ وَهُمْ يُمَارُونَ. This contradicts what you said yesterday, هٰذا بِخِلَافِ ما قُلْتَهُ أَمْسِ.

Contradiction, *n.* A gainsaying, مُمَارَة ـ مُنَاقَضَة ـ مُعَارَضَة ـ مُضَادَدَة ـ تَكْذِيب ـ تَنَاقُض ـ إِنْكَار ـ نَكْث ـ رَدُّ كَلَامٍ ـ نَقْضُ كَلَامٍ ـ جَوَاب. Inconsistency, خِلَاف ـ مُخَالَفَة ـ مُنَاقَرَة ـ تَنَاقُر ـ عَدَمُ ٱتِّفَاقٍ. Without —, indubitably, بِلا مُمَارَاةٍ ـ مِنْ كُلِّ بُدٍّ ـ بِلا ٱعْتِرَاضٍ ـ بِلا شَكٍّ ـ مَا فِيهِ كَلَامٌ.

Contradictious, *a.* *See* Captious, *a.*

Contradictiousness, *n.* *See* Captiousness, *n.*

Contradictive, *a.* Contrary, مُنَاقِض ـ مُكَذِّب ـ مُتَدَافِع ـ مُتَنَاقِر ـ مُخَالِف ـ شَكِس. Given to cavil, عَنِيد ـ مُعَانِد ـ شَرِس.

Contradictorily, *ad.* مُنَاقَضَةً ـ بِمُمَارَاةٍ ـ بِٱلْمُضَادَّةِ ـ بِٱلنَّكْثِ.

Contradictoriness, *n.* Contrariety, إِخْتِلَاف ـ تَنَاقُض ـ ضِدِّيَّة.

Contradictory, *a.* مُخَالِف ـ مُتَنَاقِض ـ مُتَدَافِع. The two sayings are —, تَدَافَعَ ٱلْكَلَامَانِ.

Contradistinction, *n.* فَرْق ـ تَفْرِيق ـ تَمْيِيز. In — to, بِخِلَافِ ـ بِعَكْسِ.

Contradistinctive, *a.* مُمَيِّز ـ فَارِقٌ بَيْنَ ـ مُفَرِّق.

Contradistinguish, *v.t.* فَرَقَ بَيْنَ [2] ـ مَيَّزَ ـ مِن.

Contra-indicate, *v.t.* دَلَّ عَلَى ٱلْخِلَافِ [2].

Contra-indication, *n.* دَلِيلٌ عَلَى ٱلْخِلَافِ.

Contralto, *n.* المَثْنَى.

Contraries, *n.* أَضْدَاد ـ تَنَاقُض.

Contrariety, *n.* Opposition, مُخَالَفَة ـ مُضَادَّة ـ مُعَاكَسَة. Inconsistency, مُنَاقَرَة ـ تَنَاقُر ـ عَدَمُ ٱتِّفَاقٍ ـ قِلَّةُ وَفْقٍ. Captiousness, صُعُوبَة ـ إِلْتِوَاء ـ شَرَاسَة.

Contrarily, *ad.* }
Contrariwise, } بِٱلْخِلَافِ ـ بِٱلضِّدِّ ـ بِٱلْعَكْسِ ـ بِعَكْسٍ.

Contrariness, *n.* *See* Contrariety, *n.*

Contrary, *a.* Adverse to, مُخَالِفٌ ل ـ ضِدٌّ ـ نَقِيض ـ مُضَادِدٌ ل ـ مُنَاقِض. Inconsistent, غَيْرُ مُوَافِقٍ ـ مُنَاقِر ـ لا يَتَّفِقُ مَع. Captious, مُلْتَوٍ ـ شَرِيس ـ شَكِس ـ صَعْب. To be — to, oppose, خَالَفَ ـ عَانَدَ ـ ضَادَّ. To be —, captious, شَكِسَ ـ ـ شَرِسَ ـ ـ تَلَوَّى ـ أَصْعَبَ. The wind was —, الرِّيحُ كَانَتْ مُضَادَّةً. Contrary to nature, مُغَائِرٌ لِلطَّبِيعَةِ. They act — to the orders of the government, يَعْمَلُونَ ما يُخَالِفُ أَحْكَامَ ٱلدَّوْلَةِ. He is of the — part, هُوَ مِنْ فَرِيقِ ٱلضِّدِّ. Each one of them is — to the other, كُلُّ وَاحِدٍ مِنْهُمْ ضِدُّ صَاحِبِهِ. On the —, إِنَّمَا ـ بِعَكْسٍ ـ بِٱلْعَكْسِ ـ بِٱلْخِلَافِ ـ بِٱلضِّدِّ.

Contrary, *n.* A thing of opposite qualities, خِلَاف ـ ضِدٌّ ـ عَكْس.

Contrast, *v.t.* مَيَّزَ ـ مِن ـ قَابَلَ ـ مع.

Contrast, *v.i.* تَمَيَّزَ ـ إِخْتَلَفَ ـ تَبَايَنَ.

Contrast, *n.* إِخْتِلَاف ـ فَرْق ـ تَبَايُن ـ تَضَادٌّ. There is a great — between the two cities, بَيْنَ ٱلْمَدِينَتَيْنِ بَوْنٌ بَعِيدٌ عِنْدَ ٱلْمُقَابَلَةِ.

Contravallation, *n.* خَنْدَقٌ وَمَتَارِيسُ حَوْلَ قَلْعَةٍ أَوْ مَدِينَةٍ لِمَنْعِ أَهْلِهَا عَنِ ٱلْخُرُوجِ مِنْهَا.

Contravene, *v.t.* To oppose, عَارَضَ ـ خَالَفَ ـ نَقَضَ [2] ـ ـ تَعَدَّى. To obstruct, مَنَعَ ـ.

Contravention, *n.* مُخَالَفَة ـ مُعَارَضَة ـ مُضَادَدَة ـ تَعَدٍّ.

Contretemps, *n.* صُعُوبَة ـ مُصِيبَة ـ عَارِضَة ـ عَائِق ـ مَانِع.

Contributable, *a.* مِمَّا يُدْفَعُ ـ يُعْطَى.

Contributary, *a.* As to a superior chief, يَدْفَعُ جِزْيَةً إِلَى ـ مِنْ أَهْلِ ٱلْخَرَاجِ ; to a stream, رَافِد ـ مَصَبٌّ فِي *pl.* رُفَّد.

Contribute, *v.t.* To give, وَهَبَ *aor.* يَهَبُ ـ دَفَعَ ـ أَعْطَى. To aid in, أَمَدَّ ـ عَلَى ـ عَاوَنَ ـ عَلَى ـ سَاعَدَ ـ عَلَى ـ أَوْزَعَ ـ بِ. *See also under to* Conduce, *v.i.*

Contribute, *v.i.* To give a part, أَعْطَى حِصَّةً ـ أَخَصَّ. To conduce to, إِسْتَدْرَجَ ـ عَاوَنَ ـ سَاعَدَ. *See also under to* Conduce, *v.i.*

Contribution, *n.* Aid, دَفْع ـ إِمْدَاد ـ إِعَانَة. A tax, جَالِيَة ـ ضَرِيبَة ـ تَكْلِيف ـ غَرَامَة. A share, حِصَّة *pl.* حِصَص. An impost, تَكَالِيف. Indirect contributions, رُسُومَات ; personal contributions, تَكَالِيف شَخْصِيَّة. To levy — upon, يَضَعُ *aor.* وَضَعَ عَلَى ـ أَغْرَمَ ـ غَرَّمَ. They made a charitable —, أَعْطُوا ـ وَزَّعُوا صَدَقَةً ـ تَبَرَّعُوا بِٱلْعَطَاءِ. A charitable —, صَدَقَة ـ حَسَنَة. A sum, مَبْلَغ.

Contributive, *a.* } Aiding, رَافِد ـ مُوَزِّع ـ مُمِدّ ; impelling,
Contributory, } دَافِع ـ دَفَّاع.

Contributor, *n.* رَافِد ـ مُمِدّ. A writer, كَاتِب ـ مُؤَلِّف.

Contrite, *a.* نَدْمَان ـ مَوْطُوّ ـ تَائِب ـ خَاشِع ـ مُخْبِت ـ مُنْسَحِقُ ٱلْقَلْبِ ـ مَكْسُورُ ٱلْقَلْبِ ـ مُنْكَسِرُ ٱلْقَلْبِ ـ مُتَأَسِّف.

Contritely, *ad.* بِقَلْبٍ مُنْكَسِرٍ ـ بِتَلَهُّفٍ ـ تَأَسُّفًا.

Contriteness, *n.* } تَأَسُّف ـ نَدَامَة ـ إِنْكِسَارُ ٱلْقَلْبِ ـ خَبْتَة
Contrition, } تَوْبَة ـ تَلَهُّف.

Contrivable, *a.* يُصْنَعُ ـ يُخْتَرَعُ ـ يُتَدَبَّرُ ـ مِمَّا يُحْتَالُ.

Contrivance, *n.* وَصِيلَة ـ حِيلَة ـ إِبْدَاع ـ إِيجَاد ـ إِخْتِرَاع ـ تَرْتِيب ـ تَدْبِير.

Contrive, *v.t.* and *i.* To invent, project, أَوْجَدَ ـ أَبْدَعَ ـ إِخْتَرَعَ ـ جَعَلَ ـ عَمِلَ حِيلَةً ـ دَبَّرَ ـ أَحْدَثَ. He contrived to get out from, صَحَّ لَهُ ٱلْخُرُوجُ مِن. He contrived it so that..., دَبَّرَ ٱلْأَمْرَ حَتَّى.

Contriver, *n.* ذُو حِيلَةٍ ـ مُحْتَال ـ بَادِع ـ مُخْتَرِع ـ مُبْدِع.

Control, *v.t.* To govern, قَيَّدَ ـ سَاسَ ـ ضَبَطَ ـ حَكَمَ عَلَى. To check, ضَبَطَ ـ مَنَعَ ـ قَمَعَ ـ حَاسَرَ. To overlook, manage, بَاشَرَ ـ نَظَرَ إِلَى.

Control, *n.* Authority, مَكِينَة ـ مُعَامَلَة ـ أَمْر ـ حُكُومَة. A check, كَبْح ـ قَمْع ـ عَائِق ـ ضَبْط ـ تَقْيِيد. Superintendence, مُبَاشَرَة ـ نَظَارَة ـ إِدَارَة ـ نَظَر. A counter-register, دَفْتَر ٱلْمُقَابَلَةِ ـ لِتَحْقِيقِ دَفْتَرٍ آخَر. A — office, قَلَمُ ٱلْمُحَاسَبَةِ.

Controllable, *a.* تَطْبِيعُهُ ـ يُقْمَعُ ـ يُضْبَطُ ـ يُكْبَحُ ـ مِذْعَان ـ لَيِّنُ ٱلْأَعْطَافِ ـ مُمْكِن.

Controller, *n.* ضَابِط ـ أَمِين ـ مُدَبِّر ـ مُبَاشِر ـ نَاظِر ـ مُفَتِّش ـ مُحَاسِبْجِي ـ مُحَاسِب ـ مُدِير ـ مُسْتَوْفٍ. Controller of the finances, مُحَاسِبُ ٱلْمَالِيَّةِ.

Controllership, *n.* مُبَاشَرَة ـ مُدِيرِيَّة ـ وَظِيفَةُ ٱلْمُسْتَوْفِي.

Controlment, *n.* *See* Control, *n.*

Controversial, *a.* مُتَعَلِّقٌ بِٱلْمُجَادَلَةِ وَٱلْمُبَاحَثَةِ.

Controversialist, *n.* مُجَادِل ـ مُبَاحِث ـ مِجْدَال.

Controversially, *a.* بِٱلْمُجَادَلَةِ ـ بِٱلْمُبَاحَثَةِ.

Controversy, *n.* Debate, مُبَاحَثَة ـ مُنَاظَرَة ـ مُجَادَلَة ـ مُشَاجَرَة. A quarrel, مُنَازَعَة ـ مُعَالَجَة. A suit at law, طَلَبٌ شَرْعِيّ ـ دَعْوَة ـ خُصُومَة. To have a — with, خَاصَمَ. A controverted point, شَجْر.

Controvert, *v.t.* To argue against, نَاظَرَ فِي ـ شَاجَرَ ـ خَالَفَ. To reply to, رَدَّ عَلَى. To deny, نَكِرَ ـ كَذَّبَ.

Controvertible, *a.* فِيهِ نِزَاعٌ ـ فِيهِ مُنَاظَرَةٌ ـ فِيهِ تَنَازُعٌ.

Controvertist, *n.* } مُجَادِل ـ مُبَاحِث ـ مُنَاظِر.
Controverter, }

Contumacious, *a.* Obstinate, عَنِيد ـ مَرِيد ـ مَارِد ـ مُعَانِد ـ عَدِيمُ ٱلطَّاعَةِ ـ عَاصٍ. Perverse, شَرِس ـ شَكِس.

Contumaciously, *ad.* مُعَانَدَةً ـ بِعِنَادٍ ـ مُتَمَرِّدًا.

Contumaciousness, *n.* } مُعَانَدَة ـ عِنَاد ـ مَرَد ـ تَمَرُّد ـ عَدَمُ
Contumacy, } ٱلطَّاعَةِ. Disobedience to a summons of the law, مُعَاصَاةُ ٱلشَّرْعِ.

Contumelious, *a.* Haughtily reproachful, هَاتِك ـ نَمَّام ـ شَتَّام ـ مُبَهْدِل ـ مُهِين. Producing reproach, مُفْضِح ـ فَاحِش ـ عَارٌ.

Contumeliously, *ad.* بِهَوَانٍ ـ تَحْقِيرًا ـ بِبَهْدَلَةٍ. To treat —, سَافَهَ.

Contumeliousness, *n.* } نَهَاكَة ـ شَتِيمَة ـ هَوَان ـ إِهَانَة ـ شَتْم
Contumely, } تَحْقِير ـ إِسْتِهْزَاء.

Contuse, *v.t.* To bray, سَحَقَ ـ دَقَّ ـ هَرَسَ. To bruise, رَضْرَضَ ـ دَشْدَشَ ـ هَرَسَ.

Contusion, *n.* رَضْرَضَة ـ ضَعْضَعَة ـ دَشَّة ـ خَبْطَة.

Conundrum, *n.* أُحْجِيَّة *pl.* أَحَاجِيّ ـ لُغْز *pl.* أَلْغَاز.

Convalescence, *n.* نَقَهٌ ـ نُقُوه ـ إِفَاقَةٌ مِنَ ٱلْمَرَضِ ـ شِفَاء ـ مُتَوَجِّهٌ إِلَى ـ إِنْتِقَهٌ ـ إِتِّجَاهٌ إِلَى ٱلصِّحَّةِ. He is in a state of —, تَنْشَنْشَ مِنْ مَرَضِهِ ـ ٱلْإِفَاقَةِ. The compliment generally addressed to one in a state of —, ٱلْحَمْدُ لِلّٰهِ عَلَى ٱلْعَافِيَةِ. *Ans.* ٱللّٰهُ يُعَافِيكَ ـ ٱللّٰهُ يُسَلِّمُكَ.

Convalescent, *a.* ناقِه *pl.* نُقَّه ـ بارِئٌ مِنْ مَرَضِهِ ـ مُتَّجِهٌ لِلصِّحَّةِ ـ قائِمٌ مِنَ ٱلْفِراشِ.

Convene, *v.t.* جَمَعَ ـ اِسْتَدْعَى ب ـ أَمَرَ بِالاجْتِماعِ ـ حَشَدَ.

Convene, *v.i.* Of many, اِجْتَمَعُوا ـ اِحْتَفَلُوا ـ اِحْتَشَرُوا ـ اِحْتَشَدُوا ـ تَحَشَّدُوا.

Convenience, *n.* } Fitness, مُوافَقَة ـ مُناسَبَة ـ مُلاءَمَة ـ وَفْق. **Conveniency,** } Commodiousness, نَفَس ـ وَسْع ـ تَوْفِيق ـ هِينَة ـ فُسْحَة ـ بَحْبَحَة ـ اِنْشِراح ـ راحَة. Utility, طائِل ـ عائِدَة. Ease, هِينَة. A useful thing, مَصْلَحَة *pl.* مَصالِح. The conveniences of a house, أَعْتِدَةُ ٱلدّار. Furnished with all the conveniences, مَفْرُوش بِسائِرِ ٱلْمُناسَباتِ ـ مُجَهَّز بِجَمِيعِ ٱللَّوازِم. At his —, leisurely, عَلَى مَهْلِهِ.

Convenient, *a.* Fit, مُوافِق ـ مُناسِب ـ لائِق. Proper, واجِب ـ لازِم. Commodious, ذُو نَفَسٍ ـ واسِع ـ وَسِيع ـ فَسِيح ـ شَرِح. Furnished with conveniences, مُجَهَّز بِجَمِيعِ ٱلْمُناسَباتِ. To be — to, to suit, صَلَحَ ل ـ قانَى. More — to than, أَعْوَن عَلَى ـ مِن. It is more — for thee, أَشْبَهُ بِكَ. And when a — day arrived, وَإِن كانَ يَوْمٌ مُوافِقٌ. When I have a — time I will send for you, إِذا حَصَلَتْ عَلَى فُرْصَةٍ أَسْتَدْعِيكَ. He will come to you if he finds a — opportunity, سَيَأْتِيكُمْ إِذا تَيَسَّرَ لَهُ ٱلْوَقْتُ. To deem —, اِسْتَحْسَنَ ـ اِسْتَصْوَبَ ـ رَأَى مُناسِبًا ـ تَحَسَّنَ عِنْدَ. Convenient for the matter or occasion, سَهِيلٌ لِما تَقْتَضِيهِ ٱلْمَصْلَحَةُ.

Conveniently, *ad.* Suitably, مُوافَقَةً ـ بِوَجْهٍ مُناسِبٍ. Properly, كَالْواجِبِ ـ كَما يَنْبَغِي. Easily, عَلَى طِيبَةٍ ـ عَلَى هِينَةٍ وَسَعَةٍ. He sought an opportunity how he might — do it, صارَ يُحاوِلُ فُرْصَةً كَيْفَ يَقْضِيهِ.

Convent, *n.* A Christian —, دَيْر *pl.* دُيُورَة. A — of darwishes, خانَقاه *pl.* خَوانِق ـ تَكِيَّة.

Conventicle, *n.* جَماعَةٌ شِيعَةٍ ـ جَماعَةُ ٱلْمُعْتَزِلَةِ.

Convention, *n.* The act of calling together, حَشْد ـ حَشْر ـ تَجْمِيع ـ جَمْع. An assembly, مَجْمَع ـ اِجْتِماع ـ مَحْفَل ـ دِيوان. An agreement, شَرْط *pl.* شُرُوط ـ لائِحَةٌ ٱتِّفاقِيَّةٌ ـ عَهْد ـ مُشارَطَة ـ اِتِّفاق عَلَى ـ مُقاوَلَة ـ قَوْل. A verbal —, مُقاوَلَةٌ شِفاهِيَّةٌ ـ وَقَرار لِسانًا. A written —, مُقاوَلَةٌ مُحَرَّرَةٌ. The — which it is intended to hold, المُؤْتَمَرُ ٱلْمُرادُ عَقْدُهُ.

Conventional, *a.* } By agreement, اِتِّفاقِيٌّ ـ شَرْطِيٌّ. Agreed **Conventionary,** } upon by use, عُرْفِيٌّ ـ اِصْطِلاحِيٌّ ـ مُعْتاد ـ حُكْمُ ٱلْعادَةِ. Conventional language, عُرْض.

Conventionalism, *n.* عادَة *pl.* عادات ـ اِصْطِلاح ـ حُكْمُ ٱلْعادَةِ.

Conventionally, *ad.* By agreement, شَرْطًا ـ بِالْمُقاوَلَةِ. According to usage, اِصْطِلاحًا ـ بِمُوجَبِ ٱلْعادَةِ ـ اِعْتِيادًا.

Conventual, *a.* دَيْرِيٌّ ـ مُتَعَلِّقٌ بِالدَّيْرِ ـ راهِبِيٌّ ـ رَهْبانِيٌّ.

Converge, *v.i.* آلَ إِلَى *aor.* يَؤُولُ ـ تَقارَبَ ـ مالَ إِلَى ـ تَوَجَّهَ إِلَى ـ قَصَدَ إِلَى ـ ضَرَبَ إِلَى.

Convergence, *n.* مَمال إِلَى ـ أَيْلُولَة ـ تَقارُب.

Convergent, *a.* } مُتَقارِب ـ مائِل إِلَى ـ آلٍ إِلَى ـ قاصِد **Converging,** } ضارِب إِلَى ـ مَرْكَزٍ واحِدٍ.

Conversable, *a.* مُتَكَلِّم ـ أَنِيس ـ صاحِبُ ٱلْأُلْفَةِ ـ صاحِب عِشْرَةٍ.

Conversant, *a.* Acquainted with, خَبِير ب ـ مُطَّلِعٌ عَلَى ـ واقِف عَلَى ـ ماهِر فِي ـ مُتَعَرِّف ب. Having intercourse with, مُتَأَنِّس ب. To be — with, clever in, اِفْتَنَّ فِي.

Conversation, *n.* Familiar discourse, خِطاب ـ مُخاطَبَة ـ مُكالَمَة ـ مُعاشَرَة ـ مُحادَثَة ـ مُحاوَرَة ـ مُباسَطَة ـ مُلاقَشَة. Intercourse, مُخالَطَة ـ مُعاشَرَة ـ مُصاحَبَة ـ صُحْبَة ـ مُقارَنَة ـ مُباشَرَة. Behaviour, تَصَرُّف ـ سِيرَة ـ سُلُوك ـ مُعامَلَة ـ مِشْيَة. Experience, اِطِّلاع عَلَى ـ خِبْرَة ـ اِخْتِبار. Cheerful —, أُلْفَة ـ عِشْرَة ـ مُباسَطَة. Good —, a holy life, أَعْمالٌ صالِحَةٌ ـ سِيرَةٌ حَسَنَةٌ. Criminal —, زِناءٌ.

Conversational, *a.* Fluent, مُتَكَلِّم ـ بَلِيغ. Done in mutual conversation, اِنْقَضَى بِالْمُكالَمَةِ.

Conversazione, *n.* جَمْعِيَّةٌ لِمُباحَثَةِ ٱلْعُلُومِ وَٱلْمَعارِفِ.

Converse, *v.i.* تَحادَثَ ـ حَدَّثَ ـ حَكَى ـ حاكَى ـ تَكَلَّمَ ـ لَقَشَ. To hold — with, have intercourse with, صاحَبَ ـ عاشَرَ.

Converse, *n.* An inverted proposition, عارِضَة ـ عَكْس ـ قَلْب ـ قَضِيَّةٌ مَقْلُوبَةٌ. *See also* Conversation, *n.*

Converse, *a.* Opposite, ضِدّ ـ عَكْس. Reciprocal, مُتَبادِل ـ مُقابِل.

Conversely, *ad.* بِغَيْرِ وَجْهٍ ـ بِالضِّدِّ ـ بِالْعَكْسِ.

Conversion, *n.* The act of changing, تَحْوِيل ـ تَبْدِيل. The being changed, اِسْتِحالَة ـ إِحالَة ـ اِنْقِلاب ـ قَلْب. Change of manners, with amelioration, إِنابَة ـ تَوْبَة ـ اِهْتِداء ـ رُجُوع عَنِ ٱلْمَناهِي. Change from one religion to another, تَمَذْهُب ـ تَمَلُّل ـ هِدايَة ـ قَلْبُ ٱلدِّيانَةِ. Conversion to Christianity, تَنَصُّر; to Islâm, تَمَسْلُم ـ إِسْلام. Conversion of the public debt, تَحْوِيلُ ٱلدُّيُونِ ٱلْمِيرِيَّةِ. Operations towards the — of the public debt, مُعامَلاتُ تَحْوِيلِ ٱلدُّيُونِ ٱلْمِيرِيَّةِ.

Convert, *n.* One who has reformed, تائِب. A proselyte,

دَخَلَ فِي . To become a —, proselyte, to, دَخِيل ـ رَاجِع
He became a — to the religion of . . . , تَدَيَّنَ بِدِيَانَةِ ٱ .

Convert, *v.t.* To transmutate, غَيَّرَ ـ حَوَّلَ ـ قَلَبَ ـ أَحَالَ ـ أَعَادَ . To — into an inferior form, مَسَخَ . To turn from a bad to a good life, رَدَّ ـ (or) رَجَّعَ ـ عَنِ ٱلْمَحَارِمِ ـ تَوَّبَ ـ أَتَابَ ـ رَدَّ عَنِ ٱلْمَنَاهِي . To turn one, as from one religion to another, رَجَّعَ إِلَى ـ قَلَبَ إِيمَانَهُ ـ رَدَّ إِلَى ـ هَدَى . To appropriate to any use, اِسْتَعْمَلَ ـ أَفَادَ بِ ـ لِ ـ خَصَّصَ لِ . He converted it into an oratory, صَيَّرَهُ مَسْجِدًا . To be converted into, صَارَ . To be converted to, اِنْقَلَبَ إِلَى .

Convert, *v.i.* اِرْتَدَّ ـ اِسْتَحَالَ ـ اِنْقَلَبَ ـ تَبَدَّلَ ـ رَجَعَ ـ تَغَيَّرَ .

Convertibility, *n.* / Convertibleness, } إِمْكَانُ ٱلتَّحْوِيلِ ـ قَابِلِيَّةُ ٱلتَّبْدِيلِ .

Convertible, *a.* Transmutable, قَابِلٌ ـ يُصْرَفُ ـ يَتَغَيَّرُ ـ يَنْقَلِبُ ٱلتَّحْوِيلَ . So much alike that one may be used for the other, مَعْنًى وَاحِدٌ ـ مُطَابِقٌ ـ مُوَافِقٌ ـ يُسْتَعْمَلُ بَدَلَ ـ مُتَرَادِفٌ . Convertible into money, يُصْرَفُ بِٱلدَّرَاهِمِ . Convertible terms, مُتَرَادِفَاتٌ ـ أَلْفَاظٌ مُتَرَادِفَةٌ .

Convertibly, *ad.* بِٱلتَّرَادُفِ ـ بِوَجْهِ ٱلتَّحْوِيلِ وَٱلْقَلْبِ .

Convex, *a.* مُقَبَّبٌ ـ مُحَدَّبٌ ـ أَحْدَبُ .

Convexity, *n.* / Convexness, } تَحَدُّبٌ ـ حَدَبَةٌ .

Convexly, *ad.* فِي صُورَةٍ مُقَبَّبَةٍ ـ فِي هَيْئَةٍ مُحَدَّبَةٍ .

Convexo-concave, *a.* مُحَدَّبٌ مِنْ نَاحِيَةٍ وَمُقَعَّرٌ مِنْ أُخْرَى .

Convexo-convex, *a.* أَحْدَبُ مِنَ ٱلنَّاحِيَتَيْنِ .

Convey, *v.t.* To transport, نَقَلَ ـ جَلَبَ ـ حَمَلَ ـ نَوَّلَ ـ لِ ـ أَعْطَى ـ فِي يَدِ ـ أَخَذَ ـ جَاءَ بِ . To hand, سَلَّمَ ـ إِلَى ـ أَلْقَى ـ إِلَى ـ نَقَلَ لِ ـ نَاوَلَ . To deliver, transfer to, To — across, عَبَّرَ ـ أَمَرَّ ـ بِ . To send, أَرْسَلَ ـ شَيَّعَ . To —, as information, to, أَفَادَ ـ دَخَّلَ ـ أَدْخَلَ . To impart to, into, To give, وَهَبَ *aor.* يَهَبُ ـ مَنَحَ ـ أَعْطَى . To — away, أَزَالَ ـ شَالَ بِ ـ رَفَعَ . To — one's self away, اِبْتَعَدَ ـ اِنْتَقَلَ ـ تَنَقَّلَ ـ تَوَرَّبَ ـ تَجَنَّبَ ـ تَبَعَّدَ . To be conveyed, moved,

Conveyable, *a.* يُجْلَبُ ـ يُحْمَلُ ـ يُنْقَلُ .

Conveyance, *n.* The act of removing, نَقْلٌ ـ اِنْتِقَالٌ ـ شَيَلَانٌ . A passage, way, سِكَّةٌ ـ طَرِيقٌ ـ مَعْدًى ـ مَعْبَرٌ ـ مَمَرٌّ . The instrument by which anything is conveyed, مِنْقَلَةٌ ـ مِنْقَلٌ ـ نَقَّالَاتٌ *pl.* نَقَّالَةٌ . Delivery from one to another, تَدَاوُلٌ ـ تَنَاوُلٌ . The act of transferring, as of property, تَسْلِيمٌ ـ تَحْوِيلٌ . A deed of —, حُجَّةُ تَحْوِيلٍ . A carriage, عَجَلَةٌ ـ عَرَبَانَةٌ ـ عَرَبِيَّةٌ .

Conveyancer, *n.* مُفَقَّهٌ فِي صِنَاعَةِ تَسْطِيرِ ٱلْحُجَجِ لِتَحْوِيلِ ٱلْأَمْلَاكِ وَنَقْلِهَا .

Conveyancing, *n.* صِنَاعَةُ تَسْطِيرِ ٱلْحُجَجِ لِتَحْوِيلِ ٱلْأَمْلَاكِ وَنَقْلِهَا .

Conveyer, *n.* نَقَّالٌ ـ حَمَّالٌ ـ شَيَّالٌ ـ رَسُولٌ *pl.* رُسُلٌ . *See also* Messenger, *n.*

Convict, *n.* One found guilty, مُجْرِمٌ ـ مُذْنِبٌ ـ خَاطِئٌ ـ ٱلذَّنْبُ مُثْبَتٌ عَلَيْهِ . A prisoner, مَحْبُوسٌ *pl.* مَحْبُوسُونَ .

Convict, *v.t.* To prove guilty, أَثْبَتَ (or) ثَبَّتَ عَلَى ـ ٱلْجُرْمَ . To be convicted of, ثُبِتَ عَلَى . To confute, نَاقَضَ ـ رَدَّ عَلَى ـ أَلْزَمَهُ ٱلرَّأْيَ ـ أَقْنَعَ ـ غَلَّطَ ـ أَبْطَلَ قَوْلَهُ . To convince, حَجَّ ـ حَجَّتْهُمْ ضَمَائِرُهُمْ . They were convicted by their own consciences,

Conviction, *n.* Detection of guilt, إِثْبَاتُ ٱللَّوْمِ ـ إِلْزَامُ ٱلْجُرْمِ . Confutation, نَقْضٌ ـ اِنْتِقَاضٌ . The state of being convinced, إِلْزَامٌ ـ إِقْنَاعٌ . I have the — that . . . , مُحَقَّقٌ عِنْدِي وَمُؤَكَّدٌ أَنَّ .

Convictive, *a.* مُقْنِعٌ ـ مُلْزِمٌ .

Convince, *v.t.* To force another to admit, حَجَّ ـ أَقْنَعَ ـ أَلْزَمَ . To prove against, أَثْبَتَ عَلَى ـ ثَبَّتَ عَلَى . To be convinced, اِقْتَنَعَ ـ اِلْتَزَمَ .

Convincible, *a.* إِقْنَاعُهُ مُمْكِنٌ ـ إِثْبَاتُهُ مُمْكِنٌ ـ إِلْزَامُهُ مُمْكِنٌ ـ يُقْنَعُ .

Convincingly, *ad.* إِقْنَاعًا ـ بِحُجَّةٍ ـ بِإِلْزَامٍ ـ بِإِقْنَاعٍ .

Convivial, *a.* عِيدِيٌّ ـ أَنِيسٌ . A — entertainment, ضِيَافَةٌ ـ مَأْدُبَةٌ ـ مُنَادَمَةٌ ـ وَلِيمَةٌ .

Conviviality, *n.* غِبْطَةٌ ـ مَسَرَّةٌ ـ إِنْسٌ ـ نُعُومَةٌ ـ فُكَاهَةٌ ـ عَيْشٌ وَعِشْرَةٌ .

Convocate, *v.t.* جَمَعَ ـ أَمَرَ بِٱلِٱجْتِمَاعِ ـ حَشَدَ ـ حَشَرَ .

Convocation, *n.* The act of calling together, اِجْتِمَاعٌ ـ جَمْعٌ ـ أَمْرٌ بِٱلِٱجْتِمَاعِ . An assembly, مَجْمَعٌ ـ مَجْلِسٌ ـ مَحْفَلٌ ـ دِيوَانٌ .

Convoke, *v.t.* *See* Convocate, *v.t.*

Convolute, *a.* / Convoluted, } مُلَفَّفٌ ـ مَلْفُوفٌ ـ مَطْوِيٌّ ـ طَوِيٌّ .

Convolution, *n.* لَيَّةٌ ـ لَفٌّ ـ لَفَّةٌ ـ تَلْفِيفٌ ـ طَيٌّ *pl.* أَطْوَاءٌ .

Convolve, *v.t.* لَفَّ ـ طَوَى .

Convolvulus, *n.* سُوسَنٌ بَرِّيٌّ . The *Convolvulus Cairicus* of Forskäl, سِتُّ ٱلْحُسْنِ .

Convoy, *v.t.* خَفَرَ ـ غَفَرَ ـ رَافَقَ ـ لِأَجْلِ ٱلْحِمَايَةِ .

Convoy, *n.* غَفَرٌ ـ خَفَرٌ ـ حِفْظٌ ـ بَذْرَقَةٌ ـ مُرَافَقَةٌ . A — of ships of war with merchantmen, تَسْيِيرُ مَعَ مَرَاكِبَ مَرَاكِبُ حَرْبٍ ـ مَرَاكِبُ مُحَافِظَةٌ ـ تُجَّارٌ لِلْغَفَرِ . To sail under a —, سَافَرَ تَحْتَ ٱلْحِفْظِ .

Convulse, *v.t.* To shake violently, ـ رَجْرَجَ ـ رَجَّ ² ـ أَرْجَفَ
زَلْزَلَ ـ زَعْزَعَ ـ هَزَّ ² ـ هَزْهَزَ ـ حَرَّكَ ـ بَرْكَلَ. To overturn, destroy, قَلَبَ ـ أَخْرَبَ ـ هَدَمَ ². To be convulsed, shaken, اِرْتَجَّ ـ تَرَجْرَجَ ـ تَزَلْزَلَ ـ اِنْهَزَّ ـ اِرْتَجَفَ. To be convulsed, agitated, troubled, اِرْتَجَّ ـ تَخَبَّطَ ـ اِضْطَرَبَ. To be convulsed with laughter, اِنْبَعَجَ مِنَ ٱلضَّحِكِ. When the earth shall be convulsed with violent convulsions, إِذَا رُجَّتِ ٱلْأَرْضُ رَجًّا.

Convulsion, *n.* Any great commotion, ـ هَزَّة ـ اِرْتِجَاج ـ رَجّ
اِلْتِوَآء ـ خَضَّة ـ زَلْزَلَة ـ رَجْفَة ـ رِجْز. A —, as of the muscles, لَقْوَة ـ لَوًى ـ ٱلْأَعْصَابِ. Convulsions, fits, صَرْع. Dying convulsions, فُوَاق.

Convulsive, *a.* Producing commotion, مُرِجّ ـ مُرْجِف. Spasmodic, صَرْعِيّ ـ مُتَشَنِّج.

Cony, *n.* A rabbit, أَرْنَب بَلَدِيّ. A jerboa, يَرْبُوع *pl.* يَرَابِيعُ.

Coo, *v.i.* As of a dove, ـ ² هَدَرَ ـ ² نَاحَ ـ تَرَنَّمَ ـ قَرْقَرَ ـ ² سَجَعَ
غَنَّى ـ ² هَتَفَ.

Cooing, *n.* ـ هَدْر ـ نَوْح ـ تَرْنِيم ـ تَرَنُّم ـ سَجْع ـ قَرْقَرَة
تَغَرُّد ـ هَتْف.

Cooing, *a.* مُغَنٍّ ـ سَجِيع ـ سَاجِع.

Cook, *n.* طَاهٍ ـ طَبَّاخ *pl.* طَبَّاخُونَ. A public or market —, شَوَّآء ـ طَعَّام. A — room, مَطْبَخ. A — shop, دُكَّان شَوَّآء.

Cook, *v.t.* To dress victuals, طَبَخَ ²; to be cooked, اِنْطَبَخَ. To — thoroughly, نَضَّجَ; to be so cooked, نَضِجَ ². To — to a rag, هَرَّأَ ـ هَرَّدَ; to be so cooked, تَهَرَّأَ ـ هَرِدَ ². To be cooked, thoroughly done, اِسْتَوَى. To —, to prepare, حَضَّرَ ـ أَعَدَّ. Half-cooked, of food, نِيّ ـ أَسْلَعُ ². Over-cooked, هَرِئٌ.

Cookery, *n.* The science of, صِنَاعَةُ ٱلطَّبْخِ. Cooking, طَبْخ ـ طِبَاخَة.

Cool, *a.* Somewhat cold, طَرِيّ ـ رَطِب ـ بَارِد. Deliberate, بَارِدُ ٱلْمِزَاجِ ـ فَاتِر ـ فَطِن ـ وَقُور ـ رَزِين ـ مُتَفَكِّر. Not ardent, فَاتِر. Indifferent, غَيْرُ مُبَالٍ. The — of the day, towards evening, بُرُودَةُ ٱلْعَشِيَّةِ ـ هُبُوبُ رِيحِ ٱلْعَشِيَّةِ. The air is —, ـ ² بَرِدَ ٱلْهَوَآءُ
بُرِدَتِ ٱلدُّنْيَا.

Cool, *v.t.* To allay heat, بَرَّدَ ـ طَرَّى ـ رَطَّبَ. To quiet, سَكَّنَ ـ أَهْدَأَ. *See also under to* Refresh, *v.t.*

Cool, *v.i.* To grow less hot, تَطَرَّى ـ بُرِدَ ². To grow less ardent, بُرِدَتْ غَيْرَتُهُ ـ تَرَاخَى ـ اِرْتَخَى. To be —, composed, تَوَقَّرَ ـ اِتَّقَرَ. To become indifferent to, فَتَرَ عَنْ ².

Cooler, *n.* A cooling medicine, دَوَآء مُبَرِّد. A vessel for cooling, آلَةُ ٱلتَّبْرِيدِ.

Cool-headed, *a.* Deliberate; *see under* Cool, *a.*

Cooling, *a.* بَارِد ـ بَرُود. *See also under* Refreshing, *a.*

Coolly, *ad.* عَلَى ٱلْبُرُودَةِ. Without passion, بِسُكُونٍ ـ بِإِرْوَادٍ
ـ ٱلْبَالِ. Leisurely, عَلَى مَهْلٍ ـ رُوَيْدًا ـ مَهْلًا. *See also* Deliberately, *ad.*

Coolness, *n.* طَرَاوَة ـ بُرُودَة. Want of affection, قِلَّةُ مَحَبَّةٍ. Want of zeal, فُتُور ـ رَخَاوَة ـ قِلَّةُ غَيْرَةٍ. Deliberation, رَزَانَة. Courage, جَسَارَة. قُرَّةُ عَيْنٍ.

Coolie, *n.* } اِسْمُ ٱلْحَمَّالِ فِي بِلَادِ ٱلْهِنْدِ.
Cooly, }

Coom, *n.* Soot, سَوَاد.

Coop, *n.* A hen coop, خُنّ *pl.* خِنَنَة ـ خُمّ *pl.* خِمَمَة ـ خَامّ ـ
قَنُّ ٱلدَّجَاجِ ـ خُنُّ ٱلْفِرَاخِ. A — for sheep, مَرَاح.

Coop, *v.t.* To shut up in a coop, ² حَطَّ فِي ـ ² جَعَلَ فِي خُمّ ـ خُنّ. To shut up in a narrow compass, ـ ضَيَّقَ عَلَى ـ حَبَسَ ² ـ حَصَرَ ².

Cooper, *n.* بَرَامِيلِيّ.

Cooperage, *n.* The business of a cooper, صَنْعَةُ ٱلْبَرَامِيلِيِّ. A place of —, مَعْمَلُ ٱلْبَتَاتِي. The charge for cooper's work, حَقُّ ٱلْبَرَامِيلِيِّ.

Co-operate, *v.i.* سَاعَدَ ـ عَمِلَ مَعَ ـ ² اِتَّفَقَ مَعَ ـ فِي ـ اِتَّحَدَ
اِقْتَرَنَ بِـ ـ فِي ـ عَاوَنَ ـ مَعَ ـ فِي. To — with for, عَضَدَ بِـ ـ عَلَى ².

Co-operation, *n.* ـ عَوْن ـ مُعَاوَنَة ـ مُسَاعَدَة ـ اِتِّفَاقٌ فِي عَمَلٍ
اِنْضِمَامُ ٱلْمُعَاوَنَةِ ـ اِقْتِرَان.

Co-operative, *a.* } قُرَنَآء *pl.* قَرِين ـ مُسَاعِدٌ عَلَى ـ فَاعِلٌ مَعَ.
Co-operator, *n.* } Co-operative stores, حَوَاصِلُ شَرَاكَةٍ.

Co-ordinate, *a.* مِنْ مَرْتَبَةٍ وَاحِدَةٍ ـ مِنْ دَرَجَةٍ وَاحِدَةٍ.

Co-ordinately, *ad.* بِمُسَاوَاةِ ٱلرُّتْبَةِ ـ عَلَى ٱلسَّوِيَّةِ.

Co-ordinates, *n.* The two —, ٱلْخَطَّانِ ٱلْمُرَتَّبَانِ.

Co-ordination, *n.* ذَاتُ مَرْتَبَةٍ مَعَ ـ وَحْدَةُ ٱلرُّتْبَةِ مَعَ.

Coot, *n.* دُجَاجَةُ ٱلْمَآءِ.

Cop, *n.* شُوشَة ـ رَأْس.

Copaiba, *n.* } بَلَسَمُ ٱلتَّعْقِيبَةِ.
Copaiva, }

Copal, *n.* سَنْدَرُوس بِلَّوْرِيّ.

Coparcenary, *n.* شِرْكَةٌ فِي ٱلْإِرْثِ.

Coparcener, *n.* شَرِيكٌ فِي ٱلْإِرْثِ.

Copartner, *n.* زُمَلَآء *pl.* زَمِيل ـ رَفِيق ـ شَرِيك. To become — with, خَالَطَ ـ شَارَكَ.

Copartnership, *n.* ـ اِشْتِرَاك ـ شِرْكَة ـ خُلْطَة ـ مُفَاوَضَة

جَمْعِيَّة ـ رُفَاقَة. Copartnership in one thing exclusive of the rest, شِرْكَةُ ٱلْعِنَانِ.

Cope, *n.* A cap, تَرَابِيشُ *pl.* تَرْبُوش ـ طَرْطُور. An ecclesiastical vestment, بَدْرَشِين ـ بَدْرَشِيل ـ غَفَّارَة. The — or vault of heaven, قُبَّةُ ٱلسَّمَآء.

Cope, *v.i.* To equal, إِسْتَقْرَنَ ـ مَاثَلَ ـ بَارَى ـ حَاذَى. To contend with, قَاتَلَ. To overcome, غَلَبَ ـِ.

Copenhagen, *n.* كُوبَنْهَاك.

Copier, *n.* *See* Copyer, *n.*

Coping, *n.* Of a building, مَشَارِفُ *pl.* مَشْرَف ـ شُرْفَة; of a wall, أَفَارِيزُ *pl.* إِفْرِيز ـ أَكْنَان *pl.* كِنٌّ ـ طَنَف ـ طَاق ـ زِيف ـ عُلْوَة.

Copious, *a.* غَزِير ـ عَمِيم ـ وَفِيٌّ ـ وَافٍ ـ فَيَّاض ـ جَمٌّ ـ كَثِير ـ زَائِد ـ فَائِض ـ نَهِير. Copious, of water, غَدَق ـ غَمِير; of rain, نَدَاء. To be —, قَاضَ ـ أَفَاضَ ـ غَزُرَ ـ زَخَرَ ـ كَثُرَ; of rain, أَغْدَقَ ـ غَدِقَ; of water, غَمُرَ. A — language, لُغَةٌ وَاسِعَةٌ. A — spring, عَيْنٌ بَجِيسٌ. The rain was —, غَدِقَ ٱلْمَطَرُ.

Copiously, *ad.* بِفَيْضٍ ـ بِكَثْرَةٍ ـ بِغَزَارَةٍ ـ بِٱتِّسَاعٍ ـ وَفْرَةً.

Copiousness, *n.* بَرَكَة ـ كَثْرَة ـ فَضْلَة ـ فَيْض ـ زِيَادَة ـ غَزَارَة; of a language, وُسْع (سَعَة *or*) لُغَة.

Copper, *n.* The metal, نُحَاس ـ نُحَاس ـ صُفْر ـ صَاد ـ قِطْر. A vessel made of —, حِلَّة *pl.* حِلَل ـ قِدْر *pl.* قُدُور ـ أَخْمَر. دَسْت *pl.* دُسُوت ـ خَلْقِين.

Copperas, *n.* قَلْقَدِيس ـ نَاجٌ أَخْضَرُ ـ نَاج ـ قَلْقَنْت.

Copper-coloured, *a.* أَصْفَرُ نُحَاسِيٌّ.

Copper-plate, *n.* صَفِيحَةُ نُحَاسٍ مَنْقُوشَةٌ لِلطَّبْعِ.

Coppersmith, *n.* نَحَّاس *pl.* نَحَّاسُون ـ صَفَّار.

Coppery, *a.* نُحَاسِيٌّ ـ صُفْرِيٌّ.

Coppice, *n.* / Copse, غَابَة ـ دَغَل ـ خِيس ـ غَيْطَلَة ـ خَمَر.

Copt, *n.* قِبْطِيٌّ *pl.* قَبَاطِيٌّ *and* أَقْبَاط.

Coptic, *a.* قِبْطِيٌّ.

Copula, *n.* A — in logic, عَلَاقَةٌ بَيْنَ ٱلْمُسْنَدِ وَٱلْمُسْنَدِ إِلَيْهِ.

Copulate, *v.t.* زَوَّجَ ـ قَارَنَ ـ جَمَعَ ـ وَصَلَ ـ ب *aor.* يَصِلُ.

Copulate, *v.i.* To unite sexually, تَنَاكَحَ ـ جَامَعَ; of beasts and birds, تَسَافَدَ ـ سَفَدَ عَلَى ٱلْأُنْثَى. They copulated, of beasts, تَسَافَدُوا ـ تَدَافَنُوا.

Copulation, *n.* Sexual —, تَنَاكُح ـ مُجَامَعَة; of beasts, سِفَاد ـ ضِرَاب ـ نِزَآء. To make advances towards —, of beasts, قَفَطَ ـِ.

Copulative, *a.* عَاطِف ـ مُتَّصِل ـ مُقْتَرِن; a — conjunction, حَرْفُ عَطْفٍ.

Copy, *n.* A transcript, أَمْثِلَة *pl.* مِثَال ـ مَنْقُول مِن ـ نُسْخَة *pl.* نُسَخ. One of many books, نُسْخَة. That from which anything is copied, قَاعِدَة ـ أَصْل ـ دُسْتُور. A fair —, مُبَيَّضَة; a foul or rough —, مُسَوَّدَة ـ مُسْوَدَّة.

Copy, *v.t.* To transcribe, إِسْتَنْسَخَ ـ نَقَلَ ـ نَسَخَ ـ أَخَذَ ـ إِقْتَصَى ب ـ ضَاهَى ـ تَقَيَّلَ ـ قَلَّدَ ـ تَمَثَّلَ ب ـ صُورَة. To imitate, نَقْلًا مِن ـ بَارَى. Copied from, نَقْلًا مِن.

Copy-book, *n.* A book to copy from, كِتَاب قَوَاعِدِ ٱلْخَطِّ. A book to copy into, كِتَابٌ لِلنَّسْخِ فِيهِ. Copies first made by children at school, تَنَاشِير.

Copyer, *n.* / Copyist, A transcriber, كَاتِب ـ وَرَّاق ـ نُسَّاخ *pl.* نَاسِخ ـ كَتَبَة *pl.* مُبَيِّضُ ٱلْأَوْرَاقِ. An imitator, مُقَلِّد. A plagiary, سَرَّاق ـ مُنْتَحِل.

Copyhold, *n.* حُجَّةُ ٱلْتِزَامٍ ـ تَعْرِيفَاتُ ٱلْإِلْتِزَامِ.

Copyholder, *n.* مُؤْجِر ـ مُسْتَأْجِر ـ مُلْتَزِم.

Copyright, *n.* إِمْتِيَازُ ٱلْمُؤَلِّفِ ـ بَرَآءَةُ كِتَاب. Having the — of, of a book, صَاحِبُ بَرَآءَةِ تَأْلِيف. *See also* Patent, *n.*

Copyright, *a.* Of a book, تَأْلِيف ذُو بَرَآءَةٍ.

Coquet, *v.i.* تَلَاطَفَ ـ تَظَرَّفَ ـ تَدَلَّلَ ـ دَلَّ ـ عَرِمَ; of a woman, تَغَنَّجَت ـ غَنِجَت. *See also to* Flirt, *v.i.*

Coquet, *v.t.* غَازَلَ ـ دَعَبَ ـ لَاطَفَ.

Coquetry, *n.* دَلَال ـ تَدَلُّل ـ دَلّ ـ شُكُول *pl.* شِكْل ـ شَنِيقَة ـ غُنْج ـ غِنَاج ـ عُجْب. To use —, of a woman, غَنِجَت ـ تَغَنَّجَت.

Coquette, *n.* / Coquettish, *a.* عَنِجَة ـ مَغْنُوجَة ـ مُتَدَلِّلَة ـ شَكِلَة. *See also* Flirt, *n.*

Coracle, *n.* قُفَّة *pl.* قُفَف.

Coral, *n.* مُرْجَان ـ بُسَّذ. Black coral, so called, يَسَر.

Coralline, *a.* Of coral, مُرْجَانِيٌّ.

Coralloid, *a.* / Coralloidal, كَٱلْمُرْجَانِ.

Corbel, *n.* (In architecture), زِينَةٌ بِشَكْلِ قُفَّةٍ.

Cord, *n.* مَرَس ـ أَحْبَال *pl.* حَبْل ـ بَنْد ـ رُسُن *pl.* رَسَن. The small — for ornamenting dresses, قِيطَان ـ شَرِيط. Tent —, طُنُب. The spinal —, خَيْطُ ٱلرَّقَبَةِ ـ نُخَاع. A maker of —, rope, صَانِعُ ٱلْحِبَالِ; of ornamental —, حَبَّاك.

Cord, *v.t.* حَبَلَ ـ رَبَطَ بِحَبْلٍ ـ شَدَّ بِحَبْلٍ.

Cordage, *n.* حِبَال ـ قُلُوس.

Cordial, *n.* A strengthening medicine, دَوَآءٌ مُفَرِّحٌ ـ سُلْوَان ـ مُفَرِّح ـ مُنْعِش ـ إِكْسِيرٌ مُفَرِّحٌ ـ ٱلْقَلْبِ. Anything that comforts, مُفَرِّح ـ مُنْعِش.

Cordial, *a.* Reviving, مُقَوٍّ ـ مُنْعِش. Sincere, قَلْبِيٌّ ـ صَمِيم ـ خَالِص.

Cordiality, *n.* صَمِيمَة ـ خُلُوص ـ صِدْق ـ مَحْض ـ وُدّ.

Cordially, *ad.* قَلْبًا وَقَالَبًا ـ بِخُلُوصٍ ـ بِإِخْلَاصٍ ـ بِمَحْضٍ ـ مِنْ صَمِيمِ ٱلْقَلْبِ. To love —, أَمْحَضَ ـ ٤ مَحَضَ.

Cordon, *n.* A — of soldiers, صَفُّ عَسْكَرٍ. Cordon Sanitaire, حَاجِزٌ حَوْلَ مَكَانٍ مُصَابٍ بِعَدْوَى صِيَانَةٌ عَنْ إِعْدَآءِ ٱلدَّآءِ ـ حَاجِزٌ تَحَفُّظِيٌّ.

Cords, *n.* } قُمَاشٌ مُضَلَّعٌ يُشْبِهُ ٱلْقَطِيفَةَ ٱلْخَشِنَةَ.
Corduroy, }

Cordwain, *n.* سِخْتِيَان ـ حَوْرَة.

Cordwainer, *n.* خَفَّاف ـ صِرْمَاتِيٌّ ـ أَسْكَاف.

Core, *n.* The heart, قَلْب ـ أَفْئِدَة *pl.* فُؤَاد. The inner part of a fruit, قَلْب ـ لُبّ *pl.* لُبُوب. The — of a boil, بَيْضَة; the matter in a sore, مِدَّة ـ قَيْح. The heart's —, جُلْجُلان ـ حَبَّةُ ٱلْقَلْبِ.

Co-regent, *n.* شَرِيكٌ فِي ٱلنِّيَابَةِ عَنِ ٱلسَّلْطَنَةِ.

Corelation, *n.* مُطَابَقَةٌ فِي ٱلنِّسْبَةِ ـ إِشْتِرَاكٌ فِي ٱلنِّسْبَةِ.

Co-respondent, *n.* شَرِيكٌ ـ مُدَّعًى عَلَى ـ مَعَ رَفِيقٍ فِي ٱلْعَمَلِ ـ فِي ٱلْعَمَلِ.

Coriaceous, *a.* كَٱلْجِلْدِ ـ مِنْ جِلْدٍ.

Coriander, *n.* The seed, جُلْجُلان ـ تِقْدَة; the plant, كُزْبَرَة.

Cork, *n.* The tree, نَوْعٌ مِنَ ٱلشَّجَرِ ـ فُلّ ـ فَلِّين. A stopple, سِدَادَة ـ سِدَاد ـ صِبَار ـ صِمَام *coll.* صِمَامَة ـ صِمَاد.

Cork, *v.t.* ٢ سَدَّ ـ بِسِدَادَةٍ ـ ٢ سَدَّ ـ أَصَمَّ ـ ٤ صَمَّ ـ أَصْبَرَ. To be corked, إِنْسَدَّ ـ إِسْتَدَّ. Corked, مَسْدُود.

Corkscrew, *n.* بَرِّيمَة ـ مِبْرَم.

Cormorant, *n.* قَاقُ ٱلْمَآءِ.

Corn, *n.* Grain generally, طَعَام ـ حَبّ *pl.* حُبُوب. Wheat, growing in the ear, حِنْطَة ـ بُرّ ـ قَمْح. Grain yet unreaped, زَرْع ـ دَخْس. Indian —, ذُرَة. An excrescence on the foot, بَثْرَةٌ (or قَرْحَةٌ) فِي ٱلْقَدَمِ ـ ثَآلِيلُ *pl.* ثُؤْلُول *pl.* بَثَرَات.

Corn, *v.t.* To salt, مَلَّحَ.

Corn-chandler, *n.* بَيَّاعُ حِنْطَةٍ ـ قَمَّاح ـ طَعَامِيٌّ.

Cornea, *n.* طَبَقَةُ ٱلْعَيْنِ.

Cornel, *n.* The tree, شَجَرَةُ ٱلْقَرَانِيَا; the fruit of the —, قَرَاصِيَة ـ حَبُّ ٱلشَّوْمِ.

Cornelian, *n.* The stone, عَقِيق *pl.* عَقَائِق.

Corneous, *a.* صُلْبٌ كَٱلْقَرْنِ ـ قَرْنِيٌّ ـ رَوْقِيٌّ.

Corner, *n.* An angle, رُكْن *pl.* أَرْكَان ـ زَاوِيَة *pl.* زَوَايَا ـ قُرْنَة *pl.* قُرَانِي. A secret place, مَحَلٌّ فِي ٱلْخَفَآءِ ـ مَكْمَن. The utmost limit, أَقْصَى ـ حَدّ ـ طَرَف. The — of the eye, مَحْجِر ـ مَاق ـ ٱلْعَيْنِ. The —, as of a street, عَطْفَة ـ مُنْعَطَف. The four corners of the globe, أَطْرَافُ (or أَقْطَارُ) ٱلدُّنْيَا ٱلْأَرْبَعَةُ. From all corners, مِنْ كُلِّ نَاحِيَةٍ ـ مِنْ كُلِّ فَجٍّ عَمِيقٍ. Tied at the four corners, مَرْبُوطٌ بِأَرْبَعَةِ أَطْرَافٍ. To look at one from the — of the eye, ٤ نَظَرَ إِلَى ـ بِطَرَفِ ٱلْعَيْنِ.

Corner-stone, *n.* حَجَرُ ٱلزَّاوِيَةِ.

Cornet, *n.* A musical instrument, بُوق ـ صُور ـ شَبُّور. An officer in a cavalry regiment, مُلَازِمٌ ثَانٍ فِي عَسْكَرِ ٱلْأَسَاوِرَةِ (or ٱلْخَيَّالَةِ).

Corn-factor, *n.* *See* Corn-chandler, *n.*

Cornice, *n.* رَفّ *pl.* رُفُوف ـ زَيْف ـ طَنَف *pl.* أَطْنَاف ـ شُرَّافَة ـ إِفْرِيز ـ شُرَف.

Corn-stack, *n.* حِنْطَة كُدْس *pl.* أَكْدَاس.

Corn-stalk, *n.* سَاقُ ٱلسُّنْبُلِ *pl.* سُوُوق.

Cornucopia, *n.* قَرْنُ ٱلْكَثْرَةِ وَهُوَ عِبَارَةٌ عَنْ خِصْبِ ٱلْغِلَالِ.

Corny, *a.* Producing corn, حِنْطَاوِيٌّ. *See also* Corneous, *a.*

Corolla, *n.* كِمَامَة ـ بُرْعُومَة ـ بُرْعُوم ـ وَرَقُ ٱلزَّهْرِ.

Corollary, *n.* Inference, نَتِيجَة ـ حَاصِل.

Corona, *n.* The — of a flower, سَطْحُ ٱلزَّهْرِ. A halo round the sun or moon, هَالَة ـ دَوَّارَة ـ نُدْأَة ـ طُفَاوَة. A crown of light, إِكْلِيلُ أَنْوَارٍ. Corona Borealis, ٱلْفَكَّةُ.

Coronal, *n.* A crown, تَاج ـ إِكْلِيل. *See also* Crown, *n.*

Coronation, *n.* تَجْلِيس ـ تَمْلِيك ـ تَتْوِيج ـ مُبَايَعَة. The — oath, ٱلْيَمِينُ بِٱللّٰهِ عِنْدَ ٱلْمُبَايَعَةِ. Coronation-day, عِيدُ (or تَذْكَارُ) جُلُوسِ ٱلْمَلِكِ.

Coroner, *n.* ضَابِطٌ يُقِيمُهُ ٱلْمَلِكُ لِلْبَحْثِ عَمَّنْ مَاتَ عَنْ غَيْرِ حَتْفِ أَنْفِهِ.

Coronet, *n.* تَاجُ ٱلْأُمَرَآءِ ـ تُوَيْج. A garland, إِكْلِيلٌ مِنْ زَهْرٍ.

Corporal, *n.* The inferior military officer, اون باشي. The covering for the chalice, لِفَافَة ـ شَوْشَفَة ـ شُوشِبَّة.

Corporal, *n.* Belonging to the body, جَسَدِيٌّ ـ جِسْمِيٌّ ـ بَدَنِيٌّ ـ جُسْمَانِيٌّ. Material, مَادِّيٌّ ـ هَيُولِيٌّ ـ هَيُولَانِيٌّ. Corporal punishment, عُقُوبَةُ ٱلسَّوْطِ ـ تَأْدِيبُ ٱلضَّرْبِ ـ ضَرْب ـ عُقُوبَةٌ جَسَدِيَّةٌ ـ مُجَازَاةٌ بَدَنِيَّةٌ.

Corporality, *n.* } Bodily substance, جِسْمَانِيَّة; materiality,
Corporeity, } مَادِّيَّة.

Corporally, *ad.* بِٱلْجَسَدِ ـ فِي ٱلْبَدَنِ.

Corporate, *a.* United in a body, مُنْضَمٌّ ـ مُتَأَلِّف ـ مُتَجَمِّع ـ مُتَّحِد ـ مُتَّفِق. A — body, authorised by charter, جَمَاعَةٌ ذَاتُ بَرَاءَةٍ.

Corporation, *n.* A body constituted by law, جَمَاعَةٌ شَرْعِيَّةٌ مُقِيمَةٌ عَلَى بَرَاءَةٍ. A trade —, حِرْفَةٌ *pl.* حِرَف ـ صِنْف *pl.* أَصْنَاف.

Corporeal, *a.* *See* Corporal, *a.*

Corps, *n.* A body of troops, كَتِيبَة *pl.* كَتَائِب ـ قَنْبَلَة ـ جَمِيع ـ وَضِيمَة *pl.* طَابُور *pl.* طَوَابِير ـ آلَاى. The diplomatic —, الشُّفَرَاءُ أَجْمَعُ ـ ٱلسُّفَرَاءِ. The consular —, القَنَاصِلُ قَاطِبَةً ـ القَنَاصِلُ كَافَّةً. An irregular —, فِرْقَةُ عَسْكَرٍ غَيْرُ مَنْظُومَةٍ ـ بَاشِي بُوزُوك.

Corpse, *n.* مَيِّت *pl.* جُثَث ـ جُثَّة *pl.* جِيَف ـ جِيفَة *pl.* جَنَائِز ـ جِنَازَة ـ مَيْتُون. The matter which exudes from a —, غَيْنَة.

Corpulence, *n.* / Corpulency, } سِمَن ـ ضَخَامَة ـ بَدَانَة ـ جُسْمَانِيَّة.

Corpulent, *a.* بَدِين ـ أَضْخَم ـ ضَخْم ـ بَدَنِيّ ـ جُسْمَانِيّ ـ جَسِيم ـ سَمِين ـ شَخِيص. To be —, ضَخُمَ [2].

Corpus Christi, *n.* The festival of, عِيدُ ٱلْقُرْبَانِ ـ عِيدُ ٱلْجَسَدِ ٱلْمُقَدَّس.

Corpuscle, *n.* هَبَاء *pl.* أَهْبَاء ـ ذَرَّة *pl.* ذَرَّات ـ هُنَامَة.

Corpuscular, *a.* هَبَائِيّ ـ ذَرِّيّ.

Correct, *v.t.* To chastise, أَدَّبَ ـ قَاصَّ ـ عَزَّرَ ـ زَجَرَ [2] ـ حَدَّ [2] ـ قَاصَصَ. To amend, صَحَّحَ ـ ضَبَطَ [2] ـ صَلَّحَ ـ أَصْلَحَ. To temper, أَصْلَحَ ـ لَطَّفَ ـ عَدَّلَ.

Correct, *a.* Painstaking, minute, مُدَقِّق ـ مُحَرِّر ـ مُنَقِّح. Accurate, صَحِيح ـ مُصَحَّح ـ مَضْبُوط. Proper, لَائِق ـ مُنَاسِب. Upright, مُسْتَقِيم ـ مُقْسِط. He is very — in keeping his accounts, هُوَ مُدَقِّقٌ فِي تَقْيِيدِ حِسَابَاتِهِ. To be —, accurate, proper, just, حَقَّ ـ صَحَّ.

Correction, *n.* Punishment, قِصَاص ـ تَوْبِيخ ـ تَعْنِيف ـ تَعْزِير ـ تَأْدِيب. Emendation, تَهْذِيب ـ تَنْقِيح ـ تَحْرِير ـ تَثْقِيف ـ ضَبْط ـ إِصْلَاح ـ تَصْحِيح ـ مُعَالَجَة. House of Correction, حَبْس ـ مَحْبَس لِتَهْذِيب. Reprehension, مَلَامَة ـ عَذْل. Correction, as of noxious qualities, تَلْطِيف ـ تَعْدِيل ـ إِصْلَاح.

Correctional, *a.* تَأْدِيبِيّ ـ مُتَعَلِّق بِٱلتَّهْذِيب ـ إِصْلَاحِيّ.

Corrective, *a.* Amending, مُصْلِح. Attempering, مُلَطِّف ـ كَاسِر ـ مُعَدِّل.

Corrective, *n.* دَوَاءٌ مُعَدِّل ـ مُعَالَجَة ـ عِلَاج.

Correctly, *ad.* Accurately, بِضَبْطٍ ـ بِتَدْقِيقٍ ـ بِتَنْقِيحٍ ـ بِٱلتَّحْرِيرِ ـ حَقًّا. Uprightly, بِقِسْطٍ ـ بِٱسْتِقَامَةٍ. Properly, fitly, مُنَاسَبَةً ـ بِلِيَاقَةٍ. More correctly, so and so, وَٱلصَّوَابُ كَذَا وَكَذَا.

Correctness, *n.* Accuracy, إِزْعَان ـ تَحْرِير ـ صِحَّة ـ حَقِيقَة ـ قِسْط ـ إِحْكَام ـ دِقَّة ـ ضَبْط. Uprightness, إِسْتِقَامَة.

Corrector, *n.* One who revises, مُصَحِّح ـ مُصْلِح.

Correlate, *n.* / Correlative, } نَسِيب ـ لَازِمٌ وَمَلْزُوم.

Correlation, *n.* عَلَاقَةٌ وَمُنَاسَبَةٌ ـ مُنَاسَبَة ـ تَنَاسُب.

Correlative, *a.* مُتَنَاسِب ـ ذُو جِهَةٍ جَامِعَةٍ. Correlative nouns, أَسْمَاءٌ مَوْصُولَةٌ. To be — to, نَاسَبَ.

Correspond, *v.i.* To suit, طَابَقَ ـ نَاسَبَ ـ شَاكَلَ ـ لَأَمَ. To — by letter, كَاتَبَ ـ رَاسَلَ. The present year, A.D. 1878, corresponds with the year 1295 of the al-Hijrah, سَنَةُ ٱلنَّصَارَى ٱلْحَالِيَّةُ وَهِيَ ١٨٧٨ مُوَافِقَةٌ لِسَنَةِ ١٢٩٥ مِنَ ٱلْهِجْرَةِ. They corresponded, by letter, with one another, of many, تَكَاتَبُوا.

Correspondence, *n.* Suitableness, مُوَافَقَة ـ مُطَابَقَة ـ مُنَاسَبَة. Relation, تَعَلُّق ـ عَلَاقَة ـ إِرْتِبَاط ـ صِلَة. Intercourse, مُصَاحَبَة ـ مُخَالَطَة ـ مُشَارَكَة ـ مُعَاشَرَة ـ مُدَاخَلَة. News, خَبَر. Correspondence by letter, مُكَاتَبَة ـ مُرَاسَلَة. Official —, مُرَاسَلَاتٌ مُحَرَّرَاتٌ رَسْمِيَّةٌ ـ رَسْمِيَّةٌ.

Correspondent, *a.* مُوَافِق ـ مُطَابِق ـ مُنَاسِب ـ طَبِيق.

Correspondent, *n.* One who corresponds by letter, مُرَاسِل ـ مُكَاتِب. An agent, عَامِل *pl.* عَمَلَة ـ مُعَامِل. Anything which corresponds to another, طِبَاقَة. One who gives or writes news, مُخْبِر.

Corridor, *n.* رِوَاق *pl.* أَرْوَاق *and* أَرْوِقَة ـ مَمْشَى.

Corrigenda, *n.* غَلَطَاتٌ تَحْتَاجُ إِلَى ٱلْإِصْلَاحِ.

Corrigible, *a.* جَدِيرٌ بِٱلتَّصْلِيحِ ـ مِمَّا يُصْلَحُ.

Corroborant, *a.* *See* Corroborative, *a.*

Corroborate, *v.t.* To confirm, عَزَّزَ ـ قَرَّرَ ـ أَيَّدَ ـ عَضَدَ [2] ـ ثَبَّتَ. To strengthen, سَدَّدَ ـ شَدَّدَ ـ قَوَّى ـ مَكَّنَ ـ عَضَدَ [2] ـ عَزَّرَ ب.

Corroboration, *n.* تَشْيِيد ـ تَشْدِيد ـ تَسْدِيد ـ تَأْيِيد ـ تَعْضِيد ـ تَثْبِيت ـ تَقْوِيَة ـ تَمْكِين ـ تَعْزِيز.

Corroborative, *a.* مُثَبِّت ـ مُؤَيِّد ـ مُشَدِّد ـ مُشِيد ـ مُقَوٍّ.

Corrode, *v.t.* To eat away by degrees, قَرَضَ ـ سَرَفَ [2] ـ أَكَلَ [2] ـ رَعَى. To —, as the moth, لَحَسَ; as the cankerworm, تَأَكَّلَ ـ أُكِلَ ـ قُرِضَ ـ سُرِفَ. To be —, خَرَبَ; by worms, قَرِدَ.

Corrodent, *a.* } أَكَّال ـ آكِل ـ قَارِض ـ سَارِف ـ مُسْرِف ـ
Corrosive, } Corrosive sublimate, زِئْبَق مُصَعَّد أَكَّال ـ سُلَيْمَانِيّ.

Corrodible, *a.* مَأْكُول ـ مِمَّا يُؤْكَل ـ يُسْرَف.

Corrosion, *n.* إِبْلَآء ـ لَحْس ـ أُكَال ـ سِرَاف ـ سَرَف.

Corrosive, *a.* *See* Corrodent, *a.*

Corrosively, *ad.* مِثْلَ ٱلْأَكَّالِ ـ كَٱلْأَكَّالِ ـ سَرَفًا.

Corrugate, *v.t.* To contract, قَبَض ـ. To wrinkle, furrow, أَمْحَلَ ـ خَدَّ ² ـ غَضَّنَ. To be corrugated, contracted, تَقَبَّضَ; to be wrinkled, shrivelled, furrowed, تَعَكَّشَ ـ خَدَّدَ ـ تَخَدَّدَ ـ تَكَمَّشَ ـ تَغَضَّنَ. Corrugated, مُخَدَّد ـ مُتَخَدِّد ـ مُتَغَضِّن. Corrugated iron, ٱلْحَدِيدُ ٱلْمُتَغَضِّنُ (or ٱلْمُتَخَدِّدُ).

Corrugation, *n.* The act of, خَدٌّ ـ تَغْضِين. The being corrugated, تَغَضُّن ـ تَخَدُّد ـ إِنْقِبَاض.

Corrupt, *v.t.* To make putrid, to vitiate, فَسَّخَ ـ أَمْذَرَ ـ عَفَّنَ ـ أَفْسَدَ ـ شَحَّمَ ـ عَفَّنَ. To deprave, أَفْسَدَ ـ أَرْدَأَ ـ فَسَّقَ ـ فَسَّدَ ـ أَسَاءَ ـ أَخْبَثَ ـ أَغْوَى ـ أَغَشَّ. To bribe, رَشَا ² ـ بَرْطَلَ. To become —, putrid, عَفِنَ ـ خَبُثَ ² ـ تَفَسَّخَ ـ إِنْفَسَخَ ـ تَعَفَّنَ ـ تَمَذَّرَ ـ شَحِمَ ². To become —, depraved, إِنْفَسَدَ ـ خَبُثَ ² ـ أَخْبَثَ.

Corrupt, *a.* Putrid, عَفِن ـ مَعْفُون ـ مَذِر ـ مُتَعَفِّن ـ مُشَحَّم ـ فَاسِد ـ مُفَسَّخ ـ مُكَرَّج ـ عَاطِل. Depraved, فَاسِد ـ رَذِيل ـ دَنِيّ ـ خَبِيث ـ شِرِّير ـ عَاثٍ ـ فَاسِق ـ فَسَّاق.

Corrupter, *n.* One who corrupts, مُخْبِث ـ عَاثٍ ـ مُفَسِّخ ـ مُفْسِد ـ مُعَطِّل. A briber, رَاشٍ ـ مُبَرْطِل.

Corruptibility, *n.* Capacity of becoming corrupt, تَفَسُّخ ـ فَسَاد ـ قُبُولُ ٱلْفَسَادِ; of being bribed, إِمْكَانُ ٱلْمُرَاشَاةِ.

Corruptible, *a.* Capable of corruption, قَابِلُ ٱلْفَسَادِ ـ فَاسِخ ـ فَانٍ. That may be bribed, يُتَبَرْطَل.

Corruptibly, *ad.* بِنَوْعٍ فَاسِدٍ.

Corruption, *n.* The separation of the parts of a substance, بِلًى ـ رَمٌّ. Putrefaction, عُفُونَة ـ تَفَسُّخ ـ رِمَّة ـ بَلَآء ـ فَسَاد. Depravity, خُبْث ـ خَسَاسَة ـ شَنَاعَة ـ خَبَاثَة ـ دَخَل ـ رَدَآءَة ـ سُوء. A cause of —, مَفْسَدَة *pl.* مَفَاسِدُ. A bribe, رِشْوَة ـ بَرْطِيل. The matter in a sore, غَثِيث ـ قَيْح ـ مِدَّة. Perversion, as of the text of a book, عَكْس ـ تَحْرِيف ـ تَصْحِيف.

Corruptive, *a.* مُحَرِّض ـ مُفْسِد ـ أَفْسَدُ ـ مُفَسِّخ.

Corruptly, *ad.* بِفَسَادٍ ـ شَنَاعَةً ـ بِخُبْثٍ.

Corruptness, *n.* *See* Corruption, *n.*

Corse, *n.* *See* Corpse, *n.*

Corselet, *n.* زَرَدِيَّة.

Corset, *n.* قُورْسِيتَة ـ نِطَاقٌ عَرِيضٌ تَلْبِسُهُ ٱلنِّسَآء.

Cortège, *n.* مَحْفَل ـ وَكْبَة ـ مَوْكِب ـ خَدَمٌ وَحَشَمٌ ـ حَشَمَة ـ دَائِرَة.

Cortes, *n.* إِسْمُ ٱلْمَجْلِسِ ٱلْأَعْظَمِ فِي دَوْلَتَيْ إِسْبَانِيَا وَبُورْتُوغَال.

Cortical, *a.* قِشْرِيّ ـ لِحَائِيّ ـ أَدِيمِيّ.

Corticated, *a.* مِثْلَ ٱللِّحَآء.

Corticose, *a.* كَثِيرُ ٱللِّحَآء.

Coruscant, *a.* بَارِق ـ بَرَّاق ـ لَمَّاح.

Coruscate, *v.i.* أَشَعَّ ـ تَنَوَّرَ ـ لَمَحَ ـ بَرَقَ ² ـ تَلَأْلَأَ ـ لَأْلَأَ.

Coruscation, *n.* لَمْحَة ـ بَرَقَان ـ رَيْق ـ تَلَأْلُؤ ـ شَعْشَعَة ـ ضِيَآء ـ رَوْنَق.

Corvette, *n.* بَارِجَة صَغِيرَة ـ قُورْوِيتَة.

Cosey, *a.* رَيِّح ـ نَزِه ـ نَعِيم ـ أَنِيق.

Co-signatary, *n.* A — to, مُوَقِّعٌ عَلَى ـ مَعَ *pl.* مُوَقِّعُونَ. The — states to the treaty, ٱلدُّوَلُ ٱلْمُوَقِّعَةُ عَلَى ٱلشَّرْطِ مَعًا.

Cosily, *ad.* فِي أُنْسٍ ـ بِٱلنِّعْمَةِ ـ بِنَزَاهَةٍ ـ بِرَاحَةٍ.

Cosmetic, *n.* A beautifying lotion, غُسْلَة ـ غِسْل مُحَسِّن ـ أَبُو ٱلْمَحَاسِنِ ـ مَآءُ ٱلْجَمَالِ ـ مُجَمِّلَة.

Cosmical, *a.* Relating to the world, مُتَعَلِّق بِٱلْكُرَةِ ـ دُنْيَوِيّ ـ كُرَوِيّ ـ فَلَكِيّ. Rising and setting with the sun, مَا يَطْلُعُ وَيَغِيبُ مَعَ ٱلشَّمْسِ.

Cosmogony, *n.* خِلْقَةُ ٱلْعَالَمِ ـ رَأْيٌ فِي تَكْوِينِ ٱلْعَالَمِ.

Cosmographer, *n.* عَارِف بِرَسْمِ ٱلدُّنْيَا وَأَحْوَالِهَا.

Cosmographic, *a.* } مِمَّا يَنْتَسِبُ إِلَى رَسْمِ ٱلْعَالَمِ وَأَحْوَالِهِ.
Cosmographical, }

Cosmography, *n.* عِلْمُ ٱلْبَحْثِ عَنْ نِظَامِ ٱلْعَالَمِ وَمَا فِيهِ مِنَ ٱلْمَوْجُودَاتِ.

Cosmologist, *n.* عَالِمٌ بِقَوَاعِدِ ٱلْخَلِيقَةِ.

Cosmology, *n.* عِلْمُ قَوَاعِدِ ٱلْخَلِيقَةِ ـ عِلْمُ ٱلْخِلْقَةِ.

Cosmopolitan, *n.* } شَائِعُ ٱلْوَطَنِ ـ مَنْ يَتَّخِذُ كُلَّ ٱلْبِلَادِ وَطَنًا لَهُ.
Cosmopolite, }

Cosmorama, *n.* مَنَاظِرُ بُلْدَانٍ تُشَاهَدُ بِنَاظُورٍ.

Cost, *n.* The price of anything, قِيمَة ـ سِعْر ـ كُلْفَة ـ مَصْرُوف. Expense, charge, نَفَقَة ـ مَصْرُوف ـ خَرْج. Loss, ضَيَاع ـ خُسْرَان ـ خَسَارَة ـ تَلَف ـ مَضَرَّة. Luxury, إِفْرَاط ـ فُضُول. At my —, expense, عَلَى كِيسِي. I did it to my —, فَعَلْتُهُ خَسَارَةً لِي. To count the —, حَسَبَ حِسَابَ ـ حَسَبَ نَفَقَةً. Prime —, ثَمَن. A lawyer's bill of costs, قَائِمَةُ حِسَابِ وَكِيلٍ ـ ٱلدَّعْوَى ـ أُجْرَةُ وَكِيلِ دَعْوَى وَإِجَارَتِهِ. A judgment with costs,

حُكْمٌ عَلَى ٱلْمُدَّعَى عَلَيْهِ يُلْزِمُهُ بِدَفْعِ نَفَقَةِ ٱلدَّعْوَى; a judgment without costs, حُكْمٌ عَلَى ٱلْمُدَّعِي يُلْزِمُهُ بِدَفْعِ نَفَقَةِ دَعْوَاهُ. He paid the costs of the suit, دَفَعَ مَصَارِيفَ ٱلدَّعْوَى.

Cost, *v.t.* and *i.* بَلَغَتْ قِيمَتُهُ ـ تَكَلَّفَ ـ كَلَّفَ ـ قَامَ. It — me a great deal of anxiety, كَلَّفَنِي مَشَقَّةً بَلِيغَةً. How much did your horse — you? كَمْ كَلَّفَكَ ـ كَمْ بَلَغَتْ قِيمَةُ حِصَانِكَ حِصَانُكَ. It — him his life, كَانَ بَاعِثَ مَوْتِهِ. It — him an eye, سَبَّبَ عَوَرَهُ. To — one, to spend upon, أَنْفَقَ عَلَى.

Costal, *a.* جَنْبِيٌّ ـ ضِلْعِيٌّ.

Costermonger, *n.* مُتَسَبِّب.

Costive, *a.* مُنْقَبِضُ ٱلْبَطْنِ ـ مُحْتَبِس ـ مِجْعَار.

Costiveness, *n.* اِنْقِبَاض ـ اِحْتِبَاس.

Costliness, *n.* نَفَاسَة ـ عَظَامَة ـ غَلَاء ـ خَطَر.

Costly, *a.* ثَمِين ـ فَاخِر ـ سَنِيّ ـ نَفِيس ـ مُكَلِّف ـ خَطِير.

Costly garments, أَفْخِرَة.

Costume, *n.* زِيّ *pl.* أَزْيَاء ـ كِسْوَة ـ سَمْت ـ كُسَم.

Cot, *n.* A bed, مَنَام. *See also* Cottage, *n.*

Cote, *n.* A sheep-cote, مُرَاحُ ٱلْغَنَمِ ـ صِيرَة ـ حَظِيرَة. A pigeon's —, بُرْجُ حَمَامٍ ـ قَادُوسُ حَمَامٍ.

Cotemporary, *a.* *See* Contemporary, *a.*

Coterie, *n.* فِرْقَة ـ شَمْل ـ شِرْذِمَة.

Cotillon, Cotillion, *n.* ضَرْبٌ مِنَ ٱلرَّقْصِ.

Cottage, *n.* كُوخ *pl.* أَكْوَاخ ـ خُصّ *pl.* خِصَاص ـ حِفْش *pl.* أَحْفَاش ـ بَيْتٌ صَغِيرٌ.

Cottager, *n.* / Cotter, } قَاطِنُ ٱلْكُوخِ *pl.* قُطَّان *and* قَاطِنَة.

Cotton, *n.* The down of the cotton plant, قُطْن ـ عُطْب. Dressed —, حَلِيج. Cloth made of —, قُمَاشٌ مِنْ ـ خَام ـ بَزّ ـ قُطْنِيّ. A — pod, عُقْز. Cotton seeds, بِزْرُ ٱلْقُطْنِ. A — plantation, مَقْطَنَة. To teaze —, نَدَفَ ٱلْقُطْنَ. To remove the seeds from —, حَلَجَ ٱلْقُطْنَ. A teazer of —, نَدَّاف. One who removes the seeds from —, حَلَّاج. The instrument for removing the seeds from —, مِحْلَاج. The art of removing the seeds from —, حِلَاجَة. Cotton print, چِيت. *See also to* Gin, Teaze, *v.t.*

Cotyledon, *n.* أُذُن *pl.* آذَان.

Cotyledonous, *a.* ذُو آذَانٍ.

Couch, *v.i.* To lie down, اِضْطَجَعَ ـ اِتَّكَى ـ اِنْسَرَحَ; of a beast, رَبَضَ; especially of a camel, بَرَكَ ـ نَاخَ.

Couch, *v.t.* To make to lie down, أَقَرَّ ـ أَضْجَعَ ـ أَرَاحَ. To comprise, clothe, أَفْرَغَ ـ فِي ـ كَسَا ـ سَبَكَ. To comprise under, include, اِحْتَوَى عَلَى ـ ضَمَّنَ ـ شَمَلَ. To — a lance, سَدَّدَ ٱلرُّمْحَ ـ شَرَّرَ ٱلرُّمْحَ. He couched his argument in graceful language, أَفْرَغَ ٱلدَّلِيلَ فِي قَالِبِ ٱلْإِتْقَانِ وَعُذُوبَةِ ٱلْأَلْفَاظِ.

Couch, *n.* A seat of repose, مَضْجَع ـ طَرَّاحَة ـ مِسْنَد ـ وِسَاد. A bed, فِرَاش ـ مَرْقَد ـ مَقْعَد ـ أَرَائِك *pl.* أَرِيكَة.

Couchant, *a.* ضَاجِع ـ ضَجِيع ـ رَابِض ـ مُضْطَجِع ـ مُضْجِع.

Cough, *n.* قُحْب ـ سُعَال ـ سُعْلَة. A slight —, سُعَيْرَة; a violent —, سُعَالٌ سَاعِلٌ. The — of a horse or camel, قُحَاب.

Cough, *v.i.* سَعَلَ ـ قَحَبَ.

Could, *aux. verb*, He —, قَدَرَ عَلَى ـ أَمْكَنَهُ ـ فِي طَاقَتِهِ أَنْ. Could I? أَقْدَرْتُ. Could they...? أَوَ كَانَ لَهُمْ أَنْ ـ أَطَاقَ.

See also under Able, *a.*

Coulter, *n.* مَدِيَة *pl.* مُدًى ـ نَوْرَج ـ سِكَّة ـ مِحْرَاث.

Council, *n.* An assembly for consultation, نَدِيّ *pl.* أَنْدِيَة ـ دِيوَانُ مَشُورَةٍ ـ مَشُورَة ـ شُورَى ـ مَحْفَل ـ مُؤْتَمَر ـ مَجْمَع. To hold a —, عَقَدَ مَشُورَةً ـ عَقَدَ مَجْمَعًا. The place where a — is held, دَارُ ٱلنَّدْوَى ـ مَجْلِس ـ مُنْتَدًى.

A cabinet council, مَجْمَعُ مُدَبِّرِي ٱلْمَمْلَكَةِ.

A council of ministers, مَجْلِسُ وُكَلَاء.

A council of war, مَجْمَعٌ حَرْبِيٌّ ـ مَجْمَعٌ عَسْكَرِيٌّ.

A local council, مَجْلِسٌ مَحَلِّيٌّ.

A municipal council, مَجْلِسٌ بَلَدِيٌّ.

A member of a council, عُضْوُ مَجْلِسٍ *pl.* أَعْضَاء.

A privy council, مَجْمَعٌ خَاصٌّ.

An ecumenical council, مَجْمَعٌ عَامٌّ ـ مَجْمَعٌ عُمُومِيٌّ.

An executive council, مَجْلِسُ ٱلْإِجْرَاآتِ.

Counsel, *n.* Advice, مَشُورَة ـ شُورَى ـ نُصْح ـ نَصِيحَة ـ رَأْي. Consultation, اِئْتِمَار ـ مُؤَامَرَة ـ تَشَاوُر ـ مُشَاوَرَة. Prudence, cunning, اِحْتِيَال ـ حِيلَة ـ إِرْب. Design, غَايَة ـ قَصْد. One that pleads a cause, مُحَامٍ ـ مُحْتَجّ. To ask — of, in any matter, اِسْتَفْتَى ـ فِي. To take the — of, أَصْغَى إِلَى. They took — together, of many, تَشَاوَرُوا ـ تَذَاكَرُوا. By way of —, عَلَى وَجْهِ ٱلنَّصِيحَةِ.

Counsel, *v.t.* نَصَحَ ـ أَشَارَ عَلَى ـ بِ ـ اِرْتَأَى لِ. To warn, نَبَّهَ ـ عَلَى ـ حَذَّرَ.

Counsellor, *n.* One who gives advice, مُشِير ـ نَاصِح. Member of a Council, أَحَدُ أَرْبَابِ مَشُورَةٍ. A solicitor, مُفْتٍ ـ فَقِيه. An advocate, وَكِيلُ دَعْوَى ـ مُحَامِي ٱلدَّعَاوِي *pl.* مُحَامُونَ.

Count, *v.t.* To number, أَحْصَى ـ عَدَّ ـ حَسَبَ. To

reckon, حَسِبَ ـ حَسَبَ ². To esteem, اِعْتَقَدَ ـ اِعْتَدَّ بِ ـ اِعْتَبَرَ. To impute to, نَسَبَ ² إِلَى ـ أَسْنَدَ إِلَى ـ عَزَا إِلَى ². I — it of no value, أَحْسِبُهُ لَا قِيمَةَ لَهُ. To be counted, reckoned, اِعْتَدَّ.

Count, *v.i.* To — upon, to rely upon, اِتَّكَلَ عَلَى ـ اِعْتَمَدَ عَلَى.

Count, *n.* A title of nobility, قُونْت ـ اِسْمُ شَرَفٍ. *See also* Account, *n.*

Countenance, *n.* The system of the features, face, وَجْه ـ مُحَيًّا ـ مَنْظَر ـ سِيمَاء ـ سَحْنَة ـ هَيْئَة ـ مَرْآة ـ طَلْعَة. Look, air, رَزَانَةُ ٱلْمَرْآةِ ـ سَمْت ـ رُؤْيَة. Figure, صُورَة. Calmness of aspect, ... Support, patronage, عِنَايَة ـ رِعَايَة ـ اِلْتِفَات ـ تَوَجُّه ـ حِمَايَة ـ ظَهْر. A pleasant —, مَرْآة وَسِيمَة ـ مَنْظَر بَهِيج. Having a pleasant —, طَلِيقُ ٱلْوَجْهِ. You put him out of — by your question, أَخْجَلْتَهُ بِسُؤَالِكَ. He must be kept in — or he will certainly fail, بِدُونِ مُظَاهَرَةٍ فَيُقَصِّرُ لَا مُحَالَةَ. He put on a good —, was persevering, تَثَبَّتَ ـ أَظْهَرَ ٱلثَّبَاتَ ـ تَجَلَّدَ.

Countenance, *v.t.* To support, أَصْلَحَ إِلَى ـ شَدَّدَ ـ أَيَّدَ ـ سَنَّدَ ـ حَثَّ ² ـ أَزَّ ² ـ قَالَ ب ² ـ شَدَّ أَزْرَهُ ². To encourage, stimulate, ... ـ أَرْغَبَ ـ عَلَى. I did not — his conduct, مَا أَحْمَدْتُ مَسْعَاهُ ـ مَا ٱسْتَحْسَنْتُ سُلُوكَهُ. To approve, اِسْتَصْوَبَ.

Counter, *n.* Any article used to count with, تَذْكِرَة *pl.* تَذَاكِر. A metal —, فَلْس *pl.* فُلُوس. A reckoner, حَسِيب ـ حَاسِب. A table on which goods are shown, بَنْك ـ مَائِدَةُ ٱلدُّكَّانِ.

Counter, *ad.* بِٱلضِّدِّ ـ ضِدّ ـ مُخَالَفَةً ـ مُنَاقَضَةً ـ نَكْثًا. To run — to, نَاقَضَ ـ ضَادَّ ـ خَالَفَ. *See also to* Counteract, *v.t.*

Counteract, *v.t.* خَيَّبَ ـ نَاقَضَ ـ عَارَضَ ـ خَالَفَ ـ عَاكَسَ.

Counteraction, *n.* عَكْس ـ مُعَارَضَة ـ مُخَالَفَة ـ مُعَاكَسَة ـ تَخْيِيب ـ مُنَاقَضَة.

Counteractive, *a.* مُبْطِل ـ مُنَاقِض ـ مُخَالِف ـ مُعَاكِس ـ مُخَيِّب.

Counterbalance, *n.* مُوَازَنَة ـ مُعَادَلَة ـ مُسَاوَاة.

Counterbalance, *v.t.* وَازَنَ ـ عَادَلَ ـ سَاوَى.

Counter-charm, *n.* فَكُّ ٱلسِّحْرِ.

Counter-check, *n.* A check, مَانِع; a reproof, تَوْبِيخ.

Counterdraw, *v.t.* نَقَلَ ٱلرَّسْمَ ² ـ حَوَّلَ ٱلرَّسْمَ.

Counter-evidence, *n.* شَهَادَة مُنَاقِضَة ـ تَنَاقُض.

Counterfeit, *a.* Forged, مُلَبَّس ـ مُقَلَّد ـ صِنَاعِيّ ـ مُمَوَّه ـ مُزَوَّر ـ زُور ـ مَغْشُوش. Deceitful, مُدَاهِن ـ مُوَالِس ـ غَابِن ـ غَاشّ. Counterfeit money, زَغَل ـ غِشّ.

Counterfeit, *n.* An impostor, مُتَحَيِّل ـ دَجَّال. A forgery, تَمْوِيه ـ بَهْرَجَة ـ تَزْوِير ـ غِشّ. A maker of — money, زُغْلِيّ.

Counterfeit, *v.t.* To forge, مَوَّهَ ـ لَبَّسَ ـ قَلَّدَ ـ زَوَّرَ ـ غَشَّ ². To imitate, to resemble, تَقَيَّلَ ـ قَلَّدَ. To — coin, ضَرَبَ دَرَاهِمَ زَيْف ـ زَائِفَة. Counterfeited, مَغْشُوش ـ مُزَوَّر ـ مُمَوَّه.

Counterfeiter, *n.* A — of coin, زُغْلِيّ.

Countermand, *n.* أَمْر مُنَاقِض ـ حُكْم مُخَالِف.

Countermand, *v.t.* To revoke an order, نَقَضَ ٱلْأَمْرَ ² ـ أَبْطَلَ ـ غَيَّرَ ٱلْأَمْرَ ـ ٱلْأَمْرَ. To oppose, نَاقَضَ ـ ضَادَّ ـ خَالَفَ.

Countermarch, *v.i.* جَالَ ² ـ تَرَاجَعَ.

Countermarch, *n.* A march backward, جَوْل ـ رَجْعَة ـ تَرَاجُع. A change, as of position, حَوْل ـ تَحَوُّل ـ اِنْقِلَاب ـ تَغَيُّر.

Countermark, *n.* A second mark on goods, نِيشَان شِرْكَة يُوضَع عَلَى ٱلْبِضَاعَةِ. Mark, as of the Goldsmiths' Company, سِمَة ـ دَمْغَة.

Countermine, *n.* لَغْم ضِدّ لَغْم آخَر. Opposition, مُعَادَاة ـ مُضَادَّة.

Countermine, *v.t.* حَفَرَ لَغْمًا ضِدّ لَغْم آخَر ـ. To defeat, as of a project, عَكَسَ ـ أَفْسَدَ ـ أَبْطَلَ ـ خَيَّبَ.

Countermovement, *n.* حَرَكَة مُخَالِفَة لِحَرَكَةٍ أُخْرَى.

Countermure, *n.* حَائِط مَبْنِيّ مُقَابِلَةَ حَائِط آخَر لِلْمُحَافَظَةِ.

Counternegotiation, *n.* مُعَامَلَة مِنْ جَانِبٍ آخَر ـ مُكَاتَبَة وَمُكَالَمَة عَلَى غَيْرِ وَجْهٍ.

Counterpane, *n.* لِحَاف *pl.* لُحُف.

Counterpart, *n.* طِبْق ـ قَطِيع ـ قَسِيمُ ٱلشَّيْءِ ـ شَقِيق ـ شَقِيقَة. He is my brother and the — of myself, هُوَ أَخِي وَشَقِيقُ نَفْسِي.

Counterplot, *n.* تَعَصُّب ضِدّ تَعَصُّب ـ حِيلَة ضِدّ حِيلَةٍ.

Counterpoise, *v.t.* وَازَنَ ـ سَاوَى ـ عَادَلَ.

Counterpoise, *n.* مُسَاوَاة ـ مُعَادَلَة ـ مُوَازَنَة.

Counter-poison, *n.* بَادْزَهْر ـ تِرْيَاق ـ دِرْيَاق ـ عِلَاج.

Counter-pressure, *n.* ٱلتَّضَادّ فِي ٱلدَّفْعِ ـ ضَغْط.

Counter-project, *n.* قَصْد (or) نِيَّة خِلَافَ نِيَّةٍ أُخْرَى.

Counter-revolution, *n.* رُجُوع إِلَى ٱلْحَالِ ٱلْأَوَّلِ ـ مُخَالَفَةُ ٱلْعِصْيَانِ.

Counterscarp, *n.* جِهَة بَرَّانِيَّة مِنْ جِدَارِ ٱلْخَنْدَقِ مُقَابِلَة لِلْقَلْعَةِ.

Countersign, *v.t.* شَهَادَة بِإِمْضَاء آخَر ـ وَقَّعَ عَلَى ـ (or) أَمْضَى.

Countersign, *n.* A military watchword, أَمْر يَوْمِيّ ـ بَارُولَة. A countersignature, إِمْضَاء شَهَادَة بِإِمْضَاء آخَر.

Countersink, *v.t.* جَوَّفَ ٱلشَّيْءَ لِإِدْخَالِ رَأْسِ ٱلْمِسْمَارِ.

Countersink, *n.* مِثْقَب تَثْقُب ٱلشَّيْءَ لِإِدْخَالِ رَأْسِ ٱلْمِسْمَارِ.

Counter-statement, *n.* إِفَادَة ضِدّ إِفَادَةٍ أُخْرَى ـ تَقْرِير مُتَضَادّ.

Counter-tenor, *n.* طَبَقَة فِي ٱلْغِنَاء مُتَوَسِّطَة.

Counter-tide, *n.* مَدٌّ وَجَزْرٌ مُتَصَادِمَانِ ـ تَيَّار.

Countervail, *v.t.* كَافَى ـ عَادَلَ ـ وَازَنَ ـ قَامَ مَقَامَ ² ـ نَابَ ـ مَنَابَ أَجْرَى مَجْرَى.

Countervail, *n.* مُعَادَلَة ـ مُكَافَاة.

Counter-work, *v.t.* ضَادَدَ ـ قَاوَمَ.

Countess, *n.* كُونْتِيسَة ـ زَوْجَةُ ٱلْكُونْت. *See* Count, *n.*

Counting-house, *n.* / Counting-room, } مَكْتَب.

Countless, *a.* لا عَدَدَ لَهُ ـ لا يُحْصَى.

Countrify, *v.t.* (ٱلرِّيفِ *or*) إِسْتَهْوَى-عَيْشَةَ ٱلْحَاضِرَةِ. Countrified, مُتَرَيِّف.

Country, *n.* A tract of land, region, أَمْصَار ـ دِيَار ـ إِيَالَة ـ قُطْر *pl.* نَاحِيَة ـ نَوَاحِي *pl.* أَقْلِيم ـ أَقَالِيمُ *pl.* أَرْض ـ أَرَاضِي ـ بِلاد. Rural parts, رُسْتَاق ـ سَوَاد ـ رِيف *pl.* أَرْيَاف. Native —, مَنْبِت ـ مَنْشَأ ـ مَسْقِطُ ٱلرَّأْسِ ـ مَأْلَف ـ مَوْلِد ـ وَطَن. The inhabitants of any region, القُطَّان ـ السُّكَّان ـ أَهْلُ ٱلْبِلادِ. He went to live in the —, تَرَيَّفَ.

Country, *a.* Rural, رِيفِيّ; of a mountainous part, جَبَلِيّ. Rude, خَشِن ـ جَافٍ ـ فَلَّاح ـ غَلِيظ.

Country-bred, *n.* مُرَبَّى فِي ٱلرِّيفِ.

Countryman, *n.* One born in the same country as another, مِنْ وَطَنٍ ـ ذَاتُ ـ مِنْ بَلَدٍ وَاحِدٍ. A rustic, خَلَاوِيّ ـ فَلَّاح. What — are you? مِنْ أَيِّ بَلَدٍ أَنْتَ.

Country-house, *n.* / Country-seat, } قَصْرٌ فِي ٱلرِّيفِ.

County, *n.* وِلَايَة *pl.* وِلَايَات ـ أَقْلِيم *pl.* أَقَالِيمُ ـ إِيَالَة ـ عَمَل *pl.* أَعْمَال.

Coup-d'Etat, *n.* مَلْعُوبٌ مِنْ مَلاعِيبِ ٱلْحُكْمِ.

Coup-de-grace, *n.* ضَرْبَةُ ٱلْمَوْتِ.

Coup-de-main, *n.* هَجْمَة ـ كَبْسَة.

Coup-de-soleil, *n.* ضَرْبَةُ ٱلشَّمْسِ. Struck with —, مَضْرُوبُ ٱلشَّمْسِ.

Couple, *n.* زَوْج *or* زَوْجَانِ *pl.* أَزْوَاج ـ إِثْنَانِ ـ قَرِينَانِ ـ زَكَا ـ زَوْ. A male and its female, ذَكَرٌ وَأُنْثَاهُ.

Couple, *v.t.* To join together, وَصَلَ-ب ـ قَرَنَ-ب ـ ثَنَّى ـ جَعَلَ-أَزْوَاجًا ـ زَوَّجَ ـ يَصِل *aor.* To marry, أَنْكَحَ ـ زَوَّجَ.

Couple, *v.i.* To copulate, تَزَاوَجَ ـ تَنَاكَحَ ـ تَسَافَدَ. *See also to* Copulate, *v.i.*

Couplet, *n.* Two verses, بَيْتَانِ مِنَ ٱلشِّعْرِ ـ ذُو بَيْتٍ. A pair, زَوْج ـ إِثْنَانِ.

Coupling, *n.* That which couples, وَصْلَة ـ عُلْقَة ـ رَابِطَة ـ وَصْل.

Coupon, *n.* كُوبُون *pl.* كُوبُونَات. The — falling due, الكُوبُونُ ٱلْمُسْتَحَقّ. The bank undertakes to realize all coupons, البَنْكُ يَقْبِضُ سَائِرَ ٱلْكُوبُونَاتِ.

Courage, *n.* عَارِضَة ـ عَارِض ـ حَمَاسَة ـ بَأْس ـ بَطْش ـ إِقْدَام ـ عَزْم ـ نَشَاط ـ هِمَّة ـ جَرَاءَة ـ جَسَارَة ـ شَجَاعَة. His — fled, طَارَ فُؤَادُهُ.

Courageous, *a.* ذُو عَارِضٍ ـ شَدِيدُ ٱلْعَارِضَةِ ـ بَطَل ـ جَرِيء ـ مِقْدَام ـ نَشِيط ـ جَسُور ـ عَزُوم ـ شُجَاع. To be —, جَسَرَ ² ـ شَجُعَ ².

Courageously, *ad.* إِقْدَامًا وَجَلادَةً ـ بِشَجَاعَةٍ ـ بِجَسَارَةٍ ـ بِجَرَاءَةٍ.

Courier, *n.* A messenger, بَرِيد *pl.* بُرُد ـ سَاعٍ *pl.* سُعَاة.

Course, *n.* A race, ضَمَّة ـ حُضْر ـ شَوْط *pl.* أَشْوَاط ـ طَلَق. A race-ground, حَلْبَة ـ مِضْمَار ـ مِشْوَار ـ مِيدَان. Progress, وَجْهَة ـ طَيَّة ـ رُحْلَة ـ سَيْر ـ جَرْيٌ. A track, line, مَدْرَج ـ سَبِيل ـ مَسْلَك ـ مَذْهَب. Process, as of time, interval, خِلال ـ غُضُون ـ أَثْنَاء ـ مَمَرّ ـ مُرُور. Succession, order of succession, تَرَاوُح ـ تَنَاوُب ـ تَعَاقُب. Method, قِدَّة ـ مِدَاد ـ أُسْلُوب ـ نَمَط ـ طِرَاز ـ طِرْز. Way of acting, طَرِيقَة ـ أُسْلُوب. Order, way, custom, طَوْر ـ طَرْز ـ شَأْن ـ طَرِيقَة ـ عَادَة. Means, way, وَسِيلَة ـ طَرِيق. Orderly structure, مُشَاكَلَة ـ نِظَام. A row, طَبَقَة *pl.* طَبَقَات *and* طِبَاق. A series of dishes placed on a table, مُدَّةُ طَعَامٍ ـ سِمَاط. Course of a torrent, مَدْرَجُ سَيْلٍ. A — of lectures, جُمْلَةُ خُطَبٍ ـ بَابُ دَرْسٍ. Course of exchange, سِعْرُ ٱلْمُعَامَلَةِ ـ مُرَابَحَة ـ تَفَاوُتُ ٱلْقَامْبِيُو. Everything in its —, كُلُّ أَمْرٍ فِي دَوْرِهِ. Everyone in his —, turn, كُلُّ وَاحِدٍ فِي دَوْرِهِ. In the —, space, of, فِي ظَرْفِ. In the natural —, عَلَى جَارِي ٱلْعَادَةِ ـ عَلَى ٱلْمَعْهُودِ. Of —, certainly, جَيْرِ ـ لا بُدَّ ـ لا مُحَالَةَ ـ عَلَى كُلِّ حَالٍ ـ أَلْبَتَّةَ.

To follow one's own course, مَضَى عَلَى طَرِيقَتِهِ ². He is following his own course, هُوَ عَلَى طَرِيقَتِهِ. Follow your own course, إِمْضِ عَلَى سُنَنِكَ. You follow the wrong course, لَمْ تَأْخُذْ بِوَجْهِ ٱلْأَمْرِ.

To shape one's course towards, ضَرَبَ إِلَى ².

To take a direct course, إِعْتَزَمَ ٱلطَّرِيقَ.

Course, *v.t.* To pursue, دَأْدَأَ ـ قَفَا ² ـ إِقْتَفَى ـ جَدَّ فِي ². To hunt, طَارَدَ ـ إِصْطَادَ ـ تَصَيَّدَ. To force طَلَبَ ² ـ تَبِعَ ² to run, تَشَوَّطَ ـ أَعْدَى ـ جَرَّى ـ رَكَّضَ.

Course, *v.i.* To run, سَرَى ² ـ إِنْطَلَقَ ـ جَرَى ². To glide,

عَامَ or يَعُومُ. The stars coursed along, عَامَتِ ٱلنُّجُومُ. The ship coursed along, عَامَتِ ٱلسَّفِينَةُ.

Courser, *n.* A race-horse, فَرَسٌ مِحْضَارٌ ـ غِمار *pl.* غَمْر ـ حَمُوم ـ قَانِص ـ صَيَّاد. A hunter, جِيَاد *pl.* جَوَاد ـ مِحْضِير.

Courses, *n.* The — of women, حَيْض ـ طِمْث ـ عَذِرَة.

Court, *n.* The place where a prince resides, دَار ـ دَارُ ٱلْوِلَايَةِ ـ قَصْرُ ٱلْمَلِكِ ـ مَقَرُّ ٱلْمَلِكِ ـ ٱلسَّلْطَنَةِ. The king's palace, قَصْرُ ٱلْمَلِكِ. A palace, سَرَايَا. A hall where justice is administered, دَارُ ٱلْقَضَآءِ ـ مَحْكَمَة. The open space before a house, سَاحَة *pl.* سَاحَات ـ فِنَآء; round a house, a compound, صَحْن ـ رِوَاق ـ وَصِيد ـ أَصِيد. A hall, سُدَّة ـ أَحْوَاش *pl.* حَوْش ـ إِيوَان ـ فُسْحَة. A royal — or hall, دَائِرَة ـ حِبَآء ـ خَوَل ـ ٱلْمَلِكِ. The retinue, as of a prince, حَشَمٌ وَخَدَمٌ ـ تَوَابِعُ ـ حَاشِيَة ـ مَعِيَّة. The sovereign, with his council, officers, *etc.*, الدَّوْلَةُ ـ الْمَلِكُ وَأَرْبَابُ ٱلدَّوْلَةِ. The persons assembled for the administration of justice, مَجْلِسُ ٱلشَّرْعِ ٱلشَّرِيفِ. An assembly, مَجْلِس ـ مَجْمَع ـ نَادٍ. The art of pleasing, مُلَاطَفَة ـ مُدَارَاة ـ مُخَالَقَة ـ مُدَاجَاة. To pay — to any one, إِسْتَعْطَفَ ـ إِسْتَخَارَ ـ إِسْتَجْلَبَ ـ تَوَدَّدَ إِلَى أَلِفَ (or أَحْدَثَ) مَحْكَمَةً ـ تَمَلَّقَ ـ إِسْتَمَالَ. To institute a —, مَحْكَمَةً. To bring into —, رَفَعَ ـ إِلَى ٱلْمَحْكَمَةِ ـ أَحْضَرَ ـ إِلَى ٱلْمَحْكَمَةِ. *See also* Tribunal, *n.*

A civil court, مَحْكَمَةُ حُقُوقٍ.

A criminal court, مَحْكَمَةُ ٱلْجِنَايَاتِ.

Admiralty court, مَحْكَمَةٌ تَحْتَكِمُ فِي أُمُورٍ مُخْتَصَّةٍ بِٱلْبَحْرِ وَٱلْبَحْرِيَّةِ.

Court of Chancery, مَحْكَمَةُ عَدَالَةٍ ـ مَحْكَمَةٌ تَحْتَكِمُ فِي سَائِرِ ٱلْحُقُوقِ.

Court of Probate and Divorce, مَحْكَمَةٌ لِتَحْقِيقِ ٱلْوَصِيِّ وَلِإِجْرَآءِ ٱلْقَضَآءِ بِٱلطَّلَاقِ.

Court, *v.t.* To woo, تَوَدَّدَ إِلَى ـ ² صَبَا إِلَى ـ ² كَلِفَ بِ. To solicit, ² طَلَبَ ـ حَاوَلَ ـ إِسْتَعْطَفَ ـ إِلْتَمَسَ مِن. He courted foreigners, إِسْتَعْطَفَ ٱلْأَجَانِبَ.

Court-card, *n.* وَرَقَةُ لَعِبٍ مُزَوَّقَةٌ.

Court-day, *n.* يَوْمُ جُلُوسِ ٱلْمَحْكَمَةِ ـ نَهَارُ قِيَامِ ٱلْقَضَآءِ. The court-days will be open, تُقَامُ أَيَّامُ ٱلْقَضَآءِ.

Court-dress, *n.* المَلَابِسُ ٱلرَّسْمِيَّةُ لِمُوَاجَهَةِ ٱلْمَلِكِ.

Courteous, *a.* لَطِيف ـ أَدِيب ـ أَنِيس ـ بَاشّ ـ كَيِّس ـ بَشُوش ـ ظَرِيف. To be — to, ² رَفَقَ ـ تَلَطَّفَ لِ ـ أَقْبَلَ عَلَى ـ أَوْجَهَ ـ وَجَّهَ ـ بِ or عَلَى. A — man, رَجُلٌ مُتَّصِفٌ بِٱلْأَخْلَاقِ ٱلْمَرْضِيَّةِ.

Courteously, *ad.* بِظَرَافَةٍ ـ بِلَطَافَةٍ ـ بِأَدَبٍ ـ بِبَشَاشَةٍ ـ بِإِنْسٍ.

Courtesan, *n.* قِحَاب *pl.* قَحْبَة ـ فَاحِشَة ـ فَاجِرَة ـ زَانِيَة ـ شَرْمُوطَة.

Courtesy, *n.* Civility, ظَرْف ـ لُطْف ـ إِنْس ـ تَأَدُّب ـ بَشَاشَة ـ إِكْرَام ـ رِعَايَة. A bow made by women, إِنْحِنَآء ـ رَسْمُ سَلَامِ ٱلنِّسَآءِ ـ ٱلنِّسَآءِ. An act of —, kindness, فَضْل ـ مَعْرُوف ـ كَرَم.

Courtesy, *v.i.* She courtesied, إِنْحَنَتْ ـ سَلَّمَتْ.

Courtier, *n.* An attendant at a prince's court, جَلِيسُ ٱلْمَلِكِ *pl.* جُلَسَآء ـ نَدِيمُ ٱلْمَلِكِ *pl.* نُدَمَآء ـ مُلَازِمُ بَابِ ٱلسُّلْطَانِ. One who solicits the favour of another, مُسْتَعْطِف ـ مُسْتَمِيل ـ مُدَاخِل ـ مُسْتَجْلِب.

Court-like, *a.*
Courtly, } *See* Courteous, *a.*

Courtliness, *n.* *See* Courtesy, *n.*

Court-martial, *n.* مَحْكَمَةٌ عَسْكَرِيَّةٌ ـ دِيوَانُ حَرْبٍ.

Court-plaister, *n.* لَزْقَةٌ (or لَزُوق) حَبَرَةٍ.

Courtship, *n.* Solicitation of favour, إِسْتِخَارَة ـ إِسْتِجْلَاب ـ إِسْتِعْطَاف ـ إِسْتِمَالَة. Wooing, كَلَف ـ صَبَابَة ـ صُبُوّ. Civility, بَشَاشَة ـ لَطَافَة ـ مُؤَانَسَة.

Cousin, *n.* An uncle's son, إِبْنُ عَمٍّ. Aunt's son, إِبْنُ خَالَةٍ.

Cove, *n.* A small bay, جُوَن *pl.* جُونَة ـ خَوْر *pl.* خُؤُور. A place of shelter, مَلْجَأ ـ مُسْتَذْرًى. A man, fellow, حَرِيف *pl.* حُرَفَآء ـ رَجُل.

Covenant, *n.* مُشَايَعَة ـ مِيثَاق ـ مُبَايَعَة ـ عَقْد ـ عَهْد ـ حِلْف ـ ذِمَام *pl.* ذِمَّة ـ إِتِّفَاق ـ شَرْط. The writing containing the —, حُجَّة ـ صَكّ ـ وَثِيقَة ـ سِجْل ـ سِجِلّ. Those with whom a — is made, أَهْلُ ٱلذِّمَّةِ. He broke the —, ² خَانَ ٱلْعَهْدَ. They entered into a reciprocal — to, تَعَاهَدُوا عَلَى ـ تَعَاقَدُوا عَلَى.

Covenant, *v.i.* To agree, stipulate with, وَاثَقَ ـ وَاطَأَ ـ عَلَى ـ تَشَارَطَ مَعَ ـ إِشْتَرَطَ ـ عَاهَدَ.

Covenant, *v.t.* To grant by covenant, أَقْرَضَ ـ لَهُ حَسَبَ ٱلْوَعْدِ. To promise, أَوْعَدَ ـ وَعَدَ ـ بِ aor. يَعِدُ.

Covenantee, *n.* مِنْ أَهْلِ ٱلذِّمَّةِ.

Covenanter, *n.* مُعَاهِد ـ مُشَارِط ـ مُوَاثِق.

Cover, *v.t.* To overspread with something else, كَفَّرَ ـ كَفَرَ عَلَى ـ أَغْشَى ـ غَشَّى عَلَى ـ ² غَمَّ ـ أَطْبَقَ عَلَى ـ ² سَتَرَ ـ أَكَنَّ ـ ² كَمَّ ـ غَطَّى ـ ² غَطَا ـ شَمِلَ ـ جَلَّلَ ـ عَالَى ـ بِ ـ عَلَى. To conceal, أَخْفَى ـ ² حَجَبَ ـ ² سَتَرَ ـ ² غَمَّ. To be sufficient for, كَافَأَ ـ وَفَى aor. يَفِي. To shelter, protect, أَجَارَ ـ ² حَجَبَ ـ ² حَضَنَ ـ رَخَّمَ. To incubate, ² حَمَى ـ ² صَانَ ـ ² خَفَرَ ـ بِ.

— ـَ نَزَقَ ² — قَعَا ². To —, as of a horse, رَنَدَ عَلَى ٱلْبَيْضِ ². To copulate, سَفَدَ ـَ — نَزَا عَلَى ². To —, to overflow, إِنْتَعَى. To — one's self, as with a veil, تَبَرْقَعَ. غَمَرَ ² — غَطَا عَلَى ². She endeavoured to — her deformities, حَاوَلَتْ سَتْرَ مَا لَهَا مِنَ ٱلْعَيْبِ. To be covered, overspread, إِغْتَطَى — تَغَطَّى — إِنْغَمَّ. To be covered, hid, إِحْتَجَبَ — حُجِبَ — إِغْتَمَّ — إِنْغَمَّ. To —, as the mouth of a bottle, *etc.*, with, ـَ فَدَمَ عَلَى-بِ.

Cover, *n.* Anything put over another, طَبَق — طِبَاق *pl.* أَطْبَاق. غِطَاء *pl.* أَغْطِيَة — سِتْر — طِبَاقَة — أَخْفِيَة *pl.* خِفَاء — أَغْطِيَة. A — for the body, سِتَارَة — سُتْرَة. Concealment, veil, pretext, مَلْجَأ — مُسْتَدْرًى — مَأْوًى. عِلَّة — حِيلَة — خِفَاء — تَوْرِيَة. Shelter, The — (boards) of a book, دَفَّتَا كِتَاب. The — of a table, غِطَاء ٱلْمَائِدَة. A — to shoot from, دَرِيئَة. *See also* Covert, *n.*

Covered, *part.* and *a.* مُغَطًّى — مُغَشًّى. Covered love, مُمَاذَقَة.

Covered-way, *n.* سَابَاط *pl.* سَوَابِيط مُسْتَحْكَم.

Covering, *n.* غِطَاء — لِبْس — كِسَاء — رِدَاء — غِشَاء.

Coverlet, *n.* لِحَاف *pl.* لُحُف — جُلّ.

Covert, *a.* Sheltered, مَسْتُور — مُتَوَارٍ — مُحْتَجِب. Concealed, خَفِيّ — مَكْتُوم. Private, insidious, مَدْسُوس — دَاسّ. A — thing, خَفَاء.

Covert, *n.* A place to hide in, مَحْجَر — مَكْمَن — غِيَابَة — مَخْبَأ. A refuge, مَلْجَأ. A shade, ظِلّ. A — for wild beasts, عَرِينَة — عِرِّيسَة. A shelter, سِتَارَة — سِتْر. A thicket, covert of trees, خَمَر. A burrow, جُحْر — سَرَب. *See also under* Defence, *n.*

Covertly, *ad.* خِفْوَة — خُفْيَة — عَلَى خَفَاء — بِٱسْتِتَار — بِٱخْتِجَاب.

Coverture, *n.* The — of a married woman, إِرْتِبَاط ٱلْمَرْأَة بِزَوْجِهَا حَسَبَ ٱلنَّامُوس.

Covet, *v.t.* and *i.* نَافَسَ فِي — تَنَافَسَ فِي — شَرِهَ إِلَى — ـَ وَلِعَ بِ. *aor.* يَوْلَعُ — طَمِعَ فِي or بِ — ـَ حَرَصَ عَلَى — ـَ جَشِعَ — تَشَهَّى. To make to —, أَطْمَعَ-فِي — أَوْلَعَ-بِ. A coveted thing, مَطْمَع — طَمَع. Coveting, طَمَعًا فِي.

Covetable, *a.* مُشْتَهًى — مِمَّا يُطْمَعُ فِيهِ — مِمَّا يُحْرَصُ عَلَيْهِ شَيْء.

Covetous, *a.* مُولَع بِ — حَرِيص — طَامِع — جَشِع — طَرِف — طَمَّاع — طَمِع — شَرِه عَلَى — مُبْتَغٍ — بَاغٍ — رَائِم. Desirous for, رَاغِب — مُتَطَلِّب.

Covetously, *ad.* بِطَمَع — بِشَرَاهَة — بِحِرْص — بِجَشَع.

Covetousness, *n.* جَشَع — طَمَاع — وُلُوع — وَلَع — حِرْص — طَمَع.

Covey, *n.* A brood, حَضْنَة. A flight of birds, سِرْب مِنَ ٱلطَّيْر.

Cow, *n.* بَقَرَة *pl.* بَقَرَات *coll.* بَقَر.

Cow, *v.t.* To intimidate, ـَ رَعَبَ — رَوَّعَ — خَوَّفَ — ـَ كَسَرَ قَلْبَ.

Coward, *n.* رَعْشَن — خَوَّار — أَجْوَف — فَشِل — هَلُوع — زُمَّل — جُبَنَاء *pl.* جَبَّان — جَبِين.

Coward, *a.* } ذُو هَلَع — ذُو فَشَل — رِعْشِيش — إِجْفِيل —
Cowardly, } جَبَّان — خَشِل فَشِل — رَعِيب.

Cowardice, *n.* جُبْن — حَيَالَة — هَلَع — فَشَل — جَبَانَة. To accuse of —, جَبَّنَ.

Cowardly, *ad.* بِهَلَع — بِجَبَانَة — جَبَانَة. To act —, ـُ جَبُنَ.

Cow-dung, *n.* بَعْر — جِلَّة — دَبْلَة.

Cower, *v.i.* ـِ خَرَّ ² — خَثَا ٱلتُّرَاب ² — إِنْحَنَى.

Cowherd, *n.* رَاعِي بَقَر *pl.* رُعَاة.

Cowhide, *n.* جِلْد بَقَر. To —, ـَ نَزَلَ عَلَى-بِٱلْقُرْبَاج.

Cow-house, *n.* حَظِيرَة ٱلْبَقَر — زَرِيبَة ٱلْبَقَر.

Cowl, *n.* قَلَنْسُوَة *pl.* قَلَاسٍ and قَلَانِس.

Cow-parsnip, *n.* إِسْفَنْدِلْيُون — إِسْفَنْدِفِلْيُون.

Cowpox, *n.* جُدَرِيّ ٱلْبَقَر.

Cowry, *n.* حِرْج *pl.* أَحْرَاج — وَدَعَة *pl.* وَدَعَات. Cowries, جَنًى.

Cowslip, *n.* زَهْر ٱلرَّبِيع.

Cows' lungwort, *n.* بُوصِير — لَبِيدَة بَيْضَاء.

Coxcomb, *n.* A fop, مُتَبَلْتِع — مُتَحَذْلِق — غَنْدُور. The plant, مُخْمَلِيَّة.

Coxcombry, *n.* تَبَلْتُع — تَحَذْلُق — تَغَنْدُر — غَنْدَرَة.

Coxcomical, *a.* مُتَحَذْلِق — مُتَبَلْتِع — شَيِّق — مُغَنْدِر — غَنْدُورِيّ.

Coy, *a.* Modest, مَحْجُوب — مُتَصَاوِن — حَيِيّ — مُحْتَشِم. Reserved, مُنْقَبِض — رَزِين — نَازِه ٱلنَّفْس — عَاقِل. To be —, modest, إِحْتَشَمَ. *See also* Reserved, *a.*

Coyly, *ad.* Modestly, بِحَيَاء — بِنَزَاهَة. With reserve, بِرَزَانَة.

Coyness, *n.* نَزْهَة — تَصَاوُن — حِشْمَة.

Cozen, *v.t.* ـَ مَسَحَ — مَكَرَ بِ ² — ـِ غَبَنَ — إِحْتَالَ عَلَى — ـَ خَدَعَ — غَشَّ ².

Cozener, *n.* مَكَّار — غَابِن — مُحْتَال — خَادِع — غَاشّ — غَشَّاش.

Cozily, *ad.* *See* Cosily, *ad.*

Cozy, *a.* *See* Cosey, *a.*

Crab, *n.* The animal, سَرَطَان *pl.* سَرَطَانَات — عَقْرَب ٱلْمَاء — أَبُو جَلَنْبُو — سَلَطْعُون. A kind of wild apple, زَعْرُور. The sign of the zodiac, بُرْج ٱلسَّرَطَان.

Crab, *a.* } Harsh, peevish, عُتُلّ — عَفَنْقَس — لَئِيم — شَكِس —
Crabbed, } شَرِس — فَظّ — صَعْب — ٱلْخُلُق. Of style, ضَيِّق — عَسِر — حَصِر — طَلِق.

Crabbedly, *ad.* بِفَظَاظَةٍ ـ بِمَلَامَةٍ ـ بِشَكَاسَةٍ.

Crabbedness, *n.* Peevishness, فَظَاظَة ـ عِفِنْقَسَة ـ مَلَامَة ـ شَكَاسَة; of style, حَصَر ـ عَدَمُ ٱنْطِلَاقٍ.

Crack, *n.* A sudden sharp sound, طَقْطَقَة ـ قَعْقَعَة ـ صَلْصَلَة. A chink, شَعْب ـ فَتّ ـ وُتُور *pl.* وَقْرَة *and* وَقَرَات ـ فَصْمَة ـ شُقُوق *pl.* شَقّ ـ فُلُوج *pl.* فَلْج ـ أَفْلَاق *pl.* فَلَق ـ صُدُوع *pl.* صَدْع. The place of a —, مَكْسِر. Cracks in the hands or feet, as from cold, شُقُوق.

Crack, *v.t.* To produce a sharp noise, صَوَّتَ ـ فَقَّعَ. To break into chinks, with separation of parts, ـ فَلَجَ ـ فَصَّ ـ فَلَّعَ ـ شَقَّ ـ صَدَعَ; without separation of parts, فَصَمَ ـ فَلَقَ ـ شَقَّقَ. To —, as of a flea between the fingers, فَرَكَ. To break, هَشَمَ ـ كَسَرَ ـ هَصَمَ. To — a joke, دَعَبَ ـ مَزَحَ ـ هَزَلَ. To — the joints, as is done in a Turkish bath, طَقْطَقَ. *See also to* Craze, *v.t.*

Crack, *v.i.* To emit a sharp sound, قَصَفَ ـ تَفَرْقَعَ ـ فَقَّعَ ـ صَرَخَ ـ تَصَوَّتَ ـ طَقْطَقَ. To break into chinks, with separation of parts, اِنْفَلَعَ ـ تَفَلَّعَ; without separation, اِنْفَصَمَ ـ تَهَدَّمَ ـ تَهَكَّمَ ـ تَشَقَّقَ ـ اِنْشَقَّ ـ تَصَدَّعَ. To fall to ruin, تَكَسَّرَ ـ طَارَ شُعَاعًا.

Crack, *a.* First rate, أَعْلَى ـ أَخْيَرُ ـ أَحْسَنُ مَا يَكُونُ.

Crack-brained, *a.* مَجْنُون ـ فِي عَقْلِهِ هَبْتَة ـ أَبْلَه ـ أَحْمَق ـ غَبِيّ.

Cracker, *n.* A boaster, طِرْمَاذ ـ فَجَّاس ـ مِهْذَار ـ جَخِيف. A kind of squib, شَارُوخ بَارُودٍ *pl.* سَارُوخ *pl.* سَوَارِيخ ـ فَشَّار *pl.* شَوَارِيخ. A kind of biscuit, نَوْعٌ مِنَ ٱلْبَقْسَمَاطِ ٱلرَّقِيقِ. Nut-crackers, مُكَسِّرُ (*or* كَاسُورَةُ) ٱلْجَوْزِ.

Crackle, *v.i.* تَفَرْقَعَ ـ زَقْزَقَ ـ قَرْقَطَ ـ فَقَّعَ; as hard snow under the feet, خَشَفَ.

Crackling, *n.* تَصَوُّت ـ تَقَرْقُط ـ تَفَقُّع ـ عَقْعَقَة; of snow under the feet, خَشْفَة.

Cradle, *n.* A — for children, مَرْجُوحَة *pl.* أَرَاجِيح ـ أُرْجُوحَة *pl.* مَرَاجِيح ـ مَهْد *pl.* مُهُود. The frame for a ship, قَوَامٌ لِمَرْكَبٍ. Infancy, طُفُولِيَّة. To rock (*v.t.*) as a —, هَزْهَزَ ـ دَبْدَبَ. From the — to the grave, مِنَ ٱلْمَهْدِ إِلَى ٱللَّحْدِ.

Cradle, *v.t.* To put into a cradle, يَضَعُ *aor.* وَضَعَ فِي ٱلْمَهْدِ.

Craft, *n.* A trade, كَار ـ صَنْعَة ـ حِرْفَة ـ مِهْنَة. Dexterity, خُبْث ـ دَهَاء ـ شَطَارَة ـ رَشَاقَة ـ خِفَّة ـ لَبَاقَة. Cunning, حِيلَة ـ مَكِيدَة ـ تَلْبِيس ـ فَنّ ـ خَدِيعَة. A small ship, زَوْرَق *pl.* زَوَارِق ـ فَلُوكَة. A ship, سَفِينَة ـ مَرْكَب *pl.* مَرَاكِب.

Craftily, *ad.* بِحِيلَةٍ ـ بِتَلْبِيسٍ ـ بِكَيْدٍ ـ بِفَنٍّ.

Craftiness, *n.* حِيلَة ـ خُبْث ـ مَكِيدَة ـ اِحْتِيَال ـ دَهَاء.

Craftsman, *n.* ذُو حِرْفَةٍ ـ ذُو صَنْعَةٍ ـ ذُو مِهْنَةٍ ـ مُحْتَرِف.

Crafty, *a.* شَاطِر ـ ذُو كَيْدٍ ـ خَبِيث ـ حُوَالِيّ ـ دَاهٍ ـ أَرِب. How — he is! مَا أَحْوَلَهُ.

Crag, *n.* As of a rock, أَكَمَة ـ حَذَارَى *pl.* حِذْرِيَة ـ قِرْنَاس ـ صَخْرَة *pl.* صَخَرَات. *See also* Nape, *n.*

Cragged, *a.* / **Craggy,** وَعِير ـ وَعْر ـ غَلَاظ ـ قَدْفَد ـ كَلَد ـ حَزْن ـ مُصْخِر ـ صَخِر.

Cragginess, *n.* غِلَظ ـ وُعُور ـ حُزُونَة.

Cram, *v.t.* To overfill, وَسَقَ *aor.* حَفَلَ ـ زَعَبَ ـ أَطَفَّ ـ شَحَنَ ـ حَشَا ـ يَسِقُ. To —, as with food, أَقْعَمَ ـ أَبْشَمَ ـ أَشْبَعَ. To —, as a room with people, حَشَرَ ـ زَحَمَ ـ أَغَصَّ. To be crammed, overfilled, اِتَّسَقَ ـ اِحْتَفَلَ ـ شَحِنَ; with food, اِحْتَشَى ـ اِتَّخَمَ ـ فَقِمَ. A —, as of people, غَمْرَة ـ قَصْفَة. Crammed, as with people, غَاصّ. *See also to* Crowd, Stuff, *v.t.*

Cramp, *n.* A spasm, تَقَبُّض ـ تَشَنُّج. A restraint, تَحْرِيج ـ طَوْقَة ـ عَقْفَاء ـ مَانِع. A shackle, قَيْد *pl.* قُيُود. A — iron, كَلَّاب *pl.* كَلَالِيب.

Cramp, *v.t.* To pain with cramps, قَبَّضَ ـ شَنَّجَ. To restrain, ضَيَّقَ عَلَى ـ زَنَقَ ـ مَنَعَ ـ حَظَرَ عَلَى ـ حَرَّجَ. To straiten, زَنَقَ عَلَى.

Cramp-fish, *n.* رَاعِدَة ـ رَعَّاد.

Crampoons, *n.* For hoisting weights; *see under* Crane, *n.*

Cranberry, *n.* نَوْعٌ مِنَ ٱلْفَاكِهَةِ.

Crane, *n.* The bird, كُرْكِيّ *pl.* غَرَانِيق *or* غِرْنِيق *pl.* غَرْنُوق ـ كَرَاكِيّ ـ وَزّ عِرَاقِيّ ـ لَكْلَك. A machine for lifting heavy weights, دُولَاب (*or* آلَة) لِرَفْعِ ٱلْأَثْقَالِ ـ مِسْمَاك. A siphon, قَصَّابَة ـ قَصَبَة ـ مِضَخَّة ـ أُنْبُوب.

Crane's-bill, *n.* The plant, نَوْعٌ مِنَ ٱلنَّبَاتِ ـ إِبْرَةُ ٱلرَّاعِي.

Cranial, *a.* مُتَعَلِّقٌ بِٱلْجُمْجُمَةِ.

Cranioclast, *n.* An instrument for breaking the cranium of a fœtus, مِفْدَغ.

Craniologist, *n.* عَالِمٌ بِمَا يَتَعَلَّقُ بِٱلْجُمْجُمَةِ.

Craniology, *n.* عِلْمُ ٱلْبَحْثِ عَنِ ٱلْجُمْجُمَةِ.

Craniometer, *n.* مِقْيَاسُ ٱلْجَمَاجِمِ.

Cranium, *n.* قِحْف ـ جُمْجُمَة *pl.* جَمَاجِم.

Crank, *a.* Bold, شُجَاع. Stout, strong, قَوِيّ ـ مَتِين. Unsafe, likely to upset, قَلَّاب.

Crank, *n.* An instrument to turn with, مِلْوَى. A twist, لَيَّة — لَفَّة. A conceit, أُغْلُوطَة *pl.* أَغَالِيط — أُحْجِيَّة *pl.* أَحَاجِي.

Crankle, *v.t.* *See* Crinkle, *v.t.*

Crannied, *a.* مُفَلَّل — مَفْتُوت — ذُو وُفُورٍ — مُثَقَّب — مَنْخُور. A — house, بَيْتٌ وَقِيرٌ.

Cranny, *n.* A chink, fissure, فَتٌّ — مَخْرَف — تَثَقُّب — تَشَقُّق — وَتْرَة *pl.* وُتُور. A secret place, مَخْبَأ *pl.* مَخَابِئ. *See also* Fissure, *n.*

Crape, *n.* گُرِيشَة — بُرُنجِك. Mourning, لِبْسُ ٱلْحِدَادِ — لِبْسُ ٱلْحُزْنِ — لِبْسُ ٱلسَّوَادِ.

Crapulence, *n.* Drunkenness, سُكْر.

Crapulent, *a.* }
Crapulous, } Drunken, سَكِير — سِكِّر — سَكْرَان — سَكِر.

Crash, *v.i.* وَجَبَ *aor.* يَجِبُ — خَرَّ — نَقَضَ.

Crash, *v.t.* *See* Crush, *v.t.*

Crash, *n.* }
Crashing, } A loud sound, as of things falling or breaking, وَجْبَة — خَرِير — نَقْض. To make a loud —, أَرَّ.

Crass, *a.* غَلِيظ — خَشِن.

Crassitude, *n.* غِلْظَة — خُشُونَة — غِلَاظَة.

Cratch, *n.* A manger, مَعْلَف — مِذْوَد.

Crate, *n.* قَفَص *pl.* أَقْفَاص.

Crater, *n.* Of a volcano, فَمُ جَبَلِ نَارٍ. An abyss, هُوَّة — جَوْبَة.

Craunch, *v.t.* لَاكَ — خَضَدَ — قَرَضَ — قَرْقَشَ — قَرَشَ.

Cravat, *n.* رِبَاطٌ (*or* مِنْدِيلٌ) لِلرَّقَبَةِ.

Crave, *v.t.* To entreat, أَلْحَفَ — أَلَحَّ عَلَى — اِلْتَمَسَ — تَضَرَّعَ إِلَى. To long for, تَنَافَسَ فِي — نَافَسَ فِي — تَشَهَّى — تَمَنَّى — تَطَلَّبَ.

Craven, *n.* *See* Coward, *n.*

Craving, *n.* تَنَافُس — إِشْتِيَاق — شَوْق — حَنِين.

Craving, *a.* حَنَّان — مُشْتَاق — طَامِعٌ فِي.

Craw, *n.* حَوْصَلَة *pl.* حَوَاصِل.

Crawfish, *n.* نَوْعٌ مِنَ ٱلسَّرَطَانِ — سَلْطَعُون.

Crawl, *v.i.* To creep, زَحَفَ — حَبَا — دَبَّ. To move slowly and weakly, دَبَى — دَلَفَ. To — or climb up, تَسَنَّقَ — تَشَعْلَقَ. He came crawling, جَآءَ حَبْوًا. He crawls along the ground, يَزْحَفُ عَلَى ٱلْأَرْضِ. A crawling gait, دِبَّة. A crawling thing, دَبَّة — دَبِيب *pl.* دَوَابّ.

Crayon, *n.* A kind of pencil, حَجَرُ تَبَاشِيرِ لِلرَّسْمِ — قَلَمُ تَبَاشِيرِ.

Craze, *v.t.* To impair the brain, هَتَرَ — أَجَنَّ — جَنَّنَ — أَحْمَقَ. To break, رَضَّ — سَحَقَ — دَقَّ.

Craziness, *n.* Derangement of the brain, هُتْر — هَتَرَة — خُرْق — ضَعْفُ عَقْلٍ — بَلَاهَة — سَخَافَة. Feebleness, want of strength, مَخَافَة — عَدَمُ صِحَّةٍ — ضَعْف.

Crazy, *n.* Deranged in mind, مُضَعْضَع — مَأْفُون — أَبْلَهُ — مُفَنَّد — فِي عَقْلِهِ هَبْتَة. Broken, rickety, سَقِيم — مُعَطَّل — مُخَسَّر. Feeble, عَلٌّ — مِسْقَام — دَنِف — يَفِن — نَحِيف — ضَعِيف.

Creak, *v.i.* صَرَفَ — أَطَّ — صَرَّ — صَرْصَرَ — زَقْزَقَ — زَيَّقَ. A creaking noise, أَطِيط — صَرِير — صَرِيف — نَقِيض.

Cream, *n.* Of milk, قُشَادَة — قُشَادَة — قِشْدَة — زُبْد. The best of anything, زُبْدَة — لُبّ — خُلَاصَة — جَوْهَر — مَحْض. Clotted —, لَبَنٌ نَمِيرٌ. *See also under* Choice, *a.*

Cream, *v.i.* Of milk, أَمْخَضَ ٱللَّبَنُ — عَلَتِ ٱللَّبَنَ ٱلْقِشْدَةُ. To — in small clots, تَمَّرَ ٱللَّبَنُ.

Cream, *v.t.* To remove the cream, صَرَّحَ ٱلْقِشْدَةَ عَنِ ٱللَّبَنِ — مَخَضَ ٱللَّبَنَ. Creamed milk, مَخُوض — مَخِيض.

Cream-faced, *a.* Pale, هَلِعُ ٱلْمَنْظَرِ. *See also* Cowardly, *a.*

Creamy, *a.* ذُو قِشْدَةٍ — زُبْدِيٌّ. To be —, of milk, كَثَعَ — كَثَّعَ — أَمْخَضَ.

Crease, *v.t.* غَضَّنَ — ثَنَى — كَمَّشَ. To be creased, تَغَضَّنَ. *See also to* Rumple, *v.t.*

Crease, *n.* كَسْر — غَرّ *pl.* غُرُور — غَضْن *pl.* غُضُون — خِنْث *pl.* أَخْنَاث — ثِنْي — تَقَبُّض — تَكْمِيش — طَيّ *pl.* أَطْوَآء. He folded the garment in its creases, طَوَى ٱلثَّوْبَ عَلَى أَخْنَاثِهِ.

Create, *v.t.* To bring into existence, بَرَأَ — فَطَرَ — جَبَلَ — خَلَقَ — كَوَّنَ — أَوْجَدَ — أَبْدَأَ — جَعَلَ — اِفْتَطَرَ. To cause, جَعَلَ — سَبَّبَ — أَحْدَثَ. To invest with a new character or office, نَصَبَ — وَظَّفَ — قَلَّدَ — وَلَّى — أَقَامَ مَقَامَ. Created, existing, مَوْجُود.

Creation, *n.* The act of conferring existence, بَرْء — إِبْدَاع — جَبْل — فِطْرَة — اِفْتِطَار — فَطْر — تَكْوِين — خَلْق. The universe, الفَلَكُ — البَرِيَّةُ — العَالَمُ — الخَلْقُ — الخَلِيقَةُ. Investing with a new office, تَوْلِيَة — نَصْب — تَقْلِيد — تَوْظِيف. Formation, making, صَيْرُورَة. The — of Bulgaria into an independent province, صَيْرُورَةُ بُلْغَارِيَا إِمَارَةً مُسْتَقِلَّةً.

Creative, *a.* Having the power to create, بَارِئٌ — بَدِيع — فَاطِر — مُبْدِع — مُكَوِّن — مُوجِد — خَالِق.

Creator, *n.* The —, God, البَارِئُ — الفَاطِرُ — المُبْدِئُ — الخَالِقُ — الخَلَّاقُ. *See also* Creative, *a.*

Creature, *n.* A created being, مَفْطُور — مَبْرُوء — مَخْلُوق *pl.* مَخْلُوقَات. An animal not human, بَهِيمَة *pl.* بَهَائِم — حَيَوَانٌ غَيْرُ نَاطِقٍ *pl.* حَيَوَانَات. A general word for man, عَبْد *pl.* عِبَاد —

إنسان. Any thing created, كائن pl. كائنات — حادث pl. حوادث. The Creation, الخليقة.. The creatures of God, خليقة الله. A poor —, مسكين pl. مساكين — منحوس — ميشوم. A nasty —, خنزير pl. خنازير — خبيث.

Credence, n. Belief, إعتقاد — إعتماد — ثقة — تصديق. Letters of —, تقارير — تمسّك — سند — شهادة — وثيقة. To give — to, صدّق.

Credenda, n. عقائد.

Credent, a. معتقد — واثق — متصدّق.

Credential, n. حجّة — وثيقة. Credentials, تقارير. The credentials appointing him ambassador, الطرس المؤذن له بنصبه سفيرا. *See also under* Credence, n.

Credibility, n. لياقة — إمكان التصديق به — إحتمال الإعتماد به.

Credible, a. محلّ الإعتقاد — جدير بالتصديق — ومما يصدّق — معقول.

Credibly, ad. يقينا — إعتمادا — بتصديق — بإعتقاد.

Credit, n. Belief, يقين — إعتقاد — تصديق. Honour, كرامة — حشمة — ثناء — حمد. Good opinion, جاه — عرض — إعتبار الظنّ ب. Testimony, شهادة — إسناد — سند — إستناد. Trust in money matters, دين — نسيئة — قرض. Influence, إمكان — نفوذ — قوّة — مقدرة — طاقة. To give one —, to lend to, أسلف — دين — أقرض. On —, بالطلوق — بالنسيئة — بالدين. To put to the — of, قيّد - في محصول. A letter of —, ورقة براءة الإعتماد. A letter of — from a sovereign, حوالة — حوالة. To give one a letter of — upon, أعطى - ورقة حوالة — حوّل - على. The public —, أمانة الدولة فيما يختصّ بالإستقراض. The — allowed in a budget, مرتّبات مفروضة. Ordinary —, مرتّبات المصارف العاديّة. Supplementary —, مرتّبات فضلة. Extraordinary —, مرتّبات فوق العادة. To open a — with, فتح حسابا مع. To sell upon —, باع بالدين — أدان. I sold it on —, بعته بأجرة (or بنظرة or بنسيئة). To buy or take upon —, أخذ - بالدين — إستدان. He took it on —, أخذه دينا. To deal with one on —, داين. They dealt together on —, تداينوا. He asked for —, تديّن — إستنسأ. To be a — to, صار افتخارا ل.

Credit, v.t. To believe, إعتقد — أيقن — صدّق - في or ب or على. To confide in, إعتمد على — يثق aor. وثق ب — إستند إلى. To admit as a debtor, أقرض — أعطى - نسيئة — نسأ — أنسأ — أدان.

Creditable, a. Laudable, حسين — مديح — معتبر — حميد — مبرور — مشكور — جميل.

Creditableness, n. جمال — حسن — حمد.

Creditably, ad. حسنا — جيّدا — حمدا.

Creditor, n. صاحب الحقّ — مدين — مستدين — ناسئ pl. أصحاب — صاحب الدين. To refer a — to another for payment, أحال الغريم. I transferred his debt, that is, the money for which he was my —, to another for payment, أحلته بدينه.

Credulity, n. سداجة — غرارة — سرعة الإعتقاد — تزبّد.

Credulous, a. سريع — سانج — نقوع أذن — غرير — متزبّد الإعتقاد. To be —, to believe a thing hastily, تزبّد.

Creed, n. Belief, مذهب — إيمان — إعتقاد. Form of —, قانون إيمان — صورة إيمان — شهادة. An article of belief, عقيدة pl. عقائد. The Apostles' —, صورة إيمان — إيمان الرسل. The Nicene —, القانون النيقوي. The Athanasian —, قانون لمار أثناسيوس.

Creek, n. An inlet, خور pl. خؤور — جونة pl. جون — شرم pl. شروم — خليج pl. خلجان.

Creeky, a. Full of creeks, كثير الجون — كثير الخؤور.

Creep, v.i. To move as a worm, دبّ — حبا — زحف — دجّ. To move slowly; (*see under to* Crawl, *v.i.*) To grow along the ground, عرّش — إنبسط — إنفرش — تعكّش — عكش. To — in or into, أدغل في — إندسّ في. To — out, as from a hole, إنساب; to escape, إنسلّ. To —, as children, درج. To — into, as a disease, دبّ في. It crept into his veins, دبّ في عروقه. A creeping gait, درجان — دبّة.

Creeper, n. A crawling thing, حشرة pl. حشرات — دبّة — دبيب pl. دوابّ. A creeping plant, عشب — عشبة — فريش — نبات معرّش — أثيث — مفرّش — دغل. Creeping stalks, حبل pl. حبال.

Creepingly, ad. بانسلال — بدبيب.

Cremation, n. إحراق — حرق.

Crenated, a. مفلّل — محزّز — محزوز — مفروض.

Creole, n. فرنجيّ مولود في جزائر أميريكا.

Creosote, n. مقطّر القطران.

Crepitate, v.i. تكتك — فقّع.

Crepitation, n. تكتكة — تفقيع.

Crepuscule, n. شفق — سدف — سحر.

Crepuscular, a. } فجريّ — شفقيّ.
Crepusculous, }

Crescent, *a.* Crescive, } مُتَزايِد ـ نابِت ـ زَكِيٌّ ـ زاكٍ ـ ناشِئٌ ـ نام.

Crescent, *n.* هِلال *pl.* أَهِلَّة. Crescent-shaped, مُهَلَّل. Crescent-shaped buildings, حَنِيَّة. The —, as the arms of the Ottoman Empire, called by the Turks, آى وَيَلْدِيز.

Cress, *n.* Water —, قُرَّةُ ٱلْعَيْنِ ـ رَشادُ ٱلْمَآء ـ حُرْف ـ حِدَّة ـ گَرْسُون.

Cresset, *n.* قِنْدِيل ـ مَشْعَلَة ـ مَشْعَل ـ نَفّاط. The bearer of a —, مَشاعِلِيٌّ.

Crest, *n.* Of a helmet, رِيشُ ٱلْخُوذَةِ; of a cock, عَفْرَى ـ عُرْف ـ قُلَّةُ جَبَلٍ ـ نَمَغَة; of a mountain, جِذْرِيَة *pl.* حَذارَى ـ عِفْرِيَة ـ رَأْسُ جَبَلٍ. Pride, spirit, عِزَّةُ ٱلنَّفْسِ ـ شَهامَة ـ كِبْر ـ غَطْرَسَة. The crests of waves, غَوارِبُ ٱلْمَآء *sing.* غارِب.

Crested, *a.* Having a crest, as of a cock, *etc.*, ذُو عُرْفٍ ـ لَهُ شُوشَة ـ ذُو وَفْرَةٍ.

Crestfallen, *a.* مُبْلِس ـ مُخْمِد ـ مُنْفَلّ ـ مُذَلَّل ـ مُدَوَّخ ـ مَخْيُوب ـ مَعْيُوب ـ فَشِيل.

Cretaceous, *a.* طَباشِيرِيٌّ ـ مِنَ ٱلْجِيرِ.

Crevasse, *n.* جَوْبَة ـ سُلُوع *pl.* سِلْع ـ هُوَّة ـ لُجَّة.

Crevice, *n.* فَلَق ـ فَتّ ـ شُقُوق *pl.* شَقّ ـ وَقْرات *pl.* وَقْرَة ـ أَنْلاق. A house full of crevices, بَيْتٌ مُوَقَّرٌ.

Crew, *n.* A company, عُصْبَة ـ زُمْرَة ـ فَوْج ـ قَوْم ـ حِزْب. A ship's company, بَحْرِيَّة ـ نُوتِيَّة ـ أَهْلُ ٱلسَّفِينَةِ.

Crib, *n.* A manger, مِذْوَد ـ مَعْلَف. A cradle, مَهْد ـ أُرْجُوحَة. A cottage, حِفْش *pl.* أَحْفاش ـ خُصّ *pl.* خِصاص ـ كُوخ *pl.* أَكْواخ.

Crib, *v.t.* To steal, تَسَرَّقَ ـ ـ سَرَقَ ـ مِن *or* ل. To confine, ـ حَبَسَ.

Cribbage, *n.* نَوْعٌ مِنْ أَلْعابِ وَرَقِ ٱلشَّدَّةِ.

Cribble, *n.* A sieve, غَرابِيلُ *pl.* غِرْبال ـ مِنْسَف.

Cribration, *n.* غَرْبَلَة ـ نَسْف.

Crick, *n.* The noise of a door, *etc.*, جَلْنَبْلَق ـ صَرْصَرَة ـ صَرِيف. A stiffness in the neck, تَشَنُّجٌ فِي ٱلرَّقَبَةِ.

Cricket, *n.* The insect, جُنْدَبُ ٱلسَّرّارِ ـ أَصْدآء *pl.* صَدًى ـ جُدْجُد *pl.* جَداجِد ـ صَرْصَر ـ صَرّارُ ٱللَّيْلِ ـ أَبُو دِرْدان. The game, لَعِبُ ٱلصَّوْلَجانِ وَٱلْكُرَةِ. A low stool, إِسْكَمْلَة. To chirp like a —, صَرَّ.

Crier, *n.* A public —, مُنادٍ ـ صارِخ ـ بَرّاح. The — of a mosque, مُؤَذِّن.

Crim. Con. *n.* فِسْق ـ زِنآء.

Crime, *n.* جَرِيمَة ـ جُناح ـ جِنايات *pl.* جِنايَة ـ مَعَرَّة ـ إِثْم ـ خَطِيئَة ـ مَسآءَة ـ ذُنُوب *pl.* ذَنْب ـ جُرُوم *pl.* جُرْم. A great —, كَبائِر *pl.* كَبِيرَة ـ عَظائِم *pl.* عَظِيمَة. A capital —, ذَنْبٌ يَسْتَحِقُّ ٱلْقَتْلَ. To commit a —, أَذْنَبَ ـ خَطِئَ ـ أَخْطَأَ. To commit a — against, جَنَى عَلَى ـ جانَى. To accuse of a —, تَذَنَّبَ عَلَى ـ إِسْتَذْنَبَ. He accused him of having committed a —, جانَى عَلَيْهِ ـ جَنَى عَلَيْهِ جِنايَةً ـ تَجَنَّى عَلَيْهِ.

Crimea, *n.* القِرْم.

Criminal, *a.* Unlawful, ذُنُوبِيٌّ ـ مُخالِفٌ لِلشَّرْعِ ـ حَرام. Criminal conversation, زِنآء. A — tribunal, مَحْكَمَةُ ٱلْجِنايَةِ. Criminal judicature, إِدارَةُ ٱلْأُمُورِ ٱلْجِنائِيَّةِ. Criminal procedure, مُحاكَمَةُ ٱلْأُمُورِ ٱلْجِنائِيَّةِ. A — matter, مادَّةٌ جِنائِيَّةٌ. Criminal cases, الدَّعاوَى ٱلْجِنائِيَّةُ وَٱلْجَزائِيَّةُ.

Criminal, *n.* مُذْنِب ـ جَرِيم ـ مُجْرِم ـ جُناة *pl.* جانٍ ـ خُطاة *pl.* خاطِئ.

Criminality, *n.* لَوْمَة ـ إِثْم ـ جَرِيمَة.

Criminally, *ad.* جِنايَةً ـ بِإِجْرام ـ جُرْمًا.

Criminate, *v.t.* To accuse of a crime; (*see under* Crime, *n.*) To — one's self, تَذَنَّبَ عَلَى نَفْسِهِ ـ إِسْتَذْنَبَ نَفْسَهُ.

Crimination, *n.* شِكايَة ـ تُهْمَة ـ قَذْف ـ جَنَى عَلَى ـ جِنايَة ـ إِتِّهام.

Criminatory, *a.* مُدِلٌّ عَلَى ٱلذَّنْبِ ـ مُتَّهِم.

Crimp, *a.* مُنْكَسِر ـ هَشِيم. *See also* Brittle, Crisp, *a.*

Crimp, *n.* مُعَرِّص ـ حَيّال.

Crimp, *v.t.* To form with plaits or ridges, جَمَّرَ ـ عَقَصَ. To decoy, وَقَّعَ ـ أَغْوَى. *See also to* Curl, *v.t.*

Crimple, *v.t.* To squeeze, دَعَكَ. To contract, wrinkle, كَمَّشَ ـ ضَمَّ. To plait, ثَنَى.

Crimson, *n.* قِرْمِز ـ لَوْنٌ قِرْمِزِيٌّ.

Crimson, *a.* قِرْمِزِيٌّ.

Crimson, *v.t.* To dye with —, صَبَغَ بِٱلْقِرْمِزِ.

Crimson, *v.i.* إِحْمَرَّ.

Cringe, *v.i.* لَكِعَ ـ تَمَلْمَلَ ـ تَمَسْكَنَ ـ تَماوَتَ ـ تَذَلَّلَ.

Cringe, *n.* لَكَع ـ لَكاعَة ـ تَذَلُّل.

Cringle, *n.* A twig, غُصْنَة ـ خُصْلَة. A ring in a bolt-rope, حَلْقَة.

Crinkle, *v.t.* أَبْرَمَ ـ طَوَى ـ لَوَى.

Crinkle, *v.i.* تَعَقَّدَ ـ تَلَوَّى ـ إِنْطَوَى ـ إِلْتَوَى.

Crinkle, *n.* تَلَوٍّ ـ تَبَرُّم ـ طَيَّة ـ أَطْوآء *pl.* طَيّ.

Crinoline, *n.* فُسْطانٌ تَحْتانِيٌّ مُبَطَّنٌ بِمُقَوِّيات.

Crinose, *n.* ذُو شَعْرٍ ـ أَشْعَرُ.

Cripple, *n.* One disabled, مُعَطَّل ـ عاجِز. Lame, أَقْزَلُ ـ عارِج ـ مَشْطُوح ـ سَطِيح. To walk like a —, قَزَلَ ـ. *See also under* Lame, *a.*

Cripple, *v.t.* To make lame, أَعْرَجَ. To disable, خَبَلَ ـ عَطَّلَ ـ سَقَّطَ ـ مُخَبَّل ـ مُعَطَّل ـ عاجِز. Crippled, disabled, عَجَّزَ ـ خَبَّلَ.

Crisis, *n.* As of a disease, بُحْران. The point at which any affair comes to its height, حَوْمَة ـ غَمْرَة. A difficulty, مُشْكِلَة. A financial —, حالُ بُحْرانٍ ٱلْمالِيَّةِ. A ministerial —, حالُ بُحْرانٍ عِنْدَ وُزَراءِ ٱلدَّوْلَةِ.

Crisp, *v.t.* To curl, جَعَّدَ ـ عَكَّفَ. To twist, أَبْرَمَ ـ ثَنَى. To make brittle, صَيَّرَ سَرِيعَ ٱلْعَطَبِ.

Crisp, | Curled, مُجَعَّد ـ جَعْد ـ مَعْكُوف ـ مُتَعَكِّف

Crispate, *a.* | Brittle, هَشٌّ ـ هَشِيم ـ واهٍ ـ هَشُّ ٱلْمَكْسِرِ.

Crispy, | Crisp paste, قَراقِيش. *See also to* Frizzle, *v.t.*

Crispation, *n.* The act of curling, تَعْكِيف ـ تَجْعِيد; the being curled, جُعُودَة ـ تَعَكُّف.

Crisping-pin, *n.* آلَةُ ٱلتَّجْعِيدِ ـ مِعْكَف.

Crispness, *n.* As of the hair, جَعادَة ـ عُكُوفَة. *See also* Brittleness, *n.*

Cristate, *a.* *See* Crested, *a.*

Criterion, *n.* عَلامَةٌ بِها يُحْكَمُ عَلَى شَيْءٍ ـ دَلالَة ـ أَمارَة ـ مِعْيار ـ قِسْطاس ـ قِياس.

Critic, *n.* One skilled in judging of literature, نَطِس *pl.* نُطُس ـ نُقّاد ـ ناقِد *pl.* نُقّاد ـ جِهابِذَة *pl.* جِهْبِذ ـ تَحارِيرُ *pl.* نِحْرِير ـ مُباحِث ـ مُحَكِّم ـ فَيْصَلِيّ ـ فَوارِسُ *pl.* فارِس. An examiner, A censurer, ناعٍ ـ مُنَدِّد ب ـ قادِحٌ فِي ـ هاجٍ ـ مُعَقِّب ـ عَيّابَة ـ مُخَطِّئ.

Critical, *a.* Exact, مُدَقِّق ـ مَضْبُوط ـ مُحْكَم. Belonging to criticism, إِنْتِقادِيّ ـ نَقْدِيّ. Inclined to find fault, مُتَعَقِّب ـ نَمّام ـ مُماحِك. Decisive, مَفْصُول ـ بَتِّيّ. Dangerous, خَطِير ـ مُخْطِر ـ مَقْرُونٌ بِٱلْخَطَرِ. Producing a crisis, حَدُّ ٱلْفَصْلَيْنِ. A — period, أَيّامٌ مُشْكِلَةٌ. A — situation, مَوْقِعٌ مُشْكِلٌ ـ صُعُوبَة. Critical affairs, أَحْوالٌ مُشْكِلَةٌ ـ صُعُوبات.

Critically, *ad.* Exactly, بِضَبْطٍ ـ بِإِتْقانٍ ـ بِتَدْقِيقٍ ـ بِإِحْكامٍ.

Criticalness, *n.* Exactness, إِتْقان ـ دِقَّة ـ تَدْقِيق ـ إِحْكام ـ ضَبْط.

Criticise, *v.t.* نَقَدَ [2] ـ إِنْتَقَدَ ـ تَعَقَّبَ عَلَى ـ بَيَّنَ ما فِيهِ مِنَ ٱلصَّحِيحِ وَٱلْغَلَطِ. To comment upon, شَرَحَ ـ أَوَّلَ ـ عَبَّرَ. To censure, لامَ [2] ـ قَدَحَ ـ نَعَى عَلَى ـ نَدَّدَ ب. He made a speech criticising the policy of the government, أَلْقَى مَقالَةً نَدَّدَ فِيها بِسِياسَةِ ٱلدَّوْلَةِ.

Criticism, *n.* مَعاب ـ إِنْتِقاد ـ نَقْد. *See also* Critique, *n.*

Critique, *n.* إِنْتِقاد ـ تَنْدِيد ـ حَطٌّ فِي ـ تَخْطِئَة ـ تَعَقُّب ـ تَفْصِيل وَتَمْيِيز.

Croak, *n.* | Of frogs, نَقِيق; of ravens, عاقٍ عاقٍ ـ غَقٌّ ـ

Croaking, | نَعِيب ـ نَغِيق ـ نَعِيق ـ نُعاق ـ نَعَبان.

Croak, *v.i.* As a frog, نَقَّ; as a raven, نَعَقَ ـ نَعَبَ.

Croaker, *n.* One who always feigns to be sick, مُتَمارِض; one who is always finding fault, نَمّام; a grumbler, نَقّاق ـ مَقِت.

Croatia, *n.* ٱلْخَرْوات ـ خَرْواتِيا. The Ban of —, بانُ ٱلْخَرْواتِ.

Croceous, *a.* زَعْفَرانِيّ.

Crock, *n.* An earthen pot, قِدْر *pl.* قُدُور ـ بُرْمَة *pl.* بِرام *and* بُرَم ـ بَرْنِيَّة *pl.* بَرانِيّ.

Crockery, *n.* كاشِي ـ عَجَمِي ـ فَخّار ـ خَزَف. A seller of —, خَزَفِيّ ـ خَزّاف.

Crocodile, *n.* تِمْساح *pl.* تَماسِيح ـ ٱلْفِرْعَوْنُ. Crocodile tears, دَمْعٌ مُذاق.

Crocus, *n.* زَعْفَران ـ كُرْكُم. *See also under* Saffron, *n.*

Croft, *n.* حَقْل جَنْبَ ٱلْبَيْتِ.

Croisade, *n.* *See* Crusade, *n.*

Croises, *n.* جِهادِيَّةُ ٱلصَّلِيبِ.

Cromlech, *n.* رَجِيمَة *pl.* رَجائِم ـ أَكَمَة *pl.* إِكام *and* أُكُم.

Crone, *n.* An old ewe, ٱلْعَجُوزُ مِنَ ٱلنِّعاجِ; an old woman, شَهْرَبَة ـ عَجُوز ـ دَرْدَبِيس.

Crony, *n.* قَدِيم *pl.* قُدَماء ـ خِدْن *pl.* أَخْدان ـ أَلِيف *pl.* نُدَماء ـ نَدِيم *pl.* عُشَراء ـ عَشِير ـ أُلَفاء.

Crook, *n.* A shepherd's —, عَصا ٱلرّاعِي ـ مِعْقال ـ قُرْصُوف ـ ٱلرّاعِي. Anything bent, a bending, إِنْحِناء ـ تَعَوُّج. Any crooked instrument, عُقّافَة ـ خُطّاف ـ كُلّاب *pl.* كَلالِيب.

Crook, *v.t.* To bend, لَوَى ـ حَنا [2] ـ حَجَنَ ـ عَقَفَ ـ عَقَّفَ ـ قَبا [2] ـ قَوَّسَ ـ عَوَّجَ. To pervert, أَعْسَفَ ـ أَغْوَى ـ أَزاغَ.

Crook-backed, *a.* أَقْطَن ـ أَقْوَس ـ مَحْدُوب; from age, مَعْقُوف.

Crooked, *a.* Not straight, bent, أَعْقَف ـ مُتَعَقِّف ـ مُنْحَنٍ ـ مُقَوَّس ـ أَحْجَن ـ مُعَقْرَب ـ أَعْوَج ـ مُعَوَّج. Crooked, of a horn, لَفْت; having — horns, أَلْفَت. Having a — bill, أَحْجَن ٱلْمِنْقارِ. A — stick, عَصًا مُعَوَّجَة. Having — hands and feet, أَعْسَم. Winding, مُلْتَوٍ. Perverse, شَكِيس ـ شَكِس. Wicked, فاسِق ـ فاجِر. Confused, مُلْتَبِس. To be —, bent, إِنْعَقَفَ ـ تَعَوَّجَ ـ لَوِيَ ـ عَوِجَ.

Crookedly, *ad.* Not straight, بِٱنْعِقَافٍ ـ بِٱلْتِوَآءٍ ـ بِٱعْوِجَاجٍ ـ بِغَيْرِ ٱسْتِقَامَةٍ. Not uprightly, بِشَكَاسَةٍ. Perversely, بِتَعَنُّتٍ.

Crookedness, *n.* Curvity, عِوَجٌ ـ ٱنْعِقَافٌ ـ ٱنْحِنَآءٌ ـ ٱعْوِجَاجٌ. Deformity, دَانٌ ـ عَيْبٌ ـ شَيْنٌ. Perversity, شَكَاسَةٌ. Want of integrity, خِيَانَةٌ ـ نِفَاقٌ ـ فِسْقٌ ـ عَدَمُ ٱسْتِقَامَةٍ.

Crop, *n.* Produce, harvest, كُدْسٌ ـ حَصِيدٌ ـ غَلَّةٌ ـ مَحْصُولٌ. The first stomach of a fowl, مِقْشَلَةٌ ـ جِرِّيَّةٌ ـ قِرِّيَّةٌ ـ نَوْطَةٌ ـ نُوْدَةٌ ـ غَرْغَرَةٌ ـ حَوْصَلَةٌ *pl.* حَوَاصِلُ. The season of the crops, مَوْسِمُ ٱلْغَلَّاتِ (*or* ٱلْغِلَالِ).

Crop, *v.t.* To cut off the top, قَلَمَ ـ قَرْطَمَ ـ قَرَضَ ـ بَرَى. To reap, حَصَدَ.

Crop-eared, *a.* مَقْطُوعُ ٱلْآذَانِ ـ قَصْيَا *and* قَصْوَآءُ *fem.* أَقْصَى.

Crop-full, *a.* مُحَوْصَلٌ ـ مَشْحُونٌ.

Crop out, *v.i.* To project, أَشْرَفَ. To manifest itself, ظَهَرَ ـ بَانَ.

Crop-sick, *a.* مَغْثُومٌ.

Crosier, *n.* عَصَا ٱلْأُسْقُفِ ـ عُكَّازَةٌ *pl.* عَكَاكِيزُ.

Croslet, *n.* صُلَيْبٌ.

Cross, *n.* As that on which CHRIST suffered, صَلِيبٌ *pl.* صُلْبَانٌ. A line drawn through another, خَطٌّ مُصَلَّبٌ. Suffering, trial, مُعَانَاةٌ ـ مِحْنَةٌ *pl.* مِحَنٌ ـ بَلِيَّةٌ ـ تَجْرِبَةٌ ـ رَزِيَّةٌ *pl.* رَزَايَا ـ مُصِيبَةٌ *pl.* مَصَائِبُ. Cross, an order of merit, *etc.*, نِيشَانُ ٱلْٱفْتِخَارِ. Grand —, نِيشَانُ ٱلْٱفْتِخَارِ مِنَ ٱلدَّرَجَةِ ٱلْأُولَى ـ نِيشَانُ شَرَفٍ. To make the sign of the —, صَلَّبَ ـ رَسَمَ ٱلصَّلِيبَ. To hang on a —, صَلَبَ. A — in love, خَيْبَةٌ فِي ٱلْعِشْقِ.

Cross, *a.* Transverse, مُعْتَرِضٌ ـ مُصَلَّبٌ. Oblique, مُنْحَرِفٌ ـ مُنْكَسِرٌ. Wry, أَحْوَلُ *fem.* حَوْلَآءُ ـ زُعْرُورٌ ـ مُعَرْبِدٌ. Adverse to, مُضَادٌّ لِ ـ مُخَالِفٌ لِ ـ مُعَاكِسٌ لِ. Peevish, شَرِسٌ ـ مُتَفَرْعِنٌ ـ جَمُوحٌ ـ مُتَمَرِّدٌ. Intractable, مُلْتَوٍ ـ مُكَرَّرُ ٱلْحَنَقِ. Contradictory, مُتَنَاقِضٌ ـ مُتَضَادٌّ ـ عَسِرٌ ـ حَرُونٌ. Unfortunate, شَقِيٌّ ـ نَحِسٌ. They played at — purposes, تَخَالَفُوا فِي ٱلْعَمَلِ بِمَرَامٍ وَاحِدٍ. To be —, ill-natured, عَرْبَدَ.

Cross, *prep.* Athwart, عَرْضًا ـ ٱعْتِرَاضًا; from side to side, over, عَبْرَ ـ قَطْعًا. *See also* Athwart, Across, *prep.*

Cross, *v.t.* To lay across, شَبَّكَ ـ صَلَّبَ. To sign with the —, صَلَّبَ عَلَى ـ رَسَمَ بِٱلصَّلِيبِ. To cancel, مَحَا ـ أَبْطَلَ ـ نَسَخَ. To pass over, عَبَرَ ـ قَطَعَ ـ جَزَعَ ـ أَجَازَ; to make another to — over, to transport to the other side, عَبَّرَ ـ قَطَّعَ. To thwart, عَارَضَ ـ عَاكَسَ ـ تَعَرَّضَ لِ ـ عَطَّلَ. To hinder, مَنَعَ. To come between, حَالَ بَيْنَ وَبَيْنَ. To —, as a cheque, كَتَبَ عَلَى مُعْتَرِضًا. To contradict, rebut, أَدْحَضَ ـ نَاقَضَ ـ ضَادَّ. To — the sea, خَاضَ ٱلْبَحْرَ ـ سَافَرَ ـ أَبْحَرَ. To — the legs, تَوَرَّكَ. To sit cross-legged, جَلَسَ مُتَرَبِّعًا ـ قَعَدَ مُتَرَبِّعًا ـ تَرَبَّعَ فِي جُلُوسِهِ. He crossed the valley, قَطَعَ ٱلْوَادِي عَرْضًا.

Cross, *v.i.* To lie athwart, تَصَالَبَ ـ تَقَاطَعَ ـ ٱعْتَرَضَ. To be inconsistent with, تَعَاكَسَ ـ تَنَاقَضَ.

Cross-action, *n.* دَعْوَى تُعَاكِسُ دَعْوَى أُخْرَى ـ حُجَّةٌ عَلَى حُجَّةٍ.

Cross-bar, *n.* خَشَبَةٌ ـ عَارِضَةٌ *pl.* عَوَارِضُ. *See also under* Bar, *n.*

Cross-bars, *n.* Lattice-work, تَشَبُّكٌ ـ تَشْبِيكٌ.

Cross-bill, *n.* The bird, طَائِرٌ أَجْنَحُ ٱلْمِنْقَارِ.

Cross-bow, *n.* قَوْسٌ ـ قَذَّافَةٌ.

Cross-breed, *n.* جِنْسٌ خِلْطٌ مِلْطٌ.

Cross-bun, *n.* رَغِيفٌ مُصَلَّبٌ.

Cross-examination, *n.* فَحْصٌ بِٱلْمُغَالَبَةِ ـ نَصٌّ ـ فَحْصٌ مُوَقَّعٌ.

Cross-examine, *v.t.* فَحَصَ بِٱلْمُغَالَبَةِ ـ نَصَّ ـ ٱمْتَحَنَ بِٱلْأُغْلُوطَاتِ.

Cross-eyed, *a.* أَحْوَلُ *fem.* حَوْلَآءُ.

Cross-grained, *a.* Of wood, خَشَبٌ أَخْشَبُ. Perverse, مُتَغَشْمِرٌ ـ مُتَعَفْرِتٌ ـ صَعْبٌ ـ شَكِسٌ ـ شَرِسٌ. To be —, perverse, شَكُسَ.

Crossing, *n.* A hindrance, مَانِعٌ ـ مُعَارَضَةٌ; a passage across, مَعْبَرٌ ـ مَقْطَعٌ.

Cross-legged, *ad.* مُتَرَبِّعًا. *See under* Cross, *v.t.*

Crossly, *ad.* Peevishly, بِشَكَاسَةٍ. Oppositely, بِتَعَارُضٍ ـ بِمُعَارَضَةٍ ـ بِتَضَادٍّ. Athwart, بِتَشْبِيكٍ ـ بِتَصْلِيبٍ ـ ٱعْتِرَاضًا.

Crossness, *n.* Peevishness, شَكَاسَةٌ ـ تَمَرُّدٌ ـ عَرْبَدَةٌ ـ شَرَاسَةٌ ـ زَعَارَةٌ ـ مُشَاغَبَةٌ ـ عَفْرَتَةٌ ـ فَرْعَنَةٌ ـ زَعَّارَةٌ *vulg.*

Cross-question, *v.t.* *See to* Cross-examine, *v.t.*

Cross-trees, *n.* قَوْرَجْنَةٌ.

Cross-way, *n.* مِفْرَقٌ; a short way, مَشْعَبٌ. The place where a road divides, مُتَفَرَّقٌ.

Cross-wind, *n.* كَوْسٌ ـ رِيحٌ مُشَارِكٌ ـ رِيحٌ نَكْبَآءُ.

Cross-wise, *ad.* *See* Across, *ad.*

Crotch, *n.* عُقَّافَةٌ ـ كُلَّابٌ *pl.* كَلَالِيبُ.

Crotchet, *n.* A mark in music, عَلَامَةٌ فِي رَسْمِ فَنِّ ٱلْمُوسِيقَةِ. A whim, خَيَالٌ ـ هُوِيَّةٌ ـ هَوًى *pl.* أَهْوَآءٌ.

Crotchety, *a.* Having whims, مُتَخَيِّلٌ ـ مُلْتَوٍ. To be —, تَلَوَّى ـ تَخَيَّلَ. *See also* Whimsical, *a.*

Crouch, *v.i.* To stoop low, لَطَأَ بِ ـ أَلْبَدَ ـ خَرَّ ـ سَجَدَ ; as an animal, رَبَضَ ـ تَلَبَّدَ. To bend servilely, تَمَاوَتَ ـ تَذَلَّلَ ـ تَمَسْكَنَ ـ تَخَضَّعَ.

Croup, *n.* The buttocks of an animal, كِفْل ـ رِدْف ـ عَجُز ـ مُؤَخَّر. The disease, نَوْعٌ مِنَ ٱلْخُنَاقِ.

Croupier, *n.* Overseer of a gaming house, نَاظِرُ مَلْعَبِ ٱلْقِمَارِ.

Crow, *n.* The bird, غَاق ـ قَيْقَان *pl.* قَاق ـ زِيْغَان *pl.* زَاغ ـ فَيْق ـ غِرْبَان *pl.* غُرَاب ـ اِبْنُ بَرِيحٍ. The voice, as of a cock, صِيَاح ـ صَقْع ـ صُقَاع. *See also* Crowbar, *n.*

Crow, *v.i.* As a cock, صَاحَ ـ صَقَعَ. To exult over, إِعْتَزَّ بِ. To boast, تَبَاهَى بِ ـ أُعْجِبَ بِ ـ يَزْهُو *aor.* زَهِيَ ـ تَاهَ ـ إِفْتَخَرَ.

Crowbar, *n.* مِخَلّ *pl.* أَمْخَال.

Crowd, *n.* A multitude of things together, جُمُوم ـ جَمٌّ ـ كَوْثَر ـ سِرْب ـ غِمَار ـ غَمْرَة ـ غَمٌّ ـ مَوْكِب ـ زَحْم ; of people, تَرَاكُم ـ زِحَام ـ اِزْدِحَام ـ غَابَة ـ جَوْقَة ـ مَحْشَر ـ لَبِيكَة ـ أَسْرَاب *pl.* جَمْع. The common people, الْأَوْبَاشُ ـ عَامَّةُ ٱلنَّاسِ ـ الطَّغَام. A — of roughs, غَوْغَآءُ. A moving —, سَائِرَة. The people met together in crowds, النَّاسُ حَشَدُوا وَتَجَمْهَرُوا. They came in crowds, confusedly, جَاؤُوا فِي هَوْشٍ وَبَوْشٍ. To get through the —, يَلِجُ *aor.* وَلَجَ غَابَةَ ٱلْجَمْعِ ـ شَقَّ ٱلزِّحَامَ.

Crowd, *v.t.* To fill confusedly, حَشَرَ ـ زَحَمَ. To — with people, as of a room, لَزَّزَ ـ ضَغَطَ ـ أَغَصَّ. To press together, لَبَّدَ ـ كَبَّسَ. To — sail, أَقْلَعَ جَمِيعَ ٱلْأَشْرِعَةِ. They crowded together, تَزَاحَمُوا. The people crowded me, زَحَمَنِي ٱلنَّاسُ.

Crowd, *v.i.* To swarm, شُحِنَ بِ ـ غَصَّ بِ ـ تَرَاكَمَ. The shore was crowded with them, غَصَّ بِهِمِ ٱلسَّاحِلُ. The people crowded together, تَحَطَّمَ ٱلنَّاسُ ـ تَضَايَقُوا ـ اِزْدَحَمُوا ـ تَقَاصَفُوا. To be crowded with, غَصَّ بِ.

Crowding, *n.* اِزْدِحَام. In order to prevent —, لِمَنْعِ ٱلْاِزْدِحَامِ.

Crown, *n.* Of the head, قُرْصُ ٱلرَّأْسِ ـ يَافُوخ ـ هَامَة ـ نَصْلَة. The ornament of imperial dignity, تَاج *pl.* تِيجَان ـ إِكْلِيل *pl.* أَكَالِيل. A garland, إِكْلِيلُ زَهْرٍ. A reward, ثَوَاب ـ مَثُوبَة ـ جَزَآء. The top of anything, قُمَّة ـ قُنَّة ـ قُرْص ـ شُنْخُوب ـ أَعْلَى ٱلشَّيْءِ ـ ذِرْوَة ـ قُلَّة. Royalty, مُلْك ـ دَوْلَة ـ سَلْطَنَة. Honour, كَرَامَة ـ سُدَّة ـ عِزّ ـ شَرَف ـ جَاه ـ رِفْعَة. The shaven — of a priest, رَشْمَة. The — of a hat, قُرْصُ بُرْنَيْطَةٍ. A five-shilling piece, سِكَّةُ خَمْسَةِ شِيلِينَاتٍ.

Crown, *v.t.* To invest with a crown, كَلَّلَ ـ تَوَّجَ. To dignify, شَرَّفَ ـ أَجَلَّ ـ أَعَزَّ ـ أَوْجَهَ ـ كَبَّرَ ـ أَمَّرَ. To recompense, أَثَابَ ـ أَنْهَى ـ أَتَمَّ. To perfect, finish, جَازَى ـ كَافَى ـ أَنْجَزَ ـ قَضَى ـ خَتَمَ. The end crowns the work, خَتْمُ ٱلْأُمُورِ عَاقِبَتُهَا. To be crowned, as a king, تَكَلَّلَ ـ تَتَوَّجَ. A crowned head, مَلِك *pl.* مُلُوك ـ سُلْطَان *pl.* سَلَاطِين ـ تَاجْ دَار. The hills were crowned with plants, إِعْتَمَّتِ ٱلْجِبَالُ بِٱلنَّبَاتِ. It will be crowned with success, يَكُونُ مَقْرُونًا بِٱلنَّجَاحِ.

Crown-glass, *n.* بِلَّوْرٌ مِنَ ٱلصِّنْفِ ٱلْأَعْلَى.

Crown-lands, *n.* (ٱلْهُمَايُونِيَّةُ *or*) ٱلْأَرَاضِي ٱلسُّلْطَانِيَّةُ. Crown and state lands, ٱلْأَرَاضِي ٱلسُّلْطَانِيَّةُ وَٱلْمِيرِيَّةُ.

Crowning, *a.* Finishing, مُتَمِّم ـ آخِر ـ خَيْرُ ٱلْعَاقِبَةِ.

Crucial, *a.* Transverse, مُشَبَّك ـ مُصَلَّب. Painful, مُؤْلِم ـ أَلِيم. Difficult, مُشْكِل. Trying, مُجَرِّب ـ مُخْتَبِر ـ مُبْتَلٍ.

Cruciate, *v.t.* To torture, أَوْجَعَ ـ أَمَضَّ ـ شَقَّ عَلَى ـ عَذَّبَ ـ آلَمَ.

Crucible, *n.* مِذْوَب ـ بَوَادِق *pl.* بُودَقَة ـ بَوَاطِق *pl.* بُوطَقَة.

Crucified, *a.* مَصْلُوب ـ مُصَلَّب.

Crucifier, *n.* صَالِب ـ مُصَلِّب.

Crucifix, *n.* A cross, صُلْبَان *pl.* صَلِيب. The image of one crucified, صُورَةُ ٱلْمَصْلُوبِ.

Crucifixion, *n.* The act of, صَلْب ـ تَصْلِيب ; the being crucified, تَصَلُّب.

Cruciform, *a.* بِصُورَةِ صَلِيبٍ.

Crucify, *v.t.* صَلَبَ. To cause to be crucified, صَلَّبَ.

Crude, *a.* Raw, نِيءٌ. Raw, —, مُلَغْوَس ـ نِيءٌ ـ خَام ـ فِجّ. Not well digested, غَيْرُ مَرِيءٍ ـ وَخِيم. Not well digested, as in the intellect, رَكِيك ـ غَيْرُ مَنْسُوقٍ ـ ذُو وَكْسٍ ـ سَخِيف ـ غَيْرُ جَزْلٍ.

Crudely, *ad.* Hastily, بِدُونِ تَدَبُّرٍ ـ بِتَهَوُّرٍ. Without deliberation, بِلَا تَرَوِّيَةٍ ـ بِتَثْبِيتَةٍ ـ بِلَا تَرَوٍّ. Imperfectly, عَلَى وَكْسٍ.

Crudity, *n.* Indigestion, وَخَامَة ـ أَخْلَاطٌ فِجَّة. Unripeness, فَجَاجَة ـ نُيُوء. Imperfection, defect, وَكْس.

Crudeness, *n.* Unripeness, فَجَاجَة. Rawness, نُيُوء. Defect, وَكْس ـ نُقْصَان ـ قُصُور.

Cruel, *a.* Of man, مُتَغَشْمِر ـ جِلْف ـ عَنِيف ـ فَظّ ـ جَائِر ـ قَاسٍ ـ أَمْرَار *pl.* مُرّ ; of things, قَاسٍ ـ ظَالِم ـ جَافٍ ـ لَظّ ـ وَجِيع ـ أَلِيم. For his — conduct when he was governor, لِمَا ٱرْتَكَبَ مِنَ ٱلْقَسَاوَةِ حِينَ كَانَ وَالِيًا.

Cruelly, *ad.* بِعُنْفٍ ـ بِجَفَآءٍ ـ بِفَرْعَنَةٍ ـ بِغَشْمَرَةٍ ـ بِجَلَافَةٍ ـ بِقَسَاوَةٍ ـ بِظُلْمٍ.

Cruelty, *n.* جَلَافَة ـ جَفَآء ـ فَظَاظَة ـ جَوْر ـ صَرَامَة ـ عَنَف.

ظُلْم — قَساوة. He vented his cruelty upon . . . , تَشَفَّى مِن — شَفَى غَلِيلَهُ مِن.

Cruet, *n.* قِنِّينَة — شِيشَة *pl.* شِيَش — حُنْجُور. Cruet-stand, آنِيَةُ ٱلْأَبَازِيرِ — مِقْرَحَة.

Cruise, *v.i.* To voyage, سَافَرَ — جَالَ فِي ٱلْبَحْرِ — أَبْحَرَ. To — for plunder, قَرْصَنَ — زَمْلَطَ. To — along a coast, أَبْحَرَ حَوْلَ ٱلشُّطُوطِ.

Cruise, *n.* A voyage, سَفَرٌ بَحْرًا; a — for plunder, زَمْلَطَة — قَرْصَنَة.

Cruiser, *n.* A guard vessel, بَارِجَةٌ مُحَافِظَةٌ عَلَى — سَفِينَةٌ رَاقِبَةٌ ٱلشُّطُوطَ. A pirate, قُرْصَان — زَمْلُوط.

Crumb, *n.* / Crum, } The soft part of bread, لُبُّ ٱلْخُبْزِ — لُبَاب. A particle of bread, فُتَات — خُشَارَة. A particle, كُسَارَة — كِسَر *pl.* كِسْرَة.

Crumble, *v.t.* Of bread, فَتَّتَ — فَتَّ — ثَرَدَ. To break into small pieces, generally, كَسَّرَ — فَتَّتَ — حَطَمَ — بَسَّ. To demolish, هَدَمَ — هَدَّ.

Crumble, *v.i.* To fall to pieces, إِنْفَتَّ — تَفَتَّتَ — إِنْحَتَّ — تَكَسَّرَ. Crumbled, مَفْتُوت — فَتِيت.

Crumb-cloth, *n.* سُفْرَة.

Crumminess, *n.* هَشُوشَة — تَحَنُّم.

Crummy, *a.* Of bread, كَثِيرُ ٱللُّبِّ — لُبِّيّ — هَشّ. Fragile, مُسْتَرْخٍ — رَخْو — ذُو تَحَنُّم. To be —, fragile, رَخِيَ. To be —, as of bread, هَشَّ.

Crumpet, *n.* نَوْعٌ مِنَ ٱلْقَطَائِفِ.

Crumple, *v.t.* جَعْلَكَ — أَذَالَ — اِبْتَذَلَ — دَعَكَ — نَهَكَ — كَمَّشَ — رَضْرَضَ — مَعَكَ. *See also to* Rumple, *v.t.*

Crumple, *v.i.* تَكَمَّشَ — تَقَلَّصَ — إِنْقَبَضَ — تَقَبَّضَ — تَرَضْرَضَ. *See also to* Rumple, *v.i.*

Crupper, *n.* Of a horse's harness, بَرْطِيز — طَفَر — أَثْفَار *pl.* ثَفَر — قَسْقُون — بَرَاطِيز *pl.*

Crupper, *v.t.* لَبَّسَ-ٱلْقَسْقُونَ — أَثْفَرَ.

Crural, *a.* مُخْتَصٌّ بِٱلسَّاقِ — سَاقِيّ. The — vein, ٱلصَّافِنُ.

Crusade, *n.* جِهَادٌ فِي سَبِيلِ دِينِ ٱلنَّصَارَى.

Crusader, *n.* مُجَاهِدٌ نَصْرَانِيٌّ.

Cruse, *n.* جَام — فِلْجَان — فِنْجَان *pl.* فَنَاجِينُ — كُوز *pl.* أَكْوَاز.

Cruset, *n* *See* Crucible, *n.*

Crush, *v.t.* To squeeze between, ضَغَطَ — هَمَزَ. To bruise, هَرَسَ — سَهَكَ — سَحَقَ — دَقَّ — رَضَّ — رَضَخَ. To — stones, رَضَخَ. To — to powder, طَحَنَ — دَقَّقَ. To beat down, دَوَّخَ — أَذَلَّ — قَهَرَ — هَدَّ — دَكَّ. To subdue, قَهَرَ — أَذَلَّ — إِنْتَصَرَ عَلَى. A crushing instrument, مِرْضَخَة — مِدَقّ. He crushed and destroyed them, طَحَنَهُمْ فَأَهْلَكَهُمْ.

Crush, *v.i.* To be broken, إِنْسَحَقَ — إِنْدَقَّ — تَرَضَّخَ — إِنْحَطَمَ — إِنْكَسَرَ.

Crush, *n.* Collision, مُصَادَمَة — مُلَاطَمَة. A — of people, غَمْرَة *pl.* غَمَرَات — إِزْدِحَام — كَظِيظ. Ruin, هَلَكَة — قَصْفَة — تَلَف — هَلَاك.

Crust, *n.* The outer part of bread, قِرْفَةُ (or) قِشْرَةُ ٱلرَّغِيفِ. A — of dry bread, عَسْمَة — جِلْف *pl.* جِلَفَة. Any hard outward covering, قِشْرَة — وَجْه — أَدِيم — بَشَرَة. The — over a wound, غَضَنَة — جُلْبَة. A — of clay, قُلَاع. The pastry of a pie, ٱلْعَجِينُ.

Crust, *v.t.* To cover with a —, لَبَّسَ-بِقِشْرَةٍ. To overlay with, لَبَّسَ-بِ.

Crust, *v.i.* To become hard, صَلُبَ — صَلَبَ — جَمَدَ. To become covered with a —, تَلَبَّسَ بِقِشْرَةٍ.

Crustacea, *n.* ٱلْحَيَوَانَاتُ ذَوَاتُ قِشْرٍ.

Crustaceous, *a.* ذُو قِشْرٍ.

Crustily, *ad.* *See* Crossly, *ad.*

Crusty, *a.* Of bread, كَثِيرُ ٱلْقِشْرِ. Hard and dry, جَفِيف — نَاشِف — يَابِس. *See also* Peevish, Cross, *a.*

Crutch, *n.* تُكَأَة — عُكَّازَة *pl.* عَكَاكِيزُ. To use a —, تَعَكَّزَ.

Crutch, *v.t.* To support, سَنَدَ — رَفَدَ — دَعَمَ.

Cry, *v.i.* and *t.* To speak loudly, إِسْتَهَلَّ — أَشَادَ — زَأَطَ — عَيَّطَ — صَرَخَ — زَعَقَ — صَاحَ — صَوَّتَ. To call importunately, to complain, هَتَفَ — شَكَا — صَرَخَ. To cry, as an eagle, or a camel, هَدَرَ. To cry or shout out to, as to cattle, نَادَى-بِ — دَعَا بِ — دَعَا; to summon, أَيَّهَ-بِ. To utter lamentations, أَعْوَلَ — وَلْوَلَ — نَحَبَ — نَاحَ. To shed tears, بَكَى — دَمَعَ — ذَرَفَتْ عَيْنُهُ.

To cry down, to depreciate, صَاحَ عَلَى — فَضَحَ — قَبَّحَ — وَكَسَ — إِسْتَخَفَّ — هَتَكَ — يَكِسُ aor.

To cry down, to prohibit, نَهَى — حَظَرَ — حَظَرَ عَلَى — مَنَعَ — حَرَّمَ.

To cry for help, إِسْتَصْرَخَ — إِسْتَغَاثَ — إِسْتَنْصَرَ — إِسْتَعَانَ.

To cry out, to exclaim, نَادَى — صَرَخَ. To cry out, to complain of, تَضَجَّرَ مِن — تَشَكَّى مِن. To cry out against, to censure, لَامَ — ذَمَّ — عَيَّبَ.

To cry up, to praise, صَاحَ بِ — فَضَّلَ — كَبَّرَ — فَخَّرَ — فَخَّمَ —

— زَيَّدَ. To cry up, to raise the price, رَفَعَ — مَدَحَ
نَادَى بِٱلْمَزَادِ.

Cry, *n.* A lamentation, نُوَاح — عَوِيل — نَحِيب — وَلْوَلَة. A weeping, تَدَمُّع — بُكَآء. Clamour, outcry, عِيَاط — صِيَاح — صَيْحَة — زَيْطَة — صُرَاخ. Cry, of a vulture, camel, *etc.*, هَدَر. An exclamation of wonder, نِدَآءُ ٱلتَّعَجُّبِ — شَهْقَة. The cry of a vender, مُنَادَاة — نِدَآءُ ٱلْبَاعَةِ. An importunate cry, a cry for help, إِسْتِعَانَة — إِسْتِنْصَار — إِسْتِغَاثَة — إِسْتِصْرَاخ. The crying, as of dogs, نُبَاح — هَرِير; of birds, تَغْرِيد — زَقْزَقَة — صُدَاح — صَدْح. A cry of joy, زَغْرَطَة — إِهْلَال — إِسْتِهْلَال.

Crying, *a.* Notorious, مُشَاع — مَشْهُور. Great, كَبِير — عَظِيم. A — shame, عَيْنُ ٱلْعَارِ.

Crypt, *n.* رَفّ *pl.* رُفُوف — طَاقَة — سَهْوَة *pl.* سِهَآء — مِشْكَاة *pl.* مَشَاكٍ.

Cryptogamous, *a.* نَبَاتٌ مَكْتُومُ ٱلتَّنَاسُلِ.

Cryptogamy, *n.* تَنَاسُلٌ مَكْتُومٌ.

Crystal, *n.* The mineral, مِلْحُ ٱلْقَاقِ — حَجَرُ ٱلْبِلَّوْرِ. Crystal glass, بِلَّوْر — مَهَاة *pl.* مَهَيَات *and* مَهَوَات.

Crystal, *a.* Crystalline, } بِلَّوْرِيّ — مَهَوِيّ. Clear, صَافٍ — شَفَّاف — مَهْوٌ. A crystalline humour in the eye, رُطُوبَةٌ زُجَاجِيَّةٌ فِي ٱلْعَيْنِ.

Crystallization, *n.* تَبَلْوُر — إِنْجِمَادُ ٱلْجَوْهَرِ فِي هَيْئَةِ حَجَرِ ٱلْبِلَّوْرِ.

Crystallize, *v.t.* بَلْوَرَ — جَوْهَرَ — صَيَّرَ مِثْلَ ٱلْبِلَّوْرِ — جَمَّدَ.

Crystallize, *v.i.* تَجَوْهَرَ — صَارَ مِثْلَ ٱلْبِلَّوْرِ.

Crystallized, *a.* مُتَجَوْهِر — مُجَوْهَر.

Cub, *n.* The young of a beast, جِرْو *pl.* جِرَآء — شِبْل *pl.* شِبَال *and* أَجْرَآء. The — of a fox, هِجْرِس *pl.* هَجَارِس — ثُعَيْلِب; of a bear, وَلَدُ ٱلدُّبِّ.

Cub, *v.i.* She cubbed, نُتِجَتْ — وَلَدَتْ — خَلَّفَتْ; (from the verbs, نُتِجَ — وَلَدَ *aor.* يَلِدُ — خَلَّفَ.)

Cubature, *n.* إِخْرَاجُ ٱلْمُكَعَّبِ — تَكْعِيب.

Cube, *n.* كَعْب *pl.* كُعُوب — مُكَعَّب.

Cube, *v.t.* كَعَّبَ.

Cube, *v.i.* صَارَ كَعْبًا.

Cubeb, *n.* كَبَابَةٌ صِينِيَّةٌ — كَبَابَة.

Cubic, *a.* Cubical, } كَعْبِيّ — مُكَعَّب. Cubical equation, مُعَادَلَةٌ مُكَعَّبَةٌ. Cubical number, عَدَدٌ مُكَعَّبٌ — مُكَعَّب.

Cubiform, *a.* بِصُورَةِ ٱلْكَعْبِ — مُكَعَّب.

Cubit, *n.* مِرْفَق *pl.* مَرَافِق — ذِرَاع *pl.* أَذْرُع *and* ذُرْعَان — ذِرَاعٌ هَاشِمِيّ. To measure with the —, ذَرَعَ. Measuring with the —, تَذَرُّع. Selling by the —, مُذَارَعَة. This garment is a — long, هٰذَا ٱلثَّوْبُ ذِرَاعٌ. The instrument of cubital measurement, ذِرَاع.

Cubital, *a.* ذِرَاعِيّ.

Cuboid, Cuboidal, *a.* بِشَكْلِ ٱلْكَعْبِ — شَبِيهُ ٱلْكَعْبِ.

Cuckold, *n.* عَكْرُوت — قَوَّاد — قُنْدُع — قَرْطَبَان — ٱلتَّيْس — قَرْنَان. A tame —, دَيُّوث — صَقُور — صَقَّار.

Cuckold, *v.t.* دَيَّثَ — صَيَّرَ قَوَّادًا.

Cuckoo, *n.* وَقْوَق — طَاطُوِي — وَقُوق — كُوكُو.

Cucumber, *n.* خِيَار — تَرْعُوز — عَجُّور — فَقُّوس — قِثَّآء. The squirting —, *elaterium*, قِثَّآءُ ٱلْحِمَارِ.

Cud, *n.* جِرَّة — جَرَّة. To chew the —, نَشْوَرَ — إِجْتَرَّ — إِشْتَرَّ — مَضَغَ. To chew the — of reflection, تَأَمَّلَ. To repent of, نَدِمَ عَلَى.

Cuddle, *v.t.* To embrace, تَعَانَقَ — عَانَقَ — كَامَعَ.

Cuddle, *v.i.* To squat, قَرْفَصَ — ثَبَجَ.

Cuddle, *n.* An embrace, مُعَانَقَة.

Cuddy, *n.* A small cabin, كَمَرَةٌ صَغِيرَةٌ.

Cudgel, *n.* هِرَاوَة *pl.* هَرَاوَى — دَبُّوس — عَصًا. To take up the cudgels for, حَامَى عَن — قَاتَلَ عَن.

Cudgel, *v.t.* زَكَأَ — قَدَعَ بِ — مَتَأَ بِ — صَمَعَ — عَصَا — ضَرَبَ بِٱلْعَصَا. A cudgelling, ضَرْبٌ بِعَصًا — قَدْع.

Cue, *n.* The end or tail of anything, غَايَة — طَرَف — خِتَام — ذَنَب — آخِر — ذَيْل. Humour, مُرَاد — شَوْق — خُلُق — خَاطِر. A hint, إِشَارَة — رَمْز — كِنَايَة — تَلْمِيح — تَعْرِيض — تَلْوِيح. A billiard cue, صَوَالِج *pl.* صَوْلَجَانُ ٱلْبِلْيَارْدُو. I am not in the cue for . . ., لَيْسَ لِي خَاطِرٌ فِي. He took his cue from him, followed his hint, أَخَذَ ٱلْإِشَارَةَ مِنْهُ — إِمْتَثَلَ رَمْزَهُ.

Cuff, *n.* A blow, ضَرْبَة — لَكْم — لَكْز — لَبْز; a — on the ear, لَطْم — كَفّ. The — of a sleeve, وُصْلَةٌ فِي طَرَفِ كُمٍّ.

Cuff, *v.t.* To beat, لَطَمَ — لَبَزَ — لَكَزَ — لَكَمَ — ضَرَبَ كَفًّا.

Cuirass, *n.* دِرْع — زَرَدِيَّة — نَثْلَة. To arm with a —, دَرَّعَ — زَرَّدَ. *See also under* Armour, *n.*

Cuirassier, *n.* لَابِسُ دِرْعٍ — مُتَدَرِّع.

Cuish, *n.* دِرْعٌ لِلْفَخِذَيْنِ.

Cuisine, *n.* Cookery, صُفْرَة — طِبَاخَة — طَبْخ. A kitchen, مَطْبَخ.

Culinary, *a.* طَبَّاخِيّ — مُخْتَصّ بِٱلطَّبِيخِ — مُتَعَلِّق بِٱلْمَطْبَخِ.

Cull, *v.t.* To select, نَقَّى — تَنَقَّى — إِنْتَقَى. To gather, لَمَّ — جَمَعَ.

Cullender, *n.* مِصْفاة ـ مُنْخُل.

Cullion, *n.* A mean fellow, خَسِيس ـ خَبِيث.

Cully, *n.* A dupe, مُغَفَّل ـ مُغْتَرّ.

Cully, *v.t.* غَشَّ ² ـ غَرَّ ².

Culm, *n.* A stalk, ساق *pl.* سُوُوق *and* سُوق. A kind of coal, جِنْسٌ مِنَ ٱلْفَحْمِ ٱلْمَعْدِنِيّ.

Culminiferous, *a.* ذُو ساقٍ ـ ذُو سُوُوقٍ.

Culminate, *v.i.* Of the sun, تَكَبَّدَتِ ٱلشَّمْسُ. To come to a point, إِنْتَهَى إِلَى ـ لَحِقَ ـ وَرَدَ إِلَى *aor.* يَرِدُ.

Culmination, *n.* As of the sun, تَكَبُّد. The highest point, أَعْلَى. Stature, قَدّ.

Culpable, *a.* مُخْطِئ ـ مُجْرِم ـ مَلُوم ـ جانٍ. To be —, جَرَمَ ـ أَذْنَبَ ـ اِلْتَأَمَ.

Culpableness, *n.* } خَطَأ ـ جُرْم ـ جِنايَة ـ قَباحَة ـ شَرّ ـ ذَنْب.
Culpability, }

Culpably, *ad.* خَطَأً ـ بِإِجْرام ـ بِجِنايَةٍ ـ بِلَوْم ـ بِقَباحَةٍ. To act —, أَخْطَأَ ـ جَرَمَ ـ أَذْنَبَ.

Culprit, *n.* مُشْتَكًى عَلَيْهِ ـ مُدَّعًى عَلَيْهِ ـ خاطِئ *pl.* خُطاة ـ مُذْنِب.

Culter, *n.* *See* Coulter, *n.*

Cultivable, *a.* Of the soil, مِمَّا يُحْرَثُ ـ يُفْلَحُ; of improvement, مِمَّا يُحْكَم ـ يُعْمَر.

Cultivate, *v.t.* As of the soil, خَدَمَ ² ـ فَلَّجَ ² ـ فَلَحَ ـ حَرَثَ ٱلْأَرْضَ ². To rear plants or trees, رَبَّى ـ نَبَّتَ ـ اِسْتَنْبَتَ. To improve, أَرْصَنَ ـ جَوَّدَ ـ رَقَّى ـ سَنَّى ـ أَحْسَنَ ـ أَحْكَمَ ـ أَصْلَحَ. To — the arts, مارَسَ ٱلْعُلُومَ ـ أَتْقَنَ ٱلْعُلُومَ. To —, as of the mind, حَكَّمَ ـ خَرَّجَ ـ فَقَّهَ ـ أَدَّبَ. To —, as the friendship of, اِسْتَرْضَى ـ تَرَضَّى ـ دارَى صُحْبَةً ـ جامَلَ ـ خالَقَ ـ أَلْطَفَ ـ دارَى ـ تَوَدَّدَ إِلَى. A cultivated, flourishing, country, أَرْضٌ عامِرَةٌ. A well — people, قَوْمٌ حَسَنُوا ٱلتَّمَدُّنِ. They have successfully cultivated music, نَجَحُوا فِي إِتْقانِ ٱلْمُوسِيقَة ما أَمْكَنَ.

Cultivation, *n.* } Tillage, as of the soil, تَعْمِير ـ خِدْمَة ـ حِراثَة ـ فِلاحَة. Melioration in general,
Culture, } تَجْوِيد ـ تَعْمِير ـ عِمارَة ـ إِتْقان ـ بُنْيان ـ تَرْبِيَة ـ إِحْكام ـ تَرْبِيَة ـ تَنْبِيه ـ تَخْرِيج ـ تَأْدِيب. Cultivation of literature, إِتْقانُ ٱلْعُلُومِ وَٱلْفُنُون. Study, diligence, مُمارَسَة.

Cultivator, *n.* A tiller of the soil, حَرّاث ـ فَلّاح ـ زَرّاع. An improver in general, مُجَوِّد ـ مُصْلِح ـ مُتْقِن. One who studies, perseveres, مُمارِس ـ طالِب *pl.* طُلّاب.

Culture, *v.t.* *See to* Cultivate, *v.t.*

Culverin, *n.* قُلُومْبُر ـ قُلُورِينَة.

Culvert, *n.* جِسْرٌ عَلَى مَجْرًى ـ مُقَبَّبٌ عَلَى سِكَّةٍ.

Cumber, *v.t.* To embarrass, عَرْبَسَ ـ أَعاقَ ـ عَوَّقَ ـ لَخَمَ ـ عَنَّتَ ـ شَقَّ عَلَى ² ـ وَرَّطَ. To involve in difficulty, لَبَّكَ عَلَى ـ أَجْحَرَ ـ لَبَّكَ ² ـ شَوَّشَ ـ حَيَّرَ. To distract, أَنْصَبَ ـ أَهَمَّ ـ أَعْنَتَ ـ أَتْعَبَ.

Cumbersome, *a.* } Troublesome, لاخِم ـ مُلَبِّك ـ مُهِمّ ـ مُعَنِّت ـ مُوَرِّط ـ مُرْهِق ـ ناصِب.
Cumbrous, }
Burdensome, شاقٌّ عَلَى ـ ثَقِيل.

Cumbrance, *n.* عَوْق ـ عَنَت ـ تَعْوِيق ـ لَخْمَة ـ تَلْبِيك ـ وَرْطَة ـ ثِقْل ـ تَعَب ـ عَرْبَسَة ـ لَبْكَة.

Cumfrey, *n.* The plant, آذانُ ٱلْحِمارِ.

Cumin, *n.* كَمُّون.

Cumulation, *n.* The act of, رَكْم ـ كَدْس ـ تَكْدِيس ـ تَكْوِيم ـ جَمْع. A heap, تَراكُم ـ اِرْتِكام ـ رُكام.

Cumulative, *a.* Augmenting, مُزَيِّد ـ مُكَثِّر. Strengthening, confirmative, مُشَدِّد ـ مُثَبِّت. A — vote, رَأْيُ ٱلْأَكْثَرِين.

Cumulatively, *ad.* بِٱرْتِكامٍ ـ اِرْتِكامًا ـ مَعًا.

Cumulus, *n.* Of clouds, تُراكُمُ ٱلسَّحابِ ـ رُكامُ سَحابٍ ـ تَراكُم ـ ٱلسَّحابُ فِي شَكْلِ ٱلْمَخْرُوطِ.

Cuneal, Cuneate, *a.* } شَرْخِيّ ـ عَلَى شَكْلِ ٱلسَّفِينِ. Cunei-
Cuneiform, Cuniform, } form character, كِتابَةُ ٱلنَّصْلِ ـ ٱلْخَطُّ ٱلْأَشُورِيّ.

Cunning, *a.* Skilful, نِحْرِير ـ خَبِير ـ ماهِر ـ حاذِق. Performed with art, مَوْضُون ـ مُتْقَن ـ دَقِيق ـ رَفِيع ـ مَعْمُولٌ بِحِيلَةٍ وَصَنْعَةٍ. Sly, داهٍ ـ مُحْتال ـ مَكّار ـ خَدّاع ـ باقِعَة ـ ذُو كَيْدٍ ـ حُوالِيّ. A — piece of art, work, مَوْضُونَة.

Cunning, *n.* } Subtlety, دَهاء ـ حِيلَة ـ اِحْتِيال ـ مَكْر ـ خُدْعَة. Skill, خِبْرَة ـ عِلْم ـ نُكْر ـ دِرايَة ـ
Cunningness, } حِذْق ـ لَباقَة ـ مَهارَة ـ مَعْرِفَة.

Cunningly, *ad.* Skilfully, بِصَناعَةٍ ـ بِمَهارَةٍ ـ بِخِبْرَةٍ. Artfully, غَدْرًا ـ بِحِيلَةٍ ـ اِحْتِيالًا.

Cup, *n.* قَدَح *pl.* أَقْداح ـ كَأْس *pl.* كَأْسات ـ طاس *pl.* طاسات; a small —, غُرُف ـ فِنْجان (properly, فِلْجان) *pl.* فَناجِينُ. The — of a flower, كُمُّ ٱلزَّهْرَةِ. The glass used in cupping, مِحْجَمَة ـ جامُ ٱلْحِجامَةِ. Sending the — round in a banquet, مُناقَلَةُ ٱلْكَأْسِ. *See also* Calyx, *n.*

Cup, *v.t.* To bleed by scarification, حَجَمَ ². To be cupped, اِحْتَجَمَ.

Cup-bearer, *n.* سَاقِي ٱلرَّاحِ.

Cupboard, *n.* خِزَانَةٌ *pl.* خَزَائِنُ ـ دُولَابٌ *pl.* دَوَالِيبُ ـ قَيْطُون.

Cupidity, *n.* حِرْص ـ طَمَع ـ شَرَاهَة.

Cupola, *n.* قُبَّة *pl.* قُبَب ـ كِتْر.

Cupper, *n.* حَجَّام ـ مَصَّاص.

Cupping, *n.* حِجَامَة.

Cupping-glass, *n.* قَارُورَةُ ٱلْحَجَّامِ ـ مِحْجَمَة. *See also under* Cup, *n.*

Cupreous, *a.* مِنْ صُفْرٍ ـ صُفْرِيّ.

Cupriferous, *a.* مُوَلِّدُ ٱلصُّفْرِ.

Cur, *n.* A dog, كَلْب ـ كَلْبٌ لا خَيْرَ فِيهِ. A worthless fellow, سُفْلِيّ ـ لَئِيم ـ وَغْدٌ نَذْل.

Curable, *a.* مُدَاوَاتُهُ مُمْكِنَةٌ ـ يُعَالَجُ ـ قَابِلُ ٱلشِّفَآء.

Curableness, *n.* إِمْكَانُ ٱلشِّفَآءِ ـ قَابِلِيَّةُ ٱلْمُعَالَجَةِ ـ إِمْكَانُ ٱلْمُدَاوَاةِ.

Curacy, *n.* The office of a curate, نِيَابَةٌ عَنِ ٱلْخُورِيِّ; a benefice, خُورَنَة.

Curate, *n.* Deputy of a vicar, نَائِبُ ٱلْخُورِيِّ; a parish priest, خُورِيّ *pl.* خَوَارِنَة.

Curative, *n.* طِبِّيّ ـ شِفَائِيّ ـ مُدَاوٍ ـ إِسَائِيّ ـ عِلَاجِيّ.
Curative treatment, طِبّ ـ أَسَاوَة.

Curator, *n.* نَاظِر ـ حَافِظ ـ أَمِين ـ مُدِير.

Curb, *v.t.* To restrain, of a horse, أَحْكَمَ ـ ‹ كَبَحَ ـ ‹ قَدَعَ. To restrain, ‹ كَفَّ عَن ـ ‹ مَنَعَ ـ ‹ زَجَرَ ـ ‹ رَدَعَ ـ ‹ صَدَّ ـ ‹ قَرَعَ. To — one's self, إِسْتَمْسَكَ ـ تَمَاسَكَ.

Curb, *n.* Of a bridle, حَكَمَة ـ حَلَقُ ٱللِّجَامِ. A curb-chain, مِسْحَلَان. Restraint, مَنْع ـ حَدّ ـ صَدّ ـ قَدْع ـ رَدْع. The frame round a well, جُول ـ جَال.

Curb-stone, *n.* حَجَرُ حَافَةِ ٱلْمَمْشَى ـ جُولُ ٱلْمَمْشَى.

Curculio, *n.* دُودَة ـ سُوسُ ٱلتَّمْرِ.

Curd, *n.* حَلِيبٌ مُجَبَّن ـ حَلِيبٌ رَائِب ـ حَالُوم ـ لَبَنٌ مُتَخَثِّر.

Curdle, *v.t.* Of milk, عَقَّدَ (*or* جَمَّدَ *or* رَوَّبَ *or* جَبَّنَ) ٱلْحَلِيبَ.
To coagulate, عَقَّدَ.

Curdle, *v.i.* Of milk, تَمَذَّرَ ـ ‹ رَابَ ـ تَخَثَّرَ. To coagulate, إِنْعَقَدَ ـ ‹ جَمَدَ. His blood curdled, ‹ قَرِسَ (*or* تَقَرَّسَ) دَمُهُ.

Cure, *v.t.* To heal, ‹ شَفَى ـ أَشْفَى ـ عَافَى ـ دَاوَى صَحَّحَ ـ عَالَجَ ـ أَصَحَّ ـ طَيَّبَ. To prepare for preservation, حَيَّقَ ـ تَبَّلَ; with salt, مَلَّحَ. 187 cases of them were treated and cured, عُولِجَ ١٨٧ مِنْهُمْ.

Cure, *n.* A remedy, أَسُوّ *pl.* آسِيَة ـ شِفَآء ـ إِسَآء ـ مَصَحَّة ـ شِفَآء ـ أَسْو ـ إِبْرَآء ـ عِلَاج ـ أَدْوِيَة *pl.* دَوَآء. The act of healing, مُدَاوَاة ـ طِبّ. A church benefice, عُهْدَةُ ٱلْخُورِيِّ.

Cureless, *a.* لا يُعَالَجُ ـ عُقَام ـ مُعْضِل ـ عُضَال.

Curer, *n.* A healer, حَكِيم ـ مُعَالِج ـ طَبِيب ـ شَافٍ.

Curfew, *n.* قَرْعُ جَرَسٍ عِنْدَ ٱلْمَسَآءِ عَلَامَةً لِإِطْفَآءِ ٱلنَّارِ فِي جَمِيعِ ٱلْبُيُوتِ.

Curiosity, *n.* Inquisitiveness, تَفَحُّص ـ إِسْتِقْرَآء ـ إِسْتِقْصَآء ـ تَجَسُّس. Intrusiveness, تَدَاخُل ـ فُضُول. A rarity, نَادِرَة *pl.* نَوَادِرُ ـ غَرِيبَة *pl.* غَرَائِبُ ـ فُرْجَة ـ تُحْفَة *pl.* تُحَف.

Curioso, *n.* مُحِبُّ ٱلْغَرَائِبِ ـ رَاغِبٌ فِي ٱلتُّحَفِ.

Curious, *a.* Inquisitive, حَفِيّ ـ مِتْيَاح ـ مُتَجَسِّس ـ مُتَفَحِّص. Intrusive, فُضُولِيّ ـ عِرْنِيض ـ مِخْلَط ـ تَيَّاح ـ مِتْيَح. Elegant, nice, غَرِيب ـ عَجِيب ـ نَادِر ـ بَدِيع ـ مُعْجِب.

Curiously, *ad.* Studiously, بِتَجَسُّسٍ ـ بِتَفَحُّصٍ ـ بِٱسْتِقْرَآءٍ ـ بِٱسْتِقْصَآءٍ ـ بِتَقَصٍّ. Elegantly, بِمَلَاحَةٍ ـ بِظَرَافَةٍ ـ بِلَطَافَةٍ ـ بِنَفَاسَةٍ. With skill, بِمَهَارَةٍ ـ بِفَنٍّ.

Curl, *n.* Of the hair, غَدِيرَة *pl.* غَدَائِرُ ـ تَجْعِيدَة ـ قُصَّابَة *pl.* قَصَائِبُ ـ ضَفِيرَة *pl.* ضَفَائِرُ. A lock of hair, خُصْلَة. An undulation, تَمَوُّج ـ أَمْوَاج *pl.* مَوْج. A flexure, إِلْتِوَآء ـ فَتْلَة ـ تَعْوِيجَة.

Curl, *v.t.* Of the hair, ‹ فَتَلَ ٱلشَّعْرَ ـ جَعَّدَ ـ ‹ عَقَصَ ـ قَصَّبَ ـ أَبْرَمَ ٱلشَّعْرَ. To raise in waves, مَوَّجَ. To — up, as heat or cold does, شَفْشَفَ.

Curl, *v.i.* Of the hair, إِنْبَرَمَ ـ تَعَقَّصَ ـ ‹ جَعُدَ ـ تَقَرَّنَ ـ تَجَعَّدَ. To rise in undulations, تَمَوَّجَ. To twist itself, إِنْفَتَلَ ـ إِلْتَفَّ. To dry up, as by the effects of cold, *etc.*, تَشَفْشَفَ.

Curlew, *n.* The bird, ضَرْبٌ مِنَ ٱلْعَصَافِيرِ ـ كُرْكِي.

Curliness, *n.* جُعُودَة ـ جَعَادَة.

Curling-irons, *n.* }
Curling-tongs, } آلَةٌ لِتَجْعِيدِ ٱلشَّعْرِ.

Curly, *a.* Of the hair, جَعْد ـ مُقَصَّب ـ أَحْجَنُ. *See also* Ripply, *a.*

Curmudgeon, *n.* رَذِيل ـ نَذْل ـ وَغْد ـ خَسِيس ـ لَئِيم.

Currant, *n.* The fruit of the currant tree, عِنَبُ ٱلثَّعْلَبِ. A small dried grape, نَوْعٌ مِنَ ٱلزَّبِيبِ ٱلنَّاعِمِ ـ كِشْمِش ـ عُجْد.

Currency, *n.* Circulation, دَوَرَان ـ سُرًى ـ رَوَاج ـ مُدَاوَلَة. General reception, قَبُول ـ أَخْذ ـ تَدَاوُل ـ مُعَامَلَةٌ بِ. Dissemination, إِشَاعَة. Continuance, مُدَاوَمَة ـ إِسْتِمْرَار. General esteem, تَنْزِيلٌ عَامٌّ ـ إِعْتِبَار. Paper —, قَوَائِمُ نَقْدِيَّة. To give — to, as of a report, *etc.*, إِشْتَهَرَ ـ ‹ شَهَرَ ـ أَشَاعَ بِ ـ سَيَّرَ. To acquire —, ‹ شَاعَ ـ إِشْتَهَرَ.

Current, *a.* Circulatory, سالِك – جارٍ – مُتَعامِلٌ ب – مُتَداوِل. Generally received, مَقْبُول – رائِج – عابِر. General, جائِز – غالِب – شامِل – عُمُومِيٌّ – عامٌّ. Estimable at, مُعامَلٌ ب – مُتَداوَلٌ ب – مُعْتَبَر ب. Current coin, مُعامَلات. Current accounts, حِساباتٌ جارِيَةٌ. Price —, السِّعْرُ ٱلرّائِجُ. Current affairs, الأُمُورُ ٱلجارِيَةُ. At the — rate, بِٱلسِّعْرِ ٱلرّائِجِ. The — fashion, الزِّيُّ ٱلمَعْهُودُ – الزِّيُّ ٱلاعْتِيادِيُّ – الرّائِجُ (or ٱلمَأْلُوفُ or ٱلمُسْتَعْمَلُ). The — month, الشَّهْرُ ٱلحاضِرُ – الشَّهْرُ هٰذا ٱلشَّهْرُ ٱلجارِي. Current proverbs, جَوائِبُ ٱلأَمْثالِ. To make —, رَوَّجَ – جَوَّزَ. To be —, راجَ [2]. The sovereign is now — at one hundred piastres, اللِّيرَةُ ٱلأَنْكِلِيزِيَّةُ دارِجَةٌ ٱلآنَ بِمِائَةِ قِرْشٍ.

Current, *n.* A running stream, سَيْل *pl.* سُيُول – مَسِيل – مَجْرًى. Progress in the motion of the sea, تَيّار – جارُوف – جُراف. Progression, تَوْر – تَواتُر – تَوالٍ – تَتابُع – سُلُوك – جَرَيان. The — of events, تَعاقُبُ ٱلحَوادِثِ – جَرَيانُ ٱلأُمُورِ.

Curricle, *n.* عَرَبَةٌ خَفِيفَةٌ بِعَجَلَتَيْنِ.

Curriculum, *n.* بابُ دَرْس.

Currier, *n.* مُهَيِّئُ ٱلجُلُودِ لِلدِّباغَةِ – جِلْوَدِيٌّ. A currier's knife, مِبْشَع – مِحْلاة.

Currish, *a.* نَظٌّ – شَكِس.

Curry, *n.* The Indian dish, رُزٌّ مُفَلْفَلٌ مِنْ طَبِيخِ ٱلهِنْدِ.

Curry, *v.t.* Of a horse, *etc.*, حَسَّ [2] ٱلحِصانَ – فَرْجَنَ. To dress leather, دَبَغَ [2, 3] – أَبْشَرَ – بَشَرَ [2]. To — favour with one, داری – اِسْتَمالَ – تَحَبَّبَ إِلَى – تَوَدَّدَ إِلَى – اِسْتَعْطَفَ. To prepare with condiments, فَلْفَلَ.

Curry-comb, *n.* مِحَسَّة – فِرْجَوْن.

Curse, *v.t.* To execrate, لَعَنَ – سَبَّ [2] – دَعا عَلَى [2] – شَتَمَ [2].

Curse, *v.i.* To utter oaths, آلَى – حَلَفَ – أَقْسَمَ. *See also under* Curse, *n.*

Curse, *n.* A wish of evil, دُعاءٌ عَلَى – سَبّ – شَتْم. A malediction, لَعْنَة. An oath, حَلْف. May the — of God rest upon him! لَعْنَةُ ٱللّٰهِ عَلَيْهِ. To invoke a — upon, باهَلَ. They invoked curses on each other, of many, باهَلَ بَعْضُهُمْ بَعْضًا – تَباهَلُوا.

Cursed, *a.* Hateful, مَبْهُول – مَدْعُوٌّ عَلَيْهِ – شَنِيع – كَرِيه. Unholy, مَلْعُون – لَعِين – مَقْبُوح – بَغِيض – فَظِيع – مُرْد. Vexatious, شاقٌّ – مُضْجِر. حَرام – دَنِس – نَجِس – قَذِر.

Cursedly, *ad.* Vilely, بِفَظاظَةٍ – بِكَراهَةٍ – كُرْهًا.

Curser, *n.* حالِف – حَلّاف. *See also* Blasphemer, *n.*

Cursive, *a.* Of writing, خَطٌّ تَعْلِيقِيٌّ.

Cursorily, *ad.* بِدُونِ رَوِيَّةٍ – بِتَساهُلٍ – بِسُرْعَةٍ – بِخِفَّةٍ.

Cursory, *a.* مُتَساهِل – بِلا إِمْعانٍ – خَفِيف.

Curst, *a.* *See* Cursed, *a.*

Cursus, *n.* *See* Course, *n.*

Curt, *a.* Short, قَصِير. Uncourteous, جافٍ – فَظٌّ.

Curtail, *v.t.* To cut off a part, جَدَعَ [3] – خَذَمَ [2] – حَسَمَ [2] – بَتَرَ [2] – قَرْطَمَ. To shorten, قَصَّرَ. A curtailed dog, كَلْبٌ أَبْتَرُ. *See also to* Abbreviate, *v.t.*

Curtailment, *n.* As of letters in a word, تَرْخِيم. The act of shortening, تَقْصِير. *See also* Abbreviation, *n.*

Curtain, *n.* حِجاب *pl.* حُجُب – سِجاف – سَجْف *pl.* سُجُوف and أَسْجاف – سَدْل *pl.* سُدُول – سِتْر *pl.* سُتُور – سُتْرَة – سِتارَة; a musquito —, نامُوسِيَّة. To draw a —, جَرَّ [2] ٱلسَّجْفَ. To let down or lower, as of a —, سَدَلَ [2, 3] – أَسْدَلَ. Bed-curtains, كِلَّة. A —, in fortification, حِجاب – حِجابُ ٱلاسْتِحْكام.

Curtain, *v.t.* أَسْجَفَ – أَسْدَلَ – حَجَبَ [2]. A curtained girl, one kept secluded, خِدْر – أُخْدُور.

Curtsy, *n.* *See* Courtesy, *n.*

Curvated, *a.* } مائِل – مُقَوَّس – مُقَنْطَر – مَحْنِيٌّ – مُنْحَنٍ –
Curved, } مُعَوَّج – أَحْجَن – مُحَرَّن. A — stick, حَنْفاءُ.

Curvation, }
Curvature, *n.* } عِوَج – عَوَج – مَيْل – اِنْحِناء – تَقَوُّس – اِعْوِجاج. A — in the back, قَطَن.
Curve, }

Curve, *v.t.* حَرَّدَ – أَطَرَ [2] – حَجَنَ [2] – حَنا [2] – قَوَّسَ – عَوَّجَ.

Curve, *v.i.* تَأَطَّرَ – تَحَجَّنَ – مالَ [2] – اِنْحَنَى – تَقَوَّسَ – اِعْوَجَّ.

Curvet, *v.i.* شَبَّ [2, 3] – وَثَبَ *aor.* يَثِبُ – نَطَّ [2] – طَفَرَ [2] – قَفَزَ [2]. A curvetting horse, حِصانٌ قافِزٌ *pl.* خُيُولٌ قَوافِزُ.

Curvet, *n.* وَثْب – وُثُوب – شُبُوب – شِباب – نَطّ – طُفُور – قَفْزَة.

Curvilinear, *a.* ذُو خُطُوطٍ مُنْحَنِيَةٍ.

Cushat, *n.* حَمامَةٌ مُطَوَّقَةٌ.

Cushion, *n.* A pillow, مِخَدَّة – وِسادَة *pl.* وَسائِدُ *and* وُسُد. A seat, a support, مِسْنَد – مَقْعَد. To —, to prop up with a —, وَسَّدَ.

Cusp, *n.* The two cusps of the new moon, طَرَفا ٱلهِلالِ; *sing.* طَرَف.

Custard, *n.* نَوْعٌ مِنَ ٱلحَلْواءِ.

Custard-apple, *n.* نَوْعٌ مِنْ ثَمَرِ بِلادِ ٱلهِنْدِ – سَفَرْجَلٌ هِنْدِيٌّ.

Custodian, *n.* ناظِر – أَمِين – مُدِير.

Custody, *n.* Imprisonment, عَقْس – صَبْر – سَجْن – حَبْس.

Guardianship, حِفْظ ـ مُحَافَظَة ـ ذَوْد ـ حِمَايَة ـ خِفَارَة ـ صَوْن ـ حِرَاسَة ـ صِيَانَة. To take into —, مَسَكَ ـ قَبَضَ عَلَى. To give one into —, حَبَسَ ـ سَلَّمَ إِلَى يَدِ.

Custom, *n.* Habit, manner, وَضْع *pl.* أَوْضَاع ـ طَوْر *pl.* أَطْوَار ـ عَادَة *pl.* عادات *and* عَوَائِد ـ طَرْز ـ رَسْم ـ شِنْشِنَة ـ دَأْب ـ خَصْلَة ـ دَرْبَة. Established manner, ضَابِطَة ـ قَانُون *pl.* قَوَانِين. Established habit, like second nature, خَلِيقَة ـ خِلْقَة. Purchasing constituents, زُبُونَة. According to —, حُكْمَ ٱلْعَادَةِ. According to their —, حَسَبَ طَرِيقَتِهِمِ ٱلْإِعْتِيَادِيَّةِ. A seller with a good — or customers, بَيَّاع ـ مُنَفِّق. As had been the —, عَلَى ما جَرَتْ بِهِ ٱلْعَادَةُ.

Customable, *a.* / Customary, Usual, مَعْهُود ـ إِعْتِيَادِيّ ـ رَسْمِيّ ـ مَأْلُوف ـ دُسْتُورِيّ. Frequent, habitual, تَوَاتُرِيّ ـ إِعْتِيَادِيّ ـ أَكْثَرِيّ ـ أَغْلَبِيّ. Is it — to...? هَلْ مِنَ ٱلْعَادَةِ أَن.

Customarily, *ad.* فِي ٱلْغَالِبِ ـ حُكْمَ ٱلْعَادَةِ ـ حَسَبَ ٱلْعَادَةِ ـ غَالِبًا.

Customer, *n.* شَرِيّ ـ عَمِيل ـ مُشْتَرٍ ـ زُبُون *pl.* زَبَائِنُ *and* زُبُونَات.

Custom-house, *n.* فُرْضَة *pl.* فُرَض ـ مَمْكَس ـ دِيوَانُ ٱلْكُمْرُكِ ـ كُمْرُك *pl.* كُمْرُكَات *or* گمارك. A custom-house officer, مَكَّاس ـ مُبَاشِرُ ٱلْكُمْرُكِ ـ مُدِيرُ ٱلرُّسُومَاتِ. Custom-house revenues, حَاصِلَاتُ ٱلْكُمْرُكِ; — dues, رُسُومَاتُ ٱلْكُمْرُكِ (or ٱلْفُرْضَةِ). Free of the —, مُعَافُ ٱلْكُمْرُكِ.

Custos-Rotulorum, *n.* أَمِينُ ٱلسِّجِلَّاتِ.

Cut, *v.t.* قَرْضَبَ ـ قَضَبَ ـ صَرَمَ ـ أَبَتَّ ـ حَذَمَ ـ قَطَعَ ـ قَطَّ ـ قَدَّدَ ـ قَدَّ ـ حَسَمَ ـ جَزَمَ ـ بَتَّ. To cut, as with scissors, قَرَضَ ـ قَصَّ. To cut, mend, a pen, بَرَى ٱلْقَلَمَ ـ قَلَمَ ٱلْقَلَمَ. To hew trees, قَضَبَ ـ إِحْتَطَبَ ـ شَجَرَ ـ ٱلشَّجَرَ. To carve, نَقَرَ ـ نَحَتَ. To form by cutting, فَصَّلَ. To divide, by cutting or passing through, فَلَعَ ـ فَرَقَ ـ فَصَلَ ـ فَلَقَ ـ شَطَرَ. To pierce with an uneasy sensation, شَقَّ عَلَى ـ أَوْجَعَ ـ أَضْجَرَ. To —, intersect, قَطَعَ ـ صَلَّبَ. To cut, as an acquaintance, هَجَرَ ـ صَرَمَ. To abstain from visiting one, أَجْفَرَ. To be cut, تَقَطَّعَ ـ إِنْقَطَعَ. To cut one's self, تَقَطَّعَ. To cut in two, قَسَمَ ـ نَصَّفَ ـ شَطَرَ. To cut a (grand) figure, تَغَطْرَسَ ـ أَقْمَحَ بِأَنْفِهِ ـ تَعَظَّمَ ـ تَشَبَّعَ.

To cut anything awkwardly, to spoil in cutting, أَفْرَى ـ فَرَى.

To cut lots, أَلْقَى ٱلْقُرْعَةَ ـ إِقْتَرَعَ.

To cut down, to lessen, أَنْقَصَ ـ نَقَّصَ. To hew, as trees; *see under to* Cut. *See also to* Reduce, *v.t.*

To cut off, to amputate, بَتَرَ ـ جَزَعَ. To cut off a piece from, إِخْتَذَفَ ـ حَذَفَ ـ بَتَكَ. To lop, shear, جَزَّ. To separate, to dismember, قَطَعَ ـ فَصَلَ ـ بَعَّضَ. To destroy, أَخْنَى عَلَى ـ تَخَرَّمَ ـ إِخْتَرَمَ ـ إِغْتَالَ ـ إِجْتَاحَ ـ إِسْتَأْصَلَ ـ عَاقَ ـ حَالَ بَيْنَ ـ وَبَيْنَ ـ سَدَّ عَلَى ـ أَهْلَكَ. To intercept, سَدَّ عَلَى ـ مَنَعَ. To put an end to, قَضَى ـ أَنْهَى ـ أَنْجَزَ. To cut off an heir, the inheritance from, أَحْرَمَهُ ٱلْمِيرَاثَ. To cut off delay, عَجَّلَ ـ بَادَرَ ـ أَسْرَعَ. To cut off the occasion, قَطَعَ ٱلْفُرْصَةَ. To be cut off, إِنْجَزَّ. To be cut off, amputated, إِنْبَتَرَ ـ صَلِمَ.

To cut out, to shape, قَطَعَ ل ـ فَصَّلَ ـ شَكَّلَ ـ صَوَّرَ ـ جَبَّلَ. To contrive, دَبَّرَ ـ نَوَى ـ إِنْتَدَّ ـ إِبْتَدَأَ ـ إِخْتَرَعَ. To debar, مَنَعَ ـ أَحْرَمَ ـ نَفَا ـ عَن ـ رَدَّ ـ عَن. To excel, بَرَعَ ـ سَبَقَ ـ بَرَزَ ـ فَاقَ ـ فَضَلَ. To be cut out for, adapted to, طُبِعَ عَلَى ـ فُطِرَ عَلَى.

To cut short, to interrupt, أَقْطَعَ ـ صَرَفَ ـ عَن ـ صَدَّ ـ صَرَمَ.

To diminish from, قَلَّلَ ـ نَقَّصَ ـ صَغَّرَ.

To cut up, to divide into pieces, قَصَّبَ ـ قَطَّعَ ـ جَزَّرَ ـ شَرَّحَ.

To give pain to, أَوْجَعَ ـ آلَمَ ـ أَضْجَرَ. To joint, عَضَا.

Cut, *v.i.* To be sharp, حَدَّ ـ إِحْتَدَّ. To make way by dividing, as shoots the soil, to sprout, طَلَعَ ـ نَبَتَ ـ أَشْطَأَ; as a tooth, شَكَأَ ـ شَقَأَ. To cut and run, فَرَّ ـ وَلَّى هَارِبًا ـ تَفَلَّتَ ـ إِنْفَلَتَ ـ إِنْسَلَّ ـ نَجَا مِن.

Cut, *n.* The action of a sharp instrument, حَسْم ـ بَتْر ـ بَتّ ـ قَطْع ـ قَطّ ـ قَدّ. A piece, a cutting, قِطْعَة ـ جَذّ *pl.* أَجْذَاذ ـ شِقْفَة *pl.* شِقَف ـ شُقَف. A slice, شَرِيحَة ـ شَرْحَة. A wound, with the nails, خَمْش ـ خَدْش. A —, wound, كَلْم *pl.* كُلُوم ـ جُرْح *pl.* جُرُوح. A channel, gap, ditch, تُرْعَة *pl.* تُرَع ـ جَدْوَل *pl.* جَدَاوِل ـ مَجْرَى *pl.* مَجَارِي. A cutting, shred, جِتَّة ـ بَتَّة ـ قِطْعَة ـ بَضْعَة. A near passage, طَرِيق أَقْرَب. A printed picture, نَقْش *pl.* نُقُوش ـ صُورَة *pl.* صُوَر. Fashion, shape, سَحْنَة ـ هَيْئَة ـ تَفْصِيل ـ طَرْز ـ خَلْق ـ زِيّ ـ صُورَة. To draw cuts, lots, أَلْقَى ٱلْقُرْعَةَ ـ إِقْتَرَعَ.

Cutaneous, *a.* / Cuticular, جِلْدِيّ ـ أَدِيمِيّ. A — eruption, قُوبَة ـ بُثُور ـ قُوبَاء.

Cute, *a.* *See* Acute, *a.*

Cuticle, *n.* The outer skin, جِلْد ـ قِشْرَة ـ بَشَرَة.

Cutlass, *n.* يَطَغَان.

Cutler, *n.* بَائِعُ سَكَاكِينَ ـ سَكَاكِينِيّ ـ سَكَّان.

Cutlery, *n.* خُرْدَة ـ آلَاتُ ٱلْقَطْعِ.

Cutlet, *n.* شَرِيحَةُ لَحْمٍ *pl.* شَرائِحُ.

Cutpurse, *n.* طَرَّار ـ نَشَّال ـ لَصّ *pl.* لُصُوص ـ حَرامِيّ *pl.* حَرامِيَّة.

Cutter, *n.* A cutting instrument, مِفْصَل ـ مِقْطَع ـ مِبْضَع. A boat, صَنْدَل ـ فَلُّوكَة.

Cut-throat, *n.* قَتَّال ـ فاتِك.

Cutting, *a.* Sharp, قاطِع ـ صارِم ـ حادّ. Vexing, ناكِي ـ أَلِيم ـ مُضْجِر ـ مُغِيظ. The — teeth, الثَّنايا ـ الأَسْنانُ ٱلْقَوادِمُ.

Cutting, *n.* A shred (*see under* Cut, *n.*) A piece cut off, نُحاتَة ـ نُجارَة ـ قُطاعَة ـ بُرايَة. A cutting, as from a tree, قِطْع *pl.* قُطَع *pl.* قَطِيع ـ قِطاع.

Cuttle, *n.* The fish, سِيبِيدَج ـ أُخْطُبُوط ـ سِيبِيَآء; the liquor which it emits, زَبَدُ ٱلْبَحْرِ.

Cutwater, *n.* مِنْقارُ ٱلْمَرْكَبِ.

Cwt., *n.* عِبارَة عَنِ ٱلْقِنْطارِ.

Cyanometer, *n.* مِيزانُ ٱلزُّرْقَةِ.

Cyclamen, *n.* فقيلاسُوس ـ وَلْف ـ بَخُورُ مَرْيَمَ.

Cycle, *n.* A period of years, دَوْر *pl.* أَدْوار. The solar —, الدَّوْرُ ٱلشَّمْسِيّ. The lunar —, الدَّوْرُ ٱلْقَمَرِيّ.

Cyclical, *a.* مُتَعَلِّق بِٱلدَّوْرِ ـ دَوْرِيّ.

Cycloid, *n.* شِبْهُ ٱلدَّائِرَةِ.

Cycloidal, *a.* شَبِيهُ ٱلدَّائِرَةِ.

Cyclone, *n.* كُوس.

Cyclopean, *n.* Gigantic, جَبَّارِيّ ـ عَظِيم.

Cyclopedia, *n.* مَجْمَعُ كُلِّيَّاتِ ٱلْعُلُومِ ـ كِتابُ كُلِّيَّاتٍ.

Cyclops, *n.* جَبَّارٌ أَعْوَرُ.

Cygnet, *n.* فُون ـ بَجَعٌ صَغِيرٌ.

Cygnus, *n.* The constellation, الدَّجاجَةُ ـ الطَّائِرُ, (the four stars of which are called, الفَوارِسُ).

Cylinder, *n.* أُسْطُوانَة *pl.* أَساطِين ـ سارِيَة ـ عِماد *pl.* عُمُد. A smoothing —, آلَةُ ٱلصَّقْلِ ـ مَدْرُونَة. A — for rolling the roofs of houses, مِحْدَلَة.

Cylindrical, *a.* أُسْطُوانِيّ ـ بِشَكْلِ ٱلأُسْطُوانَةِ.

Cymbal, *n.* صَنْج *pl.* صُنُوج.

Cynic, *n.* A snarlish man. *See* Cynic, *a.*

Cynic, *a.* } Snappish, surly, فَظّ ـ جافٍ. Depreciatory,
Cynical, } مُسْتَهْزِئ ـ مُسْتَخِفّ.

Cynically, *ad.* بِجَفاء ـ بِٱسْتِخْفافٍ ـ بِفَظاظَةٍ.

Cynicalness, *n.* }
Cynicism, } إِسْتِهْزاء ـ إِسْتِخْفاف ـ جَفاء ـ فَظاظَة.

Cynosure, *n.* The north star, الكَوْكَبُ ٱلشَّمالِيّ. That which attracts attention, نَصْبُ ٱلْعُيُونِ ـ جاذِبُ ٱلنَّظَرِ ـ مَطْمَحُ ٱلنَّظَرِ.

Cypher; *see* Cipher.

Cypress, *n.* The tree, سَرْو ـ عَرْعَر.

Cyprian, *a.* Of Cyprus, قُبْرُسِيّ. Licentious, فاحِش ـ قَبِيح.

Cyprus, *n.* The island, جَزِيرَةُ قُبْرُسَ.

Cyst, *n.* حُصَّالَة *pl.* حَواصِل ـ مَثانَة *pl.* مَثانات. Cysts, pimples, خُراج.

Cystose, *a.* ذُو مَثاناتٍ ـ ذُو حَواصِلَ.

Cystotomy, *n.* جِراحَةُ ٱلْمَثاناتِ ـ جِراحَةُ ٱلأَكْياسِ.

Czar, *n.* قَيْصَرُ ٱلرُّوسِ ـ لَقَبُ سُلْطانِ ٱلْمَسْقُوبِ ـ چار.

Czarina, *n.* لَقَبُ زَوْجَةِ سُلْطانِ ٱلْمَسْقُوبِ ـ چارِيچَة.

Czarowitz, *n.* نَجْلُ قَيْصَرِ ٱلرُّوسِ ـ شاهْزادَهُ ٱلْمَسْقُوبِ.

D.

Dab, *n.* A small lump of anything, قِطْعَة ـ بَتْكَة ـ فِرْزَة ـ لَطْمَةٌ خَفِيفَةٌ ـ ضَرْبَةٌ لَيِّنَةٌ. A gentle blow, شِقْفَة ـ حِتَّة. A dab of fat, شَحْمَة. A dab of butter, سَمْنَة. An expert, شاطِر ـ ماهِر.

Dab, *v.t.* To strike, لَطَسَ [2] ـ لَطَشَ [2]. To dry up, dabbing, نَشَّفَ ـ مَسَّحَ. To — with clay, or lime, or tar, دَمَّ [2] ـ دَمَّمَ.

Dabble, *v.t.* To moisten, wet, بَلَّ [2] ـ رَطَّبَ.

Dabble, *v.i.* To play, as in water, تَمَرَّغَ (or تَبَرْبَطَ) فِي ٱلْمَآء ـ لَعِبَ فِي ٱلْمَآءِ. To do in a superficial manner, وَهَنَ *aor.* يَهِنُ ـ وَهَنَ فِي. To meddle, تَعَانَى ـ تَعَاطَى.

Dabbler, *n.* A superficial meddler, غُمْلُوج ـ فَرَّار ـ وُهَّن *pl.* واهِن.

Dabbling, *n.* Superficial meddling, فَرْفَرَة ـ وَهْن.

Dabblingly, *ad.* بِفَرْفَرَةٍ ـ بِوَهْنٍ.

Dabster, *n.* شاطِر ـ أُسْتاذ.

Dad, Daddy, *n.* أَبِي ـ يا أَبِي ـ يا أَباتاه.

Daffodil, *n.* خُنْثَى ـ بَرْوَاق ـ سِيراس.

Daft, *a.* *See* Crazy, *a.*

Dagger, *n.* خَنَاجِرُ *pl.* خَنْجَر ـ حَرْبَة. To look daggers, تَجَهَّمَ ـ أَكْبَى وَجْهَهُ. To be at daggers drawn, at enmity, جاهَرَ بِٱلْعَداوَةِ. They were at daggers drawn, تَبادَوا بِٱلْعَداوَةِ ـ تَجاهَرُوا بِٱلْعَداوَةِ.

Daggle, *v.i.* تَلَوَّثَ.

Daguerrotpye, *n.* التَّصْوِيرُ بِواسِطَةِ ٱلنُّورِ عَلَى صَحِيفَةٍ مَطْلِيَّةٍ.

Dahlia, *n.* زَهْرٌ فِي هَيْئَةِ ٱلنَّجْمِ.

Daily, *a.* كُلَّ يَوْمٍ ـ يَوْمِيٌّ. The — administration, ٱلْخِدْمَةُ ٱلْيَوْمِيَّةُ. Daily pay, يَوْمِيَّة. Daily bread, ٱلْقُوتُ ٱلْيَوْمِيُّ. A — newspaper, غَزِيتَةٌ تُطْبَعُ كُلَّ يَوْمٍ.

Daily, *ad.* يَوْمًا فَيَوْمًا ـ كُلَّ يَوْمٍ. We expect him daily, نَتَرَقَّبُهُ كُلَّ يَوْمٍ.

Daintily, *ad.* Nicely, بِلَطافَةٍ. Exquisitely, بِكَمالِ ٱلظَّرافَةِ. Deliciously, بِكَمالِ ٱللَّذَّةِ. Fastidiously, بِتَنَعُّمٍ ـ بِتَدَلُّلٍ. To eat —, نَهَكَ مِنَ ٱلطَّعامِ ـ.

Daintiness, *n.* Elegance, لَطافَة ـ ظَرافَة ـ لَذَّة. Softness, تَأَنُّق ـ تَنَيُّق ـ نِيقَة ـ تَدَلُّل ـ نَعْمَة. To be or to affect —, تَأَنَّقَ.

Dainty, *n.* Pleasing, elegant, نَفِيس ـ مُفْتَخِر ـ لَذِيذ ـ ناعِم. Effeminate, مُدَلَّل ـ خانِق. Squeamish, نَفُور ـ مُتَأَنِّق ـ

تَنَوَّقَ ـ طَرَزَ فِي ـ تَأَنَّقَ ـ تَجَوَّدَ ـ مُكْرِه. To be —, squeamish, تَنَيَّقَ. Dainty food, أَكْلٌ نَفِيسٌ. Dainties, نَفائِسُ ـ لَذَّات ـ رَغائِبُ.

Dairy, *n.* لَبَّانَة ـ مَلْبَن. Dairy-maid, لَبَّانَة.

Dais, *n.* مَحارِيبُ *pl.* مِحْراب ـ إِيوان ـ مَسْرَبَة.

Daisy, *n.* بَيْضَةٌ مَقْلِيَّةٌ ـ زَهْرُ ٱللُّؤْلُؤ.

Dale, *n.* أَوْدِيَة *pl.* وادٍ ـ أَذْناب *pl.* ذَنَب ـ وِهاد *pl.* وَهْدَة.

Dalliance, *n.* مُلاعَبَة ـ مُلاطَفَة ـ تَدَلُّل ـ دَلَل ـ دالَّة ـ غَزَل.

Dally, *v.t.* and *i.* To fondle, تَدَلَّلَ ـ دَلَّ ـ هانَغَ ـ غازَلَ ـ لاعَبَ ـ تَمَلَّقَ ـ تَلَطَّفَ. To delay, تَمَهَّلَ ـ تَوَقَّفَ ـ تَأَخَّرَ. One who dallies after women, غَزِلُ نِسآء.

Dalmatia, *n.* دَلْماتِيا.

Dam, *n.* A mother, أُمٌّ ـ والِدَة. A mole to confine water, مُسَنّاة ـ أَحْباس *pl.* حِبْس ـ أَشْذاب *pl.* شَذَب ـ عَرِم ـ عَرِمَة *coll.* ـ جِدار ـ جِدْر. A fence, مُسَنَّوات *pl.* سَدّ ـ أَسْداد *pl.*

Dam, *v.t.* سَدَّ عَلَى ـ سَدَّ [2] ـ عَمَدَ ـ سَكَرَ [2] ـ سَكَّرَ. To be dammed, إِسْتَدَّ ـ إِنْسَدَّ.

Damage, *n.* Detriment, مَضَرَّة ـ ضَرَر ـ عُوار ـ أَسْقاط *pl.* سَقْط. Wrong, ضَيْم ـ ضامَة. Damages, *pl.* مَضارّ ـ خَسارَة ـ تَعْطِيل. Damages, a fine, غَرامَة ـ غُرْم. Reparation, as of —, مُجازاة ـ مُكافاة ـ تَعْوِيضُ ٱلْخَسارَةِ ـ وَفاءُ ٱلْحَقِّ. To assess damages, قَدَّرَ ٱلتَّضْمِيناتِ. To be liable to damages, لَزِمَ ـ بِٱلتَّضْمِينِ. To make good, as of a —, عَوَّضَ ـ جازَى ـ كافَى.

Damage, *v.t.* To injure, عَطَّلَ ـ خَسَّرَ ـ آذَى ـ أَضَرَّ ـ ضارَّ. To wrong, إِسْتَضامَ ـ ضامَ. Many ships have been damaged by the storm, مَراكِبُ كَثِيرَةٌ تَعَطَّلَتْ مِنَ ٱلنَّوْءِ. To be damaged, of goods, عابَ. Damaged, of goods, ذاتُ عُوارٍ. To have some part damaged, إِخْتَلَّ مِنْهُ. *See also to* Injure, *v.t.*

Damageable, *a.* مَحِلٌّ لِلْعُوارِ ـ قابِلُ ٱلْمَضَرَّةِ ـ يُخْسَرُ.

Damascene; *see* Damson, *n.*

Damascus, *n.* الشّامُ ـ دِمَشْقُ ٱلشّامِ.

Damask, *n.* The silk, مُشَجَّر. Venetian —, كِمْخا.

Damask, *v.t.* To weave into flowered work, نَقَّشَ ـ شَجَّرَ.

Damasked, *a.* مُنَقَّش ـ مُشَجَّر.

Damaskeen, *v.t.* To inlay steel with gold, نَزَّلَ (or سَقَّطَ) ٱلذَّهَبَ فِي ٱلْفُولاذِ.

Dame, *n.* عَوْن *pl.* أَعْوان — سَيِّدَة — مَوْلاة — سِتّ *pl.* سِتّات — خاتُون *pl.* خَواتِين.

Damn, *v.t.* To consign to eternal punishment, عَذَّبَ — سَحَتَ — أَدْخَلَ جَهَنَّمَ — قَضَى عَلَى بِالْهَلاكِ ٱلْأَبَدِيّ — جَهَّنَمَ. To sentence, دانَ *aor.* يَدِينُ — حَكَمَ عَلَى بِ — قَضَى عَلَى بِ. To curse, لَعَنَ — أَبادَ بِلَعْنَةٍ. To deride, عَيَّرَ. To — with faint praise, إِسْتَقَلَّ.

Damnable, *a.* لَعِين — مُسْتَحِقّ ٱلسَّحْتِ — بائِر — هالِك. Hurtful, مُضِرّ — مُؤْذٍ. Damnable novelties, بِدَعٌ هَلاكٍ.

Damnably, *ad.* بِلَعْنَةٍ — بِسَحْتٍ — فِي حُورٍ وَبُورٍ — سَحْتًا.

Damnation, *n.* Eternal punishment, قِصاصُ جَهَنَّم — دَيْنُونَة — عَذابُ جَهَنَّم — هَلاكٌ أَبَدِيّ — جَهَنَّم. Condemnation, دَيْنُونَة — مَلْعَنَة — سَحْت.

Damnatory, *a.* مُحْتَوٍ عَلَى ٱلْحِرْمانِ — مُسْحِت.

Damned, *a.* Consigned to eternal punishment, مِنَ ٱلْهالِكِينَ — مِنْ أَهْلِ جَهَنَّم. Condemned, مُدان. Cursed, لَعِين — مَلْعُون. The — in hell, أَهْلُ جَهَنَّم.

Damnify, *v.t.* *See to* Damage, Injure, *v.t.*

Damning, *a.* مُسْحِت — مُبِيد. Damnatory evidence against, شَهادَةٌ مُثْبِتَةٌ عَلَى.

Damp, *a.* بَلّ — نَدِيّ *pl.* أَنْدِياء — رَطِب — طَرِيّ — مَبْلُول — نَدْيان. To be or become —, إِبْتَلَّ — إِنْبَلَّ — تَرَطَّبَ — تَنَدَّى. *See also* Muggy, *a.*

Damp, *v.t.* } To moisten, بَلَّ — نَدَّى — أَنْدَى — رَطَّبَ — طَرَّى. To depress, فَتَّرَ — أَفْتَرَ — ضَعَّفَ — أَخْمَدَ — بَرَّدَ. He damped his energy, بَرَّدَ هِمَّتَهُ.
Dampen, }

Damp, *n.* } Moisture, بَلَل — نَداوَة — رُطُوبَة — طَراوَة. To throw a damp over, to discourage, فَتَّرَ — أَخْمَدَ — بَرَّدَ — أَغْبَى.
Dampness, }

Damper, *n.* A furnace valve, لَوْلَبُ مَدْخَنَةٍ — غِطاءُ لَوْلَبٍ; as of a pianoforte, جِلْدٌ مُخَفِّضُ ٱلصَّوْتِ. A check, تَفْتِير — مُطْفِئُ ٱلْغَيْرَةِ — مُبَرِّدَةٌ لِلْهِمَّةِ.

Dampish, *a.* يَضْرِبُ إِلَى ٱلرُّطُوبَةِ.

Damps, *n.* Noxious vapours, أَبْخِرَة (*or* بُخاراتٌ) ضارَّةٌ.

Damsel, *n.* سُتَيْتَة — بِنْت *pl.* بَنات — جارِيَة *pl.* جَوارٍ.

Damson, *n.* بُرْقُوقَة *coll.* بُرْقُوق — إِجّاصَة *coll.* إِجّاص.

Dance, *v.i.* زَفَنَ — رَقَصَ — أَرْقَصَ. To make to —, رَقَّصَ. To skip, حَجَلَ — عَرْقَصَ. To flutter about, هَفَتَ. To — attendance upon, لَزِمَ — جَدَمَ — إِسْتَقادَ لِ. To dandle, *v.t.* دَلَّلَ — رَقَّصَ.

Dance, *n.* زَفْنَة — رَقْصَة. The — of the darâwîsh, سَماع.

Dancer, *n.* راقِص — رَقّاص *fem.* راقِصَة — رَقّاصَة — جِنْكِيّ *fem.* جِنْكِيَّة. A female professional —, عالِمَة *pl.* عَوالِمُ — غازِيَة *pl.* غَوازِي. A rope —, جانْباز — بَهْلَوان.

Dancing, *n.* رَقْص — زَفْن. A — master, مُعَلِّمُ ٱلرَّقْصِ.

Dandelion, *n.* هِنْدَبَةٌ بَرِّيَّة — كُبَيْباتُ ٱلشِّتاءِ — سِنُّ ٱلْأَسَدِ — سَلاطَةٌ مُرَّة.

Dandiprat, *n.* قُزْعَة — خَنْبَس.

Dandle, *v.t.* رَقَّصَ — دَلَّلَ.

Dandler, *n.* مُدَلِّل.

Dandruff, *n.* نَبّاغ — نُباغَة — وَبَغ — حَزاز — هِبْرِيَة. Having —, وابِغ.

Dandy, *n.* *See* Coxcomb, *n.*

Dandyism, *n.* تَصَلُّف — غَنْدَرَة.

Dane, *n.* A native of Denmark, مِنْ أَهْلِ دانِيمارْكَ.

Danger, *n.* عَطَب — مُخاطَرَة — خَطَر *pl.* أَخْطار. To expose one's self to —, أَخْطَرَ (*or* خاطَرَ) بِنَفْسِهِ. To be in — of, to be obnoxious to, كانَ مُسْتَوْجِبًا لِ. To be in —, كانَ فِي خَطَرٍ. They encountered or braved dangers, رَكِبُوا ٱلْأَخْطارَ. There is — that..., يُخْطَرُ أَنْ. One who courts —, مُغاوِر. When they saw he was getting into —, لَمّا رَأَوْا إِلْمامَ ٱلْخَطَرِ بِهِ. He is out of —, as of sickness, هُوَ أَشْفَى عَلَى ٱلْخَطَرِ.

Dangerous, *a.* مُخْطِر — خَطِير — مُعْطِب — خَطِر — ذُو خَطَرٍ. A — place, مَعْطَب *pl.* مَعاطِبُ — مَهْلَكَة *pl.* مَهالِكُ. Travelling became —, صارَ ٱلسَّفَرُ خَطَرًا. It is certainly —, هُوَ مُخْطِرٌ لا مُحالَةَ. Very —, full of dangers, كَثِيرُ ٱلْأَخْطارِ.

Dangerously, *ad.* خَطَرًا — مَعَ خَطَرٍ.

Dangle, *v.i.* To hang loosely, إِسْتَرْخَى — تَدَلَّى — تَرَجَّحَ. To hang upon, إِسْتَقادَ لِ — تَعَلَّقَ بِ — تَذَبْذَبَ — تَدَنْدَلَ. To make to —, ذَبْذَبَ.

Dangler, *n.* A — after women, زِيرُ نِساءٍ — غالُّ ٱلنِّساءِ — غَنْدُور.

Dangling, *a.* مُتَذَبْذِب — مُسْتَرْخٍ — مُتَدَلِّل — مُتَدَنْدِل.

Danish, *a.* مِنْ دانِيمارْكَ — دانِيمارْكِيّ.

Dank, Dankish; *see* Damp, *a.*

Danube, *n.* The river, نَهْرُ ٱلطُّونَةِ.

Danubian, *a.* مُتَعَلِّقٌ بِأَطْرافِ ٱلطُّونَةِ. The — principalities, أَلْمَمْلَكَتانِ وَهُما ٱلْأَفْلاقُ وَٱلْبُغْدانُ.

Daphne, *n.* The shrub, شَجَرَةُ ٱلْغارِ.

Dapper, *a.* خَفِيف — فَلْتان — نَشِيط.

Dapple, *a.* } أَرْقَط *fem.* رَقْطآء — أَبْلَق — مُنَقَّط — زَرْزُورِيّ —
Dappled, } مُرَقَّش — أَبْرَش.

Dapple, *v.t.* نَقَّطَ — رَقَّشَ — زَرْقَشَ.

Dapple-gray, *a.* أَنْمَر *fem.* نَمْرآء *pl.* نُمْر — زَرْزُورِيّ.

Dardanelles, *n.* خَلِيجُ چَنَاق قَلْعَة.

Dare, *v.i.* To venture upon, جَسَرَ عَلَى [2] — تَجَاسَرَ — اِسْتَجْرَأَ — تَجَرَّأَ عَلَى *or* بِ. He does not — to . . . , لَا يَجْسُرُ أَن. Will any of you —? أَفَيَجْتَرِئُ أَحَدٌ مِنْكُمْ. I — say, لَعَلَّ — رُبَّمَا. A dare-devil, مُتَهَوِّر — سَادِر. *See also* to Venture, *v.i.*

Dare, *v.t.* To defy, فَتَكَ [2] — بَارَزَ — تَجَاسَرَ عَلَى.

Daring, *a.* مُغَامِر — سَنْدَرِيّ — مُكَبِّس — جَرِيء — جَسُور — مُتَجَاسِر — مُجْتَرِئ — شُجَاع. To be —, شَجُعَ [2].

Daring, *n.* Boldness, جَسَارَة — شَجَاعَة — سَنْدَرَة — جَرَآءَة. Impudence, وَقَاحَة.

Daringly, *ad.* Courageously, بِسَنْدَرَةٍ — بِشَجَاعَةٍ — بِجَسَارَةٍ. Impudently, وَقَاحَةً — بِوَقَاحَةٍ.

Dark, *a.* Not light, مُكْفَهِرّ — دَجْن — أَغْطَش — ظَلِم — مُظْلِم; becoming —, عَتِم. Of a — colour, قَاتِم — عَاتِم — غَامِق — غَلِقُ ٱللَّوْنِ. Not perspicuous, غَلِق — غَمِيس — مُتَشَابِه. Obscure, مُغْلَق — مُبْهَم — مُلْتَبِس. Intricate, مُشَبَّك. Ignorant, أَخْرَق — جَاهِل — غَشِيم. Gloomy, دَجِيّ — دَجْن — ظُلْمَانِيّ. Secret, خَفِيّ — مَكْنُون. Evil, شَنِيع — فَاحِش. Dark sayings, أَلْغَاز. Dark blue, لَازُوَرْدِيّ. Dark green, زَيْتُونِيّ. Dark brown, أَسْمَر. A — lantern, فَانُوسُ ٱلْحَرَامِيِّ. A — night, لَيْلَةٌ دَجْنٌ. A — day, يَوْمٌ دَجْنٌ — يَوْمٌ دَجْنٍ. A — place, مَظْلَمَة. The — ages, دُهُورُ ٱلْجَهْلِ — قُرُونُ ٱلْجَهَالَةِ. While it was yet —, وَٱلظَّلَامُ بَاقٍ. To be in the —, not to know of, جَهِلَ — غَبِيَ عَن — لَبِسَ. له خبر ب. To be —, غَطِشَ — ظَلِمَ. To grow —, أَغْسَى — غَسَا [2] — أَغْبَسَ — أَغْطَشَ — أَغْشَى — أَظْلَمَ — عَتِمَ — أَعْتَمَ.

Dark, *n.* Evening, عَشَآء — عَشِيَّة — عَتَمَة — مَسَآء. Till —, إِلَى وَقْتِ ٱلْمَسَآءِ. *See also* Darkness, *n.*

Dark-coloured, *a.* أَسْوَدُ ٱللَّوْنِ — أَسْمَر — يَضْرِبُ إِلَى ٱلسَّوَادِ — قَاتِم.

Darken, *v.t.* To deprive of light, أَغْطَشَ — قَتَمَ — أَظْلَمَ — أَعْتَمَ — أَظْلَمَ عَلَى — عَتَّمَ عَلَى. To obscure, as clouds the sun, حَجَبَ [2]. To perplex, شَبَّكَ — شَبَّهَ. To sully, طَبَّعَ — قَذَّعَ. To make dark-coloured, جَعَلَ غَلِقَ ٱللَّوْنِ — جَعَلَ قَاتِمًا. He rendered it —, confused, to him, شَبَّهَهُ عَلَيْهِ.

Darken, *v.i.* To grow dark, أَغْطَشَ — أَظْلَمَ — أَعْتَمَ — اِكْفَهَرَّ. To become blacker, اِسْوَدَّ.

Darkish, *a.* Rather dark, not light, يَضْرِبُ إِلَى ٱلْعُتْمَةِ. Dusky-coloured, قَتَام — يَضْرِبُ إِلَى ٱلسَّوَادِ — أَقْتَم.

Darkling, *n.* أَخْرَق — غَبِيّ — جَاهِل — غَشِيم.

Darkly, *ad.* In the dark, فِي ٱلظُّلْمَةِ. Stupidly, بِخُرْقٍ — بِغَشَمٍ — فِي ٱلْعَمَى. In an uncertain way, فِي لُغْزٍ — عَلَى ٱلْعَمَايَةِ. *See also* Obscurely, *ad.*

Darkness, *n.* Absence of light, غَيْهَب — غَبَس — دَجْن — قُتْمَة — عَتَم — عَتَمَة — ظُلْمَة — ظَلَام. Want of perspicuity, اِنْغِلَاق — اِشْتِبَاه — اِلْتِبَاس. Ignorance, خُرْق — جَهْل — غَبَاوَة — حَمَاقَة — جَاهِلِيَّة. Darkness, as of colour, قُتْمَة — خُطْبَة — غُبْس; of sight, غَمَش; of the night, جِنّ — غَبَش — جَنَان — سُدْفَة. Evil, عَشَاوَة — شَنَاعَة — خَبَاثَة — سُوء — شَرّ. Secrecy, سِرّ — خَافِيَة. The blackness of —, قَتَامُ ٱلظَّلَامِ. There is no —, concealment, in this matter, لَا جِنَّ بِهٰذَا ٱلْأَمْرِ.

Darksome, *a.* ظُلْمَانِيّ. *See also* Dark.

Darling, *a.* } مَحْبُوب — عَزِيز — وَحِيد — مَعْشُوق — عَيْن —
Darling, *n.* } أَعَزُّ ٱلْجَمِيعِ. (The feminine formed by suffixing ة.)

Darn, *v.t.* رَفَأَ — رَفَا [2] — رَتَأَهُ فِي نَظِيرِ نَسِيجِهِ. To mend, patch, أَصْلَحَ — رَقَّعَ.

Darn, *n.* رَفْو — تَصْلِيحٌ بِشَكْلِ ٱلنَّسْجِ. A patch, رُقْعَة. The place of a —, مَرْفَأ.

Darnel, *n.* شَلِيم — شَيْلَم — زُوَّان — زُوَان.

Darner, *n.* رَفَّآء.

Darning, *n.* رَفْو.

Dart, *n.* The weapon, حَرْبَة *pl.* حِرَاب — زَرَّاقَة — مِزْرَاق — عَنَزَة — سَهْم *pl.* أَسْهَام. He pierced him with a —, زَرَقَهُ بِمِزْرَاقٍ.

Dart, *v.t.* To throw, رَمَى — طَرَحَ — طَرَّحَ — رَشَقَ [2].

Dart, *v.i.* To shoot, رَمَى *aor.* يَرْمِي. To emit, أَظْهَرَ — أَبْرَزَ. To run rapidly, سَطَا [2] — فَرَّ — أَسْرَعَ — وَلَّى. To spring forth, to leap, تَفَلَّتَ — فَزَّ. To — upon, وَثَبَ عَلَى *aor.* يَثِبُ — سَطَا بِ [2] *aor.* يَسْطُو — قَحَمَ فِي — اِنْقَضَّ عَلَى.

Darting, *a.* *See under* Shooting, *a.*

Darwish, *n.* دَرْوِيش *pl.* دَرَاوِيش.

Dash, *v.t.* To strike, لَطَمَ — صَدَمَ. To — about, as of water, خَضْخَضَ. To sprinkle, رَشَّ. To mingle, مَزَجَ — خَلَطَ. To cancel, مَحَا [2] — نَسَخَ [2] — أَبْطَلَ. To break to pieces, هَشَمَ — حَطَّمَ تَحْطِيمًا — رَضْرَضَ — طَرْطَشَ — كَسَّرَ. To —, as the wind a ship, قَصَفَ. To — one's self against, صَدَمَ. To — against one another, صَادَمَ. To — down, أَهْبَطَ. To — upon, to attack,

هَجَمَ عَلَى ـ يَقَعُ .aor وَقَعَ بِ ـ يَسْطُو .aor سَطَا بِ. He dashed his foot against a stone, عَثَرَتْ رِجْلُهُ عَلَى ـ صَدَمَ بِحَجَرٍ رِجْلَهُ. To — one's hopes, رَمَى ـ فِي ـ قَطَعَ أَمَلَهُ ـ آيَسَ. حَجَرِ الإِيَاسِ.

Dash, *v.i.* To scatter, تَشَتَّتَ ـ اِنْتَشَرَ. To run quickly, to flee, هَرَبَ ـ فَرَّ ـ أَغَارَ. To flow, سَالَ ـ سَرَبَ ـ مَجَّ. To — through the water, as a ship, مَخَرَ. To — through thick and thin, مَا بَالَى بِالْمَوَانِعِ ـ تَهَوَّرَ. To — together, as the waves, اِلْتَطَمَ ـ اِعْتَلَجَ. The waves dashed against the ship, لَطَمَتِ الْأَمْوَاجُ الْمَرْكَبَ. The waves dashed against each other, تَزَاحَمَتِ ـ اِعْتَلَجَتِ الْأَمْوَاجُ ـ الْأَمْوَاجُ.

Dash, *n.* A blow, ضَرْبَة ـ لَطْمَة ـ كَبَّة. A collision, وَقْعَة ـ مُصَادَمَة. A mark thus (—), شَرْطَة ـ خَطّ. An infusion of something, قَلِيلٌ مِن ـ مِن ـ قَطْرَة ـ ذَرَق. To cut a —, تَكَبَّرَ ـ تَفَاخَرَ ـ تَفَخَّرَ ـ شَمَخَ ـ تَعَظَّمَ.

Dash-board, *n.* حَاجِزٌ لِلطِّينِ.

Dashing, *a.* Rushing, سَرِيع ـ سَيَّال ـ طَيَّار ـ مَجُوج ـ مَجَّاج. Precipitate, rash, مُتَهَالِك ـ هَيِّر ـ مُتَهَوِّر. Bold, نَجِيب ـ شُجَاع ـ بَطَل. Foppish, ostentatious, مُتَظَرِّف ـ مُتَفَاخِر ـ مُتَبَاهٍ.

Dastard, *n.* *See* Coward, *n.*

Dastard, *a.* *See* Cowardly, *a.*

Dastardize, *v.t.* أَفْزَعَ ـ خَوَّفَ ـ جَبَّنَ.

Dastardly, *ad.* *See* Cowardly, *ad.*

Data, *n. pl.* مَعْلُومَات ـ مُقَدِّمَات ـ مَوْضُوعَات.

Date, *n.* An epoch, تَارِيخ *pl.* تَوَارِيخ. Duration, مُدَّة ـ دَوَام ـ اِسْتِمْرَار. End, إِتْمَام ـ عَاقِبَة ـ آخِر. The fruit, تَمْر; a single —, تَمْرَة *coll.* تَمْر *pl.* تُمُور *and* تُمْرَان; when very young, طَلْع; while green, بَلَح ـ رَمَخ ـ جِدَال; while unripe, سُيَّاب ـ سَيَاب; when turning red, بُسْر; when quite ripe, تَمْر ـ رُطَب. Fresh dates, تَمْرٌ رَطِيب; a dry —, قَسْبَة *coll.* قَسْب; dry dates pressed in baskets, تَمْرٌ مُعَفَّس ـ عَجْوَة. A — stone, جَرِيمَة ـ نَوَى *pl.* أَنْوَاء ـ نَوَاة *pl.* نَوًى. The pellicule round a date-stone, قِطْمِير. A bunch of dates, كِبَاسَة *pl.* كَبَائِس; a bag for dates, قَوْصَرَة; a dish made of dates and clarified butter, خَبِيص. The depression in a date-stone from which the germ springs, نِقْرَة ـ نَقْرَة. A date-tree, نَخْلَة *pl.* نَخْل *and* نَخِيل. Out of —, obsolete, (of words), مُمَات ـ غَرِيب; not in use, غَيْرُ مُسْتَعْمَلٍ ـ هَامِد.

Date, *v.t.* أَرَّخَ ـ وَضَعَ (or خَطَّ) التَّارِيخَ عَلَى ـ يَضَعُ .aor.

Date, *v.i.* To begin, originate from, اِبْتَدَأَ فِي ـ حَدَثَ مِن ـ شَرَعَ فِي.

Dated, *part.* مُؤَرَّخ.

Dateless, *a.* بِلَا تَأْرِيخٍ ـ مِنْ غَيْرِ تَأْرِيخٍ ـ غَيْرُ مُؤَرَّخٍ.

Dative, *a.* In one's gift, مُتَصَرِّف ـ ذُو ـ صَاحِب ـ مَوْلَى. The — case, بَابُ الْمَجْرُورِ.

Datum, *n.* مَوْضُوع. *See also* Data, *n.*

Datura, *n.* جَوْزُ مَاثِلٍ.

Daub, *v.t.* To besmear, طَلَا ـ طَلَّى. To soil, لَوَّثَ. To smudge, طَبَّعَ. To — with mud or plaster, طَانَ ـ دَمَّ; with dirt, وَسَّخَ ـ لَوَّثَ; with pitch, زَفَّتَ ـ طَيَّنَ. To do coarsely, لَخْمَطَ ـ زَرْوَطَ ـ خَبَّصَ ـ خَرِقَ فِي. To flatter, مَلَّقَ ـ قَرَّظَ. To be daubed, made dirty, تَوَسَّخَ ـ تَلَوَّثَ; to be flattered, تَمَلَّقَ. *See also to* Smear, *v.t.*

Daub, *n.* A coarse painting, تَصْوِيرٌ دُونٌ ـ صُورَةٌ مِنْ دُونٍ (or خَشِنٌ). A smear, تَطْلِيَة. A smudge, طَبْعَة ـ بُقْعَة.

Dauber, *n.* One who smears, does things coarsely, خَرِق ـ زَرْوَاط ـ لَخْمَاط ـ مُخَبِّص ـ أَخْرَق. A poor painter, رَسَّامٌ أَخْرَق ـ رَسَّامٌ دُونٌ (or غَشِيمٌ). A flatterer, مَلِق.

Daubing, *n.* Coarse painting, تَصْوِيرٌ دُونٌ (or خَشِنٌ). Flattery, مَلَق.

Dauby, *a.* Sticky, لَزِج ـ دَبِق.

Daughter, *n.* A female child, اِبْنَة ـ خَبَأَة or بِنْت *pl.* بَنَات; a little —, بُنَيَّة. A girl, صَبِيَّة *pl.* صَبَايَا. A daughter-in-law, كَنَّة ـ اِمْرَأَةُ الاِبْنِ *pl.* كَنَائِن. A grand-daughter, بِنْتُ الْبِنْتِ or بِنْتُ الاِبْنِ ـ رَبِيبَة *pl.* رَبَائِب. Daughters, virgins, بَنَاتٌ عَذَارَى ـ بَنَاتٌ أَبْكَار.

Daughterly, *a.* كَمَا يَلِيقُ بِالاِبْنَةِ.

Daunt, *v.t.* To frighten, جَفَّلَ ـ فَزَّعَ ـ هَيَّبَ ـ خَوَّفَ ـ أَرْهَبَ ـ خَجَّلَ ـ أَخْجَلَ. To discourage, أَخْمَدَ ـ أَفْتَرَ ـ كَسَرَ قَلْبَهُ ـ كَسَرَ عَزْمَهُ.

Dauntless, *a.* ذُو بَطْشٍ ـ مُغَامِر ـ شُجَاع ـ جَسُور ـ مُكَبِّس ـ لَا يُخَافُ.

Dauphin, *n.* بِكْرُ مَلِكِ فَرَانْسَا.

Dauphiness, *n.* Wife of the Dauphin, زَوْجَةُ بِكْرِ مَلِكِ فَرَانْسَا.

Davit, *n.* آلَةٌ لِرَفْعِ قَارِبٍ أَوْ مِرْسَاةٍ مِنَ الْبَحْرِ ـ مَتَافُورَة.

Daw, *n.* زَاغ *pl.* زِيغَان ـ قُعْقُع.

Dawdle; *see to* Dally, *v.i.*

Dawn, *v.i.* أَفْجَرَ ـ سَحَرَ ـ أَضْحَى ـ أَفْصَحَ ـ فَصَحَ.

اِبْتَدَأَ — شَرَعَ — شَقَّ ٱلْفَجْرُ — أَصْبَحَ — اِنْفَجَرَ. To open, begin, Till the day dawns, إِلَى أَنْ يَنْفَجِرَ ٱلنَّهَارُ.

Dawn, *n.* طُلُوعُ — ٱلصَّبَاحُ — فَجْر — مَبْرَقُ ٱلصُّبْحِ — ضَحْوَة — سَحَر — بَرِيمُ ٱلصُّبْحِ. — شَقُّ ٱلْفَجْرِ — ٱلنَّهَارِ; early —, غَبَش; tint of —, The beginning of anything, بَدْءٌ — اِبْتِدَاءٌ. To rise at —, بَكَّرَ — تَسَحَّرَ.

Day, *n.* نَهَار *pl.* أَنْهُر — يَوْم *pl.* أَيَّام. To-day, اليَوْمَ. It is day, dawn, طَلَعَ ٱلنَّهَارُ — طَلَعَ ٱلضَّوْءُ — أَصْبَحَ ٱلصَّبَاحُ. Good day to you! (on meeting), نَهَارُكَ مُبَارَكٌ — نَهَارُكَ سَعِيدٌ; (Response), اللّٰهُ يَحْفَظُكَ — اللّٰهُ يُبَارِكُ فِيكَ. Good day! Good bye! فِي أَمَانِ ٱللّٰهِ. That same day was Friday, وَكَانَ ذَٰلِكَ ٱلْيَوْمُ ٱلْجُمْعَةَ. He left the same day, خَرَجَ مِنْ يَوْمِهِ. To fix a day, عَيَّنَ يَوْمًا. To wish one good day, صَبَّحَ. To have had one's day, رَأَى عِزَّهُ *aor.* يَرَى — حَظَّ بِيَوْمِهِ. To lose a day, ضَيَّعَ يَوْمًا. To lose the day, to come short, غُلِبَ — خَسِرَ. To turn day into night and night into day, جَعَلَ ٱلنَّهَارَ لَيْلًا وَٱللَّيْلَ نَهَارًا. To advance, of the day, عَلَا ٱلنَّهَارُ *aor.* يَعْلُو. Who has won the day, been the conqueror? لِمَنِ ٱلْفَلْجُ. Days, *n. pl.* Time, epoch, زَمَان — جِيل — أَيَّام — عُمْر — عَصْر. The five supplementary days to make up the Muslim year, المُسْتَرَقُ. Days of grace, delay, أَيَّامُ سَمَاحٍ. Evil days, أَيَّامُ نَحْسٍ — أَيَّامُ رَدِيئَةٌ — أَيَّامُ شَرٍّ. High days and holidays, أَيَّامُ فَرَحٍ وَعِيدٍ. In the days of old, فِي قَدِيمِ ٱلْعَصْرِ وَٱلْأَوَانِ — فِي قَدِيمِ ٱلْأَيَّامِ — قَدِيمًا. In those days, يَوْمَئِذٍ — فِي تِلْكَ ٱلْأَيَّامِ. One's young days, أَيَّامُ ٱلصِّبَاءِ — أَيَّامُ ٱلشَّبَابَةِ. Some days, *adv.* بَعْضَ أَيَّامٍ. The best days of a thing, أَيَّامُ حَدَاثَتِهِ. Within a few days, بَعْدَ أَيَّامٍ قَلِيلَةٍ. Within these few days, مُنْذُ أَيَّامٍ قَلِيلَةٍ. Now-a-days, فِي هٰذِهِ ٱلْأَيَّامِ — فِي ٱلْأَيَّامِ ٱلْحَاضِرَةِ — فِي هٰذَا ٱلزَّمَنِ. To shorten one's days, قَصَّرَ عُمْرَهُ — قَصَّرَ أَيَّامَهُ.

A fast day, يَوْمُ صَوْمٍ — يَوْمُ صِيَامٍ.

A feast day, festival, يَوْمُ عِيدٍ — عِيد *pl.* أَعْيَاد.

A fine day, يَوْمٌ بَهِيجٌ — يَوْمٌ صَحْوٌ — يَوْمٌ يَوْمٌ — نَهَارٌ أَنْهَرُ.

A given day, يَوْمٌ مَعْلُومٌ — يَوْمٌ مُعَيَّنٌ.

A lucky day, يَوْمُ حَظٍّ — يَوْمٌ مُبَارَكٌ.

All day, طُولَ ٱلنَّهَارِ.

An unfortunate day, يَوْمٌ كَاسِفٌ.

Break of day, شَقُّ ٱلْفَجْرِ.

Broad day, وَسَطُ ٱلنَّهَارِ — النَّهَارُ.

By day, فِي ٱلنَّهَارِ — نَهَارًا.

By the day, بِٱلْيَوْمِ.

Christmas day, عِيدُ ٱلْمِيلَادِ.

Day after day, كُلَّ يَوْمٍ — يَوْمًا فَيَوْمًا.

Day by day, مِنْ يَوْمٍ إِلَى يَوْمٍ — يَوْمٌ بِيَوْمٍ — يَوْمًا فَيَوْمًا.

Day and night, نَهَارًا وَلَيْلًا.

Day of battle, وَاقِعَة — يَوْمُ مُحَارَبَةٍ — يَوْمُ قِتَالٍ — يَوْم.

Day of grace, delay, يَوْمُ سَمَاحٍ; time for repentance, مُهْلَةٌ لِلتَّوْبَةِ.

Decline of day, زَوَالُ ٱلنَّهَارِ.

During the day, بِٱلنَّهَارِ — فِي ٱلنَّهَارِ — نَهَارًا — فِي مُدَّةِ ٱلنَّهَارِ.

Every day, *adv.* كُلَّ يَوْمٍ.

Every day, *a.* Usual, مُعْتَاد.

Every two or three days, كُلَّ يَوْمَيْنِ أَوْ ثَلَاثَةٍ.

From that day, يَوْمَئِذٍ — مِنْ ذَٰلِكَ ٱلْيَوْمِ.

From this day forth, مِنَ ٱلْيَوْمِ وَرَائِحًا — مِنَ ٱلْيَوْمِ وَصَاعِدًا.

In one day's time, during a day, فِي مُدَّةِ يَوْمٍ; a day hence, مِنْ بَعْدِ يَوْمٍ.

In the face of day, فِي ٱلنَّهَارِ — فِي ضَوْءِ ٱلنَّهَارِ.

New year's day, نُورُوز — رَأْسُ ٱلسَّنَةِ.

On a certain day, ذَاتَ يَوْمٍ مِنَ ٱلْأَيَّامِ — يَوْمًا مِنَ ٱلْأَيَّامِ — فِي يَوْمٍ مَا.

On that day, يَوْمَئِذٍ — فِي ذَٰلِكَ ٱلْيَوْمِ.

One day or other, يَوْمًا مِنَ ٱلْأَيَّامِ.

Open day, النَّهَارُ.

Order of the day, (military), الأَمْرُ ٱلْيَوْمِيُّ; proceedings for the day, تَرْتِيبُ إِجْرَاءِ ٱلْأُمُورِ لِلْيَوْمِ.

Peep of day, طُلُوعُ ٱلْفَجْرِ — غَبَش.

Settling day, يَوْمُ حِسَابٍ — يَوْمُ ٱلْمُحَاسَبَةِ.

Since the day of . . . , مُنْذُ يَوْمِ.

Some day, فِي يَوْمٍ مَا — يَوْمًا مِنَ ٱلْأَيَّامِ.

The day of Judgment, يَوْمُ ٱلدِّينِ — يَوْمُ ٱلدَّيْنُونَةِ — يَوْمُ ٱلْقِيَامَةِ — يَوْمُ ٱلْحِسَابِ.

The day after, *ad.* فِي ٱلْغَدِ — غَدًا — اليَوْمَ ٱلثَّانِيَ.

The day before, *ad.* فِي ٱلْيَوْمِ ٱلسَّابِقِ.

The day following, *ad.* / The next day, } فِي ٱلْيَوْمِ ٱلْقَادِمِ — فِي ٱلْيَوْمِ ٱلثَّانِي — غَدًا.

The third day, *ad.* فِي ٱلْيَوْمِ ٱلثَّالِثِ.

The very day, *ad.* ذَاتَ ٱلْيَوْمِ — اليَوْمَ بِعَيْنِهِ.

This day, to-day, *ad.* هٰذَا ٱلنَّهَارَ — اليَوْمَ.

This day fortnight, *ad.* عُقْبَ خَمْسَةَ عَشَرَ يَوْمٍ.

This day twelvemonth, *ad.* عُقْبَ سَنَةٍ.

This day week, *ad.* عُقْبَ أُسْبُوعٍ ـ عُقْبَ جُمْعَةٍ.

This many a day, *ad.* مُنْذُ أَيَّامٍ شَتَّى.

This very day, *ad.* هٰذَا ٱلْيَوْمَ بِعَيْنِهِ.

Time of day, *ad.* السَّاعَةُ ـ الْوَقْتُ.

To-day, *ad.* هٰذَا ٱلنَّهَارَ ـ الْيَوْمَ.

Within a day or two, مِنَ ٱلْآنَ إِلَى يَوْمٍ أَوْ ـ بَعْدَ يَوْمٍ أَوْ يَوْمَيْنِ يَوْمَيْنِ.

Working day, يَوْمُ شُغْلٍ.

Day-book, *n.* دَفْتَرٌ يَوْمِيٌّ ـ دَفْتَرُ تَسْوِيدٍ ـ دَفَاتِرُ .pl دَفْتَر.

Daybreak, *n.* *See* Dawn, *n.*

Day by day, *ad.* دَائِمًا ـ كُلَّ يَوْمٍ ـ يَوْمًا فَيَوْمًا.

Day-dream, *n.* وَهْمِيَّاتٌ .pl وَهْمِيَّةٌ ـ غُرُورٌ ـ تَخَيُّلٌ ـ تَصَوُّرٌ.

Day-labour, *n.* شُغْلٌ يَوْمِيٌّ ـ شُغْلُ نَهَارٍ.

Day-labourer, *n.* أَجِيرٌ يَوْمِيٌّ ـ فَعَلَةٌ .pl فَاعِلٌ.

Daylight, *n.* نَهَارٌ ـ ضَوْءٌ ـ نُورٌ.

Daysman, *n.* مُصَالِحٌ ـ وَسِيطٌ.

Dayspring, *n.* الْفَجْرُ ـ شَقُّ ٱلْفَجْرِ.

Day-star, *n.* نَجْمُ ٱلصُّبْحِ ـ الزُّهَرَةُ ـ كَوْكَبُ ٱلصُّبْحِ.

Day's-work, *n.* Work of the day, شُغْلٌ يَوْمِيٌّ.

Daytime, *n.* نَهَارٌ ـ وَقْتُ ٱلنَّهَارِ. In the —, نَهَارًا ـ فِي ٱلنَّهَارِ.

Daze, *v.t.* / Dazzle, } To overpower the sight with light, جَهَّرَ ـ أَسْدَرَ ـ غَشِيَ ٱلْعَيْنَ ـ خَطِفَ ٱلْبَصَرَ ـ ٱلْبَصَرَ ـ أَبْهَلَ ـ غَطْمَشَ ـ زَغْلَلَ ٱلنَّظَرَ ـ أَخَذَ ٱلْبَصَرَ. To astound, أَسْدَرَتِ ـ أَخَذَ ٱلْعَقْلَ ـ أَدْهَشَ. The sun dazzled his eye, جَهَرَتِ ٱلشَّمْسُ عَيْنَهُ ـ ٱلشَّمْسُ عَيْنَهُ.

Dazzle, *v.i.* To be overpowered with light, تَجَهَّرَ ـ سَدِرَ ـ تَزَغْلَلَ ـ تَغَطْمَشَ ـ إِنْغَبَشَ. To be astounded, تَحَيَّرَ ـ إِنْدَهَشَ.

Dazzled, *a.* As with light, مُغَطْمَشٌ ـ مَجْهُورُ ٱلْبَصَرِ ـ سَدِرٌ. Astounded, مَدْهُوشٌ ـ مُتَحَيِّرٌ.

Dazzling, *a.* مُغَطْمِشٌ خَاطِفُ ٱلْبَصَرِ ـ مُسْدِرٌ.

Dazzlingly, *ad.* بِنَوْعٍ يَخْطَفُ ٱلْبَصَرَ ـ بِسَدَرٍ ـ سَدَارَةً.

Deacon, *n.* شَمَامِسَةٌ .pl شَمَّاسٌ.

Deaconess, *n.* شَمَّاسَاتٌ .pl شَمَّاسَةٌ.

Deaconry, *n.* / Deaconship, } وَظِيفَةُ ٱلشَّمَّاسِ ـ دَرَجَةُ ٱلشَّمَّاسِ.

Dead, *a.* Destitute of life, مَيِّتٌ *pl.* أَمْوَاتٌ *and* مَوْتَى *and* مَيِّتُونَ ـ مَيِّتٌ *fem.* مَيِّتَةٌ *pl.* مَيِّتُونَ ـ مَرْحُومٌ ـ مُتَوَفًّى. Inanimate, مَوَاتٌ ـ عَدِيمُ ٱلْحَاسِّيَّةِ ـ بِلَا حِسٍّ ـ خَامِدٌ ـ جَامِدٌ. Impotent, عَاجِزٌ ـ عَجِيزٌ ـ حَرِيكٌ ـ كَسِيحٌ. Inactive, lazy, كَاهِلٌ ـ عَاجِزٌ ـ وَانٍ ـ كَسْلَانُ ـ قَلِيلُ ٱلْمُرُوَّةِ. Torpid, languid, تَفُوهٌ ـ مَلِيخٌ. Cold, without emotion, بَارِدٌ. Tasteless, فَاتِرٌ ـ مَجْفُوفٌ ـ ذَابِلٌ. Withered, of plants, مِنْ غَيْرِ لَذَّةٍ ـ بِلَا طَعْمَةٍ ـ مَاتَتْ ـ يَابِسٌ; of a member of the body, يَابِسٌ. Complete, entirely, كُلِّيًّا ـ بَتَّةً ـ بِٱلْمَرَّةِ ـ بِٱلتَّمَامِ. Dead drunk, سَكْرَانُ ـ سَكِرٌ ـ أَعْمَى. A — level, سَهْلٌ تَامٌّ ـ مُسَاوَاةٌ كَامِلَةٌ. A — calm, هُدُوٌّ كَامِلٌ. Dead, as of a market, كَاسِدٌ. Uninhabited, خَالٍ مِنَ ٱلسُّكَّانِ ـ قَفْرٌ. Feigning to be —, مُتَمَاوِتٌ. Half —, كَٱلْمَيِّتِ ـ نِصْفُ مَيِّتٍ. Twice —, مَيِّتٌ مُضَاعَفًا. A — fire, نَارٌ غَيْرُ مُشْتَعِلَةٍ ـ نَارٌ خَامِدَةٌ. A — sound, صَوْتٌ خَفِيضٌ. Dead silence, سُكُوتٌ تَامٌّ. Dead stock, صَامِتٌ. The — of night, نِصْفُ ٱللَّيْلِ. The — of winter, أَشَدُّ ٱلشِّتَاءِ. The — season, الْمَوْسِمُ ٱلْكَاسِدُ. A — body, جَنَازَةٌ *pl.* جَنَائِزُ ـ مَيْتَةٌ. To pretend to be —, تَمَاوَتَ. To fall down —, سَقَطَ بَغْتَةً مَيِّتًا. He became as one —, صَارَ كَٱلْمَيِّتِ. Only speak well of your —, أُذْكُرُوا أَمْوَاتَكُمْ بِٱلْخَيْرِ. The —, *pl.* الْمَوْتَى ـ الْأَمْوَاتُ ـ أَهْلُ ٱلْقُبُورِ.

Dead-colouring, *n.* بِطَانَةٌ ـ أَوَّلُ دَهْنَةٍ.

Deaden, *v.t.* To assuage, سَكَّنَ ـ خَفَّفَ ـ هَدَّأَ ـ أَخْمَدَ. To retard, to weaken, أَضْعَفَ ـ ثَبَّطَ عَنْ ـ أَخَّرَ. To render vapid, صَبَّرَ مِنْ غَيْرِ لَذَّةٍ ـ مَسَخَ. To —, of a sound, خَفَّضَ.

Dead-eye, *n.* بُوغَاتَةٌ ـ بَكَرَةٌ ذَاتُ ثَلَاثَةِ ثُقُوبٍ.

Dead-letter, *n.* جَوَابٌ مُهْمَلٌ. Dead-letter Office, مَحَلُّ حِفْظِ ٱلْجَوَابَاتِ ٱلْمُهْمَلَةِ.

Dead-light, *n.* غِطَاءُ ٱلطَّاقَةِ.

Deadliness, *n.* مُهْلِكَةٌ. Venom, سَمٌّ.

Deadly, *a.* مُمِيتٌ ـ قَاتِلٌ ـ مُهْلِكٌ. Anything —, مُهْلِكَةٌ. A — poison, سَمٌّ نَاقِعٌ مُمِيتٌ. A — wound, جُرْحٌ مُمِيتٌ. A — enemy, عَدُوٌّ سَخِيتٌ.

Deadlock, *n.* وَرْطَةٌ ـ صُعُوبَةٌ ـ مُعْضِلَةٌ.

Dead-march, *n.* لَحْنٌ مُحْزِنٌ تَعْزِفُهُ مُوسِيقَةُ ٱلْعَسْكَرِ وَقْتَ جِنَازَةِ أَحَدِهِمْ.

Deadness, *n.* Want of life, مَمَاتٌ ـ مَوَاتٌ. Frigidity, بَرْدٌ ـ بُرُودَةٌ. Langour, ضَعْفٌ ـ عَجْزٌ ـ عَيٌّ. Want of ardour, عَدَمُ ٱلْغَيْرَةِ ـ عَدَمُ ٱلْمُرُوَّةِ. Vapidness, as of liquors, مَسَاخَةٌ ـ عَدَمُ لَذَّةٍ. Deadness of trade, كَسَادٌ.

Dead-reckoning, *n.* تَقْوِيمُ ٱلْمَسَالِكِ.

Dead-water, *n.* الْمَاءُ ٱلرَّاكِدُ خَلْفَ ٱلسَّفِينَةِ ٱلْمَاخِرَةِ.

Dead weight, *n.* A heavy burden, حِمْلٌ ثَقِيلٌ. Weight, as of a slaughtered animal, وَزْنُ ٱلْحَيَوَانِ ٱلْمَذْبُوحِ جُمْلَةً.

Deaf, *a.* Wanting sense of hearing, أَصَمّ ـ أَصْلَخ ـ أَصْلَج *fem.* صَمَّآء *pl.* صُمّ *and* صُمَّان ـ أُطْرُوش ـ أَطْرَش *fem.* طَرْشَآء *pl.* طُرْش. Unwilling to hear, لا يَسْمَعُ ـ مارِد ـ مَرِيد. To be or become —, صَمَّ ـ طَرِشَ. To pretend to be —, تَصَامَّ ـ تَصَالَخَ ـ تَطَارَشَ. To be — to, تَصَامَّ عَن. Deaf to reason, to all considerations, لا يَسْمَعُ نِدَآءً وَلا يَبْغِي ٱهْتِدَآءً.

Deafen, *v.t.* To make deaf, أَصَمَّ. To stun, صَدَعَ ـ صَخَّ. To make less harsh, لَيَّنَ ـ خَفَّضَ.

Deafness, *n.* طَرَش ـ وَقْر ـ صَمَم ـ صَلَخ ـ صَلَج; a slight —, وَقْر. It is nothing but simulated —! صَمام صَمام.

Deal, *n.* A part, quantity, مِقْدار ـ جُزْء ـ عِدَّة ـ كَمِّيَّة ـ قَدْر ـ حِصَّة. Pine wood, صَنَوْبَر. A — board, تَخْتَة (or) لَوْح صَنَوْبَر. Distribution, as of playing cards, تَفْرِيق. A great —, كَثِير ـ جَمّ. Snow is a great — whiter than paper, اَلثَّلْجُ أَكْثَرُ بَياضًا مِنَ ٱلْقِرْطاسِ بِزِيادَةٍ. I have heard a great — concerning him, بَلَغَتْنِي أَشْيَآءُ كَثِيرَةٌ عَنْهُ. Not so much as that by a great —, أَقَلُّ مِنْ ذٰلِكَ كَثِيرًا. It is your —, التَّفْرِيقُ لَكَ.

Deal, *v.t.* To distribute, فَرَّقَ ـ قَسَمَ ـ أَعْطَى ـ وَزَّعَ. To — cards, فَرَّقَ ٱلْأَوْراقَ. To — blows, ضَرَبَ. To — out to, فَرَّقَ عَلَى ـ قَسَمَ عَلَى.

Deal, *v.i.* To traffic, تاجَرَ ـ بَاعَ وَٱشْتَرَى *fut.* يَبِيعُ. To behave, مَشَى ـ سَلَكَ. You have to — with a cheat, مُعامَلَتُكَ مَعَ غَشَّاشٍ. He deals with them as with sons, يُعامِلُهُمْ كَٱلْبَنِينَ. Why have you so dealt with us? لِمَ فَعَلْتَ بِنا هٰكَذا؟ According as God has dealt to all, حَسَبَ ما قَسَمَ ٱللّٰهُ لِلْجَمِيعِ.

To deal by or with, to behave towards, دَارَى ـ رَعَى ـ عَامَلَ ـ صَنَعَ بِ.

To deal deceitfully with, خَانَ ـ عَامَلَ بِٱلْحِيلَةِ ـ إِحْتَالَ عَلَى *aor.* يَخُونُ.

To deal harshly with, قَاسَحَ ـ عَنَفَ عَلَى ـ أَسَآءَ إِلَى ـ ظَلَمَ عَلَى.

To deal in, to sell, تَسَبَّبَ بِ ـ بَاعَ. To deal in, to practise, مَارَسَ ـ تَعَانَى ـ تَعَاطَى. To deal in, to consist of, إِشْتَمَلَ ـ إِحْتَوَى عَلَى ـ عَلَى.

To deal kindly with, عَامَلَ بِٱلطِّيبِ ـ أَحْسَنَ إِلَى.

To deal with, to settle with, إِنْفَصَلَ مَعَ ـ تَسَاوَى مَعَ. To deal with, to discuss, تَكَلَّمَ فِي ـ بَاحَثَ عَن. To deal with, to contend with, جَادَلَ ـ نَازَعَ.

Dealer, *n.* A trader, تاجِر *pl.* تُجَّار ـ مُتَسَبِّب ـ بَيَّاع *pl.* بَاعَة *and* بَيِّع *and* بَيَّاعُون. A shop-keeper, بَقَّال *pl.* بَقَّالَة ـ فاتِح ـ دُكَّانِيّ. One who has to do with anything, مُباشِر ـ مُعامِل. A — at cards, مُفَرِّقُ وَرَقِ ٱللَّعِبِ. A plain —, أَمِين ـ صادِق. A double —, مَكَّار ـ غَشَّاش خائِن. A wholesale —, بَيَّاع بِٱلْجُمْلَةِ. A retail —, بَيَّاع بِٱلْمُفَرَّقِ ـ بَيَّاع بِٱلتَّقْطِيعِ ـ بَقَّال.

Dealing, *n.* Practice, intercourse, مُعاشَرَة ـ مُعامَلَة ـ مُخالَطَة. Trade, أَخْذٌ وَعَطَآءٌ ـ تِجارَة. Conduct, أَفْعال ـ سُلُوك ـ سِيرَة. Plain —, إِسْتِقامَة ـ صَداقَة ـ صَفاوَة. Double —, مَكْر ـ رِيَآء ـ غِشّ ـ خِيانَة. These have no dealings with those, هٰؤُلآءِ لا يُعامِلُونَ أُولٰئِكَ. To have dealings with, عَامَلَ ـ صَارَفَ.

Dean, *n.* Of a cathedral, رَئِيسُ أَكْلِيرُسِ ٱلْكَنِيسَةِ ٱلْمَطْرانِيَّةِ; of a university, ناظِرٌ فِي ٱلْمَدارِسِ ٱلْعامَّةِ. The Dean and Chapter, رَئِيسُ أَكْلِيرُوسِ ٱلْكَنِيسَةِ ٱلْمَطْرانِيَّةِ وَأَهْلِ مَجْمَعِها. A rural —, قِسِّيس ناظِرٌ عَلَى ٱلْأَكْلِيرُوسِ فِي كُورَةٍ مِنَ ٱلْأَرْيافِ.

Deanery, *n.* The residence of a dean, دارُ ٱلْقِسِّيسِ ٱلْمَذْكُورِ أَعْلاهُ; the office of a dean, وَظِيفَةُ ٱلْقِسِّيسِ ٱلْمَذْكُورِ.

Dear, *a.* Beloved, عَزِيز ـ مَحْبُوب ـ أَحِبَّآء *pl.* حَبِيب ـ وَحِيد *pl.* أَعِزَّآء. Of high price, غالٍ ـ غَلِيّ. Costly, precious, نَفِيس ـ ذُو قِيمَةٍ ـ ثَمِين. My dear! my darling! يا قَلْبِي ـ يا عَيْنِي ـ يا مَحْبُوبِي. Oh dear! واه واه. My dear Sir (as in the address of a letter), عِزَّتْلُو أَفَنْدِم ـ جَنابُ ٱلسَّيِّدِ. To be —, high priced, غَلا. To sell —, أَغْلَى بِ. To make —, أَغْلَى. To be —, precious, نَفُسَ. To be —, valued, عَزَّ ـ تَعَزَّزَ. To hold —, أَعَزَّ ـ عَزَّزَ.

Dearly, *ad.* At a high price, بِٱلْغالِي. Fondly, بِوِدادٍ ـ بِمَحَبَّةٍ. Dearly beloved, حَبِيب ـ وَحِيد ـ أَعِزَّآء *pl.* أَعَزّ. I sold it —, at a high price, بِعْتُهُ بِٱلْغالِي.

Dearness, *n.* High price, غَلَآء ـ غُلْوَآء. Fondness, وِداد ـ مَحَبَّة. Lovingness, عِشْق.

Dearth, *n.* Scarcity, قِلَّة ـ عُقْر ـ قَحْط ـ جَدْب ـ جَوْجَة ـ جُوع. Non-existence, عَدَمُ وُجُودٍ. There came a — over all the land, أَتَى جُوعٌ عَلَى كُلِّ ٱلْأَرْضِ.

Death, *n.* Extinction of life, مُوات ـ حُتُوف ـ حَتْف ـ فَيْظ ـ وَفاة *pl.* وَفَيات ـ مَنا ـ مَنِيَّة ـ مَوْت. The period of —, أَجَل. Manner of —, مِيتَة. A corpse, مَيْتَة ـ مَيِّت. Destruction, هَلاك. Epidemical disorder, وَبَآء ـ جارِف ـ مُوتان. Man labours and goes about, and his end is —, المَرْءُ يَسْعَى وَيَطُوفُ وَعاقِبَتُهُ ٱلْحُتُوفُ. To be the — of, cause —, أَماتَ ـ مَوَّتَ ـ قَتَلَ. To be at the point of —, أَقَصَّ ٱلْمَوْتَ. It is a case of life or —, هٰذا ٱلْأَمْرُ يَؤُولُ إِمَّا إِلَى ٱلْحَياةِ أَوْ إِلَى ٱلْمَوْتِ. To face —, أَقْبَلَ عَلَى ٱلْمَوْتِ ـ وَاجَهَ ٱلْمَوْتَ. To grieve one's self to —, مَاتَ مِنْ غَمِّهِ ـ قَاسَى ٱلْمَوْتَ ٱلْأَحْمَرَ. To put to —, قَتَلَ ². To condemn to —, قَضَى عَلَى ـ بِٱلْمَوْتِ ـ. To expose one's self to or not to fear —, إِسْتَمَاتَ. Death stared him in the face, to be at death's door, أَقَصَّ ٱلْمَوْتُ. He struck him till he was at the point of —, ضَرَبَهُ حَتَّى أَقَصَّهُ مِنَ ٱلْمَوْتِ.

Accidental death, مَوْتٌ قَضَائِيٌّ ـ مَوْتٌ عَارِضِيٌّ.

At the point of death, فِي ٱلنَّزْعِ ـ جَرِيضٌ. Such an one escaped at the point of death, أَفْلَتَ فُلَانٌ جَرِيضًا.

Civil death, إِسْقَاطُ حُقُوقِ ٱلْمُذْنِبِ وَإِعْدَامُهُ مَرَاتِبَهُ.

Death by strangulation, ٱلْمَوْتُ شَنْقًا ـ ٱلْمَوْتُ ٱلْأَسْوَدُ.

Easy death, مَوْتٌ مِنْ غَيْرِ أَلَمٍ ـ مَوْتٌ هَيِّنٌ.

In life and in death, فِي ٱلدُّنْيَا وَٱلْآخِرَةِ ـ فِي ٱلْحَيَاةِ وَٱلْمَوْتِ.

Natural death, ٱلْمَوْتُ ٱلطَّبِيعِيُّ ـ ٱلْمَوْتُ ٱلْأَبْيَضُ. He died a —, مَاتَ حَتْفَ أَنْفِهِ.

Pangs of death, Agonies of death, } سَكْرَةُ ٱلْمَوْتِ ـ نَزْعُ ٱلْمَوْتِ ـ فُوَاقُ ٱلْمَوْتِ.

Premature or untimely death, ٱلْمَوْتُ فِي ٱلصِّبَاءِ ـ ٱلِٱخْتِصَارُ.

Quick death, مَوْتٌ سَرِيعٌ ـ مَوْتٌ جَهِيزٌ ـ مَوْتٌ مُذْعِتٌ.

Sentence of death, حُكْمُ ٱلْمَوْتِ ـ إِعْلَامٌ بِٱلْقَتْلِ.

Sudden death, مَوْتٌ بَغْتَةً ـ مَوْتٌ فُجَاءَةً ـ مَوْتُ ٱلْفَوَاتِ.

To the death, حَتَّى ٱلْمَوْتِ.

The angel of death, مَلَكُ ٱلْمَوْتِ ـ عِزْرَائِيلُ. The Summoner of death, طَارِقُ ٱلْمَنَايَا.

Violent death, ٱلْمَوْتُ قَتْلًا ـ ٱلْمَوْتُ ٱلْأَحْمَرُ.

Worthy of death, مُسْتَحِقُّ ٱلْمَوْتِ.

Deathbed, *n.* The bed of death, فِرَاشُ ٱلْمَوْتِ. Sickness to death, مَرَضُ ٱلْمَوْتِ.

Death-bell, *n.* جَرَسٌ يَقْرَعُونَهُ عِنْدَ ٱلْجِنَازَةِ.

Death-blow, *n.* ضَرْبٌ قَاتِلٌ.

Deathless, *a.* غَيْرُ مَيِّتٍ ـ لَا يَمُوتُ ـ خَالِدٌ ـ بَاقٍ; of God, حَيٌّ.

Death-like, *a.* In the image of death, بِصُورَةِ ٱلْمَوْتِ. Motionless, عَدِيمُ ٱلْحَرَكَةِ ـ خَافِتٌ ـ سُبَاتِيٌّ. Gloomy, هَائِلٌ ـ كَئِيبٌ.

Death-rattle, *n.* حَشْرَجَةٌ ـ تَنَازُعٌ ـ جَرَضٌ ـ غُصَصُ ٱلْمَوْتِ. To have the —, حَشْرَجَ.

Death's-door, *n.* أَجَلٌ ـ مُشْرِفٌ عَلَى ٱلْمَوْتِ.

Death's-head, *n.* رَأْسُ مَيِّتٍ.

Death-struggle, *n.* حَالَةُ ٱلنَّزْعِ.

Death-warrant, *n.* حُكْمُ ٱلْمَوْتِ ـ أَمْرُ ٱلْقَتْلِ.

Death-watch, *n.* دُوَيْبَّةٌ يَأْخُذُ ٱلْغُشَمَاءُ صَرِيرَهَا عَلَامَةً لِلْمَوْتِ.

Debar, *v.t.* ذَادَ ـ عَنْ *aor.* يَذُودُ ـ حَجَزَ ² ـ حَجَبَ ² ـ مَنَعَ ـ سَدَّ عَلَى ² ـ نَهَى ـ عَنْ ـ أَخْرَقَ ـ عَنْ ـ حَبَسَ ـ عَنْ ـ تَحَبَّسَ ـ إِحْتَجَبَ. To be debarred, or to debar one's self, إِحْتَجَزَ ـ إِمْتَنَعَ ـ عَلَى.

Debark, *v.t.* طَلَّعَ ـ مِنَ ٱلْمَرْكَبِ ـ أَخْرَجَ ـ مِنَ ٱلْمَرْكَبِ ـ نَزَّلَ ـ إِلَى ٱلْبَرِّ.

Debark, *v.i.* نَزَلَ إِلَى ٱلْبَرِّ ـ طَلَعَ مِنَ ٱلْمَرْكَبِ ².

Debarkation, *n.* Causing to land, إِخْرَاجٌ مِنَ ـ تَنْزِيلٌ إِلَى ٱلْبَرِّ ٱلْمَرْكَبِ; landing, or being landed, طُلُوعٌ مِنَ ـ نُزُولٌ إِلَى ٱلْبَرِّ ٱلْمَرْكَبِ.

Debase, *v.t.* To degrade, عَزَلَ ـ عَنْ ـ وَطَّى. To make mean, أَخْبَثَ ـ أَفْسَدَ ـ أَحْقَرَ ـ أَهَانَ ـ ذَلَّلَ ـ رَذَّلَ. To corrupt, خَسَّرَ. To adulterate, as coin, زَغَلَ ـ شَقْلَ ـ أَفْسَلَ. To — one's self, to be debased, تَرَذَّلَ.

Debasement, *n.* Degradation from office, عَزْلٌ. The act of making vile, إِحْتِقَارٌ ـ تَرْذِيلٌ ـ ذُلٌّ ـ إِهَانَةٌ. The being made vile, إِحْتِقَارٌ ـ هَوَانٌ ـ هُونٌ ـ رَذَالَةٌ. Adulteration, as of coin, غِشٌّ ـ زَغَلٌ ـ شَقْلَةٌ.

Debasing, *a.* مُهِينٌ ـ مُرَذِّلٌ.

Debatable, *a.* فِيهِ خِلَافٌ ـ إِنْكَارُهُ مُمْكِنٌ ـ فِيهِ نِزَاعٌ.

Debate, *v.t.* To inquire into, فَحَصَ ـ بَحَثَ عَنْ ـ بَاحَثَ ـ تَفَحَّصَ عَنْ ـ عَنْ. To dispute with, جَادَلَ ـ تَنَازَعَ مَعَ ـ نَازَعَ ـ حَاوَرَ ـ رَاجَعَ ـ تَعَالَجَ مَعَ.

Debate, *v.i.* To deliberate, تَقَاوَلَ ـ تَشَاوَرَ. To dispute, تَجَادَلَ ـ إِعْتَرَضَ. To discuss, speak about, تَكَلَّمَ فِي ـ تَشَاجَرَ. They debated the matter, إِئْتَمَرُوا ٱلْأَمْرَ.

Debate, *n.* Dispute, مُنَاظَرَةٌ ـ مُشَاجَرَةٌ ـ مُجَادَلَةٌ ـ مُنَازَعَةٌ. Discussion, مُحَاوَرَةٌ ـ مُرَاجَعَةٌ ـ بَحْثٌ ـ مُبَاحَثَةٌ ـ إِئْتِمَارٌ ـ مُذَاكَرَةٌ ـ كَلَامٌ فِي. To open a —, فَتَحَ بَحْثًا. To resume a —, عَادَ إِلَى (or) رَجَعَ إِلَى) ٱلْمُبَاحَثَةِ ².

Debater, *n.* مُؤْتَمِرٌ ـ خَطِيبٌ ـ مُتَكَلِّمٌ ـ مُبَاحِثٌ.

Debating, *a.* مُبَاحِثٌ. A — society, جَمَاعَةُ مُبَاحِثِينَ.

Debauch, *n.* Debauchery, } إِنْهِمَاكٌ فِي ـ دَعَارَةٌ ـ فِسْقٌ وَفَسَادٌ ـ هَوَاسٌ فُسُوقٌ ـ ٱللَّذَّاتِ. A drunken revel, مُنَادَمَةٌ.

Debauch, *v.t.* To corrupt, أَفْسَدَ ـ أَخْبَثَ ـ أَغْوَى ـ خَسَّرَ ـ فَسَّقَ. To violate, فَضَحَ ـ هَتَكَ. He led a debauched life, إِنْهَمَكَ فِي ٱللَّذَّاتِ ـ عَاشَ عَيْشًا مُسْرِفًا.

Debauchee, *n.* فَجَّارٌ ـ فَلَاتِيٌّ ـ نَاحِشٌ ـ زَانٍ ـ فَاجِرٌ ـ فَاسِقٌ.

Debaucher, *n.* مُفْجِرٌ ـ مُفْسِدٌ ـ مُضِلٌّ. A seducer, غَاوٍ ـ مُفْضِحٌ.

Debauchment, *n.* The act of vitiating, إِفْساد; of violation, فَضْح ـ هَتْك.

Debenture, *n.* صَكّ ـ تَحْوِيل ـ تَمَسُّك *pl.* صِكاك *and* صُكُوك.

Debilitate, *v.t.* أَضْعَفَ ـ أَعْجَزَ ـ أَعْيَى ـ أَوْهَنَ ـ وَهَّنَ.

Debilitated, *part.* كَسِيح ـ نَهِيك ـ مَضْعُوف ـ مَوْهُون ـ ضَعِيف *pl.* ضِعاف *and* ضُعَفَآءُ.

Debilitating, *a.* مُضْعِف.

Debility, *n.* نَقْص قُوَّة ـ ضَعْف ـ عَجْز ـ عَيآء ـ كَسَح ـ وَهْن; of the mind, قِلَّة ٱلْعَقْلِ ـ هَبَنَّة ـ خُرْق.

Debit, *n.* ذِمامَة ـ ذِمَّة. The — side of an account, حِساب ٱلدُّيُونِ ٱلَّتِي عَلَى أَحَدٍ. To carry to one's —, قَيَّدَ فِي حِسابِ ٱلدُّيُونِ ٱلَّتِي عَلَيْهِ.

Debonair, *a.* شَلَبِيّ ـ كَيِّس ـ ظَرِيف ـ لَطِيف.

Debouch, *v.i.* خَرَجَ ² (كَما مِنْ وادٍ أَوْ مَضِيقٍ) ـ خَرَجَ ²; of water, صَبَّ ².

Debouchure, *n.* Of a river, فَمُ نَهْرٍ ـ فِراض.

Débris, *n.* Ruins, fragments, as of a house, أَنْقاض ـ بَقايا ـ خَراب ـ رَدْم; of a fortune or army, بَقايا; of a repast, حُتات ـ فَواضِل. Detritus, جُفآء.

Debt, *n.* Money owed, دَيْن *pl.* دُيُون ـ غَرامَة ـ قَرْض ـ مَغْرَم ـ مَغْرَم. Obligation, قَرْض *pl.* قُرُوض ـ لازِمَة ـ حَقّ ـ عُهْدَة. The — of nature, وَفاة ـ مَوْت. A bad —, دَيْن ضِمار ـ دَيْنٌ تَحْصِيلُهُ بَعِيدٌ. Doubtful —, دَيْنٌ تَحْصِيلُهُ مَشْكُوك. A good —, دَيْن مَأْمُون. National or public —, دَيْنُ ٱلدَّوْلَةِ ـ دُيُونٌ مِيرِيَّةٌ ـ قَرْضُ ٱلْمَمْلَكَةِ. Funded —, دُيُونٌ مُنْتَظِمَةٌ. Floating —, دُيُونٌ مُتَفَرِّقَةٌ ـ غَيْرُ مُنْتَظِمَةٍ. Debt payable, دَيْن ـ قَرْض. Debt receivable, مَطْلُوب. The balance of a —, فَضْلُ ٱلدَّيْنِ. Unified —, ٱلدَّيْنُ ٱلْمُتَّحِدُ. To transfer a —, حَوَّلَ ٱلدَّيْنَ. To be in —, عَلَيْهِ دَيْنٌ ـ مَدْيُون ـ إِسْتَدانَ. To extinguish or pay off a —, هَلَكَ ٱلدَّيْنَ ـ وَفَى ٱلدَّيْنَ *aor.* يَفِي. To acknowledge a —, أَقَرَّ بِٱلدَّيْنِ. A — is owing to him, لَهُ دَيْنٌ. I was burdened with —, رَكِبَنِي ٱلدَّيْنُ. To forgive one a —, عَفَا لَهُ عَنِ ² ٱلدَّيْنِ. To pay one a —, أَوْفَى ٱلدَّيْنَ ـ نَقَدَ لِ ². To extend the time to one, as to pay a —, مَطَلَ بِ ² ـ ماطَلَ. Debts owed to and owed by one, ٱلدُّيُونُ ٱلَّتِي لَهُ وَعَلَيْهِ. He paid the — of nature, تُوُفِّيَ.

Debtor, *n.* غَرِيم *pl.* غُرَمآء ـ مُغْرَم ـ مَدْيُون ـ دائِن. A certain creditor had two debtors, كانَ لِمُدايِنٍ مَدْيُونانِ. He is — to, bound to, ٱلْحَقُّ عَلَيْهِ أَنْ ـ مَلْزُومٌ بِ. To press a —; *see to* Dun, *v.t.*

Début, *n.* A beginning, بَدْء; of a discourse, مَطْلَع; a first stage or scene, أَوَّلُ فَصْلٍ ـ أَوَّلُ طابَقٍ.

Débutant, *n.* بادِئ.

Débutante, *n.* شارِعَة ـ بادِئَة.

Decade, *n.* عَشْر ـ عَشْرَة.

Decadence, *n.* | **Decadency**, } إِتْلاف ـ فَناء ـ مَحاق ـ زَوال.

Decagon, *n.* and *a.* ذُو عَشْرَةِ أَضْلاعٍ ـ مُعَشَّرُ ٱلْأَضْلاعِ.

Decalogue, *n.* ٱلْوَصايا ٱلْعَشْرُ ـ ٱلْعَشْرُ وَصايا ـ ٱلْعَشْرُ كَلِماتٍ.

Decamp, *v.i.* To move off, to march away, إِرْتَحَلَ ـ رَحَلَ ² ـ زَمَطَ ² ـ إِنْفَلَتَ ـ تَفَلَّتَ مِن ـ إِنْسَلَّ. To escape, عَزَلَ عَن ² ـ تَطَفَّشَ.

Decampment, *n.* تَطْفِيش ـ تَعْزِيل ـ رَحِيل ـ إِرْتِحال.

Decant, *v.t.* سَكَبَ ² (or) صَبَّ ² (or) فَرَّغَ مِنْ إِناءٍ إِلَى إِناءٍ.

Decanter, *n.* قِنِّينَة *pl.* قَنانِيّ.

Decapitate, *v.t.* ضَرَبَ عُنُقَ ² ـ رَمَى رَقَبَةَ ² ـ ضَيَّعَ رَأْسَ ².

Decapitation, *n.* ضَرْبُ ٱلرَّقَبَةِ ـ رَمْيُ ٱلرَّقَبَةِ.

Decarbonize, *v.t.* أَخْرَجَ ٱلْمادَّةَ ٱلْفَحْمِيَّةَ مِن.

Decasyllabic, *a.* ذُو عَشْرِ تَهْجِياتٍ.

Decay, *n.* Failure, wasting away, إِتْلاف ـ فَناء ـ مَحاق ـ زَوال ـ هُبُوط ـ خَراب ـ ضُمُور ـ ضُمْر ـ إِتْلاف; of the bodily powers, ضُمُور; of plants, ذَبْل ـ ذُبُول. Rottenness, as of meat, rope, *etc.*, عُفُونَة; caries, as of the bones, رِمَّة.

Decay, *v.i.* خَرِبَ ـ تَدَمَّرَ ـ بَلِيَ ² ـ فَنِيَ ² ـ فَنَى ² ـ آلَ إِلَى ٱلزَّوالِ *fut.* يَؤُولُ; of plants, ذَبَلَ ²; of meat, تَعَفَّنَ ـ عَفِنَ ² ـ عَفَنَ ²; of rope, *etc.*, عَفِنَ ². To become carious, رَمَّ ² ـ بَلِيَ ². To cause to —, أَفْنَى.

Decayed, *a.* Spoilt, مُضْمَحِلّ ـ خَراب ـ مَتْلُوف. Rotten, رُمام ـ رَمِيم. Putrid, عَفِن ـ مُعَفَّن. Withered, ذابِل.

Decaying, *a.* ذابِل ـ فانٍ.

Decease, *n.* *See* Death, *n.*

Decease, *v.i.* *See to* Die, *v.i.*

Deceased, *a.* *See* Dead. "The deceased," speaking of one dead, ٱلْمَرْحُوم.

Deceit, *n.* غَدْر ـ خِيانَة ـ خُبْث ـ مَكْر ـ خِداع ـ تَغابُن ـ غِشّ ـ كَيْد *pl.* كُيُود ـ غَبْن ـ رِئآء ـ مُرآءاة. The — or deceitfulness, as of the world, riches, *etc.*, غُرُور.

Deceitful, *a.* صاحِب ـ خائِن ـ خَدّاع ـ خادِع ـ خَبِيث ـ غَرُور ـ غَشّاش ـ غَدّار ـ حِيلَة. Beauty is —, ٱلْحُسْنُ غِشٌّ. The heart is — above all things, ٱلْقَلْبُ أَخْدَعُ مِنْ كُلِّ شَيْءٍ.

Deceitfully, *ad.* بِغِشٍّ ـ بِخُبْثٍ ـ بِخِيانَةٍ ـ بِغُرُورٍ ـ بِغَدْرٍ. To act —, خاتَلَ. To act — with, غَدَرَ بِ ².

Deceitfulness, *n.* خَدِيعَة. *See also* Deceit, *n.*

Deceive, *v.t.* To cheat, خَدَعَ ـ مَكَرَ بِ ـ راوَغَ ـ أَغْوَى ـ غَشَّ ² ـ خَتَلَ ² ـ غَبَنَ ـ غَرَّ ² ـ جَوَّنَ. To cause to err, غالَطَ ـ ضَلَّلَ ـ أَضَلَّ. To —, as with vain hopes, أَغَرَّ بِ. To — one of his expectations, خَيَّبَ ظَنَّهُ. To — one's self, خَدَعَ ـ أَضَلَّ ـ غَوَى ـ غَشَّشَ نَفْسَهُ ـ نَفْسَهُ. To be deceived, انْخَدَعَ ـ انْغَشَّ.

Deceiver, *n.* خائِن ـ مَكّار ـ مَكَرَة *pl.* ماكِر ـ خَتّال ـ رَوّاغ ـ غَشّاش ـ خَدّاع ـ دَجّال.

December, *n.* دِيسَمْبَر ـ كانُونُ ٱلْأَوَّل.

Decency, *n.* حِشْمَة ـ مُناسَبَة ـ لِياقَة ـ ٱلْمُتَوَجِّب ـ أَدَب ـ هَيْئَة.

Decent, *a.* Proper, fit, مُناسِب ـ لائِق ـ أَدَبِيّ. Moderate, مُقْتَصِد ـ مُعْتَدِل ـ مُتَوَسِّط. Sufficing for, كافٍ ل.

Decently, *ad.* كَما يَلِيقُ ـ بِأَدَبٍ ـ بِلِياقَةٍ ـ بِٱحْتِشامٍ. I never saw him — dressed, لَمْ أَرَهُ مُحْتَشِمًا مِثْلَ ٱلنّاسِ بِلِباسِهِ قَطُّ.

Deceptibility, *n.* قابِلِيَّةُ ٱلِٱخْتِيالِ.

Deceptible, *a.* مُعَرَّضٌ لِلِٱخْتِيالِ ـ يُغْبَنُ.

Deception, *n.* A fraud, حِيلَة ـ غُرُور ـ خَدِيعَة; a phantom, خَيال. *See also* Deceit, *n.*

Deceptive, *a.* غَرّار. *See also* Deceitful, *a.*

Decide, *v.t.* To determine, أَجْمَعَ ـ قَطَعَ ـ بَتَّ ² ـ فَتَحَ ـ فَصَلَ ـ أَنْهَى ـ جَزَمَ بِ ـ قَرَّرَ. To — on, عَلَى ـ اعْتَزَمَ عَلَى ـ أَجْمَعَ عَلَى ـ تَعَمَّدَ ـ أَزْمَعَ عَلَى ـ جَزَمَ عَلَى ـ اعْتَمَدَ عَلَى ـ عَزَمَ عَلَى. To — judicially, فَصَلَ ـ سَجَّلَ بِ ـ قَضَى. To — judicially, in favour of, حَكَمَ لِ ² ـ سَجَّلَ بِ. To — against, سَجَّلَ ـ حَكَمَ عَلَى ² ـ بَتَّ عَلَى ² ـ افْتاتَ عَلَى عَلَى. To —, as between two litigants, فَتَحَ بَيْنَ. I am decided on an affair, أَنا مُزْمِعٌ عَلَى أَمْرٍ. They decided, after deliberation, to ..., اِئْتَمَرُوا عَلَى *or* بِ. The Government decided to ..., قَرَّرَ رَأْيُ ٱلدَّوْلَةِ عَلَى. It was decided at the Congress, قُرِّرَ عَلَيْهِ فِي ٱلْمُؤْتَمَرِ. They formed a council and it was decided that ..., عَقَدُوا مَجْلِسًا وَٱسْتَقَرَّ رَأْيُهُمْ عَلَى أَنْ.

Decided, *a.* Firm, determined, صِنْدِيد *pl.* صَنادِيد ـ رَبِيّ ـ مُقَرَّر ـ زَمِيع. Unequivocal, مُحْكَم ـ واضِح ـ صَرِيح. Unless he appears —, إِنْ لَمْ يُظْهِرِ ٱلْعَزِيمَةَ. A — matter, أَمْرٌ مَجْزُومٌ.

Decidedly, *ad.* بَتَّةً ـ حَتْمًا ـ قَطْعًا ـ ٱلْبَتَّةَ ـ مِنْ غَيْرِ شَكٍّ ـ حَتْمًا جَزْمًا.

Deciduous, *a.* ساقِط ـ نِفاض.

Decimal, *a.* أَعْشارِيّ. Decimal fractions, كُسُورٌ أَعْشارِيَّة. Decimal arithmetic, حِسابٌ أَعْشارِيّ. Decimal numbers, عَشَرات.

Decimal, *n.* عَشَرَة *pl.* عَشَرات ـ أَعْشارِيّ ـ كَسْرٌ أَعْشارِيّ ـ أَعْشارِيٌّ مُسَلْسَل. A — point, إِشارَةٌ أَعْشارِيَّة. A recurring —, أَعْشارِيٌّ مُسَلْسَل.

Decimate, *v.t.* To take the tenth, عَشَرَ ² ـ عَشَّرَ. To kill one in ten, قَتَلَ مِنْ كُلِّ عَشَرَةٍ واحِدًا ².

Decimation, *n.* تَعْشِير ـ عَشْر. Killing one in ten, قَتْلُ نَفَرٍ مِنْ كُلِّ عَشَرَةِ أَنْفارٍ.

Decipher, *v.t.* شَرَحَ ـ فَسَّرَ ـ بَيَّنَ ـ قَرَأَ ² ـ حَلَّ ² ـ اسْتَخْرَجَ.

Decipherable, *a.* قابِلُ ٱلتَّفْسِيرِ ـ يُفَسَّرُ ـ يُسْتَخْرَجُ ـ يُحَلُّ.

Decipherer, *n.* شارِح ـ مُفَسِّر ـ مُسْتَخْرِج.

Deciphering, *n.* شَرْح ـ تَفْسِير ـ حَلّ ـ اسْتِخْراج.

Decision, *n.* Determination, قَرار ـ جَزْم ـ حَزْم ـ عَزِيمَة ـ بَتّ. Judgment, فَصْل ـ حُكْم ـ حُكُومَة. A judicial —, حُكْم *pl.* حُكُوم. The — of a consultative meeting, اِئْتِمار. A written —, سِجِلّ. A — by a Mufti, فَتْوَى. Energy, رُسُوخ ـ رَصانَة ـ زِمام. To apply for a judicial — to, اسْتَفْتَى ـ اسْتَقْضَى. According to the — of ..., بِناءً عَلَى قَرارِ. He confirmed the —, سَجَّلَ عَلَى ٱلْقَرارِ. Without coming to any —, بِدُونِ قَرارٍ عَلَى شَيْءٍ.

Decisive, *a.* حَتْمِيّ ـ بَتِّيّ ـ فاصِل ـ قاطِع ـ شافٍ. A — proof, بُرْهانٌ قاطِع. A — battle, واقِعَةٌ فاصِلَة. Decisive acts, أَعْمالٌ قَطْعِيَّة.

Decisively, *ad.* حَزْمًا ـ جَزْمًا ـ عَلَى ٱلْوَجْهِ ٱلْقَطْعِيِّ ـ بَتَّةً.

Deck, *v.t.* To adorn, حَسَّنَ ـ زَيَّنَ. To furnish, فَرَشَ ². To decorate, as with an order, قَلَّدَ ـ وَجَّهَ بِ ـ وَشَّحَ. To — with gold, حَلَّى بِٱلذَّهَبِ. To — one's self, تَزَيَّنَ ـ تَزَخْرَفَ. She decked herself with ornaments, تَحَلَّتْ.

Deck, *n.* Of a ship, ظَهْرُ مَرْكَبٍ ـ سَطْحُ مَرْكَبٍ ـ سَقِيفَةُ سَفِينَةٍ. Between decks, بَيْنَ ٱلْأَنْبارات. Flush —, ظَهْرٌ مُسَطَّح. كوگرته Fore —, ناحِيَةُ ٱلظَّهْرِ عِنْدَ مُقَدَّمِ ٱلْمَرْكَبِ. Quarter —, ناحِيَةُ ٱلظَّهْرِ عِنْدَ مُؤَخَّرِ ٱلْمَرْكَبِ. Main —, بِلاوْرَة. Orlop —, طاوُلُون. Poop —, قَصْر. On —, فَوْقُ ـ فِي ظَهْرِ ٱلْمَرْكَبِ ـ طُولُون.

Decked, *a.* Adorned, مُزَخْرَف ـ مُحَسَّن ـ مُزَيَّن.

Decker, *n.* An adorner, مُزَخْرِف ـ مُزَيِّن. Of a ship, ذُو أَنْبارٍ. A two-decker, قَپاق; three-decker, ذُو ثَلاثَةِ أَنْبارات.

Declaim, *v.i.* تَكَلَّمَ ـ خَطَبَ ² ـ بالَغَ فِي ٱلْكَلامِ.

Declaimer, *n.* مُتَكَلِّم ـ مُبَالِغ ـ خَطِيب ـ مِهَتّ ـ هَتَّات.

Declamation, *n.* مُبَالَغَةٌ فِي ٱلْكَلَامِ ـ خَطَابَة ـ شَذْوٌ.

Declamatory, *a.* هَتَّاتِيّ ـ مُبَالِغ ـ مِفَنّ.

Declarable, *a.* مِمَّا يَفُوهُ بِهِ ـ يُعْلَنُ ـ يُشْرَحُ.

Declaration, *n.* An affirmation, تَثْبِيت ـ تَقْرِير. A proclamation, ـ تَأْوِيل ـ إِيضَاح. An explanation, تَصْرِيح ـ إِشْتِهَار ـ إِعْلَان تَفْسِير. An avowal, testimony, إِقْرَار ـ شَهَادَة. A statement, description, وَصْف ـ إِفَادَة ـ قِصَّةُ أُمُورٍ. A — of war, تَصْرِيح إِعْلَانٌ بِٱلْحَرْبِ ـ إِشْهَارُ ٱلْحَرْبِ ـ بِٱلْعَدَاوَةِ.

Declarative, *a.* مُعَبِّرٌ عَن ـ مُصَرِّح ـ مُبَيِّن. Declarative of, expressing, مُدِلٌّ عَلَى ـ كَاشِفٌ عَن.

Declaratory, *a.* مُقَرِّر ـ مُثَبِّت.

Declare, *v.t.* To make plain, صَرَّحَ ب ـ بَيَّنَ. To affirm, قَرَّرَ ـ نَادَى ب ـ أَعْلَنَ. To make known, أَثْبَتَ ـ أَكَّدَ ـ صَرَّحَ ب عَرَّفَ. To testify, شَهِدَ. To explain, فَسَّرَ. To tell, state, أَفَادَ ـ قَصَّ عَلَى ـ أَخْبَرَ ب ـ حَكَى. To — judicially, حَكَمَ ب. To — war against, أَشْهَرَ ٱلْحَرْبَ ـ نَصَبَ ٱلْحَرْبَ ل. To — against, ظَهَرَ عَلَى ـ صَرَّحَ بِٱلْحَرْبِ عَلَى ـ عَلَى. To — one's self, بَيَّنَ نَفْسَهُ ـ أَشْهَرَ نَفْسَهُ.

Declaredly, *ad.* عَلَانِيَةً ـ تَقْرِيرًا ـ إِقْرَارًا. *See also* Avowedly, *ad.*

Declension, *n.* Decay, زَوَال ـ نَقْص ـ ٱنْحِطَاط ـ هُبُوط. Inflection of nouns, تَصْرِيف ـ صَرْف. A —, تَصَارِيفُ *pl.* تَصْرِيف. Declensions, مُتَصَرِّفَات. *See also* Declination, *n.*

Declinable, *a.* مُنْصَرِف ـ يَنْصَرِفُ. Not —, غَيْرُ مُنْصَرِفٍ.

Declination, *n.* A slope, leaning, حُدُور ـ صَبَب *pl.* أَصْبَاب ـ مَيْل ـ ٱنْحِرَاف. Going from a straight line, نُزُول ـ تَسَفُّل. North —, ٱلْمَيْلُ ٱلشَّمَالِيُّ. South —, إِنْصِرَاف ـ إِنْعِرَاج ٱلْمَيْلُ ٱلْجَنُوبِيُّ.

Decline, *v.i.* To lean downwards, إِنْحَدَرَ ـ إِنْصَبَّ ـ إِنْحَنَى ـ إِنْحَدَرَ ـ إِنْحَنَى. To deviate, مَالَ إِلَى تَحْتُ ـ إِلَى تَحْتُ ـ إِسْتَمَالَ. To —, as from a way, حَادَ عَن ـ عَدَلَ عَن ـ إِنْعَرَجَ عَن زَاغَ فِي ـ أَقْرَنَ عَن ـ جَارَ عَن ـ ضَلَّ عَن. To decay, يَؤُولُ *fut.* آلَ إِلَى ٱلزَّوَالِ ـ تَدَمَّرَ ـ فَنِيَ. He declined from justice, عَالَ فِي ـ مَاجَ عَنِ ٱلْحَقِّ ـ جَنِفَ عَنِ ٱلْحَقِّ عَالَ عَنِ ٱلْحَقِّ ـ ٱلْحُكْمِ. To cause to —, lean, أَمَالَ. To cause to —, deviate, أَجَارَ عَن ـ أَزَاغَ ـ زَاغَ. The sun has declined, زَالَتِ ٱلشَّمْسُ. He declined from the road, إِنْعَرَجَ عَنِ ٱلطَّرِيقِ.

Decline, *v.t.* To shun, refuse, أَضْرَبَ عَن ـ إِسْتَنْكَفَ مِن ـ أَعْرَضَ عَن ـ أَبَى. To shun, إِجْتَنَبَ ـ أَعْرَضَ عَن. To —, as of nouns, صَرَّفَ ـ أَعْرَبَ. Do not — his proposal, لَا تُعْرِضْ عَنْ عَرْضِهِ. *See also to* Refuse, *v.t.*

Decline, *n.* A leaning, مَيْل ـ إِنْحِنَاء ـ حُدُور. Decay, زَوَال ـ تَنَاقُص ـ إِسْرَاف. Consumption, the disease, سُلَّة ـ سُحَاف دَاءُ ٱلسُّلِّ. To be in a —, سُلَّ. In a —, مَسْلُول. To die in a —, مَاتَ مَسْلُولًا.

Declivitous, *a.* حَطُوط ـ مُنْصَبّ ـ هَبُوط.

Declivity, *n.* صَبَب ـ صَبِيب ـ حُدُور ـ حُطُوط ـ هُبُوط *pl.* أَصْبَاب. A slippery —, زُحْلُوقَة.

Decoct, *v.t.* To boil, طَبَخَ ـ أَغْلَى ـ غَلَى. To extract by boiling, إِسْتَخْرَجَ بِٱلْغَلَيَانِ. To digest, هَضَمَ.

Decoction, *n.* The act of boiling, غَلَيَان. A —, as of plants, *etc.*, مَاء ـ مَطْبُوخ ـ طَبِيخ.

Decollate, *v.t.* ضَيَّعَ (*or*) قَطَعَ رَأْسَ ـ ضَرَبَ عُنُقَ.

Decollation, *n.* ضَرْبُ ٱلْعُنُقِ ـ قَطْعُ ٱلرَّأْسِ.

Decolour, *v.t.* أَزَالَ ٱللَّوْنَ ـ بَيَّضَ ـ قَصَرَ.

Decolorant, *n.* شَوْرَى ـ مُبَيِّض.

Decompose, *v.t.* حَلَّ (*or*) فَكَّ ٱلتَّرْتِيبَ ـ حَلَّ.

Decompose, *v.i.* إِنْحَلَّ (*or*) إِنْفَكَّ ٱلتَّرْتِيبُ ـ تَحَلَّلَ ـ إِنْحَلَّ.

Decomposed, *a.* Dissolved, مَفْكُوكُ ٱلْأَجْزَاءِ ـ مَحْلُول. Decayed, rotten, مَفْسُود ـ مَفْسُوخ.

Decomposition, *n.* إِنْفِكَاك ـ فَكّ ـ إِنْحِلَال ـ حَلّ; of the blood, فَسَادُ ٱلدَّمِ.

Decompound, *v.t.* رَكَّبَ ثَانِيَةً ـ رَكَّبَ.

Decompound, *a.* مُرَكَّبٌ ثَانِيَةً.

Decorate, *v.t.* زَخْرَفَ ـ وَشَّحَ ـ رَقَّشَ ـ زَوَّقَ ـ زَوَّرَ ـ فَنَّ زَيَّنَ ـ حَسَّنَ; as with colours, دَبَّجَ. To — one's self, تَزَخْرَفَ. To —, as with an order, وَجَّهَ (*or*) أَنْعَمَ عَلَى) بِنِيشَانِ ٱفْتِخَارٍ.

Decoration, *n.* The act of, تَحْسِين ـ تَوْشِيح ـ تَزْيِين; especially with colours, تَدْبِيج. An embellishment, تَزْوِيقَة ـ زُخْرُف زِينَة; especially with colours, دِيبَاج. An order of honour, نِيشَانُ ٱفْتِخَارٍ ـ نِيشَانُ شَرَفٍ. Having a —, order, حَائِزٌ نِيشَانٍ ٱفْتِخَارٍ. Decorations, tracery, ٱلدَّوَاخِلُ وَٱلْخَوَارِجُ.

Decorative, *a.* زَوَّاق ـ مُحَسِّن ـ مُزَخْرِف ـ مُزَيِّن.

Decorator, *n.* As of houses, زَوَّاق. Decorators, of houses, زَوَقَة. *See also* Decorative, *a.*

Decorous, *a.* مُوَافِقٌ لِلْأَدَبِ ـ مُنَاسِب ـ لَائِق ـ حِشْمِيّ وَٱلْحِشْمَةِ.

Decorticate, *v.t.* قَشَرَ ـ حَرَمَ ـ جَرَدَ ـ عَزَمَ.

Decortication, *n.* تَقْشِير ـ تَجْرِيم ـ تَجْرِيد ـ عَزم.

Decorum, *n.* اَلنَّامُوسُ ٱلظَّاهِرُ ـ هَيْبَة ـ حِشْمَة ـ لِيَاقَة ـ أَدَب.

Decoy, *v.t.* To allure into a snare, أَوْقَعَ بِٱلْفَخِّ ـ إِصْطَادَ ـ تَصَيَّدَ. To allure, خَدَعَ ـ جَذَبَ ـ أَغْوَى.

Decoy, *n.* A lure to catch fowls, تَطْمِيعَة ـ حِيلَةٌ لِلطَّيْرِ. A — beast, أَكِيلَة ; a — bird, مَطْمَع.

Decrease, *v.t.* أَنْقَصَ ـ نَقَّصَ ـ قَلَّلَ. To — by cutting off from, غَضَّ مِن ـ حَطَّ مِنَ ٱلثَّمَنِ. To — a price, أَسْقَطَ ٱلثَّمَنَ. To lessen, صَغَّرَ.

Decrease, *v.i.* To grow less, خَفَّ ـ قَلَّ ـ نَقَصَ ـ إِنْتَقَصَ. To —, as in price or income, هَبَطَ ـ إِنْحَطَّ. The waters continue to —, كَانَتِ ٱلْمِيَاهُ تَنْقُصُ نَقْصًا مُتَوَالِيًا.

Decrease, *n.* The act of becoming less, إِنْتِقَاص ـ نُقْصَان ـ نَقْص ـ زَوَال ـ حَوْر ـ هُبُوط. The — of the moon, نُقْصَانُ ٱلْقَمَرِ.

Decree, *v.t.* To determine judicially, حَكَمَ بِ ـ قَضَى ـ سَبَقَ ـ أَتَاحَ ـ حَتَمَ بِ ـ سَجَّلَ بِ. To —, to predetermine, قَدَّرَ عَلَى ـ نَفَّذَ. To — that such and such a thing be done by one, قَطَعَ عَلَيْهِ كَذَا. To be decreed, predetermined, تَقَدَّرَ.

Decree, *n.* An edict, حَتْم ـ حُكْم ـ حُتُوم *pl.* قَضَاء *pl.* أَقْضِيَة ـ تَقْدِير ـ قَدَر. A — of a Mufti, فَتْوَى. A —, as of God, أَحْكَام. Against the — of the king, ضِدَّ أَحْكَامِ ٱلْمَلِكِ ـ أَمْرٌ. The decrees of God, اَلْمَقَادِيرُ ـ اَلْقَضَاءُ وَٱلْقَدَرُ ـ اَلتَّقْدِيرَاتُ ٱلْإِلٰهِيَّةُ. To ask one for a —, إِسْتَقْضَى.

Decreed, *a.* Ordered, مَفْرُوض ; as of God, مُقَدَّر. A thing —, مُتَاح ـ مُتَاح.

Decrement, *n.* *See* Decrease, *n.*

Decrepit, *a.* فَحْم ـ فَحُوم ـ هَرِم *pl.* هَرِمُون ـ عَاجِز ـ حَطِم ـ ضَعِيف. A — old man, هِمٌّ. A — old woman, هِمَّة.

Decrepitate, *v.i.* تَكَتَّكَ ـ فَقَّعَ. *See also to* Crackle, *v.i.*

Decrepitation, *n.* تَكْتَكَة ـ تَفْقِيع.

Decrepitness, *n.*
Decrepitude,
} فُحُومَة ـ فَحَامَة ـ هَرَم ـ فَنَاء.

Decretal, *a.* قَضَائِيٌّ ـ حُكْمِيٌّ.

Decretal, *n.* A Pope's letter, فَتْوَى مِنَ ٱلْبَابَا ـ أَمْرٌ بَابَاوِيٌّ. A book of decretals, كِتَابُ أَوَامِرَ.

Decretory, *a.* بَتِّيٌّ ـ قَاطِع ـ بَتِّيٌّ ـ حَتْمِيٌّ.

Decrial, *n.* مَذَمَّة ـ ذَمٌّ ـ تَقْبِيح ـ إِسْتِقْلَال.

Decrier, *n.* لَوَّام ـ هَاتِك ـ مُذِمٌّ ـ مُسْتَقِلّ.

Decrustation, *n.* تَقْشِير ـ تَنْزِيعُ ٱلْبَشَرَةِ.

Decry, *v.t.* بَوَّزَ ـ ذَمَّ ـ لَامَ ـ إِسْتَقَلَّ.

Decubation,
Decumbence, *n.*
Decumbency,
} ضُجُوع ـ إِنْبِطَاح.

Decumbent, *a.* مُضْطَجِع ـ مُنْضَجِع ـ مُنْبَطِح.

Decuple, *n.* Tenfold, عَشَرَةُ أَضْعَافٍ. To —, عَشَّرَ.

Decurion, *n.* اون باشى ـ قَائِدُ عَشَرَةٍ.

Decurrent, *a.* مُمْتَدُّ ٱلْعُرُوقِ إِلَى تَحْتُ.

Decussate, *v.t.* شَبَّكَ.

Dedicate, *v.t.* To set apart, أَفْرَزَ ـ خَصَّصَ. To consecrate, قَدَّسَ ـ نَذَرَ. To — to pious uses, سَبَّلَ. To vow, give, نَذَرَ ـ أَهْدَى. To —, as of a church, كَرَّسَ. To — a book to, جَعَلَ كِتَابًا عَلَى ٱسْمِ فُلَانٍ. He dedicated it to God, قَدَّسَهُ لِلّٰهِ.

Dedication, *n.* The act of setting apart, إِفْرَاض ـ تَخْصِيص. Consecration, تَكْرِيس ـ تَقْدِيس. The act of vowing, نَذْر ; as to pious uses, تَسْبِيل. Self-dedication to religious worship, تَجَرُّدٌ لِلْعِبَادَةِ. Dedication of a book, خُطْبَةٌ (*or* رِسَالَةٌ) إِلَى مَنْ جُعِلَ ٱلْكِتَابُ عَلَى ٱسْمِهِ ـ تَخْصِيصُ كِتَابٍ ـ خُطْبَةٌ (*or* رِسَالَةٌ).

Dedicator, *n.* One who consecrates, مُكَرِّس ـ مُقَدِّس. A — of a book, مَنْ يَجْعَلُ كِتَابَهُ عَلَى ٱسْمِ غَيْرِهِ.

Dedicatory, *a.* مَوْضُوعٌ عَلَى ٱسْمِ فُلَانٍ. A — epistle, رِسَالَةٌ مِنْ مُصَنِّفٍ إِلَى مَنْ جَعَلَ كِتَابَهُ عَلَى ٱسْمِهِ.

Deduce, *v t.* To infer, إِسْتَنْتَجَ ـ إِسْتَدَلَّ. To —, as problems from principles, فَرَّعَ.

Deducement, *n.* حَاصِل ـ إِسْتِدْلَال ـ نَتِيجَة.

Deducible, *a.* To be inferred from, اَلْإِسْتِدْلَالُ ـ يُسْتَنْتَجُ مِنْ ـ مِنْهُ مُمْكِنٌ.

Deducive, *a.* إِسْتِدْلَالِيٌّ.

Deduct, *v.t.* طَرَحَ ـ قَطَعَ مِن ـ شَالَ مِن ـ أَسْقَطَ.

Deduction, *n.* An inference, حَاصِل ـ إِسْتِدْلَال ـ نَتِيجَة. The act of deducting, إِسْقَاط ـ طَرْح. Abatement, as of price, هَبْط ـ هُبُوط ـ سَمَاح.

Deductive, *a.* *See* Deducible, *a.*

Deed, *n.* An act, فَعْلَة ـ فِعْل *pl.* أَفْعَال ـ عَمَل *pl.* أَعْمَال ـ صَنِيعَة *pl.* صَنَائِع ـ قَضِيَّة *pl.* قَضَايَا. A legal writing, سِجِلّ *pl.* سِجِلَّات ـ صَكّ *pl.* صُكُوك. A good —, فَعَال. Good deeds, أَفْعَالٌ خَيْرِيَّةٌ ـ أَعْمَالٌ حَسَنَةٌ ـ خَيْرَاتٌ وَحَسَنَاتٌ. Evil deeds, أَعْمَالٌ مَرْدُودَةٌ ـ أَفْعَالٌ قَبِيحَةٌ ـ آثَام ـ ذُنُوب. Illustrious deeds, أَعْمَالٌ مَبْرُورَةٌ ـ مَحَامِدُ ـ أَفْعَالٌ حَمِيدَةٌ. A title —, حُجَّة *pl.* حُجَج ـ سَنَد *pl.* سَنَدَات. To draw up a —, كَتَبَ حُجَّةً. To execute a —, أَمْضَى ٱلْحُجَّةَ وَخَتَمَ عَلَيْهَا. To witness a —, شَهِدَ بِإِمْضَاءِ حُجَّةٍ وَكَتَبَ شَهَادَتَهُ بِذٰلِكَ ـ. In —, in very —, فِي ٱلْحَقِيقَةِ ـ حَقِيقَةً. It was a good — on his part, كَانَتْ مِنْهُ فَعْلَةٌ حَسَنَةٌ.

Deem, *v.t.* حَسِبَ ـ ظَنَّ ـ خَمَّنَ.

Deep, *a.* Far down, قَعِيرٌ ـ قَعُورٌ ـ عَمِيقٌ; as of water, or the sea, غَمْرٌ ـ غَمِيرٌ ـ عَمِيقٌ ـ نَقِيرٌ. Dug, نَقِيرٌ. Obscure, مُعَمًّى ـ مُشْتَبِهٌ ـ غَلِقٌ ـ مُشْكِلٌ. Secret, خَفِيٌّ ـ مَسْتُورٌ. Sagacious, خَبِيرٌ ـ خَارِقٌ ـ مَاهِرٌ ـ نَبِيهٌ ـ شَاطِرٌ. Deep-coloured, أَدْكَنُ *fem.* دَكْنَاءُ *pl.* دُكْنٌ. Of a — red, أَحْمَرُ زَاهِرٌ. A well twenty feet —, بِئْرٌ عُمْقُهَا عِشْرُونَ قَدَمًا. A — sleep, نَوْمٌ عَمِيقٌ ـ سُبَاتٌ. A — sound, صَوْتٌ عَمِيقٌ. Deep matters, عَمَائِقُ. To be —, profound, عَمُقَ. To have a — voice, جَرِمَ.

Deep, *n.* The sea, اليَمُّ ـ الباحَةُ ـ البَحْرُ ـ العُمْقُ. An abyss, هَاوِيَةٌ. The — of night, سُكُوتُ ٱللَّيْلِ ـ نِصْفُ ٱللَّيْلِ.

Deepen, *v.t.* أَعْمَقَ ـ عَمَّقَ ـ غَوَّطَ ـ قَعَّرَ.

Deeply, *ad.* To a low depth, عَلَى عُمْقٍ. Much, greatly, جِدًّا ـ كَثِيرًا. To be — in debt, وَقَعَ تَحْتَ حِمْلِ ٱلدُّيُونِ *aor.* يَقَعُ. To be — in love, تَعَشَّقَ ـ اِنْهَمَكَ فِي ٱلْعِشْقِ. To look — into, تَبَحَّرَ فِي ـ عَمَّقَ ٱلنَّظَرَ فِي ـ تَعَمَّقَ فِي. To go — into a thing, تَعَمَّقَ فِي. He was — in love with her, عُلِّقَ بِهَا.

Deep-mouthed, *a.* صَارِخٌ ـ صَيِّتٌ ـ مُتَرَقِّعٌ.

Deep-musing, *a.* Pensive, فَكِيرٌ ـ فَكُورٌ ـ ظَنُونٌ.

Deepness, *n.* *See* Depth, *n.*

Deep-read, *a.* عَالِمٌ ـ مِفَنٌّ.

Deer, *n.* ظَبْيٌ *fem.* ظَبْيَةٌ *pl. masc.* ظِبَاءٌ *pl. fem.* ظَبْيَاتٌ ـ شَادِنٌ. A — cover, كِنَاسٌ.

Deer-stalking, *n.* صَيْدُ (*or*) خَتْلُ ٱلظِّبَاءِ.

Deface, *v.t.* To disfigure, خَرَّبَ ـ هَدَمَ ـ شَوَّهَ ـ قَبَّحَ. To erase, طَلَسَ ـ مَحَا ـ طَمَسَ.

Defacement, *n.* Disfigurement, تَقْبِيحٌ ـ خَرْبٌ ـ تَشْوِيهٌ. Erasement, تَطْلِيسٌ ـ تَطْمِيسٌ ـ مَحْوٌ.

Defacer, *n.* A disfigurer, مُقَبِّحٌ ـ مُشَوِّهٌ; an eraser, نَاسِخٌ ـ مَاحِقٌ.

Defalcation, *n.* Subtraction, حَسْمٌ ـ طَرْحٌ. Pilfering, إِسْلَالٌ ـ سِرْقَةٌ ـ اِخْتِلَاسٌ.

Defamation, *n.* فِرْيَةٌ ـ تَشْرِيرٌ ـ شَتْمٌ ـ غَمْزٌ بِ ـ نَقْرَى ـ طَعْنٌ فِي ٱلْعِرْضِ ـ قَذْفٌ ـ اِفْتِرَاءٌ.

Defamatory, *a.* مُفْرٍ ـ نَمِيمِيٌّ ـ هَتْكِيٌّ ـ مُفْتَرٍ عَلَى ـ نَمٌّ ـ قَذْفِيٌّ.

Defame, *v.t.* هَتَكَ ـ غَمَزَ بِ ـ أَقْمَزَ فِي ـ نَقَرَ ـ شَرَّرَ ـ هَتَرَ ـ اِفْتَرَى عَلَى ـ هَتَّرَ ـ نَمَّ ـ عَيَّرَ ـ أَقْرَشَ بِ ـ جَرَّسَ بِ ـ طَعَنَ فِي عِرْضِهِ ـ. To be defamed, اِنْهَتَكَ ـ تَعَيَّرَ.

Defamer, *n.* لَمَّازٌ ـ نَمٌّ *pl.* أَنِمَّاءُ ـ شَتَّامٌ ـ هَمَّازٌ ـ هَامِزٌ.

Default, *n.* Failure, قُصُورٌ ـ نَقِيصَةٌ. Omission, إِهْمَالٌ ـ فَوْتٌ ـ فَوَاتٌ ـ خَلَلٌ ـ اِسْتِنْكَافٌ. Default of appearance, عَدَمُ ظُهُورٍ ـ عَدَمُ حُضُورٍ. In — of payment, إِنْ لَمْ يُوَفِّ. To allow judgment to go by —, سَيَّبَ دَعْوَاهُ لِلْقَضَاءِ بِدُونِ مُحَاجَجَةٍ. Judgment by —, حُكْمٌ غِيَابِيٌّ.

Defaulter, *n.* A criminal, مُذْنِبٌ ـ خَاطِئٌ *pl.* خُطَاةٌ. An absentee, غَائِبٌ. One who fails to account for money, نَاهِبُ مَالٍ ـ مُخْتَلِسُ ٱلدَّرَاهِمِ ـ رَجُلٌ مُسِلُّ ٱلْمَالِ.

Defeasible, *a.* مُمْكِنٌ إِبْطَالُهُ ـ قَابِلُ ٱلنَّسْخِ.

Defeat, *n.* Overthrow, كَسْرَةٌ ـ اِنْكِسَارٌ ـ هَزِيمَةٌ. Frustration, خَيْبَةٌ ـ تَخْيِيبٌ ـ عَنَاقٌ. The bringing to nought, تَبْطِيلٌ.

Defeat, *v.t.* To overcome, فَلَّلَ ـ أَنْجَحَ بِ ـ كَسَرَ ـ غَلَبَ ـ عَلَى ـ اِنْتَصَرَ عَلَى. To rout, هَزَمَ. To frustrate, مَنَعَ ـ خَيَّبَ ـ عَوَّقَ عَنْ ـ لَجَّ فَحَجَّهُ ـ فَحَجَّ. To — in litigation, لَجَّ فَحَجَّهُ ـ غَلَبَ فِي ٱلْمُحَاجَجَةِ. To be defeated, overcome, اِنْفَلَّ ـ اِفْتَلَّ ـ اِنْكَسَرَ ـ اِنْغَلَبَ.

Defecate, *v.t.* صَفَّى ـ أَصْفَى.

Defecation, *n.* تَخْلِيصٌ ـ تَصْفِيَةٌ.

Defecated, *a.* مُصَفًّى.

Defect, *n.* Deficiency, خَلَلٌ ـ وَكْسٌ ـ قُصُورٌ ـ نَقْصٌ ـ نَقِيصَةٌ ـ نُقْصَانٌ. A flaw, عَيْبٌ *pl.* عُيُوبٌ ـ عَوَارٌ. An error, زَلَّةٌ ـ غَلَطٌ ـ سَقَطٌ *pl.* أَسْقَاطٌ ـ غَلْطَةٌ. To hide a —, as in the sale of an article, دَلَّسَ فِي ٱلْبَيْعِ ـ تَدَلَّسَ. He concealed the — in selling, دَلَّسَ فِي ٱلْبَيْعِ.

Defection, *n.* Failure, خَيْبَةٌ ـ فَشَلٌ ـ خُسْرَانٌ. Abandonment, تَخْلِيَةٌ ـ اِرْتِدَادٌ عَنْ ـ تَرْكٌ. Revolt, طُغْيَانٌ ـ عِصْيَانٌ ـ تَمَرُّدٌ.

Defective, *a.* Imperfect, قَاصِرٌ ـ غَيْرُ كَامِلٍ ـ نَاقِصٌ. Having flaws, عَائِبٌ ـ مَعْيُوبٌ ـ مُعَوَّرٌ ـ سَقِيمٌ. To be —, have flaws, سَقِمَ ـ عَابَ *aor.* يَعِيبُ. To render —, عَيَّبَ ـ وَكَسَ *fut.* يَكِسُ. A — verb, فِعْلٌ نَاقِصٌ.

Defectively, *ad.* بِعَدَمِ كَمَالٍ ـ بِنُقْصَانٍ ـ بِقُصُورٍ.

Defectiveness, *n.* *See* Defect, *n.*

Defence, *n.* Protection, مُحَامَاةٌ ـ حِمَايَةٌ ـ عِصْمَةٌ ـ صِيَانَةٌ. Resistance, دِفَاعٌ ـ مُقَاوَمَةٌ ـ مُعَانَّةٌ ـ مُدَافَعَةٌ ـ مُحَافَظَةٌ. Vindication, بَرَاءَةٌ ـ تَبْرِئَةٌ ـ جَوَابٌ. A plea, pleading, اِحْتِجَاجٌ. A fortification, حِصْنٌ *pl.* حُصُونٌ ـ تَحْصِينٌ. In — of, ذَبًّا عَنْ. A — against the cold, صِيَانَةٌ عَنِ ٱلْبَرْدِ ـ لِحِمَايَتِهِ ـ مُحَامَاةٌ عَنْ دَفِيٌّ. To make a —, as to justify one's self, اِحْتَجَّ. The prisoner's —, جوابُ ٱلْمُذْنِبِ. To appear for the —, تَوَكَّلَ لِلْمُحاماةِ ٱلْمُدَّعَى عَلَيْهِ. To call a witness for the —, إِسْتَشْهَدَ شاهِدًا مِنْ طَرَفِ ٱلْمُدَّعَى عَلَيْهِ. They heard his —, إِسْتَمَعُوا ٱحْتِجاجَهُ.

Defenceless, *a.* Unprotected, غَيْرُ مَحْمِيّ. Unarmed, غَيْرُ مُسَلَّحٍ. Unfortified, غَيْرُ مُحَصَّنٍ. Harmless, غَيْرُ مُضِرٍّ.

Defend, *v.t.* To protect, حاطَ ب – صانَ-عَن – عَصَمَ – حَمَى – أَحْمَى. To fortify, حَصَّنَ. To fight for, to resist, قاوَمَ – قاتَلَ عَن – دافَعَ. To vindicate, بَرَّرَ – أَبْرَأَ. To advance pleas against, إِحْتَجَّ عَلَى. To —, protect, one's self, تَحَرَّمَ – تَحَمَّى – إِعْتَصَمَ – تَمَنَّعَ.

Defend, *v.i.* To make opposition, ضادَدَ – قاوَمَ; to reply to, جاوَبَ.

Defendable, *a.* *See* Defensible, *a.*

Defendant, *n.* The party accused, المُدَّعَى عَلَيْهِ – المُجِيبُ. *See also* Defender, *n.*

Defended, *a.* مَعْصُوم – مَحْمِيّ – مَنْصُور – مَحْرُوس – مَصُون.

Defender, *n.* A protector, مُحامٍ – حامٍ – عاصِم. One who resists, مُقاوِم – مُدافِع. A supporter, ظَهْر – ظَهِير – خَفِير. A guard, غَفر – حارِس – حافِظ.

Defense, *n.* *See* Defence, *n.*

Defensible, *a.* That may be protected, المُحاماةُ عَنْهُ مُمْكِنَةٌ – مُحافَظَتُهُ مُمْكِنَةٌ. Justifiable, مَعْذُور – يُبَرَّأُ – مُبَرَّأٌ – إِثْباتُ صَواب – حَقِّهِ مُمْكِنٌ.

Defensive, *a.* Protecting, حامٍ – مَحْمِيّ. Repelling, دافِع – دِفاعِيّ – دَفّاع. Defensive armour, زَرَد – عُدَّةٌ مُحامِيَةٌ. A — alliance, إِتِّفاقٌ دَفّاعِيّ. Defensive operations, تَدابِيرُ دَفّاعِيَّةٌ. Defensive measures, أَسْبابٌ دِفاعِيَّةٌ. Defensive war, مُحارَبَةٌ دِفاعِيَّةٌ. On the —, فِي حالَةِ ٱلدِّفاعِ. He will keep on the — to the end, يَسْتَمِرُّ عَلَى ٱلدِّفاعِ إِلَى ٱلنِّهايَةِ.

Defensive, *n.* A safeguard, مُحافَظَة – صِيانَة. To act on the —, قامَ بِٱلدِّفاعِ[2].

Defensively, *ad.* بِٱلدِّفاعِ وَٱلْمُحافَظَةِ.

Defer, *v.t.* To postpone, تَعَوَّقَ – طاوَلَ – جارَّ – آنَى – سَوَّفَ – أَبْطَأَ – أَمْهَلَ – أَبْقَى-إِلَى – عَن. He deferred paying him the debt, أَجَّرَهُ ٱلدَّيْنَ. Don't — to pay the debt, لا تُؤَخِّرْ عَنِ ٱلْوَفاءِ. Hope deferred maketh the heart sick, الرَّجاءُ ٱلْمُماطَلُ يُمْرِضُ ٱلْقَلْبَ.

Defer, *v.i.* To submit to, رَعَى – إِسْتَمَعَ ل – قَبِلَ – أَطاعَ ل.

Deference, *n.* مُهاوَدَة – رِعايَة – إِمْتِثالٌ ب – قُبُول. To pay — to, تَهَشَّمَ – هَشَّمَ. In — to, إِكْرامًا ل – مُراعاةً ل.

Deferent, *a.* ناقِلٌ وَحامِلٌ.

Deferential, *a.* صاحِبُ رِعايَةٍ – خاشِع – مُذْعِن.

Deferentially, *ad.* بِمُهاوَدَةٍ – بِإِذْعانٍ – بِرِعايَةٍ.

Defiance, *n.* A challenge, طَلَبُ شَرٍّ – طَلَبٌ لِلْمِيدانِ – بِمُعانَدَةٍ – إِسْتِدْعاءٌ لِلْمِيدانِ. Contempt, شَتْم – تَعْيِير. Out of —, بِخِلافٍ – مِنْ غَيْرِ مُراعاةٍ. In — of, تَمَرُّدًا. To set at —, عانَدَ – خالَفَ. *See also* to Defy, *v.t.*

Deficience, *n.* } A falling short, نَقِيصَة – نُقْصان – نَقْص – عَدَمُ وُجُودٍ – عَدَمُ كِفايَةٍ.
Deficiency, } Want, حَوْر – نُقْصانٌ كُلِّيٌّ. A total —, عَدَم – حَوْبَة. Stupidity, خُرْق – عَوَز. We have recourse to God for preservation from — after redundance, نَعُوذُ بِاللّٰهِ مِنَ ٱلْحَوْرِ بَعْدَ ٱلْكَوْنِ. *See also* Defect, *n.*

Deficient, *a.* Falling short, ناقِص. Wanting in, without, عَدِيم – نَقَصَ[2]. Stupid, أَخْرَق. Weak, ضَعِيف. To be —, إِنْتَقَصَ – دُونَ. To be — in, عَدِمَ – عَوِزَ. More — than, أَنْقَصُ مِن.

Deficit, *n.* Amount short, مَبْلَغٌ ناقِص; of revenue, نُقْصانٌ فِي ٱلْإِيرادِ. To cover a —, سَدَّ ٱلنُّقْصانَ[2]. To leave a —, نَقَصَ ٱلْإِيرادَ[2].

Defier, *n.* A challenger, بادٍ – مُدَّعٍ. A contemner, مُعَيِّر.

Defile, *v.t.* To pollute, أَفْسَدَ – نَجَّسَ – دَنَّسَ. To dirty, لَطَّخَ – لَوَّثَ – وَسَّخَ. To ravish, أَفْسَدَ – أَوْقَعَ – فَضَحَ. To debauch, أَخْبَثَ.

Defile, *v.i.* To march in file, سارُوا صَفًّا – سارُوا طابُورًا.

Defile, *n.* A narrow pass, بُوغاز – مَضِيق – خانِق.

Defilement, *n.* The act of defiling, إِفْساد – تَنْجِيس – تَدْنِيس. The state of being defiled, خَباثَة – نَجاسَة – دَناسَة – فَضِيحَة.

Defiler, *n.* مُفْسِد – مُدَنِّس – مُفَسِّد.

Definable, *a.* تَعْبِيرُهُ مُمْكِنٌ – قابِلُ ٱلْوَصْفِ – تَعْرِيفُهُ مُمْكِنٌ – مِمّا يُوصَفُ.

Define, *v.t.* To limit, حَدَّدَ. To —, of a word, حَدَّ. To explain, عَبَّرَ – فَسَّرَ – أَوْضَحَ – وَصَفَ *fut.* يَصِفُ. To appoint, عَيَّنَ.

Defined, *a.* Limited, مَحْدُود. Explained, مُفَسَّر – مَوْصُوف. Appointed, مُعَيَّن.

Definite, *a.* Having fixed limits, مَحْدُود. Certain, مَحْكُوم – مُحَقَّق – مُقَرَّر – مُؤَكَّد – مَعْلُوم. Fixed, appointed, مُعَيَّن – مَعْهُود. The — article, لامُ ٱلتَّعْرِيفِ – أَداةُ ٱلتَّعْرِيفِ.

Definitely, *ad.* Precisely, بِتَأْكِيدٍ — بِٱلتَّحْقِيقِ — بَتَّةً — إِحْكَامًا — بِٱلتَّحْدِيدِ.

Definiteness, *n.* بَيَان — تَبْيِين — تَبَيُّن — تَصْرِيح.

Definition, *n.* وَصْف — تَعْرِيف — تَحْدِيد.

Definitive, *a.* Determinate, قَطْعِيّ — شَافٍ — حَتْمِيّ — بَتِّيّ.

Definitively, *ad.* بَتَّةً — قَطْعًا — جَزْمًا — حَتْمًا جَزْمًا. Should the Government decide on the Eastern question —, إِذَا كَانَتِ ٱلدَّوْلَةُ تَجْزِمُ بِبَتِّ ٱلْمَسْأَلَةِ ٱلشَّرْقِيَّةِ.

Definitiveness, *n.* بَتّ — إِثْبَات — حَتْم — جَزْم.

Deflect, *v.t.* حَرَّفَ 2 — عَطَفَ عَن — حَرَّفَ.

Deflect, *v.i.* ٱنْحَرَفَ — ٱنْعَطَفَ — عَدَلَ عَن. The road deflected, عَدَلَ ٱلطَّرِيقُ.

Deflection, *n.* تَحْرِيف — ٱنْحِرَاف — ٱنْعِطَاف — ٱنْحِطَاط — عَدْل — عُدُول.

Defloration, *n.* Violation of chastity, طَمْث — عَزْر — إِزَالَةُ ٱلْبَكَارَةِ.

Deflour, *v.t.* } **Deflower**, } طَمَثَ 2 — ٱبْتَكَرَ ٱلْجَارِيَةَ — ٱبْتَسَرَ ٱلْجَارِيَةَ — عَزَرَ — أَزَالَ بَكَارَتَهَا.

Defluxion, *n.* نَزْلَة.

Defoliation, *n.* نَفْضُ ٱلْأَوْرَاقِ — سَقْطُ ٱلْأَوْرَاقِ — إِسْقَاطُ ٱلْأَوْرَاقِ.

Deform, *v.t.* شَقَّحَ — قَبَّحَ — عَكَّسَ — سَمَّجَ — وَحَّشَ — بَشَّعَ — شَوَّهَ. *See also to* Deface, *v.t.*

Deformation, *n.* The act of, شَقْح — تَقْبِيح — تَوْحِيش — تَعْكِيس.

Deformed, *a.* شَقِيح — بَشِيع — مَمْسُوخ — مَسْخُوط — بَشِيع. A — countenance, وَجْهٌ كَزٌّ — قَبِيحُ ٱلْوَجْهِ — قَبِيح.

Deformity, *n.* Ugliness, شَقَاحَة — وَحْش — بَشَاعَة — سَمَاجَة — قَبَاحَة. An unnatural shape, سَقَط.

Defraud, *v.t.* ضَامَ — ظَلَمَ — ٱسْتَضَامَ — مَكَرَ بِ 2 — غَبَنَ — غَدَرَ بِ 2. He defrauded him of his right, بَخَسَهُ حَقَّهُ — ظَلَمَهُ حَقَّهُ. *See also to* Cheat, *v.t.*

Defrauded, *a.* مَضِيم — مُسْتَضَام — مَغْبُون — مَظْلُوم.

Defrauder, *n.* ضَائِم — غَدَّار — غِدِّير — مَكَّار — ظَالِم — غَابِن.

Defraudment, *n.* غَبْن — غَدْر — ضَيْم — ظُلْم — غَبْن.

Defray, *v.t.* أَوْفَى — حَمَلَ ٱلْكُلْفَةَ — دَفَعَ ٱلْمَصْرُوفَ — قَامَ بِٱلنَّفَقَةِ 2.

Defrayer, *n.* حَامِلُ ٱلْكُلْفَةِ — دَافِعُ ٱلْمَصْرُوفِ.

Defrayment, *n.* وَفَاء — دَفْعُ ٱلْمَصْرُوفِ.

Deft, *a.* Dextrous, مَاهِر — صَاحِبُ مِهْنَةٍ — دَرِب — شَاطِر.

Deftly, *ad.* بِمِهْنَةٍ — مَهَارَةً — بِدِرَايَةٍ — بِغَايَةِ ٱلْإِتْقَانِ — بِشَطَارَةٍ.

Deftness, *a.* مِهْنَة — مَهَارَة — دُرَايَة — شَطَارَة.

Defunct, *a.* and *n.* Dead, مَيِّت — مُتَوَفَّى — مَرْحُوم. *See also under* Dead, *a.*

Defy, *v.t.* To challenge, دَعَا لِلْقِتَالِ 2 — ٱسْتَدْعَى لِلْمَيْدَانِ. To brave, جَسَرَ عَلَى 2. To contemn, عَيَّرَ — ٱسْتَهْزَأَ بِ — هَزِئَ بِ. He defied the army of the enemy, عَيَّرَ جُنُودَ ٱلْعَدُوِّ.

Degeneracy, *n.* } **Degenerateness**, } دَنَاءَة — ٱنْحِرَافٌ عَنِ ٱلصَّلَاحِ — فَسَادُ ٱلْحَالِ — عَنْ نَجَابَةِ ٱلْأَصْلِ — ٱنْفِسَاد — تَلَف — ٱنْحِطَاط — تَغْيِيرٌ عَنْ طِيبَةِ ٱلْأَصْلِ.

Degenerate, *a.* } **Degenerous**, } مُنْحَرِفٌ عَنْ طِيبَةِ ٱلْأَصْلِ. Mean, دَنِيء — خَسِيس — حَقِير — رَكِيك.

Degenerate, *v.i.* تَغَيَّرَ عَنْ طِيبَةِ ٱلْأَصْلِ — ٱنْفَسَدَ — ٱنْحَرَفَ عَنْ — نَجَابَةِ ٱلْأَصْلِ. To — into, turn into, ٱنْقَلَبَ — آلَ إِلَى *aor.* يَؤُولُ. He has degenerated, ٱنْحَطَّ عَنْ قِيمَتِهِ ٱلسَّابِقَةِ (*or* عَنْ مَقَامِهِ ٱلسَّابِقِ).

Deglutition, *n.* بَلْع — ٱبْتِلَاع.

Degradation, *n.* The act of depriving, as of rank, إِسْقَاطٌ مِن — حَطٌّ مِن — عَزْل — تَعْزِيل. Making base, تَرْذِيل — تَخْسِيس. Baseness, رَذَالَة — خَسَاسَة — عَيْب — عَار. A wearing away, سَحْق — نَهْك.

Degrade, *v.t.* To reduce in office, *etc.*, حَطَّ عَنِ ٱلْمَقَامِ 2 — أَسْقَطَ — وَضَعَ مِن *fut.* يَضَعُ — عَزَلَ. To debase, رَذَّلَ — خَسَّسَ. To dishonour, أَخْزَى — عَيَّبَ. To — one by speech, ٱغْتَمَطَ — غَمَطَ. To — one's self, تَرَذَّلَ — تَذَلَّلَ.

Degraded, *a.* Lowered in rank, *etc.*, مُنْحَطٌّ عَن — مُنَزَّلٌ مِن — مَعْزُول. Low, vile, سَاقِط — رَذِيل — سُفْلِيّ — ذَلِيل — سَفِيل.

Degrading, *a.* مُرَذِّل — مُهِين — خَازٍ — فَضَّاح.

Degree, *n.* A step, دَرَجَة *pl.* دَرَجَات. Honour, dignity, مَرْتَبَة *pl.* مَرَاتِب — رُتْبَة *pl.* رُتَب. Station, مَنْزِلَة — شَأْن *pl.* شُؤُون. Quantity, مِقْدَار — قَدْر. An astronomical —, دَرَجَة *pl.* دَرَجَات. A — for learning, رُتْبَةٌ لِلْعِلْمِ. To take one's —, ٱسْتَحْصَلَ عَلَى رُتْبَةٍ. Of high —, صَاحِبُ حَسَبٍ وَنَسَبٍ — مِنْ رُتْبَةِ ٱلْأَرْبَابِ. Of higher —, أَعْظَمُ دَرَجَةً. Of low —, سُفْلِيّ — فَقِير. In the highest —, لِلْغَايَةِ — بَتَّةً. In some —, نَوْعًا — فِي بَعْضِ ٱلْأَحْوَالِ. By degrees, دَرَجَات — دَرَجَةً — عَلَى ٱلتَّدْرِيجِ — دَرَجَةً دَرَجَةً — شَيْئًا فَشَيْئًا.

Dehort, *v.t.* لَفَتَ عَن — نَصَحَ عَن — رَدَّ عَن 2 — صَرَفَ عَن.

Dehortation, *n.* نَصْحٌ عَن — رَدٌّ عَن.

Dehortatory, *a.* نَاصِحٌ عَن — مُصَرِّفٌ عَن.

Deification, *n.* تَأْلِيه.

Deify, *v.t.* أَلَّهَ.

Deign, *v.i.* To condescend, تَلَطَّفَ ـ تَفَضَّلَ ـ تَنَزَّلَ.

Dei Gratia, بِعِنايَةِ ٱللّٰهِ تَعالَى.

Deism, *n.* الاِعْتِقادُ بِوُجودِ ٱللّٰهِ فَقَطْ وَإِنْكارُ ٱلْوَحْيِ وَٱلْأَدْيانِ جَمِيعًا.

Deist, *n.* مُعْتَقِدٌ بِوُجودِ ٱللّٰهِ فَقَطْ وَناكِرُ ٱلْوَحْيِ وَجَمِيعِ ٱلْأَدْيانِ.

Deistical, *a.* مُتَعَلِّقٌ بِٱلاِعْتِقادِ بِوُجودِ ٱللّٰهِ فَقَطْ مَعَ إِنْكارِ ٱلْوَحْيِ وَجَمِيعِ ٱلْأَدْيانِ.

Deity, *n.* God, ٱللّٰهُ ـ رَبُّ ٱلْعالَمِينَ. A fabulous god, آلِهَة *or* إِلٰهٌ *pl.* آلِهَةٌ. A goddess, إِلاهَة. The Godhead, الإِلاهَة ـ الأُلُوهِيَّة ـ اللّاهُوت.

Deject, *v.t.* To sadden, أَهَمَّ ـ هابَطَ ـ أَحْزَنَ ـ أَغَمَّ ـ أَكْأَبَ. To discourage, أَخْمَدَ ـ ـ كَسَرَ عَزْمَهُ ـ خَمَّدَ.

Dejected, *a.* Downcast, كَئِيب ـ مُهْتَبِط ـ مَحْزُون ـ مُكَدَّر ـ مَغْمُوم ـ مُكْتَئِب. To be —, إِنْقَطَعَ قَلْبُهُ ـ ـ كَئِبَ ـ اِهْتَبَطَ.

Dejectedly, *ad.* بِٱنْقِطاعِ ٱلْقَلْبِ ـ بِغَمٍّ ـ بِحُزْنٍ ـ بِٱهْتِباطٍ.

Dejectedness, *n.* } كَآبَة ـ حُزْن ـ غَمّ ـ عَدَمُ ٱنْبِساطٍ ـ عَدَمُ
Dejection, } نَشاطٍ.

De jure, ad. شَرْعًا ـ بِٱلْإِرْثِ وَٱلْإِسْتِحْقاقِ.

Delator, *n.* غَمّاز ـ نَمّام.

Delay, *v.t.* To retard, عَقَّبَ ـ عَوَّقَ ـ أَخَّرَ ـ أَلْبَثَ ـ لَبَّثَ ـ أَعاقَ. To defer, أَبْقَى ـ حَذَفَ ـ إِلَى غَيْرِ وَقْتٍ ـ ـ أَنَّى ـ آنَى ـ تَرَكَ ـ إِلَى.

Delay, *v.i.* تَلَبَّثَ ـ تَراخَى ـ أَبْطَأَ ـ جارَ ـ ـ لَبِثَ ـ قَصَّرَ فِي ـ تَمَهَّلَ فِي. To be tardy in, تَوانَى عَنْ ـ ـ أَنَى ـ تَعَوَّقَ ـ تَراخَى. The rain delayed, تَراخَى ٱلْمَطَرُ. He delayed paying me my due, عَقَّبَنِي حَقِّي. I will not — to return, لا أَلْبِثُ أَنْ أَعُودَ.

Delay, *n.* A stop, فَتْرَة ـ تَوَقُّف. Postponement, إِبْقاء ـ تَأْخِير ـ إِيناء ـ تَطْوِيل. The being tardy, بُطْء ـ تَعَوُّق ـ تَوانٍ ـ تَأَخُّر. Space of time, مُطاوَلَة ـ مُهْلَة. Delay allowed for paying a debt, مُدَّة قانُونِيَّة ـ مُهْلَة ـ مِطال ـ مُماطَنَة. Legal —, مُدَّة قانُونِيَّة. Without —, بِدُونِ إِمْهالٍ. To grant — to, طَوَّلَ عَلَى ـ أَمْهَلَ ـ فِي ـ أَمَدَّ ـ طَوَّلَ ـ فِي. To ask for —, إِسْتَمْهَلَ. With the least possible —, أَوَّلَ ما يَكُونُ.

Delectable, *a.* بَهِيّ ـ لَذِيذ ـ مُطْرِب ـ نَزِه ـ نَعِيم ـ أَنِيق.

Delectable things, مُشْتَهِيات.

Delectably, *ad.* بِنِعْمَةٍ ـ بِسُرُورٍ ـ بِحَظٍّ.

Delectation, *n.* سُرُور ـ تَمَتُّع ـ أُنْس ـ نِعْمَة ـ حَظّ.

Delegate, *v.t.* نَصَبَ ـ عَيَّنَ ـ وَكَّلَ ـ نَوَّبَ ـ وَفَّدَ ـ فَوَّضَ ـ اِسْتَنابَ.

Delegate, *n.* } مُتَوَكِّل ـ نُوّاب *pl.* نائِب ـ رَسُول ـ وافِد
Delegated, *a.* } ـ مَأْمُورِيَّة. Delegated power, وُكَلاء *pl.* وَكِيل. وَكالَة. To be — on the part of . . . , ناب عن.

Delegation, *n.* The act of giving authority to another, تَوْفِيد ـ تَوْكِيل. Those delegated, المُتَوَكِّلُونَ ـ الوُكَلاء ـ نِيابَة ـ وَكالَة.

Delete, *v.t.* أَزالَ ـ مَحا ـ ـ نَسَخَ ـ ـ طَمَسَ.

Deleterious, *a.* مُتْلِف ـ مُهْلِك. Deadly, مُضِرّ ـ ضارّ; of climate, وَبِيل.

Deleteriousness, *n.* Harmfulness, أَذِيَّة ـ ضامَة ـ مَضَرَّة; of climate, وَبال ـ وَبَلَة.

Delf, *n.* The ware, كاشِيّ ـ تَجَمِّي.

Deliberate, *v.i.* To — on attentively, نَظَرَ فِي ـ تَبَصَّرَ ـ مَلِيًّا ـ أَبْرَمَ ـ تَأَمَّلَ فِي ـ اِقْتَصَدَ. To — with, take counsel of, إِسْتَشارَ ـ ذاكَرَ ـ تَشاوَرَ مَعَ. They deliberated together, تَفاوَضُوا. They deliberated on the matter, إِئْتَمَرُوا ٱلْأَمْرَ.

Deliberate, *a.* Circumspect, مُتَنَبِّه ـ بَيِّن. Considered, حاتِك ـ قَصْدِيّ ـ عَنْ قَصْدٍ ـ مُلاحَظ ـ مُتَأَمَّل. Designed, قَصْدِيّ ـ عَنْ قَصْدٍ ـ مُلاحَظ. Slow, بَطِيء.

Deliberately, *ad.* Intentionally, عَنْ قَصْدٍ ـ بِٱلاِخْتِيارِ ـ تَعَمُّدًا ـ بِتَأَنٍّ ـ عَلَى مَهَلٍ ـ رُوَيْدًا ـ عَلَى مُكْثٍ. Slowly, قَصْدًا ـ عَمْدًا. To act —, إِسْتَأْنَى ـ تَأَنَّى.

Deliberateness, *n.* } Slowness, أَناة ـ بَطاءة ـ تَأَنٍّ. Mutual
Deliberation, } consultation, مُشاوَرَة ـ مُفاوَضَة ـ إِئْتِمار ـ مُذاكَرَة ـ مُلاحَظَة ـ مُطالَعَة. Design, إِقْتِصاد ـ قَصْد. To act with —, تَأَنَّى. To take into —, باحَثَ.

Deliberative, *a.* مُتَشاوِر ـ مُشاوِر. A — assembly, مَجْلِس ـ دِيوانُ مَشْوَرَةٍ ـ ٱئْتِمار. *See also* Deliberate, *a.*

Delicacy, *n.* That which delights the taste, طَعْم ـ ذَوْق ـ لَذَّة. Minute accuracy, دِقَّة ـ ضَبْطٌ كُلِّيٌّ. Softness of manner, ظَرافَة ـ لَطافَة. Fineness of texture, رَفاعَة ـ رِقَّة. Modesty, حُسْن ـ حَياء ـ أَدَب. Weakness, ضُعْف ـ رِقَّة ـ نَحافَة. Tenderness, رِفْق ـ رِقَّةُ قَلْبٍ ـ حِنَّة ـ شَفَقَة. Delicacies, of meats, مَطائِب ـ طَعامٌ فاخِرٌ لَذِيذٌ. Fragility, رِخْوَة ـ رِقَّة. There is neither sweetness nor — in her countenance, ما عَلَى وَجْهِها حَلاوَةٌ وَلا طُلاوَةٌ.

Delicate, *a.* Dainty, tasty, طَيِّب ـ لَذِيذ ـ طَعِم. Fine, light, رَفِيع ـ خَفِيف. Accurate, مُدَقِّق. Soft, of manner, لَطِيف ـ أَدِيب ـ ظَرِيف. Weak, ضَعِيف ـ عَلِيل ـ نَحِيف. Fine, of texture, رَفِيع ـ ناعِم. Fragile, easily broken, رَخْو ـ مُسْتَرْخٍ.

Fastidious, مُتَأَنِّق ـ مُتَرَفِّهٌ وَمُتَنَعِّمٌ. A —, soft, life, فَنَق ـ عَيْشٌ مُفانِقٌ. A — matter, أَمْرٌ دَقِيقٌ. To be —, weak, عَلَّ ـ ءِ إِعْتَلَّ. To be —, fastidious, تَأَنَّقَ.

Delicately, *ad.* Neatly, بِٱلتَّدْقِيقِ ـ بِدِقَّةٍ. Softly, kindly, بِظَرافَةٍ ـ بِلَطافَةٍ. Tenderly, بِرِفْقٍ. Effeminately, بِدَلالٍ ـ بِٱلتَّأَنُّقِ ـ بِٱلتَّفْنِيقِ. To bring up —, فَنَّقَ. To live —, تَنَعَّمَ ـ ٢ أَكَلَ ٱلْمَآكِلَ ٱلْفاخِرَةَ. To feed —, أَفْنَقَ ـ تَفَنَّقَ ـ تَناعَمَ ـ مُتَرَفِّهًا.

Delicious, *a.* Of taste, لَذِيذ; of smell, شَمُوم ـ مُقَتَّر ـ عَذِق ـ عَطِر; of situation or prospect, نَزِيه ـ نَهِيج ـ نَزِه. Attractive, desirable, شَهِيٌّ ـ مُشْتَهًى. Sweet, as of a voice, حُلْوٌ ـ رَقِيق; of a life, نَعِيم ـ تَرِف. To be —, لَذَّ ـ ءِ طابَ *aor.* يَطِيبُ. It was — to him, طابَتْ بِهِ نَفْسُهُ ـ لَذَّ بِهِ.

Deliciously, *ad.* بِحَلاوَةٍ ـ بِتَنَعُّمٍ ـ بِكَمالِ ٱللَّذَّةِ.

Deliciousness, *n.* Of flavour, لَذَّة; of fragrance, فَوْغَة ـ فَغْمَة ـ رائِحَة ـ عِطْر; of life, مَحْظُوظِيَّة ـ بَحْبَحَة ـ سُرُور ـ حَظٌّ; of situation, نُزْهَة ـ بَهْجَة; of manner, *etc.*, طَلاوَة. Sweetness, حَلاوَة.

Delight, *n.* سُرُور ـ تَمَتُّع ـ غِبْطَة ـ نَعِيمَة ـ حُبُور ـ قُرَّةُ عَيْنٍ ـ إِنْبِساط ـ فَرَح ـ حَظٌّ. A cause of —, مَسَرَّة *pl.* مَسارٌّ ـ فُرْحَة. With increased —, مَعَ مَزِيدِ ٱلسُّرُورِ. Delights, تَنَزُّهات. To take — in, سُرَّ بِ.

Delight, *v.t.* أَعْجَبَ ـ أَبْهَجَ ـ ٢ بَسَطَ ـ أَفْرَحَ ـ ٢ سَرَّ ـ ٢ راقَ ـ شَجَّبَ ـ بِ ـ سَلَّى ـ ءِ شَرَحَ خاطِرَهُ. It did not — me, ما راقَنِي.

Delight, *v.i.* إِنْشَرَحَ خاطِرُهُ ـ إِنْحَظَّ ـ تَغَبَّطَ ـ ءِ فَرِحَ ـ إِغْتَبَطَ ـ إِنْبَسَطَ ـ سُرَّ. To — in, سُرَّ بِ ـ تَمَتَّعَ بِ ـ ءِ عاجَ بِ ـ ءِ فَرِحَ بِ ـ مِن. To —, enjoy, one's self, تَغَبَّطَ ـ تَنَزَّهَ. He was delighted with the place, تَأَنَّقَ ٱلْمَكانَ.

Delighted, *a.* Greatly pleased, مَحْظُوظ ـ مَغْبُوط ـ مُغْتَبِط ـ فِي غايَةِ ٱلسُّرُورِ ـ مَسْرُور.

Delightful, *a.* مُفْرِح ـ بَهِيج ـ نَزِيه ـ نَزِه ـ نَعِيم ـ أَنِيق ـ مُطْرِب ـ مُفْرِح ـ مُتْرِف. A — place, مَنْزَهَة. The interview was —, كانَ ٱلْإِجْتِماعُ أَنِيقًا. To be —, ءِ نَزِهَ ـ ٢ حَلا. To esteem —, إِسْتَحْلَى.

Delightfully, *ad.* تَمَتُّعًا ـ بِحَظٍّ ـ بِكَمالِ ٱللَّذَّةِ ـ بِتَنَعُّمٍ. The evening passed off —, إِنْتَهَتِ ٱللَّيْلَةُ عَلَى أَكْمَلِ حَظٍّ وَسُرُورٍ.

Delightsome, *a.* *See* Delightful, *a.*

Delineament, *n.* تَصَوُّر ـ رَسْم.

Delineate, *v.t.* To draw, صَوَّرَ ـ ٢ رَسَمَ ـ شَكَّلَ ـ مَثَّلَ. To describe, وَصَفَ *fut.* يَصِفُ.

Delineation, *n.* The act of drawing, تَسْطِير ـ تَصْوِير ـ رَسْم ـ

Description, تَعْرِيف ـ وَصْف. A drawing, رَسْم *pl.* رُسُوم ـ تَخْطِيط ـ صُورَة.

Delineator, *n.* A painter, رَسّام ـ مُصَوِّر. A describer, واصِف.

Delinquency, *n.* زَلَّة ـ غَلْطَة ـ خَطاءٌ ـ تَقْصِير ـ جُناح ـ قَباحَة ـ عَثْرَة. To be guilty of a —, إِرْتَكَبَ جُناحًا. To regard as a —, ءِ جَنَحَ. He fell into a great —, ءِ زَلَّ زَلَّةً قَبِيحَةً.

Delinquent, *a.* }
Delinquent, *n.* } مُجْرِم ـ صاحِبُ جُناحٍ ـ مُذْنِب ـ خاطِئٌ.

Delirious, *a.* مَجْنُون ـ طائِش ـ مُفْنِد ـ هَذّار ـ هَذِر ـ هَذّاءٌ. To be —, جُنَّ ـ أَفْنَدَ ـ ءِ ٢ هَذَرَ ـ ءِ طاشَ ـ ءِ هَذَى.

Delirium, *n.* طَيَشان ـ هَذَر ـ هَتْرَة ـ هَتْر ـ فَنَد ـ هُذاءٌ ـ جُنُون.

Delirium-tremens, *n.* رُعاشٌ مَعَ جُنُونٍ حاصِلٍ مِنْ إِفْراطِ ٱلسُّكْرِ.

Deliver, *v.t.* To rescue from, خَلَّصَ ـ مِن ـ أَنْقَذَ ـ مِن ـ نَقَّذَ ـ مِن ـ نَجَّى ـ مِن ـ سَلَّمَ ـ مِن. To set at liberty, ٢ فَكَّ ـ أَطْلَقَ ـ أَعْتَقَ. To give over to, وَضَعَ ـ عِنْدَهُ *aor.* ـ ءِ دَفَعَ ـ إِلَى ـ ناوَلَ ـ سَلَّمَ ـ لِ ـ أَعْطَى ـ لِ ـ أَبْقَى ـ إِلَى ـ يَضَعُ. To utter, ءِ لَفَظَ بِ ـ ٢ قالَ ـ تَكَلَّمَ عَن ـ ءِ عَرَضَ ـ ٢ قَصَّ عَن ـ حَدَّثَ عَن ـ ٢ فاهَ بِ. To — a woman, to bring to bed, وَلَّدَ. To — fire, to fire, أَطْلَقَ ـ ءِ ضَرَبَ. To — up, to return, ءِ رَجَعَ ـ ٢ رَدَّ.

Deliverance, *n.* The act of releasing, إِنْقاذ ـ عِتْق ـ إِطْلاق ـ تَخْلِيص. Release, إِسْتِسْلام ـ سَلامَة ـ نَجاة ـ خَلاص. Surrender, إِطاعَة ـ إِلْقاءٌ ـ تَسْلِيم. The act of giving over, تَسْلِيم. Utterance, نُطْق بِ ـ تَوَّه بِ ـ تَكَلُّم ـ كَلام ـ قَصَص ـ تَقْرِير ـ نُطْق.

Deliverer, *n.* مُنَجٍّ ـ مُخَلِّص.

Delivery, *n.* Surrender, تَسْلِيم. Utterance, mode of speaking, تَقْرِير ـ نُطْق ـ تَلَفُّظ. The act of bringing forth children, نِفاس ـ وِلادَة. The act of distributing, تَوْزِيع.

Dell, *n.* وادٍ ـ نَفانِف *pl.* نَفْنَف ـ نَفْناف ـ وِهاد *pl.* وَهْدَة *pl.* أَوْدِيَة.

Delta, *n.* تَراكُمُ ٱلْأَجْرافِ فِي هَيْئَةٍ مُثَلَّثٍ عِنْدَ مَصَبِّ نَهْرٍ.

Deludable, *a.* يُغَرُّ ـ يُغْوَى ـ يُخْدَعُ.

Delude, *v.t.* جَوَّنَ ـ أَخْدَعَ ـ ءِ ٢ خَتَلَ ـ راوَغَ ـ أَغْوَى ـ غَشَّشَ ـ ءِ غَبَنَ. To be deluded, إِنْخَدَعَ ـ إِنْغَشَّ ـ إِنْغَوَى ـ غُبِنَ.

Deluder, *n.* غَشّاش ـ خَدّاع ـ خائِن ـ دَجّال ـ غَرّار ـ خَتّال.

Deluding, *n.* *See* Delusion, *n.*

Deluge, *n.* An overflowing of water, فَيَضان ـ غَمِير ـ فَيْضُ ماءٍ ـ طُغْيانُ مِياهٍ ـ سَيْل. The — of Noah, طُوفانُ نُوحٍ ـ ٱلطُّوفانُ. Exuberance, كَثْرَة ـ مُبالَغَة ـ فَرْط ـ فُضُول.

Deluge, *v.t.* To overflow, غَمَرَ ‍ـ غَطَا عَلَى. To drown, أَغْرَقَ ‍ـ غَرَّقَ. To overwhelm, surround on all sides, أَشْمَلَ ‍ـ إِشْتَمَلَ عَلَى.

Delusion, *n.* The act of deluding, مُرَاوَغَة ‍ـ إِخْدَاع ‍ـ إِغْوَآء ‍ـ تَجْوِين ‍ـ غِشّ. Error from false views, ضَلَال ‍ـ صَابَة ‍ـ غُرُور ‍ـ غَوَايَة ‍ـ غَيّ. A false fancy, خَيَال بَاطِل ‍ـ وَهْمٌ *pl.* أَوْهَام بَاطِلَة. False hope, غُرُور.

Delusive, *a.* فَارِغ ‍ـ بَاطِل ‍ـ غُرُور ‍ـ غَرَّار.

Delve, *v.t.* حَفَرَ ‍ـ نَبَشَ ‍ـ عَزَقَ.

Delver, *n.* حَفَّار ‍ـ حَفَّار بِمِعْزَقَةٍ ‍ـ نَكَّاش ٱلْأَرْضِ.

Demagogism, *n.* حُكُومَةُ ٱلْأَرَاذِلِ ‍ـ حُكُومَةُ ٱلْأَوْبَاشِ.

Demagogue, *n.* مُهَيِّجُ أَسَافِلِ ‍ـ رَئِيسُ عُصْبَةٍ مِنَ ٱلشَّعْبِ ‍ـ قَائِدُ ٱلْأَوْبَاشِ ‍ـ ٱلشَّغْب.

Demain, *n.* / Demesne, An estate, مُلْك ‍ـ أَمْلَاك ‍ـ عَقَار.

Demand, *v.t.* To claim, إِدَّعَى بِ. To ask of with authority, طَالَبَ‑بِ ‍ـ إِقْتَرَحَ عَلَى‑أَل... ‍ـ طَلَبَ مِن. To inquire of, إِسْتَفْهَمَ ‍ـ إِسْتَخْبَرَ مِن ‍ـ تَعَرَّفَ ‍ـ أَنْشَدَ ‍ـ نَشَدَ ‍ـ سَأَلَ‑مِن. To require, need, إِحْتَاجَ إِلَى ‍ـ إِسْتَدْعَى ‍ـ دَعَا بِ ‍ـ مِن. To exact, إِقْتَضَى. He agreed to all the conditions demanded of him, رَضِيَ بِكُلِّ مَا أُوجِبَ عَلَيْهِ مِنَ ٱلشُّرُوطِ.

Demand, *n.* A claim, دَعْوَى *pl.* دَعَاوَى ‍ـ إِدِّعَآء. A — with authority, عَرْض ‍ـ طَلَب ‍ـ إِسْتِدْعَآء ‍ـ إِسْتِعْلَام ‍ـ إِقْتِرَاح. A thing asked, مَطْلُوب ‍ـ مَطْلَب; a thing required, لُزُوم ‍ـ حَاجَة ‍ـ إِحْتِيَاج. Inquiry, سُؤَال ‍ـ مَسْأَلَة ‍ـ إِسْتِفْهَام. Formal —, إِسْتِعْلَامٌ رَسْمِيٌّ ‍ـ مُطَالَبَةٌ رَسْمِيَّةٌ. To make a formal — on, طَالَبَ‑رَسْمًا. On —, حِينَ ٱلتَّقْدِيمِ ‍ـ عِنْدَ ٱلْمُطَالَبَةِ. To make a — upon, طَلَبَ مِن ‍ـ إِرْتَجَعَ إِلَى. To satisfy, as of demands, وَفَّى ‍ـ أَوْفَى. To be in —, مَطْلُوب ‍ـ مَرْغُوب. He will not come down in his demands, لَا يَنْقُصُ مِنِ ٱقْتِرَاحَاتِهِ.

Demander, *n.* طَالِب ‍ـ مُدَّعٍ.

Demarkation, *n.* The act of marking a limit, تَعْيِين ‍ـ تَحْدِيد. A limit, حَدٌّ فَاصِلٌ *pl.* حُدُودٌ فَاصِلَةٌ. A line of —, ٱلْحُدُود ‍ـ حَدٌّ فَاصِل ‍ـ حُدُود.

Demean, *v.t.* To behave, سَلَكَ سُلُوكًا ‍ـ عَمِلَ ‍ـ مَشَى ‍ـ تَصَرَّفَ ‍ـ تَصَرَّفَ. To —, degrade, one's self, تَرَذَّلَ ‍ـ تَحَاقَرَ.

Demeanour, *n.* تَصَرُّف ‍ـ سِيرَة ‍ـ حَرَكَة ‍ـ أَوْضَاع وَحَرَكَات ‍ـ سُلُوك ‍ـ مُعَامَلَة.

Dementate, *v.t.* أَجَنَّ ‍ـ جَنَّنَ ‍ـ هَتَرَ.

Demented, *n.* مَجْنُون ‍ـ مُسْلَبُ ٱلْعَقْلِ ‍ـ مُسْتَلَبُ ٱلْعَقْلِ ‍ـ مُصَاب. To become —, جُنَّ ‍ـ إِخْتَلَّ عَقْلُهُ.

Dementia, *n.* هَتْرَة ‍ـ خَلَلٌ فِي ٱلْعَقْلِ ‍ـ جُنُون ‍ـ جِنَّة.

Demerit, *n.* قِلَّةُ ٱسْتِحْقَاقٍ ‍ـ نُقْصَان ‍ـ عَيْب ‍ـ تَقْصِير ‍ـ قُصُور.

Demi, *a.* نِصْف.

Demi-brigade, *n.* نِصْفُ لِوَآء.

Demigod, *n.* مَعْبُودٌ نِصْفُهُ إِلَهٌ وَنِصْفُهُ بَشَرٌ.

Demi-john, *n.* دَبَّة *pl.* دِبَاب ‍ـ دَمَجَانَة.

Demi-lune, *n.* طَابِيَةٌ فِي شَكْلِ هِلَالٍ.

Demisable, *a.* يُؤَجَّر ‍ـ جَائِزٌ إِيجَارُهُ.

Demise, *n.* Death, مَنِيَّة ‍ـ مَوْت ‍ـ وَفَاة. A lease, إِيجَار. A bequest, خَلَف ‍ـ وَصِيَّة.

Demise, *v.t.* To lease, أَجَرَ ‍ـ آجَرَ. To bequeath to by will, خَلَّفَ‑بِ ‍ـ وَصَّى لِ‑بِ.

Demission, *n.* *See under* Degradation, *n.*

Democracy, *n.* Government by the people, حُكْمٌ جُمْهُورِيٌّ ‍ـ حُكُومَةُ ٱلْعَوَامِّ ‍ـ قِيَامُ ٱلْجُمْهُورِ بِٱلْحُكْمِ.

Democrat, *n.* تَابِعُ ٱلْحُكْمِ ٱلْجُمْهُورِيِّ.

Democratic, *a.* / Democratical, مُتَعَلِّقٌ بِحُكُومَةِ ‍ـ مُخْتَصٌّ بِٱلْحُكْمِ ٱلْجُمْهُورِيِّ ٱلْعَوَامِّ.

Demolish, *v.t.* أَخْرَبَ ‍ـ رَمَى ‍ـ هَدَّ ‍ـ مَحَقَ ‍ـ هَوَّرَ ‍ـ هَدَمَ ‍ـ خَرَّبَ. To be demolished, تَهَدَّمَ ‍ـ تَخَرَّبَ ‍ـ إِنْهَدَمَ ‍ـ إِنْهَدَّ.

Demolition, *n.* خَرَاب ‍ـ إِنْهِدَام ‍ـ هُدُود ‍ـ هَوْر ‍ـ هَدْم ‍ـ هَدّ ‍ـ تَخْرِيب.

Demon, *n.* عِفْرِيت *pl.* عَفَارِيت ‍ـ قُطْرُب *pl.* قَطَارِب ‍ـ غُول *pl.* أَغْوَال and غِيلَان ‍ـ جَانّ *pl.* جِنَّان ‍ـ جِنِّيّ *fem.* جِنِّيَّة *coll.* جِنّ ‍ـ شَيْطَان *pl.* شَيَاطِين. *See also under* Devil, *n.*

Demoniac, *a.* / Demoniacal, Influenced by demons, possessed, مُشَجَّع ‍ـ سَعِر ‍ـ مَسْكُون ‍ـ مَلْبُوس ‍ـ مُصَاب. Pertaining to demons, مُتَعَلِّقٌ بِٱلْجِنِّ ‍ـ عِفْرِيتِيّ. Demoniacal possession, سُعْر.

Demoniac, *n.* One possessed, مَسْكُون ‍ـ مَلْبُوس ‍ـ مُصَاب ‍ـ مَسْعُور.

Demonism, *n.* شِرْك ‍ـ عِبَادَةُ ٱلشَّيَاطِينِ ‍ـ ٱلِٱعْتِقَادُ بِٱلشَّيَاطِينِ.

Demonology, *n.* بَحْثٌ عَنِ ٱلشَّيَاطِينِ وَٱلْجِنِّ.

Demonstrable, *a.* إِثْبَاتُهُ مُمْكِنٌ ‍ـ إِيضَاحُهُ مُمْكِنٌ ‍ـ يُبَرْهَنُ.

Demonstrably, *ad* / Demonstratively, إِثْبَاتًا ‍ـ إِظْهَارًا ‍ـ بِدَلِيلٍ وَاضِحٍ.

Demonstrate, *v.t.* To prove, بَرْهَنَ ‍ـ أَوْضَحَ ‍ـ أَثْبَتَ ‍ـ بَيَّنَ. To exhibit to, عَرَضَ‑عَلَى ‍ـ بَيَّنَ‑لِ ‍ـ فَرَّجَ‑عَلَى ‍ـ أَرَى ‍ـ أَرَاءَى.

Demonstration, *n.* Proof, بَيِّنَة ـ إِثْبات ـ بُرْهانٌ قاطِعٌ ـ دَلِيلٌ واضِحٌ ـ إِيضاح ـ إِراءة ـ إِرآءٌ. Exhibition, عُرُوض ـ إِبانَة. A movement, حَرَكَة. A hostile —, حَرَكَةٌ لِإِخافَةِ ٱلْعَدُوِّ. A collected crowd, حَشْد ـ قَوْمٌ حاشِدٌ ـ حَشْد. They made a —, collected themselves together, إِحْتَشَدُوا ـ تَحَشَّدُوا. They made a — against, تَحَشَّدُوا عَلَى; in favour of, تَحَشَّدُوا ل.

Demonstrative, *a.* Conclusive, مُثْبِت ـ إِيضاحِيٌّ ـ تأكِيدِيٌّ. Indicative, دَلِيل ـ دالٌّ ـ دَلِيلِيٌّ. Excessive in the manifestation of ..., مُفْرِطٌ فِي بَيانِ ٱلْ ـ مُبالِغٌ فِي إِظْهارِ ٱلْ...; of warmth, zeal, كَثِيرُ ٱلْحَرارَةِ. The — pronoun, إِسْمُ ٱلْإِشارَةِ ـ الضَّمِيرُ ٱلدَّالُّ. Demonstrative science, تَعْلِيمٌ بِإِراءَةِ ٱلْأَشْيَاءِ ٱلَّتِي يَتَكَلَّمُ عَنْها ٱلْمُعَلِّمُ.

Demonstrativeness, *n.* Excess in the manifestation of ..., مُبالَغَةٌ فِي إِظْهارِ ٱلْ.... Excessive warmth, حَرارَةٌ مُفْرِطَةٌ ـ كَثْرَةُ حَرارَةٍ.

Demonstrator, *n.* A prover, مُبَرْهِن ـ دَلِيل ـ مُثْبِت. A — of anatomy, مُعَلِّمُ ٱلتَّشْرِيحِ بِواسِطَةِ إِراءَةِ أَجْزاءِ ٱلْجَسَدِ.

Demonstratory, *a.* *See* Demonstrative, *a.*

Demoralization, *n.* The act of demoralizing, إِفْسادُ ٱلْآدابِ ـ إِفْساد ـ تَخْسِير ـ إِعْدامُ حُسْنِ ٱلْأَخْلاقِ. The being demoralized, عَدَمُ حُسْنِ ٱلْأَخْلاقِ ـ فَساد ـ مَفْسُودُ ٱلسِّيرَةِ. The — of an army, its being demoralized, عَدَمُ ٱلطَّاعَةِ وَٱلْإِنْتِظامِ وَٱلْأَمانَةِ فِي ٱلْعَسْكَرِ. A source of —, مَفْسَدَة.

Demoralize, *v.t.* أَعْدَمَ حُسْنَ ٱلْأَخْلاقِ ـ أَفْسَدَ ـ خَسَّرَ ـ أَفْسَدَ فِي ٱلْآدابِ. To — an army, أَعْدَمَ ٱلطَّاعَةَ وَٱلْإِنْتِظامَ وَٱلْأَمانَةَ فِي ٱلْعَسْكَرِ.

Demoralizing, *a.* مُبْطِلُ حُسْنِ ٱلْأَخْلاقِ ـ مُفْسِد ـ مُخَسِّر.

Demotic, *a.* دارِج ـ عادِيٌّ.

Demulcent, *n.* عِلاجٌ مُلَيِّنٌ ـ مُلَيِّن.

Demur, *v.i.* To hesitate, يَعِيُّ *aor.* عَيَّ ـ تَضَرَّبَ ـ تَمَخْطَرَ ـ إِرْتابَ ـ تَشَكَّكَ فِي. To —, to doubt, تَوَقَّفَ ـ إِخْتارَ. To decline, إِعْتَرَضَ.

Demur, *n.* شُبْهَة ـ تَضَرُّب ـ تَوَقُّف ـ تَرَدُّد ـ تَمَخْطُر. Doubt, رَيْب ـ شَكّ. Without —, بِلا تَوَقُّفٍ ـ بِلا تَرَدُّدٍ.

Demure, *a.* Grave, مُتَوَقِّر ـ وَقُور ـ مَحْجُوب ـ أَدِيب. Affectedly —, مُتَصَنِّعٌ بِٱلْحَياءِ. To be —, grave, تَوَقَّرَ ـ سَمَتَ ^2^.

Demureness, *n.* Gravity, وَقار ـ رَزانَة ـ سَمْت. Affected gravity, تَصَنُّع ـ تَظاهُرٌ بِٱلْحِشْمَةِ. To affect —, تَصَنَّعَ بِٱلْخَجَلِ ٱلْخَجَلَة.

Demurrage, *n.* أُجْرَةٌ تُدْفَعُ غَرامَةً لِتَأْخِيرِ سَفَرِ ٱلْمَرْكَبِ عَنْ مِيعادِهِ.

Demurrer, *n.* One who hesitates, مُتَرَدِّد ـ مُتَمَخْطِر ـ مُتَضَرِّب. A —, in law, إِعْتِراضٌ مِنْ أَحَدِ ٱلْخَصْمَيْنِ لِحُكْمٍ ٱسْتِنادًا عَلَى حُجَّةٍ ما.

Demy, *n.* Of the size of paper, قَطْعٌ مِنَ ٱلْقِرْطاسِ أَصْغَرُ مِنَ ٱلْقَطْعِ ٱلْمُتَوَسِّطِ. A — of a college, مُلازِمُ دارِ ٱلْفُنُونِ.

Den, *n.* *pl.* وَكْر ـ وُكُور ـ زَرِيبَة ـ زَرْب *pl.* زُرُوب ـ سَرَب *pl.* أَسْراب ـ جُحْر *pl.* جِحَرَة ـ مَغارَة. He betook himself (to his —), إِنْسَرَبَ فِي ـ تَسَرَّبَ إِلَى.

Denationalize, *v.t.* أَسْقَطَ حَقَّهُ فِي ٱمْتِيازاتِ ٱلْأُمَّةِ.

Denaturalize, *v.t.* To render unnatural, جَعَلَ مُخالِفًا لِلطَّبِيعَةِ ـ مَسَخَ.

Dendrology, *n.* عِلْمُ ٱلْبَحْثِ عَنِ ٱلْأَشْجارِ.

Denegation, *n.* إِنْكار.

Deniable, *a.* يُنْكَرُ ـ إِنْكارُهُ مُمْكِنٌ.

Denial, *n.* Negation, إِنْكار ـ نَكِير. Refusal, إِباءَة ـ رَدَّة ـ إِبايَة ـ إِمْتِناع. Denial of bounty received, جَحْد ـ جُحُود ـ تَجْدِيف. Denial of God, كُفْرٌ بِٱللّٰهِ. A flat —, إِنْكارٌ كُلِّيٌّ (or بَتِّيٌّ). In — of what was reported of him, تَكْذِيبًا لِما شاعَ عَنْهُ.

Denier, *n.* مُنْكِر.

Denigrate, *v.t.* *See to* Blacken, *v.t.*

Denization, *n.* The act of making a citizen, إِدْخالُ ٱلْأَجْنَبِيِّ فِي ٱمْتِيازاتِ ٱلرَّعِيَّةِ.

Denizen, *n.* A foreigner having the rights of a citizen, أَجْنَبِيٌّ حائِزٌ ٱمْتِيازاتِ ٱلرَّعِيَّةِ. A dweller, ساكِن *pl.* سُكّان. The denizens of the air, الطُّيُورُ; of the water, السَّمَكُ; of the forest, الوُحُوش.

Denizenship, *n.* حالَةُ ٱلْأَجْنَبِيِّ ٱلْحائِزِ ٱمْتِيازاتِ ٱلرَّعِيَّةِ.

Denmark, *n.* دانِيمَرْك ـ دَنِمِيرْك.

Denominable, *a.* قابِلُ ٱلتَّسْمِيَةِ ـ يُتَسَمَّى.

Denominate, *v.t.* لَقَّبَ ـ بِ ـ دَعا ^2^ ـ سَمَّى ـ بِ ـ سَمَّى.

Denomination, *n.* The act of denominating, تَلْقِيب ـ تَسْمِيَة. A name, لَقَب *pl.* أَلْقاب ـ إِسْم *pl.* أَسْماء *pl. pl.* أَسامِيُّ. A sect, مِلَّة *pl.* مِلَل ـ فِرْقَة *pl.* فِرَق ـ طائِفَة *pl.* طَوائِف ـ شِيعَة *pl.* أَشْياع.

Denominative, *a.* لَقَبِيٌّ ـ عَلَمِيٌّ ـ تَعْرِيفِيٌّ.

Denominator, *n.* (In arithmetic), مَخْرَجُ ٱلْكُسُورِ ـ مَخْرَج. One who denominates, مُسَمٍّ ـ لَقّاب.

Denotable, *a.* الدَّلالَةُ (or الدُّلُولَةُ) عَلَيْهِ مُمْكِنَةٌ ـ يُعَبَّرُ عَنْهُ.

Denotation, *n.* دِلالَة ـ دُلُولَة ـ إِعْلام ـ تَبْيِين ـ إِشْعار.

Denotative, *a.* مُشِيرٌ إِلَى ـ دَلِيلٌ عَلَى.

Denote, *v.t.* عَبَّرَ بِ *or* عَن ـ دَلَّ عَلَى ² ـ أَشَارَ إِلَى ـ أَشَّرَ ـ بَيَّنَ ـ عَلَّمَ عَلَى. This denotes . . . , هٰذا عِبارَةٌ عَن .

Denouement, *n.* عاقِبَة ـ نَتِيجَة ـ خِتام ـ حاصِل .

Denounce, *v.t.* To accuse, اِتَّهَمَ بِ ـ اِشْتَكَى عَلَى بِ . To threaten, رَعَبَ ـ أَرْعَدَ ـ هَدَّدَ . To — a treaty, to give notice of dissolving it, أَعْلَنَ بِفَسْخِ ٱلْمُعاهَدَةِ .

Denouncement, *n.* تَوَعُّد ـ تَرْعِيد ـ تَرْعِيب ـ تَهْدِيد . The — of a treaty, إِعْلانُ بِفَسْخِ مُعاهَدَةٍ .

Denouncer, *n.* An accuser, مُتَّهِم ـ شاكٍ ـ مُشْتَكٍ عَلَى .

Dense, *a.* Thick, كَثِيف . Compact, حَصِيف ـ مُكْتَنِز ـ وَثِيج ـ صَمِيم . Multitudinous, وافِر ـ كَثِير . Having a denser population, أَوْفَرُ أَهْلًا (*or* شَعْبًا) . *See also* Compact, *a.*

Densely, *ad.* *See* Thickly, *ad.*

Denseness, *n.* / Density, — Thickness, كَثافَة . Compactness, وَثاجَة ـ اِكْتِناز . Numerousness, وَفْر ـ كَثْرَة .

Dent, *n.* An indentation, هَزْمَة ـ أَثَر *pl.* أُثُور ـ قَوْب ـ نُكْتَة .

Dent, *v.t.* هَزَمَ ـ أَخْلَفَ عَلامَةً فِي ـ قَوَّبَ ـ ² نَكَتَ .

Dental, *a.* سِنِّيّ ـ مُخْتَصّ بِٱلْأَسْنانِ . A — letter, حَرْف سِنِّيّ .

Dentate, *a.* / Dentated, — مُسَنَّن ـ ذُو أَسْنانٍ . *See also* Serrated, *a.*

Dentiform, *a.* بِصُورَةِ ٱلْأَسْنانِ ـ مَسْنُونٌ كَٱلْأَسْنانِ .

Dentifrice, *n.* سَنُون ـ دَوآءٌ لِلْأَسْنانِ ـ دَوآءٌ لِتَنْظِيفِ ٱلْأَسْنانِ .

Dentist, *n.* طَبِيبُ ٱلْأَسْنانِ .

Dentistry, *n.* طِبُّ ٱلْأَسْنانِ .

Dentition, *n.* طُلُوعُ ٱلْأَسْنانِ .

Dentoid, *a.* *See* Dentiform, *a.*

Denudation, *n.* تَشْلِيح ـ تَعْرِيَة ـ تَجْرِيد .

Denudate, *v.t.* / Denude, — جَرَّدَ ـ عَرَّى ـ أَعْرَى مِن . To be denudated, تَجَرَّدَ ـ اِنْجَرَدَ .

Denunciate, *v.t.* *See to* Denounce, *v.t.*

Denunciation, *n.* *See* Denouncement, *n.*

Denunciator, *n.* *See* Denouncer, *n.*

Denunciatory, *a.* Accusatory, مُتَّهِم ـ شاكٍ . Threatening, مُرْعِب ـ مُرْعِد ـ مُهَدِّد .

Deny, *v.t.* To declare untrue, أَكْذَبَ ـ كَذَّبَ ـ أَنْكَرَ ـ اِسْتَنْكَرَ . Not to acknowledge, جَحَدَ ـ جَدَفَ بِ . To refuse to grant, أَعْدَمَ ـ رَدَّ فِي ² ـ عَزَّ . To — God, ² كَفَرَ بِٱللّٰهِ . To disown, رَفَضَ ² . It is denied here that . . . , كُذِّبَ هُنا أَن .

Deobstruent, *a.* مُفَتِّحٌ لِلسُّدَدِ .

Deodand, *n.* دِيَة *pl.* دِيات ـ عَقْل *pl.* عُقُول .

Deodorize, *v.t.* أَزالَ ٱلرَّوائِحَ ٱلْخَبِيثَةَ .

Deodorizer, *n.* مُزِيلُ ٱلرَّوائِحِ ٱلْخَبِيثَةِ .

Depaint, *v.t.* To paint, صَوَّرَ ـ نَقَّشَ . To describe, وَصَفَ *fut* يَصِفُ .

Depart, *v.i.* To go away from, بَرِحَ مِن ـ بَرِحَ ـ تَسَرَّحَ ـ سافَرَ ـ تَرَحَّلَ مِن ـ اِرْتَحَلَ عَن ـ اِنْفَصَلَ عَن ـ تَوَجَّهَ إِلَى ـ مَضَى ـ ذَهَبَ ـ اِنْتَقَلَ ـ سارَ *aor.* يَسِيرُ . To — from, to relinquish, تَرَكَ ² ـ حادَ عَن ـ فارَقَ ـ اِنْصَرَفَ عَن ـ اِفْتَرَقَ عَن . To — this life, تُوُفِّيَ ـ ² ماتَ . To —, pass away, as of heat or cold, زالَ *fut.* يَزُولُ ـ سَقَطَ ² . His spirit departed, جادَتْ نَفْسُهُ . The departed one, (the object of God's mercy), المَرْحُومُ . He departed this life, اِنْتَقَلَ إِلَى دارِ ٱلْبَقآءِ . The heat has departed from us, سَقَطَ عَنّا ٱلْحَرُّ .

Departing, *n.* *See* Departure, *n.*

Department, *n.* What appertains to, as to any science, *etc.*, مُخْتَصّ بِ ـ ما يَتَعَلَّقُ بِ . An office, as a branch of administration, قَلَم *pl.* أَقْلام ـ نَظارَة ـ إِدارَة ـ دائِرَة . The Foreign Office —, الدّائِرَةُ ٱلْخارِجِيَّةُ . The different departments, الدَّوائِرُ ٱلْمُخْتَلِفَةُ . The heads of departments, رُؤُوسُ ٱلدَّوائِرِ . Service, office, وَظِيفَة ـ خِدْمَة ـ مَنْصَب ـ إِدارَة ـ شُغْل . A province, أَقْلِيم *pl.* أَقالِيمُ ـ عَمَل *pl.* أَعْمال . *See also* Administration, *n.*

Departmental, *a.* مُتَعَلِّقٌ بِنَظارَةٍ ـ مُخْتَصٌّ بِقَلَمٍ ـ مُتَعَلِّقٌ بِإِدارَةٍ .

Departure, *n.* A going away, بُرُوح ـ رَحْل ـ رَحِيل ـ اِنْسِراح ـ اِنْطِلاق ـ ذَهاب ـ تَوَجُّه ـ سَفَر . A declining from, اِنْحِراف عَن ـ تَباعُد عَن . A separation, فِراق ـ مُفارَقَة ـ اِنْفِصال . Abandonment, تَرْك ـ هَجْر . Death, حِمام ـ مَوْت ـ وَفاة . Point of —, مَفْصِل .

Depasture, *v.t.* *See to* Graze, *v.t.*

Depend, *v.i.* To hang from, اِنْتاطَ بِ ـ عَلَى *or* تَعَلَّقَ بِ ـ تَدَلَّى مِن . To be connected with, تَعَلَّقَ بِ ـ تَبِعَ ـ اِخْتَصَّ بِ . To rely on, اِسْتَنَدَ إِلَى ـ اِعْتَمَدَ عَلَى ـ اِتَّكَلَ عَلَى . Man's happiness depends on his knowledge of the truth, سَعادَةُ ٱلْإِنْسانِ مَنُوطَةٌ بِمَعْرِفَةِ ٱلْحَقِّ . This depends on what you wish, هٰذا مَوْقُوفٌ عَلَى إِرادَتِكَ ـ هٰذا مُفَوَّضٌ إِلَيْكَ . Their departure depends upon . . . , سَفَرُهُمْ مُوَقَّفٌ عَلَى . That does not — upon me, هٰذا ما هُوَ فِي يَدِي ـ لَيْسَ ذٰلِكَ تَحْتَ حُكْمِي وَلا تَصَرُّفِي . It depended upon so and so, تَعَلَّقَ عَلَى كَذا . Depend upon it, لا شَكَّ ـ لِيَكُنْ عِنْدَكَ يَقِينًا . To make to — upon, عَلَّقَ بِ . I made the freedom of my slave to — on my death, عَلَّقْتُ عِتْقَ عَبْدِي بِمَوْتِي .

Dependence, *n.* } Connexion, مُلازَمَة – عَلاقَة – تَعَلُّق. Sub-
Dependency, } jection, إِتْباع – إِذْعان – مُتابَعَة – طاعَة. Reliance, وَثِيقَة – إِعْتِماد – إِتِّكال – تَوَكُّل عَلَى. A dependent state or territory, مُلْحَقَة *pl.* مُلْحَقات – تابِعَة *pl.* تَوابِع. Dependencies, مُلْحَقات – تَعَلُّقات. To keep in a state of —, أَلْزَمَ بِٱلْمُتابَعَةِ. There is no — to be placed in them, لا رُكُونَ إِلَيْهِمْ.

Dependent, *a.* Hanging from, أَجْنَف – مُتَناطٌ بِ – مُتَّكِل – مُعْتَمِدٌ عَلَى – مُتَعَلِّق بِ – مُتَدَلٍّ مِن. Relying on, مُعْتَمِدٌ عَلَى – مُسْتَنِدٌ إِلَى – عَلَى. Supplementary, إِضافِيّ. Connected with, مُتَعَلِّق بِ – مِنَ ٱلْزام. Subjected to, تَحْتَ أَمْرِ – تابِع – تَحْتَ حُكْمِ – تَحْتَ يَدِ – مَنُوطٌ بِ – مَوْقُوفٌ عَلَى. To be — upon, to be subjected to, وَقَفَ عَلَى – أَناطَ بِ – [2] ناطَ بِ *aor.* يَقِفُ – أُوقِفَ عَلَى.

Dependent, *n.* تابِع *pl.* تابِعُونَ – تَبَع *pl.* أَتْباع. Dependents, أَلْزام.

Depict, *v.t.* To —, as in the mind, تَصَوَّرَ. Depicted in the mind, مُتَصَوَّر *See also to* Depaint, *v.t.*

Depilate, *v.t.* مَرَّطَ – نَتَفَ (أَزالَ *or*) ٱلشَّعْرَ.

Depilation, *n.* نَتْفُ ٱلشَّعْرِ – إِزالَةُ ٱلشَّعْرِ – تَمْرِيط – مَرْط.

Depilatory, *n.* نُورَة – دَلُوك – جَمُوش. To use the — on one's self, تَنَوَّرَ.

Depletion, *n.* The act of emptying, إِنْفاد – تَفْرِيغ – إِفْراغ. Blood-letting, فِصادَة – فَصْد.

Deplorable, *a.* Sad, يُرْثَى لَ – كَئِيب – مُحْزِن – حَزِين. Contemptible, حَقِير. In a — state, فِي حالَةٍ يُرْثَى لَها.

Deplorably, *ad.* فِي حالَةٍ يُرْثَى – بِطَرِيقَةٍ مُحْزِنَةٍ – بِنَوْعٍ مُحْزِنٍ لَها. *See also* Sadly, *ad.*

Deplore, *v.t.* تَأَسَّفَ – تَوَجَّعَ عَلَى – تَحَزَّنَ عَلَى – ـ حَزِنَ عَلَى – ـ هَنَّ عَلَى – [2] ناحَ عَلَى – ـ فَجَعَ – ـ بَكَى عَلَى – عَلَى.

Deplorer, *n.* باكٍ عَلَى – حَزِينٌ عَلَى – مُتَأَسِّفٌ عَلَى.

Deploy, *v.t.* To expand a body of troops, [2] نَشَرَ (or صَفَّحَ or مَدَّدَ) ٱلْعَسْكَرَ.

Deploy, *v.i.* To be expanded, of a body of troops, أَنْتَشَرَ (or تَصَفَّحَ or تَمَدَّدَ) ٱلْعَسْكَرُ.

Deplumation, *n.* As of feathers, تَنْتِيف.

Deplume, *v.t.* نَتَّفَ.

Deponent, *a.* A — verb, فِعْلٌ بِصِيغَةِ ٱلْمَجْهُولِ فِي مَعْنَى ٱلْمَعْلُومِ.

Deponent, *n.* A witness, شاهِدٌ يَشْهَدُ بِشَهادَتِهِ رَسْمًا – شاهِد وَيَمِينًا. One who makes a statement, صاحِبُ إِفادَةٍ – صاحِبُ تَقْرِيرٍ.

Depopulate, *v.t.* خَرَّبَ – قَلَّلَ ٱلسُّكَّانَ – أَخْلَى مِنَ ٱلسُّكَّانِ – صَيَّرَ ٱلْبِلادَ قَفْرَةً – ٱلْبِلادَ.

Depopulation, *n.* خَرابُ ٱلْبِلادِ – تَقْلِيلُ ٱلسُّكَّانِ – إِزالَةُ ٱلسُّكَّانِ.

Deport, *v.t.* To carry away, أَبْعَدَ – [2] نَقَلَ. To — one's self; *see to* Behave, *v.i.* *See also to* Banish, *v.t.*

Deportation, *n.* A carrying away, إِبْعاد – نَقْل. The being carried away, إِنْتِقال. Banishment, نَفْي.

Deportment, *n.* *See* Behaviour, *n.*

Deposable, *a.* تُرْفَعُ عَنْهُ وَظِيفَتُهُ – يُخْلَعُ عَنْهُ مَنْصِبُهُ – يُعْزَلُ.

Deposal, *n.* خَلْع – عَزْل.

Depose, *v.t.* To lay down, وَضَعَ *fut.* يَضَعُ – [2] حَطَّ. To dethrone, divest of office, نَزَّلَ مِنَ ٱلْمَنْصِبِ – عَزَّلَ – ـ عَزَلَ – وَضَعَ مِنَ ٱلْوَظِيفَةِ *aor.* يَضَعُ. To give a written testimony, ـ شَهِدَ خَطًّا وَتَقْرِيرًا – أَفادَ – قَرَّرَ. To witness, ـ شَهِدَ.

Deposed, *a.* Degraded, مَخْلُوع – خَلِيع – مَعْزُول. To be —, عُزِلَ.

Deposit, *n.* A trust, أَمانَة – وَضِيعَة – وَدِيعَة. A pledge, رَهْن – رَهِينَة. An accumulation, إِلْتِئام – تَراكُم. Dregs, ثُفْل – رُسُوب – تَجْبِير – حُثالَة. To leave a —, dregs, أَثْفَلَ – تَرَسَّبَ. In —, as a —, عَلَى سَبِيلِ ٱلْأَمانَةِ. The bank receives deposits of cash, ٱلْبَنْكُ يَقْبَلُ عِنْدَهُ ٱلنُّقُودَ عَلَى سَبِيلِ ٱلْأَمانَةِ. A mineral —, سَيْب *pl.* سُيُوب – رَكِيزَة *or* رِكْزَة *pl.* رِكاز. *See also* Depository, *n.*

Deposit, *v.t.* To lay in a place, وَضَعَ *fut.* يَضَعُ – وَدَعَ *fut.* يَدَعُ – إِسْتَحْفَظَ عِنْدَ – وَدَعَ عِنْدَ. To lodge with, as for safety, إِسْتَوْدَعَ – وَضَعَ أَمانَةً عِنْدَ – سَلَّمَ إِلَى. To leave, as a sediment, أَثْفَلَ – رَسَّبَ – ثَعَّا. He deposited the corpse in the grave, ضَمَّنَ ٱلْمَيِّتَ ٱلْقَبْرَ. The corpse was deposited in the grave, تَضَمَّنَ ٱلْقَبْرُ ٱلْمَيِّتَ.

Depositary, *n.* أَمِين – مُسْتَوْدَع – وَكِيل. The depositaries of power, أَرْبابُ ٱلْحُكُومَةِ.

Deposition, *n.* A throwing down, طَرْح – رَمْي – تَسْقِيط. Testimony, شَهادَةٌ رَسْمِيَّةٌ – شَهادَة – تَقْرِيرٌ رَسْمًا. Dethronement, deprivation, as of office, وَضْعٌ مِن – خَلْع – عَزْل.

Depositor, *n.* واضِعُ أَمانَةٍ – وادِع.

Depository, *n.* مَأْمَن – مَخْزَن – مُسْتَوْدَع.

Depôt, *n.* A place of deposit, حَوْصَلَة *pl.* حَواصِل – مُسْتَوْدَع. A magazine, مَخْزَن *pl.* مَخازِن. A place for the residue of a military corps, مَحَلُّ بَقِيَّةِ ٱلْآلايِ – بَقِيَّة. A railway station, مَحَطَّةُ سِكَّةِ ٱلْحَدِيدِ – مَحَطَّة.

Depravation, *n.* تَخْبِيث – إِفْساد – إِغْواء.

Deprave, *v.t.* أَفْسَدَ ـ أَغْوَى ـ أَرْدَأَ ـ أَخْبَثَ ـ ٢ فَسَّخَ. To be depraved, يَشْرُّ .aor شَرَّ ـ ٤ فَجَرَ ـ ٢ فَسَخَ ـ ٤ شَقُحَ.

Depraved, *a.* فُجَّار .pl فاجِر ـ رَدِيءٌ ـ دَنِيٌّ ـ شَنِيع ـ شَقِيح. To be —, ٢ شَرَّ. A — man, رَجُلُ ٱلسَّوْءِ ـ رَجُلُ سَوْءٍ.

Depravement, *n.* } خُبْث ـ دَنَآءَة ـ شَنَاعَة ـ شَقَاحَة
Depravity, } فَساد ـ شَرّ ـ رَدَآءَة.

Deprecate, *v.t.* To pray to be delivered from, اِسْتَغْفَرَ ـ اِسْتَعَاذَ بِ ـ يَعُوذُ .aor عَاذَ بِ ـ اِسْتَعْفَى. To — wrath, to pray for mercy, اِسْتَرْحَمَ. To — or intercede with for another, تَشَفَّعَ إِلَى-بِ ـ ٢ شَفَعَ إِلَى-بِ. To regret, تَأَسَّفَ عَلَى ـ ٢ حَسِرَ عَلَى.

Deprecation, *n.* اِعْتِذار ـ اِسْتِعْفَآء ـ اِسْتِغْفار ـ عَوْذ ـ مَعاذ. Intercession, شَفاعَة. Prayer, دُعَآء ـ اِبْتِهال.

Deprecatory, *a.* } بِٱلِٱبْتِهالِ ـ تَضَرُّعِيّ ـ اِعْتِذارِيّ ـ اِسْتِغْفارِيّ ـ
Deprecative, } شَفاعِيّ.

Depreciate, *v.t.* Of price, بَخَسَ ـ أَهْبَطَ ـ نَزَّلَ ـ ٢ بَخَسَ. To disparage, اِسْتَقَلَّ ـ يَكِسُ .fut وَكَسَ. *See also to* Decry, *v.t.*

Depreciate, *v.i.* يَكِسُ .aor وَكَسَ ـ يَكِسُ ـ ٢ تَلِفَ ـ ٢ خَسِرَ.

Depreciation, *n.* The act of lessening, اِسْتِقْلال ـ وَكْس ـ تَهْبِيط ـ تَنْزِيل. The being depreciated, خَسارَة ـ تَلَف ـ نُقْصان ـ وَكْس.

Depreciative, *a.* } مُنْكِرُ قِيمَتِهِ ـ مُنْكِرُ فَضْلِهِ ـ مُصَغِّر ـ مُسْتَقِلّ.
Depreciator, *n.* }

Depredate, *v.t.* أَخْرَبَ ـ ٤ سَلَبَ ٱلْأَمْوالَ ـ اِنْتَهَبَ ـ ٢ نَهَبَ.

Depredation, *n.* غارَة ـ خَسارَة ـ نَهْب ـ سَلْب.

Depredator, *n.* ظالِم ـ سالِب ـ نَهّاب.

Depress, *v.t.* To lower, وَطَّأَ ـ أَنْزَلَ ـ نَزَّلَ ـ ٤ حَطَّ; of the voice, ٤ خَفَضَ. To deject, أَحْزَنَ ـ آلَمَ ـ أَغَمَّ. To discourage, أَذَلَّ ـ أَخْضَعَ ـ ٢ كَسَرَ عَزْمَهُ ـ أَخْمَدَ. To humble, أَذَلَّ ـ أَخْضَعَ. To press down, ٢ حَزَقَ ـ ٢ كَبَسَ.

Depressed, *a.* Humbled, مَخْضُوع ـ مُخْتَضِع. Sad, sorrowful, مَغْمُوم ـ حَزِين ـ مَكْرُوب ـ كَرِيب. Depressed, of a market, غَيْرُ رائِجٍ ـ كاسِد. To be —, brought low, اِنْخَفَضَ ـ تَخَفَّضَ. To be —, sad, اِكْتَرَبَ ـ ٢ كَتَبَ ـ اِكْتَأَبَ.

Depressing, *a.* } Saddening, مُغِمّ ـ مُضِيق ـ مُكْرِب ـ مُحْزِن.
Depressive, }

Depression, *n.* The act of pressing down, حَزْق ـ كَبْس; of lowering, تَوْطِئَة ـ تَنْزِيل ـ خَفْض. A sinking of the surface, نَقْرَةٌ غائِطٌ ـ خافِضَة ـ وِهادٌ. A — on any part of the face, ثَقْلَة ـ قَلْت .pl تِلات. Lowness of spirits, غَمّ ـ حُزْن ـ كَدَر. Depression in trade, عَدَمُ رَواجٍ ـ كَساد. The being lowered, اِنْحِطاط. Depression of the horizon, اِنْحِطاطُ ٱلْأُفُقِ; of the pole, اِنْحِطاطُ ٱلْقُطْبِ.

Deprivable, *a.* يُعَرَّى عَنْهُ ـ يُعْزَلُ ـ تَحْتَ ٱلْعَزْلِ ـ يُرْفَعُ عَنْهُ.

Deprivation, *n.* The act of depriving of, إِعْدام ـ رَفْعٌ عَنْ. The being deprived, loss, فُقُود ـ تَحَرُّم ـ عَدَم ـ حِرْمان. The act of deposing, تَعْزِيل; the being deposed, عَزْل.

Deprive, *v.t.* To take from, أَفْقَدَ ـ عَرَّى-مِنْ ـ أَعْدَمَ ـ ٢ خَطِفَ-عَنْ. To — of holy orders, بَطَّلَ كَهْنُوتَهُ. Those who had been deprived of these privileges, ٱلَّذِينَ كانُوا مَحْرُومِينَ مِنْ هٰذِهِ ٱلْمَنافِعِ.

Depth, *n.* Measure downwards, عَماقَة ـ عُمْق ـ غُمُورَة. A deep place, هُوَّة. Extent, مِقْدار ـ وَسْع ـ سَعَة ـ مَسافَة. The middle, as of a season, وَسَط. Acuteness, دِقَّة ـ ذِهْن. Astuteness, حِيلَة ـ إِرْبَة ـ إِرْب. Abstruseness, عُسْر ـ عِياص. Depth of soil, عُمْقُ أَرْضٍ. The —, as of the sea, غَمْر; as of a wound, غَوْر. The lowest —, دَرْك ـ دَرَك. The unbounded depths of space, مَسافاتُ ٱلسَّمَآءِ ٱلْغَيْرُ مُتَناهِيَةٍ. The depths of eternity, عَماقَةُ ٱلْأَزَلِ. To be so much in —, قَدْرُهُ كَذا ـ عُمْقُهُ كَذا. To be out of one's —, in water, لَمْ يَكُنْ لَهُ ـ ٤ عُمْقٌ عَلَى-ٱلْمَآءِ قَرارٌ. To go out of one's —, as in matters of science, *etc.*, ٤ خاضَ ٱلْغَمَراتِ.

Depthless, *a.* بِلا قَعْرٍ ـ عَدِيمُ ٱلْقَعْرِ.

Depurate, *v.t.* نَظَّفَ ـ أَصْفَى ـ صَفَّى.

Depuration, *n.* تَنْظِيف ـ تَنْقِيَة ـ تَصْفِيَة.

Deputation, *n.* The act of deputing, sending, إِرْسال ـ تَوْكِيل ـ تَفْوِيض. The persons deputed, وَفْد ـ مَبْعُوثُون ـ وُكَلآء ـ وَكالَة .pl أَوْفاد. He made a speech to the — that waited upon him, أَلْقَى خِطابًا إِلَى ٱلْوَفْدِ ٱلَّذِينَ وَفَدُوا عَلَيْهِ.

Depute, *v.t.* To send to, وَفَّدَ-إِلَى ـ أَرْسَلَ-إِلَى ـ فَوَّضَ-إِلَى. To appoint, as an agent, وَكَّلَ ـ أَجْرَى-فِي ـ جَرَّى ـ اِسْتَنابَ. To be deputed, تَوَكَّلَ.

Deputed, *a.* مُوَكَّل ـ مَوْكُول. Sent, مُوفَد ـ مُرْسَل.

Deputy, *n.* A substitute, نَقِيب .pl نُقَبآء ـ نائِب .pl نُوّاب ـ أَجْرِيآء .pl جَرِيّ. A commissioner, قائِمُ مَقامٍ ـ وُكَلآء .pl وَكِيل ـ عُمّال .pl عامِل ـ مُجِيز. To act as — for, ٤ نابَ عَنْ.

Derange, *v.t.* To put out of order, خَبَطَ ـ شَوَّشَ ـ لَبَّكَ ـ لَخْبَطَ ـ خَرْبَطَ ـ خَلَّطَ ـ هَوَّشَ ـ خَبَّلَ. To —, as of the constitution, ٤ أَخَذَ فِي ـ ٢ حَرَفَ ٱلْمِزاجَ. To — the mind, ٢ هَتَرَ. To be deranged, put out of order, تَشَوَّشَ ـ اِخْتَلَّ ـ اِرْتَبَكَ ـ

تَلَخْبَطَ ـ تَخَرْبَطَ ـ تَخَبَّطَ ـ تَخَبَّلَ. To be deranged, in constitution, إِخْتَلَّ ـ إِخْتَلَّ مِزَاجُهُ. To be deranged, crazy, أَفْنَدَ ـ ٤ فَنِدَ.

Deranged, *a.* Out of order, مُرْتَبِكٌ ـ مُتَشَتِّتٌ ـ مُتَهَوِّشٌ ـ مُتَشَوِّشٌ ـ مُلَخْبَطٌ ـ مُخَبَّطٌ ـ مُخْتَلٌّ. Of the health, مُخْتَلٌّ وسقام; of the mind, مُفْنِدٌ.

Derangement, *n.* Disorder, تَشْوِيش ـ إِرْتِبَاك ـ خَلَل ـ خَرْبَطَة ـ لَخْبَطَة ـ تَخْلِيط. Insanity, جُنُون ـ فَنَد.

Derelict, *a.* مُسَيَّب ـ مَتْرُوك.

Dereliction, *n.* The act of forsaking, هِجْرَان ـ تَرْك; of coming short, عَدَمُ إِيفَآء ـ إِهْمَال ـ قُصُور.

Deride, *v.t.* شَاقَحَ ـ ٤ خَنَثَ ـ تَسَخَّرَ بِ ـ ٤ سَخِرَ مِن ـ تَضَاحَكَ عَلَى ـ إِسْتَهْزَأَ بِ ـ ٤ ضَحِكَ مِن *or* بِ ـ فَلَحَ بِ.

Derider, *n.* سُخَرَة ـ مُسْتَهْزِئ ـ هُزَأَة ـ مُخَاتِل ـ مُسْخَرَاتِيّ ـ مُمَازِح.

Derision, *n.* مَسْخَرَة ـ إِسْتِهْزَآء ـ سُخْر. An object of contempt, ضُحْكَة ـ سُخْرَة.

Derisive, *a.* } **Derisory**, } سُخْرَة ـ ضَاحِكٌ عَلَى ـ مُسْتَهْزِئ ـ خَانِث ـ هُزَأَة.

Derisively, *ad.* بِٱسْتِهْزَآء ـ بِهُزُوءٍ.

Derivable, *a.* Obtainable, إِقْتِبَاسُهُ ـ الإِسْتِحْصَالُ عَلَيْهِ مُمْكِنٌ مُمْكِنٌ. That may be made to descend from, نَسَبُهُ إِلَى ـ مُمْكِنٌ. Deducible from, الإِسْتِدْلَالُ مِن ـ مُمْكِنٌ. Derivable, as a word, from ..., إِشْتِقَاقُهُ مِن ـ مُمْكِنٌ.

Derivation, *n.* A drawing from, إِسْتِخْرَاج ـ إِسْتِحْصَال ـ أَخْذ. A source, مَبْدَأ ـ مَخْرَج ـ مَنْشَأ ـ مَنْبَع ـ أَصْل. Tracing a word to its root, وَجْهُ ٱلْٱشْتِقَاقِ ـ إِشْتِقَاق. A branch, product, فَرْع ـ شُعْبَة. Deduction, إِسْتِنْتَاج. Descent, of birth, إِنْتِسَاب ـ نَسَب.

Derivative, *a.* Derived, إِشْتِقَاقِيّ ـ مُشْتَقّ. Deduced, مُسْتَخْرَج ـ مَأْخُوذ.

Derivative, *n.* A derived noun, كَلِمَةٌ مُشْتَقَّةٌ ـ إِسْمٌ مُشْتَقٌّ.

Derive, *v.t.* To obtain from, إِقْتَبَسَ ـ مِن ـ إِسْتَحْصَلَ ـ مِن ـ أَصْدَرَ ـ عَن ـ ٤ أَخَذَ ـ مِن. To deduce from, إِسْتَخْرَجَ ـ مِن ـ إِسْتَنْتَجَ ـ مِن ـ أَصْدَرَ ـ مِن. To —, as a word from a root, إِشْتَقَّ ـ مِن. To —, as descent, from, نَسَّبَ ـ إِلَى ـ نَسَّلَهُ إِلَى ـ ٤ نَسَبَ. To be derived from, of descent, إِسْتَنْسَبَ إِلَى ـ إِنْتَمَى إِلَى. To say of one's self that he derives his descent from, تَنَسَّبَ إِلَى. To be derived, as of a word, أُشْتُقَّ. I hope you will — much pleasure from ..., أَرْجُو أَنْ تَنْشَرِحَ كُلَّ ٱلْإِنْشِرَاحِ مِن. Problems were derived from this fundamental axiom, تَفَرَّعَتْ مِنْ هٰذَا ٱلْأَصْلِ مَسَائِلُ.

Derogate, *v.t.* and *i.* To lessen, إِسْتَخَفَّ ـ أَقَلَّ. To detract from, to be impaired or dishonoured by, أُسْتُقِلَّ بِ ـ ثُلِمَ بِ ـ أُسْتُهِينَ بِ. To impair, إِسْتَخَفَّ ـ إِسْتَقَلَّ ـ ٤ ثَلَمَ. This derogates from the truth, هٰذَا يَثْلِمُ ٱلْحَقَّ. This derogates from his honour, هٰذَا يَثْلِمُ عِرْضَهُ.

Derogation, *n.* The act of lessening, إِسْتِقْلَال ـ إِسْتِخْفَاف. Detraction, ثَلْم ـ إِسْتِثْلَال ـ نَمِيمَة ـ ضَرَر ـ مَضَرَّة.

Derogative, *a.* } **Derogatory**, } Injurious, ثَالِم ـ مُضِرّ ـ مُسْتَقِلّ. Unworthy, غَيْرُ لَائِقٍ ـ غَيْرُ مُنَاسِبٍ ـ قَبِيح ـ رَدِيّ.

Derogatorily, *ad.* ثَلْمًا ـ بِٱسْتِقْلَالٍ ـ إِسْتِقْلَالًا.

Derrick, *n.* زُرْنُوق ـ نَعَامَة.

Dervish, *n.* *See* Darwish, *n.*

Descant, *v.i.* أَكْثَرَ ٱلْقَوْلَ ـ تَكَلَّمَ ـ أَطَالَ ٱلْكَلَامَ ـ بَالَغَ فِي ٱلْكَلَامِ ـ ٤ سَابَ فِي ٱلْكَلَامِ.

Descend, *v.i.* To go down, سَفَلَ ـ ٤ إِنْحَدَرَ ـ ٤ نَزَلَ ـ ٤ هَبَطَ. To slope downwards, إِنْحَطَّ. To sink, إِنْغَمَسَ ـ ٤ غَاصَ. To —, as from ancestors, تَنَاسَلَ مِن ـ كَانَ مِن ذُرِّيَّةِ ـ إِنْتَسَبَ إِلَى. To proceed from, خَرَجَ مِن ـ ٤ صَدَرَ مِن ـ ٤. To fall to by inheritance, وَرِثَ *fut.* يَرِثُ. To — to particulars, in speaking, فَصَّلَ ٱلْمَادَّةَ ـ حَكَى بِٱلتَّفْصِيلِ ـ تَفْصِيلًا ـ رَوَى عَن ـ ٤ *aor.* يَرْوِي. To cause to —, go down, نَزَّلَ ـ أَنْزَلَ ـ أَهْبَطَ. To — by degrees, تَنَزَّلَ. I kept descending, مَا زِلْتُ أَنْزِلُ. The rain descended, ٤ جَآءَ ٱلْغَيْثُ. He descended from the mountain, ٤ هَبَطَ مِنَ ٱلْجَبَلِ.

Descend, *v.t.* نَزَّلَ ـ أَنْزَلَ.

Descendant, *n.* Offspring, نَسَب ـ مِنْ ذُرِّيَّةِ *pl.* أَنْسَاب ـ وَلَد ـ ابْن. A — of the Prophet, شَرِيف *pl.* شُرَفَآء ـ سَيِّد *pl.* سَادَة. Descendants, آل ـ أَوْلَاد ـ ذُرِّيَّة ـ نَسْل ـ أَنْسَال.

Descendent, *a.* Falling, نَازِل ـ هَابِط. Sinking, غَائِط ـ مُتَسَفِّل. Proceeding from, مُسْتَخْرَجٌ مِن ـ مُتَنَاسِلٌ مِن ـ مُنْبَثِقٌ مِن.

Descendible, *a.* That may be passed down, يَنْزِلُ مِنْهُ ـ يُنْزَلُ ـ مِمَّا ـ ٱلْهُبُوطُ مِنْهُ مُمْكِنٌ. Descendible by inheritance, يُوَرَّثُ ـ يُورَثُ.

Descension, *n.* The act of descending, نُزُول ـ هُبُوط. Descension of the stars, تَغَرُّبُ ٱلْكَوَاكِبِ. Right —, تَغَرُّبٌ ٱسْتِوَائِيٌّ. Oblique —, تَغَرُّبٌ مَائِلٌ.

Descent, *n.* The act of coming down, حَطٌّ مِن ـ نُزُول ـ هُبُوط. Degradation, عَزْل ـ حَطٌّ عَنِ ٱلْمَقَامِ ـ إِنْحِطَاطٌ مِنْ مَرْتَبَةٍ. A declivity, مُنْعَرَج ـ حُدُور ـ صَبَب ـ دُحْرَيْجَة. An invasion, غَزْو ـ غَزاة ـ دُخُول عَلَى ـ غارَة. A proceeding from, صُدُورٌ مِن ـ إِسْتِخْراجٌ مِن ـ إِنْبِثاقٌ مِن. Family origin, نَسْل ـ نَسَب ـ أَصْل. Offspring, أَوْلاد ـ ذُرِّيَّة ـ خَلَف. A place of —, مَهْبَط. Not of pure —, of mixed parentage, مُوَلَّد.

Describable, *a.* يُتَصَوَّرُ ـ قابِلُ ٱلْوَصْفِ ـ وَصْفُهُ مُمْكِنٌ.

Describe, *v.t.* To represent by words or figures, نَعَتَ = ـ اِتَّصَفَ ـ وَصَفَ *fut.* يَصِفُ ـ صَوَّرَ. To delineate, رَسَمَ [2]. To formulate, as in a document, نَصَّ [2]. To — to, مَثَّلَ-ل. To explain, فَسَّرَ ـ شَرَحَ = ـ عَبَّرَ. To recount, رَوَى عَن *aor.* يَرْوِى ـ ذَكَرَ [2] ـ حَدَّثَ. He described himself as, وَصَفَ نَفْسَهُ بِ. To be described, وُصِفَ ـ اِتَّصَفَ. It is described thus, رُوِىَ كَذا ـ يُوْرَى كَذا.

Describer, *n.* راوٍ ـ مُتَّصِف ـ واصِف ـ مُعَبِّرٌ عَن.

Description, *n.* The act of describing, بَيَان ـ وَصْف ـ اِتِّصاف ـ تَعْرِيف. Qualities described, أَوْصاف. A recital, رِوايَة ـ حِكايَة ـ حَدِيث. Exposition, تَعْبِير ـ شَرْح. Delineation, رَسْم. A sort, kind, شَكْل ـ نَوْع *pl.* أَنْواع ـ جِنْس *pl.* أَجْناس. Quality of personal character, خِلَّة ـ صِفَة. Description of a man's form, colour, *etc.*, حِلْيَة.

Descriptive, *a.* تَعْبِيرِىٌّ ـ وَصْفِىٌّ. Delineative, تَرْسِيمِىٌّ. Descriptive geometry, هَنْدَسَةٌ إِيضاحِيَّةٌ. A — catalogue, فِهْرِسٌ مَشْرُوحٌ بِٱلتَّفْصِيلِ.

Descriptively, *ad.* مُوَضَّحًا ـ بِٱلتَّفْصِيلِ ـ وَصْفًا.

Descry, *v.t.* To see at a distance, عايَنَ-مِنْ ـ أَدْرَكَ-مِنْ بَعِيدٍ. To discover, يَجِدُ *fut.* وَجَدَ ـ كَشَفَ عَن = ـ اِطَّلَعَ عَلَى ـ بَعِيدٍ.

Desecrate, *v.t.* To pollute, نَجَّسَ ـ دَنَّسَ.

Desecration, *n.* تَنْجِيس ـ تَدْنِيس.

Desert, *n.* Merit, اِسْتِئْهال ـ أَهْلِيَّة ـ لِياقَة ـ اِسْتِحْقاق.

Desert *v.t.* To abandon, دَشَّرَ ـ تَرَكَ [2] ـ هَجَرَ [2] ـ اِنْصَرَفَ عَن. To resign, give up, سَلَّمَ ـ تَخَلَّى عَن. To — from the army, فَرَّ مِنَ ٱلْخِدْمَةِ ٱلْعَسْكَرِيَّةِ [2] ـ هَرَبَ مِنَ ٱلْعَسْكَرِيَّةِ [2]. To apostatize from, اِرْتَدَّ عَن ـ خانَ [2].

Desert, *n.* A wilderness, صَحْراء ـ فَلاة *pl.* فَلَوات *and* فَلًا ـ بَرِّيَّة ـ قِفار ـ قَفْر *pl.* بَوادٍ ـ بادِيَة *pl.* دَهْناء ـ بِيد *pl.* بَيْداء ـ بَرارِى *pl.* A waterless —, فَدْفَد. The — in which the Israelites lost their way, التِّيه. A denizen of the —, بَدَوِىٌّ *pl.* بَداوَى (*vulg.* بِدْوان) ـ أَهْلُ ٱلْبَدْوِ. He passed the night in the —, باتَ ٱلْقَفْرَ =.

Desert, *a.* Wild, barren, قَفْر ـ وَحْش ـ مُسْتَوْحِش ـ أَقْفَرُ. Desert land, أَرْضٌ قَفْرٌ. Solitary, uninhabited, خالٍ مِنَ ٱلسُّكّانِ ـ مَهْجُور.

Deserted, *a.* Abandoned, مَهْجُور ـ مَتْرُوك. A — place or region, قَفْرَة *pl.* قَفَرات ـ خَرِب ـ خَراب. A — house, مَنْزِلٌ قَواء. To be —, left solitary, اِسْتَوْحَشَ ـ أَوْحَشَ.

Deserter, *n.* A — from the army, فارٌّ (*or* هارِبٌ) مِنَ ٱلْعَسْكَرِيَّةِ. One who forsakes a cause, مُنْصَرِفٌ عَن ـ مُرْتَدٌّ ـ خائِن.

Desertion, *n.* The act of abandonment, هَجْر ـ اِنْصِرافٌ عَن ـ تَرْك. Desertion from the army, فِرارٌ (*or* هَرِيبَةٌ) مِنَ ٱلْعَسْكَرِيَّةِ. The act of deceitfully forsaking a cause, اِرْتِداد ـ خِيانَة.

Deserts, *n.* *See* Merit, *n.*

Deserve, *v.t.* اِسْتَحَقَّ ـ اِسْتَوْجَبَ ـ اِسْتَأْهَلَ ـ حَقَّ ل = ـ صَلَحَ ل = [2].

Deserved, *a.* مُسْتَأْهَل ـ مُسْتَحَقّ.

Deservedly, *ad.* اِسْتِحْقاقًا ـ حَقًّا ـ بِٱلْواجِبِ.

Deserving, *a.* مُسْتَأْهِل ـ أَهْلٌ ل ـ مُسْتَحِقٌّ ـ واجِب ـ لائِقٌ بِ. To deem —, أَهَّلَ-بِ. Deserving of confidence, أَخُو ثِقَةٍ. To be —; *see to* Deserve, *v.t.*

Deshabille, *n.* لِبْسٌ خَفِيفٌ ـ تَخْفِيفَة.

Desiccant, *n.* نَشّافَة ـ دَواءٌ مُنَشِّف.

Desiccate, *v.t.* جَفَّفَ ـ نَشَّفَ.

Desiccation, *n.* تَجْفِيف ـ تَنْشِيف.

Desideratum, *n.* مَطْلُوب ـ أَمْرٌ مَطْلُوبٌ ـ بَغِيَّة ـ بُغْيَة.

Design, *v.t.* To sketch, صَوَّرَ ـ رَسَمَ [2]. To originate, أَوْجَدَ. To arrange, نَظَّمَ ـ رَتَّبَ. To purpose, عَمَدَ = ـ تَنَوَّى ـ تَعَزَّمَ ـ تَعَمَّدَ ـ نَوَى أَن = ـ قَصَدَ = ـ هَمَّ بِ [2]. To — for, خَصَّصَ-ل ـ فَرَضَ-ل = ـ أَعَدَّ-ل ـ عَيَّنَ-ل. I — to..., أَنا مُزْمِعٌ بِ *or* إِلَى.

Design, *n.* A delineation, تَصْوِير ـ رَسْم. A purpose, نِيَّة ـ مَرام ـ مَرائِر *pl.* مَرِير ـ أَغْراض *pl.* غَرَض ـ عَزِيمَة ـ عَمْد ـ مَقاصِدُ *pl.* مَقْصَد ـ قَصْد ـ مُراد ـ عَزْم ـ مَطْلَب. To have a — upon one's life, هَمَّ بِهِ [2].

Designable, *a.* That may be delineated, يُتَصَوَّرُ ـ يُرْسَمُ. That may be purposed, يُقْصَدُ. That may be originated, إِيجادُهُ مُمْكِنٌ.

Designate, *v.t.* To indicate, دَلَّ إِلَى [2] ـ أَشارَ إِلَى. To appoint, عَيَّنَ. To name, دَعا-بِ [2] ـ سَمَّى ـ سَمَّى-بِ. To distinguish, مَيَّزَ.

Designate, *a.* } Appointed to, مَنْصُوبٌ لَدَى ـ مُعَيَّنٌ لَدَى.
Designated, } Named, مُسَمًّى.

Designation, *n.* The act of pointing out, دَلالَة ـ دَلّ ـ دَلُولَة; of an appointing, تَعْيِين; of distinguishing, تَمْيِيز. Import, مَضْمُون. The act of naming, تَسْمِيَة. A name, اِسْم ـ لَقَب.

Designedly, *ad.* Purposely, بِقَصْدٍ ـ قَصْدًا ـ عَمْدًا.

Designer, *n.* A sketcher, رَسَّام ـ مُصَوِّر. A contriver, مُدَبِّر ـ مُرَتِّب. A plotter, (غايَةٍ *or*) صاحِبُ حِيلَةٍ ـ فَتَّان. Designers, schemers, أَرْبابُ ٱلْغاياتِ.

Designing, *n.* The art of delineating, عِلْمُ ٱلرَّسْمِ ـ الرَّسْمُ.

Designing, *a.* Artful, حَوَّال ـ قاصِدُ ٱلشَّرِّ ـ مَكَّار ـ غَدَّار ـ صاحِبُ حِيلَةٍ ـ أَرِيب ـ فَتَّان ـ حِيَلِيٌّ.

Desirable, *a.* شَهِيٌّ ـ شائِق ـ مَطْلُوب ـ مُشْتاقٌ إِلَيْهِ ـ مُتَمَنًّى ـ مَرْغُوب. I deem it — that it should be so, يا لَيْتَ ذٰلِكَ.

Desirably, *ad.* عَلَى أَتَمِّ ٱلْمَرامِ.

Desire, *n.* A wish, شَوْق ـ هُوِيَّة ـ أَهْواء *pl.* هَوًى ـ شَهْوَة *pl.* مُراد ـ إِرادَة ـ إِشْتِياق ـ نَفْس ـ رَغَبات *pl.* رَغْبَة ـ أَشْواق. Eager —, غَرام. An object, purpose, مَقْصُود ـ مَطْلُوب ـ مَرام ـ بُغْيَة. Hope, رَغْبَة ـ رَجاء ـ أَمَل ـ تَمَنٍّ. A prayer, إِلْتِماس ـ تَمَنٍّ. Lust, شَهْوَة *pl.* شَهَوات. Longing —, حَنِين. I have no — for it, ما لِي فِيهِ رَغْبَةٌ. An object of —, مُنْيَة ـ مُنْوَة ـ *pl.* مُنًى ـ رَغْبَة ـ رَغِيبَة *pl.* رَغائِبُ. Let him have his —, دَعْهُ يَمْلِكُ مُرادَهُ. They have a — to improve, يَتَمَنَّوْنَ لَوْ يَسْتَفِيدُونَ. The objects of — on the part of Russia, مَطامِحُ ٱلرُّوسِيَّةِ. As was desired, عَلَى ما يُرامُ مِنَ ٱلْإِقْبالِ ـ كَٱلْمَرْغُوبِ. To have a — for, إِشْتاقَ إِلَى. To excite — in, أَطْمَعَ ـ فِي ـ أَرْغَبَ ـ فِي ـ ² شاقَ ـ إِلَى ـ شَوَّقَ ـ إِلَى ـ أَنْفَسَ ـ أَغْرَمَ.

Desire, *v.t.* To wish for, إِرْتَغَبَ فِي ـ ² رَغِبَ فِي ـ ² رَغِبَ ـ إِسْتَحَبَّ ـ ² هَوِيَ ـ إِشْتاقَ إِلَى ـ أَرادَ ـ إِشْتَهَى ـ أَحَبَّ. To like, ² طَمِعَ فِي ـ ب *or* ² حَنَّ إِلَى. To long for, ² حَنَّ إِلَى. To covet, ² طَمِعَ فِي ب *or*. To design, رامَ *aor.* يَرُومُ. To —, or request of, ² طَلَبَ ـ مِن ـ سَأَلَ ـ مِن *aor.* يَسْأَلُ. To hope for, ² أَمَلَ ـ تَمَنَّى أَنْ. To make one to —, أَرْغَبَ فِي ـ مَنَّى ـ ب ـ رَغَّبَ ـ فِي ـ شَهَّى. To — a thing to be brought, ² دَعا ب. To intreat, تَرَجَّى ـ قَنَعَ إِلَى ـ ² طَلَبَ إِلَى. He desired nothing but ..., ما رامَ شَيْئًا غَيْرَ. The desired result did not follow, لَمْ يُنْتِجِ ٱلْمَطْلُوبَ. Affairs in the town are not what could be desired, لَيْسَتِ ٱلْأَحْوالُ فِي ٱلْمَدِينَةِ كَما يَنْبَغِي.

Desired, *a.* Asked for, مَطْلُوب. Wished for, مُراد ـ شَهِيٌّ ـ مَرْغُوب. A — object, رَغِيبَة ـ رَغْبَة *pl.* رَغائِبُ.

Desirous, *a.* Wishing for, شَوّاق ـ شَيِّق ـ شاءٍ ـ مُشْتاقٌ إِلَى. Intent upon, راغِبٌ فِي. Hoping, مُتَمَنٍّ. Longingly desirous, حَنّانٌ ل ـ مُغْرَمٌ ب. To be —, إِشْتاقَ إِلَى ـ تَشَوَّقَ. To make one — of, أَوْلَمَ ـ ب ـ أَغْرَمَ ـ ب ـ أَغْرَى ـ ب. To be made — of, أُغْرِمَ ب ـ أُولِمَ ب.

Desist, *v.i.* To cease from, أَزالَ ـ ² جَبَأَ عَن ـ ² كَفَّ عَن ـ ² قَعَدَ عَن ـ تَوَقَّفَ عَن ـ ² تَرَكَ ـ إِنْقَطَعَ عَن. I will not —, لا أَبْرَحُ. He did not — from reviling me, ما جَبَأَ عَنْ شَتْمِي. He will not — from his evil doing, لا يَنْفَكُّ عَنْ قُبْحِ فِعْلِهِ.

Desistance, *n.* تَبْطِيل ـ إِنْقِطاع ـ تَرْك ـ كُفُوفٌ عَن ـ تَوَقُّفٌ عَن ـ فَراغ.

Desk, *n.* A writing table, بِشْتَخْتَة ـ مَكْتَبَة. A pulpit, مِنْبَر.

Desolate, *v.t.* To deprive of inhabitants, أَخْلَى ـ مِنَ ٱلسُّكّانِ. To lay waste, دَمَّرَ ـ أَهْدَمَ ـ خَرَّبَ ـ أَخْرَبَ ـ وَحَّشَ ـ أَقْفَرَ ـ أَهْلَكَ. To be or become —, إِسْتَوْحَشَ ـ تَوَحَّشَ ـ تَخَرَّبَ.

Desolate, *a.* Laid waste, مُدَمَّر ـ مَهْدُوم ـ خَراب ـ خَرِب. Destitute of people, خالٍ مِنَ ٱلسُّكّانِ. Desert, أَقْفَر ـ قَفْر. Solitary, مَتْرُوك ـ مُتَوَحِّش. A —, waste, a ruined place, house, country, خَراب *pl.* خَرابات ـ خَرِبَة *pl.* خِرَب.

Desolately, *ad.* إِسْتِيحاشًا ـ وَحْشَةً ـ تَوَحُّشًا.

Desolation, *n.* The act of laying waste, دِمار ـ إِخْراب ـ هَلاك. A desolate state, خَرابَة ـ وَحْشَة. Sadness, كَآبَة ـ غَمّ ـ حُزْن. Dreariness, قَفْر.

Despair, *n.* قُنُوط ـ قَنَط ـ قَطْعُ ٱلرَّجاءِ ـ يَأْسَة ـ يَأْس.

Despair, *v.i.* ² قَنِطَ. To — of, أَيِسَ مِن *aor.* يَأْيَسُ ـ يَئِسَ مِن ـ قَطَعَ ٱلْأَمَلَ مِن ـ ² قَطَعَ ٱلرَّجاءَ مِن ـ إِسْتَيْأَسَ مِن ـ يَئِسَ *aor.* قَطَعَ ٱلْعَشَمَ مِن. To cause to —, آيَسَ ـ أَيْأَسَ.

Despairer, *n.* }
Despairing, *a.* } قانِط ـ قَنِط ـ يَؤُوس ـ يَؤُس ـ آيِس.

Despatch, *n.* *See* Dispatch, *n.* and *v.t.*

Desperado, *n.* مَجْنُون ـ مُتَهالِك ـ مُتَهَوِّر.

Desperate, *a.* Hopeless, يَؤُوس ـ مِنْ غَيْرِ رَجاءٍ ـ قانِط. Rash, مَطْيُور ـ طائِش ـ سادِر ـ مُسْتَخْبِط ـ مُتَهَوِّر. Irrecoverable, لا يُتَداوَى ـ لا يُتَعَوَّضُ ـ مَتْلُوف. To be —, rash, تَهَوَّرَ ـ تَهالَكَ. A — undertaking, قُحْمَة *pl.* قُحَم.

Desperately, *ad.* Without hope, بِقَطْعِ ٱلرَّجاءِ ـ مِنْ غَيْرِ رَجاءٍ ـ بِقَنَطٍ. Furiously, بِغَشْمَرَةٍ ـ مِنْ غَيْرِ عَقْلٍ ـ بِتَهَوُّرٍ. Much, جِدًّا ـ بِمُبالَغَةٍ ـ كَثِيرًا ـ بِشِدَّةٍ.

Desperation, *n.* Rashness, هَيَجان ـ إِعْتِساف ـ حُمُوٌّ ـ تَهَوُّر. They fought with —, قاتَلُوا قِتالَ ٱلْمُسْتَخْبِطِينَ. *See also* Despair, *n.*

Despicable, *a.* دَنِيء ـ حَقِير ـ قَزِم ـ شَقِيٌّ ـ أَهْوَنُ ـ خَزٍ ـ خَسِيس ـ لَئِيم ـ هَوان ـ رَذِيل. To be —, ² قَزِمَ ـ ² خَزِيَ. Mean, poor, مِسْكِين. *See also* Contemptible, *a.*

Despicableness, *n.* قَزَم ـ خَزْيَة ـ ذُلّ ـ ذِلَّة ـ رَذَالَة ـ خَسَاسَة ـ دَنَآءَة ـ حَقَارَة. Meanness, poverty, مَسْكَنَة.

Despicably, *ad.* بِهَوَانٍ ـ خَزْيَةً ـ بِرَذَالَةٍ ـ حَقَارَةً.

Despisable; *see* Despicable, *a.*

Despise, *v.t.* أَهَانَ ـ حَقَّرَ ـ قَزَّدَ ـ قَزَمَ ـ قَادَحَ ـ إِغْتَمَصَ ـ إِسْتَخَفَّ ـ ذَلَّ ـ رَذَّلَ ². To esteem one lightly, إِسْتَحْقَرَ ـ إِسْتَثْقَلَ. To — death, هَانَ عَلَيْهِ ٱلْمَوْتُ ².

Despised, *a.* هَوَان ـ مَهِين ـ مُحْتَقَر ـ حَقِير. To be —, تَحَاقَرَ ـ حُقِرَ ـ هَانَ ².

Despiser, *n.* مُزْدَرٍ ـ مُتَهَاوِن ـ حَاقِرٌ نَاقِرٌ.

Despite, *n.* Malignity, إِزْدِرَآء ـ زِرَايَة ـ سَخِيمَة ـ كَيْد ـ حِقْد ـ عَدَاوَة ـ غَرَض ـ بُغْض ـ رَغْمُ أَنْفٍ ـ نَفْسَانِيَّة. In — of, رَغْمًا ـ عَلَى رَغْمِ أَنْفِ ـ فِي وَجْهِهِ ـ مُخَالَفَةً. To do — to, to lightly esteem, تَسَخَّمَ عَلَى ـ ازرى ب ـ إِزْدَرَى ب.

Despiteful, *a.* Malicious, حَقُود ـ غَدِير ـ حَسِك ـ حَنِك ـ مُسَخَّم ـ خَبِيث.

Despitefully, *ad.* بِٱزْدِرَآءٍ ـ بِرَدَآءَةٍ ـ بِخَبَاثَةٍ ـ حِقْدًا.

Despoil, *v.t.* To strip, بَطَّلَ ـ شَلَّحَ ـ جَرَّدَ ـ عَرَّى. To plunder, نَهَبَ ـ أَنْهَبَ ـ سَلَبَ ² ـ أَعْدَمَ ـ ظَلَمَ.

Despoiler, *n.* سَلَّاب ـ نَهَّاب.

Despoliation, *n.* }
Despoilment, } سَلْب ـ نَهْب ـ تَشْلِيح ـ شَلْح.

Despond, *v.i.* To lose hope, قَنِطَ ـ إِنْكَسَرَ قَلْبُهُ ـ إِنْفَلَقَ ـ غَمَّهُ ـ قَطَعَ ٱلرَّجَآءَ مِن. To — about, أَيِسَ مِن.

Despondency, *n.* قَنَط ـ يَأْس ـ قَطْعُ ٱلْأَمَلِ ـ إِيَاس.

Despondent, *a.* }
Desponding, } قَنِط ـ قَانِط ـ يَؤُوس ـ مِنْ غَيْرِ رَجَآءٍ ـ مَأْيُوس.

Despondently, *ad.* قَنَطًا ـ بِقَطْعِ ٱلرَّجَآءِ ـ بِيَأْسٍ.

Despot, *n.* A — sovereign, حَاكِمٌ مُتَسَلِّطٌ بِسُلْطَانٍ مُطْلَقٍ ـ حَاكِمٌ ٱسْتِبْدَادِيّ ـ قَهَّار. A tyrant, جَبَّار ـ جَائِر ـ ظَالِم.

Despotic, *a.* }
Despotical, } إِسْتِقْلَالِيّ ـ مُطْلَق ـ جَبَّارِيّ. Tyrannical, جَائِر ـ عَنِيف ـ ظَلَّام ـ بَاغٍ.

Despotically, *ad.* إِسْتِقْلَالًا ـ بِمُطْلَقِ ٱلْإِرَادَةِ ـ إِطْلَاقًا. Tyrannically, بِجَوْرٍ ـ عَنْفًا وَجَبْرًا ـ ظُلْمًا. To behave —, severely, towards, عَنُفَ ب ² ـ ظَلَمَ.

Despotism, *n.* حُكْمٌ مُطْلَقٌ ـ حُكُومَةٌ مُسْتَقِلَّةٌ. Tyranny, جَوْر ـ بَغْي ـ ظُلْم ـ عَنْف.

Despumation, *n.* جُفَال ـ رِغَاوَة ـ رَغْوَة.

Desquamation, *n.* تَقَشُّر ـ تَقْشِير.

Dessert, *n.* نَقْل ـ فَاكِهَة.

Destemper, *n.* لَوْنٌ مَحْلُولٌ بِٱلْمَآءِ وَٱلصَّمْغِ ـ تَرْبِيَة.

Destinate, *v.t.* *See to* Destine, *v.t.*

Destinate, *a.* مُعَيَّن ـ مَنْصُوب ـ مَأْمُور.

Destination, *n.* The act of putting to a purpose, تَخْصِيص ـ تَعْيِين. The being put to a purpose, إِسْتِعْمَال. A design, object, غَايَة ـ مَقْصُود ـ مَرَام ـ غَرَض. A place to be reached, مَعَاد ـ رِحْلَة ـ مَرْجِع ـ جِهَة.

Destine, *v.t.* To mark out for, عَيَّنَ ـ ل ـ خَصَّصَ ـ ل ـ أَعَدَّ ـ ل. To doom, قَدَّرَ عَلَى ـ كَتَبَ ٱلنَّصِيبَ ب ² ـ قَضَى عَلَى ـ ب.

Destined, *a.* Marked out for, مُعَيَّنٌ ل ـ مُخَصَّصٌ ل. Bound for, سَائِرٌ إِلَى ـ مُسَافِرٌ إِلَى ـ رَائِدٌ إِلَى ـ وَارِدٌ إِلَى. Doomed, مُقَدَّرٌ عَلَى ـ مَكْتُوبُ ٱلنَّصِيبِ ب ـ نَصِيبُهُ. Destined to become, أَنْ يَصِير.

Destiny, *n.* The power that destines, ٱلْقَضَآءُ وَٱلْقَدَرُ ـ ٱلتَّقْدِيرُ. Lot, fate, نَصِيب ـ بَخْت ـ مُقَدَّر ـ قِسْمَة ـ مَا كُتِبَ عَلَى. An evil —, سُوءُ بَخْتٍ ـ قِلَّةُ نَصِيبٍ ـ ٱلْجَبِين. It was my —, إِسْتَوْفَى مَا كُتِبَ عَلَيْهِ. He underwent his —, كَانَ مُقَدَّرًا عَلَيَّ. He fulfilled his —, he died, قَضَى نَحْبَهُ.

Destitute, *a.* Wanting, عَدِم ـ عَدِيمٌ مِن ـ خَالٍ مِن ـ عَارٍ مِن. Abandoned, مَتْرُوك ـ مَهْجُور ـ مُدَشَّر. Friendless, عَدِيمُ ٱلرَّفِيقِ ـ بِلَا مُعِينٍ. Poor, عَوِز ـ مُحْتَاج ـ فَقِير ـ مَسْكِين. To be —, without, عَطِلَ مِن ـ خَلَا مِن ² ـ عَدِمَ مِن. To be —, solitary, تَوَحَّشَ. To make —, أَعْدَمَ. Verily, he is very —, إِنَّهُ لَعَوِزٌ لَوِزٌ.

Destitution, *n.* Want, عَدَم ـ حِرْمَان ـ عَوَز. Poverty, فَقْر ـ إِفْتِقَار ـ مَسْكَنَة. Destitution befell him, أَصَابَهُ عَوَزٌ.

Destroy, *v.t.* To lay waste, أَسْحَقَ ـ أَبَادَ ـ دَمَّرَ ـ خَرَبَ ـ خَرَّبَ. To demolish, هَدَّ ² ـ تَوَّهَ ـ هَدَمَ ـ رَمَى. To annihilate, أَفْنَى ـ لَاشَى ـ أَتْلَفَ. To — an army, قَرَضَ ـ ٱلْعَسْكَرَ ـ مَحَقَ ٱلْعَسْكَرَ. To kill, هَلَكَ ـ أَهْلَكَ ـ قَتَلَ ² ـ مَوَّتَ ـ جَرَزَ ² ـ أَبَادَ. To consume, أَذْهَبَ ـ ضَيَّعَ ـ أَتْلَفَ.

Destroyer, *n.* هَادِم ـ مُخَرِّب ـ مُبِيد ـ هَالِك. A killer, جَارِز ـ قَاتِل ـ هَالِك.

Destructibility, *n.* فَنَآء ـ تَهْلُكَة ـ مَهْلَكَة ـ تُهْلُوك.

Destructible, *a.* يُهْلَكُ ـ مِمَّا يَفْنَى ـ يُهْدَمُ ـ يُخْرَبُ ـ يَتَلَاشَى. Consumable, as with fire, يَحْتَرِق.

Destruction, *n.* The act of destroying, laying waste, هَدْم ـ تَدْمِير ـ إِسْحَاق ـ تَخْرِيب; of annihilating, إِعْدَام ـ إِفْنَآء ـ إِبَادَة; of killing, قَتْل ـ إِهْلَاك. The state of being إِتْلَاف;

destroyed, laid waste, تَدَمُّر ـ دَمار ـ خَرابَة ـ خِرْبَة; of being annihilated, تَلاشٍ ـ فَناءٌ ـ عَدَم; of being slain, اِنْقِتال ـ هَلاك. Perdition, ruin, هَلاك ـ تَوًى. Death, مَوْت. Self-destruction, suicide, قَتْلُ ٱلْإِنْسانِ نَفْسَهُ.

Destructive, *a.* Ruinous, مُخَرِّب ـ مُبِيد ـ مُهْلِك. Injurious, ضارٌّ ـ مُضِرٌّ. Killing, قاتِل ـ مُهْلِك ـ هالِك. Destructive, as of a disease, جارِف.

Destructively, *ad.* بِنَوعٍ مُهْلِك ـ تَخْرِيبًا ـ إِبادَةً ـ إِهْلاكًا.

Destructiveness, *n.* خاصَّةٌ مُضِرَّةٌ ـ خاصَّةٌ مُبِيدَةٌ ـ إِهْلاك ـ صِفَةٌ قَتّالَةٌ. A cause of —, مُهْلِكَة ـ مَضَرَّة.

Desuetude, *n.* إِلْغاءٌ ـ مَنْسِيَّة ـ بُطْلانُ (or زَوالُ) ٱلْاِسْتِعْمالِ ـ عَدَمُ ٱلْأُلْفَةِ ـ عَدَمُ ٱلْاِعْتِيادِ ـ نِسْيٌ. To fall into —, نَسِيَ ـ أُلْغِيَ ـ ²زالَ عَنِ ٱلْاِسْتِعْمالِ ـ ²بَطَلَ ٱسْتِعْمالُهُ ـ أُفْرِطَ. Gone into —, مَهْجُور.

Desultorily, *ad.* مِنْ غَيْرِ تَقَيُّدٍ ـ مِنْ غَيْرِ تَرْتِيب ـ عَنْ غَفْلَةٍ ـ عَلَى بابِ ٱللّٰهِ ـ كَيْفَما كانَ.

Desultoriness, *n.* Carelessness, عَدَمُ إِقْدام ـ عَدَمُ تَقَيُّدٍ; incoherence, عَدَمُ تَرْتِيب ـ عَدَمُ تَتابُع. *See also* Incoherence, *n.*

Desultory, *a.* Without order, عَدِيمُ ٱلتَّرْتِيبِ; incoherent, مُقَلْقَل ـ مِنْ غَيْرِ تَتابُع. Versatile, قَلّاب. *See also* Incoherent, *a.*

Detach, *v.t.* To separate from, أَفْرَزَ-مِن ـ أَفْرَدَ-مِن ـ إِبْعَدَ-مِن ـ اِقْتَصَّ-مِن ـ فَصَّ-مِن ـ فَصَلَ-مِن. To unloose, فَكَّ ـ ²حَلَّ. To — or send out a party of soldiers, أَرْسَلَ سَرِيَّةً. To be detached, to — one's self, اِنْفَصَّ ـ اِنْبَتَلَ ـ تَبَتَّلَ ـ اِعْتَزَلَ عَن.

Detached, *a.* Alone, مُنْفَرِد. Loosened, مُنْفَكّ.

Detachment, *n.* A part, بَعْض ـ أَجْزاءٌ *pl.* جُزْءٌ. A — of soldiers, طَلِيعَة *pl.* طَلائِع ـ سَرِيَّة *pl.* سَرايا ـ شَكِيكَة *pl.* شَكائِك ـ جَرِيدَة.

Detail, *v.t.* To state in detail, شَرَحَ-شَرْحًا ـ حَكَى-تَفْصِيلًا ـ فَصَّلَ ـ ²قالَ-تَفْصِيلًا ـ ²قَصَّ عَلَى-بِٱلتَّفْصِيلِ ـ مُفَصَّلًا. To — troops, as for a particular duty, عَيَّنَ ٱلْعَسْكَرَ لِ.

Detail, *n.* A minute narration, شَرْحٌ مُفَصَّلٌ ـ تَفْصِيل. A selection of troops, فِرْقَةٌ مُعَيَّنَةٌ مِنَ ٱلْعَسْكَرِ. In —, بِٱلتَّفْصِيلِ ـ تَفْصِيلًا ـ شَرْحًا. The affair with all its details, المادَّةُ بِكافَّةِ تَفَرُّعاتِها. The details, الجُزْئِيّات.

Detain, *v.t.* To keep something back from, مَنَعَ عَنْهُ آ... ـ ضَبَطَ عَنْهُ آ... ـ حَبَسَ عَنهُ آ... To hold one back, restrain, ²ثَبَرَ-عَن ـ كَفَعَ-عَن ـ ²كَفَّ-عَن ـ أَوْقَفَ ـ مَنَعَ-عَن ـ وَقَّفَ-عَن. To keep late, عَوَّقَ. To — in custody, ضَبَطَ ـ ²حَصَرَ ـ حَبَسَ. To — what belongs to another, مَخْلَسَ ـ اِخْتَلَسَ. To —, as from departure, ²حَجَزَ-عَن. *See also under to* Delay, *v.t.*

Detainder, *n.* أَمْرٌ شَرْعِيٌّ بِتَسْلِيمِ مالٍ مَحْجُوزٍ لِأَجْلِ دَيْنِ صاحِبِهِ.

Detained, *a.* Kept late, مُوَقَّف ـ مُبْطَأٌ بِهِ. Kept in custody, مَمْسُوك ـ مَضْبُوط ـ مَحْبُوس. Restrained, مَحْجُوز ـ مَمْنُوع ـ مَوْقُوف.

Detainer, *n.* A preventer, مُوَقِّف ـ مانِع. One who keeps forcible possession of another's goods, حاجِزُ مالِ ٱلنّاسِ غَصْبًا.

Detect, *v.t.* أَفْشَى ـ كَشَفَ ـ كَشَفَ عَن. To be detected, تَكَشَّفَ ـ اِنْكَشَفَ.

Detection, *n.* إِظْهار ـ كَشْفٌ عَن.

Detective, *a.* كاشِف ـ كَشّاف.

Detective, *n.* قارِيَة *pl.* قَوارِي ـ دَسِيس *pl.* دَواسِيس ـ داسُوس ـ كَشّاف ـ مُفَتِّش ـ بَصّاص.

Detector, *n.* *See* Detective, *n.*

Detention, *n.* Delay, the being delayed, تَوْقِيف. Restraint, قَفْع ـ ثَبْر ـ ضَبْط ـ مَنْع. Imprisonment, سَجْن ـ حَبْس. A place of detention, a prison, سِجْن ـ مَحْبَس. Illegal —, تَوْقِيف عَلَى خِلافِ ٱلْقانُونِ ـ مِنْ غَيْرِ حَقٍّ. *See also under* Delay, *n.*

Deter, *v.t.* أَخْرَقَ-عَن ـ عَفَقَ-عَن ـ يَهِقُ *aor.* وَهَقَ-عَن ـ أَمْسَكَ ـ مَنَعَ ـ ²حَجَبَ ـ عَوَّقَ-عَن.

Deterge, *v.t.* نَظَّفَ ـ مَسَحَ ـ مَشَّحَ.

Detergent, *n.* A purgative medicine, دَواءٌ مُسْهِلٌ ـ جَلّاب. A cleansing medicine, دَواءٌ مُنَقٍّ.

Deteriorate, *v.t.* To spoil, أَتْلَفَ ـ أَفْسَدَ ـ خَسَّرَ ـ فَسَّقَ ـ فَسَّدَ. To change into, حَوَّلَ-إِلَى ـ قَلَبَ-إِلَى ـ صَيَّرَ.

Deteriorate, *v.i.* To spoil, اِنْفَسَدَ ـ أَخْلَفَ عَن ـ ²خَلَفَ ـ تَلِفَ. To change to, اِنْقَلَبَ إِلَى ـ يَؤُولُ *aor.* آلَ إِلَى.

Deterioration, *n.* اِنْفِساد ـ تَلَف ـ خُسْران.

Determent, *n.* عَوْق ـ عائِق ـ تَعْوِيق ـ مانِع ـ مَنْع.

Determinable, *a.* That may be fixed, مِمّا يُعَيَّنُ ـ مِمّا يُحَدَّدُ; that may be abolished, ended, مِمّا يَبْطُلُ ـ مِمّا يَنْفَسِخُ.

Determinate, *v.t.* To fix bounds, حَدَّدَ.

Determinate, *a.* Limited, مَحْدُود. Fixed, مُقَرَّر ـ مَقْطُوع. Appointed, مُعَيَّن. Definite, مَعْلُوم. Defined, مُفَصَّل ـ مَفْرُوض. A — noun, مَعْرِفَة.

Determination, *n.* Direction to a certain end, مَمال ـ مَيْل ـ زَوْر. A design, عَزِيمَة ـ عَزْم ـ قَصْد ـ نِيَّة. Resolution, إِقْدام ـ زَماع ـ

— فَتْوَى — جَزْم — عَزِيمَة — عَارِفَة — عَارِض . A judicial decision, فَتْوَى. Limitation, تَحْدِيد — حُجْة. The fixing of the meaning of a word, بَيَان مَعْنَى ٱللَّفْظ. The act of lapsing, إِنْقِطَاع — تَتِمَّة. Determination of blood to the head, صُعُودُ ٱلدَّمِ إِلَى ٱلدِّمَاغِ. Any rush, as of fumes, *etc.*, حُمَيًّا. I admire your —, حَبَّذَا عَزِيمَتُكَ. To come to a —, أَزْمَعَ عَلَى.

Determinative, *a.* That which decides, confirms, مُنْجِز — بَتِّيّ — إِثْبَاتِيّ; which limits, مُعَيِّن — مُحَدِّد; which explains, مُبَيِّن — تَعْرِيفِيّ.

Determinatively, *ad.* بَتَّةً — عَزْمًا جَزْمًا — عَزْمًا.

Determine, *v.t.* To terminate, أَنْجَزَ — أَتَمَّ — قَضَى — أَنْهَى. To settle, فَصَلَ — خَتَمَ — قَرَّرَ — ثَبَّتَ — جَزَمَ. To order, قَضَى بِ — حَكَمَ عَلَى — حَكَمَ بِ. To limit, حَدَّدَ. To influence, lead one to, حَمَلَ-عَلَى — أَلْجَأَ-إِلَى — أَلْزَمَ-إِلَى — مَيَّلَ-إِلَى — أَمَالَ-إِلَى. To estimate, as of a price, قَدَّرَ. To fix the signification of a word, عَرَّفَ ٱللَّفْظَ — بَيَّنَ مَعْنَى ٱللَّفْظِ. He had determined, كَانَ قَدْ جَزَمَ.

Determine, *v.i.* To come to an end, نَجَزَ — إِنْقَضَى — إِنْتَهَى — تَمَّ. To —, or resolve, upon, عَزَمَ عَلَى — أَزْمَعَ عَلَى — تَعَمَّدَ — إِعْتَمَدَ عَلَى — تَعَزَّمَ عَلَى — إِعْتَزَمَ عَلَى — حَتَمَ عَلَى — إِعْتَزَمَ. He determined to travel, أَزْمَعَ عَلَى ٱلسَّفَرِ. I am determined on . . . , أَنَا مُزْمِعٌ عَلَى. And when the affair is determined on, وَإِذَا عُزِمَ عَلَى ٱلْأَمْرِ.

Determined, *a.* Having a fixed purpose, عَازِمٌ عَلَى — مُزْمِعٌ عَلَى. Resolute, رَبِيّ — زَمِيع — عَزُوم — شَدِيدُ ٱلْعَارِضَةِ — حَمِيس — صِنْدِيد. To be —, تَرَبَّى. He was — to . . . , كَانَ مُصَمِّمًا عَلَى. He continued — upon . . . , لَمْ يَزَلْ مُصِرًّا عَلَى.

Detersion, *n.* تَغْسِيل — تَنْظِيف.

Detersive, *a.* غَسَّال — مُنَظِّف.

Detest, *v.t.* كَرِهَ — بَغَضَ — شَنَأَ بِ — غَمِرَ عَلَى. They detested one another, of many, تَبَاغَضُوا — تَشَانَؤُوا.

Detestable, *a.* مَلْعُون — كَرِه — مَكْرُوه — شَنِيع — لَعِين — مَنْفُور — مُنْفِض. To be —, شَنِئَ.

Detestably, *ad.* قَبَاحَةً — بِٱلْكُرْهِ — شَنَاءَةً — شَنَاةً.

Detestation, *n.* Hatred, شَنِيئَة — شَنَاءَة — غُمُور — بِغْضَة — غَمَر. Enmity, بُغْض — عَدَاوَة — خُصُومَة. An object of —, شَنَاءَة — شَنَائِيَة.

Detested, *a.* مَبْغُوض — مَقْبُوح — مَنْفُور. Applied to a man, مَشْنُوٌّ — مَشْنُوءٌ.

Detester, *n.* شَانِئٌ *pl.* شُنَّاءٌ.

Dethrone, *v.t.* حَطَّ-عَنْ كُرْسِيِّ ٱلْمُلْكِ — عَزَلَ-عَنِ ٱلسَّلْطَنَةِ — عَزَلَ — خَلَعَ — خَلَعَ-عَنِ ٱلسَّلْطَنَةِ. To be dethroned, deposed, عُزِلَ — خُلِعَ.

Dethronement, *n.* عَزْلٌ عَنِ ٱلْمَمْلَكَةِ — خَلْعٌ عَنِ ٱلسَّلْطَنَةِ.

Detinue, *n.* *See* Detainder, *n.*

Detonate, *v.t.* فَقَّعَ.

Detonate, *v.i.* إِنْفَقَعَ.

Detonating, *a.* فَقَّاع. Detonating powder, مَعْجُونٌ كِيمَاوِيٌّ فَقَّاعٌ.

Detonation, *n.* إِنْفِقَاع — فَقْع.

Detour, *n.* دَوْرَة — لَفَّة. We have made a long —, دُرْنَا دَوْرَةً كَبِيرَةً.

Detract, *v.t.* To — from, to cut off from, غَضَّ-مِن — إِسْتَقَلَّ — إِسْتَخَفَّ. To depreciate, حَذَفَ-مِن — أَنْدَرَ-مِن. To defame, شَنَعَ — هَتَكَ — فَضَحَ — جَرَّسَ بِ.

Detraction, *n.* إِفْتِرَاء — ذَمّ — نَمِيمَة.

Detractive, *a.* | Detractious, — فَاضِح — مُذِمّ — نَمَّام — هَاتِك — هَتَكِيّ — مُجْلِبُ ٱلنَّمِيمَةِ.

Detractor, *n.* نَمَّام — فَضَّاح — لَمَّاز — غَمَّاز.

Detriment, *n.* غُصَّة — غَصَاصَة — وَكْس — نَقْص — نُقْصَان — مَضَرَّة — ضَرَر — نَقِيصَة — عَوَار — خَسَارَة — خَلَل. To cause — to, خَسَّرَ — أَضَرَّ — وَكَسَ — غَضَّض.

Detrimental, *a.* مُخَسِّر — مُضِرّ — ضَارّ.

Detritus, *n.* جُفَاءٌ — جُرُف.

Detrude, *v.t.* كَبَسَ.

Detruncate, *v.t.* شَذَّبَ — قَضَبَ.

Detrusion, *n.* تَكْبِيس — كَبْس.

Deuce, *n.* The devil, إِبْلِيس — ٱلشَّيْطَانُ. The —, as at cards, ٱلْإِثْنَانِ; at dice, دُوبَارَة.

Deuteronomy, *n.* The book of, سِفْرُ تَثْنِيَةِ ٱلْاشْتِرَاعِ.

Devastate, *v.t.* وَحَّشَ — خَرَّبَ — هَدَّمَ — هَدَمَ. To be devastated, خَرِبَ — خُرِبَ — إِسْتَوْحَشَ — أَوْحَشَ.

Devastation, *n.* The act of laying waste, إِخْرَاب — هَدْم — إِتْلَاف — تَخْرِيب. The being laid waste, وَحْشَة — خَرِب — خَرَاب.

Develop, *v.t.* To unfold, بَسَطَ — مَدَّ — نَشَرَ. To expose to view, أَرَى — أَظْهَرَ — عَرَضَ-عَلَى ٱلْبَصَرِ. To explain, فَسَّرَ — فَصَّلَ — شَرَحَ. To disclose, كَشَفَ عَن — أَجْهَرَ — أَذَاعَ.

Develop, *v.i.* To extend, إِتَّسَعَ. To progress, تَقَدَّمَ — تَرَوَّجَ. It developed into, عَادَ إِلَى — صَارَ.

Development, *n.* The act of budding, branching, نَبَات — تَفَرُّع. Disclosure, كَشْف. Propagation, إِنْتِشَار. Explanation, تَفْصِيل — تَفْسِير. Extent, إِمْتِدَاد — سَعَة. The act of unfolding, نَشْر —

تَنْشِير ; of furthering, تَوْسِيع ـ تَرْوِيج. A solution, result, ـ خِتام نَتِيجَة. The — of commerce, تَرْوِيجُ ٱلتِّجارَةِ.

Deviate, *v.i.* To stray, ـ ضَلَّ ـ ـ تاهَ ـ تاهَ. To — from, ـ زاغَ عَن ـ جارَ عَن ـ حادَ عَن. To digress in, أَلْوَى ب. To —, as from a purpose, عَرْقَلَ ـ كَفَّ عَن ـ عَدَلَ عَن ـ ضَرَبَ عَن. To err, sin, ـ ضَلَّ ـ أَخْطَأَ فِي ـ غَوَى. To cause to —, ـ تَوَّهَ ـ أَضَلَّ ـ أَزاغَ ـ ضَلَّلَ ـ أَغْوَى ـ تَيَّهَ. Deviating, شاذٌّ ـ تائه. He deviated from the truth, حاصَ عَنِ ٱلْحَقِّ.

Deviation, *n.* The act of straying, ـ حَيْدَة ـ ٱنْحِراف ـ حَيْص ـ غَيَّة ـ غَوَى ـ طُغْيان ـ زَلَّة ـ سَقَط ـ ضَلالَة. Error, تَوْه ـ زَوْغ.

Device, *n.* The act of devising, إِخْتِراع ـ إِيجاد. A scheme, ـ تَرْتِيب ـ أَسْباب *pl.* سَبَب ـ تَدْبِير. A stratagem, trick, ـ كَيْد ـ بِدْعَة ـ حِيَل *pl.* حِيلَة ـ رُوَيْغَة ـ مَكِيدَة. An emblem, ـ رَسْم صُورَة ـ إِشارَة ـ عَلامَة ـ نِيشان.

Devil, *n.* The, ـ ٱلْخَطّاف ـ شَياطِين *pl.* ٱلشَّيْطان ـ إِبْلِيس ٱللَّعِين. A crafty fellow, شَيْطان ـ شُطّار *pl.* شاطِر. To send to the —, ـ سَخِطَ عَلَى. The blue devils, كُرَب ـ سَوْداء. Speak of the — and his horns will appear: the following Arabic proverbs express the drift of the English, إِذا ذَكَرْتَ ٱلذِّئْبَ أَعِدَّ لَهُ ٱلْقَضِيبَ *i.e.,* If you speak of the wolf prepare a stick for him. أُذْكُرِ ٱلْكَلْبَ وَفِي يَدِكَ عَظْمٌ *i.e.,* If you speak of a dog have a bone in your hand for him.

Devilish, *a.* خَبِيث ـ مَلْعُون ـ جَهَنَّمِيٌّ ـ شَيْطانِيٌّ. Wicked, مُسَمَّم ـ حَسِك ـ حَقُود ـ شَنِيع ـ شِرِّير. Malevolent, حَقُود.

Devilry, *n.* شَيْطَنَة.

Devious, *a.* دَوّار ـ ضالٌّ ـ مُنْحَرِف ـ تائه ـ شاذٌّ.

Devisable, *a.* That may be contrived, originated, ـ مِمّا يُتَدَبَّرُ مِمّا يُوجَدُ ـ مِمّا يُخْتَرَعُ. That may be drawn, مِمّا يُتَصَوَّرُ. That may be bequeathed by will, جائِزٌ لِلْوَصِيِّ أَنْ يُوصَّى بِهِ.

Devise, *v.t.* To contrive, originate, إِبْتَدَأَ ـ إِخْتَرَعَ ـ أَوْجَدَ. To plan, دَبَّرَ ـ فَصَّلَ ـ رَتَّبَ. To draw, رَسَمَ. To — a way, دَبَّرَ سَبِيلًا. To bequeath to, أَوْصَى ل ـ ب ـ أَوْصَى ـ ب. To — mischief, تَفَكَّرَ بِٱلْإِثْمِ (*or* بِٱلشَّرِّ). To — evil against, ـ زَبَى ـ شَرًّا زَبَّى ل ـ بِشَرّ.

Devise, *v.i.* To plan, meditate, تَأَمَّلَ فِي ـ إِفْتَكَرَ فِي ـ تَدَبَّرَ.

Devise, *n.* A gift by will, خَلَف مُوَصًّى ـ وَصِيَّة. A will, وَصِيَّة.

Devisee, *n.* وارِثٌ تَحْتَ ٱلْوَصِيَّةِ ـ أَوْصِياء *pl.* وَصِيٌّ.

Deviser, *n.* مُفَصِّل ـ مُدَبِّر ـ مُخْتَرِع.

Devisor, *n.* مُوَصٍّ.

Devoid, *a.* Empty, فاضٍ ـ فارِغ ـ خالٍ. Deprived of, ـ عارٍ مِن مُتَعَرٍّ مِن ـ عَدِيم ـ غَيْرُ مالِكٍ. To be — of, without, ـ عَدِمَ ـ خَلا ٱلْمَكانُ مِن. The place was — of inhabitants, تَعَرَّى مِن ٱلنّاسِ. A land — of inhabitants, أَرْضٌ خاوِيَةٌ.

Devoir, *n.* حَقٌّ ـ واجِب ـ لازِمَة.

Devolution, *n.* تَحْوِيل ـ إِنْتِقال ـ نَقْل.

Devolve, *v.t.* To roll down, دَحْرَجَ. To deliver over, ـ حَوَّلَ سَلَّمَ ـ نَقَلَ.

Devolve, *v.i.* To roll down, تَدَحْرَجَ. To fall into, to be made over to, يَقَعُ *aor.* وَقَعَ ل ـ تَحَوَّلَ إِلَى ـ إِنْتَقَلَ إِلَى. It devolved upon me to . . . , صارَ لِي أَن.

Devote, *v.t.* To apply specially to, ـ حَصَرَ ـ ل ـ خَصَّصَ ـ ل. To give up by vow, قَدَّمَ ـ نَذَرَ. To doom to evil, ـ أَعْطَى ـ لِلشَّرِّ سَخِطَ عَلَى ـ قَضَى عَلَى ـ بِٱلشَّرِّ ; to curse, لَعَنَ. To consecrate to, حَرَّمَ ـ ل. To — to pious uses, وَقَفَ ـ ل ـ أَوْقَفَ ـ ل يَقِفُ *aor.* To — one's self to an affair, تَجَرَّدَ لِلْأَمْرِ ـ تَبَتَّلَ إِلَى ; to religious worship, تَجَرَّدَ لِلْعِبادَةِ. What end have you in view in devoting your time to that study? ما غايَةُ مَطْمَحِكَ فِي قَصْرِكَ ٱلزَّمَنَ عَلَى هٰذِهِ ٱلْمُطالَعَةِ.

Devoted, *a.* Ardent for, كَثِيرُ ٱلرَّغْبَةِ فِي ـ حامٍ فِي ـ حَرِيصٌ عَلَى. Zealous, مُتَعَصِّب ـ غَيُور. Attached, ـ مُحِبٌّ ـ أَوِدّاء *pl.* وَدِيد. To be wholly —, given up, to, تَبَتَّلَ إِلَى ـ إِنْقَطَعَ إِلَى.

Devotedness, *n.* Excessive attachment, فَرْطُ ٱلْمَحَبَّةِ. *See also* Devotion, *n.*

Devotee, *n.* A devout person, نَذِير ـ نُسّاك *pl.* ناسِك *pl.* سائح ـ عَبَدَة *pl.* عابِد ـ زُهّاد *pl.* زاهِد ـ نُذُر. One submissively attached, خَدّام ـ مُتَعَصِّب ل ـ أَسِير ـ مُتَحَمِّس ـ حَمِس. Ragged devotees, أَصْحابُ ٱلْخِرَقِ.

Devotion, *n.* The state of being solemnly set apart to, ـ تَحْرِيمٌ ل تَقْدِيمٌ ل. Piety, تَقْوَى ـ زُهْد ـ نُسُك ـ تَزَهُّد. Worship, عِبادَة. Strong attachment, تَعَصُّب ل ـ عَلاقَة ـ إِنْقِياد ـ حَمَس. Submissive attachment to, إِسارَةٌ ل. Application to, ـ تَقَيُّدٌ ب إِنْقِطاعٌ إِلَى ـ عِنايَةٌ ب ـ رَغْبَةٌ فِي. Devotions, ـ عِبادَة ـ صَلاة دُعاء. He performed his devotions, أَجْرَى عِبادَتَهُ ـ صَلَّى وَسَجَدَ.

Devotional, *a.* مُتَعَلِّقٌ بِٱلصَّلاةِ ـ مُتَعَلِّقٌ بِٱلْعِبادَةِ. *See also under* Religious, *a.*

Devotionally, *ad.* بِرَجَب ـ بِهَيْبَةٍ ـ بِطَرِيقَةِ ٱلْعِبادَةِ.

Devour, *v.t.* To eat up ravenously, ـ زَقَمَ ـ شَرَسَ ـ أَقاتَ. To eat up everything, إِقْتَمَّ ـ قَمَّ. To destroy, هَلْقَمَ ـ هَرَسَ أَخْرَبَ ـ أَفْنَى ـ هَرَسَ ـ هَدَمَ. To consume, as of fire,

أَفْنَى – حَرَقَ ﺡ – أَحْرَقَ . To —, of a wild beast, إِفْتَرَسَ . To eat, eat up, أَكَلَ ².

Devourer, n. } Devouring, a. } بَلَّاعٌ – أَكُولٌ – أَكَّالٌ – آكِلٌ . A destroyer, مُخَرِّبٌ – هَارِسٌ – هَيْذَامٌ . Ravenous, of beasts, مُفْتَرِسٌ – خَاطِفٌ .

Devout, a. Pious, وَرِعٌ – وَرِيعٌ – نَاسِكٌ – قَانِتٌ – مُتَّقٍ . Earnest in worship, وَقُورٌ فِي ٱلْعِبَادَةِ – مُتَعَبِّدٌ – حَمِسٌ . To lead a — life, نَسَكَ ² – تَنَسَّكَ . To be —, as towards God, قَنِتَ لِ ².

Devoutly, ad. عَلَى سَبِيلِ ٱلتَّقْوَى – بِتَعَبُّدٍ – وَرَعًا – بِٱلزُّهْدِ . Much, جِدًّا – لِلْغَايَةِ – كَثِيرًا .

Devoutness, n. *See* Devotion, n.

Dew, n. نَدًى – نَدًى – طِلَالٌ *pl.* طَلٌّ – لَثٌّ – لَثًى . A fall of —, رَشْحَةٌ .

Dew, v.t. أَرَشَّ – نَدَّى .

Dewberry, n. نَوْعٌ مِنَ ٱلْعُلَّيْقِ .

Dewdrop, n. قَطْرَةُ نَدًى .

Dewiness, n. نَدَاوَةٌ .

Dewlap, n. طَنْطَلَةُ ٱلْبَقَرِ – لُغْدُودٌ – لُغْدٌ – غَبْغَبٌ – غَبَبٌ .

Dewy, a. نَدْيَانُ – مَبْلُولٌ بِٱلطَّلِّ – نَدِيٌّ .

Dexter, n. اليَمِينُ .

Dexterity, n. مَعْرِفَةٌ – حَذَاقَةٌ – خِفَّةٌ – لَبَاقَةٌ – مَهَارَةٌ – مِهْنَةٌ . Cunning, حِيلَةٌ – صَنْعَةٌ – إِرْبٌ .

Dexterous, a. حُوَّلٌ قُلَّبٌ – أَرِيبٌ – مُدَرَّبٌ – أَرِبَ بِ – شَاطِرٌ – حَاذِقٌ بِاذِقٌ – نَشِيطٌ – حَذِقٌ – نَبِيهٌ – مَاهِرٌ . To be —, أَرِبَ – لَبِقَ ².

Dexterously, ad. بِغَايَةِ ٱلْإِتْقَانِ – بِمَهَارَةٍ – بِحَذَاقَةٍ – بِإِرْبٍ .

Dextral, a. يَمِينِيٌّ – يَمِينٌ .

Dhámmah, n. The vowel point so called, ضَمَّةٌ – ضَمٌّ .

Diabetes, n. سَلَسٌ – بُوَالٌ – تَقْطِيرٌ .

Diabolic, a. } Diabolical, } *See* Devilish, a.

Diachylon, n. لَزْقَةٌ مُلَيِّنَةٌ – لَزْقَةٌ .

Diaconal, a. مُخْتَصٌّ بِٱلشَّمَامِسَةِ – شَمَامِسِيٌّ .

Diacritical, a. Serving to discriminate, مُفَرِّقٌ بَيْنَ – مُمَيِّزٌ . A — vowel point, حَرَكَةٌ . To mark with — points, أَعْجَمَ – شَكَلَ ² .

Diadem, n. عِصَابَةُ ٱلْمَلِكِ – إِكْلِيلٌ – تِيجَانٌ *pl.* تَاجٌ .

Diæresis, n. نُقْطَتَانِ عَلَى حَرْفِ عِلَّةٍ تَدُلَّانِ عَلَى ٱلنُّطْقِ بِهِ .

Diagnosis, n. Of a disease, إِسْتِدْلَالٌ عَلَى مَرَضٍ – تَمْيِيزُ ٱلْمَرَضِ – تَشْخِيصُ ٱلْمَرَضِ – تَحْقِيقٌ مِنْهُ .

Diagnostic, a. Of disease, دَلِيلٌ (or دَالٌّ) عَلَى مَرَضٍ .

Diagnostic, n. Of disease, عَلَامَةُ مَرَضٍ *pl.* عَلَامٌ *and* عَلَامَاتٌ .

Diagonal, n. خَطٌّ مُسْتَقِيمٌ مِنْ زَاوِيَةٍ إِلَى زَاوِيَةٍ – خَطُّ ٱلزَّاوِيَةِ .

Diagonal, a. مُسْتَقِيمٌ مِنْ زَاوِيَةٍ إِلَى زَاوِيَةٍ .

Diagonally, ad. مِنْ زَاوِيَةٍ إِلَى زَاوِيَةٍ .

Diagram, n. A mathematical —, شَكْلٌ رِيَاضِيٌّ ; a geometrical —, شَكْلٌ هَنْدَسِيٌّ . A plan, صُورَةٌ – رَسْمٌ *pl.* رُسُومٌ .

Dial, n. A sun-dial, سَاعَةُ شَمْسٍ – دَرَجَاتٌ – مِزْوَلَةٌ – مُقَنْطَرَةٌ . A horizontal —, سَاعَةٌ بَسِيطَةٌ ; a vertical —, سَاعَةٌ مُنْحَرِفَةٌ . A — plate, مِينَاءٌ . The needle of a —, مِيلٌ .

Dialect, n. A —, لُغَةٌ *pl.* لُغَاتٌ – لِسَانٌ *pl.* أَلْسِنَةٌ . Pronunciation, كَلَامٌ – لِسَانٌ – نُطْقٌ .

Dialectic, a. } Pertaining to a dialect, مُتَعَلِّقٌ بِعِبَارَاتِ لِسَانٍ . Dialectical, } Logical, مِنْ عِلْمِ ٱلْمَنْطِقِ – مَنْطِقِيٌّ .

Dialectician, n. مِنْطِيقٌ – مِنْ أَهْلِ ٱلْمَنْطِقِ .

Dialectics, n. مُتَفَرِّعَاتٌ مَنْطِقِيَّةٌ .

Dialist, n. مَاهِرٌ فِي صِنَاعَةِ سَاعَاتِ ٱلشَّمْسِ .

Dialogistic, a. } Dialogistical, } عَلَى سَبِيلِ ٱلسُّؤَالِ – عَلَى طَرِيقِ ٱلْمُحَاوَرَةِ وَٱلْجَوَابِ .

Dialogue, n. مُحَادَثَةٌ – مُجَاوَبَةٌ – مُحَاوَرَةٌ – مُكَالَمَةٌ – مُخَاطَبَةٌ – مُرَاجَعَةٌ . They held a —, of many, حَاوَرُوا – تَجَاوَبُوا – تَحَاوَرُوا – جَاوَبَ بَعْضُهُمْ بَعْضًا .

Diameter, n. قُطْرٌ – قُطْرُ ٱلدَّائِرَةِ .

Diametral, a. قُطْرِيٌّ .

Diametrical a. قُطْرِيٌّ . Direct, عَدِلٌ – مُسْتَقِيمٌ .

Diametrically, ad. قُطْرًا . Altogether, wholly, بِٱلْكُلِّيَّةِ – بِٱلْمَرَّةِ – بَتَّةً . Two points — opposed to one another, نُقْطَتَانِ مُتَقَابِلَتَانِ .

Diamond, n. The stone, أَلْمَاسٌ . A —, at cards, دِينَارٌ . A glazier's —, أَلْمَاسُ ٱلزُّجَاجِ . A rough —, أَلْمَاسٌ خَشِيبٌ . A out —, أَلْمَاسٌ مَنْحُوتٌ . A rose —, أَلْمَاسٌ رُوزَةٌ . A — cutter, حَكَّاكُ ٱلْأَلْمَاسِ . Diamond-dust, حُكَاكَةُ أَلْمَاسٍ . Diamond cut —, مُقَابَلَةٌ .

Diapason, n. الطَّامَّةُ ٱلْكُبْرَى .

Diaper, n. بَفْتَةٌ مَشْغُولَةٌ عَلَى ٱلطَّارَةِ – قُمَاشٌ بِشُغْلِ ٱلطَّارَةِ .

Diaper, v.t. رَقَّمَ – رَقَّشَ .

Diaphaneity, n. شُفُوفٌ – شَفَافَةٌ .

Diaphanous, a. شَفَّافٌ . To be —, شَفَّ ﺡ .

Diaphoresis, n. تَكْثِيرُ ٱلْعَرَقِ – رَشْحٌ .

Diaphoretic, a. مُعَرِّقٌ – مُرَشِّحٌ . A — medicine, دَوَاءٌ مُعَرِّقٌ .

Diaphragm, *n.* حِجَابٌ ـ حِجَابُ ٱلْقَلْبِ (*or* ٱلْكَبِدِ) ـ حِلْب ٱلْجَوْفِ.

Diarist, *n.* كَاتِبُ دَفْتَرٍ يَوْمِيّ.

Diarrhœa, *n.* ذَرَبٌ ـ رِقَّةُ بَطْنٍ ـ ذَرِب ـ خِلْفَة ـ سُلَاح ـ إِسْهَال ـ ٱلْبَطْنِ.

Diary, *n.* رُوزْنَامَة ـ دَفْتَرٌ يَوْمِيّ ـ يَوْمِيَّة.

Diathesis, *n.* Predisposition to disease, قَرِيحَةٌ لِمَرَضٍ مَا.

Diatribe, *n.* مُنَاقَرَةٌ مُتَطَاوِلَةٌ ـ نَوَاقِرُ.

Dibble, *n.* وِعْزَقَةٌ صَغِيرَةٌ.

Dibble, *v.t.* عَزَقَ ـ حَفَرَ وَغَرَسَ بِٱلْمِعْزَقَةِ.

Dice, *n.* كَعْب ـ أَزْهَار *pl.* زَهْر ـ زَيْن ـ زَاقَات *pl.* زَاقَة *pl.* كِعَاب. To play at —, لَعِبَ بِٱلْكِعَابِ ـ قَمَرَ.

Dicephalous, *a.* ذُو رَأْسَيْنِ.

Dicky, *n.* A shirt front, صَدْرُ قَمِيصٍ. A seat behind a carriage, مَقْعَدٌ فِي مُؤَخَّرِ ٱلْعَرَبِيَّةِ.

Dictate, *v.t.* To direct, prescribe, كَتَبَ لِ ـ بِ ـ أَمَرَ ـ فَرَّضَ عَلَى ـ أَفْرَضَ عَلَى ـ عَلَّمَ. To suggest, advise, أَشَارَ عَلَى ـ بِ. To repeat word by word for another to write them down, قَرَأَ عَلَى ـ أَمْلَى عَلَى ـ أَكْتَبَ ـ مَلَّى. To ask one to —, إِسْتَكْتَبَ ـ إِكْتَتَبَ. To write what is dictated, إِكْتَتَبَ.

Dictate, *n.* A suggestion, impulse, تَلْقِين ـ إِرْشَاد ـ رَأْي ـ تَحْرِيض. An order, قَاعِدَة ـ وَصِيَّة ـ أَمْر. The dictates of conscience, سَرَائِرُ ٱلضَّمِيرِ.

Dictation, *n.* An order, حُكْم ـ أَمْر. Repetition to another what to write, تَمْلِيَة ـ إِكْتَاب; what is thus written, إِمْلَاء.

Dictator, *n.* مُسْتَبِدٌّ بِٱلْأَمْرِ ـ وَلِيُّ ٱلْأَمْرِ طُرًّا ـ حَاكِمٌ مُطْلَق.

Dictatorial, *a.* } Dogmatical, حُكْمِيّ ـ عَقِيدِيّ. Unlimited,
Dictatory, } as in power, مُسْتَقِلّ ـ مُطْلَق ـ مُسْتَبِدّ.
See also Arrogant, *a.*

Dictatorially, *n.* As of power, إِسْتِقْلَالًا ـ إِطْلَاقًا ـ إِسْتِبْدَادًا. Arrogantly, بِتَكَبُّرٍ ـ تَفَخُّمًا ـ تَحَكُّمًا ـ بِتَطَاوُلٍ. To act — towards, تَطَاوَلَ عَلَى.

Dictatorship, *n.* مَنْصِبُ ٱلْحَاكِمِ ٱلْمُطْلَقِ.

Dictatrix, *n.* مُسْتَبِدَّةٌ بِٱلْأَمْرِ ـ وَلِيَّةُ ٱلْأَمْرِ طُرًّا ـ حَاكِمَةٌ مُطْلَقَةٌ.

Diction, *n.* Mode of enunciation, إِجْرَاءُ ٱلتَّلَفُّظِ ـ تَلَفُّظ ـ تَقْرِير. Style, phraseology, نَظْم ـ كَلَام ـ قَوْل ـ أَلْفَاظ ـ عِبَارَة ـ نَصّ. He uses good —, هُوَ حَسَنُ ٱلْعِبَارَةِ.

Dictionary, *n.* قَوَامِيسُ *pl.* قَامُوس ـ كِتَابُ ٱللُّغَةِ.

Dictum, *n.* أَقْوَال *pl.* قَوْل ـ أَمْثَال *pl.* مَثَل ـ مَقَالَة.

Didactic, *a.* }
Didactical, } مُؤَدِّب ـ مُرْشِد ـ مُتَعَلِّقٌ بِٱلْعِلْمِ ـ تَعْلِيمِيّ.

Didactylous, *a.* ذُو أُصْبُعَيْنِ فِي قَدَمٍ.

Diddle, *v.t.* غَدَرَ بِ ـ مَسَّحَ.

Die, *v.i.* To lose life, إِنْتَقَلَ ـ فَاقَ بِنَفْسِهِ ـ فَاظَ ـ حَتَفَ ـ شَرِبَ مِنْ ـ قَضَى نَحْبَهُ ـ مِنْ دَارِ ٱلْفَنَاءِ إِلَى دَارِ ٱلْبَقَاءِ ـ مَاتَ ـ تُوُفِّيَ ـ أَتَتْهُ ٱلْمَنِيَّةُ ـ كَأْسِ ٱلْحِمَامِ. To — of, مَاتَ مِنْ ـ تُوُفِّيَ فِي ـ مَاتَ حَتْفَ فِيهِ. To — a natural death, مَاتَ حَتْفَ أَنْفِهِ. To — suddenly, مَاتَ بَغْتَةً ـ مَاتَ فُجَاءَةً. To — as a criminal, to be killed, مَاتَ قَتِيلًا. To cause to —, to put to death, أَمَاتَ ـ مَوَّتَ. To languish, يَنِي *aor.* وَنَى ـ ضَنِيَ ـ فَتَرَ ـ تَفَاتَرَ. To wither, ذَبَلَ ـ ذَوَى. To — to, رَكَنَ ـ مَاتَ عَنْ. To — away, as of the sea, مَاتَ. He died sixty years old, مَاتَ عَنْ سِتِّينَ سَنَةً. He died leaving brothers, مَاتَ عَنْ أُخْوَةٍ. He died leaving a brother and sister, مَاتَ عَنْ أَخٍ وَأُخْتٍ.

Die, *n.* *See* Dice, *n.*

Die, *n.* A stamp for coining money, سِكَّة ـ سِكَاك *pl.* سَكّ *pl.* سِكَك. A —, in backgammon, فُصُوص *pl.* فَصّ.

Diet, *n.* Food, أَكْل ـ غِذَاء ـ قُوت ـ طَعَام. Regulated —, تَدْبِيرُ ٱلْأَكْلِ ـ طَعَامٌ مُرَتَّب. Allowance of provisions, جِرَايَة. An assembly, مَجْلِسُ شُورَى ـ جَمْعِيَّة.

Diet, *v.t.* To feed, أَطْعَمَ ـ قَاتَ. To regulate one's —, رَتَّبَ لِ ـ ٱلطَّعَامَ. To — one's self, to eat by rule, أَكَلَ بِٱلْقَانُونِ. To eat sparingly, أَكَلَ قَلِيلًا ـ أَكَلَ بِٱلتَّقَشُّفِ ـ زَهِدَ فِي ٱلْأَكْلِ.

Dietary, *a.* } مُتَعَلِّقٌ بِٱلْمَأْكُولَاتِ ـ مُتَعَلِّقٌ بِٱلْأَكْلِ. Dietetics,
Dietetic, } *n.* قَوَاعِدُ ٱلْأَكْلِ.

Dietary, *n.* تَقْوِيمُ ٱلْمَأْكُولَاتِ ـ قَاعِدَةُ ٱلْأَكْلِ.

Differ, *v.i.* To be distinguished from, إِمْتَازَ مِنْ ـ إِفْتَرَقَ مِنْ ـ إِخْتَلَفَ ـ إِنْمَازَ مِنْ ـ تَمَيَّزَ مِنْ. To be at variance, تَنَازَعَ ـ تَضَادَّ. To cause to —, to distinguish, فَرَّقَ بَيْنَ ـ بَيَّنَ. To — from, خَالَفَ. One man differeth from another in disposition, رَجُلٌ يَمْتَازُ عَنْ رَجُلٍ فِي ٱلشِّيمَةِ. *See also to* Disagree, *to* Quarrel, *v.i.*

Difference, *n.* Distinction, إِمْتِيَاز ـ تَفَاوُت ـ فَصْل ـ فَرْق ـ مُخَالَفَة ـ خِلَاف ـ إِفْرَاز ـ إِخْتِلَاف. A dispute, شَوَاش ـ مُعَانَدَة ـ مُخَاصَمَة ـ مُنَازَعَة. A ground of —, سَبَبُ ٱلْمُنَازَعَةِ ـ بَاعِثُ ٱلشَّوَاشِ. To make up, of a —, صَالَحَ. There is no — between us and them, لَا فَرْقَ بَيْنَنَا وَبَيْنَهُمْ. Making a —, مُمَيِّز. The settlement of a —, تَسْوِيَةُ ٱلْخِلَافِ.

Different, *a.* Dissimilar, مُتَبَايِن ـ مُتَغَايِر ـ مُتَفَاوِت ـ آخَر ـ مُخْتَلِف. Various, شَتَّى ـ أَجْنَاس. Of — kinds, أَنْوَاع. Of — sorts, مِنْ أَصْنَافٍ مُخْتَلِفَة.

Differential, *a.* مُتَعَلِّقٌ بِٱلتَّفَاوُت. Differential duties, التَّفَاوُت بَيْنَ ٱلْمَكْسِ ٱلْمَفْرُوضِ عَلَى ٱلْبِضَاعَةِ ٱلْبَلَدِيَّةِ وَٱلْأَجْنَبِيَّة.

Differently, *ad.* خِلَاف ـ بِٱخْتِلَاف ـ بِتَفَاوُت. He acted —, فَعَلَ بِخِلَافِ ذٰلِكَ.

Difficult, *a.* Hard to be done, عَوِيص ـ عَسِير ـ صَعْب ـ مُعْضِل ـ مُشْكِل ـ غَمِض ـ غَلِق. Hard to be understood, مُشْكِل ـ عَسِير ـ عَسِرُ ٱلْفَهْم ـ عَسِير. Distressing, شَاقّ ـ فَظِيع. Difficult in disposition, شَرِيس ـ شَرِس ـ قَرِطِيّ ـ صَعْب ـ عَزِق ـ عارم ـ وَعِر ـ شَرَاس ـ نَظّ ـ شَكِس. Intricate, مُلْتَوٍ. Rugged, stony, وَعِر. To be —, hard, to be done, تَعَاسَرَ ـ تَعَسَّرَ ـ ² عَسُرَ ـ تَعَصَّى ـ أَصْعَبَ ـ ² صَعُبَ ـ إِسْتَعْسَرَ. To be — to understand, إِغْتَاصَ عَلَى ـ إِسْتَصْعَبَ عَلَى ² ـ غَمُضَ. To find —, to be — to, صَعُبَ عَلَى ـ أَعْوَصَ عَلَى ـ يَعِزُّ *aor.* وَعُرَ عَلَى. To make — to one, عَسَّرَ عَلَى ـ غَمَّضَ عَلَى. To make —, hard to be understood, to, غَمَّضَ عَلَى. To deem —, distressing, إِسْتَفْظَعَ ـ فَظِعَ بِٱلْأَمْرِ. It was — for him, تَعَسَّرَ عَلَيْهِ ـ إِلْتَوَى عَلَيْهِ ـ تَعَذَّرَ عَلَيْهِ ـ تَعَاسَرَ عَلَيْهِ. It is not — for us to understand, مَا يَعِزُّ فَهْمُهُ عَلَيْنَا. It is not — for them, لَيْسَ مِنَ ٱلصَّعْبِ عَلَيْهِمْ. A — question, مَطْلَبٌ وَعِرٌ. Great difficulties, مُشْكِلَاتٌ كُلِّيَّة.

Difficulty, *n.* A hard thing to be done, مُشْكِلَة ـ عُسْرَة ـ صُعُوبَة. A difficult affair, أَمْرٌ ـ مِحْنَة ـ عَوِيص ـ أَمْرٌ ذُو عُسْرَةٍ ـ عَجْز ـ عِيَاص ـ مُشْكِلَة ـ مَعْسَرَة ـ مُشْكِل. Obscurity in meaning, غُمُوض. It is not without —, لَمْ يَخْلُ مِنْ صُعُوبَةٍ. Distress, بَلَاء ـ مَشَقَّة ـ ضِيقَة ـ مُصِيبَة ـ مُضَايَقَة ـ ضَنْك. Difference, عَاقَة ـ مُمَانَعَة ـ مُخَالَفَة. Opposition, an obstacle, إِعْتِرَاض ـ مَانِع. To be in a —, كَانَ فِي ضَنْكٍ ـ ضَاقَ بِ ـ ٱلْأَمْرُ ـ حَصِرَ. To be in difficulties, want, إِحْتَاجَ ـ أَعْسَرَ ـ إِفْتَكَرَ; of money, تَعَسَّرَتْ عَلَيْهِ ٱلدَّرَاهِمُ ـ أَفْلَسَ. To be in difficulties, through commission of a crime, تَضَايَقَ مِنْ خَوْفِ ٱلْعِقَابِ. To raise difficulties, إِعْتَرَضَ. To place difficulties in the way of . . . , عَضَلَ عَلَى ـ ² عَضَلَ. With difficulty, عَلَى كُرْهٍ. After —, God will give ease, سَيَجْعَلُ ٱللّٰهُ بَعْدَ عُسْرٍ يُسْرًا. Surrounded with complications and difficulties, مُقْتَرِنٌ بِٱلْمَشَاكِلِ وَٱلْمَصَاعِبِ.

Diffidence, *n.* Want of confidence, عَدَمُ ٱعْتِمَادٍ ـ عَدَمُ أَمْنِيَّةٍ ـ شُبْهَة. Bashfulness, حَيَاء ـ خَجَل.

Diffident, *a.* Wanting confidence, عَدِيمُ ٱلْأَمْنِيَّةِ ـ عَدِيمُ ٱلْإِعْتِمَادِ. Bashful, خَجِل ـ حَيِيّ.

Diffidently, *ad.* بِحَيَاء ـ خَجَلًا ـ بِغَيْرِ أَمْنِيَّةٍ.

Difformity, *n.* تَشَوُّه ـ تَفَاوُت ـ إِخْتِلَاف ـ عَدَمُ مُشَابَهَةٍ.

Diffuse, *v.t.* To pour out, صَبَّ ² ـ أَفَاضَ ـ سَكَبَ ². To spread, نَشَرَ ـ إِشْتَهَرَ ـ شَهَرَ ـ نَشَرَ ² ـ أَشَاعَ بِ. To disperse, شَتَّتَ ـ مَذَّرَ. To spread, as of rays, أَشَعَّ. To —, as of sweet odours, تَضَيَّعَ ـ تَنَسَّمَ بِ ـ شَاعَ ² ـ عَمَّ. To be diffused through, The sun diffused its beams, أَشَعَّتِ ٱلشَّمْسُ. To be diffused, spread, إِنْتَشَرَ.

Diffusely, *ad.* Widely, إِمْتِدَادًا ـ إِنْتِشَارًا ـ سَعَةً. With a superabundance of words, بِٱلتَّطْوِيلِ ـ بِٱلْمُبَالَغَةِ ـ تَفْصِيلًا بِطُولِ ٱلْكَلَامِ.

Diffuseness, *n.* Of language, إِطَالَةٌ فِي ٱلْكَلَامِ ـ تَفْصِيل ـ قَالٌ وَقِيلٌ.

Diffusibility, *n.* قَابِلِيَّةُ ٱلْإِشَاعَةِ ـ قَابِلِيَّةُ ٱلْإِنْتِشَارِ.

Diffusible, *a.* شَائِع ـ بَائِع ـ إِشَاعَتُهُ مُمْكِنَةٌ ـ إِنْتِشَارُهُ مُمْكِنٌ.

Diffusion, *n.* The act of spreading, إِشَاعَة ـ إِنْتِشَار ـ إِذَاعَة. Dispersion, تَشَتُّت ـ تَشْتِيت. Extension, إِمْتِدَاد. The act of pouring, صَبّ ـ إِفَاضَة.

Diffusive, *a.* Spreading, مَدِيد ـ مُمِدّ ـ مُنْتَشِر. Diffusive, of discourse, مُفَصَّل ـ مُطِيل ـ مُبَالِغ. A — smell, فَوْحَة.

Diffusiveness, *n.* *See* Diffuseness, *n.*

Dig, *v.t.* As with a spade, حَفَرَ ـ إِحْتَفَرَ ـ ² عَزَقَ. To thrust in, أَدْخَلَ ـ ² سَلَكَ. To —, as of a hole, ² نَقَبَ. To excavate, ² نَقَرَ. To — up, as of a treasure, corpse, *etc.*, ² نَبَشَ ـ نَبَّشَ. What is dug out of a hole, mine, *etc.*, حَفِير ـ حَفِيرَة. A place of digging, مَحْفَر.

Digest, *n.* A — of laws, مَجْمُوعُ فَتَاوِي ـ خُلَاصَةُ فَتَاوِي ـ دُسْتُورٌ (or مَجْمُوعَةُ) سُنَنٍ. Digest, in a general sense, نَسَق.

Digest, *v.t.* To —, of food, هَضَمَ. To systematize, ² نَسَقَ ـ نَظَّمَ ـ ذِهْنًا ـ رَتَّبَ ـ عَقْلًا ـ نَسَّقَ. To arrange in the mind, To consider, تَأَمَّلَ فِي. To be digested, systematized, تَنَاسَقَ ـ تَرَتَّبَ ـ تَنَسَّقَ.

Digester, *n.* One who sets in order, مُنَسِّق ـ مُنَظِّم ـ مُرَتِّب.

Digestibility, *n.* سُهُولَةُ ٱلْهَضْمِ ـ قَابِلِيَّةُ ٱلْإِنْهِضَامِ.

Digestible, *a.* يَنْهَضِمُ ـ سَهْلُ ٱلْهَضْمِ.

Digestion, *n.* Of food, إِنْهِضَام ـ هَضْم. Arrangement, تَرْتِيب ـ تَنْظِيم ـ تَنْسِيق.

Digestive, *a.* هَضُوم ـ هَاضِم. The — power, ٱلْقُوَّةُ ٱلْهَاضِمَة.

Digger, *n.* حَافِر *pl.* حَوَافِر. A — up, as of a treasure, corpse, *etc.*, نَبَّاش. A grave —, حَفَّار.

Digging, *n.* The act of, حَفْر ; the place of, مَحْفَر . What is dug up, ثُلَّة ـ حُفَارَة . Copper diggings, مُنَقَّرَاتُ ٱلنُّحَاسِ .

Dight, *v.t.* *See to* Dress, Adorn, *v.t.*

Digit, *n.* The measure, إِصْبَع . A number below ten, عَدَدٌ دُونَ ٱلْعَشَرَةِ .

Digital, *a.* مُتَعَلِّقٌ بِٱلْأَصَابِعِ ـ إِصْبَعِيٌّ .

Digitalis, *n.* زَهْرُ ٱلْكَشَاتِبِينِ .

Dignified, *a.* Invested with dignity, صَاحِبُ مَنْزِلَةٍ ـ مُشَرَّف ـ وَرُتْبَةٍ . Exalted, عَالٍ ـ مُرْتَفِع . Dignified in bearing, وَجِيهٌ ـ صَاحِبُ وَقَارٍ ـ وَجِيه .

Dignify, *v.t.* To make illustrious, عَزَّزَ ـ أَجَلَّ ـ شَرَّفَ . To give rank or a decoration to, وَجَّهَ ـ بِنِيشَانٍ شَرَّفَ ـ أَنْعَمَ عَلَى ـ بِرُتْبَةٍ .

Dignitary, *n.* مِنْ أَهْلِ ٱلْمَرَاتِبِ ـ مِنَ ٱلْأَكَابِرِ ـ مِنَ ٱلْأُمَرَاءِ . The dignitaries of the Church, أَرْبَابُ ٱلرُّتَبِ ٱلْكَنَائِسِيَّةِ . The dignitaries of the state, أَرْكَانُ (or عِلْيَةُ or أَفَاخِمُ) ٱلدَّوْلَةِ .

Dignity, *n.* Elevation, عُلُوٌّ ـ رِفْعَة . Position, honour, جَاهٌ ـ كَرَامَة ـ جَنَاب ـ حَضْرَة ـ شَأْن ـ قَدْر ـ جَلَال ـ عِزّ ـ شَرَف ـ مَقَام . Rank, office, مَنْصِب ـ مَقَام ـ مَنْزِلَة ـ مَرْتَبَة . Dignity of deportment, هَيْبَة ـ وَقَار . To speak with —, تَكَلَّمَ بِهَيْبَةٍ . Such an one has rank and —, فُلَانٌ ذُو جَاهٍ . Of exalted —, رَفِيعُ ٱلْقَدْرِ وَٱلشَّأْنِ .

Digress, *v.i.* To deviate from, ٱنْحَرَفَ عَن ـ تَجَنَّبَ مِن ـ تَبَاعَدَ عَن ـ تَنَحَّى عَن ـ أَضْرَبَ عَن ـ حَادَ عَن . To wander, as in a speech, أَلْوَى بِ ـ أَضْرَبَ عَن . To — from a purpose, أَضْرَبَ عَن ـ كَفَّ عَن .

Digression, *n.* Deviation, تَنَحٍّ ـ ٱبْتِعَاد ـ تَجَنُّب ـ ٱنْحِرَاف . A wandering in speech, ٱلْتِفَات . A subject introduced by way of digression, دَخِيل . That occurred by way of —, وَقَعَ ذَلِكَ عَلَى وَجْهِ ٱلِٱسْتِطْرَادِ .

Digressive, *a.* خَارِج ـ دَخِيل ـ ٱلْتِفَاتِيّ .

Dike, *n.* A fosse, خَنْدَق *pl.* خَنَادِق . A weir, سَدٌّ ـ عَرِم ـ رَصِيف ـ بَنْد ـ مُسَنَّاة .

Dilacerate, *v.t.* مَزَّقَ ـ جَرَحَ ـ خَرَشَ .

Dilaceration, *n.* جِرَاحَة ـ جُرْح ـ خَرْشَة ـ خَرْش .

Dilapidate, *v.t.* هَدَّ ـ هَدَّمَ ـ خَرَّبَ ـ هَدَمَ . To be dilapidated, ٱنْهَدَّ ـ ٱنْهَدَمَ .

Dilapidation, *n.* The act of, خَرَاب ـ تَهْدِيم ـ هَدْم ; the state of, تَهَدُّم ـ خَرِبَة ـ ٱنْهِدَام .

Dilatability, *n.* قَابِلِيَّة ـ قَابِلِيَّةُ ٱلِٱمْتِدَادِ ـ قَابِلِيَّةُ ٱلِٱنْبِسَاطِ ٱلِٱمْتِطَاطِ .

Dilatable, *a.* مِمَّا يَنْبَسِطُ ـ يَتَنَدَّحُ ـ مِمَّا يَمْتَطُّ ـ مِمَّا يَمْتَدُّ .

Dilatation, *n.* The act of, مَدٌّ ـ مَطٌّ ـ بَسْط ـ نَدْح ; the being dilated, ٱنْبِسَاط ـ ٱتِّسَاع ـ ٱمْتِطَاط ـ ٱمْتِدَاد ـ تَنَدُّح . Dilatation of the heart, joy, ٱنْشِرَاحُ ٱلْقَلْبِ ـ سُرُور ـ حُبُور .

Dilate, *v.t.* To spread out, بَسَطَ ـ شَرَعَ ـ نَدَحَ ـ مَأَى ـ مَطَّ ـ مَدَّ . To speak upon at great length, فَصَّلَ ـ شَرَحَ ـ طَوَّلَ فِي .

Dilate, *v.i.* To swell out, expand, ٱتَّسَعَ ـ ٱمْتَدَّ ـ تَنَدَّحَ ـ ٱنْبَسَطَ ـ ٱمْتَطَّ . To speak at great length, سَابَ فِي ٱلْكَلِمِ ـ أَفَاضَ فِي ٱلْكَلَامِ ـ ٱنْدَفَعَ فِي ٱلْكَلَامِ . To —, of a part of the body, تَفَشَّجَ ـ تَمَأَّى . There is no need to —, لَا لُزُومَ إِلَى إِطَالَةِ ٱلْكَلَامِ .

Dilatorily, *ad.* بِكَسَلٍ ـ بِتَوَقُّفٍ ـ مُرَاخَاةً ـ بِبَطَاءَةٍ .

Dilatoriness, *n.* كَسَل ـ تَوَقُّف ـ مُرَاخَاة ـ بَطَاءَة .

Dilatory, *a.* كَسْلَان ـ وَقَّاف ـ مُتَرَاخٍ ـ قَعِيد ـ بَطِيء . To be —, تَكَاسَلَ ـ كَسِلَ ـ تَوَقَّفَ ـ بَطُؤَ ـ تَرَاخَى .

Dilemma, *n.* وَرْطَة ـ لَبْكَة ـ حَصَر ـ صُعُوبَة ـ إِبْلَاس ـ مُشْكِلَة . To be in a —, تَوَرَّطَ فِي وَرْطَةٍ ـ أَبْلَسَ ـ قُطِعَ بِهِ .

Dilettante, *n.* رَاغِبٌ فِي ٱلصَّنَائِعِ وَٱلْفُنُونِ ـ مُولَعٌ بِٱلصَّنَائِعِ .

Dilettanteism, *n.* رَغْبَةٌ فِي ٱلصَّنَائِعِ وَٱلْفُنُونِ ـ وُلُوعٌ بِٱلصَّنَائِعِ .

Diligence, *n.* Application, هِمَّة ـ جُهْد ـ مُلَازَمَة ـ كَدٌّ ـ جِدٌّ ـ ٱهْتِمَام . Haste, رَوْجَة ـ عَجَلَة ـ سُرْعَة . To use —, to be quick, أَسْرَعَ ـ ٱسْتَعْجَلَ ـ تَسَرَّعَ . *See also* Assiduity, *n.*

Diligent, *a.* Industrious, عَمَّال ـ عَمُول . Assiduous, لَبِيب *pl.* أَلِبَّاءُ ـ حَفِيل ـ مُدَاوِم ـ كَدُود ـ صَاحِبُ ٱجْتِهَادٍ ـ مُجْتَهِد ـ مُجِدٌّ ـ مُوَاظِبٌ عَلَى . A man — in his business, رَجُلٌ مُجْتَهِدٌ فِي عَمَلِهِ . To be —, assiduous, in, كَدَّ فِي ـ أَقَامَ عَلَى ـ ٱهْتَمَّ بِ ـ بَلَغَ فِي ـ أُولِعَ بِ ـ تَقَيَّدَ بِ ـ مَارَسَ .

Diligently, *ad.* بِجِدٍّ ـ بِهِمَّةٍ ـ بِجُهْدٍ ـ بِتَقَيُّدٍ ـ بِٱهْتِمَامٍ . To search — for, فَحَصَ بِٱلتَّدْقِيقِ عَن .

Dill, *n.* رَازِيَانَج ـ شِمَار ـ شِبِتٌّ ـ سِبِتٌّ .

Dilucidate, *v.t.* بَيَّنَ ـ شَرَحَ ـ أَوْضَحَ .

Dilucidation, *n.* شَرْح ـ بَيَان ـ إِيضَاح .

Diluent, *n.* and *a.* Making less strong, مُلَطِّف . Dissolvent, مُحَلِّل .

Dilute, *v.t.* To make less strong, خَفَّفَ ـ لَطَّفَ . To — with, قَطَّعَ بِ ; To —, as wine with water, شَجَّ بِ ـ عَرَّقَ بِ ; as milk with water, مَذَقَ بِ . To be diluted with, تَقَطَّعَ بِ ـ تَلَطَّفَ بِ . To dissolve, حَلَّ .

Diluted, *a.* Made less strong, مُلَطَّف ـ مُخَفَّف . Diluted, of milk, مَذِيق ; diluted, of wine, مَمْزُوج ـ مُعَرَّق .

Dilution, *n.* The act of making less strong, تَخْفِيف ـ تَلْطِيف ; of dissolving, حَلّ .

Diluvian, *a.* / Diluvial, } Relating to a flood, مُتَعَلِّق بِالسَّيْلِ ـ سَيْلِيّ . Relating to Noah's flood, مُخْتَصّ بِالطُّوفَانِ ـ مُتَعَلِّق بِطُوفَانِ نُوح .

Diluvium, *n.* جُرُف ـ طِينُ ٱلْإِبْلِيز .

Dim, *a.* Not seeing clearly, كَلِيلُ ٱلْبَصَرِ ـ فَاتِرُ ٱلْبَصَرِ ـ عَشٍ . Not bright, ظَلِم ـ عَتِم ـ غَشَش . Obscure, مُكَدَّر ـ كَدِر ـ مُكَدَّر . To grow —, of the sight, كَسَفَ ـ عَمِشَ . His eyes became —, كَلَّتْ عَيْنَاهُ عَنِ ٱلنَّظَرِ ـ تَغَطَّشَتْ عَيْنُهُ . The gold became —, إِكْدَرَّ ٱلذَّهَبُ . A — prospect, مَنْظَر كَدِر .

Dim, *v.t.* To cloud, أَخْمَدَ ـ حَجَبَ . To render dull, كَدَّرَ .

Dimension, *n.* سَعَة ـ إِمْتِدَاد ـ مَسَاحَة ـ قَدْر . The three dimensions, length, breadth, and depth, الطُّولُ وَٱلْعَرْضُ وَٱلْعُمْقُ . He took all the dimensions of the house, قَاسَ جِهَاتِ ٱلْبَيْتِ أَجْمَعَ .

Dimensionless, *a.* غَيْرُ مُتَنَاهٍ ـ بِلَا حَدّ .

Diminish, *v.t.* To make less, غَضَّ ـ نَقَّصَ ـ قَلَّلَ ـ بَخَسَ ـ أَنْقَصَ . To make smaller, صَغَّرَ ـ أَصْغَرَ . To make less strong, heavy, خَفَّفَ . To — in price, أَهْبَطَ ٱلثَّمَنَ ـ بَخَسَ ـ أَرْخَصَ . To —, of the voice, خَفَضَ ـ غَضَّ . To — to, to make easy to, خَفَّفَ-عَلَى . To —, to shorten, قَصَّرَ . To — one's pride, رَذَلَ ـ كَسَرَ نَفْسَهُ .

Diminish, *v.i.* To grow less, غَاضَ ـ تَغَضْغَضَ ـ غَضْغَضَ ـ إِنْتَقَصَ ـ نَقَصَ ـ قَلَّ . To grow smaller, تَصَاغَرَ ـ صَغُرَ . To grow less heavy, خَفَّ . To —, as in price, إِنْحَطَّ ـ غَاضَ ـ رَخُصَ ـ بَخُسَ . You shall not — ought of it, لَا تَنْقُصُوا مِنْهُ .

Diminution, *n.* The act of making less, تَنْقِيص ـ تَقْلِيل ; of making smaller, تَصْغِير ; of making less heavy, تَخْفِيف ; of lessening in price, إِسْقَاطُ ٱلثَّمَنِ ـ بَخْس . The state of becoming less, تَقَلُّل ـ نُقْصَان ـ نَقْص ـ تَغَضْغُض ; of becoming smaller, تَصَغُّر ; of becoming less heavy, تَخَفُّف ; lower in price, غَيْض إِنْحِطَاطُ ٱلثَّمَنِ ـ ٱلثَّمَن .

Diminutive, *a.* Small, صَغِير *fem.* صَغِيرَة *pl. masc.* and *fem.* صِغَار ; short, قَصِير ; little, قَلِيل ـ جُزْئِيّ . A — noun, إِسْم مُصَغَّر . In the form of a — noun, مُصَغَّرَة . To change a noun into the — form, صَغَّرَ . Very —, صُغَيِّر .

Diminutively, *ad.* تَصْغِيرًا .

Diminutiveness, *n.* صَغَارَة ـ قِلَّة ـ دِقَّة ـ صِغَر .

Dimissory, *a.* مُتَضَمِّن رُخْصَة ـ مُتَضَمِّن رُخْصَة بِٱلذَّهَاب .

Dimity, *n.* بَفْتَة هِنْدِيَّة .

Dimly, *ad.* Darkly, ظُلْمًا ـ عَتْمًا . With dim sight, عَمَشًا ـ كَسْفًا . As through a parable, فِي لُغْزٍ .

Dimness, *n.* Obscurity, ظُلْمَة ـ عَتْم ـ غَبَس . Weakness of sight, عَمَش ـ عَمَاشَة ـ طَشَاش ـ غَطَش . Want of brightness, كَدَر ـ تَكَدُّر . Having — of sight, أَغْطَش . *See also under* Dim, *a.*

Dimple, *n.* A — in the cheeks, فَحْصَة ـ غَمَّازَة *pl.* غَمَّازَات ـ طَابَةُ ٱلْحُسْنِ ـ نُونَة ـ فَحْصَة ; in the chin, نَقْرَة *pl.* نُقَر نُقْرَة فِي ٱلْخَدِّ . She has dimpled fingers, عُقَدُ أَيْدِيهَا مَطْمُورَاتٌ (a phrase used in Egypt).

Dimple, *v.t.* خَدَّ . To be dimpled, تَخَدَّدَ .

Din, *n.* صَوْت ـ صَرِير ـ صَرْصَرَة ـ صَرَّة ـ جِسّ . It made a —, صَرْصَرَ ـ صَرَّ ـ إِصْطَرَّ .

Din, *v.t.* To strike with continued sounds, صَوَّتَ ـ ضَرَبَ . To din, as into one's ears, كَرَّرَ-عَلَى .

Dinâr, *n.* The coin, دِينَار *pl.* دَنَانِير .

Dine, *v.i.* تَغَدَّى .

Dine, *v.t.* غَدَّى ـ إِسْتَغْدَى .

Ding-dong, *n.* صَرْصَرَة ـ صَوْتُ ٱلْأَجْرَاسِ .

Dingey, *n.* A small boat, قَارِب *pl.* قَوَارِب .

Dinginess, *n.* A dusky hue, سُمْرَة . Meanness, حَقَارَة .

Dingle, *n.* وَهْدَة *pl.* وِهَاد .

Dingy, *a.* Of a dusky colour, أَسْمَر ـ أَغْبَس . Mean, sullied, قَبِيح ـ كَدِر ـ وَسِخ ـ حَقِير .

Dining-room, *n.* غُرْفَة *pl.* غُرَف ـ بَيْتُ ٱلسُّفْرَةِ ـ مَكَانُ ٱلْغَدَاءِ .

Dint, *n.* The mark of a blow, إِنْبِعَاج ـ أَثَر . Force, قُوَّة ـ شِدَّة . By — of study, بِٱلْمُوَاظَبَةِ عَلَى ٱلدَّرْسِ . *See also* Dent, *n.*

Dint, *v.t.* بَعَجَ ـ أَثَّرَ فِي . To be dinted, إِنْبَعَجَ . *See also to* Dent, *v.t.*

Diocesan, *a.* مُتَعَلِّق بِأَبْرَشِيَّةِ ٱلْأُسْقُف .

Diocesan, *n.* أُسْقُف *pl.* أَسَاقِفَة *and* أَسَاقِف ـ أُسْقُفُ ٱلْأَبْرَشِيَّةِ .

Diocese, *n.* أَبْرَشِيَّة أُسْقُف ـ أَبْرَشِيَّة .

Diorama, *n.* دَائِرَة مَنْقُوشَة يُغَيِّرُ ٱلنُّورُ أَلْوَانَهَا وَهِيَ تَدُورُ عَلَى نَفْسِهَا .

Dip, *v.t.* To immerse into, غَمَتَ-فِي ـ غَمَسَ-فِي ـ بَلَّ-فِي ـ نَقَعَ-فِي ـ غَطَسَ-فِي . To make wet in, غَمَتَ-فِي . To dip, or take out, as with a ladle, غَرَفَ . To dip colours to by way of salute, حَيَّى- (سَلَّمَ عَلَى- *or*) بِحَطِّ ٱلْبَيْرَقِ .

Dip, *v.i.* To sink into, إِنْغَمَسَ فِي ـ غَمَسَ فِي ـ غَاصَ فِي ـ غَاطَ فِي . To incline downwards, مَالَ إِلَى تَحْت ـ إِنْصَبَّ ـ

– قَلَّبَ ٱلْأَوْرَاقَ. To dip into a book, to turn the leaves, إِنْحَطَّ. To dip, as of a star, ـ غَمَسَ, ـ لَمَحَ إِلَى.

Dip, *n.* An immersion, غَطْسَة ـ غَمْتَة ـ غَمْسَة. A quantity taken out from a liquid, غَرْفَة. Inclination, مَيْل ـ صَبَب. Declination, إِنْحِطَاط. A glance, لَمْحَة. A tallow candle, شَمْعَة مِنْ شَحْم. To take a —; *see to* Bathe, *v.i.*

Diphthong, *n.* اِزْدِوَاجُ حَرْفَى عِلَّةٍ فِى هِجَآءٍ وَاحِدٍ.

Diploma, *n.* مَنْشُور ـ بَرَآءَة *pl.* بَرَآات ـ تَقَارِير. The royal seal affixed to a —, تَوْقِيعُ هُمَايُونِىٌّ.

Diplomacy, *n.* Science of international procedure, عِلْمُ ٱصْطِلَاحَاتِ ٱلْمَمَالِكِ ـ فَنُّ ٱلْبُولِيتِيقَةِ بَيْنَ ٱلدُّوَلِ. The diplomatic corps, طَقْمُ ٱلسُّفَرَآءِ ـ أَرْبَابُ ٱلسِّفَارَةِ. Prudence in management of affairs, بَصِيرَةٌ فِى ٱلْإِدَارَةِ.

Diplomatic, *a.* Relating to diplomacy, مُتَعَلِّق بِٱصْطِلَاحَاتِ ٱلْمَمَالِكِ بَيْنَ بَعْضِهَا ـ سِفَارِىٌّ. The — corps, وُكَلَآءُ ٱلْمَمَالِكِ. Prudent in management, بَصِيرٌ فِى إِدَارَةِ ٱلْأُمُورِ. Diplomatic measures, وَسَائِطُ سِفَارِيَّة.

Diplomatically, *ad.* Through official correspondence, فِى سَبِيلِ ٱلْمُخَابَرَاتِ ٱلرَّسْمِيَّةِ ـ فِى سَبِيلِ ٱلْمُكَاتَبَةِ وَٱلْمُكَالَمَةِ ٱلرَّسْمِيَّةِ. Skilfully, prudently, بِتَبَصُّرٍ وَٱحْتِذَارٍ.

Diplomatist, *n.* مَاهِرٌ فِى أُصُولِ ٱلسِّفَارَةِ ـ مِنْ أَهْلِ ٱلسِّيَاسَةِ ـ دِيبْلُومَات ـ وَٱلْمُكَاتَبَةِ وَٱلْمُكَالَمَةِ ٱلرَّسْمِيَّةِ. Prudent in management, حَاذِقٌ فِى إِدَارَةِ ٱلْأُمُورِ.

Dipper, *n.* خَاشُوقَة ـ مِغْرَفَة.

Dipping, *n.* *See* Dip, *n.*

Dipping-needle, *n.* إِبْرَةُ ٱلْإِنْحِطَاطِ مِغْنَاطِيسِيَّة.

Dire, *a.* فَظِيع ـ هَائِل ـ مَهُول ـ مَخُوف ـ مُرْعِب ـ شَدِيد ـ مُرْهِب.

Direct, *a.* Straight, مُسْتَقِيم ـ عَدِل ـ عَدُول. Upright, مُقَوَّم ـ قَوِيم *pl.* قِيَام ـ قَيِم. From the origin, أَصْلِىٌّ. Direct, of descent, أَبًا عَنْ جَدٍّ. Without intermediation, مِنْ غَيْرِ وَسَائِطَ. Not ambiguous, وَاضِح ـ بَيِّن ـ صَرِيح. Downright, sincere, نَصُوح. Peremptory, بَتِّىٌّ ـ قَاطِع. Tending to an end, قَاصِد. Direct taxes, ٱلرُّسُومَاتُ ٱلَّتِى تُفْرَضُ عَلَى ٱلنُّفُوسِ دُونَ ٱلْكُمْرُكِ وَغَيْرِهِ ـ مِنَ ٱلضَّرَائِبِ ٱلْمِيرِيَّةِ ـ ضَرَائِبُ شَخْصِيَّة. To give one the lie —, كَذَّبَ ـ بَتًّا حَتْمًا. *See also* Straight, *a.*

Direct, *v.t.* To point out to, as the road, ـ ع دَلَّ ـ عَلَى ـ عَرَّفَ ـ ع نَصَّ ـ عَلَى ـ أَشَارَ بِ ـ إِلَى ـ أَرَى. To order, ـ ع أَمَرَ ـ بِ ـ أَوْصَى ـ بِ ـ أَشَارَ بِ ـ عَلَى. To guide, as to a meaning, أَفْهَمَ ـ أَرْشَدَ ـ إِلَى. To guide, أَرْشَدَ ـ هَدَى. To oversee, ـ رَتَّبَ ـ بَاشَرَ ـ ع سَاسَ. To manage, ـ نَظَرَ ـ إِلَى ـ كَشَفَ عَلَى ـ دَبَّرَ. To address, as of a letter, عَنْوَنَ. To send to, أَرْسَلَ ـ إِلَى ـ وَفَدَ ـ إِلَى ـ سَيَّرَ ـ إِلَى. To aim at, قَصَدَ ـ نَوَى. All minds continue to be directed to . . . , لَمْ تَزَلِ ٱلْخَوَاطِرُ مُوَجَّهَةً نَحْوَ.

Direct, *ad.* رَأْسًا. He sent it — to the administration, أَرْسَلَهُ إِلَى ٱلْإِدَارَةِ رَأْسًا. They requested that the newspaper should be sent to them —, طَلَبُوا أَنْ تُرْسَلَ لَهُمُ ٱلْجَرِيدَةُ رَأْسًا. Direct from him, رَأْسًا مِنْهُ. *See also* Directly, *ad.*

Direction, *n.* The act of pointing out, تَعْرِيف ـ دَلَالَة ـ دُلُولَة ـ إِشَارَة بِ. Line of motion or aim, نَاحِيَة ـ جِهَة ـ صَوْب ـ مَيْل إِلَى ـ تَوَجُّه إِلَى. Order, command, وَصِيَّة ـ أَمْر ـ تَنْبِيه. Oversight, superintendence, تَصَرُّف ـ نَظَارَة ـ إِدَارَة ـ سِيَاسَة ـ مُبَاشَرَة. Ultimate aim, نِهَايَة ـ حَدّ ـ مَقْصُود. Arrangement, تَرْتِيب ـ تَدْبِير. The — of the wind, مَرَادُ ٱلرِّيحِ. To ask for —, إِسْتَدَلَّ. To give the — of to, صَرَّفَ ـ فِى. To have the — of, تَصَرَّفَ فِى.

Directive, *a.* Guiding, هَادٍ ـ مُرْشِد ـ سَائِس ـ إِرْشَادِىٌّ. Arranging, مُدَبِّر ـ تَدْبِيرِىٌّ.

Directly, *a.* In a straight line, عَلَى ـ عَلَى سَوَآءٍ ـ بِٱسْتِقَامَةٍ ـ قَوَامًا ـ إِعْتِدَالًا ـ ٱسْتِوَآءً. Without intermediation, بِلَا وَاسِطَةٍ ـ رَأْسًا. Immediately, حَالًا ـ فِى ٱلْحَالِ ـ ٱلسَّاعَةَ. Directly from the department, مِنَ ٱلْإِدَارَةِ رَأْسًا. Plainly, بِصَرَاحَةٍ.

Directness, *n.* Straightness, إِسْتِقَامَة ـ إِسْتِوَآء ـ إِعْتِدَال. Plainness, downrightness, صَرَاحَة ـ نُصُوح.

Director, *n.* One who orders, أَمِير. A guide, هَادٍ *pl.* هُدَاة ـ دَلِيل *pl* أَدِلَّآءُ. A manager, سَائِس ـ مُدَبِّر ـ نَاظِر ـ مُدِير. A factor, عَامِل *pl.* عُمَّال. A spiritual —, مُعَلِّمُ ٱلذِّمَّةِ. Director of a company, مُدِيرُ شِرْكَةٍ *pl.* مُدِيرُونَ.

Directorial, *a.* مُتَعَلِّق بِٱلْإِدَارَةِ وَٱلنَّظَارَةِ.

Directorship, *n.* In general, سِيَاسَة ـ نَظَارَة ـ إِدَارَة ـ مُبَاشَرَة; of a company, إِدَارَةُ شِرْكَةٍ ـ مُدِيرِيَّة.

Directory, *n.* A rule, قَاعِدَة *pl.* قَوَاعِدُ ـ قَانُون *pl.* قَوَانِينُ. A book of directions, دُسْتُور ـ كِتَابُ تَنْبِيهَاتٍ ـ كِتَابُ مُرْشِدٍ. A book of names of persons and their residence, فِهْرِسُ أَسَامِى أَهْلِ مَحَلٍّ وَعَدَدِ مَسَاكِنِهِمْ. The — or council of a committee of management, مَجْلِسُ إِدَارَةٍ.

Direful, *a.* *See* Dire, *a.*

Direfully, *ad.* فَظَاعَةً ـ هَوْلًا ـ تَخْوِيفًا ـ بِرَهْبَةٍ.

Dirge, *n.* مَرْثَاة ـ مَرْثِيَة *pl.* مَرَاثٍ ـ نُدْبَة.

Dirham, *n.* The coin, دِرْهَم *pl.* دَرَاهِمُ.

Dirk, n. *See* Dagger, n.

Dirk, v.t. *See to* Dagger, v.t.

Dirt, n. Filth, أُفّ — رِجْس — قَذَر — دَنَس — نَجَاسَة — دَنَاسَة — وَسَخ. Ordure, دَبَال — خَرْءٌ. Dust, غُبَار — تُرَاب. Want of cleanliness, وَسَخ. Sweepings, زُبَالَة. Mud, طِين — وَحَل. The — of the streets, طِينُ ٱلْأَسْوَاقِ. Mire and dirt, حَمْأَةٌ وَطِينٌ.

Dirt, v.t. To make dirty, دَنَّسَ — قَذَّرَ — وَسَّخَ — لَوَّثَ. To soil, طَبَّعَ.

Dirt, v.i. To contract —, تَوَسَّخَ — تَلَوَّثَ — تَطَبَّعَ.

Dirtily, ad. Foully, أُفًّا — قَذَرًا — بِدَنَاسَةٍ. Obscenely, خَنًا — قَذْعًا — فُحْشًا.

Dirtiness, n. Obscenity, رَفَث — خَنًا — قَذَع — خَنَايَة — فِسْق — فَحَاشَة. *See also* Dirt, n.

Dirty, a. Unclean, رَجِس — قَذِر — دَنِس — نَجِس — وَسِخ. Mean, حَقِير — ذَلِيل — رَذْل. Obscene, خَنٍ — فَاسِق — رَفَث. Of a — tongue, بَذِيءُ ٱللِّسَانِ. To be —, foul, دَنِسَ — تَدَنَّسَ — تَوَسَّخَ. To be —, soiled, طَبِعَ — تَطَبَّعَ. To be —, obscene, in speech, رَفَثَ فِي ٱلْكَلَامِ.

Disability, n. Want of power, عَجْز — عَدَمُ قُدْرَةٍ — قِلَّةُ قُوَّةٍ. Unfitness, عَدَمُ مَصْلَحَةٍ — عَدَمُ قَابِلِيَّةٍ. Want of privileges, عَدَمُ ٱلْٱمْتِيَازَاتِ.

Disable, v.t. To deprive of strength, أَعْجَزَ — أَضْعَفَ. To maim, جَدَعَ. To hinder, مَنَعَ. To impair, mar, جَحَفَ — عَطَّلَ — خَسَّرَ.

Disabled, a. Deprived of power, عَاجِز — عَدِيمُ ٱلْقُوَّةِ. Impaired, سَقَط — مُعَطَّل. Maimed, أَجْدَع — مُجَدَّع.

Disablement, n. Weakness, قِلَّةُ قُوَّةٍ — عَجْز.

Disabuse, v.t. أَزَالَ عَنِ ٱلْغَلَطِ — نَبَّهَ عَلَى حَقِيقَةِ ٱلشَّيْءِ.

Disaccommodate, v.t. أَضْجَرَ — شَوَّشَ عَلَى — ثَقَّلَ عَلَى.

Disaccommodation, n. Want of preparation, عَدَمُ ٱسْتِعْدَادٍ — قِلَّةُ عَتَادٍ.

Disaccustom, v.t. To abstain from accustoming one to, اِجْتَنَبَ عَنْ تَدْرِيبِ ب. To — one's self, أَبَى ٱلتَّعَوُّدَ عَلَى *aor.* يَأْبَى — خَرَقَ ٱلْعَادَةَ — بَطَّلَ ٱلْعَادَةَ — اِجْتَنَبَ عَنِ ٱلتَّدَرُّبِ عَلَى.

Disacknowledge, v.t. نَكِرَ — طَرَدَ — اِمْتَنَعَ عَنِ ٱلْقَبُولِ ب.

Disadvantage, n. Loss, injury, إِجْحَاف — تَلَف — خُسْرَان — ضَرَر. Hindrance, مَانِع — عَائِقَة *pl.* عَوَائِق. At a —, with loss, بِخَسَارَةٍ; under impediment, تَحْتَ حَصْرٍ — تَحْتَ عُسْرٍ.

Disadvantage, v.t. To injure, أَضَرَّ — أَخْسَرَ — أَجْحَفَ بِ.

Disadvantageous, a. Injurious, ضَارّ — مُضِرّ; losing, خَاسِر. Not favourable to success, غَيْرُ مُوَافِقٍ لِلنَّجَاحِ.

Disadvantageously, ad. بِخَسَارَةٍ — خَسَارَةً — بِضَرَرٍ.

Disaffect, v.t. To make less friendly, to estrange, آنَى — جَنَّبَ — بَرَّدَ مَحَبَّتَهُ نَحْوَ — اِخْتَزَعَ — أَبْعَدَ. To make disaffected, أَفْسَدَ — اِسْتَفْسَدَ — أَفْتَنَ — فَتَنَ.

Disaffected, a. Having alienated affections, مُتَهَاجِرٌ عَنِ ٱلْمَحَبَّةِ — مُعْتَنِف. Dissatisfied with, سَاخِطٌ عَلَى — غَيْرُ رَاضٍ ب. Rebellious, مُقَاوِم — مَفْتُون — مَارِد — عَاصٍ *pl.* عُصَاة. To be — to, rebellious, عَصَى عَلَى — خَرَجَ عَلَى — لَوَى عَن. To be —, discontented, with, ضَجَّ مِن. The Amir treats his subjects in a way to render them —, ٱلْأَمِيرُ يَسْتَفْسِدُ رَعِيَّتَهُ.

Disaffection, n. Dislike, سُخْط — إِعْتِيَاف — إِسْتِكْرَاه. Rebellion, طُغْيَان — تَمَرُّد — عِصْيَان — فَسَاد. A cause of —, مَفْسَدَة.

Disaffirm, v.t. نَكَرَ — أَبْطَلَ.

Disaggregation, n. إِنْفِصَالُ ٱلْأَجْزَاءِ — شَذّ — شُذُوذ.

Disagree, v.i. To be discordant, تَبَايَنَ — تَفَاوَتَ — إِخْتَلَفَ — تَغَايَرَ. To be at variance, تَخَالَفَ — إِخْتَلَفَ. They disagreed among themselves, تَعَالَجُوا — تَنَاجَزُوا — إِخْتَلَفُوا. To — with, as of food, *etc.*, لَا يُلَائِمُ — شَوَّشَ — ضَرَّ — لَا يُوَافِقُ. To — with, as of a place or climate, to dislike it, جَوِيَ عَن — (*or* مِن) — إِجْتَوَى — لَا يُوَافِقُ. To — to, as to a proposition, أَبَى عَنِ ٱلْقَبُولِ ب. This food disagrees with me, هٰذَا ٱلطَّعَامُ لَا يُلَائِمُنِي. I found the country to — with me, جَوِيَتْ نَفْسِي. He found it to — with him, جَوِيَتْ نَفْسُهُ مِنْهُ (*or* عَنْهُ). He found it (a place) to — with him, جَوِيَهُ — إِجْتَوَاهُ. *See also* to Differ, v.i.

Disagreeable, a. Unpleasant to the mind, مَكْرُوه — كَرِيه — لَيْسَ بِحَسَنٍ. Offensive, سَيِّئ — غَيْرُ مَرْضِيٍّ. Disgusting, كَرِيه — مُتَقَزِّز. Fractious, بَشِع — بَشِيع — شَرِس. Disagreeable things, مَكَارِهُ. To be —, cross, بَشِعَ — شَكُسَ. *See also* Unpleasant, a.

Disagreeableness, n. Unpleasantness, كَرَاهَة — مَكْرُوهَة. Crossness, peevishness, بَشَاعَة — شَرَاسَة — شَكَاسَة. Absence of pleasure, عَدَمُ بَهْجَةٍ — عَدَمُ ٱنْبِسَاطٍ. *See also* Unpleasantness, n.

Disagreeably, ad. *See* Unpleasantly, ad.

Disallow, v.t. Not to permit, أَسْقَطَ — مَا قَبِلَ. To refuse, أَبَى — رَفَضَ. To prevent, مَنَعَ. Disallowed by the learned, مَرْفُوضٌ مِنَ ٱلْعُلَمَاءِ.

Disallowable, *a.* غَيْرُ مُرَخَّصٍ ـ غَيْرُ جائِزٍ.

Disallowance, *n.* Refusal to permit, عَدَمُ قُبُولٍ ـ إِسْقاط. Refusal, رَفْض ـ إِبايَة. Prohibition, مَنْع.

Disanimate, *v.t.* بَرَّدَ حَمِيَّتَهُ ـ أَخْمَدَ حُمَّتَهُ.

Disannul, *v.t.* *See to* Annul, *v.t.*

Disapparel, *v.t.* عَرَّى ـ شَلَّحَ ـ جَرَّدَ.

Disappear, *v.i.* إِخْتَفَى ـ غابَ. To pass away, زالَ 2. To make to —, غَيَّبَ. The man disappeared in the crowd, ذَهَبَ ٱلرَّجُلُ فِي ٱلْقَوْمِ. His person nearly disappeared from those who were in the ship, كادَ يَغِيبُ شَخْصُهُ عَمَّنْ كانَ فِي ٱلسَّفِينَةِ.

Disappearance, *n.* غُيُوب ـ غِيابَة ـ غِياب. Passing away, ذَهاب ـ زَوال.

Disappoint, *v.t.* To defeat, of expectation, أَغْوَى ـ شَمَّتَ ـ خَيَّبَ ـ إِسْتَغْوَى. To frustrate, عَنَّقَ ـ عَوَّقَ-عَن ـ أَعْدَمَ ـ خَيَّبَ ـ بَطَّلَ.

Disappointed, *a.* Defeated of expectation, خائِب ـ مَخْيُوب ـ مُشَمَّت ـ مَقْطُوعٌ بِهِ. Frustrated, مَخْذُول ـ مَفْشُول ـ مُعَوَّقٌ عَن. To be —, خابَ ـ قُطِعَ بِهِ. She was — at his absence, خابَ أَمَلُها مِنْ غِيابِهِ. They returned —, رَجَعُوا شَمائِي. He who is fainthearted will be —, (*prov.*) مَنْ هابَ خابَ. These hopes have been —, عُقِمَتْ هٰذِهِ ٱلْأَمانِي.

Disappointing, *a.* خَيّاب.

Disappointment, *n.* خَيْبَة ـ شِمات ـ عَناقَة ـ عَناق. Frustration, تَبْطِيل ـ تَعْطِيل. Faintheartedness is a cause of —, (*prov.*) الْهَيْبَةُ خَيْبَةٌ.

Disapprobation, *n.* عَدَمُ ٱلرِّضَى بِ ـ عَدَمُ ٱسْتِحْسانٍ ـ إِسْتِقْباح. Censure, مَلامَة ـ مَذَمَّة. I expressed my — of it, صَرَّحْتُ بِما أَنْكَرْتُ عَلَيْهِ.

Disappropriate, *v.t.* جَرَّدَ-مِنْ مَتاعِهِ ـ جَرَّدَ-مِن ـ جَرَّدَ.

Disapproval, *n.* *See* Disapprobation, *n.*

Disapprove, *v.t.* To — of, أَنْكَرَ عَلَى ـ إِسْتَوْحَشَ ـ إِسْتَقْبَحَ. To censure, ذَمَّ 2 ـ لامَ 2. To reject, رَفَضَ 2.

Disapprovingly, *ad.* مَذَمَّةً ـ تَذْمِيمًا ـ إِنْكارًا عَلَى ـ إِسْتِقْباحًا.

Disarm, *v.t.* To deprive of arms, أَخَذَ 2 ـ نَزَعَ ٱلسِّلاحَ مِن ـ قَلَعَ-ٱلسِّلاحَ ـ ٱلسِّلاحَ مِن. To — one's anger, أَسْكَنَ ـ هَدَّأَ غَضَبَهُ ـ حَمِيَّتَهُ. To — a ship, رَفَعَ مِنَ ٱلْمَرْكَبِ ٱلْمَدافِعَ وَسائِرَ ٱلْعُدَّةِ. To lower the military force, قَلَّلَ (*or* نَزَّلَ) ٱلْقُوَّةَ ٱلْعَسْكَرِيَّةَ.

Disarmament, *n.* The act of giving up arming, تَبْطِيلُ ٱلتَّسْلِيحِ ـ تَرْكُ ٱلتَّسَلُّحِ. The — of a castle, رَفْعُ ٱلْمَدافِعِ وَسائِرِ ٱلْعُدَّةِ مِنْ قَلْعَةٍ.

Disarrange, *v.t.* لَخْبَطَ ـ خَبَّطَ ـ خَبَّلَ ـ خَلَّطَ ـ شَوَّشَ ـ لَبَّكَ ـ خَبَّصَ. To be disarranged, تَشَوَّشَ ـ إِلْتَبَكَ ـ إِرْتَبَكَ.

Disarrangement, *n.* تَخْلِيط ـ تَشْوِيش ـ إِرْتِباك ـ إِلْتِباك ـ تَلْبِيك ـ تَخْبِيص ـ لَخْبَطَة.

Disarray, *v.t.* To undress, شَلَّحَ ـ جَرَّدَ. To put out of order, شَتَّتَ ـ بَدَّدَ. To overthrow, غَلَبَ عَلَى ـ قَهَرَ.

Disarray, *n.* Disorder, تَبْدِيد ـ تَشَتُّت ـ تَشْتِيت ـ تَشْوِيش ـ عَدَمُ نِظامٍ.

Disassociate, *v.t.* *See to* Dissociate, *v.t.*

Disaster, *n.* داهِيَة ـ مَصائِبُ *pl.* مُصِيبَة ـ بَوائِقُ *pl.* بائِقَة ـ دَواهِي *pl.* ـ بَلاء ـ مَنْحُوسَة.

Disastrous, *a.* سَوْء ـ مَنْحُوس ـ نَحِس. Suffering, as from a disaster, مُصابٌ بِ. *See also* Calamitous, *a.*

Disastrousness, *n.* بَلِيَّة ـ تَعاسَة ـ مَنْحُوسَة ـ بَلاء.

Disavouch, *v.t.* / Disavow, } نَفَا 2 ـ أَنْكَرَ ـ جَهِلَ ـ جَحَدَ.

Disavowal, *n.* / Disavowment, } إِنْكارُ بِ ـ جَهْلٌ بِ ـ جَهْل ـ جُحُود ـ جَحْد.

Disband, *v.t.* To scatter, فَضَّ 2 ـ مَذَّرَ ـ شَتَّتَ ـ وَزَّعَ. To — troops, صَرَفَ (*or* فَضَّ 2) ٱلْعَساكِرَ.

Disband, *v.i.* To be scattered, تَمَذَّرَ ـ تَوَزَّعَ ـ تَشَتَّتَ. To be disbanded, of troops, تَفَضَّضَ (*or* إِنْفَضَّ) ٱلْعَسْكَرُ (*or* ٱلْجَيْشُ).

Disbark, *v.t.* *See to* Disembark, *v.t.*

Disbelief, *n.* Unbelief, عَدَمُ إِيمانٍ. Refusal of belief, زَنْدَقَة ـ إِنْكار ـ كُفْر.

Disbelieve, *v.t.* Not to believe, قَلَّ إِيمانُهُ بِ ـ لا يُؤْمِنُ بِ ـ ما صَدَّقَ. To deny, أَنْكَرَ ـ كَذَّبَ بِ ـ كَفَرَ بِ 2 ـ فَجَرَ 2 ـ أَفْجَرَ.

Disbeliever, *n.* One of little faith, قَلِيلُ ٱلْإِيمانِ. An unbeliever, كافِر *pl.* كُفّار ـ فاجِر *pl.* فُجّار ـ زِنْدِيق *pl.* زَنادِقَة.

Disbowel, *v.t.* *See to* Disembowel, *v.t.*

Disburden, *v.t.* To unload, حَطَّ 2 ٱلْأَحْمالَ عَن. To divulge, أَعْلَنَ ـ أَفْشَى بِ ـ أَفْشَى. *See also to* Unburden, *v.t.*

Disburse, *v.t.* دَفَعَ ـ أَنْفَقَ عَلَى ـ صَرَفَ.

Disbursement, *n.* دَفْع ـ مَصْرُوف ـ نَفَقَة ـ مَصْرَف ـ خَرْج ـ دَراهِمَ.

Disburser, *n.* صاحِبُ ٱلْخَرْجِ.

Disc, *n.* *See* Disk, *n.*

Discard, *v.t.* طَرَحَ بِ ـ طَرَحَ ـ طَرَدَ 2 ـ نَفَّى ـ نَفَا 2 ـ دَشَّرَ ـ أَصْرَفَ. Discarded, مَطْرُود ـ مَرْدُود ـ نَفِيّ.

Discern, *v.t.* To see, رَأَى *aor.* يَرَى ـ أَدْرَكَ-بِٱلنَّظَرِ ـ لاحَ 2. To perceive by the mind, أَدْرَكَ ـ فَطَنَ ـ شَعَرَ بِ 2.

Discern, *v.i.* To distinguish, فَصَّلَ بَيْنَ — فَرَزَ بَيْنَ — مَيَّزَ بَيْنَ. Can I — between good and evil, هَلْ أُمَيِّزُ بَيْنَ ٱلطَّيِّبِ وَٱلرَّدِيءِ.

Discerner, *n.* فاطِن — ناقِد — مُمَيِّز — رَقِيب.

Discernible, *a.* As by the sight, يُدْرِكُهُ ٱلنَّظَرُ — يُرَى — مَرْئِيٌّ ; as by the mind, يُدْرَكُ — يُشْعَرُ بِهِ.

Discernibly, *ad.* عِيانًا — عَرْضَ عَيْنٍ — أَمامَ ٱلْعُيُونِ.

Discerning, *a.* عاقِل — بَصِير — فَطِين — فاطِن — فَطِن — فارِق — حاذِق — نَبِيه — زَكِيُّ ٱلْعَقْلِ.

Discerningly, *ad.* بِفَراسَةٍ — بِعَقْلٍ — بِفِطْنَةٍ — بِتَمْيِيزٍ.

Discernment, *n.* فِطْنَة — عَقْل — فَراسَة — تَمْيِيز.

Discharge, *v.t.* To disburden, نَزَّلَ — حَطَّ ٱلْأَحْمالَ عَن — أَنْفَضَ — حَوَّلَ ٱلْأَحْمالَ عَن — ٱلْأَحْمالَ عَن ; of a ship's cargo, فَرَّغَ — نَزَّلَ وَسْقَ ٱلْمَرْكَبِ — ٱلْوَسْق. To let off, as of a gun, قَوَّسَ ب — أَطْلَقَ. To dismiss, send away, صَرَفَ — رَدَّ. To discard, طَرَدَ — نَفَى — دَشَّرَ ; from an office, عَزَلَ عَن. To —, as of a soldier, to give him a — from service, أَعْفاهُ مِن — رَخَّصَ لِ — فِي ٱلتَّقاعُدِ عَنِ ٱلْعَسْكَرِيَّةِ — ٱلْخِدْمَةِ ٱلْعَسْكَرِيَّةِ. To liberate, سَيَّبَ — أَطْلَقَ. To emit, أَبْرَزَ — أَخْرَجَ ; of water, نَزَّ ; of blood, فاحَ ; of a sore, فَزَّ ; of flames, ٱلْتَهَبَ — تَلَهَّبَ. To —, as a river its waters, صَبَّ. To acquit, أَبْرَأَ مِن. To set free from an obligation, عَفا عَن — بَيَّضَ وَجْهَهُ. To — a debt, قَضَى ٱلدَّيْنَ — أَوْفَى ٱلدَّيْنَ — وَفَى ٱلدَّيْنَ *aor.* يَفِي. To perform, أَتَمَّ — عَمِلَ ب — كَمَّلَ — قَضَى. To — one's duties, عَمِلَ ما عَلَيْهِ — قامَ بِواجِباتِهِ. To — one's mind, أَفْشَى ما فِي قَلْبِهِ. To — one's religious duties, فَرَّضَ. The pustule discharged what was in it, عَزَّتِ ٱلْقَرْحَةُ.

Discharge, *v.i.* *See in preceding article under* To emit.

Discharge, *n.* Emission, إِطْلاق — إِخْراج — إِبْراز ; matter emitted, خُرُوج — نَفْي — الخارِجُ مِن — الصّادِرُ مِن. Dismissal, صَرْف — طَرْد ; from office, تَعْزِيل — عَزْل. Acquittal, as from a crime, تَبْرِئَة — إِبْراء مِن. Release, as from an obligation, عَفْوٌ عَن. Discharge, as from the military service, رُخْصَةٌ لِلتَّقاعُدِ عَنِ ٱلْعَسْكَرِيَّةِ. Performance, إِقامَةٌ ب — إِكْمال — إِتْمام — العَمَلُ ب. Discharge of fire-arms, رَمْيٌ — إِطْلاقُ ٱلْبَنادِقِ — تَفْرِيغُ ٱلْمَدافِعِ — ٱلْمَدافِع تَقْوِيس. The issue from a sore, قَيْح — صَدِيد ; of waters, as by a river, سَكْب — صُبُوب — صَبّ. A receipt, وُصُول — رَجْعَة. Exemption, مُعافاة. One, as of a soldier, *etc.*, having his —, مُتَقاعِد. Discharge pay, راتِبُ ٱلْمُتَقاعِدِ.

Discharge-pipe, *n.* صُنْبُور لِمَنْعِ فَيَضانِ ٱلْماءِ فِي صِهْرِيجٍ.

Discharging-rod, *n.* قَضِيبٌ يَمُرُّ بِهِ ٱلسَّيّالُ ٱلْكَهْرَبائِيُّ صِيانَةً لَهُ عَنْ صَدْمَةِ ٱلْأَجْسامِ.

Disciple, *n.* تِلْمِيذ *pl.* تَلامِيذ. A follower, تابِع *pl.* تابِعُونَ. A — or apostle of Christ, حَوارِيٌّ *pl.* حَوارِيُّونَ. One trained, educated, خِرِّيج. He is the — of such an one, هُوَ خِرِّيجُ فُلانٍ.

Disciple, *v.t.* تَلْمَذَ.

Discipleship, *n.* تَلْمَذَة.

Disciplinable, *a.* قابِلُ ٱلتَّأْدِيبِ — قابِلُ ٱلتَّخْرِيجِ — قابِلُ ٱلتَّعْلِيمِ.

Disciplinarian, *n.* مُؤَدِّب — ضابِطٌ فِي ٱلتَّعْلِيمِ وَٱلتَّأْدِيبِ.

Disciplinary, *a.* تَأْدِيبِيٌّ — تَعْلِيمِيٌّ.

Discipline, *n.* The act of rendering experienced, حَنْك — تَحْنِيك. Education, دَرْس — تَعْلِيم — تَخْرِيج. Cultivation, تَأْدِيب. Order, نِظام — نَظْم — تَرْتِيب — ضَبْط. Chastisement, تَأْدِيب — قِصاص — مُجازاة.

Discipline, *v.t.* To educate, أَدَّبَ — عَلَّمَ — دَرَّسَ — خَرَّجَ. To keep in order, نَظَّمَ — دَبَّرَ — ضَبَطَ. To chastise, أَدَّبَ. To train, حَنَّكَ — يَرُوضُ *aor.* راضَ. He disciplined him in polite accomplishments, خَرَّجَهُ فِي ٱلْأَدَبِ. One disciplined, trained, by another, خِرِّيج. To be disciplined, kept in order, كانَ — تَهَذَّبَ تَحْتَ ٱلضَّبْطِ. Age disciplined him, حَنَّكَتْهُ ٱلسِّنُّ. Disciplined officers, ضُبّاطٌ مُحَنَّكَةٌ.

Disclaim, *v.t.* *See to* Disavow, *v.t.*

Disclaimer, *n.* One who disclaims, مُنْكِر — ناكِر — جاحِد. A —, in law, عَرْضٌ رَسْمِيٌّ يَتَضَمَّنُ ٱلْإِعْلانَ بِٱلْجَحْدِ وَٱلْإِنْكارِ.

Disclose, *v.t.* To uncover, كَشَفَ عَن. To reveal, أَشْهَرَ — بادَى ب — أَبْدَى — أَشاعَ — أَجْهَرَ — أَذاعَ ب — يَبُوحُ *aor.* باحَ ب — بادَاهُ — أَبْدَى لَهُ ٱلْأَمْرَ — شَرَحَ. He disclosed the affair to him, صَرَّحَ بِٱلْأَمْرِ. He disclosed what was in himself, صَرَّحَ بِما فِي نَفْسِهِ. I disclosed my secret to him, أَفْضَيْتُ إِلَيْهِ بِسِرِّي. His bosom disclosed the secret, فاضَ صَدْرُهُ بِٱلسِّرِّ. To become disclosed, تَفَشَّى — يَفْشُو *aor.* فَشا.

Disclosure, *n.* إِظْهار — إِفْشاء — إِعْلانٌ ب — كَشْفٌ عَن — كَشْف وَإِفْشاء — تَصْرِيح.

Discolour, *v.t.* To change the colour, بَدَّلَ ٱللَّوْنَ. To stain, طَبَّعَ — فَسَخَ ٱللَّوْنَ.

Discolour, *v.i.* To change colour, خَسَفَ — (or بارَ ٱللَّوْنُ) تَغَيَّرَ ٱللَّوْنُ.

Discomfit, *v.t.* كَسَرَ — قَهَرَ — غَلَبَ — هَزَمَ — أَهْرَبَ — ظَفِرَ عَلَى.

Discomfiture, *n.* غَلَبَة — كَسْر — قَهْر — هَزِيمَة.

Discomfort, *n.* Disquiet, زَحْمَة ـ أَذِيَّة ـ إِضْطِراب ـ كَأْبَة ـ كَدَر. Grief, pain, غَمّ ـ كَرْب ـ وَجَع.

Discomfort, *v.t.* أَكْأَبَ ـ كَدَّرَ ـ زَحَمَ ـ آذَى بِ. To grieve, pain, أَحْزَنَ ـ أَغَمَّ ـ أَوْجَعَ ـ وَجَّعَ.

Discommode, *v.t.* شَوَّشَ عَلَى ـ أَتْعَبَ ـ ثَقَّلَ عَلَى ـ صَدَّعَ.

Discommodious, *a.* مُزاحِم ـ ضَيِّق ـ غَيْرُ مُناسِب.

Discompose, *v.t.* To ruffle, خَبَّلَ ـ قَلَّقَ ـ هَيَّجَ. To put out of order, لَبَّكَ ـ حَرَّفَ ـ عَكَسَ ـ قَلْقَلَ ـ أَفْسَدَ ـ خَرْبَطَ ـ لَخْبَطَ.

Discomposure, *n.* إِضْطِراب ـ تَقَلْقُل ـ حَيْرَة ـ حَيْرَةٌ وَفَشَلٌ. In a state of utter —, فِي حَيْرَةٍ وَفَشَلٍ.

Disconcert, *v.t.* To frustrate, أَفْنَى ـ أَبْطَلَ ـ عَكَسَ ـ خَيَّبَ ـ أَعْدَمَ. To unsettle, of the mind, حَيَّرَ ـ خَبَلَ ـ كَدَّرَ ـ أَغْفَلَ ـ قَلْقَلَ ـ قَلَّقَ. To be disconcerted, put out, تَقَلْقَلَ; in speaking, تَوَعَّرَ. Disconcerted, in a state of perplexity, muddle, فِي حَيْرَةٍ وَفَشَلٍ.

Disconnect, *v.t.* فَصَلَ ـ حَلَّ ـ فَكَّ ـ فَرَقَ.

Disconnection, *n.* عَدَمُ ٱرْتِباطٍ ـ إِنْفِصال ـ إِفْتِراق ـ فَصْل.

Disconsolate, *a.* لا يَتَعَزَّى ـ لا يَتَسَلَّى ـ حَزِين ـ مُكَدَّر ـ مَكْسُورُ ٱلْخاطِرِ. To be —, كانَ آيِسًا ـ تَوَحَّشَ ـ كَئِبَ.

Disconsolately, *ad.* بِوَحْشَةٍ ـ بِأَيْسٍ ـ إِياسًا ـ كَأْبَةً.

Disconsolateness, *n.* وَحْشَة ـ كَأْبَة ـ أَيْس.

Discontent, *n.* Want of contentment, عَدَمُ قَناعَةٍ ـ عَدَمُ ٱلرِّضاءِ بِ. Displeasure, opposition, كَراهَة ـ مُضادَّة ـ إِعْتِراض ـ مُعانَدَة. Sourness of spirit, مَرارَةُ نَفْسٍ.

Discontent, *v.t.* To displease, أَغْضَبَ ـ كَسَرَ خاطِرَهُ. To vex, disquiet, فَجَّعَ ـ عَنَّى ـ حَسَّرَ. The people were discontented with him, ضَجَّتْ مِنْهُ ٱلرَّعِيَّةُ.

Discontented, *a.* Not satisfied, كارِهٌ ـ غَيْرُ قانِعٍ ـ غَيْرُ مُرْتَضٍ ـ غَيْرُ مَبْسُوطٍ. Soured in spirit, مُرُّ ٱلنَّفْسِ. Displeased with, غَضْبانُ عَلَى ـ مَحْسُورٌ مِنْ ـ مُغْتاظٌ مِنْ. To be —, displeased, with, إِغْتاظَ مِنْ. To be vexed with, حَسِرَ مِنْ ـ كانَ مُحَسَّرًا مِنْ. Those who are discontented with the government, المُتَذَمِّرُونَ عَلَى ٱلْحُكْمِ.

Discontentment, *n.* *See* Discontent, *n.*

Discontinuance, *n.* كَفٌّ عَنْ ـ إِنْقِطاع ـ فَراغَة ـ تَرْك ـ قَطْع.

Discontinue, *v.t.* بَطَّلَ ـ قَطَعَ ـ أَتْرَكَ.

Discontinue, *v.i.* To leave off, إِنْقَطَعَ عَنْ ـ كَفَّ عَنْ ـ بَطَّلَ. To desist from, زالَ عَنْ *aor.* يَزُولُ ـ إِنْتَهَى عَنْ. *See also under to* Cease, *v.i.*

Discontinuity, *n.* إِنْقِطاع ـ إِنْفِصال ـ عَدَمُ ٱتِّصالٍ.

Discontinuous, *a.* مُنْفَصِل ـ مُنْقَطِع ـ عَدِيمُ ٱلِاتِّصالِ.

Disconvenience, *n.* *See* Inconvenience, *n.*

Discord, *n.* إِخْتِلاف ـ شَواش ـ نِزاع ـ إِنْشِقاق ـ مُنازَعَة ـ خُصُومَة ـ مُخاصَمَة. Disagreement of sounds, إِخْتِلافُ ٱلْأَصْواتِ ـ عَدَمُ أَنْغامٍ. There is — among them, بَيْنَهُمْ شَواشٌ. To stir up —, هَيَّجَ ٱلْخُصُومَةَ ـ هَيَّجَ ٱلْخِصامَ. Civil —, إِخْتِلالاتٌ داخِلِيَّةٌ.

Discordance, *n.*, **Discordancy,** إِخْتِلاف ـ مُغايَرَة ـ عَدَمُ ٱتِّفاقٍ ـ قِلَّةُ مُوافَقَةٍ.

Discordant, *a.* مُخالِف ـ غَيْرُ مُطابِقٍ ـ مُخْتَلِف. Inharmonious, عَدِيمُ ٱلْأَنْغامِ. Discordant sounds, تَنافُر. Their expression of opinion was —, تَفَرَّقَتْ كَلِمَتُهُمْ. Their opinions were —, تَفَرَّقَتْ آراؤُهُمْ.

Discordantly, *ad.* مُغايَرَةً ـ بِغَيْرِ ٱتِّفاقٍ ـ بِغَيْرِ مُوافَقَةٍ. Inharmoniously, بِغَيْرِ أَنْغامٍ ـ بِٱلتَّنافُرِ ـ مِنْ دُونِ أُلْفَةٍ.

Discount, *n.* إِسْقاط ـ إِسْتِقْطاع ـ إِسْتِنْزال ـ حَسْم. Interest taken in advance, فَرْط. Rate of —, سِعْرُ ٱلْفائِدَةِ. At a low rate of —, بِإِسْقاطٍ زَهِيدٍ.

Discount, *v.t.* سَقَّطَ ـ إِسْتَقْطَعَ ـ إِسْتَنْزَلَ ـ حَسَمَ ـ أَسْقَطَ.

Discountable, *a.* فِي حالَةِ ٱلْإِسْقاطِ.

Discounted, *a.* مَسْقُوط.

Discountenance, *v.t.* To be averse from, جَفا عَنْ ـ ما قَبِلَ بِ ـ إِعْتَرَضَ لِ. To — or discourage, of a person, أَخْمَدَ هِمَّتَهُ; of a thing, إِمْتَنَعَ عَنْ ـ لَمْ يَرْضَ بِ ـ نَكِرَ ـ عَطَّلَ.

Discourage, *v.t.* To —, of a person, أَخْمَدَ هِمَّتَهُ ـ كَسَرَ قَلْبَهُ ـ أَفْتَرَ غَيْرَتَهُ ـ صَدَّ قَلْبَهُ عَنْ ـ أَذابَ قَلْبَهُ ـ ضَيَّقَ نَفْسَهُ ـ أَرْعَبَ. Lest they be discouraged, لِئَلَّا يَفْشَلُوا. To be discouraged, فَشِلَ. *See also to* Discountenance, *v.t.*

Discouraged, *part.* حَشِلٌ فَشِلٌ ـ فَشِل ـ مُنْكَسِرُ ٱلْقَلْبِ. To be —, ضاقَتْ نَفْسُهُ ـ ذابَ قَلْبُهُ ـ فَتَرَتْ غَيْرَتُهُ ـ إِرْتَعَبَ ـ فَشِلَ.

Discouragement, *n.* The act of, تَخْمِيدُ ٱلْهِمَّةِ ـ تَصْدِيدُ ٱلْقَلْبِ ـ تَفْتِيرُ ٱلْغَيْرَةِ; the state of being discouraged, ضِيقُ ٱلنَّفْسِ ـ فَشَل ـ حالَةُ ٱلْفَشَلِ ـ إِرْتِعاب ـ فُتُور. A cause of —, سَبَبُ تَعْطِيلٍ.

Discouraging, *a.* مُخْمِدُ ٱلْهِمَّةِ ـ مُضَيِّقُ ٱلنَّفْسِ ـ مُذِيبُ ٱلْقَلْبِ.

Discouragingly, *ad.* بِضِيقَةِ نَفْسٍ ـ بِقِلَّةِ رَجاءٍ ـ بِفُتُورٍ ـ بِفَشَلٍ.

Discourse, *n.* Conversation, حَدِيث ـ مُحاكاة ـ مُحادَثَة ـ قَوْل ـ كَلام ـ مَقالَة. A dissertation, خِطاب ـ خُطْبَة *pl.*

خُطَب — مُباحَثَة — مَقالَة — عِبارَة . A sermon, خُطْبَة — وَعْظ — مَوْعِظَة . To pronounce a —, أَلْقَى مَقالَةً .

Discourse, v.i. To talk, تَحَدَّثَ — تَكَلَّمَ . To — with or to, حادَثَ — كالَمَ — خاطَبَ . To — upon, ذَكَرَ ² — حَدَّثَ فِي — بَحَثَ عَن = . To preach, وَعَظَ aor. يَعِظُ .

Discourse, v.t. فاهَ بِ ² — نَطَقَ بِ = .

Discourteous, a. جافٍ — فَظٌّ — غَلِيظ — قَلِيلُ ٱلْأَدَبِ — خارِجٌ عَنِ ٱلْأَدَبِ . He is very —, إِنَّهُ لَفَظٌّ بَظٌّ .

Discourteously, ad. بِفَظاظَةٍ — بِجَفاءٍ — بِقِلَّةِ أَدَبٍ . To act — to, أَساءَ ٱلْأَدَبَ فِي حَقِّهِ .

Discourtesy, n. فَظاظَة — جَفاء — قِلَّة أَدَب .

Discous, a. قُرْصِيٌّ — فِي صُورَةِ ٱلْقُرْصِ .

Discover, v.t. To uncover, أَكْشَفَ — كَشَفَ . To lay open to view, أَظْهَرَ — أَرَى . To espy, أَدْرَكَ — أَنْظَرَ — رَمَقَ ² . To invent, أَوْجَدَ — اِخْتَرَعَ — أَبْدَعَ — أَجَدَّ — أَبْدَأَ . To find, وَجَدَ aor. يَجِدُ . To find out, كَشَفَ عَن = — ظَهَرَ عَلَى = — اِطَّلَعَ عَلَى . To — or elicit by careful search, اِسْتَنْبَطَ . *See also to* Disclose, v.t.

Discoverable, a. That may be found out, مِمَّا يُكْشَفُ عَلَيْهِ ; that may be invented, مِمَّا يُخْتَرَعُ ; that may be found, مِمَّا يُوجَدُ .

Discoverer, n. One who finds out, كَشّاف — كاشِفٌ عَلَى . An inventor, مُبْتَدِع — بادِع — مُبْدِع .

Discovery, n. The act of bringing to light, كَشْف — كَشْفٌ عَن . What is found, وُجُود — جِدَة — وُجْد . Invention, اِخْتِراع — إِيجاد — إِنْشاء . Discoveries, اِكْتِشافات — مُكْتَشَفات .

Discredit, n. خِزْيَة — قِلَّة ٱعْتِبارٍ — خُمُول — عارٌ — شَيْن — بَوار — عَدَمُ ٱعْتِبارٍ . To bring — upon, أَخْزَى — جَلَبَ ٱلْإِهانَةَ = ² عَلَى — أَعْرَضَ لِلْإِهانَةِ . To fall into —, of a person, خَمَلَ ² — خَزِيَ aor. يَخْزَى — قَلَّ ٱعْتِبارُهُ = ; of a thing, بارَ aor. يَبُورُ .

Discredit, v.t. Not to believe, ما صَدَّقَ فِي — كَذَّبَ . To bring into disrepute, أَخْزَى — فَضَحَ = — أَخْمَلَ — أَبارَ . To hold in contempt, اِسْتَهانَ بِ .

Discreditable, a. فَضِيح — خَزٍ — قَبِيح — فاحِش .

Discreditably, ad. فَضاحَةً — قَباحَةً — بِخِزْيَةٍ . To act —, أَقْبَحَ — خَزِيَ aor. يَخْزَى .

Discreet, a. حازِم — بَصِير — مُتَعَقِّل — عاقِل .

Discreetly, ad. حَزْمًا — بِعَقْلٍ — بِفَرْزَنَةٍ . To act —, تَحَزَّمَ . He answered —, أَجابَ بِعَقْلٍ .

Discreetness, n. *See* Discretion, n.

Discrepance, n. / Discrepancy, } اِخْتِلاف — مُغايَرَة — فَرْق — تَناقُض — مُضادَّة .

Discrepant, a. / Discrete, } مُناقِض — مُخالِف — ضِدٌّ — مُغايِر .

Discretion, n. Judiciousness, عَقْل — حَزْم — حِذْر — بَصِيرَة . Age or years of —, رُشْد . Moderation, مُحاسَبَة — تَقْسِيط — اِعْتِدال . They surrendered themselves at —, أَذْعَنُوا وَسَلَّمُوا — سَلَّمُوا أَنْفُسَهُمْ مِنْ غَيْرِ مُشارَطَةٍ . To arrive at the years of —, بَلَغَ رُشْدَهُ ² — بَلَغَ أَشُدَّهُ ² . To use one's own —, عَمِلَ عَلَى = خِيارِهِ — صَنَعَ عَلَى خاطِرِهِ = — فَعَلَ ما ٱسْتَحْسَنَهُ = .

Discretional, a. / Discretionary, } Voluntary, اِخْتِيارِيٌّ . At one's discretion, عَلَى هَواهُ . Discretionary power, as of a judge, سَعَةٌ حُكْمِيَّةٌ . Unlimited — power, رُخْصَةٌ تامَّةٌ — سَعَةٌ كامِلَةٌ .

Discretive, a. مُمَيِّز — مُجَرِّد — مُفَرِّقٌ بَيْنَ .

Discriminate, v.t. To mark, عَيَّنَ عَلَى — رَقَّمَ .

Discriminate, v.i. To distinguish between, فَرَزَ = — أَفْرَزَ — تَنَقَّدَ — عَرَفَ بَيْنَ = — مَيَّزَ — أَفْرَدَ — فَصَلَ بَيْنَ = .

Discriminating, a. مُمَيِّز — مُفْرِز . Discerning, حازِم — حَزِيم .

Discriminately, ad. بِإِفْرازٍ — بِٱمْتِيازٍ — بِتَمْيِيزٍ .

Discrimination, n. Discernment, تَمْيِيز — إِفْراز . Distinction, فَصْل — إِفْراق — تَفْصِيل . *See also* Discernment, n.

Discriminative, a. مُمَيِّز — مُفْرِز — بَيانِيٌّ — تَعْرِيفِيٌّ .

Discriminator, n. مُمَيِّز — صاحِبُ ٱمْتِيازٍ — ناقِد pl. نُقّاد .

Disculpate, v.t. بَيَّضَ وَجْهَهُ — أَبْرَأَ — بَرَّرَ .

Disculpation, n. The act of, تَبْيِيضُ وَجْهٍ — تَبْرِير — إِبْراء .

Discumber, v.t. *See to* Disencumber, v.t.

Discursion, n. تَرَدُّد — عَيْل — دَوْرَة .

Discursive, a. / Discursory, } Roving, عَيّار — دَوّار . Irregular, غَيْرُ مَضْبُوطٍ — غَيْرُ قِياسِيٍّ . Argumentative, اِسْتِدْلالِيٌّ — مُسْتَنْتِج . By way of digression, عَلَى وَجْهِ ٱلِاسْتِطْرادِ .

Discursively, ad. Irregularly, مِنْ غَيْرِ قِياسٍ . Argumentatively, اِسْتِدْلالًا — اِسْتِنْتاجًا — بِٱلتَّبَرْهُنِ .

Discursiveness, n. Irregularity, عَدَمُ قِياسٍ . Reasoning, اِسْتِدْلال — تَبَرْهُن . Digression, اِسْتِطْراد .

Discus, n. قُرْصٌ مِنْ حَدِيدٍ يُلْعَبُ بِهِ .

Discuss, v.t. To examine into, فَحَصَ عَن = — باحَثَ عَن — فاوَضَ — بَحَثَ عَن = — ناضَلَ — خاضَ فِي ² — أَبْرَمَ — تَكَلَّمَ فِي . To separate into parts, حَلَّ ² — حَلَّلَ — صَرَّفَ .

Discussion, n. Examination, مُفاوَضَة — إِبْرام — مُباحَثَة — تَفاوُض — فَحْص — مُذاكَرَة — مُناضَلَة . The act of separating, تَحْلِيل — حَلّ — تَصْرِيف . To hold a — with . . . , تَقاوَلَ مَعَ —

ذاكر - باحث - فاوض. A warm —, مذاكرة حادّة. The discussions of the council, مذاكرات المجلس. A subject under —, موضوع مبحوث عنه - موضوع بحث.

Discussive, *a.* } Dispersing, محلّل - مصرّف - مشتّت.
Discutient, }

Disdain, *n.* Scorn of what is mean, أنفة - حميّة - ترفّع عن - ازدراء - استخفاف - إهانة - استحقار. Contempt, عزّة النفس - هوان. To excite to —, آنف.

Disdain, *v.t.* To be above doing, استحى - حمي عن or من - ازدرى. To contemn, ترفّع عن - تجالّ عن - تعظّم عن - من - استخفّ ب - استهزأ ب - أهان. His soul disdained, was above, the thing, شرفت نفسه عن الشيء. I would have disdained to . . . , كنت أستنكف من أن.

Disdainful, *a.* مزدرٍ ب - حميّ الأنف - أنف - أنوف - مستخفّ ب - مهين. Proud, جبريّ - متكبّر. To be —, تكبّر - تفخّر - ترفّع - تجالّ.

Disdainfully, *ad.* احتقارًا - بازدراء - بهوان - إهانة - أنفة.

Disease, *n.* داء *pl.* أدواء - وجع *pl.* أوجاع - سقم *pl.* أسقام - سقام - مرض *pl.* أمراض. A corrupt state of morals, فساد. The — peculiar to a country, تخمة *pl.* تخمات *and* تخم. A chronic —, دنف. An incurable —, عياء. A slight —, خطفة - خطف. A protracted —, ضنى - زمانة. A wearying —, عضال - عضيل. The remains of a —, غبّر المرض. His — increased, اشتدّ مرضه. To have a —, مرض - سقم - ضني.

Disease, *v.t.* To make ill, ألمّ - مرّض - أوجع - أسقم. To make corrupt, أفسد.

Diseased, *a.* Having a disease, مريض - سقيم *pl.* سقام - دئ - مرضى *pl.* مراضى *and* مرضى. Vitiated, فاسد. He was — in his feet, أصابه مرض في رجليه.

Disembark, *v.t.* أخرج - (أنزل - or نزّل -) من المركب. Of a cargo, وضع الوسق *aor.* يضع.

Disembark, *v.i.* نزل من المركب - أقبل إلى البرّ.

Disembarkation, *n.* } The act of bringing on shore, إخراج (or إنزال or تنزيل) من المركب; of
Disembarking, }
coming on shore, نزول من المركب - إقبال إلى البرّ.

Disembarrass, *v.t.* To extricate from difficulty, أفرج - من - حمل الثقلة عن - فرّج - من. To extricate from, خلّص - من - أخرج - من. To — one's self from, تخلّص من - خرج من - تفرّج من.

Disembarrassment, *n.* The act of, تخليص - إفراج - تفريج; the being extricated, تخلّص - تفرّج - فرج - راحة - فرج.

Disembellish, *v.t.* جرّد - من الزينة.

Disembellishment, *n.* تجريد الزينة.

Disembitter, *v.t.* أزال عن - المرارة.

Disembodied, *a.* Without a body, بلا جسد - عديم الجسد. Dispersed, شذّ - متبدّد - مفترق. Not incorporated, غير منضمّ.

Disembody, *v.t.* To divest of a body, جرّد - من الجسد. To discharge troops, صرف العساكر.

Disembogue, *v.t.* صبّ - سكب.

Disembogue, *v.i.* انسكب - انصابّ - انصبّ.

Disemboguement, *n.* } انصباب - صبّ - صبيب - سكب.
Disembouchure, }

Disembowel, *v.t.* أقلع منه الأحشاء - أخرج المصارين - فرّغ الأحشاء.

Disembroil, *v.t.* حلّ (or أسكن) المنازعة - حلّ النزاع. To free one from, أفرج - من.

Disemploy, *v.t.* *See to* Dismiss, *v.t.*

Disenchant, *v.t.* To free from sorcery, فكّ - (or حلّ -) من السحر; from false views, فتح عينه - أزال عن - الوهم.

Disenchantment, *n.* As from sorcery, فكّ (or حلّ) السحر; from false views, إزالة الأوهام عن.

Disencumber, *v.t.* To free from, خلّص - من - نجّى - من. To — of clothes, شمّر. To clear of impediments, سلّك. To empty, فرّغ - فضّى. To — one's self of clothing, تشمّر.

Disencumbrance, *n.* Freedom from, خلاص من - نجاة من. The act of clearing, as of a road, تسليك; as of a house, تفضية - تفريغ; of clothing, تشمير.

Disengage, *v.t.* To free from, فكّ - من - نجّى - من - حلّ - من. To separate from, أفرز - أفصل - فصل - من. To extricate from, خلّص - من. To withdraw from, رجع - عن - ردّ - عن. To —, free, disentangle one's self, تفرّج من - تخلّص من.

Disengaged, *a.* Separated, منفرد - منفصل. Liberated, مخلّص - مفرّج. At leisure, أفرغ - فاضٍ - فارغ - بطّال. *See also under* Leisure, *n.*

Disengagement, *n.* The act of releasing, حلّ - فكاك - إعتاق; of separating, إفراز - فصل. The being released, خلاص - تخلّص - انحلال - انفكاك. The being at leisure, بطالة - فراغ.

Disennoble, v.t. حَطَّ-عَنْ ² (or عَزَلَ-وِنْ) — جَرَّدَ-وِنَ ٱلشَّرَفِ رُتْبَةُ ٱلشَّرَفِ.

Disenrol, v.t. مَحَا ٱسْمَهُ وِنَ ٱلدَّفْتَرِ ².

Disenslave, v.t. / Disenthrall, } See Disinthrall, v.t.

Disentangle, v.t. To free, loose, solve, فَكَّ ² — حَلَّ ². To make plain, أَوْضَحَ — شَرَحَ. To — the hair, سَرَّحَ ٱلشَّعْرَ; ravelled thread, حَلَّ ٱلْخَيْطَ ٱلْمُعَرْقَلَ. To reduce to order, نَظَّمَ. To clear up, كَشَفَ — شَرَحَ — حَلَّ ٱلْمُشْكِلَاتِ ². To — one's self from, خَلَصَ وِن — تَخَلَّصَ وِن.

Disentanglement, n. / Disentangling, } The act of freeing, تَخْلِيص — حَلّ — فَكّ; of clearing up, تَوْضِيح — تَشْرِيح; of putting in order, تَنْظِيم.

Disenter, v.t. To — a corpse, أَخْرَجَ مَيْتًا وِنَ ٱلْقَبْرِ. To dig up out of the ground, نَبَشَ.

Disenthrone, v.t. See to Dethrone, v.t.

Disentrance, v.t. صَحَّى-وِنَ ٱلْغَيْبَةِ.

Disesteem, n. إِسْتِقْلَال — إِسْتِخْفَاف — إِسْتِلَام — قِلَّةُ ٱعْتِبَارٍ — إِسْتِحْقَار.

Disesteem, v.t. إِسْتَحْقَرَ — إِسْتَقَلَّ — إِسْتَلَامَ — إِسْتَخَفَّ — إِسْتَهَانَ.

Disfavour, n. قِلَّةُ قُبُولٍ. He did him a —, صَنَعَ بِهِ صَنِيعًا قَبِيحًا. See also Disesteem, n.

Disfavour, v.t. أَظْهَرَ ٱلْعَدَاوَةَ ل — عَارَضَ — هَجَرَ ². See also to Disesteem, v.t.

Disfiguration, n. The act of disfiguring, تَعْيِيب — شَيْن — تَشْوِيه — تَشْنِيع — تَقْبِيح; the state of being disfigured, سَمَاجَة — عَكْس — قَبَاحَة.

Disfigure, v.t. To make ugly, deformed, شَانَ — عَابَ — شَوَّهَ — سَمَّجَ — قَبَّحَ — شَنَّعَ — يَشِينُ aor. To put out of order, شَوَّشَ — لَبَّكَ — عَكَسَ. To change, غَيَّرَ.

Disfigured, a. سَيِّئٌ — قَبِيح — سَمِج — مُعَيَّب — مَمْسُوخ — بَشِع. To be —, سَمُجَ ². Not to be in accord, إِنْعَكَسَ — إِلْتَبَكَ — إِشْتَكَسَ.

Disfigurement, n. بَشَاعَة — قَبَاحَة — سَمَاجَة.

Disfranchise, v.t. حَرَمَ-عَنِ ٱلْحَقِّ بِٱلِانْتِخَابِ وَغَيْرِهِ وِنَ ٱلْحُقُوقِ ٱلْبَلَدِيَّةِ.

Disfranchisement, n. حِرْمَانٌ عَنِ ٱلْحَقِّ بِٱلْمُبَايَعَةِ وَغَيْرِهَا وِنَ ٱلْحُقُوقِ ٱلْبَلَدِيَّةِ.

Disgorge, v.t. مَجَّ ² — قَذَفَ — إِسْتَفْرَغَ.

Disgorgement, n. إِسْتِفْرَاغ — قَذْف.

Disgrace, n. Want of favour, نُزُولٌ وِنَ ٱلْعَيْنِ — سُقُوطٌ وِنَ ٱلنَّظَرِ. Opprobrium, عَوْرَة — عَار — سُبَّة — خِزْيَة — خِزْيٌ — سُوءُ ٱلتَّوَجُّهِ. A crying —, عَيْنُ ٱلْعَارِ. To be in — with, سَقَطَ ² — نَزَلَ وِنْ عَيْنِهِ — وِنْ نَظَرِ. To be a — to, كَانَ عَارًا ل. He held it a — to . . ., he was above . . ., شَرُفَ عَنْ ² — تَرَفَّعَ عَنْ.

Disgrace, v.t. To bring to shame, خَذَلَ — أَخْزَى — أَخْجَلَ. To — by exposing one's vices, فَضَحَ. To put out of one's favour, غَضِبَ عَلَى — أَسْقَطَ-وِنْ نَظَرِهِ. Disgraced, مَحْرُوم — مَطْرُود. To be disgraced, exposed, إِنْفَضَحَ. Do not — your position, لَا تُهِنْ مَقَامَكَ. See also to Depose, v.t.

Disgraceful, a. دَلِيل — قَبِيح — مَعِيب — خَزْيَانُ — خَزٍ — دَنِيٌّ ². A — act, فَضِيحَة pl. فَضَائِحُ — عَيْب pl. عُيُوب. See also Shameful, a.

Disgracefully, ad. عَيْبًا — قَبَاحَةً — بِٱلْعَارِ.

Disgracious, a. See Discourteous, a.

Disguise, n. A dress to conceal, لِبْسٌ لِلتَّخَفِّي — لِبْسُ تَبْدِيلٍ — لِبْسُ تَنْكِيرٍ. A false colouring, وَشْي — شِيَة. Anything covering one, سِتْر — غَيَابَة.

Disguise, v.t. To put one on an unusual habit, أَلْبَسَ-لِبْسَ نَكَّرَ — تَنْكِير. To conceal, كَتَمَ ² — أَخْفَى — وَارَى. To cover with a false colouring, وَشَى aor. يَشِي — لَبَّسَ. To — one's self, تَنَكَّرَ. He disguised himself in woman's clothes, تَنَكَّرَ بِزِيِّ ٱلنِّسَاءِ — تَوَارَى بِلِبْسِ ٱلنِّسَاءِ. He disguised his chagrin under a show of boldness, أَخْفَى ٱلْكَمَدَ وَأَظْهَرَ ٱلْجَلَدَ. Disguised in, مُتَنَكِّرٌ فِي.

Disguisedly, ad. تَنَكُّرًا — مُتَنَكِّرًا — بِتَوَارٍ — بِتَبْدِيلٍ.

Disguisement, n. False appearance, شِيَة — هَيْئَةُ ٱلتَّنَكُّرِ — تَلْبِيس.

Disgust, n. Aversion, as from food, عَدَمُ — قَرَف — تَطَعُّم — إِشْمِئْزَاز — عَوَاف — عَوَف ٱلذَّوْقِ. Aversion, ضَجَر — أَنَفَة — مَلَل — صُدُود — قَرَف — كَرَاهَة — تَقَزُّز — إِعْتِيَاف — سَآمَة. To have a —, as for food, إِعْتَافَ — قَرِفَ. To hold in —, إِشْمَأَزَّ — تَقَرَّفَ وِن — سَئِمَ وِن — إِسْتَكْرَهَ — كَرِهَ — كَرِهَ-إِلَى — آنَفَ.

Disgust, v.t. To — one with, (أَنَّفَ- or) وِن نَفَّرَ — قَرَّفَ-بِ — أَسْأَمَ-وِن. To take away, as of one's appetite, أَسْقَطَ شَهْوَةَ ٱلنَّفْسِ — سَدَّ نَفْسَهُ ² — ٱلنَّفْس. To put one out of conceit of, زَهَّدَ-فِي — صَدَّ-عَن ². He saw a thing which disgusted him, رَأَى أَمْرًا شَنِعَ بِهِ (or إِسْتَشْنَعَهُ) aor. يَرَى.

Disgusted, a. مُشْمَئِزٌ — نَافِر — ضَجِر. To be — with, بَرِمَ بِ — شَنِعَ بِ — تَقَزَّزَ وِن — إِشْمَأَزَّ وِن — أَنِفَ وِن — تَبَرَّمَ بِ

تَضَجَّرَ بِ . He was — with the food and the country, إِعْتَنَفَ ٱلطَّعَامَ وَٱلْبِلَادَ.

Disgusting, *a.* مُقْرِف _ كَرِيه _ كُرِه . *See also* Obscene, *n.*

Disgustingly, *ad.* بِكَرَاهَةٍ _ أَنَفَةً _ إِينَافًا _ إِعْتِنَافًا _ إِشْمِئْزَازًا .

Dish, *n.* The vessel, صَحْفَة *pl.* صِحَاف _ قِصْعَة _ طَبَق *pl.* أَطْبَاق _ سُلْطَانِيَّة _ صَحْن *pl.* صُحُون _ أَجَّر *pl.* أَنَاجِر _ تَبْسِي *pl.* تَبَاسِي . Cooked food, طَبِيخ *pl.* أَطْبِخَة . Dishes served up a second time, عُوَادَة . To dish up, حَطَّ ٱلطَّعَامَ عَلَى ٱلسُّفْرَةِ ² .

Dishabille, *n.* تَخْفِيفَة _ فُضُل . In —, لَابِسُ تَخْفِيفَةٍ .

Dish-cloth, *n.* }
Dish-clout, } مِمْسَحَة *pl.* مَمَاسِح .

Dishearten, *v.t.* آيَسَ _ أَيْأَسَ _ صَدَّ ² قَلْبَهُ _ أَضَاقَ نَفْسَهُ _ أَذَابَ قَلْبَهُ _ بَرَّدَ هِمَّتَهُ . To be disheartened, فَشِلَ ² _ ضَاقَتْ نَفْسُهُ _ ذَابَ قَلْبُهُ ² .

Disheartening, *a.* مُؤْيِس _ مُؤَيِّس _ مُضَيِّقُ ٱلنَّفْسِ _ مُذِيب _ مُحْزِنُ ٱلْقَلْبِ .

Dishevel, *v.t.* شَعَّثَ . To be dishevelled, تَشَعَّثَ _ تَعَكَّشَ . Having a dishevelled head of hair, ثَائِرُ ٱلرَّأْسِ _ ثَائِرُ ٱلشَّعْرِ _ مَنْفُوشُ ٱلشَّعْرِ .

Dishing, *a.* *See* Concave, *a.*

Dishonest, *a.* Knavish, خَاطِف _ غَابِن _ غَادِر _ خَاتِر _ غَاشّ . False, زُور _ غِشّ _ كَذَّاب _ مُزَوَّر . Lewd, فَاسِق _ فَاسِد _ رَفِث . A — person, خَبِيث . Dishonest gain, رِبًا _ خَطْف .

Dishonestly, *ad.* Knavishly, بِخَتْرٍ _ خُتُورًا _ بِغَبَانَةٍ . Falsely, مُتَزَوِّرًا _ زُورًا _ تَزْوِيرًا . Lewdly, بِرَفَثٍ _ بِفَسَادٍ . To behave — towards, خَتَرَ ² _ غَبَنَ ² _ غَشَّ ² . To consider —, إِسْتَغَشَّ . To lead one to be dishonest, أَغَشَّ .

Dishonesty, *n.* Want of probity, قِلَّةُ ذِمَّةٍ _ خَتْر _ خُتُور _ غَبْن . Falseness, غِشّ _ زُور _ تَزْوِير _ مَكْر . Lewdness, رَفَث _ فِسْق _ فُجُور .

Dishonour, *n.* Reproach, عَار _ عَيْب _ شَيْن _ خِزْي _ هَوَان .

Dishonour, *v.t.* To disgrace, أَخْزَى _ أَهَانَ _ عَيَّبَ . To bring into disrepute, to shame, فَضَحَ ² _ شَانَ ² _ عَرَّ ² _ كَسَرَ عِرْضَهُ ² _ خَرَقَ حُرْمَتَهُ ² . To violate chastity, فَضَحَ ² . To be dishonoured, disgraced, إِسْوَدَّ وَجْهُهُ _ خَزِيَ *aor.* يَخْزَى _ إِسْتَخْزَى . To — a bill, رَفَضَ ٱلتَّحْوِيلَ ² .

Dishonourable, *a.* خَزٍ _ قَبِيح _ فَاحِش _ يُعِرّ _ عَيْب _ عَار . A — act, فَضِيحَة _ فُضُوحَة _ فَضَاحَة _ خِزْيَة _ فَاحِشَة . Dishonourable doings, قَبَائِح _ مَعَايِب .

Dishonourably, *ad.* بِشَيْنٍ _ بِعَارٍ _ بِقَبَاحَةٍ . To act —, أَقْبَحَ .

Dishumour, *n.* وَعْقَة _ شَرَاسَة _ شَكَاسَة .

Disinclination, *n.* عَدَمُ ٱلرَّغْبَةِ فِي _ عَدَمُ مَيْلٍ إِلَى . Aversion, كَرَاهَة .

Disincline, *v.t.* أَمَالَ عَلَى _ أَمَالَ عَن _ نَفَّرَ عَن . To be disinclined for, زَهِدَ فِي ² _ رَغِبَ عَن ² _ مَالَ عَن ² _ كَرِهَ ² _ أَضْرَبَ عَن .

Disinclose, *v.t.* شَرَحَ ² _ فَتَحَ ² .

Disincorporate, *v.t.* فَسَخَ ² _ نَقَضَ ² _ حَلَّ ² .

Disincorporation, *n.* فَسْخ _ نَقْض _ حَلّ _ فَكّ .

Disinfect, *v.t.* طَهَّرَ _ أَزَالَ ٱلْعُفُونَةَ مِن . To — one's self, تَطَهَّرَ . To be disinfected, طَهُرَ ² .

Disinfection, *n.* تَطْهِير _ إِزَالَةُ عُفُونَةٍ .

Disingenuous, *a.* حِيَلِيّ _ مُرَاءٍ _ مَاكِر _ رَدِيءُ ٱلنِّيَّةِ .

Disingenuously, *ad.* مُرَاآةً _ بِمَكْرٍ _ بِمُرَايَاةٍ _ بِغَدْرٍ .

Disingenuousness, *n.* مُرَاآة _ مُرَايَاة _ نِفَاق _ غَدْر _ فَنّ _ مَكْر .

Disinherit, *v.t.* مَنَعَ مِنَ ٱلْإِرْثِ ² _ حَرَمَ ٱلْإِرْثَ ² .

Disintegrable, *a.* يَتَشَعَّثُ _ قَابِلُ ٱنْفِصَالِ ٱلْأَجْزَاءِ .

Disintegrate, *v.t.* شَعَّثَ _ حَلَّ تَرْكِيبَ ٱلْأَجْزَاءِ ² .

Disintegration, *n.* تَشْعِيث _ تَحْلِيلُ ٱلْأَجْزَاءِ .

Disinter, *v.t.* أَخْرَجَ مِنَ ٱلْقَبْرِ _ نَبَشَ .

Disinterested, *a.* مُقْسِط _ مُسْتَقِيم _ رَحِيبُ ٱلصَّدْرِ _ خَالِي ٱلْغَرَضِ _ خَالِصُ ٱلْعَلَاقَةِ ; of gain, مُنَزَّه عَنِ ٱلطَّمَعِ .

Disinterestedly, *ad.* بِٱسْتِقَامَةٍ _ مِنْ غَيْرِ غَرَضٍ _ مُتَبَرِّعًا . To act —, أَقْسَطَ . To do a thing —, تَبَرَّعَ بِ .

Disinterestedness, *n.* تَبَرُّع _ قِسْط _ إِسْتِقَامَة _ عَدَمُ غَرَضٍ _ نَزَاهَة _ نَزَاهِيَة .

Disinterment, *n.* The — of a body, إِخْرَاجُ جُثَّةٍ مِنَ ٱلْقَبْرِ . The act of digging out of the ground, تَنْبِيش _ نَبْش .

Disinthrall, *v.t.* سَيَّبَ _ أَطْلَقَ _ خَلَّصَ _ أَعْتَقَ .

Disinthrallment, *n.* The act of, إِطْلَاق _ إِعْتَاق _ تَخْلِيص .

Disjoin, *v.t.* فَتَّقَ _ فَتَقَ ² _ فَصَّ مِن ² _ إِفْتَصَّ مِن _ فَصَلَ عَن ² _ أَفْرَقَ _ فَكَّكَ . To be disjoined from, إِنْفَصَلَ عَن _ إِنْفَكَّ مِن _ تَفَتَّقَ عَن _ إِنْفَتَقَ عَن _ إِنْفَصَّ مِن .

Disjoint, *v.t.* To put out of joint, فَسَخَ ² _ فَكَّ ² _ خَلَّعَ . *See also to* Disjoin, *v.t.*

Disjoined, *a.* }
Disjointed, } Disconnected, مُنْفَصِل _ مُفَصَّل _ مُقَطَّع . Inconsistent, لَا يَتَّفِقُ مَعَ _ غَيْرُ مُوَافِقٍ . Confused, مُشَوَّش _ غَيْرُ مُقْتَرِنٍ _ مُشْتَبِك _ مُعَقَّد . Out of joint, مَخْلُوع _ مَفْكُوك . To become —, تَخَلَّعَ .

Disjunct, *a.* مُنْفَرِد ـ مُنْفَصِل .

Disjunction, *n.* إِفْرَاق ـ عَدَمُ ٱتِّصَالٍ ـ إِنْفِصَال .

Disjunctive, *a.* إِنْفِصَالِيٌّ ـ فَاصِل ـ مُفَرِّق . A — proposition, قَضِيَّةٌ مُنْفَصِلَةٌ . A — particle, عَطْفٌ مُنْفَصِلٌ .

Disjunctively, *ad.* Separately, إِنْفِصَالًا ـ إِفْتِرَاقًا ـ إِنْفِرَادًا . Unconnectedly, مِنْ غَيْرِ ٱقْتِرَانٍ .

Disk, *n.* As of the sun, قُرْص ـ فَانُوس ـ فِتَاق ـ جَوْنَة .

Dislike, *n.* كَرَاهَة ـ إِعْتِيَاف ـ عَوَاد ـ عَوْد ـ ضِغْن ; especially of a place or climate, إِجْتِوَاء ـ جَوًى . I only gave up such an one on account of my — of him, مَا تَرَكْتُ فُلَانًا إِلَّا عَوَادًا مِنْهُ .

Dislike, *v.t.* عَافَ *aor.* يَعَافُ ـ قَبَّحَ ـ ضَغِنَ عَلَى ـ جَبَأَ ـ ; of a place, إِجْتَوَى ـ كَرِهَ ـ إِعْتَنَفَ .

Dislocate, *v.t.* To put out of joint, فَسَخَ ـ فَكَّ ـ خَلَعَ .
See also to Displace, *v.t.*, *and under* Joint, *n.*

Dislocate, *a.* } **Dislocated,** } مَفْكُوك ـ مَخْلُوع . To become —, إِنْفَكَّ ـ إِنْخَلَعَ ـ إِنْفَرَكَ ـ إِنْفَسَخَ . The limb became —, إِنْفَكَّ (or إِنْخَلَعَ) ٱلْعُضْوُ .

Dislocation, *n.* The act of, فَكّ ـ خَلْع ـ فَسْخ . A state of —, فَكَك .

Dislodge, *v.t.* To drive out, عَزَلَ ـ عَن ـ أَزَاحَ ـ طَرَدَ ـ أَخْرَجَ .
To be dislodged, إِنْخَلَعَ ـ طُرِدَ ـ أُخْرِجَ ـ إِعْتَزَلَ عَن .

Disloyal, *a.* غُدَر ـ غِدِّير ـ غَدَّار ـ غَادِر ـ خَتِير ـ خَاتِر ـ خَائِن . To be — to, خَتَرَ ـ . He was — to the compact, خَتَرَ بِٱلْعَهْدِ .

Disloyally, *ad.* بِغَدْرٍ ـ بِخِيَانَةٍ ـ بِخَتْرٍ . To act — towards, خَانَ *aor.* يَخُونُ ـ غَدَرَ بِ or عَلَى ـ غَادَرَ ـ غَدِرَ ـ خَتَرَ .

Disloyalty, *n.* خَوْز ـ غَدْر ـ خِيَانَة ـ خَوْن ـ خُتُور ـ خَتْر .

Dismal, *a.* Horrible, مُزْعِج ـ مَخُوف ـ مُرْعِب ـ هَائِل ـ مَهُول . Gloomy, ظُلْمَانِيٌّ ـ مُظْلِم ـ حَزِين . Sullen, وَعْق . Mournful, حَزِين ـ كَرِيب . Of a — countenance, مُشْتَمُّ ٱلْوَجْهِ . Saddening, مُكَدِّر ـ صَعْب ـ مُغِمّ .

Dismally, *ad.* تَوَحُّشًا ـ بِوَحْشَةٍ ـ بِكَرْبٍ ـ بِحُزْنٍ .

Dismantle, *v.t.* To strip, خَلَعَ ـ أَنْزَعَ ـ حَرَّمَ . To — a town of its fortifications, هَدَّ ٱلْمَصَانِعَ ـ هَدَمَ ٱلْحُصُونَ . To — a ship, أَخْرَجَ ٱلْمَدَافِعَ وَعُدَّةَ ٱلْحَرْبِ مِنْ مَرْكَبٍ .

Dismask, *v.t.* كَشَفَ وَجْهَهُ ـ أَزَاحَ ٱلْغِمَاءَ عَن .

Dismast, *v.t.* To break the masts, كَسَرَ ٱلصَّوَارِي . To remove the masts from ..., خَلَعَ (or رَفَعَ) ٱلصَّوَارِيَ مِن .

Dismay, *v.t.* أَدْهَشَ ـ أَفْزَعَ ـ هَوَّلَ ـ أَرْعَبَ ـ خَوَّفَ .

Dismay, *n.* فَزَع ـ خَوْف ـ دَهَش ـ هَوْل ـ رُعْب .

Dismember, *v.t.* To cut off a member, حَسَمَ ـ بَتَكَ . To cut up into members, قَطَعَ عُضْوًا مِن ـ عُضْوًا ـ عَضَّى . To sever, صَرَمَ ـ صَرَّمَ ـ أَفْرَزَ . To deprive one of membership, أَخْرَجَ ـ مِنَ ٱلْجَمْعِيَّةِ .

Dismemberment, *n.* The — of a limb, قَطْعُ عُضْوٍ ـ بَتْكُ عُضْوٍ مِن . Cutting up into members, تَعْضِيَة . Deprival of membership, إِخْرَاجُ عُضْوٍ مِنَ ٱلْجَمْعِيَّةِ .

Dismiss, *v.t.* To send away, سَرَّحَ ـ صَرَفَ ـ رَدَّ ـ خَلَّى عَن ـ دَشَّرَ ـ طَرَدَ . To discard, نَفَى ـ نَفَا ـ طَرَدَ ـ دَشَّرَ ـ أَطْلَقَ ـ أَرْسَلَ . To — from office, عَزَلَ ـ خَلَعَ . To divorce, خَلَعَ ـ سَرَّحَ ـ أَطْلَقَ . He dismissed the assembly, صَرَفَ ٱلْمَحْفِلَ .

Dismissal, *n.* The act of sending away, permission to depart, إِذْن ـ رُخْصَة ; of discharging, deprivation, طَرْد ـ خَلْع ـ تَعْزِيل ـ عَزْل .

Dismissed, *a.* Permitted to depart, مُرَخَّص ـ مَأْذُون . Discarded, مَطْرُود . Discharged from office, مَعْزُول ـ مُسَرَّح ـ مَخْلُوع .

Dismissive, *a.* Permitting to depart, مُرَخِّص لِ ـ فِي ٱلِٱنْصِرَافِ ـ آذِنٌ لِ ـ فِي . Removing, مُعَزِّل ـ خَالِع .

Dismount, *v.i.* To alight, تَرَجَّلَ ـ نَزَلَ عَن ـ أَعْلَى عَن ـ حَوَّلَ عَن .

Dismount, *v.t.* To make to alight, أَرْجَلَ . To throw off from, قَلَبَ ـ عَن ـ أَكَبَّ ـ عَن ـ طَرَحَ ـ عَن . To — a cannon, حَطَّ ٱلْمِدْفَعَ عَنْ جَرَّارِهِ .

Disobedience, *n.* مُمَارَدَة ـ مَعْصِيَة ـ عِصْيَان ـ مُعَانَدَة ـ عِنَاد ـ عَدَمُ إِطَاعَةٍ . An act of —, an evil action, سَيِّئَة *pl.* سَيِّئَات ـ خَطِيئَة *pl.* خَطَايَا ـ خَطَاء ـ مَسَاءَة . Acts of —, مَسَاوٍ . Disobedience to parents, عُقُوق . Disobedience to a parent is (like) the bereavement of him who is not (really) bereft of his child, ٱلْعُقُوقُ ثُكْلُ مَنْ لَمْ يَثْكَلْ . To commit an act of —, خَطِئَ ـ أَسَاءَ ـ أَخْطَأَ .

Disobedient, *a.* عَاصٍ *pl.* عُصَاة ـ مُرِيد *pl.* مُرَدَاء ـ مَرِيد ـ مُعَانِد ـ مَارِد ـ عَاقٌّ لِ . Disobedient to parents, عَاقٌّ . To be — to parents, عَقَّ وَالِدَيْهِ . How — he is to his father, مَا أَعَقَّهُ لِوَالِدِهِ .

Disobediently, *ad.* بِعَدَمِ إِطَاعَةٍ ـ مُعَانَدَةً ـ بِمُمَارَدَةٍ .

Disobey, *v.t.* عَانَدَ ـ عَاصَى ـ إِسْتَعْصَى عَلَى ـ خَالَفَ ـ تَمَرَّدَ عَلَى ـ عَقَّ . To — parents, عَقَّ ٱلْوَالِدَيْنِ .

Disobligation, *n.* قِلَّةُ مَعْرُوفٍ ـ إِسَاءَة .

Disoblige, *v.t.* أَسَاءَ إِلَى ـ عَامَلَ ـ بِٱلْمَأْلُوفِ .

Disobliging, *a.* سَيِّئ ـ عَدِيمُ ٱلْمَعْرُوفِ .

Disobligingly, *ad.* بِقِلَّةِ مَعْرُوفٍ ـ بِإِسَآءَةٍ.

Disorder, *n.* Want of order, عَدَمُ ٱنْتِظَامٍ ـ بَلْبَلَة ـ ارْتِبَاك ـ الْتِبَاك ـ تَخْلِيط ـ تَشْوِيش ـ لَخْبَطَة. Tumult, هَوْشَة ـ غَاغَة ـ رَجَّة ـ غَلْغَلَة ـ ارْتِجَاج. Revolt, فِتْنَة ـ فَسَاد ـ إِخْتِلَال. Irregularity of manners, vice, فِسْقٌ وَفَسَادٌ ـ دَعَارَة. Perturbation, حَيْرَة ـ كَدَرُ ٱلْبَالِ ـ إِضْطِرَاب. A malady, سَقَام ـ سَقَم ـ مَرَض *pl.* أَمْرَاض ـ دَآء *pl.* أَدْوَآء. A cause of —, مَفْسَدَة. In complete —, مُكَدَّرُ ٱلْبَالِ وَمُضْطَرِبُ ٱلْأَحْوَالِ. To throw into —, لَبَّكَ ـ بَلْبَلَ ـ شَوَّشَ. To be thrown into —, إِخْتَلَّ ـ تَشَوَّشَ ـ إِرْتَبَكَ ـ إِلْتَبَكَ.

Disorder, *v.t.* To throw into confusion, لَبَّكَ ـ شَوَّشَ ـ هَوَّشَ ـ خَلَطَ ـ فَسَدَ ـ خَبَّطَ ـ خَبَّلَ ـ خَرْبَطَ. To disturb, as of the mind, كَدَّرَ ـ حَيَّرَ ـ شَوَّشَ. To make sick, أَسْقَمَ ـ أَمْرَضَ ـ أَغْمَى ـ أَضَرَّ. To be disordered, made sick, إِخْتَلَّ ـ مَرِضَ ـ أَسْقَمَ ـ تَشَوَّشَ. His health became disordered, إِخْتَلَّ مِزَاجُهُ. His affair was —, إِرْتَبَكَ أَمْرُهُ ـ إِضْطَرَبَ أَمْرُهُ. Thy affairs are in —, مَالَ سَرْجُكَ. Wine disorders the intellect, ٱلْخَمْرُ يُخَالِطُ ٱلْعَقْلَ.

Disordered, *a.* In intellect, خَبْل ـ مَخْبُول; in health, مِسْقَام ـ مَرِيض. Thrown into confusion, مُرْتَبِك ـ مُبَدَّد ـ مُشَوَّش ـ مُلَخْبَط. To be in a — state, of an affair, مَالَ سَرْجُهُ. His stomach became —, إِخْتَلَطَتْ نَفْسُهُ. His mind became —, إِخْتَلَطَ عَقْلُهُ. Their affair became —, إِخْتَلَطَ عَلَيْهِمْ أَمْرُهُمْ. The being — (in these several senses), خِلَاط ـ إِخْتِلَاط.

Disorderly, *a.* Confused, عَدِيمُ ٱلنِّظَامِ ـ قَلِيلُ ٱلتَّرْتِيبِ ـ مُتَقَلِّب ـ مُلْتَبِك ـ مُشَوَّش. Lawless, vicious, فَاسِد ـ رَذِيل ـ فَاجِر ـ مُعَاب. A —, or bawdy, house, بَيْتُ قِحَابٍ ـ مَاخُورُ ٱلزُّنَاة. To walk, act, —, سَلَكَ بِلَا تَرْتِيبٍ ².

Disorderly, *ad.* Confusedly, بِٱخْتِلَالٍ ـ فِي خَلَلٍ ـ مِنْ غَيْرِ نِظَامٍ ـ بِٱلْتِبَاكٍ ـ بِٱرْتِبَاكٍ. Without law, بِلَا قَاعِدَةٍ ـ مِنْ غَيْرِ نَامُوسٍ.

Disorganization, *n.* The act of disorganizing, تَبْدِيدُ ٱلنِّظَامِ; the state of being disorganized, تَبَدُّدُ ٱلنِّظَامِ ـ إِخْلَال ـ إِفْسَاد ـ فَسَاد ـ خَلَلٌ فِي ٱلتَّرْكِيبِ ـ إِخْتِلَال. A cause of —, مَفْسَدَة. To be in a state of —, إِخْتَلَّ ـ إِسْتَفْسَدَ.

Disorganize, *v.t.* فَرَّقَ شَمْلَهُمْ ـ أَفْسَدَ ـ فَسَخَ ـ حَلَّ ٱلتَّرْكِيبَ ². They were disorganized, فَسَدَتْ سِيرَتُهُمْ وَأَخْلَاقُهُمْ. A disorganized party, قَذِر.

Disorganizer, *n.* نَاقِضُ نِظَامٍ ـ مُفْسِد ـ مُفْسِخ ـ مُفْتِن.

Disown, *v.t.* To deny, أَنْكَرَ ـ جَحَدَ ـ رَدَّ ². To renounce, turn off, نَفَا ² ـ نَفَى ـ رَفَضَ ـ طَرَدَ ². Disowned, نَفِيٌّ ـ مَطْرُود.

Disparage, *v.t.* إِسْتَقَلَّ ـ إِسْتَخَفَّ بِ ـ قَلَّلَ ـ ذَمَّ ² ـ ذَلَّ ² ـ عَيَّبَ. He disparaged him in his eyes, قَلَّلَهُ فِي عَيْنِهِ. To be disparaged, أُسْتُقِلَّ ـ أُسْتُخِفَّ بِهِ ـ ذَلَّ *aor.* يَذِلُّ.

Disparagement, *n.* The act of, إِسْتِقْلَال ـ إِسْتِخْفَاف ـ تَقْلِيل ـ ذَمّ ـ عَيْب ـ إِذْلَال. The being disparaged, ذُلّ ـ مَذَلَّة ـ ذِلَّة.

Disparager, *n.* }
Disparaging, *a.* } مُسْتَقِلّ ـ مُسْتَخِفّ ـ مُقَلِّل ـ مُذِمّ ـ مُهِين ـ مُذِلّ.

Disparagingly, *ad.* بِٱسْتِقْلَالٍ ـ بِٱسْتِخْفَافٍ ـ بِمَذَلَّةٍ ـ بِإِهَانَةٍ ـ إِذْلَالًا.

Disparity, *n.* تَفَاوُت ـ عَدَمُ مُسَاوَاةٍ ـ فَرْق ـ إِخْتِلَاف.

Dispart, *v.t.* *See to* Disjoin, *v.t.*

Dispassionate, *a.* Calm, رَزِين ـ رَكِين. Impartial, مُقْسِط ـ مُسْتَقِيم ـ مِنْ غَيْرِ مُحَابَاةٍ.

Dispassionately, *ad.* Calmly, بِرَزَانَةٍ ـ بِوَقَارٍ ـ حِلْمًا.

Dispatch, *v.t.* To send, أَسَارَ ـ أَوْفَدَ ـ وَفَّدَ ـ وَجَّهَ ـ أَرْسَلَ. To transmit to, نَفَّذَ-إِلَى ـ أَنْفَذَ-إِلَى. To put to death, قَتَلَ ² ـ مَوَّتَ. To send, as a legate, to, فَرَطَ-إِلَى ² ـ فَرَّطَ-إِلَى ـ أَفْرَطَ. To perform quickly, أَنْجَزَ ـ أَسْرَعَ فِي ـ عَمِلَ-بِسُرْعَةٍ. To perform, صَنَعَ ـ أَجَازَ ـ أَنْفَذَ ـ أَتَمَّ.

Dispatch, *n.* Speedy performance, سُرْعَة ـ سَرَاح ـ عَجَلَة. The act of sending off, سَرْح ـ وَفْد ـ تَوْجِيه ـ تَوْفِيد ـ إِرْسَال. A letter, تَحْرِير *pl.* تَحْرِيرَات ـ مَكْتُوب *pl.* مَكَاتِيبُ ـ رَقِيم. An official —, خَطٌّ رَسْمِيٌّ *pl.* خُطُوطٌ رَسْمِيَّةٌ. Telegraphic dispatches, حَوَادِثُ ٱلتِّلِغْرَافِ. Official dispatches, تَحْرِيرَاتٌ رَسْمِيَّةٌ.

Dispel, *v.t.* دَفَعَ ـ سَاقَ ² ـ أَزَاحَ ـ أَزَالَ. To —, as wind the clouds, سَفَرَ-عَن. To cause to pass away, as of sorrow, *etc.*, أَذْهَبَ ـ فَرَّجَ. To be dispelled, of grief, إِنْفَرَجَ ـ تَفَرَّجَ.

Dispend, *v.t.* *See to* Expend, *v.t.*

Dispensable, *a.* مِمَّا يُسْتَغْنَى عَنْهُ ـ غَيْرُ ضَرُورِيٍّ.

Dispensary, *n.* مَخْزَنُ ٱلْأَدْوِيَةِ ـ وَكَالَةُ ٱلدَّوَآءِ ـ صَيْدَلِيَّة. *See also under* Chemist, *n.*

Dispensation, *n.* Distribution, تَقْسِيم ـ تَوْزِيع ـ تَفْرِيق. A system, as of rules, نَسَق ـ فَرَائِضُ ـ تَرْتِيب ـ قَوَانِينُ. The will or decree of God, أَمْرُ ٱللّٰهِ ـ قَدَرُ ٱللّٰهِ. The dealings of God with His creatures, ٱلْحِكْمَةُ ٱلْإِلٰهِيَّةُ ـ عَزَائِمُ ٱللّٰهِ ـ تَدَابِيرُ ٱللّٰهِ. Exemption from, فُسْحَة ـ سَمَاحٌ مِن. Permission, the making allowable, تَحْلِيل. The Christian —, تَدْبِيرُ ٱللّٰهِ ٱلْمُعْطَى عَلَى يَدِ سَيِّدِنَا عِيسَى ـ ٱلنَّصْرَانِيَّة. Permission, إِجَازَة.

Dispensative, *a.* } Permitting, مُجِيز ـ مُسَامِح ـ مُحَلِّل ل ـ
Dispensatory, } مُعْفٍ عَن.

Dispensatory, *n.* أَقْرَابَاذِينَات ـ كِتَابٌ فِي تَرْكِيبِ ٱلْأَدْوِيَةِ.

Dispense, *v.t.* To divide out in portions, وَزَّعَ ـ قَسَّمَ-عَلَى ـ قَسَّمَ-بَيْنَ. To administer, مَنَحَ ـ أَعْطَى ـ قَدَّمَ ل. To — with, to do without, اِسْتَغْنَى عَن ـ فَضَلَ عَن ـ أَغْنَى عَن. To allow, سَامَحَ ـ عَفَا عَن ـ صَفَحَ عَن. No one who wishes to have full knowledge of ... can — with it, لا يُمْكِنُ ٱلْاِسْتِغْنَاءُ عَنْهُ لِمَنْ يَرِيدُ أَنْ يَكُونَ لَهُ ٱطِّلَاعٌ تَامٌّ عَلَى.

Dispenser, *n.* A distributor, مُفَرِّق ـ مُوَزِّع ; a giver, واهب ـ مَانِح ـ مُعْطٍ. A director, والٍ ـ مُدَبِّر ـ مُدِير ـ مُبَاشِر.

Dispeople, *v.t.* *See to* Depopulate, *v.t.*

Disperse, *v.t.* شَرَّدَ ـ بَدَّدَ ـ نَشَرَ ـ أَشَتَّ ـ نَثَّرَ ـ نَفَّرَ ـ شَتَّتَ ـ بَثَّ ـ بَذَرَ. To —, make to fly, as wind the dust, or as straw from wheat, ذَرَى. To —, as wind the clouds, سَفَرَ-عَن. The wind dispersed it, ذَرَتْهُ ٱلرِّيحُ. To —, to cause to pass away, أَزَالَ.

Dispersed, *a.* مُشَتَّت ـ بَثّ ـ شَرِيد ـ شَتّ ـ مَنْثُور. To be —, تَشَتَّتَ ـ تَفَصَّصَ ـ اِنْفَضَّ ـ اِنْتَثَرَ ـ تَنَثَّرَ ـ تَمَذَّرَ. To be —, as of news, اِسْتَفَاضَ. They went away —, ذَهَبُوا شَعَاعًا. They were — in all directions, تَفَرَّقُوا شَذَرَ مَذَرَ. To be —, as of an odour, فَغَ.

Dispersedly, *ad.* عَلَى حَالَةِ ٱلتَّفَرُّقِ ـ شَذَرَ مَذَرَ ـ نَشْرًا.

Dispersion, *n.* The act of scattering, تَفْرِيق ـ تَبْدِيد ـ تَشْتِيت ; the state of being scattered, شَتّ ـ اِنْتِشَار ـ تَفَرُّق ـ تَشَرُّد ـ تَنَفُّض. The causing to cease, إِزَالَة ; the act of ceasing, زَوَال.

Dispersive, *a.* Scattering, مُفَرِّق ـ مُبَدِّد. Causing to cease, مُنَبِّه.

Dispirit, *v.t.* *See to* Dishearten, *v.t.*

Dispiriting, *a.* *See* Disheartening, *a.*

Displace, *v.t.* To remove from its place, فَضَّ ـ نَقَلَ ـ رَفَعَ-مِنْ مَحَلِّهِ ـ حَوَّلَ-مِنْ مَكَانِهِ ـ لَبَّكَ. To disorder, لَبَّكَ ـ خَرْبَطَ ـ شَوَّشَ. To put out of office, عَزَلَ ـ رَفَعَ-مِنَ ٱلْمَنْصِبِ. To become displaced, put out of place, اِنْفَضَّ ـ اِنْتَقَلَ ـ زَاحَ عَنْ مَوْضِعِهِ *aor.* يَزِيحُ. To be displaced, put out of office, عُزِلَ. *See also to* Dislodge, Disorder, Depose, *v.t.*

Displacement, *n.* The act of, تَحْوِيل ـ فَضّ ـ نَقْل ـ رَفْع. Deprivation of office, تَعْزِيل ـ خَلْع.

Displant, *v.t.* قَلَعَ ـ اِسْتَأْصَلَ.

Display, *v.t.* To exhibit, عَرَضَ ـ جَلَّى ـ أَرَى ـ أَظْهَرَ ـ أَوْرَى ـ أَبْدَى ـ يَأْتِي *aor.* أَتَى ب ـ أَظْهَرَ. To manifest, أَوْرَى. To spread out, بَسَطَ ـ نَشَرَ ـ فَرَشَ ـ أَظْهَرَ. To be displayed, اِنْتَشَرَ ـ اِفْتَرَشَ ـ اِنْبَسَطَ. To be spread out, اِنْعَرَضَ ـ جَلَا. To — courage, جَسَرَ. To — eloquence, تَفَصَّحَ. To — one's finery in dress, of a woman, تَبَرَّجَتْ. He displayed the thing to him, عَرَضَ لَهُ ٱلشَّيْءَ. The praiseworthy design which he displayed, ٱلْقَصْدُ ٱلْجَمِيلُ ٱلَّذِي أَبْدَاهُ.

Display, *n.* Exhibition, إِظْهَار ـ عَرْض ـ عُرُوض ـ إِرَاءَة ـ تَوْرِيَة. Parade, طَنْطَنَة ـ زِينَة ـ وَكْبَة. Display of goods, عَرْضُ بِضَاعَةٍ. To make an ostentatious — of, اِفْتَخَرَ ب ـ تَبَاهَى ب.

Displease, *v.t.* أَسَاءَ إِلَى ـ أَسْخَطَ ـ سَاءَ فِي عَيْنِ *aor.* يَسُوءُ ـ سَخِطَ. To be displeased with, to dislike, أَغَمَّ ـ أَغَاظَ ـ كَدَّرَ عَلَى ـ اِسْتَقْبَحَ ـ اِسْتَكْرَهَ. To be displeased, dissatisfied, with a place, ضَاقَتْ نَفْسُهُ مِنَ ٱلْمَكَانِ ـ مَا طَابَ لَهُ ٱلْمَوْضِعُ. To be displeased, angry, with, غَضِبَ عَلَى ـ اِغْتَاظَ عَلَى. To be displeased, vexed, اِغْتَمَّ ـ اِنْغَبَنَ ـ اِنْقَهَرَ ـ سَخِطَ ـ تَسَخَّطَ ـ تَكَرَّهَ ـ تَغَضَّبَ. He is displeased with you, خَاطِرُهُ مُغَيَّرٌ عَلَيْكَ. He was displeased with you, كَانَ سَاخِطًا عَلَيْكَ. I displeased the man (by what I did), سُؤْتُ ٱلرَّجُلَ. It was my intention to — him, أَرَدْتُ مَسَاءَتَهُ.

Displeasing, *a.* Disagreeable, غَيْرُ مَقْبُولٍ ـ مَكْرُوه ـ كَرِيه. Offensive, سَيِّئ. Causing vexation, مُغِمّ.

Displeasure, *n.* كَآبَة ـ كَدَر ـ سُخْط ـ غُبْن ـ تَكَرُّه. A cause of —, مَسْخَطَة ـ مَسَاءَة *pl.* مَسَاوٍ. A state of disgrace, سُقُوط ـ نُزُولٌ مِنَ ٱلْعَيْنِ ـ مِنَ ٱلنَّظَرِ. *See also* Disapprobation, Dislike, *n.*

Disport, *n.* } بَحْبَحَة ـ اِنْشِرَاح ـ كَيْفِيَّة ـ تَنَزُّه ـ لَعِب.
Disportment, }

Disport, *v.i.* لَعِبَ ـ تَنَزَّهَ ـ تَكَيَّفَ ـ تَبَحْبَحَ.

Disposable, *a.* That may be arranged, مِمَّا يَتَنَظَّمُ ـ مِمَّا يَتَرَتَّبُ. Free to use, at command, حَالٍ ـ حَاضِر ـ تَحْتَ ـ قَابِلُ ٱلتَّسْوِيَةِ ـ ٱلْيَدِ. Disposable effects, مُحَلَّلَات.

Disposal, *n.* The act of regulating, تَنْظِيم ـ تَرْتِيب. Order, نِظَام ـ اِنْتِظَام ـ نَسَق. Direction, superintendence, مُبَاشَرَة ـ إِدَارَة ـ تَصَرُّف ـ أَمْر ـ رَأْي ـ كَيْف ـ اِخْتِيَار. Option, power, تَصَرُّف ـ أَمْر. To be at the — of, under the order of, فِي يَدِ ـ يَد ـ حُكْم ـ تَحْتَ يَدِ ـ تَحْتَ حُكْمِ ـ فِي حَيْطَةِ تَصَرُّفِ ـ فِي تَصْرِيفِ. He placed it at his —, جَعَلَهُ فِي تَصَرُّفِهِ. They are entirely at his —, هُمْ تَحْتَ تَصَرُّفِهِ بِٱلْكُلِّيَّةِ (or بَتَّةً). To leave a sum at the — of, أَبْقَى مَبْلَغًا تَحْتَ ٱلطَّلَبِ. To be at one's own —, فِي تَصَرُّفِ نَفْسِهِ.

Dispose, *v.t.* To place, وَضَعَ *aor.* يَضَعُ. To arrange, نَظَّمَ – رَتَّبَ – ضَبَطَ. To incline, أَمَالَ – مَيَّلَ – أَلْوَى. To arrange in layers, as stones, *etc.*, رَصَفَ. To — favourably towards, عَطَفَ-عَلَى. To prepare for, أَحْضَرَ-ل – هَيَّأَ-ل – أَعَدَّ-ل. To — of, to give away to, وَهَبَ-ل – أَنَالَ – أَنْعَمَ عَلَى-ب *aor.* يَهَبُ – أَعْطَى. To apply to any purpose, اِسْتَعْمَلَ – تَسَبَّبَ ب-إِلَى. To get rid of, تَخَلَّصَ مِن – أَلْقَى ب. To sell, بَاعَ. To — of, to settle satisfactorily, سَدَّدَ. He disposed of his daughter in marriage to him, زَوَّجَهُ بِنْتَهُ – زَوَّجَ بِنْتَهُ لَهُ.

Disposed, *a.* Arranged, مُنَظَّم – مُرَتَّب – مُنَسَّق. Inclined to, مُنْعَطِف عَلَى – مَطْبُوع عَلَى – مَائِل إِلَى – مُمِيل ل. To be —, inclined to, اِنْعَطَفَ عَلَى – مَالَ إِلَى – أَخَالَ إِلَى – أَرَادَ. To be favourably — to, عَطَفَ – تَعَطَّفَ عَلَى – لَوَى عَلَى. To be rightly —, to be turned in the right direction, أَسَدَّ – صَارَ سَدِيدًا – تَسَدَّدَ. He was — thereto by nature, طُبِعَ عَلَى ٱلشَّيْء. He is becoming more — to . . . , يَزْدَادُ مَيْلًا إِلَى. If you are — to go, إِذَا أَرَدْتُمْ أَنْ تَذْهَبُوا. This speech is — in regular order, is coherent, هٰذَا ٱلْكَلَامُ آخِذٌ بَعْضُهُ بِحُجَزِ بَعْضٍ.

Disposer, *n.* A giver, وَهَّاب – وَاهِب. A director, مُرَتِّب – مُدِير – مُدَبِّر. A master, صَاحِبُ ٱلْأَمْرِ – وَالٍ. The Sovereign —, God, ٱلْمُقَدِّرُ. The —, Giver, God, ٱلرَّزَّاقُ. The Incliner of hearts, God, ٱلْمُحَرِّفُ ٱلْقُلُوبِ.

Disposition, *n.* Order, نَسَق – تَرْتِيب – نِظَام – اِصْطِلَاح. Aptitude, سَجِيَّة – قَرِيحَة – طِيَّة. Inclination, خَاطِر – مَيْل. Temper of mind, غَرِيزَة – شِيمَة *pl.* شِيَم – مَشْرَب – لَيٌّ – طَبِيعَة *pl.* طَبَائِعُ – خَلَّة – خَلِيقَة – خَصْلَة *pl.* خِصَال – فِطْرَة – ضَرِيبَة. Of a gracious —, حَلِيمُ ٱلطَّبْعِ. A bad —, خَصْلَةٌ رَدِيئَةٌ. The dispositions of a treaty, ٱلْأَحْكَامُ ٱلْمُنْدَرِجَةُ فِي مُعَاهَدَةٍ. To place at the — of, خَلَّى-فِي تَصَرُّفِ. He is of a generous —, إِنَّهُ لَكَرِيمُ ٱلضَّرِيبَةِ. Men are created of diverse dispositions, خُلِقَ ٱلنَّاسُ عَلَى ضَرَائِبَ شَتَّى.

Dispossess, *v.t.* To deprive, جَرَّدَ – سَلَبَ – أَعْرَى – عَرَّى – خَلَعَ.

Dispossession, *n.* خَلْع – تَجْرِيد – سَلْب – تَعْرِيَة.

Dispraise, *n.* جَدْب – عَيْب – مَذَمَّة – لَوْم – بَذَاءٌ – اِسْتِقْلَال.

Dispraise, *v.t.* ذَمَّ – جَدَبَ – بَذَأَ – اِسْتَقَلَّ. To be dispraised, اِسْتَذَمَّ.

Disproof, *n.* تَبْطِيل – رَدّ – تَنَاقُض – مُنَاقَضَة.

Disproportion, *n.* قِلَّةُ مُنَاسَبَةٍ – عَدَمُ مُسَاوَاةٍ – فَرْق – تَفَاوُت.

Disproportion, *v.t.* جَعَلَ فِي-مِنَ ٱلتَّفَاوُتِ – أَبْطَلَ ٱلْمُنَاسَبَةَ.

Disproportionable, Disproportional, Disproportionate, *a.* غَيْرُ – عَدِيمُ ٱلتَّنَاسُبِ – فِيهِ تَفَاوُتٌ – مُهَنْدَم.

Disproportionably, *ad.* بِٱلتَّفَاوُتِ – إِفْرَاطًا – بِغَيْرِ تَنَاسُبٍ.

Disprovable, *a.* مِمَّا يُنَاقَضُ – يُكَذَّبُ.

Disprove, *v.t.* كَذَّبَ – أَبْطَلَ قَوْلَ – رَدَّ عَلَى – نَاقَضَ.

Disputable, *a.* فِيهِ نَظَرٌ – فِيهِ خِلَافٌ – يُرَدُّ عَلَيْهِ – فِيهِ نِزَاعٌ – فِيهِ مَنَازِعُ (*or* تَنَازُعٌ).

Disputant, *n.*, **Disputer**, مُنَازِع – مُجَادِل – جَدِل – لَادّ – مُتَحَجِّج – مُشَاجِر – مُبَاحِث. An opponent, خَصِم *pl.* خَصِمُونَ – خَصِيم *pl.* خُصَمَاءُ.

Disputation, *n.* جِدَال – مُنَاقَشَة – مُنَاظَرَة – مُشَاجَرَة – مُنَاقَرَة – نِزَاع – مُجَادَلَة; debate, مُبَاحَثَة.

Disputatious, *a.* أَلَدّ *pl.* لُدّ *and* لِدَاد – خَصِم – خَصِيم – ذُو – شَرِس – شَرِيس – مِغْلَاق. *See also under* Disputant, *n.*

Dispute, *v.t.* To deny, مَا قَبِلَ ب – كَذَّبَ – رَدَّ عَلَى – نَكِرَ. To fight for, ضَارَبَ عَن – قَاتَلَ عَن – دَافَعَ عَن – مَانَعَ عَن – حَامَى عَن. To —, as of a debt, أَلَطَّ – نَكِرَ.

Dispute, *v.i.* To contend with, جَادَلَ – نَازَعَ – لَدَّ – حَاجَّ – خَاصَمَ. To — with one another, of many, تَجَادَلُوا. To answer one another disputingly, of many, رَاجَعُوا – رَادُّوا. To discuss, تَكَلَّمَ فِي – بَحَثَ عَن. They disputed together, of many, اِخْتَصَمُوا – تَنَازَعُوا.

Dispute, *n.* مُرَادَدَة – جِدَال – مُخَاصَمَة – مُعَارَكَة – مُشَاجَرَة – مُرَادَّة. A disputed point, شَجْر *pl.* شِجَار. Is he going to renew the —? هَلْ هُوَ عَازِمٌ أَنْ يُجَدِّدَ ٱلْجِدَالَ. A — arose between . . . , وَقَعَتْ مُشَاجَرَةٌ بَيْنَ. The — about it will end in blows, ٱلْجِدَالُ عَلَيْهِ يَنْتَهِي إِلَى ٱلْجِلَادِ.

Disputer, *n.* *See* Disputant, *n.*

Disqualification, *n.* The act of disqualifying, إِزَالَةُ ٱلْأَهْلِيَّةِ – إِسْقَاطُ ٱلْأَهْلِيَّةِ. Want of qualification, سَقْط – عَدَمُ أَهْلِيَّةٍ.

Disqualify, *v.t.* To deprive of fitness, أَسْقَطَ-مِن – أَزَالَ أَهْلِيَّتَهُ – ٱلْأَهْلِيَّةَ. To degrade, أَسْقَطَ. To deprive of power, عَاجَزَ – خَلَعَ-مِنَ ٱلِاسْتِطَاعَةِ – أَعْجَزَ.

Disquiet, *v.t.* أَزْعَجَ – زَعَّجَ – أَهَمَّ – كَدَّ – عَنَّى – أَضْجَرَ – قَلْقَ. To unsettle, أَفَزَّ. To be disquieted, أُحِمَّ – تَعَنَّى – تَضَجَّرَ – ضَجِرَ – اِضْطَرَبَ – تَصَدَّعَ – قَلِقَ – اِزْدَعَجَ – اِنْزَعَجَ. The affair disquieted him, قَاسَاهُ (*or* عَنَاهُ) ٱلْأَمْرُ. I was disquieted, تَعَنَّيْتُ.

Disquiet, n. } — نَكَد — عَنآء — هَمّ — إِضْطِراب — زَعَج — ضَجَر
Disquietude, } — تَضَجُّر — قَلْقَلَة — نَكْبَة .

Disquieting, a. مُعِنّ — مُتَضَجِّر — مُضْجِر — مُقْلِق — مُزْعِج .

Disquisition, n. إِيراد — مُباحَثَة — بَحْث .

Disregard, n. Omission of notice, — تَهاوُن — غُفُول — سَهْو — عَدَم — إِسْتِقْلال — عَدَمُ ٱعْتِنآء — إِهْمال. The act of slighting, — عَدَمُ ٱمْتِثال. إِسْتِحْقار — عَدَمُ ٱعْتِبار — رِعايَة. A failing to obey, مُعانَدَة — عَدَمُ مُمانَعَة. His — of . . . , إِسْتِخْفافُهُ بِ .

Disregard, v.t. To neglect, — ² غَفَلَ عَن — يَسْهُو aor. سَها عَن or فِي — إِسْتَقَلَّ — إِسْتَخَفَّ بِ. To slight, سَيَّبَ — تَصَرَّفَ — تَهاوَنَ بِ. ما ٱعْتَنَى فِي — ما حَسَبَ لَهُ حِسابًا — إِبْتَذَلَ — إِسْتَحْقَرَ. To disobey, إِسْتَعْصَى عَلَى — عانَدَ. To — one's self, تَهاوَنَ نَفْسَهُ. *See also to* Neglect, v.t.

Disregardful, a. Negligent, سَهْوان — ساهٍ — مُتَهاوِن — غافِل.

Disobedient, عاقّ لِ — مُعانِد. He is — of all considerations, advice, *etc.*, لا يَسْمَعُ نِدآء وَلا يَبْغِي ٱهْتِدآء. To be — of one, to be unmindful of him, ساهَى.

Disregardfully, ad. Negligently, بِتَهاوُنٍ; with slight, — إِسْتِحْقارًا بِٱحْتِقارٍ.

Disrelish, n. Distaste, عَدَمُ ذَوْقٍ — عَدَمُ تَلَذُّذٍ; dislike, — إِسْتِكْراه كَراهَة.

Disrelish, v.t. To dislike the taste of, ما ٱسْتَلَذَّ — إِسْتَقْبَحَ طَعْمَهُ. To have a disgust for, ² نَفَرَ قَلْبُهُ مِن — إِسْتَكْرَهَ — ² كَرِهَ ذَوْقَهُ.

Disrepair, n. إِضْمِحْلال — ضَعْضَعَة. In —, مُتَضَعْضِع — مُحْتاجٌ إِلَى ٱلتَّعْمِير. To be in —, تَضَعْضَعَ.

Disreputable, a. مُبْتَذَل. *See also* Disgraceful, a.

Disreputation, n. *See* Disgrace, Disrepute, n.

Disrepute, n. تَبَذُّل — عَدَمُ ٱعْتِبار — صِيتٌ رَدِيٌّ. To fall into —, إِنْفَضَحَتْ شُهْرَتُهُ — إِنْثَلَمَ صِيتُهُ.

Disrespect, n. سَفَه — عَدَمُ ٱحْتِرام — إِهانَة — قِلَّةُ كَرامَة.

Disrespectful, a. وَقِيح — ضِدُّ ٱلأَدَب — قَلِيلُ ٱلأَدَب. To be — to, تَوَقَّحَ عَلَى — عامَلَ بِقِلَّةِ أَدَب.

Disrespectfully, ad. بِوَقاحَةٍ — بِغَيْرِ ٱحْتِرام — بِغَيْرِ أَدَب.

Disrobe, v.t. جَرَّدَ ٱلثِّياب — شَلَحَ ثِيابَهُ. To — one's self, خَلَعَ ثِيابَهُ عَن بَدَنِهِ — شَلَحَ ثِيابَهُ.

Disroot, v.t. *See to* Eradicate, v.t.

Disrupt, a. } مَكْسُور — مَشْقُوق — مَفْرُوج — مَشْرُوم — مَفْتُوق.
Disrupted, } To be —, تَفَلَّقَ — إِنْشَرَمَ — تَشَرَّمَ.

Disruption, n. A breaking asunder, — فَلْج — فَتْق — ثَغْر — فَسْخ — فَلْج — خَلَّة — ثَغْر — شَقّ; a rent, شَقّ. A violent commotion, a calamitous occurrence, عَرْقُ ٱلقِرْبَة.

Dissatisfaction, n. Disapproval, سَخَط — عَدَمُ رِضآء. Disappointment, vexation, كَسْرُ ٱلخاطِر — قَهْر — كَرْب. A cause of —, مَسْخَطَة pl. مَساخِط. To express —, تَسَخَّطَ — ² سَخِطَ. He showed his — to . . . , أَظْهَرَ إِنْكارَهُ لِ.

Dissatisfactory, a. غَيْرُ مَرْضِيٍّ — مَسْخُوط; not sufficing, غَيْرُ كافٍ.

Dissatisfy, v.t. To discontent, ² كَسَرَ خاطِرَهُ — أَسْخَطَ. To anger, أَغْضَبَ — أَغَمَّ — أَغاظَ. To be dissatisfied with, not to approve of, لَمْ يَرْضَ بِ — تَسَخَّطَ — ² سَخِطَ عَلَى. To be vexed with, تَضَجَّرَ مِن — ² حَرِدَ عَلَى — إِنْحَسَرَ مِن. He was dissatisfied with his gift, تَسَخَّطَ عَطآءَهُ.

Dissect, v.t. To cut in pieces, قَطَّعَ — شَرَّحَ. To cut up, of a slaughtered animal, ² قَصَّبَ. To examine minutely, دَاقَّ — ² فَحَصَ بِٱلتَّدْقِيقِ — ٱلنَّظَرَ فِي.

Dissectible, a. قابِلُ ٱلتَّشْرِيح — يُشَرَّح.

Dissecting, n. تَشْرِيح. A — knife, سِكِّينٌ لِلتَّشْرِيح. A — room, بَيْتٌ لِلتَّشْرِيح.

Dissection, n. The act of cutting up, تَشْرِيح. Nice examination into, فَحْصٌ مُدَقَّق — مُداقَّةٌ فِي.

Dissector, n. تَشْرِيحْجِي — مُشَرِّح.

Dissemblance, n. إِخْتِلافُ ٱلصُّورَة — فَرْق — عَدَمُ مُشابَهَة.

Dissemble, v.t. To hide, أَخْفَى — ² كَتَمَ. To feign, — إِصْطَنَعَ — تَمَثَّلَ بِ.

Dissemble, v.i. To conceal by false pretences, — تَنَكَّرَ — رآءَى — تَخَدَّعَ. The others present dissembled with him, رآءَى مَعَهُ باقِي ٱلحاضِرِين.

Dissembler, n. مُرآءٍ pl. مُراؤُون — مُنافِق — مَكَّار.

Disseminate, v.t. — أَشاعَ بِ — ² نَشَرَ — ² بَثَّ — ² بَذَرَ — بَعْزَقَ. To —, as of slanders, among, ² فَشَّ بَيْنَ. Disseminated, مُشاع — شائِع.

Dissemination, n. The act of, — نَشْر — إِنْتِشار — نَشْر — إِشاعَة — نِثار — تَفْرِيق. A thing in a state of —, شائِعَة pl. شَوائِع.

Disseminator, n. ناشِر — مُشِيع.

Dissension, n. فِتْنَة — شَواش — نِزاع — مُشاجَرَة — إِنْشِقاق. To cause —, حَرَّشَ. To cause — between, قَرَّشَ — أَشْرَى بَيْنَ. There was — among the people, إِشْتَجَرَ ٱلقَوْمُ بَيْنَ. Civil or internal dissensions, إِخْتِلالاتٌ داخِلِيَّة.

Dissensious, a. فَتّان — مُوقِعُ ٱلفِتَن — شَرِيس — مُشاقّ.

Dissent, *v.i.* To disagree with, إِخْتَلَفَ عَن ـ شَاجَرَ ـ خَالَفَ. To separate from, إِنْفَرَدَ عَن ـ خَرَجَ مِن ـ تَشَرَّى عَن ـ إِفْتَرَقَ عَن.

Dissent, *n.* Disagreement, تَفَاوُت ـ مُضَادَّة ـ إِخْتِلَاف. Separation from, إِنْفِرَادٌ مِن ـ خُرُوجٌ مِن ـ إِفْتِرَاقٌ عَن. A dissenting body, شِيْعَة ـ شُرَاة ـ فِرْقَةٌ مِنَ ٱلْخَوَارِجِ.

Dissenter, *n.* One who disagrees with another, مُخَالِفٌ ل ـ مُعَانِدٌ ل. A sectarian, خَارِجِيٌّ *pl.* خَوَارِجُ ـ مِنْ أَهْلِ ٱلْمُعْتَزِلَةِ ـ شِيعِيٌّ *pl.* شِيْعَة ـ شَارٍ *pl.* شُرَاة. An English —, مُنْفَصِلٌ عَنِ ٱلْكَنِيسَةِ ٱلْإِنْكِلِيزِيَّةِ ٱلسُّلْطَانِيَّةِ. Dissenters from ..., مُنْفَصِلُونَ مِن.

Dissentient, *a.* and *n.* غَيْرُ قَابِلٍ بِ ـ مُخَالِف.

Dissertation, *n.* كَلَام ـ مُبَاحَثَة ـ عِبَارَة ـ مَقَالَة.

Dissertator, *n.* خَطِيب ـ خَاطِب ـ مُبَاحِث.

Disserve, *v.t.* عَامَلَ بِرَدَاءَةٍ ـ أَسَاءَ إِلَى ـ أَضَرَّ ـ ضَارَّ ـ ضَامَ.

Disservice, *n.* مُعَامَلَة ـ أَذِيَّة ـ مَسَاءَة ـ سُوء ـ ضَامَة ـ ضَاجَّة رَدِيئَة.

Disserviceable, *a.* جَائِر ـ مُضِرّ ـ ضَارّ.

Dissever, *v.t.* أَفْرَدَ ـ أَفْرَقَ ـ فَصَلَ ـ فَتَقَ. To — from, قَطَعَ مِن. To be dissevered, إِنْفَتَقَ ـ تَفَتَّقَ.

Disseverance, *n.* إِنْفِصَال ـ إِفْتِرَاق ـ مُفَارَقَة ـ فُرْقَة.

Dissident, *a.* *See* Dissentient, *a.*

Dissimilar, *a.* غَيْر ـ مُخْتَلِف ـ غَيْرُ مُمَاثِلٍ ـ غَيْرُ مُشَابِهٍ ـ غَيْرُ مُتَشَابِهٍ ـ مُجَانِس.

Dissimilarity, *n.* } **Dissimilitude**, } مُخَالَفَة ـ قِلَّةُ مُجَانَسَةٍ ـ عَدَمُ مُشَابَهَةٍ ـ تَفَاوُت.

Dissimulation, *n.* غِشّ ـ مُوَارَبَة ـ نِفَاق ـ مُرَايَاة ـ تَوْرِيَة. To use —, وَارَبَ ـ دَاهَنَ ـ أَدْهَنَ. To use — with, إِدْهَان.

Dissimulator, *n.* مُدَاهِن ـ مُنَافِق ـ مَكَّار ـ مُرَاؤُونَ *pl.* مُرَاءٍ.

Dissipate, *v.t.* To scatter, فَرَّقَ ـ شَتَّتَ ـ بَذَّرَ ـ بَدَّدَ. To —, as the wind the clouds, سَفَرَ عَن ـ أَزَالَ. To waste, أَسْرَفَ ـ بَذَّرَ مَالَهُ ـ أَتْلَفَ مَالَهُ. To — one's wealth, أَبَادَ ـ أَتْلَفَ. To — the mind, أَضَاعَ ٱلْعَقْلَ ـ أَتْلَفَ ٱلْفِكْرَ. To be —, dispersed, تَبَذَّرَ ـ تَبَدَّدَ. To be —, wasted, تَلِفَ ـ ضَاعَ.

Dissipated, *a.* Scattered, مُتَشَتِّت ـ مُتَبَدِّد. Debauched, مُنْهَمِكٌ فِي ٱللَّذَّاتِ ـ فَاجِر ـ شِرِّير ـ خَاسِر ـ فَاسِق.

Dissipation, *n.* The act of dispersing, تَفْرِيق ـ تَبْذِير ـ تَشْتِيت. Loss, waste, إِسْرَاف ـ إِبَادَة ـ إِتْلَاف. Profligacy, فِسْق ـ عَيْشٌ مُسْرِف ـ إِنْهِمَاكٌ فِي ٱللَّذَّاتِ ـ فُجُور. Dissipation of the mind, طَيَشَانُ ٱلْعَقْلِ ـ ضَيَاعُ ٱلْفِكْرِ.

Dissociability, *n.* وَحْشَة ـ عَدَمُ ٱلْمُؤَانَسَةِ ـ عَدَمُ ٱلْأُنْسَةِ ـ تَوَحُّش.

Dissociable, *n.* مُخَالِف ـ عَدِيمُ ٱلْإِقْتِرَانِ ـ عَدِيمُ ٱلْمُحَاذَاةِ.

Dissocial, *a.* مُتَوَحِّش ـ جَافٍ ـ عَدِيمُ ٱلْأُنْسِ ـ غَيْرُ أَنِيسٍ.

Dissociate, *v.t.* أَبْطَلَ ٱلْإِتِّصَالَ بَيْنَ ـ فَصَلَ بَيْنَ ـ فَرَقَ بَيْنَ. To — one's self from, شَرَدَ عَن ـ شَذَّ عَن ـ أَشَذَّ.

Dissociation, *n.* The act of, إِبْطَالُ ـ تَفْصِيلُ بَيْنَ ـ تَفْرِيقُ بَيْنَ ٱلْإِتِّصَالِ بَيْنَ; the being dissociated, شُذُوذ ـ شُرُود.

Dissoluble, *a.* That may be melted, يَذُوبُ ـ يَنْحَلُّ; that may be abrogated, يَبْطُلُ ـ يَنْتَقِضُ; that may be broken up, يَنْفَضُّ.

Dissolute, *a.* مَعْكُوس ـ زَانٍ ـ فَاجِر ـ فَاسِق ـ فُجَّار ـ دَاعِر. To lead a — life, إِنْفَرَطَ ـ غَمَطَ ـ دَعِرَ.

Dissolutely, *ad.* بِفِسْقٍ ـ فُجُورًا ـ بِفُرُطٍ ـ بِخُبْثٍ ـ دَعَارَةً.

Dissoluteness, *n.* إِنْهِمَاك ـ فُجُور ـ فِسْق ـ فُرُط ـ دَعَر ـ دَعَارَة ـ خُبْث ـ فِي ٱللَّذَّاتِ.

Dissolution, *n.* Liquefaction, إِذَابَة ـ تَحْلِيل ـ تَصْعِيد. The destruction of a compound, إِنْحِلَال. Putrefaction, فَسَاد ـ تَفَسُّخ ـ عُفُونَة. The breaking up, as of an assembly, نَقْض ـ فَضّ ـ عَزْل. Separation of partnership, إِبْطَالُ ٱلشَّرِكَةِ. Dissolution of a marriage compact, فَسْخُ ٱلزِّيجَةِ. Destruction, إِبْطَال ـ إِبَادَة ـ إِزَالَة. Death, مَوْت ـ حِمَام ـ مَنِيَّة ـ وَفَاة. They demanded the — of parliament, طَلَبُوا حَلَّ مَجْلِسِ ٱلشُّورَى.

Dissolvable, *a.* *See* Dissoluble, *a.*

Dissolve, *v.t.* To melt, ذَوَّبَ ـ حَلَّ ـ مَشَّ ـ صَهَرَ. To liquefy, of butter, and such like, سَيَّحَ ـ سَلَأَ ـ أَذَابَ. To disunite, destroy, خَرَّبَ ـ أَزَالَ ـ أَفْسَخَ ـ أَبْطَلَ ـ ذَوَّبَ. To break up, as of an assembly, نَقَضَ ـ فَضَّ. To break up, as of a partnership, حَلَّ ـ أَبْطَلَ. The council will not be dissolved this year, لَا يَنْفَضُّ ٱلْمَجْلِسُ هٰذِهِ ٱلسَّنَةَ.

Dissolve, *v.i.* To separate, إِنْقَطَعَ ـ تَشَتَّتَ. To be melted, تَفَسَّخَ ـ تَحَلَّلَ ـ إِنْحَلَّ ـ ذَابَ. To be abrogated, broken, إِنْحَلَّ ـ بَطَلَ. To be broken up, as of a partnership, إِنْفَسَخَ. To sink away, إِضْمَحَلَّ ـ إِنْحَطَّ.

Dissolvent, *a.* Which liquefies other substances, مُحَلِّل ـ مُسَيِّح ـ مُذَوِّب; in a state of liquefaction, ذَائِب.

Dissolvent, *n.* مُذَوِّب ـ مُحَلِّل.

Dissonance, *n.* إِخْتِلَاف ـ عَدَمُ ٱلْإِتِّحَادِ ـ عَدَمُ ٱلْمُطَابَقَةِ ـ تَفَاوُت.

Dissonant, *a.* مُخْتَلِف ـ غَيْرُ مُجَانِسٍ ـ غَيْرُ مُطَابِقٍ.

Dissuade, *v.t.* رَدَّ مِن ـ رَجَّعَ عَن ـ لَفَتَ عَن ـ هَارَ عَن ـ أَضْرَبَ عَن ـ مَنَعَ عَن.

Dissuasion, *n.* إِضْرَابٌ عَن ـ نُصْحٌ عَن ـ رَدٌّ مِن.

Dissuader, *n.* *See* Dissuasive, *a.*

Dissuasive, *a.* مُحَذِّرٌ عَن ـ مُنَبِّهٌ عَلَى ـ نَصُوحٌ عَن ـ مُرْجِعٌ عَن ـ مُضْرِبٌ عَن.

Dissuasively, *ad.* تَرْجِيعًا ـ تَحْذِيرًا ـ رَدًّا ـ تَرْدَادًا.

Dissunder, *v.t.* فَضَّ [2]. To be dissundered, إِنْفَضَّ.

Dissundered, *a.* مَفْضُوض ـ فَضِيض.

Dissyllabic, *a.* ذُو تَهَجِّيَتَيْنِ ـ ذُو حَرَكَتَيْنِ.

Dissyllable, *n.* كَلِمَةٌ مُرَكَّبَةٌ مِنْ حَرَكَتَيْنِ.

Distaff, *n.* رُكَّة ـ عِرْنَاس ـ فَلْكَة.

Distain, *v.t.* *See to* Stain, *v.t.*

Distance, *n.* Space between bodies, بُعْد ـ مَسَافَة ـ أَمْت ـ. Remoteness, in time, مُدَّة ـ شَيْع. A separation, بُعَاد ـ طَرَح ـ تَفَاوُت ـ مُفَاصَلَة ـ فَاصِلَة. Reserve, بُرُود ـ حِذْر. Being at a —, absence, تَبَاعُد ـ غُرْبَة. He came from a —, جَآءَ مِنْ بَعِيدٍ. I saw him from a —, رَأَيْتُهُ مِنْ بَعِيدٍ. There is a day's — between them, بَيْنَهُمْ مَسِيرَةُ يَوْمٍ. There is a — of 20 days between us, بَيْنَنَا مَسَافَةُ عِشْرِينَ يَوْمًا. I sat at a — from him, جَلَسْتُ بَعِيدًا مِنْهُ. What is the — between thee and al-Basrah? مَا ٱلْمَسَافَةُ مَا بَيْنَكَ وَبَيْنَ ٱلْبَصْرَةِ. To go to a —, abroad, تَغَرَّبَ ـ غَرَّبَ ـ غَرُبَ [2] ـ; to move away, إِبْتَعَدَ ـ تَجَنَّبَ.

Distance, *v.t.* To leave behind, as in a race, *etc.*, بَاعَدَ ـ رَاخَى ـ سَبَقَ [2] ـ تَقَدَّمَ. To place at a —, غَرَّبَ ـ أَقْصَى. To excel, بَرَعَ ـ بَرَّزَ عَلَى ـ فَضَلَ عَلَى [2] ـ يَرُوقُ *aor.* رَاقَ عَلَى.

Distant, *a.* Remote in place, بَعِيد ـ بَاعِد ـ قَاصٍ; of time, بَعِيد ـ مَدِيد. Reserved, حَرِيص ـ حَذِر ـ بَارِد. Travelling, absent, مُغَرِّب. To be —, بَعُدَ [2] ـ تَبَاعَدَ ـ إِسْتَبْعَدَ; to be very —, أَقْصَى. To be far — from, as from one's own people, تَقَصَّى عَن ـ قَصَى عَن [2]. A —, or far-reaching aim, نِيَّةٌ بَعِيدَةٌ. You are not — from us, مَا أَنْتَ مِنَّا بِبَعِيدٍ. The town is 24 hours — from us, ٱلْمَدِينَةُ تَبْعُدُ عَنَّا ٢٤ سَاعَةً. The time is not far — when it will be said . . . , قَدْ دَنَا وَقْتٌ يُقَالُ فِيهِ. *See also* Reserved, *a.*

Distantly, *ad.* Remotely, مِنْ بُعْدٍ; with reserve, بِبُرُودَةٍ ـ إِحْتِرَاسًا.

Distaste, *n.* *See* Dislike, Disrelish, Disgust, *n.*

Distaste, *v.t.* *See to* Disrelish, Disgust, Dislike, *v t.*

Distasteful, *a.* Unpleasant to the taste, كَرِيهٌ لِلذَّوْقِ. Offensive, مُمِلّ ـ مُقْرِف ـ كَرِيه.

Distemper, *n.* Disease, مَرَض ـ عِلَّة ـ دَآء. Disorder, إِلْتِبَاك ـ تَشْوِيش ـ إِرْتِبَاك. Disease in cattle, جَائِحَة ـ فَصْلُ ٱلْبَهَائِمِ. Bad temper, شَكَاسَة ـ شَرَاسَة. The mixing of colours with something besides oil or water, تَخْلِيطُ ٱلْأَلْوَانِ بِدُهْنٍ غَيْرَ ٱلْمَآءِ وَٱلزَّيْتِ. A — of gum copal, دُهْنُ سِنْدَرُوسٍ.

Distemper, *v.t.* To disease, أَعَلَّ ـ أَمْرَضَ. To disorder, لَبَّكَ ـ شَوَّشَ. To mix colours with something beside oil or water, خَلَطَ ٱلْأَلْوَانَ بِدُهْنٍ غَيْرَ ٱلْمَآءِ وَٱلزَّيْتِ [2]; as with gum copal, حَلَّ بِدُهْنِ ٱلسِّنْدَرُوسِ [2].

Distemperature, *n.* Bad temperature, شُؤْبُوبُ ٱلطَّقْسِ ـ طَقْسٌ رَدِيءٌ.

Distempered, *a.* Diseased, مَرِيض ـ مَعْلُول. Ruffled, مُضْطَرِب. Diseased, of cattle, مُصَابٌ بِٱلْجَائِحَةِ.

Distend, *v.t.* طَوَّلَ ـ مَطَّ [2] ـ بَسَطَ [2] ـ وَسَّعَ ـ نَدَحَ. To — with air, نَفَخَ فِي. To be distended, stretched out, إِفْتَرَشَ ـ إِنْبَسَطَ ـ تَنَدَّحَ ـ إِمْتَطَّ. Distended with wind, swollen, مَنْفُوخ. Distended bellies, بُطُونٌ نَاتِئَةٌ.

Distensibility, *n.* قَابِلِيَّةُ ٱلْإِمْتِدَادِ ـ قَابِلِيَّةُ ٱلْإِنْبِسَاطِ; capacity of being inflated, قَابِلِيَّةُ ٱلْإِنْتِفَاخِ. *See also* Dilatability, *n.*

Distensible, *a.* يَمْتَدُّ ـ يَنْبَسِطُ; that may be inflated, يَنْتَفِخُ. *See also* Dilatable, *a.*

Distention, *n.* The act of distending, مَطّ ـ بَسْط ـ نَدْح ـ تَطْوِيل ـ تَوْسِيع; the being distended, إِتِّسَاع ـ إِمْتِدَاد ـ تَنَدُّح. The act of inflating, نَفْخ; the being inflated, إِنْتِفَاخ.

Distich, *n.* بَيْتُ شِعْرٍ *pl.* أَبْيَات.

Distil, *v.t.* To let fall in drops, مَصَّلَ ـ رَشَحَ ـ قَطَّرَ. To draw out by distillation, أَخْرَجَ ـ أَقْطَرَ ـ قَطَّرَ ـ صَعَّدَ. Distilled water, مَآءٌ مُقَطَّرٌ.

Distil, *v.i.* To fall in drops, يَشِلُ *aor.* وَشَلَ ـ رَشَحَ ـ قَطَرَ [2] ـ نَطَّ ـ قَطَّرَ. To use a still, إِسْتَعْمَلَ ٱلْأَنْبِيقَ.

Distillable, *a.* مِمَّا يُصَعَّدُ ـ قَابِلُ ٱلتَّخْرِيجِ ـ قَابِلُ ٱلتَّقْطِيرِ.

Distillation, *n.* The act of distilling, تَخْرِيج ـ تَصْعِيد ـ تَقْطِير ـ إِخْرَاج; the thing distilled, قَطْرَان ـ مُقَطَّر ـ رُوح ـ مُصَعَّد. Exudation, تَرَشُّح.

Distiller, *n.* خَرَّاج. A — of liquors, spirits, خَرَّاجُ ٱلْعَرَقِ ٱلْأَنْبَرِيِّ.

Distillery, *n.* مَعْمَلُ ٱلتَّقْطِيرِ.

Distinct, *a.* Marked out, مَعْلُوم ـ مَرْقُوم ـ مُعَيَّن. Different, مُمَيَّز ـ مَفْرُوز ـ مُمْتَاز ـ مُفَرَّق ـ بَيِّن ـ مُتَبَايِن. Separate, ظَاهِر ـ وَاضِح ـ صَرِيح ـ بَيِّن ـ مُنْفَصِل. Special, خَاصّ. Clear, بَيِّن. Sundry, شَتَّى. A — part or portion, فِرْزَة. To make —, clear, أَنْصَحَ ـ أَنْصَحَ ـ سَرَّحَ بِ ـ أَصْرَحَ ـ أَوْضَحَ. To be —, clear, إِنْصَرَحَ ـ إِنْتَصَحَ ـ

صَرَّحَ . To make — from, مَازَ-مِن ـ . This affair became — to me, فَرَقَ لِي هٰذَا ٱلْأَمْرُ . He did not make the word —, مَا أَقَاضَ بِٱلْكَلِمَةِ .

Distinction, *n.* The act of distinguishing, تَمْيِيز ـ تَبْيِين ـ تَفْصِيل ـ تَفْرِيق . A difference, فَصْل ـ فَرْق ـ إِمْتِيَاز . Fame, شَأْن ـ إِشْتِهَار ـ إِسْم ـ سِمْع ـ صِيتَة ـ صِيت . A mark of —, عَلَامَةُ ٱفْتِخَار ـ نِيشَانُ شَرَف . Of —, renowned, مُمْتَاز ـ مُعْتَبَر ـ مَشْهُور . For distinction's sake, لِأَجْلِ ٱلتَّمْيِيز . Without —, بِلَا ٱسْتِثْنَاء ـ عَلَى ٱلسَّوِيَّةِ ـ بِلَا فَرْق . To make a —, to distinguish between, مَيَّزَ بَيْنَ . To prefer, فَضَّلَ-عَلَى ـ إِسْتَحْسَنَ ـ قَدَّمَ-عَلَى .

Distinctive, *a.* That marks a difference, بَيَانِيّ ـ تَعْرِيفِيّ ـ حَزْم ـ صَاحِبُ فِرَاسَةٍ . Judicious, مُبَيِّن ـ مُفَارِق ـ مُمَيِّز ـ مُفْرِز . Clear, وَاضِح ـ عِيَان ـ رَائِق .

Distinctively, *ad.* / Distinctly, } Clearly, جَهْرًا ـ عَلَانِيَةً ـ بِوُضُوحٍ ـ صَرَاحَةً . Separately, إِفْتِرَاقًا ـ إِنْفِرَاقًا ـ إِنْفِرَادًا ـ عِيَانًا .

Distinctness, *n.* Clearness, صَرَاحَة ـ رَوْق ـ بَيَان ـ إِيضَاح ـ وُضُوح . Point, حَدّ . Precision, دِقَّة .

Distinguish, *v.t.* To note difference from, مَيَّزَ-مِن ـ مَازَ-مِن ـ أَفْرَزَ ـ فَرَزَ ـ فَرَقَ بَيْنَ ـ فَصَلَ بَيْنَ ـ أَمَازَ-مِن . To — particularly, to characterize, خَصَّصَ ـ أَخَصَّ . To — by description, وَصَفَ *aor.* يَصِفُ . To discern, أَدْرَكَ ـ فَطِنَ ـ أَفْرَزَ . To prefer, as over another, قَدَّمَ-عَلَى ـ فَضَّلَ-عَلَى . To treat with honour, أَكْرَمَ . To give a mark of honour to, أَحْسَنَ إِلَى-بِنِيشَانٍ وَشَّحَ-بِرُتْبَةِ شَرَفٍ ـ وَجَّهَ-بِرُتْبَةِ شَرَفٍ ـ ٱفْتِخَارٍ . He distinguished him in his love, خَصَّهُ بِٱلْوُدِّ . Until you can — white from black, حَتَّى يَتَبَيَّنَ لَكَ ٱلْأَبْيَضُ مِنَ ٱلْأَسْوَدِ . To — one's self by, أَظْهَرَ ٱلْفَضْلَ فِي ـ كَسَبَ شُهْرَةً بِ ـ إِشْتَهَرَ بِ . He distinguished himself above his contemporaries, تَمَيَّزَ عَنْ أَقْرَانِهِ . He distinguished himself in it, قَامَ بِهِ بِتَمْيِيزٍ . To be —, distinct, تَمَيَّزَ ـ إِمْتَازَ . *See also under* Distinct, *a.*

Distinguishable, *a.* يُمَيَّزُ ـ تَمْيِيزُهُ مُمْكِنٌ . Worthy of regard, أَهْلٌ لِلْإِكْرَامِ ـ مُسْتَحِقُّ ٱلْإِحْتِرَامِ .

Distinguished, *a.* Separated, مَفْرُوز ـ مُمَيَّز . Eminent, مَشْهُور ـ مَعْرُوف ـ مَعْلُوم ـ صَاحِبُ شُهْرَةٍ ـ مُعْتَبَر ـ مُمْتَاز . Well known, لَوْذَعِيّ ـ بَارِعٌ فِي ٱلْعِلْمِ ـ ذُو سَمَاعٍ . Distinguished for learning, Distinguished people, the upper classes, ٱلْخَاصَّة . One of the — men, مِنْ أَفْرَادِ ٱلرِّجَالِ . He belongs to one of the — Greek families, هُوَ مِنْ إِحْدَى ٱلْعَائِلَاتِ ٱلْمُمْتَازَةِ بَيْنَ ٱلْيُونَانِ .

Distinguishingly, *ad.* بِٱمْتِيَازٍ ـ بِتَمْيِيزٍ .

Distort, *v.t.* To twist, أَبْرَمَ ـ عَوَّجَ ـ لَوَّى . To wrest, as of a meaning, عَكَسَ ـ حَرَّفَ ـ صَحَّفَ . To —, as of a word, with the tongue, لَفَتَ-بِٱللِّسَانِ . To — the countenance, عَبَّسَ قَطَّبَ وَجْهَهُ ـ إِخْتَلَجَ بِوَجْهِهِ ـ ٱلْوَجْهَ . To — to a bad meaning, أَنْمَشَ . To be distorted, of the mouth, ضَجِمَ ; of any member, عَسِمَ .

Distorted, *a.* Twisted, مُعَوَّج ـ مُبْرَم ـ مُلْتَوٍ . To be —, twisted, إِلْتَوَى ـ إِنْعَاجَ ـ تَعَوَّجَ ـ عَوِجَ ـ لَوِيَ ; of a meaning, تَصَحَّفَ ; of the joints, أَفْدَعُ .

Distortion, *n.* The act of twisting, إِبْرَام ـ تَلْوِيَة ـ تَعْوِيج ; the being distorted, لَيَّة ـ لِوَاء ـ بَرَم ـ عِوَج ـ حَوَل . The wresting, as of a meaning, تَصْحِيف ـ تَعْكِيس ـ تَحْرِيف ; the being wrested, إِنْحِرَاف ـ تَحَرُّف ـ عَكْس . Distortion, as of the face, تَعْبِيس ; of the wrist or ankle-joint, فَدَع .

Distract, *v.t.* To draw off from, فَتَلَ-عَن ـ أَفْنَظَ-عَن ـ أَضْرَبَ-عَن ـ صَرَفَ-عَن ـ شَجَرَ-عَن ـ كَفَتَ-عَن . To perplex, قَلْقَلَ ـ أَدْهَشَ ـ شَوَّشَ ـ حَيَّرَ . To make negligent, أَغْفَلَ . To preoccupy, غَيَّبَ ـ لَهَى-عَن ـ شَغَلَ . To turn off the attention from, أَلْهَى-عَن . To be distracted, perplexed, تَحَيَّرَ ـ كَدِرَ .

Distracted, *a.* Drawn off from, مَشْجُورٌ عَن ـ مَفْتُولٌ عَن ـ مَضْرُوبٌ عَن ـ مَصْرُوفٌ عَن . Perplexed, حَائِر ـ مُتَحَيِّر ـ مُضْطَرِب ـ حَيْرَان . Preoccupied, غَائِبٌ عَنْ نَفْسِهِ .

Distractedly, *ad.* Perplexedly, بِٱضْطِرَابٍ ـ مُتَحَيِّرًا ـ بِدَهَشٍ ـ فِي حَيْرَةٍ وَفَشَلٍ ـ بِشَجَرٍ .

Distracting, *a.* / Distractive, } Perplexing, مُؤْلِم ـ مُضْجِر ـ مُتَحَيِّر ـ حَيِّر ـ مُقْطِع ـ مُوجِع .

Distraction, *n.* The act of drawing off from, فَتْلٌ عَن ـ شَجْرٌ عَن ـ صَرْفٌ مِن . Preoccupation, غَيْبَةُ ٱلْعَقْلِ . Confusion of mind, سُرُوحُ ٱلْعَقْلِ ـ شَتَاتُ ٱلْعَقْلِ . Disordered reason, perturbation of mind, جُنُون ـ خَلَلٌ فِي ٱلْعَقْلِ ـ إِخْتِلَال . Trouble, perplexity, شَجَر ـ إِضْطِرَاب ـ كَدَر ـ حَيْرَة . Without —, بِدُونِ ٱرْتِبَاكٍ . Something to draw off the mind, مَلْهًى *pl.* مَلَاهٍ .

Distrain, *v.t.* ضَبَطَ ٱلْأَمْتِعَةَ لِوَفَاءِ ٱلْكِرَاء .

Distraint, *n.* ضَبْطُ ٱلْأَمْتِعَةِ لِوَفَاءِ ٱلْكِرَاء .

Distress, *n.* Suffering, شِدَّة ـ كَدَر ـ إِضْطِرَاب ـ بُؤْس ـ بَلِيَّة ـ مِحْنَة ـ ضِيق ـ ضَجَر ـ حَصْر ـ كَرْب ـ مَشَقَّة . Want, فَقْر ـ ضَرُورَة ـ إِحْتِيَاج ـ مُضَايَقَة ـ حَصْر ـ إِعْسَار ـ ضَنْك . In —, troubled, مُضْطَرِب ; in want, عَائِل ـ عَائِز ـ مُحْتَاج ـ فَقِير . *See also* Distraint, *n.*

Distress, *v.t.* To put to straits, ضَيَّقَ عَلَى — ضَايَقَ. To grieve, أَهَمَّ — ² شَجَبَ — فَجَّعَ — أَحْزَنَ — أَبْلَى — ⁼ عَزَّ عَلَى. It distressed me to annoy you, ⁼ عَزَّ عَلَيَّ أَنْ أَسُوءَكَ. How greatly does he — me, ما أَغَمَّهُ إِلَيَّ. Your doing so distresses me, عَزَّ عَلَيَّ أَنْ تَفْعَلَ كَذَا. It distresses me that you are going away, عَزَّ عَلَيَّ أَنَّكَ ذاهِبٌ. I am distressed by what befell you, عَزَزْتُ بِما أَصابَكَ. Such a matter distressed me, عَزَّ عَلَيَّ كَذا.

Distressful, *a.* }
Distressing, } كَرِيبٌ — مُحِسٌ — مُضْجِرٌ — صَعْبٌ — شَاقٌّ — مُحْزِنٌ — فاجِعٌ — فَظِيعٌ. In — circumstances, بائِسٌ. Most —, أَفْجَعُ. This is more — to me than that...., هٰذا أَعَزُّ عَلَيَّ مِنْ أَنْ — هٰذا ٱلْأَمْرُ أَبْرَحُ عَلَيَّ مِنْ أَنْ. The news was very —, كانَ ٱلْخَبَرُ مُغِمًّا جِدًّا.

Distributable, *a.* تَقْسِيمُهُ مُمْكِنٌ — قابِلُ ٱلتَّوْزِيعِ.

Distribute, *v.t.* To divide among, فَرَّقَ-بَيْنَ — وَزَّعَ-عَلَى — إِقْتَسَطَ — قَسَّمَ-بَيْنَ. The letters are distributed every morning, تَتَوَزَّعُ ٱلْمَكاتِيبُ كُلَّ صَباحٍ.

Distribution, *n.* تَقْسِيمٌ — تَفْرِيقٌ — تَوْزِيعٌ.

Distributive, *a.* تَوْزِيعِيٌّ — تَقْسِيمِيٌّ. Distributive justice, قِسْمَةُ ٱلْحَقِّ.

Distributively, *ad.* تَوْزِيعًا — تَفْرِيقًا — تَقْسِيمًا.

District, *n.* Limits, حُدُودٌ — تُخُومٌ. A tract, إِقْلِيمٌ *pl.* أَقالِيمُ — دائِرَةٌ — ناحِيَةٌ *pl.* نَواحِي — إِيالَةٌ — كُورَةٌ *pl.* كُوَرٌ — كَنَفٌ *pl.* أَكْنافٌ. A region, territory, إِقْلِيمٌ — بَلَدٌ *pl.* بُلْدانٌ — قُطْرٌ *pl.* أَقْطارٌ — أَرْضٌ. A quarter, as of a town, مَحَلَّةٌ *pl.* مَحَلَّاتٌ — حارَةٌ *pl.* حاراتٌ.

Distrust, *v.t.* إِتَّهَمَ بِ — ² شَكَّ فِي — تَشَكَّكَ فِي — تَرَيَّبَ فِي — إِسْتَخْوَنَ. To be wary of, إِحْتَرَزَ مِنْ — تَوَقَّعَ مِنْ.

Distrust, *n.* شَكٌّ — إِرْتِيابٌ — إِسْتِخْوانٌ — إِتِّهامٌ — تَوَهُّمٌ.

Distrustful, *a.* مُرِيبٌ — ذُو رِيبَةٍ — مُرْتابٌ فِي. *See also* Diffident, *a.*

Disturb, *v.t.* To trouble, vex, إِسْتَفَزَّ — قَلَّقَ — أَزْعَجَ — أَضْجَرَ. To hinder, عَجَّزَ — عَطَّلَ — ⁼ مَنَعَ — ⁼ صَدَعَ — أَفَزَّ. To put out of order, لَبَّكَ — أَفْسَدَ — شَوَّشَ — خَبَّطَ — خَبَّلَ. To be disturbed, vexed, إِنْزَعَجَ — تَضَجَّرَ. To be hindered, تَعَطَّلَ — تَصَدَّعَ. To be thrown into disorder, إِلْتَبَكَ — إِرْتَبَكَ — تَشَوَّشَ — تَخَبَّطَ — تَخَبَّلَ — تَخَرْبَطَ. They continue to do what will — the public tranquillity, لَمْ يَزالُوا يَرْتَكِبُونَ ما يُخِلُّ بِٱلرَّاحَةِ ٱلْعُمُومِيَّةِ.

Disturbance, *n.* Tumult, فَسادٌ — فِتْنَةٌ — إِخْتِلالٌ — غاغَةٌ — بَلْبَلَةٌ. Vexation, ضَجَرٌ — إِضْطِرابٌ — زَعَجٌ — إِنْزِعاجٌ — كَدَرٌ. Hindrance, تَعْطِيلٌ — تَصَدُّعٌ. To create a —, حَرَّشَ. To incite — among, أَغْرَى بَيْنَ. In a state of great —, فِي غايَةِ ٱلْإِضْطِرابِ. *See also* Tumult, *n.*

Disturber, *n.* مُضْجِرٌ — ضَرَّابُ فِتَنٍ — ساعٍ بِٱلْفَسادِ. A — of the public peace, مُقَلِّقُ ٱلنَّاسِ.

Disunion, *n.* }
Disunity, } Want of union, عَدَمُ ٱتِّفاقٍ — عَدَمُ ٱتِّحادٍ. Separation, إِنْفِصالٌ — شَتٌّ — إِفْتِراقٌ — إِنْفِرادٌ. Discord, نِزاعٌ — شَواشٌ.

Disunite, *v.t.* To separate, فَصَلَ — ⁼ فَرَقَ ². To — from, فَصَّ-مِنْ ² — إِقْتَصَّ-مِنْ. To cause discord between, قَرَّشَ بَيْنَ — أَشْرَى بَيْنَ. To be disjoined from, إِنْفَصَّ مِنْ.

Disunite, *v.i.* إِنْفَرَقَ — تَفَرَّقَ — إِفْتَرَقَ — إِنْفَصَّ — تَخَلَّعَ.

Disusage, *n.* }
Disuse, } إِلْغاءٌ — تَرْكٌ — عَدَمُ ٱسْتِعْمالٍ.

Disuse, *v.t.* أَبْطَلَ ٱسْتِعْمالَهُ — ² تَرَكَ ٱسْتِعْمالَهُ. Disused, obsolete; *see under* Antiquated, *a.*

Disvalue, *v.t.* إِسْتَقَلَّ — إِسْتَحْقَرَ — إِسْتَخَفَّ.

Ditch, *n.* A hole, حُفْرَةٌ *pl.* حُفَرٌ — جُبٌّ *pl.* جِبابٌ — هُوَّةٌ. A — round a fortification, خَنْدَقٌ *pl.* خَنادِقُ; round a tent to keep the rain off, نَأْيٌ *or* نُؤْيٌ *or* نِئْيٌ *pl.* نُؤِيٌّ *or* نِئِيٌّ *or* آنْآءٌ. He filled the valley with ditches, ⁼ جَعَلَ ٱلْوادِيَ جِباباً جِباباً.

Ditch, *v.t.* To make ditches in, ⁼ جَعَلَ-جِباباً جِباباً. To make a —, as round a fort, خَنْدَقَ. To dig round, ⁼ حَفَرَ حَوْلَ.

Ditcher, *n.* حافِرٌ — حَفَّارٌ — جَبَّابٌ. A digger of trenches, خَنْدَقْجِي — لَغَمْجِي.

Ditheism, *n.* عِبادَةُ مَعْبُودَيْنِ — زَنْدَقَةٌ.

Dittied, *a.* مُرَتَّبٌ فِي مَقامَةٍ.

Ditto, *a.* and *n.* كَذٰلِكَ — مِثْلَ ذٰلِكَ — مِثْلُهُ — شَرْحُهُ.

Ditty, *n.* أُغْرُودَةٌ *pl.* أَغارِيدُ — أُغْنِيَةٌ *pl.* أَغانِيُّ *and* أَغانٍ.

Diuresis, *n.* بُوالٌ — سَلَسُ ٱلْبَوْلِ.

Diuretic, *a.* مُدِرٌّ لِلْبَوْلِ. A —, مَبْوَلَةٌ — مُدِرٌّ — مُسْتَدِرٌّ.

Diurnal, *a.* نَهارِيٌّ — يَوْمِيٌّ. *See* Daily, *a.*

Diurnally, *ad.* يَوْمًا فَيَوْمًا — كُلَّ يَوْمٍ.

Diuturnal, *a.* باقٍ — مُسْتَدامٌ — دائِمٌ.

Divan, *n.* (*properly* Dîwân,) A couch, دِيوانٌ *pl.* دَواوِينُ. (It means also a Council, when it is generally written دِيوانُ مَشْوَرَةٍ). The —, or Ministry of the Sublime Porte, ٱلْبابُ ٱلْعالِي — ٱلْحُكُومَةُ ٱلسَّنِيَّةُ.

Divaricate, *v.i.* تَفَرَّعَ فَرْعانِ — تَشَعَّبَ شُعْبانِ — تَفاجَّ — إِنْفَرَجَ.

Divaricate, *v.t.* قَسَمَ-فَرْعَيْنِ — ⁼ ² فَجَّ.

Dive, *v.i.* To —, as into water, ² غاصَ فِي — ⁼ غَطَسَ فِي. To —

into, to give one's self up to, غَرِقَ فِي ـ . To — deeply into an affair, غَاصَ (or تَعَمَّقَ) فِي ٱلشَّيْءِ. To make to —, غَوَّصَ . A place for diving, مَغَاص.

Dive, *n.* غَطْسَة ـ غَوْصَة.

Diver, *n.* One who dives, غَطَّاس ـ غَوَّاص ـ غَائِص ; the bird, غَوَّاصَة ـ غَمَّاسَة.

Diverge, *v.i.* تَشَعَّبَ ـ تَفَرَّقَ إِلَى عِدَّةِ جِهَاتٍ ـ تَفَاجَى ـ تَفَاجَّ إِلَى عِدَّةِ جِهَاتٍ مِنْ مَرْكَزٍ وَاحِدٍ. To turn aside, ٱنْحَدَرَ ـ تَشَجَّرَ ـ ٱنْكَفَتَ.

Divergence, *n.* A departure from a point, تَفَاجٍ ـ تَفَاجٌّ. A difference, تَفَاوُت ـ تَبَايُن. A turning aside, ٱنْحِدَار ـ تَشَجُّر ـ ٱنْكِفَات.

Divergent, *a.* } Departing from a point, مُتَفَاجٍ ـ مُتَفَاجٌّ.
Diverging, } Different, مُخَالِف ـ مُغَايِر ـ مُخْتَلِف.

Divers, *a.* كَثِير ـ بَعْض ـ عَدِيد ـ شَتَّى. Divers matters, أَشْيَاءُ شَتَّى.

Diverse, *a.* مُخْتَلِف ـ مُتَنَوِّع. A body composed of — people, قَوْمٌ شَتَّى.

Diversely, *ad.* ٱخْتِلَافًا ـ بِٱخْتِلَافٍ ـ مُتَنَوِّعًا.

Diversification, *n.* The act of making into various forms, وَضْعُ ٱلشَّيْءِ عَلَى ـ تَشْكِيل ـ تَصْوِيرٌ فِي صُوَرٍ مُخْتَلِفَةٍ ـ تَصْرِيف أَنْحَاءَ شَتَّى ; of language, تَفْنِين. Variety, تَنَوُّع. Alteration, تَغْيِير. *See also* Variegation, *n.*

Diversiform, *a.* ذُو أَشْكَالٍ مُتَنَوِّعَةٍ ـ ذُو هَيْآتٍ مُخْتَلِفَةٍ.

Diversify, *v.t.* To make various, جَعَلَ ـ مُتَنَوِّعًا ـ صَرَّفَ ـ صَيَّرَ ـ فِي أَشْكَالٍ مُخْتَلِفَةٍ. To change, alter, غَيَّرَ ـ بَدَّلَ. To —, as of language, فَنَّنَ.

Diversion, *n.* The act of turning aside, فَتْل عَنْ ـ تَنْكِيبٌ عَنْ ـ نُكُوب ـ حَرْف ـ صَرْف ـ شَجْرٌ عَنْ ; the being turned aside, ٱنْصِرَاف ـ ٱنْحِرَاف. Sport, بَحْبَحَة ـ لَهْو ـ إِسْمَاد ـ سُمُود ـ تَكْيِيف ـ تَفَرُّج ـ نَفَس ـ تَنَزُّه ـ ٱنْشِرَاح. Whatever diverts one from a pursuit, مَلْهًى *pl.* مَلَاهٍ ـ عُلَالَة. A place of —, مَكَانُ فَرْجٍ. In war, a feint against the enemy, غِلَاط ـ مُغَالَطَة ـ مُشَاغَلَة.

Diversity, *n.* Difference, تَغَايُر ـ تَفَاوُت ـ فَرْق ـ ٱخْتِلَاف. Variety, أَنْوَاع ـ تَنَوُّع.

Divert, *v.t.* To turn one aside from, أَلَاثَ ـ فَتَلَ ـ عَنْ ـ شَجَرَ ـ عَنْ ـ عَجَزَ ـ عَنْ ـ أَضْرَبَ ـ عَنْ ـ كَفَتَ ـ عَنْ ـ لَاثَ ـ عَنْ رَدَّ ـ عَنْ ـ صَرَفَ ـ عَنْ ـ أَمَالَ ـ عَنْ. To — the thoughts of another to something else, أَلْهَى ـ بِ ـ عَنْ ـ شَغَلَ ـ عَنْ ـ صَدَّ ـ عَنْ.

To amuse, شَرَحَ خَاطِرَهُ ـ سَلَّى ـ أَطْرَبَ ـ أَسْمَدَ ـ سَمَّدَ. He diverted the property from the intended object of the owner, صَرَفَ ٱلْمَالَ عَنْ مَقْصَدِ صَاحِبِهِ. To — one's self with, be drawn off by, ٱلْتَهَى بِ ـ لَهَا بِ. To be diverted, amused, سَمَدَ ـ ٱنْبَسَطَ ـ ٱنْشَرَحَ ـ تَبَحْبَحَ ـ تَفَرَّجَ. To be diverted, turned off, from, تَشَجَّرَ عَنْ ـ ٱنْصَرَفَ عَنْ ـ ٱنْكَفَتَ عَنْ.

Diverting, *a.* Amusing, مُبْسِط ـ مُفَرِّح ـ مُسَلٍّ ـ مُطْرِب.

Divertisement, *n.* لَعْبَة ـ لَعِب ـ لَهْو ـ تَسْلِيَة ـ تَنَزُّه ـ تَفَرُّج.

Divertive, *a.* Tending to turn off, مُصْرِف عَنْ ـ مُشَجِّرٌ عَنْ.

Divest, *v.t.* نَزَعَ عَنْ ـ ٱ ... ـ رَفَعَ عَنْ ـ ٱ ... ـ عَرَّى ـ جَرَّدَ. To — one's self, to be divested, ٱنْجَرَدَ ـ شَلَحَ ـ تَجَرَّدَ ـ تَعَرَّى.

Divesture, *n.* تَشْلِيح ـ تَجْرِيد ـ تَعْرِيَة.

Divide, *v.t.* To part into different pieces, قَسَمَ ـ قَطَّعَ ـ جَزَّأَ. To separate, فَرَّقَ بَيْنَ ـ فَصَلَ بَيْنَ. To — among, وَزَّعَ ـ بَيْنَ ـ شَطَّرَ ـ نَصَّفَ. To — into two, فَرَّقَ ـ عَلَى ـ قَسَّمَ ـ بَيْنَ or عَلَى. To — or disunite by discord, رَمَى ٱلْإِنْشِقَاقَ بَيْنَ ـ حَرَّشَ بَيْنَ. To — with another, حَاصَصَ. To be divided into parts, تَجَزَّأَ ـ ٱفْتَرَقَ ـ ٱنْفَصَلَ. To be divided, separated, تَقَسَّمَ ـ تَقَطَّعَ. *See also to* Distribute, *v.t.*

Dividedly, *ad.* شَذَرَ مَذَرَ ـ بِعَدَمِ ٱتِّفَاقٍ ـ بِعَدَمِ ٱتِّحَادٍ.

Dividend, *n.* A portion, نَصِيب *pl.* قِسْم ـ حِصَص *pl.* حِصَّة ـ أَنْصِبَة. The share of interest on a share, فَائِدَة ـ تَمَتُّعٌ بِٱلْحِصَّةِ ـ ٱلْحِصَّةِ. The —, in arithmetic, ٱلْمَقْسُوم.

Divider, *n.* قَسَّام ـ مُفَرِّق ـ مُقَسِّم.

Divination, *n.* عِلْمُ ٱلتَّخْزِيرِ ـ تَفَاؤُل ـ عِيَافَة ـ كِهَانَة ـ ضَرْبُ ٱلرَّمْلِ ـ فَتْحُ ٱلْفَأْلِ.

Divine, *a.* Godly, إِلٰهِيّ ـ لَاهِيّ. Supremely excellent, سَنِيّ ـ لَاهُوت ـ إِلٰهَة. The — nature, Godship, ٱلْأَفْضَلُ ـ ٱلْأَعْلَى. Divine power, ٱلْقُدْرَةُ ٱلْإِلٰهِيَّةُ. Divine inspiration, وَحْيٌ.

Divine, *n.* A theologian, مُعَلِّمُ ٱللَّاهُوتِ ـ مُعَلِّمُ ٱلْإِلٰهِيَّاتِ. A priest, قَسّ *pl.* قِسِّيسُونَ *and* قُسُوس.

Divine, *v.t.* To predict, أَنْذَرَ ـ بِ ـ أَنْبَأَ ـ بِ ـ أَوْعَدَ ـ بِ ـ خَبَّرَ ـ بِٱلْغَائِبِ. To guess, خَمَّنَ. To tell by divination to, كَهَنَ لِ. *See also to* Augur, *v.t.*

Divine, *v.i.* To practise divination, فَتَحَ ٱلْفَأْلَ ـ تَكَهَّنَ ـ ضَرَبَ ٱلرَّمْلَ. *See also to* Augur, *v.i.*

Divinely, *ad.* In a Godlike manner, بِٱلْقُوَّةِ ـ مِنْ عِنْدِ ٱللّٰهِ ـ ٱلْإِلٰهِيَّةِ. Excellently, بِأُسْلُوبٍ ـ بِبَرَاعَةٍ ـ عَلَى أَحْسَنِ مِنْوَالٍ ـ فَائِقٍ.

Diviner, *n.* A predicter, عَرَّاف ـ نَبِيٌّ. A soothsayer, كاهِن ـ فاتِحُ ٱلْفَأْلِ ـ ضَرَّابُ رَمْلٍ ـ عائِف ـ مُتَفائِل.

Diving-bell, *n.* قُبَّةٌ بِشَكْلِ ٱلْجَرَسِ مُجَهَّزَةٌ بِعُدَّةٍ مَخْصُوصَةٍ يَنْزِلُ فِيها ٱلنَّاسُ لِيَكْشِفُوا عَلَى قَعْرِ ٱلْبَحْرِ ـ قُبَّةٌ لِلْغَطْسِ.

Divinity, *n.* The divine nature, اللَّاهُوت ـ الإِلاهَة. God, اللّٰه. A false God, إِلٰه ـ إِلٰهَة *pl.* آلِهَة. The science of theology, عِلْمُ ٱلْكَلامِ ـ عِلْمُ ٱللَّاهُوتِ ـ عِلْمُ ٱلْإِلٰهِيَّاتِ.

Divisibility, *n.* إِنْقِسام ـ قابِلِيَّةُ ٱلْإِنْقِسامِ.

Divisible, *a.* تَقْسِيمُهُ مُمْكِنٌ ـ قابِلُ ٱلْإِنْقِسامِ ـ يَنْقَسِمُ.

Division, *n.* A dividing into parts, جَزْء ـ تَجْزِئَة ـ تَقْطِيع ـ تَقْسِيم. The being divided, تَجَزُّؤ ـ إِنْقِسام ـ تَقَطُّع. A portion, جُزْء *pl.* أَجْزاء ـ قِسْم *pl.* أَقْسام. A partition, فاصِلَة *pl.* فَواصِل ـ حِجاب. A party, طائِفَة ـ فِرْقَة ـ جَماعَة. A — of an army, مُجَنَّبَة ـ كَتِيبَة *pl.* كَتائِب ـ فِرْقَة ـ طابُور *pl.* طَوابِير ـ لِواء. Discord, إِنْشِقاق ـ إِخْتِلاف ـ خُصُومَة ـ عَداوَة ـ فِتْنَة. The rule of —, in arithmetic, التَّقْسِيمُ ـ القِسْمَةُ. A — of a book, فَصْل *pl.* فُصُول. The place of a —, مَقْسِم. To ask for a —, إِسْتَقْسَمَ. To go to a —, of a council, إِعْلانُ أَعْضاءِ مَجْلِسٍ بِما أَجْمَعُوا عَلَيْهِ مُنْفَرِدًا.

Divisional, *a.* Belonging to the division of a body of troops, مُتَعَلِّقٌ بِكَتِيبَةٍ ـ مُتَعَلِّقٌ بِفِرْقَةٍ; of a district, مُتَعَلِّقٌ بِحارَةٍ ـ مُتَعَلِّقٌ بِمَحَلَّةٍ ـ مَحَلِّيّ. A — command, رِئاسَةُ لِواءٍ ـ إِمارَةُ لِواءٍ.

Divisor, *n.* المَقْسُومُ عَلَيْهِ. A common —, المَقْسُومُ عَلَيْهِ ٱلْمُشْتَرَكُ.

Divorce, *n.* | **Divorcement**, } Repudiation, تَسْرِيح ـ سَراح ـ طَلاق ـ إِطْلاق ـ تَطْلِيق. The act of separating, تَفْصِيل ـ تَفْرِيق.

Divorce, *v.t.* To separate, of married persons, سَرَّحَ ـ طَلَّقَ ـ أَطْلَقَ.

Divorced, *a.* مَرْدُود ـ مُطَلَّق ـ بائِن. To be — from, طَلَقَ ² مِن. A — woman, إِمْرَأَةٌ طالِقٌ ـ إِمْرَأَةٌ طالِقَةٌ ـ خَلِيَّةٌ ـ مَرْدُودَة. (In the present day the last phrase denotes a divorced woman who is taken back by her husband.) She was — from her husband, طُلِّقَتْ مِنْ زَوْجِها.

Divulge, *v.t.* أَذاعَ بِ ـ سَمَّعَ بِ ـ أَعْلَنَ بِ ـ أَفْشَى ـ أَشاعَ ـ إِشْتَهَرَ ـ شَهَّرَ ـ أَذاعَ. To —, as of a secret, باحَ بِ *aor.* يَبُوحُ ـ بَذَلَ ² بِ; to —, as of a secret, to, أَفْضَى إِلَى ـ بِ. I divulged my secret to him, أَفْضَيْتُ إِلَيْهِ بِسِرِّي. To be divulged, ـ شاعَ ـ تَفَشَّى ـ يَفْشُو *aor.* فَشا ـ إِشْتَهَرَ ـ إِسْتَعْلَنَ ـ فاضَ ٱلْخَبَرُ. Divulged, مَشْهُور ـ مُسْتَفِيض ـ شائِع ـ مُشاع.

Divulger, *n.* مُشِيع ـ مُشْتَهِر ـ مَذِيل ـ بُؤُوح.

Dizen, *v.t.* See to Bedizen, *v.t.*

Dizziness, *n.* دُوار ـ سَدَر ـ مَيَد ـ رَنَح ـ دَوَخ.

Dizzy, *a.* سَدِر ـ مُرَنَّح ـ دائِخ ـ مُدَوَّخ. To make —, رَنَّحَ ـ دَوَّخَ. He is —, هُوَ مُدارٌ بِهِ ـ هُوَ دائِخٌ.

Do, *v.t.* To perform, عَمِلَ ـ فَعَلَ ـ أَتَى بِ ـ إِتَّخَذَ ـ جاءَ بِ *aor.* يَجِيءُ. To exert power, to attempt, كادَ ـ سَعَى *aor.* يَسْعَى. To accomplish, أَنْهَى ـ أَنْجَزَ ـ نَجَزَ ² ـ قَضَى. To cheat, غَدَرَ ² ـ خَدَعَ ـ جَوَّنَ ـ غَشَّ ². To cook, طَبَخَ ². I did a good thing, جِئْتُ بِشَيْءٍ حَسَنٍ. He does nothing but..., لَمْ يَزَلْ ـ ما لَهُ إِلَّا ـ ما يَفْعَلُ إِلَّا. What do you wish me to do, ماذا تُرِيدُ أَنْ أَفْعَلَ. He did thus, فَعَلَ كَذا ـ جاءَ كَذا. He did his business, قَضَى حاجَتَهُ. I did it and it was done, فَعَلْتُهُ فَٱنْفَعَلَ. To be done, performed, إِنْفَعَلَ; to be accomplished, إِنْتَهَى ـ إِنْقَضَى.

He can do it, هُوَ فِي طاقَتِهِ ـ يَقْدِرُ أَنْ يَفْعَلَهُ ـ يَطِيقُ عَلَيْهِ ـ يَسْتَطِيعُ عَلَيْهِ ـ أَمْكَنَ فُلانًا ٱلْأَمْرُ.

He cannot do it, لا طاقَةَ لَهُ بِهِ ـ لا يَقْدِرُ أَنْ يَفْعَلَهُ ـ يَعْجِزُ عَنْهُ ـ لا يَسْتَطِيعُ عَلَيْهِ.

He may do it, عَلَّهُ يَفْعَلُهُ ـ لَعَلَّ يَفْعَلُهُ.

He may not do it, عَلَّهُ ما يَفْعَلُهُ ـ لَعَلَّ ما يَفْعَلُهُ.

He must do it, لا بُدَّ أَنْ يَفْعَلَهُ ـ يَلْزَمُ أَنْ يَفْعَلَهُ ـ عَلَيْهِ أَنْ يَفْعَلَهُ لا مَحالَةَ.

He must not do it, فِعْلُهُ مَمْنُوعٌ عَلَيْهِ ـ فِعْلُهُ مُحَرَّمٌ عَلَيْهِ ـ لا يَنْبَغِي لَهُ أَنْ يَفْعَلَهُ.

He shall do it, لا بُدَّ أَنْ يَفْعَلَهُ ـ يَفْعَلُهُ عَلَى رَغْمِ أَنْفِهِ ـ يُلْزَمُ بِفِعْلِهِ.

He shall not do it, لا يُرَخَّصُ فِي فِعْلِهِ ـ يُمْنَعُ عَنْ فِعْلِهِ ـ يُضْطَرُّ إِلَى ٱلْكَفِّ عَنْهُ.

He will do it, يَفْعَلُهُ ـ سَيَفْعَلُهُ.

He will not do it, لا يَفْعَلُهُ ـ يَكُفُّ عَنْهُ ـ يَتْرُكُهُ.

To do again, to repeat, ثَنَّى ـ كَرَّرَ ـ أَعادَ.

To do away with, to abolish, نَسَخَ ـ أَسْقَطَ ـ أَبْطَلَ.

To do badly by, to treat badly, أَساءَ إِلَى ـ آذَى.

To do evil to, شارَّ ـ جارَّ ـ أَساءَ إِلَى.

To do good to, أَحْسَنَ إِلَى ـ لَطَفَ ² بِ ـ أَنْفَضَلَ عَلَى.

To do something to one, فَعَلَ بِ. May God do (something evil) to him, فَعَلَ ٱللّٰهُ بِهِ.

To do two things at a time, قَرَنَ بَيْنَ.

To do up, to repair, أَصْلَحَ ـ رَمَّمَ ـ طَبَّقَ. To fold up, طَوَى ـ ـِ.

To do up, as of a parcel, صَرَّ ²; as of a bale or box, حَزَمَ. To deprive of strength, أَعْجَزَ ـ أَعْيَى ـ دَمَّرَ قُوَّتَهُ. To ruin, أَهْلَكَ ـ فَقَعَ ² ـِ.

To do wrong to, ظَلَمَ ـ ـِ ² جارَ عَلَى ـ تَعَدَّى عَلَى.

To have done with, as of the perusal of a book, *etc.*, فَرَغَ مِن ².

To have to do with, to have business with, لَهُ ـ لَهُ شُغْلٌ مَع مُعامَلَةٌ مَع. What have I to do with you? ما لِي وَلَكَ.

Have nothing to do with that man, إِيَّاكَ وَذٰلِكَ ٱلرَّجُل.

Do, *v.i.* To act, behave, تَصَرَّفَ ـ عَمِلَ ـِ ² سَلَكَ سُلُوكًا ـ مَشَى ـِ. To suit, لاقَ بِ ـ ناسَبَ ـ وافَقَ ـ قابَلَ ـِ. To be in a state of..., كانَ فِي حالِ ٱل... How do you do? كَيْفَ حالُكَ ـ أَنْتُمْ كَيْفَ.

What can he do? ماذا فِي طاقَتِهِ ـ ماذا يَقْدِرُ أَنْ يَفْعَلَ.

What have I to do? ماذا عَلَيَّ مِنَ ٱلشُّغْلِ ـ ماذا لِي أَنْ أَفْعَلَهُ ـ أَيُّ مَشْغَلَةٍ قُدّامِي.

What ought she to do? ماذا يَجِبُ ـ ماذا يَنْبَغِي لَها أَنْ تَفْعَلَ عَلَيْها مِنَ ٱلْعَمَلِ.

What must they do? ما ٱلَّذِي ـ ماذا يَجِبُ عَلَيْهِمْ مِنَ ٱلْعَمَلِ تَفْرِضُهُ ٱلضَّرُورَةُ عَلَيْهِمْ.

What shall I do? ماذا أَفْعَلُ. What good thing shall I do? أَيَّ صالِحٍ أَعْمَلُ.

What will he do? ماذا سَيَفْعَلُ ـ ماذا يَفْعَلُ.

What will you have me to do, ماذا تُرِيدُ أَنْ أَفْعَلَ.

To do badly, شَنَّعَ ـ أَقْبَحَ.

To do evil, فَعَلَ ٱلشَّرَّ ـ أَقْبَحَ فِي ٱلْعَمَلِ ـ أَساءَ فِي ٱلْعَمَلِ ـ أَساءَ ـِ.

To do good, فَعَلَ ٱلْخَيْرَ ـ أَحْسَنَ فِي ٱلْعَمَلِ ـِ.

To do well, to prosper, سَعِدَ ـ نَجَحَ ـ أَنْجَحَ ـِ. To perform well, أَحْسَنَ فِي ٱلْعَمَلِ. You will do well if..., لَتَفْعَلَ نِعِمّا تَفْعَلُ إِذا ـ حَسَنًا إِذا.

To do without, إِسْتَغْنَى عَن ـ غَنِيَ عَن ـِ.

To do wrong, to act oppressively, ظَلَمَ ـ ـِ ² جارَ. To err, زَلَّ ـ ضَلَّ ـِ ـِ. *See also* To do evil, *supra*.

Docibility, *n.* }
Docility, } قابِلِيَّةُ ٱلتَّعْلِيمِ وَٱلتَّعَلُّمِ.

Docible, *a.* قابِلُ ٱلتَّعْلِيمِ وَٱلتَّعَلُّمِ.

Docile, *a.* Tractable, رِخْوٌ ـ طَوْعٌ ـ لَيِّن ـ ذَلُول ـ جَنِيب ـ طَوْعُ ٱلْعِنانِ ـ ٱلْعِنانِ. *See also* Docible, *a.* and Tame, *a.*

Docility, *n.* لَيان ـ مُلاءَمَة ـ ذُلُول ـ لِينَة. *See also* Tameness, *n.*

Dock, *n.* The plant, العِرْقُ ٱلْمُسْهِلُ. A place for shipping, حَوْضٌ لِلْمَراكِبِ ـ حَوْض. The standing place of a criminal in court, مَقامٌ مَخْصُوصٌ بِٱلْمُجْرِمِينَ فِي مَحْكَمَةٍ. The stump of a tail, جَدَعَةُ ذَنَبٍ. A dry —, حَوْضٌ لِلْمَراكِبِ لا ماءَ فِيهِ. A wet —, حَوْضٌ لِلْمَراكِبِ مَمْلُوٌّ مِنَ ٱلْماءِ. A repairing —, حَوْضٌ لِتَرْمِيمِ ٱلْمَراكِبِ.

Dock, *v.t.* *See to* Curtail, *v.t.* A docked horse, حِصانٌ أَبْتَرُ.

Docket, *n.* A mark, إِشارَة ـ عَلامَة ـ عِنْوان. A list of cases or parties, as before a court, جَدْوَلُ (or فِهْرِسُ) دَعاوَى.

Docket, *v.t.* To mark, رَقَمَ عَلَى ـ عَيَّنَ عَلَى ـ عَنْوَنَ. To index, فَهْرَسَ.

Docking, *n.* The — of a ship, إِدْخالُ مَرْكَبٍ فِي ٱلْحَوْضِ. The — of the tail, بَتْر.

Dockyard, *n.* تَرْسَخانَه *pl.* تَرْسَخانات.

Doctor, *n.* A teacher, مُدَرِّس ـ مُعَلِّم. A physician, نِطِّيس *pl.* نَطاسِيّ ـ نِطاسِيّ ـ طَبِيب *pl.* أَطِبّاءُ and أَطِبَّة ـ حَكِيم ـ مُداوٍ. Any learned man, عَلِيم *pl.* عُلَماءُ ـ عالِم ـ شَيْخ ـ حَكِيم.

Doctor of Civil Law (D.C.L.), فَقِيه ـ مُدَرِّس عُلُومِ ٱلْفِقْهِ *pl.* فُقَهاءُ.

Doctor of Divinity (D.D.), مُدَرِّس ٱللّاهُوتِ ـ مُدَرِّس ٱلْإِلٰهِيّاتِ.

Doctor of Laws (LL.D.), فَقِيه ـ مُدَرِّس عُلُومِ ٱلشَّرْعِ.

Doctor of Medicine (M.D.), طَبِيب ـ مُدَرِّس عِلْمِ ٱلطِّبِّ.

Doctor of Music (Mus. D.), مُدَرِّس عِلْمِ ٱلْأَلْحانِ (or ٱلْمُوسِيقَى).

Doctor of Philosophy (Ph. D.), حَكِيم ـ مُدَرِّس عِلْمِ ٱلْحِكْمَةِ.

Doctor, *v.t.* To administer medicine, عالَجَ ـ داوَى. To practise physic, تَعاطَى ٱلطِّبَّ ـ إِسْتَعْمَلَ ٱلطِّبَّ.

Doctoral, *a.* مُتَعَلِّقٌ بِرُتْبَةِ ٱلْمُدَرِّس.

Doctorate, *n.* }
Doctorship, } مَنْصَبُ ٱلْمُدَرِّسِ ـ رُتْبَةُ ٱلْمُدَرِّسِ.

Doctor's-Commons, *n.* مَأْمُورِيَّةُ ٱلْوَصِيِّ وَإِقامَةُ ٱلْوُكَلاءِ لِتَنْفِيذِها.

Doctrinaire, *a.* ذِهْنِيٌّ ـ نَظَرِيٌّ.

Doctrinal, *n.* Appertaining to teaching, مُتَعَلِّقٌ ـ تَعْلِيمِيٌّ بِٱلتَّعْلِيمِ. Pertaining to religious principles, مُتَعَلِّقٌ بِعَقائِدِ ٱلدِّينِ.

Doctrinal, *n.* *See* Doctrine, *n.*

Doctrinally, *ad.* حَسَبَ ٱلْعَقائِدِ ـ عَلَى مِنْوالِ ٱلتَّعْلِيمِ.

Doctrine, *n.* Teaching, تَعْلِيم ـ تَدْرِيس. A law, principle, قانُون *pl.* قَوانِينُ ـ قاعِدَة *pl.* قَواعِدُ. A tenet, عَقِيدَة *pl.* عَقائِدُ ـ قاعِدَة *pl.* قَواعِدُ ـ إِعْتِقاد ـ رَأْي *pl.* آراءُ. A body of doctrines, مَذْهَب *pl.* مَذاهِبُ ـ إِعْتِقاد *pl.* إِعْتِقادات.

Document, *n*. A written paper, صَحِيفَة ـ كِتَاب. A legal —, حُجَّة *pl.* حُجَج ـ صَكّ *pl.* صُكُوك ـ سِجِلّ *pl.* سِجِلَّات.

Documentary, *a*. Written, مُحَرَّر ـ مَكْتُوب. Relating to law or official papers, مُتَضَمِّنٌ عَلَى ٱلْخُطُوطِ ـ مُحْتَوٍ عَلَى ٱلسِّجِلَّاتِ ٱلرَّسْمِيَّةِ.

Dodder, *n*. The plant, كُشُوث.

Dodecagon, *n*. / **Dodecahedron**, } شَكْلٌ ذُو ٱثْنَتَي عَشَرَ ضِلْعٍ وَٱثْنَتَي عَشَرَةَ زَاوِيَةٍ.

Dodge, *v.t.* To evade, تَفَلَّتَ مِن ـ 2 لَاذَ مِن. To overreach, حَاوَلَ ـ إِحْتَالَ عَلَى.

Dodge, *v.i.* To escape by evasion, زَلَّ *aor.* يَزِلُّ ـ إِنْسَلَتَ ـ إِحْتَالَ ـ إِسْتَعْمَلَ ٱلْحِيلَةَ. To quibble, تَلَوَّعَ ـ إِنْسَلَّ مِنْ بَيْنَ ـ تَحَوَّلَ.

Dodge, *n*. A starting aside, تَجَنُّب. A trick, evasion, حِيلَة ـ دُوَّلَاب ـ كَيْد ـ خَدِيعَة.

Dodger, *n*. مَكَّار ـ خَدَّاع ـ حَيَّال ـ مُلَوِّع.

Dodo, *n*. إِسْمُ طَيْرٍ كَبِيرٍ لَا وُجُودَ لَهُ ٱلْآنَ.

Doe, *n*. The female of the deer, ظَبْيَة *pl.* ظَبَيَات; of the rabbit or hare, أَرْنَبَة *pl.* أَرَانِب.

Doe-skin, *n*. The skin of the female deer, جِلْدُ ٱلظَّبْيَةِ. A kind of cloth, ضَرْبٌ مِنَ ٱلْجُوخِ.

Doer, *n*. فَاعِل *pl.* فَعَلَة ـ عَامِل *pl.* عُمَّال. The — of a thing, صَاحِبُ ٱلْأَمْرِ. Doer, as of an offence, crime, مُرْتَكِب.

Doff, *v.t.* أَخْلَعَ ـ رَفَعَ-عَن ـ 2 شَالَ-عَن ـ نَزَعَ ـ شَلَحَ.

Dog, *n*. كَلْب *fem.* كَلْبَة *pl.* كِلَاب. A hunting dog, ضِرْو *fem.* ضِرْوَة *pl.* ضِرَاء *and* أَضْرٍ ـ سَلُوقِيّ ـ سَلُوقِيَّة ـ كَلْبُ صَيْدٍ. Bull-dog, or a dog with a large head, (these two Arabic words are of the vulgar dialect,) كَلْبٌ جُعَايِيّ ـ دِرْوَاس *pl.* دَرَاوِيس. Dog, as a term of reproach, كَلْب. A gay dog, or fellow, مَخْلُوع ـ بَطْرَان. A loose dog, or fellow, فَالِت. Dog, a lump, as of iron, سَبِيكَة *pl.* سَبَائِك. An andiron, سَاج *pl.* سَاجَات. The constellation Sirius, ٱلشِّعْرَى ٱلْيَمَانِيَّة ـ ٱلشِّعْرَى. The lesser Dog, Procyon, ٱلشِّعْرَى ٱلشَّامِيَّة. The two dogs, Sirius and Procyon, are called, ٱلشِّعْرَيَانِ. A rearer of dogs, or having dogs, كَالِب ـ كَلَّاب. To train (a dog) for the chase, ضَرَّبَ-عَلَى ٱلصَّيْدِ. A (dog) with long ears, أَغْضَف *pl.* غُضْف. To treat like a dog, قَرَفَ عَلَى ـ عَامَلَ-مُعَامَلَةَ ٱلْكَلْبِ ـ غَلَّظَ عَلَى. To go to the dogs, هَلَكَ.

Dog, *v.t.* To follow continually, رَصَدَ ـ 2 تَرَصَّدَ لِ ـ رَاقَبَ.

Dog-cheap, *a*. رَخِيصٌ لِلْغَايَةِ ـ أَبْخَسُ ثَمَنٍ.

Dog-days, *n*. أَيَّامُ ٱلشِّعْرَى.

Doge, *n*. Of Venice, إِسْمُ رَئِيسِ مَشْيَخَةِ ٱلْبُنْدُقِيَّةِ سَابِقًا.

Dog-fish, *n*. كَلْبُ ٱلْبَحْرِ.

Dogged, *a*. Stubborn, خَشِنُ ٱلْجَانِبِ ـ صَعْب ـ شَكِس ـ لَا يَسْمَعُ نِدَاءً وَلَا يَبْغِي ٱهْتِدَاءً. Determined, زَمِيت ـ صِنْدِيد.

Doggedly, *ad*. Stubbornly, بِخُشُونَةٍ ـ بِوَعْرَةٍ. With determination, بِجَزْمٍ ـ تَزْمِيعًا ـ بِتَزْمِيعٍ.

Doggerel, *n*. إِسْتِهْجَان ـ سَجْعٌ مِنْ غَيْرِ وَزْنٍ. A writer of —, شُعْرُور.

Doggerel, *a*. Mean, vile, حَقِير ـ خَسِيس.

Doggish, *a*. Churlish, جَافٍ ـ شَكِس ـ عَنِيف.

Doggishness, *n*. جَفَاء ـ شَكَاسَة ـ عُنْف ـ شَرَاسَة.

Dogma, *n*. A religious tenet, عَقِيدَةٌ دِينِيَّةٌ. A rule, admitted truth, قَاعِدَة *pl.* قَوَاعِد ـ قَوْلٌ مُثْبَت ـ قَوْلٌ مُسَلَّم. Dogmas, a set of articles of belief, مَذْهَب *pl.* مَذَاهِب ـ إِعْتِقَاد *pl.* إِعْتِقَادَات.

Dogmatic, *a*. / **Dogmatical**, } Pertaining to a dogma, إِعْتِقَادِيّ ـ مُتَعَلِّقٌ بِٱلْاعْتِقَادَاتِ. Positive, قَاطِع. Arrogant, تَائِه ـ مُتَجَبِّر ـ مُتَكَبِّر ـ مُتَغَطْرِف. *See also* Arrogant, *a*.

Dogmatically, *ad*. Positively, مُحَكَّمًا ـ بِفَصْلٍ ـ بِتَحَكُّمٍ ـ قَطْعًا ـ فَصْلًا ـ بَتَّةً. Arrogantly, بِتِيهٍ ـ بِتَغَطْرُفٍ ـ بِتَجَبُّرٍ. *See also* Arrogantly, *ad*.

Dogmatics, *n*. Doctrinal theology, عِلْمُ ٱلْعَقَائِدِ ٱلدِّينِيَّةِ.

Dogmatism, *n*. Peremptoriness, إِسْتِحْكَام ـ فَصْل. Arrogance, تِيه ـ غَطْرَفَة ـ تَكَبُّر. *See also* Arrogance, *n*.

Dogmatist, *n*. / **Dogmatizer**, } A positive teacher, حَاتِم ـ مُعَلِّمٌ فَاصِلٌ. A confident asserter, مُدَّعٍ مُتَغَطْرِف ـ جَبَّار ـ جِبِّير ـ تَائِه ـ تَيَّاه ـ مُعْجَبٌ بِنَفْسِهِ.

Dogmatize, *v.i.* تَاهَ ـ تَغَطْرَفَ فِي ٱلْآرَاءِ ـ تَجَبَّرَ فِي رَأْيِهِ.

Dogsbane, *n*. خَانِقُ ٱلْكَلْبِ.

Dog's-grass, *n*. نَيِّل ـ نِيل.

Dog-rose, *n*. زَهْرُ ٱلْعُلَّيْقِ.

Dog's-ear, *n*. The ruffled leaf, as of a book, مَطْوِيّ *pl.* مَطَاوٍ ـ ثَنْي ـ طَيّ *pl.* أَطْوَاء.

Dog-star, *n*. (Sirius). *See under* Dog, *n*.

Dog-tooth, *n*. *See under* Canine, *a*. *and* Tooth, *n*.

Dog-trot, *n*. حَجَاجَة ـ لَبْك.

Dog-watch, *n*. نَوْبَةٌ مِنْ نَوْبَتَيْنِ عِنْدَ حُرَّاسِ ٱلسَّفِينَةِ مُدَّةُ كُلٍّ مِنْهُمَا سَاعَتَيْنِ فَقَطْ بَدَلَ أَرْبَعِ سَاعَاتٍ وَذٰلِكَ بَيْنَ ٱلسَّاعَةِ ٱلرَّابِعَةِ وَٱلثَّامِنَةِ بَعْدَ ٱلظُّهْرِ.

Doily, *n*. نَشَّافَةٌ صَغِيرَةٌ.

Doings, *n.* أَفْعَال ـ أَعْمَال ـ عَمَائِل ـ صَنَائِعُ ـ قَضَايَا ـ سِيَر ـ حَرَكَات ـ حَوَادِثُ. Sayings and doings, أَقْوَالٌ وَأَفْعَالٌ.

Festivities, مَوْسِم ـ فَرَح ـ طَنْطَنَة ـ فَنْطَزِيَّة.

Doit, *n.* مِصْرِيَّة ـ فَلْس *pl.* فُلُوس.

Dole, *n.* A pittance, كَفَف. A share, portion, حِصَّة ـ رَاتِب. Charity, حَسَنَة ـ صَدَقَة. To distribute doles to, أَحْصَصَ.

Dole, *v.t.* To deal out to one grudgingly, نَفِسَ-عَلَى.

Doleful, *a.* Sorrowful, مَكْرُوب ـ حَزِين ـ كَئِيب ـ مَغْمُوم. Causing grief, كَرِيب ـ مُحْزِن ـ مُغِمّ ـ مُضَيِّق. Gloomy, as of an abode, مُسْتَوْحِش ـ مُتَوَحِّش. Gloomy, dejected, مَلُول ـ مَكْسُورُ ٱلْخَاطِرِ. A — lamentation, مَرْثَاة. *See also* Gloomy, *a.*

Dolefully, *ad.* غَمًّا ـ بِغَمّ ـ مَلَلًا ـ بِمَلَلٍ ـ بِحُزْنٍ.

Dolesome, *a.* *See* Doleful, *a.*

Doll, *n.* عَرُوسَةٌ تَلْعَبُ بِهَا ٱلْأَطْفَالُ ـ بِنْت *pl.* بَنَات.

Dollar, *n.* رِيَال *pl.* رِيَالَات. Spanish —, رِيَالٌ أَبُو مِدْفَعٍ.

Dolorous, *a.* *See* Doleful, *a.*

Dolorously, *ad.* *See* Dolefully, *ad.*

Dolour, *n.* *See* Grief, *n.*

Dolphin, *n.* دُخَس ـ دُلْفِين ـ دُرْفِين ـ بِنْتُ ٱلْبَحْرِ *pl.* بَنَات.

Dolt, *n.* } Doltish, *a.* } طَنْبَل ـ فَسْفَاس ـ بَهِيم *pl.* بَهَائِم ـ أَحْمَق *pl.* حُمْق ـ عَبِيط ـ قَلِيلُ ٱلْعَقْلِ.

Doltishness, *n.* طَنْبَلَة ـ حَمَاقَة ـ قِلَّةُ عَقْلٍ.

Domain, *n.* Territory, مَمْلَكَة ـ مَمَالِكُ ـ أَرَاضِي. An estate, أَعْقَار ـ مُلْك ـ أَرَاضِي ـ رِزْق ـ اِلْتِزَام.

Dome, *n.* A cupola, قُبَّة *pl.* قُبَب. A palace, سَرَايَا ـ قَصْر *pl.* قُصُور. A mosque, جَامِع ـ جَوَامِعُ. A church, كَنِيسَة *pl.* كَنَائِسُ.

Domed, *a.* مُقَبَّب.

Domestic, *a.* Belonging to the house, بَيْتِيّ ـ مُتَعَلِّقٌ بِٱلْبَيْتِ ـ أَهْلِيّ. Remaining much at home, دَارِيّ. Made at home, مَصْنُوعٌ فِي ٱلْبَيْتِ. Private, not public, خَاصٌّ غَيْرُ عَامٍّ. Domestic, not foreign, بَلَدِيّ ـ دَاخِلِيّ. A — animal, not imported, حَيَوَانٌ أَهْلِيّ. Domestic, opposed to wild, tame, دَاجِن ـ إِنْسِيّ ـ مَأْنُوس ـ ذَلُول ـ ذَلُولِيّ.

Domestic, *n.* A dependant of the family, عَيِّل *pl.* عِيَال *and* عَيَائِل. A servant, خَادِم *pl.* خُدَّام ـ خُدَّام ـ أَجِير *pl.* أُجَرَاء ـ خِدْمَتْكَار *pl.* خِدْمَتْكَارِيَّة.

Domesticate, *v.t.* أَنَّسَ.

Domestication, *n.* تَأْنِيس.

Domesticity, *n.* Tameness, ذِلّ ـ أُنْس. Keeping at home, دَارِيَّة ـ تَضْرِيبٌ فِي ٱلْبَيْتِ.

Domicile, *n.* مَسْكَن ـ مَقَام ـ مَوْطِن ـ مَقَرّ ـ قَرَار. Original —, وَطَن.

Domicile, *v.t.* أَقَرَّ-فِي ـ أَسْكَنَ. To be domiciled, سَكَنَ ـ أَوْطَنَ بِ ـ أَقَامَ فِي.

Domiciliary, *a.* Pertaining to a house, مُخْتَصٌّ بِٱلْبَيْتِ. Domiciliary visits, دُخُولُ ٱلْبُيُوتِ لِلِٱسْتِكْشَافِ.

Domiciliation, *n.* The act of, إِسْكَان ـ إِقَامَة.

Dominant, *a.* Ruling, مُسْتَوْلٍ ـ مُتَسَلِّط ـ ضَابِط. Predominant, غَالِب. The — religion, مَذْهَبُ ٱلْأَكْثَرِينَ.

Dominate, *v.t.* To rule over, حَكَمَ عَلَى ـ تَسَلَّطَ عَلَى. To prevail over, قَوِيَ عَلَى ـ تَغَلَّبَ عَلَى ـ اِسْتَوْلَى عَلَى.

Domination, *n.* Rule, تَسَلُّط ـ حُكُومَة ـ مُلْك ـ إِمَارَة. Tyranny, جَيْف ـ ظُلْم ـ جَوْر.

Domineer, *v.i.* To rule with arrogance, بَطِرَ ـ تَاهَ *aor.* يَتِيهُ ـ تَسَلَّطَ عَلَى ـ تَجَبَّرَ ـ تَفَرْعَنَ. To — over, تَسَلَّطَ عَلَى-بِجَبْرٍ ـ تَسَلَّطَ بِجَبْرٍ ـ تَجَبَّرَ عَلَى ـ قَهَرَ ـ ظَلَمَ عَلَى ـ تَطَاوَلَ عَلَى.

Domineering, *a.* تَيَّاه ـ تَائِه ـ مُتَجَبِّر ـ مُتَحَكِّم ـ بَطِر ـ جَبَّار.

Dominical, *a.* Pertaining to Sunday, أَحَدِيّ ـ يَدُلُّ عَلَى يَوْمِ ٱلْأَحَدِ. The — letter, ٱلْحَرْفُ ٱلْأَحَدِيُّ.

Dominican, *n.* A — friar, رَاهِبٌ دُومِينِيقَانِيّ.

Dominion, *n.* Supreme authority, سُودَد ـ سُلْطَة ـ سُلْطَان ـ حُكُومَة ـ سَلْطَنَة ـ سِيَادَة ـ مَلَكُوت ـ مَمْلَكَة. Territory, إِيَالَة ـ وِلَايَة *pl.* وِلَايَات ـ أَرَاضِي. To exercise —, سَلَطَ. To exercise — over, مَلَكَ عَلَى ـ سَادَ عَلَى. To give the — to, سَلَّطَ ـ رَأَّسَ-عَلَى ـ أَمْلَكَ ـ مَلَّكَ. Under the — of the Sublime Porte, تَحْتَ سُودَدِ ٱلْبَابِ ٱلْعَالِي.

Domino, *n.* A dress of disguise, لِبْسُ تَبْدِيلٍ. The game, نَوْعٌ مِنَ ٱلْقِمَارِ ـ لَعْبُ ٱلدُّومِينُو.

Don, *v.t.* To put on, لَبِسَ ـ تَلَبَّسَ بِ.

Donation, *n.* } Donative, } عَطَا ـ عَطَاء ـ أَعْطِيَة *pl.* عَطِيَّة *pl.* عَطَايَا ـ مَوْهَبَة *pl.* مَوَاهِبُ ـ هَدِيَّة ـ إِنْعَام ـ تَقْدِمَة.

See also under Subscription, *n.*

Done, *part.* To be made, اِنْفَعَلَ ـ اِنْعَمَلَ ـ صُنِعَ. To be — by, to originate with, صَدَرَ عَن. To be —, cooked, اِنْطَبَخَ. Half-done, raw, نِيّ. It was —, carried into execution, جَرَى ٱلْعَمَلُ بِهِ. *See also* to Cook, *v.t.*

Done, *int.* حَبَّذَا ـ قَبِلْتُ ذٰلِكَ ـ رَضِيتُ ـ طَيِّب.

Donee, *n.* ٱلْمَوْهُوبُ لَهُ ـ ٱلْمُعْطَى لَهُ.

Donjon, *n.* حُجْرَة ـ قَلْعَة. *See also* Prison, *n.*

Donkey, *n.* *See* Ass, *n.*

Donkey-engine, *n.* حِمار ــ دُولابُ بُخارِيٌّ صَغِيرٌ فِي ٱلْبَواخِرِ.

Donor, *n.* مُعْطٍ ــ واهِبٌ ــ مُنْعِمٌ. A liberal —, وَهّابٌ. *See also under* Subscriber, *n.*

Doom, *n.* A sentence, قَضاءٌ ــ حُكْمٌ ــ شَرْعٌ. Fate, نَصِيبٌ ــ قِسْمَةٌ. Ruin, هَلاكٌ ــ إِتْلافٌ.

Doom, *v.t.* To sentence, condemn, قَضَى عَلَى ــ حَكَمَ عَلَى ــ أَوْقَعَ. To fix the fate of, قَدَّرَ عَلَى ــ أَوْقَعَ عَلَى-ب ــ دانَ عَلَى-ب.

Doom's-day, *n.* يَوْمُ ٱلدِّينِ ــ يَوْمُ ٱلدَّيْنُونَةِ.

Doom's-day-Book, *n.* كِتابُ فِهْرِسِ ٱلْعَقاراتِ ٱلَّتِي كانَتْ فِي يَدِ أَصْحابِ ٱلْمُلْكِ مِنَ ٱلْإِنْكِلِيزِ قَبْلَ ٱسْتِيلاءِ ٱلنُّورْمَنْدِيِّينَ عَلَى بِلادِهِمْ.

Door, *n.* باب *pl.* أَبْواب ــ بابٌ. The street —, بابُ ٱلْحارَةِ. A back —, بابُ سِرٍّ. An entrance, دِهْلِيزٌ ــ مَدْخَلٌ ــ ٱلسِّلْكُ. Folding doors, مِصْراعانِ; the half of a folding —, مِصْراعٌ. To open, as of a —, فَتَحَ ــ أَشْرَعَ. To shut, as of a —, أَطْبَقَ ــ سَدَمَ ــ رَدَّ ــ رَتَّجَ ــ سَكَّ. A wedge to keep a — open, سَكَن. To turn out of doors, طَرَدَ مِنَ ٱلْبَيْتِ. To lay a thing at one's —, to charge with, خَطَّأَ-ب ــ أَتْهَمَ-ب. To half open a —, فَتَحَ ٱلْبابَ نِصْفَ فَتْحٍ. In doors, فِي ٱلْبَيْتِ. Out of doors, فِي ٱلْخارِجِ. Door, access, مَوْرِد ــ مَنْفَذ ــ دُخُول ــ بابٌ إِلَى.

Door-keeper, *n.* بَوّاب ــ حارِسُ ٱلْبابِ.

Door-post, *n.* أُسْكُفَّة *pl.* أَسْكاف. The two door-posts, ٱلْأُسْكُفَّتانِ.

Dormant, *a.* Sleeping, هاجِع ــ نائِم. Stationary, واقِف. To lie —, not used, تَعَطَّلَ ــ تَوَقَّفَ. *See also* Sleeping, *a.*

Dormer-window, *n.* قَيْمَرِيَّة ــ قَمَرِيَّة ــ مَمْرَق ــ مَنْوَر ــ كُوَّة.

Dormitive, *n.* دَواءٌ مُنَوِّمٌ.

Dormitory, *n.* قاعَةُ ٱلنَّوْمِ ــ مَنامَة ــ مَنام.

Dormouse, *n.* زَبابَة *coll.* زَباب *pl.* زَبابات.

Dorsal, *a.* ظَهْرِيٌّ.

Dose, *n.* As of medicine, شَرْبَة ــ أَخْذَة. A quantity, قَدْر ــ مِقْدار ــ كَمِّيَّة.

Dose, *v.t.* To make one to take, as of medicine, *etc.*, شَرَّبَ ــ أَشْرَبَ. To make up into doses, جَزَّأَ.

Dossil, *n.* A —, as of lint, فَتِيلَة *pl.* فَتائِلُ.

Dot, *n.* نُقْطَة *pl.* نُقَط.

Dot, *v.t.* نَقَّطَ. To put the dots on letters in writing, رَقَّشَ ــ رَقَّشَ ــ أَعْجَمَ ــ شَكَلَ. The act of dotting, تَرْقِيش ــ رَقْش ــ شَكْل. The dotted letters of the Arabic alphabet, حُرُوفُ ٱلْمُعْجَمِ.

Dotage, *n.* خَرَف ــ خَرَفَةُ عَقْلٍ; imbecile talk, هَتْرَة.

Dotal, *a.* مُتَعَلِّقٌ بِٱلْمَهْرِ ــ مَهْرِيٌّ.

Dotard, *n.* شَيْخٌ خَرْفانٌ ــ خَرِف ــ مُفْنِد ــ مُفَنَّد. To make a — of, to deem a —, فَنَّدَ.

Dotation, *n.* The act of endowing, تَوْقِيف. An endowment, وَقْف *pl.* أَوْقاف.

Dote, *v.i.* To become silly, فَنِدَ ــ خَرِفَ ــ أَفْنَدَ ــ أَهْتَرَ. To be desperately in love, تَدَلَّهَ بِٱلْعِشْقِ. To — upon, to love, وَدَّ ــ حَبَّ ــ عَشِقَ. To love amorously, عَشِقَ.

Doter, *n.* *See* Dotard, *n.*

Dotingly, *ad.* With silliness, خَرَفًا ــ بِهُتْرٍ. With great fondness, بِكَثْرَةِ ٱلتَّوَدُّدِ.

Double, *a.* Two-fold, مُضاعَف. A — flower, زَهْرٌ مُكَبَّسٌ. A — chin, لُغْد. A — portion, نَصِيبُ ٱثْنَيْنِ. He shall be rewarded —, يُعَوَّضُ ضِعْفَيْنِ. He has received — for . . . , قَبِلَ ضِعْفَيْنِ عَن. Worthy of — honour, أَهْلٌ لِكَرامَةٍ مُضاعَفَةٍ. Deceitful, مَكّار ــ خَدّاع ــ خَبِيث. A — sole, نَعْل ــ خَصْف ــ خَصِيف. Capable of a — meaning, مُحْتَمِلُ ٱلضِّدَّيْنِ.

Double, *n.* Twice the quantity, ضِعْف *pl.* أَضْعاف. The fellow to, the like, بَدِيد ــ وَصْل ــ خَطِير ــ شِبْه ــ شَبِيه. This is the — of that, هٰذا خَطِيرٌ لِهٰذا. To be repaid —, أُضْعِفَ. Double or quits, تَكُونُ ٱلْمُراهَنَةُ بَيْنَنا أَمّا عَلَى ضِعْفِ ٱلْمُقامَرَةِ وَأَمّا عَلَى ٱلسَّواءِ.

Double, *v.t.* To make two-fold, ضاعَفَ ــ أَضْعَفَ ــ ضَعَّفَ. To — sew, to stitch, ضَرَّبَ. To —, or give — to, ضاعَفَ ل. To fold, ثَنَى ــ طَبَّقَ ــ طَوَى ــ طَوَى-طاقَيْنِ. To —, to sail round, سافَرَ حَوْلَ ــ جازَ ــ أَجازَ. To —, of a letter, *etc.*, طَوَى ــ شَدَّ. To — up, by folding and sewing, غَبَنَ ــ كَبَنَ ــ خَبَنَ.

Double, *v.i.* To increase two-fold, تَضاعَفَ. To become folded, اِنْثَنَى ــ تَثَنَّى ــ اِنْطَوَى. To turn back, or wind, اِلْتَفَّ ــ صَرَفَ ــ جالَ ب *aor.* يَجُولُ.

Double, *ad.* بِضِعْفٍ ــ إِضْعافًا ــ بِتَضْعِيفٍ.

Double-barrelled, *a.* Of a gun, بارُودَةٌ مُزْدَوِجَةٌ.

Double-breasted, *a.* Of a coat, سُتْرَةٌ مَثْنِيَّةُ ٱلصَّدْرِ.

Doubled, *a.* Made two-fold, مُضَعَّف ــ مُضاعَف. Folded, مَثْنِيّ ــ مَطْوِيّ; of a letter, مَشْدُود ــ طَوِيّ. The sentence, judgment, was — twice, تَكَرَّرَ ٱلْحُكْمُ مَرَّتَيْنِ.

Double-dealer, *n.* صَيِّغ ــ خائِن ــ مَكّار.

Double-dealing, *n.* مَوْغ ــ خِيانَة ــ مَكْر.

Double-entendre, n. مُحْتَمِلُ ٱلضِّدَّيْنِ — تَوْرِيَة — مِعْرَاض — تَعْرِيض. To use —, عَرَّضَ.

Double-entry, n. زِنْجِير (vulg. جِنْزِير) — سِلْسِلَة — حِسَابٌ — حِسَابٌ مُزَوَّج — ٱلزِّنْجِيرِ.

Double-faced, a. ذُو وَجْهَيْنِ — مُوَجَّه.

Double-minded, a. ذُو رَأْيَيْنِ — مُتَقَلْقِل — مُتَحَيِّر — مُتَزَعْزِع — قَلَّاب.

Doubleness, n. The being two-fold, تَضَاعُف; the being folded, تَثَنٍّ. Hypocrisy, ضَوْغ — مُرَاياة.

Doubler, n. مُضَعِّف — مُثَنٍّ — مُزَوِّج.

Doublet, n. A fellow, pair, بَدِيل — شَبِيه — زَوْج. The garment, يَلَكْ — أَزْبَنَة pl. زَبُون. A counterfeit stone, جَوْهَرَة زَغَل.

Double-tongued, a. ذُو لِسَانَيْنِ — خَائِن.

Doublets, n. Pairs, أَزْوَاج. They are —, هُمَا زَوْجٌ — هُمَا زَوْجَانِ.

Doubling, n. A fold, غَرٌّ — ثَنْيٌ — طَيٌّ pl. أَطْوَاء. An artifice, حِيلَة — كَيْد. A sailing round, سَفَرٌ حَوْلَ — جَوْل بِ.

Doubloon, n. سِكَّةُ ٱلدَّبْلُونِ.

Doubly, ad. إِضْعَافًا — تَضْعِيفًا — عَلَى ضِعْفٍ.

Doubt, v.t. To question, شَكَّ فِي aor. يَشُكُّ — تَشَكَّكَ فِي — تَمَارَى فِي — مَارَى — اِخْتَلَجَ فِي — تَخَالَجَ فِي. To suspect, اِتَّهَمَ بِ — اِتَّهَمَ — اِرْتَابَ بِ — تَرَيَّبَ بِ. I doubted about the question, كُنْتُ مُرْتَابًا فِي ٱلْمَسْأَلَةِ. I —, am in — of, you, أَنَا مُتَحَيِّرٌ فِيكُمْ.

Doubt, v.i. To hesitate, تَمَارَى — تَشَكَّكَ — اِرْتَابَ — رَابَ ـِ — شَكَّ ². To suspect, اِتَّهَمَ — تَشَكَّكَ — أَوْهَمَ. Some of them doubted, بَعْضُهُمْ شَكُّوا. Whoever doubts, أَلَّذِي يَرْتَابُ. Why did you —? لِمَاذَا شَكَّكْتَ. He doubted within himself, اِرْتَابَ فِي نَفْسِهِ. They doubted among themselves, اِرْتَابُوا فِي أَنْفُسِهِمْ. He doubted respecting his affair, اِرْتَبَكَ فِي أَمْرِهِ.

Doubt, n. Uncertainty of mind, شَكٌّ — مِرْيَة — شُبْهَة pl. شُبَهٌ — تُهَمَة — رِيبَة — رَيْب — مَوْهِمَة — شُكُوك pl. Suspicion, رِيبَة — تُهْمَة. I relieved him from — respecting the question, شَفَيْتُهُ عَنِ ٱلْمَسْأَلَةِ. To have doubts, اِشْتَبَهَ. Doubt, a mystery, غَيْب pl. غِيَاب. Without —, بِلَا شَكٍّ — بِلَا رَيْبٍ — لَا رَيْبَ — مِنْ غَيْرِ شُبْهَةٍ — لَا جَرَمَ — حَقًّا — كُلَّ بُدٍّ. There is no — that ..., لَا شَكَّ أَنْ.

Doutable, a. *See* Doubtful, a.

Doubter, n. مُتَّهِم — مُرْتَاب — مُشْتَبِه.

Doubtful, a. Uncertain, مُتَّهَم — مُخَيِّل — مُشْتَبِه — مُحْتَ — مُشْتَبِه — مُلْتَبِس. Ambiguous, قَرِينُ ٱلرَّيْبِ — ٱلشَّكّ — مُبْهَم — مُعَقَّد — مَشْكُوك. That cannot be depended on, لَا ثِقَةَ بِ. To be — to, اِشْتَبَهَ عَلَى. To make — to, شَبَّهَ عَلَى. To be —, شُكَّ فِيهِ. Anything —, شَكْل pl. أَشْكَال. Something to be suspicious of, ذُو رِيبَةٍ. This is not a — affair, هٰذَا أَمْرٌ لَا يُحِيلُ. A — affair, أَمْرٌ مَشْكُوكٌ فِيهِ — أَمْرٌ مَشْكُوك. Doubtful, giving rise to doubt, رَائِب. They were —, كَانُوا فِي شَكٍّ مُرِيبٍ.

Doubtfully, ad. بِٱرْتِيَابٍ — بِشَكٍّ — إِشْتِبَاهًا — بِرَيْبٍ.

Doubtfulness, n. Hesitation, تَرَدُّد — شُبْهَة. Suspicion, تَوَهُّم — مَوْهِمَة — شُبْهَة — مِرْيَة. Uncertainty, عَدَمُ ثَبَاتٍ. Ambiguity, اِلْتِبَاس. *See also* Doubt, n.

Doubtless, ad. / Doubtlessly, } لَا جَرَمَ — لَا وَهْمَ. *See also* Without doubt, *under* Doubt, n.

Douceur, n. حُلْوَان — حَلَاوَة.

Douche, n. صَبُّ مَاءٍ عَلَى ٱلْبَدَنِ — نَطُول.

Dough, n. عَجِين; a piece of, عَجِينَة. Dough, till made into bread, خُبْزَة. Unleavened —, فَطِير. To make —, عَجَنَ ـِ ².

Dough-faced, a. شَاحِبُ ٱلْوَجْهِ — شَاحِبُ ٱللَّوْنِ.

Dough-nut, n. كُبَّةُ عَجِينٍ مَطْبُوخَةٌ بِٱلسَّمْنِ.

Doughtily, ad. بِشَجَاعَةٍ — بِجَسَارَةٍ — عَنْتَرَةً — بِبَطَالَةٍ.

Doughtiness, n. شَجَاعَة — جَسَارَة — عَنْتَرَة — بَطَالَة.

Doughty, a. بَطَل — جَسُور — جَذَع — شُجَاع — رَجَّال.

Doughy, a. Like dough, مِثْلَ ٱلْعَجِينِ — نِيء. Soft, طَرِيّ — رَخْو. Pale, مُصْفَرّ — أَصْفَر. Doughy-mouthed, ذُو فَمٍ رَخْوٍ.

Douse, v.t. غَطَسَ فِي ـِ — أَغْطَّ فِي.

Douse, v.i. غَطَسَ فِي ـِ — اِنْغَطَّ فِي.

Dove, n. A turtle-dove, يَمَامَة coll. يَمَام — سُتَيْتِيَّة — قُمْرِيّ pl. قَمَارِي — دَرْغَل — تَرْغَل — صُلْصُل. A collared turtle —, فَاخِتَة. *See also under* Pigeon, n.

Dove-cot, n. / Dove-house, } بُرْجُ يَمَام. Dove's-nest, تِمْرَاد pl. تَمَارِيدُ.

Dove-like, a. حَلِيم — وَدِيع — سَلِيم.

Dover's-powder, n. دَوَاءٌ مُنَوِّم.

Dovetail, n. تَعْشِيق — تَعْشِيقُ ٱلْخَشَبِ فِي بَعْضِهِ — ذَكَرٌ وَأُنْثَى.

Dovetail, v.t. عَشَّقَ — عَشَّقَ فِي بَعْضِهِ.

Dovetail, v.i. As of wood, تَعَشَّقَ — تَعَشَّقَ فِي بَعْضِهِ. To coincide, طَابَقَ — وَافَقَ — اِتَّفَقَ.

Dowager, n. أَرْمَلَة pl. أَرَامِلُ. The queen —, ٱلْمَلِكَةُ ٱلْأَرْمَلَة.

Dowdy, n. A —, بَذَّة — بَلِيَّة. Slovenliness, بَذَاذَة — بَذْبَذَة.

Dowdy, a. / Dowdyish, } بَذّ. To be —, بَذَّ aor. يَبَذُّ. A — appearance, هَيْئَةٌ بَذَّةٌ.

Dowel, v.t. رَكَّبَ ٱلْخَشَبَ بِعَصَافِيرَ.

Dowel, *n.* عُصْفُور *pl.* عَصَافِيرُ.

Dower, *n.* مُهُور *pl.* مَهْر — عُقْر — صُدْق *pl.* صَداق — شَبْر — بِيَاق.
A woman having a large —, مَهِيرَة. To give a — to, مَهَرَ ² — أَمْهَرَ. Dowered, *fem.* مَمْهُورَة.

Dowerless, *a.* مِنْ غَيْرِ مَهْرٍ — بِلا صَداقٍ.

Down, *prep.* and *ad.* Below, تَحْتَ — أَسْفَلَ. From a higher to a lower place, بِنُزُولٍ — لِتَحْتَ — إِلَى تَحْتَ. Down the street, طُولَ الطَّرِيقِ — فِي الطَّرِيقِ. Down the river, — فِي النَّهْرِ سَافَرَ فِي — قَلَعَ فِي النَّهْرِ. He sailed — the river, مَعَ التَّيَّارِ النَّهْرِ. The sun is —, غَرَبَتِ الشَّمْسُ. My watch is —, سَاعَتِي وَقَفَتْ — سَاعَتِي. The wind is —, سَكَنَتِ الرِّيحُ ² — وَانْتَهَتْ — هَدَأَتِ الرِّيحُ. Up and —, جَوْلانًا — تَرَدُّدًا — هُنَا وَهُنَالِكَ. Upside —, مَنْكُوس — مَعْكُوس — مَقْلُوب. Get — quickly, أَسْرِعْ وَانْزِلْ. Down to this time, إِلَى يَوْمِنَا هٰذَا — إِلَى هٰذَا الْآنَ.

To be tossed up and down, إِنْتَقَضَ.

To boil down, ذَوَّبَ- (or سَبَخَ-) بِالْغَلَيَانِ.

To bring down, from a higher to a lower place, أَنْزَلَ — نَزَّلَ. To hit, أَصَابَ.

To burn down, أَحْرَقَ-بَتَّةً (or بِالْكُلِّيَّةِ). To be burnt down, إِحْتَرَقَ بِالْمَرَّةِ (or بَتَّةً).

To come down, descend from, هَبَطَ مِنْ ². To come down upon, to abuse, صَعِدَ بِ- وَنَزَلَ.

To fall down, وَقَعَ *aor.* يَقَعُ — سَقَطَ ²; as from a higher to a lower place, خَرَّ ².

To fall down on one's knees, رَكَعَ; as in worship, خَرَّ سَاجِدًا ².

To go down, as to a place, نَزَلَ. To stop, وَقَفَ *aor.* يَقِفُ.

To go up and down, تَاهَ — تَرَدَّدَ.

To knock down, to upset, كَبَّ ². To throw down, أَوْقَعَ.

To let down, as of a curtain, سَجَفَ — أَسْجَفَ.

To look down upon, as from a height, أَطَلَّ عَلَى — أَشْرَفَ عَلَى — إِطَّلَعَ مِنْ.

To run down, to abuse, عَيَّبَ — فَضَحَ — هَتَكَ — إِسْتَقَلَّ.

To run against, to come into collision with, صَدَعَ — صَادَمَ.

To throw, or cast, down, خَبَطَ — أَسْقَطَ — أَوْقَعَ.

To walk up and down, تَرَدَّدَ.

To wander up and down, تَاهَ — تَمَشَّى.

Down, *a.* Dejected, مَكْسُورُ الْخَاطِرِ — مَحْزُون — مُكَدَّر — مَغْمُوم.

Down, *n.* An open plain, قَاع *pl.* قِيعَان — صَاعَة — مَيْدَان. The soft plumage of fowls, زَغَب — سُخَام — دَبَب. The soft hair of the goat, مِرْعِزَّى. Gossamer, جَالِحَة *pl.* جَوَالِحُ. The ups and downs of life, تَقَلُّبَاتُ الدَّهْرِ — طَوَائِحُ الزَّمَنِ.

Downcast, *a.* *See* Down, *a.*

Downfall, *n.* Overthrow, ruin, نَكْبَة — زَوَال — سُقُوط — هَلاك. A — of rain, نَوْء *pl.* أَنْوَاء — أُسْكُوب — وَابِل. *See also* Overthrow, *n.*

Downhaul, *n.* جِنْدَرِيسَة.

Downhill, *n.* صَبَب — حُدُور.

Downhill, *a.* Sloping, هَبُوط — مُنْصَبّ — صَبِيب.

Downlooking, *a.* Dejected, مُنْقَطِعُ الْقَلْبِ — مُهْتَبِط. Gloomy, sad, كَرِيب — حَزِين.

Downpour, *n.* *See under* Downfall, *n.*

Downright, *a.* Frank, نَاصِح — صَافٍ — خَالِص — سَلِيم. *See also under* Flat, *a.*

Downright, *ad.* Frankly, بِنَصَاحَةٍ — بِصَفَاوَةٍ — بِاسْتِقَامَةٍ.

Downrightness, *n.* Frankness, نُصُوح — صَفَاوَة — إِسْتِقَامَة.

Downs, *n.* Hilly poor ground, أَكَمَات — صَحْرَاء.

Down-sitting, *n.* جُلُوس — قُعُود.

Down-trod, *a.* / Down-trodden, } مَدُوس — مَدُوسٌ عَلَيْهِ.

Downward, *ad.* *See* Down, *ad.*

Downward, *a.* نَازِل — مَائِلٌ إِلَى أَسْفَلَ — ضَارِبٌ إِلَى أَسْفَلَ. From his loins —, مِنْ حَقْوَيْهِ إِلَى تَحْتُ.

Downy, *a.* أَدَبُّ *fem.* دَبَّاء — أَزَبُّ *fem.* زَبَّاء. A — young bird, فَرْخٌ أَزْغَبُ. A — man, رَجُلٌ زَغِبٌ. A — neck, رَقَبَةٌ زَغْبَاء. A — cucumber, قِثَّاءٌ أَزْغَبُ. Soft, نَاعِم — مَلِس. Having — hair, زَغِبُ الشَّعْرِ.

Dowry, *n.* *See* Dower, *n.*

Doxological, *a.* مُتَعَلِّقٌ بِالتَّسْبِيحِ وَالتَّمْجِيدِ.

Doxology, *n.* سَبْحَلَة — حَمْدَلَة — التَّسْبِيحُ لِلّٰهِ.

Doxy, *n.* قَحْبَة — زَانِيَة.

Doyen, *n.* The oldest ambassador at a court, السَّفِيرُ الْأَقْدَمُ عَهْدًا فِي السِّفَارَةِ.

Doze, *v.i.* خَفَقَ ² — أَخْفَقَ — نَعَسَ.

Doze, *v.t.* To spend, lose, ضَيَّعَ — صَرَفَ- بِالْبَاطِلِ.

Dozen, *n.* دَسْتَة — دَزِّينَة *pl.* دَزِّينَات — إِثْنَا عَشَرَ. By the —, very common, مُرَطْرَط.

Doziness, *n.* خُفُوق — نُعَاس.

Dozing, *a.* خَافِق — نَاعِس — نَعْسَانُ.

Dozing, *n.* A doze, خَفْقَة — نَعْسَة. A nod in —, خَفْقَة.

Dozy, *a.* نَعْسانٌ . Heavy, dull, ثَقِيلٌ .

Drab, *n.* A sluttish woman, بَذِيَّةٌ ـ بَذَّةٌ . A harlot, قَحْبَةٌ *pl.* قِحاب . A — colour, لَوْنٌ سِنْجابِيٌّ .

Drab, *a.* Of the colour, سِنْجابِيٌّ .

Drabble, *v.t.* *See to* Draggle, *v.t.*

Drabble, *v.i.* *See to* Draggle, *v.i.*

Drachma, *n.* إِسْمُ ٱلدِّرْهَمِ عِنْدَ ٱلْيُونانِيِّينَ ـ دِرْخَم .

Draff, *n.* *See* Dregs, *n.*

Draffy, *a.* *See* Dreggy, *a.*

Draft, *n.* A bill drawn for money, وَرَقَةُ حَوالَةٍ ـ حَوالَةٌ . A drink, شَرْبَةٌ ـ نَطْلَةٌ . A composing —, for children, صُمْتَةٌ . A rough sketch, مُسَوَّدَةٌ ـ تَسْوِيدٌ . A detaching of soldiers, تَجْرِيدُ ٱلْعَساكِرِ . A detachment of soldiers, جَرِيدَةٌ *pl.* جَرائِدُ ـ فِرْقَةٌ مِنَ ٱلْعَسْكَرِ . To make a —, rough sketch, سَوَّدَ . *See also under* Cheque, *n.*

Draft, *v.t.* To draw a rough copy, سَوَّدَ . To draw, رَسَمَ [2] ـ صَوَّرَ . To detach soldiers, جَرَّدَ ٱلْعَسْكَرَ ; as on special service, عَيَّنَ فِرْقَةً مِنَ ٱلْعَسْكَرِ لِأَمْرٍ مَخْصُوصٍ .

Drafts, *n.* Checkers, لَعْبُ ٱلدَّامَةِ ـ دامَةٌ . A draft-board, تَخْتَةُ ٱلدَّامَةِ .

Drag, *v.t.* To harrow, of land, مَهَّدَ ـ مَهَّدَ بِٱلنَّوْرَجِ ـ سَلَفَ [2] ـ جَرَّ [2] ـ سَحَبَ ـ إِخْتَلَجَ ـ خَلَجَ [2] ـ تَلَعَ . To draw along, . To draw forcibly, إِعْتَنَفَ ـ إِجْتَذَبَ ـ عَتَلَ [2] ـ جَذَبَ . To —, as a ship its anchor, جَرَّ [2] .

Drag, *v.i.* To trail along the ground, إِنْجَرَّ ـ تَدَلَّى عَلَى ٱلْأَرْضِ ـ تَمَشَّى ـ تَزَحَّفَ ـ إِنْسَحَبَ ـ عَلَى ٱلْأَرْضِ . To proceed slowly, دَلَفَ . He dragged himself along the ground, زَحَفَ عَلَى ـ تَزَحَّفَ ـ ٱلْأَرْضِ . He dragged his garment along the ground, أَسْبَلَ ثَوْبَهُ . To be dragged, drawn, إِنْسَحَبَ ـ إِنْجَرَّ ـ أُجْتُذِبَ . To fish with a drag-net, إِصْطادَ بِمِجْرَفَةٍ .

Drag, *n.* A drag-net, مِجْرَفَةٌ *vulg.* جَرَّافَةٌ . A harrow, مِسْلَفَةٌ ـ نَوْرَجٌ . A hook, خُطّافٌ ـ كَلالِيبُ *pl.* كُلّابٌ ـ عُقّافَةٌ . A small cart, نَقَّالَةٌ بِعَجَلَتَيْنِ . The — of a carriage, مُسْكَةٌ (or ضابِطَةٌ) ٱلْجَرْمِ ; of a railway, فَرْمَلَةٌ . An incumbrance, of a thing, عائِقٌ ـ عَوْقٌ ـ تَعْوِيقٌ ; of a person, ثِقْلٌ ـ مُبْرِمٌ . To be a — upon one, ثَقُلَ عَلَيْهِ [2] .

Draggle, *v.t.* To dirty by trailing, وَسَّخَ بِٱلْجَرِّ ـ وَعَّرَ جَرًّا . To dirty, وَعَّرَ ـ وَسَّخَ . He dragged his garment, أَسْبَلَ ثَوْبَهُ فِي ٱلْوَعْرِ .

Draggle, *v.i.* To be dirtied by trailing, تَوَسَّخَ بِٱلْجَرِّ ـ تَوَعَّرَ جَرًّا .

Draggle-tail, *n.* مُوَعَّرُ ٱلثَّوْبِ ـ مُسْبِلُ ٱلثَّوْبِ ; of a woman, فُضُلٌ .

Drag-net, *n.* مِجْرَفَةٌ ـ مِجْرَفٌ *vulg.* جَرَّافَةٌ .

Dragoman, *n.* (correctly, *Tarjumán*), تَرْجُمانٌ *pl.* تَراجِمُ *and* تَراجِمَةٌ .

Dragon, *n.* A winged serpent, تِنِّينٌ . The constellation —, ٱلتِّنِّينُ .

Dragon-fly, *n.* ذُبابٌ فارِسِيٌّ .

Dragonish, *a.* } Furious, مُتَفَرْعِنٌ ـ جافٍ ـ قاسٍ ـ عَنِيفٌ .
Dragon-like, }

Dragon's-blood, *n.* القاطِرُ ـ دَمُ ٱلْأَخَوَيْنِ ـ دَمُ ٱلْغَزالِ ـ عَنْدَم ـ دَمُ ٱلثُّعْبانِ ـ قَطْرٌ مَكَّةَ *vulg.* ٱلْمَكِّيُّ . The juice of —, صَبِيبٌ .

Dragoon, *n.* عَسْكَرِيٌّ يُقاتِلُ راجِلًا وَراكِبًا .

Dragoon, *v.t.* To harass, حَرَّشَ ـ نَهَكَ ـ أَجْهَدَ . To force to submit, طَوَّعَ ـ كَسَرَ ـ أَخْضَعَ .

Dragooning, *n.* تَطْوِيعٌ ـ بَغْيٌ ـ ظُلْمٌ ـ قَهْرٌ .

Drain, *n.* A trench, لُغْمٌ . A ditch, حُفْرَةٌ . A channel for water, مَثْعَبٌ *pl.* مَثاعِبُ ـ مَجْرًى *pl.* مَجارٍ ; for carrying off rain-water, a spout, مِرْزابٌ ـ مِيزابٌ ـ مِزْرابٌ . A sink, إِرْدَبَّةٌ ـ بَلّاعَةٌ *pl.* بَلالِيعُ ـ بالُوعَةٌ *pl.* بَلُوعَةٌ ـ بَوالِيعُ ـ مَصَبٌّ *pl.* مَصابُّ .

Drain, *v.t.* To open a — or passage for water, فَتَحَ مَجْرًى . To exhaust, empty, dry up, نَشَّفَ ـ فَرَّغَ ـ نَزَحَ . To drink the last drop, as out of a cup, قَرَعَ جَبْهَتَهُ بِٱلْإِناءِ (*lit.* He hit his forehead with the cup). To — a marsh, نَشَّفَ ٱلْبَطِيحَةَ . To — the wealth of a country, أَفْنَى (or أَنْفَدَ) أَمْوالَ ٱلْبَلَدِ .

Drain, *v.i.* To filter, تَشَلْشَلَ ـ نَضَّ . To run, جَرَى . To be emptied, نُزِحَ . To be dried up, تَنَشَّفَ .

Drainage, *n.* Flow, إِنْصِبابٌ ـ جَرَيانٌ . A system of drains, تَرْتِيبٌ لِإِساحَةِ فُضُولِ ٱلْماءِ فِي ٱلْمَسالِكِ .

Draining, *n.* Making drains for —, تَسْلِيكُ فُضُولِ ٱلْماءِ فِي مَجارٍ .

Drainings, *n.* *See* Dregs, *n.*

Drake, *n.* بَطٌّ ; one —, بَطَّةٌ *coll.* بَطٌّ *pl.* بِطاط .

Dram, *n.* The weight, دِرْهَمٌ *pl.* دَراهِمُ . A drink of ardent spirits, فِنْجانُ عَرَقٍ ـ شَرْبَةُ عَرَقٍ .

Drama, *n.* تَقْلِيدُ ٱلسِّيرَةِ ـ سِيرَةٌ يُشَخِّصُها أَهْلُ ٱلتِّياترو بِٱلتَّقْلِيدِ .

Dramatic, *a.* } مُخْتَصٌّ بِٱلسِّيَرِ ٱلْمُبْكِيَةِ أَوِ ٱلْمُضْحِكَةِ يُشَخِّصُها
Dramatical, } مُخْتَصٌّ بِٱلْعابٍ ـ أَهْلُ ٱلتِّياترو بِٱلتَّقْلِيدِ ٱلتِّياترو .

Dramatically, *ad.* تَقْلِيدًا ـ بِٱلتَّقْلِيدِ فِي ٱلتِّياترو .

Dramatist, *n.* مُؤَلِّفُ سِيَرٍ يُشَخِّصُها أَهْلُ ٱلتِّياترو بِٱلتَّقْلِيدِ .

Dramatize, *v.t.* رَتَّبَ ٱلسِّيرَةَ لِلتَّقْلِيدِ فِي ٱلتِّيَاتْرُو.

Drape, *v.t.* As with cloth, *etc.*, عَلَّقَ – أَرْسَلَ عَلَى-ٱلسِّجَافَ عَلَّقَ عَلَى-بِٱلسِّجَافِ – عَلَى-بِ.

Draper, *n.* بَزَّاز – جُوخِيّ *pl.* جُوخِيَّة. The occupation of —, بِزَازَة.

Drapery, *n.* Cloth-work, أَصْنَافُ جُوخٍ وَبَفْتَةٍ وَغَيْرِهَا. Hangings, سِجْف *pl.* سِتَارَة – أَسْجَاف. An ornamentation, زِينَة.

Drastic, *a.* Purgative, مُسْهِل. Strong, شَدِيد – قَوِيّ.

Draught, *n.* The act of drawing, سَحْب – جَذْب – جَرّ. The quantity of fish caught at one haul, صَيْدَةُ سَمَكٍ. A sink, بَالُوعَة – مَخْرَج. A current of air, اِنْطِلَاقٌ (or مَمَرٌّ or مَجْرَى) ٱلْهَوَآءِ – مَلْعَبُ ٱلْهَوَآءِ. The depth to which a ship sinks when laden, غُرْفَة – نُغْبَة – قِيَاسُ ٱنْغِمَاسِ ٱلْمَرْكَبِ فِي ٱلْمَآءِ عِنْدَ شَحْنِهِ – غَاطِس. A medicine that is swallowed, بَلُوع. A summary, وَجِيز – إِيجَاز. An evening —, غَبُوق. Of —, drawing, جَارّ. *For other meanings see under* Draft, *n.*

Draught-horse, *n.* حِصَانٌ جَارٌّ – مَطِيَّة *pl.* مَطَايَا.

Draughtsman, *n.* A piece at checkers, حَجَرَةُ ٱلدَّامَةِ. A designer, رَسَّام – مُصَوِّر.

Draw, *v.t.* To drag, جَلَبَ – سَحَبَ – اِخْتَلَجَ – خَلَجَ – جَرَّ – جَذَبَ. To inhale, as of smoke, شَرِبَ. To suck, مَصَّ – رَضِعَ. To attract, جَذَبَ – جَلَبَ. To describe, وَصَفَ *aor.* يَصِفُ. To delineate, صَوَّرَ – رَسَمَ. To derive from, جَلَبَ-مِن – حَصَّلَ. To gain, اِكْتَسَبَ – رَبِحَ. To obtain, حَصَّلَ – اِجْتَنَى. To —, as of water, اِسْتَقَى. To —, as from a barrel, أَخْرَجَ-مِن. To entice, أَضَلَّ – جَلَبَ. To — a sword, سَلَّ ٱلسَّيْفَ. To — blood, أَخَذَ مِن-دَمًا – فَصَدَ. To —, as of a curtain, to let down, أَسْبَلَ – سَجَفَ – أَسْجَفَ – فَرَضَ; to open it, فَتَحَ – شَالَ-عَن – شَدَّ. To — money from, أَخَذَ (or تَسَلَّمَ) فُلُوسًا مِن. To —, to sink into the water, اِغْتَرَفَ – غَرِقَ مَآءً.

To draw along, جَرَّ – سَحَبَ.

To draw aside, to take apart, أَخَذَ-مِن – أَخْلَى (or اِسْتَخْلَى) بِ بَيْنَ. To cause to err, تَوَّهَ – أَضَلَّ.

To draw away, to disengage, فَكَّ-مِن – أَعْتَقَ-مِن. To lead astray, طَوَّحَ – تَيَّهَ – أَغْرَ – اِجْتَالَ – أَضَلَّ.

To draw back, to prevent, حَصَرَ – أَمْسَكَ. To draw behind, جَلَبَ-إِلَى وَرَآءِ – خَلَّفَ – أَخْلَفَ. To draw back from, as through cowardice, خَامَ عَن. They drew back, through cowardice, in the fight, خَامُوا فِي ٱلْقِتَالِ.

To draw down, to cause to come down, أَنْزَلَ – نَزَّلَ. To cause to fall upon, جَلَبَ عَلَى; as of a curtain, أَسْجَفَ – أَسْبَلَ.

To draw forth, to make to come out, أَخْرَجَ. To pull out, as of a sword or dagger, أَسْلَتَ. To spread out, بَسَطَ – نَشَرَ.

To draw from, as an enemy from a position, by stratagem, especially by a feigned retreat, اِسْتَطْرَدَ لَهُ.

To draw in, to make to enter, أَدْخَلَ. To contract, قَصَّرَ – ضَيَّقَ – شَدَّ. To inveigle, جَوَّنَ – غَشَّشَ – حَاوَلَ. To restrain, أَمْسَكَ – عَوَّقَ-عَن – عَكَفَ-عَن – عَكَّ-عَن.

To draw off, as of shoes, *etc.*, قَلَعَ – خَلَعَ. To pull aside, جَنَّبَ. To print, طَبَعَ. To take out of, as from a barrel, اِسْتَخْرَجَ – أَخْرَجَ. To draw off, as by distillation, صَعَّدَ – أَخْرَجَ. To draw off the attention of one from, شَغَلَ-عَن – أَلْهَى-عَن – سَهَّى-مِن.

To draw on, as of clothes, لَبِسَ. To occasion, سَبَّبَ – صَارَ – صَارَ عِلَّةً ل – سَبَبًا ل.

To draw out, as of a tooth, قَلَعَ; as of a thorn, نَقَشَ – اِنْتَقَشَ. To pull out of, أَخْرَجَ. To make a rough sketch, سَوَّدَ. To delineate, describe, رَسَمَ – وَصَفَ *aor.* يَصِفُ. To make to unfold, to talk of, كَشَفَ-عَن – حَمَلَ-عَلَى ٱلْبَقَاقِ – جَعَلَ-يُبَقْبِقُ. To draw out, to fish out, as from the sea, اِصْطَادَ. To pick out, نَقَّى. To select, appropriate, اِتَّخَذَ ل. To muster, as of soldiers, جَمَّعَ – حَشَدَ – صَفَّفَ. To prolong, as of time, طَوَّلَ; of speech, أَطَالَ ٱلْكَلَامَ. To draw out, as drink for guests, *etc.*, اِسْتَقَى. To draw out the soul to, أَنْفَقَ نَفْسَهُ ل.

To draw over, to make to pass over, عَبَّرَ – أَقْطَعَ. To persuade to, حَمَلَ-عَلَى – أَغْرَى-بِ. To convert to an opinion, هَدَى – رَدَّ-إِلَى.

To draw or sew together, خَيَّطَ. To assemble, حَشَدَ – جَمَّعَ. To combine, to join, ضَمَّ – وَصَّلَ.

To draw up, as in a bucket, نَدَلَ-مِن – اِسْتَقَى. To form into line, صَفَّ – صَفَّفَ – أَقَامَهُمْ صَفًّا. To draw up, to formulate, of a document, *etc.*, نَصَّ. To make to stop, as carriages, *etc.*, وَقَّفَ – أَوْقَفَ. To call to account, طَالَبَ – حَاسَبَ. To indite, شَرَطَ: he drew up the treaty, شَرَطَ ٱلْمُعَاهَدَةَ. To be drawn up, as into line, تَصَفَّفَ – اِصْطَفَّ: a body of soldiers was drawn up for him, اِصْطَفَّتْ لَهُ فِرْقَةٌ مِنَ ٱلْعَسَاكِرِ. To haul on land, بَلَّطَ – شَطَّطَ – سَحَبَ-إِلَى ٱلْبَرِّ. To organize, رَتَّبَ – رَكَّبَ – أَنْشَأَ. Drawn up, formulated,

مَنْصُوص. The treaty which was drawn up between ..., المُعاهَدَةُ ٱلَّتِى أُبْرِمَتْ بَيْنَ. *For to* Delineate, Describe, *see under* To draw out.

Draw, *v.i.* To pull or be pulled, إِنْسَحَبَ ـ إِنْجَرَّ ـ إِنْجَذَبَ. To practise drawing, صَوَّرَ ـ رَسَمَ. To —, as a blister, إِشْتَغَلَ ـ عَمِلَ فِى ـ أَخَذَ فِى ـ جَذَبَ ـ مَصَّ ـ جَلَبَ. To —, as a chimney, fire, تَوَقَّدَ سَرِيعًا ـ إِشْتَعَلَ جَيِّدًا.

To draw back, to go behind, تَأَخَّرَ ـ تَخَلَّفَ; aside, إِجْتَنَبَ.

To fail of, قَصَّرَ عَن ـ تَخَلَّفَ عَن ـ تَقَصَّرَ فِى. To retrograde, as from the truth, *etc.*, مَالَ عَن. To feel less interest in, تَرَاخَى عَن. To retreat, تَقَهْقَرَ.

To draw near, as of time, إِقْتَرَبَ ـ حَانَ. To approach, أَقْبَلَ ـ إِقْتَرَبَ مِن ـ تَقَدَّمَ إِلَى ـ دَنَا مِن ـ عَلَى.

To draw off, to retire, إِنْصَرَفَ ـ إِجْتَنَبَ ـ تَجَنَّبَ. To cease to participate in, رَفَعَ يَدَهُ مِن ـ تَجَنَّبَ.

To draw on, to approach; *see supra* To draw near.

To draw one's self in, إِنْدَسَّ; of a snail, *etc.*, into its shell, قَبَعَ.

To draw one's self up, as with pride, شَمَخَ ـ أَشْمَخَ بِأَنْفِهِ.

To draw together, to close up, as of a wound, ضَمَّ ـ خَتَمَ ـ تَقَبَّضَ ـ طَابَ; of a flower, طَبَّقَ ـ قَبَعَ. To contract, إِنْقَبَضَ. To get on well, to agree, together, of many, إِتَّفَقُوا ـ أَحْسَنُوا ٱلسُّكْنَى مَعًا ـ سَكَنُوا مَعًا بِوَفْقٍ ـ سَكَنُوا مَعًا.

To draw up, to stop, وَقَفَ *aor.* يَقِفُ.

Draw, *n.* As of fish, صَيْدَة ـ صَيْد.

Drawable, *a.* That may be dragged, يَنْجَرُّ. Payable by ..., as a cheque, يُدْفَعُ مَبْلَغُ ٱلْحَوالَةِ مِنْ فُلَانٍ. That may be sketched, مِمَّا يُتَصَوَّرُ.

Drawback, *n.* A defect, want, نُقْصَان ـ حَاجَة ـ حَوْبَة. Discount, إِسْقَاط. Refunded, as of a duty, إِسْقَاط ـ سَمَاح.

Drawbridge, *n.* قَنْطَرَةٌ تُفْتَحُ وَتُغْلَقُ ـ جِسْرٌ يُرْفَعُ وَيُوضَعُ.

Drawee, *n.* المَسْحُوبُ عَلَيْهِ ـ دَافِعُ ٱلْحَوالَةِ ـ المُحَوَّلُ عَلَيْهِ.

Drawer, *n.* Of a bill, صَاحِبُ ٱلْحَوالَةِ. One who draws drinks, مُسْتَقِى; of water, سَاقِى مَآءٍ ـ مُسْتَقِى مَآءٍ. A —, as of a bureau, دَرَجَة *pl.* أَدْرَاج *or* دَرَج. A chest of drawers, صِوان *pl.* أَصْوِنَة. A draughtsman, رَسَّام ـ مُصَوِّر. Drawers, under-trousers, لِبَاس تَحْتَانِىّ ـ سَرَاوِيل.

Drawing, *n.* A pulling, جَرّ ـ جَذْب ـ سَحْب. A sketching, تَرْسِيم ـ تَصْوِير. A picture, رَسْم *pl.* رُسُوم ـ صُورَة *pl.* صُوَر *or* تَصَاوِير. Drawing, as of bonds to be paid off, إِقْتِرَاع *pl.* إِقْتِرَاعَات.

Drawing, *a.* Pulling, جَارّ. A good — grate, مِيقَاد.

Drawing-master, *n.* مُعَلِّمُ ٱلرَّسْمِ.

Drawing-room, *n.* صَالُون ـ بَيْتُ ٱلْقُعُودِ ـ بَيْتُ ٱلدِّيوَانِ.

Drawl, *v.i.* قَرْتَنَ ـ إِهْتَمَسَ فِى كَلَامِهِ ـ أَبَدَّ مَنْطِقَهُ ـ قَطَّعَ كَلَامَهُ.

Drawn, *a.* Equal, قِرْن *pl.* أَقْرَان ـ مُسَاوٍ ـ مُسْتَوٍ. Moved aside, مُتَجَنَّب. Melted, مُذَاب ـ مُذَوَّب. A — battle, قِتَال لَا يُعْرَفُ مِنْهُ ٱلْغَالِبُ مِنَ ٱلْمَغْلُوبِ ـ غَيْرُ قَاطِعٍ. A — game, سَوَآء ـ صِحَّة مِنَ ٱلْجِهَتَيْنِ.

Draw-plate, *n.* مِسْحَب ـ مِسْفَن ـ سَفَن ـ طَرِيدَة. To pass through a —, سَلَكَ ٱلطَّرِيدَةَ.

Draw-well, *n.* بِئْر *pl.* أَبْيَار.

Dray, *n.* }
Dray-cart, } عَرَبِيَّةٌ لِنَقْلِ ٱلْبَضَائِعِ ٱلثَّقِيلَةِ.

Dray-horse, *n.* بِرْذَوْن *pl.* بَرَاذِين ـ حِصَان جَارّ.

Drayman, *n.* سَائِقُ عَرَبِيَّةِ ٱلْبَضَائِعِ ٱلثَّقِيلَةِ.

Drazel, *n.* *See* Drab, *n.*

Dread, *n.* Great fear, خَشَاة ـ خَشْيَان ـ جَفْلَة ـ دَهْشَة ـ مَرْعَبَة ـ تَدْهِيش ـ مَخُوف ـ خَوْف ـ رُعْب. A cause of —, مَرْعَبَة.

Dread, *a.* }
Dreadful, } هَائِل ـ مُهَوِّل ـ مُرْعِب ـ فَظِيع ـ مُخِيف. A — occurrence, مُفْظِع. A —, horrifying, thing, هِيَلَة. How — it is! مَا أَهْوَلَهُ.

Dread, *v.i.* أَشْفَقَ ـ خَشِىَ مِن ـ تَخَشَّى ـ خَشِىَ ـ خَافَ ـ تَخَوَّفَ ـ فَزِعَ مِن. This is what I most — for you, أَخْوَفُ مَا أَخَافُ عَلَيْكُمْ كَذَا.

Dreaded, *a.* مُهَوَّل ـ مَخُوف. A — road, طَرِيقٌ مَخُوفٌ. A — thing, أَمْرٌ مَخُوفٌ.

Dreadfully, *ad.* Fearfully, هَوْلًا ـ فَظَاعَةً ـ تَخْوِيفًا. Excessively, كَثِيرًا ـ لِلْغَايَةِ.

Dreadfulness, *n.* *See* Dread, *n.*

Dreadless, *a.* سَنْدَرِىّ ـ نَجِيد ـ جَسُور ـ شُجَاع.

Dreadnaught, *n.* A cloth with long pile, جُوخٌ طَوِيلُ ٱلزِّغْبِرِ ـ سُتْرَةٌ طَوِيلَةُ ٱلزِّغْبِرِ. A coat made of —, لِبَاد ـ جُوخ جِنْفَاصِى ـ سُتْرَةٌ جِنْفَاصِى.

Dream, *n.* As in sleep, رُؤْيَا *pl.* رُؤًى ـ حُلْم *pl.* أَحْلَام ـ مَنَام *pl.* مَنَامَات. An idle fancy, وَهْم *pl.* أَوْهَام ـ تَوَهُّم ـ وَهْمِيَّة *pl.* وَهْمِيَّات. He saw in a —, نَظَرَ فِى حُلْمٍ. And, lo! it was a —, وَإِذَا هُوَ حُلْمٌ.

Dream, *v.i.* To think in sleep, حَلَمَ ـ إِحْتَلَمَ. To fancy, تَوَهَّمَ ـ تَخَيَّلَ ـ تَصَوَّرَ. I dreamt good dreams of thee, رَأَيْتُ عَنْكَ رُؤًى حَسَنَةً.

Dream, *v.t.* حَلَمَ بِ or عَن — تَحَلَّمَ عَن — رَأَى مَنَامًا. He dreamt a —, حَلَمَ حُلْمًا.

Dreamer, *n.* One who dreams, مُحْتَلِم — حَالِم — حِلْمَان. A visionary, مُخَرِّف — صَاحِبُ ٱلْأَحْلَام. An idler, كَسْلَان *pl.* كَسَالَى.

Dreamful, *a.* *See* Dreamy, *a.*

Dreamless, *a.* غَيْرُ حَالِم — عَدِيمُ ٱلْأَحْلَام.

Dreamy, *a.* Full of dreams, كَثِيرُ ٱلْأَحْلَام. Visionary, خَارِف — مُهَوِّس — خَرْفَان. *See also* Moody, *a.*

Drear, *a.* } مُسْتَوْحِش — مُغِمّ — مُحْزِن — كَئِيب. *See also*
Dreary, } Dismal, Cheerless, *a.*

Drearily, *ad.* بِوَحْشَةٍ — بِحَوْبَةٍ.

Dreariness, *n.* خَوْبَة — وَحْشَة — حُزْن — غُدْم.

Dredge, *n.* A net, شَبَكَة — مِصْيَدَة. A scoop for removing sand or mud, مِجْرَفَة *pl.* مَجَارِف ; (*vulg.* جُرَّافَة *pl.* جَرَارِيف).

Dredge, *v.t.* To sprinkle flour over, رَشَّ — رَشَّ بِدَقِيقٍ دَقِيقًا عَلَى. To catch with a net, إِصْطَادَ بِشَبَكَةٍ. To remove with a dredge, جَرَفَ. Dredging flour, لُوَاث — لُوَاثَة.

Dredger, *n.* One who fishes with a net, صَيَّادٌ بِشَبَكَةٍ. One who removes sand, شَيَّالٌ بِمِجْرَفَةٍ. *See also* Dredge, *n.*

Dredging-box, *n.* مِرَشَّةُ ٱلدَّقِيقِ — مِرَشَّةُ ٱللُّوَاثِ.

Dredging-machine, *n.* جُرَّافَة *vulg.* كَرَّاكَة.

Dregginess, *n.* *See* Dregs, *n.*

Dreggy, *a.* عَكِر — مُتَرَسِّب — كَدِير. To be —, عَكِرَ. To make —, أَعْكَرَ.

Dregs, *n.* رُسُوب — دُرْدِيّ — حُثَالَة — حُفَالَة — ثُفْل — نَجِير طِحْل. Dregs of wine, عَكَرُ (or طِينُ) ٱلنَّبِيذِ — نِطْل ; of oil, عَكَر ٱلزَّيْت. The — of the people, أَسْقَاط — ٱلْأَوْبَاش — ٱلسَّفِلَة أَرَاذِلُ ٱلنَّاسِ — ٱلنَّاس.

Drench, *v.t.* To wet thoroughly, بَلَّ — خَضَّلَ — عَمَّ بِٱلْمَاءِ. To purge violently, أَسْهَلَ (or أَمْشَى) بَطْنَهُ لِلْغَايَةِ.

Drench, *n.* A purge, جُلَّاب — شَرْبَة — دَوَاءٌ مُسْهِل. A wetting, إِبْتِلَال — بَلَّة.

Dress, *n.* Clothing, مَلْبُوس — لُبُوس — لِبْس *pl.* زِيّ — لِبَاس — مَلْبَس — كِسْوَة — ثِيَاب. A suit, as of clothes, حُلَّة — طَقْم. A lady's gown, فُسْطَان *pl.* فَسَاطِين ; a lady's outer robe, قِنْبَاز — تَخْلِيلَة. Fine clothes, خِلَعٌ فَاخِرَة — زِينَة. Taste, as in —, مَلَابِس — مَلْبُوس — هِنْدَام. Official or full —, مَلَابِس رَسْمِيَّة — ٱلْخِدْمَةِ ٱلرَّسْمِيَّةِ. Court —, مَلَابِسُ ٱلْحُضُورِ أَمَامَ ٱلْمَلِكِ. A low —, فُسْطَانٌ لَا يَسْتُرُ ٱلْعَوْرَةَ ٱلْمُخَفَّفَةَ (or ٱلْعُنُقَ وَٱلذِّرَاعَيْنِ) ; a high —, فُسْطَانٌ يَسْتُرُ ٱلْعَوْرَةَ ٱلْمُخَفَّفَةَ (or ٱلْعُنُقَ وَٱلذِّرَاعَيْنِ).

An every-day or working —, مَلْبُوس — مِيدَاعَة — فَضْلَة — فُضُل ٱلشُّغْلِ.

Dress, *v.t.* To clothe, أَلْبَسَ — لَبَّسَ — كَسَا — كَسَى بِ. To deck, حَسَّنَ — زَخْرَفَ — زَيَّنَ. To cook, طَبَخَ. To prepare, هَيَّأَ. To trim, هَنْدَمَ — أَصْلَحَ — سَرَّحَ. To work, manipulate, عَالَجَ. To —, make straight, as of a line of soldiers, صَفَّفَ — نَظَّمَ — سَوَّى. To —, of a wound, عَالَجَ — ضَمَدَ — أَسَا ٱلْجُرْحَ — يَأْسُو *aor.* دَاوَى ٱلْجُرْحَ. To curry a horse, سَاسَ ٱلْحِصَانَ — تَمَّرَ ٱلْحِصَانَ. To —, as of leather, دَبَغَ. To — hemp, نَفَشَ ٱلْقِنَّبَ. To —, of silk, طَبَخَ. To —, as a weaver his cloth with the sprinkling instrument, سَاجَ *aor.* يَسُوجُ — نَسِيجَهُ بِٱلْمِسْوَجَةِ. To — a salad, تَوَّبَلَ ٱلْبَقْلَةَ. To — up, to falsify, وَشَى *aor.* يَشِي. To — out, to adorn, زَيَّنَ. To — out a ship with flags, زَيَّنَ ٱلْمَرْكَبَ بِٱلْبَيَارِقِ. To — one's self, لَبِسَ — تَكَسَّى.

Dress, *v.i.* To come straight, تَنَظَّمَ — تَسَوَّى ; as of troops, إِصْطَفَّ. To — one's self with care, تَهَنْدَمَ فِي ٱلْمَلْبُوسِ.

Dresser, *n.* One who dresses much, غَنْدُور — لَبَّاس. A kitchen table, مَائِدَةُ ٱلْمَطْبَخِ. A — of wounds, آسِي ٱلْجُرُوحِ — مُدَاوِي ٱلْجُرُوحِ.

Dressing, *n.* The act of clothing, إِلْبَاس — إِكْسَاء ; of ornamenting, زَخْرَفَة — تَزْيِين. A trimming, تَصْلِيح — تَسْرِيح — هِنْدَام. A manipulating, مُعَالَجَة. A covering for a wound, مُدَاوَاةُ ٱلْجُرْحِ — مَرَاهِم *pl.* مَرْهَم — ضِمَاد. A liquid covering, شَرْبَة — دَهْنَة. A whipping, تَأْدِيب. Dressing, for cloth, سَوْج. Seasoning for food, تَوَابِل — أَبَازِير — فَحًا. Sauce, مَرَقَة. Curative treatment, مُعَالَجَة.

Dressing-case, *n.* شَرِيط *pl.* شَرَائِطُ — عَتِيدَة *pl.* عَتَائِدُ — بِشَاخْتَة آلَاتِ ٱلزِّينَةِ.

Dressing-gown, *n.* جُبَّةُ ٱلْبَيْتِ.

Dressing-room, *n.* حُجْرَةُ (or بَيْتُ) ٱللُّبْسِ.

Dressing-table, *n.* مَائِدَةٌ مَفْرُوشَةٌ عَلَيْهَا آلَاتُ ٱلزِّينَةِ.

Dress-maker, *n.* خَيَّاطَة *pl.* خَيَّاطَات.

Dressy, *a.* Dressing much, لَبَّاس. A — woman, إِمْرَأَةٌ صَائِرَةٌ خُصْلَةً وَعُنْقُودًا. Gaudy, لَامِع — جَلِيّ — بَاهٍ.

Dribble, *v.i.* To drop slowly, قَطَرَ — نَطَفَ. To slaver, رَالَ — جَرَى ٱلرُّوَالُ مِنْ فَمِهِ. He dribbled his urine, فَشْفَشَ — أَشْغَى بِبَوْلِهِ — بِبَوْلِهِ. The dribbling of urine, شَغًا — تَشْغِيَة.

Driblet, *n.* حُتّ — هُتَامَة — دُقَاقَة — دُقَاق — يَسِير — حِتَّة *pl.* حِتَت. In driblets, شَيْئًا فَشَيْئًا.

Dried, *a.* Free from moisture, مُنَشَّف. Dried up, as by the sun, يابِس ـ شَرْيَز ـ شَزٌّ. Withered, مَجْفُوف.

Drier, *n.* *See* Dryer, *n.*

Drift, *n.* Purpose, aim, مَطْلُوب ـ غَرَض ـ مَقْصَد ـ مَقْصُود. Impulse, حَثٌّ. Meaning, import, فَحْوَى *pl.* فَحاوِى ـ مَنْحًا ـ مَضْمُون. A portion of land or sand which the water has carried away, تَيْهُور ـ جُرُف. Drift, rubbish, قَشِيش ـ قُشاش. A — of snow, كُومَة ثَلْج. Drift, rubble, لُقاطَة ـ أَنْلَم ـ أَنْلَب. The passage between shafts in a mine, مَسْلَك بَيْنَ ٱلنَّواقِيرِ فِى مَعْدِنٍ.

Drift, *v.t.* To drive into heaps, رَكَمَ ² ـ كَوَّم. To urge, أَلَتَّ ـ ساقَ ² ـ حَرَّضَ ـ عَلَى ـ أَنْفَس ـ إِسْتَفَزَّ ـ عَلَى.

Drift, *v.i.* To float, عامَ ². To accumulate in heaps, إِرْتَكَمَ ـ تَكَوَّمَ ـ تَراكَمَ.

Drift-wood, *n.* حَطَبٌ عائِمٌ عَلَى وَجْهِ ـ قُشاشُ ٱلْماءِ ـ أَتِيُّ ٱلْماءِ.

Drill, *n.* A tool for boring, مِخْراز ـ بَرِّيمَة ـ مِثْقَب. A furrow, خَطٌّ *pl.* خُطُوط ـ خُدَّة *pl.* خُدَد. Exercise, تَعْلِيم. Military —, تَمْرِينٌ عَلَى ٱلْأُصُولِ ٱلْعَسْكَرِيَّةِ ـ تَعْلِيمُ ٱلْعَسْكَرِ. The stuff, قُماش مِن كَتّان.

Drill, *v.t.* To bore, خَرَقَ ـ ² ـ خَزَمَ ـ ² ـ خَرَمَ ـ ² ـ نَقَبَ ². To exercise, عَلَّمَ; of troops, مَرَّنَ ـ عَلَى ٱلْأُصُولِ ٱلْعَسْكَرِيَّةِ.

Drill, *v.i.* To sow in furrows, زَرَعَ خُطُوطًا ². To flow, سَرَبَ ².

Drill-box, *n.* An instrument for sowing seeds, مِذْرَة.

Drill-plough, *n.* مِهْرَب.

Drink, *n.* شُرُوب ـ أَشْرِبَة *pl.* شَراب ـ شَرِيب. Drinks, أَشْرِبَة. One —, شَرْبَة. To take a — of, شَرِبَ شَرْبَةً مِن ـ عَرِقَ مِن.

Drink, *v.t.* شَرِبَ ². To —, of a bird, نَغَبَ ـ ². To — long draughts, عَبَّ ². To — small quantities at a time, to sip, تَجَرَّعَ ـ تَرَمَّقَ ـ تَمَزَّزَ ـ مَزَّ ². To — eagerly, غَمَجَ ـ ². To — hard, أَكْثَرَ ٱلشُّرْب. To — in turn with, فاوَضَ ـ فِى ٱلشُّرْب. To — with or to one, شارَبَ. To — to one, شَرِبَ ـ شَرِبَ لَهُ مُحَبَّةً فِيهِ. To absorb, نَشَّفَ ـ تَشَرَّبَ. To swallow, بَلَعَ ـ. To — off or up, تَمَعَ ـ شَرِبَهُ كُلَّهُ ـ إِقْتَمَعَ ـ تَمَعَ. To give another to —, أَشْرَبَ ـ شَرَّبَ ـ أَسْقَى ـ سَقَى.

Drink, *v.i.* To — to excess, أَكْثَرَ ٱلشُّرْب ـ سَكِرَ. It drinks flat, شَرْبَةٌ بارِدٌ ـ شُرْبُهُ مَسِيخ. They drank round, of many, شَرِبُوا بِٱلدَّوْر.

Drinkable, *a.* شَرِيب ـ مَشْرُوبِىّ.

Drinker, *n.* One who drinks much, شَرّاب ـ شارِب. A drunkard, سِكِّير ـ شَرّاب.

Drinking, *n.* The act of —, شُرْب. Intoxication, سَكْرَة. A — room, مَشْرَب. A bout of —, سَكْرَة.

Drinking-horn, *n.* قَدَح *pl.* أَقْداح ـ كَأْس ـ كاسَة ـ مِشْرَبَة.

Drip, *v.i.* To fall in drops, قَطَرَ ² ـ تَقَطَّرَ ـ تَنَقَّطَ. To cause to —, قَطَّرَ ـ أَنْقَطَ ـ أَقْطَرَ. To —, as of blood from a sword, شَلْشَلَ بِ ـ تَشَلْشَلَ بِ.

Drip, *n.* A drop, نُقْطَة ـ قَطْرَة. The cornice over a door, سَقِيفَة ـ كِنَّة.

Dripping, *n.* Dripping fat, عُرام ـ عَرْم ـ جَمِيل ـ جُمالَة ـ ٱلدُّهْنُ ٱلْمُتَقَطِّرُ مِنَ ٱللَّحْمِ ٱلْمَشْوِىّ.

Dripping-pan, *n.* صَحْنٌ لِلْجُمالَةِ ـ صَحْنٌ لِلْعُرام.

Drip-stone, *n.* وِصْفاةٌ لِلْماءِ.

Drive, *n.* An excursion in a carriage, شَمُّ ٱلْهَواءِ ـ سَيْرٌ فِى عَرَبِيَّةٍ (or رِياضَةٌ) فِى عَرَبِيَّةٍ. The place of driving, مَسِيرُ ٱلْعَرَبِيّات ـ مُتَنَزَّهُ ٱلْعَرَبِيّات.

Drive, *v.t.* To force by pressure, دَسَرَ ² ـ دَفَرَ ² ـ دَفَعَ ـ دَفَشَ ². To chase, طَرَدَ ² ـ رَوَّحَ ـ ساقَ ². To urge to, حَرَّضَ ـ عَلَى ـ عَجَّلَ ـ أَسْرَعَ ـ أَعْجَلَ. To hurry, حَرَّكَ ـ عَلَى ـ حَثَّ ² ـ عَلَى. To —, as of beasts, كَدَسَ ـ كَدَشَ ـ كَدْكَدَ ـ ساقَ ²; of sheep, قَتَّ ²; of a carriage, ساقَ ٱلْعَرَبانَةَ ²; of a nail, سَمَّرَ. To make to walk on, مَشَّى. To — one to do a thing, أَضْطَرَّ ـ إِلَى ـ أَلْزَمَ ـ بِ. To be driven, impelled, تَدافَعَ. To be driven to do, أُلْزِمَ بِ ـ أُضْطُرَّ إِلَى. I am driven to ..., أَنا مُدْفَعٌ إِلَى ـ أَنا مُضْطَرٌّ إِلَى.

To drive a bargain with, شارَطَ.

To drive away, to disperse, بَثَّ ² ـ شَرَّدَ; as wind the clouds, ساقَ ²; as flies, and such like, طَرَدَ ² ـ كَشَّ ² ـ كَشْكَشَ; of birds, زَجَرَ ². To turn off, صَرَفَ ـ عَن ـ طَرَدَ ² ـ نَفَى ـ دَشَّرَ. To check, زَجَرَ ². The wind drove away the clouds, سافَتِ ٱلرِّيحُ ٱلسَّحاب. Driven away flying, شَرِيدٌ طَرِيدٌ.

To drive back, to make to return, رَجَّعَ ـ رَدَّ ².

To drive forward, زَجَى ـ أَزْجَى.

To drive hard, as of horses, قَنَّعَ ـ قَنْزَعَ.

To drive in, to make to enter, أَدْخَلَ; of a nail, سَمَّرَ. He drove in the tent-peg, ضَرَبَ ٱلْوَتَد ـ.

To drive on, to make to walk on, مَشَّى. To urge forward, ساقَ ².

To drive out, to expel, طَرَدَ ² ـ أَخْرَجَ. To put away, باعَدَ.

Drive, *v.i.* To be forced along, إِنْطَلَقَ ـ إِنْدَفَعَ. To be urged, إِنْساقَ ـ إِحْتَثَّ. To direct, as of horses, ساقَ ². To — on, to carry on, stick to, أَدْمَنَ عَلَى ـ إِسْتَمَرَّ عَلَى ـ جَدَّ فِى ² ـ لَبِعَ ².

To —, as a carriage, over, ساقَ ٱلْعَرَبانَةَ عَلَى ². To tend to, مالَ إِلَى – يَؤُولُ aor. آلَ إِلَى. What are you driving at? ماذا مَضْمُونُكَ – غايَتُكَ. To let —, let go, سَيَّبَ.

Drivel, *v.i.* To slaver, رَالَ – رَوَّلَ – جَرَى ٱلرُّوالُ مِنْ فَمِهِ. To dote, فَنِدَ – أَفْنَدَ – أَهْتَرَ. To drop, تَنَقَّطَ – تَقَطَّرَ.

Drivel, *n.* Slaver, لُعاب – رُوال. A simpleton; *see* Driveller, *n.*

Driveller, *n.* مَجْنُون – عَبِيط – أَبْلَهُ – مُهْتِر.

Driver, *n.* سَوّاق – سائِق { A camel —, جَمّال; a donkey —, حَمّار; a sheep —, غَنّام.

Drizzle, *v.t.* طَشَّ ² – رَشَّ ².

Drizzle, *v.i.* نَفْنَفَ ٱلْمَطَرُ – رَشَّتِ ٱلسَّماءُ ² – نَضَّ ٱلْمَطَرُ.

Drizzle, *n.* رَذاذ – نَفْنُوف – نَفْناف – رَشَّة – طَشِيش – طَشّ.

Drizzling, *a.* طَلّ – رَذاذ. A — rain, مُنَفْنِف – راشّ – ناضّ.

Droll, *n.* } نُكات – أَهْبَل – هَزِل – مُضْحِك. A — speech,
Droll, *a.* } نُكْتَة pl. نُكَت.

Drollery, *n.* تَهْذار – مُزاح – هُزالَة – مَسْخَرَة.

Drogeman, *n.* *See* Dragoman, *n.*

Dromedary, *n.* جَمَلٌ هِيرِيٌّ – جَمّاز – هُجُن pl. هَجِين. A courier mounted on a —, هَجّان.

Drone, *n.* The male bee, ذَكَرُ ٱلنَّحْلِ. A sluggard, عَفْشَل – كِسْلان – وَنّاب. A hum, طَنِين – رَنِين – رَنّ – دَنْدَنَة – غُنان.

Drone, *v.i.* To idle, تَكاسَلَ – كَسِلَ.

Dronish, *a.* Idle, كِسْلان – عَفْشَل.

Droop, *v.i.* To languish, تَخَنَّثَ – خَنِثَ – وَنَى aor. يَنِي – تَوانَى. To —, from disease, ضَنِيَ. To —, of a flower, ذَبَلَ ². To pine with grief, تَأَسَّفَ – إِكْتَرَبَ – مَرِضَ حُزْنًا. To grow weak, ضَعُفَ ².

Drooping, *a.* Languishing, مُتَوانٍ – خَنِث – وانٍ; as of a plant, ذابِل – ذَبِل. Pining, مُتَأَسِّف – مُكْتَرِب.

Droopingly, *ad.* بِتَوانٍ – بِكَلالٍ – بِخَنَثٍ.

Drop, *n.* A —, of fluid, نُقْطَة pl. نُقَط – قَطْرَة pl. قَطَرات. Drop, of a tear, دَمْعَة pl. دُمُوع. An ear-ring, قُرْط pl. قُرُوط. The — of a gallows, فَخُّ ٱلْمِشْنَقَةِ. Drop by —, قَطْرَةً قَطْرَةً; little by little, شَيْئًا فَشَيْئًا.

Drop, *v.t.* To let fall in drops, قَطَّرَ – نَقَّطَ. To let fall, سَاقَطَ – أَسْقَطَ – وَقَّعَ – طَرَحَ. To let go, تَرَكَ ² – تَخَلَّى عَن. To leave out, أَسْقَطَ. To desist, إِنْقَطَعَ عَن – زالَ عَن ² – كَفَّ عَن ². To — anchor, طَرَحَ ٱلْأَنْجَرَ – رَمَى ٱلْمِرْساةَ. She dropped a courtesy to, خَرَّتْ لِ-تَحِيَّةً.

Drop, *v.i.* To fall in drops, قَطَرَ ² – نَطَفَ ² – تَنَقَّطَ – تَقَطَّرَ.

To fall, وَقَعَ aor. يَقَعُ – سَقَطَ ². To — or fall from a higher to a lower place, خَرَّ ². To sink out of notice, إِنْقَرَضَ – نُسِيَ. To — or fall down dead, سَقَطَ بَغْتَةً مَيِّتًا ² – إِضْمَحَلَّ. To — down, go lower, نَزَلَ. To — in, to enter, دَخَلَ ². To — off, to become less, إِنْتَقَصَ – نَقَصَ ²; in number, قَلَّ; to pass away, زالَ ². To — astern, إِنْتَقَلَ (or) تَخَلَّفَ إِلَى مُؤَخَّرِ ٱلْمَرْكَبِ.

Dropping, *n.* تَقَطُّر – قَطْر – قَطَران. Droppings, قُطارَة.

Dropping, *a.* Falling in drops, قاطِر; in many drops, مِقْطار.

Drop-scene, *n.* سِتارَةُ ٱلْمَلْعَبِ فِي تِياترو.

Dropserene, *n.* The disease of the eye, كُمْنَة.

Dropsical, *n.* مُحْتَبِن – مَحْبُون – أَحْبَنُ fem. حَبْناءُ ² – حَبِين – مُسْتَسْقٍ.

Dropsicalness, *n.* } إِسْتِسْقاءٌ ² – حَبَن. To have the —, حَبِنَ –
Dropsy, } إِسْتَسْقَى – إِحْتَبَنَ. He had — in the belly, سَقِيَ بَطْنُهُ. Having — in the belly, بَطْنٌ سَقٍ. A man having the —, إِنْسانٌ مُسْتَسْقٍ.

Dross, *n.* } Scum of metals, رَغْوَةُ ٱلْمَعادِنِ – خَبَث. Rust,
Drossiness, } صَدأ. Refuse, حُثالَة – سُقاطَة – خُشارَة.

Drossy, *a.* كَثِيرُ ٱلرَّغْوَةِ – خَبِثِيّ.

Drought, *n.* Want of rain, قَحْط – جَدْب.

Droughty, *a.* عَطْشان – ناشِف. Thirsty, مُسَوِّف – ساهِف – عَطْشان.

Drove, *n.* A herd, قَطِيع – قَشِيشَة – قَشاشَة – قِطاع pl. أَقْطاع and قَطِيع – عُمُومَة – زَحْمَة – زَحْم. A crowd, as of people, سِرْب pl. أَسْراب; a moving crowd, سائِرَة – لَبِيكَة.

Drover, *n.* سَوّاق – سائِق.

Drown, *v.t.* To suffocate in water, غَرَّقَ – أَغْرَقَ. To cover with water, غَطَّا عَلَى – بِٱلْماءِ – غَمَرَ بِٱلْماءِ ².

Drown, *v.i.* To be suffocated in water, غَرِقَ – إِسْتَغْرَقَ.

Drowned, غَرِيق – غارِق – غَرِق. To be drowned, absorbed, in, فاضَ – إِنْغَمَرَ – إِنْهَمَكَ فِي. To be overflowed, إِنْغَمَرَ. Death by drowning, مَوْتُ ٱلْغَمَرِ. Safe from drowning, آمِنٌ مِنَ ٱلْغَرَقِ. He saved a drowning man, أَنْجَى غَرِيقًا.

Drowse, *v.i.* *See to* Doze, *v.i.*

Drowsily, *ad.* Sleepily, بِنُعاسٍ. Sluggishly, بِتَهامُلٍ – بِكَسَلٍ – بِلا مُبالاةٍ.

Drowsiness, *n.* Sleepiness, نُعاس – كَرَى – خَفَقان – ثِقَل. Laziness, كَسَل. The overpowering influence of —, غَيْطَلَة.

Drowsy, *a.* Sleepy, ناعِس – نَعْسان – كَرْيان – خافِق. Lulling,

مُهَدًى — مُهْدِئٌ. Stupid, بَلِيد — ثَقِيلُ ٱلدَّمِ. To be —, sleepy, نَعَسَ ـُ. *See also* Sleepy, *a.*

Drub, *n.* ضَرْب — وَكْز — كَبْسَة.

Drub, *v.t.* ضَرَبَ — وَكَزَ *aor.* يَكِزُ — سَوَّطَ — سَلَخَ ـَ ـُ.

Drubbing, *n.* ضَرْبُ عَصًا — تَرْبِيَة.

Drudge, *v.i.* To labour in a mean office, سَفَلَ فِي ٱلخِدْمَةِ ـُ — كَانَ مِنْ أَحْقَرِ ٱلخَدَّامِينَ — إِشْتَغَلَ شُغْلَ ٱلذُّلِّ. To toil hard in . . . , كَدَّ فِي ـُ.

Drudge, *n.* خَادِمُ ٱلأَشْغَالِ ٱلدَّنِيئَةِ — مِنْ أَحْقَرِ ٱلخَدَّامِينَ — مِنْ أَسَافِلِ ٱلخَدَمِ.

Drudgery, *n.* خِدْمَةٌ دَنِيئَةٌ — شُغْلٌ حَقِيرٌ.

Drug, *n.* Of substances used in medicine, عَقَّار *pl.* عَقَاقِيرُ — دَوَآء — عِلَاج. An ingredient, جُزْءٌ مِن *pl.* أَجْزَآء. A thing slow of sale, مَتَاعٌ كَاسِدٌ — مَتَاعٌ لَا يُبَاعُ. Something deceptive, غِشّ. Drugs, paltry goods, سَقَطُ ٱلمَتَاعِ.

Drug, *v.t.* To administer drugs, عَالَجَ بِعِلَاجٍ — أَسْقَى دَوَآءً. He dosed, drugged, him, to excess, أَفْرَطَ فِي سَقْيِهِ ٱلأَدْوِيَةَ. To falsify, غَشَّ ـُ — وَشَى *aor.* يَشِي.

Drugget, *n.* مِسْح *pl.* مُسُوح — لَبَّاد — لِبْدَة.

Druggist, *n.* صَيْدَلَانِيٌّ *pl.* صَيَادِلَة — عَطَّار. The trade of a —, عِطَارَة.

Druid, *n.* كَاهِنٌ وَثَنِيٌّ مِنْ كَهَنَةِ ٱلإِنْكِلِيزِ ٱلقُدَمَآءِ *pl.* كَهَنَة.

Drum, *n.* دَبْدَبَة *pl.* دَبَادِب — طَبْل *pl.* طُبُول — تُرُمْبِيطَة. A small —, نَاقُور. A small box, عُلْبَة *pl.* عُلَب; a maker of such, مُعَلِّب. To beat, as of a —, قَرَعَ ـَ — دَبْدَبَ — طَبَّلَ — نَقَرَ — دَقَّ ٱلطَّبْلَ ـُ. The head or skin of the —, رَقَّةُ ٱلطَّبْلِ. The — of the ear, صِمَاخ.

Drum, *v.t.* To — out of a regiment, طَرَدَ مِنَ ٱلخِدْمَةِ ٱلعَسْكَرِيَّةِ ـُ بِدَقِّ ٱلطَّبْلِ إِهَانَةً لَهُ. *See also under* Drum, *n.*

Drum-major, *n.* مُقَدَّمُ ٱلطَّبَّالِينَ.

Drummer, *n.* طَبَّال *pl.* طَبَّالُونَ.

Drum-stick, *n.* مَلْوِينَة *pl.* مَلَاوِينَات; called in Egypt, زَخْمَة ٱلطُّرُمْبِيطَةِ. The — of a fowl, رِجْلُ ٱلطَّيْرِ ٱلمَطْبُوخَةِ دُونَ ٱلفَخْذِ.

Drunk, *a.* سَكِر — سَكْرَان *pl.* سُكَارَى; dead —, سَكِر *pl.* سَكَارَى; always —, سِكِّير. To be —, سَكِرَ ـَ. To make another —, سَكَّرَ. To be made —, as by wine, *etc.*, أَسْكَرَ. To pretend to be —, تَسَاكَرَ.

Drunkard, *n.* شَرَّاب — سِكِّير — سَكُور — سِكِّير *pl.* سَكَارَى.

Drunken, *a.* سَكْرَان. *See also* Drunk, *a.*

Drunkenness, *n.* سُكْر. A fit of —, سَكْرَة. Feigned —, تَسَاكُر. To recover from —, أَفَاقَ (or) إِسْتَفَاقَ مِنَ ٱلسُّكْرِ.

Druze, *a.* and *n.* دُرْزِيٌّ *pl.* دُرُوز.

Dry, *a.* Having no moisture, جَافّ — يَابِس — صَمِيل — صَامِل. Not rainy, قَسِيّ. Not juicy, غَيْرُ طَرِيّ — تَارِز. Thirsty, سَاهِف — عَاطِش — عَطْشَان. Insipid, عَدِيمُ ٱللَّذَّةِ — تَافِه. Void, عَارٍ — عَدِيم. Barren, جَرِد — غَيْرُ مُثْمِرٍ — عَاقِر. Uncivil, stiff, مُقَاطِع — بَارِد. Dry, of bread, يَابِس — نَاشّ — نَسَس; of herbs or herbage, جَفِيف. Anything that has been dried, جُفَاف. Separate what is — from what is damp thereof, إِعْزِلْ جُفَافَهُ مِنْ رَطْبِهِ. Dry bread, bread without anything to eat with it, عَيْشٌ حَافّ — قَفِير. He ate — bread, أَكَلَ خُبْزًا قَفَارًا ـُ. A — morsel, لُقْمَةٌ يَابِسَةٌ. A — wind, رِيحٌ لَافِحَةٌ. To have a — skin, صَوْمَلَ.

Dry, *v.t.* To free from moisture, يَبَّسَ — جَفَّفَ — نَشَّفَ. To hang out to dry, نَشَرَ ـُ — شَرَى ـِ — أَشَرَّ — شَرَّرَ. To suck up, تَشَرَّبَ.

Dry, *v.i.* To become free from moisture, جَفَّ ـِ — نَشَفَ ـَ — يَبِسَ *aor.* يَيْبَسُ and يَابَسُ — تَنَشَّفَ. To wither, as of the hand, *etc.*, عَقَمَ ـُ; as of grass, يَبِسَ *aor.* يَابَسُ. The waters were dried up from the land, قَلَّتِ ٱلمِيَاهُ مِنْ وَجْهِ ٱلأَرْضِ. The streams had dried up, قَدْ جَفَّتْ جَدَاوِلُ ٱلمِيَاهِ.

Dryad, *n.* جِنِّيَّة *pl.* جِنِّيَّات.

Dryer, *n.* مُجَفِّف — مُنَشِّف.

Dry-goods, *n.* أَمْتِعَةُ ٱلبَزَّازِ.

Dryly, *ad.* Coldly, بِبُرُودَةٍ. Severely, بِشِدَّةٍ — بِسَخَطٍ. Sarcastically, بِتَهَكُّمٍ — بِنُكْرٍ. Uncourteously, مِنْ غَيْرِ لَطَافَةٍ.

Dryness, *n.* Want of moisture, يُبُوسَة — جُفُوف. Thirst, جُوَاد — ظَمَآء — عَطَش — لَهَث. Drought, قَحْط. Want, as of ornament, *etc.*, عُرْيَة — تَعَرٍّ — عَدَم. Want of ardour, feeling, بُرُودَة — عَدَمُ حَاسِّيَّةٍ — مُرُوَّةٍ. Barrenness, يُبُوسَة — مُحُولَة — عُقْر.

Dry-nurse, *n.* حَاضِنَة.

Dry-rot, *n.* رِمَّة.

Dry-salter, *n.* One who deals in salted meats, بَيَّاعُ ٱلمَلُوحَةِ.

Dry-shod, *a.* جَافُّ ٱلأَقْدَامِ — غَيْرُ مُبَلَّلِ ٱلأَحْذِيَةِ.

Duad, *n.* إِتِّحَادُ ٱثْنَيْنِ — مُثَنًّى.

Dual, *a.* and *n.* مُثَنًّى. The act of making —, تَثْنِيَة.

Dualism, *n.* The doctrine of, ٱلإِثْنَيْنِيَّة — ٱلثَّنَوِيَّة.

Dualist, *a.* }
Dualistic, } ثَنَوِيّ — مُخْتَصّ بِٱلثَّنَوِيَّةِ.

Duality, *n.* إِثْنَيْنِيَّة.

Dub, v.t. To strike, ضَرَبَ. To confer, as a title, on, قَلَّدَ-بِ — وَجَّهَ-بِ — ... جَعَلَ-فِي رُتْبَةِ آلـ. To call or name, سَمَّى — سَمَّى-بِ. He dubbed him a knight, جَعَلَهُ كَوالِيرَ.

Dub, v.i. To make a quick noise by repeats, طَقْطَقَ.

Dubious, a. Uncertain, مُشْتَبِهٌ — تَحْتَ ٱلشَّكِّ. Confused, ambiguous, غَلِق — غامِض — مُلْتَبِس — مُشْكِل — مُبْهَم. A — affair, غَفِيَة. To render — to, شَبَّهَ-عَلَى — عَمَّى-عَلَى. *See also* Doubtful, a.

Dubiously, ad. مُتَوَهِّمًا — بِشَكٍّ — بِرَيْبٍ — بِرِيبَةٍ.

Dubiousness, n. غِمَّة — شُبْهَة. *See also* Doubt, n.

Dubitation, n. *See* Doubt, n.

Ducal, a. مُتَعَلِّقٌ بِإِمارَةِ ٱلْأُمَرَآءِ — إِمارَةُ ٱلدُّوكِ.

Ducat, n. A Venetian —, دُوكَةٌ pl. دُوكات. A —, بُنْدُقِيٌّ pl. بَنادِقَة. A Levant —, شَرِيفِيٌّ — مَحْبُوب pl. مَحابِيبُ.

Duchess, n. إِمْرَأَةُ دُوكٍ — دُوشِيسَة.

Duchy, n. إِيالَةُ ٱلدُّوكِ.

Duck, n. The waterfowl, بَطَّةٌ coll. بَطٌّ. A plunge into the water, غَطْسَةٌ فِي ٱلْمَآءِ. A kind of cloth, قُماشٌ مِنْ كَتّانٍ أَسْمَرُ. To make ducks and drakes of money, أَسْرَفَ ٱلْفُلُوسَ باطِلًا — أَسْرَفَ.

Duck, v.t. To plunge into the water, قَمَسَ-فِي ٱلْمَآءِ — غَطَسَ-فِي ٱلْمَآءِ.

Duck, v.i. إِنْغَمَسَ فِي — غَطَسَ فِي.

Ducking, n. The act of —, غَطْسٌ (or قَمْسٌ) فِي ٱلْمَآءِ. A sousing, غُطُوس — إِنْغِماس.

Duckling, n. فَرْخُ ٱلْبَطِّ pl. فُرُوخ.

Duck-weed, n. طُحْلُب.

Duct, n. A tube, أُنْبُوب pl. أَنابِيبُ. A canal, مَجْرًى pl. مَجارٍ. The ducts of the udder, السَّواعِدُ. The ducts of the kidneys, or the two spermatic ducts, الحالِبانِ. The medullary ducts of the windpipe, الشَّوارِبُ.

Ductile, a. That may be beaten out, يُتَطَرَّقُ — مِمّا يُمَطَّلُ. Pliant, easily bent, لَيِّن. Of an easy disposition, — جَنِيب — رَخْوُ ٱلْعِنانِ — طَوْعُ ٱلْعِنانِ — لَيِّن — سَهْلُ ٱلْخُلُقِ.

Ductileness, n. }
Ductility, } Quality of being easily beaten out, — تَطَرُّق قابِلِيَّةُ ٱلْمَطْلِ; of being easily bent, — إِنْحِنآء — لِينَة. Ductility, of disposition, — طَرِيقَة — خُضُوع — لِينَة — لِيان — لِينَةُ ٱلْجانِبِ — سُهُولَةُ ٱلْخُلُقِ.

Duds, n. Old clothes, خُلْقان — أَخْلاق — رِثّ — خُرَق.

Due, a. Due from, owed by, as of money, مَطْلُوبٌ — مَدْيُونٌ بِ — مِن; as service of any kind, واجِبٌ عَلَى — مَلْزُومٌ بِ — مُقْتَضًى. Proper, suitable, مُناسِب — لائِق — مُوافِق. In — time, at the appointed time, فِي ٱلْوَقْتِ ٱلْمُعَيَّنِ. Till he pay all that was — to him, حَتَّى يُوفِيَ كُلَّ ما كانَ لَهُ عَلَيْهِ. In — season, at its proper time, فِي حِينِهِ. To be —, proper, حَقَّ — وَجَبَ aor. يَجِبُ. The debt falling —, الدَّيْنُ ٱلْمُسْتَحِقُّ.

Due, n. One's right, حَقٌّ pl. حُقُوق. A tax, مَكْس pl. مُكُوس — ضَرِيبَة pl. ضَرائِبُ — رَسْم pl. رُسُوم — مَعْلُوم — عَوائِدُ. He gave to every one his —, أَعْطَى كُلَّ ذِي حَقٍّ حَقَّهُ. To every one was given his —, أُعْطِيَ كُلُّ ذِي حَقٍّ حَقَّهُ. To take more than one's —, إِسْتَفْضَلَ. To take all one's — from, إِنْتَصَفَ مِن.

Duel, n. مُبارَزَة — قِتالٌ بَيْنَ ٱثْنَيْنِ.

Duel, v.i. تَبارَزا — تَقاتَلا.

Dueller, n. }
Duellist, } مُبارِز — مُقاتِل.

Duelling, n. مُبارَزَة — قِتالٌ بَيْنَ ٱثْنَيْنِ.

Duenna, n. An old woman, مُسِنَّة — شَجُوز — عَجُوزَة pl. عَجائِزُ. A governess, مُعَلِّمَة — قَهْرَمانَة.

Duet, n. Of singing, غِنآءٌ لِمُغَنِّيَيْنِ مَعًا; of instrumental music, أَلْحانٌ لِعازِفَيْنِ مَعًا.

Dug, n. ثَدْيُ ٱلْحَيَوانِ pl. ثُدِيٌّ — بِزٌّ pl. بِزاز.

Duke, n. أَمِيرُ ٱلْأُمَرآءِ — دُوك. Grand —, الدُّوكُ ٱلْأَعْظَمُ.

Dukedom, n. مَقامُ ٱلدُّوكِ — إِيالَةُ (or إِلْتِزامُ) ٱلدُّوكِ.

Dulcet, a. Sweet, harmonious, مُطْرِب — مُنْعِش — حُلْوٌ — لَذِيذٌ لِلسَّمْعِ.

Dulcification, n. تَحْلِيَة.

Dulcify, v.t. أَحْلَى — حَلَّى.

Dulcimer, n. سِنْطِير — سَنْطُور — قانُون.

Dull, a. Stupid, أَخْرَقُ — عَرِيضُ ٱلْوِسادِ — فُطارِكٌ — سَقِيطَة — بَلِيد — أَحْمَقُ — قَلِيلُ ٱلْعَقْلِ. Not quick, بَطِيءٌ — كاهِل — مُهْمِل. Dull of hearing, ثَقِيلُ ٱلسَّمْعِ. Sad, حَزِين — كَئِيب — مَغْمُوم. Not exhilarating, مُصْعِب — صَعْب — مُمِلّ — مُزَعِّل. Blunt, كَهام — كَلِيل. Not bright, مُكَمَّدٌ — أَرْبَدُ — أَكْدَرُ — غَيْرُ لامِعٍ — عَتِم — ظَلِم. Dull, of colour, أَرْبَدُ — كُمَيْت — عَتِم; a — colour, لَوْنٌ عَتِمٌ — كُمْتَة. Dull of apprehension, قَلِيلُ ٱلْفَهْمِ — بَلِيد. Dull, as of a market, كاسِد. Dull, of a day, the weather, غَبِس — عَمِس. A — market, سُوقٌ راقِدَةٌ — سُوقٌ كاسِدَةٌ. The market was —, حَمُقَتِ ٱلسُّوقُ — رَقَدَتِ ٱلسُّوقُ. The man was — owing to lack of purchasers, أَكْسَدَ ٱلرَّجُلُ. To be —, of the weather, غَبِسَ — عَمِسَ. To be —, blunt, كَلَّ — إِنْثَلَمَ. To be —, dim, تَكَدَّرَ. *See also* Dim, a.

Dull, *v.t.* To make stupid, بَلَّهَ ـِ جَعَلَ أَبْلَهَ ـ أَبْلَهَ . To blunt, ثَلَّمَ ـِ جَعَلَ كَلِيلًا ـ غَلَّظَ ٱلْحَدَّ . To sadden, كَدَّرَ ـ أَغَمَّ ـ أَحْزَنَ . To make less bright, كَدَّرَ ـ قَتَمَ ـُ أَخْمَدَ . *See also to* Dim, *v.t.*

Dull, *v.i.* To grow less bright, تَكَدَّرَ ـ أَظْلَمَ ـ خَمَدَ ـُ . To grow blunt, كَلَّ ـِ ـ إِنْثَلَمَ .

Dullard, *n.*
Dull-head, } حِمار ـ مَجْنُون ـ بَلِيد ـ أَحْمَق ـ ثَوْر ـ أَخْرَق .

Dullness, *n.* Stupidity, بَلَه ـ خُرْق ـ بَلاهَة ـ جَهالَة ـ بَلادَة ـ حَماقَة . Slowness of comprehension, قِلَّة فَهْمٍ ـ قِلَّة إِدْراكٍ . Bluntness of edge, كَلّ ـ غِلاظَة حَدّ . Sluggishness, قِلَّة مُرُوءَة ـ تَكاسُل ـ تَهاوُن . Want of brightness, كَدَر ـ تَكَدُّر . Dullness, as of weather, غَبَس ـ عُمُوس ; of trade, كَساد ـ كَسادُ ٱلتِّجارَةِ . *See also* Dimness, *n.*

Duly, *ad.* Properly, according to rule, كَما يَجِبُ ـ بِمُوجِبِ ٱلْقَوانِينِ . Regularly, constantly, اِسْتِمْرارًا ـ بِٱلْإِدْمانِ ـ بِٱلْمُواظَبَةِ . In its proper time, بِوَقْتِهِ ـ فِي حِينِهِ .

Dumb, *a.* Without speech, بَكِيم *pl.* أَبْكام ـ أَبْكَمُ *pl.* بُكْم *and* بُكْمان ـ أَخْرَسُ *pl.* خُرْس . Silent, صَمُوت ـ سِكِّيت ـ ساكُوت . To strike —, خَرَّسَ . To be —, بَكِمَ ـَ ـ خَرِسَ ـَ . Deaf and —, صَمٌّ وَأَخْرَسُ . He makes the deaf to hear and the — to speak, جَعَلَ ٱلصُّمَّ يَسْمَعُونَ وَٱلْخُرْسَ يَتَكَلَّمُونَ .

Dumb-bells, *n.* مُسْكَتانِ ثَقِيلَتانِ تُسْتَعْمَلانِ لِتَرْوِيضِ ٱلْمَفاصِلِ ـ آلاتُ ٱلتَّرْوِيضِ ـ وَأَلْيافُ ٱلْجِسْمِ .

Dumbly, *ad.* بِخَرَسٍ ـ بِسُكُوتٍ ـ بِبَكَمٍ ـ خَرَسًا .

Dumbness, *n.* بَكَم ـ خَرَس . Silence, سُكُوت ـ ساكِتَة .

Dumb-show, *n.* لَعْبُ ٱلْإِيماءِ .

Dumb-waiter, *n.* مِنْقَلَة تُوضَعُ عَلَيْها ٱلْمَأْكُولاتُ لِلسُّفْرَةِ .

Dumfound, *v.t.* أَعْقَرَ ـ خَبَّلَ ـ حَيَّرَ . To be dumfounded, عَقِرَ ـَ ـ تَحَيَّرَ ـ تَخَبَّلَ .

Dummy, *n.* A dumb figure, تَقالِيدُ *pl.* تَقْلِيد ـ صُورَة تَقْلِيدٍ ـ تِمْثال *pl.* تَماثِيلُ ـ شَخْص *pl.* أَشْخاص .

Dumpish, *a.* Melancholy, كَئِيب . Sad, حَزِين ـ مَغْمُوم ـ مَهْمُوم ـ مَكْسُورُ ٱلْخاطِرِ .

Dumpishness, *n.* عَدَمُ نَشاطٍ ـ حُزْن ـ غَمّ ـ كَآبَة .

Dumpling, *n.* كُبَّة عَجِينٍ *pl.* كُبَب .

Dumps, *n.* *See* Dumpishness, *n.*

Dumpy, *a.* مُؤَنَّف ـ إِزَب ـ مُكَبْتَل ـ قُصَيِّر وَنَكِث ـ مَجْمُوع ـ حِنْزاب .

Dun, *a.* Of the colour, أَشْهَبُ *fem.* شَهْباءُ *pl.* شُهْب ـ أَرْمَك ـ أَكْمَت ـ دَبْس . A — colour, رُمْكَة ـ شُهْبَة .

Dun, *n.* An importunate creditor, مِعْسَر ـ مُناصّ ـ طَلّابُ ٱلدَّيْنِ . A demand for payment, تَنْقِيش ـ مُناصَّة ـ إِعْسارٌ بِٱلدَّيْنِ ـ مُطالَبَةُ ٱلدَّيْنِ . *See also under* Dun, *a.*

Dun, *v.t.* To urge for debt, أَعْسَرَ ٱلْغَرِيمَ ـ أَنْقَشَ عَلَى ـ نَصَّ ـُ ـ ناصَّ ـ اِقْتَضَى . He dunned him for such a sum, صادَرَهُ عَلَى كَذا مِنَ ٱلْمالِ .

Dunce, *n.*
Dunder-pate, } *See* Dullard, Blockhead, *n.*

Dune, *n.* A low hill of sand, حَجَب *pl.* حِجاب ـ تَلُّ رَمْلٍ *pl.* تِلال .

Dung, *n.* سَماد ـ رَوْثَة ـ سِرْجِين ـ دَمان ـ دَبال ـ زِبْل . Dung of camels, sheep, and goats, بَعَر ـ جَلَّة ; of the ox kind, خِثْي . A piece of dry —, دُبْلَة . A cake made of — and straw for fuel, سَياع ـ جَلَّة ـ جُلَّة . To throw such cakes on the wall to dry, سَيَّعَ . Bird's dung, شَخْط ـ ذَرْق .

Dung, *v.t.* سَمَّدَ ـ عَذَّنَ ـ دَبَلَ ـُ ـ دَمَنَ ـُ ـ زَبَلَ ـُ .

Dung, *v.i.* To void excrement, راثَ *aor.* يَرُوثُ ـ دَمَّنَ ـ تَغَوَّطَ .

Dungeon, *n.* مَحْبَس ـ سِجْن ـ حَبْس .

Dung-fork, *n.* مِذْرًى لِلزِّبْلِ .

Dung-hill, *n.* A heap of dung, مَزْبَلَة . A mean abode, مَسْكَن حَقِير .

Dung-hill, *a.* Mean, دَنِيء ـ حَقِير ـ ذَلِيل . A — cock, أَبُو يَقْظان ـ دِيكُ ٱلْمَزْبَلَةِ *pl.* دُيُوك .

Dungy, *a.* مُزَبَّل ـ نَجِس ـ قَذِر ـ مَذِر .

Dung-yard, *n.* مَزْبَلَة ـ حَوْش لِلزِّبْلِ .

Dunnage, *n.* حُصُر أَوْ أَلْواح تُوضَعُ تَحْتَ ٱلْبِضاعَةِ فِي مَرْكَبٍ لِحِفْظِها مِنَ ٱلْبَلَلِ ـ أَمْتِعَة لِصِيانَةِ ٱلْوَسْقِ عَنِ ٱلْبَلَلِ .

Dunning, *n.* *See* Dun, *n.*

Duo; *See* Duet, *n.*

Duodecimo, *n.* طَلْحِيَّة مِنَ ٱلْوَرَقِ مَطْوِيَّة عَلَى ٱثْنَيْ عَشَرَ وَجْهًا . In —, فِي ٱلْقَطْعِ (or ٱلْفَصْلِ) ٱلثّانِي عَشَرَ .

Duodenum, *n.* أَعْلَى ٱلْأَعْفاجِ .

Dupe, *n.* زَبُون *pl.* زَبائِنُ ـ غَرِير *pl.* أَغِرّاءُ .

Dupe, *v.t.* مَسَخَ ـ مَكَرَ بِ ـُ ـ غَشَّ ـُ .

Duplex, *a.* *See* Double, *a.*

Duplicate, *v.t.* *See to* Double, *v.t.*

Duplicate, *n.* A — copy, صُورَة ثانِيَة ـ نُسْخَة ثانِيَة . A fellow, شَبِيه ـ نَظِير ـ زَوْج .

Duplication, *n.* The act of doubling, تَضْعِيف ـ تَثْنِيَة . A fold, طَيّ *pl.* أَطْواء ـ عُرُوض ـ طَيَّة .

Duplicature, *n.* A fold; *see preceding.*

Duplicity, *n.* نِفَاق ـ رِيَآءٌ ـ مُوَالَسَة .

Durability, *n.* / **Durableness**, } إِسْتِمْرَار ـ بَقَآءٌ ـ دَوَام ـ إِسْتِقَامَة ـ إِسْتِدَامَة .

Durable, *a.* مُسْتَمِرٌّ ـ مُسْتَدِيم . This cloth is not —, هٰذَا ٱلْجُوخُ لَيْسَ لَهُ دَوَامٌ . Strong, مَتِين .

Durably, *ad.* بِٱسْتِمْرَارٍ ـ بِدَوَامٍ ـ بِٱسْتِدَامَةٍ .

Dura Mater, *n.* أُمُّ ٱلرَّأْسِ .

Durance, *n.* سِجْن ـ حَبْس ـ إِحْتِبَاس .

Duration, *n.* Continuance, إِسْتِمْرَار ـ دَوَام ـ قِيَام ـ بَقَآءٌ . Length of time, طُول ـ دَوْر ـ مُدَّةٌ ـ مُدَّةُ بَقَآءٍ .

Duress, *n.* جُبُور ـ إِجْبَار ـ إِجْتِبَار ـ جَبْر .

During, *prep.* فِي غُضُونِ ـ بِطُولِ ـ فِي مُدَّةِ ـ بَيْنَ ـ فِي أَثْنَآءِ . During the days, فِيمَا بَيْنَ ٱلْأَيَّامِ . They came — the affair, جَاؤُوا فِي أَثْنَآءِ ٱلْأَمْرِ .

Dusk, *a.* Tending to darkness, مُكْمَدٌّ ـ مُسْوَدٌّ ـ عَتِم .

Dusk, *n.* The twilight of the morning, شَقُّ ٱلْفَجْرِ ـ سَحَر ; of the evening, شَفَقُ ٱلْغُرُوبِ ـ عِشَآءٌ ـ مَلَس ـ مُلَيْسَآء . To become —, مَلَسَ ٱلظَّلَامُ [2]. *See also* Duskiness, *n.*

Duskily, *ad.* / **Duskishly**, } ظُلْمَةً ـ عَلَى ٱلْعَتَمَةِ . *See also* Darkly, *ad.*

Duskiness, *n.* Of colour, خُطْبَة ـ سُمْرَة . Darkness, عَتَمَة ـ ظُلْمَة ـ مَلَس .

Duskish, *a.* / **Dusky**, } Of colour, أَسْمَرُ ـ خُطْبَانِيٌّ ـ أَخْطَبُ ـ أَغْبَسُ . Of a — bay colour, of a horse, وَرْدٌ أَغْبَسُ ـ سَمَنْد . *See also* Dusk, *a.*

Dust, *n.* Dry particles of earth, غُبْرَة ـ عَفَر ـ عَفْر ـ عَفَار ـ غُبَار ـ تُرْب ـ تُرَاب . Dust raised by the wind, عَجَاج ـ عَجَاجَة . Dust in motion, لَهَب . Dust in the air, غَبًا ـ غَبْيَة . Fine particles of —, such as arises from flour, *etc.*, سَفْسَاف . Dust from pounding, جُرَاشَة . Sweepings, زُبَالَة ـ سُبَاطَة . Dust of metals or stones on being filed or wrought, قُرَاضَة ـ بُرَادَة . Covered with —, مُعَفَّر . Dust, the grave, تُرْبَة *pl.* تُرَب : (this last word means also a cemetery). To throw — in the eyes of, مَكَرَ بِ [2]. To raise —, أَرْهَجَ ٱلْغُبَارَ ـ أَغْبَرَ ـ غَبَّرَ . Time reduced them to —, طَحَنَتْهُمُ ٱلْمَنُونُ . To roll one in the —, عَفَّرَ ـ عَفَرَ . He dragged his garment in the —, إِعْتَفَرَ ثَوْبَهُ فِي ٱلتُّرَابِ . To be rubbed, or rolled, or filled with —, إِنْعَفَرَ ـ إِعْتَفَرَ .

Dust, *v.t.* To throw — upon, عَفَّرَ ـ غَبَّرَ . To clear from —, as of clothes, نَفَّضَ ـ نَفَضَ [2]. To wipe off —, مَسَّحَ ـ مَسَحَ . To — or wipe anything, as — with a cloth, *etc.*, مَسَحَ بِ .

Dust-coloured, *a.* أَغْبَرُ ـ أَبْغَثُ ـ أَعْفَرُ . A dust colour, غُبْرَة ـ غُبْشَة ـ غُفْرَة ـ كُتْمَة . To become —, إِغْبَرَّ ـ بَغِثَ .

Duster, *n.* نَشَّافَة ـ مِمْسَحَة *pl.* مَمَاسِح .

Dustiness, *n.* تَعَفُّر ـ إِعْتِفَار ـ غَبَرَة .

Dustman, *n.* زَبَّال .

Dusty, *a.* مُعَفَّر ـ مُغَبَّر . To be —, تَعَفَّرَ ـ إِعْتَفَرَ ـ تَغَبَّرَ .

Dutch, *a.* فَلَمَنْكِيٌّ ـ مِنْ فَلَمَنْك . The high Dutch tongue, لِسَانُ ٱلنَّمْسَةِ . Low —, لِسَانُ ٱلْفَلَمَنْكِ .

Dutch-tiles, *n.* كَاشَانِيٌّ .

Duteous, *a.* / **Dutiful**, } Performing what is due, وَافٍ بِكُلِّ مَا يَجِبُ عَلَيْهِ ـ مُنْقَاد ـ وَافِي ٱلْوَاجِبَاتِ . Obedient, respectful, طَائِع ـ مُطِيع ـ مُكْرِم ـ مُبَجِّل . *See also under* Obedient, *a.*

Duteousness, *n.* / **Dutifulness**, } Obedience, إِمْتِثَال بِ ـ إِنْقِيَادٌ لِلْوَاجِبَاتِ . Obedience, submission, طَاعَة ـ خُضُوع ـ إِذْعَان ـ إِنْقِيَاد .

Dutiable, *a.* مَا يُدْفَعُ عَلَيْهِ مَكْس ـ عَلَيْهِ كُمْرُك .

Dutifully, *ad.* بِإِطَاعَةٍ ـ بِٱمْتِثَالٍ ـ بِرِعَايَةٍ ـ مُرَاعَاةً . *See also* Obediently, *ad.*

Duty, *n.* That which is due, وَاجِبَة *pl.* وَاجِبَات ـ وَاجِبٌ ـ فُرُوض ـ عَلَى ـ لَازِمٌ عَلَى ـ رَسْم *pl.* رُسُوم . A religious —, فَرْض *pl.* فُرُوض ـ فَرِيضَة *pl.* فَرَائِضُ . Obedience, إِطَاعَة ـ إِنْقِيَاد . Respect, رِعَايَة ـ إِحْتِرَام ـ تَحِيَّة . Service, خِدْمَة . Business of a soldier, as on guard, خَفَر ـ غَفَر . A tax, فُرْضَة ـ مَكْس ـ كُمْرُك ـ رَسْم *pl.* رُسُوم . My —, مَا يَجِبُ عَلَيَّ . To be one's —, وَجَبَ عَلَيْهِ *aor.* يَجِبُ . To make it the — of another, وَجَّبَ-عَلَى ـ أَوْجَبَ-عَلَى . To discharge the duties of religion, فَرَّضَ . This is my —, هٰذَا حَقٌّ عَلَيَّ . We have done what it was our — to do, عَمِلْنَا مَا كَانَ يَجِبُ عَلَيْنَا . We should prefer — to pleasure, عَلَيْنَا أَنْ نُفَضِّلَ ٱلْفُرُوضَ عَلَى ٱللَّذَّاتِ . The — on such articles as these is high, ٱلْكُمْرُكُ عَلَى مِثْلِ هٰذِهِ ٱلْأَصْنَافِ كَثِيرٌ . Tobacco duties, ضَرَائِبُ ٱلدُّخَانِ . It is not permitted to levy any duties or taxes on goods which are in transport through the country to another place, لَا يَسُوغُ أَنْ يُوخَذَ عَلَى ٱلْبَضَائِعِ ٱلَّتِي تَمُرُّ فِي ٱلْوِلَايَةِ مُرْسَلَةً إِلَى جِهَةٍ أُخْرَى شَيْءٌ مِنَ ٱلْعَوَائِدِ أَوِ ٱلرُّسُومَاتِ .

Dwarf, *n.* عُشَيْب ـ عَشَبَة ـ مُقَرْقَم (the latter two words express the male and female,) عَاكِل *pl.* عُكْل ـ كُوتِيٌّ ـ هَنْقَب ـ هَبَنَّق ـ قَزَعَة ـ جُوجَة ـ حَنْبَس .

Dwarf, *a.* / **Dwarfish**, } Very small, صَغِير ـ قُصَيِّر ـ قَصِيرُ ٱلْقَامَةِ ـ إِزْب.

Dwarfishness, *n.* قِصَرُ ٱلْقَامَةِ ـ صِغْر.

Dwell, *v.i.* To reside in a land, ثَوَى ≈ ـ مَتَنَ بِ ² ـ بَلَدَ ـ أَحَالَ بِ ـ أَقَامَ بِ ـ ثَوَى فِي ≈ ; as in a house, سَكَنَ ² ـ أَقَامَ بِ. They dwelt together, سَكَنُوا مَعًا. To continue on, أَدْمَنَ عَلَى ـ إِسْتَمَرَّ عَلَى ـ دَامَ ². To continue speaking, أَطَالَ فِي ٱلْكَلَامِ ـ دَامَ مُتَكَلِّمًا ².

Dweller, *n.* سَاكِن *pl.* سُكَّان ـ مُقِيم ـ قَاطِن *pl.* قُطَّان *and* قَاطِنَة ـ سَكْنَى *and* نَزِيل ـ مِنْ أَهْلِ.

Dwelling, *n.* The act of residing, سُكْنَى ـ إِقَامَة. An abode, مَثْوًى *pl.* مَثَاوٍ ـ وَطَن ـ مَسْكَن *pl.* مَسَاكِنُ ـ مَوْطِن *pl.* مَوَاطِنُ ـ مَقَام ـ مَحَلّ ـ مَأْوًى ـ مَأْوٍ ـ دَار *pl.* دِيَار.

Dwelling-house, *n.* بَيْت *pl.* بُيُوت ـ مَقْعَد *pl.* مَقَاعِدُ ـ دَار *pl.* دِيَار ـ مَنْزِل *pl.* مَنَازِلُ.

Dwelling-place, *n.* *See* Dwelling, *n.*

Dwindle, *v.i.* To become less, in bulk, صَغُرَ ² ـ قَلَّ ≈ ـ تَصَاغَرَ ; in number, قَلَّ ≈ ; in either, نَقَصَ ² ـ تَنَقَّصَ ـ إِنْتَقَصَ. To degenerate, خَسَّ ـ خَسِرَ ـ تَلِفَ. To — to nothing, زَالَ ² ـ إِضْمَحَلَّ ـ تَلَاشَى. To — in health, ضَعُفَ ².

Dwindle, *v.t.* To make less, قَلَّلَ ـ نَقَّصَ ـ صَغَّرَ.

Dye, *v.t.* صَبَغَ ² ـ صَبَّغَ. To — the hands or nails with hennah, خَضَبَ ≈ ـ حَنَّى. To be dyed with, إِصْطَبَغَ بِ. To colour, لَوَّنَ. He dyed his hair black, صَبَغَ شَعَرَهُ بِٱلسَّوَادِ.

Dye, *n.* صِبْغ ـ صِبَاغ ـ صِبْغَة. A colour, لَوْن *pl.* أَلْوَان. Hair-dye, خِضَاب ـ كَتَم. Dyed, مُصَبَّغ ـ مَصْبُوغ ; of the hair or hands, مَخْضُوب ـ مُخَضَّب.

Dye-house, *n.* مَصْبَغَة.

Dyeing, *n.* The art of, صِبَاغَة.

Dyer, *n.* صَبَّاغ *pl.* صَبَّاغَة *and* صَبَّاغُونَ.

Dying, *a.* Mortal, يَمُوتُ ـ مَائِت ـ فَانٍ. Near to death, مُشْرِف عَلَى ٱلْمَوْتِ. At death, عِنْدَ ٱلْمَوْتِ ـ عِنْدَ ٱلْمَمَاتِ. A — speech, خِطَابُ ٱلْمُشْرِفِ عَلَى ٱلْمَوْتِ. A — confession, إِقْرَارُ ٱلْمَائِتِ.

Dyke, *n.* *See* Dike, *n.*

Dynameter, *n.* آلَةٌ يُقَاسُ بِهَا مَدُّ مَنْظَرِ ٱلنَّظَّارَاتِ.

Dynamics, *n.* عِلْمُ تَحْرِيكِ ٱلْأَجْرَامِ.

Dynastic, *a.* مُلُوكِيّ ـ مُتَعَلِّق بِسِلْسِلَةِ مُلُوكٍ ـ مُتَعَلِّق بِدَوْلَةٍ.

Dynasty, *n.* نَسْل ـ دَوْلَة *pl.* دُوَل ـ سِلْسِلَةُ مُلُوكٍ ـ آل مُلُوكٍ.

Dysenteric, *a.* إِسْهَالِيّ ـ مُتَعَلِّق بِٱلنَّزِيفِ.

Dysentery, *n.* دِيسَنْطَرِيَا ـ إِسْهَال ـ نَزِيف.

Dyspepsia, *n.* عُسْرُ ٱلْهَضْمِ ـ وَخَامَة ـ بَرَدَة. *See also* Indigestion, *n.*

Dyspeptic, *a.* مُسَبِّبُ ٱلْوَخَامَةِ ـ مُتَعَلِّق بِعُسْرِ ٱلْهَضْمِ.

Dyspeptic, *n.* وَخِم ـ وَخِيم ـ وَخُوم *pl.* وِخَام *and* وَخَامَى.

Dyspnœa, *n.* قِطْع ـ قُطْع. To have —, قُطِعَ.

Dysury, *n.* عُسْرُ ٱلْبَوْلِ.

E.

Each, *a.* كُلٌّ مِن – كُلٌّ – أَحَدٌ – كُلّ واحِدٍ. They love — other, كُلّ واحِدٍ – أَحَدُهُمْ يُحِبُّ ٱلآخَرَ – كُلٌّ مِنْهُمْ يُحِبُّ ٱلآخَرَ – مِنْهُمْ يُحِبُّ ٱلآخَرَ – يُحِبُّونَ بَعْضُهُمُ ٱلبَعْضَ. They asked after — other's welfare, سَأَلَ كُلُّ واحِدٍ صاحِبَهُ عَنْ سَلامَتِهِ. Each of these kings, كُلُّ مَلِكٍ مِنْ هٰؤُلاءِ ٱلْمُلُوكِ. Each of the two gardens, كِلْتا ٱلْجَنَّتَيْنِ.

Eager, *a.* Ardently wishing, راغِبٌ فِي – شَوّاق – مُشْتاقٌ إِلَى – حَرِيص – غَيْرانُ – تائِقٌ إِلَى – مُشْتَهٍ. Vehement, حَمِيس – شَدِيدُ ٱلحَرارَةِ. Hot in disposition, حامٍ – حارٌّ. He was — to work, حارِصٌ عَلَى ٱلعَمَلِ. Eager for gain, حَرِيصٌ عَلَى ٱلكَسْبِ. Eager for study, راغِبٌ فِي ٱلدَّرْسِ.

Eagerly, *ad.* With desire, بِرَغْبَةٍ – بِشَوْقٍ – بِغَيْرَةٍ – بِٱشْتِياقٍ – بِشِدَّةٍ. Vehemently, حَماسَةً – بِحَرارَةٍ – بِحُرْقَةٍ – بِحِرْصٍ – كُلِّيًّا.

Eagerness, *n.* Earnestness, غَيْرَة – رَغْبَة. Ardent wishing, شَوْق – تَوْق. Vehemence, حَماسَة – حِرْص – حَرارَة – حُمَيّا – شِدَّة.

Eagle, *n.* The bird, نَسْر *pl.* نُسُور. The constellation, النَّسْرُ – ٱلطّائِرُ – النَّسْرُ ٱلواقِعُ.

Eagle-eyed, *a.* شايِهُ ٱلبَصَرِ – خارِقُ ٱلنَّظَرِ – نَظّار.

Eagle-stone, *n.* حَجَرُ ٱلبَهْتِ – حَجَرُ ٱلنَّسْرِ.

Eaglet, *n.* فَرْخُ ٱلنَّسْرِ *pl.* فُرُوخ.

Ear, *n.* سَمْع *pl.* أَسامِعُ – مِسْمَع *pl.* مَساوِعُ – أُذُن *pl.* آذان. The two ears, الأُنْثَيانِ – الأُذُنانِ. A long —, أُذُنٌ شَرْفاءُ – شُرافِيَّة – أُذانِيٌّ; having pendulous ears, أُذُنٌ شُرافِيَّةٌ; having small ears, سُكاكَة – أَسَكُّ *fem.* سَكّاءُ. The tip, as of the —, شَحْمَةُ ٱلأُذُنِ – قُوف. The circuit of the —, سِتارُ ٱلأُذُنِ. The orifice, as of the —, صِماخ. The interior or concha of the —, مَحارَةٌ (or صَحْنُ) ٱلأُذُنِ. Having the ears slit or perforated, أَخْرَمُ – مُخَرَّم – أَخْرَبُ – مَخْرُوب. Ear, the power of hearing, القُوَّةُ ٱلسّامِعَةُ. Power of judging of harmony, قُوَّةُ تَمْيِيزِ ٱلأَلْحانِ. The privilege of being readily heard, ready access, دالَّة – جُرْأَة – تَقَرُّب – قُبُول – مَنْزِلَة. He has the — of the king, هُوَ لَهُ مَنْزِلَةٌ عِنْدَ – لَهُ سَمْعٌ عِنْدَ ٱلمَلِكِ – مَقْبُولٌ عِنْدَ ٱلمَلِكِ ٱلمَلِكِ. Indicative of a person, *e.g.* they drew all the city about his ears, هَيَّجُوا أَهْلَ ٱلمَدِينَةِ كُلَّها عَلَيْهِ. To give — to, to listen to, أَنْصَتَ إِلَى – أَذِنَ ل – تَسَمَّعَ ل – إِلَى or ٱسْتَمَعَ ل; to obey, أَصْغَى إِلَى – ٱمْتَثَلَ ل – ٱنْقادَ ل. To reach the ears, to come to the knowledge of, بَلَغَ – طَرَقَ مَسْمَعَ. To set by the ears, قَرَّشَ بَيْنَ – حَرَّضَ عَلَى ٱلجِدالِ – رَمَى ٱلفِتْنَةَ بَيْنَ – هَيَّجَ ٱلخُصُومَةَ بَيْنَ – جَعَلَهُمْ يَتَخانَقُونَ. To prick up the ears, as of a horse, *etc.*, أَنْصَبَ ٱلآذانَ; to be attentive to, ٱكْتَنَتَ إِلَى. He came pricking up his ears, جاءَ ناشِرًا أُذُنَيْهِ. To pull or ring the ears, عَرَكَ أُذُنَهُ – أَذَنَهُ. He was up to the ears in, غَرِقَ فِي – ٱنْهَمَكَ فِي. To turn a deaf — to, لَمْ يَسْمَعْ ل – لَمْ يَلْتَفِتْ إِلَى or ل. To have one's ears about one, تَنَبَّهَ عَلَى. To whisper in the — of one, كَتَّ فِي أُذُنِهِ – قَرَّ فِي أُذُنِهِ – وَشْوَشَ. A ringing in the ears, دَوِيّ – صَرِيرُ ٱلأُذُنِ.

Ear, *n.* An ear of corn, سُنْبُلَة *pl.* سَنابِلُ; of rice or millet, سَبَلَة or سَبُولَة *pl.* سُبُول. To put forth ears, سَنْبَلَ. The time of earing, حَصاد.

Ear, *v.t.* To reap, حَصَدَ. To plough, عَمِلَ ٱلأَرْضَ – فَلَحَ.

Ear, *v.i.* To put forth ears, سَنْبَلَ. The barley was in ear, الشَّعِيرُ كانَ مُسْبِلًا. The wheat was full in the ear, حَبَّلَ ٱلقَمْحُ – ٱمْتَلأَ ٱلسُّنْبُلُ قَمْحًا. To become full, of ears of wheat, *etc.*, حَبَّلَ ٱلزَّرْعُ.

Earings, *n.* Ropes to fasten sail, أَعاوِيلُ.

Earlap, *n.* The tip of the ear; *see under* Ear, *n.*

Earl, *n.* أَمِير – ٱسْمُ شَرَفٍ فِي بِلادِ ٱلإِنْكِلِيزِ أَعْلَى مِنْ بارُونٍ – أَرْل.

Earldom, *n.* ٱمْتِيازاتُ ٱلأَرْلِ. *See under* Earl, *n.*

Earless, *n.* بِلا آذانٍ.

Earliness, *n.* The being beforehand, مُبادَرَة – تَقَدُّم – سَبْق; of time of the day, بُكُور – تَبْكِير – تَبَكُّر.

Earl-Marshal, *n.* أَمِيرٌ مُفَوَّضٌ بِكُلِّ ما يَخْتَصُّ بِٱلعَساكِرِ عِنْدَ ٱلتَّبْجِيلِ ٱلرَّسْمِيِّ.

Ear-lock, *n.* خُصْلَة *pl.* خُصَل.

Early, *a.* Prior in time, أَوَّلُ – قَبْلَ ٱلأَوانِ – سابِق. Early, as in the morning, باكِر – بَدْرِيٌّ. Ancient, قَدِيم. Precocious, مُبادِر – عاجِل – بَكِير – قَبْلَ ٱلأَوانِ. Early ripe, مُبْكار. The — rain, المَطَرُ ٱلمُبَكِّرُ (*see also under* Rain). To rise —, بَكَّرَ. Early in life, فِى ٱلْغُلامِيَّةِ. Early in the day, فِى ٱلصَّباحِ – فِى ٱلضُّحَيَّةِ. Early for the season, قَبْلَ ٱلْأَوانِ – قَبْلَ وَقْتِهِ. Trees that produce — fruits, مُبَكِّر.

Early, *ad.* بُكْرَةً – بِتَبَكُّرٍ – تَبْكِيرًا. He rose —, بَكَّرَ – إِسْتَيْقَظَ باكِرًا – بَكَّرَ صَباحًا.

Ear-mark, *n.* عَلامَةٌ فِى ٱلْأُذُنِ.

Earn, *v.t.* To gain by labour, حَصَّلَ – ربح ‒ كسب. To earn for, إِسْتَأْهَلَ – إِسْتَحَقَّ. To merit, هَبَشَ – حَبَشَ ل. He earns his bread by his labour, يَعِيشُ مِنْ كَدِّهِ.

Earnest, *a.* Ardent in pursuit, مُجِدٌّ فِى – حَرِيصٌ عَلَى – غَيْرانُ – حَمِسٌ. Zealous, ذُو هِمَّةٍ فِى – مُتَبَذِّل – راغِبٌ فِى – صاحِبُ غَيْرَةٍ. Decided, صِنْدِيد – رَسِيٌّ – زَمِيع. Not in jest, لَيْسَ بِمَزْحٍ بَلْ مِنْ جِدٍّ – مِنْ جِدٍّ – جِدِّيٌّ : Not in jest but in —, عَمْدًا. Earnest desire, شَوْق ; earnest endeavour, إِجْتِهاد. I did it seriously and in —, فَعَلْتُهُ عَمْدًا عَلَى عَيْنٍ.

Earnest, *n.* Something paid in advance, عُرْبُون – مُسْكان. A first fruit, باكُورَة. To give an — to, عَرَّبَ – عَرْبَنَ – مَسَّكَ – أَعْطَى عُرْبُونًا.

Earnestly, *ad.* Zealously, بِهِمَّةٍ – بِحِرْصٍ – بِغَيْرَةٍ. Attentively, بِدَوَرانِ بالٍ – بِتَقَيُّدٍ – بِرَغْبَةٍ. To pray to, or beseech —, إِبْتَهَلَ – تَضَرَّعَ إِلَى – إِلَى. To apply one's self — to the worship of God, تَبَتَّلَ إِلَى ٱللّٰهِ. To apply one's self — to any work, جَهَدَ فِى (جاهَدَ *or* اِجْتَهَدَ *or*).

Earnestness, *n.* Zeal, جِدٌّ – غَيْرَة – رَغْبَة – حَمَس – حَرارَة. Care, solicitude, تَقَيُّد – إِهْتِمام – إِعْتِناء. Foresight, إِمْعانُ ٱلنَّظَرِ.

Earnings, *n.* Wages, كِراء – مَكْسَب – أُجارَة.

Ear-picker, *n.* مِنْكاش – هِلال.

Ear-ring, *n.* قُرْط *pl.* قِراط *or* أَقْراط *or* قُرُوط – حَلَق *pl.* حَلَقات. To adorn one with ear-rings, قَرَّطَ. To wear —, تَقَرَّطَ. Wearing —, مُقَرَّط. An ear-drop, شَنْف *pl.* شُنُوف.

Ear-shot, *n.* مَدَى ٱلسَّمْعِ – طُولُ ٱلسَّماعِ. Within —, يُسْتَمَعُ – فِى مَدَى ٱلسَّمْعِ.

Earth, *n.* Mould, تُرْب – تُراب – أَرْض ; moist —, ثَرَى – تُرابٌ نَدٍ (*or* نَدِيٌّ) ; rich —, أَرْضٌ طَيِّبَةُ ٱلتُّرْبَةِ – أَرْضٌ سَمِينَةٌ ; the best kind of —, أَطْيَبُ ٱلتُّرْبِ. The globe, الكُرَةُ – العالَمُ – الدُّنْيا. Land, country, بَرٌّ – بَلَد – دِيار. The inhabitants of the —, سُكّانُ ٱلدُّنْيا – أَهْلُ ٱلدُّنْيا. The surface of the —, وَجْهُ ٱلْأَرْضِ. Fullers' —, بَيْلُون. Potters' —, فَخّار. Scum of the —, dregs of the people, أَسافِلُ ٱلنّاسِ. Clay, طِين.

Earth, *v.t.* To hide in the —, دَفَنَ – أَخْفَى فِى ٱلْأَرْضِ. To — up, سَدَّ. To — over, كَوَّمَ ٱلتُّرابَ عَلَى.

Earth, *v.i.* *See to* Burrow, *v.i.*

Earth-board, *n.* لِسانُ ٱلْفَدّانِ.

Earth-born, *a.* أَرْضِىٌّ – دُنْيَوِىٌّ.

Earth-bound, *a.* }
Earth-bred, } Low, grovelling, حَقِير – خَسِيس – سُفْلِىٌّ.

Earthen, *a.* مِنْ طِينٍ – مِنْ فَخّارٍ – خَزَف. Earthen vessels, خَزَف.

Earthiness, *n.* Like earth, تُرابِيَّة ; taste of earth, طَعْمُ تُرابٍ.

Earthliness, *n.* حُبُّ ٱلدُّنْيا – دُنْيَوِيَّة.

Earthly, *a.* عالَمِىٌّ – دُنْيَوِىٌّ – أَرْضِىٌّ.

Earthly-minded, *a.* مُفْتَكِرٌ فِى ٱلْأَرْضِيّاتِ.

Earthly-mindedness, *n.* حُبُّ ٱلدُّنْيا – حُبُّ ٱلْأَرْضِيّاتِ.

Earth-nut, *n.* بَلْبُوس – قُلْقاسُ ٱلْيَهُودِيَّةِ.

Earthquake, *n.* زَلْزَلَة – رَجْفَة *pl.* زَلازِلُ. A violent —, زِلْزال.

Earth-work, *n.* A bastion of earth, طابِيَة *pl.* طَوابِى. An embankment, مِتْراس – مِتْرَس – سَدٌّ.

Earth-worm, *n.* خَراطِين – شَحْمَةُ ٱلْأَرْضِ.

Earthy, *a.* تُرابِىٌّ.

Ear-trumpet, *n.* بُوقٌ لِلْأُذُنِ – آلَةٌ لِلسَّماعِ.

Ear-wax, *n.* أُفّ – وَسَخُ ٱلْآذانِ.

Earwig, *n.* أَبُو مِقَصّ – دَخّالُ ٱلْأُذُنِ – عُقْرُبان.

Ear-witness, *n.* شاهِدٌ عَلَى شَىْءٍ مِنَ ٱلسَّمْعِ فَقَطْ – سامِع.

Ease, *n.* Freedom from pain, *etc.*, فَرَج – خَفْض – راحَة – قَرار. Rest after labour, إِسْتِراحَة – راحَة. Ease and plenty, سَعَةُ ٱلْعَيْشِ – نِعْمَة – تَرَفُّه – يَسار – فَنَق – خَفْض. Freedom from stiffness, إِنْبِساط – مُلاءَمَة – لَطافَة – سَعَة – شَلَبَنة. Contentment, إِنْبِساط – راحَةُ قَلْبٍ. Facility, هَوْن – هِينَة – سُهُولَة – يُسْر. He is at — regarding . . . , هُوَ رَخِىٌّ (*or* مُرْتاحُ) ٱلْبالِ مِنْ. They have a life of —, هُمْ فِى خَفْضٍ مِنَ ٱلْعَيْشِ – طَرَف. Walk at your —, أَمْشِ عَلَى هَوْنِكَ. At —, happy, مَبْسُوط – مَسْرُور – مُبْتَهِج. You are quite at — about your affair, أَنْتَ فِى نَفَسٍ مِنْ أَمْرِكَ. Take your —, sit as you please, أَقْعُدْ عَلَى هَوْنِكَ. Ease in speech, فَصاحَة – بَلاغَة. To live a life of —, أَفْنَقَ – تَفَنَّقَ. *See also* Rest, *n.*

Ease, *v.t.* To free from pain, سَكَّنَ (*or* هَدَّأَ) ٱلْوَجَعَ عَن. To lighten, as a burden, خَفَّضَ عَن – سَهَّلَ عَلَى ; of trouble, فَرَّجَ عَن – فَرَجَ عَن. To give rest to, أَراحَ – رَيَّحَ. To quiet,

هَدَّأَ – أَهْدَأَ. To reassure, أَقَرَّ – خَفَّضَ. To make to go slowly, جَعَلَ يَمْشِي رُوَيْدًا – أَمْهَلَ – أَرْوَدَ.

Easeful, *a.* *See* Easy, *a.*

Easel, *n.* مَنْصَبُ ٱلْمُصَوِّرِ.

Easeless, *a.* قَلِقٌ – غَيْرُ مُرْتَاحٍ – مُضْطَرِبٌ – قَلْقَالٌ.

Easement, *n.* Help, مُسَاعَدَةٌ – مُعَاوَنَةٌ. Relief, comfort, فَرَجٌ – تَسَلٍّ – جَبْرُ ٱلْخَاطِرِ. Facilitation, تَسْهِيلٌ.

Easily, *ad.* With facility, سَهْلًا – بِسُهُولَةٍ – يَسْرًا. Gently, رُوَيْدًا – عَلَى مَهْلٍ – مَهْلًا – عَلَى ٱلْهُوَيْنَى – بِإِرْوَادٍ. He did it — and gently, فَعَلَ سَهْوًا رَهْوًا – أَرْوَدَ فِي ٱلْأَمْرِ. He is not — provoked, لَا يَحْتَدُّ.

Easiness, *n.* Facility, مَيْسَرَةٌ – يَسَارَةٌ – يُسْرٌ – سُهُولَةٌ. Easiness of disposition, لَطَافَةٌ – سَدَاجَةٌ – دَمَاثَةٌ. Readiness of speech, فَصَاحَةٌ – بَلَاغَةٌ.

East, *n.* The —, مَطْلَعُ ٱلشَّمْسِ – ٱلْمَشْرِقُ – ٱلشَّرْقُ. To go towards the —, شَرَّقَ. Going towards the —, مُشَرِّقٌ.

East, *a.* شَرْقِيٌّ – مَشْرِقِيٌّ.

Easter, *n.* ٱلْعِيدُ ٱلْكَبِيرُ – ٱلْبَاعُوثُ – ٱلْفِصْحُ: (Muslims call it ٱلِٱسْتِشْفَاءُ).

Easterly, *a.* يَضْرِبُ إِلَى ٱلشَّرْقِ – شَرْقِيَّةٌ – شَرْقِيٌّ.

Eastern, *a.* شَرْقِيٌّ – مَشْرِقِيٌّ. The — countries, ٱلْأَقْطَارُ ٱلشَّرْقِيَّةُ – بُلْدَانُ ٱلشَّرْقِ – أَرَاضِي ٱلشَّرْقِ.

Eastward, *ad.* نَحْوَ ٱلْمَشْرِقِ – عَلَى نَاحِيَةِ ٱلشَّرْقِ. Going —, تَشْرِيقًا.

Easy, *a.* At ease, مُطْمَئِنٌّ – مُنْشَرِحُ ٱلصَّدْرِ – فِي رَاحَةٍ – مُرْتَاحٌ – مَبْسُوطُ ٱلْخَاطِرِ. Not difficult, سَمْحٌ – سَهْلٌ – سَهِلٌ – أَهْوَنُ. Complaisant, مُلَاطِفٌ – صَاحِبُ مَعْرُوفٍ – ذُو أُنْسٍ – لَيِّنٌ. Of an — temper, سَهْلُ ٱلْخُلُقِ – سَهْلٌ – ذَلُولٌ – دَمِيثٌ. Credulous, نَقُوعُ أُذُنٍ – غِرِّيرٌ – سَاذِجٌ – مُتَزَيِّدٌ (or مُغَفَّلٌ). An — life, عَيْشٌ مُفَانِقٌ – عَيْشٌ رَطْبٌ. Easy circumstances, جِدَةٌ. It is not an — matter, لَيْسَ مِنَ ٱلسَّهْلِ – لَيْسَ مِنَ ٱلْأُمُورِ ٱلسَّهْلَةِ. It is — for them to do what they ought, يَتَيَسَّرُ لَهُمْ أَنْ يَأْتُوا بِمَا يَلْزَمُهُمْ. O my Lord! make (things) — and do not make them difficult, يَا رَبِّ يَسِّرْ وَلَا تُعَسِّرْ. To be —, not difficult, سَهُلَ – تَيَسَّرَ – تَسَهَّلَ. To make — to, يَسَّرَ عَلَى – سَهَّلَ عَلَى – رَوَّضَ لِ – هَوَّنَ عَلَى. *See also under* Ease, *n.*

Eat, *v.t.* Of food, عَلَسَ – أَقَاتَ – أَكَلَ. To make one eat, آكَلَ. To give to eat, لَقَّمَ – أَكَّلَ. To eat what comes to hand, تَنَمَّشَ. To make one eat his words, أَنْكَرَ. To corrode, أَكَلَ – قَرَضَ – سَرَفَ. To eat up, to devour, قَمَّ – اِقْتَمَّ.

Eat, *v.i.* تَنَاوَلَ ٱلْمَطْعَمَ. To eat heartily, أَكَلَ بِٱلْوَحَمِ – أَكَلَ بِٱلِٱشْتِهَاءِ. To eat daintily, تَنَهَّكَ مِنَ ٱلطَّعَامِ – تَأَنَّقَ فِي ٱلْمَطْعَمِ.

Eatable, *a.* يُؤْكَلُ – أُكُلٌ – عَلُوسٌ.

Eatable, *n.* أُكَالٌ. Eatables, مَأْكُولٌ – طَعَامٌ – قُوتٌ – مَأْكُولَاتٌ.

Eater, *n.* One who eats, آكِلٌ; a great —, مِطْعَمٌ – أَكَّالٌ. A corrosive, أُكَالٌ. One who eats with another, أَكِيلٌ.

Eating, *n.* The act of, أَكْلٌ – مَأْكَلٌ.

Eating-house, *n.* مَطْعَمٌ – مَأْكَلٌ – مَوْضِعُ ٱلطَّعَامِ *pl.* مَوَاضِعُ – لُوكَنْدَةٌ.

Eaves, *n.* طَنَفٌ *pl.* طُنُوفٌ – رَفْرَفُ ٱلسَّطْحِ – كُنَّةٌ *pl.* كُنَنٌ.

Eavesdrop, *v.i.* اِسْتَمَعَ خَلْفَ ٱلْبَابِ – تَسَمَّعَ عَلَى خَفَاءٍ.

Eavesdropper, *n.* سَامِعٌ مُخْتَفٍ – مُتَسَمِّعٌ خِفْيَةً.

Ebb, *v.i.* To flow back, جَزَرَ – اِنْجَزَرَ. To decline, decay, نَقَصَ – اِضْمَحَلَّ – زَالَ – فَنِيَ. To — and flow, جَزَرَ وَمَدَّ.

Ebb, *n.* The — tide, جَزْرٌ – اِنْجِزَارٌ. Decline, decay, فَنَاءٌ – اِضْمِحْلَالٌ – زَوَالٌ. The becoming less, نُقْصَانٌ – تَقَلُّلٌ. The — and flow, ٱلْجَزْرُ وَٱلْمَدُّ.

Ebb-tide, *n.* ٱلْجَزْرُ.

Ebon, Ebony, *a.* مِنْ سَاسَمٍ – مِنْ آبْنُوسٍ.

Ebony, *n.* سَاسَمٌ – آبْنُوسٌ.

Ebriety, *n.* }
Ebriosity, } *See* Drunkenness, *n.*

Ebulliency, *n.* }
Ebullition, } A boiling, boiling over, غَلَيَانٌ – فَوَرَانٌ. An outburst, تَفَوُّرٌ – سَوْرَةٌ – ثَوَرَانٌ – فَوَرَانٌ.

Ebullient, *a.* غَالٍ – ثَائِرٌ.

Eburnean, *a.* Of ivory, عَاجِيٌّ – مِنْ سِنِّ ٱلْفِيلِ.

Eccentric, *a.* }
Eccentrical, } Deviating from the centre, خَارِجٌ عَنِ ٱلْمَرْكَزِ – مُنْحَرِفٌ عَنِ ٱلْمَرْكَزِ. Irregular, مِنْ غَيْرِ قِيَاسٍ – بِغَيْرِ طَرِيقَةٍ – بِلَا قَانُونٍ. An — person, غَرِيبُ ٱلطَّبْعِ.

Eccentric, *n.* }
Eccentric-wheel, } قُرْصَةٌ أَوْ عَجَلَةٌ خَارِجَةٌ عَنْ مَرْكَزِ دَائِرَتِهَا.

Eccentricity, *n.* Having a different centre, خُرُوجٌ عَنِ ٱلْمَرْكَزِ – عَدَمُ مُطَابَقَةِ ٱلْمَرْكَزِ. Irregularity, عَدَمُ قَانُونٍ – عَدَمُ قَاعِدَةٍ; of disposition, غَرَابَةُ ٱلطَّبْعِ.

Ecclesiarch, *n.* رَئِيسٌ كَنَائِسِيٌّ – مِنْ رُؤَسَاءِ ٱلْكَنِيسَةِ.

Ecclesiastic, *a.* }
Ecclesiastical, } كَنَائِسِيٌّ – أَكْلِيرِيكِيٌّ – رُوحَانِيٌّ. An — tribunal, مَحْكَمَةٌ رُوحَانِيَّةٌ.

Ecclesiastic, *n.* قَسٌّ *pl.* قُسُوسٌ – قِسِّيسٌ *pl.* قِسِّيسُونَ *and* قُسُسٌ – وَاحِدٌ مِنَ ٱلْإِكْلِيرُوسِ.

Ecclesiasticus, *n.* The book of, سِفْرُ ٱلْحِكْمَةِ.

Ecclesiological, *a.* مُتَعَلِّقٌ بِبِنَاءِ ٱلْكَنَائِسِ وَتَزْيِينِهَا.

Ecclesiology, *n.* عِلْمُ بِنَاءِ ٱلْكَنَائِسِ وَتَزْيِينِهَا.

Ecclesiologist, *n.* مَاهِرٌ فِي عِلْمِ بِنَاءِ ٱلْكَنَائِسِ وَتَزْيِينِهَا.

Echelon, *n.* An — of soldiers, تَصْفِيفُ ٱلْعَسَاكِرِ فِي هَيْئَةِ ٱلدَّرَجَاتِ.

Echinus, *n.* The sea —, تُوتِيَةُ ٱلْبَحْرِ ـ تُوتِيَا ـ قُنْفُذُ ٱلْبَحْرِ.

Echo, *n.* دَوِيٌّ ـ رَكَّاءُ ـ صَدًى ـ إِبْنَةُ ٱلْجَبَلِ ـ بِنْتُ صَفَا. Repetition, as of another's words, مُعَاد ـ تَصْدِيق ـ تَكْرِير. I heard the returned sound of the —, سَمِعْتُ رَدَّةَ ٱلصَّدَى.

Echo, *v.t.* أَدْوَى ـ أَصْدَى.

Echo, *v.i.* تَصَدَّى.

Eclaircissement, *n.* تَخْرِيج ـ بَيَان ـ تَصْرِيح ـ إِيضَاح.

Eclat, *n.* جَلَاءٌ ـ صِيت ـ فَخْر ـ وَكْبَة ـ نَامُوس وَشَرَف ـ صِيتَة.

Eclectic, *a.* تَفْصِيلِيٌّ ـ إِنْتِخَابِيٌّ وَٱخْتِيَارِيٌّ.

Eclecticism, *n.* أُصُولُ ٱلتَّفْصِيلِ ـ إِنْتِخَاب ـ تَفْصِيل.

Eclectics, *n.* شِيعَةٌ مِنَ ٱلْفَلَاسِفَةِ ٱلْأَقْدَمِينَ صَنَّفُوا لِنُفُوسِهِمْ عَقَائِدَ مُنْتَخَبَةً مِنْ عَقَائِدِ غَيْرِهِمْ.

Eclipse, *n.* A total —, إِنْكِسَاف ـ كُسُوف ـ خُسُوف; a partial —, خُسُوف. An — of the sun, كُسُوفُ ٱلشَّمْسِ; of the moon, خُسُوفُ ٱلْقَمَرِ.

Eclipse, *v.t.* كَسَفَ ـ. To surpass, فَاقَ ـ يَرُوقُ *aor.* رَاقَ عَلَى ـ بَرَزَ عَلَى. To extinguish, أَطْفَأَ. To cloud, darken, أَبْهَمَ ـ أَظْلَمَ عَلَى. Eclipsed, as of the moon, مُنْكَسِف; of the sun, مُنْكَسِفَة. Surpassed, مَغْلُوب.

Eclipse, *v.i.* إِنْكَسَفَ ـ خَسَفَ ـ. The moon was eclipsed, خَسَفَ ٱلْقَمَرُ ـ; the sun was eclipsed, كَسَفَتِ ٱلشَّمْسُ. To be eclipsed, swallowed up, خُسِفَ بِهِ.

Ecliptic, *n.* طَرِيقُ ٱلشَّمْسِ فِي وَسَطِ مِنْطَقَةِ ـ سَمْتُ ٱلشَّمْسِ ٱلْبُرُوجِ.

Eclogue, *n.* غِنَاءُ ٱلرُّعَاةِ ـ قَصِيدَةٌ فِي مَدْحِ ٱلرِّيفِ.

Economic, *a.* / **Economical,** } Saving, مُقْتَصِد ـ قَتُور. Relating to good management, مُخْتَصٌّ بِحُسْنِ ٱلْإِدَارَةِ ـ سِيَاسِيٌّ ـ تَدْبِيرِيٌّ. To be —, saving, قَتَرَ ـ. To be — in, إِقْتَصَدَ فِي.

Economically, *ad.* إِقْتِصَادًا ـ بِٱلْإِقْتِصَادِ ـ بِقَتْرٍ.

Economics, *n.* عِلْمُ حُسْنِ ٱلسِّيَاسَةِ ـ عِلْمُ ٱلتَّدْبِيرِ ـ عِلْمُ ٱلْإِدَارَةِ.

Economist, *n.* One who is frugal, مُقْتَصِد ـ قَتُور. Learned in economy, مُدَرِّسٌ فِي عِلْمِ ٱلتَّرْتِيبِ ـ مُدَرَّبٌ فِي عِلْمِ ٱلْإِدَارَةِ.

Economize, *v.t.* تَقَنَّى ـ نَفِسَ بِ.

Economize, *v.i.* To be frugal, as in expenditure, *etc.*, قَتَرَ فِي ـ يَفِرُ *aor.* وَفَرَ ـ إِقْتَصَدَ فِي.

Economy, *n.* Management, تَرْتِيب ـ مُدَارَاة ـ تَدْبِير ـ سِيَاسَة. A system, شَاكِلَة ـ طَرِيقَة ـ أُصُول ـ نَسَق. Frugality, قُتُور ـ إِقْتِصَاد ـ قَتْر. To live with —, عَاشَ بِٱلتَّقَنِّي ـ تَقَنَّ ـ إِقْتَصَدَ. Political —, عِلْمُ أُصُولِ ثَرْوَةِ ـ تَدْبِيرُ ٱلْمَمْلَكَةِ فِي مَعِيشَتِهِ. Animal —, عِلْمُ تَدْبِيرِ ٱلْجَسَدِ ٱلْمَمْلَكَةِ. Vegetable —, عِلْمُ ٱلتَّدْبِيرُ تَدْبِيرِ ٱلنَّبَاتِ. Economy is half a livelihood, (Arab prov.), ٱلتَّدْبِيرُ نِصْفُ ٱلْمَعِيشَةِ.

Ecstasied, *a.* In a state of ecstasy, *a.* فِي حَالٍ ـ مُتَوَجِّدٌ بِ مُسْطُول ـ ٱلْوَجْدِ.

Ecstasy, *n.* Rapture, إِنْذِهَال ـ إِنْسِطَال ـ مُكَاشَفَة ـ وَجْد. A paroxysm, بُرَحَاءُ. To be in an —, إِنْسَطَلَ ـ تَوَجَّدَ بِ. An — of joy, غَايَةُ ٱلْفَرَحِ.

Ecstatic, *a.* مُسْلِبُ ٱلْعَقْلِ ـ مُذْهِل ـ مُشْتَهٍ ـ مُوَجِّد بِ ـ سَابِي ٱلْقَلْبِ.

Ecstatically, *ad.* بِٱنْسِطَالٍ ـ بِوَجْدٍ.

Ecumenic, *a.* / **Ecumenical,** } مَسْكُونِيٌّ ـ عُمُومِيٌّ ـ عَامٌّ.

Edacious, *a.* بَلَّاع ـ هِبْلَع ـ أَكَّال.

Edacity, *n.* إِلْهَاف ـ شَرَه ـ قَرَم ـ بَلَاعَة.

Eddy, *n.* A back current, تَيَّار. A whirlpool, دَوَّارَةُ مَاءٍ ـ دَوَّار. An — of wind, جَوَلَانُ ٱلْهَوَاءِ ـ جَوْلَان. Eddying, *a.* دَوَّار ـ أَجْوَل.

Eddy, *v.i.* دَارَ ـ جَوَّلَ.

Edematous, *a.* / **Edematose,** } وَارِم.

Eden, *n.* The garden of —, أَرْضُ عَدْنٍ ـ جَنَّةُ عَدْنٍ.

Edentate, *a.* / **Edentated,** } مِنْ غَيْرِ أَسْنَانٍ ـ مَقْلُوعُ ٱلْأَسْنَانِ.

Edge, *n.* The cutting part of a blade, حَرْف ـ ذُبَاب ـ زِرٌّ ـ حَدٌّ. A brink, حَافَة ـ حَرْف ـ طَرَف ـ شُفْر. A rim, border, كَنَف ـ أَنْيَار *pl.* نِير ـ حَوَاجِبُ *pl.* حَاجِب ـ حُتْر *pl.* حِتَار ـ حَوَاشٍ *pl.* حَاشِيَة ـ أَكْنَاف *pl.* The edges of the eyelid, حِتَارُ ٱلْعَيْنِ. Sharpness of mind, حِدَّةُ عَقْلٍ ـ نَبَاهَة ـ حِذْق. Sharpness of appetite, سِنَّةُ ٱلنَّفْسِ ـ وَحَم. To set (the teeth) on —, أَضْرَسَ. His teeth were set on —, ضَرِسَتْ أَسْنَانُهُ. To draw near to the — of..., شَفَّرَ عَلَى. To take off the —, to blunt, ثَلَّمَ ـ ثَلَمَ.

Edge, *v.t.* To border, كَنَفَ ـ أَنَارَ ـ نَيَّرَ. To border or surround with, دَوَّرَ-بِ ـ أَحَاطَ-بِ. To — with fringe, سَجَّفَ. To sharpen, حَدَّدَ ـ أَحَدَّ ـ ذَبَّبَ. To incite, حَرَّضَ ـ هَيَّجَ ـ. To — in, to intrude, دَسَّ ٤ ـ أَغْمَدَ ـ أَدْخَلَ. أَنْهَضَ.

Edge, v.i. To move off sideways, اِبْتَعَدَ عَنْ عُرْضٍ ـ تَجَنَّبَ ـ تَطَرَّفَ ـ تَعَرَّضَ.

Edged, a. Sharp, قَاطِع ـ حَادٌّ. A two-edged sword, سَيْفٌ ذُو حَدَّيْنِ.

Edgeless, a. See Blunt, a.

Edge-tool, n. آلَةٌ جارِحَةٌ ـ آلَةٌ ذاتُ حَدٍّ pl. آلات.

Edgewise, ad. مِنَ ٱلْجَنْبِ ـ مِنَ ٱلطَّرَفِ.

Edging, n. سِجاف ـ حاشِيَة ـ أَنْيار pl. نِير ـ طِراز ـ كِنار ـ دائر.

Edible, a. See Eatable, a.

Edict, n. مَنْشُور ـ تَنْبِيه ـ فِرْمان ـ أَمْر ـ حُكُومَة ـ حُكْم.

Edification, n. The act of building up, بُنْيَان. Instruction, training, تَعْلِيم ـ إِصْلاح ـ تَرْقِيَة ـ تَهْذِيب ـ تَرْبِيَة. To —, لِلْبُنْيانِ ـ لِلْخَيْرِ.

Edifice, n. عِمارَة pl. عَمائِرُ ـ بِناءٌ pl. أَبْنِيَة ـ بُنْيان. Public edifices, أَبْنِيَةٌ مِيرِيَّةٌ.

Edify, v.t. To build up, بَنَى ـ. To instruct, train, هَذَّبَ ـ رَبَّى ـ أَصْلَحَ ـ عَلَّمَ ـ رَقَّى.

Edifying, a. Building up, مَا هُوَ لِلْبُنْيانِ. Instructive, improving, مُفِيد ـ تَعْلِيمِيٌّ ـ مُرَقٍّ ـ تَهْذِيبِيٌّ.

Edile, n. مُدِيرُ ٱلْعَمائِرِ.

Edileship, n. إِدارَةُ ٱلْعَمائِرِ.

Edit, v.t. To superintend the printing of another's book, بَاشَرَ طَبْعَ كِتابِ غَيْرِهِ. To publish a book, أَبْرَزَ (or أَظْهَرَ) كِتابًا.

Edition, n. The publication of a book, نَشْرُ ـ طَبْعُ كِتابٍ (or إِبْرازُ كِتابٍ). The number of a book published at once, ما يُطْبَعُ مِنْ نُسْخَةٍ فِي مَرَّةٍ واحِدَةٍ ـ طَبْعَة. A copy, exemplar, نُسْخَة ـ طَبْعَة ـ ٱلتَّرْتِيبُ ٱلْأَوَّلُ. The first —, أَوَّلُ طَبْعَةٍ ـ ٱلدَّفْعَةُ ٱلْأُولَى. He printed a new —, طَبَعَ مَرَّةً أُخْرَى.

Editor, n. One who superintends the printing of another's book, مُدِيرُ ـ مُباشِرُ طَبْعِ كِتابِ غَيْرِهِ. The superintendent of a press, مَطْبَعَة. The — of a newspaper, مُحَرِّرُ (or صاحِبُ) وَرَقَةِ أَخْبارٍ ـ مُحَرِّرُ (or مُنْشِئُ) جَرِيدَةٍ. Editors of journals, كُتَّابُ ٱلْجَرائِدِ.

Editorial, a. مُتَعَلِّقٌ بِمُباشَرَةِ طَبْعِ ٱلْكُتُبِ. An — article, مَقالَةٌ مِنْ قَلَمِ صاحِبِ ٱلْجَرِيدَةِ.

Editorship, n. وَظِيفَةُ مُدِيرٍ ـ وَظِيفَةُ مُباشِرِ طَبْعِ ٱلْكُتُبِ ـ مُحَرِّرِيَّة ـ جَرِيدَة.

Educate, v.t. To teach and cultivate, عَلَّمَ ـ دَرَّسَ ـ أَدَّبَ ـ دَرَّبَ ـ رَبَّى ـ نَشَّأَ ـ وَلَّدَ ـ هَذَّبَ ـ وَأَدَّبَ ـ رَبَّى. To train, وَلَّدَ.

Educated, a. Trained, well-taught, ماهِر ـ مُعَلَّم ـ مُدَرَّب ـ مُدَرَّس.

Education, n. The act of teaching, تَعْلِيم ـ تَدْرِيس; the being taught, instructed, عِلْم ـ تَعَلُّم ـ تَدَرُّس. The act of training, cultivation, تَأْدِيب ـ تَرْبِيَة ـ تَهْذِيب; the being cultivated, educational powers, عِلْم ـ مُمارَسَة ـ مَهارَة. He who attends to the — of his children will triumph over those who envy him (prov.) مَنْ أَدَّبَ أَوْلادَهُ أَرْغَمَ حُسَّادَهُ. Compulsory —, ٱلتَّعْلِيمُ جَبْرًا.

Educational, a. مُتَعَلِّقٌ بِٱلتَّعْلِيمِ وَٱلدَّرْسِ ـ عِلْمِيٌّ. An — establishment, مَكْتَب ـ مَدْرَسَة. An — course, دَرْس pl. دُرُوس ـ تَدْرِيس.

Educator, n. مُهَذِّب ـ مُعَلِّم ـ مُدَرِّس.

Educe, v.t. أَنْتَجَ ـ أَصْدَرَ ـ اِسْتَخْرَجَ. To — by maceration, صَوَّلَ.

Eduction, n. إِخْراج ـ إِنْتاج ـ إِصْدار ـ اِسْتِخْراج; by maceration, تَصْوِيل.

Eductor, n. مُنْتِج ـ مُصْدِر ـ مُسْتَخْرِج.

Edulcorate, v.t. صَفَّى ـ حَلَّى.

Eel, n. سَمَكُ ٱلْحَيَّاتِ ـ ثُعْبانُ ٱلسَّمَكِ ـ أَنْقَلِيس; called also in Syria, نونو. The electric —, رَعَّادَة ـ رَعَّاد.

Eel-pot, n. كُنَّةٌ لِصَيْدِ سَمَكِ ٱلْحَيَّاتِ ـ شَبَكَةٌ لِلْأَنْقَلِيس.

E'en, ad. See Even, ad.

E'er, ad. See Ever, ad.

Effable, a. مِمَّا يُوصَفُ ـ يُنْطَقُ بِهِ.

Efface, v.t. To obliterate, أَبْطَلَ ـ أَزالَ ـ أَعْدَمَ. To erase, طَلَسَ ـ ٤ مَحَا. To — from the memory, أَزاحَ-(or أَزالَ-) مِنَ ٱلْبالِ.

Effaceable, a. يُطْمَسُ ـ يُطْلَسُ ـ يُمَّحِي ـ يُمْحَى.

Effacement, n. The act of obliteration, تَعْدِيم ـ إِزالَة ـ إِبْطال; of erasement, مَحْوٌ ـ نَسْخ ـ تَمْحِيق.

Effect, n. As produced by a cause, أَثَر ـ مَجْمُوع pl. أُثُور and آثار ـ فِعْلٌ فِي pl. أَفْعال. A consequence, نَتِيجَة ـ ثَمَرَة. Drift, meaning, عِبارَة ـ مَحَطٌّ ـ مَغْناة ـ مَعْنًى ـ فَحْوَى. Necessary consequence, لازِم ـ لازِمَة. A purpose, قَصْد ـ غايَة ـ غَرَض. Power, force, قُوَّة ـ مُكْنَة. A good —, فائِدَة ـ صَدَد ـ شَأْن ـ ثَمَرَةٌ خَيْرِيَّةٌ ـ نَتِيجَةٌ حَسَنَةٌ ـ مَنْفَعَة ـ نَفْع. A bad —, ثَمَرَةٌ وَخِيمَةٌ ـ نَتِيجَةٌ سَوْءٌ ـ ضَرَر ـ مَضَرَّة. To produce an — upon, نَفَذَ فِي ـ عَمِلَ فِي ـ ٤ أَخَذَ فِي ـ أَثَّرَ فِي. To produce an —

upon, as of medicines or persons, إِشْتَغَلَ فِي ـ نَجَعَ فِي. To produce an —, to be successful, نَجَعَ ـ. In —, حَقًّا ـ فِي ٱلْوَاقِعِ ـ فِي ٱلْحَقِيقَةِ. Of no —, مِنْ غَيْرِ فَائِدَةٍ ـ بَاطِلًا ـ عَبَثًا. To this —, meaning, أَعْنِي ـ بِهٰذَا ٱلْمَضْمُونِ. To carry into —, أَجْرَى ـ قَضَى. To take —, to make an impression, أَثَّرَ; to hit, as of a mark, أَصَابَ. To gain —, to be observed, أُعْتُبِرَ. To become of no —, زَهَقَ ـ بَطَلَ ـ سَقَطَ. Cause and —, عِلَّةٌ وَأَثَرٌ ـ لَازِمٌ وَمَلْزُومٌ.

Effect, *v.t.* To do, صَنَعَ ـ فَعَلَ ـ نَجَعَ ـ أَنْجَعَ فِي ـ نَجَعَ فِي. To cause, سَبَّبَ. To accomplish, أَتَمَّ ـ كَمَّلَ ـ أَنْهَى ـ أَنْفَذَ. To gain, as an end, نَالَ ـ أَصَابَ. To be effected, done, صُنِعَ ـ إِنْعَمَلَ; to be occasioned, تَسَبَّبَ; to be accomplished, تَكَمَّلَ ـ تَتَمَّمَ ـ أَنْتَهَى. He effected the thing, carried it out, overcame it, تَمَكَّنَ مِنَ ٱلْأَمْرِ ـ إِسْتَمْكَنَ مِنَ ٱلْأَمْرِ. *See also to* Do, *v.t.*

Effectible, *a.* يُعْمَلُ ـ يُصْنَعُ ـ فِعْلُهُ مُمْكِنٌ ـ مِمَّا يُجْرَى.

Effective, *a.* Having effect, فَعَّالٌ ـ مُؤَثِّرٌ ـ مُقْتَدِرٌ فِي ٱلْفِعْلِ; of a speech, شَخْشَحَانٌ ـ قَوِيٌّ. Real, حَقِيقِيٌّ. Present, ready, as of troops, حَاضِرٌ ـ مُسْتَعِدٌّ. Energetic, مُتَبَذِّلٌ ـ شَهْمٌ *pl.* شِهَامٌ. Useful, نَافِعٌ. Effective soldiers, عَسْكَرٌ جَرَّارٌ. Effective in speech, سَدَادٌ فِي ٱلْكَلَامِ; in action, سَدَادٌ فِي ٱلْأَفْعَالِ.

Effectively, *ad.* إِسْتِحْكَامًا ـ بِنُفُوذٍ ـ كَمَا يَنْبَغِي ـ بِٱلْوَجْهِ ـ تَأْثِيرًا ـ ٱلْمَطْلُوبِ.

Effectiveness, *n.* إِيثَارٌ ـ تَأْثِيرٌ ـ إِسْتِحْكَامٌ ـ فَاعِلِيَّةٌ ـ نُفُوذٌ.

Effector, *n.* فَاعِلٌ ـ صَانِعٌ ـ مُسَبِّبٌ.

Effects, *n.* مَحَاشٌ ـ أَسْبَابٌ ـ مَتَاعٌ *pl.* أَمْتِعَةٌ. Household —, أَثَاثٌ ـ مَتَاعُ ٱلْبَيْتِ. Landed property, عِقَارٌ ـ أَمْلَاكٌ.

Effectual, *a.* Operative, مُؤَثِّرٌ ـ عَامِلٌ فِي ـ فَعَّالٌ. Producing the effect, كَافٍ *pl.* كُفَاةٌ ـ بَالِغٌ ـ نَفَّاذٌ ـ نَافِذٌ ـ نَفِيذٌ. Powerful, قَوِيٌّ. Compact, solid, مُؤَيَّدٌ ـ مَتِينٌ ـ صَارِمٌ. Useful, نَافِعٌ ـ نَفَّاعٌ.

Effectually, *ad.* حَسَبَ ٱلْمُرَادِ ـ حَقًّا ـ بِتَأْثِيرٍ ـ سَدَدًا ـ سِدَادًا. To do —; *see to* Effectuate, *v.t.*

Effectuate, *v.t.* To achieve, fulfil, أَجْرَى ـ أَتَمَّ ـ قَضَى ـ كَمَّلَ. *See also to* Achieve, *v.t.*

Effeminacy, *n.* Excessive softness, خِنَاثَةٌ ـ خَنَثٌ ـ تَدَلُّلٌ ـ تَأْنِيثٌ. Wantonness, دِعَارَةٌ ـ عَهَرٌ.

Effeminate, *a.* خَنِيثٌ ـ مُخَنَّثٌ ـ مُتَدَلِّلٌ ـ مُؤَنَّثٌ ـ أَنِيثٌ.

Effeminate, *v.t.* خَنَّثَ ـ صَيَّرَ مِثْلَ ٱلنِّسَاءِ.

Effeminately, *ad.* بِتَخَنُّثٍ ـ بِٱلتَّفْنِيقِ ـ بِٱلتَّدَلُّلِ. To act —, تَخَنَّثَ.

Effeminateness, *n.* *See* Effeminacy, *n.*

Effendi, *n.* More correctly, Efendi, أَفَنْدِي *pl.* أَفَنْدِيَّةٌ.

Effervesce, *v.n.* فَارَ. To make to —, أَفَارَ. *See also* Boil, *v.i.*

Effervescence, *n.* فَوْرٌ ـ فَوَرَانٌ.

Effervescent, *a.* فَائِرٌ ـ مَفُورٌ.

Effervescible, *a.* يَفُورُ.

Effete, *a.* Barren, عَقِيمٌ ـ عَاقِرٌ ـ عَاجِزٌ. Worn out, كَهَامٌ ـ كَهِيمٌ ـ سَحِيقٌ.

Efficacious, *a.* *See* Effective, Effectual, *a.*

Efficaciously, *ad.* *See* Effectively, Effectually, *ad.*

Efficacy, Efficience, *n.* Efficiency, } *See* Effect, Effectiveness, *n.*

Efficiently, *ad.* *See* Effectively, Effectually, *ad.*

Effigy, *n.* حِلْيَةٌ ـ تِمْثَالٌ ـ شَبِيهٌ ـ شَكْلٌ ـ صُورَةٌ. They burnt him in —, أَحْرَقُوا صُورَتَهُ حَقَارَةً بِهِ. They hung him in —, عَلَّقُوا تِمْثَالَهُ حَقَارَةً بِهِ وَدَلَالَةً عَلَى أَنَّهُ مُسْتَحِقُّ ٱلشَّنْقِ.

Effloresce, *v.i.* Of flowers, أَزْهَرَ ـ زَهَرَ; of metals, تَجَوْهَرَ.

Efflorescence, *n.* نَبْتَةٌ. Of flowers, إِزْهَارٌ; of metals, عَرَقُ ٱلْمَعَادِنِ ـ مَنْبُوتُ ٱلْمَعَادِنِ ـ تَجَوْهُرُ ٱلْمَعَادِنِ. An — on the skin, حَلًا ـ حَلًا.

Efflorescent, *a.* Of flowers, مُزْهِرٌ; of metals, مُتَجَوْهِرٌ.

Effluence, *n.* A flowing out, ثُجُوجٌ ـ صَبٌّ; that which issues, مَثْجٌ ـ ثَجِيجٌ ـ إِنْصِبَابٌ.

Effluent, *a.* ثَجَّاجٌ ـ صَابٌّ ـ مُنْصَابٌّ.

Effluvium, *n.* فَوْحَةٌ ـ هَبَاءٌ *pl.* أَهْبَاءٌ ـ بُخَارٌ *pl.* بُخَارَاتٌ ـ تَعَفُّنٌ.

Efflux, Effluxion, *n.* } *See* Effluence, Effluvium, *n.*

Effort, *n.* سَعْيٌ ـ جَدٌّ ـ جُهْدٌ ـ إِجْتِهَادٌ ـ كَدٌّ ـ هِمَّةٌ. Strenuous —, مَسْعَاةٌ ـ سَعْيٌ بَلِيغٌ ـ غَيْرَةٌ كَامِلَةٌ. With the utmost —, بِأَقْصَى سَعْيٍ وَغَيْرَةٍ. To make an — to, سَعَى فِي *aor.* يَسْعَى. To use all one's efforts, بَذَلَ ـ عَمِلَ كُلَّ جُهْدِهِ غَايَةَ هِمَّتِهِ. All our efforts have been in vain, صَارَ تَعَبُنَا بَاطِلًا بِٱلْكُلِّيَّةِ.

Effortless, *a.* بِدُونِ سَعْيٍ ـ مِنْ غَيْرِ ٱجْتِهَادٍ.

Effrontery, *n.* وَقَحٌ ـ وَقَاحَةٌ ـ قِلَّةُ حَيَاءٍ ـ سَفَاهَةٌ.

Eft, *n.* *See* Newt, *n.*

Effulgence, *n.* رَوْنَقٌ ـ بُلْجَةٌ ـ سُطُوعٌ ـ ضِيَاءٌ ـ لَمَعَانٌ.

Effulgent, *a.* زَهِيٌّ ـ نَيِّرٌ ـ مُنِيرٌ ـ سَاطِعٌ ـ بَهِيٌّ ـ مُتَلَأْلِئٌ ـ مُضِيءٌ.

Effuse, *v.t.* أَرَاقَ ـ ²سَفَكَ ـ ²سَكَبَ ـ ²صَبَّ. To be effused, إِنْسَكَبَ ـ إِنْسَفَكَ ـ إِنْصَبَّ ـ ²صَبَّ. To extract by maceration, صَوَّلَ. Effused, مَسْفُوكٌ ـ سَفِيكٌ.

Effusion, *n.* The act of effusing, إِرَاقَةٌ ـ سَكْبٌ ـ صَبٌّ ـ سَفْكٌ; what is effused, مَا سُفِكَ ـ مُسْتَرَاقٌ ـ صَبِيبٌ. Waste, consumption, سَفْكٌ ـ إِسْرَافٌ ـ تَلَفٌ. An —, shedding, of blood, إِرَاقَةُ ٱلدِّمَاءِ ـ ٱلدَّمِ. An — of bounty, جُودٌ ـ سَخَاءٌ ـ سَخَاوَةٌ ـ إِجَادَةٌ. The continuance of the —, shedding, of blood, دَوَامُ إِرَاقَةِ ٱلدِّمَاءِ.

Effusive, *a.* فَيَّاضٌ ـ فَائِضٌ ـ سَفُوكٌ.

Effusively, *ad.* سَفْكًا ـ بِفَيْضٍ.

E.G. مَثَلًا ـ مِثَالُ ذٰلِكَ.

Egad! *int.* فِي ذِمَّتِي وَدِينِي ـ عَلَى ذِمَّتِي ـ وَحَيَاتِكَ.

Egg, *n.* بَيْضَةٌ *coll.* بَيْضٌ *pl.* بَيْضَاتٌ. The yelk of an —, ذَهَبٌ (*or* صَفَارُ) ٱلْبَيْضِ ـ غِرْقِدٌ ـ قَيْقَيٌّ; the white of an —, بَيَاضُ ٱلْبَيْضِ. To lay eggs, بَاضَتْ. To hatch, of eggs, نَقَصَ ـ نَقَسَ. A hatched —, بَيْضَةٌ نَقَصَةٌ (*or* مَفْقُوصَةٌ). A new-laid —, بَيْضَةٌ طَرِيَّةٌ; a rotten —, بَيْضَةٌ مَذِرَةٌ. To sit on eggs, ²رَقَدَ عَلَى ـ ²حَضَنَ ٱلْبَيْضَ ـ ٱلْبَيْضِ. To boil or poach, of eggs, ²سَلَقَ; a boiled egg, بَيْضَةٌ مَسْلُوقَةٌ. A seller of eggs, بَيَّاضٌ. Eggs of fish, spawn, بَطَارِخُ ـ سَرْءٌ. Eggs of the silkworm, بِزْرٌ. Broken egg-shells, حُطَامٌ.

Egg, *v.t.* To incite, حَرَّضَ ـ هَيَّجَ.

Egg-cup, *n.* ظَرْفٌ لِلْبَيْضِ *pl.* ظُرُوفٌ.

Egg-plant, *n.* بَاذِنْجَانٌ أَسْوَدُ.

Eglantine, *n.* عُلَّيْقُ ٱلْكَلْبِ ـ وَرْدٌ جَبَلِيٌّ ـ جُلَّنِسْرِينُ ـ عَبَالٌ.

Egoism, *n.* تَفْضِيلُ ٱلذَّاتِ ـ أَنَانِيَّةٌ. *See also* Selfishness, *n.*

Egotist, *n.* / Egotistic, *a.* / Egotistical, *a.* } مُفَضِّلٌ ذَاتَهُ بِٱلْأَنَانِيَّةِ ـ مُتَنَانٍ. *See also* Selfish, *a.*

Egotise, *v.i.* تَأَنَّى.

Egregious, *a.* جَسِيمٌ ـ كَبِيرٌ ـ خَارِقُ ٱلْعَادَةِ ـ فَائِقٌ *pl.* فُوقَاءُ. An — crime, كَبِيرَةٌ *pl.* كَبَائِرُ ـ قَبَاحَةٌ *pl.* قَبَائِحُ. An — error, mistake, غَلْطَةٌ كَبِيرَةٌ ـ خَطَأٌ جَسِيمٌ. He could not have made a more —, لَمْ يَقْدِرْ أَنْ يَأْتِيَ بِغَلَطٍ أَعْظَمَ مِنْ هٰذَا.

Egregiously, *ad.* جِدًّا ـ فَوْقَ ٱلْعَادَةِ ـ لِلْغَايَةِ.

Egress, *n.* / Egression, } The act of going out, ذَهَابٌ ـ إِنْطِلَاقٌ ـ خُرُوجٌ. Liberty to quit, رُخْصَةٌ ـ تَرْخِيصٌ. Place of —, مَخْرَجٌ. Places of —, مَفَارِجُ.

Egret, *n.* The bird, دَنْكَلَةٌ بَيْضَاءُ. The down of seeds, جَالِحَةٌ.

Egrette, *n.* A tuft of feathers, شُوشَةٌ ـ رِيشَةٌ. The ornament, رِيشَةٌ. An — given for valour and worn on the turban in time of war, جَلَنْك ـ شَلَنْك.

Egypt, *n.* مِصْرُ ـ دِيَارُ مِصْرَ ـ بَرُّ مِصْرَ. Upper —, صَعِيدُ مِصْرَ. Central —, ٱلْأَقْلِيمُ ٱلْوَسْطَانِيُّ مِنْ مِصْرَ. Lower —, ٱلْأَقْلِيمُ ٱلْبَحْرِيُّ مِنْ مِصْرَ.

Egyptian, *a.* مِنْ مِصْرَ ـ مِصْرِيٌّ. A native of Egypt, مِصْرِيٌّ *pl.* مِصْرِيُّونَ *and* مَصَارَى *and* مَصَارِوَةٌ ـ إِبْنُ مِصْرَ *pl.* أَوْلَادُ مِصْرَ.

Eh! *int.* يَا ـ أَيْ.

Eider, *n.* / Eider-duck, } ضَرْبٌ مِنَ ٱلْبَطِّ بِرِيشٍ نَاعِمٍ.

Eider-down, *n.* زَغَبُ (*or* سُخَامُ) ٱلْبَطِّ ٱلْمَذْكُورِ.

Eight, *a.* ثَمَانِيَةٌ *fem.* ثَمَانٍ. Eight men, ثَمَانِيَةُ رِجَالٍ; eight days, ثَمَانِيَةُ أَيَّامٍ. Eight women, ثَمَانِي نِسْوَةٍ. I saw — women, رَأَيْتُ ثَمَانِيَ نِسْوَةٍ. I saw —, رَأَيْتُ ثَمَانِيًا. Eight by —, ثَمَانِيَةٌ فِي ثَمَانِيَةٍ ـ ثَمَانِيَةٌ بِثَمَانِيَةٍ.

Eighteen, *a.* ثَمَانِيَةَ عَشَرَ. I have with me — men, عِنْدِي ثَمَانِيَةَ عَشَرَ رَجُلًا. I have with me — women, عِنْدِي مِنَ ٱلنِّسَاءِ ثَمَانِيَ عَشْرَةَ ٱمْرَأَةً.

Eighteen-mo, *n.* تَفْصِيلُ ٱلطَّلْحِيَّةِ ثَمَانِيَةَ عَشَرَ صَفِيحَةً.

Eighteenth, *a.* ٱلثَّامِنَ عَشَرَ *fem.* ٱلثَّامِنَةَ عَشْرَةَ.

Eightfold, *a.* قَدْرُهُ ثَمَانِ مَرَّاتٍ ـ ثَمَانِيَةُ أَضْعَافٍ.

Eighth, *a.* ٱلثَّامِنُ *fem.* ٱلثَّامِنَةُ.

Eighth, *n.* ثُمْنٌ *pl.* أَثْمَانٌ.

Eighthly, *ad.* ثَامِنًا.

Eightieth, *a.* ٱلثَّمَانُونَ.

Eightscore, *a.* ثَمَانُونَ.

Eighty, *a.* ثَمَانُونَ.

Either, *conj.* إِمَّا ... إِلَّا. Either speak thou what is good or be silent, إِمَّا أَنْ تَتَكَلَّمَ بِٱلْخَيْرِ وَإِلَّا فَٱسْكُتْ. He will — punish them or he will turn unto them with forgiveness, (Kur.), إِمَّا يُعَذِّبُهُمْ وَإِمَّا يَتُوبُ عَلَيْهِمْ. I will — live in the house or sell it, إِمَّا أَسْكُنُ ٱلْبَيْتَ وَإِمَّا أَبِيعُهُ.

Either, *a.* and *pr.* كِلَا *fem.* كِلْتَا ـ كِلَانِ *fem.* كِلْتَانِ ـ هٰذَا *fem.* هٰذِهِ وَتِلْكَ ـ وَذَاكَ. Either the one or the other, إِمَّا ٱلْوَاحِدُ أَوِ ٱلْآخَرُ ـ إِمَّا هٰذَا أَوْ ذَاكَ. On — side, on both sides, عَلَى ٱلْجَانِبَيْنِ ـ مِنْ هُنَا وَمِنْ هُنَاكَ. Either of you, of many, أَيٌّ مِنْكُمْ ـ أَحَدُكُمْ; of two, أَيٌّ مِنْكُمَا.

Ejaculate, *v.t.* To utter, نَطَقَ بِـ ـ تَفَوَّهَ بِـ ـ ²فَاهَ بِـ ـ نَبَذَ نَبْذًا (*or* أَلْقَى صَوْتًا) وَقَالَ. To cry out, ²صَرَخَ بِـ ـ ²صَرَخَ ـ ²صَرَخَ بِـ بَغْتَةً ـ وَقَالَ.

Ejaculation, *n.* Utterance, صَوْت ـ نُطْق ـ تَفَوُّه. A short prayer, دُعَيَّة ـ دُعَآء. Speech without premeditation, فَلْتَة ـ نَبْذَة ـ بُدَاهَة.

Ejaculatory, *a.* Sudden, مِنْ فَوْر. Suddenly uttered, مُرْتَجَل ـ نَبِيذ ـ مَنْطُوق بِهِ عَلَى ٱلْبَدِيهَة.

Eject, *v.t.* To drive out, أَخْرَجَ ـ طَرَدَ ـ طَرَحَ. To exile, نَفَى. To turn out of an office, عَزَلَ. To — from the mouth, إِسْتَفْرَغَ ـ نَطَقَ.

Ejection, *n.* The act of driving out, إِخْرَاج ـ طَرْد ـ طَرْح. Ejection by stool, بِرَاز; by vomiting, إِسْتِفْرَاغ.

Ejectment, *n.* A writ to deprive of possession, حُكْمٌ شَرْعِيٌّ بِإِخْرَاجِ أَحَدٍ مِنْ تَصَرُّفِهِ.

Ejector, *n.* مُغْتَصِب ـ ضَابِطُ مُلْكِ غَيْرِهِ.

Eke, *v.t.* To make up, سَدَّ مَسَدَّ ـ سَدَّ. To prolong, طَوَّلَ.

Elaborate, *v.t.* To do with skill, care, *etc.*, to beautify, زَخْرَفَ ـ زَوَّقَ ـ حَسَّنَ; of speech, ضَرَّجَ ٱلْكَلَامَ. To work out by study, إِسْتَنْبَطَ. To perfect, أَرْصَنَ ـ كَمَّلَ ـ أَكْمَلَ.

Elaborate, *a.* } Done with skill, beautified, مُزَخْرَف ـ مُزَوَّق ـ
Elaborated, } مُحَسَّن; of speech, مُضَرَّج. Highly finished, كَامِل ـ مُكَمَّل ـ مُحْكَم ـ مُرْصَن. Elicited by study, مُسْتَنْبَط.

Elaborately, *ad.* With skill, care, well, بِإِرْصَانٍ ـ بِٱلْحُكْمِ; of speech, بِٱلتَّضْرِيجِ. As elicited by research, بِكَمَالٍ ـ بِتَحْكِيمٍ ـ إِسْتِنْبَاطًا.

Elaborateness, *n.* إِرْصَان ـ كَمَال ـ تَفْصِيل.

Elaboration, *n.* تَكْمِيل ـ تَحْكِيم ـ إِرْصَان; of speech, تَضْرِيج.

Elaborator, *n.* One who perfects, beautifies, مُزَخْرِف ـ مُرْصِن ـ مُكَمِّل; of language, مُضَرِّج. One who elicits ideas, *etc.*, by research, مُسْتَنْبِط.

Elapse, *v.i.* بَرِحَ ـ مَرَّ ـ مَضَى ـ زَالَ ـ حَالَ.

Elastic, *a.* } إِذَا ٱنْحَنَى أَوِ ٱمْتَدَّ رَجَعَ ـ يَمُدُّ وَيَتَقَلَّصُ ـ مُمْتَغِط
Elastical, } إِلَى حَالَتِهِ ٱلْأُولَى. Made of (gum) —, مِنْ لَسْتِيك. *See also under* India rubber, *n.*

Elastic, *n.* لَسْتِيك.

Elasticity, *n.* خَاصِّيَّةُ ٱلِٱمْتِغَاطِ وَٱلتَّقَلُّصِ.

Elate, *a.* غِطْرِيس ـ جَبَرِيّ ـ مُتَكَبِّر ـ مَغْرُور.

Elate, *v.t.* نَفَخَ ـ كَبَّرَ. To be elated, إِسْتَكْبَرَ ـ إِنْتَفَخَ ـ تَكَبَّرَ.

Elation, *n.* إِسْتِكْبَار ـ شَمْخَرَة ـ غَطْرَسَة ـ جَبَرِيَّة ـ تَكَبُّر.

Elbow, *n.* مِرْفَق *pl.* مَرَافِق ـ كُوع *pl.* أَكْوَاع *and* كِيعَان ـ عَكْس. An angle, flexure, عَوْجَة ـ عَطْفَة ـ قُرْنَة. The — or knee of a horse or other beast, مَثْنَى *pl.* مَثَانٍ. The — of a chair, يَدُ كُرْسِيّ ـ مَسْنَدُ كُرْسِيّ. An — chair, كُرْسِيّ بِمَسْنَدَيْنِ لِلذِّرَاعَيْنِ. The inner side of the —, مَأْبِد. The bend of the —, مَعْطِفُ ٱلْمِرْفَقِ. To be at the —, near, to one, قَرُبَ مِنْ ـ وَقَفَ عِنْدَ *aor.* يَقِفُ.

Elbow, *v.t.* To push with the —, قَصَفَ ـ دَفَعَ بِٱلْكُوعِ. To — against, صَدَمَ. To bend, عَوَّجَ ـ عَطَفَ ـ ثَنَى.

Elbow, *v.i.* To bend, إِنْثَنَى ـ تَقَوَّسَ.

Elbow-chair, *n.* *See under* Elbow, *n.*

Elbow-room, *n.* Room for the elbows, سَعَةٌ لِلذِّرَاعَيْنِ. Room, space, فُسْحَة ـ مَكَان ـ سَعَة ـ رُحْب.

Elder, *n.* The tree, خَمَان ـ أَقْطِي.

Elder, *a.* الأَقْدَمُ عُمْرًا ـ الأَكْبَرُ سِنًّا ـ الأَوَّل. Aly the son of 'Umar the —, عَلِيُّ بْنُ عُمَرَ ٱلْكَبِيرِ. He is my — brother, هُوَ أَخِي ٱلْأَكْبَرُ. She is my — sister, هِيَ أُخْتِي ٱلْكُبْرَى. Elder women, عَجَائِز. The young and the —, *pl.* الأَحْدَاثُ وَٱلشُّيُوخُ.

Elder, *n.* شَيْخ *pl.* شُيُوخ *and* مَشَائِخ. Elders, ancestors, أَسْلَاف. The ancients, الأَوَائِل ـ الأَقْدَمُونَ. The — of a church, شَيْخُ ٱلْكَنِيسَةِ.

Eldership, *n.* Seniority, شَيْخُوخَة ـ شُيُوخِيَّة ـ شُيُوخَة. The elders of a church, مَشَائِخُ كَنِيسَةٍ.

Elderly, *a.* قَادِمٌ عَلَى ٱلشُّيُوخِيَّةِ ـ مُتَوَسِّطُ ٱلْهَرَمِ. *See also* Middle-aged, *a.*

Eldest, *n.* الأَكْبَرُ ـ الكَبِير. The — brother, الأَخُ ٱلْأَكْبَرُ. An — son, بِكْر *pl.* أَبْكَار. He is the — brother, هُوَ ٱلْأَخُ ٱلْبِكْرُ.

Elecampane, *n.* The plant, زَنْجَبِيلٌ شَامِيٌّ ـ رَاسِن ـ جَنَاح ـ جَاسِيم.

Elect, *v.t.* إِنْتَخَبَ ـ إِصْطَفَى ـ إِخْتَارَ. To —, as for a sovereignty, بَايَعَ. To prefer, فَضَّلَ عَلَى ـ إِسْتَحْسَنَ. He was elected, recognized, by them, عَقَدُوا لَهُ. He was elected Khalifah, بُويِعَ بِٱلْخِلَافَةِ. *See also to* Choose, *v.t.*

Elect, *a.* } مُخْتَصّ ـ مُخْتَار ـ مُنْتَخَب ـ مُصْطَفَى. The —
Elected, } people of God, مُخْتَارُوا ٱللّٰهِ. One — of God, صَفِيُّ ٱللّٰهِ ـ صَفْوَةُ ٱللّٰهِ مِنْ خَلْقِهِ.

Electicism, *n.* *See* Eclecticism, *n.*

Election, *n.* The act of choosing, نُخْبَة ـ إِخْتِيَار ـ إِنْتِخَاب ـ خِيرَة ـ إِصْطِفَآء. Election, by swearing allegiance to, مُبَايَعَة. Election, as by God, إِصْطِفَآء وَٱجْتِبَآء. Election of members to a parliament, إِنْتِخَابُ ٱلْأَعْضَآءِ لِمَجْلِسِ ٱلشُّورَى (or ٱلْمَبْعُوثِينَ) رَسْمًا. A general —, إِنْتِخَابٌ عَامٌّ رَسْمِيٌّ. A day of general —, يَوْمٌ مِنْ أَيَّامِ ٱلِٱنْتِخَابِ ٱلْعَامِّ ٱلرَّسْمِيِّ. Mode of —, أُصُولُ ٱلِٱنْتِخَابِ.

Electioneer, *v.i.* سَعَى فِي إِقْنَاعِ ٱلْمُنْتَخِبِينَ أَنْ يَقِيمُوهُ وَكِيلاً عَنْهُمْ فِي مَجْلِسِ ٱلْمَبْعُوثِينَ.

Electioneer, *n.* مُدَرَّبٌ فِي أُمُورِ ٱلْإِنْتِخَابِ.

Electioneering, *n.* سَعْيٌ فِي إِجْرَاءِ ٱلْأُمُورِ ٱلْمُتَعَلِّقَةِ بِٱنْتِخَابِ ٱلْوُكَلَاءِ لِمَجْلِسِ ٱلشُّورَى.

Elective, *a.* حائزُ حَقِّ ٱلْإِنْتِخَابِ ـ خَيْرِيٌّ ـ خَيِّرٌ ـ إِنْتِخَابِيٌّ. An — government, حُكُومَةٌ مَبْنِيَّةٌ عَلَى أُصُولِ ٱلْإِنْتِخَابِ. Elective affinity, خاصِّيَّةُ ٱقْتِرَانِ ٱلْمَعَادِنِ بِبَعْضِ ٱلْمَوَادِّ دُونَ غَيْرِهَا.

Electively, *ad.* بِٱلْمُبَايَعَةِ ـ إِخْتِيَارًا ـ خِيَرَةً ـ بِٱلْإِنْتِخَابِ.

Elector, *n.* One who has the elective franchise, حائزُ حَقِّ مُنْتَخِبٍ ـ ٱنْتِخَابِ ٱلْوُكَلَاءِ لِمَجْلِسِ ٱلشُّورَى. An — of Germany, أَمِيرٌ جِرْمَانِيٌّ كَانَ قِدَمًا لَهُ حَقٌّ فِي مُبَايَعَةِ أَمْبَرَاطُورِ جِرْمَانِيَا.

Electoral, *a.* مَا لِلْأَعْضَاءِ مِنْ حَقِّ ٱلْإِنْتِخَابِ ـ مُتَعَلِّقٌ بِٱلْإِنْتِخَابِ.

Electoral list, دَفْتَرُ أَسَامِي ٱلْمُنْتَخِبِينَ.

Electorate, *n.* مَقَامُ ٱلْأَمِيرِ ٱلْحَائِزِ حَقَّ ٱلْمُبَايَعَةِ فِي جِرْمَانِيَا.

Electress, *n.* زَوْجَةُ أَوْ أَرْمَلَةُ ٱلْأَمِيرِ ٱلْحَائِزِ حَقَّ ٱلْمُبَايَعَةِ فِي جِرْمَانِيَا.

Electric, *n.* مَادَّةٌ كَهْرَبَائِيَّةٌ ـ جِسْمٌ كَهْرَبَائِيٌّ.

Electric, *a.* } Electrical, } كَهْرَبَائِيٌّ *fem.* كَهْرَبَائِيَّةٌ. Electric fluid, ٱلسَّيَّالُ ٱلْكَهْرَبَائِيُّ. Electric attraction, ٱلْكَهْرَبَائِيَّةُ ٱلْجَاذِبِيَّةُ.

Electrician, *n.* أُسْتَاذُ عِلْمِ ٱلْكَهْرَبَائِيَّةِ.

Electricity, *n.* ٱلْكَهْرَبَائِيَّةُ. The science of —, عِلْمُ ٱلْكَهْرَبَائِيَّةِ.

Electrifiable, *a.* مَا تَقُومُ (or تَسِيلُ) فِيهِ ٱلْكَهْرَبَائِيَّةُ ـ مِمَّا يُكَهْرَبُ.

Electrified, *a.* سَائِلَةٌ فِيهِ ٱلْكَهْرَبَائِيَّةُ ـ مُكَهْرَبٌ.

Electrify, *v.t.* As with electricity, كَهْرَبَ ـ جَعَلَ (or أَسَالَ) فِيهِ ٱلْكَهْرَبَائِيَّةَ. To excite, حَرَّكَ ـ إِسْتَفَزَّ ـ أَثَارَ ـ إِسْتَثَارَ.

Electrifying, *a.* Of electricity, مُكَهْرِبٌ. Highly exciting, مُحَرِّكٌ ـ مُهَيِّجٌ ـ مُسْتَفِزٌّ ـ مُسْتَثِيرٌ.

Electrification, *n.* تَكَهْرُبٌ ـ إِسَالَةُ ٱلْكَهْرَبَائِيَّةِ فِي شَيْءٍ.

Electrize, *v.t.* *See to* Electrify, *v.t.*

Electro-chemistry, *n.* عِلْمُ ٱلْكَهْرَبَائِيَّةِ ٱلْكِيمَاوِيَّةِ.

Electro-magnetic, *a.* مُتَعَلِّقٌ بِٱتِّحَادِ ٱلسَّيَّالِ ٱلْكَهْرَبَائِيِّ مَعَ ٱلْمَغْنَاطِيسِ ـ كَهْرَبَائِيٌّ مَغْنَاطِيسِيٌّ.

Electro-plate, *v.t.* As with silver, طَلَى بِٱلْفِضَّةِ بِوَاسِطَةِ ٱلْكَهْرَبَائِيَّةِ.

Electro-plated, *a.* As with gold, مُذَهَّبٌ بِوَاسِطَةِ ٱلْكَهْرَبَائِيَّةِ; as with silver, مُفَضَّضٌ (or مُمَوَّهٌ بِفِضَّةٍ) بِوَاسِطَةِ ٱلْكَهْرَبَائِيَّةِ.

Electro-telegraph, *n.* ٱلتِّلِغْرَافُ ٱلْكَهْرَبَائِيُّ.

Electrometer, *n.* مِيزَانُ ٱلْكَهْرَبَائِيَّةِ.

Electron, *n.* Amber, كَهْرَبَا. An alloy of gold and silver, خِلْطٌ مِنَ ٱلذَّهَبِ وَٱلْفِضَّةِ.

Electrotype, *n.* سِكَّةٌ ـ قَالِبُ صُورَةٍ مُمَوَّهٌ بِوَاسِطَةِ ٱلْكَهْرَبَائِيَّةِ ـ سِكَّةٌ مُكَهْرَبَةٌ ـ كَهْرَبَائِيَّةٌ.

Electrotype, *v.t.* رَغَّلَ قَالِبَ ٱلصُّورَةِ بِوَاسِطَةِ ٱلْكَهْرَبَائِيَّةِ ـ كَهْرَبَ ٱلسِّكَّةَ.

Electrum, *n.* *See* Electron, *n.*

Electuary, *n.* لَعُوقَةٌ *pl.* لَعُوقَات ـ مَعْجُونٌ *pl.* مَعَاجِينُ.

Eleemosynary, *a.* مُتَعَلِّقٌ بِٱلْحَسَنَةِ وَٱلصَّدَقَةِ ـ مَا يُعْطَى صَدَقَةً.

Elegance, *n.* ظَرَافَةٌ ـ جَمَالٌ ـ نَضْرَةٌ ـ لَبَقَةٌ ـ لَبَقٌ ـ صَبَاحَةٌ ـ مَلَاحَةٌ ـ حُسْنٌ ـ إِنَاقَةٌ ـ لَطَافَةٌ; of language, فَصَاحَةٌ وَبَلَاغَةٌ ـ ظَرَافَةٌ فِي ٱلْكَلَامِ; of personal shape, رَشَاقَةُ ٱلْقَامَةِ ـ إِصْطِلَاحٌ ـ حُسْنُ ٱلصُّورَةِ. To act with or to affect —, تَظَرَّفَ.

Elegant, *a.* Especially of a place, صَبِيحٌ ـ صَبْحَانُ ـ مَلِيحٌ *pl.* مِلَاحٌ ـ نَزِلٌ ـ لَطِيفٌ ـ ظَرِيفٌ ـ جَمِيلٌ ـ نَاضِرٌ; in personal shape, ظَرِيفُ ٱلصُّورَةِ ـ رَشِيقُ ٱلْقَامَةِ ـ صَيِّرٌ شَيِّرٌ; in style, فَصِيحٌ ـ بَلِيغٌ. An — or witty speech, نَادِرَةٌ ـ لَطِيفَةٌ. Elegant in movement, of a man or boy, بُلْبُلٌ. To consider —, إِسْتَظْرَفَ. An — scholar, أَدِيبٌ ـ لَوْذَعِيٌّ. Elegant scholars, orators, فَوَقَةٌ. He was — in speech, أَظْرَفَ فِي ٱلْعِبَارَةِ.

Elegantly, *ad.* بِلَطَافَةٍ ـ لَبَقَةً ـ بِبَرَاعَةٍ ـ بِظَرَافَةٍ. To do anything —, أَظْرَفَ فِي.

Elegiac, *a.* } Elegiacal, } رَاثٍ ـ مُتَعَلِّقٌ بِٱلْمَرْثِيَةِ ـ مُرِثٌّ.

Elegiast, *n.* } Elegist, } شَاعِرٌ مُرِثٌّ (or رَاثٍ) لِلْمَيِّتِ.

Elegy, *n.* مَرْثَاةٌ ـ مَرْثِيَةٌ *pl.* مَرَاثٍ. To compose or deliver an —, رَثَى (or رَثَّى) ٱلْمَيِّتَ.

Element, *n.* The constituent part of a thing, عُنْصُرٌ *pl.* عَنَاصِرُ. A principle, substance, إِسْطَقِسٌ *pl.* إِسْطَقِسَات ـ جَوْهَرٌ. Origin, foundation, أَصْلٌ ـ أَسَاسٌ ـ مَبْدَأٌ *pl.* مَبَادِئُ ـ مَنْشَأٌ *pl.* مَنَاشِئُ. A simple substance, جِسْمٌ بَسِيطٌ. A cause, medium, ذَرِيعَةٌ *pl.* ذَرَائِعُ ـ وَسِيلَةٌ. Atmosphere, هَوَاءٌ *pl.* أَهْوِيَةٌ ـ جَوٌّ. Matter, property, مَادَّةٌ ـ خُصُوصٌ. Ascertained quantity, كَمٌّ ـ كَمِّيَّةٌ مَعْلُومَةٌ. Water, مَاءٌ. The proper habitation of anything, مَوْطِنٌ ـ مَكَانٌ ـ مَوْضِعٌ. Elements, first principles, أُصُولٌ ـ مَبَادِئُ ـ أَرْكَانٌ ـ قَوَاعِدُ. Primary substance, جِذْرُ (or أَسَاسُ) ٱلْمَادَّةِ. The four elements, ٱلْعَنَاصِرُ ٱلْأَرْبَعُ ـ ٱلْأَرْبَعُ عَنَاصِرَ. The science of the elements of theology, عِلْمُ أُصُولِ ٱلدِّينِ. To be in one's —, كَانَ مَبْسُوطًا ـ حَصَلَ عَلَى ٱلْبَهْجَةِ ـ كَانَ فِي بَيْتِ أُنْسِهِ. To be out of one's —, إِسْتَوْحَشَ ـ إِسْتَغْرَبَ . A war of the elements, زَوْبَعَة ـ قُرْتُنَة . The consecrated elements, القُرْبَانُ ٱلْمُقَدَّسُ . A light —, عُنْصُرٌ خَفِيفٌ ; a heavy —, عُنْصُرٌ ثَقِيلٌ .

Elemental, *a.* Pertaining to the (four) elements, عُنْصُرِيٌّ . An — body, عُنْصُرِيَّة .

Elementariness, *n.* / Elementarity, } The being rudimental, إِبْتِدَائِيَّة ـ أَصْلِيَّة ; of the quality of the (four) elements, عُنْصُرِيَّة .

Elementary, *a.* Primary, rudimental, مُخْتَصٌّ بِٱلْأُصُولِ وَٱلْقَوَاعِدِ ـ مُخْتَصٌّ بِٱلْمَبَادِئِ . An elementary (book), مَدْخَل ـ مِنْهَاج ـ كِتَابٌ مُسَهِّلٌ . Elementary schools, مَكَاتِبُ ٱبْتِدَائِيَّة .

Elemi, *n.* The gum, صِمْغُ ٱلزَّيْتُونِ ـ صِمْغٌ لَامِيٌّ .

Elephant, *n.* فِيل *fem.* فِيلَة *pl.* فُيُول *and* أَفْيَال . An — keeper, فَيَّال . The goad for an —, مِقْمَعَة .

Elephantiasis, *n.* دَآءُ ٱلْفِيلِ ـ جُذَام . Having —, مَجْذُوم .

Elephantine, *a.* Pertaining to elephants, مُخْتَصٌّ بِٱلْأَفْيَالِ ـ فِيلِيٌّ . Huge, عَظِيم ـ جَسِيم .

Elevate, *v.t.* To raise from a lower to a higher point, أَسْمَى ـ رَفَعَ ـ أَعْلَى ـ عَلَّى . To set upright, ²سَمَا بِ ـ نَصَبَ ² ـ أَقَامَ . To raise morally, أَصْلَحَ ـ أَفَادَ ـ رَقَّى ـ هَذَّبَ ـ سَنَّى . To raise in dignity, شَرَّفَ ـ عَظَّمَ ـ رَفَّعَ ـ عَزَّزَ ـ أَعَزَّ ـ عَلَّى . To cheer, فَرَّحَ ـ سَرَّ² . To — the voice, رَفَعَ (or جَهَرَ) ٱلصَّوْتَ . To be elevated, raised, from a lower to higher point, تَسَمَّى ـ إِرْتَفَعَ ; to be set upright, أُقِيمَ ـ إِنْتَصَبَ ; to be ennobled, تَعَلَّى ـ تَعَظَّمَ ـ تَشَرَّفَ . To be elevated, high, شَهَقَ ـ إِرْتَفَعَ ـ تَعَلَّى . His ambition elevated him, طَمَتْ بِهِ هِمَّتُهُ .

Elevated, *a.* High, مُرْتَفِع ـ شَاهِق ـ عَالٍ ـ نَابِه ـ سَامٍ ـ سَمِيٌّ . An — place, شَرَف . To be — above, إِسْتَعْلَى عَلَى .

Elevation, *n.* The act of raising from a lower to a higher place, تَرْفِيع ـ إِعْلَآء ـ تَعْلِيَة ; the being so raised, إِرْتِفَاع ـ تَعَلٍّ . The act of setting upright, إِقَامَة ـ نَصْب ; the being set upright, قِيَام ـ إِنْتِصَاب . The act of promotion, تَعْظِيم ـ تَرْقِيَة ـ تَشْرِيف ; the being promoted, عَظَمَة ـ شَرَف ـ عُلُوُّ شَأْنٍ ـ رِفْعَة ـ مَنْزِلَة . Height, عُلُوٌّ ـ إِرْتِفَاع ـ شُهْقَة ـ سُمُوٌّ . A hill, تَلّ *pl.* تِلَال ـ أَكَمَة *pl.* أَكَمَات ـ كُومَة *pl.* أَكْوَام . Exaltation of mind, فَخْرُ ٱلْعَقْلِ . Elevation of the soul to God, إِبْتِهَالُ ٱلرُّوحِ إِلَى ٱللّٰهِ . Elevation of the host, إِرْتِفَاعُ ٱلْقُرْبَانِ . The front view of a building, صُورَةُ وَاجِهَةِ بِنَآءٍ . Elevation, improvement, of a department, إِرْتِقَآء (or إِسْتِتْبَابُ) ٱلْإِدَارَةِ .

Elevator, *n.* مُقِيم ـ مُرَفِّع . An —, muscle, عَضَلَةٌ مُحَرِّكَةٌ . The surgical instrument, آلَةُ جَرَّاحٍ لِرَفْعِ كِسَرِ ٱلْعِظَامِ مِنَ ٱلْجُمْجُمَةِ ٱلْمُسْتَجِهَةِ . A lift, سُمُكٌ *pl.* سِمَاكٌ .

Élève, *n.* تِلْمِيذ *pl.* تَلَامِيذ ـ خِرِّيج .

Eleven, *a.* أَحَدَ عَشَرَ *fem.* إِحْدَى عَشْرَةَ .

Eleventh, *a.* الحَادِي عَشَرَ *fem.* الحَادِيَةَ عَشْرَةَ . In the — year فِي ٱلسَّنَةِ ٱلْحَادِيَةِ عَشَرَ .

Elf, *n.* جِنِّيٌّ *fem.* جِنِّيَّة *coll.* جِنٌّ .

Elfin, *a.* / Elfish, } جِنِّيٌّ .

Elicit, *v.t.* To draw out, أَخْرَجَ ـ إِسْتَخْرَجَ . To deduce from, إِسْتَنْتَجَ مِن ـ أَنْتَجَ مِن . To — fire from flint with a steel, قَدَحَ بِٱلزِّنَادِ . To bring to light, أَظْهَرَ ـ أَشْهَرَ ـ أَعْلَنَ . To — thanks, إِسْتَوْجَبَ ٱلشُّكْرَ .

Elide, *v.t.* حَذَفَ ـ إِحْتَذَفَ . To be elided, حُذِفَ . Elided, مَحْذُوف .

Eligibility, *n.* / Eligibleness, } Capacity of being elected, قَابِلِيَّةُ ٱلْإِنْتِخَابِ ـ لِيَاقَةٌ بِٱلنُّخْبَةِ ـ إِسْتِهَالُ ٱلْإِصْطِفَاءِ ـ مُخْبَة . Fitness, لِيَاقَة ـ مَصْلَحَة ـ مُنَاسَبَة . Merit, إِسْتِحْقَاق . Preponderance in favour, رُجْحَانِيَّة ـ تَفَوُّق ـ فَضِيلَة .

Eligible, *a.* Capable of being elected, يُنْتَخَبُ ـ أَهْلٌ لِلنُّخْبَةِ . Desirable, proper, مُوَافِق ـ لَائِق ـ مُنَاسِب . Very —, superior, أَفْضَلُ ـ أَنْسَبُ ـ مُرَجَّح ـ أَخْيَرُ . Fitted for, worthy of, مَرْآةٌ . He is — for this, هُوَ مَرْآةٌ بِهٰذَا .

Eligibly, *ad.* بِوَجْهٍ خَيْرٍ ـ بِٱلْمُنَاسَبَةِ ـ لِيَاقَةً ـ بِلِيَاقَةٍ .

Eliminate, *v.t.* To draw out, أَخْرَجَ . To cause to disappear, أَزَالَ .

Elimination, *n.* إِخْرَاج ـ إِزَالَة .

Elision, *n.* حَذْف . Elision in order to soften in pronunciation, تَسْهِيل .

Elite, *n.* أَفْضَلُ ـ أَحْسَنُ ـ عِينَة ـ زُبْدَة ـ مُخْبَة .

Elixir, *n.* إِكْسِير . The essence of anything, جَوْهَر ـ خُلَاصَة . Spirit, رُوح ـ عَنْبَرِيَّة .

Elk, *n.* ضَرْبٌ مِنَ ٱلْإِيَّلِ .

Ell, *n.* ذِرَاع *pl.* أَذْرُع .

Ellipse, *n.* An oval figure, شَكْلٌ إِهْلِيلَجِيٌّ ـ بَيْضِيُّ ٱلشَّكْلِ ـ أَلِيبْسِي ـ قِطْعٌ نَاقِصٌ .

Ellipsis, *n.* Elision, تَسْهِيل ـ حَذْف ـ تَقْدِير ; *in poetry*, تَقْطِيع .

Ellipsoid, *n.* جِسْمٌ إِهْلِيلَجِيُّ ٱلشَّكْلِ ـ قِطْعٌ نَاقِصٌ مُجَسَّمٌ .

Elliptic, *a.* / Elliptical, } Oval, إِهْلِيلَجِيٌّ ـ بَيْضِيُّ ٱلشَّكْلِ ـ بَيْضِيٌّ . Having something omitted, مَحْذُوفٌ مِنْهُ ـ تَقْدِيرِيٌّ ; *in rhetoric*, تَضَمُّنِيٌّ .

Elm, *n.* بُوقِيصَا ـ شَجَرَةُ ٱلْبَقِّ ـ دَرْدَار.

Elocution, *n.* Utterance, تَكَلُّم ـ نُطْق ـ كَلَام. Mode of utterance, بَيَان ـ بَلَاغَة ـ فَصَاحَة. Fluent speech, نَصّ ـ فَنّ.

Elocutionary, *a.* مُتَعَلِّقٌ بِٱلْبَيَانِ ـ خُطَبِيٌّ.

Elocutionist, *n.* خَطِيب ـ مُتَكَلِّم *pl.* خُطَبَآءُ.

Eloge, *n.* *See* Elegy, *n.*

Elongate, *v.t.* To lengthen, أَطَالَ ـ طَوَّلَ. To remove farther, أَبْعَدَ.

Elongate, *v.i.* To recede, حَالَ ـ تَنَحَّى ـ اِبْتَعَدَ.

Elongation, *n.* The act of lengthening, إِطَالَة ـ تَطْوِيل. Distance, اِبْتِعَاد ـ بُعْد. Elongation, in astronomy, اِبْتِعَادُ سَيَّارَةٍ عَنِ ٱلشَّمْسِ حَسَبَ ٱلرُّؤْيَةِ مِنَ ٱلْأَرْضِ.

Elope, *v.i.* فَرَّ. He eloped with the woman, فَرَّ مَعَ ٱلْمَرْأَةِ خُفْيَةً. The woman eloped with the man, فَرَّتْ مَعَ ٱلرَّجُلِ خُفْيَةً. The two eloped, فَرَّا خُفْيَةً.

Elopement, *n.* مَفَرٌّ خَفِيٌّ ـ فِرَارٌ خَفِيٌّ.

Eloquence, *n.* بَلَاغَة ـ فَصَاحَة ـ بَيَان ـ شِقْشِقَة. To speak with —, تَفَصَّحَ. Eloquence is lawful incantation, (*prov.*) البَيَانُ سِحْرٌ حَلَالٌ. Eloquence is man's ornament, (*prov.*) جَمَالُ ٱلرَّجُلِ فَصَاحَةُ لِسَانِهِ. To affect —, تَفَصَّحَ.

Eloquent, *a.* ذُو شِقْشِقَةٍ ـ طَلْقُ (or طَلِقُ) ٱللِّسَانِ ـ فَتِيقُ ٱللِّسَانِ ـ لَوْذَعِيٌّ ـ بَلِيغ ـ كَلْمَانِيٌّ ـ فَصِيح *pl.* فُصَحَآءُ ـ طَلْقٌ ذَلْقٌ ـ مِنْطِيق ـ مِصْقَع.

Eloquently, *ad.* بِبَلَاغَةٍ ـ بِبَيَانٍ ـ بِفَصَاحَةٍ ـ بِشِقْشِقَةٍ. He spoke —, اِنْطَلَقَ لِسَانُهُ ـ أَفْصَحَ ٱلْقَوْلَ.

Else, *pr.* and *a.* غَيْر ـ أَحَد ـ سِوَاهُ. No one —, لَا غَيْرَ. There is one God, there is none —, اَللّٰهُ وَاحِدٌ لَيْسَ آخَرُ سِوَاهُ. He is God, there is none —, هُوَ ٱللّٰهُ لَيْسَ آخَرُ. That is nothing — but . . . , لَيْسَ ذٰلِكَ إِلَّا. I went no where —, مَا ذَهَبْتُ إِلَى غَيْرِ مَكَانٍ.

Else, *ad.* إِلَّا ـ وَإِلَّا ـ مَا ذَا وَإِلَّا فَ . . . . Either three days of rain or — three days of fine weather, إِمَّا ثَلَاثَةَ أَيَّامِ مَطَرٍ أَوْ ثَلَاثَةَ أَيَّامِ صَحْوٍ. Remember what I told you or — I will come to you, أُذْكُرْ مَا قُلْتُ لَكَ وَإِلَّا فَإِنِّي آتِيكَ.

Elsewhere, *ad.* فِي مَكَانٍ آخَرَ ـ فِي غَيْرِ مَكَانٍ.

Elucidate, *v.t.* فَصَّلَ ـ بَيَّنَ ـ أَوْضَحَ ـ شَرَحَ. To — a doubt, حَلَّ ٱلشَّكَّ ـ خَرَّجَ ٱلشَّكَّ.

Elucidation, *n.* The act of elucidating, إِيضَاح ـ تَصْرِيح ـ بَيَان ـ تَفْسِير. Elucidation of a doubt, حَلُّ مُشْكِلَةٍ ـ تَخْرِيجُ ٱلشَّكِّ.

Elucidator, *n.* شَارِح ـ مُفَصِّل ـ مُبَيِّن.

Elucidatory, *a.* تَفْسِيرِيٌّ ـ تَصْرِيحِيٌّ ـ إِيضَاحِيٌّ.

Elude, *v.t.* تَفَلَّتَ مِن ـ نَجَا مِن ـ لَاذَ (or لَاذَ) مِن ـ نَجَّى ـ تَجَنَّبَ مِن ـ فَرَّ مِن ـ اِحْتَذَرَ مِن. To cause to —, نَجَّى ـ جَنَّبَ ـ خَلَّصَ مِن.

Eludible, *a.* يُلَاذُ (or يُلَاذُ) مِنْهُ ـ يُنْجَى مِنْهُ.

Elusion, *n.* Escape, هَرِيبَة ـ لَوَاذٌ مِن. Evasion by artifice, خَدِيعَة ـ مُحَاوَلَة.

Elusive, *a.* Evasive, خَدَّاع ـ مُحْتَال.

Elusory, *a.* غَرَّار ـ غَاشّ.

Elves, *pl.* *See* Elf, *n.*

Elysian, *a.* سَعِيد ـ نَعِيم.

Elysium, *n.* جَنَّة ـ نَعِيم.

Emaciate, *v.t.* عَجَفَ ـ سَخَّفَ ـ أَذَابَ ـ هَزَّلَ ـ هَزَلَ ـ نَحَّفَ ـ أَنْحَفَ. To —, as a fever does, هَبَطَ ـ نَهَكَ; as old age, أَنْحَصَ.

Emaciate, *v.i.* To grow emaciated, هَزَلَ ـ اِخْتَلَّ جِسْمُهُ ـ بَرَدَتْ عِظَامُهُ ـ بَرَدَ مُخُّهُ ـ ذَابَ جِسْمُهُ; as through a fever, اِنْتَهَكَ; as through age, نَحَصَ.

Emaciated, *a.* رِكّ ـ نَحِيف ـ خَاسِف ـ مَهْزُول ـ مُخْتَلّ; through sickness, مَنْهُوك; through age, نَاهِق.

Emaciation, *n.* Leanness, هُزَال ـ هَزَال ـ نَحَافَة ـ خَسْف ـ عَجَف. *See also* Leanness, *n.*

Emanant, *a.* مُنْبَثِقٌ مِن ـ صَادِرٌ مِن ـ خَارِجٌ مِن.

Emanate, *v.i.* تَفَرَّعَ مِن ـ صَدَرَ عَن ـ خَرَجَ مِن ـ اِنْبَثَقَ مِن ـ اِشْتَقَّ مِن. To cause to —, أَخْرَجَ مِن ـ أَصْدَرَ عَن.

Emanation, *n.* The causing to proceed from, إِيرَاد ـ أَصْدَار; what proceeds, اِشْتِقَاق ـ وُرُود ـ صُدُور. *See also* Effluvium, *n.*

Emanative, *a.* صَادِرٌ عَن ـ مَائِلٌ إِلَى ٱلصُّدُورِ عَن.

Emancipate, *v.t.* حَرَّرَ ـ فَكَّ ـ سَيَّبَ ـ أَعْتَقَ ـ أَطْلَقَ. To be emancipated, تَحَرَّرَ ـ أُطْلِقَ ـ عَتَقَ.

Emancipated, *a.* مُحَرَّر ـ مَعْتُوق. An — slave, طَلِيق *pl.* طُلَقَآءُ ـ عَتِيق *pl.* عُتَقَآءُ ـ سَائِبَة.

Emancipation, *n.* The act of —, إِطْلَاق ـ عِتَاقَة ـ إِعْتَاق ـ تَحْرِير; the being emancipated, عَتَاق ـ عَتَاقَة ـ عِتْق ـ حُرِّيَّة. The — of slaves, إِطْلَاقُ ٱلرَّقِيقِ ـ رَفْعُ ٱلْأَسْرِ.

Emancipator, *n.* مُعْتِق ـ سَاعٍ فِي إِطْلَاقِ ٱلرَّقِيقِ.

Emasculate, *v.t.* To weaken, هَبَطَ ـ أَضْعَفَ ـ أَخْمَلَ. To render effeminate, خَنَّثَ. *See also to* Castrate, *v.t.*

Emasculate, *a.* } Castrated, مَسْلُول ـ مَطْوُوش ـ خَصِيّ *pl.*
Emasculated, } خُصًى. Weakened, فَسْخ ـ كَسِيم ـ خَامِل ـ ضَعِيف ـ عَاجِز. Effeminate, مُخَنَّث.

Emasculation, *n.* Weakness, عَجْز ـ مَعْجِزَة ـ ضَعْف ـ فَسْخ ـ كَشْح . *See also* Castration, *n.*

Embale, *v.t.* حَزَمَ ٱلْبِضَاعَة ـ حَزْم .

Embalm, *v.t.* صَبَّرَ ـ حَنَّطَ . To be embalmed, تَحَنَّطَ . The perfumes used in embalming, حِنَاط ـ حَنُوط .

Embalmer, *n.* مُصَبِّر ـ مُحَنِّط .

Embank, *v.t.* To close with a bank, سَدَّ ². To raise a bank, قَوَّمَ سَدًّا ـ ² رَصَفَ رَصِيفًا . To raise a bank, rampart, against, أَقَامَ مِتْرَاسًا عَلَى .

Embankment, *n.* The act of raising, as of a bank, تَرْصِيف ـ تَقْوِيم . A bank for fortification, مِتْرَسَة *pl.* مَتَارِس . Any mass of stones joined together, or the masonry along the side of a river, رَصِيف ـ رَصَف .

Embargo, *n.* حُكْم ـ مَنْعُ ٱلْمَرَاكِبِ عَنِ ٱلْخُرُوجِ مِنَ ٱلْمِينَا بِتَوْقِيفِ مَرْكَب . To place an — upon, وَقَّفَ . To raise an —, رَفَعَ ٱلتَّوْقِيف .

Embark, *v.i.* As on a ship, نَزَلَ ٱلْمَرْكَب ـ رَكِبَ فِي ٱلسَّفِينَة . To — in an affair, بَاشَرَ فِي ـ تَوَهَّطَ فِي ـ ٱرْتَكَبَ ـ رَكِبَ أَمْرًا ـ ٱشْتَبَكَ فِي .

Embark, *v.t.* To cause to go on board ship, رَكَّبَ فِي ٱلسَّفِينَة ـ نَزَّلَ فِي ٱلْمَرْكَب . To engage another, as in any undertaking, أَشْغَلَ فِي ـ وَهَّطَ فِي ـ شَبَكَ فِي .

Embarkation, *n.* The act of going on board ship, نُزُولٌ فِي ٱلْمَرْكَب ـ رُكُوبٌ فِي ٱلْمَرْكَب ; of putting on board, تَنْزِيلٌ فِي ٱلْمَرْكَب .

Embarrass, *v.t.* As in one's movement, to hinder, زَحَمَ ـ عَوَّقَ ـ لَحَمَ ـ لَبَكَ ـ شَبَكَ ـ حَبَسَ . To perplex, حَيَّرَ ـ ² رَبَكَ ـ أَحَمَّ ـ تَوَّهَ ـ أَجْهَدَ ـ شَوَّشَ عَلَى . To muddle, شَوَّشَ ـ عَرْبَقَ ـ خَبَّصَ ـ لَبَّكَ . To cause to blush, أَخْجَلَ .

Embarrassed, *a.* Perplexed, مُضْطَرِب ـ حَائِر ـ حَيْرَانُ . In a muddle, مُشَوَّش ـ مُرْتَبِك ـ مُلْتَبِك . In — circumstances, in want, فِي أَزَقِ ٱلْعَيْشِ ـ مُحْتَاج ـ عَائِل ـ مَحْصُور . To be —, put to the blush, خَجِلَ .

Embarrassing, *a.* Perplexing, مُشَبِّك ـ مُقْلِق ـ مُحَيِّر ـ مُكَدِّر ـ مُلَبِّك ـ مُعَوِّق .

Embarrassment, *n.* A strait, ضَيْقَة ـ صُعُوبَة ـ عَجْز . A hindrance, مَانِع ـ عَائِق *pl.* عَوَائِق ـ مُعَارَضَة . Confusion, blushing, خَجَل ـ حَيَاء . Perplexity of mind, خَبَال ـ حَيْرَة ـ تَوَه ـ خَبْلَة . Trouble, كَدَر ـ ضَجَر ; muddle, ٱرْتِبَاك ـ عَرَاقِيلُ ـ لَبْكَة ـ غَلَبَة ـ خَلَل . Straitness of circumstances, جُهْد ـ شِدَّة ـ أَزَقُ ٱلْعَيْشِ . In a state of utter —, مُكَدَّرُ ٱلْبَالِ مُضْطَرِبُ ٱلْأَحْوَالِ .

Embassy, *n.* The office of ambassador, سِفَارَة ; the residence of an —, مَحَلّ إِقَامَةِ ٱلْإِيلْجِي ـ دَارُ ٱلسِّفَارَة ; the officials attached to an —, مَأْمُورُوا ٱلسِّفَارَة وَخَدَمُهَا .

Embattle, *v.t.* To draw up troops in battle array, صَفَّ ٱلْجَيْش ² رَتَّبَ ٱلْعَسَاكِرَ لِلْمُقَاتَلَة ـ لِلْقِتَال . To furnish with battlements, رَكَّبَ شُرُفَات .

Embattle, *v.i.* ٱصْطَفَّ . The troops were embattled, ٱصْطَفَّ ٱلْجَيْشُ لِلْقِتَال .

Embattled, *a.* Arranged, as in order of battle, مُصْطَفّ ـ مُصَفَّف . Having battlements, عَلَيْهِ شُرُفَات .

Embay, *v.t.* أَدْخَلَ فِي خَلِيج .

Embed, *v.t.* طَابَقَ عَلَى ٱلـ... ـ أَحَاطَ عَلَى ٱلـ... . To fix firmly, أَرْسَخَ ـ قَرَّرَ ـ مَكَّنَ ـ ضَبَطَ .

Embedded, *a.* Deposited, مَوْضُوع ـ مُقِيم . Surrounded, مُطْبُوق عَلَيْهِ ـ مُحَاطٌ بِهِ ; fixed firmly, رَاسِخ ـ ثَابِت ـ مَكِين .

Embellish, *v.t.* زَوَّقَ ـ حَسَّنَ ـ جَمَّلَ ـ زَخْرَفَ ـ زَيَّنَ ـ ² فَنَّنَ ـ تَرَقَّشَ ـ بَرْقَشَ ـ دَبَّجَ . To — one's self or to be embellished, زَخْرَفَ ـ تَحَسَّنَ ـ تَجَمَّلَ . To — one's speech, (رَمَّقَ or بَزَّرَ or) رَقَّشَ ٱلْكَلَام . To —, with a false colouring, with lies, زَوَّرَ . *See also to* Adorn, *v.t.*

Embellishment, *n.* The act of embellishing, تَحْسِين ـ تَزْيِين ـ تَجْمِيل . Ornament, زِينَة ـ زُخْرُف ـ بَرْقَشَة ; of speech, بَزْر (or تَبْزِير or تَرْوِيق) ٱلْكَلَام . *See also* Adornment, *n.*

Ember-days, *n.* بَرَمُون ـ أَيَّامٌ مِنَ ٱلْأُسْبُوعِ ٱلْأَوَّلِ مِنَ ٱلْفُصُولِ ٱلْأَرْبَعَةِ مُعَيَّنَة لِرَسْمِ ٱلْإِكْلِيرُوس .

Ember-week, *n.* أُسْبُوعُ بَرَمُون ـ أُسْبُوعٌ مِنَ ٱلْأَسَابِيعِ ٱلْأُوْلَى مِنَ ٱلْفُصُولِ ٱلْأَرْبَعَةِ فِيهِ يُرْسَمُونَ طُلَّابُ ٱلْوَظِيفَةِ ٱلْإِكْلِيرِيكِيَّة .

Embers, *n.* جَمَرَات ـ رَمَادٌ حَارّ ـ حَال ـ مَلَّة .

Embezzle, *v.t.* سَرَقَ ـ أَسَلَّ ـ ٱخْتَلَسَ ـ زُورًا .

Embezzlement, *n.* سِرْقَة ـ ٱخْتِلَاس .

Embezzler, *n.* سَارِق ـ سَلَّابَة ـ رَجُل مُسِلّ .

Embitter, *v.t.* *See to* Imbitter, *v.t.*; *also under* Bitter, *a.*

Emblaze, *v.t.* / **Emblazon,** } To adorn with heraldic figures, نَقَّشَ (or رَسَمَ) عَلَامَاتِ ٱلشَّرَفِ وَهِيَ ٱلْآرْمَا عَلَى لَوْحٍ أَوْ غَيْرِه . To adorn, فَنَّنَ ـ بَرْقَشَ ـ زَخْرَفَ .

Emblazoner, *n.* نَقَّاش ـ رَسَّام ـ نَقَّاش (or رَسَّام) عَلَامَاتِ ٱلشَّرَفِ وَهِيَ ٱلْآرْمَا .

Emblazonry, *n.* نَقْش ـ بَرْقَشَة ـ نَقْشُ أَوْ رَسْمُ ٱلْآرْمَا .

Emblem, *n.* A sign, رَمْز *pl.* رُمُوز — كِنَايَة — كُنْوَة *pl.* كُنًى — إِشَارَة — مِثَال — عِبَارَة. An example, نَمُوذَج — عِبْرَة *pl.* عِبَر.

Emblematic, *a.* } رَمْزِيّ — كَانٍ عَن *pl.* كَانُونَ *and* كُنَاة —
Emblematical, } مُشِيرٌ إِلَى.

Emblematically, *ad.* بِالرَّمْز — فِي مِثَال — بِنَوْعٍ رَمْزِيّ.

Emblematist, *n.* مُرَتِّبُ ٱلرُّمُوزِ وَمُصَوِّرُهَا.

Emblematize, *v.i.* } صَوَّرَ رَمْزًا — إِمْتَثَلَ ب- بِٱلرُّمُوزِ.
Emblemize, }

Emblements, *n.* غَلَّاتُ ٱلْمَزَارِعِ — مَحْصُولَاتُ ٱلْأَرَاضِي.

Embloom, *v.t.* حَسَّنَ-بِٱلْكِمَام — أَشْمَلَ-بِٱلنَّوَاوِير.

Embodied, *a.* In a body, مُحْتَوٍ عَلَى جَسَدٍ — مُجَسَّم. Formed into a corporation, مُجْمَل — جَمِيع — مُجْتَمِع. Included in, مُنْدَرِجٌ فِي. An — number of men, قَوْمٌ جَمِيعٌ (or مُجْتَمِعٌ).

Embodiment, *n.* The putting into a body, تَجْسِيم. The collecting into a body, إِجْمَال — تَجْمِيع — جَمْع. The act of infolding, inclusion, تَدْرِيج. A speciality, خَاصِّيَّة — خُصُوصَة. An exact resemblance, ذَات — عَيْن. The — of pride, عَيْنُ ٱلْكِبْرِيَاء.

Embody, *v.t.* To give a body to, جَسَّمَ. To collect into a body, جَمَّعَ. To inclose, أَدْرَجَ — دَرَّجَ. To unite, as into a mass, ضَمَّ-إِلَى — جَمَعَ-فِي — أَدْخَلَ-إِلَى.

Embody, *v.i.* To unite, as in a body, تَجَمَّعَ — إِتَّحَدَ — إِجْتَمَعَ. To become infolded, إِنْضَمَّ — إِنْطَمَّ — إِنْدَرَجَ.

Embolden, *v.t.* جَسَّرَ — جَرَّأَ — شَجَّعَ — شَيَّعَ. To be emboldened, to dare, تَجَاسَرَ — إِجْتَرَأَ عَلَى — تَجَرَّأَ. To be bold, تَشَجَّعَ — تَجَرَّأَ — إِسْتَجْرَ — تَجَرَّرَ — جَرُؤَ. To — one's self, تَجَرَّرَ.

Em-bon-point, *n.* سِمَن. A woman with —, حُبَيْكَة.

Emborder, *v.t.* *See to* Border, *to* Edge, *v.t.*

Embosom, *v.t.* *See to* Imbosom, *v.t.*

Emboss, *v.t.* جَعَلَ-مُسَنَّمًا — طَرَّزَ — سَنَّمَ — عَبَّأَ.

Embossed, *a.* مُسَنَّم — مُطَرَّز — مُعَبًّا.

Embossment, *n.* تَطْرِيز — تَسْنِيم — تَعْبِئَة.

Embottle, *v.t.* *See to* Bottle, *v.t.*

Embouchure, *n.* As of a river, فِرَاض — بُوغَاز *pl.* بَوَاغِيزُ — مَصَبّ (or فَم) نَهْر; of a cannon, فَمُ مِدْفَع.

Embowel, *v.t.* أَخْرَجَ ٱلْأَحْشَاء.

Embowelment, *n.* إِخْرَاجُ ٱلْأَحْشَاء.

Embower, *v.t.* أَحَاطَ-بِأَشْجَار — عَرَّشَ.

Embower, *v.i.* To lodge in a bower, أَقَامَ — سَكَنَ ٱلْعَرِيشَ بِمُشَجَّرٍ.

Embrace, *v.t.* As in the arms, ضَمَّ-إِلَى صَدْرِهِ — عَانَقَ — إِعْتَنَقَ — إِحْتَضَنَ. To kiss, قَبَّلَ — بَاسَ. To comprehend, inclose, إِحْتَوَى عَلَى — تَضَمَّنَ — حَوَى — شَمَلَ — إِشْتَمَلَ عَلَى. To admit, قَبِلَ — إِتَّخَذَ — سَلَّمَ ب — رَضِيَ ب. To —, as of a religion, دَخَلَ فِي. To — a party, to be joined with, إِنْضَمَّ إِلَى. To — an opportunity, رَصَدَ ٱلْفُرْصَةَ — إِنْتَهَزَ (or إِفْتَرَصَ) فُرْصَةً. To — an offer, قَبِلَ ٱلْعُرُوضَ. They embraced one another, of many, تَحَاضَنُوا — تَعَانَقُوا.

Embrace, *n.* } A clasp with the arms, ضَمَّة — حِضَانَة —
Embracement, } مُعَانَقَة. An inclosure, إِحَاطَة — جِدَار. Union, إِتِّحَاد — مُجَامَعَة. A kiss, قُبْلَة — بَوْسَة.

Embracer, *n.* One who embraces in the arms, حَاضِن — مُعَانِق. One who embraces a religion, دَخِيلٌ فِي مَذْهَب.

Embrasure, *n.* طَاقٌ لِلْمِدْفَع *pl.* طَاقَات — مَزْغَل *pl.* مَزَاغِل.

Embrocate, *v.t.* To rub with, نَطَلَ-ب — طَلَى-ب.

Embrocation, *n.* The act of, نَطْل — تَطْلِيَة. A liniment, نَطُول — طِلَاء.

Embroider, *v.t.* أَعْلَمَ — طَرَّزَ — سَوَّجَ — زَرْكَشَ. To —, as in colours, نَقَّشَ-ب. Embroidered with gold, مُطَرَّز (or مُزَرْكَش) بِٱلذَّهَب.

Embroiderer, *n.* طَرَّاز — مُطَرِّز — مُزَرْكِش.

Embroidery, *n.* طِرَاز — تَطْرِيز.

Embroil, *v.t.* To confuse, خَلَّطَ — لَبَّكَ — شَوَّشَ — خَبَّصَ. To set at loggerheads, قَرَّشَ بَيْنَ — رَمَى ٱلْفِتْنَةَ بَيْنَ. To be embroiled, confused, تَلَبَّكَ — إِلْتَبَكَ.

Embroilment, *n.* The act of confusing, تَلْبِيك — تَشْوِيش — تَخْبِيص. Dissension, إِرْتِبَاك — شِقَاق — فِتْنَة — خَلَل.

Embrue, *v.t.* *See to* Imbrue, *v.t.*

Embryo, *n.* } Of an animal, عُلُوق — جَنِين *pl.* أَجِنَّة; of a
Embryon, } plant, نَشْأ — شَكِير *pl.* شُكُر.

Embryology, *n.* عِلْمُ ٱلْبَحْثِ عَنِ ٱلْجَنِينِ وَٱلشَّكِيرِ.

Emendable, *a.* قَابِلُ ٱلْإِصْلَاحِ — مِمَّا يُصْلَحُ — يُصَحَّحُ — يُعَالَجُ.

Emendation, *n.* The act of emending, تَصْحِيح — إِصْلَاح — تَضْبِيط — مُعَالَجَة. The being emended, إِسْتِتْبَاب. Correctness, صِحَّة — ضَبْط — إِحْكَام *See also* Correction, Correctness, *n.*

Emendator, *n.* } مُصْلِح — مُصَحِّح — مُعَالِج.
Emendatory, *a.* }

Emerald, *n.* زُمُرُّد; of —, زُمُرُّدِيّ. Emerald type, ضَرْبٌ مِنَ ٱلْحُرُوفِ ٱلدَّقِيقَةِ ٱلْمُسْتَعْمَلَةِ فِي ٱلطِّبَاعَةِ.

Emerge, *v.i.* To — from, طَلَعَ مِن — بَرَزَ — خَرَجَ مِن — ظَهَرَ مِن. To appear, ظَهَرَ — بَيَّنَ — لَاحَ.

Emergence, *n.* } The act of rising out of, بُرُوزٌ مِن – خُرُوجٌ مِن –
Emergency, } طُلُوعٌ مِن. A sudden occurrence, فُجَاءَةٌ – حالٌ – إِيجاب – ضَرُورة. A pressing necessity, صُدْفَة – حادِثَة – عِنْدَ وُقُوعِ ٱللُّزُومِ – عِنْدَ ٱلحاجَةِ. In case of —, صُعُوبَة – لُزُوم – إِنْ دَعَتِ ٱلحاجَةُ إِلَى.

Emergent, *a.* Rising out of, بارِزٌ مِن – خارِجٌ مِن – طالِعٌ مِن. Unexpected, باغِت – غَيْرُ مَعْهُودٍ – فُجائيٌّ. Urgent, مُهِمٌّ – مُلْزُوم – لازِم – ضَرُورِيٌّ.

Emergently, *ad.* بِٱللُّزُوم – بِٱلضَّرُورَةِ.

Emerods, *n.* *See* Hemorrhoids, *n.*

Emery, *n.* سَنْفَرَة – سَفِيرَة – دَهْنَج – سُنْبَاذَج.

Emetic, *n.* } مُسَبِّبُ ٱلاِسْتِفْراغ – مُطَرِّش – مُقَيِّئٌ – قَيُوءٌ.
Emetic, *a.* }

Emeu, *n.* The bird, ضَرْبٌ مِنَ ٱلطَّيْرِ.

Emeute, *n.* شَغْب – فَساد – فِتْنَة – قَوْمَة.

Emication, *n.* لَمْحَة – شَرارَة.

Emiction, *n.* Of urine, تَبَوُّل – تَشْغِيَة – شَغًا.

Emigrant, *n.* One leaving a place for another, جالٌّ – مُهاجِر – رَحِيل. One who leaves his home to settle elsewhere, مُهاجِرُ وَطَنِهِ لِيَسْكُنَ فِي غَيْرِ بِلادِهِ *pl.* مُهاجِرُون.

Emigrate, *v.t.* To — from, سافَرَ مِن – تَرَكَ ² – هَجَرَ ² – جَلَا عَن. To leave one's home to settle elsewhere, هَجَرَ وَطَنَهُ لِيَسْكُنَ فِي ² غَيْرِ بِلادِهِ.

Emigration, *n.* As from one place to another, جَلْوٌ – جَلاءٌ – مُهاجَرَة. The act of leaving to settle elsewhere, هِجْرَة – هَجْر – هِجْرَةٌ مِنَ ٱلوَطَنِ لِلسُّكْنَى فِي غَيْرِ بِلادِهِ.

Eminence, *n.* } Height, اِرْتِفاع – سُمُوٌّ – نِيَاف – عُلُوٌّ – عَلَاءٌ.
Eminency, } High ground, رَبَاءٌ. An — for observation or scouts, مَرْبَأَة – مَرْبَأ. A hill, قُنَّة – دَبَّة – كَثِيب *pl.* قُنَن *and* قُنُون – رَبْوَة – رَباوَة – تَلّ *pl.* تِلال. Exalted rank, مَعَلاة – جَلالَة – عِزّ – عِزَّة – نَجابَة – شَرَف – فَضْل – عَلاء – عُلَى – اِسْم – شَأْن – شُهْرَة. Reputation, عُلُوُّ مَرْتَبَةٍ – عُلُوُّ شأْنٍ – رِفْعَة – ذِكْر – صِيتَة – صِيت. Superior qualifications, بَراعَة. The title of a Cardinal, نِيافَة.

Eminent, *a.* High, مُرْتَفِع – شامِخ – سَمِيّ – شاهِق – ناشِز – صاحِبُ مَرْتَبَةٍ – عالِي ٱلمَقام – عَزِيز – عالٍ. High in rank, مُنِيفُ ٱلشَّأْنِ – سَنِيٌّ – نَجِيب – شَرِيف – سام. Celebrated, فاضِل – مُمْتاز – شَهِير – مُعْتَبَر – مَشْهُور. Eminent for learning, بارِعٌ فِي ٱلعِلْمِ – لَوْذَعِيّ; for piety, مَشْهُورٌ بِٱلتَّقْوَى. To be or to become — in, بَرَعَ فِي ² – اِسْتَعْلَى فِي – عَلِيَ فِي ². To make —, شَرَّفَ – عَزَّزَ. To be noble, شَرُفَ ². To become —, تَشَرَّفَ – عَزَّ – تَعَزَّزَ. An — man, اِبْنُ جَلاءٍ. To be —, in a general sense, بَرَعَ ².

Eminently, *ad.* Conspicuously, بِجَلالَةٍ – بِشُهْرَةٍ – عِزَّةً – بِعِزٍّ. In a high degree, فِي أَقْصَى دَرَجَةٍ – كَثِيرًا – جِدًّا – لِلْغايَةِ – بِغايَةِ ما يَكُونُ. In a superior or pre-eminent manner, بِبَراعَةٍ.

Emir, *n.* (*Properly* Amir), أَمِير *pl.* أُمَرَاءُ.

Emissary, *n.* One sent on a mission, رَسُول *pl.* رُسُل *and* رُسَلاءُ – رائِد *pl.* رُوَّاد – ساعٍ *pl.* سُعاة. A spy, جاسُوس *pl.* جَواسِيس – مُتَجَسِّس. One authorized, مَأْمُورٌ.

Emission, *n.* The act of sending forth, إِطْلاق – إِخْراج – إِبْراز; what is emitted, مَخْرَج – خُرُوج – بُرُوز. Circulation, the act of, إِعْلان – نَشْر; what is circulated, عَلانِيَة – اِنْتِشار. *Emissio seminis*, نُزالَة – إِنْزال – إِمْناءٌ.

Emit, *v.t.* To send out, أَصْدَرَ – أَبْرَزَ – أَظْهَرَ – أَخْرَجَ. To put into circulation, أَذاعَ بِ – نَشَرَ ². To —, of an odour, فاحَ ².

Emmenagogue, *n.* مُحَدِّرٌ لِلطَّمْث.

Emmet, *n.* نَمْلَة *coll.* نَمْل *pl.* نِمال. *See also* Ant, *n.*

Emollescence, *n.* لَيان.

Emolliate, *v.t.* To soften, أَلانَ – لَيَّنَ. *See also to* Effeminate, *v.t.*

Emollient, *n.* مُلَيِّن. An —, دَواءٌ مُلَيِّن.

Emollition, *n.* تَلْيِين.

Emolument, *n.* Income, advantage, مَنْفَعَة – فائِدَة – مَدْخَل – نَفْع. Gain, مَكْسَب – رِبْح – رَباح – رَبَح. Salary, عُلُوفَة – خِدْمَة – راتِب – وَظِيفَة. Monthly —, شَهْرِيَّة.

Emolumental, *a.* Producing profit, مُكْسِب – مُكَسِّب.

Emotion, *n.* اِضْطِراب – حَرَكَة – هِياج – رَوْعَة – رَوْع – طَرَب. An — of fear, رَوْعَة – رَهْبَة – رَهَبُوت; of liveliness, طَرَب – خِفَّة; of pity, شَفَقَة; of admiration, تَعَجُّب – رَوْق. To excite the — of fear in, أَرْهَبَ – رَوَّعَ; of pity in one for, حَنَّنَ-عَلَى; of admiration, أَعْجَبَ – عَجَّبَ – راقَ ². *See also* Sentiment, *n.*

Emotional, *a.* } مُحَرِّك – مُرَوِّج – باعِثٌ عَلَى. (For "Emotional,"
Emotive, } of the different feelings, add to either of these adjectives, in the construct form, the appropriate noun from the preceding, prefixing the article ال; *e.g.* (باعِثٌ عَلَى ٱلتَّعَجُّبِ).

Empale, *v.t.* To inclose with pales, أَقامَ حَيْزًا – أَحاطَ-بِحِظارٍ – حَوْلَهُ. To drive a stake through a man, خَوْزَقَ.

Empalement, *n.* The act of inclosing with pales, إِحاطَةٌ بِحِظارٍ – إِقامَةُ حَيْزٍ حَوْلَ. Death by —, خَوْزَقَة.

Empannel, *n.* *See* Panel, *n.*

Empannel, *v.t.* *See to* Impannel, *v.t.*

Empark, *v.t.* أَحْدَقَ-بِحَدِيقَةٍ ـ أَحاطَ-بِبُسْتانٍ.

Emperor, *n.* أَمْبِراطُور ـ پادِشاه ـ سُلْطان ـ سُلْطانُ ٱلسَّلاطِينِ ـ قَيْصَر *pl.* قَياصِرَة.

Emphasis, *n.* As on a word, إِمالَةُ ٱلصَّوْتِ بِقُوَّةٍ عَلَى كَلِمَةٍ فِي عِبارَةٍ دُونَ غَيْرِها ـ تَطْنِيب ـ تَوْكِيد ـ تَفْظِيع. Stress of utterance, تَطْنِيب.

Emphasize, *v.t.* طَنَّبَ ـ وَكَّدَ ـ فَظَّعَ.

Emphatic, *a.* / Emphatical, شَدِيد ـ قَوِيٌّ ـ ذُو تَأْثِيرٍ ـ مُؤَثِّر ـ تَوْكِيدِيٌّ ـ مُقَرِّر. *See also* Decisive, *a.*

Emphatically, *ad.* تَقْرِيرًا ـ بِتَوْكِيدٍ. *See also* Decisively, *ad.*

Emphysema, *n.* تَوَرُّم ـ نُفاخ ـ سِلْعَة.

Empire, *n.* Imperial power, دَوْلَة ـ سَلْطَنَة ـ سُلْطان ـ سُلْطَة. Dominion, command, أَمْرٌ وَنَهْيٌ ـ سُلْطان ـ حُكْم ـ حُكُومَة. Extent of territory, دَوْلَة ـ وِلايَة ـ مَلَكُوت ـ سَلْطَنَة ـ مَمْلَكَة. The British —, المَمالِكُ ٱلْأَنْكِلِيزِيَّة. The Ottoman —, المَمالِكُ ٱلْعُثْمانِيَّة.

Empiric, *n.* ٱلَّذِي يَتَعاطَى حِرْفَةً أَوْ صَنْعَةً بِدُونِ ٱتْقانِها ـ عارِفٌ بِ-بِٱلْخِبْرَةِ وَٱلتَّجْرِبَةِ فَقَط لا بِٱلْعِلْمِ وَٱلْمُطالَعَةِ. An impostor, فَشّار ـ غَشّاش ـ كَذّاب.

Empirical, *a.* مُرَتَّب (or مُسْتَعْمَل) بِدُونِ ـ إِمْتِحانِيٌّ فَقَط تَيَقُّنٍ وَتَفَنُّنٍ. Deceptive, غاشّ ـ كَذّاب.

Empirically, *ad.* بِٱلتَّجْرِبَةِ فَقَط لَيْسَ بِٱلْإِتْقانِ وَٱلْمُطالَعَةِ.

Empiricism, *n.* تَعاطِي حِرْفَةٍ أَوْ صَنْعَةٍ بِدُونِ ٱتْقانٍ وَمَهارَةٍ.

Emplaster, *v.t.* يَضَعُ *aor.* وَضَعَ (or حَطَّ [2]) لَزْقَةً عَلَى ـ مَرْهَمَ.

Emplastic, *a.* دَبِق ـ لَزِج.

Employ, *v.t.* To keep at work, أَشْغَلَ-بِ ـ شَغَّلَ ـ خَدَّمَ. To engage in service, إِسْتَخْدَمَ ـ أَعْمَلَ ـ إِعْتَمَلَ. To give an office to, أَقامَ-فِي مَنْصِبٍ ـ أَعْطَى-وَظِيفَةً. To use as a means, تَصَرَّفَ بِ ـ إِسْتَعْمَلَ. To use, أَعْمَلَ; he employed his hand, أَعْمَلَ يَدَهُ. To —, as an agent, وَلَّى ـ أَنابَ ـ وَكَّلَ. To — one's self in, تَصَرَّفَ بِ ـ إِشْتَغَلَ بِ ـ تَعاطَى. To — one's property in, صَرَفَ مالَهُ فِي. He employed all his energies in, إِعْتَنَى فِي ـ بَذَلَ ٱلْمَقْدُورَ وَصَرَفَ ٱلْمَجْهُودَ فِي.

Employ, *n.* وَظِيفَة ـ شُغْل ـ عَمَل ـ أَشْغُولَة. An office, مَنْصِب ـ مَنْزِلَة. Service, خِدْمَة. A trade, حِرْفَة ـ صَنْعَة ـ كار. Government —, employments, الوَظائِفُ ٱلْمِيرِيَّة. Civil —, الوَظائِفُ ٱلْعُمُومِيَّة. *See also* Business, *n.*

Employé, *n.* مُسْتَخْدَم ـ مَأْمُور.

Employed, *a.* At work, مُشْتَغِل ـ مَشْغُول. Employed by, in the service of, مُسْتَخْدَمٌ عِنْدَ ـ فِي خِدْمَةِ. They are — day and night, نَهارًا وَلَيْلًا عَلَيْهِمْ شُغْل.

Employer, *n.* مُسْتَخْدِم ـ مُخَدِّم ـ مُشَغِّل. Employer and employed, خادِمٌ وَمَخْدُومٌ.

Employment, *n.* Use, صَرْف ـ بَذْل. *See also* Employ, *n.*

Empoison, *v.t.* *See to* Poison, *v.t.*

Emporetic, *a.* جارٍ فِي ٱلسُّوقِ.

Emporium, *n.* A place of trade, مَرْكَزُ تِجارَةٍ ـ مَحَلُّ تِجارَةٍ. A port, بَنْدَر *pl.* بَنادِرُ.

Empoverish, *v.t.* *See to* Impoverish, *v.t.*

Empower, *v.t.* To authorize, قَدَّرَ-عَلَى ـ صَرَّفَ-فِي ـ وَلَّى ـ فَوَّضَ ٱلْأَمْرَ إِلَى ـ سَلَّطَ. To enable, مَكَّنَ ـ قَدَّرَ-عَلَى ـ أَمْكَنَ. To be empowered, تَصَرَّفَ فِي.

Empress, *n.* أَمْبِراطُورَة ـ مَلِكَة ـ زَوْجَةُ سُلْطانٍ.

Emprise, *n.* *See* Enterprise, *n.*

Emptiness, *n.* فُرُوغ ـ فَراغ ـ فِرْغ ـ خَوًى ـ خَواء ـ بَها.

Empty, *a.* Void, فارِغ ـ خالٍ ـ خِلْوٌ ـ خاوٍ ـ خَلِيٌّ ـ باءٍ. Empty, of a house, not inhabited, قاوٍ; unfurnished, غَيْرُ مُنَجَّدٍ ـ غَيْرُ مَفْرُوشٍ ـ غَيْرُ مُجَهَّزٍ. Hungry, جَوْعان ـ خَمِيصُ ٱلْبَطْنِ. Vain, باطِل ـ عَبَث. They sent him away —, أَرْسَلُوهُ فارِغًا. I found the house —, وَجَدْتُ ٱلدّارَ مُخْلِيَةً. An — space, خَلْوَة. To be —, إِسْتَخْلَى ـ أَخْلَى ـ خَلا [2] يَخْلُو *aor.* فَضا ـ أَفْضَى. To be unoccupied, نَفِدَ ـ خَوِيَ *aor.* يَخْوَى ـ كانَ فارِغًا.

Empty, *v.t.* To exhaust, أَنْفَدَ ـ فَرَّغَ ـ أَفْرَغَ. To make unoccupied, أَخْلَى. To drink up all, قَمَعَ ـ إِقْتَمَعَ.

Empty, *v.i.* إِنْصابَ ـ إِنْصَبَّ ـ إِنْسَكَبَ. A place where a river empties itself, مَصَبّ *pl.* مَصابُّ.

Empty-handed, *a.* يَدُهُ فارِغَةٌ ـ صِفْرُ ٱلْيَدَيْنِ ـ فارِغُ ٱلْيَدِ.

Empty-headed, *a.* أَحْمَق ـ جاهِل ـ بَلِيد.

Empurple, *v.t.* لَوَّنَ-أُرْجُوانِيًّا (or فِرْفِيرِيًّا or بِرْفِيرِيًّا).

Empyrean, *a.* Relating to the heavens, مُتَعَلِّقٌ بِفَلَكِ ٱلْأَفْلاكِ ـ يُنْسَبُ إِلَى سَماءِ ٱلسَّمٰواتِ (or بِٱلْعَرْشِ or بِٱلْأَطْلَسِ). The purest, أَصْفَى (or أَنْقَى) ما يَكُونُ.

Empyrean, *n.* العَرْش ـ فَلَكُ ٱلْأَفْلاكِ ـ سَماءُ ٱلسَّمٰواتِ.

Empyreumatic, *a.* / Empyreumatical, آتٍ بِرائِحَةِ ٱلنّارِ (or ٱلْمُحْرَقَةِ).

Emulate, *v.t.* تَفاضَلَ ـ نافَسَ ـ غَبَطَ ـ سامَى ـ خايَرَ ـ بارَى ـ تَغايَرَ عَلَى ـ عارَضَ ـ مَعَ. To — with envy, نافَسَ-فِي. To imitate, إِمْتَثَلَ بِ ـ إِقْتَفَى بِ. They emulated one another, of many, تَفاخَرُوا ـ تَباهَوْا.

Emulation, *n.* مُنافَسَة ـ مُخايَرَة ـ مُساماة ـ مُباراة ـ مُفاضَلَة ـ مُسابَقَة. To provoke to —, أَغارَ ـ حَرَّضَ-عَلَى ٱلْمُباراةِ.

Emulative, *a.* } **Emulator,** *n.* } مُخايِر ـ مُغايِر ـ مُنافِس ـ مُفاضِل ـ غابِطٌ ل ـ مُبارٍ.

Emulgent, *a.* Emptying, مُفَرِّغ ـ مُنْفِذ ـ مُخْرِج.

Emulgent, *n.* A remedy to excite a flow of bile, دَوَآءٌ مُكَثِّرُ ٱلصَّفْرآءِ.

Emulous, *a.* *See* Emulative, *a.*

Emulously, *ad.* مُخايَرَةً ـ بِمُنافَسَةٍ ـ مُغايَرَةً ـ مُباراةً.

Emulsion, *n.* مُسْتَحْلَب.

Emulsive, *a.* مُلَيِّن.

Enable, *v.t.* *See to* Empower, *v.t.*

Enablement, *n.* The act of enabling, تَمْكِين ـ تَقْدِير. Ability, قُوَّة ـ قُدْرَة ـ مَقْدِرَة ـ إِسْتِطاعَة.

Enact, *v.t.* To make or pass, as of a law, *etc.*, حَكَمَ ب ² ـ قَضَى ب ـ يَضَعُ *aor.* وَضَعَ قانُونًا ـ شَرَعَ ـ سَنَّ ² ـ أَمَرَ ب ². To carry out, أَجْرَى ـ أَنْجَزَ ـ أَمْضَى.

Enactive, *a.* قَضائِيٌّ ـ حُكْمِيٌّ ـ شارِع ـ واضِع.

Enactment, *n.* The act of passing, as of a law, *etc.*, وَضْع ـ شَرْع ـ سَنّ. A law, سُنَّة *pl.* سُنَن ـ شَرِيعَة *pl.* شَرائِع ـ قانُون *pl.* قَوانِين. Performance, إِمْضآء ـ إِنْفاذ.

Enactor, *n.* شارِع *pl.* شُرَّع ـ حاكِمٌ ب ـ واضِع. A performer, مُجْرٍ ـ صُنّاع *pl.* صانِع.

Enamel, *n.* زَرْنِشان ـ المِينآء.

Enamel, *v.t.* رَكَّبَ-بِٱلْمِينآءِ.

Enameller, *n.* مُرَكِّبُ ٱلْمِينآءِ ـ مِيناجِي.

Enamelling, *n.* The art of, تَرْكِيب ٱلْمِينآءِ ـ حِرْفَةُ تَرْكِيبِ ٱلْمِينآءِ.

Enamour, *v.t.* أَغْرَمَ ـ إِشْتَهَى ـ عَشِقَ-فِي. To — through the face, (رَمَتْ *fem.*) رَمَى-بِسَهْمِ ٱلْوَجْهِ (*or* ٱللَّحْظِ). To be enamoured with, تَوَجَّدَ ب ـ أُغْرِمَ ب.

Encage, *v.t.* *See to* Cage, *v.t.*

Encamp, *v.i.* أَقامَ ـ حَوَّلَ ـ حَطَّ ² ـ نَزَلَ. *See also to* Camp, *v.i.*

Encamp, *v.t.* ضَرَبَ خَيْمَةً. *See also to* Camp, *v.t.*

Encampment, *n.* مَضْرَبُ خِيَم; of soldiers, مُعَسْكَر. *See also* Camp, *n.*

Encase, *v.t.* *See to* Incase, *v.t.*

Encashment, *n.* Of cheques, صَرْفُ ٱلْحَوالاتِ بِٱلدَّراهِمِ.

Encaustic, *a* مُرَسَّخُ ٱلْأَلْوانِ بِواسِطَةِ ٱلنَّارِ.

Enceinte, *a.* With child, حامِلَة ـ حُبْلَى *pl.* حَبالَى.

Enceinte, *n.* An inclosure, حَظِيرَة ـ دائِر.

Encephalic, *a.* مُتَعَلِّق بِٱلْمُخِّ ـ مُخْتَصّ بِٱلرَّأْسِ ـ مُخاعِيّ.

Enchafe, *v.t.* *See to* Chafe, Fret, Irritate, *v.t.*

Enchain, *v.t.* To fix the attention, أَفْتَنَ ـ سَبَى ٱلْعَقْلَ ـ أَخَذَ ٱلْعَقْلَ ². *See also to* Chain, *v.t.*

Enchainment, *n.* The act of binding with chains, زَنْجَرَة ـ رَبْط ـ بِسَلاسِل ـ سَلْسَلَة; of binding, رَبْط ـ تَقْيِيد. The being bound, إِرْتِباط ـ تَقَيُّد ـ تَسَلْسُل. The fixing of the attention, إِفْتان ـ سَبْيُ ٱلْعَقْلِ ـ أَخْذُ ٱلْعَقْلِ ².

Enchant, *v.t.* As with sorcery, سَحَرَ ـ سَحَّرَ. To enrapture, أَغْرَمَ ـ سَحَرَ ـ أَفْتَنَ ـ سَبَى ٱلْقَلْبَ ـ أَخَذَ ٱلْعَقْلَ ². *See also to* Charm, *v.t.*

Enchanted, *a.* Bewitched, مَسْحُور. Enraptured, مَسْلُوب ٱلْعَقْلِ ـ مُفْتَن ـ مَسْلُوبُ ٱلْقَلْبِ ـ فِي غايَةِ ٱلسُّرُورِ.

Enchanter, *n.* A sorcerer, ساحِر *pl.* سَحَرَة ـ سَحّار *pl.* سَحّارُون. A fascinator, فَتّان ـ مُحَيِّرُ ٱلْعَقْلِ.

Enchanting, *a.* مُفْتِن ـ مُحَيِّر ـ يَسْلُبُ ٱلْعَقْلَ ـ يَسْلُبُ ٱلْقَلْبَ.

Enchantingly, *ad.* بِنَوْعٍ مُفْتِنٍ ـ بِوَجْدٍ ـ بِنَوْعٍ يَسْلُبُ ٱلْعَقْلَ.

Enchantment, *n.* The act of, سِحْر; the being bewitched, رِباط ـ سِحْر. Extreme delight, غايَةُ ٱلسُّرُورِ ـ نَعِيم ـ حَيْرَة. A charm, fascination, طَلاوَة. Lawful —, ٱلسِّحْرُ ٱلْحَلالُ. He who learneth a process of astrology (or astronomy) learneth a process of —, مَنْ تَعَلَّمَ بابًا مِنَ ٱلنُّجُومِ تَعَلَّمَ بابًا مِنَ ٱلسِّحْرِ. Verily there is a kind of eloquence which is —, إِنَّ مِنَ ٱلْبَيانِ لَسِحْرًا.

Enchantress, *n.* ساحِرَة ـ سَحّارَة. A charming woman, إِمْرَأَةٌ ذاتُ بَهآءٍ وَكَمالٍ.

Encharged, *a.* Ordered, مَأْمُور. Entrusted with, أَمِينٌ عَلَى ـ مُوَكَّلٌ عَلَى ـ مُفَوَّض. *See also under to* Charge, *v.t.*

Enchase, *v.t.* To infix, as jewels, رَصَّعَ ـ رَكَّبَ ـ نَضَّدَ. To chisel, adorn with embossed work, نَقَّشَ. Pearls enchased in coral, ٱللُّؤْلُؤُ مُنَضَّدٌ فِي ٱلْمَرْجانِ.

Enchasement, *n.* The act of, تَرْصِيع ـ تَرْكِيب ـ تَنْضِيد; the being enchased, تَرَصُّع ـ تَنَضُّد ـ تَرَكُّب.

Enchisel, *v.t.* *See to* Chisel, *v.t.*

Enchorial, *a.* *See* Demotic, *a.*

Encircle, *v.t.* أَحاطَ-ب ـ كَنَفَ ـ أَدارَ-ب ـ أَحْدَقَ-ب.

Encircled, *a.* مُدارٌ ب ـ مُحاطٌ ب ـ مُحْدَقٌ ب.

Enclasp, *v.t.* *See to* Clasp, *v.t.*

Enclitic, n. إمالة.

Enclose, v.t. *See to* Inclose, *v.t.*

Enclosure, n. *See* Inclosure, *n.*

Encomiast, n. }
Encomiastic, a. } قصّال – وصّاف – واصف – مدّاح – مادح.

Encomium, n. حمد – وصف pl. أوصاف – مدح – تثنية – ثناء. To pronounce an — upon, نبّى – ثنّى – أثنى على.

Encompass, v.t. To surround with, أحاط-ب – أحدق-ب – طاف – حفّ ب – أدار-ب – اشتمل-على. To go round, حفّ ب. To hem in, حاصر – حصر – دار حول – تطوّف حول – حوّل. He is encompassed by difficulties, هو محفوف بالمشكلات.

Encompassment, n. The act of surrounding with, إحاطة ب – حفاف ب – حفّ ب – إحداق ب – إدارة ب; of going round, دوران.

Encore, ad. مرّة أخرى – ثانية – أيضًا.

Encore, int. كرّر – ثانية ثانية – ما شاء الله ما شاء الله.

Encore, v.t. طلب-ثانية بالاستحسان – استعاد. It was encored, طلب تكريره.

Encounter, n. A meeting, ملاقاة – مقابلة – مصادفة. A battle, وقائع pl. وقيعة – مضاربة – وقاع – مواقعة – براز – مبارزة – مجادلة. A dispute, مناظرة – معارضة – مصارعة – مقاتلة. The place of an —, ملتقى.

Encounter, v.t. To meet, as face to face, التقى ب – ركب – لاقى – قابل – صادف – أصاب. To meet in a hostile manner, to fight, ناظر – صارع – قاتل – ضارب – بارز. To — in dispute, جادل – عارض. To brave, لاهى ب – قحم في – تغرّر. To undergo, ابتلى ب – ركب – ارتكب – احتمل. To try to overcome, سعى في دفع – دافع. We encountered a violent wind, حكمتنا ريح عاصفة. A party from the town encountered him, قابله قوم من البلد.

Encounter, v.i. To meet, التقى. They encountered one another, in fight, of many, تجادلوا – تصارعوا – تقاتلوا – تبارزوا; in dispute, تنازعوا – تشاجروا. His eyes encountered the eyes of so-and-so, وقعت عينه على عين فلان. His soldiers are not able to — the soldiers of..., ليس عساكره بكفوة لمواقعة عساكر فلان.

Encourage, v.t. To embolden, جرّأ – شجّع. To animate, شيّع – حرّض-على – أغار-على. To stimulate to, شجّع-على – روّج – حرّك-على – شاق – شوّق-في. Your success encourages me, لقد شاقني توفيقك. To be encouraged to, اجترأ – تجرّأ على – على. *See also to* Countenance, *v.t.*

Encouragement, n. The act of emboldening, تشجيع; of animating, تحريض – إغارة; of stimulating, ترويج – تشييع – وجه – نصر – عون – إعانة – سند. Support, تشويق.

Encourager, n. }
Encouraging, a. } Animating, محرّك – محرّض – مرغّب – مشوّق. Aiding, محام – معين على – مساعد. His affairs are now in a more — state, أموره الآن في أسرّ حال.

Encouragingly, ad. Promising success, على رواج – استنجاحًا – على نجاح.

Encrimson, v.t. *See to* Crimson, *v.t.*

Encroach, v.t. To infringe upon, trespass, تعدّى – اعتدى على – اختلس – جاز على – جار على – همط – تجرّأ على – على – أجحف ب – أطال اليد على.

Encroacher, n. مختلس – جائز – جائر – هامط.

Encroachingly, ad. باعتداء – باختلاس – إجحافًا – بجحف – بإطالة اليد – بجوز – بجور.

Encroachment, n. إجحاف – جحف – همط – اختلاس – إطالة اليد – جوز – جور – اعتداء. Encroachment on the Egyptian territory, التعدّى على الحدود المصرية.

Encumber, v.t. *See to* Cumber, *v t.*

Encumbrance, n. *See* Cumbrance, *n.*

Encyclical, a. General, عمومي. An — letter, نشرة – منشور – مكتوب تبعث منه نسخ إلى جملة أناس.

Encyclopedia, n. كتاب كلّيات – مجمعة العلوم والمعارف – دائرة المعارف – المعارف.

Encyclopedian, a. مشتمل على كلّيات المعارف.

Encyclopedist, a. مؤلّف كتاب كلّيات المعارف.

Encysted, a. Inclosed in a cyst, متضمّن في مثانة.

End, n. The extreme point, طرف – حدود pl. حدّ – غبّ – تمام – نهاية. A result, منتهى – آخرة – عاقبة. A conclusion, وقوف – انقطاع – قطع – اختتام – ختام – إتمام. Cessation, انقضاء – إنجاز – قضاء. Accomplishment, توقّف. A design, مطلوب – مرام – مطلب – غرض – مراد – مقصود – مقصد. A fragment, قصدة pl. قصد – قطعة pl. قطع. A cause of death, سبب ممات; death, وفاة – موت. The end, as of a sentence, مقطع; of a book, ختام – خاتمة. The ends and sides of a house, حدود بيت – نواحي البيت وجهاته. They borrow his name to accomplish their own ends, يستعيرون اسمه لتنفيذ أغراضهم. A private end, مراد خفي – غرض مخصوص.

At an end, تمّ – انتهى.

At the latter end, عِنْدَ ٱلطَّرَفِ ٱلْآخِيرِ.

End on, عَلَى طَرَفِهِ ـ عَجُزُهُ فِي صَدْرِهِ.

From beginning to end, مِنَ ٱلْبَدْءِ إِلَى ـ مِنْ أَوَّلِهِ إِلَى آخِرِهِ ٱلنِّهَايَةِ.

In the end, فِي نِهَايَةِ ٱلْأَمْرِ ـ فِي آخِرِ ٱلْأَمْرِ.

Odds and ends, أَقْمِشَةٌ pl. قُمَاش ـ حِثْت. To pick up —, قَمَّشَ.

On end, upright, بِٱسْتِقَامَةٍ ـ اِنْتِصَابًا ـ قِيَامًا. To set on end, قَيَّمَ ـ نَصَبَ ².

The end of time, الدَّهْرُ ـ الْقِيَامَةُ ـ السَّاعَةُ ـ اِنْقِرَاضُ ٱلزَّمَانِ.

The farther end, الْحَدُّ ٱلْأَبْعَدُ ـ الطَّرَفُ ٱلْأَقْصَى.

The large end, الطَّرَفُ ٱلْأَكْبَرُ.

The lower end, الطَّرَفُ ٱلتَّحْتَانِيُّ ـ الطَّرَفُ ٱلْأَوْطَى.

The upper end, الطَّرَفُ ٱلْفَوْقَانِيُّ ـ الطَّرَفُ ٱلْأَعْلَى.

There is an end of it! وَٱلسَّلَامُ.

To the end, إِلَى ٱلْاِنْتِهَاءِ ـ إِلَى ٱلنِّهَايَةِ.

To the end that, كَيْ ـ لِأَجْلِ أَنْ ـ لِ ـ لِكَيْ ـ حَتَّى أَنْ. To the end that you may know, لِكَيْ تَعْلَمَ.

To the end of one's life, طُولَ ٱلْحَيَوٰةِ ـ مُدَّةَ ٱلْعُمْرِ.

Without end, never ending, أَبَدِيٌّ ـ دَائِمٌ ـ بِلَا حَدٍّ.

World without end, إِلَى أَبَدِ ٱلْآبِدِينَ ـ إِلَى دَهْرِ ٱلدَّاهِرِينَ.

To attain or compass one's end, بَلَغَ أَرَبَهُ ² ـ نَالَ مُرَادَهُ ـ فَلَجَ ².

To be at or come to an end, تَمَّ ـ اِنْتَهَى.

To be at one's wits' end, دَهِشَ ـ تَحَيَّرَ.

To bring to an end, تَمَّمَ ـ أَنْجَزَ ـ اِخْتَتَمَ ـ خَتَمَ.

To draw near one's end, death, أَشْرَفَ عَلَى ـ أَقْضَ إِلَى ٱلْمَوْتِ ٱلْمَمَاتِ.

To make one's hair stand on end, قَرَّنَ شَعْرَهُ. His hair stood on end, قَبَّ ² شَعْرُ رَأْسِهِ; of a horse, dog, *etc.*, اِزْبَأَرَّ شَعْرُهُ.

To no end, in vain, عَبَثًا ـ بَاطِلًا.

To put an end to, to prevent, سَدَّ ² ـ مَنَعَ.

To put an end to one's life, قَتَلَ ² نَفْسَهُ.

To serve one's ends, قَصَدَ مَرَامَهُ.

To stand on end, upright, اِنْتَصَبَ ـ تَنَصَّبَ ـ اِقْتَنَّ.

End, *v.t.* To terminate, أَنْجَزَ ـ خَتَمَ ـ كَمَّلَ ـ أَتَمَّ ـ أَنْهَى.

To put to death, قَتَلَ ² ـ أَمَاتَ.

End, *v.i.* To come to an end, اِخْتَتَمَ ـ تَمَّ ـ اِنْتَهَى. To cease, ذَهَبَ ـ اِنْقَطَعَ ـ زَالَ ². To be ended, accomplished, اِنْقَضَى ـ تَقَضَّى. *See also to* Cease, *v.i.*

Endamage, *v.t.* *See to* Damage, *v.t.*

Endanger, *v.t.* عَرَّضَ لِلْخَطَرِ ـ خَاطَرَ بِ. To — one's self, جَازَفَ ـ تَعَرَّضَ لِ ـ خَاطَرَ (or أَخْطَرَ) بِنَفْسِهِ.

Endangerment, *n.* *See* Danger, *n.*

Endear, *v.t.* جَعَلَ مَحْبُوبًا عِنْدَ ـ جَعَلَ عَزِيزًا عِنْدَ ـ أَعَزَّ عِنْدَ. To be endeared to, عَزَّ عَلَى.

Endearment, *n.* مَوَدَّةٌ ـ وِدَادٌ ـ مَحَبَّةٌ ـ تَوَدُّدٌ ـ تَحَبُّبٌ.

Endeavour, *n.* عَزْمٌ ـ سَعْيٌ ـ اِجْتِهَادٌ ـ جُهْدٌ ـ جِدٌّ ـ هِمَّةٌ ـ اِهْتِمَامٌ ـ إِقْدَامٌ ـ مَسْعَاةٌ. We have used all possible endeavours, صَرَفْنَا ٱلْمَسَاعِيَ ٱلْمُمْكِنَةَ. In all his endeavours, فِي جَمِيعِ مَسَاعِيهِ. He continues his endeavours to bring about an arrangement between the two parties, لَمْ يَزَلْ سَاعِيًا فِي ٱلتَّوْفِيقِ بَيْنَ ٱلطَّرَفَيْنِ.

Endeavour, *v.i.* جَدَّ ² فِي ـ اِجْتَهَدَ فِي ـ سَعَى فِي.

Endecagon, *n.* ذُو أَحَدَ عَشَرَ ضِلْعًا.

Endemial, Endemic, *a.*, Endemical, } مُسْتَوْلٍ عَلَى مَحَلٍّ ـ خُصُوصِيٌّ ـ مُخْتَصٌّ بِ. An — disease, تَخَمَةٌ pl. تَخَمَات.

Endemically, *ad.* بِٱسْتِيلَاءٍ.

Endenizen, *v.t.* صَيَّرَ ٱلْغَرِيبَ مِنْ أَهْلِ ٱلْبِلَادِ ـ جَعَلَ مِنْ تَبَعِيَّةٍ. *See also under* Denizen, *n.*

Ending, *n.* *See* End, *n.*

Endive, *n.* الْبَقْلَةُ ٱلْمُبَارَكَةُ ـ الْهِنْدَبَا ـ هِنْدَب.

Endless, *a.* Having no end, غَيْرُ مُتَنَاهٍ ـ عَدِيمُ ٱلْحَدِّ. Perpetual, everlasting, أَبَدِيٌّ ـ دَائِمٌ. Having neither beginning nor end, سَرْمَدِيٌّ.

Endlessly, *ad.* بِلَا ٱنْقِطَاعٍ ـ أَبَدًا ـ دَائِمًا ـ إِلَى مَا لَا نِهَايَةَ لَهُ ـ اِسْتِمْرَارًا ـ بِدَوَامٍ.

Endlessness, *n.* أَبَدِيَّةٌ ـ دَوَامٌ ـ اِسْتِمْرَارٌ ـ بَقَاءٌ.

Endlong, *ad.* عَلَى طَرَفِهِ ـ عَلَى ٱلطَّرَفِ.

Endorse, *v.t.* *See to* Indorse, *v.t.*

Endorsement, *n.* *See* Indorsement, *n.*

Endow, *v.t.* To settle a pension upon, جَعَلَ لِ ـ رَتَّبَ لِ; for pious purposes, وَقَفَ *aor.* يَقِفُ ـ أَوْقَفَ عَلَى or لِ. To multiply to, أَمْلَكَ ـ كَثَّرَ لِ ـ أَنْعَمَ عَلَى بِ. To supply with, غَنَّى بِ ـ غَنِيَ بِ. To be plentifully endowed with, جَهَّزَ بِ ـ تَغَنَّى بِ. *See also to* Dower, *v.t.*

Endowment, *n.* The act of endowing, تَرْتِيبُ لِ ـ وَهْبُ لِ ـ جَعْلُ لِ; of a pious settlement, تَوْقِيفٌ. What is settled, رَاتِبَةٌ *pl.* رَوَاتِبُ; of a pious gift, وَقْفٌ *pl.* أَوْقَافٌ. Endowments, qualities, فَضَائِلُ ـ مَوَاهِبُ ـ شَمَائِلُ.

End-piece, *n.* طَرَف ـ رَأْس.

Endue, *v.t.* *See to* Indue, *v.t.*

Endurance, *n.* The act of bearing, إِحْتِمال ـ تَحَمُّل ـ تَرَكُّب ـ. Patience, صَبْر ـ شَهامَة ـ عَزاءٌ ـ طاقَة. Continuance, بَقاءٌ ـ إِسْتِمْرار ـ دَوام ـ ثُبُوت.

Endure, *v.t.* To bear, أَطاقَ عَلَى ـ إِحْتَمَلَ ـ تَحَمَّلَ. To — patiently, إِصْطَبَرَ ـ تَصَبَّرَ ـ تَعَزَّى. To —, to be patient with, صابَرَ. To — the loss of patiently, to be comforted, سَلا عَن *aor.* يَسْلُو. I endured harshness from him, قاسَيْتُ مِنْهُ شِدَّةً. *See also to* Brook, *v.t.*

Endure, *v.i.* To last, دامَ ² ـ إِسْتَدامَ ـ بَقِيَ ـ ثَبَتَ ². To — a long time, طالَ ². To make to —, أَدامَ. *See also to* Last, *v.i.*

Enduring, *a.* Bearing, مُحْتَمِل ـ مُتَحَمِّل ـ راكِب. Suffering, مُكابِد. Patient, صَبُور ـ صابِر. Lasting, ثابِت ـ باقٍ ـ صُلْب ـ راهِن.

Endwise, *ad.* On end, قِيامًا ـ وُقُوفًا ـ إِنْتِصابًا. End first, بِتَقْدِيمِ ٱلْعَجُزِ عَلَى ٱلصَّدْرِ ـ عَلَى طَرَفِهِ ـ بِتَقْدِيمِ ٱلْمُؤَخَّرِ.

Enema, *n.* *See* Clyster, *n.*

Enemy, *n.* عَدُوٌّ *pl.* أَعْداءٌ. An opponent, litigant, خَصْم *or* خَصِيم *pl.* خُصُوم *and* أَخْصام. An enemy's ship, مَرْكَبُ ٱلْعَدُوِّ. The —, the devil, ٱلشَّيْطانُ ٱللَّعِينُ. An open —, عَدُوٌّ مُبِينٌ. A private —, خَصِيم. A public —, عَدُوُّ ٱلدَّوْلَةِ. To seize from the —, قَبَضَ عَلَى ٱلْعَدُوِّ. They are your enemies, هُمْ لَكُمْ عَدُوٌّ. They treat them like enemies, يُعامِلُونَهُمْ مُعامَلَةَ ٱلْعَدُوِّ.

Energetic, *a.* } Vigorous, ذُو عارِضٍ ـ شَدِيدُ ٱلْعارِضِ ـ سُعاوِيٌّ ـ
Energetical, } فَعّال ـ صارِم ـ مُبْتَذِل ـ مُتَبَذِّل. Efficacious, مُؤَثِّر. Powerful, شَدِيد ـ قَوِيٌّ. Energetic terms, أَلْفاظٌ أَكِيدَةٌ. Energetic language, كَلامٌ جازِمٌ ـ لِسانٌ مُؤَكَّدٌ ـ لِسانٌ قَطْعِيٌّ.

Energetically, *ad.* Vigorously, مُتَبَذِّلًا ـ بِجِدَّةٍ وَشِدَّةٍ. Effectually, تَأْثِيرًا. Powerfully, بِشِدَّةٍ ـ بِقُوَّةٍ.

Energy, *n.* Power, قُوَّة ـ شِدَّة ـ جِدَّة. Efficacy, عَمَل ـ فِعْل ـ تَأْثِير. Vigour, شَوْكَة ـ مُرُوَّة ـ جَهْد ـ شَهامَة ـ عارِضَة ـ عارِض ـ صَرامَة ـ جِدّ. To act with —, تَشَدَّدَ ـ صَرَمَ ². To act with —, throw one's self into, إِنْدَفَعَ فِي ـ مَضَى فِي.

Enervate, *v.t.* To weaken, أَضْعَفَ; of the action of disease, أَخْمَلَ ـ أَوْهَنَ ـ وَهَّنَ. To deprive of vigour, أَفْتَرَ ـ خَبَطَ. To be enervated, in action, وَهَنَ *aor.* يَهِنُ ـ خَمَلَ ² ـ فَشِلَ; by disease, فَتَرَ ـ إِهْتَبَطَ ـ ضَعُفَ ². To be weakened, generally, تَضَعَّفَ.

Enervated, *a.* فَشِل ـ نَهِيك ـ نَهُوك. *See also* Weak, *a.*

Enervating, *a.* مُهْبِط ـ مُفْتِر ـ مُضْعِف ـ مُخْمِل ـ مُوَهِّن.

Enervation, *n.* The act of —, إِفْتار ـ تَوْهِين ـ إِخْمال ـ إِضْعاف; the being enervated, فَشَل ـ فَتْر ـ وَهَن ـ ضَعْف ـ خُمُول.

Enfeeble, *v.t.* *See to* Enervate, Weaken, *v.t.*

Enfeebled, *a.* *See* Enervated, *a.*

Enfeebling, *a.* *See* Enervating, *a.*

Enfeeblement, *n.* *See* Enervation, *n.*

Enfeoffe, *v.t.* أَقْطَعَ ل ـ إِقْطاعَةً ـ أَعْطَى ـ ٱلْتِزامًا ـ أَزْعَمَ ـ ٱلزَّعامَةَ ـ إِعْطاءٌ.

Enfeoffment, *n.* The act of giving in feoff, تَزْعِيم ـ إِقْطاعَة ـ إِلْتِزام. A feoff, زَعامَة ـ إِلْتِزام ـ تَقْطِيع ـ بِٱلْتِزام. The deed of —, حُجَّةُ ٱلِٱلْتِزامِ.

Enfilade, *n.* A row, line, صَفّ ـ سَطْر.

Enfilade, *v.t.* To rake with shot along a line, أَطْلَقَ ٱلنّارَ عَلَى طُولِ ٱلصَّفِّ.

Enforce, *v.t.* To strengthen, ثَبَّتَ ـ أَكَّدَ. To compel, أَلْزَمَ ـ أَكْرَهَ ـ عَلَى ـ أَلْجَأَ ـ إِلَى ـ إِضْطَرَّ ـ إِلَى. To put into execution, أَمْضَى ـ أَنْفَذَ ـ أَجْرَى. This law is not enforced now, هٰذِهِ هٰذا ٱلْقانُونُ غَيْرُ جارٍ ٱلْآنَ ـ ٱلشَّرِيعَةُ لَيْسَتِ ٱلْآنَ بِمُسْتَعْمَلَةٍ.

Enforcement, *n.* The act of strengthening, تَأْكِيد ـ تَشْيِيد ـ تَثْبِيت. Compulsion, إِلْجاءٌ ـ إِكْراه ـ إِغْصاب ـ إِضْطِرار. Execution, إِنْفاذ ـ إِجْراءٌ. Sanction, إِحْكام ـ تَقْرِير ـ رِضاءٌ ـ رُخْصَة.

Enfranchise, *v.t.* To liberate, أَعْتَقَ ـ حَرَّرَ. To make a free citizen, خَصَّهُ ² بِٱمْتِيازاتِ ٱلْأُمَّةِ ـ جَعَلَ ـ ٱبْنَ بَلَدٍ. To invest with rights and privileges, أَنالَ ـ ٱمْتِيازاتٍ وَحُقُوقًا.

Enfranchisement, *n.* The act of liberating, إِعْتاق ـ تَحْرِير; the being free, حُرِّيَّة ـ عَتاق. The act of investing with citizenship, تَخْصِيص بِٱلِٱمْتِيازاتِ ٱلْمَدَنِيَّةِ. Giving rights and privileges, إِعْطاءٌ ٱمْتِيازاتٍ وَحُقُوقٍ.

Engage, *v.t.* To enjoin, charge, عَهِدَ إِلَى. To make, cause, جَعَلَ. To wager, أَشْرَطَ ب ـ أَرْهَنَ. To enlist, as into the army, أَدْخَلَ ـ ٱلْعَسْكَرِيَّةَ ـ جَنَّدَ. To — to work, إِسْتَخْدَمَ. To induce, جَلَبَ ² ـ جَعَلَ. To appoint, إِتَّخَذَ ـ جَعَلَ. To occupy, أَشْغَلَ ـ شَغَّلَ. To hire, إِسْتَأْجَرَ ـ أَكْرَى. To promise, أَوْعَدَ ـ عَهِدَ. To — in an affair, شَبَكَ ـ فِي ـ أَشْغَلَ ـ فِي ـ وَهَتَ ـ فِي *aor.* يَهِتُ ـ أَشْرَكَ ـ فِي. To betroth, خَطَبَ ². To fight, حارَبَ ـ واقَعَ ـ هَجَمَ عَلَى ـ قاتَلَ ـ بارَزَ. To be engaged in, إِشْتَغَلَ ب ـ تَصَرَّفَ فِي ـ إِنْتَبَطَ فِي ـ تَقَيَّدَ ب ـ تَهَوَّتَ فِي ـ إِنْشَبَكَ فِي. To — another to . . ., عاهَدَ ـ إِلَى. He is engaged to marry such an one, هُوَ مَخْطُوبٌ لِفُلانَةٍ. He is engaged in trade, شُغْلَهُ ٱلْمُتَاجَرَةُ. They engaged to meet at..., تَوَاعَدُوا إِلَى. To — one's self, as by promise, تَعَهَّدَ. To — one's self to marry, تَعَهَّدَ بِٱلنِّكَاحِ.

Engage, *v.i.* To bind one's self to, أَلْزَمَ نَفْسَهُ بِ — عَهِدَ فِي — تَضَمَّنَ — اِلْتَزَمَ بِ. To — in deeply, خَاضَ فِي. To embark in an affair; (*see preceding article*). They engaged, fought, of many, تَحَارَبُوا — تَبَارَزُوا — تَقَاتَلُوا.

Engaged, *a.* At work, مَشْغُول. Under promise, عَهِد. Mixed up with, مُشْتَبِكٌ فِي — دَاخِلٌ فِي. Betrothed, مَخْطُوب. At war, مُحَارِب — مُقَاتِل. Zealous, مُتَبَذِّل — مُبْتَذِل. An — ring, خَاتَمُ ٱلْخِطْبَةِ. Engaged in, مُشْتَغِلٌ فِي — مُقَيَّدٌ بِ.

Engagedly, *ad.* بِٱنْهِمَاكٍ — بِتَبَذُّلٍ.

Engagedness, *n.* تَبَذُّل — انْهِمَاك — اِشْتِغَال — شُغْل.

Engagement, *n.* Obligation, إِكْرَاه — إِلْزَام. A promise, مُعَاقَدَة — عَهْد — مُقَاوَلَة — اِرْتِبَاط — مُعَاهَدَة — عَقْد. Security, تَكَفُّل — ضَمَان. Engagement of the attention, اِشْتِغَالُ ٱلْبَالِ. A fight, conflict, مُحَارَبَة — مُقَاتَلَة — مُبَارَزَة — وَقِيعَة — يَوْم — وَقْعَة. Business, مَشْغَلَة — شُغْل — تَعَلُّقَات — عُلَق. A promise to marry, خِطْبَة — خِطْب. To stand to one's —, وَفَى بِمَا وَعَدَ بِهِ, *aor.* يَفِي — عَهِدَ وَعْدَهُ.

Engaging, *a.* Pleasing, مُنْبَسِط — ذُو طَلَاوَةٍ — ذُو حَظٍّ — مُؤْنِق — حَبَّذَا — يَسْلُبُ ٱلْعَقْلَ — جَاذِبُ ٱلْقَلْبِ. What an — woman she is! مَا حَبَّذَا ٱلْمَرْأَةُ.

Engarland, *v.t.* *See to* Garland, *v.t.*

Engarrison, *v.t.* *See to* Garrison, *v.t.*

Engender, *v.t.* To beget, أَوْلَدَ — وَلَّدَ. To produce, أَصْدَرَ — وَلَّدَ — سَبَّبَ — أَحْدَثَ — أَوْجَدَ — أَنْشَأَ. To implant in, ... عَرَّقَ فِي ٱلْ — ضَرَبَ فِي ٱلْ ...

Engender, *v.i.* To be begotten, تَوَلَّدَ — وُلِدَ. To come from, كَانَ سَبَبًا — نَشَأَ مِن — وُجِدَ مِن — صَدَرَ مِن.

Engild, *v.t.* *See to* Gild, *v.t.*

Engine, *n.* دُولَاب *pl.* دَوَالِيبُ — مَاكِنَة — مَنْجَنِيق. A tool, آلَة *pl.* آلَات. A means, وَاسِطَة *pl.* وَسَائِطُ — وَسِيلَة *pl.* وَسَائِلُ. A tool, in a bad sense, حِيلَة — دَسِيسَة. An — for projecting, مِرْمًى *pl.* مَرَامٍ. An — for throwing fire, مِرْمَى نِيرَانٍ; for raising water, a water-wheel, نَاعُورَة — سَاقِيَة. A fire —, آلَةٌ بُخَارِيَّةٌ لِإِطْفَاءِ ٱلْحَرِيقِ. An — for throwing stones, مَنْجَنِيق. A steam —, وَابُور — بَاخِرَة — مَاكِنَةُ ٱلْبُخَارِ. A condensing —, آلَةٌ لِتَحْوِيلِ ٱلْبُخَارِ مَاءً. A stationary —, بَاخِرَةٌ ثَابِتَةٌ. A locomotive —, بَاخِرَةٌ جَرَّارَةٌ. A marine —, بَاخِرَةُ مَرْكَبٍ.

Engine-driver, *n.* سَائِقُ ٱلْبَاخِرَةِ.

Engineer, *n.* مُهَنْدِس *pl.* مُهَنْدِسُونَ. A military —, مُهَنْدِسٌ عَسْكَرِيٌّ. A civil —, مُهَنْدِسٌ مَدَنِيٌّ — مُهَنْدِسُ ٱلْحَوَاضِرِ. A mechanical —, مُهَنْدِسُ ٱلدَّوَالِيبِ — مُهَنْدِسُ ٱلْمَاكِنَاتِ. A mining —, مُهَنْدِسُ ٱلْمَعَادِنِ.

Engineering, *n.* هَنْدَسَة.

Engineering, *a.* مُتَعَلِّقٌ بِٱلْهَنْدَسَةِ.

Engine-house, *n.* مَحَلُّ ٱلْوَابُورِ — بَيْتُ ٱلْبَاخِرَةِ.

Engine-man, *n.* مُلَازِمُ ٱلْبَاخِرَةِ.

Enginry, *n.* *See* Engineering, *n.*

Engird, *v.t.* *See to* Encompass, *to* Gird, *v.t.*

Engirt, *a.* Surrounded, مُحَاط.

Engladden, *v.t.* *See to* Gladden, *v.t.*

England, *n.* مَمْلَكَةُ ٱلْإِنْكِلِيزِ — بِلَادُ ٱلْإِنْكِلِيزِ — إِنْكِلْتَرَةُ.

English, *n.* The — language, لِسَانُ ٱلْإِنْكِلِيزِ — ٱلْإِنْكِلِيزِيَّةُ. The — people, أُمَّةُ ٱلْإِنْكِلِيزِ — أَهْلُ إِنْكِلْتَرَةَ — ٱلْإِنْكِلِيزُ.

English, *v.t.* To turn into —, تَرْجَمَ إِلَى ٱللُّغَةِ ٱلْإِنْكِلِيزِيَّةِ.

Englut, *v.t.* اِبْتَلَعَ — أَسَاغَ — تَلَهَّمَ — هَلْقَمَ.

Engorge, *v.t.* *See to* Gorge, *v.t.*

Engorgement, *n.* The act of engorging, إِشْبَاع; the being engorged, شِبَع — قُقُوم — فَقْم.

Engraft, *v.t.* *See to* Ingraft, *v.t.*

Engrail, *v.t.* نَقَّطَ — بَقَّعَ — نَقَّشَ.

Engrailment, *n.* The — round a coin, زِنْجِيرُ ٱلسِّكَّةِ.

Engrain, *v.t.* To dye in grain, صَبَغَ صَبْغًا — صَبَّغَ نَمَشًا — صَبَغَ صِبَاغًا مُنَمَّشًا. To dye, as with colours, أَرْقَطَ — صَبَغَ — لَوَّنَ. To variegate, دَبَّجَ.

Engrapple, *v.t.* *See to* Grapple, *v.t.*

Engrasp, *v.t.* *See to* Grasp, *v.t.*

Engrave, *v.t.* To cut with a graver, نَقَشَ — نَقَّشَ — قَلَّمَ. To impress, as upon the mind, طَبَعَ — خَتَمَ — أَرْسَخَ.

Engravement, *n.* تَنْقِيش — نَقْش.

Engraver, *n.* نَقَّاش *pl.* نَقَّاشُونَ.

Engraving, *n.* The act of, تَنْقِيش — نَقْش; a print, نَقْش *pl.* نُقُوش — مَنْقُوش — رَسْم *pl.* رُسُوم — صُورَة *pl.* صُوَر. The art of —, نَقْش — نِقَاشَة. A tool for —, قَلَم *pl.* أَقْلَام.

Engross, *v.t.* To seize, ضَبَطَ — أَخَذَ — اِتَّخَذَ. To occupy the attention of one, أَكْلَفَ — شَغَلَ — أَلْهَى. To write in an official hand, كَتَبَ بِخَطٍّ دِيوَانِيٍّ. To be engrossed in, اِسْتَغْرَقَ فِي — خَاضَ فِي — تَكَلَّفَ بِ.

Engrosser, *n.* One who monopolizes, حَوَّاط. A fair hand-[w]riter, خَطَّاط.

Engrossing, *n.* } Engrossment, } The act of seizing, أَخْذ ـ ضَبْط ـ إِتِّخاذ ; of occupying, تَكْلِيف ; of writing in official [h]and, كِتابَةٌ بِخَطٍّ دِيوانِيٍّ. Official handwriting, خَطٌّ دِيوانِيٌّ.

Engrossing, *a.* مُكَلِّف. An — task, شُغْلٌ شاغِلٌ.

Engulph, *v.t.* أَغْرَقَ ـ فِي ـ وَرَّطَ ـ فِي ـ = خَسَفَ بِ. To be en[gul]phed in, تَوَرَّطَ فِي ـ اِسْتَغْرَقَ فِي ـ = غَرِقَ فِي ـ اِنْخَسَفَ بِ.

Engulphment, *n.* The act of, إِغْراق ـ تَوْرِيط ـ خَسْف ; the being engulphed, تَوَرُّط ـ اِسْتِغْراق ـ اِنْخِساف.

Enhance, *v.t.* To raise, رَفَعَ ـ عَلَّى ـ كَبَّرَ ـ عَظَّمَ =. To — a price, أَزادَ الثَّمَنَ ـ أَغْلَى.

Enhancement, *n.* The act of, رَفْع ـ تَعْلِيَة ـ تَكْبِير ـ تَعْظِيم ; the being raised, رِفْعَة ـ كِبْر ـ تَعَظُّم. The act of raising a price, تَزْيِيدُ الثَّمَنِ ـ إِغْلاء. *See also* Aggravation, *n.*

Enigma, *n.* A riddle, لُغْز *pl.* أَلْغاز ـ أُحْجِيَّة ـ أُدْعِيَّة ـ أُلْقِيَّة ـ تَعْمِيَة ـ حَزُّورَة. An obscure expression, اِلْتِباس ـ مُعَمًّى ـ إِيهام. I propose to you an —, أُحاجِيكَ أُحْجِيَّةً ـ أُداعِيكَ ـ أُعْطِيكَ حَزُّورَةً.

Enigmatic, *a.* } Enigmatical, } Containing a riddle, مُتَضَمِّنُ اللُّغْزِ ـ بِهِ أُلْقِيَّة ـ مُعَمًّى ـ فِيهِ أُحْجِيَّة ـ مُحْجِيَة. Ambiguous, بَعِيدٌ ـ مُبْهَم ـ غامِض ـ مُغْلَق ـ مُعَقَّد ـ مُعَمًّى ـ مُلْتَبِس عَنِ الفَهْمِ. To make —, عَمَّى.

Enigmatically, *ad.* بِالْتِباسٍ ـ لُغْزًا.

Enigmatist, *n.* مُصَنِّفُ الحَزُّوراتِ ـ مُرَتِّبُ الأَلْغازِ.

Enigmatize, *v.i.* اِسْتَعْمَلَ الحَزُّورَةَ ـ = عَقَدَ الأَلْغازَ.

Enjoin, *v.t.* أَشارَ عَلَى ـ بِ ـ أَفْرَضَ لِ ـ = فَرَضَ عَلَى ـ فَرَّزَ عَلَى ـ أَمَرَ ـ بِ 2 ـ نَبَّهَ عَلَى ـ أَوْصَى ـ بِ ـ = عَهِدَ إِلَى. He did according to what is enjoined in the book of God, = عَمِلَ بِما فِي كِتابِ اللهِ.

Enjoinment, *n.* Command, direction, تَنْبِيه ـ أَمْر ـ عَهْد.

Enjoy, *v.t.* اِلْتَذَّ بِ ـ اِسْتَمْتَعَ بِ ـ تَمَتَّعَ بِ ـ أَمْتَعَ بِ ـ تَلَذَّذَ بِ ـ اِبْتَهَجَ بِ ـ تَنَعَّمَ بِ ـ تَهَنَّأَ بِ. To — one's self, تَنَعَّمَ ـ تَبَحْبَحَ ـ تَكَيَّفَ ـ تَمَتَّعَ. To — the company of, تَمَتَّعَ بِصُحْبَتِهِ. To — privileges, تَمَتَّعَ بِالاِمْتِيازاتِ وَالحُقُوقِ ـ تَشَرَّفَ بِ. To — the possession of wealth, تَوَسَّعَ فِي. To obtain possession of, حازَ 1 ـ اِقْتَنَى ـ حَصَّلَ. I enjoyed myself at home, تَهَنَّيْتُ فِي البَيْتِ.

Enjoyable, *a.* مُكَيِّف ـ لَذِيذ ـ يُلْتَذُّ بِ ـ مُفْرِح ـ فَرِح.

Enjoyment, *n.* Pleasure, غِبْطَة ـ نِعْمَة ـ فَكاهَة ـ تَنَعُّم ـ تَمَتُّع ـ تَلَذُّذ ـ لَذَّة ـ تَبَحْبُح. Possession, تَصَرُّف ـ حَوْز ـ اِقْتِناء. To be in a state of —, اِغْتَبَطَ. *See also* Pleasure, *n.*

Enkindle, *v.t.* *See to* Kindle, *v.t.*

Enlarge, *v.t.* To make larger, كَبَّرَ ـ عَظَّمَ. To expand, مَدَّ 2 ـ بَسَطَ 2. To widen, make commodious, وَسَّعَ ـ أَوْسَعَ. To exaggerate, بالَغَ فِي ـ أَطْنَبَ فِي. To release, أَطْلَقَ ـ أَعْتَقَ ـ حَرَّرَ. To — the mind, وَسَّعَ العَقْلَ ; the heart, (رَحَّبَ *or* أَرْحَبَ) القَلْبَ.

Enlarge, *v.i.* To grow large, كَبُرَ 2 ـ عَظُمَ 2. To increase, = زادَ ـ تَكَثَّرَ ـ اِزْدادَ. To grow, نَما 2. To expatiate, أَفاضَ فِي ـ طالَ فِي الكَلامِ 2.

Enlargement, *n.* The act of making large, تَكْبِير ـ تَعْظِيم ; of becoming large, كِبَر ـ نُمُوّ ـ عِظَم. The act of expansion, مَدّ ـ تَوْسِيع ; the being expanded, اِمْتِداد ـ سَعَة. The act of exaggerating, مُجاوَزَة ـ إِطْناب ـ مُبالَغَة. The being prolonged, of speech, طُول كَلام ـ فَيَضانُ الكَلامِ. The act of releasing, إِطْلاق ـ تَحْرِير ; the being at large, حُرِّيَّة ـ طَلْق ـ طُلُوق.

Enlighten, *v.t.* To shed light, نَوَّرَ ـ أَنارَ ـ أَضاءَ. To instruct, هَذَّبَ ـ عَلَّمَ ـ فَطَّنَ ـ فَهَّمَ ـ أَفْهَمَ. To give to understand, بَيَّنَ لِ ـ أَشْعَرَ ـ بِ ـ أَطْلَعَ ـ عَلَى. To — the understanding of, أَنارَ عَقْلَهُ.

Enlightened, *a.* Having clear views, عارِف ـ فَطِين ـ فاطِن ـ مُطَّلِع ـ عالِم.

Enlightener, *n.* مُبَيِّن ـ مُفَهِّم ـ مُسْتَنِير ـ مُنِير.

Enlightenment, *n.* The act of enlightening, mentally, تَهْذِيب ـ تَعْلِيم ; the being enlightened, فَنّ ـ ذِهْن ـ عِلْم ـ فِطْنَة. The act of informing, إِطْلاع عَلَى ـ تَعْرِيف ـ تَفْهِيم ـ إِفادَة ; the being informed, عِلْم ـ وُقُوف عَلَى ـ طُلُوع عَلَى.

Enlink, *v.t.* To bind, قَيَّدَ ـ رَبَطَ = 2. *See also to* Link, *v.t.*

Enlist, *v.t.* To register, كَتَبَ 2. To —, as soldiers, جَنَّدَ ـ قَيَّدَ فِي دَفْتَرِ العَسْكَرِيَّةِ. To draw in to a cause, جَلَبَ 2 = ـ أَدْخَلَ فِي ـ جَعَلَ مِنْ حِزْبٍ ـ = قَيَّدَ. To — soldiers, جَنَّدَ الجُنُودَ. They were enlisted together, as in a party, تَحَزَّبُوا.

Enlist, *v.i.* To become a soldier, دَخَلَ فِي العَسْكَرِيَّةِ 2 ـ تَجَنَّدَ.

Enlistment, *n.* The act of enrolling, inscribing, تَكْتِيب. A roll, فِهْرِس ـ دَفْتَر. The act of enlisting soldiers, تَجْنِيد ـ تَقْيِيد ـ دُخُول فِي العَسْكَرِيَّةِ ; the being enlisted, تَجَنُّد ـ فِي العَسْكَرِيَّةِ.

Enliven, *v.t.* To cheer, فَكَّهَ ـ سَرَّ 2 ـ أَفْرَحَ ـ أَبْسَطَ ـ أَبْهَجَ. To make nimble, نَشَّطَ ـ حَذَّقَ. To make gay, طَرَّبَ ـ أَطْرَبَ. I was enlivened by his narrative, اِسْتَرْوَحْتُ إِلَى حَدِيثِهِ.

Enlivener, *n.* }
Enlivening, *a.* } فَكِه ـ مُطْرِب ـ مُبْهِج ـ سارّ ـ مُفْرِح ـ يَشْرَحُ ٱلصَّدْرَ ـ مُبَسِّط.

Enmarble, *v.t.* صَيَّرَ كَٱلْمَرْمَرِ.

En masse, *ad.* قاطِبَةً ـ مَعًا ـ بِٱلْكُلِّيَّةِ ـ بِٱلْجُمْلَةِ ـ جُمْلَةً.

Enmesh, *v.t.* To catch in a net, أَخَذَ فِي شَبَكَةٍ ـ إِحْتَبَلَ. To entangle, شَبَّكَ ـ ـ شَبَكَ.

Enmity, *n.* عُدْوان ـ بُغْض ـ خُصُومَة ـ عَداوَة ـ ذاتُ ٱلْبَيْنِ. For amending the state of — subsisting between them, لِإِصْلاحِ ذاتِ ٱلْبَيْنِ; (ذاتُ ٱلْبَيْنِ also means a state of concord). They showed open — towards each other, of many, تَجاهَرُوا بِٱلْعَداوَةِ ـ تَبادَرُوا بِٱلْعَداوَةِ. To bear —, أَحْتَنَ. He showed open — to him without cause, جاهَرَهُ بِٱلْعَداوَةِ بِدُونِ سَبَبٍ.

Ennoble, *v.t.* رَفَعَ إِلَى رُتْبَةِ ٱلشَّرَفِ ـ شَرَّفَ. To be ennobled by, تَشَرَّفَ بِ.

Ennui, *n.* زَعَل ـ مَلالَة ـ مَلال. He experienced — from the thing, أَمَلَّ عَلَيْهِ ٱلْأَمْرُ.

Enormity, *n.* An outrage, great crime, ذَنْبٌ ـ كَبائِرُ *pl.* كَبِيرَة ـ فَضاحَة ـ شَناعَة ـ فَواحِشُ *pl.* فاحِشَة ـ جُرْمٌ عَظِيمٌ ـ جَسِيمٌ خِيانَة.

Enormous, *a.* Beyond limits, مُتَجاوِزُ ٱلْحَدِّ ـ مُفْرِط ـ مُجاوِز. Immense, لِلْغايَةِ ـ عَظِيم ـ كُلِّيّ ـ كَبِير ـ جَسِيم.

Enormously, *ad.* كَثِيرًا ـ فَوْقَ ٱلْحَدِّ ـ بِلا حَدٍّ ـ لِلْغايَةِ.

Enormousness, *n.* تَفاوُت ـ فَرْط ـ جَسامَة ـ عِظَم.

Enough, *a.* وافٍ ـ كافٍ. Enough for him, كِفايَتُهُ. A dirham is — for thee, حَسْبُكَ دِرْهَمٌ. Let that be — for thee, حَسْبُكَ ذٰلِكَ.

Enough, *n.* بُلْغَة ـ حَسْب ـ كِفايَة. More than —, شُباعَة. Enough to support life, سِداد.

Enough, *ad.* وَفْرَةً ـ كِفايَةً ـ بُلْغَةً ـ شُبْعَةً. (The following comprise sentences on the three preceding articles). To have had — of, شَبِعَ مِن. The place is large — for both of them, يَسَعُ ٱلْمَكانُ كِلاهُما. This is not — for us, هٰذا لا يَكْفِينا. And that was not —, وَما كَفَى ذٰلِكَ. We have had — to eat, أَكَلْنا وَشَبِعْنا. The place is not large — for them, لا يَكْفِيهِم ٱلْمَحَلُّ. He is well — to go out, لَهُ مِنَ ٱلْعافِيَةِ ما يُمَكِّنُهُ مِنَ ٱلْخُرُوجِ مِنَ ٱلْبَيْتِ. He is always ready — to speak, converse, ذُو مُسْتَعِدٍّ دائمًا لِلْمُكالَمَةِ. It is done well —, كَفَى ما فِيهِ مِنْ طِيبَةِ ٱلصَّنِيعِ. It is —, يَكْفِي هٰذا ـ هٰذا بِزِيادَةٍ (*vulg.* بَسّ). Is it not — for you that ...? أَلَنْ يَكْفِيكُمْ أَنْ. I have —, يَكْفِينِي ما عِنْدِي ـ حَسْبِي مالِي ـ لِي كَثِيرٌ عِنْدِي ما ـ لِي قَدْرُ ما يَكْفِينِي وَزِيادَةٌ ـ يَفْضُلُ عَنِّي. I have more than —, يَزِيدُ عَنِ ٱلْكِفايَةِ.

Enquire, *v.i.* *See to* Inquire, *v.t.*

Enrage, *v.t.* أَثارَ عَصَبَهُ ـ أَغْضَبَ ـ أَغاظَ ـ غاظَ ـ مَقَطَ.

Enraged, *a.* غَضْبانُ ـ ثائِر ـ ساخِط. To be —, ثارَ ـ اِغْتاظَ ـ غَضِبَ ـ غَضْبَةً. To be — by, تَغَضَّبَ مِن.

Enrank, *v.t.* *See to* Rank, *v.t.*

Enrapture, *v.t.* *See to* Charm; *also the next article.*

Enravish, *v.t.* To send into an ecstasy, رَمَى فِي حالِ ٱلْوَجْدِ ـ سَلَبَ قَلْبَهُ ـ حَيَّرَ عَقْلَهُ ـ أَغْرَمَ. To enrapture, وَجَدَ بِ ـ سَرَّ غايَةَ ٱلسُّرُورِ. To be enravished, in an ecstasy, تَوَجَّدَ بِ ـ اِنْسَطَلَ. *See also* Ecstasy, *n.*

Enravishment, *n.* Excess of delight, وُفُورُ ٱلْحَظِّ ـ غايَةُ ٱلسُّرُورِ وَٱلتَّلَذُّذِ.

Enregister, *v.t.* *See to* Register, *v.t.*

Enrheum, *v.t.* زَكَّمَ ـ أَزْكَمَ ـ زَكَمَ. To be enrheumed, تَرَشَّحَ ـ اِسْتَهْوَى.

Enrich, *v.t.* To make rich, أَثْرَى ـ مَوَّلَ ـ أَغْنَى ـ أَوْجَدَ. To make fruitful, أَخْصَبَ. To increase, أَكْثَرَ ـ كَثَّرَ. To ornament, زَخْرَفَ ـ دَبَّجَ ـ زَيَّنَ; as with jewels, رَصَّعَ بِ. To —, of a language, بَحَّرَ ـ أَوْسَعَ. To be enriched, made rich, تَمَوَّلَ ـ اِسْتَغْنَى بِ ـ تَغانَى ـ اِغْتَنَى. To be fertilized, خَصَبَ. To be increased, تَكَثَّرَ ـ زادَ. To be extended, as of a language, اِتَّسَعَ. To be ornamented, تَزَخْرَفَ ـ تَزَيَّنَ.

Enrichment, *n.* The act of enriching, إِيجاد ـ إِغْناء; the being enriched, وَجْد ـ غَناء ـ اِسْتِغْناء. Fertilization, the act of, إِخْصاب; the being fertile, خِصْب. The act of —, as of a language, تَوْسِيع; the being so enriched, سَعَة ـ تَوَسُّع.

Enripen, *v.t.* *See to* Ripen, *v.t.*

Enrobe, *v.t.* *See to* Robe, Don, Dress, *v.t.*

Enrol, *v.t.* As in a register, قَيَّدَ فِي ـ سَجَّلَ فِي ـ كَتَبَ فِي دَفْتَرٍ. To involve, أَدْرَجَ ـ لَفَّ. To be registered in ..., تَقَيَّدَ فِي ـ سُجِّلَ فِي ـ كُتِبَ فِي. To be involved, wrapped, اِنْدَرَجَ ـ اِلْتَفَّ.

Enrolment, *n.* The act of, تَقْيِيد ـ تَكْتِيب ـ تَسْجِيل. A record, دَفاتِرُ *pl.* دَفْتَر ـ مَدارِجُ *pl.* مُدْرَج ـ سِجِلّ ـ مَحْضَر.

Enroot, *v.t.* غَرَسَ ـ أَصَّلَ.

En route, *ad.* عازِم ـ قابِل ـ فِي ٱلطَّرِيقِ. En route to Egypt, قاصِدٌ مِصْرَ.

Ens, *n.* *See* Entity, *n.*

Ensample, *n.* *See* Example, *n.*

Ensanguine, *v.t.* شَحَّطَ-بِٱلدَّمِ ـ دَمَّى ـ ضَرَّجَ-بِٱلدَّمِ .

Ensconce, *v.t.* خَبَّأَ ـ أَخْفَى ـ حَجَبَ ². To be ensconced, إِخْتَبَأَ ـ إِحْتَجَبَ .

Enseal, *v.t.* *See to* Seal, *v.t.*

Enseam, *v.t.* *See to* Seam, *v.t.*

Ensear, *v.t.* *See to* Sear, *v.t.*

Ensemble, *n.* Union, harmony, إِتِّفَاق ـ جُمْلَة . General appearance, صُورَة ـ هَيْئَة ـ طَرْز ـ مَنْظَر عَامّ .

Enshield, *v.t.* *See to* Shield, *v.t.*

Enshrine, *v.t.* To place in a shrine, وَضَعَ-فِي مِحْرَاب (or فِي مَزَار) *aor.* يَضَعُ . To preserve with affection, حَفَظَ-بِعِزٍّ وَٱحْتِرَام . *See also to* Cherish, *v.t.*

Enshroud, *v.t.* *See to* Shroud, *v.t.*

Ensiform, *a.* فِي هَيْئَةِ سِنَانِ ٱلرُّمْحِ ـ مُؤَنَّف . The — cartilage, غُلْغُل ـ رَهَابَة .

Ensign, *n.* A flag, عَلَم *pl.* أَعْلَام ـ رَايَة *pl.* رَايَات ـ بَيْرَق *pl.* بَيَارِق ـ لِوَآء *pl.* أَلْوِيَة . The great —, ٱلسَّنْجَقُ ٱلْكَبِير . A mark, as of distinction, عَلَامَة ـ نِيشَان ـ إِشَارَة . An — bearer, رَافِعُ ٱلْبَيْرَق ـ حَامِلُ ٱللِّوَآء . The rank below that of a lieutenant, مُلَازِم ثَانٍ .

Ensigncy, *n.* مَنْصَبُ حَامِلِ ٱللِّوَآء ـ رُتْبَةُ ٱلْمُلَازِمِ ٱلثَّانِي .

Enslave, *v.t.* To make a slave of, عَبَّدَ ـ إِعْتَبَدَ ـ إِسْتَعْبَدَ ـ إِسْتَرَقَّ . To reduce to submission, ضَبَطَ ـ قَهَرَ ـ طَوَّعَ ـ أَخْضَعَ . To — by love, إِسْتَهْوَى .

Enslavement, *n.* The act of, إِسْتِرْقَاق ـ إِعْتِبَاد ـ إِسْتِعْبَاد . Slavery, رِقّ ـ عُبُودِيَّة . The act of making submission, إِخْضَاع ـ قَهْر ـ ضَبْط ـ تَطْوِيع . Submissiveness, خُضُوع ـ خُشُوع ـ مُسَامَحَة .

Enslaver, *n.* مُسْتَعْبِد ـ مُعَبِّد ـ مُسْتَرِقّ . A seizer, allurer, سَالِبُ ٱلْإِخْتِيَار ـ سَالِب .

Ensnare, *v.t.* *See to* Entrap, *v.t.*

Ensue, *v.i.* To follow as a consequence, نَتَجَ ـ صَدَرَ ² ـ حَصَلَ ² ـ جَآءَ مِن *aor.* يَجِيءُ .

Ensuing, *a.* آتٍ ـ قَابِل . The — year, ٱلسَّنَةُ ٱلْقَابِلَة .

Ensure, *v.t.* *See to* Insure, *v.t.*

Entablature, *n.* صَفُّ ٱلْبِنَآءِ فَوْقَ عَمُودٍ ـ سَطْحُ ٱلْعَمُودِ .

Entail, *n.* An estate limited to particular heirs, مُلْكٌ مَوْقُوف وَقْفٌ مَرْبُوطٌ وَمَحْبُوس (or مَحْجُور) لا تَرِثُهُ إِلَّا وُرَّاثٌ مَخْصُوصُون . The rule of —, قَاعِدَةُ ٱلْوَقْفِ ٱلْمَرْبُوط . To cut off an —, حَلَّ ² (or أَبْطَلَ) ٱلْوَقْفَ ٱلْمَرْبُوط .

Entail, *v.t.* To settle property on by entail, أَوْقَفَ-ل ـ أَحْبَسَ- (or رَبَطَ ² -) ل . To cause, to occasion, سَبَّبَ ـ أَنْتَجَ ـ جَلَبَ ² .

Entailed, *a.* Settled by entail, مَرْبُوط ـ مَوْقُوف وَمَحْبُوس .

Entailment, *n.* The act of entailing, رَبْطُ ـ تَوْقِيفُ مُلْكٍ ل ـ تَحْبِيسُ مُلْكٍ ل ـ مُلْكٌ ل . The act of causing, تَسْبِيب ـ إِنْتَاج .

Entangle, *v.t.* To twist so as not to be easily separated, شَبَّكَ ـ عَقَّدَ . To perplex, حَيَّرَ ـ شَوَّشَ . To ensnare by captious questions, أَوْقَعَ ـ إِصْطَادَ-بِكَلَام . He was entangled in the rope, إِرْتَبَطَ فِي ٱلْحَبْلِ ـ إِحْتَبَلَهُ ٱلْحَبْل . To be entangled, as of the hair, إِشْتَبَكَ ـ تَعَقَّدَ ـ تَلَبَّدَ . To be twisted, knotted, تَعَكَّشَ ـ تَعَسَّرَ .

Entanglement, *n.* The act of, تَشْبِيك ; the being entangled, تَشَبُّك ـ تَشْوِيش ـ مُشَابَكَة . Perplexity, تَحَيُّر ـ تَشْوِيش ; of the hair, تَعَكُّس ـ تَلَبُّد . Difficulties, عَرَاقِيل .

Entente, *n.* مُحَادَثَة . *Entente cordiale*, مُوَافَقَة ـ مُحَادَثَة قَلْبِيَّة خَالِصَة .

Enter, *v.t.* سَلَكَ ² ـ دَخَلَ ² . To penetrate, as into a wood, خَشَّ فِي ² . To pierce, أَنْفَذَ ـ نَفَذَ ² . To pass into, دَخَلَ ² ـ دَخَلَ ـ سَلَكَ ـ فَاتَ إِلَى جَوًّا ² ـ عَبَرَ إِلَى جَوًّا ² . To admit, أَدْخَلَ . To write down, كَتَبَ ² . To enrol, كَتَبَ-فِي ² ـ دَوَّنَ ـ دَرَّجَ ـ قَيَّدَ-فِي كِتَاب ـ دَفْتَر . To — into an understanding with, تَشَارَطَ مَعَ-عَلَى ـ إِتَّفَقَ مَعَ-عَلَى ـ عَاهَدَ-عَلَى . To — the lists against, دَخَلَ ٱلْمَيْدَانَ مَعَ ² ـ قَاتَلَ . I entered the house, دَخَلْتُ ٱلْبَيْتَ (or إِلَى or فِي ٱلْبَيْتِ) . It never entered my thoughts before, لَمْ أَنْدَهِشْ بِهِ مِن قَبْلُ .

Enter, *v.i.* To go or come in, فَاتَ ² ـ دَخَلَ ² ـ سَلَكَ ² (or عَبَرَ ² إِلَى جَوًّا) . To — into, as into a religion, دَخَلَ فِي ² . To be a component part of, جُزْءٌ مِن ـ دَخَلَ فِي . To — upon, شَرَعَ فِي ² ـ بَدَأَ بِ ² ـ دَخَلَ فِي ² . To — into details, فَصَّلَ . To — into a contract with, شَارَطَ-عَلَى ـ قَاوَلَ-عَلَى ـ إِتَّفَقَ مَعَ-عَلَى .

Entering, *n.* *See* Entrance, *n.*

Entering, *a.* شَارِعٌ فِي ـ آخِذٌ فِي .

Enteritis, *n.* إِلْتِهَابُ ٱلْأَمْعَآء .

Enterprise, *n.* قَصْد ـ عَزْم ـ تَعَاطٍ ـ مُبَاشَرَة ـ عَزِيمَة ـ عَمَل . An important —, مُهِمَّة ـ نَدْب *pl.* نُدُوب . An industrial —, تَعَاطٍ صِنَاعِيّ . Enterprises, مَشْرُوعَات . He undertook different costly but profitless enterprises, أَخَذَ فِي مَشْرُوعَاتٍ مُكَلِّفَةٍ لا

نَفَعَ بِهَا . A man of great —, طَلَّاعُ ٱلثَّنَايَا – طَلَّاعُ ٱلْمَجْدِ . See also Undertaking, n.

Enterprising, a. مُمَارِسُ ٱلْأُمُورِ – جَسُور – نَدِب – مِتَصَدِّى ٱلْمُهِمَّةِ.

Entertain, v.t. To receive as a guest at table, أَوْلَمَ – آوَى – ضَيَّفَ. To receive with welcome, تَلَقَّى بِ – رَحَّبَ بِ – اِقْتَبَلَ بِٱلْإِكْرَامِ. To converse with, خَاطَبَ – حَاكَى – حَادَثَ – كَالَمَ – تَخَاطَبَ مَعَ. To amuse, سَلَّى – لَهَّى – أَحْظَى. To — in the mind, أَضْمَرَ. To admit, yield assent, قَبِلَ – سَلَّمَ. To be entertained, as a guest, تَضَيَّفَ. To be amused, اِحْتَظَّ – اِنْبَسَطَ – اِبْتَهَجَ – تَسَلَّى. To ask one to be entertained by him as a guest, اِسْتَضَافَ – تَضَيَّفَ.

Entertainer, n. One who receives company, مُؤَدِّب – آدِب – مُسَلٍّ – مُضَيِّف – مُضَايِفِيٌّ – ضَيَّاف. One who diverts, مُبَسِّط – مُسَلٍّ.

Entertaining, a. Amusing, مُفَرِّح – مُطْرِب – مُبْهِج – مُسَلٍّ – مُفَكِّه.

Entertainingly, ad. بِتَسَلٍّ – بِتَنَزُّهٍ.

Entertainment, n. A feast, عُزُومَة – ضِيَافَة – وَلِيمَة – مَأْدُبَة. Hospitable reception, تَرْحِيب – إِنْزَال – حُسْنُ ٱلْمُلَاقَاةِ – قُبُول. Amusement, فُرْجَة – تَنَزُّه – تَسَلٍّ – تَسْلِيَة – لَهْو. Retaining, as in the mind, إِضْمَار. Acceptance, تَسْلِيم بِ – قُبُول. A place of —, festivity, دَارُ وَلِيمَةٍ – دَارُ ٱلضِّيَافَةِ; for strangers, مَنْزِلٌ لِلْغُرَبَاءِ. A place of —, amusement, مَكَانُ فَرَجٍ – مَرْسَح pl. مَرَاسِح. To give an —, feast, اِتَّخَذَ مَأْدُبَةً.

Enthrall, v.t. See to Enslave, Inthrall, v.t.

Enthrone, v.t. To place on a throne, as of a king, أَجْلَسَ عَلَى كُرْسِيِّ ٱلْمَمْلَكَةِ. To — a bishop, أَجْلَسَ ٱلْأُسْقُفَ عَلَى كُرْسِيِّ ٱلْأَبْرَشِيَّةِ. To be enthroned, جَلَسَ عَلَى ٱلْكُرْسِيِّ.

Enthronement, n. The act of, إِجْلَاس – إِجْلَاسٌ عَلَى ٱلْكُرْسِيِّ عَلَى سَرِيرِ ٱلْمُلْكِ; the being enthroned, جُلُوسٌ عَلَى ٱلْكُرْسِيِّ.

Enthusiasm, n. Zeal, هَيَجَان – حُمَيَّا – حَمَاسَة – حَمَس – غَيْرَة – تَعَصُّب – حَرَارَة. Excessive admiration, عَجَبٌ زَائِدٌ – إِطْنَابٌ فِي ٱلتَّعَجُّبِ – فَرْطُ ٱلتَّحْسِينِ. See also under Fanaticism, n.

Enthusiast, n. / Enthusiastic, a. / Enthusiastical, a. } Zealous, غَيُور – مُتَعَصِّب – حَمِس. Having excessive admiration, مُسْتَعْجِب. To be —, zealous, حَمِسَ – تَحَمَّسَ. To make —, هَيَّجَ – أَغَارَ. See also under Fanatical, a.

Enthusiastically, ad. بِحَمَاسَةٍ – بِحَرَارَةٍ – بِغَيْرَةٍ – بِحِدَّةٍ وَشِدَّةٍ. To act —, تَحَمَّسَ.

Enthymeme, n. بُرْهَانٌ مُوجَزٌ.

Entice, v.t. To incite to, حَثَّ عَلَى – حَرَّضَ عَلَى – أَغْرَى بِ. To allure, جَلَبَ – جَذَبَ – تَمَلَّقَ – رَاوَدَ. To — blandishments, of a woman, هَنَّدَ – رَاوَدَ. To lead astray, خَدَعَ – ضَلَّلَ – أَضَلَّ – أَغْوَى. To be enticed, led astray, اِنْغَوَى – اِنْخَدَعَ. See also to Allure, v.t.

Enticement, n. The act of, instigation, حَثّ – تَحْرِيض – إِغْرَاء. Allurement, تَطْمِيع – جَلْب – جَذْب; by blandishment, تَهْنِيد. The act of leading astray, تَضْلِيل – إِغْوَاء.

Enticer, n. / Enticing, a. } مُهَنِّد – خَادِع – مُغْرٍ – مُغْوٍ – جَاذِب – جَالِب. Enticing words, كَلَامٌ مَلِقٌ. See also Allurer, n.

Enticingly, ad. With instigation, تَحْرِيضًا – بِإِغْرَاء. Alluringly, بِتَطْمِيعٍ – بِجَذْبٍ; especially of a woman, بِتَهْنِيدٍ.

Entire, a. All, أَجْمَعُ – جَمِيع – كُلّ fem. جَمْعَاءُ. Perfect, complete, تَمَام – كَامِل – تَامّ. Whole, سَالِم – صَحِيح – صَافٍ. Clear. An — horse, حِصَان pl. حُصُن. The — number or quantity, ٱلْجُمْلَة – ٱلْكُلّ. To make —, perfect, أَتَمَّ – رَصَنَ – كَمَّلَ. To be —, تَمَّ – صَحَّ – رَصُنَ.

Entirely, ad. Wholly, بِٱلتَّمَامِ – بِٱلْكُلِّيَّةِ – جُمْلَةً – كَافَّةً – بِرُمَّتِهِ – عَلَى ٱلْكَمَالِ وَٱلتَّمَامِ – بَتَّةً – عَلَى وَجْهِ ٱلْكَمَالِ. At once, together, بِٱلْمَرَّةِ – جُمْلَةً.

Entireness, n. / Entirety, } كُلِّيَّة – كَافَّة. In its —, بِكُلِّيَّتِهِ.

Entitle, v.t. To confer a right to, أَعْطَى حَقًّا لِ – أَوْجَبَ لِ – أَعْطَى أَمْرًا بِ aor. يُعْطِي. To give permission to, أَجَازَ لِ أَنْ – رَخَّصَ لِ فِي. To give a title, name, to, سَمَّى بِ – سَمَّى. To be entitled to, to have the right to, to deserve, صَارَ حَقِيقًا بِ – اِسْتَأْهَلَ – اِسْتَوْجَبَ – اِسْتَحَقَّ. To be entitled, named, دُعِيَ بِ – تَسَمَّى بِ – تَسَمَّى.

Entitled, a. Having a right, لَهُ حَقّ – مُسْتَوْجِب – مُسْتَحِقّ. Deserving, مُسْتَأْهِل – مُسْتَوْجِب – مُسْتَحِقّ – ٱلْحَقُّ لِ. Named, مُسَمًّى.

Entity, n. كَائِن pl. كَائِنَات – مَوْجُود pl. ٱلْمَوْجُودَاتُ (τὰ ὄντα).

Entomb, v.t. دَفَنَ – وَضَعَ فِي تُرْبَةٍ aor. يَضَعُ.

Entombment, n. The act of, دَفْن.

Entomological, a. مُتَعَلِّقٌ بِٱلْبَحْثِ عَنِ ٱلْحَشَرَاتِ.

Entomologist, n. عَالِمٌ بِطَبَائِعِ ٱلْحَشَرَاتِ.

Entomology, n. عِلْمٌ يَبْحَثُ عَنْ طَبَائِعِ ٱلْحَشَرَاتِ.

Entozoa, n. ٱلدِّيدَانُ ٱلْمَوْجُودَةُ فِي أَحْشَاءِ سَائِرِ ٱلْحَيَوَانَاتِ.

Entrails, n. أَحْشَاء – أَمْعَاء – أَمْصِرَة – مَصَارِين.

Entrance, *n.* The act of entering, عُبُور ـ سُلُوك ـ دُخُول. The right of entering, إِذْنٌ بِٱلدُّخُولِ ـ حَقٌّ بِٱلدُّخُولِ. An opening, passage, مَنْفَذ ـ باب ـ زَرْب ـ مَدْخَل. A hall, دِهْلِيز *vulg.* دُرْقاعَة. A commencement, ٱلِٱبْتِدآء ـ شُرُوع. A taking possession, ضَبْط ـ قَبْض ـ ٱتِّخاذ. Entrance-money, دُخُول فِي دَراهِمُ لِلدُّخُولِ. The wider —, ٱلمَدْخَلُ ٱلأَوْسَعُ.

Entrance, *v.t.* *See to* Enravish, *to* Charm, *v.t.*; *also under* Trance, *n.*

Entrancement, *n.* حالُ ٱلوِجْدانِ ـ وُجْد.

Entrap, *v.t.* To insnare, to catch in a trap, حَبَلَ ـ تَحَبَّلَ ـ أَخَذَ-فِي فَخٍّ ـ اِصْطادَ-فِي شَبَكَةٍ ـ صادَ-فِي شَرَكٍ ـ اِحْتَبَلَ. To catch one by artifice, أَوْقَعَ. Her husband entrapped her, اِحْتَبَلَها زَوْجُها. She entrapped him (with her love), captivated him, حَبَلَتْهُ فُلانَةُ.

Entreat, *v.t.* To beg, تَضَرَّعَ ـ طَلَبَ إِلَى ـ قَنَعَ ـ تَرَجَّى ـ رَجا ـ تَمَنَّى مِن ـ اِبْتَهَلَ إِلَى ـ إِلَى. To treat, عامَلَ.

Entreatingly, *ad.* مُتَضَرِّعًا ـ بِٱبْتِهالٍ ـ بِتَضَرُّعٍ.

Entreaty, *n.* ٱلْتِجآء ـ اِبْتِهال ـ تَضَرُّع ـ رَجآء ـ اِلْتِماس ـ تَمَنٍّ.

Entrée, *n.* Freedom of access, إِجازَةٌ ـ رُخْصَةٌ فِي ٱلدُّخُولِ بِٱلدُّخُولِ. Entrées, of dishes, أَوائِلُ ٱلأَطْعِمَةِ.

Entremets, *n.* ما يُؤْكَلُ بَعْدَ ٱلمَشْوِي وَقَبْلَ ٱلنُّقْلِ.

Entrepot, *n.* حاصِل *pl.* حَواصِلُ ـ مَحَلُّ إِيداعِ ٱلأَمْتِعَةِ ـ مَحَطَّةٌ (or) مَحَطُّ ٱلتِّجارَةِ.

Entry, *n.* An —, as in a book, كِتابَةٌ فِي دَفْتَرٍ ـ تَقْيِيد ـ تَدْوِين. A bill of —, فِهْرِسُ وَسْقِ ٱلمَرْكَبِ يُعْرَضُ عَلَى ناظِرِ ٱلكُمْرُكِ عِنْدَ دُخُولِهِ ٱلمِينا دَرْج. *See also* Entrance, *n.*

Entwine, *v.t.* شَبَّكَ ـ عَقَّدَ ـ عَلَّقَ ـ حَبَّكَ ـ وَشَجَ. To be entwined, اِنْعَقَدَ ـ تَحَبَّكَ ـ اِنْشَبَكَ ـ يَشِجُ *aor.* وَشَجَ.

Enumerate, *v.t.* عَدَّدَ ـ عَدَّ ـ حَسَبَ ـ أَحْصَى. To be enumerated, اِعْتَدَّ ـ حُسِبَ. He enumerated the dirhams one by one, عَدَّ ٱلدَّراهِمَ أَفْرادًا وِحادًا.

Enumeration, *n.* حِساب ـ تَعَدُّد ـ عَدٌّ ـ إِحْصآء ـ تَعْداد. Reckoning one by one, ٱلعَدُّ أَفْرادًا وِحادًا. An — of the attributes of God, تَنْسِيق.

Enumerative, *a.* مُعَدِّد ـ تَعْدِيدِيٌّ.

Enunciate, *v.t.* To utter, تَلَفَّظَ بِ ـ نَطَقَ بِ ـ تَلَفَّظَ. To declare, relate, ذَكَرَ ـ أَعْلَنَ ـ بَيَّنَ ـ صَرَّحَ بِ.

Enunciation, *n.* Utterance, تَلَفُّظ ـ نُطْق ـ تَلْفِيظ. A declaration, إِيضاح ـ إِعْلان بِ ـ تَصْرِيح بِ ـ ذِكْرٌ وَبَيان.

Enunciative, *a.* }
Enunciatory, } مُوَضِّح ـ مُصَرِّح بِ ـ مُبَيِّن ـ تَصْرِيحِيٌّ.

Enunciatively, *ad.* عَلانِيَةً ـ بِبَيانٍ ـ بِإِيضاحٍ.

Envassal, *v.t.* *See to* Enslave, *v.t.*

Envelop, *v.t.* As of a letter, *etc.*, لَفَّ ـ أَظْرَفَ ـ شَمَلَ ـ طَوَى-فِي ـ أَدْمَجَ ـ غَلَّفَ ـ أَغْلَفَ. To — in a dress, أَلْبَسَ. To — one's self in, اِشْتَمَلَ بِ. To be enveloped, اِغْتَلَفَ.

Envelop, *n.* }
Envelope, } In a general sense, ظَرْف *pl.* ظُرُوف ـ مِلَفٌّ ـ لِفافَة ـ غُلُف *pl.* غِلاف. A sheath, غِلاف *pl.* غُلُف. The — of grain produce, حافَةُ ٱلزَّرْعِ; of wheat, قُنْبُع. The — of a letter from the Sultan, خَرِيطَة. To put a letter in an —, غَلَّفَ مَكْتُوبًا. Under —, فِي ظَرْفٍ.

Envelopment, *n.* تَغْلِيف ـ تَلْفِيف ـ لَفّ.

Envenom, *v.t.* To poison, سَمَّ. To — a wound, by protracting its cure, أَزْمَنَ ٱلجُرْحَ. To enrage, أَثارَ ـ أَغْضَبَ. To render more hot, bitter, مَرَّرَ ـ أَضْرَمَ ـ أَجَّجَ ـ أَحْمَى.

Enviable, *a.* مَطْمُوعٌ فِيهِ ـ مَرْغُوبٌ فِيهِ ـ مُحَرِّكٌ إِلَى ٱلحَسَدِ ـ شَهِيٌّ ـ ما يَبْعَثُ عَلَى ٱلحَسَدِ. Enviable things, مَراغِبُ ـ مَطامِعُ.

Envier, *n.* }
Envious, *a.* } حاسِد ـ حَسُود ـ حَسُود ـ آنِهٌ.

Enviously, *ad.* حَسَدًا ـ بِحَسَدٍ.

Enviousness, *n.* *See* Envy, *n.*

Environ, *v.t.* To surround with, أَحْدَقَ بِ ـ أَحاطَ بِ. *See also to* Encompass, Surround, *v.t.*

Environing, *a.* مُكْتَنِف ـ مُحْدِق ـ مُحِيط.

Environment, *n.* تَكْنِيف ـ إِحْداق ـ إِحاطَة.

Environs, *n.* أَطْراف ـ نَواحِي ـ حَوالَي ـ حَرَى. In the — of, حَوْلَ ـ بِحَراةِ. The — of a town or village, سَوادُ ـ مَحْجَر ـ رَساتِيق.

Envoy, *n.* An ambassador, سَفِير *pl.* سُفَرآء ـ إِيلْچِي *pl.* إِيلْچِيَّة. A messenger, delegate, وَكِيل ـ رَسُول. A special —, سَفِيرٌ مَخْصُوص. An — extraordinary, سَفِيرٌ فَوْقَ ٱلعادَةِ. Envoy extraordinary and plenipotentiary, سَفِيرٌ مَخْصُوصٌ وَمُرَخَّص.

Envoyship, *n.* وَظِيفَةُ ٱلسَّفِيرِ ـ سِفارَة.

Envy, *n.* حَسِيدَة ـ حَسادَة ـ حَسَد ـ مُنافَسَة ـ نَفَس ـ بَغْيٌ. For —, out of —, حَسَدًا.

Envy, *v.t.* حَسَدَ عَلَى ـ نافَسَ فِي ـ غارَ عَلَى ـ بَغَى عَلَى ـ حَسَّدَ.

Eolian-harp, *n.* آلَةٌ تَعْزِفُ ٱلرِّيحُ بِها.

Eolipile, *n.* مِيزَانُ ٱلْبُخَارِ – مِيزَانٌ تُوزَنُ بِهِ قُوَّةُ ٱلْبُخَارِ.

Eon, *n.* A divine power or emanation, قُوَّةٌ مُجَرَّدَةٌ قَائِمَةٌ بِذَاتِهَا أَزَلِيَّةُ ٱلْوُجُودِ.

Epact, *n.* الزِّيَادَةُ فِي ٱلسَّنَةِ ٱلشَّمْسِيَّةِ عَنِ ٱلْقَمَرِيَّةِ.

Eparch, *n.* وَالٍ *pl.* وُلَاةٌ – وَالِيَةٌ – حَاكِمٌ *pl.* حُكَّام – قَائِد *pl.* قُوَّاد.

Eparchy, *n.* حُكُومَةُ ٱلْقَائِدِ – إِيَالَةٌ – وِلَايَةٌ.

Epaule, *n.* زَاوِيَةُ طَابِيَةٍ.

Epaulement, *n.* تُرْس – مِتْرَاس – مِتْرَس.

Epaulet, *n.* رُمَّانَةٌ مِنْ شَرِيطٍ أَوْ قَصَبٍ تُوضَعُ عَلَى – أَبُولِت ٱلْكَتِفِ.

Epergne, *n.* إِنَاءٌ فَاخِرٌ (or حِلْيَةٌ) لِزِينَةِ ٱلسُّفْرَةِ.

Epha, *n.* The Hebrew measure, إِيفَة.

Ephemera, *n.* مَا يَدُومُ إِلَّا يَوْمًا – ٱبْنُ يَوْمٍ (or سَاعَةٍ).

Ephemeral, *a.* } Short-lived, زَائِل – فَانٍ. *See also* Ephemera, *n.*
Ephemeric, }

Ephemeris, *n.* تَقْوِيم.

Ephemeron, *n.* *See* Ephemera, *n.*

Ephialtes, *n.* حِمَارُ ٱللَّيْلِ.

Ephod, *n.* أَفُود.

Epic, *a.* قَاصُّ ٱلْقِصَصِ. An — poem, قَصِيدَةٌ فِي مَدْحِ سِيَرِ ٱلْأَبْطَالِ.

Epicure, *n.* } بَطِر – شَهَّاءٌ – شَهْوَانٌ – شَهْوَانِيٌّ – مُتَلَذِّذ – بَطِن – بِطْنَانِيٌّ.
Epicurean, *a.* }

Epicurism, *n.* لَذَّة – تَمَتُّعُ ٱلنَّفْسِ بِٱللَّذَّاتِ ٱلْبَدَنِيَّةِ – بِطْنَة.

Epicurism banishes intelligence, (*prov.*) ٱلْبِطْنَةُ تُذْهِبُ ٱلْفِطْنَةَ.

Epicurize, *v.i.* تَلَذَّذَ بِ – عَاشَ فِي ٱلشَّهَوَاتِ – تَبَطَّنَ – عَاشَ مُتَرَفِّهًا.

Epicycloid, *n.* شَكْلٌ فِي هَيْئَةِ ٱلْقَوْسِ.

Epidemic, *a.* } جَامِع – عَامٌّ.
Epidemical, }

Epidemic, *n.* وَبَاء – وَافِدٌ – مَرَضٌ وَافِدٌ – مَرَضٌ مُعْدٍ – جَارِف.

Epidermis, *n.* بَشَرَة.

Epigastric, *a.* مُخْتَصٌّ بِرَأْسِ ٱلْمَعِدَةِ.

Epigastrium, *n.* رَأْسُ ٱلْمَعِدَةِ.

Epigee, *n.* } *See under* Perigee, *n.*
Epigeum, }

Epiglottis, *n.* لَهَاة *pl.* لَهًا – طُعْمَة – غَلْصَمَة – طَنْطَلَة.

Epigram, *n.* A phrase comprising much in a few words, عِبَارَةٌ مُلَخَّصَةٌ – عِبَارَةٌ وَجِيزَةٌ. A witticism, لَطِيفَة *pl.* لَطَائِفُ. A sharp speech, نُكْتَة *pl.* نُكَت.

Epigrammic, *a.* } Concise, جَامِع – وَاجِز. Witty, لَطِيف. Sharp, نَكَّات.
Epigrammatical, }

Epigrammatist, *n.* A writer of epigrams, مُؤَلِّفُ ٱللَّطَائِفِ (or ٱلنُّكَتِ). A concise writer, مُؤَلِّفٌ جَامِعٌ. A sharp writer, مُؤَلِّفُ نُكَتٍ.

Epigraph, *n.* كِتَابَة – عُنْوَان.

Epilepsy, *n.* صَرْع – خَبَل.

Epileptic, *a.* صَرِيع – مَصْرُوع – مُخَبَّل.

Epilogistic, *a.* مُخْتَتِم.

Epilogue, *n.* خَاتِم – خَاتِمَة.

Epiphany, *n.* عِيدُ ٱلتَّجَلِّي – عِيدُ ٱلْغِطَاسِ – عِيدُ ظُهُورِ ٱلسَّيِّدِ ٱلْمَسِيحِ.

Epiphysis, *n.* The — of a bone, نُشُوءُ عَظْمٍ مِنْ عَظْمٍ ثَانٍ.

Episcopacy, *n.* أَسْقُفِيَّة.

Episcopal, *a.* } أَسْقُفِيٌّ. Episcopal ordination, ٱلرِّسَامَةُ عَلَى يَدِ أَسْقُفٍ.
Episcopalian, }

Episcopalian, *n.* مِنْ أَهْلِ كَنِيسَةٍ أَسْقُفِيَّةٍ.

Episcopalianism, *n.* *See* Episcopacy, *n.*

Episcopally, *ad.* عَلَى يَدِ أَسْقُفٍ – بِأَمْرِ أَسْقُفٍ – حَسَبَ ٱلْقَوَانِينِ ٱلْأَسْقُفِيَّةِ.

Episcopate, *n.* مَنْصِبُ ٱلْأَسْقُفِ – مَقَامُ ٱلْأَسْقُفِ.

Episode, *n.* فِقْرَة – إِسْتِطْرَاد – حَادِث – وَقْعَة.

Episodic, *a.* } مُتَضَمِّنُ ٱلْفِقْرَةِ – إِسْتِطْرَادِيٌّ – حَادِثِيٌّ.
Episodical, }

Epistle, *n.* رُقْعَة *pl.* رِقَاع – رِسَالَة *pl.* رَسَائِلُ – مَكْتُوب *pl.* مَكَاتِيبُ.

Epistolary, *a.* بِٱصْطِلَاحِ ٱلرَّسَائِلِ – إِنْشَائِيٌّ. Epistolary style, إِصْطِلَاحُ ٱلْإِنْشَاءِ. An — correspondence, مُكَاتَبَة – مُرَاسَلَة.

Epistolize, *v.i.* أَنْشَأَ ٱلْمَكَاتِيبَ – كَتَبَ رَسَائِلَ.

Epistrophe, *n.* تَكْرِير – تَكْرِرَة.

Epitaph, *n.* عُنْوَانُ قَبْرٍ – كِتَابَةٌ عَلَى قَبْرٍ.

Epithalamium, *n.* قَصِيدَةٌ فِي مَدْحِ ٱلزَّوَاجِ – غِنَاءٌ لِلْعُرْسِ.

Epithet, *n.* وَصْف *pl.* أَوْصَاف – نَعْت *pl.* نُعُوت – صِفَة *pl.* صِفَات. A surname, لَقَب *pl.* أَلْقَاب. *See also* Surname, *n.*

Epitome, *n.* مُخْتَصَر – مُجْمَل – إِجْمَال – وَجْز – مُوجَز – إِيجَاز.

Epitomist, *n.* مُوجِز – مُجْمِل.

Epitomize, *v.t.* أَوْجَزَ – إِخْتَصَرَ.

Epitomizer, *n.* *See* Epitomist, *n.*

Epizoon, *n.* *See* Epizoa, *n.*

Epizoa, *n.* / **Epzoans,** } دِيدانٌ تَعِيشُ فِي باطِنِ جَمِيعِ ٱلْحَيَوانات *sing.* دُودَة *coll.* دُوْد — قُمَّل — قَمْل. The — of fish, قَمْلَةُ ٱلْقِرْش.

Epizooty, *n.* The disease, جائِحَةُ ٱلْقُمَّل.

Epoch, *n.* عَصْر — زَمان — تَوارِيخ *pl.* تارِيخ — وَقْت.

Epode, *n.* خاتِمَةُ قَصِيدَةٍ.

Epopée, *n.* *See* Epic, *n.*

Epsom-salt, *n.* مِلْحٌ أَنْكِلِيزِيّ.

Epulary, *a.* مُتَعَلِّقٌ بِوَلِيمَةٍ — ضِيافِيّ.

Epuration, *n.* تَصْفِيَة — تَنْقِيَة.

Equability, *n.* / **Equableness,** } مُساواة — سَوآء — إطِّراد — نَسَق.

Equable, *a.* مُعْتَدِل — مُساوٍ. Of an — temper, مُلائِم — لَيِّنُ ٱلْجانِبِ — لَيِّن — وَقُور.

Equably, *ad.* عَلَى حَدٍّ — اِعْتِدالًا — بِمُساواةٍ.

Equal, *a.* Like, similar, مُماثِل — نَدِيد — نَظِير — قَرِين — عَدِيل — مُساوٍ — مُساوِيٌّ — مِثْل — أَكْفاء *pl.* كُفْؤ — كُفُوّ — قِرْن — نِدّ. Equable, even, عادِل — مُعْتَدِل. Impartial, fair, مُقْسِط — مُسْتَوٍ — عَلَى عَيْنٍ — عَلَى حَدٍّ. Uniform, عادِل — مُسْتَقِيم. Capable of, لائِق ل — قابِلٌ ل — قادِرٌ عَلَى — مُعِيدٌ ل. In just proportions, نَظِير. Smooth, أَمْلَس — سَهْل — مُمَهَّد — ناعِم. Equal in stature and form, قَطِيع *pl.* قُطَعاء. They are —, هُمْ عَلَى سَوِيَّةٍ. There is none — to him, لا كِفاءَ لَهُ. They are not — to it, ضاقَ عِنْدَهُمْ ٱلشَّيْءُ. He is — to his father, سَدَّ مَسَدَّ أَبِيهِ. It is — to me whether you go or stay, سَوآءٌ عَلَيَّ ذَهَبْتَ أَوْ قَعَدْتَ. I made the two —, سَوَّيْتُ بَيْنَهُما. They two were or became —, اِسْتَوَيا — تَساوَيا. You have made them — to us, ساوَيْتَهُمْ بِنا.

Equal, *n.* قَرِين *pl.* قُرَناء — قِرْن *pl.* أَقْران — مَسَدّ — بَوآء. They are equals, هُمْ بَوآءٌ. He is without an —, ما — بِلا نَظِير. To be the — of one in, حاكَى — فِي. ما لَهُ مُحاكٍ — لَهُ مَثِيل. I was his — in the matter, حاكَيْتُهُ فِي ٱلْأَمْرِ. Such an one has met his —, رُمِيَ فُلانٌ بِحَجَرِهِ.

Equal, *v.t.* To make — to or with, أَقْرَنَ — ل — سَوَّى — ب. To make smooth, مَلَّسَ — مَهَّدَ — بَسَطَ — ساوَى — سَوَّى. To match, أَلْحَقَ — لَحِقَ — حاكَى. To become —, اِسْتَوَى; to become —, كانَ — اِسْتَقْرَنَ ل — ساوَى to, ماثَلَ. To be — to, fit for, مُعِيدًا ل. She equals her mother in beauty, لَها مِنَ ٱلْجَمالِ ما. Such an one is — to the sun in beauty, فُلانٌ يُحاكِي — يُعادِلُ أُمَّها ٱلشَّمْسَ حُسْنًا.

Equality, *n.* / **Equalness,** } مُساواة — مُناسَبَة — مُناظَرَة — سَوآء — كَفاءة — كُفْء — سَوِيَّة. Equality of rights, مُساواةُ ٱلْحُقُوقِ — تَساوِي ٱلْحُقُوقِ. They shall continue to enjoy perfect — in rights and privileges, يَبْقَوْنَ مُتَمَتِّعِينَ بِمُساواةٍ تامَّةٍ فِي ٱلْحُقُوقِ وَٱلْاِمْتِيازاتِ.

Equalization, *n.* إِقْران — تَعْدِيل — تَسْوِيَة.

Equalize, *v.t.* عَدَّلَ بَيْنَ — عَدَّلَ — سَوَّى بَيْنَ.

Equally, *ad.* عَلَى — سَوآءً — سَوِيَّةً — عَلَى ٱلسَّوِيَّةِ — بِٱلسَّوِيَّةِ — حَدَّ سَوَى. I divided it among them —, قَسَمْتُهُ عَلَيْهِمْ بِٱلسَّوِيَّةِ.

Equangular, *a.* مُتَساوِي ٱلزَّوايا.

Equanimity, *n.* صَبْر — حِلْم — رَصانَة — رَزانَة — قَرار — وَقار.

Equanimous, *a.* ثابِتُ ٱلْقَلْبِ — صاحِبُ صَبْرٍ — صَبُور — وَقُور — رَزِينُ ٱلْعَقْلِ.

Equation, *n.* Equalization, تَعْدِيل — تَسْوِيَة; the being equal, مُعادَلَة. Equation, in algebra, مُقابَلَة. Equation of time, تَعْدِيلُ زَمَنِ ٱلسّاعَةِ وَزَمَنِ ٱلشَّمْسِ — تَعْدِيلُ ٱلزَّمَنِ.

Equator, *n.* خَطُّ ٱلْاِسْتِواءِ.

Equatorial, *a.* مَنْسُوبٌ إِلَى خَطِّ ٱلْاِسْتِواءِ.

Equatorial, *n.* نَظّارَةٌ اِسْتِوائِيَّةٌ.

Equerry, *n.* سِلاحْدار. Chief —, أَمِيرُ آخُور.

Equestrian, *a.* أَسْوارِيّ — فُرُوسِيّ.

Equestrian, *n.* فارِس *pl.* فُرْسان — راكِب *pl.* رُكّاب.

Equiangular, *a.* مُتَساوِي ٱلزَّوايا.

Equidistant, *a.* مُتَساوٍ فِي ٱلْبُعْدِ. A place — between two parties, مَكانٌ عَدْلٌ بَيْنَ فَرِيقَيْنِ.

Equilateral, *a.* مُتَساوِي ٱلْأَضْلاعِ.

Equilibrate, *v.t.* عادَلَ — وازَنَ.

Equilibration, *n.* تَعْدِيل — مُعادَلَة — مُوازَنَة.

Equilibrity, *n.* / **Equilibrium,** } اِعْتِدال — بَزْو — مُوازَنَة — تَوازُن. In —, عَلَى ٱلْمِيزانِ — عَلَى ساجَةٍ. Political —, مُوازَنَةٌ سِياسِيَّةٌ — مُوازَنَةٌ دُوَلِيَّةٌ.

Equimultiple, *n.* مُساوٍ مَثَلِيّ.

Equine, *a.* مِنْ جِنْسِ ٱلْحِصانِ — حِصانِيّ.

Equinoctial, *a.* مَنْسُوبٌ إِلَى اِعْتِدالِ ٱللَّيْلِ وَٱلنَّهارِ — مَنْسُوبٌ إِلَى خَطِّ ٱلْاِسْتِواءِ — اِسْتِوائِيّ. The — line, خَطُّ ٱلْاِسْتِواءِ. The — colure, دائِرَةُ ٱلْاِعْتِدالَيْنِ — سَمْتُ ٱلْاِعْتِدالِ. An — gale, نَوْءٌ رِيحُ ٱلْاِعْتِدالِ.

Equinox, *n.* اِعْتِدال — اِعْتِدالُ ٱللَّيْلِ وَٱلنَّهارِ. The vernal —, الْاِعْتِدالُ ٱلرَّبِيعِيّ; the autumnal —, الْاِعْتِدالُ ٱلْخَرِيفِيّ.

Equip, *v.t.* To prepare, هَيَّأَ — أَعَدَّ. To furnish, جَهَّزَ —

تَجَهَّزَ لِ. To dress one in, لَبَّسَ ـ وَشَّحَ. To — one's self with arms, تَجَهَّزَ بِٱلْأَسْلِحَةِ ـ تَأَدَّى ـ آدَى ٱلْآدَاتِ ـ تَشَذَّرَ بِٱلسِّلَاحِ. To — a fleet, عَمَّرَ عِمَارَةً. To be equipped, as for battle, تَشَذَّرَ. To — for, أَهَّبَ ـ لِ. To — one's self for, تَأَهَّبَ لِ.

Equipage, *n.* Retinue, حَشَمٌ ـ وَشِيظٌ ـ خَدَمٌ ـ حَشَمٌ وَخَدَمٌ ـ تَبَعٌ. Accoutrements, baggage, أَدَاةٌ ـ أَثَاثٌ ـ عَمَائِرُ ـ أَسْبَابٌ ـ أَدَوَاتٌ ـ لَوَازِمُ.

Equipment, *n.* The act of, إِعْدَادٌ ـ تَجْهِيزٌ ـ جِهَازٌ ـ تَعْمِيرٌ ـ تَحْضِيرٌ ـ تَسْلِيحٌ. The being equipped, جِهَازٌ. Warlike equipments, مُهِمَّاتٌ عَسْكَرِيَّةٌ وَذَخَائِرُ حَرْبِيَّةٌ.

Equipoise, *n.* *See* Equilibrium, *n.*

Equipollence, *n.* }
Equipollency, } مُسَاوَاةُ ٱلْقُوَّةِ.

Equipollent, *a.* مُسَاوِي ٱلْقُوَّةِ.

Equiponderance, *n.* مُسَاوَاةُ ٱلثِّقْلِ.

Equiponderant, *a.* مُتَعَادِلٌ فِي ٱلْوَزْنِ ـ مُسَاوِي ٱلثِّقْلِ.

Equiponderate, *v.i.* سَاوَى فِي ٱلثِّقْلِ ـ وَازَنَ.

Equitable, *a.* عَدْلٌ ـ عَادِلٌ ـ مُقْسِطٌ ـ قَوَامٌ ـ مُسْتَقِيمٌ ـ ذُو إِنْصَافٍ ـ مُنْصِفٌ.

Equitableness, *n.* *See* Equity, *n.*

Equitably, *ad.* بِعَدَالَةٍ ـ بِإِنْصَافٍ ـ بِٱلصَّوَابِ. To act —, عَدَلَ.

Equitation, *n.* *See* Horsemanship, *n.*

Equity, *n.* عَدَالَةٌ ـ عَدْلٌ ـ سَوَآءٌ ـ قِسْطٌ ـ إِنْصَافٌ ـ نَصَفٌ. To act with —, أَنْصَفَ ـ عَدَلَ. Court of —, مَحْكَمَةُ ٱلْإِنْصَافِ.

Equivalence, *n.* Of power, مُسَاوَاةُ ٱلْمَقْدِرَةِ; of value, مُسَاوَاةُ ٱلْقِيمَةِ. Equality, مُعَادَلَةٌ ـ مُسَاوَاةٌ.

Equivalent, *a.* As in power, مُسَاوٍ بِٱلْقُوَّةِ; in value, مُسَاوٍ بِٱلْقِيمَةِ. In a general sense, مُسَاوٍ ـ بَوَآءٌ ـ بَزْوٌ. To be — to, سَاوَى.

Equivalent, *n.* عِوَضٌ ـ بَدَلٌ ـ عَدْلٌ ـ عَائِضٌ ـ مَعُوضَةٌ ـ خَلَاصٌ. To give an — for, أَعَاضَ عِوَضَهُ ـ إِعْتَاضَ بِ ـ عَنْ.

Equivocal, *a.* ذُو مَعْنَيَيْنِ ـ مُغْلَقٌ ـ مُبْهَمٌ ـ مُشْكِلٌ ـ مُشْتَبِهٌ. An — expression, تَوْجِيهٌ ـ مِعْرَاضٌ. To use — expressions, عَرَّضَ.

Equivocally, *ad.* بِٱشْتِبَاهٍ ـ بِشُبْهَةٍ ـ بِتَوْجِيهٍ ـ بِٱلْتِبَاسٍ.

Equivocate, *v.i.* إِحْتَالَ ـ لَوَى ـ صَاغَ. To — in a matter, تَحَوَّلَ (or إِحْتَالَ) فِي ٱلْأَمْرِ.

Equivocalness, *n.* }
Equivocation, } تَوْجِيهٌ ـ صَوْغُ ٱللِّسَانِ ـ شُبْهَةٌ ـ تَصْوِيفٌ ـ تَحَوُّلٌ ـ إِحْتِيَالٌ ـ إِلْتِبَاسٌ ـ إِشْتِبَاهٌ.

Equivocator, *n.* }
Equivocatory, *a.* } مُحْتَالٌ ـ مُرَاوِغٌ pl. مُرَاوِغُونَ ـ مُرَآءٍ ـ صَوَّاغٌ ـ صَيِّغٌ.

Equivoke, *n.* }
Equivoque, } إِحْتِيَالٌ ـ مِعْرَاضٌ ـ تَوْجِيهٌ ـ شُبْهَةٌ.

Era, *n.* عَصْرٌ ـ تَارِيخٌ. The — of the al-Hijrah, تَارِيخُ ٱلْهِجْرَةِ. The Christian —, تَارِيخُ ٱلْمَسِيحِ ـ تَارِيخُ ٱلْمِيلَادِ.

Eradicable, *a.* مِمَّا يُزَالُ ـ مِمَّا يُقْلَعُ ـ مِمَّا يُسْتَأْصَلُ.

Eradicate, *v.t.* To root out, إِسْتَأْصَلَ ـ جَثَّ ـ قَلَعَ ـ ثَلَعَ ـ إِسْتَجْذَرَ ـ إِجْتَاحَ ـ جَحَا ـ قَعَرَ. To destroy, سَحَتَ ـ أَسْحَتَ ـ دَمَّرَ ـ أَهْلَكَ ـ أَفْنَى. To be eradicated, rooted up, إِنْجَذَرَ ـ إِنْجَثَّ ـ إِنْقَعَرَ ـ تَقَوَّبَ.

Eradication, *n.* The act of pulling up by the roots, جَحْوٌ ـ جَثٌّ ـ إِسْتِئْصَالٌ ـ تَقْوِيبٌ. Destruction, تَدْمِيرٌ ـ سَحْتٌ ـ إِزَالَةٌ ـ إِفْنَآءٌ.

Eradicative, *a.* مُجْتَاحٌ ـ مُزِيلٌ ـ قَلَّاعٌ. Curative, عِلَاجِيٌّ ـ شَافٍ ـ شِفَائِيٌّ.

Erasable, *a.* That may be obliterated, يُمْحَقُ ـ يُنْسَخُ. That may be scratched out, يُطَرْمَسُ ـ يُطَلَّسُ.

Erase, *v.t.* To obliterate, مَحَا ـ مَحَقَ ـ طَمَسَ ـ نَسَخَ. To scratch out, طَرْمَسَ ـ طَلَّسَ. To — with a stroke of the pen, شَطَبَ. To be obliterated, إِمَّحَى ـ طَمَسَ ـ تَمَحَّقَ; to be scratched out, تَطَرْمَسَ ـ إِنْطَلَسَ.

Erasement, *n.* }
Erasion, } The act of obliterating, مَحْوٌ ـ طَمْسٌ ـ نَسْخٌ ـ مَحْقٌ; of scratching out, طَرْمَسَةٌ ـ طَلْسٌ ـ قَشْطٌ.

Eraser, *n.* نَاسِخٌ ـ طَامِسٌ. One who scratches out, مُطَرْمِسٌ ـ طَالِسٌ. A knife for scratching out, مِقْشَطٌ.

Erastian, *n.* صَاحِبُ ٱلْاِعْتِقَادِ بِأَنَّ لِلدَّوْلَةِ حَقَّ ٱلتَّصَرُّفِ فِي ٱلْأُمُورِ ٱلْكَنَائِسِيَّةِ.

Erastianism, *n.* ٱلْاِعْتِقَادُ بِأَنَّ لِلدَّوْلَةِ حَقَّ ٱلتَّصَرُّفِ فِي ٱلْأُمُورِ ٱلْكَنَائِسِيَّةِ.

Erasure, *n.* As with a stroke of the pen, شَطْبَةٌ; a scratching out, طَرْمَسَةٌ ـ مَقْشُوطٌ.

Ere, *ad.* Sooner than, قَبْلَ أَنْ. *See also under* Rather, *ad.*

Ere, *prep.* قَبْلُ. Ere now, مِنْ قَبْلُ ـ قَبْلًا ـ قَبْلَ ـ قَبْلَ ٱلْآنَ. Ere long, عَنْ قَرِيبٍ.

Erebus, *n.* مَمْلَكَةُ ٱلظَّلَامِ ـ بَرْزَخٌ.

Erect, *a.* Upright, جَاذِلٌ ـ مَنْهُوضٌ ـ قَيِّمٌ ـ قَائِمٌ pl. قِيَامٌ ـ قَوِيمٌ pl. قِيَامٌ ـ قَوَامٌ ـ مُنْتَصِبٌ. To be —, إِقْتَنَّ ـ إِسْتَقَنَّ. To stand —, جَذَلَ ـ إِسْتَجْذَلَ ـ إِنْتَصَبَ ـ تَنَصَّبَ ـ

إِنْتَهَضَ ـ ء نَهَضَ . He slept during the night — on the back of his beast, بَاتَ يَسْتَجْذِلُ عَلَى ظَهْرِ دَابَّتِهِ ء .

Erect, *v.t.* To raise and set up, نَصَبَ ‏² ـ نَصَّبَ ـ قَوَّمَ ـ أَنْشَأَ ـ عَمَّرَ ـ ء بَنَى . To establish, أَقَامَ ـ رَفَعَ ـ ء . To build, شَيَّدَ ـ أَسَّسَ .

Erectable, *a.* إِنْتِصَابُهُ مُمْكِنٌ ـ يَرْتَفِعُ ـ يُنْصَبُ .

Erection, *n.* The act of setting up, إِقَامَة ـ تَنْصِيب ـ نَصْب ; of standing erect, إِنْتِصَاب ـ تَنَصُّب ـ إِرْتِفَاع ـ رَفْع ـ تَقْوِيم ; of building, بُنْيَان ـ بِنَآء ـ تَعْمِير . A building, بِنَآء ; قِيَام . The act of establishing, إِمْضَآء ـ تَشْيِيد ـ تَأْسِيس ـ إِنْشَآء ـ عِمَارَة .

Erective, *a.* مُقَوِّم ـ مُنَصِّب .

Erectly, *ad.* عَلَى خَطٍّ مُسْتَقِيمٍ ـ نَصْبًا ـ قِيَامًا .

Erectness, *n.* قِيَام ـ إِنْتِصَاب .

Ere long, *ad.* *See* Ere, *prep.*

Eremite, *n.* نَاسِك ـ زُهَّاد *pl.* زَاهِد ـ رَابِط ـ رُبُط *pl.* رَبِيط *pl.* ـ مُتَوَحِّد ـ نُسَّاك .

Ere now, *ad.* *See* Ere, *prep.*

Erewhile, *ad.* مُنْذُ مُدَّةٍ يَسِيرَةٍ ـ عَنْ قَرِيبٍ ـ حِينًا .

Ergo, *ad.* بِنَآءً عَلَى ذٰلِكَ ـ إِذًا ـ لِذٰلِكَ .

Ergot, *n.* The fungus, عَاهَةُ ٱلْحُبُوبِ .

Ermine, *n.* قَاقُم .

Erode, *v.t.* أَكَلَ ‏² ـ ء رَعَى ـ ‏² سَرَفَ . To — as a moth, عَثَّ ‏² ـ تَسَوَّسَ . To be eroded, أُكِلَ ـ سُرِفَ ; as by a moth, سُوِّسَ ـ سَاسَ ‏² . *See also to* Corrode, *v.t.*

Erosion, *n.* سَرَاف ـ سَرْف ـ تَسَوُّس ـ سِيَاس . *See also* Corrosion, *n.*

Erosive, *a.* *See* Corrosive, *a.*

Erotic, *a.* مُغَزِّل ـ غَزَل ـ عِشْقِيّ ـ عِشْقِيّ ; of speech or poetry, مُغَزِّل ـ غَزَل .

Erpetologist, *n.* مُتَفَرِّغٌ لِعِلْمِ ٱلْهَوَامِّ .

Erpetology, *n.* عِلْمُ ٱلْهَوَامِّ .

Err, *v.i.* To go astray, ضَلَّ ء ـ زَاغَ عَنْ ء ـ تَاهَ ء ـ حَادَ عَنْ ء . To be seduced, غَوَى ء . To make a mistake, غَلِطَ ء ـ أَخْطَأَ ـ إِخْتَالَ ـ ضَلَّلَ ـ أَضَلَّ ـ أَغْوَى ـ زَلَّ ‏² ـ أَسْقَطَ . To cause to err, . To err through ignorance, جَهِلَ ء . To charge with erring, ضَلَّلَ . To feign to err, تَضَالَّ .

Errand, *n.* رَسَائِلُ *pl.* رِسَالَة ـ مَآلِكُ *pl.* مَأْلُكَة ـ أَلُوكَة ـ خِدْمَةُ ٱلرَّسُولِ ـ رَسُولِيَّة . To send one on an —, وَجَّهَ فِي . He communicated an — to him, أَلَاكَهُ ـ أَلُوك . One sent on an —, رَسُول . I have a secret — to you, لِي كَلَامٌ سِرٌّ إِلَيْكَ .

Errant, *a.* Wandering, دَوَّار ـ ضَالّ ـ سَائِح ـ تَايِه ـ مُتَحَيِّر ـ عَيَّار ـ جَائِر ـ سَيَّاح . Restless, خُرَجَةٌ وُلَجَةٌ . The — or wandering stars, ٱلْكَوَاكِبُ ٱلْمُتَحَيِّرَةُ ـ ٱلْخُنَّسُ .

Errantry, *n.* Wandering, عَيْل ـ مُطُور ـ دَوَرَان ـ سِيَاحَة ـ تَوْه . *See also under* Knight, *n.*

Erratic, *a.* مُلْتَوٍ . To be —, تَلَوَّى . *See also* Errant, *a.*

Erratically, *ad.* تِيهًا ـ بِغَيْرِ ضَبْطٍ ـ بِلَا نِظَامٍ ـ مُتَحَيِّرًا .

Erratum, *n.* } زَلَّة ـ خَطِيئَة ـ خَطَآء ـ سَهْو ـ تَصْحِيف ـ
Errata, } أَسْقَاط *pl.* سَقَط . The — and their correction, ٱلْخَطَآءُ وَٱلصَّوَابُ .

Errhine, *n.* سَعُوط .

Erring, *a.* Blundering, مِغْلَاط ـ مُغَفَّل ـ سَاهٍ . Wandering, straying, ضَالّ ـ ضَلُول ـ غَوِيّ ـ غَاوٍ ـ غَيَّان ـ مُضَلَّل ـ ضِلِّيل . Sinful, مُذْنِب ـ أَثِيم ـ خَاطِئ .

Erroneous, *a.* غَيْرُ صَحِيحٍ ـ غَيْرُ مَضْبُوطٍ ـ غَلَط ـ سَقَط .

Erroneousness *n.* } A mistake, هَفْوَة ـ خَطَآء ـ تَصْحِيف ـ سَهْو ـ
Error, } زَلَّة ـ أَسْقَاط *pl.* سَقَط ـ غَلَط ـ هَفَوَات *pl.* A shortcoming, تَقْصِير ـ قُصُور . A deviation, ضَلّ ـ طُغْيَان ـ إِثْم ـ ذَنْب . A false opinion, ضَلَال ـ غُرُور ـ غَيّ . A sin, ضِلَّة . Persisting in —, مُضَلَّل . To charge one with —, غَلَّطَ . Having errors in it, غَلَط ـ مَغْلُوط ـ مُغَلَّط . An — and its correction, خَطَآءٌ وَتَصْحِيحُهُ ـ سَهْوٌ وَصَوَابُهُ .

Erroneously, *ad.* بِعَدَمِ صِحَّةٍ ـ بِقِلَّةِ ضَبْطٍ ـ سَهْوًا ـ غَلْطَةً .

Errorist, *n.* نَاشِرُ ٱلْغُرُورِ ـ مُضَلِّل .

Erse, *n.* لِسَانُ أَهْلِ أَسْكُوتْلَانْدَ ٱلْقَدِيمُ .

Erst, *ad.* At first, قَبْلُ ـ أَوَّلًا . Formerly, فِيمَا مَضَى ـ سَابِقًا .

Erstwhile, *ad.* وَقْتًا مِنَ ٱلْأَوْقَاتِ .

Eruca, *n.* The plant, جِرْجِير .

Eructate, *v.i.* تَدَشَّى ـ تَكَرَّعَ ـ تَجَشَّأَ ـ أَفَشَّ ـ فَشَّ ء .

Eructation, *n.* The act of, تَدَشٍّ ـ تَكَرُّع ـ تَجَشُّؤ ـ جُشَآء .

Erudite, *a.* مِنْ ـ عَلَّام ـ عَالِم ـ مُفَنّ ـ حَاذِق ـ لَوْذَعِيّ ـ عَلَّامَة ـ أَهْلُ ٱلْعِلْمِ .

Eruditely, *ad.* بِكَمَالِ ٱلْمَعْرِفَةِ ـ بِعِلْمٍ ـ بِفَنٍّ .

Erudition, *n.* مَعْرِفَة ـ مُدَارَسَة ـ عِرْفَان ـ عِلْم ـ فَنّ .

Eruption, *n.* A breaking out, خُرُوج ـ طُلُوع ـ سُرُوح ـ سَرْح ـ هَيَجَانٌ (or فَوْرَةٌ or فَوَرَانٌ or ثَوَرَانٌ) جَبَلِ نَارٍ ; as of a volcano, صُدُور . An — on the skin, حَلّ ـ حَصْبَة . *See also under* Skin, *n.*

Eruptive, *a.* Breaking out, مُنْشِئ ـ مُصْدِر ـ سَرَّاح ـ سَارِح .

Eryngo, *n.* شَقَاقُل ـ قِرْصَعْنَة ـ قِرْصَنَّة .

Erysipelas, *n.* رَشْكِين ـ وَرَشْكِين ـ حُمْرَة .

Erysipelatous, *a.* حُمْرِيّ ـ مِثْلَ ٱلْوَرَشْكِينِ ـ شَبِيهُ ٱلْحُمْرَةِ .

Escalade, *n.* تَسَوُّرٌ بِٱلسَّلَالِمِ ـ تَسَلُّق .

Escalade, *v.t.* تَسَوَّرَ ـ تَسَلَّقَ .

Escapade, *n.* فَلْتَة .

Escape, *v.t.* To evade, فَازَ مِن ـ سَلِمَ مِن ـ نَجَا مِن ـ تَخَلَّصَ مِن ـ لَازَ مِن ـ سَهَا عَن ـ فَاتَ. To — one's notice, فَاتَ ـ سَهَا عَن. It has escaped my memory, ضَلَّ عَنِّي ـ رَاحَ مِنْ بَالِي. To — a danger, نَفَذَ مِنَ ٱلْخَطَرِ. To — shipwreck, سَلِمَ مِنَ ٱلْغَرَقِ. The word escaped me, فَرَطَتِ ٱلْكَلِمَةُ مِنِّي سَهْوًا. Every escaped word becomes relevant, (*prov.*) لِكُلِّ سَاقِطَةٍ لَاقِطَةٌ. Having once escaped the disease they were anxious not to expose themselves to it again, بَعْدَ أَنْ نَجَوا مَرَّةً مِنَ ٱلْمَرَضِ صَارُوا حُرَّاصًا عَلَى أَنْ لَا يَعْرِضُوا أَنْفُسَهُمْ لَهُ مَرَّةً أُخْرَى. The thing escaped me, I neglected it, فَاتَنِي ٱلْأَمْرُ. To make to —, to save, نَجَّى ـ أَنْجَى ـ أَنْقَذَ ـ خَلَّصَ.

Escape, *v.i.* To flee, flee from, فَرَّ ـ هَرَبَ ـ إِنْفَلَتَ ـ إِنْسَلَّ ـ إِنْهَزَمَ. To allow to —, أَفْلَتَ ـ هَرَّبَ.

Escape, *n.* The getting free, unharmed, نَجَاة ـ مَنْجَاة ـ فَوْز ـ صِيَانَة ـ خَلَاص. Flight, هِجْرَة ـ فَوْز ـ إِنْهِزَام ـ فَلْت ـ فِرَار ـ هَرَب. A fire —, (ٱلْحَرِيقِ *or*) آلَةُ نَجَاةٍ مِنَ ٱلنَّارِ. A narrow —, خَلَاصٌ بِٱلْجَهْدِ. A place of —, مَفَازَة ـ مَنَاص. There is no — from it, لَا مَنَاصَ مِنْهُ.

Escapement, *n.* The — of a watch, مِيزَانُ سَاعَةٍ.

Escarp, *v.t.* جَعَلَ مُنْحَدِرًا ـ صَيَّرَ صَبُوبًا ـ مَيَّلَ ـ جَرَفَ ـ صَيَّرَ جُرُفًا.

Escarpment, *n.* The act of, تَمْيِيل ـ صَيْرُورَةُ ٱلْمَكَانِ مُنْحَدِرًا. A slope, مُنْحَدِر ـ مُنْحَدَر ـ جُرُف ـ صَبَب ـ حَدُور ـ مَيْل. The — of a bastion, حَائِطُ ٱلْخَنْدَقِ مِنْ نَاحِيَةِ ٱلْقَلْعَةِ.

Eschalot, *n.* بَصَلٌ صَغِيرٌ.

Eschar, *n.* قِشْرَةُ ٱلْجُرْحِ ـ غَضَنَة ـ جُلْبَة. *See also* Scab, *n.*

Escharotic, *a.* حَرَّاق ـ مُحْرِق.

Escheat, *n.* إِنْتِقَالُ ٱلْمَتْرُوكَاتِ إِلَى مَنْ هُوَ أَوْلَى بِهَا أَوْ إِلَى ٱلْمِيرِي لِعَدَمِ وَارِثٍ لَهَا.

Escheat, *v.i.* إِنْتَقَلَتِ ٱلتَّرِكَاتُ إِلَى مَنْ هُوَ أَوْلَى بِهَا أَوْ إِلَى ٱلْمِيرِي لِعَدَمِ وَارِثٍ لَهَا.

Escheatable, *a.* تَرِكَاتٌ تَنْتَقِلُ إِلَى مَنْ هُوَ أَوْلَى بِهَا أَوْ إِلَى ٱلْمِيرِي لِعَدَمِ وَارِثٍ لَهَا.

Eschew, *v.t.* تَحَرَّزَ مِن ـ إِحْتَذَرَ مِن ـ تَنَحَّى عَن ـ إِجْتَنَبَ.

Escort, *n.* خَفَر ـ تَخْفِير ـ مُرَافَقَة ـ *vulg.* تَغْفِير ـ غَفَر.

Escort, *v.t.* To — to, رَافَقَ ـ (*or* أَوْصَلَ) إِلَى. To guard, خَفَّرَ ـ *vulg.* غَفَّرَ.

Escritoire, *n.* بِشْتَخْتَة ـ مَكْتَبَة.

Escritorial, *a.* مُخْتَصّ بِبِشْتَخْتَةٍ ـ مُتَعَلِّق بِٱلْمَكْتَبَةِ.

Esculapian, *a.* مُتَعَلِّق بِٱلطِّبِّ وَٱلطِّبَابَةِ.

Esculent, *a.* *See* Eatable, *a.*

Esculent, *n.* مَأْكُول ـ مِمَّا يُؤْكَلُ. Esculents, مَأْكُولَات ـ مُؤَاكِل.

Escutcheon, *n.* A coat of arms, عَلَامَةُ نَسَبٍ مَنْقُوشَةٌ ـ آرْمَا; of a ship, مَوْضِعُ كِتَابَةِ ٱسْمِ ٱلْمَرْكَبِ.

Esophagus, *n.* حَلْق ـ مَرِيء ـ مَسْرَط ـ بُلْعُوم ـ مَبْلَع.

Esoteric, *a.* دَاخِل ـ بَاطِن ـ بَاطِنِيّ. An — signification, بَطْن.

Espalier, *n.* The tree, شَجَرَةٌ مُعَرَّشَةٌ; the frame of an —, عَرِيش ـ مُشَبَّكَة.

Espalier, *v.t.* عَرَّشَ.

Especial, *a.* خَاصّ ـ مَخْصُوص; first, chief, أَوْلَى. *See also* Special, *a.*

Especially, *ad.* عَلَى ـ خُصُوصًا ـ خَاصَّةً ـ لَا سَيَّمَا ـ لَا سِيَّمَا ٱلْخُصُوصِ.

Espial, *n.* تَجَسُّس.

Espionage, *n.* تَجْسِيس.

Esplanade, *n.* سَاحَة ـ فُسْحَةٌ مُتَّسِعَةٌ ـ صَاعَة ـ صَاع ـ مِيدَان.

Espousal, *n.* Betrothal, خِطْبَة ـ خِطْب.

Espousals, *n.* Marriage, نِكَاح ـ زِيجَة ـ عَقْدُ ٱلزَّوَاجِ.

Espouse, *v.t.* To betroth, خَطَبَ ـ شَبَكَ بِٱلزِّيجَةِ. To marry, نَكَحَ ـ زَوَّجَ. To join a party, تَعَصَّبَ مَعَ ـ إِلْتَزَمَ ـ قَارَنَ ـ إِلْتَصَقَ بِ. *See also to* Marry, Defend, *v.t.*

Espousement, *n.* As of a cause, إِلْتِزَام ـ تَعَصُّب لِ. *See also* Espousals, *n.*

Esprit de corps, *n.* حَمِيَّة ـ غَيْرَة; of soldiers, ٱلنَّامُوسُ ٱلْعَسْكَرِيُّ.

Espy, *v.t.* To see at a distance, لَمَحَ ـ لَاحَ ـ أَبْصَرَ مِنْ بَعِيدٍ. To discover, كَشَفَ عَن ـ أَظْهَرَ ـ أَجْهَرَ ـ أَفَاشَ. To discover, as of a spy, تَجَسَّسَ ـ جَسَّ. He sent him to — the country, أَرْسَلَهُ لِيَتَجَسَّسَ ٱلْبِلَادَ.

Esquire, *n.* An armour bearer, حَامِلُ سِلَاحٍ ـ سِلَاحْدَار. The title of a gentleman, نَجِيب ـ سَيِّد *pl.* سَادَة ـ أَغَا *pl.* أَغَاوَات ـ بَيْك *pl.* بَيْكَات.

Esquisse, *n.* مُسَوَّدَة ـ رَسْم.

Essay, *v.t.* To endeavour, كَادَ ـ سَعَى فِي ـ جَدَّ فِي. To try, جَرَّبَ ـ إِخْتَبَرَ ـ إِمْتَحَنَ ـ رَازَ. *See also to* Assay, *v.t.*

Essay, *n.* An attempt, سَعْي ـ جِدّ ـ جَهْد. A trial, إِخْتِبَار ـ إِمْتِحَان ـ تَجْرِبَة ـ خِبْرَة. A short treatise, نُبْذَة ـ مَقَالَة ـ رِسَالَة.

Essayist, *n.* كاتِب رَسائِل ـ مُؤَلِّف مَقالات.

Esse, *n.* كَوْن. In —, مَوْجود.

Essence, *n.* The nature of a thing, كُنْه ـ كَوْن ـ ماهِيَّة ـ جَوْهَر ـ ذات ـ عَيْن ـ خاصَّة ـ حَقِيقَة. The chief properties, مَضْمُون ـ زُبْدَة ـ فَحْوَى ـ خُلاصَة. Gist, import, لُبّ ـ نِهاد ـ رُوح. Spirit, رُوح. A perfume, دُهْن ـ عِطْر *pl.* عُطُور. Essence of roses, عِطْرُ الوَرْدِ. The Divine Essence, ذاتُ اللّٰه.

Essential, *a.* Constituent, necessary, جَوْهَرِيّ ـ ذاتِيّ ـ عَيْنِيّ. Important, ضَرُورِيّ ـ مُهِمّ ـ لازِم ـ أَصْلِيّ. The — attributes, الصِفاتُ الذاتِيَّة. An — difference, فَرْق جَوْهَرِيّ.

Essentiality, *n.* / Essentialness, لُزُوم ـ أَصْلِيَّة ـ جَوْهَرِيَّة ـ ذاتِيَّة. Importance, لُزُوم ـ ضَرُورِيَّة ـ ضَرُورَة ـ مُهِمَّة.

Essentially, *ad.* مِنْ ذاتٍ ـ فِي الجَوْهَرِ ـ بِالذاتِ ـ فِي الذاتِ ـ طَبْعًا ـ الجَوْهَر. Radically, wholly, أَصْلًا ـ بَتَّة.

Establish, *v.t.* To fix firmly, شَيَّدَ ـ مَكَّنَ ـ قَرَّرَ ـ رَكَزَ ² ـ أَصَّلَ ـ أَيَّدَ ـ أَحْكَمَ ـ رَسَّخَ ـ أَثْبَتَ ـ أَكَّدَ. To confirm, to prove, أَوْجَدَ ـ أَنْشَأَ ـ أَسَّسَ. To found, بَرْهَنَ ـ حَقَّقَ ـ أَثْبَتَ. To set on foot, أَبْدَأَ ـ أَقامَ ـ عَقَدَ. To fix, as a salary, *etc.*, عَيَّنَ ـ رَتَّبَ. To set up, نَصَبَ ². To settle one in a country or place, إِسْتَعْمَرَ فِي. To — in business, رَتَّبَ لِ صَنْعَة. To —, as of a law, شَرَعَ ـ أَقامَ (or قَرَّرَ) سُنَّة ـ سَنَّ ². To put in order, نَسَّقَ ـ نَظَّمَ ـ رَتَّبَ. To be established, put in order, تَرَتَّبَ. To be established, confirmed, proved, تَبَرْهَنَ ـ تَحَقَّقَ. To be established, firmly fixed, تَشَيَّدَ ـ تَمَكَّنَ ـ مُكِّنَ ـ اِرْتَكَزَ ـ إِسْتَقامَ ـ رَسَخَ ـ تَحَكَّمَ. To be established, as in one's favour, مَكُنَ عِنْدَ ².

Established, *a.* Firm, مَكِين ـ مُقَرَّر ـ أَصِيل ـ وَكِيد. Organized, مُنْشَأ ـ مُنْعَقِد ـ مَوْقُوف. Proved, مُحَقَّق ـ مُبَرْهَن ـ مُثْبَت. An — fact, أَمْر مُقَرَّر ـ أَمْر مُحَقَّق. The — Church, الكَنِيسَة الرَسْمِيَّة السُلْطانِيَّة.

Establishment, *n.* The act of fixing firmly, تَقْرِير ـ رَكْز ـ إِحْكام ـ إِثْبات ـ تَأْكِيد ـ تَأْيِيد ـ تَمْكِين. The being fixed firmly, شَيْد ـ قَرار ـ ثَبات ـ رُسُوخ ـ اِرْتِكاز. The act of confirming, proving, تَحْقِيق ـ إِثْبات; of founding, تَأْسِيس ـ إِيجاد ـ إِنْشاء; of setting on foot, إِقامَة ـ تَعْقِيد ـ عَقْد; of fixing, as of a salary, تَعْيِين ـ تَرْتِيب; of strengthening, تَشْيِيد ـ تَقْوِيَة ـ تَحْكِيم. House and servants, *etc.*, بَيْت وَخَدَم ـ دائِرَة ـ أَتْباع. The Established Church, الكَنِيسَة السُلْطانِيَّة الرَسْمِيَّة. A ready arrangement for serving, *etc.*, تَرْتِيب حاضِر ـ عُدَّة. A warehouse, مَخْزَن *pl.* مَخازِن ـ حَوْصَل (*vulg.* حاصِل) *pl.* حَواصِل.

Establishment in life, profession, خِدْمَة. The public establishments, foundations, التَأْسِيسات الأَمِيرِيَّة; the public buildings, الأَبْنِيَة الأَمِيرِيَّة. Benevolent establishments, تَأْسِيسات خَيْرِيَّة. *See also* Institution, *n.*

Estafet, *n.* / Estafette, إِسْتِعْجالَة ـ ساعٍ ـ قاصِد ـ بَرِيد.

Estate, *n.* State, حال *pl.* أَحْوال ـ شَأْن ـ مَقام ـ دَأْب. Degree, rank, طَبَقَة ـ مَنْزِلَة ـ دَرَجَة ـ مَرْتَبَة ـ رُتْبَة. Property, income, مَدْخُول ـ مَنال ـ مال. Landed —, عُقْدَة *pl.* عُقَد ـ عِقار ـ أَمْلاك ـ مُلْك. The state, the public, الجُمْهُور ـ الدَوْلَة. The estates of the realm, أَرْكانُ الدَوْلَةِ. An — yielding much revenue, ضَيْعَة كَثِيرَة الرَيْع.

Esteem, *v.t.* To value highly, رَغِبَ فِي ـ أَعَزَّ ـ اِعْتَبَرَ ـ اِلْتَفَتَ إِلَى ـ أَكْرَمَ ـ كَرَّمَ. To respect, honour, وَقَّرَ ـ كَرَّمَ. To hold, consider, ظَنَّ ـ حَسِبَ ـ أَعَدَّ ². To — greater, better, than, فَضَّلَ عَلَى ـ اِسْتَصْلَحَ. I — Zaid more than 'Umar, زَيْدٌ عِنْدِي أَفْضَلُ مِنْ عُمَرَ.

Esteem, *n.* إِكْرام ـ اِلْتِفات ـ مُراعاة ـ عِزَّة ـ نَظَر ـ اِعْتِبار ـ رِعايَة ـ اِحْتِرام. To be held in — by, عَزَّ عَلَى ـ تَوَقَّرَ عِنْدَ. To hold in light —, اِسْتَخَفَّ.

Esteemable, *a.* / Estimable, Valuable ذُو قِيمَة ـ ثَمِين. Worthy of esteem, مَرْغُوب ـ مُسْتَحِقّ الإِكْرام ـ أَهْل لِلعِزَّة ـ مُعْتَبَر ـ عَزِيز ـ فاخِر ـ فِيه.

Esthetics, *n.* عِلْمُ المَلاحَة ـ الجَمال ـ فَلْسَفَة الذَوْقِ وَالجَمالِ.

Estimableness, *n.* لِياقَة ـ قِيمَة ـ اِسْتِحْقاق ـ اِعْتِبار.

Estimably, *ad.* بِوَجْهِ الاِعْتِبارِ.

Estimate, *v.t.* To reckon, عَدَّ ² ـ أَعَدَّ ـ حَسَبَ ² ـ قَدَّرَ ـ خَمَّنَ. *See also to* Esteem, *v.t.*

Estimate, *n.* / Estimation, Computation, تَعْداد ـ حِساب ـ تَخْمِين ـ تَقْدِير. Value, ثَمَن ـ قِيمَة. To hold in light —, اِسْتَحْقَرَ ـ اِسْتَقَلَّ ـ اِبْتَذَلَ ـ زَهِدَ. Held in mean —, مُبْتَذَل. *See also* Esteem, *n.*

Estimator, *n.* عَدّاد ـ مُحاسِب.

Estival, *a.* صَيْفِيّ.

Estivation, *n.* تَصْيِيف.

Estop, *v.t.* To impede and nullify by one's own act, أَسْقَطَ وَأَبْطَلَ مِن تِلْقاءِ نَفْسِهِ. *See also to* Bar, Stop, *v.t.*

Estoppel, *n.* فِعْلٌ أَوْ قَوْلٌ مِنْ طَرَفِ المُدَّعِي يَمْنَعُهُ عَنِ الاِحْتِجاجِ.

Estovers, *n.* ضَرُورِيّات ـ لَوازِم.

Estrade, *n.* A level place, مَيْدان ـ ساحَة ـ صاع ـ سَهْل.

Estrange, *v.t.* To keep at a distance, غَرَّبَ ـ بَعَّدَ ـ أَبْعَدَ. To alienate the heart from, أَمَالَ ٱلْقُلُوبَ عَن ـ نَفَّرَ ٱلْقَلْبَ مِن ـ أَحَالَ-عَن ـ صَرَفَ-عَن ـ رَغَّبَ ٱلضَّمَائِرَ عَن. To withdraw from, حَرَفَ-عَن. May God — him! (from good), أَبْعَدَهُ ٱللّٰهُ. To be estranged, placed at a distance, تَبَاعَدَ ; to be turned from, إِرْتَدَّ عَن. He became more estranged therefrom every day, زَادَ فِي كُلِّ يَوْمٍ تَبَاعُدًا عَنْهُ. They were estranged from one another, of two, تَبَايَنَا ; of many, تَبَايَنُوا.

Estrangement, *n.* Alienation, إِبْعَاد ـ تَبَاعُد ـ تَبَايُن ـ تَنْفِير ـ تَغْرِيب ـ إِبْتِعَاد. Diminution of friendship, فُتُورٌ فِي ٱلرِّفْقِ ـ بُرُودَةٌ فِي ٱلْمُصَاحَبَةِ. He caused — between them, أَلْقَى ٱلْوَحْشَةَ بَيْنَهُمْ.

Estrapade, *n.* شُبُوبُ ٱلْخَيْلِ ـ شُبُوب.

Estray, *n.* A strayed animal, سَائِبَة ـ عَيَّار ـ عَائِر.

Estuary, *n.* فَمُ نَهْرٍ ـ خَوْر.

Estuate, *v.i.* To simmer, جَاشَ *aor.* يَجِيشُ. *See also to* Boil, Rage, *v.i.*

Esurient, *a.* Hungry, جَوْعَانُ ـ جَائِع.

Etc., *Et cætera,* *n.* And so forth, هَلُمَّ جَرًّا ـ وَغَيْرَ ذٰلِكَ ـ إِلَى آخِرِهِ ـ وَٱلْبَاقِي ـ وَمَا شَابَهَهُ *contracted into* إلخ *and* اه.

Etch, *v.t.* *See to* Engrave, *v.t.*

Etching, *n.* *See* Engraving, *n.*

Eternal, *a.* Without beginning or ending, دَائِم ـ قَدِيم ـ صَمَد ـ أَزَلِيٌّ أَبَدِيٌّ ـ أَبَدُ ٱلْآبَادِ ـ أَزَلُ ٱلْآزَالِ ـ قَيَّام ـ سَرْمَدِيٌّ. Unchangeable, لَا يَحُولُ ـ دَائِمٌ عَلَى حَالِهِ ـ لَا يَتَغَيَّرُ. The Eternal, God, ٱلْقَيُّومُ. Life —, ٱلْخُلُودُ. To be —, دَامَ ـ إِسْتَدَامَ.

Eternally, *ad.* إِلَى دَهْرِ ٱلدَّاهِرِينَ ـ إِلَى أَبَدِ ٱلْآبَادِ ـ أَبَدًا ـ أَزَلِيَّةً ـ سَرْمَدًا ـ دَائِمًا. It is thine —, هُوَ لَكَ سَرْمَدًا.

Eternity, *n.* دَوَام ـ بَقَاء ـ أَبَد ـ أَبَدِيَّة ـ أَزَلِيَّة ـ أَزَل ـ سَرْمَد.

Eternize, *v.t.* أَدَامَ-أَبَدًا ـ أَبَّدَ.

Etesian, *a.* مَوْسِمِيٌّ ـ مُتَعَلِّقٌ بِٱلْمَوْسِمِ. An — wind, رِيحُ مَوْسِمٍ.

Ether, *n.* The air between heaven and earth, فَلَكُ ٱلْأَثِيرِ ـ أَثِير ـ نَفْنَاف. The spirit so called, رُوحُ لُقْمَانَ ـ رُوحُ ٱلْعَرَقِ.

Ethereal, *a.* / **Ethereous,** } Of ether, air, هَوَائِيٌّ ـ أَثِيرِيٌّ. Spiritual, bright, heavenly, سَمَاوِيٌّ ـ نُورَانِيٌّ ـ رُوحَانِيٌّ.

Etherealize, *v.t.* / **Etherize,** } To convert into ether, صَيَّرَ-رُوحًا لُقْمَانِيًّا. To spiritualize, جَعَلَ-رُوحَانِيًّا.

Ethereally, *ad.* نُورَانِيَّةً ـ رُوحَانِيَّةً.

Ethic, *a.* / **Ethical,** } مُتَعَلِّقٌ بِعِلْمِ ٱلْأَخْلَاقِ ـ أَدَبِيٌّ. Ethical studies, دَرْسُ (or عِلْمُ) ٱلْأَدَبِيَّاتِ.

Ethically, *ad.* حَسَبَ قَوَانِينِ ٱلْأَدَبِ.

Ethics, *n.* عِلْمُ ٱلْأَخْلَاقِ ـ عِلْمُ ٱلْآدَابِ ـ آدَاب.

Ethiop, *n.* / **Ethiopian,** } حَبَشِيٌّ *coll.* حَبَشَة.

Ethnarch, *n.* شَيْخُ بَلَدٍ ـ رَئِيسُ قَوْمٍ.

Ethnic, *a.* / **Ethnical,** } حَنَفِيٌّ ـ أُمَمِيٌّ ـ وَثَنِيٌّ.

Ethnographer, *n.* / **Ethnographist,** } عَالِمٌ بِٱلْجِنْسِيَّةِ.

Ethnographic, *a.* / **Ethnographical,** } مُخْتَصٌّ بِٱلْجِنْسِيَّةِ.

Ethnological, *a.* مُتَعَلِّقٌ بِعِلْمِ ٱلْبَحْثِ عَنِ ٱلطَّوَائِفِ.

Ethnology, *n.* عِلْمُ ٱلْبَحْثِ عَنِ ٱلطَّوَائِفِ.

Ethological, *a.* *See* Ethic, Ethical, *a.*

Etiolate, *v.t.* قَصَرَ ـ بَيَّضَ.

Etiolate, *v.i.* إِبْيَضَّ.

Etiolation, *n.* تَبْيِيض ـ قَصْر.

Etiquette, *n.* ٱلْعَوَائِدُ ٱلرَّسْمِيَّةُ ـ قَوَانِينُ ٱلْمُعَاشَرَةِ ـ سِيَرٌ وَآدَابٌ ـ تَكْلِيف ـ ٱلرُّسُومُ ٱلتَّشْرِيفِيَّةُ ـ ٱلْجَارِيَةُ. To stand upon —, إِعْتَنَى بِٱلرُّسُومِ ـ إِعْتَنَى بِإِجْرَاءِ ٱلْقَوَانِينِ. Not to stand upon —, كَانَ (صَارَ or تَصَرَّفَ or) بِدُونِ تَكْلِيفٍ. Court —, قَاعِدَةُ ٱلتَّشْرِيفَاتِ.

Etymological, *a.* مُخْتَصٌّ بِأُصُولِ ٱلْكَلَامِ ـ تَصْرِيفِيٌّ ـ إِشْتِقَاقِيٌّ.

Etymologically, *ad.* بِوَجْهِ ٱلْاِشْتِقَاقِ ـ إِشْتِقَاقًا.

Etymologist, *n.* عَالِمٌ بِأُصُولِ ٱلْكَلَامِ وَفُرُوعِهِ.

Etymologize, *v.i.* To search into the derivation of words, بَحَثَ عَنِ ٱشْتِقَاقِ ٱلْكَلَامِ. To treat of etymology, تَكَلَّمَ فِي عِلْمِ أُصُولِ ٱلْكَلَامِ.

Etymology, *n.* The science of, عِلْمُ أُصُولِ ٱلْكَلَامِ ـ ٱلْاِشْتِقَاقُ. Root and derivation, أَصْلٌ وَٱشْتِقَاقٌ ـ وَٱشْتِقَاقِهِ.

Etymon, *n.* أَصْل *pl.* أُصُول ـ كَلِمَةٌ جَامِدَةٌ غَيْرُ مُشْتَقَّةٍ.

Eucharist, *n.* The Lord's Supper, سِرُّ ٱلْقُدَّاسِ ـ ٱلْإِفْخَارِسْتِيَّا ـ ٱلْعَشَاءُ ٱلرَّبَّانِيُّ ـ ٱلْقُرْبَانُ. *See also under* Sacrament, *n.*

Eucharistic, *a.* / **Eucharistical,** } Expressive of thanks, مُتَضَمِّنُ ٱلشُّكْرِ. Pertaining to the Lord's Supper, مُتَعَلِّقٌ بِٱلْإِفْخَارِسْتِيَّا ـ قُرْبَانِيٌّ ـ قُدَّاسِيٌّ.

Eudiometer, *n.* مِيزَانُ هُبُوبِ ٱلْهَوَاءِ.

Eulogist, *n.* وَصَّاف ـ قَصَّال ـ مَدَّاح.

Eulogistic, *a.* / **Eulogistical,** } إِمْتِدَاحِيٌّ ـ مُقَصَّل ـ ثَنَائِيٌّ ـ مَدْحِيٌّ. A — poem in praise of women, غَزَل ـ تَشْبِيب ـ مَغْزَل.

Eulogistically, *ad.* مَدحًا ـ بِٱلْمَدحِ ـ بِٱلتَّشْبِيَةِ ـ بِٱلثَّنَاءِ .

Eulogium, *n.* / Eulogy, } تَبْجِيل ـ ثَنَاءٌ ـ ذِكْرٌ بِٱلْجَمِيلِ ـ مَدْح ; especially of the living, تَقْرِيظ .

Eulogize, *v.t.* فَضَّلَ ـ مَدَحَ ـ قَرَّظَ ـ أَثْنَى عَلَى ـ عَسَلَ ـ كَبَّرَ ـ ذَكَرَ بِٱلْجَمِيلِ ; especially of the living, قَرَّظَ .

Eunuch, *n.* خَصِيٌّ *pl.* خِصْيَان ـ مَخْصِيٌّ ـ طَوَاشِي *pl.* طَوَاشِيَة .

Eunuch, *v.t.* *See to* Castrate, *v.t.*

Eunuchism, *n.* حَالَةُ ٱلْخَصِيِّ .

Euphemism, *n.* حُسْنُ تَعْبِيرٍ .

Euphemistic, *a.* مُلَطِّفُ ٱلْكَلَامِ ـ مُحَسِّنُ ٱلْعِبَارَةِ .

Euphonic, / Euphonical, *a.* / Euphonious, } رَقِيقُ ٱللَّفْظِ ـ حُلْوُ ٱلصَّوْتِ .

Euphonism, *n.* لَحْنٌ مَلْحُونٌ ـ ٱتِّفَاقُ ٱلْأَصْوَاتِ .

Euphony, *n.* رِقَّةُ ٱلتَّلَفُّظِ ـ حُسْنُ ٱلصَّوْتِ .

Euphorbium, *n.* لُبَانَةٌ مَغْرِبِيَّةٌ ـ فَرْبِيُون .

Euphrasy, *n.* زَهْرٌ يُعَالَجُ بِهِ ٱلرَّمَدُ ـ فَرَاسِيُون .

Euphrates, *n.* The river, ٱلْفُرَاتُ .

Euphuism, *n.* عِبَارَةٌ مُبَالَغَةٌ ـ كَلَامٌ مُفَنٌّ ـ كَلَامٌ مُبَالَغٌ .

Euphuist, *n.* مُفَنٌّ فِي ٱلْكَلَامِ ـ مُبَالِغ .

Eurasian, *a.* and *n.* ٱلْمَوْلُودُ مِنْ أَبٍ أُورُوبَاوِيٍّ وَأُمٍّ هِنْدِيَّةٍ ـ مُسْتَوْرَبٌ *or* مُسْتَوْرِبٌ ـ مُوَلَّد .

Euroclydon, *n.* رِيحٌ شَرْقِيَّةٌ زَوْبَعِيَّةٌ .

Europe, *n.* بِلَادُ أُورُوبَا ـ أُورُبَّا . Throughout — generally, بِٱلدِّيَارِ ٱلْأُورُوبَاوِيَّةِ عَلَى ٱلْعُمُومِ . Central —, أَوَاسِطُ أُورُبَّا .

European, *a.* مِنْ أَهْلِ أُورُبَّا ـ أُورُوبَاوِيٌّ .

Eurus, *n.* The east wind, شَرْقِيٌّ ـ ٱلرِّيحُ ٱلشَّرْقِيَّةُ .

Euthanasy, *n.* مِيتَةٌ قَرَّارَةٌ ـ ٱلْمَوْتُ ٱلْأَبْيَضُ .

Eutychian, *n.* تَابِعُ أُوطِيخُوسَ *pl.* تُبَّاعٌ .

Eutychian, *a.* مَنْسُوبٌ إِلَى أُوطِيخُوسَ .

Evacuant, *n.* An — medicine, جُلَّاب ـ دَوَاءٌ مُسْهِلٌ .

Evacuate, *v.t.* To empty, أَفْرَغَ ـ فَرَّغَ ـ أَخْلَى . To — by stool, أَفْرَغَ ـ أَبْرَزَ ـ غَابَ . To withdraw from, خَرَجَ مِنْ ـ طَلَعَ مِنْ ـ تَنَحَّى عَنْ ـ عَنْ . The soldiers must — the fortresses, يَلْزَمُ أَنَّ ٱلْعَسَاكِرَ تُخْلِي ٱلْقِلَاعَ .

Evacuation, *n.* The act of ejecting, تَفْرِيغ ـ إِخْلَاءٌ ; the being evacuated, خَلَاءٌ . Evacuation by stool, بَرَاز ـ مَجْلِس ـ إِفْرَاغ ; by vomiting, إِسْتِطْلَاق ـ إِسْتِفْرَاغ . Withdrawal from, طُلُوعٌ مِنْ ـ خُرُوجٌ مِنْ . Abolition, إِبْطَال ـ نَسْخ . Excrement, بَرَاز ـ خِرَاءٌ ـ خَرَاءٌ .

Evade, *v.t.* To escape from, خَرَجَ مِنْ ـ لَاذَ مِنْ ـ تَفَلَّتَ مِنْ . To elude by craft, تَوَارَى عَنْ ـ زَاغَ مِنْ ـ تَوَارَبَ مِنْ . To practice artifice in, إِحْتَالَ فِي ـ تَحَوَّلَ فِي . To get in by evasion, إِنْزَبَقَ فِي ـ إِنْدَسَّ فِي .

Evade, *v.i.* إِنْفَلَتَ مِنْ ـ إِنْسَلَّ مِنْ .

Evaluation, *n.* *See* Valuation, *n.*

Evagation, *n.* عَيَل ـ مَطُور ـ سِيَاحَة ـ سَفَر .

Evanescence, *n.* Disappearance, فِرَار ـ غِيَاب . Departure from sight or possession, فَنَاءٌ ـ زَوَال ـ عَدَمُ بَقَاءٍ .

Evanescent, *a.* عَدِيمُ ٱلْبَقَاءِ ـ فَرَّار ـ زَائِل ـ فَانٍ . To be —, زَالَ ـ فَنِيَ .

Evanescently, *ad.* بِزَوَالٍ ـ بِعَدَمِ قَرَارٍ .

Evangelical, *a.* مُطَابِقٌ ٱلْإِنْجِيلِ ـ إِنْجِيلِيٌّ .

Evangelically, *ad.* حَسَبَ ٱلْإِنْجِيلِ ـ بِأُسْلُوبٍ إِنْجِيلِيٍّ ـ إِقْتِدَاءً بِٱلْإِنْجِيلِ .

Evangelism, *n.* بِشَارَةٌ بِٱلْإِنْجِيلِ .

Evangelist, *n.* مُبَشِّرٌ بِٱلْإِنْجِيلِ ـ إِنْجِيلِيٌّ *pl.* إِنْجِيلِيُّونَ .

Evangelize, *v.t.* بَشَّرَ بِٱلْإِنْجِيلِ ـ هَدَى إِلَى ٱلْإِنْجِيلِ .

Evangelize, *v.i.* بَشَّرَ بِٱلْإِنْجِيلِ ـ نَشَرَ وَأَشَاعَ ٱلْإِنْجِيلَ . They were evangelized by ..., دُعُوا إِلَى ٱلنَّصْرَانِيَّةِ عَلَى يَدِ .

Evaporable, *a.* مُصَعَّد ـ يُصَعَّدُ ـ مِمَّا يَتَحَوَّلُ وَيَصِيرُ بُخَارًا .

Evaporate, *v.t.* To convert into vapour, صَعَّدَ ـ صَيَّرَ بُخَارًا .

Evaporate, *v.i.* To pass off in vapour, بَخَرَ ـ تَصَعَّدَ مِنْ ـ وَصَارَ بُخَارًا . To be dissipated, تَلِفَ ـ إِنْزَاحَ ـ ذَهَبَ .

Evaporative, *a.* Converting into vapour, مُصَعِّد ـ مُحَوِّلٌ إِلَى ٱلْبُخَارِ . Dissipating, مُتْلِف ـ مُذْهِب .

Evasion, *n.* رُوَيْغَة ـ حِيلَة *pl.* حِيَل ـ مُحَاوَلَة ـ كَتْمُ ٱلنِّيَّةِ . To practice —, إِحْتَالَ . He has no means of —, لَا حِيلَةَ لَهُ . I have no means of —, لَا حِيلَةَ بِيَدِي .

Evasive, *a.* حِيَلِيٌّ . An — answer, جَوَابُ مُحَاوَلَةٍ .

Evasively, *ad.* بِرُوَيْغَةٍ ـ بِحِيلَةٍ ـ بِٱلْمُحَاوَلَةِ ـ بِكَتْمِ ٱلنِّيَّةِ .

Evasiveness, *n.* *See* Evasion, *n.*

Eve, *n.* The evening before a holiday, لَيْلَةُ عِيدٍ ـ عَشِيَّةُ عِيدٍ . *See also* Evening, *n.*

Eve, *n.* The wife of Adam, حَوَّاءُ .

Even, *n.* *See* Evening, *n.*

Even, *a.* Smooth, level, بَسَاط ـ بَسِيط ـ سَطِيح ـ مُسَطَّح ـ مُمَهَّد . Uniform, مُسَاوٍ ـ مُعَادِل ; in weight, مُوَازِن . Calm, سَاكِن ـ هَادٍ . Even-tempered, رَصِين ـ وَقُور ـ حَلِيم . Not odd, زَوْج ـ زَكًا (*vulg.* جوز). To be — with, to treat as one is treated,

قابَلَ-بِمِثْلِ ما صَنَعَ ـ كافَى-عَلَى ما صَنَعَ ـ عاوَضَ-بِمِثْلِ ما صَنَعَ. We are —, neither owes the other anything, ما لِأَحَدٍ مِنَّا شَيْءٌ عَلَى ٱلْآخَرِ. Odd or —, فَرْدٌ أَوْ زَوْجٌ ـ خَسا أَوْ زَكا. To be —, equal, إِسْتَوَى. To be —, smooth, إِنْسَطَحَ.

Even, *v.t.* To make —, level, سَطَحَ ² ـ سَطَّحَ ـ ساوَى ـ عادَلَ ـ مَهَّدَ ـ بَسَطَ ². To make —, equal, سَوَّى. To balance, وازَنَ. To make — that which was odd, شَفَعَ ².

Even, *ad.* بَلْ وَ ـ حَتَّى ـ أَيْضًا. I ate the fish — to its head, أَكَلْتُ ٱلسَّمَكَةَ حَتَّى رَأْسَها. Even the children saw him, حَتَّى (بَلْ وَ *or*) ٱلْأَطْفالُ نَظَرَتْهُ. How can you do it when — I am not equal to it? كَيْفَ تَسْتَطِيعُ أَنْ تَصْنَعَهُ مَعَ أَنِّي لَسْتُ بِقادِرٍ عَلَى ذٰلِكَ. None came to him, not — his father, لَمْ يَجِئْهُ أَحَدٌ حَتَّى وَلا (بَلْ وَلا *or*) أَبُوهُ. Even reason proves it, الرَّأْيُ بِعَيْنِهِ يُبَرْهِنُ ذٰلِكَ. It is — so, هُوَ حَقًّا هٰكَذا ـ هُوَ وَٱللّٰهِ كَذٰلِكَ. Even so, نَعَمْ.

Even-handed, *a.* Just, impartial, عادِلٌ ـ مُنْصِفٌ ـ عَدِيمُ ٱلْمُحاباةِ.

Evening, *n.* Nightfall, رَواحٌ ـ عِشاءٌ ـ مَساءٌ ـ عَشِيَّةٌ *pl.* عَشايا *and* عَشِيّاتٌ. The late part of the —, عَشِيٌّ. To converse together in the —, سامَرَ. To be —, أَمْسَى. To wish the — to, مَسَّى. Good —! مَساءُ ٱلْخَيْرِ; *Reply*: يُسْعِدُ ٱللّٰهُ مَساءَكَ. Good — to thee! مَسّاكَ ٱللّٰهُ بِٱلْخَيْرِ. Yesterday in the —, مَساءَ أَمْسِ. A place to spend an —, مُمْسَى. In the morning and —, صَباحًا وَمَساءً. I came to him late in the —, جِئْتُهُ عَشِيَّةً ـ أَتَيْتُهُ ٱلْعَشِيَّةَ. They travelled in the —, سارُوا رَواحًا.

Evening, *a.* مَسائِيٌّ ـ عَشَوِيٌّ. An — party, مُسامَرَةٌ. Evening prayer or service, صَلاةُ ٱلْمَساءِ. An — journey, رَوْحَةٌ.

Evenly, *ad.* Equally, إِعْتِدالًا ـ بِٱلِٱعْتِدالِ ـ بِٱلسَّوِيَّةِ. Smoothly, بِٱنْسِطاحٍ ـ بِٱسْتِواءٍ ـ بِتَمْهِيدٍ ـ بِتَسْطِيحٍ. Impartially, عَدْلًا ـ بِلا مُحاباةٍ.

Even-minded, *a.* وَقُورٌ ـ رَصِينٌ ـ رَكِينٌ.

Evenness, *n.* Regularity, تَسْوِيَةٌ ـ مُساواةٌ ـ إِعْتِدالٌ ـ سِواءٌ ـ إِسْتِواءٌ. Smoothness, بَساطَةٌ ـ تَمَهُّدٌ ـ تَمْهِيدٌ ـ تَسْطِيحٌ ـ إِنْسِطاحٌ. Calmness of mind, رَصانَةٌ ـ وَقارٌ ـ سَكِينَةٌ ـ رَواقُ بالٍ.

Even-song, *n.* صَلاةُ ٱلْمَساءِ.

Event, *n.* An incident, أَمْرٌ *pl.* أُمُورٌ ـ حادِثَةٌ *pl.* حَوادِثُ ـ واقِعَةٌ *pl.* وَقائِعُ ـ قَضِيَّةٌ *pl.* قَضايا ـ وُقُوعٌ ـ حَدَثٌ *pl.* أَحْداثٌ ـ حالٌ *pl.* أَحْوالٌ ـ ما جَرَى. The place of an —, مَوْقِعٌ *pl.* مَواقِعُ. A consequence, حاصِلٌ ـ طائِلٌ ـ نَتِيجَةٌ ـ آخِرَةٌ ـ عاقِبَةٌ. A supposed —, مَحْذُورٌ. In the — of, إِذا ـ إِنْ ـ إِنْ كانَ. At all events, عَلَى كُلِّ حالٍ ـ أَلْبَتَّةَ. Distressing events, حَوادِثُ باهِظَةٌ.

Eventful, *a.* ذُو حَوادِثَ مُهِمَّةٍ ـ مَمْلُوٌّ مِنْ وَقائِعَ كَثِيرَةٍ.

Eventide, *n.* وَقْتُ ٱلْمَساءِ ـ مَساءٌ ـ مُمْسَى ـ إِمْساءٌ.

Eventilate, *v.t.* *See to* Ventilate, *v.t.*

Eventual, *a.* واقِعٌ بِ ـ مُعاقِبٌ. The — result, الحاصِلُ.

Eventuality, *n.* Prevision of future events, حُسْنُ ٱلتَّبَصُّرِ بِٱلْوَقائِعِ. The eventualities, الأَحْوالُ ٱلْمُحْتَمَلَةُ. In this —, بِهٰذا ٱلْمَآلِ.

Eventually, *ad.* عاقِبَةً ـ نِهايَةَ ٱلْأَمْرِ ـ بِٱلْعاقِبَةِ.

Eventuate, *v.i.* خَرَجَ ² ـ حَصَلَ مِنْ ² ـ تَعَقَّبَ ـ نَتَجَ مِنْ ² ـ تَأَتَّى مِنْ.

Ever, *ad.* Always, دائِمًا ـ إِسْتِمْرارًا ـ أَبَدًا ـ فِي كُلِّ حِينٍ. Ever since that day, مِنْ يَوْمِهِ ـ مُنْذُ ذٰلِكَ ـ مُذْ ـ مُنْذُ. Ever and anon, كُلَّ ذِي وَقْتٍ ـ كُلَّ ساعَةٍ ـ المَرَّةَ بَعْدَ ٱلْمَرَّةِ. For ever and ever, إِلَى أَبَدِ ٱلْآبِدِينَ ـ إِلَى دَهْرِ ٱلدّاهِرِينَ. He knows it now if ever he will know it, إِنْ لَمْ يَعْرِفْهُ ٱلْآنَ لا يَعْرِفُهُ أَبَدًا. I believe you now more than ever, أُصَدِّقُكَ ٱلْآنَ حَقَّ ٱلتَّصْدِيقِ. I am as much your friend now as ever I was, أَنا صاحِبُكَ ٱلْآنَ كَما كُنْتُ قَبْلًا. I scarcely ever met a man equal to him, قَلَّما وَجَدْتُ نَظِيرَهُ أَصْلًا. He was the wisest man who ever lived, كانَ أَحْكَمَ مِمَّنْ وُجِدَ بَتَّةً. He talks without ever letting any one know what he means, يَهْذِرُ كَلامًا كَثِيرًا بِدُونِ أَنْ يُعَرِّفَ أَحَدًا بِمَعْناهُ أَبَدًا. Though he ask ever so much I will not give it to him, مَهْما كَرَّرَ ٱلطَّلَبَ فَلا أُعْطِيهِ لَهُ. Be they ever so many, بِقَدْرِ ما (مَهْما *or*) كانُوا كَثْرَةً. As soon as ever he had done it he was sorry, بِحالِ عِنْدَما قَضاهُ تَأَسَّفَ ـ ما تَمَّهُ حَزِنَ.

Evergreen, *n.* حَيُّ ٱلْعالَمِ ـ جَنْبَةٌ ـ شَجَرَةٌ دائِمَةُ ٱلْخُضْرَةِ ـ خَضِرٌ.

Everlasting, *a.* دائِمٌ ـ دائِمُ ٱلْقَرارِ ـ صَمَدٌ ـ قَيّامٌ ـ سَرْمَدِيٌّ ـ خالِدٌ ـ أَبَدِيٌّ ـ مُؤَبَّدٌ ـ باقٍ. The Everlasting, God, القَيُّومُ ـ الباقِي ٱلْأَبَدِيُّ. To be —, دامَ ² ـ إِسْتَدامَ. From — to —, مِنَ ٱلْأَزَلِ إِلَى ٱلْأَبَدِ. The present state of existence is of limited duration, but the final state of existence is —, الدُّنْيا أَمَدٌ وَٱلْآخِرَةُ أَبَدٌ.

Everlastingly, *ad.* دائِمًا ـ إِسْتِمْرارًا ـ بِلا ٱنْقِطاعٍ ـ سَرْمَدًا.

Everlastingness, *n.* أَبَدِيَّةٌ ـ سَرْمَدِيَّةٌ.

Everliving, *a.* حَيٌّ قَيُّومٌ ـ حَيٌّ لا يَمُوتُ.

Evermore, *ad.* فِي ما بَعْدُ ـ إِلَى ٱلْأَبَدِ ـ أَبَدًا.

Eversion, *n.* As of the eyelid, شَتَرَةُ ٱلْجَفْنِ. An overturning, إِنْقِلابٌ.

Evert, *v.t.* عَكَسَ ـ قَلَبَ.

Every, *a.* كُلّ. Every one, كُلّ وَاحِدٍ ـ كُلّ أَحَدٍ ـ كُلٌّ. Every man, كُلّ رَجُلٍ. Every woman, كُلّ آمْرَأَةٍ. All men, كُلّ النَّاسِ. Every cup, كُلّ كَأْسٍ. Every day, كُلّ يَوْمٍ. Every other day, كُلّ غِبَّ يَوْمَيْنِ ـ مَرَّةً كُلّ يَوْمَيْنِ; *vulg.* يَوْم أَيْوَا وَيَوْم لا. Every one for himself and God for all, كُلّ واحِدٍ لِنَفْسِهِ وَٱللّٰهُ كُلٌّ بِنَفْسِهِ وَٱلْكُلّ بِٱللّٰهِ ـ لِلْجَمِيعِ.

Every-day, *a.* مُعْتاد ـ عادِيٌّ ـ يَوْمِيٌّ.

Everywhere, *ad.* أَيْنَما كانَ ـ فِي أَيّ مَحَلّ كانَ ـ فِي كُلّ مَكانٍ.

Evict, *v.t.* To turn out, أَخْرَجَ ـ طَرَدَ. To dispossess, عَرَّى ـ سَلَبَ ـ خَلَعَ.

Eviction, *n.* Ejection, إِخْراج ـ طَرْد. Dispossession, تَجْرِيد ـ خَلْع ـ تَعْرِيَة.

Evidence, *n.* Witness, شَهادَة. Proof, بَيِّنَة ـ دِلالَة ـ دَلِيل. Authority, support, إِسْناد *pl.* أَسانِيدُ. إِثْبات ـ حُجَّة ـ بُرْهان. Clear —, حُجَّة صَرِيحَة. A witness, شاهِد *pl.* شُهُود. To bear or give —, شَهِدَ عَلَى. To call on one to give — to . . . , أَشْهَدَ-عَلَى. To establish, as by —, أَكَّدَ ـ أَثْبَتَ. To quote in — of, أَسْنَدَ-إِلَى.

Evidence, *v.t.* To give testimony for, شَهِدَ ل ; against, شَهِدَ عَلَى. To prove, confirm, بَيَّنَ ـ بَرْهَنَ ـ دَلَّ عَلَى ـ أَظْهَرَ أَثْبَتَ.

Evident, *a.* Clear, صَرِيح ـ جَلِيّ ـ مُبَيَّن ـ مُبِين ـ بَيِّن ـ ساطِع ـ مَعْلُوم ـ مُسْتَبْصَر. Notorious, واضِح ـ ظاهِر ـ باهِر ـ مَجْهُور بِهِ. To be —, بانَ ـ إِسْتَبانَ ـ صَرَّحَ ـ إِنْصَرَحَ ـ تَجَلَّى ـ تَبَيَّنَ. To make —, بَيَّنَ ـ أَصْرَحَ ـ صَرَّحَ ب. It is — that . . . , مِنَ ٱلْمَعْلُومِ أَنْ.

Evidently, *ad.* مُعايَنَةً ـ عِيانًا ـ بَيانًا ـ جِهارًا ـ جَهْرَةً ـ جَهْرًا.

Evil, *a.* Wicked, بَشِع ـ بَشِيع ـ شَنِيع ـ شِرِّير *pl.* أَشْرار ـ فاحِش ـ أَسْوَأُ *pl.* سُوءٌ ـ فاجِر ـ قَبِيح ـ سَيِّئ ـ خَلِيع ـ أَثِيم رَدِيّ. Miserable, شَقِيّ ـ مَنْحُوس. Calamitous, مَشْؤُوم *pl.* مَشائِيمُ ـ شَرّ ـ نَحِس ـ فاجِع. Evil speech, سَقَطُ ٱلْكَلامِ. To be —, wicked, خَلُعَ ـ ساءَ *aor.* يَسُوءُ ـ شَنُعَ. To do —, أَساءَ ـ شَرَّ *aor.* يَشُرُّ. A man of an — disposition, رَجُل سُوءٍ ـ بَشِيعُ ٱلْخُلْقِ. The — eye, إِصابَة ـ ٱلنَّظَرُ ـ العَيْنُ. The — one, the devil, إِبْلِيس ـ الشَّيْطانُ ٱللَّعِينُ. It is an — way, ساءَ سَبِيلًا. He did —, behaved badly, أَساءَ فِي فِعْلِهِ.

Evil, *n.* A crime, شَرّ *pl.* شُرُور ـ سُوءٌ ـ سَيِّئَة *pl.* سَيِّئات ـ إِثْم *pl.* آثام ـ خَطاءٌ *pl.* خَطايا ـ فَساد. A misfortune, آفَة *pl.* آفات ـ بَلاءٌ ـ داهِيَة ـ مِحْنَة *pl.* مِحَن ـ بَلِيَّة *pl.* بَلايا ـ مُهِمَّة.

The king's —, خَنازِيرُ ـ يَرَقان ـ سِلْعَة. The — deed, العَمَلُ السُّوءُ. A cause of —, مَشائِمُ *pl.* مَشْأَمَة ـ مَفْسَدَة ـ مَنْحَسَة. They are of the people who do actions that are causes of — and not of good, هُمْ مِنْ أَهْلِ ٱلْمَفاسِدِ لا ٱلْمَصالِحِ.

Evil, *ad.* بِرَداءَةٍ ـ بِسُوءٍ ـ شَرًّا.

Evil-affected, *a.* } غُضابِيّ ـ مُفْسِد ـ غَضْبان.
Evil-disposed, }

Evil-doer, *n.* شِرِّير ـ فاعِلُ شَرٍّ ـ مُذْنِب ـ مُجْرِم ـ خَلِيع *pl.* أَشْرار ـ لَعِين. Evil-doers, أَهْلُ ٱلشَّرِّ وَٱلْفَسادِ.

Evil-eye, *n.* العَيْنُ ـ النَّظَرُ.

Evil-eyed, *a.* حَسُود.

Evil-favoured, *a.* بَشِع ـ وَحِش ـ شَنِيع ـ كَرِه ـ قَبِيح.

Evil-minded, *a.* خَبِيث ـ حَقُود.

Evil-speaking, *n.* نِمْلَة ـ قَذْف ـ إِفْتِراءٌ ـ إِغْتِياب ـ نَمِيمَة.

Evil-worker, *n.* *See* Evil-doer, *n.*

Evince, *v.t.* To show, manifest, أَوْضَحَ ـ بَيَّنَ ـ أَجْهَرَ ـ أَظْهَرَ. To prove, بَرْهَنَ ـ أَثْبَتَ.

Evincible, *a.* قابِلُ ٱلْبُرْهانِ ـ مِمّا يُثْبَتُ ـ قابِلُ ٱلْإِيضاحِ.

Evincibly, *ad.* بِوَجْهِ ٱلْإِيضاحِ.

Evincive, *a.* مُبَيِّن ـ مُثْبِت ـ مُثَبِّت ـ مُظْهِر.

Eviscerate, *v.t.* إِسْتَدْلَقَ ٱلْأَحْشاءَ ـ أَخْرَجَ ٱلْمَصارِينَ.

Evitable, *a.* يُحْتَمَلُ ٱلْإِجْتِنابُ مِنْهُ ـ الفِرارُ مِنْهُ مُمْكِنٌ ـ الإِحْتِرازُ مِنْهُ مُحْتَمَلٌ.

Evocation, *n.* The act of calling forth, إِحْضار ـ إِسْتِدْعاءٌ ; of occasioning, إِسْتِجْلاب ـ تَسْبِيب.

Evoke, *v.t.* To call forth, أَحْضَرَ ـ إِسْتَدْعَى. To appeal, رَفَعَ الدَّعْوَى إِلَى. To occasion, إِسْتَجْلَبَ ـ سَبَّبَ.

Evolation, *n.* طَيَران.

Evolution, *n.* An act of opening out, فَتْح ـ بَسْط ـ نَشْر. Separation from, إِسْتِفْراد ـ تَفَرُّد. Progression, إِسْتِدْراج ـ تَقَدُّم. Concatenation, سِلْسِلَة ـ مُتابَعَة. Extraction of roots, as in algebra, إِسْتِخْراجُ ٱلْجُذُورِ. The development of a curved line, إِنْتِشارُ خَطٍّ مُنْحَنٍ. A movement of troops, حَرَكَة (*or*) تَحْرِيك ٱلْعَساكِرِ.

Evolutionary, *a.* Of troops, مُتَعَلِّق بِحَرَكاتِ ٱلْعَساكِرِ.

Evolve, *v.t.* To open out, فَرَشَ ـ فَتَحَ ـ بَسَطَ ـ نَشَرَ. To disentangle, فَكَّ ـ حَلَّ. To emit, أَصْدَرَ ـ أَخْرَجَ.

Evolve, *v.i.* To open itself, إِنْفَجَأَ ـ إِنْفَتَحَ ـ تَفَتَّحَ ; as of a flower, فَغَرَ ـ فَغَمَ. To — or disclose itself, تَبَيَّنَ ـ إِجْتَهَرَ.

Evolvement, *n.* *See* Evolution, *n.*

Evulsion, *n.* خَلْع ـ قَلْع ـ اِخْتِلَاج.

Ewe, *n.* شاةٌ أُنْثَى ـ شاة ـ نِعاج *pl.* نَعْجَة ـ أُمُّ ٱلْأَمْوَالِ.

Ewer, *n.* إِبْرِيق *pl.* أَبارِيق ـ كُوز *pl.* أَكْوَاز ـ جَرَّة *pl.* جِرار ـ قُدَاف. Ewer and basin, إِبْرِيقٌ وَطَسْتٌ.

Exacerbate, *v.t.* To increase, ثَقَّلَ ـ شَدَّدَ. To irritate, هَيَّجَ ـ أَوْغَرَ ـ أَغْضَبَ ـ أَلْغَضَبَ ; as of a disease, زَادَ فِي ـ حَدَّدَ.

Exacerbation, *n.* The act of increasing, إِثْقال ـ تَشْدِيد ; of irrritating, إِيغار ـ إِغْضَاب ; as of a disease, تَزْيِيد ـ تَحْدِيد.

Exacerbescence, *n.* شِدَّة ـ حِدَّة.

Exact, *a.* Perfect, correct, كامِل ـ صَحِيح ـ تامٌّ ـ تَمام. Accurate, مَضْبُوط ـ مُدَقِّق ; as in an art, مُتَعَمِّد. Careful, مُعْتَنٍ ـ حَرِيص. To be —, scrupulous, تَحَوَّنَ. To be scrupulously — in, as in an art, *etc.*, تَعَمَّدَ فِي.

Exact, *v.t.* To demand authoritatively of, طَالَبَ ـ بِ ـ اِقْتَضَى ـ أَلْزَمَ ـ بِ ـ أَوْجَبَ. To take from violently, اِقْتَرَحَ عَلَى ـ بِ.

Exacter, *n.* } بَلَّاص ـ مُكَلِّف ـ عَصَّار ـ مُسْتَلْزِم. Extortioner, extortionate, خاطِف ـ ظالِم.
Exacting, *a.* }

Exaction, *n.* The act of demanding, as by force, مُطالَبَةٌ بِ ـ اِقْتِضاءٌ بِ ـ اِسْتِلْزام. The act of seizing violently, اِقْتِراحٌ بِ ـ اِخْتِلاس. A forcible seizure, an extortion, بَلْص ـ ظُلْم ـ خُلْسَة ـ سَلَب. A tax, خَراج.

Exactitude, *n.* *See* Exactness, *n.*

Exactly, *ad.* Accurately, بِضَبْطٍ ـ بِدِقَّةٍ ـ بِغايَةِ ٱلْإِتْقانِ ـ تَحْكِيمًا. Perfectly, بِٱلتَّمامِ ـ بِٱلْكَمالِ ـ عَلَى عَيْنٍ. Exactly, like, عَيْنًا ـ طَبْقًا.

Exactness, *n.* Accuracy, تَحْكِيم ـ ضَبْط ـ دِقَّة ـ إِتْقان ـ هِنْدام. Perfect likeness, مُطابَقَةٌ كُلِّيَّةٌ. Justice, قِسْط ـ عَدالَة ـ سَوَاءٌ. Exactness, as in an art, تَعَمُّد.

Exactor, *n.* An —, as of tribute, مُلْتَزِم ـ ماكِس. *See also* Exacter, *n.*

Exaggerate, *v.t.* To enlarge, عَظَّمَ ـ زَادَ فِي ـ كَبَّرَ ; as in speaking or describing, بالَغَ فِي ـ جاوَزَ بِ ـ أَطْنَبَ فِي ـ أَفْرَطَ فِي.

Exaggerate, *v.i.* To amplify, as in speech, تَزَيَّدَ فِي ـ اِسْتَزادَ فِي. He exaggerates in his talk, يَسْتَزِيدُ (or يَزِيدُ) ـ يُطْنِبُ فِي ٱلْكَلامِ فِي حَدِيثِهِ.

Exaggeration, *n.* إِفْراط ـ إِزادَة ـ مُجاوَزَة ـ مُبالَغَة ـ إِطْناب. Based on —, مَحْمُولٌ عَلَى ٱلْمُبالَغَةِ.

Exalt, *v.t.* To raise, أَقامَ ـ عَلَّى ـ رَفَعَ. To — in dignity, رَفَعَ مَقامَهُ ـ فَخَّرَ ـ فَخَّمَ ـ عَظَّمَ ـ رَقَّى ـ عَلَّى ـ عَزَّزَ. To extol, شَكَرَ فِي ـ حَمَّدَ ـ حَمِدَ ـ كَبَّرَ ـ مَجَّدَ ; immoderately, أَطْرَأَ. To — one's self, تَكَبَّرَ ـ تَرَفَّعَ ـ تَعَزَّزَ ـ عَزَّ. To — one's self over, to domineer over, تَطاوَلَ عَلَى. To become exalted, raised, تَعَلَّى ـ عَلِيَ.

Exaltation, *n.* Height, عُلُوٌّ ـ اِرْتِفاع. The act of raising, promoting, تَرْقِيَة ـ تَرْفِيع ـ تَفْخِيم ـ تَعْزِيز. High position, جَدٌّ ـ عُلُوٌّ ـ عِزٌّ ـ رِفْعَة ـ فَخْر ـ عَظَمَة.

Exalted, *a.* High, سَنِيٌّ ـ سَمِيٌّ ـ سامٍ ـ مُرْتَفِع. High, as in rank or dignity, عالِي ٱلشَّأْنِ ـ شَرِيف ـ سَنِيّ ـ عَزِيز. The most — aims, أَعْلَى ٱلْهِمَمِ. Exalted, of God, مُتَبارِك.

Examen, *n.* } Investigation, مُعايَنَة ـ فَحْص ـ بَحْث ـ مُوازَنَة ـ تَجَسُّس ـ تَدْقِيق ـ تَفَحُّص. Interpellation, in a judicial sense, اِسْتِنْطاق. Pondering, اِطِّلاعٌ عَلَى ـ تَأَمُّل. Trial, اِمْتِحان ـ تَجْرِبَة. Self —, اِمْتِحانُ ٱلنَّفْسِ ـ فَحْصُ ٱلضَّمِيرِ. Post-mortem —, كَشْفُ ٱلْأَطِبَّاءِ عَلَى جُثَّةِ ٱلْمَيِّتِ لِتَحْقِيقِ سَبَبِ ٱلْمَوْتِ. On or upon —, مِنْ بَعْدِ ٱلْمُعايَنَةِ ـ إِذا صارَ ٱلْفَحْصُ ـ عُقْبَ ٱلْمُطالَعَةِ. Under —, judicially, تَحْتَ ٱلِٱسْتِنْطاقِ. Among those who were brought up for judicial —, مِنْ جُمْلَةِ مَنْ أُحْضِرُوا لِلِٱسْتِنْطاقِ. To condemn without —, حَكَمَ عَلَى ـ بِدُونِ تَحْقِيقِ ٱلْجَرِيمَةِ. To undergo an —, اِمْتُحِنَ. To prepare one's self for an —, اِسْتَعَدَّ لِلِٱمْتِحانِ. The — of the school, اِمْتِحانُ ٱلْمَدْرَسَةِ. Examination papers, or subjects on which candidates are examined, مُجازات.
Examination, }

Examinator, *n.* } An investigator, مُطَّلِع ـ مُتَفَحِّص ـ مُفَتِّش ـ مُخْتَبِر. A discusser, باحِث. One appointed to examine others, أَمِينٌ عَلَى ٱلِٱمْتِحانِ.
Examiner, }

Examine, *v.t.* To inquire into, فَتَّشَ ـ تَفَحَّصَ عَنْ ـ أَغارَ فِي ـ بَحَثَ عَنْ ـ اِسْتَقْصَى فِي ـ فَحَصَ عَنْ ـ عَنْ *or* عَلَى. To consider, تَأَمَّلَ ـ اِطَّلَعَ عَلَى. To try, test, اِمْتَحَنَ ـ اِخْتَبَرَ. To discuss, تَبَحَّثَ عَنْ ـ بَحَثَ عَنْ. To try, as of weights, coin, *etc.*, اِعْتَبَرَ ـ عَيَّرَ. To — into carefully, تَفَرَّسَ فِي ـ حَرَّرَ فِي ـ دَقَّقَ عَلَى ـ تَصَفَّحَ فِي. To — judicially, اِسْتَنْطَقَ. The Government is still examining the accused, ما زالَتِ ٱلْحُكُومَةُ تَسْتَنْطِقُ ٱلْمُتَّهَمِينَ.

Example, *n.* An instance, قَبِيل ـ مِثال *pl.* أَمْثِلَة. A pattern, model, عِبَر *pl.* عِبْرَة ـ قاعِدَة ـ مِثال ـ أُنْمُوذَج. An — to be followed, قِدْوَة. An —, as applied to punishment, مُثْلَة. To set or show an —, أَعْطَى (or أَظْهَرَ) قِدْوَةً. To take as an —, اِسْتَعْبَرَ ـ تَبِعَ ـ اِقْتَضَى بِ ـ تَسَنَّنَ بِ ـ اِعْتَبَرَ. To follow the — of, اِقْتَضَى بِ ـ أَثَرَهُ. To make an — of, جَعَلَ ـ عِبْرَةً لِمَنْ يَعْتَبِرُ ـ مَثَّلَ بِ.

To make a public — of, أَمْثَلَ-جَهْرًا . To punish, as an —, إِقْتِدَآءٌ بِ — إِمْتِثَالٌ بِ . For —, مَثَلًا . After the — of, أَمْثَلَ. And as an —, or instance, of the kind, وَمِنْ هٰذَا ٱلْقَبِيلِ . They followed this —, course, also, نَهَجُوا هٰذَا ٱلْمِنْهَاجَ أَيْضًا .

Exanimate, *a.* مَيِّت — مَوَات .

Exanthema, *n.* *See* Eruption, *n.*

Exarch, *n.* نَقِيب *pl.* نُقَبَآءُ — نائِب *pl.* نُوَّاب — والٍ *pl.* وُلَاة .

Exarchate, *n.* وِلَايَة — نِيَابَة — إِدَارَةُ نَقِيب .

Exasperate, *v.t.* أَسْخَطَ — أَغَاظَ — هَيَّجَ — حَرَّبَ — حَرَّشَ . To be exasperated, تَحَرَّشَ .

Exasperate, *a.* } مَغْضُوب — مُغْتَاظ — مُحَرَّب — مُحَرَّش .
Exasperated, }

Exasperation, *n.* The act of exasperating, تَحْرِيب — تَحْرِيش — إِسْخَاط — إِغَاظَة — تَهْيِيج ; the being exasperated, غَيْظ — تَحَرُّش — غَضَب — سُخْط . *See also* Exacerbation, Exacerbescence, Aggravation, *n.*

Ex cathedra, ad. Pronounced upon by a professor, بِفَصْلِ ٱلْمُدَرِّسِ — عَنْ حُكْمِ ٱلْأُسْتَاذِ .

Excavate, *v.t.* To make hollow, غَاطَ ² — نَقَرَ فِي ² — جَوَّفَ — نَبَشَ ² . To dig, حَفَرَ ² — نَقَبَ ² — حَفَرَ ² — إِحْتَفَرَ .

Excavation, *n.* The act of hollowing, نَقْر — تَجْوِيف — حَفْر . A hollow, غَوْط — حُفْرَة — جُوبَة — إِحْتِفَار — وَقْب . The act of digging, نَبْش — نَقْب — حَفْر .

Excavator, *n.* نَبَّاش — حَفَّار .

Exceed, *v.t.* To go beyond, جَاوَزَ بِ — جَاوَزَ — أَفْرَطَ فِي — جَاوَزَ ٱلْحَدَّ — شَطَّ فِي ² — أَسْرَفَ فِي . To surpass, to excel, زَادَ فَضْلًا ² — نَافَ عَلَى ² — أَنَافَ عَنْ — أَنَافَ عَلَى — فَاقَ عَلَى ² . He exceeded him in generosity, سَبَقَهُ فِي ٱلْكَرَمِ . It exceeded what he desired, زَادَ عَلَى مَا أَرَادَ . He exceeded the proper bounds of speech, أَسْرَفَ فِي ٱلْكَلَامِ . It exceeded the thing as much again, زَادَ عَلَى ٱلشَّيْءِ ضِعْفَهُ .

Exceed, *v.i.* To be redundant, زَادَ *aor.* يَزِيدُ — إِزْدَادَ . To — due bounds, to act extravagantly or immoderately, أَفْرَطَ . To — in wrong doing, طَغَى *aor.* يَطْغَى . He exceeds, or exaggerates, in his discourse, يَسْتَزِيدُ فِي حَدِيثِهِ . He exceeded the due bounds, is excessive or immoderate, in loving him, أَفْرَطَ فِي حُبِّهِ . He exceeded the due bounds towards him in speech, أَفْرَطَ عَلَيْهِ فِي ٱلْقَوْلِ . He exceeded all in riches, تَعَاظَمَ عَلَى ٱلْكُلِّ فِي ٱلْغِنَى . To — in wrong against, تَعَدَّى عَلَى .

Exceeding, *a.* عَظِيمٌ جِدًّا — كَثِيرٌ جِدًّا . *See also* Excessive, *a.*

Exceedingly, *ad.* كَثِيرًا — جِدًّا — لِلْغَايَةِ — بِزِيَادَةٍ . Exceedingly white, أَبْيَضُ جِدًّا . Exceedingly fair, beautiful, جَمِيلٌ جِدًّا . He was — happy to meet him, إِغْتَبَطَ بِلِقَائِهِ كُلَّ ٱلْإِغْتِبَاطِ .

Excel, *v.t.* بَرَزَ عَلَى — بَرَعَ ² — بَسَقَ عَلَى ² — أَفْضَلَ-فِي — فَضَلَ ² — عَنْ — بَهَرَ ² — رَاقَ عَلَى *aor.* يَرُوقُ — أَنْجَحَ بِ — فَاقَ ² — نَافَ عَلَى ² . You did not —, surpass, me, لَا أَنْفَصَلْتَ عَنِّي . To make one to —, فَضَّلَ — أَفْخَرَ .

Excel, *v.i.* بَهَرَ ² . To — in, بَسَقَ فِي ² .

Excellence, *n.* } Redundancy, glory, فَضْل — فَضِيلَة *pl.* فَضَائِل — فَخْر — بَرَاعَة — جَوْد . Goodness, كَرَم — خَيْرَة —
Excellency, }
pl. خَيْرَات — كَمَال . Excellency of rank or position, نَجَابَة — عِزّ — مَزِيَّة — نَبَالَة . The title of honour, جَنَاب — حَضْرَة — عِزَّتْلُو — شَرَف .

Excellent, *a.* Of great worth, فائِق *pl.* فُوَقَآءُ — فاضِل — مِفْضَال . Good, benevolent, خَيِّر — خِيَار — صاحِبُ فَضِيلَةٍ . Charming, لَذِيذ — طَيِّب ; of rank, نَجِيب — حَبَّذَا . Excellent, of food, أَشْرَفُ — بارِع — فاخِر . Eminent, نَبِيل . How — it is! مَا أَطْيَبَهُ . An — thing or action, فاضِلَة *pl.* فَوَاضِلُ .

Excellently, *ad.* لِلْغَايَةِ — بِبَرَاعَةٍ — فِي غَايَةِ ٱلْإِتْقَانِ .

Except, *v.t.* To take out from, إِسْتَثْنَى-مِنْ — حَاشَى-مِنْ . To object to, رَفَضَ ² — إِعْتَرَضَ عَلَى — مَا قَبِلَ — أَنْكَرَ .

Except, *v.i.* تَعَرَّضَ لِ .

Except, *prep.* } مَا خَلَا — خَلَا عَنْ — غَيْرَ — عَدَا — مَا عَدَا — سِوَى .
Excepting, } No one — you came to me, مَا جَآءَنِي سِوَاكَ .

The company came — Zaid, جَآءَ ٱلْقَوْمُ غَيْرَ زَيْدٍ .

Except, *conj.* Unless, غَيْرَ أَنْ — لَوْلَمْ — لَوْلَا — إِذْ لَمْ — إِلَّا أَنْ . Except ye return, أَنْ لَمْ تَرْجِعُوا . We have no more than this, — we go and buy food, لَيْسَ عِنْدَنَا أَكْثَرُ مِنْ هٰذَا إِلَّا أَنْ نَذْهَبَ وَنَبْتَاعَ طَعَامًا .

Exception, *n.* The act of excepting, إِخْرَاج — ثَنْوَى — إِسْتِثْنَآءٌ — إِسْتِبْقَآءٌ — مُحَاشَاة — تَشْذِيذ — إِشْذَاذ ; something excepted, ثُنْيَا — شاذٌّ — مُسْتَخْرَج — شُذُوذ — مُحَاشَى — مُسْتَبْقَى — مُسْتَثْنَى . Exception against, objection, إِعْتِرَاضٌ لِ — مُضَادَّة — رَدٌّ عَلَى . Legal —, إِعْتِرَاضٌ شَرْعِيٌّ . Without —, بِدُونِ — بِدُونِ ٱسْتِثْنَآءٍ — كُلُّهُمْ قَاطِبَةً — مُحَاشَاةٍ . With the — of, سِوَى — مَا عَدَا . To make one or a thing an —, أَخْرَجَ-عَنِ ٱلْقَاعِدَةِ . To take — to, إِعْتَرَضَ لِ . And with the — of these things, وَمَا عَدَا هٰذِهِ ٱلْأَشْيَآءِ .

Exceptionable, *a.* مُعْتَرَضٌ فِيهِ — يُلَامُ — يُرْفَضُ — يُعَابُ .

Exceptional, *a.* مُخَالِفُ ٱلْعَادَةِ — إِسْتِثْنَائِيٌّ . Exceptional clauses, شُرُوطٌ ٱسْتِثْنَائِيَّةٌ . An — or extraordinary phrase, كَلِمَةٌ فَاذَّةٌ (or) شَاذَّةٌ .

Exceptionally, *ad.* بِوَجْهِ ٱلِٱسْتِثْنَآءِ .

Exceptious, *a.* شَكِس ـ شَرِيس ـ مُشَاجِر ـ مُعْتَرِض .

Exceptive, *a.* حَاوِى (or) مُتَضَمِّنُ ٱلِٱسْتِثْنَآءِ .

Excern, *v.t.* صَوَّلَ .

Excerpt, *n.* عِبَارَةٌ مُنْتَخَبَةٌ . Excerpta, مُنْتَخَبَات .

Excess, *n.* Superfluity, شُطُوط ـ نَيِّف ـ مُبَالَغَة ـ مُجَاوَزَة ـ زِيَادَة ـ كَثْرَة ـ رَيْم ـ فُضُول *pl.* فَضْل ـ إِحْتِفَال ـ تَجَاوُز . What is left, بَقِيَّة . Excess beyond proper limits, إِفْرَاط ـ فَرْط ـ فُرُط ـ سَرَف ـ طُغْيَان . Excess in demanding, شَطَط . Wrongdoing, فُرُط . Intemperance, absence of moderation, عَدَمُ ٱعْتِدَالٍ ; in drinking, إِنْهِمَاكٌ فِى ٱلْخُمُور ـ سُكْر ; gluttony and lasciviousness, رَفَش ـ إِرْفَاش . Violence, عَنْف ـ شِدَّة . Excess of profit over expenditure, رَبَاح ـ رِبْح . To be in — of, of number, تَعَدَّدَ عَلَى . To be in —, more than, أَفْضَلَ عَنْ ـ ²فَضَلَ . There is no deficiency in it nor —, لَا بَخْسَ فِيهِ وَلَا شَطَطَ . It is in — of, هُوَ مُنَافٌ ل . Excess without excellence, فُضُولٌ بِلَا فَضْلٍ . To be given to —, in eating, drinking, *etc.*, أَرْفَشَ ـ ²رَفَشَ .

Excessive, *a.* Extreme, فَاضِل ـ مُفْرِط ـ مُتَجَاوِز ـ مُتَجَاوِزُ ٱلْحَدِّ ـ زَائِد . Vehement, عَنِيف ـ عَنِف ـ شَدِيد .

Excessively, *ad.* Extremely, بِمَا يَفُوقُ ـ لِلنِّهَايَةِ ـ لِلْغَايَةِ ـ فَوْقَ ٱلْحَدِّ ـ بِإِفْرَاطٍ ـ ٱلْحَدِّ . Greatly, كَثِيرًا ـ جِدًّا .

Excessiveness, *n.* *See* Excess, *n.*

Exchange, *v.t.* To — one thing for another, بَادَلَ ـ تَبَادَلَ ـ بَدَّلَ ـ بِ ـ عَاوَضَ ـ قَايَضَ ـ فِى ـ قَاوَضَ (or) دَاكَشَ . To — commodities, to barter, شَارَى ـ بَايَعَ ـ عَارَضَ ـ بِٱلْبَيْعِ ـ بَادَّ . To — one coin for other money, صَرَفَ ـ بِ . To — or change into, أَبْدَلَ ـ بِ ـ بَدَّلَ ـ بِ . I exchanged the gold for dirhams, صَرَفْتُ ٱلذَّهَبَ بِٱلدَّرَاهِمِ . He has exchanged his sin for repentance, كَفَّرَ ذَنْبَهُ بِٱلتَّوْبَةِ . I exchanged the garment for another, بَدَّلْتُ ٱلثَّوْبَ بِغَيْرِهِ . To — words with, كَالَمَ ـ حَادَثَ ـ سَامَرَ . They exchanged forgiveness, of many, تَغَافَرُوا ـ تَسَامَحُوا ـ سَامَحَ بَعْضُهُمْ بَعْضًا ـ تَصَافَحُوا ٱلذُّنُوبَ .

Exchange, *n.* The act of giving one thing for another, مُبَادَلَة ـ إِبْدَال ـ بَدَال ـ مُقَايَضَة ـ مُعَاوَضَة . Change, as of place, *etc.*, تَبْدِيل . Barter, مُشَارَاة ـ مُبَايَعَة ـ بِدَاد ـ مُبَادَدَة . Exchange, as of coin, صَرْف . An —, where merchants meet, مَحَلُّ مُجْمَعِ ٱلتُّجَّارِ . A stock —, بُورْس . A bill of —, كَمْبِيَالَة ـ وَرَقَةُ حَوَالَةٍ ـ سَفَاتِج *pl.* سُفْتَجَة . Course of —, تَفَاوُتُ ٱلْكَامْبِيُو ـ مُرَابَحَة . Rate of —, قِيمَة . Exchange of prisoners, مُبَادَلَةُ ٱلْأَسْرَآءِ . Exchange of notes, correspondence, تَعَاطِى ٱلْمُحَرَّرَاتِ . Exchange of thoughts, تَرَآءٍ ـ تَعَاطِى ٱلْآرَآءِ . He took it from him in —, أَخَذَهُ مِنْهُ بَدَلًا . To give one a bill of —, سَفْتَجَ .

Exchangeability, *n.* مُكْنَة ـ إِمْكَانُ ٱلتَّبْدِيلِ ـ إِمْكَانُ ٱلْمُبَادَلَةِ ٱلْمُعَاوَضَة .

Exchangeable, *a.* مِمَّا يُبَادَلُ ـ قَابِلُ ٱلْمُبَادَلَةِ .

Exchanger, *n.* *See* Banker, *n.*

Exchequer, *n.* خَزِينَةُ ٱلْمِيرِى ـ بَيْتُ ٱلْمَالِ ـ خَزْنَةُ ٱلْمُلْكِ . Chancellor of the —, نَاظِرُ ٱلْمَالِيَّةِ . Court of —, مَحْكَمَةُ مَالِ ٱلْخَزْنَةِ . Exchequer bills, تَحْوِيلُ (or) حَوَالَةُ ٱلْخَزْنَةِ .

Excisable, *a.* تَحْتَ ـ يَدْفَعُ ٱلْفُرْضَةَ ـ تَحْتَ ٱلتَّكَالِيفِ ٱلْوَضِيعَةِ .

Excise, *n.* وَضِيعَة ـ مَكْس ـ تَكَالِيفُ مِيرِيَّةٌ ـ رُسُومَات ـ فُرْضَة ـ إِحْتِسَاب . Excise dues, تَكَالِيفُ ٱلِٱحْتِسَابِ . Excise office, إِدَارَةُ ٱلِٱحْتِسَابِ ـ الِاحْتِسَابُ . Excise officer, أَحَدُ مَأْمُورِى ٱلِٱحْتِسَابِ .

Exciseman, *n.* أَحَدُ مَأْمُورِى ٱلِٱحْتِسَابِ ـ مَكَّاس .

Excision, *n.* The act of cutting off, جَزْر ـ قَطْع ـ تَبْتِيت . Extirpation, destruction, تَخْرِيب ـ إِزَالَة ـ إِفْنَآء . *See also* Excommunication, *n.*

Excitability, *n.* هَيَجَان ـ فَرْطُ ٱلِٱسْتِعْدَادِ ـ فَزَازَة ـ فُزُوزَة ـ سُرْعَة ـ رَوْجَة ـ بَادِرَة .

Excitable, *a.* سَرِيعُ ٱلْفَزَازَةِ ـ سَرِيعُ ٱلْهَيَجَانِ .

Excitant, *n.* تَحْرِيض ـ مُسَبِّبُ ٱلْحَرَكَةِ ـ تَحْرِيك .

Excitation, *n.* إِسْتِفْزَاز ـ تَحْرِيض ـ تَحْضِيض ـ ثَوْر ـ ثَوَرَان .

Excitative, *a.* } Stimulative, مُحَرِّض ـ مُحَرِّك ـ مُسْتَفِزّ ـ مُرَغِّب ـ هَامِك ـ مُهَيِّج . Occasioning,
Excitatory, } مُحْدِث ـ مُسَبِّب .

Excite, *v.t.* To urge, stimulate, أَنْهَضَ ـ حَرَّضَ ـ عَلَى ـ حَضَّضَ ـ أَحْمَى ـ عَلَى ـ حَثَّ ـ عَلَى ـ ²حَثَّ ـ أَثَارَ ـ إِسْتَفَزَّ ـ هَيَّجَ ـ أَحْدَثَ ـ سَبَّبَ ـ حَرَّكَ ـ إِلَى ـ رَوَّجَ ـ أَغْوَى ـ أَلَّبَ . To occasion, To —, as of a tumult, فَتَنَ ـ شَغَّبَ ـ أَوْقَعَ . To — one to wish for or strive after a thing, رَغَّبَ ـ فِى . To — to anger, أَهَاجَ ـ أَغْضَبَ ـ غَضَّبَهُ . To — to study, رَغَّبَ ـ فِى (or) حَثَّ ـ عَلَى ٱلدَّرْسِ . To be excited, تَهَيَّجَ ـ هَاجَ ـ ²فَارَ ـ ²ثَارَ ـ إِحْتَثَّ . They excited one another, of many, تَحَاضُّوا ـ تَحَاثُّوا . Excited with, هَائِجٌ (or) مُغْرًى بِ . He excited the surmises of the people, أَثَارَ هَوَاجِسَ ٱلنَّاسِ .

Excitement, *n.* Stimulation, إِغْرِيَة ـ حَضّ ـ حَثّ ـ ثَوْر ـ

The act of occasioning, تَسْبِيب ـ إِحْدَاث. A cause of — or stimulation, أَطْمَعَة ـ مَرَاغِب pl. مَرْغَبَة ـ سَبَبٌ لِلْحَرَكَةِ. Disturbance, صَجَاج ـ شَغْب ـ ثَوْرَة. Wait till this — is over, إِنْتَظِرْ حَتَّى تَسْكُنَ هٰذِهِ ٱلثَّوْرَةُ. In the highest state of —, فِي أَعْلَى دَرَجَةٍ مِنَ ٱلْهَيَجَانِ. The — which he caused still continues, ٱلتَّهَوُّرُ ٱلَّذِي بَعَثَهُ بَاقٍ.

Exciter, *n.* } Exciting, *a.* } *See* Excitative, *a.*

Exclaim, *v.i.* هَتَفَ ـ ضَجَّ ـ صَاتَ *aor.* يَصُوتُ ـ صَدَّ ـ تَوَجَّعَ ـ تَأَلَّمَ ـ أَلَّ; as from pain, صَرَخَ ـ وَلْوَلَ.

Exclaimer, *n.* صَارِخ ـ صَائِت ـ صَوَّات ـ صَرَّاخ.

Exclamation, *n.* نِدَاء ـ صَرْخَة ـ صُرَاخ ـ ضَجَّة. An — of pain, تَوَجُّع ـ صَجَاج ـ تَأَلُّم ـ أَلِيل ـ أَلّ; of surprise, شَهْقَة; of fear, تَهْوِيلَة ـ تَرْعِيب ـ رَعْب. An emphatical utterance, تَفْظِيع. A note of —, عَلَامَةُ ٱلتَّعَجُّبِ.

Exclamative, *a.* } Exclamatory, } صَارِخ ـ صَائِت ـ ضَاجّ.

Exclude, *v.t.* To reject, طَرَدَ ـ رَفَضَ ـ رَدَّ. To prevent one from, مَنَعَ ـ حَدَّ ـ عَن ـ عَوَّقَ ـ عَن ـ صَدَّ ـ عَن. To keep one out from, صَدَّ. To eject, أَخْرَجَ ـ نَفَا ـ مِن. To deny or refuse to one, حَرَمَ ـ أَحْرَمَ. He excluded him from the thing, denied it to him, أَحْرَمَهُ (or) حَرَمَهُ ٱلشَّيْءَ. He excluded him from the affair, أَخْرَجَهُ مِنَ ٱلْأَمْرِ. It excluded what was behind, came after, it, سَدَّ مَا وَرَاءَهُ. To be excluded, rejected, رُفِضَ ـ أُطْرِدَ. To be prevented, إِمْتَنَعَ ـ تَعَوَّقَ; to be kept out from, صُدَّ عَن; to be put out, ejected, إِنْتَفَى ـ أُخْرِجَ. *See also to* Except, *v.t.*

Excluded, *a.* Turned off, rejected, مَطْرُود ـ مَرْفُوض ـ مَرْدُود ـ مَمْنُوع ـ مَحْدُودٌ عَن ـ مُمْتَنِع ـ مُنْحَصِر ـ مُخْرَج. Prevented, مَصْدُودٌ عَن ـ مُنْتَفٍ مِن. Denied, مَحْرُوم. Shut out from, مَصْدُودٌ عَن ـ مُنْتَفٍ مِن. Cast away, abandoned, مَرْفُوض ـ رَفِيض.

Exclusion, *n.* The act of rejecting, طَرْد ـ رَفْض ـ رَدّ; of being rejected, نَفْي ـ إِطْرَاد ـ إِرْتِدَاد. The act of ejecting, إِخْرَاج; of being ejected, خُرُوج ـ إِنْتِفَاء. The act of preventing from, مَنْع ـ تَعْوِيقٌ عَن ـ صَدٌّ عَن; of being prevented, تَمَنُّع ـ إِنْحِصَار. The act of refusing anything to one, مَحْرَمَة ـ حِرْم; of being refused, تَحَرُّم ـ حِرْم. To the — of, مَا عَدَا ـ دُونَ.

Exclusive, *a.* Debarring, مَانِع ـ مُسَدِّد ـ مُعَوِّق. Consorting only with the higher classes, شَاذٌّ عَنِ ٱلصُّحْبَةِ وَٱلْمُخَالَطَةِ إِلَّا مَعَ ٱلْخَوَاصِّ. This is — of that, هٰذَا دُونَ ذٰلِكَ. An — privilege, إِمْتِيَازٌ مُنْحَصِرٌ pl. إِمْتِيَازَاتٌ مُنْحَصِرَةٌ. Their — privileges, ٱلْإِمْتِيَازَاتُ ٱلْمُنْحَصِرَةُ فِيهِمْ. *See also* Reserved, *n.*

Exclusive, *n.* *See preceding paragraph, second sentence.*

Exclusively, *ad.* Uniquely, apart, إِنْفِرَادًا وَٱنْحِصَارًا. As excepting others, دُونَ غَيْرِهِ ـ مَا عَدَا. To apply one's self — to, تَفَرَّغَ لِ ـ تَصَدَّى لِ. I addressed myself — to the affair, تَفَرَّغْتُ (or) تَصَدَّيْتُ لِلْأَمْرِ. To confine one's self — to a thing, تَخَلَّى بِ ـ تَفَرَّغَ بِ. Confine yourself — to the matter, أَخْلِ بِٱلْأَمْرِ. To act — of, تَفَوَّتَ عَلَى ـ فِي ـ فَاتَ ـ بِ. He brought the thing to pass — of him, إِفْتَاتَ عَلَيْهِ بِٱلشَّيْءِ ـ فَاتَهُ بِٱلشَّيْءِ. He followed his own opinion in the matter — of him, إِفْتَاتَ عَلَيْهِ ـ تَفَوَّتَ عَلَيْهِ فِي ٱلْأَمْرِ ـ فِي ٱلْأَمْرِ. *See also under* Exception, *n.*

Exclusiveness, *n.* As in conduct, ٱلْمُحَاشَاةُ مِنَ ٱلصُّحْبَةِ وَٱلْمُخَالَطَةِ إِلَّا مَعَ ٱلْخَوَاصِّ. *See also under* Reserve, *n.*

Excogitate, *v.t.* أَوْجَدَ ـ إِخْتَرَعَ ـ أَبْدَعَ.

Excogitation, *n.* إِيجَاد ـ إِخْتِرَاع ـ إِبْدَاع.

Excommunicable, *a.* مُسْتَحِقُّ ٱلْحِرْمَانِ ـ مُتَعَرِّضٌ لِلْحِرْمَانِ.

Excommunicate, *v.t.* To exclude, as from church communion, قَطَعَ ـ عَنْ شِرْكَةِ ٱلْكَنِيسَةِ ـ حَرَمَ. To be excommunicated, قُطِعَ عَنْ شِرْكَةِ ٱلْكَنِيسَةِ ـ حُرِمَ.

Excommunication, *n.* قَطْعٌ عَنْ شِرْكَةِ ٱلْكَنِيسَةِ ـ حِرْمَان ـ حِرْم.

Excoriate, *v.t.* To gall, جَحَشَ ـ سَلَخَ ـ سَلَقَ ـ عَقَرَ ـ سَحَجَ. To —, as with a lash, سَلَقَ ـ بِ. To be excoriated, صَرِدَ ـ إِنْسَلَقَ ـ إِنْعَقَرَ. Excoriated, مَسْحُوج ـ سَحِيج.

Excoriation, *n.* The act of, عَقْر ـ سَلْق ـ سَحْج ـ سَلْخ. A gall, سَلِيقَة ـ إِنْسِحَاج ـ مَسْحَج. The scar of an —, عُقْرَة.

Excortication, *n.* تَقْشِير ـ عَرْم ـ شَذْب ـ قَلْف.

Excrement, *n.* خَرَاء ـ خُرْء ـ دِمْن ـ بَدًا ـ بِرَاز ـ غَائِط. To void —, خَرِئَ ـ تَغَوَّطَ. To soil one's self with one's own —, تَصَوَّقَ.

Excremental, *a.* } Excrementitious, } خَرَائِيّ ـ بِرَازِيّ ـ دِمْنِيّ.

Excrescence, *n.* أُنْبُوبَة ـ فُضُولَة ـ قَمِيعَة ـ جَمًا. An — on the eyelid, a sty, قَمَع. A pimple, حَبّ pl. حُبُوب ـ بَثْر pl. بَثْرَة pl. بَثَرَات ـ بُثُور. A superfluity, زِيَادَة. A fleshy —, فُضُولَةُ ٱللَّحْمِ.

Excrescent, *a.* مُسْتَدْرَك ـ زَائِد ـ نَاتِئ.

Excrete, *v.t.* أَخْرَجَ ـ صَوَّلَ.

Excretion, *n.* رَشْح (or) خُرُوجُ ٱلْمَوَادِّ ـ تَصْوِيل.

Excretive, *a.* } Excretory, } رَشَّاح ـ مُخْرِج ـ مُصَوِّل. An excretory duct, مَجْرَى رَشَّاح.

Excruciate, *v.t.* آلَمَ ـ عَذَّبَ.

Excruciating, *a.* أَلِيم ـ مُعَذِّب.

Excruciation, *n.* إِيلام ـ تَعْذِيب.

Exculpate, *v.t.* بَيَّضَ وَجْهَهُ ـ بَرَّرَ ـ ² عَفَى عَن ـ بَرَّأَ ـ ² عَذَرَ. *See also to* Excuse, *v.t.*

Exculpation, *n.* تَبْيِيضُ ٱلْوَجْهِ ـ تَزْكِيَة ـ بَرَآءَة ـ تَبْرِئَة ـ تَبْرِير.

Exculpatory, *a.* مُبَيِّضُ ٱلْوَجْهِ ـ مُبَرِّر.

Excursion, *n.* A ramble, طِيَّة ـ مَطُور ـ سِياحَة. An — for pleasure, تَفْسِيح ـ سَيْرَة لِلتَّنَزُّهِ. A warlike —, غَزْوَة ـ غَزاة *pl.* غَزَوات ـ غارَة. A digression, إِعْتِراض ـ إِلْتِفات. To make a hostile — on, ² غارَ عَلَى. To send on a hostile —, غَزَّى ـ إِسْتَغارَ عَلَى ـ أَغارَ عَلَى.

Excursionist, *n.* A holiday maker, مُعَيِّد. *See also* Tourist, *n.*

Excursive, *a.* مُتَجَوِّل ـ جَوّال ـ إِسْتِطْرادِيّ ـ عَيّار.

Excursively, *ad.* مُعايَرَةً ـ عِيارًا ـ بِٱلْإِسْتِطْرادِ.

Excursus, *n.* A dissertation, مَقالَة ـ مُباحَثَة.

Excusable, *a.* مُعَذَّر ـ ذُو عُذْرٍ ـ مَعْذُور ـ مُعْتَذِر ـ أَهْلٌ لِلْعُذْرِ. His faults are more — than those of his brother, هُوَ مَعْذُورٌ فِي غَلَطِهِ أَكْثَرَ مِنْ أَخِيهِ. To be —, إِعْتَذَرَ ـ أَعْذَرَ.

Excusableness, *n.* تَعَذُّر.

Excusably, *ad.* عُذْرًا ـ إِعْذارًا ـ إِعْتِذارًا.

Excusatory, *a.* إِعْتِذارِيّ ـ مُعْذِر.

Excuse, *v.t.* To pardon, ² عَذَرَ ـ تَجاوَزَ عَن ـ جاوَزَ عَن ـ سامَحَ ـ أَعْذَرَ ـ عَذَرَ فِي *or* عَلَى. To disengage from an obligation, ² عَذَرَ ـ ² عَفا عَن ـ ² رَخَّصَ بِ ـ ² حَلَّ مِن ـ سامَحَ بِ. To — one's self, إِعْتَذَرَ ـ تَعَذَّرَ ـ إِعْتَلَّ. To — one's self to, إِعْتَذَرَ إِلَى *or* مِن. To remit, as of a debt, ² عَفا عَن ـ سامَحَ بِ. To ask to be excused, إِسْتَعْذَرَ. To use excuses, تَعَلَّلَ. A disposition to —, عَذِيرَة. I pray you to — me, from attendance, *etc.*, أَسْأَلُكَ أَنْ تُعْفِيَنِي.

Excuse, *n.* An apology, عُذْر *pl.* أَعْذار ـ إِعْتِذار ـ عِذْرَة *pl.* عِذَر ـ مَعْذِرَة *pl.* مَعاذِر ـ إِسْتِعْفاء. A plea, حُجَّة ـ تَعَلُّل. A legitimate —, عُذْرٌ مُعْتَبَر ـ عُذْرٌ صَحِيح. To make excuses, تَعَذَّرَ ـ تَعَلَّلَ. One who receives an —, عاذِر ـ عَذِير *pl.* عُذُر. That is only an —, هٰذا تَعَلُّلٌ فَقَط ـ هٰذِهِ حُجَّةٌ فَقَط. They are without —, هُمْ بِلا عُذْرٍ. Urging as an — that..., مُتَعَلِّلًا بِأَن. He begged me to accept his —, إِعْتَذَرَ إِلَيَّ. He urged an — for his crime, إِعْتَذَرَ مِنْ ذَنْبِهِ. Though he make many excuses I will not forgive him, لا أُسامِحُهُ وَإِنْ أَبْدَى ٱعْتِذاراتٍ كَثِيرَةً.

Exeat, *n.* بِطالَة.

Execrable, *a.* رَجِيم ـ كَرِيه ـ شَنِيع ـ لَعِين ـ مَلْعُون.

Execrably, *ad.* شَرًّا ـ كُرْهًا ـ كَراهَةً ـ شَناعَةً.

Execrate, *v.t.* إِسْتَشْنَعَ ـ ² كَرِهَ ـ ² نَفَرَ مِن ـ ² لَعَنَ ـ ² سَبَّ. *See also to* Curse, *v.t.*

Execration, *n.* بَغاضَة ـ كُرْه ـ لَعْنَة ـ لَعْن ـ سَبّ. *See also* Curse, *n.*

Execute, *v.t.* To perform, أَنْهَى ـ أَتَمَّ ـ أَمْضَى ـ أَنْفَذَ ـ أَنْجَزَ ـ أَجْرَى ـ أَنْجَزَ ـ أَكْمَلَ ـ ² فَعَلَ ـ ² عَمِلَ بِهِ. To punish capitally, ² قَتَلَ ـ أَجْرَى ٱلْمَوْتَ عَلَى. He executed his orders, إِهْتَدَى لِأَمْرِهِ. To — an order, ² قامَ بِأَمْرٍ. It was executed, ² جَرَى ٱلْعَمَلُ بِهِ. He declared that the treaty should be executed and respected, قالَ أَنَّ ٱلْمُعاهَدَةَ يَكُونُ مَعْمُولًا بِها وَمَرْعِيَّةَ ٱلْإِجْرَآءِ.

Executer, *n.* مُنَفِّذُ ٱلْأَمْرِ ـ مُجْرٍ ـ مُنْفِذ.

Execution, *n.* Performance, عَمَل ـ إِنْهاء ـ إِتْمام ـ قَضاء. The act of carrying out, إِجْرآء ـ ٱلْإِجْرآءُ فِعْلًا. Capital punishment, قَتْل. Slaughter, إِعْدام ـ قَتْلٌ وَذَبْح. A writ of —, حُكْمٌ إِعْلامِيّ. A warrant of —, حُكْمٌ بِٱلْقَتْلِ. To put or carry into —, أَمْضَى ـ أَجْرَى. To do —, to kill, ² قَتَلَ. To order a person for —, ² أَمَرَ بِقَتْلِهِ. The — of the order depends upon that, إِجْرآءُ ٱلْحُكْمِ مُتَوَقِّفٌ عَلَى ذٰلِكَ. It must be put into — at once, يَنْبَغِي وَضْعُهُ فِي مَوْقِعِ ٱلْإِجْرآءِ حالًا.

Executioner, *n.* جَلّاد ـ سَيّاف ـ مَشاعِلِيّ.

Executive, *a.* مُنْهِي ٱلْأَوامِرِ ـ مُنَفِّذُ ٱلْأَحْكامِ ـ إِجْرائِيّ. Executive power, حُكُومَةٌ إِجْرائِيَّة. Executive authority, السُّلْطَةُ ٱلْإِجْرائِيَّة.

Executive, *n.* المَأْمُورِيَّة ـ المَأْمُورُونَ بِإِجْرآءِ ٱلْأَحْكامِ.

Executor, *n.* وَصِيّ *pl.* أَوْصِياء ـ وَكِيلٌ عَلَى ٱلْوَصِيَّةِ *pl.* وُكَلاء.

Executorial, *a.* مُتَعَلِّقٌ بِٱلْوَصِيّ.

Executorship, *n.* وَكالَةٌ عَلَى وَصِيَّةٍ ـ وِصايَة.

Executrix, *n.* وَكِيلَةٌ عَلَى وَصِيَّةٍ ـ إِمْرَأَةٌ مُوَصِّيَة.

Exegesis, *n.* تَعْبِير ـ إِيضاح ـ شَرْح ـ تَفْسِير.

Exegetical, *a.* تَعْبِيرِيّ ـ إِيضاحِيّ ـ شَرْحِيّ.

Exegetically, *ad.* تَفْسِيرًا ـ بِٱلتَّعْبِيرِ ـ إِيضاحًا.

Exemplar, *n.* A pattern, أُنْمُوذَج ـ قُدْوَة ـ مِثال. A model for imitation, إِسْوَة *pl.* أُسًى ـ أُدْمَة ـ إِمام ـ أُنْمُوذَج. A copy, نُسْخَة *pl.* نُسَخ ـ نَقْل. An — for writing by, قاعِدَةُ خَطٍّ. To follow as an —, إِمْتَثَلَ بِ ـ إِقْتَضَى بِ.

Exemplarily, *ad.* حَسَنًا ـ عِبْرَةً ـ بِوَجْهٍ مُعْتَبَرٍ ـ إِسْتِجابًا ـ حَمْدًا.

Exemplariness, *n.* صَلَاح ـ فَضِيلَة ـ حُسْن .

Exemplary, *a.* أَحْسَنُ ـ جَمِيل ـ أَمْثَلُ ـ مُسْتَحِقّ ٱلِٱقْتِفَاء ـ أَفْضَل ـ حَمِيد .

Exemplification, *n.* The act of, إِيضَاح ـ تَشْرِيح ـ تَمْثِيل . A copy, مَثَل ـ صُورَة ـ نُسْخَة . An instance, مِثَال *pl.* أَمْثِلَة ـ قَبِيل .

Exemplify, *v.t.* تَمَثَّلَ بِ ـ بِأَمْثَالٍ (or شَرَحَ ـ or أَوْضَحَ ـ or فَسَّرَ) .

E.g. *Exempli gratiâ, ad.* مَثَلًا .

Exempt, *a.* سَالِمٌ مِن ـ مُسْتَثْنَى ـ مُنَزَّهٌ عَن ـ مُعَاف ـ مُبَرَّأٌ عَن ـ مُنْفَصِل مِن . He is — from blame, هُوَ خَالٍ مِنَ ٱلْمَلَام . He is — from the crime, هُوَ بَرِيءٌ مِنَ ـ مَا عَلَيْهِ لَوْمٌ ٱلذَّنْب . He is — from the work, هُوَ مُعَافٌ مِنَ ٱلشُّغْلِ .

Exempt, *v.t.* To excuse from, عَفَا ـ عَن ـ أَعْفَى ـ مِن *aor.* يَعْفُو . To make an exception of, إِسْتَثْنَى عَلَى . To free, as from blame, بَرَّأَ ـ مِن . To secure one against, سَلَّمَ ـ مِن ـ أَمَّنَ ـ مِن . To be exempted, excused, عُفِيَ عَن ; to be excepted, أُسْتُثْنِيَ . To ask to be —, excused, إِسْتَعْفَى . Exempt thou me from this, أَعْفِنِي مِنْ هٰذَا .

Exemption, *n.* The act of excepting, إِسْتِثْنَاء ; of excusing, إِعْفَاء . The being exempted, excused, مُعَافَاة ـ عَفَاء ; the being justified, بَرَاءَة . Scope for action, فُسْحَة . Asking for —, to be excused, إِسْتِعْفَاء .

Exequatur, *n.* تَقَارِيرُ قُنْصُلٍ ـ بَرَاءَةُ قُنْصُل .

Exequies, *n.* جِنَازَة .

Exercisable, *a.* That may be used, يُعْمَلُ ـ مِمَّا يُسْتَعْمَلُ ; that may be carried out, مِمَّا يُجْرَى .

Exercise, *n.* Use, تَصَرُّف ـ فِعْلٌ بِ ـ إِسْتِعْمَال . Practice, إِدْمَان ـ مُمَارَسَة ـ مُمَارَرَة . Execution, إِجْرَاء ـ إِيفَاء ـ قَضَاء ـ إِتْمَام . A task, شُغْل ـ فَرِيضَة *pl.* فَرَائِض . The exercising of soldiers, تَمْرِينٌ عَلَى ٱلْأُصُولِ ٱلْعَسْكَرِيَّةِ ـ تَعْلِيمُ (or تَدْرِيبُ) ٱلْعَسَاكِرِ . A lesson, دَرْس *pl.* دُرُوس . Bodily —, رِيَاضَة ـ رِيَاضَةٌ جَسَدِيَّة . Pious exercises, مُرَاقَبَةُ ٱلْعِبَادَةِ ـ إِجْرَاءُ ٱلْعِبَادَةِ ـ دُعَاء ـ ٱلرِّيَاضَة . Foot —, سَيْر ـ تَمَشٍّ ـ تِمْشَاء ـ مَشْي ; horse —, فَرَاسَة ـ فُرُوسِيَّة . To take —, رَوَّضَ نَفْسَهُ ; of a walk, تَمَشَّى . In the — of his functions, فِي إِجْرَاءِ وَظِيفَةِ مَأْمُورِيَّتِهِ .

Exercise, *v.t.* To use, تَصَرَّفَ فِي ـ إِسْتَعْمَلَ ـ أَعْمَلَ . To manifest, أَظْهَرَ ـ أَبْدَى . To employ, أَشْغَلَ . To train, رَاضَ *aor.* يَرُوضُ ـ رَوَّضَ ـ دَرَّبَ ; of soldiers, دَرَّبَ ـ رَوَّضَ ـ عَلَّمَ . To drill, مَرَّنَ ـ عَلَى ٱلْأُصُولِ ٱلْعَسْكَرِيَّةِ . I — myself, أَنَا أُدَرِّبُ نَفْسِي . To —, as of a trade or profession, عَمِلَ ـ تَعَاطَى . To — authority over, تَسَلَّطَ عَلَى . To — one's right, تَصَرَّفَ فِي حَقِّهِ ; one's judgment, رَاوَدَ رَأْيَهُ ـ أَدْرَكَ ذِهْنَهُ . To — patience towards, طَوَّلَ بَال ـ عَلَى ـ صَبَرَ عَلَى . To — or train one's self, دَرَّبَ نَفْسَهُ . Through exercising himself he became trained to distinguish between good and evil, بِسَبَبِ ٱلتَّمَرُّنِ صَارَ مُدَرَّبًا عَلَى ٱلتَّمْيِيزِ بَيْنَ ٱلْخَيْرِ وَٱلشَّرِّ . To — one's self in, to apply one's self to, تَصَرَّفَ فِي ـ تَمَرَّنَ عَلَى ـ وَاظَبَ عَلَى ـ أَدْمَنَ عَلَى . Exercised, trained, مُدَرَّب ـ مُعَوَّد ـ مُمَرَّن .

Exercitation, *n.* *See* Exercise, *n.*

Exergue, *n.* مَحَلُّ ٱلْكِتَابَةِ فِي ٱلسِّكَّةِ .

Exert, *v.t.* To use, to employ, صَرَفَ ـ بَذَلَ ـ أَظْهَرَ . To carry out, أَوْفَى ـ أَمْضَى ـ أَجْرَى ـ إِسْتَعْمَلَ ـ أَبْدَى ـ أَرَى . To — one's self, كَدَّ ـ جَدَّ فِي ـ إِجْتَهَدَ ـ أَجْهَدَ ـ سَعَى *aor.* يَسْعَى ـ تَأَرَّبَ بِ ـ بَذَلَ ٱلْجَهْدَ . To — one's self to the uttermost in, بَذَلَ كُلَّ جُهْدِهِ فِي .

Exertion, *n.* Use, صَرْف ـ بَذْل . Effort, هِمَّة ـ جِدّ ـ سَعْي ـ إِجْتِهَاد . Exercise, execution, إِيفَاء ـ إِجْرَاء .

Exfoliate, *v.i.* إِنْقَشَرَ ـ تَقَشَّرَ ـ إِنْحَسَرَ .

Exfoliation, *n.* إِنْقِشَار ـ تَقَشُّر ـ إِنْحِسَار .

Exhalable, *a.* مِمَّا يُصَعَّدُ ـ فَائِح ـ مِمَّا يَفُوحُ :

Exhalation, *n.* The act of, تَصْعِيد ـ تَصْوِيل . A vapour, بُخَار ـ آلّ ـ فَيْح ـ فَوْح ـ تَنَسُّم . A sweet —, فَوْحَة ـ تَرَوُّح ـ فَوَحَان .

Exhale, *v.t.* To draw out, to extract, أَخْرَجَ مِن ـ صَوَّلَ ـ صَعَّدَ . To — sweet odours, فَاحَ *aor.* يَفُوحُ ـ تَرَوَّحَ ـ فَاحَ ـ تَفَوَّحَ . It exhaled the fragrance, تَرَوَّحَتِ ٱلرَّائِحَةُ .

Exhaust, *v.t.* To end, come to the end of, أَنْفَدَ ـ أَسْرَفَ ـ أَذْهَبَ ; as of strength, أَفْرَغَ . To lose, أَتْلَفَ . To —, as a well, نَشَفَ ـ نَكَزَ ـ نَزَفَ ـ نَزَحَ ـ نَفِدَ . To empty, فَرَّغَ ـ قَعَّفَ . To drink all, إِقْتَمَعَ ـ قَمَعَ . To — the soil, أَنْفَدَ طِيبَةَ ٱلْأَرْضِ ـ جَعَلَ ٱلْأَرْضَ عَاقِرَةً . To — the patience of, أَزَالَ مِنَ ـ ٱلصَّبْرَ . To — one's wealth, أَفْنَى (or أَنْفَدَ) مَالَهُ . To — a subject, إِسْتَقْصَى فِي مَادَّةٍ ـ إِسْتَوْعَبَ ٱلْمَادَّةَ . To be exhausted, dried up, نُزِفَ ـ نُزِحَ . To be exhausted from want of blood, نُزِفَ دَمُهُ . To be exhausted, consumed, ذَهَبَ ـ نَفِدَ . To be exhausted, worn out, as by fatigue, أَعْيَى ـ أَفْنَجَ ـ تَعَيَّى .

Exhausted, *a.* As of a well, مَنْزُوف ـ نَاكِز ـ نَكُوز ; from loss of blood, مَنْزُوف ـ نَزِيف ـ نَزِف ; of strength, مُعْيٍ *fem.* مُعْيِيَة ـ كَلِيل ـ مُتْعَب ـ مُتَلَاشٍ .

Exhaustion, *n.* The act of ending, إنْفاد ; of spending, إسْراف – إذْهاب ; as of a well, نَزْف – نَزْح – نَكْز – تَنْشِيف ; of strength, تَضْعِيف . The act of emptying, تَفْرِيغ ; of a subject, إسْتِيعاب – إسْتِقْصآء . The state of being ended, إنْقِضآء – نَفَد – خُلُوص ; of being dried up, نَزْح – تَنَزُّف ; of weakness from loss of blood, تَنَزُّفُ ٱلدَّمِ . Weakness, وَهْن – ضَعْف – عِيّ – كَلال – كَلالَة . Emptiness, فَراغ – خَوًى .

Exhaustive, *a.* مُسْتَقْصٍ – حالٌ وَمُوضِحٌ .

Exhaustless, *a.* دائم – لا يُفْرَغُ – لا يَنْفَدُ – لا يُفْنَى .

Exhereditate, *v.t.* *See to* Disinherit, *v.t.*

Exhibit, *v.t.* To show, أَرَى (*vulg.* وَرَّى) – عَرَضَ-عَلَى – فَرَّجَ – قَدَّمَ . To demonstrate, أَشْرَحَ – بَيَّنَ . To display, as of courage, *etc.*, أَظْهَرَ – إمْتَثَلَ – أَبْدَى . To administer, as of medicine, أَعْطَى – سَقَى .

Exhibit, *n.* حُجَّة – سَنَد .

Exhibition, *n.* The act of showing, عَرْض – تَوْرِيَة – تَفْرِيج – تَقْدِيم . A show, or a place of —, display, مَعْرِض – فُرْجَة . A pageant, مَوْكِب . An exposition, شَرْح – إيضاح . An international —, مَعْرِضٌ عامٌّ . Administration, as of medicines, سَقْي – إسْقآء . An allowance from a college, راتِبٌ مِنْ مَدْرَسَة .

Exhibitioner, *n.* An — at a college, صاحِبُ راتِبٍ مِنْ مَدْرَسَة .

Exhibitive, *a.* مُشْرِح – مُفَرِّج – مُبَيِّن – مُرٍ .

Exhilarant, *a.* *See* Exhilarating, *a.*

Exhilarant, *n.* مُفَرِّح – مَسَرَّة *pl.* مَسارٌّ .

Exhilarate, *v.t.* أَبْسَطَ – سَرَّ – أَبْهَجَ – أَفْرَحَ – فَرَّحَ . To be exhilarated, سُرَّ – تَبَجْبَجَ – إبْتَهَجَ – إسْتَبْشَرَ – فَرِحَ – تَغَبَّطَ .

Exhilarating, *a.* مُشْرِحُ ٱلخاطِرِ – سارٌّ – مُفَرِّح – مُفْرِح . An — medicine, سُلْوان – دَوآءٌ مُفَرِّحٌ .

Exhilaration, *n.* The act of, إبْهاج – شَرْحُ ٱلخاطِرِ – تَفْرِيح . Joy, merriment, فَرَح – سُرُور – إبْتِهاج – غِبْطَة .

Exhort, *v.t.* To advise, persuade, وَعَظَ-عَلَى – نَصَحَ – أَنْذَرَ *aor.* يَعِظُ – نَبَّهَ – أَشارَ-عَلَى-بِ . To urge, حَرَّضَ – رَغَّبَ .

Exhortation, *n.* The act of persuading, نُصْح – نَذِير – إنْذار – تَنْبِيه . Advice, counsel, مَوْعِظَة – نَصِيحَة . A discourse, sermon, وَعْظ – مَوْعِظَة – خُطْبَة . To deliver an —, خَطَبَ – وَعَظَ مَوْعِظَة .

Exhortatory, *a.*
Exhorter, *n.* } مُرَغِّب – مُحَضِّض – ناصِح – واعِظ .

Exhumation, *n.* تَنْبِيش – نَبْش .

Exhume, *v.t.* نَبَّشَ – نَبَشَ .

Exigence, *n.*
Exigency, } Want, need, ضَرُورَة – إحْتِياج – حاجَة – لُزُوم . A pressing necessity, مُقْتَضِيَة – لُزُوم – إقْتِضآء . A difficulty, صُعُوبَة . A condition, حال – أَحْوال . The — of the case, مُقْتَضَى ٱلحالِ – ضَرُورِيَّةُ ٱلمَوْقِعِ . The exigencies of politics often lead to the abolition of treaties, إنَّ مُقْتَضِياتِ ٱلسِّياسَةِ تُبْطِلُ ٱلمُعاهَداتِ مِرارًا . Political exigencies, ٱلأَحاجِي ٱلسِّياسِيَّة . According to the exigencies of the case, عَلَى مُقْتَضَى ظُرُوفِ ٱلحالِ .

Exigible, *a.* مِمَّا يُطالَبُ بِهِ – مِمَّا يَقْتَضِي .

Exile, *n.* The act of, نَفْي – طَرْد ; one banished, نَفِيّ – طَرِيد – مَطْرُود . A place of —, مَحَلُّ ٱلنَّفْيِ مَنْفًى . He fled from his place of —, فَرَّ مِنْ مَنْفاهُ .

Exile, *v.t.* طَرَدَ – نَفَى – نَفا .

Exinanition, *n.* *See* Inanition, *n.*

Exist, *v.t.* To be, وُجِدَ – كانَ . To continue to be, ظَلَّ – ثَبَتَ – إسْتَمَرَّ . To cause to —, أَوْجَدَ – كَوَّنَ . To — or feed on, عاشَ مِن – إقْتاتَ بِ – تَقَوَّتَ بِ .

Existence, *n.* Being, وُجُود – كَوْن . Life, عُمْر – حَياة . Continuance, بَقآء – دَوام – إسْتِمْرار . A being, كائن *pl.* كائنات – قائم – مَوْجُود . To bring into —, إخْتَرَعَ – أَحْدَثَ – أَوْجَدَ . Eternal —, خُلُود – خُلْد . A comfortable —, تُرْفَة – نِعْمَة – سَعَةُ ٱلعَيْشِ .

Existent, *a.*
Existing, } Being, مَوْجُود – كائن . Having life, حَيّ . Under — circumstances, نَظَرًا لِلأَحْوالِ ٱلحاضِرَة وَٱلحالَة هٰذِهِ . The — agreements, ٱلشُّرُوطُ ٱلحالِيَّة .

Exit, *n.* Departure, إنْطِلاق – ذَهاب – رَحْل – خُرُوج . A passage, باب – مَخْرَج – مَعْبَر . Death, مَوْت – مَمات . Places of —, مَفارِجُ .

Ex-minister, *n.* وَزِيرٌ سابِقًا .

Exodus, *n.* The — of the Israelites, خُرُوجُ بَنِي إسْرائيلَ مِنْ مِصْرَ . The book of —, سِفْرُ ٱلخُرُوجِ .

Ex-official, *a.* رَسْمِيّ .

Ex-officio, *ad.* بِصِفَةٍ رَسْمِيَّةٍ – بِوَجْهِ ٱلمَأْمُورِيَّةِ .

Exonerate, *v.t.* To — from blame, بَرَّأَ . *See to* Exculpate, *v.t.*

Exoneration, *n.* The act of, تَبْرِئَة ; the being exonerated, بَرآءَة . *See also* Exculpation, *n.*

Exonerative, *a.* مُبَرِّئ .

Exorbitance, *n.*
Exorbitancy, } Excessiveness, زِيادَة – إفْراط – فَرْط – سَرَف ; of price, غَلآء . An enormity, كَبِيرَة – فَظاعَة – عُتِيّ – عُتُوّ .

Exorbitant, *a.* Excessive, مُفْرِط ـ مُتَجاوِز ـ فَوْقَ ٱلْحَدِّ. The demand is —, الطَّلَبُ مُتَجاوِزٌ. To be — in, أَفْرَطَ فِي; of a price, غَالَى فِي. To buy at an — price, غَالَى بِهِ. I sold it at an — price, بِعْتُهُ بِٱلْغَالِي.

Exorcise, *v.t.* عَزَمَ عَلَى ـ اِسْتَقْسَمَ.

Exorcism, *n.* تَعْزِيم ـ اِسْتِقْسام.

Exorcist, *n.* مُعَزِّم ـ مُسْتَقْسِم.

Exordial, *a.* اِفْتِتاحِيٌّ ـ مُسْتَفْتِح.

Exordium, *n.* فاتِحَة ـ دِيباجَة ـ مُقَدِّمَة ـ أَنْسام *pl.* نَسَم. To begin any speech, *etc.*, with an —, اِفْتَتَحَ بِ.

Exornation, *n.* تَزْيِين. *See* Embellishment, *n.*

Exoteric, *a.* خارِجِيٌّ ـ ظاهِرِيٌّ. An — signification, ظَهْر.

Exotic, *a.* أَجْنَبِيٌّ ـ مَجْلُوب ـ غَرِيب.

Exotic, *n.* An — plant, نَبْتٌ مَجْلُوبٌ ـ نَباتٌ غَرِيبٌ.

Exoticism, *n.* أَجْنَبِيَّة ـ اِنْجِلاب ـ غَرابَة.

Expand, *v.t.* To spread out, بَسَطَ ـ نَشَرَ ـ بَطَحَ. To stretch, وَسَّعَ ـ مَطَّ ـ مَدَّ ـ مَدَّدَ ـ مادَدَ ـ سَطَحَ. To level, سَطَحَ. To spread, as of the wings, نَاعَ ـ بَسَطَ ـ نَهَضَ. To enlarge, كَبَّرَ. To be expanded, spread out, اِنْبَسَطَ ـ اِنْتَشَرَ ـ تَبَطَّحَ. To be —, stretched, اِمْتَطَّ ـ اِتَّسَعَ ـ اِمْتَدَّ ـ تَمَدَّدَ.

Expand, *v.i.* To open out, as a flower, اِنْفَغَرَ ـ فَغَمَ ـ تَفَغَّمَ ـ تَفَتَّحَ.

Expanse, *n.* A wide extent of level space, اِتِّساع ـ كَثِيف ـ صَفِيحَة ـ بَسِيط ـ بَطْح ـ سَطِيح; of water, بَلالِيق *pl.* بُلْقُوق; of the sea or the night, دَجْداج ـ الرَّقِيع ـ أَدِيمُ ٱلسَّماءِ; of the sky, الصَّنِيع.

Expansibility, *n.* } Expansibleness, } قابِلِيَّة ـ قابِلِيَّةُ ٱلِاتِّساعِ ـ إِمْكانُ ٱلِانْبِساطِ ـ ٱلِامْتِدادِ.

Expansible, *a.* } Expansile, } قابِلُ ٱلِاتِّساعِ ـ يَمْتَدُّ.

Expansion, *n.* The act of spreading out, بَطْح ـ نَشْر ـ بَسْط; of stretching, تَوْسِيع ـ تَمْطِيط ـ تَمْدِيد; of levelling, سَطْح; of enlarging, تَكْبِير; as of the wings, بَسْطُ (or نَهْضُ) ٱلْأَجْناحِ. The state of being spread out, تَبَطُّح ـ اِنْتِشار ـ اِنْبِساط; of being stretched, اِتِّساع ـ اِمْتِطاط ـ اِمْتِداد. Width, عَرْض ـ سَعَة. Size, حَجْم ـ جِرْم. *See also* Expanse, *n.*

Expansive, *a.* Having power to expand, لَهُ قُوَّةٌ ـ ذُو قُوَّةِ ٱلِامْتِدادِ ـ ٱلِامْتِدادُ. Wide, واسِع ـ وَسِيع ـ رَغِيب ـ مُتَّسِع.

Expansiveness, *n.* تَمَدُّد ـ اِمْتِداد. *See also* Expansibility, *n.*

Ex parte, *a.* غَرَضِيٌّ ـ مِنْ أَحَدِ ٱلطَّرَفانِ فَقَط.

Expatiate, *v.i.* To dilate upon, اِنْدَفَعَ فِي ـ أَفاضَ فِي ـ وَسَّعَ فِي ـ اِفْتَنَّ فِي ـ فَصَّلَ ـ أَطالَ ٱلْكَلامَ فِي.

Expatiation, *n.* إِفاضَةُ كَلامٍ فِي ـ إِطالَةُ كَلامٍ ـ تَفْصِيل ـ تَوْسِيع ـ تَفَنُّن ـ اِمْتِداد ـ تَفْسِيح.

Expatriate, *v.t.* أَجْلَى ـ غَرَّبَ. To — one's self, or to be expatriated, جَلا ـ أَجْلَى ـ تَغَرَّبَ ـ تَطَفَّشَ. (The last word applies to secret expatriation of one's self.)

Expatriation, *n.* The act of, إِجْلاءٌ ـ جَلاءٌ ـ تَغْرِيب; the being away from one's country, إِجْلاءٌ ـ تَغَرُّب.

Expect, *v.t.* To wait for, anticipate, رَقَبَ ـ راقَبَ ـ اِرْتَقَبَ ـ لَوَى عَلَى ـ تَرَبَّصَ ـ تَوَقَّفَ ـ تَرَقَّبَ ـ اِنْتَظَرَ ـ اِنْتَظَرَل ـ اِسْتَنْظَرَ. To hope, أَمَلَ ـ تَمَنَّى. You are come sooner than you were expected, قَدِمْتَ قَبْلَ ٱلْوَقْتِ ٱلْمُنْتَظِرِ. He expected to receive something from him, اِنْتَظَرَ أَنْ يَأْخُذَ شَيْئًا مِنْهُ. He acted his part better than was expected, عَمِلَ ما عَلَيْهِ أَفْضَلَ مِمّا كانَ يُنْتَظَرُ مِنْهُ. Are you not expecting him? أَما أَنْتَ بِمُنْتَظِرٍ لَهُ.

Expectance, } Expectancy, *n.* } Expectation, } The act of expecting, اِنْتِظار ـ رُقُوب ـ تَرَقُّب ـ تَوَقُّف ـ اِسْتِنْظار ـ تَرَصُّد. The thing expected, مَأْمُول ـ مُنْيَة ـ اِنْتِظار. Hope, أَمَل ـ رَجاءٌ.

Expectant, *a.* } Expectant, *n.* } Expecter, *n.* } مُنْتَظِر ـ مُسْتَنْظِر ـ مُتَرَقِّب.

Expectorant, *a.* قاطِعُ (or دافِعُ) ٱلْبَلْغَمِ.

Expectorant, *n.* دَواءٌ يَقْطَعُ ٱلْبَلْغَمَ.

Expectorate, *v.t.* نَخَمَ ـ تَنَخَّمَ ـ تَنَخَّعَ.

Expectoration, *n.* The act of, نَخْم ـ تَنَخُّم ـ تَنَخُّع; the matter discharged, نُخاعَة ـ نُخامَة ـ بُصاق ـ تُفال ـ بَلْغَم.

Expectorative, *a.* *See* Expectorant, *a.*

Expedience, *n.* } Expediency, } مُناسِب ـ اِقْتِضاءٌ ـ إِيجاب ـ مُوافَقَة ـ لِياقَة ـ حالَةُ ٱلْإِيجابِ.

Expedient, *a.* مُناسِب ـ لازِم ـ مُقْتَضٍ ـ ضَرُورِيٌّ. It is not —, suitable, for me, لا يُوافِقُنِي. This will be more —, useful, for you, هٰذا يَنْفَعُكُمْ. It is more —, better, for us, إِنَّهُ خَيْرٌ لَنا. All things are lawful to me, but all things are not —, كُلُّ ٱلْأَشْياءِ تَحِلُّ لِي لٰكِنْ لَيْسَ كُلُّ ٱلْأَشْياءِ تُوافِقُ.

Expedient, *n.* Means, تَدْبِير ـ طَرِيق ـ وَسِيلَة ـ واسِطَة ـ باب ـ مَخْلَص ـ سَبِيل. A stratagem, حِيلَة *pl.* حِيَل. The expedients of war, أَبْوابُ ٱلْحَرْبِ.

Expediently, *ad.* مُوافَقَةً ـ فِي مَحَلِّهِ ـ بِمُناسَبَةٍ.

Expedite, *v.t.* To facilitate, يَسَّرَ ـ هَوَّنَ ـ سَهَّلَ. To hasten, عَجَّلَ ـ أَسْرَعَ. To send, ـ بَعَثَ ـ سَيَّرَ ـ أَسارَ ـ سَرَّحَ ـ سَرَحَ ـ أَرْسَلَ.

Expeditely, *ad.* *See* Expeditiously, *ad.*

Expedition, *n.* Haste, عَجَلَة ـ رَوْجَة ـ سُرْعَة ـ سَراح. An enterprise, عَزِيمَة ـ رَحِيل. The act of sending, ـ تَسْيِير ـ تَبْلِيغ ـ إِرْسال. Any detachment sent out for a specific purpose, ـ جَرِيدَة ـ تَجْرِيدَة. A warlike —, مَغْزاة ـ غَزَوات *pl.* غَزاة ـ غَزْوَة ـ سِيرَة. An — of discovery, نَفِيضَة. To dispatch a warlike —, ـ أَغْزَى ـ غَزَى. The great military expeditions, (a book so called,) كِتاب اَلسِّيَرِ اَلْكَبِير. The story or memorable deeds of a warlike —, المَغازِي.

Expeditionary, *a.* Dispatched, مُرْسُول ـ سَيّار; of war, ـ غازٍ ـ غَزَوِيّ ـ غَزِيّ ـ غُزاة *pl.* غازٍ An — force, غَزَوِيّ.

Expeditious, *a.* Quick, وَحِيز ـ وَجْز ـ سَرِيع *pl.* سُرْعان. Nimble, ـ رَشِيق ـ نَشِط ـ شَمِير. To be —, quick, وَجَزَ *aor.* يَجِزُ ـ أَفاجَ ـ أَسْرَعَ ـ اِسْتَعْجَلَ. To be nimble, شَمْلَلَ ـ تَشَمَّرَ.

Expeditiously, *ad.* ـ بِخِفَّةٍ ـ بِٱلْعَجَلِ ـ عَلَى عَجَلَةٍ ـ بِسُرْعَةٍ ـ بِشَمْلَلَةٍ.

Expel, *v.t.* To drive out, ـ دَفَعَ ـ أَخْرَجَ ـ سَيَّرَ ـ طَرَدَ. To be expelled, اِنْدَفَعَ ـ أُخْرِجَ ـ اِطَّرَدَ ـ اِنْطَرَدَ. To order to be expelled, أَطْرَدَ.

Expellable, *a.* يُدْفَعُ ـ يُخْرَجُ ـ يُطْرَدُ.

Expelled, *a.* مَخْرُوج ـ مَطْرُود.

Expend, *v.t.* ـ بَذَلَ ـ أَنْفَقَ ـ تَكَلَّفَ ـ صَرَّفَ ـ صَرَفَ. To be expended, lost, consumed, تَصَرَّفَ ـ ذَهَبَ. *See also to* Spend, *v.t.*

Expenditure, *n.* Waste, ـ سَرَف ـ إِتْلاف ـ تَلَف ـ خَرْج ـ إِسْراف. These matters lead to —, هٰذِهِ ٱلْأُمُورُ مُوجِبَةٌ لِإِسْرافٍ. *See also next article.*

Expense, *n.* Expenditure, cost, مَصْرَف ـ خَرْج ـ صَرْف *pl.* مَصارِف ـ نَفَقَة ـ مَصْرُوف. Expenditure, wear, tear, ـ سَرَف ـ جَيْب ـ كِيس ـ خَرْج ـ إِتْلاف ـ تَلَف ـ إِسْراف. Cost, purse, كِيس ـ جَيْب. Damage, مَضَرَّة ـ ضَرَر. Cost, value, قِيمَة. At a great — of time and money, مَعَ بَذْلِ ٱلتَّعَبِ ٱلْبَلِيغِ وَٱلْمَصْرُوفِ ٱلْوافِرِ. They promised to provide the expenses, تَعَهَّدُوا بِإِعْطاءِ ٱلْمَصارِيفِ. After he had paid their expenses, بَعْدَ أَنِ ٱسْتَوْفَى مَصارِيفَهُمْ. The expenses are greater than the revenue, المَصارِيفُ تَزِيدُ عَلَى ٱلْإِيرادِ. At the —, cost, of, عَلَى كِيسِ; at his —, عَلَى كِيسِهِ. At the —, to the hurt of, one, لِضَرَرِهِ. Free of —, gratuitously, مَجّانًا ـ عَفْوًا.

Current expenses, مَصارِفُ عادِيَّةٌ ـ مَصارِفُ جارِيَةٌ.

Daily expenses, مَصارِفُ يَوْمِيَّةٌ.

Estimated expenses, مَصارِفُ مُخَمَّنَةٌ.

Necessary expenses, مَصارِفُ مُقْتَضِيَةٌ.

Petty expenses, نَفَقاتٌ مُتَفَرِّقَةٌ.

Share of expenses, تَبْدِيد.

Unlooked for expenses, مَصارِفُ غَيْرُ مَأْمُولَةٍ.

Unnecessary expenses, مَصارِفُ غَيْرُ لازِمَةٍ ـ مَصارِفُ زائِدَةٌ.

To curtail expenses, قَلَّلَ (or خَفَّفَ) ٱلْمَصارِيفَ.

To defray the expense of, تَكَلَّفَ بِٱلْمَصْرُوفِ ـ صَرَفَ عَلَى.

To meet or defray an expense, ـ دَفَعَ ٱلْمَصْرُوفَ ـ سَدَّ مَصارِيفَ.

To pay each a share of expenses, بَدَّدَ. The company contributed something each to the expenses, بادَّ ٱلْقَوْمُ.

To put a person to expense, كَلَّفَ بِمَصْرُوفٍ.

Expenseless, *a.* مِنْ غَيْرِ ـ مِنْ غَيْرِ مَصْرُوفٍ ـ بِدُونِ كُلْفَةٍ ـ نَفَقَةٍ.

Expensive, *a.* Requiring much expense, ـ ذُو كُلْفَةٍ ـ مِنْفاق ـ مُكَلِّف. Costly, ـ نَفائِس *pl.* نَفِيس ـ مُنْفِس ـ ذُو قِيمَةٍ ـ غالٍ ـ ثَمِين. An — journey, سَفْرَةٌ ذاتُ كُلْفَةٍ. An — dress, لِبْسٌ ثَمِينٌ.

Expensively, *ad.* بِكُلْفَةٍ عَظِيمَةٍ ـ بِمَصْرُوفٍ وافِرٍ.

Expensiveness, *n.* *See* Expense, *n.*

Experience, *n.* Trial, إِمْتِحان ـ تَجْرِبَة. Knowledge gained by —, مَعْلُومات ـ وُقُوف ـ خِبْرَة ـ إِخْتِبار ـ إِلْمام ـ إِدْراك. A man of —, مُجَرِّبُ ٱلْأُمُورِ ـ مُدَرَّب; a man without —, ـ مُجَدِّد ـ غَشِيم. To have —, knowledge, of, تَكَرَّرَ فِي ـ تَدَرَّبَ بِ. He has — in the English and Arabic languages, لَهُ إِلْمامٌ بِٱلْإِنْكِلِيزِيَّةِ وَٱلْعَرَبِيَّةِ. Long — improves the understanding, طُولُ ٱلتَّجارِبِ زِيادَةٌ فِي ٱلْعَقْلِ.

Experience, *v.t.* To try, إِمْتَحَنَ ـ جَرَّبَ. To undergo, ـ أَدْرَكَ ـ أَصابَ. To make another to —, أَذاقَ. I came to — difficulty, أَدْرَكْتُ ٱلْجَهْدَ. He experienced such a thing from him, رَأَى مِنْهُ كَذا. He has experienced adversity, ذاقَ ٱلْبَأْسَ. We experienced a storm, أَصابَنا نَوْءٌ. He experienced joy, حَصَلَ عِنْدَهُ اِسْتِبْشار ـ سُرُور. To —, to meet with, لاقَى ـ أَدْرَكَ. To —, as a consequence, اِسْتَعْقَبَ ـ إِعْتَقَبَ.

Experienced, *a.* Versed, ـ خَبِيرٌ بِ ـ مُدَرَّب ـ لَبِيقٌ بِ ـ مُدَرِّس ـ مُنَجِّد ـ مُوَقَّف ـ أَرِيبٌ بِ ـ مُجَرَّب ـ مُلَقَّح

ماهِر. Experienced persons, أَهْلُ ٱلْخِبْرَةِ. Experienced in ..., مُتَبَحِّرٌ فِي.

Experiment, *n.* إِمْتِحَان ـ تَجْرِبَة ـ خِبْرَة. By way of —, tentatively, بَيْنَ مَحْظُورٍ وَمَحْذُورٍ. To test by —, إِخْتَبَرَ.

Experiment, *v.t.* إِمْتَحَنَ ـ جَرَّبَ.

Experiment, *v.i.* To know by trial, تَخَبَّرَ ـ إِخْتَبَرَ.

Experimental, *a.* By way of testing, تَجْرِبِيٌّ. Derived from experience, مُجَرَّب ـ مُمْتَحَن. مُحَقَّقٌ بِٱلتَّجْرِبَةِ.

Experimentalist, *n.* / Experimenter, *n.* مُمْتَحِن ـ مُجَرِّب ـ مِنْ أَهْلِ ٱلتَّجْرِبَةِ ـ كَشَّاف.

Experimentally, *ad.* بِوَجْهِ ـ بِٱلِٱمْتِحَانِ ـ بِٱلْخِبْرَةِ ـ بِٱلتَّجْرِبَةِ ٱلِٱمْتِحَانِ.

Experimentative, *a.* *See* Experimental, *a.*

Expert, *a.* مُدَرَّب ـ دَرِبٌ ب ـ لَبِيقٌ ب ـ مُفِيد ـ أَرِيب ـ بارِع ـ خَبِيرٌ ب ـ مُتَوَقِّف ـ مُجَرَّب ـ مُدَرِّس ـ حُوَّلٌ قُلَّب ـ شَمَلِيل ـ ماهِرٌ ب ـ حَذِق. He was — in the thing, أَرِبَ ب بِٱلشَّيْءِ.

Expert, *n.* كَشَّاف ـ أَهْلُ خِبْرَةٍ.

Expertly, *ad.* بِبَراعَةٍ ـ بِحِذْقٍ ـ بِمَعْرِفَةٍ ـ بِٱخْتِبارٍ. Very —, بِغايَةِ ٱلْإِتْقانِ.

Expertness, *n.* شَطارَة ـ مُمارَسَة ـ بَراعَة ـ نَشْط ـ حِذْق ـ مَهارَة.

Expiable, *a.* يُعْفَى عَنْهُ ـ يُكَفَّرُ.

Expiate, *v.t.* To atone for, كَفَّرَ عَنْ. To — from an oath, حَلَّلَ ـ حَلَّلَ ٱلْيَمِينَ. To — for, by paying blood money, عَقَلَ عَنْ ـ وَدَى *aor.* يَدِي.

Expiation, *n.* The act of atoning, تَكْفِير; as of an oath, تَحْلِيل; of a murder, by money, وَدْي. The means of —, كَفَّارَة. Blood money, غِوَر ـ إِغْيار ـ دِيَة.

Expiatory, *a.* إِغْيارِيٌّ ـ إِسْتِغْفارِيٌّ ـ تَكْفِيرِيٌّ.

Expiration, *n.* The act of breathing out, تَنْفِيس ـ فَوْحَة ـ إِخْراجُ ٱلنَّفَسِ. Vapour, بُخار (*vulg.* بُواخ). Cessation, تمام ـ غُلُوق. Termination, as of a lease, *etc.*, إِنْقِضاء ـ إِنْتِهاء ـ نُزُوع. The last breath, آخِرُ نَفَسٍ ـ تَسْلِيمُ ٱلرُّوحِ ـ آخِرُ ٱلْأَجَلِ ـ نَيْط. At the — of ..., عِنْدَ ٱنْقِضاءِ.

Expiratory, *a.* نَفَسِيٌّ ـ مُتَعَلِّقٌ بِٱلتَّنَفُّسِ.

Expire, *v.i.* To breathe out, تَنَفَّسَ ـ أَخْرَجَ ٱلنَّفَسَ. To come to an end, فَرَغَ ـ إِنْقَضَى ـ تَمَّ ـ إِنْتَهَى. To terminate, as of a lease, *etc.*, غَلِقَ. To die, ماتَ ـ سَلَّمَ ٱلرُّوحَ. He expired, فاظَ ـ تُوُفِّيَ. And when 40 years were expired, وَلَمَّا كَمَلَتْ أَرْبَعُونَ سَنَةً.

Expiscate, *v.t.* *See to* Investigate, *v.t.*

Explain, *v.t.* أَوَّلَ ـ شَرَحَ ـ خَرَّجَ ـ عَبَّرَ ـ بَيَّنَ ـ فَسَّرَ ـ فَصَّلَ ـ فَتَحَ ـ وَضَّحَ. To — in a different language, تَرْجَمَ. To ask one to —, إِسْتَفْسَرَ.

Explainable, *a.* قابِلُ ٱلْإِيضاحِ ـ قابِلُ ٱلتَّفْسِيرِ ـ يُشْرَحُ.

Explanation, *n.* The act of making plain, إِيضاح ـ تَعْرِيف ـ تَفْسِير ـ تَأْوِيل ـ تَعْبِير ـ تَخْرِيج ـ شَرْح. Interpretation, meaning, مَعْناة ـ مَضْمُون ـ مَحَطّ ـ عِبارَة ـ تَأَوُّل ـ تَفَسُّر; into another language, تَرْجَمَة. Exposition, as of motives, إِسْتِيضاح ـ إِسْتِفْهام. To ask for an —, إِسْتَوْضَحَ ـ إِسْتَفْهَمَ. Reconciliation, مُصالَحَة.

Explanatory, *a.* ذُو تَأْوِيلٍ ـ مُبَيِّن ـ مُوَضِّح ـ إِيضاحِيٌّ ـ فِيهِ تَعْرِيف.

Expletive, *n.* مُبالَغَة ـ حَشْو ـ إِشْباع ـ كَلِمَةٌ زائِدَةٌ.

Expletive, *a.* / Expletory, مُبالَغَة ـ حاشٍ ـ زائِد.

Explicable, *a.* *See* Explainable, *n.*

Explicate, *v.t.* To unfold, بَسَطَ [2] ـ فَتَحَ ـ نَشَرَ [2]. *See also to* Explain, *v.t.*

Explication, *n.* نَشْر ـ بَسْط ـ تَنْصِيص. *See also* Explanation, *n.*

Explicative, *a.* / Explicatory, *See* Explanatory, *a.*

Explicit, *a.* قاطِع ـ ظاهِر ـ صَرِيح ـ بائِن ـ واضِح ـ مُظْهَر.

Explicitly, *ad.* بَتَّةً ـ إِيضاحًا ـ حَتْمًا ـ صَراحَةً ـ قَطْعًا.

Explicitness, *n.* إِيضاح ـ صَراحَة ـ حَتْم.

Explode, *v.i.* To burst, as with a noise, ثارَ [2] ـ طَقَّ [2] ـ سَقَطَ [2] ـ إِضْمَحَلَّ ـ تَلاشَى. To come to naught, تَفَقَّعَ ـ إِنْفَقَعَ.

Explode, *v.t.* To cause to burst with a report, فَقَّعَ ـ أَطْلَقَ ـ ثَوَّرَ. To treat with contempt, إِسْتَقْبَحَ ـ إِسْتَهْوَنَ ـ إِسْتَوْحَشَ. To reduce to naught, لاشَى ـ أَبْطَلَ ـ أَسْقَطَ.

Exploit, *n.* صَنِيعَة *pl.* صَنائِعُ ـ فِعْل *pl.* أَفْعال ـ سَطْوَة *pl.* سَطَوات. An outrage, قَباحَة *pl.* قَبائِحُ ـ رَذالَة ـ كَبِيرَة.

Explorate, *v.t.* / Explore, تَجَسَّسَ ـ كَشَفَ عَنْ ـ تَحَرَّى ـ تَنَطَّسَ ـ تَهَمَّمَ ـ تَنَفَّضَ ـ نَفَضَ [2]. An exploring party, a vanguard, نَفِيضَة.

Exploration, *n.* The act of, تَحَرٍّ ـ كَشْفٌ عَنْ ـ نَفْض ـ تَنَفُّض. Result of —, وِجْدان ـ وُجُود ـ إِسْتِيفاع ـ إِنْتِفاع.

Explorator, / Explorer, *n.* / Exploratory, *a.* مُتَحَرٍّ ـ رُوَّاد *pl.* رائِد ـ نافُوض ـ مُتَنَطِّس ـ مُكْتَشِف ـ سَفَّار ـ مُتَجَسِّس.

Explosion, *n.* A burst, ثَوْرَة ـ طَلْقَة ـ فَقْعَة; the coming to naught, تَلاشٍ ـ اِضْمِحْلال.

Explosive, *a.* يَفْرَقِعُ ـ يَنْفَقِعُ ـ يَنْطَلِقُ ـ يَطُقُّ ـ ذُو ثَوْرَة.

Exponent, *n.* An expositor, مُوَضِّح ـ مُفَسِّر ـ مُبَيِّن. *In algebra,* إِسٌّ ـ جِذْر.

Export, *v.t.* نَقَلَ ٱلْبِضاعَةَ إِلَى ٱلْخارِجِ [2].

Export, *n.* تِجارَةٌ مَنْقُولَةٌ إِلَى ٱلْمَمالِكِ ٱلْأَجْنَبِيَّةِ. Exports, ما يَخْرُجُ مِنْ أَمْتِعَةٍ إِلَى ٱلْخارِجِ ـ الخارِجُ مِن ـ إِخْراجات. Export trade, تِجارَةٌ خارِجَة. The exports from Egypt, ما خَرَجَ مِنْ مِصْرَ مِنَ ٱلْبَضائِعِ. What is the chief — of England? مَا أَخَصُّ ٱلْبِضاعَةِ ٱلَّتِي تَخْرُجُ مِنْ أَنْكِلْترا.

Exportation, *n.* إِخْراج ـ نَقْلُ ٱلْبِضاعَةِ إِلَى ٱلْمَمالِكِ ٱلْأَجْنَبِيَّةِ.

Exporter, *n.* تاجِرٌ يُخْرِجُ ٱلْبِضاعَةَ إِلَى ٱلْمَمالِكِ ٱلْأَجْنَبِيَّةِ.

Exposé, *n.* بَيان ـ لائِحَة ـ تَقْرِير ـ بَيانُ حالٍ.

Expose, *v.t.* To bare, uncover, شَمَّرَ عَن ـ أَعْرَى ـ عَرَّى. To lay open to view, جَلَا [2] ـ جَلَّى ـ أَظْهَرَ ـ عَرَضَ ـ كَشَفَ. To place towards, عَرَضَ- (or) وَجَّهَ- نَحْوَ. To explain, make known, شَهَرَ ب ـ صَرَّحَ ب. To make one liable to, عَرَّضَ-ل ـ أَلْجَأَ-إِلَى. To — to ridicule, فَضَحَ ـ هَتَكَ ـ عَيَّرَ ـ عَيَّبَ. To — to the sun, شَمَّسَ. To — one's self to, تَعَرَّضَ ل ـ غَرَّرَ بِنَفْسِهِ ل; to danger, خاطَرَ بِنَفْسِهِ ـ جازَفَ. To —, cast away, رَمَى. To —, as of a criminal, أَقامَ-لِلنّاسِ; *to march him up and down as a disgrace,* جَرَّسَ ـ جَرَّسَ. To make one to be liable to, عَرَّضَ-ل. The sun became exposed to view, تَجَلَّتِ ٱلشَّمْسُ. The house is exposed to the east wind, البَيْتُ مُقابِلُ ٱلرِّيحِ ٱلشَّرْقِيَّةِ. To be exposed, disgraced, اِنْفَضَحَ. To be exposed to, in danger of, كانَ تَحْتَ ٱلضَّرَرِ ـ كانَ هَدَفًا ل ـ كانَ مُسْتَهْدِفًا ل. I exposed the commodity for sale, عَرَضْتُ ٱلْمَتاعَ لِلْبَيْعِ. He exposed them to the sword, عَرَّضَهُمْ عَلَى ٱلسَّيْفِ. He exposed himself to destruction, عَرَّضَ نَفْسَهُ لِلْهَلاكِ. He was exposed to a variety of diseases, تَعَرَّضَ لِأَنْواعِ ٱلْأَمْراضِ.

Exposedness, *n.* *See* Exposure, *n.*

Exposition, *n.* An explanation, تَعْبِير ـ إِفادَة ـ بَيان ـ عَرْض ـ تَصْرِيح ـ شَرْح ـ إِظْهار ـ عِبارَة ـ تَفْسِير. Openness, صَراحَة ـ اِنْبِساط. *See also* Exhibition, *n.*

Expositive, *a.* } **Expository,** *a.* } **Expositor,** *n.* } مُوَضِّح ـ مُفَسِّر ـ مُبَيِّن ـ كَشّاف ـ شارِح ـ مُتَرْجِم.

Ex post facto, ad. بَعْدَ ٱلْواقِعَةِ ـ بَعْدُ. An — law, قانُونٌ مَوْضُوعٌ لِمُجازاةِ ٱلذُّنُوبِ عَقِبَ وُقُوعِها.

Expostulate, *v.i.* To — with, to chide gently, عاتَبَ. To point out to by way of advice, نَبَّهَ-عَلَى ـ نَذَّرَ-ب ـ أَنْذَرَ-ب. To contend with, نازَعَ ـ ناقَرَ. To bandy words with, حاضَرَ. To beseech, تَضَرَّعَ إِلَى.

Expostulation, *n.* The act of chiding, عِتاب ـ مُعاتَبَة; of advising, إِنْذار ـ نُصْح ـ نَصاحَة ـ تَنْبِيه; of contending, مُناقَرَة ـ مُنازَعَة; of beseeching, تَضَرُّع.

Expostulator, *n.* } **Expostulatory,** *a.* } مُنْصِح ـ مُنَبِّه عَلَى ـ مُعاتِب.

Exposure, *n.* The act of baring, تَشْمِير ـ تَعْرِيَة; of laying open to view, شَرْح ـ كَشْف ـ تَبْيِين; of exposing one's vices, فَضْح. The being laid open, اِنْشِراح ـ اِنْكِشاف ـ بَيان. The act of making liable to, إِلْجاءٌ إِلَى ـ تَعْرِيض ل. Liability, تَعَرُّض ل. Danger, ضَرَر ـ خَطَر. Situation, مَحَلّ ـ مُنْتَهًى ـ مَعْرُوض ـ مَقام ـ مَوْضِع. Disclosure تَصْرِيح ب.

Expound, *v.t.* وَضَّحَ ـ فَصَّلَ ـ فَسَّرَ ـ عَبَّرَ ـ شَرَحَ.

Expounder, *n.* *See* Expositor, *n.*

Express, *v.t.* To utter, لَفَظَ ب ـ تَفَوَّهَ ب ـ فاهَ ب [2] ـ نَطَقَ ب [2]. To — in words, to describe, وَصَفَ *aor.* يَصِفُ ـ أَعْرَبَ ـ صَرَّحَ ب ـ شَرَحَ ـ بَيَّنَ ـ عَبَّرَ ب *or* عَلَى. To — clearly, To draw, represent by figure, *etc.,* رَقَمَ [2] ـ صَوَّرَ ـ مَثَّلَ ـ شَبَّهَ. To squeeze out, عَصَرَ. To — in writing, رَقَمَ [2] ـ كَتَبَ [2]. To — sorrow, حَزِنَ ـ تَحَزَّنَ ـ اِنْغَمَّ; joy, فَرِحَ ـ اِسْتَبْشَرَ. To — one's mind, فاهَ بِما فِي ضَمِيرِهِ [2] ـ تَفَتَّحَ فِي ٱلْكَلامِ. Words cannot — it, تَقْصُرُ عَنْ وَصْفِهِ ٱلْأَقْوالُ. It expresses so and so, يُعَبِّرُ عَنْ كَذا وَكَذا. Expressed juice, عَصِير ـ عُصارَة.

Express, *n.* A special messenger, ساعٍ مَخْصُوص *pl.* سُعاة ـ قاصِد ـ بَرِيد.

Express, *a.* Plain, ظاهِر ـ بائِن ـ واضِح ـ صَرِيح. Special, مَخْصُوص ـ مُعَيَّن. Decisive, بَتِّيّ ـ قاطِع ـ قَطْعِيّ. For the — purpose of ..., لِغايَةِ أَن.

Expressible, *a.* As in words, قابِلُ ٱلنُّطْقِ ب ـ يُلْفَظُ ب; in writing, مِمّا يُكْتَب; in figure, يُتَصَوَّرُ ـ يَرْتَسِمُ. That may be made clear, يُصَرَّحُ. That may be squeezed out, عَصِيرَة.

Expression, *n.* The act of squeezing out, عَصْر; what is squeezed out, عَصِير. The act of uttering, نَطْق ـ تَلَفُّظ. A word uttered, a word, عِبارَة ـ كَلِمَة ـ مَقالَة ـ لَفْظ. Figure, representation, مَثَل ـ صُورَة ـ هَيْئَة. Tone, مَقامَةُ ٱلْغِناءِ ـ صَوْت. Mode of speech, نَوْعٌ مِنَ ٱلْكَلامِ ـ فَنٌّ مِنَ ٱلْكَلامِ ـ عِبارَة. He has a good —, utterance, هُوَ حَسَنُ ٱلْأَداءِ ـ هُوَ حَسَنُ ٱلْعِبارَةِ. Manner, generally, عِبَارَةٌ ـ لَفْظَةٌ. A sentence, وَجْهٌ ـ وَضْعٌ ـ طَوْرٌ. The act of describing, بَيَانٌ ـ تَعْبِيرٌ ـ شَرْحٌ ـ وَصْفٌ. In algebra, كَمِّيَّةٌ ـ كَمٌّ. Beyond all —, يَعْجِزُ عَنْ وَصْفِهِ ٱللِّسَانُ ـ لا يُوصَفُ. To be choice in one's expressions, جَاءَ بِكَلَامٍ دَقٍّ ـ إِفْتَنَّ فِي ٱلْكَلَامِ.

Expressionless, *a.* Cold, insipid, تَافِهٌ ـ بَارِدٌ ـ سَقِيطَةٌ. Without, unpossessed of..., خَالٍ مِنْ ـ بِغَيْرِ, *followed by the appropriate nouns.*

Expressive, *a.* Indicating, دَلِيلٌ ـ مُعْتَرِفٌ بِ ـ دَالٌّ عَلَى ـ مُفِيدٌ بِ ـ دَلَالِيٌّ ـ عَلَى. Pointed, of language, نَبَّارٌ ـ حُدَّادٌ. Full of meaning, شَدِيدُ ٱلتَّعْبِيرِ ـ كَثِيرُ ٱلْمَعْنَى ـ كَلَامٌ بَلِيغٌ.

Expressively, *ad.* } بِبَلَاغَةٍ ـ بِشِدَّةِ تَعْبِيرٍ.
Ex-pressivo, }

Expressiveness, *n.* قُوَّةُ لَفْظٍ ـ بَلَاغَةُ كَلَامٍ.

Expressly, *ad.* Formally, decidedly, قَطْعًا وَجَزْمًا ـ حَتْمًا ـ بَتًّا. Openly, جَهْرًا ـ عَلَانِيَةً ـ عِيَانًا. Specially, خَاصَّةً ـ بِٱلْخُصُوصِ.

Exprobate, *v.t.* عَيَّرَ ـ بِ ـ عَاتَبَ ـ بِ ـ لَامَ ².

Exprobation, *n.* عَارٌ ـ تَعْيِيرٌ ـ عِتَابٌ ـ لَوْمٌ.

Expropriate, *v.t.* ضَبَطَ ² (أَخَذَ or قَبَضَ or) أَمْوَالَ ٱلنَّاسِ ـ إِسْتَمْلَكَ أَمْلَاكَ ٱلنَّاسِ.

Expropriation, *n.* The act of, ضَبْطُ (أَخْذُ or قَبْضُ or) مَالِ ٱلنَّاسِ ـ إِسْتِمْلَاكُ مُلْكِ ٱلنَّاسِ.

Expugn, *v.t.* فَتَحَ ـ ضَبَطَ.

Expugnation, *n.* فَتْحٌ ـ ضَبْطٌ.

Expulsion, *n.* The act of, دَفْعٌ ـ طَرْدٌ ـ تَخْرِيجٌ ـ إِخْرَاجٌ. See also Exile, *n.*

Expulsive, *a.* مُخْرِجٌ ـ طَارِدٌ ـ دَافِعٌ.

Expunge, *v.t.* أَبْطَلَ ـ طَلَسَ ـ مَحَا ². See also to Erase, *v.t.*

Expurgate, *v.t.* نَظَّفَ ـ صَفَّى ـ نَقَّحَ.

Expurgation, *n.* The act of, تَنْظِيفٌ ـ تَصْفِيَةٌ ـ تَنْقِيحٌ.

Exquisite, *a.* Peculiarly fine, زَكِيٌّ ـ لَطِيفٌ ـ أَنْفَسُ ـ نَفِيسٌ ـ بَهِيٌّ ـ خَالِصٌ. Dainty, of a person, مُتَأَنِّقٌ. Acute, painful, أَلِيمٌ ـ ثَقِيلٌ ـ شَدِيدٌ ـ حَادٌّ. An — thing, مَفْخَرَةٌ.

Exquisite, *n.* See Dandy, *n.*

Exquisitely, *ad.* بِأَتَمِّ مِنْوَالٍ ـ بِكَمَالٍ ـ حَسَنًا.

Exquisiteness, *n.* Nicety, حُسْنٌ ـ لَطَافَةٌ ـ تَمَامٌ ـ كَمَالٌ ـ نَفَاسَةٌ. Violence, حِدَّةٌ ـ شِدَّةٌ. Daintiness, of a person, تَأَنُّقٌ.

Exsanguious, *a.* بِلا دَمٍ.

Exscind, *v.t.* حَذَفَ ـ بَتَرَ ² ـ جَزَعَ.

Exsertile, *a.* يُطْرَدُ ـ يُخْرَجُ ـ يُدْفَعُ.

Exsiccant, *a.* See Exsiccative, *a.*

Exsiccate, *v.t.* يَبَّسَ ـ جَفَّفَ ـ نَشَّفَ.

Exsiccation, *n.* تَيْبِيسٌ ـ تَجْفِيفٌ ـ تَنْشِيفٌ.

Exsiccative, *a.* مُيَبِّسٌ ـ مُجَفِّفٌ ـ مُنَشِّفٌ.

Exsudation, *n.* عَرَقٌ ـ تَرَشُّحٌ.

Extant, *a.* بَاقٍ ـ كَائِنٌ ـ مَوْجُودٌ.

Extemporaneous, } مُقْتَرَحٌ ـ إِرْتِجَالِيٌّ ـ مُرْتَجَلٌ ـ مُقْتَضَبٌ.
Extemporary, *a.* } An — speech, فَلْتَةٌ ـ إِقْتِرَاحٌ ـ إِرْتِجَالٌ.
Extempore, } An — poem, شِعْرٌ مُقْتَضَبٌ.

Extemporaneousness, *n.* بُدَاهَةٌ ـ إِرْتِجَالٌ.

Extemporarily, *ad.* } عَلَى بَدِيهٍ ـ بَدِيهًا ـ بِٱلْبُدَاهَةِ ـ فَلْتَةً
Extempore, } صَخْرَةً بَحْرَةً. To speak —, إِرْتَجَلَ.

Extemporize, *v.i.* إِرْتَجَلَ ـ إِقْتَرَحَ ـ إِفْتَلَتَ ـ إِبْتَدَهَ. To — in verse, قَالَ ² ٱلشِّعْرَ عَلَى ٱلْبَدِيهَةِ ـ أَنْشَدَ ٱرْتِجَالًا.

Extemporizer, *n.* مُقْتَرِحٌ ـ مُقْتَضِبٌ ـ مُرْتَجِلٌ.

Extend, *v.t.* To stretch out, مَدَّ ² ـ جَذَبَ ² ـ نَدَحَ. To open out, بَسَطَ ² ـ نَشَرَ ² ـ شَرَحَ. To elongate, مَدَّ ² ـ أَطَالَ ـ طَوَّلَ. To widen, أَوْسَعَ ـ وَسَّعَ. To enlarge, كَبَّرَ ـ عَظَّمَ ; in numbers, أَكْثَرَ ـ كَثَّرَ. To bestow, مَنَحَ ـ وَهَبَ *aor.* يَهَبُ ـ أَكْرَمَ عَلَى بِ ـ أَعْطَى. To spread abroad, نَشَرَ ² ـ بَثَّ ² ـ أَفَاشَ ـ أَذَاعَ. To be extended, stretched out, إِجْتَذَبَ ـ إِمْتَدَّ ; to be extended, opened out, إِنْتَشَرَ ـ إِنْبَسَطَ ; to be extended, elongated, إِسْتَطَالَ ـ إِمْتَدَّ ; to be extended, widened, إِتَّسَعَ ـ إِسْتَوْسَعَ ; to be extended, enlarged, كَبُرَ ² ; in numbers, تَكَثَّرَ. *See also to* Stretch, *v.t.*

Extend, *v.i.* To reach to, لَحِقَ بِ ـ وَصَلَ إِلَى *aor.* يَصِلُ. To include, إِنْضَمَّ عَلَى ـ إِشْتَمَلَ عَلَى ـ شَمِلَ. To last, دَامَ ². To —, or stretch one's self at full length, تَسَطَّحَ ; on the stomach, إِنْبَطَحَ ; on the back, إِنْسَطَحَ. To — the arms, as when waking, تَمَطَّأَ ـ تَمَطَّى. To — over, أَحَاطَ. The skin then became extended, ثُمَّ عَرَضَ عَلَى ٱلْجِلْدِ مِنَ ٱلْمَدِّ (or ثُمَّ تَمَدَّدَ ٱلْجِلْدُ). To — to, as a disease, *etc.*, to be communicated to, سَرَى إِلَى *aor.* يَسْرِي.

Extendible, *a.* } تَوْسِيعُهُ مُمْكِنٌ ـ قَابِلُ ٱلِٱنْبِسَاطِ ـ يَمْتَدُّ.
Extensible, }

Extensibility, *n.* } إِمْكَانُ ـ قَابِلِيَّةُ ٱلتَّوْسِيعِ ـ قَابِلِيَّةُ ٱلتَّمْدِيدِ
Extensibleness, } ٱلنَّشْرِ.

Extensile, *a.* See Extendible, *a.*

Extension, *n.* The act of stretching out, جَذْبٌ ـ مَدٌّ ـ تَمْدِيدٌ ـ نَدْحٌ ; the being stretched out, إِجْتِذَابٌ ـ إِمْتِدَادٌ. The act of opening out, نَشْرٌ ـ بَسْطٌ ; the being opened out, إِنْتِشَارٌ ـ إِنْبِسَاطٌ. The act of elongating, إِطَالَةٌ ـ تَطْوِيلٌ ; the being elongated, length, طُوْل ـ إِسْتِطَالَة ـ تَطَوُّل. The act of widening, تَوْسِيع; the being widened, width, عُرْض ـ إِتِّسَاع ـ سَعَة. The act of enlarging, تَعْظِيم ـ تَكْبِير; the being large, size, عِظَم ـ كُبْر. The act of spreading abroad, إِذَاعَة ـ بَثّ ـ نَشْر. Extension of time, as for payment, مُهْلَة ـ مُدَّة. Extension, as of territory, by seizure, حَوْز. Extension of trade, إِتِّسَاعُ ٱلتِّجَارَةِ. Extension of a law, making it general, تَعْمِيمُ قَانُونٍ. Owing to excess of —, مِنْ زِيَادَةِ ٱلتَّمَدُّدِ.

Extensive, *a.* Wide, مَدِيد ـ رَحِيب ـ وَسِيع ـ وَاسِع. Large, كَثِير ـ وَافِر ـ كَبِير ـ عَظِيم. Long, مَدِيد ـ طَوِيل. Numerous, كَثِير ـ وَافِر. An — tract of land, مَمْدُوحَة.

Extensively, *ad.* Widely spread abroad, اذاعةً. Widely, بِاتِّسَاعٍ. Much, greatly, جِدًّا ـ كَثِيرًا. He or it is — known, هُوَ مَشْهُورٌ ـ عِرْفَانُهُ مَنْشُورٌ ـ ذَائِعُ ٱلشُّهْرَةِ.

Extensiveness, *n.* / **Extent**, *n.* } Of bulk, قَدّ ـ قَدْر ـ مِقْدَار ـ حَجْم ـ جِرْم; of length, طُوْل; of distance, طُوْل ـ مَسَافَة; of width, إِتِّسَاع ـ عُرْض ـ سَعَة. Largeness, size, كُبْر ـ عِظَم. Number, كَثْرَة ـ عَدَد. Extent, as of time, طُوْل.

Extenso, *ad.* In —, عَلَى طُولِهِ ـ تَمَامًا وَكَمَالًا.

Extenuate, *v.a.* To make slender, fine, رَقَّقَ ـ دَقَّقَ ـ حَسَّرَ. To weaken, أَضْعَفَ ـ ضَعَّفَ. To lessen, صَغَّرَ ـ أَقَلَّ ـ خَفَّفَ. To make rare, opposed to dense, أَمَاعَ. To palliate, أَعْذَرَ ـ إِعْتَلَّ عَلَى-بِ ـ عَذَرَ.

Extenuated, *a.* Weak, ضَعِيف. Lessened, مُخَفَّف ـ مُقَلَّل. Slender, دَقِيق ـ رَقِيق.

Extenuating, *a.* Lessening, مُقَلِّل ـ مُخَفِّف. Exculpatory, عَاذِر ـ مُعْذِر. Extenuating circumstances, مَعَاذِيرُ.

Extenuation, *n.* The act of lessening, تَخْفِيف ـ تَقْلِيل; of making weak, إِضْعَاف. Loss of flesh, عَجَف ـ نَحَافَة. An excuse, تَعَلُّل ـ إِعْتِذَار ـ عُذْر. Extenuation of punishment, تَخْفِيفُ عَذَابٍ. In — of, تَخْفِيفًا بِ.

Exterior, *a.* Apparent, طَرَفَانِيّ ـ ظَاهِر ـ بَارِز ـ ضَاحٍ. Outside, بَرَّانِيّ ـ خَارِجِيّ ـ خَارِج. Foreign, أَجْنَبِيّ ـ خَارِجِيّ. *See also* Outward, *a.*

Exterior, *n.* The outside, الظَّاهِرُ ـ الخَارِجُ. Exterior appearance, هَيْئَةٌ ظَاهِرَةٌ.

Exterminate, *v.t.* أَدْمَرَ ـ إِسْتَقْلَعَ ـ أَبَادَ ـ جَذَرَ ـ إِسْتَأْصَلَ ـ أَزَالَ ـ مَحَقَ ـ أَعْدَمَ ـ سَحَطَ.

Extermination, *n.* The act of, مَحْق ـ إِسْتِقْلَاع ـ إِسْتِئْصَال ـ سَحْط ـ جَذْر ـ إِزَالَة ـ إِعْدَام ـ إِبَادَة ـ دَمَار.

Exterminator, *n.* / **Exterminatory**, *a.* } مُعْدِم ـ دَامِر ـ مُزِيل ـ مُبِيد ـ مُسْتَقْلِع.

External, *a.* *See* Exterior, *a.*

Externally, *ad.* On the outside, فِي ٱلخَارِجِ. Apparently, فِي الظَّاهِرِ.

Externals, *n.* Outward appearance, هَيْئَةٌ ظَاهِرَةٌ. Dress, مَلْبُوسَات. Outward things, أُمُورٌ ظَاهِرَةٌ ـ أُمُورٌ خَارِجَةٌ. Worldly matters, أُمُورٌ جِسْمَانِيَّةٌ ـ أُمُورٌ دُنْيَوِيَّةٌ. Outward courtesies, أُمُورٌ رَسْمِيَّةٌ.

Extinct, *a.* Of a light, مُطْفَأٌ. Existing no more, مَعْدُوم ـ مُنْدَرِسُ ٱلآثَارِ ـ عَدِيمُ ٱلوُجُودِ ـ مُنْمَحٍ.

Extinction, *n.* The act of putting out, as of a candle or fire, إِطْفَاء ـ إِبَاخَة ـ إِهْمَاد; the being put out, هُمُود ـ طُفُوء. The act of putting an end to, إِبَادَة ـ إِفْنَاء ـ إِزَالَة ـ إِعْدَام. Cessation, destruction, إِنْقِرَاض ـ إِنْعِدَام ـ زَوَال ـ عَدَم. The act of deprivation, as of hope, *etc.*, فَسْخ ـ إِبْطَال ـ إِلْغَاء; the being so deprived, إِنْفِسَاخ ـ لَغْو. Extinction, as of a debt, وَفَاء ـ إِسْتِهْلَاك ـ إِفْتِدَاء دَيْنٍ ـ إِيفَاء.

Extinguish, *v.t.* To —, as of a candle, أَطْفَأَ; of a fire, أَخْبَى ـ أَهْلَكَ ـ أَبَادَ ـ أَزَالَ. To destroy, cause to cease, أَهْمَدَ ـ أَبَاخَ. To —, as of a debt, إِسْتَهْلَكَ (يَفِي or) وَفَى *or* إِفْتَدَى) دَيْنًا *aor.* To be extinguished, quenched, إِنْطَفَأَ ـ هَمَدَ ـ طَفِيَ. The fire was very speedily extinguished, أُطْفِئَتِ ٱلحَرِيقَةُ بِغَايَةِ ٱلسُّرْعَةِ. It was about to be extinguished, كَادَ يَنْطَفِئُ.

Extinguishable, *a.* That may be quenched, يَنْطَفِئُ ـ يُطْفَأُ ـ يُزَالُ ـ يُبَادُ ـ يُبَاخُ ـ يُهْمَدُ. That may be destroyed, يُفْنَى.

Extinguisher, *n.* One who extinguishes, quenches, مُبِيخ ـ مُطْفِئٌ. The —, as of a lamp, مُطْفِئٌ.

Extinguishment, *n.* The — as of a light, fire, إِخْبَاء ـ إِطْفَاء ـ إِبْطَال ـ إِزَالَة ـ إِبَاخَة; as of a debt, اسْتِهْلَاكُ دَيْنٍ. Destruction, إِعْدَام. *See also* Extinction, *n.*

Extirpate, *v.t.* *See to* Exterminate, Eradicate, *v.t.*

Extirpation, *n.* *See* Extermination, Eradication, *n.*

Extirpator, *n.* *See* Exterminator, *n.*

Extol, *v.t.* فَخَّرَ ـ مَدَحَ ـ فَخَّمَ ـ عَظَّمَ ـ كَبَّرَ ـ مَجَّدَ. To — above another, فَضَّلَ-عَلَى. To — one's self, تَكَبَّرَ ـ تَفَخَّمَ ـ تَفَخَّرَ. To be extolled, تَمَجَّدَ. May he be extolled, جَلَّ جَلَالُهُ.

Extort, *v.t.* To seize unjustly, إِغْتَصَرَ ـ إِخْتَلَسَ ـ سَلَبَ ـ إِخْتَطَفَ ـ إِغْتَسَرَ. To bring out, أَخْرَجَ. To — a confession from, إِسْتَقَرَّ-عَلَى ـ قَرَّرَ-عَلَى.

Extortion, *n.* Unjust seizure, oppression, إختلاس ـ إختطاف ـ ظلم ـ تطاول ـ إغتصار ـ تعسّف ـ عسف ـ جور. Excess in demanding, إفراط في الطلب.

Extortionary, *a.* } Of a person, مختلس ـ عصّار ـ طاغٍ ـ
Extortionate, *a.* } داعس ـ خاطف pl. خاطفون ـ ظالم ـ
Extortioner, *n.* } جائر. Extortionate in demand, طلوب ـ طلّاب ـ مفرط في الطلب. To be —, tyrannical, towards, ظلم ـ بغى على ـ عسف ـ تعسّف. To be — in, أفرط في.

Extra, *a.* Excessive, زائد ـ فاضل. Beyond, without, خارج عن.

Extra, *n.* زيادة pl. زيادات ـ زائدة pl. زوائد ـ فضل pl. فضول ـ فضيلة ـ فضلة.

Extract, *n.* A substance drawn from another, سلالة ـ مسن ـ روح ـ دهن pl. دهان ـ إستخراج. A quotation from a book, تلخيص ـ إقتباس ـ بند مستخرج ـ منقول. An epitome, مختصر. Choice extracts, منتخبات. To quote extracts from, إقتبس من ـ نقل عن ـ إمتثل ب.

Extract, *v.t.* To distil from, صوّل ـ من ـ مسن ـ من ـ أخرج ـ نقذ ـ (or) أنقذ ـ من. To pull out, إستخرج ـ من ـ إختلج ـ خلج. قلع ـ قلّع; as a thorn from the flesh, *etc.*, To select, إنتخب ـ نقّى. To —, get out of one, as information, *etc.*, by inquiry, إستشفّ من. He did not — anything from him, ما استشفّ منه شيئا. To make an abridgment of, إختصر ـ لخّص. To — the root of a number, إستخرج جذر عدد.

Extraction, *n.* The act of distilling, تصويل ـ إستخراج; of drawing out, إخراج ـ إستخراج ـ تقليع. Acquisition, تحصيل. Selection, إنتخاب ـ تنقية. Lineage, أصل ـ نسب ـ نسل ـ ذرّية. Of noble —, كريم الأصل. Of German —, نمساوي الأصل. *In algebra*, إستخراج الجذر.

Extractive, *a.* يستخرج ـ يخرج ـ يقلع.

Extractor, *n.* The instrument, ملزم ـ كلّاب pl. كلاليب.

Extradition, *n.* تسليم الفرار واسترداده. An — treaty, معاهدة على تسليم الفرار واسترداده.

Extra-judicial, *a.* غير رسمي ـ عرفي ـ خارج عن قوانين الشرع.

Extra-judicially, *ad.* خارج (or في خارج) ـ على باب عرفي ـ على منوال غير رسمي ـ قوانين الشرع.

Extra-mundane, *a.* غير دنيوي ـ خارج عن الدنيا.

Extraneous, *a.* Foreign, غريب ـ أجنبي ـ خارجي. Not intrinsic, ملحق. Contrary, مخالف.

Extra-official, *a.* غير رسمي ـ خارج عن القوانين الرسمية.

Extra-officially, *ad.* خارج القوانين الرسمية.

Extraordinarily, *ad.* خارج ـ بنوع غريب ـ فوق العادة (or في خارج) العادة.

Extraordinariness, *n.* غرابة ـ نادرة ـ عجيبة ـ أعجوبة.

Extraordinary, *a.* Out of the regular order, خارج ـ فوق العادة ـ بعيد ـ عن العادة. Rare, strange, طرآني ـ طرآن ـ نادر ـ غريب. Wonderful, عجيب ـ غريب. Large, numerous, عظيم ـ كثير. Special, مخصوص ـ مستثنى. Ambassador —, سفير فوق العادة. An — (good) man, نسيج وحده. A thing not less —, أمر ليس بأقلّ غرابة. How — it is! سبحان من كذا.

Extraordinary, *n.* طارئ pl. طرآء ـ أمر فوق (or مادّة or وارد) العادة. An — phrase, speech, word, كلمة فاذّة ـ فذّة ـ شاذّة.

Extra-parochial, *a.* خارج عن المحلّ ـ خارج عن الأبرشيّة.

Extra-professional, *a.* خارج عن الوظيفة ـ خارج عن الصنعة.

Extra-professionally, *ad.* خارج (or في خارج) الصنعة (or الوظيفة).

Extra-territorial, *a.* خارج عن الحكومة ـ خارج عن الحدود.

Extra-tropical, *a.* خارج عن دائرتي ـ خارج عن المنطقة الجدي والسرطان.

Extravagance, *n.* } The going beyond limits, تعدّ ـ جواز.
Extravagancy, } Prodigality, تبذير ـ بذر ـ فرط ـ تفريط ـ إسراف ـ بعزقة. Folly, حماقة ـ جنون ـ (or خباط) إختلال العقل.

Extravagant, *a.* Excessive, مبالغ ـ مفرط. Prodigal, مسرف ـ مبذر ـ شاطر. Wild, irregular, سائب ـ غير مضبوط ـ منفاق ـ خيالي. To be —, prodigal, in, أسرف ـ بذر ـ أفرط في.

Extravagantly, *ad.* Prodigally, تبذيرا ـ بإسراف ـ ببعزقة. Wildly, بتيهان ـ تيها ـ بخيال ـ بجنون ـ بخباط العقل. To act — in, أفرط في.

Extravaganza, *n.* غرابة ـ أعجوبة.

Extravasate, *v.t.* طفح. To be extravasated, طفح.

Extravasation, *n.* The act of, تطفيح; the being extravasated, طفح ـ طفوح.

Extreme, *a.* Very great, more, أعظم ـ أقصى ـ غاية ـ أزيد. Utmost, أقصى ـ آخر. Unbearable, لا يطاق. Very pressing, urgent, ضروري ـ مهمّ للغاية ـ أهمّ ما يكون. Rigorous, severe, حدّاد ـ شديد ـ قاس ـ صعب. Extreme joy, غاية السرور. Extreme cold, زمهرير ـ برد شديد للغاية ـ برد لا يطاق. The — ends of the earth, أقاصي الأرض. An — party, أصحاب الآراء القصوى.

Extreme, *n.* An end, أَمَد ـ مُنْتَهًى ـ نِهَايَة ـ آخِر ـ غَايَة. Excess, إِفْرَاط ـ فَرْط. A crisis, قُطُوع ـ شِدَّة. Avoid extremes, كُنْ مُتَوَسِّطًا ـ إِجْتَنِبِ ٱلْإِفْرَاطَ.

Extremely, *ad.* لِلنِّهَايَةِ ـ لِلْغَايَةِ ـ جِدًّا. Extremely knowing, حَقُّ عَلِيمٍ. This is the — learned man, هٰذَا ٱلْعَالِمُ حَقُّ ٱلْعَالِمِ ـ هٰذَا ٱلْعَالِمُ جِدُّ ٱلْعَالِمِ.

Extreme unction, *n.* ٱلْمَسْحَة ـ مَسْحَةُ ٱلْمَرْضَى ـ دُهْنُ ٱلْمَرْضَى ـ ٱلْمَسْحَةُ ٱلْأَخِيرَةُ.

Extremity, *n.* An end, أَمَد ـ نِهَايَة ـ آخِر ـ غَايَة. A limit, حَدّ. A brink, شَفًا *pl.* أَشْفَاء ـ طَرَف *pl.* أَطْرَاف. The — of a garment, ذَيْل *pl.* أَذْيَال. The extremities of the body, أَطْرَافُ ٱلْجَسَدِ. Violence, شِدَّة ـ شُؤُوبَة. The crisis of a difficulty, أَشَدُّ ٱلضِّيقِ ـ عِزُّ ٱلضِّيقَةِ. He is at the last —, dying, هُوَ عَلَى رَمَقٍ مِنَ ٱلْحَيٰوةِ. To drive to —, أَجْبَرَ عَلَى ٱلْعِقَابِ; to cause to despair, أَيْأَسَ ـ آيَسَ. To proceed to extremities, إِتَّخَذَ أَقْصَى ٱلْوَسَائِطِ.

Extricable, *a.* تَفْرِيجُهُ مُمْكِنٌ ـ يُفْرَجُ ـ مِمَّا يُخَلَّصُ.

Extricate, *v.t.* أَخْرَجَ مِن ـ ² نَقَذَ ـ نَقَّذَ- *or* تَنَقَّذَ- *or* مِن ـ فَرَّجَ مِن ـ أَفْرَجَ مِن ـ إِسْتَنْقَذَ ـ خَلَّصَ مِن; as from a difficulty, To — one's self, أَنْقَذَ نَفْسَهُ مِن ـ تَخَلَّصَ مِن ـ ² خَرَجَ مِن.

Extrication, *n.* The act of, إِخْرَاج ـ إِسْتِنْقَاذ ـ تَنْقِيذ ـ نَقْذ ـ تَفْرِيج مِن ـ تَخْلِيص مِن ـ مِن; the being extricated, تَخَلُّص ـ فَرَج ـ سَلَامَة ـ فُرْجَة.

Extrinsic, *a.* } **Extrinsical**, } عَرَضِيٌّ ـ مُلْحَق ـ خَارِجِيٌّ ـ خَارِج. The things — to the mind, ٱلْأُمُورُ ٱلْخَارِجِيَّةُ, as opposed to those which are called ٱلْأُمُورُ ٱلذِّهْنِيَّةُ, or things intrinsic to the mind.

Extrude, *v.t.* دَفَعَ ـ ² طَرَدَ ـ أَخْرَجَ.

Extrusion, *n.* The act of, دَفْع ـ طَرْد ـ إِخْرَاج; the being extruded, إِنْدِفَاع ـ طَرْد ـ خُرُوج.

Extuberance, *n.* نُتُوَّة ـ نُتُوء ـ حَدَب ـ حَيْدَة ـ حَيْد.

Extuberant, *a.* نَاتِئٌ ـ أَحْدَب.

Extumescence, *n.* نُفَاخ ـ تَوَرُّم ـ وَرَم.

Exuberance, *n.* } **Exuberancy**, } وُفُور ـ وَفْرَة ـ إِفْرَاط ـ كَثْرَة ـ فُضُول ـ بُذَارَة ـ بَرَكَة. Fertility of soil, خِصْب.

Exuberant, *a.* مُفْرِط ـ زَائِد ـ فَائِض ـ وَافِر ـ فَاضِل; of soil, خَصِيب ـ أَرْض كَرَم. Exuberant land, أَرْض مُخْصِبَة.

Exuberantly, *ad.* وَفْرَة ـ بِبُذَارَةٍ ـ بِإِفْرَاطٍ.

Exudation, *n.* مِغْفَار *pl.* مَغَافِير ـ رَشْح ـ صَبِيب ـ لَثًى ـ عَرَق ـ رَشَحَان.

Exude, *v.i.* ² عَرِقَ ـ أَلْثَى ـ تَرَشَّحَ ـ أَرْشَحَ ـ ² رَشَحَ. To cause to —, رَشَّحَ.

Exulcerate, *v.t.* ² قَرَّحَ.

Exulcerate, *v.i.* تَقَرَّحَ ـ تَهَدَّأَ ـ ² غَبِرَ.

Exulceration, *n.* The act of, قَرْح; the being ulcerated, تَهَدُّأ ـ تَقَرُّح ـ قَرْح. *See also* Ulceration, *n.*

Exult, *v.i.* ² جَذِلَ ـ ² طَرِبَ ـ إِهْتَزَّ طَرَبًا ـ إِبْتَهَجَ ـ تَهَلَّلَ. To — over a person, ² شَمِتَ بِ ـ إِسْتَشَرَّ.

Exultant, *a.* } **Exulting**, } مَسْرُور ـ مَمْنُون ـ مُبْتَهِج. Triumphing over an enemy, شَمَّات ـ شَامِت.

Exultation, *n.* طَرَب ـ جَذَل ـ سُرُور ـ إِبْتِهَاج ـ تَهَلُّل. Triumphing over a person, شَمَات ـ شَمَاتَة.

Exultingly, *ad.* مُتَهَلِّلًا ـ بِمَمْنُونِيَّةٍ وَسُرُورٍ; as over an enemy, بِشَمَاتٍ ـ شَمَاتَة.

Exuviæ, *n.* سَبِيٌّ ـ مِسْلَاخ ـ سُلَاخَة.

Eye, *n.* طَرْف ـ طَرَف ـ بَاصِرَة ـ (كَحْمَة in the dialect of al-Yemen) ـ عَيْن *pl.* عُيُون *and* أَعْيَان *and* أَعْيُن *pl.pl.* أَعْيُنَات. Sight, ٱلْمُبْصِرَة ـ حَاسَّةُ ٱلْبَصَرِ ـ نَظَر ـ بَصَر ـ نَظَرَان. The sense of sight, Look, countenance, مَنْظَر ـ وَجْه. Observation, تَأَمُّل ـ مَذْهَب ـ رَأْي ـ نَظَر ـ بَصِيرَة ـ مُلَاحَظَة. Opinion, Guidance, دَلِيل. The eye, as of a needle, خُرْتَة ـ خُرْت ـ سَمّ (or سُمّ) ـ عَيْنُ ٱلْإِبْرَةِ ـ خَرْمُ ٱلْإِبْرَةِ ـ ٱلْخِيَاطِ. The eye of an elephant, عَيْنُ ٱلْفِيلِ. The eye of a plant, لُبْلُوب ـ عُقْدَة ـ عَيْن ـ زِرّ. Dimness in the eye, كَرْسَاف. As far as the eye can reach, مَدَى تَذْرَ ٱلْبَصَرِ. For the sake of your eyes, إِكْرَامًا لِعَيْنَيْكَ. In the twinkling of an eye, فِي لَحْظَةٍ ـ فِي طَرْفَةِ عَيْنٍ ـ فِي لَمْحَةِ بَصَرٍ. What the eye does not see the heart does not grieve for, مَا لَا تَرَاهُ ٱلْعَيْنُ لَا يُوجِعُ بِهِ ٱلْقَلْبُ. With tears in one's eyes, مُتَدَمِّع ـ بَاكٍ. Pleasant to the eyes, بَهِجٌ لِلْعُيُونِ. With the naked eye, بِمُجَرَّدِ ٱلنَّظَرِ.

Ball of the eye, مُقْلَةُ ٱلْعَيْنِ.

Black of the eye, حَدَقَةُ ٱلْعَيْنِ.

Circumference of the eye, مَحْجِرُ ٱلْعَيْنِ.

Coats or tunics of the eye, طَبَقَاتُ ٱلْعَيْنِ.

Dry matter from the eye, غَمَصُ ٱلْعَيْنِ.

Fluid matter from the eye, رَمَصُ ٱلْعَيْنِ.

Inner corner of the eye, مَأْقُ ٱلْعَيْنِ ـ ٱلْمَأْقُ, *dual* مَاقَانِ *pl.* أَمَاق.

Intense whiteness of the white and intense blackness of the pupil of the eye, حَوَرُ ٱلْعَيْنِ.

Outer corner of the eye, لَحْظُ ٱلْعَيْنِ ـ لِحَاظُ ٱلْعَيْنِ *dual* لَحْظَانِ *pl.* أَلْحَاظ.

Pupil of the eye, بُؤْبُؤ (or) إِنْسانُ or ناظِرُ ٱلْعَيْنِ.

Slit of the eye, مَشَقُّ ٱلْعَيْنِ.

Having an evil eye, حَمِيُّ ٱلْعَيْنِ. An evil eye, نَظْرَة — لَغْطَة.

Having beautiful eyes, أَبْرَجُ fem. بَرْجاءُ pl. بُرْجٌ.

Having black eyes, أَدْعَجُ fem. دَعْجاءُ pl. دُعْجٌ.

Having contracted or small eyes, أَحْوَصُ fem. حَوْصاءُ pl. حُوصٌ — ذُو حَوَصٍ.

Having large eyes, أَجْحَمُ fem. جَحْماءُ pl. جُحْمٌ.

Having one eye only, أَعْوَرُ fem. عَوْراءُ pl. عُورانٌ and عِيرانٌ.

Having sore eyes, أَغْمَصُ fem. غَمْصاءُ pl. غُمْصٌ.

Having squinting eyes, أَحْوَلُ — أَزْغَلُ fem. زَغْلاءُ pl. زُغْلٌ.

Having weak eyes, أَعْمَشُ fem. عَمْشاءُ pl. عُمْشٌ.

To be fixed, as of the eyes, in death, شَقَّ. The eyes of the dying man were fixed, شَخَصَ (or) شَقَّ بَصَرُ ٱلْمَيِّتِ.

To cast an eye over, to read over, هَذَّ — أَلْقَى ٱلنَّظَرَ عَلَى.

To fix the eyes upon, لَتَأَ إِلَى — أَمْعَنَ ٱلنَّظَرَ فِي — شَخَصَ بِبَصَرِهِ إِلَى.

To give an eye to, تَقَيَّدَ عَلَى — أَلْقَى ٱلنَّظَرَ عَلَى.

To have an eye to, to aim at, سَعَى إِلَى — تَعَمَّدَ — تَنَوَّى.

To have one's eyes about one, تَنَبَّهَ عَلَى — تَذَرَّبَ.

To hide the eyes from, سَتَرَ عَيْنَيْهِ عَنْ.

To lift up the eyes, رَفَعَ ٱلْأَعْيُنَ.

To look at, as with a malignant eye, لَطَحَ بِ — لَعَطَ بِ.

To offend the eye, أَسَاءَ ٱلنَّظَرَ.

To pluck out the eye, بَخَصَ (or) بَخَزَ or عَوَّرَ or فَقَأَ ٱلْعَيْنَ. To have the eye plucked out, إِنْفَقَأَتْ (or) تَفَقَّأَتْ ٱلْعَيْنُ.

To shut the eyes, أَغْمَضَ (or) غَمَّضَ ٱلْعُيُونَ.

To shut the eyes to, غَمِيَ عَنْ — غَمَّضَ عَيْنَهُ عَنْ. To shut the eye to one that he may not notice you, أَغْمَضَ عَلَيْهِ.

To smite with the evil eye, شَزَرَ — إِشْتَشْرَفَ — تَعَيَّنَ.

To turn the eyes from, غَضَّ ٱلنَّظَرَ عَنْ — غَضَّ ٱلطَّرْفَ عَنْ — صَرَفَ ٱلنَّظَرَ عَنْ.

To wipe the eyes, مَسَحَ ٱلْعُيُونَ. To wipe the tears off the eyes, مَسَحَ ٱلدُّمُوعَ عَنِ ٱلْعُيُونِ.

Eye, *v.t.* أَعْيَنَ — نَظَرَ إِلَى — أَبْصَرَ — تَطَلَّعَ إِلَى.

Eyeball, *n.* المُقْلَة — مُقْلَةُ ٱلْعَيْنِ.

Eyebolt, *n.* فُرْضَة pl. فُرَض — خابُور.

Eyebright, *n.* فراسيون. *See also* Euphrasy, *n.*

Eyebrow, *n.* حاجِب pl. حَواجِبُ — رِواقُ ٱلْعَيْنِ. To knit the eyebrows, عَرْقَصَ ٱلْحَواجِبَ. Having sparse eyebrows, أَمْلَطُ ٱلْحاجِبَيْنِ. Having arched eyebrows, أَزَجُّ fem. زَجّاءُ pl. زُجٌّ. Having the eyebrows joined, أَلَفُّ — أَقْرَنُ (or) مَقْرُونُ ٱلْحَواجِبِ.

Eyeglass, *n.* A telescope, نَظّارَة — دُرْبِين. A single spectacle, بِلَّوْرَة نَظّارَة.

Eyelash, *n.* هُدْبُ ٱلْعَيْنِ pl. أَهْداب.

Eyeless, *a.* أَعْمَى fem. عَمْياءُ pl. عُمْيٌ.

Eyelet-hole, *n.* / Eyelet, } عَيْن — فَتْحَة — بَخْش — نَقْب — بَخْش. To make — in, عَيَّنَ —.

Eyelid, *n.* جَفْن pl. أَجْفان. The edge of the —, شُفْرُ ٱلْعَيْنِ. The inner part of the —, حِمْلاقُ ٱلْعَيْنِ. To contract, as of the —, أَغْضَى.

Eye-salve, *n.* كُحْل. To anoint the eyes with —, كَحَلَ ٱلْعُيُونَ (or) ٱلْأَعْيُنَ.

Eye-service, *n.* خِدْمَةُ ٱلْعَيْنِ — خِدْمَةُ ٱلْأَجِيرِ.

Eyeshot, *n.* مَدَى ٱلْبَصَرِ.

Eyesight, *n.* بَصَر — نَظَر — نَظَران. *See also* Eyeshot, *n.*

Eyesore, *n.* كُرْه — كَراهِيَة — قَذًى فِي ٱلْعَيْنِ.

Eye-string, *n.* لِيفَةُ ٱلْعَيْنِ pl. أَلْيَاف.

Eye-tooth, *n.* ناب pl. أَنْيَاب and نُيُوب.

Eye-witness, *n.* شاهِد — مُعايِن. We know it from having been eye-witness to it, تَحَقَّقَ لَدَيْنا بِٱلْمُشاهَدَةِ.

Eyre, *n.* دَوْر — دائِرَة.

Eyry, *n.* وَكْرُ (or) عُشُّ ٱلنَّسْرِ.

F.

Fabaceous, *a.* مِنْ فَصِيلَةِ ٱلْفُولِ.

Fabian, *n.* Delaying, مُتَأَخِّر. Cautious, cowardly, خَشْل — جَبَّان — مُتَحَفِّظ — فَشِل — فَشْل.

Fable, *n.* A story with a moral, مَثَل — أَحَادِيثُ *pl.* حَدِيث — أَمْثَال *pl.* A legend, أُسْطُورَة *pl.* أَسَاطِيرُ — حَدِيث *pl.* أَحَادِيثُ — خُرَافَة *pl.* خُرَافَات — حِدِّيثَى. Fables, foolish tales, رُطَزَات — خُزَعْبَلَات — خُرَافَات. A lie, كَذْب. Old wives fables, الخُرافاتُ ٱلْعَجَائِزِيَّة. A teller of fables or stories, رَجُل حَدُوث — رَجُل — حِدِّيث — مُحَدِّث.

Fable, *v.t.* To invent stories, أَحْدَثَ ٱلْأَحَادِيثَ. To devise, إِخْتَرَعَ — أَحْدَثَ.

Fable, *v.i.* To tell stories, إِقْتَصَّ — تَحَدَّثَ. To lie, كَذَبَ.

Fabler, *n.* رَجُل حِدِّيث.

Fabric, *n.* A building, عِمَارَة — بِنَآء. Structure, form, هَيْئَة — تَرْكِيب — تَرْتِيب — مَجْمُوع. Cloth, especially cotton, قُمَاش *pl.* أَقْمِشَة.

Fabricate, *v.t.* To construct, صَنَعَ — بَنَى. To weave, نَسَجَ. To invent, أَنْشَأَ — اِبْتَدَعَ — إِخْتَرَعَ. To — falsely, to forge, إِخْتَرَعَ-بَاطِلًا — سَطَّرَ. To — a lie, إِفْتَرَى كَذِبًا. To — a lie against one, إِفْتَرَى عَلَى-كَذِبًا.

Fabrication, *n.* The act of building, بِنَآء; of constructing, إِنْتِصَاص — إِنْشَآء — تَرْكِيب — تَعْمِير; of weaving, نَسْج. A forgery, fiction, بِدْعَة — فِرْيَة — إِفْتِرَآء — إِخْتِرَاعٌ بَاطِلٌ. Lies, fables, أَسَاطِيرُ.

Fabricator, *n.* A builder, constructor, صَانِع — مِعْمَار — بَانٍ. A forger, مُخْتَرِع — صَاحِبُ بِدْعَةٍ; of lies, a defamer, فَرِيٌّ — مُفْتَرٍ — مِفْرَى.

Fabulist, *n.* مُصَنِّفُ ٱلْأَمْثَالِ — مُؤَلِّفُ ٱلْأَحَادِيثِ.

Fabulous, *a.* Feigned, invented, تَصْنِيفِيٌّ — أَسَاطِيرِيٌّ — خُرَافِيٌّ — مِنْ قَبِيلِ ٱلْأَكَاذِيبِ وَٱلْأَسَاطِيرِ.

Fabulously, *ad.* تَزْوِيرًا — تَخَرُّفًا — إِخْتِرَافًا.

Façade, *n.* واجِهَة — وَجْه *pl.* وُجُوه.

Face, *n.* Visage, طَلْعَة — مَنْظَر — وَجْه *pl.* وُجُوه *vulg.* وِش. Appearance, هَيْئَة — مَنْظَر — صُورَة. Superficies, أَدِيم — سَطْح. Mien, سِيمَآء — صُورَة — شَكْل — مَرْآة. Side, surface, صَفْحَة *pl.* صَفَحَات — صَفِيحَة — وَجْهَة. State, as of affairs, كَيْفِيَّة — مَاهِيَّة — حال. Boldness, شَجَاعَة — حَمَاسَة — جُرْأَة — جَسَارَة. brazen —, وَجْهٌ بَلِيطٌ — سَفِيه. Having a distorted —, صَعِر. Having two faces, as a cloth, مُوَجَّه — وَجِيه; hypocritical, مُرَآء *pl.* مُرَاؤُونَ — مُنَافِق. Face to —, مُوَاجَهَةً. I saw him — to —, نَظَرْتُهُ وَجْهًا لِوَجْهٍ. I spoke to him — to —, كَلَّمْتُهُ مُشَافَهَةً — كَلَّمْتُهُ فَمًا لِفَم. The accused was — to — with his accusers, كَانَ ٱلْمَشْكُوُّ عَلَيْهِ مُوَاجَهَةً مَعَ ٱلْمُشْتَكِينَ. He looked at his — in the water, تَرَآءَى فِي ٱلْمَآءِ. In the — of, before, أَمَامَ — فِي حَضْرَةِ; in opposition to, مُعَانَدَةً — مُقَاوَمَةً — عَلَى إِكْرَاهِ. Unknown to such an one by —, غَيْرُ مَعْرُوفٍ بِٱلْوَجْهِ عِنْدَ فُلَانٍ. To tell one anything to his —, عَيَّنَ لِ.

To fall on the face, خَرَّ عَلَى وَجْهِهِ.

To hide the face, حَجَبَ وَجْهَهُ.

To make faces, تَلَوْلَقَ — كَشَّرَ وَجْهَهُ — إِخْتَلَجَ بِوَجْهِهِ.

To put a good face on a matter, إِحْتَمَلَ-بِٱلْجَدِّ — تَجَاسَرَ عَلَى.

To set one's face against, جَعَلَ وَجْهَهُ ضِدَّ ٱلشَّيْءِ.

To set one's face to go to, ثَبَّتَ وَجْهَهُ لِيَنْطَلِقَ إِلَى.

To set one's face towards جَعَلَ وَجْهَهُ نَحْوَ — جَعَلَ وَجْهَهُ إِلَى — ضَرَبَ إِلَى.

To smite, as on the face, لَطَمَ — لَطَحَ — لَطَشَ.

To turn black in the face, إِسْوَدَّ لَوْنُهُ.

To turn pale in the face, إِصْفَرَّ.

To turn red in the face, إِحْمَرَّ لَوْنُ وَجْهِهِ.

To turn the face from, صَدَّ عَن — وَلَّى عَن-بِوَجْهِهِ — فَتَلَ عَن.

To withstand to the face, قَاوَمَ-مُوَاجَهَةً.

Face, *v.t.* To stand opposite to, وَاجَهَ — قَابَلَ — جَابَى — جَايَا. To oppose, تَعَرَّضَ لِ — قَاوَمَ — إِعْتَرَضَ. To put a facing on, طَبَّقَ-عَلَى — لَبَّسَ-بِ — خَصَفَ. To — danger, إِقْتَحَمَ — خَاضَ ٱلْأَخْطَارَ — ٱلْأَخْطَارَ. To — about, أَدَارَ ٱلْوَجْهَ. They were facing each other, were — to —, of many, تَنَاظَرُوا. The house faces the square, ٱلْبَيْتُ تُجَاهَ (or وُجَاهَ) ٱلْمَيْدَانِ. He faced him, was opposite to him, جَايَاهُ.

Faced, *a.* Having faces or sides, مُصَفَّح — مُضَفَّح.

Facet, *n.* رُكْن *pl.* أَرْكَان — وُجَيْه — صُفَيْق — سُنَيْنَة — دُفَيْفَة. Cut in facets, مُحَرَّف — مُرَكَّن — مُقَرَّن.

Facetiæ, *n.* هُزالات ـ مَلاحات ـ لَطائف.

Facetious, *a.* لَطِيف ـ مُهَرِّج ـ مُسْخِر ـ دَعّاب ـ داعِب ـ مُضْحِك ـ مَلِيح. To be —, هَزَلَ ـ دَعَبَ ـ مَزَحَ.

Facetiously, *ad.* مَزْحًا ـ هَزْلًا ـ بِلَطافَةٍ ـ بِمَلاحَةٍ.

Facetiousness, *n.* لَطافَة ـ دُعابَة ـ مِزاح ـ هَزْل.

Facial, *a.* مُتَعَلِّق بِٱلْوَجْهِ ـ وَجْهِيّ. The — angle, زاوِيَةُ ٱلْوَجْهِ.

Facile, *a.* Easy, هَيِّن ـ أَهْوَن ـ سَهْل. Of — disposition, سَهْل ـ مُلائِم ـ لَيِّنُ ٱلْجانِبِ ـ ٱلْخُلْق. *See also* Easy, *a.*

Facilitate, *v.t.* قَدَّرَ ـ هَوَّنَ ـ يَسَّرَ ـ سَهَّلَ. To — to one, قَدَّرَ عَلَى ـ هَوَّنَ عَلَى ـ أَسْمَحَ لِ.

Facilitation, *n.* تَيْسِير ـ تَسْهِيل.

Facility, *n.* Ease, هَوْن ـ سُهُولَة ـ هَيْئَة. Dexterity, إِسْتِعْداد ـ نَشاط ـ شَطارَة ـ حِذْق. Facility, as in speech, فَصاحَة ـ سُهُولَة. Affability, لِين ـ رِفْق ـ أَفْضال ـ مُسامَحَة. Facilities, تَسَهُّل ـ تَسْهِيلات.

Facing, *n.* The part that is before or opposite, صَدَد ـ حِذاء ـ دُهْنَة. A covering, إِسْتار ـ غِطاء ـ كِساء. A coating, قُبالَة. A — on a soldier's coat, عَلَمٌ مُلَوَّنٌ عَلَى أَكْمام *pl.* أَعْلام ـ تَلْبِيس. The military movement, تَحْوِيلُ ٱلْوَجْهِ ـ بَدْلَةُ ٱلْعَسْكَرِ وَأَطْرافِها وَرِتْبَتِها.

Facing, *a.* Opposite, مُقابِل ـ ناظِر ـ تُجاهَ ـ وُجاهَ. *See also* Opposite, *a.*

Fac-simile, *n.* عَيْن ـ تَقْلِيد ـ طِبْق ـ تَقْلِيدٌ عَيْنًا.

Fact, *n.* A deed, فِعْل *pl.* أَفْعال ـ واقِعَة ـ حادِثَة *pl.* حَوادِث ـ قَضِيَّة *pl.* قَضايا ـ كائِنَة. The thing particularly alluded to, المَصْلَحَة ـ الأَمْر. Reality, حَقِيقَة. A matter of —, واقِع ـ جَهْرَة ـ أَمْرٌ أَعْرَف. A known —, أَمْرٌ حَقِيقِيّ ـ أَمْرٌ مُحَقَّق ـ حَقًّا ـ فِي ٱلْواقِعِ. Contrary to —, ضِدُّ ٱلْواقِعِ. In —, جِدًّا ـ حَقِيقَةً. But the — is, إِلَّا أَنَّ ٱلْواقِعَ هُوَ. To state a —, بَيَّنَ ـ ٱلْواقِعَ. Matter of —, of a person, صاحِبُ جِدٍّ ـ جِدِّيّ. That was an accomplished —, دَخَلَ فِي خَبَرِ كانَ. *See also* Act, *n.*

Faction, *n.* A party, حِزْب *pl.* أَحْزاب ـ فِرْقَة *pl.* فِرَق ـ عُصْبَة. Dissension, revolt, شَغْب ـ فِتْنَة ـ فَساد.

Factionist, *n.* مُفْسِد ـ أَهْلُ فَسادٍ ـ فَتّان ـ مُتَعَصِّب عَلَى ـ عاصٍ *pl.* عُصاة.

Factious, *a.* Quarrelsome, أَلَدّ *pl.* لُدّ *and* لِداد ـ شِرِّير ـ شَرِس ـ شَكِس. *See also* Factionist, *n.*

Factiously, *ad.* بِلَدَدٍ ـ بِفِتْنَةٍ وَفَسادٍ ـ بِتَجَسُّس.

Factiousness, *n.* Quarrelsomeness, لَدَد ـ شَراسَة ـ شَكاسَة. *See also* Faction, *n.*

Factitious, *a.* Artificial, صِناعِيّ ـ مُصَنَّع ـ إِصْطِناعِيّ ـ عَمَلِيّ.

Factitiously, *ad.* صُنْعًا ـ عَمَلًا ـ تَقْلِيدًا ـ إِصْطِناعًا.

Facto, *a.* A *de facto* government, حُكُومَةٌ فاعِلَة ـ حُكُومَةٌ جارِيَة.

Factor, *n.* An agent, عامِل *pl.* عُمّال ـ جَرِيّ *pl.* أَجْرِياء ـ وَكِيل *pl.* وُكَلاء ـ مُتَصَرِّف. A —, in arithmetic, أَصْلُ ٱلْحاصِلِ. The two factors, المَضْرُوبانِ. A broker, سِمْسار *pl.* سَماسِرَة ـ دَلّال.

Factorage, *n.* وَكالَة ـ أُجْرَة ـ سَمْسَرَة ـ دِلالَة.

Factory, *n.* An inn of merchants, خانُ تُجّارٍ. A manufactory, مَعْمَل.

Factotum, *n.* كَتْخُدا ـ كَتْخُدای.

Faculty, *n.* Ability, قابِلِيَّة ـ طاقَة ـ قُدْرَة ـ مُكْنَة ـ قُوَّة. Dexterity, حِذْق ـ خِفَّة ـ مَعْرِفَة; of the mind, قَرِيحَة ـ عَقْل ـ دِرايَة ـ فِطْنَة ـ قُوَّةٌ ذِهْنِيَّة. Efficacy, quality, فاعِلِيَّة ـ خاصِّيَّة. Authority, مَقْدِرَة ـ سُلْطَة. A privilege, حَقّ ـ مِنْحَة ـ شَأْن. A property, خاصَّة ـ خاصِّيَّة. The faculties of the soul, قُوَى ٱلنَّفْسِ. A corps of savants, جَماعَةٌ مِنَ ٱلْعُلَماءِ. A body of professional men, مُعَلِّمُوا فَنٍّ ـ أَرْبابُ صِنْفٍ.

Dean of a faculty, رَئِيسُ صِنْفٍ (*or* فَنٍّ).

Faculty of Medicine, الطِّبّ (صِنْفُ *or*) فَنُّ.

Faculty of Arts, صِنْفُ ٱلْفُنُونِ ٱلْأَدَبِيَّةِ وَٱلْحِكَمِيَّةِ.

The faculty of hearing, القُوَّةُ ٱلسّامِعَةُ.

The faculty of judging, خاصَّةُ ٱلْإِدْراكِ وَٱلتَّمْيِيزِ.

The faculty of seeing, القُوَّةُ ٱلْباصِرَةُ.

The faculty of speech, خاصَّةُ ٱلنُّطْقِ وَٱلْكَلامِ.

Facund, *a.* Of speech, بَلِيغ ـ صاحِبُ كَلامٍ ـ فَصِيح.

Facundity, *n.* سُهُولَةُ ٱلْكَلامِ ـ بَلاغَة ـ فَصاحَة.

Faddle, *v.i.* عَبِثَ ـ تَهابَلَ.

Fade, *v.i.* To wither, فَنِيَ ـ ذَبَلَ ـ ذَوَى ـ يَبِسَ *aor.* يَيْبَس ـ نَشَفَ ـ فَتَرَ. To grow weak, ضَعُفَ ـ تَضَعَّفَ ـ. To lose colour, خَسَفَ ـ نَحُفَ ـ عَجِفَ ـ عَجَزَ ـ. إِنْكَشَفَ ٱللَّوْنُ ـ تَفَسَّخَ (*or* إِنْفَسَخَ) لَوْنُهُ ـ زالَ (*or* فَسِخَ) ٱللَّوْنُ. To cause to —, of colour, فَسَّخَ. I fear its colour will —, أَخافُ مِنْ فَسْخِ لَوْنِهِ. We all — as the leaf, نَذْبُلُ كَوَرَقَةٍ. Faded, رَمِد ـ فاسِخ ـ أَرْمَدُ. A faded garment, ثَوْبٌ فاسِخٌ.

Fadeless, *a.* غَيْرُ زائِلٍ ـ لا يَذْبُلُ.

Fading, *a.* زائِل ـ فانٍ; of colour, مُتَفَسِّخ ـ فاسِخ.

Fæcal, *a.* *See* Fecal, *a.*

Fæces, *n.* Settlings, رُسُوب. Excrement, غائِط ـ بِراز ـ دِمْن ـ خَرْء.

Fag, *v.t.* To make to drudge, سَخَّرَ ـ أَكَلَّ ـ عَسَفَ. To be fagged, tired, تَعِبَ ـ تَعَيًا ـ أَعْيا ـ كَلَّ ـ يَتْنِين *aor.* آنَ.

Fag, *v.i.* To strive, سَعَى ـ كَدَّ [2].

Fag, *n.* مُسَخَّر.

Fag-end, *n.* As of a rope, جِذْقَة. Refuse, حُثَالَة. The coarse end of a web of cloth, حَاشِيَةُ ٱلْقُمَاشِ.

Fagot, *n.* As of sticks, جُرْزَةٌ وَقُودٍ *pl.* جُرَز ـ حِزْمَةٌ وَقِيدٍ ـ حِزْمَةُ حَطَبٍ.

Fagot, *v.t.* حَزَمَ ـ شَدَّ [2].

Fail, *v.i.* To become deficient, نَقَصَ [2] ـ قَلَّ [2]; as water from a well, *etc.*, إِنْقَطَعَ. To cease, إِنْقَطَعَ ـ إِنْتَهَى. To perish, فَنِيَ ـ تَلَاشَى ـ زَالَ [2]. To vanish away, نَفِدَ. To languish, ضَعُفَ [2] ـ نَحُفَ [2] ـ عَجِفَ ـ أَعْيَى. Not to succeed, أَخَلَّ بِ ـ خَابَ ـ تَقَصَّرَ فِي ـ أَقْصَرَ عَن ـ قَصَّرَ ـ قَصَرَ عَن [2] ـ قَصَّرَ فِي ـ لَمْ يَنْجَحْ. To become bankrupt, أَفْلَسَ ـ إِنْكَسَرَ. His heart failed him, ذَهَبَ فُؤَادُهُ. His sword failed in its effect, خَانَ [2] سَيْفُهُ. They did not — to keep the feast, مَا زَالُوا يُعَيِّدُونَ. Silver failed from the country, فَرِغَتِ ٱلْبِلَادُ مِنَ ٱلْفِضَّةِ. He failed to carry out his duty, قَصَّرَ فِي إِجْرَاءِ ٱلْوَاجِبِ عَلَيْهِ.

Fail, *v.t.* To neglect or desert, أَهْجَرَ ـ تَرَكَ [2] ـ أَهْمَلَ. He will not — you, لَا يُهْمِلُكَ. Time would — me were I to tell of..., يُعْوِزُنِي ٱلْوَقْتُ إِنْ أَخْبَرْتُ عَن ....

Fail, *n.* قُصُور ـ خَيْبَة ـ عَدَمُ حُصُولٍ. Without —, ٱلْبَتَّةَ ـ عَلَى كُلِّ حَالٍ ـ لَا جَرَمَ. He will drive him out without —, طَرْدًا يَطْرُدُهُ. Day by day without —, يَوْمًا فَيَوْمًا بِلَا ٱنْقِطَاعٍ.

Failing, *n.* The act of coming short, إِنْقِطَاع ـ قُصُور. Weakness, imperfection, خَسِيفَة ـ نَقِيصَة ـ عَيْب ـ قُصُور. A bad habit, مَخْزِيَة *pl.* مَخْزِيَات ـ خَزْيَة ـ عَادَةٌ رَدِيَّةٌ ـ قَبَاحَة.

Failing, *a.* مُضْمَحِلّ ـ فَانٍ ـ زَائِل.

Failing, *ad.* In the place of, فِي مَقَام ـ مَكَانَ ـ عِوَضًا عَن.

Failure, *n.* Cessation of supply, إِنْقِطَاع ـ قُطُوع. Want of success, خُسْرَان ـ عَدَمُ حُصُولٍ ـ خَيْبَة ـ فَشَل. Destitution, إِنْقِرَاض. Insolvency, كَسْرَة ـ فَلَس. *See also* Failing, *n.*

Fain, *a.* Glad, سَارّ ـ فَرِح. Wishful, مُشْتَاقٌ إِلَى. He would — have..., نَافَسَ فِي ـ تَنَافَسَ فِي ـ إِشْتَهَى أَن ـ تَمَنَّى أَن.

Fain, *ad.* بِفَرَحٍ ـ بِكُلِّ ٱشْتِهَاءٍ. I would — be...; would that I...! يَا لَيْتَنِي.

Faint, *a.* Languid, كَاهِل ـ مُعْيٍ *fem.* مُعْيِيَة *pl.* مَعَايَى *and* مَعَايَا ـ نَحِيف ـ مُضْنًى ـ ضَعِيف *vulg.* عَيَّان. In a swoon, مَغْشِيّ ـ مُغْمًى عَلَيْهِ. Not clear, indistinct, خَفِيفُ ٱلْبَيَانِ ـ رَكِيك. Not loud, خَفِيّ ـ رَقِيق ـ خَفِيض. Not clear to the sight, مُبْهَم ـ خَفِيّ ـ غَيْرُ بَيِّنٍ ـ غَيْرُ مُظْهَرٍ. Not vigorous, فَاتِر ـ بَارِد.

Faint, *v.i.* To swoon, غُشِيَ عَلَيْهِ ـ أُغْمِيَ عَلَيْهِ. To —, from languor, as of a sick person, غُمِيَ ـ أُغْمِيَ. To sink with fatigue, تَلَاشَى ـ أَعْيَا ـ إِضْمَحَلَّ ـ إِنْزَهَلَ ـ إِنْكَسَرَ. Lest they — by the way, لِئَلَّا يَخُورُوا فِي ٱلطَّرِيقِ. *See also to* Swoon, *v.i.*

Faint-hearted, *a.* ضَعِيفُ ٱلْقَلْبِ ـ خَائِف ـ فَشِل. To be —, فَشِلَ.

Faint-heartedly, *ad.* بِضُعْفِ قَلْبٍ ـ بِفَشَلٍ ـ بِجَبَانَةٍ.

Faint-heartedness, *n.* فَشَل ـ خَوْف ـ ضُعْفُ قَلْبٍ ـ جَبَانَة.

Fainting, *n.* A swoon, غَشْي ـ غَشْيَة. A — from languor or sickness, إِغْمَاء. A breaking down, إِضْمِحْلَال ـ تَلَاشٍ ـ إِنْكِسَار. A fit of —, غَشْيَان ـ غَشْيَة.

Faintish, *a.* مِنْ بَابِ ٱلْغَشَيَانِ ـ غَمِّيّ.

Faintly, *ad.* Coldly, negligently, بِبُرُودَةٍ ـ بِرَخَاوَةٍ ـ بِتَهَاوُلٍ ـ بِفُتُورٍ ـ بِٱلتَّكَاسُلِ. Weakly, بِضُعْفٍ ـ بِكَلَالٍ. Timidly, بِفَشَلٍ ـ جَبَانَةً ـ مَخَافَةً. Not distinct, إِبْهَامًا.

Faintness, *n.* Languor, كَلّ ـ كَلَال ـ إِعْيَاء ـ فَتَر ـ ضُعْف. Timidity, ضُعْفُ قَلْبٍ ـ فَشَل ـ خَوْف. Lightness of colour, بَيَاض ـ رِقَّة ـ قِلَّة. Indistinctness, as of colour, *etc.*, رَكَاكَة ـ بَيَانٍ ـ بُهْمَة.

Fair, *a.* Beautiful, بَهِيج ـ جَمِيل ـ حَسِين ـ ظَرِيف ـ أَنِيق. White, as in complexion, أَبْيَض *fem.* بَيْضَاء. Clear, صَافٍ ـ شَفَّاف. Pleasing to the eye or mind, جَيِّد ـ حَسَن ـ خَيِّر ـ مَرْضِيّ ـ كَيِّس ـ مَلِيح ـ طَيِّب. Not cloudy, صَاحٍ ـ صَحْو ـ صَافٍ. Equitable, عَدِل ـ سَوِيّ ـ مُسْتَوٍ ـ مُسْتَقِيم. Candid, مُقْسِط ـ أَمِين ـ خَالِص. Favourable, as of a wind, مُوَافِق ـ مُسَاعِد ـ طَيِّب ـ عَدِل. Sufficient, وَافٍ ـ كَافٍ. Sweet, gentle, عَذْب ـ حَلِيّ ـ حُلْو. Civil, لَطِيف ـ ظَرِيف. Fit, proper, مُنَاسِب ـ مُوَافِق. A — bargain, شَرْطٌ مُعْتَدِلٌ ـ مُبَايَعَةٌ مُعْتَدِلَةٌ. A — demeanour, أَدَب ـ إِنْسَانِيَّة. Fair weather, طَقْسٌ صَحْوٌ. He is in a — way to succeed, هُوَ فِي سَبِيلِ ٱلنَّجَاحِ. Her younger sister is fairer than she, أُخْتُهَا ٱلصَّغِيرَةُ أَحْسَنُ مِنْهَا. To be fair (weather), صَحَا [2] ـ أَصْحَى. By — means or foul, طَوْعًا أَوْ كَرْهًا ـ بِٱلطِّيبِ أَوْ بِٱلْغَصْبِ ـ بِٱلرِّضَاءِ أَوْ بِٱلْغَصْبِ.

Fair, *n.* A stated market, سُوق *pl.* أَسْوَاق ـ مَوْسِم *pl.* مَوَاسِمُ. A handsome woman, عَيْطَمُوس *pl.* عَطَامِيس ـ إِمْرَأَةٌ لَطِيفَةٌ ـ إِمْرَأَةٌ بَارِعَةٌ فِي ٱلْجَمَالِ ـ ٱلشَّمَائِلِ. The female sex, ٱلنِّسَاء.

Fair, *ad.* } Appropriately, بِمُنَاسَبَةٍ ـ بِمُوَافَقَةٍ ـ حَسَنًا.
Fairly, } Honestly, بِخُلُوصٍ ـ بِصَدَاقَةٍ ـ بِصَفَاءٍ ـ حَقًّا.

بِٱلسَّوِيَّةِ – بِقَ . Without violence, بِدُونِ عَكْسٍ – طَوْعًا –
بِٱلطَّ. Completely, بِكَمالٍ – تَمَامًا – بَتَّةً – تَكْمِيلًا . Gently,
عَلَى مَهْلٍ – رُوَ . To act —, أَقْسَطَ – قَسَطَ = – اِقْتَصَدَ فِي –
اِسْتَوَى – = قَصَدَ . To act — by, تَوَثَّبَ بِ – أَحْسَنَ بِ.

Fairness, *n.* Beauty, جَمَالٌ – حُسْنٌ – طَرَافَةٌ – بَهْجَةٌ . Candour,
قِسْـ – اِسْتِقَامَةٌ – خُلُوصٌ – صَفَآءٌ – صَلَاحٌ – أَمَانَةٌ . Justice,
عَدْ . Whiteness, بَيَاضٌ.

Fair-spoken, *a.* حُلْوُ ٱللِّسَانِ – عَذْبُ ٱلْكَلَامِ.

Fairy, *n.* عَيْهَرَةٌ – شَهَامٌ – جِنِّيَّةٌ *pl.* سِعْلَاةٌ – سَعَالٍ . The fairies, ٱلسَّعَالِي.

Fairy, *a.* مُتَعَلِّقٌ بِٱلْجِنِّ . Fairy tales, قِصَصُ ٱلْجِنِّيَّاتِ . Fairy land, عَبْقَرٌ.

Fairy-like, *a.* مِثْلُ ٱلسِّحْرِ – مِثْلُ صَنْعِ ٱلْجِنِّ.

Faith, *n.* Belief, إِيمَانٌ – اِعْتِمَادٌ . Trust, confidence, عُمْدَةٌ –
عِمَادٌ – وَثِيقَةٌ – ثِقَةٌ – اِعْتِمَادٌ – اِسْتِنَادٌ . A religion, creed,
دِينٌ *pl.* أَدْيَانٌ – مَذْهَبٌ *pl.* مَذَاهِبُ – إِيمَانٌ . Fidelity,
أَمَانَةٌ – وَفَآءٌ – اِسْتِقَامَةٌ – صِدْقٌ . A promise, وَعْدٌ – عَهْدٌ –
قَوْلٌ . An article of the —, قَاعِدَةُ ٱلْإِيمَانِ – عَقِيدَةٌ *pl.* عَقَائِدُ .
To have —, confidence, in, اِعْتَمَدَ عَلَى ; to believe in, صَدَّقَ –
آمَنَ بِ . To give — to, to believe in, صَدَّقَ – فِي *or* بِ *or* عَلَى .
To break one's —, = نَقَضَ عَهْدَهُ . To act in good — towards,
اِسْتَنَامَ إِلَى . In good —, حَقًّا . Unshaken —, اِعْتِمَادٌ كُلِّيٌّ .
Unspotted —, integrity, اِسْتِقَامَةٌ كُلِّيَّةٌ . On my —! وَدِينِي –
عَلَى ذِمَّتِي . In — whereof, تَقْرِيرًا وَشَهَادَةً بِذٰلِكَ.

Faithful, *a.* Firm in adherence to the truths of religion, مُؤْمِنٌ
pl. مُؤْمِنُونَ – أَهْلُ إِيمَانٍ – مُعْتَقِدٌ . Of true fidelity, صَادِقٌ –
مُسْتَقِيمٌ – ذُو وَفَآءٍ – صَالِحٌ – أَمِينٌ . Conformable to truth, صَحِيحٌ –
حَقِيقِيٌّ – مَضْبُوطٌ . The body of the —, ٱلْمُؤْمِنُونَ *fem.* ٱلْمُؤْمِنَاتُ.

Faithfully, *ad.* Believingly, تَصْدِيقًا – بِإِيمَانٍ – اِعْتِقَادًا .
Truly, loyally, بِأَمَانَةٍ – بِوَفَآءٍ – صِدْقًا – بِٱسْتِقَامَةٍ – بِصَلَاحٍ .
Completely, تَمَامًا – تَكْمِيلًا – بَتَّةً . With perfect confidence,
بِٱتِّكَالٍ كُلِّيٍّ . To deal —, = عَمِلَ بِأَمَانَةٍ . To deal — with,
خَالَصَ – صَافَى . To speak —, تَكَلَّمَ بِٱلْحَقِّ.

Faithfulness, *n.* Belief, إِيمَانٌ . Trust, تَوَكُّلٌ – اِتِّكَالٌ . Integrity, صَدَاقَةٌ – اِسْتِقَامَةٌ – صَلَاحٌ – أَمَانَةٌ . Correctness, صِحَّةٌ –
ضَبْطٌ . With all —, fidelity, بِكُلِّ أَمَانَةٍ.

Faithless, *a.* Without belief, كَافِرٌ *pl.* كُفَّارٌ – زِنْدِيقٌ *pl.* زَنَادِقَةٌ –
مُلْحِدٌ – غَيْرُ مُؤْمِنٍ . Perfidious, خَاتِرٌ – غِدِّيرٌ – غَدَّارٌ – خَائِنٌ .
Vacillating, فَرَّارٌ – نَوِسٌ – فَائِلُ ٱلرَّأْيِ – قَلِقٌ . False to duty,
عَدِيمُ ٱلْوَفَآءِ . Unchaste, untrue, عَدِيمُ ٱلْعِفَّةِ وَٱلصَّدَاقَةِ.

Faithlessly, *ad.* Without belief, بِٱلْحَادٍ – بِزَنْدَقَةٍ – بِكُفْرٍ .
Perfidiously, بِخِيَانَةٍ – بِغَدْرٍ . Without respect to duty, بِعَدَمِ
وَفَآءٍ . Unchastely, بِعَدَمِ عِفَّةٍ . To act — to, غَدَرَ = – غَدَرَ بِ =.

Faithlessness, *n.* Unbelief, كُفْرٌ – زَنْدَقَةٌ – إِلْحَادٌ . Perfidy, خَتْرٌ –
خُتُورٌ – خِيَانَةٌ – غَدْرٌ – نَكْثُ ٱلْعَهْدِ . Disregard of duty, عَدَمُ
وَفَآءٍ . Unchastity and falseness, عَدَمُ ٱلْعِفَّةِ وَٱلصَّدَاقَةِ.

Fake, *n.* A coil of a rope, مِكْوَرَةُ حِبَالٍ – تَوْشِيعُ حِبَالٍ.

Fakir, *n.* فَقِيرٌ *pl.* فُقَرَآءُ – دَرْوِيشٌ *pl.* دَرَاوِيشُ.

Falcate, *a.* } In the form of a scythe, بِصُورَةِ ٱلْمِنْجَلِ . Crescent-
Falcated, } shaped, مُهَلَّلٌ.

Falchion, *n.* حُسَامٌ – سَيْفٌ – يَطَقَانٌ.

Falcon, *n.* بَازٌ *or* بَازٍ *pl.* بُزَاةٌ – بَازِيٌّ – كُرَّزٌ . A large white or
royal —, شَاهِينٌ *pl.* شَوَاهِينُ . A falcon's perch, نُقَّازٌ . To hunt
with a —, تَصَقَّرَ.

Falconer, *n.* بَيْزَارٌ – صَقَّارٌ.

Falconet, *n.* مِدْفَعٌ صَغِيرٌ.

Falconry, *n.* تَصَقُّرٌ – صَنْعَةُ ٱلْبَيْزَارِ.

Fall, *v.i.* To drop from a higher to a lower place, سَقَطَ [2] –
طَرَّ – خَرَّ [2] – = وَقَعَ [2] *aor.* يَقَعُ . To —, as of a wall, قَعِفَ = –
هَبَطَ = [2] ; as a leaf from a tree, اِنْتَثَرَ ; as words from the mouth,
سَقَطَ [2] – تَفَوَّهَ بِ . To apostatize, كَفَرَ = – أَلْحَدَ – اِرْتَدَّ عَنِ
ٱلدِّينِ . To come to an end, فَنِيَ = – زَالَ [2] . To die, to be put to
death, مَاتَ [2] – قُتِلَ . To be degraded, اِنْعَزَلَ – اِنْحَطَّ عَنِ
ٱلْمَرْتَبَةِ . To decrease, قَلَّ [2] – نَقَصَ [2] . To descend, نَزَلَ = . To
ebb, جَزَرَ = – نَقَصَ [2] . To decrease, as in price, هَبَطَ = [2] –
غَاضَ = – رَخُصَ [2] . To be rejected, اِرْتَدَّ – رُفِضَ . To fall, as
of the wind, هَدَأَ = – تَهَدَّأَ – سَكَنَ [2] . To languish, ضَعُفَ [2] –
رَكَّ [2] . To be born, as of lambs, وُلِدَ . The value of Government
paper has fallen, نَزَلَ سِعْرُ ٱلْأَوْرَاقِ ٱلْمَالِيَّةِ = . Railway bonds have
fallen, نَزَلَ سِعْرُ أَوْرَاقِ سِكَّةِ ٱلْحَدِيدِ = . He fell from heaven,
خَرَّ مِنَ ٱلسَّمَآءِ = [2] . He fell prostrate worshipping God, خَرَّ لِلّٰهِ
سَاجِدًا . His countenance fell, سَقَطَ وَجْهُهُ [2] . The wall fell on
them, سَقَطَ ٱلسُّورُ عَلَيْهِمْ [2] . She let her hair — over her shoulders,
أَسْبَلَتْ (or أَرْخَتْ) شَعْرَهَا عَلَى أَكْتَافِهَا . He has fallen from
Scylla into Charybdis, هَرَبَ مِنَ ٱلدُّبِّ وَقَعَ فِي ٱلْجُبِّ = . To
cause to —, to throw down, وَقَّعَ – أَوْقَعَ – أَسْقَطَ – رَمَى = . To
let —, to drop, سَاقَطَ – سَيَّبَ . It fell from my hand, سَلَتَ
مِنْ يَدِي . To threaten to —, as of a wall, اِنْقَضَّ.

To fall a laughing, نَقَعَ مِنَ ٱلضَّحِكِ = [2].

To fall a sacrifice to for one, صَارَ قَتِيلًا لِأَجْلِهِ =.

To fall asleep, رَقَدَ ـ نَامَ.
To fall astern, تَخَلَّفَ.
To fall away, to grow lean, نَحِفَ ـ نَحُفَ. To revolt, مَرَدَ ـ خَرَجَ عَلَى ـ عَصَى عَلَى. To decline from religion, اِرْتَدَّ عَنِ ٱلدِّينِ. To sink into wickedness, خَبُثَ ـ أَخْبَثَ. To languish, نَحِفَ ـ وَنَى aor. يَنِي ـ فَتَرَ. To perish, زَالَ ـ فَنِيَ ـ تَلَاشَى. To fade, as of a colour, خَسَفَ ـ فَسَخَ ٱللَّوْنُ.
To fall back, to recede, أَدْبَرَ ـ تَأَخَّرَ ـ تَخَلَّفَ. To fall back from a promise, نَقَضَ ٱلْوَعْدَ ـ خَانَ ٱلْعَهْدَ.
To fall back upon, to join, اِنْضَمَّ إِلَى ـ لَحِقَ ـ أَلْحَقَ. To rely upon, اِسْتَنَدَ إِلَى ـ اِتَّكَلَ عَلَى.
To fall backwards, سَقَطَ إِلَى ٱلْوَرَآءِ ـ وَقَعَ عَلَى ظَهْرِهِ aor. يَقَعُ.
To fall behind; *see to* Fall back.
To fall below, سَفَلَ ـ وَقَعَ تَحْتُ aor. يَقَعُ.
To fall down, to fall, سَقَطَ ـ وَقَعَ aor. يَقَعُ. To fall down in worship, خَرَّ سَاجِدًا ـ سَجَدَ. Many fell down slain, سَقَطَ كَثِيرُونَ قَتْلَى.
To fall foul of, to collide with, صَدَمَ ـ أَصَابَ ـ صَدَعَ. To contend with, تَصَارَعَ ـ صَارَعَ مَعَ ـ قَاوَمَ.
To fall in, as soldiers into line, اِصْطَفَّ. To tumble down, as of a ceiling, هَبَطَ ـ اِنْخَفَسَ.
To fall in love, عَشِقَ ـ تَعَلَّقَ قَلْبُهُ بِحُبِّ.
To fall in with, to concur, قَابَلَ ـ وَافَقَ. To comply with, قَبِلَ ـ اِرْتَضَى بِ ـ قَابَلَ. To meet, لَاقَى.
To fall into, as a river into the sea, صَبَّ فِي.
To fall into, to be absorbed in, اِنْهَمَكَ فِي ـ غَطَسَ ـ خَاضَ فِي. To fall into reproach, سَقَطَ فِي ٱلتَّعْيِيرِ.
To fall into a passion, اِغْتَاظَ ـ غَضِبَ ـ تَخَلَّقَ ـ ثَارَ غَضَبًا.
To fall into error, زَلَّ ـ أَخْطَأَ ـ غَلِطَ.
To fall off, as a leaf from a tree, اِنْتَثَرَ; as of a bond or chain, تَخَلَّعَ. To be broken off, اِنْقَطَعَ ـ اِنْتَقَضَ. To decrease, قَلَّ ـ اِنْتَقَصَ. To revolt, اِرْتَدَّ. To abandon, تَرَكَ ـ هَجَرَ.
To fall off, as of the hair, اِنْحَصَّ ـ تَحَاتَّ ـ تَسَاقَطَ ـ اِنْحَصَّ.
To fall on, to begin, اِبْتَدَأَ بِ ـ شَرَعَ فِي. To attack, هَجَمَ ـ عَلَى ـ وَقَعَ بِ aor. يَقَعُ. Fall thou on . . . ! دُونَكَ ـ عَلَيْكَ بِ.
To fall out, to quarrel, تَنَازَعَ ـ تَشَاجَرَ ـ تَجَادَلَ ـ تَخَاصَمَ. To happen, حَدَثَ ـ جَرَى ـ وَقَعَ aor. يَقَعُ. To go aside from, تَجَنَّبَ عَن ـ تَنَحَّى عَن ـ طَلَعَ مِن.

To fall over, to be tossed, spilt, اِنْكَبَّ ـ اِنْقَلَبَ.
To fall over to, join, اِتَّحَدَ مَعَ ـ صَاحَبَ ـ اِلْتَصَقَ بِ.
To fall short, to be less than required, نَقَصَ ـ اِنْتَقَصَ. To fall short of doing, أَلَا فِي aor. يَأْلُو ـ أَلَّى فِي ـ قَصَّرَ فِي ـ أَخَلَّ بِ ـ أَجْحَفَ بِ ـ تَخَلَّفَ عَن. He did not fall short in the matter, لَمْ يُقَصِّرْ فِي ٱلْأَمْرِ ـ لَمْ يَأْلُ فِي ٱلْأَمْرِ. He considered him to have fallen short (of his duty), اِسْتَزَادَهُ. He wrote a letter complaining of his having fallen short (of his duty), كَتَبَ إِلَيْهِ كِتَابَ ٱسْتِزَادَةٍ.
To fall suddenly upon, اِعْتَفَقَ ـ هَجَمَ عَلَى ـ اِطَّلَعَ عَلَى ـ طَلَعَ عَلَى.
To fall to, to apply one's self to, لَازَمَ ـ اِجْتَهَدَ فِي. To begin, أَخَذَ فِي ـ شَرَعَ بِ. To fall to one's lot, صَارَ مِنْ نَصِيبِهِ ـ كَانَ حِصَّتَهُ.
To fall through, to come to nothing, خَابَ ـ تَلَاشَى *vulg.* مَا طَلَعَ رَأْسًا.
To fall under, to be subjected to, اِخْتَضَعَ لِ. To be comprehended in, اِنْدَرَكَ فِي ـ تَضَمَّنَ فِي. To become the subject matter of . . . , صَارَ مَادَّةَ (or مَنْشَأَ) آ . . . ـ صَارَ مَوْضُوعَ آ. To be ranged with, اِنْتَسَبَ إِلَى ـ أُعِدَّ مَعَ.
To fall upon, to attack, هَجَمَ عَلَى ـ حَمَلَ عَلَى ـ أَبْرَى بِ ـ اِحْتَمَلَ عَلَى. They fell, stumbled, one upon another, عَثَرُوا بَعْضُهُمْ بِبَعْضٍ.
Fall, *n.* The act of falling or tumbling, وَقْعَة ـ سَقْطَة ـ سِقَاط ـ سُقُوط ـ وُقُوع ـ وَقْع. Overthrow, هَلَاك ـ دَمَار ـ اِنْهِدَام. Downfall, degradation, عَزْل ـ اِنْحِطَاط ـ سُقُوط ـ خَرَاب. Decline of power, اِنْحِطَاطُ ٱلْقُوَّةِ ـ نُقْصَانُ ٱلْقُدْرَةِ ـ ضَعْف. Diminution of value, بَخْس ـ رُخْص. A — of water, مَآء ـ سَلِيلُ ـ اِنْحِدَارُ مَآءٍ ـ اِنْصِبَابُ مَآءٍ. A cataract, شَلَّال pl. شَلَّالَات. The — of the leaf, اِنْتِشَارُ ٱلْوَرَقِ. A —, as of rain or dew, سَقِيط. A — of rain, مَطَر ـ تَقْطِيرُ مَطَرٍ. A declivity, حُدُور ـ حَدَب pl. حِدَاب ـ زُحْلُوقَة ـ صَبَب pl. أَصْبَاب. A —, as into sin, خَطِيئَة ـ زَلَّة ـ زِنَآء. Adultery, هَلَاك ـ تَلَف. Loss, خَسَارَة ـ تَلَف. Emptying, running into, اِنْصِبَاب فِي. Autumn, الخَرِيف. There has been a great — in the Government bonds, عَرَضَ بَخْسٌ فَاحِشٌ عَلَى أَوْرَاقِ مَالِيَّةِ ٱلدَّوْلَةِ. The place of a —, مَسْقَط.
Fallacious, *a.* Delusive, خَدَّاع ـ غَرَّار ـ خَلَّاب. Sophistical, سَفْسَطِيّ.
Fallaciously, *ad.* بِخِدَاعٍ ـ غُرُورًا ـ غِرَّةً ـ اِغْتِرَارًا.

Fallacy, *n.* A delusion, خديعة ـ غواية ـ ضلال ـ أرو ـ غرّ. A sophism, سفسطة ـ سفسطة ـ مغالطة.

Fallen, *a.* Wicked, أشرار *pl.* شرير ـ طالح ـ آثم. A — woman, زانية. Fallen fruit, سقاط. Degraded, سفلي ـ ذليل ـ رذيل. Ruined, مهدوم ـ هلك.

Fallibility, *n.* عرضة للغلط ـ إمكان الغلط.

Fallible, *a.* تحت الغلط ـ قابل الخطاء.

Falling-sickness, *n.* *See* Epilepsy, *n.*

Fallopian, *n.* The — tubes, حاليا الرحم.

Fallow, *a.* Of the colour, غبساء *fem.* أغبس ـ أدريون ـ مزعفر *pl.* غبس. Fallow land, left to rest, أرض مرتاحة. Uncultivated land, أرض بلقع ـ أرض بلا حرث ـ بلقع.

Fallow, *v.t.* To plough, حرث ـ ٢.

Fallow-crop, *n.* المحصول من أرض غير مزروعة.

Fallow-deer, *n.* ضرب من الظباء.

False, *a.* Not true, لا صدق ـ لا أصل له ـ مزور ـ زور ـ كاذب ـ نبه. Unfounded, بلا أصل ـ باطل. Supposititious, بديل ـ رزق ـ بدل ـ بذل. Deceiving expectation, غرار ـ خلاب ـ عارية ـ بذل ـ بدل. Perfidious, خائن ـ خاتر. Hypocritical, مرآء ـ ذو خداع. Counterfeit, مصنوع ـ مموه ـ بهرج ـ ذو لسانين ـ ذو وجهين ـ عملي. A — witness, شاهد زور ; false testimony, كذاب ـ شهادة زور. A — alarm, رجة كاذبة. A — report, خبر كاذب. False money, فلوس زغل ـ دراهم مزيفة. A — key, مفتاح مقلد. A — diamond, ألماس كذاب. False sleeves, أكمام عارية. False hair, شعر عارية ـ واصلة ـ قرزل. A — syllogism, قياس كاذب. A — balance, موازين غش. A — oath, يمين الزور. False apostles, رسل كذبة. They said, it is —, فقالوا أنه كذب.

False, *ad.* Falsely, باطلا ـ بخيانة ـ زورا ـ كذبا. To play one —, to deal falsely by, غدر ب ـ ٢. To swear —, حلف زورا ـ حلف على فجرة. Falsely so called, الكاذب. To speak —, زور كلامه ـ تزور ـ قال باطلا ـ آثم.

False-hearted, *a.* خائن ـ خاتر.

Falsehood, *n.* A lie, زور *pl.* أزوار ـ أكذوبة *pl.* أكاذيب ـ كاذبة. *See also* Falseness, *n.*

False-keel, *n.* سهم قاعدة السفينة.

Falseness, *n.* Want of truth, بهتان ـ زور ـ كذب. Perfidy, duplicity, مراياة ـ غدر ـ خيانة ـ ألس ـ ختور ـ ختر.

Falsetto, *n.* صوت مصنع ـ تصنيع ألحان.

Falsification, *n.* The act of counterfeiting, تزييف ـ تزوير ـ تقليد ـ تمويه ـ تغشيش. Perversion of meaning, تصحيف.

Falsifier, *n.* دجال ـ مزور ـ مموه ـ مزيف ; of coin, زغلي.

Falsify, *v.t.* To counterfeit, زور ـ غش ٢ ـ زيف ـ موه. To prove to be false, أبطل ـ كذب. To —, as of a document, حرف. To colour, as with lies, وشى *aor.* يشي ـ غش ٢. To distort, as of a meaning, صحف ـ تصحيف على.

Falter, *v.i.* To hesitate in speech, تطرم ـ عقد ـ اعتقل ـ توقف في الكلام ـ لكن ـ تعثر (or عثر ٢) في كلامه ـ لسانه. To —, as in one's answers, تلجلج ـ ارتك. To hesitate, to be doubtful, تضرب ـ تمخطر. To come short of, قصر في ـ تزعزع ـ قلق ـ نقص عن ٢. To —, of the motions of the body, انحل عزمه ـ تفشل ـ فشل ـ ارتج. To — in one's resolution, *See also to* Hesitate, Stammer, *v.i.*

Falteringly, *ad.* With stammering, بلكن ـ بتأتأة ـ بعولك. With hesitation, بقلق ـ بتضرب ـ بتمخطر. Irresolutely, بفشل.

Fame, *n.* Renown, صيتة ـ صيت ـ شهرة ـ سمع ـ اسم ـ ذكر ـ سمع. Reputation, ناموس ـ صيت ـ عرض. Report, خبر ـ صوت ـ رواية. A house of ill —, ماخور ـ بيت قحاب. His — has gone abroad, ذهب سمعه في الناس.

Famed, *a.* جليل ـ مشهور ـ شهير ـ مذاع الذكر ـ مصيت.

Fameless, *a.* عديم الشهرة ـ مجهول.

Familiar, *a.* Affable, حليم ـ لطيف ـ خير ـ أنيس. Not formal, عشير ـ سكن ـ دخلل ـ دخلل ـ مثافن ـ آنس *pl.* عشراء. Well known, معلوم ـ معروف. Accustomed to, معتاد على. Easy, متيسر ـ سهل ـ هين. A — spirit, تابع ـ رجل جان ـ عفريت ـ روح ردي ٢ ـ جان. A man having a — spirit, جان. To be —, intimate, with, واصل ـ عاشر. To deal in a — manner with, باسط.

Familiar, *n.* An intimate friend, إلف *pl.* آلاف *fem.* إلفة ـ جليس ـ وصيل ـ أنساء *pl.* أنيس ـ ألفاء *pl.* أليف ـ آلفة ـ عشير ـ صاحب *pl.* أصحاب or صحبان.

Familiarity, *n.* Intimacy, friendship, معاشرة ـ مؤانسة ـ مباسطة ـ مواصلة ـ جمعة ـ صحبة ـ ألفة ـ إلف ـ عشرة. Knowledge, شعر ـ خبر ـ علم. Looseness of talk or manners, مزاحة. Familiarity breeds contempt, المزاحة تذهب المهابة. A friendly — exists between them, بينهم مباسطة.

Familiarize, *v.t.* To accustom to, أنس ـ مع ـ عود ـ على. To make easy to, هون ـ ل ـ سهل ـ ل.

Familiarly, *ad.* Without ceremony, بلا تكليف ـ بمباسطة. Easily, بيسر ـ يسرا ـ بسهولة ـ سهلا. To treat one —, openly, cheerfully, باسط.

Family, *n.* A household, بَيْت ـ أَهْل ـ عِيال *pl.* عِيالات بَيْت. (The arabicized word فامِيلِيَة is now often used in the East to denote high families, or the families of the upper classes.) Lineage, نَسَب ـ نَسْل ـ نَجْل ـ آل. A tribe, طائِفَة ـ قَبِيلَة. A generation, جِيل *pl.* أَجْيال. Relatives, أَهْل وَعِيال. Children, أَوْلاد. Wife and children, زَوْجَة وَأَوْلاد. A species, نَوْع *pl.* أَنْواع ـ جِنْس *pl.* أَجْناس. Nobility, نَجابَة ـ شَرافَة. Of high —, اِبْنُ أَكابِر. A poor man with a large —, بَوْشِيّ. A — man, صاحِبُ ٱلْعِيالِ. In the — way, حامِلَة ـ حَبالَى *pl.* حُبْلَى. To work, as for one's —, عالَ عِيالَهُ *aor.* يَعُولُ ـ كَسَمَ ـ كَدَسَ ل. To have a large —, أَعالَ ـ عالَ *aor.* يَعُولُ. The human —, بَنِي آدَمَ ـ البَشَرُ. A — man, one having a — to support, مُعَيَّل ـ مُعِيل.

Famine, *n.* مَجاعَة ـ لَزْبَة ـ جَدْب ـ غَلاء ـ قَحْط ـ مَسْغَبَة.

Famish, *v.t.* مَوَّتَ بِٱلْجُوعِ (*or* جُوعًا) ـ جَوَّعَ ـ غَرَّثَ.

Famish, *v.i.* جاعَ [2] ـ أَسْغَبَ ـ سَغَبَ [2].

Famishment, *n.* مَجاعَة ـ سَغابَة ـ سُغُوب ـ سَغْب.

Famous, *a.* جَلِيل ـ باهٍ ـ جُهُور ـ ذو صِيت ـ ذو سَماع ـ مَشْهُور ـ شَهِير ـ مُصِيت; specially of wine, عاتِق ـ عاتِك. To become —, أَصاتَ. To be — for, اِشْتَهَرَ بِ.

Famously, *ad.* With renown, بِجَلالٍ ـ بِصِيتٍ ـ شُهْرَةً. Well, عَلَى أَحْسَنِ مِنْوالٍ ـ عَلَى ٱلْكَمالِ ـ فِي غايَةِ ٱلْإِتْقانِ ـ عَلَى عَيْنٍ.

Famousness, *n.* See Fame, *n.*

Fan, *n.* A — for cooling the face or blowing the fire, مِرْوَحَة *pl.* مَراوِح. A winnowing —, مِذْراة ـ مِرْفَش *vulg.* مِذْرَى.

Fan, *v.t.* To blow the face or fire, رَوَّحَ عَلَى بِمِرْوَحَةٍ ـ رَوَّحَ. To winnow, ذَرَّى. To — one's self, تَرَوَّحَ.

Fanatic, *n.* / **Fanatic**, *a.* / **Fanatical**, *a.* } Enthusiastic, strict, over-zealous, أَحْمَسُ *pl.* حُمْس ـ مُفْرِطُ ٱلْغَيْرَةِ ـ مُتَعَصِّب ـ مُتَحَمِّس; in religion, أَحْمَسُ فِي ٱلدِّيانَةِ ـ أَحْمَسُ ـ مُفْرِطٌ فِي ٱلْغَيْرَةِ عَلَى ـ مُتَدَيِّنٌ فَوْقَ ٱلْحَدِّ ـ مُتَعَصِّبٌ فِي ٱلدِّينِ. To be —, حَمِسَ [2]; specially in religion, حَمِسَ فِي ٱلدِّينِ. To be — in favour of, تَعَصَّبَ ل; against, تَعَصَّبَ عَلَى.

Fanatically, *ad.* With over zeal or strictness, بِحَمَسٍ ـ بِغَيْرَةٍ زائِدَةٍ ـ بِعَصَبِيَّةٍ ـ بِتَعَصُّبٍ; especially in religion, بِحَمَسٍ فِي ٱلدِّينِ ـ بِعَصَبِيَّةٍ دِينِيَّةٍ. To act —, تَحَمَّسَ; in religion, تَحَمَّسَ فِي ٱلدِّينِ.

Fanaticism, *n.* Excess of zeal, rigour, غَيْرَة ـ تَعَصُّب ـ حَمَس ـ غَيْرَةٌ مُفْرِطَةٌ ـ زائِدَةٌ; in religion, إِفْراطٌ فِي ـ حَمَسٌ فِي ٱلدِّينِ ـ عَصَبِيَّةٌ دِينِيَّةٌ ـ ٱلْغَيْرَةُ ٱلدِّينِيَّةُ.

Fanaticize, *v.t.* To lead one to excess of zeal, أَلْجَأَ إِلَى ٱلْحَمَسِ ـ حَمَلَ عَلَى فَرْطِ ٱلْغَيْرَةِ ـ أَغْرَى بِٱلتَّعَصُّبِ; specially in religion, حَمَلَ ـ أَغْرَى بِٱلْعَصَبِيَّةِ ٱلدِّينِيَّةِ ـ أَلْجَأَ إِلَى ٱلْحَمَسِ فِي ٱلدِّينِ ـ عَلَى ٱلْفَرْطِ فِي ٱلْأُمُورِ ٱلدِّينِيَّةِ.

Fanciful, *n.* Capricious, مُخَبَّل ـ مُتَلَوِّن ـ طائِر ـ مُلْتَوٍ. Imaginative, مُتَوَهِّم ـ مُشْتَبِه ـ مُتَخَيِّل ـ مُتَقَلْقِل. To be —, capricious, تَلَوَّى.

Fancifully, *ad.* بِوَهْمٍ ـ وَهْمًا ـ بِٱشْتِباهٍ ـ بِٱلتَّخَيُّلِ ـ بِتَلَوُّنٍ.

Fancy, *n.* Imagination, أَوْهام *pl.* وَهْم ـ تَخَيُّل ـ خَيْل ـ خِيلَة ـ تَصَوُّر ـ تَوَهُّم. The faculty of —, الحِسُّ ٱلْمُشْتَرَكُ. An imaginative opinion, طَيْرُورَة ـ وَسْواس ـ خَيال. A thought, conception, تَخْمِين ـ زَعْم ـ ظَنّ ـ رَأْي ـ فِكْر. A delusion, وَهْمِيَّة *pl.* وَهْمِيّات. A whim, أَهْواء *pl.* هَوًى ـ هُوِيَّة. Inclination, fondness, شَوْق ـ رَغْبَة ـ مَيْل ـ غَرَض ـ نِيَّة. To take a — to one, رَغِبَ فِي ـ مالَ إِلَى. To show a —, love, for, تَوَدَّدَ إِلَى. To captivate the — or love of, تَوَدَّدَ. A — ball, لَيْلَةُ رَقْصٍ يَتَزَيَّا ٱلرّاقِصُونَ وَٱلرّاقِصاتُ فِيها بِزِيِّ ٱلْمُلُوكِ ٱلْقُدَماءِ وَمَلابِسِ ٱلْأُمَمِ ٱلْمُخْتَلِفَةِ. Fancy goods, التُّحَفُ مِنَ ٱلْأَمْتِعَةِ. A — man, a dangler after women, عَلُّ ٱلنِّساءِ. A sweetheart, عاشِق. A — price, قِيمَةُ ٱلتُّحَفِ.

Fancy, *v.t.* To imagine, خالَ [2] ـ ظَنَّ [2] ـ تَوَهَّمَ ـ تَخَيَّلَ ـ تَصَوَّرَ ـ زَعَمَ [2] ـ رَأَى *aor.* يَرَى. To be pleased with, وَدَّ [2] ـ راقَ [2] ـ تَعَلَّقَ بِحُبِّ ٱلـ... ـ اِبْتَهَجَ بِ ـ اِسْتَسَرَّ بِ. I —, لَعَمْرِي. I fancied, خَطَرَ [2] ـ يَقَعُ *aor.* وَقَعَ فِي مَظِنَّتِي ـ تَصَوَّرَ لِي ـ تَخَيَّلَ لِي بِبالِي. I — he is going away, أَرَى أَنَّهُ مُنْطَلِقٌ.

Fandango, *n.* ضَرْبٌ مِنَ ٱلرَّقْصِ.

Fane, *n.* هَيْكَل ـ مَسْجِد ـ مَعْبَد.

Fanfaronade, *n.* إِطْناب ـ تَفاخُر.

Fang, *n.* A tusk, أَنْياب *pl.* ناب ـ مِخْلَدان *dual* مِخْلاد. The fangs of any animal, صَلاقِيمُ. Talons, مَخالِبُ *pl.* مِخْلَب ـ كَلالِيبُ *pl.* كُلّاب ـ خَطاطِيفُ. The root of a tooth, صِنْخُ سِنٍّ *pl.* أَصْناخ.

Fanged, *a.* Having tusks, ذو أَنْيابٍ ـ أَنْيَبُ; having claws, ذو كَلالِيبَ; having roots, as a tooth, ذو أَصْناخٍ.

Fangless, *a.* Without tusks, بِلا أَنْيابٍ; without claws, بِلا مَخالِبَ; without roots, as of a tooth, بِلا أَصْناخٍ.

Fan-light, *n.* طاقٌ فِي شَكْلِ نِصْفِ دائِرَةٍ.

Fanlike, *a.* فِي شَكْلِ ٱلْمِرْوَحَةِ.

Fantasia, *n.* مَقامَةٌ مِنَ ٱلْمُوسِيقَى مُطْرِبَةٌ جِدًّا.

Fantasm, *n.* خَيالَة ـ هُوِيَّة ـ طَيْف.

Fantastic, *a.* } Whimsical, مُتَخَيِّل ـ خَيَالِيّ ـ مُلْتَوٍ. Strange,
Fantastical, } غَرِيب ـ عَجِيب. *See also* Fanciful, *a.*

Fantastically, *ad.* Strangely, بِنَوْعٍ عَجِيبٍ ـ بِنَوْعٍ غَرِيبٍ. *See also* Fancifully, *ad.*

Fantasy, *n.* *See* Fancy, *n.*

Fantoccini, *n.* قَرَه كُوز ـ خَيَالاتِي.

Far, *a.* Distant, قاصٍ *pl.* أَقْصَآء *fem.* قاصِيَة ـ قَصِيّ ـ نَزِيح ـ بَعِيد ـ قَذِيف. His place is — off, مَكانُهُ بَعِيدٌ. How — (free) is God (from every imperfection!) حاشَى لِلّٰهِ. How — it is from being right! مَا أَبْعَدَهُ مِنَ ٱلصَّوابِ. To be — off, بَعُدَ ².

Far, *ad.* عَلَى بُعْدٍ ـ عَلَى نُزُوحٍ ـ نَزْحًا. How — did you go? إِلَى أَيْنَ وَصَلْتَ ـ كَمْ بَعُدْتَ فِي ٱلذَّهابِ. As — as he is able, عَلَى قَدْرِ طاقَتِهِ. Far from thanking he began to abuse me, بَدَلَ أَنْ يَشْكُرَنِي ٱبْتَدَأَ يَشْتُمُنِي. You pushed the matter too —, أَفْرَطْتَ (*or* فَرَّطْتَ) فِي ٱلْأَمْرِ. Far be it! هَيْهاتَ. Far be it from such an one! حاشَى لِفُلانٍ. Far be it from me to…, مَعاذَ ٱللّٰهِ مِنْ أَنْ ـ حاشَى لِي أَنْ. It was by — the most splendid sight I ever beheld, كانَ مَنْظَرًا مِنْ أَبْهَجِ ما رَأَيْتُ قَطّ.

As far as, to, إِلَى. As far as my opinion goes, نَظَرًا لِرَأْيِي.

As far as the eye can reach, قَدْرَ مَدَى ٱلْبَصَرِ.

By far, جِدًّا ـ بِكَثْرَةٍ ـ بِكَثِيرٍ.

Far better, أَفْضَلُ جِدًّا. Far within, فِي ٱلدَّاخِلِ جِدًّا.

From far, مِنْ بَعِيدٍ. How far? إِلَى أَيْنَ.

Far and wide, ٱنْتِشارًا ـ مِنْ كُلِّ جانِبٍ.

Farce, *n.* A comedy, تَهْرِيج ـ مَضْحَكَة ـ حِكايَةٌ مُضْحِكَةٌ. Nonsense, تَفاهَة ـ هَذَر ـ عَبَث.

Farce, *v.t.* To stuff, حَشَى ـ. Farced cucumbers, خِيارٌ مَحْشِيٌّ.

Farcical, *a.* سُخْرِيّ ـ مَسْخَرَة ـ مُهَرِّج ـ مُضْحِك.

Farcically, *ad.* بِمَسْخَرَةٍ ـ سُخْرَةً ـ تَهْرِيجًا ـ إِضْحاكًا.

Fardel, *n.* بَرْذَعَة *pl.* بَرَاذِع.

Fare, *v.i.* To travel, سارَ ـ رَحَلَ ـ عَبَرَ ². To be in a state, good or bad, صارَ عَلَى حالَةٍ ٱلْ… ـ كانَ فِي حالِ ٱلْ…. To feed, eat, live, عاشَ ـ ٱغْتَذَى. To — well, to succeed, أَفْلَحَ ـ نَجَحَ. To — badly, live on poor food, تَقَشَّفَ ـ ٱغْتَذَى بِقُوتٍ خَشِنٍ; not to succeed, خابَ *aor.* يَخِيبُ.

Fare, *n.* Food, مَعِيشَة ـ مَأْكُولات ـ طَعام ـ قُوت. Price of passage, by land, أُجْرَةُ ٱلطَّرِيقِ; by sea, نَوْلُون. A passenger, مُسافِر *pl.* مُسافِرُون. A bill of —, نَشْرَةُ أَشْكالِ ٱلطَّعامِ. Living on poor —, مُتَقَشِّف; on good —, مُتَنَعِّم.

Farewell, *n.* An adieu, وِداع ـ تَوْدِيع. A departure, رَحِيل ـ سَفَر ـ ذَهاب. To bid — to, وَدَّعَ ـ وادَعَ.

Farewell, *int.* (The following are some of the forms in common use, as uttered to the person or persons leaving:) تِمُّوا فِي حِراسَةِ ٱللّٰهِ ـ خَلَّيْناكُمْ بِٱلْعافِيَةِ ـ أَوْدَعْناكُمْ ـ نَرَى وَجْهَكُمْ فِي خَيْرٍ. The ordinary complimentary replies are: مَعَ ـ مَحْمُولَ ٱلسَّلامَةِ ـ فِي أَمانِ ٱللّٰهِ ـ بِٱلْأَمانِ ـ ٱلسَّلامَة. *See also under* Adieu, *int.*

Far-famed, *a.* مَشْهُورٌ عِنْدَ ٱلْبَعِيدِ وَٱلْقَرِيبِ.

Far-fetched, *a.* أَبْعَدُ ـ بَعِيد ـ مُلْتَبِس.

Farina, *n.* The pollen of flowers, إِبار ـ كُشّ. Flour of grain, دَقِيق.

Farinaceous, *a.* دَقِيقِيّ ـ ذُو دَقِيقٍ.

Farm, *n.* Land occupied by a farmer, ٱلْتِزام ـ عُقْرَى ـ عَقار. Cultivated land, مَزْرَعَة. Land taken on hire, قَطِيعَة ـ إِجارَة.

Farm, *v.t.* To rent for a price, أَكْرَى ـ أَجَّرَ ـ آجَرَ ـ أَقْطَعَ. To cultivate land, أَفْلَحَ ـ زَرَعَ ².

Farmer, *n.* One who takes land on hire, مُسْتَأْجِر ـ مُلْتَزِم. One who cultivates land, أَرِيس ـ فَلّاح ـ جَوّار ـ أَكّار ـ بَيّار ـ أَهْلُ زِراعَةٍ ـ حارِث.

Farming, *n.* فَلاحَة ـ زِراعَة.

Farmhouse, *n.* بَيْتُ أَهْلِ ٱلزِّراعَةِ ـ مَسْكَنُ ٱلْأَكّارِ.

Farm-offices, *n.* ٱلمَعالِفُ وَٱلْأَنابِيرُ ٱلْمُتَعَلِّقَةُ بِمَزْرَعَةٍ.

Farmost, *a.* ٱلْأَقْصَى ـ ٱلْأَبْعَدُ.

Farm-yard, *n.* حَوْشُ مَزْرَعَةٍ.

Farness, *n.* بُعْد.

Faro, *n.* ضَرْبٌ مِنْ لَعِبِ ٱلْقِمارِ.

Farraginous, *a.* مُهَرَّج ـ مُخَبَّص ـ مُخْتَلِط.

Farrago, *n.* خَلِيط ـ شَمْل ـ خِلْط. A — of nonsense, هَمْرَجَة ـ لَغْوٌ ـ خَطْلَبَة.

Farrier, *n.* نَعْلَبَنْد ـ مُبَيْطِر ـ بَيْطار.

Farriery, *n.* بَيْطَرَة.

Farrow, *n.* A litter of pigs, بَطْنُ خَنانِيصَ. A young pig, خِنَّوْص *pl.* خَنانِيص.

Farrow, *v.i.* وَلَدَتِ ٱلْخِنْزِيرَةُ ـ وَلَدَتْ (*or* وَضَعَتْ) خَنانِيصَ.

Far-sighted, *a.* Having long sight, مَدِيدُ ٱلْبَصَرِ ـ طَوِيلُ ٱلنَّظَرِ. Prudent, ذُو فِراسَةٍ ـ بَصِير. A — eye, عَيْنٌ غَرِبَةٌ.

Far-sightedness, *n.* Long sight, بَصَرٌ مَدِيدٌ ـ نَظَرٌ طَوِيلٌ. Foresight, فِراسَة ـ تَعَقُّل ـ ٱمْتِدادُ بَصَرٍ.

Fart, *v.i.* حَبَقَ ـ فَقَعَ ² ـ وَكَعَ ² ـ ضَرَطَ ²; without noise, فَسا ².

Fart, *n.* حَبْقَة ـ ضَرْط ـ ضُراط; without noise, فُساء.

Farter, *n.* فَسَّاءٌ — ضَرَّاط.

Farther, *a.* أَقْصَى — أَبْعَدُ — أَنْزَحُ.

Farther, *ad.* Farther off, إِلَى مَكَانٍ أَبْعَدَ. To move — off, تَبَاعَدَ. When they had gone a little —, لَمَّا مَضَوا قَلِيلًا. Thus far shalt thou come and no —, إِلَى هُنَا تَأْتِي وَلَا تَتَعَدَّى. He made as though he would have gone —, تَظَاهَرَ كَأَنَّهُ مُنْطَلِقٌ إِلَى مَكَانٍ أَبْعَدَ.

Farthest, *a.* الأَقْصَى — الأَبْعَدُ — الأَنْزَحُ. *See also* Uttermost, *a.*

Farthing, *n.* سِكَّةٌ مِنْ نُحَاسٍ ثَمَنُهَا رُبْعُ ٱلْپَنْي مِنَ ٱلسِّكَكِ ٱلْانْكِلِيزِيَّةِ. A —, figuratively, فَلْس *pl.* فُلُوس.

Farthingale, *n.* فُسْطَانٌ نَاتِئٌ.

Fasces, *n.* بَلْطَة.

Fascinate, *v.t.* سَلَبَ ‹ — فَتَنَ — سَحَرَ — إِسْتَهْوَى — فَتَلَ — سَلَبَ قَلْبَهُ — عَقْلَهُ. *See also to* Charm, *v.t.*

Fascinating, *a.* يَسْلُبُ ٱلْقَلْبَ — يَسْلُبُ ٱلْعَقْلَ — مُفْتِن. *See also* Charming, *a.*

Fascination, *n.* جَاذِبِيَّة — سِحْر — رِبَاط — طَلَاوَة. *See also* Charm, *n.*

Fascine, *n.* حُزْمَةٌ *pl.* حُزَم — خُصَلٍ *pl.* جُرْزَةُ قُضْبَانٍ *pl.* جُرَز.

Fashion, *n.* Form, فِطْرَة — شَكْل — هَيْئَة — صُورَة — وَجْهَة — كَيْفِيَّة. The outer — of a man, خَلْق — خِلْقَة; the inward — of a man, disposition, خُلُق. Cut, as of clothes, زِيّ — كَسْم — هَيْئَة. Way, manner, نَمَط — أُسْلُوب — مِنْوَال — طَرِيق — قَاعِدَة. Custom, طَوْر — دَأْب — وَتِيرَة — سِمَة — عَادَة. People of —, الكُبَرَاء — الأَكَابِر. The old —, of dress, الزِّيُّ ٱلْعَتِيقُ; the present —, زِيُّ ٱلْيَوْمِ — زِيُّ ٱلْوَقْتِ. In the —, عَلَى زِيِّ ٱلْوَقْتِ.

Fashion, *v.t.* To create, فَطَرَ ‹ — جَبَلَ ‹. To —, as by moulding, فَطَرَ ‹. To form, شَكَّلَ — صَوَّرَ. To — in the rough, خَشَّبَ. To be fashioned, تَصَوَّرَ — تَشَكَّلَ.

Fashionable, *a.* Established by custom, مُعْتَادٌ — حَسَبَ ٱلْعَادَةِ عَلَيْهِ. According to the mode, بِحَسَبِ ٱلْعَادَةِ. As belonging to the gentry, مِنَ ٱلْأَنْجَبَاءِ — مُعْتَبَر — مِنَ ٱلْكُبَرَاءِ.

Fashionably, *ad.* عَلَى كَسْمِ ٱلْيَوْمِ — بِحَسَبِ ٱلْعَادَةِ.

Fashioner, *n.* فَاطِر — مُصَوِّر — مُشَكِّل — صَانِع.

Fast, *v.i.* To abstain from food, صَامَ *aor.* يَصُومُ.

Fast, *n.* Abstinence from food, صَوْم — صِيَام. To eat after a —, فَطَرَ. To break a — upon, أَفْطَرَ عَلَى — فَطَرَ عَلَى ‹. A breaking of a —, فِطْر. The festival of the breaking of the — just before Ramadhân, عِيدُ ٱلْفِطْرِ. Breaking —, مُفْطِر. The food taken to break a —, فُطُور.

Fast, *a.* Firm, ثَابِت — رَاسِخ — رَاسٍ — رَصِين — مَرْصُون — مُسْتَحْكَم — مُوثَق — رَاكِز — مَضْبُوط — مُقَرَّر — مُحْكَم — مَتِين — مُلْتَصِق بِ — مُتَعَلِّق مَعَ. Solid, مَتِين. Adhering to, مُتَعَلِّق مَعَ. Speedy, مُسْتَعْجِل — مِسْرَع — سَرِيع — طَيَّار — عَصُوف. Resolute, رَسِيّ — شَدِيد — صِنْدِيد. Very —, to do good or evil, مِسْرَاع. My horse runs faster than yours, حِصَانِي أَجْرَى مِنْ حِصَانِكَ. *See also* Dissolute, *a.*

Fast asleep, غَارِقٌ فِي ٱلنَّوْمِ.

To make fast, to tie, رَبَطَ ‹ — ضَبَطَ ‹.

To hold fast, as in the hand, تَمَسَّكَ بِ. To hold to unswervingly, تَمَسَّكَ بِٱلْإِقْرَارِ.

To play fast and loose, إِحْتَالَ — تَحَوَّلَ — تَلَوَّى.

Fast, *ad.* Swiftly, عَاجِلًا — بِسُرْعَةٍ — سُرْعَةً *vulg.* قَوَام. Firmly, إِحْكَامًا — بِثَبَاتٍ — بِمَتَانَةٍ. Fast by, near, بِقُرْبِ — قُرَيْبَ — عِنْدَ — دُونَ. To go too —, as of a clock, تَقَدَّمَ. My watch is —, سَاعَتِي مُسْبِقَةٌ.

Fasten, *v.t.* To make firm, وَكَّدَ — أَثْبَتَ — مَكَّنَ — أَرْصَنَ — أَمْتَنَ. To — to, to conjoin, أَوْصَلَ بِ — لَصِقَ بِ ‹. To bind, رَبَطَ مَعَ ‹ — زَمَّ ‹ — زَمَّمَ — رَبَطَ ‹ — عَقَلَ ‹ — شَدَّ ‹. To tie to, رَبَطَ مَعَ ‹. To shut, غَلَقَ ‹ — عَقَدَ مَعَ ‹ — قَيَّدَ مَعَ. To — a door, أَغْلَقَ. To — on, lay hold of, قَبَضَ بِ ‹ — أَمْسَكَ بِ — تَرَّسَ ٱلْبَابَ ‹. To — itself on the mind, طُبِعَ فِي ٱلْعَقْلِ — دَخَلَ ٱلْعَقْلَ ‹. To —, as with nails, سَمَّرَ. He fastened his eyes upon him, تَفَرَّسَ فِيهِ. The snake fastened on his hand, نَشِبَتِ ٱلْحَيَّةُ فِي يَدِهِ.

Fastening, *n.* رِبَاط — قَيْد *pl.* قُيُود. A — of a door, غَلَق — مِغْلَاق.

Fast-handed, *a.* *See* Covetous, Close-fisted, *a.*

Faster, *ad.* *See under* Fast, *a.*

Fasti, *n.* حَوَادِثُ — وَقَائِعُ.

Fastidious, *a.* مُتَأَنِّق — مَلُول. *See also* Dainty, *a.*

Fastidiously, *ad.* إِسْتِنْكَافًا — مُتَأَنِّقًا — بِمَلَالٍ.

Fastidiousness, *n.* تَأَنُّق — إِسْتِنْكَاف — مَلَّة — مَلَال.

Fasting, *a.* As from food, صَائِم *pl.* صِيَام.

Fasting, *ad.* عَلَى ٱلرِّيقِ. He drank it —, شَرِبَهُ عَلَى ٱلرِّيقِ. He is —, *i.e.*, has not breakfasted, هُوَ عَلَى ٱلرِّيقِ — هُوَ رَيِّقٌ.

Fastness, *n.* The state of being fast, إِحْكَام — رُسُوخ — رَصَانَة — ثَبَات — إِمْكَان. Security, إِطْمِئْنَان — أَمَان. A strong place, fortress, حِصْن *pl.* حُصُون — حَصِين — قَلْعَة *pl.* قِلَاع. Fastnesses, مَصَانِعُ.

Fastuous, *a.* *See* Disdainful, *a.*

Fat, *a.* Plump, سَمِين ـ شَحِيم ـ شَخِيص ـ ذُو وَدَك. Corpulent, مُجَسَّم ـ جَسِيم ـ ضِخَام *pl.* ضَخْم ـ فَعْم. Greasy, دَسِم ـ دَهِين ـ زَفِر ـ زَهِم. Dull, stupid, بَلِيد ـ أَخْرَق. Fertile, مَرِيع ـ مُخْصِب ـ أَمْرَاع *pl.* A — man, شَحِيم ـ ضَخَام. A beast that soon fattens on fodder, مُبْدان. A — waddling man, هُداكِر; woman, هُدَكُورَة. To be —, plump, سَمِنَ ـ ² شَحُمَ ـ ² ضَخُمَ.

Fat, *n.* Suet, grease, سَمْن ـ دُهْن ـ زُهْم ـ شَحْم. The — of the intestines, ثَرْب; round the kidneys, كُظْر. A bit of —, شَحْمَة ـ سَخْفَة. The — of the land, دَسَمُ ٱلْأَرْضِ. A vat, دَنّ ـ خابِيَة. Layers of —, as on the flanks, سَحَائِف.

Fat, *v.t.* and *i.* *See to* Fatten.

Fatal, *a.* Proceeding from destiny, مَحْتُوم ـ مُقَدَّر. Deadly, مُبْطِل ـ مُعْدِم ـ مُهْلِك ـ مُمِيت ـ مائِت ـ مُزِيل. Unfortunate, سُوء ـ نَحِس ـ مَشْؤُوم.

Fatalism, *n.* مَذْهَبُ ٱلْقَدَرِيَّةِ.

Fatalist, *n.* قَدَرِيّ *pl.* قَدَرِيَّة ـ القائِلُ بِٱلْقَضَاءِ وَٱلْقَدَرِ.

Fatality, *n.* Invincible necessity, قَضَاء وَقَدَر ـ تَقْدِير. Tendency to danger, مُخَاطَرَة. Unfortunateness, نَحْس ـ شُؤْم ـ شَأْم. Mortality, هَلَكَة ـ قاضِيَة ـ مَوْت. A cause of misfortune, مَنْحَسَة ـ مَشْأَمَة.

Fatally, *ad.* Mortally, بِٱلْهَلاكِ ـ هَلاكًا ـ هُلْكَ ٱلْهُلْكِ. By the decree of fate, بِٱلْقَدَرِ. To end —, to come to ruin, ﺓ هَلَكَ. To die from the effects of, ² مَاتَ مِن.

Fata Morgana, *n.* سَراب ـ آل.

Fate, *n.* Predestination, كِتاب ـ مَقْدِرَة ـ قَضَاء وَقَدَر. Peculiar destiny, good or bad, نَصِيب ـ قِسْمَة. Death, أَجَل ـ مَنِيّ ـ مَوْت. A happy —, حَظّ ـ جَدّ. An end, عَاقِبَة.

Fated, *a.* Predestined, مَكْتُوب ـ مَقْضِيّ ب ـ مُقَدَّر عَلَى.

Fates, *n.* أَصْحَابُ ٱلْقَضَاءِ وَٱلْقَدَرِ.

Father, *n.* A male parent, أَب ـ والِد *pl.* آباء. An ancestor, جَدّ *pl.* أَجْداد. A contriver, author, مُخْتَرِع ـ مُبْدِع ـ مُوجِد. Father and mother, الوالِدان. Father! oh —! يا أَبَتاهُ. The almighty —, God, اللّٰهُ تَعَالَى. Our fathers, forefathers, آباؤُنا ـ جُدُودُنا ـ أَجْدادُنا ـ أَسْلافُنا. A putative —, أَبُو المَظْنُون. Our — in God, أَبُونا. A — of a family, صاحِبُ عِيال. From — to son, أَبًا عَنْ جَدّ. To be gathered to one's fathers, تُوُفِّيَ وَٱدُّفِنَ ـ إِضْطَجَعَ مَعَ آبائِهِ. Like — like son, الوَلَدُ سِرُّ أَبِيهِ.

Father, *v.t.* To adopt, تَبَنَّى. To admit the fatherhood of a child, إِسْتَقَرَّ بِٱلْأَبُوَّةِ. To — upon, to ascribe to, ﺓ ² نَسَبَ إِلَى.

Fatherhood, *n.* أَبُوَّة ـ أُبُوَّة.

Father-in-law, *n.* أَبُو زَوْجٍ أَوْ زَوْجَةٍ ـ حَمُو ـ حَمًا ـ حَم.

Fatherland, *n.* وَطَن.

Fatherless, *a.* لا أَبَا لَهُ ـ بِلَا أَب ـ يَتِيم.

Fatherly, *a.* Parental, أَبَوِيّ ـ وَالِدِيّ. Tender, compassionate, حَنَّان ـ شَفُوق.

Fathership, *n.* *See* Fatherhood, *n.*

Fathom, *n.* The measure, قامَة *pl.* قامَات ـ باع *and* بَوْع *pl.* أَبْواع. Penetration, بَصِيرَة ـ فِراسَة ـ إِمْعان.

Fathom, *v.t.* To sound, قَاسَ عُمْقَ ٱلْمَاءِ بِٱلْبَلَدِ ـ ﺓ قَاسَ. To penetrate into, ﺓ بَحَثَ ـ ﺓ فَحَصَ ـ ² غاصَ فِي ـ تَعَمَّقَ فِي. To master, إِنْتَهَى إِلَى ـ أَدْرَكَ. They fathomed and found twenty fathoms, قاسُوا فَوَجَدُوا عِشْرِينَ قامَةً.

Fathomable, *a.* That may be sounded, يُقاس; that may be comprehended, يُدْرَك.

Fathomless, *a.* Without bottom, لا يُقاس. Incomprehensible, لا يُعْرَف ـ لا يُدْرَك.

Fatigue, *n.* Weariness, خَوْزَلَة ـ كَلال ـ كَلّ ـ إِعْيَاء ـ أَيْن. Toil, زَحْمَة ـ تَعَب ـ نَهَاكَة ـ كَدّ.

Fatigue, *v.t.* To weary, أَعْيَا ـ أَتْعَبَ ـ عَسَفَ ـ أَكَلَّ. To harass, ضَجَّرَ ـ أَكَدَّ ـ أَجْهَدَ ـ ﺓ نَهَكَ. To be fatigued, weary, أَعْيَا ـ تَعَنَّى ـ ﺓ تَعِبَ ـ ﺓ كَلَّ ـ آنَ. Fatigued, مُعْيِي *vulg.* عَيَّان.

Fatiguing, *a.* شاقّ ـ مُتْعِب.

Fatling, *n.* مَعْلُوف ـ مُسَمَّن ـ مُقْمًا ـ مُؤَوَّم.

Fatness, *n.* Plumpness, سَمَانَة ـ سِمَن ـ عَرَم ـ نُعُومَة ـ وَدَك. Corpulence, ضِخَم ـ جَسَامَة ـ ضَخَامَة. Fertility, خِصْب ـ بَرَكَة ـ خَيْر.

Fatten, *v.t.* To make fat, سَمَّنَ ـ عَلَّفَ ـ أَوَّمَ ـ أَقْمَأَ. To enrich, as of land, زَبَّلَ ـ سَبَّخَ.

Fatten, *v.i.* To grow fat, تَسَمَّنَ ـ ﺓ سَمِنَ ـ ﺓ قَمَأَ.

Fattening, *a.* مُسْمِن ـ مُسَمِّن.

Fattish, *a.* Somewhat fat, سَمِينٌ نَوْعًا ـ يَضْرِبُ إِلَى ٱلسِّمَنِ; somewhat corpulent, ضَخْمٌ (or ضَخَمٌ) نَوْعًا ـ يَضْرِبُ إِلَى ٱلْجَسامَةِ.

Fatty, *a.* زَهِم ـ دَسِم ـ زَفِر ـ دَهِن.

Fatuity, *n.* هَمَاجَة ـ جُنُون ـ بَلادَة ـ حَمَاقَة.

Fatuous, *a.* هَمِج ـ أَحْمَق ـ بَلِيد ـ طائِش.

Faubourg, *n.* حارَةٌ بَرَّانِيَّةٌ ـ ضَوَاحِي *pl.* ضاحِيَةُ مَدِينَةٍ.

Fauces, *n.* حَلْق ـ مَزْرَد. A swelling in the —, دَغْر ـ عُذْرَة.

Faucet, *n.* قَناة ـ بُلْبُل *vulg.* بَزْبُوز *and* بُلْبُول.

Faugh, *int.* تُوْه ـ عَزِّ ـ أُفًّا .

Fault, *n.* An imperfection, defect, عَيْب *pl.* عُوار ـ سَقَط ـ عُيُوب ـ نَقِيصَة *pl.* نَقَائِص . An error, زَلَّة ـ عَثْرَة ـ قُصُور ـ غَلَط ـ سَهْو . A crime, sin, خَطِيَّة *pl.* خَطَايَا ـ خَطَآء ـ سَقَط ـ سَيِّئَة *pl.* سَيِّئَات ـ إِسَآءَة . To commit a —, خَطِئَ ـ أَخْطَأَ . To find — with, جَدَبَ ـ تَعَقَّبَ ـ لَامَ ـ إِسْتَخْطَأَ ـ ذَمَّ . To be at —, تَحَيَّرَ . In —, خَاطِئٌ . I found no — in him, لَمْ أَجِدْ فِيهِ شَيْئًا . To be free of —, خَلَا مِنَ ٱلْعَيْبِ .

Fault-finder, *n.* عَيَّاب ـ هَاجٍ ـ عَذُول ـ جَادِب ـ قَادِح .

Faultily, *ad.* بِنَقِيصَةٍ ـ بِسَقَطٍ ـ بِعَيْبٍ ـ بِخَطَآءٍ .

Faultiness, *n.* Wrong doing, مَسَآءَة ـ إِسَآءَة . *See also* Fault, *n.*

Faultless, *a.* Without defect, لا عَيْبَ فِيهِ ـ تَامٌّ ـ بِلا عَيْبٍ ; of make, كَامِل ـ مُخْتَلِق ـ خَلِيق . Free from crime, بَرِئٌ ـ مُنَزَّهٌ عَنِ ٱلْخَطَآءِ ـ نَقِيٌّ . To be —, خَلَا مِنَ ٱلْعَيْبِ .

Faultlessly, *ad.* بِلا عَيْبٍ ـ بِكَمَالٍ ـ تَمَامًا ـ بِلا قُصُورٍ .

Faultlessness, *n.* Freedom from defect, عَدَمُ عَيْبٍ ـ عَدَمُ قُصُورٍ ; freedom from crime, error, نَزَاهَة ـ نَقَاوَة ـ بَرَآءَة . Perfection, كَمَالَة ـ تَمَامَة .

Faulty, *a.* Defective, سَقِيم ـ مَعْيُوب ـ مَعِيب ـ سَاقِط ـ مُعَوَّر ـ سَقَط ـ غَيْرُ مَضْبُوطٍ ـ غَيْرُ صَحِيحٍ ـ غَلَط . Erroneous, نَاقِص . Guilty of a crime, ذَمِيم ـ مَذِيم ـ جَرِيم ـ مُذْنِب ـ خَاطِئٌ .

Faun, *n.* نَسْنَاس *pl.* نَسَانِيس ـ نَوْعٌ مِنَ ٱلْجِنِّ .

Fauna, *n.* وُحُوشٌ وَحَيَوَانَاتٌ .

Fauteuil, *n.* كُرْسِيٌّ *pl.* كَرَاسِيُّ ـ صَنْدَلِيٌّ .

Faux pas, *n.* مَسَآءَة ـ زَلَّة ـ خَطَآء .

Favour, *n.* Kind regard, تَوْفِيق ـ لُطْف ـ إِشْبَال ـ رِفْق ـ نِعْمَة ـ فَوَاضِل *pl.* فَاضِلَة ـ فَيْض . A kindness, قَبُول ـ تَوَجُّه ـ هِبَة ـ إِنْعَام ـ حِبْوَة . A gift, عِنَايَة ـ إِحْسَان ـ كَرَم ـ مَعْرُوف . Aid, countenance, مُسَاعَدَة ـ مَدَد ـ ظَهْر ـ سَنَد . A —, a token of love, رُخْصَة ـ إِذْن . Permission, إِشَارَةُ قَبُولٍ ـ إِشَارَةُ حُبٍّ . The favours of a lady, وَصْلُ ٱلْمَرْأَةِ . A wedding —, إِشَارَةُ ٱلْعُرْسِ . He might do me that — if he would, هُوَ يَقْدِرُ عَلَى ذٰلِكَ ٱلْمَعْرُوفِ مَعِي لَوْ شَآءَ . By or with your —, رُخْصٌ ـ عَنْ إِذْنِكَ . The state of being in —, حُظْوَة . Under — of..., بِعِنَايَةِ ـ لِي إِنْ بِوَاسِطَةِ ـ مَدَدًا مِنْ ـ بِمُسَاعَدَةِ .

To ask a favour of, إِسْتَعْطَفَ ـ عَلَى ـ تَرَجَّى ـ مِنْ .

To consider as a favour, أَعَدَّ ـ مَعْرُوفًا .

To curry favour with, إِسْتَعْطَفَ ـ تَحَبَّبَ إِلَى ـ تَوَدَّدَ إِلَى .

To decide in favour of, حَكَمَ لِ .

To do one a favour, أَسْدَى إِلَى ـ تَفَضَّلَ عَلَى ـ صَنَعَ مَعَ ـ مَعْرُوفًا .

To favour one with, أَلْطَفَ ـ بِ ـ تَفَضَّلَ عَلَى ـ بِ ـ أَحْظَى ـ بِ .

To find favour with, نَالَ نِعْمَةً عِنْدَ ـ وَجَدَ نِعْمَةً عِنْدَ *aor.* يَجِدُ ـ حَظِيَ عِنْدَ .

To get into favour with, نَالَ رِضًى مِنْ قِبَلِ ـ عَلَا شَأْنُهُ عِنْدَ .

To load with favours, غَمَّرَ ـ بِٱلْإِحْسَانِ ـ أَفَاضَ عَلَى ـ مِنَ ٱلنِّعَمِ ـ أَجْزَلَ عَلَى ـ بِٱلْعَطَآءِ .

To restore to favour, رَدَّ ـ إِلَى مَقَامِهِ ـ عَفَا عَنْ .

Favour, *v.a.* To regard with kindness, حَنَّ (*or* تَحَنَّنَ) ـ أَشْبَلَ ـ تَعَطَّفَ عَلَى ـ خَارَ لِ ـ أَشْبَى عَلَى ـ رَفَقَ بِ ـ عَلَى (*or* بِ) لَطُفَ لِ . To assist, نَصَرَ ـ أَعَانَ ـ سَاعَدَ . To esteem in preference to another, خَصَّ ـ أَحْظَى عَلَى ـ حَابَى أَصْلَحَ إِلَى ـ تَفَضَّلَ عَلَى . To be useful to, do kindness to, أَخَصَّ . To incline towards, وَدَّ ـ لَوَى إِلَى ـ مَالَ إِلَى . Favour me with your company, تَفَضَّلْ عَلَيَّ (*or* أَكْرِمْ عَلَيَّ) بِرِفْقَتِكَ . Favour me, do me the favour, أَعْمَلْ مَعِي ٱلْمَعْرُوفَ . The most highly favoured nation clause, in treaties, البَنْدُ فِي مُعَامَلَةِ قَوْمٍ بِمَنْزِلَةِ أَفْضَلِ ٱلْمِلَلِ .

Favourable, *a.* Kind, لَطِيف ـ مُتَفَضِّل ـ مُنْعِم ـ كَرِيم ـ مَنَّان . Conducive to, نَافِعٌ لِ ـ مُسَاعِد ـ مُعَاوِن ـ طَائِل . Convenient, مُنَاسِب ـ مُوَافِق . To be — to, in favour of, رَضِيَ عَلَى ـ تَعَصَّبَ لِ . A — wind, رِيحٌ مُوَافِقَةٌ ـ رِيحٌ عَدِلَةٌ . A — opportunity, فُرْصَةٌ جَيِّدَةٌ .

Favourably, *ad.* With kindness, بِكَرَمٍ ـ بِفَضْلٍ ـ بِرِفْقٍ . Prosperously, بِنَجَاحٍ ـ بِإِقْبَالٍ ـ بِتَوْفِيقٍ . Well, حَبَّذَا ـ حَسَنًا ـ سَدِيدًا ـ إِجَادَةً . To progress —, to prosper, of a person, أَفْلَحَ ; of a thing, نَجَحَ ـ أَنْجَحَ ; of the health, تَدَرَّجَ إِلَى ٱلصِّحَّةِ . He regarded him —, نَظَرَ إِلَيْهِ بِعَيْنِ ٱلْقَبُولِ ـ نَظَرَ إِلَيْهِ بِوَجْهٍ مَرْضِيٍّ .

Favourer, *n.* ظَهْر ـ حَامٍ ـ مُعِينٌ لِ ـ مُسَاعِد .

Favourite, *n.* The most loved, المَرْغُوبُ ـ المَحْبُوبُ . A particular friend, companion, جَلِيس ـ نَدِيم . A royal —, قُرْبَان ـ نَدِيمُ ٱلْمَلِكِ .

Favourite, *a.* Preferred, مُسْتَحَبٌّ ـ مُسْتَفْضَل ـ مُسْتَحْسَن .

Favouritism, *n.* مُرَاعَاةُ ٱلْخَوَاطِرِ ـ مُحَابَاة .

Favouring, *a.* طَائِل ـ مُتَعَصِّبٌ لِ ـ مُعِينٌ لِ ـ مُسَاعِدٌ لِ .

Fawn, *n.* A young deer, فَرْخُ ٱلظَّبْيِ *pl.* أَفْرَاخ . A servile cringe, مُصَانَعَة ـ مُدَاهَنَة ـ تَذَلُّل ـ لَكْع ـ لَكَاعَة .

Fawn, *v.n.* As a dog with its tail, بَصْبَصَ بِذَنَبِهِ . To — upon, to flatter servilely, مَلَّقَ ـ دَاهَنَ ـ رَاشَى ـ تَذَلَّلَ لِ ـ صَانَعَ .

To bring forth a —, وَلَدَتِ ٱلظَّبْيَةُ .

Fawner, *n.* } — دائمُ ٱلمِشْطِ — مَلّاق — مُتَمَلِّق — حُمَدَة
Fawning, *a.* } مُتَذَلِّل.

Fawning, *n.* *See* Fawn, *n.*

Fawningly, *ad.* بِتَذَلُّلٍ — بِتَبَصْبُصٍ — بِتَمَلُّقٍ — بِمُداهَنَةٍ.

Fay, *n.* *See* Fairy, *n.*

Fealty, *n.* إطاعَة — صَداقَة — بَيْعَة. To swear — to, بَايَعَ.

Fear, *n.* Dread, خِيفَة — رَهْبَة — رَهَب — رَوْع — رُعْب — خَوْف — فَزَع — رُوْعَة — خَشْيَة — مَفْزَعَة — فُزْعَة. An object of —, أَلَّذِي يُخَافُ مِنْهُ — مَخَافَة — مَوْضُوعُ خَوْفٍ — مَخُوف. Anxiety, خَوْف — فَجَر — قَلَق. Reverence, مَهَابَة — خَشْيَة — هَيْبَة. The — of God, تَقْوَى — تُقًى — تُقاة — مَخَافَةُ ٱللّٰهِ. For — of, lest, لِئَلَّا — خَوْفًا مِنْ أَن — مَخَافَةَ أَن. We are in constant — of…, فِي كُلِّ مُدَّةٍ لَنا بَلِيَّةٌ مِن.

Fear, *v.t.* To be afraid of, فَزِعَ مِن — خَافَ مِن — هَابَ — خَوَّفَ — أَفْزَعَ. To frighten, خَشِيَ مِن *aor.* يَخْشَى — اِخْتَشَى. To — God, خَشِيَ ٱللّٰهَ — اِتَّقَى — اِتَّقَى ٱللّٰهَ. To venerate, اِخْتَشَى — رَجَبَ.

Fear, *v.i.* To be afraid, خَافَ — اِرْتَعَبَ — فَزِعَ — أَشْفَقَ — اِضْطَرَبَ — وَجِلَ *aor.* يَوْجَلُ — رَاعَ *aor.* يَرُوعُ. To be anxious, خَافَ — قَلِقَ. To fear for, خَافَ عَلَى. He feared that the soldiers might rise against their officers, أَشْفَقَ مِنْ أَنْ تَقُومَ ٱلْعَسَاكِرُ عَلَى ضُبَّاطِها.

Fearful, *a.* Timorous, خائف — مُتَهَيِّب — نَخِيب — رَعِيب — مَخُوف — مَخِيف — فُزْعَة — خَوِيف — مَرْعُوب — مُفْزِع. Terrible, مَرْهُوب — هائل — فَظِيع — مَهاب. Fearful sights, things, مَخاوِف. Of a — heart, خائفُ ٱلْقَلْبِ. Why are ye so —? ما بالُكُمْ خائفِينَ هٰكَذا.

Fearfully, *ad.* Timorously, خَشْيَةً — بِرُعْبٍ — بِخَوْفٍ — اِرْتِعابًا — فَزَعًا. Terribly, تَرْعِيبًا — تَهْوِلًا — هَوْلًا. Wonderfully, عَجَبًا.

Fearfulness, *n.* Timidity, خِيفَة — رُعْب — نَخَب. Dread, فَزَع — خَوْف — رِعْدَة. Anxiety, قَلَق — ضَجَر. *See also* Fear, *n.*

Fearing, *a.* خَائِف *pl.* خُوَّف *and* خِيَّف — فَزِع — فازِع. God —, مُتَّقٍ.

Fearless, *a.* جَسُور — شُجاع — بَطَل — جَرِيء *or* أَجْرَاء. To be —, شَجُعَ ². أَجْرَأ.

Fearlessly, *ad.* بِلا خَوْفٍ — بِجَراءَةٍ — بِجَسارَةٍ — بِشَجاعَةٍ.

Fearlessness, *n.* جَرَاءَة — جَسارَة — شَجاعَة — عَنْتَرَة — بَطَالَة.

Fear-naught, *n.* *See* Dreadnaught, *n.*

Feasibility, *n.* } إمْكانُ ٱلإجْرَاءِ — قَابِلِيَّة — إمْكان.
Feasibleness, }

Feasible, *a.* إجْرَاءُهُ مُمْكِنٌ — يُصْنَعُ — يَصِير — مُمْكِن.

Feast, *n.* A banquet, وَلِيمَة — مَأْدُبَة — ضِيافَة. A religious anniversary, عِيد *pl.* أَعْيَاد. To prepare a —, اِصْطَنَعَ مَصْنَعَةً — حَضَّرَ وَلِيمَةً — اِتَّخَذَ مَأْدُبَةً — صَنَعَ ضِيافَةً. To keep a —, عَيَّدَ.

Feast, *v.t.* To entertain at a —, أَوْلَمَ — أَضَافَ.

Feast, *v.i.* To eat sumptuously, تَلَذَّذَ — تَبَحْبَحَ — تَضَيَّفَ — اِنْبَسَطَ بِٱلأَكْلِ وَٱلشُّرْبِ — تَنَعَّمَ مُتَرَفِّهًا.

Feaster, *n.* An entertainer, ضَيَّاف — مُؤْدِب. A guest, ضَيْف *pl.* ضُيُوف. One keeping a festival, مُعَيِّد.

Feastful, *a.* *See* Festive, *n.*

Feat, *n.* An exploit, صَنِيعَة *pl.* صَنائع — فِعْل *pl.* أَفْعال — عَمِلَة *pl.* عَمائل. A trick, لُعْبَة — دُعابَة — حِرْفَة — سَطْوَة — حِيلَة.

Feather, *n.* رِيشَة *pl.* أَرْياش *and* رِياش *coll.* رِيش. A kind, species, party, جِنْس — نَوْع — شَكْل — فِرْقَة. Bombast, فَخْر — اِفْتِخار. A downy —, زَغْبَة *coll.* زَغَب — رِيش ناعِم. An ostrich —, رِيش نَعام — حَمِيلَة — زِفّ. Cast feathers, نُسال. A — broom, مِنْسَغَة. A — in one's cap, مَفْخَرَة — اِفْتِخار. The feathers of an arrow, آذانُ ٱلسَّهْمِ. To put forth the first feathers, شَوَّكَ. To brush with a — broom, نَسَغَ. To bristle up the feathers, تَنَفَّشَ. To be in high —, بَطِرَ — اِطْمَأَنَّ — اِبْتَهَجَ — تَغَبَّطَ. To show the white —, جَبُنَ ² — أَظْهَرَ ٱلْجَبَانَةَ. To pluck out the feathers, نَتَفَ — نَتَّفَ.

Feather, *v.t.* To adorn with feathers, زَيَّنَ بِرِيشٍ. To — one's nest, جَمَّعَ مَالًا. To — an oar, أَصْلَحَ ٱلْمِقْذافَ — عَدَّلَ ٱلْمِقْذافَ وَهُوَ قَاذِفٌ. To —, as of an arrow, رَيَّشَ.

Feather-bed, *n.* فِراشٌ مِنْ رِيشٍ — مَنامٌ مِنْ رِيشٍ.

Feathered, *a.* Having feathers, ذُو رِيشٍ. Figured with feathers, مُرَيَّش. The — tribe, ٱلطُّيُورُ.

Featherfew, *n.* ضَرْبٌ مِنَ ٱلزَّهْرِ.

Featherless, *a.* بِلا رِيشٍ. Plucked of its feathers, مَنْتُوفُ ٱلرِّيشِ.

Feathery, *a.* Having feathers, ذُو رِيشٍ. Resembling feathers, رِيشِيّ — مِثْلَ ٱلرِّيشِ.

Feature, *n.* Appearance, form, رُؤْيَة — مَنْظَر — هَيْئَة. A line or lineament of the face or hand, سِرار *pl.* أَسِرَّة. An outline, رَسْم — خَطّ *pl.* خُطُوط. Features, the countenance, مُحَيًّا — وَجْه — طَلْعَة. Points, subjects of a case, أَبْواب — مَوادّ — بَواعِث.

Featly, *ad.* بِنَشاطٍ.

Febrifuge, *n.* دَواءٌ لِلْحُمَّى — دافِعُ ٱلْحُمَّى.

Febrile, *a.* حُمِّيّ.

February, *n.* فَبْرَار ـ شَهْرُ شباطَ ـ شُبَاط.

Fecal, *a.* Containing dregs, مُتَرَسِّب ـ عَكِر ; containing excrement, برازِىٌّ ـ دِمْنِىٌّ.

Feces, *n.* Dregs, ثُفْل ـ رُسُوب. Excrement, دِمْن ـ براز.

Fecit, Done by such an one, شُغْلُ فُلانٍ.

Fecula, *a.* The flour of plants, دَقِيقُ ٱلْأَزْهارِ. Starch, نَشَآء ـ نَشَا.

Feculence, *n.* / **Feculency**, } Dregs, رُسُوب ـ عَكَر. Muddiness, رَنَق ـ كَدَر.

Feculent, *a.* Dreggy, مُرَسِّب ـ عَكِر. Muddy, رَنِق ـ أَكْدَرُ. To be —, عَكِرَ. To make —, أَعْكَرَ.

Fecund, *a.* Of a woman, ضَانِئٌ ; of land, خَصِيب ـ كَرِم ; of a year, أَزَبُّ. To be —, of a woman, ضَنِيَتِ ٱلْمَرْأَةُ ; of land, أَخْصَبَتِ ٱلْأَرْضُ.

Fecundate, *v.t.* To impregnate, أَحْبَلَ. To make fruitful, أَثْمَرَ ـ ثَمَّرَ. To —, as of a palm-tree, by means of the spadix of the male tree, لَقَّحَ ـ أَلْقَحَ ـ مَقَّ ـ أَبَّرَ ـ أَبَرَ. One who fecundates palm-trees, لَقَّاح. The fecundating matter of flowers, لَقاح.

Fecundation, *n.* The act of impregnating, of trees, *etc.*, إِلْقاح ـ إِحْبال ; of making fruitful, إِثْمار ـ تَثْمِير ; as of a palm-tree, إِبَارَة ـ إِبَار ـ تَلْقِيح.

Fecundity, *n.* Of a woman, ضَنًى ; of soil, خِصْب ـ بَرَكَة ـ غَنِيمَة.

Fed, *v.t.* *See to* Feed, *v.t.*

Fed, *a.* Well fed with fodder, مَعْلُوف ـ عَلِيف. Fattened, مُسَمَّن ـ مُعَلَّف.

Federal, *a.* Collective, united, مُجْتَمِع ـ مُتَّحِد ـ إِتِّحادِىٌّ. A — government, حُكُومَةٌ مُجْتَمِعَةٌ ـ حُكُومَة مُتَحالِف ـ حُكُومَةٌ مُتَحالِفَةٌ ـ جُمْهُورِيَّة.

Federal, *n.* / **Federalist**, } مُتَعَصِّبٌ لِلْحُكُومَةِ ٱلْمُجْتَمِعَةِ (*or* ٱلْجُمْهُورِيَّةِ).

Federalism, *n.* تَحالُف ـ أُصُولُ ٱلْحُكُومَةِ ٱلْجُمْهُورِيَّةِ.

Federate, *a.* *See* Confederate, *a.*

Federation, *n.* *See* Confederation, *n.*

Federative, *a.* *See* Confederate, *a.*

Fee, *n.* A reward, perquisite, حُلْوَان ـ أُجْرَة ـ أَجْر ـ نُبْلَة ـ عَائِدَة ـ مَعْلُوم *pl.* عَوائِدُ. An estate in trust, زَعَامَة ـ ٱلْتِزام ـ وَقْفٌ تَحْتَ ـ قَطِيعَة ـ إِقْطاع. Fee-simple, مُلْك. Fee-tail, وَقْفٌ تَحْتَ ٱلشُّرُوطِ. A broker's —, دَلَالَة. Fees of office, رُسُوم. To give land in — to, أَقْطَعَ لِ ـ إِقْطاعًا. To hold in —, تَصَرَّفَ بِٱلْمُلْكِ.

Fee-farm, *n.* قَطَاعَة ـ ٱلْتِزام.

Fee, *v.t.* جَازَى ـ أَجَّرَ.

Feeble, *a.* Weak, رَكِيك ـ مَنْهُوك ـ ضَعِيف *pl.* ضُعَفَاءُ. Worn out, tired, عاجِز. Ailing, sickly, عَلِيل. To be —, weak, ضَعُفَ ـ تَضَعَّفَ ; to be ailing, إِعْتَلَّ. To make —, أَضْعَفَ.

Feeble-minded, *a.* وَهِن ـ فائِلُ ٱلرَّأْيِ. To be —, وَهَنَ *aor.* يَهِنُ.

Feebleness, *n.* Weakness, ضُعْف ـ رَكَاكَة ـ فَيْلُولَة. Weariness, إِعْيَاء ـ عَجْز. Defect, نُقْصان. Want of fullness, dimness, رَكَاكَة. Unstableness, عَدَمُ ثَبَاتٍ. Flimsiness, سَخَافَة ـ عَدَمُ مَتَانَةٍ.

Feebly, *ad.* بِضُعْفٍ ـ بِرَخَاوَةٍ ـ بِعَجْزٍ.

Feed, *v.t.* To give food to, غَذَّى ـ بِ ـ غَذَا ـ بِ ـ غَذَّى ـ طَعَّمَ ـ أَطْعَمَ ـ أَكَّلَ ـ قاتَ. To supply with means of subsistence, أَطْعَمَ ـ رَزَقَ. To pasture, as of a flock, أَرْعَى. To satiate, to supply with enough, أَشْبَعَ. To nourish, رَبَّى. To supply with, جَهَّزَ ـ بِ. To be fed, supplied with food, تَغَذَّى ـ إِغْتَذَى بِ. To — upon, تَقَوَّتَ بِ ـ رَعَى. To be fed upon, إِقْتَاتَ بِ.

Feed, *v.i.* To eat, أَكَلَ ـ إِقْتَاتَ بِ. To live upon, إِقْتَاتَ بِ ـ تَقَوَّتَ بِ ـ عَاشَ بِ ـ رَعَى ; of cattle, رَعَى ـ تَرَعَّى ـ إِرْتَعَى. To graze, رَعَى. To flow into, صَبَّ فِى.

Feed, *n.* A supply, as of fodder, عَلَف ; of food, أَكْلَة ـ طَعَام ـ مأْكُول. Pasture, رَعْى ـ رِعَايَة.

Feeder, *n.* An eater, آكِل ـ أَكِيل *pl.* أَكَلَة. A great eater, أَكَّال. One who gives food, مُطْعِم. A fattener, as of cattle, مُسَمِّن ـ مُعَلِّف. An affluent stream, رافِد *pl.* رَوَافِدُ. An encourager, مُساعِد ـ مُعِينٌ عَلَى. A pastor, راعٍ ـ وَطَّاس *pl.* رُعَاة.

Feel, *v.t.* As by the touch, جَسَّ ـ لَامَسَ ـ لَمَسَ ـ مَسَّ. To —, by lightly pressing the hand on a thing, رَكَّ ـ جَرَّبَ ـ ٱلشَّىْءَ بِيَدِهِ. To try, to sound, إِمْتَحَنَ ـ جَرَّبَ. To have a sense of, عَلِمَ ـ عَرَفَ ـ شَعَرَ بِ ـ حَسَّ بِ. To — the pulse, جَسَّ ٱلنَّبْضَ. To — one's way, as with the hands, عَوَّثَ ـ تَلَمَّسَ ; to be cautious, إِحْتَذَرَ ـ عَسَّ. Come here that I may — you, تَقَدَّمْ لِأَجُسَّكَ.

Feel, *v.i.* To experience, حَسَّ ـ شَعَرَ. To — to the touch, to — like, ظَهَرَ لِلْمَسِّ كَأَنَّهُ. To — for, to pity, حَسَّ لِ ـ شَفِقَ عَلَى ـ تَحَنَّنَ ـ حَنَّ عَلَى ـ أَشْفَقَ عَلَى ـ شَفَقَ عَلَى ـ إِسْتَعْطَفَ عَلَى. To — pleasure, إِبْتَهَجَ ـ إِسْتَسَرَّ. To — pain, تَأَلَّمَ ـ حَسَّ بِٱلْوَجَعِ. To — sleepy, نَعَسَ. To — cold, بَرَدَ. To — hot, حَمَّ ـ سَخُنَ.

Feel, *n.* The act of touching, جَسّ ـ مَسّ ـ مُلَامَسَة ـ لَمْس. The sense of feeling, القُوَّةُ اللَّامِسَة.

Feeler, *n.* The — of an insect, قَرْن *pl.* قُرُون. One who compassionates, رَقِيقُ ٱلْقَلْبِ ـ شَفِيق ـ مُشْفِق. A test, تَجْرِبَة.

Feeling, *n.* The sense of touch, مَسّ ـ مُلَامَسَة ـ لَمْس. Sensibility, رِقَّةُ قَلْبٍ ـ حَنِيَّة ـ شَفَقَة. Apprehension, إِشْعَار بِ ـ عِلْم ـ تَفَهُّم ـ فَهْم ـ إِدْرَاك. State of —, heart, mind, خَاطِر ـ حَالَة ـ قَلْب. Impression, تَأَثُّر ـ تَأْثِير. Good —, friendship, صُحْبَة ـ مَحَبَّة. Countenance, support, مُعَاضَدَة ـ ظَهْر ـ مُعَاوَنَة. Right —, أَفْكَار صَالِحَة. Wrong —, أَفْكَار فَاسِدَة. Fellow-feeling, إِشْتِرَاكُ ٱلْمُتَصَاحِبِ. To have no —, to be past —, فَقَدَ ٱلْحِسّ ـ عَدِمَ ٱلْحِسّ. To hurt one's feelings, كَدَّرَ خَاطِرَهُ ـ أَغَمَّ. *See also* Emotion, Sense, Sentiment, *n.*

Feeling, *a.* Tender, مُتَحَنِّن ـ رَؤُوف ـ شَفِيق ـ شَفُوق. Affecting, مُرِقُّ ٱلْقَلْبِ ـ مُحَنِّن. Effective, مُؤَثِّر. Yearning, حَانّ ـ حَنَّان.

Feelingly, *ad.* Tenderly, بِشَفَقَةٍ ـ بِحِنِّيَّةٍ; so as to be felt, greatly, لِلْغَايَةِ ـ تَأْثِيرًا ـ جِدًّا.

Feet; *see* Foot, *n.*

Feign, *v.t.* To make a show of, تَظَاهَرَ بِ ـ تَخَيَّلَ بِ. To dissemble, تَمَثَّلَ بِ ـ إِصْطَنَعَ. To devise, أَوْجَدَ ـ إِخْتَرَعَ. To — one's self sick, تَمَارَضَ; mad, تَظَاهَرَ بِٱلْجُنُونِ; sorrowful, تَظَاهَرَ بِٱلْحُزْنِ; drunk, تَسَاكَرَ; elegance, grace, *etc.*, تَظَرَّفَ ـ تَظَارَفَ. To — to flee before an enemy, إِسْتَطْرَدَ لِ. To — one's self another person, تَنَكَّرَ. They feigned themselves righteous, تَرَآءَوْا أَنَّهُمْ أَبْرَار. *See also to* Pretend, Sham, *v.i.*

Feigned, *a.* غِشّ ـ مُصْطَنَع ـ مُخْتَلِف. A — name, إِسْم مَأْخُوذ (or مُتَّخَذ).

Feignedly, *ad.* بِٱلْكَذِبِ ـ بِتَصَنُّعٍ ـ إِصْطِنَاعًا ـ بِتَخَيُّلٍ ـ غِشًّا.

Feigner, *n.* A dissembler, مُرَآءٍ *pl.* مُرَاؤُون ـ مُنَافِق ـ مَاكِر ـ مُتَصَنِّع ـ مُدَار.

Feigning, *n.* حِيلَة ـ غِشّ ـ تَصَنُّع ـ تَخَيُّل.

Feint, *n.* A false attack, خَدْعَة ـ حِيلَة. Anything feigned, مُفْتَعِلَة. To make a —, إِحْتَالَ. To make a — against, إِفْتَعَلَ عَلَى ـ إِحْتَالَ عَلَى. To make a — of retiring from an enemy, and then turning upon him, إِسْتَطْرَدَ لِ; a — of that kind, إِسْتِطْرَاد.

Feldspar, *n.* }
Feldspath, } ضَرْب مِنْ حَجَرِ ٱلصَّوَانِ.

Felicitate, *v.t.* To congratulate, بَرَّكَ ـ بَارَكَ ـ هَنَّأَ ـ حَيَّى. To — on, for, بَارَكَ ـ فِي ـ لِ or هَنَّأَ ـ بِ. *See also to* Congratulate, *v t.*

Felicitation, *n.* مُبَارَكَة ـ تَبْرِيك ـ تَحِيَّة ـ هَنَآء. *See also* Congratulation, *n.*

Felicitous, *a.* Happy, مُبَارَك ـ سَعِيد ـ مَسْعُود. To the point, فِي مَحَلِّهِ ـ مُؤَثِّر ـ سَدِيد. He is — in speech, إِنَّهُ لَذُو سَدَادٍ.

Felicitously, *ad.* Happily, بِإِقْبَالٍ ـ نَعِيمًا ـ بِسَعَادَةٍ. To the point, فِي مَحَلِّهِ ـ سَدِيدًا.

Felicitousness, *n.* As of a speech, لَطَافَة ـ سَدَاد. *See also* Felicity, *n.*

Felicity, *n.* إِقْبَال ـ هَنَآء ـ حَظّ ـ بَرَكَة ـ سَعْد ـ أَمْن ـ نَعِيم ـ سُعُود. Eternal —, جَنَّاتُ ٱلنَّعِيمِ ـ سَعَادَة أَبَدِيَّة.

Feline, *a.* مَنْسُوب لِلْهِرِّ ـ مُتَعَلِّق بِٱلْقِطِّ.

Fell, *a.* Cruel, savage, ظَالِم ـ رِزَام ـ جَائِر ـ عَنِيف; of a war, *etc.*, عَقِيم ـ عُقَام.

Fell, *v.t.* To throw down, هَوَّرَ ـ رَمَى ـ طَرَحَ ـ لَبَطَ بِ ـ أَوْقَعَ ـ أَهْبَطَ. To —, as of trees, قَطَعَ.

Felloe, *n.* The — of a wheel, أُطْرَةُ عَجَلَةٍ *pl.* أُطَر.

Fellow, *n.* One of a pair, صِنْو *dual* صِنْوَانِ *pl.* صِنْوَان ـ زَوْج *pl.* أَزْوَاج ـ شَفْع ـ شَقِيق. Alike, match, حَرِيف ـ بَدِيد ـ ضِعْف *pl.* أَضْعَاف ـ وَصْل *pl.* أَوْصَال ـ شَبِيه *pl.* أَشْبَاه ـ نِدّ ـ شِبْه ـ قَرِين ـ نَدِيد. This is the — of that, هٰذَا خَطِير لِهٰذَا. A member, عُضْو *pl.* أَعْضَآء. A — of the Royal Academy, عُضْو مِنْ أَعْضَآءِ مَجْلِسِ ٱلْمُصَوِّرِينَ ٱلسُّلْطَانِيِّ. A companion, رَفِيق ـ رُفَقَآء ـ صَدِيق ـ أَلِيف. A man, in contempt, حَرِيف *pl.* حُرَفَآء ـ هٰذَا. An associate, شَرِيك *pl.* شُرَكَآء. Like this —, مِثْلَ هٰذَا. A turbulent —, مُفْسِد. A bed-fellow, ضَجِيع ـ كَمِيع. A school-fellow, رَفِيق فِي ٱلتَّلْمَذَةِ ـ أَحَدُ ٱلتَّلَامِيذِ. My good — ! يَا صَاحِ ـ يَا صَاحِبِي. He's a good —, لَا بَأْسَ بِهِ ـ أَنْعِمْ بِهِ ـ حَبَّذَا. Zaid is a good —, حَبَّذَا زَيْدٌ. Poor fellow! يَا مِسْكِينُ. Low fellows of the baser sort, رِجَال رُذَلَآء مِنْ أَهْلِ ٱلسُّوقِ ـ أَوْبَاش. A fine —, آدَمِيّ *pl.* أَوَادِمُ. An odd —, or amusing, مُطْرِب ـ مُفَرِّح. A quaint —, عَجِيب ـ غَرِيب ـ نُكْتَة. Such an one has not his —, فُلَانٌ لَيْسَ لَهُ خَطِير. To be hail — well met with, سَاوَى ـ كَانَ مَعَ ـ فِي طَبَقَةٍ وَاحِدَةٍ. It is like a — to the Nile, or like another Nile, كَأَنَّهُ صِنْوُ ٱلنِّيلِ. He distinguished himself from his fellows, contemporaries, تَمَيَّزَ عَنْ أَقْرَانِهِ.

Fellow-citizen, *n.* رَفِيق فِي ٱلرَّعِيَّةِ *pl.* رُفَقَآء.

Fellow-commoner, *n.* زَمِيل (or شَرِيك) فِي ٱلتَّلْمَذَةِ *pl.* زُمَلَآء.

Fellow-countryman, *n.* مِنْ بَلَدٍ وَاحِدٍ . His —, مِنْ ذاتِ بَلَدَتِهِ . Our fellow-countrymen, أَبْنَاءُ وَطَنِنا .

Fellow-creature, *n.* مِنْ جِنْسِنا . Our fellow-creatures, أَمْثَالُنا ـ نُدَائُدُنا .

Fellow-feeling, *n.* رِقَّة ـ مُوافَقَةُ الطِّباعِ ـ إِشْتِرَاكُ ٱلْمُصَاحَبَةِ .

Fellow-heir, *n.* شَرِيكٌ فِي ٱلْمِيرَاثِ .

Fellow-labourer, worker, *n.* حَرِيف *pl.* حُرَفاء ـ مُجَاهِدٌ ـ مُعَاوِل ـ عاوِلُون *pl.* عاوِل مَعَ (رَفِيقِي) ـ مَعَ (غَيْرِهِ) .

Fellow-member, *n.* مِنْ أَهْلِ ٱلـ ... ـ شَرِيكٌ فِي ٱلْعُضْوَةِ ـ رَفِيق .

Fellow-prisoner, *n.* مأْسُورٌ مَعَ (رَفِيقِي) *pl.* مأْسُورُون .

Fellow-servant, *n.* رَفِيقٌ فِي ٱلْخِدْمَةِ .

Fellow-soldier, *n.* رَفِيقٌ فِي ٱلْعَسْكَرِيَّةِ ـ مُتَجَنِّدٌ مَعَ (رَفِيقِي) .

Fellow-sufferer, *n.* مُتَأَلِّمٌ بِأَلَمٍ واحِدٍ ـ شَرِيكٌ فِي ٱلْبَلَاءِ .

Fellow-traveller, *n.* رَفِيق *pl.* رُفَقاء ـ رَفِيقٌ فِي ٱلسَّفَرِ .

Fellow, *v.t.* To match, زَوَّجَ-بِ ـ زَوَّجَ-إِلَى . To suit, وَافَقَ ـ قَارَنَ ـ عَادَلَ .

Fellowship, *n.* Companionship, intercourse, أُلْفَة ـ عِشْرَة ـ صُحْبَة ـ شِرْكَة ـ مُؤَانَسَة ـ إِتِّفاق ـ مُقارَنَة ـ مُعَاشَرَة . A society, أَهْل ـ جَمَاعَة ـ جَمْعِيَّة . The — of a college, راتِبُ مَدْرَسَةٍ *pl.* رَوَاتِب . To have — with, أَلِفَ ـ صَاحَبَ ـ عَاشَرَ .

Felo-de-se, *n.* قَتْلُ ٱلنَّفْسِ عَمْدًا ـ قَتْلُ ٱلنَّفْسِ .

Felon, *n.* A criminal, مُذْنِب ـ مُجْرِم ـ ذُو جُنَاحٍ ـ خَبِيث . One worthy of death, مُسْتَوْجِبُ ٱلْمَوْتِ . One condemned, مَقْضِيٌّ عَلَيْهِ ـ تَحْتَ ٱلدَّيْنُونَةِ . A whitlow, داحُوس ـ صُدَاعُ ٱلْأَصَابِعِ .

Felonious, *a.* فاسِد ـ شِرِّير ـ فاحِش ـ فاجِر ـ مُجْرِم .

Feloniously, *ad.* شَرًّا ـ إِذْنابًا ـ إِجْرامًا ـ جُرْمًا . To act —, تَجَرَّمَ ـ اِرْتَكَبَ ٱلْإِثْمَ ـ أَذْنَبَ ـ أَجْرَمَ .

Felony, *n.* جُرْمٌ كَبِيرٌ ـ ذَنْبٌ جَسِيمٌ ـ قَبِيحَة .

Felt, *n.* لِبْد *pl.* أَلْبَاد ـ لَبَّاد . A maker or seller of —, لُبُودِيٌّ .

Felt, *v.t.* لَبَّدَ ـ أَلْبَدَ .

Felucca, *n.* فَلُوكَة ـ فُلَيْكَة .

Female, *n.* A woman, اِمْرَأَة *pl.* نِسَاء . Any creature of the — sex, أُنْثَى *pl.* إِنَاث *or* أَنَاثَى . This is a (male) bird and its —, هٰذا طائِرٌ وَأُنْثاهُ . A — flower, زَهْرٌ مُؤَنَّثٌ . A — screw, لَوْلَبٌ أُمٌّ .

Female, *a.* مُؤَنَّث ـ نِسَائِيٌّ . The — sex, nature, الأَنَاثَة ; womankind, النِّسَاء ـ الحَرِيمُ . The — apartments, الحَرِيمُ ـ الحَرَمُ . Female studies, instructions, تَعْلِيماتٌ نِسائِيَّةٌ . The — population, الإِناثُ .

Feme covert, *n.* اِمْرَأَةٌ مُزَوَّجَةٌ ـ زَوْجَة .

Feme sole, *n.* اِمْرَأَةٌ غَيْرُ مُزَوَّجَةٍ .

Feminine, *a.* Of the female gender, مُؤَنَّث . Soft, womanly, مُخْتَصٌّ بِٱلنِّسَاءِ ـ مُتَعَلِّقٌ بِٱلنِّسَاءِ ـ مَطْرُوقَة . Pertaining to women, Like a woman, effeminate, مُخَنَّث ـ خُنْثَى . Delicate, tender, لَطِيف ـ مُلائِم ـ رَفِيع . The — gender, الجِنْسُ ٱلْمُؤَنَّثُ .

Femoral, *a.* مُتَعَلِّقٌ بِٱلْفَخِذِ ـ فَخِذِيٌّ .

Fen, *n.* رَدْغ *pl.* غِيَال ـ غُيُول ـ أَجَمَة ـ مُسْتَنْقَع ـ بَطِيحَة .

Fence, *n.* A defence, حِمَايَة ـ صِيَانَة ـ مُدَافَعَة . An inclosure, حائِط ـ حَجْر ـ جِدْر ـ إِحَاطَة . A barrier, سَدّ ـ حاجِز . A wall, دَرَابْزِين *pl.* حِيطان . A hedge, سِيَاج *pl.* سُوج ; of pales, a palisade, دَرَابْزِين .

Fence, *v.t.* To fortify, حَصَّنَ . To protect, صَانَ [2]. To surround with, أَحَاطَ-بِ . To hedge, سَيَّجَ . To inclose with a fence, حَوَّطَ ـ جَدَرَ [2].

Fence, *v.i.* To —, as with sword and shield, لَعِبَ ـ تَطَاعَنَ بِٱلسَّيْفِ وَٱلتُّرْسِ . To —, as with words, *etc.*, إِحْتَالَ ـ تَحَوَّلَ . A fenced city, مَدِينَةٌ مُحَصَّنَةٌ . It formed a — between the two, حَجَزَ بَيْنَهُما [2].

Fencer, *n.* A — with arms, مُتَطَاعِن ـ سَيَّاف ; with words, مُحَاوِل . To fence or stop us, سَدَّ [2].

Fencible, *a.* يُصَانُ ـ يُحَامَى عَنْهُ .

Fencibles, *a.* عَسَاكِرُ رَدِيف .

Fencing, *n.* Materials for making fences, لَوَازِمُ لِلْجِدَارِ . The art of making fences, تَسْيِيج ـ صِنَاعَةُ ٱلتَّحْوِيطِ ; of using the foil, مُسَايَفَة ـ فَنُّ لَعِبِ ٱلسَّيْفِ . Fencing with words, مُحَاوَلَة ـ إِحْتِيَال .

Fencing-master, *n.* مُعَلِّمُ ٱلْمُسَايَفَةِ .

Fencing-school, *n.* مَدْرَسَةٌ لِتَعْلِيمِ ٱلْمُسَايَفَةِ .

Fend, *v.t.* To ward off, to repel, دَفَعَ ـ رَدَّ [2] ـ جَنَّبَ ـ جَنَّبَ [2].

Fend, *v.i.* To shift off, زَالَ عَن ـ تَجَنَّبَ [2]. To steer clear of, تَجَنَّبَ مِن .

Fender, *n.* A — to keep ships from touching, قَرْمِيلَة . The — of a fire-place, حاجِزٌ لِلنَّارِ .

Fenestral, *a.* مُتَعَلِّقٌ بِٱلطَّاقَةِ .

Fennel, *n.* بَسْبَاس ـ رَازِيَانَج ـ شَمَر .

Fenny, *a.* رَادِغ ـ غِيَاضِيٌّ ـ أَجَمِيٌّ .

Fenugreek, *n.* حُلْبَة ـ حُلْبَة *coll.* حُلْب .

Feodal, *a.* *See* Feudal, *a.*

Feoff, *v.t.* To invest with the fee of land, أَقْطَعَ لِ ـ مَلَّكَ-عَلَى .

Feoffee, *n.* المُتَصَرِّف بِالزَّعَامَة ـ صاحِبُ الاِلتِزام ـ زَعِيم.

Feoffer, *n.* } Feoffor, } مُقْطِع ـ صاحِبُ المُلك.

Feoffment, *n.* اِلتِزام ـ زَعامَة ـ وَدِيعَة.

Feracious, *a.* Fruitful, مُخْصِب ـ مُثْمِر.

Ferial, *a.* مُتَعَلِّق بِالأَعْيَاد.

Ferine, *a.* *See* Ferocious, *a.*

Ferment, *n.* The state of boiling, غَلَيَان; of fermentation, إِخْتِمار. Agitation, tumult, هَيَجَان ـ اِضْطِراب ـ اِخْتِلال ـ فِتْنَة ـ غَوْغَاء or غَوْغَاء.

Ferment, *v.t.* To leaven, خَمَّ ـ ﹶ خَمَرَ ـ ﹸ فَتَقَ. To excite, حَرَّضَ ـ هَيَّجَ.

Ferment, *v.i.* To be in a state of leaven, تَخَمَّرَ ـ اِخْتَمَرَ; of agitation, اِهْتَاجَ ـ تَهَيَّجَ ـ اِضْطَرَبَ.

Fermentability, *n.* قَابِلِيَّة التَّخَمُّر.

Fermentable, *a.* قَابِل التَّخْمِير ـ يَتَخَمَّر ـ يَخْتَمِر.

Fermental, *a.* خَامِر ـ مُخَمِّر.

Fermentation, *n.* The act of leavening, تَخْمِير; the being fermented, تَخَمُّر ـ اِخْتِمار. State of agitation, tumult, حَرَكَة ـ فِتْنَة ـ شَغْب ـ هَيَجَان. Vinous —, تَخَمُّر النَّبِيذ. Doughy —, تَخَمُّر العَجِين. Putrefactive —, تَعَفُّن ـ اِنْفِساد.

Fermentative, *a.* *See* Fermental, *a.*

Fermented, *a.* مُخْتَمِر ـ مُتَخَمِّر. Fermented liquors, مُسْكِرات ـ مُسَكِّرات.

Fern, *n.* بَطَارِس ـ سَرْخَس.

Ferny, *a.* مَمْلُوّ مِنْ بَطَارِس ـ سَرْخَسِيّ.

Ferocious, *a.* Savage, wild, مُتَوَحِّش ـ وَحْشِيّ. Cruel, جَائِر ـ غَاشِم. Fierce, كَاسِر ـ ضَارٍ *pl.* ضَوارٍ. A — dog, كَلْب عَنِيف ـ مُكْفَهِرّ. Ferocious animals, ضَوَارٍ.

Ferociously, *ad.* Savagely, بِوَحْشَة ـ مُتَوَحِّشًا. Cruelly, بِعُنْف ـ بِجَوْر ـ بِصَرَامَة. Fiercely, بِافْتِراس ـ بِضَرَاوَة.

Ferociousness, *n.* } Ferocity, } Savageness, wildness, وَحْشَة. Cruelty, جَوْر ـ عُنْف ـ صَرَامَة. Fierceness, اِفْتِراس ـ ضَرَاوَة.

Ferreous, *a.* مِثْل الحَدِيد ـ مِنْ حَدِيد.

Ferret, *n.* The animal, اِبْنُ عِرْس *pl.* بَنَاتُ عِرْس ـ عِرْسَة ـ عُرَيْسَة. Woollen tape, شَرِيط مِنْ صُوف.

Ferret, *v.t.* To hunt, look about, for, فَتَّشَ عَلَى ـ اِصْطَادَ. To discover, ﹷ كَشَفَ عَلَى ـ ﹷ ظَهَرَ عَلَى.

Ferriage, *n.* أُجْرَة العُبُور.

Ferriferous, *a.* مُوَلِّد الحَدِيد.

Ferruginous, *a.* مَخْلُوط بِحَدِيد ـ حَدِيدِيّ.

Ferrugo, *n.* The — of plants, يَرَقَان.

Ferrule, *n.* زُجّ *pl.* زِجَاج ـ حَلْقَة. To put a — to, أَزَجَّ ـ زَجَّجَ.

Ferry, *n.* A place for passing a river, مَعْبَر *pl.* مَعَابِر. Right of passage, حَقّ العُبُور.

Ferry, *v.t.* أَقْطَعَ ـ عَدَّى ـ عَبَّرَ.

Ferry-boat, *n.* مِعْبَر ـ مِعْبَرَة.

Ferry-man, *n.* غَادِف المِعْبَر ـ غَادِف.

Fertile, *a.* Fruitful, productive, خَصِيب ـ مُثْمِر ـ ثَمْرَاء ـ غَزِير ـ مُنْبِت ـ كَرَم. Ready, مُسْتَعِدّ ـ صاحِبُ تَدْبِير. A — mind, عَقْل مُثْمِر. A — district, رِيف *pl.* أَرْيَاف. Fertile land, أَرْض مَكْرُومَة (or كَرِم). To be —, fruitful, أَخْصَبَ ـ أَرْيَفَ ـ خَصُبَ.

Fertility, *n.* Fruitfulness, بَرَكَة ـ إِثْمار ـ غَزَارَة ـ خِصْب. Readiness, اِسْتِعْداد ـ سُرْعَة ـ إِيجاد.

Fertilize, *v.t.* أَغْزَرَ ـ نَبَّتَ ـ خَصَّبَ.

Fertilization, *n.* The act of, تَنْبِيت ـ تَغْزِير ـ تَخْصِيب. The action of the pollen on plants, تَلْقِيم.

Fertilizer, *n.* مُغَزِّر ـ مُنَبِّت ـ مُخَصِّب.

Ferule, *n.* A stick, rod, عَصًا *pl.* عُصِيّ and عِصِيّ ـ سَوْط ـ عَصَا الأَدَب.

Ferule, *v.t.* ﹸ عَصَا ـ عَصَا ـ ﹷ ضَرَبَ.

Fervency, *n.* Ardency, as in prayer, حَرَارَة. Eagerness, warmth, غَيْرَة ـ حِدَّة ـ حَمِيَّة ـ حَمَس ـ حَمَاسَة. Desire, شَوْق ـ اِشْتِياق. Partizanship, تَعَصُّب.

Fervent, *a.* Warm, حَارّ ـ سَخِين ـ سُخْن. Ardent in devotion, صَاحِبُ حَرَارَة فِي التَّعَبُّد ـ مُتَحَمِّس (or حَمِس) فِي الدِّين ـ مُجْتَهِد ـ غَيُور ـ حَمِيس ـ مُلْتَهِب فِي العِبَادَة. Zealous, حَنَّان ـ مُشْتَاق إِلَى. Longing, هَائِج ـ ذُو حَمِيَّة. Fervent in spirit, حَارّ بِالرُّوح. Fervent zeal, غَيْرَة كُلِّيَّة. To be —, تَحَمَّسَ ـ ﹷ حَمِسَ. *See also* Devoted, *a.*

Fervently, *ad.* بِحَمَس ـ بِحَمِيَّة ـ بِحَرَارَة ـ بِاشْتِيَاق كُلِّيّ. To act — in, تَحَمَّسَ فِي. *See also* Devotedly, *ad.*

Fervid, *a.* *See* Fervent, *a.*

Fervidly, *ad.* *See* Fervently, *ad.*

Fervidness, *n.* } Fervour, } *See* Fervency, *n.*

Festal, *a.* *See* Festive, *a.*

Fester, *v.i.* To suppurate, أَمَدَّ ـ دَمَّلَ ـ تَقَرَّحَ ـ تَقَيَّحَ. To putrefy, تَعَفَّنَ. To become evil, mischievous, شَرَّ aor. يَشَرُّ — ² فَسَدَ — أَفْسَدَ.

Fester, *n.* شَافَة — دُمَّل — قَرْحَة.

Festival, *n.* A religious commemoration, عِيد pl. أَعْيَاد. A public —, مَوْسِم pl. مَوَاسِم. A private —, فَرَح pl. أَفْرَاح. An entertainment, وَلِيمَة pl. وَلَائِم — مَأْدُبَة pl. مَآدِب. To keep a —, عَيَّدَ. To offer one the compliment appropriate to a —, عَيَّدَ ل — عَيَّدَ. عَايَدَ عَلَى — عَايَدَ. *Usual compliments on such occasions:*— كُلَّ سَنَةٍ وَأَنْتَ — عَلَيْكَ أَبْرَكُ ٱلْأَعْيَادِ ; Ans. مُبَارَكٌ عَلَيْكَ ; أَعْوَامٌ عَدِيدَةٌ وَأَيَّامٌ مَدِيدَةٌ — وَأَنْتَ سَالِمٌ ; Ans. سَالِمٌ ; Ans. وَأَنْتَ بِخَيْرٍ.

Festive, *a.* Pertaining to a festival, عِيدِيٌّ — مُتَعَلِّقٌ بِٱلْعِيدِ. Joyous, بَجْبُوح — مُبْتَهِج — مُطْرِب — مُفْرِح — فَرِح.

Festivity, *n.* Mirth, غِبْطَة — سُرُور — طَرَب — فَرَح. *See also* Festival, *n.*

Festoon, *n.* A — of flowers, إِكْلِيلُ زَهْرٍ — أَشْرَاج pl. شَرَجُ زَهْرٍ pl. أَكَالِيل.

Festoon, *v.t.* To adorn with festoons, زَيَّنَ-بِأَشْرَاجِ زَهْرٍ — زَيَّنَ-بِأَكَالِيلَ مِنْ زَهْرٍ. To tie in festoons, (رَبَطَ- or) -رَكَّبَ بِهَيْئَةِ ٱلْأَغْصَانِ وَٱلْأَزْهَارِ.

Fetal, *n.* Relating to a fetus, جَنِينِيٌّ — مُتَعَلِّقٌ بِجَنِينٍ.

Fetch, *v.t.* To bring, جَآءَ ب aor. يَجِيءُ — أَحْضَرَ. To derive anything from, أَصْدَرَ-عَنْ — إِشْتَقَّ-مِنْ. To —, as from a place, ² نَقَلَ — ² شَالَ ب — رَفَعَ — ² جَلَبَ-مِنْ. To — away, To — a breath, تَنَفَّسَ. To — down, ² حَطَّ — أَهْبَطَ — نَزَّلَ. To — a compass, to turn, ² دَارَ : we fetched a compass, دُرْنَا. To —, as of a price, أَصَابَ — جَآءَ ب — يُبَاعُ ب. *See also to* Bring, *v.t.*

Fetch, *n.* A stratagem, حِيلَة — مَكِيدَة — دُولَاب.

Fête, *n.* *See* Feast, Festival, *n.*

Fetich, *n.* An African idol, صَنَمٌ مِنْ أَصْنَامِ أَفْرِيقِيَّةَ — فَتِيش pl. أَصْنَام.

Fetichism, *n.* عِبَادَةُ ٱلْفَتِيشِ.

Fetid, *a.* أَذْفَر — سَنِخ — زَنِخ — مُعَفَّن — مُنْتِن ; of the breath, أَبْخَر — أَمْذَح. To be —, سَنِخَ — زَنِخَ — نَتَنَ — أَنْتَنَ.

Fetidness, *n.* نَتَانَة — عُفُونَة — زَنَخَة — سَنَخَة — دَفَر ; of the mouth, بَخَر.

Fetlock, *n.* ثُنَّة pl. ثُنَن. The part covered by the —, أُمُّ ٱلْقِرْدَانِ. The — joint, ٱلْحَوْشَب.

Fetor, *n.* *See* Fetidness, *n.*

Fetter, *n.* كَبْل pl. كُبُول — صِفَاد — صِفَاد pl. أَصْفَاد — رِبَاط — قَيْد pl. قُيُود.

Fetter, *v.t.* To shackle, زَنْجَرَ — قَيَّدَ — أَصْفَدَ — ² صَفَدَ — كَبَّلَ — ² رَبَطَ. Fettered, مُقَيَّد. *See also to* Restrain, *v.t.*

Fetterless, *a.* عَتِيق — بِغَيْرِ قُيُودٍ.

Fetus, *n.* جَنِين pl. أَجِنَّة — حَبَل. The membrane covering the —, سَلًى pl. أَسْلَاء.

Feud, *n.* A contention, مُشَاجَرَة — مُعَارَضَة — خُصُومَة — نِزَاع — مُنَازَعَة — شِقَاق.

Feud, *n.* A — of land, إِقْطَاع — اِلْتِزَام — زَعَامَة.

Feudal, *a.* Relating to feuds, مُتَعَلِّقٌ بِٱلِٱلْتِزَامَاتِ. A — possession, اِلْتِزَام. A — lord, زَعِيم pl. زُعَمَآء — صَاحِبُ زَعَامَةٍ.

Feudalism, *n.* } أُصُول — الشُّرُوطُ ٱلْمُتَعَلِّقَةُ بِٱلِٱلْتِزَامَاتِ
Feudal-system, } ٱلْإِقْطَاع.

Feudality, *n.* حَالَةُ ٱلزَّعَامَةِ.

Feudalization, *n.* إِدْخَالٌ تَحْتَ شُرُوطِ ٱلِٱلْتِزَامَاتِ.

Feudary, *a.* } مُلْتَزِم — مُسْتَوْدَع — زَعِيم.
Feudatory, *n.* }

Fever, *n.* حُمَّى pl. حُمَّيَات — سُخُونَة — حُمَّة ; of cattle, حُمَام. To have a —, حُمَّ — اِنْحَمَّ — ² سَخُنَ. I have a —, حُمِمْتُ حُمَّى. He got a — from eating (certain) food, حُمَّ عَلَى طَعَامٍ. The — rose, ثَارَتِ ٱلْحُمَّى. The — continued upon him, صَلُبَتِ ٱلْحُمَّى عَلَيْهِ — رَكِبَتْهُ ٱلْحُمَّى. Having a —, سُخْنَان — سَاخِن — مَحْمُوم. He caught a —, أَخَذَتْهُ ٱلسُّخُونَةُ. He has had three attacks of —, تَوَاصَلَتْ عَلَيْهِ ٱلسُّخُونَةُ ثَلَاثَ مَرَّاتٍ. Fever, inquietude, ضَرَبَة — قَلَق — شَغَب — اِضْطِرَاب. To put one in a —, to disquiet, أَقْلَقَ — خَالَجَ — أَكَابَ — أَزْعَجَ.

Ague fever, حُمَّى رَاجِفَة.

Burning fever, حُمَّى مُحْرِقَة.

Hectic fever, حُمَّى ٱلدِّقِّ.

Inflammatory fever, حُمَّى ٱلْتِهَابِيَّة.

Intermittent fever, حُمَّى دَوْرِيَّة.

Puerperal fever, حُمَّةُ ٱلنِّفَاسِ — حُمَّةُ ٱلْوِلَادَةِ.

Quartan fever, حُمَّى ٱلرِّبْعِ — رِبْع.

Quotidian fever, حُمَّى نَائِبَة — حُمَّى وَاظِبَة — حُمَّى يَوْمِيَّة.

Remittent fever, حُمَّى لَازِمَة — حُمَّى دَائِمَة — حُمَّى مُطْبِقَة.

Scarlet fever, حُمَّةٌ حَصَبِيَّة.

Tertian fever, حُمَّى غِبٍّ — سُخُونَةٌ مُثَلِّثَة — غِبّ.

Feverfew, *n.* The plant, شُجَيْرَة — وِينَادِيق — ضَرْبٌ مِنَ ٱلْأُقْحُوَانِ مَرْيَم.

Feverish, *a.* Having fever, مَحْمُوم — سَاخِن. Disquieted, قَلِق — مُضْطَرِب.

Feverishly, *ad.* بِحَرَارَةٍ.

Feverishness, *n.* حُمَّة — حَرَارَة.

Few, *a.* بَعْض — يَسِيرَة — قَلَائِل — قَلِيلُون — قَلِيل. Few there be who find it, قَلِيلُونَ هُمُ ٱلَّذِينَ يَجِدُونَهُ. A few sick persons, قَلِيلُونَ مِنَ ٱلْمَرْضَى. Are they few who will be saved? أَقَلِيلٌ هُمُ ٱلَّذِينَ يَخْلُصُون. For a few days, لِأَيَّامٍ قَلِيلَةٍ. It seemed to him but a few days, كَانَتْ فِي عَيْنَيْهِ كَأَيَّامٍ قَلِيلَةٍ. In a few words, بِإِيجَازٍ — بِٱلِٱخْتِصَارِ. Some few, بَعْض. Not a few, عَدَدٌ لَيْسَ بِقَلِيلٍ. Fewer than…, أَقَلُّ مِن.

Fewness, *n.* قِلَّة.

Fez, *n.* The country, فَاس. A red skull cap, طَرْبُوش *pl.* طَرَابِيش.

Fiasco, *n.* خَيْبَة — عَدَمُ تَوْفِيقٍ.

Fiat, *n.* أَمْر — حُكْم.

Fib, *n.* زُور — كَاذِبَة — كَذِب — كِذْبَة.

Fib, *v.i.* كَذَبَ.

Fibber, *n.* كَاذِب *pl.* كَذَّاب — كُذَّب.

Fibre, *n.* As of plants, لِيفَة *coll.* لِيف *pl.* أَلْيَاف — فَتِيل — نَسِيج — نَسِيجَة. The capillary root of a plant, عُسْلُوج *pl.* عَسَالِيج. A rope of —, مَسَد *pl.* مِسَاد — وَشِيجَة.

Fibrous, *a.* لِيفِيّ — مِنْ لِيفٍ — ذُو أَلْيَافٍ. A — substance, نَسِيجَة — نَسِيج — لِيف.

Fibula, *n.* القَصَبَةُ ٱلصُّغْرَى.

Fickle, *a.* مُرْتَاب — طَائِش — مُقَلْقِل — مُتَلَوِّن — فَرَّار — ارْتَاب — خَفَّ. To be —, فَرْفَار — سَفِيه — هَوَائِيّ — حَالَاتِيّ — طَاشَ *aor.* يَطِيشُ. Fickle women, سَوَّآءُ لَوَّآءُ. تَلْقَل

Fickleness, *n.* تَلَوُّن — نَاقِلَة — سَفَه — طَيْرَة — فَرْفَرَة — طَيْش — طَيَشَان.

Fictile, *a.* Made by art, مَجْبُولٌ بِفَنٍّ — مَصْنُوعٌ بِصِنَاعَةٍ; of pottery, فَخَّار. A — vase, فَخَّارَة *coll.* فَخَّار.

Fiction, *n.* The act of inventing, نَشْأَة — تَصْنِيف — اخْتِرَاع. A tale, خُرَافَة *pl.* خُرَافَات. A lie, زُور — كَذِب — كَاذِبَة. A legal —, فَرْضٌ قَانُونِيٌّ غَيْرُ صَحِيحٍ. Anything feigned, مُفْتَعَلَة. A myth, إِسْمٌ مِنْ غَيْرِ جِسْمٍ.

Fictitious, *a.* Feigned, غِشّ — مُصَنَّع. Imaginary, خَيَالِيّ — مِنْ غَيْرِ أَصْلٍ — مُبْدَع. False, كَاذِب — مُزَوَّر. A — name, إِسْمٌ عَارِيَةٌ — إِسْمٌ مُصْطَنَعٌ.

Fictitiously, *ad.* اصْطِنَاعًا — بِتَصَنُّعٍ — تَزْوِيرًا.

Fid, *n.* The tool, مِبْرَم. A support, clamp, ضَبَّة.

Fiddle, *n.* كَمَانْجَة — رَبَابَة — رَبَاب.

Fiddle, *v.i.* To play the —, ضَرَبَ ٱلْكَمَانْجَةَ. To trifle, تَهَابَلَ — لَعِبَ — عَبِثَ. To — away one's time, صَرَفَ ضَيَّعَ أَوْقَاتَهُ — وَقْتَهُ.

Fiddle-faddle, *n.* هَذَر — مَسْخَرَة — تَخْرِيفَة — عَبَث — تَفَاهَة.

Fiddler, *n.* A player on a fiddle, كَمَانْجِي — ضَرَّابُ ٱلْكَمَانْجَةِ رَبَابِيّ *pl.* رَبَابِيَّة.

Fiddle-stick, *n.* قَوْسُ كَمَانْجَةٍ *pl.* قِسِيّ *and* أَقْوَاس. *See also* Nonsense, *n.*

Fiddle-string, *n.* وَتَر *pl.* أَوْتَار.

Fidelity, *n.* *See* Faithfulness, *n.*

Fidget, *v.i.* تَقَلْقَلَ — تَمَوَّرَ — تَرَقَّصَ. To —, to torment, one's self, تَعَذَّبَ — تَعَنَّفَ.

Fidget, *n.* تَقَلْقُل — تَمَوُّر — تَرَقُّص.

Fidget, *n.* } Restless, أَفْزَاز *pl.* فَزّ — عَزْهَل — وُلَجَةٌ خُرَجَةٌ —
Fidgety, *a.* } نَمِل — مَوَّار. A — woman, إِمْرَأَةٌ نَمْلَى.

Fiducial, *a.* حَقِيقِيّ — ذُو وَفَآءٍ — أَمِين.

Fiducially, *ad.* أَمَانَةً.

Fiduciary, *n.* وَكِيل — مُسْتَوْدَع — أَمِين.

Fie, *int.* أُفّ — تُوه — أُفّ. Fie upon you! أُفٍّ عَلَيْكَ. Fie for shame! عَيْبٌ عَلَيْكَ.

Fief, *n.* Land held of a superior; *see* Feud, *n.*

Field, *n.* A cultivated space, ضَيْعَة *pl.* ضِيَاع — مَزْرَعَة *pl.* مَزَارِع — حَقْل *pl.* حُقُول — غَيْط *pl.* غِيطَان; of about an English acre in extent, فَدَّان *pl.* فَدَادِين. An open space, خَلَاء — صَحْرَآء — فَضَآء. Extent, compass, سَعَة. Subject-matter, مَوْضُوع — مَادَّة. The surface of a shield, وَجْهُ تُرْسٍ. The ground on which anything is drawn, أَرْضِيَّة. A battle, مُقَاتَلَة — حَرْب — مُحَارَبَة. A —, as of battle, مَيْدَانُ ٱلْحَرْبِ — مَعْرَكَة — مَيْدَان — مَعْرَك — مَوْقِع. The scope of a telescope, قُطْرُ نَظَّارَةٍ. A hunting ground, مَصَاد — مُتَصَيَّد — مُصْطَاد. An open place for exercise, مَيْدَان. To bring into the —, as of soldiers, أَبْرَزَ فِي مَيْدَانِ ٱلْحَرْبِ مِنَ ٱلْعَسَاكِرِ. To take the —, بَرَزَ فِي ٱلْمَيْدَانِ. To keep the —, لَزِمَ ٱلْمَيْدَانَ. To drive off the —, هَزَّبَ — كَسَرَ — فَلَّلَ — أَنْزَ. Field of operations, مَيْدَانُ حَرَكَاتِ ٱلْعَسْكَرِ; of an army, مَيْدَانُ ٱلْعَمَلِ. He is able to bring 50,000 men into the —, قَادِرٌ أَنْ يُبْرِزَ خَمْسِينَ أَلْفًا مِنَ ٱلْمُقَاتِلِينَ فِي مَيْدَانِ ٱلْحَرْبِ.

Field-book, *n.* دَفْتَرُ مُهَنْدِسٍ يُقَيِّدُ فِيهِ ٱلْمَسَافَاتِ وَٱلْأَبْعَادَ إِلَخ.

Field-day, *n.* يَوْمُ عَرْضٍ — يَوْمُ كَشْفٍ عَلَى ٱلْعَسَاكِرِ عُمُومًا (ٱلْعَسْكَرِ *or* ٱلْجُنْدِ).

Field-marshal, *n.* مُشِيرُ ٱلْعَسْكَرِ ـ قائِدُ ٱلْعَساكِرِ.

Field-mouse, *n.* فَأْرُ ٱلْغَيْطِ ـ قَدَاد.

Field-officer, *n.* ضابِطٌ فِي أَعْلَى دَرَجَةٍ مِنَ ٱلْقُولِ أَغاسِي.

Field-piece, *n.* مِدْفَعٌ عَلَى جَرَّارٍ *pl.* مَدافِعُ.

Field-sports, *n.* Of hunting, *etc.*, الصَّيْدُ وَٱلْقَنْصُ; of athletic exercises, الرِّيَاضَاتُ.

Field-works, *n.* إِسْتِحْكَامَاتٌ خَفِيفَةٌ.

Fiend, *n.* A demon, شَيْطان ـ جان ـ عِفْرِيت *pl.* عَفارِيتُ *pl.* شَياطِينُ. A malicious person, شِرِّير ـ خَبِيث ـ مُسْخَم.

Fiendish, *a.* / Fiendlike, } شَيْطانِيٌّ ـ حَنِك ـ حَسِك ـ غِدِّير ـ مُسْخَم.

Fiendishness, *n.* غَمَر ـ غِمْر ـ سُخْمَة ـ حَنَك ـ شَيْطَنَة.

Fierce, *a.* Savage, مُتَوَحِّش ـ وَحِش. Cruel, قاسٍ. Insolent, overbearing, مَرِيد ـ بَطِر ـ عاتٍ. Passionate, هائِج ـ أَضَرّ ـ أَسِف ـ حُدَاد. Strong, violent, قَوِيّ ـ شَدِيد. A — wind, رِيحٌ عاصِفَةٌ. A — fire, نارٌ لَهْبَى. A — countenance, وَجْهٌ جافٍ; having a — countenance, جافِي ٱلْوَجْهِ. Fiercer than wolves, أَحَدُّ مِنَ ٱلذِّئابِ.

Fiercely, *ad.* Violently, بِغَشْمَرَةٍ ـ بِحِدَّةٍ ـ بِشِدَّةٍ.

Fierceness, *n.* Ferocity, تَوَحُّش ـ وَحْشَة. Insolent overbearing, مُرُود ـ عُتُوّ ـ بَطَر. Cruelty, عَنَف ـ قَساوَة. Violence, غَشْمَرَة ـ حِدَّة ـ شِدَّة. Fierceness of anger, حُمُوُّ ٱلْغَضَبِ ـ رِجْز; of the wind, عُصُوف; of a fire, سُخْنَة ـ لَهَبان; of a countenance, جَفَآء. Impetuosity, وَقْعَة ـ حُمَيَّا ـ سَوْرَة ـ تَهَوُّر.

Fieriness, *n.* As of heat, حَرارَة ـ لُهاب ـ نارِيَّة; of temper, حُمُوُّ ٱلْغَضَبِ ـ تَهَوُّر ـ رِجْز.

Fiery, *a.* Burning like fire, مُلْتَهِب ـ مُتَّقِد ـ كَٱلنَّارِ ـ مُحْرِق. Passionate, أَسِف ـ حُدَاد ـ هائِج. Pungent, ذَفِر ـ حادّ ـ حامِز. A — flame, لَهِيبُ نارٍ. A — oven, تَنُّورُ نارٍ.

Fife, *n.* مِزْمار ـ صَفَّارَة ـ ناى.

Fife, *v.i.* دَقَّ بِٱلنَّاى ـ زَمَّرَ.

Fifer, *n.* ضارِبٌ بِٱلنَّاى ـ زَمَّار.

Fifteen, *a.* خَمْسَةَ عَشَرَ *fem.* خَمْسَ عَشْرَةَ.

Fifteenth, *a.* The —, الخامِسُ عَشَرَ *fem.* الخامِسَةَ عَشْرَةَ. A — part, خُمْسُ عُشْرٍ.

Fifth, *a.* خامِس *fem.* خامِسَة.

Fifth, *n.* A — part, خُمْس ـ خُمُس ـ خَمِيس *pl.* أَخْماس. Three fifths of the debt, ثَلٰثَةُ أَخْماسٍ مِنَ ٱلدَّيْنِ.

Fifthly, *ad.* خامِسًا.

Fiftieth, *a.* الخَمْسُون.

Fiftieth, *n.* الخَمْسُون.

Fig, *n.* The tree, شَجَرَةُ ٱلتِّينِ ـ تِينَة; the fruit, بَلَس ـ تِينَة *coll.* تِين *pl.* تِينات. Indian —, the prickly pear, the tree, صَبَّار; the fruit, صُبَّيْرَة *coll.* صُبَّيْر *pl.* صُبَّيْرات. Young green figs, فِجّ. He does not care a — for him, لا يُلْقِي إِلَيْهِ بالاً ـ يَسْتَقِلُّهُ ـ ما يُبالِي بِهِ ـ لا يَعْتَنِي بِهِ ٱلْبَتَّةَ. To — one's self out, to pretend, تَصَنَّعَ; to deck one's self out, تَزَيَّنَ ـ تَظَرَّفَ.

Fight, *n.* A battle, مُعارَكَة ـ مُضارَبَة ـ مَغْزاة ـ غَزاة. A row, هَوْشَة ـ هَيْشَة ـ غَيْشَرَة ـ نِزاع. حَرْب ـ وَقْعَة ـ مُحارَبَة *pl.* قِتال ـ هَوْشات. The place of a —, مَعْرَك ـ مَوْقِع. The thick of the —, جاحِمُ ٱلْحَرْبِ. A stand-up —, مُجاهَرَة.

Fight, *v.i.* To contend in battle with, قاتَلَ ـ تَحارَبَ ـ عارَكَ ـ ضارَبَ. To contend, نازَعَ. To strive, كَدَّ ـ إِجْتَهَدَ. To go forth to —, or to plunder, غَزَا *aor.* يَغْزُو. To — shy of, through cowardice, خَامَ عَن. To — for one's family, دافَعَ (or قاتَلَ) عَنِ ٱلْعِيالِ. To — together, of many, تَعارَكُوا ـ تَضارَبُوا. To — for the faith, جاهَدَ فِي سَبِيلِ ٱللّٰهِ. To — it out, with battle, قَضَى ٱلدَّعْوَى بِقِتالٍ. To — to the death, إِسْتَحْنَطَ.

Fight, *v.a.* عارَكَ ـ تَقاتَلَ مَعَ ـ قاتَلَ.

Fighter, *n.* A fighting man, غازٍ *pl.* غُزاة ـ مُقاتِل ـ مُحارِب ـ ضارِب. Fighters, fighting men, مُقاتِلُ ـ مُقاتِلَة.

Fighting, *n.* See Fight, *n.*

Fighting, *a.* مُقاتِل ـ مُحارِب ـ حَرْبِيّ.

Fig-leaf, *n.* وَرَقُ تِينَةٍ. A covering for the private parts, سِتْرُ ٱلْعَوْرَةِ.

Figment, *n.* بِدْعَة ـ إِخْتِراع ـ خُرافَة ـ خَيال.

Figurability, *n.* قابِلِيَّةُ ٱلتَّصْوِيرِ ـ إِمْكانُ ٱلتَّشْكِيلِ.

Figurable, *a.* يُتَصَوَّرُ ـ قابِلُ ٱلتَّصْوِيرِ ـ تَشْكِيلُهُ مُمْكِنٌ.

Figurant, *n.* لاعِبٌ (or لَعِيبٌ) دَخِيلٌ.

Figurante, *n.* جارِيَةٌ لَعُوبٌ دَخِيلٌ.

Figurate, *a.* ذُو شَكْلٍ مَخْصُوصٍ.

Figuration, *n.* تَصْوِير ـ تَشْكِيل.

Figurative, *a.* إِسْتِعارِيّ ـ رَمْزِيّ ـ مَجاز ـ مَجازِيّ.

Figuratively, *ad.* إِسْتِعارَةً ـ رَمْزًا ـ مَجازًا. To describe anything —, مَثَّلَ بِ. He used a word —, إِسْتَعارَ لَفْظًا.

Figure, *n.* Form, شَكْل *pl.* أَشْكال ـ صُورَة *pl.* صُوَر. Appearance, شَخْص ـ هَيْئَة ـ وَجْه ـ شِبْهٌ ـ مَنْظَر. A statue, تِمْثال *pl.* تَماثِيلُ ـ مَنْقُوش ـ أَشْخاص *pl.* Arrangement, نِظام ـ تَرْتِيب ـ تَنْظِيم. A model, عَيِّنَة ـ قِياس. A — denoting a number, عَدَد ـ رَقْم. A mathematical —, شَكْل *pl.* أَشْكال. A rhetorical —, مَثَل *pl.*

إشارة ـ رمز ـ كناية ـ عبارة *pl.* عبارات ـ أمثال. Eminence, صيتة ـ صيت. To cut a —, in ridicule, صار مسخرة. To cut a great —, as in boasting, *etc.*, تعظم ـ تفخر ـ تفاخر. To cut a mean —, تحقر ـ تذلل. To describe by —, مثل ـ ب. *See also* Metaphor, Symbol, Trope, *n.*

Figure, *v.t.* To make into shape, صور ـ شكل. To draw, رسم ـ صور. To cover with different figures, برقش ـ لون ـ رقم ـ نقش. To symbolize, مثل ـ ب. To write figures, رقم. To — to one's self, تخيل ـ تصور ـ امتثل. To foreshow, أخبر ب ـ أنذر ب ـ أنبأ ب.

Figure, *v.i.* To be mentioned, with praise, ذكر بالجميل ـ ذكر; with dispraise, ذكر بالقبيح.

Figured, *a.* Variegated, منقش ـ مصور ـ مشجر ـ مخلب ـ مشكل. To be —, تصور ـ تشكل.

Figure-head, *n.* تمثال في مقدم المركب.

Filaceous, *a.* ذو أخياط ـ ذو ليف.

Filament, *n.* خيط ليفة ـ ليفة; a fine shoot, عسلوج *pl.* عساليج.

Filamentous, *a.* مثل العسلوج ـ مثل الخيط ـ ذو ليف.

Filatory, *n.* A machine for spinning threads, آلة الفتالة.

Filature, *n.* The act of reeling, فتالة; the place for reeling, معمل الفتالة.

Filbert, *n.* بندق ـ فندق *pl.* بنادق.

Filch, *v.t.* اختلس ـ استرق ـ ألمى على ـ أسل ـ سل.

Filcher, *n.* رجل مسل ـ سلابة ـ نشال.

Filchingly, *ad.* اختلاسا ـ بسرق ـ باختلاس.

File, *n.* The tool, مبرد *pl.* مبارد ـ مسحل. A thread or wire on which to string papers, سلك تربط به الأوراق. A bundle of papers, ربطة ورق. A collection, جملة ـ مجمعة. A list, فهرس ـ دفتر. A —, as of soldiers, صف *pl.* صفوف. A —, as of camels, mules, *etc.*, قطار *pl.* قطر *and* قطرات. To arrange in —, صفف ـ صف. To be in —, اصطف. Rank and —, أنفار.

File, *v.t.* To cut with a —, برد. To — papers, ضم (*or* ربط) الأوراق في سلك *or* سلك. To collect, جمع ـ جمع. To — off, by files, or twos, (*v.i.*), انصرفوا ثناء ـ انصرفوا مثنى ـ انصرفوا صفوفا.

Filial, *a.* واجب على البنين ـ بنوي. Filial love, محبة الابن لوالديه.

Filially, *ad.* مثل البنين.

Filiation, *n.* The relation of a child to its parent, بنوة. Adoption, تبن ـ تبنية. Settling the paternity of a bastard, قضاء بأبوية النغيل.

Filiform, *a.* رفيع كالخيط ـ مثل الخيط.

Filigree, *n.* مصاغ مخرم.

Filigreed, *a.* مخرم.

Filings, *n.* برادة ـ سحالة; of gold, قراضة; of iron, فسالة.

Fill, *v.t.* To make full, أفعم ـ فعم ـ أفعم ـ صفق ـ أصفق ـ ملأ ـ ملأ ـ شحن ـ طم ـ كظم. To satisfy, أشبع. To supply, أمد ب. To — to overflowing, أطفح ـ أفاض. To stuff, حشا *aor.* يحشو. To complete, تمم ـ كمل. To —, as a garrison with soldiers, أشحن. To — to the brim, أغرض ـ أطفح. To — or — up, of an office, appointment, عين ل. The Indians filled the country, الهنود ملأوا الأرض. He filled the hungry, أشبع الجياع. The wind filled the house, ملأت الريح كل البيت.

To fill a seat, to be a member of, كان من أهل ـ كان عضوا في المجلس.

To fill an office, do the duties of, خدم ـ قام ب ـ أنفذ.

To fill in, as of a well, *etc.*, طم ـ كبس. To add to, زاد في ـ ألحق ب.

To fill up, as of time, مضى ـ عدى. To fill up deficiencies, كمل النقائص. To block up, سد. They fill up the place of their ancestors, يسدون مسد أسلافهم. He sketched a book and did not fill it up, رسم كتابا ولم يحشه. To be filled, made full, تملأ ـ امتلأ ـ فعم. It was filled up, انطم ـ انسد ـ تكبس.

To fill out, to expand, وسع ـ مدد.

To fill with joy, أملأ فرحا.

To fill with pain, أبلى بالأوجاع.

To fill with shame, أشبع خزيا.

To fill with wealth, أشبع مالا.

Fill, *v.i.* To become full, تملأ ـ امتلأ ـ فعم ـ افعوعم. To grow larger, كبر. To increase in flesh, تسمن ـ سمن. To —, to pervade, as of a scent, أفعم ـ فاح ـ فغ.

Fill, *n.* Satiety, شبع ـ شبع ـ كفاية.

Fillet, *n.* A — for the head, خبيبة ـ صوقعة ـ شعرية ـ ضماد ـ ضمادة ـ عصابة ـ عصاب ـ سيدارة; as for a wound, ضماد. A — in architecture, قضيب *pl.* قضبان; chapiters and their fillets, رؤوس وقضبانها. A joint, as of meat, شريحة ـ شرحة ـ قطعة ـ شقة. Filleted with silver, حواليه قضبان من فضة.

Fillibeg, *n.* فُسْتَانٌ يَلْبَسُهُ بَعْضُ مِنْ رِجَالِ أَسْكُوتْلَانْد.

Fillip, *n.* زَنْجَرَة ـ طَقْطَقَة *vulg.* نَقْفَة. To give a — to, to excite to, حَرَّضَ-عَلَى ـ أَنْهَضَ.

Fillip, *v.t.* زَنْجَرَ ـ طَقْطَقَ *vulg.* نَقَفَ.

Filly, *n.* A young mare colt, مُهْرَة. *See also* Colt, Foal, *n.*

Film, *n.* A pellicle, فَوْف *pl.* أَفْوَاف ـ دُوَايَة. A — over the eye, غِشَاوَة ـ سَبَلَة ـ سُحْبَة ـ ظَفَرَة.

Film, *v.t.* To cover with a film, (قِشْرَةً *or*) مَدَّ عَلَى-دُوَايَةً.

Filmy, *a.* Covered with films, ذُو دُوَايَةٍ ـ ذُو أَفْوَافٍ.

Filose, *a.* لِيفِيٌّ ـ مِثْلَ ٱلْخَيْطِ.

Filter, *n.* A strainer, مِصْفَاة ـ مِبْزَل ـ مِشْخَل ـ مِشْعَل *pl.* رَاوُوق ـ مَصَافٍ.

Filter, *v.t.* صَفَّى ـ رَوَّقَ ـ بَزَلَ.

Filter, *v.i.* To trickle, تَقَطَّرَ ـ تَنَقَّطَ ـ نَضَّ.

Filtering-paper, *n.* وَرَقُ ٱلتَّرْشِيحِ ـ مِصْفَاةٌ مِنْ وَرَقٍ.

Filth, *n.* Dirty matter, دَنَس ـ دَنَاسَة ـ وَسَخ ـ لَوْث ـ وَكَب ـ قَذَر ـ رِجْس ـ نَجَاسَة. Ordure, خَرْء ـ نَجَاسَة ـ بِراز. Obscenity, خَنَايَة ـ فِسْق ـ فَحَاشَة ـ فُحْش ـ رَفَث ـ قَذَع.

Filthily, *ad.* Dirtily, نَجَسًا ـ نَجَاسَةً. Obscenely, فُحْشًا ـ خَنًا ـ بِفِسْقٍ.

Filthiness, *n.* *See* Filth, *n.*

Filthy, *a.* Dirty, وَسِخ ـ نَجِس ـ قَذِر ـ رَجِس ـ مَذِر. Obscene, بَذِئُ ٱللِّسَانِ ـ فَاسِق ـ خَنٍ ـ رَفِث. Filthy lucre, رِبْحٌ قَبِيحٌ. A — speech, كَلَامٌ خَنٍ. A — action, فَاحِشَة. To be —, دَنِسَ. To make —, دَنَّسَ.

Filtrate, *v.t.* and *i.* *See to* Filter, *v.t.* and *i.*

Filtration, *n.* The act of, تَصْفِيَة ـ تَرْوِيق ـ بَزْل; of dropping, تَقَطُّر ـ نَضِيض ـ نَضّ ـ تَنَقُّط.

Fimbriate, *a.* ذُو سِجَافٍ ـ مُنَيَّر ـ مُكَنَّف.

Fimbriate, *v.t.* نَيَّرَ ـ كَنَّفَ.

Fin, *n.* جَنَاحُ سَمَكَةٍ *pl.* أَجْنِحَة; fins, *pl.* زَعَانِف.

Finable, *a.* تَحْتَ ٱلْغَرَامَةِ ـ يُغَرَّمُ.

Final, *a.* Last, آخِر ـ أَخِير. Decisive, قَاطِع ـ فَاصِل ـ بَتِّيّ. A — cause, عِلَّةٌ غَائِيَّةٌ; a — or original cause, سَبَبٌ أَصْلِيٌّ; a — or valid cause, سَبَبٌ حَقِيقِيٌّ.

Finale, *n.* عَاقِبَة ـ آخِر.

Finality, *n.* أَوَاخِر ـ آخِرَة ـ دُبُر.

Finally, *ad.* Lastly, أَخِيرًا ـ أَخِرَةً ـ بِأَخَرَةٍ. Completely, لِلْغَايَةِ ـ بَتَّةً ـ تَمَامًا. Hopelessly, إِيَاسًا ـ مِنْ غَيْرِ رَجَاءٍ ـ بِقُنُوطٍ. In the last place, ثُمَّ ـ حَاصِلُ ٱلْكَلَامِ ـ ٱلْحَاصِلُ ـ أَخِيرًا.

Finance, *n.* Financial matters, أُمُورٌ مَالِيَّةٌ. Knowledge of —, عِلْمٌ بِٱلْأُمُورِ ٱلْمَالِيَّةِ. Experienced in —, مُتَقَلِّبٌ فِي ٱلْمَصَالِحِ ٱلْمَالِيَّةِ. The finances of a country, its revenue, مَدْخُولُ ٱلْمِيرِي. Government —, or revenue and expenditure, إِيرَادُ ٱلدَّوْلَةِ وَمَصْرُوفُهَا ـ مَال ـ ٱلْأَمْوَالُ ٱلْمِيرِيَّةُ. The public finances, أُمُورُ مَالِيَّةِ ٱلدَّوْلَةِ ٱلْمِيرِي. Minister of —, نَاظِرُ ٱلْأُمُورِ ٱلْمَالِيَّةِ. The — department, نَظَارَةُ ٱلْمَالِيَّةِ.

Financial, *a.* مُخْتَصٌّ بِٱلْأُمُورِ ٱلْمَالِيَّةِ ـ مَالِيٌّ. A — statement, — returns, قَوَائِمُ مَالِيَّةٌ. Financial condition, ٱلْحَالُ ٱلْمَالِيُّ. Financial transactions, مَصَالِحُ مَالِيَّةٌ ـ مُعَامَلَاتٌ مَالِيَّةٌ. The success of its (of a country) — position, نَجَاحُ أَحْوَالِهَا ٱلْمَالِيَّةِ. A — operation, عَمَلِيَّةٌ مَالِيَّةٌ. Financial reform, تَسْوِيَةُ ٱلْمَصَالِحِ ٱلْمِيرِيَّةِ. And thereupon the — affairs began to decline and fall, وَمِنْ ثَمَّ أَخَذَتِ ٱلْمَصَالِحُ ٱلْمَالِيَّةُ فِي ٱلْٱنْحِطَاطِ وَٱلْبَخْسِ. The causes of the — pressure, أَسْبَابُ عُسْرِ ٱلْأَحْوَالِ ٱلْمَالِيَّةِ.

Financially, *ad.* نَظَرًا لِلْمَالِيَّةِ ـ فِيمَا يَتَعَلَّقُ بِٱلْأُمُورِ ٱلْمَالِيَّةِ.

Financier, *n.* عَالِمٌ بِأُصُولِ ٱلْأُمُورِ ٱلْمَالِيَّةِ وَإِدَارَتِهَا.

Finch, *n.* شُرْشُور ـ نُغَّ.

Find, *v.t.* وَجَدَ *aor.* يَجِدُ ـ لَقِيَ ـ لَاقَى. To encounter, meet, صَادَفَ. To invent, أَوْجَدَ ـ إِخْتَرَعَ. To attain, reach, أَصَابَ ـ أَدْرَكَ ـ حَصَّلَ ـ بَلَغَ. To discover, ظَهَرَ عَلَى ـ كَشَفَ عَنْ. To experience, أَصَابَ ـ إِمْتَحَنَ ـ جَرَّبَ. I sought him but I could not — him, طَلَبْتُهُ فَمَا وَجَدْتُهُ. Who can — a faithful man, ٱلرَّجُلُ ٱلْأَمِينُ فَمَنْ يَجِدُهُ.

To find accusation against, وَجَدَ عَلَيْهِ شِكَايَةً *aor.* يَجِدُ.

To find convenient, إِسْتَلْيَقَ ـ إِسْتَوْفَقَ ـ إِسْتَحْسَنَ.

To find fault with, عَاتَبَ ـ لَامَ.

To find guilty, وَجَدَ-مُجْرِمًا *aor.* يَجِدُ ـ سَجَّلَ عَلَى ـ حَكَمَ عَلَى.

To find in, to supply with, أَعْطَى ـ أَعَالَ ـ جَهَّزَ-بِ ـ أَمَدَّ-بِ; with food, قَاتَ ـ غَذَّى ـ أَطْعَمَ.

To find insufficient, إِسْتَقَلَّ.

To find it in one's heart to, to desire, إِشْتَاقَ إِلَى.

To find occasion, إِنْتَهَزَ فُرْصَةً ـ إِفْتَرَصَ ٱلْفُرْصَةَ.

To find one's self, وَجَدَ حَالَهُ *aor.* يَجِدُ.

To find one's way to, to enter, دَخَلَ.

To find out, to discover, ظَهَرَ عَلَى ـ كَشَفَ عَنْ. To unriddle, شَرَحَ ـ حَلَّ.

To find pleasure, إِنْبَسَطَ ـ إِبْتَهَجَ ـ وَجَدَ مَسَرَّةً ـ إِسْتَلَذَّ ـ تَكَيَّفَ.

To find too large, إِسْتَكْبَرَ ـ إِسْتَعْظَمَ; too small, إِسْتَصْغَرَ.

To find to one's liking, اِسْتَطَابَ — أَطَابَ — اِسْتَلَذَّ — اِنْبَسَطَ مِن — جَآءَ عَلَى خَاطِرِهِ *aor.* يَجِيءُ.

Finding, *n.* Discovery, كَشْفٌ عَلَى — ظُهُورٌ عَلَى. The regaining what was lost, وُجُود — جِدَة — وِجْدَان. A verdict, قَضَا — حُكْم — حَتْم.

Fine, *a.* Not coarse, رَفِيع — رَقِيق. Refined, pure, صَافٍ — خَالِص. Thin, رَكِيك — سَخِيف. Sharp, مُذَرَّب — حَادّ. Transparent, clear, رَائِق — شَفَّاف. Pleasant, of a day or night, رَوْح. A — day, نَهَارٌ أَنْهَرُ. Exquisite, perfect, بَارِع — كَامِل — فَاخِر — فَاضِل. Beautiful, جَمِيل — حَسَن. Splendid, نَفِيس. Smooth, أَمْلَس — أَخْلَق — سَهْل. Soft, نَاعِم. عَظِيم — جَلِيل. Of weather, مُصْحٍ — صَاحٍ — صَحْو. Of taste, لَذِيذ. Dexterous, مَاهِر — حَاذِق *vulg.* شَاطِر. Rare, خَاصّ — نَادِر. Fine, in style, eloquent, فَصِيح — ذُو بَلَاغَة. A — mind, عَقْلٌ زَكِيٌّ. Of fine, refined, manners, لَطِيف — ذُو أَدَب. The — arts, الفُنُونُ ٱلظَّرِيفَة. To be —, in texture, رَفُعَ; of weather, صَحَا — أَصْحَى. To be soft, نَعِمَ. To be —, thin, رَقَّ — اِسْتَرَقَّ. The weather has become —, طَابَ ٱلزَّمَانُ. We shall have — weather to-day, سَيَصْحُو لَنَا ٱلنَّهَار.

Fine, *n.* A penalty, غَرَامَة — جَرِيمَة — مَعَرَّة — أَثَام — أَرْش. The exaction of a —, مُصَادَرَة. In —; *see* Finally, *ad.*

Fine, *v.t.* To punish with a —, غَرَّمَ — أَغْرَمَ — أَثْبَتَ عَلَى غَرَامَةً. To be fined in, اِلْتَزَمَ بِ. To — or refine, as of metals, مَحَّصَ — رَوَّقَ; of sugar, كَرَّرَ; of wine or other liquors, شَخَّلَ; of butter, أَخْلَصَ — كَشَدَ. To make —, thin, رَقَّقَ.

Finedraw, *v.t.* To make fine, رَفَا — رَقَّقَ. To rectify, أَصْلَحَ.

Fine-fingered, *a.* خَفِيفُ ٱلْيَدِ.

Finely, *ad.* Beautifully, حَسَنًا — بِظَرَافَة — حَبَّذَا. Perfectly, بِكَمَال. Dexterously, بِخِفَّة *vulg.* بِشَطَارَة. Gaily, بِٱنْبِسَاط — بِبَهْجَة. Neatly, بِرِفْق.

Fineness, *n.* Minuteness, رِقَّة — دِقَّة — رَفَاعَة. Thinness, رِكَّة — سَخَافَة. Sharpness, حِدَّة — رَهَافَة. Elegance, ظَرَافَة — نُضُور — فَخْر. Splendour, جَلَال — جَمَال — حُسْن — مَلَاحَة — لَطَافَة — فَضِيلَة. Ingenuity, حَذَاقَة — حِذْق — مَهَارَة — نَشْط *vulg.* شَطَارَة. Purity, نَقَاوَة — صَفْو — خُلُوص — مَحْض. Showiness, رَوْنَق — بَهَآء.

Finer, *n.* صَائِغ — مُصَفٍّ. *See also* Refiner, *n.*

Finery, *n.* Fine dress, appearance, بَهَآء — زِينَة — طِرَاز. A place where metals are refined, مَعْمَلٌ يُرَوِّبُونَ فِيهِ ٱلْمَعَادِن. A sugar —, مَعْمَلُ سُكَّر.

Fine-spun, *a.* Drawn to a thread, دَقِيق — رَفِيع — مِثْلَ ٱلْخَيْط. Sophistical, مُفَنَّن — سَفْسَطِيٌّ *or* سِفِسْطِيٌّ — غَشَّاش.

Finesse, *n.* مَكْر — حِيلَة *vulg.* شَطَارَة.

Finesse, *v.i.* اِسْتَعْمَلَ ٱلْحِيَل — تَحَوَّلَ — اِحْتَالَ. The best finessing is not to finesse, الحِيلَةُ فِي تَرْكِ ٱلْحِيَل.

Fin-footed, *a.* ذُو غِشَآء بَيْنَ ٱلْأَصَابِع — مُكَفَّف.

Finger, *n.* إِصْبَع *pl.* أَصَابِع — أُصْبُوع *pl.* أَصَابِيع. The fingers, البَنَان. The forefinger, الدَّعَّاءَة — السَّبَّابَة — المُسَبِّحَة; the middle —, الوُسْطَى; the third or ring —, البِنْصِر; the little —, الخِنْصِر. The tips of the fingers, بَنَانٌ مُخَرَّف — التَّطَارِيف. The joints of the fingers, بَرَاجِم — قَصَب. The bones of the fingers, كِعَاس — ٱلْعَآء — سُلَامَى. The interstices between the fingers, شُتْرَة. The space between the little and ring —, البُصْم; between the ring and middle finger, العَتَب; between the middle and forefinger, الرَّتَب. Having six fingers, أَغْنَس. Finger, skill, فَنّ. To point the — at, as in contumely, صَبَعَ بِ *or* عَلَى. To crack the joints, as of the fingers, فَرْقَعَ — فَقَّعَ. The — of God, القُدْرَةُ ٱلْإِلٰهِيَّة — الحِكْمَةُ ٱلْإِلٰهِيَّة.

Finger, *v.t.* To put one's finger into, عَالَقَ فِي. To take hold of with the fingers, قَبَصَ — نَبَضَ — قَرَزَ — قَمَزَ — قَبَا. To handle, مَسَّ — جَسَّ. To toy with, لَعِبَ بِ. To steal, سَرَقَ — أَسَلَّ. To play, as on a musical instrument, دَقَّ — لَعِبَ.

Finger-board, *n.* The — of a violin, يَدُ كَمَانْجَة.

Fingered, *a.* ذُو أَصَابِع.

Finger-glass, *n.* إِنَآءٌ لِغَسْلِ ٱلْأَنَامِلِ عَلَى ٱلسُّفْرَة *pl.* آنِيَة.

Finger-post, *n.* أَرَم *pl.* آرَام — صُوَّة *pl.* أَصْوَآء — عَلَم *pl.* أَعْلَام.

Finial, *n.* زِينَةٌ مِنْ حَجَرٍ فِي قِمَّةِ بِنَآء.

Finical, *a.* تَافِه — مُتَلَوِّن — مُتَصَنِّع — صَنِع — مُتَحَذْلِق — مُتَبَلْتِع — مُتَأَنِّق.

Finically, *ad.* بِتَلَوُّن — بِتَحَذْلُق — بِتَصَنُّع — تَبَلْتُعًا — بِتَأَنُّق.

Fining-pot, *n.* بُوطَة — بُوطَقَة — بُودَقَة.

Finings, *n.* Materials for clarifying, مَوَادُّ ٱلتَّصْفِيَة.

Finis, *n.* خِتَام — آخِر — نِهَايَة — تَمَام.

Finish, *v.t.* خَتَمَ — أَنْهَى — اِخْتَتَمَ — أَكْمَلَ; as of a task, قَضَى — فَرَغَ مِن. To perfect, كَمَّلَ بِكَمَال. To polish, صَقَلَ. To do for, to destroy, أَتْلَفَ — أَبَادَ. They have just finished dinner, إِنَّمَا ٱلْآنَ فَرَغُوا مِنْ غَدَائِهِم.

Finish, *v.i.* اِنْتَهَى — اِنْقَضَى.

Finish, *n.* صِقَال ــ كَمال.

Finisher, *n.* A polisher, صَيْقَل ــ صَقَّال. One who is scrupulously neat in his workmanship, مُتَعَنِّد.

Finite, *a.* Limited, مُتَنَاهٍ ــ مَحْدُود. Atomic, ذُو هَبَآء ــ جُزْئِيٌّ.

Finitely, *ad.* With limitation, حَدًّا ــ تَحْدِيدًا. To a degree only, جُزْءًا ــ دَرَجَةً.

Finiteness, *n.* Limitedness, حَدٌّ مَوْقُوف ــ حَدٌّ; of a particle, جُزْئِيَّة.

Finless, *a.* (سَمَكٌ) بِلا جَنَاحٍ (*or*) زَعَانِف.

Finlike, *a.* مِثْلَ جَنَاحِ ٱلسَّمَكِ.

Finned, *a.* (سَمَكٌ) ذُو جَنَاحٍ ــ ذُو زَعَانِف.

Finnikin, *n.* The pigeon, حَمَامَةٌ ذَاتُ شُوشَةٍ (*or*) مُتَوَّجَةٌ.

Finny, *n.* The — tribe, ٱلْحُوتُ ــ ٱلسَّمَكُ. *See also* Finned, *a.*

Fin-toed, *a.* *See* Fin-footed, *a.*

Fir, *n.* صَنَوْبَر. A — tree, صَنَوْبَرَة. A — cone, صَنَوْبَر ــ جَوْزُ صَنَوْبَرٍ.

Fire, *n.* نَار ــ وَقْد ــ وَبِيصَة *pl.* نِيرَان *and* أَنْوَار. Anything burning, نَار ــ وَقِيد. A conflagration, حَرِيقَة ــ إِحْرَاق ــ حَرَق. The — of hell, نَارُ جَهَنَّمَ ــ سَعِير. Flame, lustre, ضِيَآء ــ لَمْع ــ رَوْنَق. Warmth of disposition, ardour, غَيْرَة ــ وَجْد ــ حَمِيَّة. Liveliness of imagination, حِدَّةُ ٱلْعَقْلِ ــ حِدَّةُ ٱلتَّصَوُّرِ ــ حَرارَة. The — of love, صَبَابَة. An incendiary —, إِحْرَاقٌ قَصْدًا. St. Anthony's —, حُمْرَة ــ رَشْكِين. Full of — for, مُغْرًى ب. He will never set the Thames on —, هُوَ لا يَرْكُض ٱلْمِحْجَنَ (*lit.* He will not kick the hooked stick, *i.e.* will do nothing surprising.) Owing to the fierceness of the — and its extension, لِشِدَّةِ ٱلْتِهَابِ ٱلنَّارِ وَٱمْتِدَادِهَا. The — ran, extended, سَرَتِ ٱلنَّارُ.

To add fuel to fire, آكَلَ ٱلنَّارَ. To embitter, أَضْرَمَ ــ أَجَّجَ ــ أَحْمَى ــ مَرَّرَ.

To ask fire or light from another, إِسْتَقْبَسَ نَارًا مِن.

To be on or to take fire, إِلْتَهَبَ ــ إِضْطَرَمَ ــ إِشْتَعَلَ ــ تَشَعَّلَ ــ إِسْتَوْقَدَ ــ إِتَّقَدَ ــ تَضَرَّمَ. To be inflamed with, أُغْرِمَ ب. The fire broke out in every direction, إِنْتَشَرَتِ ٱلنَّارُ مِنْ كُلِّ جَانِبٍ.

To carry fire and sword through a country, أَبَادَ ــ أَخْرَبَ.

To get fire from one, ـ قَبَسَ نَارًا مِن.

To give fire to another to light, قَبَسَ ـ نَارًا.

To go through fire and water for, إِسْتَخْطَ لِأَجْلِ.

To keep up a fire, as of soldiers, تَتَابَعُوا عَلَى إِطْلَاقِ ٱلنَّارِ.

To make or light a fire, أَوْقَدَ ــ أَضْرَمَ نَارًا ــ شَعَلَ نَارًا.

To miss fire, كَذَبَ.

To put out, as of a fire, أَهْمَدَ ــ أَخْبَى ــ أَطْفَأَ.

To set on fire; *see below* to Fire, *v.t.*

To spread like wildfire, أَسْرَعَ فِي ٱلسَّيْرِ كَٱلْتِهَابِ ٱلنَّارِ ــ كَٱلنَّارِ.

To stand fire, لا يُخَافُ (*or* لا يُهَابُ) إِطْلَاقَ ٱلنَّارِ.

To strike fire, as with a flint and steel, زَنَدَ ٱلنَّارَ ــ زَنَدَ ــ قدح.

Fire, *v.t.* To light or kindle, as of a fire, أَضْرَمَ ــ إِسْتَضْرَمَ ــ وَقَدَ. To set on fire, أَضْرَمَ ــ بِٱلنَّارِ ــ ضَرَبَ ــ بِٱلنَّارِ ــ أَشْعَلَ ــ شَعَّلَ. To inflame, أَغْرَمَ ــ أَنْهَضَ ــ أَشْعَلَ ــ حَرَّضَ ــ أَغْرَى. To animate, أَحْمَى ــ عَلَى. To discharge, as of firearms, أَطْلَقَ ــ قَوَّسَ ــ ضَرَبَ. To cauterize, كَوَى ــ نَارَ. Their muskets are fi[red] with a flint, بَنَادِقُهُمْ تُقْدَحُ بِٱلصَّوَّانِ.

Fire, *v.i.* أَطْلَقَ. The guns will have been firing for th[ree] hours when the clock strikes seven, قَدْ مَضَتْ ثَلَاثُ سَاعَاتٍ وَٱلْمَدَافِعُ تُطْلَقُ حِينَ تَدُقُّ ٱلسَّاعَةُ سَبْعًا تَكُونُ. *See also under* p[re]*ceding article,* To be on fire, *and to* Discharge, *v.t.*

Firearms, *n.* أَدَوَاتٌ نَارِيَّةٌ ــ أَسْلِحَةٌ نَارِيَّةٌ ــ أَسْلِحَةُ ٱلنَّارِ.

Fireball, *n.* A grenade, قُنْبُرَة ــ كُلَّةٌ مِثْلَ ٱلرُّمَّانَةِ. A mete[or], شِهَاب *pl.* شُهُب.

Fire-board, *n.* طَبَقُ ٱلْكَانُونِ.

Firebrand, *n.* A lighted stick, ضِرَامَة ــ ضِرْمَة ــ شُعْلَة *pl.* شُعَل ــ جِذْوَة ــ شِهَاب. A stirrer up of contention, مِحَشُّ حَرْبٍ ــ أَبُو ٱلْعِصْيَانِ. *See also* Fire-eater, *n.*

Fire-brick, *n.* آجُرٌّ لا تُؤَثِّرُ فِيهِ ٱلنَّارُ *pl.* آجُورٌ.

Fire-bucket, *n.* دَلْوٌ تُسْتَعْمَلُ عِنْدَ إِطْفَآءِ ٱلْحَرِيقَةِ *pl.* دِلَاءٌ.

Fire-clay, *n.* طِينٌ (*or* طُفَال) لا تُؤَثِّرُ فِيهِ ٱلنَّارُ.

Fire-company, *n.* شِرْكَةٌ تَتَكَفَّلُ بِخَسَائِرِ ٱلْحَرِيقِ.

Fire-damp, *n.* هَوَآءٌ ذُو نُورَةٍ يَتَوَلَّدُ فِي ٱلْمَعَادِنِ.

Fire-eater, *n.* شُعْلَةُ نَارٍ ــ فَتَّان ــ أَبُو ٱلْعِصْيَانِ ــ مِحَشُّ قِتَالٍ.

Fire-engine, *n.* طُلُمْبَة ــ تُرُمْبَةٌ لِإِطْفَآءِ ٱلْحَرِيقَةِ *pl.* طُلُمْبَات. They brought four fire-engines, أَحْضَرُوا أَرْبَعَ طُلُمْبَاتٍ.

Fire-escape, *n.* آلَةٌ لِلنَّجَاةِ مِنَ ٱلنَّارِ (*or* ٱلْحَرِيقَةِ).

Firefly, *n.* أَبُو حُبَاحِبَ ــ حُبَاحِبُ.

Fire-hook, *n.* خُطَّافٌ لِهَدْمِ ٱلْبُيُوتِ عِنْدَ وُقُوعِ حَرِيقَةٍ.

Fire-irons, *n.* عُدَّةُ ٱلْكَانُونِ.

Firelock, *n.* بُنْدُقِيَّة *pl.* بَنَادِقُ ــ تَفَنْكَة ــ بَارُودَة ــ مُكْحَلَة *pl.* مَكَاحِلُ.

Fireman, *n.* طُلُمْبَهجِي ــ نَفَرٌ مِنْ أَهْلِ ٱلْإِطْفَآءِ.

Fire-master, *n.* طُلُمْبَهجِي بَاشِي ــ مُدِيرٌ عَلَى ٱلْإِطْفَآءِ.

Fire-new, *a.* جَدِيدٌ خَالِصٌ.

Fire-office, *n.* مَكْتَبُ إدارةِ ٱلشَّرِكَةِ ٱلَّتِي تَتَكَفَّلُ بِخَسائِرِ ٱلْحَرِيقِ.

Firepan, *n.* A pan for fire, مِجْمَرَة *pl.* مَجامِرُ — مَوْقِد. The — of a musket, قالِيَة — بَيْتُ ٱلذَّخِيرَةِ — جُرْنُ ٱلْقَدَّاحَةِ.

Fireplace, *n.* إِرَة *pl.* أَراةٌ — كانُون *pl.* كَوانِينُ — مَوْقِد.

Fire-plug, *n.* لَوْلَبُ ٱلْمآءِ لِإِطْفاءِ ٱلْحَرِيقِ.

Fire-proof, *a.* لا تُؤَثِّرُ ٱلنّارُ فِيهِ.

Fire-screen, *n.* حاجِزٌ لِلنّارِ — دَرَّى لِلنّار.

Fire-ship, *n.* سَفِينَةٌ حَرّاقَةٌ.

Fire-shovel, *n.* مِجْرَفَة *pl.* مَجارِفُ.

Fireside, *a.* Near the fire, جَنْبَ ٱلنّارِ. Home, كِنٌّ — الوَطَنُ.

Fireside, *a.* Belonging to home, كِنِّيٌّ — وَطَنِيٌّ.

Fire-stick, *n.* *See* Firebrand, *n.*

Firewood, *n.* حَطَب — شُعْلَة — وَقِيد — وَقُود; small —, شِيَاع; dry —, جَزْل. A collector or seller of —, حَطّابَة *pl.* حَطّاب.

Fire-works, *n.* أَلْعابُ ٱلْبارُودِ — لَعِبُ ٱلنّارِ — شَعْوَذَةٌ بِٱلنّارِ.

Fire-worship, *n.* عِبادَةُ ٱلنّارِ.

Fire-worshipper, *n.* عابِدُ ٱلنّارِ *pl.* عَبَدَة.

Firing, *n.* The act of cauterizing, كَيٌّ — وِسام — نار; of setting fire to, إِضْرام — إِشْعال — إِيقاد. Discharge, as of firearms, ضَرْب — إِطْلاق. *See also* Firewood, *n.*

Firkin, *n.* A fourth part of a barrel, رُبْعُ بَتِيَّةٍ. A small cask, بَرْمِيلٌ صَغِيرٌ.

Firm, *a.* Firmly fixed, أَكِيد — واثِق — وَكِيد — رَصِين — راسٍ — مُحْكَم — راسِخ — مَكِين *pl.* مُكَناءُ. Compact, مَفْتُول. Hard, solid, صُلْب — مَتِين — تَمِيم — صَمِيم — جامِد. Resolute, حَمِيس — حَمِس — رَبِيٌّ — شَدِيد — راسِخ — ذُو حَزْمٍ. Solid, not fluid, جامِد. Firm in judgment, حَصِيف. Firm land, terra firma, يَبَس. Firm-footedness, ثَبْتُ ٱلْقِيامِ. Hard and strong, جَدْل. To make —, أَحْكَمَ — أَثْبَتَ — أَرْسَى — رَصَنَ ² — أَرْصَنَ — وَثَّقَ — أَوْثَقَ — مَكَّنَ. To be or be made —, وَثُقَ *aor.* يَوْثُقُ — رَسا *aor.* يَرْسُو — رَسَخَ — تَقَرَّرَ — ثَبُتَ ² — تَمَكَّنَ — رَصُنَ ². To be —, resolute, تَرَسَّى — رَسا *aor.* يَرْسُو. He is — in his religion, هُوَ صُلْبٌ فِي دِينِهِ.

Firm, *n.* An association, شِرْكَة. A member of a —, شَرِيك *pl.* شُرَكاءُ.

Firmament, *n.* الرَّقِيعُ — الفَلَكُ — العَلْياءُ.

Firmamental, *a.* فَلَكِيٌّ — مُخْتَصٌّ بِٱلرَّقِيعِ — مُتَعَلِّقٌ بِٱلْفَلَكِ.

Firmân, (more correctly, Farmân,) *n.* فِرْمان *pl.* فَرامِينُ.

Firmly, *ad.* Fixedly, إِحْكامًا — بِرُسُوخٍ — بِمَتانَةٍ. Resolutely, بِحَمَسٍ — بِرُسُوخٍ — بِصَلابَةٍ — مُتَشَدِّدًا — بِحَزْمٍ — بِحَتْمٍ. Firmly made, compacted, رَصِيف — رَصِين — مُرَصَّن. To build —, أَرْصَنَ — شَيَّدَ.

Firmness, *n.* إِحْكام — إِتْقان — رُسُوخ — وَثاقَة — رَصانَة — ثَبْت. Stability, ثُبُوت — ثَبات — إِسْتِمْرار. Resolution, صَلابَة — عَزْم — مُرُوءَة — رَوْقَة — إِقْدام — صَلابَة — حَماسَة — حَمَس. To act with —, تَحَمَّسَ — تَشَدَّدَ — تَرَسَّى.

First, *a.* أَوَّل *pl.* أَوَّلُونَ and أَوائِلُ; *fem.* أُولَى *pl.* أُوَل and أُوَّل.

First, in time, أَقْدَمُ — قَدِيم — أَوَّل. Highest in dignity, مُقَدَّم — الأَعْظَمُ — الأَكْبَرُ — رَئِيس. The — part of anything, أَنْفُ ٱلشَّيْءِ. At — thought, بادِئَ ٱلرَّأْيِ — بَدْءَ ٱلرَّأْيِ. He did it at — thought, فَعَلَهُ فِي بادِئِ ٱلرَّأْيِ.

First, *ad.} In the — place, أَوَّلًا — أَوَّلَ بَدْءٍ — بادِئَ بَدْءٍ. At —,
Firstly, } at the —, فِي ٱلْبَدْءِ — إِبْتِداءً. You at — thought to wrong us, أَنْتَ بادِئَ ٱلرَّأْيِ تُرِيدُ ظُلْمَنا. As at the —, كَٱلأَوَّلِ. I will begin with him —, أَبْدَأُ بِهِ أَوَّلًا. I did it — of all, فَعَلْتُهُ أَوَّلَ كُلِّ شَيْءٍ.

First-born, *a.* The eldest, الأَكْبَرُ *fem.* الكُبْرَى.

First-born, *n.* بِكْر *pl.* أَبْكار.

First-comers, *n.* Those who are foremost for action, سَرَعانُ ٱلنّاسِ; those who come first, السّابِقُونَ.

First-cousin, *n.* اِبْنُ عَمٍّ لَحًّا *pl.* أَبْناءٌ; *fem.* بِنْتُ خالَةٍ لَحًّا *pl.* بَنات.

First-floor, *n.* الطَّبَقَةُ ٱلثّانِيَةُ.

First-fruits, *n.* باكُورَة *pl.* باكُورات. First results, أَوَّلُ نَتِيجَةٍ — أَوَّلُ ثَمَرَةٍ.

Firstling, *n.* بِكْر *pl.* أَبْكار. The firstlings of the flocks, أَبْكارُ ٱلْغَنَمِ.

First-rate, *a.* بارِع — فائِق — الأَعْلَى — أَعْلَى.

Firth, *n.* خَوْر *pl.* خُؤُور.

Fiscal, *a.* مُخْتَصٌّ بِٱلْمالِيَّةِ — مُتَعَلِّقٌ بِبَيْتِ ٱلْمالِ — مِيرِيٌّ.

Fish, *n.* سَمَكَة, *coll.* سَمَك, *pl.* سَمَكات. A large —, حُوتَة, *coll.* حُوت, *pl.* حِيتان. A small —, سُمَيْكَة — هَفّ. A flying —, وَطْواطُ ٱلْبَحْرِ. A — skin, غَضْبَة. A condiment made of —, صِيرٌ صِحْناءُ. The disagreeable smell of —, سَهَكَةُ ٱلسَّمَكِ. The man of the —, Jonah, صاحِبُ ٱلْحُوتِ. A shell-fish, أُطُوم. Dried —, سَمَكٌ مُقَدَّدٌ. The spawn of —, شِصّ *pl.* شُصُوص.

Fish, *v.t.* To catch, as of —, إِصْطادَ — قَبَضَ عَلَى. To strengthen, شَيَّدَ — مَسَكَ ب. To search for, تَقَعَّرَ عَلَى — تَطَلَّبَ — فَتَّشَ عَن. To — out; *see to* Find, *v.t.*

Fish, *v.i.* To attempt to catch —, تَصَيَّدَ ـ إِصْطَادَ ٱلسَّمَكَ .

Fish-bone, *n.* شَوْكَةُ ٱلسَّمَكِ *coll.* شَوْك ـ حَسَك *coll.* حَسَكَة *and* حُسَاكَة .

Fish-day, *n.* A day of abstinence from flesh, يَوْمُ قُطَاعَةٍ .

Fisher, *n.* } صَيَّادُ ٱلسَّمَكِ *pl.* صَيَّادُونَ .
Fisherman, }

Fishery, *n.* The business of fishing, صَيْدُ ٱلسَّمَكِ . A place of —, مَصْيَد ; what is taken in fishing, صَيْد ـ مَصِيد . Pearl —, fishing, الغِيَاصَة ـ الغَوْصُ عَلَى ٱلدُّرَرِ . *See also under* Pearl, *n.*

Fishing-boat, *n.* صَيَّادِ ٱلسَّمَكِ (قارِب *pl.* قَوارِب *or*) زَوْرَق *pl.* زَوارِق .

Fishing-tackle, *n.* لِصَيْدِ ٱلسَّمَكِ (آلات *or*) عُدَّة .

Fish-kettle, *n.* طَاجِرَةُ ٱلسَّمَكِ ـ طاجِنٌ لِطَبْخِ ٱلسَّمَكِ .

Fish-pond, *n.* حَوْضٌ لِلسَّمَكِ ـ بِرْكَةٌ فِيهَا سَمَكٌ .

Fish-market, *n.* سُوقُ ٱلسَّمَكِ .

Fishmonger, *n.* بَيَّاعُ ٱلسَّمَكِ ـ سَمَّاك .

Fish-wife, *n.* } بَيَّاعَةُ ٱلسَّمَكِ ـ سَمَّاكَة .
Fish-woman, }

Fish-slice, *n.* } مِشْرَحُ ٱلسَّمَكِ .
Fish-trowel, }

Fishy, *a.* Of fish, مِثْلَ ٱلسَّمَكِ ـ حُوتِيٌّ . Suspicious, مَعْرُوف ـ نَطِف ـ تَهِيم .

Fissile, *a.* سَهْلُ (قابِلُ *or*) ٱلإِنْشِقَاقِ ـ يَتَشَرَّمُ .

Fissility, *n.* سُهُولَةُ ٱلتَّشَرُّمِ ـ سُهُولَةُ ٱلإِنْشِقَاقِ .

Fissure, *n.* A rent, split, نَفَذ ـ شَرْم *pl.* شُرُوم ـ عَوْرَة *pl.* عَوْرات ـ وَقْرَة *pl.* وَقَرات ـ فَلْق *pl.* أَفْلاق ـ فَلَج *pl.* أَفْلاج ـ شَقّ *pl.* شُقُوق . A chink, فَتّ . A chasm, سِلْم *pl.* سُلُوم . Houses full of fissures, بُيُوتٌ عَوِرَةٌ .

Fissure, *v.t.* شَقَّقَ ـ شَقَّ ـ وَقَرَ ـ شَرَمَ . To be fissured, تَشَقَّقَ ـ اِنْشَقَّ .

Fist, *n.* يَدٌ مَطْبُوقَةٌ ـ جُمْعُ ٱلْكَفِّ ـ الجُمْعُ . As much as can be held in the —, قُبْضَة *pl.* قُبْضات ـ حَفْنَة *pl.* حَفَنات .

Fist, *v.t.* To strike with the —, لَكَمَ . To hold in the —, قَبَضَ عَلَى ـ مَسَكَ بِ ـ ضَبَطَ .

Fisticuffs, *n.* مُلاكَمَة ـ مُلَقَّمَة .

Fistula, A pipe, reed, أُنْبُوب ـ قَلَم . *Fistula in ano,* عَجَن ـ نَاسُور ـ فَنْتُورَة . *Fistula lachrymalis,* عِرْقُ ٱلعَبَرَاتِ ـ نَاسُور ـ دَمَّع ـ نَاسُورُ ٱلعَيْنِ . To have — *in ano,* أَعْجَنَ .

Fistular, *a.* Hollow like a pipe, أَجْوَفُ كَٱلأُنْبُوبِ .

Fistulate, *v.i.* To become a fistulous sore, تَنَسَّرَ ـ صَارَ نَاسُورًا .

Fistuliform, *a.* In the form of tubes, فِي شَكْلِ ٱلأَنَابِيبِ ـ فِي صُورَةِ ٱلْقَصَبِ .

Fistulous, *a.* } Relating to a fistulous sore, نَاسُورِيٌّ . *See also*
Fistulose, } Fistular, *a.*

Fit, *n.* A paroxysm, سِنْخ *pl.* أَسْنَاخ ـ مُوم ـ دَوْر ـ نَوْبَة . A sudden attack, rush, هُجُوم ـ حُمَيَّا . A fit, as in epilepsy, صَرْع ـ صَرْعَة . A swoon, غَشْيَة ـ مَوْتَة . A whim, هَوِيَّة ـ خَيَال . Fits, convulsions, تَشَنُّج . A cut, shape, تَفْصِيل . A cold fit, as of fever, بُرَدِيَّة ـ نُفْضَة ـ نُفَاض . Having epileptic fits, صَرِيع ـ مَصْرُوع . A hot fit, of fever, سُخُونَة . Subject to epileptic fits, مَحَلٌّ لِلصَّرْعِ . A fit of fever, عِكَاك ; of passion, حُمَيَّا ـ هَمْرَة ـ غَضَب ـ هَيَجَان ; of drunkenness, خَمْرَة ـ سَكْرَة . The fit, whim, took him, تَحَيَّلَ بِهِ ـ تَلَوَّى بِهِ .

A good fit, of clothes, تَفْصِيل ; a bad fit, بِلا (بِدُونِ *or*) تَفْصِيلٍ .

By fits and starts, كَرَّةً وَفَرَّةً .

Fainting fit, غَشْيَان ـ غَشْيَة .

Hysterical fit, خَفَقَان .

Shivering fit, رَجَفَان ـ رِعْشَة .

Fit, *a.* Suitable, proper, وَاجِب ـ مُطَابِق ـ مُوَافِق ـ مُنَاسِب . Suitable to, capable of, خَلِيقٌ لِ ـ جَدِيرٌ لِ *or* بِ *or* بِأَنْ ـ قَمِينٌ لِ *or* بِ *or* أَنْ ـ صَالِحٌ لِ ـ مَحَلٌّ لِ . To be fit for, equal to, اِسْتَقْرَنَ لِ . Fit to eat, يُؤْكَلُ ـ أُكُل . Fit to be seen, لائِق ـ حُشْمِيّ . Fit for publication, لائِقٌ بِٱلنَّشْرِ . It is not fit that, لا يَحِقُّ أَنْ ـ لا يَجْمُلُ أَنْ . It is not fit that he should live, لا يَجُوزُ أَنْ يَعِيشَ . It is fit that ..., مِنَ ٱلْوَاجِبِ أَنْ ـ وَمِنَ ـ يَحِقُّ أَنْ ـ ٱلْمُقْتَضَى أَنْ . If you think fit, إِنْ حَسُنَ لَدَيْكَ ـ إِنْ أَعْجَبَكَ .

Fit, *v.t.* To suit one thing to another, وَفَّقَ ـ لِ ـ طَابَقَ . To make fit, أَصْلَحَ ـ جَعَلَ ـ مُنَاسِبًا . To fit, by beating, as of iron, *etc.*, طَرَّقَ ; as with a plane, نَجَّرَ . To judge fit, capable of, أَهَّلَ ـ لِ . To fit, as of clothes, فَصَّلَ ـ قَطَّعَ ـ قَطَعَ . To fit out, or up, with, جَهَّزَ ـ بِ . To fit up, to furnish, a house, جَهَّزَ بَيْتًا بِٱلأَثَاثِ . To fit out a fleet, جَهَّزَ مَرَاكِبَ حَرْبِيَّةً ـ عَمَّرَ عِمَارَةً . To be fitted up, furnished, تَجَهَّزَ .

Fit, *v.i.* To suit, لَبِقَ ـ نَاسَبَ ; as of a dress, لَبِقَ بِ ـ جَاءَ عَلَى ـ خَالَ عَلَى ـ صَلَحَ لِ *aor.* يَجِيءُ . This dress does not fit you, هٰذِهِ ٱلْبَدْلَةُ مَا تَجِيءُ عَلَيْكَ . *See also to* Suit, *v.t.* and *i.*

Fitch, *n.* *See* Vetch, *n.*

Fitful, *a.* مُرْتَبِك ـ مُزَعَّج ـ فَرَّار ـ مُتَلَوِّن . *See also* Capricious, *a.*

Fitly, *ad.* بِلِيَاقَةٍ ـ مُلَاءَمَةً ـ مُوَافَقَةً ـ بِالصَّوابِ . A word — spoken, كَلِمَةٌ مَقُولَةٌ فِي مَحَلِّهَا . Fitly framed together, مُرَكَّبٌ مَعًا ـ مُرَكَّبٌ مَعًا وَمُقْتَرِنٌ .

Fitness, *n.* Suitableness, مُلَاءَمَة ـ مُوَافَقَة ـ لِيَاقَة ـ مُنَاسَبَة . Capability, أَهْلِيَّة ـ صَلَاحِيَة ـ إِسْتِقْرَان . *See also* Suitableness, *n.*

Fitting, *a.* As of clothes, مَفْصُول ـ لَبِيقٌ بِ . *See also* Fit, *a.*

Fittings, *n.* لَوَازِمُ ـ مُتَعَلِّقَات ـ مُلْحَقَات .

Fitz, *prefix,* لَقَبٌ يَدُلُّ عَلَى النَّغَلِ .

Five, *a.* خَمْسَةٌ *fem.* خَمْس . Five men, خَمْسَةُ رِجَالٍ ; five women, خَمْسُ نِسْوَةٍ . The — fingers, المُخَمَّسُ . They came in fives, (مُخَمَّسَ *or*) جَاؤُوا خُمَاسَ .

Five-barred, *a.* As of a gate, بَابٌ ذُو خَمْسِ عَوَارِضَ .

Five-cornered, *a.* مُخَمَّسُ الزَّوَايَا ـ مُخَمَّس .

Fivefold, *a.* خَمْسَةُ أَضْعَافٍ .

Fives, *n.* The game of, ضَرْبٌ مِنَ اللَّعِبِ بِالطَّابَةِ . A disease in horses, خَنَازِيرُ الخَيْلِ ـ الخَنَازِيرُ الَّتِي تَظْهَرُ فِي الخَيْلِ .

Fix, *v.t.* To set firmly, مَتَّنَ ـ أَرْسَخَ ـ أَحْكَمَ ـ مَكَّنَ ـ قَرَّرَ . To set up, أَوْقَفَ ـ أَقَامَ ـ نَصَّبَ ـ ² نَصَبَ . To fix, to hang, as of a door, عَلَّقَ . To make fast, أَرْسَى ـ أَرْسَخَ . To put into its place, رَكَّبَ . To fix for, as a task, ـ قَطَعَ عَلَى . To fix firmly in the ground, ـ غَرَزَ ـ ² رَكَزَ . To appoint, عَيَّنَ . To determine, ـ فَصَلَ ـ ـ خَتَمَ ـ حَدَّدَ ـ قَرَّرَ . To deprive of volatility, جَمَّدَ . To fix upon, to choose, إِنْتَخَبَ ـ إِخْتَارَ . To fix the eyes upon, أَمْعَنَ النَّظَرَ فِي ـ ـ رَنَا إِلَى . To be fixed, set firmly, تَقَرَّرَ ـ تَمَكَّنَ ; to be made fast, إِرْتَسَى ـ ـ رَسَخَ ـ تَرَسَّى ; to be set upright, إِنْتَصَبَ ; to be set firmly in the ground, إِرْتَكَزَ ; to be appointed, تَعَيَّنَ ; to be deprived of volatility, أَجْمَدَ ـ ² جَمَدَ ; to be determined, تَقَرَّرَ ـ تَحَدَّدَ ـ ² ثَبَتَ . To be fixed upon, chosen, أُنْتُخِبَ ـ أُخْتِيرَ ـ أُسْتُخِيرَ . To have the eyes immoveably fixed, ـ شَخَصَ بِبَصَرِهِ . Death was fixed on his limbs, ² بَرَدَ المَوْتُ عَلَى مُضْطَاهُ .

Fix, *v.i.* To remain permanent, ـ قَرَّ ـ ـ رَسَخَ . To cease to wander, إِسْتَقَامَ . To lose volatility, أَجْمَدَ ـ ² جَمَدَ .

Fix, *n.* A difficulty, وَرْطَة ـ بَلَاء ـ مُشْكِلَة ـ حَيْرَة . To be in a fix, إِسْتَحَارَ ـ تَحَيَّرَ ـ تَوَرَّطَ ; to put one into a fix, حَيَّرَ ـ أَوْرَطَ ـ (وَرَّطَ *or*) فِي وَرْطَةٍ ـ ² شَقَّ عَلَى .

Fixation, *n.* The act of setting firm, إِرْسَاخ ـ تَقْرِير ـ إِحْكَام ; of setting up, إِقَامَة ـ تَنْصِيب ـ رَكْز . *See also* Fixedness, *n.*

Fixed, *a.* Firm, مَكِين ـ رَصِين ـ مُقَرَّر ـ مُسْتَحْكَم . Settled, as in a place, مُسْتَمِرّ ـ مُقِيم ـ مُسْتَقِرّ . Determined, ثَبْت ـ مُحَدَّدٌ عَلَى ـ مُسْتَمِرٌّ فِي ـ ثَبْتُ الجَنَانِ . Appointed, مُعَيَّن . Concreted, جَمَد ـ جَامِد . To be —, to persist in, ² ثَبَتَ فِي ـ أَدْمَنَ عَلَى ـ وَاظَبَ عَلَى ـ إِسْتَمَرَّ فِي . Ink will not become — on greasy parchment, الرَّقُّ الدَّهِينُ لَا يَرْسَخُ فِيهِ الحِبْرُ . A — star, كَوْكَبٌ ثَابِتٌ ـ ثَوَابِتُ *pl.* ثَابِتَة . Fixed alkali, حُرُض ـ القِلْي ـ خِلْم . Fixed principles, أُصُول رَاسِخَة .

Fixedly, *ad.* Firmly, بِمَتَانَةٍ ـ بِثُبُوتٍ ـ بِثَبَاتٍ ; without wandering, إِسْتِمْرَارًا ـ بِإِسْتِمْرَارٍ .

Fixedness, *n.* The state of being firm, قَرَار ـ ثَبَات ـ رُسُوخ ـ ثَبْت ـ ثَبَاتَة ـ مَتَانَة ـ تَحَكُّم ; of purpose, ثَبْت ـ ثَبَاتَة . Residence, إِقَامَة ـ سُكْنَى ـ إِسْتِمْرَار . Want of volatility, جُمُود ـ جَمْد .

Fixity, *n.* Coherence, عَدَمُ تَغْيِيرٍ ـ إِلْتِصَاق ـ لُزُوق .

Fixture, *n.* Position, ضِعَة ـ حَال ـ وَضْع . Something attached to a building not to be removed, مَتَاعٌ غَيْرُ ـ مُلْحَقَةٌ غَيْرُ مَنْقُولَةٍ ـ أَمْتِعَةٌ غَيْرُ مَنْقُولَةٍ *pl.* مَنْقُولٍ .

Fizz, *v.i.* ـ ² فَارَ ـ يَفُورُ *aor.* ثَارَ .

Flabbiness, *n.* إِرْتِخَاء ـ ثَلْمَطَة ـ خُنْث ـ خَرَع ـ خَبْخَبَة ـ رَخَاوَة ـ لِينَة ـ رَخْوَة ـ إِنْدِيَال .

Flabby, *a.* رَخْو ـ رَخّ ـ خَرِيع ـ سَبِل . Of a plant, ذَوِيّ . A soft — man, مَخْلُوع . To be —, تَخَبْخَبَ ـ إِرْتَخَى ـ ² هَشَّ ـ إِسْتَرْخَى ـ يَرْخَى *aor.* رَخِيَ ـ ـ لَانَ ـ تَخَرْخَرَ . Of a plant, fruit, *etc.*, ـ ذَوَى ـ ² قَبَّ .

Flaccid, *a.* *See* Flabby, *a.*

Flaccidity, *n.* }
Flaccidness, } *See* Flabbiness, *n.*

Flag, *v.i.* To hang loose, إِسْتَرْخَى ; (*see also* To be Flabby, *under* Flabby, *a.*) To be or become remiss in, أَلَا فِي ـ ـ مَلَّ مِن ـ إِسْتَرْخَى فِي ـ تَرَاخَى عَن ـ يَأْلُو *aor.* . To become cool, uninterested, تَفَاتَرَ ـ ² فَتَرَ . To droop, as in health, ² ضَعُفَ ; of a plant, ـ ذَوَى ـ أَلْوَى . He did not —, لَمْ يُقَصِّرْ ـ لَمْ يَأْلُ . He does not — in his endeavours to..., لَمْ يَمِلَّ مِنْ مَسْعَاتِهِ لِ .

Flag, *v.t.* To let fall into feebleness, ² هَبَطَ ـ أَضْعَفَ . To pave, بَلَّطَ ـ فَرَّشَ بِ ـ ² فَرَشَ بِ .

Flag, *n.* The rush, حَلْفَاء . The wild iris, يَاسَمِين بَحْرِيّ . A stone for paving, بَلَاطَة *coll.* بَلَاط . An ensign, رَايَة *pl.* رَايَات ـ لِوَاء *pl.* أَلْوِيَة ـ بَيْرَق *pl.* بَيَارِق ـ عَلَم *pl.* أَعْلَام ـ سَنْجَق *pl.* سَنَاجِق . To hoist a —, ² نَصَبَ البَيْرَقَ ـ أَلْوَى . To lower a —, ² حَطَّ البَيْرَقَ لِ ; in compliment to, نَزَّلَ اللِّوَاءَ . To strike a —, in submission, نَزَّلَ اللِّوَاءَ عِبَارَةً عَنِ التَّسْلِيمِ .

Flagellant, *n.* سَائِطٌ نَفْسَهُ ـ جَالِدُ نَفْسِهِ .

Flagellate, *v.t.* جَلَدَ ـ ‍ سَاطَ *aor.* يَسُوطُ .

Flagellation, *n.* جَلْدٌ بِٱلسِّيَاطِ .

Flageolet, *n.* نای ـ نُوْرَة .

Flagginess, *n.* *See* Flabbiness, *n.*

Flaggy, *a.* *See* Flabby, *a.*

Flagitious, *a.* شَرِيرٌ ـ أَشَرُّ ـ خَبِيثٌ ـ شَنِيعٌ ـ فُجَّار *pl.* فاجر لِلْغَايَةِ .

Flagitiously, *ad.* فَضَاحَةً ـ بِخَبَاثَةٍ ـ بِفُجُورٍ .

Flagitiousness, *n.* فَضَاحَة ـ خَبَاثَة ـ خُبْث ـ فُجُور .

Flag-officer, *n.* سِنْجَق ـ أَمِيرُ ٱلْبَحْرِ .

Flag-ship, *n.* مَرْكَبُ ٱلسَّنْجَقِ ـ مَرْكَبُ أَمِيرِ ٱلْبَحْرِ .

Flagon, *n.* شِيَش *pl.* شِيشَة ـ قَمَاقِمُ *pl.* قُمْقُم ـ فاثُور .

Flagrancy, *n.* Notoriousness, شُهْرَة ـ وُضُوح . Enormity, تَفَاوُت ـ فَرْط ـ عَظَامَة .

Flagrant, *a.* Notorious, مَجْهُورٌ بِ ـ مَشَاع ـ مَشْهُور . Enormous, كَبِير ـ عَظِيم ـ مُجَاوِز ـ مُفْرِط .

Flagrantly, *ad.* Notoriously, جِهَارًا ـ جَهْرَةً ـ شُهْرَةً . Enormously, إِفْرَاطًا ـ لِلْغَايَةِ .

Flag-staff, *n.* سَارِي ٱللِّوَاء ـ لِوَايَة .

Flag-stone, *n.* بَلَاطَة *coll.* بَلَاط *pl.* بَلَاطَات .

Flail, *n.* مِرَضَّة ـ مِدْوَس ـ طِرْبِيل . A thrashing wagon, نَوْرَج *pl.* نَوَارِجُ .

Flake, *n.* A —, as of wool, كُوكَة ; of snow, كِسْف *pl.* كِسْفَةُ ثَلْج ـ رُقْعَةُ ثَلْجٍ ; of fire, شَرَارَة . A layer, طَبَق *pl.* أَطْبَاق ـ مَثْنَاة *pl.* مَثَانٍ ـ صَفِيحَة *pl.* صَفَائِحُ . In flakes, صَفَائِحَ صَفَائِحَ . It snowed in flakes, (كِسَفًا كِسَفًا or) ثَلَجَتِ ٱلسَّمَاءُ صَفَائِحَ صَفَائِحَ .

Flake, *v.i.* To peel off, إِنْقَشَرَ ـ تَقَشَّرَ .

Flake, *v.t.* جَعَلَ صَفَائِحَ صَفَائِحَ ـ .

Flake-white, *n.* إِسْفِيدَاج .

Flakiness, *n.* تَرْتِيبُ ٱلْأَطْبَاقِ ـ هَيْئَةُ ٱلصَّفِيحَةِ .

Flaky, *a.* ذُو أَطْبَاقٍ ـ ذُو صَفَائِحَ .

Flam, *n.* غَدْر ـ غِشّ ـ زُور ـ كِذْبَة .

Flam, *v.t.* غَدَرَ ـ غَبَنَ ـ غَشَّ .

Flambeau, *n.* شُعْلَة ـ مِشْعَلَة ـ مِشْعَل *pl.* مَشَاعِلُ .

Flame, *n.* شِهَاب *pl.* شُهْبَان ـ لَهَب ـ لُهَابَة ـ لَهْبَة *pl.* لَهَب . The —, of fire, شُعْلَة ـ شُعْلُول . Ardour, حَرَارَة ـ وَجْد ـ غَيْرَة ـ حِدَّةُ ٱلْمِزَاجِ . The — of love, نَارُ ٱلْمَحَبَّةِ ـ هَوًى ـ جَوًى . To be in flames, إِلْتَهَبَ ـ تَلَهَّبَ . To commit to the flames, أَوْقَدَ ـ أَحْرَقَ . To make to break out into flames, أَشْعَلَ ـ لَظَّى ـ أَلْهَبَ ـ لَهَّبَ .

Flame, *v.i.* To burn with a —, إِحْتَدَمَ ـ تَلَظَّى ـ لَظِيَ ـ إِلْتَهَبَ ـ تَلَهَّبَ ـ شَعَلَ . To break out into a passion, شَاطَ غَضَبًا .

Flame-coloured, *a.* لَوْنُ ٱللَّهِيبِ .

Flameless, *a.* بِلَا لَهِيبٍ .

Flamen, *n.* كَاهِن *pl.* كَهَنَة .

Flaming, *a.* Burning with a blaze, مُشْتَعِل ـ مُلْتَهِب ـ مُلْتَظٍّ . Bright, بَرَّاق ـ لَامِع ـ مُنِير . Red, أَحْمَر . Violent, مُتَهَوِّر ـ شَدِيد . Exciting, مُهَيِّج ـ مُحَرِّض . Excessive, مُبَالِغ ـ مُفْرِط .

Flamingly, *ad.* Brightly, لَمْعًا ـ بِلَمَعَانٍ ـ بِضِيَاءٍ . With vehemence, تَهَوُّرًا ـ شَدِيدًا . Successfully, عَلَى عَيْنٍ ـ بِنَجَاحٍ .

Flamingo, *n.* مُحَامَة *coll.* مُحَام .

Flaminical, *a.* مُتَعَلِّقٌ بِٱلْكَاهِنِ ـ كَهَنُوتِيّ .

Flammability, *n.* سُرْعَةُ ٱلْإِلْتِهَابِ ـ إِلْتِهَاب .

Flammeous, *a.* مِثْلُ ٱللَّهِيبِ ـ لَهِيبِيّ .

Flammiferous, *a.*
Flammivomous, } مُلَظٍّ ـ مُلْهِب .

Flamy, *a.* *See* Flaming, *a.*

Flanch, *n.* إِضَافَة ـ ثِنْيَة .

Flange, *n.* The — of a wheel, حَاجِب *pl.* حَوَاجِبُ ـ شُفْرُ ٱلْعَجَلَةِ (حَافِيَة or حِفَاف or) ٱلْعَجَلَةِ . *See also* Flanch, *n.*

Flank, *n.* A side, جَنَاح ـ طَرَف ـ جَانِب . The —, as of an army, جَنَاح ـ مُجَنِّبَة ; the two flanks, as of an army, ٱلْمُجَنِّبَتَانِ ـ جَنَاحَانِ ; the right —, ٱلْمَيْمَنَة ; the left —, ٱلْمَيْسَرَة . The — of a mountain, كِتْفُ ٱلْجَبَلِ . The — of a man, ٱلْخَاصِرَةُ *dual* ٱلْخَاصِرَتَانِ *pl.* ٱلْخَوَاصِرُ . In —, عَلَى جَنْبٍ . Large in the —, ضَخْمُ ٱلْخَوَاصِرِ . The — of a bastion, حِجَابُ ٱلطَّابِيَةِ . Length of the flanks, in a horse, صَقَل .

Flank, *v.t.* To attack the —, هَجَمَ عَلَى جَنَاحِ ٱلْجَيْشِ ـ طَرَّفَ . To defend the —, حَمَى جَنَاحَ ٱلْجَيْشِ . To defend, دَافَعَ ـ دَفَعَ عَنْ ـ حَمَى . To pass round the side of, مَرَّ عَلَى جَانِبِهِ . They surrounded him on his two flanks, أَحَاطُوا بِهِ مِنْ جَانِبَيْهِ .

Flank, *v.i.* To border, كَانَ عَلَى ٱلْجَنْبِ ـ إِتَّصَلَ بِ ـ تَاخَمَ .

Flanking, *a.* Attacking the flank, مُطَرِّف . A — battery, طَابِيَةٌ مُطَرِّفَةٌ .

Flannel, *n.* فَانِلَة ـ صُوف .

Flap, *n.* Any cloth hanging loose, ذَيْل *pl.* أَذْيَال ـ أُرْخِيَّة . A slap, لَطْم ـ خَفْق . A —, as of the wing, دَفْدَفَة ـ رَفْرَفَة . The — of the ear, شَحْمَةُ ٱلْأُذُنِ ; of a coat or other garment, ذَيْل

pl. آذْيَال; of a pocket, فَم ـ باب. The two flaps of a pair of shoes, أُذْنَا ٱلْمَرْكُوب. A fly-flap, مِكَشَّة.

Flap, *v.t.* To slap, خَفَقَ ² ـ صَقَعَ ـ صَفَعَ ـ سَفَعَ ـ لَطَمَ. To —, as of the wings, دَفَّ ² ـ دَفْدَفَ ـ إِسْتَدَفَّ ـ رَفْرَفَ. To — away, as of flies, كَشَّ ² ـ وَزَّعَ.

Flap, *v.i.* To dangle, تَدَنْدَلَ ـ تَدَلَّى. To flutter, خَفَقَ ² ـ إِخْتَفَقَ.

Flap-eared, *a.* غَاضِف.

Flapping, *n.* A fluttering, خُفُوق ـ خَفَقَان.

Flapping, *a.* As of the wing, خَفَّاق.

Flare, *v.i.* To flutter, as of a light, خَفَقَ ٱلسِّرَاجُ ². To glitter, تَلَأْلَأَ ـ تَنَوَّرَ ـ دَرَأَ ـ لَمَحَ. To make a show, إِفْتَخَرَ ـ تَفَخَّرَ. To — up, break out, أَفَاضَ ـ فَاضَ. To — out into a passion, إِحْتَمَقَ ـ إِحْتَمَى غَضَبًا.

Flare, *n.* A fluttering, خَفَقَان; a glittering, لَمَعَان ـ رَيْق ـ تَنَوُّر. A flare-up, breaking out, إِفَاضَة ـ حُمَيًّا. A row, disturbance, شَغَب ـ تَأَلُّب. To create a flare-up among, شَغَبَ عَلَى.

Flaring, *a.* Making a display, مُتَكَبِّر ـ مُفْتَخِر ـ مُتَعَجْرِف. Apparent, manifest, بَارِز. *See also* Gaudy, *a.*

Flaringly, *ad.* With ostentation, مُتَكَبِّرًا ـ بِٱفْتِخَارٍ ـ تَعَجْرُفًا; with glitter, بِبَرَقَانٍ ـ بِشَعْشَعَةٍ. *See also* Gaudily, *ad.*

Flash, *n.* A sudden burst of light, تَحَلُّج ـ صَلُود ـ صَلِيد ـ بَرْقَة ـ شَفِيقَة ـ بَرَقَة ـ بَرِيق. A — of lightning, شَفِيقَةُ بَرْقٍ. A — of wit, لَطِيفَة ـ أُضْحُوكَة ـ نُكْتَة. A transient state, سَاعَة ـ مُهْلَة. A — of the eye, لَمْحَة ـ نَظْرَة ـ تَبْرِيقُ ٱلْعَيْنِ. Adulterating matter, غِشّ.

Flash, *v.i.* To flame, تَحَلَّجَ ـ ٱلْتَهَبَ ـ تَلَهَّبَ ـ بَرَقَ ². To burst out, أَفَاضَ ـ فَاضَ. He flashed with his eyes, بَرَقَ بِعَيْنَيْهِ. To — upon the mind, خَطَرَ بِٱلْبَالِ ². It flashed upon his mind, خَطَرَ بِبَالِهِ ـ يَخْفَى aor. خَفِيَ لَهُ. To —, as with anger, of the eye, زَمْهَرَتْ عَيْنُهُ.

Flash, *a.* Counterfeit, غِشّ ـ زَغَل ـ مُقَلَّد ـ مُزَوَّر.

Flash-house, *n.* بَيْتُ ٱلسُّرَّاقِ ـ مَاوَى ٱللُّصُوصِ.

Flashily, *ad.* With ostentation, تَكَبُّرًا ـ إِفْتِخَارًا ـ بِٱفْتِخَارٍ ـ إِسْتِكْبَارًا.

Flashings, *n.* حِجَاب *pl.* حُجُب.

Flashy, *a.* Gaudy, فَاخِر ـ جَلِيّ. Insipid, فَاتِر ـ تَافِه ـ بِلَا مَعْنَى.

Flask, *n.* قَوَارِير *pl.* قَارُورَة ـ قَنَانِيّ *pl.* قَنِّينَة ـ سَفَط ـ حُنْجُور ـ قِزَازَة ـ قَارُورَة. A — for wine, صُرَاحِيَّة; for powder, مُذْخَر ـ وِعَاءُ لِلْبَارُودِ.

Flasket, *n.* قَصْعَة *pl.* قِصَاع ـ زِنْبِيل.

Flat, *a.* Level, مُسْتَوٍ ـ سَوَآء ـ سَطِيح ـ مُسَطَّح. Prostrate, صَرِيع ـ مَتْلُول ـ تَلِيل. Insipid, بَاطِل ـ فَاتِر ـ تَافِه ـ بِلَا لَذَّةٍ. Downright, قَطْعِيّ ـ مُطْلَق ـ قَاطِع ـ بَتّ. A — lie, كَذْبٌ سَقِيطَة ـ سُمَاق. Dejected, مَغْمُوم. Dull, stupid, أَخْرَق ـ غَبِين. Flat, of a market, كَاسِد. A — sound, جِسٌّ جِرْمٌ. A — roof, سَطْح *pl.* سُطُوح. Flat wine, عَسِيقَة. A — slab, طَابِق *pl.* طَوَابِق *and* طَوَابِيق. A — nose, فَطَسَة. Having a — nose, أَفْطَس *fem.* فَطْسَآء.

Flat, *ad.* In a level position, إِنْسِطَاحًا ـ سَطْحًا; in a prostrate position, إِنْصِرَاعًا ـ تَلًّا. To fall —, as to the ground, كَبَا ل ². To lie —, تَسَطَّحَ ـ إِنْسَطَحَ. To throw down —, سَطَحَ ـ تَكَبَّى. To make to lie down —, or to make —, سَطَّحَ.

Flat, *n.* A level piece of ground, سَهْل *pl.* سُهُول ـ بَسِيطَة. Low land, غَوْطَة ـ وَطَآء. A floor, طَبَقَة *pl.* طَبَقَات. A shoal, صَفْح ـ سَرْب *pl.* أَسْرَاب. The broad side, as of a blade, عُرْض ـ صَفْحَة *pl.* صِفَاح. A broad boat, مَاعُونَة ـ صَنْدَل ـ صَنْدَال. A dunce, ثَوْر ـ حِمَار ـ أَحْمَق ـ أَخْرَق. A —, in music, عَلَامَةُ ٱلْخَفْضِ فِي ٱلْمُوسِيقَى. He struck him with the — of the sword, أَصْفَحَهُ بِٱلسَّيْفِ ـ ضَرَبَهُ بِصَفْحِ ٱلسَّيْفِ.

Flat, *v.t.* and *i.* *See to* Flatten, *v.t.* and *i.*

Flat-bottomed, *a.* سَطِيحُ ٱلْقَرَارِ ـ ذُو قَعْرٍ مُسَطَّحٍ.

Flat-fish, *n.* سَمَكَةٌ مُسَطَّحَةٌ عَرِيضَةٌ.

Flat-iron, *n.* مِكْوَى *pl.* مَكَاوٍ.

Flatly, *ad.* Downrightly, بَتَّةً ـ قَطْعًا ـ تَمَامًا ـ لِلْغَايَةِ ـ بِٱلْمَرَّةِ. Without spirit, بِفُتُورٍ ـ بِبُرُودَةٍ. *See also* Flat, *ad.*

Flatness, *n.* Evenness, سَطْح ـ تَسْطِيح ـ إِنْسِطَاح ـ تَسْوِيَة ـ سَوَآء. Insipidity, قِلَّةُ لَذَّةٍ ـ فُتُور ـ تُفُوه ـ تَفَاهَة. Stupidity, غَبَاوَة ـ حَمَاقَة ـ خُرْق. Flatness, as of a market, كَسَاد ـ عَدَمُ رَوَاجٍ; of sound, إِنْخِفَاض ـ خَفْض. Depression, إِنْخِفَاض. Flatness of mind, غَمّ ـ كَدَر ـ حُزْن.

Flat-nosed, *a.* أَفْطَس.

Flatten, *v.t.* To make flat, بَسَطَ ـ سَوَّى ـ سَطَّحَ. To beat down to the ground, هَبَطَ ² ـ سَطَحَ ـ تَكَبَّى. To dispirit, هَابَطَ ـ أَغَمَّ ـ كَسَرَ عَزْمَهُ ـ أَخْمَدَ. To —, as in music, خَفَضَ. To make insipid, مَسَخَ.

Flatten, *v.i.* To become flat, إِنْبَسَطَ ـ إِنْسَطَحَ ـ تَسَطَّحَ. To become insipid, dull, تَفِهَ ـ خَسَّ *aor.* يَخَسُّ.

Flatter, *v.t.* To praise excessively, أَطْرَأَ ـ فَرَطَ ـ قَرَّظَ ـ مَانَى ـ حَاوَلَ ـ تَلَيَّنَ ل ـ صَانَعَ ـ دَاهَنَ ـ دَالَى. To wheedle, مَلَّقَ.

تَلَطَّفَ ب. To —, by way of comfort, طَيَّبَ خَاطِرَهُ – رَفَأَ ـ.
To —, as with promises, مَنَّى ب – عَلَّلَ بِٱلْمَوَاعِيدِ. To —
one's self, to think, ظَنَّ – خَمَّنَ. To — one's self to one's self,
مَلَّقَ نَفْسَهُ لِنَفْسِهِ.

Flatterer, *n.* } مُمَلِّق – مَلِق – مَلَّاق – دائم ٱلْمَشْط. A
Flattering, *a.* } wheedler, wheedling, مُرَاوِض عَلَى –
مُتَلَطِّف – مُتَلَيِّن ل – ب. Flattering lips, شَفَاهٌ مَلِقَةٌ. Flattering words,
أَقْوَالٌ مُشْتَمِلَةٌ عَلَى ٱلتَّمَلُّقِ. A — likeness, صُورَةٌ مُفْرِطَةٌ فِي
ٱلْحُسْنِ. Encouraging, مُرَغِّب – مُشَوِّق; by way of praise,
مادِح. A flatterer of women, غَزِل.

Flatteringly, *ad.* اِسْتِحْسَانًا – بِتَمَلُّقٍ – بِإِطْرَاءٍ.

Flattery, *n.* Adulation, تَقْرِيظ – تَفْرِيط – إِطْرَاء – تَمَلُّق –
تَمَلَّاق. Wheedling, مُدَاهَنَة – مُصَانَعَة – مُحَاوَلَة. The — of
the tongue, مَلَقُ ٱللِّسَانِ.

Flattish, *a.* Somewhat flat, مُسَطَّحٌ نَوْعًا; somewhat dull,
تافِهٌ نَوْعًا.

Flatulence, *n.* } Of wind, رِيح – رِيحَة – نَفْخَة – زَفِيرَة. Vanity,
Flatulency, } عَبَث – باطِل. Flat colic, قُولَنْجٌ رِيحِيٌّ.
The — of children, أُمُّ ٱلصِّبْيَانِ.

Flatulent, *a.* Of wind, نَفَّاخ – رِيحِيٌّ. Vain, تافِه – باطِل.
A — tumour, نُفْخَة.

Flatulently, *ad.* كَأَنَّهُ بِهِ نَفْخَةٌ.

Flatus, *n.* A puff, رِيحَة – نَفْخَة.

Flat-wise, *ad.* عَلَى ٱلصَّفْحِ – عُرْضًا.

Flaunt, *v.t.* To display ostentatiously, بِتَفَخُّرٍ – أَظْهَرَ – اِفْتَخَرَ ب –
تَبَاهَى ب.

Flaunt, *v.i.* To exhibit one's self ostentatiously, تَبَاهَى – اِفْتَخَرَ –
تَغَنْدَرَ. To strut, as in walking, تَكَفَّأَ – تَخَطَّلَ – تَخَطَّلَ فِي
مِشْيَتِهِ.

Flaunt, *n.* Something hanging loose, أُرْجِيحَة – ذَيْل. Display
for show, تَفَخُّر – اِفْتِخَار.

Flaunting, *a.* Of a person, مُتَكَبِّر – غَنْدُور – مُتَزَخْرِف. *See*
also Gaudy, *a.*

Flavour, *n.* An agreeable taste, لَذَّة – ذَوْق. An agreeable
smell, عِطْر – رَائِحَة. Taste, طَعْم. Smell, عَرْف – نَشْوَة. A
modicum, *soupçon*, عِرْق.

Flavour, *v.t.* To give a taste to with, فَوَّحَ ب – تَبَّلَ ب –
حَيَّقَ ب. To give a scent to with, عَطَّرَ ب. To —, to taste
of..., طَعْمُهُ كَطَعْمِ ...

Flavouring, *n.* Seasoning for food, تابِل – قِزْح.

Flavourless, *a.* Without taste, غَيْرُ ذِي نَفَسٍ – تافِه – مَلِيخ –
بِلا لَذَّةٍ; without smell, بِلا رَائِحَةٍ.

Flavorous, *a.* Pleasant to the taste, لَذِيذ; pleasant to the smell,
عَطِر – شَمُوم – طَيِّبُ ٱلرَّائِحَةِ. Generous, as of wine, ذُو نَفَسٍ.

Flaw, *n.* A crack, شَقّ *pl.* شُقُوق – فَتّ *pl.* فُتُوت – كُسُور.
A defect, خَلَل – عَوَار – قُصُور – نُقْصَان – سَقَط – عَيْب *pl.*
عُيُوب. A — in precious stones, عَيْب *pl.* عُيُوب. A gust of
wind, نَفْخَة – هُبُوبُ رِيحٍ – مَهَبّ.

Flawed, *a.* *See* Flawy, *a.*

Flawless, *a.* عَيْب – بِدُونِ قُصُورٍ – بِلا عَوَارٍ – كَامِل – تَامّ.

Flawy, *a.* Having flaws, ذُو عُيُوبٍ – مَعْيُوب – ذُو عَوَارٍ –
مُعَوَّر; of precious stones, ذُو عُيُوبٍ. Gusty, ذُو هُبُوبٍ –
هَبُوب.

Flax, *n.* The plant, كَتَّان – نَبَاتُ ٱلْكَتَّانِ. The fibres of —,
كَتَّان. Cloth of —, قُمَاشُ كَتَّانٍ. Fine —, كَتَّانٌ خَاصّ.

Flax-comb, *n.* مِسْرَحُ (or مِسْرَحَةُ) ٱلْكَتَّانِ.

Flax-dresser, *n.* مَشَاقِيّ.

Flaxen, *a.* Of flax, كَتَّانِيّ – مِنْ كَتَّانٍ. Fair, as of the hair,
أَشْهَب – أَشْقَر *fem.* شَقْرَاء *pl.* شُقْر.

Flax-seed, *n.* بِزْرُ كَتَّانٍ.

Flay, *v.t.* To skin, جَلَّدَ – سَلَقَ ² – سَلَخَ ² –.

Flayer, *n.* مُجَلِّد – سَلَّاخ *pl.* سَلَّاخُون. When a cow dies the
flayers multiply, (*prov.*) إِذَا سَقَطَتِ ٱلْبَقَرَةُ كَثُرَتِ ٱلسَّلَّاخُونَ.

Flea, *n.* عِدَام *pl.* عُدُم – بُرْغُوث *pl.* بَرَاغِيث. To kill, of
a —, فَرَكَ ².

Flea, *v.t.* To hunt for fleas, فَلَّى ٱلْبَرَاغِيثَ.

Flea-bane, *n.* حَشِيشَةُ ٱلْبَرَاغِيثِ – طُبَّاق مِدْيَنِيّ.

Flea-bite, *n.* The bite of a flea, قَرْصُ ٱلْبُرْغُوثِ – لَسْع
ٱلْبَرَاغِيثِ. A trifle, شَيْءٌ جُزْئِيٌّ – ضَرَرٌ خَفِيفٌ – تَفَاهَة.

Flea-bitten, *a.* Bitten by fleas, مَقْرُوصٌ مِنَ ٱلْبَرَاغِيثِ. Spotted,
as with flea-bites, مُحَبَّر.

Fleam, *n.* نَشْتَرُ ٱلْبَيْطَارِ.

Fleck, *v.t.* } To spot, زَرْقَشَ – نَقَّطَ; to daub, stain, بَقَّعَ – طَبَّعَ.
Flecker, }

Flection, *n.* *See* Flexion, *n.*

Fledge, *v.t.* رَيَّشَ – لَبَّسَ بِٱلرِّيشِ.

Fledgeling, *n.* فَرْخٌ أَزْغَبُ.

Flee, *v.i.* To run away, لَاذَ ² – اِنْفَلَتَ – أَقْنَبَ – اِنْهَزَمَ –
فَرَّ – شَرَدَ ² – هَرَبَ ² – وَلَّى هَارِبًا. To — away in terror,
أَجْفَلَ. To — in disorder, نَفَرَ ². To — to, لَاذَ ب – إِلَى ².

o make to —, هَرَّبَ — ‎ ‎هَزَمَ — نَفَّرَ — أَنْفَرَ — أَفَرَّ — أَفَرَّ بِهِ . To avoid, حَادَ عَنْ — اِجْتَنَبَ — أَتْنَبَ . أَهْرَبَ

Fleece, *n.* جِزَّة *pl.* جِزَز *or* جَزَائِز . The order of the Golden Fleece, نِيشَانُ ٱلْجِزَّةِ ٱلذَّهَبِيَّةِ .

Fleece, *v.t.* To shear, قَصَّ — جَزَّ . To plunder, سَلَبَ — نَهَبَ .

Fleecer, *n.* As of wool, جَزَّاز — قَصَّاص . A despoiler, نَهَّاب — سَلَّاب .

Fleecy, *a.* ذُو صُوف — صُوفِيٌّ .

Fleer, *v.t.* To mock, تَسَخَّرَ مِن — سَخِرَ مِن — فَلَّحَ بِ — اِسْتَهْزَأَ بِ .

Fleer, *n.* هَزْو — سُخْرِيَّة — اِسْتِهْزَآء .

Fleeringly, *ad.* سُخْرَةً — بِٱسْتِهْزَآء .

Fleet, *a.* Quick, swift, مُعَجَّل — مِزَاق — مِرْآس — طَيَّار — طَائِر — سَرِيع . A — horse, فَرَسٌ سَرِيعٌ . *See also* Fleeting, *a.*

Fleet, *n.* A — of ships, دُونَنْمَا — عِمَارَة — شُوَن — أَسَاطِيلُ . The — was dispersed and some of the ships were captured, تَفَرَّقَتِ ٱلْأَسَاطِيلُ كُلُّهَا وَأُخِذَ بَعْضُهَا . All the — has arrived, ٱلشُّوَنُ (or ٱلْعِمَارَةُ) وَصَلَتْ قَاطِبَةً .

Fleet, *v.i.* To pass quickly, سَرُعَ .

Fleet, *v.t.* To do quickly, تَسَرَّعَ إِلَى — أَسْرَعَ فِي .

Fleeting, *a.* سَرِيعُ ٱلزَّوَالِ — زَائِل — فَانٍ — عَاجِل — أَعْجَلُ .

Fleetingly, *ad.* بِعَدَمِ بَقَآء — بِزَوَالٍ — بِسُرْعَةٍ .

Fleetly, *ad.* اِسْتِعْجَالًا — عَجَلًا — بِسُرْعَةٍ .

Fleetness, *n.* خِفَّة — سُرْعَة — عَجَلَة .

Fleming, *n.* A native of Flanders, مِنْ أَهْلِ ٱلْفَلَمَنْك .

Flemish, *a.* مَنْسُوبٌ إِلَى ٱلْفَلَمَنْك — مِنَ ٱلْفَلَمَنْك .

Flesh, *n.* Animal food, زَفَر — لَحْم *or* لَحَم *pl.* لُحُوم . The body, ٱلْجَسَدُ — ٱلْجِسْمُ — ٱلْبَدَن . Being, وُجُود . Man, إِنْسَان — مِنْ آدَم — مِنْ بَنِي بَشَرٍ — ٱبْنُ بَشَرٍ . Animal nature, حَيَوَان — ٱلْجِنْسُ ٱلْحَيُّ . Human nature, طَبِيعَةٌ بَشَرِيَّةٌ — نَاسُوت — إِنْسَانِيَّة . Carnality, lusts of the —, أَشْوَاقٌ نَفْسَانِيَّةٌ — شَهْوَةُ ٱلْجَسَدِ — لَذَّاتٌ جَسَدَانِيَّةٌ . Kindliness, شَفَقَة — تَرَحُّم — حِلْم — رِقّ . Life in the world, عُمْرٌ فَانٍ — حَيَاةُ ٱلدُّنْيَا . Relationship, نَسَب — نَسْل — قَرَابَة — مِنْ قَرَابَةٍ . Raw —, لَحْمٌ نِيّ . A lump of —, لَحْمَة . An arm of —, قُوَّةٌ إِنْسَانِيَّةٌ . Fed on —, of beasts, مُلْحَم . The — placed as a bait for wild beasts, لُحْمَة .

Flesh, *v.t.* To initiate, أَدْخَلَ فِي . To try, test, جَرَّبَ . To accustom, دَرَّبَ بِ — دَرَّجَ إِلَى . To glut, شَبَّعَ .

Flesh-brush, *n.* فُرْشَةٌ لِحَكِّ ٱلْجِلْدِ .

Flesh-colour, *n.* لَوْنُ ٱلْجَسَدِ .

Flesh-hook, *n.* مِنْشَل *pl.* مَنَاشِل — مِنْشَال .

Fleshiness, *n.* Fatness, سِمَن — سَمَانَة — عَزْم . Corpulence, ضَخَامَة — جَسَامَة — جُسْمَانِيَّة .

Fleshliness, *n.* Carnal appetites, شَهَوَاتُ ٱلْجَسَدِ — نَفْسَانِيَّة .

Fleshly, *a.* Corporeal, جَسَدَانِيٌّ — جِسْمَانِيٌّ . Human, بَشَرِيٌّ . Animal, حَيَوَانِيٌّ . Carnal, شَهْوَانِيٌّ .

Flesh-pot, *n.* قِدْرَة *pl.* قُدُور — جِلَّة — طِنْجِرَة *pl.* طَنَاجِير .

Fleshy, *a.* رَضْرَاض — غَضَنْفَر — مُلَحَّم — لَحِيم — سَمِين — ضَخْم — ضُخَام . To be —, لَحُمَ — ضَخُمَ . Fleshy or quivering buttocks, كَفَلٌ رَضْرَاض .

Fletch, *v.t.* To —, as of arrows, رَاشَ *aor.* يَرِيش — رَيَّشَ .

Fletcher, *n.* A —, as of arrows, رَيَّاش — مُرَيِّش .

Fleur-de-lis, *n.* زَنْبَق — زَهْرُ ٱلزَّنْبَقِ .

Flew; *pret. of to* Fly, *v.i.*; *q.v.*

Flex, *v.t.* حَنَّى — قَوَّسَ — ثَنَى .

Flexibility, *n.* Pliancy, قَابِلِيَّةُ ٱلتَّعْوِيجِ — سُرْعَةُ ٱلتَّعَوُّجِ — رُطُوبَةُ ٱلْخُلُقِ — لَيَانُ ٱلْجَانِبِ . Pliancy of temper, لِيَانَة — لِينَة — مُيَاسَرَة — دَمَاثَة — خُضُوع .

Flexible, *a.* Pliant, لَيِّن — رَطْب — رَطِيب — يَنْحَنِي — سَهْل — ٱلْعُطُوف — يَتَعَوَّجُ ; of a tree, مُغْدَوْدِن — قَصْلَة ; of a bow, سَمْحَة — غَلْفَق — دَمِيث — أَمْلَدُ . Pliant in disposition, سَادِج — سَهْلُ ٱلْعُطُوفَةِ — لَيِّنُ ٱلْجَانِبِ — مُيَاسِر . Comprehensive in meaning, كَثِيرُ ٱلْمَعَانِي — مَعْنَوِيٌّ . To be —, لَانَ — رَطُبَ ; to make pliant, رَطَّبَ — لَيَّنَ . To be —, compliant to, عَطَفَ إِلَى ; to make —, compliant, خَفَّضَ — اِسْتَعْطَفَ .

Flexibleness, *n.* *See* Flexibility, *n.*

Flexibly, *ad.* *See* Pliantly, *ad.*

Flexile, *a.* *See* Flexible, *a.*

Flexion, *n.* The act of bending, عَطْف — تَعْوِيج — ثَنْي . *See also* Flexure, *n.*

Flexor, *n.* A — muscle, عَضَلَةٌ مُعَطِّفَةٌ .

Flexuous, *a.* / Flexuose, } Bending, winding, ذُو ٱعْوِجَاجٍ وَمَعَاطِف — مُعَوَّج — ذُو مَحَانٍ .

Flexure, *n.* ٱلْحِنَآء — عِوَج — عَوْجَة — حِنَايَة . Any — of the members, of the groin, armpit, *etc.*, مَغْبِن *pl.* مَغَابِنُ .

Flicker, *v.i.* رَعِشَ — اِخْتَفَقَ — خَفَقَ — رَفْرَفَ — رَأْرَأَ — اِضْطَرَبَ — خَطَرَ — اِرْتَعَشَ .

Flickering, *n.* رَعْش — خَفَقَان — خَفْق — رَفْرَفَة — رَأْرَأ — اِرْتِعَاش .

Flickering, *a.* مُضْطَرِب ـ مُرْتَعِش ـ خافِق ـ مُرَفْرِف ـ مُرَأْرِئ.

Flickeringly, *ad.* رَفْرَفَةً ـ اِرْتِعاشًا ـ بِخَفَقانٍ.

Flier, *n.* One who flees, شارِد ـ فارّ ـ هارِب. The —, as of a wheel, جَناح *pl.* أَجْنِحَة. The balance, as of a wheel, رَقّاص.

Flight, *n.* The act of running away, فَرّ ـ مَفَرّ ـ فُرُور ـ هُرُوب ـ شُرُود. A rout, هَزِيمَة ـ هِزِّيمَى. A flying, طَيَران. A movement, سَيْر ـ حَرَكَة. A flock, as of birds, وِرْد ـ حَوْم ـ سِرْب *pl.* أَسْراب. A volley, طَلْقَة ـ ضَرْبَة. The space past by flying, طَيْرَة ـ مَسافَةُ ٱلطَّيَرانِ. A series, floor, طَبَقَة *pl.* طَبَقات. The —, as of an arrow, the height to which it ascends, غَلْوَة. A sally, as of the mind, طَيْرَة ـ طَيْش. A — of fancy, تَخَيُّل ـ تَوَهُّم. A place of —, a retreat, مَفَرّ. The era of the Flight, the al-Hijrah, تارِيخُ ٱلْهِجْرَةِ. To take —, to run away, اِنْهَزَمَ ـ فَرَّ. To put to —, to defeat, كَسَرَ ـ فَلَّلَ ـ أَفَرَّ ـ هَزَّمَ ـ هَزَمَ ـ فَلَّ ـ هَرَّبَ. To be put to —, to be defeated, اِنْكَسَرَ. Put to —, فَلّ *pl.* فُلُول *and* أَفْلال. A bad omen from the — of birds, إِطِّيَرَة. To draw a bad omen from the — of birds, تَطَيَّرَ ـ إِطَّيَّرَ. To wing one's —, اِنْطَلَقَ ـ وَثَبَ *aor.* يَثِبُ.

Flightiness, *n.* Of the mind, قِلَّةُ ثَباتٍ ـ خِفَّةُ عَقْلٍ ـ طَيْرَة ـ تَلَوُّن ـ طَياشَة ـ طَيَشان.

Flighty, *a.* Of the mind, خَفِيفُ ٱلْعَقْلِ ـ ذُو طَيْرَةٍ ـ مُتَخَيِّل ـ أَخْطَل. He became —, طارَ طائِرُهُ.

Flimsily, *ad.* As of texture, بِسَخافَةٍ ـ بِرِقَّةٍ. Superficially, بِرَثاثَةٍ. Weakly, بِضَعْفٍ. *See also under* Slightly, *ad.*

Flimsiness, *n.* Weakness of texture, رِقَّة ـ سُخْف ـ سَخافَة ـ عَدَمُ مَتانَةٍ; as of language, رَثاثَة ـ رَكاكَة.

Flimsy, *a.* Weak in texture, سَخِيف ـ رَخْو ـ عَدِيمُ ٱلْمَتانَةِ. Weak, ضَعِيف. Worn out, رَثّ ـ رَثِيث. Flimsy language, كَلامٌ رَثٌّ (*or* رَكِيك). To be —, سَخُفَ ـ رَثَّ ـ رَخُوَ *aor.* يَرْخُو.

Flinch, *v.i.* To —, as from danger, جَبَأَ عَن ـ جَفَلَ عَن; through cowardice, خامَ عَن. To draw back from, اِرْتَدَّ مِن ـ اِنْقَبَضَ مِن. To abandon, تَرَكَ.

Fling, *v.t.* To throw, رَمَى *aor.* يَرْمِي ـ أَلْقَى ـ بِ. To — at, رَشَقَ ـ بِ ـ رَمَى ـ بِ ـ أَلْقَى ـ بِ. To baffle, defeat, خَيَّبَ ـ أَخْجَلَ. To defeat, غَلَبَ عَلَى ـ ظَفِرَ بِ. To scatter, بَدَّدَ ـ شَتَّتَ. To — away, أَلْقَى ـ طَرَحَ ـ تَرَكَ. To — down, أَوْقَعَ ـ أَهْبَطَ; to prostrate, جَفَأَ بِهِ ـ أَجْفَأَ بِهِ. To — or give up, تَخَلَّى عَن ـ تَرَكَ ـ هَجَرَ ـ اِسْتَعْفَى مِن. To — open, أَرْحَبَ ـ فَتَحَ. To — into the teeth of one, عَيَّرَ ـ بِ ـ رَمَى ـ بِقَبِيحٍ ـ سَبَّ ـ حَسَكَ عَلَى. *See also to* Cast, *v.t.*

Fling, *n.* A throw, رَشْقَة ـ رَمْيَة *pl.* رَمَيات. A sneer, رَمْيَة بِقَبِيحٍ ـ نَوادِر ـ تَهَكُّم. Will, liberty, مَشِيئَة ـ إِجْراءُ ٱلْخاطِرِ ـ هَوًى. *See also under* Swing, *n.*

Flint, *n.* A — stone, حَصْوَة ـ حَجَرُ صَوّانٍ ـ صَوّان ـ صَوّانَة *pl.* حَصاة. The — of a musket, صَوّانَة ـ صَلّاطَة ـ مِظَرَّة; of a tinder-box, قَدّاحَة. Flint and steel, زِناد ـ مِقْدَحٌ وَقَدّاحَةٌ. Harder than —, أَصْلَبُ مِنَ ٱلصَّوّانِ. To strike light, as with a — and steel, قَدَحَ بِ ـ اِقْتَدَحَ بِ.

Flint-glass, *n.* بِلَّوْر.

Flint-hearted, *a.* قاسٍ ـ عَنِيف ـ جافٍ.

Flinty, *a.* Of flint, مِنْ صَوّانٍ ـ صَوّانِيّ. Flinty soil, containing pebbles, أَرْضٌ مَحْصاةٌ ـ أَرْضٌ حَصِيَةٌ. A — rock, صَوّانُ ٱلصَّخْرِ. Very hard, صَلِيب ـ مَتِين. *See also* Flint-hearted, *a.*

Flip, *n.* شَرابٌ مُرَكَّبٌ مِنَ ٱلسُّكَّرِ وَٱلْبُوزَةِ ـ بُوزَةٌ بِٱلسُّكَّرِ.

Flippancy, *n.* Talkativeness, خَطَل ـ فَرْفَرَة ـ بَقَق ـ كَثْرَةُ كَلامٍ. Pertness, فَرْط ـ سَفاهَة.

Flippant, *a.* Loquacious, بَيْذار ـ بَذِر ـ كِلْمانِيّ ـ بَقّاق ـ غَلْباوِيّ ـ لَقّاش. Pert, سَفِيه ـ مُفْرِط. A — tongue, لِسانٌ طَلِقٌ. A — person, هُذَرَةٌ بُذَرَةٌ.

Flippantly, *ad.* With loquacity, بِفَرْفَرَةٍ ـ بِخَطَلٍ ـ بِكَثْرَةِ كَلامٍ. Pertly, بِسَفاهَةٍ ـ بِوَقاحَةٍ.

Flippantness, *n.* *See* Flippancy, *n.*

Flirt, *v.t.* To toss, نَثَرَ ـ رَمَى *aor.* يَرْمِي; of water, رَشَّ. To move, حَرَّكَ.

Flirt, *v.i.* To gibe at, نَقَّرَ بِ ـ هَزَأَ بِ. To — about, حامَ ـ طارَ ـ رَفْرَفَ ـ تَرَدَّدَ. To coquet, تَدَلَّلَ ـ شَكَّلَ ـ تَشَكَّلَ ـ تَشَكَّلَتْ ـ تَغَنَّجَتْ ـ تَعاجَبَ; of a woman, غَنِجَتْ ـ تَغَنَّجَتْ.

Flirt, *n.* A jerk, خَضَّة ـ نَخْعَة. A coquette, مُتَدَلِّلَة ـ شَكِلَة ـ غَنِجَة ـ مُعْجَبانَة ـ مُغَنِّجَة.

Flirtation, *n.* Coquetry, شِكْل ـ غُنْج ـ تَدَلُّل ـ غَزَل ـ تَعَجُّبَة.

Flit, *v.i.} / **Flitter,** To flutter, vibrate, خَفَقَ ـ حامَ ـ رَفْرَفَ. To move about, of anything light, هَفَتَ. To flee away, طارَ. To move away, اِنْتَقَلَ. To — by, مَرَّ يَطِفُّ.

Flitch, *n.* A — of bacon, شِقَّةُ خِنْزِيرٍ مُمَلَّحَةٌ.

Flitter-mouse, *n.* The bat; *see* Bat, *n.*

Flitting, *a.* Variable, changing, فَرّار ـ طَيّار ـ طائِر ـ هافِت.

Float, *n.* Anything floating, شَيْءٌ طافٍ; as of grass, weeds, *etc.*, سَبْخَة. A cork used in angling, عَوّامَة. An inflated skin used for floating, عامَة — طَوْف *pl.* أَطْوَاف. A raft, رَمَث — مَالِج — مَالَق. A trowel, مَالِج — مَالَق. The — عِمَامَة — كَلَك *pl.* أَكْلَاك as of a wheel, دَوَّارَة *pl.* دَوَّارات.

Float, *v.t.* To cause to swim upon, عَوَّمَ عَلَى — أَسْبَحَ عَلَى. To make to —, floating, جَعَلَهُ يَطْفُو. To convey across, عَبَّرَ. To cover, as with water, غَمَرَ. To smooth with a float, صَقَّلَ بِالْمَالِج. To make current, ready of sale, رَوَّجَ. To — a loan, عَقَدَ قَرْضًا وَرَوَّجَهُ. A floating dress to keep one afloat, لِبَاسُ الطَّفْوِ.

Float, *v.i.* To swim on the surface, عَامَ — غَفَا — طَفَا فَوْقَ. To — in suspense, تَقَلَّبَ فِي الْآرَاءِ — تَرَدَّدَ — تَضَرَّبَ. To be current, ready for sale, *etc.*, رَاجَ *aor.* يَرُوجُ.

Floatage, *n.* كُلَّمَا يَطْفُو — سَابِحَة.

Float-boards, *n.* أَجْنِحَةُ الدُّولَابِ.

Floating, *a.* } عَوَّام — طَافٍ. Floating debt, دُيُونٌ غَيْرُ مُنْتَظِمَةٍ —
Floaty, } دُيُونٌ مُتَفَرِّقَةٌ.

Floating-bridge, *n.* جِسْرٌ عَوَّامٌ.

Flocculence, *n.* تَسَبُّخ — تَشَعُّث — تَلَبُّد.

Flocculent, *a.* سَبِيخ — مُتَشَعِّث — مُتَلَبِّد.

Flock, *n.* A flight, herd, سِرْب *pl.* أَسْرَاب — قَطِيع *pl.* قِطَاع; especially of sheep and cattle at pasture, رَعِيَّة *pl.* رَعَايَا. A multitude, فَوْج *pl.* أَفْوَاج — حَوْم — عَمٌّ *pl.* عُمُومَة — جَمَاعَة. A —, as of wool, سَبِيخَة — صُوفَة — جَزِيزَة.

Flock, *v.i.* To come together, of many, اِلْتَمُّوا — تَكَأْكَأُوا — اِجْتَمَعُوا.

Flock-bed, *n.* فِرَاشٌ مِنْ صُوفٍ — فِرَاشٌ مَحْشِيٌّ بِصُوفٍ.

Flock-paper, *n.* أَوْرَاقٌ مُزَرْكَشَةٌ بِالْقَطِيفَةِ.

Flocky, *a.* سَبِيخ — ذُو تَشَعُّثٍ — ذُو تَلَبُّدٍ.

Floe, *n.* A — of ice, قِطْعَةُ جَلِيدٍ — كُومَةُ ثَلْجٍ.

Flog, *v.t.* جَلَدَ — سَاطَ *aor.* يَسُوطُ — سَوَّطَ. To order to be flogged, جَلَّدَ.

Flogger, *n.* سَوَّاط — جَلَّاد.

Flogging, *n.* ضَرْب — سَوْط — جَلْد.

Flood, *n.* The — of Noah, الطُّوفَانُ — طُوفَانُ نُوحٍ. An inundation, طُوفَان — غَمِير — فَيَضَان — فَيْض. Flow, as of the tide, مَدٌّ — مَاءٌ. A large body of water, غَمْرَة — نَهْر — بَحْر. A great quantity, كَثْرَة — وَفْرَة.

Flood, *v.t.* To inundate, غَمَرَ — غَطَا عَلَى — طَبَّقَ — طَمَّ — غَرَّقَ. To — with, أَفَاضَ عَلَى.

Flood-gate, *n.* مُسَنَّاة *pl.* مُسَنَّيَات — حَاجِز — سَدّ *pl.* سُدُود.

Flooding, *n.* Excessive flow of the menses, إِسْتِحَاضَة. A woman subject to —, مُسْتَحَاضَة.

Flood-mark, *n.* عَلَامَةُ عُلُوِّ الْمَدِّ.

Flook, *n.* A — of an anchor, شُعْبَةُ مِرْسَاةٍ.

Floor, *n.* The bottom of a room or house, أَرْض — بَلَاط — أَرْضِيَّة — الْبَيْتِ. A flooring of wood, تَخْشِيبَة. A story, دَوْر *pl.* أَدْوَار — طَبَقَة *pl.* طَبَقَات. The ground-floor, الطَّبَقَةُ السُّفْلَى — الْأَدْمَنُ. A house of one —, دَارٌ ذَاتُ طَبَقَةٍ وَاحِدَةٍ.

Floor, *v.t.* To cover the — with, فَرَشَ بِ — أَفْرَشَ بِ. To — with stone, بَلَّطَ; with wood, تَخَّتَ — خَشَّبَ. To prostrate, اِعْتَفَرَ — عَفَرَ — أَهْبَطَ — أَوْقَعَ — صَرَعَ — أَجْفَأَ بِهِ — جَفَأَ بِهِ.

Floor-cloth, *n.* مُشَمَّعٌ أَرْضِيَّةٌ.

Flooring, *n.* *See* Floor, *n.*

Flop, *v.t.* To clip the wings, قَصَّ الْجَنَاحَ. *See also to* Flap, *v.t.*

Flora, *n.* An account of flowers, شَرْحُ الْأَزْهَارِ. The botany of a country, نَبَاتَاتُ بَلَدٍ — النَّبَاتَاتُ الْمُخْتَصَّةُ بِبَلَدٍ مَا.

Floral, *a.* مُخْتَصٌّ بِالْأَزْهَارِ — زَهْرِيٌّ.

Florence, *n.* The city of, مَدِينَةُ فِيُورَنْسَة — الْفَلُورَانْس.

Florentine, *n.* The stuff, خَزٌّ; the silk, إِسْتَبْرَق.

Florescence, *n.* زَهْر — إِزْهَار.

Floret, *n.* زُهَيْرَة *pl.* زُهَيْرَات — زُهَيْرَةٌ مُفْرَدَةٌ.

Floriculture, *n.* تَرْبِيَةُ الْأَزْهَارِ.

Florid, *a.* Ruddy, أَحْمَرُ قَرَّاص — قُنَاع — أَشْقَر. Flowery, زَاهِر — مُزْهِر. Showy, بَهِيّ — بَرَّاق — مُرَوْنَق. Bright in colour, نَاضِر; in writing, style, مُفَنَّن — بَلِيغ. To be —, bright, نَضَرَ — أَنْضَرَ.

Floridity, *n.* } Ruddiness, شُقْرَة. Brightness, نَضْر. Showi-
Floridness, } ness, بَهَاء — رَوْنَق — زَهْرَة. Of speech, writing, مُبَالَغَة — تَفَنُّن.

Floriferous, *a.* حَامِلُ الْأَزْهَارِ.

Floriform, *a.* بِصُورَةِ الزَّهْرِ.

Florin, *n.* اِسْمُ سِكَّةٍ مِنَ الْفِضَّةِ.

Florist, *n.* أَزْهَرِيٌّ.

Floscular, *a.* } مُرَكَّبٌ مِنَ الزُّهَيْرَاتِ.
Flosculous, }

Floscule, *n.* *See* Floret, *n.*

Floss, *n.* Of silk, مُشَاقَةُ الْحَرِيرِ; of wool, مُشَاقَةُ الصُّوفِ.

Flotage, *n.* *See* Floatage, *n.*

Flotation, *n.* تَسْبِيح — عَوْم.

Flotilla, *n.* A little fleet, دُونَنْمَةٌ صُغَيْرَةٌ; a fleet of small ships, دُونَنْمَةُ مَرَاكِبَ صِغَارٍ.

Flotsam, *n.* | **Flotsom**, | ما يطفو على ظهر البحر من الاموال المباحة . سوائب على وجه البحر ـ وفضلات الغرق .

Flounce, *v.t.* To deck with a —, زين بتغريج .

Flounce, *v.i.* To —, as in the water, غاص 2. To move about, تقلب .

Flounce, *n.* The —, as of a dress, تغريج . A sudden jerk, خضة ـ نخعة .

Flounder, *v.i.* As in mud, *etc.*, اختبط ـ ضل ـ وحل ; in speech, اعتقل لسانه ـ هرج . A floundering in speech, عقلة .

Flounder, *n.* The fish, نوع من السمك .

Flour, *n.* دقيق ـ طحين ـ طحن . Coarse-ground —, سميذ ـ جريش . The — sprinkled on a board to prevent the paste from sticking, لوانة ـ لواث .

Flour, *v.t.* To grind, طحن ـ دق 2. To sprinkle with —, رش بدقيق 2.

Flourish, *v.t.* To brandish, as of a sword, شهر ـ اجل ـ اهب . To — a trumpet, نفخ في البوق . To beautify, in needlework, زين ـ برج ـ طرز ; in language, زوق الكلام . To adorn, زين .

Flourish, *v.i.* As of a plant, to grow, نبت ـ نشر 2 ـ نما 2. To flower, ازهر ـ نور ـ ورد ـ اوشع ـ استكهل . To be in a prosperous state, سعد ـ استفلح ـ افلح ; of a country, عمر 2. To bounce, boast, افتخر ـ هلج . To use florid language, تفنن (or بالغ) في الكلام . To make an irregular prelude, as in music, دندن . He shall — as a flower, يزهر كالزهر .

Flourish, *n.* A parade of words, مبالغة ـ تزويق الكلام . Splendour, عز ـ رونق . Show, افتخار ـ مباهاة . A — of the pen, تداوير في الكتابة . A — of trumpets, هتاف الابواق .

Flourishing, *a.* Happy, سعيد . Well peopled, عمران . Flowering, زاهر ـ مورد . Prosperous, فالح ـ ناجح . To be in a — state, of a country, عمر 2. To put into a — state, عمر 2. A — state, عمارة . A — country, بلاد معمورة ـ ارض عامرة .

Flourishingly, *ad.* With growth, بنمو . Prosperously, بنجاح ـ في النعيم ـ نعمة ـ توفيقا ـ بتوفيق .

Flout, *v.t.* ازدرى ب ـ تسخر ب ـ حشم 2 ـ استهزأ ب ـ ضحك من .

Flouter, *n.* هزأة ـ سخرة ـ حاشم ـ ناقر .

Floutingly, *ad.* استهزاء ـ باستهزاء ـ بسخرية ـ نقرا .

Flow, *v.i.* To move on, as of water, تفوض ـ ساح *aor.* يسيح ـ جرى ـ سرب 2 ـ يسرب ـ سال *aor.* يسيل ـ زرب ـ يسيب ـ ساب *aor.* يسيب . To rise, as the tide, *etc.*, علا 2 ـ مد الماء 2. To melt, انحل ـ انسلاب ـ كثر 2 ـ ذاب 2. To — with, to abound, ملئ ب ـ زخر ب . To —, as of tears, *etc.*, همى ـ انثعب ـ سفح ; as rain from the clouds, انهل ; as water from a fountain, or a water finding vent, انبجس ـ تفجر ـ انفجر ; as blood from a wound, سفح ـ فر ـ فار 2 ـ ثج ; as matter from a sore, غشق ـ نج ; as time, مر 2 ـ جرى ـ مضى . To — or proceed from, نشأ من 2 ـ صدر من ـ انبثق من . To — into, as of water, انسكب في ـ انصب في ـ صب في 2. To ebb and —, جزر ومد 2. To —, of speech, بلغ 2. His tears flowed, ذاب 2 دمعه . To make to —, to move, as water, فجر 2 ـ بجس ـ سيح ـ اذاب ـ ذوب ـ اسال ـ سيل ـ فجر . To make fluid, اذاب ـ ذوب . To make a vent for, as for water, فجر . To cause to —, as in different channels, صرف . *See also to* Issue, *v.i.*

Flow, *v.t.* *See to* Float, *v.a.*

Flow, *n.* A stream, current, سيل ـ سيلان ـ سيلة . Abundance, وفور ـ فرط ـ بركة ـ كثرة ـ وفرة . Ease, سهولة . Flow of language, بلاغة . Flow of soul, انشراح ـ انفتاح القلب ـ انعطاف الصدر .

Flower, *n.* Of a tree, نور *pl.* انوار ـ نورة ـ نوار *pl.* نواوير ; of shrubs, زهرة ـ ورود *pl.* ورد *coll.* زهر *pl.* ازهار ـ فقاح . Any —, فاغية ـ حنون . A nosegay, زهر (صحبة or باقة or) ربطة . An ornament, زينة . The best part of anything, جوهر ـ خلاصة ـ زبدة ـ عنبرة *pl.* عنابر . The — of the troops, (افضل or) نخبة العسكر . The — of youth, (عنفوان or) عنفو الشباب . The — of age, (الكهولة or الرجولة or) الرجولية ـ كمال الرجولية . To close, as of a —, قبع .

Flower, *v.i.* To bloom, ازهر ـ ورد ـ نور . To froth, ازبد ـ ارغى ـ جفأ . To simmer, جاش *aor.* يجيش .

Flower, *v.t.* To embellish, زخرف ـ زين ب ـ زركش ـ نقش .

Flowerage, *n.* The being in flower, ازهار ; flowers, ازهار ـ زهر .

Flower-bed, *n.* مربع زهر *pl.* مربعات .

Flower-bud, *n.* جمة *pl.* جمم ـ زر الزهر . *See also* Bud, *n.*

Flower-de-luce, *n.* زنبق .

Flower-dust, *n.* *See* Pollen, *n.*

Flower-garden, *n.* دقر ـ روضة *coll.* روض *pl.* رياض .

Flower-gentle, *n.* *See* Amaranth, *n.*

Floweret, *n.* زهيرة *pl.* زهيرات .

Floweriness, *n.* Of flowers, بركة ازهار ; as of speech, رونق ـ فن ـ زينة . Embellishments, تزيينات .

Flower-leaf, *n.* ورق زهر *pl.* اوراق .

Flowerless, *a.* غَيْرُ مُنَوِّرٍ ـ بِدُونِ زَهْرٍ.

Flower-pot, *n.* قِحْفٌ لِلزَّهْرِ *pl.* قُحُوف *and* أَقْحَاف.

Flower-stalk, *n.* سَاقُ زَهْرٍ *pl.* سُوُوق.

Flower-stand, *n.* قَاعِدَةٌ لِلزَّهْرِ.

Flowers, *n.* The menses, طَمْث ـ حَيْض.

Flowery, *a.* مُنَوِّر ـ أَنْوَر ـ مُنِير ـ أَزْهَر ; of speech, بَدِيع ـ زَاهِر ـ بَلِيغ. A — or flowered dress, ثَوْبٌ مُبَرَّج.

Flowing, *a.* Of water, سَائِل ـ أَسْيَاح *pl.* سَيْح ـ سَرِب ـ ثَعْب. Of speech, فَصِيح ـ بَلِيغ. Fluid, ذَائِب. Abounding, غَنِيّ ـ كَثِير ـ مُوفُور. Hanging down, of hair, *etc.*, مُسْدَل. A — garment, ثَوْبٌ طَوِيلٌ مُسْدِلٌ. A — style, نَصٌّ مُسْتَرْسِل ـ بَسِيط. Flowing water, سَرِب. *See also* Fluent, *a.*

Flowingly, *ad.* With volubility, بِبَلَاغَةٍ ـ بِسُهُولَةٍ ; with abundance, بِكَثْرَةٍ ـ بِغَزَارَةٍ.

Fluctuate, *v.i.* To move to and fro, مَارَ ² ـ تَرَجْرَجَ ـ ارْتَجَّ ـ تَمَوَّجَ ـ خَبَّ ² ـ تَرَدَّدَ ـ تَمَوَّرَ. To be irresolute, تَضَرَّبَ ـ إِحْتَارَ ـ ذَبْذَبَ. The value of money and shares has fluctuated, تَغَيَّرَتْ قِيمَاتُ النُّقُودِ وَالْأَسْهَامِ. To — or vacillate between, تَذَبْذَبَ بَيْنَ.

Fluctuating, *a.* As in a state of commotion, مُتَمَوِّر ـ مُرْتَجّ ـ مُتَمَوِّج. Uncertain, عَدِيمُ الْقَرَارِ ـ فَرَّار. Irresolute, مُتَرَدِّد ـ مُضْطَرِب ـ مُذَبْذَب ـ حَيْرَان.

Fluctuation, *n.* Restlessness, تَمَوُّج ـ مَوْر ـ ارْتِجَاج ـ تَرَدُّد. Irresolution, تَقَلُّب ـ تَضَرُّب ـ حَيْرَة ـ ذَبْذَبَة. The fluctuations of money value, تَغَيُّرَاتُ قِيمَاتِ النُّقُودِ ; of public opinion, تَغَيُّرُ أَفْكَارِ النَّاسِ. To undergo —, تَغَيَّرَ وَتَحَوَّلَ.

Flue, *n.* A passage for smoke, مَجْرَى ـ مَدْخَنَة ـ دَاخُون ـ مَنْفَذُ الدُّخَانِ ـ لِلدُّخَانِ. Down, very fine hair, هِبْرِيَة ـ زَغَب ـ سُخَام.

Fluency, *n.* Of liquids, أَمَاعَة ـ تَمَوُّع ـ مَيْع ; of language, بَلَاغَة ـ فَصَاحَة ـ سُهُولَةُ كَلَامٍ. Flowing, سَيَلَان.

Fluent, *a.* Flowing, جَارٍ ـ سَرِب ـ سَائِل. In speech, سَلَّاق ـ بَلِيغ ـ فَصِيح ـ مِسْلَاق ـ مِسْلَق. A — orator, خَطِيبٌ مِسْلَقٌ. *See also* Fluid, *a.*

Fluent, *n.* A stream, سَيْل ـ سَرِب.

Fluently, *ad.* Volubly, بِبَلَاغَةٍ ـ بِسُهُولَةٍ.

Fluid, *a.* A liquid, مَائِع *pl.* مَوَائِع. Melting, ذَائِب. Flowing, جَارٍ ـ سَرِب ـ سَائِل. To be or become —, مَاعَ ـ تَمَوَّعَ ; to melt, *v.i.* ذَابَ ². To make —, أَذَابَ ـ ذَوَّبَ.

Fluid, *n.* جِسْمٌ سَيَّالٌ ـ سَيَّالَة ـ مَائِع.

Fluidity, *n.* }
Fluidness, } تَمَوُّع ـ مَيْع ـ أَمَاعَة.

Fluke, *n.* Of an anchor, شُعْبَةُ الْمِرْسَاةِ.

Flummery, *n.* The food, حَرِيرَة ـ لَبَنَة. Nonsense, تَفَاهَة ـ لَغْو ـ عَبَث. Flattery, تَمَلُّق.

Flunkeyism, *n.* Base conduct, رَذَالَة ـ خَسَاسَة ـ سَفَالَة ـ تَذَلُّل.

Flunkey, *n.* A low fellow, خَسِيس ـ رَذِيل ـ سَفِلَة *pl.* سَفِيل ـ خِسَاس *and* أَخِسَّاءُ. A servant, خَادِم ـ خَدَّام.

Fluor, *n.* The spar, نَوْعٌ مِنَ الْمَرْمَرِ.

Flurried, *a.* مُقْلَق ـ مُتَحَيِّر ـ مُتَضَجِّر ـ مُضْطَرِب. To be —, خَفَّ ـ تَحَيَّرَ ـ إِسْتَطَارَ.

Flurry, *n.* Bustle, agitation, ضَجِيج ـ دَوْشَة ـ إِضْطِرَاب ـ زَعَج ـ حَيْرَة. *See also* Gust, *n.*

Flurry, *v.t.* أَضْجَرَ ـ أَدْهَشَ ـ أَقْلَقَ ـ أَعْجَلَ ـ إِسْتَخَفَّ ـ أَخَذَ عَقْلَهُ ² ـ حَيَّرَ ـ أَزْعَجَ ـ كَدَّرَ عَلَى. To be flurried, خَفَّ ـ تَضَجَّرَ ـ إِضْطَرَبَ ـ إِسْتَطَارَ. I flurried him so that he could not draw his sword, أَعْجَلْتُهُ عَنِ اسْتِلَالِ سَيْفِهِ.

Flush, *a.* Fresh, full of vigour, جَدِيد ـ صُلْب ـ صَلِيب. Affluent, كَثِير ـ فَائِض ـ نَهِير ـ وَافِر. Level, سَوَاءٌ ـ مُسَطَّح ـ مُسْتَوٍ. Flush of money, rich, كَثِيرُ الْمَالِ ـ غَنِيّ ـ مُدَرْهَم. Spending, مُضَيِّع ـ مُسْرِف.

Flush, *n.* A glow, فَوْرَة ـ حُمْرَة ـ شُقْرَة. Freshness, نَضَارَة ـ زَهْو ـ رَعْرَعَة. A flow, rush, فَوْر ـ فَوَرَان ـ هَيَجَان ـ حُمَيَّا. Abundance, كَثْرَة ـ بَرَكَة. A — of water, فَجْرَةُ مَاءٍ ; a — of joy, فَوْرَةُ الْفَرَحِ. The — of youth, حُمَيَّا الشَّبَابِ.

Flush, *v.t.* To cause to glow, أَفَارَ ـ لَوَّنَ ـ حَمَّرَ. To excite the spirits, أَنْفَسَ ـ خَضْخَضَ. To cause delight to, فَرَّحَ ـ سَرَّ ². To inspire one with such a thing, فَتَحَ عَلَى ـ بِكَذَا. To cover, fill, as with water, طَمَّ ².

Flush, *v.i.* To become red, ruddy, شَقِرَ ـ إِشْقَرَّ ـ إِحْمَرَّ. To —, mantle, فَارَ ². To flow with violence, إِنْفَجَرَ. To be gay, beautiful, لَمَعَ ـ حَسُنَ ـ نَضَرَ ². The fumes of the cup flushed to his head, سَارَتْ فِيهِ حُمَيَّا الْكَأْسِ.

Flush-deck, *n.* ظَهْرُ مَرْكَبٍ مُسَطَّحٌ ـ سَقِيفَةُ مَرْكَبٍ مُسَطَّحَةٌ.

Flushing, *n.* A glow, as in the face, فَوْرَة ـ شُقْرَة ـ حُمْرَة.

Fluster, *n.* *See* Flurry, *n.*

Fluster, *v.t.* *See to* Flurry, *v.t.*

Flustered, *a.* *See* Flurried, *a.*

Flute, *n.* The instrument, مِزْمَار ـ زَمَّارَة ـ شَبَّابَة. The — of

46

a column, تَخْرِيم ـ تَخْطِيط. To play the —, عَزَفَ ـ زَمَّرَ. A player on the —, عازِفُ ٱلشَّبَّابَةِ ـ زَمَّار ٱلشَّبَّابَة.

Flute, *v.t.* To hollow, جَوَّفَ ـ حَفَرَ. To make flutes, as in a column, خَطَّطَ ـ خَرَّمَ.

Fluting, *n.* In architecture, تَخْرِيم ـ تَخْطِيط.

Flutter, *v.t.* *See to* Flurry, *v.t.*

Flutter, *v.i.* Of the wings, رَفْرَفَ ـ فَرْفَرَ ـ أَخْفَقَ ـ هَفَا. To vibrate, خَفَقَ. To palpitate, خَفَقَ. To — about, as a moth round a candle, تَهَافَتَ. To — about, as in the air, هَفَتَ. The flag fluttered, خَفَقَتِ ٱلرَّايَةُ. They — about to find causes, يَتَهافَتُونَ عَلَى أَسْبابٍ.

Flutter, *n.* }
Fluttering, } A —, as of the wings, هَفَّة ـ هَفْوان ـ رَفْرَفَة ـ خَفَقانُ ٱلْجَناحِ; of the heart, *etc.*, خَفَقان. A — about, هَفَات. *See also* Flurry, *n.*

Fluttering, *a.* Hovering, سالِم ـ حائِم ـ مُرَفْرِف. Agitating, مُحَيِّر ـ مُقْلِق ـ مُزْعِج ـ ضَجّاج.

Fluviatic, *a.* }
Fluvial, } مَنْسُوبٌ إِلَى نَهْرٍ ـ حاصِلٌ مِنْ نَهْرٍ ـ نَهْرِيٌّ. Fluvial deposit, alluvium, غِرْيَل ـ غِرْيَن.

Flux, *n.* A flowing, فَيْض ـ جَرَيان ـ سَيَلان. Looseness, as of the bowels, إِسْهال. A concourse, مُزاحَمَة ـ ٱزْدِحام. A moving, transit, مُرُور. A substance to aid the melting of metals, مادَّةٌ كِيماوِيَّةٌ لِصَهْرِ ٱلْمَعادِنِ. Bloody —, إِسْهالُ ٱلدَّمِ. A — from the nose, رُعاف. The — and reflux of the tide, ٱلْمَدُّ وَٱلْجَزْرُ.

Flux, *v.t.* To melt, fuse, أَماعَ ـ أَذابَ ـ ذَوَّبَ ـ صَهَرَ.

Fluxibility, *n.* قابِلِيَّةُ ٱلذَّوَبانِ (*or* ٱلِٱنْصِهارِ).

Fluxion, *n.* A flowing, جَرَيان ـ سَيَلان. Runnings, نَوازِل. In mathematics, ٱلْفَضْل. *See also* Flux, *n.*

Fluxional, *a.* }
Fluxionary, } مُخْتَصٌّ بِعِلْمِ ٱلْفَضْلِ ـ فَضْلِيٌّ.

Fly, *v.i.* To move with the wings, طارَ ـ جَدَفَ. To pass away swiftly, فَرَّ ـ أَسْرَعَ ـ سَرُعَ. To pass away, as of time, زالَ ـ ٱنْقَضَى. To fly, as of a flag, تَنَشَّرَ ـ ٱنْتَشَرَ (*or* ٱنْتَشَرَ) ٱلْبَيْرَقُ. To cause to fly, أَطارَ ـ طَيَّرَ. حَمَلَ رايَةً ـ رَفَعَ بَيْرَقًا. To let fly, to release, أَطْلَقَ; to discharge, as of firearms, أَطْلَقَ ـ ضَرَبَ. *See also to* Flee, *v.i.*

To fly about, as of dust, تَمَوَّرَ ـ مارَ. To move about hither and thither, تَرَدَّدَ; as anything light in the air, هَفَتَ; as a moth round a light, تَهافَتَ.

To fly or to become spread abroad, شاعَ ـ ٱشْتَهَرَ ـ ٱنْتَشَرَ *aor.* يَشِيعُ.

To fly asunder, تَطايَرَ ـ ٱنْشَقَّ بَغْتَةً ـ ٱنْصَدَعَ ـ تَصَدَّعَ.

To fly at anything, قَفَزَ ـ يَثِبُ *aor.* وَثَبَ عَلَى ـ هَجَمَ عَلَى ـ ثاوَرَ ـ ٱنْطَبَقَ عَلَى ـ طَفَّ عَلَى ـ عَلَى.

To fly away, طارَ.

To fly back, ٱرْتَدَّ طائِرًا ـ ٱرْتَدَّ.

To fly for one's life, فَرَّ.

To fly for refuge to, ٱلْتَجَأَ إِلَى. To fly for refuge to God against. . . . , عاذَ (*or* تَعَوَّذَ *or* ٱسْتَعاذَ) بِٱللّٰهِ مِن.

To fly in the face of, عانَدَ ـ أَغاظَ ـ خالَفَ.

To fly into a passion, ٱغْتاظَ ـ يَثُورُ *aor.* ثارَ ٱلْغَضَبُ.

To fly into fragments, تَطايَرَ.

To fly off with, طارَ بِ.

To fly open, يَثُورُ *aor.* ثارَ مَفْتُوحًا ـ ٱنْفَتَحَ بَغْتَةً.

To fly out, as into a passion, *etc.*, يَثُورُ *aor.* ثارَ. To fly out suddenly, as a seed from a fruit, *etc.*, قَفَزَ ـ نَتَرَ.

To fly up, as a bird from the ground, يَثُورُ *aor.* ثارَ.

Fly, *v.t.* To shun, ٱحْتَذَرَ ـ ٱجْتَنَبَ. To escape from, فَرَّ ـ مِن ـ نَجا مِن ـ مِن. To fly a flag, رَفَعَ بَيْرَقًا ـ نَشَرَ رايَةً.

Fly, *n.* The insect, ذُباب ـ ذُبابَة *pl.* ذُبٌّ *and* ذِبّان *and* أَذِبَّة; *vulg.* دِبّان *pl.* دِبّانَة. A Spanish fly, ذُبابٌ هِنْدِيٌّ ـ ذُرارِيح *pl.* ذُرَّاح ـ ذُرَّنُوح *pl.* ذَرارِيحُ. A gad-fly, ذُبابٌ ـ نُعَرَة ـ ٱلْخَيْلِ. A small carriage, عَرَبِيَّةٌ صَغِيرَةٌ. The fly of a wheel, رَقّاصَةُ عَجَلَةٍ.

Fly-bane, *n.* حَشِيشَةٌ قاتِلَةُ ٱلذِّبّانِ.

Fly-blow, *v.t.* To — meat, سَرَأَتِ ٱلذُّبابَةُ فِي ٱللَّحْمِ.

Fly-blow, *n.* دُقْط *pl.* أَدْقاط ـ جَيْهَر ـ جَيْهُور ـ (*or* سَرْءٌ) سَرْأَةٌ ـ بَيْضَةُ ذُبابَةٍ ـ ٱلذُّبابَةِ.

Fly-flap, *n.* مِنَشَّة *pl.* مِنَشّات ـ مِكَشَّة.

Flying, *a.* As with wings, طائِر. Floating, عائِم ـ طافٍ. Expanded, مَنْشُور. Waving, خافِق. Light, خَفِيف. Moving, حَرِك ـ نَقّال. Fleeing, مُنْهَزِم ـ فَرّار. To come off with — colours, ظَفِرَ ـ ٱظَّفَرَ. Flying-artillery, مَدافِعُ عَلَى عِجالٍ. Flying-bridge, جِسْرٌ طافٍ ذاتُ ٱلرَّفِيفِ ـ سَرِيعَةُ ٱلسَّيْرِ ـ جِسْرٌ مِنْ خَشَبٍ مُمْتَدَّةٌ عَلَى زَوارِقَ. Flying-buttress, بَغْلَةُ حائِطٍ مُجَوَّفَةٌ. Flying-camp, سَرِيَّةٌ خَفِيفَةٌ ـ فِرْقَةٌ سَيّارَةٌ.

Flying-fish, *n.* سَمَكٌ طائِرٌ ـ سَمَكٌ ذُو أَجْنِحَةٍ ـ سَمَكٌ مُجَنَّحٌ.

Fly-leaf, *n.* وَرَقَةٌ بَيْضاءُ *pl.* أَوْراق ـ وَرَقَةُ ٱلْمُجَلَّدِ *pl.* أَوْراق.

Fly-speck, *n.* خَرْءُ ٱلذِّبّانِ *pl.* خُرُوءٌ.

Fly-wheel, *n.* عَجَلَةٌ رَقّاصَةٌ.

Foal, *n.* فَلُوٌّ *and* فُلُوٌّ *and* فِلْوٌ *fem.* فَلُوَّة *pl.* أَفْلاء. The — of

…n ass, دُبَّل ـ عُيَيْر . A young horse, مُهْر . Having a —, مُفْلٍ, *fem.* مُفْلِيَة.

Foal, *v.i.* Of a mare, وَلَدَتِ ٱلْفَرَسُ ; of an ass, وَلَدَتِ ٱلْحِمَارَةُ.

Foam, *v.i.* To throw out froth, ـ جَفَأَ ـ أَجْفَأَ ـ أَزْبَدَ ـ رَغَى ـ أَرْغَى. To — as the sea, غَطْمَطَ ـ تَغَطْغَطَ ـ غَطْغَطَ. To — at the mouth, as a camel, ـ لَغَمَ. To — with rage, أَزْبَدَ مِنَ ٱلْغَيْظِ. He spoke until the two sides of his mouth foamed, تَكَلَّمَ حَتَّى زَبَّبَ شِدْقَاهُ. The cooking-pot frothed or foamed, جَفَأَتِ ٱلْقِدْرُ.

Foam, *n.* Froth, scum, رَغْوَة ـ ثُفْل ـ زَبَد ـ جُفَآء ـ فُوَارَة. Foam from the mouth of a camel, لُغَام. The — of wine, فَوْرَة.

Foamingly, *ad.* With foam, إِرْغَآء ـ رَغْوًا ـ تَرْغِيَة ; with rage, غَيْظًا ـ بِغَضَب.

Foamy, *a.* / Foaming, } Having froth, مُزْبِد ـ مُرْغ. A — sea, بَحْر قَلَّاس ـ بَحْر مُزْبِد.

Fob, *n.* جَيْبَة ـ جُيُوب *pl.* جَيْب فِي جَانِبِ ٱلثَّوْبِ *pl.* جِيَاب.

Fob, *v.t.* To trick, غَشَّ ² ـ خَدَعَ.

Focal, *a.* Belonging to the focus of a telescope, مُتَعَلِّق بِقُطْرِ ٱلنَّظَّارَةِ ; to the burning focus, مُتَعَلِّق بِنُقْطَةِ ٱلِٱحْتِرَاقِ.

Focus, *n.* The — of a telescope, قُطْرُ ٱلنَّظَّارَةِ (أَيْ نُقْطَةُ ٱجْتِمَاعِ ٱلضَّوْءِ وَشِدَّتِهِ) ; the burning —, مَحْرَق ـ نُقْطَةُ ٱلِٱحْتِرَاقِ. A centre, مَرْكَز.

Fodder, *n.* Dry —, عَلُوفَة *pl.* عَلَف ـ حَشِيش ـ عَلِيق ; green —, عُشْب. A seller of —, عَلَّاف. Fed with —, مَعْلُوف. To collect —, تَعَلَّفَ ـ حَشَّ ².

Fodder, *v.t.* عَلَفَ ـ عَلَّفَ ـ أَعْلَفَ ـ حَشَّ ².

Foe, *n.* / Foeman, } خَصْم *pl.* خُصُوم ـ عَدُوّ *pl.* أَعْدَآء.

Fœtus, *n.* *See* Fetus, *n.*

Fog, *n.* ضَبَاب ـ عَمَآء ـ سَدِيم ; a fog, ضَبَابَة.

Fog-bank, *n.* تَكَاثُفُ ٱلضَّبَابِ فِي ٱلْبَحْرِ.

Foggily, *ad.* Mistily, بِضَبَابَةٍ ; darkly, فِي عَمًى ; uncertainly, فِي لُغْزٍ.

Fogginess, *n.* عَمَآء ـ ضَبَابَة.

Foggy, *a.* Misty, مُضَبَّب ـ مُغَيِّم ـ شَيْبَان. Dull, stupid, أَخْرَق ـ غَشِيم ـ غَمِيس. A — day, يَوْم أَشْيَب ـ يَوْم شَيْبَان ـ يَوْم ضَبَاب. The day was —, أَضَبَّ ٱلْيَوْمُ. The atmosphere was —, أَضَبَّتِ ٱلسَّمَآءُ.

Fogy, *n.* أَخْرَق ـ غَشِيم ـ مَغْرُور ـ مُعَانِد.

Foh, *int.* بَشْ ـ أُفّ ـ آخ.

Foible, *n.* A weakness, عَيْب ـ نَقِيصَة ـ رَكَاكَة ـ نُقْصَان. A folly, جَهْل ـ جَهَالَة. A youthful —, غَمْرَة *pl.* غَمَرَات ـ شَبِيبَة. That of which one is tenacious, ضِنّ.

Foil, *v.t.* To defeat, غَلَبَ ـ أَفْلَجَ عَلَى. To prevent, مَنَعَ ـ أَمْسَكَ. To frustrate, خَيَّبَ ـ عَنَقَ.

Foil, *n.* A defeat, تَخْيِيب ـ كَسْرَة. A blunt sword, سَيْف أَفْلَف. Leaf gilding, صَفِيحَة ذَهَبٍ لِعِلْمِ ٱلسَّاطِعِ. The — under a precious stone to set it off, فُوِيَة. Contrast, تَبَايُن ـ فَرْق. A tool, means, بَاب ـ وَاسِطَة.

Foin, *v.t.* طَاعَنَ.

Foin, *n.* طَعْنَة.

Foist, *v.t.* حَشَا ² ـ أَدْخَلَ زُورًا ـ أَدْخَلَ خُلْسَةً (or خُفْيَةً) أَدْرَجَ. To — upon, to deceive, مَكْرَبَ ². *See also to* Interpolate, *v.t.*

Foisty, *a.* *See* Fusty, *a.*

Fold, *n.* A pen for sheep, حَظِير ـ زَرِيبَة ـ مُرَاح ـ مَرْبِض. A flock of sheep, غَنَم (or قَطِيع) سِرْب. A limit, حَدّ *pl.* حُدُود. A plait in a dress, طَيَّة ـ أَطْوَآء *pl.* طَيّ ـ غُرُوض ـ غَبْن ـ ثَنِيَّة. The — of a door, مِصْرَاع *pl.* مَصَارِيع. The — of a leaf in a book, مَطْوًى *pl.* مَطَاوٍ. A — or folding of the arms, تَكْتِيف ٱلْأَيَادِي. The same quantity added, ضِعْف *pl.* أَضْعَاف. Two-fold, مُضَاعَف. A hundred —, مِئَةُ ضِعْفٍ. The sheep were inclosed in the —, إِنْزَرَبَتِ ٱلْغَنَمُ فِي ٱلزَّرْبِ. I made a — for the sheep, زَرَبْتُ لِلْغَنَمِ. The night cast the folds of its darkness over the earth, أَلْقَى ٱللَّيْلُ أَخْتَانَهُ عَلَى ٱلْأَرْضِ. To make two —, three —, or many —, ضَعَّفَ ـ ضَاعَفَ.

Fold, *v.t.* To —, as of sheep, أَدْخَلَ ٱلْغَنَمَ فِي ـ زَرَبَ ٱلْغَنَمَ ² ٱلزَّرِيبَةَ. To pen up, زَرَبَ ² ـ قَيَّدَ ـ رَبَّضَ. To —, of cloth, لَفَّ ² ـ أَطْبَقَ ـ طَبَّقَ ـ ثَنَى ـ طَوَى ـ غَبَنَ. To — up, To — a letter, لَفَّ ² (or طَوَى) مَكْتُوبًا. To —, as in a letter, to inclose, أَدْرَجَ. To — the arms, تَكَتَّفَ ـ كَتَّفَ ٱلْأَيَادِي. To — in the arms, إِحْتَضَنَ ـ حَضَنَ ² ـ عَانَقَ. To — one's self up in . . ., تَلَفَّفَ فِي.

Folder, *n.* One who folds paper, طَوَّآء. A paper-knife, مِطْوًى ٱلْوَرَقِ.

Folding, *n.* A sheet folded, of a book, إِضْمَامَة مِنْ كِتَابٍ *pl.* أَضَامِيم ـ كُرَّاس *pl.* كَرَارِيس. A manner of —, طَيَّة. A — of a door, مِصْرَاع *pl.* مَصَارِيع ; a door with two foldings, بَاب ذُو مِصْرَاعَيْنِ. The inside, ضِمْن. I transmitted it within the —

of my letter, أَنْفَذْتُهُ ضِمْنَ (or فِي طَيِّ) كِتَابِي. I found it in the — of the book, وَجَدْتُهُ فِي طَيِّ ٱلْكِتَابِ.

Foliaceous, *a.* Leafy, ذُو أَوْرَاقٍ ـ وَرِق. Having scales, ـ ذُو قُشُورٍ قِشْرِيٌّ.

Foliage, *n.* شَجْرَآءُ ـ أَوْرَاقُ ٱلشَّجَرِ.

Foliate, *v.t.* To beat into a thin plate, صَفَّحَ. To cover with a thin plate, غَشَّى بِصَفِيحَةٍ.

Foliation, *n.* The beating into plates, تَصْفِيحٌ; the covering with thin plates, تَغْشِيَةٌ بِصَفَائِحَ. The leafing of plants, تَوْرِيقُ ٱلْأَشْجَارِ. The layering of leaves, تَطَبُّقُ ٱلْأَوْرَاقِ.

Foliferous, *a.* حَامِلُ أَوْرَاقٍ.

Follicle, *n.* كُمٌّ *pl.* أَكِمَّةٌ *and* أَكَامِيمُ.

Folio, *n.* A volume, مُجَلَّدٌ *pl.* مُجَلَّدَاتٌ ـ مُصْحَفٌ *pl.* مَصَاحِفُ. A leaf with a certain number of inscribed lines, قِطْعَةٌ *pl.* قِطَعٌ. A page, صَحِيفَةٌ *pl.* صَحَائِفُ. A book in —, كِتَابٌ فِي قِطَعِ ٱلْكَامِلِ.

Folk, *n.* خَلْقٌ ـ عَالَمٌ ـ طَائِفَةٌ ـ أُنَاسٌ.

Folk-lore, *n.* أَحَادِيثُ ٱلطَّوَائِفِ.

Follow, *v.t.* To go after, ـ قَفَا ـ ² اِتَّقَفَى ـ تَلَا ـ ² خَلَفَ ـ ² لَحِقَ ـ تَبِعَ ـ ² أَتْبَعَ. To come after, to succeed, ² خَلَفَ. To — one after another, تَتَابَعَ ـ تَرَادَفَ. To — a road, ² سَلَكَ ٱلطَّرِيقَ. To — or — up, to run after, ـ تَلَقَّفَ بِ ـ ² لَحِقَ بِ. To accompany, رَافَقَ ـ صَاحَبَ. To attend on, as a dependent, ² خَدَمَ ـ ² تَبِعَ ـ ² لَزِمَ بِ. To succeed in order of time, ² تَبِعَ ـ عَاقَبَ ـ تَعَقَّبَ ـ ² عَقَبَ. To imitate, اِمْتَثَلَ ـ تَمَثَّلَ بِ ـ اِحْتَذَى ـ اِقْتَدَى بِ ـ اِحْتَذَى بِ. To obey, أَطَاعَ ـ أَذْعَنَ لِ ـ اِمْتَثَلَ أَمْرَهُ. To pursue, as an object of desire, ² طَلَبَ ـ ² سَعَى فِي ـ ² جَدَّ فِي طَلَبِ. To — in turns, of many, تَحَاشَوا ـ تَعَاقَبُوا ـ تَدَاوَلُوا. To attach one's self to, حَازَبَ ـ ² ظَرَبَ بِ. To — the traces of, ـ ² تَقَفَّرَ ـ قَفَرَ اِقْتَفَى أَثَرَهُ ـ اِقْتَفَرَ. To — with the eyes, أَثَارَ. To — a course of study, وَاظَبَ عَلَى ٱلدَّرْسِ. To — up, to reiterate, عَقَّبَ: He followed up one prayer by another, عَقَّبَ بِصَلَاةٍ بَعْدَ صَلَاةٍ. To — or mind other people's business, تَدَاخَلَ (or اِنْحَشَرَ) فِي شُغْلِ ٱلْغَيْرِ. To — a profession, كَانَ ـ ² عَمِلَ ـ تَعَاطَى: He follows the profession of a doctor, هُوَ طَبِيبٌ ـ يَتَعَاطَى ٱلطِّبَّ. To —, in the sense of conforming to, عَلَى: The people — the religion of their forefathers, ٱلنَّاسُ عَلَى دِينِ أَجْدَادِهِمْ. He follows, comes after, such an one, هُوَ يَتْلُو فُلَانًا. The night follows the day, يَخْلُفُ ٱللَّيْلُ ٱلنَّهَارَ. The people followed one another, تَتَابَعَ ٱلْقَوْمُ. He followed his instructions, اِقْتَدَى لِأَمْرِهِ. He followed his own opinions, ² رَكِبَ رَأْيَهُ. To be made to — uninterruptedly, تَدَارَكَ: the tidings followed one another uninterruptedly, تَدَارَكَتِ ٱلْأَخْبَارُ. *See also to* Succeed, *v.t.*

Follow, *v.i.* To be consequent upon, ـ ² نَتَجَ مِن ـ عَاقَبَ ² صَدَرَ مِن. To come after; (*see preceding article*). This act will be followed by the capture of the country, هٰذَا ٱلْعَمَلُ يُعَقِّبُ إِنَّ هٰذَا ٱلْعَمَلَ يُعْقِبُ فَتْحَ ٱلْبِلَادِ ـ بِفَتْحِ ٱلْبِلَادِ. To — on, to continue, أَدْمَنَ عَلَى ـ وَاظَبَ عَلَى.

Follower, *n.* One who follows, تَابِعٌ *pl.* تَبَعٌ *and* تَبَعٌ ـ تُبَّاعٌ *pl.* أَتْبَاعٌ ـ لَاحِقٌ; one who comes after another, ـ قَفِيٌّ ـ عَاقِبٌ قَفِيَّةٌ. An attendant, مُلَازِمٌ ـ خَدَّامٌ ـ تَابِعٌ. A disciple, scholar, تِلْمِيذٌ *pl.* تَلَامِيذُ. A companion, رَفِيقٌ ـ صَاحِبٌ. A partisan, مِنْ جَمَاعَةِ آل... ـ مِنْ حِزْبِ آل... ـ مُتَعَصِّبٌ لِ.

Following, *n.* A retinue, أَلْزَامٌ ـ حَشَمٌ.

Following, *a.* Coming after, ـ مُتَعَاقِبٌ ـ تَابِعٌ ـ عَاقِبٌ تَالٍ. Next, مُقْبِلٌ ـ قَابِلٌ. The — day, اليَوْمَ ٱلثَّانِي ـ فِي ٱلْغَدِ. The — part of a discourse, سِيَاقٌ. The preceding and — parts of a discourse, سِيَاقُ ٱلْكَلَامِ وَسِيَاقُهُ.

Folly, *n.* جَهْلٌ ـ حُمْقٌ ـ بَلَهٌ ـ جُنُونٌ ـ سَفَهٌ ـ خُرْقٌ. A foolish act, بَلَادَةٌ ـ حَمَاقَةٌ ـ رُعُونَةٌ. A youthful —; *see* Foible, *n.*

Foment, *v.t.* To apply warm lotions to, هَبَّلَ ـ كَمَّدَ. To excite, أَثَارَ ـ هَيَّجَ ـ أَشْعَلَ ـ قَوَّمَ ـ حَرَّكَ ـ أَضْرَمَ.

Fomentation, *n.* The act of bathing with lotions, ـ تَكْمِيدٌ تَهْبِيلٌ. A warm lotion, كِمَادٌ. Instigation, ـ حَثٌّ ـ تَحْرِيضٌ حَضٌّ ـ هِيَاجٌ.

Fomenter, *n.* An instigator, مُهَيِّجٌ ـ مُحَرِّكٌ ـ مُقَوِّمٌ ـ مُحَرِّضٌ.

Fond, *a.* Silly, foolish, أَهْبَلُ ـ أَبْلَهُ ـ هَوْهَآءُ ـ عِبِّيثٌ. Foolishly tender, مُتَدَلِّلٌ. Loving, وَدُودٌ ـ وَدٌّ. To be — of, to like, أَحَبَّ ـ أَحَبَّ ـ ² وَدَّ ـ اِشْتَهَى ـ ² هَوِيَ. To make one — of, تَوَدَّدَ إِلَى.

Fondle, *v.t.* دَلَّلَ ـ لَاطَفَ ـ ² لَطَفَ بِ.

Fondler, *n.* مُدَلِّلٌ ـ مُلَاطِفٌ.

Fondling, *n.* مَحْبُوبٌ *fem.* مَحْبُوبَةٌ.

Fondly, *ad.* Dotingly, بِهَتْرٍ ـ بِجُنُونٍ ـ بِبَلَاهَةٍ. Vainly, ـ بَاطِلًا عَبَثًا. Tenderly, بِرِفْقٍ ـ بِحِنِّيَّةٍ. Lovingly, ـ بِعِشْقٍ ـ بِغَرَامٍ بِحُبٍّ.

Fondness, *n.* Weakness, folly, جُنُونٌ ـ بَلَادَةٌ ـ جَهْلٌ. Tender passion, وُدٌّ ـ مَحَبَّةٌ ـ غَرَامٌ ـ عِشْقٌ. Fondling, تَدْلِيلٌ. Liking, اِشْتِهَآءٌ ـ شَوْقٌ ـ وُدٌّ ـ مَرْضَاةٌ ـ رِضًى. To show — for, تَوَدَّدَ إِلَى.

Font, *n.* A baptismal —, جُرْنُ ٱلْمَعْمُودِيَّةِ.

Fontal, *a.* Pertaining to a source, يَنْبُوعِيٌّ.

Fontanel, *n.* An issue, كَيَّة – كَيٌّ *pl.* كَيَّات. The joining in e skull, يافوخ – أَكْلِيلِيٌّ.

Food, *n.* طَعَام – عَيْش – مَعِيشَة – أَقْوَات *pl.* قُوت – *pl.* غِذَآء *pl.* أَغْذِيَة. To ask for —, اِسْتَقَاتَ. Excel- nt —, أَطَايِبُ ٱلْمَأْكُولِ – أَطْعِ حَسَنٌ. One who lives on good —, سَيِّئُ ٱلْغِذَآء ; on bad —, جَيِّدٌ لِلْأَكْلِ. Good for —, أَلْغِذ.

Fool, *n.* جاهِل *pl.* جُهَّال – أَحْمَق *pl.* حُمْق – مَجْنُون *pl.* – أَبْلَه *pl.* بُلْه – أَهْبَل. A buffoon, لَقِس – ثَوْر – مَجانِ – هَزِل – أُضْحُوكَة – مازِح – مَسْخَرَة – مَسْخَراتِيّ – مُضْحِك. To ake a — of, ضَحِكَ عَلَى – سَخِرَ مِن – تَسَخَّرَ ب – or مِن. To play the —, سَاخَفَ – نَوَكَ – سَفُهَ – سَفِهَ ². نَقَس. pril —, مَلْعُوب – كَذْبَة. To make an April — of, لَعِبَ عَلَيْهِ مَلْعُوبًا فِي أَوَّلِ شَهْرِ نِيسَار.

Fool, *v.t.* To impose upon, مَكَرَ ب ². To infatuate, أَجَنَّ –. To — one with promises, غَشَّمَ بِٱلْبَاطِلِ. To — one of hat he possessed, سَلَبَ مالَهُ بِحِيلَةٍ ² – اِمْتَخَطَ ما فِي يَدِهِ.

Fool, *v.i.* To trifle, عَبِثَ ; as in talk, أَهْجَرَ فِي مَنْطِقِهِ. To — away one's time, ضَيَّعَ ٱلزَّمَن – ضَيَّعَ أَوْقَاتِهِ. To play the —; *see under* Fool, *n.*

Foolery, *a.* بَلَاهَة – باطِل – عَبَث – جَهَالَة – خُرْق. To talk —, nonsense, أَهْجَرَ – أَهْذَرَ.

Foolhardiness, *n.* تَهَوُّر – هَجْعَمَة – مُجازَفَة.

Foolhardy, *a.* مُتَهَوِّر – يَهْفُوف.

Foolish, *a.* Stupid, جاهِل *pl.* جُهَّال – سَفِيه – أَخْرَق – أَحْمَق. Vain, contemptible, باطِل – تافِه. A — action, حَماقَة.

Foolishly, *ad.* Absurdly, بِبَلَاهَةٍ – بِجَهَالَةٍ – سَفَهًا – بِخُرْقٍ – بِجُنُونٍ. Vainly, باطِلًا – عَبَثًا. Wickedly, شَرًّا – شَنَاعَةً. To act —, فَعَلَ بِغَبَاوَةٍ – سَفِهَتْ نَفْسُهُ – سَفِهَ.

Foolishness, *n.* *See* Folly, *n.*

Foolscap, *n.* The paper, وَرَقٌ دِيوَانِيٌّ.

Fool's-errand, *n.* A vain pursuit, مَسْعاةٌ باطِلَةٌ – سَعْيٌ باطِلٌ.

To send on a —, وَجَّهَ فِي ٱلْمُحَالِ.

Foot, *n.* The lower end of the leg, رِجْل *dual* رِجْلانِ *pl.* أَرْجُل – قَدَم *pl.* أَقْدام. The — of an animal, قائِمَة *pl.* قَوائِم ; the same, having claws, كَفّ *pl.* كُفُوف. The —, as of a mountain, جَرّ – قاعِدَة – أَسْفَل – ذَيْل – حَضِيض – سَفْح ; of a pillar, أَساس ; of a candlestick, قائِمَة (or عَمُود) الشَّمْعَدانِ. Having large feet, أَرْجَل. The act of walking, تَمْشَآء – مَشْي – رُجْلَة. Infantry, عَسْكَرٌ مُشاةٌ (or رَجَّالَة). State, condition, حال – شَأْن. Foot, of a verse, جُزْء *pl.* أَجْزَآء ; feet, in poetry, رُكْن *pl.* أَرْكان. A plan, scheme, تَرْتِيب – نِظام – تَدْبِير – تَفاعِيل. A step, خَطْوَة *pl.* خَطَوات. A — measure, قَدَم *pl.* أَقْدام. A garden 40 feet long by 50 wide, بُسْتانٌ طُولُهُ أَرْبَعُونَ قَدَمًا وَعَرْضُهُ خَمْسُونَ.

At foot of . . . , فِي ذَيْلِ آ. . . – فِي أَسْفَلِ آ. . .

Bare-foot, حافٍ *pl.* حُفاة. Bare-footedness, حِفايَة.

Cloven-foot, ظِلْف *pl.* ظُلُوف *and* أَظْلاف.

Club-foot, حَنَف – فَدَغ. Club-footed, أَحْنَف.

Foot by foot, بِٱلتَّدْرِيجِ – قَدَمًا قَدَمًا.

On foot, on the feet, عَلَى ٱلرِّجْلِ ; walking, ماشٍ. Going on, عَمَّال – جارٍ. They followed him on foot, تَبِعُوهُ مُشاةً.

To be on one's feet, وَقَفَ *aor.* يَقِفُ – قامَ واقِفًا ² – اِنْتَصَبَ عَلَى قَدَمَيْهِ.

To fall at one's feet, وَقَعَ عَلَى رِجْلَيْهِ *aor.* يَقَعُ – تَوَاقَعَ عَلَى رُكْبَتَيْهِ.

To go on foot, رَجِلَ – اِرْتَجَلَ.

To put one's foot into, as into a difficulty, تَلَبَّكَ فِي – اِلْتَبَكَ فِي – اِرْتَبَكَ فِي – تَوَرَّطَ فِي.

To rest first on one foot and then on the other, رَاوَحَ بَيْنَ قَدَمَيْهِ.

To set on foot, to institute, شَرَعَ ب – اِبْتَدَأَ ب – اِخْتَرَعَ – أَنْشَأَ.

To set one on his feet, to succour, أَغاثَ – أَصْلَحَ – قَوَّمَ – قَيَّمَ.

Trodden under foot, مُداس.

Foot, *v.i.* To walk, مَشَى – سَارَ – اِرْتَجَلَ. To dance, رَقَصَ ² – زَفَنَ.

Foot, *v.t.* To tread under foot, دَاسَ ². To spurn, اِحْتَقَرَ – اِسْتَخَفَّ ب. To settle, أَثْبَتَ – قَرَّرَ. To —, to add up, جَمَعَ.

Foot-ball, *n.* طابَة. To play at —, لَعِبَ ٱلطَّابَةَ. To make a — of, تَلَاعَبَ بِهِ.

Foot-boy, *n.* غُلام *pl.* غِلْمان – وَلَد *pl.* أَوْلاد.

Foot-bridge, *n.* جِسْرٌ لِلرَّجَّالَةِ فَقَطْ.

Footed, *a.* ذُو أَرْجُلٍ. Four-footed, ذُو أَرْبَعِ قَوائِمَ *pl.* ذَوَاتُ ٱلْأَرْبَعِ.

Foot-fall, *n.* خَطْوَة *pl.* خَطَوات – خَطْو.

Foot-guards, *n.* عَساكِرُ حُرّاس – خَفَرٌ مُشاةٌ – عَساكِرُ مُشاةٌ خاصَّةٌ.

Foot-hold, *n.* مَوْطَأٌ – مَوْضِعٌ أَمِينٌ لِلْقَدَمِ.

Footing, *n.* Ground for the feet, مَكانٌ لِوَضْعِ ٱلرِّجْلِ – مَوْطَأٌ – وَطْأَةُ قَدَمٍ. A foundation, basis, أَساس – مُسْنَد – جِذْر. Possession, hold, حَوْز – اِمْتِلاك. Walk, مَسِير – مِشْيَة –

مَشْيٌ. A road, track, أَثَر ـ طَرِيق. State, حال. To get a — in a place, تَمَكَّنَ فِي ـ إِسْتَقَرَّ فِي ـ إِسْتَمْكَنَ فِي. To be on a — of equality with, قَارَنَ ـ فِي ٱلْمُعَامَلَةِ. To be on a —, كَانَ عَلَى حَالَةٍ: We are not on this — with you, لَسْنَا مَعَكُمْ فِي هٰذَا ٱلْمَقَام. He placed the soldiers on a war —, جَعَلَ ٱلْعَسْكَرَ عَلَى أُهْبَةِ ٱلْحَرْبِ. On a perfect — of equality, عَلَى قَدَمِ مُسَاوَاةٍ تَامَّةٍ. They are on the same —, هُمْ عَلَى قَانُونٍ وَاحِدٍ. On the same —, in the same way, عَلَى ذَاتِ ٱلْمِنْهَاجِ. On the — of..., عَلَى مِنْهَاجِ آلْ. To place on a firm —, أَتْقَنَ ـ أَحْكَمَ. *See also under* Friendly, *a.*

Footless, *a.* Of men, بلا أَرْجُلٍ; of quadrupeds, بلا قَوَائِمَ.

Footman, *n.* A servant, خادِم *pl.* خُدَّام. A wedge to keep a door open, شَرْخٌ لِلْبَابِ ـ سَنَّادَة. *See also* Foot-soldier, *n.*

Foot-mark, *n.* أَثَرُ ٱلْأَقْدَامِ *pl.* آثار.

Foot-pace, *n.* سِيْرَةُ ماشٍ ـ مِشْيَة.

Foot-pad, *n.* قاطِعُ ٱلطَّرِيقِ *pl.* قُطَّاع ـ اِبْنُ ٱلطَّرِيقِ.

Foot-passenger, *n.* ماشٍ *pl.* مُشَاة ـ راجِل *pl.* رَجَّالَة ـ ظَلَم *pl.* ظُلُوم.

Foot-path, *n.* مَمْشًى.

Foot-print, *n.* *See* Footmark, *n.*

Foot-post, *n.* ساعٍ *pl.* سُعَاة ـ بَرِيد.

Foot-rasp, *n.* مِحَكّ ـ دَلُوك.

Foot-rope, *n.* حَبْلُ مِرْقَاةٍ. A — to ascend palm-trees, كَرّ *pl.* كُرُور ـ مِصْعَاد.

Foot-rot, *n.* دَآءٌ فِي قَوَائِمِ ٱلْغَنَمِ.

Foot-rule, *n.* عِيَار ـ مِقْيَاس ـ قِيَاس.

Foot-soldier, *n.* عَسْكَرِيٌّ رَاجِلٌ *pl.* عَسَاكِرُ رَجَّالَة.

Foot-sore, *a.* عارِج. To be —, عَرِجَ.

Foot-stalk, *n.* شِرَاك *pl.* شُرُك.

Footstall, *n.* غُرَيْفَة *pl.* غُرَيْفَات ـ نَعْل.

Footstep, *n.* قَدَم *pl.* أَقْدَام ـ خُطْوَة *pl.* خُطُوَات. A trace, وَطْأَة. Notice, إِشَارَة ـ عَلَامَة. To follow the — of, to imitate, اِمْتَثَلَ ب. To trace the footsteps, قَفَرَ ـ تَقَفَّرَ ـ اِقْتَفَى.

Foot-stool, *n.* مَوْطِئٌ or مَوْطَأٌ *pl.* مَوَاطِئ.

Foot-stove, *n.* مِسْخَنَةٌ لِلرِّجْلَيْنِ.

Fop, *n.* مُتَصَلِّف ـ بَلْتَعَانِيّ ـ مُتَنَطِّس ـ مُتَحَذْلِق ـ غَنْدُور ـ أَبْلَهُ ـ مُتَكَيِّس.

Foppery, *n.* } تَصَلُّف ـ تَبَلْتُع ـ تَنَطُّس ـ تَحَذْلُق ـ غَنْدَرَة ـ بَلَاهَة.
Foppishness, }

Foppishly, *ad.* بِتَبَلْتُعٍ ـ بِغَنْدَرَةٍ ـ بِبَلَاهَةٍ. To act —, تَصَلَّفَ ـ تَغَنْدَرَ ـ تَكَيَّسَ.

For, *prep.* Because of, for to, in hope of, لِأَجْلِ ـ لِ ـ بِسَبَبِ ـ لِأَجْلِ أَنْ ـ لِأَنَّ ـ لِكَوْنِ ـ بِسَبَبِ أَنْ. With regard to, نَظَرًا لِ ـ اِعْتِبَارًا لِ ـ إِلَى ـ بِٱلنِّسْبَةِ. In the character of, كَأَنَّ ـ كَ. In the place of, as representing, عَنْ ـ عِوَضًا عَنْ ـ بِٱلنِّيَابَةِ عَنْ. For the interest of, مِنْ أَجْلِ ـ لِأَجْلِ خَيْرِ ـ مَحَبَّةً بِ ـ لِإِفَادَةِ. With the intention of going to, as to a certain place, إِلَى ـ نَحْوَ ـ إِلَى جِهَةِ. In account or in solution of, فِي ـ عَنْ. In exchange for, بَدَلًا عَنْ. Since, مُنْذُ ـ مُذْ. In search of, فِي طَلَبِ. On the side of, a partisan of, مِنْ حِزْبِ. In recompense of, جَزَآءً لِ ـ مُكَافَأَةً لِ. For all, notwithstanding, مَعَ أَنْ ـ وَمَعَ أَنْ ـ وَلَوْ أَنْ. For your sake, لِأَجْلِكَ ـ مِنْ جَرَاكَ ـ مِنْ جَرَّاكَ (or جَرَّائِكَ) ـ مِنْ جَرَّائِكَ ـ مَحَبَّةً فِيكَ. For pity of, رَحْمَةً لِ. For the present, ٱلْآنَ ـ فِي هٰذَا ٱلْوَقْتِ. For ever, أَبَدًا ـ إِلَى ٱلْأَبَدِ. For God's sake, لِلّٰهِ. For the most part, عَلَى ٱلْأَغْلَبِ ـ عَلَى ٱلْأَكْثَرِ ـ غَالِبًا. That is for thee, ذٰلِكَ لَكَ. I have not spoken to him for a month, مَا كَلَّمْتُهُ مُذْ شَهْرٍ. It is impossible for me to do it, لِي عَلَى فِعْلِهِ (or لا إِمْكَانَ) لا طَاقَةَ ـ لا يُمْكِنُنِي أَنْ أَصْنَعَ ذٰلِكَ. He went from this for Egypt, سَافَرَ مِنْ هُنَا مُتَوَجِّهًا إِلَى مِصْرَ. We sailed from Egypt for Malta, قَلَعْنَا مِنْ مِصْرَ إِلَى جِهَةِ مَالْطَة. He is for us, هُوَ مِنْ حِزْبِنَا ـ هُوَ مِنْ طَرَفِنَا ـ هُوَ مَعَنَا. It is not for you to do such a thing, لَيْسَ لَكَ عَلَاقَةٌ بِعَمَلِ ذٰلِكَ. He is tall for his age, هُوَ طَوِيلُ ٱلْقَامَةِ نَظَرًا لِعُمْرِهِ. I cannot do it for my life, لا أَقْدِرُ أَنْ أَصْنَعَ ذٰلِكَ وَلَوْ أَحْيَانِي. Oh! for a better knowledge of myself, يَا لَيْتَ لِي مَعْرِفَةً أَفْضَلَ بِنَفْسِي. I got it for nothing, اِقْتَنَيْتُهُ بِلَا شَيْءٍ (or مَجَّانًا). He believes it for true, هُوَ مُصَدِّقٌ بِأَنَّهُ حَقٌّ. They left him for dead, تَرَكُوهُ كَأَنَّهُ مَيِّتًا. As for me I cannot go, أَمَّا أَنَا فَمَا أَسْتَطِيعُ أَنْ أَذْهَبَ.

For, *conj.* *See* Forasmuch, *conj.*

Forage, *n.* *See* Fodder, *n.*

Forage, *v.t.* To look about for, فَتَّشَ ـ فَتَّشَ عَنْ. To seek for fodder, رَادَ ـ اِرْتَادَ (or اِرْتَادَ or إِسْتَرَادَ) ٱلْكَلَأَ ـ يَرُودُ *pl.* رَادَ. *See also to* Fodder, *v.t.*

Forager, *n.* An explorer for food, رائِد *pl.* رُوَّاد *and* رَادَة.

Foramen, *n.* خَرْق *pl.* خُرُوق ـ خُرْم ـ خُرْبَة *pl.* خُرُوب ـ نَقْبَة.

Foraminated, *a.* أَخْرَق ـ ذُو خُرُوق ـ أَخْرَب ـ ذُو خُرُوب ـ مَثْقُوب.

Foray, *n.* غَزْو *pl.* غَزَوَات ـ غَارَة. *See also* Incursion, *n.*

Forbear, *v.i.* To be patient, صَبَرَ ـ اِصْطَبَرَ ـ تَحَمَّلَ. To restrain one's self, تَمَاسَكَ ـ اِسْتَمْسَكَ ـ تَقَمَّعَ.

Forbear, *v.t.* To bear with, صَبَرَ عَلَى ـ . To intermit, جَبَأَ عَن ـ . To cease from, إِنْتَهَى عَن . To abstain from, عَدَلَ ـ تَقَعَّدَ عَن ـ إِمْتَنَعَ عَن ـ تَجَنَّبَ ـ أَنْحَجَزَ عَن ـ عَن . He forbore to go out, كَفَّ عَن ـ أَبَدَّ عَن ـ عَدَلَ عَنِ ٱلْخُرُوجِ . To cause one to —, مَنَعَ عَن .

Forbearance, *n.* Patience, صَبْر ـ أَنَاة ـ تَحَمُّل . Intermission, إِهْمَال ـ فَتْرَة ـ إِنْقِطَاع ـ تَوَقُّف . Avoidance, إِجْتِنَاب ـ إِمْتِنَاع ـ إِحْتِرَاز . Lenity, رَحْمَة ـ رَأْفَة ـ شَفَقَة ـ حِلْم . Bearing and forbearing, or —, التَّحَمُّلُ وَٱلتَّحَلُّمُ . With great —, بِطُولِ ٱلْأَنَاةِ . To treat with —, حَلُمَ عَن ـ تَحَلَّمَ عَن ـ تَحَمَّلَ ـ إِحْتَمَلَ .

Forbearing, *a.* صَبَّار ـ حَلِيم ـ صَبُور ـ صَبِير . To make —, حَلَّمَ .

Forbearingly, *ad.* Patiently, بِصَبْرٍ وَتَحَمُّلٍ . With avoidance, إِحْتِرَازًا ـ إِمْتِنَاعًا .

Forbid, *v.t.* نَهَى ـ رَدَعَ ـ حَرَّمَ ـ عَزَرَ ـ عَزَرَ عَن ـ نَهَى عَن ـ حَرَّمَ عَلَى ـ مَنَعَ ـ رَدَّ . To — anything to, حَظَرَ عَلَى ـ حَدَّ عَلَى ـ رَدَّ عَن . To be forbidden, حَرُمَ . To be forbidden to, حَرُمَ عَلَى . I forbade food to the sick man, حَمَيْتُ ٱلْمَرِيضَ ٱلطَّعَامَ (or مِنَ ٱلطَّعَامِ) . God —! مَعَاذَ ٱللّٰهِ ـ اللّٰهُ لَا يُقَدِّرُ ـ حَاشَا لِلّٰهِ ـ مَعَاذَةَ وَجْهِ ٱللّٰهِ . Their religion forbids them to cross the sea, يَنْهَاهُمْ مَذْهَبُهُمْ عَنْ سَفَرِ ٱلْبِحَارِ .

Forbiddance, *n.* عَزْر ـ تَوَقُّف ـ إِنْقِطَاع ـ إِمْتِنَاع .

Forbidden, *a.* مَحْظُور ـ مُحَرَّم ـ مَعْزُور ـ مَحْدُود ـ مَمْنُوع . Anything —, حَرَام *pl.* مَحَارِمُ ـ حُرْمَة ـ حُرْم ـ سُحْت . Forbidden things, مَنَاهِي . This is — to thee, هٰذَا حِجْرٌ عَلَيْكَ . This is rigorously — thee, هٰذَا حِجْرٌ عَلَيْكَ حِجْرًا مَحْجُورًا .

Forbidding, *a.* Preventing, مَانِع *pl.* مَنَعَة ـ مَنَّاع ـ مَنُوع . Repulsive, كَرِيه ـ وَحِش *pl.* أَوْحَاش ـ مَمْقُوت ـ مُقْرِف . One who has the power of commanding and —, صَاحِبُ أَمْرٍ وَنَهْيٍ . *See also* Hideous, *a.*

Forbiddingly, *ad.* Repulsively, بِقَبَاحَةٍ ـ كَرَاهَةً ـ شَنَاعَةً .

Force, *n.* Strength, قُدْرَة ـ قُوَّة ـ شِدَّة ـ حَوْل ـ حَيْل . Violence, قُهْرَة ـ قَهْر ـ رَغْم ـ غَصْب ـ جُبُور ـ جَبْر ـ إِقْتِدَار . Efficacy, فَاعِلِيَّة ـ قُوَّة . Validity, صِحَّة . Impetuosity, حَمِيًّا ـ دَفْعَة ـ شِدَّة ـ بَطْش ـ سَوْرَة . Power of resistance, مَتَانَة ـ صَلَابَة . Penetrating —, نَفَذ . By main —, غَصْبًا ـ عَزًّا بَزًّا ـ جَبْرًا . He took him by —, أَخَذَهُ عَلْوًا (or عَنْوَةً) . A military —, عَسْكَر *pl.* عَسَاكِرُ ـ جُنْد *pl.* جُنُود ـ جُوْل *pl.* أَجْوَال ـ جُوَل . Military forces, أَفْوَاج ـ جُيُوش ـ عَسَاكِرُ . Naval forces, دُونَنْمَا ـ مَرَاكِبُ حَرْبِيَّةٌ ـ مَرَاكِبُ . The treaties which are still in —, المُعَاهَدَاتُ ٱلَّتِي لَمْ يَزَلْ عَمَلُهَا جَارِيًا . A large military —, قُوَّةٌ عَظِيمَةٌ مِنَ ٱلْعَسَاكِرِ . To take by — from, غَصَبَ ـ مِن ـ إِغْتَصَبَ ـ مِن . To ask or demand a (military) — from, إِسْتَجَاشَ .

Force, *v.t.* To compel, أَلْجَأَ ـ إِلَى ـ أَلْزَمَ ـ بِ ـ اِضْطَرَّ ـ إِلَى ـ كَلَّفَ ـ إِلَى *or* أَن ـ إِغْتَصَبَ ـ عَلَى ـ غَصَبَ ـ عَلَى . To —, with violence, إِسْتَكْرَهَ ـ أَكْرَهَ ـ عَلَى ـ قَهَرَ ـ شَدَّ عَلَى ـ دَسَرَ ـ غَلَبَ عَلَى ـ أَجْبَرَ ـ عَلَى . To overpower, قَهَرَ ـ قَاهَرَ . To ravish, قَهَرَ ٱمْرَأَةً ـ اِفْتَضَّ ـ اِفْتَرَعَ ـ هَتَكَ . To storm, فَتَحَ ـ اِفْتَتَحَ . To — back, رَجَّعَ ـ رَدَّ . To — from or out of, أَخْرَجَ ـ مِن ـ نَفَى ـ مِن ـ طَرَدَ ـ مِن . To cause to ripen prematurely, إِسْتَبْكَرَ نُضْجَهُ ـ أَنْضَجَ ـ قَبْلَ ٱلْوَقْتِ . To — one's self, تَجَلَّدَ ـ غَصَبَ عَلَى نَفْسِهِ ـ غَصَبَ نَفْسَهُ . To —, to stuff, as with meat, حَشَا ـ بِلَحْمٍ . To be forced, compelled, to . . ., أَلْزَمَ بِ ـ أُضْطُرَّ إِلَى .

Forced, *a.* Compelled, مَلْزُوم ـ مَغْصُوب . Ripened prematurely, نَاضِج (or مُنْضَج) قَبْلَ ٱلْوَقْتِ . Forced labour, سُخْرَة . One — to do — labour, سُخْرَة . To make to do — labour, سَخَّرَ . Forced meat, حَشْو ـ لَحْمٌ لِلْحَشْوِ .

Forcedly, *ad.* *See* Forcibly, *ad.*

Forceful, *a.* *See* Forcible, *a.*

Forceps, *n.* كُلَّاب *pl.* كَلَالِيبُ .

Forcible, *a.* Strong, شَدِيد ـ قَوِيّ ـ قَدِير . Efficacious, ذُو فَاعِلِيَّةٍ ـ نَافِذ ـ مُؤَثِّر . Emphatic, بَلِيغ ـ شَدِيدُ ٱلتَّعْبِيرِ . Impetuous, مُتَهَوِّر ـ سَرِيع . Done or suffered by force, غَصْبِيّ ـ مَغْصُوب . How — it is! مَا أَشَدَّهُ .

Forcibly, *ad.* Powerfully, بِقُوَّةٍ ـ بِشِدَّةٍ . Efficaciously, تَأْثِيرًا ـ بِفَاعِلِيَّةٍ . Emphatically, بِبَلَاغَةٍ ـ بِشِدَّةِ ٱلتَّعْبِيرِ . With violence, عَلْوًا ـ قَهْرًا ـ بِبَطْشٍ ـ بِٱلْقُوَّةِ ٱلْقَاهِرَةِ ـ عَزًّا بَزًّا ـ غَصْبًا ـ عَلَى رَغْمِ ٱلْأَنْفِ ـ عَنْوَةً .

Forcing-pit, *n.* دُرَاوَةٌ لِإِنْمَاءِ ٱلنَّبَاتَاتِ .

Forcing-pump, *n.* طُلُمْبَة ـ تُرُمْبَة .

Ford, *n.* طَبْع *pl.* أَطْبَاع ـ مَخَاضَة *coll.* مَخَاض *pl.* مَخَائِضُ *and* مَخَاضَات ـ مَقْطَع *pl.* مَقَاطِعُ .

Ford, *v.t.* خَاضَ *aor.* يَخُوضُ ـ خَوْض ـ اِخْتَاضَ ـ عَبَرَ ٱلْمَآءَ . To make to —, أَخَاضَ ـ أَقْطَعَ ـ قَطَعَ ـ خَوْضًا . Their horses forded the water, خَاضَتْ خَيْلُهُمُ ٱلْمَآءَ . The party made their horses — the water, أَخَاضَ ٱلْقَوْمُ خَيْلَهُمُ ٱلْمَآءَ .

Fordable, *a.* مُخَاض ـ مُخْتَاض ـ قَابِلُ ٱلْخَوْضِ . The water was —, أَخَاضَ ٱلْمَآءُ .

Fordo, *v.t.* To undo, to destroy, خَرَّبَ ـ أَهْلَكَ .

Fore, *a.* أَدْنَى ـ سَابِق ـ فِي رَأْسٍ ـ مُقَدَّم ـ مُتَقَدِّم ـ أَوَّلُ.

Fore, *ad.* مُتَقَدِّمًا ـ أَوَّلًا ـ سَابِقًا. Fore and aft of a ship, مِنْ مُقَدَّمِ ٱلْمَرْكَبِ إِلَى مُؤَخَّرِهِ. To the —, ready, حَاضِر ـ عَتِيد ـ أَعَدُّ.

Fore, *n.* The — part of anything, أَدْنَى ـ قُبَالَة ـ قُبْل ـ صَدْر. The — and aft of a ship, مُقَدَّمُ ٱلْمَرْكَبِ وَمُؤَخَّرُهُ.

Fore-appointed, *a.* مُقَدَّر ـ مُعَيَّنٌ سَابِقًا.

Fore-arm, *v.t.* حَضَّرَ ـ لِلْوَاقِعِ ـ سَلَّحَ ـ قَبْلَ ٱلْحَاجَةِ. To caution, حَذَّرَ ـ نَبَّهَ ـ عَلَى.

Fore-arm, *n.* ذِرَاع *pl.* أَذْرُع ـ سَاعِد *pl.* سَوَاعِد.

Forebode, *v.t.* To prognosticate, وَعَدَ بِ ـ أَوْعَدَ ـ نَبَّأَ بِ *aor.* يَعِدُ ـ دَلَّ عَلَى *aor.* يَدُلُّ.

Forbodement, *n.* } عَلَامَة ـ دَلَالَة ـ إِشَارَة ـ مَوْعِد *pl.* مَوَاعِد.
Foreboding, } To have a — of, أَحَسَّ بِ ـ وَجَدَ *aor.* يَجِدُ.

Foreboding, *a.* Prognosticating, مُشِيرٌ بِ ـ مُوعِد. Sinister, calamitous, مَنْحُوس ـ نَحِس.

Forebodingly, *ad.* بِإِحْسَاسٍ ـ بِٱسْتِدْلَالٍ.

Forebrace, *n.* بَرَاسِيَا تَرْنْكِيت.

Forecast, *v.t.* To project, قَصَدَ ـ نَوَى ـ هَمَّ بِ [2]. To calculate, as of the consequences, *etc.*, ... حَسَبَ حِسَابَ ٱلـ [2]. To provide against, اِفْتَكَرَ فِي ٱلْعَوَاقِبِ. To — devices against, دَبَّرَ عَلَى ـ تَدَابِير.

Forecast, *n.* حِسَابُ ٱلْعَوَاقِبِ ـ بَصِيرَة.

Forecastle, *n.* مَوْضِعٌ مُرْتَفِعٌ فِي مُقَدَّمِ سَطْحِ ـ سَلُوقِيَّةُ ٱلْبَحْرِيَّةِ ٱلْمَرْكَبِ.

Forechosen, *a.* مُخْتَارٌ قَبْلًا (or سَابِقًا).

Forecited, *a.* سَابِق ـ سَالِفُ ٱلذِّكْرِ ـ مَقُول ـ مُشَارٌ إِلَيْهِ ـ مَذْكُور.

Foreclose, *v.t.* To preclude, مَنَعَ ـ مِنْ ـ أَعَاقَ ـ عَنْ ـ حَجَبَ [2]. To — a mortgage, أَغْلَقَ ٱلرَّهْنَ.

Foreclosure, *n.* Preclusion, مَنْع ـ إِعَاقَة ـ حَجْب. The — of a mortgage, إِغْلَاقُ ٱلرَّهْنِ.

Fore-deck, *n.* سَطْحُ مُقَدَّمِ ٱلْمَرْكَبِ.

Foredoom, *v.t.* قَضَى ـ عَلَى ـ قَدَّرَ ـ عَلَى ـ أَعَدَّ ـ سَابِقًا لِ.

Fore-end, *n.* الطَّرَفُ ٱلْأَقْرَبُ ـ القِسْمُ ٱلْأَدْنَى.

Forefather, *n.* جَدّ *pl.* أَجْدَاد ـ سَلَف *pl.* أَسْلَاف.

Forfend, *v.t.* *See to* Forbid, *v.t.*

Forefinger, *n.* الشَّاهِدُ ـ السَّبَّابَةُ. *See also under* Finger, *n.*

Forefoot, *n.* يَدُ ٱلْبَهَائِمِ وَٱلْوُحُوشِ ـ يَد *pl.* أَيَادِي.

Forefront, *n.* مُقَدَّمَة ـ قُبَالَة ـ قُبْل ـ صَدْر.

Forego, *v.t.* سَيَّبَ ـ نَزَلَ عَنْ ـ سَلَّمَ ـ فَاتَ [2] ـ تَرَكَ [2] ـ كَفَّ عَنْ [2].

Foregoing, *a.* مُتَقَدِّم ـ سَابِق ـ سَالِف *pl.* سُلَّاف.

Foregone, *a.* Formed beforehand, مُقَرَّرٌ سَابِقًا ـ مُتَّخَذٌ سَابِقًا. A — conclusion, نَتِيجَةٌ سَابِقَةُ ٱلِاسْتِنْتَاجِ.

Foreground, *n.* The front part, قُبَالَة ـ صَدْر. The — of a picture, صَدْرُ ٱلرَّسْمِ.

Forehand, *n.* *See* Forefoot, *n.*

Forehand, *a.* *See* Beforehand, *a.*

Forehead, *n.* جَبْهَة *pl.* جِبَاه ـ جَبِين *pl.* جُبُن. The part of the — where the hair grows, نَاصِيَة. Breadth of —, جَبَة. Having a large —, أَجْبَهُ ـ أَجْلَحُ ـ أَجْلَهُ. Impudence, وَقَاحَة ـ قِلَّةُ حَيَاءٍ ـ سَفَاهَة.

Foreign, *a.* Not native, غَرِيب *pl.* غُرَبَاء ـ أَجْنَبِيٌّ *pl.* أَجَانِب. Imported, مُجْتَلَب ـ جَلْب. Adventitious, عَرَضِيٌّ. External to, without, beyond, خَارِجٌ عَنْ. Foreign affairs, أُمُورٌ خَارِجِيَّةٌ. Recent — news, خَبَرٌ مُغَرِّبٌ. Is there any — news? هَلْ مِنْ مُغَرِّبَةِ خَبَرٍ. Has any — news reached you? هَلْ جَاءَكُمْ مِنْ مُغَرِّبَةِ خَبَرٍ.

Foreigner, *n.* غَرِيب *pl.* غُرَبَاء ـ أَجْنَبِيٌّ *pl.* أَجَانِب.

Foreignness, *n.* The state of being a stranger, جَنَبَة ـ جَنْبَة. Strangeness, غَرَابَة. Remoteness, improbability, بُعْد. Want of relation, مُبَايَنَة ـ عَدَمُ مُوَافَقَةٍ ـ عَدَمُ مُنَاسَبَةٍ.

Forejudge, *v.t.* To conceive, judge, beforehand, سَبَقَ ذِهْنُهُ [2] ـ اِسْتَبَقَهُ بِٱلْحُكْمِ ـ حَكَمَ [2] فِي ـ قَبْلًا ـ إِلَى.

Foreknow, *v.t.* عَلِمَ ٱلْغَيْبَ ـ عَلِمَ ـ سَابِقًا ـ سَبَقَ [2] فَعَرَفَ.

Foreknowledge, *n.* عِلْمُ ٱلْغَيْبِ ـ عِلْمٌ سَابِقٌ. His —, عِلْمُهُ ٱلسَّابِقُ.

Foreland, *n.* أَنْفُ جَبَلٍ ـ رَأْس *pl.* رُؤُوس.

Forelay, *v.t.* To entrap, كَمَنَ لِ ـ اِصْطَادَ. *See also to* Forecast, *v.t.*

Forelock, *n.* نَاصِيَة ـ قُصَّة *pl.* قُصَص. To take time by the —, اِغْتَنَمَ ٱلْفُرْصَةَ ـ اِفْتَرَصَ ٱلْأُمُورَ ـ سَبَقَ [2] إِلَى ٱلْأَمْرِ.

Foreman, *n.* A head man, رَئِيس ـ نَاظِر ـ مُبَاشِر ـ مُقَدَّم. One who holds the reins, a leader, ضَابِطُ ٱلزِّمَامِ.

Foremast, *n.* صَارِي مُقَدَّمِ ٱلْمَرْكَبِ.

Forementioned, *a.* } *See* Forecited, Foregoing, *a.*
Forenamed, }

Foremost, *a.* First, أَقْدَمُ ـ أَوَّلُ *pl.* أَوَّلُونَ *fem.* أُولَى *pl.* أُوَّلُ. First in position, dignity, كَبِير ـ رَئِيس ـ مُقَدَّم. First and —, أَوَّلًا ـ أَوَّلًا بِأَوَّلٍ. Head —, عَلَى رَأْسِهِ ـ اِنْكِرَاسًا. First, as in a race, سَابِق *pl.* سُبَّاق. To fall into head —, اِنْكَرَسَ فِي.

Forenoon, *n.* صَحْوَةُ ٱلنَّهَارِ ـ ضَحْوَة ـ صُبْحِيَّة ـ صَباح.

Forensic, *a.* مُتَعَلِّقٌ بِٱلْمَحَاكِمِ ـ مُخْتَصٌّ بِٱلْمَحْكَمَةِ.

Foreordain, *v.t.* ء = سَبَقَ فَأَعَدَّ ـ ٤ أَمَرَ بِ ـ قَبْلًا ـ ء فَرَضَ ـ قَبْلًا.

Foreordained, *a.* مَفْرُوضٌ قَبْلًا ـ مُعَيَّنٌ سَابِقًا ـ كُتِبَ مُنْذُ ٱلْقَدِيمِ.

Foreordination, *n* قِسْمَة ـ قَدَر ـ تَقْدِير.

Fore-part, *n.* الأَدْنَى ـ القِسْمُ ٱلْأَوَّلُ ـ مُقَدَّم.

Fore-rank, *n.* A — of soldiers, أَوَّلُ صَفٍّ ـ وَجْهُ ٱلْعَسْكَرِ ٱلْعَسْكَرِ.

Fore-recited, *a.* *See* Forecited, *a.*

Forerun, *v.t.* To precede, تَقَدَّمَ ـ ٤ = سَبَقَ.

Forerunner, *n.* A harbinger, مُبَشِّر ـ بَشِير. A prognostic, عَلَامَةٌ سَابِقَةٌ ـ دَلِيل ـ بُشَارَة ـ بُشْرَى. One who outruns, سَابِق *pl.* سُبَّاق.

Foresaid, *a.* *See* Forecited.

Foresail, *n.* تَرِنْكِيت ـ تَرِينْكَة.

Foresee, *v.t.* سَبَقَ فَرَأَى ـ تَأَوَّلَ. To perceive, أَبْصَرَ ـ ٤ بَصُرَ ـ أَبْصَرَ بِ. To bear in mind, to be cautious of, وَعَى إِلَى. One cannot — everything, حَسْبُنَا كُلَّ شَيْءٍ إِلَّا ٱلزَّلَقَ فِي ٱلصَّيْفِ (prov.) *Literally:* We have provided against everything but slipping (or skating) in summer.

Foreseen, *a.* سَبَقَهُ ٱلْإِدْرَاكُ ـ مَعْرُوفٌ سَابِقًا.

Foreshadow, *v.t.* كَانَ رَمْزًا لِ ـ أَشَارَ إِلَى ـ قَبْلَ ٱلْوُقُوعِ.

Foreshorten, *v.t.* Of drawn figures, قَصَّرَ ٱلرَّسْمَ.

Foreshortening, *n.* تَقْصِيرُ ٱلرَّسْمِ.

Foreshow, *v.t.* To predict, تَنَبَّأَ بِ ـ أَوْعَدَ ـ يَعِدُ *aor.* وَعَدَ بِ.

Foreside, *n.* *See* Fore-part, *n.*

Foresight, *n.* Foreknowledge, عِلْمُ ٱلْغَيْبِ ـ عِلْمٌ سَابِقٌ. Penetration, نَظَرٌ فِي ـ نَبَاهَة ـ ذَكَاء ـ فِطْنَة. Prudence, بَصِيرَة ـ رُشْد ـ عَوَاقِبِ ٱلْأَمْرِ.

Foreskin, *n.* قُلْفَة ـ غُرْلَة ـ غُلْفَة.

Forest, *n.* غَرِيف *pl.* غُرُف ـ غَابَة ـ أَجَمَة *pl.* أَجَمَات ـ حَرَش *pl.* أَحْرَاش ـ غَيْضَة *pl.* غِيَاض.

Forest, *a.* مُتَعَلِّقٌ بِٱلْغِيَاضِ ـ مِثْلَ ٱلْحَرَشِ ـ غَرِيفِيٌّ. A — tree, شَجَرَةُ ٱلْغَرِيفِ *coll.* شَجَر.

Forestall, *v.t.* To anticipate, ٤ = سَبَقَ. To engross the mind, شَغَلَ ٱلْبَالَ. To — goods, حَوَّطَ عَلَى (*or* إِسْتَبَقَ شِرَى) ٱلْبَضَائِعِ.

Forestaller, *n.* As on goods, حَوَّاط ـ سَبَّقٌ فِي شِرَاءِ ٱلْبَضَائِعِ.

Forestalling, *n.* Of goods, تَحْوِيطٌ عَلَى (*or* سَبْقٌ إِلَى شِرَاءِ) ٱلْبَضَائِعِ.

Forester, *n.* An inhabitant of a forest, سَاكِنُ ٱلْغَابَةِ *pl.* سُكَّان. A keeper of a forest, حَارِسُ ٱلْأَجَمَةِ.

Foretaste, *v.t.* To have a — of, ٤ = سَبَقَ فَٱسْتَطْعَمَ. To anticipate, ء = حَسَّ بِ ـ قَبْلًا.

Foretaste, *n.* إِسْتِطْعَامٌ سَابِقٌ ـ لَذَّةُ ٱلتَّمَتُّعِ. Anticipation, حَسٌّ مُتَقَدِّمٌ. He had in this world a — of beatitude, ٤ ذَاقَ فِي ٱلدُّنْيَا نَوْعًا مِنَ ٱلسَّعَادَةِ ٱلْأَبَدِيَّةِ.

Foretell, *v.t.* To — to, أَخْبَرَ بِٱلْغَيْبِ ـ أَنْذَرَ بِ ـ أَنْبَأَ بِ ـ ٤ سَبَقَ فَأَخْبَرَ بِ ـ ٤ سَبَقَ فَقَالَ لِ.

Foretell, *v.i.* To prophesy of, تَنَبَّأَ بِ ـ نَبَّأَ بِ.

Foreteller, *n.* نَبِيٌّ *pl.* أَنْبِيَاء.

Forethought, *n.* أَسْبَقُ فِكْرٍ ـ فِكْرٌ سَابِقٌ. Provident care, بَصِيرَة ـ نَظَرٌ فِي عَوَاقِبِ ٱلْأَمْرِ.

Foretoken, *v.t.* ٤ دَلَّ عَلَى ـ بَشَّرَ بِ. *See also to* Foreshadow, *v.t.*

Foretoken, *n.* إِشَارَة ـ عَلَامَة ـ دَلَالَة; foretokens, تَبَاشِير.

Foretooth, *n.* ضَاحِكَة *pl.* ضَوَاحِكُ ـ سِنٌّ مِنَ ٱلْأَرْبَعِ *pl.* أَسْنَان ٱلَّتِي فِي مُقَدَّمِ (*or* أَدْنَى) ٱلْفَمِ.

Foretop, *n.* The — of a ship, بَاش چِنَاقلغِي. *See also* Forelock, *n.*

Foretop-gallant sail, *n.* قُمَاش بَابَا فَنْقُو بُرُوَّة.

Foretopmast, *n.* بَابَا فَنْقُو بُرُوَّة.

Foretopsail, *n.* قُمَاش غَابِيَة بُرُوَّة.

Foreward, *s.* المُتَقَدِّمُ ـ الأَدْنَى. A vanguard, سُلَافُ ٱلْعَسْكَرِ ـ قَادِمَة.

Forewarn, *v.t.* To put one on his guard, نَبَّهَ عَلَى ـ قَبْلًا ـ أَنْذَرَ بِ ـ حَذَّرَ مِن. To show, point out to, أَرَى. To tell to one beforehand, ٤ قَالَ لِ ـ قَبْلًا. Forewarned forearmed, المُحْتَذِرُ مَصُونٌ.

Forewarning, *n.* تَحْذِيرٌ (*or* تَنْبِيهٌ) مُتَقَدِّمٌ.

Forewoman, *n.* مُبَاشِرَة ـ نَاظِرَة ـ رَئِيسَة.

Forewheel, *n.* العَجَلَةُ ٱلْمُتَقَدِّمَةُ.

Forfeit, *v.t.* To lose by an offence, ء = جَلَبَ عَلَى نَفْسِهِ ٱلْخَسَارَةَ ٤ سَقَطَ مِنْ مَنْزِلَتِهِ عِقَابًا مُجَازَاةً بِجُرْمِهِ: he forfeited his position, ء فَضَحَ نَفْسَهُ ـ ضَيَّعَ كَرَامَتَهُ بِجَرِيرَتِهِ. To — one's own credit, To — one's word, ء رَجَعَ فِي كَلَامِهِ ـ ٤ = نَقَضَ (*or* خَالَفَ) وَعْدَهُ. To make to —, جَرَّمَ. The pledge was forfeited (owing to foreclosure), ء غَلِقَ ٱلرَّهْنُ فِي يَدِ ٱلْمُرْتَهِنِ ـ ء غَلِقَ ٱلرَّهْنُ. To declare a pledge to be forfeited, أَغْلَقَ ٱلرَّهْنَ.

Forfeit, *n.* A penalty, جَرِيمَة ـ غَرَامَة ـ قِصَاص ـ نَكَال. That which is lost by an offence, عُقُوبَةُ ٱلْجِنَايَةِ. A —, as of a mortgage, غَلِقُ ٱلرَّهْنِ. The game of forfeits, لَعِب ـ لَعِبُ ٱلْمَغَالِقِ ٱلْغُلُوقِ.

Forfeit, *a.* Lost by crime, fine, *etc.*, مُغَرَّمٌ عُقُوبَةَ ٱلْجِنَايَةِ. All his property shall be —, or forfeited, يُوخَذُ مِنْهُ ما لَهُ مِنَ ٱلْمَالِ غَرَامَةً. *See also* Forfeitable, *a.*

Forfeitable, *a.* Liable to seizure, ضَبْطُهُ مُمْكِنٌ وَجائِزٌ; of a foreclosure, غَلْقُهُ (or غُلُوقُهُ) مُمْكِنٌ.

Forfeiture, *n.* The act of forfeiting, as through an offence, إِغْتِرام (or غرامة) ٱلْجِنَايَةِ. What is forfeited; also, the — of a pledge; also a penalty, fine; *see under* Forfeit, *n.*

Forfend, *v.t.* To protect against, سَلَّمَ-مِن — حَمَى-مِن. God —! اللّٰهُ لا يُقَدِّرُ — يا سَاتِرُ! — أَسْلَمَ-مِن.

Forge, *n.* A blacksmith's furnace, كُورُ ٱلْحَدَّادِ *pl.* أَكْوَار. The act of forging, مَطَالَة.

Forge, *v.t.* To form by hammering, مَطَلَ — طَرَقَ — دَقَّ. To invent, صَنَعَ — اِبْتَدَعَ — إِخْتَرَعَ — أَنْشَأَ. To counterfeit, قَلَّدَ — زَوَّرَ. To — in the name of, as of poetry, *etc.*, صَنَعَ-عَلَى. To — lies, إِفْتَرَى كَذِبًا — لَفَّقَ كَذِبًا — إِخْتَرَعَ باطِلًا. To — a lie against one, إِفْتَعَلَ عَلَى-كَذِبًا — إِفْتَرَى عَلَى-كَذِبًا. Handwritings are forged, الخُطُوطُ تُفْتَعَلُ. This Kurân could not have been forged, وَمَا كَانَ هٰذا ٱلْقُرْآنُ أَنْ يُفْتَرَى (*Kur.* x. 38). A forged writing, كِتابَةُ ٱفْتِرَاءٍ — مُفْتَعَل.

Forger, *n.* As of iron, طَرَّاق — مَطَّال. A falsifier, مُزَوِّر — مُفْتَرِي كَذِبٍ — مُقَلِّد — مُلَفِّقُ كَذِبٍ — مُؤَلِّفُ ٱلْكَذِبِ. A — of money, مُزَيِّف.

Forgery, *n.* Smith's work, شُغْلُ ٱلطَّرَّاقِ — مَطَالَة. Falsification, إِفْتِرَاءٌ — تَقْلِيد — تَزْوِير.

Forget, *v.t.* To lose memory of, ذَهَبَ عَلَى — نَاسَى — نَسِيَ. To slight, إِسْتَحْقَرَ — إِسْتَقَلَّ. To neglect, سَهَا عَن *aor.* يَسْهُو — أَهْمَلَ — غَفَلَ عَن — ذَهَلَ عَن. To cause to —, not to remember, أَنْسَى — نَسَّى; to cause to —, neglect, أَغْفَلَ-عَن — أَذْهَلَ-عَن — غَفَّلَ. To — one's self, to fail in what was due, نَقَصَ فِي ٱلْوَاجِبِ. To pretend to —, تَغَافَلَ. To forgive and —, صَفَحَ عَنِ ٱلْمَعْصِيَةِ وَما ذَكَرَهَا فِي ما بَعْدُ. I forgot the thing, ضَلَلْتُ ٱلشَّيْءَ. Do not — to bring your account, لا تَنْسَ أَنْ تُحْضِرَ مَعَكَ قائِمَةَ ٱلْحِسابِ.

Forgetful, *a.* Not remembering, نَسْيَان — ذاهِل — ساهٍ — غَبِيٌّ. Negligent, مُتَوَانٍ — مُتَهاوِل — سَهْوَان — غَبِين — غَبِيٌّ. He is very — of his duty, هُوَ نَسِيٌّ وَاجِبَاتِهِ.

Forgetfully, *ad.* Without remembering, نِسْيانًا — بِذُهُولٍ. Negligently, إِهْمالًا — سَهْوًا — بِغَبَاوَةٍ.

Forgetfulness, *n.* The losing remembrance, ذُهُول — مَنْسِيَّة — سُهُوٌّ — سَهْو — غَبَاوَة — غُفُول — غَفْلَة. Negligence, نِسْيان — تَهامُل — تَوانٍ — إِهْمَال. An instance of —, سَهْوَة.

Forget-me-not, *n.* The flower, آذَانُ ٱلْفَارِ.

Forgive, *v.t.* To pardon, صَفَحَ عَن — عَفَا عَن — سَامَحَ — سَمَحَ لَهُ — تَجاوَزَ عَن — غَفَرَ لِ — إِغْتَفَرَ. To —, of a debt, فَاتَ لَهُ ٱلدَّيْنَ — بِٱلدَّيْنِ. It is nobler to — an injury than to revenge it, العَفْوُ عَنِ ٱلأَذَى أَجَلُّ مِنَ ٱلإِنْتِقام.

Forgiveness, *n.* Pardon, سِماح — مُسامَحَة — عَفْوٌ — غَفْر — غُفْران — مُعَافاة — مَغْفِرَة — غِفْرَة. A forgiving disposition, غَفِيرَة. To ask — of, إِسْتَغْفَرَ مِن or لِ.

Forgiving, *a.* عَفُوٌّ — صَفُوح — غَفُور — غَفَّار. The very —, (God), العَفُوُّ — الغَفَّارُ.

Fork, *v.t.* To pitch with a —, أَذْرَى-بِمِذْرَاةٍ. To dig, حَفَرَ. To sharpen, سَنَّ — ذَرَّبَ.

Fork, *v.i.* To shoot into branches, إِنْشَعَبَ — تَشَعَّبَ. To — out, to give, pay, أَعْطَى — دَفَعَ — أَدَّى.

Fork, *n.* A pitchfork, مِذْرَى — مِذْرَاة. A flesh —, مِنْشَل. A table —, مِلْقَط *pl.* مَلاقِطُ — شَوْكَة *pl.* أَشْوَاك — فِرْتَيْكَة *pl.* فِرْتَيْكَات. A winnowing —, عَضْم *pl.* أَعْضِمَة. The prong of a —, سِنُّ ٱلشَّوْكَةِ *pl.* أَسْنَان.

Forked, *a.* } Having prongs, ذُو شُعَبٍ. Forked lightning,
Forky, } بَرْقٌ مَفْلُوقٌ — بَرْقٌ مُتَشَعِّبٌ.

Forkedness, *n.* تَشَعُّب — تَفَرُّع.

Forlorn, *a.* Forsaken, مَتْرُوك — مُتَوَحِّش — مَخْذُول. Wretched, despairing, بائِس — مُبْتَئِس — مَنْحُوس — شَقِيٌّ. One of the — hope, شُرْطَة *pl.* شُرَط — فِدَاوِيٌّ *pl.* الفِدَاوِيَّة. The — hope, المُسْتَحْنِطُونَ. To be —, تَأَيَّمَ — تَوَحَّشَ. *See also* Lorn, *a.*

Forlornness, *n.* The being forsaken, وَحْشَة — وَحْدَة. Wretchedness, نَحْس — شَقَا — شَقَآءٌ — شَقَاوَة — شِقَاوَة.

Form, *n.* Shape, طَرْز — صِيغَة — ماهِيَّة — هَيْئَة *pl.* هَيْآت — صُورَة *pl.* صُوَر — شِبْه — شَكْل *pl.* أَشْكَال — صِفَة *pl.* صِفَات — تَصْوِير *pl.* تَصاوِيرُ. Symmetry, هِنْدام. A pattern, model, مِثال *pl.* أَمْثِلَة — حِيلَة — ضَرْب — صِيغَة — صِياغَة — بِنْيَة. Method, arrangement, نِظام — إِنْتِظام — تَرْتِيب. Manner, order, رَسْم *pl.* رُسُوم — قانُون *pl.* قَوانِينُ — أُسْلُوب — مِنْوال. A ceremony, تَكْلِيف *pl.* تَكالِيف — قاعِدَة *pl.* قَواعِدُ. A bench, صُفَّة *pl.* صُفَّات — دَكَّة *pl.* دِكَك — مَصْطَبَة *pl.* مَصاطِبُ. In the — of, فِي صُورَةِ — بِشَكْلِ — عَلَى ضَرْبِ. He treated the affair in proper —, باشَرَ ٱلْمَصْلَحَةَ بِمُوجِبِ ٱلْقَوانِينِ. In the usual —, حَسَبَ ٱلأُصُولِ ٱلْمُعْتادَةِ. In legal —, شَرْعًا — حَسَبَ ٱلنَّهْجِ

ٱلشَّرْعِيّ. For form's sake, لِعُيُونِ ٱلنَّاسِ – لِأَجْلِ ٱلصُّورَةِ فَقَطْ. The — of a government, صُورَةُ (or هَيْئَةُ) حُكُومَةٍ. Without —, waste, خَرِب – خَرَاب. Form, appearance, as of the countenance, مَنْظَر. Mould it according to this —, fashion, إِضْرِبْهُ عَلَى طَبْعِ هٰذَا.

Form, v.t. To make, صَنَعَ – جَبَلَ – صَوَّرَ. To create, أَوْجَدَ مِنَ ٱلْعَدَمِ – خَلَقَ – كَوَّنَ – جَبَلَ – بَرَأَ – فَطَرَ. To produce, invent, إِخْتَرَعَ – إِبْتَدَعَ. To adjust, نَظَّمَ – رَتَّبَ. To shape, فَصَّلَ – شَكَّلَ – صَاغَ aor. يَصُوغُ – صَوَّرَ. To train, دَرَّبَ – خَرَّجَ. To bring up, رَبَّى. To —, as the mind of another, هَذَّبَ – عَلَّمَ. To — in one's own mind, to imagine, تَصَوَّرَ – تَخَيَّلَ. To —, as a project, نَوَى أَنْ – عَزَمَ عَلَى. To — into, صَيَّرَ. They formed themselves into a secret committee, إِجْتَمَعُوا فِي خَلْوَةٍ لِلْمُذَاكَرَةِ. According to the new forms, بِمُوجَبِ ٱلْإِصْطِلَاحَاتِ ٱلْجَدِيدَةِ.

Formal, a. According to form, حَسَبَ ٱلرُّسُومِ – رَسْمِيّ. Ceremonious, كَثِيرُ ٱلتَّكَالِيفِ – مُتَكَلِّف – مُدَقِّق. Methodical, exact, مُدَقِّق – مَضْبُوط – مُحْكَم. External, خَارِجِيّ – ظَاهِر فَقَطْ – بَرَّانِيّ. Decisive, قَطْعِيّ. Special, خَاصّ – مَخْصُوص. Reserved, cool, بَارِد – كَتُوم – طَرِيق. A — denial, تَكْذِيبٌ قَطْعِيّ. Formal or decisive language, لِسَانٌ قَطْعِيّ – إِفَادَةٌ قَطْعِيَّةٌ – كَلَامٌ بَتٌّ.

Formalism, n. دِقَّةٌ فِي ٱلطُّقُوسِ بِٱلظَّاهِرِ فَقَطْ – مُرَايَاة.

Formalist, n. مُدَقِّقٌ فِي ٱلطُّقُوسِ – مُنَافِق – مُرَاءٍ pl. مُرَاؤُونَ بِٱلظَّاهِرِ فَقَطْ.

Formality, n. Prescribed form, رَسْم pl. رُسُوم – رَسْمِيَّة – عَادَة pl. عَوَائِد. Ceremony, تَبْجِيل – تَوْجِيب pl. تَوْجِيبَات – تَبْجِيلَات – ظَاهِر – شِبْه – سِيمَة. Outward form, تَكْلِيف pl. تَكَالِيف. Order, method, قَاعِدَة pl. قَوَاعِد – قَانُون pl. قَوَانِين. Legal —, مُعَامَلَةٌ قَانُونِيَّةٌ – مُعَامَلَةٌ نِظَامِيَّةٌ. The obligatory formalities, ٱلْقَوَانِينُ ٱللَّازِمَةُ – ٱلْمُعَامَلَاتُ ٱلْمُقْتَضِيَةُ. A simple —, مُعَامَلَةٌ رَسْمِيَّةٌ فَقَطْ. An absurd —, رَسْمٌ وَاهٍ. The formalities of justice, ٱلْمُعَامَلَاتُ ٱلرَّسْمِيَّةُ ٱلْحُكْمِيَّةُ. Intrinsic formalities, شَرَائِطُ أَسَاسِيَّةٌ; extrinsic formalities, مُعَامَلَاتٌ قَلَمِيَّةٌ رَسْمِيَّةٌ. Executionary formalities, مُعَامَلَاتٌ إِجْرَائِيَّةٌ رَسْمِيَّةٌ. He observed the necessary formalities, أَجْرَى ٱلْمُعَامَلَاتِ ٱلْمُقْتَضِيَةَ ٱلرَّسْمِيَّةَ وَكُلَّهَا.

Formally, ad. According to form, حَسَبَ – بِمُوجَبِ ٱلرُّسُومِ – رَسْمًا – ٱلْقَوَانِينِ. Ceremoniously, بِتَكَالِيفَ. In appearance only, بِٱلظَّاهِرِ فَقَطْ. Decidedly, قَطْعًا – بَتَّةً – جَزْمًا. To deny —, أَنْكَرَ بَتَّةً وَقَطْعًا. To protest —, decidedly, قَامَ ٱلْحُجَّةَ حَسَبَ عَلَى جَزْمًا. To protest in due form, أَقَامَ ٱلْحُجَّةَ حَسَبَ ٱلْأُصُولِ ٱلْمُعْتَادَةِ. The act — states that ..., مُسَطَّرٌ فِي ٱلسَّنَدِ صَرِيحًا أَنْ.

Formalize, v.t. See to Formulate, v.t.

Formation, n. The act of forming, صُنْع – تَفْطِير – فَطْر – فِطْرَة – تَصْوِير – تَشْكِيل – تَفْصِيل – تَصْوِير – جَبْل – عَمَل; of shaping, تَصْوِير – تَشْكِيل – تَفْصِيل; of creating, إِيجَادٌ مِنَ ٱلْعَدَمِ – تَكْوِين – خَلْق; of arranging, تَرْتِيب – تَنْظِيم; of collecting, تَجْمِيع – جَمْع; of inventing, إِحْدَاث – إِيجَاد – إِخْتِرَاع. Production, in a passive sense, فِطْرَة – تَرْكِيب. Organism, تَحَدُّث – حُدُوث – حُصُول – خِلْقَة – جِبْلَة – تَرَكُّب. Formation of a ministry, تَشْكِيلُ ٱلْوُزَرَاءِ.

Formative, a. مُكَوِّن – صَانِع – جَابِل – مُشَكِّل – فَاطِر. In grammar, زَائِد.

Formative, n. In grammar, حَرْفٌ زَائِدٌ pl. حُرُوفٌ زَائِدَةٌ.

Formed, a. Made, مَصْنُوع; created, مَخْلُوق – مَفْطُور; shaped, مُهَنْدَم – مُصَوَّر – مُشَكَّل. Well formed, صَيِّر. To be —, shaped, تَشَكَّلَ – تَصَوَّرَ. To be — into, to become, صَارَ.

Former, n. One who forms, مُصَوِّر – مُكَوِّن – جَابِل – صَانِع – فَاطِر.

Former, a. Preceding, سَابِق – مُقَدَّم – سَالِف pl. سُلَّاف. First, أَوَّل pl. أَوَّلُونَ fem. أُولَى pl. أُوَل. Past, مَاضٍ. Mentioned before, مَذْكُورٌ آنِفًا – سَابِقُ ٱلذِّكْرِ. To make — to, سَلَّفَ. To be — to, سَلَفَ. A — people, قَوْمٌ سُلَّاف. The — people, the ancients, ٱلْأَوَّلُونَ – ٱلْأَوَائِل. In — times, فِي قَدِيمِ ٱلزَّمَانِ وَسَالِفِ ٱلْعَصْرِ وَٱلْأَوَانِ.

Formerly, ad. سَابِقًا – سَالِفًا – مِنْ قَبْلُ – مُتَقَدِّمًا – قَبْلًا – فِيمَا سَبَقَ. Formerly one of the members of the council, مِنْ أَعْضَاءِ ٱلْمَجْلِسِ سَابِقًا. Formerly Dutch consul in Egypt, قُنْصُلُ ٱلْفَلَمَنْكِ فِي مِصْرَ سَابِقًا.

Formication, n. تَنَمُّل.

Formidable, a. Terrifying, فَظِيع – مَهُوب – مَخُوف – مَهُول – هَائِل. Powerful, قَاهِر – قَهَّار. Large, عَظِيم. A — thing or event, جُلَّى pl. جُلَل – جَلَل pl. أَجْلَال.

Formidableness, n. The quality of exciting dread, هَيْبَة – هَوْل – مَهَابَة. Powerfulness, قُوَّة – حَيْل – حَوْل. Largeness, عَظَامَة – عِظَم – كَثْرَة.

Formidably, ad. بِنَوْعٍ فَظِيعٍ – فَظَاعَةً – بِفَزَعٍ – بِهَوْلٍ.

Formless, a. لَيْسَ لَهُ صُورَةٌ – عَدِيمُ ٱلشَّكْلِ – خَشِيب. Simple, مُجَرَّد.

Formula, n. A prescribed form, قَاعِدَةٌ مَعْلُومَةٌ رَسْمِيَّةٌ. Model, form, ضَرْب ـ قاعِدَة ـ صُورَة ـ شَكْل. Arrangement, ـ تَرْتِيب وَجْه ـ نِظام. The — of an oath, صُورَةُ يَمِينٍ. The opening — of letters, الدِّيبَاجَة. A prescription, as of a physician, وَصْفَة. A — of faith, صُورَةُ إيمانٍ ـ قانُونُ ٱلإيمانِ. *See also* Form, *n.*

Formulary, *n.* A book of prescribed forms, ـ دَسْتُورُ ٱلعَمَلِ كِتابُ طُقُوسٍ ـ كِتابُ صَلَواتٍ. A — of prayers, كِتابُ قَوانِينَ.

Formulate, *v.t.* To enounce, تَلَفَّظَ بـ ـ نَطَقَ بـ. To — a question, أَلَّفَ مَسْأَلَةً. To — a judgment, أَصْدَرَ حُكْمًا. To draw up, of a document, *etc.*, نَصَّ ². Formulated, مَنْصُوص.

Fornicate, *v.i.* *See under next article.*

Fornication, *n.* زِناءٌ ـ زِنًى ـ عِهْر ـ فُجُور; a single act of —, زَنْيَة ـ فَجْرَة. To commit —, زَنَى *aor.* يَزْنِي. He committed — with her, فَجَرَ بِها ـ زَنَى بِها ـ عاهَرَ بِها ². She committed —, زَنَت ـ فَجَرَت. Idolatry, عِبادَةُ ٱلأَصْنامِ.

Fornicator, *n.* زانٍ *pl.* زُناة ـ عاهِر; *fem.* زانِيَة *pl.* ـ زَوانٍ فاجِر *pl.* فُجّار.

Forray, *n.* *See* Foray, *n.*

Forsake, *v.t.* To desert, تَرَكَ ² ـ تارَكَ ـ هَجَرَ ² ـ فارَقَ. To give up, إِنْحَجَزَ عَن ـ تَخَلَّى عَن. To cast off, طَرَدَ ². His reason forsook him, ذَهَبَ عَقْلُهُ. *See also to* Abandon, *v.t.*

Forsaken, *a.* *See* Abandoned, *a.*

Forsooth, *ad.* هَيْهاتَ ـ وَحَياتِكَ ـ لا رَيْبَ ـ حَقًّا.

Forswear, *v.t.* To deny on oath, أَنْكَرَ ـ (رَفَضَ ² *or*) بِقَسَمٍ. To declare one's self guiltless of on oath, تَبَرَّأَ مِن ـ بِقَسَمٍ.

Forswear, *v.i.* To swear falsely, حَلَفَ ـ حَنِثَ فِي ٱلْيَمِينِ زُورًا. Forsworn, حانِث.

Fort, *n.* قَلْعَة ـ حِصار ـ حِصْن *pl.* حُصُون ـ مَعاقِل *pl.* مَعْقِل *pl.* قُلُوع *and* قِلاع. A small —, قُلَيْعَة.

Forte, *n.* شَطارَة ـ فَنّ.

Forth, *ad.* Onward in time, ـ مِن بَعْدِ ـ فِيما بَعْدُ ـ وَصاعِدًا لِقُدّامٍ. From that time —, مِن ذٰلِكَ ٱلوَقْتِ. Forward in place, لِقُدّامٍ. Abroad, بَرًّا ـ فِي ٱلخارِجِ. Out into view, ـ عِيانًا عَلانِيَةً. With currency, إِشاعَةً ـ مَشاعًا. Plainly, in detail, تَفْصِيلًا ـ صَراحَةً. And so —, إِلَى آخِرِهِ ـ وَهَلُمَّ جَرًّا.

To bring forth, *v.t.* To produce, أَصْدَرَ ـ أَحْدَثَ; of plants, حَمَلَ; of a woman, وَلَدَت *aor.* تَلِدُ.

To come forth, بَرَزَ ² ـ خَرَجَ ². Come forth! هَلُمَّ خارِجًا.

To put forth, to drive out, طَرَدَ ² ـ أَخْرَجَ. To put forth, of leaves, وَرَقَ *aor.* يَرِقُ ـ أَخْرَجَ ٱلأَوْراقَ. To extend, as the hand, *etc.*, مَدَّ ² ـ بَسَطَ ² ـ بَسَّطَ.

To set forth, to declare, أَصْرَحَ ـ أَوْضَحَ. To set forth on a journey, سافَرَ ـ شَرَعَ فِي ٱلسَّفَرِ. To set forth, as in writing, to draw up, نَصَّ ².

Forthcoming, *a.* مُزْمِعُ ٱلظُّهُورِ ـ مَوْجُود ـ حاضِر. Not —, عائِز.

Forthissuing, *a.* مُنْبَثِق ـ بارِز ـ صادِر ـ خارِجٌ مِن.

Forthwith, *ad.* بِلا تَوانٍ ـ عَلَى ٱلفَوْرِ ـ فِي ٱلحالِ ـ حالًا.

Fortieth, *a.* الأَرْبَعُونَ.

Fortification, *n.* A work of defence, ـ إِسْتِحْكامات *pl.* إِسْتِحْكام قَلْعَة ـ حِصْن ـ حِصار. A fortified place, as of refuge, ـ مَلاذ مَعاقِل *pl.* مَعْقِل. The act of fortifying, تَحْصِين. The science of —, عِلْمُ ٱلإِسْتِحْكاماتِ ـ فَنُّ ٱلتَّحْصِينِ. The act of strengthening, تَأْكِيد ـ تَشْدِيد ـ تَشْيِيد. A rampart, كانِفَة.

Fortifier, *n.* One who strengthens, مُؤَكِّد ـ مُشَيِّد ـ مُشَدِّد. An engineer, مُحَصِّن ـ مُهَنْدِس.

Fortify, *v.t.* To erect works of defence around, ـ حَصَّنَ ـ أَحْكَمَ حَصَّنَ بِٱلإِسْتِحْكاماتِ. To invigorate, strengthen, قَوَّى ـ شَيَّدَ. To — one's self by, لاذَ بـ ². To — or nerve one's self, ـ تَحَصَّنَ تَجَلَّدَ. To be fortified, defended against attack, حَرُزَ ². To — one's self against, to be in a state of preparation against, تَحَرَّزَ إِحْتَرَزَ مِن ـ مِن.

Fortiori, *ad.* A —, بِٱلطَّرِيقِ ٱلأَوْلَى.

Fortitude, *n.* ـ مُرُوَّة ـ تَصَلُّب ـ صَلابَة ـ نَجْدَة ـ إِقْدام ـ جَراءَة تَصَلَّبَ ـ تَجَرَّأَ. To act with —, بَأْس.

Fortnight, *n.* مُدَّةُ خَمْسَةَ عَشَرَ يَوْمًا ـ جُمْعَتانِ ـ أُسْبُوعانِ. A — hence, عُقْبَ جُمْعَتَيْنِ. A — ago, ـ مُنْذُ جُمْعَتَيْنِ مُنْذُ خَمْسَةَ عَشَرَ يَوْمًا.

Fortress, *n.* *See* Fort, Fortification, *n.*

Fortuitous, *a.* حُدُوثِيّ ـ إِعْتِراضِيّ ـ تَصادُفِيّ ـ إِتِّفاقِيّ ـ عَرَضِيّ. A — occurrence, عَوارِض *pl.* عارِض. *See also* Accidental, *a.*

Fortuitously, *ad.* إِعْتِراضًا ـ مُصادَفَةً ـ إِتِّفاقًا. An occurrence befell him —, إِعْتَرَضَهُ (عَرَضَهُ *or*) عارِضٌ.

Fortuitousness, *n.* } عارِض ـ مُصادَفَة ـ تَصادُف ـ إِتِّفاق *pl.*
Fortuity, } حادِثَة ـ عَوارِض. *See also* Accident, *n.*

Fortunate, *a.* Happy, ـ مَرْزُوق ـ حَظِيظ ـ حَظِيّ ـ بَخِيت مُفْلِح ـ فالِح ـ سَعْد. Successful, مَسْعُود ـ مُبارَك ـ سَعِيد. To be — in an affair, حَظَّ فِي ٱلأَمْرِ *aor.* يَحَظُّ. A — or prosperous man, رَجُلٌ غَضِيرُ ٱلنّاصِيَةِ.

Fortunately, *ad.* لِلّٰهِ ـ عَلَى حَظٍّ ـ مِن بَرَكَةٍ ـ مِن بَخْتٍ ٱلحَمْدُ.

Fortune, *n.* The good or ill which befalls one, ـ قَدَر ـ بَخْت

طالِع — قِسْمَة — نَصِيب . Prosperity, جَدّ — نُعْم — نَعْمَة — إِقْبَال . Good —, صَوَاب — فَوْز — فَلَاح . Success, سُعُود . Bad —, تُوَلَة — نَكْبَة — سَوْءُ بَخْتٍ . دَهْرٌ مُوافِقٌ — حَظٌّ — بَخْت . State, حَال — شَأْن — حَالَة . Means of living, مَعِيشَة . Possessions, أَمْوَال — أَمْلَاك — أَرْزَاق .

A gentleman of fortune, صَاحِبُ وَجْدٍ — غَنِيٌّ pl. أَغْنِيَاءُ .

A handsome fortune, رِزْق — غَنَاء — وَجْد .

A turn of bad fortune, دَبْرَة ; of good fortune, دَوْلَة .

By good fortune he..., وَمِنْ سَعَادَتِهِ أَن — بِسَعْدِهِ — وَمِنْ بَخْتِهِ — لِلّٰهِ ٱلْحَمْدُ نَهُوَ .

To brave fortune, عَارَكَ ٱلدَّهْرَ .

To follow a person's fortunes, لَازَمَ - فِي ٱلرَّخَاءِ وَٱلشِّدَّةِ .

To have a fortune, كَانَ صَاحِبَ غَنَاءٍ — تَغَنَّى .

To make a fortune, تَقَرَّشَ مَالًا — إِكْتَسَبَ غَنَاءً .

To run out of one's fortune, ضَيَّعَ (or أَسْرَفَ) مَالَهُ .

To seek one's fortune, سَعَى فِي طَلَبِ ٱلرِّزْقِ (or ٱلْحَظِّ) .

To tell one's fortune, أَرَى - بَخْتَهُ — فَتَحَ لَهُ ٱلْفَأْلَ .

Fortune-hunter, *n.* In the way of matrimony, طَالِبُ ٱلزِّيجَةِ مَعَ ٱمْرَأَةٍ لِأَجْلِ مَالِهَا .

Fortune-teller, *n.* فَتَّاحُ ٱلْفَأْلِ .

Fortune-telling, *n.* فَتْحُ ٱلْفَأْلِ .

Forty, *a.* أَرْبَعُونَ .

Forum, *n.* An open space, مَيْدَان — فُسْحَة — صَحْرَاء . A law-court, مَحْكَمَة .

Forward, *a.* Antecedent, أَوَّل — سَالِف — مُتَقَدِّم . Earnest, غَيُور pl. غُيُر — حَامٍ — مُجْتَهِد — مُجِدٌّ — جَادٌّ . Presumptuous, impudent, قَلِيلُ ٱلْحَيَاءِ — مُتَكَبِّر — وَقِح . Early (ripe), بَدْرِيّ — قَبْلَ ٱلْأَجَلِ — بَكِير . Quick, مُبَادِر — مُعَجِّل . Getting on, مُفْلِح — دَارِج . *See also* Intermeddling, *a.*

Forward, *ad.* In front, قُبُلًا — مُتَقَدِّمًا . Progressively, تَدْرِيجًا — بِٱلتَّدْرِيجِ . Do not put yourselves —, لَا تُقَدِّمُوا .

Forward, *v.t.* To make to go onward, قَدَّمَ — عَجَّلَ . To send to, أَوْصَلَ - إِلَى — بَعَثَ - إِلَى — أَنْفَذَ - إِلَى — أَرْسَلَ - إِلَى . To make to ripen, أَنْضَجَ .

Forwardly, *ad.* Eagerly, بِجِدٍّ — بِحَرَارَةٍ — إِجْتِهَادًا . Promptly, بِخِفَّةٍ — بِسُرْعَةٍ — عَلَى ٱلْفَوْرِ . Boldly, بِشَجَاعَةٍ — بِجَرَاءَةٍ . Impudently, بِوَقَاحَةٍ — بِسَفَاهَةٍ .

Forwardness, *n.* Eagerness, حَرَارَة — هِمَّة — غَيْرَة — حَمِيًّا . Alacrity, إِسْتِعْجَال — مُبَادَرَة — خِفَّة — سُرْعَة . Want of modesty, قِلَّةُ حَيَاءٍ — وَقَاحَة .

Fosse, *n.* A moat, خَنْدَق pl. خَنَادِق . To surround with a —, خَنْدَقَ حَوْلَ — خَنْدَق .

Fossil, *a.* مُتَحَجِّر .

Fossil, *n.* Any metal or mineral found in the earth, رِكَاز — سَيْب pl. سُيُوب — رَكِيزَة . Any fossilized substance, مُتَحَجِّرَة pl. مُتَحَجِّرَات .

Fossiliferous, *a.* مَا فِيهِ مِنَ ٱلْبَقَايَا ٱلْمُتَحَجِّرَة . Fossiliferous ground, أَرْضٌ فِيهَا بَقَايَا مُتَحَجِّرَة .

Fossilist, *n.* مِنْ أَهْلِ ٱلْعِلْمِ بِٱلْمُتَحَجِّرَاتِ .

Fossilize, *v.t.* صَيَّرَ - كَٱلْحَجَرِ .

Fossilize, *v.i.* تَحَجَّرَ .

Foster, *v.t.* To nurse, support, حَضَنَ [2] — رَبَّى — غَذَّى — أَعَالَ . To persist in, تَشَجَّعَ عَلَى — أَصَرَّ عَلَى . To encourage, أَيَّدَ — قَدَّمَ — أَعَانَ . *See also under to* Entertain, *v.t.*

Fosterage, *n.* تَرْبِيَة — حَضَانَة .

Foster-brother, *n.* رَضِيع . His —, أَخُوهُ بِلِبَانِ أُمِّهِ .

Foster-child, *n.* رَبِيب pl. رَبَائِب — مَرْبُوب fem. مَرْبُوبَة — مُرَبَّاة fem. مُرَبَّى .

Foster-dam, *n.* مُرْضِعَة — رَبِيبَة — رَابَّة — حَاضِنَة .

Foster-daughter, *n.* *See fem. under* Foster-child, *n.*

Foster-father, *n.* رَبِيب — حَاضِن pl. أَرِبَّاء .

Fostering, *n.* *See* Fosterage, *n.*

Fosterling, *n.* *See* Fosterchild, *n.*

Foster-mother, *n.* *See* Foster-dam, *n.*

Foster-sister, *n.* رَضِيعَة . Her —, أُخْتُهَا بِلِبَانِ أُمِّهَا .

Fother, *v.t.* سَدَّ [2] - بِمُشَاقَةٍ أَوْ بِأَقْمِشَةٍ أَوْ بِغَيْرِهَا .

Fought, *part. of to* Fight, *q v.* A hard-fought battle, مَلْحَمَة — حَرْبٌ عَلَى سَاقٍ .

Foul, *n.* Dirty, نَجِس — مُلَوَّث — وَسِخ — قَذِر — مَذِر — دَنِس . Turbid, كَدِير — كَدِر — مُكَدَّر . Impure, polluted, قَبِيح — ذَمِيم — شَتِيم — دَنِيء — نَجِس . Abominable, خَبِيث — فَاحِش — كَرِيه — شَنِيع . Wicked, سُوءٌ — فَاسِد — قَبِيح — شِرِّير . Ugly, بَشِيع — بَشِع . Unjust, جَائِف — ظَالِم — ظَلِم . Not bright, مُغَيَّم — مُكَدَّر . Contrary, مُخَالِف — عَكْس . A — action, سَيِّئَة pl. سَيِّئَات — قَبِيحَة pl. قَبَائِح — فَاحِشَة pl. فَوَاحِش — فِعْلٌ فَاحِشٌ — فَعْلَةٌ سَيِّئَة . Foul dealing, حِيلَة — غَدْر — مَكْر ; a cheat, trick, خَدِيعَة . To be —, unseemly, سَمُجَ [2] — شَنُعَ [2] . To judge to be —, to loathe, إِسْتَقْذَرَ — تَقَذَّرَ — إِسْتَشْنَعَ . To run — of, come into concussion with, لَطَمَ — صَدَمَ : They ran — of each other, of many, تَلَاطَمُوا — تَصَادَمُوا ; of two,

تَفَحَّشَ (or أَفْحَشَ) فِي — language, To talk . تَلَاطَمَا — تَصَادَمَا
ٱلْكَلَامِ — أَبْذَأَ . *See also* Obscene, *a.*

Foul, *v.t.* To soil, pollute, قَذَرَ ² — قَذَّرَ — سَخَّمَ — دَنَّسَ — وَسَّخَ — لَوَّثَ — نَجَّسَ . To —, as of a rope, *etc.*, عَكَسَ — لَوَى . To — one's self, تَصَوَّكَ — تَصَوَّقَ .

Foul, *v.i.* To become —, dirty, تَوَسَّخَ — سَخِمَ ² — قَذِرَ ; of liquids, كَدَرَ ² — تَكَدَّرَ ; of a rope, *etc.*, اِنْعَكَسَ — تَلَوَّى .

Foully, *ad.* Dirtily, بِنَجَاسَةٍ — بِوَسَاخَةٍ . Odiously, كَرَاهَةً — شَنَاعَةً — شَتَامَةً — قَبَاحَةً . Obscenely, مُتَفَحِّشًا . Deceitfully, غَدْرًا — خِيَانَةً . Unlawfully, ظُلْمًا — بِجَوْرٍ .

Foul-mouthed, *a.* / **Foul-spoken,** — بَذِيءٌ — مِلْحَب — مِلْدَغ — لَغَّاز — لَمَّاز — فَاحِشُ ٱللِّسَانِ — زَفِرُ ٱللِّسَانِ . *See also* Obscene, *a.*

Foulness, *n.* Dirtiness, قَذَر — دَنَس — دَنَاسَة — وَسَخ . Odiousness, فُحْش — فَحَاشَة — شَنَاعَة — دَنَاءَة — قَبَاحَة . Turbidity, كَدَر . Scoundrelism, villainy, خُبْث — خَبَاثَة . Unseemliness, سَمَاجَة . Deformity, ugliness, قَشَف — بَشَاعَة — كَرَاهَة . Dishonesty, خِدَاع — غَدْر — خِيَانَة — مَكْر .

Found, *v.t.* To lay a foundation, كَرَّسَ — أَسَّسَ — وَضَعَ ٱلْأَسَاس *aor.* يَضَعُ . To build, بَنَى — عَمَّرَ — شَيَّدَ . To establish, أَقَامَ — أَوْقَفَ — نَصَبَ ² — أَنْشَأَ . To cast, as of metal, صَاغَ *aor.* يَصُوغُ — أَفْرَغَ — سَبَكَ . To fix firm, رَسَّخَ — أَثْبَتَ .

Foundation, *n.* Basis, as of an edifice, أَسَاس . The act of laying a —, تَكْرِيس — تَأْسِيس . A stand for anything, قِيَام — قَاعِدَة *pl.* قَوَاعِدُ — مَغْرِز — رُكْن . Rise, origin, أَصْل — مَنْشَأ — مَبْدَأ . Establishment, revenue for any particular purpose, وَقْف *pl.* أَوْقَاف .

Foundationer, *n.* صَاحِبُ رَاتِبٍ .

Foundationless, *a.* Without foundation, بِلَا أَسَاسٍ . Not true, لَا وَجْهَ لَهُ — غَيْرُ صَحِيحٍ .

Founded, *a.* Established, built, مُؤَسَّس — مُعَمَّر . Well-founded, true, صَحِيح — مُحَقَّق — مُتَحَقِّق . Founded on a rock, مُؤَسَّس عَلَى ٱلصَّخْرِ .

Founder, *n.* A builder, مُؤَسِّس — بَنَّاء . One who establishes a revenue for some particular purpose, مُوقِفُ أَوْقَافٍ . One who originates, بَادٍ — مُبْدِع — مُخْتَرِع — مُنْشِئ — أَصْل . A caster, سَبَّاك . Lameness, عَرَج — عَتْرَسَة — سَقَط .

Founder, *v.t.* Of a horse, تَعَتْرَسَ عَلَى فَرَسٍ — أَسْقَطَ .

Founder, *v.i.* To sink, غَرِقَ — غَطَسَ . To fail, خَابَ ; to — or fail in, قَصَّرَ عَنْ ² — تَقَاصَرَ عَنْ .

Foundry, *n.* / **Foundery,** The act of casting, of metals, صَوْغ — سَبْك . A place for, مَسْبَك — دَارُ ٱلسَّبْكِ .

Foundling, *n.* حَمِيل *fem.* حَمِيلَة — لَقِيط *pl.* لُقَطَاء — مَلْقُوط — مَنْبُوذ — مِنْ أَبْنَاءِ ٱلدَّهَالِيزِ .

Foundress, *n.* One who endows, مُوقِفَةُ ٱلْأَوْقَافِ .

Fount, *n.* / **Fountain,** A spring, فَوَّارَة — مَنْبَع — يَنْبُوع *pl.* يَنَابِيعُ — عَيْن *pl.* عُيُون . A basin of springing water, فِسْقِيَّة *pl.* فَسَاقِي — شَاذِرْوَان . A drinking —, سَبِيل *pl.* سُبُل . An original, source, مَنْبَع — أَصْل — مَنْشَأ — مَبْدَأ . Fountain-head, مَنْبَع *pl.* مَنَابِعُ — رَأْسُ عَيْنٍ . A — of type, صِنْفٌ كَامِلٌ مِنَ ٱلْأَحْرُفِ لِلطَّبْعِ .

Four, *a.* and *n.* أَرْبَعَةٌ *fem.* أَرْبَعٌ . Four and — together, or — at a time, أَرْبَعَةً أَرْبَعَةً — رُبَاعَ . He is one of —, هُوَ رَابِعُ أَرْبَعَةٍ . A word of — letters, رُبَاعِيٌّ .

Four-cornered, *a.* *See* Four-sided, *a.*

Fourfold, *a.* أَرْبَعَةُ أَضْعَافٍ . To make —, ضَاعَفَ أَرْبَعَ مِرَارٍ .

Four-footed, *a.* ذُو أَرْبَعِ قَوَائِمَ . Quadrupeds, ذَوَاتُ ٱلْأَرْبَعِ .

Fourscore, *a.* ثَمَانُونَ .

Four-sided, *a.* / **Four-square,** مُرَبَّع . To make —, رَبَّعَ .

Fourteen, *a.* أَرْبَعَةَ عَشَرَ *fem.* أَرْبَعَ عَشْرَةَ .

Fourteenth, *a.* ٱلرَّابِعُ عَشَرَ *fem.* ٱلرَّابِعَةَ عَشْرَةَ . This is the —, هٰذَا ٱلرَّابِعُ عَشَرَ *fem.* هٰذِهِ ٱلرَّابِعَةَ عَشْرَةَ .

Fourth, *a.* رَابِع *fem.* رَابِعَة . A — part, رُبْع *pl.* أَرْبَاع .

Fourthly, *ad.* رَابِعًا .

Four-wheeled, *a.* ذُو أَرْبَعِ عَجَلَاتٍ .

Fowl, *v.i.* To catch birds, اِصْطَادَ (or تَصَيَّدَ) ٱلطُّيُورَ .

Fowl, *n.* A bird, طَائِر or طَيْر *pl.* طُيُور . A domestic hen, دَجَاجَة *coll.* دَجَاج *pl.* دَجَاجَات or دُجُج . *See also* Hen, *n.*

Fowler, *n.* صَيَّادُ ٱلطُّيُورِ — صَيَّاد .

Fowling-piece, *n.* بُنْدُقِيَّة *pl.* بَنَادِقُ .

Fox, *n.* ثَعْلَب *pl.* ثَعَالِبُ — أَبُو ٱلْحُصَيْنِ . A male —, ثُعْلُبَان — ذَكَرُ ٱلثَّعْلَبِ ; a female —, ثَعْلَبَة — ثَعْلَبٌ أُنْثَى . A fox's cub, هِجْرِس — ثُعَيْلِب — مُعَاوِيَة . A sly fellow, مُحْتَال — نَصَّاب — حَيَّال — شَيْطَان .

Fox-chase, *n.* صَيْدُ ٱلثَّعْلَبِ *pl.* صُيُود — طَرْدُ ٱلثَّعْلَبِ .

Fox-glove, *n.* The plant, ٱلْجَرْسَة .

Fox-hound, *n.* سَلُوقِيٌّ صَيَّادُ ٱلثَّعْلَبِ .

Fox-hunt, *n.* / **Fox-hunting,** صَيْدُ ٱلثَّعْلَبِ *pl.* صُيُود .

Foxy, *a.* مِثْلَ ٱلثَّعْلَبِ.

Fracas, *n.* غاغَة ـ شَغْب ـ رَجَّة ـ طَشَّة. To excite a — among, شَغَبَ فِي ². *See also* Disturbance, Row, *n.*

Fraction, *n.* The act of breaking, تَكْسِير ـ كَسْر ـ فَضّ. A broken part, كِسْر *pl.* كُسُور ـ فَضَض ـ فُضَاض. Fractions, كُسُور. Vulgar —, الكَسْر. Decimal —, كَسْر إعْشارِيّ. A small part, جُزْء *pl.* أَجْزاء. The reduction of fractions by a common divisor, الحَطّ (وَهُوَ تَحْوِيلُ ٱلْكَسْرِ إلَى أَبْسَطِ ما يُمْكِنُ ٱلتَّغْيِيرُ بِهِ).

Fractional, *a.* جُزْئِيّ ـ كَسْرِيّ.

Fractious, *a.* باسِل ـ وَعِق ـ شَكِس ـ شَرِس.

Fractiously, *ad.* بِشَراسَة ـ بِوَعَقَة.

Fractiousness, *n.* بَسالَة ـ وَعَقَة ـ شَراسَة ـ شَكاسَة.

Fracture, *n.* كَسْر *pl.* كُسُور ـ كَسْرَة ـ كَسْر ـ آمَّة. A simple —, كَسْر. A compound —, كَسْر اقْتِرانِيّ; an imperfect —, وَثْأ; سائِخ. A state of —, or of dislocation, فَكَك. A —, as of the skull, سَلْعَة ـ شَجَّة ـ حَرْضَة. To reduce, as of a —, جَبَرَ ² ـ جَبَّرَ.

Fracture, *v.t.* كَسَرَ ـ كَسَّرَ. To be fractured, إنْكَسَرَ.

Fragile, *a.* سَرِيعُ ٱلْعَطَبِ ـ قَصِم ـ واهٍ ـ مُسْتَرْخٍ ـ رَخْو ـ حَطِم. To be —, رَخِيَ *aor.* يَرْخُو. To make —, راخَى ـ أَرْخَى.

Fragilely, *ad.* بِرَخاوَة ـ بِرِخْوَة.

Fragility, *n.* سُرْعَةُ ٱلْعَطَبِ ـ إفات ـ رَخاوَة ـ رِخْوَة.

Fragment, *n.* رَضْح ـ قِطْعَة *pl.* قِطَع ـ كِسْرَة *pl.* كِسَر ـ هُتامَة ـ فَضَض ـ نُفاض ـ قُشام ـ قُشامَة ـ شَقَف ـ شَقْفَة *pl.* شُقَف. Fragments, as of food, خُشارات ـ كِسَر ـ فُتات; as of a song, *etc.*, نُبْذَة *pl.* نُبَذات. Fragments of anything, فُتات ـ دُقاق ـ رُفات. To break into fragments, رَضَحَ ـ كَسَّرَ ـ رَفَتَ ². To be broken into fragments, تَكَسَّرَ ـ إرْفَتَّ ـ رَفَتَ ². To become broken into fragments, إسْتَطارَ ـ تَطايَرَ.

Fragmentary, *a.* جُزْئِيّ ـ مُرَكَّب مِنَ ٱلْأَجْزاء.

Fragrance, *n.* } خَمْرَة ـ فَوْغَة ـ فَغْمَة ـ شَمِيم ـ فَغْوَة ـ
Fragrancy, } راحَة ـ طِيب ـ عِطْر. The — of the odour of wine, فَغْمَةُ رِيحِ ٱلْخَمْرِ ـ طَيَّبَ ـ أَفْغَمَ. To scatter a —, عَطَّرَ.

Fragrant, *a.* أَرِج ـ عَذِق ـ شَمُوم ـ مُعَطَّر ـ مُقَتَّر. To exhale — odours of, تَنَسَّمَ بِ.

Fragrantly, *ad.* بِعِطْر ـ بِزَكاءِ ٱلرّائِحَة.

Frail, *a.* That easily breaks, حَطِم. Liable to decay, واهٍ ـ فانٍ ـ سَرِيعُ ٱلزَّوالِ. Weak, عاجِز ـ ضَعِيف. Of easy virtue, سَرِيعُ ٱلزَّنْوِ. The world is a present — good; the righteous and unrighteous eat thereof, الدُّنْيا عَرَضٌ حاضِرٌ يَأْكُلُ مِنْها ٱلْبَرُّ وَٱلْفاجِرُ.

Frail, *n.* A basket, زِنْبِيل *pl.* زَنابِيل ـ قُطْف ـ مِقْطَف ـ سَلَّة *pl.* سِلال and سَلّات.

Frailly, *ad.* بِرَخاوَة ـ بِضَعْف.

Frailness, *n.* Weakness, want of coherence, سُرْعَةُ ٱلْحَطْمِ ـ رِخْوَة ـ رَكاكَة ـ رَخاوَة. Infirmity, عَجْز ـ ضِعْف ـ وَهْن. Transitoriness, زَوال ـ فَناء.

Frailty, *n.* Liableness of falling, sinning, سُرْعَةُ ٱلزَّلَلِ. The — of human nature, ضِعْفُ ٱلطَّبِيعَةِ ٱلْبَشَرِيَّةِ.

Frame, *v t.* To make, form, صَنَعَ ـ فَطَرَ ² ـ جَبَلَ ² ـ صَوَّرَ. To draw up, as in writing, نَصَّ ². To regulate, adjust, نَظَّمَ ـ وَفَّقَ. To compose, put together, شَكَّلَ ـ رَتَّبَ ـ رَكَّبَ. To invent, إخْتَرَعَ ـ إبْتَدَعَ. To — into poetry, قَصَدَ. To build, بَنَى ـ عَمَّرَ. To put into a —, فَرْوَزَ ـ رَكَّبَ فِي فَرْواز. To — deceit, إخْتَرَعَ غِشًّا. Framed, drawn up, as in a document, مَنْصُوص. Framed together, مُرَكَّب مَعًا. To — a speech so that its parts may be coherent, لَفَّقَ.

Frame, *n.* The construction of parts, تَوٌّ ـ بَنْيٌ ـ بُنْيَة ـ تَرْكِيب ـ جِبِلَّة ـ جِبْلَة. A —, as of a picture, دائِرَة ـ فَرْواز *pl.* فَراوِز. Arrangement, تَرْتِيب ـ تَنْسِيق ـ نِظام. Form, shape, هَيْئَة ـ شَكْل ـ صُورَة. Of large —, build, of a man, جُرَنْفِس. Frame of mind, حال ـ خاطِر. A stand, قاعِدَة ـ دَسْتَكاه. The bodily —, الجَسَد ـ الجِسْم ـ البَدَن.

Franc, *n.* The coin, فَرَنْك *pl.* فَرَنْكات.

France, *n.* مَمْلَكَة فَرَنْسا.

Franchise, *n.* A privilege, إمْتِياز *pl.* إمْتِيازات. Immunity, مُعافاة ـ إعْفاء. A privileged district, مَلْجَأ مُعْفًى. Electoral —, الإمْتِيازُ بِٱنْتِخابِ ٱلْأَعْضاءِ لِمَجْلِسِ ٱلشُّورَى.

Franchise, *v.t.* حَرَّرَ ـ أَعْفَى مِن.

Franchisement, *n.* تَحْرِير ـ إعْفاء.

Franciscan, *n.* A — monk, راهِبٌ مِنْ أَخَوِيَّةِ مار فَرَنْسِيس.

Francolin, *n.* دُرّاج. The male —, دَيْلَم.

Frangibility, *n.* سُرْعَةُ ٱلإنْكِسارِ. *See also* Fragility, Frailness, *n.*

Frangible, *a.* سَرِيعُ ٱلإنْكِسارِ ـ واهٍ. *See also* Fragile, Frail, *a.*

Frank, *n.* The name given by Orientals to Europeans, فِرَنْجِيّ *coll.* فِرَنْج.

Frank, *a.* Candid, sincere, ناصِح ـ سَلِيم ـ صادِق ـ مُخْلِص ـ صافٍ.

Frank, *n.* A writing which exempts from postage, صَحٌّ بِخَلاصَةِ أُجْرَةِ ٱلْبُوسْطَةِ. A free letter, مَكْتُوبٌ خالِصُ أُجْرَةِ ٱلْبُوسْطَةِ.

Frank, *v.t.* To — a letter, وَضَعَ صَحًّا عَلَى ٱلْمَكْتُوبِ *aor.* يَضَعُ بِخَلاصَةِ أُجْرَةِ ٱلْبُوسْطَةِ.

Frankincense, *n.* كُنْدُر ـ لُبَان ـ حَصَآءُ لُبَانٍ ـ قُنْقِ.

Franklin, *n.* A freeholder, صَاحِبُ إِلْتِزَامٍ ـ مُلْتَزِم.

Frankly, *ad.* Candidly, بِإِخْلَاصٍ ـ بِسَذَاجَةٍ ـ بِنُصُوحٍ ـ صِدْقًا ـ بِتَفَتُّحٍ فِي ٱلْكَلَامِ ـ بِإِطْلَاقٍ ـ إِطْلَاقًا. Without reserve, بِصَدَاقَةٍ ـ بِٱنْبِسَاطٍ. To act — with, خَالَصَ ـ صَافَى ـ إِنْبَسَطَ إِلَى.

Frankness, *n.* Ingenuousness, إِنْبِسَاط ـ نُصُوح ـ خُلُوص ـ صِدْق ـ سَذَاجَة ـ صَفَآء.

Frantic, *a.* Mad, مُصَاب ـ مَجْنُون. Furious, سَاخِط ـ غَضُوب ـ هَائِج ـ مُغْتَاظ ـ مُسَرْسَم ـ مُتَهَوِّر.

Franticly, *ad.* بِجُنُونٍ ـ بِسَخْطٍ ـ بِغَيْظٍ ـ بِتَهَوُّرٍ.

Franticness, *n.* جُنُون ـ سَخْط ـ غَيْظ ـ غَضَب ـ تَهَوُّر.

Fraternal, *a.* أَخَوِيّ.

Fraternally, *ad.* إِخَآءً ـ بِتَآخٍ ـ مِثْلَ ٱلْأُخُوَّةِ.

Fraternity, *n.* The relation of a brother, أُخُوَّة. A society, brotherhood, مَعْشَر ـ جَمَاعَة ـ جَمْعِيَّة ـ أَخَوِيَّة. A — of friars, جَمَاعَةُ رُهْبَانٍ.

Fraternization, *n.* تَآخٍ ـ تَوَاخٍ ـ مُؤَاخَاة ـ وِخَآء.

Fraternize, *v.i.* تَآخَى ـ تَوَخَّى ـ تَوَاخَى. To — with, آخَى *vulg.* وَاخَى.

Fratricidal, *a.* مُتَعَلِّقٌ بِقَتْلِ ٱلْأَخِ.

Fratricide, *n.* The murder of a brother, قَتْلُ ٱلْأَخِ. The murderer of a brother, قَاتِلُ أَخِيهِ.

Fraud, *n.* بَخْس ـ إِرْب ـ مَكْر ـ غَدْر ـ غَبْن ـ حِيلَة ـ دُولَاب *pl.* دَوَالِيبُ ـ خِيَانَة. To use — towards, بَخَسَ ـ.

Fraudful, *a.* } Defrauding of right, بَاخِس ـ ظَالِم. Deceitful,
Fraudulent, } غَدَّار ـ خَادِع ـ خَدَّاع ـ غَشَّاش. Treacherous, خَاتِر ـ خَائِن ـ غَادِر.

Fraudfully, *ad.* } Wrongfully, بِبَخْسٍ ـ ظُلْمًا. Perfidiously,
Fraudulently, } بِغَدْرٍ ـ بِخِيَانَةٍ ـ بِحِيلَةٍ.

Fraudless, *a.* بِلَا خِيَانَةٍ ـ صَالِح ـ خَيِّر.

Fraudlessly, *ad.* بِلَا خِيَانَةٍ ـ بِصَلَاحٍ.

Fraudlessness, *n.* عَدَمُ ٱلْحِيلَةِ ـ صَفَاوَة ـ صَلَاح.

Fraught, *a.* مُفْعَم ـ مَمْلُوٌّ ـ مَشْحُون ـ كَثِير. Fraught with danger, خَطِير ـ كَثِيرُ ٱلْخَطَرِ.

Fray, *n.* A — in a garment, occasioned by a thorn, *etc.*, جَذْبَة ـ عَلْقَة. *See also* Affray, Fracas, *n.*

Fray, *v.t.* To rub, نَفَشَ ـ نَقَّشَ ـ حَكَّ. To frighten away, أَزْعَجَ ـ طَرَدَ ـ أَجْفَلَ. To break, to mar, ثَلَمَ ـ شَجَّ. A frayed wooden peg, and such like, شَجِيج.

Fray, *v.i.* To rub, fret, إِنْتَفَشَ.

Freak, *n.* جُنُون ـ جِنَّة ـ هَزْل ـ لَهْو ـ خَيَال ـ هَوِيَّة ـ عَبْثَة. *See also* Whim, *n.*

Freakish, *a.* هَوَائِيّ ـ هَزِل ـ مُمَازِح ـ عِبِّيث. *See also* Skittish, Frisky, *a.*

Freakishly, *ad.* عَلَى هَوَآءِ ٱلنَّفْسِ ـ بِمَزْحٍ.

Freakishness, *a.* مُمَازَحَة ـ مُهَاوَاة ـ جُنُون ـ عَبَث.

Freckle, *n.* كَلَف ـ نَمَش *pl.* أَنْمَاش.

Freckle, *v.t.* بَقَّعَ ـ بِنَمَشٍ.

Freckle, *v.i.* نَمِشَ ـ. Freckled, ذُو نَمَشٍ ـ أَنْمَش *fem.* نَمْشَآءُ *pl.* نُمْش ـ نَمِش.

Freckly, *a.* Marked with spots, أَنْمَش ـ مُنَمَّر ـ مُنَقَّش ـ مُرَقَّط.

Free, *a.* At liberty, مُطْلَق ـ مَعْتُوق ـ حُرّ *pl.* أَحْرَار. Permitted, مُبَاح ـ جَائِز ـ مُجَاز ـ مُرَخَّص ـ حَلَال ـ جَارٍ ـ مَأْذُون. Unrestrained, مُخَيَّر ـ مُطْلَقُ ٱلْحُرِّيَّةِ. Licentious, نَالِت ـ زَفِر ـ. Frank, صَادِق ـ مُخْلِص ـ صَافٍ. Liberal, سَخِيّ ـ كَرِيم ـ جَوَاد. Exempt from, فِي حِلٍّ مِنْ ـ سَلِيمٌ مِنْ ـ مُعْفًى مِنْ. Guiltless, بَرِيٌّ مِنْ ـ بَرِيُّ ٱلذِّمَّةِ. Free from admixture, صِرْف ـ بَحْت ـ مَحْض ـ خَالِص ـ صَرِيح. Quit of, فِي حِلٍّ مِنْ. Without cost, مَجَّانًا ـ بِلَا شَيْءٍ ـ بِدُونِ كُلْفَةٍ. Free with one's tongue, طَلِقُ ٱللِّسَانِ ـ ذَلِقٌ ـ طَلَقٌ. Voluntary, إِخْتِيَارِيّ ـ بِٱلرِّضَآءِ. Unconnected, disconnected, مَفْرُوز ـ تَوًّا ـ لِوَحْدِهِ ـ مُنْفَصِل. Free, eager to go, as of a horse, شَرِيّ. Free, as of a translation, طَلِيق. A — country, بِلَادٌ حُرَّةٌ. To be —, safe, from, سَلِمَ مِنْ ـ; to make — from, سَلَّمَ ـ مِنْ. To make —, allowable, أَبَاحَ. To get —, away, إِنْفَلَتَ ـ تَفَلَّتَ ـ فَلَتَ ـ. To be — of, clear of admixture, بَحُتَ مِنْ ـ خَلَصَ مِنْ ـ; to make — or clear from, خَلَّصَ ـ مِنْ ـ أَخْلَصَ. To be — from, quit of, as of an obligation or troublesome affair, *etc.*, حَلَّ مِنْ ـ; to make to be quit of, حَلَّ ـ مِنْ ـ. To declare one's self — from, تَسَلَّمَ مِنْ. You are perfectly —, in perfect safety, أَنْتَ فِي أَوْسَعِ ٱلْأَمَانِ. He is — to speak, هُوَ حُرٌّ فِيمَا يَقُولُهُ. I am — from, guiltless of, have nothing to do with . . . , أَنَا خَالٍ مِنْ. Free from anxiety, خَالٍ لَهُ ـ مِنَ ٱلْهَمِّ. To be —, familiar, with, تَأَنَّسَ بِ ـ بَاسَطَ. To make — with, to exceed, جَاوَزَ ـ أَفْرَطَ فِي ـ وَجَّهَ عِنْدَ. To make one's self too —, تَجَاسَرَ. To be —, disengaged, تَفَرَّغَ ـ تَخَلَّى مِنَ ٱلشُّغْلِ ـ تَفَضَّى. *See also* Liberal, *a.*

Free, *v.a.* To set at liberty, أَعْتَقَ ـ فَكَّ ـ أَفْلَتَ ـ سَيَّبَ. To make —, حَرَّرَ. To exempt from, عَفَا لِ ـ عَنْ. To clear from, to justify, بَرَّأَ ـ مِنْ. To make to pass away, to put an end to, أَزَالَ. To — from impurities, خَلَّصَ ـ صَفَّى. To free from pain, (of God,) مَصَحَ ; (otherwise,) أَزَالَ عَنِ ٱلْوَجَعَ . To — one from another person, قَضَّى مِن ; to be so freed, إِنْقَضَى مِن — To —, as from trouble, فَرَّجَ عَن — فَرَجَ عَن ; تَفَصَّى مِن. to be so freed, or free from care, إِنْفَرَجَ — تَفَرَّجَ . He freed me from my anxiety, سَلَّانِي عَنْ هَمِّي . *See also preceding article, and to* Exempt, *v.t.*

Free-agency, *n.* إِخْتِيار — إِرَادَةٌ مُطْلَقَةٌ . Of his own —, مِنْ تِلْقَاءِ نَفْسِهِ .

Freebooter, *n.* لِصّ *pl.* لُصُوص — سارِق *pl.* سُرَّاق — قاطِعُ ٱلطَّرِيقِ *pl.* قُطَّاع .

Freebooting, *n.* شَلْح — سَرِقَة — سَلْب — نَهْب .

Free-born, *a.* حُرٌّ *pl.* أَحْرار — حُرُّ ٱلْأَصْلِ .

Free-city, *n.* مَدِينَةٌ حُرَّةٌ — مَدِينَةٌ مُمْتَازَةٌ — مَدِينَةٌ ذَاتُ ٱمْتِيَازاتٍ .

Free-cost, *n.* عَدَمُ تَكْلِيفٍ . At —, مَجّانًا .

Freedman, *n.* مُحَرَّر — مَعْتُوق — عَتِيق — طَلِيق *pl.* طُلَقَاء .

Freedom, *n.* حُرِّيَّة . The being at liberty, عِتْق — طَلْق . Permission, إِذْن — إِجازَة — رُخْصَة — دُسْتُور . Facility in doing, سُهُولَة — طَلْق . Clearness from impurities, بُحُوتَة — بَحْت — خَلاصَة — صَرَاحَة . Freedom of will, إِخْتِيار — تِلْقَاءُ ٱلنَّفْسِ . Exemption, مُعافاة — إِنْتِفاء — بَرَاءَة . Freedom from care, فُرْجَة — تَفَرُّج — راحَةُ بالٍ ; from anxiety, trouble, مَسْلاة — تَسَلٍّ . Freedom of action, حُرِّيَّةُ ٱلْعَمَلِ . Freedom of the city, أَمانَةُ ٱلْبَلَدِ — إِمْتِيازُ ٱبْنِ ٱلْبَلَدِ . *See also* Liberty, *n.*

Freehearted, *a.* سَخِيٌّ — رَحِيبُ ٱلصَّدْرِ — جَوَاد — صاحِبُ مُرُوَّةٍ .

Freeheartedness, *n.* سَخَاوَة — جُود — مُرُوَّة — رُحْبُ ٱلصَّدْرِ .

Freehold, *a.* and *n.* مُلْك *pl.* أَمْلاك .

Freeholder, *n.* صاحِبُ مُلْكٍ .

Free-liver, *n.* مُسْرِف *pl.* مُسْرِفُون — مُتَنَعِّم .

Free-living, *n.* عَيْشٌ مُسْرِفٌ — تَنَعُّم .

Freely, *ad.* Plentifully, بِوَفْرَةٍ — بِكَثْرَةٍ . Generously, بِجُودٍ — بِسَخاوَةٍ . Openly, جِهارًا . Flowingly, بِسُهُولَةٍ . Optionally, إِخْتِيارًا — خِيارًا — بِٱلْخِيارِ . Without restraint, بِحُرِّيَّةٍ . Gratuitously, مُتَبَرِّعًا — مَجّانًا . Without cost, مَجّانًا — بِلا شَيْءٍ . To speak —, openly, إِنْبَسَطَ فِي ٱلْكَلامِ — تَكَلَّمَ جَهْرَةً . To do a thing —, unasked, تَبَرَّعَ بِ . To treat one —, openly, as in conversation, *etc.*, باسَطَهُ .

Freeman, *n.* حُرٌّ *pl.* أَحْرار — إِبْنُ بَلَدٍ .

Freemason, *n.* فِرْمَسِيُونِيٌّ *coll.* الفِرْمَسِيُون .

Freemasonry, *n.* طَرِيقَةُ ٱلْفِرْمَسِيُونِ .

Freeness, *n.* Candour, صَفَاء — خُلُوص — صِدْق . Liberality, سَخاوَة — جُود — كَرَم . Familiarity, إِنْبِساط — عَدَمُ تَكْلِيفٍ — مُباسَطَة . *See also* Freedom, *n.*

Free-port, *n.* مِينا مُعافاةٌ عَنِ ٱلرُّسُومِ — مِينا مُمْتَازَةٌ .

Free-spoken, *a.* مُتَكَلِّمٌ جِهارًا — طَلْقُ ٱللِّسانِ — مُنْبَسِطٌ فِي ٱلْكَلامِ . To be — with, إِنْبَسَطَ إِلَى .

Free-stone, *n.* حَجَرٌ لِلْبِناء — حَجَرٌ رَمْلِيٌّ .

Freethinker, *n.* } دَهْرِيٌّ *pl.* دَهْرِيُّون — مُلْحِد *pl.* مَلاحِدَة —
Freethinking, *a.* } زِنْدِيق *pl.* زَنادِقَة .

Freethinking, *n.* زَنْدَقَة — إِلْحاد — طَرِيقَةُ ٱلدَّهْرِيِّينَ .

Free-tongued, *a.* *See* Free-spoken, *a.*

Free-trade, *n.* تِجارَةٌ مُطْلَقَةٌ .

Free-will, *n.* إِرادَةٌ مُطْلَقَةٌ — إِخْتِيارٌ كُلِّيٌّ . To do anything of one's —, تَبَرَّعَ بِ .

Free-will, *a.* مُتَبَرِّع — إِخْتِيارِيٌّ . A — offering, تَبَرُّع *pl.* تَبَرُّعات .

Free-woman, *n.* حُرَّة *pl.* حَرائِر .

Freeze, *v.t.* قَرَّسَ — أَقْرَسَ — جَمَّدَ — ثَلَّجَ .

Freeze, *v.i.* قَرِسَ — ثَلِجَ — جَمَدَ — أَجْلَدَ . The water froze, قامَ ٱلْماءُ . The ground froze or became frozen, أَجْلَدَتِ ٱلْأَرْضُ .

Freezing, *a.* قَرِيس — قارِس . A — night, لَيْلَةٌ ذَاتُ قَرْسٍ .

Freezing point, دَرَجَةُ ٱلْجُمُودِ .

Freight, *v.t.* To load, شَحَنَ — شَحَنَ بِ — حَمَّلَ — أَوْسَقَ . To — or hire a ship, إِسْتَأْجَرَ (*or*) إِسْتَكْرَى مَرْكَبًا .

Freight, *n.* The load, as of a ship, شَحْنَة — وَسْقَة — حَمْل . What is paid for the hire of a ship, نَوْل — نَوْلُون .

Freighter, *n.* As of a ship, مُؤَجِّرُ مَرْكَبٍ — مُكْرِي مَرْكَبٍ .

French, *a.* فَرَنْساوِيٌّ — فَرَنْسِيز . The — language, اللِّسانُ ٱلْفَرَنْساوِيُّ .

French-beans, *n.* لُوبِيا .

Frenchify, *v.t.* شَرَّبَ مِنْ طَبائِعِ ٱلْفَرَنْساوِيِّينَ .

Frenetic, *a.* *See* Frantic, *a.*

Frenzied, *a.* خَبِل — أَخْبَلُ — مُخَبَّل — مَجْنُون . To make —, خَبَّلَ .

Frenziedly, *ad.* بِخَبالٍ — بِجُنُونٍ .

Frenzy, *n.* خَبْل — خَبال — جُنُون — سِرْسام . To be in a —, خَبِلَ .

Frequence, *n.* } Common occurrence, تِكْرار — تَكَرُّر — كَثْرَةٌ
Frequency, } كَثْرَةُ وُقُوعٍ .

Frequent, *a.* مُكَرَّر — كَثِيرُ ٱلْوُقُوعِ — مُعْتاد .

Frequent, *v.t.* آلَفَ ـ أَلِفَ ـ اِخْتَلَفَ إِلَى ـ تَعَهَّدَ ـ اِعْتَادَ *aor.* آلَفَ ـ تَرَدَّدَ إِلَى ـ يُؤَالِفُ. To — a person, لَازَمَ *aor.* يُؤَالِفُ. A frequented road, دَرْبٌ مَسْلُوكٌ; a — house, بَيْتٌ مَطْرُوقٌ. A — port, مِينَةٌ وَرَّادَةٌ.

Frequentation, *n.* تَرَدُّدٌ إِلَى ـ اِخْتِلَافٌ إِلَى ـ تَعَهُّدٌ.

Frequentative, *a.* مُتَعَهِّدٌ ـ مُكَرِّرٌ. A — verb, فِعْلٌ فَعَّالٌ.

Frequenter, *n.* مُتَعَهِّدٌ ـ إِلْفٌ إِلَى ـ مُتَرَدِّدٌ.

Frequently, *ad.* طَالَمَا ـ آوِنَةً ـ عَرَكَاتٍ ـ عَرْكَةً بَعْدَ عَرْكَةٍ ـ دَفَعَاتٍ ـ كَثِيرًا ما ـ مِرَارًا. He did it —, كَثُرَ ذٰلِكَ مِنْهُ. More —, مِرَارًا أَكْثَرَ.

Frequentness, *n.* *See* Frequency, *n.*

Fresco, *n.* Coolness, بُرُودَةٌ; *al fresco*, فِي ٱلْبُرُودَةِ. A painting in —, تَصْوِيرٌ عَلَى حائطٍ مُدَمَّمٍ بِٱلْجِصِّ. To paint in —, (*v.t.*) صَوَّرَ عَلَى حائطٍ مُدَمَّمٍ بِٱلْجِصِّ.

Fresh, *a.* Cool, بارِدٌ. Moist, succulent, juicy, green, غَضِيرٌ ـ رَطِيبٌ ـ رَطْبٌ. Not salt, حَلُوٌّ ـ حُلْوٌ ـ عَذْبٌ. Green, recent, غَضِيضٌ ـ غَضٌّ ـ طَرِيٌّ ـ أَخْضَرُ ـ غَضِيرٌ. Fresh, vigorous, غَرِيضٌ. Fresh, of a horse, شَرِيٌّ. Sweet, not stinking, غَرِيضٌ. Not faded, نَضِرٌ ـ زاهٍ. Brisk, as of a wind, قَوِيٌّ ـ شَدِيدٌ. New, جَدِيدٌ. Recent, مُسْتَجِدٌّ ـ حَدِيثٌ. Fresh oil, زَيْتٌ طَرِيٌّ. Fresh water, ماءٌ عَذْبٌ. Fresh bread, خُبْزٌ طَرِيٌّ. Fresh news, أَخْبارٌ طارِئَةٌ (or مُسْتَجِدَّةٌ).

Fresh, *n.* *See* Freshet, *n.*

Freshen, *v.t.* To revive, as from fatigue, أَرَاحَ. To brighten, repair, صَلَّحَ ـ صَفَّى; of colours, جَنْدَرَ. To make cool, رَطَّبَ ـ بَرَّدَ. To sweeten, حَلَّى. To invigorate, شَدَّدَ ـ قَوَّى.

Freshen, *v.i.* To grow fresh, sweet, حَلَا [ع]. To grow cool, بَرُدَ [ع]. To grow humid, juicy, green, طَرُوَ *aor.* يَطْرُو ـ طَرِيَ *aor.* يَطْرَى ـ تَرَطَّبَ ـ رَطُبَ [ع]. To grow strong, as of wind, *etc.*, اِشْتَدَّ ـ قَوِيَ [ي].

Freshet, *n.* سَيْلٌ *pl.* سُيُولٌ ـ اِزْدِيادٌ ـ فَيَضانٌ ـ فَيْضٌ.

Freshly, *ad.* Coolly, بِبُرُودَةٍ ـ بِطَرَاوَةٍ. Newly, حَدَاثَةً ـ جِدَّةً ـ اِسْتِجْدادًا. Strongly, بِقُوَّةٍ ـ بِشِدَّةٍ.

Freshness, *n.* Coolness, طَرَاوَةٌ ـ بُرُودَةٌ. Newness, حَدَاثَةٌ ـ جِدَّةٌ. The commencement of anything, جِدْثَانٌ. Vigour, نَضَارَةٌ ـ طَرَاوَةٌ ـ رُطُوبَةٌ ـ طَرَاءٌ ـ طَرَآءَةٌ. Freedom from staleness, حُمَيًّا ـ حَدَاثَةٌ; from saltness, حَلَاوَةٌ ـ عُذُوبَةٌ. Strength, as of the wind, شِدَّةٌ ـ عُصُوفٌ. Freshness of youth, شَبَابٌ.

Fret, *v.t.* To wear away by rubbing, عَرَكَ [ع] ـ بَرَى [ي] ـ بَلَّى ـ أَبْلَى ـ أَكَلَ [ع]. To vex, أَضْجَرَ ـ أَحْنَقَ ـ أَغَاظَ ـ أَزْعَجَ ـ نَجَّزَ. To —, as of moths, عَثَّ [ع]. To form into raised work, نَقَشَ [ع] ـ حَفَرَ [ي]. The rag or other substance bound round a nail, *etc.*, to keep it from fretting, نُوتٌ ـ نُوَّةٌ. *See also to* Chafe, *v.t.*

Fret, *v.i.* To become worn away, corroded, اِنْبَرَى ـ أُكِلَ ـ بَلِيَ [ي]. To be in commotion, agitation, اِضْطَرَبَ ـ تَقَلْقَلَ. To be chafed, vexed, قَلِقَ [ي] ـ اِضْطَرَبَ ـ اِغْتَاظَ ـ اِنْزَعَجَ ـ غَرِيَ [ي]. To be fretted, as by moths, عُثَّ. One who frets himself to death about anything, باخِعٌ عَلَى. Fret not thyself, لا تَغْرَ. To — one's self to death, بَخَعَ نَفْسَهُ [ي].

Fret, *n.* Commotion of temper, اِضْطِرابٌ ـ اِنْزِعاجٌ ـ زَعَجٌ ـ قَلَقٌ. The stop of a musical instrument, مُلَمَّسَةٌ ـ عَتَبٌ ـ دَسْتَانٌ *pl.* دَسْتانات. A — in architecture, نَقْشٌ *pl.* نُقُوشٌ.

Fretful, *a.* Peevish, نَكِدٌ ـ شَرِسٌ ـ شَكِسٌ ـ وَعِقٌ. To be —, شَكُسَ [ع] ـ نَكِدَ [ي]; to be — with, شَاكَسَ.

Fretfully, *ad.* بِنَكَدٍ ـ بِشَرَاسَةٍ ـ بِشَكَاسَةٍ.

Fretfulness, *n.* نَكَدٌ ـ شَرَاسَةٌ ـ شَكَاسَةٌ ـ وَعَقَةٌ.

Fretter, *n.* *See* Termite, *n.*

Fretting, *n.* Agitation, اِنْزِعاجٌ ـ اِضْطِرابٌ ـ قَلَقٌ. *See also* Fretfulness, *n.*

Fret-work, *n.* حَفْرٌ ـ نَقْرٌ ـ نَقْشٌ; especially such as tracery on gypsum, within and without a building, الدَّواخِلُ وَٱلْخَوارِجُ.

Friability, *n.* }
Friableness, } هَشَاشَةٌ ـ تَحَطُّمٌ.

Friable, *a.* فَرِيكٌ ـ هَشٌّ ـ ذُو تَحَطُّمٍ.

Friar, *n.* راهِبٌ *pl.* رُهْبانٌ.

Friarlike, *a.* }
Friarly, } مِثْلُ ٱلرَّاهِبِ ـ راهِبِيٌّ.

Friar's-cowl, *n.* The plant, آذانُ ٱلْفِيلِ.

Friary, *n.* دَيْرٌ *pl.* دُيُورٌ.

Fribble, *v.i.* *See to* Trifle, *v.i.*

Fricandeau, *n.* لَحْمَةٌ مُحَمَّرَةٌ.

Fricassee, *n.* يَخْنَةٌ. A fricasseed fowl, يَخْنَةُ دُجاجَةٍ.

Friction, *n.* The act of rubbing, حَكٌّ ـ تَدْلِيكٌ ـ دَلْكٌ ـ تَفْرِيكٌ ـ تَحْكِيكٌ. A rubbing, حَكٌّ ـ دَعْكٌ ـ عَرْكَةٌ. A thing with which one rubs himself, دَلُوكٌ. To use — on one's self, تَدَلَّكَ.

Friday, *n.* يَوْمُ ٱلْجُمْعَةِ ـ ٱلْجُمْعَةُ. Good —, الْجُمْعَةُ ٱلْكَبِيرَةُ ـ جُمْعَةُ ٱلْآلامِ.

Fried, *a.* مَقْلِيٌّ. Fried food, قَلِيَّةٌ *pl.* قَلَايا. One who fries, قَلَّاءٌ.

Friend, *a.* خِلٌّ *pl.* أَخِلَّةٌ ـ خَلِيلٌ *pl.* خُلَّانٌ (*fem.* خَلِيلَةٌ *pl.*

(خلا — مُحِبٌّ — حَبِيب *pl.* أَحْبَاب *and* أَحِبَّآءُ *and* أَحِبَّةٌ
حَبِيبَة *pl.* حَبَائِبُ *and* حَبِيبَات — صَدِيق *pl.* أَصْدِقَآءُ *and*
صُدّ *and* صُدْقَان — صَاحِب *pl.* أَصْحَاب . A sincere —, خِلْص
خُلْصَان — خِدْن *pl.* خُدْنَان — خِلّ *and* خَلِيل . A helper,
مُعِ — مُسَاعِد . To make friends with, after a rupture, صَالَحَ —
تَصَالَحَ . To be a — to; *see to* Befriend, *v.t.*; *also* Quaker, *n.*

Friendless, *a.* وَحِيد — مَتْرُوك — مُحْتَاج — مُسَيَّب .

Friendliness, *n.* Kindness, رَأْفَة — فَضْل — حِلْم — إِحْسَان —
مَحَبَّة . *See also* Familiarity, *n.*

Friendly, *a.* مُحِبٌّ — صَدِيق — أَنِيس . Suitable, مُوافِق —
مُنَاسِب . To be — with, عَاشَرَ — وَاصَلَ — صَادَقَ . To treat in
— manner, as in conversation, *etc.*, بَاسَطَ . The — governments,
الدُّوَل ٱلْمُتَحَابَّة . His relations with them continue on the
same — footing, لَمْ تَزَلْ عَلَاقَتُهُ مَعَهُمْ عَلَى ٱلْأُلْفَةِ وَٱلْوِدَادِ . In
— way, بِصُورَةٍ وِدَادِيَّةٍ .

Friendship, *n.* خُلَّة — أُلْفَة — جُمْعَة — مُوَاصَلَة — خُلُولَة —
مُوَادَّة — مُوَالَاة — مُحَابَّة — صُحْبَة — مُصَاحَبَة — مَحَبَّة .

Frieze, *n.* In architecture, شُرْفَة *pl.* شُرَف — إِفْرِيز *pl.* أَفَارِيز .
The nap on cloth, خَمِيلَة — زِئْبِر . A kind of coarse woollen cloth,
قُمَاش مِنْ صُوفٍ مُزَأْبَر .

Frieze, *v.t.* To adorn with friezes, شَرَّفَ — زَيَّنَ بِأَفَارِيز . To —
cloth, أَخْمَلَ — زَأْبَرَ .

Frigate, *n.* The ship, فَرْقَاطَة .

Fright, *n.* رَوْع — ذُعْر — دَهْش — هَوْل — وَحْشَة — فَزَع —
خَوْف . A fit of —, رَوْعَة — دَهْشَة — وَحْشَة — وَهْرَة . To take —
and run away, جَفَلَ — ² نَدَّ — ² نَفَرَ — ² شَرَدَ . A — and
running away, شُرُود — نُفُور — جُفُول . Anything ugly, قَبَاحَة —
سَمَاجَة .

Fright, *v.t.* } To terrify, دَهَّشَ — أَدْهَشَ — ذَعَرَ — أَذْعَرَ —
Frighten, } خَشَّى — رَوَّعَ — أَفْزَ — أَرْعَدَ — أَرْهَبَ — أَرْعَبَ —
فَزَّعَ — أَفْزَعَ — خَوَّفَ ; in the sense of disabling, أَقْطَعَ . To —
away, أَجْفَلَ — شَرَّدَ . To be frightened, رَهِبَ — إِنْدَهَشَ —
نَزَ — تَفَزَّعَ — فَزِعَ — خَافَ *aor.* يَخَافُ . He was frightened at
him, خَافَ مِنْهُ — تَخَوَّفَهُ . Frightened, terrified, مَخْلُوع — مَرْعُوب .

Frightful, *a.* Terrifying, ذَعِر — هَائِل — مُرْعِب — مَهُول —
مُفْزِع — مَخُوف — مُقْطِع . Disastrous, فَظِيع — نَحِس — مَنْحُوس .
Ugly, كَرِيه — سَمِج — قَبِيح .

Frightfully, *ad.* بِنَوْعٍ فَظِيع — إِفْزَاعًا — تَفْزِيعًا — إِقْشِعْرَارًا .
Greatly, جِدًّا — لِلْغَايَةِ .

Frightfulness, *n.* The quality of frightening, هَوْل — وَحْشَة .
Ugliness, كَرَاهَة — سَمَاجَة — قَبَاحَة . Disastrousness, نَحْس —
سُوء — فَظَاعَة .

Frigid, *a.* Cold, مَقْرُور — بَارِد . Dull, stupid, أَخْرَق — تَافِه —
بَارِد — فَارِغ ٱلْبَالِ — عَدِيمُ ٱلْمَحَبَّةِ . Without affection,
The — zone, المِنْطَقَةُ ٱلْجَامِدَةُ . *See also* Cold, Freezing, *a.*

Frigidness, *n.* } بُرُودَة . *See also* Coldness, *n.*
Frigidity, }

Frigidly, *ad.* بِبُرُودَةٍ . *See also* Coldly, *ad.*

Frill, *n.* كُشْكُش *pl.* كَشَاكِش . Frilling, كَشَاكِش — زِينَة .

Frill, *v.t.* رَكَّبَ كَشَاكِش .

Fringe, *n.* The trimming, سِجَاف — هُدَّاب — طِرَاز — شَرَارِيب .
Edging, نِيرِ *pl.* أَنْيَار — كَنَف *pl.* أَكْنَاف — خَرَج .

Fringe, *v.t.* To — with trimming, طَرَّزَ — سَجَّفَ — خَرَّجَ ; with
edging, نَيَّرَ — كَنَّفَ .

Fringy, *a.* ذُو شَرَارِيب — مُزَيَّن بِسِجَاف .

Frippery, *n.* Paltry goods, سَقَطُ ٱلْمَتَاعِ . Old clothes, ثِيَابٌ
رِثَاثٌ ; traffic in —, شِرَآءُ ٱلْأَخْلَاقِ وَبَيْعُهَا . A shop of —, دُكَّانُ
عُتُقِيٍّ . Nonsense, trash, تَفَاهَة — عَبَث — حَقَارَة .

Frippery, *a.* Trashy, تَافِه — عِبِّيث — حَقِير — سَقَط .

Frise, *n.* Chevaux-de-frise, حَسِيكَة .

Frisk, *v.i.* مَرِحَ — عَنْظَزَ — قَفَزَ — ² نَطَّ .

Frisk, *n.* مِرَاح — عَنْظَزَة — قَفْزَة — نَطَّة .

Frisket, *n.* قَرْوَازُ ٱلْمَطْبَعَةِ .

Friskiness, *n.* مَرَحَان — تَعَنْظُز — قَفَزَان .

Frisky, *a.* مَرِح — مَرِيح — نَطَّاط — أَلُوب — فَلْتَان ; of a horse,
مِمْرَاح — نَطَّاط .

Frith, *n.* خَوْر *pl.* خُؤُور — خَلِيج *pl.* خُلْجَان .

Fritter, *n.* A cake, عُومَة — زَلَابِيَة — زُنْكُلَة — زَلُوبِيَة —
عَجِينٌ مَقْلِيٌّ . A fragment, كُسَارَة — هُشَامَة — جِذَّة . A shred,
شُقَّة *pl.* شُقَق . An egg —, omelet, عُجَّة .

Fritter, *v.t.* To break into fragments, رَضَحَ — رَضَخَ — كَسَّرَ .
To — away, ضَيَّعَ — أَتْلَفَ .

Frivolity, *n.* } Triflingness, سُخْف — تَفَهٌ — سَخَافَة — طَفَافَة ;
Frivolousness, } of disposition, سَخَافَة — تَفَاهَةُ عَقْلٍ — سُخَافَة
عَقْلٍ — خِفَّةُ عَقْلٍ — هَزْل .

Frivolous, *a.* Of a person, سَخِيفُ ٱلْعَقْلِ — سَخِيف — عِبِّيث —
هَزِل — تَافِهُ ٱلْعَقْلِ — تَفَاتِفُ *pl.* تَفْتَاف ; of a thing, سَخِيف —
عَبِث — تَافِه — طَفِيف — صَغِير — بَاطِل — بَهْرَج — زَهِيد .

Frivolously, *ad.* بِسَخَافَةٍ — بِهَزْلٍ — بِمَزَاحٍ — بَاطِلًا — بِتَفَهٍ .
One who talks —, هَيْذَارَةٌ بَيْذَارَةٌ — هُذَرَةٌ بُذَرَةٌ .

Friz, *v.i.* } عقص ـ جعّد ـ عكّف ـ . To —, as heat or cold
Frizzle, } does, شَفْشَف .

Frizzle, *v.i.* تجعّد ـ عقص ـ تعكّف . To become frizzled, as by heat or cold, تشفشف .

Frizzly, *a.* مجعّد ـ جعد ـ معكّف .

Fro, *ad.* Hindward, إلى وراء ـ إلى خلف ـ إلى دبر . To go to and fro, تردّد ـ أدبر وأقبل . Moved and carried to and fro by every wind, مضطرب ومحمول بكل ريح . A leaf driven to and fro, ورقة متطاردة . They reel to and fro and stagger like a drunken man, يتمايلون ويترنحون مثل السكران .

Frock, *n.* A dress for children, ضرب من الملبوس للأولاد ـ فسطان .

Frock-coat, *n.* سورتو ـ سِتارة *pl.* سترة فوقانية .

Frog, *n.* The animal, علجوم *pl.* عداميل ـ شرنوغ ـ نقّاق ـ ضفدع *pl.* ضفادع ـ فدّادة ـ فدّاد ـ نقّاقة . The — of a horse's hoof, نسر *pl.* نسور . A button, زرّ *pl.* أزرار . To croak as a —, نقّ .

Frog-bit, *n.* The plant, قصعة الماء .

Frolic, *n.* مزاحة ـ هزالة ـ مزح ـ لعب ـ لهو .

Frolic, *v.i.* هزل ـ لعب ـ مزح .

Frolicsome, *a.* ملاعب ـ هزل ـ لعّاب ـ لعبان .

Frolicsomeness, *n.* هزل ـ تلعّب ـ مزاح .

From, *prep.* As issuing —, من عند ـ عن ـ من . From me, من عندي ; from him, من عنده ; from them, من عندهم . (*Note.*—The word عند is declinable only after the preposition من ; in all other cases it preserves the adverbial form عند). Since, منذ ـ مذ . From above, من فوق ـ من العلى . From afar, من مسافة بعيدة ـ من بعد . From off, عن ـ من . From within, من داخل . From hence, — these premises, من هنا ـ من ذلك ـ من هذا . From, copied —, نقلاً عن . From first to last of it, من أوله إلى آخره . From father to son, أباً عن جدّ . From bygone days, من القديم . From all eternity, من الأزل . From ignorance, عن جهل . From day to day, يوماً فيوماً . To be — home (residence), خرج من البيت .

Frondescence, *n.* أوان التوريق ـ توريق .

Frondiferous, *a.* ورّاق ـ حامل ورق .

Frondose, *a.* حامل أوراق وأزهار معاً .

Front, *n.* A face, or frontage, وجه *pl.* وجوه ; the part opposite, مقابلة ـ حيال ـ حذاء . The fore part of anything, أدنى ـ وجه ـ مقدّمة ـ قدّام ـ حيال ـ قبال . The van, as of an army, طليعة ـ مجنّبة ـ نظيرة . A cause, origin, أصل ـ سبب . I stood in — of him, قمت حياله . He sat in — of him, قعد بحياله . In the —, facing, مجاياة ـ صدد . In front, before, قبلاً ـ متقدّماً ; opposite, مجاياة ـ قبال . He passed by me, being in front, opposite, to me, مرّ بي مجاياة .

Front, *v.t.* To oppose face to face, جبه . To stand opposite to, جاياً ـ قابل ـ واجه ـ وازى . He fronted him, جاياه .

Front, *v.i.* To stand foremost, تقدّم . To have the face turned to..., توجّه إلى .

Frontage, *n.* The front part, حيال ـ قبال ـ وجه .

Frontal, *a.* متعلّق بالجبين ـ جبيني . The — bone, العظم الإكليلي .

Frontal, *n.* A bandage for the head, عصابة *pl.* عصب . A —, in architecture, قوصرة . A Jewish phylactery, عصابة *pl.* عصائب ـ حرز *pl.* أحراز .

Frontier, *n.* حدّ *pl.* حدود . The — of a kingdom, حدود مملكة .

Frontier, *a.* على حدوده ـ حديد ـ محادّ . A frontier-way of access to a country, ثغر البلاد . A scientific —, حدود علمية .

Fronting, *a.* مقابل ـ حذاء ـ بحيال . He sat — him, جلس بحذائه . My house is — his, داري حذاء داره . He is — you, هو حذاءك .

Frontispiece, *n.* The — of a book, أول كتاب ـ عنوان كتاب ; of a building, قبالة (or وجه) بناء .

Frontless, *a.* Shameless, قليل الحياء ـ سفيه ـ وقيح ـ وقح .

Frontlet, *n.* *See* Frontal, *n.*

Frost, *n.* ضريب ـ صقيع ـ قرس ـ قريس . Hoar-frost, صقيع ـ سقيط الندى ـ سقيط . To cover with —, أصقع ; to be covered with —, أصقع ـ صقع . The earth was covered with —, صقعت الأرض .

Frost, *v.t.* To cover with sugar, لبّس بسكّر .

Frost-bitten, *a.* مضروب (or مصاب) بالصقيع ـ مبرود .

Frosted, *a.* Covered with frost, صقع عليه ; of the hair, رشّ ـ أشيب ـ عليه الشيب . Covered with sugar, ملبّس بسكّر .

Frostily, *ad.* ببرودة ـ بصقعة .

Frostiness, *n.* The state of being frosty, صقعة .

Frosting, *n.* As of sugar, التلبيس بسكّر .

Frosty, *a.* Freezing, صاقع ـ مصقع ـ صقع . Of the hair, أشيب . Grizzled, of animals, منمّر .

Froth, *n* Foam, رغوة ـ رغاوة ـ زبد ـ جفال . The — from a boiling pot, فوارة ـ جفاء ; of milk, زبد اللبن ـ رغوة ـ ثمالة .

Twaddle, كَلامٌ فِي ٱلْهَوآءِ ـ عَبَث ـ هُجْر ـ لَغْوٌ. To sip —, يُسِرُّ حَسْوًا فِي ٱرْتِغَاءٍ. He conceals a sipping in drinking the —, إِرْتَغَى; (*prov.*) applied to a person who says one thing and means another.

Froth, *v.i.* أَرْغَى ـ رَغَى ـ أَزْبَدَ. The cooking-pot has frothed, أَجْفَتِ ٱلْقِدْرُ. *See also to* Foam, *v.i.*

Froth, *v.t.* زَبَدَ [2].

Frothiness, *n.* Scumminess, رِغَاوَة ـ إِرْغَاء. Emptiness, nonsense, بُطْل ـ هَلْس ـ تَفَاهَة. Frothy speeches, بُطَّالات.

Frothy, *a.* Scummy, مُزْبِد ـ رِغْوِيّ. Vain, تافِه ـ هافِت ـ بَهْرَج ـ باطِل. He was — in his talk, بَطَلَ فِي حَدِيثِهِ [2]. A — speaker, مُتَبَطِّل.

Frouziness, *n.* Mustiness, عُفُونَة ـ تَفَل; especially of the hair, جُفُول ـ شَعَث.

Frouzy, *a.* Musty, bad, رَدِيء ـ مُعَفَّن. A — man, رَجُلٌ تَفِلٌ; woman, اِمْرَأَةٌ تَفِلَةٌ. To be or become —, of the hair, جَفَلَ [2] ـ تَشَعَّثَ. To make —, شَعَّثَ. To be —, musty, تَفِلَ.

Froward, *a.* خَشِن ـ عَنِيد ـ مُتَجَبِّر ـ وَعِق ـ جامِح ـ جَمُوح ٱلجانِبِ. To be —, to act frowardly, شَرَسَ [2] ـ شَكِسَ ـ عَنَدَ [2].

Frowardly, *ad.* عِنادًا ـ بِعِنادٍ ـ تَجَبُّرًا ـ تَمَرُّدًا.

Frowardness, *n.* تَجَبُّر ـ عِناد ـ شَكاسَة ـ وَعْقَة ـ جُمُوح طَبْعٌ نَكِدٌ.

Frown, *n.* As on the face, قَطْب ـ عَبْس ـ جُهُومَة ـ بَسالَة غَضَن *pl.* غُضُون. Displeasure, سُخْط.

Frown, *v.i.* Of the features, عَبَسَ ـ تَجَهَّمَ ـ بَسَلَ [2] ـ بَسَرَ [2] ـ تَقَطَّبَ ـ كَبَا وَجْهُهُ [2] ـ عَبَّسَ ـ كَلَحَ ـ تَعَبَّسَ ـ وَجْهُهُ عَرْقَصَ جَبِينَهُ ـ قَطَّبَ بَيْنَ عَيْنَيْهِ. To be displeased, سَخِطَ ـ تَسَخَّطَ.

Frown, *v.t.* To — at, to rebuke, express displeasure at, تَسَخَّطَ ـ شَتَمَ [2] ـ سَخِطَ.

Frowning, *a.* As of the face, قاطِبُ ٱلْوَجْهِ ـ جَهْم ـ باسِل. Repelling, threatening, شَتِيم ـ بَشِعُ ٱلْوَجْهِ ـ قَطُوب ـ عَبَّاس ساخِط.

Frowningly, *ad.* As of the face, بِجَبِينٍ مُعَبَّسٍ ـ بِوَجْهٍ مُقَطَّبٍ. Repulsively, كَراهَةً ـ بِتَسَخُّطٍ ـ شَتْمًا ـ سُخْطًا.

Frowy, *a.* *See* Frouzy, *a.*

Frozen, *n.* جامِد ـ قَرِس ـ قارِس. Frozen ground, أَرْضٌ مَضْفُوعَةٌ. To become —, أَجْلَدَ. The ground was —, أَجْلَدَتِ ٱلأَرْضُ.

Frutescence, *n.* أَوانُ ٱلتَّثْمِيرِ ـ تَثْمِير.

Fructiferous, *a.* ثَمْرآء ـ مُثْمِر ـ ثَمِير. A — tree, شَجَرَةٌ ثَمْرآء. A — soil, أَرْضٌ ثَمْرآء.

Fructification, *n.* *See* Fecundation, *n.*

Fructify, *v.t.* To make fruitful, أَغْزَرَ ـ نَبَّتَ ـ خَصَّبَ.

Fructify, *v.i.* أَثْمَرَ ـ أَخْصَبَ ـ أَرْيَفَ. It (of a tree) blossoms but does not —, يُنَوِّرُ وَلا يُرْبِي.

Frugal, *a.* مُعْتَدِل ـ قَتُور ـ مُقْتَصِد. To be — in, إِقْتَصَدَ فِي ـ إِعْتَدَلَ فِي. *See also* Economical, *a.*

Frugality, *n.* إِعْتِدال ـ إِقْتِصاد. To use the blessings of Providence with — is our duty and interest, التَّصَرُّفُ بِخَيْراتِ ٱلْعِنايَةِ ٱلإِلٰهِيَّةِ بِٱلاِقْتِصادِ واجِبٌ عَلَيْنا وَنافِعٌ لَنا. *See also* Economy, *n.*

Frugally, *ad.* بِٱعْتِدالٍ ـ بِٱقْتِصادٍ.

Frugiferous, *a.* *See* Fructiferous, *a.*

Fruit, *n.* The product of a tree, ثَمَرَة ـ أَثْمار ـ ثِمار *pl.* ثَمَر *and* ثَمَرات ـ فاكِهَة *pl.* فَواكِهُ. Advantage, مَنْفَعَة ـ فائِدَة. Consequence, عاقِبَة ـ إِسْتِفادَة ـ نَتِيجَة. Produce, حاصِل ـ مَحْصُول ـ حَصائِلُ *pl.* حَصِيلَة. The — of the womb, حَمْل ـ ثَمَرَةُ ٱلْبَطْنِ. Fruits laid on the table after dinner, نُقْل. A stone —, ثَمَرَةٌ ذاتُ نَواةٍ. A dry —, ثَمَرَةٌ يابِسَةٌ. To preserve —, make them into preserves, رَبَّى ـ عَمِلَ مُرَبَّى. They shall eat the — of their doings, سَيَأْكُلُونَ ثَمَرَ أَفْعالِهِمْ.

Fruit, *v.i.* *See to* Fructify, *v.i.*

Fruiterer, *n.* فَكْهانِيّ ـ فاكِهانِيّ *pl.* فَكْهانِيَّة.

Fruitery, *n.* A loft for fruit, حاصِلُ (or مُسْتَوْدَعُ) ٱلأَثْمارِ. Fruit, in general, فَواكِهُ ـ ثَمَرات.

Fruitful, *a.* Productive, خَصِب ـ ثَمْرآء ـ مُثْمِر ـ خَصِيب; of grain, مُغِلّ; in herbage, مُرِيع. Abundant, كَثِير ـ غَزِير. Broad, of a subject, واسِع. Profitable, نافِع ـ مُفِيد. A — woman, اِمْرَأَةٌ نَثُورٌ ـ اِمْرَأَةٌ نَفُوضٌ ـ نَسُولَة. To be —, of land, أَخْصَبَ ـ أَثْمَرَ; of a woman, نَثَرَتْ [2].

Fruitfully, *ad.* بِبَرَكَةٍ ـ وَفْرَةً ـ إِخْصابًا ـ بِكَثْرَةٍ.

Fruitfulness, *n.* Productiveness, غَنِيمَة ـ بَرَكَة ـ خِصْب; of a woman, نِثار ـ نَثْر ـ نَفْض.

Fruition, *n.* حُصُولٌ عَلَى ٱلْمَرامِ ـ نَيْل ـ حَوْز ـ تَنَعُّم ـ تَمَتُّع.

Fruitless, *a.* Barren of fruit, عاقِر ـ غَيْرُ مُثْمِرٍ. Vain, باطِل ـ بِلا فائِدَةٍ ـ غَيْرُ نافِعٍ ـ لا طائِلَ فِيهِ. Fruitless trees, شَجَرٌ مُتَخَلِّلٌ. All his efforts were —, ذَهَبَ ٱجْتِهادُهُ سُدًى ـ حَبِطَتْ أَعْمالُهُ. To be —, vain, حَبِطَ; to render —, vain, أَحْبَطَ.

Fruitlessly, *ad.* سُدًى ـ بِلا فائِدَةٍ ـ باطِلًا.

Fruitlessness, *n.* Defect of fruit, عَدَمُ ٱلثَّمَرَةِ; of profit, قِلَّةُ نَفْعٍ ـ قِلَّةُ فَائِدَةٍ ـ بُطْلَانُ ـ عَدَمُ طَائِلٍ.

Fruit-tree, *n.* *See under* Fructiferous, *a.*

Fruity, *a.* Tasting of fruit, طَعْمُهُ كَطَعْمِ ٱلْفَاكِهَةِ.

Frumentatious, *a.* Like grain, مِثْلَ ٱلْحَبِّ ـ حُبُوبِيٌّ ـ قَمْحِيٌّ.

Frumenty, *n.* عَصِيدَةٌ.

Frump, *n.* A testy woman, سَلِيطَةٌ ـ سِلْقَةٌ *pl.* سِلْقَان ـ عَاهِرَةٌ. A jeer, jest, هُزْوٌ ـ نُقُورَةٌ ـ قَارِصَةٌ.

Frustrate, *v.t.* To prevent, مَنَعَ ـ عَجَّزَ عَن ـ عَوَّقَ عَن. To balk, خَيَّبَ ـ أَعْجَزَ ـ عَنَّتَ. To nullify, أَبْطَلَ ـ أَعْدَمَ. To be frustrated, balked, خَابَ *aor.* يَخِيبُ.

Frustrate, *a.* مُنْعَدِمٌ ـ بَاطِلٌ ـ خَائِبٌ.

Frustration, *n.* The act of balking, تَخْيِيبٌ ـ عِنَاتٌ; of preventing, مَنْعٌ ـ تَعْوِيقٌ; of nullifying, إِبْطَالٌ ـ إِعْدَامٌ. The being balked, disappointed, خَيْبَةٌ; the being prevented, تَعَوُّقٌ ـ إِمْتِنَاعٌ; the being nullified, بُطْلَانٌ ـ عَدَمٌ. The — of one's hopes, شَمَاتَةٌ.

Frustrative, *a.* مُخَيِّبٌ ـ مُبْطِلٌ ـ مُعْدِمٌ.

Frustrum, *n.* شَكْلٌ نَاقِصٌ. The — of a cone, مَخْرُوطٌ نَاقِصٌ; of a pyramid, هَرَمٌ نَاقِصٌ.

Fry, *v.t.* To cook in a pan, قَلَى ـ قَلًا. Fried, مَقْلُوٌّ ـ مَقْلِيٌّ.

Fry, *v.i.* As in a frying-pan, يُقْلَى. To be in a state of heat or agitation, حَمِيَ ـ إِضْطَرَبَ.

Fry, *n.* That which is fried, قَلِيَّةٌ *pl.* قَلَايَا. A swarm of small fish, صِيرٌ ـ بَسَارِيَةٌ. A swarm, سُرْبَةٌ *pl.* سُرَبٌ ـ كَثْرَةٌ.

Frying-pan, *n.* طَاجِنٌ *pl.* طَوَاجِنُ ـ مِقْلًى ـ مِقْلَاةٌ *pl.* مَقَالِي. He jumped out of the — into the fire (*prov.*) هَرَبَ مِنَ ٱلدُّبِّ وَقَعَ فِي ٱلْجُبِّ.

Fucus, *n.* A kind of seaweed, ضَرْبٌ مِنْ صُوفِ ٱلْبَحْرِ.

Fuddle, *v.t.* أَسْكَرَ ـ سَكَّرَ.

Fuddle, *v.i.* سَكِرَ.

Fuddled, *a.* مَسَّهُ سُكْرٌ ـ سَكْرَانُ.

Fudge, *n.* Nonsense, لَغْوٌ ـ عَبَثٌ. Fudge! أُفٌّ ـ أُفٌّ وَتُفٌّ.

Fuel, *n.* ضِرَامٌ ـ ضَرَمٌ ـ وَقِيدٌ ـ وُقُودٌ ـ حَطَبٌ ـ إِرَاثٌ ـ ثِقَابٌ ـ حُرَاقٌ ـ مَأْكُولُ ٱلنَّارِ. Dry —, جَزْلٌ. Small —, شِيَاعٌ ـ مَشْيُوعٌ. To collect —, حَطَبَ ـ إِحْتَطَبَ.

Fuel, *v.t.* وَضَعَ وَقِيدًا عَلَى ٱلنَّارِ *aor.* يَضَعُ ـ حَشَّ ٱلنَّارَ.

Fugacious, *a.* Volatile, طَيَّارٌ. *See also* Fugitive, *a.*

Fugaciousness, *n.* } Volatility, قَابِلِيَّةُ ٱلتَّطْيِيرِ. *See also* Fugitiveness, *n.*
Fugacity, }

Fugh! *int.* } أُفٌّ ـ تُفٌّ ـ تُوهْ ـ عَزْوَى. Fugh! it was not so, عَزْوَى مَا كَانَ كَذَا.
Foh! }

Fugitive, *a.* Running away, فَارٌّ ـ فَرَّارٌ ـ شَارِدٌ ـ هَارِبٌ ـ فَلٌّ *pl.* فُلُولٌ. Fleeting, زَائِلٌ ـ غَيْرُ ثَابِتٍ ـ سَرِيعُ ٱلزَّوَالِ. Vagabond, هَامِلٌ ـ ضَالٌّ. A — detachment, of soldiers, كَتِيبَةٌ فَرَّى.

Fugitive, *n.* فَرٌّ (this word is masc. and fem., sing., dual, and plural) ـ فَارٌّ ـ شَارِدٌ *pl.* شُرَّدٌ ـ هَارِبٌ. A — slave, آبِقٌ *pl.* أُبَّقٌ *and* أُبَّاقٌ.

Fugitiveness, *n.* Fleetingness, عَدَمُ بَقَاءٍ ـ سُرْعَةُ زَوَالٍ ـ عَدَمُ ثُبُوتٍ.

Fulcrum, *n.* مُغْرِزٌ ـ مُسْنَدٌ ـ مَرْكَزٌ *pl.* مَرَاكِزُ.

Fulfil, *v.t.* To perform, فَعَلَ ـ عَمِلَ ـ أَجْرَى ـ قَضَى. To complete, أَتَمَّ ـ تَمَّمَ ـ أَكْمَلَ ـ كَمَّلَ. To finish, نَجَّزَ ـ أَنْجَزَ. To verify, حَقَّقَ ـ ثَبَّتَ. To —, as of a promise, وَفَى ب *aor.* يَفِي ـ عَهِدَ وَعْدَهُ ـ أَوْفَى ب; of a payment, أَدَّى. *See also to* Accomplish, *v.t.*

Fulfilment, *n.* The act of performance, execution, فِعْلٌ ـ عَمَلٌ ـ إِجْرَاءٌ ـ قَضَاءٌ; of completing, إِتْمَامٌ ـ إِكْمَالٌ ـ تَكْمِيلٌ; of bringing to an end, إِنْجَازٌ ـ تَنْجِيزٌ; of verification, تَحْقِيقٌ ـ إِثْبَاتٌ. The — of a promise, وَفَاءُ وَعْدٍ; of a payment, أَدَاءٌ ـ تَأْدِيَةٌ.

Fulgency, *n.* } شَعْشَعَةٌ ـ رَوْنَقٌ ـ جَلَالَةٌ ـ لَمَعَانٌ ـ سُطُوعٌ. *See also* Effulgence, *n.*
Fulgor, }

Fulgent, *a.* } بَهِيٌّ ـ لَامِعٌ ـ سَاطِعٌ ـ جَلِيٌّ. *See also* Effulgent, *a.*
Fulgid, }

Fuliginous, *a.* دَخِنٌ ـ أَدْخَنُ ـ دُخَانِيٌّ.

Full, *a.* Replete, مُفْعَمٌ ـ مَشْحُونٌ ـ شَاحِنٌ ـ مَمْلُوٌّ ـ مُمْتَلِئٌ ـ مَلْآنُ *fem.* مَلْآنَةٌ *pl.* مِلَاءٌ. Full to the brim, مَوْفُورٌ ـ طَامٍ ـ أَفْعَمُ ـ فَائِضٌ. Abounding in, زَائِدٌ ـ فَائِضٌ ـ غِلٌّ ـ غَلِيلٌ ـ كَثِيرٌ. Fat, سَمِينٌ. Sated, أَكْتَمُ ـ شَبْعَانُ; full of food, كَثِيءٌ ـ كَشِيٌّ. Stuffed, مَحْشِيٌّ ـ مَحْشُوٌّ. Complete, كَامِلٌ ـ تَامٌّ; as of full weight, of a coin, قَائِمٌ. Absolute, as of power, مُطْلَقٌ ـ كُلِّيٌّ. Strong, قَوِيٌّ ـ شَدِيدٌ. Full, as of weight, وَافٍ ـ كَافٍ ـ مُسْتَوْفٍ. Full, ample, as of a dress, سَابِغٌ ـ وَاسِعٌ. Full, as ears of wheat, لَبِيبٌ ـ سَمِينٌ ـ غَلِيظٌ. Full, bushy, لَثِيثٌ ـ جَثِلٌ. Full, thick, كَثِيفٌ. Detailed, مُفَصَّلٌ. Solid, مُصْمَتٌ. Full of days, مُسِنٌّ ـ طَاعِنٌ فِي ٱلسِّنِّ. Of full age, أَشُدٌّ: until he attains full age, حَتَّى يَبْلُغَ أَشُدَّهُ. Three full years, ثَلَاثُ سَنَوَاتٍ كَامِلَةٍ. Full of business, كَثِيرُ ٱلْأَشْغَالِ. Full of play, لَعَّابٌ. Full of nonsense, عِبِّيثٌ. The full moon, بَدْرٌ ـ

قَمْرٌ تامٌّ. One who has full power in ..., مُطْلَقُ ٱلْإِرَادَةِ فِي. Full (official) dress, مَلابِسُ رَسْمِيَّةٌ: to be in full dress, لَبِسَ ٱلْمَلابِسَ ٱلرَّسْمِيَّةَ. Full pay, مَعاشٌ كامِلٌ. To have full knowledge of, وَقَفَ عَلَى-وُقُوفًا كُلِّيًّا aor. يَقِفُ. To be full, replete, كانَ مَلآنًا — تَمَلَّأَ — تَنَعَّمَ — ² نَعُمَ. To be full, as of ears of wheat, etc., إِسْتَغْلَظَ — ² سَمِنَ — لَبَّبَ — حَبَّلَ ٱلزَّرْعُ. To make full, as of a garment, أَوْسَعَ — أَسْبَغَ. To be —, as a boil, تَقَصَّعَ. To be full to overflowing, ² طَفَحَ. The country has become full of them, إِمْتَلَأَتِ ٱلْبِلادُ مِنْهُمْ.

Full, n. The state of satiety, شَبَعٌ. Completeness, كَمالٌ — وَفاءٌ — تَغْلِيقُ ٱلْحِسابِ. In full of all demands, تَمامَةٌ — تَمامٌ — وافٍ. In full, completely, بِٱلْكُلِّيَّةِ — بِٱلْمَرَّةِ — إِتْمامًا — بَتَّةً.

Full, ad. Quite, بِٱلْكُلِّيَّةِ — بَتَّةً. Exactly, ضَبْطًا — بِدِقَّةٍ — فِي غايَةِ ٱلْإِتْقانِ. Full little, قَلِيلًا جِدًّا. Full well he knew, ² عَرَفَ جَيِّدًا (or حَقَّ ٱلْمَعْرِفَةِ). Full many, كَثِيرٌ — كَثِيرُونَ. Full many a ..., كَمْ مِنَ ٱلْ....

Full, v.t. To —, as of cloth, ² قَصَرَ — ² خَبَطَ — خَبَّطَ.

Full-blown, a. فَغُومٌ. A — rose, فَغْرٌ — وَرْدَةٌ مُفَتَّحَةٌ.

Full-bodied, a. Bulky, شَخِيصٌ. As of wine, رَحِيقٌ.

Full-eared, a. سَنابِلُهُ مَلآنَةٌ — مُلَبَّبُ ٱلسَّنابِلِ.

Full-formed, a. فَعْمٌ.

Fuller, n. A — of cloth, قَصّارٌ — مُقَصِّرٌ. A fuller's hammer, مِقْصَرَةٌ — مِيجَنَةٌ — كُذَيْنَقٌ.

Fuller's-earth, n. بَيْلُونٌ.

Fullery, n. مَقْصَرَةٌ.

Full-grown, a. Of plants or men, كَهْلٌ pl. كُهْلانٌ — مُكْتَهِلٌ. To be —, إِكْتَهَلَ.

Full-manned, a. كامِلٌ (or مُكَمَّلٌ) ٱلشَّحْنَةِ — مَشْحُونٌ.

Fulling-mill, n. دُولابُ ٱلْقَصّارِ.

Fullness, n. Repletion, مَلْءٌ — إِمْتِلاءٌ — فَعامَةٌ — فَيْضٌ — شَحْنٌ. Completion, كَمالٌ — تَمامٌ. Satiety, إِمْتِلاءٌ — شَبَعٌ. Force, قُوَّةٌ — بِذْءٌ. Breadth, as of a dress, سُبُوغٌ — سَعَةٌ. Fullness of heart, joy, مِلْءُ ٱلزَّمانِ — كَمالُ ٱلْمَسَرَّةِ — فَوَرانُ ٱلْقَلْبِ. The — of time, إِتْمامُ ٱلْمِيعادِ. The — of the sea, زَخْرَةُ ٱلْبَحْرِ.

Full-orbed, a. مُقَرَّصٌ — مُدَوَّرٌ — دائِرٌ — قُرْصِيٌّ.

Fully, ad. Entirely, تَمامًا — بِٱلْكُلِّيَّةِ. Perfectly, فِي غايَةِ ٱلْإِتْقانِ — بِٱلْكَمالِ — تَكْمِيلًا — كَما يَلِيقُ. Properly, بِلِياقَةٍ. Conformably, تَطْبِيقًا. To be — come, of time, وَصَلَ aor. يَصِلُ — ² حَضَرَ — إِنْقَضَى. Fully persuaded, مُتَيَقِّنٌ. Fully able, قادِرٌ عَلَى.

Fulminate, v.i. To thunder, أَرْعَدَ. To express denunciations, أَرْعَدَ وَأَبْرَقَ — ² رَعَدَ وَبَرَقَ — تَسَخَّطَ — ² سَخِطَ. Fulminating against, مُرْعِدٌ عَلَى. The Government continues to —, لَمْ تَزَلِ ٱلدَّوْلَةُ تُرْعِدُ وَتُبْرِقُ.

Fulminate, v.t. To issue, publish, نادَى بِ — أَشْهَرَ. To utter denunciations against, ² لَعَنَ — تَسَخَّطَ عَلَى — ² سَخِطَ عَلَى. To explode, فَقَّعَ — نَوَّرَ — أَطْلَقَ.

Fulminating-powder, n. بارُودٌ مُزَنْبَقٌ — مَعْجُونٌ كِيماوِيٌّ فَقّاعٌ.

Fulmination, n. Denunciation, لَعْنٌ — تَسَخُّطٌ — سَخَطٌ. Explosion, إِطْلاقٌ — تَنْوِيرٌ. The — of ecclesiastical censures, مُناداةٌ بِعُقُوباتٍ كَنائِسِيَّةٍ.

Fulminatory, a. مُرْعِدٌ وَمُبْرِقٌ — مُرْعِدٌ — مُرْعِبٌ — ساخِطٌ.

Fulsome, a. Offensive, gross, فاحِشٌ — مُقْرِفٌ — مَكْرُوهٌ — كَرِيهٌ. Rank, مُنْتِنٌ — مُعَفَّنٌ. Coarse, غَلِيظٌ. Fulsome praise, إِطْراءٌ.

Fulsomely, ad. بِغَلاظَةٍ — بِفُحْشٍ — بِكَراهَةٍ. To praise —, أَطْرَى.

Fulsomeness, n. كَراهِيَةٌ — فُحْشٌ — غَلاظَةٌ — كَراهَةٌ.

Fulvid, a. }
Fulvous, } زَعْفَرانِيٌّ — أَصْفَرُ.

Fumble, v.i. To do awkwardly, ² خَرِقَ — ² خَرُقَ — تَغَفَّلَ — طَنْبَلَ. To grope with the hands, عَيَّثَ — عَيْثٌ.

Fumbler, n. } عِفْشٌ — مُتَغَفِّلٌ — مُعَيِّثٌ — أَخْرَقُ — خَرِقٌ
Fumbling, a. } طَنْبَلٌ — عَكِسٌ. See also Clumsy, a.

Fumblingly, ad. مِثْلَ — بِعَفَشٍ — تَغَفُّلًا — تَعْيِيثًا — بِخُرْقٍ — ٱلطَّنْبَلِ.

Fume, n. Smoke, دُخانٌ. Vapour, بُخارٌ pl. أَبْخِرَةٌ and بُخاراتٌ. The —, as of passion, هَيَجانٌ — حِمَرَّةٌ — حُمَيّا. Conceit, زَهْوٌ — كِبْرِياءٌ. The fumes of the cup mounted into his head, صارَتْ فِيهِ حُمَيّا ٱلْكَأْسِ.

Fume, v.i. To smoke, أَدْخَنَ — دَخَّنَ — ² دَخَنَ. To yield vapour, ² بَخَرَ. To be in a rage, ² حَمِيَ أَنْفُهُ — إِحْتَمَى غَضَبًا — إِغْتاظَ.

Fume, v.t. To smoke, دَخَّنَ; to perfume, بَخَّرَ.

Fumiferous, a. ذُو بُخارٍ — مُدَخِّنٌ — داخِنٌ.

Fumigate, v.t. To smoke, عَثَّنَ — دَخَّنَ — عَثَنَ; to perfume, بَخَّرَ. To — one's self, تَبَخَّرَ.

Fumigation, n. The act of perfuming, تَبْخِيرٌ. The emission of perfume or vapour, بَخْرٌ. Any substance for —, دُخْنَةٌ — ذَرِيرَةٌ — بَخُورٌ.

Fumitory, n. The plant, بَقْلَةُ ٱلْمَلِكِ — ٱلشّاهْتَرَجُ — شاهْتَرَجٌ.

Fumy, a. See Fumiferous, a.

Fun, *n.* Sport, هَذَر ـ هَزْل ـ مِزاح ـ لَعِب ـ نُعُومَة. Serious — or joking, الهَزْلُ ٱلَّذِى يُرادُ بِهِ ٱلْجِدُّ. To have —, sport, لَعِبَ. To make — of, هَزَأَ ب ـ شَمَّعَ ب ـ مِن *or* ب *or* مِن ضَحِكَ ـ عَلَى *or* ب ـ سَخِرَ ب ـ شاقَحَ.

Funambulist, *n.* بَهْلَوان.

Function, *n.* Action, خِدْمَة ـ فِعْل ـ عَمَل. A faculty, قُوَّة ـ حاسَّة *pl.* حَواسّ. An office, مَأْمُورِيَّة ـ خِدْمَة ـ مَنْصِب ـ وَظِيفَة. An employment, شُغْل. Public or official functions, خِدْمَة رَسْمِيَّة ـ مَأْمُورِيَّة رَسْمِيَّة. To enter upon the functions of ..., شَرَعَ فِى إِجْرَاءِ مَأْمُورِيَّةِ ٱلْ... To fulfil the functions of ..., أَجْرَى مَأْمُورِيَّةَ ٱلْ... The animal functions, الحَرَكاتُ ـ حَرَكاتُ ٱلْجَسَدِ ـ الحَواسّ ـ الحَرَكاتُ ٱلْحَيَوانِيَّة. The mental functions, الحَرَكاتُ ٱلْعَقْلِيَّة ـ ٱلذِّهْنِيَّة.

Functional, *a.* مُخْتَصّ بِٱلْحَرَكاتِ ـ فِعْلِىّ ـ عَمَلِىّ.

Functionally, *ad.* Operatively, نَظَرًا لِلْعَمَلِ ـ حَرَكَةً ـ بِٱلْعَمَلِ. Officially, رَسْمًا.

Functionary, *n.* مَأْمُور *pl.* مَأْمُورُون. High functionaries, المَأْمُورُونَ ٱلْمُكَرَّمُونَ ـ أَوْلِيَاءُ ٱلْأُمُورِ ـ أَصْحابُ ٱلْمَناصِبِ ٱلْعَلِيَّة. A public —, صاحِبُ مَنْصِبٍ رَسْمِىّ.

Fund, *n.* Stock, resource, ذَخِيرَة ـ خَزِينَة ـ كَنْز. Stock, capital, أَصْلُ مالٍ ـ رَأْسُ مالٍ (*vulg.* رَسْمال). The public funds, خَزِينَةُ ٱلدَّوْلَةِ ـ المالِيَّة. A sinking —, مَبْلَغٌ لِإِلْغاءِ قَرْضٍ وَٱسْتِهْلاكِهِ.

Fund, *v.t.* To consolidate a debt, عَيَّنَ مَبْلَغًا لِوَفاءِ ٱلدَّيْنِ. To place, as money in the public funds, وَضَعَ ـ *aor.* يَضَعُ ـ فِى ٱلدُّيُونِ ٱلْمِيرِيَّةِ.

Fundament, *n.* إِسْت ـ دُبُر ـ مَقْعَد.

Fundamental, *a.* مُؤَسِّس ـ أَساسِىّ ـ أَصْلِىّ. A — principle, قاعِدَةٌ أَساسِيَّةٌ. A — point, مادَّةٌ جَوْهَرِيَّةٌ. A — law, نِظامٌ مُؤَسِّس.

Fundamentally, *ad.* Primarily, عَلَى أَساسٍ ـ تَأْسِيسًا ـ عَلَى عَنْ أَصْلٍ ـ ٱلْأُصُولِ. Necessarily, مِنَ ٱللُّزُومِ ـ بِٱلضَّرُورَةِ.

Fundamentals, *n.* قَواعِدُ أَصْلِيَّةٌ ـ أَرْكان ـ أُصُول.

Funded, *a.* مُنْتَظِم. A — debt, دَيْنٌ مُنْتَظِمٌ.

Funebrial, } مُتَعَلِّقٌ بِدَفْنِ ٱلْمَوْتَى ـ جِنائِزِىّ. Mournful,
Funeral, *a.* } مُحْزِن ـ حَزِين. A — service, رُتْبَةُ لِدَفْنِ
Funereal, } ٱلْمَوْتَى. A — oration, نُدْبَة ـ مَرْثاة. To pronounce a — oration, رَثَى ٱلْمَيِّتَ.

Funeral, *n.* جِنازَة *pl.* جَنائِزُ. His — was conducted with the greatest solemnity and respect, شُيِّعَتْ جِنازَتُهُ بِغايَةِ ٱلْاِحْتِفالِ وَٱلْإِكْرام. His — was attended by a large company, حَضَرَ دَفْنَهُ جَمٌّ غَفِيرٌ ـ شُيِّعَتْ جِنازَتُهُ بِجَمٍّ غَفِيرٍ.

Fungosity, *n.* عِلَّةٌ ناشِئَةٌ فِى ٱلْأَجْسامِ شِبْهَ ٱلْإِسْفَنْجِ.

Fungous, *a.* Like a mushroom, spongy, إِسْفَنْجِىّ ـ مِثْلَ ٱلْفُطْرِ. Excrescent, فاضِل.

Fungus, *n.* A mushroom, فُطْر *pl.* فَطارَى ـ عَرْهُون *pl.* عَراهِين. Mouldiness, عُفُونَة. A fleshy excrescence, عُشُّ ٱلْغُرابِ ـ فَضْلَةٌ فِى ٱللَّحْمِ.

Funicle, *n.* خَيْطُ قِنَّبٍ ـ دُبارَة.

Funnel, *n.* A chimney, داخِنَة *pl.* دَواخِن. A tunnel for fluids, قَمْع ـ إِسْكابَة. A pipe, قَناة. The — of a mill, دَلْو ـ قادُوس.

Funnel-shaped, *a.* فِى شَكْلِ ٱلْقَمْعِ ـ بِصُورَةِ ٱلْإِسْكابَةِ.

Funny, *a.* Droll, of a person, لَطِيف ـ مُهَرِّج ـ مُضْحِك ـ مَسْخَرَة. A — or ridiculous thing, أُضْحُوكَة ـ مَسْخَرَة.

Fur, *n.* Fine soft hair, وَبَر *pl.* وِبار ـ فَرْوَة *pl.* فَرَوات. Skin, جِلْد *pl.* جُلُود. The — of the ermine, سِنْجاب; of the marten, سَمُّور. A tunic lined with fur, فَرْوَة *pl.* فِرَاء *and* فَرَوات ـ جُبَّة مُفَرّاة. Morbid matter, as on the tongue, وَسَخ. Hard coating, as in boilers, *etc.*, رُسابَة ـ قُرَّة. Having no fur, أَصْقَف. A seller of fur, فَرّاء. To wear fur, اِفْتَرَى.

Fur, *v.t.* To line with fur, بَطَّنَ بِفَرْوَةٍ ـ فَرَّى. To cover with morbid matter, وَسَّخَ. To board, تَخَّتَ.

Furbelow, *n.* تَعْرِيج *pl.* تَعارِيج *and* تَعْرِيجات.

Furbelow, *v.t.* زَيَّنَ بِتَعارِيجَ.

Furbish, *v.t.* جَلَّى ـ صَقَلَ ـ جَلَى.

Furbisher, *n.* صَيْقَل *pl.* صَياقِل ـ صَقّال ـ هالِكِىّ.

Furcate, *a.* } مُتَشَعِّب ـ ذُو شُعَبٍ.
Furcated, }

Furfuraceous, *a.* Scurfy, ذُو حَزازٍ ـ ذُو هِبْرِيَةٍ.

Furious, *a.* Vehement, raging, مَسْعُور ـ سَعِير ـ هائِج ـ هَيّاج ـ مُتَهَوِّر. Strong, عاصِف ـ قَوِىّ ـ شَدِيد. Exasperated, حارِد ـ غَضُوب ـ ساخِط ـ مُتَحَرِّش ـ حَرْدان. Mad, مَجْنُون. To be —, exasperated, اِغْتاظَ ـ تَسَخَّطَ ـ تَهَوَّرَ ـ سَخِطَ. A — sea, بَحْرٌ زَخّار ـ بَحْرٌ زاخِر.

Furiously, *ad.* Vehemently, سُعُورًا ـ هِياجًا. With force, بِعَصَبٍ ـ تَسَخُّطًا ـ بِسَخَطٍ. With exasperation, بِعُنْفٍ ـ بِشِدَّةٍ وَسُخْطٍ. Madly, بِجُنُونٍ. He drives —, يَسُوقُ بِجُنُونٍ.

Furiousness, *n.* Vehemence, حِدَّة ـ شِدَّة ـ سُعُور ـ هِياج; as of the sea, زُخُور ـ زَخْر. Rage, غَضَب ـ سُخْط. Madness, جُنُون.

Furl, *v.t.* To — a sail, طَوَى ٱلْقِلْعَ ـ.

Furlong, *n.* فَرْسَخ *pl.* فَرَاسِخُ.

Furlough, *n.* رُخْصَةٌ بِٱلْغِيَابِ.

Furlough, *v.t.* رَخَّصَ لِ-بِٱلْغِيَابِ.

Furnace, *n.* An oven, وَطِيسٌ ـ سَاعُور. A — where bricks are made; also the — of a bath, أَتُّون *pl.* أَتَاتِينُ. A — lined with brick, شَاخُورَة. A blacksmith's —, كِيرٌ *pl.* أَكْيَار ـ كُورٌ *pl.* أَكْوَار ـ مِجْمَرَة *pl.* مَجَامِرُ.

Furnish, *v.t.* To supply, provide with, أَمَدَّ-بِ ـ جَهَّزَ-بِ ـ زَوَّدَ-بِ ـ أَعَدَّ-لِ. To — with, as with tools, or other requirements, for, أَهَّبَ-لِ. To —, as of a house, فَرَشَ ـ نَجَّدَ ـ أَثَّثَ. To — a place with what is necessary, عَمَّرَ (or جَهَّزَ) ٱلْمَكَانَ بِمَا ٱحْتَاجَ إِلَيْهِ. To — with arms, سَلَّحَ. To be furnished, supplied, تَجَهَّزَ ـ تَأَهَّبَ; of a house, إِنْفَرَشَ ـ تَنَجَّدَ.

Furnisher, *n.* A — of household furniture, فَرَّاش ـ نَجَّاد ـ بَيَّاعُ ٱلْأَثَاثِ.

Furniture, *n.* Apparatus, أَدَاة ـ مَتَاع *pl.* أَمْتِعَة ـ مَعَاش. Household —, مَتَاعُ ٱلْبَيْتِ ـ نِجَاد ـ مَرَمَّةُ ٱلْبَيْتِ ـ ثُمّ ـ جَهَاز. Decoration, زُخْرُف ـ تَزْيِين ـ أَثَاثُ ٱلْبَيْتِ ـ فَرْشُ ٱلْبَيْتِ. Old —, رِثَّة (or سَقَط) ٱلْمَتَاعِ. A seller of old —, سَقَطِيّ.

Furrier, *n.* فَرَّاء.

Furriery, *n.* فِرَاوَى.

Furring, *n.* A lining of fur, بِطَانَةُ فَرْوَةٍ; of boards, فَرْش ـ تَخْشِيب ـ تَخْتِيت.

Furrow, *n.* As made by the plough, خُدَّة *pl.* خُدَد ـ أُخْدُود *pl.* أَخَادِيدُ. A trench, حُفْرَة *pl.* حُفَر ـ أُخْدُود. A — in the sea made by a ship, شَجّ. A wrinkle, غَضْن *pl.* غُضُون.

Furrow, *v.t.* To — land, عَزَقَ ـ فَلَجَ ـ خَدَّ. To —, as a ship the sea, مَخَرَ ـ شَجَّ. To wrinkle, غَضَّنَ. To be furrowed, of land, تَخَدَّدَ; of the sea, شُجَّ. His flesh was furrowed, تَخَدَّدَ لَحْمُهُ. Furrowed land, أَرْضٌ مُشَطَّبَةٌ ـ أَرْضٌ مَعْزُوقَةٌ. The horses furrowed the ground with their hoofs, جَرَّتِ ٱلْخَيْلُ ٱلْأَرْضَ بِسَنَابِكِهَا.

Furry, *a.* ذُو فَرْوَةٍ ـ وَبِر.

Further, *a.* Additional, أَزْيَدُ ـ أَكْثَرُ *vulg.* كَمَان. More distant, أَبْعَدُ ـ أَقْصَى. Till — orders, إِلَى أَنْ ـ إِلَى أَنْ يَصْدُرَ أَمْرٌ جَدِيدٌ ـ يُعْطَى أَمْرٌ مُسْتَجِدٌّ. Further confirmation respecting . . . , مُبَالَغَةٌ ٱلتَّحْقِيقِ عَنْ

Further, *ad.* Moreover, ثُمَّ ـ زِدْ عَلَى ذٰلِكَ ـ وَمَا عَدَا ذٰلِكَ ـ أَيْضًا ـ مِنْ دُونِ ذٰلِكَ ـ غَيْرَ ذٰلِكَ.

Further, *v.t.* رَوَّجَ ـ رَقَّى ـ دَرَّجَ ـ قَدَّمَ ـ أَعَانَ ـ سَاعَدَ.

Furtherance, *n.* تَدْرِيج ـ تَرْوِيج ـ مُسَاعَدَة ـ مُعَاوَنَة.

Furtherer, *n.* مُدَرِّج ـ مُغِيث ـ مُسَاعِد ـ مُعِين.

Furthermore, *ad.* *See* Further, *ad.*

Furthermost, *a.* }
Furthest, } ٱلْأَبْعَدُ ـ ٱلْأَقْصَى.

Furtive, *a.* مَسْتُور ـ خَفِيّ ـ مَسْرُوق.

Furtively, *a.* خِفْيَةً ـ بِٱسْتِرَاقٍ. To look — at, رَنَا ـ رَنَقَ ٱلنَّظَرَ إِلَى ـ سَارَقَ ٱلنَّظَرَ إِلَى ـ رَامَقَ. One who listens —, مُسْتَرِق. To do anything —, إِسْتَرَقَ.

Furuncle, *n.* دُمَّل *pl.* دَمَامِلُ ـ حَبَّة *pl.* حُبُوب.

Fury, *n.* A violent rushing, هِيَاج ـ هَيَجَان ـ حُمَيَّا. Vehemence, شِدَّة ـ جِدَّة ـ قُوَّة. Rage of passion, تَهَوُّر ـ سُخْط ـ غَضَب ـ جُنُون ـ سُعُور; as of the sea, زَخْر ـ زُخُور. A shrew, عَاهِرَة ـ إِمْرَأَةٌ فَحْلَةٌ ـ خَطَّالَة ـ عَاجِرَة.

Furze, *n.* رَتَم ـ رَتِيمَة ـ وَزَّال.

Furzy, *a.* رَتَمِيّ ـ ذُو وَزَّالٍ ـ ذُو رَتِيمَةٍ.

Fuscous, *a.* كَدِر ـ كَابٍ.

Fuse, *v.t.* حَلَّ ـ سَبَكَ ـ ذَوَّبَ ـ أَذَابَ.

Fuse, *v.i.* تَمَيَّعَ ـ تَحَلَّلَ ـ ذَابَ ـ مَاعَ.

Fuse, *n.* A pipe for shell, grenades, *etc.*, فَوْشِيق *pl.* فَوَاشِيقُ ـ أَبُو قَصَبَةٍ ـ صَارُوخ *pl.* صَوَارِيخُ. A squib, فَشَكَة *coll.* فَشَك.

Fusee, *n.* A small firelock, مِكْحَلَةٌ (or بُنْدُقِيَّةٌ) صَغِيرَةٌ. The cone, as of a watch or clock, دُولَاب *pl.* دَوَالِيبُ.

Fusibility, *n.* قَابِلِيَّةُ ٱلْإِذَابَةِ ـ ذَوَبَان ـ إِنْسِبَاك ـ سَيَحَان.

Fusible, *a.* }
Fusil, } قَابِلُ ٱلْإِذَابَةِ ـ يَنْسَبِكُ ـ يَنْحَلُّ.

Fusiform, *a.* فِي شَكْلِ ٱلْمِغْزَلِ.

Fusileer, *n.* حَامِلُ بُنْدُقِيَّةٍ (or مِكْحَلَةٍ).

Fusion, *n.* The act of melting, حَلّ ـ سَبْك ـ تَسْيِيح ـ إِذَابَة. Union, إِتِّحَاد ـ إِتِّفَاق ـ إِمْتِزَاج.

Fuss, *n.* بَعْثَرَة ـ شَغْب ـ بَعْثَرَة ـ عَجِيج ـ لَشْلَشَة ـ فَرْفَرَة ـ إِضْطِرَاب ـ قَرْقَعَة ـ غَوْغَاء ـ فَشْفَشَة. To make a — about, to magnify, إِسْتَعْظَمَ. They made a great — about or around him, as with attentions, حَشَدُوا لَهُ.

Fuss, *v.i.* To make a —, عَجَّ ـ ضَجَّ ـ فَرْفَرَ ـ لَشْلَشَ ـ إِضْطَرَبَ ـ تَبَعْثَرَ ـ تَبَعْثَرَ ـ نَفَشَ رُوحَهُ.

Fussy, *a.* مُتَبَعْثِر ـ مُتَبَعْثِر ـ عَجَّاج ـ فَرْفَار ـ مُتَحَبِّل.

Fust, *n.* As of a pillar, أُسْطُوَانَةُ عَمُودٍ ـ طُولُ ٱلْعَمُودِ. A musty smell, عُفُونَة.

Fust, *v.i.* To become musty, تَعَفَّنَ.

Fustian, *n.* The cloth, أَلاجَة ـ قُماشٌ مِنْ قُطْنٍ وَكَتّانٍ. A swelling style, لَغْوٌ ـ تَفَنُّن ـ طَرْمَذَة ـ العَظائِمُ. To talk —, طَرْمَذَ ـ ² نَفَخَ فِي ٱلْكَلامِ ـ تَكَلَّمَ بِٱلْعَظائِمِ.

Fustian, *a.* Made of —, مِنَ ٱلاجَةِ ـ مِنْ قُطْنٍ وَكَتّانٍ. Bombastic, طِرْماذ ـ مُتَنَفِّخ ـ مَفِنٌّ.

Fustiness, *n.* عُفُونَة ـ عَفَن ـ نَتانَة.

Fusty, *a.* مُعَفَّن ـ عَفِن ـ ونَتِن.

Futile, *a.* لا طائِلَ لَهُ ـ باطِل ـ عَبَث.

Futility, *n.* عَدَمُ طائِلَةٍ ـ بُطْل ـ عَبَث.

Futtocks, *n.* The — of a ship, أَطْواقُ ٱلْمَرْكَبِ ٱلْمُتَوَسِّطَةُ.

Future, *a.* To come hereafter, مُزْمِع ـ قابِل ـ آتٍ ـ مُسْتَقْبِل. To be in the —, إِسْتَقْبَلَ. The — tense of a verb, المُضارِعُ ـ المُسْتَقْبِلُ. Indicative — (tense), مُضارِعٌ مَرْفُوعٌ; apocopate —, مُضارِعٌ مَجْزُومٌ.

Future, *n.* المُسْتَقْبِلُ ـ جَيّآت ـ وَتّى. In —, for the —, مِنَ ٱلآنَ وَصاعِدًا ـ فِيما بَعْدُ. A wide opening is made thereby for its —, فَتَحَتْ بِذٰلِكَ طَرِيقًا واسِعًا لِمُسْتَقْبِلِ حالِها.

Futurity, *n.* الزَّمَنُ ٱلْمُقْبِلُ. The unknown of the —, الغَيْبُ. To all —, إِلَى أَبَدِ ٱلآبِدِينَ ـ إِلَى أَبَدِ ٱلآبادِ ـ إِلَى ٱلأَبَدِ.

Fy! *int.* تُفٍّ ـ أُفٍّ. Fy upon him! أَفًّا لَهُ وَتُفًّا ـ أُفِّهْ. Fy upon you! عَيْبٌ عَلَيْكَ.

G.

Gab, *n.* The mouth, tongue, لِسان ـ كَلام. The gift of the —, لِسانٌ طَلِقٌ.

Gab, *v.i.* *See to* Gabble, *v i.*

Gabble, *v.i.* فَضْفَضَ (or نَرْثَرَ) ـ ² هَذَرَ ـ ³ سابَ فِي ٱلْكَلامِ. To — over, زَخْلَفَ فِي ٱلْكَلامِ ـ ³ هَذْرَمَ ـ هَذْرَمَ فِي ٱلْكَلامَ.

Gabble, *n.* لَبْلَبَة ـ هَيْنام ـ هَذَر ـ بَقّ ـ الشَّيُوبُ فِي ٱلْكَلِمِ ـ هَذْرَمَة ـ فَضْفَضَة ـ ثَرْثَرَة.

Gabbler, *n.* بَقّاق ـ هُذارِم ـ فَضْفاض ـ فَشّار ـ ثَرْثار ـ مِهْذار.

Gabion, *n.* قُفَّةٌ مَمْلُوَّةٌ تُرابًا تُوضَعُ فِي بِناءِ ٱلاسْتِحْكاماتِ ٱلْخَفِيفَةِ ـ قُفَّةٌ مِنْ قُفَفِ ٱلطّابِيَةِ *pl.* قُفَف.

Gable, *n.* حائِطٌ جَمَلُونٍ.

Gable-end, *n.* طَرَفُ ٱلْجَمَلُونِ.

Gabriel, *n.* جِبْرِيلُ ـ جِبْرائِيلُ; called also in the Kurân, ٱلرُّوحُ ـ رُوحُ ٱلْقُدُسِ ـ ٱلأَمِينُ.

Gad, *n.* A wedge, سَفَن ـ شَرْخ *pl.* شُرُوخ. A graving-tool, مِنْقاش. A punch, مِثْقَب.

Gad, *v.i.* To gad about, تَرَدَّدَ ـ تَطَوَّفَ ـ ² دارَ ـ ³ هامَ ـ طَوَّفَ. To gad about among, ² طافَ بِ (or بَيْنَ).

Gadabout, *n.} دَوّار ـ خَرّاجٌ وَلّاجٌ ـ طَوّاف ـ وُلَجَةٌ خُرَجَةٌ; of a female, زَلِزَة ـ طَوّافَة.

Gadder, Gadabout women, سَوّآءُ لَوّآءُ.

Gad-fly, *n.* نُعَرَة ـ ذُبابُ ٱلْخَيْلِ ـ زَنابِيرُ *pl.* زُنْبُور.

Gaff, *n.* A hook, خُطّاف *pl.* خَطاطِيف ـ كُلّاب *pl.* كَلالِيب. Of a ship, باسْتُون ـ جارِيَة.

Gaffer, *n.* إِخْتِيار ـ شَيْخ *pl.* شُيُوخ.

Gaffle, *n.* مِهْمازٌ يُشَدُّ فِي رِجْلِ ٱلدِّيكِ لِلْمُبارَزَةِ.

Gag, *v.t.* حَطَّ عُقْلَةً فِي فَمِهِ ـ ² كَعَمَ ـ ² شَجَرَ فاهُ.

Gag, *n.* عُقْلَة ـ كِعام ـ شِجار.

Gage, *n.* A pledge, عَرَبُون ـ رَهِينَة ـ رَهْن. A measure, قِياس.

Gage, *v.t.* To pledge, ² رَهَنَ. To measure, ³ قاسَ ـ عايَرَ.

Gaiety, *n.* *See* Gayety, *n.*

Gaily, *ad.* Cheerfully, بِٱبْتِهاجٍ ـ بِفَرَحٍ ـ بِغِبْطَةٍ. Splendidly, بِبَهآءٍ ـ بِجَلالٍ ـ بِفَخْرٍ.

Gain, *n.* Profit, كَسْب ـ مَكْسَب; in trade, رَباح ـ رِبْح ـ فَوائِضُ ٱلْمالِ. A return, مَرْجُوع ـ رِجْعَة. Earnings, حُباشَة ـ خَيْر ـ فائِدَة ـ مَنْفَعَة ـ نِفاع *pl.* نَفْع. An advantage, حَبْش. Progress, تَقَدُّم ـ تَدَرُّج ـ تَرَقٍّ ـ نَجاح ـ إِفْلاح. Greedy of —, مُوْلَعٌ بِٱلْكَسْبِ. To make or get —; *see under next article.*

Gain, *v.t.* To acquire, إِسْتَقْرَفَ ـ إِكْتَسَبَ ـ ³ حَصَلَ عَلَى ـ ² رَبِحَ فِي (or أَفْضَلَ. To — in trade, ² فازَ بِ ـ إِقْتَنَعَ ـ ³ نالَ (فِي) ٱلتِّجارَةِ. To win, ³ غَلَبَ ـ ² ظَفِرَ بِ ـ ² فازَ بِ. To reach, ² بَلَغَ ـ ² لَحِقَ. To earn, ² حَبَشَ ـ حَبَّشَ. To draw over, as to a party, ³ جَذَبَ-إِلَى ـ أَرْضَى-لِ ـ أَقْبَلَ-عَلَى. To — another's affections, ³ مَلَكَ قَلْبَهُ ـ تَوَدَّدَ-إِلَى. To —, as one's ends, ² بَلَغَ مَقْصُودَهُ ـ ³ نالَ مُرادَهُ ـ أَنْفَذَ ـ ³ نَفَذَ ـ ² فازَ بِ. To — ground, تَقَدَّمَ ـ أَفْلَحَ. To make to —, أَكْسَبَ ـ كَسَّبَ ـ أَرْبَحَ.

Gain, *v.i.* To advance, to — ground, تَقَدَّمَ ـ تَدَرَّجَ ـ ² فازَ. To get deeper into a matter, تَعَمَّقَ فِي . To — on, to outstrip, سَابَقَ . To — upon, to prevail against, قَوِيَ ـ ظَفِرَ بِ ـ غَلَبَ عَلَى . To obtain influence with, تَدَاخَلَ مَعَ ـ إِسْتَمْلَكَ عَلَى .

Gainer, n. مُسْتَفِيد ـ مُنْتَفِع ـ رَابِح ـ كَاسِب ـ كَسُوب . The Muslims were the gainers, had the best of it, فَكَانَ ٱلْفَوْزُ لِلْمُسْلِمِينَ .

Gainful, a. فِيهِ مَكْسَبٌ ـ نَافِع ـ مُفِيد ـ رَبِيح ـ رَابِح .

Gainsay, v.t. To deny, أَكْذَبَ ـ كَذَّبَ ـ أَنْكَرَ ـ نَكَرَ . To oppose, إِعْتَرَضَ عَلَى ـ قَاوَمَ ـ نَاقَضَ ـ ضَادَّ ـ خَالَفَ .

Gainsayer, n. مُعْتَرِضٌ عَلَى ـ مُقَاوِم ـ مُضَادّ ـ مُنَاقِض ـ مُنْكِر .

Gainsaying, n. مُقَاوَمَة ـ مُضَادَّة ـ مُنَاقَضَة ـ إِنْكَار ـ نُكْر ـ إِعْتِرَاض .

Gairish, a. بَهِيّ ـ مُنِير ـ نَيِّر .

Gairishness, n. جَلْوَة ـ بَهَآء .

Gait, n. مِشْيَة ـ سَمْت pl. سُمُوت ـ سِيرَة . An affected —, خَطَرَان ـ تَغَيُّف ـ إِبْزَآء . To walk with an affected —, تَغَيَّفَ ـ خَطَرَ .

Gaiter, n. جُرْمُوق ـ ضَرْبٌ مِنَ ٱلْجَوْرَبِ .

Gala, n. عِيد ـ فَرَح ـ مَوْسِم . A — day, يَوْمُ فَرَحٍ .

Galactometer, n. عِيَار (or مِعْيَارُ) ٱللَّبَنِ .

Galaxy, n. A brilliant assembly, إِحْتِفَالٌ بَهِيّ ـ مَوْكِبٌ جَلِيلٌ . See also Milky-way, n.

Galbanum, n. بِيرْزَد ـ قِنَّة .

Gale, n. A strong wind, رِيحٌ عَاصِفَةٌ ـ زَفْزَافَة ـ زَفْزَفَة . A light breeze, نَسِيم ـ نَسَم pl. أَنْسَام . It blew a —, زَفَّتِ ٱلرِّيحُ ـ زَفْزَفَتِ ٱلرِّيحُ .

Galena, n. رَصَاص ـ عَلَابِيّ .

Galilean, n. مِنْ أَرْضِ ٱلْجَلِيلِ ـ جَلِيلِيّ .

Galilee, n. ٱلْجَلِيلُ .

Galiot, n. سَفِينَةٌ صَغِيرَةٌ ـ فَلُوكَة .

Galipot, n. صَمْغُ ٱلصَّنَوْبَرِ ـ رَاتِينَج ـ قَلْفُونَة .

Gall, n. Bile, مِرَّة ـ مَرَارَة ـ صَفْرَآء . Rancour, مَرَارَة ـ حِقْد ـ بُغْض ـ ضِغْن . An excoriation, سَلِيقَة ـ خَدْش . A — on the back of a horse, دَبَر pl. أَدْبَار ; on the shoulders, مِكْتَاف .

Gall, v.t. As of the skin, سَلَقَ ـ كَدَحَ ـ خَدَشَ ـ عَقَرَ ; as by a saddle, عَقَرَ . To vex, أَضْجَرَ ـ أَقْلَقَ ـ صَدَّعَ . To be galled, excoriated, إِنْعَقَرَ ـ إِنْسَلَقَ ـ صَرِدَ . To be galled, vexed, تَصَدَّعَ ـ تَقَلَّقَ ـ تَضَجَّرَ . Galled, of a horse, دَبِر ـ أَدْبَر ـ صَرِد .

Gallant, n. A wooer, عَاشِق pl. عُشَّاق . A courtier of ladies, غُنْدُور ـ عَلُّ ٱلنِّسَآءِ pl. أَعْلَال ـ زِيرُ نِسَآءٍ ـ تَلَّآءُ ٱلنِّسَآءِ . A sprightly blade, ظَرِيف ـ شَلَبِيّ . A seducer, زَانٍ ـ خَدَّاع .

Gallant, a. Brave, شُجَاع ـ شَجِيع ـ بَئِيس ـ جَسُور ـ بَطَل . Magnanimous, noble, نَبِيل ـ حُرّ ـ شَرِيف ـ رَحِيبُ ٱلصَّدْرِ .

Gallánt, a. Polite, أَدِيب ـ ظَرِيف . Attentive to ladies, تُبَّع ـ تِبْع ـ عَلُّ ٱلنِّسَآءِ pl. أَعْلَال ـ غُنْدُور pl. غَنَادِرُ .

Gallantly, ad. Bravely, بِشَجَاعَةٍ ـ جَسَارَةً ـ شَجَاعَةً .

Gallántly, ad. Politely, بِظَرَافَةٍ ـ كَٱلْعَلِّ ـ تَلَطُّفًا .

Gallantness, n. كَمَال ـ شَمَائِلُ ـ فَضَائِلُ .

Gallantry, n. Bravery, بَطَالَة ـ بَأْس ـ جَسَارَة ـ شَجَاعَة ـ بُطُولَة . Generosity, رَحْبُ ٱلصَّدْرِ ـ غَيْرَة ـ مُرُوءَة . Politeness, شَلَبْنَة ـ أَدَب ـ ظَرَافَة . Lewdness, فَسَاد ـ فِسْق ـ رَفَث ـ فُحْش .

Gall-bladder, n. مَرَارَة .

Galleon, n. سَفِينَةٌ إِسْبَانِيُولِيَّةٌ ذَاتُ ثَلْثَةِ أَنَابِرَ .

Gallery, n. A covered walk, قَيْسَارِيَّة ـ رِوَاق pl. أَرْوِقَة and رُوُق . A portico, دِهْلِيز pl. دَهَالِيزُ ـ أُسْطُوَانَة pl. أَسَاطِينُ . The — round the minaret of a mosque or any similar building, شُرْفَة pl. شُرُفَات ـ شُرَّافَة pl. شُرَّافَات . The — of a church or any such platform, مَحْفِل pl. مَحَافِل . The —, as of a mine, مَجَاز ـ دِهْلِيز . The quarter — of a ship, جُنَيْنَةُ ٱلْمَرْكَبِ ; the stern —, رِوَاقُ مُؤَخَّرِ ٱلْمَرْكَبِ . A — of pictures, مَجْمَعُ صُوَرٍ .

Galley, n. The ship, قَارِب pl. قَوَارِبُ . A printer's galley, بِرْوَاز vulg. قَرْوَاز لِلْأَحْرُفِ .

Galley-slave, n. مُجْرِمٌ مَحْكُومٌ عَلَيْهِ بِٱلْقَذْفِ ـ مُذْنِبٌ قَذَّافٌ .

Gall-fly, n. دُودَةُ ٱلْعَفْصِ .

Galliard, n. مَخْلُوع ـ بَطْرَان .

Gallic, a. French, فَرَنْسَاوِيّ . Belonging to galls, عَفْصِيّ ـ مُتَعَلِّقٌ بِٱلْعَفْصِ .

Gallic-acid, n. حَامِضُ ٱلْعَفْصِ .

Gallican, n. See Gallic, a.

Gallicanism, n. لَفْظَةٌ فَرَنْسَاوِيَّةٌ .

Gallicize, v.t. See to Frenchify, v.t.

Galligaskins, n. شَخْشِير pl. شَخَاشِيرُ .

Gallinaceous, a. دُجَاجِيّ ـ مِنْ جِنْسِ ٱلدَّجَاجِ .

Gallinipper, n. نَامُوسَة coll. نَامُوس ـ بَعُوضَة coll. بَعُوض .

Gallipot, n. وِعَآء pl. أَوْعَاة or أَوْعِيَة .

Gall-nut, n. عَفْص . A seller of gall-nuts, عَفْصِيّ . To put — into, أَعْفَصَ .

Gallon, n. كَالَن وَهُوَ مِكْيَالُ ٱلْمَوَائِعِ يَسَعُ نَحْوَ ١١٢٠ دِرْهَمًا .

Galloon, *n.* Of gold thread, قَصَبٌ أَصْفَرُ ; of silver thread, قَصَبٌ أَبْيَض .

Gallop, *v.i.* رَكَضَ ـ ~ رَمَحَ [2].

Gallop, *v.t.* رَكَّضَ ـ [2] رَكَضَ ـ رَمَّحَ .

Gallop, *n.* رَكْضَة ـ رَمْحَة .

Galloper, *n.* رامِح ـ راكِض .

Galloping, *a.* Swift, طَيَّار ـ سَرِيع ـ شَمَّرِيٌّ ـ شَمَرِيٌّ .

Galloway, *n.* حُصَانٌ قَصِيرُ ٱلْقَدِّ ـ قَلَهْزَم .

Gallows, *n.* A gibbet, مَشْنَقَة . Braces, شِمار ـ شِناط .

Galvanic, *a.* غَلْوانِيٌّ . A — battery, بَطَّارِيَّة ـ طَقْمٌ غَلْوانِيٌّ ـ غَلْوانِيَّة .

Galvanism, *n.* الكَهْرَبائِيَّة ٱلْكِيماوِيَّة ـ الغَلْوانِيَّة .

Galvanist, *n.* أُسْتاذُ ٱلْكَهْرَبائِيَّةِ ٱلْكِيماوِيَّةِ ـ ماهِرٌ فِي عِلْمِ ٱلْغَلْوانِيَّةِ .

Galvanize, *v.t.* أَثَّرَ فِي بِواسِطَةِ ٱلطَّقْمِ ٱلْغَلْوانِيِّ .

Gamble, *v.i.* To play for money, ~ لَعِبَ ٱلْقِمارَ .

Gambler, *n.* لَعَّاب ـ قِمَرَاتِيٌّ ـ لَعِيبُ قِمارٍ ـ لَعِيب ـ خَلِيع ; a —, as in stocks, مُقامِر *pl.* مُقامِرُونَ . To become a notorious —, خَلُعَ [2]. *See also* Gamester, *n.*

Gambling, *n.* لَعِبُ قِمارٍ ـ خَلاعَة ; as on the stocks, مُقامَرَة .

Gambling, *a.* مُتَعَلِّقٌ بِلَعِبِ ٱلْقِمارِ ـ قِماراتِيٌّ ; as on the stocks, مُقامِر .

Gamboge, *n.* ضَرْبٌ مِنَ ٱلصَّمْغِ أَخْضَرُ ٱللَّوْنِ يَدْخُلُ فِي ٱلْأَدْوِيَةِ وَفِي ٱلصِّباغَةِ ـ ٱلْمُسْهِلَةِ ـ كوتا كنبا .

Gambol, *n.* *See* Frisk, *n.*

Gambol, *v.i.* *See to* Frisk, *v.i.*

Gambrel, *n.* The hind leg of a horse, رِجْلُ ٱلْحِصانِ *dual* رِجْلانِ .

Game, *n.* Play, لَعِب ـ تَسَلٍّ . Jest, fun, هَزْل ـ مُزاح . Insult, هُزُوءَة . An arrangement, shuffle, تَدْبِير ـ قِدْيَة ـ بَرْمَة . A match or a game at play, لُعْبَة ; as at cards, دَسْت *pl.* دُسُوت . Animals hunted, صَيْد . Mettle, مُرُوءَة . A — that two can play at, something that cuts both ways, دَوْرٌ مُشْتَرَكٌ . A — of chance, قِمار . A losing —, لَعِبٌ خاسِرٌ . A drawn —, لَعِبٌ غَيْرُ قاطِعٍ . To beat up for —, حاشَ ٱلصَّيْدَ [2]. To throw up the —, فاتَ [2] (or تَرَكَ [2]) ٱللُّعْبَةَ . To make — of, إِسْتَهْزَأَ بِ ـ شاقَحَ ـ ~ ضَحِكَ مِن . The —, as at cards, is mine, لِي (الدَّسْتُ or) الدَّوْرُ . The — is against me, عَلَيَّ (الدَّسْتُ or) الدَّوْرُ .

Game, *a.* Ready to brave, بَطَل ـ جَسُور . Fighting, مُقاتِل .

Game, *v.i.* ~ لَعِبَ ٱلْقِمارَ . To — away, ضَيَّعَ فِي لَعِبِ ٱلْقِمارِ . To —, or play at hazard with another, خالَعَ .

Game-cock, *n.* دِيكٌ مُرَبًّى لِلْمُقاتَلَةِ .

Gamekeeper, *n.* ناظِرُ (or حارِسُ) ٱلصَّيْدِ .

Gamesome, *a.* مُحِبُّ ٱلْمُزاحِ وَٱللَّعِبِ ـ لَعِيب . *See also* Frolicsome, *a.*

Gamester, *n.* مُقامِر ـ لَعَّابُ ٱلْقِمارِ ـ مُخالِع ـ خَلِيع ـ قِماراتِيٌّ .

Gaming, *n.* لَعِبُ قِمارٍ ـ مُقامَرَة .

Gaming-house, *n.* بَيْتُ لَعِبِ ٱلْقِمارِ .

Gammon, *n.* As of bacon, كِتْفُ (or فَخْذُ) لَحْمِ خِنْزِيرٍ مُمَلَّحٌ . Imposition, مَسْح ـ مَكْر .

Gammon, *v.t.* As of bacon, دَخَّنَ وَمَلَّحَ . To impose upon, فازَبَ ـ [2] مَسَحَ ـ [2] مَكَرَبِ . To beat, to overcome, غَلَبَ عَلَى . To fasten a bowsprit to the stem of a ship, ~ رَبَطَ باشْتُونًا إِلَى مُقَدَّمِ ٱلْمَرْكَبِ .

Gamut, *n.* دائِرَةُ ٱلْمُوسِيقَى ـ دُرٌّ مُفَصَّلٌ .

Gander, *n.* وَزَّة ـ وَزٌّ ـ إِوَزٌّ *coll.*

Gang, *n.* زُمْرَة ـ طائِفَة ـ شِرْذِمَة ـ جَماعَة ـ حَلْقَة ; as of workmen, وَرْشَة .

Gang-board, *n.* تَخْتَةُ ٱلْإِسْكَلَةِ .

Ganglion, *n.* ضَواة ـ سِلْعَة ـ غُدَّة ـ عُقْدَة . A — under the skin, خَنازِيرُ .

Ganglionic, *a.* مُتَعَلِّقٌ بِٱلسِّلْعَةِ ـ مِنْ داءِ ٱلْغُدَّةِ .

Gangrene, *n.* أَكِلَة ـ أُكال .

Gangrene, *v.i.* تَأَكَّلَ ـ ~ أَكِلَ .

Gangrenous, *a.* ذُو أُكالٍ .

Gangue, *n.* رِكاز ـ سُيُوب ـ الحِجارَةُ ٱلْمُحْتَوِيَةُ عَلَى ٱلْمَعادِنِ .

Gangway, *n.* دَرَجُ (or سُلَّمُ) ٱلْمَرْكَبِ .

Gannet, *n.* ضَرْبٌ مِنَ ٱلطُّيُورِ .

Gantlet, *n.* The punishment, عَذابٌ عَسْكَرِيٌّ . To run the —, to brave, تَغَرَّرَ ـ غَرَّرَ بِنَفْسِهِ ـ غَنْتَرَ .

Ganymede, *n.* A cup-bearer, ساقِي ٱلرَّاحِ *pl.* سُقاة .

Gaol, *n.* سِجْن ـ حَبْس . *See also* Jail, *n.*

Gaoler, *n.* سَجَّان . *See also* Jailer, *n.*

Gap, *n.* A rent, fissure, خَرْق *pl.* خُرُوق ـ فَلْج *pl.* أَفْلاج ـ شَقّ *pl.* شُقُوق . An opening, خَلَّة ـ خَلَل *pl.* خِلال ـ ثَغْر *pl.* ثُغُور . A lacuna, خَلَل *pl.* خِلال ـ نُقْصان . To stop, as of a —, سَدَّ [2]. To stand in the —, وَقَفَ فِي ٱلثَّغْرِ *aor.* يَقِفُ ; to aid, defend, حامَى ـ عاوَنَ . O God, supply his family with that which is good, filling up the gap of him whom they have lost, اللّٰهُمَّ أَخْلِفْ عَلَى أَهْلِهِ بِخَيْرٍ وَٱسْدُدْ خَلَّتَهُ .

Gape, *v.i.* To yawn, تَثاوَبَ ـ تَثَأَّبَ ـ تَثاءَبَ ـ ثُئِبَ . To open in a breach, اِنْفَتَحَ ـ اِنْشَقَّ ـ اِنْفَرَجَ . To stare with astonishment, اِنْذَهَلَ عَجَبًا ـ ² بَهَتَ ـ غَرَا . To stare at, حَمْلَقَ . To — after, to desire, اِشْتَهَى ـ = لَمِقَ إِلَى ـ = شَفَنَ إِلَى ـ إِلَى تَمَنَّى .

Gape, *n.* A yawn, تَثَاؤُب ـ ثُؤَبَآء ـ ثَأْب . An opening of the mouth, غَرْوٌ . A stare, شُفُون ـ حَمْلَقَة .

Gaper, *n.* A yawner, مُتَثَاوِب . A starer, شَافِن .

Garb, *n.* Dress, كِسْوَة ـ لِبَاس ـ أَثْيَاب ـ رِدَآء . Fashion of dress, زِيٌّ ـ كِمَّة ـ كِسْم . Appearance, form, بِلَالَة ـ خِيَر ـ هَيْئَة ـ صُورَة ـ شَبَه ـ شَكْل . Truly, his — is beautiful, إِنَّهُ لَحَسَنُ ٱلْبِلَلِ .

Garbage, *n.* Refuse, عَفْشَة ـ حُثَالَة ـ سُقَاطَة ـ خُشَارَة . Entrails, مَصَارِينُ .

Garble, *v.t.* To sift, غَرْبَلَ ـ نَقَّى ـ نَخَلَ = ² . To dress up, تَصَحَّفَ عَلَى ـ صَحَّفَ . يَشِي *aor.* وَشَى . To misrepresent,

Garbler, *n.* A sifter, مُنَقٍّ ـ مُغَرْبِل . A misquoter, مُصَحِّف ـ صَحَّاف .

Garbles, *n.* سُقَاطَة ـ نُقَاوَة ـ حُثَالَة .

Garden, *n.* جَنَّة ـ غَيْط ـ رِيَاض *pl.* رَوْضَة ـ حَدَائِق *pl.* حَدِيقَة ـ جِنَان *pl.* . A walled —, حَدِيقَة ـ مَحَاجِرُ *pl.* مَحْجِر . A flower —, بُسْتَان *pl.* بَسَاتِينُ . A small —, جُنَيْنَة . Garden stuff, vegetables, قُطَانِي ـ خُضَر ـ بَقْل .

Garden, *v.i.* فَلَحَ ٱلْبُسْتَانَ = .

Gardener, *n.* بُسْتَانِيٌّ ـ غَيْطَانِيٌّ .

Gardening, *n.* خِدْمَةُ ٱلْجِنَانِ ـ فَلْحُ ٱلْبَسَاتِينِ .

Gargarism, *n.*, Gargle, — A wash, غَرْغَرَة . A gargle in the throat of a dying person, غَرْغَرَة . *See also* Death-rattle, *n.*

Gargle, *v.t.* To wash with a —, تَمَخْمَضَ بِ ـ تَغَرْغَرَ بِ ـ غَرْغَرَ . To —, rattle, as the throat of a dying person (*v.i.*), غَرْغَرَ .

Gargoyle, *n.* مَآزِيبُ *pl.* مِيزَاب .

Garish, *a.* *See* Gaudy, *a.*

Garishness, *n.* *See* Gaudiness, *n.*

Garland, *n.* أَكَالِيلُ *pl.* إِكْلِيلٌ مِنْ زَهْرٍ ـ رُعْلَة .

Garland, *v.t.* زَيَّنَ ـ بِأَكَالِيلَ مِنْ زَهْرٍ .

Garlic, *n.* ثُومٌ ـ فُومٌ ; a clove, as of —, فُصُوص *pl.* فَصٌّ ـ حُبُوب *pl.* حَبَّة .

Garment, *n.* A dress, كِسَآء ـ لِبَاس ـ مَلْبُوس ـ سِرْبَال ـ رِدَآء ـ بَذْلَة (this last is commonly used now for a new suit of clothes). An outer —, خِلْعَة ـ ثَوْب *pl.* أَثْيَاب . An under —, worn next the skin, غِلَالَة ـ شِعَار *pl.* شُعُر . A white —, or a white piece of cloth, سَحْل *pl.* سُحُول *and* سُحُل . An old —, such as is used for work, or a worn-out —, مِبْذَلَة ـ مِعْوَز ـ بِذْلَة *pl.* مَبَاذِلُ . A woman's outer wrapper, مِلْحَفَة ـ جِلْبَاب : when walking or riding, حَبَرَة . Worn-out garments, جُرُود .

Garner, *n.* هُرْيٌ *pl.* أَهْرَآء ـ شُونَة *pl.* شُوَن ـ أَنْبَار *pl.* أَنْبَارَات .

Garner, *v.t.* كَدَّسَ ـ ² خَزَنَ .

Garnet, *n.* حَجَرٌ سَيْلَان *pl.* أَحْجَار ـ مَقِيق .

Garnish, Garnishment, *n.*, Garniture, — زِينَة ـ زَخْرَفَة ـ حِلْيَة ـ حَلْيٌ .

Garnish, *v.t.* زَيَّنَ ـ حَسَّنَ ـ زَخْرَفَ ـ حَلَّى .

Garnisher, *n.* مُزَخْرِف ـ مُحَسِّن ـ مُحَلٍّ .

Garret, *n.* A room under a roof, عُلِّيَّة *pl.* عَلَالِيّ ـ غُرْفَة *pl.* غُرَف . The highest story, الطَّبَقَةُ ٱلْعُلْيَا ـ الغُرْفَة .

Garrison, *n.* A fortress furnished with troops, قَلْعَةٌ مَشْحُونَةٌ . A body of troops in a fort, عَسَاكِرُ مُسْتَحْفِظَة ـ شِحْنَةٌ عَسْكَرٍ ـ وَضَائِعُ ـ الْمُحَافِظُونَ . A fortified place, حِرْز *pl.* أَحْرَاز ـ حِرْزٌ ـ حِصْن *pl.* حُصُون ـ قِلَاع *pl.* قَلْعَة ـ حَرِيزٌ . A barrack, قَاعَةُ ٱلْعَسَاكِرِ ـ قِشْلَة .

Garrison, *v.t.* To fortify, حَصَّنَ . To fill with soldiers, جَعَلَ = عَسَاكِرَ فِي ـ أَشْحَنَ بِعَسَاكِرَ .

Garrote, *n.* خَنْق .

Garrote, *v.t.* خَنَقَ ـ ² خَنَّقَ .

Garrotter, *n.* خَنَّاق ـ خَانِق .

Garrulity, *n.* إِسْهَاب ـ فَرْفَرَة ـ بَقٌّ ـ الشَّيُوبُ فِي ٱلْكَلِمِ ـ كَثْرَةُ كَلَامٍ ـ فَشْر ـ بَقْبَقَة ـ إِسْهَام .

Garrulous, *a.* قَوَّال ـ مِفْوَه ـ فَيِّه ـ فَاهٍ ـ نَثِر ـ بَقَّاق ـ كِلْمَانِيٌّ . Noisy, clamorous, of a woman, مُجَلِّبَة ـ جَلَّابَة . To be —, بَقَّ *aor.* يَبِقُّ ـ بَقْبَقَ ـ بَقَّ كَلَامًا ـ أَسْهَبَ ـ أَسْهَمَ ـ فَشَرَ ـ = سَابَ فِي ٱلْكَلِمِ .

Garter, *n.* رِبَاطٌ لِلسَّاقِ . The Order of the Garter, النِّيشَانُ ٱلْأَشْرَفُ ٱلْمَعْرُوفُ بِنِيشَانِ ٱلْكَارْتَر .

Garter, *v.t.* ² رَبَطَ ـ بِرِبَاطِ ٱلسَّاقِ . To invest one with the Order of the Garter, وَشَّحَ ـ بِنِيشَانِ ٱلْكَارْتَر .

Gas, *n.* غَاز .

Gasconade, *n.* فَشْر ـ خَرْطَة ـ اِفْتِخَار ـ بَطَر . *See also* Brag, *n.*

Gasconade, *v.i.* فَشَرَ ـ تَفَخَّرَ ـ اِفْتَخَرَ ـ = بَطِرَ . *See also* to Brag, *v.i.*

Gaseous, *a.* Aeriform, رُوحِيٌّ ـ هَوَائِيٌّ . In the form of gas, مِنْ غَازٍ .

Gash, *n.* كَلْم *pl.* كِلام – جُرْح *pl.* جُرُوح – شَقّ *pl.* شُقُوق.

Gash, *v.t.* كَلَمَ – خَمَشَ – جَرَحَ – شَقَّ 2.

Gasification, *n.* التَّحْوِيلُ إِلَى غازٍ.

Gasify, *v.t.* صَيَّرَ غازًا.

Gasket, *n.* حَبْلٌ يُرْبَطُ بِهِ الشِّراعُ – ماتّه.

Gaskins, *n.* شَخْشِير *pl.* شَخاشِيرُ.

Gas-light, *n.* ضَوْءُ الغازِ.

Gas-meter, *n.* مِيزانُ الغازِ.

Gasometer, *n.* خَزِينَةُ الغازِ.

Gasometry, *n.* عِلْمُ صَنْعَةِ الغازِ وَوَزْنِهِ.

Gasp, *v.i.* To — for breath, فاقَ 2 – تَنَفَّسَ الصُّعَداءَ – إِلْتَهَثَ – شَهِقَ – شَهَقَ. To pant, إِبْتَهَرَ. To long for, حَنَّ إِلَى – إِشْتاقَ إِلَى – إِسْتَحَنَّ إِلَى.

Gasp, *n.* شُهْقَة – شُهاق – تَنَفُّس – نَفَس – فُواق – إِبْتِهار. The last —, آخِرُ نَفَسٍ – عَشْف – طِنْءٌ. To give the last —, صَعَقَ. One who is at the last —, رامِق – مُرامِق. He is at the last —, هُوَ عَلَى رَمَقٍ مِنَ الحَيٰوةِ.

Gate, *n.* باب *pl.* أَبْواب. The — of a street, quarter, or the way into a place, دَرْب *pl.* دُرُوب. A large — with a wicket, رِتاج *pl.* رُتُج *and* رَتائِجُ. A wicket —, بُوَيْبَة – خَوْخَة – خادِعَة. To let one go his own —, تَمَهَّلَ. Go your own —, إِسْتَقْلِحْ بِأَمْرِكَ. To shut, as of a —, غَلَّقَ – رَدَّ 2 – صَكَّ 2.

Gather, *n.* A plait, fold, غَضْن *pl.* غُضُون – سَفَّة – سَفِيفَة – طَيَّة *pl.* أَطْواءٌ – ثِنْيَة. A — in or of the hair, عَقِيصَة – عِقْصَة.

Gather, *v.t.* To bring together, collect, جَبَى – حَشَدَ 2 – أَلَّفَ – لَمَّ 2 – ضَمَّ 2 – اِلْتَقَطَ – جَمَعَ – جَمَّعَ. To pluck, قَطَفَ – قَطَّفَ. To —, as of fruit, خَرَفَ 2 – جَنَى – إِجْتَنَى. To pick out, لَقَطَ 2. To draw into gathers, غَضَّنَ – كَمَّشَ. To know by inference, إِسْتَدَلَّ – إِسْتَنْتَجَ. To — or collect one's ideas, جَمَعَ حَواسَّهُ. To — courage, تَجَلَّدَ – تَشَجَّعَ – تَشَدَّدَ – شَدَّ حَيْلَهُ 2 – قَوَّى قَلْبَهُ. To — strength, get in better health, تَعافَى – تَوَجَّهَ إِلَى الصِّحَّةِ – اِنْجَبَرَتْ صِحَّتُهُ. He gathered, inferred, good therefrom, تَوَسَّمَ فِيهِ الخَيْرَ. Spilt milk cannot be gathered up again, اللَّبَنُ المُهْراقُ لا يُجْمَعُ أَيْضًا; *or*, as a proverb, كَسْرُ الزُّجاجَةِ لا يُشْعَبُ *lit.* Broken glass cannot be restored.

Gather, *v.i.* To collect together, إِحْتَشَدَ – إِنْضَمَّ – إِجْتَمَعَ. To — around, to throng, of many, إِحْتَشَدُوا – تَزاحَمُوا – اِرْتَكَمُوا – تَكَأْكَأُوا. To —, as pus, تَقَيَّحَ – أَمَدَّ – تَدَمَّلَ. It may be gathered, learnt, from …, يُسْتَفادُ مِن.

Gatherer, *n.* جامِع – حاشِد; of corn, شامِلُ (*or* حَصّادُ) القَمْحِ; of fruit, جانٍ – قاطِف; of taxes, جابٍ – جامِعُ الخَراجِ.

Gathering, *n.* A collection, جَمْعِيَّة – جَماعَة. A tumour, دُمَّلَة – سِلْعَة. A social —, أُلْفَة – شَمْل *pl.* شُمُول. Gatherings of grapes and other fruit, قُطُوف. There was a great —, meeting, of …, اِلْتَأَمَتْ جَمْعِيَّةٌ كَبِيرَةٌ مِن.

Gaud, *n.* حِلْيَة *pl.* حِلًى – زِينَة *pl.* زِيَن.

Gaudily, *ad.* بِمُباهاةٍ – بِزَهْوٍ.

Gaudiness, *n.* زَهْو – زَهْوَة – مُباهاة – فَخارَة.

Gaudy, *a.* زاهٍ – جَلِيّ – مُفْتَخِر. Of a — colour, زاهِي اللَّوْنِ.

Gauge, *v.t.* *See to* Gage, *v.t.*

Gauge, *n.* *See* Gage, *n.*

Gauger, *n.* Of measures, كَيّال; of land, مَسّاح.

Gauging-rod, *n.* جَدْوَلُ القِياسِ – قَصَبَةُ القِياسِ – مِقْياس.

Gaul, *n.* *See* Gallican, *n.*

Gaunt, *a.* شَخِيت – شَخْت – نَحِيف – هَزِل. Gaunt in the legs, شَخْتُ الجُزارَةِ.

Gauntliness, *n.* شُخُوتَة – نَحافَة – هُزال.

Gauntlet, *n.* كَفٌّ حَدِيدٍ *pl.* كُفُوف. To throw down the — to, طَلَبَ لِلْقِتالِ – بَرَزَ إِلَى الحَرْبِ مَعَ 2. To take up the —, حَرَّكَ الشَّرَّ مَعَ – بَرَزَ لِ 2 – غَرَّرَ بِنَفْسِهِ – تَغَرَّرَ – عَنْتَرَ.

Gauze, *n.* سُنْدُس – قَزّ. Wire —, حِباكٌ مِنْ سِلْكٍ.

Gavel-kind, *n.* مِيراثٌ يَرِثُونَهُ البَنُونَ عَلَى السَّوِيَّةِ.

Gawk, *n.* A simpleton, أَخْرَقُ – أَحْمَقُ – بَلِيد – حِمار.

Gawky, *a.* }
Gawky, *n.* } أَخْرَقُ – غَشِيم – أَخْبَلُ – قَلِيلُ المَعْرِفَةِ. *See also* Clumsy, *a.*

Gay, *a.* Lively, سارّ – مَسْرُور – مَغْبُوط – فَرْحانُ – هَشٌّ بَشٌّ – مَبْسُوط – بَشُوش – مُبْتَهِج – جَذْلانُ – مُكَيِّف. Cheering, مُفْرِح – مُجَذِّل – مُكَيِّف. Fine, showy, جَلِيل – مُرَوْنَق – ناضِر – جَلِيّ. Meretricious, بَشِيع – فاحِش. To be gay, cheerful, أَغْبَطَ – اِنْغَبَطَ – تَغَبَّطَ – تَفَسَّحَ – اِنْبَسَطَ – اِبْتَهَجَ – تَكَيَّفَ. *See also* Gaudy, *a.*

Gayety, *n.* Cheerfulness, سُرُور – غِبْطَة – فَرَح – اِنْبِساط – جَذَل – بَهْجَة – كَيْف. Gratification, لَذَّة *pl.* لَذّات – شَهْوَة *pl.* شَهَوات. The gaieties of the world, حُطامُ الدُّنْيا.

Gayly, *ad.* Merrily, اِغْتِباطًا – بِغِبْطَةٍ – بِسُرُورٍ – بِانْبِساطٍ – بِفَرَحٍ. Splendidly, بِاحْتِفالٍ. *See also* Gaudily, *ad.*

Gayness, *n.* Show, اِحْتِفال – وَكْبَة – رَوْنَق – زِينَة.

Gaze, *v.i.* بَرَقَ بِعَيْنَيْهِ – هَطَعَ. To — at, رَنَّقَ – تَعَيَّنَ –

ـ أَعْيَنَ ـ ² نَقَدَ إِلَى ـ ـِ لَمَقَ إِلَى ـ رَامَقَ ـ ² رَمَقَ ـ ٱلنَّظَرَ إِلَى تَفَرَّسَ فِي.

Gaze, *n.* نَظَر ـ لَمْق ـ هُطُوع ـ هَطْع ـ رَمْق ـ رَنْق.

Gazeful, *a.* } Gazer, *n.* } مُتَفَرِّس ـ نَظَّار ـ هاطِع.

Gazelle, *n.* غَزَال *pl.* غِزْلَة *or* غِزْلان ـ ظَبْيٌ *pl.* أَظْب.

Gazette, *n.* An official —, صَحِيفَةُ ٱلْأَخْبارِ ٱلرَّسْمِيَّةِ *pl.* صُحُف *and* صَحائِف. *See also* Newspaper, *n.*

Gazette, *v.t.* أَدْرَجَ-فِي صَحِيفَةِ ٱلْأَخْبارِ ٱلرَّسْمِيَّةِ. To be gazetted, اِنْدَرَجَ فِي صَحِيفَةِ ٱلْأَخْبارِ ٱلرَّسْمِيَّةِ.

Gazetteer, *n.* A dictionary of geography, كِتابُ تَقْوِيمِ ٱلْبُلْدانِ.

Gazing-stock, *n.* أُضْحُوكَة ـ عِبْرَة. To make a — of, ـَ جَعَلَ-عِبْرَةً.

G.C.B., حائزُ نِيشَانِ ٱلرُّتْبَةِ ٱلْأُولَى مِنَ ٱلنِّيشانِ ٱلْمَعْرُوفِ بِنِيشانِ ٱلْباث.

G.C.H., حائزُ نِيشَانِ ٱلرُّتْبَةِ ٱلْأُولَى مِنَ ٱلنِّيشانِ ٱلْمُسَمَّى بِنِيشَانِ صَلِيبِ هَنُورَةَ ٱلْمُفْتَخِرِ.

G.C.M.G., حائزُ نِيشانِ ٱلرُّتْبَةِ ٱلْأُولَى مِنَ ٱلنِّيشانِ ٱلْمُسَمَّى بِنيشانِ حَضْرَةِ مَخائيلَ وَحَضْرَةِ جِرْجِيس.

Gear, *n.* Apparatus, طَقْم ـ أَشْيَآء ـ عُدَّة ـ أَداة. In —, شاغِل; out of —, بَطَّال ـ سَاقِط. To throw out of —, ـ عَطَّلَ أَوْقَفَ ـ أَبْطَلَ. To put into —, شَغَّلَ ـ أَصْلَحَ. *See also* Head-gear, *n.*

Gear, *n.* } Geer, } A toothed wheel, عَجَلَةٌ مُسَنَّنَةٌ.

Gearing, *n.* Machinery, أَداة ـ دَوالِيب.

Gee! *int.* يا أَللّٰهُ ـ دَه.

Gehenna, *n.* جَهَنَّمُ ـ ٱلْجَحِيمُ.

Gelable, *a.* يَصِيرُ هُلامًا.

Gelatine, *n.* هُلام.

Gelatine, *a.* } Gelatinous, } هُلامِيٌّ.

Gelatinate, *v.t.* صَيَّرَ-هُلامًا.

Geld, *v.t.* طَوَّشَ ـ ² جَبَّ ـ ـِ خَصَى.

Gelding, *n.* خَصِيٌّ ـ مَخْصِيٌّ ـ طَوَاشِي *pl.* طَواشِيَة. A gelt horse, حِصانٌ مَخْصِيٌّ ـ فَرَسٌ مَجْبُوبٌ.

Gelid, *a.* بارِدٌ لِلْغايَةِ.

Gelly, *n.* هُلام. *See also* Jelly, *n.*

Gem, *n.* A bud, بُرْعُوم ـ باقِل *pl.* بَراعِيمُ. A precious stone, جَوْهَرَة *pl.* جَواهِرُ. The —, stone, of a ring, فَصّ *pl.* فُصُوص.

Gem, *v.t.* To adorn with gems, رَكَّبَ-(رَصَّعَ- *or*) بِجَوَاهِرَ.

Gem, *v.i.* To bud, أَبْقَلَ ـ بَرْعَمَ ـ تَزَرَّرَ.

Geminate, *v.t.* *See to* Double, *v.t.*

Gemination, *n.* *See* Doubling, *n.*

Gemini, *n.* The constellation, ٱلْجَوْزَآء.

Gemmary, *a.* جَوْهَرِيٌّ ـ مُتَعَلِّقٌ بِٱلْجَواهِرِ.

Gemmate, *a.* } Gemmiferous, } حامِلُ بَراعِيمَ ـ ذُو بَراعِيمَ.

Gemmation, *n.* بَرْعَمَة.

Gemmy, *a.* Full of gems, جَوْهَرِيٌّ ـ مُرَصَّعٌ بِٱلْجَواهِرِ.

Gendarme, *n.* قَوَّاس *pl.* قَوَّاسَة ـ شُرْطِيٌّ *pl.* شُرْطِيَّة.

Gendarmerie, *n.* شُرْطَة ـ جَلاوِزَة.

Gender, *n.* جِنْس *pl.* أَجْناس. The masculine —, ٱلْمُذَكَّر; the feminine —, ٱلْمُؤَنَّث; the common —, ٱلْمُسْتَوِى.

Gender, *v.t.* To beget, occasion, وَلَّدَ ـ أَنْتَجَ ـ سَبَّبَ.

Genealogical, *a.* نَسَبِيٌّ. A — tree, شَجَرَة ـ شَجَرَةُ ٱلنَّسَبِ.

Genealogist, *n.* نَسَّاب ـ عَلَّام ـ عَلَّامَة.

Genealogize, *v.i.* ² نَسَبَ-ٱلنَّسَبَ ـ ـِ رَوَى ٱلْأَنسابَ *aor.* يَرْوِى.

Genealogy, *n.* نَسَب *pl.* أَنْساب ـ سِلْسِلَة *pl.* سَلاسِلُ ـ شَجَرَة ـ ذُرِّيَّة.

General, *a.* شامِل ـ كُلِّيٌّ ـ عُمُومِيٌّ ـ جامِع ـ عامٌّ. A — principle, قاعِدَةٌ عُمُومِيَّةٌ. General remarks, مُلاحَظاتٌ عُمُومِيَّةٌ. A — officer, أَمِيرُ ٱلْعَسْكَرِ *pl.* أُمَرَآء ـ باشا ضابِطُ ٱلْعَسْكَرِ *pl.* باشَاوات ـ ضُبَّاطُ ٱلْعَسْكَرِ ـ جِنِرال *vulg.* جَنْنار. In a — point of view, عَلَى ٱلْعُمُومِ ـ عُمُومًا. In — use, دارِج ـ مُسْتَعْمَلٌ عُمُومًا. Of more — utility, أَعَمُّ فائِدَةً. To be —, common, ² عَمَّ; to affect all, اِشْتَمَلَ عَلَى ٱلْجَمِيعِ. To make —, عَمَّمَ: The disease became — among them, تَفَشَّا فِيهِمِ ٱلْمَرَضُ ـ عَمَّهُمُ ٱلْمَرَضُ. The rain was — over the land, ² عَمَّ ٱلْمَطَرُ ٱلْأَرْضَ.

Adjutant-General, مَأْمُورٌ عُمُومِيٌّ عَلَى إِدارَةِ فِرْقَةٍ مِنَ ٱلْعَسْكَرِ.

Attorney-General, وَكِيلُ ٱلدَّوْلَةِ فِي ٱلدَّعاوَى ٱلْجِنائِيَّةِ.

Commissary-General, أَمِينُ ٱلنُّزُلِ لِفِرْقَةٍ مِنَ ٱلْعَسْكَرِ.

Quartermaster-General, مَأْمُورٌ عُمُومِيٌّ عَلَى حَرَكاتِ فِرْقَةٍ مِنَ ٱلْعَسْكَرِ وَمُعَسْكَرِهِمْ.

Solicitor-General, وَكِيلُ ٱلدَّوْلَةِ فِي ٱلدَّعاوَى ٱلْحُقُوقِيَّةِ.

General, *n.* The main part, ٱلْأَجَمُّ ـ ٱلْأَكْثَرُ ـ ٱلْأَغْلَبُ ـ ٱلْأَكْبَرُ. A head, chief, ناظِر ـ رَأْس ـ رَئِيس. A —, as of a religious community, رَئِيسٌ عامٌّ. The commander of an army, قائِدُ جُنُودٍ *pl.* قُوَّاد ـ أَمِيرُ عَسْكَرٍ ـ جِنِرال *vulg.* جَنْنار. A —, one of that rank in the army, فَرِيق ـ أَمِيرُ لِوَآء. In —, عَلَى ٱلْعُمُومِ ـ عامَّةً ـ فِي ٱلْأَكْثَرِ.

Brigadier-General, أَمِيرُ لِوَآءٍ مُوَقَّتٌ.

Lieutenant-General, فَرِيقٌ عَسْكَرٍ ـ فَرِيقٌ.

Major-General, مِيرُ لِوَآءٍ ـ أَمِيرُ لِوَآءٍ.

Generalissimo, *n.* أَمِيرُ أُمَرَآءِ ٱلْعَسَاكِرِ ـ رَئِيسُ رُؤَسَآءِ ٱلْعَسَاكِرِ ـ سَرْدَارٌ أَكْرَمُ.

Generality, *n.* The bulk, أَكْثَرِيَّةٌ ـ الأَكْثَرُ ـ الجُمْهُورُ ـ الأَغْلَبُ; especially of men, جَمَّانٌ ـ جَنَانٌ. A general matter, قَضِيَّةٌ قَضِيَّةٌ كُلِّيَّةٌ ـ عُمُومِيَّةٌ. This is what is stated by the —, هٰذَا قَوْلُ ٱلْجُمْهُورِ. To utter generalities; *see to* Generalize, *v.i.*

Generalization, *n.* إِطْلَاقٌ ـ تَعْمِيمٌ.

Generalize, *v.i.* عَمَّ ـ ² بَحَثَ فِي عَامَّةٍ ـ تَكَلَّمَ عَلَى ٱلْعُمُومِ فِي ٱلْكَلَامِ.

Generalize, *v.t.* أَطْلَقَ ـ عَلَى ـ عَمَّمَ.

Generally, *ad.* Wholly, عَلَى ٱلْعُمُومِ ـ غَالِبًا ـ بِٱلْجُمْلَةِ ـ عُمُومًا. Without specification, عَلَى ٱلْإِطْلَاقِ ـ إِطْلَاقًا ـ عَلَى ٱلْإِجْمَالِ ـ بِلَا تَخْصِيصٍ. It has become well known —, صَارَ مِنَ ٱلْمَعْلُومِ عِنْدَ ٱلْخَاصِّ وَٱلْعَامِّ. It is — admitted, مَقْبُولٌ وَمُسَلَّمٌ عِنْدَ ٱلْبَيِّنِ لَدَى ٱلْخَاصِّ وَٱلْعَامِّ. It is — thought, غَلَبَ عَلَى ٱلظَّنِّ ٱلْخَاصِّ وَٱلْعَامِّ.

Generalness, *n.* كُلِّيَّةٌ ـ عُمُومِيَّةٌ. Frequency, تَكْرَارٌ ـ كَثْرَةٌ ـ كَثْرَةُ وُقُوعٍ.

Generalship, *n.* The office of a general, رُتْبَةُ أَمِيرِ ٱلْعَسْكَرِ (or ٱلْجِنِرَالِ). Military skill, تَدْبِيرٌ عَسْكَرِيٌّ ـ فَنٌّ عَسْكَرِيٌّ.

Generant, *n.* دَاعٍ لِ ـ مُوَلِّدٌ ـ مُوَرِّثٌ ـ بَاعِثٌ ـ عِلَّةٌ ـ سَبَبٌ.

Generate, *v.t.* To procreate, وَلَّدَ ـ أَوْلَدَ ـ أَنْسَلَ. To produce, أَنْتَجَ ـ سَبَّبَ. To occasion, حَصَّلَ ـ ² دَعَا إِلَى ـ أَحْدَثَ.

Generation, *n.* The act of procreating, وِلَادَةٌ ـ تَوْلِيدٌ ـ إِنْسَالٌ; of producing, occasioning, تَسْبِيبٌ ـ تَحْصِيلٌ ـ إِحْدَاثٌ ـ إِيرَاثٌ ـ إِنْتَاجٌ. A race, أُمَّةٌ *pl.* أُمَمٌ ـ قَبِيلَةٌ *pl.* قَبَائِلُ ـ آلٌ *pl.* أَيَالٌ. Progeny, نَسْلٌ *pl.* أَنْسَالٌ ـ ذُرِّيَّةٌ. Succession, سِلْسِلَةٌ. An age, دَهْرٌ *pl.* دُهُورٌ ـ عَصْرٌ *pl.* أَعْصَارٌ ـ قَرْنٌ *pl.* قُرُونٌ. The people of an age, جِيلٌ *pl.* أَجْيَالٌ. From — to —, إِلَى دَوْرٍ فَدَوْرٍ. A good —, progeny, خَلَفُ صِدْقٍ; a bad —, خَلَفُ سَوْءٍ. Past generations, القُرُونُ ٱلْخَالِيَةُ (or ٱلسَّالِفَةُ).

Generative, *a.* The — organs, أَعْضَآءُ ٱلتَّنَاسُلِ. *See also* Generant, *a.*

Generator, *n.* One who begets, مُوَلِّدٌ ـ وَالِدٌ. A steam boiler, قَزَانُ ٱلْبُخَارِ *pl.* قَزَانَاتٌ.

Generic, *a.* } General, شَامِلٌ. Comprehending a genus, جِنْسِيٌّ.
Generical, } A — quality, جِنْسِيَّةٌ. A — noun, إِسْمُ جِنْسٍ. A collective — noun, إِسْمُ جِنْسٍ جَمْعِيٌّ.

Generically, *ad.* حَسَبَ ٱلْجِنْسِيَّةِ ـ نَظَرًا لِلْجِنْسِ ـ جِنْسًا.

Genericalness, *n.* جِنْسِيَّةٌ.

Generosity, *n.* } Munificence, سَخَآءٌ ـ كَرَامَةٌ ـ فَضْلٌ ـ خَيْرٌ ـ
Generousness, } سَمَاحَةٌ ـ جُودٌ ـ سَخَاوَةٌ. Nobleness, نُبْلَةٌ ـ عُلُوُّ جَانِبٍ. Magnanimity, مُرُوَّةٌ ـ شَهَامَةٌ ـ نَجَابَةٌ. Words replete with —, أَقْوَالٌ نَاطِقَةٌ بِٱلْفَضْلِ.

Generous, *a.* Munificent, مِفْضَالٌ ـ سَخِيٌّ ـ كَرِيمٌ ـ جَوَادٌ ـ ذُو خَيْرٍ ـ رَحِيبُ ٱلصَّدْرِ ـ سَمُوحٌ ـ فَضَّالٌ. Noble, حُرٌّ *pl.* أَحْرَارٌ ـ نَبِيلٌ *pl.* نِبَالٌ ـ نَجِيبٌ *pl.* نُجَبَآءُ. Magnanimous, ذُو مُرُوَّةٍ ـ شَهِيمٌ. Fruitful, of soil, خَصِيبٌ ـ كَرِمٌ. Generous to, مِفْضَالٌ عَلَى. Of good quality, جَيِّدٌ. Generous wine, شَرَابٌ ذُو نَفَسٍ. A — action, مَكْرُمَةٌ *pl.* مَكَارِمُ. A — quality, مَأْثُرَةٌ *pl.* مَآثِرُ. The — (people), ذَوُو ٱلْفَضْلِ. To be —, munificent, كَرُمَ ـ ² تَكَرَّمَ ـ ² سَخِيَ ـ تَسَخَّى ـ ² جَادَ. To be — to; *see under* Bounteous, *a.*

Generously, *ad.* *See* Munificently, Bountifully, *ad.*

Genesis, *n.* Creation, تَكْوِينٌ ـ خَلْقٌ ـ خِلْقَةٌ. The book of —, سِفْرُ ٱلْخَلِيقَةِ ـ سِفْرُ ٱلتَّكْوِينِ.

Genet, *n.* حِصَانٌ صَغِيرٌ ـ قَلَهْزَمٌ.

Geneva, *n.* The town, بَلَدُ جِنِيفٍ (or جِنِيوَةُ). The spirit; *see* Gin, *n.*

Genevese, *n.* مِنْ أَهْلِ جِنِيفٍ (or جِنِيوَةَ).

Genial, *a.* Contributing to production, مُوجِبٌ ـ بَاعِثٌ ـ مُوَلِّدٌ. Cheerful, بَشُوشٌ ـ فَرِحٌ ـ فَرْحَانُ. Native, natural, طَبِيعِيٌّ ـ أَصْلِيٌّ ـ عَرِيقٌ. Favourable, مُوَافِقٌ. A — climate, هَوَآءٌ مُوَافِقٌ ـ طَقْسٌ مُعْتَدِلٌ.

Genially, *ad.* بِبَشَاشَةٍ ـ بِفَرَحٍ ـ بِسُرُورٍ ـ بِٱنْبِسَاطٍ.

Genialness, *n.* Naturalness, عِرْقٌ ـ أَعْرَاقٌ. Favourableness, مُوَافَقَةٌ.

Geniculation, *n.* Knottiness, إِنْعِقَادٌ ـ تَعَقُّدٌ ـ أُنْبُوبَةٌ ـ أَنَابِيبُ.

Genital, *a.* مُتَعَلِّقٌ بِٱلتَّنَاسُلِ.

Genitals, *n.* أَعْضَآءُ (or آلَاتُ) ٱلتَّنَاسُلِ.

Genitive, *n.* جَرٌّ ـ خَفْضٌ ـ إِضَافَةٌ. A noun in the — is called مُضَافٌ إِلَيْهِ; governing the —, مُضَافٌ.

Genitor, *n.* أَبٌ ـ مُوَلِّدٌ ـ وَالِدٌ.

Genius, *n.* A demon, جِنِّيٌّ or جَانٌّ *fem.* جِنِّيَّةٌ *coll.* جِنٌّ. The genii, الْجِنُّ. *See also* Demon, *n.*

Genius, *n.* Nature, disposition, جِبِلَّةٌ ـ طَبِيعَةٌ ـ قَرِيحَةٌ ـ خِلْقَةٌ ـ طَوِيَّةٌ ـ خُلْقٌ. Mental power, ذَكَآءٌ ـ ذِهْنٌ ـ فِطْنَةٌ ـ إِدْرَاكٌ ـ عَقْلٌ. A man of —, ذَكِيٌّ ـ ذِهْنٌ ـ ذُو قَرِيحَةٍ ـ لَوْذَعِيٌّ ـ صَاحِبُ فِطْنَةٍ.

Genteel, *a.* Of persons, أَدِيب ـ صاحِبُ أَدَب ـ مُحْتَشِم ـ ظَرِيف ـ لَطِيف ـ لِطاف *pl.* لُطَفاء ; of things, لَطِيف. Shabby —, لُطْفُ دَجَّال.

Genteelly, *ad.* بِلَطافَةٍ ـ بِظَرافَةٍ ـ بِتَرْبِيَةٍ ـ بِأَدَب.

Genteelness, *n.* ظَرافَة ـ لَطافَة ـ إِحْتِشام ـ تَرْبِيَة.

Gentian, *n.* جانْطِيان ـ جِنْتِيانَة.

Gentile, *n.* A pagan, infidel, كافِر *pl.* كُفّار *and* كافِرُون ـ أَجْنَبِيٌّ ـ عَبَدَةُ ٱلأَوْثانِ. The Gentiles, pagans, خارِجِيٌّ *pl.* خَوارِجُ ـ وَثَنِيٌّ.

Gentilism, *n.* Paganism, عَبَدَةُ ٱلأَوْثانِ.

Gentility, *n.* Of birth, نَجابَة ـ شَرَف ـ شَرافَة. *See also* Genteelness, *n.*

Gentle, *a.* Well-born, أَصِيل ـ نَجِيب ـ شَرِيفُ ٱلأَصْلِ. Soft, meek, حَلِيم ـ رَفِيق ـ وَدِيع ـ لَيِّن ـ دَمِيث ـ خَوّارُ ٱلعِنانِ ـ لَطِيف. Soothing, مُهْدِئٌ. A — pace, إِرْواد ـ خَفْض. A — beast, دابَّةٌ سَمْحَةٌ. A — voice, صَوْتٌ خَفِيضٌ. To be —, رَفُقَ ـ حَلُمَ ². To be — to, deal gently with, أَرْوَدَ ـ تَلَطَّفَ ل ـ ذَلَّ. To be —, tame, تَسَهَّلَ عَلَى ـ ساهَلَ ـ ياسَرَ ـ تَلَطَّفَ ل ـ تَأَنَّسَ ـ أَسْمَحَ ـ سَمُحَ.

Gentle-folks, *n.* أَغْنِياء ـ أَكابِر ـ أَشْراف.

Gentleman, *n.* Of gentle birth; *see under* Gentle, *a.* As a term of complaisance, خَواجَة *pl.* خَواجات ـ أَفَنْدِي ـ آغا ـ سَيِّد. A gentleman's —, a servant, خَدّام ـ تابِع. A —, in derision, خَواجَةٌ دَجّال. The gentlemen, messieurs, الحَضَرات.

Gentlemanlike, *a.* }
Gentlemanly, } شَلَبِيٌّ ـ أَدِيب ـ لَطِيف ـ ظَرِيف.

Gentlemanlike *n.* *See* Genteelness, *n.*

Gentleness, *n.* Tameness, سَماحَة ـ أُنْس ـ ذِلّ. Meekness, softness, رَأْفَة ـ وَداعَة ـ لَيان ـ لِينَة ـ رِفْق ـ حِلْم ـ دَماثَة ـ مُساهَلَة ـ تَوَدُّد ـ لَطافَةُ طَبْع ـ بَشاشَة. Gentle dealing, إِرْواد.

Gentleness, as of voice, رَخامَة ـ رِقَّة ـ خَفْض.

Gentlewoman, *n.* Of noble birth, إِمْرَأَةٌ ـ خاتُونٌ شَرِيفَةُ ٱلأَصْلِ ـ بِنْتُ أَشْراف. A woman of polite manners, a lady, سِتٌّ *pl.* سِتّات ـ سَيِّدَة *pl.* سَيِّدات ـ خاتُون *pl.* خَواتِينُ.

Gently, *ad.* Tenderly, بِرَشاقَةٍ ـ بِلَطافَةٍ ـ بِرِقَّةٍ. Without precipitation, بِتَأَنٍّ ـ عَلَى مَهْلٍ ـ مَهْلًا ـ رُوَيْدًا. The party marched —, سارَتِ ٱلقَوْمُ رُوَيْدًا. To treat —, أَرْوَدَ ـ حَلُمَ عَن ² ـ تَرَفَّقَ ب ـ تَحَلَّمَ عَن.

Gentoo, *n.* مِنْ أَهْلِ ٱلهِنْدِ ـ هِنْدِيٌّ.

Gentry, *n.* الخاصَّة ـ الأَكابِرُ طائِفَةُ (*or* طَقْمُ) ٱلأَشْراف. The — and the common people, الخاصَّةُ وَٱلعامَّةُ.

Genuflexion, *n.* سَجْدَة ـ سُجُود ـ رُكُوع ـ خُرُور ـ رَكْعَة *pl.* رَكَعات.

Genuine, *a.* صَرِيح ـ خالِص ـ صافٍ ـ أَصِيل ـ حَقّانِيٌّ ـ حَقِيقِيٌّ. To be —, خَلَصَ ² ـ حَقَّ ². *See also under* Pure, *a.*

Genuinely, *ad.* صَراحَةً ـ بِخُلُوصٍ ـ بِصَفاوَةٍ.

Genuineness, *n.* حَقِيقَة ـ صَراحَة ـ خالِصَة ـ صِحَّة ـ صَفاء.

Genus, *n.* جِنْس *pl.* أَجْناس ـ قَبِيل *pl.* قَبائِلُ. Genus comprehends many species, الجِنْسُ يَشْمَلُ أَنْواعًا شَتَّى.

Geocentric, *a.* }
Geocentrical, } ما حاذَى مَرْكَزُهُ مَرْكَزَ كُرَةِ ٱلأَرْضِ.

Geodesy, *n.* عِلْمُ ٱلمَساحَةِ.

Geognosy, *n.* عِلْمُ تَرْكِيبِ ٱلأَرْضِ.

Geogony, *n.* عِلْمُ ٱلبَحْثِ فِي فِطْرَةِ ٱلأَرْضِ.

Geographer, *n.* مُهَنْدِسٌ جُغْرافِيٌّ ـ عالِمٌ بِهَيْئَةِ ٱلأَرْضِ ـ جُغْرافِيُّون *pl.* جُغْراف.

Geographic, *a.* }
Geographical, } جُغْرافِيٌّ ـ مُتَعَلِّقٌ بِهَيْئَةِ ٱلأَرْضِ. Its — position, مَوْقِعُهُ ٱلجُغْرافِيُّ.

Geographically, *ad.* نَظَرًا لِلجُغْرافِيَةِ ـ حَسَبَ قَوانِينِ ٱلجُغْرافِيَةِ.

Geography, *n.* جُغْرافِيَة ـ عِلْمُ رَسْمِ ٱلأَرْضِ. Physical —, جُغْرافِيَةٌ طَبِيعِيَّةٌ. Political —, جُغْرافِيَةٌ مُلْكِيَّةٌ.

Geological, *a.* مُتَعَلِّقٌ بِعِلْمِ ٱلحِجارَةِ وَٱلمَعادِنِ وَطَبَقاتِها.

Geologist, *n.* أَهْلُ عِلْمِ ٱلحِجارَةِ وَٱلمَعادِنِ.

Geologize, *v.t.* بَحَثَ عَنْ تَرْكِيبِ ٱلحِجارَةِ وَٱلمَعادِنِ.

Geology, *n.* عِلْمُ ٱلحِجارَةِ وَٱلمَعادِنِ ـ عِلْمُ طَبَقاتِ ٱلأَرْضِ.

Geomancer, *n.* خَطّاط ـ رَمّال.

Geomancy, *n.* عِلْمُ ٱلرَّمْلِ ـ عِلْمُ ٱلخَطِّ.

Geometer, *n.* مَسّاح ـ مُهَنْدِس ـ هَنْدَسِيٌّ.

Geometral, }
Geometric, *a.* }
Geometrical, } هَنْدَسِيٌّ. Geometrical ratio, نِسْبَةٌ هَنْدَسِيَّةٌ. Geometrical proportion, تَناسُبٌ هَنْدَسِيٌّ ـ تَزايُدٌ وَتَناقُصٌ هَنْدَسِيٌّ.

Geometrically, *ad.* عَلَى قَوانِينِ ٱلهَنْدَسَةِ.

Geometrician, *n.* *See* Geometer, *n.*

Geometrize, *v.t.* To perform geometrically, حَسَبَ ـ حَسَّبَ ² قَوانِينِ ٱلهَنْدَسَةِ.

Geometry, *n.* عِلْمُ ٱلهَنْدَسَةِ ـ هَنْدَسَة ـ مَساحَة.

George, *n.* The medallion of the Order of the Garter, إِيقُونَةٌ مَنْقُوشٌ عَلَيْها تِمْثالُ حَضْرَةِ جِرْجِيس وَهُوَ راكِبٌ عَلَى حِصانٍ ـ إِيقُونَةُ حَضْرَةِ ـ يَحْمِلُها ٱلحائِزُونَ نِيشانَ ٱلكَرْتِرِ ٱلكُلِّيِّ ٱلشَّرَفِ جِرْجِيس.

Georgic, *n.* قَصِيدَةٌ فِي مَدْحِ ٱلفَلاحَةِ.

Georgic, *a.*
Georgical, } مُتَعَلِّقٌ بِٱلْفِلَاحَةِ.

Georgium-Sidus, *n.* سَيَّارَةُ هِرْشَل.

Geranium, *n.* إِبْرَةُ ٱلرَّاعِي.

Gerfalcon, *n.* شَاهِين *pl.* شَوَاهِين.

Germ, *n.* A seed-bud, بِذْر *pl.* بُذُور ـ شُكْر *pl.* شُكَيْر ـ نَشْأ ـ بَارِض ـ نَبْت *coll.* نَبَات. Origin, first principle, أَسَاس ـ أَصْل ـ طَلْع ـ طُلُوع.

German, *n.* and *a.* A native of Germany, نَمْسَاوِيّ *pl.* نَمْسَاوِيَّة.

German, *a.* A cousin — on the brother's side, or first cousin, اِبْنُ عَمٍّ لَحًّا; on the sister's side, اِبْنُ خَالَةٍ لَحًّا. A female cousin-german, شَقِيقَة.

Germanic, *a.* نَمْسَاوِيّ.

Germanism, *n.* عِبَارَةٌ نَمْسَاوِيَّة.

German-silver, *n.* مَعْدِنٌ أَبْيَض ـ مَعْدِن.

Germany, *n.* نَمْسَا ـ بِلَادُ ٱلنَّمْسَا ـ جَرْمَانِيَا.

Germen, *n.* See Germ, *n.*

Germinal, *a.* بِذْرِيّ ـ نَبْتِيّ ـ مُتَعَلِّقٌ بِٱلشُّكَيْر.

Germinant, *a.* نَابِت ـ بَاذِر ـ شَاكِر.

Germinate, *v.t.* To sprout, نَبَتَ ² ـ أَبْرَضَ ـ بَرَّضَ ـ أَلْحَسَ; of seeds, قَصَّعَ.

Germination, *n.* إِلْحَاس ـ تَبْرِيض ـ تَنْبِيت; of seeds, تَقْصِيع.

Gerund, *n.* إِسْمُ فَاعِلٍ.

Gestation, *n.* حَمْل ـ مُدَّةُ ٱلْحَمْلِ.

Gestatory,
Gestic, *a.*
Gesticulatory, } حَرَكَاتِيّ ـ مُوْمِئ. Making ridiculous gestures, مَسْخَرَاتِيّ.

Gesticulate, *v.i.* تَحَرَّكَ ـ إِسْتَعْمَلَ ٱلْإِيمَآء. To — ridiculously, تَمَسْخَرَ.

Gesticulate, *v.t.* To make signs to, أَوْمَأَ إِلَى ـ أَشَارَ إِلَى.

Gesticulation, *n.* The act of making gestures, signs, إِيمَآء; of making ridiculous gestures, مَسْخَرَة ـ هُزْأَة.

Gesticulator, *n.* One who makes signs, مُوْمِئ. One who makes ridiculous gestures, سُخْرَة ـ هُزْأَة.

Gesture, *n.* A motion, nod, وَمْأ ـ إِيمَآء ـ حَرَكَة ـ إِشَارَة. Position, وَضْع. An amorous —, غَزَل ـ دُلّ ـ شِكْل ـ غُنْج ـ غُنَاج. To make amorous gestures, تَغَنَّجَ; of a woman, تَشَكَّلَتْ ـ شَكِلَتْ ـ تَدَلَّلَتْ ـ تَغَنَّجَتْ. A woman who makes amorous gestures, شَكِلَة ـ غَانِجَة ـ مِغْنَاج. Gestures, أَوْضَاع.

Gesture, *v.t.* أَظْهَرَ بِٱلْحَرَكَاتِ ـ شَوَّرَ إِلَى.

Get, *v.a.* To acquire, obtain, قَنَى ـ إِقْتَنَى ـ فَازَ بِ ² ـ كَسَبَ ـ إِكْتَسَبَ ـ حَصَّلَ. To gain, كَسَبَ ـ رَبِحَ. To attain, فَازَ بِ ² ـ أَدْرَكَ ـ حَصَلَ عَلَى ² ـ لَحِقَ ². To win, أَصَابَ ـ ظَفِرَ بِ ـ حَظِيَ بِ ـ إِمْتَلَكَ. To beget, نَسَلَ ² ـ وَلَدَ *aor.* يَلِدُ. To learn, حَفِظَ ـ تَعَلَّمَ. To have possession of, مَلَكَ ـ فَازَ بِ ² ـ ل. To catch, as of a disease, أُصِيبَ بِ ـ وَصَلَ إِلَى ـ تَسَلَّمَ. To receive, as of a letter, إِرْتَكَبَ ـ إِعْتَرَى *aor.* يَصِلُ. To get, to prevail on, to ..., رَغَّبَ فِي ـ حَمَلَ عَلَى ـ أَلْزَمَ بِ ـ إِضْطَرَّ إِلَى ـ أَغْصَبَ بِ. To make to do, جَعَلَ أَن. To draw, جَذَبَ. To catch, as of game, إِصْطَادَ. To get a thing made, إِصْطَنَعَ; to order a thing from one, وَصَّى بِ. To get a thing mended, أَصْلَحَ ـ رَمْرَمَ. To get one into one's power, تَسَلَّطَ عَلَى ـ تَضَبَّطَ. To get or squeeze something out of one, قَصَّعَ مِن ـ آ... To get one to tell, to pump, ... تَجَسَّسَ مِن ـ آ.... To get one employed, شَغَّلَ ـ قَعَّدَ ـ حَطَّ فِي مَنْصِبٍ ². To get by heart, حَفِظَ ـ حَفِظَ غَيْبًا. To get one's self to, to go to, ذَهَبَ إِلَى ـ إِنْطَلَقَ إِلَى. To get one's self up, to adorn one's self, تَزَيَّنَ ـ تَزَخْرَفَ. To get one home, جَذَبَ إِلَى ٱلْبَيْتِ. Get thee gone! إِذْهَبْ ـ إِنْقَلِعْ.

(*Note.*—The verb "Get" throughout the following examples is in the *active* or *transitive* voice; *e.g.* "To get away," means to get one or something away.)

To get advantage of, إِنْتَصَرَ عَلَى ـ غَلَبَ ـ فَازَ بِ ².

To get along, as on a road, سَلَكَ ² ـ مَشَّى. To make to improve, to push forward, أَفَادَ ـ رَوَّجَ ـ قَدَّمَ ـ أَنْجَحَ ـ وَفَّقَ.

To get away, نَقَلَ ² ـ أَبْعَدَ ـ شَالَ بِ.

To get back, to make to return, إِسْتَرَدَّ ـ رَجَّعَ ـ رَدَّدَ. To get possession of anew, إِرْتَدَّ ـ إِعْتَادَ ـ عَادَ حَصَلَ عَلَى ² ـ مَلَكَ ثَانِيَةً ².

To get down, to prostrate, أَجْفَأَ بِهِ ـ كَبَّ ² ـ أَكَبَّ ـ أَهْبَطَ ـ أَوْقَعَ. To bring down, نَزَّلَ ـ أَهْبَطَ. To swallow, إِلْتَقَمَ ـ إِبْتَلَعَ.

To get forward; *see* To get along.

To get hold of, ضَبَطَ ـ قَبَضَ بِ. To get hold and carry off, سَلَبَ ².

To get in, to make to enter, أَدْخَلَ ـ أَخَشَّ; as a thread into a needle, سَلَكَ ² ـ وَسَّقَ ـ عَبَّأَ. To take in, as cargo, شَحَنَ. To collect, as a harvest, حَصَدَ ². To collect, to ask for payment, إِجْتَزَى ـ طَلَبَ غَلْقَ ٱلْحِسَابِ ².

To get off, as of a dress, خَلَعَ ـ نَزَعَ ـ شَلَحَ. To save one from, سَلَّمَ-مِن ـ خَلَّصَ-مِن ـ أَنْقَذَ-مِن. To float, as a ship, ـ ء صَرَفَ ـ أَجْرَى. To put into circulation, أَسْبَحَ ـ عَوَّمَ ـ رَوَّجَ.

To get on, as of a dress, ء لَبِسَ. To improve one, push forward; *see* To get along.

To get out, as of a stain, أَزَالَ ـ ٤ مَحَا. To cause one to come out, أَخْرَجَ. To extricate from, أَنْقَذَ-مِن ـ أَفْرَجَ-مِن ـ خَلَّصَ-مِن ـ فَرَّجَ-مِن. To get out, as of a tooth, قَلَّعَ; as of a thorn, ء نَتَفَ ـ ء نَتَعَ.

To get out of one, to sound, ...تَجَسَّسَ مِن-آل.

To get over, to make to cross, عَبَّرَ. To cure, ـ ء شَفَى-مِن أَطَابَ ـ أَبْرَأَ-مِن. To extricate; *see under* To get out.

To get under, as of a fire, أَطْفَأَ ـ أَهْمَدَ. To master, ـ ء قَمَعَ ـ ء ضَبَطَ أَكَبَّ ـ أَوْقَعَ ـ أَجْفَأَ بِ ـ جَفَأَ. To prostrate,

To get up, to make to arise, أَقَامَ. To make to go up, أَصْعَدَ. To originate, أَبْدَأَ ـ أَقَامَ ـ عَقَدَ ـ أَنْشَأَ. To arrange, ـ نَسَّقَ نَظَمَ ـ رَتَّبَ. To build, ء بَنَى ـ عَمَّرَ. To be got up, of a meeting, *etc.*, تَحَشَّدَ ـ تَشَكَّلَ.

Get, *v.i.* To be on the way to, to become ء كَانَ يَصِيرُ; *vulg.* شَمَّالِ يَصِير. (The idea of *getting to be* is almost always expressed in Arabic by different forms of the verb, as is also the case sometimes in English; *e.g.* To redden, *i.e.* to become red. The equivalents for the Arabic will be generally found in this Lexicon in the ordinary English passive form *to be*.... In almost every such case the Arabic has the additional force of *to become*...)

(*Note.*—The verb "Get," in the subjoined examples, *when not followed by a particle making it transitive*, is used throughout in an *intransitive* sense.)

To get at, to find, reach, وَصَلَ إِلَى ـ ٤ بَلَغَ ـ ٤ حَصَلَ عَلَى *aor.* يَصِلُ. To find, encounter, وَجَدَ *aor.* يَجِدُ ـ لَاقَى.

To get above a thing, فَاقَ عَلَى ـ ٤ فَاقَ.

To get along, to advance, تَقَدَّمَ. To prosper, تَوَفَّقَ ـ أَفْلَحَ.

To get away, to leave, ء ذَهَبَ ـ إِنْصَرَفَ ـ ء مَضَى. To escape, ء فَلَتَ ـ تَفَلَّتَ ـ إِنْفَلَتَ. To float (*v.i.*), ٤ طَفَا ـ ٤ عَامَ.

To get back, to return, ء قَدِمَ مِن ـ ٤ عَادَ إِلَى ـ ء رَجَعَ.

To get better, as in health, تَجَبَّرَ ـ شُفِيَ. To improve, ـ إِصْطَلَحَ إِسْتَتَبَّ.

To get between, ٤ دَخَلَ بَيْنَ.

To get clear, as of the weather, ء صَحَتِ ٱلدُّنْيَا ـ أَصْحَى ـ ٤ صَحَا.

To get clear of, to become disentangled from, ـ إِنْعَتَقَ مِن إِنْفَصَى مِن ـ تَفَصَّى مِن ـ تَمَلَّصَ مِن ـ تَخَلَّصَ مِن. To be rid of,

To get clear of debt, تَبَرَّأَ مِنَ ٱلدَّيْنِ ـ أَوْفَى ٱلدَّيْنَ.

To get down, to descend, ٤ هَبَطَ ـ إِنْحَدَرَ ـ ء نَزَلَ.

To get forward; *see* To get along.

To get home, وَرَدَ عَلَى (or وَصَلَ إِلَى *aor.* يَصِلُ) ٱلْبَيْتِ *aor.* يَرِدُ.

To get on; *see* To get along.

To get in, to enter, ٤ فَاتَ إِلَى جَوًّا ـ ٤ دَخَلَ إِلَى. To get in the way, as of danger, جَازَفَ ـ تَعَرَّضَ لِ.

To get loose, to run away, ء جَفَلَ ـ ء فَرَّ ـ إِنْفَلَتَ ٤. To become slack, إِرْتَخَى ـ إِنْحَلَّ.

To get off, as from a chair, ٤ قَامَ عَن ـ ء نَزَلَ عَن ـ ٤ قَعَدَ عَن.

To dismount, تَرَجَّلَ عَن ـ حَوَّلَ ـ ء نَزَلَ عَن.

To get on, to mount, رَكِبَ عَلَى ـ ء رَكِبَ. *See also* To get along.

To get out; *see* To get away, *and* To get clear of.

To get out of the way of, to move aside, إِنْحَرَفَ ـ تَجَنَّبَ. To secrete one's self, تَطَفَّشَ ـ إِخْتَفَى.

To get over, to cross, أَجَازَ ـ ء قَطَعَ ـ ء عَبَرَ. To recover, ـ تَجَبَّرَ ـ تَسَلَّى عَن ـ تَأَسَّى عَن ـ تَعَافَى ـ شُفِيَ. To be consoled for, تَعَزَّى (or تَصَبَّرَ) عَن. To accomplish, أَنْجَزَ ـ أَنْفَذَ. To travel over, ٤ سَلَكَ ـ ء عَارَ فِي ـ يَسِيحُ *aor.* سَاحَ فِي. To peruse, ء قَرَأَ ـ طَالَعَ ـ ٤ تَلَا.

To get through; *see* To get over, *and* To get clear of.

To get tiresome to, ء زَعِلَ مِن ـ ٤ عَنَا ٱلْأَمْرُ عَلَى.

To get together, to assemble, تَحَشَّدُوا ـ إِجْتَمَعُوا.

To get to sleep, ء نَامَ ـ أَغْفَى ـ ٤ رَقَدَ.

To get up to, to overtake, أَلْحَقَ ـ أَدْرَكَ. To be equal to, سَاوَى ـ إِسْتَقْرَنَ لِ. To ascend, ء صَعِدَ.

Gewgaw, *n.* *See* Bauble, *n.*

Geyser, *n.* فَوَّارَةُ مَآءٍ غَالٍ.

Ghastful, *a.* Frightful, هَائِلٌ ـ مُرْعِبٌ ـ فَظِيعٌ.

Ghastliness, *n.* Horror of countenance, وَحْشَةٌ ـ هَوْلُ ٱلْمَنْظَرِ وَجْهٍ. Paleness, صُفَارُ ٱلْوَجْهِ ـ سَوَادُ ٱلْوَجْهِ.

Ghastly, *a.* Pale, مُصْفَرٌّ ـ أَصْفَرُ ٱلْوَجْهِ ـ أَسْوَدُ ٱلْوَجْهِ.

Ghaut, *n.* جِبَالٌ *pl.* جَبَلٌ ـ تِهَامَةٌ.

Ghee, *n.* سَمْنٌ *pl.* سُمْنَانٌ. A seller of —, سَمَّانٌ.

Gherkin, *n.* ضُغْبُوصٌ *pl.* ضَغَابِيصُ.

Ghost, *n.* A spectre, خَيَالٌ *pl.* أَخْيِلَةٌ ـ زَوْلٌ *pl.* أَزْوَالٌ ـ طَيْفٌ *pl.* طُيُوفٌ. Soul, spirit, رُوحٌ *pl.* أَرْوَاحٌ ـ نَفْسٌ *pl.* نُفُوسٌ. To give up the —, أَسْلَمَ ٱلرُّوحَ ـ ء فَاظَ نَفْسَهُ. The Holy Ghost, ٱلرُّوحُ ٱلْقُدُسُ.

Ghostly, *a.* Spectral, خَيالِيٌّ . Spiritual, رُوحانِيٌّ ـ رُوحِيٌّ .

Ghoul, *n.* / **Ghole**, } غُول *pl.* غِيلان *and* أَغْوال .

Giant, *n.* جَبّار *pl.* جَبابِرَة ـ عَوْن *pl.* أَعْوان .

Giant, **Giant-like**, *a.* **Giantly**, } Like a giant, كَالْجَبّارِ ـ جَبّار . Large, عَظِيم ـ جَبّار ـ أَكْبَر ـ كَبِير .

Giantess, *n.* جَبّارَة *pl.* جَبّارات .

Giantship, *n.* جَبَرُوت ـ جَبَرُوَّة .

Giaour, *n.* كافِر *pl.* كُفّار ـ كاوُر .

Gibber, *v.i.* بَرْطَمَ ـ هَمْرَجَ ـ غَذْمَرَ .

Gibberish, *n.* غَذْمَرَة ـ لَغْوٌ ـ هَمْرَجَة . To speak — to, رَطَنَ ل ².

Gibbet, *n.* مِشْنَقَة *pl.* مَشانِق .

Gibbet, *v.t.* صَلَبَ ـ شَنَقَ ².

Gibbose, *a.* **Gibbous**, } مُحَرَّن ـ ناتِئٌ ـ أَحْدَبُ ـ مُقَوَّب . To be —, تَحَدَّبَ ـ نَتَأَ .

Gibbosity, *n.* **Gibbousness**, } نَتأ ـ نُتُوءٌ ـ تَحَدُّب ـ تَقَوُّس .

Gib-cat, *n.* قِطٌّ عَجُوزٌ .

Gibe, *v.t.* To assail with scorn, نَقَرَ ² ـ قَرَصَ ب ² ـ اِسْتَهْزَأَ ب ـ سَخِرَ مِن ـ ضَحِكَ عَلَى *or* مِن .

Gibe, *n.* قارِصَة *pl.* قَوارِص ـ نَقْر ـ نَقْرَى ـ مَسْخَرَة ـ هُزْؤٌ .

Giblets, *n.* سَقَطُ الطُّيُورِ *vulg.* عِفْشُ الطُّيُورِ .

Gibraltar, *n.* جَبَلُ طارِق . The Straits of —, بَحْرُ زُقاقِ سَبْتَة ـ الزُّقاق ـ بُوغازُ جَبَلِ طارِق .

Giddily, *ad.* With vertigo, بِمَيْدٍ ـ بِدَوْخ . Carelessly, بِتَهامُلٍ ـ بِغَفْلَةٍ .

Giddiness, *n.* Vertigo, مَيْد ـ دُوار ـ دَوْخَة ـ هُدام ـ رَنْح . Changeableness, دَوْخ ـ طَيْرَة ـ طَيْرُورَة ـ فَرْفَرَة ـ ناقِلَة ـ اِنْقِلاب . Wantonness, طَيْش ـ طَيَشان . To be affected with —, vertigo, مادَ ² ـ داخَ ². He has —, بِهِ دَوْخَة .

Giddy, *a.* Vertiginous, دائِخ ـ مَدُورٌ بِهِ . Thoughtless, wild, أَثْوَل ـ طائِش ـ أَطْيَر ـ مَطْيُور ـ مُتَغافِل . Unsteady, unsettled, خُرَجَة وُلَجَة ـ نُعَرَة فِي رَأْسِهِ ـ فَرْفار ـ مُتَقَلْقِل ـ قُلَّب ـ مُتَحَيِّر ـ عَدِيمُ السُّكُونِ . To be —, unsteady, طاشَ *aor.* يَطِيشُ . To render —, unsteady, أَطاشَ . To be —, with vertigo, مادَ ² ـ داخَ ². To make so —, رَنَّحَ ـ دَوَّخَ .

Giddy-brained, *a.* **Giddy-headed**, } خَرِيم ـ أَطْيَر ـ طائِش ـ كاهِل ـ أَثْوَل ـ مَجْنُون ـ مَلْطُوش . To be —, ثالَ *aor.* يَثُولُ ـ طاشَ *aor.* يَطِيشُ .

Gift, *n.* A present, هَدِيَّة *pl.* أَعْطِيَة ـ هِبَة ـ عَطاء *or* عَطا ـ *pl.* هَدايا ـ عَطِيَّة مَجّانِيَّة ـ مَوْهِبَة *pl.* مَواهِبُ . A voluntary —, benefit, سَيْب *pl.* سُيُوب . A small —, عُطَيٌّ . A fine present, تُحْفَة *pl.* تُحَف . An oblation, sacrifice, قُرْبان *pl.* قَرابِينُ ـ ضَحِيَّة *pl.* ضَحايا . A small present, لُطْفَة . A — without compensation, (the vulgar word is), جَبَا . A bribe, بِرْطِيل ـ رَشْوَة . A talent, قَرِيحَة ـ فَضِيلَة *pl.* فَضائِل ـ صِفَة *pl.* صِفات . A charitable —, زَكاة ـ صَدَقَة . To make a free —, تَبَرَّعَ بِالْعَطاء .

Gifted, *a.* As with talents, مُزَيَّن ب ـ مُفَضَّل ب ـ مُوَشَّح ب . Talented, فاضِل ـ مُفَضَّل ـ فَضّال ـ مِفْضال . To be — with something, أُوتِيَ كَذا .

Gig, *n.* A whirligig, دُوّارَة ـ هَرِيرَة . A small carriage, عَرَبانَة صَغِيرَة . A small boat, فَلُوكَة خَفِيفَة ـ قارِب *pl.* قَوارِب ـ قائِق .

Gigantic, *a.* Like a giant, عَوْنِيٌّ ـ كَالْجَبّارِ . Enormous, كَبِيرٌ (*or* عَظِيمٌ) لِلْغايَةِ .

Giggle, *n.* ضَحِكَة ـ كَتْكَتَة ـ هَأْهَأَة ـ قَهْقَهَة .

Giggle, *v.i.* ضَحِكَ ـ هَأْهَأَ ـ كَتْكَتَ ـ قَهْقَهَ .

Giggler, *n.* ضَحّاك ـ بُهْلُول ـ مُكَتْكِت ـ مُقَهْقِه .

Gigot, *n.* فَخِذ *pl.* أَفْخاذ .

Gild, *v.t.* To — with gold, طَلَى بِالذَّهَبِ ـ ذَهَّبَ ـ مَوَّهَ ـ مَوَّهَ (*or* لَطَخَ) بِالذَّهَبِ . To adorn, زَيَّنَ ـ زَخْرَفَ . To — a bait for, حَلَّى (*or* حَلَّأَ) ل .

Gilder, *n.* مُمَوِّه ـ طَلّاء ـ مُذَهِّب .

Gilding, *n.* طَلاء ـ تَذْهِيب . Gold-wash for —, دُجال ـ غُراب .

Gill, *n.* The measure, جِلّ وَهُوَ مِكْيالُ الْمَوائِعِ يَسَعُ ٣٥ دِرْهَمًا .
The gills of a fish, رِئَةُ السَّمَكِ ـ نَخْشُوشُ السَّمَكِ .

Gilly-flower, *n.* مَنْثُور ; the yellow —, خِيرِيّ .

Gilt, *a.* Overlaid with gold, مُذَهَّب ـ مُمَوَّه (*or* مَلْطُوخ) بِالذَّهَبِ .

Gimbal, *n.* The — for a compass, حَلْقَة لِلْبُوصْلَة (*or* لِبَيْتِ الْإِبْرَة) .

Gimcrack, *n.* Trivial or worthless mechanism, آلَة بَطّالَة ـ دُولاب لا طائِلَ فِيهِ . *See also* Trifle, *n.*

Gimlet, *n.* مِثْقَب ـ مِخْرَز ـ عَتَلَة ـ بَرِّيمَة ـ مِلْخَش .

Gimp, *n.* ضَرْبٌ مِنَ الْقَيْطانِ (*or* الْمُخَرَّجِ) .

Gin, *n.* The spirit, رُوحُ حَبِّ الْعَرْعَرِ ـ رُوحُ حَبِّ الْكُوكَلانِ ـ ضَرْبٌ مِنَ الْعَرَقِ . A trap, حِبالَة *pl.* حَبائِل ـ مِصْيَدَة ـ فَخّ *pl.* فِخاخ . An instrument for cleaning cotton of its seed, مِحْلَج .

Gin, *v.t.* To clean cotton of its seed, حَلَجَ ‎ِ ‎ُ. To snare, صَادَ *aor.* يَصِيدُ — اِصْطَادَ. To change one's mind, عَدَلَ عَنْ ‎ِ.

Ginger, *n.* جَنْزَبِيل — زَنْجَفِيل — زَنْجَبِيل.

Ginger-beer, *n.* شَرَابُ زَنْجَبِيلٍ.

Ginger-bread, *n.* كَعْكُ زَنْجَبِيلٍ.

Ginger-wine, *n.* شَرَابُ (or خَمْرُ) ٱلزَّنْجَبِيلِ.

Ginger-bread-work, *n.* Ornamental work, ٱلدَّوَاخِلُ وَٱلْخَوَارِجُ — شُغْلٌ مُزَخْرَفٌ — صَنْعَةٌ مُشَكَّلَةٌ. Fragile work, شُغْلٌ خَفِيفٌ — صَنْعَةٌ حَطِمَةٌ — شُغْلٌ هَشُّ ٱلْمَكْسِرِ (or سَرِيعُ ٱلْعَطَبِ).

Gingerly, *ad.* Carefully, بِٱحْتِيَاطٍ — بِخِفَّةٍ — عَلَى مَهْلٍ.

Gingham, *n.* ضَرْبٌ مِنَ ٱلْقُمَاشِ.

Gingival, *a.* مُخْتَصٌّ بِٱللِّثَاتِ.

Gingle, *v.i.* *See* Jingle, *v.i.*

Gipsy, *n.* غُجْرِيٌّ *pl.* غُجْر: called in Egypt, نَوَرِيٌّ *coll.* نَوَر; in Kasruân, قَرَبَاتِيٌّ *pl.* قَرَبَاتِيَّة; in Aleppo, زُطِّيٌّ *coll.* زُطّ; in Damascus, ضَرَّابُ فَالٍ; in Mesopotamia, مُطْرِبِيٌّ *pl.* مَطَارِبَة.

Gipsies, called in Turkey, چِنْگَنَة.

Gipsy, *a.* Like a gipsy, غُجْرِيٌّ. Brown, أَسْمَرُ *fem.* سَمْرَآءُ *pl.* سُمْر.

Giraffe, *n.* زَرَافَةٌ *pl.* زَرَافِيُّ and زَرَافِي.

Girandole, *n.* مَنَارَةٌ *pl.* مَنَائِرُ — ثُرَيَّا *pl.* ثُرَيَّات.

Gird, *n.* A blow, ضَرْبَةٌ. A taunt, قَارِصَةٌ — نَقْرَةٌ. A hoop, مِنْطَق. *See also under* Hoop, *n.*

Gird, *v.t.* To bind with a girdle, حَزَمَ ‎ِ — زَنَّرَ. To — with a bandage, شَدَّ ‎ُ — عَصَّبَ بِعِصَابَةٍ. To — with a hoop, نَطَّقَ بِمِنْطَقَةٍ. To inclose, أَحَاطَ بِ — حَاصَرَ. To — up, كَمَّشَ. To dress, لَبَّسَ. To — one's own loins with, تَزَنَّرَ بِ — شَدَّ ‎ُ حَقْوَيْهِ بِ — وَسَطَهُ بِ. To — another with a sword, قَلَّدَ بِسَيْفٍ. To — one's self with a sword, تَقَلَّدَ بِسَيْفٍ. *See also under to* Hoop, *v.t.*

Girder, *n.* عَارِضَةٌ *pl.* عَوَارِض — خَشَبَةٌ *pl.* خَشَبَات.

Girdle, *n.* حِزَامٌ *pl.* أَحْزِمَةٌ and حِزَامَات — زُنَّار *pl.* زَنَانِير — مِنْطَقَةٌ. A lady's —, حِيَاصَةٌ — حِزَام. A leather — worn by servants, سَبْتَة. A — with a pouch for money, كَمَر. The zodiack, مِنْطَقَةُ ٱلْبُرُوجِ.

Girdle, *v.t.* *See to* Gird, *v.t.*

Girl, *n.* جَارِيَةٌ *pl.* جَوَارٍ — صَبِيَّةٌ *pl.* صَبَايَا — بِنْتٌ *pl.* بَنَات — بِنْتَة. A servant —, جَارِيَةٌ *pl.* جَوَارٍ — خَدَّامَةٌ *pl.* خَدَّامَات.

Girlhood, *n.* جَرَآءٌ — جَرَايَةٌ — جَرَآئِيَّةٌ — طُفُولِيَّةٌ — صَبَآءٌ.

Girlish, *a.* مِثْلَ ٱلصَّبِيَّةِ. Light, giddy, فَرَّارَةٌ — آنُولَةٌ — طَائِشَةٌ.

Girlishness, *n.* جَرَايَةٌ — جَرَائِيَّةٌ.

Girth, *n.* Of a saddle, وَلَمٌ — وَضِين — ضَفِير — شِكَال *pl.* شُكُل. A fore or belly —, بِطَان; a hind —, حَقَب; the breast —, سِنَاف — لَبَب — تَصْدِير.

Gist, *n.* خُلَاصَةٌ — نَصٌّ — لُبٌّ — زُبْدَةٌ. The — of a speech, نَصُّ ٱلْكَلَامِ — زُبْدَةُ ٱلْعِبَارَةِ.

Give, *v.a.* To bestow, أَعْطَى — وَهَبَ لِ *aor.* يَهَبُ. To — to with kindness, سَامَحَ بِ — سَمَحَ لِ ‎َ — أَنْعَمَ عَلَى بِ — أَكْرَمَ عَلَى بِ — أَهْدَى إِلَى — اِمْتَنَّ عَلَى بِ — أَرْزَقَ بِ — بَذَلَ بِ. To hand to, نَالَ لِ ‎َ — نَوَّلَ عَلَى — أَنَالَ. To pay, as of a price, أَعْطَى; to buy at a price, اِشْتَرَى بِ. To pay to, دَفَعَ ‎َ — دَفَعَ إِلَى ‎َ. To grant, confer, مَنَحَ ‎َ ‎ُ — مَنَّ — أَنْعَمَ عَلَى بِ. To deliver to, سَلَّمَ إِلَى — أَدَّى لِ — أَوْصَلَ لِ. To show, أَبْدَى — أَعْلَنَ — أَظْهَرَ — بَيَّنَ. To amount to, بَلَغَ إِلَى ‎ُ — صَارَ مَبْلَغُهُ ‎ِ. To — one as good as he brings, of evil, قَابَلَ بِٱلْقَبِيحِ. Give thou! هَاتِ. Shall we — or not —? أَنُعْطِي أَمْ لَا نُعْطِي.

To give again, رَجَّعَ — رَدَّدَ.

To give a good account of the enemy, to commit havoc among them, كَانَ ذَا شَوْكَةٍ فِي ٱلْعَدُوِّ.

To give an answer, أَجَابَ — اِسْتَجَابَ — رَدَّ جَوَابًا ‎ُ.

To give away, make a present of, تَبَرَّعَ بِ — أَعْطَى هَدِيَّةً — أَهْدَى — بَخْشَشَ.

To give back, to restore, أَعَادَ — رَدَّ ‎ُ — رَجَّعَ.

To give chase to, طَارَدَ — تَبِعَ ‎َ — لَاحَقَ.

To give credit to, of money, أَدَانَ — أَقْرَضَ — أَعَارَ — سَلَّفَ. To believe, صَدَّقَ.

To give a denial to, أَنْكَرَ — كَذَّبَ — أَكْذَبَ.

To give forth, to enounce, أَنْشَأَ — لَفَظَ بِ ‎ِ — تَفَوَّهَ بِ — قَالَ ‎ُ. To publish, نَادَى بِ — أَشَاعَ بِ — أَذَاعَ بِ. To publish, as of a book, بَرَّزَ — نَشَرَ ‎ُ ‎ِ.

To give ear, or a hearing to, اِسْتَمَعَ لِ — تَنَصَّتَ لِ — أَصْغَى إِلَى — سَمِعَ مِن ‎َ — أَذِنَ لِ ‎َ.

To give in, as of an account, عَرَضَ ‎ِ — قَدَّمَ — أَعْطَى بَيَانَ ٱلـ....

To give in charge, to intrust with, أَوْدَعَ لِ — اِسْتَوْدَعَ لِ — آمَنَ عَلَى — اِسْتَأْمَنَ عَلَى. To give in charge to the police, سَلَّمَ لِلضَّبْطِيَّةِ.

To give in to, to submit to, قَنَعَ إِلَى ‎َ — اِنْقَادَ إِلَى — سَلَّمَ إِلَى — تَذَلَّلَ لِ.

To give it, as of a judgment, against, to decide against, حَكَمَ عَلَى ‎ُ: He gave it against him in the affair, تَفَوَّتَ عَلَيْهِ فِي ٱلْأَمْرِ.

To give it, as of a judgment, for, to decide in favour of, ² حَكَمَ ل.

To give leave to; *see below*, To give permission to.

To give off, to emit, أَخْرَجَ ـ أَصْدَرَ ـ أَبْرَزَ; of sparks, أَبْرَزَ ٱلشَّرَارَ.

To give out, to distribute, فَرَّقَ-بَيْنَ ـ وَزَّعَ-عَلَى ـ إِقْتَسَطَ. *See also* To give forth.

To give one's self out for, إِدَّعَى بِ ـ تَظَاهَرَ بِ ـ تَصَلَّفَ بِ.

To give over, as a charge, to another, سَلَّمَ-إِلَى ـ فَوَّضَ-إِلَى. To cease to do, إِنْقَطَعَ عَن ـ إِنْفَتَرَ مِن ـ زَالَ عَن *aor.* يَزُولُ ـ بَطَّلَ. To give over, to despair of, أَيِسَ مِن *aor.* يَأْيَسُ ـ قَطَعَ ٱلْيَأْسَ مِن. To give over, to resign, renounce, نَزَلَ ـ ² تَرَكَ ـ عَن. To make to give over, or to restore, إِسْتَرَدَّ.

To give permission to, أَذِنَ ل-فِي ـ رَخَّصَ ل ـ جَوَّزَ ـ سَوَّغَ ـ أَذِنَ-فِي.

To give place, room, to, وَسَّعَ ل ـ فَسَحَ ل. *See also below*, To give way to.

To give rise to, سَبَّبَ ـ أَنْشَأَ ـ أَصْدَرَ. To give rise to misgivings, أَثَارَ ٱلْهَوَاجِسَ.

To give one the slip, تَطَفَّشَ مِن ـ إِنْفَلَتَ مِن ـ ² نَجَا مِن.

To give suck to, أَرْضَعَ ـ أَرْغَثَ.

To give up, to deliver over, سَلَّمَ. To relinquish, ² تَرَكَ ـ تَخَلَّى عَن ـ إِنْتَهَى عَن: He gave up his right, ² تَرَكَ حَقَّهُ. To resign, as of a claim, نَزَلَ عَن ـ ² تَرَكَ. To give up, as not being able to do, عَجَزَ عَن ـ إِنْقَشَّ عَن.

To give one's self up, إِسْتَسْلَمَ ـ أَسْلَمَ.

To give one's self up to an affair, تَوَلَّعَ بِ ـ تَجَرَّنَ لِلْأَمْرِ ـ تَفَرَّغَ ل ـ وَاظَبَ عَلَى ـ ² جَدَّ فِي ـ إِنْكَبَّ عَلَى.

To give thanks, to thank one, تَشَكَّرَ ل ـ ² شَكَرَ ل.

To give the lie to; *see* To give a denial to.

To give to understand, أَفْهَمَ ـ فَهَّمَ ـ أَخْبَرَ-بِ ـ أَعْلَنَ ـ أَفَادَ.

To give way to, to yield to, سَلَّمَ ل ـ أَذْعَنَ ل ـ طَاوَعَ.

Give, *v.i.* To become loose, لَانَ ـ إِرْتَخَى ـ إِسْتَرْخَى.

To give in, to yield, إِسْتَسْلَمَ ـ أَسْلَمَ.

To give off, or over, to cease, ² كَفَّ عَن ـ تَمَّ ـ إِنْقَطَعَ عَن ـ ² بَطَلَ.

To give way, to move aside, تَجَنَّبَ ـ تَنَحَّى. To listen to, to be beguiled, إِنْخَدَعَ. To break, to become loose, إِنْقَطَعَ ـ إِرْتَخَى ـ إِنْفَلَتَ. To relent, لَانَ ـ رَحِمَ. To be treacherous to, خَانَ *aor.* يَخُونُ: His legs gave way under him, خَانَتْهُ رِجْلَاهُ. He cannot give way on the Eastern Question, لا يُمْكِنُهُ أَنْ يَتَسَاهَلَ فِي ٱلْمَسْأَلَةِ ٱلشَّرْقِيَّةِ.

Given, *a.* Given or addicted to, ... مُدْمِنُ ٱل ـ مَطْبُوعٌ عَلَى.

To be —, addicted, to, تَدَرَّبَ بِ ـ دَرِبَ بِ ـ لَوِيَ عَلَى ـ تَعَاطَى ـ تَعَلَّثَ بِ. Given to, characterized by, مَطْبُوعٌ عَلَى.

Given to wine, مُدْمِنُ ٱلْخَمْرِ. To be — up to, absorbed in, إِغْتَرَقَ فِي ـ غَرِيَ بِ.

Giver, *n.* وَاهِب ـ مَنَّان ـ مَانِح ـ مُعْطٍ; a large —, وَهَّاب.

God, the bounteous —, أَللّٰهُ ٱلْوَهَّابُ.

Gives, *n.* *See* Fetters, *n.*

Gizzard, *n.* حَوْصَلَة *pl.* حَوَاصِل ـ جِرِّيَّة ـ مِقْشَلَة ـ قَانِصَة *pl.* قَوَانِص. To fret one's —, قَتَلَ نَفْسَهُ غَمًّا ـ بَخَعَ نَفْسَهُ ².

Glabrous, *a.* أَمْلَس. *See also* Smooth, *a.*

Glacial, *a.* جَامِد ـ مَثْلُوج ـ مُثْلِج.

Glacier, *n.* جَبَلُ ثَلْجٍ ـ وَادٍ مُثْلِج *pl.* أَوْدِيَة.

Glacis, *n.* A slope, نَزْلَة ـ صَبَب ـ حُدُور. The — of a fortification, صَبَبُ ٱلِٱسْتِحْكَام.

Glad, *a.* فَرْحَان *fem.* فَرْحَانَة *pl. fem.* فَرَاحَى ـ فَرِح ـ بَهِيج ـ سَارّ ـ مَبْسُوط ـ مَسْرُور ـ مُفْرِح ـ مَفْرُوح. To be —, بَهِجَ ـ سُرَّ بِ. To be — of, فَرِحَ بِ ـ سُرَّ ـ إِبْتَهَجَ ـ فَرِحَ ـ إِنْبَسَطَ مِن ـ تَكَيَّفَ بِ. We are — that..., قَدْ سَرَّنَا بِأَنْ.

We are — of what is mentioned in..., قَدْ سَرَّنَا مَا ذُكِرَ فِي.

Gladden, *v.t.* أَبْهَجَ ـ ² سَرَّ ـ أَفْرَحَ ـ فَرَّحَ ـ أَنْزَهَ. To be gladdened, إِسْتَسَرَّ.

Glade, *n.* عَرْقَة ـ فَضَاء ـ فَتْق.

Gladiate, *a.* مُسَيَّف ـ سَيْفَان *fem.* سَيْفَانَة ـ فِي شَكْلِ ٱلسَّيْفِ.

Gladiator, *n.*
Gladiatorial, *a.*
Gladiatory, *a.*
} سَائِف ـ سَيَّاف.

Gladiolus, *n.* The flower, دَلْبُوث ـ كسيفون.

Gladly, *ad.* عَلَى ٱلرَّأْسِ وَٱلْعَيْنِ ـ بِٱلْفَرَحِ ـ بِحَظٍّ ـ بِسُرُورٍ.

Gladness, *n.* إِنْبِسَاط ـ سُرُور ـ فَرَح ـ فَرْحَة ـ بَهْجَة ـ طَرَب; a source of —, فُرْجَة ـ مَسَرَّة.

Gladsome, *a.* Causing gladness, مُطْرِب ـ مُبْهِج ـ مُنَزِّه ـ مُفَرِّح ـ مُفْرِح. *See also* Glad, *a.*

Gladsomeness, *n.* *See* Gladness, *n.*

Glair, *n.* The white of an egg, زُلَالُ ٱلْبَيْضِ ـ بَيَاضُ ٱلْبَيْضِ.

Glair, *v.t.* To smear with the white of an egg, ² دَهَنَ-بِبَيَاضِ ٱلْبَيْضِ.

Glairy, *a.* مِثْلُ بَيَاضِ ٱلْبَيْضِ.

Glamour, *n.* شَزْر ـ تَعَيُّن ـ سِحْر.

Glance, *n.* A sudden dart of light, لَمْعَة ـ شُعَاعَة. A shot with the eye, رَمْزُ ٱلْعَيْنِ ـ طَلَّة ـ لَمْحَة ـ لَحْظَة ـ رَمْق ـ نَظْرَة. A — in hatred, شَزْر. At a —, فِي طَرْفَةِ عَيْنٍ ـ فِي لَحْظَةٍ. At first —, فِي ٱلْحَالِ ـ حَالاً ـ عِنْدَ أَوَّلِ رَمْقٍ.

Glance, *v.i.* To dart a ray of light, لَمَعَ ـ لَمَحَ. To fly off obliquely, طَارَ ـ قَفَزَ ـ ترَّ. To view with a sudden cast of the eye, تَبَصَّرَ ـ رَمَقَ ـ رَامَقَ. To — at, as with the eye, لَحَظَ إِلَى ـ أَلْمَحَ إِلَى ـ لَمَحَ إِلَى ـ رَنَّقَ ٱلنَّظَرَ إِلَى ـ رَامَقَ ـ أَلْحَظَ. To refer to lightly, ذَكَرَ طَرَفًا ـ أَشَارَ إِلَى. To — at in enmity, شَزَرَ. To censure, عَذَلَ ـ وَشَى بِ *aor.* يَشِي ـ لَامَ ـ ذَمَّ.

Glancingly, *ad.* تَلْمِيحًا ـ بِرَمْزِ ٱلْعَيْنِ ـ لَحْظًا.

Gland, *n.* غُدَّة ـ ذِرْبَة *pl.* ذِرَب ـ لَوْزَة *pl.* لَوْزَات ـ عُقْدَة *pl.* عُقَد. The glands of the throat, ٱلْجَوْزَانِ; of the groin, ٱلشُّعْرَانِ. A swollen —, سِلْعَة *pl.* سِلَع.

Glanders, *n.* عِلَّةُ ٱلْمِنْقَافَا ـ سِقَاوَة ـ ذُبَيْةُ ٱلْخَيْلِ.

Glandiferous, *a.* Bearing acorns, حَامِلُ ٱلْبَلُّوطِ; bearing nuts, حَامِلُ جَوْزٍ.

Glandular, *a.* }
Glandulous, } مِثْلَ ٱلذِّرْبَةِ ـ مُتَعَلِّقٌ بِٱلْغُدَّةِ.

Glans, *n.* A swollen gland, سِلْعَة *pl.* سِلَع. *Glans penis*, عُكْبُر ـ حَشَفَة ـ قِرْقِم ـ فَيْشَلَة ـ كَمَرَة *pl.* كَمَر; the bridle of the *glans penis*, وَتَرَة. An acorn, بَلُّوط.

Glare, *n.* Bright light, لَمَعَان ـ ضِيَآء ـ جَلَآء ـ جَهْر. A piercing look, هُطُوع ـ هَطْع ـ شُفُون. A viscous substance, تَرِبَة ـ غِرَآء. *See also* Glair, *n.*

Glare, *v.i.* To shine brightly, جَهَرَ ـ تَجَلَّى. To look with staring eyes, هَطَعَ ـ شَفَنَ ـ فَصَّصَ بِعَيْنِهِ. To — or stare at, هَطَعَ إِلَى ـ شَفَنَ إِلَى.

Glaring, *a.* Dazzling, لَامِع ـ مُسْدِر. Notorious, مَجْهُورٌ بِهِ ـ وَاضِح ـ ظَاهِر. Atrocious, فَظِيع ـ كَبِير ـ فَاحِش ـ فَاجِر.

Glaringly, *ad.* Openly, notoriously, عَلَانِيَةً ـ بِوُضُوحٍ ـ جَهْرًا.

Glass, *n.* قِزَاز ـ زَجَاج ـ زِجَاج ـ زُجَاج ـ أَسْر. A — vessel, قِنِّينَة *pl.* قَنَانِي ـ أَقْدَاح *pl.* قَدَح ـ نُهَاة ـ زُجَاجَة ـ قَوَارِير *pl.* قَارُورَة. A — of wine, قَدَحُ (or كَأْسُ or قَارُورَةُ) خَمْرٍ. Glasses, spectacles, عُيَيْنَات ـ عُوَيْنَات ـ عُيُون. A pane of —, لَوْحُ قِزَازٍ *pl.* أَلْوَاح.

Burning glass, زُجَاجَةٌ حَرَّاقَةٌ.

Cheval glass, مِرْآةُ طُولِ ٱلشَّخْصِ.

Coloured glass, زِجَاجٌ مُلَوَّنٌ.

Crown glass, }
Flint glass, } بِلَّوْر ـ زُجَاجٌ عَالٍ.

Cupping glass, قَارُورَةُ ٱلْحَجَّامِ ـ مِحْجَمَة.

Hour glass, سَاعَةُ رَمْلٍ ـ رَمْلِيَّة.

Looking glass, مِرْآة *pl.* مَرَايَا ـ سَجَنْجَل.

Magnifying glass, زُجَاجَةٌ مُكَبِّرَةٌ.

Minifying glass, زُجَاجَةٌ مُصَغِّرَةٌ.

Plate glass, زُجَاجُ ٱلْمِرْآةِ ـ بِلَّوْر.

Spy glass, نَظَّارَة.

Stained glass, زُجَاجٌ مُدَبَّجٌ ـ زِجَاجٌ مُلَوَّنٌ.

Watch glass, زُجَاجَةُ ٱلسَّاعَةِ.

Weather glass, مِيزَانُ ٱلْهَوَآءِ.

Glass, *a.* Made of —, بِلَّوْرِيّ ـ زُجَاجِيّ.

Glass, *v.t.* To cover with —, فَرَشَ زُجَاجًا.

Glass-blower, *n.* زَجَّاج.

Glass-blowing, *n.* زِجَاجَة.

Glasses, *n.* Spectacles, عُوَيْنَات ـ عُيَيْنَات.

Glass-furnace, *n.* شَاخُورَةُ ٱلزَّجَّاجِ.

Glass-house, *n.* } Where glass is made, مَعْمَلُ زُجَاجٍ. Having
Glass-works, } much glass, كَثِيرُ ٱلزُّجَاجِ.

Glassiness, *n.* زُجَاجِيَّة.

Glass-wort, *n.* قِلْي ـ أُشْنَان ـ غُوَّلَان. *See also* Alkali, *n.*

Glass-work, *n.* قِزَاز ـ زُجَاج.

Glassy, *a.* يُشْبِهُ ٱلزُّجَاجَ ـ زُجَاجِيّ.

Glauber's salt, *n.* مِلْحٌ إِنْكِلِيزِيٌّ مُسْهِلٌ.

Glaucous, *a.* أَخْضَرُ *fem.* خَضْرَآءُ *pl.* خُضْر.

Glaze, *v.t.* To furnish with glass, زَوَّجَ. To polish, دَلَّصَ ـ سَجَّلَ ـ صَقَلَ; as of paper, زَرَّزَ. To coat with glass, as of pottery, طَلَا بِٱلزُّجَاجِ.

Glaze, *n.* طَلْيَةٌ مِنَ ٱلزُّجَاجِ.

Glazier, *n.* زَجَّاج.

Gleam, *n.* لَمْعَة ـ شُعَاع ـ لَمْع ـ بَرَقَان ـ سَطْع ـ رَنَّة ـ رَفّ. A — of hope, ذَرَّةٌ مِنَ ٱلْأَمَلِ.

Gleam, *v.i.* لَمَعَ ـ تَلَأْلَأَ ـ بَرَقَ ـ إِرْتَفَّ ـ رَفَّ ـ سَطَعَ.

Gleaming, *a.* لَامِع ـ سَاطِع ـ رَفِيف.

Glean, *v.t.* To scrape together, قَمَّشَ ـ قَمَشَ ـ لَقَطَ. To pick up here and there, إِلْتَقَطَ ـ تَلَقَّطَ. To —, as after harvest, صَيَّفَ ـ إِنْتَقَى ـ لَمَّ ٱلْقَشَّ ـ قَشَّ ـ إِلْتَقَطَ; of a vineyard, عَلَّلَ.

Gleaner, *n.* صَيَّاف ـ لَمَّامُ ٱلْقَشِّ.

Gleaning, *n.* The act of, اِلْتِقاط ـ تَشْيِيف ; of grapes, تَعْلِيل. What is gleaned, لُقَاط ; of grapes, خُصَاصَة ـ عُلَالَة.

Glebe, *n.* Soil, أَرْض *pl.* أَرَاضِي. The — of a church, أَرْض مُخْتَصَّة بِكَنِيسَةٍ.

Glebous, *a.* / Gleby, } مَمْلُوٌّ مِنَ مَدَرٍ ـ طَانٍ *fem.* طَانَة.

Glee, *n.* Mirth, فَرَح ـ سُرُور ـ اِنْبِسَاط ـ بَهْجَة. A song, نَشِيد *pl.* أَنْشَاد ـ نِشْدَة.

Gleeful, *a.* / Gleesome, } Merry, مَسْرُور ـ فَرْحَانُ ـ مَغْبُوط. Gladdening, سَارٌّ ـ مُنَزِّه ـ مُفَرِّح ـ مُفْرِح.

Gleet, *n.* The — from a sore, وَرَى ـ وَغْي ـ غِذٌّ ـ غَثِيثَة ـ قَيْح.

Glen, *n.* عَرْقَة ـ وَهْدَة *pl.* وِهَاد ـ نَفْنَف *pl.* نَفَانِف ـ جَوَّة ـ وَادٍ *pl.* أَوْدِيَة.

Glib, *a.* Smooth, أَمْلَس *fem.* مَلْسَاء ـ أَخْلَق ـ طَلِق. Voluble, طَلِق. A — tongue, لِسَانٌ طَلِقٌ. Having a — tongue, طَلِقُ اللِّسانِ.

Glibly, *ad.* بِسُرْعَةٍ ـ بِسُهُولَةٍ. To talk —, اِفْتَرَشَ ٱللِّسَانَ ـ سَابَ فِي ٱلْكَلِمِ.

Glibness, *n.* Smoothness, خُلْقَة ـ زَلَق. Volubility, تَفَوُّه ـ سُهُولَةُ لِسانٍ ـ سُيُوبُ ٱلْكَلِمِ ـ طَلَقُ ٱللِّسانِ.

Glide, *v.i.* To shoot or pass quickly, زَلَّ *aor.* يَزِلُّ ـ سَبَحَ. To flow, سَالَ *aor.* يَسِيلُ ـ سَاحَ *aor.* يَسِيحُ ـ حَبَا *aor.* يَحْبُو ـ جَرَى. To —, as a bird along the ground, سَفَّ. To go at a gliding pace, زَفَّ. To — away, as of time, مَرَّ ـ مَضَى. To — out, to escape imperceptibly, اِنْسَلَّ ـ اِنْفَلَتَ ـ فَاتَ. To — into, to become, صَارَ. The stars glide along the firmament, النُّجُومُ تَسْبَحُ فِي ٱلْفَلَكِ. The ship glided through the waters, تَشَمَّرَتِ ٱلسَّفِينَةُ فِي ٱلْمَاءِ. His life glided away, زَلَّ عُمْرُهُ. To —, to flow gently, نَضَّ. *See also to* Course, *v.i.*

Glimmer, *v.i.* لَمَحَ ـ أَشَعَّ ـ طَفْطَفَ ـ أَضَاءَ. *See also to* Gleam, *v.i.*

Glimmering, *n.* لَمْح ـ لَمْعَة ـ شَعْشَعَة.

Glimpse, *n.* A faint light, لَمْحَة ـ لَمْعَة ـ شَعْشَعَة. A transitory view, لَمْحَة ـ لَوْحٌ إِلَى. To take a — at, لَمَحَ إِلَى.

Glisten, / Glister, *v.i.* / Glitter, } لَمَحَ ـ لاحَ ـ أَلَاحَ ـ اِلْتَمَعَ ـ لَمَعَ ـ بَرَقَ ـ سَطَعَ ـ دَلَصَ. To —, as of fruit, بَصَّ *aor.* يَبِصُّ ; as a colour, رَفَّ ـ اِرْتَفَّ. To make to —, دَلَّصَ. He glistened with his eyes, بَرَقَ بَصَرُهُ ـ بَرَقَ بِعَيْنَيْهِ.

Glitter, *n.* رَفّ ـ رَيْق ـ دَلِيص ـ بَرَقَان ـ لَمَعَان ـ جَلَاء.

Glistening, *a.* / Glittering, } لَمُوح ـ لَمَّاح ـ نَيِّر ـ مُنِير ـ لامِع ; of a colour, رَفِيف. A — sword, سَيْفٌ بَارِقٌ.

Gloaming, *n.* The twilight of the morning, سَحَر ; of the evening, عِشَاء.

Gloat, *v.i.* هَطَعَ ـ شَفَنَ.

Globate, *a.* / Globated, / Globose, / Globous, } كُرَوِيٌّ ـ كُرِيٌّ ـ مُطَوَّب ـ مُكَبْكَب ـ مُكَبَّب ـ مُدَعْبَل.

Globe, *n.* كُرَة *pl.* كُرَات ـ كُورَة *pl.* كُوَر. The world, العالَمُ ـ الدُّنْيا. The terrestrial —, كُرَةُ ٱلْأَرْضِ ; the celestial —, كُرَةُ ٱلسَّمَاءِ. The — of the eye, مُقْلَةُ ٱلْعَيْنِ.

Globular, *a.* *See* Globate, *a.*

Globule, *n.* كُرَةٌ صَغِيرَةٌ *pl.* كُرَات ـ حَبٌّ *pl.* حُبُوب ـ حَبَّة *pl.* حَبَّات.

Globulous, *a.* *See* Globate, *a.*

Glomerate, *v.t.* كَبَّبَ.

Glomeration, *n.* The act of, تَكْبِيب. A ball, كُرَة ـ كُبَّة.

Gloom, *n.* Darkness, قَتَم ـ قَتَام ـ دُجًا ـ دُجَى ـ دُجْيَة ـ عَتَمَة ـ ظُلْمَة ـ غَبَش ـ قَلَق. Heaviness of mind, كَدَر ـ غَمٌّ ـ كَآبَة.

Gloomily, *ad.* Darkly, ظُلْمَةً ـ بِغَبَشٍ. Sadly, sullenly, بِكَدَرٍ ـ بِكَآبَةٍ ـ بِحُزْنٍ ـ بِعُبُوسٍ.

Gloominess, *n.* *See* Gloom, *n.*

Gloomy, *a.* Dark, قَاتِم ـ ظُلْمَانِيّ ـ دَجِيٌّ ـ مُظْلِم. Sad, مُكَدَّرُ ٱلْخَاطِرِ ـ كَئِيب ـ مَغْمُوم. Dull, as of the weather, عاتِم ـ مُغَيِّم. Sullen, austere, عابِس. A — day, يَوْمٌ قَتَامٌ. To be —, of the weather, قَتِمَ ـ تَدَجَّى ـ عَتَمَ. To be —, sad, كَيِبَ ـ أَكْأَبَ ـ تَكَدَّرَ خاطِرُهُ. To be —, austere, عَبَسَ ـ تَعَبَّسَ.

Gloria in excelsis Deo! int. المَجْدُ لِلّٰهِ فِي ٱلْأَعَالِي.

Glorification, *n.* The act of, ذِكْر ـ تَمْجِيد ـ تَحْمِيد ـ تَبْجِيل ـ تَجْلِيل. Praise, إِثْنَاء ـ مَدْح ـ ثَنَاء. The attainment of everlasting happiness, نَيْلُ ٱلسَّعَادَةِ ٱلْأَبَدِيَّةِ. Self —, فَخْر ـ اِفْتِخار ـ تَكَبُّر ـ تَعَظُّم.

Glorify, *v.t.* Of God, ذَكَرَ ـ سَبَّحَ ـ مَجَّدَ ـ أَجَلَّ ـ حَمِدَ. To praise, eulogize, أَثْنَى عَلَى ـ عَظَّمَ ـ فَخَّرَ ـ أَعَزَّ. To — one above another, فَخَّرَ عَلَى ـ أَفْخَرَ عَلَى. To — one's self, اِفْتَخَرَ ـ تَكَبَّرَ ـ تَبَاهَى بِذَاتِهِ ـ تَمَخَّا. To be glorified, تَمَجَّدَ.

Glorious, *a.* جَلِيل ـ ذُو ٱلْجَلالِ ـ ماجِد ـ مَجِيد ـ حَمِيد ـ عَزِيز. Noble, مُفَخَّم ـ فَاخِر ـ شَرِيف ـ أَعَزُّ ـ مَمْدُوح ـ مُعَظَّم. Most —, أَجَلُّ ـ أَمْجَدُ ـ أَعَزُّ ـ. Grand, beautiful, بَهِيٌّ. Glorious things, أَمْجاد. Most — is God, ٱللّٰهُ تَعَظَّمَ (or تَعَاظَمَ). A — sovereign, مَلِكٌ أَعَزُّ. To be or to become —, عَزَّ ـ تَعَزَّزَ.

Gloriously, *ad.* عَلَى ـ جَلَالَةٍ ـ بِحَمْدٍ ـ بِجَلَالٍ ـ بِعِزٍّ ـ عِزَّةً أَعْلَى مِثْوَالٍ.

Glory, *n.* Brightness, جَلَآءٌ ـ بَهَآءٌ. Praise, تَمْجِيدٌ ـ تَسْبِيحٌ ـ فَخْرٌ ـ ذِكْرٌ ـ ثَنَآءٌ ـ مَجْدٌ. Grandeur, honour, جَلَالٌ ـ جَلَالَةٌ ـ شَرَفٌ ـ جَاهٌ ـ عِزٌّ. Renown, صِيتٌ ـ صِيتَةٌ. Felicity, as in heaven, طُوبَى ـ نَعِيمٌ ـ سَعَادَةٌ أَبَدِيَّةٌ ـ سَعَادَةٌ. Beauty, بَهَآءٌ. A halo, طُفَاوَةٌ ـ هَالَةٌ. Arrogance, نَخْوَةٌ ـ كِبْرٌ ـ تَشَامُخٌ ـ غُرُورٌ. Love of — and pomp, حُبُّ ٱلْفَخْرِ وَٱلنَّخْوَةِ. To acquire —, تَكَبَّرَ. اِسْتَعْلَى ـ يَعْلَى *aor.* عَلَى.

Glory, *v.i.* تَكَبَّرَ ـ اِفْتَخَرَ ـ تَشَامَخَ ـ تَعَالَى. I gloried in it, فَخَرْتُ بِهِ.

Gloss, *n.* Superficial lustre, تَلَأْلُؤٌ ـ صِقَالٌ ـ جَلَآءٌ ـ دَلَاصَةٌ. A specious signification, تَصْحِيفٌ ـ شِيَةٌ ـ وَشْيٌ. A signification, تَعْبِيرٌ ـ تَفْسِيرٌ ـ شَرْحٌ ـ بَيَانٌ ـ مَعْنًى ـ تَأْوِيلٌ. A note, حَاشِيَةٌ *pl.* حَوَاشٍ. To make glosses upon, to explain, أَوَّلَ ـ شَرَحَ ـ بَيَّنَ ـ فَسَّرَ ـ عَبَّرَ. To write glosses or notes, as on a margin, حَشَّى.

Gloss, *v.t.* To polish, صَقَلَ ـ جَلَّى ـ دَلَّصَ. To give a specious signification to, تَصَحَّفَ عَلَى ـ يَشِي ـ وَشَى *aor.* To — over, to palliate, سَتَرَ ـ كَفَّرَ.

Glossarial, *a.* مُتَضَمِّنٌ عَلَى شَرْحٍ وَبَيَانٍ.

Glossary, *n.* كِتَابُ شَرْحِ ٱلْكَلِمَاتِ ـ مِصْبَاحٌ فِي غَرِيبِ ٱلشَّرْحِ كِتَابُ ٱلتَّعْرِيفَاتِ ـ وَٱلِاصْطِلَاحَاتِ.

Glossiness, *n.* *See* Gloss, *n.*

Glossographer, *n.* مُحَشٍّ ـ كَاتِبُ حَوَاشٍ.

Glossologist, *n.* مُفَسِّرٌ ـ شَارِحٌ.

Glossology, *n.* شَرْحُ ٱلْكَلِمَاتِ وَٱلِاصْطِلَاحَاتِ.

Glossy, *a.* مَجْلُوٌّ ـ دَلِيصٌ ـ دِلَاصٌ ـ مَصْقُولٌ ـ لَمُوحٌ ـ لَامِعٌ. To be —, دَلَصَ.

Glottis, *n.* زَرْدَمَةٌ ـ غَلْسَمَةٌ.

Glove, *n.* كَفٌّ *pl.* كُفُوفٌ. To throw down the glove; *see* Gauntlet, *n.*

Glove, *v.t.* لَبِسَ ٱلْكُفُوفَ.

Glow, *v.t.* To shine, لَمَحَ ـ اِلْتَمَعَ ـ لَمَعَ. To be red, اِحْمَرَّ. To be hot, حَرَّ ـ أَحَرَّ ـ حَمِيَ ـ سَخُنَ. To — with zeal, حَمِيَتْ فِيهِ ٱلْغَيْرَةُ ـ اِحْتَمَى غَيْرَةً. To — with passion, اِحْتَمَى اِحْتَرَقَ غَيْظًا ـ حَمِيَ أَنْفُهُ ـ غَضَبًا. The oven glowed with heat, حَمِيَ ٱلْوَطِيسُ. The day glowed with heat, حَرَّ ٱلنَّهَارُ. The fire glowed, حَرَّتِ ٱلنَّارُ.

Glow, *n.* Heat, حَرٌّ ـ حَرَارَةٌ ـ حُمُوٌّ. Redness, اِحْمِرَارٌ ـ حُمْرَةٌ. Brightness of colour, زَهْوَةٌ ـ زُهْرَةٌ. Zeal, غَيْرَةٌ. Beauty, force, fascination, طَلَاوَةٌ ـ طُلَاوَةٌ. Passion, حَمِيٌّ ـ حُمَيًّا. The — of the sky at sunrise or sunset, نَدِيٌّ; at sunset, شَفَقٌ. His diction has the — of beauty, عَلَى مَنْطِقِهِ طُلَاوَةُ ٱلْحُسْنِ. *See also* Redness, *n.*

Glowing, *a.* Shining, burning, مُلْتَمِعٌ ـ لَامِعٌ. Bright, of colour, مُغَيَّارٌ ـ مُتَحَمِّسٌ ـ حَمِسٌ. Ardent, بَهِيٌّ ـ زَهِيٌّ. Eulogistic, مَادِحٌ ـ مُطْنِبٌ. Red, أَحْمَرُ *fem.* حَمْرَآءُ *pl.* حُمْرٌ. A — coal, جَمْرَةٌ. To describe in — colours, كَبَّرَ ـ فَضَّلَ ـ أَطْنَبَ فِي ـ أَثْنَى عَلَى.

Glow-worm, *n.* أَبُو حُبَاحِبٍ ـ سِرَاجُ ٱلْقُطْرُبِ ـ حُبَاحِبٌ ـ يَرَاعٌ.

Gloze, *v.* and *n.* *See* Flattery, *n.*

Glue, *n.* غِرَآءٌ ـ لِزَاقٌ.

Glue, *v.t.* غَرَّى ـ غَرَا. To — to, stick to, أَلْزَقَ بِ. Glued, مَغْرُوٌّ.

Gluey, *a.* دَبِقٌ ـ لَزِجٌ. *See also* Glutinous, *a.*

Glum, *a.* Austere, sullen, شَرِسٌ ـ عَبُوسٌ ـ عَنِيفٌ ـ وَعِقٌ ـ نَكِدٌ. To be — with, عَنَّفَ ـ أَعْنَفَ. To look —, عَبَسَ ـ تَعَبَّسَ.

Glume, *n.* The calix of certain plants, بُرْعُومٌ *pl.* بَرَاعِيمُ ـ كِمَامَةٌ. Husk, chaff, قَشٌّ ـ حُثَالَةٌ.

Glut, *v.t.* To cloy, أَشْبَعَ ـ أَتْخَمَ ـ قَرَّفَ. To disgust, أَسَامَ. To overload, طَفَحَ ـ أَفَاضَ ـ أَنْعَمَ. To —, as a market, أَزَادَ فَوْقَ ٱللُّزُومِ ـ طَفَحَ. To be glutted, choked up with, as a wound with blood, *etc.*, شَرِقَ بِ. To — the eyes; *see to* Gloat, *v.i.*

Glut, *n.* Over-plenty, طُفُوحٌ ـ زِيَادَةٌ ـ كَثْرَةٌ ـ وُفُورٌ ـ وَفْرَةٌ.

Gluten, *n.* مَادَّةٌ لَزِجَةٌ ـ نَشَآءٌ.

Glutinate, *v.t.* *See to* Glue, *v.t.*

Glutination, *n.* إِلْزَاقٌ ـ تَلْزِيقٌ ـ تَغْرِيَةٌ.

Glutinative, *a.* } صَمْكُوكٌ ـ دَبِقٌ ـ لَزِجٌ. To be or become —,
Glutinous, } تَلَزَّجَ ـ تَدَبَّقَ ـ تَمَطَّطَ ـ تَسَعَّبَ.

Glutinousness, *n.* لُزُوجَةٌ ـ تَغْرِيَةٌ.

Glutton, *n.* أَكِيلٌ ـ أَكُولٌ ـ عَلْدَمٌ ـ نَهِمٌ ـ جُرَافٌ ـ سُرَاطِيٌّ ـ هِبْلَاعٌ ـ هِلْقَمٌّ. The animal, نَوْعٌ مِنَ ٱلْحَيَوَانَاتِ.

Gluttonize, *v.i.* هَلْقَمَ ـ لَهِمَ ـ نَهِمَ ـ شَرِهَ.

Gluttonous, *a.* شَرِهٌ ـ شَرْهَانُ ـ نَهِيمٌ ـ نَهِمٌ ـ مِلْهَمٌ ـ لَهُومٌ ـ حَرِيصٌ.

Gluttonously, *ad.* مِثْلَ ٱلْعَلْدَمِ ـ بِنَهَامَةٍ ـ بِشَرَهٍ.

Gluttony, *n.* نَهَمٌ ـ نَهَامَةٌ ـ شَرَهٌ.

Glycerine, *n.* خُلَاصَةُ ٱلدِّهانِ وَٱلسَّمْنانِ.

Glyph, *n.* The — of a column, خَطٌّ عَلَى عَمُودٍ *pl.* خُطُوط.

Glyphography, *n.* فَنُّ نَقْلِ ٱلصُّوَرِ إِلَى مَعْدِنٍ بِواسِطَةِ ٱلكَهْرَبائِيَّةِ.

Glyptics, *n.* حِكاكَة ـ فَنُّ حَكِّ ٱلحِجارَةِ ـ فَنُّ نَقْشِ ٱلجَواهِرِ.

Gnar, *v.i.* } **Gnarl**, } To snarl, هَرَّ ـ تَمَزَّعَ. To — at, هَرَّ إِلَى.

Gnarled, *a.* } **Gnarly**, } أَعْقَدُ ـ ذُو عُقَدٍ ـ مُعَقَّد. *See also* Knotted, *a.*

Gnash, *v.t.* To — the teeth, قَرْقَطَ (*or* صَرَّ بـ *or* فَرَعَ) ٱلأَسْنَانَ.

Gnashing, *n.* As of the teeth, قَرْقَطَةُ (*or* صَرِيرُ) ٱلأَسْنانِ.

Gnat, *n.* بَقَّة *coll.* بَقّ ـ بَعُوضَة *coll.* بَعُوض ـ بَرْغَش ; in Egypt called نامُوسَة *coll.* نامُوس.

Gnaw, *v.t.* To —, as of a bone, لَاكَ ـ عَرَقَ. To —, as a rat gnaws, قَرَضَ ـ قَرَّضَ. To corrode, أَكَلَ. He gave the dog a bone to —, عَظَمَ ٱلكَلْبَ.

Gnome, *n.* *See* Demon, *n.*

Gnomon, *n.* As of a dial, عَقْرَبُ ساعَةِ ٱلشَّمْسِ ـ مِيْل.

Gnomonics, *n.* فَنُّ ٱلقَواعِدِ ٱلبَسِيطَةِ.

Gnostic, *n.* شِيْعَةٌ مِنَ ٱلخَوارِجِ عِنْدَ ٱلنَّصَارَى ٱلأَقْدَمِيْنَ.

Gnu, *n.* نَوْعٌ مِنَ ٱلحَيَوانَاتِ يُشْبِهُ ٱلأَيِّلَ ٱلفَتَ ٱلقُرُونِ وَذَيْلُهُ مِثْلَ ذَيْلِ ٱلحِصانِ.

Go, *v.i.* To move, walk, سَعَى ـ مَضَى ـ سَارَ *aor.* يَسِيرُ ـ سَافَرَ ـ ذَهَبَ. To leave, go away, سَلَكَ ـ مَشَى ـ مَرَّ ـ مَشَى ـ سَلَكَ. To pass, as of coin, رَاجَ ـ إِنْتَقَلَ ـ إِنْطَلَقَ. To make progress, تَقَدَّمَ ـ تَرَقَّى ـ تَدَرَّجَ. To go, in pregnancy, حَبِلَت ـ حَمَلَت. To reach, وَصَلَ إِلَى *aor.* يَصِلُ ـ بَلَغَ ـ حَصَّلَ. To decay, إِضْمَحَلَّ ـ زَالَ ـ نَحِفَ. To work, as of a machine, إِشْتَغَلَ ـ مَشَى. To be about to ..., كَادَ ـ هَمَّ بـ ـ وَشَكَ أَن *aor.* يُوشِكُ ـ رَاحَ ; (*On this latter signification see under* About, *ad.*) Here goes it! Now or never! أَمَّا هَلَكَ أَمَّا مَلَكَ. Who goes there? مَنْ هُوَ هٰذا ; (the phrase used by sentinels in the Turkish and Egyptian armies is كِيْم دِرْ أَو.) He went his way, مَضَى سَبِيلَهُ. Go from me! إِلَيْكَ عَنِّي. Go to! هَلُمَّ.

To go about, here and there, تَرَدَّدَ ـ طَوَّفَ ـ جَالَ فِي ـ دَارَ ـ حَارَ *aor.* يَحُورُ. To begin, شَرَعَ فِي ـ إِبْتَدَأَ. To put one's hand to, أَلْقَى يَدَهُ فِي. To go about one's business, أَلْزَمَ (*or* بَاشَرَ) شُغْلَهُ. To endeavour, إِجْتَهَدَ ـ سَعَى ـ جَدَّ.

To go abroad, as from one's house, خَرَجَ ـ طَلَعَ. To leave for foreign parts, تَغَرَّبَ. To spread, as of news, إِنْبَثَّ ـ إِنْتَشَرَ ـ شَاعَ ـ ذَاعَ *aor.* يَذِيعُ ـ فَاشَ. To depart on a journey, سَفَرَ ـ سَافَرَ عَن.

To go after, follow, pursue, لَحِقَ ـ تَبِعَ ـ أَتْبَعَ.

To go again, to return, تَرَدَّدَ ـ رَجَعَ.

To go against, to oppose, ضَادَّ ـ عَارَضَ ـ عَانَدَ ـ خَالَفَ. To go to war with, حَارَبَ. To strike against, صَدَمَ.

To go along, to walk on, سَارَ *aor.* يَسِيرُ ـ مَشَى ـ سَلَكَ. To go or walk along, as by a river, شَطَأَ ـ أَشْطَأَ. To go along with, to accompany, رَافَقَ ـ إِسْتَصْحَبَ. To go along with one to, أَوْصَلَ إِلَى. Go along with you! أَخِّرْ عَنِّي ـ إِذْهَبْ ـ إِنْقَلِعْ ـ البَعِيدَ ـ إِمْضِ سَبِيلَكَ.

To go aside, حَايَدَ ـ تَجَنَّبَ.

To go astray, to lose one's way, ضَلَّ ـ زَاغَ ـ تَاهَ. To stray, as a loose animal, عَارَ. To get loose, إِنْفَلَتَ.

To go away, to walk off, ذَهَبَ ـ إِنْطَلَقَ ـ إِنْتَقَلَ. To leave, بَرِحَ مِن. He went away from his place, زَالَ عَنْ مَكانِهِ. I will not go away until..., لَا أَبْرَحُ حَتَّى.

To go away with, to take off, ذَهَبَ بـ ـ إِنْطَلَقَ بـ ـ مَضَى بـ ; as by force, سَلَبَ.

To go back, to return, تَرَدَّدَ ـ رَجَعَ ـ تَرَاجَعَ ـ تَرَادَّ.

To go back again, رَجَعَ ثانِيَةً ـ عَادَ ٱلكَرَّةَ.

To go backwards, behind, أَدْبَرَ. To walk backwards, تَقَهْقَرَ.

To go before, to precede, سَبَقَ ـ إِسْتَقْدَمَ ـ تَقَدَّمَ.

To go behind, to follow, تَبِعَ ـ أَتْبَعَ.

To go between, to pass between, جَازَ بَيْنَ. To interpose, دَخَلَ بَيْنَ ـ تَوَاسَطَ.

To go beyond, عَدَّى ـ عَبَرَ ـ جَازَ.

To go by, to pass by or near, مَرَّ بـ ـ مَرَّ عَلَى. To go along, not to call at, مَضَى بـ ـ فَاتَ. To follow, copy, imitate, تَبِعَ ـ تَمَثَّلَ بـ ـ إِتَّبَعَ. To observe as a rule, تَسَنَّنَ بـ ـ طَابَقَ ـ إِسْتَقْعَدَ عَلَى ـ سَلَكَ بِمُقْتَضَى.

To go by the board, انْكَسَرَ مِنْ أَسْفَلِهِ.

To go down, descend, نَزَلَ ـ سَفَلَ ـ هَبَطَ. To set, as of the sun, غَابَ ـ غَرَبَ. To be accepted, approved, قُبِلَ ـ سُلِّمَ بـ ـ رَضِيَ عَن ـ أَسْتُحْسِنَ. To sink, غَرِقَ ـ إِسْتَغْرَقَ. To stop, as of a watch, وَقَفَ *aor.* يَقِفُ. To pass away, مَالَ إِلَى ٱلزَّوالِ ـ زَالَ.

To go down in the world, to become poor, إِفْتَقَرَ ـ أَعْوَزَ.

To go far, in distance, بَعُدَ ـ إِبْتَعَدَ. To go towards supplying, سَدَّ مَسَدَّ كَذا.

To go for, to call for, or upon, طَلَبَ ـُ مَرَّ بِ ـُ or عَلَى ـ إِسْتَدْعَى بِ. To pass for, to be worth, as coin, سَاوَى. To be deemed, قِيلَ عَنْهُ أَنَّهُ ـ إِشْتَهَرَ بِ. To be used as, أُسْتُعْمِلَ كَ. It goes for, is worth, nothing, لا يُسَاوِي شَيْئًا. It goes for, counts for, nothing, لا يُعَدُّ شَيْئًا ـ لا يُعْتَدُّ بِهِ.

To go forth, to go out, خَرَجَ ـُ. To become circulated, إِنْبَثَّ ـ ذَاعَ aor. يَذِيعُ ـ إِنْتَشَرَ.

To go forward, to advance, تَقَدَّمَ. To happen, جَرَى ـِ ـ رَدَفَ ـِ.

To go from, to quit, تَرَكَ ـُ ـ فَارَقَ ـ ذَهَبَ ـَ عَنْ.

To go halves with, نَاصَفَ ـ شَاطَرَ.

To go hard with, to be difficult to, إِسْتَصْعَبَ عَلَى. To be in great danger, كَانَ عَلَى خَطَرٍ عَظِيمٍ.

To go ill with, أَذِيَ ـَ ـ تَأَذَّى: It went ill with him on their account, تَأَذَّى بِسَبَبِهِمْ. It will go ill with him, يُلَاقِي شَرًّا.

To go in, to enter, دَخَلَ ـُ ـ فَاتَ إِلَى جَوًّا ـُ. To go in to, خَشَّ فِي ـ دَخَلَ إِلَى ـِ.

To go in and out, تَرَدَّدَ ـ سَاحَ aor. يَسُوحُ. To do the business of life, سَلَكَ ـُ ـ سَعَى ـَ ـ سَارَ aor. يَسِيرُ.

To go mad, جُنَّ ـ تَجَنَّنَ ـ خَبِلَ ـَ.

To go near to, إِقْتَرَبَ مِنْ ـ دَنَا مِنْ aor. يَدْنُو.

To go off, to die, سَلَّمَ ٱلرُّوحَ ـ مَاتَ ـُ ـ تُوُفِّيَ. To explode, فَقَعَ ـَ ـ تَفَقَّعَ.

To go on, to continue, إِسْتَمَرَّ ـ أَدْمَنَ ـ ظَلَّ عَلَى ـُ ظَلَّ ـُ ـ وَاظَبَ ـ مَا بَرِحَ ـَ. To go onward, تَقَدَّمَ. The affairs went on, followed one another, تَتَالَتِ ٱلْأُمُورُ.

To go on foot, ذَهَبَ مَاشِيًا ـ إِنْطَلَقَ رَاجِلًا ـ تَرَجَّلَ ـ رَجِلَ ـَ.

To go out, as of a place, طَلَعَ مِنْ ـُ خَرَجَ مِنْ ـُ. To be extinguished, إِنْطَفَى. To go out from, to revolt against, لَوَى عَنْ ـِ ـ عَصَى عَلَى ـِ خَرَجَ مِنْ أَمْرِهِ ـُ. To go out of one's religion, إِرْتَدَّ عَنْ دِينِهِ. To cease, زَالَ ـُ.

To go over, to cross, as of a stream, قَطَعَ ـَ ـ عَبَرَ ـُ ـ تَعَدَّى ـ جَازَ ـُ. To go over to another party, دَاخَلَ ـ صَارَ دَخِيلًا فِي ـ رَافَقَ. To go over, to travel over, سَاحَ ـ عَارَ فِي ـِ ـ عَالَ فِي ـِ aor. يَسِيحُ. To read over, قَرَأَ ـُ ـ طَالَعَ.

To go round, to walk or travel round, حَفَّ بِ ـُ ـ طَافَ حَوْلَ ـُ ـ إِسْتَدَارَ (or دَارَ) حَوْلَ; of a bird or a dog round a place, حَاتَ بِ aor. يَحُوتُ. To whirl round, إِسْتَدَارَ ـ دَارَ ـُ. He went round the house, دَارَ بِٱلْبَيْتِ. He went round with him, دَارَ بِهِ.

To go through, to suffer, أُصِيبَ بِ ـ إِنْصَاقَ بِ ـ إِحْتَمَلَ. To read over, قَرَأَ ـ طَالَعَ ـُ.

To go through with, to accomplish, أَتَمَّ ـ أَنْهَى ـ كَمَّلَ ـ قَضَى ـِ.

To go to, قَدِمَ عَلَى ـ أَقْبَلَ عَلَى ـ تَقَدَّمَ إِلَى ـِ.

To go to nothing, هَلَكَ ـِ ـ تَلَاشَى.

To go to the dogs, خَرِبَ ـَ ـ هَلَكَ ـِ.

To go to the wall, خَسِرَ ـ غُلِبَ ـَ.

To go to the war, إِنْطَلَقَ إِلَى ٱلْحَرْبِ. To go to war with, قَاتَلَ ـ حَارَبَ.

To go under, to pass under, مَرَّ مِنْ تَحْتُ ـُ. To go under a name, تَسَمَّى.

To go up, to ascend, إِسْتَعْلَى ـ طَلَعَ ـُ ـ صَعِدَ ـَ. To become more, إِزْدَادَ ـ زَادَ ـِ. The price of the shares is going up, سِعْرُ ٱلْأَسْهَامِ لَمْ يَزَلْ فِي ٱرْتِفَاعٍ.

To go up against, to go to war with, حَارَبَ ـ بَارَزَ.

To go up and down, to wander, تَرَدَّدَ ـ أَقْبَلَ وَأَدْبَرَ.

To go upon, to follow as a rule; *see under* To go by.

To go a-walking, تَمَشَّى.

To go well with one, أَنْجَحَ ـ حَسُنَ إِلَيْهِ ـُ ـ كَانَ خَيْرٌ لَهُ.

To go with, to accompany, صَحِبَ ـَ ـ رَافَقَ. To go with to, أَوْصَلَ إِلَى. To agree with, نَاسَبَ ـ وَافَقَ.

To go without, to do without, إِسْتَغْنَى عَنْ ـ فَضَلَ عَنْ ـُ.

To let go, خَلَّى ـ أَفْلَتَ ـ سَيَّبَ. To let go anchor, أَلْقَى ٱلْمِرْسَاةَ.

Go, *n.* A turn, دَوْرٌ ـ دَفْعَةٌ. Energy, مُرُوَّةٌ. To have a go, قَضَى حَاجَتَهُ ـِ. Here's a pretty go! مَا شَاءَ ٱللّٰهُ ـ يَا سَلَامُ!

To be all the go, of a thing, أُسْتُحِنَّ عَلَيْهِ. It is no go, عَبَثٌ ـ خَيْبَةٌ ـ بَاطِلٌ.

Goad, *n.* مِسْوَقَةٌ *pl.* مَسَاوِقُ ـ مِنْخَاسٌ ـ مِنْخَزٌ ـ مِهْمَزٌ.

Goad, *v.t.* To — cattle, طَعَنَ ـُ ـ هَمَزَ ـِ ـ شَمَّصَ ـ نَكَزَ ـُ ـ نَخَزَ ـُ ـ نَخَسَ بِ ـُ. To stimulate, أَنْهَضَ ـ حَثَّ ـُ.

Goal, *n.* The starting post at a race, قَصَبُ ـ أَمَدُ ـ ٱلْحَبْلِ ٱلسِّبَاقِ; the winning post, أَمَدٌ *pl.* آمَادٌ ـ غَايَةٌ *pl.* غَايَاتٌ. Any point to be reached, أَمَدٌ ـ جِهَةٌ ـ مَرْجِعٌ ـ رُحْلَةٌ. Scope, object to be reached, شَوْطٌ *pl.* أَشْوَاطٌ ـ مَبْلَغٌ ـ غَايَةٌ ـ نِيَّةٌ ـ مَقْصُودٌ. To attain, as of the —, أَصَابَ. The — is remote, (of the long extent of hope), ٱلشَّوْطُ بَطِينٌ.

Goat, *n.* مَاعِزٌ *fem.* مَاعِزَةٌ *coll.* مَاعِزٌ ـ مَعْزٌ ـ تَيْسٌ *pl.* تُيُوسٌ and أَتْيَاسٌ. A she —, عَنْزٌ ـ عَنْزَةٌ *pl.* عِنَازٌ and عُنُوزٌ. A mountain —, بَدَنٌ *pl.* بُدُونٌ ـ بَدَنٌ ـ وَعِلٌ ـ ثَيْتَلٌ ـ رَمِيٌّ *fem.* رَمِيَّةٌ *pl.* رَمَايَا ـ وَعِلٌ *pl.* أَوْعَالٌ.

Goat-herd, *n.* مَعَّازٌ *pl.* مَعَّازَةٌ ـ تَيَّاسٌ.

Goatish, *a.* Like a goat, تَيْسِيٌّ — مِثْلَ ٱلتَّيْسِ. Lustful, شَهْوَانِيٌّ.

Goat's-grass, *n.* The plant, مُرَيْر.

Go-between, *n.* مُصْلِح — مُتَوَسِّط — وَسِيط — دَرَج — مِقْرَع. Of a woman who corresponds with men seeking women in marriage, مُرَاسِل.

Gob, *n.* } **Gobbet**, } زَقْم — زُخْمَة — دُبْلَة *pl.* دُبَل — لُقْمَة *pl.* لُقَم. To make into a —, دَبَّلَ.

Gobble, *v.t.* To swallow hastily, اِلْتَهَمَ — ـَ لَهِمَ — اِلْتَقَمَ — ـَ لَقِمَ — اِغْتَذَمَ — ـَ شَذِمَ — ² زَقَمَ — ـَ زَرِدَ — هَلْقَمَ.

Gobble, *v.i.* To —, as of a turkey, نَقْنَقَ — ـِ قَاقَ.

Gobbler, *n.* A greedy eater, هِبْلَاع — هَبَلَّع — مُتَغَذِّم. A turkey-cock, دِيكٌ هِنْدِيٌّ *pl.* دُيُوكٌ هِنْدِيَّةٌ.

Gobelin, *n.* Tapestry, طِرَاز.

Goblet, *n.* رِفْد *pl.* أَرْفَاد — مِرْفَد — قَدَح *pl.* أَقْدَاح.

Goblin, *n.* جِنِّيٌّ *coll.* جِنٌّ — مَارِد — عِفْرِيت *pl.* عَفَارِيت — غُول *pl.* غِيلَان *and* أَغْوَال.

Go-by, *n.* اِنْحِرَاف — جَوَاز — اِنْصِرَاف. To give one the —, أَجَازَ — ² جَازَبَ. *See also under* to Cut, *v.t.*

Go-cart, *n.* دَرَّاجَة — دَرَّجَة — حَالَة — حَال. He is made to walk in a —, يُدَرَّجُ عَلَى ٱلْحَالِ.

GOD, *n.* اَللّٰهُ; the Lord, اَلرَّبُّ. God, to whom belong might and majesty, اَللّٰهُ عَزَّ وَجَلَّ. God, the sovereign Creator, اَلْبَارِئُ تَعَالَى. The Pitiful, the Compassionate, اَلرَّحْمٰنُ ٱلرَّحِيمُ. The Creator, اَلْخَالِقُ ٱلْخَلَّاقُ. The Almighty, اَلْقَادِرُ عَلَى كُلِّ شَيْءٍ. The Lord of the worlds, رَبُّ ٱلْعَالَمِينَ. The Protector, اَلسَّاتِرُ. The Beneficent, اَلْجَوَادُ. The Provider, اَلرَّزَّاقُ. The Lord of the day of Judgment, مَالِكُ يَوْمِ ٱلدِّينِ. The Omniscient, عَالِمُ ٱلْغَيْبِ. By God! وَٱللّٰهِ — تَٱللّٰهِ — بِٱللّٰهِ. Good God! سُبْحَانَ ٱللّٰهِ — يَا رَبِّ — اَللّٰهُ ٱللّٰهُ — بِٱللّٰهِ — لَا حَوْلَ وَلَا قُوَّةَ إِلَّا بِٱللّٰهِ.

For God's sake! عَلَيْكَ بِٱللّٰهِ — بِٱللّٰهِ. For the sake of God, حُبًّا بِٱللّٰهِ — لِلّٰهِ — لِوَجْهِ ٱللّٰهِ.

God bless you, اَللّٰهُ يُبَارِكُ فِيكَ — فِي أَمَانِ ٱللّٰهِ.

God damn him, لَعَنَهُ ٱللّٰهُ — ـَ لَعْنَةُ ٱللّٰهِ عَلَيْهِ.

God forbid! يَا سَاتِرُ — اَللّٰهُ لَا يُقَدِّرُ — اَلشَّرُّ بَعِيدٌ.

God grant! إِنْ شَاءَ ٱللّٰهُ.

God save the Queen! لِتَحْيَ ٱلْمَلِكَةُ.

God speed! فِي أَمَانِ ٱللّٰهِ.

God speed the plough! بَرَكَةُ ٱللّٰهِ عَلَى ٱلْفِلَاحَةِ.

God the Father, Son, and Holy Ghost, one God world without end, اَللّٰهُ ٱلْآبُ وَٱلِابْنُ وَٱلرُّوحُ ٱلْقُدُسُ إِلٰهٌ وَاحِدٌ إِلَى دَهْرِ ٱلدَّاهِرِينَ.

In God's name, بِسْمِ ٱللّٰهِ. *See also above*, For God's sake.

Oh God! يَا أَللّٰهُ — اَللّٰهُمَّ.

Please God, God willing, إِنْ أَرَادَ ٱللّٰهُ — بِإِذْنِهِ تَعَالَى — إِنْ شَاءَ ٱللّٰهُ.

Thank God! اَلْحَمْدُ لِلّٰهِ — لِلّٰهِ ٱلْحَمْدُ.

There is but one God, لَا إِلٰهَ إِلَّا ٱللّٰهُ.

Trust in God, تَوَكَّلْ عَلَى ٱللّٰهِ — عَلَيْكَ عَوْنَ ٱللّٰهِ.

Would to God! يَا لَيْتَ.

God, *n.* A heathen deity, إِلٰهٌ *or* إِلَاهٌ *pl.* آلِهَة.

God-child, *n.* فَلْيُون *fem.* فَلْيُونَة — اِبْنُ ٱلْمَعْمُودِيَّةِ *fem.* بِنْتُ ٱلْمَعْمُودِيَّةِ.

God-daughter, *n.* *See preceding article.*

Goddess, *n.* A deity, إِلَاهَة — مَعْبُودَة. A sweetheart, مَعْشُوقَة.

Godfather, *n.* إِشْبِين *pl.* أَشَابِين — عَرَّاب. To stand — to, عَمَّدَ — وَقَفَ لِ-إِشْبِينًا *aor.* يَقِفُ.

Godhead, *n.* The Divine nature, اَلرُّبُوبِيَّةُ — اَللَّاهُوتُ. *See also* God, *n.*

Godless, *a.* مُلْحِد — زِنْدِيق *pl.* زَنَادِقَة — فَاجِر *pl.* فُجَّار — كَافِر *pl.* كُفَّار.

Godlessly, *ad.* بِٱلْإِلْحَادِ — بِفُجُورٍ — بِزَنْدَقَةٍ.

Godlessness, *n.* إِلْحَاد — زَنْدَقَة — فُجُور — نِفَاق.

Godlike, *a.* Divine, إِلٰهِيٌّ — رَبَّانِيٌّ. Supernatural, يَفُوقُ ٱلطَّبِيعَةَ.

Godliness, *n.* وَرَع — وُرُوع — زُهْد — تَزَهُّد — صَلَاح — دِيَانَة — نُسْك — تَعَبُّد — تَدَيُّن — تَقْوَى. *See also* Piety, *n.*

Godly, *a.* Devout, pious, وَرِع — دَيِّن — مُتَدَيِّن — مُتَّقٍ. To be —, practise godliness, تَنَسَّكَ — وَرِعَ *aor.* يَرِعُ — تَزَهَّدَ — اِتَّقَى. Cleanliness is next to godliness, (*prov.*) اَلطُّهُورُ شَطْرُ ٱلْإِيمَانِ. (*lit.* Purification is part of faith.)

Godmother, *n.* عَرَّابَة — إِشْبِينَة *pl.* إِشْبِينَات. To stand — to; *see under* Godchild, *n.*

Godsend, *n.* خَيْرٌ مِنَ ٱللّٰهِ — سَعَادَة — حَظٌّ — بَخْت.

Godship, *n.* *See* Godhead, *n.*

Godson, *n.* *See* Godchild, *n.*

Godward, *ad.* لِلّٰهِ — نَظَرًا لِلّٰهِ — لَدَى ٱللّٰهِ.

Goggle, *v.i.* ـُ شَنَفَ بِعَيْنَيْهِ — دَوَّرَ عَيْنَيْهِ — اِلْتَفَتَ بِعَيْنَيْهِ.

Goggle-eyed, *a.* لَفُوتُ ٱلْعَيْنَيْنِ.

Goggles, *n.* Glasses to cure squinting, عُيَيْنَات (*vulg.* عُوَيْنَات)

عُوَيْنَاتٌ لِلصِّيَانَةِ عَنِ ٱلْغَبَرَةِ (or ٱلْغُبَار) ; against dust, لِلْأَحْوَلِ ; blinkers for horses, رَفَارِيفُ ـ غَمَائِمُ .

Gogglet, *n.* كُوز *pl.* أَكْوَاز .

Going, *n.* A walking, مَشْيٌ ـ رَحِيلٌ ـ سِيرَةٌ . Pregnancy, حَمْل ـ حَبَل . Departure, مُضِيٌّ ـ مُضُوٌّ ـ إِنْطِلَاق . Conduct, سُلُوك ـ سِيرَة . The going-down of the sun, غُرُوبُ ٱلشَّمْسِ .

Goings-on, تَصَرُّفَات ـ أَعْمَال ـ أَفْعَال ـ حَرَكَات ـ أُمُور .

Goitre, *n.* غُدَدَة ـ سِلْعَة *pl.* سِلَع ـ ضَوًى ـ ضَوَاة . To have goitres, ضَوِيَ . Having goitres, مَسْلُوع .

Gold, *n.* ذَهَب *pl.* ذُهُوب and ذُهْبَان ـ الصَّفْرَاء . Money, فُلُوس ـ دَرَاهِم . Wealth, مَال ـ غَنَاء . Liquid —, زِرْيَاب ـ دُجَال ـ ذَوْبُ ٱلذَّهَبِ ـ مَاءُ ٱلذَّهَبِ . Gold-wash for gilding, غُرَاب . Gold and silver, الأَحْمَرُ وَٱلأَبْيَضُ . Particles of —, شَذْر . Not all is gold that glitters, مَا كُلُّ مُدَوَّرٍ ـ مَا كُلُّ مُشَعْشَعٍ ذَهَبٌ جَوْزٌ وَلَا كُلُّ مُسْتَطِيلٍ مَوْزٌ (*lit.* Not everything round is a walnut, nor everything oblong a plantain.) The Gold Coast, بِلَادُ ٱلتِّبْرِ ـ سَوَاحِلُ ٱلذَّهَبِ .

Gold-beater, *n.* مُوَرِّقُ ٱلذَّهَبِ . Goldbeater's skin, لَزْقَةُ مُوَرِّقِي ٱلذَّهَبِ .

Gold-dust, *n.* تِبْر ـ نُضَار .

Gold, *a.* / Golden, Of gold, مِنْ ذَهَبٍ ـ ذَهَبِيٌّ . Shining, أَجُوج ـ سَاطِع ـ لَامِع . Yellow, أَصْفَر ـ أَصْفَرُ ذَهَبِيٌّ . Happy, خَفِيظ ـ سَعِيد . A — age, أَيَّامُ عِزٍّ ـ أَيَّامُ تَرَقٍّ . A — opportunity, فُرْصَةٌ ثَمِينَةٌ ـ فُرْصَةٌ جَيِّدَةٌ . The — rule, the rule of proportion, القَوَاعِدُ ٱلأَرْبَعَةُ ٱلْمُتَنَاسِبَةُ . Golden opinions, حُسْنُ ٱلظَّنِّ .

Goldfinch, *n.* زُقَيْقِيَّة ـ دُنُورَة ـ زَقَاقِيَّة .

Goldfish, *n.* سَمَكٌ لَوْنُهُ كَلَوْنِ ٱلذَّهَبِ ـ سَمَكُ مُرْجَانٍ .

Gold-lace, *n.* قَصَبٌ أَصْفَرُ . Gold-laced, مُخَطَّطٌ بِقَصَبٍ أَصْفَرَ ـ مُقَصَّب .

Gold-leaf, *n.* وَرَقُ ذَهَبٍ *pl.* أَوْرَاق .

Goldsmith, *n.* صَائِغ *pl.* صَاغَة and صَوَّاغ ـ سَيَّاغ ـ فَتَّان ـ جَوْهَرِيٌّ ـ مُوَّاغ . To model as a —, صَاغَ *aor.* يَصُوغُ . The art of the —, صِيَاغَة .

Gold-thread, *n.* خَيْطٌ مِنْ قَصَبٍ أَصْفَرَ .

Gold-wire, *n.* سِلْكٌ مِنَ ٱلذَّهَبِ .

Golf, *n.* لَعِبُ ٱلصَّوْلَجَانِ .

Golosh, *n.* جُرْمُوق *pl.* جَرَامِيق (Properly, the name of a shoe worn over the boot called a خُفّ).

Gondola, *n.* قَارِب *pl.* قَوَارِب ـ زَوْرَق *pl.* زَوَارِق ـ قَائِق *pl.* قَائِقَات .

Gondolier, *n.* مَلَّاحُ ٱلْقَارِبِ ـ قَائِقْجِي *pl.* قَائِقْجِيَّة .

Gone, *part.* Ruined, خُسْرَان ـ ضَالٌّ ـ ضَائِع . Dead, مَيِّت .

Gone with child, حُبْلَى ـ حَامِلَة . Gone in years, هَرِم ـ مُسِنٌّ ـ شَيْخ . Too far gone, utterly spoilt, خَرَاب ـ مُعَفَّنٌ لِلْغَايَةِ .

Gong, *n.* نَاقُوس *pl.* نَوَاقِيس . The mallet of a —, وَبِيلَة .

Gonorrhœa, *n.* سَيَلَانٌ فِرَنْجِيٌّ ـ نُزُولُ ٱلْمَنِيِّ .

Good, *a.* خَيْر ـ حَسِين ـ حَسَن ـ جَيِّد ـ مَلِيح *pl.* مِلَاح ـ طَيِّب ـ مُسْتَطَاب . Sound, صَحِيح ـ سَالِم . Valid, جَائِز . Wholesome, طَيِّب : of water, مَجُوع ـ نَجِيع . Pleasant to the taste, لَذِيذ ـ طَعِم . Useful, نَافِع ـ طَائِل ـ مُفِيد . Qualified for, مُوَافِقٌ ل ـ أَهْلٌ ل ـ خَلِيقٌ ل ـ جَدِيرٌ ب . Pious, مَشْمُولٌ بِٱلْخَيْرِ ـ مُتَدَيِّن ـ دَيِّن ـ صَالِح . Benevolent, جَوَاد ـ زَكِيٌّ ـ كَرِيم ـ خَيِّر . Quiet, سَاجٍ ـ قَرَّار ـ سَاكِن *pl.* سُكَّان . Handy, dexterous, مَاهِر ـ مُدَرَّب ـ شَاطِر . A — man, رَجُلٌ خَيِّرٌ . A — workman, أُسْتَاذ . A — name, صِيتٌ حَسِينٌ . A — turn, مَعْرُوف ـ جُود ـ إِحْسَان ـ خَيْر . Good breeding, أَدَب ـ حُسْنُ ٱلأَخْلَاقِ ـ ظَرَافَة . Good understanding, concord, وَفْق ـ إِتِّفَاق . A — deal, جَمّ ـ كَثِير ـ جِدًّا . A — while, مُدَّةٌ طَوِيلَةٌ ـ بُرْهَةٌ مَدِيدَةٌ . A — way, far, بَعِيد ـ قَصِيّ . In — earnest, بِجِدٍّ ـ مِنْ جِدٍّ . As — as, as if, كَأَنَّ ـ كَمِثْلِ .

Good Friday; (*see* Friday). He spoke that which was no —, unprofitable, نَطَقَ بِمَا لَا طَائِلَ تَحْتَهُ . It is not — that . . ., لَا يَجْمُلُ أَنْ . Good qualities, مَحَامِدُ ـ مَحَاسِنُ . *See also under* Well, *a.*

Good-bye ! فِي أَمَانِ ٱللّٰهِ .

Good for nothing, of a person, خِشْبٌ قِشْبٌ ; of a thing, لَا نَفْعَ فِيهِ ـ بَطَّال ـ هُوَ غَيْرُ طَائِلٍ . It is good for nothing, مَا هُوَ بِطَائِلٍ . He is good for nothing, لَيْسَ هُوَ بِلُحْمَةٍ وَلَا سَدَاةٍ ; (*lit.* He is neither woof nor warp.) (*For* Good-morning, day, evening, *see under the several nouns.*)

Good news, بَشَارَة .

Good sense, عَقْلٌ وَتَمْيِيزٌ .

Good works, حَسَنَات ـ خَيْرَات .

In good sooth, وَٱللّٰهِ ـ عَلِمَ ٱللّٰهُ ـ حَقًّا .

Well and good, حَبَّذَا ـ طَيِّب ـ حَسَنًا .

To be or become good, useful, healthy, طَابَ ـ صَحَّ . To be good, benevolent, جَادَ *aor.* يَجُود ـ أَحْسَنَ .

To be as good as one's word, قَامَ بِوَعْدِهِ ـ عَهِدَ ـ وَفَى وَعْدَهُ *aor.* يَفِي .

To be good for, نَفَعَ ل ـ صَلَحَ ل .

To be good to, جادَ ² إلى ـ أَحْسَنَ بِ or إلى ـ أَصْلَحَ إلى ـ أَفْضَلَ (or تَفَضَّلَ) عَلَى.

To hold good, to be valid, صَحَّ ـِ. To be held good by one, صَحَّ ـِ عِنْدَهُ.

To make good, to perform, أَنْفَذَ ـ أَنْجَزَ ـ أَتَمَّ ـ أَكْمَلَ ـ أَدَّى ـ أَمْضَى. To establish, prove, قَرَّرَ ـ حَقَّقَ ـ ثَبَّتَ ـ أَثْبَتَ ـ أَيَّدَ ـ أَوْضَحَ ـ بَرْهَنَ. To compensate for, عَوَّضَ-عَن. *See also under* Amends, *n.*

To think too good for, نَفِسَ-عَلَى ـَ.

Good, *n.* خَيْر ـ صَلاح. Advantage, مَنْفَعَة ـ نَفْع ـ طائِل ـ فائِدَة. The chief —, السَّعادَةُ ٱلعُظْمَى ـ الخَيْرُ ٱلأَعْظَمُ. The public —, مَنْفَعَةُ ٱلجَمِيعِ ـ الخَيْرُ ٱلعامُّ. One possessing little or no —, قَلِيلُ ٱلخَيْرِ ـ لا خَيْرَ فِيهِ.

Good, *ad.* حَبَّذا. As —, just as —, عَلَى سَوِيَّةٍ. *See also under* Well, *ad.*

Good! *int.* طَيِّب ـ مَلِيح ـ حَبَّذا ـ ما شاءَ ٱللّٰهُ ـ ما أَحْسَنَهُ.

Good-breeding, *n.* أَدَب ـ حُسْنُ ٱلأَخْلاقِ ـ ظَرافَة.

Good fellow, *n.* عَشِير *pl.* عُشَراء ـ نَدِيم *pl.* نُدَماء ـ أَلِيف *pl.* أُلَفاء.

Good-fellowship, *n.* أُلْفَة ـ عِشْرَة ـ مُنادَمَة ـ أُدْمَة.

Good-humour, *n.* كَيْف ـ حُبُور ـ بَشاشَة. To be in —, بَشَّ *aor.* يَبَشُّ ـ تَفَكَّهَ ـ اِنْبَسَطَ. To put into —, حَبَّرَ ـ أَحْبَرَ ـ كَيَّفَ ـ سَرَّ ² ـ أَبْسَطَ ـ نَكَّهَ ـ بَسَطَ ². He was in — with him, بَشَّ بِهِ ـِ ـ بَشْبَشَ بِهِ.

Good-humoured, *a.* بَشٌّ ـ هَشٌّ ـ بَشِيش ـ يَحْبُور ـ مُتَكَيِّف ـ عَلَى ٱلحَشِيشَةِ.

Goodliness, *n.* رَوْقَة ـ أَناقَة ـ كِياسَة ـ بَهاء ـ بَهْجَة ـ طَلاوَة ـ جَمال ـ حُسْن ـ صَلاح.

Goodly, *a.* أَنِيق ـ رائِق ـ بَهِيج ـ بَهِيّ ـ مَلِيح *pl.* مِلاح ـ جَمِيل ـ حَسِين ـ فاخِر. To be —, حَسُنَ ² ـ ظَرُفَ ². To make —, حَسَّنَ. To consider —, اِسْتَحْسَنَ.

Good man, *n.* صاحِبُ ٱلبَيْتِ ـ رَبُّ ٱلبَيْتِ.

Good-mannered, *a.* ظَرِيف ـ أَدِيب ـ شَلَبِيّ.

Good nature, *n.* لُطْف ـ حُسْنُ خُلْقٍ ـ كَرَم ـ سَماحَة ـ سُمُوحَة.

Good-natured, *a.* كَرِيم ـ مُحْسِن ـ ذُو كَرَم ـ وَدِيد ـ صاحِبُ مَعْرُوفٍ; of a beast, وَدِيع ـ سَمِيح.

Good-naturedly, *ad.* بِسَماحَةٍ ـ بِكَرَمٍ ـ بِتَجَمُّلٍ ـ بِحُسْنِ ٱلطَّوِيَّةِ.

Goodness, *n.* Quality of what is good, طِيبَة. Validity, صِحَّة ـ حَقّ. Strength, قُوَّة. Uprightness, صَلاح ـ اِسْتِقامَة. Sweetness of disposition, حِلْم ـ ظَرافَة ـ حُسْنُ ٱلشِّيَمِ. Kindliness, لُطْف ـ كَرَم ـ جَوْدَة ـ فَضْل ـ إِحْسان. The — of God, لُطْفُ ٱللّٰهِ. Goodness, as of meat, دَسَم ـ وَدَك. Goodness of soil, خَصْبَة ـ خِصْب. Have the —, إِعْمَلِ ٱلمَعْرُوفَ ـ تَفَضَّلْ ـ كَلِّفْ خاطِرَكَ ـ مِنْ فَضْلِكَ. I wish to —!, يا لَيْتَ. For goodness' sake, بِٱللّٰهِ عَلَيْكَ ـ مِنْ حِلْمِكَ. My —!, أَمانْ يا رَبّ.

Goods, *n.* Moveables, property, أَمْوال ـ أَرْزاق. Furniture, أَشْياء ـ أَثاث ـ أَمْتِعَة ـ جِهاز. Merchandize, سِلَع ـ أَمْتِعَة ـ أَسْباب ـ تِجارَة ـ أَصْناف. Goods of a dangerous nature, such as are forbidden on railways, *etc.*, المَناهِي مِنَ ٱلأَصْنافِ ـ الأَصْنافُ ٱلمَمْنُوعُ نَقْلُها. The perishing — of the world, حُطامُ ٱلدُّنْيا. Confiscation of —, غَرامَةُ ٱلمالِ. To waste one's —, بَذَّرَ أَمْوالَهُ.

Good-wife, *n.* رَبَّةُ ٱلبَيْتِ ـ صاحِبَةُ ٱلبَيْتِ.

Good-will, *n.* Benevolence, حُسْنُ إِرادَةٍ ـ خَيْر ـ كَرَم. Custom, customers, زَبُونَة.

Goody, *n.* والِدَة.

Goody, *a.* مُتَجَوِّد ـ مُتَأَنِّق.

Goose, *n.* The bird, إِوَزَّة *coll.* إِوَزّ ـ وَزَّة *coll.* وَزّ. A tailor's —, مِكْواة.

Gooseberry, *n.* عِنَبُ ٱلثَّعْلَبِ ـ كُشْبُرَة إِفْرَنْجِيَّة. Gooseberry-fool, كُشْبُرَة مُصَفّاة وَمُحَلّاة.

Goose-quill, *n.* رِيشُ ٱلإِوَزِّ.

Gopher, *n.* The wood, خَشَبُ جُفْرٍ.

Gordian, *a.* Very intricate, مُعَقَّد ـ عَوِيص. To cut the — knot, حَلَّ ² ٱلمُشْكِلَةَ ـ فَكَّ ² ٱلعُقْدَةَ جَبْرًا.

Gore, *n.* Clotted blood, دَم ـ دَمٌ مُجَمَّد. The — of a dress, شِعاب ـ شُعَب *and* شُعْبَة *pl.* دَخارِيص ـ دِخْراص *pl.* دِخْرِصَة ـ بَنِيقَة *pl.* بَنائِق. To add a — to a dress, بَنَّقَ (or طَبَّبَ) ٱلثَّوْبَ.

Gore, *v.t.* To stab with the horns, ناطَحَ ـ نَطَحَ ـَ. To piece with a —, بَنَّقَ. Gored land, *i.e.* land joined to other land, أَرْضٌ مَبْنُوقَة.

Gorge, *n.* The throat, حُلْقُوم ـ مَزْرَد. A narrow pass, مَضِيق *pl.* مَضائِق ـ خانِق *pl.* خَوانِق ـ شَقّ *pl.* شُقُوق ـ بُوغاز.

Gorge, *v.t.* أَشْبَعَ ـ مَلَأَ ـَ. To be gorged, فَقِمَ ـَ. *See also* to Glut, *v.t.*

Gorgeous, *a.* لامِع ـ عَظِيم ـ مُزَخْرَف ـ فاخِر ـ بَهِيّ ـ زاهٍ.

Gorgeously, *ad.* بِبَهاءٍ ـ بِجَلالٍ ـ بِفَخْرٍ.

Gorgeousness, *n.* زَخْرَفَة ـ بَهاء ـ فَخْر ـ جَلال.

Gorget, *n.* Armour for the throat, طَوْق. A surgical knife, مِبْضَع ـ مِشْرَطَة.

Gorgon, *n.* A demon, عِفْرِيتٌ *pl.* عَفَارِيتُ.

Gorilla, *n.* قِرْدٌ يُشْبِهُ رَجُلًا وَحْشِيًّا — نَوْعٌ مِنَ ٱلْقِرْدِ.

Gormand,
Gormander, *n.*
Gormandizer, } *See* Glutton, *n.*

Gormandize, *v.i.* ٢ قَفَشَ. *See also to* Gluttonize, *v.i.*

Gorse, *n.* *See* Furze, *n.*

Gory, *a.* مُلَوَّثٌ (or مَلْطُوخٌ or مُضَرَّجٌ) بِٱلدَّمِ — دَمِيٌّ.

Goshawk, *n.* نَوْعٌ مِنَ ٱلصَّقْرِ.

Gosling, *n.* فَرْخُ ٱلْوَزَّةِ *pl.* أَفْرَاخٌ.

Gospel, *n.* إِنْجِيلٌ *pl.* أَنَاجِيلُ. The four Gospels, ٱلْأَرْبَعَةُ أَنَاجِيلَ.

Gospel, *a.* *See* Evangelical, *a.*

Gospeler, *n.* *See* Evangelist, *n.*

Gossamer, *n.* رِيقُ ٱلشَّيْطَانِ — جَالِجَةٌ — سُهَامٌ — سُهُمٌ — خَيْتَعُورٌ — لُعَابُ (or رِيقُ) ٱلشَّمْسِ.

Gossip, *n.* A tattler, فُضُولِيٌّ — بَقَّاقٌ — لِسَانٌ طَلِقٌ — فَشَّارٌ; especially of a woman, زَلِزَةٌ. One who goes about among his neighbours, طَوَّافٌ. Tattle, بَقٌّ — قِيلٌ وَقَالٌ — لَقْشٌ. *See also* Godfather *and* Godmother, *n.*

Gossip, *v.i.* ٢ بَقَّ — زَخْلَفَ فِي ٱلْكَلَامِ — هَذْرَمَ — ٢ سَابَ فِي ٱلْكَلِمِ.

Got, *part.* *See to* Get, *v.t.*

Goth, *n.* One of the Goths, غُوطِيٌّ. A barbarian, clown, هَمَجٌ — جَافٍ — فَظٌّ — غَلِيظٌ — وَحْشٌ — فَلَّاحٌ.

Gothic, *a.* Pertaining to the Goths, غُوطِيٌّ. The — style of architecture, ٱلْبِنَاءُ عَلَى هَنْدَسَةٍ غُوطِيَّةٍ.

Gothicize, *v.t.* To bring back to barbarism, ٢ رَدَّ-إِلَى حَالِ ٱلْهَمَجِ.

Gouge, *n.* إِزْمِيلٌ — إِزْمِيلٌ مُدَوَّرُ ٱلشَّفْرِ.

Gouge, *v.t.* ٢ نَقَرَ-بِإِزْمِيلٍ. To — one's eyes, ٢ فَقَأَ عَيْنَيْهِ. To have the eyes gouged out, of one person, إِنْفَقَأَتَا عَيْنَاهُ.

Gourd, *n.* قَرْعَةٌ *coll.* قَرْعٌ — يَقْطِينَةٌ *coll.* يَقْطِينٌ.

Gourmand, *n.* بَطِنٌ. *See also* Glutton, *n.*

Gout, *n.* The disease, نِقْرِسٌ. Rheumatic —, دَآءُ ٱلْمَفَاصِلِ.

Gout, *n.* Taste, طَعْمٌ — لَذَّةٌ.

Gouty, *a.* Having gout, مُصَابٌ بِٱلنِّقْرِسِ; of a — nature, مِنْ عِرْقِ ٱلنِّقْرِسِ.

Govern, *v.t.* To rule over, ٢ مَلَكَ عَلَى — ٢ رَعَى — ٢ حَكَمَ عَلَى — تَسَلَّطَ عَلَى — إِسْتَوْلَى عَلَى. To direct, سَاسَ *aor.* يَسُوسُ — قَادَ *aor.* يَقُودُ — دَارَى — دَبَّرَ. To —, as in grammar, ٢ عَمِلَ فِي. To turn, as of a helm, أَدَارَ — دَوَّرَ. To cause to —, مَلَّكَ-عَلَى — سَلَّطَ-عَلَى — أَمْلَكَ.

Govern, *v.i.* To exercise authority, تَوَلَّى — سَلَطَ ٢ — قَامَ ٢ بِٱلْحُكُومَةِ.

Governable, *a.* وَدِيعٌ — طَيِّعٌ — مِمَّا يُحْكَمُ عَلَيْهِ.

Governance, *n.* Management, إِدَارَةٌ — ضَبْطٌ — تَدْبِيرٌ — سِيَاسَةٌ — قِيَادَةٌ.

Governess, *n.* A female teacher, مُعَلِّمَةٌ — قَهْرَمَانَةٌ.

Government, *n.* Controul, حُكْمٌ — حُكُومَةٌ — وِلَايَةٌ — إِيَالَةٌ — إِيَالَةٌ. Administration, تَدْبِيرٌ — إِدَارَةٌ — سِيَاسَةٌ — قِيَادَةٌ. System of rule, أُصُولُ إِدَارَةٍ — أُصُولُ حُكُومَةٍ. An empire, دَوْلَةٌ *pl.* دُوَلٌ — سَلْطَنَةٌ — حُكُومَةٌ. The administrators of a —, وُكَلَاءُ ٱلدَّوْلَةِ. The science of —, فَنُّ ٱلسِّيَاسَةِ. Government of nouns, إِضَافَةُ ٱلْإِسْمِ إِلَى ٱلْإِسْمِ.

Absolute government, حُكُومَةٌ مُطْلَقَةٌ.

Central government, حُكُومَةٌ مَرْكَزِيَّةٌ.

Independent government, حُكُومَةٌ مُسْتَقِلَّةٌ.

Monarchical government, حُكُومَةٌ مُنْفَرِدَةٌ (or مَلَكِيَّةٌ).

Provincial government, لِوَآءٌ — سَنْجَقٌ — إِيَالَةٌ; one of large extent, وِلَايَةٌ.

Provisional government, حُكُومَةٌ مُوَقَّتَةٌ.

Republican government, حُكُومَةٌ جُمْهُورِيَّةٌ.

Governmental, *a.* سِيَاسِيٌّ — مُتَعَلِّقٌ بِٱلْحُكُومَةِ. Governmental power, أَمْرٌ سِيَاسِيٌّ — قُوَّةٌ سِيَاسِيَّةٌ.

Governor, *n.* A ruler, وَالٍ *pl.* وُلَاةٌ — ضَابِطٌ *pl.* ضُبَّاطٌ — مُتَصَرِّفٌ — حَاكِمٌ *pl.* حُكَّامٌ. A chief, قَائِدٌ *pl.* قَادَةٌ *and* قُوَّادٌ — رَئِيسٌ *pl.* رُؤَسَآءُ. A director, حَافِظٌ — مُدَبِّرٌ — أَمِينٌ — نَاظِرٌ. A Deputy —, وَالِي — وَلِيٌّ وِلَاءٍ — وَالٍ — قَائِمُ مَقَامٍ — مُتَسَلِّمٌ. Governor-General, وَلَاةٌ. Governor of a province, حُكْمَدَارٌ — وَالِي وِلَايَةٍ. To be — over, إِسْتَوْلَى عَلَى — ٢ حَكَمَ عَلَى — ٢ رَأَسَ عَلَى. To make — over, وَلَّى-عَلَى — رَأَّسَ-عَلَى — أَمَّرَ-فِي. To be made — over, تَأَمَّرَ عَلَى — إِرْتَأَسَ عَلَى — تَرَأَّسَ عَلَى. Governor, a contrivance for regulating machinery, مِفْتَاحٌ لِتَشْدِيدِ سُرْعَةِ ٱلدَّوَالِيبِ وَتَخْفِيفِهَا.

Governorship, *n.* Authority, directorate, إِمَارَةٌ — نَظَارَةٌ — أَمَانَةٌ — مُحَافَظَةٌ — تَصَرُّفٌ. Office of a governor, وِلَايَةٌ *pl.* وَلَايَا.

Gown, *n.* A loose robe for men or women, قَنْبَسٌ *vulg.* قُنْبَازٌ *pl.* قَنَابِزُ — مِنْتَانَةٌ — يَلَكٌ. A woman's —, فُسْتَانٌ *pl.* فَسَاتِينُ. A priest's —, كَثُونَةٌ. An academical —, فَرُّوجٌ *pl.* فَرَارِيجُ — فَرَاجِيَّةٌ — حُلَّةٌ *pl.* حُلَلٌ (the best words which I can find to express the idea. Muhammad is said to have prayed in a فَرُّوج of خَزٌّ or silk). A night-gown, قَمِيصُ ٱلنَّوْمِ.

Gownsman, *n.* One who wears a gown, لابِسُ ـ صاحِبُ حُلَّةٍ فَرُّوجٍ. An elegant scholar, أَدِيب. One who wields a pen, صاحِبُ ٱلْقَلَمِ. A member of a university, مِنْ أَهْلِ مَدْرَسَةِ ٱلْعُلُومِ وَٱلْفُنُونِ.

Grab, *n.* A sudden seizure, خَطْفَة. A — anchor, مِرْساةٌ صَغِيرَةٌ.

Grab, *v.t.* خَطِفَ ـ اِخْتَطَفَ ـ سَلَبَ.

Grace, *n.* Favour, كَرَم ـ عِنَايَة ـ لُطْف ـ إِحْسَان ـ نِعْمَة. Kindness, bounty, تَوْفِيق ـ فَضْل. Aid, support, عَضُد ـ عَوْن ـ تَأْيِيد. Benevolence, blessing, فَيْض ـ جُود ـ بَرَكَة. Pardon, عَفْو ـ سَمَاح ـ غُفْرَان ـ صَفْح ـ مَرْحَمَة ـ رَحْمَة. A benefit conferred, إِنْعَام ـ نِعْمَة *pl.* نِعَم ـ مِنَّة *pl.* مِنَن ـ فَضْل *pl.* أَفْضَال. A virtue, فَضِيلَة *pl.* فَضَائِل ـ صَلاح. Elegance, صَبَاحَة ـ حُسْن ـ لَطَافَة ـ ظَرَافَة ـ حَلاوَة ـ طُلاوَة ـ جَمَال ـ رَوْنَق ـ بَرَاعَة. An ornament, زِينَة *pl.* زِيَن ـ حِلْيَة *pl.* حُلًى. A privilege, اِمْتِيَاز *pl.* اِمْتِيَازَات. A prayer before meals, دُعَآءٌ (or شُكْرٌ) قَبْلَ ٱلْأَكْلِ ـ بَسْمَلَة. Grace, as a title, سَعَادَة ـ جَنَاب. *See also under* Favour, *n.*

A grace issued by a university, أَمْر ـ تَنْبِيه.

An act of grace, pardon, عَفْوٌ وَصَفْحٌ.

By the grace of God, بِعِنَايَةِ ٱللّٰهِ تَعَالَى ـ بِتَوْفِيقِهِ سُبْحَانَهُ وَتَعَالَى.

Day of grace, of obtaining pardon, أَمَدُ ٱلتَّوْبَةِ. Days of delay, أَيَّامُ سَمَاحٍ.

With a bad grace, بِعَدَمِ رِضَآءٍ ـ كُرْهًا ـ عَنْفًا.

With a good grace, حَسَنًا ـ بِحُسْنِ رِضَآءٍ ـ بِلُطْفٍ ـ بِبَشَاشَةٍ.

To be in one's good graces, لَهُ جَاهٌ عِنْدَهُ ـ هُوَ مُقَرَّبٌ عِنْدَهُ.

To say grace, صَلَّى عَلَى ٱلطَّعَامِ ـ بَارَكَ (or بَرَّكَ) عَلَى ٱلطَّعَامِ.

To sue for grace, اِسْتَرْحَمَ ـ اِسْتَغْفَرَ.

Grace, *v.t.* To adorn, ظَرَّفَ ـ حَسَّنَ ـ جَمَّلَ ـ زَخْرَفَ ـ زَيَّنَ. To honour, شَرَّفَ ـ بَجَّلَ. To —, to honour, one with, as with a decoration, *etc.*, أَنْعَمَ عَلَى ـ بِ ـ وَشَّحَ ـ بِ ـ وَجَّهَ ـ بِ.

Graceful, *a.* صَبَاحَانُ ـ صَبِيح ـ لَطِيف *pl.* لِطَاف ـ جَمِيل ـ ظَرِيف ـ رَشِيق ـ حُلْوُ ٱلشَّمَائِلِ.

Gracefully, *ad.* بِظَرَافَةٍ ـ بِحَلاوَةٍ ـ بِطُلاوَةٍ ـ بِجَمَالٍ.

Gracefulness, *n.* طُلاوَة ـ جَمَال ـ حَلاوَة ـ مَلاحَة ـ ظَرَافَة ـ رَشَاقَة.

Graceless, *a.* Wicked, أَبْتَر ـ خَاسِر ـ خَبِيث ـ فَاحِش ـ شِرِّير.

Gracious, *a.* Merciful, رَؤُوف ـ رَحِيم ـ حَنَّان ـ شَفِيق ـ شَفُوق. Benevolent, خَيِّر ـ مُحْسِن ـ كَرِيم. Expressive of kindness, ظَرِيفُ ٱلْمَعَانِي ـ مِنْعَام ـ ظَرِيف ـ لَطِيف ـ مُطَيِّب. To be — to, رَفَقَ بِ or عَلَى. May God be — to thee, نَعِمَ ٱللّٰهُ بِكَ. The Gracious (God), ٱلْحَنَّان ـ ٱلرَّؤُوف ـ ٱلرَّحِيم.

Graciously, *ad.* بِلُطْفٍ ـ بِلَطَافَةٍ ـ بِتَطْيِيبِ ٱلْخَاطِرِ.

Graciousness, *n.* إِحْسَان ـ إِنْعَام ـ كَرَم ـ لُطْف ـ حَلاوَة ـ رِفْق.

Gradation, *n.* Regular process, تَدْرِيج ـ اِسْتِدْرَاج. A grade, دَرَجَة *pl.* دَرَجَات ـ مَرْتَبَة ـ مَقَام. Series, طَبَقَة ـ سِيَاقَة. By —, عَلَى ٱلتَّدْرِيجِ ـ دَرَجَةً دَرَجَةً ـ تَدْرِيجًا.

Gradational, *a.* }
Gradatory, } وَاقِعٌ دَرَجَةً دَرَجَةً ـ تَدْرِيجِيٌّ.

Grade, *n.* دَرَجَة ـ مَرْتَبَة ـ طَبَقَة ـ رُتْبَة.

Gradient, *n.* A slope, حُدُور ـ صَبَب *pl.* أَصْبَاب.

Gradient, *a.* Moving by steps, مُتَدَرِّج. Sloping, هَبُوط.

Gradual, *a.* تَدْرِيجِيٌّ ـ مُتَدَرِّج.

Gradually, *ad.* عَلَى ٱلتَّدْرِيجِ ـ دَرَجَةً دَرَجَةً. It has been — increasing, تَزَايَدَ شَيْئًا فَشَيْئًا. To move —, اِسْتَدْرَجَ.

Graduate, *v.t.* To honour, as with an academical or other degree, وَجَّهَ بِرُتْبَةٍ. To mark with degrees, قَسَّمَ دَرَجَاتٍ ـ دَرَّجَ. To temper, عَادَلَ ـ عَدَّلَ.

Graduate, *v.i.* To receive a degree, وُجِّهَ بِرُتْبَةٍ. To pass gradually, تَدَرَّجَ.

Graduate, *n.* As of a university, ذُو رُتْبَةٍ مِنْ مَدْرَسَةٍ جَامِعَةٍ; one permitted to practise a profession, مَأْذُون ـ مُجَاز.

Graduation, *n.* The act of conferring degrees, تَوْجِيهُ ٱلْمَرَاتِبِ; receiving a degree, تَوَشُّحٌ بِرُتْبَةٍ ـ تَنَاوُلُ رُتْبَةٍ.

Gradus, *n.* كِتَابُ ٱلْمَبَادِئِ.

Graft, *n.* A scion inserted, غَرْز *pl.* غُرُوز ـ طُعْم ـ تَطْعِيم.

Graft, *v.t.* To insert a scion, غَرَزَ ـ طَعَّمَ ـ أَطْعَمَ ـ لَقَّمَ. To be grafted, طَعِمَ. To insert into, أَدْخَلَ ـ فِي ـ ضَمَّ ـ إِلَى ـ أَسْلَكَ ـ فِي.

Grafting, *n.* غَرْز ـ تَطْعِيم ـ إِطْعَام ـ تَلْقِيم.

Grain, *n.* A single seed of wheat, قَمْحَة. Corn, wheat, قَمْح ـ حِنْطَة ـ طَعَام *pl.* أَطْعِمَة. Grain for sowing, بَذْر. The seed of any pulse, حَبَّة *coll.* حَبّ *pl.* حُبُوب. Produce, ثَمَرَة ـ غَلَّة. A — in weight, قَمْحَة *pl.* قَمْحَات ـ شَعِيرَة ـ حَبَّة. The — of wood, جَوْهَرُ ٱلْخَشَبِ. Disposition, عِرْق ـ خُلْق ـ طَبْع. Wood of a good —, عُودٌ طَيِّبُ ٱلْمَكْسِرِ. The wavy — of a sword, دَرِيٌّ. Against the —, with contrariety, بِٱلْعَكْسِ ـ كُرْهًا: He did it against the —, فَعَلَهُ عَلَى تَكَرُّهٍ.

To cut across the grain, of wood, قَطَعَ - عَكَسَ جَوْهَرَ ٱلْخَشَبِ.

To dye in grain, of wood, صَبَغَ - شِبْهَ جَوْهَرِ ٱلْخَشَبِ — نَقَشَ - شِبْهَ عُرُوقِ ٱلشَّجَرِ.

To go against the grain of another, عَاكَسَ. To go against one's own grain, تَكَرَّهَ - كَرِهَ.

Grain, v.t. To form into grains, حَبَّبَ. To paint in imitation of the grains of wood, صَبَغَ - صَبَغَ جَوْهَرَ ٱلْخَشَبِ — صَبَغَ - (or دَبَّجَ or زَوَّقَ) بِهَيْئَةِ — نَقَشَ - بِهَيْئَةِ عُرُوقِ ٱلشَّجَرِ عُرُوقِ ٱلشَّجَرِ.

Grain, v.i. To form itself into grains, تَحَبَّبَ.

Grained, a. Painted in imitation of the grains of wood, مَصْبُوغٌ مَصْبُوغٌ (or مُدَبَّجٌ or مَنْقُوشٌ) بِهَيْئَةِ عُرُوقِ — صَبْغُ جَوْهَرِ ٱلْخَشَبِ ٱلشَّجَرِ. Made into grains, مُحَبَّبٌ. Made rough, مُخَشَّبٌ — أَخْشَبُ. Ingrained, given to, مَطْبُوعٌ عَلَى.

Grainer, n. مُدَبِّجُ (or زَوَّاقُ) ٱلْخَشَبِ.

Graining, n. صَبْغُ (or دَبْجُ or تَزْوِيقُ) ٱلْخَشَبِ بِهَيْئَةِ عُرُوقِ ٱلشَّجَرِ.

Grains, n. Dregs, رُسُوبٌ — حُثَالَةٌ — عَكَرٌ. *See also* Dregs, n.

Grallic, a. Having long legs, سَقَّاقٌ.

Gram, n. The pulse, the chick-pea, حِمَّصٌ — حِمِّصٌ. A single grain of —, حِمَّصَةٌ.

Gramercy! int. أَصْبِرْ عَلَى — عَنْ إِذْنِكَ.

Gramineal, n. } Gramineous, } حَشِيشِيٌّ — عُشْبِيٌّ.

Graminivorous, a. آكِلُ حَشِيشٍ.

Grammar, n. The science of, عِلْمُ ٱلنَّحْوِ — ٱلنَّحْوُ; a book of —, كِتَابُ نَحْوٍ وَصَرْفٍ.

Grammarian, n. نَحْوِيٌّ — نَاحٍ pl. نُحَاةٌ.

Grammar-school, n. مَدْرَسَةُ ٱلْعُلُومِ — مَكْتَبُ ٱلْمَعَارِفِ — رُشْدِيَّةٌ.

Grammatic, a. } Grammatical, } صَرْفِيٌّ — نَحْوِيٌّ.

Grammatically, ad. عَلَى قَوَاعِدِ ٱلنَّحْوِ. To inflect, decline, or conjugate —, صَرَّفَ.

Grampus, n. سَمَكٌ مِنْ جِنْسِ حُوتٍ — نَوْعٌ مِنَ ٱلسَّمَكِ ٱلْكَبِيرِ — يُونُسُ.

Granary, n. هُرْيٌ pl. أَهْرَآءٌ — صَوْنَةٌ — شُونَةٌ pl. شُوَنٌ — أَنْبَارٌ pl. أَنْبَارَاتٌ. An underground —, مَطْمُورَةٌ pl. مَطَامِيرُ.

Grand, a. Great, عَظِيمٌ — كَبِيرٌ. Magnificent, splendid, جَلِيٌّ — سُلْطَانِيٌّ — مُفَخَّمٌ — بَهِيٌّ — فَاخِرٌ — جَلِيلٌ. Noble, نَبِيلٌ — سَامٍ — شَرِيفٌ — جَلِيلٌ. A — assembly, مَوْكِبٌ بَاهِرٌ.

Grandam, n. An old woman, عَجُوزَةٌ pl. عَجَائِزُ. *See also* Grandmother, n.

Grandchild, n. As applied generally to a son's son and a daughter's son, حَفِيدٌ pl. حَفَدَةٌ and حُفَدَآءُ — سِبْطٌ pl. أَسْبَاطٌ (but in vulgar usage the former is applied to a son's son and the latter to a daughter's son).

Grand-daughter, n. حَافِدَةٌ; a son's daughter, بِنْتُ ٱبْنٍ; a daughter's daughter, بِنْتُ بِنْتٍ.

Grand-duchess, n. غَرَانْدُوشِيسْ.

Grand-duke, n. غَرَانْدُوكْ.

Grandee, n. عَيْنٌ pl. أَعْيَانٌ — كَبِيرٌ pl. أَكَابِرُ — أَمِيرٌ pl. أُمَرَآءُ — شَرِيفٌ pl. شُرَفَآءُ. The grandees, ٱلْأَكَابِرُ — ٱلْأَعْيَانُ — ٱلْأَشْرَافُ — عُظَمَاتُ ٱلْقَوْمِ.

Grandeur, n. Greatness, excellency, عَظَمَةٌ — جَلَالٌ — هَيْبَةٌ — عُلُوٌّ. Stateliness, حِشْمَةٌ — إِحْتِشَامٌ — أُبَّهَةٌ. Magnificence, دَوْلَةٌ — سَلْطَنَةٌ — عِزٌّ — إِحْتِفَالٌ.

Grandfather, n. جَدٌّ pl. أَجْدَادٌ; great —, أَبُو جَدٍّ.

Grandiloquence, n. تَفَنُّنٌ فِي ٱلْكَلَامِ — هَتْهَتَةٌ — ٱلْعَظَائِمُ فِي ٱلْكَلَامِ.

Grandiloquent, a. هَتْهَاتٌ — كَتَّاتٌ — مُتَفَنِّنٌ — مِفَنٌّ.

Grand-juror, n. عُضْوٌ مِنْ أَعْضَاءِ ٱللَّجْنَةِ ٱلْمُنْتَخَبَةِ تَحْتَ قَسَمٍ لِتَمْيِيزِ ٱلدَّعَاوَى عِنْدَ إِعْرَاضِهَا أَوَّلَ بَدْءٍ عَلَى ٱلْمَحْكَمَةِ. *See also under* Juror *and* Jury, n.

Grand-jury, n. لَجْنَةٌ تَمْيِيزِ ٱلْجِنَايَاتِ عِنْدَ إِعْرَاضِهَا أَوَّلَ بَدْءٍ عَلَى ٱلْمَحْكَمَةِ. *See also under* Jury, n.

Grandmother, n. جَدَّةٌ: a father's mother, أُمُّ ٱلْأَبِ; a mother's mother, أُمُّ ٱلْأُمِّ.

Grand-seignior, n. The Sultân of Turkey, سُلْطَانُ دَوْلَةِ آلِ عُثْمَانَ.

Grand-nephew, n. إِبْنُ ٱبْنِ لِأَخٍ.

Grandsire, n. *See* Grandfather, n.

Grandson, n. حَفِيدٌ — حَافِدٌ; a son's son, إِبْنُ ٱبْنٍ; a daughter's son, إِبْنُ بِنْتٍ.

Grand Vizier, n. (More correctly Grand Wazîr), ٱلصَّدْرُ ٱلْأَعْظَمُ.

Grange, n. حَوْشٌ pl. حِيشَانٌ — دَارُ ٱلْمَزْرَعَةِ وَحَيِّزُهَا. *See also* Farm, n.

Graniferous, a. حَامِلُ حُبُوبٍ.

Granite, n. حَجَرُ صَوَّانٍ.

Granite, a. } Granitic, } مِثْلَ حَجَرِ ٱلصَّوَّانِ — مِنْ حَجَرِ صَوَّانٍ.

Granivorous, a. آكِلُ ٱلْحُبُوبِ — مُقْتَاتٌ بِٱلْحُبُوبِ.

Grant, v.t. To concede, قَنَعَ إِلَى — أَجَابَ بِ — سَلَّمَ بِ —

جَوَّزَ – رَضِيَ بِ – قَبِلَ – أَقْرَضَ لِ – مَنَحَ. To bestow, فَرَضَ لِ – وَهَبَ لِ aor. يَهَبُ – أَعْطَى. To give to, out of kindness, أَنْعَمَ عَلَى-بِ – أَكْرَمَ عَلَى-بِ – أَحْسَنَ إِلَى-بِ. To listen to, to give in answer to a request, أَجَابَ – أَصْغَى إِلَى دُعَآئِهِ دُعَآءَهُ. To —, as of a concession of land, أَقْطَعَهُ قَطِيعَةً. To —, to commit to, فَوَّضَ-إِلَى. He granted him what he requested, آتَاهُ بِمَا سَأَلَ. It shall be granted, given, them, يُمْنَحُ لَهُمْ. To — a delay, مَهَّلَ – أَخَّرَ-إِلَى مُدَّةٍ. To transfer, نَقَلَ. To take for granted, صَدَّقَ – اتَّخَذَ-صَادِقًا.

Grant, *n.* The act of granting, إِقْرَاض – مَنْح – وَهْب – تَفْوِيض – إِعْطَآء; out of kindness, إِحْسَان – إِنْعَام. A thing granted, هِبَة – مَوْهِبَة – مِنْحَة – مِنَح *pl.* عَطِيَّة – عَطَايَا *pl.*; as of land, قَطِيعَة – اِلْتِزَام. Special appropriation, تَخْصِيص. Admission, تَسْلِيم. The deed of a —, حُجَّة – سَنَد. A — of land, طُعْمَة – عُقْرَة. To make a — to, أَوْقَفَ-لِ – خَصَّصَ-لِ.

Granted, *ad.* Granted that, سَلَّمْنَا أَنْ – فَرَضْنَا أَنْ.

Grantee, *n.* مُلْتَزِم – مُمْتَنِح.

Grantor, *n.* مُعْطٍ – مُفَوِّض – وَاهِب – مَانِح.

Granular, Granulary, *a.* Granulate, } Like grains, مُحَبَّب – حُبُوبِيٌّ. Rough, خَشِن – أَخْشَب – خَشِب.

Granulate, *v.t.* To form into grains, حَبَّبَ. To make rough, خَشَّنَ.

Granulate, *v.i.* To form itself into grains, تَحَبَّبَ. To become rough, خَشُنَ – تَخَشَّنَ.

Granulation, *n.* Making into grains, تَحْبِيب. The process of healing, الأَخْذُ فِي الْجَبْرِ.

Granule, *n.* حَبَّة *pl.* حُبُوب; a particle, هُنَامَة – حُتْرَة *vulg.* حُتَّة.

Granulous, *a.* حُبُوبِيٌّ – ذُو حُبُوبٍ.

Grape, *n.* عِنَبَة (or حَبَّة مِنْ عِنَبٍ) *coll.* عِنَب *pl.* أَعْنَاب. A bunch of grapes, عُنْقُودُ عِنَبٍ *pl.* عَنَاقِيدُ. Sour grapes, حُصْرُم. A — seed, فَصَاة *coll.* فَصًا – فِرْصِد – فِرْصِيد – بِزْرَةُ عِنَبٍ *coll.* بِزْر. Grapes with small seeds, عِنَبٌ مُخَرْدَقٌ. Made of grapes, عِنَبِيٌّ. A seller of grapes, عَنَّاب. A — vine, دَالِيَة *pl.* دَوَالٍ. To gather or produce grapes, عَنَّبَ. A small bunch or raceme of grapes, خُصْلَةُ عِنَبٍ.

Grapery, *n.* ذُرًى لِلدَّوَالِي.

Grape-shot, *n.* مِرْمَاةٌ مِنْ حَدِيدٍ أَوْ رَصَاصٍ فِي شَكْلِ عَنَاقِيدِ الْعِنَبِ; *in Turkish,* صالقم.

Graphic, *a.* Graphical, } Pertaining to writing, مُتَعَلِّقٌ بِالْخَطِّ. Descriptive, تَعْبِيرِيٌّ – وَصْفِيٌّ. Accurate, مُدَقِّق – كَامِل – مَضْبُوط. Embellished, of speech, *etc.,* مُحَبَّر.

Graphically, *ad.* Descriptively, accurately, بِدِقَّةٍ – وَصْفًا.

Grapline, *n.* Grapnel, } A small anchor, مِرْسَاةٌ صَغِيرَةٌ.

Grapple, *v.t.* To close with in contest, صَارَعَ – تَشَبَّثَ بِ. To lay hold of with grappling-irons, تَمَسَّكَ-بِكَلَالِيبَ – تَشَبَّثَ بِ-بِكَلَالِيبَ. *See also to* Grasp, *v.t.*

Grapple, *v.i.* They grappled, as wrestlers, of many, تَصَارَعُوا – اِصْطَرَعُوا; of two, تَصَارَعَا – اِصْطَرَعَا.

Grapple, *n.* A seizing, ضَبَاطَة – قَبْض; A wrestling, contest, مُصَارَعَة. A hook, كُلَّاب *pl.* كَلَالِيبُ. A hooked stick, مِحْجَن – مِحْجَنَة.

Grappling-irons, *n.* عُوْدَقَة – كَلَالِيبُ.

Grasp, *v.t.* To seize and hold, أَضَبَّ عَلَى – تَشَبَّثَ بِ – أَضَبَّ عَلَى – قَبَضَ – أَمْسَكَ بِ – ضَبَطَ. To hold, أَمْسَكَ – مَسَكَ – ضَمَّ عَلَى – تَحَاوَى – اِحْتَوَى عَلَى. To snatch away, خَطِفَ – سَلَبَ. He grasped all the property, ضَمَّ عَلَى الْمَالِ.

Grasp, *n.* Gripe, ضَبْط – قَبْض – مَسْكَة – ضَبٌّ – إِضْبَاب – ضَبَاطَة. Possession, ضَبْط – تَصَرُّف – يَد – حَوْز. Embrace, inclosure, إِحَاطَة – اِحْتِوَآء. The matter has come into your —, صَارَ الشَّيْءُ فِي قَبْضَتِكَ (or فِي قَبْضَةِ يَدِكَ).

Grasping, *a.* Avaricious, طَمَّاع. One who takes everything within his grasp, ضَمْضَام.

Grass, *n.* Herbage, whether green or dry, كَلَأ – أَبٌّ *pl.* أَوُبٌّ – نَبَات. Green —, عُشْب; dry —, حَشِيش. Dog's —, نُيِّل – ثِيِّل. To send (a horse) to —, مَذَى – أَمْذَى.

Grass, *v.t.* To cover with —, لَبَّسَ- (or صَفَّحَ-) بِخَضَارِيَ – فَرَشَ-بِخُضْرَةٍ.

Grass, *v.i.* To be covered with —, كَلَأَ – مَجَلَ – أَعْشَبَ.

Grass-green, *a.* أَخْضَرُ *fem.* خَضْرَآءُ *pl.* خُضْر.

Grass-grown, *n.* مُعْشَوْشِب – عَشِب – مُعْشِب.

Grasshopper, *n.* جَرَادَة *coll.* جَرَاد.

Grassiness, *n.* خَضَار – خُضَّارَى – خَضِر – عَشَابَة.

Grass-plot, *n.* خُضْرَة *pl.* خُضَر – رَوْضَة خُضَّارَى.

Grass-widow, *n.* One whose husband is absent, مُغِيبَة – مُغِيب.

Grassy, *a.* خَضِر – مُعْشَاب – مُكْلِئٌ – مُعْشِب. A — meadow, مَرْغَة. Grassy land, أَرْضٌ مُكْلَأَةٌ.

Grate, *n.* A lattice, شَعَرِيَّة ـ شَبَابِيكُ *pl.* شُبَّاكَة ـ مُشَبَّكُ ـ. A fire —, كَانُون *pl.* كَوَانِينُ ـ مَوْقِد ـ. A good drawing —, مُخْزَم ـ مِيقَاد.

Grate, *v.t.* To rub, حَكَّ ـ قَضَّ ـ حَرَقَ. To wear away, أَغَمَّ ـ كَدَّرَ ـ سَحَقَ ـ نَهَكَ ـ أَفْرَزَ ـ نَحَتَ. To vex, حَرَقَ. To lattice, شَبَّكَ. To — the teeth, أَضْجَرَ ـ أَزْعَجَ ـ ٱلْأَسْنَانَ.

Grate, *v.i.* To make a harsh noise, اِصْطَرَّ ـ صَرَّ ـ صَرَفَ ـ صَرْصَرَ. To —, as a key in a rusty lock, صَلَّ *aor.* يَصِلُّ. To be grated by, as the teeth by gravel or any hard substance in eating, قَضَّ مِن *aor.* يَقَضُّ. To — on the ear, صَرَّ لِلْأُذُنِ.

Grateful, *a.* Thankful, شَكُور ـ مَمْنُون ـ قَنِيع ـ قَنُوع ـ. Agreeable, لَطِيف *pl.* لِطَاف ـ نَزِيه ـ حَسَن ـ مُرَاعِي ٱلْجَمِيلِ. Pleasant to the taste, لَذِيذ.

Gratefully, *ad.* Thankfully, بِشُكْرٍ ـ تَشَكُّرًا ـ بِقُنُوعٍ. Pleasantly, بِلَطَافَةٍ ـ حَسَنًا.

Gratefulness, *n.* Pleasantness, طَلَاوَة ـ لَطَافَة ـ لُطْف ـ نِعْمَة ـ حُسْن; to the taste, لَذَّة. *See also* Gratitude, *n.*

Grater, *n.* مِبْشَرَة ـ مِحَكَّة.

Gratification, *n.* The act of pleasing, إِفْرَاح ـ تَفْرِيح ـ رَوْق. That which affords pleasure, مَسَرَّة. Pleasure, satisfaction, بَهْجَة ـ أَجْر ـ خَاطِر ـ فَرْحَة ـ وُدّ ـ فَرَح ـ سُرُور. Recompense, عِوَض ـ ثَوَاب ـ مُكَافَاة ـ جَزَاء.

Gratify, *v.t.* To satisfy, أَرْضَى ـ أَقْنَعَ. To please, رَاقَ *aor.* يَرُوقُ ـ أَعْجَبَ ـ فَرَّحَ ـ أَبْهَجَ ـ سَرَّ ـ وَادَّ ـ حَلَا لِ. To recompense, جَازَى ـ عَوَّضَ عَن ـ كَافَى خَيْرًا. It gratified me, رَاقَنِي ـ حَلَا لِي ـ حَلِيَ فِي عَيْنِي (or فِي صَدْرِي). This is what gratifies, satisfies, me, هٰذَا مَا طَالَبَتْ بِهِ نَفْسِي.

Grating, *a.* Rubbing, creaking, مُصَلْصِل ـ صَرَّار ـ صَرِيف. Offensive, كَرِه. To be grating, offensive, to one, كَرِهَهُ ـ اِسْتَكْرَهَهُ.

Grating, *n.* A harsh sound of rubbing, صَلَّة ـ صَرْصَرَة ـ صَرِير. Lattice work, مُشَبَّك ـ شُبَّاكَة.

Gratingly, *ad.* With a harsh noise, بِصَرْصَرَةٍ ـ بِصَرِيرٍ. Offensively, اِسْتِكْرَاهًا ـ بِكَرَاهَةٍ.

Gratis, *ad.* تَبَرُّعًا ـ بِلَا بَدَلٍ ـ بِلَا مُكَافَاةٍ ـ بِلَا عِوَضٍ ـ مَجَّانًا *vulg.* مُتَبَرِّعًا ـ بَلَاش. To give —, what was not obligatory, أَعْطَى مَجَّانًا ـ تَبَرَّعَ بِ.

Gratitude, *n.* حَمْد ـ تَشَكُّر ـ شُكْرَان ـ شُكْر.

Gratuitous, *a.* Granted without claim, بِلَا ثَمَنٍ ـ مَجَّان. Voluntary, إِخْتِيَارِيّ. Without proof, غَيْرُ مُبَرْهَنٍ ـ بِدُونِ إِثْبَاتٍ ـ بَاطِل ـ بِلَا أَصْلٍ.

Gratuitously, *ad.* Gratis, تَبَرُّعًا ـ تَفَضُّلًا ـ مَجَّانًا. Without proof, بِغَيْرِ بُرْهَانٍ. Voluntarily, اِخْتِيَارًا ـ مِنْ تِلْقَاءِ نَفْسِهِ. He did it —, without its being incumbent on him, فَعَلَهُ مُتَبَرِّعًا.

Gratuity, *n.* A free gift, سَيْب *pl.* سُيُوب ـ إِنْعَام ـ إِحْسَان ـ عَطِيَّة. A douceur, رِفْد ـ حُلْوَان. He gave him a —, حَلَاهُ. By way of —, عَلَى سَبِيلِ ٱلْإِحْسَانِ.

Gratulate, *v.t.* *See to* Congratulate, *v.t.*

Gratulation, *n.* *See* Congratulation, *n.*

Gratulatory, *a.* *See* Congratulatory, *a.*

Gravamen, *n.* مَادَّةُ ٱلشِّكَايَةِ ـ أَصْلُ قَبَاحَةٍ. *See also* Grievance, *n.*

Grave, *n.* A pit or place for the dead, ضَرِيح *pl.* ضَرَائِحُ ـ ضَرِيحَة ـ قَبْر *pl.* قُبُور. A separate compartment in a —, لَحْد *pl.* لُحُود. A place of sepulture, مَرْقَد. *See also* Cemetery, *n.*

Grave, *a.* Heavy, ثَقِيل ـ رَزِين. Important, عَظِيم ـ مُهِمّ. Serious, solemn, of a person, رَكِين ـ رَصِين ـ رَزِين ـ سَاكِنُ ٱلطَّائِرِ ـ تَوَقُّر ـ اِتِّقَر ـ وَقُور. Implying danger, خَطِير. To be —, serious, سَمَتَ: He became —, وَقَعَ طَائِرُهُ *aor.* يَقَعُ. They have exposed themselves to — questioning, أَوْجَبُوا عَلَى أَنْفُسِهِمْ مَسْئُولِيَّةً خَطِيرَةً. Grave matters, مُهِمَّات.

Grave, *v.t.* To engrave, نَقَشَ ـ نَقَرَ. To —, or careen a ship, قَلْفَطَ *vulg.* جَلْفَطَ.

Grave-clothes, *n.* كَفَن *pl.* أَكْفَان *and* كُفُونَات. To wrap in —, كَفَّنَ.

Grave-digger, *n.* تُرَبِيّ ـ حَفَّار ـ نَبَّاش.

Gravel, *n.* Sand, sea-sand, سِهْلَة. Fine pebbles, رَضْرَاض ـ حَصًى ـ حَصْبَاء ـ قِضَّة ـ قَضَض ـ قَضّ. The disease, سِهْلَة ـ حَصَاة.

Gravel, *v.t.* To cover with —, فَرَشَ بِحَصًى ـ حَصَّبَ ـ رَمَّلَ. To puzzle, اِلْتَوَى عَلَى ـ حَيَّرَ. To be gravelled, puzzled, تَحَيَّرَ.

Gravelled, *a.* Covered with gravel, مَفْرُوش بِحَصًى ـ مُحَصَّب. Puzzled, مُتَحَيِّر.

Gravelly, *a.* Abounding in gravel, حَصِب ـ قَضِض ـ سَهِل ـ مَحْصَبَة ـ أَرْض سَهِلَة ـ حَاصِب ـ مُحَصَّب. Gravelly soil, قِضَّة ـ أَرْض حَصِبَة. A — and pebbly river-bed, نَهْر ذُو سِهْلَةٍ وَذُو رَضْرَاضٍ. To be —, قَضَّ *aor.* يَقَضُّ. The soil was —, حَصِبَتِ ٱلْأَرْضُ.

Gravely, *ad.* بِأَنَاةٍ ـ بِهَيْبَةٍ ـ بِرَزَانَةٍ ـ بِوَقَارٍ.

Graven, *a.* مَنْقُوش ـ مَنْحُوت. A — image, تِمْثَال مَنْحُوت *pl.* تَمَاثِيل.

Graveness, *n.* *See* Gravity, *n.*

Graver, *n.* An engraver, نَقَّاش ـ نَقَّار. A graving tool, مِنْقَاش. A — of ships, جِلْفَاط ـ جِلِّفَاط *vulg.* قِلْفَاط.

Grave-stone, *n.* رُجْمَة *pl.* رُجَم *and* رِجَام.

Graveyard, *n.* مَقْبَرَة ـ تُرْبَة *pl.* تُرَب ـ مَرْقَد.

Gravid, *ad.* حُبْلَى ـ حَامِلَة.

Graving, *n.* The act of engraving, نَقْش ـ نَقْر; of careening, جَلْفَطَة ـ جِلْفَاط *vulg.* قَلْفَطَة *and* قِلْفَاط. A — dock, حَوْض لِلْجَلْفَطَة (or لِلْقَلْفَطَة).

Gravitate, *v.i.* To tend towards the centre, اِنْجَذَبَ إِلَى ٱلْمَرْكَز ـ مَالَ إِلَى ٱلْمَرْكَز. To tend, as matter, towards other matter, اِنْجَذَبَ وَتَجَاذَبَ.

Gravitation, *n.* As towards the centre, اِنْجِذَاب إِلَى ٱلْمَرْكَز ـ مَيَلَان إِلَى ٱلْمَرْكَز. Tendency of matter to other matter, اِنْجِذَاب وَتَجَاذُب.

Gravity, *n.* Weight, ثَقَالَة ـ ثِقَل ـ وَزْنَة. Sedateness, سَمْت ـ أَنَاة ـ وَقَار ـ سَكِينَة ـ رَزَانَة. Importance, أَهَمِّيَّة ـ هَيْمَنَة. Greatness, جَسَامَة ـ عَظَامَة. Difficulty, شِدَّة. Danger, خَطَر ـ مُخَاطَرَة. Atrocity, قَبَاحَة ـ فُحْش. Specific —, ثِقَلَة ذَاتِيَّة. Grievousness, فَظَاعَة ـ وَبَال.

Gravy, *n.* مَرَق ـ مَرَقَة ـ وَدَك ـ دَسَم.

Gray, *a.* White with black, أَشْمَط *fem.* شَمْطَآء *pl.* شُمْطَان *and* شُمْط ـ أَشْهَب *fem.* شَهْبَآء *pl.* شُهْب. Hoary, شَائِب ـ شَيِّب ـ أَشْيَب ـ مُشَيَّب. Having — eyes, أَزْرَق *fem.* زَرْقَآء *pl.* زُرْق. A — beard, لِحْيَة شَيْبَآء ـ لِحْيَة سَلَق بِلَبَن. To grow —, hoary, شَابَ; to make —, أَشَابَ.

Gray, *n.* One that is —, of a horse, *etc.*, أَشْهَب ـ أَشْهَب ـ أَدْهَم; a — horse, حِصَان أَشْهَب *pl.* حُصُن شُهْب. A — mare, فَرَسَة شَهْبَآء ـ شَهْبَآء.

Graybeard, *n.* An old man, اِخْتِيَار ـ شَائِب ـ عَجُوز *pl.* عَجَائِز *pl.* اِخْتِيَارِيَّة. *See also under* Gray, *a.*

Grayhound, *n.* كَلْب سَلُوقِيّ ـ سَلُوقِيّ.

Grayish, *a.* Tending to grayness, يَضْرِبُ إِلَى ٱلشَّمَط; to hoariness, مَائِل إِلَى ٱلشَّيْبَة.

Grayness, *n.* Whiteness with blackness, شَهَب ـ شُهْبَة ـ شَمَط. Hoariness, مَشِيب ـ شَيْبَة ـ شَيْب. Grayness, as of the eyes, زُرْقَة.

Graze, *v.t.* To rub, or rub off, as of the skin, سَحَجَ ـ سَحَّجَ ـ قَشَرَ ـ قَشَطَ. To feed on grass, حَشَّ. To pasture, of cattle, أَرْعَى. To be grazed, abraded, اِنْسَحَجَ ـ اِنْقَشَطَ.

Graze, *v.i.* To pasture, feed on grass, رَعَى: The cattle grazed, رَعَتِ ٱلْمَاشِيَة (or تَرَعَّتْ or اِرْتَعَتْ).

Grazier, *n.* A cutter or supplier of grass, حَاشّ *pl.* حُشَّاش. A shepherd, رَاعٍ *pl.* رُعَاة.

Grazing, *a.* Feeding on grass, رَاعٍ ـ حَاشّ.

Grazing, *n.* Feeding on grass, رَعْي ـ مَرْعَى. A place of —, مَرْعًى ـ مَرْعَاة.

Grease, *n.* شَحْم ـ زَفَر ـ دُهْن ـ دَسَم ـ وَدَك ـ إِهَالَة. The — of bones, صَلِيب. An under cap to preserve the head-dress from —, عَرَقِيَّة ـ صِقَاع ـ غِفَارَة. The smell of —, عَرَن ـ غَمَر.

Grease, *v.t.* دَهَنَ ـ مَسَحَ بِشَحْم. To daub with —, زَفَّرَ ـ لَوَّثَ بِدُهْن. To —, as of a skin, *etc.*, سَلَقَ.

Greasiness, *n.* دُهْنِيَّة ـ دُهْن. Dirtiness, foulness, دَرَن. Greasiness of the head, هِبْرِيَة.

Greasy, *a.* Fatty, دُهْنِيّ ـ شَحِيم ـ دَهِن ـ زَفِر ـ زَهِم. Daubed with grease, مُلَوَّث بِٱلدُّهْن. Foul, as with grease, دَرِن. Greasy food, زَفِر. His hand is —, يَدُهُ زَهِمَة. A man having — hair, رَجُل مُدْهَان. To be —, foul, as with grease, دَرِنَ ـ أَدْرَنَ. To make —, foul, أَدْرَنَ.

Great, *a.* Large, عَظِيم ـ كَبِير ـ جَسِيم. Broad, wide, وَاسِع. Many, numerous, عَدِيد ـ كَثِيرُ ٱلْعَدَد. Mighty, powerful, عَزّ ـ قَدِير ـ قَادِر ـ كَثِيرُ ٱلْمِقْدَار ـ عَزِيز ـ ذُو عِزَّة. Long in duration or in length, طَوِيل ـ مَدِيد ـ مُمْتَدّ. Much, جَزِيل. Important, عَظِيم ـ مُهِمّ. Involving danger, خَطِير. Of high rank, جَلِيلُ ٱلشَّأْن ـ عَظِيمُ ٱلشَّأْن ـ فَخِيم ـ عَالٍ ـ سَامٍ ـ شَرِيف. Renowned, مَشْهُور ـ جَلِيل. Wonderful, عَجِيب ـ غَرِيب. Learned, حَاذِق ـ عَالِم ـ أَدِيب. Difficult, صَعْب ـ عَسِير ـ ثَقِيل. Familiar with, لَهُ عِشْرَة مَعَ ـ مُصَاحِب ـ مُقَرَّب مِن. Chief, أَعْظَم ـ أَصْلِيّ ـ أَوَّل. Pregnant, حُبْلَى ـ حَامِلَة. A — man of the age, فَائِقُ ٱلْأَقْرَان ـ وَحِيدُ ٱلْعَصْر ـ فَرِيدُ ٱلْعَصْر ـ مُمْتَازُ ٱلزَّمَان. In a — measure, بِٱلْأَكْثَر ـ كَثِيرًا. A — deal, مِقْدَار كُلِّيّ ـ كَثِير ـ جَمّ. How — he is! مَا أَجَلَّهُ. How —! مَا أَعْظَمَ. Who so — as he is? أَيّ عَظِيم مِثْلُهُ. So — as this, مِقْدَار هٰذَا. Alexander the Great, إِسْكَنْدَر ذُو ٱلْقَرْنَيْن ـ إِسْكَنْدَرُ ٱلرُّومِيّ. An affair of — moment, جَلَل *pl.* أَجْلَال ـ مُهِمَّة ـ عَظِيمَة. A — sin, كَبِيرَة *pl.* كَبَائِر. It is one of the greatest calamities, إِنَّهَا لَإِحْدَى ٱلْكُبَر. To become —, عَزَّ ـ تَعَزَّزَ ـ كَبُرَ ـ عَظُمَ. To make —, أَعَزَّ ـ عَزَّزَ ـ عَظَّمَ ـ كَبَّرَ ـ أَعْظَمَ.

To esteem or describe as —, أَكْبَرَ ـ اِسْتَعْظَمَ . To assume — airs, إِسْتَكْبَرَ ـ تَكَبَّرَ ـ تَعَزَّزَ. To be of — moment, عَظُمَ ².

Great, *n.* The mass, الكُلِّيَّة ـ الجُمْلَة. The —, people of distinction, الأَشْرَافُ ـ الأَكَابِرُ.

Greatest, *a.* الأَعْظَمُ ـ الأَكْبَرُ. This man was the — of all, كانَ هٰذا الرَّجُل أَعْظَمَ الكُلّ.

Greatly, *ad.* In a great degree, بِزِيادَةٍ ـ جَمًّا ـ كَثِيرًا ـ جِدًّا. With force, بِقُوَّةٍ ـ بِشِدَّةٍ ـ عِزَّةً. Magnanimously, بِرَحْبِ ـ بِكَرَمِ ـ الصَّدْرِ. Bravely, بِشَجاعَةٍ.

Greatness, *n.* In bulk, جَسامَة ـ كِبْر ـ عَظامَة ـ عِظَم. Width, largeness, سَعَة. Extent, مُدَّة ـ إِمْتِداد. Multitude, جَزْل ـ جَمّ ـ عُمُومَة ـ كَثْرَة ـ جِدّ ـ عِزَّة. Exaltedness, illustriousness, عَظَمَة ـ سُمُوّ ـ شَرَف ـ نَجابَة ـ نَبالَة ـ جَلالَة. Magnificence, عَظَمَة ـ بَهاء ـ جَلالَة ـ عِزّ ـ أَثُول. Importance, هَيْمَنَة ـ أَهَمِّيَّة. Strength, power, قُوَّة ـ شِدَّة ـ عِزَّة ـ عِزّ. Atrociousness, فَظاعَة ـ خَباثَة ـ شَناعَة.

Greave, *n.* Armour for the legs, ساق *pl.* سِيقان.

Greaves, *n.* The sediment of tallow, رُسُوب (*or* ثُفْل) ـ حُثالَة الدُّهْنِ.

Grebe, *n.* The bird, نَوْعٌ مِنَ الطُّيُورِ.

Greece, *n.* Ancient —, يُونانِسْتان ; modern —, بِلادُ الرُّومِ.

Grecian, *a.* and *n.* } Of the ancients, يُونانِيٌّ ; (modern), رُومِيٌّ
Greek, } *coll.* الرُّومُ *or* الأَرْوامُ. The ancient Greeks, بَنُو الأَصْفَرِ ـ الرُّومُ.

Grecism, *n.* اِصْطِلاحٌ رُومِيٌّ ـ لُغَةٌ يُونانِيَّةٌ.

Greed, *n.* *See* Greediness, *n.*

Greedily, *ad.* Ravenously, بِلَعْصٍ. Gluttonously, بِشَراهَةٍ ـ بِشَوْقٍ ـ بِرَغْبَةٍ زائِدَةٍ ـ رَغْبَةً. Eagerly, بِحِرْصٍ. Grudgingly, بِضِنِّينٍ.

Greediness, *n.* Voracity, إِلْهاف ـ شَرَه ـ قَرَم. Covetousness, طَمَع ـ حِرْص ـ طَماع ـ لَهَج ـ وُلُوع. Eagerness, شَوْق ـ رَغْبَة.

Greedy, *a.* Voracious, شَهْوانُ ـ حَرِيص ـ أَكُول ـ مِبْطان ـ شَرِهٌ ـ جارُوف. Covetous, شَهْوانِيٌّ ـ طامِع ـ حَرِيص ـ لَهِج. Greedy or eager for, حَرِيصٌ عَلَى ـ راغِبٌ بِ ـ مُولَعٌ بِ. Grudging, ضَنِين. To be —, eager for, أَلْهَفَ لِ ـ شَرِهَ عَلَى ـ حَرَصَ عَلَى. To be — of, addicted to, لَهِجَ بِ ـ قَرِمَ إِلَى.

Greedy-guts, *n.* *See* Glutton, *n.*

Greek, *n.* *See* Grecian, *a.* and *n.*

Greek-fire, *n.* نِفْط ـ ضَرْبٌ مِنَ الصَّوارِيخِ النّارِيَّةِ المائِيَّةِ.

Green, *a.* Of the colour, أَخْضَرُ *fem.* خَضْراءُ *pl.* خُضْر. Green like an emerald, زُمُرُّدِيٌّ. Deep —, أَخْضَرُ حانِئٌ. Fresh, undecayed, أَخْضَرُ ـ نَضِر ـ زاهٍ ـ غَضِير. Fresh, recent, طَرِيٌّ ـ أَخْضَرُ ـ جَدِيد. Verdant, نَضِر ـ أَخْضَرُ ـ خَضِر. Unripe, فِجٌّ ـ جاهِل ـ أَخْرَق ـ خَرِق. Inexperienced, غَيْرُ يانِع ـ غَيْرُ ناضِج ـ عَجَمِيٌّ. Green herbage, خَضار. Green land, أَرْضٌ مَخْضَرَةٌ. To become —, إِخْضَرَّ ; to make —, خَضَّرَ. The — substance which overspreads stale water, نَوْر ـ نَوْرُ المَاءِ ـ طُحْلُب ـ عَرْمَض ـ غَلْفَق.

Green, *n.* The colour, خُضْرَة. A — plant, خَضْرَة *pl.* خُضَر.

Green-eyed, *a.* Envious, حَسُود ـ حَسّاد.

Greengage, *n.* قَلْبُ الطَّيْرِ ـ إِجّاص فِرَنْجِيّ.

Greengrocer, *n.* بَقّال *pl.* بَقّالَة.

Greenhand, *n.* } أَخْرَق ـ خَرِق ـ جاهِل ـ أَبْلَهُ ـ عَجَمِيٌّ ـ
Greenhorn, } زَبُون *pl.* زَبائِن ـ غَبِيٌّ.

Greenhouse, *n.* بَيْتٌ (*or* ذَرَى) لِلنَّباتِ.

Greenish, *a.* مُخْضَرٌّ ـ مائِلٌ إِلَى الخُضْرَةِ ـ يَضْرِبُ إِلَى الخُضْرَةِ.

Greenishness, *n.* Of a colour, إِخْضِرار. Inexperience, خَرَق ـ جاهِلِيَّة ـ جَهالَة ـ جَهْل.

Greenly, *ad.* Newly, جِدَّةً ـ حَداثَةً. With simplicity, بِخُرْقٍ ـ بِجَهْلٍ ـ جَهالَةً.

Greenness, *n.* Viridity, خُضْرَة. Immaturity, فَجاجَة ـ عَدَمُ يَنْع. Vigour, زَهْوٌ ـ صِحَّة ـ نَجادَة. Newness, حَداثَة ـ جِدَّة.

Green-room, *n.* Of a theatre, خَلْوَةٌ لِأَهْلِ الدُّنْيا تَرَوْ.

Greens, *n.* Vegetables, خُضَر ـ خَضار ـ بُقُول ـ قُطْنِيَّة ـ قَطانِي.

Green-sickness, *n.* داءُ الرُّماعِ.

Greensward, *n.* خَضِر ـ يَخْضُور ـ مَخْضَرَة ـ مَرْج.

Greenweed, *n.* صَفْراءُ.

Greet, *v.t.* To salute, حَيَّا ـ سَلَّمَ عَلَى. To congratulate, هَنَّأَ ـ بارَكَ. To address, خاطَبَ ـ حادَثَ ـ سامَرَ. To welcome, رَحَّبَ بِهِ ـ أَقْبَلَ عَلَى ـ بَشْبَشَ بِ. To — with..., تَلَقَّى بِ. They send greeting, يُهْدُونَ سَلامًا.

Greeting, *n.* A salutation, تَحِيَّة ـ سَلام ـ تَسْلِيم. A welcome, تَرْحِيب ـ إِقْبال. I met him with the — of welcome, لَقِيتُهُ بِالتَّرْحِيبِ.

Gregarian, *a.* Belonging to the herd, مُتَعَلِّقٌ بِالقَطِيعِ.

Gregarious, *a.* عايِشُونَ أَقْطاعًا ـ مُتَكائِنُونَ وَعايِشُونَ سِرْبًا سِرْبًا.

Gregariously, *ad.* أَقْطاعًا ـ سِرْبًا سِرْبًا ـ كَأْكَأَةً ـ تَكَأْكُؤًا.

Gregariousness, *n.* المَعِيشَةُ أَسْرابًا ـ تَكَأْكُؤ ـ كَأْكَأَة.

Gregorian, *a.* مُتَعَلِّقٌ بِغْرِيغُور. The — year, عِدَّةُ أَيّامِ السَّنَةِ

عَلَى حِسَابِ ٱلْأَفْرَنْجِ. Gregorian chaunt, ضَرْبٌ مِنَ ٱلتَّرْتِيلِ مَنْسُوبٌ إِلَى ٱلْبَابَا غَرِيغُورَ ٱلْأَوَّلِ.

Grenade, n. قُنْبُرَة pl. قَنَابِرُ — كُلَّةٌ مِثْلَ ٱلرُّمَّانَةِ.

Grenadier, n. One who throws grenades, ضَرَّابُ قَنَابِرَ. A picked soldier, شُرْطِيٌّ pl. شُرْطَةٌ — عَسْكَرِيٌّ مُنْتَخَبٌ.

Grey, Greyness, etc. See Gray, Grayness.

Greyhound, n. See Grayhound, n.

Griddle, n. ماجور pl. مَوَاجِيرُ.

Gridiron, n. مُصَبَّع — مِشْوًى.

Grief, n. غَمٌّ pl. غُمُوم — حُزْن — حَسْرَة — تَلَهُّف — شَجَب — تَأَسُّف — مَشَقَّة — أَلَم — هَمٌّ — كَرْب — كَدَر — كَآبَة — مَلَال. There is no joy that is not followed by a —, مَا مِنْ فَرْحَةٍ إِلَّا بَعْدَهَا تَرْحَةٌ. To come to —, to be ruined, تَلِفَ — هَلَكَ. To cause —; see to Grieve, v.t.

Grievance, n. A cause of grief, ضَيْم pl. ضُيُوم — مَشَقَّة. A misfortune, آفَة pl. آفَات — مُصِيبَة pl. مَصَائِبُ. A complaint, شَكْوَى — شَكِيَّة pl. شَكَايَا. The setting forth of grievances, as in a petition, اِقْتِرَاح pl. اِقْتِرَاحَات. To set forth one's grievances to, اِشْتَكَى إِلَى — تَشَكَّى إِلَى. To present a petition of grievances to..., قَدَّمَ ٱلْاِقْتِرَاحَاتِ إِلَى.

Grieve, v.t. أَكَابَ — آسَفَ — فَجَعَ — أَشْجَرَ — شَجَبَ — أَهَمَّ — غَمَّ — أَغَمَّ — أَحْزَنَ — كَدَّرَ. To make to weep, أَبْكَى.

Grieve, v.i. كَئِبَ — اِنْغَمَّ — تَأَسَّفَ — اِكْتَرَبَ — حَزِنَ. To lament, شَجِنَ — بَكَى — تَرِحَ — تَلَهَّفَ عَلَى. To — for, حَسِرَ عَلَى. To affect to —, تَغَامَّ. We are grieved to learn that..., يَهُمُّنَا أَنْ نَعْلَمَ.

Grieving, part. كَئِيب — حَزِين — أَسِيف. Weeping, بَاكٍ.

Grievingly, ad. In a manner causing grief, حُزْنًا — تَكْدِيرًا — إِيسَافًا — بِشَجَبٍ.

Grievous, a. Afflictive, فَاجِع — كَرِيب — شَاقّ — مُؤْلِم — مُحْزِن — بَائِس. Oppressive, جَائِر — قَاهِر — ظَالِم. Atrocious, فَاحِش — شَنِيع — فَظِيع — عَظِيم. More —, afflictive, أَدْهَى. To be —, afflictive, بَئِسَ.

Grievously, ad. Painfully, بِوَجَعٍ — بِحُزْنٍ — تَأَسُّفًا — بِتَلَهُّفٍ. Atrociously, بِفَحَاشَةٍ — بِنَوْعٍ شَنِيعٍ — فَظَاعَةً.

Grievousness, n. Gravity, heinousness, وَبَال — فَظَاعَة.

Griffin, n. A fabulous animal, عَنْقَاءُ. See also Greenhorn, n.

Grig, n. A small eel, أَنْقَلِيس صَغِير. A merry creature, بَطِر.

Grill, v.t. To broil, شَوَى — شَوَّى. To vex, أَزْعَجَ — أَضْجَرَ. To scorch (of the sun), صَقَرَ. Grilled meat, شِوَاء — شَوِيّ.

Grilling, a. Vehemently hot, مُسْمَقِرّ — حَارٌّ لِلْغَايَةِ. The — heat of the sun, صَقَرَات.

Grim, a. مَهُول — كَالِح — مُكْلَح — شَتِيم — مُقَطِّب — بَشِع — بَشِيع.

Grimace, n. لَهَع — كَشْر — كِشْرَة. To make grimaces, اِخْتَلَجَ بِوَجْهِهِ. To make grimaces at, كَاشَرَ — تَلَايَقَ فِي — تَلَوْلَقَ فِي.

Grime, n. دَرَن — وَسَخ — دَنَس — دَنَاسَة.

Grime, v.t. See to Begrime, v.t.

Grimly, ad. تَبَشُّعًا — بِبَشَاعَةٍ.

Grimness, n. كُلُوح — كُمُوس — قَبَاحَة — عُبُوسَة — بَشَاعَة.

Grimy, a. دَرِن — أَدْرَن — وَسِخ — دَنِس.

Grin, v.i. كَلَحَ — كَشَرَ. To — at, كَاشَرَ — كَالَحَ. To —, in laughing, so as to show the teeth, اِزْمَهَرَّ — كَشَرَ عَنْ أَسْنَانِهِ.

Grin, n. كُلَاح — كُلُوح — كِشْرَة — كَلْحَة. What an ugly — he has! مَا أَقْبَحَ كَلْحَتَهُ.

Grind, v.t. To — to powder, طَحَنَ — طَحَّنَ — سَحَقَ. To — coarsely, جَشَّ — أَجَشَّ — جَرَشَ — حَدَّدَ — أَحَدَّ. To sharpen, دَرَّبَ — سَنَّ. To — on a stone, شَرْشَرَ. To — to a point, سَنَّ. To —, as with the teeth, خَرَقَ بِٱلْأَسْنَانِ — صَلْقَمَ. To oppress, تَعَدَّى عَلَى — ظَلَمَ — بَغَى عَلَى — قَاهَرَ.

Grind, v.i. To perform the act of grinding, طَحَنَ. To be rubbed together, ground, تَطَحَّنَ; as on a stone, تَشَرْشَرَ. To be sharpened, سُنَّ — سُنِّنَ — اِنْحَدَّ.

Grinder, n. One who grinds or sharpens, سَنَّان. One who polishes, صَقَّال. An instrument for polishing, مِصْقَلَة. A whetstone, صُلَّبِيَّة — صُلَّبِيّ — مِسَنّ. A molar tooth, ضِرْس pl. أَضْرَاس — طَاحِنَة pl. طَوَاحِنُ: the grinders, the molar teeth, ٱلْعَوَارِقُ.

Grinding, n. A — noise, صُرُوف — صَرِير.

Grindstone, n. مِسَنّ — حَجَرُ مِسَنٍّ.

Grinning, part. Showing the teeth in laughing, مُزْمَهِرّ.

Gripe, v.t. To seize, hold fast, تَشَبَّثَ بِ — قَبَضَ — ضَبَطَ. To squeeze, حَزَقَ — عَصَرَ — قَرَصَ. To give pain to the bowels, أَمْغَصَ. See also to Grasp, v.t.

Gripe, v.i. To feel the colic, مُغِصَ — أَصَابَهُ ٱلْمَغَصُ. To be overreaching, طَمَعَ — قَسَّ.

Gripe, n. A grasp, تَشَبُّث — يَدٌ — ضَبْط — ضَبَاطَة — مَسْكَة. A squeeze, عَصْرَة — قَرْصَة. Tenaciousness, avarice, حَزَق — طَمَاعَة — ضِنَّة.

Gripes, n. Of the bowels, مَغْص — مَغَص — قُولَنْج. Having —, مَمْغُوص.

Griping, *a.* Overreaching, طَمَّاع ـ حُزُقّ ـ ضَنِين. Like colic, قُولَنْجِ ـ مَغْصِيّ.

Griping, *n.* *See* Gripe, Gripes, *n.*

Grippe, *n.* *See* Catarrh, *n.*

Grisette, *n.* صَبِيَّة *pl.* صَبَايَا.

Grisly, *a.* *See* Grim, *a.*

Grist, *n.* Corn for grinding, حِنْطَةٌ لِلطَّحْن. A supply, ذَخِيرَة. Gain, profit, مَنْفَعَة ـ رِبْح. To bring — to the mill, to make gain, إِسْتَشَفَّ ـ رَبِحَ. To bring — to another's mill, to make him to profit, أَرْبَحَ.

Gristle, *n.* غُرْضُوف ـ غُضْرُوف.

Gristly, *a.* غُضْرُوفِيّ.

Grist-mill, *n.* طَاحُون *pl.* طَوَاحِين ـ جارُوشَة.

Grit, *n.* Any sharp minute substance, gravel, sand, حَصَب ـ حَصْبَة ـ حَصًى ـ رَمْل; a single atom of —, حَصَبَة. The coarse part of meal, جَرِيش; grit, of wheat, cleaned and pounded, بُرْغُل. Firmness, صَلَابَة.

Grittiness, *n.* رَمْلِيَّة ـ كُوفَة ـ مَحْصَبَة.

Gritty, *a.* مُرَمَّل ـ حَصِب. Gritty food or wheat, طَعَامٌ مُرَمَّل.

Grizzle, *n.* *See* Gray, *n.*

Grizzled, *a.* *See* Gray, *a.*

Grizzly, *a.* *See* Grayish, *a.*

Groan, *n.* Groaning, } حَنّ ـ نَحِيط ـ أَنَانَة ـ أَنِين ـ أَنَّة ـ نَئِيط ـ أُنَان ـ نِيَاحَة ـ نَوْح.

Groan, *v.i.* To moan, نَأَطَ ـ نَحَطَ ـ نَاحَ ـ حَنَّ ـ أَنَّ *aor.* يَئِنّ ـ تَأَوَّهَ ـ أَنَحَ. To — or creak, as of a tree, *etc.*, حَنَّ.

Groaning, *a.* نَائِح ـ أَنَّان ـ آنّ ـ حَنَّان. Of a tree, حَنَّان.

Groat, *n.* Four pence, عِبَارَةٌ عَنْ ثَمَانِيَنَ فِضَّة. Proverbially, a small sum, فَلْس.

Groats, *n.* سَوِيق ـ شَعِيرٌ مَجْرُوش ـ طَحِينُ شَعِير.

Grocer, *n.* بَقَّالَة وَعَطَّارَة *pl.* بَقَّالٌ وَعَطَّار.

Grocery, *n.* Groceries, عَطَّارَة. The — business, عِطَارَة.

Grog, *n.* (صَرْف or) عَرَقٌ مَمْزُوجٌ بِمَاءٍ بِلَا سُكَّر.

Groggery, *n.* خَمَّارَة.

Groggy, *a.* Tipsy, سَكْرَان ـ سَكْرَانُ مُلَكَّك. Hobbling, أَقْزَل. He was —, tipsy, مَسَّهُ سُكْر.

Grogram, *n.* سُنْدُس.

Groin, *n.* The — of the body, رُفْغ *pl.* أَرْفَاغ ـ حِنُّ الْوَرِك. The —, as of an arch, حَالِب *pl.* حَوَالِب ـ أَرْنَبَة ـ أَرْنَمَة ـ سِلِسْلَة.

Groined, *a.* Of a building, مُسَلْسَل.

Groom, *n.* One who tends horses, سَائِس *pl.* سَاسَة *and* سُيَّاس. A servant, خَادِم *pl.* خُدَّام ـ غُلَام. A — of the Bedchamber, حَاجِب *pl.* حُجَّاب ـ آغَا *pl.* أَغَوَات. A bridegroom, عَرِيس *pl.* عَرَائِس.

Groom, *v.t.* سَاسَ الدَّوَابَّ *aor.* يَسُوسُ ـ حَسَّ.

Groomwell, *n.* The plant, نَكْش.

Grooming, *n.* حَسّ ـ سِيَاسَةُ الدَّوَابّ.

Groove, *n.* مَحَزّ ـ قَوْب ـ تَقْوِيب ـ تَجْوِيف ـ نَقْر ـ تَخْطِيط ـ زِيق. To go on in the same —, إِسْتَمَرَّ عَلَى.

Groove, *v.t.* حَزَّ ـ قَوَّبَ ـ جَوَّفَ ـ نَقَرَ ـ خَطَّطَ. Grooved or ridged, مُشَطَّب.

Grope, *v.i.* To feel along, as in the dark, تَلَمَّسَ ـ عَيَّثَ ـ تَعَسْعَسَ. He groped for the wall, or along the wall, تَلَمَّسَ الْحَائِطَ.

Groping, *n.* تَلَمُّس ـ تَعَسْعُس.

Gropingly, *ad.* تَلَمُّسًا ـ بِتَعَسْعُسٍ ـ تَعْيِيثًا.

Gros-de-Naples, إِسْتَبْرَق.

Gross, *a.* Bulky, ضَخْم *pl.* ضِخَام ـ ضُخَام ـ جَسِيم ـ أَضْخَم. Thick, coarse, ثَخِين ـ غَلِيظ ـ خَشِن ـ سَمِج. Rude, فَظّ ـ غَلِيظ ـ خَشِن ـ سَمِج. Obscene, حَنِي ـ بَذِيّ ـ رَفَث ـ فَاحِش ـ قَبِيح. Stupid, بَلِيد ـ أَخْرَق ـ أَحْمَق ـ غَلِيظ ـ هِلْبَاجَة. Entire, مَجْمُوع ـ غَيْرُ مُنْقَسِم. To be —, foul, obscene, سَمُجَ. How — of him! مَا أَسْمَجَ فِعْلَهُ.

Gross, *n.* The whole bulk, جُلّ ـ جُمْهُور ـ مَجْمُوع. Twelve dozen, إِثْنَتَا عَشْرَةَ دَسْتَةً فِرَنْجِيَّةً عِبَارَةٌ عَنْ مِئَةٍ وَأَرْبَعَةٍ وَأَرْبَعِينَ. The — part, أَكْثَر ـ أَشَدّ ـ أَغْلَب. In the —, رُزْمَةٍ فِي الْجُمْلَةِ. By the —, بِالرُّزْمَةِ.

Grossly, *ad.* Coarsely, بِغِلَاظَةٍ ـ بِفَظَاظَةٍ ـ بِسَمَاجَةٍ. Palpably, إِيضَاحًا ـ ظَاهِرًا. Greatly, كَثِيرًا ـ بِإِفْرَاطٍ.

Grossness, *n.* Bulkiness, جَسَامَة ـ ضَخَامَة. Thickness, coarseness, ثُخْن ـ غِلَاظَة ـ غِلَاظَة ـ سَمَاجَة. Rudeness, فَظَاظَة. Obscenity, قَذَع ـ رَفَث ـ خَنَايَة ـ فَحَاشَة ـ شَنَاعَة ـ خَشَانَة. Stupidity, خُرْق ـ بَلَادَة ـ حَمَاقَة.

Gross-weight, *n.* وَزْنٌ مُجْمَل.

Grot, *n.* Grotto, } مَغَارَة *pl.* مَغَارَات ـ كَهْف *pl.* كُهُوف. *See also* Cave, *n.*

Grotesque, *a.* عَجِيبٌ غَرِيبٌ ـ خَيَالِيّ. Grotesque things, عَجَائِب ـ تَعَاجِيب.

Grotesquely, *ad.* أُعْجُوبَةً ـ بِنَوْعٍ غَرِيبٍ.

Grotesqueness, *n.* غَرَابَة ـ أُعْجُوبَة. *See also* Strangeness, *n.*

Ground, *n.* Soil, land, حَضِيض ـ بَرّ ـ أَرْض *pl.* أَرَاضِي. Country, بَلَد *pl.* بُلْدَان ـ نَاحِيَة *pl.* نَوَاحِي. An estate, عِقَار ـ أَرْض *pl.* أَرَاضِي. The — of a painting, أَرْضِيَّة. A first principle, مَبْدَأ *pl.* مَبَادِئ ـ أَصْل *pl.* أُصُول ـ قَاعِدَة *pl.* قَوَاعِد. A foundation, أَسَاس. A proof, بُرْهَان ـ إِثْبَات ـ أَصْل. A place of action, مَوْقِع ـ مَيْدَان *pl.* مَيَادِين. A cause, plea, عِلَّة ـ سَبَب *pl.* أَسْبَاب ـ مُوجِب ـ بَاعِث ـ دَعْوَى. A source, مَنْشَأ ـ مَخْرَج ـ مَنْبَع. The bottom, قَعْر. Distance, بُعْد ـ مَسَافَة.

He has no — or pretension, لا أَصْلَ لَهُ وَلا فَصْلَ. Pretension, claim, دَعْوَى.

Above ground, عَلَى وَجْهِ ٱلْأَرْضِ ـ عَلَى ٱلْأَرْضِ. Plainly, *ad.* عِيَانًا ـ عَلَانِيَة.

A piece of ground, حَقْل *pl.* حُقُول ـ عَرْصَة *pl.* عِرَاص and عَرَصَات.

Consecrated ground, أَرْض مُكَرَّسَة.

Even with the ground, فِي مُسَاوَاةِ ٱلْأَرْضِ ـ مُسْتَوٍ مَعَ ٱلْأَرْضِ.

Fishing ground, مَأْخَذُ ٱلسَّمَكِ ـ مُصْطَادُ (or مَصَادُ) ٱلسَّمَكِ ـ مُتَصَيَّدُ ٱلسَّمَكِ.

Low ground, صَاعَة ـ صَاع ـ حَضِيض ـ سَافِل ـ سَفْح. Low and level ground, غَوْر.

Not without grounds, بِحَقّ ـ لَيْسَ بِلا سَبَب.

On very good grounds, إِسْتِنَادًا إِلَى دَلَائِل قَوِيَّة.

Rising ground, رَبَاء ـ رَبْو ـ رَبِيئَة.

Under ground, تَحْتَ ٱلْأَرْضِ. A room under ground, سِرْدَاب *pl.* سَرَادِيب.

To bite the ground, إِنْغَلَبَ ـ لَحَسَ ٱلتُّرَاب.

To break the ground, to begin, إِسْتَفْتَحَ ـ إِفْتَتَحَ ـ شَرَعَ فِي.

To burn to the ground, أَحْرَقَ بَتَّة.

To dispute the ground, to contend against, نَازَعَهُ ـ عَارَضَهُ وَقَاوَمَهُ.

To fall to the ground, or earth, سَقَطَ عَلَى ٱلْأَرْضِ. To fail, خَابَ ـ سَقَطَ.

To gain ground, to advance, تَرَقَّى ـ أَنْمَى ـ نَمَى ـ تَقَدَّمَ. To overcome, غَلَبَ.

To give ground, to surrender, retire, أَدْبَرَ ـ إِنْقَهَرَ ـ إِرْتَجَّ ـ إِنْكَسَرَ ـ تَقَهْقَرَ ـ سَلَّمَ.

To go upon sure ground, بَنَى عَلَى ٱلْيَقِين.

To keep, or maintain, one's ground, تَثَبَّتَ ـ ثَبَتَ ـ رَسَخَ ـ تَأَرَّضَ. He still maintains the same ground, لَمْ يَزَلْ مُصِرًّا عَلَى رَأْيِهِ ٱلسَّابِق.

To keep one's self in the background, تَجَنَّبَ ـ أَضْرَبَ عَنْ ـ دَفَنَ نَفْسَهُ ـ تَسَتَّرَ ـ إِجْتَنَبَ.

To keep another in the back ground, جَانَبَ ـ جَنَّبَ.

To lose ground, to go back, أَدْبَرَ ـ تَأَخَّرَ. To lose, خَسَرَ. To be defeated, كَانَتِ ٱلدَّائِرَةُ عَلَيْهِ ـ إِنْكَسَرَ.

To put under ground, to bury, دَفَنَ. To hide, as in the ground, دَسَّ.

To stand one's ground; *see above,* To keep one's ground.

To take up one's ground, to hold, إِتَّخَذَ بِ ـ تَمَسَّكَ بِ; as of troops, تَصَافُّوا ـ تَحَصَّرُوا.

To throw into the back ground, not to take notice of, تَغَمَّدَ ـ غَمَّدَ.

To throw one's self on the ground, إِنْبَطَحَ ـ تَلَبَّطَ.

Ground, *v.t.* To lay on the —, بَطَحَ. To found, كَرَّسَ ـ أَسَّسَ. To originate, أَبْدَعَ ـ أَبْدَأَ ـ أَجَدَّ. To fix firmly, أَرْصَنَ ـ قَرَّرَ ـ أَرْسَخَ. To teach, عَلَّمَ ـ مَرَّنَ. To —, as of a ship, بَلَّطَ: He grounded the ship, بَلَّطَ (or شَطَّطَ) ٱلسَّفِينَة.

Ground, *v.i.* To run aground, of a ship, جَنَحَ: The ship grounded, جَنَحَتِ ٱلسَّفِينَة. *See also under to* Root, *v.i.*

Groundage, *n.* حَقُّ ٱلْمَرْسَى ـ حَقُّ ٱلْمَرْسَى.

Grounded, *a.* Founded, built, مَبْنِيّ ـ مُتَأَسِّس ـ مُؤَسَّس. Taught, مُتَعَلِّم ـ مُدَرَّس ـ مُمَرَّن. Aground, مَجْنُوح ـ مُبَلَّط. Grounded in science, رَاسِخٌ فِي ٱلْعِلْمِ. *See also* Rooted, *a.*, and *to* Root, *v.i.*

Ground-floor, *n.* أَرْض ـ أَسْفَلُ ٱلْبَيْتِ. A room on the —, مَنْدَرَة.

Ground-ivy, *n.* خَمَاقِسُوس ـ قِسُوس ـ حَبَلُ ٱلْمَسَاكِين.

Groundless, *a.* بَاطِل ـ بِدُونِ أَسَاس ـ لا أَصْلَ لَهُ وَلا فَصْلَ.

Groundlessly, *ad.* بِلا سَبَب ـ بَاطِلًا.

Groundlessness, *n.* بُطْلان ـ بُطُول ـ عَدَمُ ٱلْأَصْلِ ـ عَدَمُ إِثْبَات.

Groundling, *n.* One of the vulgar, سُفْلانِيّ ـ سُوقِيّ.

Ground-nut, *n.* عَبْدُ ٱللَّذِيذ ـ حَبُّ ٱللَّذِيذ.

Ground-plan, *n.* رَسْمُ ٱلْأَرْضِيَّة ـ صُورَةُ ٱلْأَرْضِ.

Ground-plot, *n.* مَقَامُ ٱلْبِنَايَة ـ عَرْصَةُ ٱلْبِنَايَة.

Ground-rent, *n.* كِرَاءُ ٱلْعَرْصَة ـ كِرَاءُ ٱلْأَرْضِ.

Grounds, *n.* Dregs, رُسُوب ـ عَكَر ـ ثُفْل ـ تَجْبِير.

Groundsel, *n.*, **Groundsill,** } The plant, بَابُونَجُ ٱلطُّيُور. The sill of a door, عَتَبَة *pl.* عَتَبَات.

Ground-swell, *n.* طَيَّارَة.

Ground-work, *n.* مَبْدَأ ـ مَصْدَر ـ أَصْل ـ قَاعِدَة ـ أَسَاس.

Group, *n.* A cluster, جَمَاعَة ـ جَمْع ـ إِضْمَامَة ـ حُزْمَة ـ جُمْلَة ـ كُوم *pl.* أَكْوَام. A package of money, أَمَانَة *pl.* أَمَانَات ـ صُرَّةُ أَمَانَة.

Group, *v.t.* ضَمَّ ـ كَوَّمَ ـ لَمَّ ـ جَمَّعَ.

Group, *v.i.* إِنْضَمَّ ـ تَكَوَّمَ ـ إِجْتَمَعَ ـ تَجَمَّعَ.

Grouse, *n.* The bird, قَطَاةٌ *coll.* قَطًا *pl.* قَطَوَات ـ كُدْرِيٌّ *coll.* كُدْرِيَّةٌ. A long-tailed —, جُونِيٌّ *pl.* جُونِيَّةٌ.

Grout, *n.* Coarse ground meal, جَرِيش. Plaster, سَارُوج ـ شَارُوق.

Grove, *n.* حِرْش ـ غَابَة ـ مُشْجِر ـ غَيْضَة.

Grovel, *v.i.* To creep on the earth, دَبَّ ـ حَبَا *aor.* يَحْبُو. To be mean, ذَلَّ *aor.* يَذِلُّ ـ تَذَلَّى ـ تَحَاقَرَ ـ إِحْتَقَرَ.

Groveller, *n.* } دَنِيٌّ ـ حَقِير ـ ذَلِيل.
Grovelling, *a.* }

Grow, *v.i.* To vegetate, نَمَى ـ أَنْمَى ـ نَبَتَ ـ أَنْبَتَ. To — up or advance, نَشَأَ. To make progress, تَقَدَّمَ ـ تَرَقَّى. To multiply, زَادَ ـ إِزْدَادَ ـ كَثُرَ ـ تَكَثَّرَ. To — in stature, طَالَ ـ إِسْتَطَالَ. To — up into a youth, شَبَّ. To become greater, larger, كَبُرَ ـ عَظُمَ. To — in years, كَبِرَ ـ إِسْتَسَنَّ. To —, to appear, as of the teeth, *etc.*, طَلَعَ. To — up, to be brought up, amongst, نَشَأَ فِي. To — or arise out of a thing, صَدَرَ عَن ـ نَشَأَ مِن ـ نَتَجَ ـ أَنْبَعَ ـ إِسْتَنْبَتَ. To begin to —, أَخَذَ فِي ٱلنُّمُوِّ ـ إِبْتَدَأَ يَنْمُو. To become, to — into, صَارَ. To — into a habit of, تَطَبَّعَ بِطَبْعِ كَذَا ـ تَطَبَّعَ عَلَى. To — out of the habit of, تَرَكَ ٱلْعَادَةَ ـ خَرَقَ ٱلْعَادَةَ. To — towards, to become near, دَنَا مِن ـ تَقَارَبَ. To — upon one, to become more given to, رَسَخَ فِي ـ تَطَبَّعَ فِي ـ إِنْطَبَعَ عَلَى. To — red, إِحْمَرَّ; white, إِبْيَضَّ; green, إِخْضَرَّ; yellow, إِصْفَرَّ; black, إِسْوَدَّ. Whereunto will this grow? مَا عَسَى أَنْ يَصِيرَ هٰذَا. Joseph has grown since I last saw him, شَبَّ يُوسُفُ مُذْ رَأَيْتُهُ آخِرَ مَرَّةٍ. The place was all grown over with thorns, غَطَّى ٱلْعَوْسَجُ وَجْهَ ٱلْمَكَانِ. What grows of itself, of produce, زَرِيع.

Grow, *v.t.* To cause to —, نَبَّتَ ـ نَمَّى ـ أَنْبَتَ. To raise, to cultivate, رَبَّى ـ خَدَمَ: He grows quinces, هُوَ يُرَبِّي ٱلسَّفَارِجَ.

Grower, *n.* A cultivator, مُرَبٍّ ـ زَرَّاع.

Growing, *a.* Vegetating, increasing, نَامٍ ـ نَاشِئٌ. A — lad, نَاشِئٌ *pl.* نَشَأٌ ـ نَوَاشِئُ; a — girl, نَاشِئَةٌ *pl.* نَوَاشِئُ.

Growl, *n.* As of a dog, *etc.*, هَدِير ـ هَدِير ـ هَمْهَمَة ـ هَبْهَبَة. The — of a camel when being laden, رُغَاءٌ; a camel so growling, رَاغٍ.

Growl, *v.i.* As a dog, *etc.*, هَدَرَ ـ هَدَّرَ ـ هَمْهَمَ ـ هَبْهَبَ. To — as a camel when being laden, رَغَا *aor.* يَرْغُو. To — at, هَرَّ إِلَى. *See also to* Grumble, *to* Roar, *v.i.*

Growl, *v.a.* To express by growling, مَغْمَغَ.

Growler, *n.* } Of a beast, هَادِر ـ هَدَّار ـ هِمْهِيم ـ هَبْهَاب.
Growling, *a.* } *See also* Grumbler, *n.*

Growth, *n.* Increase, نَشْأَةٌ ـ نَمَاءٌ ـ نَمِيَّة ـ نَبْتَة. Consequence, result, حَاصِل ـ مَحْصُول ـ نَتِيجَة. Origin, مَصْدَر ـ مُنْتَسَب ـ مَبْدَأ ـ أَصْل. Of home —, بَلَدِيٌّ ـ وَطَنِيٌّ; of foreign —, خَارِجِيٌّ ـ أَجْنَبِيٌّ. The — of trade, (تَرْوِيج or) إِتِّسَاعُ ٱلتِّجَارَةِ. The — of a disease, زِيَادَةُ ٱلْمَرَضِ.

Grub, *n.* A worm, دُودَةٌ ـ شَحْمَةُ ٱلْأَرْضِ *coll.* دُود *pl.* دِيدَان. A dwarf, هَبَنْقَ ـ نُغَاش ـ عَشِيب. A student, مُدَرِّس. Food, طَعَام ـ أَكْل.

Grub, *v.t.* To — the ground, (نَكَشَ or نَبَشَ or) قَلَعَ ٱلْأَرْضَ.

Grub, *v.i.* To dig, عَزَقَ ـ حَفَرَ. To — up, to eradicate, إِسْتَأْصَلَ ـ جَثَّ ـ قَلَعَ. To — up, as out of the ground, نَبَشَ عَن ـ نَبَّشَ عَن. To — up, to discover, كَشَفَ عَن ـ إِطَّلَعَ عَلَى.

Grubber, *n.* نَبَّاش.

Grub-street, *a.* Poor, mean, حَقِير ـ دَنِيٌّ ـ سُفْلِيٌّ.

Grudge, *v.i.* To repine, مَرْمَرَ ـ تَمَرْمَرَ ـ تَذَمَّرَ ـ تَقَمْقَمَ. To be reluctant, تَمَنَّعَ ـ إِشْمَأَزَّ ـ شَنَأَ. To be envious, ضَغِنَ ـ غَلَّ صَدْرُهُ.

Grudge, *v.t.* To envy the enjoyment of something by another, نَفِسَ عَلَى ـ حَسَدَ ـ حَسَدَ عَلَى. To do reluctantly, تَجَبَّرَ بِ ـ تَرَدَّدَ فِي. To be niggardly of a thing to, ضَنَّ عَلَى بِ ـ نَفِسَ عَلَى بِ.

Grudge, *n.* Enmity, حِقْد ـ ضِغْن ـ غِلٌّ ـ بُغْض ـ كَيْد. Reluctance, مُكَاشَحَة ـ حَرَق ـ تَأَخُّر ـ تَرَدُّد ـ إِمْتِنَاع. To bear a — against, حَقَدَ عَلَى. They entertained mutual grudges, of many, تَحَاقَدُوا.

Grudgingly, *ad.* عَنْ ضَغِينَةٍ ـ عَنْ حَرَقٍ ـ بِدَمْدَمَةٍ ـ بِغِصَّةٍ ـ بِتَرَدُّدٍ ـ بِٱمْتِنَاعٍ ـ بِكَرَاهِيَةِ خَاطِرٍ.

Gruel, *n.* Of flour, (سَمِيذ or) طَعَامٌ مِنْ سَمِيذٍ. Spoon-diet, سِكْبَاج ـ أَمْوِيَة.

Gruff, *a.* عَبُوس ـ شَرِيس ـ شَكِس; of the voice, أَبَحّ ـ مُخِين.

Gruffly, *ad.* بِعُبُوسٍ ـ بِشَرَاسَةٍ; with a gruff voice, بِبُحَّةٍ ـ بِصَوْتٍ مُخِينٍ.

Gruffness, *n.* Surliness, سَخْط ـ عُبُوس ـ شَرَاسَة ـ شَكَاسَة; of voice, بُحَّة. There is — in his voice, فِي صَوْتِهِ بُحَّةٌ.

Grum, *a.* Morose, وَعِق ـ مُحْكَان ـ عَنِيف; of countenance, شَتِيم.

Grumble, *v.i.* To mutter, murmur, مَرْمَرَ ـ بَرْبَرَ ـ دَمْدَمَ ـ هَدَرَ.

To —, as of a camel, ضَجَّ ـ ﺭ. To rumble, قَرْقَرَ. To — at, complain of, إِشْتَكَى ب ـ تَشَكَّى ب.

Grumbler, *n.* }
Grumbling, *a.* } شَكِس ـ مُتَشَكٍّ ـ مُدَمْدِم.

Grumbling, *n.* دَمْدَمَة ـ بَرْبَرَة ـ تَذَمُّر ـ هَدِير. A rumbling, قَرْقَرَة.

Grume, *n.* Clotted blood, دَمٌ جَامِدٌ. Matter, pus, عَثِيثَة ـ مِدَّة. *See also under* Clot, *n.*

Grumly, *ad.* Morosely, بِعُنْف ـ بِوَعْثَة.

Grumous, *a.* Clotted, مُجَمَّد ـ جَامِد. Mattery, عَثِيث ـ قَيِّحِيّ.

Grunt, *v.i.* To —, like a pig, قَاعَ ـ قَبَعَ ـ ﺭ نَخَرَ ـ ﺭ.

Grunt, *n.* قَبْع ـ قِبَاع ـ نَخْر ـ نَخِير.

Grunting, *a.* نَخَّار.

Guiacum, *n.* The gum, صَمْغُ خَشَبِ ٱلْأَنْبِيَاءِ ـ بَلَسَان.

Guano, *n.* ذَرْق ـ شَخْط.

Guarantee, *n.* Security for performance, ضَمَان ـ كَفَالَة ـ قَبَالَة. One who guarantees, زَعِيم *pl.* زُعَمَاءُ ـ كَفِيل *pl.* كُفَلَاءُ ـ ضَامِن *pl.* ضُمَّان. A reciprocal —, كَفَالَةٌ مُتَقَابِلَةٌ. A party —, كَفَالَةٌ مُشْتَرِكَةٌ. A stipulated —, كَفَالَةٌ مَشْرُوطَةٌ. Constitutional guarantees, نِظَامَاتٌ مُؤَسَّسَةٌ ـ تَأْمِينَاتٌ مَشْرُوطَةٌ. Security, أَمَان ـ أَمَانَة. He took from them the necessary —, أَخَذَ مِنْهُمُ ٱلْكَفَالَةَ ٱللَّازِمَةَ. Satisfactory guarantees, ٱلتَّأْمِينَاتُ ٱلْكَافِيَةُ.

Guarantee, *v.t.* تَضَمَّنَ ـ تَكَفَّلَ ب ـ كَفَلَ ب ـ ضَمِنَ ـ ﺭ. To — against, أَمَّنَ ـ مِن ـ آمَنَ ـ مِن ـ قَعَدَ ب. To — a treaty, تَكَفَّلَ بِمُعَاهَدَةٍ ـ تَضَمَّنَ. To — the integrity of a state, صِيَانَةُ ٱلْمَمْلَكَةِ مِنَ ٱلْإِجْحَافِ ـ حَفِظَ. To — the rights of…, أَمَّنَ حُقُوقَ ٱلـ... وَٱمْتِيَازَاتَهُ ـ حُقُوقَ. To — the possession of…, ٱلـ... وَتَصَرُّفَهُ. To ask for a —, security, إِسْتَأْمَنَ. The guaranteeing Powers, ٱلدُّوَلُ ٱلْكَافِلَةُ. On guaranteed security, عَلَى كَفَالَةٍ مَضْمُونَةٍ مِنَ ٱلتَّعَرُّضِ.

Guarantor, *n.* *See* One who guarantees, *under* Guarantee, *n.*

Guaranteeship, *n.* كَفَالَة ـ قَبَالَة ـ ضَمَان.

Guard, *n.* Security against loss or attack, أَمَان ـ أَمَانَة ـ. A sentinel, watch, خَفَر ـ خَفِير *pl.* خُفَرَاءُ *vulg.* حِرَاسَة ـ خَفْر. حَارِس *pl.* حُرَّاس *or* حَرَس. Protection, غَفْر ـ حُرَّاس ـ حَارِس ـ حَرَس ـ. Vigilance, حَذَر ـ صَوْن ـ صِيَانَة ـ مُحَافَظَة ـ حِفْظ ـ نُبْه ـ تَيَقُّظ. The — or hilt, as of a sword, قَبِيعَة *pl.* قَبَائِعُ ـ مِقْبَضَة. A watch-guard, بَنْدُ ٱلسَّاعَةِ. The — of a railway train, گوُمْسَار; the guard's van, سِبِنْسَة. A — or fender, حَائِل ـ حَاجِز. A — over the custom-house, وَقَّاف.

An advanced guard, the van, as of an army, طَلِيعَة ـ مُجَنَّبَة ـ سُلَافُ ٱلْعَسْكَرِ.

Body-guard, of a sovereign, حُرَّاسُ ٱلسُّلْطَانِ.

Coast-guards, خُفَرَاءُ ٱلْكُمْرُكِ ـ حُرَّاسُ ٱلْبَرِّ.

Foot-guards, عَسَاكِرُ مُشَاةٌ خَاصَّةٌ.

Grenadier-guards, عَسَاكِرُ مُشَاةٌ مُنْتَخَبَةٌ ـ شُرْطَة.

Guard of honour, رِفْقَةٌ عَسَاكِرَ لِلتَّبْجِيلِ (*or*) لِلِاحْتِفَالِ.

Horse-guards, عَسْكَرٌ مِنَ ٱلْفُرْسَانِ ٱلْخَاصَّةِ ـ خَيَّالَةٌ خَاصَّةٌ. The office of the Commander-in-chief, إِدَارَةُ ٱلسِّرْعَسْكَرِيَّةِ ـ ٱلسِّرْعَسْكَرِيَّةُ.

Life-guards, كَتِيبَةٌ عَسَاكِرَ خَاصَّةٌ ـ حَرَس ـ شُرَط.

Main-guard, ٱلْخَفَرُ ٱلْكَبِيرُ.

National guards, عَسَاكِرُ مُسْتَحْفِظَةٌ ـ عَسَاكِرُ مُحَافِظَةُ ٱلْمَمْلَكَةِ.

Rear-guard, مُؤَخَّرُ ٱلْجَيْشِ.

To be on or to mount guard, قَامَ بِٱلنَّوْبَةِ ـ أَجْرَى ٱلْخَفَرَ.

To be on one's guard against, حَذِرَ مِن ـ تَنَبَّهَ عَلَى ـ نَذِرَ ب ـ ﺭ ـ إِحْتَمَى مِن ـ تَحَفَّظَ مِن ـ تَوَقَّى مِن ـ تَحَرَّزَ مِن.

To put a person on his guard against, نَبَّهَ ـ عَلَى ـ أَنْذَرَ ـ ب ـ حَذَّرَ ـ مِن.

To be off one's guard, تَغَافَلَ عَن ـ تَغَفَّلَ.

To throw a person off his guard, أَغْفَلَ ـ عَن ـ غَفَّلَ.

To relieve guard, قَامَ مَكَانَ ـ غَيَّرَ (*or* ـ ﺭ بَدَّلَ) ٱلنَّوْبَةَ (*or*) ٱلْخَفَرَ ٱلسَّابِقَ.

Guard, *v.t.* To defend, إِحْتَفَظَ ب ـ حَفِظَ ـ ﺭ صَانَ ـ عَن ـ. يَحُوطُ *aor.* حَاطَ ب ـ أَحْمَى ـ حَمَى ـ ﺭ حَرَسَ ـ ﺭ. To watch, نَطَرَ. To guard against; *see under last article*, To be on one's guard against, *and* To put a person on his guard against.

Guard, *v.i.* To be in a state of caution or vigilance, إِحْتَرَزَ ـ إِحْتَمَى ـ تَحَرَّسَ ـ تَحَفَّظَ ـ إِحْتَرَسَ ـ تَنَبَّهَ.

Guard-boat, *n.* فَلُوكَةُ ٱلنَّوْبَةِ ـ فَلُوكَةٌ حَارِسَةٌ.

Guard-chamber, *n.* بَيْتُ ـ مَحَلُّ نَوْبَةِ ٱلسَّرَايَةِ ـ بَيْتُ ٱلْحَرَسِ خَفَرِ (*or* غَفَرِ) ٱلْقَصْرِ.

Guardedly, *ad.* بِعَقْلٍ ـ بِتَحَفُّظٍ ـ بِٱحْتِرَازٍ.

Guardedness, *n.* Circumspection, تَنَبُّه ـ تَحَفُّظ ـ حَذَر ـ إِحْتِرَاز ـ إِحْتِرَاس.

Guard-house, *n.* *See* Guard-room, *n.*

Guardian, *n.* As of an orphan, مُجِيز ـ وَكِيلُ ٱلْقُصَّرِ ـ وَصِيٌّ ـ وَكِيلُ ٱلْيَتَامَى. A keeper, حَافِظ *pl.* حُفَّاظ ـ حَارِس *pl.* حُرَّاس ـ حَفِيظ. One who keeps watch, نَاطِر *pl.* نَوَاطِيرُ ـ نَاطُور. One intrusted with the administration of any concern, overseer, أَمِين ـ أَمِينٌ عَلَى ـ مُتَصَرِّف ـ مُبَاشِر. A — angel, مَلَاكٌ حَارِسٌ ـ قَعِيد.

Guardianship, *n.* The office of guardian, وَكَالَة ـ وِصَايَة. Protectorate, صِيَانَة ـ حِمَايَة.

Guardless, *a.* لا حِمَايَةَ لَهُ ـ غَيْرُ مُحَصَّنٍ.

Guard-room, *n.* غَفَر ـ بَيْتُ ٱلْحَرَسِ. *Turkish,* قَرَه قَوْل.

Guard-ship, *n.* مَرْكَبُ حَافِظِ ٱلْمِينَا.

Guava, *n.* ضَرْبٌ مِنَ ٱلْفَاكِهَةِ.

Gudgeon, *n.* The fish, بِسَارِيَّة. One easily gulled, أَحْمَقُ ـ سَخِيفُ ٱلْعَقْلِ ـ أَبْلَهُ. *See also* Greenhorn, *n.*

Gudgeon, *v.t.* *See to* Gull, *v.t.*

Guebre, *n.* A fire-worshipper, عَابِدُ نَارٍ *pl.* عُبَّادٌ ـ گَبْر.

Guelder-rose, *n.* أَنْلُوس.

Guerdon, *n.* إِجَارَة ـ ثَوَاب ـ مُكَافَاة ـ أَجْر.

Guerdon, *v.t.* أَجَرَ ـ ٤ ـ كَافَى ـ ٤ أَثَابَ.

Guerdonless, *a.* بِدُونِ ثَوَابٍ ـ بِلا مُكَافَاةٍ ـ بِلا أَجْرٍ.

Guerilla, *n.* عَسْكَرِيٌّ مِنْ غَيْرِ نِظَامٍ *pl.* عَسَاكِرُ ـ بَاشِي بُوزُق.

Guerilla, *a.* مِثْلَ ٱلْبَاشِي بُوزُق ـ غَيْرُ نِظَامِيٍّ.

Guess, *v.t.* and *i.* To conjecture, حَزَرَ ـ ٤ حَزَرَ ـ تَوَهَّمَ ـ خَمَّنَ. To find out, in guessing, أَصَابَ فِي تَخْمِينِهِ ـ أَصَابَ فِي حَزْرِهِ.

Guess, *n.* قِيَاس ـ حَدْس ـ حَزْر ـ تَخْمِين.

Guest, *n.* One who comes to visit another, نَزِيل *pl.* نُزُل ـ ضَيْف *pl.* ضِيفَان ـ حِلال *pl.* حُلَّال. An invited —, دَعِيٌّ *pl.* دُعَوَاء. An uninvited —, ضَيْفَن *pl.* ضَيَافِنُ ـ قَرْوَاش ـ طُفَيْلِيٌّ ـ ضُيُوف. To accommodate a —, ضَافَ ـ ٤ نَزَّلَ ـ أَنْزَلَ ـ وَارِش ـ رَاشِي. To be the — of one, تَضَيَّفَ عِنْدَهُ. Guests, حُشَمَاء. Preparation for a —, نُزُل ـ نُزْل.

Guest-chamber, *n.* مَنْزِل ـ نَوِيّ. A public — for visitors, مَنْزِل خَانَه ـ دَارُ ٱلْمُسَافِرِينَ.

Guidage, *n.* A present for guiding, أُجْرَةُ دِلَالَةٍ.

Guidance, *n.* Direction, دِلَالَة ـ هِدَايَة. Teaching, advice, نَصِيحَة ـ تَعْلِيم. Supervision, ضَبْط ـ سِيَاسَة ـ إِدَارَة ـ تَدْبِير ـ قِيَادَة. Happy —, رَشَاد ـ هُدًى ـ تَوْفِيق.

Guide, *v.t.* To direct, point out the way, دَلَّ ـ ٤ دَلَّ ـ عَلَى. To — in the right way, هَدَى ـ أَرْشَدَ ـ رَشَّدَ. To teach, عَلَّمَ. To direct, manage, سَاسَ ـ ٤ ضَبَطَ ـ ٤ قَادَ ـ دَبَّرَ. To — to attainment, وَفَّقَ. To be guided, directed in the way, إِنْدَلَّ ـ إِنْدَلَّ عَلَى. To be guided aright, led in the way of salvation, إِهْتَدَى ـ تَهَدَّى ـ رُشِدَ. He was guided by his orders, إِهْتَدَى بِأَمْرِهِ.

Guide, *n.* As on a journey, دَلِيل *pl.* أَدِلَّة ـ بَيْذَق ـ بَذْق. A teacher, director, مُرْشِد ـ هَادٍ. A commander, قَائِد *pl.* قُوَّاد. An overseer, manager, أَمِين *pl.* أُمَنَاء ـ مُدَبِّر ـ سَائِس. Instructions, وَصَايَا ـ تَعْلِيمَات ـ أَمْر. A driver, سَائِق *pl.* سَاقَة.

Guide-book, *n.* كِتَابُ دُسْتُورِ ٱلسَّفَرِ ـ كِتَابُ دَلِيلٍ.

Guideless, *a.* بِلا دَلِيلٍ.

Guide-post, *n.* مَعْلَم *pl.* مَعَالِمُ ـ صَدَح ـ صَارِيَةٌ لِلدِّلَالَةِ; of stones, عَوَّة. *See also under* Post, *n.*

Guidon, *n.* رَايَةُ ٱلْخَيَّالَةِ ـ أُمُّ ٱلرُّمْحِ. *See also under* Pennon, *n.*

Guild, *n.* صِنْف *pl.* أَصْنَاف ـ أَخَوِيَّة ـ مَجْمَع.

Guilder, *n.* سِكَّةٌ فَلَمَنْكِيَّةٌ تُسَاوِي عَشَرَةَ غُرُوشٍ.

Guild-hall, *n.* Hall of a guild, دَارُ أَصْنَافٍ. The hall of the mayor, دَارُ شَيْخِ ٱلْبَلَدِ.

Guile, *n.* خِيَانَة ـ حِيلَة ـ مَكْر ـ غَبْن ـ غَدْر ـ أَرَب.

Guileful, *a.* غَشَّاش ـ خَائِن ـ غَدَّار ـ مَكَّار.

Guilefully, *ad.* بِغِشٍّ ـ بِخِيَانَةٍ ـ بِمَكْرٍ.

Guilefulness, *n.* *See* Guile, *n.*

Guileless, *a.* مُخْلِص ـ صَادِق ـ بَسِيط ـ سَلِيم ـ نَصُوح ـ لا غِشَّ فِيهِ.

Guilelessly, *ad.* بِلا غِشٍّ ـ بِخُلُوصٍ ـ بِسَلَامَةِ قَلْبٍ ـ بِنُصُوحٍ.

Guilelessness, *n.* صَفَاء ـ خُلُوص ـ سَلَامَةُ قَلْبٍ ـ نُصُوح.

Guillotine, *n.* آلَةٌ لِضَرْبِ أَعْنَاقِ ٱلْمُجْرِمِينَ.

Guillotine, *v.t.* قَطَعَ رَأْسَهُ ـ ٤ ضَرَبَ عُنُقَهُ.

Guilt, *n.* A crime, إِثْم *pl.* آثَام ـ جُرْم ـ جُنَاح ـ ذَنْب *pl.* ذُنُوب ـ لَوْمَة ـ إِثْم. Guiltiness, خَطِيئَة *pl.* خَطَايَا ـ قَبَاحَة ـ جَرِيمَة.

Guiltily, *ad.* إِثْمًا ـ بِجُنَاحٍ ـ بِإِثْمٍ.

Guiltiness, *n.* *See under* Guilt, *n.*

Guiltless, *a.* بَرِيء *pl.* أَبْرِيَاء ـ بَرِيءُ ٱلذِّمَّةِ ـ مَعْصُوم ـ زَكِيّ ـ لا ذَنْبَ لَهُ ـ لا جُنَاحَ لَهُ. To be — of, بَرِئَ مِن. To declare one's self — of, تَبَرَّأَ مِن. To hold —, بَرَّأَ ـ أَبْرَأَ.

Guiltlessly, *ad.* بِعِصْمَةٍ ـ بِبَرَاءَةٍ ـ بِلا ذَنْبٍ.

Guiltlessness, *n.* بَرَاءَة ـ بَرَاءَةُ ٱلذِّمَّةِ ـ عِفَّة ـ عِصْمَة.

Guilty, *a.* خَاطِئٌ *pl.* خَوَاطِئُ ـ جَانٍ ـ أَثِيم ـ جَرِيم ـ مُجْرِم ـ مُذْنِب. To be —, إِرْتَكَبَ ذَنْبًا ـ أَذْنَبَ ـ أَخْطَأَ. To own one's self —, أَقَرَّ بِذَنْبِهِ ـ تَذَنَّبَ عَلَى. To accuse as —, خَطَّأَ ـ إِسْتَذْنَبَ. To acknowledge one's self to be — falsely, تَخَاطَأَ. To be — of, deserving, death, إِسْتَوْجَبَ ٱلْمَوْتَ. We are verily — in respect of our brother, حَقًّا إِنَّنَا مُذْنِبُونَ إِلَى أَخِينَا.

Guinea, *n.* جِنِيَه (سِكَّةٌ تُسَاوِي ١٢٥ غِرْشًا) *pl.* جِنِيهَات. The — coast, بِلَادُ ٱلتِّبْرِ.

Guinea-fowl, *n.* }
Guinea-hen, } غِرْغِرَة *coll.* غِرْغِر ـ حَبِيشَة *coll.* حَبِيش.

Guinea-pig, *n.* خِنْزِيرٌ هِنْدِيٌّ *pl.* خَنَازِيرُ هِنْدِيَّةٌ.

Guinea-worm, *n.* دُودَةٌ رَفِيعَةٌ كَٱلْخَيْطِ تَثْوِى تَحْتَ ٱلْبَشَرَةِ *pl.* دِيدَان.

Guise, *n.* Manner, habit, عَادَة ـ طَرْز ـ طَرِيقَة ـ باب ـ شَكْل; of dress, زِيّ. Appearance, بُلْلَة ـ صُورَة ـ وَجْه ـ هَيْئَة ـ كَيْفِيَّة.

Guitar, *n.* قِيثَارَة ـ طُنْبُور.

Guitarist, *n.* ضَرَّابُ ٱلْقِيثَارَةِ ـ طُنْبُورَانِيّ.

Gules, *n.* اللَّوْنُ ٱلْقِرْمِزِيُّ فِي رَسْمِ ٱلْآرْمَا. *See* Coat-of-Arms, *under* Arms, *n.*

Gulf, *n.* As of the sea, خَلِيج *pl.* خُلْجَان ـ جُون. A frith, شَرْم *pl.* شُرُوم ـ خَوْر *pl.* خُؤُور. An abyss, لُجّ ـ هُوَّة. A whirlpool, دُرْدُور ـ دَوَّامَةُ ٱلْبَحْرِ *coll.* دُوَّام.

Gulfy, *a.* ذُو خُلْجَانٍ. Deep, عَمِيق ـ قَعِير.

Gull, The bird, نَوْرَزَة ـ جُنْقُلَة *pl.* جَنَاقِل. One easily cheated, غَبِيّ ـ غَرِير *pl.* أَغِرَّآء ـ زَبُون *pl.* زَبَائِن *and* زَبُونَات. A trick, مَكْر ـ خِدَاع ـ حِيلَة ـ خَدْعَة.

Gull, *v.t.* مَسَّحَ ـ مَكْرَب ـ [2] اِحْتَالَ عَلَى ـ خَدَعَ ـ غَشّ [2].

Gullet, *n.* عُضْرُوط ـ سِلْجَان ـ مَزْرَد ـ بُلْعُوم ـ حَلْق.

Gullibility, *n.* غَرَارَة ـ سَخَافَة ـ حَمَاقَة.

Gullible, *a.* غِرّ *pl.* أَغْرَار ـ غَرِير *pl.* أَغِرَّآء ـ سَخِيفُ ٱلْعَقْلِ.

Gully, *v.t.* خَانِق *pl.* خَوَانِق ـ شَقّ *pl.* شُقُوق ـ سَيْل *pl.* سُيُول ـ وَادٍ *pl.* أَوْدِيَة.

Gully, *v.t.* شَقّ [2] ـ حَفَرَ ـ جَوَّفَ.

Gully-hole, *n.* نَفَذ ـ فَم ـ بَالُوعَة.

Gulp, *v.t.* عَبّ [2] ـ سَرَطَ [2] ـ تَسَرَّطَ ـ لَقِمَ ـ اِلْتَقَمَ ـ بَلَعَ ـ لَهِمَ ـ هَلْقَمَ ـ تَزَبَّدَ.

Gulp, *n.* سَرْطَان ـ جُرْعَة *pl.* جُرَع ـ بُلْعَة ـ شَرْبَة. To take — after — from a vessel, غَتّ [2] فِي ٱلْإِنَآءِ.

Gum, *n.* Of the teeth, عَمْر ـ عُمْر ـ قَيْدُ ٱلْأَسْنَانِ ـ لِثَة *pl.* لِثَات ـ لَحْمُ ٱلْأَسْنَانِ. The part of the teeth where the gums grow, the alveolar process, دُرْدُر *pl.* دَرَادِر ـ المَنَاصِب. A receding of the gums, سُلَاق. A thin —, لِثَةٌ حَمِشَةٌ.

Gum, *n.* The substance, صَمْغ *pl.* صُمُوغ. Long slender twisted —, or a piece of —, صُعْرُور *pl.* صَعَارِير. A tear of —, صُعْرُورَة ـ صَمْغَة. The gum-arabic tree, سَمُر ـ طَلْح. To produce —, أَصْمَغَ. To scarify a tree to let the — flow, اِصْطَمَغَ.

Gum-ammoniac, وُشَّق ـ أُشَّق ـ قِنَاوُشَق.

Gum-arabic, صَمْغٌ عَرَبِيٌّ ـ صَمْغٌ سَنَارِيٌّ.

Gum-copal, سِنْدَرُوس ـ سِنْدَرُوسٌ بِلَّوْرِيٌّ.

Gum-dragon, صَمْغٌ ظُفْر.

Gum-elastic, الصَّمْغُ ٱلْمُغِيطُ.

Gum-lac, صَمْغُ ٱللَّكِّ.

Gum-resin, عِلْك *pl.* عُلُوك.

Gum-tragacanth, كَثِيرَآء.

Gum, *v.t.* To stick with —, صَمَّغَ ـ أَلْزَقَ بِٱلصَّمْغِ. To make to stick to, أَلْصَقَ بِ.

Gum-arabic, *n.* *See under* Gum, *n.*

Gum-boil, *n.* دُمَّلَةٌ فِي ٱللِّثَةِ.

Gum-lac, *n.* *See under* Gum, *n.*

Gummiferous, *a.* صَمْغَان ـ أَبُو صَمْغٍ ـ صَمَّاغ.

Gumminess, *n.* لُزُوجَة ـ تَدَبُّق.

Gummous, *a.* }
Gummy, } صَمْغِيّ ـ لَزِج ـ دَبِق. To be or become —, تَدَبَّقَ.

Gumption, *n.* فِرَاسَة ـ مُرُوَّة.

Gum-resin, *n.* *See under* Gum, *n.*

Gum-tragacanth, *n.* *See under* Gum, *n.*

Gum-tree, *n.* The — of America, إِسْمُ شَجَرَةٍ كَبِيرَةٍ تَنْبُتُ بِأَمِيرِيكَا.

Gun, *n.* A musket, بُنْدُق *coll.* بُنْدُقِيَّة ـ مَكَاحِل *pl.* مُكْحُلَة *pl.* بَنَادِق ـ بَارُودَة. A cannon, مِدْفَع *pl.* مَدَافِع ـ طُوب *pl.* أَطْوَاب. They fired 15 guns for his rank and 72 guns for the years of his age, أَطْلَقُوا خَمْسَةَ عَشَرَ مِدْفَعًا لِمَنْصِبِهِ وَٱثْنَيْنِ وَسَبْعِينَ مِدْفَعًا عَلَى عَدَدِ سِنِي عُمْرِهِ. Heavy guns, مَدَافِعُ ضَخِمَةٌ. Light guns, مَدَافِعُ خَفِيفَةٌ.

A gun *en barbette*, مِدْفَعٌ أَكْشَفُ *pl.* مَدَافِعُ كُشْفَآء ـ مَدَافِعُ بِلَا ـ مَزْغَل ـ مِدْفَعٌ مَنْصُوبٌ عَلَى سَطْحِ ٱلسُّورِ.

A gun in position, مِدْفَعٌ مَضْمُون *pl.* مَدَافِعُ مَضْمُونَة.

Gun-barrel, *n.* مَاصُورَة *pl.* مَوَاصِير.

Gun-boat, *n.* فَلُوكَةٌ حَرْبِيَّةٌ *pl.* فَلُوكَات ـ فَلُوكَةٌ بِمِدْفَعَيْنِ ـ لَنْجُون *pl.* لَنْجُونَات.

Gun-carriage, *n.* جَرَّارُ ٱلْمِدْفَعِ ـ خَشَبَةُ ٱلْمِدْفَعِ ـ قُنْدَاق *pl.* قَنَادِق.

Gun-cotton, *n.* حَلِيجٌ بَارُودِيٌّ ـ قُطْنُ ٱلْبَارُودِ.

Gun-fire, *n.* Morning —, مِدْفَعُ ٱلصَّبَاحِ; evening —, مِدْفَعُ ٱلْمَسَآءِ.

Gunnel, *n.* *See* Gunwale, *n.*

Gunner, *n.* طُوبْجِي *or* طُبْجِي *pl.* طُبْجِيَّة.

Gunnery, *n.* عِلْمُ ٱلطُّبْجِيَّةِ ـ عِلْمُ ٱلْأَطْوَابِ.

Gunpowder, *n.* بَارُود.

Gun-room, *n.* طارِمَةٌ (or مَقْعَدٌ) فِي بارِجَةٍ مُعَدَّةٌ لِلضُّبّاطِ وَخَواصِّ الضُّبّاطِ مِنَ البَحْرِيَّةِ. Gun-room officers, (or المَقْعَدِ) أَهْلُ الطّارِمَةِ المَذْكُورَةِ.

Gun-shot, *n.* A shot from a gun, ضَرْبَةُ مِدْفَعٍ. Range of a —, مَسافَةُ ضَرْبَةِ المِدْفَعِ ـ ضَرْبَة ـ مَدَى ضَرْبَةِ المِدْفَعِ. A — wound, إِصابَةُ ضَرْبَةِ مِدْفَعٍ أَوْ بارُودَةٍ.

Gun-smith, *n.* *See* Armourer, *n.*

Gun-smithery, *n.* صِناعَةُ الأَسْلِحَةِ.

Gun-stock, *n.* قُنْداقُ البارُودَةِ ـ خَشَبُ البُنْدُقِيَّةِ.

Gun-stock, *n.* Of a musket, قُنْداقُ المِكْحَلَةِ.

Gun-tackle, *n.* بَكَرُ المَدافِعِ ـ عُدَّةُ المَدافِعِ.

Gunter's-scale, *n.* جَدْوَلٌ مُفِيدٌ لِتَسْهِيلِ الحِساباتِ الهَنْدَسِيَّةِ ـ جَدْوَلُ كُنْتَر.

Gunwale, *n.* (or مِشْفَرُ شُفْرُ or حاجِزُ) القارِبِ. A false —, (called in the Persian Gulf, بَرْضَة or بَرْدَة).

Gurgle, *v.i.* تَجَرْجَرَ. To — as any liquid when being decanted, صَوَّتَ بِقٍّ بِقٍّ ـ بَقْبَقَ ـ خَرَّ.

Gurgling, *n.* As of a stream, تَجَرْجُر; as made by a liquid when decanted, غَرْغَرَة ـ بَقْبَقَة ـ خَرِير. The — noise of a camel, رُغاءٌ.

Gurgling, *a.* As a stream, خارٌّ ـ مُتَجَرْجِر.

Gush, *v.i.* ثارَ ـ تَصَبَّبَ ـ أَثَجَّ ـ ثَجَّ ـ اِنْبَجَسَ ـ اِنْفَجَرَ ـ اِنْصَبَّ ـ تَدَفَّقَ ـ *aor.* يَثُورُ.

Gush, *n.* دُفْقَة *pl.* دُفَق ـ ثَوْر ـ ثَجِيج.

Gushing, *a.* As of a stream, دَفّاق ـ ثَجّاج ـ ثَجُوج ـ مُنْبَجِس; of a fountain, فَوّار.

Gusset, *n.* بِنَقَة ـ بَنِيقَة ـ نُفّاجَة ـ نِفاجَة ـ نُفْجَة ـ لِبْنَة. To put a — into, بَنَّقَ.

Gust, *n.* نَفْخَة *pl.* نَفَخات ـ تَلْقِيحَة ـ هُبُوب ـ مَهَبّ ـ زَفْزَفَة ـ نُخْرَة.

Gustatory, *a.* ذائِق ـ مُتَعَلِّقٌ بِالذَّوْقِ.

Gusto, *n.* اِبْتِهاج ـ تَلَذُّذ ـ حَظّ.

Gusty, *a.* ذُو زَفْزَفَةٍ ـ هَبِيب ـ هَبُوب.

Gut, *n.* Of the intestines, مَعًى *pl.* أَمْعاء ـ مَصِير *pl.* أَمْصِرَة and مُصْران and مَصارِين. The small guts, الأَعْفاجُ. Gut, for fishing, حَرِيرٌ لِلصِّنّارَةِ. A channel, خَلِيج. He drank until he filled his guts, شَرِبَ حَتّى مَلأَ مَصارَّهُ. *See also* Intestines, *n.*

Gut, *v.t.* أَخْرَجَ المَصارِينَ ـ جَوَّفَ. To clear out, فَرَّغَ.

Gutta-serena, *n.* كُمْنَة.

Gutter, *n.* A passage for water, قَناة ـ مَجْرًى ـ قَصَبَة; for dirty water, بالُوعَة ـ بَلُّوعَة. To roll about in the —, as a drunken man, تَرَنَّحَ ـ اِرْتَبَخَ. To take one from the —, أَخَذَ مِنَ المَزْبَلَةِ.

Gutter, *v.t.* قَعَّرَ ـ وَقَّرَ ـ نَقَرَ فِي ـ نَطَفَ.

Gutter, *v.i.* As a candle, نَطَفَ ـ سالَ.

Guttural, *a.* مُتَعَلِّقٌ ـ يُنْسَبُ لِلحَلْقِ ـ مِنَ الحَلْقِ ـ حَلْقِيٌّ ـ حَنْجَرِيٌّ ـ بِالحَلْقِ.

Guttural, *n.* A — letter, حَرْفٌ حَلْقِيٌّ. The — letters, الحُرُوفُ الحَلْقِيَّةُ.

Gutturally, *ad.* مِنَ الحَلْقِ.

Gutturalness, *n.* حَلْقِيَّة.

Guy, *n.* A steadying rope, حَبْلٌ سَنَدٍ. One dressed preposterously, تُرْتُعٌ. A laughing-stock, أُضْحُوكَة ـ سُخْرَة ـ لُعْبَة.

Guzzle, *v.i.* أَفْرَطَ فِي الشُّرْبِ ـ شَرِبَ.

Guzzle, *v.t.* بَلْعَمَ ـ بَلِعَ ـ شَرِبَ.

Guzzler, *n.* شِرِّيب ـ شَرّاب ـ بَلْعَم ـ بُلَع ـ هِبْلاع ـ سُرَط.

Gymnasium, *n.* A place of exercise, wrestling, مَعْرَكَة ـ مَحَلٌّ لِلرِّياضَةِ. A school of science, دارُ الفُنُونِ ـ مَدْرَسَة.

Gymnast, *n.* رِياضِيٌّ.

Gymnastic, *a.* رِياضِيٌّ.

Gymnastics, *n.* رِياضَةُ البَدَنِ ـ نِقاز.

Gymnosophist, *n.* فَيْلَسُوفٌ مُتَقَشِّفٌ *pl.* فَلاسِفَةٌ مُتَقَشِّفُون ـ مُتَفَلْسِف.

Gynarchy, *n.* حُكُومَةُ امْرَأَةٍ.

Gynecian, *a.* مُتَعَلِّقٌ بِالحَرَمِ ـ مُتَعَلِّقٌ بِالنِّساءِ.

Gynecium, *n.* حَرَم.

Gyp, *n.* مُحافِظُ الأَدَبِ.

Gypseous, *a.* }
Gypsine, } مِنْ جِصٍّ ـ جِصِّيٌّ ـ جِبْسِيٌّ.

Gypsum, *n.* جِصّ ـ جِبْس ـ شارُوق ـ شِيد. A — pit, جَصّاصَة. A preparer of —, جَصّاص. To plaster with —, شادَ *aor.* يَشِيدُ. Plastered with —, مَشِيد.

Gypsy, *n.* *See* Gipsy, *n.*

Gyral, *a.* عاكِف ـ دائِر ـ دَوّار ـ جائِل ـ فاتِل.

Gyrate, *v.i.* عَكَفَ ـ جالَ ـ فَتَلَ ـ دارَ ـ اِسْتَدارَ.

Gyration, *n.* عُكُوف ـ جَوَلان ـ جَوَلان ـ دَوْر ـ دَوَران.

Gyratory, *a.* *See* Gyral, *a.*

Gyrfalcon, *n.* نَوْعٌ مِنَ البازِ.

Gyve, *v.t.* To shackle, صَفَدَ ـ أَصْفَدَ ـ قَيَّدَ.

Gyves, *n.* Fetters for the legs, صِفاد ـ مِصْفاد ـ قُيُودٌ لِلرِّجْلَيْنِ.

H.

Ha! *int.* سُبْحَانَ ٱللّٰهِ ـ يَه يَه.

Habeas Corpus, *n.* أَمْرٌ شَرْعِيٌّ بِتَسْلِيمِ ٱلشَّخْصِ ٱلْمَسْجُونِ لِأَيِّ سَبَبٍ كَانَ وَحَيْثُمَا كَانَ.

Haberdasher, *n.* بَزَّاز *pl.* بَزَّازُون.

Haberdashery, *n.* بِزَازَة ـ قُمَاش *pl.* أَقْمِشَة.

Habergeon, *n.* دِرْع *pl.* دُرُوع.

Habiliments, *n.* ثِيَاب ـ كِسْوَة ـ لِبْس.

Habit, *n.* As of body, خِلْقَة ـ مِزَاج ـ طَبْع ـ جِبْلَة ـ جِبِلَّة. Dress, زِيّ ـ مَلْبُوس ـ كِسْم ـ ثَوْب ـ خِلْعَة. Custom, إِجْرِيَّآء ـ دُرْبَة ـ دَأْب ـ وَضْع ـ خُلُق ـ عَادَة *pl.* عَادَات. A riding —, بَدْلَةُ ٱلرُّكُوب. That is her —, custom, ذَلِكَ ـ ذَلِكَ دَأْبُهَا مِنْ دَأْبِهَا. A bad — of body, قَشَف. To get into the — of, تَعَوَّدَ عَلَى ـ طُبِعَ عَلَى. To be of a bad — of body, ـ قَشِفَ.

Habit, *v.t.* *See to* Clothe, Dress, *v.t.*

Habitable, *a.* قَابِلُ ٱلسُّكْنَى ـ يُسْكَنُ فِيهِ.

Habitableness, *n.* قَابِلِيَّةُ ٱلسُّكْنَى فِيهِ.

Habitant, *n.* *See* Inhabitant, *n.*

Habitat, *n.* Home, place, habitation, مَوْطِن ـ ٱلْوَطَنُ ٱلْأَصْلِيّ *pl.* مَوَاطِنُ ـ سَكِينَة *pl.* سَكِينَات ـ مَوْلِد. Place where anything is to be found, مَوْقِع.

Habitation, *n.* Residence in a place, إِقَامَة ـ قُعُود ـ حُلُول ـ قُطُون ـ سُكْنَى. A dwelling, مَحَلَّة *pl.* مَحَلَّات ـ مَقَام *pl.* مَقَامَات ـ مَقْعَد *pl.* مَقَاعِد ـ مَسْكَن *pl.* مَسَاكِن ـ بَيْت *pl.* بُيُوت. To place one in a —, أَسْكَنَ.

Habitual, *a.* Acquired by habit, مَأْلُوف عَلَى ـ مَطْبُوعٌ عَلَى ـ مُدْمِنٌ عَلَى ـ مُعَوَّدٌ عَلَى ـ مُعْتَاد. According to habit, إِعْتِيَادِيّ. His — walk, سَيْرُهُ ٱلْمُعْتَادُ.

Habitually, *ad.* عَادَةً ـ مِرَارًا ـ إِعْتِيَادًا.

Habituate, *v.t.* وَطَّنَ ـ عَلَى ـ مَرَّنَ ـ عَلَى ـ دَرَّى ـ (or أَدْرَى ـ) ب ـ طَبَّعَ ـ عَلَى ـ عَوَّدَ ـ عَلَى ـ دَرَّبَ ـ ب ـ دَرَّجَ ـ إِلَى ـ مَارَزَ. To — one's self to . . . , دَرِبَ ب ـ تَدَرَّبَ ب ـ دَرِيَ ب ـ تَعَوَّدَ عَلَى ـ تَطَبَّعَ ب ـ تَوَطَّنَ عَلَى ـ تَمَرَّنَ عَلَى. He is habituated to it, هُوَ دَرِبٌ بِهِ. Habituated, ضَارٍ ـ مَوَارِنُ *pl.* مَارِن. A dog habituated to the chase, كَلْبٌ ضَارٍ بِٱلصَّيْدِ. He became habituated to the thing, مَرَنَ عَلَى ٱلشَّيْءِ.

Habituation, *n.* As of another, تَعْوِيد ـ تَدْرِيب ـ تَمْرِين; of one's self, تَدَرُّب ـ تَعَوُّد ـ تَمَرُّن ـ تَطَبُّع.

Habitude, *n.* عَادَة ـ مُمَارَزَة ـ دُوبَة.

Hacienda, *n.* *See* Farm, *n.*

Hack, *v.t.* To cut to pieces, قَطَّعَ ـ فَرَمَ. To cut one awkwardly, to injure, of a person, قَحَطَ ـ خَدَشَ ـ خَمَشَ; of a thing, خَرَّبَ ـ أَعْدَمَ ـ أَتْلَفَ. To use in common, عَفَسَ. To notch, فَلَّ ـ حَزَّ ـ إِحْتَزَّ.

Hack, *n.* The horse, دَابَّة ـ بِرْذَوْن ـ كُدْش كَدِيش *coll.* A notch, حَزّ ـ فَلّ *pl.* فُلُول. A cut, جُرْح ـ قَطْع ـ ثَلْم. A — writer, مُلَازِمُ ٱلتَّأْلِيفِ وَٱلْكِتَابَةِ. A — carriage, عَرَبِيَّةُ ٱلزُّقَاقِ.

Hackle, *v.t.* To dress, as of flax or hemp, مَشَطَ ـ سَرَّحَ ـ نَتَفَ. To tear asunder, خَرَقَ ـ هَتَكَ ـ مَزَّقَ.

Hackle, *n.* Raw silk, قَزّ. Anything flimsy, سَخَافَة ـ مُشَاقَة.

Hackney, *n.* A hired horse, حِصَانٌ مُسْتَأْجَرٌ; a — carriage, عَرَبَةٌ لِلْكِرَآءِ. *See also under* Hack, *n.*

Hackney, *v.t.* To use much, عَفَسَ. To make trite, عَكَّ ب ـ كَرَّرَ: He hackneyed it in his speech, لَجْلَجَهُ فِي كَلَامِهِ.

Hackneyed, *a.* Used often, فُضُل. Trite, of speech, مَقُول ـ مَطْرُوق.

Had, (*pret. of to* Have), I had, or would, rather, أَرْجَحُ ـ أَحْسَنُ عِنْدِي. *See to* Have, *v.t.*

Haddock, *n.* نَوْعٌ مِنَ ٱلسَّمَكِ.

Hades, *n.* ٱلْجَحِيمُ ـ عَالَمُ ٱلْأَمْوَاتِ.

Hadj, *n.* (Properly al-Hajj), the pilgrimage to Makkah, ٱلْحَجُّ ـ ٱلْحِجَّةُ.

Hadji, *n.* (Properly Hâjj), a pilgrim to Makkah, حَاجّ *fem.* حَاجَّة *pl.* حُجَّاج.

Haft, *n.* مِقْبَضَة ـ مِقْبَض. *See also* Handle, *n.*

Haft, *v.t.* أَقْبَضَ ـ رَكَّبَ لِ ـ يَدًا.

Hag, *n.* A shrew, خَطَّالَة ـ سَلِيطَة ـ سِلْقَة *pl.* سُلْقَان ـ كُوكُوبَة. *See also* Witch, *n.*

Haggard, *n.* A hawk, بَاشِق *pl.* بَوَاشِق.

Haggard, *a.* Wan, خَاسِف ـ شَاحِب ـ هَزِيل. Ugly, قَبِيح ـ بَشِع ـ فَظِيع. To look —, شَحَبَ ـ خَسَفَ.

Haggardliness, *n.* خَسِيفَة ـ خَسْف ـ هُزَال ـ شُحُوبَة.

Haggardly, *ad.* In an ugly manner, بِبَشَاعَةٍ ـ بِفَظَاعَةٍ. Wanly, بِخَسِيفَةٍ ـ بِشُحُوبَةٍ ـ بِهُزَالٍ.

Haggis, *n.* مَحْشُوٌّ ـ مَحْشِيٌّ.

Haggish, *a.* Like a hag, كَٱلسَّلِيطَةِ ـ كَٱلْعَطْلَةِ. A — tongue, سَلِيطَةُ ٱللِّسَانِ.

Haggle, *v.t.* *See to* Hackle, *v.t.*

Haggle, *v.i.* As in bargaining, بَايَعَ ـ شَارَطَ ـ شَارَى. To hesitate, in speech, تَمَخْطَرَ ـ تَصَرَّبَ. To cavil, تَحَجَّجَ ـ تَعَالَجَ. They haggled together in their talk, تَجَاذَبُوا أَطْرَافَ ٱلْكَلَامِ.

Haggler, *n.* مُعَالِج ـ مُجَاذِب.

Haggling, *n.* مُجَاذَبَة ـ مُعَالَجَة.

Hagiography, *n.* The sacred writings, ٱلْكُتُبُ ٱلْمُقَدَّسَة.

Haha, *n.* خَنْدَقٌ دُونَ حُدُودٍ.

Haik, *n.* A waist-wrapper, حِقَاءٌ ـ حَقْوَة ـ حَقْوٌ.

Hail, *n.* حَبُّ ٱلْغَمَامِ ـ حَبَّةُ ٱلْمُزْنِ ـ سَقِيطُ ٱلسَّحَابِ ـ أَسْنَانُ ٱلْعَجُوزِ ـ بَرَد ـ ضَرِيب ـ إِغْرِيض ـ حَبُّ قُرّ.

Hail, *v.t.* To call, صَاحَ بِ aor. يَصِيحُ ـ صَوَّتَ بِ ـ نَدَا ² ـ نَدَنَا. To salute, سَلَّمَ عَلَى.

Hail, *v.i.* To fall in —, نَزَلَ ٱلْبَرَدُ ـ. To be hailed upon, بُرِدَ: The ground was hailed upon, بُرِدَتِ ٱلْأَرْضُ.

Hail! *int.* حَيَّاكَ ٱللّٰهُ ـ ٱلسَّلَام.

Hail, *n.* A salutation, تَحِيَّة ـ تَسْلِيم ـ سَلَام. A call, دَعْوَة ـ صَيْحَة ـ نَدْوٌ. Range of voice, مَدَى ٱلصَّوْتِ.

Hail-fellow, *n.* صَاحِب ـ زَمِيل *pl.* زُمَلَاءُ ـ نَدِيم *pl.* نُدَمَاءُ. To be — well met with, آلَفَ *aor.* يُؤَالِفُ ـ وَاصَلَ.

Hailstone, *n.* حَبَّةُ بَرَدٍ *pl.* حُبُوب.

Hair, *n.* شَعَر ـ شَعْر *pl.* شِعَار *and* شُعُور. A single —, شَعْرَة *pl.* شَعَرَات. A very fine —, شُعَيْرَة. A head of —, جُمَّة *pl.* جُمَم ـ شُوشَة. The — on the forehead, طُرَّة ـ نَاصِيَة. Hair on the pubes or podex, شِعْرَة ـ إِسْب. False —, a chignon, قَرْزَل ـ قُنْزُعَة *or* قَنْزَعَة *or* قَنَزَعَة. The — which comes off in combing, مُرَاطَة. Hair in locks, braided with silk, and hanging down the back, عُقُوص. Hair like bristles, هُلْب. Hair of animals, شَعَر ـ صُوف; the downy — on animals, وَبَر *pl.* وُبُور ـ وَبَرَة *pl.* أَوْبَار. Horse —, سَبِيب ـ سَيْب. To pluck off the —, نَتَفَ ٱلشَّعَرَ ـ. To remove the — from the body with boiling water, سَمَطَ ² ـ; with tweezers, نَمَّصَ ـ مَرَّطَ ² ـ مَرَطَ; in a general way, to remove all the —, سَمَّدَ ٱلشَّعَرَ. To unloose, of the —, سَرَّحَ. To fall off, of the —, تَمَرَّطَ. Having scanty —, أَزْعَرُ ـ أَنَطُّ ـ نَطٌّ. To stand on end, of the — of a man or woman, قَبَّ شَعْرُ رَأْسِهِ ²; of animals, ٱزْبَارَّ شَعْرُهُ. To a —, precisely, بِضَبْطٍ ـ بِدِقَّةٍ ـ فِي غَايَةِ ٱلْإِتْقَانِ ـ بِٱلتَّمَامِ.

Hair, *a.* } *See* Hairy, *a.*
Haired, }

Hair-brained, *a.* مُتَهَوِّر ـ مَجْنُون ـ مُهَوَّس ـ خَرِيم.

Hair-breadth, *a.* عَجِيب ـ مُشْرِف عَلَى. A — escape, عَسِيرُ خَلَاصٍ بِٱلْعُسْرِ ـ نَجَاةٌ بِٱلْجَهْدِ ـ ٱلْخَلَاص.

Hair-brush, *n.* فُرْشَةٌ لِلشَّعْرِ.

Hair-cloth, *n.* مِسْح ـ قُمَاشٌ مِنْ شَعْرٍ.

Hair-dresser, *n.* مُزَيِّن. A female —, مَاشِطَة ـ مَشَّاطَة.

Hair-dye, *n.* خِضَاب.

Hairiness, *n.* شَعْرَانِيَّة ـ شَعَر.

Hair-lace, *n.* عِصَابَة.

Hairless, *a.* أَمْلَطُ ـ أَجْرَدُ ـ أَمْرَدُ. Hairless and shining, of the body, أَمْرَطُ ـ أَدْلَصُ ـ أَزْلَقُ. Hairless and beardless, جُرْدٌ مُرْدٌ.

Hair-pencil, *n.* قَلَمُ شَعْرٍ *pl.* أَقْلَام.

Hair-pin, *n.* مِدْرَاةٌ لِلشَّعْرِ ـ مِشْقَاة *pl.* مِدْرَاوَات.

Hair-powder, *n.* ذَرُورٌ لِلشَّعْرِ.

Hair-sack, *n.* بَلَاس *pl.* بُلُس.

Hair's-breadth, *n.* أَقَلُّ ـ أَدْنَى ـ رِقَّةُ شَعْرَةٍ.

Hair-splitting, *n.* شَقُّ ٱلشَّعْرَةِ ـ دِقٌّ ـ دِقَّة ـ تَجَوُّد ـ تَنَوُّق.

Hair-splitting, *a.* Of a person, دَقِيق ـ مُدَقِّقٌ لِلْغَايَةِ *pl.* دِقَاق.

Hair-splitting subtilties, مَدَاقُّ (*or* دَقَائِقُ) ٱلْأُمُورِ.

Hair-stroke, *n.* خَطٌّ رَفِيعٌ ـ قَلَمٌ رَفِيعٌ.

Hairy, *a.* Having much hair, مُشْعِر ـ شَعْرَانِيٌّ ـ شَعِر ـ أَزَبُّ ـ أَشْعَرُ. Having much hair on the face, قِنْعَاث; on the body, قِنْعَاث. Made of hair, شَعِر ـ مِنْ شَعْرٍ. To be —, شَعِرَ ـ ؞ ـ تَشَعَّرَ. To grow —, to get hair, of a child, تَشَاعَرَ.

Hake, *n.* نَوْعٌ مِنَ ٱلسَّمَكِ.

Halberd, *n.* مِطْرَد *pl.* مَطَارِدُ ـ رُمْح *pl.* أَرْمَاح.

Halberdier, *n.* رَمَّاح ـ رَامِح.

Halcyon, *n.* *See* Kingfisher, *n.*

Halcyon, *a.* Peaceful, happy, مَغْبُوط ـ سَعِيد.

Hale, *a.* Robust, قَوِيّ *pl.* أَقْوِيَاءُ ـ مُتَعَافٍ ـ ضَلِيع.

Hale, *v.t.* *See to* Haul, *v.t.*

Half, *n.* نِصْف *pl.* أَنْصَاف ـ شَطْر *pl.* أَشْطُر *and* شُطُور ـ شَطِير ـ نَصِيف. Half-and-half, anything diluted, مَمْزُوج. The cloven — of anything, شَقِيقَة ـ شَقِيق ـ شِقَق .pl شِقَّة ـ شِقّ.

To go halves with one, شَارَكَ ـ نَاصَفَ. To drink the —, as of a glass, نَصَفَ ². The reduction of the war indemnity to one —, تَقْلِيلُ غَرَامَةِ ٱلْحَرْبِ إِلَى ٱلنِّصْفِ.

Half, *a.* نِصْف. Half green, — dry, شَمِيط.

Half-blood, *n.* } مِنْ أَحَدِ ٱلْأَبَوَيْنِ ـ نَسْلٌ مِنْ وَالِدَيْنِ مُخْتَلِفَيْنِ.
Half-blood, *a.* } Sons of one mother by different fathers, and children of different mothers by one father, صِنْوَانٌ وَغَيْرُ صِنْوَانٍ.

Half-blooded, *a.* Base, ignoble, مَغْسُود ـ سَفِيل ـ دَنِيّ ².

Half-breed, *n.* and *a.* *See* Half-blood, *n.* and *a.*

Half-brother, *n.* صِنْو *pl.* أَصْنَاء ـ أَخٌ مِنْ أَحَدِ ٱلْأَبَوَيْنِ.

Half-caste, *n.* and *a.* مُوَلَّد. *See also* Eurasian, *n.*

Half-cock, *n.* Of fire-arms, نِصْفُ دَرَجَةٍ ـ أَوَّلُ دَرَجَةٍ.
To be at half-cock, كَانَ عَلَى نِصْفِ صِلَةٍ ـ كَانَ عَلَى ٱلْوَصِيلَةِ ـ كَانَ مَرْفُوعًا دَرَجَةً وَاحِدَةً.
To bring to half-cock, رَفَعَ ـ دَرَجَةً وَاحِدَةً ـ وَصَّلَ ـ إِلَى نِصْفِ صِلَةٍ.
To bring back to half-cock, رَجَّعَ ـ دَرَجَةً وَاحِدَةً.

Half-dead, *a.* بَيْنَ حَيٍّ وَمَيِّتٍ ـ كَٱلْمَيِّتِ. To be — with fright, مَدْهُوش ـ مَرْعُوب.

Half-full, *a.* شَطْرَان *fem.* شَطْرَى ـ نَصْفَان *fem.* نَصْفَى.

Half-holiday, *n.* بَطَالَةُ نِصْفِ نَهَارٍ.

Half-moon, *n.* تَرْبِيعُ ٱلْقَمَرِ.

Half-pay, *n.* نِصْفُ مَعَاشٍ ـ نِصْفُ مَاهِيَّةٍ (or شَهْرِيَّةٍ). To be on —, صَاحِبُ نِصْفِ مَعَاشٍ. To put on —, رَتَّبَ لِـ نِصْفَ مَاهِيَّةٍ. *See also under* Retired, *a.*

Half-penny, *n.* سِكَّةٌ أَنْكِلِيزِيَّةٌ مِنْ نُحَاسٍ تُسَاوِي رُبْعَ ٱلْقِرْشِ.

Half-pennyworth, *n.* بِقِيمَةِ ٱلسِّكَّةِ ٱلْمَذْكُورَةِ.

Half-quarterly, *a.* and *ad.* فِي كُلِّ سِتَّةِ أَسَابِيعَ ـ كُلَّ شَهْرٍ وَنِصْفٍ.

Half-seas-over, *a.* سَكْرَانُ ـ مُلْتَكٌّ. To be —, مَسَّهُ ٱلسُّكْرُ.

Half-sister, *n.* أُخْتٌ مِنْ أَحَدِ ٱلْأَبَوَيْنِ *pl.* أَخَوَات.

Half-way, *n.* نِصْفُ ٱلطَّرِيقِ. A — house, مَنْزِلٌ ـ خَانٌ وَاسِطٌ عَلَى نِصْفِ ٱلطَّرِيقِ.

Half-witted, *a.* أَبْلَهُ ـ سَخِيفُ ٱلْعَقْلِ ـ جَاهِل.

Half-yearly, *a.* and *ad.* فِي كُلِّ سِتَّةِ أَشْهُرٍ.

Halibut, *n.* نَوْعٌ مِنَ ٱلسَّمَكِ.

Halidom, *n.* مَرْيَمُ ٱلْعَذْرَاءُ.

Hall, *n.* A court, courtyard, صَحْن *pl.* أَصْحَان. A vestibule, دِهْلِيز *pl.* دَهَالِيزُ ـ سُدَّة. A large upper apartment in a house, مَقْعَد; a similar one on the lower floor, مَنْظَرَة. A royal —, سُدَّةُ ٱلْمَلِكِ. A — of justice, مَحْكَمَة ـ دَارُ ٱلْوِلَايَةِ. A college, مَدْرَسَة *pl.* مَدَارِس. Any building of a corporation, دَار. A — or place of meeting, دَارُ نَدْوَةٍ ـ مُنْتَدًى ـ نَادٍ.

Hallelujah, *n.* سُبْحَانَ ٱللّٰهِ ـ تَهْلِيل ـ هَلَلِينَة. To sing —, ذَكَرَ ² ـ هَلَّلَ.

Halliards, *n.* } أَحْبَال ـ قَنْدَلِيسَى ـ مَنطارى ـ جَنْدَرِيسَى
Halyards, } دِقَاق.

Halloo, *v.i.* صَوَّتَ ـ صَيَّحَ ـ صَاحَ ـ.

Halloo, *v.t.* To shout to, صَيَّحَ عَلَى ـ صَوَّتَ عَلَى. To encourage, instigate, to..., أَغْرَى ـ عَلَى ـ أَضْرَى ـ بِـ.

Halloo, *n.* صِيَاح ـ صَيْحَة.

Halloo! *int.* هُوه ـ يَاهُو. Halloo! gently! رُوَيْدًا ـ عَلَى مَهْلٍ.

Hallow, *v.t.* To sanctify, بَارَكَ ـ قَدَّسَ. To consecrate, كَرَّسَ.

Hallow-e'en, *n.* لَيْلَةُ تَذْكَارِ جَمِيعِ ٱلْقِدِّيسِينَ.

Hallow-mass, *n.* عِيدُ ٱلْقِدِّيسِينَ ـ عِيدُ جَمِيعِ ٱلْقِدِّيسِينَ.

Hallucination, *n.* Delusion, شُبْهَة ـ طَيْف ـ وَهْمِيَّة ـ تَوَهُّم ـ هَشْرَة ـ هَبْتَة ـ طَيْشَان. False hope, غُرُور.

Halo, *n.* A circle round the sun or moon, طُفَاوَة; round the moon, هَالَة *pl.* هَالَات ـ دَوَّارَة (or دَارَة) ٱلْقَمَرِ ـ تَحْجِير. The moon was surrounded by a —, حَجَّرَ ٱلْقَمَرُ تَحْجِيرًا.

Halser, *n.* *See* Hawser, *n.*

Halt, *v.i.* To limp, ظَلَعَ ـ خَمَعَ ـ عَرِجَ ـ غَمَزَ فِي ـ. To stop, وَقَفَ *aor.* يَقِفُ ـ تَوَقَّفَ ـ حَطَّ ² ـ حَجَلَ ـ مَشَّيَهُ. To hesitate, تَضَرَّبَ ـ تَمَخْطَرَ; in speech, تَطَرَّمَ ـ أُعْتُقِلَ لِسَانُهُ. *See also to* Falter, *v.i.*

Halt, *v t.* To stop another, وَقَّفَ ـ أَوْقَفَ.

Halt, *a.* Limping, lame, ظَالِع ـ خَامِع ـ أَعْرَجُ *fem.* عَرْجَاءُ *pl.* عُرْج ـ سَقَط. A — affair, أَمْرٌ عَرِيجٌ.

Halt, *n.* A limping, ظَلْع ـ خُمَاع ـ عَرَجَان ـ عُرُوج. A stop in marching, حَطّ ـ تَوَقُّف ـ نُزُول. A place of halting, مَحَطّ ـ مَحَطَّة ـ مَنْزِل *pl.* مَنَازِل.

Halter, *n.* One who hesitates, مُتَضَرِّب ـ مُتَرَدِّد. The — of a horse, رَسَن *pl.* أَرْسَان ـ مِقْوَد *pl.* مَقَاوِدُ ـ جِنَاب ـ رُسُن. A rope for hanging, خِنَاق.

Halter, *v.t.* To — a horse, رَسَنَ ² ٱلْفَرَسَ ـ. To confine, حَبَسَ ـ.

Halting, *n.* *See* Halt, *n.*

Halting, *a.* *See under* Halter, *n.*

Haltingly, *ad.* Limpingly, بِخُمَاعٍ ـ كَٱلْأَعْرَجِ. With indecision, بِتَضَرُّبٍ ـ بِحُبْسَةٍ.

Halve, *v.t.* نَصَّفَ ـ شَطَّرَ ـ شَطَرَ ². To break into two pieces,

قَصَّدَ. To be halved, تَنَصَّفَ; to be broken in halves, تَقَصَّدَ — إِنْقَصَدَ. To go halves with, شَاطَرَ — نَاصَفَ. To cry halves, إِدَّعَى بِٱلنِّصْفِ.

Halyards, *n.* *See* Halliards, *n.*

Ham, *n.* The — of the leg, مَأْبِض — لُبَّةُ ٱلسَّاقِ. The thigh of a hog salted, فَخِذُ خِنْزِيرٍ مُمَلَّحٍ.

Hames, *n.* The — of a horse's collar, سِمْط *pl.* سُمُوط.

Hamlet, *n.* قَسَّة — ضُيَيْعَة — قُرَيَّة.

Hammer, *n.* A small —, مِطْرَقَة *vulg.* شاكوش. A — for breaking stones, صَوْقَر — مِقْرَاع — مِعْوَل *pl.* مَعَاوِل. A smith's —, مِرْزَبَّة *pl.* مَرَازِب — بِسْطَاب. A wooden —, مِيتَدَة. The — of a musket, مَقْلَب; the — and cock, زِنَاد. To come to the —, to auction, وَقَعَ بِٱلْمَزَادِ *aor.* يَقَعُ. To bring to the —, to sell by auction, حَطَّ بِٱلْمَزَادِ ².

Hammer, *v.t.* To drive in, as a nail, سَمَّرَ. To strike, as with a —, طَرَقَ ² — دَقَّ ². To beat out, مَطَلَ ². To — at, strive after, لَجَّ فِي ² — كَدَّ فِي ². To — at one, أَلَثَّ عَلَى — لَجَّ ² — إِنْتَرَمَ عَلَى.

Hammer-cloth, *n.* مِفْرَشَةُ مَقْعَدِ سَائِقِ ٱلْكَرُّوسَةِ.

Hammering, *n.* The noise of the hammer, طَرْق — دَقّ. Endeavour, كَدّ — جَهْد. Importunity, تَصْدِيع — إِقْتِرَاح — لَجَاجَة.

Hammock, *n.* أُرْجُوحَة — جُوجْخَانَة — بَرَانْدَة.

Hamper, *n.* A basket, زَنْبِيل *pl.* زَنَابِيل — جَوْلَق *pl.* جَوَالِق — وَهْق — سَلَّة *pl.* سِلَال. A hindrance, عُرْضَة — جُونَة — ثُنَّة عَائِق.

Hamper, *v.t.* To hinder, حَجَزَ ² — عَارَضَ — أَمْسَكَ. To perplex, شَبَّكَ — قَلَّقَ — لَبَّكَ — حَيَّرَ. To be hampered, hindered, إِشْتَبَكَ — إِحْتَجَبَ — إِنْحَجَزَ.

Hamstring, *n.* عُرْقُوب — عَصَبُ ٱلْفَخِذِ.

Hamstring, *v.t.* أَعْرَجَ — عَرْقَبَ — عَقَرَ ² — عَقَّرَ. Hamstrung, مَعْقُور — عَقِير.

Hand, *n.* Of a human being, كَفّ *pl.* أَكُفّ *and* كُفُوف — يَد *dual* يَدَانِ *pl.* أَيْدٍ *and* أَيَادٍ. The foreleg, as of a horse, *etc.*, يَد *pl.* أَيَادٍ. The measure, شِبْر *pl.* أَشْبَار. A side, quarter, طَرَف *pl.* أَطْرَاف — جَانِب *pl.* جَوَانِب — جَنْب *pl.* جُنُوب — صَوْب — نَاحِيَة *pl.* نَوَاحٍ. Intervention, agency, يَد — تَدَاخُل — مُدَاخَلَة. Power, قُوَّة — يَد — مُكْنَة. Possession, management, مُلْك — تَصَرُّف — أُسْلُوب. Manner, نَمَط — نَوْع — طَرِيقَة. Authority, سُلْطَة — سَطْوَة — رِئَاسَة. Labour, performance, شُغْل — صَنْعَة — عَمَل. An agent, workman, صَانِع *pl.* صُنَّاع — فَاعِل *pl.* فَعَلَة — شَاغِل *pl.* شَوَاغِل. A mode of writing, كِتَابَة — خَطّ *pl.* خُطُوط. An individual, شَخْص *pl.* أَشْخَاص — نَفَر *pl.* أَنْفَار. A —, as of a watch, عَقْرَب *pl.* عَقَارِب. A — at cards, دَسْتَة. A good — at, أُسْتَاذ — مَاهِرٌ فِي. He is my right —, هُوَ ثِقَتِي — هُوَ سَنَدِي. Bear a hand! be quick! ٱلسَّرْعَ ٱلسَّرْعَ — عَلَى البَعِيدُ — إِلَيْكَ عَنِّي. Hands off! شَيّ. By his —, means, بِوَاسِطَتِهِ — يَدِهِ. I left a copy of it in his hands, تَرَكْتُ صُورَةً مِنْهُ لَدَيْهِ. He has tied the hands of the Government, so that it cannot act, حَجَزَ ٱلدَّوْلَةَ عَنِ ٱلْعَمَلِ.

At hand, ready, حَاضِر — عَتِيد — قَرِيب.

Clean hands, innocence, عِصْمَة — بَرَاءَة.

Hour-hand, of a watch, عَقْرَبُ ٱلسَّاعَةِ.

Minute-hand, of a watch, عَقْرَبُ ٱلدَّقَائِقِ.

Second's-hand, of a watch, عَقْرَبُ ثَوَانِي ٱلسَّاعَةِ.

In hand, of work, مَشْرُوعٌ فِيهِ — فِي ٱلْيَدِ. Submissive, مُطِيع — مُنْقَاد.

Near or nigh at hand, دُونَ — قَرِيب.

Off hand, at once, حَالاً — بِٱلْمَرَّةِ. Careless, ذَاهِل — مُغَفَّل. Haughty, شَامِخ — مُتَكَبِّر.

On hand, going forward, in progress, تَحْتَ ٱلْإِدَارَةِ — فِي ٱلْمُطَالَعَةِ. Unsold, غَيْرُ مَبِيعٍ مِنَ ٱلْكَسَادِ. In stock, مَوْجُود — فِي ٱلْمَخْزَنِ.

Out of hand, finished, تَمَّ — خَلَصَ — إِنْقَضَى.

Large hand, in writing, خَطّ ثُلُث — خَطّ ثُلُثِيّ.

Round hand, in writing, خَطّ نَسْخ.

Running hand, in writing, خَطّ رِقَاع — رُقْعَة.

Short-hand, stenography, خَطّ إِشَارَةٍ.

Text hand, in writing, خَطّ ثُلُث رَفِيع.

Second-hand, used, مُسْتَعْمَل. Quoted from, نَقْلاً عَنْ.

The left hand, اليُسْرَى — اليَدُ ٱلْيُسْرَى.

The right hand, اليُمْنَى — اليَدُ ٱلْيُمْنَى.

With a strong hand, forcibly, عَنْفًا — قَهْرًا — جَبْرًا.

A hand-to-hand fight, حَرْبُ كِفَاحٍ.

A note of hand, تَحْوِيل — تَمَسُّك.

A shake of the hand, مُصَافَحَة.

Clapping of hands, صَفْق — تَصْفِيق.

From hand to mouth, in straitened circumstances, فِي ضِيقَةٍ — بِتَقَشُّفٍ — قَشْفًا.

Hands and arms, of a woman, or those parts of her which are exposed, المُجَرَّد — مَعَارِي. How beautiful are the hands and arms of this woman! مَا أَحْسَنَ مَعَارِيَ هٰذِهِ ٱلْمَرْأَةِ. A young woman having fine hands and arms, جارِيَةٌ حَسَنَةُ ٱلْعَوْرَةِ (ٱلْمُجَرَّدِ or ٱلْمُعَرَّاةِ or).

Hand in hand, بِٱتِّفاقٍ — اِتِّفاقًا . Unitedly, يَدٌ لِيَدٍ — يَدٌ فِي يَدٍ.

Hand over hand, quickly, بِٱلْعَجَلِ — بِسُرْعَةٍ — بِخِفَّةٍ.

On all hands, مِنْ كُلِّ جانِبٍ — مِنْ كُلِّ طَرَفٍ.

On the one hand, عَلَى ٱلْجانِبِ ٱلْواحِدِ — مِنْ طَرَفٍ واحِدٍ.

On the other hand, عَلَى — وَما عَدا ذٰلِكَ فَ... — هٰذا وَأَنْ ٱلْجانِبِ ٱلْآخَرِ.

Sleight of hand, شَعْوَذَة (vulg. شَعْبَذَة).

Under one's hand and seal, بِإمْضائِهِ وَخَتْمِهِ.

Under one's hand, signature, بِتَوْقِيعِهِ — بِإمْضائِهِ.

To be a good hand at, كانَ ماهِرًا فِي — مَهَرَ فِي — اِتَّقَنَ فِي — كانَ أُسْتاذًا فِي.

To be hand and glove with, آلَفَ: They are hand and glove with one another, هُمْ سَدًى وَلُحْمَةٌ.

To be in good hands, كانَ فِي حِفْظٍ: He is in good hands, they take care of him, يَعْتَنُونَ بِهِ.

To be off one's hands, خَلَصَ مِن — تَفَصَّى مِن.

To bind the hands behind the back, كَتَفَ; the bandage used therein, كِتاف. To bind one hand and foot, to oblige to, أَلْزَمَ-ب.

To bring up by hand, رَبَّى-بِدُونِ مُرْضِعَةٍ.

To carry things with a high hand, تَفَرْعَنَ — تَجَبَّرَ.

To change hands, أَحالَ — تَحَوَّلَ.

To come to hand, وَرَدَ إِلَى — يَفِدُ aor. وَفَدَ إِلَى — يَصِلُ aor. وَصَلَ aor. يَرِدُ.

To drive four in hand, ساقَ ٱلْعَرَبانَةَ بِزَوْجَيْنِ مِنَ ٱلْخَيْلِ.

To get the upper hand of, غَلَبَ عَلَى — اِسْتَعْلَى (عَلا or) عَلَى — فازَ-ب. To cause another to get the better hand of, أَفازَ-ب — غَلَّبَ-عَلَى.

To give the hand, to give in marriage, زَوَّجَ-ب — زَوَّجَ. To give one's hand to, to marry, تَزَوَّجَ ب.

To hang on hand, of goods, ما يُباعُ.

To have a hand in a matter, تَداخَلَ — تَدَخَّلَ.

To have one's hand in, at work, هُوَ عامِلٌ — هُوَ مَشْغُولٌ.

To have the upper hand, فازَ — رَأَسَ — سَلَطَ — عَلا.

To hold with a firm hand, تَشَدَّدَ عَلَى — أَمْسَكَ ب — ضَبَطَ — تَشَبَّثَ ب.

To kiss a person's hand, قَبَّلَ يَدَهُ.

To kiss the hand to, قَبَّلَ يَدَهُ تَسْلِيمًا عَلَى.

To lay hands upon, to seize, قَبَضَ ب — مَسَكَ ب — ضَبَطَ — بَطَشَ ب. To lay hands upon, to ordain, قَلَّدَ — رَسَمَ.

To lay the hand on, to find, لَاقَى — لَقِيَ — يَجِدُ aor. وَجَدَ.

To lay violent hands upon, أَعْنَفَ — اِغْتَصَبَ — اِخْتَلَسَ.

To lay violent hands on one's self, قَتَلَ نَفْسَهُ.

To lend one a hand, ساعَفَ — ساعَدَ — عاوَنَ.

To lift up the hand against, عاصَى — رَفَعَ ٱلْيَدَ عَلَى — عَصَى عَلَى.

To live from hand to mouth, تَقَشَّفَ — ضاقَ عَلَيْهِ مَعاشُهُ — قَشِفَ. A hand-to-mouth life, عِيشَةٌ ضَيِّقٌ — ضَيِّقَةٌ — تَقَشُّفٌ.

To put the last hand to, finish, أَتَمَّ — كَمَّلَ.

To receive a benefit at one's hands, إِسْتَكْرَمَ مِن — إِسْتَفادَ مِن.

To send a letter by hand, أَنْفَذَ مَكْتُوبًا عَلَى يَدِ شَخْصٍ.

To set or put one's hand to paper, to sign, وَقَّعَ عَلَى — عَلَّمَ ب — أَمْضَى.

To shake hands with, صافَحَ-بِيَدِهِ: They shook hands, of many, تَصافَحُوا.

To stretch out the hand, as in begging, إِسْتَكَفَّ.

To stretch out the hand to, مَدَّ يَدَهُ إِلَى — يَسْدُو aor. سَدا إِلَى-بِيَدِهِ.

To strike hands, in token of a bargain, صَفَقَ يَدَهُ بِٱلْبَيْعَةِ — صَفَقَ عَلَى يَدِهِ.

To take a thing in hand, تَشَمَّرَ لِ — شَرَعَ فِي — أَلْقَى يَدَهُ فِي.

To take one by the hand, to assist, ساعَدَ — دَرَّجَ — عاوَنَ.

To take with the hand, تَعاطَى — تَناوَلَ — اِسْتَلَمَ-بِٱلْيَدِ.

To try one's hand, جَرَّبَ — يَسْعَى aor. سَعَى إِلَى.

To wash one's hands of, رَفَعَ يَدَهُ مِن.

To write a good hand, كانَ خَطّاطًا — كَتَبَ خَطًّا حَسِينًا.

Hand, *v.t.* To deliver to, سَلَّمَ-إِلَى — أَسْلَمَ-إِلَى — قَبَّضَ; to give from — to —, ناوَلَ-لِ — قَبَّضَ.

Hand-ball, *n.* طابَة *pl.* طابات — كُرَة *pl.* كُرًى *and* كُرات.

Hand-barrow, *n.* نَقّالَة.

Hand-book, *n.* A manual, دُسْتُور *pl.* دَساتِيرُ — كِتابٌ مُخْتَصَرٌ — كِتابٌ مُجْمَلٌ. *See also* Guide, *n.*

Hand-breadth, *n.* شِبْر *pl.* أَشْبار — قُبْضَة *pl.* قُبْضات.

Handcraft, *n.* } Handicraft, } حِرْفَة *pl.* حِرَف — سِكافَة — صِناعَة *pl.* صَنائِعُ — صَنْعَة.

Handcraftsman, *n.* مُحْتَرِف — إِسْكاف *pl.* أَساكِفَة — صاحِبُ حِرْفَةٍ — صانِع *pl.* صُنّاع.

Hand-cuff, *n.* جامِعَة — غُلّ *pl.* أَغْلال — قَيْدٌ لِلْيَدَيْنِ.

Hand-cuff, *v.t.* قَيَّدَ يَدَيْهِ.

Handed, *a.* Having two hands, ذُو يَدَيْنِ.

Empty-handed, فَارِغُ ٱلْيَدِ – صِفْرُ ٱلْيَدَيْنِ.

Double-handed, / Two-handed, } Using both hands alike, أَعْسَرُ يَسَرٌ.

Left-handed, أَعْفَكُ – أَعْسَرُ *fem.* عَسْرَآءُ. To be —, عَسِرَ.

One-handed, having lost one hand, أَكْتَعُ – مَشْلُول *fem.* كَتْعَآءُ *pl.* كُتْع – عَاجِزٌ عَنْ يَدٍ – عَاجِزٌ عَنْ ذِرَاعٍ.

Open-handed, liberal, سَخِيٌّ – جَوَاد – بَسِيطُ ٱلْيَدَيْنِ *fem.* سَخِيَّة; *pl. m.* أَسْخِيَآءُ *pl. fem.* سَخِيَّات

Right-handed, أَيْمَنُ.

Single-handed, by one's self, بِمَعْزَلٍ عَنْ غَيْرِهِ – لِوَحْدِهِ – ٱنْفِرَادًا.

Handful, *n.* عَامَة *pl.* عَام – جُمْعَة – قُمْزَة *pl.* قُمَز – كَفّ – قُبْضَة – كَمْشَة – حَفْنَة *pl.* حَفَنَات – كُفُوف *pl.* A small number, as of men, شِرْذِمَة *pl.* شَرَاذِيمُ – بَعْض – قَلَائِل. To take up a —, كَمَشَ.

Handicap, *n.* نَوْعٌ مِنَ ٱلْمُسَابَقَةِ.

Hand-gallop, *n.* رَمْحٌ (*or*) رَكْضٌ خَفِيفٌ.

Handily, *ad.* Dexterously, بِحِذْقٍ – بِإِتْقَانٍ. Conveniently, مُوَافَقَةً – وَفْقًا – عَلَى لِيَاقَةٍ.

Handiness, *n.* Dexterity in performance, حِذْق – إِتْقَان – فَنّ – مَهَارَة. Utility, طَائِل – عَائِدَة.

Handiwork, *n.* / Handy-work, } عَمَل – شُغْل – صَنْعَة.

Handkerchief, *n.* مَحْرَمَة *pl.* مَحَارِمُ – مِنْدِيل *pl.* مَنَادِيلُ. A — used by female mourners, مِعْوَز – عَذَبَة.

Handle, *v.t.* To touch, feel, جَسَّ – مَسَّ – لَمَسَ. To manage, دَبَّرَ – بَاشَرَ – اِسْتَعْمَلَ. To lay hold of, مَسَكَ – مَسَكَ بِ. To — a subject, ذَكَرَ – أَوْضَحَ – بَيَّنَ – تَكَلَّمَ فِي – بَحَثَ عَنْ. To treat, of a person, عَامَلَ – صَنَعَ بِ. To — a pen, خَطَّ. To — a harp, ضَرَبَ ٱلْعُودَ. To — a sword, سَايَفَ. To — an oar, مَسَكَ ٱلْمِجْدَافَ.

Handle, *n.* A haft, عُرْوَة – مِقْبَض – قَبْضَة – فِعَال *pl.* فُعُل – نِصَاب *pl.* نُصُب – مِمْسَكَة – يَد. A — to turn with, مِلْوًى. An ear-shaped —, أُذُن *pl.* آذَان. The — of a cup or basket, عُرْوَة *pl.* عُرًى. An instrument for a purpose, آلَة – وَسِيلَة – وَاسِطَة. A — to a name, لَقَب – كُنْيَة; as of a decoration, اِسْمُ شَرَفٍ – لَقَبُ شَرَفٍ. To fix a — to, أَقْبَضَ. *See also* Haft, *n.*

Handling, *n.* The act of touching, لَمْس – مَسّ. Management, إِدَارَة – تَدْبِير – مُبَاشَرَة. Treatment of a subject, ذِكْر – بَحْث – مُبَاحَثَة. Skill, صِنَاعَة.

Handmaid, *n.* أَمَة *pl.* آمٍ (properly a slave, but as a — in relation to God) – جَارِيَة *pl.* جَوَارٍ – خَادِمَة *pl.* خَادِمَات. A little —, أُمَيَّة.

Handmill, *n.* رَحًى *pl.* أَرْحَآءُ – طَاحُون *pl.* طَوَاحِينُ – جَارُوشَة.

Handrail, *n.* دَرَابْزِين.

Hand-saw, *n.* مِنْشَارٌ صَغِيرٌ – مِنْشَارٌ بِقَبْضَةٍ.

Handsome, *a.* Becoming, لَائِق – قَرِيف. Pretty, حَسِين – نَزِق – صَبِيح – كَيِّس. Elegant, سُبْحَانٌ – مَلِيح – جَمِيل – ظَرِيف – لَطِيف. Ample, وَاسِع – عَظِيم – كَبِير. Liberal, كَرِيم – مِكْرَام. A — action, مَكْرُمَة *pl.* مَكَارِمُ. A — fortune, وُجْد – جَدّ – نِعْمَة – حَظّ. Having a — fortune, صَاحِبُ جَدٍّ.

Handsomely, *ad.* Gracefully, بِظَرَافَةٍ – حَسَنًا – صَبَاحَةً – بِلَطَافَةٍ. Liberally, بِجُودٍ – بِكَرَمٍ – بِسَخَاوَةٍ.

Handsomeness, *n.* Gracefulness, جَمَال – طَلَاوَة – صَبَاحَة – ظَرَافَة – حُسْن. Liberality, كَرَم – جُود – سَخَاوَة.

Handspike, *n.* عَتَلَة *coll.* عَتَل – هِرَاوَة *pl.* هَرَاوَى.

Hand-vice, *n.* كَلْبَتَان.

Handwriting, *n.* قَلَم *pl.* أَقْلَام – خَطّ *pl.* خُطُوط.

Handy, *a.* Dexterous with the hand, صَنَعُ ٱلْيَدَيْنِ – أَرِيب – حَاذِق – مَفَنّ – حَذِق – مَاهِر. Easy to be got at, at hand, يَقْرُبُ تَنَاوُلُهُ – عَتِد – عَتِيد. To be — at, مَهَرَتْ يَدُهُ فِي *or* بِ. Convenient, لَائِق – مُنَاسِب – مُوَافِق – طَائِل. To be —, in doing, أَتْقَنَ فِي – أَرِبَ بِ. To be —, useful, for, صَلَحَ لِ. A — woman, اِمْرَأَةٌ صَنِيعَةُ ٱلْيَدَيْنِ. A — thing, مَصْلَحَة *pl.* مَصَالِحُ.

Hang, *v.t.* To suspend, سَمَّطَ – نَاطَ بِ – سَمَطَ – عَلَّقَ بِ *or* عَلَى. To — by the neck, شَنَقَ. To —, as a room, with, زَيَّنَ بِ – فَرَشَ بِ. To — something round the neck of one, طَوَّقَ بِ – قَلَّدَ بِ. To — out, as clothes to dry, نَشَرَ – شَرَّى. To — up, as on a cross, صَلَبَ – صَلَّبَ. To — meat out to dry, عَرَّصَ ٱللَّحْمَ.

Hang, *v.i.* To be suspended, تَعَلَّقَ – تَسَمَّطَ – اِنْتَاطَ. To bend forward, اِنْحَنَى – مَالَ.

To hang or hover about, to frequent, تَرَدَّدَ – لَازَمَ – تَعَهَّدَ.

To hang back, as from anything, اِجْتَنَبَ – تَجَنَّبَ – تَرَاخَى عَنْ.

To hang fire, كَذَّبَ.

To hang in doubt, to hesitate, تَضَرَّبَ – تَرَدَّدَ – تَمَخْطَرَ.

To hang loose, to dangle, تَدَلَّى – تَرَجَّحَ – اِسْتَرْخَى.

To hang on to, to adhere to, لَازَمَ ـ تَعَلَّقَ بِ: The snake hung on to his hand, تَعَلَّقَتِ ٱلْحَيَّةُ بِيَدِهِ.

To hang over, to be deferred, تَأَخَّرَ ـ إِسْتَأْخَرَ. To overlook, overtop, أَشْرَفَ عَلَى. To be absorbed in, إِسْتَغْرَقَ فِي ـ كَلِفَ بِ.

To hang together, of many persons, تَلَاتَبُوا ـ تَحَزَّبُوا.

To hang upon a person's words, إِسْتَحَبَّ ـ أَصَاخَ لِ ـ أَنْصَتَ إِلَى كَلَامَهُ (أَحَبَّ or).

Hanger, *n.* (*Properly* Khánjar), a short sword, خَنْجَر *pl.* خَنَاجِرُ.

Hang-dog, *n.* فُجَّار ـ خَبِيث.

Hanger-on, *n.* A follower, تَابِع *pl.* تُبَّاع ـ مِنْ أَلْزَامِ فُلَانٍ. A parasite, طُفَيْلِيٌّ ـ لَقْلُوق *pl.* لَقَالِيقُ. A — of women, زِيرُ نِسَاءٍ ـ عَلُّ ٱلنِّسَاءِ *pl.* أَعْلَال.

Hangings, *n.* بِسَاط ـ سَجِف ـ سِدَافَة.

Hangman, *n.* شَنَّاق ـ جَلَّاد ـ مَشَاعِلِيٌّ.

Hangnail, *n.* نَسْر *pl.* نُسُور.

Hank, *n.* As of thread, ثُلَّة *pl.* ثُلَل. The ring, as of a sail, حَلْقَة.

Hanker, *v.t.* To — after, to long for, تَنَافَسَ فِي ـ هَوِيَ ـ إِشْتَهَى ـ إِشْتَاقَ إِلَى ـ إِشْتَاقَ. *See also to* Long for, *under to* Long, *v.i.*

Hankering, *n.* تَنَافُس فِي ـ هَوِيَّة ـ شَوْق ـ إِشْتِيَاق.

Hankeringly, *ad.* إِشْتِيَاقًا ـ بِهَوِيَّةٍ ـ بِٱشْتِيَاقٍ.

Hap, *n.* / Haphazard, } عَارِض ـ أَعْرَاض *pl.* عَرَض ـ أَحْدَاث *pl.* حَدَث *pl.* عَوَارِضُ. *See also* Chance, *n.*

Haphazard, *a.* عَرَضِيٌّ. A — frontier, حَدٌّ عَرَض ـ حَدٌّ عَرَضٍ.

Hapless, *a.* عَدِيمُ ٱلْبَخْتِ ـ مَشْؤُوم ـ مَنْحُوس ـ نَحِس.

Haply, *ad.* يُمْكِنُ ـ عَسَى ـ لَعَلَّ ـ رُبَّمَا.

Happen, *v.i.* To come to pass, جَاءَ ـ حَدَثَ ـ صَدَرَ *aor.* يَجِيءُ ـ حَصَلَ ـ إِعْتَرَضَ ـ إِتَّفَقَ ـ جَرَى ـ صَارَ. To — to, إِعْتَرَضَ لِ ـ عَرَضَ لِ ـ جَرَى عَلَى ـ يَقَعُ *aor.* وَقَعَ لِ. To — to one unexpectedly, to take him by surprise, بَادَهَ ـ بَدَهَ. To — to, as a misfortune, أُصِيبَ بِ ـ نَزَلَ بِ ـ إِعْتَرَى. To — to suddenly, إِسْتَعَرَّ. To — to afterwards, رَدِفَ: The event happened to them afterwards, رَدِفَهُمُ ٱلْأَمْرُ. About to —, مُزْمِع ـ قَرِيبُ ٱلْوُقُوعِ. Should it — that …, إِذَا فَرَضَ أَنْ. Tell you us what will —, or what things will —, أَعْلِمُونَا ٱلْمُسْتَقْبَلَاتِ. It happened that I was there, إِتَّفَقَ أَنِّي كُنْتُ هُنَاكَ.

Happily, *ad.* By good fortune, مِنْ ـ مِنْ يُمْنٍ ـ مِنْ بَخْتٍ. Cleverly, بِفِطْنَةٍ ـ بِحِذْقٍ ـ بِٱتْقَانٍ ـ بِخِفَّةٍ ـ سَعْدٍ. In a state of happiness, فِي غِبْطَةٍ ـ فِي حَظٍّ. To the point, بِإِصَابَةٍ ـ سَدَدًا ـ سَدَادًا.

Happiness, *n.* State of enjoyment, نَعِيم ـ حَظٌّ ـ بَهْجَة ـ غِبْطَة ـ هَنَاءَة ـ سُعُودَة ـ سُعُود ـ حُظْوَة ـ يُمْن ـ سَعَادَة. Good fortune, تَوْفِيق ـ نِعْمَة ـ نُعْم ـ خَيْرُ نَصِيبٍ ـ طَالِع ـ بَخْت. Prosperity, Eternal —, سَعَادَةٌ أَبَدِيَّةٌ ـ نَعِيم ـ طُوبَى.

Happy, *a.* In a state of enjoyment, سَعِيد ـ مَسْعُود ـ مَغْبُوط ـ مُفْلِح ـ فَالِح ـ مَحْبُور ـ حَظِيظ ـ طَيِّبُ ٱلنَّفْسِ. Successful, Felicitous, clever, حَذِق ـ لَطِيف ـ مَاهِر ـ نَاجِح. To the point, سَدِيد. Verily he has a — faculty of hitting the right thing, إِنَّهُ لَذُو سَدَادٍ. To be —, طَابَتْ ـ إِبْتَهَجَ ـ إِغْتَبَطَ ـ طَرِبَ ـ حَبِرَ ـ سَعِدَ ـ نَفْسُهُ. To make —, حَبَّرَ ـ أَسْعَدَ ـ أَطْرَبَ. May you be —, طُوبَاكَ ـ طُوبَى لَكَ. I am —, تَقَرُّ عَيْنِي. A — or jolly set, حَابُور.

Harangue, *n.* خُطْبَة ـ مَقَالَة *pl.* خُطَب.

Harangue, *v.i.* خَطَبَ ـ أَلْقَى مَقَالَةً.

Harangue, *v t.* خَاطَبَ ـ أَلْقَى مَقَالَةً لِ.

Haranguer, *n.* مُلْقِي مَقَالَةٍ ـ خَطِيب ـ خَاطِب.

Harass, *v.t.* To fatigue, أَعْيَا ـ أَكَدَّ ـ عَسَفَ ـ أَتْعَبَ ـ أَزْعَجَ ـ نَهَكَ ـ أَجْحَفَ بِ ـ أَكَلَّ. To vex, annoy, أَضْجَرَ ـ أَكْرَبَ ـ ضَارَّ ـ آذَى. To — with attacks, عَاكَسَ ـ تَحَارَشَ عَلَى. To be harassed, fatigued, تَعِبَ ـ تَعْيَا ـ أَعْيَا. To be harassed, vexed, تَضَجَّرَ ـ إِكْتَرَبَ ـ إِنْزَعَجَ; as by attacks, تَحَرَّشَ بِ.

Harassing, *n.* عِكَاس وَمِكَاس.

Harassing, *a.* Vexatious, شَاقٌّ ـ مُضْجِر ـ فَاجِع.

Harbinger, *n.* مُبَشِّر ـ بَشِير ـ مُخَبِّر.

Harbour, *n.* A haven for ships, مَرْسًى ـ مِينَا *pl.* مِيَن *pl.* بَنَادِرُ *pl.* بَنْدَر ـ مَرْفَأ ـ مُكَلَّأ ـ مَرَاسٍ. A place of safety, refuge, مَنْجَاة ـ مَلَاذ ـ مَلْجَأ. Inspectorship of harbours and lighthouses, رِئَاسَةُ ٱلْمَرَاسِي وَٱلْمَنَارَاتِ.

Harbour, *v.t.* To lodge, أَنْزَلَ ـ آوَى. To — in the mind, كَتَمَ ـ أَسَرَّ ـ أَضْمَرَ. They are always harbouring designs to destroy him, يَتَلَبَّسُونَ بِٱلْفِتَنِ لِخَرَابِهِ.

Harbourer, *n.* One who receives and protects, خَفِير ـ مَأْوٍ ـ حَامٍ.

Harbourless, *a.* مِنْ غَيْرِ مِينَا.

Harbour-master, *n.* رَئِيسُ ٱلْمِينَا ـ شَهْبَنْدَر.

Hard, *a.* Firm, solid, صُلْب ـ مَتِين ـ صَمِيم ـ سَلِيط ـ جَدْل ـ صَلِيد ـ صَلِيب. Difficult, صَعْب ـ عَسِير ـ عَسِر ـ مُشْكِل; of a journey, عَطُوف. Distressing, شاقّ ـ ناصِب ـ مُتْعِب ـ مُغِمّ ـ مُحْزِن. Cruel, oppressive, عَسِر ـ شَدِيد ـ عَنِيف ـ قاسٍ ـ قَسِيّ ـ جافٍ ـ ظالِم. Austere, of a life, زاهِد ـ زِهِّيد ـ مُتَقَشِّف. Obstinate, عَنِيد ـ كَنُود ـ خَشِنُ ٱلْجانِبِ. Callous, of the hands, جاسٍ. Dry, ناشِف ـ يابِس. Not plentiful, يَسِير ـ قَلِيل. Severe, of the weather, شَدِيد ـ قاسٍ. Avaricious, بَخِيل ـ لَئِيم *pl.* لِئام. Hard, of a letter, مُفَخَّم. Hard to deal with, مَرِيد ـ شَكِس ـ عَنِيد. Hard gold, ذَهَبٌ كَزٌّ. Hard water, ماءٌ ثَقِيل. Hard, of stone, صَلْد ـ صَلُود ـ صَلِيد. A — matter, مُشْكِلَة ـ أَمْرٌ عَسِرٌ. A —, dissolute, life, غَمْط ـ فِسْق ـ عَيْشٌ مُسْرِف. A —, wretched, life, قَشَف ـ عَيْشٌ مُتَقَشِّف. To be or become —, firm, solid, تَصَلَّبَ ـ صَلُبَ [2]. To be —, difficult, distressing, صَعُبَ [2] ـ إِسْتَعْسَرَ ـ تَعَسَّرَ ـ عَسُرَ [2]. To be — upon one, شاقَّ ـ شَدَّ عَلَى [2] ـ عَسَّرَ عَلَى. To lead a —, poor, life, تَقَشَّفَ. To make —, difficult, صَعَّبَ ـ عَسَّرَ. Whosoever is — upon others, God will be — upon him, مَنْ شَدَّدَ شَدَّدَ ٱللّٰهُ عَلَيْهِ. The times were —, عَسُرَ ٱلزَّمانُ [2].

Hard, *ad.* Near, قَرِيب. Laboriously, شَدِيدًا ـ بِكَدٍّ. Fast, بِسُرْعَةٍ ـ بِٱلْعَجَلِ. Nearly, تَقْرِيبًا. Hard by, قَرِيبٌ مِنْ ـ بِصَدَدِ. To rain —, تَصَوَّبَ ٱلْمَطَرُ ـ تَمَطَّرَ صَبُوبًا. To drink —, أَفْرَطَ فِي ٱلشُّرْبِ. To work —, إِشْتَغَلَ بِشِدَّةٍ. To try —, بَذَلَ [2] جُهْدَهُ. They rowed — to bring the boat to land, جَذَفُوا بِشِدَّةٍ لِيُرْجِعُوا ٱلسَّفِينَةَ إِلَى ٱلْبَرّ. His house was — by the mosque, كانَ بَيْتُهُ بِصَدَدِ ٱلْجامِعِ. The treasury is very — up, ٱلْخَزِينَةُ فِي عُسْرٍ عَظِيمٍ.

Hard-drinking, *n.* سُكْر.

Hard-earned, *a.* مَحْبُوشٌ بِكَدٍّ.

Harden, *v.t.* To make hard, صَلَّبَ. To make firm, ثَبَّتَ ـ مَكَّنَ ـ أَرْصَنَ; as rain the ground, *etc.*, عَزَّزَ. To —, of the heart, شَدَّدَ [2]: Harden thou their hearts, أُشْدُدْ عَلَى قُلُوبِهِمْ. To make impudent, سَفَّهَ ـ جَعَلَهُ سَفِيهًا. To make stubborn, شَرَّدَ. Anything which hardens the heart, مَقْساة: Sin hardens the heart, ٱلذَّنْبُ مَقْساةٌ لِلْقَلْبِ. The rain has hardened the ground, عَزَّزَ ٱلْمَطَرُ ٱلْأَرْضَ.

Harden, *v.i.* To be or become hard, صَلُبَ [2] ـ صَلُبَ ـ أَصْلَدَ. To become hard, as of bricks, *etc.*, إِسْتَحْجَرَ. To become firm, رَصُنَ [2] ـ تَمَكَّنَ ـ ثَبَتَ [2] ـ إِسْتَقَرَّ. To — one's self, to behave with firmness, تَصَلَّبَ ـ تَشَدَّدَ ـ تَأَتَّبَ ـ تَشَجَّعَ. To — one's own heart, أَقْسَى قَلْبَهُ; as against one, غَلَّظَ قَلْبَهُ عَلَى. To harden, to become dry, جَفَّ [2] ـ نَشَفَ [2] ـ تَنَشَّفَ.

Hard-favoured, Hard-featured, *a.* Hard-visaged, } كَرِيهُ ٱلْمَنْظَرِ ـ بَشِع ـ شَيِّهٌ ـ أَشْوَهُ *fem.* شَوْهاءُ *pl.* شُوْه ـ مُشَوَّهٌ ـ بَشِعُ ٱلْوَجْهِ.

Hard-fisted, *a.* خَسِيس ـ بَخِيل.

Hard-handed, *a.* Having hard hands, جاسِئُ ٱلْيَدَيْنِ.

Hard-hearted, *a.* عَسُوف ـ قاسٍ ـ قاسِي ٱلْقَلْبِ.

Hard-heartedly, *ad.* بِقَساوَةٍ ـ بِعَنْفٍ.

Hard-heartedness, *n.* عَنْف ـ قَساءٌ ـ قَساوَة ـ جَفاء.

Hardihood, *n.* Bravery, عارِضَة ـ عارِض ـ بَسالَة ـ شَجاعَة ـ جَسارَة ـ جَراءَة ـ نَجْدَة ـ إِقْدام ـ تَشَجُّع. Impudence, مُجازَفَة ـ وَقاحَة ـ سَفاهَة ـ سُوءُ أَدَبٍ.

Hardily, *ad.* Bravely, بِبَسالَةٍ ـ شَجاعَةً ـ بِجَسارَةٍ. Impudently, وَقاحَةً.

Hardiness, *n.* *See* Hardihood, *n.*

Hard-laboured, *a.* Abstruse, مُبْهَم ـ مُشْكِل ـ مُعَقَّد ـ غَلِق ـ مُغْلَق.

Hardly, *ad.* With difficulty, كُرْهًا ـ صَعْبًا ـ بِعُسْرٍ ـ بِصُعُوبَةٍ. Harshly, بِعَنْفٍ ـ بِقَساوَةٍ. What one can — believe, ما لا يُكادُ يُصَدِّقُهُ أَحَدٌ. I had — opened the door when he knocked, لَمْ أَفْتَحِ ٱلْبابَ إِلَّا وَقَدْ طَرَقَهُ ـ فَتَحْتُ ٱلْبابَ وَهُوَ يَطْرُقُهُ. How — shall a rich man enter the kingdom of heaven, إِنَّهُ يَعْسُرُ أَنْ يَدْخُلَ غَنِيٌّ إِلَى مَلَكُوتِ ٱلسَّمٰواتِ. He — escaped, نَجا [2] بِطُوفِ نَفْسِهِ. *See also* Scarcely, *ad.*

Hard-mouthed, *a.* جاسِئُ ٱلْفَمِ.

Hardness, *n.* Firm texture, صَلابَة ـ صَلادَة ـ مَتانَة. Toughness, شِدَّة ـ حِدَّة ـ جُسُوء ـ جَسْأَة. Injustice, عَدَمُ إِنْصافٍ ـ جَوْر. Harshness of temper, عَنْف ـ خُشُونَة; of voice, جُشَّة; of visage, عُبُوس. Hardness to be understood, عُسْر ـ صُعُوبَة ـ إِبْهام ـ إِشْكال. Unfeelingness, قَساوَةُ قَلْبٍ ـ عَدَمُ ٱلْحاسِّيَّةِ. Avarice, بُخْل ـ إِمْساك. Scarcity, جَدْب ـ مَحْس ـ شِدَّة. Trials, مَشَقَّات. Boldness, resolve, ثَبات ـ إِقْدام. Callosity, ثَفَن ـ جَسْأَة ـ كُنُوب.

Hards, *n.* Tow, مُشاقَة.

Hardship, *n.* Severe toil, تَعَب ـ عَناء. A trial, difficulty, عَتَبَة ـ مَشَقَّة ـ شَدِيدَة. Oppression, جَوْر ـ بَغْي ـ ظُلْم ـ مَظْلَمَة. He endured hardships, إِحْتَمَلَ ٱلْمَشَقَّاتِ. He considered the matter a —, إِسْتَصْعَبَ ٱلْأَمْرَ. The matter was a — to him, أَصْعَبَ عَلَيْهِ ٱلْأَمْرُ.

Hardware, *n.* خُرْدَة.

Hardwareman, *n.* خُرْدَجِي *pl.* خُرْدَجِيَّة.

Hardy, *a.* Brave, شَجِيع – شَهْم – بَطَل – جَرِئٌ – جَسُور. Robust, شَدِيدٌ – قَوِيٌّ – ضَلِيع – صُلْب – فَصَافِص. Indomitable, صُلْبُ ٱلْمَعَاجِم – عَزِيز – ذُو عَارِضَةٍ – ٱلْعَارِض – بَاقٍ. Enduring, دَائِم – دَيُوم. A — plant, نَبَاتٌ رَاهِنٌ – نَبَاتٌ دَيُومٌ – أُغْرُوَان.

Hard-won, *a.* مُسْتَحْصَل بِٱلْجَهْد.

Hard-working, *a.* شَغَّال – عَمَّال – فَعُول – مُتَبَذِّل.

Harebell, *n.* The flower, ٱلْجَرَسَة.

Hare, *n.* أَرْنَب *fem.* أَرْنَبَة *pl.* أَرَانِب. A young —, خِرْنِق *pl.* خَرَانِق.

Harebrained, *a.* *See* Hairbrained, *a.*

Harelip, *n.* شَرَمُ ٱلشَّفَة.

Harelipped, *a.* أَشْرَمُ ٱلشَّفَة.

Harem, *n.* (*properly* Háram *or* Harîm), حُرُم – حُرَم – حَرَم *pl.* أَحْرَام *pl.* حَرِيم.

Haricot, *n.* يَخْنَة – لُوبِيَةٌ بِلَحْم.

Haricot-bean, *n.* لُوبِيَة. The speckled —, لُوبِيَةٌ رَقْطَاء.

Hark, *v.i.* *See to* Hearken, *v.i.*

Hark! *int.* صَهْ – أَنْصِتْ.

Harlequin, *n.* مُهَرِّج – سُخْرِيٌّ – سُخْرَة.

Harlequinade, *n.* أُضْحُوكَة – مَسْخَرَة.

Harlot, *n.* A prostitute, قَحْبَة – سَوَّاقَة – عَاهِرَة *pl.* قِحَاب.

Harlotry, *n.* فِسْقٌ وَفَسَادٌ – زِنَاء – عِهْر.

Harm, *n.* Enmity, injury, ضَيْم – ضِجَاج – بَأْس – إِجْحَاف – أَذًى – مَضَرَّة – ضَرَر – مُضَاجَّة – مَسَاءَة – ضَامَة. Damage, عَوَار. A defeat, عَيْب. Oppression, ظُلْم – جَوْر. I did not say so to thy —, as disapproving of it, مَا قُلْتُ هٰذَا لِشَرِّكَ. There is no — in it, لَا حَرَجَ فِيهِ – لَا بَأْسَ فِيهِ.

Harm, *v.t.* إِسْتَضَامَ – ـ ضَامَ – آذَى – ـ حَكَرَ – أَجْحَفَ بِ – أَسَاءَ إِلَى-فِي – ضَاجَّ – ضَارَّ – أَضَرَّ – ضَرَّ. To be harmed, تَأَذَّى – إِنْضَرَّ. To be harmed by, إِنْضَرَّ مِن.

Harmattan, *n.* The hot wind so called, حَرُور – بَارِح – سَمُوم.

Harmful, *a.* مُسْتَضِيم – مُضِرٌّ – مُؤْذٍ – ضَارٌّ.

Harmfully, *ad.* بِمَضَرَّةٍ – بِضَرَرٍ – بِمَسَاءَةٍ – إِجْحَافًا.

Harmfulness, *n.* *See* Harm, *n.*

Harmless, *a.* Doing no harm, لَا يَضُرُّ – لَا ضُرَّ (*or* ضَرَّ) فِيهِ. Receiving no harm, لَا ضَيْمَ عَلَيْهِ – سَلِيم – غَيْرُ مُضَام. Tame, وَدِيع – أَنِيس. Simple, سَاذِج – مَسْكِين. *See also* Scatheless, *a.*

Harmlessly, *ad.* Without hurt, بِلَا مُضَاجَّةٍ – بِلَا مَضَرَّةٍ. Innocently, بِبَرَاءَةٍ – بِسَلَامَةِ قَلْب – بِنِيَّةٍ خَالِصَةٍ.

Harmlessness, *n.* عَدَمُ ضَرَرٍ. Innocence, عِصْمَة. Tameness, أُنْس. Simpleness, سَذَاجَة – مَسْكَنَة.

Harmonic, *a.* } Concordant, مُتَنَاسِب – مُتَطَابِق. Musical, sweet, لَذِيذٌ لِلسَّمْع – مُطْرِب – ذُو نَغْمَةٍ.
Harmonical, }

Harmonica, *n.* أَجْرَاسٌ مِنَ ٱلْبِلَّوْر تُقْرَعُ عَلَى نَغْمَةٍ مُطْرِبَةٍ.

Harmonically, *ad.* بِأُلْفَةٍ – بِأَنْغَامٍ – طِبْقَ قَوَاعِدِ ٱلْأَنْغَامِ ٱلْأَصْوَاتِ.

Harmonics, *n.* The science of musical sounds, عِلْمُ قَوَاعِدِ ٱلْأَلْحَانِ. Consonances, أَنْغَام – مَقَامَات.

Harmonious, *a.* Of sound, لَذِيذٌ لِلسَّمْع – مُطْرِب – ذُو نَغْمَةٍ – مَوْزُون – سَوِيٌّ – مُهَنْدَم – مُتَتَابِع – حَسَن. Symmetrical, – مَنْظُوم – حَسِين. In accord, مُتَطَابِق – مُتَّفِق. Well arranged, نَسَق – مُنَسَّق.

Harmoniously, *ad.* Musically, sweetly, بِنَوْعٍ مُطْرِب – بِنَغْم – بِأَلْحَانٍ. In accord, بِمُطَابَقَةٍ – بِٱتِّفَاقٍ. Symmetrically, بِنَسَقٍ – بِنِظَامٍ – حَسَنًا – بِوَزْنٍ – بِهَنْدَامٍ.

Harmonium, *n.* أُرْغُنٌّ (*or* أُرْغُنُونٌ) صَغِيرٌ.

Harmoniousness, *n.* *See* Harmony, *n.*

Harmonist, *n.* Of music, عَالِمٌ بِٱلْأَلْحَانِ. An arranger, مُطَبِّق – مُؤَلِّف – مُوَفِّق.

Harmonize, *v.t.* To make symmetrical, سَوَّى – هَنْدَمَ. To arrange, رَتَّبَ – نَظَّمَ – وَفَّقَ – نَسَّقَ. To cause to agree, طَابَقَ – صَالَحَ – أَصْلَحَ بَيْنَ – أَوْفَقَ-بِ – بَيْنَ.

Harmonize, *v.i.* To be in accord, of many, تَطَابَقُوا – إِتَّفَقُوا; specially of sounds, تَآلَفُوا.

Harmony, *n.* Musical concord, أُلْفَة – طَرَب – نَغْم – إِلْحَان ٱلْأَصْوَاتِ. Agreement, مُطَابَقَة – مُوَافَقَة – إِتِّفَاق. Symmetry, نِظَام – مُوَازَنَة – هَنْدَام. Union, إِتِّحَاد – وِفَاق. Good order, إِنْتِظَام. A — of the Sacred Scriptures, كِتَابُ تَنْسِيقِ ٱلْأَسْفَارِ ٱلْمُقَدَّسَةِ.

Harness, *n.* Arms, armour, زَغَامَة – سِلَاح – آلَة *pl.* آلَات. Furniture, as for a horse or carriage, طَقْم – عُدَّة.

Harness, *v.t.* To arm, سَلَّحَ. To saddle, as of a horse, or to prepare a carriage, طَقَّمَ – عَلَّقَ. He harnessed the horses to the carriage, رَبَطَ ٱلْخَيْلَ إِلَى ٱلْعَرَبَةِ ‏ـ ‎²‎.

Harp, *n.* جُنْك – عِيدَان *pl.* عُود – قِيثَارَة – كَنَّارَة.

Harp, *v.i.* To play on the —, ضَرَبَ ٱلْجُنْكَ (*or* ٱلْعُودَ). To — upon, to repeat, كَرَّرَ – كَرْكَرَ – ² عَكَّ بِ.

Harper, *n.* } **Harpist,** } ضارِبٌ بِٱلْعُودِ ـ عَوَّاد .

Harpoon, *n.* خُطَّاف *pl.* خَطاطِيفُ ـ عَرَكٌ .

Harpoon, *v.t.* رَمَى ٱلْخُطَّافَ عَلَى .

Harpooner, *n.* رامٍ بِٱلْخُطَّافِ ـ عَرَكِيٌّ .

Harpsichord, *n.* قانُون *pl.* قَوانِينُ .

Harpy, *n.* A kind of demon, غُولَةٌ ـ عَيْهَرَةٌ . An extortioner, plunderer, باغٍ *pl.* بُغاةٌ ـ سَلَّاب . A set of harpies, فِرْقَةٌ باغِيَةٌ .

Harridan, *n.* عاهِرَةٌ ـ إِمْرَأَةٌ فَحِلَةٌ ـ خَطَّالَةٌ .

Harrier, *n.* The dog, ضِرْوٌ *fem.* ضِرْوَةٌ *pl.* ضِراءٌ . The bird, أَبْرَقُ تَنَّارٍ .

Harrow, *n.* مِسْلَفَةٌ ـ مِهْرَبٌ .

Harrow, *v.t.* To — the soil, أَسْلَفَ (or سَلَفَ) ٱلْأَرْضَ . To lay waste, خَرَّبَ ـ دَمَّرَ ـ جَفَا . To harass, vex, فَجَّعَ ـ أَحْجَفَ بِ ـ نَشْغَرَ .

Harrower, *n.* One who harrows the soil, حَرَّاث ـ سالِفُ ٱلْأَرْضِ .

Harrowing, *a.* Causing horror, فَظِيعٌ ـ يُقَطِّعُ ٱلْقَلْبَ ـ مُخِيفٌ .

Harry, *v.t.* *See to* Harass, *v.t.*

Harsh, *a.* Rough to the touch, خَشِنٌ ـ أَحْرَشُ ـ شَرِسٌ . Austere, جافٍ ـ غَلِيظٌ ـ قاسٍ ـ شَرِيسٌ ـ عَنِيفٌ . Severe, عَنِيفٌ ـ فَظٌّ . Harsh to the ear, أَبَحُّ ـ أَجَشُّ ; to the taste, حامِضٌ ـ حامِزٌ ـ حادٌّ ـ حِرِّيفٌ . A man having a — voice, أَبَحُّ ٱلصَّوْتِ ـ رَجُلٌ أَجَشُّ ٱلصَّوْتِ . The lute was — in sound, بَحَّ ٱلْعُودُ *aor.* يَبَحُّ . To be —, cruel, فَظَّ ـ قَسَحَ .

Harshly, *ad.* Roughly, cruelly, بِغَلاظَةٍ ـ بِعُنْفٍ ـ بِقَسْرٍ ـ بِجَفاءٍ . Roughly to the ear, بِبُحَّةٍ ـ بِجَشَشٍ ـ بِجُشَّةٍ . To treat —, قَرَفَ عَلَى ـ أَعْنَفَ ـ عَنَفَ عَلَى or بِ ـ ضايَقَ ـ عاسَرَ ـ غَلَظَ عَلَى ـ قادَرَ ـ قاسَرَ .

Harshness, *n.* To the taste, حَرارَةٌ ـ حُمُوضَةٌ ـ حَمازَةٌ ـ حَرافَةٌ ـ مَرارَةٌ ; to the ear, صَرِيفٌ ـ بُحَّةٌ ـ جَشَشٌ ـ جُشَّةٌ ; to the touch, شَراسَةٌ ـ خُشُونَةٌ ـ حُرْشَةٌ . Roughness of temper, قَساحَةٌ ـ غِلاظَةٌ ـ غِلَظٌ ـ مُعاسَرَةٌ ـ فَظاظَةٌ ـ بَفاظَةٌ . Violence, جَفاءٌ ـ قَساوَةٌ ـ عُنْفٌ .

Harslet, *n.* } **Haslet,** } مِعْلاقُ ٱلْخِنْزِيرِ .

Hart, *n.* إِيَّلٌ *pl.* أَيائِلُ ـ أَرْيَلُ .

Hartshorn, *n.* The horn of a hart, قَرْنُ ٱلْإِيَّلِ . Sal ammonia, مِلْحُ ٱلنُّشادِرِ ـ نُشادِر . Spirit of —, رُوحُ ٱلنُّشادِرِ .

Hartswort, *n.* كاشِمٌ ـ ٱلْجُذانُ رُومِيٌّ .

Harum-scarum, *a.* *See* Hairbrained, *a.*

Harum-scarum, *ad.* شَذَرَ مَذَرَ .

Haruspice, *n.* عَرَّاف *pl.* عَرَّافَةٌ .

Harvest, *n.* The season, زَمَنُ ٱلْحِصادِ ـ حِصاد . The — crop, حَصِيدَةٌ ـ مَحْصُودٌ . Effects, consequence, عَواقِبُ ـ نَتائِجُ . Result, حَصِيلَةٌ ـ حاصِلٌ ـ مَحْصُول . The product of any growth, حَصِيدٌ ـ ثَمَرَةٌ ـ غِلَّةٌ .

Harvest, *v.t.* To gather the —, حَصَدَ ـ أَحْصَدَ . To save, وَفَّرَ ـ تَقَنَّى .

Harvest-home, *n.* The song, غِناءُ ٱلْحَصَّادِينَ .

Harvest-moon, *n.* البَدْرُ فِي أَوانِ ٱلْحِصادِ .

Hash, *v.t.* To mince, قَطَّعَ ـ ناعَمَ ـ نَعَّمَ ـ فَرَمَ .

Hash, *n.* Minced meat, لَحْمٌ مَفْرُومٌ . The dish, يَخْنَةٌ ـ حَشْوٌ . A — of meat and boiled wheat, هَرِيسَةٌ . A medley, شَمْلٌ . A muddle, شَواش ـ تَهَوُّش ـ اِلْتِباك . To make a — of a matter, لَبَّكَ ـ شَوَّشَ ـ هَوَّشَ .

Haslet, *n.* *See* Harslet, *n.*

Hasp, *n.* عُرْوَةٌ *pl.* عُرًى ـ مِشْبَكٌ ـ بُكْلَةٌ *pl.* بُكَل . *See also* Clasp, *n.*

Hasp, *v.t.* شَبَكَ . *See also to* Clasp, *v.t.*

Hassock, *n.* A — for praying upon, مَسْنَدُ ٱلرُّكُوعِ ـ مَجْثًى *pl.* مَساجِدُ ـ مَسْجِد *pl.* مَسانِدُ . *See also* Footstool, *n.*

Haste, *n.* Celerity, وِشاكٌ ـ وُشْكٌ ـ رَوْحَةٌ ـ سُرْعَةٌ ـ إِيفاد ـ وَفْز ـ فَوْر ـ اِسْتِعْجال ـ عَجَلَةٌ ـ عَجَل . Impatience, جَزَع ـ طَيْش ـ قِلَّةُ صَبْرٍ ـ جُزُوع . Asperity, حِدَّةٌ . All — was made to..., بُودِرَ إِلَى .

Haste, *v.t.* } **Hasten,** } To cause to make —, أَوْفَضَ ـ أَوْفَزَ ـ اِسْتَفَزَّ ـ أَعْجَلَ ـ عَجَّلَ ـ نَكَّظَ ـ أَنْكَظَ . To ask another to —, اِسْتَعْجَلَ . To be hastened, put into a state of preparation, اِسْتَوْفَزَ ـ اِسْتَوْفَدَ .

Haste, *v.i.* } **Hasten,** } أَفاجَ ـ أَوْشَكَ ـ يُوشِكُ *aor.* وَشُكَ ـ زَفَّ ـ أَسْرَعَ ـ اِسْتَعْجَلَ ـ طارَ ـ أَوْفَضَ . To — to be before another, بادَرَ . He hastened with it, بادَرَ بِهِ . He hastened to it, بادَرَ إِلَيْهِ . Hasten ye to perform the prayer of sunset before the rising of the evening star, بادِرُوا بِصَلاةِ ٱلْمَغْرِبِ قَبْلَ طُلُوعِ ٱلنَّجْمِ . He hastened to get before him to the goal, بادَرَهُ إِلَى ٱلْغايَةِ . They hastened together, striving who should be first, تَبادَرُوا ـ بادَرُوا بَعْضُهُمْ بَعْضًا . Hasten! make —! أَسْرِعْ ـ هَيْتَ ـ أَسْرِعْ . Hasten thou to us, خالِي بِكَ ; hasten ye to us, خالِي بِكُمْ . It is not prudent to — to a decision, لَيْسَ مِنَ ٱلْحَزْمِ أَنْ نُسْرِعَ إِلَى ٱلْجَزْمِ .

Hastily, *ad.* In a hurry, بِسُرْعَةٍ ـ عَلَى ٱلْعَجَلِ ـ عَلَى إِيفَازٍ. Precipitately, بِقِلَّةِ صَبْرٍ ـ بِطَيْشٍ ـ بِتَهَوُّرٍ. Sharply, بِحِدَّةٍ ـ بِحَمْوَةٍ. To speak —, تَكَلَّمَ فِرَاطًا. To reply to one —, without premeditation, بَدَّهَ. He spoke —, سَبَقَ مِنْهُ كَلَامٌ ². I spoke — to him, سَبَقَ إِلَيْهِ مِنِّي كَلَامٌ. Hastily-formed opinion, رَأْيٌ فَطِيرٌ.

Hastiness, *n.* Rashness, بَطْشٌ ـ بَادِرَةٌ ـ تَهَوُّرٌ. Irritability, vehemence, حَمْوَةٌ ـ شِدَّةٌ ـ حِدَّةٌ ـ بَدْرَةٌ. Hastiness leads to repentance, or sorrow; slowness to safety, (*prov.*) العَجَلَةُ نَدَامَةٌ وَٱلْمُهْلَةُ سَلَامَةٌ.

Hasty, *a.* Quick, سَرِيعٌ ـ عَجِيلٌ ـ عَجُولٌ ـ مِسْرَعٌ ـ وَشِيكٌ *pl.* سُرْعَانٌ *fem.* سَرِيعَةٌ *pl. fem.* سِرَاعٌ ـ عَجْلَانُ *pl.* عِجَالٌ. Rash, precipitate, قَلِيلُ ٱلصَّبْرِ ـ طَائِشٌ ـ مُتَهَوِّرٌ ـ هَيِّرٌ. Of a — spirit, قَصِيرُ ٱلرُّوحِ. Passionate, غَضُوبٌ ـ حَادُّ ٱلطَّبْعِ ـ سَرِيعُ ٱلْغَضَبِ. What disquieted him to such a — return? مَا ٱسْتَفَزَّهُ إِلَى وُشْكِ ٱلرُّجُوعِ.

Hasty-pudding, *n.* عَصِيدَةٌ.

Hat, *n.* A European hat, بُرْنَيْطَةٌ *pl.* بَرَانِيطُ *and* بُرْنَيْطَاتٌ ـ بُرَّيْطَةٌ *pl.* بَرَارِيطُ. (The following are the names of some of the head-dresses corresponding to our hat. The most general equivalent would be رُشَّةٌ. A round-shaped hat, كُمَّةٌ. A pointed hat, صَوْمَعَةٌ *pl.* صَوَامِعُ. A melon-shaped hat, أُرْسُوسَةٌ. A monk's hat, or cowl, قَلَنْسُوَةٌ *pl.* قَلَانِيسُ ـ بُرْطُلٌ). To send round the hat, to ask for contributions, إِسْتَمَدَّ ـ تَسَوَّلَ.

Hatch, *v.t.* To break the egg, as of a hen, فَقَصَ ـ فَقَّصَ ². To procreate, give birth to, وَلَّدَ. To contrive, أَبْدَعَ ـ إِخْتَرَعَ ـ إِبْتَدَعَ. To plot against, إِحْتَالَ عَلَى. He hatched the egg of, or originated, the sedition, فَقَصَ بَيْضَةَ ٱلْفِتْنَةِ ². *See also to* Conspire, *v.i.*

Hatch, *v.i.* To produce, as the egg the chicken, أَفْرَخَ ـ فَرَّخَ. The egg was hatched, أَفْرَخَتِ ٱلْبَيْضَةُ.

Hatch, *n.* The cover of a hold, بَابُ أَنْبَارٍ. A plot, رِبَاطِيَّةٌ ـ مُحَالَفَةٌ. *See also* Brood, *n.*

Hatchel, *n.* مُشْطٌ ـ مَشْطٌ *pl.* مُشْطٌ ـ مِشَاطٌ.

Hatchel, *v.t.* مَشَطَ ـ فَتَّكَ ـ فَكَّكَ ².

Hatches, *n.* Covers of holds in a ship, أَبْوَابُ ٱلْأَنَابِيرِ. *See also* Hatchway, *n.*

Hatchet, *n.* فَأْسٌ *pl.* فُؤُوسٌ ـ قَدُومٌ *pl.* قُدُمٌ *and* قَدَائِمُ.

Hatching, *n.* Production of young from eggs, تَفْرِيخٌ. Making lines to cross one another, as in drawing, خُطُوطٌ ـ تَخْطِيطٌ شِطْرَنْجٌ عَلَى رَسْمِ شِطْرَنْجٍ. The colours in a shield, تَلْوِينُ ٱلْآرْمَا.

Hatchment, *n.* رَسْمُ آرْمَا تُصْمَدُ عَلَى بَابِ ٱلدَّارِ حَوْلًا عَلَامَةَ ٱلْحُزْنِ عَلَى وَفَاةِ صَاحِبِهَا. *See* Coat-of-arms, *under* Arms, *n.*

Hatchway, *n.* فَمُ ٱلْأَنْبَارِ.

Hate, *v.t.* أَبْغَضَ ـ ضَغِنَ عَلَى ـ شَنَأَ ـ مَقَتَ ². To dislike, إِشْمَأَزَّ ـ كَرِهَ. To — one secretly, كَشَحَ بِ ². To — mutually, of many, تَبَاغَضُوا ـ تَضَاغَنُوا. How he hates me! مَا أَبْغَضَهُ لِي.

Hate, *n.* *See* Hatred, *n.*

Hated, *n.* مَمْقُوتٌ ـ مَشْنُوءٌ ـ مَبْغُوضٌ.

Hateful, *a.* فَظِيعٌ ـ بَغِيضٌ ـ شَنِيعٌ ـ مَقِيتٌ. To make —, بَغَّضَ. To be —, شَنُعَ ². To be — to, إِسْتَشْنَعَ ـ شَنِعَ بِ. How — he is to me! مَا أَبْغَضَهُ إِلَيَّ.

Hatefully, *ad.* بِبُغْضٍ ـ بِفَظَاعَةٍ ـ شَنَاعَةً ـ بِشَنَعٍ ـ بِمَقْتٍ.

Hatefulness, *n.* كَرَاهِيَةٌ ـ كَرَاهَةٌ ـ شَنَاعَةٌ ـ فَظَاعَةٌ.

Hater, *n.* } عَدُوٌّ ـ مَمْقُوتٌ ـ مَقِيتٌ ـ مُبْغِضٌ ـ شَانِئٌ.
Hating, *a.* }

Hatred, *n.* شَنْءٌ ـ إِبْغَاضٌ ـ بَغَاضَةٌ ـ بِغْضَةٌ ـ مَقْتٌ ـ بُغْضٌ ـ شَنَآءَةٌ ـ مُعَادَاةٌ ـ ضَغِينَةٌ. Disgust, إِشْمِئْزَازٌ ـ كُرْهٌ.

Hatter, *n.* بُرْنَيْطِيٌّ *pl.* بُرْنَيْطِيَّةٌ.

Hauberk, *n.* صُدْرَةٌ مُدَرَّعَةٌ ـ زَرَدِيَّةٌ.

Haugh, *n.* مَرْجٌ *pl.* مُرُوجٌ ـ رَبِيعَةٌ.

Haughtily, *ad.* بِغَطْرَسَةٍ ـ بِتَشَامُخٍ ـ تَكَبُّرًا ـ بِكِبْرِيَاءَ. To behave —, تَكَبَّرَ ـ تَكَابَرَ ـ تَاهَ *aor.* يَتِيهُ ـ تَجَالَّ ـ غَطْرَسَ ـ تَرَفَّعَ.

Haughtiness, *n.* غَطْرَسَةٌ ـ فُخُومِيَّةٌ ـ شَمْخَرَةٌ ـ جَبْرِيَّةٌ ـ تِيهٌ ـ تَشَامُخُ ـ تَعَظُّمٌ ـ غُرُورٌ ـ تَكَبُّرٌ ـ كِبْرِيَاءُ. Haughtiness of spirit, تَشَامُخُ ٱلرُّوحِ.

Haughty, *a.* شَامِخٌ ـ مُتَنَفِّخٌ ـ غِطْرِيسٌ ـ غِطْرِسٌ ـ جَبَرِيٌّ ـ مُتَعَظِّمٌ ـ مُتَكَبِّرٌ ـ مَغْرُورٌ. Of a — spirit, شَامِخُ ٱلرُّوحِ. To be —, تَعَظَّمَ ـ إِسْتَكْبَرَ ـ شَمَخَ أَنْفُهُ ² ـ شَمْخَرَ.

Haul, *v.t.* جَرَّ ـ جَذَبَ ² ـ سَحَبَ ². To — down, أَنْزَلَ ـ نَزَّلَ. To be hauled, of a ship, alongside another, and to be canted for the discharge of cargo into it, كُبِّسَتِ ٱلسَّفِينَةُ.

Haul, *n.* A pulling, سَحْبٌ ـ جَرَّةٌ ـ جَرٌّ ـ جَذْبَةٌ ـ جَذْبٌ. The — of a net, صَيْدٌ.

Haulm, *n.* } قَشٌّ ـ تِبْنٌ.
Haum, }

Haunch, *n.* The flank, شَاكِلَةٌ *dual* شَاكِلَتَانِ *pl.* شَوَاكِلُ ـ وَرِكٌ ـ أَعْجَازٌ *pl.* عَجُزٌ ـ حَجَبَةٌ. The crest bone of the —, عَرْقَفَةٌ. A loin or a leg, فَخِذٌ *pl.* أَفْخَاذٌ. *See also* Hip, *n.*

Haunt, *v.t.* To frequent, تَرَدَّدَ إِلَى ـ إِنْتَابَ. To go round about a place, as of birds or dogs, حَاتَ ². To stick to, لَازَمَ. To abide or live in, سَكَنَ ². To intrude upon, دَخَلَ عَلَى ـ مِنْ ²

غَيْرِ إِذْنٍ. To disturb, أَزْعَجَ ـ أَضْجَرَ ـ نَهَكَ ². The places which he used to —, الأَمَاكِنُ ٱلَّتِي كَانَ يَتَرَدَّدُ إِلَيْهَا.

Haunt, *v.i.* To go about, سَاحَ *aor.* يَسُوحُ ـ جَالَ *aor.* يَجُولُ ـ تَرَدَّدَ ـ جَوَّلَ.

Haunt, A place of resort, مَأْلَف ـ مَأْوًى ـ مَعْهَد ـ مَآب *pl.* مَآوِلُ *pl.* مَآلَ ـ مَآرِبُ. The — of a wild beast, وُجْر *pl.* وِجَار *or* أَوْجِرَة ـ سَرَب *pl.* أَسْرَاب.

Haunted, *a.* As by apparitions, فِي ضَبْطِ ٱلْجِنِّ. Troubled, afflicted by, مُبْتَلًى ب.

Hautboy, *n.* زَمَّارَة ـ مِزْمَار.

Hauteur, *n.* *See* Haughtiness, *n.*

Have, *v.t.* To possess, مَلَكَ ² ـ اِقْتَنَى ـ حَازَ ² ـ كَانَ لِ ـ عِنْدَهُ ـ لِ ـ مَعَ ـ بِ. Have? as a query, هَلْ. To have religion is to have true morality, إِحْرَازُ ٱلدِّينِ أَحْرَازُ ٱلْأَدَبِ ٱلصَّحِيحِ.

Not having had assistance I have not had success, حَيْثُ لَمْ يَكُنْ لِي إِسْعَافٌ فَمَا أَنْجَحْتُ.

Could she have had them? أَكَانَ يُمْكِنُهَا ٱلْحُصُولُ عَلَيْهِمْ.

Do you have circumspection, كُنْ مُحْتَرِزًا.

Has he no paper? أَلَيْسَ عِنْدَهُ وَرَقٌ.

Having had the disease once I would not have it a second time, مِنْ حَيْثُ أَنِّي ٱبْتُلِيتُ بِٱلدَّاءِ مَرَّةً فَمَا أُرِيدُ أَنْ أُبْتَلَى بِهِ مَرَّةً أُخْرَى.

He could have had no prudence, مَا تَأَتَّى لَهُ ٱلْحَزْمُ.

He had this disease yesterday, كَانَ بِهِ هٰذَا ٱلدَّاءُ أَمْسِ.

He might have had the politeness, كَانَ يُمْكِنُهُ ٱلْأَدَبُ.

If he have not prosperity he will not repine, إِنْ لَمْ يَتَوَفَّقْ فَلَنْ يَتَظَلَّمَ.

If we have not more caution, إِنْ لَمْ نَزِدْ حَزْمًا.

I have no father, مَا لِي (*or* مَا عِنْدِي) أَبٌ.

I have pens, عِنْدِي أَقْلَامٌ.

I shall have dinner to-day, أَنَا أَتَغَدَّى ٱلْيَوْمَ.

I will not have any, لَا أُرِيدُ شَيْئًا.

Let me have my own way, دَعْنِي وَشَأْنِي.

Let them have nothing at all, لَا تَدَعْهُمْ أَنْ يَحْصُلُوا عَلَى شَيْءٍ أَلْبَتَّةَ.

May I have this flower? هَلْ لِي أَنْ آخُذَ هٰذَا ٱلزَّهْرَ.

Nobody shall have you, لَنْ تَكُونَ لِأَحَدٍ.

Nobody will have me, مَا أَحَدٌ يُرِيدُنِي.

She might have had them, قَدْ يُمْكِنُهَا ٱلْحُصُولُ عَلَيْهِمْ.

They can have no sincerity, لَا يَتَهَيَّأُ لَهُمُ ٱلصِّدْقُ.

They may have had it, كَانَ يُمْكِنُهُمُ ٱلْحُصُولُ عَلَيْهِ.

They shall have their reward, سَيُجَازَوْنَ.

We have had the cholera, كَانَتِ ٱلْهَيْضَةُ عِنْدَنَا.

We may have rain to-day, رُبَّمَا يَكُونُ لَنَا ٱلْيَوْمَ مَطَرٌ ـ رُبَّمَا تَمْطُرُ ٱلْيَوْمَ.

You had many friends, كَانَ لَكَ أَصْحَابٌ كَثِيرُونَ.

You may have it, لَكَ أَنْ تَأْخُذَهُ.

You shall have a flogging, سَتُضْرَبُ بِٱلسَّوْطِ.

You should have wisdom, عَلَيْكَ بِٱلْحِكْمَةِ.

You would not have patience, لَمْ تُرِدْ أَنْ تَصْبِرَ.

To have about one, عِنْدَهُ ـ حَمَلَ مَعَهُ ².

To have at, to attempt, عَزَمَ عَلَى ² ـ سَعَى فِي ². Have thou at it! (try it, catch it, hold to it, *etc.*) عَلَيْكَ بِهِ.

To have away, to remove, رَفَعَ ² ـ نَقَلَ ².

To have down, to bring down, أَنْزَلَ ـ أَهْبَطَ.

To have in, to make to enter, أَدْخَلَ ـ فَوَّتَ إِلَى دَاخِلٍ.

To have on, to wear, لَبِسَ ² ـ كَانَ لَابِسًا.

To have it out, to settle an affair, with, تَدَبَّرَ مَعَهُ ـ تَسَاوَى مَعَهُ *vulg.* اِصْطَفَلَ مَعَهُ.

To have up, to make to appear, أَحْضَرَ. To make to ascend, صَعَّدَ.

To let one have a thing, فَاتَ لَهُ ² ـ تَرَكَ لَهُ ² ـ خَلَّى لَهُ.

Haven, *n.* A harbour, مَرْسًى *pl.* مَرَاسٍ ـ مِينَا *pl.* مِيَن. A place of refuge, مَلْجَأٌ ـ مَعَاذ ـ مَأْوًى. *See also* Harbour, *n.*

Haversack, *n.* رَدِيف *pl.* رِدَاف ـ حَقِيبَة ـ سَلْف *pl.* سُلُوف ـ مِزْوَد *pl.* مَزَاوِدُ ـ جُرُب *pl.* جِرَاب.

Havock, *n.* دَمَار ـ نَهْب ـ خَسَارَة ـ خَرَاب ـ عَصْف. To make — of, دَمَّرَ ـ خَرَّبَ.

Havock, *v.t.* عَصَفَ بِ ² ـ أَعْصَفَ بِ ـ دَمَّرَ ـ نَهَبَ ² ـ خَرَّبَ.

Haw, *n.* Of the hawthorn, ثَمَرُ ٱلْعَضْرِ. Hesitation in speech, هَاْهَاْ. *See also* Dale, *n.*

Haw, *v.i.* To — in speech, هَأْهَأَ. *See also to* Hesitate, *v.i.*

Haw-haw, *n.* *See* Ha-ha, *n.*

Hawk, *n.* أَبُو لَاحِقٍ ـ أَخْطَبُ ـ بُزَاة *pl.* بَازِي ـ بَاشِق *pl.* بَوَاشِقُ ـ صَقْر *pl.* صِقَار *and* صُقُور. A trainer of hawks, صَقَّار.

Hawk, *v.t.* To catch by means of hawks, اِقْتَنَصَ بِٱلصَّقْرِ ـ اِصْطَادَ بِٱلْبَازِي. To force phlegm from the throat, (*v.i.*) تَنَخَّعَ ـ تَنَخَّمَ. To — wares for sale, دَارَ يَبِيعُ كَذَا ². To proclaim abroad, بَرَّحَ ـ نَادَى بِ ـ اِشْتَهَرَ.

Hawker, *n.* A — of wares, بَيَّاع فِي ٱلْأَزِقَّةِ *pl.* بَيَّاعَة ـ عَنْقَاش ـ خُرْدَجِي ـ دَوَّار ـ حَدَّار.

Hawk-eyed, *a.* لَمَّاح ـ شايِهُ ٱلْبَصَر ـ ذُو بَصَرٍ خارِقٍ.

Hawking, *n.* With hawks, ٱلصَّيْدُ بِٱلْبازِي ـ تَصَقُّر. Forcing phlegm from the throat, تَنَخُّع ـ تَنَخُّم. Crying goods about, ٱلْبَيْعُ فِي ٱلْأَزِقَّةِ. To go a-hawking, with hawks, تَصَقَّرَ.

Hawksweed, *n.* مُرَيْرَة.

Hawse-hole, *n.* مَنْفِذُ ٱللَّبانِ ـ بَيْتُ ٱلْقَلْسِ.

Hawser, *n.* لَبان ـ قَلْس *pl.* قُلُوس.

Hawthorn, *n.* عِضَّة ـ شَجَرُ ٱلْعِضَّةِ.

Hay, *n.* Dry grass, حَشِيش; fodder, عَلَف. To give hay, as to a horse, *etc.*, أَعْلَفَ ـ ²حَشَّ. To make hay while the sun shines, إِغْتَنَمَ ٱلْفُرْصَةَ. To fail to make hay while the sun shone, (*prov.*) فِي ٱلصَّيْفِ ضَيَّعْتِ ٱللَّبَنَ (*lit.* Thou losedst the milk in summer; applied originally to a female).

Hay, *v.t.* To cut grass, ²حَشَّ ـ إِحْتَشَّ.

Hay-cock, *n.* حَشِيش (كُوم *or*) عَرَمَة *pl.* عَرَمات.

Haying, *n.* }
Haymaking, } حَشّ.

Hay-knife, *n.* مِحَشّ ـ حُشَّاش.

Hayloft, *n.* مَخْزَنُ ٱلْحَشِيشِ ـ مَتْبَنَة ـ مَتْبَن ـ تَبَّانَة.

Haymaker, *n.* حاشّ *pl.* حُشَّاش.

Haymarket, *n.* سُوقُ ٱلتِّبْنِ ـ سُوقُ ٱلْحَشِيشِ.

Hay-mow,
Hay-rick, *n.* } كُدْس حَشِيشٍ ـ بَيْدَرُ ٱلْحَشِيشِ.
Hay-stack,

Hazard, *n.* Chance, قَدَر ـ قَدَآء. An accident, عَرَضَة ـ حادِثَة ـ صِدْفَة. Danger, خَطَر ـ مُخاطَرَة ـ تَهْلُكَة. A game of chance, قِمار ـ غَرَر. To run the —, أَخْطَرَ. He forbade sales of —, نَهى عَنْ بَيْعِ ٱلْغَرَرِ.

Hazard, *v.i.* To expose one's self to danger, (أَخْطَرَ *or*) خاطَرَ بِنَفْسِهِ. He hazarded himself and his property, خاطَرَ بِنَفْسِهِ وَمالِهِ.

Hazard, *v.t.* To expose to danger or risk, أَلْقَى ـ أَخْطَرَ. He hazarded the property, أَخْطَرَ ٱلْمالَ. He hazarded his life, as a stake to death, أَخْطَرَ ٱلْمَوْتَ نَفْسَهُ.

Hazardous, *a.* ذُو خَطَرٍ ـ مُخْطِر. They embarked in — undertakings, رَكِبُوا ٱلْأَخْطارَ.

Hazardously, *ad.* بِخَطَرٍ ـ بِمُخاطَرَةٍ ـ بِنَوْعٍ مُخْطِرٍ.

Haze, *n.* Mist, ضَبابَة ـ ضَباب. *See also* Haziness, Fog, *n.*

Hazel, *n.* The tree, شَجَرَةُ ٱلْبُنْدُقِ.

Hazel, *a.* The colour, لَوْنُ ٱلْبُنْدُقِ.

Hazel-nut, *n.* جِلَّوْز ـ فُنْدُق ـ بُنْدُق.

Haziness, *n.* Mistiness, ضَباب. Obscurity of speech or meaning, إِبْهام ـ إِيْهام. Free from — (in the latter sense), خالٍ مِنَ ٱلْإِبْهامِ.

Hazy, *a.* Misty, كَدِر ـ كَدِير ـ مُغَيِّم ـ مُضِبّ. Obscure, of speech or meaning, مُبْهَم ـ مُلْتَبِس.

He, *pr.* هُوَ ـ ذاكَ. The male, ٱلذَّكَرُ. He himself, هُوَ نَفْسُهُ. I am he, أَنا هُوَ. Who is he? مَنْ هُوَ.

Head, *n.* As of the body, هامَة *pl.* هام *and* هامات ـ رَأْس *pl.* رُؤُوس. Head, as of a spear, the tip of anything, أَسَل *coll.* أَسَلَة. A number, عَدَد. The principal place, presidency, صَدْر. A principal person, زَعِيم *pl.* زُعَماء ـ رَئِيس *pl.* رُؤَساء ـ مُقَدَّم ـ كَبِير ـ أَمِير. A head man, master, lord, سَيِّد *pl.* سادَة *and* سادات. Authority, command, إِمارَة ـ مَأْمُورِيَّة ـ رِئَاسَة ـ إِدارَة. An administrator, director, ناظِر ـ مُدِير ـ مَأْمُور ـ مُباشِر. Understanding, عَقْل ـ ذِهْن ـ فَهْم ـ ذَكاوَة. Resistance, مُقاوَمَة ـ مُضادَّة. The front of anything, مُقَدَّم. A topic, مَطْلَب ـ مَبْحَث ـ مَوْضُوع ـ مَوْرِد. A source, as of a stream, مَنْبَع ـ عَيْن ـ مَصْدَر. The top of anything, رَأْس ـ قُلَّة *pl.* قُلَل ـ قِمَّة *pl.* قِمَم. The prow of a ship, صَدْرُ ٱلسَّفِينَةِ ـ مُرَجَّحَة ـ مُقَدَّمُ ٱلْمَرْكَبِ. A division, chapter, فَصْل *pl.* فُصُول ـ جُزْء *pl.* أَجْزاء. A seller of heads, رَأَّس ـ رَوَّاس. A-head, before, أَمامَ ـ قُدَّامَ. Having a large —, أَرْأَس. His sin is on his own —, ذَنْبُهُ فِي رَقَبَتِهِ. It did not enter the — of anyone, لَمْ يَخْطِرْ بِبالِ أَحَدٍ.

A crowned head, مَلِك *pl.* مُلُوك ـ سُلْطان *pl.* سَلاطِين ـ تاج دار.

A-head, per head, لِكُلِّ واحِدٍ ـ لِكُلِّ رَأْسٍ ـ رَأْسًا.

Crown of the head, قُرْعُ ٱلرَّأْسِ ـ يافُوخ ـ نَصْلَة.

Head first, foremost, عَلَى رَأْسِهِ ـ مُنْكَرِسًا. He fell head first, يَقَعُ *aor.* وَقَعَ عَلَى رَأْسِهِ شَكًّا ـ وَقَعَ مُنَكَّسَ ٱلرَّأْسِ.

Head of an arrow, سِنُّ ٱلسَّهْمِ.

Head of a cask, تُرْسُ ٱلْبَرْمِيلِ.

Head of hair, جُمَّة *pl.* جُمَم.

Head or tail? وَجْهٌ أَوْ قَفًا. *See also under* Even, *a.*

Heads I win, tails you lose, أَنْتَ تَخْسَرُ ٱلرَّأْسَ وَأَنا أَفُوزُ بِٱلذَّنَبِ.

Overhead, above, فَوْق.

Over head and ears in, مُنْهَمِك فِي ـ مُسْتَغْرِق فِي.

Over head and heels, عَجْزَهُ عَلَى صَدْرِهِ. To turn over head and heels, إِنْقَلَبَ عَجْزَهُ عَلَى صَدْرِهِ.

Under the head, chapter, of . . . , فِي فَصْلِ كَذا.

To beat a thing into the head of one, أَقْنَعَ ـ أَدْخَلَ فِي عَقْلِهِ.

To bind on the head, عَصَّبَ.

To break the head of one, دَمَّ رَأْسَهُ ـ فَضَخَ ـ شَجَّ ـ شَدَخَ ـ كَسَرَ رَأْسَهُ.

To break one's own head over, كَدَّ فِي ـ تَكَلَّفَ بِ ـ كَسَّرَ رَأْسَهُ فِي.

To bring to a head, to ripen, أَنْضَجَ. To sharpen to a point, أَنْصَلَ. To make manifest, أَظْهَرَ. To cause to suppurate and heal, دَمَّلَ ـ أَدْمَلَ.

To bring in, head and shoulders, forcibly, أَدْخَلَ غَصْبًا ـ أَسْلَكَ قَهْرًا.

To come into one's head, خَطَرَ بِبَالِهِ (or عَلَى بَالِهِ).

To come to a head, of a tumour, غَذَّ ـ أَمَدَّ. To become ripe, نَضِجَ. To break out, show itself, اِشْتَهَرَ ـ شَاعَ.

To cover one's head, as with clothes, كَبَسَ.

To forfeit one's head, جَلَبَ عَلَى نَفْسِهِ قِصَاصَ ٱلْمَوْتِ مُجَازَاةً عَلَى جُرْمِهِ.

To get ahead, سَبَقَ ـ تَقَدَّمَ.

To get into one's head, حَطَّ فِي رَأْسِهِ كَذَا ـ تَوَهَّمَ.

To give, as of a horse, his head, أَطْلَقَ ـ سَيَّبَ.

To hang down the head, حَنَا رَأْسَهُ.

To hide one's head, or one's self, تَكَمَّنَ ـ اِخْتَفَى.

To hit the right nail on the head, أَسَدَّ ـ سَدَّ ـ أَصَابَ ٱلصَّوَابَ.

To hold up one's head, رَفَعَ رَأْسَهُ.

To knock or hit on the head, رَأَسَ ـ قَمَعَ. To kill, مَوَّتَ ـ قَتَلَ.

To lay heads, to consult, together, اِئْتَمَرُوا ـ تَوَازَرُوا فِي ـ تَشَاوَرُوا.

To make head against, to oppose, تَعَرَّضَ لِ ـ قَاوَمَ; to advance, تَقَدَّمَ.

To run in one's head, لَازَمَ عَقْلَهُ ـ لَاطَ بِعَقْلِهِ.

To set a price, as on the head of one, وَضَعَ عَلَى *aor.* يَضَعُ.

To shake the head at, أَنْغَضَ ٱلرَّأْسَ إِلَى. They shall shake their heads at you, وَسَيُنْغِضُونَ إِلَيْكَ رُؤُوسَهُمْ (Kur. xvii. 53).

To stand head down, downwards, اِنْتَكَسَ.

To strike off the head, رَمَى رَقَبَتَهُ ـ ضَيَّعَ (or قَطَعَ) رَأْسَهُ.

To take a thing into one's head, حَطَّ (or دَخَّلَ) فِي رَأْسِهِ (or عَقْلِهِ).

To take the head, the principal post, تَصَدَّرَ.

To trouble one's head about, اِهْتَمَّ بِ ـ هَمَّ بِ ـ تَعَانَى.

To turn or incline the head, لَوَى بِرَأْسِهِ.

To turn a person's head, طَيَّشَ ـ حَيَّرَ ـ أَبْطَرَ.

Head, *a.* *See* Chief, *a.*

Head, *v.t.* To be at the — of, رَأَسَ عَلَى ـ قَادَ. To direct, قَضَبَ ـ شَذَّبَ ـ حَصَّلَ. To lop, of trees, أَرْشَدَ ـ دَبَّرَ. To go in front of, تَقَدَّمَ ـ قَدَمَ. To put a — to, رَكَّبَ لِ رَأْسًا ـ حَطَّ عَلَى رَأْسًا. To put a — or bottom to, as of a cask, أَقْعَرَ ـ تَرَسَ. To oppose, خَالَفَ ـ قَاوَمَ. To sail against the wind, مَخَرَ (or أَبْحَرَ) فِي فَمِ ٱلرِّيحِ. *See also to* Behead, *v.t.*

Head, *v i.* To originate, حَدَثَ. To spring or have its source, صَدَرَ ـ نَبَعَ. To be directed, led, اِنْقَادَ. To be turned towards, to face, قَابَلَ ـ وَاجَهَ. To come to a —, to ripen, نَضِجَ ـ نَضَجَ.

Headache, *n.* وَجَعُ ٱلرَّأْسِ ـ صُدَاعٌ ـ غَوْلٌ; on one side only of the head, hemicrania, شَقِيقَةٌ. To have the —, صُدِّعَ. To give the —, صَدَّعَ. Having the —, مَصْدُوعٌ. Headache from wine, خُمَارٌ ـ خُمْرَةٌ ـ خَمْرَةٌ.

Head-band, *n.* عِصَابَةٌ.

Head-borough, *n.* قَصَبَةٌ *pl.* قِصَابٌ.

Head-downwards, *a.* مَنْكُوسٌ ـ مُنَكَّسٌ.

Head-dress, *n.* } كِسْوَةُ ٱلرَّأْسِ ـ عِصَابٌ ـ عَصْبٌ ـ عَمْرَةٌ
Head-gear, } عِمَارَةٌ.

Header, *n.* A leader, رَئِيسٌ ـ مُقَدَّمٌ *pl.* رُؤَسَاءُ. A leap into the sea head foremost, غَطْسٌ فِي ٱلْبَحْرِ مُنْكَرِسًا. A fixer-on of heads, مُرَكِّبُ ٱلرُّؤُوسِ.

Headiness, *n.* Rashness, تَهَوُّرٌ. Obstinacy, عِنَادٌ ـ تَمَرُّدٌ ـ طَيْشٌ ـ عَجْرَفَةٌ.

Heading, *n.* A title, caption, عُنْوَانٌ ـ عِنْوَانٌ *pl.* عِنْوَانَاتٌ *pl.* عُنْوَانَاتٌ ـ فَصْلٌ *pl.* فُصُولٌ. To write or give a — to, عَنْوَنَ.

Headland, *n.* A promontory, أَنْفُ جَبَلٍ ـ طَنَفٌ *pl.* طُنُوفٌ ـ أَرْضٌ بِلَا حَرْثٍ. Unploughed land, رُؤُوسٌ *pl.* رَأْسٌ.

Headless, *a.* Without a head, بِلَا رَأْسٍ. Beheaded, مَقْطُوعُ ٱلرَّأْسِ. Without a chief, لَا رَئِيسَ لَهُ ـ بِدُونِ رَئِيسٍ.

Headlong, *a.* Head-foremost, مُنْكَرِسٌ. Rash, precipitate, طَرَحَ إِلَى أَسْفَلَ ـ مُتَهَوِّرٌ ـ هَيِّرٌ ـ مِغْشَمٌ. To throw —, نَكَتَ. To fall —, اِنْتَكَتَ. To fall — upon, اِنْكَرَسَ عَلَى. To fall — into, اِنْكَرَسَ فِي. To throw — into, كَبْكَبَ فِي. To proceed in a — manner, تَهَوَّرَ ـ رَكِبَ رَأْسَهُ.

Headman, *n.* رَئِيسٌ ـ عُمَّالٌ *pl.* عَامِلٌ ـ زُعَمَاءُ *pl.* زَعِيمٌ *pl.* رُؤَسَاءُ ـ مُقَدَّمٌ. A superintendent-in-chief, مُصَيْطِرٌ ـ مُسَيْطِرٌ.

Head-money, *n.* Capitation-tax, جِزْيَةٌ ـ خَرَاجٌ.

Headmost, *a.* ٱلسَّابِقُ ـ ٱلْأَوَّلُ *fem.* ٱلْأُولَى ـ ٱلْمُتَقَدِّمُ.

Head-piece, *n.* A helmet, مُقَنَّع — خُوذَة *pl.* خُوَذ. Intelligence, ذِهْن — عَقْل — فِطْنَة.

Head-quarters, *n.* As of a regiment or army, مَرْكَزُ ٱلْعَسْكَرِيَّةِ. A station of a guard or police, مَحَلُّ ٱلضَّبْطِيَّةِ. A place of resort, مَعْهَد — مَأْلَف — مَأْوَى.

Head-sea, *n.* بَحْرٌ مُضَادٌّ — بَحْرٌ مُخَالِف.

Headship, *n.* زَعَامَة — رِئَاسَة — تَقَدُّم — سِيَادَة.

Headsman, *n.* An executioner, مَشَاعِلِيّ — سَيَّاف — جَلَّاد.

Head-spring, *n.* A source, مَنْبَع — مَصْدَر — عَيْن *pl.* عُيُون.

Head-stall, *n.* عِذَارُ ٱلرَّسَنِ — رَاشِيَة. The two cheek-straps forming the —, العِذَارَانِ.

Head-stone, *n.* A corner-stone, حَجَرُ ٱلزَّاوِيَةِ. The — of a grave, حَجَرٌ فِي رَأْسِ قَبْرٍ — رُجْم *and* رِجَام *pl.* رُجْمَة.

Headstrong, *a.* Rash, سَادِر — مِغْشَم — خَرِيم — عَنِيد — مَرِيد. He acts in a — manner, غَشَمَ ٱلْأُمُورَ — يَرْكَبُ رَأْسَهُ. He prosecuted his affairs in a — manner, خَبَطَ أَمْرَهُ عَلَى غَيْرِ بَصِيرَةٍ.

Head-way, *n.* تَقَدُّم. To make —, تَقَدَّمَ.

Head-wind, *n.* رِيحٌ مُخَالِفَةٌ — كَوْس. They feared the —, خَافُوا ٱلْكَوْسَ.

Heady, *a.* *See* Headstrong, *a.*

Heal, *v.t.* To cure, غَفَرَ — أَطَابَ — أَبْرَأَ مِنَ ٱلْمَرَضِ — شَفَى مِن — عَالَجَ — دَاوَى; of a wound, لَأَمَ. To —, as of a dissension, between, لَأَمَ بَيْنَ — دَمَلَ بَيْنَ — أَصْلَحَ بَيْنَ — صَالَحَ. The remedy healed the wound, العِلَاجُ دَمَلَ ٱلْجُرْحَ.

Heal, *v.i.* To grow sound, بَرَأَ — طَابَ — لَأَمَ. To — up, of a sore, ٱلْتَأَمَ — جَلَبَ — أَنْدَبَ — قَطِبَ ٱلْجُرْحُ. Near healing, قَرِيبُ ٱلِٱلْتِئَامِ.

Healable, *a.* مِمَّا يُعَالَجُ — قَابِلُ ٱلْمُدَاوَاةِ — الشِّفَاءُ مِنْهُ مُمْكِنٌ — مِمَّا يُبْرَأُ.

Healing, *n.* The act of curing, مُعَالَجَة — مُدَاوَاة; the growing sound, ٱلْتِئَام. The act of reconciling, دَمْلٌ بَيْنَ — إِصْلَاحٌ بَيْنَ — مُصَالَحَة.

Healing, *a.* شَافٍ — مُشْفٍ — دَامِل. The — art, فَنُّ ٱلطِّبَابَةِ — الطِّبّ.

Health, *n.* Sound state of body, شِفَاء — صِحَّة — سَلَامَة — عَافِيَة. Constitution, state, أَمْزِجَة *pl.* مِزَاج — طَبْع — حَال — كَيْف. Salvation, خَلَاص — سَلَامَةُ ٱلنَّفْسِ. To recover one's —, تَصَحَّحَ — صَحَّ مِن — أَفَاقَ مِن — إِسْتَفَاقَ; as from a disease, إِشْتَفَى — تَشَفَّى. To be restored to — by such a means, إِشْتَفَى بِكَذَا. To restore to —, صَحَّحَ — أَعْفَى — عَافَى. In good —, سَالِم — بِخَيْرٍ وَعَافِيَةٍ.

In poor —, مُعْتَلُّ ٱلْمِزَاجِ — ضَعِيفُ ٱلْمِزَاجِ. To drink to one's —, شَرِبَ عَلَى صِحَّتِهِ. To your —! Your good —! مَحَبَّةٌ فِيكُمْ — هَنِيئًا — صِحَّةٌ وَعَافِيَةٌ — *Ans.* بِسَرِّكُمْ. A bill of —, تَذْكِرَةٌ صِحِّيَّةٌ — تَذْكِرَةُ ٱلْكُورَنْتِينَا. A Board of Health, مَجْلِسُ ٱلصِّحَّةِ. The public —, الصِّحَّةُ ٱلْعُمُومِيَّةُ.

Healthful, *a.* *See* Healthy, *a.*

Healthfully, *ad.* In a wholesome manner, بِمُعَافَاةٍ — بِعَافِيَةٍ — بِسَلَامَةٍ.

Healthfulness, *n.* } Salubrity, نُزْهَة — سَلَامَة; of climate, إِعْتِدَالُ
Healthiness, } هَوَاءٍ.

Healthily, *ad.* Without disease, بِصِحَّةٍ وَعَافِيَةٍ.

Healthy, *a.* Being in a sound state, صَحِيح — مُعَافًى — سَلِيم — فِي حَالَتَيِ ٱلصِّحَّةِ وَٱلْعَافِيَةِ. Conducive to health, شَافٍ — نَافِعٌ — طَيِّبٌ (or) لِلصِّحَّةِ. Salutary, rectifying, مُصْلِح. *See also* Salubrious, *a.*

Heap, *n.* A pile, رَكْم — عَرَمَة — كُومَة *pl.* أَكْوَام — صُبْرَة. A — of wheat, حِنْطَةٍ (صُبْرَةُ or) عَرَمَةٌ *coll.* عَرَم. A — of mud, جُثْمَة; of earth, a mound, تَلّ *pl.* أَتْلَال *and* تِلَال — أَكَمَة *pl.* إِكَام; of stones, رُجْمَة *pl.* رُجَم; of clouds, رُكَامُ سَحَابٍ; of sand, رُكَامُ رَمْلٍ. A round —, كُمْزَة. A — of people, a crowd, عَمٌّ *pl.* عُمُومَة — جَوْقَة — إِزْدِحَام — جَمْع — جَمَاعَة. In a —, أَكْوَامًا — إِرْتِكَامًا — مُشَوَّش — مُلْتَبِك — مُرْتَبِك. All of a —, in disorder, مُلْتَخْبِط. Confounded, مُتَحَيِّر. To strike one all of a —, حَيَّرَ — أَدْهَشَ.

Heap, *v.t.* To pile, رَكَمَ — كَدَّسَ — كَرَّسَ — كَوَّمَ — عَرَّمَ. To — on wood, كَثَّرَ ٱلْحَطَبَ. To be heaped up, تَعَقَّدَ — تَرَاكَمَ — إِرْتَكَمَ. To be heaped up together, or one upon another, رَكِبَ بَعْضُهُ بَعْضًا.

Hear, *v.t.* To perceive by the ear, سَمِعَ — إِسْتَمَعَ — تَسَمَّعَ — أَسْمَعَ. To listen to, سَمِعَ — تَسَمَّعَ إِلَى — إِسْتَمَعَ إِلَى. To — with attention, أَنْصَتَ لِ — صَغَى إِلَى *aor.* يَصْغَى — أَصْغَى إِلَى. إِسْتَحْسَبَ كَلَامَهُ — أَصْغَى إِلَى — سَمِعَ لِ. To obey, سَمِعَ — أَطَاعَ — قَامَ بِأَمْرِهِ. To try, as of a judge, فَحَصَ عَنِ ٱلدَّعْوَى — قَضَى — فَصَّلَ ٱلدَّعْوَى. To make to —, سَمَّعَ. To pretend to —, تَسَامَعَ. He said it that it might be heard, قَالَ كَذَا سُمْعَةً. Things heard, مَسْمُوعَات. When he heard, لَمَّا بَلَغَ مَسَامِعَهُ. I never heard the like of that speech, مَا سَكَّ سَمْعِي مِثْلَ ذَلِكَ — مَا ٱسْتَكَّ فِي مَسَامِعِي مِثْلُهُ — الْكَلَامِ. May God — (accept) the praise of him who praises Him! سَمِعَ ٱللَّهُ لِمَنْ حَمِدَهُ.

Hear, *v.i.* To have the sense of hearing, سَمْعًا يَسْمَعُ. To know, to listen, سَمِعَ. To — from, سَمِعَ مِن. To — of,

سَمِعَ عَن – ـَ سَمِعَ ٱلتَّكَلُّمَ بِ. He heard of..., as spoken of, To — is to obey, سَمْعًا وَطَاعَةً. We have heard that ..., قَدْ بَلَغَنَا أَنْ. The people heard of it from one another, تَسَامَعَ بِهِ ٱلنَّاسُ.

Hearer, *n.* An auditor, سَامِع *pl.* سُمَّاع – مُسْتَمِع – حَاضِر *pl.* حُضَّار. Hearers, an audience, مَحْضَر – جَمَاعَة – ٱلْحُضَّارُ. The Hearer, (of God,) ٱلسَّمِيعُ. O Thou Hearer (answerer) of prayer! يَا مُجِيبَ ٱلسُّؤَالِ. One who listens attentively, سَمَّاع.

Hearing, *n.* The sense of, سَمْع – ٱلْقُوَّةُ ٱلسَّامِعَةُ. The act of listening, سَمَاعَة – إِسْتِمَاع. A judicial trial, فَحْصُ دَعْوَى – قَضَاء.

A place of hearing, where one listens, مَسْمَع.

Dull of hearing, ثَقِيلُ ٱلسَّمْعِ.

In or within one's hearing, فِي مَسْمَعِهِ. In my hearing, وَأَنَا سَامِعٌ.

They said so in my hearing, قَالُوا ذٰلِكَ سَمْعَةَ أُذُنِي.

To give a hearing, as on a trial, ـَ فَحَصَ عَنِ ٱلدَّعْوَى.

To give one a hearing, ـَ سَمِعَ لِ.

To obtain a hearing, an audience, of such an one, ـُ حَصَلَ عَلَى ٱلْمُلَاقَاةِ مَعَ فُلَانٍ.

Hearing, *a.* سَمِيع – سَامِع. A — ear, أُذُنٌ سَامِعَةٌ – أُذُنٌ – سَمَّاعَةٌ.

Hearken, *v.t.* To listen to, أَنْصَتَ إِلَى. *See also to* Hear, *v.t.* and *i.*

Hearsay, *n.* Rumour, report, صَوْت – رِوَايَة – تَسَامُع – قَوْل – شُهْرَة.

Hearse, *n.* عَرَبَانَةٌ لِنَقْلِ ٱلْمَوْتَى – نَعْش. *See also* Bier, *n.*

Hearse-cloth, *n.* غِطَاءُ (or كِسْوَةُ) ٱلنَّعْشِ.

Heart, *n.* The organ, لُبّ *pl.* أَلْبَاب – فُؤَاد *pl.* أَفْئِدَة – قَلْب *pl.* قُلُوب. The heart's core, حَبَّةُ ٱلْقَلْبِ. The heart's blood, مُهْجَة. The mind, ٱلضَّمِيرُ – ٱلطَّوِيَّةُ. The inner part of anything, the core, قَلْب – لُبّ *pl.* لُبُوب – وَسْط. Courage, مُرُوَّة – هِمَّة – جَرَاءَة – قُوَّةُ قَلْب. Affection, inclination, حُبّ – نَفْس – وِدَاد – مَيْل – هَوًى. The — of a country, عُقْرُ ٱلْبِلَادِ. Concern, care, إِعْتِنَاء – إِهْتِمَام – رَغْبَة. Disposition, خُلُق – طَبْع. Purpose, قَصْد – نِيَّة. Conscience, ذِمَّة – ضَمِير. Memory, ذِكْر – حَافِظَة – حِفْظُ ٱلْقَلْبِ. Disease of the —, قُلَاب.

A bad heart, قَلْبٌ رَدِيءٌ. A hard heart, قَلْبٌ جَبَّارٌ. Having a bad heart, رَدِيءُ ٱلْقَلْبِ.

A good heart, قَلْبٌ سَلِيمٌ. Having a good heart, سَلِيمُ ٱلْقَلْبِ – خَالِصُ ٱلْفُؤَادِ.

At heart, having at heart, فِي حِفْظِ ٱلْقَلْبِ – حَافِظٌ عَلَى. Truly, حَقِيقَةً.

By heart, عَلَى ظَهْرِ ٱلْقَلْبِ – غَيْبًا. He knew the Kurân by heart, ـِ حَمَلَ ٱلْقُرْآنَ عَلَى ظَهْرِ لِسَانِهِ.

From the bottom of the heart, مِنْ غُشَّانِ ٱلْقَلْبِ – مِنْ صَمِيمِ – مِن صَمِيمِ ٱلْقَلْبِ – ٱلْفُؤَادِ.

Light of heart, فَرْحَان *pl.* فَرَاحَى *fem.* فَرْحَى – مَسْرُور – مَمْنُون – and فَرْحَانَة – مَحْبُور.

Sick at heart, سَقِيمُ ٱلْقَلْبِ – مَغْمُوم – مُكَدَّر.

To one's heart's content, عَلَى كَيْفِهِ – عَلَى مُرَادِهِ – عَلَى خَاطِرِهِ – إِقْتِنَاعًا.

To be of good heart, إِسْتَبْشَرَ – تَشَجَّعَ – يَثِقُ *aor.* وَثِقَ.

To be out of heart, discouraged, ـَ فَشِلَ – إِرْتَعَبَ – إِنْقَطَعَ قَلْبُهُ.

To break a person's heart, ـِ كَسَرَ قَلْبَهُ – ـِ جَرَمَ قَلْبَهُ – ـَ غَرَّقَ فِي بَحْرِ ٱلْآلَامِ.

To commune with one's own heart, فَتَّشَ قَلْبَهُ – تَكَلَّمَ فِي قَلْبِهِ.

To find it in one's heart to..., to be able to, إِسْتَطَاعَ – أَطَاقَ عَلَى.

Not to have the heart to..., مَا لَهُ قَلْبٌ أَنْ – مَا أَمْكَنَ لَهُ أَنْ.

To get by heart, ـَ حَفِظَ عَلَى ظَهْرِ قَلْبِهِ – ـَ حَفِظَ غَيْبًا.

To get at one's heart, ـِ مَلَكَ قَلْبَهُ.

To have at heart, to be inclined to, ـِ مَالَ إِلَى. To aspire to, ـَ رَغِبَ فِي – تَنَافَسَ فِي.

To set one's heart on, ـِ عَقَدَ قَلْبَهُ عَلَى – وَجَدَ بِ *aor.* يَجِدُ – ـَ جَعَلَ فِي قَلْبِهِ – يَضَعُ *aor.* وَضَعَ عَلَى قَلْبًا.

To take heart, تَشَجَّعَ – ـُ جَسَرَ – تَشَدَّدَ – تَصَلَّبَ.

To take a thing to heart, ـَ حَزِنَ عَلَى – إِنْغَمَّ عَلَى.

To unburden one's heart, ـُ سَكَبَ نَفْسَهُ – سَكَبَ قَلْبَهُ – أَفَاضَ رُوحَهُ.

To win the heart of, ـُ سَلَبَ قَلْبَهُ – ـِ مَلَكَ قَلْبَهُ.

To wring the heart of, ـَ سَحَقَ (or قَطَّعَ) قَلْبَهُ.

Heartache, *n.* Deep sorrow, غَمّ – تَأَسُّف – كَرْب. To have the —, إِكْتَرَبَ – إِنْغَمَّ.

Heartbroken, *a.* مَجْرُوحُ ٱلْقَلْبِ – غَارِقٌ فِي بَحْرِ ٱلْآلَامِ – مُنْسَحِقُ ٱلْقَلْبِ.

Heartburn, *n.* دَاءُ ٱلْمَعِدَةِ – دَاءُ ٱلْمَأْنَةِ.

Heart-burning, *n.* Discontent, عَدَمُ قَنَاعَةٍ. Secret enmity, ضِغْن – كُشَاحَة. To have — against, ـَ ضَغِنَ عَلَى. They entertained mutual —, of many, تَضَاغَنُوا.

Heartfelt, *a.* Sincere, عَنْ صَمِيمِ ٱلْقَلْبِ – سَلِيم – صَادِق – خَالِص – نَصُوح.

Hearth, *n.* The fireside, جُوب ـ مَوْقِد ـ مَوْقِدَة ـ إِرَة *pl.* أَرَاة. Home, وَطَن ـ كِنّ.

Hearth-stone, *n.* حَجَرَةُ ٱلْمَوْقِدِ ـ أُثْفِيَّة.

Heartily, *ad.* بِطِيبَةِ خاطِرٍ ـ مِنْ صَمِيمِ ٱلْقَلْبِ ـ مِنَ ٱلْقَلْبِ. Actively, بِهِمَّةٍ ـ بِرَغْبَةٍ. With appetite, بِٱشْتِهَآءٍ.

Heartiness, *n.* Sincerity, صَفَآء ـ خُلُوص ـ صِدْق. Diligence, هِمَّة ـ مُرُوَّة ـ جِدّ. Appetite, إِشْتِهَآء.

Heartless, *a.* Without spirit, قَلِيلُ ٱلْمُرُوَّةِ ـ جَبِين ـ جَبان. Harsh, قاسٍ ـ شَرِيس ـ شَرِس ـ عَنِيف.

Heartlessly, *ad.* Without spirit, بِجَبَانَةٍ. Harshly, عِنْفًا ـ بِشَرَاسَةٍ.

Heartlessness, *n.* Want of spirit, فَشَل ـ جَبَانَة. Harshness, شَرَاسَة ـ قَسَاحَة ـ عِنْف ـ قَسَاوَةُ قَلْبٍ.

Heart-rending, *a.* يَسْحَقُ (*or* يَكْسِرُ *or* يُقَطِّعُ) ٱلْقَلْبَ.

Heart-searching, *a.* كاشِفُ ٱلْقَلْبِ ـ فاحِصُ ٱلضَّمِيرِ.

Heart's-ease, *n.* The plant, زَهْرَةُ ٱلثَّالُوثِ.

Heart-sick, *a.* مُتَكَدِّرُ ٱلخاطِرِ ـ قَلِق ـ مَكْرُوب.

Heartsome, *a.* Cheerful, مَحْبُور ـ فَلْتان ـ أَلُوب ـ مَسْرُور.

Heart-stirring, *a.* مُهَيِّج ـ مُحَرِّض. Gladdening, مُفَرِّح ـ مُحَبِّر ـ مُطْرِب.

Heart-strings, *n.* أَوْتَارُ ٱلْفُؤَادِ ـ أَعْصَابُ ٱلْقَلْبِ.

Heart-whole, *a.* سَلِيمُ (*or* شافِي) ٱلْقَلْبِ.

Hearty, *a.* Sincere, نَصُوح ـ صادِق ـ خالِص ـ قَلْبِيّ. Healthy, صَلِيح ـ سَلِيم ـ قَوِيّ ـ ذو عَافِيَةٍ.

Heat, *n.* شَوْب ـ حُمَّة ـ سُخْنَة ـ سُخُونَة ـ حَرّ ـ حَمّ. Intense —, أَجَّة ـ أَجِيج. The — of fever, سُخُونَة ـ سُخْنَة. Vehemence, as of —, فَوْرَة. Heat from a fire, وَقِيد. Ardour, شِدَّة ـ رَغْبَة ـ شَوْق ـ غَيْرَة ـ مُرُوَّة. Passion, غَضَب ـ حُمَيَّا. One course at a race, شَوْط ـ أَعْراق *pl.* عَرَق ـ أَشْراف *pl.* شَرَف *pl.* أَشْواط ـ جِرْيَة. He ran a —, شَاطَ *aor.* يَشُوطُ.

Heat, *v.t.* To make hot, أَسْخَنَ ـ سَخَّنَ ـ أَحْمَى ـ أَحَمَّ ـ حَمَّمَ. To make warm with covering, دَفَّى. To warm another with anger, أَشْعَلَ-غَضَبًا ـ أَغْضَبَ; with ardour for, أَحْمَى-عَلَى ـ حَرَّكَ-إِلَى ـ حَرَّضَ-عَلَى. He warmed him with ardour for fight, أَحْمَاهُ عَلَى ٱلْقِتالِ. *See also under* Hot, *a.*

Heat, *v.i.* To be in a —, إِحْتَمَى ـ حَمِيَ. To be heated with rage, إِشْتَعَلَ غَضَبًا ـ إِحْتَمَى غَضَبًا. *See also under* Hot, *a.*

Heater, *n.* حَدِيدَةٌ حَامِيَةٌ ـ مِكْوَاة ـ مِسْخَنَة.

Heath, *n.* The shrub, خَلَنْج. An open plain, أَرْض ـ بادِيَة ـ صَحْرَآء ـ مِيدان ـ قاع ـ صاعَة ـ عاقُول.

Heath-cock, *n.* دُرَّاجَة *coll.* دُرَّاج *pl.* دَرَارِيجُ.

Heathen, *n.* } A gentile, وَثَنِيّ ـ أُمِّيّ *pl.* أُمِّيُّونَ ـ وَثَنِيُّونَ *pl.*
Heathen, *a.* } An idolater, مُشْرِك ـ عُبَّاد *pl.* عابِدُ ٱلْأَصْنامِ *pl.* مُشْرِكُونَ.

Heathendom, *n.* بِلادُ عُبَّادِ ٱلْأَصْنامِ ـ بِلادُ ٱلْكُفَّارِ ـ أَرْضُ ٱلْوَثَنِيِّينَ.

Heathenish, *a.* Like a heathen, كَٱلْوَثَنِيِّ. Rude, barbarous, فَلَّاح ـ جافٍ ـ عَجَمِيّ ـ هَمَج. Heathenish, barbarous, people, قَوْمٌ هَمَجٌ.

Heathenism, *n.* Gentilism, الأُمِّيَّة ـ الوَثَنِيَّة. Idolatry, عِبادَةُ ٱلْأَصْنامِ ـ كُفْر ـ شِرْك ـ الأَصْنامِيَّة.

Heather, *n.* *See* Heath, *n.*

Heather-bells, *n.* زَهْرُ ٱلخَلَنْجِ.

Heathery, *a.* } مِنْبَاتُ خَلَنْجٍ ـ مَخْلَنْج.
Heathy, }

Heating, *a.* مُنْتِجُ حُمُوٍّ ـ مُوَلِّدُ حَرارَةٍ.

Heave, *v.i.* To rise and fall, to flutter, خَفَقَ ـ نَهَجَ. To rise, to swell, عَلَا ـ فارَ ـ تَصَعَّدَ ـ صَعِدَ. To roll, as a ship, تَحَرَّكَ ـ تَمَايَلَ ـ إِرْتَجَّ ـ تَقَالَبَ. To feel a tendency to vomit, تَخَوَّعَ. To — in sight, نَدَرَ ـ أَشْرَفَ ـ تَبَيَّنَ. To — or haul down, أَهْبَطَ ـ أَنْزَلَ. To — to, as of a ship, صَلَّبَ ٱلْمَرْكَبَ. To — ahead, تَقَدَّمَ تَدْرِيجًا. To — astern, تَأَخَّرَ تَدْرِيجًا.

Heave, *v.t.* To lift, شَالَ ـ شَالَ بِ ـ أَشَالَ ـ رَفَعَ ـ عَلَّى. To throw, طَرَحَ ـ رَمَى *aor.* يَرْمِي. To —, as of a ship, ahead, قَدَّمَ-تَدْرِيجًا. To — astern, أَخَّرَ-تَدْرِيجًا. To — a sigh, حَنَّ ـ تَنَهَّدَ.

Heave, *n.* A rising, fluttering, خَفَقَان ـ نَهْج. A roll, as of a ship, تَقَالُب ـ إِرْتِجاج. The — of the sea, تَمَوُّجُ ٱلْبَحْرِ. A throw, cast, طَرْحَة ـ رَمْيَة. A rising, swelling, صُعُود ـ تَصَعُّد.

Heaven, *n.* The expanse above us, سَقْفُ ٱلْأَرْضِ ـ الرَّقِيعُ ـ الجَوّ ـ الجَلَدُ ـ الفَلَكُ ـ السَّمَآء. Paradise, دارُ ٱلخُلْدِ ـ الجَنَّة ـ السَّمَاوَاتُ ـ فِرْدَوْسُ ٱلنَّعِيمِ. God, اللّٰهُ تَعالَى. Happiness, سَعادَة ـ سُرُور ـ حُبُور.

Good beavens! يا لِلْعَجَبِ ـ لِلّٰهِ دَرِّي.

Thanks to heaven! لِلّٰهِ ٱلْحَمْدُ ـ الحَمْدُ لِلّٰهِ.

Would to heaven! يا لَيْتَ.

To ascend to heaven, صَعِدَ إِلَى ٱلسَّمَآءِ.

To call heaven to witness to, أَشْهَدَ ٱللّٰهَ عَلَى كَذا ـ حَلَفَ بِٱللّٰهِ عَلَى كَذا.

To move heaven and earth, بَذَلَ كُلَّ جُهْدِهِ وَسَعْيِهِ ـ قَلَّبَ ٱلدُّنْيا.

Heavenliness, *n.* Happiness in another state, سَعَادَةٌ أُخْرَاوِيَّةٌ. Delightfulness, نَعِيمٌ. Beauty, splendour, بَهَآءٌ — جَمَال — طُلَاوَة — رَوْنَق.

Heavenly, *a.* Of the firmament, فَلَكِيّ — سَمَاوِيّ — سَمَائِيّ. Divine, إِلٰهِيّ — رَبَّانِيّ — مِنَ ٱللّٰهِ. High, عَلِيّ — عُلْوِيّ. Spiritual, رُوحَانِيّ. Angelic, مَلَكِيّ. Beautiful, بَهِيّ — جَمِيل. Our — Father, أَبُونَا ٱلسَّمَاوِيّ — أَبُونَا ٱلَّذِي فِي ٱلسَّمَاوَاتِ. The — bodies, ٱلْأَجْرَامُ ٱلْفَلَكِيَّةُ.

Heavenly, *ad.* بِأُسْلُوبٍ سَمَاوِيّ.

Heavenward, *ad.* نَحْوَ ٱلسَّمَآءِ — تَوَجُّهًا إِلَى ٱلسَّمَآءِ.

Heave-offering, *n.* صَعِيدَة *pl.* صَعَائِدُ.

Heavily, *ad.* With great weight, بِثِقَلٍ. Much, جَزِيلًا — كَثِيرًا — بِشِدَّةٍ. Sorrowfully, بِكَآبَةٍ — بِحُزْنٍ — بِغَمٍّ. Slowly, بِبُطْوءٍ — رُوَيْدًا — عَلَى مَهْلٍ. They drove —, سَاقُوا بِثِقْلَةٍ. The yoke bore — upon them, ثَقُلَ عَلَيْهِمُ ٱلنِّيرُ. It rained —, تَصَوَّبَ ٱلْمَطَرُ — تَمَطَّرَتْ صُبُوبًا.

Heaviness, *n.* Weight, ثِقَل — ثَقْلَة — ثَقَالَة. Affliction, كَرْب — غَمّ — كَآبَة — حُزْن — ضِيقَة. Laziness, كَسَل. Stupidity, بَلَادَة — خُرْق — حَمَاقَة. Sleepiness, نُعَاس — ثَقْلَة — نُوَام. Heaviness in the heart of a man makes him stoop, ٱلْغَمُّ فِي قَلْبِ ٱلرَّجُلِ يَحْنِيهِ.

Heavy, *a.* Ponderous, رَزِين — ثَقِيل. Sorrowful, كَئِيب — مَغْمُوم — حَزِين — مَكْرُوب — مَلُول. Oppressive, شَاقّ — جَائِر — ظَالِم — ظَلِيم. Causing sorrow, مُحْزِن — مُغِمّ — شَاقّ. Much, كَثِير — شَدِيد — وَافِر — رُدَام. Dull, stupid, أَخْرَق — فُطَارِيّ — بَلِيد — أَحْمَق — ثَقِيلُ ٱلْعَقْلِ. Lazy, كَسْلَان — تِنْبَل. A — sluggish fellow, مُبْرِم. Not easily digested, عَسِرُ ٱلْهَضْمِ — ثَقِيل. Difficult, as of a road, وَعِر — صَعْب — عَسِير. Rich, of soil, مُخْصِب — مَرْبَع. Tedious, مُمِلّ — مُتْعِب — شَاقّ. Turbid, كَدِر — عَكِر — كَدِير. Cloudy, مُغَيَّم. Slow, بَطِيء. Large, كَبِير. Important, مُهِمّ — بَارِع — كَبِير — عَظِيم. Difficult, intricate, صَعْب — مُشْكِل. Drowsy, نَوْمَانُ — نَعْسَانُ — نَاعِس. Heavy sums, مَبَالِغُ فَاحِشَةٌ. To be —, weighty, ثَقُلَ ². To make —, ثَقَّلَ. To consider —, إِسْتَثْقَلَ. The matter is too — for you, ٱلْأَمْرُ أَعْظَمُ مِنْكَ. The demand was — upon them, كَانَ ٱلْمَطْلُوبُ ثَقِيلًا عَلَيْهِمْ. Their eyes were — with sleep, تَثَقَّلُوا بِٱلنَّوْمِ. He laid a — burden on him, ثَقَّلَ عَلَيْهِ — أَثْقَلَهُ: He imposed upon him a burden heavier than he could bear, أَبْطَرَهُ ذَرْعَهُ. To be heavier, to outweigh, رَجَحَ ² ²: He made this heavier, *i.e.* to outweigh that, رَجَّحَ هٰذَا عَلَى ذَاكَ.

Hebdomadal, *a.* }
Hebdomadary, } أُسْبُوعِيّ — كُلَّ أُسْبُوعٍ.

Hebelate, *v.t.* To stupefy, أَبْطَرَ — سَفَّهَ عَقْلَهُ — أَبْهَمَ.

Hebetude, *n.* سَفَه — غَبَن.

Hebraic, *a.* *See* Hebrew, *a.*

Hebraism, *n.* إِصْطِلَاحٌ عِبْرَانِيٌّ.

Hebraist, *n.* عَالِمٌ بِٱللِّسَانِ ٱلْعِبْرَانِيِّ.

Hebraistic, *a.* مُتَعَلِّقٌ بِٱللِّسَانِ ٱلْعِبْرَانِيِّ.

Hebraize, *v.t.* صَيَّرَ (or جَعَلَ) كَٱلْعِبْرَانِيِّ.

Hebrew, *n.* } عِبْرَانِيّ *pl.* عِبْرَانِيُّونَ — يَهُودِيّ *coll.* يَهُود. The —
Hebrew, *a.* } language, ٱللِّسَانُ ٱلْعِبْرَانِيُّ — ٱلْعِبْرِيَّةُ — ٱلْعِبْرَانِيَّةُ.

Hebrewess, *n.* عِبْرَانِيَّة — إِمْرَأَةٌ عِبْرَانِيَّةٌ *pl.* نِسَآءٌ — يَهُودِيَّة.

Hecatomb, *n.* ذَبِيحَةُ مِئَةِ ثَوْرٍ.

Hectare, *n.* قِيَاسٌ فَرَنْسَاوِيٌّ قَدْرُهُ نَحْوَ فَدَّانَيْنِ وَنِصْفِ فَدَّانٍ.

Hectic, *a.* Habitual, continual, مُعْتَاد — مَطْبُوعٌ عَلَى — دَائِم. A — fever, حُمَّى ٱلدِّقِّ — ٱلدَّمَوِيَّةُ.

Hector, *n.* جَبَّار — سَفَّاح — غِطْرِيس — مِهْيَاص.

Hector, *v.t.* تَجَبَّرَ عَلَى — سَخِطَ عَلَى.

Hector, *v.i.* To bluster, بَطِرَ — تَجَبَّرَ — غَطْرَسَ — تَنَفَّخَ — تَهَوَّرَ.

Hectoring, *n.* بَطَر — تَجَبُّر — غَطْرَسَة — تَنَفُّخ — تَهَوُّر.

Hedge, *n.* سِيَاج *pl.* سُوَج — وَشِيع; a fence, جِدَار — جَدِيرَة — حَدِيقَة. A — for protecting sheep, زَرِيبَة.

Hedge, *v.t.* To make a — to, سَيَّجَ — سَوَّجَ. To inclose in, أَحَاطَ بِ. To protect, حَفِظَ — حَامَى — خَفَرَ ². To — or thrust in, حَشَرَ ²; to prevent, حَصَرَ ².

Hedge, *v.i.* To keep back, تَمَاسَكَ — تَمَسَّكَ. To trim, to practise shifts, تَحَوَّلَ — إِحْتَالَ. To bet on both sides, وَضَعَ مُرَاهَنَةً عَلَى ٱلطَّرَفَيْنِ *aor.* يَضَعُ.

Hedgehog, *n.* شَيْهَم — شَوْهَب — لُشْتَة — حَسِيكَة — أَنْقَدُ *pl.* قَنَافِذُ قُنْفُذ.

Hedger, *n.* One who makes hedges, سَيَّاج. A shuffler, مُحْتَال — مُتَحَوِّل — قُلَّب — حُوَّل.

Hedgerow, *n.* سِيَاجُ شَجَرٍ — مُشَجَّر.

Heed, *n.* Care, إِعْتِنَآء — إِهْتِمَام — حِذْر — مُبَالَاة — حِرْس. Attention, مُلَاحَظَة — إِعْتِبَار — إِعْتِنَآء — إِلْتِفَات. To give — to, أَصْغَى إِلَى. *See also* Care, *n.*

Heed, *v.t.* To mind, بَالَى بِ — سَمِعَ لِ — أَنْصَتَ إِلَى. إِهْتَمَّ بِ — إِلْتَفَتَ إِلَى. To observe, لَاحَظَ — لَحَّ إِلَى ² — إِعْتَبَرَ. I do not — him, لَا أُبَالِيهِ — لَا أُبَالِي بِهِ.

Heed, *v.i.* تَحَفَّظَ.

Heedful, *a.* Attentive, مُعْتَنٍ ـ مُنْتَبِه. Cautious, حَذِير ـ حَرِيص ـ عاقِل. Heedful of propriety, أَدِيب.

Heedfully, *ad.* بِمُبالاةٍ ـ بِحِذْرٍ ـ بِٱنْتِباهٍ.

Heedfulness, *n.* *See* Heed, *n.*

Heedless, *a.* ساهٍ ـ مُتَعَسِّف ـ مِغْشَم ـ أَبْلَهُ ـ مُتَوانٍ ـ مُتَهامِل ـ غافِل ـ قَلِيلُ ٱلْإِعْتِناء ـ قَلِيلُ ٱلتَّمْيِيز. Not caring what he says or does, ماجِن. To be —, غَشَمَ ٱلْأُمُورَ ـ أَغْبَى. To be — of, سَهَا عَن *aor.* يَسْهُو ـ غَفَلَ عَن. To be — towards, to act heedlessly by, ساهَى ـ غَافَلَ. To feign one's self — of, تَغاطَشَ عَن.

Heedlessly, *ad.* بِتَوانٍ ـ بِتَهامُلٍ ـ بِتَغافُلٍ ـ بِبَلاهَة ـ بِسَهْوٍ ـ سُدًى. To act — in a matter, تَعَسَّفَ فِي ـ إِعْتَسَفَ فِي.

Heedlessness, *n.* بَلاهَة ـ تَعَسُّف ـ عَسافَة ـ سَهْو ـ تَهامُل ـ تَوانٍ.

Heel, *n.* Of the foot, عَقِب *pl.* أَعْقاب ـ كَعْب *pl.* كِعاب and كُعُب. The latter part, آخِر *pl.* أَواخِر. The lower end, أَسْفَل. To take to one's heels, فَرَّ ـ هَرَبَ ـ إِنْفَلَتَ ـ وَلَّى ـ عُرْضَ أَوْرَى ـ رَكِبَ أَكْتافَهُ. To be at one's heels, لَزِمَ ـ سَكَنَ فِي عَراقِيبِهِ ـ جَرَى وَرَآءَهُ ـ أَكْتافَهُ. To be out at heels, with holes in the stockings, مُخَرَّقُ ٱلْجَوارِب; to be in bad circumstances, إِفْتَقَرَ ـ إِحْتاجَ. To tread on one's heels, رَفَسَ. To trip up the heels of one, أَسْقَطَ ـ أَوْقَعَ. To stand heels upwards, إِنْتَكَسَ. Standing heels upwards, مُنْكَس ـ مَنْكُوس.

Heel, *v.t.* To — a boot, رَكَّبَ لِلنَّعْلِ كَعْبًا. To put a patch on the —, رَقَعَ كَعْبَ ٱلنَّعْلِ. To — a cock with a spur, رَكَّبَ لِلدِّيكِ شَوْكَةً مِنْ حَدِيدٍ.

Heel, *v.i.* To dance, رَقَصَ. To incline, مَالَ ـ ٱنْحَنَى ـ إِنْعَطَفَ.

Heel-rope, *n.* طِوَل ـ رِساغ ـ مِرْسَغَة *pl.* مَراسِغُ.

Heel-tap, *n.* A — to a shoe, رُقْعَةٌ فِي كَعْبِ ٱلْخُفِّ. Liquor left in a glass after drinking, شُفافَة ـ خِتام ـ بَقِيَّة.

Heel-tap, *v.t.* *See under to* Heel, *v.t.*

Heft, *n.* *See* Haft, Weight, *n.*

Heft, *v.t.* وَزَنَ *aor.* يَزِنُ ـ قَدَرَ.

Heifer, *n.* عِجْل *pl.* عُجُول and عِجال.

Heigh-ho! *int.* أَوَّاهْ ـ آه آه ـ آها.

Height, *n.* Elevation, عُلُوّ ـ رِفْعَة ـ إِرْتِفاع ـ شُهْقَة ـ عِلِّيَّة. High ground, رَبِيَّة ـ رابِيَة ـ رُبًى. Fortified heights, مَعاقِل. An eminence, hill, تَلّ *pl.* تُلُول ـ عَلايَة ـ أَكَمَة *pl.* أَكَمات. Excellence, رِفْعَة ـ عُلًى ـ نَجابَة. Completion, كَمال ـ تَمام ـ غايَة. Utmost degree, شِدَّة. The —, as of water, or the day, مَدّ ـ نِيآء. The — of happiness, كَمالُ ٱلسَّعادَةِ. The — of summer, شِدَّةُ ٱلصَّيْفِ. The —, as of a disease, بُحْران. The — of the day has come upon us, أَتانا شِدُّ ٱلنَّهارِ. To be at its —, بَلَغَ أَشُدَّهُ.

Heighten, *v.t.* To make higher, عَلَّى ـ رَفَعَ. To improve, حَسَّنَ ـ أَصْلَحَ ـ رَقَّى. To make more, larger, stronger, شَدَّدَ ـ عَظَّمَ ـ كَبَّرَ. To — a colour, شَبَّ.

Heinous, *n.* Enormous, شَدِيد ـ كَبِير ـ فَظِيع. Very wicked, أَشْنَعُ (or أَشَدُّ شَناعَةً) ـ أَخْبَثُ (or أَشَدُّ خَباثَةً). A — crime, كَبِيرَة *pl.* كَبائِرُ ـ فَظاعَة *pl.* فَظائِعُ. *See also* Atrocious, Flagitious, *a.*

Heinously, *ad.* Enormously, بِفَظاعَةٍ ـ بِإِفْراطٍ. Atrociously, بِفُجُورٍ ـ بِفُحْشٍ.

Heinousness, *n.* Enormity, وَبال ـ جَسامَة ـ فَظاعَة ـ شِدَّة. Odiousness, شَناعَة ـ خَباثَة.

Heir, *n.* وارِث *pl.* وَرَثَة. Heir apparent, وَلِيُّ عَهْدٍ. Heir presumptive, ٱلْمُقَدَّرُ لَهُ بِٱلْمُلْكِ بَعْدَ وَفاةِ ٱلسُّلْطانِ. To be heir, وَرِثَ *aor.* يَرِثُ. To appoint as heir, وَرَّثَ ـ أَوْرَثَ ـ خَلَّفَ.

Heirdom, *n.* خِلافَة ـ خَلَف; a perpetual —, تَناسُخ.

Heiress, *n.* وارِثَة *pl.* وارِثات.

Heirless, *a.* لا وارِثَ لَهُ.

Heirloom, *n.* مَتاعٌ مُخْتَصٌّ بِٱلْمِيراثِ *pl.* أَمْتِعَة ـ تِرْكَة ـ تَرِكَة *pl.* تَرِكات.

Heirship, *n.* وِراثَة ـ مِيراث.

Hejra, *n.* (More correctly *al-Hijrah*), ٱلْهِجْرَة ـ تارِيخُ ٱلْهِجْرَةِ.

Helial, *a.* } شَمْسِيٌّ. Heliacal rising, طالِعٌ بَيْنَ شُعاعِ ٱلشَّمْسِ.
Heliacal, } Heliacal setting, غائِبٌ بَيْنَ شُعاعِ ٱلشَّمْسِ.

Helical, *a.* لَوْلَبِيٌّ.

Heliocentric, *a.* ما دَلَّ عَلَى مَنْزِلَةِ ٱلنَّجْمِ عَنْ مَرْكَزِ ٱلشَّمْسِ.

Heliography, *n.* ٱلرَّسْمُ بِوَاسِطَةِ ضَوْءِ ٱلشَّمْسِ.

Heliolatry, *n.* عِبادَةُ ٱلشَّمْسِ.

Heliometer, *n.* مِقْياسُ قُطْرِ دائِرَةِ ٱلشَّمْسِ وَٱلنُّجُوم.

Heliostat, *n.* آلَةٌ دالَّةٌ عَلَى مَوْقِعِ شُعاعِ ٱلشَّمْسِ.

Heliotrope, *n.* The flower, دَوّارُ ٱلشَّمْسِ ـ أَكْرار. The large —, تُنَوِّم; the small —, صابِرٌ يَوْمًا. *See also* Blood-stone, *n.*

Helispherical, *a.* فِي هَيْئَةِ ٱلْهالَةِ ٱلْكُرَوِيَّةِ.

Helix, *n.* A spiral line, خَطٌّ مُلَوًّى ـ لَوْلَب. A coil of wire, ثَنِيٌّ مِنَ ٱلسِّلْكِ. The external ear, ٱلْمَحارَة ـ صَحْنُ ٱلْأُذُنِ.

Hell, *n.* The place of the damned, ٱلْجَحِيمُ ـ جَهَنَّمُ ـ ٱلسَّقَرُ. The grave, ٱلْقَبْرُ. The place of departed spirits, عالَمُ ٱلْأَمْواتِ ـ

الجحيم. The powers of hell, قُوَّاتُ جَهَنَّمَ. A gambling-house, قِمارخانه ـ دارُ قِمارٍ.

Hellebore, *n.* خَرْبَق.

Hellenian, *a.* / Hellenic, } يُونانِيٌّ.

Hellenism, *n.* اِصْطِلاحٌ يُونانِيٌّ.

Hellenist, *n.* Learned in Greek, عالِمٌ بِٱلْيُونانِيَّةِ. One who uses the Greek language, مُسْتَعْمِلُ ٱللِّسانِ ٱلْيُونانِيِّ.

Hellenize, *v.i.* إِسْتَعْمَلَ ٱللِّسانَ ٱلْيُونانِيَّ.

Hell-hound, *n.* اِبْنُ جَهَنَّمَ ـ مِنْ أَهْلِ جَهَنَّمَ.

Hellish, *a.* Of hell, جَهَنَّمِيٌّ. Malignant, ضاغِن ـ مُسْتَحِمّ ـ خَبِيث ـ خَنِك ـ حَسِك.

Hellishly, *ad.* مِثْلَ أَهْلِ جَهَنَّمَ ـ بِحَنَكٍ ـ بِحَسَكٍ ـ بِضِغْنٍ.

Hellishness, *n.* خَباثَة ـ شَيْطَنَة ـ سَخِيمَة ـ حَسَك ـ ضِغْن.

Helm, *n.* A tiller, سُكَّان ـ خَيْزُران ـ كُوتَل. A rudder, دَفَّة. A centre of government, صَدْرُ إِدارَةٍ ـ إِدارَة.

Helm, *n.* / Helmet, } Armour for the head, مِغْفَر ـ دَوْمَص ـ بَيْضَة ـ خُوذَة.

Helm, *v.t.* To cover with a helmet, لَبَّسَ-خُوذَةً. To steer with the —, ضَبَطَ ٱلسُّكّانَ. To direct, دَبَّرَ ـ ساسَ *aor.* يَسُوسُ ـ قادَ.

Helmsman, *n.* Of a ship, ماسِكُ ٱلدَّفَّةِ ـ ٱلْمُسْتَعْمِلُ. One who guides, مُدَبِّر ـ سائِس *pl.* ساسَة ـ قائِد *pl.* قُوّاد.

Helot, *n.* A slave, مَمْلُوك *pl.* مَمالِيك ـ أَسِير *pl.* أَسْرَى.

Helotism, *n.* Slavery, عُبُودِيَّة.

Help, *v.t.* To aid, عاوَنَ ـ ساعَفَ ـ عاضَدَ ـ عَزَّرَ ـ عَزَّ ـ ساعَدَ ـ أَغاثَ ـ أَعانَ. To supply with, أَمَدَّ-بِ. To remedy, أَصْلَحَ ـ داوَى ـ عالَجَ. To forbear, إِمْتَنَعَ عَنْ. To prevent, أَمْسَكَ ـ حَجَبَ ـ عَوَّقَ-عَنْ. To give, to hand, to, أَعْطَى ـ نَوَّلَ-لِ. To — against, عَلَى (- ساعَدَ or) عاوَنَ-. To — one's self, to take, تَناوَلَ. To ask for — from, إِسْتَعانَ ـ إِسْتَسْعَدَ ـ إِسْتَغاثَ بِ ـ إِسْتَغاثَ. To ask one for — against, إِسْتَمَدَّ-عَلَى. I cannot — it, ما عَلَيَّ مِنْهُ. It cannot be helped, لَيْسَ لِهٰذا لَيْسَ لَهُ عِلاجٌ ـ لا بُدَّ مِنْهُ ـ ٱلْأَمْرُ لا بُدَّ. If I can —, prevent, it, إِنْ قَدَرْتُ أَنْ أَمْنَعَهُ. I could not — it, it was not my fault, ما هُوَ ذَنْبِي ـ ما لِي ذَنْبٌ فِيهِ. Help yourself to..., تَفَضَّلْ إِلَى كَذا. Will you not help yourself to...? أَلا تُكَلِّفُ خاطِرَكَ أَلا تَتَفَضَّلُ إِلَى كَذا ـ إِلَى كَذا. They helped one another in the affair, تَعاوَنُوا عَلَى ٱلْأَمْرِ.

To help down, نَزَّلَ ـ أَنْزَلَ.

To help forward, دَرَّجَ ـ قَدَّمَ.

To help out, as of a difficulty, خَلَّصَ-مِنْ ـ فَرَّجَ (or أَفْرَجَ) مِنْ ـ أَنْقَذَ-مِنْ.

To help over, to help to pass over, عَدَّى ـ عَبَّرَ ـ قَطَّعَ.

To help up, to raise, رَفَعَ ـ قَيَّمَ ـ شالَ.

Help, *v.i.* To contribute to, إِسْتَدْرَجَ ـ ساعَدَ ـ عاوَنَ. To be useful to, نَفَعَ لِ ـ صَلَحَ لِ.

Help, *n.* Aid, إِعانَة ـ عَوْن ـ مَدَد ـ مُساعَفَة ـ عَزْر ـ مُعاضَدَة ـ غِياث ـ غَوْث ـ مُساعَدَة. A remedy, عِلاج ـ مُعالَجَة ـ إِصْلاح.

Helper, *n.* / Helpful, *a.* } Aider, aiding, مُساعِد ـ مُعاوِن ـ غِياث ـ ناصِر ـ ساعِد ـ مُعِين. Contributing to, مُفِيدٌ لِ ـ مُساعِفٌ لِ ـ صالِحٌ لِ ـ نافِعٌ لِ.

Helpfulness, *n.* *See* Help, *n.*

Helpless, *a.* Without help, لا مُعِينَ لَهُ ـ لا عَوْنَ لَهُ. Without strength, عاجِز. Destitute, poor, فَقِير ـ مُحْتاج. To be — to..., عَجَزَ عَنْ كَذا.

Helplessness, *n.* Want of strength, عَجْز. Poverty, إِفْتِقار ـ مَسْكَنَة.

Helpmate, *n.* / Helpmeet, } *See* Helper, *n.*

Helter-skelter, *ad.* خِلْطَ مِلْطَ ـ شَتاتَ شَتاتَ ـ شِذَرَ مِذَرَ.

Helve. *See* Haft, Handle, *n.*

Helve, *v.t.* *See* to Haft, *v.t.*

Helvetic, *a.* Pertaining to Switzerland, مُتَعَلِّقٌ بِإِسْوِيسَرَة. The — republic, جُمْهُورِيَّةُ إِسْوِيسَرَة.

Hem, *n.* The edge sewed down, كُفَّة *pl.* كُفَف ـ كَبْن. A border, كَنَف ـ حاشِيَة ـ طَرَف. The noise made by a sudden expiration of the breath, تَنَحْنُح ـ نَحْنَحَة.

Hem, *v.t.* Of sewing, كَفَّ ـ كَبَنَ. To edge, border, نَيَّرَ ـ كَنَّفَ. To — in, to confine, حاصَرَ ـ حَصَرَ ـ حَفَّ بِ.

Hemmed in, as by difficulties, *etc.*, مَحْفُوفٌ بِ.

Hem, *v.i.* To make a sudden expiration, تَنَحْنَحَ ـ أَحَّ.

Hematite, *n.* مَعْدِنُ ٱلْحَدِيدِ.

Hemicrany, *n.* شَقِيقَة.

Hemicycle, *n.* نِصْفُ دائِرَةٍ.

Hemiplegy, *n.* فالِج.

Hemipteral, *a.* ذُو أَجْنِحَةٍ نِصْفُها غِشائِيَّةٌ وَنِصْفُها جِلْدِيَّةٌ.

Hemisphere, *n.* Half of a sphere, نِصْفُ كُرَةٍ; half of the globe, نِصْفُ كُرَةِ ٱلْأَرْضِ.

Hemispheric, *a.* } عَلَى شَكْلِ نِصْفِ كُرَةٍ.
Hemispherical, }

Hemistich, *n.* مِصْرَاع *pl.* مَصَارِيعُ. The first part of the first — of a poem, صَدْر; the last part of a —, عَرُوض.

Hemlock, *n.* شَيْكُرَان ـ شَوْكُرَان.

Hemoptysis, *n.* نَفْثُ ٱلدَّمِ.

Hemorrhage, *n.* نُزُوف (or نَزْف) دَم ـ رُعَاف دَم.

Hemorrhoidal, *a.* بَوَاسِيرِيٌّ ـ بَاصُورِيٌّ. An — flux, سَيَلَانٌ بَاصُورِيٌّ.

Hemorrhoids, *n.* بَاصُور *pl.* بَوَاصِير ـ بَاسُور *pl.* بَوَاسِيرُ. Dry —, بَوَاسِيرُ غَيْرُ سَائِلَةٍ ـ بَوَاصِيرُ صُمٌّ.

Hemp, *n.* حَشِيش ـ قُنَّب. The — of which ropes are made, تِيل. Pills or potions made of — leaves, بَسْط. A chewer of —, حَشَّاش *pl.* حَشَّاشُونَ.

Hempen, *a.* مِنْ قُنَّب ـ قُنَّبِيٌّ.

Hemp-seed, *n.* قُنْبُس ـ طُلَّم ـ شَهْدَانَج.

Hemstitch, *n.* شَكَّة ـ غُرْز *pl.* غُرْزَة.

Hen, *n.* The domestic hen, دَجَاجَة *coll.* دَجَاج *pl.* دَجَاجَات (in Syria called also فَرُّوجَة *coll.* فَرُّوج *pl.* فَرَارِيج ـ فَرْخَة *coll.* فَرْخ *pl.* أَفْرَاخ). The female of any bird, أُنْثَى ٱلطَّيْرِ.

Henbane, *n.* سَيْكُرَان ـ بَنْج.

Hence, *ad.* From this place, مِنْ هُنَا. At a distance, غَائِب ـ بَعِيد. From this time, مِنَ ٱلْآنَ وَصَاعِدًا ـ فِيمَا بَعْدُ. From this cause, therefore, مِنْ ثَمَّ ـ لِأَجْلِ ذٰلِكَ ـ لِذٰلِكَ. Hence! Begone! اِنْقَلِعْ ـ إِلَيْكَ عَنِّي. Not many days —, لَيْسَ بَعْدَ هٰذِهِ ٱلْأَيَّامِ بِكَثِيرٍ. Remove these things —, اِرْفَعْ هٰذِهِ مِنْ هُنَا. Before I go —, قَبْلَ أَنْ أَذْهَبَ مِنْ هُنَا. Get ye up, let us go —, قُومُوا نَنْطَلِقْ مِنْ هُنَا.

Henceforth, *ad.* } مِنَ ٱلْآنَ وَصَاعِدًا ـ فِيمَا بَعْدُ ـ مِنَ ٱلْآنَ
Henceforward, } فِي ٱلْمُسْتَقْبِلِ ـ مُنْذُ ٱلْآنَ.

Henchman, *n.* غُلَام ـ خَدَّام.

Hen-coop, *n.* خُمّ *pl.* خِمَمَة ـ خُنّ *pl.* خِنَنَة.

Hendecagon, *n.* ذُو إِحْدَى عَشْرَ زَاوِيَةً.

Henna, *n.* (*properly* Hinnâ), the Egyptian privet, حِنَّان ـ حِنَّاء. The flower of the —, فَاغِيَة ـ حِنُّون; the leaves, حِنَّا. (In the present day the plant is called تَمْرُ ٱلْحِنَّاءِ, vulgarly, تَمْر حِنَّا.) A seller of —, حِنَّائِيٌّ *pl.* حِنَّائِيُّونَ. To dye with —, حَنَّأَ. She dyed her hand with —, حَنَّأَتْ يَدَهَا. To be dyed with —, تَحَنَّأَ.

Hen-pecked, *a.* Governed by the wife, زَوْجٌ مُتَضَعْضِعٌ.

Hepatic, *a.* مُتَعَلِّقٌ بِٱلْكَبِدِ ـ كَبِدِيٌّ. Hepatic disease, كُبَاد.

Heptade, *n.* Seven, سَبْعَة *fem.* سَبْع.

Heptaglot, *n.* كِتَابٌ فِي سَبْعَةِ أَلْسُنٍ.

Heptagon, *n.* مُسَبَّع.

Heptagonal, *a.* } ذُو سَبْعِ زَوَايَا ـ مُسَبَّعِيٌّ.
Heptangular, }

Heptarch, *n.* حَاكِمٌ مِنْ سَبْعَةِ حُكَّامٍ فِي حُكُومَةٍ وَاحِدَةٍ.

Heptarchy, *n.* حُكُومَةٌ فِي تَصَرُّفِ سَبْعَةِ مُلُوكٍ ـ حُكُومَةٌ مُسَبَّعَةٌ.

Her, *pron.* Expressed grammatically by the suffix ها: *e.g.*, her father, أَبُوهَا; he loved her, حَبَّهَا. Expressed vulgarly by the suffix to nouns of بِتَاعْهَا: *e.g.*, her book, الكِتَابُ بِتَاعْهَا.

Herald, *n.* One who proclaims, مُنَادٍ. *See also* Forerunner, Harbinger, *n.*

Heraldic, *a.* مُخْتَصٌّ بِفَنِّ عَلَامَاتِ ٱلنَّسَبِ ـ مُتَعَلِّقٌ بِٱلْآرْمَا.

Heraldic bearings, تَفْصِيلَاتُ ٱلْآرْمَا.

Heraldry, *n.* فَنُّ عَلَامَاتِ ٱلنَّسَبِ.

Heraldship, *n.* The office of an herald, وَظِيفَةُ ٱلْمُنَادِي.

Herb, *n.* عُشْب *pl.* أَعْشَاب ـ نَبْت *coll.* نَبَات. Pot-herbs, خُضْرَة ـ خَضَارَات ـ بَقْل *pl.* بُقُول ـ قُطْنِيَّة *pl.* قَطَانِي. Dry herbs, تَفِيف ـ جَفِيف. Medicinal herbs, عَقَّار *pl.* عَقَاقِيرُ.

Herbaceous, *a.* Belonging to herbs, نَبَاتِيٌّ ـ عَشِب ـ عُشْبِيٌّ. An — or yearly plant, نَبَاتٌ سَنَوِيٌّ. Producing herbage, مُعْشَاب ـ عَاشِب.

Herbage, *n.* Green —, مَرْعًى ـ غَيْث ـ رِعْيٌ ـ عُشْب ـ رُطْب. Dry —, حَشِيش ـ تِبْنٌ; whether fresh or dry, خُضَارَة ـ أَبٌّ. Tangled —, رِثَّان. To collect —, حَشَّ [2]. To produce —, أَعْشَبَ ـ عَشِبَ.

Herbal, *n.* A book on plants, كِتَابٌ فِي ٱلنَّبَاتِ. A collection of plants, مَجْمُوعُ حَشَائِشَ وَنَبَاتَاتٍ.

Herbal, *a.* *See* Herbaceous, *a.*

Herbalist, *n.* عَشَّاب ـ عَالِمٌ بِٱلْحَشَائِشِ وَٱلنَّبَاتَاتِ ـ حَشَائِشِيٌّ.

Herbarium, *n.* *See* Herbal, *n.*

Herbary, *n.* بَيْتٌ (or دَرَبِي) لِلنَّبَاتِ.

Herbescent, *a.* نَابِت.

Herbiferous, *a.* مُنْبِت.

Herbivorous, *a.* يَرْعَى ٱلنَّبَاتَ وَٱلْحَشِيشَ.

Herbless, *n.* بِلَا نَبَاتٍ ـ خَالٍ مِنَ ٱلْعُشْبِ.

Herborist, *n.* *See* Herbalist, *n.*

Herborize, *v.i.* *See to* Botanize, *v.i.*

Herbous, *a.* كَثِيرُ ٱلنَّبَاتِ ـ كَثِيرُ ٱلْعُشْبِ.

Herby, *a.* مِثْلَ ٱلنَّبَاتِ ـ مِنْ جِنْسِ ٱلْعُشْبِ.

Herculean, *a.* Very powerful, أَبُو زَيْدٍ ـ عَنْتَر ـ جَبَّار. Very difficult, جَسِيم ـ كَبِيرٌ جِدًّا ـ أَكْبَرُ. Very large, أَوْعَرُ ـ أَصْعَبُ.

Hercules, *n.* The constellation, الجَاثِي ـ الجَاثِي عَلَى رُكْبَتَيْهِ. A powerful man, جَبَّار ـ عَنْتَر ـ أَبُو زَيْدٍ.

Herd, *n.* As of cattle, قَطِيع *pl.* سِرْب *pl.* أَسْرَاب ـ صِرْمَة ـ قِطَاع *and* أَقْطَاع ـ مَوَاشِي ـ رَعِيَّة *pl.* رَعَايَا. The —, the common people, الأَوْبَاش ـ العَوَامّ ـ العَامَّة. A — of swine, قَطِيعُ خَنَازِيرَ.

Herd, *v.t.* جَمَّعَ أَسْرَابًا ـ سَرَّبَ ٱلْمَوَاشِي.

Herd, *v.i.* تَسَرَّبُوا. To associate together, تَأَلَّفُوا ـ تَرَافَقُوا ـ تَصَاحَبُوا.

Herdsman, *n.* سَائِقُ ٱلْمَوَاشِي ـ رَاعٍ *pl.* رُعَاة ـ سَاقَة *pl.* سَاقَة.

Here, *ad.* هُنَا ـ هَاهُنَا ـ فِي هٰذِهِ. In this life, فِي هٰذِهِ ٱلْحَيٰوةِ ـ ٱلْمَعِيشَةِ. Here! lo! هَاءَ. Here they two are, هَاؤُمَا. Here they are, *masc.* هَاؤُمْ; *fem.* هَاؤُنَّ. Here am I, هَٰئَذَا. Here he comes, هَا هُوَذَا. Here and there, هُنَا وَهُنَاكَ; pell-mell, شَذَرَ مَذَرَ. They were scattered — and there, تَفَرَّقُوا شَذَرَ مَذَرَ. Gray hairs are — and there upon him, رَشَّ عَلَيْهِ ٱلشَّيْبُ. That is neither — nor there, ذٰلِكَ لَا سَدَدَ فِيهِ ـ هٰذَا لَا طَائِلَ تَحْتَهُ ـ هٰذَا لَيْسَ تَحْتَ خَبَرٍ.

Hereabout, *ad.* }
Hereabouts, } هُنَا قَرِيبًا ـ بِٱلْقُرْبِ مِنْ هُنَا.

Hereafter, *n.* آخِرَة.

Hereafter, *ad.* فِي ٱلْمُسْتَقْبِلِ ـ فِيمَا بَعْدُ ـ مِنَ ٱلْآنَ ـ مِنْ بَعْدُ. What will be —, مَا هُوَ عَتِيدٌ أَنْ يَكُونَ بَعْدُ.

Hereat, *ad.* At this time, ٱلْآنَ ـ فِي هٰذَا ٱلْوَقْتِ. On this account لِذٰلِكَ ـ لِهٰذَا.

Hereby, *ad.* بِهٰذَا ـ مِنْ هٰذَا.

Hereditable, *a.* مِمَّا يُوَرَّثُ.

Hereditament, *n.* مَالٌ مَوْرُوثٌ ـ مُلْكٌ مَوْرُوثٌ ـ تُرَاث.

Hereditarily, *ad.* وِرَاثَةً.

Hereditary, *a.* مُتَوَارِث ـ أَبًا عَنْ جَدٍّ ـ إِرْثِيٌّ. An — disposition, العِرْقُ *pl.* عُرُوق عِرْق. The natural disposition is —, العِرْقُ دَسَّاسٌ. She implanted in them a bad — disposition, عَرَّقَتْ فِيهِمْ عِرْقَ سُوءٍ.

Herein, *ad.* فِي هٰذَا ـ مِنْ هٰذَا.

Hereof, *ad.* عَنْ هٰذَا.

Hereon, *ad.* }
Hereupon, } لِأَجْلِ ذٰلِكَ ـ بَعْدَ ذٰلِكَ.

Heresiarch, *n.* رَئِيسُ هَرْطَقَةٍ ـ رَئِيسُ بِدْعَةٍ ـ رَأْسُ شِيعَةٍ.

Heresy, *n.* شِيعَة *pl.* شِيَع *and* أَشْيَاع ـ بِدْعَة *pl.* بِدَع ـ ضَلَالٌ ـ هَرْطَقَة.

Heretic, *n.* }
Heretical, *a.* } خَارِجِيٌّ *pl.* خَوَارِجُ ـ رَافِضِيٌّ *pl.* رَوَافِضُ ـ مُبْتَدِعٌ ـ أَرَاتِيكِيٌّ ـ هَرَاطِقَة ـ هَرْطُوقِيٌّ *pl.* هَرَاطِقَة.

Hereto, *ad.* }
Hereunto, } For this, لِهٰذَا; thus far, إِلَى هُنَا; add to this, زِدْ عَلَى هٰذَا.

Heretofore, *ad.* مِنْ قَبْلُ ـ فِيمَا مَضَى ـ أَوَّلًا ـ سَابِقًا.

Hereupon, *ad.* عِنْدَ ذٰلِكَ.

Herewith, *ad.* مَعَ هٰذَا ـ بِهٰذَا.

Heritable, *a.* *See* Hereditable, *a.*

Heritage, *n.* تَرِكَة ـ مِيرَاث ـ إِرْث.

Hermaphrodism, *n.* }
Hermaphroditism, } خُنُوثِيَّة.

Hermaphrodite, *n.* خُنْثَى *pl.* خِنَاث.

Hermeneutic, *a.* }
Hermeneutical, } مُبَيِّن ـ مُوَضِّح ـ إِيضَاحِيٌّ ـ مُفَسِّر.

Hermeneutics, *n.* فَنُّ ٱلتَّعْبِيرِ ـ التَّفَاسِيرُ.

Hermetic, *a.* }
Hermetical, } Chemical, كِيمَاوِيٌّ. Perfectly close, مَسْدُودٌ ـ مَسْدُودٌ بِٱلتَّمَامِ (or أَصْلًا) ـ بِطِينِ ٱلْحِكْمَةِ ـ سَدٌّ مُحْكَمٌ.

Hermetically, *ad.* Chemically, عَلَى فَنِّ ٱلْكِيمِيَاءِ. Closed —, مَسْدُودٌ أَصْلًا.

Hermit, *n.* سَائِح *pl.* سَائِحُونَ ـ زَاهِد *pl.* زُهَّاد.

Hermitage, *n.* صَوْمَعَة *pl.* صَوَامِعُ ـ حُجْرَة.

Hermitess, *n.* سَائِحَة *pl.* سَائِحَات ـ زَاهِدَة *pl.* زَاهِدَات.

Hernia, *n.* قِلِّيط ـ قَرْو ـ فَتْق. Scrotal —, خُصْيَة ـ أُدْرَة; having the scrotal —, آدَرُ ـ مَأْدُور ـ قَرْوَانِيٌّ ـ أَنْفَخُ. Intestinal —, أُدْرَةٌ مَعَائِيَّةٌ. To have —, أَدِرَ.

Hernial, *a.* مُتَعَلِّقٌ بِٱلْفَتْقِ.

Hero, *n.* A great man, بَطَل *pl.* أَبْطَال ـ صِنْدِيد ـ هُمَام *pl.* هِمَام ـ بَاسِل *pl.* بُسْل *and* بُسَلَاء ـ مِقْدَام *pl.* مَقَادِيمُ. The — of a narrative, الَّذِي عَلَيْهِ ٱلْكَلَامُ ـ سَيِّد ـ أُحْدُوثَة. Such an one has become the — of a wonderful story, قَدْ صَارَ فُلَانٌ أُحْدُوثَةً.

Heroic, *a.* }
Heroical, } حَمِيس ـ أَحْمَس ـ هُمَامِيٌّ ـ بَطَلِيٌّ.

Heroically, *ad.* بِحَمَاسَةٍ ـ بِبَسَالَةٍ ـ بِشَجَاعَةٍ.

Heroine, *n.* A brave woman, مِقْدَامَة ـ بَاسِلَة ـ حَمِيسَة. The —, as of a tale, الَّتِي عَلَيْهَا ٱلْكَلَامُ ـ سَيِّدَة ـ حَمِيسَة.

Heroism, *n.* حَمَاسَة ـ بَسَالَة ـ شَجَاعَة.

Heron, *n.* صَيَّادَةٌ *pl.* صَيَّادُ سَمَكٍ ـ دَنَاكِلُ *pl.* دَنْكَلَةٌ.

Heronry, *n.* مَأْلَفُ ٱلدَّنَاكِلِ.

Hero-worship, *n.* عِبَادَةُ ٱلشَّجَاعَةِ ـ تَعْظِيمُ ٱلْأَبْطَالِ.

Herpes, *n.* جُذْمَةٌ ـ قَوَابِئُ *pl.* قُوبَآءُ ـ هَرَضٌ ـ هَرَصٌ ـ جُذَامٌ.

Herpetic, *a.* جُذَامِيٌّ.

Herring, *n.* رَنْكَةٌ ـ فَسِيخٌ. Smoked —, فَسِيخٌ مُدَخَّنٌ; salted —, فَسِيخٌ مُمَلَّحٌ. Crowded together like herrings, مَلْزُوزٌ لَزَّ ٱلْفَسِيخِ. *See also under* Sprat, *n.*

Herse, *n.* *See* Hearse, Bier, *n.*

Herself, *pr.* عَيْنُهَا ـ نَفْسُهَا ـ ذَاتُهَا. Fâtimah — took it, أَخَذَتْهَا فَاطِمَةُ بِنَفْسِهَا. She said within —, قَالَتْ فِي نَفْسِهَا.

Herzegovina, *n.* The province so called, هَرْسَكْ.

Hesitancy, *n.* *See* Hesitation, *n.*

Hesitate, *v.i.* To pause in doubt, تَعَايَا ـ يَعْيَ *aor.* عَيَّ بِ ـ تَرَدَّدَ ـ تَضَرَّبَ ـ تَمَخْطَرَ ـ تَوَقَّفَ ـ إِحْتَارَ ـ (or تَعَيَّا) بِ. To stop in speaking, تَفَرْكَ ـ يَعْيَى *aor.* عَيِيَ فِي ـ عَقِدَ ـ تَطَرَّمَ ـ تَذَبْذَبَ بَيْنَ أَمْرَيْنِ. To — between two things, أُعْتُقِلَ لِسَانُهُ ـ مَيَّلَ بَيْنَ أَمْرَيْنِ. We should — to fight them, عَلَيْنَا أَنْ نَقْعِرَ عَنْ قِتَالِهِمْ. He would not —, be backward, to …, لَا يَتَحَاشَى مِنْ أَنْ. They hesitated to return, إِمْتَنَعُوا مِنَ ٱلرُّجُوعِ.

Hesitation, *a.* Delay, doubt, تَضَرُّبٌ ـ تَرَدُّدٌ ـ تَمَخْطُرٌ ـ تَأَخُّرٌ ـ شُبْهَةٌ ـ رَهْيَاءُ ـ تَوَقُّفٌ. Stoppage in speech, حَصَرٌ ـ حُبْسَةٌ ـ عُقْدَةٌ ـ طَمْطَمَةٌ ـ عِيٌّ. One who has a — in his speech, طِمْطِمٌ. He exhibited much — in his speech, جَآءَ بِٱلْعِيِّ وَٱلشِّيِّ.

Hesperian, *a.* مَغْرِبِيٌّ or مَغْرَبِيٌّ ـ غَرْبِيٌّ.

Heterodox, *a.* شِيَعِيٌّ ـ مُخَالِفٌ لِلْحَقِّ.

Heterodoxy, *n.* شِيَعِيَّةٌ ـ خِلَافُ ٱلْحَقِّ.

Heterogeneous, *a.* غَيْرُ ـ مُخْتَلِفُ ٱلْجِنْسِ ـ مُخْتَلِفُ ٱلطِّبَاعِ مُتَجَانِسٍ.

Heterogeneousness, *n.* مُغَايَرَةٌ ـ عَدَمُ تَجَانُسٍ ـ إِخْتِلَافُ ٱلطِّبَاعِ ٱلْجِنْسِ وَٱلطَّبْعِ.

Hetmân, *n.* A Cossack general, قَائِدٌ مِنَ ٱلْقَزَاقِ ـ هَتْمَان.

Hew, *v.t.* To notch, clip, حَزَّ ². To hew, as of a tree, قَطَعَ ². To hew, of stone, نَحَتَ ² ². To hew out, نَقَرَ فِي ². To hew in pieces, قَطَّعَ. To hew down, to destroy, كَسَّرَ ـ هَدَمَ ². To hew wood, to go out to hew and collect wood, حَطَبَ ² (or إِحْتَطَبَ) حَطَبًا. To shape out, خَشَّبَ ـ شَكَّلَ ـ صَيَّرَ.

Hewer, *n.* A — of wood, مُحْتَطِبُ حَطَبٍ; a feller of trees, قَطَّاعُ شَجَرٍ. A — of stone, حَجَّارٌ ـ نَحَّاتٌ.

Hexagon, *n.* مُسَدَّسٌ ـ تَسْدِيسٌ.

Hexagonal, *a.* مُسَدَّسٌ.

Hexahedral, *a.* ذُو سِتَّةِ سُطُوحٍ.

Hexahedron, *n.* جِسْمٌ ذُو سِتَّةِ سُطُوحٍ.

Hexameter, *n.* مِصْرَاعٌ مُرَكَّبٌ مِنْ سِتَّةِ تَفَاعِيلَ.

Hexameter, *a.* }
Hexametric, } ذُو (or مُرَكَّبٌ مِنْ) سِتَّةِ تَفَاعِيلَ.

Hexangular, *a.* مُسَدَّسُ ٱلزَّوَايَا ـ ذُو سِتِّ زَوَايَا.

Hexapla, *n.* مَجْمُوعُ ٱلْكُتُبِ ٱلْمُقَدَّسَةِ فِي سِتَّةِ أَلْسُنٍ.

Hexaplar, *a.* ذُو سِتَّةِ أَعْمِدَةٍ.

Hey! *int.* An interjection of joy, بَخٍ ـ هَهْ هَهْ.

Heyday! *int.* An exclamation of surprise, آهَا ـ هَاي ـ وَاي.

Heyday, *n.* أَيَّامُ ٱلْحَظِّ ـ أَيَّامُ ٱلْعِزِّ. The — of youth, مَآءُ ـ عُنْفُوَانُ ٱلشَّبَابِ ـ ٱلشَّبَابُ.

Hiatus, *n.* A gap, فَتْحَةٌ ـ وَتْرَةٌ *pl.* وَتَرَاتٌ. A division, فَاصِلَةٌ. A pause, وَقْفَةٌ ـ وَقْفٌ. Something wanting, نُقْصَانٌ. The eliding of a letter, حَذْفٌ.

Hibernal, *a.* خَرَافِيٌّ ـ شَتَوِيٌّ ـ شَتْوِيٌّ.

Hibernate, *v.i.* To winter, تَشَتَّى ـ شَتَّى. To pass the winter in a lethargic state, شَتَّى (or يَشْتُو *aor.* شَتَا) فِي سُبَاتٍ.

Hibernation, *n.* As in a lethargic state, تَشْتِيَةٌ فِي سُبَاتٍ.

Hibernian, *a.* إِيرْلَانْدِيٌّ. A native of Ireland, مِنْ أَهْلِ إِيرْلَانْد.

Hibernicism, *n.* إِصْطِلَاحٌ إِيرْلَانْدِيٌّ.

Hiccough, *n.* }
Hiccup, *n.* }
Hickup, } حَزُوقَةٌ ـ أُفُوقَةٌ *pl.* فُوَاقٌ *pl.* أُفُوقَةٌ. Dying —, فُوَاقُ ٱلْمَوْتِ.

Hiccough, *v.i.* فَاقَ ² ـ فَاقَ ² ـ مَلَكَتْهُ ٱلْحَزُوقَةُ.

Hickory, *n.* شَجَرُ جَوْزٍ بِأَمِيرِيكَا.

Hid, *a.* Not seen or known, مَسْتُورٌ ـ مُسْتَتِرٌ ـ مَكْتُومٌ. Obscure, غَلِقٌ ـ مُعَمًّى ـ خَفِيٌّ. The matter cannot be hid, لَا يُمْكِنُ أَنْ تَخْفَى ٱلْمَادَّةُ.

Hidden, *a.* As of grief, مُكْتَمِنٌ. Inward, بَاطِنٌ. Hidden, as in the heart, مَكْنُونٌ. Concealed, as from sight, مُخْفًى عَنْ. Nothing is — from him, لَا يَخْفَى عَلَيْهِ شَيْءٌ. To be —, as in the ground, to lie concealed, إِنْدَسَّ. *See also to* Hide, *v.t.*

Hiddenly, *ad.* Secretly, عَلَى خَفَآءٍ ـ سِرًّا ـ خُفْيَةً.

Hide, *v.t.* To withdraw anything from sight, يَخْفَى *aor.* خَفَى ـ إِحْتَجَبَ ـ حَجَبَ ² ـ إِخْتَبَأَ ـ خَبَأَ ـ خَبَأَ ² ـ أَخْفَى

اِكْتَتَمَ ـ كَتَّمَ ـ ² كَتَمَ. To —, as a secret, غَبَّى ـ ² دَسَّ. To — something from another, ² كَتَمَ-عَن ـ ² طَوَى-عَن. To — something, as in the heart, ² كَنَّ-فِي ـ أَكَنَّ-فِي. To —, as the faults of another, تَغَمَّدَ ـ غَمَّدَ ـ تَكَمَّنَ. To — one's self, اِسْتَخْفَى ـ اِخْتَفَى ـ اِخْتَبأَ. He hid himself from them, اِخْتَفَى عَنْهُمْ. The sun hid itself in the clouds, تَوَارَتِ ٱلشَّمْسُ فِي ٱلسَّحَابِ. He did not — the matter from them, لَمْ يُخْفِ ٱلْأَمْرَ عَنْهُمْ.

Hide, *n.* A skin, جِلْد *pl.* جُلُود. A — of land, تُرْسٌ مِنَ ٱلْأَرْضِ *pl.* تِرَاس. Sewers of hides, or boots, خَرَّازُونَ ـ خُرُزُم. A seller of hides, أَدَّام ـ أَدَمِيٌّ. *See also under* Tanned, *a.*

Hide-and-seek, *n.* The game, طُمَّامَة ـ الفِئِل ـ الفِيَال ـ الطَّبَن ـ السُّدَّر.

Hidebound, *n.* Of an animal, مُقَلِّص ٱلْجِلْدِ; of a tree, مُقَلِّص ٱلْقِشْرَةِ.

Hideous, *a.* Frightful, مَهُول ـ مَخُوف ـ مُرْعِب ـ قَبِيح; of a place, مَهِيل. Hateful, شَنِيع ـ فَظِيع ـ فَجِيع. Ugly, كَرِيه ـ بَشِع. To be —, ² قَبُحَ. How — he is! مَا أَهْوَلَهُ.

Hideously, *ad.* قَبَاحَةً ـ بِشَنَاعَةٍ ـ بِكَرَاهَةٍ.

Hideousness, *n.* Frightfulness, وَحْشَة ـ قَبَاحَة. Hatefulness, فَظَاعَة ـ شَنَاعَة. Ugliness, كَرَاهَة ـ بَشَاعَة.

Hiding-place, *n.* مَخْبَأ *pl.* مَخَابِئُ ـ سِتْر. A refuge, مَلْجَأ ـ عَوَذ.

Hie, *v.i.* *See to* Hasten, *v.i.*

Hierarch, *n.* زَعِيمُ ٱلدِّينِ *pl.* زُعَمَاء ـ زَعِيمٌ فِي أُمُورِ ٱلدِّيَانَةِ ـ رَئِيسُ كَهَنَةٍ.

Hierarchal, *a.* / Hierarchical, Belonging to an hierarchy, مَنْسُوبٌ إِلَى مَنَاصِبَ دِينِيَّةٍ. Consisting of degrees, رُتَبِيٌّ.

Hierarchically, *ad.* عَلَى مُوجَبِ ٱلرُّتَبِ ـ عَلَى مَرَاتِبِهِمْ.

Hierarchy, *n.* Rule in sacred things, الرِّئَاسَةُ ٱلدِّينِيَّةُ. The persons forming an —, أَهْلُ ٱلْمَرَاتِبِ فِي رِئَاسَةٍ دِينِيَّةٍ. The heavenly —, الْقُوَّاتُ ٱلسَّمَاوِيَّةُ.

Hieratic, *a.* Pertaining to priests, كَاهِنِيٌّ. The — writing, قَلَمٌ كَاهِنِيٌّ (or بَرْبَاوِيٌّ).

Hierocracy, *n.* حُكُومَةٌ دِينِيَّةٌ.

Hieroglyph, *n.* / Hieroglyphic, A symbol in picture, تَصْوِيرٌ رَمْزِيٌّ. The writing of the ancient Egyptians, قَلَمٌ بَرْبَاوِيٌّ ـ قَلَمُ ٱلْمِصْرِيِّينَ ٱلْقَدِيمُ.

Hieroglyphic, *a.* / Hieroglyphical, Expressed by pictures, مُعَبَّرٌ بِٱلتَّصَاوِيرِ. Denoting the writing of the ancient Egyptians, مَنُوطٌ بِقَلَمِ ٱلْمِصْرِيِّينَ ٱلْقَدِيمِ; called in Egypt, بَرْبَاوِيٌّ.

Hieroglyphist, *n.* عَالِمٌ بِقَلَمِ ٱلْمِصْرِيِّينَ ٱلْقَدِيمِ.

Hierogram, *n.* قَلَمٌ كَاهِنِيٌّ.

Hierographic, *a.* / Hierographical, مُخْتَصٌّ بِٱلْكُتُبِ ٱلدِّينِيَّةِ.

Hieromancy, *n.* التَّفَأُّلُ مِنَ ٱلذَّبَائِحِ.

Hierophant, *n.* كَاهِن *pl.* كَهَنَة.

Higgle, *v.i.* *See to* Chaffer, Haggle, *v.i.*

Higgledy-piggledy, *n.* خَلْطَةٌ بَلْطَةٌ ـ هَرْجٌ مَرْجٌ ـ شِذَرَ مِذَرَ.

Higgler, *n.* *See* Chafferer, Haggler, *n.*

High, *a.* Lofty, مُرْتَفِع ـ رَفِيع ـ عَالٍ ـ سَامٍ. High, very —, as of a mountain, *etc.*, شَاهِق *pl.* شَوَاهِق ـ فَارِع ـ نَاشِز ـ شَامِخ *pl.* شُمَّاخ ـ سَمِيٌّ ـ نَابِه ـ بَاذِخ. Grand, سَنِيٌّ ـ رَفِيع ـ كَبِير ـ فَخِيم ـ عَظِيم. Wonderful, عَجِيب. Noble, سَنِيٌّ ـ جَلِيل ـ جَلِيلُ ٱلشَّأْنِ. Violent, as of wind, عَاصِف ـ شَدِيد ـ قَوِيٌّ. Arrogant, مَغْرُور ـ مُتَكَبِّر ـ مُتَعَظِّم. Dear, high-priced, غَالٍ. Rough, as of the sea, زَاخِر. Loud, جَهْوَر ـ جَهِير ـ جَهْوَرِيُّ ٱلصَّوْتِ. Abstruse, صَعْب ـ مُشْكِل ـ غَوِيص. High, of food, مُتَعَفِّن ـ مُعَفَّن. The Most High, اللّٰهُ عَزَّ وَجَلَّ ـ الْبَارِئُ تَعَالَى ـ اللّٰهُ ٱلْعَلِيُّ ـ الْعَلِيُّ ـ الْمُتَعَالِي. High life, عِيشَةُ ٱلْأَكَابِرِ; the people in — life, الْخَاصَّةُ ـ الْخَوَاصُّ. A — place, نَشَاز. From on —, مِنْ صُعُدٍ. Higher, more lofty, أَرْفَعُ ـ أَعْلَى. High and low, of people, أَغْنِيَاءُ وَفُقَرَاءُ ـ عَالٍ وَدُونٌ. High noon, الظُّهْرُ. High tide, مَدٌّ كَامِلٌ. The matter is too — for me, I cannot attain it, اِرْتَفَعَ ٱلْأَمْرُ فَوْقِي لَا أَسْتَطِيعُهُ. High days and holidays, أَيَّامُ عِيدٍ وَبَطَالَةٍ. High and dry, aground, مُشَطَّط ـ مَصْدُوم. To have a — opinion of, أَحْسَنَ ظَنَّهُ فِي ـ اِسْتَحْسَنَ. To speak in — terms of, مَدَحَ ـ أَثْنَى عَلَى. To ask —, dear, terms for, أَغْلَى بِ. It is — time that . . ., حَانَ ٱلْوَقْتُ لِ *aor.* يَحِينُ. The two — contracting governments, الدَّوْلَتَانِ ٱلْفَخِيمَتَانِ ٱلْمُتَعَاهِدَتَانِ. To be or to become —, lofty, ² عَلِيَ ـ ² شَهَقَ ـ ² نَشَزَ ـ اِعْتَلَى ـ تَعَلَّى ـ اِرْتَفَعَ ـ تَعَالَى. To be —, as of meat, تَعَفَّنَ. To be —, as in rank, ² عَلِيَ ـ ² شَرُفَ. The sun became —, عَلَتِ (or اِعْتَلَتِ) ٱلشَّمْسُ. To make —, to raise, عَلَّى.

High, *ad.* Aloft, إِلَى فَوْقُ ـ فَوْقُ. Greatly, كَثِيرًا. Eminently, بِشَرَفٍ ـ بِسَنَاءٍ. To carry it —, to be overbearing, ² بَطِرَ ـ تَاهَ *aor.* يَتِيهُ ـ تَشَامَخَ ـ تَكَبَّرَ. To feed or live —, عَاشَ عِيشَةَ ٱلْأَكَابِرِ. The wind blew —, ² هَبَّتِ ٱلرِّيحُ بِشِدَّةٍ ـ زَهَتِ ٱلرِّيحُ. His pulse beats —, اِضْطَرَبَ نَبْضُهُ. To set on —, to raise, ² رَفَعَ. He ascended up on —, ² صَعِدَ إِلَى ٱلْعَلَاءِ. To stand —, to be esteemed by, أُعْتُبِرَ مِن. The sea runs mountains —, إِرْتَفَعَ ٱلْبَحْرُ جِبالاً — صارَتْ أَمْواجُ ٱلْبَحْرِ كَٱلْجِبالِ.

High-blown, *a.* مَنْفُوخ.

High-born, *n.* شَرِيفُ ٱلْأَصْلِ. To be —, شَرُفَ ².

High-church, *a.* | High-churchism, *n.* } The — party, طائِفَةٌ مِنْ أَهْلِ ٱلْكَنِيسَةِ ٱلْأَنْكِلِيزِيَّةِ ٱلْمَلَكِيَّةِ ذاتُ تَعَصُّبٍ لِلْأُسْقُفِيَّةِ.

High-churchman, *n.* مِنْ أَهْلِ ٱلطّائِفَةِ ٱلْمَذْكُورَةِ.

High-coloured, *a.* Of colour, شَدِيدُ ٱللَّوْنِ. Of speech, مِفَنٌّ — مُوَشًّى.

Higher, *a.* أَعْلَى. One — than the other, ٱلْواحِدُ أَعْلَى مِنَ ٱلْآخَرِ. Taller, أَطْوَلُ. The — powers, ٱلسَّلاطِينُ ٱلْكُبْرَى. Go up —, إِرْتَفِعْ إِلَى فَوْقُ.

Highest, *a.* ٱلأَعْلَى. The —, God, ٱللّٰهُ تَعالَى — ٱلعَلِيُّ. The — parts of the city, أَعالِي ٱلْمَدِينَةِ.

Highflown, *a.* Of language, مِفَنٌّ — فَخِيم. To use — language, تَكَلَّمَ بِعَظائِمَ.

Highland, *n.* An upland, نَجْد *pl.* نُجُود *and* أَنْجاد.

Highlander, *n.* جَبَلِيٌّ — ساكِنُ ٱلْجِبالِ *pl.* سُكّانٌ.

Highlands, *n.* جِبال.

Highly, *ad.* In a high degree, بِكَثْرَةٍ — بِزِيادَةٍ — كَثِيرًا. Strongly, بِقُوَّةٍ — شَدِيدًا. Fully, بِٱلْكُلِّيَّةِ — بِٱلتَّمامِ — بَتَّةً. Proudly, تَكَبُّرًا — بِتَفَخُّمٍ. To think — of, إِسْتَصْلَحَ. *See also* High, *ad.*

High-mass, *n.* قُدّاسٌ كَبِيرٌ.

High-mettled, *a.* شَدِيدُ ٱلْحَرارَةِ — غائِر — أَنْفَسُ.

High-minded, *a.* Noble, liberal, رَحِيبٌ — نَجِيبٌ — نَبِيلٌ ٱلصَّدْرِ. Proud, arrogant, مُتَصَلِّفٌ — مَغْرُور — مُتَعَظِّم — مُتَكَبِّر. To be —, noble, شَرُفَ ²; to be —, proud, تَعَظَّمَ — تَكَبَّرَ.

Highmindedness, *n.* Nobleness, liberality, نَجابَةٌ — نَبالَة — رُحْبُ ٱلصَّدْرِ. Arrogance, تَعَظُّم — تَكَبُّر — كِبْرِياءُ — غُرُور — فَخَمِيَّة.

Highness, *n.* Dignity of rank, سُمُوٌّ — سَناءٌ — رِفْعَة. Your Highness, ٱلْحَضْرَةُ ٱلسّامِيَةُ — ٱلْجَنابُ ٱلْعالِي. H.H. the Grand Wazir, صاحِبُ ٱلدَّوْلَةِ حَضْرَةُ ٱلصَّدْرِ ٱلْأَعْظَمِ. H.H. the Khedive of Egypt, صاحِبُ ٱلسَّعادَةِ خِدِيوِي مِصْرَ ٱلْأَعْظَمِ.

High-pressure, *n.* Of steam, زِيادَةٌ فِي حَصْرِ (*or* ضَغْطِ) ٱلْبُخارِ. A — engine, باخِرَةٌ حَصْرَآء — باخِرَةٌ مَضْغُوطَةُ ٱلْبُخارِ. In a general sense, ضَغْطٌ شَدِيدٌ.

High-priest, *n.* رَئِيسُ كَهَنَةٍ *pl.* رُؤَساءُ. The modern — of the Jews, ٱلْخاخامُ ٱلْأَكْبَرُ.

High-priestship, *n.* رِئاسَةُ كَهَنُوتٍ. The modern — of the Jews, رِئاسَةُ ٱلْخاخام.

High-principled, *a.* مُدَقِّق — مُنْصِف — مُسْتَقِيم — صِدِّيق — نَبِيل *pl.* نِبال — أَهْلُ ذِمَّةٍ.

High-road, *n.* *See* Highway, *n.*

High-spirited, *a.* Generous, نَبِيل *pl.* نِبال — حُرٌّ *pl.* أَحْرار. Of a horse, طامِحٌ — حَرُون.

High-time, *n.* تَمامُ ٱلْوَقْتِ. It is —, حانَ ٱلْوَقْتُ ³.

High-treason, *n.* خُرُوجٌ — بَغْيٌ عَلَى ٱلْمَلِكِ — غَدْرٌ بِٱلْمَلِكِ عَلَى ٱلسُّلْطانِ.

Highway, *n.* شارِع *pl.* شَوارِعُ — طَرِيقٌ سُلْطانِيٌّ (*or* دَرْبٌ).

Highwayman, *n.* قاطِعُ ٱلطَّرِيقِ *pl.* قُطّاع. To be a —, قَطَعَ ٱلطَّرِيقَ.

High-water, *n.* مَدٌّ — مَدٌّ كامِلٌ.

High-water-mark, *n.* عَلامَةُ أَعْلَى ٱلْمَدِّ. To be at —, in the height of prosperity, تَبَحْبَحَ — أَحَظَّ — تَنَعَّمَ — صارَ فِي كَمالِ ٱلْفَلَجِ.

High-wrought, *a.* Finished, مُكَمَّل — مُتَمَّم. Ornate in style, مِفَنٌّ. He used — speech, رَقَّى كَلامَهُ ³.

Hilarious, *a.* مَطْرُوب — طَرِب — فَرْحان — مَسْرُور — مَغْبُوط.

Hilarity, *n.* حُبُور — بَسْطَة — نَشاط — إِنْشِراح — طَرَب — غِبْطَة.

Hill, *n.* قُنَّة — قُنَّةٌ *pl.* قُنَن *and* قُنُون — أَكَمَة *pl.* أَكَمات *and* إِكام — تَلٌّ *pl.* تِلال. High ground, an eminence, عُقاب — رُبْوَة *pl.* رُبًى — رابِيَة *pl.* رَوابٍ. Hill-forts, مَعاقِلُ. A round hill; *see* Hummock, *n.*

Hill, *v.t.* To draw earth around anything, كَوَّمَ ٱلتُّرابَ حَوْلَهُ.

Hilliness, *n.* كَثْرَةُ تِلالٍ — طِلْع.

Hillock, *n.* جُثْوَة *pl.* جُثًا — كُومَة *pl.* أَكْوام — تَلٌّ *pl.* تُلُول. A — of stones, رُجْمَة. *See also* Hill, *n.*

Hilly, *a.* جَبَلِيٌّ. The — country, ٱلْجِبال.

Hilt, *n.* مِقْبَضَة — مِقْبَض. The iron tongue which runs into the —, سِنْخ — سِيلان. *See also* Handle, *n.*

Himself, *pr.* عَيْنُهُ — ذاتُهُ — نَفْسُهُ. It is he —, هُوَ هُوَ بِعَيْنِهِ. He came in by —, دَخَلَ وَحْدَهُ ². He made it for —, صَنَعَهُ لِغَرَضِهِ (*or* لِنَفْسِهِ). He — loves you, هُوَ نَفْسُهُ يُحِبُّكُمْ. He is beside —, هُوَ مُخْتَلٌّ. When he came to —, لَمّا رَجَعَ إِلَى نَفْسِهِ. He spake for —, defended —, تَحَجَّجَ عَنْ نَفْسِهِ.

Himyaritic, *a.* حِمْيَرِيٌّ. The — language, ٱلْحِمْيَرِيَّة. The — character, ٱلْمُسْنَد.

Hind, *n.* The female of the deer, إِيَّلَة — أُنْثَى ٱلْإِيَّل. A rustic, فَلّاح *pl.* فَلّاحُون — مِنْ أَهْلِ ٱلْوَبَرِ.

Hind, *a.* / **Hinder**, } أَخِير ـ مُتَأَخِّر ـ وَرَّانِيّ . The — part of the body, the buttocks, كَفَل *pl.* أَكْفَال . The — part, as of an army, سَاقَة . The — part of anything, مُؤَخَّر ـ أُخُر . He struck the — part of his head, ضَرَبَ مُؤَخَّرَ رَأْسِهِ .

Hinder, *v.t.* To prevent, حَجَبَ ـ نَبَرَ ـ ثَبَّطَ-عَن ـ عَارَضَ ـ صَدَّ-عَن ـ عَزَرَ-عَن ـ عَزَرَ ـ يَهِقُ *aor.* وَهَقَ-عَن ـ عَكَّ ـ أَعَاقَ ـ حَجَزَ ـ تَعَرَّضَ ل ـ إِعْتَرَضَ ل ـ صَدَعَ-عَن ـ مَنَعَ ـ أَمْسَكَ ـ صَرَفَ-عَن . To make to lose time, عَطَّلَ . To be hindered, تَعَوَّقَ ـ إِحْتَجَبَ ـ إِنْحَجَزَ .

Hinderance, *n.* / **Hindrance**, } The act of impeding, تَعَرُّض ـ مُعَارَضَة ـ عَزْر ـ مَنْع ـ إِعَاقَة . That which impedes, مَانِع *pl.* مَوَانِع ـ عَائِق *pl.* عَوَائِق ـ حَاجِز ـ سَدّ *pl.* سُدُود *or* أَسْدَاد .

Hinderer, *n.* عُوَق ـ عَائِق *pl.* عُوَّق ـ عَيِّق ـ عَوْق . A — or hindrance hindered me, عَقَانِي عَاقٍ ـ عَاقَنِي عَائِق .

Hindermost, *a.* / **Hindmost**, } أَخِير ـ آخِر . They came with the — of them, جَاءُوا عَنْ آخِرِهِمْ .

Hindoo, *n.* and *a.* / **Hindû**, } A native of Hindustân, هِنْدِيّ *pl.* هُنُود .

Hindûism, *n.* دِينُ ٱلْهُنُود .

Hindustâny, *n.* The — language, اللِّسَانُ ٱلْهِنْدُسْتَانِيّ .

Hinge, *n.* On which a door hangs, عَقِب ـ جَوَارِير *pl.* جَارُور ـ وَصَل *pl.* وُصْلَة ـ رَزَّات *pl.* رَزَّة ـ أَعْقَاب *pl.* That on which anything turns, مَدَار *pl.* مَدَارَات . To be off the hinges, in disorder, إِخْتَلَّ ـ تَشَوَّشَ ـ إِنْسَبَكَ . The point on which anything hinges, فَصّ ـ مَفْصِل . The door turns on its hinges, البَابُ يَدُورُ عَلَى صَائِرِهِ .

Hinge, *v.t.* To supply with hinges, رَكَّبَ ل-أَعْقَابًا (*or* وُصَلًا) .

Hinge, *v.i.* To turn on hinges, دَارَ عَلَى مِفْصَلَاتٍ . To rest, to depend upon, تَوَقَّفَ عَلَى ـ تَعَلَّقَ ب . He will tell thee the affair from the point on which it hinges or turns, يَأْتِيكَ بِٱلْأَمْرِ مِن مَفْصِلِهِ .

Hint, *v.t.* To bring to the mind of another by a hint, أَشْعَرَ-ب ـ رَمَزَ-ب ـ أَوْعَزَ-إِلَى ـ وَمَأَ-إِلَى *aor.* يَمَأُ .

Hint, *v.i.* To — at, غَمَزَ ب ـ تَرَمَّزَ ـ وَعَزَ إِلَى *aor.* يَعِزُ ـ كَنَى عَن ـ أَكْنَى ـ وَحَى إِلَى *aor.* يَحِي . To — at obscurely, to insinuate, أَلْغَطَ ب ـ لَغَّطَ ب ـ لَغَطَ ب .

Hint, *n.* شَرْط *pl.* أَشْرَاط ـ رَمْز ـ شِعْرَة ـ غَمْز ـ وَعْز . An insinuation, إِلْغَاط ـ لِغَاط ـ لَغَط . To have a — of, to take a —, فَهِمَ ٱلْإِشَارَةَ ـ شَعَرَ بِهِ .

Hintingly, *ad.* بِشَرْطٍ ـ وَعْزًا ـ غَمْزًا ـ رَمْزًا .

Hip, *n.* The joint, وَرِك *pl.* أَوْرَاك . The hip bone, نَوْض *pl.* أَنْوَاض ـ وَرِك . The crest or head of the hip, خَرْقَفَة *dual* خَرْقَفَتَانِ ـ حَجَبَة *dual* حَجَبَتَانِ . The socket of the hip, صَدَفَة ـ خَرَابَةُ ٱلْوَرِكِ ـ خُرْبَةُ ٱلْوَرِكِ . The sinew of the hip, حَارِقَة *dual* حَارِقَتَانِ . To sprain one's hip, تَوَرَّكَ . To sprain the hip of another, وَرَّكَ . To carry, as of a child, on the hip, تَوَرَّكَ-عَلَى . Having a sprained hip, مَحْرُوق . Hip, melancholy, طَلْطَفَة ـ سَوْدَاء . Hip, the berry of the wild rose, دَلِيك *pl.* دُلُك . To have one on the hip, فَاجَأَ ـ فَجَأَ ـ وَقَعَ فِيهِ *aor.* يَقَعُ .

Hipped, *a.* As with melancholy, سَوْدَاوِيّ ـ كَرِيب .

Hippo-centaur, *n.* / **Hippo-griff**, } حَيَوَانٌ خُرَافِيٌّ نِصْفُهُ رَجُلٌ وَنِصْفُهُ حِصَانٌ .

Hippocrates, *n.* The famous physician, إِبُقْرَاط ـ بُقْرَاط .

Hippodrome, *n.* مَيْدَانُ ٱلْخَيْلِ *pl.* مَيَادِين ـ مِضْمَار .

Hippophagous, *a.* آكِلُ لَحْمِ ٱلْخُيُولِ .

Hippopotamus, *n.* فَرَسُ ٱلْبَحْرِ *pl.* أَفْرَاس *and* فُرُوس ; called also in Egypt, بِرْنِيق .

Hip-shot, *a.* Having a dislocated hip, مَحْرُوق .

Hire, *v.t.* To take on hire, إِسْتَأْجَرَ ـ أَكْرَى . To let on —, أَجَرَ ـ آجَرَ ـ كَارَى : He hired him the house, أَجَرَهُ ٱلدَّارَ . He was hired to do it for such a sum, أُوجِرَ عَلَيْهِ بِكَذَا . To bribe, رَاشَى ـ بَرْطَلَ . To bargain with for the spring, عَامَلَهُ مُرَابَعَةً ; for a month, عَامَلَهُ مُشَاهَرَةً ; for a day, عَامَلَهُ مُيَاوَمَةً . To — a vessel; *see to* Charter, *v.t.*

Hire, *n.* عُمَالَة ـ إِجَارَة ـ إِسْتِئْجَار ـ أُجْرَة ـ كِرْوَة ـ كِرَاء .

Hireling, *n.* / **Hireling**, *a.* } One who is hired, أَجِير *pl.* أُجَرَاء ـ شَاكِرِيّ *pl.* شَاكِرِيَّة .

Hirer, *n.* One who takes on hire, مُسْتَأْجِر ـ مُكْرٍ . One who lets on hire, مُؤْجِر ـ كَرِيّ .

Hirsute, *a.* مُشْعِر ـ شَعْرَانِيّ ـ أَزَبّ .

Hirsuteness, *n.* شَعْرَانِيَّة ـ شَعْر .

His, *pr.* *Expressed by the suffix* ه ; (*vulg.* بِتَاعُه). His father's horse, حِصَانُ أَبِيهِ . This is mine as well as his, هٰذَا لِي وَلَهُ . My son and his, إِبْنِي وَٱبْنُهُ . My children and his, أَوْلَادِي وَأَوْلَادُهُ .

Hispid, *a.* أَهْلَب ـ هَلِبِيّ .

Hiss, *v.i.* To — as a serpent, فَحَّ ـ فَرَّ ـ نَبَجَ ; as a kettle on the fire or hot iron plunged into water, كَتَّ . To whiz, حَفَّ ـ خَرَّ . To —, in contempt, صَفَرَ .

Hiss, *v.t.* To disapplaud, عَيَّرَ ـ صَاحَ عَلَى ـ هَلَّلَ عَلَى ـ

To explode, to treat with contempt, إِسْتَقْبَحَ — صَفَرَ عَلَى ² — إِسْتَهْزَأَ بِ — إِسْتَفْحَشَ.

Hiss, n. / Hissing, } As of a serpent, نَبِيجٌ — قَرِيرٌ — فَحِيحٌ ; of a kettle simmering, كَشِيشٌ — كَتِيتٌ. A whizzing, خَرِيرٌ — حَفِيفٌ. A — in contempt, صَفِيرٌ. An object of derision, صَفِيرٌ — سُخْرَةٌ — ضُحْكَةٌ.

Hist! int. أُسْكُتْ — صَهْ. Hist, O man! صَهْ يَا رَجُلُ.

Histology, n. عِلْمُ تَرْكِيبِ أَبْدَانِ ٱلْحَيَوَانَاتِ.

Historian, n. مُؤَرِّخٌ pl. مُؤَرِّخُونَ.

Historic, a. / Historical, } مُخْتَصٌّ بِٱلتَّوَارِيخِ — تَارِيخِيٌّ. Descriptive, تَعْبِيرِيٌّ — وَصْفِيٌّ. Historical style, نَصٌّ تَارِيخِيٌّ. The — remains of that province, آثَارُ تِلْكَ ٱلْوِلَايَةِ ٱلتَّارِيخِيَّةُ.

Historically, ad. حَسَبَ ٱلتَّوَارِيخِ — عَلَى وَجْهِ ٱلتَّارِيخِ.

Historiographer, n. كَاتِبُ ٱلْوَقَائِعِ — كَاتِبُ ٱلتَّارِيخِ.

Historiography, n. كِتَابَةُ ٱلْوَقَائِعِ — كِتَابَةُ ٱلتَّوَارِيخِ.

History, n. تَارِيخٌ pl. تَوَارِيخُ. A narrative, حَدِيثٌ pl. أَحَادِيثُ — قِصَّةٌ pl. قِصَصٌ — حِكَايَةٌ pl. حِكَايَاتٌ. An account, خَبَرٌ pl. أَخْبَارٌ. A life, biography, سِيرَةٌ pl. سِيَرٌ — تَرْجَمَةٌ pl. تَرَاجِمُ. Natural —, عِلْمُ ٱلطَّبِيعِيَّاتِ. Sacred —, تَارِيخُ ٱلنُّبُوَّةِ. Profane —, تَارِيخُ ٱلْوَقَائِعِ ٱلْعَادِيَّةِ.

Histrionic, a. / Histrionical, } مَنُوطٌ بِمَرْسَحِ ٱللَّعِبِ — مُتَعَلِّقٌ بِٱلتِّيَاتْرُو — مَرْسَحِيٌّ.

Hit, v.t. To strike, لَطَمَ — صَدَمَ — قَرَعَ بِ — صَدَعَ بِ — ضَرَبَ. To hit, as a mark, أَصَابَ — لَطَعَ. To attain, حَصَّلَ — حَصَلَ عَلَى ² — بَلَغَ ² — فَازَ بِ. To light upon, إِلْتَقَى — أَصَابَ. To taunt, jibe at, طَعَنَ فِي. To hit off, to do a thing well, أَحْكَمَ — سَدَّدَ — أَسَدَّ — إِتَّقَنَ — أَحْسَنَ. To parody, قَلَّبَ هَزْلًا — هَزَأَ بِ. He hit the target, أَصَابَ ٱلْقِرْطَاسَ. He hit the right point, أَصَابَ ٱلسَّدَادَ — أَصَابَ ٱلصَّوَابَ. He certainly hits the right nail on the head in his speech, إِنَّهُ لَيُسَدِّدُ فِي قَوْلِهِ. The bullet did not hit its aim, لَمْ تُصِبِ ٱلرَّصَاصَةُ ٱلْغَرَضَ.

Hit, v.i. To clash, تَلَاطَمَ — تَصَادَمَ. Not to miss, أَصَابَ. To succeed, نَجَحَ — أَفْلَحَ.

Hit, n. A blow, دَقَّةٌ — ضَرْبَةٌ — لَطْمَةٌ — صَدْمَةٌ. A lucky chance, إِصَابَةٌ — إِتِّفَاقٌ. Hitting a mark, إِصَابَةٌ.

Hitch, v.t. To catch, to hook, عَلَّقَ — شَبَكَ. To knot, عَقَدَ. To entangle, as a rope in a pulley, أَمْرَسَ.

Hitch, v.i. To move by jerks, as in walking, نَطَّ — حَتَكَ. To become entangled, إِشْتَبَكَ — إِنْشَبَكَ — مَرِسَ.

Hitch, n. A knot, عُقْدَةٌ. A twist in a rope, شَبْكٌ — مَرَسٌ — تَشْبِيكٌ. A difficulty, عَائِقَةٌ — صُعُوبَةٌ — وَرْطَةٌ. A jerk in walking, نَطٌّ — حَتَكَانٌ — حَتْكٌ. There is a — somewhere, لَا بُدَّ مِنْ عَائِقَةٍ.

Hithe, n. *See* Haven, n.

Hither, ad. إِلَى هُنَا — هُنَا. Come up —, إِصْعَدْ إِلَى هُنَا. Reach — your finger, هَاتِ أُصْبُعَكَ إِلَى هُنَا. Hither and thither, هُنَا وَهُنَاكَ.

Hither, a. أَقْرَبُ — أَدْنَى fem. دُنْيَا. In the — part of the land, فِي أَدْنَى ٱلْأَرْضِ. The — world, ٱلدُّنْيَا.

Hithermost, a. ٱلْأَقْرَبُ — ٱلْأَدْنَى — أَدْنَى دَنَا. The — part of the house, أَدْنَى ٱلْبَيْتِ.

Hitherto, ad. To this place, إِلَى هُنَا ; to this time, إِلَى ٱلْآنَ — حَتَّى ٱلْآنَ.

Hitherward, ad. نَحْوَ هٰذَا ٱلصَّوْبِ — إِلَى هٰذِهِ ٱلْجِهَةِ.

Hive, n. A — for bees, خَلِيَّةٌ — خَلِيُّ نَحْلٍ — جِزْعٌ pl. أَجْزَاعٌ — كُوَّارَةٌ pl. كُوَّارَاتٌ — مَعْسَلَةٌ pl. خَلَايَا. A swarm of bees, ثَوْلٌ — سُرْبَةٌ — سَرْبَةُ نَحْلٍ — خَشْرَمٌ. A — of people, عُمْرَانٌ — عَوْمَرَةٌ — سُرْبَةٌ pl. سُرَبٌ — مُشْتَارٌ.

Hive, v.i. To —, as bees, تَثَوَّلَتِ ٱلنَّحْلُ. To reside collectively, تَسَرَّبُوا — تَصَاحَبُوا — إِنْثَالُوا — تَآلَفُوا.

Hive, v.t. To put into a —, جَمَعَ فِي كُوَّارَةٍ. To collect, جَمَّعَ — جَمَعَ.

Ho! int. / Hoa! } يَا هُوَ — أَيَا — يَا. Ho, ho! run ye away, يَا يَا آهْرُبُوا.

Hoar, a. / Hoary, } White, أَبْيَضُ fem. بَيْضَاءُ pl. بِيضٌ. Gray, أَشْيَبُ fem. شَيْبَاءُ — شَائِبٌ. Mossy, ذُو أُشْنَةٍ. Mouldy, مُعَفَّنٌ. The summits of the hills were —, شَابَتْ رُؤُوسُ ٱلْآكَامِ. To grow —, شَابَ aor. يَشِيبُ — شَابَ غُرَابُهُ — طَارَ غُرَابُهُ. To make —, شَيَّبَ. Grief made him —, شَيَّبَ ٱلْحُزْنُ رَأْسَهُ. *See also* Gray, a.

Hoard, v.t. To amass, جَمَّعَ. To lay up in store, كَنَزَ — ذَخَرَ — إِدَّخَرَ — خَزَنَ ² — إِخْتَزَنَ. To — something for one's self, إِسْتَخْزَنَ.

Hoard, v.i. إِجْتَمَعَ — تَجَمَّعَ — إِكْتَنَزَ.

Hoard, n. كَنْزٌ pl. كُنُوزٌ — صَوْنَةٌ — ذَخِيرَةٌ pl. ذَخَائِرُ.

Hoar-frost, n. صَقِيعٌ — سَقِيطٌ — صَرِيدٌ — صَقْعَةٌ — صَيِّبٌ. The ground became covered with —, صُقِعَتِ ٱلْأَرْضُ.

Hoarhound, n. The plant, حَشِيشَةُ ٱلْكَلْبِ — أُنْجِيدَةٌ — فَرَاسِيُونُ.

Hoariness, n. Grayness, شَيْبٌ — مَشِيبٌ. Mossiness, أُشْنَةٌ.

Hoarse, *a.* Of the voice, أَبَحُّ ـ أَجَشُّ ـ أَجْشَرُ *fem.* بَحَّآءُ *and* بَحَّة *pl.* بُحٌّ. Having a — voice, أَبَحُّ ٱلصَّوْتِ. To have a — voice, بَحَّ ـ جَشِرَ *aor.* يَبَحُّ. To make —, أَبَحَّ. *See also* Harsh, *a.*

Hoarsely, *ad.* بِجُشْرَةٍ ـ بِصَوْتٍ مَبْحُوحٍ.

Hoarseness, *n.* بُحَّة ـ بُحَاح ـ بَحَاحَة ـ جَشَر ـ جُشْرَة.

Hoary, *a.* *See* Hoar, *a.*

Hoax, *n.* سُخْرَة ـ سَخَر ـ أُلْعُوبَة ـ مَضْحَكَة.

Hoax, *v.t.* تَلَاعَبَ بِ ـ مَكَرَ بِ ـ سَخِرَ مِن ـ ضَحِكَ عَلَى.

Hob, *n.* As of a grate, طَابِقُ مَوْقِدٍ *pl.* طَوَابِقُ.

Hobble, *v.i.* To limp, عَشَزَ ـ خَمَعَ ـ حَجَلَ ـ قَزَلَ ـ عَرَجَ.

Hobble, *n.* عَرَج ـ قَزَلَان ـ حَجَلَان ـ حَجَل. To get into a —, تَوَرَّطَ فِي وَرْطَةٍ ـ (اِنْبَلَشَ *vulg.*) أَبْلَسَ.

Hobble-de-hoy, *n.* تِنْبَل ـ غَلِيظ ـ غَشِيم ـ أَخْرَق.

Hobbler, *n.* }
Hobbling, *a.* } أَعْرَجُ ـ أَقْزَلُ ـ خَامِع ـ عَاشِز.

Hobbles, *n.* Hobbles, as for a horse, عِقَال ـ شِكَال. To put —, as on a horse, شَكَّلَ ـ شَكَلَ.

Hobby, *n.* A horse, فَرَس *pl.* أَفْرَاس. A hawk, بَازِي *pl.* بُزَاة ـ صَقْر. A favourite object, هَوِيَّة. He rode his —, fancy, رَكِبَ هَوِيَّتَهُ. *See also* Foible, *n.*

Hobby-horse, *n.* A wooden horse, فَرَسٌ مِنْ خَشَبٍ. *See also* Hobby, *n.*

Hobgoblin, *n.* تَهْوِيل ـ غُول *pl.* غِيلَان.

Hobnail, *n.* A large-headed nail, مِسْمَارٌ خَشِنٌ.

Hobnob, *ad.* عَلَى ٱلتَّنَاوُبِ ـ بِٱلدَّوْرِ.

Hobson's-choice, *n.* شَيْءٌ لَا بُدَّ مِنْهُ ـ خِيَارٌ بِٱلْجَبْرِ. It is — with me, مَا لِي مِنْهُ بُدٌّ. It is — in this matter, لَيْسَ لِهٰذَا ٱلْأَمْرِ بُدٌّ.

Hock, *n.* The joint between the knee and fetlock, عُرْقُوب ـ كُرْسُوع. Part of the thigh, مَعْطِفُ ٱلرُّكْبَةِ ـ بَطْنُ ٱلسَّاقِ. A kind of wine, ضَرْبٌ مِنَ ٱلْخَمْرِ. A swelling in the —, جَرَذ. To have such a swelling, of a horse, *etc.*, جَرِذَ.

Hock, *v.t.* *See to* Hamstring, *v.t.*

Hockey, *n.* لَعْبُ ٱلصَّوْلَجَانِ.

Hockle, *v.t.* *See to* Hamstring, *v.t.*

Hocus, *v.t.* To deceive, مَكَرَ بِ ـ سَخَرَ.

Hocus-pocus, *n.* خَدِيعَة ـ شَعْوَذَة (شعبشة *vulg.*).

Hod, *n.* قُفَّةُ ٱلسَّيَّاعِ ـ نَقِير *pl.* نُقْرَان.

Hodge-podge, *n.* Of food, طَعَامٌ نَفِيٌّ ـ أَعْلَاث ـ لَفِيف. A medley, أَخْلَاط ـ خِلْط *pl.* تَهَاوُش ـ شَمَل.

Hodiernal, *a.* يَوْمِيّ ـ مُتَعَلِّقٌ بِٱلْيَوْمِ ٱلْحَاضِرِ.

Hodman, *n.* حَامِلُ قُفَّةِ ٱلسَّيَّاعِ ـ فَعَلَة *pl.* فَاعِل ـ حَامِلُ ٱلنَّقِيرِ.

Hoe, *n.* مِعْزَقَة ـ مِجْرَفَة ـ مِقْلَب.

Hoe, *v.t.* عَزَقَ ـ جَرَفَ.

Hoe, *v.i.* جَرَفَ بِٱلْمِجْرَفَةِ ـ عَزَقَ بِٱلْمِعْزَقَةِ.

Hog, *n.* A swine, خِنْزِير *pl.* خَنَازِيرُ. A dirty fellow, نَجِس *pl.* أَنْجَاس. A scraper, مِحَكَّة ـ جَارُوف.

Hog, *v.i.* To bend, تَثَنَّى ـ اِنْعَطَفَ ـ عَوِجَ.

Hog, *v.t.* To scrape, حَكَّ ـ جَرَفَ.

Hoggish, *a.* مِثْلَ ٱلْخِنْزِيرِ. *See also* Brutish, Filthy, *a.*

Hoggishly, *ad.* كَٱلْخِنْزِيرِ. *See also* Filthily, *ad.*

Hoggishness, *n.* Filthiness, قَذَر ـ رِجْس. Gluttony, شَرَاهَة.

Hogshead, *n.* A barrel, بَرْمِيل *pl.* بَرَامِيل.

Hog-skin, *n.* جِلْدُ خِنْزِيرٍ مَدْبُوغٌ.

Hogsty, *n.* زَرِيبَةٌ لِلْخَنَازِيرِ *pl.* زَرَائِبُ.

Hoiden, *n.* A bold girl, بِنْتٌ فَرْتَعٌ ـ صَبِيَّةٌ بَلْهَآءُ ـ بِنْتٌ فَحِلَةٌ.

Hoiden, *a.* Bold, rude, قَلِيلُ ٱلْحَيَآءِ ـ سَفِيه ـ وَقِح.

Hoiden, *v.i.* To behave lightly, سَفِهَ ـ وَقُحَ *aor.* يَوْقَحُ ـ تَوَاقَحَ.

Hoist, *v.t.* To raise, lift, نَصَبَ ـ رَفَعَ ـ نَصَّبَ ـ عَلَّى. To — a flag, أَلْوَى ٱلْبَيْرَقَ.

Hoist, *n.* A lift, رَفْع ـ نَصْب. The — of a sail, نَصْبُ ٱلشِّرَاعِ. *See also under* Lift, *n.*

Hoity-toity! *int.* يَه مَه ـ مَا شَآءَ ٱللّٰهُ ـ سُبْحَانَ ٱللّٰهِ ـ هَيْهَاتَ.

Hold, *v.t.* To grasp, قَبَضَ ـ مَسَكَ ـ أَمْسَكَ بِ ـ تَمَاسَكَ بِ. To — anything together, ضَمَّ. To — firmly, ضَبَطَ. To stop, arrest, أَوْقَفَ ـ وَقَّفَ. To restrain, مَنَعَ ـ ضَبَطَ ـ أَجْبَرَ ـ أَمْسَكَ. To contain, حَصَرَ ـ اِحْتَوَى عَلَى ـ اِشْتَمَلَ عَلَى ـ وَسِعَ *aor.* يَسَعُ. To maintain, as an opinion, عَقَدَ عَلَيْهِ ٱلْقَلْبَ ـ اِعْتَقَدَ ـ آمَنَ بِ ـ اِرْتَأَى. To esteem, consider, عَدَّ ـ نَزَّلَ بِمَنْزِلَةِ كَذَا ـ حَسِبَ. To possess, حَازَ *aor.* يَحُوزُ ـ اِقْتَنَى ـ اِمْتَلَكَ ـ تَمَتَّعَ بِ ـ مَلَكَ. To —, as of an office, قَامَ فِي مَأْمُورِيَّةٍ ـ تَقَلَّدَ وَظِيفَةً. To —, to have in possession, حَازَ *aor.* يَحُوزُ. To preserve, keep, حَفِظَ ـ حَرَسَ ـ صَانَ *aor.* يَصُونُ. To confine, حَصَرَ ـ حَبَسَ. To maintain, تَمَسَّكَ بِ ـ ثَبَتَ عَلَى. To continue, اِسْتَمَرَّ ـ ظَلَّ ـ أَدْمَنَ عَلَى ـ وَاظَبَ عَلَى. Not to give way, to continue to —, مَا زَالَ مَاسِكًا بِ. The soldiers still held the position which they had taken up, العساكِرُ لَمْ تُزايِلِ ٱلْمَوْضِعَ ٱلَّذِى تَبَوَّأَتْهُ. I — this to be better than that, عِنْدِى هٰذا أَفْضَلُ مِنْ ذٰلِكَ. To cause to —, to put into the grasp of, قَبَّضَ ـ مَسَّكَ ـ (or ـ) أَمْسَكَ ـ) بِ. Hold! take hold! عِنْدَكَ.

To hold a conference, of many, إِيتَمَرُوا ـ تَذاكَرُوا ـ تَشاوَرُوا.

To hold a feast, عَيَّدَ.

To hold, as of a house, of, to rent from, إِسْتَكْرَى ـ (or ـ) كارَى ـ) مِن.

To hold (one) back from, قَبَضَ ـ عَن ـ ثَبَّطَ ـ عَن ـ كَفَّ ـ عَن.

To hold something back from, حَبَسَ ـ عَن ـ رَبَطَ ـ عَن.

To hold for, to be on the side of, تَعَصَّبَ لِ ـ تَمَسَّكَ مَع ـ مَسَكَ طَرَفَهُ.

To hold forth or out to, ناوَلَ ـ عَرَضَ ـ عَلَى ـ مَدَّ ـ لِ.

To hold one free, عَصَمَ.

To hold one guiltless, بَرَّأَ ـ أَبْرَأَ.

To hold one in, to restrain, مَنَعَ ـ ضَبَطَ ـ أَجْبَرَ; of a horse, أَلْجَمَ.

To hold one off, مَنَعَ ـ أَبْعَدَ.

To hold one's own, حَفِظَ أَمْرَهُ ـ حافَظَ عَلَى حُقُوقِهِ.

To hold one's peace or tongue, صَمَتَ ـ سَكَتَ ـ صَمَّتَ.

To hold over, to defer, أَخَّرَ ـ سَوَّفَ.

To hold to, to love, prefer, حَبَّ ـ إِسْتَحْسَنَ ـ إِسْتَفْضَلَ. To maintain, تَمَسَّكَ بِ ـ ثَبَتَ عَلَى ـ صَرَّ عَلَى. To persevere in, لَزِمَ ـ واظَبَ عَلَى. To hold to a promise, قامَ بِوَعْدِهِ ـ وَفَى وَعْدَهُ aor. يَفِى.

To hold together, to cohere, تَماسَكَ ـ إِسْتَعَزَّ.

To hold up, to raise, as from the ground, شالَ بِ ـ أَقامَ ـ رَفَعَ. To sustain, support, سانَدَ ـ أَسْنَدَ.

To hold water, ضَبَطَ ٱلْماءَ. Not to hold water, to be invalid, لا يَصِحُّ ـ لا يَصْلُحُ ـ بَطَلَ.

Hold, *v.i.* To be true, صَحَّ ـ صَلَحَ. To last, أَزْمَنَ ـ دامَ ـ إِسْتَدامَ. To stand firm, رَسَخَ ـ ثَبَتَ. To stick, تَماسَكَ ـ إِلْتَزَقَ ـ تَلَزَّجَ.

To hold back, to keep at a distance, تَباعَدَ ـ تَأَخَّرَ. To keep aloof, جانَبَ ـ تَمَنَّعَ عَن ـ تَباعَدَ. He held back in the affair, تَضَجَّعَ فِى ٱلْأَمْرِ.

To hold forth, to preach, speak, خَطَبَ ـ أَنْذَرَ ـ يَعِظُ aor. وَعَظَ.

To hold good, إِسْتَقَرَّ ـ ثَبَتَ ـ صَلَحَ ـ صَحَّ.

To hold off, إِجْتَنَبَ ـ تَجَنَّبَ ـ تَباعَدَ.

To hold on, to continue, أَدْمَنَ عَلَى ـ إِسْتَمَرَّ. To continue to adhere, ما زالَ ماسِكًا. He held on his way, إِسْتَمْسَكَ بِطَرِيقِهِ.

To hold out, to endure, إِسْتَدامَ ـ إِسْتَقامَ. Not to yield, ظَلَّ ـ إِشْتَدَّ ـ صَلُبَ ـ ثَبَتَ مُقاوِمًا ـ دافِعًا. To resist, to stand,

To hold together, of many, تَوافَقُوا ـ إِتَّحَدُوا ـ إِلْتَصَقُوا ـ إِنْضَمُّوا.

To hold up, of the weather, صَحَتِ ٱلدُّنْيا ـ يَصْفُو aor. صَفا ـ أَصْحَتِ ٱلسَّماءُ.

To hold with a person, تَراءَى بِرَأْيِهِ ـ يَرَى aor. رَأَى رَأْيَهُ ـ تَعَصَّبَ لِ ـ كانَ مِنْ حِزْبِهِ ـ وافَقَ ـ فِى.

Hold! *int.* كِفَّ ـ أَصْبِرْ عَلَىَّ ـ قِفْ ـ عِنْدَكَ.

Hold, *n.* A catch, grasp, مُسْكَةٌ ـ قَبْضٌ ـ إِمْساكٌ ـ تَمَسُّكٌ. The power of holding, قُوَّةُ ٱلْقَبْضِ ـ قُوَّةُ ٱلتَّماسُكِ. A support, رُكْنٌ ـ عُمْدَةٌ ـ مُسْنَدٌ. Power, influence, قُدْرَةٌ ـ نُفُوذٌ ـ مَقْدَرَةٌ ـ سَطْوَةٌ. A prison, حَبْسٌ ـ سِجْنٌ. The — of a ship, أَنْبارٌ; the bottom of the — of a ship, where the water collects, قِنْطاسٌ. A fort, حُجْرَةٌ pl. حُجَرٌ ـ قَلْعَةٌ ـ حِصْنٌ. Custody, حِفْظٌ.

To lay or take hold of, قَبَضَ بِ ـ أَمْسَكَ بِ. To take firm hold of, تَشَبَّثَ بِ.

To let go one's hold, خَلَّى عَن ـ أَطْلَقَ بِ ـ طَلَقَ بِ ـ سَيَّبَ.

Holdback, *n.* *See* Hindrance, Drawback, *n.*

Holder, *n.* One who holds, ماسِكٌ; one who carries, حامِلٌ; a possessor, مالِكٌ ـ حائِزٌ ـ ضابِطٌ; a tenant, مُلْتَزِمٌ. A handle, نُصُبٌ pl. نِصابٌ ـ مِقْبَضٌ ـ مِمْسَكٌ. A kettle —, جِعالَةٌ. A pen —, مُسْكَةُ قَلَمٍ. A holder-forth; *see* Haranguer, *n.*

Holdfast, *n.* A hook, a catch, عَقْرَبٌ pl. عَقارِبُ ـ كُلّابٌ ـ عُقّافَةٌ ـ خُطّافٌ. A support, عِمادٌ ـ عُمْدَةٌ ـ سَنَدٌ ـ رُكْنٌ.

Holding, *n.* Tenure, ضَبْطٌ. A farm held, إِلْتِزامٌ. A chorus, مَرَدٌّ. Power, influence, نُفُوذٌ ـ سَطْوَةٌ ـ قُوَّةٌ. Anchoring ground, مَرْبَطٌ ـ مَرْسًى.

Hole, *n.* A perforation, نَقْبٌ pl. نُقُوبٌ ـ ثُقْبٌ pl. ثُقُوبٌ ـ نُقْبَةٌ pl. نُقَبٌ ـ بُخْشٌ pl. بُخُوشٌ. A — in the ground, a ditch, حُفْرَةٌ pl. حُفَرٌ. A — in a garment, or an aperture, شَقٌّ pl. شُقُوقٌ ـ خَرْقٌ pl. خُرُوقٌ. A burrow, بَيْتٌ pl. بُيُوتٌ ـ جُحْرٌ pl. جِحَرَةٌ. The — in which a hatchet, *etc.*, is infixed, حُرْتٌ ـ حُرْتَةٌ. A hovel, مَسْكَنٌ دَنِيٌّ. A — to creep out of, an excuse, عُذْرٌ. Full of little holes, عَيِّنٌ. To make a —; *see to* Hole, *v.t.*

To pick holes in one's character, نَقَرَ ـ ثَلَمَ صِيتَهُ. He made holes in, scuttled, the ship, خَرَقَ ٱلسَّفِينَةَ.

Hole, *v.t.* To make holes in, نَقَبَ ـ خَرَقَ ـ بَخَشَ. To put holes in, as in beads, قَصَّ ـ عَيَّنَ.

Hole, *v.i.* To go into a hole or burrow, جَحَرَ ـ تَجَحَّرَ ـ إِنْجَحَرَ.

Holiday, *n.* A day of rejoicing, يَوْمُ فَرَحٍ *pl.* أَيَّام. A day of public rejoicing, مَوْسِم *pl.* مَوَاسِمُ. A festival, عِيد *pl.* أَعْيَاد. A day of exemption from labour, يَوْمَ بَطَالَةٍ *pl.* أَيَّام. A half —, تَعْطِيلُ نِصْفِ نَهَارٍ.

Holiday, *a.* لائق بِٱلْعِيدِ ـ مُخْتَصٌّ بِأَيَّامِ ٱلْفَرَحِ.

Holily, *ad.* بِقَدَاسَةٍ ـ بِطَهَارَةٍ.

Holiness, *n.* قُدْس ـ طَهَارَة ـ قَدَاسَة. Piety, تَقْوَى ـ تُقَاوَة ـ وَرَع. Sacredness, حُرْمَة. His Holiness the Pope, قَدَاسَةُ ٱلْبَابَا.

Holland, *n.* The country, مَمْلَكَةُ فَلَمَنْك ـ هُولَانْدَة. The cloth, ضَرْبٌ مِنَ ٱلْقُمَاشِ.

Hollander, *n.* مِنْ أَهْلِ فَلَمَنْك.

Hollands, *n.* *See* Gin, *n.*

Hollo, *v.i.* } عَيَّطَ ـ ـ صَرَخَ ـ ـ صَاحَ ـ صَيَّحَ ـ صَوَّتَ ـ ـ زَعَقَ.
Holla, } To — to, ـ زَعَقَ بِ ـ ـ صَاحَ بِ ـ صَوَّتَ بِ.

To — repeatedly, عَطْعَطَ.

Holloa! *int.* } يا ذا ـ أَلَا ـ يا هُو ـ هَيَّا.
Hollo! }

Hollow, *a.* Empty, خَاوٍ ـ خَالٍ ـ فَارِغ ـ بَاوٍ. Hollowed out, أَجْوَف ـ مُقَوَّب ـ مُجَوَّف ـ مُنْقَر. Of a sound, أَبَحّ. False, خَادِع ـ كَاذِب ـ غَيْرُ صَمِيمِيّ. Vain, فَارِغ ـ بَاطِل. A — tooth, ضِرْس مُسَوَّس. A — reed, قَنَاةٌ جَوْفَاءُ (or مُجَوَّفَة). A — tree, شَجَرَةٌ جَوْفَاءُ (or مُجَوَّفَة). To be —, hollowed out, ـ جَافَ تَجَوَّفَ.

Hollow, *n.* A concavity, جَوْف ـ وُقُور and وَقَرَات *pl.* وَقْرَة ـ غَوْط *pl.* أَجْوَاف ـ حُفْرَة *pl.* حُفَر ـ نُقْرَة *pl.* نُقَر. A — in a stone, وَقْب *pl.* أَوْقَاب. An empty space, خَلْوَة ـ فَرَاغ ـ خُلُوّ. A low place, غَوْر ـ خَافِضَة. The — of the hand, كَفّ; of the eye, نُقْرَةُ ٱلْعَيْنِ *pl.* نُقَر; in any part of the face, قَلْت *pl.* قِلَات. The — of the thigh, حُقُّ ٱلْفَخِذِ. A deep —, هُوَّة.

Hollow, *v.t.* غَاطَ ـ نَقَرَ فِي ـ ـ حَفَرَ ـ ـ قَعَّرَ ـ جَوَّفَ ـ جَوَّرَ ـ قَوَّبَ. To be hollowed, تَجَوَّبَ ـ تَجَوَّفَ. Hollowed out, نَقِير ـ مُجَوَّب.

Hollow, *v.i.* *See to* Hollo, *v.i.*

Hollow, *ad.* Wholly, بِٱلْمَرَّةِ ـ بَتَّةً. To beat all —, ـ كَسَرَ غَلَبَ عَلَيْهِمْ بَتَّةً ـ ٱلْجَمِيعَ كَسْرَةً فَاحِشَةً.

Hollow-eyed, *a.* مُتَقَعِّرُ ٱلْعَيْنَيْنِ ـ مُنْقَعِرُ ٱلْعَيْنَيْنِ ـ هَاجّ.

Hollow-hearted, *a.* مُنَافِق ـ عَدِيمُ ٱلْوَفَاءِ ـ خَائِن.

Hollow-heartedness, *n.* عَدَمُ وَفَاءٍ ـ خِيَانَة.

Hollowness, *n.* Concavity, تَجَوُّر ـ تَجَوُّف. Deceitfulness, عَدَمُ إِخْلَاصٍ ـ نِفَاق ـ مُرَايَاة.

Holly, *n.* The flower, شَرَابَةُ ٱلرَّاعِي.

Hollyhock, *n.* قَرْصَعْنَة ـ شُوَيْكَةُ إِبْرٰهِيمَ.

Holm, *n.* The evergreen oak, سِنْدِيَان. A river isle, جُزَيْرَةٌ فِي نَهْرٍ.

Holocaust, *n.* صَعِيدَة *pl.* صعائد ـ وُقُود ـ قُرْبَانٌ وَقُودٍ ـ ضَحِيَّة *pl.* ضَحَايَا.

Holograph, *n.* كِتَابَةٌ بِخَطِّ ٱلْمُوصِي.

Holster, *n.* غِلَاف *pl.* غُلُف (or قِرَاب) ٱلطَّبَنْجَةِ.

Holy, *a.* Wholly pure, طَاهِر ـ قُدُّوس. Sacred, sanctified, شَرِيف ـ مُبَارَك ـ مُحَرَّم ـ مُقَدَّس. Pious, قَانِت ـ مُتَّقٍ ـ دَيِّن ـ وَرِع. Pure, chaste, عَفِيف ـ صَالِح. The Holy Land, أَرْضُ فِلِسْطِينَ. The Holy One, ٱللّٰهُ ٱلْقُدُّوسُ ـ ٱلْوَحِيدُ ٱلْقُدُّوسُ. The Holy One of God, حَضْرَةُ عِيسَى ـ وَحِيدُ ٱللّٰهِ ٱلْقُدُّوسُ. The Holy Ghost, ٱلرُّوحُ ٱلْقُدُسُ. Holy writ, ٱلْكُتُبُ ٱلْمُقَدَّسَةُ ـ ٱلْكُتُبُ ٱلنَّبَوِيَّةُ. The Holy of holies, قُدْسُ ٱلْأَقْدَاسِ. Holy ground, أَرْضٌ مُقَدَّسَةٌ. To be —, قَدُسَ ـ تَقَدَّسَ. To make —, قَدَّسَ.

Holyday, *n.* عِيد *pl.* أَعْيَاد. *See also* Holiday, *n.*

Holy-office, *n.* ٱلْمَحْكَمَةُ ٱلْبَابَاوِيَّةُ.

Holy-rood, *n.* صَلِيب *pl.* صُلْبَان.

Holy-stone, *n.* حَجَرُ مَالْطَةَ.

Holy-stone, *v.t.* نَظَّفَ بِحَجَرِ مَالْطَةَ.

Holy-Thursday, *n.* عِيدُ ٱلصُّعُودِ.

Holy-week, *n.* جُمْعَةُ ٱلْآلَامِ.

Homage, *n.* As to a sovereign, بَيْعَة. Obedience, service, رِعَايَة ـ إِطَاعَة ـ خِدْمَة. Respect, إِحْتِرَام. To do — to, as to a sovereign, بَايَعَ. To reverence, كَرَّمَ ـ أَكْرَمَ ـ وَجَّهَ.

Home, *n.* One's native place with its surroundings, وَطَن *pl.* أَوْطَان ـ كِنّ *pl.* أَكْنَان ـ مَسْقَط ـ مَسْقَطُ ٱلرَّأْسِ. Aleppo is my —, or birth-place, حَلَبُ مَسْقَطُ رَأْسِي. He yearns for his —, يَحِنُّ إِلَى مَسْقَطِهِ. One's own people, أَهْل ـ خَاصَّة. A place of residence, مَوْطِن *pl.* مَوَاطِنُ ـ مَقَام ـ مَسْكَن ـ بَيْت. The place where one was brought up, مَنْشَأ. To keep at —, لَازَمَ ٱلْبَيْتَ. A keeper at —, مُلَازِمُ ٱلْبَيْتِ. To choose a —, وَطَّنَ ـ إِتَّطَنَ ـ إِسْتَوْطَنَ. The last —, the grave, ٱللَّحْدُ ـ ٱلْقَبْرُ. The eternal —, جَنَّةُ ٱلْخُلْدِ. At —, in one's house, فِي ٱلْبَيْتِ. Make yourself at —, أَجْعَلْ نَفْسَكَ كَأَنَّكَ فِي مَحَلِّكَ. To feel one's self at —, كَانَ مِنْ غَيْرِ تَكْلِيفٍ ـ طَابَتْ نَفْسُهُ فِي ٱلْمَقَامِ ـ إِسْتَكَنَّ كَأَنَّهُ فِي بَيْتِهِ. He yearned for his —, أَبَّ إِلَى وَطَنِهِ.

Home, *a.* Belonging to —, وَطَنِيٌّ. Not foreign, بَلَدِيٌّ – داخِلِيٌّ. Sincere, صافٍ – خالِص – صِدِّيق. Telling, effective, صادِق. A — thrust, حَمْلَةٌ صادِقَةٌ. A — truth, صِدْقٌ صادِقٌ.

Home, *ad.* In, within, فِي داخِلٍ. At —, in one's house, فِي ٱلْبَيْتِ. Closely, بِدِقَّةٍ. To the point, سَدِيدًا. To drive —, as a nail, أَحْكَمَ تَسْمِيرَهُ – مَكَّنَ ٱلْمِسْمارَ. To hit —, of speech, سَدَّ فِي ٱلْقَوْلِ [2]. To take —, as to one's self, أَخَذَ لِنَفْسِهِ. Is he at — think you? يا تَرَى هُوَ فِي ٱلْبَيْتِ.

Home-born, *a.* / Home-bred, } Natural, طَبِيعِيٌّ. Native, not foreign, وَطَنِيٌّ – مَوْلُودُ ٱلْأَرْضِ. A — man, داخِلِيٌّ – بَلَدِيٌّ.

Homefelt, *a.* صادِق – باطِن – ضَمِيرِيٌّ – مِنَ ٱلْقَلْبِ – قَلْبِيٌّ.

Homeless, *a.* Without a home, بِدُونِ إِقامَةٍ – لا مَأْوَى لَهُ. Destitute, عاجِز.

Homeliness, *n.* Plainness, عَدَمُ جَمالٍ. Absence of ornament, simplicity, سَذاجَة. Coarseness, خَشانَة. Domesticity, good nature, أُنْسَة.

Homely, *a.* Plain, لا جَمالَ لَهُ. Without ornament, سانِج. Coarse, خَشِن. Homely language, كَلامٌ سائِرٌ.

Home-made, *a.* Made in the house, مَصْنُوعٌ فِي ٱلْبَيْتِ – بَيْتِيٌّ. Native, not foreign, بَلَدِيٌّ – وَطَنِيٌّ.

Homeopathic, *a.* ما نِيطَ بِتَطْبِيبِ ٱلْأَمْراضِ عَلَى أُصُولِ ٱلْمَثَلِ بِٱلْمَثَلِ.

Homeopathically, *ad.* حَسَبَ قَوانِينِ ٱلطِّبِّ ٱلَّذِي يَفْرِضُ مُعالَجَةَ ٱلدَّآءِ بِمِثْلِهِ.

Homeopathist, *n.* طَبِيبٌ يُعالِجُ ٱلْأَمْراضَ بِأَدْوِيَةٍ تُجانِسُ ٱلدَّآءَ.

Homeopathy, *n.* تَطْبِيبُ ٱلْمَثَلِ بِٱلْمَثَلِ.

Homer, *n.* The Hebrew measure, حُومِر. The Greek poet, أُومِيرُسُ ٱلشّاعِرُ ٱلْيُونانِيُّ.

Homeric, *a.* مَنْسُوبٌ إِلَى أُومِيرُسَ – مُتَعَلِّقٌ بِأُومِيرُسَ.

Homesick, *a.* مَنْ بِهِ دآءُ ٱلْحَنِينِ إِلَى ٱلْوَطَنِ. Home-sickness, وَحْشَةُ ٱلْوَطَنِ – حَسْرَةٌ عَلَى ٱلْوَطَنِ – إِجْتِوآء.

Homespun, *a.* / Homespun, *n.* } نَسِيجٌ بَلَدِيٌّ – نَسْجٌ وَطَنِيٌّ.

Homestall, *n.* / Homestead, } مَقام – مَسْكَن – مَنْزِل.

Homeward, *ad.* إِلَى صَوْبِ بَلَدِهِ – نَحْوَ ٱلْوَطَنِ.

Homeward-bound, *a.* سائِرٌ (*or* راجِعٌ) إِلَى بَلَدِهِ (*or* مَمْلَكَتِهِ).

Homicidal, *a.* سافِكُ ٱلدِّمآءِ – قاتِل – مُتَعَلِّقٌ بِٱلْقَتْلِ.

Homicide, *n.* Murder, قَتْل. A murderer, قاتِل *pl.* قُتّال.

Justifiable —, قَتْلٌ جائِزٌ. Excusable —, قَتْلٌ مَعْذُورٌ. Felonious —, قَتْلٌ جِنائِيٌّ.

Homiletic, *a.* / Homiletical, } خُطَبِيٌّ – مُتَعَلِّقٌ بِٱلْوَعْظِ.

Homiletics, *n.* عِلْمُ ٱلْخُطْبَةِ (*or* ٱلْخَطابَةِ) – فَنُّ ٱلْوَعْظِ.

Homilist, *n.* خَطِيب – خاطِب – واعِظ *pl.* وُعّاظ.

Homily, *n.* خُطْبَة *pl.* خُطَب – مَوْعِظَة *pl.* مَواعِظ. A written —, a treatise, رِسالَة *pl.* رَسائِل. To read one a —, to scold, سَخِطَ [2] – عاتَبَ – عَلَى.

Hominy, *n.* جَرِيشَة – خَبِيصٌ مُرَمَّلٌ.

Hommock, *n.* تَلٌّ مُنْفَرِدٌ – تَلٌّ فارِدٌ – قَرْن *pl.* قِران *and* قُرُون.

Homocentric, *a.* مُتَجانِسُ ٱلْمَرْكَزِ.

Homogeneal, *a.* / Homogeneous, } مُتَجانِس – مُجانِس. To be — with, شاكَلَ – جانَسَ. The two things became —, تَجانَسَ ٱلشَّيْآنِ.

Homegeneousness, *n.* / Homogeneity, } إِشْتِراكُ ٱلْجِنْسِ – تَجانُس – مُجانَسَة – مُشاكَلَة. To make — with, جَنَّسَ بِ.

Homoiousian *n.* مِنْ أَهْلِ ٱلتَّشابُهِ.

Homologous, *a.* نَظِيم – مُتَشابِهُ ٱلنَّسَقِ.

Homology, *n.* مُشابَهَةُ ٱلنَّسَقِ.

Homonym, *n.* مُشْتَرَكٌ فِيهِ – نَظِيم – سَمِيٌّ – إِسْمٌ سَمِيٌّ.

Homonymous, *a.* سَمِيٌّ. The being —, homonomy, الاِشْتِراكُ.

Homousian, *n.* مِنْ أَهْلِ ٱلتَّجانُسِ.

Homophonous, *a.* مُتَشابِهُ ٱللَّحْنِ (*or* ٱلصَّوْتِ).

Hone, *n.* مِسَنٌّ. The rubbings from a hone, سَنِين.

Hone, *v.t.* سَنَّ [2] – سَنَّ عَلَى ٱلْمِسَنِّ.

Honest, *a.* Upright, أَهْلُ عِرْضٍ – صالِح – عادِل – مُسْتَقِيم. Sincere, نَصُوح – أَمِين – صادِق – مُقْسِط – جَيِّد. Firm, to be depended upon, صُلْب – أَخُو ثِقَةٍ. Chaste, عَفِيف – وَرِع. Lawful, حَلال. A man of — report, رَجُلٌ مَشْهُودٌ لَهُ.

Honestly, *ad.* Uprightly, بِصَلاحٍ – بِعَدالَةٍ – بِٱسْتِقامَةٍ. Sincerely, جَيِّدًا – بِقِسْطٍ – بِصَداقَةٍ. Chastely, بِوَرَعٍ – بِعِفَّةٍ. Lawfully, بِٱلْحَلالِ. Properly, بِلِياقَةٍ. To act —, أَقْسَطَ – قَسَطَ [2]. To act — with, by, أَجادَ إِلَى – صادَقَ – صَنَعَ حَسَنًا [2]. To live —, أَجادَ فِي سِيرَتِهِ – أَحْسَنَ فِي ٱلسِّيرَةِ – تَصَرَّفَ تَصَرُّفًا حَسَنًا.

Honesty, *n.* Uprightness, صَلاح – قِسْط – عَدالَة – إِسْتِقامَة. Sincerity, أَمانَة – إِخْلاص – صِدْق – نُصُوح. Honesty is the best policy, (prov.) *lit.* The best strategy is to forego stratagems, الحِيلَةُ فِي تَرْكِ ٱلْحِيَلِ.

Honey, *n.* عَسَل *pl.* عُسْلان – مازِيٌّ – سَدًى – طِرْيَم – ضَيْح

and مَعْسُول. Wild —, عَسَلُ ٱلْبَرِّ. Honey made from the inspissated juice of the grape, or of fresh dates, دِبْس (called in the Hijâz صَقْر). Preserved in —, مُعَسَّل. To sweeten with or preserve in —, عَسَّلَ ـ ٢ عَسَلَ. Having the colour of —, عَسَلِيّ. A gatherer of —, عاسِل.

Honey-bag, *n.* وِعَاءُ ٱلنَّحْلِ.

Honey-comb, *n.* شَهْد *pl.* شِهاد ـ قُرْصُ عَسَلٍ. The being full of small cells, تَخَلْخُل ـ تَثَقُّب.

Honey-comb, *v.t.* خَرَّقَ ـ ثَقَّبَ ـ عَيَّنَ. Honey-combed, مُعَيَّن ـ مُثَقَّب ـ ذُو خِلالٍ ـ مُتَخَلْخِل.

Honey-comb, *v.i.* تَخَلْخَلَ ـ اِنْثَقَبَ ـ تَعَيَّنَ.

Honey-dew, *n.* That found on trees, مَنّ ـ أُسْلُوب ـ تَرَنْجُبِين.

Honeyed, *a.* Covered with honey, مُعَسَّل. Honeyed words, كلامٌ مَلِقٌ ـ حديثٌ مَعْسُول.

Honeymoon, *n.* الشَّهْرُ ٱلْأَوَّلُ بَعْدَ ٱلزَّوَاجِ.

Honeysuckle, *n.* زَهْرُ ٱلْعَسَلِ.

Honied, *a.* *See* Honeyed, *a.*

Honorary, *a.* بلا أُجْرَةٍ ـ فَخْرِيّ ـ رَسْمِيٌّ فَقَط. Honorary titles, أَلْقَابٌ رَسْمِيَّةٌ (or فاخِرَة) فَقَط.

Honorarium, *n.* أُجْرَة ـ إِجَارَة ـ حُلْوَان ـ رِفْد.

Honour, *n.* Respect, فَخْر ـ عِزّ ـ شَرَفَة ـ كَرامَة ـ كَرَم. Reputation, self-respect, نَامُوس ـ عِرْض. The esteem paid to worth, تَعْظِيم ـ اِعْتِبار ـ اِحْتِرام ـ إِعْزاز ـ تَكْرِيم ـ تَبْجِيل. Fame, شُهْرَة ـ صِيت. Probity, ذِمَّة ـ اِسْتِقامَة ـ صَلاح. Dignity, وَقار ـ هشم ـ هَيْبَة ـ مَجَابَة ـ مَزِيَّة. Glory, boast, عِزّ ـ عِزَّة ـ اِفْتِخار ـ فَخْر ـ نَخْوَة. A decoration, نِيشَانُ شَرَفٍ. Chastity, عِفَّة ـ وَرَع. Military —, النَّامُوسُ ٱلْعَسْكَرِيّ. Honours, dignities, مَعَالٍ ـ مَرَاتِب ـ مَنَاصِب; ceremonies, تَشْرِيفات ـ اِحْتِفالات. Your —, as an address, حَضْرَتُكُمْ ـ جَنابُكَ. He attacked his —, نَهَكَ عِرْضَهُ ـ طَعَنَهُ فِي عِرْضِهِ. Our — has not been compromised, حُرْمَتُنا بَاقِيَةٌ عَلَيْنا. Without damage to the soldier's —, بِدُونِ إِخْلالٍ فِي نامُوسِ ٱلْعَسْكَرِ. He will maintain our — and rights, هُوَ يَصُونُ شَرَفَنَا وَحُقُوقَنا. I had the — of paying you a visit, تَشَرَّفْتُ بِٱلْقُدُومِ إِلَيْكُمْ. Do me the — of dining with me, شَرِّفْنِي وَتَغَدَّى مَعِي ـ تَفَضَّلْ لِلْغَدَاءِ عِنْدِي. On my —, عَلَى (or فِي) ذِمَّتِي. In — of, اِحْتِفالاً بِ ـ تَعْظِيماً لِ ـ إِكْرَاماً لِ. He had the — of an interview with the Sultan, حَظِيَ بِمُشَاهَدَةِ ٱلسُّلْطانِ.

A man of honour, حُرّ *pl.* أَحْرار ـ أَهْلُ ذِمَّةٍ.

An affair of honour, أَمْرٌ مُتَعَلِّقٌ بِٱلْعِرْضِ.

Court of honour, مَجْلِسٌ لِفَصْلِ ٱلدَّعَاوَى ٱلْمُتَوَطِّقَةِ بِٱلْعِرْضِ.

Lady of honour (to a queen), سَيِّدَةٌ مِنْ حَرِيمِ ٱلشُّرَفَاءِ تُلازِمُ ٱلْمَلِكَةَ.

Laws of honour, أُصُولُ ٱلْعِرْضِ وَٱلنَّامُوسِ.

The honours of war, مُحَافَظَةُ ٱلْجُنُودِ عَلَى رَايَاتِهِمِ ٱلْمَنْشُورَةِ وَأَسْلِحَتِهِمِ ٱلْمَرْفُوعَةِ. The retiring garrison evacuated the castle with the honours of war, أَخْلَى ٱلْمُسْتَحْفِظُونَ ٱلْمُسْتَسْلِمُونَ ٱلْقَلْعَةَ بِرَايَاتٍ مَنْشُورَةٍ وَأَسْلِحَةٍ مَرْفُوعَةٍ وَٱلْمُوسِيقَى تَعْزِفُ أَمَامَهُمْ.

To come off with honour, تَخَلَّصَ بِسَلامَةِ ٱلْعِرْضِ.

To do honour to; *see to* Honour, *v.t.*

To do the honours to guests, ٢ قَامَ بِإِكْرَامِ ٱلضُّيُوفِ.

Honour, *v.t.* To treat with honour, بَجَّلَ ـ أَكْرَمَ ـ كَرَّمَ ـ اِحْتَرَمَ. To render honourable, عَظَّمَ ـ هَشَّمَ ـ شَرَّفَ ـ أَوْجَهَ ـ وَجَّهَ. To entertain high respect for, عَزَّزَ ـ فَخَّمَ. To — one by, with, تَفَضَّلَ عَلَى ـ بِ ـ شَرَّفَ ـ بِ ـ أَتْقَى ـ بِ. To — a bill of exchange, قَبِلَ ٱلتَّحْوِيلَ. They honoured him with all —, أَكْرَمُوهُ غَايَةَ ٱلْإِكْرَامِ. Honoured, respected, مُعْتَبَر.

Honourable, *a.* Upright, صَاحِبُ عِرْضٍ ـ عَادِل ـ مُسْتَقِيم ـ مُكَرَّم ـ فَخِيم ـ جَلِيل ـ وَجِيه ـ أَعَزّ ـ عَزِيز ـ خَيِّر. Illustrious, شَرِيف ـ مَشْهُور ـ نَجِيب ـ مُعَظَّم. The Right Honourable (as an address), الجَنَابُ ٱلْأَفْخَم; *in Turkish*, دَوْلَتْلُو عَطُوفَتْلُو.

Honourableness, *n.* *See* Honour, *n.*

Honourably, *ad.* With honour, بِشَرَفٍ ـ بِإِكْرامٍ ـ عِزَّةً ـ بِعِزٍّ; with honesty, بِٱسْتِقامَةٍ ـ بِصَدَاقَةٍ ـ بِعَدَالَةٍ. Magnanimously, بِشَهامَةٍ ـ بِنَبَالَةٍ ـ اِقْتِدَاءً بِقَوَانِينِ ٱلْعِرْضِ. Nobly, بِرُحْبَةِ صَدْرٍ بِمُرُوَّةٍ.

Hood, *n.* A woman's head dress, مِقْنَعَة. The — of a cloak, بُرْنُس *pl.* بَرَانِيس ـ قُبَّعَة. A philosopher's —, طَيْلَسان. A monk's —, قَلَنْسُوَة *pl.* قَلانِس. A covering for the eyes, غِطَاءٌ لِلْعُيُونِ. Hood, as of a carriage, رَفْرَف ـ سَقِيفَة.

Hood, *v.t.* To dress in a —, قَلْنَسَ. *See also to* Hoodwink, *v.t.*

Hoodwink, *v.t.* To blindfold, ٢ رَبَطَ عَيْنَيْهِ ـ عَصَبَ عَيْنَيْهِ ـ أَمْسَكَ عَيْنَيْهِ. To deceive, ٢ غَشَّ ـ ٢ مَكَرَ بِ.

Hoof, *n.* نَعْل *pl.* نِعَال ـ حافِر *pl.* حَوَافِر. A cloven —, ظِلْف *pl.* ظُلُوف *and* أَظْلاف. The — of a camel, خُفّ *pl.* أَخْفاف. The — of a camel or elephant, فِرْسِن *pl.* فَرَاسِن ـ رَحًى *pl.* أَرْحَاء. The trace of a — on the ground, سَلِيقَة *pl.* سَلائِق. The feet of men and hoofs have made marks upon the road, سَلَقَتِ ٱلْأَقْدَامُ وَٱلْحَوَافِرُ ٱلطَّرِيقَ. A swelling in the —, جَرَذ. To have such a swelling, جَرِذَ.

Hoof-bound, *a.* مُضْطَرٌّ ـ مَضْرُور. To get —, اِضْطَرَّ ٱلْحَافِرُ ـ ضَاقَ عَقِبُ حَافِرِ ٱلدَّابَّةِ.

Hoofed, *a.* ذُو حَوَافِرَ.

Hook, *n.* A bent piece of iron to catch anything with, عَقْفَاءُ ـ عُقَّافَة ـ كُلَّاب *pl.* كَلَالِيبُ ـ خُطَّاف *pl.* خَطَاطِيفُ. A hooked stick, مِحْجَن. A — to hang anything upon, عِلَاقَة ـ عَلَّاقَة *pl.* عَلَالِيقُ. A fish —, شِصّ *pl.* شُصُوص ـ صِنَّارَة *pl.* صَنَانِيرُ. A reaping —, مِنْجَل ـ مِجَزّ. A grappling —, كُلَّاب ـ عَوْدَقَة. The — of a spindle, حُجْنَة. By — or by crook, عَلَى كُلِّ حَالٍ ـ مِنْ كُلِّ بُدٍّ ـ كَيْفَمَا كَانَ. To be off the hooks, to be disordered, اِلْتَبَكَ ـ تَلَخْبَطَ ـ تَشَوَّشَ; to die, تُوُفِّيَ. A — and eye, مِشْبَك *pl.* مَشَابِكُ. A flesh-hook, مِنْشَل ـ مِنْشَال.

Hook, *v.t.* To fix or catch on a hook, اِصْطَادَ ـ شَبَكَ ـ خَطِفَ. To hang on a —, عَلَّقَ ـ فِي ـ شَبَكَ ـ فِي. To —, as of a dress, شَبَكَ ـ ضَمَّ ـ قَفَلَ. To crook, حَجَنَ.

Hook, *v.i.* To become bent, تَحَجَّنَ ـ اِنْعَطَفَ ـ تَعَوَّجَ.

Hookah, *n.* A kind of pipe, حُقَّة ـ شِيشَة *pl.* شِيَش.

Hooked, *a.* Curvated, مُعَقَّف ـ مُعَوَّج ـ أَحْجَنُ. A — stick, صَوْلَجَان ـ مِحْجَن. Having a — beak, أَحْجَنُ ٱلْمِنْقَارِ. A — nose, أَنْفٌ قُعْنُبٌ.

Hookedness, *n.* حَجَن ـ تَحَجُّن.

Hoop, *n.* As of a barrel, طَوْق *pl.* أَطْوَاق ـ جُلْبَة *pl.* جُلَب ـ طَارَة *pl.* طَارَات; as of a sieve, إِطَار ـ حِتَار *pl.* حُتُر. A — for extending a skirt, عُظْمَة *pl.* عُظْمَات. A ring, حَلْقَة *pl.* حَلَق. *See also* Bustle, *n.*

Hoop, *v.t.* To — a barrel, أَحْكَمَ ٱلْبَرْمِيلَ بِطَارَاتٍ. To encircle with, أَحَاطَ ـ بِ ـ طَوَّقَ.

Hoop, *v.i.* To whoop, صَاحَ ـ صَرَخَ ـ هَلَّلَ ـ أَصَاحَ ـ صَوَّتَ.

Hooping-cough, *n.* سُعَال كَلْبِيّ.

Hoopoe, Hoopoo, *n.* The bird, هُدْهُد *pl.* هَدَاهِدُ.

Hoot, *n.* A shout of contempt, ضَحِكٌ عَلَى ـ صَفِير ـ جَلَبَة. The cry of an owl, صِيَاحُ ٱلْبُوم. A hooting owl, بُومٌ بَوَّامٌ.

Hoot, *v.i.* To shout in contempt, جَلَبَ ـ صَفَرَ. To cry, as of an owl, بَوَّمَ ـ صَاحَ ـ صَرَخَ ـ أَعْوَلَ.

Hoot, *v.t.* To drive with noises of contempt, أَجْلَبَ عَلَى ـ ضَحِكَ عَلَى ـ صَاحَ عَلَى. They hooted him in derision, صَفَرُوا لَهُ ٱسْتِهْزَاءً بِهِ.

Hop, *v.i.* To hop on one leg, نَطَّ عَلَى رِجْلٍ وَاحِدَةٍ. To skip, frisk, مَرِحَ ـ نَطَّ ـ قَفَزَ ـ وَثَبَ *aor.* يَثِبُ. To dance, رَقَصَ.

Hop, *v.t.* To cross by a hop, طَفَرَ ـ قَطَعَ. To hop the twig, to die, مَاتَ; to move off, وَلَّى هَارِبًا; to decamp, تَطَفَّشَ.

Hop, *n.* A leap, jump, طَفْرَة ـ نَطَّة ـ قَفْزَة ـ وَثْبَة. Hop, the plant, حَشِيشَةُ ٱلدِّينَارِ.

Hope, *n.* Desire and belief of future good, إِمْلَة ـ أَنَاة ـ أَمَل ـ رَجَاء ـ طُلَوَاء ـ تَرَقُّب ـ اِنْتِظَار ـ تَوَقُّع. Confidence, ثِقَة ـ اِعْتِمَاد. An object of —, أَمَل ـ رَجِيَّة ـ مُنْيَة *pl.* مُنًى. The Cape of Good Hope, رَأْسُ ٱلْعَشَمِ ٱلْخَيْرِ ـ رَأْسُ ٱلرَّجَاءِ ٱلصَّالِحِ. There is no — left for him, لَمْ يَبْقَ أَمَلٌ لَهُ. The forlorn —, شُرْطَة *pl.* شُرَط ـ ٱلْفِدَاوِيَّة ـ ٱلْمُسْتَحْنِطُونَ. Hope deferred makes the heart sick, ٱلرَّجَاءُ ٱلْمُمَاطَلُ يُمْرِضُ ٱلْقَلْبَ. In — of, عَلَى رَجَاءِ. All — of their gains was gone, خَرَجَ (or خَابَ) رَجَاءُ مَكْسَبِهِمْ. His — was disappointed, خَابَ أَمَلُهُ. There is no — left, لَمْ يَبْقَ أَمَلٌ. We have but little — of that, أَمَلُنَا فِي ذٰلِكَ ضَعِيفٌ. This scatters all — of attaining the desired end, هٰذَا يَقْطَعُ ٱلْأَمَلَ مِنَ ٱلْوُصُولِ إِلَى ٱلْمَطْلُوبِ.

Hope, *v.i.* أَمَلَ. To expect, تَرَقَّبَ ـ اِنْتَظَرَ ـ تَوَقَّعَ. To — that ..., تَمَنَّى أَنْ. To — for, رَجَا *aor.* يَرْجُو. We also — that ..., نَرْجُو أَيْضًا أَنْ. I hoped for him or it, رَجَيْتُهُ *or* رَجَوْتُهُ *or* تَرَجَّيْتُهُ. There is nothing for me to — for in him, مَا لِي فِيهِ رَجِيَّةٌ. It is hoped, يُؤَمَّلُ. As was hoped, عَلَى وَفْقِ ٱلْمَأْمُولِ وَٱلتَّمَنِّي. It is to be hoped that ..., ٱلْمَأْمُولُ أَنْ. It is hoped that it will lead to a reconciliation, ٱلْمَأْمُولُ أَنَّهُ يَؤُولُ إِلَى ٱلْمُصَالَحَةِ. That he may fulfil this our —, أَنْ يُوَفِّقَ أَمَلَنَا هٰذَا. How he goes on hoping! مَا أَطْوَلَ إِمْلَتَهُ. To cause one to — for, جَعَلَ ـ يَنْتَظِرُهُ ـ مَنَّى ـ بِ.

Hoped-for, *a.* مَأْمُول ـ يُرْتَجَى. A thing —, أَمَل ـ رَجِيَّة ـ أُمْنِيَّة ـ مُنْيَة.

Hopeful, *a.* Full of hope, آمِل ـ رَاجٍ ـ مُتَمَنٍّ ـ مُتَرَجٍّ. Promising, لَا يَضِيعُ ٱلرَّجَاءُ فِيهِ.

Hopefully, *ad.* In a manner to raise hope, بِأَمَلٍ وَرَجَاءٍ. With hope, بِرَجَاءٍ ـ عَلَى ٱلرَّجَاءِ ـ عَلَى رَجَاءٍ.

Hopefulness, *n.* مِلْءُ ٱلرَّجَاءِ ـ رَجَاءٌ فِي نَجَاحِهِ.

Hopeless, *a.* Without hope, despairing, يَئِس ـ قَانِط ـ مَقْطُوعُ ٱلْأَمَلِ. Giving no hope, لَا يُرْجَى مِنْهُ خَيْرٌ.

Hopelessly, *ad.* بِدُونِ رَجَاءٍ.

Hopingly, *ad.* بِٱلرَّجَاءِ ـ بِتَمَنٍّ ـ عَلَى ٱلرَّجَاءِ.

Hopper, *n.* One who hops, قَافِز ـ نَطَّاط ـ وَاثِب. The — of a mill, عَيْنُ (or قَادُوس) طَاحُونَةٍ. A basket for seed corn, مِبْذَرَة.

Hopple, *v.t.*
Hopples, *n.* } *See* Hobbles, *n.*

Horal, *a.*
Horary, } مُتَعَلِّقٌ بِسَاعَةٍ ـ مُخْتَصٌّ بِٱلسَّاعَةِ.

Horde, *n.* قَوْمٌ *pl.* أَقْوَام ـ قَبِيلَة *pl.* قَبَائِل ـ شِرْذِمَة ـ جَمَاعَة ـ فَوْج *pl.* أَفْوَاج. A migratory —, نَوَاقِل ـ قَوْمٌ مُهَاجِرُونَ.

Horehound, *n.* *See* Hoarhound, *n.*

Horizon, *n.* أُفُق *pl.* آفَاق ـ دَائِرَةُ ٱلْأُفُقِ. Sensible or apparent —, أُفُقٌ مَرْئِيٌّ. Real —, أُفُقٌ حَقِيقِيٌّ.

Horizontal, *a.* بَسِيط ـ أُفُقِيٌّ.

Horizontality, *n.* صِفَةُ ٱلْأُفُقِ.

Horizontally, *ad.* عَلَى حَذْوِ ٱلْأُفُقِ.

Horn, *n.* As of an animal, قَرْن *pl.* قُرُون. A drinking-cup, قَدَح *pl.* أَقْدَاح. The wind instrument, بُوق *pl.* بُوقَات ـ نَفِير ـ صُور. The — worn on the head by the women of the Lebanon, طَرْطُور ـ طَنْطُور. On the day when the — shall be blown, يَوْمَ يُنْفَخُ فِي ٱلصُّورِ (*Kur.* vi. 73.) An ink-horn, دَوَاة *pl.* دُوًى ـ نُون *pl.* نُونَان ـ مِحْبَرَة. The second horns which come up after the first, ٱلثَّوَانِي. Having crooked horns, أَلْفَتُ ٱلْقُرُونِ; having straight horns, أَنْصَبُ ٱلْقُرُونِ. A — of the moon, طَرَفُ ٱلْهِلَالِ *dual* طَرَفَا. To sound a —, نَفَخَ بِٱلصُّورِ. To butt with the horns; *see to* Butt, *v.t.*

Hornbeam, *n.* A species of wood, ضَرْبٌ مِنَ ٱلْخَشَبِ.

Hornblende, *n.* ضَرْبٌ مِنَ ٱلرُّخَامِ.

Hornbook, *n.* كِتَابُ أَلِفٍ بَاءٍ ـ كِتَابُ ٱلْأَبْجَدِيَّةِ.

Horned, *a.* Having horns, نَطَّاح ـ ذُو قُرُونٍ. Incurvated, أَخْجَنُ ـ مُقَوَّس.

Hornet, *n.* زُنْبُور *pl.* زَنَابِير ـ شُفْفُور *pl.* شَفَافِير.

Horning, *n.* Of the crescent, غُرَّةُ ٱلْهِلَالِ (*or* هِلُّ).

Hornless, *a.* أَجَمّ *pl.* جُمّ ـ لَا قُرُونَ لَهُ ـ بِلَا قُرُونٍ.

Hornpipe, *n.* The instrument, زُمَّارَة. Playing on the —, زِمَارَة. A kind of dance, ضَرْبٌ مِنَ ٱلرَّقْصِ.

Horn-work, *n.* هِلَال (*or* قَوْس) ٱلطَّابِيَةِ.

Horny, *a.* مِنْ قَرْنٍ ـ مِثْلُ ٱلْقَرْنِ. *See also* Callous, *a.*

Horological, *a.* مَا نِيطَ بِعَمَلِ ٱلْآلَاتِ لِقِيَاسِ ٱلْأَوْقَاتِ.

Horology, *n.* صِنَاعَةُ ٱلْآلَاتِ ٱلْمَذْكُورَةِ.

Horometry, *n.* قِيَاسُ ٱلْأَوْقَاتِ عَلَى حِسَابِ ٱلسَّاعَاتِ.

Horoscope, *n.* The position of the stars at the time of one's birth, طَالِع *pl.* طَوَالِعُ ـ نَجْم *pl.* نُجُوم. To interpret to one his —, كَشَفَ لَهُ طَالِعَهُ.

Horoscopy, *n.* *See* Astrology, *n.*

Horrent, *a.* Standing on end like bristles, مُنْتَفِش ـ مُقَرَّن.

Horrible, *a.*
Horrid, } مُهِيب ـ مَهُول ـ مَخُوف ـ هَائِل ـ فَظِيع. Hideous, كَرِيه ـ شَنِيع. A — thing, أَمْرٌ مُفْظِعٌ ـ جِنَايَةٌ ـ جُنَاحٌ فَظِيعٌ ـ قَبَاحَة. A — crime, مَا يُقْشَعِرُّ مِنْهُ فَظِيعَة.

Horribleness, *n.*
Horridness, } إِقْشِعْرَار ـ مَخَافَة ـ فَظَاعَة ـ مَا يُقْشَعِرُّ مِنْهُ.

Horribly, *ad.*
Horridly, } بِفَظَاعَةٍ ـ فَظَاعَةً ـ بِٱقْشِعْرَارٍ. I was — afraid, إِقْشَعْرَرْتُ ٱقْشِعْرَارًا. They shall be — afraid at you, يَقْشَعِرُّونَ عَلَيْكَ ٱقْشِعْرَارًا.

Horrific, *a.* *See* Horrible, *a.*

Horrify, *v.t.* To strike with horror, أَرْعَدَ ـ أَرْعَبَ ـ أَدْهَشَ. To disgust, كَرَّهَ ـ قَرَّفَ ـ أَقْرَفَ. To be horrified, struck with horror, إِقْشَعَرَّ; to be disgusted, كَرِهَ ـ إِشْمَأَزَّ. We were horrified by the death of . . ., قَدْ فُجِعْنَا بِوَفَاةِ فُلَانٍ.

Horror, *n.* A shivering, إِقْشِعْرَار ـ إِشْمِئْزَاز. Terror, هَوْل ـ رُعْب ـ خَوْف ـ دَهْش. Hatred, disgust, نَفْرَة ـ كَرَاهِيَة ـ بُغْضَة ـ شَنَآءَة. Trembling with —, مُقْشَعِرّ *pl.* قَشَاعِرُ. A —, such as makes the hair stand on end, إِقْشِعْرَار. The horrors of war, دَوَاهِي ٱلْحُرُوبِ.

Horse, *n.* An entire or high-bred —, حِصَان *pl.* حُصُن. A thorough-bred —, حِصَانٌ أَصِيلٌ. A — or mare, فَرَس *pl.* أَفْرَاس and فُرُوس (*vulg.* فُرْسَان) ـ خَيْل *pl.* خُيُول. A courser, جَوَاد *pl.* أَجْوَاد *or* أَجَاوِدُ. A low-bred —, هَجِين *pl.* هَوَاجِنُ. A half-bred —, مُسْهَم. A common —, a hack, بِرْذَوْن *pl.* بَرَاذِينُ. A led —, مَقْوُود ـ مَقُود ـ جَنِيبَة. A — trained for racing by being kept on short food, ضَامِر; one who so trains horses, مُضَمِّر. A gentle going —, فَرَسٌ مُعْتَاد. An ambling —, هِمْلَاج *pl.* هَمَالِيجُ. A draft —, حِصَانٌ جَارٌّ ـ مَطِيَّة *pl.* مَطَايَا. رَهْوَان *or* رَخْوَان. A fine —, حِصَانٌ نَجِيبٌ: of the finest horses, مِنْ أَنْجَبِ ٱلْخَيْلِ. A wooden —, for punishment, حِمَار. Horse, cavalry, خَيَّالَة ـ فُرْسَان. Master or Gentleman of the Horse, أَمِيرُ آخُورٍ. To mount or ride a —, رَكِبَ فَرَسًا ـ رَكِبَ عَلَى فَرَسٍ. To fall, as from a —, نَدَرَ عَنْ. To roll on the ground, of a —, تَمَرَّغَ; a rolling —, دَابَّةٌ مِرَاغَةٌ. Horse, a stand on which anything is laid, قَاعِدَة ـ تَخْتَة. A clothes' —, مِشْجَب ـ مِشْجَر. The near side of a —, يَسَارُ ٱلْفَرَسِ; the off side of a —, يَمِينُ ٱلْفَرَسِ.

Horse, *v.t.* To mount a horse, رَكِبَ فَرَسًا ـ رَكِبَ عَلَى فَرَسٍ. To mount another, رَكَّبَ ـ أَرْكَبَ.

Horseback, *n.* رُكُوبُ ٱلْفَرَسِ. He was on —, كَانَ رَاكِبًا عَلَى فَرَسٍ.

Horse-block, *n.* مَصْطَبَة (or) حَجَرُ ٱلرُّكُوبِ — سُلَّمُ ٱلرُّكُوبِ.

Horse-boat, *n.* A boat moved by horses, شَخْتُورٌ تَجُرُّهُ ٱلْخَيْلُ.

Horse-breaker, *n.* رَائِضُ ٱلدَّوَابِّ *pl.* رَاضَة or رُوَّاض.

Horse-chestnut, *n.* شَهْبَلُّوطُ ٱلْهِنْدِ.

Horse-cloth, *n.* رَخْت — طَرَّاحَة — شِعَار.

Horse-dealer, *n.* }
Horse-jockey, } مُضَارِبُ ٱلْخَيْلِ — دَلَّالُ ٱلْخَيْلِ *pl.* دَلَّالَة.

Horse-dealing, *n.* مُضَارَبَةُ ٱلْخَيْلِ — دِلَالَةُ ٱلْخَيْلِ.

Horse-dung, *n.* زِبْل.

Horse-flesh, *n.* لَحْمُ ٱلْخَيْلِ. A horse, خَيْل *pl.* خُيُول. To be a judge of —, مُدَرَّب (or) عَارِف بِٱلْخَيْلِ.

Horse-fly, *n.* نُعَرَة.

Horse-guards, *n.* Picked cavalry, عَسَاكِرُ أَسَاوِرَةٍ خَاصَّة. Office of the Commander-in-Chief, إِدَارَة (or) مَأْمُورِيَّةُ ٱلسَّرْعَسْكَرِ. The office of the —, سَرْعَسْكَرِيَّة.

Horsehair, *n.* سَبِيب — سَبِيب.

Horse-laugh, *n.* قَهْقَهَة.

Horse-leech, *n.* A large leech, عَلَقَةٌ كَبِيرَة — عَلُوقَة. A farrier, بَيْطَار.

Horse-litter, *n.* The vehicle, تَخْتُ رَوَان — تَخْت رَهْوَانٍ.

Horseman, *n.* A rider, فُرْسَان *pl.* فَارِس — أَسَاوِرُ *pl.* إِسْوَار — رُكَّاب *pl.* رَاكِب. An experienced rider, أَفْرَس. A troop of horsemen, كَتَائِب *pl.* كَتِيبَة — خَيَّالَة.

Horsemanship, *n.* فُرُوسِيَّة — فُرُوسَة — فَرَاسَة. To be skilled in —, فَرُسَ ². To pretend to —, تَفَرَّسَ. To vie with one in —, فَارَسَ.

Horse-play, *n.* لَعِبٌ جَافٍ.

Horse-pond, *n.* حَوْض *pl.* حِيَضَان — مَوْرِد *pl.* مَوَارِدُ — مَنْهَل *pl.* مَنَاهِلُ — مَسْقَاة.

Horse-power, *n.* قُوَّةُ حِصَانٍ. Five steamers, each of 500 —, خَمْسُ بَوَاخِرَ قُوَّةُ كُلٍّ مِنْهَا قُوَّةُ خَمْسِمِئَةِ حِصَانٍ.

Horse-race, *n.* مُسَابَقَةُ خَيْلٍ — سِبَاقُ خَيْلٍ. *See also* Course, Race, *n.*

Horse-radish, *n.* فُجْلٌ حَارٌّ.

Horse-shoe, *n.* نَعْلُ ٱلْحِصَانِ *pl.* أَنْعَال.

Horse-shoeing, *n.* بَيْطَرَة.

Horse-stealer, *n.* سَارِقُ ٱلْخَيْلِ — سَلَّال.

Horsetail, *n.* The plant, أَذْنَابُ ٱلْخَيْلِ.

Horsewhip, *n.* سَوْط *pl.* أَسْوَاط — مِقْرَعَة *pl.* مَقَارِعُ — كِرْبَاج.

Horsewhip, *v.t.* جَلَدَ ² — ضَرَبَ سَوْطًا — سَوَّطَ.

Horsewhipping, *n.* جَلْد — ضَرْبُ سَوْطٍ.

Horse-woman, *n.* A masculine woman, اِمْرَأَةٌ فَحْلَة — مُذَكَّرَة. An experienced female rider, فَرْسَاءُ.

Hortation, *n.* تَرْغِيب — مَوْعِظَة — نُصْح.

Hortative, *a.* }
Hortatory, } وَعْظِيٌّ — نُصْحِيٌّ.

Horticultural, *a.* مَنُوطٌ بِفَلَاحَةِ ٱلْجُنَيْنَاتِ.

Horticulture, *n.* عِلْمُ فَلَاحَةِ ٱلْجُنَيْنَاتِ.

Horticulturist, *n.* مَاهِرٌ بِفَلَاحَةِ ٱلْجُنَيْنَاتِ.

Hortus-siccus, *n.* *See* Herbarium, *n.*

Hosanna! *int.* اَلسَّبْحُ لِلّٰهِ — بَارَكَ ٱللّٰهُ — اَلْحَمْدُ لِلّٰهِ — أُوصَنَّا.

Hosanna, *n.* تَسْبِيح — حَمْدَلَة.

Hose, *n.* Stockings, جَوْرَب *pl.* جَوَارِبُ — جُرَابَات. Covering for the legs, شَخْشِير *pl.* شَخَاشِيرُ. A tube or pipe, لَزْلَب *pl.* لَوَالِبُ.

Hosier, *n.* جَوْرَبَاتِيٌّ — جَوَارِبِيٌّ.

Hosiery, *n.* أَمْتِعَةُ ٱلْجَوَارِبِيِّ.

Hospice, *n.* دَارٌ مَلْجَأ — مَأْوًى.

Hospitable, *a.* كَثِيرُ ٱلرَّمَادِ (*lit.* having much ashes) — خَصِيب — مُضِيف — مَأْوَى ٱلْغُرَبَاءِ — مُكْرِمُ ٱلضُّيُوفِ. A — roof, مَأْوَى ٱلضُّيُوفِ.

Hospitably, *ad.* بِضِيَافَةٍ.

Hospital, *n.* As for the sick, دَارٌ لِلْمَرْضَى — دَارُ مُسْتَشْفًى — اَلشِّفَاءِ — بِيمَارِسْتَان. A — for strangers, *etc.*, مَأْوًى لِلْغُرَبَاءِ. A school, مَدْرَسَة *pl.* مَدَارِسُ. A — which will contain 100 beds, مُسْتَشْفًى يَسَعُ مِئَةَ فِرَاشٍ. A foundling —, دَارٌ لِلُّقَطَاءِ.

Hospitaller, *n.* A knight —, فَوَالِيرُ مِنْ أَخَوِيَّةِ ٱلشُّرَفَاءِ ٱلَّذِينَ بَنَوْا قَدِيمًا مَأْوًى لِلْمَرْضَى وَٱلْغُرَبَاءِ فِي ٱلْقُدْسِ ٱلشَّرِيفِ.

Hospitality, *n.* إِضَافَةُ ٱلْغُرَبَاءِ — ضِيَافَة — قُبُولُ ٱلْغُرَبَاءِ. To receive with —, ضَيَّفَ — أَضَافَ — آوَى. To ask — of, اِسْتَضَافَ بِ.

Hospodar, *n.* The —, as of Wallachia or Moldavia, وَيْوُدَه — بَيْك.

Host, *n.* One who entertains another, مُضِيف. The landlord of an inn, صَاحِبُ ٱللُّوكَنْدَةِ — صَاحِبُ ٱلْمَنْزِلِ. A great number, فَوْج *pl.* أَفْوَاج — جَوْقَة. An army, جُنْد *pl.* جُنُود. Hosts, رِبِّيُون. The hosts of angels, أَجْوَاقُ ٱلْمَلَائِكَةِ — ٱلصَّافَّاتُ صَفًّا. The consecrated —, اَلْقُرْبَانُ — اَلْبُرْشَانُ ٱلْمُقَدَّسُ.

Hostage, *n.* كَفِيل *pl.* كُفَلَاءُ — رَهِين *pl.* رَهَائِنُ.

Hostel, *n.* } *See* Hotel, *n.*
Hostelry, }

Hostess, *n.* A lady who entertains, مُضِيفَة. The landlady of an inn, صاحِبَةُ ٱللُوكَنْدَةِ ـ مَوْلاةُ ٱلْمَنْزِل.

Hostile, *a.* Inimical, عادٍ ـ عَدُوٌّ ـ خَصِيم ـ مُخالِف *pl.* عادُون. Warlike, حَرْبِيٌّ ـ مُحارِب. A — incursion, غارَة ـ غَزاة *pl.* غَزَوات.

Hostilely, *ad.* Inimically, بِعَداوَةٍ ـ بِعُدْوانٍ; with war, حَرْبًا ـ بِحَرْب.

Hostility, *n.* Enmity, عَداوَة ـ مُعاداة ـ مُخاصَمَة ـ عُدْوان ـ شَرٌّ. Open —, مُجاهَرَة ـ مُباداةٌ بِٱلْعَداوَةِ. Hostilities, تَناكُث ـ أَفْعالٌ حَرْبِيَّةٌ ـ مُحارَبَة ـ حَرْب. He manifested open — to him, باداهُ بِٱلْعَداوَةِ.

Hostler, *n.* *See* Groom, *n.*

Hot, *a.* Having heat, سَخِين ـ حام ـ سُخْن ـ حارٌّ. Scorching, شَهْوانُ ـ مُحْرِق ـ حُراق ـ حِراق. Of anger, ساخِط ـ حام. Lustful, شَهِيٌّ ـ رغِيب ـ مَحْرُور ـ حَرْدانُ ـ حَرِير. Passionate, ardent, مُتَهَوِّر. Hot, of temperature, سَخْنانُ. Hot, as with pepper, pungent, حَرِيف ـ أُجاج ـ حادٌّ ـ حارٌّ ـ مُفَلْفَل. Hot bread, خُبْزٌ حارٌّ. A hot day, يَوْمٌ صائِفٌ ـ يَوْمٌ سُخْنٌ; a hot night, لَيْلَةٌ سُخْنَةٌ ـ لَيْلَةٌ صائِفَةٌ. An intensely hot day, يَوْمٌ سُخاخِينٌ; an intensely hot night, لَيْلَةٌ سُخْنانَةٌ. The horse became very hot, حَمِيَ ٱلْفَرَسُ. I became hot with anger, حَمِيتُ فِي ٱلْغَضَب. He became hot with anger, إِحْتَمَى غَضَبًا. He did it in hot blood, فَعَلَهُ لَمّا حَمِيَ قَلْبُهُ. The oven (tropically for battle) became hot, vehement, حَمِيَ ٱلْوَطِيس. To be or become hot, سَخُنَ ـ حَمِيَ ـ حَمَّ ـ حَرَّ. To make hot, سَخَّنَ ـ أَسْخَنَ.

Hotbed, *n.* A — for plants, بَيْتٌ (or ذَرًى) لِلنَّباتِ. A source, مَصْدَر ـ مَنْبَع. A centre, مَرْكَز.

Hotchpotch, *n.* } A mixture, مَخْلُوطَة ـ خَبِيصَة. *See also*
Hotch-pot, } Hodge-podge, *n.*

Hot-cockles, *n.* *See* Blindman's-buff, *n.*

Hotel, *n.* مَنْزِلٌ مُعَدٌّ لِنُزُولِ ٱلْمُسافِرِين *pl.* مَنازِلُ ـ خان ـ لُوكَنْدَة ـ هُوتِل.

Hot-headed, *a.* *See* Hair-brained, *n.*

Hot-house, *n.* As for plants, دارٌ (or ذَرًى) لِلنَّباتِ.

Hot-house, *a.* مُنْبَتٌ فِي ذَرَى ٱلنَّباتِ.

Hotly, *ad.* Vehemently, eagerly, بِحَمِيًّا ـ بِحَرارَةٍ ـ بِشِدَّةٍ ـ بِرَغْبَةٍ ـ بِطَيْشٍ ـ بِهِياجٍ ـ تَهَوُّرًا.

Hotness, *n.* *See* Heat, *n.*

Hot-press, *v.t.* صَقَلَ ـ بَيْنَ أَلْواحٍ حَدِيدٍ حامِيَةٍ[2].

Hotspur, *n.* *See* Hair-brained, *a.*

Hough, *n.* فَخِذ *pl.* أَفْخاذ.

Hough, *v.t.* عَرْقَبَ. *See also to* Hamstring, *v.t.*

Hound, *n.* سَلُوقِيٌّ ـ هَجْرَع *coll.* سَلُوقِيَّة ـ كَلْبٌ سَلُوقِيٌّ.

Hound, *v.t.* To set dogs at, أَطْلَقَ ٱلْكِلابَ عَلَى. To hunt, تَصَيَّدَ ـ إِصْطادَ. To — on, to incite to, حَرَّضَ عَلَى ـ هَيَّجَ عَلَى.

Hour, *n.* ساعَة ـ فَيْنَة *pl.* ساعات. A particular time, مَوْقِت ـ وَقْتٌ مُعَيَّنٌ ـ وَقْتٌ مَوْقُوفٌ ـ مِيعاد. At that —, ساعَتَئِذٍ ـ خَرَجَ فِي تِلْكَ ٱلسّاعَةِ[2]. He came out the same —, فِي تِلْكَ ٱلسّاعَةِ. Come to me at an early —, بَكِّرْ عَلَيَّ. A *mauvais quart d'heure*, ساعَةٌ مَلْعُونَةٌ. To keep good hours, to be home early, بادَرَ إِلَى ٱلْبَيْتِ. To keep late hours, باتَ ٱللَّيْلَ خارِجًا *aor.* يَبِيتُ. From — to —, مِنْ ساعَةٍ لِساعَةٍ.

Hour-glass, *n.* ساعَةٌ رَمْلِيَّةٌ ـ ساعَةُ رَمْلٍ.

Hour-hand, *n.* عَقْرَبُ ٱلسّاعَةِ.

Houri, *n.* حَوارِيَّة *pl.* حَوارِيّات.

Hourly, *a.* كُلَّ ساعَةٍ. Repeated often, continual, مُكَرَّر ـ مُتَمادٍ ـ مُتَّصِل.

Hourly, *ad.* كُلَّ ساعَةٍ. Repeatedly, مِرارًا ـ مَرَّةً بَعْدَ مَرَّةٍ.

House, *n.* A habitation, مَسْكَن *pl.* مَساكِنُ ـ مَقام ـ مَنْزِل *pl.* مَنازِل ـ دار *pl.* دِيار ـ مَقَرّ ـ بَيْت *pl.* بُيُوت. A race, progeny, آل *pl.* أَيال ـ بَيْت ـ أَصْل ـ سِلْسِلَة. A family, عِيال *pl.* عِيالات. A council, مَجْلِسُ أَحْكامٍ. Government —, قَصْرُ ٱلْحُكُومَةِ. A mercantile —, شِرْكَة. Obliged to keep to his —, مُلازِمُ دارِهِ.

A country house, بَيْتٌ فِي ٱلرِّيفِ.

A public house, حانُوت *pl.* حَوانِيت ـ حانَة *pl.* حانات ـ خَمّارَة *pl.* خَمامِير.

A religious house, دَيْر *pl.* دُيُورَة.

A town house, بَيْتٌ فِي ٱلْمَدِينَةِ.

The house of Israel, بَنُو إِسْرائِيل.

The house of 'Othmân, آلُ عُثْمانَ.

The Lower House, مَجْلِسُ ٱلنُّوّابِ ـ مَجْلِسُ وُكَلاءِ ٱلْأُمَّةِ (or ٱلْمِلَّةِ).

The master of a house, صاحِبُ ٱلْبَيْتِ ـ رَبُّ ٱلْمَثْوَى.

The mistress of a house, صاحِبَةُ ٱلْبَيْتِ ـ رَبَّةُ ٱلْمَثْوَى.

The two Houses of Parliament, مَجْلِسا ٱلْبَرْلَمَنْتُو.

The Upper House, مَجْلِسُ ٱلْأُمَراءِ وَٱلْأَساقِفَةِ.

To eat out of house and home, أَتْلَفَ ـ أَعْدَمَ.

To form a house, as of a board, committee, *etc.*, كَفَى عَدَدَ ٱلْأَعْضَآءِ لِعَقْدِ ٱلْمَجْلِسِ. The house was counted out, قَلَّتْ أَعْضَآءُ ٱلْمَجْلِسِ عَدَدًا لِفَصْلِ ٱلْمَسْأَلَةِ.

To keep house, كَانَ صَاحِبَ بَيْتٍ.

To keep open house, تَفَتَّحَ فِي — آوَى ٱلضُّيُوفَ فِي كُلِّ حِينٍ ٱلضِّيَافَةِ.

To keep to the house, قَبَعَ — قَصَعَ — أَضْرَبَ فِي ٱلْبَيْتِ. One who keeps to the house through laziness, ضَاجِعٌ — ضُجَعَةٌ.

To turn a house out of window, قَلَبَ (or هَوَّشَ) ٱلْبَيْتَ. The house was turned out of window, تَهَمْرَجَ (or تَقَلَّبَ) ٱلْبَيْتُ.

House, *v.t.* ضَيَّفَ — أَنْزَلَ — سَكَّنَ — آوَى.

House, *v.i.* To take shelter, reside, سَكَنَ — إِيْتَوَى — تَأَوَّى.

House-breaker, *n.* سَارِقٌ يَنْقُبُ ٱلْبُيُوتَ *pl.* سُرَّاقٌ.

House-breaking, *n.* نَقْبُ ٱلْبُيُوتِ لِلسَّرِقَةِ.

Household, *n.* أَهْلُ ٱلْبَيْتِ — عِيَالٌ — سَكَنٌ — حَشَمٌ — أَرْبِيَةٌ — أَهْلُ مَنْزِلٍ.

Household, *a.* مُتَعَلِّقٌ بِٱلْعِيَالِ — مُخْتَصٌّ بِٱلْبَيْتِ. Household stuff, أَثَاثُ بَيْتٍ — مَرَمَّةُ بَيْتٍ. Officers of the royal —, أَغْوَاتُ ٱلسَّرَايَةِ — أَرْبَابُ دَائِرَةِ ٱلْمَلِكِ.

Householder, *n.* صَاحِبُ بَيْتٍ *pl.* أَصْحَابٌ — رَبُّ بَيْتٍ *pl.* أَرْبَابٌ. The hirer of a house, مُسْتَكْرِي بَيْتٍ. Householders, those having or living in houses, رُبَّى.

Housing, *n.* A horse-cloth, رَخْتٌ — طَرَّاحَةٌ. A mounting, تَطْرِيزٌ — تَرْكِيبٌ. A shelter, مَأْوَاةٌ — مَأْوًى.

Housekeeper, *n.* One who keeps a house, صَاحِبٌ — أَبُو مَثْوًى. A female superintendent, إِمْرَأَةٌ مُهْتَمَّةٌ — أَمِينَةُ بَيْتٍ بَيْتٍ بِأُمُورِ ٱلْبَيْتِ.

Housekeeping, *n.* بَيْتٌ — تَدْبِيرُ بَيْتٍ.

House-leek, *n.* ٱلْأَبِيدُ — حَيُّ عَالَمٍ.

Houseless, *a.* *See* Homeless, *a.*

Housemaid, *n.* خَادِمَةٌ *pl.* خَادِمَاتٌ — جَارِيَةٌ *pl.* جَوَارٍ.

House-room, *n.* مَبِيتٌ — مَحَلٌّ — سَعَةٌ.

House-warming, *n.* عَذِيرَةٌ — وَكِيرَةٌ — وَكْرَةٌ. To prepare a —, وَكَرَ *aor.* يَكِرُ. To invite to a —, أَعْذَرَ — وَكَّرَ.

Housewife, *n.* مُدَبِّرَةُ بَيْتٍ — أُمُّ مَنْزِلٍ — أُمُّ ٱلْمَثْوَى. A case for female work, دُرْجٌ — حِفْشٌ.

Housewifery, *n.* إِدَارَةُ ٱلْبَيْتِ عَلَى يَدِ أُمِّ ٱلْمَثْوَى — تَدْبِيرُ بَيْتٍ.

Hove; *see under to* Heave, *v.i.*

Hovel, *n.* بَيْتٌ حَقِيرٌ — أَكْوَاخٌ *pl.* كُوخٌ — خِصَاصٌ *pl.* خُصٌّ.

Hovel, *v.t.* آوَى — أَدْخَلَ ٱلْخُصَّ.

Hover, *v.i.* As a bird, fluttering over, تَفَرَّشَ عَلَى — فَرَّشَ عَلَى — عَافَ *aor.* يَعُوفُ — سَامَ عَلَى — حَامَ عَلَى *aor.* يَحُومُ or حَوْلَ — رَفْرَفَ عَلَى; as a dog or a bird round a place, حَاتَ. To — about a subject, to hesitate, حَامَ عَلَى *aor.* يَحُومُ. To wander about or near a place, لَازَمَ — تَرَدَّدَ. He hovers about an object of his desire, يَحُومُ حَوْلَ غَرَضٍ لَهُ. The birds hovered, حَافَتِ ٱلطُّيُورُ.

Hovering, *a.* عَائِفٌ — مُتَفَرِّشٌ — مُرَفْرِفٌ.

Hoveringly, *ad.* تَفَرُّشًا — تَرَفْرُفًا.

How, *ad.* In what manner? كَيْفَ. How many or much? كَمْ. How often? كَمْ مَرَّةً. How soon? مَتَى. For what cause? لِمَاذَا — لِمَا — لِأَيِّ سَبَبٍ. How then? فَكَيْفَ. How do you do? كَيْفَ أَنْتُمْ — بِكَ. How old is he? كَمْ لَهُ مِنَ ٱلْعُمْرِ. How far is it from hence? مَا ٱلْمَسَافَةُ مِنْ هُنَا. How long will he stay there? حَتَّى مَتَى يَدُومُ هُنَاكَ — إِلَى مَتَى يَبْقَى هُنَاكَ. How now? لِمَاذَا — كَيْفَ ذَلِكَ. How is it that...? كَيْفَ صَارَ حَتَّى. How comes it that you...? مَاذَا حَمَلَكَ عَلَى أَنْ. How much do you owe to...? كَمْ عَلَيْكَ لِ. How great soever it may be, مَهْمَا كَانَ عِظَمُهَا. How could it be otherwise when...? كَيْفَ لَا وَ. How great! how grand! يَا هَيَّ. How! مَا: *e.g.* How generous Zaid is! مَا أَكْرَمَ زَيْدًا. How good you are! مَا أَحْسَنَكَ. How he talks! مَا أَبْقَهُ. How good! how beautiful! مَا شَآءَ ٱللهُ. How are the mighty fallen! كَيْفَ سَقَطَ ٱلْجَبَابِرَةُ.

Howadji, *n.* (properly *Khawdjah*, a Persian word for a man of distinction, and often applied by the natives to European travellers in the East), خَوَاجَةٌ *pl.* خَوَاجَاتٌ.

Howbeit, *ad.* وَمَعَ ذَلِكَ — وَلَكِنْ — غَيْرَ أَنَّ — وَأَمَّا.

However, *ad.* In whatever manner, بِأَيِّ وَجْهٍ كَانَ — كَيْفَمَا. At all events, مَعَ هٰذَا كُلِّهِ — كَيْفَ كَانَ — عَلَى كُلِّ حَالٍ. However it may be, مَهْمَا كَانَ — كَيْفَمَا كَانَ — أَيًّا كَانَ. However cold it may be, مَهْمَا كَانَ ٱلْبَرْدُ شَدِيدًا.

Howitzer, *n.* مِدْفَعٌ قَصِيرٌ ضَخْمٌ *pl.* مَدَافِعُ قِصَارٌ ضِخَامٌ — أُوبُوس.

Howl, *v.i.* As of a dog or wolf, عَوَى *aor.* يَعْوِي. To — at, as from cold, *etc.*, هَرَّ إِلَى. To make to —, as cold a dog, أَهَرَّ. To —, as the wind, قَصَفَ. To shout in lamentation, وَيَّلَ — وَلْوَلَ — وَهْوَهَ. To cry out, صَرَّ — صَرْصَرَ — صَرَخَ — ضَجَّ — عَيَّطَ. He does not — nor bark, مَا يَعْوِي وَمَا يَنْبَحُ. The dogs howled to one another, تَعَاوَتِ ٱلْكِلَابُ.

Howl, *v.t.* To utter with outcry, صَرْصَرَ (or صَرَّ) — صَرَخَ بِ — عَيَّطَ بِ — بِ.

Howl, *n.* / **Howling,** As of a dog, هَرِير – عَوَّة – عُوَآء ; of a camel, هَرّ ; of the wind, صَرْصَرَة ; of a human being, وَهْوَهَة – وَلْوَلَة – وَلْوَال . A cry, صَرِير – صِيَاح – صُرَاخ .

Howling, *a.* Of a dog, هَرِير – عَوَّآء ; of the wind, قَاصِف . A — wilderness, خَلَآءٌ مُسْتَوْحِش .

Howsoever, *ad.* *See* However, *ad.*

Hoy, *n.* A small vessel, فَلُوكَة *pl.* فَلُوكَات .

Hoyden. *See* Hoiden, *n.*

Hub, *n.* Of a wheel, مَرْكَزُ ٱلْبَكَرَةِ – قُبُّ ٱلْعَجَلَةِ .

Hubbub, *n.* لَجَّة – ضَجَّة – هَمْرَجَة – هَرْجٌ وَمَرْجٌ .

Huckaback, *n.* قُمَاشُ فُوطٍ خَشِنٌ .

Hucklebacked, *a.* أَحْدَبُ *fem.* حَدْبَآءُ *pl.* حُدْب .

Huckleberry, *n.* *See* Whortleberry, *n.*

Huckster, *n.* خُرْدَجِي – مُتَسَبِّب .

Huckster, *v.i.* تَعَاطَى ٱلْخُرْدَةَ – تَسَبَّبَ بِٱلْخُرْدَةِ .

Hucksterage, *n.* تَعَاطِي ٱلْخُرْدَةِ – تَسَبُّب .

Huddle, *v.t.* To do a thing precipitately, تَهَوَّرَ فِي . Not to do well, to do a thing clumsily, خَرَقَ 2 بِٱلشَّيْءِ . To — up, to cover up in haste, أَخْفَى بِعَجَلَةٍ – أَسْرَعَ إِلَى سَتْرِهِ . To throw together in confusion, لَخْبَطَ – لَبَّكَ – خَبَّصَ – شَوَّشَ – قَصَّفَ .

Huddle, *v.i.* To be huddled together, of many persons, تَقَاصَفُوا ; of many things, اِلْتَبَكُوا – تَقَصَّفُوا .

Huddle, *n.* اِلْتِبَاك – تَشْوِيش – تَقَاصُف – تَقَصُّف .

Hudibrastic, *a.* *See* Doggerel, *a.*

Hue, *n.* Colour, لَوْن *pl.* أَلْوَان . Hue and cry, جِيَاش – حَوْش . To raise a hue and cry after, صَاحَ بِٱلْحَوْشِ عَلَى *aor.* يَصِيحُ .

Huff, *n.* A swell of anger, شُوَاظ – هَيَجَانُ ٱلْغَضَبِ – حُمَيَّا ٱلْغَيْظِ ; of pride, نَفْخ – تَعَظُّم – تَكَبُّر .

Huff, *v.t.* *See to* Bully, Hector, *v.t.*

Huff, *v.i.* To swell with pride or rage, وَرِمَ (or شَمَخَ 2) بِأَنْفِهِ – وَرِمَ أَنْفُهُ *aor.* يَرِمُ – عَتَا 2 .

Huffiness, *n.* عُرَام – شَرَاسَة – شَكَاسَة .

Huffish, *a.* شَكِس – عَاتٍ *pl.* عُتَاة – مُتَكَبِّر – تَائِه .

Huffishly, *ad.* بِعُتُوٍّ – بِشَكَاسَةٍ – بِتَكَبُّرٍ .

Huffishness, *n.* شَكَاسَة – عُتُوّ – تَكَبُّر – تَوْه .

Huffy, *a.* عَارِم – عَزِق – فَرِطِيّ – شَكِس .

Hug, *v.t.* اِخْتَضَنَ بِشِدَّةٍ – عَانَقَ – ضَمَّ 2 . To hug, or congratulate, one's self, طَنَّبَ فِي حَالِهِ – سُرَّ . To hug the shore, to coast, سَافَرَ بِٱلْقُرْبِ مِنَ ٱلسَّوَاحِلِ – شَطَّأَ 2 . To hug one's self with the vain hope of, اِغْتَرَّ بِ .

Hug, *n.* اِحْتِضَان – مُعَانَقَة – حَزْق – ضَمّ .

Huge, *a.* جَسِيم – كَبِيرُ ٱلْجِرْمِ – عَظِيم – مَدِيد – مُفْرِط – خَارِجٌ عَنِ ٱلْحَدِّ .

Hugely, *ad.* لِلْغَايَةِ – فَوْقَ ٱلْحَدِّ – بِفَرْطٍ – بِكَثْرَةٍ – بِجَسَامَةٍ .

Hugeness, *n.* عِظَم – عَظَامَة – جَسَامَة .

Hulk, *n.* مَرْكَبٌ جَرِيمٌ – جِرْم . The hulks, مَرْكَبٌ لِسَجْنِ ٱلْمُجْرِمِينَ .

Hull, *n.* Of a ship, جِرْمُ مَرْكَبٍ . Hull down, الجِرْمُ مَحْجُوبٌ . *See also* Husk, *n.*

Hull, *v.t.* To pierce the hull with a cannon ball, أَصَابَ جِرْمَ ٱلْمَرْكَبِ بِمِدْفَعٍ . *See also to* Husk, *v.t.*

Hum, *v.i.* As of bees, or to utter in a low sound, دَنْدَنَ – عَنْتَرَ – زَطَّ 2 . To hum, hesitate, in speaking, هَمْهَمَ . *See also to* Buzz, *v.i.*

Hum, *v.t.* To sing in a low voice, تَنَغَّمَ فِي – نَغَمَ فِي 2 – أَغَنَّ .

Hum, *n.* / **Humming,** A sound with a pause implying doubt, هَمْهَمَة . A low buzzing sound, طَنِين – زَطّ – غُنَّة – دَنْدَنَة . A hum or humming in the ears, دَوِيّ . The valley resounded with humming, أَغَنَّ ٱلْوَادِي . *See also* Buzz, *n.*

Hum! *int.* يَا لِلْعَجَبِ – يَا .

Hum and haw, *v.i.* هَمْهَمَ – تَوَقَّفَ .

Human, *a.* آدَمِيٌّ – إِنْسَانِيٌّ – بَشَرِيٌّ – إِنْسِيٌّ . Human nature, الطَّبِيعَةُ ٱلْبَشَرِيَّةُ – نَاسُوت – إِنْسَانِيَّة . A — being, a man, آدَمِيٌّ – إِنْسَان – إِنْسِيٌّ . The — family or race, الإِنْسُ – بَنُو آدَمَ – بَنُو بَشَرٍ . He is a — being, هُوَ بَشَرٌ ; she is a — being, هِيَ بَشَرٌ ; they are — beings, هُمْ بَشَرٌ .

Humane, *a.* شَفِيق – رَحِيم – لَطِيف – كَرِيم – وَدِيع – حَلِيم – رَقِيقُ ٱلْقَلْبِ . The Humane Society, (for saving people from drowning,) الجَمْعِيَّةُ ٱلْخَيْرِيَّةُ لِإِنْقَاذِ ٱلْغَرْقَى .

Humanely, *ad.* بِإِنْسَانِيَّةٍ – بِحَنَانٍ – بِشَفَقَةٍ .

Humaneness, *n.* وَدَاعَة – حِلْم – حَنَان – رِقَّةُ قَلْبٍ .

Humanist, *n.* مُعَلِّمُ ٱلْعُلُومِ ٱلْأَدَبِيَّةِ .

Humanitarian, *n.* القَائِلُ أَنَّ فِي ٱلْمَسِيحِ طَبِيعَةً بَشَرِيَّةً فَقَطْ .

Humanitarianism, *n.* مَذْهَبُ ٱلْقَائِلِينَ أَنَّ فِي ٱلْمَسِيحِ طَبِيعَةً بَشَرِيَّةً فَقَطْ .

Humanity, *n.* Human nature, الطَّبِيعَةُ – إِنْسَانِيَّة – نَاسُوت – ٱلْبَشَرِيَّةُ – بَشَرِيَّة . Mankind, الإِنْسُ – بَنُو آدَمَ – بَنُو بَشَرٍ . Kindly disposition, tenderness, حَنَان – حُنُوّ – شَفَقَة – حِلْم – رَآفَة – رِقَّةُ قَلْبٍ . The humanities, العُلُومُ ٱلْأَدَبِيَّةُ – الأَدَبِيَّة . The claims of —, حُقُوقُ ٱلْإِنْسَانِيَّةِ . He adjured him by the claims of —, نَاشَدَهُ بِحَقِّ ٱلْإِنْسَانِيَّةِ .

Humanization, *n.* The act of, تَلْيِين ـ تَأْدِيب ـ تَأْنِيس ; the being humanized, تَأَنُّس ـ لَيَان ـ أَدَب ـ إِنْس .

Humanize, *v.t.* لَيَّنَ ـ أَدَّبَ ـ أَنَّسَ .

Humanizing, *a.* مُلَيِّن ـ مُؤَدِّب ـ مُؤَنِّس .

Humankind, *n.* *See under* Human, *a.*

Humanly, *ad.* After the ideas of mankind, حَسَبَ آرَآءِ ٱلنَّاسِ ـ كَٱلْإِنسانِ .

Humble, *a.* Not proud, خَاضِع ـ أَخْضَعُ ـ ضَارِع ـ ضَرَع ـ مُتَوَاضِع ـ خاشِع ـ مُتَخَشِّع . Low, mean, حَقِير ـ سُفْلَانِيّ ـ مَسْكِين ـ دَنِيّ 2 . To be —, خَشَعَ ـ إِخْتَشَعَ ـ تَخَشَّعَ . To occupy a — position, تَسَفَّلَ .

Humble, *v.t.* To bring low, كَسَرَ ـ خَفَضَ ـ أَخْضَعَ ـ أَضْرَعَ نَفْسَهُ . To make ignominious, أَهَانَ ـ أَذَلَّ . To — one's self, تَخَشَّعَ ـ إِتَّضَعَ . To — one's self to, خَضَعَ ل ـ إِخْتَضَعَ ل . To — one's self to God, تَضَرَّعَ لِلّٰهِ (or إِلَى ٱللّٰهِ) ـ أَخْبَتَ إِلَى ٱللّٰهِ . To be humbled, إِنْخَضَعَ .

Humble-bee, *n.* دَبْرَة *coll.* دَبْر *pl.* دُبُور .

Humbly, *ad.* بِخُضُوعٍ ـ تَضَرُّعًا ـ بِتَوَاضُعٍ ـ تَخَشُّعًا .

Humbug, *n.* An impostor, كَذَّاب ـ غَشَّاش ـ تِمْسَح ـ مِسْيَح . An imposition, تَمْسَاح ـ غِشّ .

Humbug, *v.t.* مَكْرَبَ 2 ـ مَسَّحَ . Mutually to —, مَاسَحَ .

Humdrum, *a.* Stupid, of a person, أَحْمَقُ ـ أَخْرَقُ ـ بَلِيد ; of a thing, مُمِلّ ـ شَاقّ . Wearisome, تَافِه ـ فَاتِر ـ عَدِيمُ ٱللَّذَّةِ .

Humdrum, *n.* Tediousness, تَفَاهَة ـ زَعَل ـ مَلَل ـ مَشَقَّة .

Humectate, *v.t.* نَدَّى ـ رَطَّبَ ـ بَلَّ 2 .

Humectation, *n.* The act of, تَنْدِيَة ـ تَرْطِيب ـ بَلّ .

Humeral, *a.* مَنْكِبِيّ ـ مُتَعَلِّق بِٱلْمَطْنَبِ .

Humerus, *n.* مَنَاكِبُ *pl.* مَنْكِب ـ مَطَانِبُ *pl.* مَطْنَب ـ عَظْمُ ٱلسَّاعِدِ .

Humid, *a.* رَطِب ـ بَلّ ـ نَرِيّ ـ نَدٍ ـ نَدِيّ ـ طَرِيّ . To be —, نَدِيَ ـ رَطِبَ 2 .

Humidity, *n.* } **Humidness,** } طَرَاوَة ـ نَدَاوَة ـ رُطُوبَة ـ نَرًى ـ بَلَل .

Humiliate, *v.t.* *See to* Humble, *v.t.*

Humiliation, *n.* The act of humbling, تَوْضِيع ـ إِضْرَاع ـ حَطّ ـ خَفْض ; of vilifying, degrading, تَذْلِيل ـ إِهَانَة ـ إِذْلَال . The being humiliated, ضَرَاعَة ـ خُشُوع ـ تَوَاضُع ـ وَضَاعَة ـ إِتِّضَاع ; the being vilified, ذُلّ ـ هَوَان .

Humility, *n.* Freedom from pride, تَوَاضُع ـ خُضُوع ـ وَطَآءَة .

Humming, *a.* مُنَغِّم ـ مُغَنْتِر ـ مُدَنْدِن ـ أَغَنّ . A — valley, وَادٍ مُغِنّ . A — top, دُوَّامَة مُدَنْدِنَة ـ دُوَّامَة مُنَغِّمَة . The flies made a — sound, طَنْطَنَ (or طَنَّ) ٱلذُّبَابُ .

Humming, *n.* *See* Hum, *n.*

Humming-bird, *n.* عُصْفُور مِنْ أَصْغَرِ ٱلطُّيُورِ .

Hummock, *n.* A round hill, دَبَّة *pl.* دِبَاب ـ كُثَيِّب *pl.* كُثْبَان .

Humoral, *a.* Pertaining to the humours, مَنُوط بِأَخْلَاطِ ٱلْبَدَنِ .

Humorist, *n.* } **Humorous,** *a.* } Witty, droll, مَرِح ـ أَزْوَال *pl.* زَوْل ـ فَكِه ـ رَقِيع ـ مِرِّيح *pl.* مَرْحَى *and* مِرِّيحُون ـ مُضْحِك ـ بَدِيع . A — speech, نَادِرَة ـ مُلَاحَة ـ لَطِيفَة .

Humorously, *ad.* بِهَزْلٍ ـ بِظَرَافَةٍ ـ بِلَطَافَةٍ ـ بِمِرَاحٍ ـ بِفَكَاهَةٍ .

Humorsome, *a.* Peevish, شَرِس ـ شَكِس ـ عَارِم ـ نَكِد ـ قَتِب .

Humorsomely, *ad.* Petulantly, بِشَرَاسَةٍ ـ بِشَكَاسَةٍ .

Humour, *n.* Moisture, طَرَاوَة ـ رُطُوبَة . One of the four humours of the body, خِلْط *pl.* أَخْلَاط . Matter, ichor, عَثِيث ـ سَبِيب ـ مِدَّة ـ مَادَّة . Turn of mind, disposition, سَجِيَّة ـ مَشْرَب ـ خَاطِر ـ طَبْع ـ مِزَاج . Wittiness, مَرَاحَة ـ فَكَه ـ فَكَاهَة ـ ذِهْن ـ ذَكَاوَة عَقْل . Caprice, طَلْعَة خُلُقِيّ ـ هَوِيَّة . Merriment, فَرَح ـ إِنْبِسَاط ـ مِطْرَاب . Good —, بَشَاشَة ـ فَكَاهَة ; good-humoured, لَطِيفُ ٱلطَّبْعِ ـ خَلِط ـ طَرُوب ـ مَطَارِيبُ *pl.* To put into a good —, كَيَّفَ ـ أَطْرَبَ ـ تَطَرَّبَ ـ أَفْكَهَ . To be in a good —, شَرَاسَة ـ طَبْعٌ نَكِدٌ (or شَرِسٌ) . Bad —, بَشَّ ـ تَفَكَّهَ ـ طَرِبَ ; bad-humoured, شَرِس ـ شَكِس ـ عَارِم ـ نَكِد ـ قَتِب ـ أَخْلَاقِ . To put into a bad —, نَقَّسَ ـ أَزْعَجَ ـ أَضْجَرَ ـ أَغْضَبَ ; to be in a bad —, تَزَعَّلَ ـ إِنْزَعَجَ ـ تَغَضَّبَ ـ شُوِّشَ عَلَيْهِ . Out of —, زَعْلَانُ ـ غَضْبَى ـ غَضْبَانُ *fem.* To be in a — to…, لَهُ خَاطِرٌ فِي أَن ـ يَتُوقُ *aor.* تَاقَ إِلَى أَن ـ خَطَرَ بِبَالِهِ أَن .

Humour, *v.t.* دَارَى ـ أَرْضَى ـ لَاطَفَ ـ وَادَّ ـ فَاكَهَ ـ رَاوَدَ ـ رَاعَى خَاطِرَهُ .

Hump, *n.* A — on the back, حَدَبَة . A camel's —, سَنَام *pl.* أَسْنِمَة . *See also* Bump, *n.*

Humpback, *n.* } **Humpbacked,** } أَحْدَبُ ـ أَثْبَجُ ـ أَحْنَى ٱلظَّهْرِ *fem.* حَدْبَآءُ *pl.* حُدْب . To be —, حَدِبَ .

Hunch, *n.* A protuberance, حَدَب . A thick piece, شِقَّة *pl.* شِقَق *and* شِقَاق ـ قِطْعَة كَبِيرَة . A push, دَفْعَة ـ لَكْز ـ وَكْز .

Hunch, *v.t.* To push with the fist or elbow, يَكِزُ *aor.* وَكَزَ ـ لَكَزَ 2 ـ دَفَعَ .

Hunchbacked, *a.* *See* Humpbacked, *a.*

Hundred, *n.* مِئَة ـ مِائَة *pl.* مِئَات *and* مِئُون . Belonging to hundreds, مِئَوِيّ . Two hundred, مِئَتَانِ . Three hundred, ثَلَاثُ مِئَةٍ ـ ثَلَثْمِئَةٍ . Several hundreds, عِدَّةُ مِئَاتٍ .

Hundredth, *a.* المِائَةُ — المِئَةُ. A — part, جُزْءٌ مِنْ مِئَةِ أَجْزَآءٍ.

Hungarian, *n.* and *a.* مِنْ أَهْلِ هُنْكَارِيَا — مَجَر.

Hungary, *n.* هُنْكَارِيَا — بِلَادُ ٱلْمَجَرِ.

Hung-beef, *n.* لَحْمُ بَقَرٍ مُمَلَّحٌ وَمُعَرَّضٌ.

Hunger, *n.* غَرَث — عَوَق — خَوًى — خَوَآءٌ — هَمَج — سَغَبَة — جُوع. Insatiable —, دَآءُ ٱلذِّئْبِ. Thirst, as for knowledge, etc., إِسْتِجَاعَة. A morsel to stay —, عُلَالَة.

Hunger, *v.i.* جَاعَ *aor.* يَجُوعُ — سَغِبَ — غَرِثَ. To cause to —, أَجَاعَ — غَرَّثَ. To make one's self to — intentionally, تَجَوَّعَ. To show hunger, to be insatiable, as for knowledge, إِسْتَجَاعَ.

Hungrily, *ad.* بِٱلْجُوعِ — إِسْتِجَاعَةً.

Hungry, *a.* عَوِق — لَأْحَانُ *fem.* لَأْحَى — سَاغِب — سَغْبَانُ *fem.* سَغْبَى *pl.* سِغَاب — جَوْعَانُ *pl.* جِيَاع — جَائِع *pl.* جُوَّع.

Hunks, *n.* مُبْرِم — خَبِيث — لَئِيم — خَسِيس.

Hunt, *v.t.* To take in hunting, صَادَ — قَنَصَ — حَنَشَ — اِصْطَادَ. To search for, فَحَصَ عَن — فَتَّشَ عَلَى. To — away, أَشْرَدَ — شَرَّدَ — طَرَدَ. To worry, حَرَشَ — اِحْتَرَشَ — تَحَرَّشَ.

Hunt, *v.i.* تَصَيَّدَ — حَنَشَ.

Hunt, *n.* صَيْد — قَنْص — حَنْش.

Hunter, *n.* / **Huntsman**, } صَيَّاد — صَيُود — قَنَّاص — قَنِيص *pl.* صُيَّد. A hunting-dog, كَلْب — ضِرْوٌ *fem.* ضِرْوَة *pl.* ضِرَآء — سَلُوقِيّ *pl.* سَلُوقِيَّة — صَيُود. *See also* Courser, *n.*

Hunting, *n.* تَصَيُّد — قَنْص — حَنْش.

Hunting-ground, *n.* مُصْطَاد — مَصَاد.

Huntress, *n.* صَيَّادَة — قَنَّاصَة.

Huntsmanship, *n.* تَصَيُّد.

Hurdle, *n.* A texture, as of twigs, شِبَاك — جِدَار — جِدْر *pl.* جُدُور. A — race, مِضْمَارٌ تَعْتَرِضُهُ حُزَمٌ مِنَ ٱلْعِيدَانِ تَطْفِرُهَا ٱلْجِيَادُ. *See also* Fascine, *n.*

Hurdy-gurdy, *n.* آلَةٌ مِنْ آلَاتِ ٱلْمُوسِيقَى تُشْبِهُ ٱلْقَانُونَ.

Hurl, *v.t.* رَمَى ب *aor.* يَرْمِي — رَشَقَ. To — a dart at one, زَرَقَ — بِمِزْرَاقٍ — رَشَقَ — بِٱلنَّبْلِ. To — something at, أَلْقَى — ب. To — down, أَهْبَطَ — هَبَطَ — كَوَّرَ.

Hurl, *n.* The act of throwing, رَمْي — زَرْق — رَشْق.

Hurly-burly, *n.* غَاغَة — جَلَبَة — رَجَّة — هَرْجٌ وَمَرْجٌ.

Hurra! *int.* / **Hurrah**, } يَعِيش.

Hurrah, *n.* تَهْتِيفٌ بِٱلسَّلَامِ — هُتَاف — تَحِيَّة. *See also* Huzza, *n.*

Hurrah, *v.t.* صَاحَ ب — يَعِيش — حَيَّى. The people hurrahed him, حَيَّاهُ ٱلنَّاسُ. *See also to* Huzza, *v.i.*

Hurricane, *n.* رِيحٌ زَعْزَعَانٌ — زَوْبَعَة *pl.* زَوَابِعُ — أُمُّ زَوْبَعَةٍ.

Hurried, *a.* عَجْلَانُ — مُسْتَعْجِل — عَاجِل.

Hurriedly, *ad.* بِٱسْتِعْجَالٍ — عَلَى ٱلْعَجَلَةِ. He did the thing —, before its time, عَاجَلَ ٱلشَّيْءَ عَنْ وَقْتِهِ.

Hurriedness, *n.* إِسْتِعْجَال — عَجَلَة.

Hurry, *v.t.* إِسْتَعْجَلَ — أَعْجَلَ — أَسْرَعَ — إِسْتَفَزَّ. *See also to* Hasten, *v.t.*

Hurry, *v.i.* أَفَاجَ — بَادَرَ — أَوْفَضَ — أَوْشَكَ — كَصْكَصَ — إِسْتَعْجَلَ. To — one off or away, أَلَحَّ عَلَيْهِ بِٱلذَّهَابِ. *See also to* Hasten, *v.i.*

Hurry, *n.* Haste, إِسْتِعْجَال — عَجَلَة. Commotion, غَوْغَآء — هَوْشَة — هَمْرَجَة. *See also* Haste, *n.*

Hurry-skurry, *n.* تَهَوُّر — هَرْجٌ وَمَرْجٌ — عَجَلَة.

Hurt, *n.* A pain, أَلَم — وَجَع *pl.* أَوْجَاع. An injury, ضَرَر — خَسَارَة — أَذِيَّة — أَذًى — مَضَرَّة *pl.* مَضَارّ. A wound, contusion, جُرْح *pl.* جُرُوح — رَضّ — هَرْس. A —, as from a saddle, عَقْر *pl.* عُقُور. An evil, شَرّ *pl.* شُرُور — سُوء *pl.* أَسْوَآء — إِسَآءَة.

Hurt, *v.t.* To harm, آذَى — ضَرَّ — ضَارَّ — أَضَرَّ. To injure, to behave badly to, آذَى — أَسَآءَ إِلَى. To defame, أَبَرَ — حَكَرَ. To wound, جَرَحَ. To pain, آلَمَ — أَوْجَعَ. To chafe, as of a saddle, عَقَرَ — عَقَّرَ. To — one's feelings, غَمَّ — أَغَمَّ — كَسَرَ خَاطِرَهُ. I did not say this to — you, مَا قُلْتُ هٰذَا لِشَرِّكَ.

Hurtful, *a.* Injurious, مُؤْذٍ — جَانٍ — ضَارٌّ — مُضِرّ. Painful, وَجِيع — مُؤْلِم. Destructive, مُهْلِك — مُفْسِد.

Hurtfully, *ad.* مَضَرَّةً — بِضَرَرٍ — بِنَوْعٍ مُؤْذٍ.

Hurtfulness, *n.* مَضَرَّة — ضَرَر.

Hurtless, *a.* غَيْرُ مُؤْذٍ — لَا يَضُرُّ.

Hurtlessly, *ad.* بِلَا أَذِيَّةٍ — مِنْ غَيْرِ مَضَرَّةٍ.

Hurtlessness, *n.* عَدَمُ أَذِيَّةٍ — عَدَمُ مَضَرَّةٍ.

Husband, *n.* عَشِير *pl.* عُشَرَآء — حَلِيل *pl.* حَلَائِل — قَيِّمُ ٱلْمَرْأَةِ — رَجُل *pl.* رِجَال — زَوْج *pl.* أَزْوَاج — بَعْل *pl.* بُعُول *and* بُعُولَة. A male, ذَكَر *pl.* ذُكُور. Husband and wife, زَوْجٌ وَزَوْجَةٌ.

Husband, *v.t.* To manage with frugality, دَبَّرَ — وَفَّرَ — تَقَنَّى. To till, حَرَثَ — فَلَحَ — أَكَرَ.

Husbanding, *n.* Thrift, تَوْفِير — تَقَنٍّ.

Husbandless, *a.* بِلَا زَوْجٍ.

Husbandman, *n.* فَلَّاح *pl.* فَلَّاحُون — حَرَّاث *pl.* حَرَّاثَة — أَكَّار *pl.* أَكَرَة.

Husbandry, *n.* Tillage, حِرَاثَة — فِلَاحَة — أَكْر. Frugality, تَقَنٍّ — تَوْفِير.

Hush! *int.* صَهْ ـ أَنْصِتْ.

Hush, *a.* Still, silent, صِمِّيت ـ صامِت ـ ساكِن ـ ساكِت.

Hush, *v.t.* To silence, سَكَّتَ ـ أَسْكَتَ ـ أَصَمَّ ـ أَصْمَتَ. To quiet, خَفَّضَ ـ هَدَّأَ ـ هَدَنَ ـ. To —, as a child to sleep, هَمَّمَ. To — a thing up, طَبَّقَ عَلَى ـ نَيَّمَ ـ أَغْضَى عَلَى.

Hush, *v.i.* To be still, silent, صَمَتَ ـ أَنْصَتَ ـ هَدَأَ ـ تَهَدَّأَ. The storm was hushed, هَدَأَتِ ٱلْعَاصِفَةُ.

Hush-money, *n.* رِشْوَة ـ بَرْطِيل.

Husk, *n.* قِشْرَة ـ قِشْر ـ غِمْد *pl.* غُمُود *and* أَغْمَاد. The — of wheat, قُنَّابَة; of barley, إِتْب. Having a —, قَشِر; without a —, أَقْشَرُ *fem.* قَشْرَآء. Made of the husks of the coffee-bean, قِشْرِيّ.

Husk, *v.t.* قَشَّرَ ـ قَشَرَ ـ جَرَّدَ ـ شَذَّبَ.

Huskiness, *n.* Roughness, خُشُونَة; of voice, بُحَاح ـ جُشْرَة ـ بُحَّة.

Husky, *a.* Having husks, قِشْرِيّ ـ قَشِر. Hoarse, أَبَحّ *fem.* بَحَّآء *and* بَحَّة *pl.* بُحّ. Having a — voice, أَبَحُّ ٱلصَّوْتِ.

Husking, *n.* The act of, تَقْشِير.

Hussar, *n.* عَسْكَرِيّ مِنَ ٱلْأَسَاوِرَةِ ٱلْخَفِيفَةِ *pl.* عَسَاكِر.

Hussy, *n.* عاهِرَة ـ حاسِرَة.

Hustings, *n.* مَحْفِل تُنْتَخَبُ فِيهِ ٱلْأَعْضَآء لِمَجْلِسِ ٱلشُّورَى ـ مَحْفِلُ ٱلْإِنْتِخَابِ.

Hustle, *v.t.* To push, قَصَفَ ـ دَسَعَ ـ صَكَمَ. To crowd, زَحَمَ. To shake together in confusion, لَبَّكَ ـ هَوَّشَ ـ خَبَّصَ.

Huswife, *n.* *See* Housewife, *n.*

Hut, *n.* خُصّ *pl.* أَخْصَاص ـ كُوخ *pl.* أَكْوَاخ ـ عَرِيش *pl.* عُرُش ـ مِظَلَّة.

Hut, *v.t.* To place in huts, نَزَّلَ ـ فِي أَكْوَاخٍ (or أَخْصَاصٍ) ـ سَكَّنَ ـ فِي عُرُشٍ.

Hutch, *n.* A box, صَنْدُوق *pl.* صَنَادِيق. A trap, مِصْيَدَة.

Huzza, *n.* A shout of joy, هُتَاف ـ تَهْلِيل ـ يَعِيش.

Huzza, *v.i.* هَلَّلَ ـ هَتَفَ ـ أَبْدَى أَصْوَاتَ ٱلْفَرَحِ. *See also to* Hurrah, *v.i.*

Hyacinth, *n.* The flower, سَلَب *pl.* أَسْلَاب ـ سُنْبُل *pl.* سَنَابِل; the gem, حَجَر يَمَانِيّ.

Hyads, *n.* } The constellation, ٱلتَّوَابِع ـ ٱلتَّابِعُ ٱلدَّبَرَانِ.
Hyades, }

Hyaline, *a.* زُجَاجِيّ ـ بِلَّوْرِيّ.

Hybernate, Hybernation; *See* Hibernate, Hibernation, *n.*

Hybrid, *a.* } بَغْل ـ خِلْط مِلْط ـ أَخْلَاط *pl.* خِلْطَة *fem.* خِلْط
Hybridous, *a.* } بِغَال ـ أَبْغَال *pl.* بَغْلَة *fem.*
Hybrid, *n.* }

Hybridity, *n.* خِلْط.

Hydatid, *n.* A cyst with fluid, بَثْرَة *or* بَثَرَة *pl.* بَثَرَات. An intestinal worm, دُودُ ٱلْأَمْعَآء.

Hydra, *n.* A monster with many heads, غُولٌ ذُو رُؤُوسٍ عَدِيدَةٍ. A great calamity, بَلِيَّة ـ آفَة ـ ٱلدُّهَيْمَآء ـ أُمُّ ٱلدُّهَيْمِ. The constellation, ٱلشُّجَاع.

Hydrangea, *n.* The aquatic plant, قَصْعَةُ ٱلْمَآء.

Hydrant, *n.* طُلُمْبَة ـ تُرُمْبَة.

Hydrargyrum, *n.* Quicksilver, زِئْبَق ـ زَاوُوق.

Hydrate, *n.* إِمْتِزَاجُ ٱلْمِلْحِ ٱلْمَعْدِنِيِّ بِٱلْمَآء.

Hydraulic, *a.* } مُتَعَلِّقٌ بِفَنِّ إِصْعَادِ ٱلْمَآء. Hydraulic lime,
Hydraulical, } جِيرٌ لَا يُؤَثِّرُ فِيهِ (or يَتَطَرَّقُ إِلَيْهِ) ٱلْمَآء. An — press, دُولَابٌ تُدِيرُهُ قُوَّةُ ٱلْمَآء. An — machine, for raising water for irrigation, نَاعُورَة *pl.* نَوَاعِير.

Hydraulics, *n.* عِلْمُ سَيْرِ ٱلْمِيَاهِ وَوُقُوفِهَا ـ فَنُّ رَفْعِ ٱلْمَآء.

Hydrocele, *n.* قِيلَة ـ قُلَيْطَة.

Hydrocephalus, *n.* مَآءٌ فِي ٱلرَّأْسِ ـ إِسْتِسْقَآءُ ٱلرَّأْسِ.

Hydrochlorate, *n.* ما رُكِّبَ مِنْ رُوحِ ٱلْمِلْحِ ٱلْأَخِيرِ وَأُسٍّ آخَرَ.

Hydrochloric acid, *n.* رُوح ـ حُمُوضَةُ ٱلْقُلُورِ مَمْزُوجَةً بِأُمِّ ٱلْمَآء ـ ٱلْمِلْحِ.

Hydrodynamics, *n.* عِلْمُ تَحْرِيكِ ٱلْأَجْرَامِ وَٱسْتِعْمَالِهِ فِي فَنِّ إِصْعَادِ ٱلْمِيَاهِ وَنَقْلِهَا.

Hydrogen, *n.* إِدْرُجِين ـ أُمُّ ٱلْمَآء ـ مُوَلِّدُ ٱلْمَآء ـ أَصْلُ ٱلْمَآء.

Hydrogenate, *v.t.* } شَرَّبَ ـ (or رَكَّبَ ـ) ـ مَزَجَ ـ بِأَصْلِ ٱلْمَآء
Hydrogenize, } إِدْرُجِينًا.

Hydrogenous, *a.* إِدْرُجِينِيّ ـ مُشَرَّبٌ بِٱلْإِدْرُجِينِ ـ بِهِ أَصْلُ ٱلْمَآء.

Hydrographer, *n.* رَسَّامُ ٱلْبُحُورِ وَوَاصِفُهَا.

Hydrographic, *a.* } مُتَعَلِّقٌ بِفَنِّ رَسْمِ ٱلْبُحُورِ وَوَصْفِهَا.
Hydrographical, }

Hydrography, *n.* رَسْمُ ٱلْبُحُورِ وَوَصْفُهَا.

Hydrology, *n.* عِلْمُ ٱلْبَحْثِ عَنْ كَيْفِيَّاتِ ٱلْمِيَاهِ.

Hydromel, *n.* شَرَابُ ٱلْعَسَلِ.

Hydrometer, *n.* مِيزَانُ ٱلْمَآء.

Hydrometric, *a.* } مُتَعَلِّقٌ بِمِيزَانِ ٱلْمَآء.
Hydrometrical, }

Hydrometry, *n.* فَنُّ وَزْنِ ٱلْمِيَاهِ وَكَيْفِيَّاتِهَا.

Hydropathic, *a.* مُتَعَلِّقٌ بِمُدَاوَاةِ ٱلْأَمْرَاضِ بِوَاسِطَةِ ٱلْمَآء.

Hydropathist, *n.* مُطَبِّبُ ٱلْأَمْرَاضِ بِوَاسِطَةِ ٱلْمَاءِ.

Hydropathy, *n.* مُدَاوَاةُ ٱلْأَمْرَاضِ بِوَاسِطَةِ ٱلْمَاءِ.

Hydrophanous, *a.* شَفَّافٌ مِنَ ٱلِٱبْتِلَالِ.

Hydrophobia, *n.* كَلَاب ـ دَآءُ ٱلْكَلْبِ ـ خَوْفٌ مِنَ ٱلْمَاءِ; having —, كَلِبٌ *pl.* كَلْبَى.

Hydrophobic, *a.* مُتَعَلِّقٌ بِٱلْكَلَابِ.

Hydropic, *a.* }
Hydropical, } *See* Dropsical, *a.*

Hydrostatic, *a.* }
Hydrostatical, } مُتَعَلِّقٌ بِثِقَلِ ٱلْمَاءِ وَقُوَّتِهِ. A — press, دُولَابٌ تُدِيرُهُ قُوَّةُ ٱلْمَاءِ.

Hydrostatics, *n.* مَعْرِفَةُ ثِقَلِ ٱلْمَوَائِعِ بِٱلنِّسْبَةِ إِلَى ثِقَلِ ٱلْجَوَامِدِ.

Hydrothorax, *n.* اِسْتِسْقَآءُ ٱلصَّدْرِ.

Hydrous, *a.* مَائِيٌّ.

Hydrus, *n.* A water snake, حَيَّةُ ٱلْمَآءِ.

Hyemal, *a.* Pertaining to winter, شَتَوِيٌّ.

Hyemation, *n.* *See* Hibernation, *n.*

Hyena, *n.* أُمُّ رِمَالٍ ـ أُمُّ عَامِرٍ ـ جَيْأَلُ *fem.* جَيْأَلَةُ ـ ضِبْعَان ـ
pl. ضِبَاع *fem. sing.* ضَبُع *pl.* ضُبْع *and* ضِبَاع *and* أَضْبُع *and* مَضْبَعَة.

Hygeian, *a.* مُتَعَلِّقٌ بِحِفْظِ ٱلصِّحَّةِ.

Hygiene, *n.* قَوَاعِدُ لِحِفْظِ ٱلصِّحَّةِ.

Hygienic, *a.* مُتَعَلِّقٌ بِٱلْقَوَاعِدِ لِحِفْظِ ٱلصِّحَّةِ.

Hygrometer, *n.* مِيزَانُ رُطُوبَةِ ٱلْهَوَآءِ.

Hygrometric, *a.* }
Hygrometrical, } دَالٌّ عَلَى تَحْقِيقِ رُطُوبَةِ ٱلْهَوَآءِ.

Hygrometry, *n.* فَنُّ تَحْقِيقِ رُطُوبَةِ ٱلْهَوَآءِ.

Hygroscope, *n.* مِيزَانُ رُطُوبَةِ ٱلْهَوَآءِ.

Hymen, *n.* The virginal membrane, بِنْتُ سَعْدٍ ـ خِتَام ـ
غِشَآءُ ٱلْبَكَارَةِ ـ خَاتِم. Marriage, زِيجَة ـ نِكَاح.

Hymeneal, *a.* }
Hymenean, } Pertaining to marriage, مُخْتَصٌّ بِٱلزِّيجَةِ ـ مُتَعَلِّقٌ بِٱلنِّكَاحِ.

Hymeneal, *n.* }
Hymenean, } A marriage song, قَصِيدَةٌ فِي مَدْحِ ٱلْعُرْسِ *pl.* قَصَائِدُ ـ قَصِيدَةُ فَرَحٍ.

Hymn, *n.* تَسْبِيحَة *pl.* تَسَابِيحُ ـ مَدِيحَة *pl.* مَدَائِحُ.

Hymn, *v.t.* سَبَّحَ ـ حَمِدَ ـ مَدَحَ.

Hymn, *v.i.* سَبَّحَ.

Hymnal, *n.* A book of hymns, كِتَابُ تَسَابِيحَ.

Hymnic, *a.* تَسْبِيحِيٌّ ـ مُتَعَلِّقٌ بِٱلتَّسَابِيحِ.

Hyoid, *a.* مُتَعَلِّقٌ بِٱلْعَظْمِ فِي عُكْوَةِ ٱللِّسَانِ.

Hyoscyamus, *n.* غَسْلَج ـ سَيْكُرَان ـ بَنْج.

Hyp, *n.* *See* Hypochondria, *n.*

Hyp, *v.t.* To depress the spirits, أَكْرَبَ ـ كَسَرَ خَاطِرَهُ.

Hypæthral, *a.* An — edifice, بِنَآءٌ بِلَا سَقْفٍ.

Hyperbola, *n.* قَطْعٌ زَائِدٌ.

Hyperbole, *n.* تَعْظِيم ـ مُبَالَغَة ـ إِطْرَآء ـ غُلُوٌّ.

Hyperbolic, *a.* }
Hyperbolical, } Belonging to hyperbola, مُتَعَلِّقٌ بِقَطْعٍ زَائِدٍ. Exaggerating, مُبَالِغ ـ إِطْرَائِيٌّ ـ تَعْظِيمِيٌّ.

Hyperbolically, *ad.* بِمُبَالَغَةٍ ـ إِطْرَآءً.

Hyperbolism, *n.* مُبَالَغَة.

Hyperbolist, *n.* مُبَالِغ.

Hyperbolize, *v.i.* بَالَغَ ـ هَلَّجَ.

Hyperbolize, *v.t.* أَطْرَأَ ـ عَظَّمَ ـ بَالَغَ فِي.

Hyberborean, *a.* }
Hyperborean, *n.* } سَاكِنٌ فِي أَقْصَى ٱلشَّمَالِ ـ شَمَالِيٌّ.

Hyper-critic, *n.* عَيَّاب ـ نَقَّاد ـ مُبَالِغٌ فِي ٱلنَّقْدِ.

Hyper-critical, *a.* مُبَالِغٌ فِي ٱلتَّعْيِيبِ ـ نَقَّاد.

Hyper-criticism, *n.* تَعْيِيب ـ المُبَالَغَةُ فِي ٱلنَّقْدِ.

Hyperdulia, *n.* عِبَادَةٌ لِمَرْيَمَ ٱلْعَذْرَآءِ.

Hypericum, *n.* The plant, رُمَّانُ ٱلْأَنْهَارِ.

Hyphen, *n.* (- وَهِيَ) وُصْلَةٌ *pl.* وُصَل ـ شَرْطَة.

Hypochondria, *n.* The region below the short ribs, ـ النَّاطِفَةُ
الْقُرْبُ ـ الْقُرْنُبُ ـ الْكَشْحُ ـ الْخَاصِرَةُ; the two hypochondriæ,
الْخَاصِرَتَانِ. The disease, طَفْطَفَة ـ مَرَضُ ٱلْوَهْمِ ٱلشَّدِيدِ ـ
فَسَادُ ٱلْفِكْرِ ـ سَوْدَآء.

Hypochondriac, *a.* }
Hypochondriac, *n.* }
Hypochondriacal, *a.* } سَوْدَاوِيٌّ ـ سَوْدَائِيٌّ ـ ذُو مَالِيخُولِيَا ـ مُصَابٌ بِمَرَضِ ٱلْوَهْمِ ٱلشَّدِيدِ.

Hypochondriacally, *ad.* بِكَرْبٍ ـ بِٱلسَّوْدَآءِ.

Hypochondriacism, *n.* The disease; *see under* Hypochondria, *n.*

Hypocrisy, *n.* مُرَآءَاة ـ مُرَايَاة ـ نِفَاق ـ رِئَآء ـ خُبْث ـ
مُدَاهَنَة.

Hypocrite, *n.* مُرَآءٍ *pl.* مُرَاؤُونَ ـ مُنَافِق *pl.* مُنَافِقُونَ ـ مُدَاهِن
pl. مُدَاهِنَة. To play the —, نَفَّقَ ـ دَاهَنَ.

Hypocritical, *a.* مُرَائِيٌّ ـ مُدَاهِن ـ نِفَاقِيٌّ.

Hypocritically, *ad.* بِنِفَاقٍ ـ بِمُنَافَقَةٍ ـ بِمُرَايَاةٍ.

Hypogastric, *a.* مُتَعَلِّقٌ بِأَسْفَلِ ٱلْمَأْنَةِ ـ مُخْتَصٌّ بِٱلثُّنَّةِ.

Hypogastrium, *n.* أَسْفَلُ ٱلْمَأْنَةِ ـ الثُّنَّةُ.

Hypogene, *a.* مُتَعَلِّقٌ بِصُخُورٍ مُكَوَّنَةٍ فِي بَاطِنِ ٱلْأَرْضِ.

Hypostasis, *n.* أُقْنُوم *pl.* أَقَانِيمُ.

Hypostatic, *a.* }
Hypostatical, } أُقْنُومِيٌّ.

Hypostatically, *ad.* أُقنومًا.

Hypothecate, *v.t.* أَرْهَنَ ـ رَهَنَ. I hypothecated the commodity on account of debt, رَهَنْتُ ٱلْمَتاعَ بِٱلدَّيْنِ.

Hypothecation, *n.* إِرْهان ـ رَهْن. *See also* Bottomry, *n.*

Hypothecator, *n.* راهِن.

Hypothenuse, *n.* وَتَرُ قائِمَةٍ ـ وَتَر.

Hypothesis, *n.* قِياس ـ تَخْمِين ـ تَقْدِير ـ فَرْض.

Hypothetic, *a.* / Hypothetical, } قِياسِيّ ـ فَرْضِيّ.

Hypothetically, *ad.* بِٱلتَّخْمِينِ ـ بِٱلْفَرْضِ.

Hyson, *n.* A kind of green tea, ضَرْبٌ مِنَ ٱلشّايِ ٱلْأَخْضَرِ.

Hyssop, *n.* زُوفا ـ ثُغام.

Hysteria, *n.* / Hysterics, } The disease of the womb, مَرَضُ ٱلرَّحِمِ. A nervous fluttering of the heart, خَفَقانُ ٱلْقَلْبِ.

Hysteric, *a.* / Hysterical, } Appertaining to the womb, رَحِمِيّ ; to the fluttering of the heart, مُتَعَلِّقٌ بِخَفَقانِ ٱلْقَلْبِ.

Hysteron-proteron, *n.* تَقْدِيمٌ وَتَأْخِيرٌ.

Hysterotomy, *n.* إِخْراجُ ٱلْجَنِينِ مِنَ ٱلرَّحِمِ بِٱلْآلاتِ.

Hythe, *n.* *See* Hithe, Haven, *n.*

I.

I, *pr.* أَنا. It is I, أَنا هُوَ. I am the man, أَنا هُوَ ٱلرَّجُلُ. Is it I? هَلْ أَنا هُوَ.

Iambic, *a.* مَنْظُومٌ عَلَى بَحْرِ ٱلرَّجَزِ.

Iambic, *n.* / Iambus, } The poetical foot so called, بَحْرُ ٱلرَّجَزِ. A verse of such feet, بَيْتٌ عَلَى بَحْرِ ٱلرَّجَزِ.

Ibex, *n.* ثَيْتَل *pl.* ثَياتِل ـ بَدَن *pl.* بُدُون ـ وَعِل *pl.* أَوْعال.

Ibis, *n.* لَقْلَق *or* لَقْلاق *pl.* لَقالِق.

Ice, *n.* جَلِيد ـ سَقِيط ـ قَرْث. He broke the ice, opened the subject, فَتَحَ بابَ (*or* بَحْثَ فِي) ٱلْخِطابِ. The ground became covered with ice, froze, أَجْلَدَتِ ٱلْأَرْضُ.

Ice, *v.t.* To freeze, ثَلَّجَ ـ أَقْرَسَ ـ قَرَّسَ. To cover with sugar, لَبَّسَ بِسُكَّرٍ.

Iceberg, *n.* كِسْفَةٌ كَبِيرَةٌ مِنَ ٱلْجَلِيدِ *pl.* كِسَف *and* كُسُوف *and* أَكْساف.

Ice-blink, *n.* وَمِيضٌ يُشاهَدُ فِي أُفُقِ ٱلْقُطْبِ ٱلشَّمالِيِّ مُنْعَكِسٌ عَنْ جَلِيدٍ بَعِيدٍ (وَذٰلِكَ فِي ٱلْبَحْرِ ٱلْجامِدِ).

Ice-bound, *a.* مُحاطٌ بِٱلْجَلِيدِ.

Ice-cream, *n.* بُوظَة ـ بُوزَة ـ بُوز ـ قِشْطَةٌ مُثَلَّجَة.

Ice-floe, *n.* كِسْفَةٌ مِنَ ٱلْجَلِيدِ *pl.* كِسَف *and* كُسُوف.

Ice-house, *n.* مَجْمَدَة ـ مَثْلَجَة ـ مَخْزَنُ ٱلثَّلْجِ (*or* ٱلْجَلِيدِ) ـ سِرْدابٌ لِلثَّلْجِ (*or* لِلْجَلِيدِ).

Iceland-moss, *n.* أُشْنَةٌ فِرَنْجِيَّةٌ ـ حَزازُ ٱلصَّخْرِ فِرَنْجِيّ.

Ice-plant, *n.* نَباتُ ٱلثَّلْجِ.

Ichneumon, *n.* نِمْس *pl.* نُمُوس ـ زَقْزاق.

Ichnography, *n.* رَسْمُ قاعِدَةِ بِناءٍ.

Ichor, *n.* غَثِيث ـ صَبِيب ـ صَدِيد. The — from a dead body, غَثِيثَة ـ مُهْلَة. *See also* Pus, *n.*

Ichorous, *a.* Like ichor, كَٱلْغَثِيثِ ـ كَٱلصَّبِيبِ. Watery, مَاوِيّ ـ مائِيّ.

Ichthyolite, *n.* سَمَكٌ مُتَحَجِّرٌ.

Ichthyologist, *n.* عالِمٌ بِٱلْأَسْماكِ وَخاصِّيّاتِها.

Ichthyology, *n.* عِلْمُ ٱلسَّمَكِ ـ عِلْمٌ يُبْحَثُ فِيهِ عَنْ أَنْواعِ ٱلْأَسْماكِ وَخاصِّيّاتِها.

Ichthyophagous, *a.* آكِلُ ٱلْأَسْماكِ *pl.* أَكَلَة.

Ichthyosaurus, *n.* A fish lizard, ضَبُّ ٱلْبَحْرِ.

Icicle, *n.* مَخْرُوطٌ مُسْتَطِيلٌ مِنَ ٱلْجَلِيدِ قاعِدَتُهُ فِي ٱلسَّقْفِ ـ وَمُسْتَدَقُّهُ مُتَّجِهٌ نَحْوَ ٱلْأَرْضِ ـ ذَنَل ـ ذِنْل ـ قُطْران ـ عُثْنُونٌ مِنَ ٱلْجَلِيدِ *pl.* عَثانِين.

Iciness, *n.* صَرَّة ـ زَمْهَرِير ـ قَرْس ـ قَرَس ـ قَرِيس.

Icing, *n.* As of sugar, تَلْبِيسٌ بِسُكَّرٍ.

Iconoclasm, *n.* تَكْسِيرُ ٱلصُّوَرِ وَٱلتَّماثِيلِ.

Iconoclast, *n.* كَسّارُ ٱلصُّوَرِ وَٱلتَّماثِيلِ.

Iconography, *n.* عِلْمُ ٱلرَّسْمِ وَٱلتَّصْوِيرِ.

Iconology, *n.* ٱلْبَحْثُ فِي فَنِّ ٱلرَّسْمِ وَٱلتَّصْوِيرِ.

Icosahedral, *a.* ما نِيطَ بِٱلْجِسْمِ ٱلْإِفْلاطُونِيِّ.

Icosahedron, *n.* ٱلْجِسْمُ ٱلْإِفْلاطُونِيُّ وَهُوَ ما كانَ ذا عِشْرِينَ سَطْحًا فِي شَكْلِ مُثَلَّثٍ مُتَساوِي ٱلْأَضْلاعِ.

Icteric, *a.* Having jaundice, مُصابٌ بِيَرَقانٍ ـ بِهِ يَرَقان.

Icterus, *n.* Jaundice, يَرَقان.

Icy, *a.* Very cold, ثَلِج ـ مَقْرُور ـ قارِس. Unaffectionate, بارِد ـ بِلا وُدّ. Dull, insensible, مَثْلُوجُ ٱلْفُؤادِ.

I'd, *for* I had *or* I would. I'd rather, الأَرْجَحُ ـ الأَفْضَلُ عِنْدِي. I'd rather not, لا أَوَدُّ عِنْدِي.

Idea, *n.* The form of anything in the mind, تَصَوُّر ـ تَخَيُّل ـ وَهْم *pl.* أَوْهام. Opinion, notion, رَأْي *pl.* آراء ـ رَوِيَّة *pl.* رَوايا ـ فِكْر *pl.* أَفْكار. A design, plan, رَسْم ـ صُورَة. A design, object, نِيَّة ـ مَرام ـ مُراد. Knowledge, مُطالَعَة ـ عِلْم. A subject, قَضِيَّة *pl.* قَضايا ـ أَمْر *pl.* أُمُور. A mere —, خَيال ـ تَخَيُّل. A common or general — involved in a subject, وَجْهٌ جامِعٌ. A modicum, *soupçon*, عِرْق ـ ظِنَّة. I have some — of having seen him, فِي بالِي أَنِّي رَأَيْتُهُ. To have an —, to imagine, صَوَّرَ (or) تَصَوَّرَ ل ـ خُيِّلَ ل ـ تَخَيَّلَ; to intend, رامَ *aor.* يَرُومُ ـ [2] عَزَمَ عَلَى ـ تَعَمَّدَ. To form an —, to plan, تَرَسَّمَ. To form a high — of one, اِسْتَحْسَنَ ـ عَظُمَ صَلاحُهُ فِي عَيْنِهِ [2]. To give one an — of, أَبْصَرَ بِ.

Ideal, *a.* Existing in the fancy, مُتَصَوَّر ـ تَصَوُّرِيّ ـ خَيالِيّ ـ وَهْمِيّ. Ideal as opposed to practical, نَظَرِيّ. An — image, اِرْتِسام.

Ideal, *n.* An — image, اِرْتِسام. Beau —, صُورَةُ ٱلْكَمالِ.

Idealism, *n.* The theory that everything is comprehended by the idea, مَذْهَبُ ٱلْقائِلِينَ أَنَّ ٱلأَشْياءَ كُلَّها تُدْرَكُ بِٱلتَّصَوُّرِ لا بِٱلْحِسِّ.

Idealist, *n.* A believer in idealism, مِنَ ٱلْقائِلِينَ أَنَّ ٱلأَشْياءَ كُلَّها تُدْرَكُ بِٱلتَّصَوُّرِ لا بِٱلْحِسِّ.

Ideality, *n.* قُوَّةُ ٱلتَّصَوُّرِ ـ قُوَّةُ ٱلتَّخَيُّلِ.

Idealize, *v.t.* تَصَوَّرَ ـ تَخَيَّلَ.

Ideally, *ad.* بِٱلتَّصَوُّرِ ـ تَخَيُّلاً ـ ذِهْنًا ـ بِٱلْوَهْمِ.

Idem, *n.* شَرْحُهُ ـ مِثْلُهُ.

Identic, *a.* } Identical, } ذات ـ عَيْن ـ بِعَيْنِهِ. This — thing or person, هٰذا عَيْنُهُ. The — man, ذاتُ ٱلرَّجُلِ. For this — thing, لِهٰذا عَيْنِهِ. Identical notes, تَحْرِيراتٌ مُتَّحِدَةٌ. Identical proceedings, تَبْلِيغاتٌ مُتَّحِدَةٌ مُتَشابِهَةٌ. To be — with, like, ماثَلَ.

Identically, *ad.* ذاتًا ـ عَيْنًا ـ بِعَيْنِهِ ـ اِتِّحادًا.

Identicalness, *n.* *See* Identity, *n.*

Identification, *n.* تَحْقِيق ـ تَحْقِيقُ ٱلشَّخْصِ ـ تَشْخِيص ـ تَعْيِين.

Identify, *v.t.* To prove the identity of, شَخَّصَ ـ عَيَّنَ ـ حَقَّقَ شَخْصَهُ ـ أَثْبَتَ وَحْدانِيَّتَهُ. To make the same with, مَثَّلَ بِ *or* فِي.

Identify, *v.i.* To become the same, تَمَثَّلَ. To coalesce, اِتَّحَدَ بِ ـ حازَبَ.

Identity, *n.* Perfect sameness, عِيان ـ عَيْن ـ وَحْدَة ـ وَحْدانِيَّة. Likeness, مُماثَلَة. Personal —, ذاتُ ٱلشَّخْصِ.

Ideographic, *a.* } Ideographical, } دالٌّ عَلَى ٱلتَّصَوُّرِ دُونَ ٱلتَّلَفُّظِ.

Ideological, *a.* مُتَعَلِّقٌ بِعِلْمِ ٱلْبَحْثِ عَنِ ٱلأَفْكارِ.

Ideologist, *n.* مَنْ تَفَرَّغَ لِعِلْمِ ٱلْبَحْثِ عَنِ ٱلأَفْكارِ.

Ideology, *n.* عِلْمُ ٱلْبَحْثِ عَنِ ٱلأَفْكارِ ـ عِلْمُ ٱلتَّصْدِيقاتِ وَٱلتَّصَوُّراتِ.

Ides, *n.* اليَوْمُ ٱلْخامِسُ عَشَرَ مِنْ شَهْرِ آذارَ وَتَمُّوزَ وَتَشْرِينَ ٱلأَوَّلِ وَٱلثّالِثَ عَشَرَ مِنْ سائِرِ شُهُورِ ٱلسَّنَةِ حَسَبَ تَقْوِيمِ ٱلرُّومانِيِّينَ ٱلْقُدَماءِ.

Id est, يَعْنِي ـ وَهُوَ ـ أَعْنِي.

Idiocrasy, *n.* *See* Idiosyncrasy, *n.*

Idiocy, *n.* } Idiotcy, } هَبالَة ـ بَلاهَة ـ حُمْق ـ جَهْل.

Idiom, *n.* Language, لُغَة *pl.* لُغات ـ لِسْن ـ لِسان *pl.* أَلْسُن. Peculiar expression, اِصْطِلاح ـ تَعْبِيرٌ مَخْصُوص.

Idiomatic, *a.* } Idiomatical, } لُغَوِيّ ـ مَخْصُوصُ ٱلْعِبارَةِ ـ اِصْطِلاحِيّ.

Idiomatically, *ad.* بِٱللُّغَةِ ـ اِقْتِداءً ـ اِصْطِلاحًا.

Idiosyncrasy, *n.* فِطْرَة ـ غَرِيزَة *pl.* غَرائِز ـ جِبِلَّة ـ جِبْلَة ـ سَجِيَّة *pl.* سَجايا ـ خُلْق ـ عِرْق.

Idiosyncratic, *a.* مَعْرُوق ـ عِرْقِيّ ـ مِنْ خُلْقِي ـ مِنْ سَجِيَّةٍ ـ مَنُوطٌ بِٱلطَّبِيعَةِ ـ غَرِيزِيّ ـ خُلُقِيّ.

Idiot, *n.* A natural fool, أُمِّيّ *pl.* أُمِّيُّون ـ غَبِيّ ـ أَبْلَه *fem.* بَلْهاء *pl.* بُلْه. A fool, مَعْتُوه ـ أَبْلَه ـ أَحْمَق ـ مَجْنُون. Idiots, غَيْرُ أُولِي ٱلإِرْبَةِ. To play the —, حَمُقَ [2]. To pretend to be an —, تَحامَقَ.

Idiotic, *a.* } Idiotical, } مِثْلَ ٱلأَحْمَقِ ـ غَبِيّ ـ مَعْتُوه.

Idiotically, *ad.* مِثْلَ ٱلأَحْمَقِ ـ بِغَباوَةٍ ـ بِبَلاهَةٍ.

Idiotism, *n.* *See* Idiom, *n.*

Idle, *a.* Not employed, بَطّال ـ مُعَطَّل. At leisure, فارِغ. Lazy, كَسِل ـ كَسْلان *pl.* كُسالَى. Vain, باطِل ـ عَدِيمُ ٱلْفائِدَةِ ـ فارِغ. An — word, كَلِمَةٌ بَطّالَةٌ. Idle stories, أَساطِير ـ هَذَيان ـ خُرافات. An — fellow, بَطّال ـ بَرَم *pl.* أَبْرام ـ مُبْرِم ـ دَوّار. To be —, unemployed, تَعَطَّلَ; to be lazy, كَسِلَ [2] ـ تَكاسَلَ. It is —, vain, to . . . , هُوَ مِنَ ٱلْعَبَثِ أَنْ.

Idle, *v.i.* To be —, lazy, تَكَاسَلَ – ـَ كَسِلَ . To — away one's time, *etc.*, ضَيَّعَ (or أَتْلَفَ or ـِ سَرَفَ) أَوْقَاتَهُ .

Idleness, *n.* Absence of employment, عُطْلَةٌ – تَعَطُّلٌ – بَطَالَةٌ . Laziness, كَسَلٌ . Leisure, فَرَاغَةٌ – فَرَاغٌ . Frivolousness, عَبَثٌ – تَفَاهَةٌ – بُطْلَانٌ .

Idler, *n.* كَسْلَانُ *pl.* كَسَالَى ; a worthless fellow, بَرَمٌ *pl.* أَبْرَامٌ – بَلِيدٌ – مِرْدَامٌ – رُدَامٌ – مُبْرِمٌ .

Idly, *ad.* Lazily, تَكَاسُلًا – بِكَسَلٍ . Vainly, triflingly, عَبَثًا – بَاطِلًا . To talk —, ـِ هَذَرَ – ـُ بَقَّ *aor.* يَبِقُّ – جَرْدَمَ .

Idol, *n.* مَعْبُودٌ *pl.* مَعَابِيدُ – وَثَنٌ *pl.* أَوْثَانٌ – نِدٌّ *pl.* أَنْدَادٌ – صَنَمٌ *pl.* أَصْنَامٌ . One loved to adoration, مَحْبُوبٌ *fem.* مَحْبُوبَةٌ – مَعْشُوقٌ *fem.* مَعْشُوقَةٌ . To make an —, صَنَّمَ .

Idolater, *n.* عَابِدُ ٱلْأَوْثَانِ *pl.* عَبَدَةٌ – عَابِدُ ٱلْأَصْنَامِ *pl.* عَبَدَةٌ – وَثَنِيٌّ – مُشْرِكٌ – مُشْرِكِيٌّ .

Idolatrous, *a.* مُتَعَلِّقٌ بِعِبَادَةِ ٱلْأَصْنَامِ – مُشْرِكِيٌّ – وَثَنِيٌّ .

Idolatrously, *ad.* كَعَابِدِ صَنَمٍ – بِنَوْعٍ وَثَنِيٍّ .

Idolatry, *n.* إِشْرَاكٌ – عِبَادَةُ ٱلْأَصْنَامِ – وَثَنِيَّةٌ .

Idolize, *v.t.* ـَ وَلِعَ بِ *aor.* يَلَعُ – تَجَنَّنَ بِحُبِّهِ . To be jealous of, ـِ غَارَ عَلَى .

Idyl, *n.* قَصِيدَةُ ٱلرُّعَاةِ *pl.* قَصَائِدُ – غَزَلٌ .

I.e., for *id est*, يَعْنِي – وَهُوَ – أَعْنِي .

If, *conj.* إِنْ – إِذَا – لَوْ – وَلَوْ . Even if, وَلَوْ . As if, كَأَنَّ – مِثْلَمَا . If you do (it) I will do (it), إِنْ تَفْعَلْ أَفْعَلْ . If you come to me I will come to you, إِنْ تَأْتِنِي آتِكَ . If he be in the house I will inform you, إِنْ كَانَ فِي ٱلدَّارِ أَعْلَمْتُكَ بِهِ . If it is in my power I will do it; if not you must excuse me, إِنْ كَانَ فِي طَاقَتِي عَمِلْتُهُ وَإِلَّا فَٱعْذُرْنِي . If he had listened to me he would not have been ruined, لَوْ سَمِعَ مِنِّي لَمَا أَتْلَفَ مَالَهُ . He made as if he were sick, تَمَارَضَ – تَظَاهَرَ بِٱلْمَرَضِ . If it be so, إِنْ كَانَ هٰكَذَا . If now I have found favour in your sight, إِنْ كُنْتُ قَدْ وَجَدْتُ نِعْمَةً فِي عَيْنَيْكَ . If you call them they will not hear you call, and even if they hear they will not answer you, إِنْ تَدْعُوهُمْ لَا يَسْمَعُوا دُعَآءَكُمْ وَلَوْ سَمِعُوا مَا ٱسْتَجَابُوا لَكُمْ (Kuran, xxxv. 15).

Igneous, *a.* نَارِيٌّ – مِنَ ٱلنَّارِ .

Ignescent, *a.* Emitting sparks, شَرَّارٌ .

Igniferous, *a.* مُوَلِّدُ ٱلنَّارِ .

Igniform, *a.* Like fire, مِثْلَ ٱلنَّارِ – فِي صُورَةِ ٱللَّهَبِ .

Ignigenous, *a.* Produced by fire, مُوَلَّدٌ مِنَ ٱلنَّارِ .

Ignipotent, *a.* قَادِرٌ عَلَى ٱلنَّارِ .

Ignis-fatuus, *n.* نُورٌ مُتَوَلِّدٌ مِنْ فَسَادِ ٱلْمَوَادِّ يُرَفْرِفُ عَلَى ٱلْبَطَائِحِ لَيْلًا .

Ignite, *v.t.* To kindle, أَوْقَدَ – أَشْعَلَ – شَعَّلَ – أَضْرَمَ .

Ignite, *v.i.* إِضْطَرَمَ – ـَ شَعَلَ – إِشْتَعَلَ – تَضَرَّمَ – إِسْتَوْقَدَ .

Ignitible, *a.* يُشْعَلُ – قَابِلُ ٱلْإِشْتِعَالِ .

Ignition, *n.* The act of, إِشْعَالٌ – إِضْرَامٌ – تَوْلِيعٌ ; the state of being ignited, إِشْتِعَالٌ – إِشْتِيقَادٌ – تَشَعُّلٌ .

Ignoble, *a.* وَغْلٌ – مَفْسُولٌ – سَفِلٌ – سَفِيلٌ – دَنِيٌّ – حَقِيرٌ – خَسِيسٌ – ذَلِيلٌ – رُدَامٌ . Base-born, مُدْخَلٌ .

Ignobleness, *n.* سَفَالَةٌ – دَنَآءَةٌ – حَقَارَةٌ – خَسَاسَةٌ – ذُلَالَةٌ – رَذَالَةٌ – ذِلَّةٌ .

Ignobly, *ad.* بِدَنَآءَةٍ – بِحَقَارَةٍ – بِرَذَالَةٍ .

Ignominious, *a.* شَنِيعٌ – مُعَابٌ – قَبِيحٌ – رَذِلٌ – فَاحِشٌ .

Ignominious matters, فَضَائِحُ .

Ignominiously, *ad.* بِرَذَالَةٍ – بِهَوَانٍ – بِفَضَاحَةٍ – بِشَيْنٍ .

Ignominiousness, *n.*
Ignominy, } فَضَاحَةٌ – فُضُوحٌ – شَنَاعَةٌ – ذُلٌّ – هَوَانٌ – حَقَارَةٌ – شَيْنٌ – دَنَآءَةٌ . To brand with —, ـَ فَضَحَ – ـِ حَقَّرَ – شَانَ *aor.* يَشِينُ . To be so branded, إِفْتَضَحَ .

Ignoramus, *n.* جَاهِلٌ *pl.* جُهَّالٌ – خَاطِلٌ – أُمِّيٌّ – نُغْنُغَةٌ – غَبِينٌ – أَبُو ٱلْجَهْلِ .

Ignorance, *n.* Want of knowledge, غَبَاوَةٌ – جَهْلٌ – عَدَمُ مَعْرِفَةٍ – عَدَمُ إِدْرَاكٍ – غُشُومِيَّةٌ – جَهَالَةٌ . The being illiterate, أُمِّيَّةٌ – غَبَاةٌ – عَمِيَّةٌ – غَشَمٌ – عَمًى . The time of —, paganism, ٱلْجَاهِلِيَّةُ ; one living in that time, جَاهِلِيٌّ .

Ignorant, *a.* Not knowing, غَبِيٌّ *pl.* أَغْبِيَآءُ – جَاهِلٌ بِ – عَمِيُّ ٱلْقَلْبِ – لَيْسَ لَهُ عِلْمٌ بِ – غَشِيمٌ . Illiterate, أُمِّيٌّ – غَشِيمٌ – جَاهِلٌ *pl.* جُهَّالٌ – غَبِينٌ . To be —, ـَ جَهِلَ ; to be — of..., ـَ خَفِيَ عَنْ – ـَ غَبِيَ عَنْ – ـَ جَهِلَ بِ ; to act in a foolish or — way towards, ـَ جَهِلَ عَلَى . To feign to be —, تَجَاهَلَ – تَغَاشَمَ – تَعَامَى . How — he is! مَا أَعْمَاهُ . You are not — of the events which..., لَا تَخْفَاكَ ٱلْأَحْوَالُ ٱلَّتِي . He was — of the news, غَبِيَ عَنِ ٱلْخَبَرِ . No one is — of the cause of the war, لَمْ يَجْهَلْ أَحَدٌ سَبَبَ ٱلْحَرْبِ .

Ignorantly, *ad.* بِجَهْلٍ – بِسَهْوٍ – بِغَيْرِ عِلْمٍ – بِدُونِ مَعْرِفَةٍ . To sin —, أَخْطَأَ جَهْلًا .

Ignore, *v.t.* To declare ignorance of, ـَ جَهِلَ بِ . To reject, ـُ رَدَّ – أَبَى *aor.* يَأْبَى – أَنْكَرَ .

Ilex, *n.* سِنْدِيَانٌ .

Iliac, *a.* Pertaining to the lower bowels, مُتَعَلِّقٌ بِٱلْأَعْفَاجِ – مُخْتَصٌّ بِٱلْأَمْعَآءِ ٱلدِّقَاقِ . The — passion; *see* Colic, *n.*

Iliad, *n.* An epic of Homer, قَرِيضٌ حَماسِيٌّ لِلشّاعِرِ أُومِيرُس.

Ilk, *n.* The same, عَيْن ـ ذات. Each, كُلّ. Of that ilk, of the same name, مِنْ ذاتِ ٱللَّقَب.

Ill, *a.* Bad, قَبِيح ـ فاسِد ـ رَدِيء ـ أَشْرار *pl.* شِرِّير ـ سَيِّئ. Sick, مَرِيض ـ مُعَلّ ـ مَعْلُول ـ عَلِيل ـ سَقِيم. فاحِش ـ مَنْحُوس ـ نَحِس. Unfortunate, مُشَوَّش ـ عَيّان *vulg.* ضَعِيف. Stupid, خَرِق ـ أَخْرَق. To be ill, sick, تَوَجَّع ـ عَلَّ ـ اعْتَلَّ. To make one ill, أَمْرَض ـ مَرَّض. To pretend to be ill, مَرِض ـ تَمارَض. To do one an ill turn, أَساءَ إِلَى. It went ill with him on their account, تَأَذَّى بِسَبَبِهِمْ. Why do you deal ill with me, لِماذا أَسَأْتُمْ إِلَيَّ. Ill of a fever, مَحْمُوم ـ مُعْتَرًى بِحُمَّى.

Ill, *n.* Whatever is opposed to good, رَداءة ـ شَرّ *pl.* شُرُور ـ سُوء *pl.* أَسْواء. A misfortune, شَقاوة ـ آفَة ـ بَلاء ـ داهِيَة ـ نَحْس ـ مُصِيبَة *pl.* مَصائِب. An injury, ضَرَر ـ مَضَرَّة ـ أَذِيَّة. Defeat, miscarriage, خَيْبَة ـ دائِرَةُ ٱلسَّوْء.

Ill, *ad.* Not rightly, badly, بِرَداءة ـ بِعَدَمِ لِياقَة. Wickedly, improperly, شَرًّا ـ بِقَباحَة ـ بِرَداءة. Ill at ease, مُكَدَّرُ ٱلبال ـ مَكْرُوب ـ غَيْرُ مُرْتاح. To behave ill towards, أَساءَ إِلَى ـ ضارَّ ـ آذَى. To think ill of, ظَنَّ بِهِ ٱلسَّوْء ـ ساءَ بِهِ ٱلظَّنّ *aor.* يَسُوء. To fall out ill, to miscarry, خابَ *aor.* يَخِيب ـ ما صَحَّ. To do ill, to act wickedly, أَساءَ ـ أَذَمَّ ـ أَقْبَحَ. To be ill, bad, depraved, رَدُؤَ. I wished to do you ill, أَرَدْتُ مَساءَتَكَ.

I'll, for I will; *see under* Will, *v.t.*

Ill-advised, *a.* خَرِق ـ أَخْرَق.

Ill-affected, *a.* As towards one, مُتَعَصِّب عَلَى ـ مُقاوِم لِ ـ مُضادّ. He is — towards you, هُوَ ضِدُّكَ ـ هُوَ ضَدِيدُكَ.

Illapse, *n.* Entrance upon, falling on, دُخُول إِلَى ـ وُصُول إِلَى; becoming, صَيْرُورَة ـ صَيْر.

Illation, *n.* اِسْتِدْلال ـ اِسْتِنْتاج ـ اِسْتِخْراج.

Illative, *a.* اِسْتِدْلالِيّ.

Ill-blood, *n.* نَفْسانِيَّة ـ عَداوَة ـ كَشاحَة ـ ضِغْن.

Ill-boding, *a.* ذُو تَشاؤُم ـ بِهِ تَشاؤُم.

Ill-bred, *a.* سَيِّئُ ٱلأَخْلاق ـ قَلِيلُ ٱلأَدَب ـ غَشِيم ـ ذُو غَشْمَشَمَة.

Ill-breeding, *n.* سُوءُ ٱلأَخْلاق ـ قِلَّةُ أَدَب ـ غَشْم ـ غَشْمَشَمَة.

Ill-conditioned, *a.* Weak, عاجِز ـ ضَعِيف. *See also under* Lean, *a.*

Ill-contrived, *a.* }
Ill-devised, } فاسِدُ ٱلاِخْتِراع ـ خَرِق ـ أَخْرَق.

Ill-defined, *a.* مُشْتَبِه ـ مُلْتَبِس ـ غَيْرُ مَحْدُود.

Illegal, *a.* بَسْل ـ حَرام ـ مُحَرَّم ـ ضِدُّ ٱلشَّرِيعَة ـ خِلافُ ٱلقَوانِين (or ٱلنّامُوس) ـ غَيْرُ حَلال ـ غَيْرُ جائِز. To be —, حَرُمَ.

Illegality, *n.* حُرْمَة ـ عَدَمُ جَواز ـ عَدَمُ مُوافَقَةِ ٱلقَوانِين.

Illegalize, *v.t.* حَرَّمَ ـ نَهَى ـ نَهْي.

Illegally, *ad.* بِخِلافِ ٱلقَوانِين ـ بِضِدِّ ٱلشَّرْع ـ بِعَدَمِ جَواز.

Illegalness, *n.* *See* Illegality, *n.*

Illegibility, *n.* }
Illegibleness, } تَطَلُّس ـ كَوْنُ ٱلكِتابَةِ لا تُقْرَأ.

Illegible, *a.* Not to be read, غَيْرُ مَقْرُوء ـ لا يُقْرَأ. Worn out, defaced, مَمْحُوّ ـ أَطْلَس ـ طِلْس *pl.* أَطْلاس.

Illegibly, *ad.* تَطَلُّسًا ـ عَلَى مِنْوالٍ غَيْرِ مَقْرُوء.

Illegitimacy, *n.* Bastardy, حالَةُ ٱلمُدَّعِي ـ نَغُولَة. Want of legitimacy, عَدَمُ جَواز ـ حُرْمَة.

Illegitimate, *a.* Bastard, نَغِل ـ دَعِيّ ـ مُدَّعِي ـ نَغِيل *pl.* نُغُول ـ اِبْنُ حَرام ـ اِبْنُ زِنَى. *See also* Illegal, *a. and under* Bastard, *n.*

Illegitimate, *v.t.* To declare —, bastard, صَرَّحَ بِنُغُولَتِهِ.

Illegitimately, *ad.* As a bastard, كَٱبْنِ حَرام. *See also* Illegally, *ad.*

Illegitimation, *n.* Declaration of bastardy, تَصْرِيح بِٱلنُّغُولَة. Declaring anything illegal, تَحْرِيم ـ نَهْي.

Ill-fated, *a.* نَحِس ـ مَنْحُوس ـ طالِعُهُ نَحِس ـ مَنْهُوس.

Ill-favoured, *a.* Foul, ugly, دَمِيم ـ مَسِيخ ـ قَبِيحُ ٱلمَنْظَر.

Ill-gotten, *a.* مَكْسُوب مِنَ ٱلحَرام ـ مُقْتَنًى بِٱلحَرام.

Ill-grounded, *a.* بِدُونِ أَساس ـ لا أَصْلَ لَهُ.

Illiberal, *a.* Not candid, غَيْرُ خالِصِ ٱلطَّوِيَّة. Narrow-minded, ضَيِّقُ ٱلخُلُق ـ حَوْصُ ٱلحِمار ـ حَرِق ـ ضَيِّقُ ٱلصَّدْر. Opposed to liberty, مُخالِفُ ٱلحُرِّيَّة. Mean, عَدِيمُ ٱلمُرُوَّة ـ خَسِيس ـ دَنِيء. Stingy, بَخِيل ـ مَسِيك. Illiberal measures, قَواعِدُ مُخالِفَةُ ٱلحُرِّيَّة.

Illiberality, *n.* Meanness, عَدَمُ مُرُوَّة ـ دَناءة. Narrow-mindedness, حَرَقُ ٱلصَّدْر ـ حَرَق. Stinginess, بُخْل ـ مَساكَة. Opposition to liberty, مُخالَفَةُ ٱلحُرِّيَّة.

Illiberally, *ad.* With narrow-mindedness, بِحَرَق ـ بِحَرَقِ ٱلصَّدْر. Meanly, بِخَساسَة ـ بِدَناءة. With stinginess, بِبُخْل ـ بِمَساكَة. Disingenuously, مُخادَعَة ـ بِمُراياة.

Illicit, *a.* حَرام ـ مُحَرَّم ـ مَنْهِيّ عَنْهُ. Illicit actions, مُنْكَرات ـ مَمْنُوعات ـ مَناهِي.

Illicitly, *ad.* بِغَيْرِ حَقّ ـ بِضِدِّ ٱلشَّرْع ـ بِخِلافِ ٱلشَّرْعِ وَٱلقانُون.

Illicitness, *n.* حُرْمَة ـ عَدَمُ جَواز.

Ill-imagined, *a.* *See* Ill-judged, *a.*

Illiteracy, *n.* أُمِّيَّة ـ جَهالَة ـ قِلَّةُ مَعْرِفَة.

Illiterate, *a.* قَلِيلُ ٱلْمَعَارِفِ ـ أُمَّانٌ ـ أُمِّيٌّ.

Illiterately, *ad.* بِقِلَّةِ مَعْرِفَةٍ ـ بِجَهَالَةٍ ـ بِأُمِّيَّةٍ.

Illiterateness, *n.* *See* Illiteracy, *n.*

Ill-judged, *a.* بِدُونِ بَصِيرَةٍ ـ مِنْ غَيْرِ تَدْبِيرٍ ـ أَخْرَقُ ـ خَرِقٌ ـ نَقِيضُ ٱلْعَقْلِ.

Ill-looking, *a.* بَشِعٌ ـ قَبِيحٌ ـ وَحْشٌ ـ مَسِيخُ ٱلْوَجْهِ ٱلْمَنْظَرِ.

Ill-minded, *a.* قاصِدُ ٱلرَّدِيءِ ـ حَقُود.

Ill-nature, *n.* Badness of temper, طَبْعٌ نَكِدٌ ـ عَرْبَدَةٌ ـ حِقْدٌ ـ شَرَاسَةٌ ـ عَرْبَدَةٌ ـ شَكَاسَةٌ ـ شَرُّ ٱلْأَخْلَاقِ. Crabbedness, شَرَاسَةٌ ـ عَرْبَدَةٌ ـ شَكَاسَةٌ.

Ill-natured, *a.* Bad tempered, حَقُود ـ نَكِدُ ٱلطَّبْعِ ـ بَشِيع ـ شَرِيرُ ٱلْأَخْلَاقِ; crabbed, مُعَرْبِد ـ شَرِس ـ شَكِس.

Ill-naturedly, *ad.* بِحِقْدٍ ـ بِشَكَاسَةٍ ـ بِشَرَاسَةٍ. To act —, عَرْبَدَ.

Ill-naturedness, *n.* *See* Ill-nature, *n.*

Illness, *n.* Sickness, دَآءٌ *pl.* أَدْوَآءٌ ـ دَوًى *pl.* أَدْوَآءٌ ـ سُقْم *pl.* سِقَام ـ عِلَّةٌ *pl.* عِلَل *and* عِلَّات ـ مَرَض *pl.* أَمْرَاض. After his long —, بَعْدَ مَرَضِهِ ٱلْمُزْمِنِ.

Illogical, *a.* Not according to logic, خِلَافُ قَوَاعِدِ ٱلْمَنْطِقِ. Incoherent, مَنْطِقٌ هُرَاءٌ ـ هُرَاءٌ.

Illogically, *ad.* بِخِلَافِ قَوَاعِدِ ٱلْمَنْطِقِ ـ بِهُرَاءٍ.

Illogicalness, *n.* نَقِيضُ قَوَاعِدِ ٱلْمَنْطِقِ ـ هُرَاءٌ.

Ill-omened, *a.* ذُو طَائِرٍ أَشْأَمَ ـ نَحِس ـ مَشْؤُوم.

Ill-provided, *a.* غَيْرُ مُجَهَّزٍ ـ عَدِيمُ ٱللَّوَازِمِ.

Ill-requited, *a.* بِلَا مُكَافَاةٍ ـ غَيْرُ مُثَوَّبٍ ـ غَيْرُ مُثَابٍ.

Ill-spoken of, *a.* Having a bad name, رَدِيءٌ ـ ذُو صِيتٍ رَدِيءٍ ـ رَدِيءُ ٱلصِّيتِ.

Ill-starred, *a.* مَنْهُوش ـ مَنْحُوس ـ نَحِس.

Ill-tempered, *a.* *See* Ill-natured, *a.*

Ill-timed, *a.* فِي غَيْرِ وَقْتِهِ ـ خَارِجٌ عَنْ وَقْتِهِ ـ فِي غَيْرِ مَحَلِّهِ.

Ill-treat, *v.t.* شَطَّ [2] ـ بَهْدَلَ ـ أَعْسَرَ ـ أَسَاءَ إِلَى.

Ill-treatment, *n.* شُطُوط ـ شَطٌّ ـ بَهْدَلَة ـ إِسَآءَة ـ إِعْسَار.

Ill-turn, *n.* An injurious act, قَبِيحَة *pl.* قَبَائِحُ ـ إِسَآءَة ـ سَيِّئَة. To do one an —, أَقْبَحَ إِلَى ـ أَسَاءَ إِلَى.

Illude, *v.t.* أَغْوَى ـ أَخْدَعَ ـ مَكَرَ بِ [2] ـ إِحْتَالَ عَلَى.

Ill-usage, *n.* Contempt, oppression, ظُلْم ـ إِسْتِخْفَاف ـ بَهْدَلَة ـ شُطُوط ـ شَطٌّ ـ جَفَآء. The act of spoiling, خُسْرَان ـ إِعْدَام; the being ill-used, spoilt, خُسْرَان ـ عُدْم.

Ill-use, *v.t.* To vilify, بَهْدَلَ ـ إِسْتَخَفَّ ـ شَطَّ [2]. To spoil, أَتْلَفَ ـ أَعْدَمَ ـ خَسَّرَ. Ill-used, oppressed, ذُو جَوْرٍ.

Illume, *v.t.* } **Illume**, } To brighten, أَضَآءَ ـ ضَوَّى ـ نَوَّرَ ـ أَنَارَ. To adorn, زَيَّنَ ـ زَخْرَفَ. To be illumined, brightened, تَضَوَّى.

Illuminate, *v.t.* To enlighten, instruct, عَلَّمَ ـ هَذَّبَ ـ فَطَّنَ ـ فَهَّمَ. To adorn with lamps, زَيَّنَ بِمَصَابِيحَ ـ أَوْقَدَ. To —, as of a book, زَوَّقَ ـ ذَهَّبَ ـ نَقَّشَ ـ زَخْرَفَ ـ دَبَّجَ.

Illuminated, *a.* Bright, light, مُضِيءٌ ـ ضَوِيٌّ. Adorned, as with pictures, *etc.*, مُزَوَّق ـ مَنْقُوش ـ مُزَخْرَف.

Illuminati, *n.* People claiming a superior inward light on some subject, طَائِفَةٌ تَدَّعِي بِٱلْإِلْهَامِ ٱلْبَاطِنِ ـ بَاطِنِيَّة. People bound together by an oath, مُتَحَالِفُونَ.

Illumination, *n.* The act of making luminous, تَنْوِير ـ إِضَآءَة; the being luminous, نُور ـ ضَوْءٌ. The act of instructing, إِنَارَةٌ ـ تَهْذِيب ـ تَفْهِيم ـ ٱلْعَقْلِ; the being enlightened, instructed, ذَكَآءٌ ـ فَهْم ـ نُورُ ٱلْعَقْلِ. Inspiration, وَحْي ـ إِلْهَام. A festal — with lamps, *etc.*, وَقِيد ـ زِينَةٌ بِمَصَابِيحَ ـ وَقْدَة. The act of illuminating, as of a book, *etc.*, زَخْرَفَة ـ نَقْش ـ تَزْوِيق ـ تَدْبِيج; the being illuminated, an embellishment, زُخْرُف ـ دِيبَاج ـ تَزْوِيقَة ـ تَزَاوِيقُ *pl.* تَزْوِيق ـ نَقْش.

Illuminative, *a.* مُنِير ـ مُضِيءٌ.

Illuminator, *n.* One who enlightens, مُنِير ـ مُضِيءٌ. An —, as of books, مُزَوِّق ـ زَوَّاق ـ مُزَخْرِف ـ مُذَهِّب ـ نَقَّاش.

Illusion, *n.* A false appearance, تَخَيُّل ـ تَصَوُّر ـ خَيَال. False hope, غُرُور. A deception, مَكْر ـ تَسْوِيل ـ خُدْعَة ـ حِيلَة.

Illusionist, *n.* غَاوٍ ـ غُرُورِيٌّ ـ خَيَالِيٌّ.

Illusive, *a.* } **Illusory**, } غَرَّار ـ خَيَالِيٌّ ـ غُرُورِيٌّ ـ غَاوٍ ـ يُغْوِي.

Illusively, *ad.* بِتَخَيُّلٍ ـ بِغُرُورٍ ـ بِتَسْوِيلٍ.

Illustrate, *v.t.* To elucidate, فَسَّرَ ـ شَرَّحَ ـ شَرَحَ ـ أَوْضَحَ ـ صَرَّحَ ـ بَيَّنَ. To discourse on, to interpret, عَبَّرَ عَنْ [2]. To make distinguished, أَجَلَّ ـ شَرَّفَ ـ أَعَزَّ. To explain by pictures, جَلَا بِٱلتَّصَاوِيرِ [2]. To adorn with pictures, حَسَّنَ بِٱلصُّوَرِ.

Illustrated, *a.* Expounded, مُصَرَّح ـ مُفَسَّر ـ مَشْرُوح. Distinguished, praised, مَحْمُود ـ مَمْدُوح ـ مَشْهُور. Illustrated with pictures, مُحَبَّرٌ (*or* مُرَقَّشٌ) بِٱلتَّصَاوِيرِ ـ مُزَوَّقٌ بِٱلصُّوَرِ.

Illustration, *n.* The act of explaining, تَفْسِير ـ شَرْح ـ إِيضَاح ـ تَصْرِيح. An example, عِبَارَة ـ مِثَال. A picture, تَزْوِيقَة *pl.* تَزَاوِيق ـ صُورَة *pl.* صُوَر ـ تَصْوِير *pl.* تَصَاوِيرُ.

Illustrative, *a.* Tending to explain, تَصْرِيحِيٌّ ـ إِيضَاحِيٌّ ـ شَرْحِيٌّ ـ ذُو تَأْوِيلٍ ـ مُبَيِّن.

Illustratively, *ad.* بأسلوب ـ بوجهِ التفسير ـ تبيينًا ـ بإيضاحٍ شرحيّ.

Illustrator, *n.* One who adorns with pictures, مُجبّر ـ زوّاق ـ مُزخرف ـ رقّاش.

Illustrious, *a.* مُفخّم ـ عزيز ـ أعزّ ـ جليل ـ شهير ـ سنيّ. Most — Sir, السيّدُ الكُلّيُّ الشرف ـ صاحبُ شهرةٍ ـ أمجد والجزيلُ الاحترام. To be or become —, جلّ *aor.* يجلّ ـ عزّ شرُف. To make —, عزّز ـ أعزّ ـ أجلّ ـ شرّف.

Illustriously, *ad.* بعزٍّ ـ عزّةٍ ـ بجلالٍ ـ بشهرةٍ ـ بفخرٍ ـ فخرةٍ.

Illustriousness, *n.* شرف ـ جلال ـ فخر ـ عزّة ـ عزّ ـ شأن فخرة ـ رفعة.

Ill-will, *n.* ضغن ـ حقد ـ بغض ـ عداوة. To bear — to, ضغن على ـ أبغض ـ حقد على.

I'm, *for* I am, أنا هو ـ أنا.

Image, *n.* The similitude of a person or thing, شكل *pl.* أشكال ـ شبهٌ *pl.* مشابهُ ـ دُميةٌ *pl.* دُمى ـ أيقونة *pl.* أيقونات ـ تمثال *pl.* تماثيل ـ صورة *pl.* صُور. An idol, نِدٌّ *pl.* أنداد ـ وثن *pl.* أوثان ـ صنم *pl.* أصنام. Shape, هيئة *pl.* هيئات ـ رسم. An idea, فكرة *pl.* فِكر ـ تخيّل ـ تصوّر. This is the — of him or it, هٰذا شبيهُهُ ; its express —, رسمٌ جوهريّ. Such an one is the — of you, فلانٌ شبيهُك. Sleep is the — of death, النومُ أخو الموت. A graven —, تمثالٌ منحوتٌ ; a molten —, تمثالٌ مسبوكٌ ; a standing or erect —, تمثالٌ نصبٌ ; a golden —, تمثالٌ من ذهبٍ. To make an —, idol, صنّم.

Image, *v.t.* To form, fashion, صوّر ـ شكّل. To form in idea, تصوّر ـ تخيّل ـ تخايل. It was imaged to his mind, or he imagined it, تشبّهَ لهُ ـ تصوّرَ لهُ ـ تخيّلَ لهُ. I imaged it in the mind, or fancied it, and it became imaged in the mind to me, صوّرتُهُ فتصوّرَ لي ـ خيّلتُهُ فتخيّلَ لي.

Imagery, *n.* Pictures, تماثيل ـ دُمى ـ مشابهُ ـ أيقونات ـ صُور ـ أشكال. Imaginations, تصوّرات ـ خيالات ـ تخيّلات. Figures, tropes, in discourse, مجاز *pl.* مجازات ـ عبارة *pl.* عبارات. The science of figures, علمُ البديع.

Image-worship, *n.* عبادةُ الأصنامِ ـ عبادةُ الأوثانِ ـ عبادةُ الصُوَر.

Imaginable, *a.* يتخيّل ـ يتصوّر ـ ممّا يخطرُ بالبالِ.

Imaginably, *ad.* بوجهِ التصوّرِ.

Imaginary, *a.* نظيريّ ـ خياليّ ـ وهميّ ـ تصوّريّ.

Imagination, *n.* The power of imagining, المخيّلة ـ الواهمة. The exercise of the —, مُتخيّلة. An image formed in the mind, تخيّل ـ تصوّر. An idea, خيال *pl.* أخيلة *and* خيلان ـ مُخيّل ـ تخيّل ـ تصوّر. A contrivance, إيجاد ـ اختراع ـ فطرة ـ بدعة. زعم ـ فكر.

Imaginative, *a.* خياليّ. Quick at imagining, سريعُ التخيّلِ ـ سريعُ الاختراعِ.

Imaginativeness, *n.* Quickness to imagine, سرعةُ التخيّلِ ـ سرعةُ الاختراعِ. *See also* Imagination, *n.*

Imagine, *v.t.* To form ideas in the mind, خيّل ـ تخيّل ـ تصوّر ـ توهّم ـ امتثل ـ تمثّل. To think, surmise, ظنّ ـ زعم. To contrive, أوجد ـ اخترع. I imagined, تصوّر لي ـ تخيّل لي. They — themselves to be good, يدّعون بالصلاحِ ـ يتوهّمون أنّهم من الصالحين. *See also under to* Image, *v.t.*

Imaum, *n.* (More correctly, Imâm), إمام *pl.* أيمّة *or* أئمّة.

Imband, *v.t.* حزّب. They imbanded themselves, of many, تحزّبوا.

Imbank, *v.t.* *See to* Embank, *v.t.*

Imbankment, *n.* *See* Embankment, *n.*

Imbathe, *v.t.* غسّل.

Imbecile, *n.* / Imbecile, *a.* } In mind, في عقلهِ هبتة ـ سخيفُ العقلِ ـ غبين ـ سفيه ـ أبله. To be —, طرق ـ غبن ـ سفه.

Imbecility, *n.* طرق ـ سفه ـ هبتة ـ غبانة ـ بلاهة ـ ركاكة العقلِ.

Imbed, *v.t.* أرسى ـ ركز ـ رصّع. To imbed in earth, رمس في التراب.

Imbibe, *v.t.* To drink, شرب. To suck up, نشف ـ تنشّف ـ شرّب ـ تشرّب. To receive and retain, اتّخذ ـ حصّل ـ استفاد.

Imbibition, *n.* The act of drinking, شرب ; of sucking up, نشف ـ تنشيف ـ تشريب.

Imbitter, *v.t.* To make bitter, أمرّ ـ مرّر. To make unhappy, نكّد ـ أشقى.

Imbodiment, *n.* *See* Embodiment, *n.*

Imbody, *v.t.* *See to* Embody, *v.t.*

Imborder, *v.t.* *See to* Border, Edge, *v.t.*

Imbosk, *v.t.* *See to* Embower, *v.t.*

Imbosom, *v.t.* To hold in the bosom, حضن ـ احتضن. To hold in intimacy, آلف ـ أعزّ. To surround with, أحاط ب.

Imbow, *v.t.* *See to* Bow, *v.t.*

Imbricate, *a.* / Imbricated, } Hollowed, مجوّب ـ مجوّف. Lapping over, متركّب ـ متراكب. Convolvulated, ملفّف ـ ملفوف.

Imbrication, *n.* A concave indenture, تَجَوُّب ـ تَجْوِيف . Convolution, إِلْفَاف ـ تَلَفُّف .

Imbroglio, *n.* إِلْتِبَاس ـ مُشَاجَرَة ـ فَسَاد ـ مَغْلَطَة ـ هَمْرَجَة ـ وَرْطَة ـ إِلْتِبَاك .

Imbrown, *v.t.* *See to* Brown, *v.t.*

Imbrue, *v.t.* To steep, soak, غَمَسَ ـ أَنْقَعَ ـ فِي ـ مَرَسَ . To — with blood, خَضَبَ ـ دَمَّى ـ رَمَّلَ ـ مَرَثَ ـ لَثَّ ـ لَطَخَ ـ (or) بِٱلدَّمِ .

Imbrute, *v.t.* *See to* Brutalize, Degrade, *v.t.*

Imbue, *v.t.* To cause to imbibe, شَرَّبَ ـ أَشْرَبَ . To tinge, صَبَّغَ ـ صَبَغَ . To cause to take in, learn, عَلَّمَ ـ أَشْرَبَ ـ دَرَّبَ ـ ب . He was imbued with the love of such an one, أُشْرِبَ بِحُبِّ فُلَانٍ .

Imburse, *v.t.* To supply with money, أَعْطَى ـ فُلُوسًا ـ أَمَدَّ ـ بِدَرَاهِمَ .

Imbursement, *n.* The act of imbursing money, إِمْدَادٌ بِٱلدَّرَاهِمِ . Money laid up, سَرْمَايَة ـ رَأْسُ مَالٍ .

Imitable, *a.* التَّمَثُّلُ بِهِ مُمْكِنٌ ـ يُقْتَدَى ب ـ الإِقْتِدَاءُ بِهِ مُمْكِنٌ .

Imitate, *v.t.* To follow in manners, إِحْتَذَى ب ـ إِئْتَمَّ ـ حَاكَمَ ـ إِتَّبَعَ ـ تَمَثَّلَ ب ـ إِقْتَدَى ب ـ تَسَنَّنَ ب . To counterfeit, زَوَّرَ ـ قَلَّدَ . To copy in form, to make to resemble, مَثَّلَ ـ ب ـ شَبَّهَ ـ ب .

Imitation, *n.* The act of copying, تَمْثِيل ـ تَشْبِيه ; of following, as in manners, إِهْتِدَاء ب ـ إِقْتِدَاء ب ـ مُحَاكَاة ـ مُتَابَعَة ـ تَمَثُّل ب . A copy, مَنْقُول عَن ـ نُسْخَة ـ مِثَال . A resemblance, شُبْهَة ـ مُشَاكَلَة ـ شَبَه ـ مُشَابَهَة ـ مُحَاكَاة . *See also* Counterfeit, *n.*

Imitative, *a.* تَقْلِيدِيّ ـ مُتَابِع ـ مُتَتَبِّع ـ مُخِيل لِلْإِقْتِدَاء ب .

Imitatively, *ad.* إِمْتِثَالًا ب ـ إِقْتِدَاء ب ـ مُتَابَعَةً ـ إِتِّبَاعًا .

Imitator, *n.* As in manners, مُمْتَثِل ب ـ مُقْتَدٍ ب ـ مُحَاكٍ ـ تُبَّع *pl.* تَابِع . One who copies or counterfeits, مُقَلِّد ـ مُفْتَر .

Immaculate, *a.* مُنَزَّهٌ عَنِ ٱلْعُيُوبِ ـ عَدِيمُ ٱلدَّنَسِ ـ طَاهِر ـ عَفِيف . Immaculate conception, الحَبَلُ بِلَا دَنَسٍ . The — Conception, حَبَلُ مَرْيَمَ ٱلْعَذْرَاءِ ٱلْعَفِيفُ .

Immaculately, *ad.* بِعِفَّةٍ ـ بِلَا دَنَسٍ ـ بِطَهَارَةٍ .

Immaculateness, *n.* عِصْمَة ـ عِفَّة ـ عَدَمُ دَنَسٍ ـ طَهَارَة .

Immalleable, *a.* لا يُمْطَلُ .

Immaterial, *a.* Incorporeal, غَيْرُ جَسَدِيّ ـ غَيْرُ هَيُولِي ـ مُجَرَّد ـ رُوحِيّ . Unimportant, نَقِير ـ غَيْرُ مُهِمّ ـ غَيْرُ ضَرُورِيّ ـ تَافِه ـ خَفِيف ـ يَسِير .

Immaterialism, *n.* القَوْلُ بِوُجُودِ ٱلْكَائِنَاتِ ٱلرُّوحِيَّةِ .

Immaterialist, *n.* القَائِلُ بِوُجُودِ ٱلْكَائِنَاتِ ٱلرُّوحِيَّةِ .

Immateriality, *n.* } Incorporeality, عَدَم ـ تَجَرُّد مِنَ ٱلْجَسَدِ ـ
Immaterialness, } الغَيْر ـ الخُلُوُّ مِنَ ٱلْجِسْمِ ـ ٱلْمَادَّةِ ـ رُوحِيَّة ـ ٱلْهَيُولِيَّة .

Immaterially, *ad.* As not depending on matter, بِنَوْعٍ غَيْرِ بِمُجَرَّدِ ٱلرُّوحِ ـ هَيُولِي . Without importance, مِنْ غَيْرِ ضَرُورَةٍ ـ لا مُهِمَّةَ لَهُ .

Immature, *a.* } Unripe, غَيْرُ مُسْتَوٍ ـ غَيْرُ نَاضِجٍ ـ فِجّ . Not per-
Immatured, } fect, غَيْرُ تَامٍّ . Hasty, عَاجِل ـ فَطِير . Out of its time, فِي غَيْرِ أَوَانِهِ . Beware of — opinion, إِيَّاكَ وَٱلرَّأْيَ ٱلْفَطِيرَ . The worst opinion is that which is —, (*prov.*) شَرُّ ٱلرَّأْيِ ٱلْفَطِيرُ .

Immaturely, *ad.* Before its time, قَبْلَ ٱلْأَوَانِ . Without mental digestion, بِفَطْرٍ .

Immatureness, *n.* } Unripeness, فَجَاجَة . Incompleteness, عَدَمُ
Immaturity, } نُقْصَان ـ كَمَالٍ . Hasty opinion, فَطِير .

Immeasurable, *a.* غَيْرُ ـ بِلَا قِيَاسٍ ـ لا حَدَّ ل ـ غَيْرُ مُتَنَاهٍ ـ مَحْدُودٍ .

Immeasurableness, *n.* عَدَمُ قِيَاسٍ ـ عَدَمُ حَدٍّ .

Immeasureably, *ad.* بِلَا قِيَاسٍ ـ بِدُونِ حَدٍّ . Much, very much, لِلْغَايَةِ ـ جِدًّا ـ كَثِيرًا .

Immediate, *a.* Acting without a medium, مِنْ غَيْرِ وَاسِطَةٍ ـ مُؤَثِّر ـ مُلَازِم ـ رَأْسِيّ ـ ذَاتِيّ . Proximate, efficient, الأَقْرَب . Instant, فِي ٱلْحَالِ ـ حَاضِر ـ مُؤَقَّت . Immediately following, مُتَلَاحِق ب ـ مُتَوَاصِل ب ـ تَابِع ـ أَقْرَبُ إِلَى . He requires an — answer, يَطْلُبُ جَوَابًا فِي ٱلْحَالِ .

Immediately, *ad.* Without intervention, ذَاتًا ـ بِلَا وَاسِطَةٍ ـ رَأْسًا . Instantly, مِنْ فَوْرٍ ـ عَلَى ٱلْفَوْرِ ـ حَالًا ـ فِي ٱلْحَالِ ـ السَّاعَةَ .

Immediateness, *n.* Exemption from intervening causes, ذَاتِيَّة ـ عَدَمُ تَوَسُّطٍ . Instantaneousness, فُجَاءَة ـ فَوْر .

Immedicable, *a.* لا شِفَاءَ لَهُ ـ لا يُعَالَجُ .

Immelodious, *a.* غَيْرُ مُطْرِبٍ ـ بِلَا نَغَمٍ .

Immemorial, *a.* قَدِيم ـ قَبْلَ كُلِّ تَارِيخٍ ـ لا يُعْرَفُ لَهُ زَمَنٌ . From time —, مِنْ زَمَانٍ مُنْدَرِسِ ٱلذِّكْرِ .

Immemorially, *ad.* مِنْ زَمَنٍ لا يُعْرَفُ لَهُ ذِكْرٌ ـ مِنْ قَبْلِ كُلِّ تَارِيخٍ .

Immense, *a.* Huge in bulk, عَظِيمٌ جِدًّا ; in extent, مَدِيدٌ جِدًّا ; in breadth, وَاسِعٌ جِدًّا . Without bounds, لا حَدَّ لَهُ ـ بِلَا قِيَاسٍ ـ غَيْرُ مَحْصُورٍ ـ بِدُونِ حَدٍّ . Downright, altogether, بَتِّيّ ـ كُلِّيّ .

Immensely, *ad.* بَتَّةً ـ كَثِيرًا ـ جِدًّا ـ كُلِّيًّا .

Immenseness, *n.* } عِظَم ـ إِمْتِدَادٌ كُلِّيّ ـ إِتِّسَاعٌ غَيْرُ مَحْدُودٍ ـ
Immensity, } كُبْر .

Immensurability, *n.* عَدَمُ قِيَاسٍ ـ عَدَمُ مُقَايَسَةٍ.

Immensurable, *a.* لا يُقَاسُ.

Immerge, *v.t.* } To plunge, as into a fluid, غَمَّسَ-فِي ـ أَغَطَّ-فِي ـ أَغْرَقَ-(or) ـ غَطَّسَ-or-غَمَسَ-) فِي. To be immerged, immersed, in, إِغْتَمَرَ فِي ـ إِنْغَمَرَ فِي ـ إِنْغَطَّ فِي ـ إِنْغَمَسَ فِي.
Immerse,

He immersed himself in the water, إِرْتَمَسَ (or) إِنْغَمَسَ) فِي ٱلْمَآءِ. To be immersed in a discourse, أَفَاضَ فِي ـ سَابَ فِي ٱلْكَلَامِ ٱلْكَلَامِ. They immersed themselves in the sea, of many, تَغَاطُّوا تَغَاطَسُوا فِي ٱلْبَحْرِ ـ فِي ٱلْبَحْرِ.

Immersion, *n.* The act of plunging something into, غَمْسٌ ـ غَطْسٌ ـ تَغْرِيقٌ ـ أَغْرَاقٌ. The state of being immersed, غُطُوسٌ ـ غَرَقٌ.

Immethodical, *a.* Without arrangement, بِلا نَسَقٍ ـ غَيْرُ مُهَنْدَمٍ ـ بِلا تَرْتِيبٍ ـ مُشَوَّشٌ ـ بِلا نِظَامٍ ـ غَيْرُ مُرَتَّبٍ; of a person, فَرْفَارٌ ـ طَيَّاشٌ ـ طَائِشٌ.

Immigrant, *n.* مُوَطِّنٌ ـ مُهَاجِرٌ *pl.* مُهَاجِرُونَ.

Immigrate, *v.t.* إِتَّطَنَ ـ وَطَّنَ ـ سَيَّرَ-إِلَى ٱلْمُهَاجَرَةِ.

Immigration, *n.* تَوْطِينٌ ـ مُهَاجَرَةٌ.

Imminence, *n.* A hanging over, إِشْرَافٌ عَلَى. The being at the point of occurrence, قُرْبُ ٱلْوُقُوعِ ـ إِشْرَافٌ عَلَى ـ وَشْكٌ. We prognosticated the — of war between them, قَدْ أَنْبَأْنَا بِوَشْكِ ٱلْحَرْبِ بَيْنَهُمْ.

Imminent, *a.* Overlooking, مُطِلٌّ عَلَى ـ مُشْرِفٌ عَلَى. About to happen, قَرِيبُ ٱلْوُقُوعِ ـ قَرِيبٌ ـ مُزْمِعٌ ـ مُطِفٌّ.

Immiscibility, *n.* عَدَمُ مُخَالَطَةٍ ـ عَدَمُ قَابِلِيَّةِ ٱلْمَزْجِ.

Immiscible, *a.* لا يُخْلَطُ ـ غَيْرُ قَابِلِ ٱلْمَزْجِ.

Immission, *n.* The act of sending in, إِدْخَالٌ.

Immit, *v.t.* أَدْخَلَ.

Immitigable, *a.* لا يُفَتَّرُ ـ لا يُخْمَدُ ـ لا يُنْقَصُ.

Immix, *v.t.* خَلَطَ ـ شَمَّطَ ـ مَازَجَ ـ مَزَجَ-بِ.

Immobility, *n.* Quiescence, عَدَمُ حَرَكَةٍ ـ سُكُونٌ ـ جُمُودٌ. Unchangeableness, عَدَمُ تَغْيِيرٍ. The state of being unmoved, ثَبَاتٌ. Resistance, مُدَافَعَةٌ ـ مُقَاوَمَةٌ ـ عِنَادٌ ـ مُعَانَدَةٌ.

Immoderate, *a.* مُنْتَهِزٌ ـ جَائِزُ ٱلْحَدِّ ـ زَائِدٌ ـ مُفْرِطٌ. Immoderate praise, تَقْرِيظٌ ـ تَفْرِيطٌ. To be — in, أَغْرَبَ (or) إِسْتَغْرَبَ) فِي ـ أَفْرَطَ فِي ـ إِنْتَهَزَ فِي ـ أَسْرَفَ فِي.

Immoderately, *ad.* بِزِيَادَةٍ ـ بِإِفْرَاطٍ. To act — in . . . , أَفْرَطَ فِي. To praise —, فَرَّطَ ـ قَرَّظَ.

Immoderateness, *n.* } إِسْرَافٌ ـ إِفْرَاطٌ ـ عَدَمُ ٱعْتِدَالٍ ـ إِنْتِهَازٌ.
Immoderation,

Immodest, *a.* Without shame, سَفِيهٌ ـ قَلِيلُ ٱلْحَيَآءِ. Obscene, قَبِيحٌ ـ دَاعِرٌ ـ فَاسِدٌ ـ فَاحِشٌ ـ خَنٍ ـ بَذِيٌّ ـ رَفِثٌ. To use — language, أَفْحَشَ فِي ٱلْكَلَامِ.

Immodestly, *ad.* بِلا حِشْمَةٍ ـ بِسَفَاهَةٍ ـ بِقِلَّةِ حَيَآءٍ.

Immodesty, *n.* فَحَاشَةٌ ـ فُحْشٌ ـ دَعَارَةٌ ـ سَفَاهَةٌ ـ قِلَّةُ حَيَآءٍ.

An immodest act, فَاحِشَةٌ *pl.* فَوَاحِشُ.

Immolate, *v.t.* To sacrifice, قَرَّبَ ضَحِيَّةً ـ قَدَّمَ ذَبِيحَةً ـ ذَبَحَ. To kill, قَتَلَ ـ ذَبَحَ.

Immolation, *n.* The act of sacrificing, تَقْدِيمٌ ـ ذَبْحٌ ـ تَضْحِيَةٌ; the sacrifice offered up, ذَبِيحَةٌ *pl.* ذَبَائِحُ ـ ضَحِيَّةٌ *pl.* ٱلذَّبَائِحِ ضَحَايَا. The act of killing, قَتْلٌ ـ ذَبْحٌ.

Immolator, *n.* ذَبَّاحٌ ـ ذَابِحٌ.

Immoral, *a.* Of a person, فَاسِدٌ ـ فَاجِشٌ ـ دَاعِرٌ ـ خَلِيعٌ ـ طَالِحٌ ـ سَفِيهٌ ـ فَاسِقٌ ـ فَاجِرٌ ـ قَبِيحٌ. To be —, to act immorally, فَحُشَ ـ فَسَقَ ـ أَفْجَرَ ـ فَجَرَ ـ دَعِرَ. An — action, قَبَاحَةٌ *pl.* قَبَائِحُ ـ فَحَاشَةٌ ـ خَلَاعَةٌ. To be —, vicious, خَلُعَ.

Immorality, *n.* قُبْحٌ ـ فَسَادٌ ـ فُحْشٌ ـ فُجُورٌ ـ خَلَاعَةٌ ـ دِعَارَةٌ ـ قَبَاحَةٌ ـ رَدَآءَةُ ٱلْأَخْلَاقِ ـ طَلَاحٌ ـ فِسْقٌ ـ سَفَاهَةٌ. To charge with —, فَجَّرَ.

Immorally, *ad.* بِفُجُورٍ ـ بِفَسَادٍ ـ بِرَدَآءَةِ ٱلْأَخْلَاقِ ـ بِخَلَاعَةٍ.

Immortal, *a.* Undying, عَدِيمُ ٱلْمَوْتِ ـ لا يَفْنَى ـ لا يَمُوتُ. Eternal, أَبَدِيٌّ ـ ذُو أَبَدٍ ـ سَرْمَدِيٌّ ـ مُخَلَّدٌ ـ ذُو خُلُودٍ ـ دَائِمٌ ـ بَاقٍ. The Immortal (God), ٱلْقَيُّومُ ـ ٱلْحَيُّ ـ وَاجِبُ ٱلْوُجُودِ. Of — memory, مُخَلَّدُ ٱلذِّكْرِ.

Immortality, *n.* Immortal existence, عَدَمٌ ـ عَدَمُ مَوْتٍ ـ بَقَآءٌ ـ ٱلْمَوْتِ. Perpetuity, بَقَآءٌ ـ أَبَدٌ ـ دَوَامٌ ـ خُلُودٌ.

Immortalize, *v.t.* To make immortal, صَيَّرَ-عَدِيمَ ٱلْمَوْتِ. To make perpetual, أَبْقَى ـ أَدَامَ ـ أَبَّدَ ـ أَخْلَدَ ـ خَلَّدَ.

Immortally, *ad.* With endless existence, تَأْبِيدًا ـ بِلا مَوْتٍ ـ بِدُونِ زَوَالٍ ـ أَبَدًا ـ دَائِمًا.

Immovability, *n.* } The property of not being movable, جُمُودٌ ـ عَدَمُ تَزَعْزُعٍ ـ عَدَمُ تَنَقُّلٍ. Stedfastness, رُسُوخٌ ـ ثُبُوتٌ. The property of receiving no impression, عَدَمُ تَأَثُّرٍ.
Immovableness,

Immovable, *a.* Not capable of being moved, لا ـ لا يُنْتَقَلُ يَتَزَعْزَعُ ـ يَتَحَرَّكُ. Motionless, by reason of disease, *etc.*, رَاكِزٌ ـ مُتَمَكِّنٌ ـ رَاسِخٌ ـ ثَابِتٌ ـ مُثْبِتٌ. Inert, جَامِدٌ. Firm, ثَابِتٌ. Not susceptible of tender feelings, قَاسٍ ـ عَدِيمُ ٱلرَّحْمَةِ. Immovable property, عَقَارٌ ـ مِلْكٌ ثَابِتٌ لا يَنْتَقِلُ. Receiving no impression, لا يُؤَثِّرُ فِيهِ شَيْءٌ. To be —, firm, رَسَخَ - ثَبَتَ. To become —, as a stranded ship, *etc.*, اِرْتَكَزَ. To make —, firm, أَرْسَخَ.

Immovables, *n.* Real estate, عَقَار *pl.* عَقَارَات - مِلْك *pl.* أَمْلَاك.

Immovably, *ad.* Without motion, بِدُونِ - بِلَا تَحَرُّكٍ - بِجُمُودٍ; firmly, بِرُسُوخٍ - بِثُبُوتٍ - زَعْزَعَةٍ.

Immunity, *n.* Safety, أَمْن - سَلَام - سَلَامَة. Exemption from, بَرَآءَة مِن - إِعْفَآء مِن - مُعَافَاة مِن. A charter of —, بَرَآءَة. Immunity from punishment, الأَمْنُ مِنَ الْعِقَابِ. Immunities, privileges, اِمْتِيَازَات.

Immure, *v.t.* To inclose in walls, أَحَاطَ-بِحِيطَانٍ. To confine, حَبَسَ.

Immusical, *a.* غَيْرُ مُطْرِبٍ - غَيْرُ مَلْحُونٍ; *Persian*, نَشَاز.

Immutability, *n.* / **Immutableness**, } تَنَزُّهٌ عَنِ التَّغْيِيرِ - عَدَمُ تَبْدِيلٍ - عَدَمُ تَغَيُّرٍ - ثَبَات.

Immutable, *a.* ثَابِت - عَدِيمُ التَّغْيِيرِ - غَيْرُ مُتَغَيِّرٍ - لَا يَتَغَيَّرُ.

Immutably, *ad.* بِثُبُوتٍ - بِدُونِ تَغَيُّرٍ - بِلَا تَبْدِيلٍ - بِلَا تَغْيِيرٍ.

Imp, *n.* قُطْرُب *pl.* قَطَارِب - شَيْطَان *pl.* شَيَاطِين.

Impact, *v.t.* To drive close together, كَبَسَ - رَصَّصَ - رَصَّ. To make tight, شَدَّ - حَزَقَ - وَكَّدَ.

Impact, *n.* The act of striking against another body, صِدَام - مُصَادَمَة. A shock, blow, صَدْمَة - مُصَادَمَة.

Impair, *v.t.* To make worse, spoil, أَعْدَمَ - خَرَّبَ - أَفْسَدَ - أَتْلَفَ. To weaken, أَضْعَفَ - أَوْنَى; as a disease does, وَهَّنَ - أَنْقَطَ - أَضَرَّ - ضَارَّ - أَضْعَفَ - هَبَطَ - أَفْتَرَ - أَوْهَنَ. To injure, ثَلَمَ. To be impaired, injured, wounded, اِنْثَلَمَ; to be weakened, وَهَنَ *aor.* يَهِنُ; to be injured, damaged, hurt, اِنْضَرَّ; to be spoiled, تَلِفَ - خَسَّرَ - خَسِرَ.

Impair, *n.* / **Impairment**, } Damage, a defect, خَلَل - ضَرَر - نُقْصَان - دَرَك - عَوَار - سَقْط - خُسْرَان.

Impale, *v.t.* *See to* Empale, *v.t.*

Impalpability, *n.* عَدَمُ قَابِلِيَّةِ اللَّمْسِ - غَايَةُ دِقَّةٍ.

Impalpable, *a.* دَقِيق (or نَاعِم) لِلْغَايَةِ - لَا يُلْمَسُ.

Impalpably, *ad.* بِطَرِيقَةٍ لَا تُلْمَسُ - بِوَجْهٍ لَا يُشْعَرُ بِلَمْسِهِ.

Impanation, *n.* *See* Consubstantiation, *n.*

Impannel, *v.t.* دَوَّنَ أَسْمَآءَ الْوُكَلَاءِ لِفَحْصِ جُنَاحٍ.

Imparity, *n.* *See* Disparity, *n.*

Impark, *v.t.* To inclose for a park, صَيَّرَ حَدِيقَةً.

Impart, *v.t.* To give, وَهَبَ *aor.* يَهَبُ - أَعْطَى - أَفْضَى إِلَى-بِ - أَوْقَفَ-عَلَى - أَلْقَى عَلَى. To make known to, أَفَادَ-بِ - أَخْبَرَ - أَطْلَعَ-عَلَى - عَرَّفَ-بِ. To make another a sharer in, أَعْطَى-مِن - أَشْرَكَ-فِي. To — instruction, عَلَّمَ. *See also to* Disclose, Grant, Confer, *v.t.*

Impartation, *n.* إِفْضَآء - إِفَادَة - إِعْطَآء - وَهْب.

Impartial, *a.* Free from bias, عَدِيمُ التَّعَصُّبِ - عَدِيمُ الْمُحَابَاةِ - عَدِيمُ الْغَرَضِ. Upright, equitable, مُنْصِف - مُقْسِط - مُسْتَقِيم - عَادِل.

Impartiality, *n.* Freedom from bias, عَدَم - عَدَمُ مُحَابَاةٍ - عَدَمُ غَرَضٍ - تَعَصُّبٍ. Equity, إِنْصَاف - اِسْتِقَامَة - قِسْط. To act with —, اِنْتَصَفَ - أَنْصَفَ.

Impartially, *ad.* بِقِسْطٍ - مِنْ غَيْرِ غَرَضٍ - بِدُونِ مُحَابَاةٍ - بِالْعَدْلِ - بِإِنْصَافٍ. To act —, أَقْسَطَ - قَسَطَ.

Impartible, *a.* Not divisible, لَا يَنْقَسِمُ - تَقْسِيمُهُ غَيْرُ مُمْكِنٍ. That cannot be given, لَا يُعْطَى - وَهْبُهُ غَيْرُ مُمْكِنٍ. That cannot be communicated, said, لَا يُقَالُ - لَا يُلْفَظُ بِهِ - لَا يُطْلَعُ عَلَيْهِ.

Impassable, *a.* That cannot be passed, عُبُورُهُ - سُلُوكُهُ مُحَال - غَيْرُ سَالِكٍ - غَيْرُ مُمْكِنٍ - الْمُرُورُ بِهِ غَيْرُ مُمْكِنٍ. Without a passage, لَا طَرِيقَ لَهُ - غَيْرُ نَافِذٍ.

Impassableness, *n.* عَدَمُ إِمْكَانِ - الْعُبُورُ (or الْمُرُورُ) بِهِ مُحَال - عَدَمُ التَّطَرُّقِ إِلَيْهِ - السُّلُوكُ فِيهِ.

Impassibility, *n.* / **Impassibleness**, } عَدَم - عَدَمُ الْأَلَمِ - عَدَمُ قَبُولِ الْآلَامِ - التَّأَلُّم.

Impassible, *a.* غَيْرُ مُتَأَلِّمٍ - لَا يَتَأَلَّمُ - غَيْرُ قَابِلٍ لِلْأَلَمِ.

Impassion, *v.t.* To affect with passion, desire, اِشْتَهَى - أَنْفَسَ - حَرَّضَ - حَمَّى - حَضَّضَ. To inspirit, أَوْلَعَ-بِ.

Impassionable, *a.* يَنْفَسُ - أَمَّارٌ لِلْأَهْوَآءِ.

Impassionate, *v.t.* أَغْرَمَ - اِشْتَهَى - أَنْفَسَ - أَوْلَعَ.

Impassionate, *a.* Strongly affected, عَذُور - مُنْفَس - مُوَلَّع. Without passion, بَارِد - بِدُونِ غَرَامٍ.

Impassioned, *a.* مُهَيَّج - مُحَرَّض - مُغْرَم.

Impassive, *a.* *See* Impassible, *a.*

Impassively, *ad.* مِنْ غَيْرِ تَأَثُّرٍ - بِدُونِ تَأَلُّمٍ.

Impassiveness, *n.* / **Impassivity**, } *See* Impassibility, *n.*

Impastation, *n.* The act of impasting, عَجْن; the things impasted, عَجِين.

Impaste, *v.t.* To knead, عَجَنَ. To lay on colours thick, أَفْرَطَ فِي الْأَلْوَانِ - يَزِيدُ *aor.* زَادَ فِي التَّلْوِينِ.

Impatience, *n.* قِلَّةُ صَبْرٍ - هَلَع - جُوَاظ - جُزُوع - جَزَع -

عَدَمُ تَحَمُّلٍ. Impatience is impiety, but patience is always rewarded, (*prov.*) مَنْ لَجَّ كَفَرَ وَمَنْ صَبَرَ نَالَ.

Impatient, *a.* قَلِيلُ ٱلصَّبْرِ ـ هَلُوع ـ جَازِع ـ جَزِع. To be —of, جَزِعَ مِن ـ هَلِعَ. To make one —, أَجْزَعَ. To be —, anxious, ضَجِرَ بِ (or مِن) ـ ضَاقَ صَدْرُهُ ـ جَوَّظَ. To make one —, anxious, أَضْجَرَ.

Impatiently, *ad.* بِضَجَرٍ ـ بِدُونِ صَبْرٍ ـ بِجَزَعٍ.

Impawn, *v.t.* *See to* Pawn, *v.t.*

Impeach, *v.t.* To assert or charge against, جَوَّرَ ـ إِدَّعَى عَلَى ـ أَقْرَفَ بِ ـ أَتْهَمَ بِ ـ إِشْتَكَى عَلَى. To summons, دَعَا بِ *aor.* يَدْعُو ـ إِسْتَدْعَى. To call in question, قَرَفَ بِ ـ تَشَكَّكَ فِي ـ أَتْهَمَ بِ. To attribute anything to, نَسَبَ إِلَى; by way of reproach, عَيَّرَ بِ. To denounce to the authorities, بَلَّغَ ٱلْحُكْمَ بِ ـ أَعْلَمَ ٱلْحُكْمَ بِ.

Impeachable, *a.* تَحْتَ ٱلشِّكَايَةِ ـ مُتَعَرِّضٌ لِلْاِشْتِكَاءِ عَلَيْهِ ـ مُتَّهَم ـ يُحَاكَمُ مِنْ أَجْلِهِ ـ وَمَّا يُتَّهَمُ بِهِ. Doubtful, مَشْكُوك.

Impeacher, *n.* مُجَوِّر ـ مُبَلِّغ ـ مُقْرِف ـ شَاكٍ.

Impeachment, *n.* The act of, إِشْتِكَاء ـ إِتْهَام ـ إِقْرَاف ـ تَجْوِير عَلَى. An accusation, قَرَف ـ تُهَمَة ـ شِكَايَة.

Impeccability, *n.* عِصْمَةٌ مِنَ ٱلْخَطَاءِ ـ تَنَزُّهٌ عَنِ ٱلذُّنُوبِ.

Impeccable, *a.* مَعْصُوم ـ مَعْصُومٌ مِنَ ٱلْإِثْمِ ـ مُتَنَزِّهٌ عَنِ ٱلذُّنُوبِ.

Impede, *v.t.* آنَى ـ حَجَزَ ـ خَزَلَ عَن ـ كَبَحَ عَن ـ كَبَعَ ـ عَاقَ عَن ـ عَجَزَ عَن ـ مَنَعَ عَن. To be impeded, تَمَنَّعَ ـ إِنْحَجَزَ ـ تَعَوَّقَ.

Impeder, *n.* *See* Obstructor, *n.*

Impediment, *n.* خَزْل ـ مُمَانَعَة ـ عُرْضَة ـ عَائِق *pl.* عَوَائِق ـ مَانِع *pl.* مَوَانِعُ: An —, or an impeder, hindered me, عَاقَنِي عَائِقٌ ـ عَاقَنِي عَانٍ. An obstruction, سَدٌّ *pl.* أَسْدَاد. An — in speech, عُقْدَة ـ رَتَج ـ طَمْطَمَة ـ غُتْمَة; having an — in speech, أَعْقَدُ ـ أَرْتَلُ ـ أَرَتُّ ـ طِمْطِم. Impedimenta to a traveller, وَضَائِعُ *pl.* وَضِيعَة ـ أَثْقَال. He has an — in his speech, فِي لِسَانِهِ عُقْدَة ـ فِي كَلَامِهِ رَتَج. Should they meet with no — from the Government, إِذَا لَمْ يَحْصُلْ لَهُمْ مَانِعٌ مِنَ ٱلْحُكُومَةِ.

Impedimental, *a.* عَائِق ـ مَانِع ـ حَاجِز.

Impel, *v.t.* To drive forward, دَسَرَ ـ سَاقَ *aor.* يَسُوقُ ـ سَوَّقَ ـ دَفَعَ. To excite to, هَزَّ عَلَى *aor.* يَهُزُّ ـ حَرَّضَ عَلَى ـ حَثَّ عَلَى ـ أَزَّ عَلَى ـ أَنْهَضَ عَلَى. To be impelled, driven, تَدَافَعَ. To be impelled, urged, إِنْحَثَّ.

Impellent, *a.* دَاسِر ـ دَافِع ـ سَوَّاق. Exciting, حَاثٌّ ـ مُنْهِض ـ مُحَرِّض.

Impellent, *n.* An impelling power, قُوَّةٌ دَافِعَةٌ ـ قُوَّةٌ دَاسِعَةٌ ـ قُوَّةٌ مُحَرِّكَةٌ.

Impend, *v.i.* To hang over, أَشْرَفَ عَلَى. To be near, to happen, to threaten, دَنَا ـ قَرُبَ مِن ـ عَتُدَ ـ هَمَّ بِ *aor.* يَدْنُو ـ أَوْشَكَ أَن ـ يُوشِكُ *aor.* وَشُكَ أَن. The matter impended, يُوشِكُ ٱلْأَمْرُ أَن يَكُونَ.

Impendence, *n.* / Impendency, } A hanging over, مُشْرَف ـ شَرَف ـ مُشْرِف.

Impendent, *a.* / Impending, } Hanging over, مُشْرِفٌ عَلَى. Approaching near, about to happen, قَرِيبُ ٱلْوُقُوعِ ـ هَامٌّ بِ ـ عَتِيد ـ قَرِيبٌ مِن ـ مُزْمِع. Instant, حَاضِر. An — danger, خَطَرٌ قَرِيبُ ٱلْوُقُوعِ.

Impenetrability, *n.* Quality of not being capable of being pierced, عَدَمُ ٱلنُّفُوذِ ـ كَوْنُ ٱلشَّيْءِ لَا يُمْكِنُ ٱلنُّفُوذُ فِيهِ; of not being discoverable, عِصْمَةٌ مِنَ ٱلْاِسْتِقْصَاءِ فِيهِ ـ عِصْمَةٌ مِنَ ٱلْفَحْصِ فِيهِ.

Impenetrable, *a.* Not to be pierced, لَا يَتَطَرَّقُ إِلَيْهِ ـ لَا يُنْفَذُ ـ النُّفُوذُ فِيهِ مُحَال ـ فِيهِ. Undiscoverable, بَعِيدٌ عَنِ ـ لَا يُفْحَصُ ـ لَا يُعْرَفُ ـ الْكَشْفُ عَنْهُ مُحَال ـ لَا يُدْرَكُ ـ ٱلْاِسْتِقْصَاء. Not to be moved, غَيْرُ مُؤَثِّرٍ فِيهِ ـ لَا يُؤَثِّرُ فِيهِ شَيْءٌ. Not passable, غَيْرُ سَالِكٍ. Stupid, بَلِيد ـ غَلِيظُ ٱلذِّهْنِ. An — thicket, حَرَج. How — are his judgments! مَا أَبْعَدَ أَحْكَامَهُ عَنِ ٱلْفَحْصِ.

Impenetrably, *ad.* بِنَوْعٍ لَا يُتَطَرَّقُ إِلَيْهِ ـ بِعَدَمِ نُفُوذٍ فِيهِ. As a superlative, wholly, altogether, بِٱلْكُلِّيَّةِ ـ لِلْغَايَةِ ـ بَتَّةً.

Impenitence, *n.* / Impenitency, } عَدَمُ ٱسْتِغْفَارٍ ـ عَدَمُ نَدَامَةٍ ـ عَدَمُ ٱلتَّوْبَةِ ـ قَسَاوَةُ قَلْبٍ ـ عِنَاد ـ عُتُوّ.

Impenitent, *a.* قَاسِي ـ عَتِيّ ـ عَاتٍ ـ غَيْرُ نَادِمٍ ـ غَيْرُ تَائِبٍ. An — heart, قَلْبٌ غَيْرُ تَائِبٍ ـ ٱلْقَلْبِ.

Impenitently, *ad.* بِقَسَاوَةِ قَلْبٍ ـ بِلَا تَنَدُّمٍ ـ بِعِنَادٍ ـ بِدُونِ تَوْبَةٍ.

Imperative, *a.* Having authority, decisive, أَمْرِيّ ـ حَتْمِيّ ـ قَطْعِيّ ـ بَتِّيّ. Necessary, ضَرُورِيّ. To be — upon, وَجَبَ عَلَى *aor.* يَجِبُ ـ حَقَّ عَلَى. To make something imperative upon, أَثْبَتَ عَلَى ـ أَوْجَبَ عَلَى. The — mood, الأَمْرُ ـ صِيغَةُ ٱلْأَمْرِ.

Imperatively, *ad.* With authority, decidedly, بَتَّةً ـ قَطْعًا ـ بِأَمْرٍ. With necessity, بِلُزُومٍ ـ بِضَرُورَةٍ.

Imperceivable, *a.* / Imperceptible, } Not to be perceived, لَا يُدْرَكُ ـ لَا يُعَايَنُ ـ خَفِيّ ـ خَافٍ ـ لَا يُشْعَرُ بِهِ ـ لَا يُحَسُّ بِهِ. Obliterated, مُنْدَرِس. To be —, خَفِيَ *aor.* يَخْفَى.

Imperceivableness, / Imperceptibleness, *n.* / Imperceptibility, } عَدَمُ إِشْعَارٍ ـ كَوْنُ ٱلشَّيْءِ لَا يُدْرَكُ. Want of power to perceive, عَدَمُ إِمْكَانِ ٱلْإِدْرَاكِ.

Imperceptibly, *ad.* بلا حِسٍّ ـ بِدُونِ إدراكٍ.

Imperfect, *a.* Defective, غَيْرُ كامِلٍ ـ ناقِص. Wanting, قاصِر ـ خاطِئٌ ـ غَوِيٌّ ـ غاوٍ ـ ذُو عَيْبٍ. Imperfect in shape or wanting a limb, خادِجٌ ـ مُخْدَجٌ ـ ناقِص. Having faults, liable to err, خاطِئٌ ـ غَوِيٌّ ـ غاوٍ ـ ذُو عَيْبٍ. The — tense, صِيغَةُ حالِ ٱلْمَاضِي ٱلْغَيْرِ ٱلتّامِّ. To be —, to have defects, عابَ *aor.* يَعِيبُ ـ تَعَيَّبَ.

Imperfection, *n.* Want of perfection, عَدَمُ كَمالٍ. A defect, قُصُور ـ عُيُوب *pl.* عَيْب ـ نَقائِص *pl.* نَقِيصَة ـ نُقْصان ـ خِداج ـ عَوار. A fault, ذَنْب *pl.* ذُنُوب ـ زَلَّة ـ إساءَة. An —, as in an article sold, دَرَك; the warranty of the same, ضَمانُ دَرَكٍ.

Imperfectly, *ad.* بِنَقِيصَةٍ ـ بِنَقْصٍ ـ بِدُونِ كَمالٍ.

Imperforate, *a.* } **Imperforated,** } بِدُونِ نَقْبٍ ـ غَيْرُ مُنْثَقِبٍ ـ غَيْرُ مَثْقُوبٍ ـ غَيْرُ مُسَلَّكٍ ـ مَسْدُود.

Imperforation, *n.* إنْسِداد ـ عَدَمُ تَثَقُّبٍ.

Imperial, *a.* Royal, هُمايُونِيٌّ ـ سُلْطانِيٌّ. Commanding, imposing, مُوَقَّر ـ مُهاب. The — party, الحِزْبُ ٱلْإِمْبَراطُورِيُّ. The — family, العائِلَةُ ٱلْإِمْبَراطُورِيَّةُ.

Imperial, *n.* The — of a carriage, صُنْدُوقُ ٱلْكَرُوسَةِ. A tuft of hair on the chin, سَبَلَةُ ٱلذَّقَنِ ـ مَغْفَلَة ـ عَنْفَقَة ـ عُثْنُون ـ طُرَّةُ شَعْرٍ عَلَى ٱلذَّقَنِ.

Imperialist, *n.* مِنْ حِزْبِ ٱلْإِمْبَراطُورِيَّةِ.

Imperially, *ad.* In an imperial manner, فِي طِرْزٍ سُلْطانِيٍّ ـ مِثْلَ ٱلْمُلُوكِ. Through the sovereign, بِواسِطَةِ ٱلسُّلْطانِ.

Imperil, *v.t.* *See to* Endanger, *v.t.*

Imperious, *a.* Arrogant, غِطْرِيس ـ بَطِر ـ تائِه ـ تَيّاه ـ مُتَجَبِّر ـ مُتَكَبِّر ـ عَنِيف ـ عُتاة *pl.* عاتٍ. Necessary, لا بُدَّ مِنْهُ ـ ضَرُورِيٌّ. *See also* Arrogant, Domineering, *a.*

Imperiously, *ad.* بِتِيهٍ ـ بِغَطْرَسَةٍ ـ بِبَطَرٍ ـ بِعُنْفٍ ـ بِتَجَبُّرٍ ـ بِجَوْرٍ ـ مِنْ بابِ ٱلتَّسَلُّطِ وَٱلْوَقاحَةِ ـ بِتَكَبُّرٍ. To act —, بَطِرَ ـ غَطْرَسَ ـ تَجَبَّرَ ـ تَكَبَّرَ ـ جارَ *aor.* يَجُورُ ـ عَتا ـ تاهَ *aor.* يَتِيهُ.

Imperiousness, *n.* عُنْف ـ تَجَبُّر ـ عُتُوّ ـ غَطْرَسَة ـ بَطَر ـ تِيه ـ تَكَبُّر ـ جَوْر. Necessity, ضَرُورِيَّة ـ ضَرُورَة.

Imperishable, *a.* لا يَزُولُ ـ لا يُدْرِكُهُ ٱلْهَلاكُ ـ دائِم ـ باقٍ ـ غَيْرُ فانٍ ـ غَيْرُ مُضْمَحِلٍّ ـ لا يَفْنَى.

Imperishableness, *n.* بَقاء ـ عَدَمُ فَناءٍ ـ عَدَمُ زَوالٍ.

Imperishably, *ad.* بِبَقاءٍ ـ بِمِنْوالٍ لا يُدْرِكُهُ ٱلْهَلاكُ.

Impermanence, *n.* عَدَمُ ٱسْتِقْرارٍ ـ عَدَمُ دَوامٍ ـ عَدَمُ ثُبُوتٍ ـ زَوال.

Impermeability, *n.* } **Impermeableness,** } عَدَمُ تَطَرُّقِ ٱلْماءِ ـ عَدَمُ نُفُوذِ ٱلْماءِ فِيهِ إلَيْهِ.

Impermeable, *a.* لا يُؤَثِّرُ فِيهِ ٱلْماءُ ـ لا يَتَطَرَّقُ إلَيْهِ ٱلْماءُ ـ نَفاذُهُ مُحالٌ ـ لا يَنْفُذُ فِيهِ ٱلْماءُ.

Impermeably, *ad.* بِمِنْوالٍ لا يَتَطَرَّقُ إلَيْهِ ٱلْماءُ ـ بِنَوْعٍ لا يَنْفُذُ فِيهِ ٱلْماءُ.

Impersonal, *a.* (Of a verb), صِيغَةُ ٱلْغائِبِ ٱلْمَجْهُولِ. Not denoting a person, لا يَدُلُّ عَلَى شَخْصٍ. Indistinct, unknown, مُبْهَم ـ مَجْهُول.

Impersonality, *n.* عَدَمُ شَخْصِيَّةٍ ـ عَدَمُ تَشْخِيصٍ.

Impersonally, *ad.* بِدُونِ تَعْيِينِ ٱلشَّخْصِ ـ بِعَدَمِ تَشْخِيصٍ.

Impersonate, *v.t.* To assume the person of another, تَظاهَرَ بِشَخْصِ ٱلْغَيْرِ ـ تَمَثَّلَ بِ ـ تَشَخَّصَ بِ. To represent, شَخَّصَ. To ascribe animation to inanimate bodies, صَوَّرَ كَشَخْصٍ ـ أَنْطَقَ ـ شَخَّصَ.

Impersonation, *n.* The act of ascribing animation to inanimate objects, تَشْخِيص ـ تَصْوِيرُ ٱلشَّيْءِ كَأَنَّهُ شَخْصٌ ناطِقٌ ـ إنْطاق.

Imperspicuity, *n.* عَدَمُ وُضُوحٍ ـ إبْهام.

Imperspicuous, *a.* غَيْرُ واضِحٍ ـ مُبْهَم.

Impertinence, *n.* } **Impertinency,** } Irrelevance, فُضُول ـ عَدَمُ مُناسَبَةٍ ـ فَرْط ـ خُرُوج. Obtrusiveness, لَجاجَة ـ غَطْرَسَة ـ تَطَفُّل ـ سَفاهَة ـ ضَجَر ـ تَصَدُّع ـ إلْحاح. Impudence, سَفاهَة.

Impertinent, *a.* Out of place, خارِجٌ عَنْ مَحَلِّهِ ـ فُضُولِيٌّ ـ غَيْرُ مُناسِبٍ ـ فِي غَيْرِ مَحَلِّهِ. Rude, impudent, فَظٌّ ـ وَقِح ـ قَلِيلُ ٱلْحَياءِ ـ سَفِيه ـ مُتَطَفِّل. To be — to, تَسَفَّهَ عَلَى ـ تَوَقَّحَ عَلَى.

Impertinently, *ad.* Out of place, فِي غَيْرِ مَحَلِّهِ. Intrusively, بِلا حَياءٍ ـ بِسَفاهَةٍ ـ بِفُضُولٍ ـ بِتَصَدُّعٍ ـ بِلَجاجَةٍ. Impudently, بِسَفاهَةٍ ـ بِوَقاحَةٍ.

Imperturbable, *a.* لا يُبالِي ـ لا تَتَغَيَّرُ أَحْوالُهُ ـ رَكِين ـ رَصِين. To be —, تَوَقَّرَ ـ تَرَزَّنَ ـ تَرَكَّنَ.

Imperturbation, *n.* عَدَمُ مُبالاةٍ ـ رَصانَة ـ رَكانَة.

Imperviability, *n.* *See* Imperviousness, *n.*

Imperviable, *a.* } **Impervious,** } Impenetrable, لا يَنْفُذُ فِيهِ ـ لا يُتَطَرَّقُ إلَيْهِ ـ نُفُوذُهُ مُحالٌ ـ لا يُدْخَلُ فِيهِ. That cannot be reached, لا يُمْكِنُ ٱلْوُصُولُ إلَيْهِ ـ الوُصُولُ إلَيْهِ مُحالٌ; that cannot be crossed, عُبُورُهُ مُحالٌ ـ عُبُورُهُ غَيْرُ مُمْكِنٍ. Impervious, of a woman, *in coitû*, عَفْلاءُ ـ رَتْقاءُ. *See also* Impenetrable, *a.*

Imperviously, *ad.* بِعَدَمِ ٱلنُّفُوذِ فِيهِ ـ بِمِنْوالٍ لا يُتَطَرَّقُ إلَيْهِ ـ بِنَوْعٍ لا يُدْخَلُ فِيهِ.

Imperviousness, *n.* عَدَمُ نُفُوذِ غَيْرِ جِسْمٍ ـ عَدَمُ ٱلتَّطَرُّقِ إلَيْهِ.

Impetuosity, *n.* } A rushing with violence, شِدَّة ـ جِدَّة ـ صَوْلَة. Impetuousness, } Velocity, سُرْعَة. Violence of temper, تَهَوُّر ـ حُمَيَّا ـ سَوْرَة. Fury of an attack, بَطْش ـ وَقْعَة ـ سَطْوَة. *See also* Hasty, *a.*

Impetuous, *a.* Violent, شَدِيد ـ عَنِيف ـ حَادّ. Precipitate, مُتَهَوِّر ـ هَيِّر. Swift, سَرِيع. Passionate, غَضُوب ـ هَيَّاج.

Impetuously, *ad.* With violence, بِحِدَّةٍ ـ بِشِدَّةٍ ـ بِصَوْلَةٍ. With precipitation, بِتَهَوُّر. With fury, as of an attack, بِسَطْوَةٍ ـ بِبَطْشٍ. *See also* Furiously, *ad.*

Impetus, *n.* سَطْوَة *pl.* سَطَوَات ـ هَيَجَان ـ هِيَاج ـ صَكْمَة ـ صَدْمَة. A sudden —, هَجْمَة ـ حَمْل ـ كَبْسَة ـ دَفْعَة ـ وَثْب. To give an — to, إِسْتَفَزَّ ـ دَفَعَ ـ أَوْثَبَ ـ صَكَمَ.

Impiety, *n.* عَدَمُ تَقْوَى ـ فُجُور ـ نِفَاق ـ كُفْر ـ إِلْحَاد ـ زَنْدَقَة.

Impinge, *v.t.* صَادَمَ ـ لَطَمَ فِي ـ صَكَمَ.

Impingement, *n.* مُصَادَمَة ـ لَطْم ـ صَكْم.

Impious, *a.* كَافِر ـ فُجَّار *pl.* فَاجِر ـ مُنَافِق ـ مُلْحِد ـ زِنْدِيق *pl.* زَنَادِقَة ـ كُفَّار. An — discourse, كَلَامُ كُفْرٍ. An — action, فِعْلٌ نَقِيضُ ٱلدِّينِ ـ كُفْر.

Impiously, *ad.* بِنِفَاقٍ ـ بِإِلْحَادٍ ـ بِزَنْدَقَةٍ.

Impiousness, *n.* *See* Impiety, *n.*

Impish, *a.* شَيْطَانِيّ ـ جِنِّيّ.

Implacability, *n.* } غَلِيل ـ غِلّ ـ حِقْدُهُ لَا يُلَامُ ـ غَضَبُهُ لَا يُسَكَّنُ. Implacableness, }

Implacable, *a.* شَدِيدُ ـ لَا يَهْدَأُ غَضَبُهُ ـ لَا يَعْفُو ـ مُغِلّ ـ حَقُود ـ غِلّ ـ حِقْد ـ مُدْمِنٌ عَلَى ٱلْحِقْدِ ـ ٱلْحِقْدِ. Implacable resentment, غَضَبٌ لَا يَهْدَأُ وَغِلٌّ لَا يُشْفَى.

Implacably, *ad.* بِإِدْمَانٍ ـ بِدُونِ رَحْمَةٍ ـ بِغَلِيلٍ ـ بِغِلٍّ ـ بِحِقْدٍ عَلَى ٱلْحِقْدِ.

Implant, *v.t.* To plant, أَغْرَسَ ـ زَرَعَ ـ غَرَسَ. To insert, أَدْخَلَ ـ أَسْلَكَ ـ سَلَكَ. To —, as in the nature, عَرَّقَ فِي ـ أَعْرَقَ فِي ـ ضَرَبَ فِي ـ أَحْدَثَ فِي ـ طَبَعَ فِي ـ أَشْرَبَ. He implanted in them an evil disposition, عَرَّقَ (*or* أَعْرَقَ) فِيهِمْ عِرْقَ سَوْءٍ. To be implanted, as in the nature, أُعْرِقَ فِي ـ أُشْرِبَ فِي ـ ضُرِبَ فِي. The love of him was implanted in his heart, أُشْرِبَ فِي قَلْبِهِ حُبَّهُ ; *or* أُشْرِبَ حُبَّ فُلَانٍ.

Implantation, *n.* The act of planting, زَرْع ـ إِغْرَاس ـ غَرْس. Insertion, إِدْخَال ـ إِسْلَاك ـ سَلْك. Fixing in the mind, إِشْرَاب ـ تَعْرِيق ـ إِرْسَاخ فِي ٱلْقَلْبِ ـ تَطْبِيع فِي ٱلْعَقْلِ.

Implausible, *a.* بَعِيد ـ غَيْرُ مُحْتَمَلٍ.

Implead, *v.t.* حَاكَمَ ـ رَافَعَ. Let them — one another, فَلْيُرَافِعْ بَعْضُهُمْ بَعْضًا.

Implement, *n.* آلَة *pl.* آلَات ـ أَدَاة *pl.* أَدَوَات. Implements, أَدَات ـ عُدَّة ـ أُهْبَة.

Impletion, *n.* The act of filling, مَلْأَة ـ مَلْأ ; the being filled, مِلْأَة ـ مِلَاء.

Implex, *a.* مُشْبَك ـ جَبِيل ـ أَشِبٌ ـ مُشْتَوْشِج. *See also* Complex, *a.*

Implicate, *v.t.* To cause to be involved in, شَبَكَ فِي ـ رَطَمَ فِي. To lay one open to, عَرَّضَ عَلَى.

Implication, *n.* Entanglement, إِشْتِبَاك ـ شُبْكَة ـ رَطْم. The act of inferring, إِسْتِنْتَاج ـ إِسْتِدْلَال. An inference, مَدْلُول ـ نَتِيجَة. A meaning involved though not expressed, تَلْمِيح ـ كِنَايَة ـ تَلْوِيح. Among the implications of his speech, فِي ضِمْنِ كَلَامِهِ.

Implicit, *a.* Implied, حَاصِلٌ (*or* نَاتِجٌ) مِنْ نَصِّ ٱلْكَلَامِ. Without reserve, خَالٍ مِنَ ٱلشَّكِّ ـ تَامّ ـ كَامِل ـ بَتِّيّ ـ كُلِّيّ. Implicit confidence, إِعْتِمَادٌ تَامٌّ. Implicit obedience, إِطَاعَةٌ كَامِلَةٌ.

Implicitly, *ad.* As contained in meaning, إِضْمَارًا ـ مَعْنًى. By inference, بِٱلنَّتِيجَةِ. Unreservedly, بِٱعْتِمَادٍ تَامٍّ ـ بِوَثِيقَةٍ كُلِّيَّةٍ ـ بِأَمْنِيَّةٍ كُلِّيَّةٍ ـ بِدُونِ مُبَالَاةٍ.

Implicitness, *n.* State of trusting unreservedly, أَمْنِيَّةٌ كُلِّيَّةٌ ـ إِعْتِمَادٌ كُلِّيٌّ.

Impliedly, *ad.* إِضْمَارًا ـ مَعْنًى.

Imploration, *n.* إِلْتِمَاس ـ إِبْتِهَال ـ تَضَرُّع.

Implore, *v.t.* To entreat, إِبْتَهَلَ إِلَى ـ تَضَرَّعَ إِلَى ـ قَنَعَ. To beg, ask, تَرَجَّى ـ طَلَبَ مِن ـ سَأَلَ *aor.* يَسْأَلُ ـ إِلْتَمَسَ مِن. To — assistance, إِسْتَمَدَّ ـ إِسْتَعَانَ. To — in behalf of another, إِسْتَشْفَعَ. To — one for mercy, إِسْتَرْحَمَ.

Implorer, *n.* طَالِب *pl.* طُلَّاب ـ مُلْتَمِس ـ مُبْتَهِل ـ مُتَضَرِّع.

Imploringly, *ad.* بِٱلْتِمَاسٍ ـ بِٱبْتِهَالٍ ـ بِتَضَرُّعٍ.

Implumed, *a.* } Having no feathers, بِدُونِ رِيشٍ ـ غَيْرُ مَرِيشٍ. Implumous, }

Impluvium, *n.* A shower-bath, رَشَاشَةُ مَاءٍ.

Imply, *v.t.* To contain in substance, أَضْمَرَ ـ دَلَّ عَلَى ـ مَعْنًى *aor.* يَدُلُّ ; it implies, يُسْتَدَلُّ بِهِ عَلَى ـ يُنْتَجُ مِنْهُ. To signify, يَعْنِي بِهِ ـ يَدُلُّ عَلَى ـ عَنَى بِ ـ عَنَى. It implies, signifies, يُرَادُ بِهِ. The word implied such a meaning, تَضَمَّنَتِ ٱلْكَلِمَةُ مَعْنًى كَذَا.

Impoison, *v.t.* As with poison, سَمَّ. To imbitter, أَمَرَّ ـ أَشْقَى.

Impolicy, *n.* عَدَمُ ٱلْإِحْتِيَاطِ ـ قِلَّةُ فِطْنَةٍ ـ قِلَّةُ تَبَصُّرٍ ـ سُوْءُ سِيَاسَةٍ ـ مُوَافَقَةٍ.

Impolite, *a.* مِنْ غَيْرِ وَاجِبٍ ـ جَافٍ ـ فَظٌّ ـ قَلِيلُ ٱلْأَدَبِ.

Impolitely, *ad.* خِلَافَ قَوَانِينِ ٱلْأَدَبِ ـ بِفَظَاظَةٍ ـ بِقِلَّةِ أَدَبٍ.

Impoliteness, *n.* قِلَّةُ وَاجِبٍ ـ فَظَاظَةٌ ـ قِلَّةُ أَدَبٍ.

Impolitic, *a.* لَيْسَ ذَا فِطْنَةٍ ـ عَدِيمُ ٱلْإِحْتِيَاطِ ـ قَلِيلُ ٱلتَّبَصُّرِ ـ مُخَالِفُ أُصُولِ ٱلسِّيَاسَةِ.

Impoliticly, *ad.* بِسُوْءِ ـ بِلَا فِطْنَةٍ ـ بِعَدَمِ ٱحْتِيَاطٍ ـ بِقِلَّةِ تَبَصُّرٍ سِيَاسَةٍ.

Imponderability, *n.* } كَوْنُ ـ تَنَزُّهٌ عَنِ ٱلثِّقَلِ ـ عَدَمُ ثِقَلٍ
Imponderousness, } ٱلشَّيْءِ لَا يُشْعَرُ بِثِقَلِهِ.

Imponderable, *a.* } لَا يُشْعَرُ ـ ذُو ثِقَلٍ لَا يُشْعَرُ بِهِ ـ عَدِيمُ ٱلثِّقَلِ
Imponderous, } بِثِقَلِهِ.

Imporosity, *n.* كَوْنُ ٱلشَّيْءِ خَالِيًا مِنَ ٱلْمَسَامِّ ـ عَدَمُ مَسَامَّ. Compactness, صَمَمٌ ـ كَثَافَةٌ.

Imporous, *a.* عَدِيمُ ٱلْمَسَامِّ ـ لَا مَسَامَّ لَهُ. Compact, كَثِيفٌ ـ أَصَمُّ.

Import, *v.t.* To carry, as into a country, أَدْخَلَ-إِلَى ـ جَلَبَ-إِلَى ². To imply, signify, دَلَّ عَلَى *aor.* يَدُلُّ ـ عَنَى ـ عَنَى بِ. To occasion, سَبَّبَ. To be of moment, هَمَّ ² ـ عَظُمَ ² ـ لَزِمَ.

Import, *n.* That which is brought from another country, جَلَبٌ *pl.* أَجْلَابٌ ; the imports, ٱلْبَضَائِعُ ـ ٱلدَّاخِلُ إِلَى ـ مَدْخُولَاتٌ ٱلْمُجْتَلَبَةُ. Drift, مَحَطٌّ ـ غَرَضٌ ـ فَحْوَى. Meaning, مَعْنًى ـ مَعْنَاةٌ ـ مَضْمُونٌ. Imports and exports, ٱلْأَمْوَالُ ٱلْوَارِدَةُ وَٱلْخَارِجَةُ. The — trade, ٱلتِّجَارَةُ ٱلدَّاخِلَةُ. The imports into Egypt, مَا وَرَدَ إِلَى مِصْرَ مِنَ ٱلْبَضَائِعِ. *See also* Importance, *n.*

Importable, *a.* مِمَّا يُجْلَبُ ـ جَلْبُهُ جَائِزٌ ـ إِدْخَالُهُ مُمْكِنٌ.

Importance, *n.* Consequence, هَمَامَةٌ ـ لُزُومٌ ـ عِظَمٌ ـ ضَرُورَةٌ ـ مَهَمَّةٌ. Standing, position, مَقَامٌ ـ مَنْزِلَةٌ ـ إِعْتِبَارٌ. Greatness, totality, جَسَامَةٌ ـ كُلِّيَّةٌ ـ جَمٌّ. Self-importance, صَلَفٌ ـ كِبْرِيَاءُ ـ كِبْرٌ ـ غُرُورٌ ـ تَصَلُّفٌ. A matter of —, جَلَلٌ *pl.* أَجْلَالٌ ـ أَمْرٌ مُهِمٌّ ـ أَمْرٌ بَارِعٌ ـ أَمْرٌ جَامِعٌ ; matters of —, مَصْلَحَةٌ ـ عَظَائِمُ ـ مُهِمَّاتٌ. A matter of small —, أَمْرٌ خَفِيفٌ ـ شَيْءٌ لَا طَائِلَ تَحْتَهُ ـ جُزْئِيَّةٌ. A matter of the highest —, أَمْرٌ مِنْ أَهَمِّ ٱلْمُهِمَّاتِ ـ أَهَمُّ وَأَلْزَمُ مَا يَكُونُ. To attach — to, أَعْظَمَ ـ إِسْتَعْظَمَ. To be of —, weighty, عَظُمَ ² ـ هَمَّ ². To make one's self of —, نَفَشَ رُوحَهُ ² ـ تَعَظَّمَ ـ إِسْتَكْبَرَ ـ تَصَلَّفَ. To lose one's —, سَقَطَ عَنْ مَنْزِلَتِهِ ². A man of —, رَجُلٌ عَظِيمٌ ـ صَاحِبُ مَقَامٍ. It is of no —, لَا مَهَمَّةَ تَحْتَهُ. Of the highest —, خَطِيرُ ٱلشَّأْنِ. That no — should be given to those charges, أَنْ لَا تُعْطَى مَهَمَّةٌ لِتِلْكَ ٱلشِّكَايَاتِ.

Important, *a.* Of consequence, weighty, بَارِعٌ ـ عَظِيمٌ ـ مُهِمٌّ ـ كَبِيرٌ. Having influence, صَاحِبُ نُفُوذٍ ـ صَاحِبُ ٱعْتِبَارٍ. More — than any other post, أَهَمُّ مِنْ جَمِيعِ ٱلْمَنَاصِبِ. It is most — to know it, ٱلْإِطِّلَاعُ عَلَيْهِ مِنْ أَهَمِّ ٱلْمُهِمَّاتِ. He rendered — services to the state, أَفَادَ ٱلدَّوْلَةَ فَوَائِدَ عَظِيمَةً. An — matter; *see under* Importance, *n.*

Importantly, *ad.* بِوَجْهٍ مُهِمٍّ ـ بِضَرُورَةٍ.

Importation, *n.* Of goods, إِجْلَابُ (*or*) إِدْخَالُ ٱلْبَضَائِعِ.

Importer, *n.* Of goods, جَالِبُ ٱلْبَضَائِعِ *pl.* جَلَّابَةٌ.

Importunate, *a.* لَجُوجٌ ـ مُلِحٌّ ـ مِقْشَرٌ ـ مُلِثٌّ ـ مِلْظَاظٌ. Troublesome, مُعْجِزٌ ـ مُضْجِرٌ. An — beggar, شَحَّاذٌ. He was — in his request, كَدَّ فِي طَلَبِهِ ².

Importunately, *ad.* بِإِلْحَاحٍ ـ بِلَجَاجَةٍ.

Importunateness, *n.* *See* Importunity.

Importune, *v.t.* To urge on one with frequency, لَثَّثَ عَلَى ـ أَقْرَحَ عَلَى ـ إِسْتَكَدَّ ـ أَكَدَّ ـ لَذِجَ ـ أَلْحَفَ عَلَى ـ أَلَثَّ عَلَى ـ أَمَلَّ ـ أَضْجَرَ ـ أَلَحَّ عَلَى بِ *or* لَجَّ عَلَى. To annoy, teaze, أَقْلَقَ ـ ثَقَّلَ عَلَى ـ أَزْعَجَ. To —, of a beggar, شَحَذَ. He importuned me, مَلَلْتُ مِنْهُ ـ مَلَّنِي.

Importunity, *n.* إِلْحَاحٌ ـ لَجَاجَةٌ ـ مُحَاجَاةٌ ـ إِقْتِضَاءٌ ـ إِقْتِرَاحٌ إِلْحَافٌ ـ إِلْثَاثٌ.

Imposable, *a.* مِمَّا يُلْقَى عَلَى ـ وَضْعُهُ جَائِزٌ ـ مِمَّا يُطْرَحُ عَلَى.

Impose, *v.t.* To lay on, أَلْقَى عَلَى ـ وَضَعَ عَلَى *aor.* يَضَعُ ـ كَلَّفَ-بِ ـ ضَرَبَ عَلَى ـ طَرَحَ عَلَى. To —, as contributions, فَرَضَ عَلَى-غَرَامَةً ـ رَمَى عَلَى-تَكَالِيفَ ـ حَدَّدَ عَلَى ـ غَرَّمَ. To appoint, عَيَّنَ. To —, as a task on one, سَوَّمَ-ٱلْأَمْرَ ـ جَشَّمَ ـ سَخَّرَ-بِ ـ حَمَّلَ. To —, as conditions on, شَرَطَ-عَلَى ² ـ أَشْرَطَ-عَلَى. To —, as a judgment on, حَكَمَ عَلَى-بِ ² ـ قَضَى عَلَى-بِ. To — trouble on, أَكْلَفَ. To —, as a duty or law on, فَرَضَ-عَلَى ـ وَصَّى-بِ ـ أَمَرَ-بِ ² ـ إِفْتَرَضَ-عَلَى. To impute to, نَسَبَ-إِلَى ². To — respect on towards one, هَيَّبَ-إِلَى. To —, as a task on one's self, كَلَّفَ نَفْسَهُ إِلَى ـ تَحَمَّلَ أَلْزَمَ نَفْسَهُ بِ. To cheat, delude, غَشَّ ² ـ غَبَنَ ـ مَكَرَ بِ ² ـ مَسَحَ يَحْتَالُونَ عَلَيْكَ ـ إِحْتَالَ عَلَى. They will certainly — upon you, وَلَا بُدَّ. *See also under* Impost, *n.*

Imposer, *n.* One who lays on, مُلْقٍ ـ وَاضِعٌ ; one who enjoins, فَارِضٌ ـ مُوَصٍّ.

Imposing, Grand, *a.* جَلِيلٌ ـ مَهُوبٌ ـ مَهِيبٌ ـ بَهِيجٌ ـ فَاخِرٌ.

Imposingly, *ad.* With grandeur, بِهَيْبَةٍ ـ بِجَلَالَةٍ ـ بِبَهْجَةٍ.

Imposition, *n.* The act of laying on, طَرْح ـ وَضْع ـ إِلْقَآء. An injunction, وَصِيَّة ـ فَرْض ـ أَمْر. Constraint, a forced task, ظُلْم ـ إِغْتِصَاب ـ سُخْرَة ـ تَكْلِيف. An impost, ضَرِيبَة *pl.* ضَرَائِبُ ـ رَمِيَّة ـ وَضِيعَة *pl.* وَضَائِعُ ـ مَكْس. Deceit, a trick, غَدْر ـ غِشّ ـ خِدَاع ـ حِيلَة. The — of sellers, overreaching, شَرْطُونِيَّة ـ طَمَاعِيَة ٱلْبَاعَةِ. The — of hands, وَضْعُ ٱلْأَيَادِى. The — of a name, تَسْمِيَة. *See also under* Impost, *n.*

Impossibility, *n.* عَدَمُ ٱلْإِمْكَانِ ـ عِزّ ـ عِزَّة. An impossible thing, أَمْرٌ مُحَالٌ ـ أَمْرٌ غَيْرُ مُمْكِنٍ ـ شَىْءٌ لَا يُسْتَطَاعُ.

Impossible, *a.* أَعَزُّ ـ عَزِيز ـ عَدِيمُ ٱلْإِمْكَانِ ـ غَيْرُ مُمْكِنٍ ـ لَا يُسْتَطَاعُ ـ مُحَال. That cannot happen, مُمْتَنِعُ ٱلْوُقُوعِ; that cannot be attained, مُمْتَنِعُ ٱلتَّحْصِيلِ ـ تَحْصِيلُهُ مُحَالٌ; that cannot be carried out, إِجْرَآؤُهُ مُحَالٌ ـ مُمْتَنِعُ ٱلْإِجْرَآءِ. Nothing is — to God, لَيْسَ شَىْءٌ غَيْرَ مُمْكِنٍ لَدَى ٱللّٰهِ. It is — but that offences will come, لَا يُمْكِنُ إِلَّا أَنْ تَأْتِىَ ٱلْعَثَرَاتُ. It is — to please him, لَا يُمْكِنُ إِرْضَاؤُهُ. It is — for you to do this, لَا يُمْكِنُكَ أَنْ تَعْمَلَ هٰذَا. If you wish to be obeyed do not ask what is —, إِذَا أَرَدْتَ أَنْ تُطَاعَ فَلَا تَطْلُبْ مَا لَا يُسْتَطَاعُ. It is — that …, مِنَ ٱلْمُسْتَحِيلِ أَنْ. To be —, عَزَّ ـِ.

Impost, *n.* A duty, tax, ضَرِيبَة *pl.* ضَرَائِبُ ـ رَسْم *pl.* رُسُوم ـ رَمِيَّة ـ وَضِيعَة *pl.* وَضَائِعُ ـ تَكْلِيف *pl.* تَكَالِيف ـ مَكْس *pl.* مُكُوس. To lay imposts on, أَلْقَى (or رَمَى ـِ) تَكَالِيفَ عَلَى ـ ضَرَبَ عَلَى ضَرَائِبَ ـِ. They resisted the excessive imposts upon them, رَفَضُوا زِيَادَةَ ٱلضَّرِيبَةِ عَلَيْهِمْ.

Imposthumate, *v.t.* To gather into an abscess, قَيَّحَ ـ أَمَدَّ ـ دَمَّلَ.

Imposthume, *n.* خُرَاج ـ دُمَّل *pl.* دَمَامِيلُ or دَمَامِلُ.

Impostor, *n.* مُمَسِّح ـ مُفْتَرٍ ـ خَدَّاع ـ دَجَّال ـ غَدَّار ـ كَذَّاب.

Imposture, *n.* خِدَاع ـ تِمْسَاح ـ غَدْر ـ خِيَانَة ـ مَكْر ـ غِشّ ـ حِيلَة.

Impotence, *n.* / **Impotency**, Want of power, فَسَخ ـ كَسَح ـ عَجْز ـ وَنَآء ـ نَأْنَأَة ـ ضَعْف. Incapacity of propagation, حَوْقَلَة ـ عَنَانَة ـ عِنِّينَة.

Impotent, *a.* Wanting in power, فَدْم ـ فُطَارِىّ ـ فَسِيخ ـ كَسِيح ـ عَاجِز ـ وَانٍ ـ جَهُوم ـ ضَعِيف. Incapable of propagation, حَرِيك ـ حَوْكَل ـ عَجِير ـ عَجِيز ـ عِنِّين ـ سَرِس.

Impotently, *ad.* بِعَجْزٍ ـ بِضَعْفٍ ـ بِدُونِ قُوَّةٍ.

Impound, *v.t.* As of cattle, زَرَبَ [2] فِى زَرِيبَةِ ٱلسَّائِبَات. To seize, retain, ضَبَطَ عَلَى ـِ [2] ـ أَوْقَفَ ـ حَاشَ [2].

Impoverish, *v.t.* To reduce to poverty, أَفْقَرَ. To exhaust fertility, أَتْلَفَ (or أَنْفَدَ) دَسَمَ ٱلْأَرْضِ.

Impoverishment, *n.* The act of reducing to poverty, إِفْقَار; the being reduced to poverty, فَقْر ـ فَاقَة. Exhaustion of fertility, نَفَادُ دَسَمِ ٱلْأَرْضِ ـ إِتْلَافُ خِصْبِ ٱلْأَرْضِ.

Impracticableness, *n.* / **Impracticability**, عِزَّة ـ عِزّ ـ عَدَمُ إِمْكَانٍ ـ اِمْتِنَاع. An impracticable thing, أَمْرٌ مُحَالٌ ـ أَمْرٌ غَيْرُ مُمْكِنٍ ـ شَىْءٌ لَا يُسْتَطَاعُ. Untractableness, شَكَاسَة ـ تَمَرُّد ـ عِنَاد.

Impracticable, *a.* That cannot be done, فِعْلُهُ غَيْرُ مُمْكِنٍ ـ لَا يُنَالُ ـ أَعَزُّ ـ عَزِيز ـ مُحَالٌ ـ مُمْتَنِع. Untractable, عَارِم ـ شَكِس ـ صَعْب. An — road, طَرِيقٌ غَيْرُ مُطَرَّقٍ ـ طَرِيقٌ غَيْرُ سَالِكٍ ـ طَرِيقٌ غَيْرُ نَافِذٍ. An — man, رَجُلٌ شَكِسٌ ـ رَجُلٌ. The thing was — to me, اِمْتَنَعَ ـ بَرَّقَ بِىَ ٱلْأَمْرُ. لَا يُعَاشَرُ عَنِّى ٱلشَّىْءُ.

Impracticably, *ad.* بِعِزٍّ ـ بِعِزَّةٍ.

Imprecate, *v.t.* دَعَا عَلَى [2] ـ لَعَنَ ـَ ـ سَبَّ [2]. *See also under to* Curse, *v.t.*

Imprecation, *n.* دُعَآءٌ عَلَى ـ سَبّ ـ لَعْنَة. *See also under* Curse, *n.*

Imprecatory, *a.* دَاعٍ عَلَى ـ لَعِين ـ سَابّ.

Impregnability, *n.* عِزّ ـ عِزَّة ـ مَنَاعَة.

Impregnable, *a.* عَزِيز ـ أَعَزُّ ـ فَتْحُهُ مُحَالٌ ـ مَنِيع ـ حَصِين ـ فَتْحُهُ غَيْرُ مُمْكِنٍ. To be —, عَزَّ ـِ ـ مَنُعَ [2]. *See also under* Inaccessible, *a.*

Impregnably, *ad.* بِعِزٍّ ـ بِعِزَّةٍ ـ بِٱسْتِحْكَامَاتٍ فَتْحُهَا مُحَالٌ.

Impregnate, *v.t.* To make pregnant, حَبَّلَ ـ أَحْبَلَ. To fecundate, as by pollen, أَبَّرَ ـ مَقَّ ـَ ـ أَلْقَحَ ـ لَقَّحَ. To make fruitful, ثَمَّرَ ـ أَثْمَرَ. To impart to, to saturate with, أَشْبَعَ ـ أَشْرَبَ ـ أَدْخَلَ فِى ـ مَلَأَ مِنْ ـَ.

Impregnation, *n.* The act of making pregnant, إِحْبَال; the being pregnant, حَبَل ـ حَمْل. The act of fecundating, as of trees, إِبَار ـ تَحْبِيل ـ تَلْقِيح; of filling, imparting, saturating with, إِشْبَاع ـ إِشْرَاب.

Imprescriptibility, *n.* عَدَمُ ٱسْتِحْلَالٍ مَعَ طُولِ ٱلْمُدَّةِ ـ دَوَام ـ بَتَّة.

Imprescriptible, *a.* لَا يُبْطَلُ أَبَدًا ـ مُؤَبَّد ـ بَتّ. I gave it to him as an — gift, أَعْطَيْتُهُ إِيَّاهُ عَطِيَّةً بَتًّا بَتْلًا (or بَتَّةً بَتْلَةً).

Impress, *v.t.* To mark, رَسَمَ [2] ـ رَشَمَ [2] ـ أَعْلَمَ. To stamp, as with a seal, خَتَمَ عَلَى ـِ ـ خَتَمَ; as a mark on cloth, بَصَمَ [2];

as with type, طَبَعَ ‏². To fix in, as of the mind, أَثَّرَ فِي ـ طَبَعَ فِي ـ ‏² فَعَلَ فِي ـ أَدْخَلَ فِي ـ ‏² عَمِلَ فِي. To force, as into service, سَخَّرَ; to oblige, force, ‏² قَهَرَ ـ ‏² جَبَرَ ـ عَلَى ـ اِضْطَرَّ ـ إِلَى. To be impressed, as on the mind, اِنْطَبَعَ فِي ـ أَثَّرَ فِي. Death became impressed upon him, ‏² بَرَنَ ٱلْمَوْتُ عَلَيْهِ. They became impressed, convinced, that…, اِسْتَوْلَى عَلَى أَذْهَانِهِمْ أَن….

Impress, *n.* A mark made by pressure, رَسْم *pl.* رُسُوم ـ رَشْم ـ رُشُوم ـ صُورَة ـ عَلَامَة ـ طَبْع ـ خِتَام ـ خَتْم. Character, صِفَة. It bears the — of such a thing, عَلَيْهِ أَثَرُ كذا.

Impressibility, *n.* لِينَة ـ لَيَان ـ سُهُولَةُ ٱلتَّأْثِيرِ فِيهِ.

Impressible, *a.* That can be stamped, مِمَّا يُطْبَعُ ـ يَنْطَبِعُ عَلَيْهِ ـ مِمَّا يَبْصَمُ ـ عَلَيْهِ; that easily receives an impression, سَهْلُ ٱلتَّأْثِيرِ فِيهِ ـ لَيِّن. Of an — disposition, لَيِّنُ ٱلْجَانِبِ.

Impression, *n.* The act of pressing one body upon another, رَشْم ـ بَصْم ـ طَبْع ـ تَأْثِير. A mark made by pressure; *see* Impress. An — by cautery, وَسْم. An image fixed in the mind, اِرْتِسَام ـ تَحْزِير ـ تَخْمِين ـ ظَنّ. An idea, تَأْثِير ـ أَثَرَة ـ آثَار *pl.* أَثَر. Impressions, ideas, suspicions, هَوَاجِس. The — of a seal, خَتْم. Operation, فَاعِلِيَّة. An edition, طَبْعَةُ كِتَابٍ. To make an — on one, to become indwelling in one, تَأَثَّرَ فِي ـ ‏² حَلَّ فِي *or* بِ. I have an — that he will not come to-day, أَظُنُّ أَنَّهُ لَا يَجِيءُ ٱلْيَوْمَ. These words made no — on him, هٰذَا ٱلْكَلَامُ مَا أَثَّرَ فِيهِ (*or* مَا عَمِلَ فِيهِ *or* مَا قَطَعَ فِيهِ).

Impressive, *a.* Producing an effect, مُحَرِّك ـ مُؤَثِّر; affecting, مُحَشِّ ـ مُحَشِّن ـ مُرِقّ لِلْقَلْبِ; producing reverence, مُهَيِّب.

Impressively, *ad.* تَأَثُّرًا ـ بِتَأْثِيرٍ.

Impressiveness, *n.* تَأْثِير ـ فَاعِلِيَّة.

Impressment, *n.* تَسْخِير ـ إِلْزَام ـ جَبْر.

Impressure, *n.* *See* Impress, *n.*

Imprimatur, *n.* إِجَازَةٌ لِلطَّبْعِ.

Imprimis, *ad.* أَوَّلًا.

Imprint, *v.t.* *See to* Impress, *v.t.*

Imprint, *n.* عُنْوَانُ كِتَابٍ وَتَارِيخُهُ وَمَحَلُّ طَبْعِهِ وَٱسْمُ ٱلطَّبَّاعِ.

Imprison, *v.t.* ‏² سَجَنَ ـ ‏² حَبَسَ. *See also to* Confine, *v.t.*

Imprisonment, *n.* Confinement in prison, حَبْس ـ اِحْتِبَاس ـ سَجْن. A cause of —, مَسْجَنَة. False —, اِحْتِبَاسٌ جَائِرٌ ـ حَبْسٌ جَائِرٌ. *See also* Confinement, *n.*

Improbability, *n.* عَدَمُ ٱحْتِمَالٍ.

Improbable, *a.* غَرِيب ـ لَا يُحْتَمَلُ ـ غَيْرُ مُحْتَمَلٍ ـ غَيْرُ مَعْقُولٍ ـ بَعِيدٌ عَنِ ٱلْعَقْلِ ـ بَعِيد ـ بَعِيدُ ٱلِٱحْتِمَالِ. To be —, ‏² بَعُدَ عَنِ ٱلِٱحْتِمَالِ. To regard as —, اِسْتَبْعَدَ. It is not — that…, هُوَ غَيْرُ بَعِيدٍ أَن. It is not —, هُوَ غَيْرُ بَعِيدٍ.

Improbably, *ad.* بِعَدَمِ ٱحْتِمَالٍ.

Improbity, *n.* خِيَانَة ـ شَرّ ـ قِلَّةُ ذِمَّةٍ ـ فُجُور ـ عَدَمُ ٱسْتِقَامَةٍ ـ خُبْث.

Impromptu, *ad.* عَلَى ٱلْبَدِيهَةِ. Anything done —, بَدَاهَة ـ اِقْتِرَاح ـ اِرْتِجَال فِي ٱلْكَلَامِ. Impromptu speech, بَدِيهَة. Impromptu verses, شِعْرٌ مُرْتَجَل. He is a good — speaker, ذُو بَدِيهَةٍ. A good — speaker, رَجُلٌ بَدِيهٌ. To speak —, [illegible] ـ اِقْتَرَحَ ـ اِرْتَجَلَ ـ ٱلْخُطْبَةَ.

Improper, *a.* Not appropriate, غَيْرُ لَائِقٍ ـ غَيْرُ صَائِبٍ ـ غَيْرُ مُنَاسِبٍ. Corrupt, فَاسِد. An — speech, هُتْر. *See also* Obscene, *a.*

Improperly, *ad.* فِي غَيْرِ مَحَلِّهِ ـ بِلَا مُنَاسَبَةٍ ـ بِدُونِ لِيَاقَةٍ.

Impropriate, *v.t.* To take to one's self, اِسْتَمْلَكَ ـ تَوَلَّى ـ اِتَّخَذَ لِنَفْسِهِ ـ ‏² ضَبَطَ ـ عَلَى.

Impropriation, *n.* The act of taking to one's self, اِسْتِمْلَاك ـ اِتِّخَاذ ـ اِسْتِيلَاء عَلَى. The — of ecclesiastical property, [illegible] ٱلْعَوَامِّ عَلَى أَوْقَافِ ٱلْكَنَائِسِ.

Impropriator, *n.* A lay — of tithes, [illegible] مُسْتَوْلٍ عَلَى أَوْقَافِ ٱلْكَنِيسَةِ.

Impropriety, *n.* قِلَّةُ مُنَاسَبَةٍ ـ عَدَمُ لِيَاقَةٍ. Inaccuracy, [illegible] عَدَمُ صِحَّةٍ ـ دِقَّة.

Improvable, *a.* يُصْلَحُ ـ إِصْلَاحُهُ مُمْكِن ـ قَابِلُ ٱلتَّحْسِينِ ـ يَسْتَتِبُّ.

Improvableness, *n.* } إِمْكَانُ ٱلْإِصْلَاحِ ـ قَابِلِيَّةُ ٱلتَّحْسِينِ ـ
Improvability, } قَابِلِيَّةُ ٱلِٱسْتِتْبَابِ.

Improve, *v.t.* To make better, حَسَّنَ ـ أَصْلَحَ ـ أَفَادَ. To rectify, عَدَّلَ. To push forward, قَدَّمَ ـ رَوَّجَ ـ رَقَّى. To utilize, اِسْتَفَادَ بِ ـ لِ ـ اِنْتَفَعَ بِ ـ لِ. To — by increasing, زَادَ *aor.* يَزِيدُ. To cultivate, حَسَّنَ ٱلْفِلَاحَةَ ـ ‏² فَلَحَ ـ خَصَّبَ. To fortify, شَيَّدَ ـ حَصَّنَ. To — an opportunity, ٱنْتَهَزَ ٱلْفُرْصَةَ. *See also to* Better, *v.t.*

Improve, *v.i.* To grow better, حَسُنَ ـ اِصْطَلَحَ ـ اِسْتَتَبَّ. To advance, progress, اِسْتَفَادَ ـ اِزْدَادَ ـ تَرَقَّى ـ ‏² نَمَى ـ أَنْمَى. To — in health, ‏² صَحَّ مِزَاجًا ـ تَشَفَّى ـ اِشْتَفَى. To — to rise in the market, ٱزْدَادَ ثَمَنًا ـ اِرْتَفَعَ سِعْرُهُ ـ يَرُوجُ *aor.* رَاجَ. He improves in knowledge every day, ‏² زَادَ كُلَّ يَوْمٍ عِلْمًا. To — upon, to perfect, زَادَ فِيهِ كَمَالًا ـ زَادَ فِيهِ فَضْلًا.

Improvement, *n.* The act of bettering, تَحْسِين ـ إِصْلَاح; of rectifying, تَعْدِيل; of cultivating, teaching, تَأْدِيب — تَهْذِيب — تَعْلِيم. Progress, تَرَقٍّ — تَقَدُّم. Increase, اِزْدِيَاد — زِيَادَة — نُمُوّ.

Improvement, as of a building, *etc.*, تَعْمِير — إِسْتِتْبَاب; in health, اَلتَّقَدُّمُ إِلَى ٱلصِّحَّةِ — شِفَآء. Improvements, إِصْلَاحَات — إِسْتِتْبَاب. Practice, إِنْتِفَاع — إِسْتِعْمَال. This is an — on that, هٰذَا أَكْمَلُ مِنْ ذٰلِكَ. Towards the — of the town, فِي سَبِيلِ إِصْلَاحَاتِ ٱلْمَدِينَةِ.

Improver, *n.* مُحَسِّن — مُصْلِح. A cause of fertilization, مُخَصِّب.

Improvidence, *n.* عَدَمُ ٱحْتِيَاطٍ — قِلَّةُ تَدْبِيرٍ — قِلَّةُ ٱلنَّظَرِ فِي ٱلْعَوَاقِبِ — عَدَمُ بَصِيرَةٍ.

Improvident, *a.* غَيْرُ مُتَرَوٍّ — مُتَغَافِل — قَلِيلُ ٱلتَّبَصُّرِ — لَا يَحْسِبُ لِلْعَوَاقِبِ — عَدِيمُ ٱلْبَصِيرَةِ.

Improvidently, *ad.* بِعَدَمِ تَرَوٍّ — بِتَغَافُلٍ — بِقِلَّةِ ٱلنَّظَرِ فِي ٱلْعَوَاقِبِ — بِعَدَمِ بَصِيرَةٍ.

Improvisation, *n.* إِرْتِجَال — إِقْتِرَاح.

Improvisatore, *n.* شَاعِرٌ مُرْتَجِلٌ — مُرْتَجِل.

Improvisatrice, *n.* مُرْتَجِلَة.

Improvise, *v.i.* إِرْتَجَلَ — أَنْشَدَ ٱرْتِجَالًا — 2 قَالَ ٱلشِّعْرَ عَلَى ٱلْبَدِيهَةِ.

Imprudence, *n.* غَفْلَة — عَدَمُ فِطْنَةٍ — غَبَاوَة. He will repent his —, يَنْدَمُ عَلَى تَهَوُّرِهِ.

Imprudent, *a.* مُتَهَدِّمُ — عَدِيمُ ٱلتَّبَصُّرِ — قَلِيلُ ٱلْإِحْتِيَاطِ — غَبِيٌّ — مُتَهَوِّر — قَلِيلُ ٱلْعَقْلِ — ٱلْحِجْرِ. *See also* Indiscreet, *a.*

Imprudently, *ad.* بِقِلَّةِ عَقْلٍ — بِتَغَافُلٍ — بِغَبَاوَةٍ. To act —, اِنْحَمَقَ — اِسْتَحْمَقَ — تَغَفَّلَ — غَبِيَ.

Impudence, *n.* قِلَّةُ حَيَاءٍ — طَمُولَة — وَقَاحَة — وَقَح.

Impudent, *a.* — صَفِيقُ ٱلْوَجْهِ — طَمُول — طِمْل — جَالِع — أَبَلّ — وَقِيح — وَقِح.

Impudently, *ad.* بِقِلَّةِ حَيَاءٍ — بِوَقَاحَةٍ. To act —, وَقُحَ *aor.* وَقَحَ — يَوْقُحُ. To act — to, تَوَقَّحَ عَلَى.

Impugn, *v.t.* To oppose, — نَاقَضَ — خَالَفَ — إِنْتَدَبَ لِ — قَاوَمَ — عَارَضَ. To contradict, تَعَقَّبَ — أَكْذَبَ — كَذَّبَ. His testimony was impugned, غُمِزَتْ شَهَادَتُهُ. To — one's character, حَكَرَ.

Impugner, *n.* — مُقَاوِم — مُعَارِض — مُنَاقِض — مُخَالِف — حَكِر — مُكَذِّب.

Impulse, *n.* Force communicated, a shock, — دَسْرَة — دَسْر — صَكْمَة — رَكْضَة — دَفْع — صَدْمَة. Instigation, — حَثّ — إِغْرَآء — إِسْتِفْزَاز — دَاعٍ — إِيزَاع — بَاعِث — حَضّ. To act upon —, إِنْبَعَثَ بِ — اِنْحَثَّ إِلَى. My first — was to beat him, أَوَّلُ مَا خَطَرَ بِبَالِي أَنْ أَضْرِبَهُ.

Impulsion, *n.* The act of impelling, صَدْم — دَفْع; instigation, حَثّ — إِسْتِفْزَاز — تَحْرِيك — تَحْرِيض — سَوْق — تَسْوِيق.

Impulsive, *a.* Communicating force, — سَائِق — بَاعِث — دَافِع — مُحَرِّك. Acting by impulse, حَثُوث — حَثِيث — هَيَّاج.

Impulsively, *ad.* — بِهِيَاجٍ — بِحَثٍّ — بِحُمَيَّا — بِهَيَجَانٍ — بِٱسْتِفْزَازٍ.

Impunity, *n.* عَدَمُ ٱلْقِصَاصِ — عَدَمُ ٱلْعِقَابِ. With —, — ظَلَفًا — ضَلَّةً — بَطْرًا — هَدْرًا. His blood was shed with —, ذَهَبَ دَمُهُ هَدْرًا.

Impure, *a.* Defiled with guilt, مُذْنِب — خَاطِئٌ — أَثِيم. Unholy, of things, رَجِس — نَجَس — نَجْس. Unchaste, — فَاسِق — عَاهِر — دَاعِر — قَذِر — دَنِس — غَيْرُ عَفِيفٍ. Adulterated, غَيْرُ خَالِصٍ — مَخْلُوط — مَغْشُوش. Not clear, كَدِر — غَيْرُ صَافٍ. To be —, defiled, foul, تَنَجَّسَ — نَجِسَ — دَنِسَ. To make —, نَجَّسَ — أَنْجَسَ.

Impurely, *ad.* Without purity, بِغَيْرِ طَهَارَةٍ. With foulness, بِدَعَارَةٍ — بِدَنَاسَةٍ — بِنَجَاسَةٍ.

Impureness, *n.* }
Impurity, } Want of purity, admixture, — عَدَمُ صَفَاوَةٍ — عَدَمُ خُلُوصٍ. Want of moral purity, عَدَمُ طَهَارَةٍ — جَنَابَة. Want of chastity, عَدَمُ عِفَّةٍ. Turbidity, كَدَر — عُكُور — رَنْق. Wickedness, — نَجَاسَة — إِثْم — خُبْث — شَرّ — خَبَاثَة — فُجُور. Error, خَطَآء — غَلَط — فَسَاد — سَقَط.

Imputable, *a.* — يُتَلَقَّحُ عَلَى — يُتَّهَمُ بِ — مُمْكِنٌ ٱتِّهَامُهُ بِهِ — يُنْسَبُ إِلَى.

Imputation, *n.* The act of imputing to one, — نَسْبٌ إِلَى — إِسْنَادٌ إِلَى — تَعْلِيقٌ بِ. An — of ill, — إِسْتِذْنَاب — تَذَنُّبٌ عَلَى — تَجَنٍّ عَلَى — تَلْقِيح — إِتِّهَامٌ بِ. An unproven charge, تُهْمَة. Censure, شَكْوَى — قَدْح — ذَمّ — لَوْم. Evil thought of one, سُوءُ ٱلظَّنِّ فِي.

Imputative, *a.* *See* Imputable, *a.*

Impute, *v.t.* To ascribe to, — عَلَّقَ-بِ — 2 نَسَبَ-إِلَى — حَمَّلَ-عَلَى — نَثَّى-عَلَى — أَلْقَى-عَلَى — أَسْنَدَ-إِلَى. To charge with, إِحْتَسَبَ — تَلَقَّحَ عَلَى — اِتَّهَمَ-بِ — أَتْهَمَ — 2 أَبَنَ-بِ — تَجَنَّى عَلَى — إِسْتَذْنَبَ عَلَى. To — sin to, — تَذَنَّبَ عَلَى — 2 أَثِمَ.

Imputrescible, *a.* غَيْرُ قَابِلِ ٱلْفَسَادِ — لَا يَفْسُدُ.

In, *prep.* فِي — بِ. Within, — فِي ٱلدَّاخِلِ — دَاخِل — فِي — جُوَّا. In the mean time, فِي غُضُونِ ذٰلِكَ. In order that, — حَتَّى

لِ ـ لِأَنْ ـ لِكَيْ. In case, in the event, إِذا. In that, inasmuch as, مِنْ أَجْلِ أَن ـ بِسَبَبِ أَن ـ مِنْ حَيْثُ أَن. In the power of, فِي قُدْرَةِ ـ فِي طَاقَةِ. In, in the sense of with, by, عِنْدَ: In old people, عِنْدَ ٱلْعَجائِزِ. In a continued series, عَلَى ٱلتَّوالِي. In hand, ready, present, مَوْجود ـ حاضِر; being done, مَشْرُوعٌ. نَقْدًا ـ شاغِلٌ فِيهِ ـ فِيهِ. In the name of God, بِسْمِ ٱللّٰهِ. In that year, فِي تِلْكَ ٱلسَّنَةِ. In anger, بِغَضَبٍ ـ غَضَبًا. In debt, مَدْيُونٌ. In the house, فِي (or فِي داخِلِ) ٱلْبَيْتِ. In case he should arrive I will meet him, إِذا وَصَلَ فَأُلاقِيهِ. He will be here in two years' time, يَحْضُرُ بَعْدَ عامَيْنِ. In all probability he will not come, لا يُحْتَمَلُ مَجِيئُهُ. The book is in the press, شَرَعُوا الكِتابُ تَحْتَ ٱلطَّبْعِ ـ فِي طَبْعِ ٱلْكِتابِ. To be in for, (*in* as an adverb), إِرْتَكَبَ ـ إِكْتَسَبَ.

In, *n.* باطِنٌ ـ الداخِلُ ـ الباطِنُ. The ins and outs of an affair, ٱلْأَمْرِ وَظاهِرُهُ.

Inability, *n.* Want of power, عَدَمُ ـ عَدَمُ قُوَّةٍ ـ نَأْنَأَةٌ ـ عَجْزٌ; want of skill, عَدَمُ ـ عَدَمُ حِذْقٍ ـ عَدَمُ مِهْنَةٍ ـ خُرْقٌ ; آقْتِدارٍ; want of knowledge, عَدَمُ فَنٍّ ـ خُرْقٌ ـ عَدَمُ عِلْمٍ بِ ; مَهارَةٍ; want of readiness, عَدَمُ آسْتِعْدادٍ; want of being equal to, عَدَمُ أَهْلِيَّةٍ.

Inaccessibility, *n.* / Inaccessibleness, } Quality of being beyond reach, عِزٌّ ـ عِزَّةٌ ـ تَمَنُّعٌ ـ مَناعَةٌ ـ عَدَمُ ٱلتَّطَرُّقِ إِلَيْهِ ـ إِمْتِناعُ ٱلْوُصُولِ إِلَى شَيْءٍ أَوْ مَكانٍ.

Inaccessible, *a.* That cannot be reached, لا يُتَطَرَّقُ ـ عَزِيزٌ ـ أَعَزُّ ـ مَنِيعٌ ـ الوُصُولُ إِلَيْهِ مُحالٌ ـ لا وُصُولَ إِلَيْهِ ـ لا يُقْرَبُ إِلَيْهِ ـ إِلَيْهِ شاهِقٌ. That cannot be ascended, لا يُرْقَى إِلَيْهِ ـ لا يُدْرَكُ. That cannot be attained, بُلُوغُهُ غَيْرُ مُمْكِنٍ ـ إِسْتِحْصالُهُ مُمْتَنِعٌ. Impregnable, حَصِينٌ ـ مَنِيعٌ. An — fortress, مَناعَةٌ. An — mountain, هَضْبَةٌ *pl.* هِضَب *and* هِضاب ـ جَبَلٌ مَنِيعٌ. An — man, صاحِبُ مَناعَةٍ. He is —, هُوَ فِي عِزٍّ وَمَنَعَةٍ.

Inaccessibly, *ad.* بِتَمَنُّعٍ ـ بِوَجْهٍ لا يُتَطَرَّقُ إِلَيْهِ ـ بِمَناعَةٍ ـ حَتَّى لَمْ يَكُنْ أَحَدٌ يَقْدِرُ أَنْ يَصِلَ إِلَيْهِ.

Inaccuracy, *n.* Want of accuracy or exactness, قِلَّةُ ضَبْطٍ ـ عَدَمُ تَقْيِيدٍ ـ عَدَمُ صِحَّةٍ ـ عَدَمُ دِقَّةٍ. A fault, mistake, غَلَطٌ ـ زَلَّةٌ *pl.* زَلّات ـ خَطَأٌ.

Inaccurate, *a.* غَيْرُ مُدَقِّقٍ ـ غَيْرُ صَحِيحٍ ـ غَيْرُ مَضْبُوطٍ. *See also* Imperfect, *a.*

Inaccurately, *ad.* بِقِلَّةِ ضَبْطٍ ـ بِغَيْرِ صِحَّةٍ ـ بِعَدَمِ دِقَّةٍ.

Inaction, *n.* / Inactivity, } State of rest, عَدَمُ حَرَكَةٍ ـ قَرار ـ سُكُون. Doing nothing, بَطالَةٌ ـ فَراغ. Idleness, كَسَل. Constipation, إِنْقِباض ـ سَدٌّ.

Inactive, *a.* Without motion, عَدِيمُ ٱلْحَرَكَةِ. Not working, غَيْرُ شاغِلٍ ـ بَطّال. Tardy, بَطِيءٌ. Inert, lazy, هَدَف ـ جامِد ـ كَسْلان ـ مَيّاط. Having no effect, عَدِيمُ ٱلتَّأْثِيرِ.

Inactively, *ad.* With tardiness, بِبُطْءٍ. Idly, بِبَطالَةٍ. Lazily, بِكَسَلٍ ـ بِتَهامُلٍ.

Inadequacy, *n.* / Inadequateness, } Insufficiency, عَدَمُ كِفايَةٍ. Inappropriateness, عَدَمُ مُوافَقَةٍ ـ عَدَمُ مُناسَبَةٍ. Defect, قُصُور ـ نُقْصان.

Inadequate, *a.* Insufficient, غَيْرُ وافٍ ـ غَيْرُ كافٍ. Inappropriate, غَيْرُ مُوافِقٍ ـ غَيْرُ مُناسِبٍ. Defective, ناقِص ـ قاصِرٌ عَن. To be —, or not equal to, قَصُرَ عَن. The property was — to the debts, ضاقَ ٱلْمالُ عَن.

Inadequately, *ad.* بِعَدَمِ مُناسَبَةٍ ـ دُونَ كَفاءٍ ـ بِغَيْرِ كَفاءَةٍ ـ بِقُصُورٍ ـ بِلا تَساوٍ ـ بِدُونِ كَمالٍ.

Inadhesion, *n.* عَدَمُ ٱتِّحادٍ ـ عَدَمُ ٱلْتِصاقٍ.

Inadhesive, *a.* غَيْرُ مُتَّحِدٍ ـ غَيْرُ مُلْتَصِقٍ.

Inadmissibility, *n.* عَدَمُ جَوازٍ ـ عَدَمُ قُبُولٍ ـ حَرام.

Inadmissible, *a.* قُبُولُهُ مُحالٌ ـ قُبُولُهُ غَيْرُ جائِزٍ ـ لا يُقْبَلُ.

Inadvertence, *n.* / Inadvertency, } Negligence, إِهْمال ـ تَوانٍ ـ تَغافُل ـ سَهْوٌ ـ غَفْلَةٌ ـ غَفَل. Inaccuracy, عَدَمُ دِقَّةٍ ـ خَطاءٌ ـ عَدَمُ صِحَّةٍ. At a time of —, عَلَى حِينِ غَفْلَةٍ.

Inadvertent, *a.* غَبِين ـ سَهْوانُ ـ ساهٍ ـ غافِل ـ غَفْلان. To be —, غَبِيَ. To be — of, غَفَلَ عَن ـ سَها عَن *aor.* يَسْهُو.

Inadvertently, *ad.* بِتَغافُلٍ ـ عَنْ غَفْلَةٍ ـ بِتَوانٍ.

Inaffable, *a.* غَيْرُ أَنِيسٍ.

Inalienable, *a.* In a general sense, irrevocable, بَتات ـ بَتٌّ. That may not be transferred, لا يُمْكِنُ تَحْوِيلُهُ إِلَى ـ غَيْرُ مُنْتَقِلٍ إِلَى ٱلْغَيْرِ; that may not be given away, لا يُوهَبُ ـ إِعْطاؤُهُ مَمْنُوعٌ; that may not be sold, بَيْعُهُ مَمْنُوعٌ ـ لا يُباعُ; that cannot legally be taken from its possessor, لا يَجُوزُ سَلْبُهُ مِنْ صاحِبِهِ. Continuous, جارٍ ـ مُؤَبَّد. An — charitable donation, صَدَقَةٌ جارِيَةٌ. Inalienable, in a general sense, but with special reference to property given for pious purposes, مُحَبَّس ـ مُحْبَس ـ مَحْبُوس ـ حَبِيس. An — gift, حَبِيسَة *pl.* حَبائِسُ; an — gift, or alms, صَدَقَةٌ بَتَّةٌ بَتْلَةٌ ـ صَدَقَةٌ بَتَّةٌ. To make —, of property, حَبَّسَ. He made his land an — bequest, وَقَفَ أَرْضَهُ وَقْفًا مُؤَبَّدًا *aor.* يَقِفُ. Make thou the property (itself) to remain to be —, (in perpetuity,) and assign the profits therefrom to be employed in the cause of God, or religion, حَبِّسِ ٱلْأَصْلَ وَسَبِّلِ ٱلثَّمَرَةَ.

Inalienableness, *n.* إِحْتِباس ـ عَدَمُ ٱلْإِنْتِقالِ بَتَّةً ـ بَتَّةٌ ـ إِحْباس.

Inalienably, *ad.* إِحْبَاسًا ـ تَحْبِيسًا ـ حَبْسًا ـ بَتَّةً بَتْلَةً ـ بَتَّةً.

He bequeathed the thing — in the cause of God, or religion, حَبَّسَ ٱلشَّيْءَ فِي سَبِيلِ ٱللّٰهِ.

Inane, *a.* Void, فَارِغ ـ خَالٍ ـ فَاضٍ ـ خَاوٍ.

Inanimate, *a.* لا رُوحَ لَهُ ـ غَيْرُ ذِي نَفْسٍ ـ جَامِد ـ مَوَات. Inanimate nature, عَالَمُ ٱلْجَمَادَاتِ ـ الْجَمَادَاتُ. Inanimate things, إِنَاث.

Inanition, *n.* } Emptiness, فَرَاغ ـ فَضَآء ـ خُلُوّ ـ خَوَآء ـ
Inanity, } بَاطِل ـ لَغْو ـ عَبَث. Absurdity, سَخَسَخَة. تَفَاهَة.

Inappetence, *n.* } عَدَمُ قَابِلِيَّةٍ لِ ـ عَدَمُ ٱشْتِهَآء. Want of
Inappetency, } fervour, zeal, عَدَمُ رَغْبَةٍ.

Inapplicability, *n.* عَدَمُ مُوَافَقَةٍ ـ عَدَمُ مُقَايَسَةٍ ـ عَدَمُ مُطَابَقَةٍ ـ عَدَمُ مُنَاسَبَةٍ.

Inapplicable, *a.* غَيْرُ لَائِقٍ ـ غَيْرُ مُطَابِقٍ ـ لا يَلْبَقُ بِ ـ غَيْرُ لَيْسَ بِمُوَافِقٍ ـ مُنَاسِبٍ.

Inapplication, *n.* كَسَل ـ عَدَمُ تَقَيُّدٍ ـ عَدَمُ إِقْدَامٍ ـ إِهْمَال ـ قِلَّةُ ٱجْتِهَادٍ.

Inapposite, *a.* *See* Inapplicable, *a.*

Inappreciable, *a.* Not to be estimated, تَقْدِيرُهُ غَيْرُ مُمْكِنٍ ـ تَقْدِيرُ ثَمَنِهِ (*or* قِيمَتِهِ) مُحَال. Very minute, جُزْئِيٌّ لِلْغَايَةِ ـ دَقِيقٌ لِلْغَايَةِ.

Inapprehensible, *a.* لا يَنْفَهِمُ ـ لا يُفْهَمُ ـ عُقْمِيٌّ.

Inapprehensive, *a.* مُتَهَامِل. *See also* Inattentive, *a.*

Inapproachable, *a.* *See* Inaccessible, *a.*

Inappropriate, *a.* غَيْرُ مُوَافِقٍ ـ غَيْرُ لَائِقٍ ـ غَيْرُ مُنَاسِبٍ.

Inappropriately, *ad.* بِوَجْهٍ غَيْرِ لَائِقٍ ـ بِعَدَمِ مُنَاسَبَةٍ.

Inappropriateness, *n.* قِلَّةُ مُطَابَقَةٍ ـ عَدَمُ لِيَاقَةٍ ـ عَدَمُ مُنَاسَبَةٍ.

Inapt, *a.* Not ready, غَيْرُ ـ عَدِيمُ ٱلِٱسْتِعْدَادِ ـ خَرِق ـ أَخْرَقُ ـ غَيْرُ وَجْزٍ ـ نَدْب. *See also* Inappropriate, *a.*

Inaptitude, *n.* } Want of readiness, عَدَمُ ـ عَدَمُ وُجُوزٍ ـ خُرْق
Inaptness, } ٱسْتِعْدَادٍ. *See also* Inappropriateness, *n.*

Inarch, *v.t.* طَعَّمَ غُصْنًا بِدُونِ فَصْلِهِ مِنَ ٱلشَّجَرَةِ.

Inarching, *n.* تَطْعِيمُ ٱلْغُصْنِ بِدُونِ فَصْلِهِ مِنَ ٱلشَّجَرَةِ.

Inarticulate, *a.* Of speech, غَيْرُ بَيِّنٍ ـ غَيْرُ مَلْفُوظٍ. One having — speech, مُتَغَمْغِم ـ غُتْم *pl.* غَتْمَآء *fem.* أَغْتَمُ ـ غُتْمِيٌّ. Not having joints, بِدُونِ مَفَاصِلَ ـ عَرِيٌّ ٱلْمَفَاصِلِ. *See also* Indistinct, *a.*

Inarticulately, *ad.* Of speech, بِعَدَمِ بَيَانٍ ـ بِغُتْمَةٍ ـ غَتْمًا ـ بِغَمْغَمَةٍ. To speak —, غَتِمَ ـ تَغَمْغَمَ ـ غَمْغَمَ.

Inarticulateness, *n.* } Of speech, تَلَفُّظٌ غَيْرُ ـ غَمْغَمَة ـ غُتْمَة
Inarticulation, } مُمَيَّزٍ. Want of joints, عَدَمُ ٱلْمَفَاصِلِ.

Inartificial, *a.* Not done by art, خَشِن ـ خَشِيب ـ مَخْشُوب ـ سَاذِجُ ٱلشُّغْلِ ـ خَشِنُ ٱلصِّنَاعَةِ. *See also* Artless, *a.*

Inartificially, *ad.* Without art, بِخُشُونَةٍ ـ بِقِلَّةِ صِنَاعَةٍ. *See also* Artlessly, *ad.*

Inasmuch, *ad.* Seeing that, مِنْ حَيْثُ أَنْ ـ عَلَى أَنْ ـ مِنْ أَجْلِ أَنْ ـ بِسَبَبِ أَنْ.

Inattention, *n.* قِلَّةُ ٱلْتِفَاتٍ ـ إِهْمَال ـ تَوَانٍ ـ تَغَافُل ـ غَبَاوَة ـ قِلَّةُ دَوَرَانِ بَالٍ ـ شَتَاتُ ٱلْعَقْلِ ـ قِلَّةُ ٱنْتِبَاهٍ ـ عَدَمُ تَقَيُّدٍ.

Inattentive, *a.* قَلِيلُ ـ مُتَوَانٍ ـ غَافِل ـ سَهْوَانُ ـ سَاهٍ ـ غَبِيٌّ ـ ٱلِٱلْتِفَاتِ ـ غَيْرُ مُنْتَبِهٍ. To be —, تَغَفَّلَ. To be — to, سَهَا عَنْ *aor.* يَسْهُو ـ غَبِيَ فِي.

Inattentively, *ad.* بِعَدَمِ تَقَيُّدٍ ـ بِقِلَّةِ ٱلْتِفَاتٍ ـ بِتَوَانٍ ـ بِتَغَافُلٍ.

Inaudible, *a.* غَيْرُ مَسْمُوعٍ ـ لا يُسْمَعُ.

Inaudibly, *ad.* بِصَوْتٍ لا يُسْمَعُ ـ بِوَجْهٍ غَيْرِ مَسْمُوعٍ.

Inaugural, *a.* مَا نِيطَ بِٱلِٱفْتِتَاحِ ـ رَسْمِيٌّ ـ ٱفْتِتَاحِيٌّ. An — address, خُطْبَةُ ٱلِٱفْتِتَاحِ ـ خُطْبَةٌ ٱفْتِتَاحِيَّةٌ.

Inaugurate, *v.t.* To induct, as into office, أَقْعَدَ فِي ـ أَوْلَى ـ وَلَّى ـ نَصَبَ ـ قَلَّدَ ـ رَسَمَ. To open with ceremonies, فَتَحَ رَسْمًا. To enter upon, أَخَذَ فِي ـ أَنْشَأَ بِ ـ ٱبْتَدَأَ فِي بِٱلتَّبْجِيلِ.

He was inaugurated Khalifah, بُويِعَ لَهُ بِٱلْخِلَافَةِ.

Inauguration, *n.* Induction, as into office, تَجْلِيسٌ فِي مَنْصِبٍ ـ تَقْلِيد. Enthronement, مُبَايَعَة ـ تَجْلِيس ـ تَوْلِيَةُ وَظِيفَةٍ. The —, as of a monument, تَكْرِيس. A beginning, opening, ٱفْتِتَاح.

Inauguratory, *a.* *See* Inaugural, *a.*

Inauspicious, *a.* مَنْحُوس ـ مَشْؤُوم ـ نَحِس. It was — to them, شَوُمَ عَلَيْهِمْ.

Inauspiciously, *ad.* بِنُحُوسَةٍ ـ بِنَحْسٍ ـ بِشُؤْمٍ.

Inauspiciousness, *n.* مَشْأَمَة ـ نَحْس ـ شُؤْم.

Inboard, *n.* What is stowed in a ship, مِنْ تَعْبِيَةِ (*or* مِنْ وَسْقِ) ٱلْمَرْكَبِ.

Inboard, *ad.* فِي أَنْبَارِ ٱلْمَرْكَبِ ـ فِي دَاخِلِ ٱلْمَرْكَبِ.

Inborn, *a.* } خِلْقِيٌّ ـ طَبِيعِيٌّ ـ جِبِلِّيٌّ ـ غَرِيزِيٌّ ـ ذَاتِيٌّ.
Inbred, } An — quality, سَجِيَّة *pl.* سَجَايَا ـ عِرْق *pl.* عُرُوق.

Inbreathe, *v.t.* نَفَخَ فِي.

Inca, *n.* لَقَبُ مُلُوكِ مَمْلَكَةِ بِرُوفِي جَنُوبِ أَمِيرِكَا سَابِقًا.

Incage, *v.t.* *See to* Cage, *v.t.*

Incalculable, *a.* لا يُقَدَّرُ ـ لا يُحْسَبُ ـ لا يُعَدُّ ـ لا يُحْصَى.

Incalculably, *ad.* لِلْغَايَةِ ـ بِمَا لا يُحْصَى.

Incandescence, *n.* إِسْتِحَالَةُ ٱلشَّيْءِ إِلَى بَيَاضٍ مِنْ شِدَّةِ تَأْثِيرِ ٱلنَّارِ فِيهِ.

Incandescent, *a.* شَرَّار ـ أَبْيَضُ لِشِدَّةِ عَمَلِ ٱلنَّارِ فِيهِ.

Incantation, *n.* سِحْر ـ عَزِيمَة ـ رُقْيَة. To utter an — over, عَزَمَ عَلَى ـِ ـ رَقَى *aor.* يَرْقِي.

Incantatory, *a.* سِحْرِيٌّ ـ مُتَعَلِّقٌ بِٱلْعَزَائِمِ.

Incapability, *n.* } Want of power, عَجْز ـ عَدَمُ قُدْرَةٍ ـ عَدَمُ ٱقْتِدَارٍ ـ قِلَّةُ طَاقَةٍ. Unfitness, عَدَمُ أَهْلِيَّةٍ ـ عَدَمُ لِيَاقَةٍ ـ عَدَمُ مُنَاسَبَةٍ. Ignorance, خُرْق ـ قِلَّةُ مَعْرِفَةٍ ـ جَهْل. A shortcoming, تَقْصِير. An obstacle, إِمْتِنَاع ـ عَائِق.
Incapableness, }

Incapable, *a.* Wanting in power, عَاجِزٌ عَنْ ـ عَدِيمُ ٱلْإِقْتِدَارِ ـ لَيْسَ لَهُ قُدْرَةٌ عَلَى ـ لَيْسَ كُفْوًا بِ ـ غَيْرُ. Unready, أَخْرَقُ ـ مُسْتَعِدٍّ. Ignorant, خَرِق ـ أَخْرَقُ ـ جَاهِل ـ غَبِين. Excluded from, مُنْتَهٍ عَنْ ـ مَحْرُومٌ مِن ـ مَمْنُوعٌ عَنْ. You are — of, above doing, such an action, حَاشَاكَ مِنْ ذٰلِكَ. The mind is — of estimating it, يَضِيقُ ٱلصَّدْرُ عَنْ تَقْدِيرِهِ.

Incapably, *ad.* With want of power, بِعَجْزٍ; with ignorance, بِجَهْل ـ بِغَبَانَةٍ ـ بِخُرْق; clumsily, خُرْقَةً ـ بِخُرْقٍ ـ بِعَدَمِ شَطَارَةٍ. *See also* Clumsily, *ad.*

Incapacitate, *v.t.* To deprive of power, أَعْيَا ـ عَجَّزَ ـ أَعْجَزَ ـ أَضْعَفَ; as from fear, أَقْطَعَ. To disqualify for, to prevent from, مَنَعَ عَنْ ـَ ـ حَجَزَ عَنْ ـُ. To be incapacitated, تَعَيَّا ـ تَعَايَا. To be incapacitated for, عَجَزَ عَنْ ـِ.

Incapacity, *n.* *See* Incapability, *n.*

Incarcerate, *v.t.* سَجَنَ ـُ ـ حَبَسَ ـِ.

Incarceration, *n.* The act of imprisoning, سَجْن ـ حَبْس; the being imprisoned, إِحْتِبَاس.

Incarnate, *a.* مُتَجَسِّد. To become —, تَجَسَّدَ.

Incarnation, *n.* The assumption of a body, تَجَسُّد. The thing itself, عَيْنُ ٱلشَّيْءِ. The — of impudence, عَيْنُ ٱلْوَقَاحَةِ.

Incase, *v.t.* To inclose in a case, عَلَّبَ ـ وَضَعَ فِي صَنْدُوقٍ *aor.* يَضَعُ. To surround with, أَحَاطَ بِ.

Incask, *v.t.* وَضَعَ فِي بَرْمِيلٍ *aor.* يَضَعُ.

Incatenation, *n.* *See* Concatenation, *n.*

Incautious, *a.* Unwary, قَلِيلُ ٱلْحِرْصِ ـ قَلِيلُ ٱلْإِحْتِيَاطِ ـ أَبْلَهُ ـ سَاهٍ ـ غَافِل. Imprudent, غَبِيٌّ ـ قَلِيلُ ٱلتَّبَصُّرِ. *See also* Careless, *a.*

Incautiously, *ad.* تَغَفُّلًا ـ بِدُونِ ٱحْتِيَاطٍ ـ مِنْ غَيْرِ ٱحْتِذَارٍ ـ سَهْوًا ـ بِتَهَامُلٍ. To be or to act —, تَغَافَلَ. To act — with, غَافَلَ ـ سَاهَى.

Incautiousness, *n.* غَفْلَة ـ تَغَافُل ـ سَهْو ـ عَدَمُ ٱحْتِذَارٍ ـ عَدَمُ ـ مُلَاحَظَةٍ ـ قِلَّةُ ٱحْتِيَاطٍ. *See also* Carelessness, *n.*

Incavated, *a.* *See* Concave, *a.*

Incavation, *n.* *See* Concavity, Hollow, *n.*

Incendiarism, *n.* حَرْقُ ٱلْبُيُوتِ قَصْدًا ـ ٱلْحَرْقُ قَصْدًا.

Incendiary, *n.* One who maliciously burns houses, مُحْرِقُ ٱلْبُيُوتِ قَصْدًا. A stirrer up of strife, مُحَرِّكُ ٱلْفِتَنِ ـ مُحَرِّش ـ صَاحِبُ فِتْنَةٍ ـ مِنْ أَهْلِ ٱلْفَسَادِ.

Incendiary, *a.* Exciting factions, مُفْتِن ـ مُفْسِد ـ زَارِعُ ٱلْفِتَنِ.

Incense, *n.* Gums used for incense, بَخُور *pl.* بَخَاخِيرُ ـ لُبَان ـ كُنْدُر ـ حَصَاءُ لُبَانٍ ـ كُنْكُ. The fumes of —, بَخُور. The — of flattery, مُدَاهَنَة ـ تَقْرِيظ ـ إِطْرَآء ـ تَمْلِيس ـ تَفْرِيط. Praise, ثَنَآء ـ مَدْح ـ تَنْبِيَة. Thanksgiving, شُكْر ـ شُكْرَان.

Incense, *v.t.* To perfume with incense, بَخَّرَ. To praise, مَدَحَ ـَ ـ أَثْنَى عَلَى. To flatter, دَاهَنَ ـ فَرَّطَ ـ قَرَّظَ ـ أَطْرَأَ. To irritate, هَيَّجَ ـ حَكَّرَ ـَ ـ أَغْضَبَ ـ أَغَاظَ ـ أَمَلَّ ـ أَوْغَرَ ٱلصَّدْرَ.

Incensed, *a.* Angered, مَحْكُور ـ غَضُوب ـ مُغْتَاظ. *See also* Angry, *a.*

Incentive, *a.* Inciting, مُسْتَفِزٌّ ـ مُحَرِّض ـ مُهَيِّج ـ بَاعِث ـ مُرَغِّب ـ سَائِق ـ حَاثٌّ. Encouraging, مُشَجِّع ـ مُشَوِّق ـ مُرَغِّب.

Incentive, *n.* إِسْتِفْزَاز ـ مَنْخَسَة ـ حَضّ ـ مِهْمَاز ـ بَاعِث ـ حَثّ ـ سَائِق.

Inception, *n.* بَدْء ـ أَوَّل ـ إِبْتِدَآء ـ شُرُوع ـ بَدَآءَة ـ بِدَايَة.

Inceptive, *a.* بَادِئٌ ـ شَارِع ـ إِبْتِدَائِيٌّ.

Inceration, *n.* تَشْمِيع ـ تَلْبِيس بِشَمْعٍ.

Incertitude, *n.* إِشْتِبَاه ـ رَيْب ـ إِرْتِيَاب ـ شَكّ ـ شُبْهَة. To be in a state of —, تَحَيَّرَ.

Incessancy, *n.* إِسْتِمْرَار ـ تَوَاتُر ـ تَتَابُع ـ دَوَام.

Incessant, *a.* مُسْتَمِرٌّ ـ مُتَوَاتِر ـ مُتَوَالٍ ـ مُتَتَابِع ـ بِدُونِ ٱنْقِطَاعٍ. To be —, تَوَاتَرَ ـ إِسْتَمَرَّ ـ تَوَالَى ـ دَامَ ـُ.

Incessantly, *ad.* عَلَى ٱلتَّوَالِي ـ تَوَاتُرًا ـ بِتَتَابُعٍ ـ بِلَا ٱنْقِطَاعٍ ـ بِدُونِ تَوَقُّفٍ ـ دَائِمًا ـ عَلَى ٱلدَّوَامِ ـ عَلَى ٱلْإِسْتِمْرَارِ.

Incest, *n.* ٱلْفُجُورُ فِي ٱلْقَرَابَةِ ـ زِنَآءُ ٱلْأَقَارِبِ ـ زِنَآءٌ بَيْنَ ٱلْأَقَارِبِ ـ مُفَاجَرَة ـ فِجَار ـ فِسْق.

Incestuous, *a.* Of a person, مُرْتَكِبُ ٱلْفَحْشَآءِ فِي ٱلْأَقَارِبِ ـ فَاجِرٌ بِٱلْأَقْرِبَآءِ. Illicit, حَرَام ـ فَاحِش.

Incestuously, *ad.* بِٱلْحَرَامِ. In incest, فِي ٱلْحَرَامِ.

Incestuousness, *n.* *See* Incest, *n.*

Inch, *n.* إِصْبَع *pl.* أَصَابِعُ. Twelve inches make one foot,

— ٤ مَاتَ رُوَيْدًا رُوَيْدًا . To die by inches, القَدَمُ إِثْنَا عَشَرَ أُصْبُعًا تَجَرَّعَ ٱلْمَوْتَ غُصَصًا.

Inchoate, *a.* مَبْدُوٌّ .

Inchoation, *n.* إِبْتِدَآءٌ — بَدْءٌ .

Inchoative, *a.* بادِئٌ — إِبْتِدائِيٌّ . An — (*n.*) إِبْتِدَآءٌ — مُبْتَدَأٌ .

Incidence, *n.* The act of falling, happening, — وُقُوع — إِعْتِراض لِقَآءٌ — وُرُود — وُصُول . The angle of —, زَاوِيَةُ ٱلْوُرُودِ .

Incident, *a.* Happening, وَارِد — لَقِيٌّ — واصِل — واقِع . Appertaining to, — مَرْبُوطٌ ب — مُتَوَقِّف عَلَى — مَنُوطٌ ب — مُلْحَقٌ ب مُتَعَلِّقٌ ب . *See also* Incidental, Casual, *a.*

Incident, *n.* An event, — عَوارِض .*pl* عارِض — أَعْراض .*pl* عَرَض — خَوادِث .*pl* حادِث — ما جَرَى — وَقائِع .*pl* واقِعَة — وَقْعَة . A part of a narrative, قِصَّة — قَضِيَّة — حِكايَة — أَعْراض .*pl* عَرَض . *See also* Circumstance, *n.*

Incidental, *a.* إِتِّفاقِيٌّ — عارِضِيٌّ — تَصادُفِيٌّ .

Incidentally, *a.* صِدْفَةً — إِتِّفاقًا — عَرَضًا .

Incinerate, *v.t.* أَحَالَ-رَمَادًا — صَيَّرَ-رَمَادًا .

Incineration, *n.* إِحالَةُ ٱلشَّيْءِ إِلَى رَمادٍ — تَصْيِيرُ ٱلشَّيْءِ رَمادًا .

Incipiency, *n.* بِدايَة — شُرُوع — بَدْءٌ — بادِئُ بَدْءٍ .

Incipient, *a.* شارِع — بادِئٌ — إِبْتِدائِيٌّ .

Incipiently, *ad.* فِي ٱلشُّرُوعِ — أَوَّلًا — فِي ٱلْبَدْآءَةِ .

Incircumspection, *n.* *See* Incautiousness, *n.*

Incise, *v.t.* حَزَّ ٤. *See also to* Carve, Engrave, *v.t.*

Incision, *n.* A cut, gash, notch, — حَزَّة — حَزّ — شُقُوق .*pl* شَقّ جِراحات .*pl* جِراحَة — جُرُوح .*pl* جُرْح . A wound, قُرُوض .*pl* قِراض . Light incisions for letting blood, شَطِيبَة — شَطْب . To make such incisions in, شَطَّبَ .

Incisive, *a.* صارِم — بَتّار — قاطِع . The — teeth, الثَّنايا مِنَ ٱلْأَسْنانِ .

Incisor, *n.* An — tooth, ثَنِيَّة *pl.* ثَنايا .

Incitation, *n.* — تَحْرِيض — إِسْتِفْزاز — هِياج — حَضّ — حَثّ إِغْرَآء — تَحْرِيك .

Incite, *v.t.* — حَضَّضَ — ٤ حَثَّ عَلَى — ٤ حَثَّ — ٤ أَزَّ-عَلَى حَرَّضَ — ٢ حَمَلَ-عَلَى — إِسْتَفَزَّ — أَغْرَى — هَيَّجَ — أَنْهَضَ . To spur on, إِحْتَثَّ — إِهْتاجَ — تَهَيَّجَ . To be incited, أَنْكَظَ — نَكَظَ .

Incitement, *n.* A motive, سَبَب — باعِث — سائِق . *See also* Incitation, *n.*

Inciter, *n.* داعٍ — مُحَرِّك — مُحَرِّض — مُسْتَفِزّ .

Incitingly, *ad.* بِهِياجٍ — حَثًّا — بِإِغْراضٍ — تَهْيِيجًا — إِسْتِفْزازًا .

Incivility, *n.* غِلْظَة — غِلاظَة — قِلَّةُ أُنْسٍ — قِلَّةُ أَدَبٍ .

Incivilly, *ad.* بِخُشُونَةٍ — بِغِلاظَةٍ — بِقِلَّةِ أَدَبٍ .

Inclemency, *n.* Want of mildness, عُنْف — عَسْف — شِدَّة ; want of mercy, عَدَمُ شَفَقَةٍ — قَساوَة . Of the weather, — زَمْهَرِير شِدَّة — حِدَّة .

Inclement, *a.* Wanting in mildness, فَظّ — شَدِيد — عَنِيف . Of the weather, شَدِيد — حادّ — مُزَمْهِر .

Inclinable, *a.* Leaning to, مُمِيل ل — مائِلٌ إِلَى . Disposed to, راغِبٌ فِي — مُعْطَفٌ عَلَى — مُطْرِقٌ إِلَى .

Inclination, *n.* A leaning towards, إِنْحِراف — صَغًا — مَيْلٌ إِلَى — مَيَلان — مَيْل — هَرِيَّة . Propension of mind, إِنْعِطافٌ نَحْوَ — إِلَى — أَعْطاف *or* عَواطِفُ .*pl* عَطْف — حَذْل — خاطِر — عُرْجَة — إِصْغَآء — وُدّ — مَحَبَّة . Love, affection, مَمِيل — مَمال — عِمْلَة — طَبِيَّة . The — of a balance, شَوْق — هَوًى — لَوْط . The — of a balance, عَيْن . To have an — for a thing, إِشْتاقَ إِلَى — إِنْعَطَفَ عَلَى — ٢ صَدَعَ إِلَى . *See also* Slope, *n.*

Incline, *v.t.* To cause to deviate from a certain line, — صَوَّبَ — إِسْتَمالَ ب — ٢ عَطَفَ — ٤ حَرَفَ — أَصْغَى — مَيَّلَ — أَمالَ أَشْرَى — أَرْكَنَ-إِلَى . To give a tendency to, as of the will or affections, مَيَّلَ-إِلَى — عَطَفَ-عَلَى . To — the ear to, to listen to, ٢ نَصَتَ إِلَى — أَصْغَى إِلَى . To — one's steps towards, ٢ ضَرَبَ تَوَجَّهَ إِلَى — ٢ سارَ إِلَى — إِلَى . He inclined his sight towards him, صَوَّبَ إِلَيْهِ بَصَرَهُ . *See also to* Bend, Slope, Stoop, *v.t.*

Incline, *v.i.* To deviate from an erect or parallel line, — ٢ جَنَحَ أَصْغَى — إِجْتَنَحَ — تَصَوَّبَ — إِنْحَدَرَ — إِنْعَرَجَ ; to — towards, إِنْحَرَفَ إِلَى — إِنْعَطَفَ إِلَى — ٢ مالَ نَحْوَ . To be favourably disposed to, — ٢ مالَ إِلَى — ٢ لَوَى عَلَى — ٢ وَدَّ — تَشَوَّقَ إِلَى — تَعَطَّفَ عَلَى — يَجُودُ .aor جادَ إِلَى — ٤ رَكَنَ إِلَى — ٢ غَرِضَ إِلَى ٢ رَغِبَ فِي . To —, as to an opinion, ٢ لَوَى عَلَى . To —, as a colour to some other colour, ٢ ضَرَبَ إِلَى : it inclines to blackness, يَضْرِبُ إِلَى ٱلسَّوادِ . To —, as in worship, ٤ سَجَدَ . To —, of the sun or stars, ٢ مالَ — ٢ عَرَجَ . To — towards one, as in listening, تَلَفَّتَ إِلَى . The balance inclined, عالَ ٱلْمِيزانُ *aor.* يَعُولُ . The weather inclines to fair, كانَ ٱلْجَوُّ يَصْحُو . This cloth inclines to red, هٰذا ٱلْجُوخُ يَمِيلُ (*or* يَضْرِبُ) إِلَى ٱلْحُمْرَةِ . He inclined to them, جَنَحَ إِلَيْهِمْ . The road inclined with us, ٢ إِنْعَرَجَ بِنا ٱلطَّرِيقُ . To — or to be disposed to, أَطْرَقَ إِلَى : He inclines to diversion, يُطْرِقُ إِلَى ٱللَّهْوِ .

Incline, *n.* حُدُور — حُطُوط — صَبَب — هُبُوط — مُنْعَرَج .

Inclined, *a.* Leaning, مَيّال — مائِل — مُنْحَطّ . Bent, — مُضْغًى مُعْوَجّ . To be — to, bent towards, إِنْعَوَجَ إِلَى . An — plane, سَطْحٌ مائِلٌ . To be favourably — towards one, إِسْتَعْطَفَ عَلَى ; to seek to make one so, إِسْتَعْطَفَ-عَلَى .

Incloister, *v.t.* *See to* Cloister, *v.t.*

Inclose, *v.t.* To surround, أَحَاطَ بِ ; as with a border, كَنَّفَ — اِكْتَنَفَ ; as with a hedge, سَوَّجَ — سَيَّجَ . To besiege, حَاصَرَ . To —, as with a wall of defence, حَصَّنَ . To stop up, سَدَّ ². To —, as of a letter, ظَرَّفَ — أَدْرَجَ — لَفَّ ². To — land, so as to prevent others building thereon, حَكَّرَ : such an inclosure, حِكْر *pl.* أَحْكَار . He inclosed his land, حَجَزَ ² (*or* اِحْتَجَزَ *or* حَجَّزَ) حَوْلَ أَرْضِهِ . I sent it inclosed in my letter, أَنْفَذْتُهُ ضِمْنَ (*or* فِي طَيِّ) كِتَابِي .

Inclosure, *n.* The act of inclosing, إِحَاطَة ; a place inclosed, حَدِيقَة — حُجْرَة — جِدَار — جَدِيرَة — مَحَاجِرُ *pl.* مَحْجِر . An — of pales, حَيْرَة ; of hedges, سِيَاج . An — made of canes, حِبَاك . An — for cattle, حَظِيرَة — زَرِيبَة — زَرْب . A wall, حَائِط . The — of a letter, مَا هُوَ فِي ضِمْنِ — أَوْرَاق *pl.* وَرَقَة أَوْ غَيْرُهَا فِي طَيِّ كِتَابٍ . I constructed an — for the sheep, زَرَبْتُ لِلْغَنَمِ .

Incloud, *v.t.* *See to* Darken, *v.t.*

Include, *v.t.* To reckon in, حَسَبَ فِي ². To insert, أَدْخَلَ — أَدْرَجَ — ضَمَّنَ . To comprise, شَمِلَ ² — اِحْتَوَى عَلَى — اِحْتَوَى — تَضَمَّنَ — اِشْتَمَلَ عَلَى .

Inclusion, *n.* جَمْع — إِدْرَاج — تَضْمِين — إِدْخَال .

Included, *a.* مَجْمُوع — مَشْمُول — مُضَمَّن — مُنْدَرِج — دَاخِل . What is — within a town or country, ضَامِنَة . What is — in any vessel, contents, مُضَمَّن .

Including, *a.* } **Inclusive**, } — مُشْتَمِلٌ عَلَى — مُتَضَمِّن — مُحْتَوٍ عَلَى — شَامِل — عَامّ . From Monday to Saturday inclusive, مِنَ ٱلِاثْنَيْنِ إِلَى ٱلسَّبْتِ ٱشْتِمَالًا .

Inclusively, *ad.* لَفًّا — ضِمْنًا .

Incoagulable, *a.* لَا يُجْمَدُ — تَجْمِيدُهُ غَيْرُ مُمْكِنٍ .

Incog. *ad.* } **Incognito**, } بِتَنَكُّرٍ — تَنَكُّرًا — تَسَتُّرًا — بِٱخْتِفَاءٍ . To make one's self —, تَخَفَّى — تَنَكَّرَ . He came —, جَاءَ مُتَنَكِّرًا أَعْنِي بِدُونِ إِظْهَارِ صِفَتِهِ ٱلرَّسْمِيَّةِ . *See also under to* Disguise, *v.t.*

Incogitative, *a.* عَاجِزٌ عَنِ ٱلْفِكْرِ .

Incognizable, *a.* غَيْرُ مُدْرَكٍ — لَا يُدْرَكُ — لَا يُمَيَّزُ .

Incoherence, *n.* } **Incoherency**, } Want of cohesion, عَدَمُ مُلَازَمَةٍ — عَدَمُ ٱلْتِصَاقٍ — اِنْفِكَاك — اِرْتِخَاء ; want of continuity, عَدَمُ إِلْحَاقٍ — عَدَمُ تَتَابُعٍ — عَدَمُ ٱطِّرَادٍ — عَدَمُ تَنَاسُقٍ . Incongruity, قِلَّةُ مُطَابَقَةٍ . Foolish speech, هَذَر .

Incoherent, *a.* Wanting cohesion, مُنْفَكّ — غَيْرُ مُلْتَصِقٍ — مُنْحَلّ — خَالٍ — عَدِيمُ ٱلتَّنَاسُقِ — مُرْتَخٍ — غَيْرُ مُلَازِمٍ ; wanting in continuity, غَيْرُ مُطَّرِدٍ — عَدِيمُ ٱلِٱطِّرَادِ — غَيْرُ مُتَتَابِعٍ ; separate like grains of sand, مُنْهَال ; of speech, مِنْطَق — هُرَاء — عَشْطَلَة — هُرَاء . Inconsequent, غَيْرُ مُتَلَاحِقٍ — غَيْرُ مُتَوَاصِلٍ . The language is —, الْكَلَامُ لَا يَأْخُذُ بَعْضُهُ بِأَعْنَاقِ بَعْضٍ .

Incoherently, *ad.* بِدُونِ إِلْحَاقٍ — بِلَا تَنَاسُقٍ — بِدُونِ مُلَازَمَةٍ — بِعَدَمِ تَتَابُعٍ . To speak —, هَرَأَ — فَرْفَرَ ².

Incombustibility, *n.* عَدَمُ إِمْكَانِ ٱلِاحْتِرَاقِ .

Incombustible, *a.* إِحْرَاقُهُ غَيْرُ مُمْكِنٍ — لَا يَحْتَرِقُ .

Incombustibly, *ad.* بِوَجْهٍ لَا يَحْتَرِقُ .

Income, *n.* مَاهِيَّة — إِيرَاد — مَحْصُول — دَخْل — مَدْخُول . The income of the Treasury, الْوَارِدَاتُ ٱلْمَالِيَّةُ . Income tax, أَمْلَاكِيَّة — رَسْمٌ عَلَى إِيرَادِ ٱلْأَشْخَاصِ — ضَرِيبَةٌ عَلَى ٱلْإِيرَادَاتِ .

In commendam, *ad.* تَعْيِينُ خُورِيٍّ إِلَى وَظِيفَةٍ كَنَائِسِيَّةٍ عَلَى يَدِ ٱلْحُكُومَةِ وَذَلِكَ مُوَقَّتًا إِلَى أَنْ يَتَعَيَّنَ خُورِيٌّ قَانُونِيٌّ .

Incommensurability, *n.* } **Incommensurableness**, } The quality of having no common measure, اِمْتِنَاعُ ٱلْمُقَايَسَةِ . Inequality, عَدَمُ مُسَاوَاةٍ — عَدَمُ نِسْبَةٍ . Inadequacy, عَدَمُ كِفَايَةٍ .

Incommensurable, *a.* لَا يُقَاسُ بِهِ — مُمْتَنِعُ ٱلْقِيَاسِ — مُخْتَلِفُ ٱلْقِيَاسِ — الْمُقَايَسَةُ بِهِ غَيْرُ مُمْكِنَةٍ . Unequal, inadequate, غَيْرُ مُتَنَاسِبٍ — لَا يَتَنَاسَبُ .

Incommensurably, *ad.* مِنْ غَيْرِ مُسَاوَاةٍ — بِعَدَمِ ٱلتَّنَاسُبِ — بِعَدَمِ كِفَايَةٍ .

Incommensurate, *a.* غَيْرُ كَافٍ — غَيْرُ مُتَنَاسِبٍ — غَيْرُ مُسَاوٍ — نَاقِصٌ عَنْ .

Incommiscible, *a.* لَا يُخْلَطُ — لَا يُمَازَجُ — لَا يُمْزَجُ .

Incommode, *v.t.* أَتْعَبَ — آذَى — كَلَّفَ — ضَجَّرَ — أَضْجَرَ — ثَقَّلَ عَلَى . To crowd, زَاحَمَ .

Incommodious, *a.* Giving trouble, ضَجُور — مُتْعِب — شَاقّ — غَيْرُ — غَيْرُ مُلَائِمٍ — ضَيِّق . Inconvenient, مُثْقِلٌ عَلَى — مُضْجِر — عَدِيمُ ٱلرَّحْبِ — مُنَاسِبٍ .

Incommodiously, *ad.* بِعَدَمِ مُنَاسَبَةٍ — بِعَدَمِ مُلَاءَمَةٍ — بِإِزْهَاقٍ .

Incommodiousness, *n.* The quality of causing inconvenience, عَدَمُ — ضِيقَة — زَحْمَة — تَكَلُّف — ضَجَر . Want of accommodation, عَدَمُ سَعَةٍ — عَدَمُ ٱلرَّحْبِ — عَدَمُ مُنَاسَبَةٍ — مُلَاءَمَةٍ .

Incommunicability, *n.* } **Incommunicableness**, } The quality of not being capable of being told, الْبَوْحُ بِهِ غَيْرُ مُمْكِنٍ ; of not being capable of being partaken of by another, إِشْرَاكُ ٱلْغَيْرِ فِيهِ مُحَال ; of not being transferred by contagion, عَدَمُ سِرَايَةٍ .

Incommunicable, *a.* That cannot be shared by others, غَيْرُ — إِشْرَاكُ ٱلْغَيْرِ فِيهِ مُحَال — مُشْتَرَكٍ فِيهِ ; that cannot be told, إِفْشَاؤُهُ غَيْرُ مُمْكِنٍ — الْبَوْحُ بِهِ غَيْرُ مُمْكِنٍ ; not contagious, غَيْرُ سَارٍ .

Incommunicably, *ad.* بِما لا يُباحُ بِهِ ـ بِدُونِ إِشْراكِ ٱلْغَيْرِ فِيهِ ـ بِما يَعِزُّ تَبْلِيغُهُ.

Incommunicative, *a.* مِنْ طَبْعِهِ قِلَّةُ ٱلْمُبالَغَةِ ـ حِرِّيس ـ كَتُوم ـ طِرِّيق. *See also* Reserved, *a.*

Incommutability, *n.* }
Incommutableness, } عَدَمُ ٱلتَّحْوِيلِ وَٱلِٱبْتِدالِ.

Incommutable, *a.* ما لا يُبْدَلُ.

Incommutably, *ad.* بِدُونِ إِبْدالٍ وَٱبْتِدالٍ.

Incompact, *a.* }
Incompacted, } سَخِيف ـ غَيْرُ مَتِينٍ ـ أَسْوَلُ ـ رِخْوٌ ـ هَشٌّ ـ مُخْتَلٌّ ـ خالٍ.

Incomparable, *a.* نادِرَةٌ ـ يَتِيم ـ وَحِيد ـ نادِر ـ فَرِيد ـ عَزِيز ـ واحِدُ ٱلْأَحَدِينَ ـ مُنْقَطِعُ ٱلْقَرِينِ ـ فُرادَى *pl.* فَرْد ـ ٱلدَّهْرِ ـ لَيْسَ لَهُ شَبِيهٌ ـ لا نَظِيرَ لَهُ ـ عَدِيمُ ٱلْمِثْلِ ـ بَيْهَم. The — One, God, ٱلْعَزِيزُ.

Incomparableness, *n.* Excellence beyond comparison, عِزٌّ ـ كَوْنُ ٱلشَّيْءِ مِنْ غَيْرِ شَبِيهٍ ـ نادِرَة ـ فَضْلٌ لا نَظِيرَ لَهُ ـ عِزَّة.

Incomparably, *ad.* لِلْغايَةِ ـ بِكَثِيرٍ ـ بِلا نَظِيرٍ ـ بِلا مُقايَسَةٍ. The sun is — more splendid than the moon, ٱلشَّمْسُ أَزْهَرُ مِنَ ٱلْقَمَرِ بِلا مُقايَسَةٍ.

Incompassionate, *a.* قاسِي ـ مِنْ غَيْرِ شَفَقَةٍ ـ عَدِيمُ ٱلرَّحْمَةِ ـ ٱلْقَلْبِ.

Incompassionately, *ad.* مِنْ غَيْرِ شَفَقَةٍ ـ بِعَدَمِ ٱلرَّحْمَةِ ـ بِقَساوَةٍ.

Incompatibility, *n.* Incongruity, عَدَمُ ـ تَخالُف ـ مُبايَنَة ـ إِخْتِلاف. Difference, عَدَمُ ٱلْمُشاكَلَةِ ـ قِلَّةُ وِفاقٍ ـ مُوافَقَةٍ. Antipathy, مُنافَرَة ـ تَنافُر. Incompatibility of temper, إِخْتِلافُ ٱلْمِزاجِ.

Incompatible, *a.* غَيْرُ ـ مُتَنافِر ـ مُخالِف ـ مُغايِر ـ مُناقِض. To be —, incongruous, with, لا يَتَّفِقُ مَعَ ـ لا يُطابِقُ ـ مُوافِقٍ ـ ناقَضَ ـ خالَفَ.

Incompatibly, *ad.* بِٱخْتِلافٍ ـ بِٱلتَّناقُضِ ـ بِلا ٱتِّفاقٍ.

Incompetency, *n.* Insufficiency, تَقْصِير ـ قِلَّةُ كِفايَةٍ ـ عَدَمُ كِفايَةٍ. Unfitness, عَدَمُ أَهْلِيَّةٍ. Inappropriateness, عَدَمُ صَلاحِيَةٍ. Inability, عَدَمُ ٱقْتِدارٍ ـ عَجْز. *See also* Inability, *n.*

Incompetent, *a.* Without power, عاجِز ـ غَيْرُ مُقْتَدِرٍ. Unfit for ..., غَيْرُ أَهْلٍ لِ. Not sufficient for ..., غَيْرُ كافٍ لِ.

Incompetently, *ad.* بِقِلَّةِ كِفايَةٍ ـ بِلا كِفايَةٍ ـ بِدُونِ لِياقَةٍ ـ بِٱلتَّقْصِيرِ.

Incomplete, *a.* غَيْرُ كامِلٍ ـ ناقِص. *See also* Defective, Imperfect, *a.*

Incompletely, *ad.* بِنَقْصٍ ـ بِغَيْرِ كَمالٍ. *See also* Defectively, Imperfectly, *ad.*

Incompleteness, *n.* نَقْص ـ عَدَمُ كَمالٍ. *See also* Defect, Imperfection, *n.*

Incomplex, *a.* مُجَرَّد ـ ساذِج ـ بَسِيط ـ غَيْرُ مُرَكَّبٍ.

Incompliable, *a.* Untractable, عارِم ـ شَكِس ـ صَعْب ـ فَظٌّ.

Incompliance, *n.* Untractableness, فَظاظَة ـ شَراسَة ـ شَكاسَة. Refusal of compliance, عَدَمُ رِضاءٍ ـ عِناد ـ إِباءَة.

Incompliant, *a.* مُتَأَبٍّ. To be — to, تَأَبَّى عَلَى.

Incomposite, *a.* *See* Incomplex, *a.*

Incomprehensibility, *n.* }
Incomprehensibleness, } عَدَمُ ـ كَوْنُ ٱلشَّيْءِ لا يُمْكِنُ إِدْراكُهُ ـ إِمْكانِ ٱلْإِحاطَةِ بِهِ.

Incomprehensible, *a.* يَفُوقُ ـ لا يُدْرَكُ ـ إِدْراكُهُ غَيْرُ مُمْكِنٍ ـ ٱلْإِحاطَةُ بِهِ غَيْرُ مُمْكِنَةٍ ـ غَيْرُ مُدْرَكٍ ـ يَتَجاوَزُ حَدَّ ٱلْفَهْمِ ـ ٱلْعَقْلَ.

Incomprehensibly, *ad.* بِنَوْعٍ غَيْرِ مُدْرَكٍ.

Incompressibility, *n.* كَوْنُ ٱلشَّيْءِ لا يُضْغَطُ ـ كَبْسُهُ مُحالٌ.

Incompressible, *a.* لا يُضْغَطُ ـ لا يُكْبَسُ.

Incomputable, *a.* *See* Incalculable, *a.*

Inconcealable, *a.* لا يُخْفَى.

Inconceivable, *a.* لا يُتَخَيَّلُ ـ لا يُتَصَوَّرُ ـ يَفُوقُ ٱلْوَهْمَ.

Inconceivableness, *n.* كَوْنُ ٱلشَّيْءِ لا يُتَصَوَّرُ ـ كَوْنُ ٱلشَّيْءِ يَفُوقُ ٱلْوَهْمَ.

Inconceivably, *ad.* بِدُونِ تَصَوُّرٍ ـ لِلْغايَةِ.

Inconclusive, *a.* غَيْرُ مُقْنِعٍ ـ غَيْرُ قاطِعٍ ـ غَيْرُ كافٍ.

Inconclusiveness, *n.* عَدَمُ إِقْناعٍ ـ عَدَمُ كِفايَةٍ.

Inconcoction, *n.* Unripeness, فَجاجَة ـ عَدَمُ نُضْجٍ ـ عَدَمُ ٱسْتِواءٍ.

Incondensable, *a.* That may not be thickened, لا يَجْمُدُ. That may not be shortened, لا يُوجَزُ.

Inconformity, *n.* عَدَمُ مُوافَقَةٍ ـ مُخالَفَة ـ مُغايَرَة ـ مُناقَضَة.

Incongealable, *a.* تَجْمِيدُهُ غَيْرُ مُمْكِنٍ.

Incongealableness, *n.* عَدَمُ إِمْكانِ ٱلتَّجْمِيدِ.

Incongruity, *n.* Inconsistency, عَدَمُ تَتابُعٍ ـ عَدَمُ تَوافُقٍ ـ عَدَمُ تَجانُسٍ ـ إِخْتِلاف ـ خِلاف. An absurdity, نازِيَة. A discord, وَتْنَة. An — of speech, غُجْمَة.

Incongruous, *a.* مُحال ـ مُحالٌ ب ـ مُسْتَحِيل ـ مُخالِف ـ غَيْرُ مُتَجانِسٍ ـ مُناقِض ـ غَيْرُ مُناسِبٍ; of a speaker, فَكّاكٌ ـ هَكّاكٌ. Inconsistent, not harmonizing, as with something else, غَيْرُ مُتَتابِعٍ.

Incongruously, *ad.* بِلا مُناسَبَةٍ ـ بِعَدَمِ تَتابُعٍ.

Inconscionable, *a.* بِلا ذِمَّةٍ ـ عَدِيمُ ٱلْإِخْلاصِ.

Inconsequence, *n.* عَدَمُ مُوَافَقَةٍ ـ عَدَمُ مُطَابَقَةٍ.

Inconsequent, *a.* مُضَادِدٌ ـ غَيْرُ مُطَابِقٍ ـ غَيْرُ مُوَافِقٍ.

Inconsequential, *a.* Of no importance, غَيْرُ مُهِمٍّ ـ جُزْئِيٌّ ـ مَا تَحْتَ خَبَرٍ ـ عَبَثٌ. Not following from the premises, غَيْرُ نَاتِجٍ مِنَ مُقَدِّمَاتِ ٱلْبُرْهَانِ.

Inconsiderable, *a.* جُزْئِيٌّ ـ تَافِهٌ ـ صَغِيرٌ ـ طَفِيفٌ ـ حَقِيرٌ ـ قَلِيلٌ ـ كَلَا شَيْءٍ ـ دَنِيءٌ ـ أَدْنَى.

Inconsiderableness, *n.* جُزْئِيَّةٌ ـ طَفَافَةٌ ـ ضِعَةٌ ـ صُغْرٌ ـ تَفَاهَةٌ ـ حَقَارَةٌ ـ قِلَّةٌ.

Inconsiderate, *a.* Thoughtless, مَاجِنٌ ـ مُتَهَوِّرٌ ـ مَجُونٌ ـ دِعِنٌّ *pl.* دَعِنَةٌ ـ مُتَعَسِّفٌ ـ غَافِلٌ ـ غَيْرُ ٱلْتِي. Not proper, غَيْرُ مُنَاسِبٍ. How — he is! مَا أَدْعَنَهُ.

Inconsiderately, *ad.* بِبَادِئِ رَأْيٍ ـ تَعَسُّفًا ـ بِمُجُونٍ ـ بِدَعَانَةٍ ـ بِتَغَافُلٍ ـ بِلَا بَصِيرَةٍ. To do a thing —, to act — in a matter, تَعَسَّفَ فِي ـ إِعْتَسَفَ فِي.

Inconsiderateness, *n.* | **Inconsideration,** Thoughtlessness, مَجَانٌ ـ دَعَانَةٌ ـ طَيْشٌ ـ تَغَافُلٌ ـ إِعْتِسَافٌ ـ قِلَّةٌ ـ تَمْيِيزٍ ـ قِلَّةُ فِكْرٍ. To act with — in, تَمَجَّنَ فِي ـ تَعَسَّفَ فِي.

Inconsistence, *n.* | **Inconsistency,** Contrariety, incongruity, مُبَايَنَةٌ ـ مُغَايَرَةٌ ـ مُخَالَفَةٌ ـ مُنَاقَضَةٌ ـ وَثْنَةٌ ـ فَرْقٌ. Changeableness, فَرْفَرَةٌ ـ إِنْقِلَابٌ ـ طَيْشٌ ـ طَيَشَانٌ.

Inconsistent, *a.* Contrary, مُخَالِفٌ ـ مُغَائِرٌ ـ غَيْرُ مُوَافِقٍ ـ مُنَاقِضٌ ـ مُخْتَلِفٌ. Inconstant, طَائِشٌ ـ طَيَّاشٌ. His arguments are —, دَلَائِلُهُ مُتَنَافِيَةٌ (*or* مُتَنَاقِضَةٌ). He is — with himself, هُوَ مُضَادِدٌ لِنَفْسِهِ. To be —, fickle, طَاشَ ـ. *See also* Inconstant, *a.*

Inconsistently, *ad.* Contrarily, بِتَغَايُرٍ ـ بِتَنَاقُضٍ ـ بِدُونِ مُوَافَقَةٍ; inconstantly, طَيْشًا ـ بِطَيَشَانٍ ـ بِفَرْفَرَةٍ.

Inconsolable, *a.* لَا يَتَسَلَّى ـ لَا يَتَعَزَّى.

Inconsolably, *ad.* بِدُونِ تَعَزٍّ ـ بِلَا تَسَلٍّ.

Inconsonance, *n.* | **Inconsonancy,** مُبَايَنَةٌ ـ إِخْتِلَافٌ. *See also* Disagreement, Inconsistency, Discordance, *n.*

Inconspicuous, *a.* لَا يَتَمَيَّزُ ـ غَيْرُ بَائِنٍ ـ غَيْرُ مُبِينٍ ـ مُبْهَمٌ.

Inconstancy, *n.* Instability, عَدَمُ ثَبَاتٍ ـ عَدَمُ قَرَارٍ. Fickleness, نَاقِلَةٌ ـ فَرْفَرَةٌ ـ مَجْرٌ ـ هَيْعَرَةٌ ـ خَفِيفٌ ـ طَيْشٌ ـ طَيْرَةٌ. Irresolution, سَفَهٌ ـ فَيْلُولَةٌ ـ شَكٌّ ـ تَقَلْقُلٌ.

Inconstant, *a.* Unstable, عَدِيمُ ٱلثَّبَاتِ ـ عَدِيمُ ٱلْقَرَارِ. Fickle, نَزِقٌ *pl.* نُزُوزٌ ـ عَاتِكٌ ـ مُتَلَوِّنٌ ـ قِلْقَالٌ ـ غَمْلُوجٌ ـ قَرْنَارٌ ـ عَضْبٌ ـ طَائِشٌ ـ مُتَقَلِّبٌ. Irresolute, سَفِيهٌ ـ فَائِلُ ٱلرَّأْيِ ـ قَلَّاعٌ. Unfaithful, of a man or woman, عَيْهَرٌ. To be —, flighty, خَفَّ ـ. He became —, flighty, طَارَ طَائِرُهُ ـ طَاشَ ـ *aor.* يَطِيشُ.

Inconstantly, *ad.* بِعَدَمِ ثَبَاتٍ ـ بِقِلَّةِ قَرَارٍ ـ بِفَرْفَرَةٍ ـ تَلَوُّنًا ـ تَقَلْقُلًا ـ بِطَيْشٍ.

Inconsumable, *a.* As with fire, إِحْرَاقُهُ غَيْرُ مُمْكِنٍ ـ لَا يُحْرَقُ.

Incontestable, *a.* لَا يُنْكَرُ ـ شَافٍ ـ قَاطِعٌ ـ إِنْكَارُهُ غَيْرُ مُمْكِنٍ.

Incontestably, *ad.* بِلَا نِزَاعٍ ـ بِغَيْرِ ٱعْتِرَاضٍ ـ إِطْلَاقًا.

Incontinence, *n.* | **Incontinency,** Want of restraint upon the passions, unchastity, غُلْمَةٌ ـ قِلَّةُ عِفَّةٍ ـ عَدَمُ نَزَاهَةٍ ـ عَدَمُ ضَبْطِ ٱلشَّهْوَةِ ـ إِنْهِمَاكٌ فِي ٱلْمَعَاصِي ـ دَعَارَةٌ. Incontinence of urine, إِدْرَارُ ٱلْبَوْلِ.

Incontinent, *a.* غَلِيمٌ ـ عَدِيمُ ٱلْعِفَّةِ ـ مُنْهَمِكٌ فِي ٱلْمَحَارِمِ.

Incontinently, *ad.* Unchastely, بِدُونِ عِفَّةٍ. Immediately, حَالًا ـ فِي ٱلْحَالِ ـ فِي ٱلسَّاعَةِ.

Incontrovertible, *a.* *See* Incontestable, *a.*

Incontrollable, *a.* لَا يُسَاسُ ـ لَا يَنْقَادُ ـ لَا يُقْمَعُ ـ ضَبْطُهُ مُحَالٌ ـ مُتَمَرِّدٌ ـ سَائِبٌ.

Incontrovertible, *a.* قَاطِعٌ ـ شَافٍ ـ لَا يُخْشَى عَلَيْهِ مِنْ مُنْكِرٍ ـ مُسَلَّمٌ ـ مُحَقَّقٌ.

Incontrovertibly, *ad.* إِطْلَاقًا ـ بِغَيْرِ ٱعْتِرَاضٍ ـ بِلَا نِزَاعٍ.

Inconvenience, *v.t.* ثَقَّلَ عَلَى ـ أَتْعَبَ ـ شَقَّ عَلَى ـ أَكْلَفَ. I am afraid of inconveniencing you, أَخَافُ مِنْ أَنْ أُثَقِّلَ عَلَيْكَ. I hope this will not — you, أَرْجُو أَنْ لَا يَحْصُلَ لَكَ مِنْ ذٰلِكَ ثِقْلَةٌ.

Inconvenience, *n.* | **Inconveniency,** Trouble, بَأْسٌ ـ أَذِيَّةٌ ـ إِقْلَاقٌ ـ تَعَبٌ ـ تَكَلُّفٌ ـ مَضَرَّةٌ ـ ثِقْلَةٌ. Unsuitableness, عَدَمُ مُلَاءَمَةٍ ـ عَدَمُ مُوَافَقَةٍ. A crowding, straitening, want of room, زَحْمَةٌ. There is no — in that, لَا بَأْسَ بِهِ. A serious —, such as is feared, مَحْذُورٌ ـ مَحْذُورَةٌ.

Inconvenient, *a.* Giving trouble, مُقْلِقٌ ـ مُكَدِّرٌ ـ مُتْعِبٌ ـ مُكَلِّفٌ ـ مُضِرٌّ. Unsuitable, غَيْرُ مُلَائِمٍ ـ غَيْرُ مُنَاسِبٍ ـ غَيْرُ مُوَافِقٍ ـ فِي غَيْرِ مَحَلِّهِ.

Inconveniently, *ad.* As occasioning trouble, بِزَحْمَةٍ ـ بِتَكَلُّفٍ; unsuitably, بِدُونِ مُوَافَقَةٍ; out of time or place, فِي غَيْرِ مَحَلِّهِ ـ فِي حِينٍ غَيْرِ مُنَاسِبٍ.

Inconvertibility, *n.* تَغَيُّرُهُ مُحَالٌ ـ تَبَادُلُهُ غَيْرُ مُمْكِنٍ ـ عَدَمُ إِمْكَانِ ٱلتَّحْوِيلِ; as into money, صَرْفُهُ بِٱلدَّرَاهِمِ مُحَالٌ.

Inconvertible, *a.* لَا يَتَغَيَّرُ ـ لَا يَتَحَوَّلُ; as into money, لَا يُصْرَفُ بِٱلدَّرَاهِمِ.

Inconvincible, *a.* لَا يُقْنَعُ ـ إِقْنَاعُهُ غَيْرُ مُمْكِنٍ ـ إِقْنَاعُهُ مُحَالٌ.

Inconvincibly, *ad.* بِدُونِ إِقْنَاعٍ.

Incorporal, *a.* *See* Incorporeal, *a.*

Incorporate, *v.t.* To mix together, مَزَجَ-مَعًا – خَلَطَ. To introduce into, أَدْخَلَ-فِي – أَدْرَجَ – أَدْمَجَ. To collect together, أَلَّفَ – جَمَعَ. To unite to, أَلْحَقَ-بِ – ضَمَّ-إِلَى. To make into one, أَحَّدَ. To comprise, إِحْتَوَى عَلَى. To — into a book extracts from another, عَلَّقَ.

Incorporate, *v.i.* To become mixed with, خَالَطَ – مَازَجَ –. To become united with, إِمْتَزَجَ – تَوَحَّدَ مَعَ – إِتَّحَدَ مَعَ. To be introduced into, أُدْرِجَ فِي. To be incorporated to, collected together with, إِنْضَمَّ إِلَى.

Incorporate, *a.* United in a body, مُتَّحِد – مُتَأَلِّف – مُنْضَمّ –. An — body, authorized by charter, مُجْتَمَع جَمْعِيَّة حَائِزَة بَرَاءَة.

Incorporation, *n.* The act of mixing, مَزْج – تَخْلِيط; of introducing into, إِدْمَاج – إِدْرَاج – إِدْخَال – جَمْع; of uniting to, ضَمّ إِلَى – إِلْحَاق بِ. The being incorporated, brought together, إِنْضِمَام. *See also* Corporation, *n.*

Incorporeal, *a.* رُوحِيّ – لا جَسَدَ لَهُ – غَيْرُ جَسَدِيّ – غَيْرُ هَيُولِيّ – خَالٍ مِنَ ٱلْجِسْمِ.

Incorporeally, *ad.* مِنْ غَيْرِ جَسَدٍ – رُوحِيًّا – بِعَدَمِ هَيُولَى – بِلَا جِسْمٍ.

Incorporeity, *n.* رُوحِيَّة – عَدَم جِسْمِيَّة – عَدَمُ هَيُولَى.

Incorrect, *a.* Inaccurate, ذُو غَلَطٍ – غَيْرُ مَضْبُوطٍ – غَيْرُ صَحِيحٍ. Improper, غَيْرُ لَائِقٍ – غَيْرُ مُسْتَحْسَنٍ – غَيْرُ مَمْدُوحٍ. *See also* Inaccurate, *a.*

Incorrectly, *ad.* غَلَطًا – بِلَا ضَبْطٍ – بِدُونِ تَصْحِيحٍ – بِلَا صِحَّةٍ.

Incorrectness, *n.* Inaccuracy, غَلَط – تَصْحِيف – قِلَّة ضَبْطٍ – عَدَم صِحَّةٍ. Impropriety, قِلَّة مُنَاسَبَةٍ – عَدَم لِيَاقَةٍ.

Incorrigibility, *n.* } Hopeless depravity, عُتُوّ – مُعَانَدَة – عِنَاد –
Incorrigibleness, } إِصْرَار عَلَى ٱلْمَعَاصِي.

Incorrigible, *a.* شَدِيدُ ٱلْخُبْثِ – لَا يَقْبَلُ ٱلْإِصْلَاحَ – عَاتٍ – لَا يَنْثَنِي عَنْ غَيِّهِ – مُعَانِد.

Incorrigibly, *ad.* بِلَا دَوَاءٍ – بِلَا عِلَاجٍ.

Incorrodible, *a.* غَيْرُ مَأْكُولٍ – مِمَّا لَا يُؤْكَلُ – لَا يُسْرَفُ – لَا يُقْرَضُ.

Incorrupt, *a.* Free from depravity, صَالِح – خَالِص – نَقِيّ – عَفِيف وَمُسْتَقِيم – طَاهِر – صَافٍ – صَادِق. Free from decay, غَيْرُ فَاسِدٍ – لَا يَفْسُدُ – بَاقٍ – دَائِم – لَا يَفْنَى. Not to be bribed, لَا يَقْبَلُ لَا يُرَاشَى – ٱلرِّشْوَة.

Incorruptibility, *n.* } Not being capable of decay, عَدَمُ ٱلْفَسَادِ –
Incorruptibleness, } عَدَمُ – تَنَزُّه عَنِ ٱلْفَسَادِ – عَدَمُ زَوَالٍ – بَقَاء – فَنَاء. The not receiving of bribes, إِمْتِنَاع عَنِ ٱلرِّشْوَةِ.

Incorruptible, *a.* Not subject to decay, عَدِيمُ ٱلْفَسَادِ – لَا يَفْنَى – لَا يَضْمَحِلُّ. *See also* Incorrupt, *a.*

Incorruption, *n.* } Exemption from decay, بَقَاء – عَدَمُ فَسَادٍ.
Incorruptness, } Purity, integrity, صَلَاح – إِسْتِقَامَة – صَفَاء – خُلُوص – طَهَارَة – نَقَاوَة.

Incrassate, *v.t.* To make thick, كَثَّفَ – جَمَّدَ – خَثَّرَ.

Incrassate, *v.i.* To become thick, تَكَاثَفَ – تَخَثَّرَ – جَمَدَ.

Incrassation, *n.* The act of thickening, تَجْمِيد – تَخْثِير – تَكْثِيف.

Incrassative, *a.* مُخَثِّر – مُكَثِّف.

Increase, *v.t.* As in size, جَسَّمَ – كَبَّرَ; in numbers, كَثَّرَ; in quantity, زَيَّدَ – زَادَ. To make to grow, أَنْمَى. To — by addition to, أَضَافَ-إِلَى – أَلْحَقَ-بِ. To multiply, double, ضَعَّفَ – ضَاعَفَ. To expand, وَسَّعَ – مَدَّ. To bless with increase, نَمَّى – بَارَكَ. God increased his property, زَادَهُ ٱللّٰهُ مَالًا.

Increase, *v.i.* As in size, تَجَسَّمَ – كَبُرَ; in numbers, كَثُرَ; in quantity, زَادَ *aor.* يَزِيدُ – إِزْدَادَ – تَكَاثَرَ. To —, of the moon, أَقْمَرَ; of water, مَدَّ; of seeds, زَكَا; of wealth, نَمَى; of plants, زَكَا; of wheat, أَرَاعَ. To grow, نَمَا *aor.* يَنْمُو – نَمَى. To multiply, double, تَضَاعَفَ. The affair increased in difficulty, إِزْدَادَ ٱلْأَمْرُ صُعُوبَةً. I increased in wealth, إِزْدَدْتُ مَالًا.

Increase, *n.* Growing larger in size, الْإِزْدِيَادُ جِرْمًا; in numbers, كَثْرَة – تَكَاثُر; in quantity, زِيَادَة – إِزْدِيَاد; in growth, نُمُوّ; by multiplication, ضَعْف – تَضَاعُف; by junction, إِضَافَة – إِلْحَاق. Produce, ثَمَر – مَحْصُول. Progeny, ذُرِّيَّة. To be on the —, كَانَ فِي ٱلزِّيَادَةِ. It is on the —, هُوَ فِي مَزِيدٍ. To ask one for an —, إِسْتَزَادَهُ. If I had demanded it he would have given me an —, لَوِ ٱسْتَزَدْتُهُ لَزَادَنِي.

Increasingly, *ad.* زِيَادَةً – فِي مَزِيدٍ – بِٱلزِّيَادَةِ.

Increate, *a.* غَيْرُ مَخْلُوقٍ.

Incredibility, *n.* } عَدَمُ تَصْدِيقٍ.
Incredibleness, }

Incredible, *a.* مُحَال – مُسْتَحِيل – لَا يُصَدَّقُ. Why should you believe it to be — ? لِمَاذَا يُعَدُّ عِنْدَكُمْ أَمْرًا لَا يُصَدَّقُ.

Incredibly, *ad.* بِمَا لَا يُصَدَّقُ.

Incredulity, *n.* } قِلَّة إِيمَانٍ – عَدَمُ ٱعْتِقَادٍ – قِلَّة تَصْدِيقٍ –
Incredulousness, } إِنْكَار – عَدَمُ ٱعْتِمَادٍ.

Incredulous, *a.* قَلِيلُ ٱلتَّصْدِيقِ ـ قَلِيلُ ٱلِٱعْتِقَادِ ـ قَلِيلُ ٱلْإِيمَانِ ـ مُنْكِر.

Incredulously, *ad.* بِقِلَّةِ ٱعْتِقَادٍ ـ بِقِلَّةِ تَصْدِيقٍ ـ بِقِلَّةِ إِيمَانٍ.

Increment, *n.* *See* Increase, *n.*

Increpation, *n.* سَخْط ـ تَوْبِيخ.

Incriminate, *v.t.* أَتْهَمَ ـ ب ـ إِسْتَذْنَبَ ـ عَزَى ٱلذَّنْبَ إِلَى. *See also under* Crime, *n.*

Incrust, *v.t.* لَبَّسَ ـ بِقِشْرَةٍ ـ لَبَّسَ ـ ب.

Incrustation, *n.* The act of incrusting, تَلْبِيسٌ بِقِشْرَةٍ ـ تَلْبِيس ـ ب. A crust, covering, قِشْرَة ـ غِشَآء. An — of clay, قُلاع.

Incubate, *v.i.* *See to* Brood, *v.i.*

Incubation, *n.* حَضْن ـ رَخْم ـ وُكُون.

Incubus, *n.* Nightmare, دَوْفَان ـ جَاثُوم ـ كَابُوس ـ ضَاغُوط ـ جُثَام. A dead weight, of a person, مُبْرِمٌ ثَقِيلٌ.

Inculcate, *v.t.* أَلَحَّ عَلَى ـ ب ـ طَبَعَ ـ فِي عَقْلِهِ ـ أَكَّدَ عَلَى ـ ب ـ عَلَّمَ ـ دَخَّلَ ـ فِي عَقْلِهِ.

Inculcation, *n.* تَعْلِيم ـ إِلْحَاح ـ تَأْكِيد.

Inculpable, *a.* لا ذَنْبَ لَهُ ـ ما عَلَيْهِ عِتَابٌ ـ لا يُعَابُ.

Inculpate, *v.t.* *See to* Blame, Censure, Incriminate, *v.t.*

Inculpation, *n.* *See* Blame, Censure, *n.*

Inculpatory, *a.* مُسْتَذْنِب ـ مُتْهِم.

Incumbency, *n.* A lying or resting on, إِتِّكَآءٌ عَلَى ـ إِسْتِنَادٌ إِلَى. Possession of an office, تَصَرُّف ـ إِقَامَةٌ بِمَنْصِبٍ. The — of a church, خُورَنَة.

Incumbent, *a.* Resting upon, مُسْتَنِدٌ إِلَى ـ مُتَّكِئٌ عَلَى ـ مُضْطَجِعٌ عَلَى. Obligatory, مَنُوطٌ بِ ـ لَازِم ـ وَاجِبٌ عَلَى ـ مُقْتَضًى. To be — on, حَقَّ لِ ـ وَجَبَ لِ *aor.* يَجِبُ. To make — on, أَوْجَبَ ـ ل ـ أَثْبَتَ ـ عَلَى ـ بَرَّزَ ـ عَلَى. It is most — on me, مِنْ أَهَمِّ ٱلْوَاجِبِ عَلَيَّ.

Incumbent, *n.* The — of an office, مُتَصَرِّف ـ صَاحِبُ مَنْصِبٍ; of a church, خُورِي *pl.* خَوَارِنَة.

Incumber, *v.t.* *See to* Cumber, *v.t.*

Incumbrance, *n.* *See* Cumbrance, *n.*

Incur, *v.t.* To become liable to, إِسْتَأْهَلَ ـ إِلْتَزَمَ ل ـ تَعَرَّضَ ل ـ وَقَعَ فِي *aor.* يَقَعُ ـ جَلَبَ عَلَى نَفْسِهِ. To — punishment, جَلَبَ عَلَى نَفْسِهِ ٱلْقِصَاصَ. To — expenses, تَكَلَّفَ مَصْرُوفًا ـ صَرَفَ مَصْرُوفًا. To — disgrace, وَقَعَ فِي غَضَبٍ. To — danger, أَخْطَرَ بِنَفْسِهِ.

Incurability, *n.* }
Incurableness, } كَوْنُ ٱلشَّيْءِ لا عِلَاجَ لَهُ ـ إِمْتِنَاعُ ٱلْعِلَاجِ; of a disease, كَوْنُ ٱلدَّآءِ عُقَامًا ـ كَوْنُ ٱلدَّآءِ لا عِلَاجَ لَهُ.

Incurable, *a.* Not to be cured, لا دَوَآءَ لَهُ ـ عُضَال ـ عَضِيل ـ عُقَام ـ عَيَآء ـ نَاجِس; of a disease, لا عِلَاجَ لَهُ ـ لا يُعَالَجُ ـ دَآءٌ عُضَالٌ ـ عَدِيمُ ٱلشِّفَآءِ ـ لا شِفَآءَ لَهُ. The disease which is — is stupidity, (*prov.*) ٱلدَّآءُ ٱلْعَيَآءُ ٱلْحُمْقُ.

Incurable, *n.* (عَضِيل *or* عُضَال) مُصَابٌ بِدَآءٍ ـ مُصَابٌ بِمَرَضٍ ـ عَدِيمُ ٱلشِّفَآءِ.

Incurably, *ad.* بِلا مُعَالَجَةٍ. Altogether, to the utmost, لِلْغَايَةِ ـ بَتَّةً.

Incurious, *a.* عَدِيمُ ٱلتَّفَحُّصِ ـ عَدِيمُ ٱلِٱسْتِقْصَآءِ ـ غَيْرُ سَآئِلٍ ـ سَاهٍ ـ مُتَغَافِل.

Incursion, *n.* غَزَاة ـ غَزْوَة ـ غَارَة ـ إِغَارَة *pl.* غَزَوَات. To make an — into an enemy's country, غَزَا ـ غَارَ عَلَى. To send on an —, إِسْتَغَارَ ـ عَلَى ـ أَغَارَ ـ عَلَى. They made mutual incursions, تَغَاوَرُوا. They made an — over the boundary, جَاوَزُوا ٱلْحُدُودَ.

Incursive, *a.* غَزَوِيّ ـ غَازٍ ـ مُغَاوِر ـ مُغِير. An — expedition, غَزَاة; an — troop of horse, خَيْلٌ مُغِيرَةٌ.

Incurvate, *v.t.* عَوَّجَ ـ ثَنَّى. *See also to* Bend, Curve, *v.t.*

Incurvation, *n.* The act of bending, تَعْوِيج ـ تَعْطِيف; the being bent, إِعْوِجَاج ـ إِنْعِوَاج ـ إِنْحِنَآء ـ حِنَايَة ـ إِنْثِنَآء.

Indagation, *n.* طَلَب ـ بَحْث ـ تَفْتِيشٌ عَلَى.

Indebted, *a.* Of debt, مَدْيُون; under obligation, مَمْنُون. To be indebted, in debt, إِسْتَدَانَ. I am — to you for your kindness to me, أَنَا مَدْيُونٌ لَكَ لِأَجْلِ فَضْلِكَ عَلَيَّ.

Indebtedness, *n.* Of debt, إِسْتِدَانَة ـ دَيْن; the being under obligation, مَنِّيْنَى ـ مِنَّة. To be under —, obligation, كَانَ تَحْتَ ٱلْمِنَّةِ.

Indecency, *n.* قِلَّة ـ فَحْشَآء ـ خَنَايَة ـ خَنًى ـ بَذَآءَة ـ بَذَآء ـ عَيْب ـ قِلَّةُ حِشْمَةٍ ـ أَدَب. *See also* Obscenity, *n.*

Indecent, *a.* قَلِيلُ ٱلْحِشْمَةِ ـ قَلِيلُ ٱلْحَيَآءِ ـ بَذِيء ـ خَنٍ ـ غَيْرُ لَائِقٍ ـ مُعِيب ـ فَاحِش. He narrates things quite —, يَحْكِي أُمُورًا مُخِلَّ بِٱلْأَدَبِ ـ يَخْنَى فِي مَنْطِقِهِ. Indecent speech, كَلَامٌ خَنٍ.

Indecently, *ad.* بِفَحَاشَةٍ ـ بِلا حِشْمَةٍ ـ بِقِلَّةِ حَيَآءٍ ـ بِخَنًى. To speak —, خَنِيَ فِي مَنْطِقِهِ *aor.* يَخْنَى.

Indeciduous, *a.* غَيْرُ سَاقِطٍ ـ غَيْرُ نَفَاضٍ.

Indecipherable, *a.* غَيْرُ قَابِلِ ٱلتَّفْسِيرِ ـ لا يُفَسَّرُ ـ لا يُسْتَخْرَجُ. *See also* Illegible, *a.*

Indecision, *n.* قِلَّةٌ - حَيْرَةٌ - فَرْفَرَةٌ - تَرَدُّدٌ - طَيْش - طَيَشان - قِلَّةُ عَزْمٍ - حَزْمٍ.

Indecisive, *a.* غَيْرُ بَتِّيٍّ - غَيْرُ فاصِلٍ - غَيْرُ قاطِعٍ. An — battle, واقِعَةٌ غَيْرُ فاصِلَةٍ.

Indecisively, *ad.* بِلا فَصْلٍ - بِصُورَةٍ غَيْرِ قاطِعَةٍ ; of an engagement between two contending parties, مِنْ دُونِ أَنْ يَتَّجِهَ وَجْهُ ٱلظَّفَرِ أَحَدَ ٱلفَرِيقَيْنِ.

Indecisiveness, *n.* عَدَمُ جَزْمٍ - عَدَمُ فَصْلٍ - عَدَمُ بَتَّةٍ.

Indeclinable, *a.* مَمْنُوع - غَيْرُ مُنْصَرِفٍ - لا يَنْصَرِفُ - لا يُجْرَى - مُلازِم - مَبْنِيٌّ. An — noun, إِسْمٌ مَبْنِيٌّ.

Indecomposable, *a.* لا يَنْحَلُّ - غَيْرُ مُتَحَلِّلٍ - غَيْرُ مُنْفَكٍّ ٱلتَّرْتِيبِ.

Indecorous, *a.* مُخَالِفُ ٱلأَدَبِ - غَيْرُ لائِقٍ - ذَمِيم - غَيْرُ مُناسِبٍ.

Indecorously, *ad.* بِلا حِشْمَةٍ - بِقِلَّةِ أَدَبٍ.

Indecorousness, *n.*
Indecorum, } عَيْب - قِلَّةُ حِشْمَةٍ - قِلَّةُ أَدَبٍ.

Indeed, *ad.* In reality, in truth, حَقًّا - يَقِينًا - بِلا رَيْبٍ - فِي ٱلوَاقِعِ - حَقِيقَةً - فِي ٱلحَقِيقَةِ. He is a friend —, هُوَ بِٱلحَقِيقَةِ صَدِيقٌ. They heard — and they saw —, but they don't know, سَمْعًا سَمِعُوا وَمَا دَرُوا. Indeed! can it be true? هَلْ يُمْكِنُ أَنْ يَكُونَ هٰذا صَحِيحًا - أَحَقٌّ هٰذا - يا لِلْعَجَبِ. Indeed! وَيْ. *See also under* Verily, *ad.*

Indefatigable, *a.* مُصِرٌّ عَلَى فِعْلِهِ - لا يَكِلُّ - مُدْمِن - لا يَتْعَبُ - مُوَاظِب - كَدُود - غَيْرُ فاتِرٍ - لا يَكِلُّ وَلا يَمِلُّ - لا يُعْجِزُهُ شَيْءٌ.

Indefatigableness, *n.* مُواظَبَة - عَدَمُ كُلُولٍ - عَدَمُ فُتُورٍ - كَدٌّ - إِضْرار - إِدْمان.

Indefatigably, *ad.* بِمُواظَبَةٍ - بِعَدَمِ فُتُورٍ - بِلا كُلُولٍ - مِنْ غَيْرِ كَلالٍ - بِكَدٍّ كُلِّيٍّ - بِإِدْمانٍ.

Indefeasibility, *n.* The quality of not being subject to be made void, عَدَمُ ٱلفَسْخِ - عَدَمُ ٱلإِزالَةِ - عَدَمُ ٱلبُطْلانِ - عَدَمُ إِلْغَاءٍ.

Indefeasible, *a.* لا يُفْسَخُ - لا يُزالُ - لا يُبْطَلُ - عَدِيمُ ٱلإِلْغَاءِ.

Indefeasibly, *ad.* بِلا فَسْخٍ - بِوَجْهٍ لا يَبْطُلُ - بِعَدَمِ إِلْغَاءٍ.

Indefectible, *a.* لا يَزُولُ - دائِم.

Indefective, *a.* غَيْرُ ناقِصٍ - تَامٌّ.

Indefensibility, *n.* The quality of not being capable of defence, عِزَّةُ ٱلمُحاماةِ عَنْهُ. Unjustifiableness, عِزَّةُ ٱلمُناضَلَةِ عَنْهُ. *See also* Inexcusableness, *n.*

Indefensible, *a.* Not capable of defence, مِنَ ٱلمُحَالِ ٱلمُحاماةُ عَنْهُ - مُحاماتُهُ مُسْتَحِيلَةٌ. Unjustifiable, مِنَ ٱلمُحَالِ ٱلمُناضَلَةُ عَنْهُ. *See also* Inexcusable, *a.*

Indefensibly, *ad.* بِوَجْهٍ يَتَعَزَّزُ ٱلإِسْتِنْصَارُ لَهُ. Unjustifiably, بِوَجْهٍ لا يَحِلُّ تَبْرِيرُهُ.

Indefinable, *a.* يَتَعَذَّرُ تَفْسِيرُهُ - لا يُعْرَفُ - تَفْسِيرُهُ مُحالٌ - يَسْتَحِيلُ تَعْرِيفُهُ - عَدِيمُ ٱلتَّعْرِيفِ.

Indefinably, *ad.* بِوَجْهٍ لا يُفَسَّرُ.

Indefinite, *a.* Not limited, غَيْرُ مَحْدُودٍ - غَيْرُ مُقَرَّرٍ - لَيْسَ بِمَحْصُورٍ ; not fixed, غَيْرُ مُعَيَّنٍ - غَيْرُ مُقَرَّرٍ - غَيْرُ مُعَرَّفٍ. Uncertain, obscure, مُنَكَّر - مُبْهَم - مُلْتَبِس. An — article, أَدَاةُ (or حَرْفُ) تَنْكِيرٍ. For an — time, إِلَى ما شاءَ ٱللّٰهُ.

Indefinitely, *ad.* Without limitation, بِلا حَصْرٍ - مِنْ غَيْرِ تَحْدِيدٍ. Obscurely, بِنَكِرَةٍ - بِتَنَكُّرٍ - بِٱلتِبَاسٍ.

Indefiniteness, *n.* Quality of not being defined, عَدَمُ ٱلتَّحْدِيدِ - عَدَمُ بَيانٍ ; of not being fixed, عَدَمُ تَعَيُّنٍ - عَدَمُ تَعْيِينٍ. Obscurity, نَكِرَة - اِلْتِبَاس - إِبْهام.

Indelibility, *n.* عَدَمُ مَحْوٍ - عَدَمُ ٱمِّحَاءٍ - عَدَمُ إِبْطالٍ - كَوْنُ ٱلشَّيْءِ مُسْتَحِيلَ ٱلإِنْدِرَاسِ.

Indelible, *a.* مُسْتَحِيلُ ٱلإِنْدِرَاسِ - مَحْوُهُ مُحالٌ - لا يُمْكِنُ مَحْوُهُ - لا يُبْطَلُ - عَدِيمُ ٱلإِزالَةِ.

Indelibly, *ad.* بِوَجْهٍ لا يُمْحَى - بِعَدَمِ إِزالَةٍ - بِدَوامٍ.

Indelicacy, *n.* قِلَّةُ أَدَبٍ - قِلَّةُ حِشْمَةٍ - قِلَّةُ ظَرافَةٍ - خُشُونَة - فَظاظَة.

Indelicate, *a.* Of a person, قَلِيلُ ٱلأَدَبِ - قَلِيلُ ٱلظَّرافَةِ - فَظٌّ ; of a thing; *see* Indecorous, Obscene, *a.*

Indemnification, *n.* The act of securing against loss, تَضْمِين - تَعْوِيض عَنِ ٱلخَسارَةِ. Reimbursement, as of loss, عِوَض - تَعْوِيض. An equivalent, requital, or compensation, خَلاص *pl.* أَخْلاص. A claim set up for —, دَرْك - دَرَك. An injury or evil consequence for which — is claimed, دَرَك - تَبِعَة. Whatever evil consequence or injury may ensue to thee I will be its —, that is, I will indemnify you against loss therein, ما لَحِقَكَ مِنْ دَرْكٍ (or دَرَكٍ) فَعَلَيَّ خَلاصُهُ. Whatever consequence ensue to it, of a thing sold, I will be its —, that is, I will indemnify or make it good, ما أَدْرَكَهُ مِنْ دَرَكٍ فَعَلَيَّ خَلاصُهُ - ما يَلْحَقُهُ مِنْ تَبِعَةٍ فَعَلَيَّ خَلاصُهُ. A warranty of —, as for a thing sold, ضَمانُ ٱلدَّرَكِ. *See also* Indemnity, *n.*

Indemnify, *v.t.* To secure against loss, تَكَفَّلَ لَهُ بِٱلخَسارَةِ - ضَمِنَ بِٱلخَسارَةِ. To reimburse, جازَى عَلَى ٱلخَسارَةِ -

عَوَّضَ-عَلَى - جَزَى-عَلَى. To — me for what I have undergone, لِأَجْلِ مُكَافَاةِ ٱلضَّرَرِ ٱلَّذِي تَحَمَّلْتُهُ.

Indemnity, *n.* Recompense for injury sustained, مُجَازَاة - غَرَامَة - مُقَابَلَة - تَعْوِيض - عِوَض. A war —, مُقَابَلَةُ ٱلْحَرْبِ - ٱلْحَرْبِ. In the shape of an —, مِنْ قَبِيلِ ٱلْعِوَضِ. An — in money, غَرَامَةٌ نَقْدِيَّةٌ. *See also* Indemnification, *n.*

Indent, *v.t.* To make a dent in, هَزَمَ - نَكَتَ - أَخْلَفَ. To notch, فَلَّلَ - إِحْتَزَّ - حَزَّ - سَنَّنَ - عَلَّمَ فِي. To bind to service, إِسْتَخْدَمَ-بِصَكٍّ شَرْعِيٍّ. To — upon government stores for, قَدَّمَ - إِسْتَدْعَى ٱلْمُؤْنَةَ وَٱسْتَلْزَمَهَا مِنْ مَخَازِنِ ٱلْمِيرِي رَسْمًا. قَوَائِمَ رَسْمِيَّةً لِمُدِيرِ مَخَازِنِ ٱلْمِيرِي فِيمَا أُحْتِيجَ إِلَيْهِ مِنَ ٱلذَّخِيرَةِ.

Indent, *n.* A dent, ثَوْب - أَثَر. A notch, حَزّ - فَلّ *pl.* فُلُول. A return sent in for stores, عَرْضُ قَوَائِمِ ٱلْمُؤْنَةِ (*or* ٱلذَّخِيرَةِ) تَقْوِيمُ مَطْلُوبَاتٍ - ٱللَّازِمَةِ.

Indentation, *n.* A dent, ثَوْب - أَثَر - تَضْرِيس - هَزْمَة. Dentation, تَسْنِين. *See also* Dent, *n.* and *to* Dent, *v.t.*

Indented, *a.* Notched, مُسَنَّن - مُفَلَّل - مُحْتَزّ. Bound by writings to service, مُسْتَخْدَمٌ بِمُوجِبِ ٱلصُّكُوكِ.

Indenture, *n.* صَكّ *pl.* صُكُوك - حُجَّة *pl.* حُجَج.

Independence, *n.* / Independency, } Exemption from control, حُرِّيَّة. State of not being connected with, عَدَمُ عَلَاقَةٍ بِ; of not resting upon, عَدَمُ ٱسْتِنَادٍ إِلَى; of being able to dispense with, إِسْتِغْنَاءٌ عَن. Competency of fortune, حَظّ - سِدَاد - بُلْغَة - رَفَاهِيَة - سَعَةُ عَيْشٍ. Independence, as of a state, إِسْتِبْدَاد - إِسْتِقْلَال *vulg.* إِسْتِقْلَالِيَّة. Political —, إِسْتِقْلَالٌ مُلْكِيٌّ. Rights of —, حُقُوقُ ٱلِٱسْتِقْلَالِ. To recognize the — of one, إِعْتَرَفَ بِٱسْتِقْلَالِهِ. To aspire to —, طَلَبَ ٱلِٱسْتِقْلَالَ. To acquire —, نَالَ ٱلِٱسْتِقْلَالَ. A spirit of —, حُرِّيَّةُ ٱلْأَفْكَارِ - تَفَرُّدٌ بِٱلْأَفْكَارِ. He enjoys an —, competency, هُوَ مُوسِرٌ.

Independent, *a.* Free, مُطْلَق - حُرّ. Not connected with, مَا لَهُ عَلَاقَةٌ بِ - غَيْرُ مُتَعَلِّقٍ بِ. He was —, had absolute control, over his affair, إِسْتَبَدَّ بِأَمْرِهِ. Standing by himself, قَائِمٌ بِذَاتِهِ - مُسْتَبِدّ - مُسْتَقِلٌّ بِهِ - تَفَذَّذَ بِهِ. Able to dispense with, مُسْتَغْنٍ عَن. Having a competency, رَافِه - طَائِل. An — government, دَوْلَةٌ قَائِمَةٌ بِذَاتِهَا - دَوْلَةٌ مُسْتَقِلَّةٌ. Independent of the interference of the authorities, مُسْتَقِلٌّ عَنْ مُدَاخَلَةِ ٱلْمَأْمُورِينَ. He was — of me in the affair, إِسْتَقَلَّ عَلَيَّ بِٱلْأَمْرِ.

Independent, *s.* *See* Congregationalist, *n.*

Independently, *ad.* With independence, إِسْتِبْدَادًا - بِٱسْتِقْلَالٍ. By himself, عَلَى حِيَالِهِ. Besides, وَغَيْرُ ذٰلِكَ. He would go — of that, وَمَعَ ذٰلِكَ حَتَمَ بِٱلِٱنْطِلَاقِ. He did it — of me, إِسْتَبَدَّ بِٱلْأَمْرِ دُونِي - فَعَلَهُ وَحْدَهُ (*or* بِنَفْسِهِ) بِدُونِي. Independently of, besides, فَضْلًا عَن. He acted —, followed his own opinion, إِسْتَبَدَّ بِرَأْيِهِ.

Indescribable, *a.* لَا يُعْرَفُ - لَا يُوصَفُ.

Indestructibility, *n.* عِزَّة - عَدَمُ ٱلْخَرَابِ - عَدَمُ ٱلْفَنَاءِ - عَدَمُ - ثَبَات - دَوَام - إِمْكَانُ هَدْمِ ٱلشَّيْءِ.

Indestructible, *a.* عَزِيز - هَدْمُهُ مُحَال - لَا يُفْنَى - لَا يُخْرَبُ - ثَابِت - دَيُّوم - دَائِم - إِزَالَتُهُ مِنَ ٱلْمُحَالِ - لَا يَزُولُ.

Indestructibly, *ad.* عِزَّةً - لَا يَزُولُ - بِوَجْهٍ - بِدَوَامٍ - بِثَبَاتٍ - لَا سَبِيلَ إِلَى رَدْمِهِ.

Indeterminable, *a.* That cannot be determined, تَعْيِينُهُ أَوْ تَحْدِيدُهُ مُحَالٌ; that cannot be ascertained, لَا يُسْتَطَاعُ تَحْقِيقُهُ; that cannot be ended, divided, فَصْلُهُ مُحَالٌ - لَا يُمْكِنُ فَصْلُهُ.

Indeterminably, *ad.* بِمَا لَا يُسْتَطِيعُ تَحْقِيقُهُ.

Indeterminate, *a.* غَيْرُ مُقَرَّرٍ - غَيْرُ مُحَدَّدٍ - غَيْرُ مُعَيَّنٍ - غَيْرُ مُعَرَّفٍ. An — noun, نَكِرَة. *See also* Indefinite, *a.*

Indeterminately, *ad.* مِنْ غَيْرِ تَحْدِيدٍ - بِدُونِ تَعْيِينٍ - بِلَا تَخْصِيصٍ. *See also* Indefinitely, *ad.*

Indeterminateness, *n.* / Indetermination, } عَدَمُ تَحْدِيدٍ - عَدَمُ تَعْيِينٍ - عَدَمُ تَخْصِيصٍ. Irresolution, تَرَدُّد - فَرْفَرَة - تَقَلُّبُ ٱلرَّأْيِ - قِلَّةُ حَزْمٍ. *See also* Indefiniteness, *n.*

Indevotion, *n.* قِلَّةُ تَعَبُّدٍ - عَدَمُ تَبَتُّلٍ إِلَى ٱللّٰهِ - قِلَّةُ دِينٍ - قِلَّةُ وَرَعٍ.

Indevout, *a.* قَلِيلُ ٱلتَّعَبُّدِ - غَيْرُ دَيِّنٍ - لَيْسَ بِمُتَدَيِّنٍ - قَلِيلُ ٱلْوَرَعِ.

Index, *n.* That which points out, إِشَارَةٌ إِلَى - مُشِيرٌ إِلَى - دَالٌّ (*or* دَلِيلٌ) عَلَى - عَلَامَةٌ لِ. A finger post, صُوَّة - مَعْلَم. Indication, proof, شَهَادَة - بُرْهَان. An — of a watch, عَقْرَبُ ٱلسَّاعَةِ *pl.* عَقَارِبُ; of a book, فِهْرِس *pl.* فَهَارِسُ. The forefinger, ٱلْمُسَبِّحَة - ٱلسَّبَّابَة. The —, in arithmetic, ٱلْجِذْرُ - ٱلْأُسّ.

Index expurgatorius, فِهْرِسُ ٱلْكُتُبِ ٱلْمُحَرَّمَةِ.

Index, *v.t.* فَهْرَسَ.

Indexterity, *n.* خُرْق - قِلَّةُ حِذْقٍ - عَدَمُ مَهَارَةٍ - غَلَاظَة. *See also* Clumsiness, *n.*

India, *n.* ٱلْهِنْدُ - بِلَادُ ٱلْهِنْدِ - هِنْدُسْتَان.

Indiaman, *n.* The ship, مَرْكَبٌ يُسَافِرُ إِلَى ٱلْهِنْدِ.

Indian, *a.* هِنْدُوَانِيّ - هِنْدِيّ *pl.* هُنُود. The — language, لِسَانُ ٱلْهِنْدِ. Indian fig, تِينٌ فِرَنْجِيّ - تِينٌ شَوْكِيّ - صُبَّيْر. Indian corn, ذُرًا. Indian ink, مِدَادٌ صِينِيّ - حِبْرٌ صِينِيّ.

Indian, *n.* هِنْدِيٌّ *fem.* هِنْدِيَّةٌ — إِمْرَأَةٌ هِنْدِيَّةٌ, *pl. m.* هُنُود, *pl. fem.* نِسَآءٌ هِنْدِيَّاتٌ — هِنْدِيَّات.

India-rubber, *n.* اَلصَّمْغُ ٱلْمُغِيط — لَسْتِيكْ *pl.* لَسَاتِيكْ (called in Africa مَبِيرَة).

Indicant, *n.* عَلَامَة — دَلِيل — إِشَارَة.

Indicate, *v.t.* To point out, دَلَّ إِلَى *or* عَلَى — أَشَارَ بِ *or* إِلَى — أَوْمَى إِلَى — رَمَزَ إِلَى — وَعَزَ إِلَى *or* فِي. To intimate, أَظْهَرَ — أَتَى بِ — عَبَّرَ بِ *or* عَن. To manifest, show, display, أَظْهَرَ — أَبْدَى — يَأْتِي *aor.* To explain, فَسَّرَ — عَبَّرَ عَن. To make known to, أَفَادَ — عَرَّفَ بِ — أَشْعَرَ بِ.

Indication, *n.* A showing, mark, token, دِلَالَة — دُلُولَة — دَلِيل *pl.* أَدِلَّة — إِشَارَة — بُرْهَان — نِيشَان. A trace, أَثَر. A look, semblance, رَأْوَة. An intimation, بَيِّنَة — عِبَارَة — رَمْز — إِيمَآء. Intelligence given, خَبَر — إِظْهَار — إِخْبَار — إِعْلَام — إِفَادَة. Explanation, شَرْح — تَعْبِير — تَفْسِير — بَيَان. A manifestation, شِيَة — مَظِنَّة — مَخِيلَة — إِظْهَار — عَرْض. A symptom of anything, A slight — of anything, حِسٌّ بِ. The indications of generosity appeared in him, ظَهَرَتْ فِيهِ مَخَايِلُ ٱلنَّجَابَةِ. A noun of —, إِسْمُ إِشَارَةٍ.

Indicative, *a.* Pointing out, دَلِيلِيٌّ — يَدُلُّ عَلَى — عَلَامَةٌ عَلَى — دَالٌّ عَلَى — إِشَارَةٌ إِلَى — مُظْهِر. Making known, مُعَرِّف — مُشِيرٌ بِ. Indicative of, مُعْتَرِفٌ بِ. The — mood, صِيغَة — ٱلرَّفْع — صِيغَةُ ٱلْفِعْلِ ٱلْمُطْرِدِ.

Indicatively, *ad.* إِشْعَارًا — بِصُورَةِ ٱلْإِشْعَارِ — بِصُورَةِ ٱلدَّلِيلِ.

Indicator, *n.* One or something that points out, دَلِيل — مُخْبِر. A pointer, عَقْرَب.

Indicatory, *a.* *See* Indicative, *a.*

Indict, *v.t.* طَلَبَ إِلَى ٱلْمَحْكَمَةِ — أَتْهَمَ — ٱدَّعَى عَلَى — فِي ٱلشَّرْعِ حَاكَمَ.

Indictable, *a.* مُتَعَرِّضٌ لِلشِّكَايَةِ عَلَيْهِ.

Indiction, *n.* Declaration, تَقْرِير — تَعْيِين. A cycle of fifteen years, مُدَّةُ خَمْسَ عَشْرَةَ سَنَةً.

Indictment, *n.* تُهْمَة — شِكَايَة — شَكْوَة.

Indies, *n.* المَمَالِكُ ٱلْهِنْدِيَّةُ. The East Indies, هِنْدُسْتَان — جَزَائِرُ ٱلْأُوقِيَانُوسِ ٱلْمَدْعُوَّةُ بِٱلْهِنْدِ. The West Indies, الهِنْدُ ٱلْغَرْبِيُّ.

Indifference, *n.* Freedom from prejudice, عَدَمُ مُحَابَاةٍ. Carelessness, negligence, unconcern, فُتُور — بُرُودَة — عَدَمُ رَغْبَةٍ — تَسَاهُل — تَكَاسُل — عَدَمُ مُبَالَاةٍ — تَغَافُل — عَدَمُ ٱعْتِنَاء. He showed great — in the matter, لَمْ يُبَالِ — تَسَاهَلَ فِي ٱلْأَمْرِ — غَافَلَ — عَامَلَ بِبُرُودَةٍ بِٱلْأَمْرِ. To treat one with —, coolness, سَاهَى.

Indifferent, *a.* Neutral, لَا مَعَ وَلَا عَلَى — مُنْفَرِدٌ عَنِ ٱلطَّرَفَيْنِ — مُتَسَاهِل — غَيْرُ مُبَالٍ — مُتَكَاسِل. Unconcerned, سَوَآءٌ عِنْدَهُ — تَافِه — عَدِيمُ ٱلِٱعْتِنَاء — عَدِيمُ ٱلْمُبَالَاةِ. Insipid, of a person, عَدِيمُ ٱلْمُحَابَاةِ — بِلَا غَرَضٍ. Impartial, مَا فُلَانٌ بِخَلٍّ وَلَا بِخَمْرٍ — مُتَوَسِّط — وَسَط — مُقَارِب. Of a middling quality, عَدِيمُ ٱلْغَرَضِ — عَدِيمُ — بِلَا عَصَبِيَّةٍ — بَيْنَ بَيْنَ — وَسْطَانِيٌّ. Not a partisan, غَيْرُ عَصَبِيٍّ — لَيْسَ مِنْ أَهْلِ حِزْبٍ — ٱلتَّعَصُّبِ. Not good, دُون — غَيْرُ جَيِّدٍ — رَدِيءٌ. An — action, *i.e.* which may or may not be done, فِعْلٌ مُبَاحٌ (*or* جَائِزٌ) — فِعْلٌ مُخَيَّرٌ فِيهِ. To become — to anything, تَكَاسَلَ فِي — فَتَرَ عَن. It is — to me whether you stand or sit, سَوَآءٌ عَلَيَّ قُمْتَ أَوْ قَعَدْتَ. I am — to his anger, لَا أُبَالِي بِغَضَبِهِ. He is — to his interests, هُوَ مُتَغَافِلٌ لَا يَعْتَنِي بِخَيْرِهِ — عَنْ خَيْرِهِ. He wrote it on — paper, كَتَبَهُ عَلَى وَرَقٍ دُونٍ. Indifferent matters, أُمُورٌ — أُمُورٌ خَلِيَّةُ ٱلْغَرَضِ عَادِيَّةٌ.

Indifferently, *ad.* Without making a difference, عَلَى وَجْهٍ — بِلَا غَرَضٍ — بِدُونِ مُحَابَاةٍ. Impartially, سَوَآءً — بِلَا فَرْقٍ — ٱلسَّوِيَّةِ. Tolerably, بَيْنَ بَيْنَ; not well, رَدَآءَةً — مِنْ دُونٍ. He did it — well, أَحْسَنَ فِي فِعْلِهِ بَعْضَ ٱلْإِحْسَانِ.

Indigence, *n.* حَاجَة — ضَيْقَة — أَرَب — خَلَّة — عَدَم — عَالَة — فَاقَة — فَقْر — حَوْبَة — إِحْتِيَاج.

Indigenous, *a.* بَلَدِيٌّ.

Indigent, *a.* فَقِير — عَدِيم — عَوِز — عَائِز — عَالَة *pl.* عَائِل — مُحْتَاج — صُعْلُوك *pl.* صَعَالِيك. To be —, إِحْتَاجَ.

Indigested, *a.* Not digested, غَيْرُ مَهْضُوم. Crude, raw, نِيءٌ. Not regularly disposed, غَيْرُ مُنَسَّقٍ — غَيْرُ مُرَتَّبٍ — غَيْرُ مَنْظُوم — مَخْبُوص — مُشَوَّس — فَطِير.

Indigestible, *a.* عَسِرُ ٱلْهَضْمِ — لَا يَنْهَضِمُ — مُتْخِمَة — مُتَوَخِّم.

Indigestible food, طَعَامٌ مُتْخِمَةٌ.

Indigestion, *n.* وَخَامَة — بَشَم — بَرْدَة — زَان — تُخَمَة — غَثْم — وَخَم — قِلَّةُ ٱلْهَضْمِ. To have —, تَخِمَ — إِغْتَشَمَ — بَشِمَ — وَخِمَ. Having —, بَشِر — وَخِم — وَخِيم — وَخُوم *pl.* وِخَام *and* وَخَامَى. I suffered — from the food, وَخَمْتُ مِنَ — بَشِمْتُ مِنَ ٱلطَّعَامِ. The source of all disease is —, أَصْلُ كُلِّ دَآءٍ ٱلْبَرَدَةُ ٱلطَّعَامِ.

Indignant, *a.* غَضْبَانُ — وَحِر — حَنِق — حَارِد — أَنُوف — مُحْتَنِق. To be —, غَضِبَ — أَحْنَقَ — حَنِقَ — يَحْرُ *or* يَحِرُ *aor.* وَحِرَ. To be — with, حَنِقَ عَلَى.

Indignantly, *ad.* غَضَبًا — بِشِدَّةِ غَيْظٍ — حَنَقًا — بِوَحَرٍ.

Indignation, *n.* – حِدَّة – حَبَن – غَضَب – حَنَق – وَحْر – أَنَفَة. أَغْضَب – غَيْظ – = غَاظَ. To excite the — of one, شِدَّةُ غَيْظٍ. His bosom burned with —, = فَاضَ صَدْرُهُ بِٱلْغَيْظِ.

Indignity, *n.* – شَتْم – بَهْدَلَة – عَيْبَة – إِهَانَة – وَضِيعَة – سَبَل. قَبَاحَة. To cast an — upon, بَهْدَلَ – عَيَّبَ – أَهَانَ – = حَكَرَ. To cause one to incur an —, ignominy, (خُسْفًا *or*) سَامَهُ خَسْفًا – سَامَهُ ٱلْخَسْفَ.

Indigo, *n.* نِيل – وَسِمَة – عِظْلِم. The — plant, نِيلَة.

Indirect, *a.* Not from the source, head, لا عَنْ رَأْسٍ. Not straight, أَعْوَج – مُعَوَّج – مُلْتَوٍ. Turning aside, – مُنْحَرِف إِنْحِرَافِيّ. Not straightforward, غَيْرُ مُسْتَقِيمٍ – مُحَاوِل – مُعَرَّض. Through a medium, بِوَاسِطَةٍ. Fraudulent, – حِيَلِيّ – حَوَلْوَل خَبِيث – خَدَّاع – مُحْتَال. Secret, خَافٍ – خَفِيّ. He asked such a one an — question, عَرَّضَ لِفُلَانٍ بِٱلسُّؤَالِ. An — speech, تَوْرِيَة – مِعْرَاض. An — tax, ضَرِيبَةٌ (وَضِيعَةٌ *or*) عَلَى ٱلْأَمْتِعَةِ; indirect taxes, رُسُومَات.

Indirectly, *ad.* Not from the source, عَنْ وَسِيلَةٍ – لا عَنْ رَأْسٍ. Obliquely, بِٱنْعِطَافٍ – بِعَوَجٍ – بِٱنْحِرَافٍ. In indirect terms, بِخُبْثٍ – بِٱحْتِيَالٍ. بِمُحَاوَلَةٍ – مُعَارَضَةً – تَعْرِيضًا. Unfairly, I reminded him —, ذَكَّرْتُهُ مُعَارَضَةً. He accused him —, عَرَّضَ بِتُهْمَتِهِ. I pointed it out to him —, عَرَّضْتُهُ لَهُ. To speak —, obliquely, عَرَّضَ.

Indirectness, *n.* The being through a medium, وُقُوعُ ٱلْوَاسِطَةِ. Obliquity, إِنْحِرَاف – إِعْوِجَاج – تَعَوُّج. Unfairness, عَدَمُ ٱسْتِقَامَةٍ فِيهِ – حِيلَة. Dishonesty, خُبْث – خِيَانَة. A *double entendre*, تَعْرِيض.

Indiscernible, *a.* – لا يُرَى – لا يُدْرَكُ – غَيْرُ بَيِّنٍ – لا يَتَمَيَّزُ مُبْهَم.

Indiscernibleness, *a.* إِبْهَام – عَدَمُ بَيَانٍ – حَالَةُ ٱلْإِبْهَامِ.

Indiscernibly, *ad.* إِبْهَامًا – عَلَى بُعْدٍ عَنِ ٱلْبَيَانِ – بِوَجْهٍ لا يَتَمَيَّزُ.

Indiscerptibility, *n.* مَتَانَة – عَدَمُ مُفَارَقَةٍ – عَدَمُ ٱنْفِصَالٍ.

Indiscerptible, *a.* – غَيْرُ مُنْفَرِقٍ – لا يُفْرَقُ – لا يَنْفَصِلُ – لا يَنْحَلُّ مَتِين.

Indisciplinable, *a.* لا يُذَلَّلُ – لا يُمَرَّنُ – لا يَتَأَدَّبُ.

Indiscoverable, *a.* كَشْفُهُ مُحَالٌ. *See also* Inexplicable, *a.*

Indiscreet, *a.* Inconsiderate, عَدِيمُ – مَاجِن – ضَعْضَع – ضَعْضَاع غَافِل – ٱلتَّبَصُّرِ. Meddlesome, فُضُولِيّ. Not keeping a secret, لا يَكْتُمُ ٱلسِّرَّ – مَذِيل. Indiscreet words, كَلَامٌ بِغَيْرِ تَمْيِيزٍ.

Indiscreetly, *ad.* بِلَا ٱحْتِيَاطٍ – بِغَيْرِ وَعْيٍ – بِلَا مُلَاحَظَةٍ. With meddlesomeness, بِفُضُولٍ.

Indiscretion, *n.* قِلَّةُ مُحَاسَبَةٍ – تَغَافُل – دَعَانَة – عَدَمُ تَبَصُّرٍ. An indiscreet action, قِلَّةُ عَقْلٍ – رُعُونَة – حُمُوقَة – غَبَاوَة.

Indiscriminate, *a.* بِلَا تَمْيِيزٍ – سَوَآء – بِدُونِ فَرْقٍ (تَفْرِيقٍ *or*).

Indiscriminately, *ad.* بِدُونِ تَمْيِيزٍ – عَلَى حَدٍّ سِوَى – بِلَا فَرْقٍ.

Indiscriminating, *a.* غَيْرُ فَارِقٍ – غَيْرُ مُمَيِّزٍ.

Indiscrimination, *n.* عَدَمُ تَمْيِيزٍ.

Indispensable, *a.* – أَلْزَمُ – لَازِم – مُقْتَضًى – ضَرُورِيّ – لَازِب وَاجِب – مُطْلَقُ ٱلْوُجُوبِ – لا بُدَّ مِنْهُ. The thing was —, صَارَ ٱلشَّيْءُ ضَرْبَةَ لَازِبٍ. It is — that it should be so, لا يَخْلُو ٱلْحَالُ مِنْ أَنْ يَكُونَ كَذَا.

Indispensableness, *n.* لُزُومِيَّة – إِقْتِضَآء – ضَرُورِيَّة – لُزُوم – ضَرُورَة.

Indispensably, *ad.* حَتْمًا – مِنْ كُلِّ بُدٍّ – وَلَا بُدَّ – بِٱلضَّرُورَةِ.

Indispose, *v.t.* To make averse to, – رَغَّبَ-عَن – نَفَّرَ-مِن أَمَالَ-عَن. To change one towards, غَيَّرَ-عَلَى. To disorder, شَوَّشَ – لَبَّكَ; to disorder the health, أَمْرَضَ – أَعَلَّ. *See also to* Disqualify, *v.t.*

Indisposed, *a.* Disinclined to, مُكْرَه – مُنَفَّرٌ مِن – مُرَغَّبٌ عَن – عَلِيل – مُعْتَلّ – مُنْحَرِفُ ٱلْمِزَاجِ – شَاكٍ – مَشْكُوّ إِلَى. Unwell, مُشَوَّش. To be —, unwell, يَشْكُو .aor شَكَا – إِعْتَلَّ – = عَلَّ.

Indisposition, *n.* Aversion, عَدَمُ – كَرَاهَة – رَغْبَةٌ عَن – نُفُور رَغْبَةٍ. Want of affinity, عَدَمُ – عَدَمُ مُطَابَقَةٍ – عَدَمُ تَجَانُسٍ – شَكْوَة – عِلَّة – شَكَاة مُبَايَنَة – مُوَافَقَةٍ. Disorder of the body, إِنْحِرَافُ ٱلْمِزَاجِ.

Indisputable, *a.* – يَقِين – حَقِيق – مُسَلَّم – لا نِزَاعَ فِيهِ مَا فِيهِ كَلَامٌ.

Indisputableness, *n.* حَقِيقَة – عَدَمُ مُنَازَعَةٍ.

Indisputably, *ad.* حَقِيقَةً – يَقِينًا – لا مَحَالَةَ.

Indissolubility, *n.* / **Indissolubleness**, } عَدَمُ – عَدَمُ ٱنْحِلَالٍ – عَدَمُ ٱنْفِكَاكٍ مُلَازَمَة – ٱنْفِسَاخ.

Indissoluble, *a.* لا يَنْفَرِقُ – لا يَنْفَكُّ – لا يَنْفَسِخُ – لا يَنْحَلُّ – بَتِّيّ. Binding for ever, دَائِم – بَتِّيّ. Indissoluble friendship, صُحْبَةٌ بَتَّةٌ بَتْلَةٌ – لا يَعْتَرِيهَا ٱنْفِصَالٌ. He swore an — oath, = حَلَفَ بَتَّةً.

Indissolubly, *ad.* بِدُونِ ٱنْفِكَاكٍ – بِلَا ٱنْحِلَالٍ – بَتَّةً – بَتًّا.

Indistinct, *a.* Confused, – مُشَوَّش – مُلَبَّك – مُخْتَلّ مُلْتَبِك – بِغَيْرِ تَرْتِيبٍ – مُبْهَم – مُلْخَبَط. Not clear, غَيْرُ غَيْرُ مُمَيَّزٍ – غَيْرُ صَرِيحٍ – غَيْرُ بَيِّنٍ – مُبْهَم – مُمْتَاز. Not clear intellectually, مُبْهَم – مُلْتَبِس. Indistinct, of speech, utterance, غُتْمِيّ – أَغْتَم. Indistinct speech, تَغَمْغُم. Very slight, – جُزْئِيّ خَفِيف. To be — in speech, of a drunken man, إِرْتَكَّ.

Indistinction, *n.* } Confusion, إِخْتِلَال ــ اِلْتِبَاك ــ تَشْوِيش ــ
Indistinctness, } اِخْتِلَاط. Want of clearness, عَدَمُ تَمْيِيزٍ ــ
اِلْتِبَاس ــ إِبْهَام. Confusion of meaning, عَدَمُ بَيَانٍ; of speech, غَمْغَمَة.

Indistinctly, *ad.* Not clearly, بِدُونِ بَيَانٍ. Confusedly, اِلْتِبَاكًا ــ بِٱخْتِلَالٍ. Without precision, بِٱلْتِبَاسٍ ــ بِإِبْهَامٍ. To speak —, غَمْغَمَ ــ جَمْجَمَ.

Indistinguishable, *a.* لَا يُمَيَّزُ بَيْنَهُ وَبَيْنَ ــ لَا يُفَرَّقُ بَيْنَهُ وَبَيْنَ غَيْرِهِ. غَيْرُ مُمَيَّزٍ ــ غَيْرِهِ.

Indite, *v.t.* To write, خَطَّ ــ كَتَبَ ــ حَرَّرَ ــ سَطَرَ. To compose, صَنَّفَ ــ أَلَّفَ ــ نَظَمَ. To dictate, أَمْلَى عَلَى ــ مَلَّى ــ أَكْتَبَ.

Individual, *a.* مُنْفَرِد ــ مُفْرَد ــ وَحِيد ــ وَاحِد. The — thing, ذَاتُ ٱلشَّيْءِ ــ عَيْنُ ٱلشَّيْءِ. Personal, ذَاتِيّ ــ شَخْصِيّ.

Individual, *n.* A single person, شَخْص *pl.* أَشْخَاص ــ ظَلَم *pl.* ظُلُوم; نَفَر ــ *pl.* أَنْفَار; a single thing or person, فَرْد *pl.* أَفْرَاد *fem.* فَرْدَة; a single man, مَرْء. For individuals and for the public, لِلْخَاصِّ وَلِلْعَامِّ ــ لِلْأَفْرَادِ وَلِلْعُمُوم.

Individualism, *n.* اَلتَّعَصُّبُ لِشَخْصٍ دُونَ غَيْرِهِ.

Individuality, *n.* شَخْص *pl.* أَشْخَاص ــ اِنْفِرَاد ــ أَحَدِيَّة.

Individualize, *v.t.* شَخَّصَ ــ عَيَّنَ ــ أَفَذَّ. To be individualized, تَعَيَّنَ.

Individually, *ad.* اِنْفِرَادًا ــ أَفْرَادًا ــ بِمَعْزِلٍ ــ شَذًّا ــ فُذَاذًا ــ عَلَى حِدَةٍ ــ فَرْدًا فَرْدًا ــ وَاحِدًا وَاحِدًا ــ عَلَى ٱلِٱنْفِرَادِ.

Individuate, *v.t.* شَخَّصَ ــ عَيَّنَ ــ مَيَّزَ ــ أَفَذَّ.

Individuation, *n.* تَشْخِيص ــ تَعْيِين ــ تَمْيِيز ــ إِفْذَاذ.

Indivisibility, *n.* } عَدَمُ ٱنْفِصَالٍ ــ عَدَمُ ٱنْقِسَامٍ.
Indivisibleness, }

Indivisible, *a.* لَا يَنْفَصِلُ ــ لَا يَنْقَسِمُ.

Indocible, *a.* شَرِس ــ عَنِيد ــ صَعْب ــ غَيْرُ قَابِلٍ ٱلتَّعْلِيمِ ــ مُتَمَرِّد.

Indocile, *a.* *See* Untractable, *a.*

Indocility, *n.* شَكَاسَة ــ تَمَرُّد ــ عِنَاد.

Indoctrinate, *v.t.* أَشْرَبَ ــ عَلَّمَ.

Indoctrination, *n.* تَعْلِيم ــ إِشْرَاب.

Indolence, *n.* Want of sensitiveness, عَدَمُ ــ قِلَّةُ حِسٍّ ــ جُمُود ــ ٱلتَّوَجُّع. A state of —, an unimproving condition, جُمَاد. *See also* Idleness, Laziness, *n.*

Indolent, *a.* Without feeling or pain, قَلِيلُ ٱلْحِسِّ ــ جَامِد ــ عَدِيمُ ٱلتَّوَجُّعِ. He was —, remiss, in the matter, اِنْفَشَّ عَنِ ٱلْأَمْرِ. *See also* Idle, Lazy, *a.*

Indolently, *ad.* Lazily, بِكَسَلٍ ــ بِبَلَادَةٍ.

Indomitable, *a.* That cannot be subdued, لَا يُقْهَرُ ــ عَزِيز ــ أَعَزّ; that cannot be tamed, لَا يَنْطَبِعُ ــ لَا يُغَالَبُ ــ لَا يُقْدَرُ عَلَيْهِ. Very courageous, صُلْبُ ٱلْمَعَاجِمِ ــ بَطَل ــ لَا يَتَقَعْقَعُ. Indomitable courage, عَزْمٌ لَا يَنْفَلُّ ــ بُطُولَة ــ بَطَالَة. To be —, عَزَّ.

Indomitableness, *n.* عِزَّة ــ عِزّ.

Indorse, *v.t.* To write on the back of a paper, وَقَّعَ عَلَى قَفَا ٱلْوَرَقَةِ. To assign to by indorsement of a deed, حَوَّلَ بِٱلتَّوْقِيعِ عَلَى قَفَا ٱلصَّكِّ. To — a bill of exchange, وَقَّعَ عَلَى ظَهْرِ وَرَقَةِ حَوَالَةٍ. To become liable to pay, تَضَمَّنَ. To approve, support, ظَاهَرَ ــ سَانَدَ ــ اِسْتَحْسَنَ. To — in blank, وَقَّعَ عَلَى بَيَاضٍ.

Indorsee, *n.* مُتَسَلِّمُ وَرَقَةِ حَوَالَةٍ.

Indorsement, *n.* A writing on the back of a deed, تَوْقِيعٌ عَلَى ظَهْرِ ٱلصَّكِّ; on the back of a bill of exchange, تَوْقِيعٌ عَلَى ظَهْرِ وَرَقَةِ حَوَالَةٍ. To negotiate by —, as of a deed, سَلَكَ بِٱلتَّوْقِيعِ عَلَى ظَهْرِ ٱلصَّكِّ. Support given, مُعَاوَنَة ــ إِسْنَاد ــ ظَهْر ــ اِسْتِحْسَان.

Indorser, *n.* مُوَقِّعٌ عَلَى قَفَا وَرَقَةِ ٱلْحَوَالَةِ ــ صَاحِبُ ٱلْحَوَالَةِ. A guarantor, ضَامِن.

Indrench, *v.t.* *See to* Drench, *v.t.*

Indubious, *a.* } مَا فِيهِ ــ صَحِيح ــ أَكِيد ــ حَقِيق ــ لَا رَيْبَ فِيهِ ــ
Indubitable, } لَيْسَ فِيهِ شُبْهَة ــ مَعْلُوم ــ مُسَلَّم ــ شَكّ.

Indubitably, *ad.* يَقِينًا ــ حَقًّا ــ فِي ٱلْحَقِيقَةِ ــ بِلَا شَكٍّ.

Induce, *v.t.* To prevail on, to incite to, حَرَّضَ عَلَى ــ حَضَّ عَلَى ــ أَلَحَّ عَلَى بِ ــ رَغَّبَ فِي ــ حَثَّ عَلَى ــ حَمَلَ عَلَى ــ أَغْرَى بِ. To produce, أَدَّى إِلَى ــ سَبَّبَ ــ أَنْتَجَ. To lead into, دَخَّلَ ــ أَدْخَلَ. What induced you to go, مَا دَعَاكَ إِلَى ٱلذَّهَابِ. He induces me to write, يَضْطَرُّنِي إِلَى ٱلْكِتَابَةِ. *See also to* Persuade, *v.t.*

Inducement, *n.* سَائِق ــ سَبَب ــ مُوجِب ــ دَاعٍ ــ بَاعِث.

Inducible, *a.* مِمَّا يُنْتَجُ ــ مِمَّا يَتَسَبَّبُ.

Induct, *v.t.* أَقَامَ ــ قَبَّضَ ــ جَلَّسَ فِي ــ أَقْعَدَ. He inducted him into the office, أَقَامَهُ فِي ٱلْوَظِيفَةِ. To be inducted into, أُقِيمَ فِي.

Inductibility, *n.* } Incapability of being beaten out, عَدَمُ قَابِلِيَّةِ ٱلْمَطْلِ; of being drawn out, عَدَمُ قَابِلِيَّةِ ٱلِٱمْتِدَادِ.
Inductility, }

Inductile, *a.* That cannot be beaten out, لَا يُمْطَلُ; that cannot be drawn out, غَيْرُ قَابِلٍ ٱلِٱمْتِدَادِ.

Induction, *n.* As into an office, إِقَامَة (or إِقْعَاد or تَجْلِيس) فِي مَنْصِبٍ. Enumeration of particular facts wherefrom to draw a general inference, إِسْتِقْرَآءٌ. A deduction, نَتِيجَة — قِيَاس — إِسْتِنْتَاج — إِسْتِدْلَال. To draw an — from, إِسْتَدَلَّ عَلَى-ب.

Inductional, a. } إِسْتِخْرَاجِيٌّ — إِسْتِدْلَالِيٌّ. The — sciences,
Inductive, } اَلْعُلُومُ ٱلْقِيَاسِيَّة. The — method, اَلنِّظَامُ ٱلْقِيَاسِيُّ.

Inductively, ad. بِٱلْقِيَاسِ — بِٱسْتِدْلَالٍ — إِسْتِخْرَاجًا.

Inductor, n. An installer, مُقِيم — مُجْلِس — مُدْخِل.

Indue, v.t. To clothe, كَسَى-ب — لَبَّسَ. To furnish with, وَشَّحَ-ب; to —, as with an office or decoration, قَلَّدَ-ب — وَجَّهَ-ب. To endow, supply with, أَمْلَكَ — جَهَّزَ-ب — أَنْعَمَ — أَطْعَمَ — أَعْطَى — عَلَى-ب.

Indulge, v.t. To let one have his own way, تَرَكَ-يَعْمَلُ [2] — أَرْوَدَ — سَيَّبَ — أَطْلَقَ — عَلَى هَوَاهُ. To be easy with, أَرْوَدَ — سَاهَلَ — يَاسَرَ — سَاهَلَ. To allow, رَخَّصَ ل — فَسَّحَ ل — أَطْلَقَ. To indulge, as of a child, دَلَّلَ — فَنَّقَ. To grant to, as a favour, تَفَضَّلَ عَلَى-ب — تَكَرَّمَ (or أَنْعَمَ) عَلَى-ب. He indulged his son by giving him a horse, أَنْعَمَ عَلَى ٱبْنِهِ بِفَرَسٍ. Do not — your wit, لَا تُبَالِغْ فِي ٱللَّهْوِ. He indulged himself in sin, إِنْهَمَكَ فِي ٱلْإِثْمِ.

Indulge, v.i. To yield to the enjoyment of, إِنْهَمَكَ فِي — غَاصَ فِي [2] — تَعَاطَى.

Indulgence, n. Easy treatment, تَسَاهُل — مُيَاسَرَة — مُسَاهَلَة. Fond kindness, لَطَافَة — حِلْم — إِسْتِمَالَة — تَسَاهُل — تَعَطُّف; as towards a child, مُفَانَقَة — تَدْلِيل — تَفْنِيق. Forbearance, سَتْرُ ٱلْقُصُور — عُفُوّ — مُسَامَحَة — تَسَامُح. A favour granted, نِعْمَة — فَضْل — مِنَن pl. مِنَّة. Permission, إِجَازَة — رُخْصَة. Gratification, إِنْهِمَاكٌ فِي ٱللَّذَّاتِ — حَظُّ ٱلنَّفْسِ. A papal —, تَذْكِرَةُ غُفْرَانٍ مِنَ ٱلْبَابَا — غُفْرَانٌ مِنَ ٱلْبَابَا. He spoiled him by —, حَمَلَهُ بِٱلتَّدْلِيلِ عَلَى ٱلْبَطَرِ — أَبْطَرَهُ بِٱلتَّسَاهُلِ. Indulgence in forbidden things, إِرْتِكَابُ ٱلْمَحَارِمِ.

Indulgent, a. Yielding to wishes, سَرِيعُ ٱلْمَيْلِ — مُرْضٍ — كَثِيرُ ٱلْأَلْطَافِ — مُيَاسِر — مُسَاهِل. Kind, مُحْسِن — كَرِيم. Compassionate, حَنُون — مُسَامِح. Friendship is — to faults, اَلْحُبُّ سَاتِرُ ٱلْعُيُوبِ — يَسْتُرُ ٱلْقُصُورَ.

Indulgently, ad. بِٱلْمُسَاهَلَةِ — بِٱلتَّدْلِيلِ — بِٱلتَّسَامُحِ — بِٱلتَّسَاهُلِ.

Indurate, v.t. صَلَّبَ. *See also to* Harden, v.t.

Indurate, v.i. صَلُبَ [2]. *See also to* Harden, v.i.

Indurated, a. مُصَلَّب. Indurated clay, صَلْصَال.

Induration, n. The act of, تَصْلِيب; of becoming hard, صَلَابَة. Induration of the spleen, طُحَال.

Industrial, a. مُتَعَلِّقٌ بِٱلْحِرَفِ وَٱلصَّنَائِعِ — صِنَاعِيٌّ. Industrial products, مَحْصُولَاتٌ صِنَاعِيَّة. An — school, مَكْتَبُ صَنَائِعَ.

Industrious, a. Hard working, كَدُود — فَعُول — عَمَّال — عَمِل — شَغَّال. Diligent, كَادِح — مُبْتَذِل — مُتَبَذِّل — مُجِدّ. Industrious people, أَهْلُ ٱلْكَدْحِ. To be — in, كَدَّ فِي [2] — كَدَحَ فِي [2].

Industriously, ad. بِٱجْتِهَادٍ — بِكَدٍّ — بِكَدْحٍ.

Industry, n. Work, عَمَل — سَعْي — شُغْل. Diligence, assiduity, دَوَام — إِقْدَام — جُهْد — إِجْتِهَاد — كَدْح — كَدّ. Perseverance, مُدَاوَمَة. Arts and sciences, حِرَف وَصَنَائِع.

Indweller, n. مُقِيم — سَاكِن.

Indwelling, n. حُلُولٌ فِي — إِسْكَان — سُكْنَى — إِقَامَة.

Indwelling, a. حَالٌّ فِي — مَوْجُودٌ فِي — مُقِيمٌ فِي.

Inebriant, a. مُسْكِر.

Inebriate, v.t. سَكَّرَ. *See also under* Drunk, a.

Inebriate, v.i. سَكِرَ [2].

Inebriate, n. سَكْرَ — سِكِّير.

Inebriation, n. } سُكْر.
Inebriety, }

Inedited, a. غَيْرُ مَنْشُورٍ — غَيْرُ مَبْرُوزٍ — غَيْرُ مُبْرَزٍ.

Ineffableness, n. عَدَمُ ٱلْوَصْفِ.

Ineffable, a. يَفُوقُ ٱلْوَصْفَ — عَدِيمُ ٱلْوَصْفِ — لَا يُوصَفُ — وَصْفُهُ مُحَال.

Ineffably, ad. بِنَوْعٍ لَا يُوصَفُ — بِمَا يَفُوقُ ٱلْوَصْفَ.

Ineffaceable, a. مَحْوُهُ مُحَال — وَمَا لَا يَنْمَحِي — لَا يُمْحَى — دَرْسُهُ مُحَال — لَا يُطْلَسُ.

Ineffaceably, ad. بِمَا لَا يُزَالُ — بِوَجْهٍ لَا يَمَّحِي.

Ineffective, } Producing no effect, خَالٍ عَنْ — غَيْرُ مُؤَثِّرٍ
Ineffectual, a. } — لَا فَاعِلِيَّةَ فِيهِ — اَلتَّأْثِيرِ. Useless, غَيْرُ نَافِعٍ
Inefficacious, } — غَيْرُ طَائِلٍ — لَا طَائِلَ تَحْتَهُ — بَاطِل — عَبَث — بَطَّال.

Ineffectively, } بِدُونِ نَفْعٍ — بِلَا فَاعِلِيَّةٍ — بِدُونِ تَأْثِيرٍ
Ineffectually, ad. } — بِلَا طَائِلٍ — عَبَثًا — بَاطِلًا.
Inefficaciously, }

Ineffectualness, }
Inefficacy, n. } عَدَمُ طَائِلٍ — قِلَّةُ فَاعِلِيَّةٍ — عَدَمُ تَأْثِيرٍ.
Inefficiency, }

Ineffervescent, a. عَدِيمُ ٱلْفَوَرَانِ — غَيْرُ فَائِرٍ.

Ineffervescible, a. لَا يَفُورُ.

Inefficient, a. Incapable, لَيْسَ لَهُ — عَاجِزٌ عَنْ — لَيْسَ كُفُوًّا لِ — قُدْرَةٌ عَلَى. *See also* Ineffective, a.

Inefficiently, *ad.* Incapably, بِقِلَّةِ أَهْلِيَّةٍ ـ بِعَجْزٍ. *See also* Ineffectively, *ad.*

Inelastic, *a.* جاسِئٌ ـ غَيْرُ قابِلِ ٱلْإِمْتِغاطِ ـ لا يُمَدُّ وَلا يُقْلَصُ.
To be —, stiff, جَسَأَ ـ ٢.

Inelasticity, *n.* جُسْأَةٌ ـ جَسَاءَةٌ ـ عَدَمُ ٱلْإِمْتِغاطِ.

Inelegance, *n.* | Inelegancy, غِلَظٌ ـ عَدَمُ لَطافَةٍ ـ قِلَّةُ ظَرافَةٍ (or طَلاوَةٍ) بَشاعَةٌ; of language, رَكاكَةٌ ـ هُجْنَةٌ.

Inelegant, *a.* Not becoming, لا ظَرافَةَ فِيهِ ـ عَدِيمُ ٱللَّطافَةِ ـ غَلِيظٌ ـ بَشِعٌ ـ بَشِيعٌ; of language, رَكِيكٌ ـ مُسْتَهْجَنٌ.

Inelegantly, *ad.* بِبَشاعَةٍ ـ بِقِلَّةِ ظَرافَةٍ ـ بِعَدَمِ لَطافَةٍ (or طَلاوَةٍ).

Ineligibility, *n.* Incapacity of being elected, عَدَمُ صَلاحِيَّةٍ لِلْإِخْتِيارِ ـ عَدَمُ إِمْكانِ ٱنْتِخابِهِ. Unfitness, عَدَمُ مَصْلَحَةٍ (or مُناسَبَةٍ).

Ineligible, *a.* Not capable of being elected, غَيْرُ ـ لا يُنْتَخَبُ أَهْلٍ لِلْإِنْتِخابِ. Not suitable, غَيْرُ مُناسِبٍ ـ غَيْرُ مُوافِقٍ ـ غَيْرُ لائِقٍ ـ غَيْرُ سائِغٍ.

Inept, *a.* Futile, باطِلٌ ـ عَبَثٌ ـ غَيْرُ طائِلٍ ـ غَيْرُ نافِعٍ. Unready, awkward, عَدِيمُ ٱللَّطافَةِ ـ عَدِيمُ ٱلْإِسْتِعْدادِ ـ خَرِقٌ ـ أَخْرَقُ; of a thing, سَمِجٌ.

Ineptly, *ad.* Vainly, باطِلًا ـ عَبَثًا. Awkwardly, بِخُرْقٍ ـ بِقِلَّةِ مَعْرِفَةٍ ـ بِعَدَمِ دِرايَةٍ. Unfitly, بِعَدَمِ مُناسَبَةٍ.

Ineptitude, *n.* | Ineptness, Futility, عَبَثٌ ـ عَدَمُ طائِلٍ ـ عَدَمُ نَفْعٍ. Awkwardness, خُرْقٌ ـ عَدَمُ دِرايَةٍ ـ عَدَمُ ٱسْتِعْدادٍ; of a thing, سَماجَةٌ. Unfitness, عَدَمُ مُناسَبَةٍ ـ عَدَمُ مُوافَقَةٍ.

Inequality, *n.* Difference of quantity, إِخْتِلافٌ ـ مُبايَنَةٌ ـ فَرْقٌ ـ تَفاوُتٌ ـ عَدَمُ مُساواةٍ ـ عَدَمُ ٱعْتِدالٍ; as of surface, أَمْتٌ ـ عَدَمُ بَساطَةٍ ـ عَدَمُ تَسْطِيحٍ ـ عَدَمُ تَمَهُّدٍ; of temper or of the weather, تَقَلُّبٌ ـ تَغَيُّرٌ ـ عَدَمُ ٱعْتِدالٍ. Want of regular succession, عَدَمُ ٱطِّرادٍ. Insufficiency, عَدَمُ كِفايَةٍ.

In equilibrio, ad. بِمُوازَنَةٍ ـ عَلَى ٱلْمِيزانِ ـ عَلَى سَاحَةٍ.

Inequitable, *a.* ظالِمٌ ـ غَيْرُ مُقْسِطٍ ـ غَيْرُ مُنْصِفٍ.

Inequitably, *ad.* بِلا قِسْطٍ ـ بِظُلْمٍ ـ بِعَدَمِ إِنْصافٍ.

Inerrable, *a.* *See* Infallible, *a.*

Inert, *a.* Without motion, عَدِيمُ ٱلْحَرَكَةِ ـ جامِدٌ. Inactive, sluggish, ثَقِيلٌ ـ مَيّاطٌ ـ بَلِيدٌ ـ فاتِرٌ ـ ضاجِعٌ ـ جامِدٌ ـ جامِدُ ٱلْحالِ.

Inertia, *n.* عَدَمُ حَرَكَةٍ ـ جُمُودٌ. *See also* Inertness, *n.*

Inertion, *n.* | Inertness, Want of activity, كَسَلٌ ـ جَمادٌ ـ بَلادَةٌ ـ ضُجْعَةٌ.

Inertly, *ad.* بِكَسَلٍ ـ بِبَلادَةٍ ـ بِجَمادٍ.

In esse, ad. كائِنٌ ـ بِٱلْفِعْلِ.

Inestimable, *a.* فائِقُ ٱلتَّثْمِينِ ـ عَزِيزٌ لِلْغايَةِ ـ تَثْمِينُهُ مُحالٌ ـ لا يُعْرَفُ لَهُ ثَمَنٌ ـ لا يُثَمَّنُ.

Inestimably, *ad.* بِأَغْلَى ثَمَنٍ ـ بِما يَفُوقُ ٱلتَّثْمِينَ ـ عِزَّةً لِلْغايَةِ.

Inevitability, *n.* | Inevitableness, لُزُومِيَّةٌ ـ ضَرُورَةٌ ـ لُزُومٌ ـ إِلْزامٌ ـ بُدٌّ.

Inevitable, *a.* لا بُدَّ مِنْ حُدُوثِهِ ـ لا مَفَرَّ مِنْهُ ـ لا بُدَّ مِنْهُ ـ لا يُرَدُّ ـ مُلازِمٌ ـ غَيْرُ مَرْدُودٍ ـ لا يُمْكِنُ تَجَنُّبُهُ مِنْهُ. The thing was —, لا وَهَمَ.

Inevitably, *a.* لا مَفَرَّ مِنْهُ ـ مِنْ غَيْرِ مَفَرٍّ ـ مِنْ كُلِّ بُدٍّ ـ لا وَهَمَ.

Inexact, *a.* غَيْرُ مَضْبُوطٍ ـ غَيْرُ صَحِيحٍ.

Inexactness, *n.* قِلَّةُ ضَبْطٍ ـ قِلَّةُ صِحَّةٍ.

Inexcusable, *a.* غَيْرُ مَعْذُورٍ ـ لا حُجَّةَ لَهُ ـ لا عُذْرَ لَهُ ـ بِلا عُذْرٍ.

Inexcusableness, *n.* عَدَمُ حُجَّةٍ ـ خُلُوٌّ مِنَ ٱلْعُذْرِ.

Inexcusably, *ad.* بِلا عُذْرٍ ـ بِلا ٱعْتِلالٍ ـ بِدُونِ عُذْرٍ.

Inexhausted, *a.* غَيْرُ مُنْتَهٍ ـ غَيْرُ مَنْزُوحٍ ـ غَيْرُ مَنْزُوفٍ ـ غَيْرُ نافِدٍ.

Inexhaustible, *a.* لا يَنْفَدُ ـ لا يَفْرَغُ ـ لا يُنْزَحُ ـ لا يُنْزَفُ ـ دائِمٌ ـ لا يَنْتَهِي.

Inexhaustibleness, *n.* عَدَمُ ٱلنَّفادِ ـ عَدَمُ ٱلْفُرُوغِ.

Inexistence, *n.* عَدَمٌ ـ عَدَمُ ٱلْوُجُودِ.

Inexistent, *a.* عَدِيمٌ ـ غَيْرُ مَوْجُودٍ.

Inexorability, *n.* | Inexorableness, عَدَمُ حُنُوٍّ ـ عَدَمُ لَيانٍ ـ عُنْفٌ ـ لَدٌّ ـ عَدَمُ رَحْمَةٍ.

Inexorable, *a.* أَلَدُّ *pl.* لُدٌّ *and* لِدادٌ ـ أَصَمُّ *fem.* صَمّاءُ *pl.* صُمٌّ ـ سَخِيتٌ ـ لا يَهْدَأُ غَضَبُهُ ـ لا يَلِينُ ـ عَسُوفٌ ـ شَدِيدُ ٱلْأَخْدَعِ ـ سَحْتٌ. An — man, رَجُلٌ أَصَمُّ. Such a one is —, فُلانٌ شَدِيدُ ٱلْأَخْدَعِ. Inexorable fortune, دَهْرٌ أَصَمُّ. *See also* Implacable, *a.*

Inexorably, *ad.* بِشِدَّةِ ٱلْأَخْدَعِ ـ مِنْ غَيْرِ رَحْمَةٍ.

Inexpedience, *n.* | Inexpediency, قِلَّةُ مُناسَبَةٍ ـ عَدَمُ مُلاءَمَةٍ ـ عَدَمُ مُوافَقَةٍ.

Inexpedient, *a.* لَيْسَ بِمُناسِبٍ ـ غَيْرُ مُلائِمٍ ـ غَيْرُ مُوافِقٍ ـ فِي غَيْرِ وَقْتِهِ ـ فِي غَيْرِ مَحَلِّهِ. It is — for me to go, لا يُوافِقُنِي أَنْ أَذْهَبَ.

Inexpediently, *ad.* فِي غَيْرِ مَحَلِّهِ ـ بِعَدَمِ مُناسَبَةٍ ـ بِغَيْرِ مُوافَقَةٍ.

Inexpensive, *a.* رَخِيصٌ ـ غَيْرُ ثَمِينٍ ـ غَيْرُ مُكَلِّفٍ.

Inexpensively, *ad.* بِرُخْصٍ ـ بِقِلَّةِ كُلْفَةٍ.

Inexperience, *n.* Want of experience, عَدَمُ ـ غَرارَةٌ ـ غَمارَةٌ

عَدَمُ ٱخْتِبَارٍ ـ غُشُومِيَّةٌ ـ عَدَمُ خِبْرَةٍ ـ مُمَارَسَةٍ. Want of knowledge, skill, جَهَالَةٌ ـ خُرْقٌ.

Inexperienced, *a.* Wanting experience, أَغِرَّةٌ *pl.* غَرِيرٌ ـ غِرٌّ ـ أَخْرَقُ ـ غَشِيمٌ ـ مُجَدَّدٌ ـ غَيْرُ مُدَرَّبٍ ـ غُمْرٌ. Simple, foolish, غَشِيمٌ ـ أَبْلَهُ ـ جَاهِلٌ. To be —, غَمِرَ ـ غَرَّ.

Inexpert, *a.* غَيْرُ حَاذِقٍ ـ غَيْرُ بَارِعٍ ـ غَيْرُ مَاهِرٍ ـ خَرِقٌ ـ أَخْرَقُ ـ غَيْرُ شِمْلِيلٍ.

Inexpertness, *n.* قِلَّةُ بَرَاعَةٍ ـ قِلَّةُ نَشَاطٍ ـ عَدَمُ مَهَارَةٍ ـ خُرْقٌ *vulg.* عَدَمُ شَطَارَةٍ.

Inexpiable, *a.* لا يُعْفَى عَنْهُ ـ لا يُكَفَّرُ.

Inexpiably, *ad.* بِمَا لا يُعْفَى عَنْهُ ـ بِمَا لا يُكَفَّرُ.

Inexplicability, *n.* / Inexplicableness, عَدَمُ ٱلتَّفْسِيرِ ـ غَيْبَةٌ ـ غَيْبٌ.

Inexplicable, *a.* غَيْرُ تَأْوِيلُهُ غَيْرُ مُمْكِنٍ ـ لا يُعَبَّرُ ـ لا يُشْرَحُ ـ غَائِبٌ ـ قَابِلُ ٱلتَّفْسِيرِ. To be —, beyond the reach of mental perception, تَغَيَّبَ ـ غَابَ.

Inexplicably, *ad.* بِغَيْبَةٍ ـ بِصُورَةٍ لا تُعَبَّرُ ـ بِمَا لا يُشْرَحُ.

Inexplorable, *a.* لا يُتَجَسَّسُ ـ الكَشْفُ عَنْهُ غَيْرُ مُمْكِنٍ ـ لا يُتَنَفَّضُ.

Inexpressible, *a.* يَعْجِزُ عَنْ وَصْفِهِ ٱللِّسَانُ ـ لا يُوصَفُ.

Inexpressibly, *ad.* بِوَجْهٍ يَعْجِزُ عَنْ وَصْفِهِ ٱللِّسَانُ ـ بِنَوْعٍ لا يُوصَفُ لِلْغَايَةِ.

Inexpressive, *a.* عَدِيمُ ٱلْإِيضَاحِ ـ غَيْرُ حَدِيدٍ ـ قَلِيلُ ٱلتَّعْبِيرِ ـ بِلا مَعْنَى.

Inexpressiveness, *n.* قِلَّةُ حِدَّةٍ ـ قِلَّةُ مَعْنَى ـ قِلَّةُ تَعْبِيرٍ.

Inexpugnable, *a.* حَصِينٌ ـ مَنِيعٌ ـ لا يُقْهَرُ ـ عَزِيزٌ ـ أَعَزُّ.

In extenso, *a.* حَرْفًا حَرْفًا ـ بِلا ٱخْتِصَارٍ ـ كُلِّيًّا ـ بِعِبَارَاتِهِ.

Inextinct, *a.* Of a light, غَيْرُ مُطْفَأٍ. Still existing, غَيْرُ مُنْعَدِمٍ ـ مَوْجُودٌ ـ غَيْرُ مَعْدُومٍ.

Inextinguishable, *n.* Not to be quenched, لا يُخْمَدُ ـ لا يُطْفَأُ; not to be assuaged, لا يَهْدَأُ ـ لا يَلِينُ ـ لا يَبُوخُ.

Inextricable, *a.* مُعَقَّدٌ ـ مُشْكِلٌ ـ لا يَنْحَلُّ ـ عَزِيزٌ ـ أَعَزُّ ـ مُشَوَّشٌ ـ مُشْتَبِكٌ.

Inextricably, *ad.* طُرًّا ـ بِٱرْتِبَاكٍ ـ بِٱشْتِبَاكٍ ـ بِعِزَّةٍ; wholly, لِلْغَايَةِ.

Infallibility, *n.* إِعْتِصَامٌ (or عِصْمَةٌ) عَنِ ٱلْخَطَاءِ. Certainty, حَقٌّ ـ حَقِيقَةٌ ـ يَقِينٌ. Papal —, عِصْمَةُ ٱلْبَابَا. For establishing the papal —, لِأَجْلِ إِثْبَاتِ ٱلْعِصْمَةِ لِلْبَابَا.

Infallible, *a.* مَعْصُومٌ عَنِ ٱلْخَطَاءِ. Certain, غَيْرُ مُكَذَّبٍ ـ أَكِيدٌ ـ لا رَيْبَ فِيهِ ـ يَقِينٌ ـ حَقِيقٌ.

Infallibly, *ad.* بِدُونِ خَطَاءٍ ـ بِٱعْتِصَامٍ. With certainty, مِنْ كُلِّ بُدٍّ ـ يَقِينًا ـ بِلا رَيْبٍ.

Infamous, *a.* Of a person, ذَمِيمٌ ـ مَذْمُومٌ ـ فَضِيحٌ ـ مَعْيُوبٌ ـ فَظِيعٌ ـ شَنِيعٌ ـ فَاحِشٌ ـ مَهْتُوكٌ *pl.* فَاجِرٌ ـ فُجَّارٌ; of a thing, فَظِيعٌ ـ شَنِيعٌ ـ فَاحِشٌ. O thou — fellow! يَا أَيُّهَا ٱلْفَاسِقُ ـ يَا فُسَقُ.

Infamously, *ad.* تَفَضُّحًا ـ بِفُجُورٍ ـ بِفَضَاحَةٍ.

Infamousness, *n.* / Infamy, ذَمٌّ ـ عَيْبٌ ـ فُجُورٌ ـ فَضِيحَةٌ ـ عَارٌ ـ عَزَارَةٌ ـ هَتِيكَةٌ. To expose to infamy, فَضَحَ ـ. To act with —, تَفَضَّحَ.

Infancy, *n.* طُفُولِيَّةٌ ـ طُفُولَةٌ ـ صَبَاءٌ ـ صِبًا. That was in his —, كَانَ ذٰلِكَ فِي صِبَاهُ. *See also* Beginning, *n.*

Infant, *n.* *Masc.* صَبِيٌّ *pl.* صِبْيَانٌ; *fem.* صَبِيَّةٌ *pl.* صَبَايَا ـ طِفْلٌ *pl.* أَطْفَالٌ; *fem.* طِفْلَةٌ *pl.* طِفْلَاتٌ. A child while it is a suckling, رَضِيعٌ.

Infanta, *n.* لَقَبُ بَنَاتِ مُلُوكِ إِسْپَانِيَا وَبُورْتُكَالَ دُونَ ٱلْبِكْرِ مِنْهُنَّ.

Infante, *n.* لَقَبُ أَوْلَادِ مُلُوكِ إِسْپَانِيَا وَبُورْتُكَالَ دُونَ ٱلْبِكْرِ مِنْهُمْ.

Infanticide, *n.* قَتْلُ ٱلطِّفْلِ.

Infantile, *a.* / Infantine, مَا نِيطَ بِٱلصِّبَا ـ طِفْلِيٌّ. *See also* Childish, *a.*

Infantry, *n.* عَسَاكِرُ رَجَّالَةٌ ـ عَسَاكِرُ مُشَاةٌ.

Infatuate, *v.t.* أَجَنَّ ـ حَيَّرَ ـ سَلَبَ عَقْلَهُ ـ أَفْتَنَ ـ فَتَنَ.

Infatuated, *a.* Inspired with a foolish passion, مُسْتَلَبٌ ـ مَفْتُونٌ ـ مَجْنُونٌ ـ مُتَحَيِّرُ ٱلْعَقْلِ; as with pride, مُتَحَذْلِقٌ.

Infatuation, *n.* جُنُونٌ ـ تَحَيُّرٌ ـ إِسْتِلَابُ ٱلْعَقْلِ ـ فُتُونٌ; pride, تَحَذْلُقٌ.

Infeasibility, *n.* عَدَمُ إِمْكَانٍ ـ عِزَّةٌ ـ عِزٌّ. An —, شَيْءٌ مُحَالٌ ـ شَيْءٌ غَيْرُ مُمْكِنٍ.

Infeasible, *a.* مُحَالٌ ـ عَزِيزٌ ـ أَعَزُّ.

Infect, *v.t.* To taint with disease, أَكْسَبَ ـ أَعْدَى ـ بِٱلْمَرَضِ ـ أَثَّرَ فِي ـ ٱلْمَرَضُ ـ أَصَابَ ـ بِٱلْمَرَضِ ـ ٱلدَّاءُ. To pervade, عَمَّمَ ـ خَالَطَ ـ خَامَرَ. The disease infected him, خَالَطَهُ (or خَامَرَهُ) ٱلدَّاءُ. Wine infects the intellect, ٱلْخَمْرُ يُخَالِطُ ٱلْعَقْلَ. The poison infected or pervaded him, سَرَى فِيهِ ٱلسَّمُّ. It infected, corrupted, the air, أَفْسَدَ ٱلْهَوَاءَ. He infected him with fever, أَعْدَاهُ بِٱلْحُمَّى. The people were infected, تَعَادَى ٱلْقَوْمُ. They were infected with heresy, سَرَتْ فِيهِمِ ٱلْهَرْطَقَةُ (or ٱلْبِدْعَةُ).

Infection, *n.* مُخَامَرَةٌ ـ إِصَابَةٌ ـ سِرَايَةٌ ـ عَدْوَى. Taint, عُفُونَةٌ ـ وَبَاءٌ ـ دَنَاسَةٌ ـ إِنْفِسَادٌ. Infection of the air, عُفُونَةُ ٱلْهَوَاءِ.

Infectious, *a.* مُصِيبٌ ـ سَارٍ ـ مُعْتَدٍ ـ مُعْدٍ.

Infectiously, *ad.* بِٱلسِّرَايَةِ ـ بِعَدْوَى .

Infectiousness, *n.* *See* Infection, *n.*

Infecund, *a.* Unfruitful, غَيْرُ مُثْمِرٍ . Barren, عَاقِرٌ ـ عَقِيمٌ .

Infecundity, *n.* Unfruitfulness, عَدَمُ ٱلثَّمَرَةِ ; barrenness, عُقْرٌ ـ عُقْمٌ .

Infelicitous, *a.* *See* Unhappy, *a.*

Infelicity, *n.* *See* Unhappiness, *n.*

Infer, *v.t.* إِسْتَنْتَجَ ـ إِسْتَدَلَّ . To gather, as from appearances, تَوَسَّمَ فِي : He inferred good therefrom, تَوَسَّمَ فِيهِ ٱلْخَيْرَ .

Inferable, *a.*
Inferrible, } مِمَّا يُسْتَنْتَجُ ـ مُسْتَدَلٌّ .

Inference, *n.* حَاصِلٌ ـ نَتِيجَةٌ *pl.* نَتَائِجُ ـ إِسْتِدْلَالٌ . To draw an —, إِسْتَنْتَجَ ـ إِسْتَدَلَّ . They must not draw any — from this, لَا يَنْبَغِي أَنْ يَسْتَنْتِجُوا مِنْ هٰذَا أَدْنَى طَائِلٍ .

Inferential, *a.* إِسْتِدْلَالِيٌّ .

Inferentially, *ad.* بِٱسْتِدْلَالٍ .

Inferior, *a.* Lower, سُفْلَانِيٌّ ـ سُفْلَانٌ *pl.* سَافِلٌ ـ سُفْلِيٌّ ـ أَحَطُّ ـ أَوْطَى ـ تَحْتَانِيٌّ ـ أَسَافِلُ *pl.* أَسْفَلُ . Lower in rank, دُونٌ ـ أَسْفَلُ ـ أَدْنَى ـ تَحْتَ ـ مَا دُونَ . Secondary, next to the chief person, ثِنْيٌ ـ ثُنْيَانٌ . Inferior in numbers, أَقَلُّ عَدَدًا ـ أَدْنَى . Inferior in quality, دُونٌ ـ أَدْنَى . An — man, رَجُلٌ مِنْ دُونٍ ـ رَجُلٌ دُونٌ . An — thing, شَيْءٌ دُونٌ ـ شَيْءٌ مِنْ دُونٍ . He is — to him in knowledge, هُوَ دُونَهُ عِلْمًا . This is —, or the — of that, هٰذَا دُونَ ذَاكَ . Inferior in power to him, أَدْنَى قُدْرَةً مِنْهُ . Will you take in exchange that which is — for that which is better? أَتَسْتَبْدِلُونَ ٱلَّذِي هُوَ أَدْنَى بِٱلَّذِي هُوَ خَيْرٌ (*Kur.* ii. 58.) To be —, under, سَفَلَ [2]. To accept an — position, سَفَّلَ ـ تَسَفَّلَ . To make or to pronounce to be —, سَفَّلَ .

Inferior, *n.* أَدْنَى ـ دُونٌ . A subordinate, تَحْتَ يَدِ غَيْرِهِ ـ تَحْتَ حُكْمِ غَيْرِهِ . He is my — in every thing, هُوَ دُونِي فِي كُلِّ شَيْءٍ .

Inferiority, *n.* دَنَاءَةٌ ـ سَفْلَةٌ .

Infernal, *a.* Belonging to hell, جَحِيمِيٌّ ـ جَهَنَّمِيٌّ . Accursed, detestable, شَنِيعٌ ـ مَلْعُونٌ ـ لَعِينٌ ـ خَبِيثٌ . The — machine, ٱلْآلَةُ ٱلْجَهَنَّمِيَّةُ . *See also* Fiendish, Diabolical, *a.*

Infernally, *ad.* بِشَنَاعَةٍ . Extremely, لِلْغَايَةِ .

Infertile, *a.* غَيْرُ مُنْبِتٍ ـ غَيْرُ مُثْمِرٍ ـ غَيْرُ مُخْصِبٍ . *See also* Barren, *a.*

Infertility, *n.* عَدَمُ ٱلْخِصْبِ ـ عَدَمُ ٱلثَّمَرَةِ . *See also* Barrenness, *n.*

Infest, *v.t.* To torment, ضَجَّرَ ـ أَقْلَقَ ـ آذَى . To vex with incursions, فَسَدَ [2] ـ نَهَبَ [2] ـ عَدَا عَلَى [2] ـ غَارَ عَلَى [2]. The road is infested with robbers, ٱللُّصُوصُ قَطَعُوا ٱلطَّرِيقَ ـ ٱللُّصُوصُ ـ ٱلدَّرْبُ مَمْلُوٌّ مِنْ قُطَّاعِ ٱلطَّرِيقِ ـ تَاعُوا ٱلطَّرِيقَ . The house was infested with rats, أُصِيبَ ٱلْبَيْتُ ـ عَدَتِ ٱلْجُرْذَانُ عَلَى ٱلْبَيْتِ ـ إِمْتَلَأَ ٱلْمَنْزِلُ مِنَ ٱلْجُرْذَانِ ـ بِٱلْجُرْذَانِ .

Infidel, *a.* كَافِرٌ *pl.* كُفَّارٌ ـ جَاحِدُ ٱلْإِيمَانِ ـ مُشْرِكٌ ـ مُشْرِكِيٌّ ـ مُلْحِدٌ *pl.* مَلَاحِدَةٌ .

Infidel, *a.* Containing infidelity, unbelief, مُحْتَوٍ عَلَى ٱلْكُفْرِ ـ جَاحِدُ ٱلْإِيمَانِ .

Infidelity, *n.* Disbelief of religion, كُفْرٌ ـ شِرْكٌ ـ جُحُودُ ٱلْإِيمَانِ . Breach of trust, عَدَمُ وَفَاءٍ . Treachery, غَدْرٌ ـ خِيَانَةٌ .

Infiltrate, *v.i.* رَشَحَ [2]. To — into, دَخَلَ فِي [2] ـ قَطَعَ فِي [2] ـ تَفَشَّى فِي . The ink infiltrated into the paper, تَفَشَّى ٱلْحِبْرُ فِي ٱلْكَاغِدِ .

Infiltration, *n.* رَشْحٌ .

Infinite, *a.* Boundless, لَا نِهَايَةَ لَهُ ـ لَا حَدَّ لَهُ ـ غَيْرُ مُتَنَاهٍ ـ غَيْرُ مَحْصُورٍ . Infinite in number, لَا يُعَدُّ ـ لَا يُحْصَى . Very great, immense, كَبِيرٌ لِلْغَايَةِ ـ مُطْلَقٌ ـ كُلِّيٌّ .

Infinite, *n.* كُلٌّ .

Infinitely, *ad.* Without limit, بِلَا نِهَايَةٍ . Immensely, wholly, إِطْلَاقًا ـ كُلِّيًّا ـ كَثْرَةً ـ بَتَّةً ـ جِدًّا .

Infiniteness,
Infinitude, *n.*
Infinity, } Boundless extent, عَدَمُ حَدٍّ ـ عَدَمُ حُدُودٍ ـ عَدَمُ نِهَايَةٍ . The whole, كُلِّيَّةٌ . A large quantity, كَثْرَةٌ ـ جَمٌّ . A boundless number, عَدَدٌ لَا يُحْصَى .

Infinitesimal, *a.* جُزْئِيٌّ لِلْغَايَةِ ـ لَا يَتَجَزَّأُ . An — part, جُزْءٌ لَا يَتَجَزَّأُ .

Infinitive, *a.* مَصْدَرِيٌّ . The — mood, صِيغَةُ ٱلْمَصْدَرِ . An — noun of action, إِسْمُ فِعْلٍ . An — noun of unity, إِسْمُ ٱلْمَرَّةِ ; of modality, إِسْمُ ٱلنَّوْعِ .

Infirm, *a.* Weak, مَوْهُونٌ ـ عَاجِزٌ ـ مَنْهُوكٌ ـ نَهِيكٌ ـ كَسِيحٌ ـ ضَعِيفٌ *pl.* ضُعَفَاءُ . Infirm of mind, غَبِينٌ ـ سَقِيمٌ ـ عَلِيلٌ ـ فَائِلُ ٱلرَّأْيِ ـ خَرِفٌ ـ مَأْفُونٌ ـ مَأْفُوكٌ . Irresolute, مُتَرَدِّدٌ ـ مُتَقَلْقِلٌ ـ قَلَّاعٌ . Not stable, غَيْرُ ثَابِتٍ ـ مُتَزَعْزِعٌ . To be —, weak, ضَعُفَ [2] ـ ضَعَفَ [2]. To be too — to, عَجَزَ عَنْ [2] ـ ضَعُفَ عَنْ [2]. To be —, irresolute, تَرَدَّدَ ـ تَزَعْزَعَ ـ تَقَلْقَلَ .

Infirmary, *n.* *See* Hospital.

Infirmity, *n.* Weakness, سُقْمٌ ـ عِلَّةٌ ـ وَهْنٌ ـ ذَمِيمَةٌ ـ كَسْحٌ ـ ضَعْفٌ ـ ضَنًى . A failing, تَقْصِيرٌ ـ نَقْصٌ . A chronic —, عَاهَةٌ .

Infirmity of mind, أَفْن ـ إِفْنَاد ـ غَبَانَة. Irresolution, فَيْلُولَة ـ قَرْقَرَة ـ تَقَلْقُل ـ تَرَدُّد.

Infirmness, *n.* ضَعْف. *See also* Infirmity, *n.*

Infix, *v.t.* غَرَزَ-فِي ـ أَنْشَبَ-فِي ـ رَكَزَ-فِي ـ رَكَّزَ-فِي ـ شَكَّ-فِي ـ رَزَّ-فِي. To —, so as to make to stand upright, نَصَبَ ـ نَصَّبَ. To be infixed, اِنْغَرَزَ ـ اِنْغَرَسَ ـ اِرْتَكَزَ.

Inflame, *v.t.* To kindle, أَشْعَلَ ـ أَضْرَمَ ـ أَلْهَبَ ـ أَجَّجَ ـ أَوْقَدَ. To provoke, أَغْرَمَ ـ أَثَارَ. To enrage, أَشْعَلَ-غَضَبًا ـ حَمَلَهُ عَلَى ٱلْغَضَبِ ـ أَغْضَبَ ـ أَغَاظَ. To heat the body morbidly, أَلْهَبَ ـ وَرَّمَ. To exaggerate, عَظَّمَ ـ كَبَّرَ ـ بَالَغَ فِي. To stir up, أَثَارَ ـ هَيَّجَ ـ اِسْتَفَزَّ. To be inflamed; *see under* Inflamed, *a.*

Inflame, *v.i.* حَمَّ ـ وَرِمَ *aor.* يَرِمُ.

Inflamed, *a.* In flames, مُشْتَعِل. Morbidly —, مُلْتَهِب ـ مُتَوَرِّم. To be — with rage, اِلْتَظَى ـ وَرِمَ أَنْفُهُ *aor.* يَرِمُ. To be —, excited with, أَغْرَمَ بِ ـ ثَارَ بِ *aor.* يَثُورُ.

Inflammability, *n.* }
Inflammableness, } سُرْعَة ـ قَابِلِيَّة ٱلِاضْطِرَام (*or* ٱلِالْتِهَاب) ٱلِالْتِهَاب.

Inflammable, *a.* سَرِيع ـ قَابِل ٱلِاشْتِعَال ـ سَهْل ٱلِالْتِهَاب ٱلِالْتِهَاب.

Inflammation, *n.* The act of setting on fire, إِشْعَال ـ إِلْهَاب ـ إِحْرَاق. The being in flame, اِلْتِهَاب ـ تَأَجُّج ـ إِضْرَام ـ اِضْطِرَام ـ اِشْتِعَال. Violent excitement, ثَوْرَة ـ هَيَجَان ـ هِيَاج. Febrile symptoms, سُخُونَة ـ حَرَارَة ـ حُمَّى. Disease accompanied with pain, اِلْتِهَاب. Inflammation of the brain, سَرْسَام; of the lungs, ذَاتُ ٱلرِّئَةِ; of the eye, أُخُذ; of the throat, تَعَل; of the bowels, غَلَل ـ غُلّ; of the chest, حَرْوَة ـ أُجَاج.

Inflammatory, *a.* Tending to preternatural heat, اِلْتِهَابِيّ ـ حَارّ. Exciting, حَاثّ ـ مُحَرِّك ـ مُهَيِّج.

Inflate, *v.t.* نَفَخَ ـ نَفَخَ فِي ـ دَاجَ. To elate, غَرَّ. To be inflated, as with air; also with pride, اِنْتَفَخَ. To inflate, as of the nostrils, فَنْخَرَ.

Inflation, *n.* The act of filling with air, نَفْخ; the being inflated, اِنْتِفَاخ. Haughtiness, اِنْتِفَاخ ـ تَكَبُّر ـ غَطْرَسَة ـ غُرُور ـ شَمْخَرَة. Inflation of the testicles, قَرْوَة.

Inflect, *v.t.* To bend, حَنَى ـ عَوَّجَ. To incline, عَطَفَ ـ أَمَالَ. To vary a verb or noun in its terminations, صَرَّفَ ـ غَيَّرَ آخِرَ ٱلْكَلِمَةِ ـ أَعْرَبَ. To — the voice in reading, لَحَّنَ فِي (or طَرَّبَ فِي or تَرَنَّمَ فِي) قِرَاءَتِهِ.

Inflection, *n.* The act of bending, تَعْوِيج ـ حَنْو; of inclining, عَطْف ـ إِمَالَة. Variation of nouns and verbs, تَصْرِيف ـ إِعْرَاب. Inflection of the voice, تَطْرِيب ـ تَلْحِين.

Inflective, *a.* *See* Flexible, *a.*

Inflexibility, *n.* Unyielding stiffness, عَدَمُ إِمْكَانِ ٱلِانْحِنَاءِ ـ مَتَانَة ـ صَلَابَة. Obstinacy of will or temper, تَمَرُّد ـ عِنَاد. Firmness of purpose, ثَبَات ـ مَتَانَة ـ خُشُونَة ـ وَعْقَة ـ إِصْرَار عَلَى ـ عَزِيمَة ـ إِدْمَان.

Inflexible, *a.* Not to be bent, مَتِين ـ صُلْب ـ لَا يَنْحَنِي. Unyielding, لَا يَلِين. Obstinate, عَنِيد ـ مَرِيد ـ وَعْق. Inflexible constancy, عَزْمٌ ثَابِتٌ (or شَدِيدٌ). It is my — determination, هُوَ مِنِّي صِرًّى.

Inflexibly, *ad.* بِثَبَاتٍ ـ بِإِصْرَارٍ ـ بِصَلَابَةٍ. Wholly, very, بَتَّةً ـ بِشِدَّةٍ ـ جِدًّا ـ لِلْغَايَةِ. He determined upon it —, أَصَرَّ عَلَيْهِ.

Inflexion, *n.* *See* Inflection, *n.*

Inflict, *v.t.* To bring on, أَصَابَ-بِ ـ أَجْرَى-عَلَى ـ أَبْلَى-بِ. To — with, as with a punishment, قَاصَّ-بِ ـ عَاقَبَ-بِ ـ عَذَّبَ ـ جَازَى. To — with a fine, أَغْرَمَ; with a disease, أَصَابَ-بِمَرَضٍ ـ أَمْرَضَ ـ مَرَّضَ. The punishments inflicted by the law, ٱلْمُجَازَاتُ ٱلْمُرَتَّبَةُ ٱلْقَانُونِيَّةُ.

Infliction, *n.* The act of inflicting on, إِصَابَة بِ ـ إِجْرَاء عَلَى. Punishment, عَذَاب ـ عُقُوبَة ـ عِقَاب ـ قِصَاص. A misfortune, مُصِيبَة *pl.* مَصَائِب ـ آفَة *pl.* آفَات ـ بَلِيَّة *pl.* بَلَايَا. To be inflicted with, أُبْتُلِيَ بِ.

Inflictive, *a.* مُعَاقِب ـ مُصِيب ـ قِصَاصِيّ ـ مُبْلٍ ـ حُكْمِيّ.

Inflorescence, *n.* *See* Florescence, *n.*

Influence, *n.* Effect, فَاعِلِيَّة ـ تَأْثِير ـ عَمَلٌ فِي. A motive, حُكْم ـ سُلْطَة ـ مُكْنَة ـ قُدْرَة ـ سَطْوَة. Power, دَاعٍ ـ بَاعِث. Power to do or move, نُفُوذ. Great —, نُفُوذٌ كُلِّيٌّ. Political —, نُفُوذٌ سِيَاسِيٌّ. To use one's —, بَذَلَ (or صَرَفَ) مَا لَهُ مِنَ ٱلنُّفُوذِ. They have obtained an —, صَارَتْ لَهُمْ سَطْوَةٌ رَهِينَةٌ. Preponderating —, نُفُوذٌ غَالِبٌ ـ نُفُوذٌ مُرَجَّحٌ. Under the — of ..., تَحْتَ بَاعِثِ شَيْءٍ ـ تَحْتَ تَأْثِيرِ شَيْءٍ. The — of the stars, تَأْثِيرُ ٱلْكَوَاكِبِ. His — with the ambassador increased, زَادَ نُفُوذًا لَدَى ٱلسَّفِيرِ. Nothing that any one may say will have any — upon him, لَا يَأْخُذُ فِيهِ قَوْلُ قَائِلٍ. To exercise —, أَجْرَى نُفُوذًا.

Influence, *v.t.* To have an effect upon, نَفَذَ فِي ـ أَخَذَ فِي ـ فَعَلَ فِي ـ عَمِلَ فِي ـ أَثَّرَ فِي. To lead one to, أَغْرَى-عَلَى ـ

حَمَلَ-عَلَى ـ حَثَّ-عَلَى ـ أَوْزَعَ-عَلَى. To succeed in one's influence with one, أَجْرَى نُفُوذَهُ عِنْدَهُ.

Influential, *a.* Exerting power, مُؤَثِّرٌ ـ لَهُ تَأْثِيرٌ ـ ذُو سَطْوَةٍ ـ نَافِذٌ ـ ذُو ٱعْتِبَارٍ. Of persons, صَاحِبُ نُفُوذٍ ـ لَهُ فَاعِلِيَّةٌ ٱلْكَلِمَتَيْنِ.

Influentially, *ad.* تَأْثِيرًا ـ بِٱلتَّأْثِيرِ ـ بِٱلنُّفُوذِ.

Influenza, *a.* نَزْلَةٌ عَامَّةٌ ـ زُكَامٌ عَامٌّ.

Influx, *n.* The act of flowing, جَرَيَانٌ ـ ٱنْصِبَابٌ. Introduction, وُصُولٌ ـ دُخُولٌ. An — of strangers, وُصُولُ ٱلْغُرَبَاءِ ـ جَمٌّ مِنَ ٱلْغُرَبَاءِ.

Infold, *v.t.* To wrap in, غَلَّفَ-فِي ـ لَفَّ-بِ ـ أَدْرَجَ-فِي ـ أَظْرَفَ-فِي. To — in the arms, عَانَقَ ـ ٱحْتَضَنَ. It infolded such a thing, ٱشْتَمَلَ عَلَى كَذَا.

Inform, *v.t.* As with life, to animate, أَحْيَى. To acquaint, أَطْلَعَ-عَلَى ـ أَفَادَ ـ أَعْلَمَ-بِ ـ بَصَّرَ-بِ ـ آذَنَ ـ أَذَنَ-بِ ـ بَلَّغَ-عَنْ ـ أَوْقَفَ-عَلَى ـ عَرَّفَ-بِ ـ أَشْعَرَ ـ أَنْشَى-بِ ـ أَخْبَرَ-بِ ـ أَنْهَمَ. To — against, ٱشْتَكَى ـ يَسْعَى *aor.* سَعَى بِهِ. To be informed of, أَذِنَ بِ ـ يَشِي *aor.* وَشَى-بِ-عَلَى-بِ ـ عَلِمَ بِ. We are informed (in an impersonal sense, *i.q.* we learn,) from, يُسْتَفَادُ مِنْ.

In formâ pauperis, ad. عَلَى سَبِيلِ ٱلْفُقَرَاءِ وَهِيَ فِقْرَةٌ مِنْ أَقْوَالِ ٱلشَّرْعِ تُطْلَقُ عَلَى مَنْ لَا ٱسْتِطَاعَةَ لَهُ عَلَى إِيفَاءِ نَفَقَةِ مُحَاكَمَتِهِ.

Informal, *a.* Not according to proper form, مُخَالِفُ ٱلْأُصُولِ ـ غَيْرُ رَسْمِيٍّ. Without ceremony, مِنْ غَيْرِ تَكْلِيفٍ. Defective, نَاقِصٌ.

Informality, *n.* Want of due forms, عَدَمُ ٱلرَّسْمِ ـ خِلَافُ ٱلْأُصُولِ. Want of ceremony, عَدَمُ تَكْلِيفٍ. A defect, خَطَأٌ ـ خُلْفَةٌ.

Informally, *ad.* Without due form, بِمِنْوَالٍ غَيْرِ رَسْمِيٍّ. Without ceremony, مِنْ غَيْرِ تَكْلِيفٍ.

Informant, *n.* مُفِيدٌ ـ مُعْلِمٌ بِ ـ مُعَرِّفٌ بِ ـ مُخْبِرٌ عَنْ.

Information, *n.* Intelligence, news, إِعْلَامٌ ـ عِلْمٌ ـ أَخْبَارٌ ـ خَبَرٌ. Knowledge, إِطْلَاعٌ ـ وُقُوفٌ عَلَى ـ نَبَأٌ ـ خُبْرَةٌ ـ عِلْمٌ. An accusation against, شِيَةٌ ـ وَشْيٌ ـ ٱشْتِكَاءٌ عَلَى ـ سَعْيٌ بِ. To ask — of, ٱسْتَفْهَمَ ـ تَخَبَّرَ ـ ٱسْتَخْبَرَ. I have received — of him, بَلَغَنِي عَنْهُ. To seek — from, ٱسْتَطْلَعَ مِنْ ـ ٱسْتَعْرَفَ. His desire for —, news, is great, رَغْبَتُهُ فِي ٱلْإِطْلَاعِ عَلَى ٱلْأَخْبَارِ شَدِيدَةٌ. He had no — on that matter, لَمْ يَكُنْ لَهُ مَعْلُومَاتٌ فِي ذٰلِكَ ٱلْأَمْرِ.

Informed, *a.* Having intelligence of, خَبِيرٌ بِ ـ وَاقِفٌ عَلَى ـ مُطَّلِعٌ عَلَى. Learned, عَالِمٌ ـ فَهِيمٌ ـ ذَكِيٌّ.

Informer, *n.* As of offences, غَمَّازٌ ـ مَاحِلٌ ـ وَشَاةٌ *pl.* وَاشٍ ـ سُعَاةٌ *pl.* سَاعٍ ـ جَوَاسِيسُ *pl.* جَاسُوسٌ.

In foro conscientiæ, ad. بِضَمِيرٍ صَالِحٍ ـ حَسَبَ ٱلْإِنْصَافِ.

Infraction, *n.* The act of breaking, كَسْرٌ. Violation, breach, فَسْخٌ ـ نَقْضٌ. The — of a treaty, فَسْخُ مُعَاهَدَةٍ ـ نَقْضُ عَهْدٍ.

Infractor, *n.* As of an agreement, نَاقِضٌ.

Infra-mundane, *a.* دُونَ ٱلدُّنْيَا ـ كَائِنٌ تَحْتَ ٱلْعَالَمِ.

Infrangible, *a.* لَا يَنْكَسِرُ.

Infrequence, *n.* } Infrequency, } قِلَّةُ وُقُوعٍ ـ قِلَّةٌ ـ نُدُورٌ ـ نَدْرَةٌ.

Infrequent, *a.* قَلِيلُ ٱلْحُدُوثِ ـ نَادِرُ ٱلْوُقُوعِ ـ نَادِرٌ.

Infrigidate, *v.t.* بَرَّدَ.

Infrigidation, *n.* تَبْرِيدٌ.

Infringe, *v.t.* To transgress, تَعَدَّى عَلَى ـ عَدَا ـ خَالَفَ ـ جَاوَزَ. To violate, نَقَضَ ـ فَسَخَ ـ نَكَثَ. To injure, damage, حَكَرَ ـ جَحَفَ بِ. To infringe, as of a patent, ٱفْتَرَى- (or قَلَّدَ-) بِخِلَافِ ٱلشَّرْعِ. Should one of the articles of this treaty be infringed, the entire treaty will thereby be deemed to have been infringed, إِنْ نُقِضَ بَنْدٌ مِنْ بُنُودِ هٰذِهِ ٱلْمُعَاهَدَةِ فَتَنْتَقِضُ بِذٰلِكَ ٱلْمُعَاهَدَةُ بِأَسْرِهَا.

Infringement, *n.* A violation, breach, فَسْخٌ ـ نَقْضٌ ـ نَكْثٌ. Transgression, تَعَرُّضٌ ـ تَعَدٍّ. An —, as of a patent, ٱفْتِرَاءٌ (or تَقْلِيدٌ) بِخِلَافِ ٱلشَّرْعِ. Damage done, an injury, إِجْحَافٌ ـ حَكْرٌ ـ جَحْفٌ.

Infructuose, *a.* *See* Infertile, Unfruitful, *a.*

Infrugal, *a.* *See* Extravagant, *a.*

Infundibular, *a.* فِي شَكْلِ ٱلْقِمَعِ (or ٱلْإِشْكَابَةِ).

Infuriate, *v.t.* هَيَّجَ ـ أَشْعَلَ-غَضَبًا. To be infuriated, ٱشْتَعَلَ ـ ٱلْتَظَى ـ غَضَبًا.

Infuriate, *a.* غَضْبَانُ ـ هَائِجٌ ـ مُلْتَظٍ.

Infuriation, *n.* The act of infuriating, تَهْيِيجٌ ـ إِشْعَالٌ ـ تَغْضِيبٌ; the being infuriated, غَضَبٌ ـ ٱشْتِعَالٌ ـ هَيَجَانٌ.

Infuscate, *v.t.* *See to* Darken, *v.t.*

Infuscation, *n.* تَغْتِيمٌ ـ قَتَمٌ.

Infuse, *v.t.* To pour, سَكَبَ ـ صَبَّ ـ كَتَّ. To instil, as of principles, عَرَّقَ فِي- (or أَعْرَقَ فِي- or أَفْرَغَ عَلَى-) كَذَا ـ عَلَّمَ ـ لَقَّنَ ـ أَلْقَى فِي-شَيْئًا ـ أَلْهَمَ-بِ ـ طَبَعَ-عَلَى. To soak, steep, مَرَثَ ـ أَنْقَعَ ـ نَقَعَ. To introduce, أَدْخَلَ. To implant, engender, in, أَعْرَقَ (or عَرَّقَ) فِي. He infused into them an evil disposition, عَرَّقَ فِيهِمْ عِرْقَ سَوْءٍ. The love of the calf was

infused into their hearts, أُشْرِبُوا فِي قُلُوبِهِمُ ٱلْعِجْلَ (*Kur.* ii. 87). The love of her was infused into his heart, أُشْرِبَ فِي قَلْبِهِ حُبَّهَا.
See also to Inculcate, *v.t.*

Infusibility, *n.* Capacity of being poured, قَابِلِيَّةُ ٱلْإِنْصِبَابِ. Incapacity of being fused, عَدَمُ ذَوَبَانٍ – عَدَمُ ٱنْسِبَاكٍ – عَدَمُ قَابِلِيَّةِ ٱلذَّوَبَانِ.

Infusible, *a.* That may be poured, يَنْصَبُّ – قَابِلُ ٱلْإِنْصِبَابِ. That cannot be dissolved, melted, لَا يَنْسَبِكُ – لَا يَذُوبُ – لَا يَنْحَلُّ.

Infusion, *n.* The act of pouring, صَبٌّ – سَكْبٌ; of instilling, as of principles, تَغْرِيقٌ – إِغْرَاقٌ – تَلْقِينٌ – إِفْرَاغٌ – إِلْقَاءٌ – إِلْهَامٌ. Mixtion, مَزْجٌ – إِخْلَاطٌ. The act of steeping, إِنْقَاعٌ – نَقْعٌ. The liquor in which anything has been steeped, غُسَالَةٌ – نَقُوعٌ – نَقِيعٌ. The act of inculcation, تَعْلِيمٌ – تَدْرِيبٌ – تَلْقِينٌ. What is infused, as of a quality or disposition, عِرْقٌ *pl.* أَعْرَاقٌ.

Infusive, *a.* يُنْقِعُ – يَمْزِجُ.

Infusoria, *n.* نُغَلٌ (wrongly written نُعَالٌ in the *al-Kâmûs*) – دُوَيْبَّاتٌ.

Ingathering, *n.* جَمْعٌ – حِصَادٌ – جِنَايَةٌ.

Ingenious, *a.* مَاهِرٌ *pl.* مَهَرَةٌ – لَبِيقٌ – بَدِيعٌ – حَاذِقٌ – لَبِيبٌ – عَارِفٌ – شَهْمٌ *pl.* شِهَامٌ – ذَهِينٌ – لَوْذَعِيٌّ.

Ingeniously, *ad.* بِشَهَامَةٍ – بِمَهَارَةٍ – بِكِيَاسَةٍ – بِبَرَاعَةٍ – بِغَايَةِ ٱلْإِتْقَانِ.

Ingeniousness, *n.* } ذِهْنٌ – كِيَاسَةٌ – ظَرْفٌ – بَرَاعَةٌ – لَبَقٌ –
Ingenuity, } شَطَارَةٌ *vulg.* مَهَارَةٌ – قَرِيحَةٌ.

Ingenuous, *a.* مُنْبَسِطٌ – صَدُوقٌ *pl.* صُدُقٌ – حُرٌّ *pl.* أَحْرَارٌ – زَكِيٌّ – وَفِيٌّ – صِدِّيقٌ – صَادِقٌ – سَلِيمٌ – صَفِيٌّ – نَصُوحٌ – نَزِهٌ – مُخْلِصٌ.

Ingenuously, *ad.* بِصَدَاقَةٍ – بِحُرُورَةٍ – بِوَفَاءٍ – بِخُلُوصِ جَنَانٍ. To deal — with, ٱنْبَسَطَ إِلَى – صَافَى – صَادَقَ.

Ingenuousness, *n.* كِيَاسَةٌ – مُصَافَاةٌ – صَدَاقَةٌ – نَزَهٌ – خُلُوصٌ – إِخْلَاصٌ – صِدْقٌ – وَفَاءٌ – حُرُورَةٌ – ٱنْبِسَاطٌ.

Inglorious, *n.* Bringing no glory, عَارٍ مِنَ – خَالٍ مِنَ ٱلْفَخْرِ – ٱلْمَجْدِ. Shameful, دَنِيٌّ – خَسِيسٌ – خَزٍ – ذَمِيمٌ – ذَلِيلٌ.

Ingloriously, *ad.* Without glory, بِلَا فَخْرٍ – مِنْ غَيْرِ مَجْدٍ. Ignominiously, بِخِزْيَةٍ – بِدَنَاءَةٍ.

Ingloriousness, *n.* Want of glory, عَدَمُ ٱلْمَجْدِ – عَدَمُ ٱلْفَخْرِ. Ignominy, ذِلَّةٌ – دَنَاءَةٌ – خِزْيَةٌ – مَخْزَاةٌ.

Ingot, *n.* سَبِيكَةٌ *pl.* سَبَائِكُ.

Ingraft, *v.t.* To fix deep, عَلَى *or* فِي – طَبَعَ – أَثْبَتَ فِي – أَرْسَخَ فِي – مَكَّنَ فِي. *See also to* Graft, *and to* Infuse, *v.t.*

Ingraftment, *n.* The act of grafting, غَرْزٌ – تَطْعِيمٌ – تَلْقِيمٌ; of infixing, تَثْبِيتٌ – تَمْتِينٌ – إِرْسَاخٌ – تَرْكِيزٌ.

Ingrain, *v.t.* To dye before weaving, صَبَغَ قَبْلَ ٱلنَّسْجِ. To introduce into, أَدْخَلَ فِي. To fix into, طَبَعَ عَلَى – أَرْسَخَ فِي.
See also to Infuse, *v.t.*

Ingrate, *a.* كَنَّادٌ – نَاكِرُ ٱلْإِحْسَانِ – نَاكِرُ ٱلْمَعْرُوفِ.

Ingrate, *n.* رَجُلٌ كَنَّادٌ *fem.* ٱمْرَأَةٌ كَنَّادَةٌ.

Ingratiate, *v.t.* To — one's self with, ٱسْتَعْطَفَ – ٱسْتَمَالَهُ إِلَيْهِ – مَلَكَ قَلْبَهُ.

Ingratitude, *n.* كُفْرَانٌ بِٱلنِّعَمِ – غَمْطٌ – كُنُودٌ – إِكْنَادٌ – إِنْكَارُ ٱلْمَعْرُوفِ. Ingratitude degrades man, (*prov.*) مَنْ لَمْ يَعْرِفِ ٱلْإِحْسَانَ لَيْسَ بِإِنْسَانٍ.

Ingravidate, *v.t.* *See to* Impregnate, *v.t.*

Ingravidation, *n.* *See* Impregnation, *n.*

Ingredient, *n.* جُزْءٌ *pl.* أَجْزَاءٌ. One of the ingredients, جُزْءٌ مِنَ ٱلْأَجْزَاءِ.

Ingress, *n.* Entrance, دُخُولٌ; right of entrance, إِذْنٌ بِٱلدُّخُولِ; a place of entrance, مَدْخَلٌ.

Ingression, *n.* دُخُولٌ – عُبُورٌ.

Inguinal, *a.* مُخْتَصٌّ بِٱلرَّفْغِ – مُتَعَلِّقٌ بِٱلْأَرْبِيَةِ – مُخْتَصٌّ بِٱلْحَقْوِ – ٱلْوَرِكِ.

Ingulf, *v.t.* To swallow up, وَرَّطَ فِي – خَسَفَ بِ – ٱبْتَلَعَ. To drown, غَمَرَ – أَغْرَقَ. To cast, or drive, into a gulf, حَمَلَ إِلَى خَلِيجٍ (or بُوغَازٍ). To be ingulphed, driven into a gulf, ٱنْحَمَلَ إِلَى خَلِيجٍ (or بُوغَازٍ).

Inhabit, *v.t.* As of a house, سَكَنَ – أَقَامَ فِي. To reside in a land, مَتَنَ بِ – أَحَالَ بِ – أَقَامَ بِ. To cause to —, سَكَّنَ فِي.

Inhabit, *v.i.* سَكَنَ – قَطَنَ بِ – أَوْطَنَ بِ – ٱتَّطَنَ.

Inhabitable, *a.* يُسْكَنُ – قَابِلُ ٱلسُّكْنَى.

Inhabitancy, *n.* إِقَامَةٌ – سَكِينَةٌ.

Inhabitant, *n.* سَاكِنٌ *pl.* سُكَّانٌ – قَاطِنٌ *pl.* قَاطِنَةٌ – مُقِيمٌ – مُتَوَطِّنٌ – مُسْتَقِرٌّ. The inhabitants of a country, سُكَّانُ (or أَهْلُ) ٱلْبِلَادِ. The inhabitants of the town, أَهْلُ ٱلْبَلَدِ; of the villages, country, أَهْلُ ٱلْقُرَى.

Inhabited, *a.* مَأْهُولٌ *pl.* مَآهِلُ – آهِلٌ – عَامِرٌ – عَمِيرٌ – مَعْمُورٌ – مَسْكُونٌ. The villages — by Christians, ٱلْقُرَى ٱلْمَأْهُولَةُ بِٱلنَّصَارَى.

Inhabiter, *n.* *See* Inhabitant, *n.*

Inhalation, *n.* The act of inhaling, تَنَفُّسٌ; of drawing in smoke, شُرْبُ دُخَانٍ.

Inhale, *v.t.* تَنَفَّسَ مِن. To draw in smoke, to smoke, شَرِبَ الدُّخَانَ.

Inhaler, *n.* مُتَنَفِّس. An apparatus for inhaling medicated vapours, آلَة — آلَةٌ لِاسْتِنْشَاقِ أَبْخِرَةِ ٱلْعَقَاقِيرِ وَغَيْرِهَا بِسُهُولَةِ ٱلتَّنَفُّسِ.

Inharmonious, *a.* Unmusical, غَيْرُ مُطْرِبٍ — عَدِيمُ ٱلنَّغَمِ. Discordant, مُخْتَلِف — مُخَالِف. Without order, غَيْرُ مَنْظُومٍ — مُتَشَوِّش — مُلْتَبِك — غَيْرُ مُنْتَسِقٍ.

Inharmoniously, *ad.* Unmusically, مِنْ غَيْرِ نَغَمٍ. Discordantly, إِخْتِلَافًا — اِلْتِبَاكًا — بِغَيْرِ ٱتِّفَاقٍ — مُغَايَرَةً.

Inhere, *v.i.* تَوَصَّلَ بِ — لَازَمَ — لَزِمَ بِ — طُبِعَ عَلَى — اِقْتَرَنَ بِ — اِلْتَصَقَ بِ. *See also to* Adhere, *v.i.*

Inherence, *n.* } Existence, وُجُود. Existence in, دُخُولٌ فِي — حُلُولٌ فِي. Attachment, adherence, لُزُوم — اِقْتِرَانٌ بِ — اِتِّحَادٌ بِ.
Inherency, }

Inherent, *a.* Coherent with, مُوَصَّلٌ فِي — مُلَازِمٌ لِ — لَازِبٌ بِ — مُلْتَصِقٌ بِ. Natural to, لَازِمٌ طَبْعًا. Inherent circumstances, لَوَازِمُ. Inherent power, قُوَّةٌ ذَاتِيَّةٌ. *See also* Inborn, *a.*

Inherently, *ad.* لُزُومًا — مُلَازَمَةً — طَبْعًا — لَزْمَةً.

Inherit, *v.t.* To take by descent from, وَرِثَ *aor.* يَرِثُ — وَرِثَ مِن. To cause to —, وَرَّثَ — أَوْرَثَ. He inherits this vice from his father, أَخَذَ هٰذَا ٱلشَّرَّ عَنْ أَبِيهِ *aor.* يَأْخُذُ. One who has an inherited fault, دَسَّاس.

Inheritability, *n.* إِمْكَانُ ٱلْوِرَاثَةِ — وِرَاثَة.

Inheritable, *a.* يُورَثُ — مِمَّا يُورَثُ — وِرْثِيٌّ.

Inheritably, *ad.* وِرَاثَةً.

Inheritance, *n.* The act of inheriting, رِثَة — إِرْث — وِرْث — وِرَاثَة. That which descends by —, مُوَرَّث — تُرَاث — مِيرَاث — مُلْكٌ مُوَرَّثٌ. Property by right, مُلْك.

Inheritor, *n.* وَارِث *pl.* وَرَثَة.

Inheritress, *n.* } وَارِثَة *pl.* وَارِثَات.
Inheritrix, }

Inhesion, *n.* تَوَصُّلٌ بِ — لُزُوب — لُزُوم — لُزُومٌ دَاخِلٌ.

Inhibit, *v.t.* To restrain from, رَدَّ عَن — مَنَعَ عَن — نَهَى عَن — رَدَعَ عَن. To forbid, حَدَّدَ عَن — أَخَذَ عَن — مَنَعَ عَن.

Inhibition, *n.* The act of, رَدّ — رَدْع — تَحْدِيد — مَنْع — نَهْي. A prohibition, نَهْيَة — مُمَانَعَة — حُرْمَة *pl.* حُرَم — اِمْتِنَاع.

Inhibitory, *a.* مَنُوع — مَنَّاع.

Inhospitable, *a.* Wanting in hospitality, غَيْرُ مُضِيفٍ — غَيْرُ أَبْيَضِ ٱلْمَطْبَخِ — خَصِيب (*lit.* one whose kitchen is white.) غَيْرُ مُكْرِمِ ٱلضُّيُوفِ — لَا يَقْرِي ٱلْغُرَبَاءَ. Inclement, cold, مُزَمْهِرٌ. Desolate, مُقْفِر — وَحْش.

Inhospitably, *ad.* بِلَا إِكْرَامٍ — بِلَا إِحْسَانٍ — بِلَا إِيثَارٍ.

Inhospitableness, *n.* } عَدَمُ إِكْرَامِ ٱلضُّيُوفِ — عَدَمُ إِيثَارِ ٱلْغُرَبَاءِ.
Inhospitality, } Desolateness, قَفْر — وَحْشَة.

Inhuman, *a.* قَاسِي ٱلْقَلْبِ — ظَالِم — عَسُوف — جَافٍ — فَظٌّ — عَدِيمُ ٱلشَّفَقَةِ — جَائِر.

Inhumanity, *n.* جَوْر — ظُلْم — قَسَاوَة — عَسْف — جَفَاء — فَظَاظَة.

Inhumanly, *ad.* بِجَوْرٍ — ظُلْمًا — بِعَسْفٍ — بِقَسَاوَةٍ — بِفَظَاظَةٍ.

Inhumate, *v.t.* } *See to* Bury, Inter, *v.t.*
Inhume, }

Inhumation, *n.* *See* Burial, Interment, *n.*

Inimical, *a.* Unfriendly, عَدُوٌّ — مُعَادٍ. Adverse to, مُقَاوِم — مُخَالِفٌ لِ — مُضَادٌّ لِ. Not helping, غَيْرُ مُسَاعِدٍ. Hurtful, حَكَر — ضَارٌّ — مُضِرٌّ. Preventing, مَانِع.

Inimically, *ad.* حَكْرًا — بِعَدَاوَةٍ — مُخَالَفَةً — مُضَادَّةً.

Inimitability, *n.* عَدَمُ ٱلْقُدْوَةِ — عَدَمُ إِمْكَانِ تَقْلِيدِهِ — عَدَمُ إِمْكَانِ ٱلِاقْتِدَاءِ بِهِ.

Inimitable, *a.* That cannot be imitated, غَيْرُ مُمْكِنٍ ٱلِاقْتِدَاءُ بِهِ — لَا يُمَاثَلُ — ٱلتَّمَثُّلُ بِهِ مُحَالٌ — لَا يُضَاهَى — لَا يُحَاكَى — فَائِق. Unique, فَرْد — لَا شَبِيهَ لَهُ — لَمْ يَكُنْ لَهُ كُفُؤٌ.

Inimitably, *ad.* بِدُونِ مُشَابَهَةٍ.

Iniquitous, *a.* Wicked, of a person, شِرِّير — شَرِير — أَثِيم — فَاسِد — فَاجِر — ظَالِم. Nefarious, corrupt, خَبِيث — مُنَافِق — جَائِر. An — act, خَبِيثَة *pl.* خَبَائِثُ — شَرٌّ *pl.* أَشْرَار — إِثْم *pl.* آثَام.

Iniquitously, *ad.* ظُلْمًا — بِخُبْثٍ — بِنِفَاقٍ — بِغَيْرِ إِنْصَافٍ. To act —, أَفْجَرَ — اِرْتَكَبَ جَوْرًا.

Iniquity, *n.* Want of rectitude, عَدَمُ إِنْصَافٍ. Unrighteousness, إِثْم — شَرّ — فَسَاد — فِسْق — فُجُور — جَوْر — نِفَاق. A particular act of —, إِثْم *pl.* آثَام — ذَنْب *pl.* ذُنُوب. *See also* Crimes, *n.*

Initial, *a.* Placed at the beginning, وَاقِعٌ فِي ٱلِابْتِدَاءِ. First, مُبْتَدِئ — مُقَدَّم — أَوَّل.

Initiate, *v.t.* To instruct, عَلَّمَ — عَلَّمَ ٱلْأُصُولَ. To introduce into, أَدْخَلَ فِي. To originate, اِخْتَرَعَ — أَبْدَأَ — أَوْجَدَ. To begin, بَدَأَ بِ — شَرَعَ فِي — أَنْشَأَ بِ.

Initiate, *v.i.* اِبْتَدَأَ — بَدَأَ — تَبَدَّأَ.

Initiation, *n.* Instruction in first principles, تَعْلِيمُ ٱلْأُصُولِ. Introduction into, إِدْخَالٌ فِي; the being introduced into, دُخُولٌ فِي. A beginning, بَدْء — شُرُوع — إِبْدَاء.

Initiative, *a.* }
Initiatory, } إِنْشَائِيٌّ ـ إِبْتِدَائِيٌّ . First, أَوَّلُ .

Initiative, *n.* شُرُوع ـ مُبَادَاة . He took the — in the affair, كَانَ فِي ٱبْتِدَآءِ ٱلْأَمْرِ ـ تَبَدَّأَ فِي ٱلْأَمْرِ ـ تَقَدَّمَ فِي ٱلْأَمْرِ . To take the — towards, to open the door to, فَتَحَ ٱلْبَابَ إِلَى . To be first towards, to anticipate one with, بَادَى-بِ .

Inject, *v.t.* To throw in, أَطْرَحَ ـ أَدْخَلَ ـ أَلْقَى . To — a medicinal injection, حَقَنَ .

Injection, *n.* The act of throwing in, إِطْرَاح ـ إِدْخَال ـ إِلْقَآء . A clyster, حُقْنَة . The act of making to absorb, تَشْرِيب . He gave the patient an —, حَقَنَ ٱلْمَرِيضَ .

Injudicial, *a.* يُضَادُّ قَوَانِينَ ٱلشَّرِيعَةِ ـ مُخَالِفُ ٱلشَّرْعِ .

Injudicious, *a.* عَدِيمُ ٱلرَّوِيَّةِ ـ لَا فِطْنَةَ لَهُ ـ قَلِيلُ ٱلتَّبَصُّرِ ـ أَخْرَق ـ غَبِيٌّ . An — action, غَبَاوَة ـ نَازِيَة .

Injudiciously, *ad.* بِغَبَاوَةٍ ـ بِغَيْرِ رُشْدٍ ـ بِدُونِ رَوِيَّةٍ ـ بِلَا تَبَصُّرٍ . To act — in a matter, خَرِقَ بِٱلْأَمْرِ ـ جَهِلَ بِٱلْأَمْرِ .

Injudiciousness, *n.* غَبَاوَة ـ عَدَمُ تَرَوٍّ ـ عَدَمُ تَبَصُّرٍ ـ خُرْق ـ قِلَّةُ عَقْلٍ .

Injunction, *n.* وَصِيَّة *pl.* وَصَايَا ـ أَمْر *pl.* أَوَامِرُ ـ حُكْم *pl.* أَحْكَام ـ تَنْبِيه ـ نَصِيحَة *pl.* نَصَائِحُ . They gave me the strictest and most decided injunctions to keep the peace, أَوْصُونِي بِوَصَايَا جَازِمَةٍ صَارِمَةٍ بِمُلَازَمَةِ ٱلرَّاحَةِ .

Injure, *v.t.* To harm, حَكَرَ ـ آذَى ـ ضَامَ ـ أَجْحَفَ بِ ـ أَضَرَّ ـ ضَارَّ . To damage, عَطَّلَ ـ خَسَّرَ ـ ثَلَمَ ـ أَعْدَمَ . To do injustice to, حَكَرَ ـ شَطَّ ـ أَسَآءَ إِلَى ـ جَارَ عَلَى *aor.* يَجُورُ ـ أَظْلَمَ ـ جَنَى عَلَى ـ ظَلَمَ ـ تَعَدَّى عَلَى ـ غَدَرَ بِ . He injured his character, ثَلَمَ صِيتَهُ ـ طَعَنَ فِي عِرْضِهِ . To be injured, marred, إِنْثَلَمَ . It will not — the interests of such an one, لَا يُجْحِفُ بِمَصْلَحَةِ فُلَانٍ .

Injurious, *a.* Unjust, ضَائِم *pl.* ضَامَة ـ حَكِر ـ ظَالِم ـ مُتَعَدٍّ ـ جَائِر . Hurtful, حَكِر ـ مُضِرٌّ ـ ضَارٌّ ـ مُؤْذٍ . An — man, رَجُلٌ حَكِرٌ ـ ظَلِيم . Injurious language, سَبّ ـ شَتْم . Injurious to his character, يَخُلُّ فِي أَوْصَافِهِ .

Injuriously, *ad.* With harm, بِحَكَرٍ ـ بِأَذِيَّةٍ ـ بِضَرَرٍ ; with injustice, ظُلْمًا ـ بِجَوْرٍ . To treat —, أَشَطَّ عَلَى ـ إِشْتَطَّ عَلَى . To act — in a matter, حَكَرَ ـ شَطَّ (or أَشَطَّ or إِشْتَطَّ) فِي أَمْرٍ .

Injuriousness, *n.* حَكْر ـ ضَرَر ـ مَضَرَّة ـ ضَيْم .

Injury, *n.* Harm, حَكْر ـ إِجْحَاف ـ شُطُوط ـ شَطٌّ ـ ضَيْم ـ ضَرَر ـ مَضَرَّة . Damage, عَوَار ـ خَسَارَة ـ سَقْط *pl.* أَسْقَاط . A calamity, آفَة ـ عَاهَة . Wrong, ظُلْم ـ أَذِيَّة ـ جَوْر ـ تَعَدٍّ ـ جِنَايَة ـ ضَامَة ـ ضَامٌ . Injury, damage, as in merchandize, عَوَار .

Injustice, *n.* جَوْر ـ عُدْوَان ـ ضَيْم ـ شُطُوط ـ إِعْتِدَآء ـ عَدْوٌ ـ جَيْف ـ ظُلْم . To do — to, أَشَطَّ عَلَى ـ إِشْتَطَّ عَلَى ـ ظَلَمَ . To accuse of —, ظَلَّمَ . He vied with him in — and surpassed him, شَاطَّهُ فَشَطَّهُ .

Ink, *n.* نِقْس ـ مِدَاد ـ حِبْر . A seller of —, حِبْرِيٌّ . Lint put into ink, لِيقَة . Red —, حِبْرٌ قِرْمِزِيٌّ . Indian —, حِبْرٌ صِينِيٌّ .

Ink, *v.t.* To cover with ink, دَهَنَ بِحِبْرٍ . To daub with ink, دَمَّمَ (or لَوَّثَ) بِحِبْرٍ .

Inkhorn, *n.* }
Inkstand, } مَحْبَرَة *pl.* مَحَابِرُ ـ نُون ـ دَوَاة *pl.* دُوًى and دَوَايَات .

Inkling, *n.* شِعْرَة ـ شُعُورَة ـ حِسّ . To have an — of, شَعَرَ بِ . To give an — of to, أَشْعَرَ بِ . *See also* Hint, *n.*

Inky, *a.* Like ink, مِثْلَ ٱلْحِبْرِ . Daubed with ink, مُلَوَّثٌ بِحِبْرٍ . Black, أَسْوَد ـ أَسْحَمُ ـ فَحِيم .

Inlaid, *a.* مُرَصَّع . Inlaid work, فُسَيْفِسَة ـ تَرْصِيع ـ تَرْكِيب ـ زَوَاق .

Inland, *a.* دَاخِلُ ٱلْبَرِّ ـ جَوَّا ٱلْبَرِّ ـ بَعِيدٌ عَنِ ٱلْبَحْرِ .

Inlay, *v.t.* To — with, رَصَّعَ بِ ـ رَكَّبَ .

Inlay, *n.* *See* Inlaid work, *under* Inlaid, *a.*

Inlayer, *n.* مُرَصِّع ـ مُرَكِّبُ ٱلتَّرْصِيعِ .

Inlet, *n.* A passage, بَاب ـ مَدْخَل . A bay, شَرْم *pl.* شُرُوم ـ خَلِيج *pl.* خُلْجَان ـ خَوْر *pl.* خُوُور ـ غَوْر ـ بُوغَاز .

In limine, ad. عَنْ أَصْلِهِ ـ مِنَ ٱلْبَدْءِ .

In loco, ad. فِي مَحَلِّهِ .

Inly, *ad.* Inside, فِي دَاخِلٍ ـ فِي ٱلدَّاخِلِ ـ جَوَّا . In the heart, قَلْبًا ـ فِي ٱلْبَاطِنِ ـ فِي ٱلضَّمِيرِ . Secretly, سِرًّا .

Inmate, *n.* سَاكِن *pl.* سُكَّان ـ مِنَ ٱلْأَهْلِينَ . The — of a prison, صَاحِبُ (or مِنْ أَهْلِ) سِجْنٍ . The inmates of hell, أَهْلُ (or أَصْحَابُ) ٱلنَّارِ .

Inmost, *a.* دَاخِلِيٌّ ـ دَاخِل ـ بَاطِن . *See also* Innermost, *a.*

Inn, *n.* فُنْدُق *pl.* فَنَادِقُ ـ خَان *pl.* خَانَات ـ دَارٌ لِلْمُسَافِرِينَ ـ مَنْزِل ـ لُوكَنْدَة . An — of law, مَدْرَسَةٌ لِأَهْلِ ٱلشَّرْعِ .

Inn, *v.t.* بَوَّأَ ـ أَنْزَلَ فِي ـ سَكَّنَ .

Inn, *v.i.* تَبَوَّأَ ـ أَبَآءَ بِ ـ نَزَلَ فِي .

Innate, *a.* جِبِلِّيٌّ ـ ذَاتِيٌّ ـ خِلْقِيٌّ ـ غَرِيزِيٌّ ـ طَبِيعِيٌّ . An — quality, سَجِيَّة *pl.* سَجَايَا ـ عِرْق *pl.* أَعْرَاق ـ سَلِيقَة .

Innately, *ad.* طَبْعًا ـ خِلْقَةً ـ سَلِيقَةً .

Innateness, *n.* طَبْع ـ خُلْق ـ جِبِلَّة .

Innavigable, *a.* يعزّ السّفر فيه ـ لا يسافر فيه ـ لا تمخر فيه السّفن.

Inner, *a.* باطن ـ داخل ـ داخليّ ـ جوّانيّ. The — man, النّفس ـ الرّوح ـ الضّمير. An — room, خزانة ـ عُلّيّة *pl.* عَلاليّ ـ مخدع *pl.* مخادع. An — court, دار داخليّة. Whoso maketh his — man to be good, God will make his outer man to be good, (or علانيته) من أصلح جوّانيّته (or سريرته) أصلح الله برّانيّته.

Innermost, *a.* الجوّانيّ ـ الدّاخليّ ـ الدّاخل. The — parts of the heart, مخادع القلب.

Innervation, *n.* The functions of the nervous system, خواصّ العصب.

Innerve, *v.t.* To strengthen, شدّد ـ قوّى ـ أيّد ـ شيّع. To encourage, شجّع.

Inning, *n.* A turn at play, نوبة ـ أدوار *pl.* دور ـ لعبة *pl.* نوبات. They took their innings at play by turns, تعاقبوا في اللّعبة. *See also* Ingathering, *n.*

Innkeeper, *n.* صاحب ـ خانجي ـ صاحب الخان (or الفندق) لوكندي.

Innocence, *n.* } Innocency, } Freedom from guilt, براءة الذّمّة ـ براءة ـ نقاوة يد ـ نقاوة ـ عصمة. Simplicity, candour, سلامة قلب ـ سداجة. Baptismal —, برّ المعموديّة.

Innocent, *a.* Exemption, as from crime, برئ من *pl.* أبرآء *and* أبرياء ـ بلا ذنب. Simple-minded, سليم القلب ـ سادج. An — thing, شيء لا بأس فيه. To be —, guiltless of, تبرّأ من. I am — of his blood, أنا برئ من دمه.

Innocent, *n.* One simple-minded, سادج ـ زكيّ. *See also* Idiot, Greenhorn, *n.*

Innocently, *ad.* على نيّة صافية ـ من غير قصد شرّ ـ بسلامة قلب.

Innocuous, *a.* غير مؤذ ـ غير مضرّ. *See also* Harmless, *a.*

Innocuously, *ad.* بلا مضاجرة ـ من غير مضرّة.

Innocuousness, *n.* عدم ضرر ـ عدم مضرّة. *See also* Harmlessness, *n.*

Innovate, *v.t.* أحدث ـ أبدع ـ اخترع ـ اقترح ـ أجدّ.

Innovate, *v.i.* ابتدع ـ تجدّد.

Innovation, *n.* The act of, إبداع ـ إحداث ـ اختراع ـ اقتراح. An —, حادثة ـ أحداث *pl.* حدث ـ ابتداع ـ بدعة.

Innovator, *n.* مبتدع ـ من أهل بدعة *pl.* أهل بدعة.

Innoxious, *a.* *See* Harmless, *a.*

Innuendo, *n.* غمز ـ غميزة ـ كناية. *See also* Insinuation, *n.*

Innumerability, *n.* } Innumerableness, } ما لا عدد له ـ ربوات ـ عدم عدد.

Innumerable, *a.* } Innumerous, } بلا عدد ـ لا يعدّ ـ لا يحصى ـ لا يتكيّف.

Innumerably, *ad.* خارجا عن حدّ الحساب ـ من غير عدد ـ بلا عدد.

Innutrition, *n.* عدم غذاء ـ عدم اغتذاء.

Innutritious, *a.* } Innutritive, } لا غذاء فيه ـ غير غاذ.

Inobservance, *n.* The not keeping, قلّة رعاية ـ قلّة حفظ. Neglect, carelessness, غفلة ـ غفلان ـ عدم اعتناء.

Inobservant, *a.* ساه ـ غفلان ـ غافل ـ غير راع ـ غبيّ ـ قندع.

Inobtrusive, *a.* غير فضوليّ ـ محتجب ـ وطراق ـ طريق. *See also* Reserved, Modest, *a.*

Inobtrusively, *ad.* بعدم فضول ـ باحتجاب ـ بطريقة ـ طريقة.

Inobtrusiveness, *n.* عدم فضول ـ احتجاب ـ طريقة.

Inoculate, *v.t.* طعّم ـ لقّح. To — for small pox, (or طعّم ـ) لقّح الجدري.

Inoculation, *n.* تطعيم ـ تلقيح; of the small pox, تلقيح ـ تطعيم الجدري ـ الجدري.

Inoculator, *n.* As for the small pox, مطعّم الجدري.

Inodorous, *a.* عديم الرّائحة ـ لا رائحة له.

Inoffensive, *a.* Giving no offence, بلا شرّ ـ غير مسيئ ـ بلا سيّئة. Harmless, غير مضرّ. Simple, بسيط *pl.* بسطآء ـ سادج.

Inoffensively, *ad.* In a manner not to offend, بلا شرّ ـ بلا إساءة. Harmlessly, بلا مضرّة. With simplicity, سداجة ـ ببساطة.

Inoffensiveness, *n.* Harmlessness, عدم مضرّة. *See also* Innocence, *n.*

Inofficial, *a.* غير رسميّ.

Inofficious, *a.* Not courteous, بلا إيثار ـ بلا معروف.

Inoperative, *a.* Having no operation or effect, غير ـ غير عامل ـ باطل ـ لا طائل له ـ بلا فائدة. Useless, غير مؤثّر ـ فاعل.

Inopportune, *a.* خارج عن ـ خارج عن محلّه ـ غير سائغ وقته.

Inopportunely, *ad.* خارجا عن محلّه ـ خارجا عن وقته.

Inordinacy, *n.* } Inordinateness, } زيادة ـ كثرة ـ إفراط ـ فرط.

Inordinate, *a.* جائز الحدّ ـ منتهز ـ زائد ـ مفرط. To be — in, انتهز في ـ أفرط في. Inordinate praise, تقريظ ـ تقريط.

Inordinately, *ad.* بزيادة ـ بإفراط. To praise —, فرّط ـ قرّظ.

Inorganic, *a.* } Inorganical, } Destitute of organs, غير ذي ـ عاري الأعضاء ـ أعضاء. Not found with the organs of life,

– أَجْسَامٌ غَيْرُ نَامِيَةٍ. Inorganic substances, جَمَادِيٌّ – غَيْرُ نَامٍ جَمَادَاتٌ – أَجْسَامٌ بِلَا أَعْضَاءٍ.

Inosculate, *v.t.* عَشَّقَ – أَلْحَمَ شُفْرًا بِشُفْرٍ – يَصِلُ *aor.* وَصَلَ بَيْنَ.

Inosculation, *n.* تَعْشِيقٌ – إِلْحَامُ ٱلشُّفْرَيْنِ – وَصْلُ ٱلشُّفْرَيْنِ.

In petto, ad. مَكْتُومٌ فِي ٱلْقَلْبِ – فِي ٱلضَّمِيرِ – فِي ٱلْخَاطِرِ – فِي ٱلْبَاطِنِ.

In posse, ad. مُحْتَمَلٌ – حُدُوثُهُ مُمْكِنٌ – مُمْكِنٌ – فِي ٱلْقُوَّةِ.

In propriâ persona, ad. عَيْنًا – شَخْصًا – ذَاتًا.

Inquest, *n.* An official inquiry, فَحْصٌ (or بَحْثٌ or تَحْقِيقٌ) رَسْمِيٌّ – كَشْفٌ رَسْمِيٌّ عَنْ. A coroner's —, فَحْصٌ رَسْمِيٌّ يُجْرِيهِ مَأْمُورُ ٱلْحُكُومَةِ لِلِٱطِّلَاعِ عَلَى حَالَةِ مَنْ مَاتَ مَوْتًا مُشْتَبِهًا.

Inquietude, *n.* A disturbed state of mind, بَلْبَالٌ – رَمَضٌ – أَشْغَالٌ – وَسْوَاسٌ – شُغْلُ ٱلْبَالِ – عَنَايَةٌ – إِضْطِرَابٌ – هَمٌّ – قَلَقُ ٱلْفِكْرِ. To cause one —, أَهَمَّ – ـ عَنَى. *See also* Inconstancy, *n.*

Inquire, *v.t.* To ask, ـ سَأَلَ. To — the way, إِسْتَدَلَّ – إِسْتَخْبَرَ عَنِ ٱلطَّرِيقِ.

Inquire, *v.i.* إِسْتَعْلَمَ – إِسْتَخْبَرَ – تَخَبَّرَ. To — of one about, إِسْتَفْهَمَ عَنْ – مِنْ – إِسْتَخْبَرَ عَنْ – ـ سَأَلَ عَنْ – تَصَفَّحَ فِي – ـ نَدَشَ. To — into, ـ نَشَدَ (or أَنْشَدَ) عَنْ – ـ بَحَثَ عَنْ or فِي – فَتَّشَ عَنْ or عَلَى – إِسْتَقْصَى بِ – فَاتَشَ – تَعَرَّفَ عَنْ – تَبَحَّثَ عَنْ. The two inquired of each other, تَسَاءَلَا; they inquired of one another, of many, تَسَاءَلُوا. To — of one his name, إِسْتَسْمَى أَحَدًا.

Inquirendo, n. أَمْرٌ حُكْمِيٌّ بِٱلتَّفْتِيشِ.

Inquirer, *n.* An asker, seeker, سَائِلٌ – طُلَّابٌ *pl.* طَالِبٌ – بَاغٍ *pl.* بُغَاةٌ – جَادٌّ فِي ٱلطَّلَبِ. An investigator, فَتَّاشٌ – مُفَتِّشٌ.

Inquiringly, *ad.* بِٱسْتِفْهَامٍ – عَلَى طَرِيقَةِ ٱلسُّؤَالِ.

Inquiry, *n.* The act of inquiring, مَسَائِلُ *pl.* مَسْأَلَةٌ – سُؤَالٌ – إِسْتِعْلَامٌ – إِسْتِفْهَامٌ – إِسْتِقْصَاءٌ – إِسْتِخْبَارٌ. The act of investigating, تَفَحُّصٌ – إِسْتِقْصَاءٌ – تَفْتِيشٌ – تَدْقِيقٌ – تَحْقِيقٌ. A Board of —, دِيوَانُ تَفْتِيشٍ.

Inquisition, *n.* The tribunal so called, مَحْكَمَةُ ٱلتَّفْتِيشِ عَنِ ٱلْبِدَعِ فِي أُمُورِ ٱلدِّينِ لِقِصَاصِ ٱلْمُبْتَدِعِينَ. *See also* Inquiry, *n.*

Inquisitional, *a.} Inquisitionary,} مَا نِيطَ بِٱلِٱسْتِفْهَامِ – مُخْتَصٌّ بِٱلِٱسْتِقْصَاءِ. Busy in inquiry, مُجِدٌّ فِي ٱلتَّفْتِيشِ وَٱلتَّحْقِيقِ. *See also* Inquisitive, *a.*

Inquisitive, *a.* Given to inquiry, مُجِدٌّ (or رَاغِبٌ) فِي ٱلْبَحْثِ. Curious, prying, سَآلٌ – رَجُلٌ سُؤَلَةٌ – نَقَّافٌ – نِقَافٌ – فُضُولِيٌّ – مُتَدَخِّلٌ – مُلَاوِصٌ – مُتَجَسِّسٌ. To be —, لَاوَصَ – تَجَسَّسَ – ـ لَصَّ. To be — respecting, to intermeddle with, تَدَخَّلَ فِي – تَدَاخَلَ فِي.

Inquisitively, *ad.* With inquiry, carefully, بِٱعْتِنَاءٍ – بِرَغْبَةٍ. With prying, بِفُضُولٍ – بِتَجَسُّسٍ – مُلَاوَصَةً.

Inquisitiveness, *n.* Earnestness in seeking, رَغْبَةٌ (or جِدٌّ) فِي ٱلطَّلَبِ – تَشَوُّقٌ إِلَى. Curiosity, meddling, مُلَاوَصَةٌ – سُؤُولٌ – فُضُولٌ – مُدَاخَلَةٌ.

Inquisitor, *n.* An inquirer, مُفَتِّشٌ. A judge of the Inquisition, قَاضِي مَحْكَمَةِ ٱلتَّفْتِيشِ فِي أُمُورِ ٱلدِّينِ.

Inquisitorial, *a.* مُدَقِّقٌ – مُتَجَسِّسٌ.

Inquisitorially, *ad.* بِٱلتَّدْقِيقِ – بِٱلتَّجَسُّسِ.

Inroad, *n.* An incursion, غَزَاةٌ – غَارَةٌ – غَزْوٌ. Harm, إِجْحَافٌ – ضَرَرٌ – مَضَرَّةٌ – خَسَارَةٌ. To make an — into, غَارَ عَلَى – ـ غَزَا; to harm, أَضَرَّ – أَخْسَرَ – آذَى – أَجْحَفَ بِ – ـ حَكَرَ; to lessen, قَلَّلَ. They made an — upon the border, جَاوَزُوا ٱلْحُدُودَ.

Insalubrious, *a.* وَخِيمٌ – مُتَوَخِّمٌ – وَبِيلٌ. An — country, أَرْضٌ مُتَوَخِّمَةٌ.

Insalubrity, *n.* مَضَرَّةٌ لِلصِّحَّةِ – وَخَامَةٌ – وَبَلَةٌ – وَبَالٌ.

Insane, *a.* Unsound in mind, مُصَابٌ – مَخْبُولٌ – طَائِشٌ – خَبِلٌ – مَجْنُونٌ – مَفْتُونٌ. Wild, foolish, of a thing, ضِدُّ ٱلْعَقْلِ – خَيَالِيٌّ. To be or become —, إِخْتَلَّ عَقْلُهُ – ـ جُنَّ – ـ خَبِلَ. To pretend to be —, تَجَانَنَ – تَجَانَّ. To render —, خَبَّلَ – إِخْتَبَلَ – أَجَنَّ – جَنَّنَ.

Insanely, *ad.* Madly, كَٱلْمَجْنُونِ – بِجُنُونٍ. Foolishly, بِحَمَاقَةٍ.

Insanity, *n.* خَلَلٌ فِي – جُنُونٌ – هَبَّةٌ – خَبْطَةٌ – طَيْفٌ – ٱلْعَقْلِ. Having a touch of —, مَلْمُومٌ – مَمْسُوسٌ. A touch of —, طَيْفٌ مِنَ ٱلشَّيْطَانِ. Youth is a branch of —, (*prov.*) ٱلشَّبَابُ شُعْبَةٌ مِنَ ٱلْجُنُونِ.

Insatiability, *n.*} Insatiableness,} إِسْتِجَاعَةٌ – عَدَمُ قَنَاعَةٍ – قِلَّةُ شِبَعٍ. Insatiability for knowledge, إِسْتِجَاعَةُ ٱلْعِلْمِ. *See also* Avarice, *n.*

Insatiable, *a.*} Insatiate,} لَا يَشْبَعُ – لَا يَشْبَعُ.

Insatiably, *ad.* بِقِلَّةِ قَنَاعَةٍ – مِنْ غَيْرِ شِبَعٍ.

Insatiety, *n.* *See* Insatiability, *n.*

Inscribable, *a.* يُحَرَّرُ عَلَيْهِ – يُكْتَبُ عَلَيْهِ – يُرْسَمُ عَلَيْهِ – يَعْنُونُ.

Inscribe, *v.t.* To write, ـ كَتَبَ – حَرَّرَ. To enter, as in a book, أَدْرَجَ – قَيَّدَ – دَوَّنَ. To imprint, draw, ـ رَسَمَ. To engrave, نَقَشَ – قَلَّمَ. To dedicate, as of a book, *etc.*, to one, ـ جَعَلَ عَلَى ٱسْمِ فُلَانٍ.

Inscription, *n.* That which is written, كِتَابَة – مَكْتُوب. Enrolment, تَدْوِين – تَقْيِيد – تَدْرِيج. Dedication as of a book, عُنْوَانٌ عَلَى ٱسْمِ فُلَانٍ. *See also* Dedication, *n.*

Inscriptive, *a.* عَلَيْهِ كِتَابَةٌ – مَكْتُوبٌ عَلَيْهِ.

Inscrol, *v.t.* حَرَّرَ (or) كَتَبَ عَلَى طُومَارٍ.

Inscrutability, *n.* }
Inscrutableness, } مَا لَا – عَدَمُ ٱلْإِدْرَاكِ – عَدَمُ ٱلْفَحْصِ يُفْحَصُ.

Inscrutable, *a.* لَا يُبْحَثُ – لَا يُفْحَصُ – بَعِيدٌ عَنِ ٱلْفَحْصِ – إِدْرَاكُهُ مُحَالٌ.

Inscrutably, *ad.* بِنَوْعٍ لَا يُفْحَصُ.

Insculp, *v.t.* *See to* Carve, Engrave, *v.t.*

Insecable, *a.* لَا يُقْطَعُ – لَا يُنْشَرُ.

Insect, *n.* هَامَّة – حَشَرَة *pl.* حَشَرَات – دُوَيْبَّة *pl.* دُوَيْبَّات – *pl.* هَوَامّ. The — of the earth, حَشَرَاتُ ٱلْأَرْضِ – أَحْرَاشُ ٱلْأَرْضِ. A noxious insect, سَامَّة *pl.* سَوَامّ.

Insectile, *a.* مِنْ جِنْسِ ٱلْحَشَرَاتِ.

Insection, *n.* The act of cutting, قَطْع – نَشْر.

Insectivorous, *a.* آكِلُ ٱلْحَشَرَاتِ.

Insecure, *a.* Not safe, غَيْرُ أَمِينٍ – غَيْرُ آمِنٍ; not firm, غَيْرُ مَضْبُوطٍ – غَيْرُ مُحْكَمٍ – وَاهٍ; not at rest, غَيْرُ مُرْتَاحٍ – غَيْرُ مُطْمَئِنٍّ. Doubtful, تَحْتَ ٱلرَّيْبِ. Hazardous, مُخْطِر – ذُو خَطَرٍ.

Insecurely, *ad.* مِنْ غَيْرِ ضَبْطٍ – بِعَدَمِ إِحْكَامٍ – بِعَدَمِ أَمْنَةٍ.

Insecurity, *n.* Want of safety, عَدَمُ أَمْنَةٍ; want of firmness, عَدَمُ ضَبْطٍ – عَدَمُ إِحْكَامٍ. Hazard, خَطَر – مُخَاطَرَة.

Insensate, *a.* Stupid, بَلِيد – أَحْمَق – غَبِيّ; of a thing, غَبِيّ.

Insensibility, *n.* }
Insensibleness, } Want of sensibility, عَدَمُ – عَدَمُ حِسٍّ حَاسِّيَّةٍ. Coldness, dulness, فُتُور. Want of pity, عَدَمُ ٱلشَّفَقَةِ – عَدَمُ ٱلرَّحْمَةِ. A stagnant or unimproving state, جُمُود – جَمَاد. Unimpressibility, عَدَمُ تَأَثُّرٍ. Between a state of sensibility and insensibility, بَيْنَ ٱلصَّحْوَةِ وَٱلسَّكْرَةِ. Insensibility, as from illness or disease, سَكْتَة. *See also* Indifference, *n.*

Insensible, *a.* Destitute of feeling, عَدِيمُ ٱلْحِسِّ. Cold, فَاتِر – مَثْلُوجُ ٱلْفُؤَادِ. Without pity, عَدِيمُ ٱلشَّفَقَةِ – عَدِيمُ ٱلرَّحْمَةِ. Unimpressible, فُطَارِيّ – لَا يُؤَثِّرُ فِيهِ شَيْءٌ. Insensible to reproach, لَا يُؤَثِّرُ فِيهِ ٱلتَّعْزِيرُ. Imperceptible, غَيْرُ مَحْسُوسٍ – لَا يُحَسُّ. Lifeless, dead, stupid, inert, جَامِدُ ٱلْحَالِ – جَامِد. To be —, lifeless, dull, stagnant, جَمَدَ ².

Insensibly, *ad.* Imperceptibly, عَلَى خَفَاءٍ – بِدُونِ إِدْرَاكٍ – قَلِيلًا قَلِيلًا – عَلَى ٱلتَّدْرِيجِ. By degrees, بِلَا حِسٍّ. With stagnation, inertness, بِجَمَادٍ – بِجُمُودٍ.

Insentient, *a.* عَدِيمُ ٱلنَّظَرِ – عَدِيمُ ٱلْإِدْرَاكِ. *See also* Insensible, *a.*

Inseparable, *a.* مَلْزُومٌ بِ – لَازِمٌ وَمَلْزُومٌ – لَا يَتَفَرَّقُ. An — associate, رَصِيف *pl.* رُصُف.

Inseparableness, *n.* }
Inseparability, } مُلَازَمَة – عَدَمُ ٱلْاِفْتِرَاقِ.

Inseparably, *ad.* بِمُلَازَمَةٍ – مِنْ غَيْرِ ٱنْفِرَاقٍ.

Insert, *v.t.* To put in, جَعَلَ فِي – أَدْخَلَ ². To —, as into a sheath, غَمَدَ ². To —, as one thing into another, غَلَّ فِي ². أَسْلَكَ فِي – سَلَكَ فِي ². To —, as into a sentence, or a ring into a camel's nose, خَشَّ فِي ². To —, by way of hiding, دَسَّ ². To wrap up in, to foist in, to insert as in a paragraph or sentence, أَدْرَجَ فِي. He inserted the thread into the needle, سَلَكَ ٱلْخَيْطَ فِي ٱلْإِبْرَةِ. To be inserted, foisted, إِنْدَسَّ; as into a paragraph, *etc.*, أُدْرِجَ; as into a sheath, تَغَلَّلَ. *See also to* Thrust, *v.t.*

Insertion, *n.* The act of inserting, إِدْخَال; into a paper, *etc.*, إِدْرَاج; as into a needle or one thing into another, سَلْك – سُلُوك. A kind of lace, شَرِيط – حَبِيكَة *pl.* حَبَائِك.

Inset, *v.t.* *See to* Infix, Implant, *v.t.*

Inshore, *ad.* قَرِيبٌ مِنَ ٱلشَّطِّ – قَرِيبٌ مِنَ ٱلْبَرِّ.

Inshrine, *v.t.* *See to* Enshrine, *v.t.*

Insiccation, *n.* تَنْشِيف.

Inside, *a.* بَاطِن – دَاخِلِيّ – دَاخِل.

Inside, *ad.* جَوًّا – فِي دَاخِلٍ. Inside out, بِٱلْمَقْلُوبِ. To turn — out, جَعَلَ دَاخِلَهُ خَارِجَهُ ². *See also* Within, *ad.*

Inside, *n.* بَاطِن – ضِمْن – قَلْبَة *pl.* قَلْب – جَوْف – بَطْن – جَوَّة – دَاخِل – ٱلْجَوَّانِيّ. He built the — of the walls of the house with bricks, بَنَى حِيطَانَ ٱلْبَيْتِ مِنْ دَاخِلٍ بِٱلْآجُرِّ ².

Insidious, *a.* Wily, of a person, أَحْوَل – حُوَّلِيّ قُلَّبِيّ – ذُو كَيْدٍ – خَاتِل – خَبِيث – مُخَادِع – غَدَّار – دَسَّاس – خَدَّاعِيّ; deceptive, of a thing, خَفِيّ. Imperceptible, خَفِيّ.

Insidiously, *ad.* Wilily, بِكَيْدٍ – بِغَدْرٍ – بِخِيَانَةٍ – بِخِدَاعٍ. Secretly, imperceptibly, عَلَى خَفَاءٍ – بِلَا إِدْرَاكٍ – بِلَا حِسٍّ. To act — towards, خَانَ ² – غَدَرَ بِهِ ² – خَادَعَ – خَاتَلَ.

Insidiousness, *n.* Wiliness, treachery, غَدْر – خَتْل – خِدَاع – خِيَانَة – كَيْد. Imperceptibility, عَدَمُ حِسٍّ – عَدَمُ إِدْرَاكٍ – خَفَاء – دَسِيسَة.

Insight, *n.* Sight, نَظَر ـ طِلْع . Inspection, إِطِّلَاعٌ عَلَى ـ وُقُوف ـ دِرَايَة ـ مُلَاحَظَة ـ تَرَوٍّ ـ إِمْعَان ـ نَظَارَة. Knowledge, مَعْلُومَات ـ مَعْرِفَة ـ جَلِيَّة خَبَر ـ عَلَى. To have an — into, يَقِفُ *aor.* وَقَفَ عَلَى ـ تَعَمَّقَ فِي ـ إِطَّلَعَ عَلَى.

Insignia, *n.* As of honour, عَلَامَاتُ ٱلشَّرَفِ ; of office, نَوَاشِينُ ٱلْمَأْمُورِيَّةِ.

Insignificance, *n.* / **Insignificancy**, Want of meaning, عَدَمُ مَعْنًى ; want of importance, عَدَمُ ٱعْتِبَارٍ ـ تَفَاهَة. Smallness, جُزْئِيَّة. Worthlessness, تَفَاهَة ـ حَقَارَة ـ خَسَاسَة.

Insignificant, *a.* Wanting meaning, عَدِيمُ ٱلْمَعْنَى ; wanting importance, عَدِيمُ ٱلِاعْتِبَارِ. Small, جُزْئِيٌّ ـ زَهِيد. Worthless, تَافِه ـ حَقِير ـ خَسِيس ـ بَاطِل. To be —, تَفِهَ ـِ. *See also* Trifling, *a.*

Insignificantly, *ad.* Without meaning, بِلَا مَعْنًى ; as wanting importance, بِلَا ٱعْتِبَارٍ ـ بِتَفَاهَةٍ.

Insincere, *a.* غَيْرُ صَادِقٍ ـ عَدِيمُ ٱلْوَفَآءِ ـ غَاشٌّ ـ مَكَّار ـ كَذَّاب ـ مُدَاهِن ـ نِفَاقِيٌّ ـ مُرَآءٍ. Hypocritical, خَادِع ـ خَاتِل.

Insincerely, *ad.* بِخَتْلٍ ـ بِعَدَمِ صَدَاقَةٍ ـ بِرِئَآءٍ ـ بِعَدَمِ وَفَآءٍ. To act — towards, غَشَّ ـُ خَتَلَ ـِ خَدَعَ ـَ خَدَّعَ.

Insincerity, *n.* خَتْل ـ عَدَمُ وَفَآءٍ ـ عَدَمُ صَدَاقَةٍ ـ رِئَآء ـ عَدَمُ إِخْلَاص ـ غِشّ ـ كَذِب. I acted with — towards him, خَتَلْتُهُ ـ غَشَشْتُهُ ـ رَآيَيْتُهُ ـ خَاتَلْتُهُ.

Insinuate, *v.t.* To introduce gently, دَسَّ ـُ دَحَسَ ـَ *vulg.* أَدْخَلَهُ بِلَطَافَةٍ ـ دَحَشَ. To foist in, أَدْرَجَ. To suggest by allusion, أَلْغَطَ بِ ـ عَرَّضَ ـ بِلَغْطٍ ـ رَمْزًا ـ أَخْطَرَ ـ بِٱلْبَالِ ـ وَسْوَسَ لَهُ ـ بِ ـ دَسَّ ـ بِٱلْكَلَامِ ـُ أَوْمَأَ إِلَى ـ بِ. To — one's self into the good graces of, تَحَبَّبَ إِلَى ـ تَوَدَّدَ إِلَى ـ إِسْتَعْطَفَ ـ سَعَى فِي ـَ تَحْصِيلِ مَحَبَّتِهِ ـ مَلَكَ قَلْبَهُ ـِ. To — something against one, to charge with, أَتْهَمَ ـ بِ.

Insinuating, *a.* / **Insinuative**, Stealing on the affections, أَخْلَطُ ـ مُسْلِب ـ مُسْلِبُ ٱلْقَلْبِ. Conveying insinuation, مُتَوَارٍ. Having address, رَفِيع ـ حَاذِق. More — than fever, أَخْلَطُ مِنَ ٱلْحُمَّى. An — man, خِلْط ـ خُلُط ـ خَلِط ; an — woman, خِلْطَة.

Insinuatingly, *ad.* With address, بِٱسْتِعْطَافٍ ـ بِلَطَافَةٍ ـ بِطَرِيقَةٍ تَسْلُبُ ٱلْقَلْبَ. By innuendo, إِيهَامًا ـ بِلَغْطٍ.

Insinuation, *n.* A winding in, دَسّ ـ دَحْس ـ إِدْخَال ; a foisting in, إِدْرَاج. The act of casting or charging, إِلْقَآءٌ ; of suggesting, إِخْطَارٌ بِٱلْبَالِ. The act of gaining favour, إِسْتِعْطَاف ـ تَوَدُّد. An innuendo, ظِنَّة ـ لَغْط *pl.* أَلْغَاط ـ إِيهَام ـ كِنَايَة. The casting suspicion upon, إِتِّهَام ; an accusation, تُهَمَة. Insinuations, تَوَارِيَات.

Insipid, *a.* in a general sense, غَيْرُ ذِي نَفَسٍ ـ تَفِه ـ تَافِه ; of food, مَسِيخ ـ مَلِيخ ـ بِلَا لَذَّةٍ ـ بِلَا طَعْمٍ ـ تَافِه. Of a person or discourse, سَقِيطَة ـ بَارِد ـ بِلَا طَعْمَةٍ ; of a person, مَا فُلَانٌ بِخَلٍّ وَلَا خَمْرٍ ـ مَا لَهُ خَلٌّ وَلَا خَمْرٌ. To be —, in a general sense, تَفِهَ ـَ ; of food, مَلُخَ ـُ ; to render —, مَسَّخَ ـَ. An — woman, غَابِيَة.

Insipidness, *n.* / **Insipidity**, Want of flavour, مَلْخ ـ عَدَمُ لَذَّةٍ ـ قِلَّةُ طَعْمٍ. Dullness, تُفُوه ـ تَفَاهَة ـ بُرُودَة ـ سَقَط ـ سُقَاط ـ عَدَمُ طَعْمَةٍ.

Insipidly, *ad.* بِلَا لَذَّةٍ ـ مِنْ غَيْرِ طَعْمٍ ـ بِبُرُودَةٍ ـ بِتَفَاهَةٍ.

Insist, *v.i.* To insist upon, to persevere in, أَصَرَّ عَلَى ـ لَجَّ فِي ـَ. To urge, أَلَحَّ عَلَى ـ بِ ـ إِقْتَضَى. To — upon from one, إِقْتَرَحَ عَلَى ـ بِ. To — upon one for, صَادَرَ ـ عَلَى كَذَا. He insisted upon (the payment of) such a sum from him, صَادَرَهُ عَلَى كَذَا مِنَ ٱلْمَالِ.

Insistence, *n.* إِقْتِرَاح ـ إِقْتِضَآء. *See also* Persistence, *n.*

In situ, *ad.* فِي مَحَلِّهِ ـ فِي مَحَلِّهِ ٱلْأَصْلِيِّ.

Insnare, *v.t.* *See to* Entrap, *v.t.*

Insobriety, *n.* Intemperance, excess, فَرْط ـ تَفَاوُت ـ إِرْفَاش. *See also* Drunkenness, *n.*

Insolate, *v.t.* شَمَّسَ ـ شَرَّى ـ شَرَّرَ ـ شَرَى ـِ.

Insolence, *n.* غَطْرَسَة ـ سَفَاهَة ـ وَقَاحَة ـ فَرْعَنَة. Haughtiness, جَبَرِيَّة ـ تَكَبُّر ـ بَطَر.

Insolent, *a.* قَلْطِيّ ـ مُتَفَرْعِن ـ وَقِح *pl.* وِقَاح ـ سَفِيه *pl.* سُفَهَآء. Overbearing, proud, بَطِر ـ مَارِد *pl.* مَرَدَة ـ جَبَرِيّ. To be —, بَطِرَ ـَ ـ غَطْرَسَ ـ غَطْرَفَ. To be — towards, فَرَطَ عَلَى ـ فِي ـُ. They behaved in an — or domineering manner towards those who had benefited them, بَطِرُوا مَنْ أَسْدَى إِلَيْهِمِ ٱلْمَعْرُوفَ.

Insolently, *ad.* بِفَرْعَنَةٍ ـ بِسَفَاهَةٍ ـ بِبَطَرٍ. To behave — to, بَغَى عَلَى ـِ.

Insolidity, *n.* قِلَّةُ صَلَابَةٍ ـ قِلَّةُ رَصَانَةٍ ـ رَكَاكَة ـ رِقَّة.

Insolubility, *n.* عَدَمُ ٱنْحِلَالٍ ـ عَدَمُ ذَوَبَانٍ.

Insoluble, *a.* لَا يَنْحَلُّ ـ لَا يَذُوبُ.

Insolvable, *a.* Not to be explained, لَا يُشْرَحُ ـ لَا يُعَبَّرُ ـ غَيْرُ قَابِلِ ٱلتَّفْسِيرِ. *See also* Insoluble, *a.*

Insolvency, *n.* فَلَس ـ إِفْلَاس.

Insolvent, *a. and n.* مُفْلِس *pl.* مَفَالِيس. To become —, أَبْلَطَ ـ أَفْلَسَ ـ أَبْلَطَ. To declare —, فَلَّسَ. Declared —, مُفَلَّس.

Insomuch, *ad.* حَتَّى. Insomuch that the apostle said, حَتَّى يَقُولَ ٱلرَّسُولُ.

Insouciance, *n.* *See* Neglect, *n.*

Inspect, *v.t.* To look into, to examine, ـ فَحَصَ ـ بَحَثَ ـ تَصَفَّحَ فِي ـ صَفَحَ فِي ـ إِخْتَبَرَ ـ فَتَّشَ عَن *or* عَلَى. To view, نَظَرَ ـ إِطَّلَعَ عَلَى ـ عَايَنَ ـ تَفَرَّجَ عَلَى. To superintend, بَاشَرَ ـ إِلَى. To inspect, as of an inspector, كَشَفَ عَلَى. To —, as of troops; *see under to* Review, *v.t.*

Inspection, *n.* A view, survey, نَظَر ـ تَفَرُّج ـ مُعَايَنَة. Examination, تَدْقِيق ـ فَحْص ـ بَحْث ـ التَّرَوِّي فِي ـ تَفْتِيش ـ مُعَايَنَة. Superintendence, نِظَارَة ـ مُبَاشَرَة.

Inspector, *n.* An overseer, نَاظِر *pl.* نُظَّار ـ مُدِير ـ مُبَاشِر ـ مُحْتَسِب ـ كَشَّاف ـ مُشَارِف. An — of weights and measures, مُحْتَسِب. A police —, بَصَّاص ـ مُفَتِّش ٱلضَّبْطِيَّة ـ دَيْدُبَان.

Inspectorship, *n.*
Inspectorate, } مُبَاشَرَة ـ مُدِيرِيَّة ـ نِظَارَة.

Inspirable, *a.* مِمَّا يُتَنَفَّس ـ يُتَنَفَّس.

Inspiration, *n.* The drawing in of the breath, زَفْرَة *pl.* زَفَرَات ـ نَفَس *pl.* أَنْفَاس ـ تَنَفُّس. Infusion into the mind, suggestion, وَحْي ـ إِلْهَام رَبَّانِيّ ـ إِخْطَار عَلَى ٱلْبَال ـ إِلْقَاء; Divine —, natural —, infusion of spirit, إِلْهَام. Inspiration of the devil, تَبْعَات ـ إِغْوَاء ٱلشَّيْطَان. Animation, the act of, بَعْث ـ تَرْوِيج ـ إِنْهَاض ـ تَحْرِيض.

Inspiratory, *a.* مُخْتَصّ بِٱلزَّفْرَة ـ مُتَعَلِّق بِٱلتَّنَفُّس.

Inspire, *v.i.* To draw breath, زَفَرَ ـ تَنَفَّسَ.

Inspire, *v.t.* To breathe into, نَفَخَ فِي ـ شَمَّمَ ـ هَوَّى. To —, as of the mind, to suggest, أَحْدَثَ ـ فِي ـ أَخْطَرَ ـ بِٱلْبَال ـ أَلْقَى ـ فِي ٱلذِّهْن ـ فَتَحَ عَلَى ـ ب ـ عَقْلِهِ. To —, as poetic ideas, أَلْهَمَ. To suggest supernaturally, أَوْحَى. To animate, بَعَثَ ـ حَضَّضَ ـ خَوَّفَ ـ إِسْتَفَزَّ ـ رَوَّجَ ـ حَرَّضَ. To — with fear, أَرْعَبَ ـ. To — with friendship for, أَمَالَ قَلْبَهُ إِلَى ـ حَبَّبَ ـ إِلَى. To — with security, آمَنَ ـ أَمَّنَ.

Inspired, *a.* Infused, as with poetic spirit, مُلْهَم ـ مَشْرُوب; supernaturally —, مُنَزَّل ـ مُوحَى ب. The — scriptures, الكُتُب ٱلمُنَزَّلَة. An — journal, جَرِيدَة شَبِيهَة بِٱلرَّسْمِيَّة.

Inspirer, *n.*
Inspiring, *a.* } *See* Encourager, *n.*

Inspirit, *v.t.* To give new life to, أَحْيَى ـ بَعَثَ. To animate, encourage, رَوَّجَ ـ شَجَّعَ ـ حَرَّضَ ـ بَعَثَ. To enliven, أَنْعَشَ ـ سَرَّ. They were inspirited by the presence of such an one, زَادَهُمْ إِقْدَامًا وَجَسَارَةً حُضُورُ فُلَانٍ.

Inspissate, *v.t.* كَثَّفَ ـ عَقَّدَ. To be or become inspissated, إِنْعَقَدَ ـ تَكَاثَفَ ـ كَثُفَ.

Inspissate, *a.*
Inspissated, } مُتَكَثِّف ـ كَثِيف ـ مُنْعَقِد. The — juice of the grape, دِبْس. Inspissated juice, رُبّ. To be —, تَعَقَّدَ.

Inspissation, *n.* تَكْثِيف ـ تَعْقِيد.

Instability, *n.* Want of firmness, عَدَمُ ثَبَاتٍ ـ عَدَمُ قَرَارٍ ـ ضُعْف ـ ضَعْضَعَة ـ قِلَّة رُسُوخ. Inconstancy, طَيْش ـ هَيْهَرَة ـ تَلَوُّن ـ قَرْقَرَة. *See also* Inconstancy, Fickleness, *n.*

Instable, *a.* Wanting firmness, مَا لَهُ ـ غَيْر ثَابِت ـ ضَعْضَاع ـ ضَعِيف ـ قَرَار. Inconstant, مُتَلَوِّن ـ نَرْفَار ـ طَائِش. *See also* Inconstant, Unstable, Fickle, *a.*

Instal, *v.t.* As in an office, أَجْلَسَ ـ فِي مَنْصَب. To — into, to invest with an office, مَكَّنَ ـ فِي ـ ضَبَّطَ ـ وَظِيفَة ـ أَضْبَطَ ـ مَنْصَبًا. To — one's self in, إِسْتَقَرَّ فِي ـ تَأَبَّدَ فِي ـ مَأْمُورِيَّة.

Installation, *n.* As into an office, إِقْعَاد فِي ـ إِجْلَاس فِي مَنْصَب ـ إِقَامَة فِي مَنْصَب ـ مَأْمُورِيَّة. One's —, as in a house, *etc.*, إِسْتِقْرَار.

Instalment, *n.* Part of a sum of money paid, إِسْتِنْصَاص ـ جَانِب مِنَ ٱلْمَبْلَغ ـ تَقْسِيط ـ أَقْسَاط *pl.* قِسْط. To pay one by instalments, نَقَدَ لَهُ قِسْطًا ـ نَقَدَ لَهُ ٱلدَّيْن ٱسْتِنْصَاصًا ـ بِقِسْط. To obtain payment of a debt from one by instalments, إِسْتَنْجَزَ (*or* إِسْتَخْرَجَ) ٱلدَّيْنَ مِنْهُ شَيْئًا ـ إِسْتَنَضَّ ٱلدَّيْنَ مِنْهُ بَعْدَ شَيْءٍ.

Instance, *n.* Solicitation, إِلْحَاح ـ إِسْتِدْعَاء ـ رَجَاء ـ اِلْتِمَاس ـ إِبْرَام ـ لَجَاجَة. An example, مَثَل *pl.* أَمْثَال ـ مِثَال *pl.* أَمْثِلَة. A subject, matter, خُصُوص ـ مَادَّة ـ أَمْر. As an — of this kind, وَمِنْ هٰذَا ٱلْقَبِيل. For —, مَثَلًا. In the first —, أَوَّلًا ـ اِبْتِدَاء ـ أَوَّلُ ٱلْأَمْر. At my —, عَلَى كَلِمَتِي ـ عَنِ ٱلْتِمَاسِي ـ عَنْ طَلَبِي.

Instance, *v.t.* To mention as an example, تَمَثَّلَ ب. To quote something from, اِقْتَبَسَ ـ مِن ـ نَقَلَ ـ عَن.

Instant, *n.* A moment of time, لَحْظَة ـ دَقِيقَة *pl.* دَقَائِق ـ لَمْحَة. A short period of time, تَوَّة. A particular time, وَقْت ـ زَمَان ـ دَرَجَة ـ سَاعَة. In an —, فِي لَحْظَةٍ ـ فِي لَحْظَةٍ وَاحِدَةٍ. But, only, for an —, إِلَى وَقْتٍ فَقَطْ ـ مِنَ ٱلزَّمَان. At that —, حَالًا ـ فِي ٱلْحَال ـ فِي ٱلسَّاعَة. He was here this —, كَانَ هُنَا ـ تَوَّة كَانَ هُنَا ـ ٱلسَّاعَة (*or* تَوَّة). At the — that, while, when, كُلّ سَاعَة ـ عِنْدَمَا. Every —, كُلّ سَاعَةٍ.

Instant, *a.* Importunate, لَجُوج ـ مُلِثّ. Urgent, pressing, كُلِّيّ ـ ضَرُورِيّ ـ شَدِيد ـ مُهِمّ. Present, immediate, حَالّ ـ حَاضِر ـ مُوَقَّت. Continuing or persevering in, مُعْتَكِف عَلَى ـ مُوَاظِب عَلَى.

Instantaneous, *a.* اِبْنُ سَاعَة ـ فُجَائِيّ ـ مُوَقَّت. An — occurrence, فُجَاءَة. Instantaneous death, المَوْتُ ـ مَوْتُ ٱلْفَوَاتِ بَغْتَةً.

Instantaneously, *ad.* فُجَاءَةً ـ السَّاعَةَ ـ فِي ٱلْفَوْرِ ـ فِي ٱلْحَالِ.

Instantaneousness, *n.* فَوَات ـ فُجَاءَة.

Instanter, *ad.* حَالًا ـ فِي ٱلْحَالِ.

Instantly, *ad.* With importunity, بِلَجَاجَةٍ; with perseverance, بِعُكُوفٍ ـ إِعْتِكَافًا. Directly, أَوَّلَ سَاعَةٍ ـ فِي ٱلْحَالِ ـ فِي ٱلْفَوْرِ. *See also under* Instant, *n.*

Instar, *v.t.* To set with stars, زَيَّنَ ـ (or) رَصَّعَ ـ بِنُجُوم.

Instate, *v.t.* وَضَعَ *aor.* يَضَعُ ـ حَطَّ [2].

In statu quo, *ad.* كَمَا كَانَ ـ فِي ٱلْحَالَةِ ٱلسَّابِقَةِ ـ فِي ٱلْحَالِ ٱلسَّابِقِ.

Instaurate, *v.t.* أَصْلَحَ. To be instaurated, إِسْتَتَبَّ. *See also to* Renew, Repair, Reform, Restore, *v.t.*

Instauration, *n.* The act of, إِصْلَاح; the being instaurated, إِسْتِتْبَاب.

Instead, *ad.* عِوَضًا عَن ـ مَكَانَ ـ بَدَلًا مِن ـ بَدَلَ. Instead of money he gave me goods, عِوَضًا عَنِ ٱلدَّرَاهِمِ أَعْطَانِي بَضَائِعَ. He plays — of working, يَلْعَبُ بَدَلَ أَنْ يَشْتَغِلَ. Instead of your doing this, بَدَلَ أَنْ تَفْعَلَ كَذَا. I have a man with me — of Zaid, عِنْدِي رَجُلٌ سِوَى زَيْدٍ. Instead of him, in his place, عِوَضًا عَنْهُ. Instead or in the place of, in compensation for the thing, فِي مُقَابَلَةِ ٱلشَّيْءِ.

Insteep, *v.t.* *See to* Steep, *v.t.*

Instep, *n.* صَدْرُ ٱلْقَدَمِ ـ رُسْغُ ٱلرِّجْلِ ـ جِمَارَةُ ٱلْقَدَمِ. Having a high —, طَفَنْش.

Instigate, *v.t.* To incite to, حَثَّ [2]-عَلَى ـ حَرَّضَ-عَلَى ـ حَرَّكَ-إِلَى ـ أَغْوَى-عَلَى ـ حَمَلَ-عَلَى ـ أَزَّ [2]-عَلَى ـ أَغْرَى-عَلَى ـ حَضَّضَ-عَلَى. *See also to* Incite, Stimulate, *v.t.*

Instigation, *n.* تَهْيِيج ـ تَحْرِيك ـ تَحْرِيض ـ حَثّ ـ أَزّ ـ إِغْرَاء ـ إِغْوَاء. The instigations, as of the devil, وَسْوَسَة ـ وَسْوَاس.

Instigator, *n.* مُحَرِّك ـ بَاعِث; as to evil, دَاعٍ إِلَى ٱلشَّرِّ ـ طَاغٍ *pl.* طُغَاة.

Instil, *v.t.* To infuse by drops, أَقْطَرَ ـ قَطَّرَ. To cause to imbibe, to instruct, عَلَّمَ ـ أَلْقَى ـ لَقَّنَ. *See also to* Insinuate, *v.t.*

Instillation, *n.* The act of infusing by drops, تَقْطِير. Infusion, as into the mind, تَعْلِيم ـ تَلْقِين ـ إِلْقَاء ـ فَيْض.

Instinct, *n.* حِسّ طَبِيعِيّ ـ إِحْسَاس *pl.* حِسّ ـ أَوْهَام *pl.* وَهْم ـ مَيْل طَبِيعِيّ. An instinctive movement, إِنْبِعَاثُ ٱلطَّبْعِ. The — of conscience, التَّمْيِيز. By pure —, بِمُجَرَّدِ ٱلطَّبْعِ.

Instinct, *a.* Living, moving, حَاسّ وَمُتَحَرِّك ـ حَيّ.

Instinctive, *a.* إِكْتِسَابِيّ ـ طَبِيعِيّ.

Instinctively, *ad.* بِطَرِيقِ ٱلْفَيْضِ ـ بِٱلطَّبْعِ ـ بِمَيْلٍ طَبِيعِيٍّ ـ بِمُجَرَّدِ ٱلطَّبْعِ.

Institute, *v.t.* To set up, establish, أَقَامَ ـ وَضَعَ *aor.* يَضَعُ ـ رَتَّبَ ـ جَعَلَ. To originate, أَحْدَثَ ـ أَبْدَعَ ـ أَوْجَدَ. To found, أَنْشَأَ ـ أَوْقَفَ ـ أَقَامَ. To enact, as laws, فَرَضَ ـ شَرَعَ ـ سَنَّ [2]. *See also to* Establish, Enact, *v.t.*

Institute, *n.* A rule, law, system, قَانُون *pl.* قَوَانِين ـ قَاعِدَة *pl.* قَوَاعِد ـ سُنَّة *pl.* سُنَن. An — of learned men, دِيوَانُ عُلَمَاء.

Institution, *n.* The act of setting up, قِيَام ـ وَضْع ـ نِظَام ـ تَرْتِيب. The act of origination, إِحْدَاث ـ إِبْدَاع ـ إِيجَاد; of founding, إِنْشَاء ـ تَأْسِيس ـ إِيجَاد. A system, plan, laws, قَوَاعِدُ ـ قَوَانِينُ ـ تَرْتِيب ـ نِظَام ـ نَسَق. The elements of knowledge, أُصُولُ ٱلْعِلْمِ. A school, college, مَدْرَسَة. An establishment, institute, جَمَاعَة ـ نِظَام ـ تَرْتِيب. The place, as of an establishment, دِيوَان ـ دَار ـ مَحَلّ. Useful institutions, تَنْسِيقَاتٌ خَيْرِيَّةٌ ـ نِظَامَاتٌ خَيْرِيَّةٌ.

Institutional, *a.* } مُخْتَصّ بِٱلْمَبَادِئ ـ مُخْتَصّ بِٱلْأُصُولِ وَٱلْقَوَاعِدِ.
Institutionary, } Relating to system, مُتَعَلِّق ـ نِظَامِيّ ـ مُنَسَّق ـ بِٱلتَّرْتِيبِ.

Institutive, *a.* That establishes, مُقِيم ـ وَاضِع ـ مُرَتِّب ـ مُنَسِّق ـ إِيجَادِيّ.

Institutor, *n.* One who institutes, مُنْشِئ ـ وَاضِع ـ مُوجِد. An originator, مُبْدِع ـ مُوجِد. A founder, مُؤَسِّس. *See also* Instructor, *n.*

Instruct, *v.t.* To teach, عَلَّمَ ـ أَدْرَسَ ـ دَرَّسَ. To imbue, as with useful knowledge, أَفَادَ ـ لَقَّنَ. To train, دَرَّبَ ـ مَرَّنَ. To give one knowledge of, أَعْلَمَ-بِ ـ عَرَّفَ-بِ. To order, أَوْصَى-بِ ـ أَشَارَ بِهِ عَلَى ـ أَمَرَ-بِ [2].

Instruction, *n.* The act of teaching, تَعْلِيم ـ تَدْرِيس. Precepts, تَعْلِيم *pl.* تَعَالِيمُ. Acquired knowledge, عِلْم ـ إِفَادَة. An order, تَعْلِيم ـ أَوَامِرُ *pl.* أَمْر ـ وَصَايَا *pl.* وَصِيَّة. Instructions, directions, تَعْلِيمَات. Secret instructions, تَعْلِيمَاتٌ خَفِيَّةٌ. According to given instructions, بِحَسَبِ تَعْلِيمَاتٍ مَعْلُومَةٍ. Director of public instruction, نَاظِرُ ٱلْمَعَارِفِ ٱلْعُمُومِيَّةِ.

Instructive, *a.* مُفِيدٌ لِلتَّعْلِيمِ ـ مُفِيد.

Instructively, *ad.* بِطَائِل ـ بِإِفَادَةٍ.

Instructiveness, *n.* طَائِل ـ إِفَادَة.

Instructor, *n.* أُسْتَاذ ـ مُدَرِّس ـ مُعَلِّم ـ مُعَلِّمُ تَعْلِيمٍ ـ مُمَرِّن ـ مُدَرِّب.

Instructress, *n.* قَهْرَمَانَة ـ مُعَلِّمَة.

Instrument, *n.* That with which work is performed, آلَة *pl.* آلَات; tools, apparatus, عُدَّة *pl.* عُدَد. An agent, فاعِل *pl.* فَعَلَة ـ عامِل *pl.* عُمَّال ـ وَكِيل *pl.* وُكَلَاء. A means, وَاسِطَة *pl.* وَسَائِط ـ وَسِيلَة *pl.* وَسَائِل ـ سَبَب *pl.* أَسْبَاب. A legal document, سَنَد *pl.* سَنَدَات ـ حُجَّة *pl.* حُجَج ـ بَرَاءَة. A musical —, آلَة الطَّرَب (or ٱلْمُوسِيقَى) *pl.* آلَات. A stringed musical —, عَزْف *pl.* مَعَازِف.

Instrumental, *a.* Conducive to, مُفْضٍ إِلَى ـ وَسِيلَة إِلَى ـ مُدار. Not vocal, آلاتِيّ. Aiding, نافِع ـ مُسَاعِد ـ مُعَاوِن ـ مُعِين إِلَى.

Instrumental music, مُوسِيقَى ـ عَزْف (or عَزِيف) ٱلْمَعَازِف.

Instrumentality, *n.* Means, medium, طَرِيقَة ـ وَاسِطَة ـ وَسِيلَة.

Instrumentally, *ad.* By an instrument, بِعُدَّة ـ بِآلَة. Through a medium, بِوَاسِطَة ـ بِوَسِيلَة. With musical instruments, بِآلَاتِ الطَّرَب ـ بِعَزْفِ ٱلْمَعَازِف ـ بِٱلْمُوسِيقَى.

Insubjection, *n.* }
Insubmission, } قِلَّة خُضُوع ـ عَدَمُ ٱنْقِيَاد ـ عَدَمُ إِطَاعَة ـ تَمَرُّد ـ مُعَانَدَة ـ مُخَالَفَة ـ عِصْيَان.

Insubordinate, *a.* مُعَانِد ـ عَدِيمُ ٱلْإِطَاعَة ـ عَدِيمُ ٱلِٱنْقِيَاد ـ عاصٍ *pl.* عُصَاة ـ مارِد ـ مُتَمَرِّد. To be — to, عَصَى عَلَى ـ مَارَدَ.

Insubordination, *n.* عِنَاد ـ عِصْيَان ـ مُخَالَفَة ـ قِلَّة طَاعَة ـ تَمَرُّد. An act of —, مُمَارَدَة ـ مَعْصِيَة.

Insufferable, *a.* Not to be borne, لَا يُحْتَمَل ـ أَعَزّ ـ عَزِيز ـ لَا يُطَاق. Detestable, مَنْفُور ـ مَكْرُوه ـ شَنِيع. Excessive, بَتِّيّ ـ كُلِّيّ.

Insufferably, *ad.* Beyond endurance, بِصُورَةٍ لَا تُحْتَمَل. Detestably, بِشَنَاعَة ـ بِكَرَاهَة. Excessively, بَتَّة ـ بِإِفْرَاط ـ كُلِّيًّا ـ لِلْغَايَة.

Insufficiency, *n.* Want of sufficiency, نُقْصَان ـ عَدَمُ كِفَايَة ـ قِلَّة. Inadequacy, عَدَمُ قَابِلِيَّة ـ عَدَمُ أَهْلِيَّة. Want of power, عَجْز ـ عَدَمُ ٱسْتِطَاعَة.

Insufficient, *a.* Not sufficient, قَلِيل ـ نَاقِص ـ غَيْرُ كَافٍ. Not adequate to, غَيْرُ أَهْلٍ بِ ـ عَدِيمُ. Wanting in power, عَاجِز ـ عَدِيمُ ٱلِٱسْتِطَاعَة. An — price, ثَمَنٌ بَخْس.

Insufficiently, *ad.* قِلَّة ـ بِنُقْصَانٍ ـ مِنْ غَيْرِ كِفَايَة.

Insular, *a.* }
Insulary, } Surrounded by water, sea, مُحَاط ـ مُحَاطٌ بِٱلْمَاء ـ جَزِيرَة ـ بِٱلْبَحْر. *See also* Isolated, *a.*

Insular, *n.* An islander, مِنْ أَهْلِ جَزِيرَة.

Insularity, *n.* Of an island, إِكْتِنَافُ ٱلْمَاءِ بِهِ ـ إِحَاطَةُ ٱلْمَاءِ بِهِ; the being alone, apart, فَذّ.

Insulate, *v.t.* To place in a detached situation, أَفْرَدَ. To —, by surrounding with water, حَوَّطَ ـ بِٱلْمَاء. To prevent electricity from escaping, مَنَعَ نُفُوذَ ٱلْكَهْرَبَائِيَّة. To be insulated, apart, alone, فَذَّ ـ فَذَّ عَنْ: He was insulated from his companions, فَذَّ عَنْ أَصْحَابِهِ. *See also to* Isolate, *v.t.*

Insulated, *a.* قائِمٌ بِذَاتِهِ ـ فَرْد ـ مُفْرَد ـ فَارِد ـ فَذّ *pl.* فُذُوذ. *See also* Isolated, *a.*

Insulation, *n.* The act of surrounding with water, تَحْوِيط بِٱلْمَاء; the being surrounded with water, اِحْتِيَاطُ ٱلْمَاءِ بِهِ. The act of making separate, إِفْرَاد; the being separate, فَذّ ـ اِنْفِرَاد. Electrical —, مَنْعُ ٱلسَّيَّالِ ٱلْكَهْرَبَائِيّ ـ اِنْفِرَادٌ كَهْرَبَائِيّ.

Insulator, *n.* Of electricity, حاجِزَةُ ٱلْكَهْرَبَائِيَّة (or آلَة) مَادَّة.

Insult, *n.* طَعْنَة ـ تَجْرِيس ـ بَهْدَلَة ـ إِهَانَة ـ اِنْتِهَاك ـ حَكْر ـ إِسَاءَة ـ نَقْصٌ فِي حَقِّ أَحَد. *See also* Insolence, *n.*

Insult, *v.t.* To abuse, طَعَنَ فِي عِرْضِهِ ـ اِنْتَهَكَ ـ حَكَرَ ـ أَسَاءَ إِلَى ـ تَنَقَّصَ. To outrage, بَغَى عَلَى ـ اِعْتَدَى عَلَى ـ أَغَارَ عَلَى. To make an attack upon, سَطَا بِ *or* عَلَى *aor.* يَسْطُو ـ هَجَمَ عَلَى. To — the understanding, خَالَفَ ٱلْعَقْل.

Insult, *v.i.* To behave with insolent triumph, تَاهَ *aor.* يَتِيهُ ـ اِفْتَخَرَ ـ أَزْهَى ـ زَهِيَ *aor.* يَزْهُو ـ بَطِرَ.

Insulting, *a.* مُزْدَرٍ ـ مُسْتَحْقِر ـ مُهِين ـ حَكِر ـ بَاغٍ ـ بَطِر ـ وَقِح. *See also* Insolent, *a.*

Insultingly, *ad.* بِسَفَاهَة ـ بِإِهَانَة ـ بِٱنْتِهَاك ـ بِبَطَر. To behave —, جَاءَ يَنْفُضُ مِذْرَوَيْهِ *aor.* يَجِيءُ بِفَرْعَنَة ـ بَطِرَ ـ تَعَزَّزَ.

Insuperability, *n.* }
Insuperableness, } Insurmountability, unattainableness, عِزّ ـ اِمْتِنَاع ـ مَنَاعَة ـ تَعَذُّر ـ عِزَّة. An impossibility, شَيْءٌ مُحَال ـ أَمْرٌ غَيْرُ مُمْكِن ـ أَمْرٌ مُحَال.

Insuperable, *a.* Insurmountable, الظَّفَرُ بِهِ مُحَال ـ أَعَزّ ـ عَزِيز نَوَالُهُ ـ ذُو عِزَّة ـ عَزِيز ـ أَعَزّ ـ اَلِٱنْتِصَارُ عَلَيْهِ مُحَال. Unattainable, إِدْرَاكُهُ غَيْرُ مُمْكِن ـ لَا يُنَال ـ لَا يُغَالَب ـ مُحَال. The thing was —, عَزَّ (or اِعْتَزَّ *or* تَعَزَّزَ) ٱلشَّيْءُ ـ تَعَذَّرَ ٱلْأَمْر. The matter was — to me, عَزَّ عَلَيَّ ٱلْأَمْرُ ـ بَرَّقَ بِيَ ٱلْأَمْرُ ـ تَعَذَّرَ عَلَيَّ ٱلْأَمْر.

Insuperably, *ad.* Insurmountably, unattainably, بِعِزَّة ـ بِعِزّ ـ تَعَذُّرًا. Wholly, extremely, لِلْغَايَة.

Insupportable, *a.* *See* Insufferable, *a.*

Insupportableness, *n.* عِزَّة ـ عِزّ.

Insupportably, *ad.* *See* Insufferably, *ad.*

Insuppressible, *a.* إِزَالَتُهُ غَيْرُ مُمْكِنَة ـ لَا يُقْهَر ـ عَزِيز ـ أَعَزّ.

Insuppressible rage, غَيْظٌ لَا يُكْتَم.

Insuppressibly, *ad.* بِعَدَمِ إِمْكَانِ قَهْرِهِ ـ بِعِزَّة ـ بِعِزّ.

Insuppressive, *a.* غَيْرُ مُبْطِلٍ ـ غَيْرُ مُزِيلٍ ـ غَيْرُ قَاهِرٍ.

Insurable, *a.* وِمَّا يُضَمَّنُ فِي سِكُورْتَا ـ وِمَّا يُضَمَّنُ.

Insurance, *n.* سِكُورْتَا ـ ضَمَانُ خَسَارَةٍ. *See also* Assurance, *n.*

Insurance company, شِرْكَةٌ (or كُومْپَانْيَةٌ) سِكُورْتَا (or آلتَّأْمِينِ).

Insurance office, قَلَمُ كُومْپَانْيَةِ سِكُورْتَا.

Fire insurance, ضَمَانُ (or سِكُورْتَا) آلْخَسَارَةِ مِنَ آلْحَرِيقِ.

Life insurance, ضَمَانُ (or سِكُورْتَا) مَبْلَغٍ يُدْفَعُ إِلَى وَرَثَةِ آلْمَضْمُونِ عُقْبَ وَفَاتِهِ.

Marine insurance, سِكُورْتَا آلْمَرَاكِبِ ـ سِكُورْتَا بَحْرِيَّةٌ.

Policy of insurance, سَنَدُ سِكُورْتَا.

Premium of insurance, أُجْرَةُ آلسِّكُورْتَا.

Insurance broker, سِمْسَارُ آلسِّكُورْتَا.

Insure, *v.t.* To make sure against loss, ضَمَّنَ ـ أَمَّنَ ـ مِنَ آلضَّرَرِ ـ آلْخَسَارَةِ. To — in an Insurance office, ضَمَّنَ ـ فِي سِكُورْتَا ـ سَوْكَرَ. *See also to* Assure, *v.t.*

Insure, *v.i.* To — one's goods or life, تَسَوْكَرَ ـ جَعَلَ مَالَهُ أَوْ حَيَاتَهُ فِي سِكُورْتَا.

Insurer, *n.* One who insures, مُسَوْكِر ـ سِكُورْتَاجِي. One who insures another against loss, ضَامِنُ خَسَارَةٍ *pl.* ضَمَنَة.

Insurgent, *a.* مُقَاوِم ـ عَاصٍ *pl.* عُصَاة ـ بَاغٍ *pl.* بُغَاة ـ ثَائِر *pl.* ثَائِرُونَ.

Insurgent, *n.* ثَائِر *pl.* ثَائِرُونَ ـ عَاصٍ *pl.* عُصَاة ـ بَاغٍ *pl.* بُغَاة. Insurgents, عُصَاة ـ أَهْلُ فَسَادٍ ـ أَهْلُ طُغْيَانٍ ـ أَهْلُ آلْبَغْيِ وَآلْعِصْيَانِ.

Insurmountability, *n.* *See* Insuperability, *n.*

Insurmountable, *a.* *See* Insuperable, *a.*

Insurmountably, *ad.* *See* Insuperably, *ad.*

Insurrection, *n.* هَرَج ـ فِتْنَة ـ عِصْيَان ـ طُغْيَان. To rise in, عَصَى عَلَى ـ قَامَ عَلَى. To rise in — against, طَغَى ـ هَرَجَ. To excite to —, فَتَّنَ. *See also to* Rebel, *v.i.*, Rebellion, *n.*

Insurrectional, *a.* } Insurrectionary, } شَغِب ـ هَرِج ـ قَوْمِيّ ـ عَاصٍ ـ عِصِيّ ـ ثَائِر ـ مَا نِيطَ بِقَوْمَةِ آلشَّعْبِ.

Insusceptibility, *n.* Want of capacity to feel, عَدَمُ حِسٍّ; of possibility, تَعَذُّر ـ عِزَّة ـ عَدَمُ إِمْكَانٍ; of fitness, عَدَمُ أَهْلِيَّةٍ. *See also* Incapacity, *n.*

Insusceptible, *a.* Not capable of feeling, عَدِيمُ آلْحِسِّ; apathetic, فُطَارِيّ; not capable of receiving, غَيْرُ قَابِلٍ ـ غَيْرُ عَتِيدٍ لِقُبُولِ آلشَّيْءِ ـ غَيْرُ جَدِيرٍ. Insusceptible of offence, غَيْرُ نَزِقٍ. *See also* Insensible, *a.*

Intact, *a.* غَيْرُ مَمْسُوسٍ ـ صَحِيح. His honour is —, حُرْمَتُهُ بَاقِيَةٌ عَلَيْهِ. His fame is —, مَا آنْثَلَمَ صِيتُهُ.

Intaglio, *n.* The cutting so called, نَحْت. A stone in —, حَجَرٌ مَنْحُوتٌ.

Intangibility, *n.* } Intangibleness, } عَدَمُ آلْإِحْسَاسِ ـ عَدَمُ آلشُّعُورِ بِهِ بِآللَّمْسِ بِآللَّمْسِ.

Intangible, *a.* غَيْرُ مَحْسُوسٍ ـ لَا يَشْعُرُ بِهِ آللَّمْسُ.

Integer, *n.* One, فَرْد. A whole number, عَدَدٌ صَحِيحٌ.

Integral, *a.* Whole, entire, كَامِل ـ تَامّ ـ تَمَام. Not fractional, غَيْرُ مُنْكَسِرٍ ـ غَيْرُ مُنْقَسِمٍ. Forming part of a whole, جُزْءٌ مِنَ أَجْزَاءٍ. Intact, uninjured, صَحِيح. An — molecule, جُزْءٌ لَا يَتَجَزَّأُ ـ فَرْدٌ جَوْهَرٌ. Integral calculus, حِسَابٌ تَمَامِيٌّ. A State forming an — part of the Ottoman dominions, مَمْلَكَةٌ مِنْ ذَاتِ آلْمَمَالِكِ آلْعُثْمَانِيَّةِ.

Integral, *n.* شَيْءٌ كَامِلٌ ـ شَيْءٌ صَحِيحٌ.

Integrant, *a.* Perfecting, مُكَمِّل ـ مُتَمِّم. Making part of a whole, مُرَكِّب ـ دَاخِلٌ فِي تَرْكِيبِ آلشَّيْءِ.

Integrate, *v.t.* To make entire, تَمَّمَ ـ كَمَّلَ. To restore, أَصْلَحَ ـ عَمَّرَ ـ جَدَّدَ. To be integrated, restored, إِسْتَتَبَّ.

Integration, *n.* The act of, تَكْمِيل ـ تَتْمِيم ـ تَعْمِير; the being integrated, إِسْتِتْبَاب.

Integrity, *n.* Wholeness, unbrokenness, تَمَام ـ تَمَامَة ـ صِحَّة ـ كَمَال. Purity, صَفَاء ـ صَفَاوَة. Rectitude, صَوَاب ـ هَذَب ـ عَدَالَة ـ قِسْط ـ إِسْتِقَامَة. To guarantee the — of a state, تَكَفَّلَ بِإِبْقَاءِ آلْمَمْلَكَةِ عَلَى صِحَّتِهَا بِدُونِ إِجْحَافٍ بِهَا.

Integument, *n.* غِشَاء *pl.* أَغْشِيَة ـ قِشْر *pl.* قُشُور ـ جِلْد *pl.* جُلُود ـ فُوف ـ فُوفَة.

Integumentary, *a.* Relating to integuments, قِشْرِيّ ـ غِشَائِيّ ـ مُتَعَلِّقٌ بِآلْجِلْدِ.

Intellect, *n.* ذِهْن ـ فَهْم ـ إِدْرَاك ـ عَقْل *pl.* عُقُول ـ قُوَّة مُدْرِكَة. Full of —, رَاجِحُ آلْعَقْلِ.

Intellectual, *a.* Relating to the intellect, ذِهْنِيّ ـ عَقْلِيّ. Perceived by the intellect, مَعْنَوِيّ. Having the power of understanding, نَاطِق ـ فَهِيم ـ صَاحِبُ عَقْلٍ. Knowing, well-informed, عَاقِل ـ ذَكِيّ ـ فَهِيم ـ فَطِين. To pretend to be —, تَعَاقَلَ.

Intellectualist, *n.* مَنْ يُبَالِغُ فِي سُمُوِّ آلْعَقْلِ.

Intellectually, *ad.* عَقْلًا ـ ذِهْنًا.

Intelligence, *n.* Understanding, لُبّ *pl.* أَلْبَاب ـ نُكْر ـ فِطْنَة ـ مِهْنَة ـ ذَكَاء ـ بَصِيرَة ـ نَاهِيَة ـ جَوْل ـ دَهْي ـ دَهَاء ـ فِرَاسَة ـ عَقْل ـ فَهْم ـ مَعْرِفَة. News, خَبَر ـ حَدِيث. Terms of intercourse, مُعَاشَرَة ـ عَلَاقَة ـ إِرْتِبَاط. A spiritual —, spirit, رُوح; spiritual intelligences, رُوحَانِيُّونَ ـ مَلَائِكَة. To show —,

— أَوْقَفَ عَلَى — أَعْلَمَ — أَفَادَ عِلْمًا . To give — to, تَعَقَّلَ . To ask for —, إِسْتَخْبَرَ . To have — of, تَخَبَّرَ بِ . To أَخْبَرَ live in good — with, عَاشَرَ بِحُسْنِ ٱلْوِفَاقِ . Intelligence department, قَلَمُ — قَلَمُ ٱلتَّجَسُّسِ . Intelligence office, مَأْمُورِيَّةُ ٱلْخَبَرِ ٱلتَّحْقِيقِ . To be in — with, to correspond with, عَاشَرَ — عَامَلَ ; by letter, كَاتَبَ .

Intelligencer, *n.* One who gives news, مُبَشِّر — مُخْبِر . A newspaper, جَرِيدَةُ أَخْبَارٍ — تَقْوِيمُ وَقَائِعَ .

Intelligent, *a.* خَفِيفٌ — جَزْلُ ٱلرَّأْيِ — بَنِيْن — أَرِب — أَرِيب — ذِهِن — دَهِيٌّ — أَلِبَّاءُ *pl.* لَبِيب — لَوْذَعِيٌّ — مُنَهَّاة — ٱلرُّوح — فَطِين — عَاقِل — ذَكِيٌّ — بَصِير — فَاطِن — ذَهِين . To be —, تَعَقَّلَ — ذَهِنَ — يَذْهَى *aor.* دَهِيَ — عَقَلَ — فَطِنَ — أَرِبَ . To render —, عَقَّلَ — فَطَّنَ — أَرَّبَ . To be — in …, فَطِنَ بِ — أَرِبَ بِ .

Intelligently, *ad.* بِٱتْقَانٍ — بِعَقْلٍ — بِمَعْرِفَةٍ — بِبَيَانٍ — تَعَقُّلًا .

Intelligibility, *n.* / Intelligibleness, } بَيَان — صَرَاحَة — وُضُوح .

Intelligible, *a.* يَنْفَهِمُ — مَفْهُوم — مَعْقُول — وَاضِح .

Intelligibly, *ad.* بَيَانًا — بِصَرَاحَةٍ — بِوُضُوحٍ .

Intemperance, *n.* Want of moderation, عَدَمُ ٱعْتِدَالٍ . Excess, إِفْرَاط — فَرْط — قِلَّةُ عَفَافٍ — خَلَاعَة — دِعَارَة . Immorality, فِسْق . Drunkenness, سُكْر .

Intemperate, *a.* Excessive, مَعْكُوس — مُفْرِط — فَائِض . Addicted to drunkenness, سِكِّير — شَرَّاب . Ungovernable, صَعْب — عَارِم — شَكِس — مُتَمَرِّد . Intemperate in eating, أَكُول ; in language, طَوِيلُ ٱللِّسَانِ ; of the weather, غَيْرُ — شَدِيد — غَضُوب — مُتَهَوِّر مُعْتَدِلٍ .

Intemperately, *ad.* بِزِيَادَةٍ — بِإِفْرَاطٍ — بِلَا ٱعْتِدَالٍ .

Intend, *v.t.* رَامَ — هَمَّ بِ — إِعْتَزَى — غَزَا — صَمَدَ *aor.* تَعَمَّدَ — تَنَوَّى أَنْ — نَوَى — أَرَادَ — إِعْتَمَدَ — عَزَمَ عَلَى — يَزِيمُ I intend to, أَنَا مُزْمِعٌ بِ or عَلَى . He intended to do him such a thing, أَرَادَ بِهِ كَذَا . He intends to go to the town, عَازِمٌ عَلَى ٱلْمَسِيرِ إِلَى ٱلْمَدِينَةِ . What do you — to do respecting these people? مَا أَنْتُمْ مُزْمِعُونَ مِن جِهَةِ هٰؤُلَاءِ ٱلنَّاسِ . He is intending to build a house, هُوَ يُرِيدُ أَنْ يَبْنِيَ بَيْتًا .

Intendancy, *n.* نِظَارَة — مُبَاشَرَة — أَمَانَة — مُدِيرِيَّة .

Intendant, *n.* أُمَنَاءُ *pl.* أَمِين — مُدِير — نُظَّار *pl.* نَاظِر — مُبَاشِر — شُيُوخ *pl.* شَيْخُ بَلَدٍ . The mayor of a village, عُمَّال *pl.* عَامِل كَوَاتِب *pl.* كَاتِبَة . An — of customs, أَمِينُ ٱلْكُمْرُكِ . A general —, وَكِيلٌ مُطْلَقٌ .

Intended, *a.* Designed, مَقْصُود — مُرَاد — مُصَمَّم . An — marriage, نِكَاحٌ مُصَمَّمٌ . An — husband, عَرِيس ; an — wife, عَرُوسَة . *See also* Intentional, *a.*

Inteneration, *n.* تَلْيِين .

Intense, *a.* بَالِغ — شَدِيد — عَصِيب — شَعْث . Intense heat, حَارٌّ شَدِيدٌ . An — look, حَذْلَقَة — تَحْدِيقُ ٱلنَّظَرِ — بَصَرٌ شَاخِصٌ . Of — stupidity, بَالِغٌ فِي ٱلْحُمْقِ . To become —, of a colour, إِسْتَشْرَبَ : The cloth became of an — redness, إِسْتَشْرَبَ ٱلثَّوْبُ حُمْرَةً . The darkness of the night was —, إِعْتَكَرَ ٱللَّيْلُ . *See also* Attentive, *a.*

Intensely, *ad.* To a high degree, بِمُبَالَغَةٍ — لِلْغَايَةِ — بِشِدَّةٍ . With attention, بِدَوَرَانِ بَالٍ — بِتَقَيُّدٍ — بِٱنْتِبَاهٍ . To look at —, أَحَدَّ ٱلنَّظَرَ فِي . *See also* Intently, *ad.*

Intenseness, *n.* / Intensity, } مُبَالَغَة — إِفْرَاط — فَرْط — حِدَّة — شِدَّة .

Intensify, *v.t.* شَدَّدَ . To be intensified, إِشْتَدَّ .

Intensive, *a.* مُبَالِغ . An — noun, إِسْمُ مُبَالَغَةٍ .

Intensively, *ad.* بِمُبَالَغَةٍ .

Intent, *a.* Engaged in, مُقِيمٌ عَلَى — مُتَقَيِّد بِ — كَلِفٌ بِ — مُجِدٌّ فِي — مُوَاظِبٌ عَلَى — مَشْغُولٌ بِ — شَغِلٌ بِ . To be — on, جَدَّ فِي — تَقَيَّدَ بِ — أَقَامَ عَلَى .

Intent, *n.* A design, عَزِيمَة — مَرَام — نِيَّة . Meaning, مَحَطُّ ٱلْكَلَامِ — مَعْنًى — فَحْوَى . To all intents and purposes, مِنْ كُلِّ وَجْهٍ — عَلَى كُلِّ حَالٍ . To the — that, حَتَّى — لِأَجْلِ أَنْ . With the — of travelling, بِقَصْدِ ٱلسَّفَرِ . With bad —, بِنِيَّةٍ رَدِيَّةٍ .

Intention, *n.* A design, عَمْد — نَوَى — مَرَام — عَزِيمَة — هَمّ — أَغْرَاض *pl.* غَرَض — مَقْصُود — قَصْد — نِيَّة . A meaning, مَحَطُّ ٱلْكَلَامِ — مَضْمُون — فَحْوَى — مَعْنًى . It was his —, كَانَ فِي عَزْمِهِ . What is your —? عَلَى مَا عَزَمْتَ — مَاذَا فِي نِيَّتِكَ . With what —? بِأَيَّةِ نِيَّةٍ . A good —, نِيَّةٌ خَيْرٍ — سَدَد ; a bad —, نِيَّةٌ رَدِيَّةٌ — نِيَّةُ شَرٍّ . Actions are judged by intentions, (*prov.*) ٱلْأَعْمَالُ بِٱلنِّيَّاتِ . Against their —, ضِدُّ مَا ٱنْطَوَتْ عَلَيْهِ ضَمَائِرُهُمْ .

Intentional, *a.* إِخْتِيَارِيٌّ — عَمْدِيٌّ — قَصْدِيٌّ .

Intentionally, *ad.* إِخْتِيَارًا — قَصْدًا — عَمْدًا — عَلَى بَصِيرَةٍ .

Intentioned, *a.* رَائِم — قَاصِد — طَالِب — مُتَنَوٍّ — مُعْتَمِد . Well —, قَاصِدُ خَيْرٍ ; ill —, قَاصِدُ شَرٍّ .

Intently, *ad.* Attentively, بِتَقَيُّدٍ . Steadfastly, بِإِمْعَانٍ — بِمُوَاظَبَةٍ — بِمُلَازَمَةٍ . Eagerly, بِرَغْبَةٍ . To look —, فَقَصَ بِعَيْنَيْهِ . To look at —, أَمْعَنَ ٱلنَّظَرَ فِي — حَدَّ ٱلْبَصَرَ إِلَى . My eye became — fixed on him, شَخَصَ إِلَيْهِ بَصَرِي . The sight of the dying man became — fixed, شَخَصَ بَصَرُ ٱلْمَيِّتِ ـَ. His sight became — fixed towards the sky, شَخَصَ بِبَصَرِهِ إِلَى ٱلسَّمَآءِ ـَ.

Intentness, *n.* Close application, تَقَيُّد ـ دِقَّة ـ إِمْعَان ـ جِدّ ـ مُلَازَمَة.

Inter, *v.t.* *See to* Bury, *v.t.*

Intercalar, *a.* / Intercalary, } كَبِيس ـ مُضَاف. An — year, سَنَةٌ كَبِيسَةٌ ; an — day, يَوْمٌ كَبِيس ـ يَوْمٌ زَائِدٌ.

Intercalate, *v.t.* أَدْخَلَ ـ فِي ـ أَضَافَ ـ إِلَى ـ كَبَسَ ـِ.

Intercalation, *n.* ضَمّ ـ إِضَافَة ـ كَبِيس.

Intercede, *v.i.* To plead or pray for, شَفَعَ إِلَى ـ سَأَلَ ـ فِي ـَ or ب ـ فِي or تَشَفَّعَ إِلَى ـ فِي ب. He interceded, interposed, between the people, شَفَعَ بَيْنَ ٱلنَّاسِ ـَ.

Interceder, *n.* *See* Intercessor, *n.*

Intercellular, *a.* مَا تَخَلَّلَ نَسِيجَ ٱلْبَدَنِ ـ كَائِنٌ فِي أَلْيَافِ ٱلْبَدَنِ.

Intercept, *v.t.* To seize, ضَبَطَ ـِ ـ قَبَضَ عَلَى ـِ. To — the road, قَطَعَ ٱلطَّرِيقَ ـَ. To — a letter, إِخْتَلَسَ مَكْتُوبًا. To — the light, حَجَبَ ٱلنُّورَ ـُ ـ مَنَعَ ٱلنُّورَ ـَ. To arrest, stop, وَقَّفَ ـ أَوْقَفَ.

Interception, *n.* Seizure, أَخْذ ـ ضَبْط ـ قَبْض عَلَى ; as of a letter, إِخْتِلَاس. Prevention, as of light, *etc.*, مَنْع ـ حَجْز ـ حَجْب. Stoppage, تَوْقِيف.

Intercession, *n.* The act of interceding, شَفَاعَة ـ شَفْع. Mediation, تَوَسُّط ـ وَسَاطَة. To beg the — of another, إِسْتَشْفَعَ إِلَى. I asked — through him, إِسْتَشْفَعْتُ بِهِ. I accepted his — for him, شَفَّعْتُهُ بِهِ.

Intercessor, *n.* One who intercedes, شَفِيع ـ شَافِع *pl.* شُفَعَآء ـ مُشَفِّع ـ صَاحِبُ شَفَاعَةٍ. An — whose intercession is accepted, شَافِعٌ مُشَفَّعٌ. A mediator, وَسِيط ـ مُتَوَسِّط.

Intercessory, *a.* مُتَشَفِّع.

Interchange, *v.t.* To change by giving and receiving, بَادَلَ ـ قَابَلَ ـ ب ـ عَاوَضَ. To vary, غَيَّرَ ـ بَدَّلَ. To — letters with, رَاسَلَ ـ كَاتَبَ.

Interchange, *v.i.* To succeed alternately, تَخَالَفَ ـ تَعَاقَبَ ـ تَنَاوَبَ. To change alternately, تَبَادَلَ.

Interchange, *n.* Mutual change, تَبَادُل ـ مُبَادَلَة. Alternate succession, إِخْتِلَاف ـ تَخَالُف ـ مُنَاوَبَة ـ تَنَاوُب ; of letters, correspondence, مُكَاتَبَة ـ مُرَاسَلَة ; of courtesies, تَهْنِئَاتٌ بَيْنَ وَبَيْنَ. From the date of the — of this treaty, مِنْ تَارِيخِ تَعَاطِي هٰذِهِ ٱلْمُعَاهَدَةِ. The — of the treaty took place, جَرَتْ مُبَادَلَةُ ٱلْمُعَاهَدَةِ.

Interchangeability, *n.* / Interchangeableness, } إِمْكَانُ ٱلتَّبَادُلِ ـ إِمْكَانُ ٱلْمُبَادَلَةِ.

Interchangeable, *a.* مُتَبَادِل ـ قَابِلُ ٱلْمُبَادَلَةِ.

Interchangeably, *ad.* With mutual exchange, بِٱلْمُبَادَلَةِ. Alternately, بِٱلْمُنَاوَبَةِ.

Intercipient, *a.* Obstructing, مُعْتَرِض ـ مَنَّاع ـ عَائِق ـ مَانِع.

Interclude, *v.t.* *See to* Intercept, *v.t.*

Interclusion, *n.* *See* Interception, *n.*

Intercolumniation, *n.* مَا بَيْنَ ٱلْعُمُدِ مِنَ ٱلْمَسَافَةِ فِي ٱلْبِنَآءِ.

Intercommune, *v.t.* To commune together, of many, تَقَاوَلُوا ـ تَشَاوَرُوا ـ إِيتَمَرُوا ـ تَرَاجَعُوا. To associate with, شَارَكَ ـ عَاشَرَ ـ رَافَقَ. To hold converse with the enemy, خَالَطَ ٱلْعَدُوَّ.

Intercommunicate, *v.t.* *See to* Intercommune, *v.t.*

Intercommunicate, *v.i.* To hold mutual communion, of many, تَعَاشَرُوا ـ تَخَالَطُوا. To — secretly, تَسَارُّوا. To —, as rooms, roads, يُفْضِي بَعْضُهَا إِلَى بَعْضٍ.

Intercommunication, *n.* Reciprocal communication, مُعَاشَرَة ـ أَخْذٌ وَعَطَآءٌ ـ مُخَالَطَة ; as between rooms, ways, *etc.*, مَنْفِذٌ بَيْنَ *pl.* مَنَافِذُ.

Intercommunion, *n.* Mutual participation of the Lord's Supper, إِشْتِرَاكٌ فِي مُنَاوَلَةِ ٱلْقُرْبَانِ ; between Churches, الِاشْتِرَاكُ بَيْنَ ٱلْكَنَائِسِ. *See also* Intercommunication, *n.*

Intercommunity, *n.* إِشْتِرَاك ـ شَرَاكَة.

Intercostal, *a.* مَا كَانَ بَيْنَ ٱلضُّلُوعِ.

Intercourse, *n.* مُصَاحَبَة ـ مُعَاشَرَة ـ مُخَالَطَة. Social —, أُلْفَة ـ أُنْسَة ـ أُنْس ـ أُدْمَة. Intercourse by letter, مُكَاتَبَة ـ مُرَاسَلَة. Sexual or carnal —, نِكَاح ـ جِمَاع ـ مُجَامَعَة. To hold — with, صَاحَبَ ـ عَاشَرَ ـ خَالَطَ. To hold — with by letter, كَاتَبَ ـ رَاسَلَ. To be in constant — with, وَاصَلَ ـ لَازَمَ. To have carnal — with, جَامَعَ ـ نَاكَ ـُ ـ نَكَحَ ـِ ـ أَدْخَلَ ب. *See also* Correspondence, *n.*

Intercurrent, *n.* وَاقِعٌ بَيْنَ ـ كَائِنٌ بَيْنَ.

Interdict, *v.t.* To prohibit to, حَرَمَ ـِ ٱلشَّيْءَ ـ مَنَعَ ـَ عَنْ ـ قَطَعَ ـَ عَنْ شِرْكَتِهِ ـ نَهَى ـَ عَنْ. To excommunicate, حَرَمَ ـِ ٱلْكَنِيسَةِ.

Interdict, *n.* A prohibition, مَنْعٌ عَنْ ـ نَهْي ـ حِرْمَةٌ عَنْ. A papal —, حَرْمٌ مِنَ ٱلْبَابَا بِهِ يَمْنَعُ ٱلْإِكْلِيرُوسَ عَنْ قِيَامِ ٱلصَّلَوَاتِ وَمَنْحِ ٱلْأَسْرَارِ لِلْمُؤْمِنِينَ.

Interdicted, *a.* مَحْرُوم ـ مَمْنُوع ـ مُنْهًى.

Interdiction, *n.* مَنْع ـ مُمَانَعَة ـ نَهْي.

Interdictive, *a.* مانِع – مَنَّاع.

Interdictory, *a.* يَمْنَعُ – يَنْهَى.

Interest, *v.t.* To inspire with emotion for, رَغَّبَ-فِي – أَرْغَبَ-فِي – إِسْتَمَالَ-بِ. To give a share in, أَشْرَكَ-فِي – أَدْخَلَ-فِي – نَفَعَ-بِ – خَصَّ-بِ. To touch, to move with compassion, حَنَّنَ – حَرَّكَ فِي-الشَّفَقَةَ. To — one's self for, رَغِبَ فِي – تَعَطَّفَ عَلَى – كَلِفَ بِ. To — one's self in, to take part in, تَدَاخَلَ فِي. What does this — you? ماذا لَكَ فِي هٰذا.

Interest, *s.* Concern felt in any matter, رَغْبَةٌ فِي – غَيْرَةٌ عَلَى – حُسْنُ الاِهْتِمامِ بِ. A share possessed, حِصَّةٌ *pl.* حِصَص – شِرْكٌ – نائِب. A premium paid for use of money, مُرابَحَة – رِبْح – فائدة *pl.* فَوائِد. Interest, pleasure, such as attaches to a book, *etc.*, لَذَّة – ذَوْق – تَعَجُّب. Commotion, surprise, إِرْتِجاج. Power, influence, إِعْتِبار – نُفُوذ. Connexion with an affair, عَلاقَة – غَرَض – نائِب. A part taken in favour of one, تَعَصُّبٌ لِ; against one, تَعَصُّبٌ عَلَى. An affair of great —, أَمْرٌ مُهِمٌّ. Interests, profit, advantages, نَفْع – مَنافِعُ – فائِدة *pl.* فَوائِد. Interests, what particularly concerns one, أَغْراض – مَصالِحُ. His interests are my interests, أَغْراضُهُ أَغْراضِي – ما يَنْفَعُهُ يَنْفَعُنِي وَما يَضُرُّهُ يَضُرُّنِي. Sects having different interests, طَوائِفُ مُخْتَلِفَةُ الأَغْراضِ. They care for nothing but their own interests, لا يَعْنِيهِمْ إِلَّا خَيْرُ أَطْوارِهِمْ. I have no —, part, in this matter, ما لِي عَلاقَةٌ فِي هٰذِهِ المادَّةِ. The interest of the tale — is gone, بَقِيَتِ الحِكايَةُ بِلا لَذَّةٍ – قَدْ مُسِخَتْ لَذَّةُ الحِكايَةِ. At seven per cent. —, بِفائِدَةٍ سَبْعَةٍ فِي المِئَةِ. Not by — or favouritism, لا بِالوَسائِطِ وَمُراعاةِ الخَواطِرِ. British interests, مَصالِحُ الدَّوْلَةِ الإِنْكِلِيزِيَّةِ – مَصالِحُ الإِنْكِلِيزِ – خَيْراتُ الإِنْكِلِيزِ.

High interest, فَوائِدُ جَسِيمَةٌ.

Low interest, فَوائِدُ قَلِيلَةٌ. He lends money at low interest, يُسْلِفُ دَراهِمَ بِفَوائِدَ قَلِيلَةٍ.

Material interests, فَوائِدُ مادِّيَّةٌ.

Political interests, فَوائِدُ سِياسِيَّةٌ – مَنافِعُ مَلَكِيَّةٌ.

Private interests, مَنافِعُ – ما هُوَ لِنَفْسِهِ – مَنافِعُ مَخْصُوصَةٌ خُصُوصِيَّةٌ.

Public interests, المَنافِعُ العُمُومِيَّةُ – المَنافِعُ العامَّةُ.

To attend to one's own interests, إِعْتَنَى – راعَى ما يَصْلُحُ لِنَفْسِهِ بِما يَخُصُّهُ.

To be in a person's interest, on his side, مَسَكَ – تَعَصَّبَ لِ طَرَفَهُ.

To be to a person's interest, نَفَعَ بِ – إِنْتَفَعَ مِن – أَفادَ.

To bear interest, أَعْطَى فائِدَةً.

To borrow at interest, تَدَيَّنَ بِالفائِدَةِ.

To feel an interest for one, تَعَطَّفَ عَلَى – رَغِبَ فِي – إِهْتَمَّ بِ.

To give an interest to a thing, داوَرَ – عالَجَ – رَوَّجَ – نَجَّحَ – وَشَّى – أَوْشَى.

To give one's interest to a person, وَفَّقَ – أَعانَ – نَجَّحَ – صَرَفَ نُفُوذَهُ لِأَجْلِهِ.

To have an interest, share, in an undertaking, لَهُ حِصَّةٌ فِي – لَهُ نَصِيبٌ فِي – لَهُ تَداخُلٌ فِي.

To lose one's interest in, فَتَرَ عَن.

To make interest with a person, إِكْتَسَبَ – إِسْتَمالَ-إِلَى – إِسْتَمْلَكَ – عَطَفَ-عَلَى.

To pay with interest, or usury, دَفَعَ المَبْلَغَ وَالفائِدَةَ. To requite, ضاعَفَ-لِ – جازَى.

To prejudice the interests of one, أَجْحَفَ بِمَنافِعِهِ.

To promote the interests of another, وَفَّقَ – رَوَّجَ بِ – نَفَعَ.

To put out money to interest, حَطَّ الدَّراهِمَ بِالفائِدَةِ – شَغَّلَ الفُلُوسَ.

To secure one's interest in, عَطَفَ-عَلَى – إِسْتَمالَ-إِلَى – إِكْتَسَبَ التَّوْفِيقَ مِن.

To solicit a person's interest in, تَشَفَّعَ إِلَى-فِي – تَوَسَّلَ إِلَى-فِي – إِسْتَعْطَفَ-عَلَى.

To take an interest in a thing, رَغِبَ فِي – إِشْتاقَ إِلَى – غارَ عَلَى.

Interested, *a.* Having an interest or share in, لَهُ شَرِيكٌ فِي – لَهُ حِصَّةٌ فِي – لَهُ عَلاقَةٌ فِي – نائِبٌ فِي. Feeling a concern in, لَهُ رَغْبَةٌ فِي – راغِبٌ فِي. Feeling a pleasure in, مُلْتَذٌّ بِ. Having gain from, لَهُ مَصالِحُ فِي – لَهُ فائِدَةٌ فِي. Self-interested, صاحِبُ غَرَضٍ – طَمّاع – حَرِيص – يُحِبُّ الكَسْبَ وَلا يَطْلُبُ إِلَّا المَنْفَعَةَ.

Interesting, *a.* Which moves, affects, مُرَغِّب – مُسْتَمِيل. Pleasant, لَذِيذ – لَطِيف. Captivating, مُسْلِبُ العَقْلِ – مُتَرَوِّق. Important, مُهِمّ – أَهَمّ.

Interfere, *v.t.* To intermeddle with, *or* تَداخَلَ *or*) دَخَلَ فِي – تَدَخَّلَ – قارَشَ – حَشَرَ حالَهُ فِيما لا يَعْنِيهِ. To — between so as to excite discord, دَحَسَ بَيْنَ – قَرَّشَ بَيْنَ. To interrupt, oppose, تَعَرَّضَ لِ – مَنَعَ. To injure, molest, حَكَرَ – جَحَفَ – أَجْحَفَ بِ – ضَرَّ – أَضَرَّ. They did not — with his assailant, لَمْ يَتَعَرَّضُوا لِضارِبِهِ. *See also to* Intercept, *v.t.*, *to* Intermeddle, *v.i.*

Interference, *n.* Intermeddling, ـ دُخُول ـ مُدَاخَلَة ـ تَدَخُّل ـ إِجْحَاف ـ جَحْف ـ حَكْر . Opposition, فُضُول ـ مُقَارَشَة ـ بَيْنَ تَعَرُّض ل ـ مُضَادَّة . Mediation, تَوَسُّط .

Interfering, *a.* Meddling, ـ وِعَنّ ـ مِتْيَاح ـ تَيِّحَان ـ عِرِّيْض فُضُولِيّ . Molesting, injuring, جَاحِف ـ حَكِر .

Interferingly, *ad.* ـ بِنَوْعٍ فُضُولِيّ ـ بِٱلْمُقَارَشَةِ ـ بِٱلْمُدَاخَلَةِ بِٱلْفُضُولِ .

Interfluent, *a.* جَارٍ بَيْنَ .

Interfulgent, *a.* لَامِعٌ بَيْنَ .

Interfused, *a.* Poured between, صَبِيبٌ بَيْنَ; spread between, مَنْشُورٌ بَيْنَ .

Interim, *n.* A time, midst, ـ مُدَّة ـ غُضُون ـ حِين ـ أَثْنَآء . In the —, فِي هٰذِهِ ٱلْمُدَّةِ; for a time, مُوَقَّتًا ـ وَقْتًا . He carried on the office in the —, أَجْرَى ٱلْمَأْمُورِيَّةَ مُوَقَّتًا . He came in the —, جَآءَ فِي أَثْنَآءِ ذٰلِكَ .

Interim, *a.* مُوَقَّت . An — governor, lieutenant, ـ قَائِمُ مَقَامٍ نَائِبُ ٱلْغَيْبَةِ .

Interior, *a.* Internal, جَوَّانِيّ ـ بَاطِن ـ دَاخِلِيّ ـ دَاخِل . Inland, بَعِيدٌ عَنِ ٱلْبَحْرِ ـ دَاخِلُ ٱلْبَرِّ . Internal administration, إِدَارَةٌ دَاخِلِيَّةٌ . Minister of the —, نَاظِرُ ٱلدَّاخِلِيَّةِ . Ministry of the —, نَظَارَةُ ٱلدَّاخِلِيَّةِ . Commerce of the —, ٱلتِّجَارَةُ ٱلدَّاخِلِيَّةُ .

Interior, *n.* The inside of anything, جَوْف ـ بَاطِن ـ دَاخِل . What is contained within, ضِمْن . The — of a country, دَاخِل ـ ٱلْأَطْرَافُ ٱلْبَعِيدَةُ عَنِ ٱلسَّوَاحِلِ ـ ٱلْجَوَّانِيُّ ـ ٱلْبَلَدِ .

Interjacency, *n.* The being between, وُقُوعٌ بَيْنَ . Lying near; *see* Adjacency, *n.*

Interjacent, *a.* Lying between, كَائِنٌ بَيْنَ ـ وَاقِعٌ بَيْنَ . *See also* Adjacent, *a.*

Interject, *v.t.* *See to* Insert, *v.t.*

Interjection, *n.* A word of exclamation, صَوْت *pl.* ـ أَصْوَات حَرْفُ نِدَآءٍ . To utter interjections, صَوَّتَ ـ ء ـ صَاتَ . *See also* Exclamation, *n.*

Interjectional, *a.* بِٱلنِّدَآءِ ـ صَائِت .

Interknit, *v.t.* عَقَّدَ ـ مَعَ بَعْضٍ ـ نَسَجَ ـ ء .

Interlace, *v.t.* شَبَّكَ ـ وَشَّجَ . To be interlaced, وَشَجَ *aor.* ـ يَشِجُ إِنْشَبَكَ . Interlaced, مُشَبَّك .

Interlard, *v.t.* To insert, أَدْخَلَ ـ فِي ـ أَدْرَجَ ـ فِي . To embellish, of speech, بَزَّرَ (*or* زَخْرَفَ *or* تَوَبَّلَ *or* رَمَّقَ) ٱلْكَلَامَ . To —, embellish, as with colours, *etc.*, وَشَّى ـ دَبَّجَ ـ رَقَّشَ .

Interleave, *v.t.* يَحْشُو *aor.* حَشَا طَرْحِيَّةَ وَرَقٍ أَبْيَضَ بَيْنَ كُلِّ وَرَقَتَيْ كِتَابٍ .

Interline, *v.t.* To write between lines, ء كَتَبَ بَيْنَ ٱلسُّطُورِ; of marginal notes, حَشَّى .

Interlinear, *a.* } مَكْتُوبٌ بَيْنَ ٱلسُّطُورِ . Interlinear or marginal
Interlineary, } notes, أَصْنَافُ ٱلْكِتَابِ ـ حَوَاشٍ . *See also* Interspace, *n.*

Interlineation, *n.* The act of writing between the lines, ٱلْكِتَابَةُ بَيْنَ ٱلسُّطُورِ . What is written between lines, ٱلْمَكْتُوبُ بَيْنَ ٱلسُّطُورِ .

Interlink, *v.t.* سَلْسَلَ .

Interlocution, *n.* A conference, dialogue, ـ مُكَالَمَة ـ مُسَامَرَة مُحَاوَرَة ـ مُخَاطَبَة . *In law,* إِعْلَامٌ بِفَصْلٍ ـ إِعْلَامٌ بِقَرَارٍ مُوَقَّتٍ غَيْرِ بَتِّيّ .

Interlocutor, *n.* A speaker in a dialogue, ـ مُسَاوِر ـ مُتَكَلِّم مُخَاطِب . *In law; see* Interlocution, *n.*

Interlocutory, *a.* Consisting of dialogue, مِنْ قَبِيلِ ٱلْمُحَاوَرَةِ . *In law,* مُوَقَّت ـ غَيْرُ بَتِّيّ .

Interlope, *v.i.* To come in furtively, إِنْدَسَّ . To exercise artifice against, إِحْتَالَ عَلَى . To encroach upon, ـ إِعْتَدَى عَلَى أَجْحَفَ بِ ـ تَعَدَّى عَلَى .

Interloper, *n.* One who comes in furtively, دَسِيس *pl.* دُسُس . An encroacher, مُخْتَلِس ـ جَائِز ـ جَائِر ـ هَاوِط . *See also* Intruder, *n.*

Interlude, *n.* فَصْلٌ بَيْنَ فُصُولِ ٱللَّعْبِ فِي ٱلتِّيَاتْرُو .

Interlunar, *a.* وَاقِعٌ فِي مَحَاقِ ٱلْقَمَرِ .

Intermarriage, *n.* تَزَاوُج ـ إِزْدِوَاج .

Intermarry, *v.i.* تَزَاوَجَ ـ إِزْدَوَجَ .

Intermeddle, *v.i.* To interfere with, قَارَشَ ـ تَدَاخَلَ فِي . To occupy one's self about, تَعَنَّى ـ تَعَاطَى ـ تَعَطَّى . He intermeddles with what does not concern him, يَحْشُرُ حَالَهُ فِيمَا لَا يَعْنِيهِ . *See also to* Interfere, *v.i.*

Intermeddler, *n.* } ـ فُضُولِيّ ـ وِعَنَّة *fem.* وِعَنّ ـ عِرِّيْض ـ تَيَّاح
Intermeddling, *a.* } مُتَكَلِّف .

Intermeddling, *n.* مُقَارَشَة ـ فُضُول ـ تَدَاخُل ـ مُدَاخَلَة .

Intermedial, *a.* } Lying between, وَسْطَانِيّ ـ كَائِنٌ بَيْنَ ـ مُتَوَسِّط .
Intermediate, }

Intermediately, *ad.* بِٱلْوَاسِطَةِ ـ بِٱلتَّوَسُّطِ .

Intermediation, *n.* As between parties, وَسَاطَة ـ تَوَسُّطٌ بَيْنَ .

Intermedium, *n.* وَسِيط .

Interment, *n.* *See* Burial, *n.*

Interminable, *a.* دائم ـ لا حدّ له ـ لا ينتهي ـ غير متناهٍ.

Interminably, *ad.* بلا نهايةٍ ـ دائمًا ـ بالدوام ـ بلا انقطاعٍ.

Intermingle, *v.t.* To mingle together, خلط ـ مازج ـ شمّط. To confuse, خبّص ـ لبّك ـ شبّك.

Intermingle, *v.i.* To mingle together, امتزج ـ اختلط. To be or become confused, تخبّص ـ التبك ـ تشبّك.

Intermission, *n.* Cessation for a time, توقّف ـ ونيرة ـ مُقلع ـ فترة; as between heat and cold, فصية. Intervenient time, غضون ـ وقتٌ موقّتٌ. Discontinuance, انقطاع. The — of a pulse, انقطاع النبض مدّةً من الزمان ـ فترة النبض. The — of a fever, إقلاع من الحمّى ـ قلاع *pl.* قلع. Without —, بلا توقّف ـ على الاتّصال ـ بالتوالي ـ بلا انقطاع.

Intermissive, *a.* *See* Intermittent, *a.*

Intermit, *v.t.* To cause to cease for a time, ـ ٢ قطّع ـ موقّتًا ـ أبقى ـ إلى غير وقتٍ. To postpone, أخّر ـ موقّتًا ـ وقّف.

Intermit, *v.i.* انقطع زمنًا ـ توقّف. To —, as in violence, ٢ فتر ـ ٢ خفّ ـ ارتخى.

Intermittent, *a.* تارةً ينقطع وتارةً يعود يظهر ـ مغبّ. An — fever, حمّى دائرة ـ حمّى غبّ. An — disease, مرض عداد.

Intermixture, *n.* امتزاج ـ اختلاط ـ خلط.

Intermontane, *a.* بين الجبال.

Intermundane, *a.* بين العالمين.

Intermural, *a.* في داخل الأسوار ـ في داخل الحيطان.

Internal, *a.* داخليّ ـ داخل ـ باطن. An — remedy, علاجٌ داخليّ. *See also* Interior, *a.*

Internally, *ad.* جوًّا ـ في الباطن ـ في الداخل.

International, *a.* Existing and regulating between nations, جارٍ ومرعى بين الدول. International law, rights, حقوق مليّة ـ قاعدة مللٍ ـ قاعدة دولٍ ـ حقوق دوليّة. International inquiry, تحقيقات مشتركة دوليّة. An — question, مسألة عن حقوقٍ مليّة. International trade, أخذ وعطاء بين الملل. International principles, الأصول المتعارفة بين الأمم.

Internecine, *a.* جارف ـ مهلك ـ قتّال ـ قاتل.

Internode, *n.* A knot in a cane or straw, معقِم *pl.* معاقِم ـ أنبوب *pl.* أنابيب.

Internodial, *a.* ذو أنابيب.

Inter nos, ad. فيما بيننا.

Internuncio, *n.* A message between two parties, طالع بين طرفين. An ambassador, سفير *pl.* سفراء. A papal —, نائب البابا.

Interpellation, *n.* A question put, سؤال *pl.* سؤالات ـ استفسار ـ مكالمة ـ مخاطبة ـ مقالة. An address, طلب جواب. A judicial —, استنطاق. A summons, دعوة; a suit, دعوى *pl.* دعاوى. To put an — to, سأل *aor.* يسأل ـ استفسر ـ أقبل على ـ بالكلام وطلب جوابًا; to do so judicially, استنطق.

Interpenetrate, *v.t.* ٢ نفذ ـ بين ـ أدخل ـ بين.

Interplead, *v.i.* احتجّ بمسألةٍ على الدعوى قبل فصلها.

Interpleader, *n.* استفتاء المديون القاضي لأيّ من الخصمين ينبغي أن يدفع الدين.

Interpledge, *v.t.* تعاهدوا على.

Interpolate, *v.t.* To foist in, ٢ حشا ـ أدرج. *See also to* Insert, *v.t.*

Interpolation, *n.* The act of foisting in, حشو ـ إدراج; what is interpolated, مدرج.

Interpolator, *n.* مدرج ـ حاشٍ.

Interposal, *n.* *See* Interposition, *n.*

Interpose, *v.t.* To place between, ـ ٢ جعل ـ بين ـ وسّط ـ أدخل ـ بين. To —, or offer service to, قدّم له الخدمة. To make something a means to, جعله وسيلةً إلى. To —, or bring in, the name of one, ٢ جاء باسمه ـ جاء بذكره. To — difficulties, ٢ جاء بالمشكلات.

Interpose, *v.i.* To step in as a mediator, ٢ دخل ـ توسّط بين ـ قارش ـ تداخل في ـ تدخّل في ـ بين. To mix one's self up with, To come in, to occur, as of a sentence, اعترض. To pass, revolve, ـ أحول حول ـ أحال عام. A year interposed, حال *aor.* يحول: To —, or intercede, with one in behalf of..., تشفّع إلى ـ ب *or* في. Interposing, or coming in, between, معترض. An interposed sentence, جملة معترضة. *See also to* Intervene, *v.i.*

Interposition, *n.* Interference, وساطة ـ مداخلة ـ توسّط. Mediation, مواسطة ـ توسّط. The — of a sentence, اعتراض. The coming between, دخول بين. Assistance, إمداد ـ خدمة. Intercession, تشفّع. To ask the —, assistance, of, ـ استمدّ ـ استعان ب ـ استعان.

Interpret, *v.t.* To explain the meaning of words, ترجم. To explain, expound, فسّر ـ عبّر. To take a thing in a particular sense, أوّل. To —, or take in a good sense, استحسن; in bad part or sense, استقبح ـ استصعب.

Interpretable, *a.* قابل الترجمة ـ ممّا يفسّر ـ ممّا يترجم.

Interpretation, *n.* The act of interpreting, ترجمة. Explanation, meaning, بَيَان ـ مَعْنَى ـ تَفْسِير ـ تَعْبِير ـ تَأْوِيل . The — of a dream, تَأْوِيل حُلْم . A result, عاقِبَة ـ تَأْوِيل .

Interpretative, *a.* تَفْسِيرِيّ ـ تَأْوِيلِيّ .

Interpreter, *n.* As of a language, تَرَاجِمُونَ or تَرَاجِم *pl.* تَرْجُمَان . A translator, مُتَرْجِم An expounder, مُعَبِّر ـ مُفَسِّر .

Interred, *a.* مَدْفُون ـ دَفِين . *See also to* Bury, *v.t.*

Interregnum, *n.* فَتْرَة زَمَانٍ بَيْنَ مَلِكٍ وَخَلِيفَتِهِ ـ فَتْرَة . There is an — among them, as not having a leader, أَمْرُهُمْ فَضَى بَيْنَهُمْ .

Interrex, *n.* قائِمُ مَقامِ ٱلْمَلِكِ مُدَّةَ غِيابِهِ ـ نائِبُ ٱلسَّلْطَنَةِ .

Interrogate, *v.t.* سَأَلَ *aor.* يَسْأَلُ ـ طالَبَ ـ إِسْتَفْهَمَ . To — about, طالَبَ ب ـ سَأَلَ عَن . To — judicially, إِسْتَنْطَقَ .

Interrogation, *n.* Examination by questions, إِمْتِحانٌ بِمَسَائِلَ ; judicially, إِسْتِنْطاق . A question, سُؤالات *pl.* سُؤَال ـ مُطالَبَة ـ مَسْأَلَة *pl.* مَسائِل ـ مَسائِل ـ إِسْتِفْهام . A point of —, نُقْطَة لِلْإِسْتِفْهامِ ـ عَلامَة ٱلْإِسْتِفْهامِ .

Interrogative, *a.* مُتَضَمِّنُ سُؤالٍ ـ إِسْتِفْهامِيّ .

Interrogatively, *ad.* بِطَرِيقَةِ ٱلْإِسْتِفْهامِ ـ بِٱلسُّؤالِ .

Interrogator, *n.* مُخاطِب ـ مُسْتَفْهِم ـ سائِل ; a judicial —, مُسْتَنْطِق .

Interrogatory, *n.* A question; *see* Interrogation. The — of a judge, questions asked by him and answered by the accused, مَسائِلُ (or إِسْتِنْطاقُ) ٱلْقاضِي وَجَوابات ٱلْمَتْهُومِ .

Interrogatory, *a.* *See* Interrogative, *a.*

In terrorem, ad. تَهْدِيدًا ـ تَخْوِيفًا .

Interrupt, *v.t.* To prevent, hinder, أَوْقَفَ ـ وَقَّفَ ـ عَكَظَ . To break continuity, صَرَمَ وَصْلَهُ ـ قَطَعَ ـ عَوَّقَ ـ مَنَعَ . To cause one to suspend his work, عَطَّلَ ـ أَقْعَدَ ـ عَوَّقَ . To —, in the sense of marring, أَجْحَفَ ب ـ أَخَلَّ ب . To oppose, interfere with, تَعَرَّضَ ل . To — the speech of another, قَطَعَ (or صَرَمَ) كَلامَهُ . It will not — tranquillity, لا يُخِلُّ بِٱلرَّاحَةِ .

Interruptedly, *ad.* With interruptions, hindrances, بِتَوْقِيف ـ بِتَعَرُّضٍ ـ بِمَوانِعَ . With hindrances, as from work, بِتَعْوِيقٍ ـ بِتَعْطِيلٍ . With a stoppage, as of continuity, بِٱنْقِطاعٍ . With breaches or marring, بِخَلَلٍ .

Interruption, *n.* A breaking up, as of continuity, إِنْقِطاع . A breach, خَلَل ـ خِلال . A stoppage, hindrance, عُرْضَة ـ عائِق . Opposition, interference, تَعَرُّض . An — such as hinders and mars, إِجْحاف ـ خَلَل ـ إِخْلال . An —, as of business, تَعْوِيق ـ تَعْطِيل . An — of political relations, إِنْقِطاعُ ٱلْمُواصَلاتِ ٱلسِّياسِيَّةِ ; of trade, إِنْقِطاعُ مُعامَلاتِ ٱلْأَخْذِ وَٱلْعَطاءِ . To prevent any — to the navigation of the river, لِمَنْعِ خَلَلِ ٱلسَّفَرِ فِي ٱلنَّهْرِ . It will cause the — of peace, يَكُونُ سَبَبًا لِلْإِخْلالِ بِٱلسِّلْمِ . Without —, or intervention, مِنْ غَيْرِ تَخَلُّلٍ .

Interruptive, *a.* Preventing, عائِق ـ مانِع ; causing a stoppage, suppression, مُوَقِّف ـ مُعَوِّق ـ مُعَطِّل ; marring, causing breaches, جاحِف ـ مُخِلّ ـ مُجْحِف ب .

Interruptively, *ad.* With hindrance, بِمُمانَعَةٍ ; with opposition, بِتَعَرُّضٍ ـ تَعَرُّضًا ; with arrest, as of business, بِتَعْطِيلٍ ـ تَعْوِيقًا ; with breaches of continuity, بِتَخَلُّلٍ ; as causing injury, marring, بِإِخْلالٍ ـ إِجْحافًا .

Interscapular, *a.* كائِنٌ بَيْنَ ٱلْأَكْتافِ ـ ما نِيطَ بِٱلْكاهِلِ ـ كائِنٌ بَيْنَ لَوْحَي ٱلْأَكْتافِ .

Interscribe, *v.t.* *See to* Interline, *v.t.*

Intersect, *v.t.* To divide, قَطَعَ ـ قَسَمَ . To cause to cross, to interweave, شَبَّكَ ـ نَسَجَ . To run between, as of a river, *etc.*, جَرَى بَيْنَ .

Intersect, *v.i.* To meet and cross, as of lines, إِشْتَبَكُوا ـ تَقاطَعُوا ـ نَاسَجَ بَعْضُهُ بَعْضًا .

Intersection, *n.* The act of crossing, as of lines, تَقاطُع ـ تَشابُك . A point of —, خَطٌّ (or مَحَلُّ) ٱلتَّقاطُعِ ـ مَقْطَع .

Interspace, *n.* The space between the lines, as of a book, *etc.*, أَضْعافُ ٱلْكِتابِ . Such an one made notes, or entries, in the interspaces of his book, وَقَّعَ فُلانٌ فِي أَضْعافِ كِتابِهِ .

Intersperse, *v.t.* To scatter among, بَذَرَ (or بَذَّرَ) بَيْنَ ـ بَثَّ (or بَثَّثَ) فِي . To — with jewels, رَصَّعَ بِٱلْجَواهِرِ . To be interspersed among, إِنْبَثَّ بَيْنَ ـ تَبَذَّرَ بَيْنَ . Interspersed with jewels, مُرَصَّع بِٱلْجَواهِرِ .

Interspersion, *n.* The act of, بَثّ ـ بَذْر (or تَبْذِير) بَيْنَ (or تَبْثِيث) بَيْنَ ; as with jewels, تَرْصِيع ب .

Interstellar, *a.* }
Interstellary, } مُخْتَصّ ـ كائِنٌ ما بَيْنَ ٱلْكَواكِبِ ٱلثَّابِتَةِ بِٱلنُّجُومِ .

Interstice, *n.* A space between, خِلال ـ خَلَل ـ فُرْجَة .

Interstitial, *a.* مُتَعَلِّق بِٱلْخِلالِ ـ خَلَلِيّ .

Interstratified, *a.* ما تَخَلَّلَ بَيْنَ طَبَقاتِ ٱلشَّيْءِ .

Intertexture, *n.* The act of interweaving, تَشْبِيكُ ٱلنَّسِيجِ ; the state of things interwoven, نَسِيجَة ـ مُناسَجَة ـ إِشْتِباكُ ٱلنَّسِيجِ .

Intertropical, *a.* واقِعٌ بَيْنَ مَدارِ ٱلسَّرَطانِ وَمَدارِ ٱلْجَدْيِ .

Intertwine, *v.t.* }
Intertwist, } عَقَّدَ ـ حَبَّكَ ـ شَبَّكَ ـ وَشَجَ . To be or become intertwined, وَشَجَ *aor.* يَشِجُ ـ تَحَبَّكَ ـ إِشْتَبَكَ ـ إِنْشَبَكَ .

Interval, *n.* Of time, زَمَان ـ مُدَّة ـ فَتْرَة. In the — of this time, فِي أَثْنَاءِ هٰذِهِ ٱلْمُدَّةِ. During this —, فِي خِلَالِ هٰذِهِ ٱلْمُدَّةِ. An — of place, مَسَافَة ـ قِبَآء *pl.* مَسَافَات. An intervening blank space, خِلَال. A division, مُنْفَرَج ـ إِنْفِرَاج ـ فَاصِلَة. At intervals, أَنْفَاسًا ـ خَطْرَةً بَعْدَ خَطْرَةٍ ـ بُعَيْدَاتِ بَيْنٍ : she laughed at intervals, ضَحِكَتْ خَطْرَةً بَعْدَ خَطْرَةٍ (or بُعَيْدَاتِ بَيْنٍ). A long — of time, مُلَاوَة *See also* Gap, *n.*

Intervene, *v.i.* To mix one's self in an affair, تَدَاخَلَ فِي ـ تَوَسَّطَ بَيْنَ ـ تَعَرَّضَ ـ قَارَشَ. To — as a mediator between . . . , دَخَلَ بَيْنَ [2]. To —, as an obstacle to, إِعْتَرَضَ ل ـ = عَرَضَ ل. An obstacle intervened, = عَرَضَ عَارِضٌ. To run or pass between, حَالَ بَيْنَ ـ = فَصَلَ بَيْنَ *aor.* مَرَّ بَيْنَ [2] ـ = جَرَى بَيْنَ. To divide, يَحُولُ: The river intervened between us, حَالَ النَّهْرُ بَيْنَنَا [2]. The thing intervened as an obstacle to the thing, حَالَ [2] (or إِعْتَرَضَ) ٱلشَّيْءُ دُونَ ٱلشَّيْءِ. Know ye that God intervenes between man and his heart, وَٱعْلَمُوا أَنَّ ٱللّٰهَ يَحُولُ بَيْنَ ٱلْمَرْءِ وَقَلْبِهِ (*Kur.* viii. 24.) *See also to* Interpose, *v.i.*

Intervenient, *a.* جَارٍ بَيْنَ ـ عَارِض ـ دَاخِلٌ بَيْنَ ـ وَاقِعٌ بَيْنَ. An — vacant space, خَلَل ـ رَهْو ـ خَوًى ـ خَوَآء *pl.* خِلَال.

Intervention, *n.* The coming between, دُخُول بَيْنَ. Mediation, وَسَاطَة ـ تَوَسُّط. Interference, مُقَارَشَة ـ مُدَاخَلَة. Aid, مُعَاوَنَة ـ إِسْعَاف. Intercession for, شَفَاعَة ـ تَشَفُّعٌ فِي. Armed —, وَسَاطَةٌ حَرْبِيَّةٌ ـ تَوَسُّطٌ حَرْبِيٌّ. Collective —, وَسَاطَةٌ مُشْتَرَكَةٌ. Secret —, وَسَاطَةٌ سِرِّيَّةٌ. The right of —, حَقُّ ٱلْمُدَاخَلَةِ. Non-intervention, عَدَمُ ٱلْمُدَاخَلَةِ. The principle of non-intervention, قَاعِدَةُ عَدَمِ ٱلْمُدَاخَلَةِ. Through his —, بِوَاسِطَتِهِ. With the — of the authorities, بِمُعَاوَنَةِ ٱلْمَأْمُورِيَّةِ ـ بِمُعَاوَنَةِ ٱلْحُكُومَةِ.

Intervertebral, *a.* كَائِنٌ بَيْنَ ٱلْخَرَزِ.

Interview, *n.* مُوَاصَلَة ـ مُوَاجَهَة ـ مُلَاقَاة. A colloquy, مُكَالَمَة. To have an — with, وَاجَهَ ـ لَاقَى. To have a colloquy with, كَالَمَ. He was honoured with an — with the Sultan, تَشَرَّفَ بِمُقَابَلَةِ حَضْرَةِ ٱلسُّلْطَانِ. He had an — with, or met, him, تَلَاقَى مَعَهُ.

Intervolve, *v.t.* وَشَّجَ ـ شَبَّكَ. *See also to* Intertwine, *v.t.*

Interweave, *v.t.* = نَسَجَ [2] ـ = نَسَجَ مَعَ [2].

Intestable, *a.* Not qualified to make a will, غَيْرُ صَالِحٍ أَنْ يُوصِيَ.

Intestacy, *n.* وَفَاةٌ بِلَا وَصِيَّةٍ.

Intestate, *a.* and *n.* مِنْ غَيْرِ وَصِيَّةٍ. To die —, مَاتَ عَنْ غَيْرِ وَصِيَّةٍ [2].

Intestinal, *a.* مُتَعَلِّقٌ بِٱلْأَمْعَاءِ ـ مَعَوِيٌّ.

Intestine, *a.* Internal, دَاخِلِيٌّ ـ بَاطِن ـ دَاخِل. Domestic, not foreign, بَلَدِيٌّ. Intestine war, قَوْمَةُ ٱلشَّعْبِ عَلَى بَعْضِهِمْ. *See also* Inward, *a.*

Intestine, Intestines, *n.* مَعًى ـ مَصَارِينُ *pl.* مُصْرَان and مَصِير *pl.* حَوِيَّة. A winding or coiled —, أَحْشَآء ـ أَمْعَآء *pl.* حَشًا *pl.* حَوَايَا. The blind —, cæcum, المَعَى ٱلْأَعْوَرُ. The small intestines, الْأَمْعَآءُ ٱلدَّقَائِقُ ـ الْأَعْفَاجُ. The intestines of a bird, قَانِصَة *pl.* قَوَانِصُ.

Inthral, *v.t.* *See to* Enslave, *v.t.*

Inthralment, *n.* *See* Enslavement, *n.*

Inthrone, *v.t.* *See to* Enthrone, *v.t.*

Inthronization, *n.* *See* Enthronement, *n.*

Intimacy, *n.* Close relationship, مُوَاصَلَة ـ دُخْلُل ـ حِلْف ـ صُحْبَةٌ أَكِيدَةٌ ـ صُحْبَة ـ مُصَاحَبَة. Friendship, مُخَالَطَة ـ وِصَال مَحَبَّةٌ كُلِّيَّةٌ.

Intimate, *v.t.* To hint, suggest to, = غَمَزَ بِ ـ وَحَى إِلَى ـ فِي ـ أَوْمَأَ إِلَى ـ بِ ـ أَشَارَ إِلَى ـ بِ. To make known to, أَخْبَرَ ـ بِ ـ أَفَادَ ـ عَرَّفَ ـ بِ ـ بَلَّغَ ـ عَن.

Intimate, *a.* Particular, خَاصَّة ـ خَاصّ *pl.* خَوَاصّ. Inmost, hearty, صَمِيمِيٌّ ـ خَلِيف. Whole, perfect, كَامِل ـ كُلِّيّ ـ تَمَام. An — union, إِتِّحَادٌ صَمِيمِيٌّ ـ حِلْف. Intimate relations, رَوَابِطُ صَمِيمَةٌ. An — persuasion, يَقِين. To be — with, وَاصَلَ ـ آنَسَ ـ = أَنِسَ بِ or إِلَى. He is one of our most — friends, هُوَ مِنْ حُلَفَائِنَا ـ هُوَ مِنْ أَخَصِّ أَحْبَابِنَا.

Intimate, *n.* حَلِيف *pl.* حُلَفَآء ـ حِلْف *pl.* أَحْلَاف ـ وَصِيل ـ إِلْف ـ إِلْفَة ; *fem.* آلَاف *pl.* إِلْف ـ أَنِيس ـ دَخِيل.

Intimately, *ad.* Heartily, صَمِيمًا ـ قَلْبًا. Closely, ضِمْنًا. Firmly, decidedly, جَزْمًا وَيَقِينًا. Wholly, كُلِّيًّا ـ بَتَّةً. لِلْغَايَةِ. To be — persuaded, إِقْتَنَعَ جَزْمًا وَيَقِينًا ـ تَيَقَّنَ.

Intimation, *n.* A hint, إِشَارَة ـ غَمْز ـ وَحْي ـ إِيمَآء. Information, تَعْرِيف ـ خَبَر ـ تَبْلِيغ ـ إِخْبَار ـ إِفَادَة. To cause — to be given to, أَبْلَغَ ـ إِبْلَاغًا.

Intimidate, *v.t.* To frighten, أَفْزَعَ ـ خَوَّفَ ـ أَخَافَ. To confuse, perplex, حَيَّرَ ـ أَخْجَلَ.

Intimidation, *n.* The act of frightening, تَخْوِيف ـ إِخَافَة ـ إِفْزَاع; of perplexing, تَخْجِيل ـ تَحْيِير. The being made fearful, فَزَع ـ خَوْف; of being perplexed, حَيْرَة ـ تَحَيُّر ـ خَجْلَة.

Into, *prep.* In, بِ ـ فِي. Inside, جَوًّا ـ فِي ٱلدَّاخِلِ. To, إِلَى. He went — the house, دَخَلَ إِلَى ٱلْبَيْتِ ـ دَخَلَ ٱلْبَيْتَ [2] ـ دَخَلَ جَوًّا ٱلْبَيْتِ. To turn a thing —, صَيَّرَ ـ قَلَبَ ـ إِلَى.

Intolerable, *a.* Unbearable, لا يُطَاقُ ـ لا يُحْتَمَلُ. Abhorrent, شَنِيعٌ. *See also* Insufferable, *a.*

Intolerableness, *n.* عِزَّةٌ ـ عِزٌّ. *See also* Insufferableness, *n.*

Intolerably, *ad.* Beyond endurance, بِصُورَةٍ لا تُحْتَمَلُ. Detestably, بِشَنَاعَةٍ ـ كَرَاهَةً. Excessively, بِإِفْرَاطٍ ـ كُلِّيًّا ـ لِلْغَايَةِ.

Intolerance, *n.* عَدَاوَةٌ ـ عَصَبِيَّةٌ ـ تَعَصُّبٌ. Religious —, إِفْرَاطُ ٱلْحَمَاسَةِ فِي ٱلدِّينِ ـ عَصَبِيَّةٌ دِينِيَّةٌ. To act with —, أَتَى ـ بِٱلْعَصَبِيَّةِ.

Intolerant, *a.* Of a partisan, عَصَبِيٌّ ـ مُتَعَصِّبٌ; of religious intolerance, مُفْرِطٌ فِي ٱلْحَمَاسَةِ ٱلدِّينِيَّةِ ـ أَحْمَسُ فِي ٱلدِّينِ. Impatient, قَلِيلُ ٱلصَّبْرِ ـ جَازِعٌ ـ جَزِعٌ. To be — in religion, حَمِسَ (*or* تَحَمَّسَ) فِي أُمُورِ ٱلدِّينِ. To be — of, جَزِعَ مِنْ ـ هَلِعَ.

Intolerantly, *ad.* بِعَصَبِيَّةٍ ـ بِعَدَاوَةٍ ـ بِتَعَصُّبٍ. To act —, أَتَى بِٱلْعَصَبِيَّةِ.

Intoleration, *n.* عَدَاوَةٌ ـ تَعَصُّبٌ.

Intomb, *v.t.* *See to* Bury, *v.t.*

Intonate, *v.i.* To sound, صَاتَ *aor.* يَصُوتُ ـ أَرْسَلَ ٱلصَّوْتَ. To thunder, رَعَدَتِ ٱلسَّمَآءُ. To —, of a song, بَدَأَ بِٱلْغِنَآءِ.

Intonation, *n.* إِدْرَاجٌ ـ إِرْسَالُ ٱلصَّوْتِ ـ صَوْتٌ ـ تَلَفُّظٌ. Modulation of voice, لَحْنٌ *pl.* أَلْحَانٌ ـ صَوْتٌ *pl.* أَصْوَاتٌ.

Intone, *v.t.* أَدْرَجَ ـ أَرْسَلَ ـ رَتَّلَ ـ تَلَا *aor.* يَتْلُو ـ تَرَنَّمَ بِ ـ رَتَّلَ. I intoned the Kurân, رَتَّلْتُ ٱلْقُرْآنَ. He intones the Kurân, يَتَرَنَّمُ بِٱلْقُرْآنِ. He intones the Psalms, يُرَتِّلُ ٱلْمَزَامِيرَ. *See also to* Chant, *v.t.*

Intone, *v.i.* رَجَّعَ صَوْتَهُ ـ رَنَمَ ـ تَرَنَّمَ.

Intoning, *n.* تَرْتِيلٌ ـ تِلَاوَةٌ ـ إِرْسَالٌ ـ تَرْسِيلٌ ـ إِدْرَاجٌ.

Intort, *v.t.* To twist, لَوَى ـ أَبْرَمَ.

In toto, *ad.* بِٱلْكُلِّيَّةِ ـ كُلِّيًّا ـ بَتَّةً.

Intoxicate, *v.t.* To make drunk, سَكَّرَ. To infatuate, أَفْتَنَ ـ غَرَّ. Intoxicated, سَكْرَانُ. Intoxicating liquors, مُسْكِرَاتٌ ـ سُكْرٌ. *See also under* Drunk, *and* to Infatuate, *v.t.*

Intoxication, *n.* The act of making drunk, تَسْكِيرٌ; the state of being drunk, سُكْرٌ. Intoxication produced by hemp, إِنْسِطَالٌ. A fit of —, سَكْرَةٌ. Infatuation, جُنُونٌ ـ فُتُونٌ ـ غُرُورٌ.

Intractability, *n.* } عِنَادٌ ـ مُعَانَدَةٌ ـ شَكَاسَةٌ ـ شَرَاسَةٌ ـ عَدَمُ
Intractableness, } طَاعَةٍ ـ صُعُوبَةٌ ـ تَمَرُّدٌ.

Intractable, *a.* صَعْبٌ *pl.* صِعَابٌ ـ عَنِيدٌ ـ عَانِدٌ *pl.* عُنُدٌ ـ مُتَمَرِّدٌ ـ غَيْرُ طَائِعٍ ـ شَرِسٌ ـ لا يَتَعَامَلُ ـ شَكِسٌ ـ لا يَسْمَعُ ٱلنِّدَآءَ وَلَا يَبْغِي ٱلِٱهْتِدَآءَ. To be —, تَمَرَّدَ ـ أَصْعَبَ ـ شَرِسَ ـ شَكِسَ.

Intractably, *ad.* تَمَرُّدًا ـ بِشَرَاسَةٍ ـ بِٱلْمُعَانَدَةِ ـ بِشَكَاسَةٍ.

Intramural, *a.* فِي دَاخِلِ ٱلسُّورِ ـ فِي دَاخِلِ ٱلْحِيطَانِ ـ فِي دَاخِلِ ٱلْبَلَدِ.

Intransitive, *a.* غَيْرُ مُتَعَدٍّ. An — verb, فِعْلٌ لَازِمٌ ـ فِعْلٌ مُطَاوِعٌ.

Intransitively, *ad.* بِغَيْرِ تَعَدٍّ ـ بِعَدَمِ تَعَدٍّ.

In transitu, *ad.* فِي ٱلْمُرُورِ ـ فِي أَثْنَآءِ ٱلْعُبُورِ.

Intransmissible, *a.* لا يَنْتَقِلُ.

Intransmutability, *n.* عَدَمُ إِحَالَةٍ ـ عَدَمُ ٱلتَّحَوُّلِ.

Intransmutable, *a.* لا يَتَحَوَّلُ.

Intrench, *v.t.* To make a trench around, أَقَامَ مَتَارِيسَ ـ خَنْدَقَ حَوْلَ. To fortify, حَصَّنَ ـ أَحْكَمَ. To — one's self, تَحَصَّنَ.

Intrenchment, *n.* A ditch, خَنْدَقٌ *pl.* خَنَادِقُ. A fortification for defence, مِتْرَاسٌ *pl.* مَتَارِيسُ ـ إِسْتِحْكَامٌ *pl.* إِسْتِحْكَامَاتٌ.

Intrepid, *a.* ذُو بَطْشٍ ـ جَسُورٌ ـ قَدُومٌ ـ سَنْدَرِيٌّ ـ سَبَنْدًى ـ شُجَيْعٌ ـ لا يَخَافُ. *See also* Bold, Brave, *a.*

Intrepidity, *n.* } شَجَاعَةٌ ـ بَطْشٌ ـ جَسَارَةٌ ـ إِقْدَامٌ ـ شَوْكَةٌ.
Intrepidness, } To act with —, شَجُعَ ـ جَسَرَ.

Intrepidly, *ad.* بِبَطْشٍ ـ بِجَسَارَةٍ ـ بِشَجَاعَةٍ ـ بِإِقْدَامٍ.

Intricacy, *n.* } State of being entangled, تَعْقِيدٌ ـ شَجْرٌ ـ
Intricateness, } إِرْتِبَاكٌ ـ تَشْبِيكٌ ـ شَبْكٌ ـ عِيَاصٌ ـ إِلْتِبَاكٌ ـ خَبْصٌ ـ لَخْبَطَةٌ. Perplexity, حَيْرَةٌ ـ إِخْتِلَاطٌ ـ إِلْتِبَاسٌ. A difficulty, مُشْكِلَةٌ ـ صُعُوبَةٌ.

Intricate, *a.* مُشَبَّكٌ ـ مُعَقَّدٌ ـ عَوِيصٌ ـ مُلْتَوٍ ـ شَجِرٌ ـ مُلْتَبِكٌ ـ مُشْتَبِكٌ. Perplexing, مُلْتَبِسٌ ـ مُلْبِسٌ. Difficult, صَعْبٌ ـ عَسِيرٌ. An — matter, أَمْرٌ غُمَّةٌ ـ شَجِرٌ ـ مُشْكِلَةٌ. The story is —, ٱلْحَدِيثُ ذُو شُجُورٍ. To be —, عَسُرَ ـ شَجِرَ ـ إِشْتَبَكَ ـ إِخْتَلَفَ ـ إِشْتَجَرَ ـ إِعْتَصَى ـ تَعَسَّرَ ـ تَعَاسَرَ. To make —, difficult, شَبَكَ ـ شَبَّكَ ـ عَوَّصَ. To be —, difficult, to one, تَعَسَّرَ (*or* إِسْتَعْسَرَ) ـ إِعْتَاصَ عَلَيْهِ ـ إِلْتَوَى عَلَيْهِ ـ عَلَيْهِ ـ تَشَبَّكَ عَلَيْهِ.

Intricately, *ad.* بِٱلْتِبَاسٍ ـ بِتَعْقِيدٍ ـ بِتَشْبِيكٍ ـ بِعِيَاصٍ ـ بِلَخْبَطَةٍ ـ بِخَبْصٍ ـ بِشَجْرٍ ـ إِلْتِبَاكًا ـ بِصُعُوبَةٍ.

Intrigue, *n.* A plot, artifice, دُولَابٌ *pl.* دَوَالِيبُ ـ فَسَادٌ ـ خُدْعَةٌ ـ مَكْرٌ ـ حِيلَةٌ ـ فِتْنَةٌ ـ دَسِيسَةٌ *pl.* دَسَائِسُ ـ تَصَنُّعَاتٌ ـ خَفِيَّةٌ. The plot of a play, or tale, مَضْمُونٌ ـ تَأْوِيلٌ. An amorous —, عِشْقٌ (*or* حُبٌّ) حَرَامٌ. Political intrigues, دَسَائِسُ سِيَاسِيَّةٌ. Palace intrigues, *from the Turkish*, دَسَائِسُ ٱلْأَنْدَرُونِ; دَسَائِسُ ٱلسَّرَايَةِ. To confound an —, أَزْهَقَ ـ حَمَّقَ ٱلْحِيلَةَ ٱلدَّسِيسَةَ.

Intrigue, *v.i.* To practise a stratagem, إِحْتَالَ ـ تَحَيَّلَ ـ

دَسَّ ـ عَمِلَ دَسِيسَةً. To carry on an amour with a woman, إِخْتَلَفَ إِلَى ٱمْرَأَةٍ عَلَى ٱلْخَفَاءِ وَبِٱلْحَرَامِ. To — against, إِخْتَالَ عَلَى. To — for, إِحْتَالَ لِ.

Intriguer, *n.* } صَاحِبُ دَسَائِسَ ـ مُحْتَالٌ. How intriguing,
Intriguing, *a.* } or what an intriguer, he is! مَا أَحْوَلَهُ.

Intrinsic, *a.* } Real, belonging to the essence of a thing,
Intrinsical, } ذَاتِيٌّ ـ أَصْلِيٌّ ـ حَقِيقِيٌّ ـ جَوْهَرِيٌّ. Internal, بَاطِنٌ. An — good quality, فَاضِلَةٌ *pl.* فَوَاضِلُ. The — circumstances of an affair, بَاطِنُ ٱلْأَمْرِ. He displayed to me the outward and the — state of his affair, أَفْرَشَنِي ظَهْرَ أَمْرِهِ وَبَطْنَهُ. He is experienced in the — state of affairs, هُوَ مُجَرِّبٌ بَطْنَ ٱلْأُمُورِ.

Intrinsically, *ad.* فِي نَفْسِ ٱلْأَمْرِ ـ حَقِيقَةً ـ فِي ٱلْأَصْلِ ـ ذَاتًا.

Introduce, *v.t.* To cause to enter, أَدْخَلَ ـ حَشَّ ـ فِي. To — to, present to, عَرَضَ لِ ـ قَدَّمَ ـ لِ ـ أَبْرَزَ ـ إِلَى ـ عَرَّفَ ـ بِ. To insert, سَلَكَ. To show, أَرَى ـ أَظْهَرَ. To make known, أَبْدَى ـ بَيَّنَ ـ أَظْهَرَ. To originate, أَبْدَأَ ـ أَبْدَعَ ـ إِخْتَرَعَ ـ إِبْتَدَعَ. To — a usage, سَنَّ سُنَّةً ـ أَجْرَى عَادَةً. To — reforms, أَجْرَى ٱلْإِصْلَاحَاتِ ـ أَصْلَحَ ٱلْأُمُورَ. To — a subject, فَتَحَ سِيرَةً. To — one's self, بَرَزَ ـ دَخَلَ. The ambassador introduced the officers to the Sultan, عَرَّفَ ٱلسَّفِيرُ ٱلسُّلْطَانَ بِٱلضُّبَّاطِ.

Introducer, *n.* One who introduces anything, مُدْخِلٌ ـ مُبْرِزٌ. An official —, تَشْرِيفَاتِيٌّ ـ نَاظِرُ ٱلْمُقَابَلَاتِ ٱلرَّسْمِيَّةِ. The — of foreign ambassadors, تَشْرِيفَاتِيُّ ٱلسُّفَرَاءِ ٱلْخَارِجِيَّةِ. *See also* Originator, Inventor, *n.*

Introduction, *n.* The act of bringing in, presentation, إِدْخَالٌ ـ تَعْرِيفٌ ـ تَقْدِيمٌ ـ إِبْرَازٌ. Entrance, the being presented, بُرُوزٌ ـ دُخُولٌ. An —, letter of commendation, مَكْتُوبُ تَوْصِيَةٍ ـ تَوْصِيَةٌ. The —, or way to anything, بَابٌ ـ مَدْخَلٌ. An — to a book, فَاتِحَةٌ ـ مُقَدِّمَةٌ ـ دِيبَاجَةٌ. Origination, إِبْدَاعٌ ـ إِخْتِرَاعٌ ـ إِيجَادٌ. The — of a subject, narrative, فَتْحُ سِيرَةٍ. The — of one thing into another, سَلْكٌ ـ غَلٌّ.

Introductory, *a.* Serving to introduce, of a subject, book, إِفْتِتَاحِيٌّ. An — letter, مَكْتُوبُ تَوْصِيَةٍ.

Introit, *n.* فَاتِحَةٌ. An — to the Communion Office, بَدْءُ ٱلْقُدَّاسِ.

Intromission, *n.* A sending in, إِدْخَالٌ. Intermeddling, مُقَارَشَةٌ ـ مُدَاخَلَةٌ.

Intromit, *v.t.* سَلَكَ ـ أَدْخَلَ.

Introspection, *n.* مَنْظَرَةٌ ـ كَشْفُ (or نَظَرُ) ٱلدَّاخِلِ (or ٱلْبَاطِنِ) ٱلدَّاخِلِ.

Introspective, *a.* مُرِي ـ كَاشِفٌ عَنِ ٱلدَّاخِلِ (or ٱلْبَاطِنِ) ٱلدَّاخِلَ.

Introsusception, *n.* غَلُّ ٱلْمُصْرَانِ.

Introversion, *n.* تَقْلِيبُ ٱلْخَارِجِ دَاخِلًا.

Introvert, *v.t.* قَلَبَ ٱلشَّيْءَ عَلَى قَفَاهُ ـ قَلَبَ ٱلْخَارِجَ دَاخِلًا.

Intrude, *v.i.* To — one's self, دَخَلَ بِغَيْرِ حَقٍّ ـ تَطَفَّلَ. To — upon, دَخَلَ عَلَى ـ دَمَرَ عَلَى ـ دَخَلَ بِغَيْرِ إِجَازَةٍ ـ إِعْتَرَضَ لِ ـ تَعَرَّضَ لِ ـ إِدَّخَلَ عَلَى. He intruded upon them, دَمَرَ عَلَيْهِمْ. When you wish to enter a house, beware of intruding, or entering without permission, إِذَا دَخَلْتَ ٱلدُّورَ إِيَّاكَ وَٱلدُّمُورَ. He intrudes into what does not concern him, هُوَ مُتَدَاخِلٌ فِي مَا لَا يَعْنِيهِ.

Intruder, *n.* One who intrudes himself unasked, خُضَرٌ ـ خَضِرٌ ـ دَخِيلٌ ـ طُفَيْلِيٌّ. One who intrudes into other people's affairs, فُضُولِيٌّ ـ عِرِّيضٌ ـ مُدَخِّلٌ (or مُتَدَاخِلٌ) فِي أُمُورِ غَيْرِهِ. A woman wont to intrude, or a set of intruders, دَمَّرَاءُ.

Intrusive, *a.* Of a person; (*see under* Intruder, *n.*) Intrusive rocks, صَخْرٌ فِي خِلَالِ طَبَقَاتِ ٱلْأَرْضِ.

Intrusion, *n.* The act of thrusting in without permission, إِدْخَالٌ بِلَا إِجَازَةٍ. Entrance without right, as an intruder, تَعَرُّضٌ ـ إِعْتِرَاضٌ ـ دُخُولٌ مِنْ غَيْرِ حَقٍّ ـ تَطَفُّلٌ ـ دُمُورٌ. The act of encroaching, إِجْحَافٌ ـ إِخْتِلَاسٌ ـ هَضْمٌ ـ جَوْرٌ ـ إِطَالَةُ ٱلْيَدِ. The penetration of melted matter, سَبِيكَةٌ. *See also* Interference, *n.*

Intrusively, *ad.* With intrusion of one's self, تَطَفُّلًا ـ بِتَطَفُّلٍ with interference, تَعَرُّضًا ـ بِتَعَرُّضٍ ـ بِٱلْفُضُولِ.

Intrust, *v.t.* To confide to the fidelity of, أَمِنَ ـ بِ ـ إِسْتَأْمَنَ ـ عَلَى. To — to one, as a deposit, إِسْتَحْفَظَ ـ أَمَانَةً ـ إِسْتَوْدَعَ ـ أَمَانَةً ـ أَوْدَعَ ـ عِنْدَهُ وَدِيعَةً. To — one with a secret, أَطْلَعَهُ عَلَى سِرٍّ ـ أَمِنَهُ عَلَى سِرٍّ ـ سَارَّ. To — one with an affair, commission, وَكَّلَ ـ بِٱلْأَمْرِ ـ فَوَّضَ ٱلْأَمْرَ إِلَى. To — with an appointment, to appoint, وَلَّى ـ مَنْصَبًا ـ أَوْلَى ـ مَنْصَبًا. Intrusted with, أَمِينٌ عَلَى.

Intuition, *n.* نَظَرٌ ـ مُكَاشَفَةٌ ـ إِسْتِشْرَافٌ ـ بَدِيهَةٌ ـ بُدَاهَةٌ ـ إِدْرَاكٌ بِغَيْرِ ٱلْحَوَاسِّ ـ عَقْلِيٌّ. Mental perception, بَصِيرَةٌ. A man of —, رَجُلٌ مُبَدَّهٌ.

Intuitive, *a.* حُضُورِيٌّ ـ ذُو بَدِيهَةٍ ـ بَدِيهِيٌّ ـ إِسْتِدْلَالِيٌّ ـ ذُو بَصِيرَةٍ. Intuitive perception, بَدِيهَةٌ. This is known among the — notions of intellect, هٰذَا مَعْلُومٌ فِي بَدَائِهِ ٱلْعُقُولِ. He possesses true — perception, لَهُ فِرَاسَةٌ ذَاتُ بَصِيرَةٍ.

Intuitively, *ad.* بِٱلنَّظَرِ ٱلْعَقْلِيِّ ـ بِمُكَاشَفَةٍ ـ فِي بَدَائِهِ ٱلْعُقُولِ. This is known —, هٰذَا مَعْلُومٌ فِي بَدَائِهِ ٱلْعُقُولِ.

Intumescence, *n.* / Inturgescence, } تَوَرُّم ـ وَرَم ـ نُفَاخ ـ إِنْتِفَاخ.

Intussusception, *n.* *See* Introsusception, *n.*

Intwine, *v.t.* / Intwist, } شَبَّكَ ـ وَشَّجَ ـ لَفَّفَ. To be intertwined, إِنْشَبَكَ ـ يَشِجُ *aor.* وَشَجَ.

Inuendo, *n.* A hint, تَعْرِيض ـ إِيمَآء ـ تَوْمِئَة ـ وَمْأ ـ كِنَايَة. An allusion in a suspicious sense, لَغْط *pl.* أَلْغَاط ـ تُهَمَة *pl.* تُهَم ـ ظِنَّة. *See also* Innuendo, *n.*

Inundate, *v.t.* To cover with water, غَطَّى ـ فَيَّضَ ٱلْمِيَاهِ ـ غَطَّى ٱلْمَآء آلـ... غَرَّقَ ٱلْمَآء آلـ... To fill to overflowing, غَمَرَ ـ أَفَاضَ ع. To be inundated, covered with water, تَطَبَّعَ ـ إِنْغَمَرَ بِٱلْمَآء ـ فَاضَ عَلَى ٱلْمَآء ـ بِٱلْمَآء. Inundating, carrying all before it, جَارِف ـ جَاعِف.

Inundation, *n.* As of water, سَيْل (or فَيْض or فَيَضَان) ٱلْمِيَاهِ. Overflowing abundance, كَثْرَة ـ فَيَضَان. Land not reached by inundation, (a word used in Egypt,) شَرَاقِيّ.

Inurbanity, *n.* *See* Incivility, *n.*

Inure, *v.t.* To accustom to, دَرَّبَ ـ فِي ـ مَرَّنَ ـ عَلَى ـ عَوَّدَ ـ عَلَى ـ دَرَّجَ إِلَى ـ مَارَزَ ـ وَطَّنَ ـ عَلَى ـ (or عَلَى or ب). To — one's self to, تَمَرَّنَ عَلَى ـ تَدَرَّبَ عَلَى ـ إِعْتَادَ ب. *See also to* Accustom, *v.t.*

Inure, *v.i.* To pass into use, أَسْتَعْمِلَ ـ صَارَ عَادَةً. To benefit, نَفَعَ ـ صَلَحَ ل.

Inurement, *n.* تَمَرُّن ـ مُمَارَزَة ـ تَعَوُّد ـ تَدَرُّب.

Inurn, *v.t.* يَضَعُ *aor.* وَضَعَ تُرَابَ ٱلْمَيِّتِ فِي قَبْرٍ. *See also to* Bury, *v.t.*

Inutility, *n.* عَدَمُ فَائِدَةٍ ـ عَبَث ـ عَدَمُ مَنْفَعَةٍ ـ قِلَّةُ نَفْعٍ ـ عَدَمُ طَائِلٍ.

In vacuo, ad. فِرْغًا ـ بِٱلْخَلَآءِ.

Invade, *v.t.* To attack, دَخَلَ عَلَى ـ غَزَا ـ هَجَمَ عَلَى ـ أَجْحَفَ بِ ـ بَغَى عَلَى ـ غَارَ عَلَى. To encroach upon, تَعَدَّى عَلَى. To usurp, إِسْتَوْلَى عَلَى ـ عَنْفًا. To —, as a disease, يَرِدُ *aor.* وَرَدَ عَلَى ـ إِسْتَوْلَى عَلَى ـ أَصَابَ. They invaded us on the south, غَزَوْنَا عَلَى ٱلْجَنُوبِ. *See also to* Attack, *v.t.*

Invader, *n.* غَازٍ *pl.* غُزَاة *and* غُزًّى ـ هَاجِم ـ مُتَعَدٍّ ـ بَاغٍ *pl.* بُغَاة.

Invalid, *a.* Null, void, نَقِيض ـ بَاطِل ـ بَطَّال ـ غَيْرُ صَالِحٍ ـ فَاسِد.

Invalid, *n.* One disabled by sickness, عَلِيل ـ عَاجِز *pl.* عَجَز ـ سَاقِط *pl.* سُقَّاط. An — soldier, عَسْكَرِيٌّ مُتَقَاعِدٌ ـ عَسْكَرِيٌّ عَاجِزٌ.

Invalid, *v.t.* To enrol on the list of the disabled, كَتَبَ ـ مَعَ ـ قَيَّدَ ـ فِي دَفْتَرِ ٱلسُّقَّاطِ ـ ٱلْعَاجِزِينَ.

Invalidate, *v.t.* To make null, فَسَخَ ـ نَاقَضَ ـ أَفْسَدَ ـ أَبْطَلَ. To — the testimony of a witness, جَرَحَ ٱلشَّاهِدَ ـ زَوَّرَ ٱلشَّهَادَةَ. To prove the invalidity of a thing, أَثْبَتَ عَدَمَ صَلَاحِيَةِ ٱلشَّيْءِ. A thing by which any testimony is invalidated, جُرْحَة. Hast thou anything to adduce whereby to — the testimony? هَلْ لَكَ جُرْحَة. I authorise thee to adduce anything whereby to — the testimony, أَقْصَصْتُكَ ٱلْجُرْحَةَ فَإِنْ كَانَ عِنْدَكَ مَا تَجْرَحُ بِهِ ٱلْحُجَّةَ فَهَلُمَّهَا.

Invalidity, *n.* بُطْل ـ قِلَّةُ صِحَّةٍ ـ رَكَاكَة ـ عَدَمُ صَلَاحِيَةٍ ـ بُطْلَان ـ بُطُول.

Invaluable, *a.* أَثْمَن ـ لَا يُقَيَّمُ بِثَمَنٍ ـ مَا لَهُ قِيمَةٌ.

Invariability, *n.* / Invariableness, } ثَبَات ـ قَرَار ـ قِلَّةُ تَغْيِيرٍ ـ عَدَمُ تَغْيِيرٍ ـ إِسْتِمْرَار.

Invariable, *a.* ثَابِت ـ دَائِم ـ لَا يَتَغَيَّرُ.

Invariably, *ad.* دَائِمًا ـ بِٱلدَّوَام ـ بِلَا تَغْيِيرٍ.

Invasion, *n.* Hostile entrance into a country, غَزَاة ـ غَزْوٌ ـ هُجُومٌ عَلَى ـ حَمْلَةٌ عَلَى ـ دُخُولٌ عَلَى. Infringement, violation, إِخْلَال ـ تَعْدِيَة ـ تَجَاوُز ـ إِجْحَاف ـ تَعَدٍّ. Coming in, as of a disease, ظُهُور ـ سِرَايَة ـ إِسْتِعْلَآء.

Invasive, *a.* مُتَعَدٍّ عَلَى ـ مُتَجَاوِز ـ مُجْحِف ـ جَاحِف ـ مُخْتَلِس ـ جَائِر ـ جَاثِر.

Invective, *n.* Railing speech, شَتْم ـ طَعَّان ـ طَعْن ـ بَهْدَلَة. A railing expression, سَبّ ـ شَتِيمَة ـ طَعْنَة ـ أَسَابِيب *pl.* أُسْبُوبَة.

Invectively, *ad.* بِبَهْدَلَةٍ ـ بِشَتِيمَةٍ ـ شَتْمًا ـ طَعْنًا فِي.

Inveigh, *v.i.* To rail against, حَشَكَ عَلَى ـ سَبَّ ع ـ شَتَمَ ع. They inveighed against one another, of two, شَاتَمَا ـ تَسَابَّا ـ تَشَاتَمَا; of more, تَشَاتَمُوا ـ تَسَابُّوا.

Inveigher, *n.* مُبَهْدِل ـ سَبَّاب ـ شَتَّام ـ سَبِيب ـ مِسَبّ.

Inveigle, *v.t.* To seduce, deceive, أَضَلَّ ـ أَخْدَعَ ـ أَغْوَى ـ تَحَاوَلَ عَلَى ـ ضَلَّلَ. To be inveigled, إِنْخَدَعَ ـ إِنْغَوَى. To — away, أَسَلَّ ـ أَسَلَّ ـ بِحِيلَةٍ.

Inveiglement, *n.* تَطْمِيعَة ـ حِيلَة ـ إِخْدَاع ـ إِغْوَآء.

Inveigler, *n.* حِيلِيّ ـ خَدَّاع ـ مُغْوٍ ـ غَاوٍ.

Invent, *v.t.* To devise something new, إِخْتَرَعَ ـ أَبْدَعَ ـ إِفْتَرَحَ ـ إِفْتَرَى ـ أَوْجَدَ ـ أَبْدَأَ ـ أَحْدَثَ. To fabricate falsely, (or إِخْتَرَعَ) ـ إِفْتَرَى ـ زُورًا. To frame by imagination, تَخَيَّلَ ـ خَيَّلَ. He invented or forged a lie, إِفْتَرَى كَذِبًا. He invented or forged a lie against him, إِفْتَرَى عَلَيْهِ كَذِبًا. To be invented, أُخْتُرِعَ ـ أُجِدَّ ـ تَجَدَّدَ ـ بَدَأَ.

Invention, *n.* The act of devising something new, إِبْدَاع — إِقْتِرَاح — نَشَآءَة — إِيجَاد — إِحْدَاث — إِخْتِرَاع. That which is invented, بَدِيعَة *pl.* بَدَائِعُ — إِيجَاد *pl.* إِيجَادَات — إِخْتِرَاع *pl.* إِخْتِرَاعَات. Fabricating what is untrue, إِخْتِرَاعُ زُورٍ — إِفْتِرَآءُ زُورٍ. Excogitation, تَخْيِيل — تَخَيُّل. The — of the Cross, الكَشْفُ عَنِ ٱلصَّلِيبِ. A patent of —, بَرَآءَةُ (or إِمْتِيَازُ) ٱلإِخْتِرَاعِ. A wonderful —, إِخْتِرَاعٌ عَجِيبٌ. Inventions, as of science, مُخْتَرَاعَات.

Inventive, *a.* سَرِيعُ ٱلإِبْدَاعِ — مُبْتَدِع — بَدِيع. Imaginative, سَرِيعُ ٱلتَّخَيُّلِ — مُتَخَيِّل. Lying, مُفْتَرٍ — مُزَوِّر — كَذَّاب. An — genius, بَدِيعُ ٱلعَقْلِ.

Inventor, مُبْتَدِع — مُبْدِع — مُخْتَرِع — مُحْدِث — مُنْشِئ — مُوجِد.

Inventory, *n.* دَفْتَرُ أَشْيَآءَ *pl.* دَفَاتِرُ — سِيَاقَة — فِهْرِس.

Inventory, *v.t.* فَهْرَسَ — قَيَّدَ- (or كَتَبَ-) فِي دَفْتَرٍ.

Inventress, *n.* مُوجِدَة — مُبْدِعَة — مُخْتَرِعَة — مُحْدِثَة — مُنْشِئَة.

Inverse, *a.* مَقْلُوب — مَعْكُوس — مَرْكُوس — مُرْتَكِس. Inverse ratio, نِسْبَةٌ عَكْسِيَّةٌ. Inverse proportion, تَنَاسُبٌ عَكْسِيٌّ. *See also* Mutual, *a.*

Inversely, *ad.* بِٱلْمَقْلُوبِ — بِٱلْعَكْسِ — عَكْسًا.

Inversion, *n.* The act of inverting, عَكْس — نَكْس — بَعْثَرَة — قَلْب; of turning topsy-turvy, بَعْثَرَة; the being inverted, إِنْقِلَاب — إِنْعِكَاس. Change, so that the last becomes first, تَقْدِيمٌ وَتَأْخِيرٌ. The — of the eyelid, شَتَر; to have that —, شَتِرَ; one who has it, أَشْتَرُ. The —, as of an argument, مُعَاكَسَة.

Invert, *v.t.* To turn upside-down, حَوَّلَ حَابِلَهُ عَلَى نَابِلِهِ — بَعْثَرَ — عَكَسَ — قَلَبَ — نَكَسَ — أَرْكَسَ — رَكَسَ. To change the order, تَنَكَّسَ — إِرْتَكَسَ — كَانَ حَابِلُهُ نَابِلَهُ. قَدَّمَ وَأَخَّرَ. To be inverted, إِنْعَكَسَ — إِنْقَلَبَ. *See also* Upside-down, *a.*

Invertebral, *a.* }
Invertebrate, } بِلَا فَقَارٍ — عَدِيمُ خَرَزِ ٱلظَّهْرِ.

Invertebrate, *n.* حَيَوَانٌ عَدِيمُ ٱلْفَقَارِ.

Inverted, *a.* *See* Upside-down, *a.*

Invertedly, *ad.* بِٱلْمَقْلُوبِ — بِٱلْعَكْسِ — بِحَابِلِهِ عَلَى نَابِلِهِ — بَعْثَرَةً.

Invest, *v.t.* To clothe, dress, لَبَّسَ — أَلْبَسَ. To — with an office, قَلَّدَ- مَنْصِبًا. To —, as with a decoration, وَجَّهَ- بِ. To inclose, besiege, حَاصَرَ — إِحْتَاطَ بِ. To —, as money, with a view to profit, صَرَفَ- فِي — شَغَّلَ — حَطَّ: He invested his money in articles of merchandise, صَرَفَ دَرَاهِمَهُ فِي ٱلْبَضَائِعِ.

Investigable, *a.* مِمَّا يَتَحَقَّقُ — مِمَّا يُفَتَّشُ عَنْهُ.

Investigate, *v.t.* تَبَحَّثَ عَنْ — بَحَثَ فِي — نَدَشَ — أَغَارَ فِي — فَتَّشَ عَنْ or عَلَى — تَفَحَّصَ عَنْ — إِفْتَحَصَ عَنْ — فَحَصَ عَنْ. To — the truth, جَدَّ فِي طَلَبِ ٱلْحَقِيقَةِ. To — narrowly into, تَقَعَّرَ فِي — تَعَمَّقَ فِي — تَنَطَّعَ فِي. To persevere in investigating into, تَتَبَّعَ.

Investigation, *n.* تَدْقِيق — تَفْتِيش — فَحْص — بَحْث — نَدْش — تَحْقِيق. A ground for —, مُتَفَحَّص.

Investigative, *a.* }
Investigator, *n.* } جَادٌّ فِي — مُدَقِّق — مُفَتِّش — مُتَتَبِّع — مُتَفَحِّص — ٱلطَّلَبِ.

Investiture, *n.* The act of investing, as with an office, *etc.*, تَوْجِيه — تَقْلِيد. A patent of —, بَرَآءَةُ ٱلتَّوْجِيهِ.

Investment, *n.* The act of clothing, إِكْسَآءٌ. Clothes, كِسْوَة — أَلْبِسَة — لِبَاس. A siege, مُحَاصَرَة — إِحْتِيَاط. The placing of money, تَشْغِيلُ ٱلدَّرَاهِمِ — مُعَامَلَةُ ٱلدَّرَاهِمِ. Money invested, دَرَاهِمُ مَشْغُولَةٌ.

Inveteracy, *n.* }
Inveterateness, } Deep-rooted firmness, ثَبَات — إِنْغِرَاس — ثُبُوت. Violence, شِدَّة — حِدَّة. Relentlessness, لَدَّ.

Inveterate, *a.* Deeply rooted, مُتَمَكِّن — مُنْغَرِس — لَا يُدْفَعُ — ثَابِت. Violent, حَادٌّ — شَدِيد. Relentless, أَلَدُّ *pl.* لُدٌّ *and* لِدَاد. An —, or deep-rooted disposition, عِرْق.

Inveterately, *ad.* بِعِنَادٍ — بِشِدَّةٍ — بِتَمَكُّنٍ — بِلَدَّ.

Invidious, *a.* *See* Envious, *a.*

Invidiously, *ad.* *See* Enviously, *ad.*

Invidiousness, *n.* *See* Envy, *n.*

Invigorate, *v.t.* To give vigour to, شَيَّعَ — شَدَّدَ — قَوَّى — عَزَّزَ. To restore to health, عَافَى. *See also to* Animate, *v.t.*

Invigoration, *n.* The act of, تَشْدِيد — تَشْيِيع — تَقْوِيَة — تَعْزِيز; of animating, إِحْيَآءٌ. The state of being invigorated, قُوَّة — شِدَّة — حَوْل. Health, عَافِيَة.

Invincibility, *n.* }
Invincibleness, } مَنَعَة — مَنَاعَة — عِزَّة — عِزّ; as of an argument, عَدَمُ إِمْكَانِ ٱلرَّدِّ عَلَيْهِ. *See also* Impregnability, *n.*

Invincible, *a.* Unconquerable, غَيْرُ مَقْهُورٍ — لَا يُقْهَرُ — أَعَزُّ — عَزِيز. Not to be rebutted, فِي مَنَعَةٍ. ٱلرَّدُّ عَلَيْهِ مُحَالٌ — دَفْعُهُ غَيْرُ مُمْكِنٍ. Not to be invalidated, جَرْحُهُ (or ثَلْمُهُ) مُحَالٌ — لَا جَرْحَةَ لَهُ. An — argument, بُرْهَانٌ قَاطِعٌ — حُجَّةٌ قَاطِعَةٌ. To be —, عَزَّ.

Invincibly, *ad.* مِنْ غَيْرِ إِقْهَارٍ — بِعِزَّةٍ — بِعِزٍّ. He proved it —, بَرْهَنَ- بَيَّنَهُ — بَرْهَنَ- (or ثَبَّتَ-) بِبُرْهَانٍ قَاطِعٍ.

Inviolability, *n.* }
Inviolableness, } Non-susceptibility of being broken or infringed, العِصْمَةُ مِنَ ٱلتَّعَدِّي عَلَيْهِ. Impro-

priety of being transgressed, عَدَمُ جَوَازِ ٱلتَّعَدِّى عَلَيْهِ. Sacredness, حُرْمَة. The — of ambassadors, صِيَانَةُ ٱلسُّفَرَآءِ مِنَ ٱلأَذَى. The — of the Crown, عِصْمَةُ ٱلْمَلِكِ مِنَ ٱلْمَلَامِ ـ حُرْمَةُ ٱلْمَلِكِ.

Inviolable, *a.* Not susceptible of being broken, لا يُنْقَضُ. Not to be transgressed, لا يَحِلُّ ٱلتَّعَدِّى عَلَيْهِ. Not to be profaned, حُرْمَتُهُ وَاجِبَةٌ ـ مُحَرَّمٌ ـ حَرَام ـ مَحْجُور ـ حِجْر. An — or sacred thing, حِجْرٌ ـ حُجْرِيٌّ.

Inviolably, *ad.* بِحُرْمَةٍ ـ بِلا تَعْدِيَةٍ ـ مِنْ غَيْرِ نَقْضٍ.

Inviolate, *a.* }
Inviolated, } Not broken or infringed, مَصُونٌ عَنِ (or مَعْصُومٌ مِنَ) ٱلنَّقْضِ. Uninjured, صَحِيح ـ غَيْرُ مُضَام ـ غَيْرُ مُنْثَلِمٍ ـ غَيْرُ مَجْرُوحٍ. Respected, observed, مُعْتَبَر ـ مُرْعَى. Protected from dishonour, عِرْضُهُ مَصُونٌ.

Invisible, *a.* غَائِبٌ عَنِ ٱلأَبْصَارِ ـ لا يُرَى ـ غَيْرُ مَنْظُورٍ. The — world, العَالَمُ ٱلْغَيْبُ. The visible and —, مَا يُرَى وَمَا لا يُرَى. He used to make himself — to the people, كَانَ يَغِيبُ عَنْ أَبْصَارِ ٱلنَّاسِ.

Invisibly, *ad.* مِنْ غَيْرِ أَنْ يُرَأَى (or يُرَى).

Invitation, *n.* The act of inviting, a call, إِسْتِدْعَآءٌ ـ دَعْوَةٌ. An —, as to dinner, *etc.*, عَزِيمَة ـ عَزُومَة ـ أَدْب ـ طَلَبَة.

Invitatory, *a.* إِسْتِدْعَائِيٌّ ـ مُتَضَمِّنٌ ٱسْتِدْعَآءً. An — psalm, تَسْبِحَة ـ تَسْبِيح.

Invitatory, *n.* تَسْبِحَة ـ تَسْبِيح.

Invite, *v.t.* As to a feast, دَعَا ـ ل ـ آدَبَ ـ إِلَى ـ أَدَبَ ـ إِلَى *aor.* يَدْعُو ـ كَلَّفَ ـ ل ـ عَزَمَ ـ ل. To call upon to, to solicit to, دَعَا ـ إِلَى ـ حَمَلَ ـ عَلَى. He invited him to dinner with him, دَعَاهُ لِلْغَدَآءِ مَعَهُ. He invited the general to sup with him, دَعَا ٱلْجِنْرَالَ لِيَتَعَشَّى مَعَهُ. *See also* to Instigate, *v.t.*

Invited, *a.* مَدْعُوٌّ ـ مَعْزُوم.

Inviting, *a.* *See* Pleasant, *a.*

Inviter, *n.* As to a feast, آدِب.

Invitingly, *ad.* بِطَلَاوَةٍ ـ بِنَوْعٍ لَطِيفٍ ـ بِنَوْعٍ يَسْلُبُ ٱلْعَقْلَ ـ تَرْغِيبًا.

Invocate, *v.t.* To implore, إِبْتَهَلَ إِلَى ـ تَضَرَّعَ إِلَى. *See also to* Implore, Invoke, *v.t.*

Invocation, *n.* A prayer, دُعَآء ـ صَلَاة; a single —, دَعْوَة. An address, مَقَالَة ـ مُنَاجَاة ـ مُخَاطَبَة. An — for help, إِسْتِغَاثَة. An —, charm, against evil, عَزِيمَة. A calling upon God to ward off some evil, عَوْذٌ بِٱللّٰهِ. The — of the saints, إِسْتِغَاثَةٌ بِٱلأَوْلِيَآءِ ـ صَلَاةٌ إِلَى ٱلْقِدِّيسِينَ.

Invoice, *n.* دَفْتَرُ أَشْيَآءَ ـ قَائِمَةُ أَمْتِعَةٍ ـ لائِحَةُ بِضَاعَةٍ ـ فَاتُورَة.

Invoice, *v.t.* قَيَّدَ ـ كَتَبَ قَائِمَةَ ٱلأَمْتِعَةِ (or لائِحَةَ ٱلْبِضَاعَةِ) ـ فَاتُورَةَ ٱلأَمْتِعَةِ.

Involucre, *n.* بُرْعُومَةٌ ذَاتُ أَزْهَارٍ فِى هَيْئَةِ مِظَلَّةٍ.

Invoke, *v.t.* To address in prayer, دَعَا *aor.* يَدْعُو ـ صَلَّى إِلَى. To entreat, تَرَجَّى ـ طَلَبَ إِلَى ـ إِلْتَمَسَ مِن. He invoked his assistance, إِسْتَغَاثَ بِهِ. To — God against an evil, إِسْتَعَاذَ (or تَعَوَّذَ or عَاذَ) بِٱللّٰهِ مِن; to cause one thus to — God, عَوَّذَ ـ بِٱللّٰهِ. To — the law, refer one to it, as an authority, أَسْنَدَ ـ إِلَى ٱلْقَانُونِ.

Involuntarily, *ad.* عَنْ كَرَاهِيَةٍ ـ مِنْ غَيْرِ إِرَادَةٍ ـ مِنْ غَيْرِ ٱخْتِيَارٍ ـ لا عَنْ قَصْدٍ.

Involuntary, *a.* بِغَيْرِ ٱخْتِيَارٍ ـ عَنْ غَيْرِ إِرَادَةٍ ـ بِغَيْرِ مُرَادٍ.

Involute, *a.* }
Involuted, } مُلَوْلَبٌ إِلَى ٱلدَّاخِلِ.

Involution, *n.* The act of involving, enveloping, تَلْفِيف ـ تَغْلِيف ـ شَمْل; the state of being involved, إِلْتِفَاف ـ إِغْتِلَاف. Complication, إِلْتِبَاك ـ تَشْوِيش ـ إِلْتِبَاس ـ تَعْقِيد ـ تَشْبِيك. *In mathematics*, قَاعِدَةُ حِسَابِ ٱلأَعْدَادِ وَٱلْكَمِّيَّاتِ.

Involve, *v.t.* To inwrap in, لَفَّ ـ فِى ـ أَدْمَجَ ـ فِى ـ أَدْرَجَ ـ فِى ـ غَلَّفَ ـ بِ. To surround with, أَحَاطَ ـ بِ. To bring one in to, أَدْخَلَ ـ فِى. To become afflicted with, mixed up with, as a disease, trouble, إِبْتَلَى بِ. To comprehend, inclose, إِحْتَوَى عَلَى ـ شَمَلَ ـ إِشْتَمَلَ عَلَى ـ تَضَمَّنَ. To draw in by necessary consequence, إِسْتَلْزَمَ ـ نَتَجَ. To complicate, عَقَّدَ ـ شَبَّكَ ـ لَبَّكَ ـ خَلَطَ. To — in dust, عَفَّرَ ـ غَبَّرَ. To — in smoke, دَخَّنَ. To — in darkness, غَطَّى ـ بِٱلظُّلْمَةِ. To — one in, mix him up with, شَبَّكَ ـ فِى. It involves the innocent with the guilty, يَخْلِطُ ٱلْبَرِىءَ بِٱلْمُذْنِبِ. To — a nation in war, حَمَلَ ٱلْمِلَّةَ عَلَى ٱلْمُحَارَبَةِ. To — a contradiction, نَاقَضَ ـ خَالَفَ بَعْضُهُ بَعْضَهُ ـ ضَادَدَ بَعْضُهُ بَعْضَهُ. To be involved, complicated, تَلَبَّكَ ـ إِلْتَبَكَ ـ إِنْشَبَكَ ـ إِخْتَلَطَ.

Involved, *a.* Complicated, مُشْتَبِك ـ مُلْتَبِك ـ مُعَقَّد ـ مُشَبَّك. In debt, مَدْيُون. An — sentence, تَعْقِيد.

Involvedness, *n.* The state of being involved, complicated, لَبْكَة ـ إِخْتِلَاط ـ شَبْكَة ـ لَخْبَطَة. The being in debt, دَيْن.

Involvement, *n.* The act of complicating, تَلْبِيك ـ تَشْبِيك ـ تَعْقِيد.

Invulnerability, *n.* عِزَّة ـ صِيَانَةٌ عَنِ ٱلْجُرْحِ ـ عِصْمَةٌ مِنَ ٱلْكَلْمِ; especially against weapons, عَدَمُ تَأْثِيرِ ٱلأَسْلِحَةِ فِيهِ.

Invulnerable, *a.* Not to be wounded, عَزِيز ـ لا يُجْرَحُ ـ مَعْصُوم

فِي وِقايَةٍ عَنِ ٱلْجُرْحِ – مِنَ ٱلْكَلِمِ. Which nothing can injure, لا تَأْثُّرَ فِيهِ. Which weapons cannot penetrate, ما لا يَضُرُّهُ شَيْءٌ ٱلْأَسْلِحَةِ.

Inwall, *v.t.* أَحاطَ بِحائِطٍ – أَحاطَ بِسُورٍ.

Inward, *a.* جَوّانِيٌّ – باطِنٌ – بِٱلدّاخِلِ. The — thoughts of the mind, القَلْبُ – النَّفْسُ – الباطِنُ. The — man, الضَّمِيرُ. Infixed, as of grief, *etc.*, مُتَمَكِّنٌ. He knows the — state of affairs, هُوَ مُجَرِّبٌ بَطْنَ ٱلْأُمُورِ.

Inward, *ad.* فِي ٱلدّاخِلِ.

Inwardly, *ad.* To the inward side, مِنْ داخِلٍ – إِلَى داخِلٍ. In the heart, mind, فِي – فِي ٱلضَّمِيرِ – فِي ٱلْقَلْبِ – باطِنًا – بِٱلْباطِنِ.

Inwards, *ad.* نَحْوَ ٱلدّاخِلِ – إِلَى ٱلطَّرَفِ ٱلْجَوّانِيِّ.

Inwards, *n.* *See* Intestines, Entrails, *n.*

Inweave, *v.t.* نَسَجَ بِـ ٥. Inwoven with, مَنْسُوجٌ بِـ.

Inwreathe, *v.t.* To adorn, as with a wreath, زَيَّنَ بِأَكالِيلَ مِنْ زَهْرٍ – زَيَّنَ بِـ. *See also to* Intertwine, *v.t.*

Inwrought, *a.* Woven in with, مَنْسُوجٌ بِـ.

Iodine, *n.* يُودٌ – إِيُودٌ.

Ionic, *a.* أَناطُولِيٌّ – يُونانِيٌّ. The — order, البِناءُ ٱلْأَناطُولِيُّ.

Iota, *n.* The Greek letter, حَرْفُ ٱلْياءِ بِٱلْيُونانِيَّةِ. A jot, tittle, جُزْءٌ أَصْغَرُ – ذَرَّةٌ – نُقْطَةٌ – حَرْفٌ.

Ipecacuanha, *n.* عِرْقُ ٱلذَّهَبِ ٱلْمُقَيِّئُ.

Ipso facto, ad. فِعْلًا – بِنَفْسِ ٱلْأَمْرِ.

Irascibility, *n.* }
Irascibleness, } شَكاسَةٌ – شَكَسٌ – حِدَّةُ مِزاجٍ – حِدَّةٌ.

Irascible, *a.* سَرِيعُ ٱلْغَضَبِ – غَضُوبٌ – شَرِسُ ٱلْمِزاجِ – شَكِسٌ – فَيُورٌ ٱلْحَنَقِ.

Ire, *n.* غَيْظٌ – غَضَبٌ. *See also* Anger, *n.*

Ireful, *a.* غَضْبانُ – غَضُوبٌ – ثائِرٌ. *See also* Angry, *a.*

Irefully, *ad.* بِٱلْغَضَبِ – غَضَبًا – غَيْظًا. *See also* Angrily, *ad.*

Ireland, *n.* بِلادُ إِيرْلانْدا – إِيرْلانْدا.

Iridescence, *n.* أَلْوانُ ٱلْقَوْسِ قُزَحَ.

Iridescent, *a.* مُتَلَوِّنٌ بِأَلْوانِ قَوْسِ قُزَحَ.

Iridium, *n.* ضَرْبٌ مِنَ ٱلْمَعْدِنِ أَبْيَضُ ٱللَّوْنِ نادِرُ ٱلْوُجُودِ – إِرِيدِيُوم.

Iris, *n.* The rainbow, قُسْطانَةٌ – قَوْسُ قُزَحَ. The — of the eye, قُزَحِيَّةٌ بَنَفْسَجِيٌّ. The flower, إِيرِسَاءٌ – سُوسَنٌ – سُوسَنٌ – دائِرُ ٱلْبُؤْبُؤِ. A small wild —, ياسَمِينٌ بَحْرِيٌّ. Iris-root, شِرْشُ ٱلطَّيِّبِ – إِيرِساءٌ.

Irish, *a.* إِيرْلانْدِيٌّ – مِنْ إِيرْلانْدا. The — language, لِسانُ الإِيرْلانْدِيَّةِ – إِيرْلانْدا.

Irishism, *n.* لَفْظَةٌ إِيرْلانْدِيَّةٌ – تَعْبِيرٌ إِيرْلانْدِيٌّ.

Irishman, *n.* مَرْءٌ مِنْ أَهْلِ إِيرْلانْدا – إِيرْلانْدِيٌّ.

Irishwoman, *n.* اِمْرَأَةٌ مِنْ أَهْلِ إِيرْلانْدا – إِيرْلانْدِيَّةٌ.

Irksome, *a.* مُزْعِجٌ – مُتْعِبٌ – مُمِلٌّ – مُضْجِرٌ – شاقٌّ. To be — to, أَضْجَرَ – أَزْعَجَ – أَمَلَّ.

Irksomely, *ad.* مَلَّةً – بِضَجَرٍ – بِمَلالٍ.

Irksomeness, *n.* زَعَلٌ – ضَجَرٌ – مَلالٌ – مَلالَةٌ – مَلَّةٌ.

Iron, *n.* The mineral metal, حَدِيدٌ. Tough —, or — mixed with steel, حَدِيدٌ ذَكِيرٌ – حَدِيدٌ ذَكَرٌ; soft —, حَدِيدٌ أَنِيثٌ. A flat —, مِكْواةٌ *pl.* مَكاوٍ. An — instrument, a piece of —, حَدِيدَةٌ – آلَةٌ مِنْ حَدِيدٍ. The —, or head of an arrow, نَصْلٌ *pl.* نِصالٌ *and* نُصُولٌ. Irons, chains, زِنْجِيرٌ *pl.* زَناجِيرُ – قُيُودٌ; captivity, أَسْرٌ. Cast —, حَدِيدٌ سَكْبٌ. Old —, حَدِيدٌ عَتِيقٌ. Sheet —, حَدِيدٌ صَفائِحُ – حَدِيدٌ مُصَفَّحٌ – صَفائِحُ مِنْ حَدِيدٍ. Wrought —, حَدِيدٌ مَطْرُوقٌ. Bar —, سَبِيكَةُ حَدِيدٍ *pl.* سَبائِكُ. To put one's — in the fire, to intermeddle, تَعَرَّضَ – تَدَخَّلَ.

Iron, *a.* مِنْ حَدِيدٍ. The — age, عَصْرُ ٱلْجَوْرِ وَٱلْجَهالَةِ – الجاهِلِيَّةُ.

Iron, *v.t.* As with a smoothing iron, ضَرَبَ مِكْواةً – كَوَى.

Iron-bound, *a.* Bound with iron, مَشْدُودٌ بِحَدِيدٍ – مُطَوَّقٌ بِحَدِيدٍ. Rocky, مُضْخِرٌ – صَخِرٌ. Wild, مِقْفارٌ – مُكْفَهِرٌّ.

Iron-clad, *a.* Clad in iron, لابِسٌ حَدِيدًا – مُدَرَّعٌ.

Iron-clad, *n.* Of a ship, مُدَرَّعَةٌ (or سَفِينَةٌ) بارِجَةٌ.

Iron-filings, *n.* بُرادَةُ (or) حَدِيدٍ سُحالَةُ.

Iron-founder, *n.* سَبّاكُ ٱلْحَدِيدِ.

Iron foundry, *n.* دارُ سَبْكِ ٱلْحَدِيدِ – مَسْبَكُ ٱلْحَدِيدِ.

Iron-grey, *a.* أَصْدَأُ *fem.* صَدْآءُ – شُقْرَةٌ.

Ironic, *a.* }
Ironical, } هُزْأَةٌ – ذُو هَجْوٍ. An — speech, قارِصَةٌ – هِجاءٌ *pl.* قَوارِصُ. Ironical speeches, نَوادِرُ.

Ironically, *ad.* بِنِفاقٍ – إِسْتِهْزاءً. To speak —, عَكَسَ.

Ironist, *n.* هُزْأَةٌ – هاجٍ.

Ironmonger, *n.* خُرْدَجِيٌّ *pl.* خُرْدَجِيَّةٌ.

Ironmongery, *n.* أَمْتِعَةٌ مِنْ حَدِيدٍ – خُرْدَةٌ.

Iron-mould, *n.* بُقْعَةُ صَدَأٍ.

Ironside, *n.* Intrepid, سَنْدَرِيٌّ – سَبَنْدَى – قَدُومٌ.

Ironsmith, *n.* حَدّادٌ *pl.* حَدّادُونَ. *See also* Blacksmith, *n.*

Ironstone, *n.* مَعْدِنُ حَدِيدٍ مَخْلُوطٌ بِحِجارَةٍ.

Iron-wood, *n.* ضَرْبٌ مِنَ ٱلْخَشَبِ شَدِيدُ ٱلصَّلابَةِ.

Iron-work, *n.* حَدِيدٌ – شُغْلُ حَدِيدٍ.

Iron-works, *n.* مَعْمَلُ حَدِيدٍ.

Iron-wort, *n.* The plant, سِيدِرِيتِس — سِيدِرِيتِيس.

Irony, *n.* تَهَكُّم — هُزْؤ — إِسْتِهْزَآء — نِقَاسَة — أُهْجِيَّة. *See also* Satire, *n.*

Irradiance, *n.* / Irradiancy, } بَرِيق — نُور — شَعْشَعَة — ضِيَآء — رَوْنَق — تَنْوِير — بُرُوق.

Irradiate, *v.t.* أَضَآءَ — أَنَارَ — نَوَّرَ — أَلْمَحَ. To be —, أَضَآءَ — تَنَوَّرَ — تَشَعْشَعَ — شَعْشَعَ — أَشْرَقَ — تَبَرَّقَ — بَرَّقَ — بَرَقَ ².

Irradiation, *n.* The emission of rays, تَشَعْشُع — تَبْرِيق — تَلْمَاح. Intellectual light, إِلْهَام — نُورُ ٱلْعَقْلِ — لَمَحَان — إِدْرَاكٌ عَقْلِيٌّ.

Irrational, *a.* Void of reason, عَدِيمُ ٱلْعَقْلِ — غَيْرُ نَاطِقٍ. Not according to reason, خَارِجٌ عَنْ — مُخَالِفُ ٱلْعَقْلِ — غَيْرُ مَعْقُولٍ — خِيطَةُ ٱلصَّوَاب. An — man, قَلِيلُ ٱلْعَقْلِ. An — or surd root, جِذْرٌ أَصَمُّ.

Irrationality, *n.* The quality of being void of reason, عَدَمُ ٱلنُّطْقِ — طَبِيعَةٌ غَيْرُ نَاطِقَةٍ; the quality of not being according to reason, عَدَمُ تَعَقُّلٍ — عَدَمُ صَوَابٍ — جَهَالَة.

Irrationally, *ad.* بِطَرِيقَةٍ مُخَالِفَةٍ ٱلْعَقْلِ — بِعَدَمِ مَعْقُولٍ.

Irreclaimable, *a.* Not to be reformed, إِسْتِشْبَابُهُ غَيْرُ مُمْكِنٍ — لَا يَتَهَذَّبُ — لَا يَقْبَلُ ٱلْإِصْلَاحَ — لَا يَعْتَدِلُ. Not to be reclaimed, of land, لَا يُحْيَى. Not to be tamed, لَا يَنْطَبِعُ — غَيْرُ مُنْطَبِعٍ. Hopeless, لَا يُرْجَى مِنْهُ خَيْرٌ — لَا يُؤْنَسُ.

Irreclaimably, *ad.* بِمَا لَا يَقْبَلُ — بِمَا لَا يَعْتَدِلُ — بِعَدَمِ ٱسْتِشْبَابِ ٱلْإِصْلَاحِ. Irreclaimably lost, ضَائِعٌ أَصْلًا *pl.* ضِيَاع *and* ضُيَّع.

Irreconcilable, *a.* That cannot be reconciled, appeased, أَلَدُّ — لَا يَتَصَالَحُ — لَا يَقْبَلُ ٱلْمُصَالَحَةَ. Incompatible, لَا يَتَّفِقُ مَعَ غَيْرِهِ — مُنَاقِض — مُخَالِف — غَيْرُ مُوَافِقٍ. Irreconcilable enmity, عَدَاوَةٌ دَائِمَةٌ.

Irreconcilableness, *n.* Quality of being irreconcilable, عَدَمُ إِمْكَانِ إِصْلَاحِهِ — مُخَالَفَة. Incongruity, تَخَالُف — تَضَادّ — عَدَمُ ٱتِّفَاقٍ — تَنَاقُض.

Irreconcilably, *ad.* In a manner precluding reconciliation, بِغَيْرِ مُصَالَحَةٍ. Without congruity, بِغَيْرِ ٱتِّفَاقٍ.

Irrecoverable, *a.* That cannot be recovered, تَحْصِيلُهُ ثَانِيَةً مُحَال — مَا لَا يُعَوَّضُ — مَا لَا خَلَفَ لَهُ — مُحَال. That cannot be made good again, تَعْوِيضُهُ مُحَالٌ. That cannot be repaired, لَا يُعَالَجُ — لَا يُصْلَحُ. Lost entirely, مَفْقُودٌ بَتَّةً. *See also* Incurable, *a.*

Irrecoverably, *ad.* مِنْ غَيْرِ مُدَاوَاةٍ — مِنْ غَيْرِ عِلَاجٍ. Wholly, أَصْلًا — طَرًّا — بِٱلْكُلِّيَّةِ — بَتَّةً.

Irredeemable, *a.* That cannot be redeemed, freed, إِسْتِخْلَاصُهُ مُحَال — فِدَاؤُهُ مُحَالٌ — مُحَال. *See also* Irrecoverable, Irreparable, *a.*

Irredeemably, *ad.* بِلَا فِدًى — دُونَ ٱفْتِدَآءٍ. Wholly, بَتَّةً — أَصْلًا — بِٱلْكُلِّيَّةِ — بِٱلْمَرَّةِ.

Irrefragability, *n.* As of a testimony, claim, *etc.*, عَدَمُ جُرْحَةٍ — ثِقَة — ثَبَات — عِزَّة.

Irrefragable, *a.* As of a claim, *etc.*, رَدُّهُ (*or* جَرْحُهُ) مُحَالٌ — لَا يُكَذَّبُ — مُسَلَّم — ثَابِت — عَزِيز — غَيْرُ مَرْفُوضٍ — لَا يُرَدُّ — نَقْضُهُ مُحَالٌ.

Irrefragably, *ad.* بِمَا لَا يُرَدُّ عَلَيْهِ — بِثَبَاتٍ — بِعَدَمِ جُرْحَةٍ — بِعِزَّةٍ.

Irrefutable, *a.* لَا يُرَدُّ عَلَيْهِ — إِبْطَالُهُ مُحَالٌ — لَا يُجْرَحُ.

Irrefutably, *ad.* بِثَبَاتٍ — بِمَا لَا يُرَدُّ عَلَيْهِ — بِعَدَمِ جُرْحَةٍ — عِزَّةً — بِلَا مُنَاقَضَةٍ.

Irregular, *n.* Not according to rule, غَيْرُ قِيَاسِيٍّ — شَاذٌّ — بِغَيْرِ قَانُونٍ — ضِدُّ ٱلْقَانُونِ — عَلَى غَيْرِ ٱلْقِيَاسِ. Not in order, غَيْرُ مَنْظُومٍ — غَيْرُ مَضْبُوطٍ. Against fixed principle, خِلَافُ ٱلْأُصُولِ — مُنَاقِضُ ٱلْقَوَانِينِ. Deviating from the proper course, exceptional, سَمَاعِيٌّ — شَوَاذّ. *pl.* شَاذَّة *fem.* شُذَّان *pl.* شَاذٌّ. Not appropriate, not in its proper place, of a word or sentence, غَيْرُ سَالِمِ ٱلْعَيْنَيْنِ. Dissipated, مُنْهَمِكٌ فِي ٱللَّذَّاتِ — مُعَاب — فَاسِد. Irregular soldiers, بَاشِي بُزُق — عَسْكَرٌ غَيْرُ مُنْتَظِمٍ. To be —, abnormal, out of the common course, شَذَّ ².

Irregularity, *n.* Deviation from rule or method, مُخَالَفَةُ ٱلْقَوَانِينِ — شَذّ. Want of order, عَدَمُ نَسَقٍ — عَدَمُ ٱلْإِنْتِظَامِ. Irregularity of life, فِسْقٌ وَفَسَادٌ — قِلَّةُ تَرْتِيبٍ. Irregularity of the pulse, إِضْطِرَابُ ٱلنَّبْضِ. An immoral action, vice, عَيْب — عَيْبَة *pl.* عِيَاب *and* عَيْبَات.

Irregularly, *ad.* Without rule or method, بِغَيْرِ ٱلْقِيَاسِ — مِنْ غَيْرِ تَرْتِيبٍ — بِغَيْرِ ضَبْطٍ — مِنْ غَيْرِ نِظَامٍ. Not appropriately, بِغَيْرِ مُنَاسَبَةٍ — بِشُذُوذٍ.

Irrelative, *a.* غَيْرُ مَوْصُولٍ — شَاذٌّ — غَيْرُ مُقْتَرِنٍ.

Irrelevancy, *n.* شُذُوذ — فَرْط — خُرُوج — عَدَمُ مُنَاسَبَةٍ.

Irrelevant, *a.* غَيْرُ مُنَاسِبٍ — خَارِجٌ عَنِ ٱلصَّدَدِ — فِي غَيْرِ مَحَلِّهِ — شَاذٌّ.

Irrelevantly, *ad.* بِعَدَمِ — فِي خَارِجِ ٱلصَّدَدِ — فِي غَيْرِ مَحَلِّهِ — بِشُذُوذٍ — مُنَاسَبَةٍ.

Irrelievable, *a.* لَا يُلَطَّفُ — ٱلتَّخْفِيفُ عَنْهُ مُحَالٌ.

Irreligion, *n.* / Irreligiousness, } قِلَّةُ دِينٍ — زَنْدَقَة — مُنَافَقَة — نِفَاق.

Irreligious, *a.* Of a person, مُنَافِق — غَيْرُ دَيِّن — ما لَهُ دِينٌ ; of things, مُخَالِفُ ٱلدِّيَانَةِ — ضِدُّ ٱلدِّينِ.

Irreligiously, *ad.* بِعَدَمِ دِيَانَةٍ — مِنْ غَيْرِ دِينٍ — بِمُنَافَقَةٍ — بِنِفَاقٍ.

Irremediable, *a.* لا عِلَاجَ لَهُ — لا يُدَوَى. *See also* Incurable, Irreparable, *a.*

Irremediably, *ad.* بِلا مُعَالَجَةٍ — مِنْ غَيْرِ مُدَاوَاةٍ.

Irremissible, *a.* لا يُعْفَى عَنْهُ — لا يُغْفَرُ.

Irremissibleness, *n.* عَدَمُ إِمْكَانِ غُفْرَانِهِ — عَدَمُ ٱلْإِعْفَآءِ (*or* ٱلْمُعَافَاةِ).

Irremissibly, *ad.* بِدُونِ مُعَافَاةٍ — بِدُونِ إِعْفَآءٍ — مِنْ غَيْرِ غُفْرَانٍ.

Irremovable, *a.* رَاهِن — ثَابِت — لا يَتَحَوَّلُ — لا يَتَزَعْزَعُ.

Irremovably, *ad.* بِثَبَاتٍ — بِعَدَمِ تَزَعْزُعٍ.

Irreparability, *n.* تَعَذُّرُ ٱلْمُعَالَجَةِ — عَدَمُ إِمْكَانِ مُعَالَجَتِهِ.

Irreparable, *a.* لا يُصْلَحُ — لا يُعَالَجُ. An — fault, ذَنْبٌ لا يَنْمَحِى — غَلَطٌ لا يُصْلَحُ. *See also* Irremediable, *a.*

Irreparably, *ad.* مِنْ غَيْرِ عِلَاجٍ — بِعَدَمِ مُعَالَجَةٍ. *See also* Irremediably, *ad.*

Irrepealable, *a*, *See* Irrevocable, *a.*

Irreprehensible, *a.* }
Irreproachable, } نَقِيٌّ — بِلا لَوْمٍ — لا يُلَامُ — ما عَلَيْهِ عِتَابٌ — زَكِيٌّ — مُسْتَقِيم — عَادِل. *See also* Blameless, *a.*

Irreprehensibly, *ad.* }
Irreproachably, } بِٱسْتِقَامَةٍ — مِنْ غَيْرِ لَوْمٍ — مِنْ غَيْرِ مَلَامَةٍ — بِبَرَآءَةٍ — بِنَقَاوَةٍ. *See also* Blamelessly, *ad.*

Irrepressible, *a.* مُحَالٌ (*or*) قَهْرُهُ ضَبْطُهُ. Irrepressible laughter, قَرْقَرَة.

Irrepressibly, *ad.* بِمَا لا يُقْهَرُ.

Irreproachableness, *n.* عِصْمَة — بَرَآءَة — عَدَمُ عَيْبٍ — عَدَمُ مَلَامَةٍ.

Irreprovable, *a.* بِلا لَوْمٍ. *See also* Irreprehensible, Blameless, *a.*

Irreprovably, *ad.* مِنْ غَيْرِ لَوْمٍ. *See also* Irreprehensibly, Blamelessly, *ad.*

Irresistibility, *n.* }
Irresistibleness, } عِزَّة — عِزّ — عَدَمُ إِمْكَانِ مُقَاوَمَتِهِ — عَدَمُ إِمْكَانِ مُخَالَفَتِهِ.

Irresistible, *a.* لا يَقْدِرُ أَحَدٌ عَلَى مُقَاوَمَتِهِ — لا يُقَاوَمُ — أَعَزّ — عَزِيز — لا يُغَالَبُ — لا يُقْدَرُ عَلَيْهِ. An — torrent, جُحَاف.

Irresistibly, *ad.* بِعِزٍّ — بِعِزَّةٍ. Forcibly, قَهْرًا — غَصْبًا.

Irresoluble, *a.* *See* Indissoluble, *a.*

Irresolubleness, *n.* *See* Indissolubility, *n.*

Irresolute, *a.* ما لَهُ عَزْمَةٌ وَلا — قَلِق — سَفِيه — فَائِلُ ٱلرَّأْيِ — يُقَدِّمُ رِجْلًا وَيُؤَخِّرُ أُخْرَى — مُتَرَدِّد — قَلَّاع — طَائِش — عَزِيمَة. To be —, طَاشَ *aor.* يَطِيشُ. To be — in, تَحَيَّرَ فِي — تَرَدَّدَ فِي — قَلَّبَ ٱلرَّأْيَ فِي.

Irresolutely, *ad.* بِطَيْشٍ — بِحَيْرَةٍ — بِتَرَدُّدٍ — بِغَيْرِ تَعَمُّدٍ.

Irresoluteness, *n.* }
Irresolution, } طَيْش — تَرَدُّد — عَدَمُ قَرَارٍ — سَفَهٌ — قَيْلُولَة — طَيَشَان.

Irresolvable, *a.* *See* Indissoluble, *a.*

Irrespective, *a.* Irrespective of, without regard to, بِلا نَظَرٍ إِلَى — بِغَيْرِ عَلَاقَةٍ بِ — بِلا نِسْبَةٍ إِلَى.

Irrespectively, *ad.* سِوَى — ما عَدَا.

Irresponsibility, *n.* عَدَمُ مَسْؤُولِيَّةٍ.

Irresponsible, *a.* Not answerable, غَيْرُ مُطَالَبٍ — غَيْرُ مَسْؤُولٍ. Innocent of, بَرِيٌّ مِنْ.

Irresponsibly, *ad.* مِنْ غَيْرِ مَسْؤُولِيَّةٍ.

Irretrievable, *a.* *See* Irreparable, Irremediable, *a.*

Irretrievably, *ad.* *See* Irremediably, Irreparably, *ad.*

Irreverence, *n.* تَرْكُ ٱلْحُرْمَةِ — عَدَمُ ٱحْتِرَامٍ — عَدَمُ حُرْمَةٍ — قِلَّةُ تَعَبُّدٍ.

Irreverent, *a.* قَلِيلُ ٱلتَّعَبُّدِ — عَدِيمُ ٱلِٱحْتِرَامِ — قَلِيلُ ٱلْحُرْمَةِ.

Irreverently, *ad.* بِلا تَعَبُّدٍ — بِلا حُرْمَةٍ.

Irreversible, *a.* As of a decree, *etc.*, لا يُفْسَخُ — بَتِّيٌّ. *See also* Irrevocable, *a.*

Irreversibleness, *n.* As of a decree, عَدَمُ ٱنْفِسَاخٍ — بَتٌّ. *See also* Irrevocability, *n.*

Irreversibly, *ad.* بَتَّةً — حَتْمًا جَزْمًا — بِعَدَمِ تَغْيِيرٍ.

Irrevocability, *n.* }
Irrevocableness, } عَدَمُ إِمْكَانِ تَغْيِيرِهِ — بَتَّة.

Irrevocable, *a.* لا يُرَدُّ — لا يَتَغَيَّرُ — لا يُفْسَخُ — بَتٌّ. An — decree, حَتْمٌ لا يُفْسَخُ — حَتْمٌ بَتٌّ. An — charitable gift, صَدَقَةٌ بَتَّةٌ — صَدَقَةٌ بَتَّةٌ بَتْلَةٌ. I made him an — gift, أَعْطَيْتُهُ عَطِيَّةً بَتًّا بَتْلًا. He swore an — oath, حَلَفَ بَتًّا ح.

Irrevocably, *ad.* بَتَّةً — حَتْمًا جَزْمًا — بِعَدَمِ تَغْيِيرٍ.

Irrigate, *v.t.* سَقَى — ح سَقَى.

Irrigation, *n.* The act of, تَسْقِيَة. The — of land by canals, سِقَايَةٌ (*or*) سَقْيُ ٱلْأَرْضِ بِٱلتُّرَعِ.

Irritability, *n.* Of temper, حِدَّةُ مِزَاجٍ. Susceptibility to inflammation, سُهُولَةُ ٱلِٱلْتِهَابِ — هَيْجَة.

Irritable, *a.* Of temper, غَضُوب — فَيُور — حَدِيدُ ٱلْمِزَاجِ. Susceptible of inflammation, سَهْلُ ٱلِٱلْتِهَابِ.

Irritably, *ad.* غَضَبًا — غَيْظًا — بِحِدَّةٍ.

Irritant, *a.* Inflammatory, مُسَبِّبٌ لِلِٱلْتِهَابِ — مُقْرِح.

Irritant, *n.* Of a medicine, دَوَآءٌ يُسَبِّبُ — دَوَآءٌ مُقْرِحٌ ٱلِٱلْتِهَابَ.

Irritate, *v.t.* To excite anger, أَغْضَبَ ـ أَغَاظَ ـ أَوْغَرَ. To rouse up, هَيَّجَ ـ حَرَّضَ ـ إِسْتَفَزَّ. To vex, عَجَّزَ ـ أَزْعَجَ. To chafe, عَقَرَ ـ جَرَشَ. To inflame, أَلْهَبَ.

Irritation, *n.* The act of exciting, تَهْيِيج ـ تَحْرِيض ـ إِسْتِفْزَاز ـ إِغَاظَة; the being vexed, excited, غَضَب ـ سُخْط ـ غَيْظ. Inflammation, اِلْتِهَاب ـ هَيَجَان.

Irritative, *a.* } Inflammatory, مُسَبِّبٌ ـ مُقْرِح ـ اِلْتِهَابِيٌّ
Irritatory, } لِلْاِلْتِهَاب.

Irruption, *n.* حَمْلَة ـ غَزَاة ـ هُجُوم. They made an — into the border, جَاوَزُوا الْحُدُودَ. *See also* Invasion, *n.*

Irruptive, *a.* غَازٍ ـ هَاجِم.

Ischuretic, *a.* نَافِعٌ لِقَطْعِ الْبَوْلِ.

Ischury, *n.* اِنْقِطَاعُ الْبَوْلِ.

Ishmael, *n.* إِسْمَاعِيلُ. The Ishmaelites, the sect, الإِسْمَاعِيلِيَّة.

Ishmaelite, *a.* إِسْمَاعِيلِيٌّ.

Isinglass, *n.* غِرَآءُ السَّمَكِ.

Islâm, *n.* } دِينُ الْإِسْلَامِ ـ الإِسْلَامُ.
Islamism, }

Islamitic, *a.* إِسْلَامِيٌّ.

Island, *n.* جَزِيرَةٌ *pl.* جَزَائِرُ.

Islander, *n.* مِنْ أَهْلِ جَزِيرَةٍ *pl.* أَهْلُ جَزِيرَةٍ.

Isle, *n.* جُزَيْرَةٌ *pl.* جُزَيْرَات.

Islet, *n.* جَزِيرَةٌ صَغِيرَةٌ.

Isochronal, *a.* } مُشْتَرِكُ الْوُقُوعِ وَقْتًا ـ مُتَسَاوِي الْمُدَّةِ. Iso-
Isochronous, } chronous movements, حَرَكَاتٌ مُدَّتُهَا وَاحِدَةٌ.

Isolate, *v.t.* To place detached, أَوْتَرَ ـ جَعَلَ فَذًّا ـ أَفَذَّ; to place alone, أَفْرَدَ ـ أَوْحَدَ ـ أَفَذَّ. To — one's self from, فَذَّ ـ اِنْفَرَدَ مِنْ ـ اِبْتَعَدَ مِنْ ـ عَنْ. To — by water, حَوَّطَ بِالْمَآءِ.

Isolated, *a.* Alone, فَذٌّ *pl.* فُذُوذ ـ فَارِد *fem.* فَارِدَة ـ مُنْفَرِد. Lonely, of a person, مُتَوَحِّد. Of whom no one takes notice, مَتْرُوك.

Isolation, *n.* The state of being alone, اِنْفِرَاد ـ فَذٌّ ـ إِسْتِفْذَاذ. Solitude, وَحْدَة ـ خَلْوَة.

Isoperimetrical, *a.* مُتَسَاوِي الْمُحِيطِ.

Isoperimetry, *n.* عِلْمُ الْبَحْثِ عَنِ الْأَشْكَالِ الْمُتَسَاوِيَةِ الْمُحِيطِ.

Isosceles, *a.* مُتَسَاوِي السَّاقَيْنِ. An — triangle, مُثَلَّثٌ مُتَسَاوِي السَّاقَيْنِ.

Isothermal, *a.* مُتَسَاوٍ فِي دَرَجَاتِ الْحَرَارَةِ.

Isotonic, *a.* مُتَسَاوِي الصَّوْتِ.

Israelite, *n.* يَهُودِيٌّ ـ إِسْرَائِيلِيٌّ *pl.* يَهُود.

Israelitic, *a.* } يَهُودِيٌّ ـ إِسْرَائِيلِيٌّ.
Israelitish, }

Issuable, *a.* إِصْدَارُهُ مُمْكِنٌ ـ مِمَّا يُصْدَرُ. It is — from the treasury, تَوْزِيعُهُ مِنَ الْخَزِينَةِ.

Issue, *n.* A flowing forth, خُرُوج ـ صُدُور ـ اِنْصِبَاب ـ صَبٌّ. The making to issue, إِصْدَار ـ إِخْرَاج. The place of —, مَخْرَج ـ مَخْلَص ـ مَنْفَذ ـ بَاب ـ مَصْدَر. A consequence, result, نَتِيجَة ـ ثَمَرَة ـ نِهَايَة ـ حَاصِل ـ تَأْوِيل ـ آخِرَة ـ عَاقِبَة. The act of distributing, تَوْزِيع ـ تَفْرِيق ـ تَقْسِيم ـ قَسْم; what is distributed, تَفَرُّق ـ تَوَزُّع. A spring, يَنْبُوع ـ عَيْن ـ مَنْبَع. An intentional ulcer, كَيٌّ *pl.* كَيَّة ـ كَيَّات. Offspring, أَوْلَاد ـ نَسْل ـ آل. Having an — of blood, نَازِفُ دَمٍ. The — of a loan, إِصْدَارُ قَرْضٍ. He died and left no —, مَاتَ بِغَيْرِ وَلَدٍ ـ مَاتَ وَلَمْ يُخَلِّفْ نَسْلاً ـ مَاتَ بِلَا بَنِينَ. An inquiry into a matter of fact, إِسْتِقْصَآءٌ فِي حَالِ الْوَاقِعَةِ. An — at law, مَسْأَلَةٌ شَرْعِيَّةٌ. At —, under litigation, تَحْتَ الْخِصَامِ ـ تَحْتَ النِّزَاعِ. To be at — with, خَاصَمَ ـ نَازَعَ. They were at — one with another, of many, تَخَاصَمُوا. To bring to an —, أَنْفَذَ ـ أَتَمَّ ـ أَنْهَى. To join — with, to adduce arguments against one, إِحْتَجَّ عَلَى ـ بِ: they joined issue, disputed with one another, about, إِخْتَصَمُوا فِي. The issues of life and death, مَخَارِجُ الْحَيٰوةِ وَالْمَوْتِ.

Issue, *v.i.* To flow from, جَرَى مِنْ ـ سَالَ مِنْ *aor.* يَسِيلُ ـ خَرَجَ مِنْ. To —, as blood from a wound, فَارَ ـ نَجَّ ـ سَفَحَ. To —, as matter from a sore, عَسَقَ ـ نَجَّ. To emanate from, صَدَرَ عَنْ. To come to pass, to take place, تَحَدَّثَ. To come to an end, اِنْقَضَى ـ اِنْتَهَى ـ تَمَّ. To — in, to result in, حَصَلَ ـ جَآءَ مِنْ *aor.* يَجِيءُ. Gum issues from trees, الصَّمْغُ يَرْشَحُ مِنَ الْأَشْجَارِ. A notice has been issued by the department, صَدَرَ إِشْعَارٌ مِنَ الْإِدَارَةِ.

Issue, *v.t.* To cause to come out, أَخْرَجَ. To distribute, وَزَّعَ ـ فَرَّقَ. To cause to emanate, as orders, *etc.*, أَصْدَرَ. To publish, proclaim, أَذَاعَ بِ ـ أَشْهَرَ ـ نَادَى بِ. To publish, as of a book, طَبَعَ ـ أَظْهَرَ ـ نَشَرَ ـ بَرَّزَ. To — a loan, أَصْدَرَ قَرْضًا. The loan has been issued, قَدْ صَدَرَ الْقَرْضُ. Which it is intended to —, الْمُرَادُ صُدُورُهُ. To — a decree, قَضَى قَضَاءً ـ حَكَمَ حُكْمًا.

Issueless, *a.* Of offspring, مِنْ غَيْرِ نَسْلٍ ـ بِلَا أَوْلَادٍ.

Isthmus, *n.* بَرْزَخ ـ شَبِيهُ الْجَزِيرَةِ ـ لِسَانُ أَرْضٍ بَيْنَ بَحْرَيْنِ *pl.* بَرَازِخ. The Canal of the — of Suez, تُرْعَةُ السُّوَيْسِ.

It, *pr. masc.* هُوَ; *fem.* هِيَ. As a suffix, *m.* ـهُ; *fem.* هَا. It was, كَانَ; it will be, سَيَكُونُ. It must be so, لَابُدَّ أَنْ يَكُونَ كَذَا.

It ought to be so, كَانَ يَنْبَغِي أَنْ يَكُونَ كَذَا. It is very likely, قَرِيبُ ٱلْاِحْتِمَالِ. It rains, تَمْطُرُ ٱلدُّنْيَا ـ تَمْطُرُ. It is going to rain to-day, ٱلْيَوْمَ يَصِيرُ مَطَرٌ. It never entered my thoughts before, لَمْ أَحْدُسْ بِهِ مِنْ قَبْلُ. It may happen again, رُبَّمَا يَحْدُثُ مَرَّةً أُخْرَى. It is I, أَنَا ـ أَنَا هُوَ. He walked it, مَشَى ٱلْمَسَافَةَ. It is not twilight till an hour before sunrise, لَا يَكُونُ ٱلشَّفَقُ إِلَّا قَبْلَ طُلُوعِ ٱلشَّمْسِ بِسَاعَةٍ. It was not always so, هٰذَا مَا كَانَ دَائِمًا.

Italian, *a.* مِنْ بِلَادِ إِيطَالِيَا ـ إِيطَلْيَانِيٌّ. The — language, اللِّسَانُ ٱلْإِيطَلْيَانِيُّ.

Italian, *n.* مِنْ أَهْلِ إِيطَالِيَا ـ إِيطَلْيَانِيٌّ *pl.* إِيطَلْيَانِيَّةٌ.

Italianize, *v.t.* أَغْرَقَ فِي طَبَائِعِ ٱلْإِيطَلْيَانِيَّةِ ـ صَيَّرَ إِيطَلْيَانِيًّا.

Italics, *n.* رُقْعَةٌ ـ خَطُّ رِقَاعٍ ـ حُرُوفُ ٱلْكِتَابَةِ. To write in —, كَتَبَ فِي خَطِّ رِقَاعٍ.

Itch, *n.* The disease, حِكَّةٌ ـ إِكْلَةٌ ـ جَرَبٌ ـ نَغَلَانٌ ـ أُكَالٌ. A longing desire; *see* Itching, *n.* To have the —, جَرِبَ ـ نَغِلَ ـ حَكَّ.

Itch, *v.i.* أَكَلَ ـ أَحَكَّ ـ نَغِلَ ـ رَعَى. My skin itched, جِلْدِي ٱسْتَحَكَّنِي ـ جِلْدِي أَحَكَّنِي ـ جِلْدِي يَأْكُلُنِي. My head itched, أَحَكَّنِي رَأْسِي ـ أَكَلَنِي رَأْسِي. To — for, long for, حَنَّ إِلَى ـ ٱشْتَهَى ـ تَتَوَّقَ إِلَى ـ تَاقَ إِلَى.

Itching, *n.* أُكَالٌ ـ حَكٌّ ـ جَرَبٌ. Longing desire, تِبَاقَةٌ ـ شَوْقٌ ـ هَوِيَّةٌ ـ حَنِينٌ.

Itching, *a.* Teasing, مُغْرِضٌ ـ مُضْجِرٌ ـ مُصَدِّعٌ. Itching ears, مَسَامِعُ مُسْتَحِكَّةٌ.

Itchy, *a.* جَرْبَانُ ـ أَجْرَبُ.

Item, *n.* An article, شَيْءٌ *pl.* أَشْيَاءُ ـ قَلَمٌ *pl.* أَقْلَامٌ ـ مُفْرَدَةٌ *pl.* مُفْرَدَاتٌ. A subject, مَادَّةٌ *pl.* مَوَادٌّ ـ فَصْلٌ *pl.* فُصُولٌ.

Item, *ad.* وَمِثْلُهُ ـ أَيْضًا ـ كَذٰلِكَ.

Item, *v.t.* To make a memorandum of, دَوَّنَ ـ كَتَبَ ـ ضَبَطَ ـ قَيَّدَ.

Iterate, *v.t.* عَادَ ـ أَعَادَ ـ رَجَّعَ ـ كَرْكَرَ ـ كَرَّرَ ـ ثَنَّى.

Iteration, *n.* تَرْجِيعٌ ـ إِعَادَةٌ ـ تَرْدَادٌ ـ تَرْدِيدٌ ـ تَثْنِيَةٌ ـ تَكْرَارٌ. With —, بِتَرْدِيدٍ ـ تَكْرَارًا.

Iterative, *a.* مُكَرِّرٌ ـ مُرَجِّعٌ.

Itinerant, *n.* سَيَّاحٌ ـ سَيَّارٌ ـ سَافِرٌ *pl.* سُفَّارٌ *and* أَسْفَارٌ ـ دَائِرٌ *pl.* دُوَّارٌ ـ زَائِلٌ ـ نَقِيلٌ.

Itinerant, *a.* Wandering, سَائِحٌ *pl.* سُوَّاحٌ. An —, or wandering people, نَوَاقِلُ. *See also* Itinerant, *n.*

Itinerary, *n.* A book of travels, كِتَابُ سِيرَةٍ ـ سِيرَةُ سَفَرٍ. A book of directions for travelling, عِلْمُ بَيَانِ ٱلطُّرُقَاتِ ـ دُسْتُورٌ. A list of stations, مَنَازِلُ (or) فِهْرِسُ سِيَاحَةٍ لِلسَّفَرِ.

Itinerate, *v.i.* سَاحَ *aor.* يَسِيحُ ـ عَارَفَ ـ عَالَ فِي ـ دَارَ.

Itself, *pr. masc.* هُوَ ـ *fem.* هِيَ; as a suffix, *m.* هُ; *fem.* هَا ـ نَفْسٌ ـ ذَاتٌ ـ عَيْنٌ. It is the thing —, هُوَ هُوَ عَيْنُهُ ـ هُوَ هُوَ عَيْنًا ـ هُوَ هُوَ ذَاتُهُ. Virtue itself, ٱلصَّلَاحُ بِعَيْنِهِ. The thing —, هُوَ هُوَ بِعَيْنِهِ ٱلشَّيْءُ. By —, عَلَى حِيَالِهِ ـ وَحْدَهُ.

Ivory, *n.* The tusk, سِنُّ فِيلٍ ـ حَضَنُ ٱلْفِيلِ; the substance, عَاجٌ ـ حَضَنٌ. To inlay with —, عَوَّجَ. Inlaid with — or tortoise-shell, مُعَوَّجٌ.

Ivory, *a.* مِنْ سِنِّ ٱلْفِيلِ ـ مِنْ عَاجٍ ـ عَاجِيٌّ.

Ivory-black, *n.* جَرِيشُ ٱلْأَعْظَامِ ٱلْمَحْرُوقَةِ.

Ivory-nut, *n.* ضَرْبٌ مِنَ ٱلْجَوْزِ بَاطِنُهُ يُشْبِهُ ٱلْعَاجَ.

Ivy, *n.* قِسُّوسٌ ـ حَبْلُ ٱلْمَسَاكِينِ ـ ٱلْبَقْلَةُ ٱلْبَارِدَةُ. Ground —, خَمَاقِسُّوس.

Ivied, Ivy-crowned, *a.* Ivy-mantled, } مَعْرُوشٌ بِحَبْلِ ٱلْمَسَاكِينِ ـ مُغَطًّى بِقِسُّوسٍ.

J.

Jabber, *v.i.* هَذْرَمَ ـ زَحْلَفَ فِي ٱلْكَلَامِ ـ بَقَّ. He jabbered at us, فَرَّقَ عَلَيْنَا ٱلْكَلَامَ. *See also to* Babble, Chatter, *v.i.*

Jabber, *n.* / Jabbering, } قِيلٌ وَقَالٌ ـ لَقْش ـ هَذْرَمَةٌ ـ بَقٌّ. *See also* Babble, Chatter, *n.*

Jabberer, *n.* لِسانٌ طَلِقٌ ـ فَرْفَار ـ بَقَّاق ـ بَرْبَار. *See also* Babbler, Chatterer, *n.*

Jabberingly, *ad.* بِقِيلٍ وَقَالٍ ـ بِهَذْرَمَةٍ ـ بِبَقٍّ.

Jacinth, *n.* *See* Hyacinth, *n.*

Jack, *n.* A nickname for John, لَقَبُ ٱسْمِ يُوحَنَّا (*or* يَحْيَى). An instrument to pull off boots, مِلْزَمُ ٱلْأَحْذِيَةِ (*or* ٱلْجِزْمَاتِ). An instrument for turning a spit, آلَةٌ لِتَدْوِيرِ ٱلسَّفُّودِ. The fish, سَمَكُ ٱلْكَرَاكِي. A keg, مَطَرِيَّةٌ ـ مَطَرَةٌ. The male, ٱلذَّكَرُ. The flag, بَيْرَقُ ٱلْبَوَارِجِ ـ بَيْرَقُ ٱلْمَرَاكِبِ ٱلْحَرْبِيَّةِ. A sailor, بَحْرِيٌّ *pl.* بَحْرِيَّةٌ. The — fruit, ضَرْبٌ مِنَ ٱلْفَاكِهَةِ. The Union Jack, عَلَمُ ٱلْبَوَارِجِ ٱلْأَنْكِلِيزِيَّةِ. Jack of all trades, ما يَشِذُّ عَلَيْهِ شَيْءٌ ـ مِفَنٌّ ـ صَنَّاعٌ. Jack-in-a-box, the plant, إِهْلِيلَج; the toy, عَرُوسَةٌ فِي عُلْبَةٍ. An instrument, آلَةٌ.

Jackadandy, *n.* مُتَكَيِّس ـ غَنْدُور ـ مُتَطَوِّس.

Jackal, *n.* اِبْنُ آوَى *pl.* بَنَاتُ آوَى *vulg.* وَاوِي.

Jack-a-lantern, *n.* *See* Ignis-fatuus, *n.*

Jack-a-lent, *n.* A boy, غُلَام ـ صَبِيٌّ ـ وَلَد.

Jackanapes, *n.* A stupid fellow, أَبْلَهُ ـ أَخْرَقُ ـ رَقِيعٌ ـ أَرْقَعُ ـ حِمَار.

Jackass, *n.* حِمَار *pl.* حَمِير.

Jackboots, *n.* حِذَاءٌ طَوِيلٌ (*or* جِزْمَةٌ طَوِيلَةٌ) إِلَى ٱلرُّكْبَةِ.

Jackdaw, *n.* قَاق *pl.* قِيقَان ـ زَاغ *or* زَاق *pl.* زِيغَان.

Jacket, *n.* بَدَن *pl.* أَبْدَان ـ جُبَّة *pl.* جُبَب. A man's —, جَكِيتَةٌ ـ قَبَاءٌ ـ فَرْمَلَةٌ; made of cloth, جُوخَةٌ; of stuff, رِدَاءٌ مِنْ صُوفٍ ـ قَبُّوط; of silk, مُصَرَّبِيَّة. A woman's —, مِنْتَان. A strait —, دِرْعٌ لِضَبْطِ ٱلْمَجَانِينِ.

Jack-Ketch, *n.* جَلَّاد ـ مَشَاعِلِيٌّ.

Jack-knife, *n.* سِكِّين *pl.* سَكَاكِين ـ مَطْوَى *pl.* مَطَاوِي.

Jack-pudding, *n.* بَهْلُول. *See also* Buffoon, *n.*

Jacob, *n.* The name, يَعْقُوب.

Jacobin, *n.* A demagogue, disorganiser, مِنْ أَهْلِ عُصْبَةٍ ـ فَتَّان ـ مُفْسِد.

Jacobin, / Jacobinic, *a.* / Jacobinical, } مُفْتِن ـ عَصَبِيٌّ ـ مُفْسِد.

Jacobinism, *n.* عَصَبِيَّة ـ فَسَاد.

Jacobite, *n.* A follower of the Jacobite creed, يَعْقُوبِيّ *pl.* يَعْقُوبِيَّة *or* يَعَاقِبَة.

Jacobite, *a.* Pertaining to the creed of Jacob Baradæus, مُتَعَلِّقٌ بِٱلْمَذْهَبِ ٱلْيَعْقُوبِيِّ ـ يَعْقُوبِيٌّ. The — creed, مَذْهَبُ (*or* قَاعِدَةُ إِيمَانِ) ٱلْيَعْقُوبِيَّةِ.

Jacob's ladder, *n.* The — of a ship, سُلَّمُ ٱلْغَابِيَةِ. A ladder of rope, سُلَّمٌ مِنْ حَبْلٍ.

Jacob's staff, *n.* عُكَّازَة ـ عَصًا.

Jaconet, *n.* ضَرْبٌ مِنَ ٱلشَّاشِ رَفِيعٌ.

Jaculate, *v.t.* رَمَى ـ طَرَحَ.

Jaculation, *n.* رَمْيٌ ـ طَرْح.

Jaculatory, *a.* *See* Ejaculatory, *a.*

Jade, *n.* A tired horse, دَابَّةٌ ـ حِصَانٌ مُتْعَبٌ (*or* تَعْبَانٌ) ـ دَابَّةٌ عَيَّانَةٌ *vulg.* مُعْيِيَةٌ. A low woman, عَاهِرَة ـ حَاسِرَة. The mineral حَجَرُ ٱلْيَشْبِ (called in Persian, يَشْم).

Jade, *v.t.* أَتْعَبَ ـ أَهْلَكَ ـ أَجْهَدَ ـ نَهَكَ ـ أَعْيَا.

Jadish, *a.* Unruly, restiff, نَمِل ـ شَمُوس ـ مُتَمَرِّد. Wanton, مُتَنَعِّم ـ هَوَّاس ـ دَنِس ـ شَقِيٌّ. A — horse, حِصَانٌ طَمُوحٌ ـ حِصَانٌ جِرَانٌ.

Jag, *n.* A notch, حَزٌّ *pl.* حُزُوز ـ فَلٌّ *pl.* فُلُول ـ ثَلْم ـ ثَلْمَة *pl.* ثُلَم.

Jag, *v.t.* حَزَّى ـ اِحْتَزَّ ـ فَلَّلَ ـ ثَلَّمَ. To be jagged, تَحَزَّزَ ـ اِنْثَلَمَ. *See also to* Notch, *v.t.*

Jagged, *a.* أَثْلَم ـ مُتَثَلِّم ـ فَلِيل ـ مَفْلُول ـ أَفَلُّ.

Jaggedness, *n.* تَحَزُّز ـ اِنْثِلَام ـ تَثَلُّم.

Jagger, *n.* / Jagging-iron, } قَالِبٌ لِلْفَطَائِرِ.

Jaggy, *a.* *See* Jagged, *a.*

Jaguar, *n.* نَمِرٌ أَمِيرِكَانِيٌّ.

Jah, *n.* *See* Jehovah, *n.*

Jail, *n.* سِجْن ـ حَبْس ـ مَحْبَس. *See also* Prison, *n.*

Jailer, *n.* حَبَّاس ـ سَجَّان.

Jail-bird, *n.* A prisoner, مَحْبُوس. One who is often in prison, أَلِيفُ ٱلسُّجُونِ.

Jail-fever, *n.* حُمَّى ٱلسُّجُونِ.

Jakes, *n.* كَنِيف ـ مِسْتَرَاح ـ شَشْمَة.

Jalap, *n.* جَلَبَا ـ جَلَابَا.

Jalousie, *n.* مُخَرَّم ـ شَعْرِيَّة ـ مُشَبَّك ـ شَبَّاكَة.

Jam, *n.* A pressure, squeeze, حَزْق ـ غَمْز ـ قَرْص ـ ضَغْط. A conserve of fruits, مُرَبَّى *pl.* مُرَبَّيَات ـ رِيصَال.

Jam, *v.t.* To squeeze, ـ ضَغَطَ ـ ٢ شَدَّ عَلَى ـ ـ غَمَزَ ـ ـ حَزَقَ. To press, wedge, مَكَّنَ عَلَى.

Jamb, *n.* As of a door, *etc.*, قائمة *pl.* قَوَائِم. A post, نَصِيبَة ـ خَشَبَة ـ صَوَارِي *pl.* صارى. A pillar, عَمُود *pl.* عُمُد.

Jangle, *v.i.* Of many, تَشَاجَرُوا ـ تَنَازَعُوا ـ تَجَادَلُوا; of two, تَنَازَعَا ـ تَشَاجَرَا ـ تَجَادَلَا.

Jangle, *v.t.* خَشْخَشَ ـ أَطَنَّ.

Jangle, *n.* }
Jangling, } شِقَاق ـ مُشَاجَرَة ـ مُجَادَلَة.

Janissary, *n.* The old Turkish troops so called, يَنْكِجَارِيّ *pl.* يَنْكِجَارِيَّة. The modern orderly at a Consulate, قَوَّاس *pl.* قَوَاوِيس.

Janitor, *n.* بَوَّاب ـ حاجب.

Jantily, *ad.* }
Jauntily, } Briskly, بِخِفَّةٍ ـ بِخِفَّةٍ وَنَشَاطٍ. With airs, بِتَصَلُّفٍ ـ بِبَطَرٍ ـ بِتَعَظُّمٍ.

Jantiness, *n.* }
Jauntiness, } Briskness, خِفَّة ـ نَشَاط. Levity, هَزَل ـ فَرْفَرَة ـ خِفَّةُ عَقْلٍ. To behave with —, ـ بَطِرَ ـ تَعَظَّمَ ـ تَصَلَّفَ.

Janty, *a.* }
Jaunty, } Brisk, ذُو خِفَّةٍ ـ خَفِيف ـ نَشِيط. Light, trifling, of a person, خَفِيفُ ٱلْعَقْلِ ـ هَزِل. Gay, of a thing or person, مَلِيح ـ ظَرِيف ـ لَطِيف.

Japan, *n.* The country, بِلادُ ٱلْفَغْفُورِ ـ مَمْلَكَةُ يَابَانَ ـ يَابَان (or ٱلْفَرْفُورِ). The varnish, صَمْغُ ٱللَّكِّ. Japan or Japanese work, شُغْل يَابَان. Porcelain of —, فَرْفُورِيّ ـ فَغْفُورِيّ.

Japan, *v.t.* To varnish with —, ـ ٢ دَهَنَ ـ بِٱللَّكِّ. To smear or rub with, ـ ٢ دَهَنَ ب ـ ـ طَلَى ب. To gloss, ٢ صَقَلَ.

Japanese, *a.* Of Japan, يَابَانِيّ ـ مِنْ يَابَانَ. A —, مِنْ أَهْلِ يَابَانَ. The — language, لِسَانُ يَابَان.

Japanning, *n.* Size for paper, تَرْبِيَة ـ آهَار. Varnish, دُهْن ـ دُهْن ٱللَّكِّ. The act of varnishing, تَدْهِين ـ تَطْلِيَة; of polishing, صِقَال.

Jar, *v.t.* To shake, حَرَّكَ ـ قَلْقَلَ ـ زَعْزَعَ ـ هَزَّزَ ـ فَرْفَرَ. To be jarred, تَقَلْقَلَ ـ تَزَعْزَعَ.

Jar, *v.i.* To dash, of many things, تَلَاطَمُوا ـ تَصَادَمُوا; of two things, تَلَاطَمَا ـ تَصَادَمَا. To be harsh in sound, بَجَّ *aor.* يَبُجُّ. To make a harsh noise, ـ صَرَّ ـ ـ صَرَفَ. To be discordant to, خَالَفَ ـ ضَادَدَ. It jarred on the ear, ـ صَرَّ لِلْأُذُنِ.

Jar, *n.* A shake, حَرَكَة ـ زَعْزَعَة ـ قَلْقَلَة ـ هَزَّة. A dash, مُلَاطَمَة ـ مُصَادَمَة. Dissension, شِقَاق ـ مُنَازَعَة ـ نِفَاق. A vessel, بَاطِيَة ـ خَوَابِي *pl.* خابية ـ جَوْنَة. A — with a narrow neck, جِرَار *pl.* جَرَّة. A small —, دَوْرَجَة. A — for water, زِير *pl.* أَزْيَار. A — for cooling water, مُزَمَّلَة. To be on the jar, of a door, إِنْفَتَحَ قَلِيلًا.

Jargon, *n.* Gibberish, رَطَانَة ـ لَغْو ـ غَذْمَرَة. To speak — to, ٢ رَطَنَ ل.

Jargonelle, *n.* The pear, ضَرْبٌ مِنَ ٱلْكُمَّثْرَى فاخِرٌ جِدًّا.

Jarring, *n.* *See* Dissension, *under* Jar, *n.*

Jarringly, *ad.* With discord, بِشِقَاقٍ ـ بِمُنَازَعَةٍ.

Jasmine, *n.* يَاسَمِين ـ يَاسَمُون ـ غِرْنَف. Arabian, or double —, فُلّ. Creeping —, يَاسَمِينُ ٱلتَّعْرِيشِ.

Jasper, *n.* يَصْب ـ يَشْب ـ يَشْم.

Jaundice, *n.* يَرَقَان.

Jaundiced, *a.* Having jaundice, مُصَابٌ بِيَرَقَانٍ ـ بِهِ يَرَقَانٌ. Prejudiced, envious, مُعَادٍ ـ حَسُود ـ حاسِد. To take a — view of, تَبَصَّرَ بِعَيْنِ ٱلْحِقْدِ.

Jaunt, *v.i.* To ramble about in, تَرَدَّدَ فِي ـ ـ عَالَ فِي ـ ـ غَارَ فِي. سَاحَ فِي *aor.* يَسِيحُ.

Jaunt, *n.* تَفْسِيح ـ سَيْرَةٌ لِلتَّنَزُّهِ. A pleasure —, مُطَوَّر ـ سِيَاحَة.

Jauntily, Jauntiness, Jaunty; *see* Jantily, Jantiness, Janty.

Javelin, *n.* مِزْرَاق ـ زَرَّاقَة ـ مِزَجّ. To pierce with a —, ٢ زَرَقَهُ بِمِزْرَاقٍ.

Jaw, *n.* The bone in which the teeth are fixed, لَحْي; the two jaws, لَحْيَانِ ـ فَكّ *pl.* فُكُوك. The jaws, the inside of the mouth, حَنَك. The jaws of death, رِبَاطُ (or) ٱلْمَوْتِ. The upper —, ٱلْفَكُّ ٱلْأَعْلَى; the lower —, ٱلْفَكُّ ٱلْأَسْفَلُ. Talk, قِيلٌ وَقَالٌ ـ فُشَار ـ لَبْلَبَة. Having a broken —, فَكِك. The part of the jaw nearest the nose, فُقْم.

Jaw, *v.i.* To gabble, ثَرْثَرَ ـ لَبْلَبَ ـ بَقْبَقَ. To rail, show displeasure, تَسَخَّطَ ـ ـ سَخِطَ.

Jaw, *v.t.* To scold, revile, تَسَخَّطَ عَلَى ـ ـ شَتَمَ ـ ـ سَخِطَ.

Jawbone, *n.* لَحْي *pl.* لُحِيّ ـ فَكّ *pl.* فُكُوك.

Jay, *n.* The bird, عَقْعَق *pl.* عَقَاعِق.

Jealous, *a.* Apprehensive of rivalship, غَيْرَانُ ـ مِغْيَار ـ غَيُور;

very —, شَحْشَاح . Envious, حاسِد . Suspicious, ذُو رِيبَةٍ ـ مُرِيب . To be — of, غَارَ عَلَى ². To make —, أَغَارَ . He is — of his wife, يَغَارُ عَلَى ٱمْرَأَتِهِ . To be —, envious, of, on account of, حَسَدَ-عَلَى ². To be — for, solicitous to defend, غَارَ غَيْرَةً ل ².

Jealously, *ad.* غَيْرَةً ـ بِغَيْرَةٍ . With care, بِٱحْتِذَارٍ ـ بِحَذَرٍ ـ بِدِقَّةٍ .

Jealousy, *n.* Apprehension of rivalship, غَيْرَة . Envy, حَسَد . Suspicion, شَكٌّ ـ رِيبَة ـ مَوْهِمَة . To provoke to —, أَغَارَ .

Jean, *n.* The cloth, ضَرْبٌ مِنَ ـ ضَرْبٌ مِنَ ٱلْقُمَاشِ ٱلْمَصْقُولِ ٱلدَّائِمَةِ .

Jeer, *v.i.* To utter sarcastic reflections, تَسَخَّطَ ـ سَلَطَ ² ـ سَخِرَ مِن ـ إِسْتَهْزَأَ ب ـ قَرَصَ ب ² ـ نَقَرَ ² ـ سَخِطَ ². To jeer at, بَهْدَلَ ـ ضَحِكَ مِن *or* ب *or* عَلَى .

Jeer, *v.t.* *See to* Jeer at, *in the preceding paragraph.*

Jeer, *n.* بَهْدَلَة ـ نَقْرَى ـ إِسْتِهْزَاء ـ قارِصَة .

Jeering, *n.* هُزْؤٌ ـ نَقْر ـ قَرْص .

Jeeringly, *ad.* بِبَهْدَلَةٍ ـ بِنَقْرٍ ـ بِقَرْصٍ ـ إِسْتِهْزَاءً .

Jehovah, *n.* إِهْيَا أَشَرْ إِهْيَا so given, from the Hebrew, in the *Tâju-'l-'Arûs* and the *al-Kâmus*; others abridge it into هَيَا شَرَاهيا giving it the Arabic meaning of يا حَيُّ يا قَيُّومُ . Al-Ama'iy says that the vulgar say يا هيا or, what would be more correct, يا هَيَاه . *See* Lane *under* شَرَة .

Jejune, *a.* Hungry, جائع . Dry, عَطْشَان ـ عاطِش . Barren, عاقِر ـ جارِز . Empty, فارِغ . Poor, mean, رَكِيك ـ حَقِير ـ مَسْكِين . Insipid, عَدِيمُ ٱللَّذَّةِ ـ تافِه . To be —, paltry, تَفِهَ ². *See also under* Meagre, *a.*

Jejuneness, *n.* Poverty, meanness, رَكَاكَة ـ حَقَارَة ـ تَفَه ـ مَسْكَنَة . Barrenness, قِلَّةُ ثَمَرَةٍ ـ عُقْرَة . Insipidity, عَدَمُ ٱللَّذَّةِ ـ تُفُوهَة ـ تَفَاهَة ـ قِلَّةُ لَذَّةٍ .

Jellied, *a.* Preserved with jelly, مُرَبَّب . Made into a jelly, مُجَمَّد .

Jelly, *n.* As of calves' feet, *etc.*, لُعَاب ـ هُلام . Inspissated juice of fruit, رُبٌّ . Jellies, preserved fruits, مُرَبَّبَات . Coagulated juice, عَصِيرٌ مُجَمَّدٌ ـ مَرَقَةٌ مُجَمَّدَةٌ . Jelly of salted fish, صِحْنَاة ـ صِير . To thrash or pound to a —, رَضْرَضَ ـ رَضَّ ². He beat his body to a —, رَضْرَضَ جِسْمَهُ .

Jelly-bag, *n.* كِيسٌ لِعَصْرِ ٱلْعَصِيرِ .

Jelly-fish, *n.* فَرَجُ ٱلْبَحْرِ .

Jemadar, *n.* مُلازِمٌ مِنَ ٱلضُّبَّاطِ ٱلْهِنْدِيَّةِ .

Jemmy, *n.* مُخْول *and* أَمْخَال *pl.* مُخْل ـ حَدِيدَة ـ عَمُودُ حَدِيدٍ . *See also* Bar, *n.*

Jennet, *n.* *See* Genet, *n.*

Jenny, *n.* The machine, دُولَابُ ٱلْغَزْلِ .

Jeopard, *v.t.* } أَلْقَى ـ أَخْطَرَ . To — one's self, خَاطَرَ (*or* أَخْطَرَ)
Jeopardize, } بِنَفْسِهِ . *See also to* Hazard, Endanger, Imperil, *v.t.*

Jeopardous, *a.* ذُو خَطَرٍ ـ مُخْطِر . *See also* Dangerous, Hazardous, *a.*

Jeopardy, *n.* مُخَاطَرَة ـ خَطْرَة ـ خَطَر . *See also* Danger, Hazard, *n.*

Jerboa, *n.* يَرْبُوع *pl.* يَرَابِيعُ ; *vulg.* جَرْبُوع *pl.* جَرَابِيع ـ شُورَابِيّ .

Jereed, *n.* (More correctly *Jarîd*), جَرِيد . To play the —, لَعِبَ ٱلْجَرِيدَ ².

Jeremiad, *n.* أَنِين ـ كُرْبَة ـ شَكْوَى ـ تَبْكَاء ـ مَرْثَاة .

Jerk, *v.t.* To — or spit out, مَخَعَ ب ². To push, thrust, دَفَعَ ² ـ صَدَمَ ² ـ قَصَفَ ². To throw, رَمَى ـ طَرَحَ ² *aor.* يَرْمِي . To shake, حَرَّكَ ـ هَزَّ ².

Jerk, *n.* A pushing out, مَخْع . A push, thrust, دَفْعَة ـ صَدْمَة . A cast, throw, طَرْحَة ـ رَمْيَة . A shake, هَزَّة .

Jerked-beef, *n.* لَحْمُ بَقَرٍ مُقَدَّدٌ فِي ٱلشَّمْسِ .

Jerkin, *n.* A short jacket, جُبَّة ـ دُرَّاعَة ـ مِدْرَعَة . A hawk, باز *pl.* بُزَاة ـ باشِق *pl.* بَوَاشِق ـ صَقْر *pl.* صُقُور .

Jersey, *n.* Fine wool, صُوفٌ ناعِمٌ . A woollen shirt, قَمِيصٌ مِنَ صُوف ـ قَمِيصٌ مِنَ ٱلْخَزِّ (*or* ٱلصُّوف) .

Jerusalem, *n.* أُورُشَلِيمُ ـ ٱلْقُدْسُ ٱلشَّرِيفُ ـ ٱلْقُدْسُ .

Jerusalem-artichoke, *n.* ضَرْبٌ مِنَ ٱلْكَمْأَةِ ; *vulg.* ضَرْبٌ مِنَ ٱلْكَمَايَة .

Jess, *n.* A hawk's jesses, قَيْدَا ٱلْبَازِي ـ سِبَاقَا ٱلْبَازِي .

Jessamine, *n.* *See* Jasmine, *n.*

Jest, *v.i.* هَزَلَ ² ـ هَازَلَ ـ شَمَعَ ² ـ دَعَبَ ² ـ هَرَجَ ² ـ مَرَحَ ² ـ مَزَحَ ² ـ هَذِرَ ². To — with, فاكَهَ ـ داعَبَ ـ مازَحَ ـ مازَهَ . He jested, or joked, in his talk, بَطِلَ فِي حَدِيثِهِ ². They jested together, of many, تَفَاكَهُوا ـ تَمَازَهُوا ـ تَمَازَحُوا .

Jest, *n.* عَبَث ـ دُعَابَة ـ مُزَاحَة ـ هُزَالَة ـ مَزْح . The object of laughter or —, سُخْرَة ـ أُضْحُوكَة ـ لُعْبَة . To make a — of, تَسَخَّرَ مِن ـ سَخِرَ مِن ² ـ ضَحِكَ مِن *or* ب *or* عَلَى ².

Jester, *n.* داعِب ـ هَزِل ـ مُضْحِك ـ مُسْخِر .

Jestful, *a.* } داعِب ـ دَعَّاب ـ مُلاعِب . *See also* Jocose, *a.*
Jesting, }

Jesting, *n.* شِمَاع ـ عَبَث ـ شِمَاعَة ـ هَزْل ـ مَزْه ـ مَزْح ـ بَسْط ـ مُمَازَحَة .

Jestingly, *ad.* شَمْعًا ـ بِهَزْلٍ ـ بِمَزْحٍ ـ بِمُزَاحَةٍ .

Jesuit, *n.* يَسُوعِيٌّ *pl.* يَسُوعِيَّة. A casuist, صُوفِيٌّ *pl.* صُوفِيَّة.

Jesuitic, *a.} Belonging to the Jesuits, يَسُوعِيٌّ. Crafty, أَرِيب —
Jesuitical, } ذُو كَيْدٍ — خَبِيث — حَوَالِيٌّ — دَاهٍ.

Jesuitically, *ad.* Craftily, بِتَلْبِيسٍ — بِحِيلَةٍ — بِكَيْدٍ — بِٱحْتِيَالٍ — بِخِيَانَةٍ.

Jesuitism, *n.* Craft, deceit, خَدِيعَة — خُبْث — دَهَآء — إِحْتِيَال — شَيْطَنَة. Casuistry, تَصْوِيف — تَصَوُّف.

Jesuit's-bark, *n.* *See* Cinchona, *n.*

Jet, *n.* The fossil, حَجَرٌ مُوسَى — كَهْرَبَآء سَوْدَآء. A spouting, as of water, نَوْفَرَة — نَافُورَة — فَوَّارَة. A fountain with a jet or jets of water, فَسْقِيَّة *pl.* فَسَاقِيٌّ — شَادُرْوَان.

Jet, *v.i.* *See to* Jut, *v.i.*

Jet-black, *a.* أَسْوَدُ فَحْمِيٌّ — فَحِيم — أَسْوَدُ خَالِص — أَسْوَد.

Jetsam, *n.* } إِلْقَآءُ أَثَاثِ مَرْكَبٍ فِي ٱلْبَحْرِ لِأَجْلِ تَخْفِيفِهِ فِي
Jetsom, } وَقْتِ ٱلنَّوْءِ — شَيْءٌ مَدْسُورٌ مِنَ ٱلْبَحْرِ.

Jet d'eau, *n.* نَوْفَرَة (or نَافُورَة or فَوَّارَة) مَآء.

Jetty, *n.* رَصِيف — رَصْفَة — رَصَف.

Jetty, *a.* Made of jet, مِنْ كَهْرَبَا سَوْدَآء. *See also* Jet-black, *a.*

Jew, *n.* يَهُودِيٌّ *coll.* يَهُود. To become a —, تَهَوَّدَ — هَادَ ².

Jewel, *n.* A precious stone, جَوْهَرَة *coll.* جَوْهَر *pl.* جَوَاهِر. An ornament, حِلْيَة *pl.* حُلِيّ — مَصَاغ — زِينَة. A term of endearment, عَيْن — قَلْب — عَزِيز. Covered with jewels, مُحَلًّى بِٱلْجَوَاهِرِ. A — casket, سَفَطُ جَوَاهِر.

Jewel, *v.t.* To stud with jewels, رَصَّعَ بِجَوَاهِر. To adorn with jewels, زَيَّنَ بِجَوَاهِر.

Jewelled, *a.* مُرَصَّعٌ بِجَوَاهِر.

Jeweller, *n.* جَوَاهِرْجِي — جَوْهَرِيٌّ. One who cuts jewels, حَكَّاكُ ٱلْجَوَاهِرِ.

Jewelry, *n.* جَوَاهِر — مُرَصَّعَات — مَصَاغ — حُلِيٌّ.

Jewess, *n.* يَهُودِيَّة *pl.* يَهُودِيَّات.

Jewish, *a.* يَهُودِيٌّ — مِثْلَ ٱلْيَهُودِ.

Jewry, *n.* بِلَادُ ٱلْيَهُودِيَّةِ — مَحَلُّ ٱلْيَهُودِ.

Jew's-harp, *n.* طُنْبُورٌ يُلْعَبُ بِهِ بِٱلْفَمِ وَٱلْبَاهِمِ.

Jew's-pitch, *n.* Bitumen, قَفْرُ ٱلْيَهُودِ. *See also* Bitumen, *n.*

Jezebel, *n.* A shrew, خَطَّالَة — سَلِيطَة — إِمْرَأَةٌ فَحْلَةٌ — عَاهِرَة.

Jib, *n.* The foremost sail of a ship, فَلُوق. Countenance, appearance, the cut of one's jib, هَيْئَة — وَجْه — صُورَة. Flying —, قُنْطَرَةُ ٱلْفَلُوقِ.

Jibboom, *n.* بَاشْتُون.

Jibe, *n.* *See* Jeer, *n.*

Jibe, *v.t.* *See to* Jeer, *v.t.*

Jibe, *v.i.* *See to* Jeer, *v.i.*

Jiffy, *n.* دَقِيقَة. In a —, حَالًا — عَلَى ٱلْفَوْرِ.

Jig, *n.* ضَرْبٌ مِنَ ٱلرَّقْصِ. To jig, *v.i.* رَقَصَ ² — زَفَنَ ².

Jigger, *n.* The insect, دُوَيْبَّةٌ تَدِبُّ فِي ٱللَّحْمِ. The — of a cable, آلَةٌ لِحِفْظِ ٱلْقَلْسِ.

Jihád, *n.* A war for the faith, a holy war, جِهَاد. To proclaim a —, نَادَى بِٱلْجِهَادِ.

Jill, *n.* صَبِيَّة.

Jilt, *v.t.* قَابَحَ — مَكَرَ بِ ² — غَشَّ ² — تَرَكَ بِٱلْغِشِّ ² — ضَحِكَ عَلَى or مِن or بِ ².

Jilt, *n.* مُخَادِعٌ فِي ٱلْعِشْقِ *fem.* مُخَادِعَة — عَيْهَر *fem.* عَيْهَرَة — غَشَّاش *fem.* غَشَّاشَة.

Jingle, *v.t.* To cause to sound with a sharp noise, أَطَنَّ; of a bell, دَقَّ ² — قَرَعَ ². To —, as money, arms, *etc.*, خَشْخَشَ; of rhyme, سَجَّعَ.

Jingle, *v.i.* To sound with a sharp rattle, طَنَّ ² — طَنْطَنَ; of a bell, إِنْدَقَّ; of money, *etc.*, تَخَشْخَشَ; of speech or rhyme, سَجَعَ ² — سَجَّعَ.

Jingle, *n.* } طَنِين — طَنْطَنَة; of money, arms, *etc.*, خَشْخَشَة.
Jingling, } Concordance of sounds, أُلْفَةُ ٱلْأَصْوَاتِ — سَجْع.

Job, *n.* A piece of work, شُغْلَة — حَاجَة — أَشْغُولَة. Something to be done in a given time, يَوَام — مُقَاوَلَة — مُيَاوَمَة. A mess, muddle, إِلْتِبَاك — شَوَاش — شَجَر — خَبْصَة. An arrangement for undue gains at others' expense, خِدْعَة. An affair, أَمْر — قَضِيَّة — قِصَّة. By the job, بِٱلْمُقَاطَعَةِ — بِٱلْقِطْعَةِ — بِٱلْوَاحِدِ. To make a job, muddle, of, لَبَكَ — هَوَّشَ — شَوَّشَ — خَبَصَ. To repair, أَصْلَحَ — رَمْرَمَ.

Job, *v.t.* To let out on hire, آجَرَ — أَجَرَ ² — كَارَى ². To take on hire, إِسْتَأْجَرَ — أَكْرَى. To make a job of; *see under preceding article.*

Job, *v.i.* To do jobs, إِشْتَغَلَ أَشْغَالًا — قَضَى حَاجَاتٍ ². To job on the exchange or bank, تَحَكَّرَ فِي ٱلْبُورْسِ.

Job, *n.* The patriarch of Holy Scripture, حَضْرَةُ أَيُّوب — أَيُّوبُ.

Jobation, *n.* سُخْط — شَتِيمَة — عِتَاب.

Jobber, *n.* One who does jobs, رَقَّابَة — رَجُلُ وَعْدٍ — قَاضِي حَاجَاتٍ. A broker, سِمْسَار. A — on the Stock Exchange, مُتَحَكِّرٌ (or مُحْتَكِرٌ) فِي ٱلْبُورْسِ.

Jobbing, *n.* As on the Stock Exchange, إِحْتِكَارٌ (or تَحَكُّرٌ) فِي ٱلْبُورْسِ. Brokerage, سَمْسَرَة. *See also under* Job, *n.*

Jockey, *n.* One who rides race-horses, رَكَّاب ـ رَاكِبُ جِيَادٍ ـ مَحَاضِيرَ. A horse dealer, مُضَارِبُ ٱلْخَيْلِ ـ دَلَّالُ ٱلْخَيْلِ. A trickster, حُوَّلٌ قُلَّبٌ ـ غَشَّاش ـ مَكَّار.

Jockey, *v.t.* To trick, deceive, غَشَّ ـ مَكَرَ ب. To use tricks to hide the defects of a horse, سَلَّعَ ٱلْحِصَانَ.

Jockeyism, *n.* Horse dealing, مُضَارَبَةُ ٱلْخَيْلِ ـ دَلَالَةُ ٱلْخَيْلِ. Cheating in horses, تَسْلِيعُ ٱلْخَيْلِ.

Jockeyship, *n.* Horseriding, فُرُوسِيَّة ـ فُرُوسَة ـ فَرَاسَة.

Jocose, *a.* Given to jokes, مَازِح ـ هَزِل ـ دَعَّاب ـ دَاعِب ـ لَطِيف ـ هَزْلِيّ. To be —, مَزَحَ ـ هَازَلَ ـ هَزَلَ.

Jocosely, *ad.* بِهَزْلٍ ـ هَزْلًا ـ بِمُزَاحَةٍ.

Jocoseness, *n.* هَزَالَة ـ هَزْل ـ مُزَاحَة ـ مُزَاح.

Jocular, *a.* *See* Jocose, *a.*

Jocularity, *n.* *See* Jocoseness, *n.*

Jocund, *a.* *See* Blithe, Gay, Merry, *a.*

Jocundly, *ad.* *See* Blithely, Gaily, Merrily, *ad.*

Jocundness, *n.* / **Jocundity**, } *See* Blitheness, Gaiety, Merriment, *n.*

Jog, *v.t.* To push, move, هَزْهَزَ ـ هَزَّ ـ حَرَّكَ ـ ضَغَطَ ـ تَعْتَعَ ـ زَعْزَعَ. To jog one's memory, ذَكَّرَ ـ نَبَّهَ.

Jog, *v.i.* To shake, إِنْهَزَّ ـ تَهَزْهَزَ ـ تَحَرَّكَ. To — on, travel or proceed slowly, مَشَى رُوَيْدًا رُوَيْدًا ـ سَارَ عَلَى مَهَلٍ ـ أَرْوَدَ ـ تَمَشَّى مُتَمَهِّلًا.

Jog, *n.* A push, shake, حَرَكَة ـ هَزَّة ـ ضَغْط. A — to make one do something quickly, زَفْنَة ـ إِسْتِفْزَاز. A — to the memory, تَذْكِير ـ تَنْبِيه.

Joggle, *v.t.* *See to* Jog, *v.t.*

Joggle, *v.i.* *See to* Jog, *v.i.*

Jog-trot, *n.* A slow, regular pace, سَيْرٌ (*or* سِيرَةٌ) رُوَيْدِيَّة ـ عَلَى مَهَلٍ.

John, *n.* The name, حَنَّا ـ يُوحَنَّا ـ يَحْيَى.

John Bull, *n.* لَقَبُ أُمَّةِ ٱلْانْكِلِيزِ.

John-Dory, *n.* The fish, ضَرْبٌ مِنَ ٱلسَّمَكِ.

Johnny-cake, *n.* فَطَائِرُ ذُرَةٍ.

Join, *v.t.* To bring one thing in contact with another, قَرَنَ ـ ب ـ يَصِلُ *aor.* وَصَلَ ـ ب ـ جَمَعَ بَيْنَ ـ جَمَعَ ـ أَلْحَقَ ـ ب ـ أَضَافَ ـ وَاصَلَ ـ أَلْزَقَ ـ ب. To — together, as of stones in masonry, رَصَّفَ ـ رَصَفَ. To —, to go to, to reach, overtake, أَلْحَقَ ـ لَحِقَ. To accompany, keep company with, رَافَقَ ـ إِسْتَصْحَبَ. To —, of a wound, لَحَمَ. To — one's self to, with, إِنْضَافَ إِلَى ـ إِلْتَصَقَ ب. To — one's self to, in favour of, تَعَصَّبَ ل. To become affiliated to, دَخَلَ فِي. To — in marriage, عَقَدَ ٱلزَّوَاجَ بَيْنَ ـ زَوَّجَ. They joined battle, تَحَارَبُوا. To — issue; *see under* Issue, *n.*

Join, *v.i.* To adhere, stick, لَزِجَ ب ـ إِلْتَزَقَ ب ـ لَصِقَ ب. To be contiguous to, وَلِيَ *aor.* يَلِي ـ إِتَّصَلَ ب ـ جَاوَرَ ـ قَارَبَ. To be added to, إِنْضَافَ إِلَى. To —, as of a wound, إِلْتَحَمَ. To combine, of many, إِتَّحَدُوا ـ إِتَّفَقُوا. They joined together against me, تَعَصَّبُوا عَلَيَّ. They joined in partnership, تَشَارَكُوا ـ إِشْتَرَكُوا. Some of the soldiers joined them, إِتَّصَلَ بِهِمْ بَعْضُ ٱلْعَسَاكِرِ. To be well joined together, as of masonry, *etc.*, إِرْتَصَفَ ـ تَرَصَّفَ.

Joiner, *n.* نَجَّار ـ فَيْتَق *pl.* نَجَّارُونَ.

Joinery, *n.* صَنْعَةُ ٱلنَّجَّارِ ـ نِجَارَة.

Joining, *n.* A seam, وَصْل *pl.* أَوْصَال ـ وُصْلَة. A place of —, مَوْصِل; as of a wound, crack, إِلْتِحَام.

Joint, *n.* A limb, member, إِرْب *pl.* آرَاب ـ عُضْو *pl.* أَعْضَاء. An articulation, مَفْصِل *pl.* مَفَاصِل ـ عُقْدَة *pl.* عُقَد. The knot of a plant, أُبْنَة *pl.* أُبَن ـ مَعْقِم *pl.* مَعَاقِم ـ أُنْبُوب *pl.* أَنَابِيب ـ شِلْو *pl.* أَشْلَاء ـ عِضَّةُ لَحْمٍ ـ عُقْدَة *pl.* عُقَد. A — of meat, قِطْعَةُ لَحْمٍ. The joints of the jaws فَكّ *pl.* فُكُوك. Out of —, of the limbs, أَفَكّ ـ مُخَلَّع ـ مَخْلُوع; in disorder, مُلْتَبِك ـ مُلْتَخِبَط ـ مُخَبَّص ـ مُتَهَوِّش ـ مُتَشَوِّش ـ مُشْتَجِر. To put out of —, of the limbs, خَلَّعَ ـ خَلَعَ ـ فَكَّ. To put into disorder, خَبَّصَ ـ هَوَّشَ ـ لَبَّكَ ـ شَوَّشَ. To be put out of —, of the limbs, إِنْفَكَّ ـ إِنْخَلَعَ ـ تَخَلَّعَ. All my bones are out of —, إِنْفَصَلَتْ كُلُّ عِظَامِي. To put one's nose out of —, أَسْتَحِبُّ عَلَى فُلَانٍ.

Joint, *v.t.* To form into joints, فَصَّلَ ـ عَضَّى ـ عَضَا. To cut up into joints, قَطَّعَ أَشْلَاء ـ شَقَّصَ ـ عَضَّى ـ بَعَّضَ ـ أَرَّبَ ـ شَرَّحَ ـ قَصَّبَ ـ قَطَّعَ. To make notches in, فَلَّلَ. I jointed the sheep, عَضَّيْتُ ٱلشَّاةَ.

Joint, *a.* Shared by two or more, شِرْكَة ـ مُشْتَرَك. United, acting in concert, مُتَّحِد ـ مُتَّفِق. Joint consent, تَوَافُق ـ إِتِّفَاق. Joint efforts, إِجْتِهَادٌ مُتَّحِدٌ ـ سَعْيٌ مُتَّفِقٌ. A — or common burden, expense, تَكْلِيفٌ عُمُومِيٌّ.

Jointed, *n.* Having joints, ذُو مَفَاصِلَ. Notched, مَفْلُول. Cut up into joints, مُشَرَّح ـ مُقَصَّب ـ مُؤَرَّب.

Joint-heir, *n.* شَرِيكٌ فِي ٱلْإِرْثِ ـ وَارِثٌ مَعَ غَيْرِهِ *pl.* وَارِثُونَ *pl.* شُرَكَاء.

Jointly, *ad.* In concert, سَوَآءً ـ إِشْتِرَاكًا ـ إِتِّفَاقًا ـ جُمْلَةً ـ جَمْعًا.

Jointress, *n.* A woman having a jointure, ذَاتُ مَهْرٍ ـ مَهِيرَةٌ.

Joint-stock, *n.* سَرْمَايَةٌ ذَاتُ حِصَصٍ ـ رَأْسُ مَالٍ مُشْتَرَكٌ ـ كُمْپَانِيَّةٌ ـ شِرْكَةٌ ـ شِرْكَةُ أَسْهَامٍ. A — company, سَرْمَايَةٌ مُشْتَرَكَةٌ.

Joint-tenancy, *n.* Of an estate, شِرْكَةٌ فِى ٱلْأَمْلَاكِ; of a lease, شِرْكَةٌ فِى ٱلِٱسْتِئْجَارِ.

Joint-tenant, *n.* Of an estate, شَرِيكٌ فِى ٱلْأَمْلَاكِ; of a lease, شَرِيكٌ فِى ٱلِٱسْتِئْجَارِ.

Jointure, *n.* *See* Dower, *n.*

Jointure, *v.t.* *See to* Dower, *v.t.*, *under* Dower, *n.*

Jointured, *a.* مَهِيرَةٌ ـ ذَاتُ مَهْرٍ.

Joist, *n.* جائز *pl.* جُوزَان *and* جِيزَان ـ خَشَبَةٌ مُعْتَرِضَةٌ.

Joist, *v.t.* رَكَّبَ جِيزَانًا.

Joke, *n.* لَطِيفَةٌ ـ هُزَالَةٌ ـ مُزَاهَةٌ ـ دُعَابَةٌ. A practical —, مَلْعُوبٌ ـ أُلْعُوبَةٌ ـ تَهْرِيجٌ. And the best of the — is that he found it in his pocket, وَمَا زَادَ ٱلْمَزْحَ ضَحِكًا وَجُودَةُ ٱلشَّيْءِ فِى جَيْبِهِ. To crack a —, مَزَحَ ـ هَزَلَ ـ دَعَبَ. To take a — as a —, لَيْسَ ـ مِنْ جِدٍّ. In —, بِسَبِيلِ ٱلْمَزْحِ. It is no —, إِتَّخَذَهُ هُزُوًا ـ بِهَزْلٍ. *See also* Jest, *n.*

Joke, *v.t.* فَاكَهَ ـ مَازَحَ ـ دَاعَبَ.

Joke, *v.i.* مَزَحَ ـ هَزَلَ ـ دَعِبَ. *See also to* Jest, *v.i.*

Joker, *n.* هَزِلٌ ـ دَعَّابٌ ـ دَاعِبٌ. *See also* Jester, *n.*

Joking, *n.* بَسْطٌ ـ مَزْحٌ ـ هَزْلٌ. Joking apart, مِنْ جِدٍّ ـ بِلَا مِزَاحٍ. To be inclined to —, أَطْرَقَ إِلَى ٱلْمَزْحِ.

Jokingly, *ad.* بِمُزَاحَةٍ ـ بِسَبِيلِ ٱلْمَزْحِ ـ بِهَزْلٍ.

Jole, *n.* The cheek, ٱلْخَدُّ *pl.* ٱلْخُدُودُ. The head, ٱلرَّأْسُ *pl.* ٱلرُّؤُوسُ. Cheek-by-jole, بَعْضٌ إِلَى جَانِبِ بَعْضٍ ـ خَدٌّ دُونَ خَدٍّ.

Jollification, *n.* A revel, فَرَحٌ ـ عَيْشٌ وَعِشْرَةٌ ـ مُنَادَمَةٌ.

Jollily, *ad.* بِعَيْشٍ وَعِشْرَةٍ ـ بِتَفَكُّهٍ ـ بِخَلَاعَةٍ ـ بِبَطَرٍ.

Jolliness, *n.* }
Jollity, } Festivity, بَطَرٌ ـ خَلَاعَةٌ ـ عَيْشٌ وَعِشْرَةٌ ـ تَفَكُّهٌ ـ فَكَهٌ ـ فُكَاهَةٌ. Happiness, حَبَرٌ ـ حُبُورٌ. Activity, خِفَّةٌ ـ نَشَاطٌ.

Jolly, *a.* أَهْلُ كَيْفٍ ـ مُتَفَكِّهٌ ـ مَخْلُوعٌ ـ بَطِرٌ ـ بَحْبُورٌ ـ فَكِهٌ. Plump, like one in health, سَمِينٌ ـ لَبِيخٌ ـ خَدْلٌ. A — set, حَابُور. To be —, gay, تَكَيَّفَ ـ تَفَكَّهَ ـ فَكِهَ ـ بَطِرَ ـ حَبِرَ ـ كَيِّفٌ. أَفْكَهَ ـ فَكَّهَ ـ حَبَّرَ. To make —, إِنْفَسَحَ صَدْرُهُ.

Jolly-boat, *n.* فَلُوكَةٌ صَغِيرَةٌ ـ فَلُوكَةٌ.

Jolt, *v.t.* خَضَّ ـ هَزَّ ـ زَعْزَعَ. *See also to* Jog, *v.t.*

Jolt, *v.i.* خَضَّ ـ إِهْتَزَّ ـ تَزَعْزَعَ. A jolting pace, سَيْرٌ زَعْزَعٌ. This horse jolts me, هٰذَا ٱلْحِصَانُ يَخُضُّنِى.

Jolt, *n.* خَضَّةٌ ـ زَعْزَعَةٌ ـ هَزَّةٌ. A shock, صَدْمَةٌ ـ كَبْسَةٌ.

Jolt-head, *n.* *See* Blockhead, Dunce, *n.*

Jonathan, *n.* The name, يُهُونَاثَانُ. Brother —, the people of the United States, لَقَبُ لِأَهْلِ جُمْهُورِيَّةِ أَمِيرِيكَا ٱلْمُتَّحِدَةِ.

Jonquil, *n.* قَطْمِرْبُولِيَا ـ نِسْرِينٌ.

Joseph, *n.* The, of Scripture, حَضْرَةُ يُوسُفَ; the name, يُوسُفُ.

Jostle, *v.t.* دَفَشَ ـ دَفَّشَ ـ زَحَمَ ـ قَصَفَ ـ ضَغَطَ. To — against, إِنْدَفَشَ ـ إِنْقَصَفَ ـ إِنْضَغَطَ ـ تَفَكَّسَ عَلَى. To be jostled, تَزَاحَمُوا ـ تَضَاغَطُوا. They jostled against one another, of many, إِزْدَحَمُوا.

Jostling, *n.* دَفْشٌ ـ قَصْفَةٌ ـ قَصْفٌ ـ زَحْمَةٌ ـ زِحَامٌ ـ ضَغْطٌ.

Jot, *v.t.* To set down, make a memorandum of, كَتَبَ ـ دَوَّنَ ـ قَيَّدَ ـ ضَبَطَ.

Jot, *n.* نُقْطَةٌ ـ حَرْفٌ. Not a jot or tittle, لَا حَرْفٌ وَاحِدٌ وَلَا نُقْطَةٌ وَاحِدَةٌ.

Jotting, *n.* *See* Memorandum, *n.*

Journal, *n.* A day-book, دَفْتَرُ تَسْوِيدٍ ـ دَفْتَرٌ يَوْمِىٌّ. A daily account, memorandum, أَوْرَاقٌ يَوْمِيَّةٌ ـ أَخْبَارٌ يَوْمِيَّةٌ ـ تَقْوِيمٌ يَوْمِىٌّ. The — or log of a ship, جُرْنَالُ مَرْكَبٍ ـ تَقْوِيمُ سَيْرِ ٱلسَّفِينَةِ. A newspaper, صَحِيفَةُ تَقْوِيمِ ٱلْوَقَائِعِ ـ صُحُفٌ (or صَحِيفَةٌ) أَخْبَارٍ ـ جَرَائِدُ *pl.* جَرِيدَةٌ ـ صَحَائِفُ *pl.* صَحِيفَةٌ ـ جَرِيدَةُ حَوَادِثَ ـ جَرِيدَةٌ (or صَحِيفَةٌ) رَسْمِيَّةٌ ـ جُرْنَالٌ ـ غَزِيتَةٌ. An official —, جَرِيدَةٌ عَادِيَّةٌ ـ صَحِيفَةٌ غَيْرُ رَسْمِيَّةٍ. An unofficial or ordinary —, A literary —, مَجْمُوعَةُ فُنُونٍ. To edit a —, أَنْشَأَ جَرِيدَةً. To publish a —, أَصْدَرَ صَحِيفَةً ـ طَبَعَ جَرِيدَةً وَنَشَرَهَا. To suspend a —, عَطَّلَ ٱلصَّحِيفَةَ بَتَّةً ـ عَطَّلَ ٱلْجَرِيدَةَ. To suppress a —, أَلْغَى ٱلْجَرِيدَةَ دَوَامًا. The influence of journals, نُفُوذُ ٱلْجَرَائِدِ (or ٱلصَّحَائِفِ).

Journalism, *n.* تَحْرِيرُ ٱلْجَرَائِدِ ـ تَأْلِيفُ ٱلْجَرَائِدِ (or ٱلصَّحَائِفِ) ـ إِدَارَةُ غَزِيتَةٍ.

Journalist, *n.* مُحَرِّرُ ٱلْحَوَادِثِ ـ مُحَرِّرُ صَحِيفَةٍ ـ مُؤَلِّفُ جَرِيدَةٍ ـ مُنْشِئُ غَزِيتَةٍ.

Journalize, *v.i.* كَتَبَ ٱلْأَخْبَارَ ٱلْيَوْمِيَّةَ ـ قَيَّدَ ٱلْحَوَادِثَ يَوْمِيًّا.

Journey, *n.* Travel to some distance, رَحِيلٌ ـ رَحْلٌ ـ تَرْدَادٌ ـ سُرْيَةٌ ـ سُرًى. A night —, أَسْفَارٌ *pl.* سَفَرٌ ـ مَسِيرَةٌ ـ سِيرَةٌ. A day's —, مَرَاحِلُ *pl.* مَرْحَلٌ ـ مَرْحَلَةٌ ـ مَنَاقِلُ *pl.* مَنْقَلَةٌ. Distance, بُعْدٌ ـ مَسَافَةٌ. The account, description, of a —, أَلُوكَةٌ ـ ذِكْرُ سَفَرٍ ـ سَفْرَةٌ. A month's —, مَسِيرَةُ شَهْرٍ. An errand, مَشْوَةٌ. To prepare one's self for a —, أَبَّ لِلسَّفَرِ. To set out on a —, سَافَرَ ـ يَسِيرُ *aor.* سَارَ ـ نَزَلَ. To send on a —,

= رَحَلَ ب ـ أَرْحَلَ ـ رَحَّلَ. One who makes frequent journeys, رَحَّال.

Journey, v.i. سَافَرَ فِي = ـ ذَهَبَ = ـ مَشَى ـ يَسِيرُ aor. سَارَ. To — from, عَنْ (إِرْتَحَلَ or تَرَحَّلَ or رَحَلَ =). To — by night, إِسْتَرَى.

Journeyman, n. صَانِع pl. صُنَّاع ـ صَنَائِعِيّ.

Journey-work, n. صِنَاعَة ـ صَنْعَة.

Joust, n. مُطَاعَنَةٌ رِيَاضِيَّةٌ ـ مُحَارَبَةٌ رِيَاضِيَّةٌ.

Jove, n. رَئِيسُ مَعَابِدِ ٱلرُّومَانِيِّينَ ٱلْأَقْدَمِينَ.

Jovial, a. See Jolly, a.

Jovially, ad. See Jollily, ad.

Jovialness, Jovialty, n. See Jollity, n.

Jowl, n. See Jole, n.

Joy, n. حَبْر ـ حُبُور ـ طَرَب ـ فَرَج ـ سُرُور ـ بَهْجَة ـ فَرَح ـ طِيبَةُ قَلْبٍ ـ إِنْشِرَاح. A cause of —, مَسَرَّة. A shouting for —, هُتَافُ ٱلْفَرَحِ. To have or experience —, سُرَّ ـ إِبْتَهَجَ ـ فَرِحَ = ـ إِنْشَرَحَ صَدْرُهُ. To give — to, حَبَّرَ ـ سَرَّ ² ـ فَرَّحَ ـ أَفْرَحَ. To leap for —, إِهْتَزَّ مِنَ ٱلسُّرُورِ ـ تَهَلَّلَ. To weep from —, بَكَى مِنَ ٱلْفَرَحِ =. To wish —, to congratulate, هَنَّأَ ب = ² ـ هَنَّأَ. To meet one with —, بَشَّ ب = ـ أَقْبَلَ عَلَى.

Joy, v.i. فَرِحَ = ـ إِبْتَهَجَ ـ سُرَّ ـ حَبِرَ.

Joy, v.t. شَرَحَ خَاطِرَهُ = ـ أَبْهَجَ ـ أَفْرَحَ ـ فَرَّحَ ـ سَرَّ ² ـ حَبَّرَ.

Joyful, a. Full of joy, مَفْرُوح ـ فَرِح ـ طَرِب ـ مَسْرُور ـ يَحْبُور ـ فَرْحَان. Giving joy, مُبْهِج ـ مُفْرِح ـ مُفَرِّح. Pleasant, amiable, courteous, هَشّ بَشّ ـ بَشَّاش. A — noise or shout, هُتَاف. A — mother of children, أُمُّ أَوْلَادٍ فَرْحَانَةٌ. Joyful tidings, بُشْرَى ـ بِشَارَة. To be — to, pleasing to, طَرِبَ ب =. To make one —, pleased, with, أَطْرَبَ ب. To be —, pleasant, towards one, تَبَشْبَشَ ب. To be —, make —; see to Joy, v.t. and i.

Joyfully, ad. بِسُرُورٍ ـ بِفَرَحٍ.

Joyfulness, n. See Joy, n.

Joyless, a. Void of joy, عَدِيمُ ٱلْفَرَحِ; giving no joy, غَيْرُ مُفْرِحٍ. Sad, حَزِين ـ كَرِيب ـ كَئِيب.

Joylessly, ad. بِلَا مَسَرَّةٍ ـ مِنْ غَيْرِ فَرَحٍ.

Joylessness, n. حُزْن ـ كَآبَة ـ كَآب ـ عَدَمُ سُرُورٍ ـ عَدَمُ فَرَحٍ.

Joyous, a. See Joyful, n.

Joyously, ad. See Joyfully, ad.

Joyousness, n. See Joy, Joyfulness, n.

Jubilant, a. بَطِر ـ هَاتِف. To be —, بَطِرَ = ـ هَتَفَ =. To make, أَبْطَرَ.

Jubilation, n. سُرُور ـ طَحْمَةُ فَرَحٍ ـ بَطَر ـ تَهْتِيف ـ هُتَاف ـ وَصَفَاء.

Jubilee, n. The — of the Jews, ٱلْيُوبِيل ـ ٱلْهُتَاف. The trumpet of the —, بُوقُ ٱلْيُوبِيلِ; the year of the —, سَنَةُ ٱلْيُوبِيلِ. See also Jubilation, n.

Judaic, n. }
Judaical, } See Jewish, a.

Judaism, n. The religion of the Jews, دِينُ ٱلْيَهُودِ. Conformity to Jewish rites, ٱلِامْتِثَالُ بِمَذْهَبِ ٱلْيَهُودِ.

Judaize, v.i. To conform to Judaism, ذَهَبَ مَذْهَبَ ٱلْيَهُودِ =.

Judge, n. One authorized to pass judgment, حَاكِمُ ٱلشَّرْعِ ـ حَاكِم pl. حُكَّام ـ قَاضٍ pl. قُضَاة. God the Judge, ٱللّٰهُ ـ ٱللّٰهُ ٱلدَّيَّان ـ ٱلْفَتَّاح. An umpire, arbitrator, فَيْصَل ـ فَيْصَلِيّ ـ مُفَصِّل ـ مُمَيِّز. One who has experience of any matter, عَارِفٌ ب ـ دَرِبٌ ب ـ صَاحِبُ رَأْيٍ فِي. A chief —, قَاضِي ٱلْقُضَاةِ. A commissioner —, مَأْمُورٌ مَخْصُوصٌ. The office or functions of a —, مَأْمُورِيَّةُ ٱلْقَاضِي ـ فِتَاحَة. An acting —, قَاضٍ مُوَكَّل. To appoint as —, حَكَّمَ ـ جَعَلَ قَاضِيًا ـ قَضَّى. To make one the — of anything, refer a matter to his decision, سَلَّمَ لَهُ فَصْلَ ٱلدَّعْوَى. To summon before a —, رَافَعَ (or حَاكَمَ) إِلَى ٱلْحَاكِمِ. To be appointed —, إِسْتَقْضَى. To refer a matter to the —, حَوَّلَ ٱلْمَادَّةَ إِلَى ٱلْقَاضِي. Deputy —, نَائِبُ ٱلْقَاضِي. The Book of Judges, سِفْرُ ٱلْقُضَاةِ.

Judge, v.t. To hear and decide, فَصَلَ ٱلدَّعْوَى ـ فَصَلَ =. To — between, فَتَحَ بَيْنَ = ـ حَكَمَ ب ² ـ قَضَى =. To pass sentence, قَطَعَ فِي = ـ حَكَمَ فِي ² ـ شَرَعَ عَلَى =. To —, pass sentence, in favour of, قَضَى ل = ـ حَكَمَ ل ²; against, قَضَى = عَلَى ـ حَكَمَ عَلَى ². To decide, estimate, the merits of, إِعْتَبَرَ ـ قَدَّرَ ـ قَايَسَ ـ قَاسَ =. To — of, قَالَ فِي aor. يَقُولُ ـ عَبَّرَ. To — of one by his physiognomy, تَفَرَّسَ فِي. To — favourably of one, ظَنَّ فِيهِ ٱلْخَيْرَ ² ـ إِسْتَحْسَنَ; unfavourably, ظَنَّ فِيهِ ٱلسُّوءَ ². As you — so shall you be judged, كَمَا تَدِينُ تُدَانُ. He judged what he knew not by what he knew, قَاسَ مَا لَا يَعْرِفُهُ بِمَا يَعْرِفُهُ =. Judge thou between us, إِفْتَحْ بَيْنَنَا. See also to Adjudge, Discern, v.t.

Judge, v.i. To compare facts and distinguish truth, رَأَى aor. يَرَى ـ مَيَّزَ. To form an opinion, ظَنَّ ² ـ تَصَوَّرَ. To feel, perceive, حَسَّ ب = ـ عَلِمَ مِنْ عَيْنِ ٱلْعَقْلِ =. He judged it best to..., إِسْتَحْسَنَ لَهُ أَنْ ـ تَحَسَّنَ عِنْدَهُ أَنْ.

Judge Advocate, n. مُفْتِي دِيوَانِ ٱلْحَرْبِ.

Judgeship, *n.* مَأْمُورِيَّةُ ٱلْقَاضِي — وَظِيفَةُ ٱلْقَاضِي — فِتَاحَة. Such an one was appointed to the —, فُلَانٌ وَلِيَ ٱلْفِتَاحَةَ.

Judgment, *n.* A decision, as of a judge, حُكْمٌ وَقَرَارٌ — مَحْضَر — سِجِلٌّ — فَتْوَى *pl.* فَتَاوٍ. A sentence, حُكُومَة — حُكْم — قَضَآء or قَضًا *pl.* أَقْضِيَة. An opinion, رَأْيٌ *pl.* آرَآء. A conception, ظَنٌّ. The faculty of judging, تَمْيِيز. Understanding, عَقْل — ذِهْن — فِرَاسَة. Uprightness, عَدْل — اِسْتِقَامَة — إِنْصَاف. A remarkable punishment, or catastrophe, جَلَل *pl.* أَجْلَال — جَزَآء — مُصِيبَة *pl.* مَصَائِب — بَلِيَّة *pl.* بَلَايَا. A decree, providence, حُكْم *pl.* أَحْكَام — تَقْدِيرٌ إِلٰهِيٌّ. A divine —, or statute, commanding something, أَمْرٌ إِلٰهِيٌّ; forbidding, نَهْيٌ إِلٰهِيٌّ. A man of sound —, ذَهِين — عَاقِل — صَاحِبُ عَقْلٍ — حَكِيم — رَجُلٌ لَهُ رَأْيٌ رَصِينٌ. Judgments, statutes, ordinances, فَرَائِض. The —, day of —, ٱلدَّيْنُونَة — يَوْمُ ٱلدِّينِ — يَوْمُ ٱلْحُكْمِ — ٱلدَّيْنُونَةُ ٱلْأَخِيرَةُ — يَوْمُ ٱلْمِيزَانِ. Sound —, حَزْم. In my —, عَلَى ظَنِّي — حَسَبَ رَأْيِي. Arrest of —, تَوْقِيفُ حُكْمٍ. A provisional —, قَرَارٌ مُوَقَّتٌ. I did not do it of my own —, مَا فَعَلْتُهُ بِأَمْرِي.

To act with judgment, تَعَقَّلَ; in a matter, أَصَابَ فِي ٱلْأَمْرِ.

To apply to one for a judgment, decision, إِسْتَقْضَى; for an opinion, إِسْتَفْتَى.

To exercise one's judgment in, إِرْتَأَى فِي — نَظَرَ فِي [2].

To follow one's own judgment, إِئْتَمَرَ بِرَأْيِهِ.

To have a correct judgment, أَصَابَ فِي رَأْيِهِ.

To pass or give judgment; *see to* Judge, *v.t.*

To pass judgment on one's self, حَكَمَ عَلَى نَفْسِهِ [2].

To pray judgment; *see supra*, To apply for a judgment.

To pervert or wrest judgment, عَوَّجَ ٱلْقَضَآءَ — عَوَّجَ ٱلْحُكْمَ.

To rise up in judgment against, قَامَ عَلَى-فِي ٱلْقَضَآءِ.

Judgment-hall, *n.* A pretorium, دَارُ وِلَايَةٍ — قَصْر. A court of justice, مَحْكَمَة.

Judgment-seat, *n.* Seat of the judges, كُرْسِيُّ ٱلْقُضَاةِ — مَسْنَدُ ٱلْقُضَاةِ.

Judicative, *a.* Having power to judge, مُحَكِّم — مُفَصِّل — قَاضٍ — قَضِيٌّ.

Judicatory, *n.* A court of justice, مَجْلِسُ ٱلْقَضَآءِ — مَحْكَمَة.

Judicatory, *a.* Dispensing justice, مُحَاكِم — فَاتِح — مُحَكِّم.

Judicature, *n.* The power of distributing justice, مُحَاكَمَة — حُكُومَة — قَضَآء. A court of justice, مَجْلِسُ قَضَآءٍ.

Judicial, *a.* Pertaining to a court of justice, مُنِيطٌ بِمَجْلِسِ ٱلْقَضَآءِ — مُتَعَلِّقٌ بِٱلْمَحْكَمَةِ. Inflicted as a penalty, مُجْزًى — مُجْتَزًى — جَزَآئِيّ. According to law, شَرْعِيٌّ. Judicial powers, قُوَّةُ ٱلْمُحَاكَمَةِ — حَقُّ ٱلْمُحَاكَمَاتِ. Judicial authorities, مَأْمُورِيَّةُ ٱلْمُحَاكَمَاتِ. Judicial forms, مُعَامَلَاتٌ حُكْمِيَّةٌ — أُصُول — حُكْمِيَّة — قَوَاعِدُ شَرْعِيَّةٌ. Judicial organization, تَنْظِيمَاتٌ حُكْمِيَّةٌ — تَشْكِيلَاتٌ شَرْعِيَّةٌ. A — document, حُجَّة *pl.* حُجَج — سَنَدٌ شَرْعِيٌّ — سَنَدٌ رَسْمِيٌّ. Judicial functions, مَأْمُورِيَّةٌ حُكْمِيَّةٌ — إِدَارَةُ أُمُورٍ شَرْعِيَّةٍ.

Judicially, *ad.* حُكْمًا — شَرْعًا — رَسْمًا — حَسَبَ ٱلشَّرْعِ.

Judiciary, *a.* *See* Judicial, *a.*

Judiciary, *n.* The ruling and judicial powers, ٱلْحُكَّامُ وَٱلْقُضَاةُ.

Judicious, *n.* Having sound judgment, حَكِيم — رَوِيٌّ — عَاقِل *pl.* عُقَّال — ذُو رَأْيٍ — فَطِن. Directed by reason, صَائِب — صَيُوب — مَعْقُول. A — thing, صَوَاب. A — opinion, رَأْيٌ صَائِبٌ — رَأْيٌ مُصِيبٌ.

Judiciously, *ad.* بِعَقْلٍ صَائِبٍ — بِعَقْلٍ — بِفَطَانَةٍ.

Judiciousness, *n.* Sound judgment, عَقْلٌ مُصِيبٌ — عَقْل — فِطْنَة — حُسْنُ رَأْيٍ — رُشْد. Wise arrangement, صَوَاب — حُسْنُ تَدْبِيرٍ — رَشَاد.

Jug, *n.* مِشْرَبَة — شَرْبَة — إِبْرِيق *pl.* أَبَارِيق — قُلَّة *pl.* قُلَل — كُوز *pl.* أَكْوَاز. A milk —, وِعَآءُ ٱلْحَلِيبِ.

Jug, *v.t.* سَبَّكَ — طَبَخَ-فِي إِبْرِيقٍ [2].

Juggle, *n.* A trick, حِيلَة — دَوْرَة *pl.* دَوَرَات — مَلْعُوب *pl.* مَلَاعِيب. *See also* Jugglery, *n.*

Juggle, *v.t.* To deceive, impose upon, مَسَخَ — غَبَنَ — اِحْتَالَ عَلَى.

Juggle, *v.i.* To practise jugglery, شَعْوَذَ — شَعْبَذَ.

Juggler, *n.* One who practises sleight of hand, شَعْبَذِيٌّ — مُشَعْوِذ — مُلَاعِب — مُزَغْبِر. A trickster, حُوَّلٌ قُلَّبٌ — مَكَّار.

Jugglery, *n.* Legerdemain, شَعْوَذَة *vulg.* شَعْبَذَة — مَخْرَقَة. An imposture, غِشٌّ — مَكْر — حِيلَة — خِدَاع.

Juggling, *n.* *See* Jugglery, *n.*

Jugglingly, *ad.* بِشَعْبَذَةٍ — بِمَلَاعِيب — بِحِيلَةٍ.

Jugular, *a.* زَوْرِيٌّ — حَلْقِيٌّ. The — vein, حَبْلُ ٱلْوَرِيدِ — ٱلْوَرِيد — ٱلْوَدَج *pl.* ٱلْأَوْدَاج — عِرْقُ ٱلزَّوْرِ. The two external — veins, ٱلْوَدَجَانِ.

Juice, *n.* Sap, صَبِيب — لَبَن *pl.* أَلْبَان — نُسْغَةُ شَجَرٍ. The liquid part of fruits, مَآء — عَرَق — رُطُوبَة. What is pressed out, عُصَار — عَصِير — عُصَارَة — مَآء. The juice of meat, مَرَقَة; the best part of the meat, دَسَم. The — of grapes, دِبْس. Inspissated —, رُبٌّ. Lemon —, مَآء (or عَصِيرُ) ٱللَّيْمُونِ. The cream of anything, زُبْد — خُلَاصَة.

Juiceless, *a.* Of fruits, غَيْرُ رَطِيبٍ – غَيْرُ خاضِلٍ ; of meats, غَيْرُ دَسِمٍ – بِلا مَرَقَةٍ.

Juiciness, *n.* Abundance of juice, غَضاضَةٌ – كَثْرَةُ رُطُوبَةٍ – زِيادَةُ ماءٍ ; of meat, زِيادَةُ مَرَقَةٍ. Succulence, as of plants, تَسَقٍّ – ماءٌ – رُطُوبَةٌ – غَضاضَةٌ – غُضُوضَةٌ.

Juicy, *a.* Succulent, of plants, خَضِلٌ – سَهْوَقٌ – سَوْهَقٌ – رَطِيبٌ – نَدْيانُ – غَضِيرٌ – غَضِيضٌ – غَضٌّ – خاضِلٌ ; of meat, خَضِلٌ – دَسِمٌ. To be —, of plants, رَطُبَ – غَضَّ – تَسَقَّى – إِخْضالَّ ; to make —, رَطَّبَ. To be —, of meat, دَسِمَ – تَدَسَّمَ. To make —, أَمْرَقَ.

Jujube, *n.* The fruit, عُنّابٌ ; the white — tree, زَيْزَفُونٌ – شَجَرُ ٱلْعُنّابِ ; the red, شُنْجٌ. The sweetmeat, قُرْصٌ مِنْ صَمْغٍ بِسُكَّرٍ *pl.* أَقْراصٌ.

Julep, *n.* شَرابٌ *pl.* شَراباتٌ – شُرُوبٌ.

Julian, *n.* The name, جُولْيانُوس. The — Calendar, ٱلتَّقْوِيمُ ٱلرُّومِيُّ.

July, *n.* تَمُّوزُ – جُولاي.

Jumble, *v.t.* لَخْبَطَ – شَوَّشَ – هَوَّشَ – لَبَكَ – ضَغَثَ – خَبَّصَ.

Jumble, *v.i.* تَلَخْبَطَ – اِرْتَبَكَ – تَلَبَّكَ – اِشْتَجَرَ – اِلْتَبَكَ – تَخَبَّصَ.

Jumble, *n.* اِلْتِباكٌ – لَبْكٌ – تَهْوِيشٌ – هَوْشٌ – ضِغْثٌ – لَخْبَطَةٌ – خَبْصَةٌ – شَواشٌ. A — of words, غَذْمَرَةٌ.

Jump, *v.i.* To leap, قَفَزَ – نَطَّ. To —, as a deer, to skip about, نَقَزَ. To spring, فَزَّ. To — up, نَهَضَ – اِنْتَهَضَ. To — up suddenly, فَزَّ. To — over, جَلَّبَ – نَطَّ. To — from place to place, قَزَّ. To — or agree together, of many, تَوافَقُوا – اِتَّفَقُوا. To — at, to accept gladly, قَبِلَ بِفَرَحٍ – اِرْتاحَ إِلَى – رَضِيَ بِ – حالاً *aor.* يَرْضَى. To — to a conclusion, تَهافَتَ عَلَى ٱلنَّتِيجَةِ. They naturally — at, are delighted with, war, يَرْتاحُونَ طَبْعًا إِلَى ٱلْحَرْبِ.

Jump, *v.t.* To jump over, جَلَّبَ – نَطَّ. To omit, skip, فاتَ.

Jump, *n.* قَزٌّ – قَفْزَةٌ – نَطٌّ. At a jump, بِقَفْزَةٍ واحِدَةٍ – بِٱلْمَرَّةِ.

Jumper, *n.* One who jumps, قافِزٌ *fem.* قافِزَةٌ *pl.* قَوافِزُ – نَطّاطٌ.

Junction, *n.* The act of joining, وَصْلٌ – صِلَةٌ. The point of union, مَفْصِلٌ – مَوْصِلٌ. Junction, as of the joints, أَوْصالٌ. Union, اِتِّصالٌ. Meeting, اِلْتِقاءٌ. A seam, وُصْلَةٌ. An assemblage, اِجْتِماعٌ – مَجْمَعٌ. That which joins two things, وَصِيلَةٌ. A railway —, مُلْتَقَى سِكَّةِ ٱلْحَدِيدِ.

Juncture, *n.* Union, اِتِّصالٌ – اِتِّحادٌ. A point of time, آنٌ – وَقْتٌ – ساعَةٌ. Condition, حالٌ – حالَةٌ. At that —, time, عِنْدَ ذٰلِكَ – حِينَئِذٍ – فِي ذٰلِكَ ٱلْوَقْتِ. *See also* Joint, Junction, *n.*

June, *n.* شَهْرُ جُون – حَزِيرانُ.

Jungle, *n.* غَيْطَلٌ – غَرِيفَةٌ – غَيْضَةٌ.

Junior, *a.* Younger, أَصْغَرُ عُمْرًا ; more recent, أَحْدَثُ ; inferior, دُونٌ. The — partner, ٱلشَّرِيكُ ٱلْأَحْدَثُ. He is my —, in age, هُوَ أَصْغَرُ مِنِّي عُمْرًا. Juniors should submit to their elders, يَجِبُ عَلَى ٱلْأَحْداثِ أَنْ يَخْضَعُوا لِلشُّيُوخِ.

Junior, *n.* *See* Junior, *n.*

Juniper, *n.* أَبْهَلُ – عَرْعَرٌ. The berries of the —, أَبْهَلُ – حَبُّ ٱلْعَرْعَرِ – حَبُّ ٱلْكُوكَلانِ.

Junk, *n.* A Chinese ship, مَرْكَبٌ صِينِيٌّ. A thick piece, شِلْوٌ *pl.* أَشْلاءٌ – قِطْعَةٌ. Old rope, قُماشُ أَحْبالٍ – سَقَطُ ٱلْمَرَسِ. Salt beef, لَحْمُ بَقَرٍ مُمَلَّحٌ.

Junket, *n.* } **Junketing**, } مَرَحٌ – بَطَرٌ – مُنادَمَةٌ.

Junket, *v.i.* مَرِحَ – بَطِرَ – تَفَكَّهَ – تَكَيَّفَ.

Junta, *n.* مَجْلِسٌ – شُورَى.

Junto, *n.* A cabal, party, تَعَصُّبٌ – عَصَبِيَّةٌ – عُصْبَةٌ – حِلْقَةٌ.

Jupiter, *n.* The planet, ٱلْأَحْوَرُ – ٱلْمُشْتَرِي. *See also* Jove, *n.*

Jurat, *n.* أَمِينٌ *pl.* أُمَناءُ – مَأْمُورٌ *pl.* مَأْمُورِيَّةٌ – مِنْ أَهْلِ ٱلْأَعْيانِ.

Jure divino, *ad.* مِنْ طَرَفِ ٱللّٰهِ – مِنْ تَعْيِينِ ٱللّٰهِ – مِنَ ٱللّٰهِ.

Juridical, *a.* *See* Judicial, *a.*

Juridically, *ad.* *See* Judicially, *ad.*

Jurisconsult, *n.* فَقِيهٌ *pl.* فُقَهاءُ – مُفْتٍ.

Jurisdiction, *n.* Legal authority, power, وَلاءَةٌ – وِلايَةٌ – حُكُومَةٌ – حَقُّ ٱلْمُحاكَمَةِ – حَقُّ ٱلْقَضاءِ – إِجْراءُ إِدارَةٍ. Circle of —, دائِرَةُ حُكُومَةٍ – مَوْلَوِيَّةٌ – وَلِيَّةٌ *pl.* وَلايا.

Civil jurisdiction, ٱلْمُحاكَماتُ ٱلْعادِيَّةُ – إِدارَةُ ٱلْأُمُورِ ٱلْعادِيَّةِ.

Criminal jurisdiction, إِدارَةُ ٱلْأُمُورِ ٱلْجَزائِيَّةِ.

Ecclesiastical jurisdiction, حُكُومَةٌ دِينِيَّةٌ – حُكُومَةٌ كَنائِسِيَّةٌ.

Local jurisdiction, إِدارَةُ ٱلْمُحاكَماتِ ٱلْمَحَلِّيَّةِ.

Maritime jurisdiction, مُحاكَماتُ ٱلْأُمُورِ ٱلْبَحْرِيَّةِ.

To exercise jurisdiction, أَجْرَى أَمْرَ ٱلْمُحاكَماتِ.

To go beyond the limits of one's jurisdiction, جاوَزَ دائِرَةَ حُكُومَتِهِ.

The right of jurisdiction, حَقُّ ٱلْمُحاكَماتِ – حَقُّ إِجْراءِ ٱلْمُحاكَماتِ.

Jurisdictional, *a.* مُتَعَلِّقٌ بِحُقُوقِ ٱلْمُحاكَمَةِ – مَنُوطٌ بِٱلْحُكُومَةِ.

Jurisprudence, *n.* عِلْمُ أُصُولِ ٱلْفِقْهِ ـ الفِقْهُ ـ عِلْمُ ٱلْفِقْهِ ـ عِلْمُ ٱلْفُرُوعِ.

Jurisprudential, *a.* مُتَعَلِّقٌ بِٱلْفِقْهِ.

Jurist, *n.* فَقِيهٌ *pl.* فُقَهَآءُ.

Juror, *n.* One who serves on a jury, وَكِيلٌ مُسْتَحْلَفٌ *pl.* وُكَلَآءُ مُسْتَحْلَفُونَ ـ مِنْ أَهْلِ ٱلْجُورِى. *See* Jury, *n.*

Jury, *n.* لَفْظَةٌ جُورِى تَدُلُّ عَلَى ٱلثَّنَى ـ الوُكَلَاءُ ٱلْمُسْتَحْلَفُونَ عَشَرَ مِنْ مُعْتَبَرِى أَهْلِ ٱلْبَلَدِ يَنْتَخِبُونَ رَسْمًا لِٱسْتِمَاعِ ٱلدَّعَاوِى فِى ٱلْمَحْكَمَةِ جُمْلَةً بِقَسَمٍ لِيَعْلَمُوا ٱلْقَاضِى بِرَأْيِهِمْ عَنْهَا حَسَبَ إِرْشَادِ ضَمَائِرِهِمْ بِدُونِ مُحَابَاةٍ وَإِذَا ٱتَّفَقَتْ آرَاؤُهُمْ فَصَلَ ٱلْقَاضِى ٱلْحُكْمَ شَرْعًا وَإِنْ لَمْ تَتَّفِقْ سَقَطَتِ ٱلدَّعْوَى ـ أَهْلُ ٱلْجُورِى ـ ٱلْجُورِى. A committee of awards, أَهْلُ ٱلتَّمْيِيزِ. Grand —, جُورِى ٱلتَّفْتِيشِ. Petty —, جُورِى ٱلْحُكْمِ وَٱلْقَرَارِ. Special —, جُورِى مَخْصُوصٌ. Jury of inquest, جُورِى ٱلْفَحْصِ ٱلرَّسْمِىِّ عَنْ مَوْتِ أَحَدٍ مِنْ غَيْرِ حَتْفِ أَنْفِهِ. Foreman of the —, مُقَدَّمُ ٱلْجُورِى. To serve on a —, كَانَ مِنْ أَهْلِ ٱلْجُورِى. *See also to* Impannel, *v.t.*

Juryman, *n.* *See* Juror, *n.*

Jury-mast, *n.* دَقَلٌ عَارِيَةٌ.

Jus gentium, *n.* حُقُوقُ ٱلْمِلَلِ.

Just, *a.* Perfect, تَامٌّ ـ صَحِيحٌ ـ كَامِلٌ. Accurate, مُدَقِّقٌ ـ مَضْبُوطٌ. Equitable, upright, عَادِلٌ *pl.* عُدُولٌ ـ مُسْتَقِيمٌ ـ قَوَّامٌ ـ مُقْسِطٌ. Conformable to justice, حَقٌّ ـ عَدْلٌ ـ مُطَابِقُ ٱلْإِنْصَافِ. Righteous, godly, بَارٌّ *pl.* أَبْرَارٌ ـ صَالِحٌ ـ مُتَّقٍ. Truthful, صَادِقٌ. Just to one's word, مُقِيمٌ عَلَى ٱلْعَهْدِ ـ صَاحِبُ وَفَآءٍ. Just weights, وَزْنَاتٌ حَقٌّ. Just measure, كَيْلٌ وَافٍ. A — expression, كَلِمَةٌ صَوَابٌ ـ مَضْبُوطَةٌ. Impartial, عَدِيمُ ٱلْغَرَضِ ـ عَدِيمُ ٱلْمُحَابَاةِ. It is — that . . . , حَقَّ أَنْ ـ ٢. It is — for him to . . . , يَحِقُّ عَلَيْهِ أَنْ. It was —, right, proper, حَقَّ *aor.* يَحِقُّ. To be —, accurate, دَقَّ *aor.* يَدِقُّ. To be proper, fit, صَلَحَ ـ ٣ نَاسَبَ ـ ٤. To be —, right, true, حَقَّ *aor.* يَحِقُّ. To be —, equitable in, عَدَلَ فِي ـ ٢. To be — towards, أَنْصَفَ. The — and the unjust, ٱلصَّالِحُ وَٱلطَّالِحُ.

Just, *ad.* Exactly, بِٱلتَّمَامِ ـ بِعَيْنِهِ ـ بِغَايَةِ ٱلْإِتْقَانِ. Nicely, بِضَبْطٍ ـ عَيْنًا ـ كَمَا يَنْبَغِي. Barely, تَقْرِيبًا. Just now, تَوًّا ـ حَالًا ـ السَّاعَةَ. Just so, كَذٰلِكَ. You were — the man to do this, حُقِقْتَ بِأَنْ تَفْعَلَ هٰذَا. That's — the thing, هٰذَا هُوَ بِعَيْنِهِ. Just what took place between them, عَيْنَ مَا جَرَى بَيْنَهُمْ. He —, barely, entered into the house, بِٱلْجَهْدِ دَخَلَ إِلَى ٱلْبَيْتِ. I had — spoken when he came in, بِٱلْجَهْدِ تَكَلَّمْتُ إِذْ دَخَلَ. Just tell me, فَقَطْ قُلْ لِي.

Just, *n.* *See* Joust, *n.*

Justice, *n.* The virtue of rendering to every one what is due, عَدَالَةٌ ـ عَدْلٌ ـ إِنْصَافٌ ـ قِسْطٌ. Right, حَقٌّ. Uprightness, اِسْتِقَامَةٌ. Equity, إِنْصَافٌ ـ قِسْطٌ. Impartiality, عَدَمُ ٱلْمُحَابَاةِ ـ عَدَمُ غَرَضٍ. Retribution, جَزَآءٌ ـ مُسْتَحَقٌّ. Punishment, اِنْتِقَامٌ ـ قِصَاصٌ. A civil magistrate, حَاكِمٌ *pl.* حُكَّامٌ ـ حَاكِمُ ٱلضَّبْطِيَّةِ ـ مَأْمُورُ ٱلضَّبْطِيَّةِ. Recognition, عُرْفٌ. The law, الشَّرْعُ ـ شَرْعُ ٱللّٰهِ. A tribunal of —, مَحْكَمَةٌ شَرْعِيَّةٌ ـ مَحْكَمَةٌ نِظَامِيَّةٌ. To treat one with —, أَنْصَفَ ـ عَامَلَ بِٱلْإِنْصَافِ. To administer —, قَضَى ـ ٢ حَكَمَ فِي *or* بَيْنَ ـ ٨ اِحْتَكَمَ (*or* تَحَكَّمَ). To execute — on, صَنَعَ دَيْنُونَةً عَلَى ـ دَانَ *aor.* يَدِينُ ـ أَجْرَى حُكْمًا عَلَى ـ ٢ حَكَمَ عَلَى. To deliver up to —, سَلَّمَ إِلَى ٱلْحُكُومَةِ. To render — to, to give one his right, أَنْصَفَ ـ خَلَّصَ لَهُ حَقَّهُ; to acknowledge the merits of, شَهِدَ لِ ـ ٣. Commutative —, قِسْطٌ مُبَادِلٌ. Distributive —, عَدَالَةٌ قَاسِمَةٌ. The administration of —, إِدَارَةُ ٱلْقَضَآءِ (*or* ٱلْحُقُوقِ). To be hasty in blaming is not —, (prov.) لَيْسَ مِنَ ٱلْعَدْلِ سُرْعَةُ ٱلْعَذْلِ. There is no guide like reason, and no protector like —, (prov.) لَا سَائِسَ مِثْلُ ٱلْعَقْلِ وَلَا حَارِسَ مِثْلُ ٱلْعَدْلِ.

Justice of the Peace, حَاكِمُ ٱلضَّبْطِيَّةِ.

Lord Chief Justice, قَاضِي ٱلْقُضَاةِ.

Minister of Justice, وَزِيرُ ٱلْعَدْلِيَّةِ.

Justiceship, *n.* وَظِيفَةُ ٱلْحَاكِمِ ـ مَأْمُورِيَّةُ ٱلْحَاكِمِ.

Justiciary, *n.* حَاكِمٌ ـ مُحَكِّمٌ.

Justifiable, *a.* That can be justified, لَهُ عُذْرٌ ـ يُعْتَذَرُ ـ يَتَبَرَّرُ.

Justifiable homicide, قَتْلٌ جَائِزٌ ـ قَتْلٌ مَعْذُورٌ.

Justifiableness, *n.* حَقٌّ ـ قَابِلِيَّةُ ٱلْإِثْبَاتِ بِمُطَابَقَتِهِ لِلْحَقِّ.

Justifiably, *ad.* بِٱلْحَقِّ ـ بِٱلْحَلَالِ.

Justification, *n.* The act of justifying, تَبْرِئَةٌ ـ تَزْكِيَةٌ ـ تَبْرِيَةٌ. The state of being justified, بَرَآءَةٌ ـ بَرَآءَةُ ٱلذِّمَّةِ. A defence, apology, حُجَّةٌ ـ عِذْرَةٌ. The accounting righteous, تَبْرِيرٌ. Righteousness, بِرٌّ. To plead something in —, اِحْتَجَّ بِ.

Justificative, *a.* } Tending to justify, مُبَرِّرٌ ـ بَارٌّ. Establishing,
Justificatory, } مُبَرْهِنٌ ـ مُثْبِتٌ. *Pièces justificatives*, أَوْرَاقٌ مُثْبِتَةٌ ـ سَنَدَاتٌ مُبَرْهِنَةٌ.

Justify, *v.t.* To prove innocent, بَرَّأَ ـ بَرَّرَ ـ زَكَّى. To prove the goodness of, to verify, أَيَّدَ ـ حَقَّقَ ـ ثَبَّتَ. To prove the justice of, أَثْبَتَ حَقَّهُ. To — the good opinion of, حَقَّقَ حُسْنَ ٱلظَّنِّ فِي. To be justified, proved true, بَرَّ *aor.* يَبَرُّ *and* يَبِرُّ ـ ٢ ثَبَتَ ـ تَحَقَّقَ. To — one's self, تَبَرَّرَ. To — one's self from,

بَيَّضَ ـ بَرَّرَ نَفْسَهُ مِن ـ إِنْتَصَفَ مِن ـ تَنَصَّحَ مِن ـ تَبَرَّأَ مِن وَجْهَهُ مِن. He was justified in, has a right to ..., هُوَ مَحْقُوقٌ بِأَنْ. The end justifies the means, تُبَرَّرُ ٱلْوَاسِطَةُ بِٱلْغَايَةِ. The end does not justify the means, لَا تُبَرَّرُ ٱلْوَاسِطَةُ بِٱلْغَايَةِ. Is the government justified in this aggression? هَلِ ٱلدَّوْلَةُ مُحِقَّةٌ فِي هٰذَا ٱلْفَتْكِ. He is justified in his demand, هُوَ مُحِقٌّ فِي طَلَبِهِ. We were justified in saying that ..., قَدْ صَدَقْنَا فِي قَوْلِنَا أَنْ. The financial condition does not — this burden of expenditure, أَحْوَالُ ٱلْمَالِيَّةِ لَا تُطَاوِعُهُ عَلَى حَمْلِ هٰذِهِ ٱلْمَصَارِيفِ.

Justifying, *a.* مُبَرِّر.

Justle, *v.t.* *See to* Jostle, *v.t.*

Justly, *ad.* Equitably, بِإِنْصَافٍ ـ بِعَدْلٍ ـ حَقًّا ـ بِٱلصَّوَابِ. Deservedly, حَقًّا ـ بِٱسْتِحْقَاقٍ. To act —, أَقْسَطَ ـ قَسَطَ ـِ ². To act — in, to, with, عَدَلَ فِي *or* عَلَى *or* بَيْنَ ـِ.

Justness, *n.* Exactness, إِتْقَان ـ دِقَّة ـ ضَبْط ـ إِحْكَام. Truth, حَقّ. Propriety, لِيَاقَة ـ مُنَاسَبَة. *See also* Justice, *n.*

Jut, *v.i.* To shoot out, بَرَزَ ـُ ² ـ أَشْرَفَ ـ نَتَأَ ـَ.

Jut, *n.* أَنْف ـ خَرْم ـ بُرُوز ـ نُتُوء.

Jute, *n.* تُنْبُس هِنْدِيٌّ ـ لِيف هِنْدِيٌّ.

Juvenescence, *n.* شَبَاب.

Juvenescent, *a.* شَابٌّ.

Juvenile, *a.* Youthful, فَتًى *pl.* أَفْتَاءٌ ـ صَغِير *pl.* صُغَرَاءُ. Suited to youth, لِلْأَوْلَادِ ـ لِلْجُهَّالِ.

Juvenileness, *n.* } وَلَدَنَة ـ شُبُوبِيَّة ـ شُبُوب ـ صَبَاءٌ.
Juvenility, }

Juxta-posited, *a.* قَرِيب ـ لَصِيق ـ مُقْتَرِن ـ مُتَّصِل.

Juxta-position, *n.* مُقَارَنَة ـ إِتِّصَال ـ قُرْب ـ مُقَارَبَة. To place in —, قَارَنَ ـ قَابَلَ.

K.

Kaàbah, *n.* The — of Mákkah, كَعْبَةُ مَكَّةَ ـ ٱلْكَعْبَةُ.

Kaffer, *n.* A — of South Africa, إِسْمُ بَعْضِ قَبَائِلَ فِي جَنُوبِ أَفْرِيقِيَّة.

Kale, *n.* ضَرْبٌ مِنَ ٱلْكُرُنْبِ ـ مَلْفُوف.

Kaleidoscope, *n.* نَظَّارَةُ ٱلْأَشْكَالِ وَٱلْأَلْوَانِ ٱلْجَمِيلَةِ; called in Turkish أَشْكَالْنُمَا.

Kalendar, *n.* *See* Calendar, *n.*

Kalender, *n.* *See* Calender, *n.*

Kali, *n.* *See* Alkali, *n.*

Kalif, *n.* *See* Khalifah, *n.*

Kamala, *n.* The name given in the English Pharmacopœia, (probably from an Indian source,) to the dye called *Wars.* *See* Wars, *n.*

Kamsin, *n.* *See* Khamsin, *n.*

Kangaroo, *n.* نَوْعٌ مِنَ ٱلْحَيَوَانِ ذِي كِيسٍ تَحْتَ بَطْنِهِ.

Kaw, *v.i.* *See to* Caw, *v.i.*

K.C.B., حَائِزُ ٱلدَّرَجَةِ ٱلثَّانِيَةِ مِنْ نِيشَانِ ٱلْبَاثْ.

K.C.H., حَائِزُ ٱلدَّرَجَةِ ٱلْأُولَى مِنْ نِيشَانِ هَانُوَر.

K.C.M.G., حَائِزُ ٱلدَّرَجَةِ ٱلثَّانِيَةِ مِنْ نِيشَانِ حَضْرَتَي مِيخَائِيلَ وَجِرْجِيس.

Kawwâs, *n.* قَوَّاس *pl.* قَوَّاسَة.

Keckle, *v.t.* To — a cable, شَدَّ ـُ ² ـ لَفَّ ـُ ² ٱلْمَرَسَةَ حَوْلَ ٱلْقَلْسِ ٱللَّبَّانَ.

Kedge, *n.* مِرْسَاةٌ صَغِيرَةٌ.

Kedge, *v.t.* جَرَّ ـُ ² ـ سَحَبَ ـَ.

Keel, *n.* Of a ship, قَاعِدَةُ ٱلسَّفِينَةِ. A goods' boat, مَرْكَب ـ مَعُونَة. A false —, سَهْمُ ٱلْقَاعِدَةِ. To be on an even —, of a ship, إِعْتَدَلَ ٱلْمَرْكَبُ.

Keel, *v.t.* To navigate, plough the waters, شَجَّ ـُ ² ـ مَخَرَ ـَ. To turn up the —, كَشَفَ عَنْ قَاعِدَةِ ٱلْمَرْكَبِ ـِ.

Keelage, *n.* ضَرِيبَةٌ عَلَى ٱلْمَرَاكِبِ.

Keeler, *n.* An open boat for merchandise, مَعُونَة.

Keel-haul, *v.t.* عَبَّرَهُ مِنْ تَحْتِ قَاعِدَةِ ٱلسَّفِينَةِ جَزَاءً لَهُ.

Keelson, *n.* لَوْحٌ عَلَى قَاعِدَةِ ٱلسَّفِينَةِ ـ لَوْحٌ عَلَى تَغْرِ ٱلْمَرْكَبِ ـ ٱلْبَرِيمُ.

Keen, *a.* Eager, vehement, for, حَرِيصٌ عَلَى *pl.* حِرَاص ـ تَائِقٌ إِلَى ـ رَاغِبٌ فِي ـ شَوَّاقٌ إِلَى. Sharp, of appetite, حَدِيد ـ حَادٌّ. Piercing, as of wind, مُزَمْهِر ـ خَارِق ـ نَافِذ. A — wind, حَرِيق. Bitter, sarcastic, مُؤْذٍ ـ مُرٌّ ـ جَارِح. Circumspect, مُحْتَرِز ـ حَرِيص ـ لَبِيب. Acute of intellect, حَسَّاس ـ دَرَّاك ـ فَطِين ـ ذَكِيُّ ٱلْعَقْلِ ـ فَهِيم ـ خَارِق. To be — for, eager, حَرَصَ عَلَى ـِ ². *See also* Sharp, *a.*

Keen-edged, *a.* ذَرِب ـ صارِم ـ خارِق ـ حادٌّ ـ ماضٍ. *See also* Sharp, *a.*

Keen-eyed, *a.* حَدِيدُ ٱلْبَصَرِ ـ بارِقُ ٱلنَّظَرِ ـ لَمّاح ـ شائِهٌ ـ شاهِي ٱلْبَصَرِ.

Keenly, *ad.* Eagerly, بِرَغْبَةٍ ـ بِحِرْصٍ ـ إِحْتِراصًا. Sharply, بِجِدَّةٍ. Circumspectly, بِٱلْحَذَرِ ـ تَحَذُّرًا ـ بِحِرْصٍ. With effect, بِغايَةٍ ـ بِٱلتَّدْقِيقِ ـ تَدْقِيقًا. Accurately, إِنْفِعالًا ـ بِكَمالِ ٱلتَّأْثِيرِ ـ ٱلْإِتْقانِ. *See also* Sharply, *ad.*

Keenness, *n.* Eagerness, رَغْبَة ـ شَوْق ـ تَوْق ـ حِرْص. Sharpness, as of appetite, زَمْهَرِير ـ حِدَّة ـ شِدَّة; as of wind, حِدَّة; as of intellect, ذَكاء ـ إِرْب ـ شَهامَة ـ فِطْنَة ـ ثِقاف; bitterness, as of sarcasm, أَذِيَّة ـ مَرارَة; of edge, حِدَّة ـ رَهافَة. *See also* Sharpness, *n.*

Keen-witted, *a.* ذُو إِرْبٍ ـ ثَقِيف ـ حَسّاس دَرّاك ـ دَرّاك ـ حاذِق ـ فَطِين ـ أَرِب. *See also under* Keen, *a.*

Keep, *v.t.* To hold, grasp, تَمَسَّكَ بِ ـ قَبَضَ: He kept it in his hand, مَسَكَهُ بِيَدِهِ.

To keep, to arrest, restrain, أَعاقَ ـ مَنَعَ ـ حَجَزَ ـ كَفَّ ـ أَرْتَفَ. *See also under* To keep from.

To keep, as in store, to lay up, إِدَّخَرَ ـ ذَخَرَ ـ خَزَنَ; as for use another time, خَلَّى ـ إِلَى ـ إِدَّخَرَ ـ خَبَّى: He kept them to fight with the Persian troops, كانَ يُخَبِّيهِمْ لِقِتالِ عَساكِرِ ٱلْعَجَمِ.

To keep a woman, concubine, عِنْدَهُ مَحْظِيَّةٌ ـ تَسَرَّى ـ تَسَرَّرَ.

To keep, to carry about with one, حَمَلَ ـ صَحِبَ ـ مَعَهُ: He keeps, carries, it in his pocket, يَحْمِلُهُ فِي جَيْبِهِ حَمَلَ ـ مَعَهُ.

To keep, to celebrate, ذَكَرَ ـ عَيَّدَ عِيدَ ٱلْ...: To keep Christmas, عَيَّدَ عِيدَ ٱلْمِيلادِ.

To keep, to delay, عَوَّقَ ـ أَعاقَ ـ أَخَّرَ ـ لَبَّثَ: He kept me five hours, عَوَّقَنِي ثَلاثَ ساعاتٍ.

To keep, to engage in work, خَدَّمَ ـ شَغَّلَ: He keeps a hundred workmen, يُشَغِّلُ مِئَةً مِنَ ٱلْفَعَلَةِ.

To keep, to guard, نَطَرَ ـ حافَظَ ـ حَرَسَ. To keep a fort, حافَظَ ٱلْقَلْعَةَ. Unless the Lord keep the city the watchman waketh but in vain, إِنْ لَمْ يَحْفَظِ ٱلرَّبُّ ٱلْمَدِينَةَ فَباطِلًا يَسْهَرُ ٱلْحارِسُ. To give to one to keep, take care of, إِسْتَحْفَظَ ـ عَلَى.

To keep, to have, كانَ صاحِبَ كَذا ـ لِ ـ عِنْدَ ـ مَلَكَ ـ قَعَدَ عِنْدَهُ. He keeps a garden, عِنْدَهُ جُنَيْنَةٌ. He keeps a horse, هُوَ صاحِبُ حِصانٍ. He keeps a house, هُوَ صاحِبُ بَيْتٍ. He keeps a shop, هُوَ فاتِحٌ دُكّانٍ. He keeps a school, فاتِحٌ مَدْرَسَةٍ. He keeps five men and five women servants, قَعَدَ فِي خِدْمَتِهِ خَمْسَةُ خُدّامِينَ وَخَمْسُ خُدّاماتٍ.

To keep, to hold, as of an opinion, آمَنَ بِ ـ إِعْتَقَدَ ـ إِرْتَأَى. He keeps to his opinion, هُوَ مُتَمَسِّكٌ بِرَأْيِهِ.

To keep, to hold in one's possession, حَفِظَ ـ ضَبَطَ ـ عَلَى. He kept, retained, the watch, ضَبَطَ ٱلسّاعَةَ.

To keep, to lay up in a place, رَفَعَ ـ فِي: He keeps it in a cupboard, يَرْفَعُهُ فِي خِزانَةٍ.

To keep, to leave, خَلَّى ـ تَرَكَ: He keeps the door open, يُخَلِّي (or يَتْرُكُ) ٱلْبابَ مَفْتُوحًا.

To keep, to manage, رَعَى *aor.* يَرْعَى ـ دَبَّرَ ـ ساسَ *aor.* يَسُوسُ ـ باشَرَ ـ قامَ بِ: He keeps the accounts, هُوَ يُقَيِّدُ ٱلْحِساباتِ ـ هُوَ يُدَبِّرُ ٱلْمَصْرُوفَ.

To keep, to observe, راعَى ـ إِمْتَثَلَ بِ ـ أَجْرَى ـ أَوْفَى ـ حَفِظَ: If ye love me keep my commandments, إِنْ كُنْتُمْ تُحِبُّونَنِي فَٱحْفَظُوا وَصايايَ.

To keep, to pasture, as sheep, *etc.*, رَعَى *aor.* يَرْعَى: He keeps his father's sheep, or goats, يَرْعَى ماشِيَةَ أَبِيهِ.

To keep, to protect, defend, صانَ *aor.* يَصُونُ ـ حَمَى ـ حامَى.

To keep or defend against, حَصَّنَ ـ صانَ ـ عَنْ: He kept it against the enemy, دَفَعَ ٱلْعَدُوَّ ـ صانَهُ عَنِ ٱلْعَدُوِّ. God keeps, repels, aggression from, those who have believed, إِنَّ ٱللّٰهَ يَدْفَعُ عَنِ ٱلَّذِينَ آمَنُوا.

To keep, to provide for, قامَ بِمَعِيشَتِهِ ـ إِعْتَنَى بِ *aor.* يَقُومُ. To keep or provide for one's family, عالَ *aor.* يَعُولُ ـ أَعالَ.

To keep, to reserve, خَلَّى ـ تَرَكَ ـ أَبْقَى: You have kept the best of them until now, أَبْقَيْتَ أَخْيَرَهُمْ إِلَى ٱلْآنَ. They shall keep it till to-morrow, يَكُونُ عِنْدَهُمْ تَحْتَ ٱلْحِفْظِ إِلَى غَدٍ.

To keep, to watch, to keep guard over, as over a house, field, نَطَرَ: He keeps the vineyard, يَنْطُرُ ٱلْكَرْمَ.

To keep, to watch over, إِحْتَفَظَ بِ ـ إِحْتَرَسَ عَلَى ـ حَفِظَ ـ حارَسَ ـ حَرَسَ ـ حَرَزَ ـ أَحْرَزَ: May God keep him from affliction! حَرَسَهُ ٱللّٰهُ مِنَ ٱلْبَلاءِ.

To keep at, to make to continue at, أَلْزَمَ ـ بِ ـ شَغَّلَ ـ شَغَلَ. To place, وَضَعَ *aor.* يَضَعُ ـ حَطَّ. He keeps his son at school, يُخَلِّي ٱبْنَهُ فِي ٱلْمَدْرَسَةِ.

To keep away, at a distance, بَعَّدَ ـ أَبْعَدَ. To drive away, طَرَدَ ـ دَشَّرَ. To prevent, مَنَعَ.

To keep back, to restrain, from, عَوَّقَ ـ عَنْ ـ أَعاقَ ـ عَنْ ـ شَجَرَ ـ عَنْ

To keep back by fraud, إِخْتَلَسَ . أَمْسَكَ-عَن ـ أَوْقَفَ-عَن. To keep in reserve, خَبَّى ـ أَبْقَى.

To keep by, near, one, قَرَّبَ-لِ . To keep in store, خَزَنَ ² ـ إِخْتَزَنَ . To retain with, have at hand, خَلَّى-عِنْدَهُ.

To keep charge of, حَرَسَ ² ـ أَحْرَزَ ـ حَفِظَ.

To keep company with, أَلِفَ ـ إِسْتَصْحَبَ ـ صَاحَبَ ـ عَاشَرَ ـ آلَفَ.

To keep down, to prevent from rising, مَنَعَ-عَنِ ٱلْقِيَامِ. To repress, ضَبَطَ ² ـ قَهَرَ ـ أَوْطَأَ. To keep down, as of a price, حَطَّ ² ـ سَكَّنَ ـ أَخْمَدَ (or أَسْقَطَ ٱلثَّمَنَ). To keep down, as a fever, *etc.*, سَكَّنَ ـ أَخْمَدَ.

To keep faith with, أَقَامَ عَلَى ـ حَفِظَ ٱلْمُعَاهَدَةَ مَعَهُ ـ صَادَقَ عَهْدِهِ مَعَهُ.

To keep guard, أَجْرَى ٱلنَّوْبَةَ.

To keep guard over, خَفَرَ ـ حَافَظَ ـ نَطَرَ ² ـ حَرَسَ ² خَفَرَ-عَلَى.

To keep hold of, قَبَضَ عَلَى ـ تَمَسَّكَ بِ.

To keep house, كَانَ صَاحِبَ ـ يَقُومُ *aor.* قَامَ بِمَصْرُوفِ بَيْتٍ بَيْتٍ. To keep open house, أَثْوَى ٱلضُّيُوفَ فِي كُلِّ حِينٍ ـ تَفَتَّحَ فِي ٱلضِّيَافَةِ.

To keep from, to restrain from, كَفَّ-عَن ² ـ أَعَاقَ-عَن ـ عَوَّقَ-عَن. To keep from, by engaging one in something else, شَغَلَ-عَن ـ أَقْعَدَ-عَن ـ قَعَدَ بِ-عَن ². To keep from, as a secret, كَاتَمَ-عَن ـ كَتَمَ-عَن ². To keep one from danger, وَقَى-(or حَفِظَ-) مِنَ ٱلْخَطَرِ *aor.* يَقِي. It will preserve him from danger, يَقِيهِ مِنَ ٱلْخَطَرِ.

To keep in, prevent from going out, مَنَعَ-عَنِ ٱلْخُرُوجِ. To confine, lock up, قَفَلَ عَلَى ². To keep in, by way of punishment, to imprison, حَبَسَ. To supply with, زَوَّدَ-مِن ـ سَدَّ-بِ ² ـ أَمَدَّ-بِ. To keep in, as a light, fire; *see* To keep up, *infra*.

To keep in motion, أَلْزَمَ-بِٱلْحَرَكَةِ ـ مَنَعَ-عَنِ ٱلْوُقُوفِ.

To keep off; *see* To keep at a distance, *supra*.

To keep off from; *see* To keep from, *supra*.

To keep on, to continue wearing, لَمْ يَزَلْ يَلْبَسُهُ ـ لَزِمَ لِبْسَهُ.

To keep on, as of servants, in employment, أَبْقَى-فِي ٱلْخِدْمَةِ.

To keep on, as a house, renting it, لَمْ يَزَلْ يَسْتَأْجِرُ ٱلْبَيْتَ.

To keep one's bed, لَزِمَ ٱلْفِرَاشَ.

To keep one's gravity, حَفِظَ رَزَانَتَهُ ـ رَزُنَ ².

To keep one's room, لَزِمَ ٱلْبَيْتَ ـ لَزِمَ ٱلدَّارَ.

To keep one's self, to guard one's self, وَعَى لِنَفْسِهِ ـ حَفِظَ نَفْسَهُ.

ـ حَذِرَ مِن *aor.* يَحْذَرُ. To be on one's guard against, إِحْتَذَرَ مِن. To provide for one's self, قَامَ بِمَعَاشِ نَفْسِهِ *aor.* يَقُومُ.

To keep one's promise, أَمْسَكَ عَهْدَهُ ـ أَنْجَزَ عَهْدَهُ ـ عَهِدَ ـ كَمَّلَ وَعْدَهُ ـ أَوْفَى بِقَوْلِهِ.

To keep out, not to let inside, مَنَعَ-عَنِ ² ـ حَجَزَ ٱلدُّخُولَ عَلَى ـ خَلَّى-خَارِجًا ـ ٱلدُّخُولِ. Not to let in, to be impervious to, لَا يَتَطَرَّقُ إِلَيْهِ ـ لَا يَنْفُذُ فِيهِ.

To keep silent, أَسْكَتَ ـ سَكَتَ ـ أَصْمَتَ ـ أَصَمَّ ـ أَطْرَقَ.

To keep to, غَصَبَ-عَلَى ـ أَلْزَمَ-بِ ـ سَامَ ². Keep thou to gentleness, عَلَيْكَ بِٱلرِّفْقِ.

To keep a term at college, قَضَى مُدَّةَ ٱلدَّرْسِ فِي ٱلْمَدْرَسَةِ.

To keep under, to bring into subjection, أَطَاعَ ـ أَخْضَعَ ـ أَقْمَعَ ـ قَهَرَ. *See also* To keep down, *supra*.

To keep up, to continue, مَنَعَ-عَنِ ٱلزَّوَالِ ـ أَبْقَى. To prolong, طَوَّلَ ـ مَدَّ ². To make to sit up after the time of rest, أَسْهَرَ. To keep up, as a price, قَامَ بِٱلثَّمَنِ ـ أَثْبَتَ ٱلثَّمَنَ *aor.* يَقُومُ. To keep up, as one's name, ذَكَّرَ: I have no son to keep up my name, لَيْسَ لِي ٱبْنٌ لِتَذْكِيرِ (or لِتَخْلِيدِ) ٱسْمِي.

To keep it up, to continue doing, أَدْمَنَ ـ أَدْمَنَ عَلَى: They kept up the entertainment till morning, أَقَامُوا ٱلْوَلِيمَةَ إِلَى ٱلصَّبَاحِ.

Keep, *v.i.* To remain in any state, دَامَ ـ ظَلَّ ـ يَبْقَى *aor.* بَقِيَ *aor.* يَدُومُ: It keeps as it was, ظَلَّ عَلَى حَالِهِ ـ بَقِيَ عَلَى حَالِهِ. It kept raining, ظَلَّتْ تَمْطُرُ ـ دَامَتْ (or دَوَّمَتْ) ٱلسَّمَاءُ. He keeps coming and going, يَظَلُّ مُتَرَدِّدًا. She kept crying, ظَلَّتْ بَاكِيَةً. To keep, as of meat, not to spoil, صَلُحَ ² ـ إِسْتَقَامَ ـ ظَلَّ عَلَى حَالِهِ ـ لَا يَفْسُدُ. To remain in any place, أَحَالَ بِٱلْمَكَانِ ـ أَقَامَ بِٱلْمَكَانِ ـ مَكَثَ بِٱلْمَكَانِ ². He kept there a long time, بَقِيَ هُنَاكَ زَمَانًا طَوِيلًا. He kept there a year, صَرَفَ هُنَاكَ سَنَةً. Keep where you are! hold hard! عِنْدَكَ.

To last, يَبْقَى *aor.* بَقِيَ ـ إِسْتَدَامَ ـ يَدُومُ *aor.* دَامَ ـ رَهَنَ: It will keep, last, till to-morrow, يَسْتَدِيمُ إِلَى بُكْرَةٍ ـ يَدُومُ إِلَى ٱلْغَدِ.

To continue doing, لَا بَرِحَ ـ وَاظَبَ عَلَى ـ دَاوَمَ عَلَى ـ أَدْمَنَ عَلَى ـ إِسْتَمَرَّ عَلَى ـ يَفْعَلُ. *See also to* Continue, Abide, *v.i.*

To keep away, at a distance, تَجَنَّبَ ـ إِبْتَعَدَ ـ تَبَعَّدَ ـ تَبَاعَدَ ـ غَابَ عَن ـ إِغْتَرَبَ عَن ـ إِجْتَنَبَ. To absent one's self from, مَا حَضَرَ فِي.

To keep back, behind, تَأَخَّرَ ـ قَعَدَ خَلْفَ ² ـ تَخَلَّفَ. Not to meddle with, رَفَعَ ـ أَضْرَبَ عَن ـ إِجْتَنَبَ ـ تَجَنَّبَ عَن ـ يَدَهُ عَن.

To keep close to, عَلِقَ بِ ـ إِقْتَرَبَ ـ قَرُبَ مِن ـ لَازَمَ .

To keep down, to remain below, قَعَدَ تَحْتَ . To descend lower, تَسَفَّلَ ـ نَزَلَ . To become less, نَقَصَ ـ قَلَّ . To subside, as anger, passion, إِرْتَخَى . To keep low, of price, هَبَطَ ٱلثَّمَنُ ـ ظَلَّ ٱلثَّمَنُ مَهْبُوطًا . *See also to* Abate, *v.i.*

To keep from, to abstain, كَفَّ عَن ـ تَمَسَّكَ مِن ـ إِحْتَرَزَ مِن ـ إِمْتَنَعَ عَن . Not to go near, إِجْتَنَبَ ـ تَجَنَّبَ . *See also under to* Abstain, *v.i.*

To keep in, to hide one's self, إِخْتَبَأَ ـ إِخْتَفَى ـ تَكَمَّنَ . To keep in doors, لَازَمَ ٱلْبَيْتَ . To restrain one's self, حَبَسَ ـ إِسْتَمْسَكَ ـ تَمَاسَكَ نَفْسَهُ . To keep in, as a fire, ظَلَّ شَاعِلًا .

To keep in favour with, ظَلَّ ـ إِحْتَظَى بِ ـ حَظِيَ عِنْدَهُ مَقْبُولًا عِنْدَهُ .

To keep in memory, حَفِظَ ـ تَنَبَّهَ عَلَى ـ تَذَكَّرَ .

To keep in, retain, one's place, office, إِسْتَقَامَ ـ قَعَدَ فِي مَنْصِبِهِ فِي خِدْمَتِهِ .

To keep off, at a distance, تَجَنَّبَ ـ تَبَعَّدَ ـ تَبَاعَدَ . To be delayed, تَأَخَّرَ . Not to happen, مَا صَارَ ـ لَمْ يَحْدُثْ ـ إِحْتَقَدَ .

Keep off! إِبْعَدْ عَنِّي ـ البَعِيدُ ـ أَخِّرْ عَنِّي . The rain kept off, حَقِدَ (*or* إِحْتَقَدَ) ٱلْمَطَرُ .

To keep on, to go forward, تَقَدَّمَ . To hold on, مَا زَالَ مَاسِكًا .

To keep on one's way, إِسْتَمْسَكَ بِطَرِيقِهِ . To continue doing; *see* To continue doing, *under* Keep, *v.i.*

To keep or retain one's anger, حَقِدَ ـ إِحْتَقَدَ ـ تَحَقَّدَ .

To keep out, to remain outside, ظَلَّ خَارِجًا ـ بَقِيَ بَرًّا *aor.* يَبْقَى .

To keep to, to remain shut, ظَلَّ مَغْلُوقًا . To adhere to, to be contented with, إِكْتَفَى بِ ـ إِعْتَمَدَ عَلَى ـ اسْتَقَرَّ عَلَى . To keep or cleave to without quitting, تَمَسَّكَ بِ ـ سَامَ . To keep to a particular place, as birds, أَلِفَ : The gazelles kept to the sands, أَلِفَتِ ٱلْغِزْلَانُ ٱلرَّمْلَ . He kept to the place, أَلِفَ ٱلْمَكَانَ .

To keep under, to remain below, بَقِيَ أَسْفَلَ ـ ظَلَّ تَحْتَ . *See also* To Keep down, *supra.*

To keep up, to remain above, قَعَدَ فَوْقَ . To float, طَفَا فَوْقَ ٱ... ـ عَامَ . To continue to burn, as a fire, ظَلَّ شَاعِلًا . To keep awake, to sit up, سَهِرَ . To bear up, as against adversity, بَقِيَ عَلَى ٱلشِّدَّةِ ـ عُرِفَ عِنْدَ ٱلْمُصِيبَةِ ـ عَرَفَ لِلْأَمْرِ ـ تَشَدَّدَ . To keep up one's spirits, إِحْتَمَلَ ـ صَبَرَ عَلَى تَصَلَّبَ .

To keep up with, to be equal to, مَاثَلَ ـ عَادَلَ ـ حَاكَى . To keep up with, as in walking, *etc.* أَلْحَقَ ـ لَحِقَ بِ .

Keep, *n.* A castle, blockhouse, قَلْعَة *pl.* قِلَاع ـ هُجْرَة *pl.* هُجَر . Sustenance, كُلْفَة ـ مَعِيشَة ـ قُوت . In good —, fat, سَمِين ; in bad —, رَقِيقُ ٱللَّحْمِ .

Keeper, *n.* A watch, guard, حَارِس *pl.* حُرَّاس ـ حَافِظ *pl.* حُفَّاظ . One who is entrusted with something, أَمِين . A — of a field or vineyard, نَاطُور *pl.* نَوَاطِير . The — of a prison, سَجَّان . A door-keeper, بَوَّاب . A — at home, through laziness, ضَاجِع ; on any other account, مُلَازِمُ ٱلْبَيْتِ . The — of the Great Seal, مُهْرْدَارُ ٱلْمَمْلَكَةِ ـ أَمِينُ مُهْرِ ٱلْمَمْلَكَةِ . A keeper ring, فَتْخَة حَافِظَة .

Keeping, *n.* Holding possession, ضَبْط ـ حِفْظ . Restraining, كَفّ ـ ضَبْط ـ مَنْع . Custody, حِفْظ ـ مُحَافَظَة . Due proportion, مُنَاسَبَة ـ تَنَاسُب . In —, consistent, congruous, مُتَتَابِع . To be in — with, وَافَقَ ـ نَاسَبَ . May God have you in His —, كُنْ فِي حِفْظِ ٱللّٰهِ ـ يَحْفَظُكَ ٱللّٰهُ .

Keepsake, *n.* تَذْكَار ـ تَذْكِرَة ـ تَفْكِرَة .

Keg, *n.* A small cask, بَرْمِيل صَغِير *pl.* بَرَامِيل صِغَار .

Kelp, *n.* Calcined seaweed, قَشُّ ٱلْبَحْرِ مُكَلَّس .

Kelson, *n.* قَعْرُ مَرْكَبٍ عَارِيَة .

Ken, *v.t.* To descry at a distance, شَافَ مِنْ ـ أَدْرَكَ مِنْ بَعِيد . To discover, كَشَفَ عَن ـ إِطَّلَعَ عَلَى . To know, شَعَرَ بِ ـ دَرَى بِ ـ دَرَى ـ عَرَفَ بِ .

Ken, *n.* Reach of sight, مَدَى ٱلْبَصَرِ . A view, مَنْظَر . Knowledge, مَعْرِفَة ـ طُلُوعٌ عَلَى ـ عِلْم . To be within —, sight, كَانَ فِي مَدَى ٱلْبَصَرِ .

Kennel, *n.* A — for dogs, بَيْتُ (*or* مَحَلُّ) ٱلْكِلَابِ .

Kennel, *v.t.* To — dogs, بَيَّتَ ٱلْكِلَابَ .

Kennel, *v.i.* بَاتَتِ ٱلْكِلَابُ .

Kentledge, *n.* صَابُورَةُ قَعْرِ ٱلْمَرْكَبِ .

Kept, *pret. and part. of to* Keep, *q.v.* A kept mistress: *see* Concubine, *n.*

Kerbstone, *n.* حَجَرَةُ حَاجِزٍ ـ حَجَرَةُ ٱلدَّائِرَةِ ـ حَجَرَةُ ٱلْحَاشِيَةِ ٱلْمَمْشَى .

Kerchief, *n.* كِسْوَةُ ٱلرَّأْسِ ـ عِصَاب ـ عَصْب ـ عَمْرَة .

Kerf, *n.* *See* Notch, *n.*

Kermes, *n.* (*properly* Kírmiz), حَبُّ ٱلْقِرْمِزِ ـ قِرْمِز . Mineral —, قِرْمِزٌ مَعْدِنِيٌّ .

Kern, *v.i.* *See to* Harden, *v.i.*

Kernel, *n.* The seed of a pulpy fruit, حَبٌّ ـ عَجَم ـ عَجَمَة *pl.* عَجَمٌ ـ حُبُوب . The — of a date, نَوَاة *pl.* نَوًى . The pulpy matter of a fruit, لُبٌّ *pl.* لُبُوب ـ قَلْب *pl.* قِلَبَة . A grain, حَبٌّ *pl.* حُبُوب . The — of a matter, زُبْدَةُ ٱلْمَادَّةِ . *See also* Stone, *n.*

Kernel, *v.i.* تَحَبَّبَ .

Kerneled, *a.* ذُو أَنْوَآءٍ ـ ذُو حُبُوبٍ .

Kersey, *n.* ضَرْبٌ مِنَ ٱلشَّالِ ٱلْخَشِنِ .

Kerseymere, *n.* ضَرْبٌ مِنَ ٱلْكَشْمِيرِ .

Kestrel, *n.* سُقَيْر ـ بَاشَق ـ نَوْعٌ مِنَ ٱلْبَازِ .

Ketch, *n.* A small vessel, فَلُوكَة *pl.* فَلُوكَات ـ مَرْكَب *pl.* مَرَاكِب .

Ketchup, *n.* *See* Catsup, *n.*

Kettle, *n.* قِدْر *pl.* قُدُور ـ طَاجِير ـ طَاجِرَة ـ حِلَّة *pl.* حِلَل ـ قَزَان *pl.* قَزَانَات ـ قُمْقُمَة *pl.* قُمْقُمَات . A — to heat water in, قُمْقُم *pl.* قَمَاقِمُ ـ صَحَمٌ ـ غَلَّايَة .

Kettle-drum, *n.* طَبْل *pl.* طُبُول ـ كُوس *pl.* كُوسَات . A small —, نَقَّارَة *pl.* نَقَّارَات .

Kettle-drummer, *n.* طَبَّال ـ دَقَّاقُ ٱلنَّقَّارَاتِ .

Kettle-holder, *n.* جِعَال ـ جِعَالَة *pl.* جُعُل ـ شَيَّال . *See also under* Parasite, *n.*

Key, *n.* The instrument to open and shut with, أَقْلِيد ـ مِقْلَد ـ مِقْلَاد *pl.* مَقَالِيدُ ـ مِفْتَح ـ مِفْتَاح *pl.* مَفَاتِيحُ . The — of a country, جَيْبٌ (or أَقْلِيدُ) ٱلْبِلَادِ . The — of the sea, أَقْلِيدُ ٱلْبَحْرِ . Key to the sciences, مِفْتَاحُ ٱلْعُلُومِ . Key, in music, دَرَجَةُ ٱللَّحْنِ ـ لَحْن *pl.* أَلْحَان ـ طَامَّة . Major —, ٱلطَّامَّةُ ٱلْكُبْرَى ; minor —, ٱلطَّامَّةُ ٱلصُّغْرَى . *See also* Quay, *n.*

Keyage, *n.* Wharfage, حَقُّ ٱلْأَسْكَلَةِ (or ٱلرَّصِيفِ) .

Key-board, *n.* ٱلْمَلَامِسُ ـ دَسَاتِينُ ٱلسَّنْطِيرِ .

Keyed, *a.* Having musical keys, ذُو مَلَامِسَ ـ ذُو دَسَاتِينَ . Set to a key, مُرَتَّبٌ عَلَى طَبَقَةٍ ـ مُطَبَّق . Having pieces let in to preserve from warping, مُشَيَّد .

Key-hole, *n.* خَرْقُ ٱلْقُفْلِ ـ مَنْفَذُ ٱلْمِفْتَاحِ .

Key-note, *n.* طَبَقَةُ ٱلنَّغْمِ .

Keystone, *n.* As of an arch, أَقْلِيدُ ٱلْقُبَّةِ ـ حَجَرُ أَقْلِيدِ ٱلْعَقْدِ ـ أَقْلِيدُ ٱلْعِمَارَةِ ; called by builders, رُهْبَان ـ ٱلرَّاهِبُ . A foundation, أَسَاس ـ أَصْل .

K.G., حَائِزُ نِيشَانِ ٱلْكَارْتِرِ ٱلْأَفْخَرِ .

K.H., حَائِزُ ٱلرُّتْبَةِ ٱلثَّالِثَةِ مِنْ نِيشَانِ هَانُوفِر .

Khalif or Khalifah, *n.* خَلِيف *pl.* خُلَفَآءُ ـ خَلِيفَة *pl.* خَلَائِفُ .

Khalifate, *n.* خِلَافَة .

Khamâsin, *n.* (The hot winds so called), ٱلْخَمَاسِينُ .

Khân, *n.* The title, خَان . A caravanserai, خَان *pl.* خَانَات . A — for lodging strangers, مُسَافِرْخَانَة ـ مَنْزِلٌ لِلْغُرَبَآءِ .

Khânate, *n.* مَمْلَكَةُ ٱلْخَانِ ـ دَوْلَةُ ٱلْخَانِ .

Khedive, *n.* (Pronounced in Egypt, al-Khidêwy), ٱلْخِدِيُو ـ ٱلْخِدِيوِيّ .

Kick, *n.* A blow with the foot, ضَرْبٌ ـ رَفْسَة ـ ضَرْبٌ بِٱلرِّجْلِ ـ لَبْط ـ بِٱلزَّوْجِ . A — on the backside, عَفْس ـ لَطْع . A — with the hind legs, رَمْح ; with the front legs, خَبْط .

Kick, *v.t.* رَفَسَ ـ ² ـ ضَرَبَ ـ بِٱلرِّجْلِ ـ رَمَحَ ـ ² *vulg.* لَبَطَ ـ ضَرَبَ ـ بِٱلزَّوْجِ . To — one with the hind legs, رَمَحَ ; with the front legs, especially of a camel, خَبَطَ ـ اِخْتَبَطَ ـ تَخَبَّطَ . To — on the backside, عَفَسَ ـ لَطَعَ . To — against the pricks, رَفَسَ ٱلْمَنَاخِسَ ² . To — out, أَخْرَجَ ـ عَنْفًا ـ أَخْرَجَ . To — about, كَبْكَبَ ـ خَبَطَ . To — under foot, دَاسَ *aor.* يَدُوسُ .

Kick, *v.i.* اِعْتَادَ ٱلرَّفْسَ ـ تَلَبَّطَ ـ اِلْتَبَطَ . To —, to paw the ground, خَبَطَ ٱلْأَرْضَ . The vice of kicking, رُفُوس ـ رِفَاس . A kicking beast, ذُو رِمَاحٍ ـ رَمَّام ـ رَمُوح ـ دَابَّةٌ رَفُوسٌ .

Kicking, *n.* *See* Kick, *n.*

Kid, *n.* A young goat, جَدْيٌ *pl.* جِدَآءٌ *and* جِدْيَان ; the female is called عَنَاق *pl.* عُنُوق . Kid-skin, جِلْدُ ٱلْجَدْيِ . A bundle, حُزْمَة . A wooden bowl, قَصْعَة *pl.* قِصَع *and* قَصَاعَات .

Kid, *v.i.* خَلَّفَتِ ٱلْمَاعِزَةُ .

Kidnap, *v.t.* سَلَبَ بَنِي آدَمَ ـ اِخْتَلَسَ بَشَرًا ² .

Kidnapper, *n.* خَاطِفُ ٱلنَّاسِ ـ خَالِسُ (or خَلَّاسُ) ٱلنَّاسِ .

Kidnapping, *n.* سَلْبُ بَنِي بَشَرٍ ـ اِخْتِلَاسُ ٱلنَّاسِ .

Kidney, *n.* Of the body, كُلْيَة or كُلْوَة *pl.* كُلْوَات ـ كُلْيَة *dual* كُلْيَتَانِ *pl.* كُلًى . The fat round the kidneys, كُظْر . A kind of potato, ضَرْبٌ مِنَ ٱلْبَطَاطَا . Character, خُلُق ـ طَبِيعَة . *See also under* Kind, *n.*

Kidney-bean, *n.* لُوبِيَة .

Kilderkin, *n.* بَرْمِيلٌ يَسَعُ ١٦ أَوْ ١٨ كَالَنًا . *See under* Gallon, *n.*

Kill, *v.t.* To deprive of life, قَتَلَ ـ مَوَّتَ ² . To — much, many, قَتَّلَ . To slaughter, of an ox or sheep, ذَبَحَ ; of a camel, and of a sheep, نَحَرَ ـ جَزَرَ ; of a flea, فَرَكَ ² ; of a louse, قَصَعَ ـ أَقْصَعَ ـ أَزْعَفَ ـ زَعَفَ . To — on the spot, أَقْعَصَ . To destroy, أَعْدَمَ . To — in hunting, اِصْطَادَ ـ صَيَّدَ . To —, of a colour, أَزَالَ ـ سَكَّنَ ـ كَتَمَ ² . To be killed, قُتِلَ ; through passion, أُقْتِلَ; to be slaughtered, إِنْذَبَحَ. To — one's self, قَتَلَ ² – قَتَلَ نَفْسَهُ ². To — time, قَطَعَ ٱلْوَقْتَ. Killing, mode of being killed, قِتْلَة – حَالَةٌ.

Killer, *n.* قَاتِل *pl.* قَتَّال – قُتَّال. A slaughterer, ذَابِح – ذَبَّاح.

Kiln, *n.* An oven, قَمِين *pl.* قُمَنَآءُ. A lime —, قَمِينُ جِيْرٍ – كَلَّاسَة. A — for pottery, قَمِينُ ٱلْفَخَّارِ.

Kiln-dry, *v.t.* طَبَخَ فِي ٱلْقَمِينِ ².

Kilogramme, *n.* كِيلُوگْرَام.

Kilometre, *n.* كِيلُومِتْر وَهُوَ عِبَارَةٌ عَنْ أَلْفِ مِتْرٍ. *See also* Metre, *n.*

Kilt, *n.* ضَرْبٌ مِنَ ٱلْفُسْطَانِ يَلْبَسُهُ أَهْلُ إِسْكُوتْلَانْد. Kilted, مُفَسْطَن.

Kimbo, *a.* Crooked, bent, مُعَوَّج – مُعَقَّف. With arms a-kimbo, مُكَتِّفُ ٱلْيَدَيْنِ – مُكَتِّف.

Kin, *n.* *See* Kindred, *n.*

Kind, *n.* A race, نَسْل – صِيغَة – نَسَب *pl.* أَنْسَاب – نَجْل. A sort, ضَرْب *pl.* ضُرُوب – نَوْع *pl.* أَنْوَاع – قِسْم *pl.* أَقْسَام – قَبِيل *pl.* قُبُل – جِنْس *pl.* أَجْنَاس – صِنْف *pl.* أَصْنَاف – شَكْل *pl.* أَشْكَال – بَاب *pl.* أَبْوَاب. Manner, way, طَرِيقَة *pl.* طَرَائِق – طَرْز – مِنْوَال – جَوْب. To arrange into kinds, صَنَّفَ. To pay in —, as of taxes, وَفَى ٱلرُّسُومَ مِنْ عَيْنِ ٱلشَّيْءِ ² *aor.* يَفِي. To pay one in —, to reciprocate one's action, عَوَّضَ – أَعَاضَ – قَابَلَ بِ. Nothing of the —, كَلَّا. Of this —, مِنْ هٰذَا ٱلْقَبِيلِ.

Kind, *a.* Benevolent, ذُو فَضْلٍ – كَرِيم – مِنْعَام – خَيِّر – مَنَّان – مُحْسِن – مُفْضِل. Benignant, حَلِيمُ ٱلطَّبْعِ – حَلِيم – رَؤُوف – لَطِيف – لَيِّنُ ٱلْقَلْبِ. To be —, benevolent, generous to, in, تَفَضَّلَ عَلَى – بِ – أَنْعَمَ عَلَى – بِ. To be —, courteous, to, تَلَطَّفَ لِ – تَلَاطَفَ لِ. You are very —, فَضْلُكَ عَلَيَّ – لَكَ ٱلْفَضْلُ. Be kind enough to present my regards to your family, مِنْ فَضْلِكَ سَلِّمْ عَلَى أَهْلِ بَيْتِكَ مِنْ طَرَفِي. He has been very — to me, أَحْسَنَ إِلَيَّ كُلَّ ٱلْإِحْسَانِ.

Kind-hearted, *a.* شَفِيق – رَقِيقُ ٱلْقَلْبِ – رَؤُوف.

Kind-heartedness, *n.* شَفَقَة – رَأْفَة.

Kindle, *v.t.* To set on fire, حَشَّ ² – أَوْهَجَ – أَلْعَجَ – أَجَّجَ – شَعَّلَ – أَشْعَلَ – أَوْقَدَ – أَضْرَمَ – سَعَّرَ – حَضَا ٱلنَّارَ ² – ٱلنَّارَ. To — a fire, أَزَّ ² (or قَادَ or أَضْرَمَ or أَوْقَدَ or وَلَّعَ) – عَلَّقَ ٱلنَّارَ. To be kindled, as of a fire, إِشْتَعَلَ – تَأَرَّثَتِ ٱلنَّارُ – تَشَعَّلَ – إِتَّقَدَ – تَوَقَّدَ – تَضَرَّمَ – إِضْطَرَمَ. To inflame, exasperate, أَضْرَمَ – أَلْهَبَ. To animate, أَنْهَضَ – إِسْتَفَزَّ – أَنْفَسَ. To — war, أَضْرَمَ نَارَ ٱلْحَرْبِ – أَثَارَ ٱلْحَرْبَ. To — strife between, أَجَّجَ بَيْنَهُمْ شَرًّا – أَلَّبَ بَيْنَ – أَرَّشَ بَيْنَ – أَرَّجَ بَيْنَ – أَرَّثَ بَيْنَ.

Kindle, *v.i.* To take fire, إِلْتَهَبَ – إِضْطَرَمَ – إِشْتَعَلَ – تَوَقَّدَ – تَضَرَّمَ. To be exasperated, إِغْتَاظَ – إِلْتَهَبَ غَيْظًا. To be animated, إِنْتَهَضَ. The war was kindled, تَضَرَّمَتِ ٱلْحَرْبُ.

Kindler, *n.* مُؤَجِّج – مُشْعِل – شَاعِل.

Kindliness, *n.* رَأْفَة – حُسْنُ ٱلِٱلْتِفَاتِ – لَطَافَة – لُطْف – مَيْل إِلَى. Kindliness is gain, (prov.) ٱلسَّمَاحُ رَبَاحٌ.

Kindly, *a.* Mild, مُسَامِح – حَلِيم – لَطِيف. To act in a — manner toward one in an affair, سَامَحَهُ فِي.

Kindly, *ad.* With good will, obligingly, بِجَمِيلٍ – بِفَضْلٍ – بِإِحْسَانٍ – بِمَعْرُوفٍ. To behave — to, إِقْتَفَى بِ. To deal —, compassionately, with, أَشْفَقَ عَلَى. To take a thing —, حَمَلَ ² – إِسْتَحْسَنَ – ٱلشَّيْءَ عَلَى ٱلْخَيْرِ.

Kindness, *n.* Benevolence, خَيْر – فَضْل *pl.* فُضُول – كَرَم – حُسْنُ ٱلِٱلْتِفَاتِ. A kind act, مَعْرُوف – عُرْف. Courtesy, جُود – شَفَقَة – رَأْفَة. Compassion, لَطَافَة – لُطْف. Mildness, gentleness, بَشَاشَة – رَآفَة – دَمَاثَة – لَطَافَة – حِلْم. To show — generosity to, أَفْضَلَ عَلَى – مَنَّ عَلَى ²; to show courtesy to, أَلْطَفَ بِ. He did him a —, صَنَعَ إِلَيْهِ مَعْرُوفًا ². Will you have the — to send this to my house, أَتَتَفَضَّلُ عَلَيَّ بِإِرْسَالِ هٰذَا إِلَى مَنْزِلِي. Have the — to tell me, مِنْ فَضْلِكَ قُلْ لِي. Have the — to hand me the inkstand and pen, تَفَضَّلْ عَلَيَّ وَقُلْ لِي – كَلِّفْ خَاطِرَكَ وَنَاوِلْنِي ٱلدَّوَايَةَ وَٱلْقَلَمَ. To thank one for his —, شَكَرَ فَضْلَهُ ².

Kindred, *n.* Consanguinity, قَرَابَة – خَابٌ. Relatives, أَقْرِبَآءُ – عِيَال – أَهْل – نَسَائِبُ – أَنْسِبَآءُ – أَقَارِبُ – أَقْرَبُونَ. Family, أَهْل.

Kindred, *a.* Allied by birth, نَسِيب *pl.* أَنْسِبَآءُ – قَرِيب. Congenial, مِنْ جِنْسٍ وَاحِدٍ – مِنْ طَبْعٍ وَاحِدٍ – مُوَافِق – مُجَانِس.

Kine, *n.* Cows, بَقَرَات.

King, *n.* A monarch, مَلِك *pl.* مُلُوك – سُلْطَان *pl.* سَلَاطِين. The — at chess, ٱلشَّاهُ – ٱلسُّلْطَانُ. King of kings, مَلِكُ ٱلْمُلُوكِ. To make one —, أَمْلَكَ – مَلَّكَ. To act like a —, تَمَلَّكَ. The Book of Kings, سِفْرُ ٱلْمُلُوكِ.

Kingcraft, *n.* The art of reigning, سِيَاسَةُ ٱلْمُلْكِ – تَمَلُّك – حُكْمُ ٱلْمَمَالِكِ.

Kingdom, *n.* دَوْلَة *pl.* دُوَل – مَمْلَكَة *pl.* مَمَالِكُ – وِلَايَة *pl.* وِلَايَات – سَلْطَنَة. In those two kingdoms, فِي تَيْنِكَ ٱلْمَمْلَكَتَيْنِ. The — of Heaven, مَلَكُوتُ ٱلسَّمَآءِ.

The animal kingdom, عالَمُ ٱلحَيَوانِ.

The mineral kingdom, عالَمُ ٱلمَعادِنِ.

The vegetable kingdom, عالَمُ ٱلنَّباتِ.

King-fisher, *n.* عُصْفُورُ ٱلدُّورِى ـ أَبو نَقّارٍ.

King-like, *a.* / Kingly, } مِثْلَ ٱلمُلُوكِ ـ مِثْلَ مَلِكٍ ـ مُلُوكِيٌّ.

King's Bench, *n.* The supreme court of law, مَحْكَمَةُ ٱلتَّمْيِيزِ. A prison, حَبْس.

King's evil, *n.* سِلَع ـ خَنازِيرُ ـ خَلَد *pl.* خُلُود. Having the —, مَسْلُوع.

Kingship, *n.* سَلْطَنَة ـ مُلْك.

Kink, *n.* فَتْلَة ـ لَيَّة.

Kink, *v.i.* تَلَوَّى ـ اِلْتَوَى.

Kino, *n.* راتِينَجُ صِينِيٌّ.

Kinsfolk, *n.* *See* Kindred, *n.*

Kinsman, *n.* قَرِيب ـ خَوَاتٌ *pl.* خاتّ ـ أَنْسِباءُ *pl.* نَسِيب *pl.* أَقْرِباءُ. He is near — to me, هُوَ قَرِيبُ ٱلقَرابَةِ مِنِّي.

Kinswoman, *n.* قَرِيبَة *pl.* قَرِيبات ـ نَسِيبَة *pl.* نَسِيبات.

Kiosk, *n.* كِشْك.

Kipper, *v.t.* To —, مَلَّحَ وَدَخَّنَ. Kippered, مُمَلَّحٌ وَمُدَخَّنٌ.

Kirk, *n.* A church, كَنِيسَة *pl.* كَنائِسُ.

Kirtle, *n.* قَرّاجَة ـ فُسْطان ـ فُسْتان.

Kiss, *n.* A —, as with the lips, بَوْسَة ـ قُبْلَة ـ بَوْس ـ لَثْمَة. To send a — to, as with the hands, أَوْمَى (or أَشارَ) بِقُبْلَةٍ إِلَى. A comfit, مُلَبَّس.

Kiss, *v.t.* As with the lips, باسَ ـ قَبَّلَ ـ أَلْثَمَ ـ لَثَمَ *aor.* يَبُوسُ. To — a woman suddenly, كافَحَ. They kissed one another, of many, تَباوَسُوا.

Kit, *n.* A small fiddle, كَمانْجَة صَغِيرَة. A small barrel of salt fish, بَرْمِيلُ سَمَكٍ مُمَلَّحٍ. Tools, آلات ـ عُدَّة. A soldier's —, لَوازِمُ ٱلعَسْكَرِيِّ. The whole — of them, كُلُّهُمْ ـ أَجْمَعُ. *See also* Kitten, *n.*

Kitchen, *n.* مَطْبَخ *pl.* مَطابِخُ. A soup —, for the poor, مَطْبَخُ ٱلطَّبِيخِ لِلْفُقَراءِ. A — garden, بُسْتانُ ٱلخُضارِ. A — maid, غَسّالَةُ ٱلصُّحُونِ. Kitchen stuff, فُضالاتُ (or خُشارُ) ٱلمَطْبَخِ.

Kite, *n.* The bird, حِدَأَة ـ مُرْزَة ـ أَبو ٱلخَطّافِ ـ أَبو ٱلصَّلْتِ *vulg.* حِدايَة. The toy, طَيّارَة. To fly a —, طَيَّرَ ٱلطَّيّارَةَ.

Kith, *n.* أَصْحاب ـ رُفَقاءُ ـ أَصْدِقاءُ. Kith and kin, أَصْدِقاءُ وَأَقْرِباءُ.

Kitten, *v.i.* خَلَفَتِ ٱلقِطَّةُ.

Kitten, *n.* جِرْوُ ٱلقِطَّةِ ـ قُطَيْط. To be in —, القِطَّةُ حامِلٌ.

Klick, *v.i.* صاتَ بِتِكْ تِكْ.

Klick, *n.* طَقْطَقَة ـ تِكَّة.

Knab, *v.t.* *See to* Apprehend, Seize, *v.t.*

Knack, *n.* Habit, عادَة. Dexterity, خِفَّة ـ مَهارَة ـ شَطارَة. To have the —, the habit of . . ., مِنْ عادَتِهِ أَنْ; to have the —, dexterity, of . . ., مِنْ مَهارَتِهِ أَنْ.

Knacker, *n.* دَلّالُ ٱلخَيْلِ ٱلسَّقَطِ.

Knag, *n.* A knot in wood, عُجَر *pl.* عُجْرَة ـ أُبْن *pl.* أُبْنَة ـ عُقْدَة *pl.* عُقَد. The shoot of a deer's horn, حَيْدَة *pl.* حُيُود.

Knaggy, *a.* Full of knot, مُعَقَّد ـ ذُو عُجَرٍ.

Knap, *n.* A protuberance, حَيْد ـ حَيْدَة *pl.* أَحْياد ـ حِدَب. A swelling, وَرَم ـ تَوَرُّم ـ نُفّاخ.

Knap, *v.t.* To bite off, عَضَّ.

Knapsack, *n.* حَقِيبَة ـ مَزاوِدُ *pl.* مِزْوَد ـ رِداف *pl.* رَدِيف.

Knar, *n.* *See* Knag, *n.*

Knarled, *a.* *See* Gnarled, *a.*

Knave, *n.* خاسِر *pl.* خُسَّر ـ خَلِيع *pl.* خُلَعاءُ ـ خَبِيث *pl.* خُبَثاءُ ـ لَعِين ـ غَدّار ـ قَبِيح *pl.* قِباح. The —, at cards, الأَعْرَجُ *pl.* العَرْجان ـ المُفَرْشَخُ.

Knavery, *n.* / Knavishness, } خَلاعَة ـ غَدْر ـ غَبْن ـ قَباحَة. To act with —, أَقْبَحَ.

Knavish, *a.* خَبِيث ـ لَعِين ـ أَشْقِياءُ *pl.* شَقِيّ ـ دَنِس ـ قَبِيح *pl.* خُبَثاءُ.

Knavishly, *ad.* بِحِيلَةٍ ـ بِغَدْرٍ ـ بِقَباحَةٍ ـ بِخَباثَةٍ.

Knead, *v.t.* As of dough, عَجَنَ; to — well, much, مَلَكَ ـ أَمْلَكَ. To — into bread, فَطَرَ ـ فَطَّرَ ـ خَبَزَ خُبْزًا ـ اِخْتَبَزَ. To be kneaded, اِنْعَجَنَ.

Kneading-board, *n.* سَقِيبَة.

Kneading-trough, *n.* مِعْجَن *pl.* مَعاجِنُ.

Knee, *n.* Of the leg, رُكْبَة *pl.* رُكَب. A — or elbow of a horse or other beast, مَثْنَى *pl.* مَثانٍ. To bow the —, in worship, رَكَعَ. To sit on one's own knees, جَثا *aor.* يَجْثُو ـ جَثَى *aor.* يَجْثِي. جَثَى عَلَى رُكْبَتَيْهِ ـ يَجْثِي. To fall down on the knees, وَقَعَ عَلَى رُكْبَتَيْهِ ـ خَرَّ عَلَى رُكْبَتَيْهِ. To make to bend the —, أَجْثَى. To sit — to — with one, جاثَى. They sat together on their knees, تَجاثَوْا عَلَى ٱلرُّكَبِ. The inner side of the —, مَأْبِض. A crook, مِحْجَن ـ مِحْجَنَة. Feeble knees, رُكَبٌ مُخَلَّعَةٌ. Having large knees, أَرْكَبُ. His knees knocked together, اِصْطَكَّتْ رُكْبَتاهُ. To dandle on the knees, دَلَّلَ عَلَى ٱلرُّكْبَتَيْنِ.

Kneed, *a.* ذُو رُكَبٍ. Having large knees, أَرْكَبُ. A hard-—camel, بَعِيرٌ مُسْتَوْقِحُ ٱلرُّكَبِ.

Knee-deep, *a.* } إِلَى ٱلرُّكْبَتَيْنِ.
Knee-high, }

Kneel, *v.i.* To bow, as in worship, رَكَعَ. To go down on the knees, خَرَّ - يَقَعُ *aor.* وَقَعَ عَلَى رُكْبَتَيْهِ - جَثَى عَلَى رُكْبَتَيْهِ - عَلَى رُكْبَتَيْهِ. To make to —, أَجْثَى. To —, as a camel, بَرَكَ - تَنَوَّخَ. To make a camel to —, أَنَاخَ - بَرَّكَ - أَبْرَكَ. To — to, to supplicate, اِبْتَهَلَ إِلَى - تَضَرَّعَ إِلَى.

Kneeling, *n.* As in worship, رُكُوعٌ; one such —, رَكْعَةٌ. A sitting on the knees, جُثُوٌّ. A place for sitting on the knees, a hassock, مَجْثًى. He performed the prayer of one —, صَلَّى رَكْعَةً; he performed two such kneelings, صَلَّى رَكْعَتَيْنِ. The —, as of a camel, بَرْكٌ.

Kneeling, *a.* Bowing, as in worship, رَاكِعٌ; sitting on the knees, جَاثٍ. Of a camel, بَارِكٌ.

Knee-pan, *n.* دَاغِصَةٌ.

Knell, *n.* The sound of a bell, دَقُّ جَرَسٍ. A funeral —, دَقُّ جَرَسِ ٱلْمَوْتِ. To toll the —, دَقَّ ٱلْجَرَسَ عِنْدَ مَوْتِ أَحَدٍ.

Knicknack, *n.* (زَهِيدٌ *or* دَقِيقٌ) شَيْءٌ طَفِيفٌ.

Knicknackery, *n.* (دَقَائِقُ *or*) خُرْدَةٌ - مَدَاقُّ ٱلْأَمْتِعَةِ.

Knife, *n.* سِكِّينَةٌ - سِكِّينٌ *pl.* سَكَاكِينُ. A maker of knives, سَكَاكِينِيٌّ - سَكَّانٌ.

Carving-knife, سِكِّينٌ لِلتَّقْطِيعِ.

Case-knife, سَاطُورٌ *pl.* سَوَاطِيرُ.

Clasp-knife, small, مِطْوًى.

Dessert knife, سِكِّينٌ صَغِيرٌ.

Fruit-knife, سِكِّينٌ لِلْفَاكِهَةِ.

Paper-knife, مِطْوَى ٱلْوَرَقِ.

Penknife, مِبْرَاةٌ - مِطْوًى *pl.* مَطَاوٍ (in Syria called, عَوَيْسِيَّةٌ).

Pocket-knife; *see* Clasp-knife.

Pruning-knife, مِشْذَبٌ - مِحْطَبٌ.

Shoemaker's paring knife, إِزْمِيلٌ.

Table-knife, سِكِّينٌ لِلسُّفْرَةِ.

Knife and fork, سِكِّينٌ وَشَوْكَةٌ.

War to the knife, مُحَارَبَةٌ عَلَى ٱلسَّاقِ.

Knife-board, *n.* لَوْحَةٌ لِجَلْوِ ٱلسَّكَاكِينِ - مِصْقَلَةُ ٱلسَّكَاكِينِ.

Knife-grinder, *n.* سَنَّانُ سَكَاكِينَ.

Knife-sharpener, *n.* A whetstone, مِسَنٌّ - مِشْحَذَةٌ.

Knife-tray, *n.* أَنَاءُ ٱلسَّكَاكِينِ.

Knight, *n.* Of the order of knighthood, قَوَالِيرُ. A nobleman, نَبِيلٌ *pl.* نِبَالٌ - أَمِيرٌ *pl.* أُمَرَاءُ. A champion, مُبَارِزٌ - مُنَاجِدٌ. The — in chess, ٱلْخَيَّالُ - ٱلْفَارِسُ.

Knight-errant, *n.* مُبَارِزٌ دَوَّارٌ.

Knight Commander of the Bath, حَائِزُ ٱلرُّتْبَةِ ٱلثَّانِيَةِ مِنْ نِيشَانِ ٱلْبَاثْ.

Knight of the Garter, حَائِزُ نِيشَانِ ٱلْكَارْتَرِ ٱلْأَفْخَمِ.

Knight Grand Cross of the Bath, حَائِزُ ٱلرُّتْبَةِ ٱلْأُولَى مِنْ نِيشَانِ ٱلْبَاثْ.

Knight of Hanover, حَائِزُ نِيشَانِ مَمْلَكَةِ هَانُوَرَ.

Knight of St. Patrick, حَائِزُ نِيشَانِ حَضْرَةِ مَارِ بَاتْرِيكَ.

Knight of the post, مُزَوِّرٌ.

Knight of the shire, حَائِزُ وَكَالَةِ ٱلْمَشُورَةِ فِي وِلَايَةٍ.

Knight of the Thistle, حَائِزُ نِيشَانِ ٱلشَّسْلِ.

Knight-errantry, *n.* إِغَارَةٌ فِي ٱلْبُلْدَانِ لِلْمُبَارَزَةِ.

Knighthood, *n.* رُتْبَةُ ٱلْقَوَالِيرِ.

Knightly, *a.* مِثْلَ قَوَالِيرَ - نَبِيلٌ *pl.* نِبَالٌ.

Knit, *v.t.* As with needles, صَنَعَ - صَنْعَ ٱلْجَوَارِبِ. To tie, رَبَطَ - جَمَعَ بَيْنَ - جَمَّعَ. To — together, to unite, قَرَنَ بَيْنَ - قَطَّبَ وَجْهَهُ - عَبَسَ وَجْهَهُ. To — the brows, عَرَّضَ حَوَاجِبَهُ. To be — together, united, اِتَّحَدَ - اِقْتَرَنَ.

Knitter, *n.* صَانِعُ ٱلْجَوَارِبِ وَمَا مَاثَلَهَا.

Knitting-needle, *n.* مِيلٌ لِصَنْعِ ٱلْجَوَارِبِ وَمَا شَاكَلَهَا *pl.* أَمْيَالٌ.

Knob, *n.* A knot, protuberance, عُجْرَةٌ *pl.* عُجَرٌ - كُعْبُرَةٌ *pl.* كَعَابِرُ - حَيْدَةٌ *pl.* حُيُودٌ. A — on a tree, سِلْعَةٌ *pl.* سِلَعٌ. The —, handle of a door, مِقْبَضُ بَابٍ - مُسْكَةُ بَابٍ. *See also* Knot, *n.*

Knobbed, *a.* } عُجَرٌ - ذُو عُجَرٍ - ذُو كَعَابِرَ - مُعَقَّدٌ. *See also*
Knobby, } Knotty, *a.*

Knobbiness, *n.* عُجَرٌ - عُجْرَةٌ - تَعْقِيدٌ.

Knock, *v.t.* To hit, strike, صَدَمَ - قَرَعَ - لَطَمَ - ضَرَبَ. To — with, strike with, قَرَعَ بِ - ضَرَبَ بِ. To — at a door, (قَرَعَ *or* دَقَّ *or*) طَرَقَ ٱلْبَابَ. He continued to — at the door, لَبِثَ يَقْرَعُ ٱلْبَابَ.

To knock about, to kick about, طَرَّدَ - رَضْرَضَ - خَبَطَ - رَفَسَ.

To put into disorder, عَثْعَثَ - شَوَّشَ - بَلْبَلَ - لَبَكَ - لَخْبَطَ.

To knock against, صَدَمَ - صَادَمَ - سَدَعَ بِ. The ass knocked against him, صَادَمَهُ ٱلْحِمَارُ. He knocked his foot against a stone, صَدَمَ بِحَجَرٍ رِجْلَهُ. They knocked one against the other, of two, تَصَادَمَا; of many, تَصَادَمُوا.

To knock away, to remove, قَلَعَ - أَبْعَدَ - شَالَ بِ - رَفَعَ.

To knock down, throw on the ground, جَفَأَ بِهِ ـ أَجْفَأَ بِهِ ـ أَوْقَعَ ـ كَبْكَبَ ـ أَكَبَّ ـ كَبَّ ـ صَرَعَ. To throw or pull down, to demolish, هَدَمَ ـ هَدَّ ـ أَسْقَطَ ـ ضَعْضَعَ.

To knock in, أَدْخَلَ ـ دَخَّلَ ; of a nail, سَمَّرَ.

To knock off, to break, كَسَرَ ـ بَعَّجَ. To finish, فَرَغَ مِن ـ أَتَمَّ ـ كَمَّلَ ـ أَنْجَزَ ـ نَجَزَ.

To knock on the head, to kill, قَتَلَ.

To knock out, قَلَّعَ ـ أَخْرَجَ.

To knock under to, تَضَعْضَعَ ل ـ اِخْتَضَعَ ل ـ تَذَلَّلَ ل.

To knock up, to tire, أَتْعَبَ ـ أَعْجَزَ ـ عَنَّى ـ أَكَلَّ ـ تَهَوَّرَ ـ أَعْيَا.

To build or run up slightly, عَشَّمَ ـ اِعْتَشَمَ. To make to get up, to awaken, أَفَاقَ ـ نَبَّهَ ـ أَيْقَظَ.

Knock, *v.i.* As of a door, دَقَّ ـ قَرَعَ ـ طَرَقَ ـ اِنْدَقَّ.

To knock about, to go here and there, سَاحَ ـ تَرَدَّدَ. To be tossed about, as of a ship at sea, اِلْتَطَمَ ـ تَعَذَّبَ.

To knock off, to give up doing, تَرَكَ ـ بَطَلَ ـ اِنْقَطَعَ.

To knock under, to give in, خَضَعَ ـ اِسْتَسْلَمَ ـ أَسْلَمَ.

Knock, *n.* } A blow, ضَرْبَة ـ مُصَادَمَة ـ صَدْمَة ـ سَطْوَة ـ سَدْع.
Knocking, } A —, as at a door, دَقّ ـ طَرْق ـ قَرْع.

Knocker, *n.* One who knocks, طَارِق ـ قَارِع. The — of a door, مِطْرَقَة.

Knock-kneed, *a.* أَصَكّ. To be —, صَكَّ.

Knoll, *n.* *See* Knell, *n.*

Knoll, *n.* A hillock, تَلّ *pl.* تِلَال ـ كُومَة *pl.* أَكْوَام ـ جُثْوَة *pl.* جُثًا.

Knop, *n.* *See* Knob, *n.*

Knot, *n.* As in cords, عُقْدَة *pl.* عُقَد ـ شَدَّة. A tie, رَبْطَة. A — in a horn, حَيْدَة *pl.* حُيُود ـ عُقْصَة. A — in a reed or straw, عُقْدَة ـ أُنْبُوب *pl.* أَنَابِيب ـ مَعْقِم *pl.* مَعَاقِم ـ كَعْب *pl.* كُعُوب. A — in wood, عُجْرَة ـ أُبْن *pl.* أُبَن ـ جُرْذ *pl.* جِرْذَان ـ عُقْدَة *pl.* عُقَد. A difficulty, مُشْكِلَة ـ صُعُوبَة ـ عُقْدَة *pl.* عُقَد ـ عُجَر. A nautical mile, مِيل *pl.* أَمْيَال. A group, كُوم *pl.* أَكْوَام ـ جَمْع ـ جُمْلَة ـ شِرْذِمَة ـ جَمَاعَة. A branch in which there are no knots, غُصْن مُتَتَابِع. To tie in a —, عَقَّدَ ـ عَقَدَ. To be tied in a —, اِنْعَقَدَ. To untie a —, حَلَّ ـ حَلَّ ٱلْعُقْدَةَ. The steamer goes ten knots an hour, تَسِيرُ ٱلْبَاخِرَةُ فِي ٱلسَّاعَةِ عَشَرَةَ أَمْيَالٍ. Free of knots, سَمْح ـ مُتَتَابِع. A gordian —, عُقْدَة لَا تَنْحَلّ. To free of knots, of wood, جَرَّدَ.

Knot, *v.t.* To tie in knots, عَقَدَ ـ عَقَّدَ.

Knot, *v.i.* To form knots, of thread, *etc.*, تَعَقَّدَ ـ اِنْعَقَدَ ; of plants, نَبَّبَ. To grow in knots, of a tree, نَبَّبَتِ ٱلشَّجَرَةُ.

Knot-grass, *n.* عَصَا ٱلرَّاعِي ـ بَطْبَاط.

Knotted, *a.* } Full of knots, of thread, *etc.*, أَعْجَرُ ـ عَجِر ـ
Knotty, } أَعْقَدُ ـ مُعَقَّد ـ مَعْقُود ; of wood, أَعْجَرُ ـ مُعَقَّد ـ ذُو أُبَنٍ ـ ذُو عُجَر. Difficult, intricate, صَعْب ـ مُشْكِل ـ عَسِير. To be —, in knots, تَعَقَّدَ ; to be —, difficult, صَعُبَ ـ تَعَصَّى ـ أَصْعَبَ. A — staff, عَصًى عَجْرَاء. A — piece of wood, خَشَبَة بَشِعَة.

Knout, *n.* سَوْط *pl.* سِيَاط ـ كِرْبَاج.

Knout, *v.t.* سَوَّطَ ـ جَلَدَ بِٱلسَّوْطِ ـ كَرْبَجَ.

Know, *v.t.* To have an idea of, أَذِنَ ب ـ شَعَرَ ب ـ دَرَى ـ وَقَفَ عَلَى ـ تَخَبَّرَ ب ـ طَلَعَ عَلَى ـ اِطَّلَعَ عَلَى ـ دَرَى ب *aor.* يَقِفُ ـ عَلِمَ ـ عَرَفَ. To —, to have experience of, بَلَا ـ اِخْتَبَرَ ـ عَرَفَ. To learn, discover, make one's self acquainted with, تَعَرَّفَ. To distinguish, مَيَّزَ ـ عَرَفَ. To have the acquaintance of, عَرَفَ ـ لَهُ مَعْرِفَةٌ ب. To — carnally, جَامَعَ ـ دَخَلَ إِلَى ـ تَمَتَّعَ ب. To cause to —, to inform, آذَنَ ب ـ آذَنَ ـ أَشْعَرَ ب ـ أَعْلَمَ ـ عَلَّمَ ـ عَرَّفَ. He knew it perfectly, عَلِمَ بِهِ حَقَّ مَعْرِفَتِهِ ـ عَرَفَهُ حَقَّ ٱلْمَعْرِفَةِ. I don't know, لَا أَدْرِي. Don't you know? أَلَا تَدْرِي. Not to —, جَهِلَ ـ جَهِلَ ب. Oh that I knew! لَيْتَ شِعْرِي. To — by heart, حَفِظَ غَيْبًا ـ حَفِظَ عَلَى ظَهْرِ قَلْبِهِ. As is well known, كَمَا هُوَ مَشْهُور. Every one knows, لَا يَخْفَى عَلَى أَحَدٍ. To make known, أَظْهَرَ ـ بَيَّنَ ـ عَرَّفَ. To — one's self, عَرَفَ نَفْسَهُ ـ ذَاقَ رُوحَهُ. To make one's self known to, تَعَرَّفَ إِلَى ـ اِسْتَعْلَنَ ل ـ عَرَّفَ بِنَفْسِهِ. Joseph was made known to his brethren, اِسْتَعْرَفَ يُوسُفُ إِلَى إِخْوَتِهِ. I came in disguise, and then made known who I was, أَتَيْتُ مُتَنَكِّرًا ثُمَّ ٱسْتَعْرَفْتُ.

Know, *v.i.* عَلِمَ ـ دَرَى ـ عَرَفَ.

Knowable, *a.* مِمَّا يُعْرَفُ ـ يُطَّلَعُ عَلَيْهِ.

Knowing, *a.* Having knowledge, وَاقِف عَلَى ـ عَالِم ـ عَارِف. Experienced, عَرِيف *pl.* عُرَفَاء ـ مُدَرَّب ـ خَبِير ـ مُدَرِّس ـ مَاهِر. Significant, مَعْنَوِيّ.

Knowingly, *ad.* Intentionally, عَمْدًا ـ قَصْدًا ـ عَنْ قَصْدٍ.

Knowledge, *n.* Information, عِلْم ـ خَبَر ـ وُقُوف عَلَى ـ شُعُور ب ـ طُلُوع عَلَى ـ مَعْرِفَة. Science, عِلْم ـ مَعْرِفَة ـ عِرْفَان. Experience, دِرَايَة ـ اِخْتِبَار ـ خِبْرَة ـ مَعْلُومَات. To have —, experience, of, تَدَرَّبَ ب. To acquire a — of, تَعَرَّفَ ـ ضَمِنَ. To seek after the — of, تَعَرَّفَ. Certain —, عِلْمُ ٱلْيَقِينِ ـ يَقِين. Carnal —, جِمَاع ـ مُجَامَعَة ـ دُخُول إِلَى. To the best of my —, عَلَى ما أَعْرِفُ يَقِينًا ـ عَلَى عِلْمِي. Without my —, مِنْ غَيْرِ مَعْرِفَتِي ـ مِنْ غَيْرِ عِلْمِي. I sought leisurely, or repeatedly, after the — of what such an one possessed until I knew it, تَعَرَّفْتُ ما عِنْدَ فُلانٍ.

Known, *part.* مَعْرُوف ـ مَعْلُوم. Spread abroad, مُشَاع. To become —, تَكَشَّفَ ـ إِنْكَشَفَ ـ إِسْتَبَانَ ـ تَبَيَّنَ ـ ، بَانَ ـ ، شَاعَ بِ. To make —, كَشَّفَ ـ ، كَشَفَ ـ إِسْتَكْشَفَ ـ تَعَرَّفَ أَشَاعَ بِ. Well known, مَشْهُور ـ مَعْلُوم. He made himself — to him, تَعَرَّفَ إِلَيْهِ.

Knuckle, *n.* Of the fingers, بُرْجُمَة *pl.* بَرَاجِم ـ بُرْجُمَات. The — of a sheep, calf, *etc.*, عُرْقُوب *pl.* عَرَاقِيب ـ قُرْعُوب.

Knuckle, *v.i.* To — under to, تَذَلَّلَ لِ ـ أَقَرَّ إِلَى ـ تَضَعْضَعَ لِ ـ إِخْتَضَعَ لِ.

Knur, Knurl, *n.* *See* Knot, *n.*

Knurly, *a.* *See* Knotty, *a.*

Kopeck, *n.* A Russian coin, سِكَّة رُوسِيَّة اِسْمُهَا كُوبِك.

K.P., *n.* حائِزُ نِيشَانِ حَضْرَةِ مار باتْرِيك.

Kraal, *n.* مَنازِلُ (*or* أَكْوَاخُ) أَهْلِ أَفْرِيقِيَّةَ ٱلْجَنُوبِيَّةِ.

Kraken, *n.* سَمَكٌ كَبِيرٌ مَجْهُول.

Krupp, *n.* A Krupp's gun, مِدْفَعُ عَمَلِ كُرُوب.

K.T., *n.* حائِزُ نِيشَانِ ٱلتَّسَلْسُل.

Kûfic, *n.* كُوفِيّ. Kûfic writing, الخَطُّ ٱلْكُوفِيُّ.

Kûran, *n.* القُرْآن ـ المُصْحَف. *See also* Alcoran, *n.*

Kyanize, *v.t.* دَهَنَ ـ بِدُهْنٍ ـ وَقَى ـ مِنَ ٱلْفَسادِ (*or* ٱلزَّنَاخَة) [2] دَمَّمَ ـ بِدِمامٍ وِقايَةً مِنَ ٱلْفَسادِ ـ وِقايَةً مِنَ ٱلزَّنَاخَة.

Kyrie eleison! يا رَبُّ ٱرْحَمْنَا.

L.

La, *int.* طَلِّعْ عَلَى ـ إِطَّلِعْ عَلَى *vulg.* إِصْغَ إِلَى.

Label, *n.* An address, ticket, عِنْوَان ـ رُقْعَة *pl.* رِقَاع *and* رُقَع ـ كِتَابَة ـ تَذَاكِرُ *pl.* تَذْكِرَة. A name, إِسْم *pl.* أَسَامِي.

Label, *v.t.* [2] كَتَبَ عَلَى ـ [2] حَطَّ عِنْوَانًا عَلَى ـ عَيَّنَ عَلَى [2] حَطَّ تَذْكِرَةً عَلَى.

Labial, *a.* شَفَهِيّ ـ شَفَوِيّ. The — letters, الحُرُوفُ ٱلشَّفَهِيَّة.

Labial, *n.* حَرْف شَفَهِيّ *pl.* حُرُوف شَفَهِيَّة.

Labiodental, *a.* ما خَرَجَ مِنْ مَقْطَعَي ٱلْأَسْنَانِ وٱلشِّفَاهِ مَعًا.

Laboratory, *n.* كَرْخانَة ـ مَعْمَل ـ مُحْتَرَف ـ مَحْرَف.

Laboring, *a.* Working, مُشْتَغِل ـ شاغِل ـ فاعِل ـ صانِع.

A — man; *see* Labourer, *n.*

Laborious, *a.* Hard working, مُتَبَذِّل ـ كَدُود ـ أَشْغَلُ ـ شَغَّال. Requiring labour, difficult, مُتْعِب ـ عَسِير ـ عَوِيص ـ مُعْضِل. *See also* Industrious, Assiduous, Difficult, Toilsome, *a.*

Laboriously, *ad.* بِصُعُوبَةٍ ـ بِكُلْفَةٍ ـ بِتَعَبٍ كُلِّيٍّ ـ بِتَعَبٍ ـ بِكَدٍّ.

Laboriousness, *n.* Difficulty, مُشْكِلَة ـ عُسْر ـ صُعُوبَة. *See also* Labour, *n.*

Labour, *n.* Exertion, effort, تَعَب *pl.* أَتْعَاب ـ مَسْعًى *pl.* مَسَاعٍ ـ سَعَاة ـ جُهْد ـ إِجْتِهَاد ـ كَدّ ـ جِدّ. Care, treatment, مُعالَجَة. Fruit of labour, تَعَب. Work done or to be done, شُغْل *pl.* أَشْغَال. Pangs of child-birth, مَخَاض ـ نِفَاس ـ وَجَع ـ طَلْقُ ٱلْوِلادَة. Fatigue, إِعْيَاء ـ كَلّ ـ كُلُول ـ تَعَب. An enterprise, مُهِمَّة ـ مُبَاشَرَة. Labour in vain, عَبَث. Forced —, سُخْرَة. Hand —, شُغْل يَدٍ. To lose one's —, to have one's — for one's pains, ضَيَّعَ تَعَبَهُ: Our — was in vain, صارَ تَعَبُنا باطِلًا. To rest from one's labours, إِسْتَراحَ مِنْ أَتْعابِهِ. She had a hard —, in child-birth, تَعَسَّرَتْ وِلادَتُها. In labour, childbirth, ماخِض.

Labour, *v.i.* To exert strength, use effort, إِجْتَهَدَ ـ ، جَهَدَ فِي ـ صَرَفَ ٱلْهِمَّةَ ـ يَسْعَى *aor.* سَعَى ـ [2] كَدَّ ـ ، تَعِبَ ـ ، عَمِلَ. To be in some difficulty, to be in a state of perplexity, from, إِرْتَبَكَ ـ تَعَسَّرَ عَلَى ـ [2] عَسَّرَ عَلَى. To — under, to suffer from, أُصِيبَ بِ ـ أُبْتُلِيَ بِ. To be in travail, childbirth, تَمَخَّضَتْ ـ [2] ، مَخِضَتْ. To — in vain, ، تَعِبَ عَبَثًا (*or* باطِلًا). He refused to —, أَبَى ٱلشُّغْلَ *aor.* يَأْبَى. However much he may — in the inquiry he will not discover it, مَهْما جَدَّ فِي طَلَبِهِ فَلا يُدْرِكُهُ. To — with one's own hands, إِشْتَغَلَ (*or* ، عَمِلَ) بِيَدَيْهِ.

Labour, *v.t.* To form with care, دَقَّقَ ـ ضَرَّجَ ـ [2] فَنَّ ـ عالَجَ. To —, or work at, أَعْمَلَ نَفْسَهُ فِي ـ إِشْتَغَلَ بِ. He laboured to destroy him, ، عَمِلَ فِي هَلاكِهِ.

Labourer, *n.* A workman, صَنائِعِيّ *pl.* صانِع ـ صِناعَة *pl.* صُنّاع ـ عَمَلَة ـ فَعَلَة *pl.* فاعِل. A female —, شَغّالَة. Labourers, فَعَلَة. One who works hard, شَغّال. A forced —, صانِعُ سُخْرَةٍ ـ عَسِيف.

A day —, فاعِل pl. فَعَلَة. A fellow —, عامِلٌ مَعَ pl. عامِلُونَ — رَفِيقٌ فِي الشُّغْلِ pl. أَرْفاق or رُفَقَاء. A field —, فَلَّاح pl. فَلَّاحُونَ. The — is worthy of his hire, الفاعِلُ مُسْتَحِقٌّ أُجْرَتَهُ.

Labyrinth, n. A maze, مَلاث. A place in which one loses his way, تِيهٌ pl. أَتْيَاه — تَيْهَاء pl. أَتاوِهَة — مَفازَة. Something very intricate, مِحْنَة — لُغز pl. أَلْغاز — مُشْكِلَة — مَغْلَطَة — غَلُوطَة — عُسْرَة.

Labyrinthian, a. Winding, تَيِّهٌ — مُتَوَّهٌ — لَوْلَبِيٌّ. Intricate, مُشَبَّكٌ — عَوِيص — مُشْكِل. See also Intricate, a.

Lac, n. The gum, صَمْغُ اللَّكِّ — لُكّ. A hundred thousand, لَكّ pl. لُكُوك.

Lace, n. Ornamental work of threads, مُخَرَّمَة — شَبِيكَة. Braid, شَرِيط — حَبَكَة. Tissue of silk or thread, قِيطان — شَرِيط. Gold —, قَصَبٌ أَصْفَرُ; silver —, قَصَبٌ أَبْيَضُ. A cord, قِيطان pl. قَيَاطِينُ — بَنْد pl. بُنُود. A string to lace with, خَيْط — سِلْك pl. سُلُوك and سِلْكَة — أَسْلاك. A leather — for a boot, سَيْر pl. سُيُور.

Lace-embroiderer, n. طَرَّاز — طَرَازِيٌّ.

Lace-man, n. }
Lace-merchant, } حَبَّاك.

Lace, v.t. To trim with ..., زَيَّنَ-ب — حَطَّ عَلَى-آ... ² — رَكَّبَ عَلَى-سِجافًا مِنَ آ... (adding the kind of lace from the preceding article). To fasten, عَقَدَ — أَسْلَكَ (or سَلَكَ) الْخَيْطَ فِي. To thrash, ضَرَبَ — نَزَلَ بِ.

Lacerable, a. That may be torn, مِمَّا يُخْرَقُ — يُمَزَّقُ.

Lacerate, v.t. To tear, شَرْمَطَ — مَزَّقَ — خَرَقَ ². To — with the nails, خَرَشَ. To wound, جَرَّحَ — كَلَمَ — جَرَحَ. To be lacerated, torn, تَشَرْمَطَ — انْخَرَقَ — تَمَشَّقَ — تَمَزَّقَ. To be lacerated, wounded, جُرِحَ.

Lacerated, a. Cut into segments, of plants, etc., ذُو — مُفَلَّع — فِلاقٍ. Also part. of to Lacerate, q.v.

Laceration, n. The act of tearing, مَزْق — خَرْق; a tear, مِزْقَة — شَقّ pl. شُقُوق — شَقِيقَة. The act of tearing with the nails, خَرْش; a tear with the nails, خَرْشَة. The act of wounding, كَلْم — جَرْح; a wound, كَلْم pl. كِلام and كُلُوم — جُرْح pl. جُرُوح and أَجْراح.

Lacerta, n. A genus of lizard, نَوْعٌ مِنَ الْوَرَلِ.

Lachrymal, a. Belonging to the — ducts, مُتَعَلِّقٌ بِشُؤُونِ الْعَيْنِ. The — ducts, شُؤُونُ الْعَيْنِ. A — fistula, ناصُورٌ (or ناسُورٌ) فِي مَاقِ الْعَيْنِ.

Lachrymatory, n. حُاجُورٌ لِلدُّمُوعِ.

Lachrymose, a. باكٍ — أَدْمَعُ — مُتَدَمِّع.

Lacing, n. A fastening, تَسْلِيك — تَشْدِيد — تَرْبِيط — تَعْقِيد. A cord for —; see under Lace, n.

Lack, v.t. To be in want of, اِحْتاجَ إِلَى — أَعْوَزَ — اِخْتَلَّ إِلَى. To be without, عَدِمَ — أَفْتَقَرَ إِلَى — تَفَقَّدَ. He lacked the thing, عَدِمَ الشَّيْءَ — أَعْوَزَهُ الشَّيْءُ. He who gives to the poor shall not —, مَنْ يُعْطِي الْفَقِيرَ لا يَحْتاجُ. Ye shall — nothing, لا تَكُونُ لَكُمْ حاجَةٌ إِلَى شَيْءٍ. If any of you — anything, let him ask me, إِنْ كانَ أَحَدُكُمْ يُعْوِزُهُ شَيْءٌ فَلْيَطْلُبْهُ مِنِّي. What lack I yet? ماذا يُعْوِزُنِي بَعْدُ. To make to —, أَعْدَمَ — أَفْقَدَ. See also to Want, v.t.

Lack, v.i. To be in want, اِحْتاجَ — عَوِزَ. To be wanting, short, قَصُرَ ² — قَلَّ — نَقَصَ. To — strength for, تَقَصَّرَ فِي — ضَعُفَ عَن ² — عَجَزَ عَن. If there should — five out of the fifty, رُبَّما نَقَصَ الْخَمْسُونَ خَمْسَةً.

Lack, n. Need, اِحْتِياج — حَوْجَة — عَوَز — حاجَة. Destitution, عَدَم. Shortcoming, deficiency, نَقِيصَة — نَقْص. For — of food, لِعَدَمِ الْقُوتِ. He died for — of food, ماتَ لِعَدَمِ الْأَكْلِ. Lack of ability, مَعْجِزَة — عَجْز.

Lackadaisical, a. مُتَغَنِّج — مُخَنَّث — خَنِيث.

Lack-a-daisy, int. }
Lack-a-day, } See Alas, int.

Lack-brain, n. حِمار — بَلِيد — ثَوْر — أَحْمَق.

Lacker, v.t. See to Lacquer, v.t.

Lackey, n. تابِع pl. تابِعُونَ — تَبِيع — خَدَّام pl. خَدَّامُونَ. See also Footman, n.

Lackey, v.i. خَدَمَ ².

Lackey, v.t. To attend upon servilely, تَضَعْضَعَ لِ — تَذَلَّلَ لِ.

Laconic, a. }
Laconical, } مُحَذِّفٌ فِي الْجَوابِ — مُقْتَصِرٌ فِي الْكَلامِ — مُوجِز — مِيجاز.

Laconically, ad. بِحَذْفِ الْكَلامِ — بِالْإِيجازِ. To speak —, حَذَفَ فِي كَلامِهِ — وَجَزَ فِي الْقَوْلِ aor. يَجِزُ.

Laconicism, n. }
Laconism, } إِيجاز — اِقْتِصارٌ فِي الْكَلامِ.

Lacquer, v.t. طَلَى-ب — دَهَنَ-ب ².

Lacquer, n. طِلاء — دُهْن.

Lactation, n. The act of suckling, إِرْضاع — لِبان — إِرْغاث.

Lacteal, a. Pertaining to milk, لَبَنِيٌّ. Conveying chyle, كَيْلُوسِيٌّ — كَيْمُوسِيٌّ.

Lacteal, n. مَجْرَى الْكَيْمُوسِ pl. مَجارٍ.

Lactean, *a.* / Lacteous, } يُشْبِهُ ٱلْحَلِيبَ ـ مِثْلَ ٱللَّبَنِ ـ لَبَنِيٌّ.

Lactescence, *n.* The milky juice of plants, لَبَنُ ٱلنَّبَاتَاتِ.

Lactescent, *a.* / Lactiferous, } لَبِن *pl.* لُبُون ـ لابِن . A — tree, لُبْنَى.

Lactic, *a.* مِنَ ٱللَّبَنِ ـ لَبَنِيٌّ.

Lactometer, *n.* مِيزَانٌ لِسَبْرِ جَوْدَةِ ٱللَّبَنِ ـ مِيزَانُ ٱللَّبَنِ.

Lacuna, *n.* فَرَاغ ـ خَلَل. To fill up the — which exists in the deed, سَدَّ ٱلْخَلَلَ ٱلْحَاصِلَ فِي ٱلْحُجَّةِ.

Lacustral, *a.* / Lacustrine, } ذُو بِطَاحٍ ـ أَبْطَحُ ـ غِيَاضِيٌّ.

Lad, *n.* حَزْوَر ـ غُلَام *pl.* غِلْمَة ـ صَبِيٌّ *pl.* صُبْيَان ـ شَابٌّ *pl.* أَشْبَاب ـ وَلَد *pl.* أَوْلَاد.

Ladder, *n.* مِرْقَاة ـ مِعْرَج *pl.* مَعَارِجُ ـ سُلَّمُ خَشَبٍ *pl.* سَلَالِمُ *and* سَلَالِيمُ. A rope —, سُلَّمُ ٱلتَّشْلِيقِ. A scaling —, مِصْعَاد. A — to ascend tall trees, مِصْمَاد ـ كَرٌّ. To ascend a —, صَعِدَ فِي ٱلسُّلَّمِ. A companion —, سُلَّمُ مَقْعَدِ (*or* دِيوَانِ) ٱلْمَرْكَبِ.

Laddie, *n.* *See* Lad, *n.*

Lade, *v.t.* To load, حَمَّلَ. To —, of a ship, شَحَنَ ـ شَحَنَ ـ بِ ـ أَوْسَقَ ـ أَوْسَقَ ـ بِ. To throw with a dipper, ladle, غَرَفَ ـ بِ ـ غَرَفَ ـ صَبَّ ـ بِمِغْرَفَةٍ. He laded the ship with cotton, أَوْسَقَ ٱلْمَرْكَبَ قُطْنًا.

Laden, *a.* Oppressed, burdened, مُحَمَّل ـ ثَقِيلُ ٱلْأَحْمَالِ. Having a full freight, غَامِد ـ مَشْحُون ـ مُوسَق.

Lading, *n.* A burden, حِمْل *pl.* حُمُول *and* أَحْمَال. A cargo, تَعْبِيَةُ مَرْكَبٍ ـ وَسْقَةُ (*or* شَحْنَةُ) مَرْكَبٍ. A bill of —, تَعْرِيفُ ٱلْوَسْقِ ـ صَكُّ ٱلشَّحْنِ; called in the Persian Gulf, سَتَمِي.

Ladle, *n.* خَاشُوقَة ـ مِغْرَفَة.

Ladle-full, *n.* غُرْفَة ـ مِلْءُ مِغْرَفَةٍ. A single act of lading out, غَرْفَة.

Lady, *n.* سَيِّدَة *pl.* سَيِّدَات ـ خَاتُون *pl.* خَوَاتِينُ ـ سِتٌّ *pl.* سِتَّات ـ خَانِم ـ مَادَامَة ـ لَيْدِي *pl.* لَيْدِيَات. My lady, (as an address), يَا سِيِّدَتِي ـ يَا سِتِّي ـ خَانِمْ أَفَنْدِي. A young —, سِتٌّ صَغِيرَةٌ ـ صُتَيْتَة ـ سُتَّي. Our Sovereign Lady the Queen, حَضْرَةُ ٱلْمَلِكَةِ ٱلْمُعَظَّمَةِ وَلِيَّةِ نِعْمَتِنَا. Our Lady, the Virgin Mary, حَضْرَةُ مَرْيَمَ ٱلْعَذْرَاءِ. The — of the house, صَاحِبَةُ ٱلْبَيْتِ. Lady, a kept woman, سَرِيَّة. A ladies' man, زِيرُ نِسَاءٍ ـ تِبْع ـ أَعْلَال *pl.* عَلُّ ٱلنِّسَاءِ ـ تِلْوُ (*or* طِلْعُ) نِسَاءٍ.

Lady-bird, *n.* / Lady-bug, } نَوْعٌ مِنَ ٱلْبَقِّ أَحْمَرُ ٱللَّوْنِ مُنَقَّطُ ٱلْأَجْنِحَةِ.

Lady-day, *n.* عِيدُ ٱلْبِشَارَةِ ٱلْوَاقِعُ فِي ٢٥ مِنْ شَهْرِ مَارِسْ أَعْنِي آذَارَ.

Lady-like, *a.* لَطِيفَة ـ مِثْلَ ٱلسِّتِّ ـ مِثْلَ ٱلْخَاتُونِ ـ خَاتُونِ. A — person, سِتٌّ لَطِيفَةٌ.

Lady-love, *n.* مَحْبُوبَة ـ حَبِيبَة ـ مَعْشُوقَة.

Ladyship, *n.* حَضْرَة. Her — the Baroness Burdett-Coutts, حَضْرَةُ ٱلْبَارُونَةِ بِرْدَطْ كُوتْس. Her —, the wife of the ambassador, حَضْرَةُ زَوْجَةِ ٱلسَّفِيرِ.

Lag, *n.* One who lags, مُتَحَوِّز ـ مُتَأَخِّر. A fag end, جِذْقَة ـ طَرَف.

Lag, *v.i.* To loiter, تَمَهَّلَ ـ تَأَخَّرَ ـ تَحَوَّزَ. To lag behind, سَقَطَ ـ إِسْتَأْخَرَ ـ غَدِرَ ـ تَغَدَّرَ. He lagged behind his companions, غَدِرَ عَنْ أَصْحَابِهِ.

Laggard, *n.* مُكَيِّث ـ مُتَأَخِّر ـ مُتَحَوِّز ـ مُسْتَأْخِر.

Laggingly, *ad.* بِتَوَقُّفٍ ـ بِتَعْوِيقٍ ـ بِتَأَخُّرٍ ـ بِمُرَاخَاةٍ.

Lagoon, *n.* / Lagune, } A pond, نَقْع *pl.* نِقَاعَة ـ مُسْتَنْقَعُ مَاءٍ ـ غَدِير *pl.* غُدْرَان *and* غُدُر. An inlet, خَوْر *pl.* خُؤُور.

Laic, *n.* عَلْمَانِيٌّ *pl.* عَلْمَانِيُّون ـ مِنْ أَهْلِ ٱلْعَوَامِّ.

Laic, *a.* / Laical, } عَوَامٌّ *pl.* عَامِّي ـ عَلْمَانِيٌّ.

Laid, *pret. and past part. of to* Lay, *q.v.* Laid up, treasured up, مَوْضُوع ـ ذَخِيرَة ـ مَذْخُور ـ مُقَوَّم. Laid up, sick, عَلِيل ـ مُلَازِمُ ٱلْفِرَاشِ ـ مَرِيض. New laid eggs, بَيْضٌ طَرِيٌّ. Laid by, put aside, reserved, مُسْتَبْقًى ـ مَرْفُوع ـ مَحْفُوظ.

Lair, *n.* Of a wild beast, سَرَب *pl.* أَسْرَاب ـ وَكْر ـ زَرِيبَة ـ مَأْوًى ـ وِجَار.

Laird, *n.* سَيِّد *pl.* سَادَة ـ مَوْلًى *pl.* مَوَالِي ـ عَيْن *pl.* أَعْيَانُ.

Laity, *n.* ٱلْعَلْمَانِيُّونَ ـ ٱلْعَوَامُّ. The clergy and —, ٱلْأَكْلِيرُوسُ وَٱلْعَوَامُّ.

Lake, *n.* Of water, بِرْكَة *pl.* بِرَك ـ بُحَيْرَة *pl.* بُحَيْرَات. The colour, لَوْنٌ أَحْمَرُ قَاتِمٌ.

Lakelet, *n.* بُحَيْرَةٌ صَغِيرَةٌ ـ مُسْتَنْقَعُ مَاءٍ ـ غَدِير *pl.* غُدْرَان *and* غُدُر.

Lama, *n.* The — of Tartary, مَعْبُودُ قَبَائِلِ ٱلْمُغُلِ. A priest of Tartary, إِمَامُ قَبَائِلِ ٱلْمُغُلِ. The South American camel, حَيَوَانٌ مَوْجُودٌ فِي أَمِيرِكَا ٱلْجَنُوبِيَّةِ.

Lamb, *n.* حَمَل *pl.* حُمْلَان *and* أَحْمَال ـ خَرُوفَة *pl.* أَخْرِفَة ـ خَارُوف *pl.* خِرْفَان ـ رُمَيْس; *vulg.* قُوزَة. Jesus, the Lamb of God that taketh away the sins of the world, يَسُوعُ (حَضْرَةُ عِيسَى) حَمَلُ ٱللّٰهِ ٱلَّذِي يَرْفَعُ خَطِيَّةَ ٱلْعَالَمِ. In — or with —, حَامِلَة *pl.* حَامِلَات (*or* حَامِل).

Lamb, *v.t.* To bring forth young, of a sheep, خَلَفَتِ ٱلنَّعْجَةُ — وَلَدَتِ ٱلشَّاةُ حَمَلًا *aor.* تَلِدُ.

Lambent, *a.* حَفِيف — هَفَّاف. A — flame, لُهَابَةٌ هَفَّافَةٌ.

Lambkin, *n.* خَرُوفٌ صَغِيرٌ.

Lamblike, *a.* Gentle, رَفِيق — وَدِيع — حَلِيم. A — beast, دابَّةٌ سَمْحَةٌ.

Lamb's-wool, *n.* صُوفُ ٱلْخِرْفَانِ. *See also under* Wool, *n.*

Lame, *a.* Unsound in limb, سَقَط — مُخَبَّل — خَبِل. Being without a limb, mutilated, أَجْدَعُ. Hobbling, خامِع — أَقْزَلُ — عاثِر. Lame in the feet by nature, أَعْرَجُ *fem.* عَرْجَاءُ *pl.* عُرْج *and* عُرْجان. Lame in the hand or arm, أَكْتَعُ; in the foot, أَقْصَعُ — أَفْدَعُ — أَحْنَفُ. A — hand, يَدٌ مَكْتُوعَةٌ; a — foot, رِجْلٌ مَقْصُوعَةٌ — فَدَع — حَنَف. Lame, so as not to be able to rise, سَطِيح. How lame he is! ما أَشَدَّ عَرَجَهُ. Imperfect, unsatisfactory, غَيْرُ مَوْزُونٍ — غَيْرُ وافٍ — عَرِيج — رَكِيك — أَخْبَل — سَقَط. A — affair, أَمْرٌ عَرِيجٌ. To be — in the legs, by nature, عَرِجَ. To be or become —, from accident, *etc.*, عَرَجَ — تَعَرَّجَ. *See also to* Hobble, Limp, *v.i.*; *also* Cripple, Hobble, *n.*

Lame, *v.t.* To make lame, أَعْرَجَ. To cripple, عَطَّلَ — خَبَّلَ. To render unsound, in a general sense, خَبَّلَ — عَجَّزَ — سَقَّطَ — إِخْتَبَلَ.

Lamellar, *a.* } Formed or disposed in plates or scales, مُرَكَّبٌ
Lamellate, } مُطَبَّقٌ صَفَائِحَ صَفَائِحَ — مُصَفَّح — بِصَفَائِحَ.

Lamellated, *a.* Covered with plates, مُغَشًّى بِصَفَائِحَ.

Lamelliform, *a.* In the form of a plate, فِي شَكْلِ صَفِيحَةٍ.

Lamely, *ad.* As if lame, بِعَرَجانٍ — بِعَرَجٍ — تَعَرُّجًا. Unsatisfactorily, بِعَدَمِ كِفَاءٍ — بِخَبَالٍ. Weakly, بِضَعْفٍ — بِرَكَاكَةٍ. To walk —, خَمَعَ — قَزَلَ.

Lameness, *n.* The being unsound, in a general sense, خَبَال. The being crippled in the feet, عَثَرَان — قَزَل. Lameness in the legs, عَرَج — عَرَجان — تَعَرُّج. Unsatisfactoriness, خَبَال — رَكَاكَة — عَدَمُ مُوَازَنَةٍ — سَقَط — عَدَمُ كِفَاءٍ.

Lament, *n.* An elegy, مَرْثَاةٌ — مَرْثِيَةٌ *pl.* مَرَاثٍ. *See also* Lamentation, *n.*

Lament, *v.i.* To express or feel sorrow, تَحَزَّنَ — أَسِفَ — تَأَسَّفَ — أَنَّ *aor.* يَئِنُّ — بَكَى — نَاحَ — تَفَجَّعَ.

Lament, *v.t.* To lament for, deplore, تَأَسَّفَ عَلَى — تَلَهَّفَ عَلَى — حَزِنَ عَلَى — نَاحَ عَلَى — بَكَى عَلَى — بَكَى. To — for the dead, رَثَى (*or* رَثَّى) ٱلْمَيِّتَ.

Lamentable, *a.* فاجِع — يُرْثَى لَهُ — كَئِيب — مُحْزِن — حَزِين.

Lamentably, *ad.* With sorrow, بِبُكَاءٍ — بِتَأَسُّفٍ — بِحُزْنٍ. In a way to cause grief, بِنَوْعٍ مُحْزِنٍ — بِطَرِيقَةٍ مُحْزِنَةٍ. Excessively, لِلْغَايَةِ.

Lamentation, *n.* أَنِين — بُكَاءٌ — حُزْن — نَحِيب — نِيَاح — نَوْح. A house of —, مَنَاحَة. Lamentation for the dead, مَرْثَاةٌ — نَوْحَةٌ. The Book of the Lamentations of Jeremiah, سِفْرُ مَرَاثِي إِرْمِيَا ٱلنَّبِيِّ.

Lamenter, *n.* مُتَشَكٍّ — شَاكٍ — نَوَّاح.

Lamented, *a.* Worthy of being —, مُسْتَحِقُّ ٱلتَّأَسُّفِ. The —, speaking of one departed, ٱلْمَرْحُومُ.

Lamina, *n.* A thin plate, صَفِيحَةٌ *pl.* صَفَائِحُ. A thin crust, قِشْرَةٌ *pl.* قِشَر. A parietal bone, صَفِيحَةٌ *pl.* صَفَائِحُ. A blade of a flower, وَرَقَةٌ.

Laminable, *a.* يُطْرَقُ صَفَائِحَ — يُصَفَّحُ.

Laminar, *a.* Consisting of thin plates, مُصَفَّحٌ — صَفَائِحُ صَفَائِحُ.

Laminate, *a.* } Plated, lying in plates, مُرَكَّبٌ صَفَائِحَ — مُصَفَّحٌ.
Laminated, }

Lamination, *n.* تَرَكُّبٌ فِي صَفَائِحَ.

Lammas, *n.* The day, أَوَّلُ شَهْرِ أُغُسْطُسَ أَعْنِي آب.

Lammer-geir, *n.* أَكْبَرُ ٱلْعِقْبَانِ.

Lamp, *n.* قِنْدِيل *pl.* قَنَادِيلُ — مِسْرَجَة — مِصْبَاح *pl.* مَصَابِيحُ. A small —, سِرَاج *pl.* سُرُج. A safety —, سِرَاجُ ٱلْأَمْنِ فِي ٱلْمَعَادِنِ. To light, as of a —, أَسْرَجَ — وَلَّعَ. *See also* Light, Lantern, *n.*

Lamp-black, *n.* سُخَام — سُخَامُ ٱلْقِنْدِيلِ.

Lamp-light, *n.* ضَوْءُ ٱلْقِنْدِيلِ.

Lamplighter, *n.* شَعَّال — شَعَّالُ ٱلْقَنَادِيلِ.

Lamp-post, *n.* قاعِدَةُ ٱلْقِنْدِيلِ.

Lampas, *n.* حَمَاةٌ فِي سَقْفِ فَمِ ٱلْفَرَسِ *vulg.* حَمْوَة.

Lampoon, *n.* تَهْجَاءٌ — هِجَاءٌ — هَجْوٌ — نَقْرَى — نُكْر.

Lampoon, *v.t.* هَجَا — نَقَرَ — أَنْشَدَ بِ — نَكَّرَ. To — mutually, هَاجَى.

Lampooner, *n.* نَاقِر — هَاجٍ — نَكِر.

Lamprey, *n.* مُورِينَة.

Lanary, *n.* A storehouse for wool, مَخْزَنٌ لِلصُّوفِ — مَصْوَفَة.

Lanate, *a.* صُوفِيّ — مِثْلُ ٱلصُّوفِ.

Lance, *n.* رُمْح *pl.* رِمَاح *and* أَرْمَاح — مِزْرَاق *pl.* مَزَارِيقُ. A maker of lances, رَمَّاح. To pierce with a —, رَمَحَ — طَعَنَ بِرُمْحٍ.

Lance, *v.t.* To pierce, as with a lancet, شَرَطَ — شَرَّطَ. To pierce with a lance, رَمَى بِسَهْمٍ — زَرَقَ بِمِزْرَاقٍ.

Lanceolate, *a.* مُؤَنَّف — مُؤَسَّل — فِي شَكْلِ ٱلرُّمْحِ.

Lancer, *n.* خَيَّالٌ رَمَّاحٌ ـ فُرْسَانٌ مَزَارِقَةٌ *pl.* فارِسٌ مِزْرَاقِيٌّ *pl.* خَيَّالَةٌ رَمَّاحَةٌ.

Lancet, *n.* For bleeding, رِيشَةٌ ـ مِسَلٌّ ـ مِفْصَد ـ مِبْضَع ـ مِبْضَعٌ ـ ٱلْفِصَادَةِ; *vulg., from the Turkish,* نِشْتَر. A — for scarification, مِشْرَاط ـ مِشْرَط *pl.* مَشَارِيطُ.

Land, *n.* As opposed to sea, بَرٌّ. Soil, أَرْض ـ تُرَاب. Dry land, يَابِسَةٌ. Country, أَرْض *pl.* أَرَاضِي ـ مَمْلَكَةٌ ـ وِلَايَةٌ ـ بَلَد *pl.* بِلاد ـ دِيَار. Ground, أَرْض ـ حَضِيض. Real estate, مُلْكٌ ـ أَمْلَاكٌ. The people of a country, أَهْلُ ٱلْبِلَادِ. Land assigned in fee simple for military service, إِقْطَاع ـ قَطِيعَة. By — and by sea, بَرًّا وَبَحْرًا. To make —, to be in sight of —, أَطْلَعَ عَلَى (or أَشْرَفَ عَلَى) ٱلْبَرِّ. To see how the — lies, أَطْلَعَ عَلَى دَبْدَبِ ٱلْحَالِ ـ ٱلْأَحْوَالِ.

A foreign land, بِلادٌ غُرْبٌ ـ مَمْلَكَةٌ أَجْنَبِيَّةٌ.

Arable land, أَرْضٌ قَابِلَةُ ٱلْحِرَاثَةِ.

Crown lands, ٱلْأَرَاضِي ٱلسُّلْطَانِيَّةُ (or ٱلْهُمَايُونِيَّةُ).

Made land, أَرْضٌ مَجْلُوبَةٌ.

Native land, وَطَن *pl.* أَوْطَان.

Pasture land, مَرْعًى ـ مَرْعَاة.

State lands, ٱلْأَرَاضِي ٱلْمِيرِيَّةُ.

The Holy Land, أَرْض (or دِيَار) فِلَسْطِينَ.

The Land of Promise, أَرْضُ ٱلْمِيعَادِ.

The mainland, أَصْلُ ٱلْبَرِّ.

Unknown or untraversed land, غُفْل ـ بِلادٌ أَغْفَالٌ.

Land, *v.t.* As from a ship, أَخْرَجَ ـ (or نَزَّلَ ـ) مِنَ ٱلْمَرْكَبِ; of a cargo, وَضَعَ ٱلْوَسْقَ *aor.* يَضَعُ.

Land, *v.i.* نَزَلَ مِنَ ٱلْمَرْكَبِ ـ أَقْبَلَ إِلَى ٱلْبَرِّ ـِ. When he landed at Bairût, لَمَّا نَزَلَ إِلَى بَيْرُوتَ. We landed at Saida and remained there three days, نَزَلْنَا إِلَى صَيْدَا وَمَكَثْنَا ثَلَاثَةَ أَيَّامٍ.

Landamman, *n.* رَئِيسُ مَجْلِسِ ٱلشُّورَى عِنْدَ أَهْلِ ٱلسُّوِيسْرَا.

Landau, *n.* عَرَبَانَةٌ ذَاتُ أَرْبَعِ عَجَلَاتٍ سَقْفُهَا يُفْتَحُ وَيُطْبَقُ.

Landaulet, *n.* عَرَبَانَةٌ صَغِيرَةٌ ذَاتُ أَرْبَعِ عَجَلَاتٍ سَقْفُهَا يَنْفَتِحُ.

Landed, *a.* Possessing land, صَاحِبُ عَقَارٍ ـ مُعْقِر. Consisting of land, أَرْضِيٌّ ـ مُتَعَلِّقٌ بِٱلْأَرَاضِي. Landed property, عَقَار ـ عِكْر. He sold his — property, بَاعَ عِكْرَهُ ـِ.

Landfall, *n.* Land first seen, إِشْرَافُ ٱلْبَرِّ. Sudden succession to property, وِرَاثَةُ مَالٍ عَنْ غَيْرِ ٱنْتِظَارٍ.

Land-force, *n.* عَسْكَر ـ عَسَاكِرُ بَرِّيَّةٌ.

Landgrave, *n.* إِسْمُ حَاكِمٍ فِي بِلَادِ ٱلنَّمْسَا. Landgravine, إِمْرَأَةُ ٱلْمَذْكُورِ.

Landgraviate, *n.* ٱلْأَرْضُ ٱلَّتِي فِي وِلَايَةِ ٱلْحَاكِمِ ٱلْمَذْكُورِ.

Land-holder, *n.* صَاحِبُ أَرَاضٍ ـ صَاحِبُ عَقَارٍ ـ مُعْقِر.

Landing, *n.* The act of putting on shore, تَنْزِيلٌ مِنَ ٱلْمَرْكَبِ; of cargo, وَضْعُ ٱلْوَسْقِ. Going on shore, طُلُوعٌ مِنَ ٱلْمَرْكَبِ. A place for —, رَصِيف ـ رَصَف. The top of a flight of stairs, بَسْطَةٌ.

Landing-place, *n.* A quay, رَصِيف ـ إِسْكَلَة *pl.* أَسَاكِلُ ـ صَقَالَة. *See also* Landing, *n.*

Land-jobber, *n.* سِمْسَارُ ٱلْأَرَاضِي ـ ضَرَّابُ تَخَامِينِ ٱلْأَرَاضِي.

Land-waiter, *n.* خَفَرُ ٱلْكُمْرُكِ.

Landlady, *n.* A lady who holds land, صَاحِبَةُ أَرَاضٍ. A woman who has tenants under her, كَرِيَّة ـ مُؤَجِّرَة. The mistress of an inn, صَاحِبَةُ لُكَنْدَةٍ ـ صَاحِبَةُ خَانٍ.

Landlock, *v.t.* حَوَّطَ حَوْلَهُ ٱلْأَرْضَ ـ أَحَاطَ بِٱلْأَرْضِ.

Landlocked, *a.* مُحِيطٌ بِٱلْبَرِّ.

Landloper, *n.* A vagrant, مُبْرِم ـ ضَالِل ـ ضَائِعٌ سَائِحٌ.

Landlord, *n.* An owner of lands, صَاحِبُ أَرَاضٍ ـ مُعْقِر. One who has tenants, a hirer, صَاحِبُ ٱلْكِرَاءِ ـ كَرِيّ ـ مُؤَجِّر. Master of an inn, صَاحِبُ لُكَنْدَةٍ ـ خَانْجِي ـ صَاحِبُ خَانٍ.

Landlubber, *n.* لَقَبُ تَعْيِيرٍ بِهِ ٱلْبَحْرِيَّةُ أَهْلَ ٱلْبَرِّ.

Landmark, *n.* A mark to bound land, تَخْم ـ مَنَار ـ عَلَم *pl.* تُخُوم. The sign of a boundary, تُخُوم. An elevated object to serve as a guide, إِشَارَة ـ مَعْلَم. To place landmarks on a land, حَجَرَ (or إِحْتَجَرَ) ٱلْأَرْضَ ـُ.

Land-office, *n.* مَكْتَبٌ لِبَيْعِ ٱلْأَرَاضِي وَشِرَائِهَا.

Landscape, *n.* A prospect of land, مَنْظَر (or مَنْظَرَة) بِلَادٍ. A picture of a —, صُورَةُ مَنْظَرَةِ بِلَادٍ. A — painter, مُصَوِّرُ ٱلْمَنَاظِرِ.

Landslide, *n.* / Landslip, هُبُوطُ أَرْضٍ ـ خُرُورُ (or خَرُّ) أَرْضٍ.

Landsman, *n.* مِنْ أَهْلِ ٱلْبَرِّ.

Land-tax, *n.* وَضِيعَةٌ عَلَى ٱلْأَرَاضِي ـ طَسْق.

Landward, *n.* نَحْوَ ٱلْبَرِّ ـ بَرًّا.

Lane, *n.* زُقَاق *pl.* أَزِقَّة; (in Egypt) خَوْخَة ـ خَوْخ. A narrow pass, خَانِق.

Langrage, *n.* / Langrel, خُرْدَةٌ تُطْلَقُ مِنَ ٱلْمَدَافِعِ لِخَرْقِ شِرَاعِ مَرَاكِبِ ٱلْعَدُوِّ وَحِبَالِهَا.

Lang syne, *ad.* مُنْذُ زَمَنٍ طَوِيلٍ. For auld —, حُبًّا بِذِكْرِ ٱلْقَدِيمِ.

Language, *n.* Speech, لُغَة ـ نُطْق ـ كَلَام. A tongue, لُغَة *pl.* لُغَات ـ لِسَان *pl.* أَلْسِنَة. A dead —, لِسَانٌ غَيْرُ ـ لِسَانٌ مَهْجُورٌ. An ancient —, لِسَانٌ قَدِيمٌ. A living —, لِسَانٌ دَارِجٌ ـ مُسْتَعْمَلٌ.

One's native —, لِسَانٌ أَصْلِيٌّ. Style, عِبَارَة ـ اِصْطِلَاح ـ إِنْشَآء. Good —, style, فَنٌّ. Bad —, abuse, بَذَآءٌ ـ ذَمٌّ ـ سَبٌّ ـ شَتْم; profane swearing, شَتْم ـ سَبٌّ. To translate, as into another —, نَقَلَ ـ إِلَى. Every one spoke in his own —, كُلُّ وَاحِدٍ تَكَلَّمَ بِلُغَتِهِ.

Languid, *a.* Without activity, ضَنًى ـ وَانٍ ـ مَلُول ـ مَتْؤُوب. Weak, ضَعِيف. Slow, بَطِيءٌ. Soft, effeminate, خَنِث ـ سَقِيم ـ فَاتِر. To be —, فَتَرَ ـ بَرَدَ ـ تَعَنَّى ـ تَثَاءَبَ ـ تَثَآءَبَ ـ تَوَنَّى ـ تَفَاتَرَ. To make —, فَتَّرَ ـ عَنَّى ـ أَوْنَى ـ بَرَّدَ. To be —, as in doing, اِسْتَرْخَى فِي ـ تَرَاخَى فِي. To be — in speech, كَلَّ فِي ٱلْكَلَامِ. To be — through walking, كَلَّ مِنَ ٱلْمَشْيِ. The war became —, رَجَعَتِ ٱلْحَرْبُ عَلَى عُقْرَةٍ.

Languidly, *ad.* With lassitude, بِخَنَثٍ ـ بِثُؤَبَآءَ ـ بِبُرُودٍ. Slowly, بِبَطَآءَةٍ. With weakness, بِضَعْفٍ ـ بِفَتْرٍ ـ بِكَلَالٍ. To walk —, سَقَطَ فِي ٱلْمَشْيِ.

Languidness, *n.* *See* Languor, *n.*

Languish, *v.i.* To be affected with languor, تَثَاءَبَ ـ بَرَدَ ـ خَنِثَ ـ تَخَنَّثَ ـ تَفَاتَرَ ـ تَعَنَّى ـ يَنِي *aor.* وَنَى ـ تَثَأَّبَ. To droop, of plants, ذَبَلَ ـ ذَوَى. To sink gradually, as under a disease, سَلَّ. A bed of languishing, فِرَاشُ ٱلضَّنَى. To pine, as under a passion, اِنْسَقَمَ ـ ضَنِيَ. To be slow, to proceed slowly, بَطُؤَ ـ طَوَّلَ ـ اِرْتَخَى ـ أَرْوَدَ. To cause to —; *see under* Languid. To — from love, أَضْنَاهُ ٱلْعِشْقُ. To — of ennui, أَهْلَكَهُ ٱلضَّجَرُ. To — from hunger, أَهْلَكَهُ ٱلْجُوعُ.

Languishing, *a.* ذَابِل ـ مُضْنًى. A — look, طَرْفٌ ـ غَضَاضَة. A — style, كَلَامٌ وَاقِفٌ (or بَارِدٌ or سَقِيمٌ or رَكِيكٌ). نَظَرٌ مَكْسُورٌ ـ ذَابِلٌ. A — voice, صَوْتٌ شَجِيٌّ.

Languishingly, *ad.* بِذُبُولٍ ـ بِشَجْوٍ ـ بِسَقَمٍ ـ بِبُرُودٍ. To look —, أَغْضَى ـ غَضَّ.

Languishment, *n.* A state of languor, ثُؤَبَآءُ. Prolongation, بَطَآءَة ـ تَمَطٍّ.

Languor, *n.* Lassitude of body, ثَأْب ـ غَضَاضَة ـ ضَعْضَعَة ـ فَتْرَة ـ فَتْر ـ مَذْل ـ كَلَال ـ كَلٌّ ـ بِرَاد ـ تَخَنُّث ـ خَنَث ـ ضَنَآء. Weakness, ضَعْف. Languor from over-drinking, خَتَر.

Laniard, *n.* } Of a ship, مَرَسَة.
Lanyard, }

Laniferous, *a.* ذُو صُوفٍ ـ مُرَبِّي ٱلصُّوفِ.

Lank, *a.* } Loose, مُسْتَرْسِل ـ مُرَهْرَط ـ رَخْو ـ سَاقِط ـ أَسِيل.
Lanky, } Lean and light of flesh, شَازِب. Thin, رَقِيق ـ دَقِيق ـ رَكِيك. To be —, lean and light, تَخَدَّدَ ـ شَزَبَ. To become —, thin, رَقَّ ـ دَقَّ *aor.* يَدِقُّ ـ رَكَّ *aor.* يَرِكُّ. Lank, flabby, سِبَاط *pl.* سَبِط ـ أَسْوَل. To be —, flabby, not crisp, أَسِلَ ـ سَبِطَ. A — fellow, زَعْرُوع.

Lankness, *n.* Leanness and lightness, شُزُوب ـ شَزْب. Flabbiness, سَبَط ـ أَسَالَة. Thinness, دِقَّة ـ رِقَّة.

Lantern, *n.* } فَانُوس *pl.* فَوَانِيس ـ فَنَار. A dark —, فَانُوس
Lanthorn, } ٱلْحَرَامِيِّ. A magic —, فَانُوس ـ خَيَالُ ظِلٍّ ـ الْمِصْبَاحُ ٱلسِّحْرِيُّ ـ خَيَالُ ظِلٍّ.

Lanthanum, *n.* لَنْثَانُومٌ وَهُوَ ضَرْبٌ مِنَ ٱلْمَعَادِنِ.

Laodicean, *a.* Lukewarm, فَاتِر.

Lap, *n.* As of a coat, أَذْيَال *pl.* ذَيْل. The part above the knees, حُجُور *pl.* حُجْر. A fold, طَيَّة ـ ثِنْي. A — with the tongue, وَلْغ ـ وُلُوغ. A — full, مِلْءُ ثَوْبٍ. I shook my —, نَفَضْتُ حُجْرِي. In the — of wealth, فِي وَسْطِ ٱلنَّعِيمِ.

Lap, *v.i.* To be turned or to bend over, اِنْطَوَى ـ تَثَنَّى ـ اِنْثَنَى. To — with the tongue, وَلَغَ بِٱللِّسَانِ *aor.* يَلَغُ *and* يَالَغُ.

Lap, *v.t.* To wrap in, لَفَّ ـ فِي ـ طَوَى ـ فِي ـ أَدْرَجَ ـ فِي. To drink by lapping, وَلَغَ فِي ٱلشَّرَابِ بِٱللِّسَانِ *aor.* يَلَغُ. To lap from, وَلَغَ فِي ٱلشَّرَابِ مِن. He did not take a —, مَا وَلَغَ وَلُوغًا. A dish to lap from, مِيلَغَة ـ مِيلَغ.

Lap-dog, *n.* كَلْبٌ صَغِيرٌ.

Lapel, *n.* طَيَّةُ صَدْرِ ٱلسُّتْرَةِ.

Lapful, *n.* مِلْءُ حُجْرٍ ـ مِلْءُ ثَوْبٍ.

Lapidary, *n.* Of precious stones, جَوَاهِرْجِيّ ـ حَكَّاك; one who sets stones in rings, فَصَّاص.

Lapidate, *v.t.* To stone, رَجَمَ.

Lapidation, *n.* رَجْمٌ بِٱلْأَحْجَارِ.

Lapideous, *a.* صُلْب ـ كَٱلْحَجَرِ.

Lapidescence, *n.* تَحَجُّر.

Lapidify, *v.t.* صَيَّرَ ـ حَجَرًا; *v.i.* صَارَ حَجَرًا ـ تَحَجَّرَ.

Lapidist, *n.* *See* Lapidary, *n.*

Lapis, *n.* حَجَر. Lapis lazuli, لَازَوَرْد ـ حَجَرُ ٱللَّازَوَرْدِ.

Lapper, *n.* One who wraps, لَفَّاف. One who laps with the tongue, وَالِغ.

Lappet, *n.* أَذْيَال *pl.* ذَيْل.

Lapse, *v.i.* To slip or glide, زَلَّ *aor.* يَزِلُّ ـ سَبَحَ ـ مَرَّ. To commit a fault, سَقَطَ ـ خَطِئَ. To — from anything, آلَ عَن *aor.* يَؤُولُ ـ ضَرَبَ عَن ـ سَقَطَ عَن. To — into, آلَ إِلَى *aor.* يَؤُولُ. To elapse, مَرَّ ـ زَالَ ـ حَالَ. To fall into something less, to come down, آلَ *aor.* يَؤُولُ ـ نَقَصَ ـ اِنْحَطَّ. To — by preëmption, سَقَطَتْ شُفْعَتُهُ ـ بَطَلَ ٱلْحَقُّ لِعَدَمِ شُفْعَتِهِ.

His right lapsed, سَقَطَ حَقُّهُ ². His demand lapsed, سَقَطَ طَلَبُهُ ². He lapsed from his station, سَقَطَ عَنْ مَنْزِلَتِهِ ². They lapsed into barbarity, رَجَعُوا إِلَى ٱلْوَحْشَةِ. To cause to —, to annul, أَسْقَطَ.

Lapse, *n.* A slipping or gliding, سَبْح — زَلّ. A slip, fault, خَطَأ — عَثْرَة — زَلَّة — قُصُور — سَهْو — تَقْصِير — سَقْطَة *pl.* سِقَاط. Falling into, سُقُوطٌ فِي; falling from, سُقُوطٌ عَن. The — of time, مُرُورُ ٱلزَّمَانِ. A — of the tongue, زَلٌّ فِي ٱلْكَلَامِ — إِسْقَاطٌ فِي ٱلْكَلَامِ. The passing of property through neglect, بُطْلَانُ ٱلْحَقِّ فِي شَيْءٍ — سُقُوط — سُقُوطُ ٱلشُّفْعَةِ — مِنْ أَجْلِ عَدَمِ ٱلتَّصَرُّفِ بِهِ. He made a — in his speech, زَلَّ فِي كَلَامِهِ — أَسْقَطَ فِي كَلَامِهِ ². He spoke without one —, تَكَلَّمَ وَمَا سَقَطَ بِكَلِمَةٍ. No one is free from a —, لَا يَخْلُو أَحَدٌ مِنْ سَقْطَةٍ.

Lapsided, *a.* غَيْرُ مُوَازِنِ ٱلْجَنْبَيْنِ.

Lapstone, *n.* مِسَنُّ ٱلْأَسَاكِفَةِ.

Lapsus-linguæ, *n.* إِسْقَاطٌ فِي ٱلْكَلَامِ — زَلَلٌ فِي ٱلْكَلَامِ.

Lapwing, *n.* طَاتُوِيت — نَبَّاح.

Larboard, *n.* ٱلْجَانِبُ ٱلْيَسَارُ مِنَ ٱلْمَرْكَبِ. Larboard! صَلَّح.

Larceny, *n.* سَرِق — سَرِقَة — سَرْقَة. To commit —, سَرَقَ ². Petty —, سَرَقَ سَرِقَةً دُونَ شِيلِينٍ ².

Larch, *n.* The tree, شَجَرَةُ ٱللَّارِيسِ — لَارِيس.

Lard, *n.* دُهْنُ ٱلْخِنْزِيرِ.

Lard, *v.t.* To smear with lard, دَهَنَ بِدُهْنِ ٱلْخِنْزِيرِ ². To season, زَوَّقَ — فَتَّنَ ² (or بَزَّرَ or قَزَّحَ). To — speech, تَبَّلَ — قَزَّحَ ٱلْكَلَامَ.

Larder, *n.* بَيْتُ ٱلْمُؤْنَةِ — دُولَاب — كِلَارُ ٱلنَّقْلِ.

Lares, *n.* مَعَابِدُ ٱلْبَيْتِ.

Large, *a.* Of great bulk, كَبِير — عَظِيم — جَسِيم. Big, corpulent, جِرْنَفْش — جِسْمَانِيّ — بَدَنِيّ — بَدِين — سَمِين. Wide, وَسِيع — وَاسِع. Large, broad, فَسِيح — عَرِيض. Copious, جَزِيل. Numerous, كَثِير — عَدِيد. Abundant, كَثِير — وَافِر — فَائِض. A large army, جَيْشٌ عَظِيمٌ. A — amount, مَبْلَغٌ عَظِيمٌ. As — as life, كَبِيرٌ كُبْرَ ٱلشَّخْصِ — طَبِيعِيّ. Large-hearted, رَحِيبُ ٱلصَّدْرِ. At large, free, مُطْلَقُ ٱلْعِنَانِ — سُدًى. With details, عَلَى ٱلتَّفْصِيلِ — تَفْصِيلًا. See also Big, *a.*

Largely, *ad.* In a large manner, فِي ٱلْبَسِيطِ — فِي ٱلْكَبِيرِ. Amply, بِٱلْكَثْرَةِ — بِسَعَةٍ — إِتِّسَاعًا — تَفَضُّلًا. Liberally, بِٱلْكَرَمِ — كَرَامَةً. Copiously, بِوُفُورٍ — بِكَثْرَةٍ — وَفْرَةً.

Largeness, *n.* Great size, جَسَامَة — عِظَم. Great extent, سَعَة. Broadness, فُسْحَة — عَرْض. Abundance, وَفْرَة — كَثْرَة — جَزْل. Numerousness, كَثْرَةُ عَدَدٍ — كَثْرَة. Corpulence, بَدَانَة — جَسَامَة — عُمُومِيَّة — شُمُول — جِسْمَانِيَّة — سِمَن. Comprehensiveness, كُلِّيَّة. Largeness of heart, رَحْبَةُ قَلْبٍ. See also Bigness, *n.*

Largess, *n.* إِحْسَان — إِنْعَام; *vulg.* بَخْشِيش. To distribute —, نَثَرَ ٱلنِّثَارَ ².

Larghetto, *ad.* } In music, عِبَارَةٌ عَنْ صَوْتٍ خَفِيضٍ (or مَهْمُوسٍ).
Largo, }

Lark, *n.* The bird, حُمَّر — قُبَّرَة — قُنْبُرَة *pl.* قَبَابِرُ — قُنْبُرَة *pl.* قَنَابِرُ — أَبُو ٱلْمَلِيحِ — دَالُوع. See also Frolic, *n.*

Lark, *v.i.* To catch larks, إِصْطَادَ ٱلْقَبَابِرَ (or ٱلْقَنَابِرَ). See also to Frolic, Sport, *v.i.*

Larrup, *v.t.* جَلَدَ — سَوَّطَ — سَاطَ ².

Larum, *n.* تَنْبِيه. See also Alarm, *n.*

Larva, *n.* } أَشْكَال *pl.* شَكْل — أُمُّ ٱلصِّبْيَانِ.
Larve, }

Larval, *a.* } فِي شَكْلِ أُمِّ ٱلصِّبْيَانِ — مَا نِيطَ بِأُمِّ ٱلصِّبْيَانِ.
Larvated, }

Laryngeal, *a.* } مُخْتَصٌّ بِٱلْحَنْجَرَةِ — مُتَعَلِّقٌ بِٱلْغَلْصَمَةِ —
Laryngean, } حَنْجَرِيّ.

Laryngites, *n.* اِلْتِهَابُ ٱلْحَنْجَرَةِ — مُغَلْصَمَة.

Laryngotomy, *n.* شَطْرُ ٱلْغَلْصَمَةِ.

Larynx, *n.* ٱلْحُنْجُور — ٱلْحَنْجَرَة — غَلْصَمَة.

Lascar, *n.* هِنْدِيٌّ (or بَحْرِيٌّ) عَسْكَرِيٌّ *vulg.* لَشْكَرِيٌّ *coll.* لَشْكَر.

Lascivious, *a.* فَاسِق — شَهْوَانِيّ — رَفِث — عَاهِر *pl.* عُهَّار. See also Libidinous, *a.*

Lasciviously, *ad.* بِفِسْقٍ — بِرَفَثٍ — بِعَهَارَةٍ.

Lasciviousness, *n.* عَهَارَة — رَفَث — فِسْق — فُجُور — دَعَارَة. They have given themselves up to —, أَسْلَمُوا نُفُوسَهُمْ لِلدَّعَارَةِ.

Lash, *n.* A stroke with a whip, ضَرْبَةُ سَوْطٍ *pl.* ضَرَبَات. A whip, سَوْط *pl.* سِيَاط — دِرَّة — كِرْبَاج. The lash of a whip, فَتِيلَة (or ثَمَرُ) ٱلسَّوْطِ (or عَذَبَةُ). A censure, scolding, تَوْبِيخ — تَقْبِيح. Satire, هَجْو — نَقْر.

Lash, *v.t.* To whip, سَاطَ ² — سَوَّطَ — جَلَدَ — قَضَبَ. To lash against, as waves, لَطَمَ — لَطَمَ. To bind fast, شَدَّ ² — رَبَطَ ². To censure, لَامَ ² — وَبَّخَ — قَبَّحَ. To satirize, هَجَا ². See also under to Dash, *v.t.*

Lash, *v.i.* To ply with the whip, إِسْتَعْمَلَ ٱلسَّوْطَ. To — out, do something extravagant, أَفْرَطَ.

Lashing, *n.* Beating, ضَرْبُ سَوْطٍ — سَوْط. The cords for binding, حَبْلَة — مَرَسَة — سَلَبَة. What is put round anything to keep it from fretting, ثُوِيّ — ثُوَّة.

Lass, *n.* بِنْت *pl.* بَنَات ـ صَبِيَّة *pl.* صَبَايا.

Lassitude, *n.* تَعَب ـ عَيَاء ـ كُلُول ـ كَلال ـ كَلّ. *See also* Languor, *n.*

Lasso, *n.* جَرَّة ـ جُرَّة.

Last, *a.* Following all others, آخِر ـ تالٍ. Preceding, ماضٍ ـ سَابِق. The — part of anything, as of an event, دُبُر *pl.* أَدْبَار ـ غِبّ ـ عَاقِبَة. The — following, as of a procession, التَّوَالِي. The — of the prophets, عَاقِبُ ٱلأَنْبِيَاء. His — state was worse than the first, كَانَتْ أَوَاخِرُهُ أَشَرَّ مِنْ أَوَائِلِهِ. He came up —, هُوَ جَاءَ أَخِيرًا. Until you have paid the — farthing, حَتَّى تُوفِيَ ٱلْفَلْسَ ٱلأَخِير. The — day, اليَوْمُ ٱلأَخِيرُ. The — evening, مَسَاءَ أَمْسِ. The — breath, آخِرُ نَفَسٍ. Last year, العَامُ ٱلْمَاضِي ـ عَامَ ٱلأَوَّلِ. The — degree, أَبْلَغُ غَايَةٍ ـ آخِرُ دَرَجَةٍ. In the — place, أَخِيرًا ـ فِي ٱلآخِرِ. At —, عَاقِبَةً ـ أَخِيرًا. To the —, إِلَى ٱلنِّهَايَةِ ـ إِلَى ٱلآخِرِ. They came with the — of them, جَاؤُوا عَنْ آخِرِهِمْ. I did not know it save at the —, ما عَرَفْتُهُ إِلَّا أَخِيرًا (*or* بِأَخَرَةٍ). He came with those who were the — of the people, جَاءَ فِي أُخْرَى ٱلْقَوْمِ.

Last, *v.i.* To continue, إِسْتَمَرَّ ـ أَزْمَنَ ـ بَقِيَ ـ ثَبَتَ ـ دَامَ ـ إِسْتَدَامَ. To — a long time, طَالَ ـ رَهَنَ. To serve for a long time خَدَمَ. To make to —, أَدَامَ ـ أَرْهَنَ. They — only for a time, هُمْ إِلَى حِينٍ فَقَطْ. This shirt will — a year, هٰذَا ٱلْقَمِيصُ يَخْدُمُ سَنَةً. A battle took place which lasted twelve hours, جَرَتْ مَلْحَمَةٌ ٱسْتَمَرَّتِ ٱثْنَتَي عَشْرَةَ سَاعَةً. *See also to* Endure, *v.i.*

Last, *ad.* }
Lastly, } أَخِيرًا ـ عَاقِبَةً ـ آخِرَةً ـ بِٱلآخِرَةِ. Lastly, in summing up, as an argument, *etc.*, الحَاصِلُ ـ وَٱلْحَاصِلُ ـ حَاصِلُ ٱلْكَلَامِ. He came —, or latterly, جَاءَ آخِرًا (*or* أَخِيرًا).

Last, *n.* The form for a shoe, قَالَبُ لِلْمَدَاسِ *pl.* قَوَالِبُ.

Last, *n.* An end, آخِر; an ending, إِتْمَام ـ عَاقِبَة. The last part, towards the end, عَقِب. A load, حِمْل. The burden of a ship, حُمُولَةُ مَرْكَبٍ ـ تَعْبِيَةُ مَرْكَبٍ. They came to the — of them, *i.e.*, all, جَاؤُوا عَنْ آخِرِهِمْ.

Lasting, *n.* The cloth, قُمَاشٌ رَاهِنٌ.

Lasting, *a.* Durable, ذُو أَبَدٍ *fem.* ذَاتُ أَبَدٍ ـ مُسْتَدِيم ـ رَاهِن ـ مُسْتَمِرّ. Permanent, ثَابِت ـ دَائِم ـ قَيُّوم ـ بَاقٍ. Fixed, durable, as a colour, مَاكِن ـ رَاهِن. A — condition, حَالَةٌ رَاهِنَةٌ. Lasting food, طَعَامٌ رَاهِنٌ. It is more — than such a thing, هُوَ أَدْوَمُ مِنْ كَذَا. The bounty of God is —, نِعْمَةُ ٱللّٰهِ رَاهِنَةٌ.

Lastingly, *ad.* بِٱسْتِدَامَةٍ ـ بِٱسْتِمْرَارٍ ـ بِدَوَامٍ ـ رَهْنًا.

Lastingness, *n.* عَدَمُ زَوَالٍ ـ إِسْتِمْرَار ـ دَوَام ـ رَهْن.

Lastly, *ad.* *See above under* Last, *n.*

Latch, *n.* Of a door, شُقَّاطَة. To leave a door on the —, خَلَّى ٱلْبَابَ عَلَى ٱلشُّقَّاطَةِ.

Latch, *v.t.* To — a door, أَوْصَدَ ٱلْبَابَ بِٱلشُّقَّاطَةِ.

Latchet, *n.* For the shoe, سَيْر *pl.* سُيُور ـ شِرْع ـ شِرَاك.

Latch-key, *n.* مِفْتَاحٌ صَغِيرٌ لِلْبَابِ ٱلْبَرَّانِيِّ يُحْمَلُ فِي ٱلْجَيْبِ.

Late, *a.* Dilatory, tardy, بَطِيء *pl.* بِطَاء ـ مَكِيث ـ لَبِيث. Not long past, قَرِيب. The —, speaking of one dead, المَرْحُوم. The —, speaking of one who formerly held an office, السَّابِق. It is getting —, فَاتَ ٱلْوَقْتُ. To sit up —, سَهِرَ. He was too — for the train, مَا لَحِقَ ٱلْقِطَارَ. Late, out of season, خَارِجٌ عَنْ وَقْتِهِ. A — spring, رَبِيعٌ مُتَأَخِّرٌ. At a — period of life, عِنْدَ أَوَاخِرِ ٱلْحَيَاةِ. The — Wazir, الوَزِيرُ سَابِقًا. Late intelligence, أَخْبَارٌ جَدِيدَةٌ. Coming — in the evening, عَاتِم. To be late, tardy, تَعَوَّقَ ـ بَطُؤَ ـ تَلَبَّثَ ـ لَبِثَ. To make —, لَبَّثَ ـ عَوَّقَ ـ أَلْبَثَ.

Late, *ad.* Past time, فَاتَ ٱلْوَقْتُ. Behindhand, تَأَخُّرًا ـ تَعَوُّقًا. Recently, مِنْ مُدَّةٍ قَرِيبَةٍ. Just before, آنِفًا ـ تَوًّا. Late in the day, فِي آخِرِ ٱلنَّهَارِ. What — he preferred, لَيْسَ لَهُ زَمَانٌ. Late in the day, ... ٱلَّذِي ٱسْتَحْسَنَهُ آنِفًا.

Lately, *ad.* فِي ٱلْمُدَّةِ ـ بِهٰذَا ٱلْقُرْبِ ـ مُنْذُ زَمَنٍ قَرِيبٍ ـ تَوًّا ـ مِنْ مُدَّةٍ قَرِيبَةٍ ـ ٱلْمُتَأَخِّرَةِ. He came — from Egypt, جَاءَ حَدِيثًا مِنْ مِصْرَ. I did not know him until —, مَا عَرَفْتُهُ إِلَّا أَخِيرًا.

Latency, *n.* خَفَاء ـ خَفِيَّة ـ دِفْن.

Lateness, *n.* A coming after the usual hour, تَأَخُّر ـ وَخْرَة. Lateness in the evening, عَتْم. Slowness, بِطَاءَة ـ بُطْء. Time far advanced, تَنَاهِي ٱلْوَقْتِ ـ فَوَاتُ (*or* فَوْتُ) ٱلْوَقْتِ. Unseasonableness, كَوْنُ ٱلشَّيْءِ فِي غَيْرِ وَقْتِهِ. The — of spring, تَأَخُّرُ ٱلرَّبِيعِ.

Latent, *a.* خَفِيّ ـ دَفِين ـ مَدْفُون. A — disease, دَاءٌ دَفِينٌ. Latent heat, حَرَارَةٌ بَاطِنَةٌ.

Later, *a.* *See* Posterior, *a.*

Lateral, *a.* جَنْبِيّ ـ مُتَعَلِّقٌ بِٱلْجَانِبِ ـ مِنْ جَانِبٍ. A — view, مَنْظَرٌ جَانِبِيّ.

Laterally, *ad.* عَلَى جَنْبٍ ـ عَنْ جَانِبٍ.

Lateran, *n.* كَنِيسَةٌ عَلَى ٱسْمِ ٱلْقِدِّيسِ يُوحَنَّا بِرُومِيَّةَ.

Lath, *n.* لَوْحٌ مِنَ ٱلْخَشَبِ *pl.* أَلْوَاح ـ صَفِيحَةٌ مِنْ خَشَبٍ *pl.* صَفَائِح; *vulg.* بَدَاوِرَة.

Lath, *v.t.* رَكَّبَ-أَلْوَاحًا مِنْ خَشَبٍ ; *vulg.* رَكَّبَ-بَدَاوِرَاتٍ.

Lathe, *n.* مِخْرَطَةٌ ـ مِخْرَطٌ ـ بَلْط. To turn on a —, خَرَطَ ـ رَكَّبَ-عَلَى ٱلْمِخْرَطَةِ.

Lather, *n.* The — of soap, رَغْوَةُ (or) زَبَدُ ٱلصَّابُونِ. Froth from profuse sweat, زَبَد.

Lather, *v.t.* As with soap, صَبَّنَ.

Lather, *v.i.* To form a foam, تَزَبَّدَ ـ أَرْغَى ـ رَغَّى.

Lathy, *a.* Like a lath, مِثْلَ ٱلصَّفِيحَةِ (or) ٱلْبَدَاوِرَةِ. Slender, دَقِيق ـ رَقِيق.

Laticostate, *a.* عَرِيضُ ٱلْأَضْلَاعِ.

Latidendate, *a.* عَرِيضُ ٱلْأَسْنَانِ.

Latifolious, *a.* عَرِيضُ ٱلْأَوْرَاقِ.

Latin, *n.* لَاتِينِيٌّ. The Latin Church, ٱلْكَنِيسَةُ ٱللَّاتِينِيَّةُ ـ ٱلْكَنِيسَةُ ٱلرُّومَانِيَّةُ. The Latin tongue, ٱللِّسَانُ ٱللَّاتِينِيُّ.

Latinism, *n.* عِبَارَةٌ لَاتِينِيَّةٌ.

Latinist, *n.* عَالِمٌ بِٱللِّسَانِ ٱللَّاتِينِيِّ.

Latinity, *n.* لَاتِينِيَّةٌ.

Latinize, *v.t.* نَقَلَ-إِلَى ٱللَّاتِينِيَّةِ.

Latish, *a.* مُتَأَخِّرٌ قَلِيلًا.

Latitat, *n.* أَمْرٌ شَرْعِيٌّ بِحُضُورِ شَخْصٍ مُخْتَفٍ.

Latitude, *n.* Breadth, عَرْض. Room, space, اِتِّسَاع ـ سَعَة. Liberty of action, وُسْع ـ رُخْصَة. The — of a place, ٱلْعَرْضُ *pl.* ٱلْعُرُوضُ. To take a —, قَايَسَ ٱلْعَرْضَ. A degree of —, دَرَجَةُ ٱلْعَرْضِ. To give one's self — in, تَوَسَّعَ فِي ـ تَرَخَّصَ فِي.

Latitudinal, *a.* مِنْ جِهَةِ ٱلْعَرْضِ.

Latitudinarian, *n.* / **Latitudinarian**, *a.* } In religion, مُتَوَسِّعٌ (or) مُتَسَاهِلٌ فِي أُمُورِ ٱلدِّينِ ـ غَيْرُ مُتَعَصِّبٍ فِي ٱلدِّيَانَةِ. Lax in views, مُهَاوِد ـ سَائِب.

Latitudinarianism, *n.* In religion, تَسَاهُلٌ فِي أُمُورِ ٱلدِّينِ. Laxness, رَخَاء ـ مُهَاوَدَة.

Latitudinous, *a.* وَسِيع.

Latrant, *a.* Barking, نَبَّاح ـ نَابِح.

Latria, *n.* عِبَادَةٌ لِلّٰهِ وَحْدَهُ.

Latrina, *n.* كَنِيف ـ مِرْحَاض ـ مُتَوَضَّأ ; *from the Turkish*, شَشْمَة *pl.* شَشَم.

Latten, *n.* Iron plates covered with tin, صَفَائِحُ مِنْ حَدِيدٍ مُصَفَّحَةٌ بِقَزْدِيرٍ.

Latter, *a.* The last of two, ٱلْأَخِيرُ ـ ٱلْآخِرُ. The last, ٱلثَّانِي. Near, late, قَرِيب. The — growth, of vegetation, خِلْفُ ٱلْعُشْبِ. In these — times, فِي هٰذِهِ ٱلْأَزْمِنَةِ ٱلْأَخِيرَةِ. *See also* Last, *a.*

Latterly, *ad.* *See* Lately, *ad.*

Lattice, *n.* Anything latticed, مُشَبَّكَة ـ شَبَكَة. A — window, شُبَّاكَة *pl.* شَبَابِيكُ.

Lattice-work, *n.* شَبَاكَة. *See also* Trellis, *n.*

Lattice, *v.t.* شَبَّكَ. Latticed, مُشَبَّك.

Laud, *n.* Praise, ذِكْر ـ حَمْد ـ مَدْح ـ ثَنَاء. Lauds, morning prayers, صَلَاةُ ٱلصَّبَاحِ ـ صَلَاةُ ٱلضُّحَى. Praise, to God, تَسْبِيح.

Laud, *v.t.* ذَكَرَ ـ فَخَّمَ ـ مَجَّدَ ; of God, سَبَّحَ. *See also to* Eulogize, *v.t.*

Laudable, *a.* مَمْدُوح ـ مَدِيح *pl.* مَدَائِح ـ حَمِيد. A — act, مِدْحَة.

Laudableness, *n.* إِسْتِحْقَاق ـ فَضْل ـ مَحْمَدَة.

Laudably, *ad.* بِوَجْهٍ حَمِيدٍ ـ بِٱسْتِحْقَاقٍ.

Laudanum, *n.* رُوحُ ٱلْأَفْيُونِ ـ دُهْنُ ٱلْأَفْيُونِ.

Laudatory, *a.* مُوَصِّف ـ مُفَضِّل ـ ثَنَائِيٌّ ـ مَدْحِيٌّ.

Laudatory, *n.* ذِكْرٌ جَمِيلٌ ـ ثَنَاء ـ مَدْح.

Laugh, *v.i.* ضَحِكَ ـ تَضَحَّكَ ـ تَضَاحَكَ. To be gay, تَبَجَّحَ ـ تَغَبَّطَ ـ إِنْبَسَطَ ـ تَكَيَّفَ. To — immoderately, قَرْقَرَ ـ قَهْقَهَ. To jest, هَزَلَ ـ مَزَحَ. To make one —, ضَاحَكَ ـ أَضْحَكَ.

To burst out laughing, إِنْبَعَجَ مِنَ ـ فَقَعَ مِنَ ٱلضَّحِكِ ٱلضَّحِكَ.

To laugh at, to mock, ضَحِكَ (or) هَزِئَ مِن ـ سَخِرَ مِن ـ ب or مِن.

To laugh at, about, ضَحِكَ مِن.

To laugh in one's face, ضَحِكَ فِي وَجْهِهِ ـ ضَحِكَ عَلَى ذَقْنِهِ.

To laugh in one's sleeve, ضَحِكَ خِفْيَةً ـ ضَحِكَ سِرًّا.

To make one laugh on the wrong side of the mouth, حَوَّلَ ضَحِكَهُ خَيَّبَ ـ إِلَى ٱلْخَيْبَةِ.

Laugh, *v.t.* To laugh one out of a thing, صَرَفَ-عَنِ ٱلْأَمْرِ. To — one to scorn, خَنَّ لَهُ بِأَنْفِهِ ـ بِوَاسِطَةِ ٱلضَّحِكِ ـ هَزَأَ ب ـ إِسْتَهْزَأَ ب ـ إِسْتَحْقَرَ.

Laugh, *n.* ضَحِكَة. A loud —, قَهْقَهَة ـ قَرْقَرَة.

Laughable, *a.* مُضْحِك. Ludicrous, ridiculous, مُسْخِر ـ سُخْرَة. A — thing, أُضْحُوكَة ـ ضُحْكَة.

Laughableness, *n.* أُضْحُوكَة.

Laughably, *ad.* بِضَحِكٍ ـ بِنَوْعٍ مُضْحِكٍ.

Laugher, *n.* ضَحَّاك ـ مِضْحَاك.

Laughing, *a.* ضَحُوك ـ ضَاحِك *pl.* ضُحَّك. Laughing gas, غَازٌ مُضْحِكٌ.

Laughing, *n.* ضَحْك ـ ضِحْك ـ ضَحِك.

Laughing-stock, *n.* مَضْحَكَة ـ أُضْحُوكَة ـ سُخْرَة. To be or become a — to, صَارَ مَضْحَكَةً لِ. A public —, مَضْحَكَةٌ مَشْهُورَةٌ.

Laughter, *n.* ضَحِكٌ ـ ضِحْكٌ ـ ضَحِكٌ. Loud —, قَرْقَرَة ـ قَهْقَهَة.

Launch, *v.t.* To move from land into water, to float, أَسْبَحَ-فِي ـ أَطْلَقَ-سَيَّبَ-شَمَّرَ ـ عَوَّمَ ـ ٱلْمَاء. To throw, رَمَى. To let go, شَمَّرَ ـ سَيَّبَ ـ أَطْلَقَ.

Launch, *v.i.* To go forth, as a ship from a place, أَقْلَعَ. To — out, to go away towards, أَبْعَدَ إِلَى. To — out, to expatiate on, إِنْدَفَعَ فِي ـ أَفَاضَ فِي. To — out, as into expenses, أَفْرَطَ فِي; as into an action, أَفَاضَ فِي ٱلْعَمَلِ. After we had launched forth, بَعْدَ مَا أَقْلَعْنَا. We launched forth towards, أَبْعَدْنَا إِلَى. To — into acts of disobedience, فَجَرَ ².

Launch, *n.* A ship's small boat, فَلُوكَة. A large boat, شَخْتُور ـ صَنْدَل. The launching of a ship, تَعْوِيمُ مَرْكَبٍ ـ إِسْبَاحُ مَرْكَبٍ. The launch of the armour-plated frigate took place last week, فِي ٱلْأُسْبُوعِ ٱلْمَاضِي جَرَى تَعْوِيمُ ٱلْفِرْقَاطَةِ ٱلْمُدَرَّعَةِ.

Launderer, *n.* غَسَّال *pl.* غَسَّالُون.

Laundress, *n.* غَسَّالَة *pl.* غَسَّالَات.

Laundry, *n.* مَغْسَلَة ـ مَغْسَل.

Laureate, *a.* Crowned with laurel, مُكَلَّلٌ بِإِكْلِيلِ ٱلدِّفْلَى. Poet —, مَلِكُ ٱلشُّعَرَاء.

Laureate, *v.t.* كَلَّلَ-بِإِكْلِيلٍ مِنَ ٱلدِّفْلَى. To make head poet, صَيَّرَ-مَلِكَ ٱلشُّعَرَاء.

Laureateship, *n.* مَنْصِبُ مَلِكِ ٱلشُّعَرَاء.

Laurel, *n.* The common —, شَجَرُ ٱلْغَارِ. The rose —, ٱلدِّفْلَى. Laurels, honour, glory, إِسْم ـ ذِكْر ـ شُهْرَة ـ شَأْن. To gather laurels, honours, تَشَرَّفَ ـ إِكْتَسَبَ ٱلشَّرَفَ ـ عَلِيَ فِي ٱلشَّرَفِ. To tarnish one's laurels, فَضَحَ صِيتَهُ ـ عَرَّ شَرَفَهُ ².

Laurustinus, *n.* The plant, ضَرْبٌ مِنَ ٱلدِّفْلَى.

Lava, *n.* مَادَّةٌ سَيَّالَةٌ مِنْ جَبَلِ نَارٍ.

Lavatory, *n.* A place for washing, مَغْسَلَة. *See also* Latrina, *n.*

Lave, *v.t.* To wash, غَسَّلَ. To bathe with, بَلَّلَ ـ بَلَّ-بِ ².

Lave, *v.i.* To lave or wash one's self, حَمَّمَ ـ إِسْتَحَمَّ ـ إِغْتَسَلَ. *See also to* Bathe, *v.i.*

Lavender, *n.* خُزَامَى ـ سُنْبُلُ خُزَامَى. Lavender water or Eau de Cologne, مُوِيَةُ ٱلْمَلِكَةِ *vulg.* مَاءُ ٱلْمَلِكَةِ ـ لَوَنْدَا.

Laver, *n.* جُرْن ـ حَوْض.

Lavish, *a.* Profuse, spending much, مُبَذِّر ـ مُسْرِف. Profusely liberal, فَاضِل ـ بَذَّال. To be —, prodigal, بَاذَرَ ـ بَذَّرَ. To be profusely liberal, بَسَطَ ٱلْيَدَ ـ تَسَخَّى ².

Lavish, *v.t.* To scatter freely, بَذَرَ ـ بَذَلَ ². To expend prodigally, أَفْرَطَ ـ أَسْرَفَ ـ أَتْلَفَ ـ بَدَّدَ ـ بَذَّرَ ـ بَاذَرَ. To — words, نَشَرَ ٱلْكَلَامَ ²; to be loquacious, سَابَ فِي ٱلْكَلَامِ ـ بَذِرَ.

Lavishly, *ad.* Excessively, بِإِفْرَاطٍ ـ تَفْرِيطًا; with prodigality, بِبَذَارَةٍ ـ بِمُبَاذَرَةٍ.

Lavishness, *n.* / Lavishment, } Excess, تَفْرِيط ـ إِسْرَاف ـ سَرَف. Prodigality, تَبْذِرَة ـ بَذَارَة ـ تَبْذِير ـ مُبَاذَرَة.

Law, *n.* The —, in an absolute sense, ٱلشَّرْعُ. Jurisprudence, ٱلْفِقْهُ. A statute, شَرِيعَة *pl.* شَرَائِعُ ـ سُنَّة *pl.* سُنَن. An ordinance, فَرِيضَة *pl.* فَرَائِضُ ـ قَانُون *pl.* قَوَانِينُ. A rule, قَاعِدَة *pl.* قَوَاعِدُ. A regulation, نِظَام *pl.* نِظَامَات. A bond, ضَابِطَة ـ رَابِطَة. A custom, عَادَة *pl.* عَوَائِدُ ـ رَسْم *pl.* رُسُوم ـ سُنَّة *pl.* سُنَن. The — of honour, ٱلنَّامُوس *pl.* ٱلنَّوَامِيس. An edict, حُكْم ـ أَمْر ـ حُكُومَة ـ تَنْبِيه. The Law and the Prophets, ٱلنَّامُوسُ وَٱلْأَنْبِيَاءُ. One learned in the law, شَرْعِيٌّ ـ فَقِيه *pl.* فُقَهَاءُ. An organic —, دُسْتُور *pl.* دَسَاتِيرُ. Laws and regulations, أَحْكَامٌ وَنِظَامَاتٌ.

To go to law with, طَلَبَ-إِلَى ٱلشَّرْعِ ـ حَاكَمَ-إِلَى ٱلشَّرْعِ ².

To have knowledge of the law, تَفَقَّهَ ـ فَقِهَ. Having a knowledge of the law, فَقِيه.

To have the law of one, أَخَذَ حَقَّهُ مِن ـ إِنْتَقَمَ مِن ².

To impose a law upon, شَرَعَ لِ.

To make a law to, سَنَّ لِ-سُنَّةً ².

To make a law to one's self, إِسْتَسَنَّ.

To make void a law, أَبْطَلَ ٱلنَّامُوسَ.

To sue at law; *see supra*, To go to law with.

To take the law into one's own hands, خَلَّصَ حَقَّهُ بِيَدِهِ.

To violate the law, تَعَدَّى ٱلشَّرَائِعَ ـ تَعَدَّى ٱلْوَصِيَّةَ.

Bye-law, نِظَامٌ مَخْصُوصٌ ـ قَاعِدَةٌ مَخْصُوصَةٌ.

Commercial laws, أُصُولٌ وَأَحْكَامٌ تِجَارِيَّةٌ ـ نِظَامَاتٌ تِجَارِيَّةٌ.

Civil laws, أَحْكَامٌ شَرْعِيَّةٌ ـ نِظَامَاتٌ حُقُوقِيَّةٌ ـ حُقُوقٌ عَادِيَّةٌ وَنِظَامِيَّةٌ.

Criminal law, قَوَانِينُ جَزَائِيَّةٌ.

Divine law, أَحْكَامٌ إِلٰهِيَّةٌ.

Fiscal laws, نِظَامَاتٌ مِيرِيَّةٌ.

Fundamental laws, قَوَانِينُ أَسَاسِيَّةٌ.

Law of retaliation, حَقُّ ٱلْقِصَاصِ.

Laws in force, نِظَامَاتٌ جَارِيَةٌ مَرْعِيَّةٌ.

Law of nations, or International law, حُقُوقُ ٱلْمِلَلِ ـ قَوَانِينُ مِلِّيَّةٌ.

Martial law, قَوَانِينُ ٱلْحَرْبِ ـ قَاعِدَةٌ حَرْبِيَّةٌ.

Municipal laws, نِظَامَاتٌ بَلَدِيَّةٌ.

Muslim or religious law, الشَّرْعُ ٱلْمُبِينُ ـ الشَّرْعُ ٱلشَّرِيفُ.

Natural laws, أَحْكَامُ ٱلطَّبِيعَةِ.

Organic laws, دَسَاتِيرُ ـ نِظَامَاتٌ أَصْلِيَّةٌ.

Police laws, نِظَامَاتُ ٱلضَّبْطِيَّةِ.

Political laws, قَوَانِينُ سِيَاسِيَّةٌ ـ نِظَامَاتٌ مُلْكِيَّةٌ.

Positive laws, نِظَامَاتٌ مُؤَسَّسَةٌ ـ قَوَانِينُ مُقَرَّرَةٌ.

Press laws, نِظَامَاتُ ٱلْمَطْبُوعَاتِ.

Prohibitive laws, نِظَامَاتٌ زَاجِرَةٌ ـ أَحْكَامُ نَهْيٍ.

The law of the strongest, القَهْرُ.

Bachelor of Laws, مُجَازُ عِلْمِ ٱلْفِقْهِ.

Doctor of Laws, مُدَرِّسُ ٱلْعُلُومِ ٱلْفِقْهِيَّةِ.

Doctor of Civil Law, مُدَرِّسُ ٱلْفِقْهِ ٱلْقَدِيمِ ـ فَقِيهٌ *pl.* فُقَهَاءُ.

Law-breaker, *n.* مُخَالِفُ ٱلشَّرْعِ.

Lawful, *a.* Conformable to law, right, permissible, مُبَاحٌ ـ مُوَافِقُ ٱلشَّرْعِ وَٱلْقَوَانِينِ ـ مَشْرُوعٌ ـ جَائِزٌ ـ حَلَالٌ ـ طِلْقٌ. Legal, شَرْعِيٌّ. To be — to, حَلَّ لِ. To make —, permissible, أَبَاحَ. To make — to, حَلَّلَ لِ ـ سَوَّغَ لِ. To consider —, اِسْتَحَلَّ. To do what is — and right, فَعَلَ حَقًّا وَعَدْلًا. To do what is not —, فَعَلَ مَا لَا يَحِلُّ فِعْلُهُ. It is —, هُوَ حِلٌّ بِلٌّ. Is it — to...? هَلْ يَحِلُّ. It is — for you, هُوَ حِلٌّ لَكَ.

Lawfully, *ad.* حَسَبَ ٱلْقَوَانِينِ ـ بِٱلْحَقِّ ـ بِٱلْحَلَالِ. It is yours —, هُوَ لَكَ طِلْقًا. To use a thing —, اِسْتَعْمَلَهُ نَامُوسِيًّا. He strove —, اِجْتَهَدَ قَانُونِيًّا.

Lawfulness, *n.* اِسْتِبَاحَةٌ ـ إِبَاحَةٌ ـ جَوَازٌ ـ حَلَالٌ ـ حِلٌّ. Accordance with law, مُطَابَقَةُ ٱلْقَوَانِينِ وَٱلشَّرْعِ.

Lawgiver, *n.* } وَاضِعُ ـ صَاحِبُ ٱلشَّرِيعَةِ ـ شَرْعٌ *pl.* شَارِعٌ
Law-maker, } النَّامُوسِ. The —, Moses, حَضْرَةُ مُوسَى عَلَيْهِ ٱلسَّلَامُ.

Lawless, *a.* Opposed to the law, مُخَالِفُ ٱلشَّرْعِ وَٱلْقَوَانِينِ. Disorderly, disobedient, مُتَمَرِّدٌ ـ مُعَانِدٌ ـ عَاصٍ *pl.* عُصَاةٌ.

Lawlessness, *n.* تَمَرُّدٌ ـ عِصْيَانٌ.

Lawn, *n.* A grass plot, مَخْضَرَةٌ ـ يَخْضُورٌ. A fine muslin, شَاشٌ.

Lawn, *a.* Made of lawn, مِنْ شَاشٍ.

Lawny, *a.* بَسِيطٌ لَيِّنٌ.

Lawsuit, *n.* دَعْوَةٌ ـ دَعْوَى *pl.* دَعَاوَى. He gained his —, كَسَبَ دَعْوَاهُ.

Lawyer, *n.* نَامُوسِيٌّ ـ فَقِيهٌ *pl.* فُقَهَاءُ ـ مِنْ أَهْلِ ٱلشَّرْعِ *pl.* أَهْلُ ٱلشَّرْعِ.

Lax, *a.* Loose, أَسِيلٌ ـ رَخٌّ ـ رَخْوٌ ـ مُرْتَخٍ. Vague, مُنْكَرٌ ـ مُبْهَمٌ. Loose, as in morals, عِتْرِيفٌ ـ مُهَاوِدٌ ـ سَائِبٌ ـ فَالِتٌ.

To be —, loose, flabby, تَخَبْخَبَ ـ اِرْتَخَى ـ رَخِيَ *aor.* يَرْخَى ـ لَانَ ـ اِسْتَرْخَى. *See also* Flabby, Loose, *a.*

Laxation, *n.* Making lax, مُرَاخَاةٌ. Laxation of the bowels, إِسْهَالٌ.

Laxative, *a.* Of medicine, مُسْهِلٌ ـ سَهُولٌ.

Laxative, *n.* A purgative medicine, مُسْهِلَةٌ ـ حَادُورٌ.

Laxativeness, *n.* إِسْهَالٌ.

Laxity, *n.* } Slackness, رَخَاءٌ ـ رَخْوَةٌ ـ خَبْخَبَةٌ ـ رَخَاوَةٌ. Laxity
Laxness, } in morals, فُسُوقٌ ـ اِنْهِمَاكٌ فِي ٱلْمَنَاهِي ـ مَيْلٌ إِلَى ٱلْفُجُورِ. Want of exactness, إِبْهَامٌ ـ تَنَكُّرٌ ـ عَدَمُ دِقَّةٍ. Lightness, as of cloth, خِفَّةٌ ـ سُخْفٌ ـ سَخَافَةٌ.

Lay, *v.t.* To put, place, جَعَلَ ـ وَضَعَ *aor.* يَضَعُ ـ حَطَّ. To — one thing upon or to another, وَصَّلَ بِ ـ وَصَلَ *aor.* يَصِلُ ـ إِلَى ـ ضَمَّ. To —, or spread out upon, بَسَطَ عَلَى. To —, spread, as on a surface, as of a colour, طَلَّى ـ وَضَعَ عَلَى. To dispose in order, رَتَّبَ ـ نَسَّقَ ـ نَظَّمَ. To set up, صَمَدَ ـ رَكَزَ ـ نَصَبَ. To prepare, أَعَدَّ ـ أَجْمَعَ ـ هَيَّأَ ـ أَحْضَرَ. To charge, as a mine, *etc.*, عَمَّرَ. To allay, أَهْدَأَ ـ لَطَّفَ ـ أَخْمَدَ ـ سَكَّنَ ـ نَوَّمَ.

To lay a cable, at the bottom of the sea, قَعَّرَ ٱلْقَلْسَ فِي ٱلْبَحْرِ.

To lay a course, رَتَّبَ ٱلْمَسِيرَ ـ رَسَمَ ٱلْمَدْرَجَ.

To lay aside, to put on one side, جَنَّبَ ـ حَطَّ عَلَى جَنْبٍ.

To give up, تَخَلَّى عَنْ ـ تَرَكَ ـ سَيَّبَ. To put up or away, رَفَعَ ـ شَالَ بِ. To take away, رَفَعَ ـ أَقَامَ ـ رَفَعَ.

To lay a table, رَصَّ ٱلْأَوَانِي ـ رَصَّ ٱلطَّعَامَ.

To lay a wager with, رَاهَنَ ـ تَغَالَبَ ـ شَارَطَ. *See also to* Bet, *v.t.*

To lay before, to submit to, قَدَّمَ إِلَى ـ عَرَضَ عَلَى. To make known to, عَلَّمَ بِ ـ أَفَادَ بِ.

To lay by, to save, تَقَنَّى.

To lay eggs, بَاضَتْ *aor.* تَبِيضُ.

To lay down, as on a table, *etc.*, حَطَّ (or وَضَعَ) عَلَى. To design, trace, رَسَمَ. To give up, surrender, تَخَلَّى عَنْ ـ سَيَّبَ ـ تَرَكَ ـ سَلَّمَ. To lay down arms, رَفَعَ ٱلسِّلَاحَ. To lay down, as a principle, law, وَضَعَ ـ سَنَّ. To explain, بَيَّنَ ـ فَسَّرَ.

To lay one's self down, اِضْطَجَعَ ـ اِنْضَجَعَ ـ رَقَدَ ـ نَامَ.

To lay down one's life, وَضَعَ نَفْسَهُ *aor.* يَضَعُ.

To lay hands on, to seize, أَمْسَكَ ـ أَلْقَى ٱلْأَيَادِي عَلَى ـ أَبْزَى بِ ـ اِحْتَمَلَ عَلَى ـ قَبَضَ عَلَى. To ordain, وَضَعَ ٱلْأَيَادِي عَلَى ـ رَسَمَ.

To lay hold of, to take with the hand, قَبَضَ ـ أَمْسَكَ بِ.

To seize, تَمَسَّكَ ب ـ بَطَشَ ب ـ قَبَضَ عَلَى. They sought to lay hold of him, طَلَبُوا أَنْ يَمْسِكُوهُ.

To lay in, as of stores, إِدَّخَرَ ـ خَزَنَ. To put inside, أَدْخَلَ ـ أَدْرَجَ-فِي ـ رَفَعَ-فِي.

To lay low, to bring down, أَهْبَطَ ـ خَبَّطَ ـ خَفَضَ.

To lay on, to place upon, وَضَعَ-عَلَى aor. يَضَعُ. To accuse of, تَهَمَ-ب. To impose, as a burden, etc., عَوَّلَ عَلَى-ٱلشَّيْء ـ نَزَّلَ عَلَى ـ سَخَّرَ-ب ـ كَلَّفَ-ب. To beat, رَمَى-عَلَى ـ ضَرَبَ. To lay it on, to do in excess, بَذَّرَ ـ أَفْرَطَ فِي ـ زَوَّدَ.

To charge immoderately, سَلَخَ ـ غَلَّى. To lay on, as of a plaster on a wound, ضَمَدَ ٱلْجُرْحَ.

To lay one's self open to, تَعَرَّضَ ل ـ إِسْتَهْدَفَ ل.

To lay open, to open, فَتَحَ. To reveal, أَذَاعَ ب ـ كَشَفَ. To lay open, reveal, something to one, عَرَضَ-ل ـ أَفْضَى إِلَى-ب.

To lay out, to spend, أَنْفَقَ ـ صَرَّفَ ـ صَرَفَ. To trace out, to arrange, سَطَحَ ـ نَظَّمَ ـ نَسَّقَ ـ رَتَّبَ. To spread, نَشَرَ ـ فَرَشَ. To lay one's self out to, to undertake, تَكَلَّفَ ب.

To lay out, as of a dead body, كَفَّنَ.

To lay over, to cover with, غَطَّى-ب ـ سَتَّرَ-ب. To put over, عَالَى-ب.

To lay siege to, أَحَاطَ ب ـ حَاصَرَ.

To lay the dust, لَبَّدَ ٱلتُّرَابَ.

To lay to, of a ship, صَلَّبَ ٱلْمَرْكَبَ.

To lay to heart, وَضَعَ-فِي قَلْبِهِ ـ جَعَلَ-فِي ٱلْقَلْبِ. To lay up in the heart, كَنَّ-فِي ٱلْقَلْبِ.

To lay together, ضَمَّ بَعْضًا ـ حَطَّ-جُمْلَةً ـ جَمَّعَ ـ جَمَعَ ـ قَرَّبَ بَعْضًا إِلَى بَعْضٍ ـ إِلَى بَعْضٍ.

To lay under, حَطَّ-أَسْفَلَ ٱلشَّيْء ـ وَضَعَ-تَحْتَ ٱلشَّيْء. To lay one under an obligation, صَيَّرَ-تَحْتَ ٱلْمِنَّةِ; vulg. صَيَّرَ-مَمْنُونًا.

To lay up, to amass, لَمَّ ـ جَمَّعَ ـ كَوَّمَ. To reserve, خَلَّى ـ أَبْقَى ـ حَفِظَ ـ خَبَّأَ. To make ill, عَطَّلَ ـ أَمْرَضَ. To disarm, of a ship, رَفَعَ مِنَ ٱلْمَرْكَبِ ٱلْمَدَافِعَ وَٱلْآلَاتِ.

To lay wait for, رَاصَدَ ـ تَرَصَّدَ ل ـ رَصَدَ ـ كَمَنَ ل ـ قَعَدَ ل.

To lay waste, دَمَّرَ ـ أَجْعَلَ-خَرَابًا ـ خَرَّبَ ـ أَخْرَبَ.

Lay, v.i. To lay eggs, بَاضَتْ aor. تَبِيضُ.

Lay, n. A song, قَصِيدَة pl. قَصَائِدُ ـ مَقَامَة pl. مَقَامَات. A layer, طَبَقَة pl. طَبَقَات. A wager, خَطَر pl. خِطَار ـ مُرَاهَنَة. A lawn, خُضْرَة.

Lay, a. Not clerical, عَلْمَانِيّ ـ عَامِّيّ.

Lay-brother, n. رَاهِب غَيْرُ مَرْسُوم.

Lay-clerk, n. قَارٍ غَيْرُ مَرْسُوم.

Lay-figure, n. تِمْثَال pl. تَمَاثِيلُ ـ تَقْلِيد pl. تَقَالِيدُ ـ صُورَةُ تَقْلِيدٍ.

Layer, n. As of stones in a wall, سَافَة pl. سَافَات ـ سَاف ـ طَاق pl. طَاقَات. A row, صَفّ pl. صُفُوف. A stratum, طَاق pl. طَاقَات ـ طَبَقَة pl. طَبَقَات. A sprig for growth, عُقْلَة pl. عُقَل ـ شَتْلَة. To dispose stones in layers, رَصَفَ. To be disposed in layers, إِطَّرَقَ.

Layering, n. Of plants, غَرْسُ ٱلْعُقَلِ (or ٱلشَّتْلَاتِ).

Layman, n. See Laic, n.

Lazaret, n. } Lazaretto, } كُوَارَنْتِينَا. To be, or to be put into the —, كَرْتَنَ.

Lazar-house, n. دَارٌ لِلْمُصَابِينَ بِٱلْوَبَاءِ.

Lazily, ad. بِتَوَانٍ ـ بِٱلْكَسَلِ ـ بِكَسَلٍ.

Laziness, n. Indolence, تَوَانٍ ـ كَسَل.

Lazy, a. كَسِل pl. كَسْلَان ـ كَسَالَى pl. كُسَالَى ـ ضَاجِع. To be —, تَوَانَى ـ تَكَاسَلَ ـ كَسِلَ.

Lazzaroni, n. رَعَاع.

Lea, n. } Ley, } A meadow, مَرْج pl. مُرُوج ـ رَوْضَة pl. رِيَاض and رِيَضَان. A plain, قَاع pl. قِيعَان ـ مِيدَان pl. مَيَادِينُ.

Leach, n. رَمَادُ ٱلْقَلْيِ.

Leach, v.t صَفَّى ٱلرَّمَادَ.

Leach-tub, n. وِعَاءٌ لِتَصْفِيَةِ ٱلرَّمَادِ.

Lead, n. The going before, تَقْدِمَة ـ سَابِقَة ـ تَقَدُّم. To take the —, to go in advance, تَقَدَّمَ ـ سَاقَ إِلَى قُدَّام. To preside, تَصَدَّرَ ـ أَنْجَحَ ب. To surpass, فَاقَ ـ بَرَزَ عَلَى. To follow the — of, قَفَا ـ لَحِقَ ـ أَتْبَعَ ـ مَشَى وَرَاءَهُ.

Lead, v.t. To be before one, سَبَقَ ـ هَدَى. To go with as leader, أَوْصَلَ ـ قَادَ ـ أَسْلَكَ ـ سَارَ ب. To guide, دَلَّ ـ أَرْشَدَ ـ هَدَى. To — in the right way, أَرْشَدَ ـ دَلَّ-عَلَى. To direct, manage, سَاسَ aor. يَسُوسُ ـ دَبَّرَ. To command, as of troops, قَادَ ـ دَبَّرَ. To — one to, to cause him to arrive at, أَوْرَدَ ـ أَفْضَى-إِلَى ـ جَاءَ ب-إِلَى aor. يَجِيءُ ـ أَدَّى-إِلَى ـ هَدَى-إِلَى. To cause to do, to instigate, حَمَلَ-عَلَى ـ دَعَا-إِلَى aor. يَدْعُو. To —, as of water, to a place, أَجْرَى ٱلْمَاءَ إِلَى. To be led, driven, to, إِنْسَاقَ إِلَى ـ سِيقَ إِلَى ـ أُضْطُرَّ إِلَى. What led you to do this thing? مَا دَعَاكَ إِلَى هٰذَا ٱلْأَمْرِ. That would — to..., كَانَ ذٰلِكَ دَعِيًّا لِ. That will — the rest to think badly of us, يَحْمِلُ ذٰلِكَ ٱلْبَاقِي عَلَى إِسَاءَةِ ٱلظَّنِّ فِينَا. The reason which led me to that, ٱلسَّبَبُ ٱلَّذِي سَاقَنِي إِلَى ذٰلِكَ.

To lead a life, سَارَ سِيرَةً ـ عَاشَ عَيْشَةً ـ سَلَكَ سُلُوكًا. To lead a good life, هَدَى ـ قَضَى حَيَاةً. To lead a quiet life, قَضَى حَيَاةً مُطْمَئِنَّةً.

To lead one a life, to be harsh to, قَاهَرَ ـ عَنَفَ عَلَى ـ قَاسَرَ.

To lead one about, جَالَ بِ ـ سَارَ بِهِ هُنَا وَهُنَاكَ ـ دَارَ بِهِ ـ دَوَّرَ.

To lead along, سَاقَ. To lead a horse along, as with the bridle, قَادَ ٱلْحِصَانَ.

To lead astray, as from the road, تَوَّهَ عَنِ ٱلطَّرِيقِ ـ ضَيَّعَ ٱلدَّرْبَ عَلَى. To cause to swerve from rectitude, أَضَلَّ ـ أَفْسَدَ ـ أَغْوَى. To be led astray, deceived, تَغَاوَى.

To lead away, to remove, ذَهَبَ بِ ـ مَضَى بِ ـ أَنْقَلَ. To be led away, إِنْسَاقَ ـ سِيقَ. To lead away captive, سَبَى aor. يَسْبِي.

To lead back, أَعَادَ ـ رَجَّعَ.

To lead forth, أَخْرَجَ ـ أَبْرَزَ.

To lead off, to carry off, remove; *see* To lead away, *supra*.

To lead on, to go with, سَارَ بِ ـ قَادَ. To instigate, حَمَلَ عَلَى ـ دَعَا إِلَى aor. يَدْعُو.

To lead out, أَخْرَجَ ـ أَبْرَزَ. He led them out as far as the castle, أَخْرَجَهُمْ خَارِجًا إِلَى ٱلْقَلْعَةِ.

To lead up, أَصْعَدَ إِلَى.

Lead, *v.i.* To go before, تَقَدَّمَ ـ سَبَقَ ـ إِسْتَقْدَمَ. To — to, أَدَّى إِلَى aor. يُؤَدِّي. To — off, to be the first, تَقَدَّمَ. This road leads to, هٰذَا ٱلطَّرِيقُ يُؤَدِّي إِلَى. This action will lead to trouble, هٰذَا ٱلْعَمَلُ يَقْتَادُ إِلَى ٱلْإِلْتِبَاكِ.

Lead, *n.* The mineral, صَرَفَان ـ عَلَابِيٌّ ـ أُسْرُبٌ ـ رَصَاص. A ship's —, بَلَد ـ إِسْقِنْدِيل. A printer's — to divide lines, رَصَاصَة *pl.* رَصَاصَات. Leads, a roof covered with —, سَطْحٌ مُصَفَّحٌ بِصَفَائِحَ مِنَ ٱلرَّصَاصِ. To heave the —, رَمَى ٱلْإِسْقِنْدِيلَ (or ٱلْبَلَدَ). A worker in —, رَصَّاص.

Black lead, أُسْرُب.

Black lead pencil, قَلَمُ رَصَاصٍ.

Pig lead, رَصَاصٌ سَكْب.

Sheet lead, رَصَاصٌ مُصَفَّحٌ ـ رَصَاصٌ صَفَائِحُ.

Sugar of lead, مِلْحُ ٱلرَّصَاصِ.

White lead, إِسْفِيدَاج. Red lead, سُنْجَاب.

Lead, *a.* Made of lead, أُسْرُبِيٌّ ـ مِنْ رَصَاصٍ.

Leaded, *a.* Loaded with lead, مُحَمَّلٌ رَصَاصًا. Having leads between the lines, بَيْنَ أَسْطُرِهِ فَوَاصِلُ مِنْ رَصَاصٍ. Set with lead, مُرَصَّعٌ بِرَصَاصٍ.

Leaden, *a.* Made of lead, أُسْرُبِيٌّ ـ مِنْ رَصَاصٍ. Dull, أَرْبَدُ ـ عَاتِم ـ كُمَيْت ـ مُكْمَدٌّ.

Leader, *n.* A guide, دَلِيل *pl.* أَدِلَّاء ـ هَادٍ ـ مُرْشِد. A manager, ضَابِطُ ٱلزِّمَامِ ـ مُدَبِّر ـ مُرَتِّب. The —, as of an army, قَائِدُ عَسْكَرٍ *pl.* قَادَة ـ رَئِيس *pl.* رُؤَسَاء ـ كَبِير *pl.* كِبَار. The — of a party, زِمَامُ ٱلْقَوْمِ. The leading horse, زِمَامُ ٱلْحُصُنِ. Head, chief, زَعِيم *pl.* زُعَمَاء ـ رَئِيس *pl.* رُؤَسَاء ـ مُتَقَدِّم. A leading article in a paper, جُمْلَةٌ سِيَاسِيَّةٌ ـ بَنْدٌ أَصْلِيٌّ فِي جَرِيدَةِ ٱلْأَخْبَارِ فِي غَازِيتَةٍ. The — of the council, زِمَامُ أَهْلِ ٱلشُّورَى. The principal orator, أَبْلَغُ ٱلْخُطَبَاءِ ـ أَفْضَلُ ٱلْمُتَكَلِّمِينَ. The — of an orchestra, مُعَلِّمُ ٱلْقُدُودِ ـ مُعَلِّمُ ٱلنَّوْبَاتِيَّةِ. The — of an insurrection, رَأْسُ ٱلْفِتْنَةِ. The principal one in asking and replying, ٱلْمُتَقَدِّمُ فِي ٱلسُّؤَالِ وَٱلْجَوَابِ.

Leadership, *n.* Headship, رِئَاسَة ـ تَقَدُّم ـ سِيَادَة. The office of being principal asker and answerer, وَظِيفَةُ ٱلْمُتَقَدِّمِ فِي ٱلسُّؤَالِ وَٱلْجَوَابِ ـ صَاحِبُ زِمَامِ ٱلْحِزْبِ.

Leading, *a.* Conducting to, مُؤَدٍّ إِلَى. The — men of the government, أَرْبَابُ ٱلْحُكُومَةِ. A — rope, حَبْلُ ٱلْخِطَامِ ـ قِيَاد.

Leading-strings, *n.* For children, مِقْوَدٌ لِحِفْظِ ٱلْأَطْفَالِ مِنَ ٱلتَّعَثُّرِ. To be in —, to be led by, إِنْقَادَ مِنْ ـ سَلَّمَ قِيَادَهُ لِ ـ أَسَاقَ مِنْ.

Leadsman, *n.* A sounder, عَسَّاس ـ رَاوِي ٱلْإِسْقِنْدِيلِ (or ٱلْبَلَدِ).

Leaf, *n.* As of a tree, وَرَقَة ـ أَوْرَاق *pl.* وَرَق. A — of paper, وَرَقَة ـ طَرْحِيَّةُ وَرَقٍ *pl.* طَرَاحِي; *called in Egypt*, فَرْخُ وَرَقٍ *pl.* أَفْرَاخ. A —, as of gold or silver, صَفِيحَة *pl.* صَفَائِح. The — of a door, صَحِيفَةُ بَابٍ *pl.* صَحَائِف ـ مِصْرَاع ـ دَرْفَةُ بَابٍ *pl.* دَرَف ـ ضَلْفَةُ بَابٍ *pl.* ضَلَف ـ فَرْدُ بَابٍ *pl.* فِرَاد. The two leaves of a door, ٱلْمِصْرَاعَانِ. The leaves of a door, رَوَاجِعُ ٱلْأَبْوَابِ. A door with two leaves, بَابٌ مِنْ دَرْفَتَيْنِ. A —, as of a table, وَصْلَة *pl.* وَصْلَات. Fallen leaves, نُفَض. Leaves blown about on the ground by the wind, سَفِير. The trees broke forth with leaves, تَفَطَّرَ ٱلشَّجَرُ بِوَرَقٍ ـ تَرَوَّحَ (or رَاحَ) ٱلشَّجَرُ. To garnish with leaves, زَيَّنَ بِوَرَقٍ. To feed, as camels, on leaves of trees, عَلِقَ.

The fall of the leaf, ٱلْخَرِيفُ ـ ٱلرَّبِيعُ ٱلْأَوَّلُ.

To beat down leaves, as from a tree, هَشَّ.

To strip a tree of its leaves, خَبَطَ (or جَرَّدَ) ٱلْوَرَقَ مِنَ ٱلشَّجَرَةِ ـ وَرَّقَ aor. يَبْرُقُ.

To take a leaf out of another's book, تَمَثَّلَ بِ ـ إِقْتَدَى بِ.

To put forth leaves; *see* to Leaf, *v.i.*

To tremble like a leaf, إِرْتَجَفَ مِثْلَ ٱلْوَرَقَةِ.

To turn a leaf down, ثَنَى وَرَقَةً.

To turn over a new leaf, أَصْلَحَ ٱلسِّيرَةَ.

To turn over the leaves of a book, قَلَّبَ ٱلْوَرَقَ – صَفَحَ ٱلْوَرَقَ.

Leaf, *v.i.* وَرَقَ *aor.* يَرِقُ – وَرَّقَ – أَوْرَقَ. To —, after a tree had been supposed to be dead, تَجَبَّرَ. Time of leafing, الوِرَاقُ.

Leaf-bud, *n.* بَاقِل.

Leafiness, *n.* كَثْرَةُ وَرَقٍ – تَوْرِيق.

Leafless, *a.* عَارٍ مِنَ ٱلْوَرَقِ – أَمْرَدُ.

Leaflet, *n.* وُرَيْقَة *pl.* وُرَيْقَات.

Leaf-stalk, *n.* سَاقُ وَرَقَةٍ *pl.* سُوُوق – ذَيْلُ ٱلْوَرَقِ *pl.* أَذْيَال.

Leafy, *a.* وَارِق – وَرِق – وَرِيق. A — tree, وَارِقَة.

League, *n.* Alliance, عَقْد – مُعَاقَدَة – حِلْف – حِلْفَة – ذِمَّة *pl.* ذِمَام – اِتِّفَاق. A party, حِزْب *pl.* أَحْزَاب. A cabal, عُصْبَة – رَبِيطَة. A — of states, مُعَاهَدَةُ مَمَالِكَ – اِجْتِمَاعُ دُوَلٍ. To join in a — with, حَالَفَ-عَلَى. To enter into a —, عَاهَدَ – عَاقَدَ. They entered into a —, of many, تَحَالَفُوا – تَرَابَطُوا – تَعَصَّبُوا. They entered into a — against, تَعَصَّبُوا عَلَى.

League, *n.* The measure, about an hour's travelling on foot, مَسَافَةُ سَاعَةٍ – سَاعَة *pl.* سَاعَات – مَلْقَة *pl.* أَمْلَاق.

League, *v.i.* They leagued together, of many, تَحَالَفُوا – تَرَابَطُوا – تَعَاهَدُوا. *See also under* League, Alliance, *n.*

Leaguer, *n.* حِلْف – حَلِيف – مُتَعَصِّب.

Leak, *n.* A seam that lets fluid pass, فَجْرَة – مَفْجَرَة – خَرْق *pl.* خُرُوق. A leaking, خَرِير. A — in a ship, خَرْقٌ فِي مَرْكَبٍ يَدْخُلُ مِنْهُ ٱلْمَاءُ; in a water-skin, نَثِيث. To spring a —, of a ship, تَخَرَّقَ (*or* ٱلْخَرْقَ) ٱلْمَرْكَبُ.

Leak, *v.i.* سَرِبَ – نَضَحَ – اِنْفَضَحَ – خَرَّ; especially of a house or roof, وَكَفَ *aor.* يَكِفُ – وَكَّفَ – دَلَفَ; of a water-skin, نَثَّ. To trickle, نَضَّ. To — out, to become known, فَشَا – ظَهَرَ.

Leakage, *n.* A leaking, as of a roof, وَكْف – وُكُوف; as of a water-skin, نَثِيث; in a more general sense, نَضْح – نُضُوح – خَرِير. Loss from —, عَوَارٌ مِنَ ٱلْخَرِيرِ. Allowance for loss by —, إِسْقَاطٌ مِنَ ٱلثَّمَنِ بَدَلَ ٱلْعَوَارِ مِنَ ٱلْخَرِيرِ.

Leaky, *a.* That leaks, يَرْشَحُ – يَخِرُّ – دَالِف; of a roof, يَكِفُ. Leaky, of a ship, مُتَخَرِّق. One who can't keep a secret, غِرْبَال – مِذْيَال – فُرُج.

Leal, *a.* صَادِق *pl.* صَادِقُون – صَدِيق *pl.* أَصْدِقَاءُ.

Lean, *a.* Thin, emaciated, نِضْو *pl.* أَنْضَاءُ – نَضِيّ *pl.* أَنْضِيَة – غَثّ – مُخْتَلّ – رَثّ – خَاسِف – عَجْفَاءُ *pl.* عِجَاف – أَعْجَف *fem.* عَجْفَاءُ *pl.* عِجَاف – مَهْزُول – ضَعِيف – نَحِيف – غِشَاث. A very — person, شَخْت – مَمْصُوص. Lean meat, لَحْمَةٌ غَثَّةٌ. Lean in the legs, مَنْهُوشُ ٱلْقَدَمَيْنِ. Lean cows, بَقَرَاتٌ رَقِيقَةُ ٱللَّحْمِ. To be or become —, عَجُفَ – خَسَفَ – نَحِشَ – نَحُفَ – غَثَّ – ذَابَ – شَفَّ جِسْمُهُ – خَلَّ (*or* اِخْتَلَّ) لَحْمُهُ – أَغَثَّ – أَعْجَفَ – سَخُفَ – أَنْحَفَ – أَخْمَصَ جِسْمُهُ. To make —, أَعْجَفَ – أَنْحَفَ – أَخْمَصَ. *See also* Barren, Infertile, *n.*

Lean, *n.* The — of meat, هَبْر – بَسِير.

Lean, *v.i.* To incline, وَكَفَ *aor.* يَكِفُ – جَنَحَ – اِجْتَنَحَ – مَالَ. To — towards, مَالَ إِلَى. To — against, اِسْتَنَدَ إِلَى – سَنَدَ إِلَى – اِتَّكَى عَلَى. To — on, as on a staff, عَشَزَ عَلَى – عَكَزَ عَلَى – اِتَّكَى عَلَى. To — or depend on, اِعْتَمَدَ عَلَى – اِتَّكَلَ عَلَى. To — to, to be disposed in favour of, لَوَى عَلَى – رَكَنَ إِلَى – تَعَطَّفَ عَلَى. To make one to — against, اِسْتَنَدَ-إِلَى.

See also to Incline, *v.i.*

Leanness, *n.* Want of flesh, خَسْف – خُلُول – غَثَاثَة – غُثُونَة – نَحَافَة. Leanness of language, meaning, كَلَامٌ رَثٌّ (*or* رَكِيكٌ). Poverty generally, مَسْكَنَة.

Lean-to, *n.* Something to lean against, مِتْكَاءٌ *pl.* مِتْكَاآت.

Leap, *v.i.* سَاوَرَ – قَزَّ – نَطَّ – نَفَزَ – قَفَزَ. To cause to —, of a horse, *etc.*, طَفَّرَ – نَفَّزَ. To —, of a horse, طَفَرَ; of hoofed animals generally, نَزَا; to cause such to —, أَنْزَى. To — up, as with joy, ثَارَ *aor.* يَثُورُ. To — upon, تَفَلَّتَ عَلَى – وَثَبَ عَلَى *aor.* يَثِبُ. To cause one to — upon, أَوْثَبَ-عَلَى. To — off, تَفَلَّتَ عَن. He leaped towards him, ثَارَ (*or* وَثَبَ) إِلَيْهِ. His heart leapt, رَقَصَ فُؤَادُهُ.

Leap, *v.t.* To — or jump over, طَفَرَ – نَطَّ عَلَى. To — or to — over a wall, سَوَّرَ – تَسَوَّرَ – تَسَوَّرَ عَلَى. To — the female, of a bird or camel, قَعَا – اِسْتَخْلَطَ; as of a horse the mare, دَمَّ ٱلْحِجْرَ – سَفَدَ – نَزَقَ; to cause a horse so to —, أَنْزَقَ.

See also to Copulate, *v.i.*, *and the preceding article.*

Leap, *n.* طَفْرَة – قَزّ – قَزَّة – نَطَّة – نَطّ – سَوْرَة – قَفْزَة – وَثْبَة; of a horse, طَفْرَة. The act of copulation, سِفَاد – سَفْد – نَزْق. At a leap, قَفْزَة – بِٱلْمَرَّةِ – قَفْزَةً وَاحِدَةً.

Leap-frog, *n.* دُبَّاح. The boy who bends his back is called, دَبَّح. He lowered his back, as in —, دَبَّحَ – دَبَّحَ.

Leap-year, *n.* سَنَةٌ كَبِيسَةٌ.

Learn, *v.i.* تَعَلَّمَ – تَدَارَسَ.

Learn, *v.t.* As a language or science, تَعَلَّمَ – دَرَسَ – دَارَسَ. To — well, thoroughly, تَعَلَّمَ-عِلْمًا. To become skilled in,

— ضَمِنَ ‹. To acquire information of, تَمَهَّرَ فِي — ‹ مَهَرَ فِي. To — under one, ‹ دَرَسَ عِنْدَ فُلَانٍ. aor. يَقِفُ وَقَفَ عَلَى. To — by heart, ‹ أَخَذَ ٱلْعِلْمَ عَنْ فُلَانٍ — تَعَلَّمَ مِنْ فُلَانٍ حَفِظَهُ عَلَى ظَهْرِ قَلْبِهِ — ‹ حَفِظَ-غَيْبًا. We learn, are informed, (in an impersonal sense), from the journals, يُسْتَفَادُ مِنَ ٱلْجَرَائِدِ.

See also to Teach, *v.t.*

Learned, *a.* حَاذِق — عَالِم *pl.* عُلَّام — عَلِيم — لَوْذَعِيّ — مِفَنّ. The —, أَهْلُ ٱلْعِلْمِ. Containing learning, مُفِيد — حَاوٍ مِنَ ٱلْعِلْمِ.

Learnedly, *ad.* بِمَعْرِفَةٍ — بِإِفَادَةٍ — بِعِلْمٍ.

Learner, *n.* تِلْمِيذ *pl.* تَلَامِيذ — طَالِبُ عِلْمٍ *pl.* طُلَّاب.

Learning, *n.* Erudition, عِلْم — فَنّ — عِرْفَان — مَعْرِفَة. Study, studying, مُدَارَسَة.

Leasable, *a.* يُؤْجَرُ.

Lease, *n.* Letting for hire, إِيجَار *pl.* إِيجَارَات. A — for a number of years, إِيجَارٌ إِلَى أَجَلٍ مِنَ ٱلسِّنِينَ; a — in perpetuity, رُقْبَى. The deed for any of these, حُجَّة *pl.* حُجَج.

Lease, *v.t.* To let on hire, آجَرَ. To — for a number of years, آجَرَ-إِلَى أَجَلٍ مِنَ ٱلسِّنِينَ. To — to, in perpetuity, of a house, أَرْقَبَهُ ٱلدَّارَ.

Leasehold, *a.* | Leasehold, *n.* } مُسْتَأْجَرٌ إِلَى أَجَلٍ مِنَ ٱلسِّنِينَ.

Leaseholder, *n.* مُسْتَأْجِرٌ إِلَى أَجَلٍ مِنَ ٱلسِّنِينَ.

Leash, *n.* A — for dogs, حَبْلَةُ (or سَلَبَةُ) ٱلْكِلَابِ. The — of a hawk, رَسَنُ ٱلْبَازِي. A brace and a half, ثَلَاثَةُ رُؤُوسٍ.

Leash, *v.t.* قَيَّدَ — ‹ ضَبَطَ — ‹ رَسَنَ ‹.

Leasing, *n.* Lying, كَذِب.

Least, *a.* and *ad.* The smallest, أَصْغَرُ *pl.* أَصَاغِرُ; *fem.* صُغْرَى *pl.* صُغَر. Of a thing, the smallest, the worst, أَدْنَى — أَحَطُّ. The —, in number, الأَقَلُّ. The — thing, أَدْنَى شَيْءٍ. Not in the —, not at all, أَصْلًا — أَبَدًا — قَطُّ. Not the —, none at all, لَا شَيْءَ أَصْلًا — لَا شَيْءَ أَبَدًا. At —, at the lowest estimate, بِٱلْقَلِيلِ — قَلَّمَا يَكُونُ — أَقَلَّ مَا يَكُونُ. They have not the — cause, لَيْسَ لَهُمْ أَدْنَى سَبَبٍ. I require at — one hundred pounds, أَحْتَاجُ إِلَى مِئَةِ لِيرَةٍ أَقَلَّ مَا يَكُونُ. If you had known what was for your good, at — on this occasion, لَوْ عَلِمْتَ خَيْرَكَ حَتَّى فِي هٰذِهِ ٱلْفُرْصَةِ. If they have kept themselves at least (specially) from drunkenness, إِذَا كَانَ قَدْ حَفِظُوا أَنْفُسَهُمْ لَا سِيَّمَا مِنَ ٱلسُّكْرِ. I am not tired in the —, (or مُتْعَب) لَيْسَ أَنَا بِتَعْبَانٍ ٱلْبَتَّةَ. I am the — of all, أَنَا أَصْغَرُ ٱلْجَمِيعِ. The — cause will inflame them, أَقَلُّ الأَسْبَابِ يُضْرِمُهُمْ.

Leather, *n.* Skin, جِلْد *pl.* جُلُود. Sheepskin, جِلْدُ — حَوَر غَنَمٍ مَدْبُوغ. Ox-hide, جِلْدُ بَقَرٍ — كُوْن.

Black leather, جِلْدٌ أَدْلَمُ — أَرَنْدَج.

Curried leather, جِلْدٌ مَدْبُوغٌ.

Morocco leather, سَخْتِيَان.

Sole leather, جِلْدُ نَعْلٍ.

Tanned leather, جِلْدٌ مَأْدُومٌ — أَدِيم.

To dress leather, ‹ دَبَغَ ٱلْجُلُودَ — ‹ أَفَقَ ٱلْجُلُودَ ‹.

Leather, *a.* } مِنْ جِلْدٍ. A leather strap, شِرَاك — سَيْر *pl.*
Leathern, } أَسْيَار سَيْرَة *pl.* سُيُور.

Leather, *v.t.* To cover with —, جَلَّدَ. To beat, ‹ جَلَدَ — ضَرَبَ — ‹ نَزَلَ بِ.

Leather-dresser, *n.* جُلُودِيّ — دَبَّاغ *pl.* دَبَّاغُونَ *and* دَبَّاغَة.

Leather-dressing, *n.* دِبَاغَة.

Leave, *n.* Permission, إِذْن — إِجَازَة — رُخْصَة — اِسْتِئْذَان — دُسْتُور. Farewell, وِدَاع. Leave, holiday, as from school, بَطَالَة.

By your leave, بِدُسْتُورِكَ — عَنْ إِذْنِكَ.

On leave, مُرَخَّصٌ لِوَقْتٍ.

On sick leave, مُرَخَّصٌ لِوَقْتٍ بِعِلَّةِ ٱلْمَرَضِ.

To ask leave of, اِسْتَأْذَنَ.

To give leave to, to permit, ‹ أَذِنَ لِ-فِي — رَخَّصَ لِ-فِي. I gave him leave to trade, أَذِنْتُ لَهُ فِي ٱلتِّجَارَةِ.

To take French leave, تَطَفَّشَ — ‹ غَابَ بِدُونِ إِذْنٍ.

To take leave of, to bid farewell to, وَدَّعَ — وَادَعَ. To take permission, تَرَخَّصَ.

Leave, *v.t.* To separate from, فَاصَلَ — فَارَقَ — تَارَكَ. To depart from, ‹ طَلَعَ — ‹ بَرِحَ — ‹ زَالَ مِن — سَافَرَ عَن — ‹ رَحَلَ عَن تَخَلَّى — ‹ تَرَكَ — ‹ رَجَعَ عَن — ‹ مَضَى مِن — عَن. To relinquish, تَجَرَّدَ ‹ فَاتَ — عَن. To abandon, ‹ هَجَرَ. To quit, as a service, عَن. To —, as property, خَلَّفَ. To —, as heat or cold, ‹ سَقَطَ عَن. To —, as a fever, أَقْلَعَ عَن. To — one's country, تَغَرَّبَ — هَاجَرَ. To — to, bequeath to, — وَصَّى لِ-بِ ‹ عَهِدَ إِلَى — خَلَّفَ-بِوَصِيَّةٍ. To separate one's self from, اِنْفَصَلَ مِن. To —, to let remain till…, أَبْقَى-إِلَى; to suffer to remain, اِسْتَبْقَى. To —, as a remainder of anything, — أَفْضَلَ مِن اِسْتَفْضَلَ مِن. I will never — you, and never forsake you, لَا أُهْمِلُكَ وَلَا أَتْرُكُكَ أَبَدًا. I left my affair in his hands, سَوَّفْتُهُ أَمْرِي — سَوَّمْتُهُ أَمْرِي. The fever left him, أَخْطَفَتْهُ ٱلْحُمَّى — زَالَتْ عَنْهُ ٱلْحُمَّى. He died leaving a brother and sister, مَاتَ عَنْ أَخٍ وَأُخْتٍ. She died leaving brothers, مَاتَتْ

أَوْرَثَهُ عَنْ إِخْوَتِهِ. He left it (as an inheritance) to his children, أَوْلَادَهُ. All that the hail had left, كُلُّ مَا تَرَكَهُ ٱلْبَرَدُ. They left the sheep with a keeper, تَرَكُوا ٱلْغَنَمَ مَعَ حارِسٍ. To be left till called for, يُحْفَظُ إِلَى حِينِ ٱلطَّلَبِ.

To leave about, as in a litter, خَلَّى-مُبَدَّدًا ـ خَلَّى-بَدَادِ.

To leave alone, to neglect, جَهِلَ ب ـ سَيَّبَ. To — by one self, تَخَلَّى عَن ـ خَلَّى ـ تَرَكَ-وَحْدَهُ. Not to meddle with, كَفَّ عَن. He was left alone, بَقِيَ وَحْدَهُ. Leave me alone, أُتْرُكْنِي ـ كُفَّ عَنِّي. If we leave him alone, إِنْ تَرَكْنَاهُ وَحْدَهُ.

He left him alone, did not meddle with him, خَلَّاهُ ـ خَلَّى عَنْهُ.

He left him alone to do as he chose, أَجَرَّهُ رَسَنَهُ.

To leave behind, to be before one, سَبَقَ. To leave behind, as at a place, تَرَكَ.

To leave it to one, to empower, صَرَّفَ-بِ ـ فَوَّضَ-إِلَى ـ فَسَّحَ لِ.

To leave off, not to put on, تَخَلَّى عَن ـ شَلَحَ. To discontinue, بَطَّلَ ـ تَرَكَ ـ إِنْقَطَعَ عَن ـ كَفَّ عَن. He left off numbering, تَرَكَ ٱلْعَدَدَ. He left off speaking, فَرَغَ مِنَ ٱلْكَلَامِ.

He left off doing kindness to him, تَرَكَ ٱلْمَعْرُوفَ مَعَهُ. Since we left off, مِنْ حِينِ كَفَفْنَا. *See also to* Cease, *v.i.*

To leave out, omit, تَرَكَ ـ أَسْقَطَ ـ ضَرَبَ عَن. To leave out, as in a reckoning, أَوْهَمَ-مِنَ ٱلْحِسَابِ ـ أَوْهَمَ. To — outside, خَلَّى-خارِجًا ـ تَرَكَ-خارِجًا.

To leave over, some part of, أَبْقَى مِن. What was left (over) of the food, ما فَضَلَ مِنَ ٱلطَّعَامِ.

To leave to one's self, to his own way, أَجَرَّهُ ـ أَطْلَقَ-إِلَى هَوَاهُ ـ رَسَنَهُ.

To leave with, to deposit with one, وَضَعَ-عِنْدَهُ *aor.* يَضَعُ ـ سَلَّمَ-إِلَيْهِ.

Leave, *v.i.* To start, to go away, ذَهَبَ ـ إِنْطَلَقَ ـ سَافَرَ ـ مَضَى. To leave off, بَطَّلَ ـ تَمَّ ـ إِنْقَطَعَ.

Leaved, *a.* Having foliage, وَارِق ـ وَرِيق ـ وَرِق. Having folds, as a door, ذو رَوَاجِعَ ـ ذو مِصْرَاعٍ; as a table, خِوَانٌ ذو وَصْلَاتٍ ـ خِوَانٌ مُرَكَّبٌ مِن وَصْلَاتٍ.

Leaven, *n.* خَمِيرَة ـ خَمِير ـ خُمْرَة.

Leaven, *v.t.* خَمَّرَ ـ خَمَرَ. To mingle with, خَالَطَ ـ خَامَرَ. He leavened his action with the leaven of zeal, خَمَّرَ عَمَلَهُ خَمِيرَةَ ٱلْغَيْرَةِ. To become leavened, إِخْتَمَرَ. He leavened the dough, خَمَّرَ ٱلْعَجِينَ.

Leavened, *a.* مُخَمَّر ـ خَمِير. Leavened bread, خُبْزٌ خَمِيرٌ. Unleavened bread, فَطِير.

Leavening, *n.* *See* Leaven, *n.*

Leavings, *n.* تَلَاوَة ـ فَضَلَات ـ فِضَال ـ بَقِيَّات ـ فُضُول.

Lecher, *n.* / Lecherous, *a.* } فاسِق ـ نَيَّاك ـ مِغْلِيم ـ غَلِم ـ شَبِق. To be —, فَسَقَ ـ شَبِقَ.

Lecherously, *ad.* بِفِسْقٍ وَفَسَادٍ ـ بِغُلْمَةٍ ـ بِشَبَقٍ.

Lecherousness, *n.* / Lechery, } فِسْق وَفَسَاد ـ غُلْمَة ـ شَبَق.

Lectern, *n.* *See* Lecturn, *n.*

Lection, *n.* A reading, قِرَاءَة ـ تِلَاوَة ـ قِرَة ـ قُرْآن. Difference in copies, إِخْتِلَاف *pl.* إِخْتِلَافَات. A copy, نُسْخَة *pl.* نُسَخ. A chapter, فَصْل *pl.* فُصُول.

Lectionary, *n.* كِتَابُ قِرَاءَاتٍ.

Lecture, *n.* A speech, harangue, خُطْبَة *pl.* خُطَب ـ مُخَاطَبَة ـ مَقَالَة ـ خِطَاب. A sermon, exhortation, خُطْبَة ـ وَعْظ ـ مَوْعِظَة. A reproof, تَوْبِيخ ـ كَرْز ـ نَصِيحَة ـ سَخْطَة. A public —, دَرْسٌ عامٌّ *pl.* دُرُوس ـ تَدْرِيس. A course of lectures, أَعْطَى دُرُوسًا عامَّةً مُتَتَابِعَةً. To give a course of public lectures, Recitation, عَرْض.

Lecture, *v.t.* To instruct, عَلَّمَ ـ دَرَّسَ. To reprimand, وَبَّخَ ـ سَخِطَ عَلَى ـ عاتَبَ.

Lecture, *v.i.* To deliver lectures, to teach, عَلَّمَ ـ دَرَّسَ. To — on, تَكَلَّمَ عَن ـ قَصَّ عَن ـ حَدَّثَ عَن. To sermonize, وَعَظَ *aor.* يَعِظُ.

Lecturer, *n.* An orator, reader, خَطِيب *pl.* خُطَبَاء ـ خَاطِب ـ قارِئٌ *pl.* قُرَّاء ـ مُدَرِّس. A preacher, وَاعِظ.

Lecture-room, *n.* مَحَلُّ ٱلدَّرْسِ ـ مَحَلُّ ٱلتَّدْرِيسِ ـ مَخْطَب.

Lectureship, *n.* مَأْمُورِيَّة ـ خِدْمَةُ ٱلْمُدَرِّسِ ـ وَظِيفَةُ ٱلْخَطِيبِ ـ ٱلتَّدْرِيسِ.

Lecturn, *n.* رَحْل *pl.* رِحَال ـ مَسْنَدُ كِتَابٍ. (In Christian churches in the East it is called, جَوْقَة *or* كُوي.) The — for the Kurân is called, رَحْلُ ٱلْمُصْحَفِ.

Led, *part. of to* Lead, *q.v.* A led horse, جَنِيبَة *pl.* جَنَائِب.

Ledge, *n.* A layer, طَبَقَة *pl.* طَبَقَات. A shelf, رَفّ *pl.* رُفُوف. A projecting —, طَنَف ـ كُنَّة. A ridge, brow, حَرْف *pl.* حُرُوف. A — of a mountain, شَاقٍ *pl.* شَوَاقٍ ـ حَيْد *pl.* حُيُود ـ طَنَف *pl.* أَطْنَاف ـ رَيْد *pl.* رُيُود. A — of rocks, رَصْفَة ـ رَصَف *pl.* رِصَاف ـ رُصُف. The — of a window, حَاجِبُ ٱلطَّاقَةِ *pl.* حَوَاجِب. A rim, border, حاجِب *pl.* حَوَاجِب.

Ledger, *n.* Of a book, دَفْتَرُ حِسَابٍ. A large flat slab, صَفِيح *pl.* صَفَائِح ـ صَفِيحَة *pl.* صُفَّاح. Ledgers of wood, صَفَائِحُ خَشَبٍ.

Lee, *n.* The opposite side to the wind, تحت ـ سُفالة الرِّيح. A place of shelter, جناح ـ مأواة ـ مأوى. I am under his —, أنا في جناحه.

Lee-gage, *n.* *See* Leeward, *n.*

Leech, *n.* The animal, علقة *coll.* علق ـ سلع *pl.* سلعة. A physician, طبيب *pl.* أطبّاء. To put on leeches, أعلق. The — took (on him), علقت العلقة به. The horse has a — in his mouth, الفرس معلق.

Leech, *v.t.* To treat, as a physician, عالج ـ داوى. To apply leeches; *see preceding article.*

Leechline, *n.* A rope to take in sail, حبلة ـ جندريسى البركاتة.

Lee-lurch, *n.* خنخ إلى سفالة الريح.

Leek, *n.* كرّاث.

Leer, *n.* ترميق ـ رمق ـ كشرة ـ كشر.

Leer, *v.i.* أضحك ـ كشر. To — at, رمق ـ رامق ـ رمق. To despise, استحقر ـ استقلّ.

Leeringly, *ad.* بكشرة ـ باستقلال ـ برمق ـ بكشر.

Lees, *n.* عكر ـ ثفل ـ دُردِيّ ـ نطل. Wine —, طين (*or*) عكر. Oil —, دُردِيّ (*or*) طحل الزيت. النبيذ.

Lee-shore, *n.* ساحل في سفالة الريح.

Leeward, *a.* and *ad.* أسفل الريح. The — side, السفالة. On the — side, في سفالة الريح.

Leeway, *n.* حيد نحو سفالة ـ حيد عن الطريق ـ انحراف الريح.

Left, *pret. of to* Leave, *q.v.*

Left, *a.* and *ad.* Opposite to the right, يسار ـ يسار ـ شمال *pl.* يسر *and* يسرة ـ أيسر. The — hand, اليسرة ـ الياسر ـ الأيسر ـ الشمال *pl.* أشمل *and* شمائل. The — hand side, الياسر ـ الأيسر ـ الشمال ـ اليسار ـ اليسرة ـ اليسار. On the — hand side, يسارا ـ يسرا. To the right and —, يمينا ويسارا. In the direction of the — side, ذات الشمال. To take one in the — side, شمل ب. The — wing of an army, ميسرة الجيش. The — bank of a river, مجرى النهر الأيسر.

Left-handed, *a.* أعفك ـ أعسر *fem.* عسراء ـ أشول. To be —, عسر. *See also* Awkward, *n.*

Left-handedness, *n.* عسر.

Leg, *n.* Of a human being, رجل *pl.* أرجل ـ ساق *pl.* سيقان. The fore leg of an animal, ذراع ـ يد *dual* يدان. The hind leg of a quadruped, رجل *pl.* أرجل *dual.* رجلان. Legs, generally, مشاة. The legs of a quadruped, ذريعات ـ مذارع. The legs of a horse, أربعة الحصان ـ قوائم الحصان. The leg of a bird, فخذ *pl.* أفخاذ; of a boot, ساق; of a table, *etc.*, رجل *pl.* أرجل ـ قائمة *pl.* قوائم. A base, stand, قعر ـ قاعدة ـ عمود. A side, as of a triangle, زاوية *pl.* زوايا. Having long legs, سوّاق. Not to have a leg to stand on, as in argument, قطع لسانه.

To be on one's legs, to stand, قام ـ نهض ـ انتهض; to make a speech, ألقى مقالة.

To be on its last legs, to draw to an end, قرب من الانتهاء ـ مال إلى الزوال.

To be on one's last legs, to be near to death, أشرف على الموت.

To catch by the leg, ارتجل.

To get on one's legs again, to recover, اشتفى ـ انجبر ـ انجبر ـ تجبّر. To recover one's former position, استشفى.

To stand on one's own legs, to be independent, قام بذاته ـ استغنى عن غيره.

Leg-rest, *n.* مسند للرجل.

Legacy, *n.* خلف موصى ـ وصيّ ـ وصيّة *pl.* وصايا. A pious —, وقف *pl.* أوقاف. To leave a — to, وصّى ل ـ ب. *See also to* Endow, *v.t.*

Legal, *a.* Laid down by law, مشروع. According to law, متعلق ـ قانوني ـ نظامي ـ شرعي. Pertaining to the law, شرعي ـ مبني على الشرع. Founded on law, بالشرع. Permissible, مأذون ـ جائز ـ مباح. Legal measures, أسباب ووسائط قانونية. A — act, معاملة قانونية. A — sale, بيع صحيح. To give a — form to, طبّق ـ حسب الأصول القانونية. The — profession, الطريقة العلمية ـ أصحاب الطريقة العلمية ـ أهل الشرع. *See also* Lawful, *a.*

Legality, *n.* The being according to law, حلال ـ حلّ; the being permissible, عدم امتناع ـ جواز ـ إباحة. To contest the — of, أنكر حلال الأمر.

Legalize, *v.t.* To make conformable to law, جعل ـ طبّق ـ وفّق ـ بالقوانين ـ الشريعة. To attest officially, صدّق ـ رسما ـ صحّح ـ رسما. To make lawful, أباح.

Legally, *ad.* حسب القوانين ـ حسب الشرع ـ شرعا ـ نظاما. Legally ordained, حسب القوانين مرسوم (*or*) مثبت.

Legate, *n.* A representative of the Pope, قاصد رسولي ـ نائب البابا.

Legatee, *n.* وارث بوصية ـ الموصى له. Residuary —, وارث حاصر.

Legateship, *n.* نيابة عن البابا.

Legatine, *n.* متعلق بنيابة البابا.

Legation, *n.* سِفَارَة. Secretary of —, كَاتِبُ سِرِّ سِفَارَةٍ. The personnel of a —, مَأْمُورِيَّةُ سِفَارَةٍ. The residence of a —, دَارُ سِفَارَةٍ.

Legato, *a.* تَنْبِيهٌ لِلْعَازِفِينَ بِخَفْضِ ٱلصَّوْتِ.

Legator, *n.* وَصِيٌّ *pl.* أَوْصِيَآءُ.

Leg-bail, *n.* فِرَارٌ مِنَ ٱلْحَبْسِ (or مِنَ ٱلضَّبْطِيَّةِ).

Legend, *n.* The inscription on a coin, *etc.*, كِتَابَةٌ — عُنْوَانُ سِكَّةٍ — عُنْوَان. A chronicle, تَارِيخٌ *pl.* تَوَارِيخُ — خَبَرٌ *pl.* أَخْبَار. A tale, قِصَّةٌ *pl.* قِصَص — حَدِيثٌ *pl.* أَحَادِيثُ. A fable, أُسْطُورَة *pl.* أَسَاطِيرُ — خُرَافَة *pl.* خُرَافَات. *See also* Fable, *n.*

Legendary, *a.* Consisting of tales, مُحَدَّث. Fabulous, أَسَاطِيرِيٌّ — خُرَافِيٌّ.

Legerdemain, *n.* شَعْوَذَة (*vulg.* شعبثة). One who practises —, مُشَعْوِذ — أَبُو ٱلْعَجَبِ. *See also* Jugglery, Juggler, *n.*

Legged, *a.* ذُو سِيقَانٍ. Two —, ذُو رِجْلَيْنِ — ذُو سَاقَيْنِ. Long —, أَرْجَلُ — سُوَّاق — أَسْوَقُ.

Leggin, Legging, *n.* جَوْرَبٌ لِلرِّجْلَيْنِ; a single —, جَوْرَبَة. Leggins, طَمَاقَات.

Legibility, *n.* } The quality of being legible, سُهُولَةُ ٱلْقِرَآءَةِ; of
Legibleness, } being decipherable, سُهُولَةُ ٱلْاِسْتِخْرَاجِ — إِنْحِلَال — سُهُولَةُ فَكِّ تَعْقِيدِ ٱلشَّيْءِ.

Legible, *a.* That can be read, يُقْرَأُ. Decipherable, يَنْحَلُّ — قَابِلُ ٱلتَّفْسِيرِ — يُسْتَخْرَجُ.

Legibly, *ad.* بِتَصْرِيحٍ — بِصَرَاحَةٍ — بَيِّنًا.

Legion, *n.* فَيْلَق *pl.* فَيَالِقُ — جَيْش *pl.* جُيُوش — جَوْقَة *pl.* أَجْوَاق — طَابُور *pl.* طَوَابِيرُ. The Order of the Legion of Honour, نِيشَانُ ٱللِّيجُون دُونُور.

Legionary, *n.* One of a legion, مِنْ أَنْفَارِ ٱلطَّابُورِ — جَيْشِيٌّ.

Legionary, *a.* مُتَعَلِّقٌ بِٱلطَّابُورِ — مُخْتَصٌّ بِٱلْجَيْشِ — جَيْشِيٌّ.

Legislate, *v.i.* سَنَّ ² — شَرَعَ ² — وَضَعَ قَانُونًا *aor.* يَضَعُ. He legislated, or enacted a law, for them, سَنَّ لَهُمْ — شَرَعَ لَهُمْ شَرْعًا سُنَّةً. *See also to* Administer, Enact, *v.t.*

Legislation, *n.* The act of making laws, وَضْعُ قَوَانِينَ. The laws laid down, ٱلْقَوَانِينُ ٱلْمَوْضُوعَة. The right of —, حَقُّ وَضْعِ ٱلْقَوَانِينِ. To reform the —, أَصْلَحَ ٱلنِّظَامَاتِ ٱلْمَوْجُودَةَ.

Legislative, *a.* نِظَامِيٌّ — قَانُونِيٌّ — اِشْتِرَاعِيٌّ. Legislative power, سُلْطَانٌ عَلَى وَضْعِ ٱلْقَوَانِينِ — قُوَّة قَانُونِيَّة. Legislative measures, تَدَابِيرُ تَنْظِيمِيَّة. A — section, دَائِرَةُ ٱلْقَوَانِينِ. A — assembly, مَجْلِس نِظَامِيَّة.

Legislator, *n.* مُشْتَرِع *pl.* مُشْتَرِعُونَ — وَاضِعُ ٱلشَّرَائِعِ — وَاضِعُ قَوَانِينَ.

Legislatorship, *n.* وَظِيفَةُ ٱلْمُشْتَرِعِ.

Legislature, *n.* أَصْحَابُ ٱلشَّرَائِعِ — دِيوَانُ أَعْضَآءِ مَجْلِسِ ٱلْقَوَانِينِ. A sitting of the —, جَلْسَة (or مُدَّةُ جُلُوسِ or مُذَاكَرَةُ) مَجْلِسِ ٱلْقَوَانِينِ.

Legist, *n.* فَقِيه *pl.* فُقَهَآءُ — مِنْ أَهْلِ ٱلْفِقْهِ.

Legitimacy, *n.* Lawfulness, حِلٌّ — حَلَال — جَوَاز. Lawful birth, حَلَال. Correctness and propriety, صِحَّة وَمُنَاسَبَة. Rightfulness, صَوَاب — صِحَّة — حَقٌّ.

Legitimate, *a.* According to law, جَائِزٌ حَسَبَ ٱلْقَوَانِينِ — شَرْعِيٌّ — مُطَابِقُ ٱلْقَوَانِينِ. Born in lawful marriage, حَلَال. Real, true, صَحِيح — حَقٌّ. In accordance with what is right, حَسَبَ ٱلْإِنْصَافِ. Legitimate authority or government, حُكُومَة مُحَقَّقَة. A — sovereign, حَاكِمٌ شَرْعِيٌّ. A — cause, سَبَبٌ مَشْرُوعٌ. A — marriage, نِكَاحٌ مَقْبُولٌ شَرْعًا — نِكَاحٌ أُصُولِيٌّ. A — child, اِبْنُ حَلَالٍ. A — wife, حَلِيلَة. Legitimate measures, أَسْبَاب مَشْرُوعَة.

Legitimate, *v.t.* To make lawful or allowable, حَلَّلَ — أَحَلَّ. To — a child, حَلَّلَ ٱلنَّغِيلَ وَأَلْحَقَهُ بِٱلنَّسَبِ ².

Legitimately, *ad.* Lawfully, حَسَبَ — حَسَبَ ٱلْقَوَانِينِ — بِصُورَةٍ شَرْعِيَّةٍ — نِظَامًا — قَانُونًا — شَرْعًا — ٱلْقَانُونِ. Genuinely, حَقًّا — بِٱلْحَلَالِ — بِٱلْحَقِّ.

Legitimateness, *n.* *See* Legitimacy, *n.*

Legitimation, *n.* The act of making lawful, تَحْلِيل; of confirming, proving, تَحْقِيق. The — of a child, تَحْلِيلُ ٱلْوَلَدِ — تَحْلِيلُ وَلَدٍ شَرْعًا — بَعْدَ مَا كَانَ نَغِيلًا وَإِلْحَاقُهُ بِٱلنَّسَبِ.

Legitimist, *n.* One who holds with the royalist party, مُتَعَصِّب لِحِزْبِ ٱلسُّلْطَانِ — مُتَعَصِّبٌ لِسِلْسِلَةِ ٱلْمُلُوكِ.

Legume, *n.* A vegetable, بَقْل *pl.* بُقُول — خُضَارَة *pl.* خُضْرَاوَات — قِطْنِيَّة *pl.* قَطَانِيّ.

Leguminous, *a.* بُقُولِيٌّ.

Leisure, *n.* فَضَآءٌ — فَضَاوَة — فَرَاغ — هَوْن — تَخَلٍّ مِنَ ٱلشُّغْلِ — وَقْت تَخَلُّعٍ مِنَ ٱلشُّغْلِ. To be at —, تَفَرَّغَ مِنَ ٱلشُّغْلِ — تَفَصَّى. To be at — from, تَفَرَّغَ مِنْ — فَرَغَ ² مِنْ. Walk at your —, اِمْشِ عَلَى هَوْنِكَ. At his —, عَلَى مَهْلِهِ. They had no —, or opportunity, to write, لَمْ تَتَيَسَّرْ لَهُمْ فُرْصَةٌ لِلْكِتَابَةِ.

Leisure, *a.* خَالٍ — فَاضٍ — فَارِغ. A — day, يَوْمٌ فَاضٍ.

Leisurely, *ad.* عَلَى مَهْلٍ — مَهْلًا — رُوَيْدًا. To look into a thing —, تَرَوَّى (or رَوَّى) فِي ٱلْأَمْرِ.

Lemma, *n.* A previous proposition, مَوْضُوعٌ سَابِقٌ.

Lemon, *n.* لَيْمُون *pl.* لَيْمُونَات. Lemon-peel, قِشْرُ ٱللَّيْمُونِ.

Lemon juice, عَصِيرُ لَيْمُونٍ. Candied —, مُرَبَّى لَيْمُونٍ. Lemon plant, verbena, أَكْمُوبْرَان ـ بَارِسْطَارِيُون ـ رَعَى ٱلْحَمَامِ ـ بَرْبِيْنَا. A — tree, شَجَرَةُ ٱللَّيْمُونِ.

Lemonade, *n.* لَيْمُونَاتَةٌ ـ شَرَابُ ٱللَّيْمُونِ.

Lemur, *n.* A Madagascar monkey, قِرْدُ جَزِيرَةِ بُوكِيسَ (أَيْ مَدَغَشْكَر).

Lend, *v.t.* سَلَّفَ ـ أَسْلَفَ ـ أَرْهَنَ ـ عَوَّرَ ـ أَعَارَ. To — one money, أَقْرَضَ ـ دَيَّنَ. To —, on condition of receiving part of the profits, قَارَضَ. To — at interest, رَابَحَ ـ أَقْرَضَ. To — at usury, سَلَّفَ بِٱلْفَائِدَةِ ـ رَابَى. To ask one to — money, تَدَيَّنَ مِنْ ـ إِسْتَقْرَضَ مِنْ. Lend me, سَلِّفْنِي ـ أَقْرِضْنِي.

To lend to on usury, أَقْرَضَ بِرِبَآءٍ.

To lend one's self to, to labour or strive in, سَعَى فِي *aor.* يَسْعَى; to lend one's self to another in a matter, تَسَبَّبَ لَهُ فِي ٱلْأَمْرِ.

To lend aid to, أَعَانَ ـ سَاعَدَ ـ أَغَاثَ.

To lend ear to, to listen to, سَمِعَ ل ـ إِسْتَمَعَ ل ـ أَصْغَى إِلَى ـ ٥.

Lendable, *a.* مِمَّا يُعَارُ ـ مِمَّا يُسَلَّفُ.

Lender, *n.* سَلَّافٌ ـ مُقْرِضٌ ـ قَرَّاضٌ. A money —, مِدْيَانٌ.

Lending, *n.* The act of —, or the thing lent, سَلَفٌ ـ سَلَفَةٌ ـ قَرْضَةٌ ـ قَرْضٌ.

Length, *n.* Extent from end to end, طُولٌ. Distance, مَسَافَةٌ. A portion of time, مُدَّةٌ. Extension, إِمْتِدَادٌ ـ سَعَةٌ ـ إِنْبِسَاطٌ. Length of days, طُولُ ٱلْعُمْرِ. Its — is about . . . , طُولُهُ قَدْرَ كَذَا.

Length and breadth, طُولٌ وَعَرْضٌ.

At great length, in detail, مُفَصَّلًا ـ تَفْصِيلًا.

At length, at last, أَخِيرًا ـ عَاقِبَةً. Profusely, in detail, تَفْصِيلًا.

Full length portrait, صُورَةٌ طُولَ ٱلشَّخْصِ.

Half length portrait, صُورَةٌ لِحَدِّ ٱلْوَسَطِ ـ صُورَةٌ لِحَدِّ ٱلْحِزَامِ.

In length and breadth, طُولًا وَعَرْضًا.

To lie at length, إِنْبَطَحَ ـ تَبَطَّحَ.

Lengthen, *v.t.* To make longer, طَوَّلَ ـ أَطَالَ. To stretch out, جَذَبَ ـ ٥ إِجْتَذَبَ ـ مَدَّ ٢ ـ مَطَّ ٢ ـ بَسَطَ ٢.

Lengthen, *v.i.* To grow long, طَالَ ٢ ـ إِسْتَطَالَ. To become stretched out, إِمْتَدَّ. To —, as the days, تَنَفَّسَ.

Lengthening, *n.* The act of making long, تَطْوِيلٌ ـ إِطَالَةٌ. Delay, مُهْلَةٌ. Extension, مَدٌّ ـ إِمْتِدَادٌ. Lengthening, as of the days, تَنَفُّسٌ.

Lengthily, *ad.* بِٱلتَّطْوِيلِ ـ تَفْصِيلًا ـ بِإِطْنَابٍ ـ بِٱلتَّسْيِيبِ فِي ٱلْكَلَامِ.

Lengthiness, *n.* طُولٌ ـ تَطْوِيلٌ.

Lengthways, *ad.* } Lengthwise, } بِٱلطُّولِ ـ طُولًا. He cut it —, قَطَعَهُ طُولًا.

Lengthy, *a.* طَوِيلٌ ـ مُفَصَّلٌ.

Leniency, *n.* } Lenity, } لَيَانٌ ـ لِينَةٌ ـ مُلَاءَمَةٌ ـ مُسَامَحَةٌ ـ شَفَقَةٌ ـ مَرْحَمَةٌ. To treat one with —, تَسَمَّحَ بِ.

Lenient, *n.* Having the quality of mildness, لَيِّنٌ ـ مُلَائِمٌ ـ مُسَامِحٌ ـ أَهْلُ سَمَاحٍ ـ شَفِيقٌ.

Leniently, *ad.* بِلِيَانَةٍ ـ بِمُسَامَحَةٍ ـ بِشَفَقَةٍ.

Lenitive, *a.* مُلَيِّنٌ.

Lenitive, *n.* دَوَآءٌ مُلَيِّنٌ.

Lens, *n.* A transparent substance, جِسْمٌ شَفَّافٌ. A glass, زُجَاجَةٌ ـ بِلَّوْرَةٌ ـ قِزَازَةٌ. The lens of the eye, (خَرَزَةٌ *or*) حَدَقَةُ ٱلْعَيْنِ.

Concavo-convex lens, بِلَّوْرَةٌ بِوَجْهٍ مُقَعَّرٍ وَوَجْهٍ مُحَدَّبٍ.

Double-concave lens, بِلَّوْرَةٌ مُقَعَّرَةُ ٱلْوَجْهَيْنِ.

Double-convex lens, بِلَّوْرَةٌ مُحَدَّبَةُ ٱلْوَجْهَيْنِ ـ قِزَازَةٌ عَدَسِيَّةُ ٱلشَّكْلِ.

Plano-concave lens, بِلَّوْرَةٌ وَجْهُهَا مُسَطَّحٌ وَقَفَاهَا مُقَعَّرٌ.

Plano-convex lens, بِلَّوْرَةٌ وَجْهُهَا مُسَطَّحٌ وَقَفَاهَا مُحَدَّبٌ.

Lent, *part. of* Lend, مُسْتَعَارٌ ـ مُسَلَّفٌ ـ مَسْلُوفٌ. Lent money, قَرْضٌ *pl.* قُرُوضٌ.

Lent, *n.* The season of, ٱلصَّوْمُ ٱلْكَبِيرُ ـ صَوْمُ ٱلْأَرْبَعِينَ.

Lenten, *n.* مُتَعَلِّقٌ بِٱلصَّوْمِ ٱلْكَبِيرِ.

Lenticular, *a.* } Lentiform, } شَلْجَمِيٌّ ـ عَدَسِيٌّ ـ بِشَكْلِ عَدَسَةٍ.

Lentil, *n.* عَدَسَةٌ *coll.* عَدَسٌ. A dish made of lentils and rice, مُجَدَّرَةٌ. Lentil broth, عَدَسِيَّةٌ.

Lentiscus, *n.* } Lentisk, } The tree, ضِرْوٌ ـ شَجَرَةُ ٱلْمُصْطَكَآءِ ـ كُمْكَام.

Leo, *n.* The constellation, بُرْجُ ٱلْأَسَدِ.

Leonine, *a.* Of the lion, أَسَدِيٌّ ـ سِبَاعِيٌّ.

Leopard, *n.* الأَزْرَقُ ـ الأَبْرَدُ. The spotted —, نَمِرٌ *pl.* نُمْرٌ *and* نِمَارٌ *and* أَنْمَارٌ.

Leper, *n.* } Leprous, *a.* } أَبْرَصُ ـ مُجَذَّمٌ ـ مَجْذُومٌ ـ مُبْتَلَى. A — hand, يَدٌ بَرْصَآءُ. *See also under* Leprosy, *n.*

Lepidoptera, *n.* دُوَيْبَّاتٌ مِنْ جِنْسِ ٱلْفَرَاشِ ـ حَشَرَاتٌ مِنْ جِنْسِ ٱلْبِشَارَةِ.

Leporine, *a.* أَرْنَبِيٌّ ـ مُخْتَصٌّ بِٱلْأَرْنَبِ.

Leprosy, *n.* بَرَصٌ ـ جُذَامٌ ـ بَلَآءٌ. To have the —, بَرِصَ ٤ ـ جُذِمَ. To afflict with —, أَبْرَصَ.

Leprous, *a.* *See* Leper, *n.*

Lepus, *n.* The constellation, ٱلْأَرْنَبَة.

Lesion, *n.* جُرْح ـ خَلَل ـ مَضَرَّة ـ ضَرَر.

Less, *a.* Smaller, أَصْغَر. Less in number, أَقَلّ ـ أَدْنَى. Less, lighter, أَخَفّ. John the Less, يُوحَنَّا ٱلْأَصْغَر. Below, under, أَسْفَل ـ تَحْتَ ـ دُونَ. Less than the least, أَصْغَرُ ٱلْجَمِيع. Neither — in number than that nor more, لا أَدْنَى مِنْ ذٰلِكَ وَلا أَكْثَر (*Kur.* lviii. 8.)

Less, *ad.* أَقَلّ. Less learned, أَقَلّ عِلْمًا. Less than, دُونَ. There is one —, wanting, يَنْقُصُ وَاحِدٌ. In — time, فِي أَقْرَب مُدَّة. Not — than that, لا أَقَلّ مِنْ ذٰلِكَ. The more I love you the — I am loved, كُلَّمَا أَحْبَبْتُكُمْ أَكْثَرَ أُحَبُّ أَقَلّ. In the course of a year, or —, if possible, فِي ظَرْفِ سَنَةٍ أَوْ أَقَلّ إِنْ أَمْكَنَ. What he has is not — than . . . , ٱلَّذِي لَهُ لا يَنْقُصُ عَنْ كَذَا.

Lessee, *n.* مُسْتَكْرٍ ـ مُسْتَأْجِر.

Lessen, *v.t.* To make smaller, صَغَّرَ ـ أَصْغَرَ. To — in number, قَلَّلَ ـ أَقَلَّ; in dignity or temper, أَغَضَّ ـ ٢ غَضَّ. To make less heavy, to lighten, أَخَفَّ ـ خَفَّفَ. To diminish, غَضْغَضَ ـ أَنْقَصَ ـ نَقَّصَ ـ ٢ غَضَّ. To bring down, to abate, أَسْقَطَ ـ أَنْزَلَ ـ نَزَّلَ. To abase, ضَعْضَعَ ـ خَفَّضَ ـ ٢. To — the voice, خَفَضَ صَوْتَهُ ـ ٢. *See also to* Diminish, Lower, *v.t.*

Lessen, *v.i.* To become less, in size, صَغُرَ ٢. To become less in number, قَلَّ ـ ٢. To become less heavy, lighter, خَفَّ ـ ٢. To diminish, become wanting, إِنْتَقَصَ ـ ٢ نَقَصَ ـ تَغَضْغَضَ.

Lesser, *a.* *See* Less, *a.* Lesser Asia, أَنَاطُول ـ آسِيَا ٱلصُّغْرَى.

Lesson, *n.* An instruction given, تَعْلِيم ـ تَدْرِيس. Something given one to learn, مِثَالَة. An admonition, عِظَة ـ وَعْظ ـ تَنْبِيه ـ مَوْعِظَة. An example, عِبْرَة ـ مُثْلَة. Correction, chastisement, تَوْبِيخ ـ تَأْدِيب. A boy's — for the day, سَبَق *pl.* أَسْبَاق ـ إِمَام. To give a —, instruction, to, دَرَّسَ ـ أَقْرَأَ. To take lessons of, from, such an one, ٢ دَرَسَ عَلَى فُلَانٍ ـ قَرَأَ عَلَى فُلَانٍ. To learn a —, ٢ دَرَسَ. He has attended my lessons assiduously, وَاظَبَ عَلَى تَدْرِيسِي. He learnt a — from the past, *or*) تَذَكَّرَ (إِتَّعَظَ *or* إِعْتَبَرَ) بِمَا مَضَى. This will be a —, example, to others, يَكُونُ عِبْرَةً لِمَنْ يَعْتَبِرُ. The money paid for a —, (experience,) is not lost money, (*prov.*) لَمْ يَضِعْ مِنْ مَالِكَ مَا وَعَظَكَ.

Lessor, *n.* كَرِيّ ـ مُؤَجِّر.

Lest, *conj.* لِئَلَّا ـ كَيْلا ـ خِشْيَةَ أَنْ ـ خَوْفًا مِنْ ـ خِيفَةَ أَنْ. Lest he should get the advantage of you, لِئَلَّا يَطْمَعَ فِيكُمْ. Lest we omit it, لِئَلَّا نَفُوتَهُ.

Let, *v.t.* To give leave to, أَذِنَ لِ ـ رَخَّصَ لِ ـ فَسَحَ لِ ـ ٢. To lease, let on hire, أَكْرَى ـ ٢ كَرَى ـ ٢ أَجَرَ ـ كَارَى. "To be let," as of a house, لِلْكِرَاءِ. They may let their lands, لَهُمْ أَنْ يُؤَجِّرُوا أَرَاضِيَهُمْ. To let, in the sense of that, لِ: Let him stand at his right hand, لِيَقِفْ عَنْ يَمِينِهِ. *See also to* Hinder, *v.t.* To let alone, تَرَكَ ـ ٢ كَفَّ عَنْ ٢. Let me alone, أُكْفُفْ عَنِّي. Let ye them alone, أُتْرُكُوهُمْ. Let thou us alone, أُتْرُكْنَا ـ مَا لَنَا وَلَكَ. Let it — this year also, أُتْرُكْهَا هٰذِهِ ٱلسَّنَةَ أَيْضًا. He let him alone, to do as he would, أَجَرَّهُ رَسَنَهُ.

To let blood, to bleed, فَصَدَ ـ ٢. To be bled, إِنْفَصَدَ.

To let down, to make to descend, دَلَّى ـ أَنْزَلَ ٢. To let down, as curtains, *etc.*, ضَرَبَ ـ أَرْخَى ـ ٢ حَدَرَ ـ ٢ سَدَلَ. They let down the boat into the sea, أَنْزَلُوا ٱلْقَارِبَ إِلَى ٱلْبَحْرِ. They let him down with ropes, دَلَّوْهُ بِحِبَالٍ. He let down his hand, خَفَضَ يَدَهُ ـ ٢. They let him down from the wall, أَنْزَلُوهُ مِنَ ٱلسُّورِ. She let down her wings, أَرْخَتْ أَجْنِحَتَهَا. Let down your nets, أَلْقُوا شِبَاكَكُمْ.

To let go, to cease to hold, سَيَّبَ ـ خَلَّى عَنْ. I will not let it go, لا أُرْخِيهِ. *See also next article.*

To let go away, to let depart, أَطْلَقَ ـ ٢ صَرَفَ. To suffer to escape, أَفْلَتَ. To let go away empty, أَطْلَقَ فَارِغًا. He will not let you go away, لا يَدَعُكُمْ تَمْضُونَ.

To let fly, to let go on the wing, أَطَارَ ـ طَيَّرَ. To let fly, as of a shot, أَطْلَقَ ـ ٢ ضَرَبَ ـ أَطْلَقَ. To dart, throw, أَطْلَقَ ـ ٢ رَمَى.

To let in, to make to enter, سَلَكَ ـ أَدْخَلَ ٢. To penetrate, as of water, *etc.*, تَطَرَّقَ إِلَى: It lets in water, يَتَطَرَّقُ إِلَيْهِ ٱلْمَاءُ. To let in, as a piece, joint, of wood, *etc.*, عَشَّقَ; as of a gore, رَصَّعَ ـ رَكَّبَ ـ نَضَّدَ ـ بَنَّقَ. To chase, as with jewels, *etc.*, رَصَّعَ.

To let loose, أَفْلَتَ ـ أَطْلَقَ. To let loose, as to pasture, أَسْرَحَ ـ سَرَّحَ. He let loose his tongue against him, أَرْسَلَ عَلَيْهِ لِسَانَهُ.

To let off, to forgive, أَصْفَحَ عَنْ ـ ٢ عَفَا عَنْ ـ سَامَحَ. To let off, as a gun, فَضَّى ـ فَرَّغَ ـ أَطْلَقَ. To let off, as of water, سَيَّبَ ـ أَجْرَى ـ أَسَالَ.

To let out, to suffer to go out, خَلَّى سَبِيلَهُ ـ أَخْرَجَ. To ask one to let him out, إِسْتَخْرَجَهُ ـ إِخْتَرَجَهُ. To divulge, بَاحَ بِ *aor.* يَبُوحُ. To let escape, أَفْلَتَ ـ أَطْلَقَ ـ سَيَّبَ. To slacken, رَاخَى ـ أَرْخَى. To enlarge, كَبَّرَ ـ وَسَّعَ. *See also to* Hire, *v.t.*

To let remain, ٢ تَرَكَ (*or* خَلَّى) فِي مَحَلِّهِ ـ أَبْقَى.

To let slip, to omit, فَاتَ *aor.* يَفُوتُ. *See also under to* Slip, *v.t.*

To let up, let go up, إِسْتَصْعَدَ ـ صَعَّدَ.

Let, *v.i.* To be taken on hire, أجر ـ إيتجر.

Let, *n.* A hindrance, مُمانَعة ـ سَدّ ـ عاقة ـ مانِع. A letting, rent, إيجار.

Lethal, *a.* Mortal, مُهلِك.

Lethargic, *a.* مَسْبُوت ـ سَبِت. *See also* Dull, Drowsy, *a.*

Lethargy, *n.* نِسْيان ـ سُبات. To be in a state of —, سُبِت.

Lethe, *n.* Forgetfulness, نِسْيان. The waters of —, ماء النِّسيان.

Lethean, *a.* Promoting forgetfulness, مُنسٍ ـ مُنسِّ.

Lethiferous, *a.* قاتِل ـ مُهلِك.

Letter, *n.* As of the alphabet, حَرْف *pl.* حُرُوف *and* أحْرُف. A — with diacritical points, حَرْف مُعْجَم; without points, حَرْف مُهْمَل. A weak —, حَرْف عِلَّة *pl.* حُرُوف. The vocal letters, الحُرُوف المَجْهُورة. The letters of the alphabet, حُرُوف الأبْجَدِيَّة. A silent —, حَرْف ساكِت. A dominical —, حَرْف الأحَد. A capital —, قَلَم ثُلُثِيّ ـ قَلَم طومار ـ حَرْف ثَخِين. An epistle, كِتاب *pl.* كُتُب ـ مَكْتُوب *pl.* مَكاتِيب ـ رِسالة *pl.* رَسائل ـ مُودّة ـ خَطّ *pl.* خُطوط ـ تَحْرِير *pl.* تَحارِير ـ وَرَقة ـ شُقّة. Letter, text, نَصّ ـ كِتاب. To the letter, حَرْفًا ـ حَرْفًا بِحَرْف. In letter and in spirit, لَفْظًا وَمَعْنًى. A letter of recommendation, مَكْتُوب تَوصِيَة. I have received the letter which you did me the honour to address to me, وَصَلَتْنِى مُشَرَّفَتُكُم. I received letters from them, أخَذْتُ مِنْهُم رَسائل. We did not receive letters, ما وَصَلَتْ إلَيْنا مَكاتِيب ـ ما وَرَدَتْ إلَيْنا رَسائل. The letter kills, but the spirit vivifies, الحَرْف يَقْتُل وَلٰكِنَّ الرُّوح يُحْيِى. *See also* Lessor, *n.*

Black letter, قَلَم قَدِيم ـ رَقْم عَتِيق.

Circular letter, مَنْشُور ـ نَشْرة ـ كِتاب مُلْحَق ـ مُلْحَق.

Dead-letter, not claimed at the post-office, مَكْتُوب مَتْرُوك.
Not in force, as of an ordinance, قانُون ـ قانُون غَيْر واقِع ـ مُلْغًى.

Dispatch of a letter, إنْفاذ كِتاب ـ إرْسال مَكْتُوب.

Paid letter, مَكْتُوب بِضَمّ (*or* خالِص) أُجْرَة البُوسْطة.

Receiver of a letter, نائل مَكْتُوب.

Registered letter, مَكْتُوب مُقَيَّد (*or* مُوَصًّى بِهِ).

Unpaid letter, مَكْتُوب بِدُون أُجْرَة البُوسْطة.

Writer of a letter, كاتِب مَكْتُوب *pl.* كَتَبَة.

To address a letter to one, حَرَّر (*or* كَتَب) مَكْتُوبًا إلَى فُلان.

To direct a letter, عَنْوَن الكِتاب.

To distribute letters, وَزَّع (*or* فَرَّق) المَكاتِيب.

To fold a letter, لَفّ² (*or* ـ طَوَى) مَكْتُوبًا.

To inclose in a letter, ـ ثَنَى ـ (*or* ـ طَوَى ـ *or* أدْرَج ـ) فِى مَكْتُوب.
I transmitted it in a letter, أنْفَذْتُهُ فِى دَرْج الكِتاب (*or* فِى طَيّ *or* فِى داخِل الكِتاب).

To post a letter, وَضَع المَكْتُوب فِى البُوسْطة *aor.* يَضَع.

Letters, *n.* Literature, العُلُوم. Belles-lettres, العُلُوم الأدَبِيَّة. A man of —, أدِيب *pl.* أُدَباء ـ صاحِب العُلُوم الأدَبِيَّة ـ لَوْذَعِيّ ـ مِن أهْل الأدَب. Letters patent, فِرْمان ـ بَراءة.

Letters of marque; *see under* Marque, *n.*

Letter, *v.t.* To stamp with letters, رَقَم².

Letter-book, *n.* دَفْتَر قَيْد نُسَخ المُكاتَبات.

Letter-box, *n.* صَنْدُوق المَكاتِيب.

Letter-carrier, *n.* مُوَزِّع المَكاتِيب.

Lettered, *a.* Stamped with letters, مُرَقَّم ـ رَقِيم ـ مَرْقُوم. Versed in literature, صاحِب عِلْم ـ عالِم ـ أدِيب. Belonging to learning, مُخْتَصّ بِالعِلْم.

Letter-founder, *n.* سَبّاك أحْرُف الطَّبْع.

Lettering, *n.* The act of impressing letters, رَقْم; what is impressed, رَقِيم ـ تَرْقِيم.

Letter-press, *n.* A press for lettering, آلة الرَّقْم. *See also* Lettering, *n.*

Letter-writer, *n.* كاتِب مُكاتَبات ـ كاتِب مَكاتِيب. A writer of literary epistles, مُنْشِئ ـ صاحِب إنْشاء. A manifold —, آلة لِمُضاعَفة المَكاتِيب.

Letting, *n.* Putting out on lease, إيجار.

Lettuce, *n.* خَسّ. Cabbage —, خَسّ مُدَوَّر. Sea —, شُبْرُم.

Leucorrhœa, *n.* رُطُوبة النِّساء.

Levant, *n.* The east, المَشْرِق ـ الأقْطار الشَّرْقِيَّة. The Ottoman dominions, المَمالِك العُثْمانِيَّة. The — trade, التِّجارة الشَّرْقِيَّة ـ تِجارة المَمالِك العُثْمانِيَّة.

Levanter, *n.* The wind, رِيح زَوْبَعِيَّة شَرْقِيَّة.

Levantine, *n.* A Frank born in the Levant, فِرَنْجِيّ مَوْلُود فِى المَمالِك العُثْمانِيَّة. A kind of stuff, خَزّ.

Levantine, *a.* مَوْلُود ـ مُتَعَلِّق بِالإفْرَنْج المَوْلُودِين فِى الشَّرْق ـ الشَّرْقِيّ.

Levator, *n.* The muscle, عَضَلة رافِعة.

Levee, *n.* A formal assembly of visitors, زِيارة ـ مَحْفِل رَسْمِيّ ـ زِيارة رَسْمِيَّة. To hold a —, اتَّخَذ (*or* اسْتَقْبَل) زِيارة رَسْمِيَّة.

Level, *a.* Even, smooth, سَهْل ـ سَهِل ـ مُسَطَّح ـ سَواء ـ مُسْتَوٍ ـ بَسِيط. Equal, عَدِيل ـ قَرِين ـ نَظِير. To be —, اعْتَدَل ـ سَهُل² ـ عادَل ـ ساوَى ـ اسْتَوَى. To be —, on the same plane, with, اسْتَوَى.

إِسْتَوَى بِ. To be — to, within the power of, كَانَ فِي طَاقَتِهِ ـ قَدَرَ عَلَى ² =. Level ground, بَسِيطَة.

Level, *v.t.* To make even, سَوَّى ـ سَطَّحَ. To lay flat, بَسَطَ ² ـ سَهَّلَ ـ بَسَّطَ. To lay smooth, مَهَّدَ. To — the ground with a roller, مَدَّدَ ٱلْأَرْضَ. To —, as difficulties, سَهَّلَ. To —, to throw down, هَدَمَ = ـ أَهْبَطَ ـ رَمَى = (or أَلْقَى) إِلَى ٱلْأَرْضِ ـ جَدَّلَ. To take levels of, قَاسَ = (or مَسَحَ =) بِٱلشَّاقُولِ ـ شَقَلَ ². To —, of a road, مَهَّدَ ـ طَرَّقَ: He will —, or take levels of, the road which it has been decided to make between Bairût and Damascus, يُمَهِّدُ ٱلطَّرِيقَ ٱلْمُقَرَّرَ فَتْحُهَا بَيْنَ بَيْرُوتَ وَدِمَشْقَ ٱلشَّامِ. To — at, take aim at..., أَقْصَدَ ـ أَشْرَعَ (or شَرَّعَ = or شَرَعَ =) نَحْوَ كَذَا ـ طَلَبَ ².

Level, *n.* A plain, مَيْدَان ـ قَاع ـ قَاعَة ـ صَاع ـ سَهْل. A flat surface, سَطْح مُسْتَوٍ ـ بَسِيطَة ـ بِسَاط ـ سَطْح. An equal state, سَوِيَّة ـ مُسَاوَاة ـ سَوَآء. Aim, رَمْيَة ـ طَلْعَة. An instrument for levelling, taking levels, قِيَاس ـ شَاقُول ـ جَدْوَل. A plan, scheme, idea, نِيَّة ـ رَسْم. Elevation, إِرْتِفَاع سَطْحِيّ ـ إِرْتِفَاع. To be on a — with, on the same elevation, سَاوَى فِي ٱلْإِرْتِفَاعِ; to be on an equality with, سَاوَى ـ نَاظَرَ. To put one's self on a — with, نَزَلَ مَنْزِلَتَهُ = ـ حَلَّ مَحَلَّتَهُ ². They are on the same —, footing, هُمْ عَلَى قَانُونٍ وَاحِدٍ.

Above the — of the sea, مُرْتَفِعٌ عَنْ مُسَاوَاةِ ٱلْبَحْرِ.

Dead level, سَطْح مُطْلَق.

On a level with, at the same elevation, مُسْتَوِي ٱلْإِرْتِفَاعِ. Equal with or to, عَلَى قَانُونٍ وَاحِدٍ ـ نَظِير ـ نَدِيد ـ كُفْؤٌ لِ.

Plumb level, زِيج ـ شَاقُول.

Spirit level, شَاقُول ذُو رُوحٍ.

Summit level, highest elevation, أَعْلَى ٱرْتِفَاعٍ.

Leveller, *n.* One who takes levels, مُقَدِّر ـ قَائِسٌ بِٱلشَّاقُولِ. That which makes things or persons equal, مُبَطِّل ـ مَسَّاح ـ مُسَوِّب ـ ٱلْمَقَامَاتِ.

Levelling, *n.* The act of making level, تَسْطِيح ـ تَسْهِيل ـ تَسْوِيَة. Levelling, as with a roller, مَدْدَرَةُ ٱلْأَرْضِ. Reduction to an equality, تَعْدِيل ـ إِسْوَآء ـ تَسْوِيَة ـ إِقْرَان. Taking levels, مِسَاحَة (or قِيَاس) بِٱلشَّاقُولِ.

Levelness, *n.* مُسَاوَاة ـ سَوِيَّة ـ سَطْح ـ سُهُول.

Lever, *n.* A bar —, عَتَلَة *pl.* عَتَل. An iron —, مُخْل *pl.* أَمْخَال *and* مُخُول. The — of a watch, نَقَّالَة سَاعَةٍ; the pendulum of a clock, رَقَّاص سَاعَةٍ. A regulator, مِيزَان.

Leverage, *n.* قُوَّةُ ٱلْمُخْلِ ـ قُوَّة عَتَلَةٍ ـ قُوَّة آلِيَّة.

Leveret, *n.* خِرْنِق *pl.* خَرَانِق.

Leviable, *n.* That may be levied from or imposed upon, مِمَّا يُفْرَضُ عَلَى ـ يُحَصَّلُ مِن مِمَّا.

Leviathan, *n.* حُوتٌ كَبِيرٌ مَجْهُولٌ ـ لاوِيَاثَان.

Levigate, *v.t.* To pound, سَحَقَ = ـ دَقَّ ². To polish, صَقَلَ ².

Levigation, *n.* The act of reducing to powder, تَدْقِيق ـ دَقّ.

Levite, *n.* لاوِيّ *pl.* لاوِيُّون.

Levitical, *a.* مُتَعَلِّق بِٱللَّاوِيِّينَ ـ لاوِيّ.

Leviticus, *n.* The book of, سِفْرُ ٱللَّاوِيِّينَ.

Levity, *n.* Lightness, want of mental gravity, قِلَّة عَقْلٍ ـ خِفَّة ـ خِفَّة عَقْلٍ ـ مُجَاهَلَة ـ خُرْق. Silliness, سَفَاهَة ـ سَفَه. Inconstancy, تَلَوُّن ـ طَيْشَان ـ طَيْرَة ـ قِلَّة ثَبَاتٍ ـ فَرْفَرَة.

Levy, *v.t.* To collect together, جَمَعَ =. To — troops, جَيَّشَ ـ إِسْتَجَاشَ ـ جَمَعَ = (or لَمَّ ²) ٱلْعَسَاكِرَ. To — troops from the town, مِنَ ٱلْمَدِينَةِ. To — contributions from, فَرَدَ = عَلَى ـ غَرَامَة ـ حَصَّلَ مِنَ ـ ٱلْغَرَائِمَ ـ طَرَحَ = عَلَى ـ ٱلضَّرَائِبَ ـ رَمَى = عَلَى ـ ٱلتَّكَالِيفَ. To — war upon, حَارَبَ. To — by compulsion, سَخَّرَ.

Levy, *n.* The act of levying troops, لَمّ ² (or جَمْع) ـ تَجْيِيش ـ عَسَاكِر; of levying contributions, تَحْصِيل. Troops raised, جَيْش ـ حَاصِل ـ مَحْصُول ـ حَصِيلَة ـ لَمَّة عَسَاكِرَ; contributions levied, حَاصِل ـ مَحْصُول ـ حَصِيلَة. A compulsory —, سُخْرَة. To demand a — of soldiers from, طَلَبَ ² مِنَ ـ ٱلْعَسَاكِرِ ـ إِسْتَجَاشَ.

Lewd, *a.* غَلِم ـ فَاسِق ـ فَالِت ـ شَهْوَان ـ قَطَامِيّ ـ هَوِس ـ مُغْلِيم. To be —, to utter — speeches, رَفَثَ ² ـ تَرَفَّثَ ـ فَحُشَ فِي ٱلْكَلَامِ ـ أَرْفَثَ.

Lewdly, *ad.* بِفُجُورٍ ـ بِفِسْقٍ وَفَسَادٍ ـ بِرَفْثٍ.

Lewdness, *n.* فَحَاشَة ـ فُجُور ـ فِسْقٌ وَفَسَادٌ ـ رَفَث. A lewd action, فَاحِشَة *pl.* فَوَاحِش.

Lewdster, *n.* فَاحِش ـ فَاجِر ـ فَاسِق ـ رَافِث ـ قَيْفَط.

Lex, *n.* شَرِيعَة ـ قَاعِدَة ـ قَانُون. *Lex talionis*, قَانُونُ ٱلثَّأْرِ ـ قَاعِدَةُ ٱلدَّخْلِ. *Lex scripta*, قَوَانِينُ وَأَحْكَامٌ مُحَرَّرَةٌ.

Lexical, *n.* لُغَوِيّ.

Lexicographer, *n.* مِنْ أَهْلِ ٱللُّغَةِ ـ صَاحِبُ كِتَابِ لُغَةٍ ـ مُؤَلِّفُ قَامُوسِ ٱللُّغَةِ.

Lexicographic, *a.* } مُتَعَلِّقٌ بِعِلْمِ ٱللُّغَةِ.
Lexicographical,

Lexicography, *n.* } عِلْمُ ٱللُّغَةِ.
Lexicology, *n.*

Lexicon, *n.* كِتَابُ لُغَةٍ.

Lexigraphic, *a.* لُغَوِيّ ـ مُعَبِّرٌ بِإِشَارَاتٍ.

Lexigraphy, *n.* عِلْمُ تَفْسِيرِ ٱلْكَلِمَاتِ.

Ley, *n.* *See* Lye, *n.*

Leyden-jar, *n.* وِعَآءُ ٱلْكَهْرَبَائِيَّةِ.

Liability, *n.* } Responsibility, مَسْئُولِيَّةٌ ـ ضَمَان ـ كَفَالَةٌ ـ ذِمَّةٌ.
Liableness, } Exposedness to, مَعْرُوض ـ تَعَرُّض ل. The being obnoxious to, deserving, إِسْتِيجَاب. Liabilities, debt, دُيُون. To acquit of —, أَحَلَّ ـ جَعَلَ ـ فِي حِلٍّ مِنْ كَذَا. To incur —, تَكَفَّلَ ـ تَضَمَّنَ. A limited — company, شِرْكَةٌ كَفَالَتُهُ مَحْدُودَةٌ (يَعْنِي كُلٌّ مِنَ ٱلْمُشْتَرِكِينَ يَضْمَنُ مَبْلَغَ سَهْمِهِ لَا غَيْر).

Liable, *a.* Responsible, كَفِيل *pl.* كُفَلَآءُ ـ ضَامِن *pl.* ضُمَنَآءُ ـ مُطَالَبٌ ب. Subject to, مُحِلٌّ ل ـ مُتَعَرِّضٌ ل. In danger of, تَضَمَّنَ ل ـ مُسْتَوْجِبٌ ل. To be — for, يُطَالَبُ ب ـ يُطْلَبُ مِن. He was —, responsible, to him for the property [received] from him, ضَمِنَ ٱلْمَالَ مِنْهُ. To be —, subject, to, تَعَرَّضَ ل. To make —, responsible, لَزَّمَ ـ ب. *See also under to* Expose, *v.t.*; *also* Subject, *a.*

Liaison, *n.* A bond of union, عِشْرَةٌ ـ أُلْفَةٌ ـ صُحْبَةٌ. Illicit connection, عَلَاقَةُ زِنَآءٍ ـ عَلَاقَةٌ خَفِيَّةٌ.

Liar, *n.* كَذَّاب *pl.* كَذَّابُونَ ـ أَثِيم ـ خَرَّاص. An habitual —, مَرَّاج ـ سَرَّاج.

Liss, *n.* ضَرْبٌ مِنَ ٱلْأَحْجَارِ ٱلصَّلْدَةِ.

Libation, *n.* سَكِيبَةٌ *pl.* سَكَائِبُ.

Libel, *n.* A defamatory writing, طَعْنٌ فِي ٱلْعِرْضِ ـ هَجْوٌ مُبَرَّزٌ مَنْشُورٌ. Defamation, نَمِيمَةٌ ـ قَذْفٌ ـ إِفْتِرَآءٌ ـ تَشْرِير.

Libel, *v.t.* To defame by writing, طَعَنَ ـ فِي ٱلْعِرْضِ ـ هَجَا ـ خَطَّأَ. To defame, طَعَنَ ـ فِي ٱلْعِرْضِ ـ جَرَّسَ ـ نَمَّ ـ هَتَّرَ ـ خَطَّأَ.

Libeller, *n.* هَاجٍ (*or* مُتَّهِم) خَطَّأ.

Libellous, *a.* مُفْتَرٍ عَلَى أَحَدٍ ـ هَتْكِيٌّ ـ فَضَّاح.

Liberal, *a.* Generous, سَخِيٌّ *pl.* أَسْخِيَآءُ ; *fem.* سَخِيَّةٌ *pl.* سَخَايَا *and* سَخِيَّات ـ جَوَاد ـ ذُو خَيْرٍ ـ مِفْضَال ـ فَضَّال. Large, abundant, وَاسِع ـ وَافٍ ـ كَافٍ. Liberal minded, رَحِيبُ ٱلصَّدْرِ. Not direct, not literal, غَيْرُ حَرْفِيٍّ ـ طَلِق ـ وَاسِع. Free born, of — birth, نَجِيب *pl.* نُجَبَآءُ ـ كَرِيم *pl.* كِرَام *and* كُرَمَآءُ ـ كَرَم ـ نَبِيل. Liberal, as in politics, ذُو حُرِّيَّةٍ ـ مُتَسَاهِل. A — government, حُكُومَةٌ مُتَسَاهِلَةٌ ـ حُكُومَةٌ حُرِّيَّةٌ. Liberal opinions, أَفْكَارٌ ذَاتُ حُرِّيَّةٍ ـ أَفْكَارٌ مُتَسَاهِلَةٌ. A — party, أَصْحَابُ ٱلْأَفْكَارِ ٱلْمُتَسَاهِلَةِ ـ حِزْبُ ٱلْحُرِّيَّةِ ـ حِزْبُ ٱلْمُتَسَاهِلِينَ. Liberal measures, تَدَابِيرُ مُتَسَاهِلَةٌ ـ تَدَابِيرُ ذَاتُ حُرِّيَّةٍ. The — arts, ٱلْعُلُومُ ٱلْعَقْلِيَّةُ ـ ٱلْفُنُونُ ٱلْعِلْمِيَّةُ. A — action, مَكْرُمَةٌ *pl.* مَكَارِمُ. To be —, generous, بَسَطَ ٱلْيَدَ ـ سَخِيَ. To be —, to act in a — or free way with one, سَامَحَهُ فِي ٱلْأَمْرِ. He was — with his property, جَادَ بِمَالِهِ. He is — with other people's property, يَجُودُ بِمَالِ غَيْرِهِ.

Liberal, *n.* One who advocates liberal measures, مِنْ حِزْبٍ عَصَبِيٍّ (*or* مُتَعَصِّبٍ) فِي ٱلْحُرِّيَّةِ ـ ٱلْمُتَسَاهِلِينَ. The liberals, أَصْحَابُ ٱلْحُرِّيَّةِ ـ ٱللِّبِيرَالُ أَعْنِي ٱلْمُتَسَاهِلِينَ.

Liberalism, *n.* Liberal principles, أُصُولُ ٱلْأَفْكَارِ ٱلْمُتَسَاهِلَةِ ـ أُصُولُ ٱلْحُرِّيَّةِ ـ ٱلتَّعَصُّبُ لِلْحُرِّيَّةِ.

Liberality, *n.* Generosity, خَيْر ـ جُود ـ سَخَاوَةٌ. Largeness of mind, رُحْبُ ٱلصَّدْرِ. Nobleness, نَجَابَةٌ ـ كَرَم ـ نَبَالَةٌ. Absence of strictness, يُسْر ـ تَسَاهُل ـ تَسَامُح.

Liberalize, *v.t.* To make liberal, generous, أَرْحَبَ (*or* رَحَّبَ) صَدْرَهُ. To free from narrow views, أَنْقَذَ ـ مِنْ شِدَّةِ ٱلتَّعَصُّبِ ـ رَحَّبَ أَفْكَارَهُ (*or* ٱلْعَصَبِيَّةِ).

Liberally, *ad.* Generously, بِسَخَاوَةٍ ـ بِكَرَمٍ. Abundantly, مَعَ زِيَادَةٍ ـ كَثِيرًا ـ بِكَثْرَةٍ. Without strictness, prejudice, طَلِقًا ـ بِدُونِ تَعَصُّبٍ (*or* عَصَبِيَّةٍ). To act —, generously, أَجْمَلَ ـ جَادَ. To let things go easily, يَسَّرَ ـ تَسَامَحَ ـ تَسَاهَلَ.

Liberate, *v.t.* To release, let go, أَعْتَقَ ـ أَطْلَقَ ـ سَيَّبَ. To let escape, أَفْلَتَ. To save, خَلَّصَ ـ خَفَرَ. To be liberated, عَتَقَ: The slave was liberated, عَتَقَ ٱلْعَبْدُ. Such an one is a liberated slave, فُلَانٌ مَوْلَى عَتَاقَةٍ.

Liberation, *n.* The act of setting free, إِطْلَاق ـ إِعْتَاق. The being set free, خَلَاص ـ عَتَاقَةٌ.

Liberator, *n.* خَفِير ـ مُخَلِّص.

Libertine, *n.* } Dissolute, فَلَتِيٌّ ـ فَاجِر ـ فَاسِق ـ خَلِيع. Im-
Libertine, *a.* } pious, زِنْدِيق *pl.* زَنَادِقَةٌ ـ مُنَافِق.

Libertinism, *n.* Dissoluteness, فِسْقٌ وَفَسَادٌ ـ فُجُور ـ فِسْق. Impiety, زَنْدَقَةٌ ـ نِفَاق.

Liberty, *n.* A free condition, حُرِّيَّةٌ ـ حُرُورِيَّةٌ. The being set at liberty, خَلَاص ـ إِنْفِكَاك ـ إِنْطِلَاق ـ عِتَاق ـ عِتْق ـ عَتَاقَةٌ. Leave, permission, رُخْصَةٌ ـ إِجَازَةٌ ـ إِذْن ـ فُسْحَةٌ. Independence, إِسْتِقْلَال ـ إِسْتِبْدَاد. A privilege, immunity, إِمْتِيَاز *pl.* إِمْتِيَازَات ـ مَزِيَّةٌ *pl.* مَزَايَا ـ مُعَافَاةٌ *pl.* مُعَافَات. Freedom of will, of action, إِطْلَاق ـ إِخْتِيَار. Leisure, وَقْت ـ مُهْلَةٌ ـ فَرَاغ ـ هَوْن ـ تَفَرُّغ. A boundary, حَدٌّ *pl.* حُدُود. Boldness, intrusion, جُرْأَةٌ ـ جَسَارَةٌ ـ إِجْتِرَآءٌ ـ إِجْتِسَار. Liberty of thought, طَلَاقَةُ ٱلْفِكْرِ. You have full — therein, ٱلْأَمْرُ لَكَ طَلِقًا ـ أَنْتَ مُطْلَقُ ٱلْإِرَادَةِ فِي ذٰلِكَ. I take the — to send you the book, أَجْتَرِئُ عَلَى إِرْسَالِ هٰذَا ٱلْكِتَابِ إِلَيْكُمْ. We take the — to ask you to do us a service, نَتَجَاسَرُ

نَحْنُ مُتَجَاسِرُونَ عَلَى تَكْلِيفِكُمْ – عَلَى ٱلتَّكْلِيفِ إِلَيْكُمْ قَضَى حَاجَةً – قَضَى غَرَضًا. He is at — to marry whom he will, هُوَ مُخَيَّرٌ بِٱلزَّوَاجِ لِمَنْ شَاءَ.

Civil liberty, إِسْتِقْلَالٌ مَدَنِيٌّ.

Individual liberty, حُرِّيَّةٌ – حُرِّيَّةُ ٱلشَّخْصِ – حُرِّيَّةُ ٱلذَّاتِ شَخْصِيَّةٌ.

Liberty of conscience, حُرِّيَّةُ ٱلْأَدْيَانِ.

Liberty of instruction, حُرِّيَّةُ ٱلتَّعْلِيمِ وَٱلتَّعَلُّمِ.

Liberty of the press, إِمْتِيَازَاتُ ٱلطَّبْعِ – حُرِّيَّةُ ٱلْمَطْبُوعَاتِ.

Natural liberty, إِسْتِقْلَالٌ طَبِيعِيٌّ.

Political liberty, إِسْتِقْلَالٌ سِيَاسِيٌّ.

Religious liberty, حُرِّيَّةُ ٱلْمَذْهَبِ – حُرِّيَّةٌ دِينِيَّةٌ.

To be at liberty, at leisure, تَفَضَّى – تَفَرَّغَ. To have permission, رُخِّصَ – أُذِنَ. To be free, released, أُطْلِقَ. To have the option, تَخَيَّرَ.

To give liberty, permission, to, رَخَّصَ لِ-فِي.

To restore to or set at liberty, ² فَكَّ – أَعْتَقَ – سَيَّبَ – أَطْلَقَ.

This man might have been set at liberty had he not appealed to the ambassador, كَانَ يُمْكِنُ أَنْ يُطْلَقَ هٰذَا ٱلرَّجُلُ لَوْ لَمْ يَكُنْ قَدْ رَفَعَ دَعْوَاهُ إِلَى ٱلسَّفِيرِ.

To take liberties, to allow one's self license, تَرَخَّصَ. To act with impertinence, سَفِهَ – سَفُهَ ² – وَقُحَ aor. يَوْقُحُ. To take liberties with one, تَوَقَّحَ عَلَى أَحَدٍ.

To take the liberty, تَجَرَّأَ – اِجْتَرَأَ – اِجْتَسَرَ – تَجَاسَرَ.

To walk at liberty, تَمَشَّى فِي رُحْبٍ.

Libidinist, *n.*
Libidinous, *a.* } شَهْوَانِيٌّ – شَبِقٌ – مِغْلِيمٌ – غَلِمٌ.

Libidinously, *ad.* بِشَهْوَةٍ – بِشَبَقٍ – بِغُلْمَةٍ.

Libidinousness, *n.* شَهْوَةٌ – شَبَقٌ – غُلْمَةٌ.

Libra, *n.* The constellation, بُرْجُ ٱلْمِيزَانِ – ٱلْمِيزَانُ.

Librarian, *n.* حَافِظٌ – أَمِينُ خِزَانَةِ كُتُبٍ – نَاظِرُ خِزَانَةِ كُتُبٍ – قَيِّمُ ٱلْكُتُبِ – كُتُبِيٌّ.

Librarianship, *n.* وَظِيفَةُ حَافِظِ كُتُبٍ.

Library, *n.* A — of books, خِزَانَةُ كُتُبٍ – خِزَانَةُ كُتُبٍ. A case for books, قِمَطْرٌ *pl.* قَمَاطِرُ.

Librate, *v.t.* وَزَنَ *aor.* يَزِنُ – وَازَنَ.

Librate, *v.i.* اِرْتَجَّ – تَرَجَّحَ – تَمَايَلَ – مَالَ.

Libration, *n.* The act of balancing, مُوَازَنَةٌ. The — of the moon, اِرْتِجَاجُ ٱلْقَمَرِ.

Libratory, *a.* مُرْتَجٌّ – مُتَرَجِّحٌ – مُتَمَايِلٌ.

License, *n.* Permission, إِجَازَةٌ – إِذْنٌ – رُخْصَةٌ. A certificate of —, تَذْكِرَةُ إِجَازَةٍ. A patent, بَرَاءَةٌ – تَقْرِيرٌ *pl.* تَقَارِيرُ. Boldness, forwardness, اِجْتِرَاءٌ – جَسَارَةٌ. Impudence, unruliness, وَقَاحَةٌ – سَفَاهَةٌ. Abuse of liberty, سُوءُ ٱسْتِعْمَالِ ٱلْحُرِّيَّةِ – شَرٌّ. Want of decorum, قِلَّةُ أَدَبٍ. Excess, فَيْضٌ – فَرْطٌ. Vicious conduct, خَلَاعَةٌ – دَعَارَةٌ – فَسَادٌ. To give free — to, رَخَّصَ لِ. To take —, تَرَخَّصَ. Poetical —, إِجَازَةٌ فِي ٱلشِّعْرِ. To grant a — to, أَجَازَ لِ.

License, *v.t.* To permit, أَذِنَ لِ – رَخَّصَ لِ – فَسَحَ لِ. To authorize, أَمْكَنَ – قَدَّرَ-عَلَى – صَرَّفَ-فِي. To give one a —, *e.g.* to teach, practise, أَجَازَ – جَوَّزَ: He granted him a license to teach all the matters he had learned from his shaikhs, أَجَازَ لَهُ جَمِيعَ مَسْمُوعَاتِهِ مِنْ مَشَايِخِهِ. (The matter or matters which one is licensed to are called, مُجَازَات).

Licensed, *n.* Permitted, مُرَخَّصٌ – مَأْذُونٌ. Having a license, صَاحِبُ تَذْكِرَةِ إِجَازَةٍ. Privileged, صَاحِبُ ٱمْتِيَازٍ – ذُو ٱمْتِيَازٍ. A — victualler, صَاحِبُ إِجَازَةٍ لِبَيْعِ ٱلْمُسْكِرَاتِ.

Licentiate, *n.* صَاحِبُ إِجَازَةٍ – مُجَازٌ. A — in theology, مُجَازُ ٱللَّاهُوتِ. A — in medicine, مُجَازُ ٱلطِّبِّ.

Licentious, *a.* Using freedom to excess, مُتَرَخِّصٌ – فَلْتَانٌ. Loose in morals, شَقِيٌّ – فَاسِقٌ – فَاجِرٌ – دَاعِرٌ – فُرُطِيٌّ. Licentious talk, كَلَامٌ خَنًى – كَلَامٌ زَفِرٌ.

Licentiously, *ad.* Without restraint, بِٱلْإِفْرَاطِ – بِتَرَخُّصٍ – بِفَلْتٍ. Immorally, بِفُجُورٍ – بِشَقَاوَةٍ – بِفِسْقٍ – بِدَعَارَةٍ.

Licentiousness, *n.* Want of restraint, عَدَمُ ٱلتَّقَنُّعِ – فَلْتٌ. Immorality, فِسْقٌ – خَلَاعَةٌ – دَعَارَةٌ – فُجُورٌ – فُرُطٌ.

Lichen, *n.* Moss, أُشْنَةٌ. Rock-moss, كَوْكَبٌ – حَزَازُ ٱلصَّخْرِ. Oak-tree —, كُشْنَةُ ٱلْعَجُوزِ. *Lichen prunastri,* حِنَّاءُ قُرَيْشٍ – ٱلْوَغْرُ – ٱلشَّيْبَةُ. *Lichen sypifer,* شَيْبَةُ ٱلْجَبَلِ.

Licit, *a.* *See* Permissible, *a.*

Licitness, *n.* *See* Lawfulness, *n.*

Lick, *v.t.* As with the tongue, لَحَفَ – لَحِسَ – لَحِكَ. To —, or lap, as a dog, لَحِسَ – لَعِقَ – لَجَنَ ² لَجِذَ. To —, as a plate, لَسِبَ – لَسَّ ². To —, as honey from off the fingers, اِلْتَطَعَ – أَلْطَعَ – لَطِعَ. To beat, overcome, غَلَبَ – أَنْجَحَ بِ. To thrash, وَزَعَ – ضَرَبَ.

To lick up, لَحِسَ: They shall lick up the dust under your feet, يَلْحَسُونَ غُبَارَ رِجْلَيْكَ. To devour, اِلْتَهَمَ.

To lick the dust, to be slain, قُتِلَ – لَحِسَ ٱلتُّرَابَ.

To lick into shape, هَنْدَمَ; of language, فَتَّقَ.

To lick over, to do a thing negligently, فَرَّطَ فِي ـ ـ عَشَمَ ـ قَصَّرَ فِي ـ تَكَاسَلَ فِي ـ تَغَفَّلَ فِي.

Lick, *n.* } A stroke with the tongue, لَعْقَة ـ لَحْكَة ـ لَحْس ـ
Licking, } لَحْسَة; of a dog, لَغْد. A beating, قَتْل ـ ضَرْب. A wipe, مَسْحَة.

Licking, *a.* لَوَاحِس *pl.* لَاحِس.

Lickerish, *a.* Eager, مُشْتَهٍ ـ تَائِق إِلَى. Lustful, شَهْوَانِيّ.

Lick-spittle, *n.* مُبَصْبِص ـ مُدَاهِن.

Licorice, *n.* سُوس. Licorice root, عِرْقُ ٱلسُّوسِ. Inspissated — juice, رُبُّ ٱلسُّوسِ. A seller of —, سَوَّاس.

Lictor, *n.* One who bears the rod and flogs in the presence of the Sultan, مِشْعَل.

Lid, *n.* غِطَاء *pl.* أَغْطِيَة.

Lie, *n.* An untruth, زُور *pl.* أَزْوَار ـ كَاذِبَة ـ كِذْبَة ـ كَذِب. To lead one to tell a —, فَجَّرَ ـ كَذَّبَ ². To give the — to, كَذَّبَ ـ كَاذَبَ ـ إِسْتَكْذَبَ. To be given to tell lies, تَكَذَّبَ. You have told me lies, كَلَّمْتَنِي بِٱلْكَذِبِ. They have spoken lies against me, تَكَلَّمُوا عَلَيَّ بِٱلْكَذِبِ.

Lie, *v.i.* To tell untruths, كَذَبَ ـ ـ مَانَ ـ أَخْلَفَ. To blend lies with truth, أَفْجَرَ ـ فَجَرَ ².

Lie, *v.i.* To be at rest, سَكَنَ ² ـ قَعَدَ ²; to cause to lie, أَقْعَدَ ـ سَكَّنَ. To lean, rest, إِتَّكَى. To lie, lie down, recline, ضَجَعَ ـ ـ إِضْطَجَعَ ـ إِنْضَجَعَ. To lie, as on a bed to sleep, رَقَدَ ² ـ نَامَ. To be spread out, إِنْبَسَطَ ـ تَمَدَّحَ ـ إِفْتَرَشَ ـ إِنْسَطَحَ. To remain, abide, مَكَثَ ² ـ بَقِيَ ـ ـ إِسْتَقَامَ. To be buried, of persons, دُفِنَ; of things, إِنْدَفَنَ ـ إِدَّفَنَ. To be situated, to look towards, نَظَرَ نَحْوَ ـ ـ نَظَرَ إِلَى ـ وَاجَهَ or *simply* نَحْوَ: it lies towards the north, وَاقِعٌ نَحْوَ ٱلشَّمَالِ ـ يَنْظُرُ نَحْوَ ٱلشَّمَالِ. To lie, to consist in, بِ: Wherein does his strength lie? بِمَاذَا قُوَّتُهُ. To lie, or lie down, as of quadrupeds, رَبَضَ ـ ـ; as of a camel, بَرَكَ ²; as a bird, جَثَمَ ². To lie, lie down, flat, تَسَطَّحَ ـ إِمْتَدَّ عَلَى طُولِهِ ـ إِنْسَطَحَ. To lie on one's back, إِسْتَلْقَى ـ إِنْبَطَحَ. إِمْتَدَّ عَلَى قَفَاهُ ـ إِسْتَلْقَى. To lie on one's stomach, إِمْتَدَّ عَلَى بَطْنِهِ; on one's breast, جَثَمَ ² ـ. To lie, to hold, as in law, جَازَ قَانُونًا ² ـ يَثْبُتُ شَرْعًا. To lie, in the sense of to be, may often be expressed by the verb كَانَ; *e.g.* it lies open, كَانَ مَفْتُوحًا. Here lies, (of the inscription on a gravestone,) هٰذَا قَبْرُ. As much as in him lies, عَلَى قَدْرِ إِمْكَانِهِ ـ حَسَبَ طَاقَتِهِ. To lie about, to be scattered, كَانُوا شَذَرَ مَذَرَ ـ تَشَتَّتَ ـ تَبَدَّدَ. To lie at anchor, رَسَتِ ٱلسَّفِينَةُ *aor.* تَرْسُو ـ رَبَطَ ² ـ أَرْسَى.

To lie at one's door, *literally,* رَبَضَ عِنْدَ ٱلْبَابِ ². To be consequent upon, تَرَتَّبَ عَلَى. To be responsible for, كَانَ عَلَى ذِمَّتِهِ.

To lie at one's heart, to be thoughtful, anxious, about, أَضْمَرَ عَلَى ـ إِهْتَمَّ بِ.

To lie at the point of death, أَشْرَفَ عَلَى ـ كَانَ عَلَى آخِرِ نَسَمَةِ ٱلْمَوْتِ.

To lie by, to be at rest, إِسْتَرَاحَ ـ إِرْتَاحَ. To let lie by, to store, as for another occasion, أَبْقَى ـ خَلَّى ـ خَبَّأَ ـ إِدَّخَرَ.

To lie close, as in layers, كَانُوا طِبَاقًا. They lie, or lay themselves, close together, تَرَاصُّوا. The stones lie close together, تَرَصَّصَتِ (or إِرْتَصَّتِ) ٱلْجَنَادِلُ. To keep silent upon, سَكَتَ عَنْ ².

To lie down, to die, تُوُفِّيَ ـ مَاتَ ² ـ أَرَاحَ. (*See also under to* Lie.) To make to lie down, نَوَّمَ ـ أَضْجَعَ; to make to lie flat, مَدَّ عَلَى طُولِهِ ² ـ مَدَّدَ ـ سَطَّحَ. To make to lie down, of a quadruped, أَرْبَضَ; of a camel, أَبْرَكَ.

To lie hard, as on the stomach, ثَقُلَ عَلَى ٱلْمِعْدَةِ ². It lay hard upon, was afflictive to, him, عَسُرَ (or تَعَسَّرَ or تَعَاسَرَ) عَلَيْهِ ² ـ ثَقُلَ عَلَيْهِ ². The word lay hard upon, was unpleasant to, him, ثَقُلَ عَلَيْهِ ٱلْقَوْلُ.

To lie in, to be confined, of a woman, وَضَعَت ـ تَلِدُ *aor.* وَلَدَت *aor.* تَضَعُ. To confine, of a woman, وَلَّدَ.

To lie in the way, to be an obstacle to, تَعَرَّضَ لِ ـ آنَى ـ سَدَّ ².

To lie in wait, to waylay, رَصَدَ ² ـ إِرْتَصَدَ. To — for, تَكَمَّنَ لِ ـ كَمَنَ لِ.

To lie on or upon, إِضْطَجَعَ عَلَى ـ إِسْتَقَرَّ عَلَى. To be regularly disposed or arranged upon, تَرَتَّبَ عَلَى. All thy want lies upon me, كُلُّ ٱحْتِيَاجِكَ عَلَيَّ. It, the decision, lies or rests with you, ٱلْأَمْرُ أَمْرُكَ.

To lie on hand, as not saleable, كَسَدَتِ ٱلْأَمْتِعَةُ مِنْ قِلَّةِ ٱلرُّغَّابِ ².

To lie over, to be deferred to, تَسَوَّفَ ـ حُذِفَ إِلَى غَيْرِ وَقْتٍ ـ تَأَخَّرَ إِلَى.

To lie to, of a ship, صَلَّبَ ٱلْمَرْكَبُ ـ تَوَقَّفَ.

To lie under, to have to suffer, إِحْتَمَلَ. To be exposed to, تَعَرَّضَ لِ ـ كَانَ تَهِيمًا ـ أُتْهِمَ ـ أُتَّهَمَ. To lie under suspicion, كَانَ تَهِيمًا ـ أُتْهِمَ.

To lie with, ضَاجَعَ. To lie with a woman, carnally, جَامَعَ ـ نَاكَ ـ ـ نَكَحَ ـ ـ دَخَلَ بِ ² ـ يَطَأُ *aor.* وَطِئَ. The matter rests with you, the option is yours, أَنْتَ ـ ٱلْأَمْرُ أَمْرُكَ ٱلْمُخَيَّرُ.

To let lie, to leave alone, خَلَّى ـ ² تَرَكَ.

Lief, *ad.* Willingly, عَلَى ٱلرَّأْسِ وَٱلْعَيْنِ ـ رِضًا. I would as — go as not, عِنْدِي ٱلرَّوَاحُ وَٱلْقُعُودُ سَوَآءٌ.

Liege, *n.* Lord, suzerain, صاحِب ـ مُلْتَزِم ـ سَيِّد. Liege man, vassal, تابِع *pl.* تَوَابِع. *See also* Suzerain, *a.*

Lien, *n.* تِباعَة *pl.* تِباعات ـ تَبِعَة *pl.* تَبِعات ـ عُلْقَة ـ عَلَاقَة ـ مَطْلُوب ـ رُهُون *and* رِهَان *pl.* رَهْن. He has a — on this house, لَهُ فِي هٰذِهِ ٱلدَّارِ عَلَاقَةٌ.

Lieu, *n.* Stead, behalf, عِوَض ـ مَحَلّ ـ بَدَل. In — of, بَدَلًا عَن. He took the thing in — of another, إِسْتَبْدَلَ ٱلشَّيْءَ بِغَيْرِهِ. He gave him money in — of it, أَعْطَاهُ دَرَاهِمَ عِوَضَ ٱلشَّيْءِ ـ بَدَّلَهُ بِهِ دَرَاهِمًا. He gave in — of it such a thing, بَدَّلَ مَكَانَهُ كَذَا ـ أَعْطَاهُ شَيْئًا فِي بَدَلِهِ. He took it from him in — of it, أَخَذَهُ مِنْهُ بَدَلًا. In —, instead, thereof, فِي مُقَابَلَةِ ذٰلِكَ.

Lieutenancy, *n.* The office of in the army, رُتْبَة (*or* وَظِيفَة) ٱلْمُلَازِم; in the navy, رُتْبَة (*or* وَظِيفَة) ٱلْيُوزْبَاشِي. The office of deputy, وَظِيفَةُ ٱلْقَائِمِ مَقَام ـ خِلَافَة ـ نِقَابَة ـ وَكَالَة ـ نِيَابَة ـ قائمَقامِيَّة. Lord-Lieutenancy, وِلَايَة ـ وَلِيَّة. Deputy Lord-Lieutenancy, وَظِيفَةُ ٱلْقَائِمِ مَقَام.

Lieutenant, *n.* A — in the army, مُلازِم *pl.* مُلازِمَة; in the navy, يُوزْبَاشِي. A deputy, نَقِيب *pl.* نُقَبَآء ـ نائِب *pl.* نُوَّاب ـ قائِمُ مَقام. Lord-Lieutenant, وَالٍ *pl.* وُلَاة ـ والي وِلايَة. Deputy Lord-Lieutenant, قائِمُ مَقامِ ٱلْوَالِي. To act as —, deputy, for, ² نَابَ عَن. To appoint as —, deputy, إِسْتَنَابَ.

Life, *n.* The faculty of existence and growth, عَيْش حَيْوة ـ حَيَاة *pl.* حَيَاوَات (*also as an intensitive,* حَيّ ـ حَيَوَان). The present —, الدُّنْيَا ـ الحَيْوة. Lifetime, عُمْر ـ عَمْر *pl.* أَعْمَار ـ مُدَّةُ ٱلْحَيَاةِ. Movement, حَرَكَة. Vivacity, نَارِيَّة ـ حَرَارَة ـ مُرُوَّة. A biography, سِيرَة *pl.* سِيَر ـ تَرْجَمَة *pl.* تَرَاجِم; a memoir, تَذْكِرَة. Events, حَوَادِث. Livelihood, مَعَاش ـ مَعِيشَة ـ عِيشَة ـ حَيَاة. Mode of living, سُلُوك ـ سِيرَة ـ عِيشَة. O that I had prepared for my [everlasting] life! يا لَيْتَنِي قَدَّمْتُ لِحَيْوتِي (*Kur.* lxxxix. 25). Verily the last abode is [the abode of] everlasting life, فَإِنَّ ٱلدَّارَ ٱلْآخِرَةَ لَهِيَ ٱلْحَيَوَانُ (*Id.* xxix. 64). To be in —, living, ² عَاشَ. May God prolong your life! أَطَالَ ٱللّٰهُ عُمْرَكُمْ ـ اَللّٰهُ يُطَوِّلُ عُمْرَكَ. I never saw it during my life, عُمْرِي مَا رَأَيْتُهُ. He has passed all his life in work, ² صَرَفَ عُمْرَهُ فِي ٱلشُّغْلِ. By my life! لَعَمْرِي; by thy life! لَعَمْرُكَ. By the — of God! لَعَمْرُ ٱللّٰهِ. She had a little life left in her, كَانَ لَهَا رَمَقٌ مِنَ ٱلْحَيَاةِ. The lives of the poets, سِيَرُ ٱلشُّعَرَآءِ.

A bad life, one who is ailing or unhealthy, سَقْطٌ ـ سَقَط ـ عَلِيل ـ عَلِيلُ (*or*) ٱلْجَسَدِ.

A good life, one who is strong and healthy, صَحِيح ـ شافٍ ـ سَلِيمُ (*or* صَحِيحُ) ٱلْجَسَدِ ـ مُتَعافٍ ـ سَلِيم.

During life, طُولَ ٱلْعُمْرِ ـ مُدَّةَ ٱلْحَيَاةِ.

Comfortable life, سَعَة ـ تُرْفَة ـ نِعْمَة ـ عَيْش مُفانِق ـ فَنَق ٱلْعَيْشِ.

Early life, infancy, طُفُولِيَّة; youth, شُبُوبِيَّة ـ شَبَاب ـ غُلُومِيَّة.

Eternal life, الحَيَاةُ ٱلسَّرْمَدِيَّةُ; eternal happiness, السَّعَادَةُ ٱلْأَبَدِيَّةُ.

For life, while he lives, مَا دَامَ فِي قَيْدِ ٱلْحَيَاةِ ـ مَا دَامَ بِٱلْحَيَاةِ.

He gave it to him for his life, عَمَّرَهُ إِيَّاهُ.

For the life of me! لَعَمْرِي.

From the life, of a picture taken, مِنَ ٱلْأَصْلِ; of a person, مِنَ ٱلشَّخْصِ.

Hard life, جُحُود ـ جَحْد ـ عُسْرُ ٱلْعَيْشِ.

High life, مَعِيشَةُ ٱلْأَكَابِرِ.

In one's life, فِي عُمْرِهِ ـ مُدَّةَ حَيَاتِهِ.

Line of life, business, شُغْل ـ حِرْفَة ـ تَعاطٍ ـ صَنْعَة.

Long life, عُمْرٌ مَدِيدٌ (*or* طَوِيلٌ).

Love of life, حَلَاوَةُ ٱلرُّوحِ ـ حُبُّ ٱلْحَيَاةِ.

Low life, that of the poor, مَعِيشَةُ ٱلْفُقَرَآءِ; of the base, مَعِيشَةُ ٱلسُّفَلَآءِ.

Manner of life, طَرِيقَة ـ سُنَّة ـ سِيرَة.

Married life, الزَّوَاجُ ـ الزِّيجَةُ ـ التَّأَهُّلُ.

Position in life, شَأْن ـ مَقَام ـ قِيَام ـ دَرَجَة ـ حَال.

Power of life and death, حَقّ ـ سُلْطَانٌ عَلَى ٱلْحَيَاةِ وَٱلْمَوْتِ ـ حَقُّ ٱلِاسْتِحْيَآءِ وَٱلْمَمَاتِ ـ السَّيْفُ.

Single life, عُزُوبَة ـ عُزْبَة.

The life to come, الآخِرَةُ ـ الحَيَوَانُ ـ الحَيَاةُ.

This present life, الدُّنْيَا ـ حَيَاةُ ٱلدُّنْيَا ـ الحَيَاةُ ٱلْحَاضِرَةُ.

Time of life, age, عُمْر ـ سِنّ ـ عَمْر.

The prime of life, عِزُّ ٱلْحَيَاةِ ـ عُنْفُوَانُ ٱلْعُمْرِ ـ شَبَاب.

To the life, of a picture, عَيْنُ ٱلشَّيْءِ ـ طِبْقُ ٱلْأَصْلِ ـ طِبْق هُوَ هُوَ.

To be between life and death, كَانَ بَيْنَ ٱلْحَيَاةِ وَٱلْمَوْتِ.

To beg for life, طَلَبَ ٱلْأَمَانَ ـ إِسْتَأْمَنَ.

To beg one's life, ² طَلَبَ عَفْوَهُ عَنِ ٱلْقَتْلِ.

To defend one's life, إِحْتَمَى ـ مَانَعَ عَنْ نَفْسِهِ.

To depart this life, ² مَاتَ ـ تُوُفِّيَ ـ أَرَاحَ.

To expose one's life, خَاطَرَ بِنَفْسِهِ.

To fly for one's life, فَازَ بِنَفْسِهِ ــ هَرَبَ لِحَيَاتِهِ.

To give life to, to make alive again, أَحْيَى ــ بَعَثَ. To inspirit, حَضَّضَ ــ أَنْهَضَ ــ أَنْفَسَ.

To keep life and soul together, تَعَيَّشَ ــ قَاسَى.

To lay down one's life, وَضَعَ نَفْسَهُ aor. يَضَعُ.

To lead a life, سَلَكَ سُلُوكًا ــ سَارَ سِيرَةً. To lead a pleasant life, تَنَعَّمَ ــ نَعِمَ.

To lead a hard life, عَاشَ عِيشَةً ضَيِّقَةً ــ اِخْشَوْشَبَ فِي عَيْشِهِ. To lead a dissolute life, فَسَقَ ــ غَمَطَ ــ تَفَشَّفَ. He led an exemplary life among them, سَارَ بِهِمْ سِيرَةً حَسَنَةً.

To restore to life, أَحْيَى ــ بَعَثَ.

To seek any one's life, طَلَبَهُ لِيَقْتُلَهُ.

To spend or pass one's life, صَرَفَ عُمْرَهُ. In the sense of to waste one's life, ضَيَّعَ عُمْرَهُ.

To take any one's life, قَتَلَ.

To throw away one's life, أَتْلَفَ حَيَاتَهُ ــ أَتْلَفَ عُمْرَهُ; to waste one's life, ضَيَّعَ عُمْرَهُ.

To try one for his life, أَقَامَ ٱلدَّعْوَى عَلَى ــ لِذَنْبٍ يَسْتَحِقُّ ٱلْقَتْلَ.

Life-annuity, n. مَعَاشٌ سَنَوِيٌّ مَا دَامَ ٱلْمُتَمَتِّعُ بِهِ فِي قَيْدِ ٱلْحَيَاةِ.

Life-assurance, n. سِكُورْتَا مُدَّةَ ٱلْعُمْرِ. *See also under* Insurance, n.

Life-blood, n. In the eyelid, خَفَقَانُ ٱلْجَفْنِ. The essential part, ٱلْجَوْهَرُ. The heart's blood, حَبَّةُ ٱلْقَلْبِ.

Life-boat, n. قَارِبُ ٱلنَّجَاةِ ــ قَارِبُ ٱلْخَلَاصِ.

Life-buoy, n. عَامَةٌ (or عَوَّامَةٌ) ٱلنَّجَاةِ ــ عَامَةٌ (or عَوَّامَةٌ) ٱلْخَلَاصِ.

Life-guards, n. شُرْطَةُ ٱلسُّلْطَانِ ــ شُرَطٌ ــ حَرَسٌ. The —, ٱلْأُرْدُوِي ٱلْهُمَايُونِيُّ ٱلْخَاصُّ.

Life-guardsman, عَسْكَرِيٌّ مِنَ ٱلْأُرْدُوِي ــ شُرْطٌ pl. شُرْطَةٌ ــ شُرْطِيٌّ ٱلْهُمَايُونِيِّ ٱلْخَاصِّ.

Life-estate, n. ٱلتَّصَرُّفُ فِي شَيْءٍ مَا دَامَ ٱلْمُتَمَتِّعُ بِهِ فِي قَيْدِ ٱلْحَيَاةِ ــ ٱلتَّصَرُّفُ فِي شَيْءٍ مُدَّةَ ٱلْعُمْرِ.

Life-insurance, n. سِكُورْتَا مُدَّةَ ٱلْعُمْرِ.

Life-interest, n. ٱلتَّمَتُّعُ بِشَيْءٍ مَا دَامَ ٱلْمُسْتَفِيدُ فِي قَيْدِ ٱلْحَيَاةِ ــ عُمْرَى ــ عَلَاقَةٌ مُدَّةَ ٱلْعُمْرِ.

Lifeless, n. Without life, لَيْسَ فِيهِ حَيَاةٌ ــ مَيِّتٌ ــ بِدُونِ حَيَاةٍ ــ هَامِدٌ. Without spirit, لَا رُوحَ لَهُ ــ جَامِدٌ ــ مَوَاتٌ. Without vigour, عَاجِزٌ ــ ضَعِيفٌ ــ وَانٍ ــ بِلَا قُوَّةٍ. Dull, not exhilarating, قَصِفٌ ــ مُمِلٌّ ــ مُضْعِبٌ. To be —, هَمَدَ.

Lifelessly, ad. In a spiritless manner, بِلَا مُرُوَّةٍ ــ بِقَصَفٍ.

Lifelessness, n. Absence of life, death, مَوْتٌ ــ عَدَمُ حَيَاةٍ. Want of power, weakness, ضَعْفٌ ــ عَجْزٌ ــ وَنًى. Dullness, وِنَاءٌ ــ عَدَمُ مُرُوَّةٍ ــ تَهَاوُنٌ ــ قَصَفٌ.

Lifelike, a. عَيْنُ ٱلشَّيْءِ ــ مِثْلُ ٱلْأَصْلِ ــ طِبْقٌ.

Lifelong, a. مُسْتَقِرٌّ مُدَّةَ ٱلْحَيَاةِ.

Life-preserver, n. An apparatus for saving life from drowning, عَامَةٌ (or عَوَّامَةٌ) ٱلنَّجَاةِ ــ عَامَةٌ (or عَوَّامَةٌ) ٱلْخَلَاصِ. A club, دَبُّوسٌ ــ نَبُّوتٌ.

Lifespring, n. يَنْبُوعُ (or مَنْبَعُ) ٱلْحَيَاةِ.

Lifetime, n. مُدَّةُ ٱلْحَيَاةِ ــ عُمْرٌ.

Lift, v.t. To raise up, رَفَعَ ــ أَشَالَ ــ شَالَ بِ ــ عَلَّى. To — up the countenance, رَفَعَ ٱلْوَجْهَ. To — up a prayer, طَلَبَ ــ تَضَرَّعَ ــ رَفَعَ صَلَوَةً. To — up the voice, صَوَّتَ ــ رَفَعَ ٱلصَّوْتَ. To — up the eyes, رَفَعَ عَيْنَيْهِ. To — one's self up, اِرْتَفَعَ. She lifted her veil, رَفَعَتْ (or كَشَفَتْ) عَنْ وَجْهِهَا ٱلْغِطَاءَ. To be lifted, اِنْشَالَ ــ اِرْتَفَعَ ــ تَعَلَّى. To be lifted up from, اِرْتَفَعَ عَنْ.

Lift, v.i. To be raised into view, رُفِعَ لِلنَّظَرِ. The thing lifted into my view, رُفِعَ لِيَ ٱلشَّيْءُ. The mirage lifted the person or figure (into view), زَالَ بِهِ ٱلسَّرَابُ ــ رَفَعَ ٱلسَّرَابُ ٱلشَّخْصَ.

Lift, n. The act of lifting, رَفْعٌ ــ شَوَلَانٌ ــ شَوْلٌ. A rise, شَائِلَةٌ ــ شَوْلَةٌ ــ رَفْعَةٌ. A machine to lift with, مِرْفَعٌ. Aid, تَأْيِيدٌ ــ مُسَاعَدَةٌ ــ مُعَاوَنَةٌ. A drive or ride, رَكْبَةٌ. Lifts, mast-ropes, مِنْتَلِيَة ــ عَيَايِيرُ ــ حَلِيَةٌ ــ حِبَالُ أَثْقَالِ ٱلْمَرْكَبِ. A dead —, extreme emergency, أَشَدُّ ٱلضِّيقِ ــ عِزُّ ٱلضِّيقَةِ. To be at a dead —, أَشْرَفَ عَلَى ٱلْهَلَاكِ.

Ligament, n. عَصَبٌ pl. عِصَابَةٌ ــ عِصَابٌ. A bond, قَيْدٌ pl. قُيُودٌ ــ رِبَاطٌ pl. رِبَاطَاتٌ.

Ligamental, a. }
Ligamentous, } مُتَعَلِّقٌ بِٱلْعَصَبِ ــ عَصَبِيٌّ.

Ligation, n. The act of binding, حَزْقٌ ــ عَقْدٌ ــ رَبْطٌ. The state of being bound, قَيْدٌ ــ اِرْتِبَاطٌ.

Ligature, n. A bandage, عَصَبٌ pl. عِصَابٌ ــ عِصَابَةٌ ــ حُفَاظٌ ــ خَبِيبَةٌ pl. خَبَائِبُ.

Light, n. That by which we see, نُورٌ ــ ضِيَاءٌ ــ ضَوْءٌ ــ ضَحْوٌ. Light, as of a candle or lamp, ضَوْءٌ ــ نُورٌ. A candle, lamp, مِصْبَاحٌ pl. مَصَابِيحُ ــ قِنْدِيلٌ pl. قَنَادِيلُ ــ سِرَاجٌ pl. سُرُجٌ. Fire, نَارٌ. Clearness, صَفْوَةٌ ــ صَفَاءٌ ــ صَفْوٌ ــ نُورٌ. Illustration, إِيضَاحٌ ــ تَشْرِيحٌ. Situation, position, طَلْعَةٌ ــ نَظَرٌ ــ مَوْقِعٌ. The dawning —, وُضُوحٌ ــ شَقُّ ٱلْفَجْرِ ــ مَبْرَقُ ٱلصُّبْحِ ــ ٱلصَّبَاحُ ــ ٱلْإِصْبَاحُ. Knowledge, عِلْمٌ ــ مَعْرِفَةٌ ــ فَنٌّ. Joy, فَرَحٌ ــ اِبْتِهَاجٌ ــ نُورُ ٱلسُّرُورِ.

The light through a crevice during sunshine, سَوْطُ باطِلٍ. The lights of the firmament, أَنْوارُ ٱلسَّماءِ. Light of Light, (God), نُورُ ٱلنُّورِ – ذُو ٱلنُّورِ. It throws — on past transactions, يُلْقِي نُورًا عَلَى ما مَضَى مِنَ ٱلْأُمُورِ.

Bad light, as of a candle, نُورٌ غَيْرُ ساطِعٍ – ضَوْءٌ عاطِلٌ. A bad light in which to view, as a picture, مَوْقِعٌ يَسُدُّ (or يَحْجُبُ) ٱلْمَنْظَرَةَ.

Borrowed light, as that of the moon, نُورُ ٱلْقَمَرِ – إِسْتِنارَةُ ٱلْقَمَرِ مُسْتَعارٌ (مِنَ ٱلشَّمْسِ).

False light, نُورٌ كَذّابٌ.

Floating light, سَفِينَةُ فَنارٍ – مَرْكَبُ مَنارَةٍ.

Good light, as of a candle, ضَوْءٌ لامِعٌ – نُورٌ مُضِيءٌ. A good light in which to view, as a picture, مَوْقِعُ ٱلنُّورِ.

The Northern lights, الأَنْوارُ ٱلشَّمالِيَّةُ.

The light of one's countenance, تَوْجِيهٌ – حُسْنُ نَظَرٍ – نُورُ ٱلْوَجْهِ.

To ask one for a light, إِسْتَضاءَ مِن – ٢ طَلَبَ ضَوْءًا مِن – إِسْتَنارَ بِ.

To bring to light, ٢ شَهَرَ بِ – جَلَّى – ٢ جَلا – أَوْضَحَ – ضَوَّى عَن – أَوْرَى – أَظْهَرَ.

To catch a gleam of light, تَضَوَّى.

To come to light, إِنْفَضَحَ – إِشْتَهَرَ – إِنْجَلَى – تَجَلَّى – ٢ جَلا.

To give light, ضَوَّى – أَضاءَ.

To light a light, أَشْعَلَ – ٢ شَعَلَ.

To place in a false light, ٢ حَرَفَ ٱلشَّيْءَ عَنْ وَجْهِهِ – ٢ عَكَسَ. To be so placed, إِنْعَكَسَ – إِنْحَرَفَ.

To put out, as of a light, أَطْفَأَ; of a fire, أَهْمَدَ – أَباخَ – أَخْبَى.

To see in a false light, أَبْصَرَ بِٱلْعَكْسِ.

To show a light, ضَوَّى – أَظْهَرَ نُورًا.

To stand in one's own light, to disappoint one's self, خَيَّبَ نَفْسَهُ – أَضَرَّ نَفْسَهُ. To keep off the light by one's self, ٢ حَجَبَ ٱلضَّوْءَ بِذاتِ شَخْصِهِ.

To strike a light, ٢ قَدَحَ نارًا بِٱلْمِقْداحِ – ٢ زَنَدَ ٱلنّارَ.

To throw light upon, of light, ضَوَّى – أَضاءَ – أَنارَ – نَوَّرَ. To explain, جَلَّى – صَرَّحَ بِ – أَوْضَحَ.

Light, *a.* Bright, giving light, مُنِيرٌ – مُضِيءٌ – نَيِّرٌ – ضَوِيٌّ. Not heavy, خَفِيفٌ *pl.* خِفافٌ. Flimsy, سَخِيفٌ – سَفِيهٌ. Nimble, سَرِيعٌ *pl.* سِرْعانٌ – حَرِكٌ – نَدِبٌ – نَشِطٌ – فَزٌّ – بُلْبُلٌ *and* سِراعٌ – خَفِيفٌ – بَطِرٌ. Easy, هَيِّنٌ – أَهْوَنُ – سَهْلٌ. Light of digestion, سَهْلُ ٱلْهَضْمِ. Light, of a colour, خَفِيفٌ – مَفْتُوحٌ – مَفْتُوحُ ٱللَّوْنِ. Gay, بَهِيجٌ – سارٌّ – مَغْبُوطٌ – بَشُوشٌ – جَذْلانُ. Giddy, trifling, أَطْيَرُ – طائِشٌ – فَرْفارٌ – أَثْوَلُ. Light, of a burden, خَفِيفٌ. Not deep in the water, غَيْرُ غَطّاسٍ فِي ٱلْماءِ – عَوّامٌ – سَبّاحٌ. Small, as of a part, جُزْئِيٌّ. Small, of little importance, تافِهٌ – لَيْسَ تَحْتَ خَبَرٍ – خَفِيفٌ – واهٍ – وَجِيزٌ. A — wind, نَسِيمٌ – رِيحٌ خَفِيفَةٌ. Light troops, عَسْكَرٌ خَفِيفٌ. A — task, شُغْلٌ هَيِّنٌ – أَشْغُولَةٌ خَفِيفَةٌ. How —, bright, it is! ما أَضْواهُ. To be —, not dark, أَنارَ – ٢ نارَ – أَضاءَ. To be —, not heavy, ٢ خَفَّ. To be —, fickle, trifling, ٢ خَفَّ – ٢ طاشَ – ٢ طارَ طائِرُهُ. To be —, gay, ٢ إِبْتَهَجَ – ٢ بَهِجَ. To be — in estimation, ٢ خَفَّ. (The same verb ٢ خَفَّ applies to being light-hearted, brisk, quick in motion, unsteady, fickle, deranged in intellect, and to be sharp, clever.) One of the scales of the balance was light, ٢ خَفَّ ٱلْمِيزانُ. He is — of hearing, فِي أُذُنِهِ خِفَّةٌ.

To make light of a thing, إِسْتَخَفَّ: He made light of him, إِسْتَخَفَّ بِهِ. He considered it light, easy to carry, إِسْتَخَفَّهُ.

To make light, as of advice, إِسْتَقَلَّ – إِسْتَحْقَرَ.

Light, *v.t.* To set on fire, أَشْعَلَ – شَعَّلَ – أَوْقَدَ – أَضْرَمَ – ٢ سَعَرَ.

To —, as of a candle, أَشْعَلَ – أَسْرَجَ – ضَوَّى. To give light, ضَوَّى – أَنارَ – نَوَّرَ – أَضا. *See also to* Kindle, *v.t.*

Light, *v.i.* To take fire, إِشْتَعَلَ – تَشَعَّلَ. To — upon, to meet with, صادَفَ – إِلْتَحَقَ بِ – ٢ عَثَرَ (or تَعَثَّرَ) عَلَى – أَصابَ. To fall upon, يَقَعُ *aor.* وَقَعَ عَلَى. To pick up, إِلْتَقَطَ.

To — off, ٢ نَزَلَ عَن. *See also to* Alight, *v.i.*

Lighten, *v.t.* To give light, ضَوَّى – نَوَّرَ – أَنارَ – أَضاءَ. To make light, not heavy, خَفَّفَ. To make easy, هَوَّنَ – سَهَّلَ. To lighten, make easy, to, سَهَّلَ عَلَى – هَوَّنَ عَلَى. To gladden, أَفْرَحَ – ٢ سَرَّ. They cast their wares into the sea to — the boat, طَرَحُوا أَمْتِعَتَهُمْ إِلَى ٱلْبَحْرِ لِيُخَفِّفُوا عَنِ ٱلسَّفِينَةِ. They began to — the ship, جَعَلُوا يُفَرِّغُونَ ٱلْمَرْكَبَ.

Lighten, *v.i.* Of lightning, بَرَقَتِ ٱلسَّماءُ – أَبْرَقَ – ٢ بَرَقَ. It lightens, الدُّنْيا تَبْرُقُ – البَرْقُ بادٍ.

Lighter, *n.* One who lights, شَعّالٌ – مُضَوِّيٌّ. A cargo boat, جَرِيمَةٌ – ماعُونَةٌ.

Lighterage, *n.* Charge for a lighter, أُجْرَةُ ٱلْماعُونَةِ.

Lighterman, *n.* مَلّاحُ ٱلْماعُونَةِ *pl.* مَلّاحَةٌ.

Light-fingered, *a.* Having industrious hands, نَبِلُ ٱلْأَصابِعِ. Given to pilfering, رَجُلٌ مُسِلٌّ – سَلّابَةٌ – طَرّازٌ – نَشّالٌ.

Light-headed, *a.* مَطْيُورٌ – أَطْيَرُ – طائِشٌ. To be —, ٢ طاشَ – ٢ طارَ طائِرُهُ – ٢ خَفَّ – ٢ طارَ عَقْلُهُ.

Light-headedness, *n.* طَيّارَةٌ – طَياشَةٌ – طَيَشانٌ.

Light-hearted, *a.* هَشٌّ بَشٌّ – مَسْرُورٌ – طَرِبٌ – فَرِحٌ – بَشُوشٌ – بَطِرٌ – يَحْبُورٌ. To be —, ٢ طَرِبَ – ٢ سُرَّ – ٢ حَبِرَ.

Light-heartedness, *n.* هَشًا ـ طَرَب ـ سُرُور ـ إنْبِسَاط ـ حُبُور ـ بَهْجَة ـ كَيْف.

Light-horse, *n.* أَسَاوِرُ خَفِيفَةٌ.

Lighthouse, *n.* مَنَار ـ مَنَارَة *pl.* مَنَاوِرُ *and* مَنَايِرُ ـ فَنَار. A fixed —, فَنَارٌ ثَابِتٌ ; a revolving —, فَنَارٌ دَوَّارٌ.

Light-infantry, *n.* عَسْكَرٌ مُشَاةٌ خَفِيفٌ.

Lightless, *a.* Without light, بِلَا ضَوْءٍ ـ مِنْ غَيْرِ نُورٍ.

Lightly, *ad.* Without weight, بِدُونِ ثِقْلٍ. With ease, بِسُهُولَةٍ. With alacrity, بِنَشَاطٍ ـ بِخِفَّةٍ. Without consideration, بِغَيْرِ تَمْيِيزٍ. With evil intent, شَرًّا. To tread — on the ground, خَفَّ عَلَى ٱلْأَرْضِ. To esteem —, إسْتَحْقَرَ ـ إسْتَقَلَّ. *See also under* Slightly, *ad.*

Light-minded, *a.* Volatile, سَفِيه ـ أَخْطَلُ ـ طَائِش ـ فَرْفَار. To be —, طَاشَ ـ سَفِهَ ـ طَارَ طَائِرُهُ.

Light-mindedness, *n.* خِفَّة ـ سَفَاهَة ـ خَطَل ـ طَيَشَان ـ فَرْفَرَة.

Lightness, *n.* State of being light, not dark, ضَوْء ـ نُور. Want of weight, خِفَّة. Agility, quickness, خِفَّة ـ نَشَاط ـ بَهْجَة ـ سُرْعَة ـ مُرُوَّة ـ إنْعَاج. Unsteadiness, خِفَّة ـ سَفَاهَة ـ خَطَل ـ عَدَمُ قَرَارٍ ـ فَرْفَرَة. Delicacy, fineness, رِقَّة. Joyfulness, إنْبِسَاط ـ كَيْف ـ سُرُور ـ حُبُور.

Lightning, *n.* بَرْق *pl.* بُرُوق. Forked —, بَرْقٌ مُتَشَعِّبٌ ـ بَرْقٌ مَفْلُوقٌ. Continued flashes of —, سَلَاسِلُ ٱلْبَرْقِ. The — appeared, it lightened, بَرَقَ ٱلْبَرْقُ. The — almost took away their sight, يَكَادُ ٱلْبَرْقُ يَخْطَفُ أَبْصَارَهُمْ. To be struck by —, أُبْرِقَ.

Lightning-conductor, *n.* }
Lightning-rod, } آلَةٌ تَقِي مِنَ ٱلصَّاعِقَةِ ـ بَرَّاقَة.

Lights, *n.* The lungs, سَحْر ـ رِئَة *pl.* رِئُون. The — of a calf, فَشَّة.

Lightsome, *a.* Giving light, نَيِّر ـ مُنِير. Gay, هَشّ بَشّ ـ طَرِب ـ مَسْرُور ـ فَرْحَان. Bright, نَضِير ـ نَاضِر ـ نَضِير. Cheering, شَارِح ـ سَارّ ـ مُطْرِب ـ مُفْرِح.

Lightsomeness, *n.* The being light, not dark, نُور ـ تَنَوُّر. Gaiety, إنْبِسَاط ـ فَرَح ـ طَرَب ـ سُرُور ـ أُنْس ـ هَشًا.

Light-witted, *a.* *See* Light-headed.

Lign-aloes, *n.* عُود ـ عُودٌ صَنْفِيٌّ ـ قُطْر ـ عُودُ ٱلطِّيبِ ـ عُودُ ٱلنَّدِّ.

Ligneous, *a.* مِثْلَ ٱلْخَشَبِ ـ خَشَبِيٌّ.

Lignification, *n.* The act of turning into wood, تَخْشِيب ; the being turned into wood, تَخَشُّب.

Ligniform, *a.* مِثْلَ ٱلْخَشَبِ.

Lignify, *v.t.* خَشَّبَ ـ صَيَّرَ خَشَبًا.

Lignify, *v.i.* تَخَشَّبَ ـ صَارَ كَٱلْخَشَبِ.

Lignite, *n.* خَشَبٌ مَعْدِنِيٌّ.

Lignum-vitæ, *n.* خَشَبُ ٱلْأَنْبِيَاءِ ـ حَطَبُ ٱلْقِدِّيسِينَ.

Like, *a.* ضَدِيد *pl.* أَضْدَاد ـ مِثْل *pl.* أَمْثَال ـ كَفِيل *pl.* كُفَلَاءُ ـ ضِرْب *pl.* أَضْرَاب ـ أَخ ـ مُمَاثِل ـ شَبِيه *pl.* شِبَاه ـ (or ضَرْب). Like, fellow, بَدِيد ـ أَخ ـ أُخْت. A little like, مُثَيْل. Equal, نَظِير ـ قِرْن ـ مُسَاوٍ. Probable, مُحْتَمَل. Like thee, سِوَاكَ ـ مَثَلُكَ ; like them, سِوَاهُمْ ـ مِثْلُهُمْ. This is like it, هٰذَا مِثْلُهُ ـ هٰذَا شَبِيهُهُ. These things are not like one another, هٰذِهِ ٱلْأَشْيَاءُ لَيْسَ هِيَ مِثْلَ بَعْضِهَا. They were like one another, تَشَابَهُوا. He is like his mother, يُشَابِهُ أُمَّهُ ـ هُوَ مِثْلُ أُمِّهِ. Who is like unto thee, مَنْ مِثْلُكَ. I have never seen anything like it, عُمْرِي مَا رَأَيْتُ شَيْئًا مِثْلَهُ. Such like things, أُمُورٌ مِثْلُ هٰذِهِ. As like as two peas, (*prov.*) مِثْلُ فُولَةٍ مَقْسُومَةٍ. Like master like man, كَمَا هُوَ ٱلسَّيِّدُ كَذٰلِكَ هُوَ ٱلْعَبْدُ. To be like, قَارَبَ ـ شَابَهَ ـ شَبُهَ بِ. To make like, سَاوَى ـ تَشَبَّهَ بِ ـ مَثَّلَ بِ.

Like, *n.* That which is like or equal, مِثْل ـ شَبِيه ـ مَثِيل. Fellow, as one of a pair, بَدِيد ـ ضَرِيب ـ ضِرْب ـ ضِرْع ـ عِدْل. This garment is the like of this, هٰذَا ٱلثَّوْبُ أَخُو هٰذَا. The like of which was never known, لَمْ يُعْهَدْ لَهُ مِثَالٌ. Probability, إحْتِمَال. The like of a thing, that which doubles it, ضِعْفُ ٱلشَّيْءِ. I shall never see his like again, لَنْ أَعْهَدَ نَظِيرَهُ قَطُّ ـ لَنْ أَرَى مِثْلَهُ قَطُّ. He had like to have done it, كَادَ فَعَلَهُ. I had like to have done it, كِدْتُ أَفْعَلُهُ. Such an one is the like of such an one, فُلَانٌ ضَرِيبُ فُلَانٍ. I have the like of your boy, عِنْدِي عِدْلُ غُلَامِكَ.

Like, *ad.* In the same manner, كَ ـ مِثَال ـ مَثَل ـ كَمِثْلِ ـ زِيّ. Probably, إحْتِمَالًا. Like a man, كَرَجُلٍ. Like as, مِثْلَمَا ـ كَأَنَّ. In like manner, كَذٰلِكَ. And the —, وَمَا شَابَهَهُ.

Like, *v.t.* To be pleased with, approve, وَدَّ ـ هَوِيَ ـ إسْتَحْسَنَ ـ أَعْجَبَ ـ إشْتَهَى ـ أَحَبَّ. To desire, wish, إشْتَهَى ـ أَرَادَ ـ رَغِبَ فِي ـ رَغِبَ ـ إرْتَغَبَ فِي. To be agreeable to, to approve of, رَضِيَ عَنْ *aor.* يَرْضَى. To like better, to prefer, إسْتَفْضَلَ. To like, in the sense of to love, as a lover, عَشِقَ. He liked the cooking, إسْتَحْسَنَ ٱلطَّبِيخَ. I did not like it, it was not to my liking, مَا إسْتَطْيَبْتُهُ ـ مَا جَاءَ عَلَى خَاطِرِي ـ مَا أَعْجَبَنِي ـ مَا جَاءَ عَلَى مَيْلِي. He liked the taste of it, إسْتَلَذَّ طَعْمَهُ. He does not like work, مَا لَهُ مَيْلٌ إلَى ٱلشُّغْلِ. The man did not like to take the woman, لَمْ يَرْضَ ٱلرَّجُلُ أَنْ

يَأْخُذُ ٱلْمَرْأَةَ. He liked, was pleased, with me, سَرَّ بِي. I liked the thing, was pleased with it, رَاقَنِي ٱلشَّيْءُ ². I should like it to be so, وَدِدْتُ لَوْ كَانَ كَذَا. I should have liked it had you done so, وَدِدْتُ لَوْ أَنَّكَ فَعَلْتَ كَذَا.

Like, *v.i.* رَانَ *aor.* يَرُونُ – جَآءَ عَلَى خَاطِرِهِ *aor.* يَجِيءُ ² – نَاسَبَ. I should like to know, يَا لَيْتَ شِعْرِي. As you like, عَلَى رِضَاكَ – عَلَى مُرَادِكَ – عَلَى خَاطِرِكَ – عَلَى كَيْفِكَ.

Likelihood, *n.* } Appearance of truth or reality, شِبْهٌ – مُشَابَهَةٌ.
Likeliness, } Probability, قُرْبٌ مِنَ – تَخْمِينٌ – إِحْتِمَالٌ – ٱلْعَقْلِ. There is no — that, لَا يُحْتَمَلُ أَنْ (or لَا يَحْتَمِلُ أَنْ). The — now is so and so, ٱلْمُتَرَجِّحُ ٱلْآنَ كَذَا.

Likely, *a.* مُحْتَمِلٌ – مِنَ ٱلْمُحْتَمَلِ – قَرِيبُ ٱلْإِحْتِمَالِ – قَرِيبٌ مِنَ ٱلْعَقْلِ. It is much more — that he will do it, ٱلْأَرْجَحُ جِدًّا أَنْ يَفْعَلَهُ. The motives — to influence him, ٱلْأَسْبَابُ جَدِيرَةٌ أَنْ تُؤَثِّرَ فِيهِ. He is a — man to do this, هُوَ جَدِيرٌ بِهٰذَا. He is the most — man for it, هُوَ أَجْدَرُ بِهِ.

Likely, *ad.* Probably, بِٱلتَّخْمِينِ – عَلَى ٱلتَّخْمِينِ – بِٱلْإِحْتِمَالِ – تَخْمِينًا. It is very —, قَرِيبُ ٱلْإِحْتِمَالِ. It is still — that he will return, لَا زَالَ رُجُوعُهُ مِنَ ٱلْمُمْكِنِ. I do not know whether it is — that the Government will reply to his letter, لَا أَدْرِي هَلْ مِنَ ٱلْمُمْكِنِ أَنَّ ٱلدَّوْلَةَ تُجَاوِبُ خَطَّهُ.

Like-minded, *a.* عَلَى رَأْيٍ – عَلَى فِكْرٍ وَاحِدٍ – عَلَى ٱهْتِمَامٍ وَاحِدٍ – وَاحِدٍ.

Liken, *v.t.* To make like, to liken to, مَثَّلَ بِ – شَبَّهَ بِ. To whom will you liken God? بِمَنْ تُشَبِّهُونَ ٱللّٰهَ. To whom shall I liken you? بِمَنْ أُشَبِّهُكَ. He shall be likened to, يُشَبَّهُ بِ.

Likeness, *n.* Similarity in appearance, مُشَابَهَةٌ – شِبْهٌ – شَكْلٌ – شَاكِلَةٌ. Equally, كَفَآءَةٌ – كِفَآءٌ. The counterpart, طِبْقٌ – عَيْنٌ. A picture, تَصْوِيرٌ *pl.* تَصَاوِيرُ – صُورَةٌ *pl.* صُوَرٌ – رَسْمٌ. There is a — between them, بَيْنَهُمْ شَبَهٌ. There is in him a — to his father, يُشْبِهُ أَبَاهُ – فِيهِ لَمْحَةٌ مِنْ أَبِيهِ. I see in you a — to him, شَبَّهْتُكَ بِهِ. To pretend to have a likeness to one, تَشَبَّهَ بِهِ. To sit for one's —, قَعَدَ حَتَّى يَتَصَوَّرَ ² (or تُؤْخَذَ صُورَتُهُ). To have one's — taken, تَصَوَّرَ.

Likewise, *ad.* In like manner, مِثْلُهُ – نَظِيرُهُ – كَذٰلِكَ. Also, أَيْضًا *vulg.* كَمَانْ. He went out and did —, خَرَجَ وَفَعَلَ كَذٰلِكَ ². He — took part in it, هُوَ أَيْضًا ٱشْتَرَكَ فِيهِ.

Liking, *n.* رِضًى – مَرْضَاةٌ – وُدٌّ – وِدٌّ – وِدَادٌ. It was to his —, كَانَ عَلَى خَاطِرِهِ; of food, أَرْضَاهُ – أَعْجَبَهُ – وَافَقَهُ – إِسْتَحْسَنَهُ – إِسْتَلَذَّهُ. To take a — to, جَادَ إِلَى ² – وَدَّ ² – تَشَوَّقَ إِلَى. To take on —, أَخَذَهُ بِٱلْخِيَارِ.

Lilac, *n.* The shrub, لَيْلَك – لَغْلَى.

Lilac, *a.* لَغْلِيٌّ.

Liliaceous, *a.* سَوْسَنِيٌّ – مُتَعَلِّقٌ بِٱلسَّوْسَنِ – مُتَعَلِّقٌ بِٱلزَّنْبَقِ – زَنْبَقِيٌّ.

Lilied, *a.* مُزَخْرَفٌ (or مُشَكَّلٌ) بِٱلزَّنْبَقِ – مُزَيَّنٌ بِٱلسَّوْسَنِ.

Liliputian, *a.* and *n.* صَغِيرٌ جِدًّا. *See also* Dwarf, *n.* and *a.*

Lily, *n.* The white —, زَنْبَقٌ. The narcissus —, زَنْبَقُ ٱلنَّرْجِسِ. The asphodel, بَرْوَقٌ – خُنْثَى. The hyacinth, خُزَامَةٌ. The blue —, سَوْسَانٌ – سَوْسَنٌ. The water —, نَيْلُوفَر – نَيْنُوفَر. The yellow —, زَنْبَقٌ أَصْفَرُ. Lily of the valley, سَوْسَن – مُضَعَّف.

Limb, *n.* Any member, جِدْلٌ *pl.* جُدُولٌ. A — of the body, عُضْوٌ *pl.* أَعْضَآءٌ ² – آرَابٌ *pl.* أَرْبٌ. A — of a slaughtered animal, بَدَنٌ *pl.* أَبْدَانٌ. The bones of the arms and legs, جُدُولٌ. A border, extremity, طَرَفٌ *pl.* أَطْرَافٌ – حَافَةٌ *pl.* حَافٌّ. A — of the moon, قِطْعَةُ ٱلْقَمَرِ: The upper —, (of the moon,) ٱلْمُحِيطُ ٱلْأَوْسَطُ; the lower —, ٱلْمُحِيطُ ٱلتَّحْتَانِيُّ. The — of a tree, غُصْنٌ *pl.* أَغْصَانٌ. A — of the law, مِنْ أَهْلِ ٱلشَّرْعِ. A — of the devil, خَبِيثٌ – شَاطِرٌ – شَيْطَانٌ. To cut up — by —, to joint, أَرَّبَ. *See also under* Member, *n.*

Limb, *v.t.* To give limbs to, وَضَعَ لِ – أَعْضَآءً *aor.* يَضَعُ. To cut a — from, قَطَعَ ² – جَذَّ ² – بَتَكَ ². To hit in a —, as the foot, أَصَابَهُ فِي رِجْلِهِ – أَصَابَ رِجْلَهُ – رَجَلَ ².

Limbed, *a.* Having limbs, ذُو أَعْضَآءٍ. Hit, مُصَابٌ.

Limber, *a.* Easily bent, pliable, رَطِيبٌ – رَطْبٌ – خَنِثٌ – لَيِّنٌ. *See also* Flexible, *a.*

Limber, *n.* } Of a gun, عَرَبَةُ ٱلْمِدْفَعِ. To limber a gun, رَكَّبَ
Limbers, } شَدَّ ٱلْمِدْفَعَ بِٱلْعَرَبَةِ ² – ٱلْمِدْفَعَ عَلَى ٱلْعَرَبَةِ.

Limberness, *n.* لِينَةٌ – خُنْثٌ. *See also* Flexibility, *n.*

Limbless, *a.* مِنْ غَيْرِ أَعْضَآءٍ – خَالٍ مِنَ ٱلْأَعْضَآءِ.

Limbo, *n.* The intermediate state, ٱلْأَعْرَافُ; called by the Christians, يَمْبُوس. A place of restraint, prison, مَحْبَسٌ – مَحْفَظٌ – سِجْنٌ.

Lime, *n.* Calcined stone, نُورَةٌ – كِلْسٌ – جِيرٌ. Slaked or quick —, كِلْسٌ مُطْفَأٌ; unslaked —, كِلْسٌ غَيْرُ مُطْفَىٍّ. Hydraulic —, كِلْسٌ جَامِدٌ – لَا يُؤَثِّرُ فِيهِ ٱلْمَآءُ. To reduce to —, كَلَّسَ. To burn to —, أَحَالَ – كِلْسًا بِٱلنَّارِ. Lime, the fruit, ضَرْبٌ مِنَ ٱللَّيْمُونِ. Lime juice, عَصِيرُ ٱللَّيْمُونِ. Burning a body with — by way of punishment, تَوْسِيطٌ. *See also* Birdlime, Linden, *n.*

Lime, *v.t.* To manure with —, سَمَّدَ ٱلْأَرْضَ بِكِلْسٍ ـ جَيَّرَ ٱلْأَرْضَ. To plaster with —, كَلَّسَ ـ جَيَّرَ ـ دَمَّمَ ـ [2] دَمَّ. To cement, أَلْحَمَ. To catch with birdlime, دَبَّقَ. Plastered with —, مُكَلَّسٌ.

Lime-burner, or plasterer, *n.* جَيَّار ـ كَلَّاس ـ مُكَلِّس.

Limekiln, *n.* أَتُون *pl.* أُتُن ـ كَلَّاسَة ـ قَمِينُ جِيْرٍ.

Lime-pit, *n.* أَتُون.

Limestone, *n.* حَجَرُ ٱلْجِيْرِ.

Lime-water, *n.* مَاءُ ٱلْجِيْرِ ـ مَاءُ ٱلْكِلْسِ.

Liming, *n.* Manuring with lime, تَسْمِيدُ ٱلْأَرْضِ بِكِلْسٍ ـ تَجْبِيرُ ٱلْأَرْضِ.

Limit, *n.* Utmost extent, حَدٌّ ـ غَايَة ـ نِهَايَة. A boundary, حُدُود *pl.* حَدٌّ ـ تُخُوم *pl.* تَخْم ـ أَزْفَة. A — of time, أَمَد. He or it reached his or its extreme —, [2] بَلَغَ أَمَدَهُ. To go beyond, exceed, the limits, تَجَاوَزَ (or جَاوَزَ or عَدَّى) ٱلْحُدُودَ. To set limits to, حَدَّدَ. To mark out the limits of a field, house, *etc.*, أَزَّفَ. Having a —, term, ذُو أَمَدٍ; *fem.* ذَاتُ. An extreme — attained, أَمَدٌ مَأْمُودٌ. The present state of existence has a —, but that which is to come is everlasting, الدُّنْيَا أَمَدٌ وَٱلْآخِرَةُ أَبَدٌ.

Limit, *v.t.* To fix limits, حَدَّدَ. To mark the boundaries of, أَزَّفَ. To set up boundary marks, أَقَامَ تُخُومًا. To confine, restrain, حَصَرَ [2] ـ أَحْصَرَ. Limited to a fixed number, مَحْدُودُ ٱلْعَدَدِ. Limited, as to time, مُؤَجَّل.

Limitable, *a.* قَابِلُ ٱلتَّحْدِيدِ ـ مِمَّا يُحَدَّدُ.

Limitary, *a.* On the boundaries, مُقِيمٌ عَلَى ٱلْحُدُودِ ـ عَلَى ٱلْحُدُودِ. To be — to, on the boundaries of, حَادَّ ـ تَاخَمَ.

Limitation, *n.* The act of bounding, تَحْدِيد; of confining, حَصْر ـ إِحْصَار. A boundary, حَدٌّ; confinement, إِنْحِصَار. A limited time, أَمَد.

Limited, *a.* Bounded, مُحَدَّد ـ مَحْدُود. Confined, restrained, مَحْصُور ـ مُنْحَصِر. Small, جُزْئِيٌّ ـ قَلِيل ـ مُخْتَصَر. Limited by law, مَشْرُوع. A — time, أَمَد.

Limitless, *a.* بِلَا حَدٍّ ـ غَيْرُ مَحْدُودٍ.

Limn, *v.t.* [2] رَسَمَ ـ صَوَّرَ.

Limner, *n.* رَسَّام ـ مُصَوِّر.

Limning, *n.* الرَّسْمُ ـ التَّصْوِيرُ.

Limp, *v.i.* To walk lamely, خَمَعَ ـ عَشَزَ ـ [2] عَرَجَ. *See also under* Lame, *a.*

Limp, *n.* خُمَاع ـ خُمُوع ـ عَشَزَان ـ عُرُوج. He has a —, بِهِ خُمَاعٌ. *See also* Limping, *n.*

Limp, *a.* رَخْوٌ ـ مُسْتَرْخٍ ـ هَشٌّ. *See also* Flaccid, *a.*

Limper, *n.* One who limps, عَاشِز ـ خَامِع ـ عَارِج.

Limpet, *n.* ضَرْبٌ مِنَ ٱلصَّدَفِ يَلْصَقُ بِٱلصُّخُورِ.

Limpid, *a.* قَرَاح ـ قَرِيح *pl.* أَقْرِحَة ـ صَافٍ *pl.* صَوَافٍ. To be —, صَفَا *aor.* يَصْفُو; to become —, تَصَفَّى; to make —, صَفَّى.

Limpidity, *n.*
Limpedness, } صَفَاء ـ صَفَاوَة.

Limping, *a.* خَامِع. *See also* Limper, *n.*

Limping, *n.* خَيْزَرَى ـ خَيْزَلَى ـ خُمَاع ـ خُمَال. *See also* Limp, *n.*

Limpingly, *ad.* بِخَيْزَرَى ـ بِخُمَاعٍ ـ كَٱلْعَارِجِ ـ عَرَجًا.

Limpness, *n.* رَخَاوَة ـ رَخَاء. *See also* Flaccidity, *n.*

Limpsy, Limsy, *a.* *See* Limp, *a.*

Limy, *a.* Glutinous, دَبِق ـ لَزِج. Calcareous, ذُو جِيْرٍ *fem.* ذَاتُ.

Linch-pin, *n.* مِحْوَرُ ٱلْعَجَلَةِ.

Linden, *n.* The tree, شَجَرَةُ ٱلزَّيْزَفُونِ. The water of the flower of the —, مَاءُ زَهْرِ ٱلزَّيْزَفُونِ.

Line, *n.* An extended mark, خَطٌّ *pl.* خُطُوط. A small cord, رَسَن *pl.* أَرْسَان ـ مَرَس *pl.* أَمْرَاس ـ حَبْل *pl.* حِبَال. A —, as of a page, سَطْر *pl.* سُطُور. A —, verse, of poetry, مِصْرَاع. A row, صَفّ *pl.* صُفُوف (*see also* Row, *n.*). A —, as of soldiers, *etc.*, صَفّ *pl.* صُفُوف; a station where such lines are drawn up, مَصَفّ *pl.* مَصَافّ. A boundary, حَدّ *pl.* حُدُود ـ تَخْم *pl.* تُخُوم. A — of fortification, خَطُّ ٱسْتِحْكَام ـ تَحْصِين ـ مَتَارِيس. An outline, contour, شَكْل ـ هَيْئَة ـ هِنْدَام ـ دَائِرَة ـ تَدْوِير. A mode, manner, شِرَاك ـ مِنْوَال ـ طَرِيقَة *pl.* طَرَائِق ـ بَاب *pl.* أَبْوَاب. Order, سِمَاط *pl.* سُمُوط ـ تَرْتِيب *pl.* تَرَاتِيبُ. Line of conduct, سِيرَة ـ سُلُوك ـ تَعَاطٍ ـ شُغْل ـ خِدْمَة. A profession, حِرْفَة. A — as of ancestry, نَسْل *pl.* أَنْسَال ـ نَجْل ـ سِلْسِلَة. The twelfth part of an inch, قَدْرُ حَبَّةِ شَعِيرٍ. A fishing —, صِنَّارَة ـ تُرٌّ. A builder's —, زِيج ـ مِطْمَر ـ زِئْبَق ـ مِطْمَار ـ تُرٌّ ـ إِمَام. An instrument to make lines with, جَدْوَل ـ مِسْطَرَة. A — where anything stops, or which separates it from something else, مَقْطَع ـ مُنْقَطَع. A ruled — on a book, جَدْوَلُ كِتَابٍ. Lines on the face, سَرَر ـ سِرَر. A — of the palms of the hand, سِرَار *pl.* أَسِرَّة *and* أَسَارِيرُ. A — in a drawing, نَمَش. Line, as of a railway, خَطّ *pl.* خُطُوط. They went away in one uniform — or manner, مَضَوْا عَلَى شِرَاكٍ وَاحِدٍ. (*See also under* Row, *n.*) That is not in my —, مَا هُوَ ـ لَيْسَ ذٰلِكَ مِنْ عَلَاقَتِي عَلَى طَرِيقَتِي. *See also* Parallel, *n.*

Branch line, of a railway, شُعْبَةٌ مِنْ سِكَّةِ حَدِيدٍ *pl.* شُعَب.

Curved line, خَطٌّ مَحْنِيٌّ — خَطٌّ مُنْحَنٍ.

Dotted line, i.e. Denoting doubt, خَطٌّ مِنْ نُقَطٍ يَدُلُّ عَلَى شَيْءٍ مُبْهَمٍ — نُقَطٌ تَدُلُّ عَلَى ٱلرَّيْبِ.

Equinoctial line, خَطُّ ٱلِٱسْتِوَآءِ.

Fishing line, صِنَّارَةٌ pl. صَنَانِيرُ.

In a line, صَفٌّ — مُصْطَفٌّ. To stand in a line, of many, إِصْطَفُّوا.

Main line, ٱلْخَطُّ ٱلْأَوْسَطُ — ٱلْخَطُّ ٱلْأَصْلِيُّ.

Meridian line, خَطُّ نِصْفِ ٱلنَّهَارِ.

Mixed line, خَطٌّ مُخْتَلِطٌ.

Right, straight, line, خَطٌّ مُسْتَقِيمٌ.

Ship of the line, بَارِجَةٌ pl. بَوَارِجُ.

Troops of the line, عَسَاكِرُ مُشَاةٌ.

To break a line, to go out of it, حَادَ عَنِ — عَدَلَ عَنِ ٱلصَّفِّ ٱلصَّفِّ. To break through a line, شَقَّ ٱلصَّفَّ.

To draw a line, as with a ruler, خَطَّ — إِسْتَطَرَ — سَطَرَ — سَطَّرَ — خَطَّطَ; to be lined, ruled, إِخْتَطَّ. To make a difference, مَيَّزَ — فَرَّقَ.

To draw up, as troops, in a line, صَفَّ — صَفَّفَ.

To drop one a line, كَتَبَ لَهُ سَطْرًا — شَيَّعَ لَهُ رُقْعَةً.

To pass the (equinoctial) line, عَبَرَ خَطَّ ٱلِٱسْتِوَآءِ.

To run a line, as of steamers, سَفَّرَ بَوَاخِرَ مُتَتَابِعَةً.

Line, v.t. To put a lining in, بَطَّنَ. To —, as with fortifications, حَصَّنَ. To — a street with soldiers, صَفَّ ٱلْعَسْكَرَ طُولَ ٱلطَّرِيقِ. Lined, having a lining, مُبَطَّنٌ.

Lineage, a. بَدَنٌ — نَسَبٌ pl. أَنْسَابٌ — نَجْلٌ — ذُرِّيَّةٌ — سِلْسِلَةٌ pl. سَلَاسِلُ.

Lineal, a. In direct descent, أَبًا عَنْ جَدٍّ. Hereditary, وِرَاثِيٌّ — وِرْثِيٌّ. Composed of lines, خُطُوطِيٌّ — مُرَكَّبٌ مِنْ خُطُوطٍ. Marked, as cloth, with crooked or wavy lines, مُعَرَّجٌ.

Lineally, ad. In a direct line, أَبًا عَنْ جَدٍّ.

Lineament, n. Form, صُورَةٌ — تَفْصِيلٌ — هَيْئَةٌ pl. هَيْئَاتٌ. Lineaments, countenance, طَلْعَةٌ — مَنْظَرٌ — وَجْهٌ — مُحَيًّا. See also Feature, n.

Linear, n. Pertaining to a line, خَطِّيٌّ — خُطُوطِيٌّ. Having lines, or streaks, of herbage, ذُو أَسْرَارٍ. In a line, linked, مُسَلْسَلٌ. Slender, of a plant, أَقْصَفُ. Fine, رَكِيكٌ — دَقِيقٌ. Linear, of lines in a drawing, ذُو نَمَشٍ fem. ذَاتُ — نَمَشِيٌّ.

Lineation, n. See Delineation, n.

Linen, n. Cloth of flax, قُمَاشُ كَتَّانٍ — كَتَّانٌ. Fine —, كَتَّانٌ خَاصٌّ. Garments of —, ثِيَابٌ مِنْ كَتَّانٍ. Dirty —, غَسِيلٌ.

Linen or cotton goods, بَزٌّ — قُمَاشٌ.

Linen, a. كَتَّانٌ — مِنْ كَتَّانٍ.

Linen-draper, n. بَزَّازٌ pl. بَزَّازُونَ — قَمَّاشٌ coll. قَمَّاشَةٌ.

Linen-press, n. خِزَانَةُ ٱلْقُمَاشِ.

Linen-trade, n. مَتْجَرُ ٱلْقُمَاشِ.

Linen-yarn, n. خِيطَانُ كَتَّانٍ.

Line-of-battle ship, بَارِجَةٌ pl. بَوَارِجُ.

Liner, n. A ship of a regular line, مَرْكَبٌ مِنْ جُمْلَةِ مَرَاكِبَ تَتَرَدَّدُ فِي أَسْفَارِهَا إِلَى جِهَةٍ وَاحِدَةٍ.

Ling, n. A kind of fish, نَوْعٌ مِنَ ٱلسَّمَكِ.

Linger, v.i. To dally, delay, تَمَهَّلَ — تَوَقَّفَ — تَأَخَّرَ — أَبْطَأَ — تَعَوَّقَ — تَوَانَى. To be prolonged, طَالَ. To languish, as under a disease, سَلَّ. To hesitate, be in doubt, تَصَرَّبَ — تَمَخْطَرَ. He lingered in his sickness, طَالَ بِهِ ٱلْمَرَضُ. While he lingered, delayed, لَمَّا تَوَانَى. To make to —, delay, أَبْطَأَ — بَطَّأَ بِهِ — أَخَّرَ.

Lingering, a. Protracted, مُمْتَدٌّ — طَوِيلٌ — مُزْمِنٌ — مُتَرَاخٍ. See also under Disease, n.

Lingering, n. Loitering, تَمَهُّلٌ — تَوَقُّفٌ — بَطَآءَةٌ — بُطْءٌ — تَوَانٍ.

Lingeringly, ad. With delay, بِتَوَانٍ — بِتَوَقُّفٍ — بِبَطَآءَةٍ.

Lingo, n. See Jargon, n.

Linguadental, a. مَا خَرَجَ مِنْ مَقْطَعَيِ ٱللِّسَانِ وَٱلْأَسْنَانِ مَعًا.

Lingual, a. لِسَانِيٌّ.

Linguiform, a. فِي صُورَةِ (or بِصُورَةِ) لِسَانٍ.

Linguist, n. مَاهِرٌ فِي ٱلْأَلْسِنَةِ.

Linguistic, a. / Linguistical, } مُتَعَلِّقٌ بِعِلْمِ ٱللُّغَاتِ.

Liniment, n. ضِمَادٌ — دِهَانٌ — مَرْهَمٌ — طِلَآءٌ — دِمَامٌ — نِثَاثٌ. To anoint with a —, دَمَّمَ — دَمَّ — نَثَّ — ضَمَدَ بِضِمَادٍ — دَهَنَ بِدِهَانٍ.

Lining, n. تَبْطِينٌ — بِطَانَةٌ. Lining leather for boots, سُلْفَةٌ.

Link, n. A part of a chain, كُلَّبٌ pl. كِلَابٌ — زَرَدٌ pl. زُرُودٌ — حَلْقَةُ سِلْسِلَةٍ pl. حَلَقٌ. Connexion, رِبَاطٌ — تَعَلُّقٌ. A step, دَرَجَةٌ — خُطْوَةٌ. A torch, مَشْعَلٌ pl. مَشَاعِلُ.

Link, v.t. To connect by links, سَلْسَلَ بِحَلَقٍ. To join in a chain, series, سَلْسَلَ. To bind, unite, جَمَعَ — وَصَّلَ — رَبَطَ.

Link-boy, n. مَشْعَلْجِي pl. مَشْعَلْجِيَّةٌ.

Linnæan, n. مَنْسُوبٌ إِلَى (or مَنُوطٌ بِ) قَاعِدَةِ لِينِيُوسَ ٱلْمَشْهُورِ بِعِلْمِ ٱلنَّبَاتِ.

Linnet, *n.* زُقَيْقِيَّة.

Linseed, *n.* } بِزْرُ ٱلْكَتَّانِ. Linseed meal, طَحِينُ بِزْرِ ٱلْكَتَّانِ.
Lintseed, } Linseed cake, عَجِينُ بِزْرِ ٱلْكَتَّانِ.

Linseed-oil, *n.* زَيْتُ بِزْرِ ٱلْكَتَّانِ.

Linsey-woolsey, *n.* Made of linen and wool, قُمَاشٌ مِنْ كَتَّانٍ وَصُوفٍ. Mean, حَقِيرٌ ـ دُونٌ ـ تَفِهٌ. Flimsy, سَخِيفٌ.

Linstock, *n.* مُسْكَةُ ٱلْفَتِيلَةِ *pl.* مُسَكٌ.

Lint, *n.* Scrapings of cloth for wounds, نُسَالَةٌ ـ كُتَيْتٌ ـ سَبِيخٌ.

Lintel, *n.* As of a door, أُسْكُفَّةٌ ـ سَاكِفٌ ـ لِجَافٌ ـ وَصِيدٌ *pl.* وُصُدٌ. The two lintels of a door, سَاكِفَا (or لِجِيفَتَا) ٱلْبَابِ ـ الْعَارِضَتَانِ.

Lion, *n.* The animal, حَيْدَرَةٌ ـ أَسَدٌ *pl.* أُسُودٌ ـ سَبُعٌ *pl.* سِبَاعٌ and سُبُوعَةٌ. A young —, سُبَيْعٌ. A lion's whelp, شِبْلٌ *pl.* شِبَالٌ. A resort of lions, مَأْسَدَةٌ. A land abounding in lions, أَرْضٌ مَأْسَدَةٌ. The constellation, بُرْجُ ٱلْأَسَدِ. An object of interest or curiosity, رَغِيبَةٌ *pl.* رَغَائِبُ ـ بَيْضَةُ ٱلْبَلَدِ ـ شُهْرَةٌ.

Lioness, *n.* سَبُعَةٌ ـ سَبْعَةٌ ـ لَبُوَةٌ and لِبْوَةٌ and لَبَاةٌ *pl.* لَبَآتٌ and لَبُوَاتٌ. A young —, سُبَيْعَةٌ.

Lion-hearted, *a.* أَسِدٌ ـ أَسِيدٌ ـ مُتَأَسِّدٌ ـ سَنْدَرِيٌّ.

Lionize, *v.t.* عَزَّزَ ـ بَالَغَ فِي ـ شَهَّرَ بَيْنَ ٱلنَّاسِ ـ صَيَّرَ بَيْضَةً ـ ٱلْبَلَدِ ـ إِسْتَنْسَرَ. To be lionized, تَعَزَّزَ ـ شُهِرَ مِنَ ٱلنَّاسِ ـ أَسْتَنْسَرَ ـ صَارَ بَيْضَةَ ٱلْبَلَدِ.

Lip, *n.* Of the mouth, شَفَةٌ *dual* شَفَتَا *pl.* شِفَاهٌ and شَفَهَاتٌ. The two lips, الْمَرَاشِفُ. The lip of a camel or horse, مِشْفَرٌ *pl.* مَشَافِرُ; of any solid-hoofed animal, جَحْفَلَةٌ *pl.* جَحَافِلُ. A small lip, شُفَيْهَةٌ. Having thick lips, غَلِيظُ ٱلشَّفَتَيْنِ ـ خُنَارِمٌ. Having large lips, أَشْفَهُ ـ شُفَاهِيٌّ. The lip of a wound, حَافَةُ ٱلْجُرْحِ *dual* حَافَتَانِ. To touch with the lips, but not to drink, لَثَمَ. To wet one's lips, take a sip, غَمَّسَ. To bring one's lips close to those of another, شَافَهَ. To strike on the lip, شَفَهَ. To make a lip, to pout, تَبَرْطَمَ ـ بَوَّزَ ـ حَرِنَ. *See also* Edge, *n.*

Lip, *v.t.* To put one's lip near to another's, to speak to, putting one's lips near to another's, شَافَهَ. To kiss, قَبَّلَ ـ بَاسَ.

Lipothymy, *n.* *See* Swoon, *n.*

Lipped, *a.* Having lips, ذُو شِفَاهٍ. *See also under* Lip, *n.*

Lippitude, *n.* Of the eyes, زِيَادَةُ غَمَصٍ ـ رَمَدٌ.

Liquefaction, *n.* The act of, حَلٌّ ـ تَذْوِيبٌ ـ إِمَاعَةٌ ـ صَهْرٌ; the being liquefied, الْحِلَالُ ـ ذَوَبَانٌ.

Liquefy, *v.t.* حَلَّ ـ ذَوَّبَ ـ أَذَابَ ـ أَمَاعَ ـ صَهَرَ.

Liquefy, *v.i.* تَحَلَّلَ ـ إِصْطَهَرَ ـ تَمَيَّعَ ـ مَاعَ ـ إِنْصَهَرَ.

Liquescency, *n.* Aptness to melt, قَرِيحَةٌ لِلذَّوَبَانِ.

Liquescent, *a.* ذَائِبٌ ـ مَائِعٌ.

Liquid, *a.* مَارِقٌ ـ ذَائِبٌ ـ مَايِعٌ ـ سَائِلٌ ـ مَآءٌ ـ صَهِيرٌ.

Liquid, *n.* خَلٌّ ـ مَايِعٌ *pl.* مَوَايِعُ ـ مَآءٌ *pl.* أَمْيَاهٌ. An inflammable —, مَايِعٌ سَرِيعُ ٱلِٱلْتِهَابِ.

Liquidate, *v.t.* To pay off a debt, أَوْفَى (or إِسْتَوْفَى) ٱلدَّيْنَ ـ غَلَّقَ ٱلْحِسَابَ ـ جَزَى ٱلدَّيْنَ.

Liquidation, *n.* Payment of debts, وَفَآءٌ (or جَزَآءٌ) دَيْنٍ. In —, تَحْتَ رُؤْيَةِ ٱلْمُحَاسِبِ ٱلرَّسْمِيِّ.

Liquidator, *n.* مَأْمُورٌ بِرُؤْيَتِهِ ـ مُوَكَّلٌ (or مَأْمُورٌ) بِٱلْمُحَاسَبَةِ ٱلْحِسَابَاتِ.

Liquidity, *n.* } إِمَاعَةٌ ـ تَمَيُّعٌ ـ مِيَاعَةٌ.
Liquidness, }

Liquor, *n.* A strong drink, spirit, عَنْبَرِيٌّ ـ عَرَقٌ عَنْبَرِيٌّ ـ شَرَابٌ مُثَلَّثٌ. Intoxicating liquors, مُسْكِرَاتٌ. *See also* Liquid, *n.*

Liquorice, *n.* *See* Licorice, *n.*

Lisp, *v.i.* طَمْطَمَ ـ تَهْتَهَ ـ تَمْتَمَ ـ لَكِنَ.

Lisp, *v.t.* تَهْتَهَ ـ تَمْتَمَ ـ لَفَظَ بِلُكْنٍ.

Lisp, *n.* } طَمْطَمَةٌ ـ تَمْتَمَةٌ ـ لُكْنَةٌ ـ لُكُونَةٌ ـ لُكْنٌ.
Lisping, }

Lisper, *n.* مُتَهْتِهٌ ـ مُتَمْتِمٌ ـ أَلْكَنُ.

Lispingly, *ad.* بِتَمْتَمَةٍ ـ بِلُكْنٍ ـ بِلُكُونَةٍ.

List, *v.t.* To border, form a border to, كَنَّفَ ـ أَنَارَ ـ نَيَّرَ. To cover with —, رَكَّبَ لـ حَاشِيَةً. *See also to* Enlist, *v.t.*

List, *v.t.* To lean, إِنْعَطَفَ ـ تَصَوَّبَ ـ إِنْحَدَرَ ـ مَالَ. To wish, شَآءَ *aor.* يَشَآءُ ـ أَرَادَ. They did to him whatever they listed, عَمِلُوا بِهِ كُلَّ مَا أَرَادُوا. The wind bloweth where it listeth, الرِّيحُ تَهُبُّ حَيْثُ تَشَآءُ. *See also to* Enlist, *to* Hearken, *vv.n.*

List, *n.* The edge of cloth, كَنَارٌ ـ حَاشِيَةٌ. A catalogue, قَائِمَةٌ ـ تَقْوِيمٌ ـ عَلَمٌ. An index, فِهْرِسٌ. A — of names, سِيَاقَةٌ أَسَامِي (or جَدْوَلُ) دَفْتَرُ أَسَامِي. An inclination to one side, مَيْلٌ ـ مَيَلَانٌ ـ إِنْحِرَافٌ ـ إِنْعِطَافٌ إِلَى جَنْبٍ. The Civil —, the income of a king, مَاهِيَّةُ ٱلْمَلِكِ ـ مَدْخُولُ ٱلسُّلْطَانِ; (*in Turkey*, الْإِيرَادُ ٱلْهُمَايُونِيُّ ـ الْخَزِينَةُ ٱلْخَاصَّةُ). The civil —, yearly stipend of functionaries, قَائِمَةُ سَنَوِيَّاتِ ٱلْمَأْمُورِيَّةِ. Soldiers on the active —, عَسَاكِرُ عَتِيدَةٌ لِلْقِتَالِ. Lists, for combat, مَعْرَكَةٌ ـ مِيدَانٌ.

Listen, *v.i.* To — attentively, أَنْصَتَ ـ تَسَمَّعَ ـ إِسْتَمَعَ.

To — to, to hear, attend to, تَسَمَّعَ ل ـ إِسْتَمَعَ ل ـ أَذِنَ ل ـ أَطَاعَ ل . To — to, pay attention to, to obey, أَنْصَتَ إِلَى ـ إِكْتَنَتَ إِلَى ـ سَمِعَ ل ـ أَذِنَ ل ـ أَصْغَى إِلَى .

Listener, *n.* سَمِيع ـ سَامِع *pl.* سَامِعُونَ ـ مُسْتَمِع .

Listening, *n.* سَمْع ـ سَمَاع ـ إِسْتِمَاع . A place for —, مَسْمَع .

Lister, *n.* One who makes a list, مُرَسِّمُ ٱلْقَائِمَةِ (*or* ٱلسِّيَاقَةِ) ـ مُعَلِّمُ ٱلْعَلَمِ .

Listless, *a.* لَا هَمَامَ لَهُ ـ فَاتِر ـ غَيْرُ مُبَالٍ ـ مُتَغَافِل ـ مُتَهَامِل ـ مُتَسَاهِل ـ تَارِك . To be —, تَرَاخَى ـ غَبِيَ ـ تَغَفَّلَ . He was — about it, تَرَاخَى فِي ٱلْأَمْرِ .

Listlessly, *ad.* بِغَيْرِ مُبَالَاةٍ ـ بِتَهَامُلٍ ـ بِتَغَافُلٍ ـ بِتَكَاسُلٍ .

Listlessness, *n.* قِلَّةُ مُرُوءَةٍ ـ تَغَافُل ـ إِهْمَال ـ تَهَامُل .

Lists, *n.* Ground enclosed for a race, حَاجِزٌ حَوْلَ ٱلْحَلْبَةِ ـ مِضْمَار ـ (*or* ٱلْمِيدَانِ) .

Litany, *n.* دُعَاءٌ عَامٌّ ـ لِيتَانِيَّة .

Literal, *a.* According to the letter, حَرْفِيٌّ ; closely following the words, لَفْظِيٌّ . A — translation, تَرْجَمَةٌ لَفْظٌ بِلَفْظٍ ـ تَرْجَمَةٌ كَلِمَةٌ بِكَلِمَةٍ .

Literalism, *n.* إِمْتِثَال بِٱلْحَرْفِ .

Literalist, *n.* مُتَمَسِّكٌ بِظَاهِرِ ٱلْأَلْفَاظِ فَقَط .

Literally, *ad.* Word for word, كَلِمَةً بِكَلِمَةٍ ـ حَرْفًا بِحَرْفٍ . According to the obvious meaning, حَسَبَ ظَاهِرِ ٱلْمَعْنَى . Without comment, بِدُونِ شَرْحٍ .

Literalness, *n.* دِقَّةُ ٱلْحَرْفِ ـ مُطَابَقَةُ ٱلْأَلْفَاظِ .

Literary, *a.* مُتَعَلِّقٌ بِٱلْعُلُومِ وَٱلْمَعَارِفِ ـ مُتَعَلِّقٌ بِٱلْكُتُبِ ـ مُخْتَصٌّ بِعِلْمِ ٱلْأَدَبِ . A — man, أَدِيب *pl.* أُدَبَاءُ ـ مُدَرِّس ـ مِنْ أَهْلِ ٱلْأَدَبِ ـ لَوْذَعِيٌّ . Literary pursuits, تَفَرُّغٌ إِلَى ٱلْعُلُومِ ـ أَشْغَالٌ أَدَبِيَّةٌ .

Literati, *n.* أَهْلُ ٱلْأَدَبِ ـ أَصْحَابُ ٱلْعِلْمِ ـ مَشَاهِيرُ ٱلْمُؤَلِّفِينَ .

Literatim, *ad.* حَرْفًا ـ حَرْفًا بِحَرْفٍ .

Literature, *n.* Science in general, ٱلْمَعْلُومَاتُ ـ ٱلْعُلُومُ ـ ٱلْعِلْمُ ـ كُتُبٌ أَدَبِيَّةٌ . Belles-lettres, عِلْمُ ٱلْأَدَبِ . Biblical —, عِلْمُ ٱلْكُتُبِ ٱلْمُقَدَّسَةِ . Authorship, تَأْلِيف . Books, ٱلْكُتُبُ ـ ٱلْمُؤَلَّفَاتُ .

Litharge, *n.* مَرْتَك ـ مُرْدَاسَنْج ـ مَرْتَك ـ مَرْتَج ; of gold, مَرْتَكٌ ذَهَبِيٌّ ; of silver, مَرْتَكٌ فِضِّيٌّ .

Lithe, *a.*
Lithesome, } لَيِّن . *See also* Flexible, *a.*

Litheness, *n.* لَيَان ـ لِينَة . *See also* Flexibility, *a.*

Lithic, *a.* مُتَعَلِّقٌ بِٱلْحَصَى .

Lithium, *n.* لِثِيُومٌ وَهُوَ ضَرْبٌ مِنَ ٱلْمَعَادِنِ .

Lithograph, *v.t.* رَسَمَ عَلَى ٱلْحَجَرِ لِلطَّبْعِ ـ طَبَعَ بِٱللِّيثُغْرَاف .

Lithograph, *n.* صُورَةٌ بِٱللِّيثُغْرَاف ـ مَطْبُوعٌ عَلَى ٱلْحَجَرِ .

Lithographer, *n.* لِيثُغْرَافْجِي .

Lithographic, *a.*
Lithographical, } لِيثُوغْرَاف .

Lithographically, *ad.* بِٱللِّيثُغْرَاف .

Lithography, *n.* صِنَاعَةُ ٱلرَّسْمِ عَلَى حَجَرٍ لِلطَّبْعِ ـ صِنَاعَةُ ٱللِّيثُغْرَاف .

Lithology, *n.* The science of stones, عِلْمٌ بِٱلْأَحْجَارِ ; of stones in the bladder, عِلْمٌ بِحَصَى ٱلْمَثَانَةِ .

Lithontriptor, *n.*
Lithotriptor, } مِسْحَقُ ٱلْحَصَى .

Lithofracteur, *n.* For crushing stones, مِرْضَخَة ـ مِدَقٌّ .

Lithotomist, *n.* جَرَّاحُ ٱلْحَصَى .

Lithotomy, *n.* جِرَاحَةُ ٱلْحَصَى .

Lithotripsy, *n.* سَحْقُ ٱلْحَصَى .

Litigant, *n.* At law, خَصِيم *pl.* خُصُوم ـ مُنَازِع *pl.* مُنَازِعُونَ ـ مُدَّعٍ ـ مُخَاصِم .

Litigate, *v.t.* To adduce arguments, plead, *etc.*, in support of any case, إِحْتَجَّ بِ . To do so against another, إِحْتَجَّ عَلَى ـ بِ .

Litigate, *v.i.* To contest a point with, لَدَّ ـ شَاجَرَ ـ لَاجَّ ـ خَاصَمَ ـ نَازَعَ ـ حَاجَّ ـ جَادَلَ . To plead, حَاجَّ . To — with one, حَاجَّ . To adduce a plea against one by way of litigation, إِحْتَجَّ بِ . He litigated with him and overcame him, حَاجَّهُ فَحَجَّهُ . He litigated with his adversary with a strong argument, إِحْتَجَّ عَلَى خَصْمِهِ بِحُجَّةٍ شَهْبَاءَ . To — mutually, of many, تَحَاجُّوا .

Litigation, *n.* مُنَازَعَة ـ مُلَاجَّة ـ مُخَاصَمَة ـ تَحَاجٌّ ـ مُحَاجَّة ـ مُشَاجَرَة ـ لِجَاج ـ خُصُومَة ـ نِزَاع ـ دَعْوَى . *See also* Lawsuit, *n.*

Litigious, *a.* أَلَدُّ *pl.* لُدٌّ *and* لِدَاد ـ ذُو مِغْلَاقٍ ـ رَجُلٌ مِغْلَاقٌ ـ شَرِس ـ لَجُوج ـ خَصُوم ـ خَصِيم ـ خَصِم ـ مِمْرَاث ـ مَرِث ـ شَرِيس ـ جُعْلِيُّ ٱلطَّبْعِ . To be — in, لَجَّ فِي .

Litigiously, *ad.* لَدًّا ـ بِمُخَاصَمَةٍ ـ بِمُنَازَعَةٍ ـ بِلَجَاجَةٍ ـ بِشَرَاسَةٍ .

Litigiousness, *n.* لَدٌّ ـ لَجَاجَة ـ شَرَاسَة ـ تَنَازُع .

Litmus, *n.* The dye of the orchilla lichen, لَوْنٌ أَزْرَقُ مُسْتَخْرَجٌ مِنَ ٱلشَّنَّةِ . Litmus paper, وَرَقٌ مُشَرَّبٌ بِزُرْقَةِ ٱلشَّنَّةِ .

Litter, *v.t.* To bring forth, وَلَدَتْ *aor.* تَلِدُ ـ وَضَعَتْ *aor.* تَضَعُ ـ خَلَّفَتْ . To scatter scraps, نَثَرَ قُصَاصَةً . To put into disorder, خَبَّطَ ـ شَوَّشَ ـ هَوَّشَ ـ عَثْعَثَ ـ خَنْحَثَ .

Litter, *n.* A frame-work for carrying the sick, *etc.*, نَعْش — مَحْمَل — نَقَّالَة — سَرِير ; a —, such as is carried by camels, *etc.*, for travelling, تَخْت رَوَان — مِحَفَّة. A dome-shaped — for one person only, carried by a camel, قُبَّة *pl.* قُبَب — هَوْدَج *pl.* هَوَادِج. A bed for horses, *etc.*, فِرَاش تِبْن لِلدَّوَابّ. A brood, وَضْع — وَلِيدَة — وُلْد. Small pieces strewn about, قُصَاصَة — تَفَارِيق. A mess, muddle, لَخْبَطَة — تَهَوُّش — شَوَاش — خَلْخَلَة — عَشْعَشَة. Lumber, of goods, سَقَط المَتَاع ; of household rubbish, سَقَط البَيْت. He put together his littered furniture, ضَمَّ تَفَارِيق مَتَاعِهِ.

Little, *a.* Small, صَغِير *pl.* صِغَار — صُغْرَان — جُزْئِيّ — دَقِيق. Little in quantity, طَفِيف — نَزْر — نَزُور — نَزِير *pl.* نُزُر — زَهِيد — قُطْرَة ; in numbers, قَلِيل *pl.* قُلُل *and* قَلِيلُون *and* أَقِلَّاء — يَسِير. Mean, contemptible, رَذِيل — شَقِيّ — حَقِير — تَفِه — تَافِه. Poor, abject, دَنِيّ — مِسْكِين. A — matter, أَمْر زَهِيد.

To be or become little, as in bulk, quantity, صَغُرَ ; in numbers, قَلَّ. To be little, contemptible, صَغُرَ. To be paltry, meagre, تَفِهَ. He became little in the eyes of men, صَغُرَ فِي عُيُون النَّاس. To be little in one's own eyes, تَصَاغَرَ. When I was little in your eyes, إِذ كُنْتَ صَغِيرًا فِي عَيْنَيْكَ.

To be too little for, صَغُرَ عَن : If the house is too little to hold you, إِنْ كَانَ المَنْزِل صَغِيرًا عَن أَن يَسَعَكُم.

To esteem little, to think light of, إِسْتَقَلَّ ; to despise, إِسْتَحْقَرَ.

To have or possess little, أَقَلَّ.

To make little, small, قَلَّلَ — صَغَّرَ — أَقَلَّ. To make little of, أَصْغَرَ. To make little, contemptible, إِسْتَقَلَّ — إِسْتَصْغَرَ.

Little, *n.* A small quantity, يَسِير — قَلِيل — قِلّ — نُضَيْض — لَطْخ — نُتْفَة — نُطْفَة — شُوَايَة. A — piece, جِزْع *pl.* جِزَعَة — غُمَيْض. A — of, لَقَط مِن — نُبْذ مِن *pl.* أَنْبَاذ — نُتَف *pl.* لُمْسَة — لُهْنَة. A few, شَمْل *pl.* أَشْمَال. A — time, مُدَّة — لَحْظَة — قَلِيل مِن ; a very — time, لُحَيْظَة — قَلِيلَة. You looked for much, it came to —, إِنْتَظَرْتُم كَثِيرًا وَإِذَا هُوَ قَلِيل. Whether he eat — or much, إِنْ أَكَلَ قَلِيلًا أَوْ كَثِيرًا. The — that he hath, القَلِيل الَّذِي لَهُ. The being content with — is to be rich, (*prov.*) القَنْع بِالقَلِيل غِنًى. The — that is left of my life, القَلِيل الَّذِي بَقِيَ مِن عُمْرِي.

Little, *ad.* قَلِيلًا — يَسِيرًا. Little by little, تَدْرِيجًا — قَلِيلًا قَلِيلًا — شَيْئًا فَشَيْئًا. For a — time, لِمُدَّةٍ يَسِيرَةٍ — لِلَحْظَةٍ. As — as possible, أَقَلّ مَا يَكُون. Not a —, لَيْسَ بِقَلِيل. Yet a — while, عَن قَلِيل — بَعْد قَلِيل. For a very — moment, نَحْو لُحَيْظَة. He possessed it for a —, أَمْسَكَهُ إِلَى قَلِيل. He went a — farther, تَقَدَّمَ قَلِيلًا. He is only a — better, مَا اعْتَدَلَ إِلَّا قَلِيلًا. They wanted but a — of not doing it, مَا كَادُوا يَفْعَلُونَهُ.

Littleness, *n.* Smallness, صِغَر — دِقَّة ; fewness of number, قِلّ — قِلَّة. Meanness, حَقَارَة — دَنَاءَة — صِغَر — تَفَه — تَفَاهَة. Smallness, as of price, ثَمَن بَخْس. Little matters, أَشْيَاء حَقِيرَة — تَفَاهَات. Littleness of mind, قِصَر العَقْل — قِلَّة العَقْل — عَدَم حَصَر الصَّدْر — رُحْب الصَّدْر.

Littoral, *a.* سَوَاحِلِيّ — مُتَعَلِّق بِالسَّوَاحِل — عَلَى شَطّ البَحْر — بِجِوَار نَهْر.

Liturgical, *a.* طَقْسِيّ — طُقُوسِيّ.

Liturgy, *n.* طَقْس — رُتْبَة طُقُوس — خِدْمَة. The Communion office, طَقْس القُدَّاس — خِدْمَة القُدَّاس.

Live, *v.i.* To have life, be alive, حَيَّ *and* حَيِيَ *aor.* يَحْيَا. To pass one's life, عَمَرَ — عَمِرَ — بَقِيَ — عَاشَ — قَضَى عُمْرَهُ. To —, as in a place, أَقَامَ فِي — مَكَثَ — ثَوَى — سَكَنَ. To — for ever, حَيِيَ إِلَى الأَبَد. To — a pleasant life, إِلْتَذَّ عَيْشًا. To lead a life, to conduct one's self, تَصَرَّفَ — سَلَكَ. It is not fit that he should —, لَا يَجُوزُ أَنْ يَعِيشَ. While he lived, وَهُوَ بَعْدُ حَيّ. Had he lived, لَوْ كَانَ حَيًّا. Let him —, لِيَحْيَ. If a man die shall he — again? إِنْ مَاتَ رَجُل أَفَيَحْيَى. Where does he —? أَيْنَ هُوَ مُقِيم. Enough to — upon, كِفَايَة لِلْمَعِيشَة. To let —, to spare, إِسْتَحْيَى — أَبْقَى — إِسْتَبْقَى. God let him —, preserved his life, أَبْقَاهُ اللّٰه. To make to —, to give life to, أَحْيَى — أَعَاشَ ; to give long life to, عَمَّرَ.

To live alone, عَاشَ وَحْدَهُ.

To live apart, عَاشَ مُنْفَرِدًا.

To live at a place, أَقَامَ فِي — سَكَنَ : He lives at Bûlâk, هُوَ مُقِيم فِي بُولَاق.

To live at the rate of..., صَرَفَ فِي مَعِيشَتِهِ نَحْوَ كَذَا — خَرَجَ قَدْر كَذَا.

To live away, a long distance, from a place, أَقَامَ فِي مَحَلّ بَعِيد مِن مَكَان.

To live from hand to mouth, ضَاقَ عَلَيْهِ مَعَاشُهُ — إِخْشَوْشَبَ.

To live honestly, uprightly, تَصَرَّفَ حَسَنًا.

To live in clover, in wealth, تَنَعَّمَ — إِسْتَلَذَّ عَيْشًا — تَفَنَّقَ — أَفْنَقَ.

To live near to one, سَاكَنَهُ — جَاوَرَهُ.

To live on, feed on, or get a livelihood by, عَاشَ مِن — أَكَلَ — إِقْتَاتَ بِ. To continue to live, تَبَقَّى — بَقِيَ — دَامَ حَيًّا.

To live a wretched life, إِخْشَوْشَبَ — تَقَشَّفَ — تَصَعْلَكَ — قَاسَى.

To live peacably with, سَالَمَ.

To live together, تَعَايَشُوا – سَكَنُوا مَعًا.

To live with one, عَايَشَ.

To live up to, to conform to, وَافَقَ – اِمْتَثَلَ – عَمِلَ بِحَسَبِ ٥.

To live up to one's income, صَرَفَ – أَنْفَقَ مَدْخُولَهُ بِتَمَامِهِ ٥ إِيرَادَهُ أَجْمَعَ.

To live with, lodge with, سَاكَنَ – عَاشَ مَعَ ٥. To be in the service of, خَدَمَ – اِسْتَخْدَمَ ².

Live, *v.t.* To lead, as of a life, عَاشَ عِيشَةً ٥ – سَلَكَ سُلُوكًا ² تَصَرَّفَ. To — down anything, عَاقَبَ. To —, to act in conformity to; *see preceding article*, To live up to.

Live, *a.* Living, حَيٌّ *pl.* أَحْيَاءٌ. A — fire, نَارٌ حَيَّةٌ. A — coal, جَمْرَةٌ – بَصٌّ نَارٍ – بَصَّةُ نَارٍ. Live stock, نَاطِقٌ. *See also* Alive, *a.*

Lived, *a.* Living, حَيٌّ. Longlived, طَوِيلُ ٱلْعُمْرِ; shortlived, قَصِيرُ ٱلْعُمْرِ.

Livelihood, *n.* تَعَيُّش – مَعِيشَةٌ – قِيَام – قَوَام – مَعَاش – عَيْش. To earn one's —, تَعَيَّشَ. The source from which a — is obtained, بَابُ ٱلرِّزْقِ – كَسْبُ ٱلْعَيْشِ. Where they may be safe to gain their —, حَيْثُ يُؤْمَنُونَ عَلَى تَحْصِيلِ مَعَاشِهِمْ.

Liveliness, *n.* Vivacity, فُرُوهَةٌ – نَشَاطٌ – حِدَّةٌ – حَرَارَةٌ – خِفَّةٌ – فَرَاحَةٌ. Cheerfulness, pleasantness, بَشَاشَةٌ.

Livelong, *a.* مُمْتَدٌّ – طَوِيل. For the — day, طُولَ ٱلنَّهَارِ.

Lively, *a.* Strong, vigorous, قَوِيٌّ – شَدِيد – عَفِيٌّ. Animated, brisk, أَلْوَب – فَلْتَان – خَفِيف – حَادٌّ – حَامٍ – نَارِيٌّ. Pleasant, courteous, بَشَّاش – بَشٌّ – هَشٌّ. Cheering, مُطْرِب – مُفْرِح. Clever, ذَكِيٌّ – مَاهِر – مُؤَلِّف. Ingenious, رَفِيع – بَدِيع. A — writer, بَدِيعٌ. To be —, فَرُهَ ². To be —, pleasant, courteous towards, بَشَّ لِ ٥.

Lively, *ad.* بِفُرُوهَةٍ – بِنَشَاطٍ – بِحِدَّةٍ – بِحَرَارَةٍ – بِخِفَّةٍ.

Live-oak, *n.* سِنْدِيَان – شَجَرَةُ ٱلْبَلُّوطِ.

Liver, *n.* One who lives, حَيٌّ – نَفْسٌ حَيَّةٌ – عَايِش. A free —, سُرُف – بَحْبُوح *pl.* بَحَابِيحُ. The organ which secretes the bile, فُؤَاد – سَوَادُ ٱلْبَطْنِ – كِبْدَة *or* كِبْد *or* كَبِد *or* كَبْد *pl.* أَكْبَاد. A segment of the —, فِلْذَةُ ٱلْكَبِدِ *pl.* أَفْلَاذ. The longitudinal ligament in the middle of the —, عَمُودُ ٱلْكَبِدِ. Having a diseased liver, مَكْبُود. To have a disease in the —, فُئِدَ. To hit on the —, فَأَدَ ٥.

Livered, *a.* Having a liver, ذُو كَبِدٍ. White-livered; *see* Coward, *n.*

Liveried, *n.* Wearing a livery, لَابِسُ كِسْمٍ مَخْصُوصٍ.

Liverwort, *n.* The plant, بَهَقُ ٱلْحَجَرِ – حَزَازُ ٱلصَّخْرِ – ٱلْحَزْوَر – جَلْدَم – حِنَّاءُ قُرَيْشٍ – كَوْكَبُ ٱلْوَعْرِ.

Livery, *n.* Delivery, تَسْلِيم. A garb for servants, كِسْمٌ مَخْصُوصٌ لِلْخَدَمِ. A garb for liverymen, كِسْمٌ مَخْصُوصٌ لِأَهْلِ ٱلْأَصْنَافِ. A collective body of liverymen, جَمَاعَةُ أَصْنَاف – أَصْنَاف.

Liveryman, *n.* مِنْ أَهْلِ أَصْنَاف.

Livery-stable, *n.* مَنْزِلٌ لِاسْتِكْرَاءِ ٱلدَّوَابِّ.

Live-stock, *n.* نَاطِق – حَيَوَانَات.

Livid, *a.* كَابٍ – كَالِح. To be — with rage, كَلَحَ ٥.

Lividness, *n.* كَبْوَة – كُلُوح.

Living, *a.* Having life, عَائِش – حَيٌّ *pl.* أَحْيَاء – فِي قَيْدِ ٱلْحَيَاةِ. Living words, أَقْوَالٌ حَيَّةٌ. Living waters, مِيَاهٌ حَيَّةٌ. A — soul, نَفْسٌ حَيَّةٌ. A — thing, ذُو نَفْسٍ. A — rock, صَخْرٌ جَامِدٌ. The land of the —, أَرْضُ ٱلْأَحْيَاءِ. The — and the dead, ٱلْأَحْيَاءُ وَٱلْأَمْوَاتُ.

Living, *n.* Means of subsistence, مَعِيشَة – مَعَاش. A benefice, مَعِيشَةٌ (*or* رَاتِبُ) ٱلْقِسِّيسِ. A place of living, إِقَامَة – مَسْكَن – مَعِيش. He used to get his — there from what some of the people of the town kindly gave him, كَانَ يَتَعَيَّشُ هُنَاكَ مِمَّا يَتَكَرَّمُ عَلَيْهِ بَعْضٌ مِنْ أَهْلِ ٱلْبَلَدِ.

Livraison, *n.* جُزْءٌ مِنْ كِتَابٍ *pl.* أَجْزَاء – كُرَّاسَة *pl.* كُرَّاس *and* كَرَارِيس.

Livre, *n.* *See* Franc, *n.*

Lixivial, *a.}
Lixivious, } مُشَرَّبٌ أُشْنَانًا – حُرُضِيٌّ – أُشْنَانِيٌّ.

Lixiviate, *v.t.* To impregnate with lixivium, شَرَّبَ أُشْنَانًا. To form into lye, صَيَّرَ أُشْنَانًا.

Lixiviate, *a.*
Lixiviated, } *See* Lixivial, *a.*

Lixiviation, *n.* إِخْرَاجُ ٱلْأُشْنَانِ مِنَ ٱلرَّمَادِ.

Lixivium, *n.* مَاءُ قِلْيٍ – مَاءُ أُشْنَانٍ.

Lizard, *n.* The reptile, وَرَل *pl.* أَوْرَال – وَرَن *pl.* أَوْرَان – ضَبٌّ *pl.* ضِبَاب – حَيَّةُ شَمْسٍ – أَبُو بُرَيْصٍ.

LL.D. (Doctor of laws), عِبَارَةٌ عَنْ رُتْبَةِ ٱلْمُتَفَقِّهِ بِٱلْقَوَانِينِ (*or* ٱلشَّرَائِعِ).

Lo! *int.* هَا – هَا هُوَذَا – إِذَا – إِذَا بِ. And lo! فَهَا.

Load, *n.* A burden, حِمْل *pl.* أَحْمَال: what a man can carry, شَيْلَةُ ٱلرَّجُلِ; a beast's —, حِمْلُ ٱلدَّابَّةِ; a ship's —, تَعْبِئَة – شِحْنَة (*or* حُمُولَة) ٱلْمَرْكَبِ – ٱلْمَرْكَب. A — or charge for a musket, or gun, عُمَارُ بَارُودَةٍ (*or* مِكْحَلَةٍ *or* مِدْفَعٍ). A — or burden on another, of a person, مُبْرِم ـ بَرَم. A — of chains, fetters, كَبْلُ قُيُودٍ. A weight, ثِقْل *pl.* أَثْقَال. To be a load upon, ثَقُلَ عَلَى.

Load, *v.t.* To put a burden on, عَلَّى بِهِ عَلَى ـ حَمَّلَ ـ تَحَمَّلَ. To —, as on the shoulder of a man, جَعَلَ عَلَى كَتِفِهِ. To — with chains, كَبَلَ بِٱلْقُيُودِ. To — a ship with, شَحَنَ ـ وَسَقَ *aor.* يَسِقُ ـ أَوْسَقَ. To —, as a gun, دَكَّ ـ شَحَنَ بِ. To —, to fill to the full, with, شَحَنَ بِ ـ غَمَرَ. To — with taxes, ثَقَّلَ عَلَى ٱلتَّكَالِيفِ. He loaded the mule with wood, حَمَّلَ ٱلْبَغْلَةَ حَطَبًا. He loaded the ship with cotton, وَسَقَ ٱلْمَرْكَبَ قُطْنًا. To bestow upon in abundance, أَفَاضَ عَلَى ـ مِن ـ أَجْزَلَ عَلَى ـ بِ.

Loading, *n.* *See* Load, *n.*

Load-star, *n.* }
Lode-star, } The pole-star, ٱلْقُطْبُ ـ ٱلْكَوْكَبُ ٱلشَّمَالِيُّ.

Loadstone, *n.* حَجَرُ ٱلْمَغْنَاطِيسِ.

Loaf, *n.* خُبْزَة *pl.* خُبْزَات. Thin cakes, the common form in which bread is used in the East, رَغِيف *pl.* أَرْغِفَة *and* رُغْفَان. A — of bread with a hole in the middle, كَعْكَة *pl.* كَعْك. A — of bread made round and thick, قُرْص *pl.* أَقْرَاص. A whole —, رَغِيفٌ حَادِرٌ. Any round and pointed mass, رَأْس *pl.* رُؤُوس. A — of sugar, قَالِبُ سُكَّرٍ ـ رَأْسُ سُكَّرٍ *pl.* قَوَالِبُ.

Loafer, *n.* بَطَّال ـ أُفَّة ـ هِبِلٌّ ـ مُبْرِم ـ لُكَع.

Loafing, *n.* تَكَاسُل ـ كَسَل ـ تَأَفُّف.

Loam, *n.* أَرْضٌ سَمِينَة ـ طِينُ ٱلْإِبْلِيزِ.

Loamy, *a.* سَمِين ـ مِثْلَ طِينِ ٱلْإِبْلِيزِ.

Loan, *n.* As of goods, سَلَف ـ عَارَة ـ عَارِيَّة; of money, قَرْض *pl.* قُرُوض ـ قِرْضَة ـ دَيْن *pl.* دُيُون. To issue a —, أَقْرَضَ ـ أَدَانَ ـ دَايَنَ ـ دَيَّنَ ـ أَصْدَرَ قَرْضًا. To grant a — to, دَايَنَ ـ دَيَّنَ. To take a — from, تَسَلَّفَ مِن. To ask a — from, إِسْتَعَارَ مِن ـ إِسْتَسْلَفَ مِن ـ إِسْتَقْرَضَ مِن ـ تَدَيَّنَ مِن. A — without interest, عِينَة. A public —, إِسْتِقْرَاضُ ٱلدَّوْلَةِ *pl.* إِسْتِقْرَاضَات. A forced —, إِسْتِقْرَاضٌ عَلَى سَبِيلِ ٱلْجَبْرِ. A — guaranteed by the mines of the country, قَرْضٌ يَكُونُ ضَمَانَهُ مَحْصُولُ مَعَادِنِ ٱلْبِلَادِ. Short loans, دُيُونٌ قَصِيرَةٌ. To contract a —, عَقَدَ ٱسْتِقْرَاضًا. In the shape of a —, عَلَى سَبِيلِ ٱلْقَرْضِ. The bond of a —, سَنَدُ ٱلْإِسْتِقْرَاضِ *pl.* سَنَدَات. Loan me, lend me, أَدِنِّي ـ إِسْلِفْنِي ـ أَقْرِضْنِي.

Loan, *v.t.* *See* to Lend, *v.t.*

Loathe, *a.* *See* Loth, *a.*

Loathe, *v.t.* To regard with aversion, عَافَ *aor.* يَعَافُ ـ أَجِمَ. To —, of food, سَئِمَ مِن ـ إِغْتَنَفَ ـ قَفِعَ عَن ـ جَشَأَ عَن ـ أَقْهَى عَن ـ قَهِيَ عَن ـ عَافَ ـ أَقْهَمَ عَن. To dislike, detest, كَرِهَ ـ إِسْتَكْرَهَ ـ تَكَرَّهَ. He loathed food, جَشَأَ عَنِ ٱلطَّعَامِ.

Loathful, *a.* }
Loathsome, } خَبِيث ـ كَرِيه ـ كُرْه ـ مَكْرُوه ـ مُقْرِف.

Loathing, *n.* Abhorrence, قَرَف ـ سَأَم ـ تَقَرُّف ـ إِعْتِيَاف; of food, عِيَافَة ـ عِيَاق ـ أَبَاءٌ مِنَ ٱلطَّعَامِ ـ أَبَاءٌ. He was affected with a — for food, أَخَذَهُ أَبَاءٌ مِنَ ٱلطَّعَامِ.

Loathingly, *ad.* بِكَرَاهَةٍ ـ بِٱعْتِيَافٍ ـ بِسَأَمٍ.

Loathsomeness, *n.* مَكْرُوهَة ـ كَرَاهِيَة ـ كَرَاهَة ـ خَبَاثَة.

Lobate, }
Lobated, *a.* }
Lobed, } ذُو أَفْلَاقٍ ـ ذُو آذَانٍ.

Lobby, *n.* A passage, سُدَّة ـ دِهْلِيز ـ مَقْطَع. An apartment on the lower floor, مَنْظَرَة. *See also* Chamber, *n.*

Lobe, *n.* As of the ear, لُغْد *pl.* أَلْغَاد ـ حَجَمَة ـ حَاجَة ـ رَوْم; the lower part of the ear —, شَحْمَةُ ٱلْأُذُنِ ـ رَوْم. Lobe of the liver, رُغَامَى ـ رُغَامِى; the greater — of the liver, زِيَادَةُ ٱلْكَبِدِ; the lesser, وَرَف. The — of a plant, أُذُن *pl.* آذَان ـ فِلْقَة ـ فَلَق *pl.* أَفْلَاق.

Lobster, *n.* أَرْبِيَان ـ زَلْعَطَانٌ بَحْرِيٌّ ـ سَلْطَعُونٌ بَحْرِيٌّ.

Lobule, *n.* فِلْقَةٌ صَغِيرَةٌ ـ أُذَيْن.

Local, *a.* مَحَلِّيٌّ. Confined to a given place, مَحْصُورٌ بِمَحَلٍّ ـ غَيْرُ شَامِلٍ. Local government, حُكُومَةٌ مَحَلِّيَّةٌ. The — press, ٱلْمَطْبُوعَاتُ ٱلْمَحَلِّيَّةُ. Items of — news, حَوَادِثُ مَحَلِّيَّةٌ.

Locality, *n.* Existence in a place, سُكْنَى ـ إِقَامَة. Limitation to a place, حَدٌّ ـ مَقَام. Situation, مَوْقِع ـ مَوْضِع. A place, مَكَان ـ مَوْضِع ـ مَحَلّ. The arrangements of a place, تَرْتِيبُ ٱلْمَحَلِّ. A place where a thing is or is met with, مَعْهَد; from whence anything is obtained, مَأْخَذ.

Localization, *n.* تَحْدِيدٌ بِدَائِرَةٍ ـ تَحْدِيد ـ حَصْرٌ فِي مَكَانٍ.

Localize, *v.t.* حَدَّدَ ـ حَصَرَ فِي مَكَانٍ. To localize a war, حَصَرَ (or حَدَّدَ) ٱلْمُحَارَبَةَ فِي مَوْقِعٍ مَخْصُوصٍ.

Locate, *v.t.* To place, مَكَّنَ ـ أَقَامَ ـ حَطَّ ـ وَضَعَ *aor.* يَضَعُ. To cause to dwell, أَقَامَ ـ أَنْزَلَ ـ بَوَّأَ.

Location, *n.* The act of placing, إِقَامَة ـ تَبْوِئَة ـ تَمْكِين ـ وَضْع ـ قِيَام. *See also* Locality, *n.*

Loch, *n.* بُحَيْرَة ـ خَلِيج *pl.* خُلْجَان. *See also* Lake, *n.*

Lock, *n.* For fastening a door, كَالُون ـ كِيلُون ـ مِغْلَق *pl.* أَقْفَال *pl.* قُفْل ـ كَوَالِين; a wooden —, ضَبَّة; the pin of a wooden —, أَسْنَان *pl.* سِنّ ٱلضَّبَّة. A — of hair, أَقْرَان *pl.* قَرْن ـ غَدَائِر *pl.* غَدِيرَة ـ حَلْقَة شَعْر ـ خُصَل *pl.* خُصْلَة ـ جُمَّة. A hanging —, a tress, سَبَائِب *pl.* سَبِيب ـ ذُؤَابَة. The — of a gun, دِيَك *pl.* دِيك ـ أَزْنِدَة *pl.* زِنَاد; *in Turkish*, چَقْمَق. The — of a stream, *etc.*, سُدُود *pl.* سَدّ ـ مَسَكَ. A — of wool, جَزِيزَة; of dyed wool, عِهْنَة. A grapple, كُلَّاب ـ عَوْدَقَة. Under — and key, مَقْفُول ـ مُقْفُول عَلَيْهِ. To pick a —, زَبَقَ ٱلْقُفْل ـ فَتَحَ ٱلْقُفْل بِٱلْكُلَّابَة ـ كَلَبَ ٱلْقُفْل.

Lock, *v.t.* To fasten with a lock, قَفَّلَ; to shut up, close, سَكَّرَ ـ أَغْلَقَ ـ غَلَّقَ. To —, close, a door, (تَرَّسَ *or* تَرَّعَ *or*) أَغْلَقَ ٱلْبَاب. To — up, قَفَلَ. To — out, قَفَّلَ عَلَى. To dam, سَكَّرَ ـ سَدَّ. To furnish, as a canal, with locks, جَعَلَ لِ ـ سُدُودًا. To restrain, حَصَرَ. To imprison, حَبَسَ. To —, to embrace, ضَمَّ إِلَى صَدْرِهِ ـ حَضَنَ. He locked the door, أَرْتَجَ ٱلْبَاب.

Lock, *v.i.* To become locked, سُكِّرَ ـ إِنْقَفَلَ ـ تَقَفَّلَ. To unite closely, إِتَّصَلَ بِ ـ إِصْطَمَّ ـ إِتَّحَدَ. They were closely locked, joined together, تَوَاصَلُوا. They were locked in each other's arms, of many, تَعَانَقُوا.

Lockage, *n.* Materials for locks, أَمْتِعَة ٱلْأَقْفَال. Locks, dams, سُدُود. Tolls for locks, مَكْس ٱلسَّدّ ـ مَكْس ٱلْمَسَكَ.

Locker, *n.* أَنْبَار ـ خِزَانَة ـ صَنْدُوق ـ دُولَاب.

Locket, *n.* The ornament, بَيْت حِجَاب ـ حُجُب *pl.* حِجَاب.

Lock-jaw, *n.* لَقْوَة.

Locksmith, *n.* A maker of locks, قَفَّال. A blacksmith, حَدَّاد *pl.* حَدَّادُون. *See also* Armourer, *n.*

Locomotion, *n.* سَيْر وَحَرَكَة ـ حَرَكَة.

Locomotive, *a.* Having the power to move something, مُجِيز ـ مُحَرِّك ـ جَوَّاز. Moving of itself, سَيَّار ـ مُتَحَرِّك.

Locomotive, *n.* The engine, لُوكُومُوتِيف ـ آلَة مُزْجِيَة.

Locum-tenens, *n.* قَائِم مَقَام ـ وَكِيل. *See also* Lieutenant, *n.*

Locus, *n.* مَوْقِع. Locus-standi, مَغْرِز. Ground, defence, حُجَّة.

Locust, *n.* The insect, جَرَادَة *coll.* جَرَاد. Eggs of the —, إِبْنُ ٱلْجَرَاد ـ سَوْء ـ سِرْأَة. The — tree, شَجَرَة ـ شَجَرَة ٱلْخُرْنُوب ٱلْخَرُّوب. A pod of the — tree, قُرُون *pl.* قَرْن خَرُّوب ـ خَرُّوبَة.

Lode, *n.* Of a mine, رِكَاز (سَيْب *or*) مَعْدِن.

Lodestone, *n.* *See* Loadstone, *n.*

Lodge, *n.* A small house, بُيُوت *pl.* بَيْت ـ مَسْكَن ـ حُجْرَة ـ حُجُورَات *and* حُجَر *pl.* مَحَلّ ـ. A den, زَرِيبَة ـ وَكْر. A cave, جُحْر ـ مَغَارَة. A meeting of freemasons, جَمَاعَة ٱلْفَرَمَسِيُّون. the place of their meeting, مَجْمَع ٱلْفَرَمَسِيُّون.

Lodge, *v.t.* To deposit, place, وَضَعَ *aor.* يَضَعُ ـ حَطَّ. To confide into the hands of, سَلَّمَ لِ ـ إِسْتَوْدَعَ ـ عِنْدَهُ. To give one a lodging, أَضَافَ ـ أَنْزَلَ ـ بَوَّأَ ـ آوَى. To give a lodgment to, to harbour, as in the mind, أَضْمَرَ ـ أَسَرَّ ـ كَتَمَ. He lodged us for three days, أَضَافَنَا ثَلَاثَة أَيَّام.

Lodge, *v.i.* To rest in a place at night, بَاتَ *aor.* يَبِيتُ. To dwell, حَلَّ ـ سَكَنَ ـ نَزَلَ. To take refuge in, تَآوَى ـ تَأَوَّى. To stop, وَقَفَ *aor.* يَقِفُ. Where do you lodge? أَيْنَ أَنْتَ سَاكِن ـ أَيْنَ أَنْتَ نَازِل. Is there room in your father's house for us to — in, هَلْ فِي بَيْتِ أَبِيكَ مَكَانٌ لَنَا لِنَبِيتَ. The birds come and — in the branches, تَأْتِي ٱلْعَصَافِيرُ وَتَتَآوَى فِي ٱلْأَغْصَانِ. How long shall vain thoughts — amongst them? إِلَى مَتَى تَبِيتُ فِي وَسْطِهِمِ ٱلْأَفْكَارُ ٱلْبَاطِلَة. The ball lodged in his shoulder, إِسْتَقَرَّتِ ٱلرَّصَاصَة فِي كَتِفِهِ.

Lodger, *n.* A wayfarer, مُسَافِر. One who hires a lodging, مُسْتَأْجِر ـ مُسْتَكْرٍ ـ كَارٍ. One who lodges in a place, نَزِيل *pl.* مَنَازِل ـ مُسَاكِن ـ سُكَّان *pl.* سَاكِن ـ مُقِيم ـ نُزُل. A fellow —, أَنْزَل ـ كَارِي. To take in lodgers, (أَجَّرَ *or*) لِلْمُسْتَأْجِرِينَ ٱلْمُسْتَأْجِرِينَ. *See also* Guest, *n.*

Lodging, *n.* A place of rest at night, مَبِيت ـ دِمَّة. A place of abode, مَنْزِل *pl.* مَنَازِل ـ سُكْنَى ـ مَحَلّ. To give a — to, نَزَّلَ ـ أَنْزَلَ ـ بَوَّأَ. To take up one's — at, نَزَلَ بِ ـ بَاتَ فِي. Have you a — for us in your house? هَلْ فِي بَيْتِكَ مَكَانٌ لَنَا لِنَبِيت. Prepare me a —, أَعِدَّ لِي مَنْزِلًا. Furnished lodgings, مَحَلَّات (حُجَر *or*) حُجَر مَفْرُوشَة. Private lodgings, (حُجَر *or*) مَحَلَّات فِي بُيُوت مَخْصُوصَة. Unfurnished lodgings, (حُجَر *or*) مَحَلَّات غَيْر مَفْرُوشَة. To let furnished lodgings, أَكْرَى حُجَرًا مَفْرُوشَة. To take furnished lodgings, إِسْتَكْرَى حُجَرًا مُؤَثَّثَة.

Lodging-house, *n.* دَار لِلنُّزُل ـ دَار لِلْمُسَافِرِين ـ دَار لِلْغُرَبَاء. To live at a —, سَكَنَ دَار ٱلنُّزُل. A — keeper, صَاحِب دَار ٱلنُّزُل.

Lodgment, *n.* The act of lodging or placing, حَطّ ـ وَضْع. Consignment, تَوْدِيع ـ تَسْلِيم. A deposit, أَمَانَة ـ وَدِيعَة. Possession, ضَبْط ـ إِسْتِحْكَام ـ حَوْز. A foothold, مَوْطِئ. A place where anything lodges, مَحَطّ ـ مَوْقِع. Matter lodged, مَوْضُوع. To effect a — in, to get possession of, حَازَ ـ إِسْتَحْكَمَ عَلَى.

Loft, *n.* A story, طَبَقَة *pl.* طَبَقَات. A gallery, شُرَّافَة *pl.* شُرَّافَات. An upper story, آخِر طَبَقَة. A corn-loft, شُونَة *pl.* أَنَابِير *pl.* أَنْبَار ـ شُوَن.

Loftily, *ad.* To a great elevation, إِرْتِفَاعًا ; haughtily, بِغَطْرَسَةٍ — تَكَبُّرًا — إِسْتِكْبَارًا . Sublimely, بِرِفْعَةٍ — بِٱرْتِفَاعٍ — بِعُلُوٍّ .

Loftiness, *n.* Height, إِرْتِفَاع — شُمُوخ — سُمُوّ — شُهْقَة . Sublimity, إِرْتِفَاع — رِفْعَة — سُمُوّ — عُلُوّ . Haughtiness, شَمْخَرَة — إِسْتِكْبَار — تَكَبُّر — كِبْرِيَاء . *See also* Elevation, Haughtiness, Height, *n.*

Lofty, *a.* High, شَاهِق — شَمَّاخ — شَامِخ — مُنِيف — نَاشِز *pl.* شَوَاهِق — مُرْتَفِع — عَالٍ — سَمِيّ — نَابِه . Haughty, proud, مُتَكَبِّر — غِطْرِيس — غَرُور — مَغْرُور — شَامِخ — شَمَّاخ . Sublime, سَنِيّ — رَفِيع — شَمِخ — عَالٍ — سَمِيّ — عَلِيّ . A — mountain, جَبَلٌ شَامِخٌ . A — purpose, نِيَّةٌ شَمَخٌ . A — place, نَشَاز . To be —, high, عَلَا — شَمَخَ ² — عَلِيَ — إِرْتَفَعَ — تَعَالَى — تَعَلَّى . To be —, haughty, إِسْتَكْبَرَ — شَمَخَ ² أَنْفُهُ — شَمْخَرَ . To be —, sublime, عَلَا ² — رَقِيَ . *See also under* High, Haughty, Elevated, *a.*

Log, *n.* As of wood, زَنْدُ حَطَبٍ — حَطَبَة — قُرْم *pl.* قُرْمَة حَطَبٍ *pl.* أَزْنَاد . A ship's —, the machine, آلَةٌ لِقِيَاسِ سَيْرِ ٱلْمَرَاكِبِ — بَرْكِيتَة (called in the Persian Gulf باطلى). A heavy fellow, بَلِيد . To heave the —, قَاسَ ² بِٱلْبَرْكِيتَةِ . Log, the day-book of a ship, جُرْنَالُ ٱلْمَرْكَبِ — دَفْتَرُ مَسِيرِ ٱلسَّفِينَةِ .

Logarithmic, *a.* } **Logarithmical**, } مُتَعَلِّقٌ بِٱلْأَنْسَابِ — مَا نِيطَ بِعِلْمِ نِسْبَةِ ٱلْأَعْدَادِ .

Logarithm, *n.* اللُّوغَرِيتْم — أَنْسَاب — عِلْمُ نِسْبَةِ ٱلْأَعْدَادِ .

Log-book, *n.* جُرْنَالُ مَرْكَبٍ — دَفْتَرُ مَسِيرِ ٱلْمَرْكَبِ .

Loggerhead, *n.* A blockhead, ثَوْر — أَبْلَه — أَحْمَق — بَلِيد . To be at loggerheads, of many, تَنَازَعُوا — تَشَاجَرُوا — تَقَاتَلُوا . He went to loggerheads with, نَازَعَ — شَاجَرَ — قَاتَلَ .

Logic, *n.* عِلْمُ ٱلْمَنْطِقِ — المَنْطِق — عِلْمُ ٱلْمَنْطِقِيَّاتِ . He spoke with false —, أَغَثَّ فِي مَنْطِقِهِ .

Logical, *a.* حَسَبَ قَوَاعِدِ ٱلْمَنْطِقِ — مَنْطِقِيّ . According to reason, مَعْقُول — مُطَابِقُ ٱلْعَقْلِ .

Logically, *ad.* حَسَبَ ٱلْمَنْطِقِ .

Logician, *n.* مُتَكَلِّم — مَنْطِقِيّ — مِنْطِيق .

Log-line, *n.* مَرَسَةُ ٱللُّكّ — حَبْلَةُ ٱلْبَرْكِيتَةِ .

Log-reel, *n.* دُولَابُ ٱللُّكّ — دُولَابُ ٱلْبَرْكِيتَةِ .

Logomachy, *n.* مُجَادَلَةٌ عَلَى لَفْظَةٍ — نِزَاعٌ فِي كَلِمَةٍ .

Logwood, *n.* بَقَّم مُوَرَّد .

Loin, *n.* صُلْب *pl.* أَصْلُب *and* أَصْلَاب *and* صِلَبَة . The son of his loins, إِبْنُ صُلْبِهِ .

Loiter, *v.i.* تَمَهَّلَ — تَوَقَّفَ — تَأَخَّرَ — تَحَوَّزَ . To — away one's time, ضَيَّعَ وَقْتَهُ . *See also to* Delay, Linger, *v.i.*

Loiterer, *n.* بَطِيءٌ — مُتَوَانٍ . One who dallies, trifles, مُبْرِم — لُكَع .

Loitering, *n.* بُطُوء — تَمَهُّل — تَوَقُّف — بِطَاء — بَطَاءَة — تَوَانٍ .

Loiteringly, *ad.* بِبُطُوءٍ — بِبَطَاءَةٍ — بِتَوَقُّفٍ — بِتَوَانٍ .

Loll, *v.i.* To lean idly, تَرَامَى — تَرَاخَى — إِتَّكَى مُتَكَاسِلًا . To — upon, تَدَلَّلَ عَلَى — إِتَّكَى عَلَى .

Loll, *v.t.* دَلَعَ ² . He lolled out his tongue, of men and animals, دَلَعَ لِسَانَهُ . His tongue lolled out, إِنْدَلَعَ (or إِدَّلَعَ) لِسَانُهُ .

Lollipop, *n.* حَلَاوَة — حَلَاوِيَات .

Lone, *a.* Separate, مُنْفَرِد . Solitary, isolated, وَحِيد — مُتَوَحِّد . Unmarried, عَازِب *pl.* أَعْزَاب *fem.* عَازِبَة *pl.* عَازِبَات . A lone forest, غَابَةٌ مُسْتَوْحِشَةٌ . A — woman, إِمْرَأَةٌ — إِمْرَأَةٌ مَتْرُوكَةٌ — مُتَوَحِّشَةٌ . A — man, one whose wife has died, أَيْمَانُ *pl.* أَيَامَى . A — woman, one who has been married or not, أَيِّمَة *pl.* أَيِّمَات . *See also* Lorn, Desolate, *a.*

Loneliness, *n.* The being alone, إِنْفِرَاد — وَحْدَة . Solitariness, خَلْوَة — وَحْدَة . Dreariness, وَحْشَة .

Lonely, *a.* } **Lonesome**, } *See* Lone, *n.*

Lonely, *ad.* Apart, إِنْفِرَادًا ; in solitariness, تَوَحُّدًا — وَحْشَةً — إِسْتِيحَاشًا .

Lonesomeness, *n.* *See* Loneliness, *n.*

Long, *a.* Not short, طَوِيل *pl.* طِوَال . Extended, مَدِيد *pl.* مُدُد . Tedious, مُسْهِب — نَفِس . Wearisome, شَاقّ . Prolix, طَوِيل — مُمِلّ . Lingering, طَوِيل — مُمْتَدّ — مُزْمِن — مُتَرَاخٍ . To be or become —, طَالَ ² — إِسْتَطَالَ ; to be dilatory, تَأَخَّرَ — تَرَاخَى — تَوَقَّفَ — بَطُؤَ ² . To consider —, إِسْتَطَالَ — عَدَّهُ ² طَوِيلًا . To make —, أَطَالَ — طَوَّلَ ; to prolong, as of life, أَبْقَى . To suffer to grow —, of the hair, رَبَّى خُصَلًا . One's — home, الدَّارُ ٱلْأَبَدِيَّةُ — البَيْتُ ٱلْأَبَدِيُّ . He lived a — time, طَالَ بِهِ ٱلْعُمْرُ . A foot —, طُولُ قَدَمٍ : It is a foot —, طُولُهُ قَدَمٌ . A — time, زَمَنٌ طَوِيلٌ . For a — time, لِزَمَنٍ مَدِيدٍ . After so — a time, بَعْدَ زَمَانٍ هٰذَا وَمِقْدَارُهُ . A — letter, having the *maddah* over it, حَرْفٌ مَمْدُودٌ . In the — run, عَاقِبَةً — عِنْدَ ٱلْعَاقِبَةِ . Long, *used as a noun*: the — and the short of the matter, خُلَاصَةُ ٱلْمَادَّةِ — نَتِيجَةُ ٱلْأَمْرِ .

Long, *ad.* A long time, زَمَانٌ طَوِيلٌ . It is — since I saw you, خَيْرُ ٱللّٰهِ مَا رَأَيْنَاكُمْ — مِنْ زَمَانٍ مَا رَأَيْتُكَ . The way is —, الطَّرِيقُ طَوِيلٌ — طَالَ ٱلطَّرِيقُ .

To ask long, for many days, سَأَلَ أَيَّامًا كَثِيرَةً .

To bear long with, تَأَنَّى لِ — تَصَبَّرَ عَلَى — صَابَرَ — تَمَهَّلَ عَلَى — إِسْتَأْنَى بِ .

As long as, مَا دَامَ: As long as I live, مَا دُمْتُ مَوْجُودًا. As long as he lives, مَا دَامَ حَيًّا. As long as the moon shall endure, إِلَى ٱضْمِحْلَالِ ٱلْقَمَرِ. As long as I see the man sitting at the door, كُلَّمَا أَرَى ٱلرَّجُلَ جَالِسًا عِنْدَ ٱلْبَابِ. I will not do it as long as there is a star in the heavens, مَا أَفْعَلُهُ مَا أَنَّ فِي ٱلسَّمَآءِ نَجْمًا. As long as there is a drop in the Euphrates, مَا أَنَّ فِي ٱلْفُرَاتِ قَطْرَةً. As long as there is rain in heaven, مَا أَنَّ فِي ٱلسَّمَآءِ سَمَآءً.

Before long, } عَنْ قَرِيبٍ.
Ere long, }

Don't be long, لَا تَتَعَوَّقْ.

How long? إِلَى أَيَّةِ مُدَّةٍ — إِلَى مَتَى.

I have long expected, طَالَ عَلَيَّ ٱلتَّرَقُّبُ.

If I delay long, إِنْ كُنْتُ أُبْطِئُ.

It is a long time that..., طَالَمَا.

Long ago, مِنْ زَمَانٍ — مُنْذُ زَمَنٍ طَوِيلٍ — قَدِيمًا.

No longer than yesterday, البَارِحَةَ — أَمْسِ.

That thy days may be long, لِكَيْ تَطُولَ أَيَّامُكَ.

The trumpet sounded long, كَانَ صَوْتُ ٱلْبُوقِ يَزْدَادُ جِدًّا.

They sit long over the wine, يُدْمِنُونَ ٱلْخَمْرَ.

When the cloud hung long over him, إِذَا تَمَادَتِ ٱلسَّحَابَةُ زَمَنًا طَوِيلًا عَلَيْهِ.

Why was he so long in coming, لِمَاذَا أَبْطَأَ عَنِ ٱلْمَجِيءِ.

Ye have dwelt long enough in this place, كَفَاكُمُ ٱلْقُعُودُ فِي هٰذَا ٱلْمَحَلِّ.

Long, *v.i.* To — for, to desire earnestly, جَادَ إِلَى *aor.* يَجُودُ — تَنَافَسَ فِي — نَافَسَ فِي — تَتَوَّقَ إِلَى — تَاقَ إِلَى — حَنَّ إِلَى — إِشْتَاقَ إِلَى — هَوِيَ. *See also to* Desire, *v.t.*

Long-boat, *n.* صَنْدَال — صَنْدَل — فَلُوكَة.

Longanimity, *n.* Composedness, وَقَار. Endurance, صَبْر — أَنَاة — تَحَمُّل.

Longe, *n.* *See* Lunge, *n.*

Long-eared, *a.* أُذَانِيّ.

Longer, *a.* أَطْوَل. A — time, زَمَنٌ أَطْوَل.

Longer, *ad.* بَعْدُ. How much longer? إِلَى مَتَى. To stay —, لَبِثَ: Don't stay — again, لَا تَعُدْ تَلْبَثْ. He could stand no —, لَمْ يَقْدِرْ بَعْدُ عَلَى ٱلْوُقُوفِ. He could bear it no —, لَمْ يَسْتَطِعْ أَنْ يَحْتَمِلَهُ بَعْدُ. You cannot be my agent any —, لَا تَقْدِرُ أَنْ تَكُونَ وَكِيلًا لِي بَعْدُ. He ought not to live any —, لَا يَنْبَغِي أَنْ يَعِيشَ بَعْدُ. Time shall be no —, لَا يَكُونُ زَمَانٌ بَعْدُ.

If they continue any time — in this state, إِنْ طَالَتْ عَلَيْهِمْ بُرْهَةٌ مَا وَهُمْ فِي هٰذِهِ ٱلْحَالَةِ.

Longest, *a.* ٱلْأَطْوَل. The — in extent, ٱلْأَطْوَلُ ٱمْتِدَادًا.

Longeval, *a.* Long-lived, طَوِيلُ ٱلْعُمْرِ.

Longevity, *n.* طُولُ ٱلْعُمْرِ — مَكْبِر — كِبْرَة — كَبْرَة.

Long-forgotten, *a.* مُنْسًى مِنْ زَمَانٍ — مَذْهُولٌ عَنْهُ. A — thing, نَسْيٌ مِنْ زَمَانٍ.

Long-headed, *a.* ذَكِيّ — عَاقِل — فَطِين — فَاطِن — فَطِن.

Long-headedness, *n.* ذَكَآء — فِرَاسَة — عَقْل — فِطْنَة.

Longing, *n.* شَوْق — هَوِيَّة — حَنِين — تِيَاقَة — تَوْق — أَنَانَة.

Longing, *a.* مُشْتَاق — مَشُوق — تَوَّاق — حَنَّان.

Longingly, *ad.* بِشَوْقٍ — بِحَنِينٍ — بِأَنَانَةٍ.

Longitude, *n.* طُول *pl.* أَطْوَال — طُولُ ٱلْبِلَادِ. Celestial —, طُولٌ سَمَاوِيٌّ. Difference of —, تَفَاضُلُ ٱلطُّولِ. The difference between two longitudes, تَفَاضُلُ ٱلطُّولَيْنِ. Lines of —, خُطُوطُ ٱلطُّولِ.

Longitudinal, *a.* بِٱلطُّولِ — طُولِيّ.

Longitudinally, *ad.* فِي ٱلطُّولِ — طُولًا.

Long-legged, *a.* Of a man, شَلَغْلَع — عَنَطْنَط — عَشَنَّق — عَشَنَّط.

Long-lost, *a.* غَائِبٌ مِنْ زَمَانٍ — ضَالٌّ مِنْ زَمَانٍ.

Long-measure, *n.* قِيَاس (or جَدْوَل) لِلطُّولِ وَٱلْمَسَافَةِ.

Long-sighted, *a.* Far seeing, غَرْبُ ٱلْعَيْنِ. A — eye, عَيْنٌ غَرْبَةٌ.

Long-sufferance, *n.* } طُولَةُ رُوحٍ — رِفْق — طُولُ أَنَاةٍ. *See also* Forbearance, *n.*
Long-suffering, }

Long-suffering, *a.* طَوِيلُ ٱلرُّوحِ — رَفِيق — آنٍ. *See also* Forbearing, *a.*

Long-tongued, *a.* Disputatious, مِغْلَاق — ذُو مِغْلَاقٍ.

Longways, *ad.* } بِٱلطُّولِ — طُولًا.
Longwise, }

Long-winded, *a.* Prolix, مُطَوِّل — نَفِس. A — story, حَدِيثٌ طَوِيلُ ٱلذَّنَبِ. He wrote a — book, كَتَبَ كِتَابًا نَفِسًا.

Loo, *n.* ضَرْبٌ مِنْ لَعِبِ ٱلْوَرَقِ.

Looby, *n.* حِمَار — ثَوْر — أَحْمَق — بَلِيد.

Look, *v.i.* To direct the eye, بَصَرَ — نَظَرَ — تَطَلَّعَ — تَشَوَّفَ. To open the eyes, فَتَحَ ٱلْعَيْنَيْنِ — بَصَّرَ. To consider, نَظَرَ — تَأَمَّلَ. To appear, seem, ظَهَرَ — بَيَّنَ — تَبَيَّنَ. A place where a thing is looked for, مَطْلَب.

To look about, round upon, one, نَظَرَ حَوْلَهُ. To see after, look for, فَتَّشَ عَلَى.

To look after, behind another, نَظَرَ وَرَآءَهُ. To attend to, نَظَرَ لِ —

اِعْتَنَى بِ ـ ؎ لَوَى عَلَى ـ اِطَّلَعَ إِلَى. To assist, سَاعَدَ ـ عَاوَنَ.

To look after one's self, اِعْتَنَى بِنَفْسِهِ.

To look at, ؎ حَدَّقَ ـ بِعَيْنِهِ ـ ؎ نَظَرَ إِلَى ـ رَامَقَ ـ رَمَقَ إِلَى ـ ² رَمَقَ ; ـ أَعْيَنَ vulg. ² شَافَ ـ ² بَصَّ لِ. To take a good look at, أَحَدَّ ٱلنَّظَرَ إِلَى ـ أَمْعَنَ ٱلنَّظَرَ فِي ـ تَفَرَّسَ فِي ـ تَعَيَّنَ. To look at one from the angle of the eyes, رَنَّقَ ٱلنَّظَرَ ـ رَنَّقَ ـ رَامَقَ إِلَى : He looked at him from the corner of the eyes, looked at him askance, رَمَقَهُ بِعَيْنِهِ. To look at lightly, glance at, رَامَقَ. To try to look at, تَعَيَّنَ.

To look away from, أَغْضَى عَن ـ اِقْتَصَرَ عَن.

To look behind another, ؎ نَظَرَ إِلَى وَرَآئِهِ. To look, one's self, behind, اِلْتَفَتَ إِلَى وَرَآءِ. Don't look behind you, لا تَلْتَفِتْ (or لا تَنْظُرْ) إِلَى وَرَائِكَ.

To look down, تَطَلَّعَ إِلَى تَحْتَ ـ نَظَرَ إِلَى تَحْتَ. To look down upon, to look at what is below, أَشْرَفَ عَلَى ـ أَطَلَّ عَلَى ; to contemn, اِسْتَحْقَرَ ـ اِسْتَخَفَّ.

To look for, seek after, فَتَّشَ عَلَى. To expect, ـ تَرَقَّبَ ـ اِنْتَظَرَ اِسْتَنْظَرَ ـ اِرْتَكَبَ.

To look forward to, to hope for, تَوَقَّعَ ـ تَمَنَّى ـ يَرْجُو aor. رَجَا.

To look ill, to appear sick, ؎ بَانَ كَأَنَّهُ مَرِيضٌ. To have a bad appearance, ² قَبُحَ ـ سَآءَ ٱلْأَمْرُ aor. ² يَسُوءُ.

To look in, or into, as into a house, تَفَرَّجَ ـ تَطَلَّعَ إِلَى ـ ؎ نَظَرَ فِي. To visit, زَارَ aor. يَزُورُ ـ ² دَخَلَ عِنْدَهُ ـ جَازَ بِ aor. عَلَى ـ ² مَرَّ بِ ـ يَجُوزُ.

To look into, to scrutinize, دَقَّقَ ـ ؎ بَحَثَ ـ تَصَفَّحَ فِي ـ تَبَصَّرَ.

To look on, or upon, be an observer, ؎ شَهِدَ ـ لَاحَظَ ـ ؎ نَظَرَ إِلَى. To esteem, ² ظَنَّ ـ ؎ ؎ حَسِبَ ـ ² عَدَّ ـ اِعْتَدَّ. To look on one with an evil eye, to envy, حَسَدَ ـ ² حَسَدَ عَلَى. Goodly to look upon, حَسَنُ ٱلْمَنْظَرِ. He was to look upon like a lion, كَانَ مَنْظَرُهُ مَنْظَرَ ٱلْأَسَدِ. To be looked upon, esteemed, ـ أُعِدَّ ـ ² ظُنَّ فِيهِ ـ حُسِبَ. To be ill looked upon, ² حُقِرَ ـ تَحَاقَرَ سَآءَ ٱلظَّنُّ فِيهِ. To be well looked upon, ـ أُعْتُبِرَ ـ أُخْتُبِرَ ² حَسُنَ ٱلظَّنُّ فِيهِ.

To look one in the face, وَاجَهَ. They looked one another in the face, of many, تَرَآءَوْا مُوَاجَهَةً ـ نَظَرُوا بَعْضُهُمْ إِلَى بَعْضٍ.

To look out, as out of a house, etc., اِطَّلَعَ إِلَى بَرًّا ـ نَظَرَ خَارِجًا. To be watchful, to take care, اِحْتَذَرَ ـ اِحْتَرَزَ ـ تَوَقَّى. To select, نَقَّى ـ اِخْتَارَ ـ اِنْتَخَبَ.

To look out for, to expect, اِنْتَظَرَ ـ اِرْتَكَبَ ـ تَرَقَّبَ.

To look out of, as out of a window, أَشْرَفَ مِن.

To look over, as from a height, أَشْرَفَ عَلَى. To read, revise, ² ؎ قَرَأَ ـ طَالَعَ. To pardon, سَامَحَ ـ ؎ صَفَحَ. To overlook, superintend, بَاشَرَ ـ ؎ نَظَرَ عَلَى ـ ؎ ² حَرَسَ.

To look sharp, تَحَذَّرَ ـ تَوَقَّى ـ أَوْعَى ـ يَعِي aor. وَعَى. To look sharp after, أَحَدَّ ٱلنَّظَرَ فِي ـ حَدَّدَ ٱلنَّظَرَ فِي.

To look steadfastly on, ؎ شَخَصَ إِلَى.

To look to, towards, ؎ نَظَرَ إِلَى. To take care of, ـ اِعْتَنَى بِ اِهْتَمَّ بِ ـ اِطَّلَعَ فِي. To look to one's self, ـ اِعْتَنَى بِنَفْسِهِ اِلْتَجَأَ إِلَى ـ اِلْتَبَطَ إِلَى. To have recourse to, إِحْتَذَرَ. To depend upon, اِتَّكَلَ عَلَى ـ اِسْتَنَدَ إِلَى ـ اِعْتَمَدَ عَلَى. To have an eye to, ؎ جَعَلَ عَيْنَهُ عَلَى ـ يَضَعُ aor. وَضَعَ عَيْنَهُ عَلَى. People's minds are still looking towards, or directed to ..., لَمْ تَزَلِ ٱلْخَوَاطِرُ مُتَشَوِّفَةً إِلَى كَذَا. Look ye to it, أَبْصِرُوا أَنْتُمْ.

To look through, into, the inside of a thing, ؎ نَظَرَ فِي دَاخِلِ ٱلشَّيْءِ.

To look through, as through a telescope, تَطَلَّعَ بِ ـ ؎ نَظَرَ بِ.

To look through, as of a book, تَصَفَّحَ ـ طَالَعَ.

To look twice, to consider carefully, تَرَوَّى جَيِّدًا ـ تَأَمَّلَ جِدًّا.

To look up, upwards, ؎ نَظَرَ إِلَى فَوْقُ. To be encouraged, ـ تَشَيَّدَ تَجَرَّأَ. To progress, تَقَدَّمَ ـ يَرُوجُ aor. رَاجَ ـ أَفْلَحَ ـ تَوَفَّقَ. The affair was looking up, رَاجَ ٱلْأَمْرُ. To expect, ـ تَرَقَّبَ ـ اِنْتَظَرَ تَرَاقَبَ. To look up to, to defer to, أَطَاعَ لِ ـ اِسْتَمَعَ لِ. To depend upon, تَوَكَّلَ عَلَى ـ اِسْتَنَدَ إِلَى ـ اِعْتَمَدَ عَلَى. One looked up to, نَظِيرَةٌ ـ نَظُورَةٌ ـ نَظُورٌ.

To look well, healthy, لَاحَتْ عَلَيْهِ لَوَائِحُ ٱلصِّحَّةِ. To have a good appearance, ؎ جَمُلَ ـ تَحَسَّنَ ـ ² حَسُنَ. He did what looked well, أَحْسَنَ. To look well to, to have an eye to, اِعْتَنَى بِ ـ جَعَلَ عَيْنَهُ عَلَى ـ ؎ جَعَلَ قَلْبَهُ إِلَى.

Look, v.t. تَطَلَّعَ إِلَى ـ ؎ نَظَرَ ـ ² بَصُرَ.

To look one down, ؎ سَخِطَ عَلَى ـ عِيَانًا ـ أَقْمَعَ ـ بِٱلنَّظَرِ.

To look one in the face, قَابَلَ ـ وَجْهًا بِوَجْهٍ ـ وَاجَهَ.

To look something out, to select, نَقَّى ـ اِنْتَقَى ـ اِخْتَارَ. To search for, فَتَّشَ عَلَى.

To look one up, search for, ² جَدَّ فِي طَلَبِهِ ـ فَتَّشَ عَلَى. To visit, زَارَ aor. يَزُورُ.

To look something over, to glance through, ؎ لَحَظَ ـ ؎ لَمَحَ إِلَى اِطَّلَعَ عَلَى ـ إِلَى. To read, ² ؎ قَرَأَ ـ طَالَعَ. To look over, as a lesson, رَاجَعَ ٱلدَّرْسَ.

Look, n. The act of looking, نَظَر ـ بَصَر ; a single —, ـ لَحْظَةٌ نَظْرَةٌ. Appearance, مَنْظَر ـ هَيْئَةٌ pl. هَيْآتٌ ـ سَمَامَةٌ ـ رَأْوَةٌ.

Looks, countenance, وَجْه ـ مَنْظَر ـ سِيمَا . Good looks, حُسْنُ ـ قَبَاحَة ـ جَمَال ـ مَلَاحَة ـ ٱلْمَنْظَرِ . Ill looks, sulkiness, وَغْفَة ـ قَبَاحَةُ ٱلْوَجْهِ . There is a — of stupidity in his face, عَلَى وَجْهِهِ رَأْوَةُ ٱلْحُمْقِ .

Looker-on, *n.* ناظِر *pl.* نُظَّارَة ـ شاهِد *pl.* شُهُود ـ مُتَفَرِّج *pl.* مُتَفَرِّجُون .

Looking, *a.* ذُو مَنْظَرٍ . Good —, ـ جُوِيْل ـ حَسَنُ ٱلْمَنْظَرِ . Ill —, وَحْش ـ سَمِيْج ـ سَمِج ـ قَبِيحُ ٱلْمَنْظَرِ . مَلِيح ـ كَيِّس

Looking-glass, *n.* مِرْآة *pl.* مَرَآءٍ *and* مَرَايا ; *vulg.* مَرَايَة .

Look-out, *n.* A place to look out from, مَرْبَأَة ـ مَرْقَب ـ مَطْلَعَة ـ عَلَم ـ مَرْقَبَة . A — built on a wall, شُونَة *pl.* شُوَن . A careful watching, نَبَاهَة ـ نُبْه ـ حِرَاسَة . A sentinel, ناطُور . A — party, شَيِّفَة .

Loom, *n.* A weaver's, نَوْل ـ مِنْسَاج ـ مِنْسَج . The web-beam, or yarn-beam, of a —, مِنْوَال ـ حَفَّة .

Loom, *v.i.* أَشْرَفَ . The cavalry loomed in the distance, came into view, أَشْرَفَتِ ٱلْخَيَّالَة . The island loomed into view, أَشْرَفَتِ ٱلْجَزِيرَةُ عَلَى ٱلْعِيَانِ .

Looming, *n.* The indistinct appearance of objects seen in particular states of the atmosphere, خَيَال مَيَال ـ سُرَاب ـ آل .

Loon, *n.* A simpleton, حِمَار ـ أَبْلَهُ ـ أَحْمَقُ .

Loop, *n.* In a general sense, شَرَج *pl.* أَشْرَاج . A — for a button, عُرْوَة *pl.* عُرًى *and* عَرَاوَى ـ زِرّ *pl.* زُرُور ـ بَنِيقَة *pl.* بَنَائِق . The loops of a sandal, أُذُنَا ٱلنَّعْلِ ; of a large bag, such as is borne by camels, عُرْوَة *pl.* عَرَاوَى : He inserted the stick into the —, سَلَكَ ٱلْعُودَ فِي ٱلْعُرْوَةِ . A tie, fold, ثِنْي *pl.* أَثْنَاء .

Loop, *v.t.* To put loops to, عَرَّى ـ زَرَّرَ . To join two extremities, ثَنَى . To put into loops, زَرَّرَ ـ زَرَّ *aor.* يَزُرُّ ـ رَكَّبَ فِي ٱلْعُرَى . To — up, زَرَّ *aor.* يَزُرُّ ـ لَفَّ ـ طَبَّقَ .

Loop, *v.i.* تَزَرَّرَ . To — up, إِلْتَفَّ ـ إِنْطَبَقَ .

Loophole, *n.* A mural aperture, سَهْوَة *pl.* سِهَاء *and* سَهَوَات ـ كُوَّة فِي سُورٍ أَوْ قَلْعَةٍ لِإِطْلَاقِ ٱلْمَكَاحِلِ ; for musketry, كُوَّة ـ رَوْشَن ـ كُوَّات مِنْهَا *pl.* (*from the Turkish*), مَزْغَل لِلْمَكَاحِلِ *pl.* مَزَاغِل . A means of escape, بَابٌ لِلْخَلَاصِ ـ مَخْلَص ـ مَنْجَاة . A — to watch from, مَرْصَدٌ فِي شَكْلِ ٱلْكُوَّةِ *pl.* مَرَاصِدُ ; called in Egypt, apparently from the Persian, دَرْخُوش *pl.* دَرَاخِيش . An excuse, pretext, عِلَّة ـ حُجَّة .

Loophole, *v.t.* To furnish with loopholes, جَعَلَ لِ ـ مَزَاغِل (or) كُوَّاتٍ لِإِطْلَاقِ ٱلْمَكَاحِلِ مِنْهَا .

Loose, *v.t.* To untie, حَلَّ ـ فَكَّ . To let go, خَلَّى عَن ـ أَطْلَقَ ـ سَيَّبَ ـ أَفْلَتَ ـ فَكَّ . To be loosed, untied, إِنْحَلَّ ـ إِنْفَكَّ . *See also to* Loosen, *n.*

Loose, *a.* Unbound, مَفْكُوك ـ مُنْفَكّ ـ مَحْلُول ـ طَلْق . Not tight, lax, هَشّ ـ لَيِّن ـ سَهْل ـ مُسْتَرْخٍ ـ مُرْتَخٍ ـ رَخْو ـ رَخّ . Incompact, سَخِيف ـ أَسْوَل . In leaves, not bound, غَيْرُ مُجَلَّدٍ ـ أَوْرَاق . Vague, مُنْكَر . Loose in the bowels, رَخْو ـ سَائِب ـ مُتَدَلٍّ ـ مُتَرَجِّج ـ مُسْهَل . Stray, عَيَّار ـ عَائِر . Hanging down, مُتَدَلٍّ . Lax, wanton, فَلَاتِيّ ـ خَلِيع ـ فَاسِق ـ فُجَّار . Unsewed, مَفْتُوق . Separate, unattached, غَيْرُ مُتَعَلِّقٍ بِ ـ مُنْفَرِد . Loose, as of the hair, مُسَرَّح ـ مَنْشُور ـ مُنْسَدِل . Loose, of texture, سَخِيف ـ رَكِيكُ ٱلنَّسْجِ ـ خَفِيف . Ample, وَاسِع ـ رَحْب ; of a garment, full, سَابِغ . Loose, of style, رَكِيك . Having —, flabby, flesh, of a woman, مُبَتَّلَة . A — metaphor, مَجَازٌ مُرْسَل . To be —, slack, رَخِيَ *aor.* يَرْخَى . To be —, ample, وَسِعَ ـ سَبَغَ *aor.* يَسَعُ . To be —, as in texture, رَكَّ ـ سَخُفَ *aor.* يَرِكُّ . To be —, wanton, فَسَقَ . To be —, in the bowels, أَخَذَهُ سَكٌّ ـ أُسْهِلَ ـ فِي بَطْنِهِ . To be —, of hair hanging down, تَسَدَّلَ ـ إِنْسَدَلَ .

To break loose, إِنْهَزَمَ ـ إِنْسَلَّ ـ إِنْفَلَتَ .

To get loose, become slack, تَرَاخَى ـ إِسْتَرْخَى ـ إِرْتَخَى . To escape, فَلَتَ ـ إِنْفَلَتَ ـ تَفَلَّتَ .

To hang loose, تَدَلَّى ـ تَرَجَّحَ ـ إِسْتَرْخَى .

To have loose stools, قَعَدَ مَقَاعِدَ رِقَاقًا ـ سَكَّ بِسَلْحِهِ .

To leave loose, of an animal, أَعَارَ .

To let loose, at large, خَلَّى عَن ـ سَيَّبَ ـ أَطْلَقَ ـ أَفْلَتَ .

I let the bird loose from my hand, أَرْسَلْتُ ٱلطَّيْرَ مِنْ يَدِي .

He let loose his tongue against him, أَرْسَلَ عَلَيْهِ لِسَانَهُ . To turn loose, of animals, أَعَارَ . To turn loose, to pasture, أَسْرَحَ ـ سَرَّحَ .

To make loose, ample, وَسَّعَ ـ أَسْبَغَ .

Loose, *v.i.* To set sail from, سَافَرَ مِن ـ أَقْلَعَ مِن .

Loose, *n.* Absence of restraint, إِطْلَاق ـ حُرِّيَّة . To give — to, to let go, to express, أَطْلَقَ . To give one's self up to, تَجَرَّدَ لِ ـ سَلَّمَ نَفْسَهُ إِلَى . To be on the —, سَابَ فِي سِيرَتِهِ *aor.* يَسِيبُ ـ كَانَ سَائِبًا فِي سِيرَتِهِ .

Loosely, *ad.* Not tightly, بِرَخَاوَةٍ . Hanging down, بِٱسْتِرْخَاءٍ ـ تَسَدُّلًا ـ إِنْسِدَالًا . With fullness, amplitude, بِسَعَةٍ ـ بِسُبُوغٍ . Carelessly, بِإِهْمَالٍ ـ تَغَافُلًا . Without order, مِنْ غَيْرِ نِظَامٍ ـ بِلَا ضَبْطٍ ـ بِلَا دِقَّةٍ . Without exactness, إِرْتِبَاكًا ـ إِلْتِبَاكًا . Wantonly, بِفَلَتٍ ـ بِفِسْقٍ ـ بِلَا هِنْدَامٍ . Vaguely, بِتَنَكُّرٍ ـ بِإِبْهَامٍ ـ تَنَكُّرًا .

Loosen, *v.t.* To untie, حَلَّ ـ فَكَّ. To make less tense, رَاخَى ـ أَرْخَى. To make softer, لَيَّنَ. To —, of a garment, وَسَّعَ ـ أَسْبَغَ. To make more ample, أَسْدَلَ ـ سَدَلَ. To relax the bowels, لَيَّنَ (or سَهَّلَ or مَشَّى) ٱلْبَطْنَ ـ أَسْهَلَ. To — one's hold, to let go, أَطْلَقَ ب ـ سَيَّبَ. To —, as ground, turn it over, قَلَّبَ ٱلْأَرْضَ. Loosen the rope for him, أَرْخِ لَهُ ٱلْحَبْلَ. Loosen his shackles, أَرْخِ لَهُ قَيْدَهُ. He loosened or slackened the tie, أَرْخَى ٱلرِّبَاطَ. He loosened the horse's tether, أَرْخَى لِلْفَرَسِ. He loosened his turban, أَرْخَى عِمَامَتَهُ.

Loosen, *v.i.* To become loose, تَرَاخَى ـ ٱرْتَخَى. To become soft, تَلَيَّنَ. To —, of the hair, or a garment, to let hang loose, أَسْدَلَ ـ سَدَّلَ ـ سَدَلَ.

Looseness, *n.* Freedom from tightness, ٱنْفِكَاكٌ ـ ٱنْحِلَالٌ. Laxity, flabbiness, رَخَاوَةٌ ـ ٱرْتِخَاءٌ ـ سَخَافَةٌ. Amplitude, as of a dress, سَعَةٌ ـ سُبُوغٌ. Falling down, as of hair down the shoulders, تَسَدُّلٌ ـ ٱنْسِدَالٌ. Looseness of the bowels, إِسْهَالٌ ـ سَكٌّ ـ لِينُ ٱلْبَطْنِ. Softness, لِينَةٌ. Vagueness, تَنَكُّرٌ. Want of exactitude, قِلَّةُ دِقَّةٍ. Negligence, تَغَافُلٌ ـ إِهْمَالٌ. Want of order, regularity, قِلَّةُ نِظَامٍ ـ قِلَّةُ ضَبْطٍ. Looseness of style, رَكَاكَةٌ ـ رِكَّةٌ. Wantonness, lewdness, عَدَمُ عِفَّةٍ ـ سَفَاهَةٌ ـ فِسْقٌ وَفَسَادٌ. He has — of the bowels, أَخَذَهُ سَكٌّ فِي بَطْنِهِ ـ أَخَذَهُ سَكٌّ.

Loose-strife, *n.* The plant lysimachus, خُوخُ ٱلْمَاءِ.

Lop, *v.t.* As of trees, شَذَبَ ـ شَذَّبَ ـ خَصَّلَ ٱلشَّجَرَ ـ قَلَّمَ ـ شَذَّبَ. عَضَدَ ٱلشَّجَرَ ـ كَسَحَ ٱلْأَشْجَارَ. To cut off anything, قَضَبَ ـ خَصَّلَ ـ ٱقْتَضَبَ.

Lop-eared, *a.* شَرَافِيَّةٌ ـ أُذَانِيٌّ.

Lopper, *n.* As of trees, عَاضِدٌ.

Lopping, *n.* What is cut off, شَذَبَةٌ ـ شَذَبٌ *pl.* أَشْذَابٌ; loppings, عَيَازِرُ ـ قِطَاعٌ.

Lop-sided, *a.* Inclined to one side, مَائِلٌ إِلَى طَرَفٍ ـ مَائِلُ ٱلْجَنْبِ.

Loquacious, *a.* كَلْمَانِيٌّ ـ ثَرْثَارٌ ـ بَقَّاقٌ ـ بَذِرٌ ـ فَرْفَارٌ ـ فَجْفَاجٌ ـ قَوَّالٌ. A — tongue, لِسَانٌ طَلِقٌ. Noisy, garrulous, of a woman, جَلَّابَةٌ ـ مُجْلِبَةٌ. To be —, بَقَّ *aor.* يَبِقُّ ـ سَابَ فِي ٱلْكَلَامِ.

Loquaciously, *ad.* بِكَثْرَةِ كَلَامٍ ـ بِبَقِيقٍ.

Loquaciousness, *n.* } فَجْفَجَةٌ ـ بَقِيقٌ ـ بَقٌّ ـ سُيُوبٌ فِي ٱلْكَلَامِ
Loquacity, } ثَرْثَرَةٌ ـ كَثْرَةُ كَلَامٍ.

Lord, *n.* God, the Supreme Lord, رَبُّ ٱلْعَالَمِينَ ـ حَضْرَةُ ٱلْمَوْلَى ـ ٱلرَّبُّ; Lord of lords, رَبُّ ٱلْأَرْبَابِ. A sovereign, chief, as of a people, غُرَّةٌ. A master, مَوْلًى *pl.* مَوَالِي ـ سَيِّدٌ *pl.* سَادَةٌ and سَادَاتٌ. A nobleman, شَرِيفٌ *pl.* شُرَفَاءُ ـ عَيْنٌ *pl.* أَعْيَانٌ ـ لُورْدٌ *pl.* لُورْدَاتٌ. Governor, وَالٍ *pl.* وُلَاةٌ. A husband, زَوْجٌ ـ بَعْلٌ. A possessor, ruler, حَاكِمٌ *pl.* حُكَّامٌ ـ ضَابِطٌ *pl.* ضُبَّاطٌ. Head, chief, رَأْسٌ ـ رَئِيسٌ ـ رَيِّسٌ *pl.* رُؤَسَاءُ. Our Lord and Saviour Jesus Christ, حَضْرَةُ عِيسَى وَحِيدِ ٱللّٰهِ ـ رَبُّنَا وَسَيِّدُنَا يَسُوعُ ٱلْمَسِيحُ. My lord, as an address in speech, حَضْرَةُ مَوْلَانَا ـ يَا سَيِّدِي. The House of Lords, مَجْلِسُ ٱلشُّرَفَاءِ ـ مَجْلِسُ ٱلْأَعْيَانِ. Our sovereign lord, the king, مَوْلَانَا ٱلْمُعَظَّمُ ـ حَضْرَةُ سَعَادَةِ مَلِكِنَا; our sovereign lady, the queen, مَوْلَاتُنَا ٱلْمُعَظَّمَةُ ـ حَضْرَةُ سَعَادَةِ ٱلْمَلِكَةِ. Lord paramount, سُلْطَانٌ. The first Lord of the Treasury, رَئِيسُ شُورَى ٱلصَّدْرُ ٱلْأَعْظَمُ ـ ٱلدَّوْلَةِ. The Lord's day, يَوْمُ ٱلْأَحَدِ. The Lord's Supper, ٱلْعَشَاءُ ٱلرَّبَّانِيُّ. To be — over, تَرَأَّسَ ـ رَأَسَ عَلَى. To make — over, سَوَّدَ ـ رَأَّسَ ـ عَلَى.

Lord, *v.i.* To rule haughtily, تَعَظَّمَ ـ تَسَلَّطَ ـ تَجَبَّرَ. The inhabitants were lorded over, tyrannized, by him, تَقَمْقَمَتْ مِنْهُ ٱلْأَهَالِي.

Lordliness, *n.* Haughtiness, تَعَظُّمٌ ـ تَسَلُّطٌ ـ تَجَبُّرٌ. Dignity, جَلَالٌ ـ عِزٌّ ـ نَبَالَةٌ ـ شَرَفٌ ـ سِيَادَةٌ. Dignity, as of deportment, وَقَارٌ ـ هَيْبَةٌ.

Lordling, *n.* غَنْدُورٌ ـ مُتَكَبِّرٌ ـ سُوَيِّدٌ.

Lordly, *a.* Becoming a lord, dignified, نَبِيلٌ ـ وَجِيهٌ ـ وُجِهٌ. Exalted, مُرْتَفِعٌ ـ عَالٍ. Imperious, مُتَكَبِّرٌ ـ جَبْرِيٌّ ـ مَغْرُورٌ. Fine, superb, فَاخِرٌ ـ مُفْتَخِرٌ ـ سَنِيٌّ ـ مُتَنَفِّجٌ.

Lordly, *ad.* *See* Haughtily, *ad.*

Lordship, *n.* Rule, وِلَايَةٌ ـ حُكُومَةٌ ـ رِئَاسَةٌ ـ سِيَادَةٌ. State of being a lord, سِيَادَةٌ ـ رُبُوبِيَّةٌ. A domain, مُلْكٌ ـ مَمْلَكَةٌ ـ أَرَاضِي ـ ٱلْتِزَامٌ. As an address, your lordship, حَضْرَتُكَ ـ غِبْطَةُ سِيَادَتِكُمْ ـ سِيَادَتُكَ.

Lore, *n.* عُلُومٌ ـ عِلْمٌ. *See also* Erudition, *n.*

Lorgnette, *n.* نَظَّارَةٌ صَغِيرَةٌ.

Lorica, *n.* *See* Cuirass, *n.*

Loricate, *v.t.* To plaster over with, طَلَى ـ ب ـ طَلَّى ـ ب ـ دَمَّمَ ـ ب.

Lorication, *n.* تَطْلِيَةٌ ب.

Loriot, *n.* The bird, صُفْرَى ـ صُفَارِى.

Lorn, *a.* مَتْرُوكٌ. *See also* Lone, Lonely, *a.*

Lory, *n.* A kind of parrot, نَوْعٌ مِنْ طَائِرِ ٱلْبَبْغَاءِ.

Lose, *v.t.* As opposed to find, أَضَاعَ ـ ضَيَّعَ ـ ضَلَّ. To miss, أَعْدَمَ ـ فَقَدَ ـ عَدِمَ. To —, as opposed to gain, خَسِرَ. To become deprived of, تَلِفَ أَعْدَمَ. To become bereft of, ثَقِلَ. To —, of a savour, فَسَدَ: The salt has lost its savour,

فَسَدَ ٱلْمِلْحُ ². To — through prodigality, أَتْلَفَ. I lost ten piastres at play, خَسِرْتُ عَشَرَةَ غُرُوشٍ فِي ٱللَّعْبِ. I have lost the key, ضَيَّعْتُ ٱلْمِفْتَاحَ. They lost the battle, خَسِرُوا ـ غُلِبُوا ـ إِنْكَسَرُوا ـ كَانَتِ ٱلدَّائِرَةُ عَلَيْهِمْ. To make to —, as opposed to gain, أَخْسَرَ ـ خَسَّرَ; specially in trade, وَكَّسَ. To become lost, ضَاعَ aor. يَضِيعُ. Your sheep that were lost are found, الغَنَمُ الضَّالَّةُ لَكَ وُجِدَتْ.

To lose a law suit, خَسِرَ دَعْوَاهُ ².

To lose an opportunity, فَقَدَ ² (or إِفْتَقَدَ or ضَيَّعَ) ٱلْفُرْصَةَ.

To lose, as of a child or relative, إِنْفَجَعَ فِي ـ فَقَدَ ² ـ ثَكِلَ ².

To lose breath, إِنْقَطَعَ نَفَسُهُ.

To lose hope of, أَضَاعَ عَشَمَهُ بِ ـ قَطَعَ ٱلْأَمَلَ مِنْ. To lose hope; *see to* Despair, *v.i.*

To lose its savour, تَلِفَ ² طَعْمُهُ. The salt has lost its savour, صَارَ ٱلْمِلْحُ بِلَا مُلُوحَةٍ ـ فَسَدَ ٱلْمِلْحُ ².

To lose itself, disappear, غَابَ ²: The water loses itself in the earth, المَآءُ يَغِيبُ فِي ٱلْأَرْضِ.

To lose one's life, خَسِرَ ² نَفْسَهُ ـ هَلَكَ ² ² ـ أَضَاعَ حَيَاتَهُ.

To lose one's pains, ضَيَّعَ تَعَبَهُ.

To lose one's self, to become confounded about a thing, طَوَّحَ نَفْسَهُ ـ تَحَيَّرَ ـ حَارَ فِكْرُهُ فِي aor. يَحُورُ. To be guilty of impropriety, تَرَكَ ٱلْأَدَبَ ² ـ قَصَّرَ فِي ٱلْأَدَبِ. To become debauched, خَلُعَ ² ـ إِنْعَكَسَ ـ تَلِفَ ². To lose one's mind, تَجَنَّنَ ـ جُنَّ ـ عَدِمَ ².

To lose one's time, ضَيَّعَ أَوْقَاتِهِ ـ ضَيَّعَ ٱلزَّمَنَ.

To lose one's way, تَاهَ ² ـ ضَيَّعَ ٱلدَّرْبَ ـ تَاهَ aor. يَتِيهُ ـ ضَلَّ ² ـ تَطَوَّحَ ـ عَنِ ٱلطَّرِيقِ. To make one to lose his way, تَيَّهَ ـ ضَيَّعَ ٱلدَّرْبَ عَلَى ـ أَضَلَّ.

To lose patience, ضَيَّعَ ٱلصَّبْرَ ـ عَدِمَ ² ٱلصَّبْرَ.

To lose sight of, no longer to see, مَا بَقِيَ ـ غَابَ ² ٱلشَّيْءُ عَنْهُ يَنْظُرُهُ. To let drop out of mind, تَرَكَ ² مِنْ بَالِهِ.

To lose teeth, سَلَّ ².

Lose, *v.i.* To become marred, vitiated, تَلِفَ ². To suffer loss, خَسِرَ ². To —, as in trade, خَسِرَ ² (or غَرِمَ ² or وَكَسَ aor. يَكِسُ) فِي ٱلتِّجَارَةِ. To — in value, إِنْحَطَّ سِعْرُهُ ـ نَزَلَ ² ـ تَلِفَ ² ـ بُخِسَ ـ خَسَّ ². To — time, as a watch, قَصَّرَ ـ تَأَخَّرَ: My watch loses, سَاعَتِي مُقَصِّرَةٌ.

Loser, *n.* خَاسِرٌ ـ خُسْرَانٌ. To be a —, خَسِرَ ².

Losing, *a.* خَاسِرٌ ـ مُتْلِفٌ. A — bargain, صَفْقَةٌ خَاسِرَةٌ. A — affair, قَضِيَّةٌ خَاسِرَةٌ.

Losingly, *ad.* بِخَسَارَةٍ.

Loss, *n.* Deprivation of what was once possessed, فَقْدٌ ـ عَدَمٌ. Loss, as in trade, خَسَارَةٌ ـ خُسْرَانٌ ـ خُسْرٌ ـ وَكْسٌ. Damage, مَضَرَّةٌ ـ ضَرٌّ ـ عَوَارٌ. Anything lost, مَفْقُودٌ. Vitiation, تَلَفٌ. Loss, as of relatives, فَقْدٌ ـ ثُكْلٌ ـ ثَكَلٌ. Deficiency, نُقْصَانٌ. Ruin, إِتْلَافٌ ـ خَرَابٌ ـ هَلَاكٌ ـ تَلَفٌ. The being backward, تَأَخُّرٌ. Loss of time, the being kept without employment, عُطْلَةٌ: He paid for his — of time, عَوَّضَ عُطْلَتَهُ. Loss of blood, نَزِيفُ دَمٍ. Profit and —, المَكْسَبُ وَٱلْخَسَارَةُ. He claims for his —, يَدَّعِي بِخَسَارَتِهِ ـ يَدَّعِي بِضَيَاعِهِ. He shall pay for his — of time, يُعَوِّضُ عُطْلَتَهُ. There shall not be the — of a single soul, لَا تَكُونُ خَسَارَةُ نَفْسٍ وَاحِدَةٍ. A dead —, خَسَارَةٌ كُلِّيَّةٌ. A cause of —, إِضَاعَةٌ. At a —, with —, بِخَسَارَةٍ.

To be at a loss, perplexed, بُهِتَ ـ إِهْتَمَّ بِ ـ تَحَيَّرَ.

To bear or suffer a loss, خَسِرَ ²; in trade, وَكَسَ aor. يَكِسُ ـ خَسِرَ ². To suffer damage, إِنْضَرَّ. To be bereaved, فَقَدَ ² ـ ثَكِلَ ².

To console for a loss, سَلَّى ـ عَنْ فَقْدِهِ. We pray that God will console his relatives for his loss, نَسْأَلُهُ تَعَالَى أَنْ يُوَلِّيَ أَهْلَهُ ٱلتَّعْزِيَةَ عَلَى فَقْدِهِ. To be consoled for the loss of one, تَسَلَّى عَنْ فَقْدِهِ.

To indemnify for a loss, عَوَّضَ ـ ٱلْخَسَارَةَ. Whatever loss you may sustain, I will indemnify you for the same, مَا لَحِقَكَ مِنْ دَرَكٍ (or تِبْعَةٍ) فَعَلَيَّ خَلَاصُهُ. *See also under to* Indemnify, *n.*

To meet with a loss, حَصَلَ لَهُ خَسَارَةٌ ² ـ لَاقَى خَسَارَةً.

To occasion another a loss, أَوْقَعَ ٱلْخَسَارَةَ عَلَى ـ أَخْسَرَ ـ خَسَّرَ.

To retrieve a loss, جَبَرَ ٱلْخَسَارَةَ ² ـ سَدَّ ٱلْخَسَارَةَ ². To retrieve one's losses, broken fortune, إِنْجَبَرَ ـ تَجَبَّرَ.

To save one from loss, سَلَّمَ ـ مِنَ ٱلْخَسَارَةِ.

Lost, *a.* Absent, غَائِبٌ. Not to be found, مَفْقُودٌ ـ ضَائِعٌ. Astray, ضَالٌّ ـ تَائِهٌ. Perplexed, حَيْرَانُ. In perdition, هَالِكٌ ـ فِي ٱلْهَلَاكِ. A — thing, مَفْقُودٌ. Her hope was —, هَلَكَ ² ² رَجَاؤُهَا. That nothing be —, لِكَيْ لَا يَضِيعَ شَيْءٌ. To be —, of a ship, إِنْكَسَرَ ٱلْمَرْكَبُ ـ غَرِقَ ². To become —, not to be found, ضَاعَ aor. يَضِيعُ. The number of the —, dead, perished, عَدَدُ ٱلضِّيَاعِ (or ٱلْمَفْقُودِينَ).

Lot, *n.* The means of determining a chance, قُرْعَةٌ ـ سُهْمَةٌ pl. قُرَعٌ. Fortune, chance, portion, طَالِعٌ ـ نَصِيبٌ pl. أَنْصَابٌ ـ بَخْتٌ ـ حِصَّةٌ pl. حِصَصٌ ـ حِزْبٌ pl. أَحْزَابٌ. A parcel, مِنْ ـ جُمْلَةٌ ـ دَسْتٌ pl. دُسُوتٌ. To draw or cast lots, قَرَعَ ² ـ أَقْرَعَ ـ سَاهَمَ. To choose or win by lot, قَرَعَ ². They cast lots among themselves, of many, تَقَارَعُوا ـ قَارَعُوا ـ تَسَاهَمُوا. The lot fell to him, كَانَتِ ٱلْقُرْعَةُ لَهُ. Taking soldiers by lot, ٱلْقُرْعَةُ ٱلْعَسْكَرِيَّةُ.

Lot, *v.t.* *See to* Allot, *v.t.*

Lote, *n.* The tree, Forskal's *Rhamnus nabeca*, سِدْرَةٌ ـ سِدْر *pl.* سُدُور ـ شَجَرَةُ ٱلنَّبَقِ. The fruit of the —, نَبَق.

Loth, *a.* Unwilling, كَارِهٌ ـ غَيْرُ رَاضٍ. To be —, to consider hard, difficult, annoying, شَقَّ ـ بَشِعَ عِنْدَهُ ـ إِسْتَكْرَهَ ـ كَرِهَ ـ صَعُبَ عَلَى ـ غَمَّ ـ عَلَى. Nothing —, مِنْ غَيْرِ كَرَاهَةٍ ـ عَلَى ٱلرَّأْسِ وَٱلْعَيْنِ ـ حَاضِرٌ ـ بِلَا ٱسْتِكْرَاهٍ.

Lotion, *n.* A washing, غَسْلَةٌ ـ غَسْل. A medicinal —, غِسْل ـ شَطْفَة.

Lottery, *n.* قُرْعَةٌ ـ نَصِيب ; (from the Italian) لُوتُو. To put into a —, حَطَّ فِي ٱلنَّصِيبِ. This is all a —, هٰذَا كُلُّهُ نَصِيبٌ.

Lotus, *n.* The plant, حَنْدَقُوقِي ـ حَنْدَقُوق.

Loud, *a.* جَهْوَرٌ (or جَهُورٌ or جَهُورِيٌّ) ٱلصَّوْتِ. A — voice, صَوْتٌ مُرْتَفِعٌ ـ صَوْتٌ عَالٍ ـ صَوْتٌ عَظِيمٌ ـ هُتَاف. Loud instruments, صُنُوجُ ٱلْهُتَافِ. He uttered it with a — voice, هَتَفَ بِهِ. I cried with a — voice, صَرَخْتُ بِصَوْتٍ عَظِيمٍ. To cry out with a — voice, عَيَّطَ ـ صَرَخَ. Loud thunder, رَعْدٌ مُطَنْطِنٌ. Loud fame, صِيتٌ مُشْتَهِرٌ ـ صِيتٌ جَلِيلٌ.

Loudly, *ad.* بِصَوْتٍ عَظِيمٍ ـ بِهُتَافٍ ـ بِصُرَاخٍ.

Loudness, *n.* جَهَارَة ـ طَنْطَنَة ـ هُتَاف ـ صُرَاخ.

Louis d'or, *n.* سِكَّةُ ٱللُّويزِيِّ.

Lounge, *v.i.* تَكَاسَلَ ـ تَضَجَّعَ. To — away the time, ضَيَّعَ ٱلْوَقْتَ. *See also to* Loll, *v.i.*

Lounge, *n.* The act of reclining lazily, تَكَاسُل ـ تَضَجُّع. A place for lounging, مَكَانُ ٱلتَّكَاسُلِ ـ مَضْجَع. A kind of sofa, طَرَّاحَة ـ مَضْجَع.

Lounger, *n.* ضُجَعَة ـ ضَاجِع ـ ضِجْعِيٌّ ـ مِكْسَال.

Louse, *n.* قَمْلَة coll. قَمْل *pl.* قَمْلَات. A wood —, حِمَارُ قَبَّانَ ـ حُمَيِّرُ جَدَّةٍ ـ أُمُّ عَلِيٍّ. A crab —, قَمْقَامَة ـ طَبُّوع. A —, such as infests plants, بَقٌّ. A wall —, بَقُّ ٱلْحِيطَانِ. To crack or kill, of a —, قَصَعَ. To search the head of another for lice, فَلَى ـ فَلَّى. To ask to have one's head searched for lice, إِسْتَفْلَى ـ تَفَالَى. Searching the head for lice, فِلَايَة. I cleared his head of lice, فَلَّيْتُ رَأْسَهُ مِنَ ٱلْقَمْلِ.

Lousiness, *n.* قَمَل.

Lousy, *a.* Swarming with lice, قَمِلٌ ـ عُلٌّ قَمِلٌ. Mean, contemptible, خَسِيس ـ ذَلِيل ـ دَنِيء ـ حَقِير ـ قَمْلِيٌّ.

Lout, *n.*
Loutish, *a.* } مَعْكُوس *pl.* مَعَاكِيس ـ خَلِيع ـ فَلَاتِيٌّ. A lazy —, مُبْرِم.

Lovable, *a.* *See* Amiable, *a.*

Love, *v.t.* To regard with affection, أَحَبَّ *aor.* يُحِبُّ ـ وَدَّ ـ إِسْتَحَبَّ ـ إِعْتَلَقَ بِ. To like, have an esteem for, هَوِيَ ـ وَدَّ ـ تَعَلَّقَ بِ ـ إِلْتَصَقَ بِ. To be amorous of, عَشِقَ. To desire, covet, affect, رَغِبَ. To be or become loved, حَبَّ. This became an object of — to me, *i.e.* I — it, حَبَّ إِلَيَّ هٰذَا ٱلشَّيْءُ. I became loved, *i.e.* an object of — to him, حَبُبْتُ إِلَيْهِ. To make one to —, حَبَّبَ إِلَى. He was madly in — with her, أُغْرِمَ بِهَا ـ أُوْلِعَ بِهَا. They — to have it so, هٰكَذَا يُحِبُّونَ. They loved one another, حَابَّ بَعْضُهُمْ بَعْضًا. He loved, preferred, him above others, إِسْتَحَبَّهُ عَلَى غَيْرِهِ. They — fine clothes, يَرْغَبُونَ فِي ٱللُّبْسِ ٱلْفَاخِرِ.

Love, *n.* Affection, مَحَبَّة ـ مَوَدَّة ـ وِدَاد ـ وُدٌّ ـ حُبٌّ ـ صُحْبَة ـ عَلَاقَة. Sincere —, خِلَّة ـ خُلَّة ـ خِلٌّ. Friendship, إِلْتِصَاق. Amorous —, غَرَام ـ هَوًى ـ عِشْق ـ جَوًى. Violent —, شَغَف ـ كَلَف. Desire, رَغْبَة. Love of self, حُبُّ ٱلذَّاتِ ـ حُبُّ ٱلنَّفْسِ. Covered —, مُمَاذَقَة. A labour of —, تَعَبُ ٱلْمَحَبَّةِ. Mutual —, مُحَابَّة ـ مُحَابَبَة. The first or last traces of —, رَسُّ ٱلْحُبِّ. Tender —, صَبَابَة. Brotherly —, مَحَبَّةٌ أَخَوِيَّةٌ. Inordinate —, مَحَبَّةٌ مُفْرِطَةٌ. Unfeigned —, مَحَبَّةٌ بِلَا رِيَاءٍ. Sick with or of —, مَرِيضٌ حُبًّا. Out of — for him, مَحَبَّةً فِيهِ ـ عَلَى حُبِّهِ. Love entered into his heart, رَسَّ ٱلْهَوَى فِي قَلْبِهِ. Love, as a term of endearment, my —, يَا عَيْنِي ـ يَا حُبَّةَ نَفْسِي ـ يَا قَلْبِي. Love, what one loves, مَحَبَّة ـ حُبَّة. Love, a beloved one, حَبِيب *fem.* حَبِيبَة ـ مَحْبُوب *fem.* مَحْبُوبَة. Love, one amorously loved, مَعْشُوق *fem.* مَعْشُوقَة. A cause of —, مَحَبَّة *pl.* مَحَابّ. Such an one was endowed with qualities attracting the — of hearts, أُوتِيَ فُلَانٌ مَحَابَّ ٱلْقُلُوبِ. The — of money is the root of all evil, مَحَبَّةُ ٱلْمَالِ أَصْلٌ لِكُلِّ ٱلشُّرُورِ. For the love of God, حُبًّا بِٱللّٰهِ ـ حُبًّا بِهِ تَعَالَى ـ لِأَجْلِ ٱللّٰهِ. To be in love, حَبَّ ـ عَشِقَ. To be in love with, إِنْشَغَفَ بِ ـ تَوَلَّعَ بِحُبِّهِ.

To fall in love, تَعَشَّقَ ـ تَغَرَّمَ حُبًّا ـ رَسَّ ٱلْهَوَى فِي قَلْبِهِ.

To get the love of another, حَبَّبَ إِلَى ـ تَوَدَّدَ إِلَى.

To inspire, amorous, love, شَغَفَ ـ عَشَّقَ.

To make love to, تَعَشَّقَ إِلَى ـ تَحَبَّبَ إِلَى ـ تَوَدَّدَ إِلَى.

To make one madly in love, أَوْلَعَ (or أَغْرَمَ) حُبًّا ـ إِسْتَهْوَى. To be made so, أُوْلِعَ حُبًّا ـ أُغْرِمَ حُبًّا.

To send one's love to, بَلِّغ ٱلسَّلَامَ وَٱلتَّحِيَّةَ إِلَى.

To smite with love, to captivate, حَبَلَ.

Love-apple, *n.* The tomato, بَاذَنْجَان فِرَنْجِيّ ـ تَمَاتِم.

Loved, *a.* A loved one, مَحْبُوب *fem.* مَحْبُوبَة ـ حَبِيب *fem.* حَبِيبَة. *See also* Lover, *n.*

Love-favour, *n.* عَلَامَةُ مَحَبَّةٍ.

Love-feast, *n.* وَلِيمَةُ ٱلْمَحَبَّةِ.

Love-knot, *n.* نِيشَانُ مَحَبَّةٍ ـ نِيشَانُ ٱلْمَحَبَّةِ.

Love-letter, *n.* رِسَالَةٌ مِنْ عَاشِقٍ إِلَى مَعْشُوقٍ.

Loveliness, *n.* Amiableness, لَطَافَة ـ وُدّ ـ مَحَبَّة. Beauty, لَطَافَة ـ حُسْن ـ ظَرَافَة ـ جَمَال ـ طَلَاوَة. Brightness, زَهْو.

Love-lock, *n.* سَبِيبَة *pl.* سَبَائِب ـ ذُؤَابَة *pl.* ذَوَائِب.

Love-lorn, *a.* مَتْرُوكٌ مِنْ حَبِيبَتِهِ *fem.* مَتْرُوكَةٌ مِنْ حَبِيبِهَا ـ عَاشِقٌ مُفَارِقٌ *fem.* عَاشِقَةٌ مُفَارِقَةٌ.

Lovely, *a.* Amiable, حُلْو ـ وَدُود ـ لَطِيف ـ أَنِيس. Charming, ظَرِيف ـ جَمِيلٌ لِلْغَايَةِ ـ خَيِّر ـ بَدِيع ـ حَبَّذَا. Beautiful, لَطِيف ـ حَسِين ـ جَمِيل. He is altogether —, كُلُّهُ مَلَاحَةٌ ـ هُوَ جَمِيلٌ لِلْغَايَةِ. A — prospect, مَنْظَرٌ بَهِيجٌ. A — flower, نَبَاتٌ زَهُوٌّ. A — garment, ثَوْبٌ زَهُوٌّ. A — song, نَشِيدٌ جَمِيلٌ (or عَذْبٌ). A — countenance, or a woman with a — countenance, زَلَفَةٌ حَسَنَةٌ. How — the thing is! حَبَّذَا ٱلْأَمْرُ. How — Zaid is! حَبَّذَا زَيْدٌ.

Lover, *n.* وِدّ *pl.* أَوُدّ ـ حَبِيب *pl.* أَحِبَّاء ـ حِبّ *pl.* أَحْبَاب. One in love, عَاشِق *pl.* عُشَّاق *and* عَاشِقُونَ *and* عَشَائِق; *fem.* عَاشِقَة *pl.* عَاشِقَات. The two lovers, *i.e.* the loving and the loved one, (masc.) ٱلْحَبِيبُ وَٱلْمَحْبُوبُ.

Love-sick, *a.* مَرِيضٌ حُبًّا ـ مُوَلَّه ـ مَتْبُول ـ تَبِيل. To be —, أَتْبَلَهُ ٱلْهَوَى ـ تَبَلَهُ ٱلْحُبُّ.

Love-sickness, *n.* وَلَهَان ـ وَلَه ـ تَبْل.

Love-suit, *n.* تَعَشُّق ـ تَحَبُّب ـ تَوَدُّد.

Love-token, *n.* تَذْكِرَةُ مَحَبَّةٍ ـ عَلَامَةُ مَحَبَّةٍ.

Loving, *a.* حَبِيب ـ وَدُود ـ مُودّ ـ مُحِبّ ـ حِبّ. Amorous, عَاشِق.

Loving-kindness, *n.* رَأْفَة ـ شَفَقَة ـ لُطْف ـ رَحْمَة ـ مَرَاحِم ـ حِلْم.

Lovingly, *ad.* بِكَمَالِ ٱلْمَحَبَّةِ ـ بِصَبَابَةٍ ـ بِمَحَبَّةٍ ـ بِوِدَادٍ ـ بِرِقَّةِ قَلْبٍ.

Lovingness, *n.* رِقَّةُ قَلْبٍ ـ صَبَابَة ـ حَنَان.

Low, *a.* Not high, وَطِيء ـ سَافِل ـ غَيْرُ مُرْتَفِعٍ. Mean, vile, خَسِيس ـ خَزِر ـ سَفِيل ـ دَنِيء ـ سُفْلَانِيّ ـ رَذِيل ـ تَفِه ـ ذَلِيل. Inferior, دُون. Deep, عَمِيق. Short, قَصِير. Low, of price, رَخِيص. Plain, level, سَاهِل. Not loud, خَفِيت ـ خَافِت ـ خَفِيّ ـ خَفِيض. Weak, مَوْهُون ـ عَاجِز ـ ضَعِيف. Depressed, sad, حَزِين ـ مَكْرُوب ـ كَرِيب. Poor, مِسْكِين ـ فَقِير. Humble, مُتَوَاضِع ـ خَشِيع ـ وَضِيع. Low, as liquid in a cask, getting low, مُقِلّ ـ مُقِلّ ـ مُتَصَوِّب. Low, of a plant with a short stalk, قَصِيرُ ٱلسَّاقِ. Low, or depressed land, خَوْر ـ غَوْر. The Low countries, Holland, بِلَادُ فَلَمَنْكَ.

Low estate, مَسْكَنَة ـ فَقْر ـ إِتِّضَاع ـ مَذَلَّة.

Low people, أَوْبَاش ـ سِفْلَة.

Low stature, قِصَرُ ٱلْقَامَةِ.

To be or to become low, not high, سَفَلَ ـ سَفُلَ ـ تَسَفَّلَ ـ صَارَ وَاطِيًا ـ تَخَفَّضَ ـ تَصَوَّبَ; weak, فَتَرَ ـ ضَعُفَ ـ تَضَعَّفَ; depressed in spirits, كَتُبَ ـ إِكْتَرَبَ ـ تَضَجَّرَ; humble, خَشَعَ ـ إِتَّضَعَ ـ إِنْغَمَّ; mean, abject, رَذُلَ. To be brought low, as in rank, إِنْحَطَّ مَنْزِلًا.

To bring low, to lay low, to overthrow, دَمَّرَ ـ أَهْبَطَ ـ خَرَّبَ.

See also to Lower, *v.t.*

Low, *ad.* With a low voice, بِصَوْتٍ خَفِيضٍ (or مُنْخَفِضٍ). Meanly, بِخَسَاسَةٍ ـ بِرَذَالَةٍ. Cheaply, بِرُخْصٍ ـ رُخْصًا. In a state of a depression of spirits, بِحُزْنٍ ـ إِكْتِرَابًا. In a state of poverty, بِفَقْرٍ ـ بِمَسْكَنَةٍ. Getting low, as liquids, بِتَنَقُّصٍ ـ تَصَوُّبًا. As low down as possible, أَسْفَلَ مَا يَكُونُ.

Low, *v.i.* To bellow, جَأَرَ ـ نَعَرَ; *vulg.* جَعَرَ. *See also to* Bellow, *v.i.*

Low-born, *a.* ذَلِيلُ ٱلنَّسْلِ ـ فَقِيرُ ٱلْأَهْلِ ـ مِنَ ٱلْفُقَرَاءِ ـ سَفِيل.

Low-bred, *a.* ذَلِيلُ ٱلتَّرْبِيَةِ ـ ذَمِيمُ ٱلْأَخْلَاقِ ـ رَذِيل ـ دَنِيء.

Lower, *v.t.* To make —, طَأْطَأَ ـ وَطَّأَ ـ سَفَّلَ. To make shorter, قَصَّرَ. To bring down, أَنْزَلَ ـ نَزَّلَ ـ سَفَّلَ. To make to descend to a — place, حَدَرَ ـ أَحْدَرَ. To depress, abase, خَفَضَ. To humiliate, أَذَلَّ ـ أَخْضَعَ ـ أَرْذَلَ ـ أَهَانَ. To let down, as of a curtain, سَدَلَ ـ أَسْدَلَ ـ أَرْخَى. To — yards, أَرْخَى ٱلزَّوَاجِعَ ـ مَايَنَ. To —, as of a price, أَهْبَطَ ـ هَبَّطَ ـ رَخَّصَ ـ خَفَّضَ ٱلثَّمَنَ; of stocks, بَخَسَ. To weaken, هَبَطَ ـ وَهَّنَ ـ أَفْتَرَ ـ أَضْعَفَ. To make less, in number, قَلَّلَ. To — one's reputation, غَضَّ مِنْهُ ـ هَتَكَ. To —, of the eyes and voice, غَضَّ. To be lowered, made less high, تَطَأْطَأَ ـ تَسَفَّلَ; shorter, إِقْتَصَرَ ـ تَقَصَّرَ; depressed, sad, إِكْتَرَبَ ـ إِنْغَمَّ; humiliated, abased, إِرْتَذَلَ ـ تَرَذَّلَ ـ أُهِينَ ـ إِخْتَضَعَ; of a price, إِنْحَطَّ ثَمَنُهُ — إِرْتَخَصَ — إِنْهَبَطَ. To — one's self to, تَضَعْضَعَ لِ. To — a flag half-mast high; *see under* Mast, *n.*

Lower, *v.i.* To fall low, إِنْحَطَّ. To become shorter, إِقْتَصَرَ. To become less, in number, قَلَّ ≈.

Lower, *v.i.* To appear dark, gloomy, of the weather, تَدَجَّى — آلَ إِلَى — ²هَمَّ بِ — تَوَعَّدَ *aor.* أَظْلَمَ — ≈ غَتَمَ. To threaten, تَوَعَّدَ — هَمَّ بِ — يَؤُولُ. To frown, قَطَّبَ بَيْنَ عَيْنَيْهِ — ≈ عَبَسَ — ² بَسَرَ.

Lower, *a.* Less low, أَنْزَلُ — أَدْنَى — دُونٌ — أَسْفَلُ — أَحَطُّ. Deeper, أَعْمَقُ. Below, or — down, تَحْتَانِيٌّ. In a — place, فِي أَسْفَلِ مَوْضِعٍ. The — pool, الْبِرْكَةُ ٱلسُّفْلَى. The — parts of the earth, أَسَافِلُ ٱلْأَرْضِ. Belonging to the — class, سُفْلِيٌّ. A rank — than that of an ambassador, رُتْبَةٌ أَحَطُّ مِنْ رُتْبَةِ ٱلسِّفَارَةِ.

Lower, *n.* Cloudiness, gloominess, غَتَمَةٌ — دُجْيَةٌ — دُجًا — غَبَشٌ — غُبُوسَةٌ. Sullenness, عُبُوسَةٌ — عَبَسٌ — بَسْرٌ — وَعْقَةٌ.

Lowering, *a.* Weakening, مُوَهِّنٌ — مُفَتِّرٌ — مُهْبِطٌ — مُضْعِفٌ. Humiliating, مُذِلٌّ — مُزْدَلٌ. Gloomy, مُظْلِمٌ — ظُلْمَانِيٌّ — دَجِيٌّ.

Loweringly, *ad.* With gloom, بِغَبَشٍ — ظُلْمَةً — بِدُجُوٍّ. With frowning, تَشَتُّمًا — تَسَخُّطًا — بِعُبُوسَةٍ — بِعَبَسٍ. Threateningly, إِهْتِمَامًا بِ — تَوَعُّدًا.

Lowermost, *a.* } Below all, تَحْتَ — أَسْفَلُ ٱلسَّافِلِينَ — الْأَسْفَلُ
Lowest, } ٱلْكُلِّ. The — of the people, السِّفْلَةُ — أَسَافِلُ ٱلنَّاسِ — أَطْرَافُ ٱلشَّعْبِ. The — place, الْمَوْضِعُ ٱلْأَخِيرُ. The — rank, الدَّرَجَةُ ٱلْأَخِيرَةُ — آخِرُ دَرَجَةٍ.

Lowing, *n.* As of cattle, نَعِيرٌ — خُوَارٌ — جُؤَارٌ — جَأْرٌ.

Lowland, *n.* وَطَآءٌ — مِيطَآءٌ — غَمْضٌ — غَمْطٌ — خَوْرٌ — حَضِيضٌ — غَوْرٌ — غَوْطٌ.

Lowlander, *n.* سُكَّانٌ *pl.* سَاكِنُ ٱلْغَوْرِ — مِنْ أَهْلِ ٱلْغَوْطِ.

Lowliness, *n.* Freedom from pride, مَسْكَنَةٌ — سَفَالٌ — وَضَاعَةٌ. Humbleness, تَوَاضُعٌ — خُضُوعٌ — خُشُوعٌ — ضَعْضَعَةٌ.

Lowly, *a.* Free from pride, مَسْكِينٌ — خَاشِعٌ — وَضِيعٌ. Humble, مُتَضَرِّعٌ — مُتَوَاضِعٌ. Poor, mean, دُونٌ — فَقِيرٌ — سَفِيلٌ — حَقِيرٌ. Lowly in heart, مُتَوَاضِعُ ٱلْقَلْبِ. To be —, تَخَشَّعَ — إِخْتَشَعَ — إِخْتَضَعَ.

Lowly, *ad.* بِخُضُوعٍ وَخُشُوعٍ — بِتَخَشُّعٍ — بِوَضَاعَةٍ.

Low-minded, *a.* سَفِيلٌ — رَذِيلٌ — خَسِيسٌ. *See also* Base, *a.*

Lowness, *n.* Want of elevation, تَسَفُّلٌ — سُفُولٌ — عَدَمُ ٱرْتِفَاعٍ. State of poverty, حَقَارَةٌ — فَقْرٌ — مَسْكَنَةٌ — عَدَمٌ. Meanness, vileness, ذِلَّةٌ — دَنَآءَةٌ — خَسَاسَةٌ — رَذَالَةٌ. Lowness, of price, هُبُوطُ ثَمَنٍ — رُخْصَةٌ. Weakness, ضَعْفٌ — وَهْنٌ. Depression of spirits, قَلَقٌ — إِضْطِرَابٌ — غَمٌّ — حُزْنٌ — كَدَرٌ. Lowness of voice, هَمْسٌ (or خُفُوتُ) ٱلصَّوْتِ — خَفْضُ ٱلصَّوْتِ. Depression, of a market, كَسَادٌ.

Low-pressure, *n.* As of a steam-engine, ضَغْطُ ٱلْبُخَارِ.

Low-spirited, *a.* *See* Dejected, *a.*

Low-water, *n.* Of the tide, جَزْرٌ كَامِلٌ.

Loyal, *a.* Obedient, مُطِيعٌ. Faithful, مُسْتَقِيمٌ — أَمِينٌ — صَادِقٌ. To be —, أَخْلَصَ. Loyal to the government, نَصُوحٌ لِلدَّوْلَةِ. He was — in his efforts, أَخْلَصَ فِي مَسَاعِيهِ. To be — to, as in friendship, *etc.*, أَخْلَصَ لَهُ ٱلنُّصُوحَ.

Loyalist, *n.* وَثِيقُ ٱلْوِدَادِ لِ — ثَابِتٌ فِي نُصُوحِهِ لِ.

Loyally, *ad.* بِٱسْتِقَامَةٍ — بِصَدَاقَةٍ — بِنُصُوحٍ.

Loyalty, *n.* إِسْتِقَامَةٌ — صَدَاقَةٌ — نُصْحٌ — نُصُوحٌ. His —, many loyal services, to the government, should not be forgotten, أَخْلَصَ لِلدَّوْلَةِ خِدَمًا وَافِرَةً لَا يَنْبَغِي أَنْ تُنْسَى.

Lozenge, *n.* The geometrical figure, مُعَيَّنٌ. A — of confectionery, أَقْرَاصٌ *pl.* قُرْصٌ مِنْ سُكَّرٍ — أَلْوَاحٌ *pl.* لَوْحُ سُكَّرٍ.

Lubber, *n.* شَلُوشٌ — غَشِيمٌ — بَلِيدٌ — مُغَفَّلٌ — عَجَمِيٌّ — أَخْرَقُ. A lazy —, مُبْرِمٌ.

Lubberly, *a.* غَلِيظٌ — قَلِيلُ ٱلْمُرُوَّةِ — بَلِيدٌ — ثَقِيلٌ — أَخْرَقُ. *See also* Awkward, *a.*

Lubric, *a.* Having a smooth surface, مَصْقُولٌ — سَهْلٌ — أَمْلَسُ.

Lubricant, *n.* مَلَاسَةٌ — صَقَالَةٌ.

Lubricate, *v.t.* To make smooth, صَقَلَ — مَلَّسَ — سَهَّلَ — ² أَمْلَسَ. To anoint, دَهَنَ².

Lubricity, *n.* Smoothness, slipperiness, سُهُولَةٌ — مَلَاسَةٌ — صَقْلٌ. Wantonness, شَهْوَانِيَّةٌ.

Lubricous, *a.* Slippery, smooth, أَمْلَسُ — أَمْلَصُ — مَصْقُولٌ. Wanton, شَهْوَانِيٌّ.

Lubrifaction, *n.* } The act of making smooth, تَمْلِيسٌ — تَسْهِيلٌ —
Lubrification, } صَقْلٌ — صِقَالَةٌ. An anointing, تَدْهِينٌ.

Lucent, *a.* ضَوِيٌّ — لَمَّاحٌ — بَارِقٌ — لَامِعٌ.

Lucern, *n.* The plant, قُرْطٌ — قَضَّةٌ — بَرْسِيمٌ.

Lucernal, *a.* مِصْبَاحِيٌّ — سِرَاجِيٌّ.

Lucid, *a.* Shining, مُنِيرٌ — لَامِعٌ — لَمَّاحٌ — بَارِقٌ — جَلِيٌّ. Translucent, شَفَّافٌ. Perspicuous, ظَاهِرٌ — مُبِينٌ — وَاضِحٌ. Clear in mind, سَالِمُ ٱلْعَقْلِ — ذَكِيٌّ. A — interval, سَاعَةُ صَحْوٍ.

Lucidness, *n.* } Brightness, ضِيَآءٌ — نُورٌ — لَمَعَانٌ — لَمْعٌ. Trans-
Lucidity, } parency, شَفَّافَةٌ. Perspicacity, بَيَانٌ — وُضُوحٌ — إِمْتِيَازٌ.

Lucifer, *n.* The planet Venus as the morning star, الزُّهَرَةُ.

Satan, الشَّيْطَان ـ إِبْلِيس. A — match, كِبْرِيتَة ـ نَبِيخَة *coll.* كِبْرِيت.

Luciferous, *a.*
Lucific, } مُنِير ـ مُنَيِّر.

Luciform, *a.* فِي هَيْئَةِ ٱلنُّور.

Luck, *n.* بَخْت ـ طَالِع ـ نَصِيب ـ قَدَر. Good —, حَظّ ـ دَهْر مُوَافِق ـ إِقْبَال. Bad —, شُؤْم ـ نَحْس ـ سُوء بَخْت ـ دَهْر مُخَالِف. A run of —, حَظّ مُتَتَابِع. By his good —, مِنْ بَخْتِهِ ـ بِسَعْدِهِ; by his ill —, مِنْ نَحْسِهِ ـ مِنْ سُوء بَخْتِهِ. To be in luck's way, رُزِقَ ٱلسَّعْدَ فِي ـ حَظَّ ـ أَحَظَّ *aor.* يَحَظُّ. To be born to good —, وُلِدَ مَحْظُوظًا. *See also* Fortune, *n.*

Luckily, *ad.* لِلّٰهِ ٱلْحَمْدُ ـ مِنْ بَرَكَةِ ـ مِنْ بَخْت.

Luckiness, *n.* *See* Luck, *n.*

Luckless, *a.* نَحِس ـ مَنْحُوس ـ مَشْؤُوم.

Lucklessly, *ad.* مِنْ قِلَّةِ بَخْت ـ مِنْ سُوء بَخْت.

Lucky, *a.* صَاحِب بَخْت ـ سَعِيد ـ حَظِيظ ـ حَظِيّ. To be —, حَظَّ *aor.* يَحَظُّ. A — moment, وَقْت مُوَافِق. In a — moment, فِي أَسَرِّ وَقْت. *See also* Fortunate, *a.*

Lucrative, *a.* كَثِير ٱلْفَائِدَة ـ فِيهِ مَكْسَب ـ مُفِيد ـ رَابِح.

Lucrative trade, تِجَارَة رَابِحَة.

Lucre, *n.* Gain, فَائِدَة ـ مَكْسَب ـ كَسْب ـ رِبْح. Filthy —, الرِّبْح ٱلْقَبِيح.

Lucubrate, *v.i.* سَهِرَ ٱللَّيَالِي فِي ٱلدَّرْس.

Lucubration, *n.* سَهَرُ ٱللَّيَالِي فِي ٱلدَّرْس. Study, دَرْس ـ مُطَالَعَة.

Luculent, *a.* *See* Luminous, *a.*

Ludicrous, *a.* يُضْحِكُ مِنْهُ ـ مُضْحِك. A — thing, سُخْرِيَّة ـ مَسْخَرَة ـ أُضْحُوكَة *pl.* أَضَاحِيك. A — tale, لَهْوُ ٱلْحَدِيث.

Ludicrously, *ad.* بِمَسْخَرَة ـ بِنَوْع مُضْحِك.

Ludicrousness, *n.* أُضْحُوكَة ـ سُخْرِيَّة.

Lues, *n.* Poison, سُمّ; venom, حُمَة.

Luff, *v.i.* لَفَّ [2]. Luff! خَيْلَك.

Lug, *v.t.* إِسْتَجَرَّ ـ جَرَّ ـ سَحَبَ [2]. To be lugged, اِنْجَرَّ. To — the ear of one, أَذَنَ.

Lug, *n.* A heavy drawing, جَرَّة. A heavy load, حِمْل ـ ثِقْل ـ ثَقِيل. A sea-worm, دُودَة ٱلْبَحْر.

Luggage, *n.* Baggage and train, ثِقْل *pl.* أَثْقَال. A — van, عَرَبِيَّة ٱلْبِضَاعَة. *See also* Baggage, *n.*

Lugger, *n.* شَخْتُور ـ فَلُوكَة بِسَارِيَة وَاحِدَة *pl.* شَخَاتِير.

Lugubrious, *n.* مَكْرُوب ـ كَرِيب ـ حَزِين.

Lugubriously, *ad.* بِكَرْب ـ بِحُزْن ـ كَرْبًا ـ بِنَوْع حَزِين.

Lukewarm, *a.* Tepid, فَاتِر. To be —, فَتَرَ [2]; to make —, فَتَّرَ. Without ardour, بَارِد ـ عَدِيمُ ٱلْغَيْرَة ـ فَاتِر. Insipid, of a person, لَا فُلَانٌ بِخَلٍّ وَلَا خَمْر.

Lukewarmly, *ad.* With indifference, بِبُرُودَة ـ بِفُتُور ـ بِفَتَر.

Lukewarmness, *n.* Tepidness, فُتُور ـ فَتَر. Want of ardour, بُرُودَة ـ فُتُور ـ عَدَمُ ٱلْغَيْرَة ـ فَتَر.

Lull, *v.t.* To calm, quiet, سَكَّنَ ـ أَهْدَأَ ـ هَدَّأَ ـ رَيَّحَ. To — to sleep, نَوَّمَ ـ هَمْهَمَ ـ هَمَّمَ.

Lull, *v.i.* To subside, سَكَنَ ـ تَهَدَّأَ ـ هَدَأَ [2]. The wind lulled, أَهْمَدَتِ ٱلرِّيحُ.

Lull, *n.* Something that quiets, or which is relied upon to give quiet, سُكْتَة ـ سَكَن. Quiescence, سُكْتَة ـ سِكْتَة. A — of the wind, هُمُودُ ٱلرِّيح; of the sea, سُجُوّ ـ غَلِينَة.

Lullaby, *n.* سُكْتَة.

Lumbago, *n.* رُمَاع ـ ظُهَار.

Lumbar, *a.* صُلْبِيّ. The — region, مَحَلُّ ٱلْأَصْلَاب. The — nerve, لَحِمَة.

Lumber, *n.* Useless furniture, عَفْش نَفْش ـ دَبْش ـ سَقَط. a piece of —, دَبْشَة ـ عَفْشَة ـ عَفْش; Household —, سَقَطُ ٱلْبَيْت. Poor, paltry goods, سَقَطُ ٱلْمَتَاع. *See also* Litter, *n.*

Lumber, *v.t.* To heap carelessly together, كَوَّمَ ـ جَمَّعَ ـ سَدَّ ـ بِسَقَط ـ مَلَأهُ عَفْشًا ـ عَفَشَ ـ أَشْغَلَ [2]. To fill with lumber, ٱلْمَتَاع. *See also to* Litter, *v.t.*

Lumber, *v.i.* To move heavily, حَبَا *aor.* يَحْبُو ـ زَحَفَ ـ دَبَّ [2].

Lumbering, *a.* Heavy, ثَقِيل. Dragging, moving heavily, حَبِيّ ـ زَاحِف.

Lumber-room, *n.* بَيْتُ سَقَطِ ٱلْمَتَاع ـ مَحَلُّ ٱلْعَفْش.

Lumbri, *n.* A worm, دُودَة *coll.* دُود.

Lumbrical, *a.* مِثْلَ ٱلدُّودَة.

Luminary, *n.* A body that gives light, مَنَارَة *pl.* مَنَائِر. An illustrious personage, شَهِيرُ عَصْرِهِ ـ مَشْهُور ـ شَهِير.

Luminiferous, مُضِيء ـ مُنِير.

Luminosity, *n.*
Luminousness, } إِسْتِنَارَة ـ تَنَوُّر ـ ضِيَاء ـ نُور. Perspicuity, اِمْتِيَاز ـ وُضُوح ـ إِيضَاح.

Luminous, *a.* Emitting light, لَمُوح ـ لَائِح ـ مُنِير ـ نَيِّر. Perspicuous, صَرِيح ـ وَاضِح ـ مُبِين.

Luminously, *ad.* With brightness, بِنُور ـ تَنَوُّرًا ـ بِضِيَاء. Perspicuously, بِكَمَالِ ٱلْوُضُوح ـ بِوُضُوح ـ بِإِيضَاح.

Lump, *n.* A mass, بَضْعَة *pl.* بِضَاع ـ دُبْلَة *pl.* دُبَل ـ قِطْعَة ـ

شُقْفَة pl. شُقَف. A — of figs, قُرْصَةُ تِينٍ; a — of clay, مَدَرَة coll. مَدَر — سِجِّيل — دَبْشَة — دَبْشَةُ طِينٍ — طِينَة; of dough, عَجِينٌ — عَجِينَة. A collection of articles, جُمْلَة — كُومَة — هِدْفَة. A — or swelling in the neck, سِلْعَة pl. سِلَع. In —, in gross, بِالْجُمْلَةِ — بِالْكُلِّيَّةِ. *See also* Gross, *n.*

Lump, *v.t.* To make into lumps, دَبَّلَ — دَبَلَ ². To throw into a mass, أَجْمَلَ. To take in the lump, أَخَذَ-جُمْلَةً — أَخَذَ-بِالْجُمْلَةِ aor. يَأْخُذُ.

Lump, *v.i.* To become lumpy, صَارَ دُبَلاً — تَعَقَّدَ.

Lumping, *a.* Heavy, large, كَبِير — جَسِيم — عَظِيم — ثَقِيل.

Lumpish, *a.* Heavy, رَصَص — ثَقِيل. Dull, بَلِيد — ثَقِيل — غَشِيم.

Lumpishly, *ad.* In a heavy manner, بِثَقَالَةٍ. Stupidly, بِخُرْقٍ — بِغَشَمٍ — بِبَلَادَةٍ.

Lumpishness, *n.* Heaviness, ثَقَالَة — ثِقَل. Stupidity, خُرْق — غَشَم — حَمَاقَة — بَلَادَة.

Lumpy, *a.* Abounding in lumps, of earth, مَمْلُوٌّ مَدَرًا — مُتَجَعِّد — وَاعِر — خَشْبَاء. Full of small lumps, مُعَقَّد — مَمْلُوٌّ دُبَلاً — مَمْلُوٌّ عُقَدًا.

Lunacy, *n.* مَجَنَّة — خَلَلٌ فِي ٱلْعَقْلِ — جُنُون — جِنَّة. Commission in —, مَأْمُورِيَّةٌ رَسْمِيَّةٌ لِفَحْصِ حَالِ ٱلْمَجَانِينِ.

Lunar, *a.*
Lunary, } قَمَرِيٌّ.

Lunar-caustic, *n.* حَجَرُ جَهَنَّمَ.

Lunar cycle, *n.* دَوْرٌ قَمَرِيٌّ.

Lunarian, *n.* سَاكِنُ ٱلْقَمَرِ.

Lunar month, *n.* شَهْرٌ قَمَرِيٌّ.

Lunar year, *n.* سَنَةٌ قَمَرِيَّةٌ.

Lunated, *a.* هِلَالِيٌّ — بِصُورَةِ ٱلْهِلَالِ.

Lunatic, *a.*
Lunatic, *n.* } مَجْنُون — مُصَاب — مُشَجَّع. A lunatic asylum, بَيْتُ ٱلْمَجَانِينِ — مُسْتَشْفَى ٱلْمَجَانِينِ — بِيمَارِسْتَان.

Lunation, *n.* شَهْرٌ قَمَرِيٌّ — دَوْرُ ٱلْقَمَرِ.

Lunch, *n.* غَدَاء — طَعَامُ ٱلظُّهْرِ — مَا يُؤْكَلُ فِي وَسَطِ ٱلنَّهَارِ.

Lunch, *v.i.* تَغَدَّى — أَكَلَ طَعَامَ ٱلظُّهْرِ ².

Lunch, *v.t.* غَدَّى.

Luncheon, *n.* *See* Lunch, *n.*

Lunette, *n.* In fortification, طَابِيَةٌ فِي صُورَةِ ٱلْهِلَالِ. A loophole to watch from, نَظَّارَة — دَرْخُوش pl. دَرَاخِيش.

Lung, *n.* رِئَة and رِيَة pl. رِئُون — سَحْر pl. سُحُور and أَسْحَار — فُؤَاد. Ulceration of the lungs, سُحَاف. Inflammation of the lungs, ذَاتُ ٱلرِّئَةِ.

Lunge, *n.* A thrust, طَعْنَة — ضَرْبَة.

Lung-wort, *n.* The plant, أُشْنَة — خَرْخَرُ ٱلصُّخُورِ — كُشَّةُ ٱلْعَجُوزِ.

Luniform, *a.* بِشِبْهِ ٱلْقَمَرِ — مِثْلَ ٱلْقَمَرِ.

Luni-solar, *a.* مَنْسُوبٌ إِلَى ٱلشَّمْسِ وَٱلْقَمَرِ مَعًا.

Lunt, *n.* *See* Linstock, *n.*

Lupin, *n.* The pulse, تُرْمُس — جِرْجِيرٌ مِصْرِيٌّ.

Lupus, *n.* The constellation, ٱلسَّبُعُ.

Lurch, *n.* A sudden roll of a ship, تَدَحْرُجٌ إِلَى جَانِبٍ — كَبَّة — خَبْطَة — خَبْط. To leave one in the —, خَلَّى-فَجْأَةً — خَيَّبَ — تَرَكَ ².

Lurch, *v.i.* To roll to one side, تَدَحْرَجَ (or ٱنْدَفَعَ) إِلَى جَنْبٍ — تَدَرْكَلَ (or تَدَرْكَبَ) جَنْبًا. *See also* to Lurk, *v.i.*

Lurch, *v.t.* To disappoint, خَيَّبَ.

Lurcher, *n.* The dog, كَلْبُ رَصِيدٍ.

Lure, *v.t.* To entice, جَلَبَ ² — أَغْوَى — رَاوَدَ. To — from, رَاوَدَ-عَنْ. To — to, رَاوَدَ-عَلَى.

Lure, *n.* As for animals, طُعْمَة — طُعْم. Something to entice, غِوَايَة — إِغْوَاء — تَطْمِيعَة.

Lurid, *a.* Gloomy, dismal, مُحْزِن — مُعْتِم — مُكَدِّر — دَجِيٌّ.

Lurk, *v.i.* To lie in wait, تَرَصَّدَ — تَكَمَّنَ. To — for, رَصَدَ ² — أَكْمَنَ ل — كَمَنَ ل — ٱرْتَصَدَ. To — in a place, to keep out of sight, تَخَفَّى — ٱخْتَبَأَ — غَابَ فِي — غَاطَ فِي.

Lurker, *n.* One who lies in ambush, رَاصِد pl. رَاصِدُون. One who lies secreted, مُسْتَخْفٍ.

Lurking-place, *n.* Where one lies hid, مُخْتَفِيَة — مَخْبَأ. The — of a wild beast, خَفِيَّة. *See also* Den, *n.*

Luscious, *a.* حُلْوٌ لِلْغَايَةِ — لَذِيذٌ لِلْغَايَةِ — لَذِيذ.

Lusciousness, *n.* غَايَةُ ٱلْحَلَاوَةِ — لَذَّة.

Lusitanian, *a.* Belonging to Portugal, مِنْ بِلَادِ بُرْتُقَال.

Lusory, *n.* Belonging to play, لَاعِب — مُتَعَلِّقٌ بِٱللَّعِبِ.

Lust, *n.* In a general sense, قَطَم. Longing desire, تَوْق — شَوْق — هَوِيَّة. Covetousness, حِرْص — طَمَع — طَمَاع. Depraved desire, شَهْوَة pl. شَهَوَات — هَوًى pl. أَهْوَاء — إِغْلَام — غُلْمَة. The lusts of the flesh, شَهَوَاتُ ٱلْجَسَدِ. To serve lusts and pleasures, ٱسْتَعْبَدَ لِشَهَوَاتٍ وَلَذَّاتٍ. Abandoned to lusts, مُنْهَمِكٌ فِي ٱللَّذَّاتِ.

Lust, *v.i.* To desire, ٱشْتَهَى. To — after, قَطِمَ — ٱشْتَهَى — هَوِيَ.

Lustful, *a.* شَهْوَانٌ – قَيْفَط – شَبِقٌ – قَطَامِيٌّ – مِغْلِيم – غَلِم. To be —, اِغْتَلَمَ – ءِ غَلِمَ. To make —, أَغْلَمَ. More — than a bear (or ape), أَزْنَى مِنْ هِجْرِسٍ.

Lustfully, *ad.* شَهْوَانِيَّةً – بِشَهْوَةٍ – بِغُلْمَةٍ.

Lustfulness, *n.* *See* Lust, *n.*

Lustily, *ad.* Strongly, بِقُوَّةٍ – بِجَرَآءَةٍ – بِعَزْمٍ شَدِيدٍ – بِحَيْلٍ; with a loud voice, بِصَوْتٍ عالٍ.

Lustiness, *n.* جِدٌّ – جَرَآءَة – قُوَّة – مُرُوَّة – صَلَابَة. *See also* Robustness, *n.*

Lusting, *n.* *See* Lust, *n.*

Lustral, *a.* مُطَهِّر.

Lustrate, *v.t.* To cleanse, غَسَلَ – نَظَّفَ – طَهَّرَ.

Lustration, *n.* وُضُوءٌ – غَسْل – تَطْهِير.

Lustre, *n.* Brilliancy, لَمَعَان – جَلَآء – رَوْنَق; of a colour, نَضْر. Polish, صَقْلَة – صِقَال. Splendour, فَخْر – بَهْجَة – رَوْنَق. Renown, صِيت – ذِكْر – اِسْم – جَلال – شُهْرَة. A chandelier with sconces, ثُرَيَّا. The —, as of cloth, مَآء.

Lustrous, *a.* Glossy, مَصْقُول – مَجْلُوّ – لَمُوح – لامِع.

Lustrously, *ad.* بِرَوْنَقٍ – بِجَلَآءٍ.

Lustrum, *n.* A period of five years, مُدَّةُ خَمْسِ سِنِينَ.

Lusty, *a.* Vigorous, قَوِيّ – صُلْب – صَلِيب – صارِم – ضَلِيع *pl.* أَقْوِيَآء. To be —, ٢ صَلُبَ. To make —, صَلَّبَ.

Lusus-naturæ, *n.* مِنْ عَجائِبِ الطَّبِيعَةِ.

Lutarious, *a.* Pertaining to mud, وَحَلِيّ – وَحِل.

Lute, *n.* كِنَارَة *pl.* كِنَارَات – عُود *pl.* عِيدَان – طُنْبُور *pl.* طَنَابِير – جُنْك.

Lute, *n.* / Luting, } Clay for coating vessels, طِينُ الحِكْمَةِ (وَهُوَ ضَرْبٌ مِنَ العَلَقِ).

Lute, *v.t.* To coat with lute, دَمَّمَ – (طَيَّنَ – or) بِطِينِ الحِكْمَةِ.

Luteous, *a.* Of a clay colour, وَحَلِيُّ اللَّوْنِ – مِنْ لَوْنِ الوَحَلِ.

Lute-string, *n.* وَتَرُ العُودِ *pl.* أَوْتَار.

Lutheran, *a.* and *n.* عَلَى مَذْهَبِ لُوتِيرُوسَ – تابِعُ لُوتِيرُوسَ.

Lutheranism, *n.* مَذْهَبُ لُوتِيرُوسَ.

Lutist, *n.* A player on the lute, ضَرَّابُ العُودِ – عَوَّاد *fem.* عَوَّادَة – طُنْبُرَانِيّ – جُنْكِيّ *fem.* جُنْكِيَّة.

Lutose, *a.* Miry, مُوَحَّل – وَحِل.

Lutulent, *a.* Muddy, turbid, كَدِير – كَدِر – رَنِق.

Luxate, *v.t.* To put out of joint; *see to* Dislocate, *v.t.*

Luxated, *a.* Put out of joint; *see* Dislocate, *a.*

Luxation, *n.* Dislocation of a joint; *see* Dislocation, *n.*

Luxuriance, *n.* / Luxuriancy, } Of vegetation, تَكَثُّف – كَثَافَة. Exuberance, كَثْرَة – وُفُور – بَذَارَة – وَفْرَة – فِرَة.

Luxuriant, *a.* Of soil, خَصِيب – أَخْصَب – كَرِم. Exuberant, وَفُور – مُتَوافِر – مُوَفَّر. Tangled, of trees or hair, أَثِيث – جَثْجَل. Luxuriant herbage, نَبَاتٌ أَثِيثٌ – ثِنَان. A — beard, (أَثِيثَةٌ or) لِحْيَةٌ جَثْلَةٌ. The land was — in herbage, أَخْصَبَتِ الأَرْضُ. To be —, exuberant, ٢ ءِ أَثَّ. To become — in herbage, اِسْتَكَّ النَّبْتُ. The meadows were —, اِسْتَكَّتِ الرِّيَاضُ.

Luxuriantly, *ad.* Of vegetation, بِتَكَثُّفٍ. Exuberantly, بِبَذَارَةٍ – بِإِفْرَاطٍ. To grow —, ءِ كَثَّ – اِلْتَفَّ.

Luxuriate, *v.i.* To grow luxuriantly; *see preceding article.* To be rich or luxuriant in, ءِ خَصِبَ – أَخْصَبَ – ءِ غَنِيَ بِ. To enjoy, تَنَعَّمَ بِ – تَمَتَّعَ بِ.

Luxurious, *a.* Living in luxury, عائِشٌ فِي – مُتَنَعِّم – مُتْرَف. Voluptuous, شَهْوَانٌ – شَهْوَانِيٌّ. Abounding in luxuries, مُتَلَذِّذ – وَفْرَةُ النَّعِيمِ – غامِرُ النُّعَمَاءِ – ذُو زَهَآءٍ. Soft, ناعِم. *See also* Effeminate, *a.*

Luxuriously, *ad.* بِزَهَآءٍ – بِالتَّنَعُّمِ. To live —, تَنَعَّمَ مُتَرَفِّهًا.

Luxuriousness, *n.* *See* Luxury, *n.*

Luxurist, *n.* مُتَنَعِّم – مُتْرَف.

Luxury, *n.* Softness of life, نَعْمَة – تُرْفَة. Sumptuousness, كُلْفَة – فَخْر – زَهَآء. Exuberance, إِفْرَاط – بَذَارَة – وُفُور – وَفْرَة. A delicacy, ذَوْق – لَذَّة *pl.* لَذَّات – نِعْمَة. Voluptuousness, لَذَّة – تَلَذُّذ. Sensuality, شَهْوَانِيَّة. The luxuries of the world, نُعَمَآءُ الدُّنْيَا.

Lyceum, *n.* مَدْرَسَة *pl.* مَدَارِس – دارُ الفُنُونِ – دارُ المَعارِفِ.

Lydian, *n.* *See* Effeminate, *a.*

Lye, *n.* مَآءُ رَمَادٍ لِلْغَسِيلِ – مَآءُ قَلِي.

Lying, *n.* Telling lies, كِذْب – كِذْبان.

Lying, *a.* كَذَّاب – دَجَّال. A — tongue, لِسانٌ كاذِبٌ.

Lying-in, *a.* والِدَة. A — hospital, دارُ لِلوِلادَةِ – دارُ لِتَوْلِيدِ الحامِلاتِ.

Lymph, *n.* لِمْفا – مادَّةٌ شَفَّافَةٌ تَسْرِي فِي أَجْسامِ الحَيَوانِ.

Lymphate, *a.* / Lymphated, } Raving, مَجْنُون – مُصاب – مَخْلُوع – مُخَلَّع.

Lymphatic, *a.* لِمْفاوِيّ – مادِّيّ.

Lymphatic, *n.* / Lymph-duct, } مَجْرَى المادَّةِ – مَجْرَى اللِّمْفا *pl.* مَجَارٍ.

Lynch, *v.t.* حاقَتْ بِهِ الأَوْبَاشُ – أَوْقَعَ الأَوْبَاشُ بِهِ شَرًّا.

Lynch-law, *n.* عُقُوبَةٌ مِنَ ٱلْأَوْبَاشِ ـ شَرْعُ ٱلْأَوْبَاشِ.

Lynx, *n.* فَهْد *fem.* فَهْدَة *pl. masc.* فُهُود *pl. fem.* فَهْدَات ـ أَبُو مُعَاوِيَة.

Lynx-eyed, *a.* شَاهِي ٱلْبَصَرِ ـ شَائِهُ ٱلْبَصَرِ.

Lyra, *n.* The constellation, ٱلنَّسْرُ ٱلْوَاقِعُ ـ ٱلسِّلْيَاقُ ـ ٱلشَّلْحَفَاةُ.

Lyre, *n.* The instrument, قِيثَارَة ـ عُود.

Lyric, *a.*
Lyrical, } غِنَائِيٌّ ـ شِعْرُ غَزَلٍ.

Lyrist, *n.* A player on the lyre, ضَرَّابُ ٱلْقِيثَارَةِ ـ ضَرَّابُ ٱلْعُودِ.

M.

M.A. (Master of Arts,) عِبَارَةٌ عَنْ مُجَازِ ٱلْعُلُومِ ٱلْأَدَبِيَّةِ.

Ma, *n.* Mother, أُمٌّ ـ وَالِدَة. My mother, as an address, يَا أُمِّي abbreviated into, يُمِّي. Ma, as an infantile expression, أُمَّة ـ مِيمَة.

Ma'am, *n.* سِتّ ـ تَخْفِيفُ لَفْظَةِ Madam, يَعْنِي سَيِّدَة أَوْ سِتّ ـ مَادَامَة ـ خَانِم ـ خَاتُون.

Mab, *n.* Queen of the fairies, مَلِكَةُ ٱلْجِنِّيَّاتِ.

Mac, *n.* عِبَارَةٌ عَنْ لَفْظَةِ بْنُ (or آبْنُ) فُلَانٍ.

Macadamize, *v.t.* رَصَفَ ـ بِٱلْحَصَى ². A macadamized road, سِكَّةٌ مَرْصُوفَةٌ بِٱلْحَصَى.

Macaroni, *n.* The paste, شَعِيرِيَّةٌ إِيطَالِيَانِيَّةٌ ـ مَعْكَرُون. A finical fellow, غَنْدُور *pl.* غَنَادِرَة ـ طَقْطُوق ـ مُتَأَنِّق.

Macaronic, *a.* Jumbled, مُعَذْمَر ـ غُذَارِم ـ مُهَوَّش ـ مُلَبَّك ـ مُخَبَّص.

Macaroon, *n.* The biscuit, كَعْكٌ بِلَوْزٍ ـ حَلَاوَةُ لَوْزٍ بِسُكَّرٍ.

Macaw, *n.* The parrot, نَوْعٌ مِنْ طَائِرِ ٱلْبَبْغَاءِ.

Maccabees, *n.* The family of the, آلُ ٱلْمَقَّابِيِّينَ.

Mace, *n.* The spice, بَزْبَازَة ـ بَسْبَاسَة. A stick, sceptre, مِخْصَرَة *pl.* مَخَاصِرُ ـ قَضِيب *pl.* قُضْبَان. A club, مِقْمَعَة ـ دَبُّوس *pl.* دَبَابِيس. An iron —, عَمُودُ حَدِيدٍ.

Mace-bearer, *n.*
Macer, } حَامِلُ ٱلْقَضِيبِ.

Macerate, *v.t.* To make lean, أَنْحَفَ. To mortify, أَمَاتَ ـ قَهَرَ ². To steep, to soften, وَدَنَ *aor.* يَدِنُ ـ لَاثَ ² ـ مَاسَ ² ـ مَرَسَ ² ـ مَرَثَ ². To — in, أَنْقَعَ ـ فِي ـ نَقَعَ ـ فِي. A vessel in which anything is macerated, مَنْقَع. The result of maceration, a tincture, نُقُوع.

Maceration, *a.* Mortification, قَهْر ـ إِمَاتَة. The act of steeping, إِنْقَاع ـ مَرْث ـ وَدْن.

Machiavelian, *a.* Crafty, cunning, خَيْدَع ـ خَادِع ـ أَخْدَعُ ـ خَدَّاع ـ مَكَّار.

Machiavelism, *n.* Cunning, craft, خَدِيعَة ـ خِدْعَة ـ خِدَاع ـ تَمَاكُر.

Machicolated, *a.* Furnished with — openings, مَا كَانَ لَهُ طَاقَاتٌ. A — window, طَاقَةٌ ذَاتُ حِجَابٍ حَصِينٍ ـ طَاقَةٌ مُحَصَّنَةٌ.

Machinal, *a.* آلِيٌّ ـ مُتَعَلِّقٌ بِٱلْآلَاتِ.

Machinate, *v.t.* To plot, تَحَيَّلَ (or تَحَوَّلَ or إِحْتَالَ) فِي ـ إِخْتَرَعَ. To — against, إِحْتَالَ عَلَى ـ تَحَيَّلَ عَلَى ـ دَسْدَسَ عَلَى.

Machination, *n.* The act of plotting, إِحْتِيَال ـ تَحَيُّل ـ دَسْدَسَة. A plot, intrigue, حِيلَة *pl.* حِيَل ـ مَكْر ـ فَسَاد ـ خِدْعَة ـ دَسِيسَة.

Machinations, دَسَائِسُ ـ مَوَاكِرُ.

Machinator, *n.* مَاكِر *pl.* مَكَرَة ـ خَادِع ـ دَسِيس ـ صَاحِبُ حِيَلٍ.

Machine, *n.* آلَة *pl.* آلَات ـ (from the Italian) مَاكِينَة *pl.* مَاكِينَات; a — with a rotatory motion, دُولَاب *pl.* دَوَالِيبُ.

Machinery, *n.* Machines collectively, آلَات ـ دَوَالِيبُ. The science of —, فَنُّ ٱلدَّوَالِيبِ. The composite parts of a machine, تَرْكِيبُ ٱلْآلَاتِ. Arrangement, تَرْكِيب ـ تَدْبِير. Means, وَسَائِط ـ وَسَائِل.

Machinist, *n.* صَانِعُ آلَاتٍ *pl.* صُنَّاع ـ صَنَّاعُ ٱلْآلَاتِ.

Mackerel, *n.* إِسْقُمْرِي ـ إِسْقُومْرِي. A — sky, سَمَآءٌ نَمْرَآءُ ـ سَمَآءٌ أَنْمَشُ ـ سَمَآءٌ مَنْقُوشٌ.

Mackintosh, *n.* قَبُّوطٌ لِلْمَطَرِ ـ رِدَآءٌ لِلْمَطَرِ *pl.* قَبَابِيطُ.

Mactation, *n.* The slaughter of a beast for sacrifice, ذَبْح.

Macula, *n.* A spot, نُقْطَة *pl.* نُقَط ـ بُقْعَة *pl.* بُقَع.

Maculate, *v.t.* نَقَّطَ ـ بَقَّعَ.

Maculate, *a.*
Maculated, } مُنَقَّط ـ مُبَقَّع.

Maculation, *n.* تَبْقِيع ـ تَنْقِيط.

Mad, *a.* Disordered in intellect, مَعْتُوه ـ مَأْلُوف ـ مَأْلُوس ـ مَفْتُون ـ مَجْنُون ـ مُشْجَع ـ مُخَبَّل ـ مُصَاب. Mad, applied to animals, أَتْوَل. Inflamed with passion, حَنِيق ـ حَنِق. Delirious or foolish, هَذِر ـ هَذَّآء ـ مَأْفُون ـ مَأْفُوك. To be —, إِسْتَجَنَّ ـ تَجَنَّن ـ جُنَّ ـ خَبِلَ. To be — against, حَنِقَ عَلَى. To be — for, تَجَنَّنَ عَلَى ـ تَهَالَكَ عَلَى. To feign one's self —, تَظَاهَرَ بِٱلْجُنُون. I was exceedingly — against them, أَفْرَطَ حَنَقِي عَلَيْهِمْ. You are mad, don't know what you say, أَنْتَ تَهْذِي. I am not mad, لَسْتُ أَهْذِي. Much book-learning hath made him mad, ٱلْكُتُبُ ٱلْكَثِيرَةُ حَوَّلَتْهُ إِلَى ٱلْهَذَيَانِ.

Madagascar, *n.* The island, جَزِيرَةُ مَدَغَشْكَار (called by the natives on the east coast of Africa بُوكِين).

Madam, *n.* خَاتُون *pl.* خَوَاتِين ـ سَيِّدَة ـ سِتّ *pl.* سِتَّات ـ خَانِم ـ مَادَامَة *pl.* مَادَامَات. Yes, Madam, نَعَم يَا سِتِّي.

Mad-brain, *n.* *See* Madcap, *n.*

Mad-brained, *a.* Foolhardy, مُتَهَوِّر ـ يَهْفُوف. Wild, foolish, of a scheme, *etc.*, ضِدُّ ٱلْعَقْلِ ـ خَيَالِيّ.

Madcap, *n.* A wild person, مَجْنُون ـ مُتَهَوِّر ـ أَفْزَاز *pl.* فَزّ ـ سَادِر.

Madden, *v.t.* To disorder the intellect, خَبَّلَ ـ خَبَلَ ـ أَخْتَبَلَ ـ أَجَنَّ ـ حَمَّقَ ـ جَنَّنَ. To — with rage, أَحْنَقَ ـ أَغَاظَ. *See also under* Mad, *a.*

Madden, *v.i.* تَجَنَّنَ ـ جُنَّ ـ خَبِلَ.

Madder, *n.* ٱلْعُرُوقُ ٱلْحُمْرُ ـ رُنَّاس ـ فُوَّةُ ٱلصَّبَّاغِين ـ فُوَّة. Dyed with —, مُفَوًّى.

Made, *part. of* Make, *q.v.* Made up, compounded, مُرَكَّب; sewn, مَخْيُوط; factitious, مُمَوَّه ـ كَذَّاب ـ مُصَنَّع ـ مَصْنُوع.

Madefy, *v.t.* To moisten, بَلَّ ـ رَطَّبَ ـ خَضَّلَ ـ نَدَّى.

Madeira, *n.* The island, جَزِيرَةُ مَدِيرَا; the wine, (خَمْرُ *or*) نَبِيذُ مَدِيرَا.

Mademoiselle, *n.* سُتَيْتَة *pl.* سُتَيْتَات ـ سِتّ صَغِيرَة.

Madhouse, *n.* مُسْتَشْفَى ٱلْمَجَانِين ـ دَارٌ لِلْمَجَانِين.

Madly, *ad.* With foolhardiness, بِجُنُونٍ ـ بِحَمَاقَةٍ ـ بِتَهَوُّرٍ ـ كَٱلْمَجْنُونِ.

Madman, *n.* One disordered in intellect, مُخَبَّل ـ مُصَاب ـ مَجْنُون ـ مُشْجَع. A foolhardy man; *see* Madcap, *n.*

Madness, *n.* The state of disordered intellect, خُلَاع ـ خَبَال ـ جُنُون ـ جِنَّة ـ خَبَل. Madness in cattle, تُوَل. Headstrong passion, غَيْظ ـ حَنَق. Rashness, تَهَوُّر. To feign —, تَظَاهَرَ ـ تَجَنَّنَ ـ بِٱلْجُنُونِ.

Madonna, *n.* The Virgin Mary, حَضْرَةُ مَرْيَم. A picture of the —, صُورَةُ حَضْرَةِ مَرْيَم.

Madrepore, *n.* عِرْقُ ٱللُّؤْلُؤ.

Madrigal, *n.* أُرْجُوزَة *pl.* أَنَاشِيد ـ نَشِيد ـ أُنْشُودَة *pl.* قَصِيدَة *pl.* قَصَائِد.

Maelstrom, *n.* دُوَّامَةُ ٱلْبَحْرِ بِٱلْقُرْبِ مِنْ سَوَاحِلِ نُرْوِيجَا.

Maestoso, *n.* عِبَارَةٌ تَدُلُّ عَلَى رَزَانَةِ ٱلصَّوْتِ فِي فَنِّ ٱلْمُوسِيقَى.

Magazine, *n.* A store, مَخْزَن *pl.* مَخَازِن ـ حَوْصَلَة *vulg.* حَاصِل *pl.* حَوَاصِل. A — for gunpowder, مَخْزَنُ ٱلْبَارُودِ ـ جَبْخَانَه. A pamphlet, publication, رِسَالَة *pl.* رَسَائِل ـ مَجَامِع *pl.* مَجَامِيع ـ جَرِيدَة *pl.* جَرَائِد. A periodical —, وِيقَاتِيَّة *pl.* وِيقَاتِيَّات ـ جَرِيدَةٌ دَوْرِيَّة.

Magdalen, *n.* A penitent prostitute, زَانِيَةٌ تَائِبَة.

Magenta, *n.* The colour, حُمْرَة.

Maggot, *n.* The insect, دُودَة *coll.* دُود *pl.* دِيدَان. A whim, خَيَال ـ هَوِيَّة.

Maggotiness, *n.* تَدْوِيد ـ خُنُوز.

Maggoty, *a.* مُدَوَّد. To become —, دَوَّدَ ـ أَدَادَ ـ خَنِزَ.

Magi, *n.* مَجُوس.

Magian, *n.* } مَجُوسِيّ *coll.* مَجُوس.
Magian, *a.* }

Magianism, *n.* مَذْهَبُ ٱلْمَجُوسِ ـ عَقَائِدُ ٱلْمَجُوسِ.

Magic, *n.* Sorcery, سِحْر. Natural —, سِحْرٌ حَلَال ـ ٱلسِّيمِيَاء. Black —, سِحْرٌ شَيْطَانِيّ.

Magic, *a.* } سِحْرِيّ ـ سَحَّار ـ سَاحِر. A — lantern, فَانُوسٌ سِحْرِيّ.
Magical, } *See also under* Lantern, *n.*

Magically, *ad.* By magic, بِٱلسِّحْرِ. Wonderfully, عَجَبًا. Instantaneously, عَلَى ٱلْفَوْرِ ـ حَالًا ـ فِي ٱلْحَالِ.

Magician, *n.* سَاحِر *pl.* سَحَرَة *and* سُحَرَاء ـ سَحَّار *pl.* سَحَّارُون.

Magisterial, *a.* Belonging to a magistrate, مُتَعَلِّقٌ بِٱلْحَاكِمِ ـ مُخْتَصٌّ بِٱلْمَأْمُورِ ـ حُكْمِيّ. Arrogant, مُتَجَبِّر ـ مَغْرُور ـ مُتَنَفِّخ.

Magisterially, *ad.* As a magistrate, حَسَبَ ٱلْمَأْمُورِيَّةِ. Arrogantly, غُرُورًا ـ بِتَجَبُّرٍ ـ بِتَأَمُّرٍ.

Magistracy, *n.* The office of a magistrate, وَظِيفَةُ ٱلْوَالِي ـ مَأْمُورِيَّةُ ٱلضَّابِطِ. The body of magistrates, وُلَاةُ ٱلْحُكُومَاتِ ـ ٱلْحُكُومَةُ ٱلنِّظَامِيَّةُ ـ ٱلْحُكَّامُ.

Magistrate, *n.* In a general sense, حَاكِم ـ مُتَوَلِّي ٱلْحُكُومَاتِ ـ مَأْمُورٌ نِظَامِيّ ـ ضُبَّاط *pl.* ضَابِط ـ حَاكِمٌ مَأْمُورٌ ـ حُكَّام *pl.* A police —, وُلَاة *pl.* وَالِي ٱلضَّبْطِيَّةِ. An officer of the judicature, قَاضٍ *pl.* قُضَاة. To bring before the —, قَدَّمَ إِلَى ٱلْحَاكِمِ ـ حَاكَمَ إِلَى ٱلْحَاكِمِ.

Magistrature, *n.* *See* Magistracy, *n.*

Magna Charta, *n.* The — of England, خَطٌّ يُثَبِّتُ حُقُوقَ ٱلرَّعِيَّةِ أُضْطُرَّ ٱلْمَلِكُ جُونُ ٱلْأَنْكِلِيزِيُّ إِلَى إِصْدَارِهِ بِٱلْعَامِ ٱلشَّرْنَاه . A charter of privileges, بَرَاءَة ـ سَنَدُ ٱمْتِيَازَاتٍ .

Magnanimity, *n.* شَرَف ـ سَعَةُ صَدْرٍ ـ عُلُوُّ هِمَّةٍ ـ رَحْبُ ٱلصَّدْرِ ـ نَجَابَة ـ نَفْس .

Magnanimous, *a.* هُمَام *pl.* هِمَام ـ رَحِيبُ ٱلصَّدْرِ ـ وَاسِعُ ٱلصَّدْرِ ـ صَاحِبُ هِمَّةٍ ـ شَرِيفُ ٱلنَّفْسِ .

Magnanimously, *ad.* بِعُلُوِّ هِمَّةٍ ـ بِسَعَةِ صَدْرٍ ـ بِرَحْبِ ٱلصَّدْرِ .

Magnate, *n.* زَعِيم *pl.* زُعَمَاءُ ـ كَبِير *pl.* أَكَابِرُ ـ عَيْن *pl.* أَعْيَان . The magnates, ٱلْأَعْيَانُ ـ ٱلْأَكَابِرُ .

Magnesia, *n.* The earth so called, مَنَازِيَا ـ مَغْنِيسِيَا . Sulphate of —, مِلْحٌ أَنْكِلِيزِيٌّ .

Magnesian, *a.* مِنْ مَغْنِيسِيَا .

Magnesium, *n.* مَغْنِيسِيُوم .

Magnet, *n.* ٱلْمَغْنَطِيس ـ حَجَرُ ٱلْمَغْنَاطِيسِ ـ حَجَرٌ مَغْنَطِيس .

Magnetic, *a.* / Magnetical, مَغْنَطِيسِيٌّ . The — needle, ٱلْإِبْرَةُ ٱلْمَغْنَطِيسِيَّةُ ـ ٱلْإِبْرَةُ . The — telegraph, ٱلتِّلِغْرَافُ ٱلْمَغْنَطِيسِيُّ .

Magnetically, *ad.* بِٱلْمَغْنَطِيسِ ـ بِوَاسِطَةِ ٱلْمَغْنَطِيسِ ـ حَسَبَ قَوَاعِدِ ٱلْمَغْنَطِيسِ .

Magnetic battery, *n.* بَطَّارِيَّةٌ مَغْنَطِيسِيَّةٌ .

Magnetic needle, *n.* ٱلْإِبْرَةُ ـ إِبْرَةٌ مَغْنَطِيس .

Magnetics, *n.* The science of magnetism, عِلْمُ ٱلْمَغْنَطِيسِ .

Magnetism, *n.* ٱلْمَغْنَطِيسِيَّةُ ـ خَاصَّةُ ٱلْمَغْنَطِيسِ . Animal —, ٱلْمَغْنَطِيسِيَّةُ ٱلْحَيَوَانِيَّةُ .

Magnetize, *v.t.* To impart the properties of a magnet, مَغْنَطَ ـ صَيَّرَ مَغْنَطِيسًا ـ أَشْرَكَ فِي ٱلْمَغْنَطِيسَ . To be magnetized, خَالَطَهُ ٱلْمَغْنَطِيسُ ـ أُشْرِبَ فِي ٱلْمَغْنَطِيسَ . *See also under to* Electrify, *v.t.*

Magnetize, *v.i.* تَشَرَّبَ (*or* شَرُبَ *or* شَرِبَ) ٱلْمَغْنَطِيسَ .

Magnetizer, *n.* مُشْرِكُ ٱلْمَغْنَاطِيسِ .

Magneto-electric, *a.* كَهْرَبَائِيَّةٌ مَغْنَطِيسِيَّةٌ .

Magneto-electricity, *n.* ٱلْكَهْرَبَائِيَّةُ ٱلْمَغْنَطِيسِيَّةُ .

Magnetometer, *n.* مِيزَانُ ٱلْمَغْنَطِيسِ .

Magnific, *a.* / Magnifical, عَظِيم ـ مُفْتَخِر ـ فَاخِر ـ نَبِيل *pl.* نُبَلَاءُ .

Magnificat, *n.* تَسْبِيحُ حَضْرَةِ مَرْيَمَ ٱلْعَذْرَاءِ .

Magnificence, *n.* Show, pomp, فَخْر ـ عِزّ ـ طَنْطَنَة ـ سَلْطَنَة ـ فَخْفَخَة ـ عَظَمَة ـ مَوْكِب ـ عِزٌّ وَجَلَال . *See also* Grandeur, Greatness, *n.*

Magnificent, *a.* Splendid, of things, مُطَنْطِن ـ مُفْتَخِر ـ فَاخِر ـ عَظِيم ; of persons, عَزِيز ـ فَخْم *pl.* فِخَام ـ جَلِيل *pl.* أَجِلَّاء ـ صَاحِبُ عِزٍّ وَجَلَالٍ ـ فَاخِر . *See also* Grand, Great, *a.*

Magnificently, *ad.* With pomp, بِجَلَالٍ ـ بِفَخْرٍ ـ بِطَنْطَنَةٍ . Admirably, بِغَايَةِ ٱلْإِتْقَانِ ـ بِفَخْرٍ ـ بِجَلَالٍ ـ بِنَوْعٍ عَجِيبٍ .

Magnifier, *n.* One who extols, مُكَبِّر ـ مُمَجِّد ـ مُسَبِّح . A magnifying glass, بِلَّوْرَةٌ مُكَبِّرَةٌ .

Magnify, *v.t.* To make great, كَبَّرَ ـ عَظَّمَ ـ عَزَّزَ . To extol or praise (God), سَبَّحَ ـ ذَكَرَ . To praise, أَثْنَى عَلَى ـ مَجَّدَ ـ فَخَّمَ ـ ذَكَرَ . To revere, رَجَّبَ ـ رَجِبَ . To exaggerate, كَبَّرَ ـ بَالَغَ فِي ; of praise, قَرَّظَ ـ أَطْرَأَ ـ قَرَّطَ . To — one's self, تَعَظَّمَ ـ كَبَّرَ نَفْسَهُ ـ تَعَزَّزَ ـ عَزَّ . To — one's self against, تَعَظَّمَ عَلَى .

Magniloquence, *n.* تَفَنُّنٌ فِي ٱلْكَلَامِ ـ مُبَالَغَةٌ فِي ٱلْكَلَامِ .

Magniloquent, *a.* مُتَفَنِّنٌ فِي ٱلْكَلَامِ ـ بَلِيغُ ٱلْكَلَامِ ـ مِفَنٌّ .

Magniloquently, *ad.* تَفَنُّنًا ـ بِتَفَنُّنٍ ـ بِٱلْمُبَالَغَةِ .

Magnitude, *n.* Greatness, size, كِبَر ـ كُبْر ـ عَظَامَة ـ عِظَم ـ قَدْر ـ قَدٌّ . Importance, هَمِيَّة ـ عِظَم ـ لُزُوم . Grievousness, قَبَاحَة ـ وَبَال . Gravity, as of a crime, شَنَاعَة ـ جَسَامَة ـ فَظَاعَة . Matters of —, importance, مُهِمَّات ـ أَجِلَال . *See also* Importance, *n.*

Magnolia, *n.* شَجَرَةُ ٱلْمَغْنُولِيَا .

Magpie, *n.* عَقْعَق *pl.* عَقَاعِقُ ـ تَعَلْقَع ـ كُنْدُش . The green —, *picus viridis*, شِقِرَّاق ـ شِقْرَاق .

Magyar, *n.* *See* Hungarian, *n.*

Mahlab, *n.* The *Prunus Mahaleb* of Linn., شَجَرَةُ ٱلْمَحْلَبِ .

Mahogany, *n.* كَابِلِي . Made of —, كَابِلِيٌّ ـ مِنَ ٱلْكَابِلِي .

Mahomet, *n.* *See* Muhammad, *n.*

Maid, *n.* / Maiden, A young unmarried woman, بِنْت *pl.* بَنَات ـ صَبِيَّة *pl.* صَبَايَا . A virgin, بِكْر *pl.* أَبْكَار ـ بَتُول ـ عَذْرَاءُ *pl.* عَذَارَى *and* عَذْرَاوَات . A — servant, جَارِيَة *pl.* جَوَارٍ ـ نَقِلَة ـ خَدَّامَة *pl.* خَدَّامَات . An old —, عَانِس *pl.* عَوَانِسُ ـ عَاهِل *pl.* عَوَاهِلُ ـ تَرِيكَة . An instrument of torture, عَذْرَاءُ ـ حِمَار . To marry an old —, تَرِكَ . *See also* Virgin, *and* Spinster, *n.*

Maiden, *a.* Belonging to a virgin, مُتَعَلِّقٌ بِٱلْعَذْرَاءِ ـ بِكْرِيٌّ ـ بَتُولِيٌّ . A — speech, مَقَالَةٌ بِكْرٌ . A — assize, طَوَافُ ٱلْقُضَاةِ لِقِيَامِ ٱلْحُكْمِ فِي بَلْدَةٍ عَلَى ٱلْمُجْرِمِينَ فَلَا يَجِدُونَ أَحَدًا . *See also* Virgin, *a.*

Maiden-hair, *n.* The plant, كُزْبَرَة ـ كُزْبَرَةُ ٱلْبِئْرِ ـ بَرْسِيَاوِشَان .

Maidenhead, *n.* / Maidenhood, عُذْرَة ـ بَكَارَة . To deprive of —, اِفْتَضَّ . He took her —, هُوَ صَاحِبُ عُذْرِهَا ـ هُوَ أَزَالَ بُكُورِيَّتَهَا .

Maiden-like, *a.* } Like a maid, بَتُولِيٌّ ـ كَٱلْعَذْرَآءِ. Modest,
Maidenly, } حَيِيٌّ *fem.* حَيِيَّةٌ.

Maid-servant, *n.* *See under* Maid, *n.*

Mail, *n.* Armour, زَرَد *pl.* زُرُود ـ دِرْع *pl.* أَدْرَاع *and* دُرُوع. A coat of —, سِرْبَال. A coat of — made of fine rings, سَكٌّ *pl.* سِكَاك *and* سُكُوك. To clad one's self in —, تَدَرَّعَ. A maker of coats of —, سَرَّاد. The art of manufacturing coats of —, سِرَادَة ـ زِرَادَة. He was in a coat of —, كان لابسًا دِرعًا حَرْشَفِيًّا. Letters conveyed by post, بُوسْطَة. A — bag, جِرَابُ مَكَاتِيبِ جُرُب *pl.* ٱلْبُوسْطَةِ.

Mail, *v.t.* To cover with mail, دَرَّعَ. To send letters by post, أَرْسَلَ ٱلْمَكَاتِيبَ بِٱلْبُوسْطَةِ.

Mail-clad, *a.* مُدَرَّع.

Mail-coach, *n.* } عَرَبَةُ ٱلْبُوسْطَةِ.
Mail-stage, }

Mailed, *a.* Protected by scales, مُدَرَّع ـ مُلَبَّس صَفَائِحَ. Spotted, speckled, مَنْقُوش ـ مُنَمَّر.

Maim, *v.t.* To cut off, جَزَمَ [2]. To disable, عَجَّزَ ـ سَقَّطَ.

Maimed, *a.* أَقْطَع *pl.* قُطْع *and* قُطْعَان.

Main, *a.* Principal, أَكْبَر ـ أَخَصّ ـ أَهَمّ ـ أَصْلِيّ ـ رَأْس ـ أَعْظَم. The —, or chief part, جُلّ ـ جُلَال. He took the — part of it, أَخَذَ جُلَّهُ (*or* جُلَالَهُ) [2]. *See also* Chief, Principal, *a.*

Main, *n.* Strength, force, زُور ـ قُوَّة ـ شِدَّة ـ حَيْل. The ocean, ٱلْبَحْر ٱلْمُحِيط ـ القَامُوس ـ البَاحَة. The — portion, مُعْظَم ـ جُلّ. The mainland, أَصْل ٱلْبَرّ. A principal conduit, مَجْرًى كَبِير. With might and —, بِٱلزُّور ـ بِأَشَدّ قُوَّةٍ. In the —, principally, خَاصَّةً ـ فِي ٱلْجُمْلَةِ ـ عَلَى ٱلْأَغْلَبِ.

Maindeck, *n.* ظَهْرُ ٱلسَّفِينَةِ ـ البِلَاوِرَة.

Mainland, *n.* البَرّ ـ أَصْلُ ٱلْبَرّ.

Mainly, *ad.* فِي ٱلْغَالِبِ ـ غَالِبًا. What we — hope, غايةُ ما نَتَمَنَّاهُ.

Mainmast, *n.* الدَّقَل ٱلْأَكْبَر.

Mainprize, *n.* إِطْلَاق بِٱلْكَفَالَةِ ـ إِطْلَاق تَحْتَ ٱلضَّمَانِ.

Mainprize, *v.t.* سَيَّبَ بِٱلْكَفَالَةِ ـ أَطْلَقَ تَحْتَ ٱلضَّمَانِ.

Mainsail, *n.* القِلْع ٱلْأَكْبَر ـ المَايِسْتَرَة.

Mainsheet, *n.* أَشْقُوتِي ٱلْمَايِسْتَرَةِ.

Maintain, *v.t.* To hold, ضَبَطَ ـ حَفِظَ [2]. To affirm, وَكَّدَ ـ ثَبَّتَ ـ قَرَّرَ. To make to continue, not to allow to cease, أَدَامَ ـ أَبْقَى. To vindicate, حَامَى عَنْ. To persist in, أَصَرَّ عَلَى ـ وَاظَبَ عَلَى ـ اِسْتَمَرَّ فِي ـ لَزِمَ بِ ـ أَدْمَنَ عَلَى. To supply with, أَنْفَقَ عَلَى ـ صَرَفَ عَلَى ـ أَمَدَّ بِ. To pay the expenses of, قَامَ بِمَعِيشَتِهِ ـ تَكَلَّفَ بِمَصْرُوفِهِ [2]. To strengthen, شَدَّدَ ـ مَتَّنَ ـ قَوَّى. To support, hold up, سَانَدَ ـ حَمَلَ ـ تَمَسَّكَ. To — in a place, قَرَّرَ ـ مَكَّنَ. To study to do, to persevere in, مَارَسَ. To — the cause of one, أَقَامَ حَقَّهُ ـ قَضَى قَضَاءَهُ ـ أَجْرَى حُكْمًا لَ. To — the laws, حَفِظَ ٱلشَّرَائِعَ. To — correspondence with, as by letter, كَاتَبَ ـ رَاسَلَ; of many, تَرَاسَلُوا. To — a conversation, أَدْمَنَ ٱلْمُحَاوَرَةَ. To — a family, عَيَّلَ.

Maintainable, *a.* That may be affirmed, مِمَّا يُقَرَّر ـ مِمَّا يُثْبَتُ. That may be kept up, قَابِلُ ٱلْإِبْقَاءِ ـ إِدَامَتُهُ مُمْكِنَةٌ. That may be vindicated, مِمَّا يُوَكَّدُ ـ مِمَّا يُحَامَى عَنْهُ.

Maintenance, *n.* The act of keeping up, قِيَام ـ دَوَام. Support, مَسْنَد ـ رُكْن ـ إِسْنَاد. Assistance, مَدَد ـ مُعَاوَنَة. Backing, تَأْيِيد ـ ظَهْر. Preservation, حِفْظ ـ ضَبْط ـ صَوْن. Persistence in, إِدْمَان عَلَى ـ مُوَاظَبَة عَلَى. Carrying out, execution, إِجْرَآء. Means of support, living, إِيرَاد ـ مَعَاش ـ مَعِيشَة ـ عِيشَة. For the — of his house, لِمَعِيشَةِ أَهْلِ بَيْتِهِ. For the — of order, لِقِيَامِ ٱلنِّظَامِ.

Maintop, *n.* جَامُورُ ٱلْغَرَانْدِي.

Mainyard, *n.* مِيزَانُ (*or* رَاجِعُ) ٱلْمَايِسْتَرَةِ.

Maize, *n.* The *holcus sorghum* of Linn., ذُرَة ـ ذُرَة صَيْفِيّ ـ قَيْظِيّ. White —, the *zea mays* of Linn., ذُرَة شَامِيّ ـ ذُرَة كِيزَان. Yellow —, ذُرَة مِصْرِيّ.

Majestic, *a.* Grand, of persons, مُلُوكِيّ ـ سُلْطَانِيّ ـ جَلِيّ ـ جَلِيل ـ صَاحِبُ هَيْبَةٍ وَوَقَارٍ; of things, بَهِيّ ـ جَلِيل ـ عَظِيم ـ فَاخِر.

Majestically, *ad.* بِأُبَّهَةٍ ـ بِجَلَالٍ ـ بِجَدّ ـ بِهَيْبَةٍ ـ بِعِزٍّ ـ عِزَّةً.

Majesty, *n.* Dignity, stateliness, حِشْمَة ـ اِحْتِشَام ـ أُبَّهَة. Magnificence, عِزَّة ـ عِزّ ـ سَلْطَنَة ـ طَنْطَنَة. Grandeur, عَظَمَة ـ جَلَال. As the title of a king, سَعَادَة. Your —, سَعَادَتُكُمْ. Her — the Queen of Great Britain, جَلَالَةُ مَلِكَةِ بِرِيتَانِيَا ٱلْعُظْمَى. God, to whom belong glory and —, ٱللّٰهُ عَزَّ وَجَلَّ. Incomparable in — is God, تَعَظَّمَ (*or* تَعَاظَمَ) ٱللّٰهُ.

Major, *a.* Greater in number, أَكْثَر ـ أَعْدَد ـ أَكْثَرُ عَدَدًا; in quantity, أَكْبَر ـ أَعْظَم ـ أَقْدَرُ قَدْرًا; in extent, أَمَدُّ مَدًّا; in height, أَعْلَى; in rank, أَشْرَف; in years, أَسَنّ ـ أَكْبَرُ عُمْرًا. A — part, كُثْر ـ كَثْرَة. Major, in music, الكُبْرَى: the — key, الطَّامَّة ٱلْكُبْرَى.

Major, *n.* A — in the army, بِيكْبَاشِي ـ نَاظِر *pl.* نُظَّار. The — of a syllogism, الكُبْرَى *pl.* الكُبَر *and* الكُبْرَيَات. Town —, ضَابِطُ إِدَارَةِ ٱلْعَسْكَرِيَّةِ فِي بَلَدٍ.

Major-domo, *n.* عامِل ـ وَكِيلُ عَلَى بَيْتٍ ـ وَكِيلُ خَرْجٍ ـ وَكِيل *pl.* عُمَّال ـ كَتْخُدا ـ كاخِيا *vulg.* كَخْيا.

Major-General, *n.* أَمِيرُ لِوَآءٍ *vulg.* لِوَآءٌ باشا.

Majority, *n.* The greater number, الأَكْثَرُ ـ كَثْرَة ـ مُعْظَم. Full age, بُلُوغٌ شَرْعِيٌّ ـ بُلُوغُ ٱلسِّنِّ. The rank of major, رُتْبَةُ ٱلْبِيكْباشِي (or أَمِيرُ ٱلْأَلْوَاء). The opinion of the —, رَأْيُ ٱلْأَكْثَرِينَ. He who has the — of votes, مَنْ فَازَ بِرَأْيِ ٱلْأَكْثَرِينَ. The — of the members to be townspeople, يَكُونُ أَكْثَرُ ٱلْأَعْضَآءِ مِنَ ٱلْأَهَالِي.

Majuscula, *n.* A capital letter, حَرْفٌ ثَخِينٌ ـ قَلَمٌ طُومَارٍ ـ قَلَمٌ ثُلُثِيٌّ.

Make, *v.t.* To do, صَنَعَ ـ عَمِلَ ـ جَعَلَ ـ فَعَلَ *vulg.* سَوَّى. To work at or in, صَنَعَ ـ عَالَجَ. To create, فَطَرَ ـ خَلَقَ ـ كَوَّنَ ـ جَبَلَ (*see also under to* Create, *v.t.*). To oblige, constrain, غَصَبَ ـ جَبَرَ ـ أَلْزَمَ ـ اِضْطَرَّ-إِلَى. To cause to become, صَيَّرَ ـ أَوَّلَ-إِلَى. To amount to, صَارَ ـ لَحِقَ ـ بَلَغَ مَبْلَغَهُ. To arrange, نَظَمَ ـ رَتَّبَ ـ نَسَّقَ. To compose, put together, رَكَّبَ. To arrive at, وَصَلَ إِلَى *aor.* يَصِلُ. To attain, نَالَ ـ أَصَابَ ـ قَارَبَ ـ لَحِقَ ـ بَلَغَ. To occasion, أَحْدَثَ ـ أَنْتَجَ ـ كَانَ سَبَبًا ل ـ سَبَّبَ ـ أَوْجَبَ. To tend towards, ضَرَبَ إِلَى. To — bread, خَبَزَ. To — a bed, صَلَّحَ ٱلْفَرْشَةَ.

To make account of, to respect, أَكْرَمَ ـ وَقَّرَ ـ اِعْتَبَرَ ـ اِحْتَرَمَ. To reckon, حَسَبَ ـ عَدَّ. To estimate, حَسِبَ.

To make amends, to excuse one's self, تَعَذَّرَ. To make amends to for, to make good to, عَوَّضَ ـ أَعَاضَ ـ جَازَى ـ كَافَى.

To make away with, to spend, أَسْرَفَ ـ ضَيَّعَ ـ أَزَالَ ـ أَعْدَمَ. To purloin, أَسَلَّ. To kill, قَتَلَ ـ مَوَّتَ.

To make away with one's self, قَتَلَ نَفْسَهُ ـ قَتَلَ حَالَهُ.

To make free with, to treat without ceremony, عَامَلَ-بِلا تَكْلِيفٍ ـ جَاوَزَ ب ـ اِسْتَأْنَسَ إِلَى ـ تَأَنَّسَ ب. To exceed in, أَفْرَطَ فِي. To act rudely towards, اِسْتَجْفَى إِلَى ـ غَلَّظَ عَلَى.

To make one free of, a member of, صَيَّرَ-مِنْ ـ صَيَّرَ-مِنْ أَهْلِ ٱلْ... أَعْضَآءِ ٱلْ....

To make good, to perform, أَنْجَزَ ـ أَنْفَذَ ـ أَتَمَّ. *See also under* To make amends, *supra*.

To make headway, تَقَدَّمَ.

To make leeway, أَدْبَرَ ـ تَأَخَّرَ.

To make into, صَيَّرَ ـ جَعَلَ. To be made into, صَارَ.

To make light, little, of, اِسْتَقَلَّ ـ اِسْتَخَفَّ. To esteem lightly, اِسْتَخَفَّ بِ ـ اِسْتَحْقَرَ.

To make love, تَعَشَّقَ.

To make love to, تَعَشَّقَ إِلَى ـ تَحَبَّبَ إِلَى ـ تَوَدَّدَ إِلَى.

To make merry; *see under* Merry, *a.*

To make money, اِكْتَسَبَ دَرَاهِمَ ـ قَرَّشَ.

To make much of, to consider much, اِسْتَعْظَمَ ـ اِسْتَكْثَرَ. To esteem highly, وَقَّرَ ـ أَكْرَمَ ـ عَزَّزَ. Not to be able to make much of, not to understand well, ما لَحِقَ بَاطِنَهُ ـ لَمْ يُحِطْ بِهِ عِلْمًا.

To make nothing of, to make light of, اِعْتَبَرَ-كَلَا شَيْءٍ ـ اِسْتَقَلَّ. Not to understand, مَا فَهِمَ ـ اِسْتَبْهَمَ ل ـ اِسْتَغْلَقَ ل.

To make off with, run away with, وَلَّى ب ـ سَلَبَ. To purloin; *see supra*, To make away with.

To make out, to decipher, قَرَأَ ـ بَيَّنَ ـ حَلَّ ـ اِسْتَخْرَجَ. To explain, بَيَّنَ ـ شَرَحَ ـ فَسَّرَ. To discover, أَكْشَفَ عَلَى ـ كَشَفَ. To find out, اِطَّلَعَ عَلَى. To prove, بَرْهَنَ ـ ثَبَّتَ. To draw up, write, نَصَّ ـ كَتَبَ ـ شَرَطَ ـ حَرَّرَ.

To make over, to transfer to, أَلْقَى-عَلَى ـ حَوَّلَ-إِلَى ـ نَقَلَ-إِلَى. To deliver over to, قَبَّضَ ـ سَلَّمَ-إِلَى.

To make a pen, بَرَى ٱلْقَلَمَ.

To make sail, شَرَعَ ٱلْقُلُوعَ ـ أَقْلَعَ.

To make sure, safe, ضَبَطَ ـ أَمَّنَ. To convince, أَقْنَعَ ـ أَرْضَى.

To make up, as of a parcel, صَرَّ ـ لَفَّ. To complete, أَكْمَلَ ـ خَلَّصَ ـ أَتَمَّ. To fabricate, اِخْتَرَعَ-زُورًا ـ اِفْتَرَى-كَذِبًا. To make fancy, تَخَيَّلَ. To arrange, نَظَمَ ـ رَتَّبَ ـ نَسَّقَ. To make up, as of cloth into clothes, خَيَّطَ ـ فَصَّلَ; to make up, as an account, حَسَبَ ٱلْحِسَابَ ـ عَمِلَ ٱلْقَائِمَةَ. To make up a difference, dispute, صَالَحَ. To supply what is wanting, كَمَّلَ ٱلنَّقَائِصَ. To compensate, أَعَاضَ ـ كَافَى ـ جَازَى. To make up, as of a medicine, عَجَنَ ـ رَكَّبَ. To amass, كَوَّمَ ـ جَمَعَ.

To make up one's mind, decide, اِعْتَمَدَ عَلَى ـ تَعَمَّدَ ـ جَزَمَ عَلَى.

To make water, to piss, طَرَقَ بَوْلَهُ ـ شَخَّ ـ بَالَ. To let in water, of a ship, نَفَذَ ٱلْمَآءُ فِي ٱلْمَرْكَبِ ـ اِنْخَرَقَ ٱلْمَرْكَبُ ـ تَطَرَّقَ ٱلْمَآءُ إِلَى ٱلْمَرْكَبِ.

Make, *v.i.* To tend, conduce to, آلَ إِلَى *aor.* يَؤُولُ ـ اِسْتَدْرَجَ.

To proceed, march, sail, سَافَرَ ـ تَقَدَّمَ ـ سَارَ ـ مَشَى.

To make against, خَالَفَ ـ اِعْتَرَضَ ـ عَاكَسَ ـ ضَادَدَ.

To make as if, صَيَّرَ ـ عَمِلَ رُوحَهُ كَأَنَّهُ ـ حَاوَلَ أَنْ ـ تَظَاهَرَ ب رُوحَهُ كَأَنَّهُ.

To make for, to conduce to, to favour, آلَ إِلَى *aor.* يَؤُولُ ـ

وَفَقَ – اِسْتَدْرَجَ. To go towards, سَافَرَ نَحْوَ – ء سَارَ إِلَى – ء ضَرَبَ إِلَى – ء سَعَى إِلَى.

To make off, run away, ٤ هَرَبَ – اِنْسَلَّ – تَفَلَّتَ – اِنْفَلَتَ. To make off with; *see preceding article, under to* Make, *v.t.*

To make up for, دَاوَى ٱلنُّقْصَانَ – ٤ قَامَ مَقَامَ – ٤ سَدَّ مَسَدَّ.

To make up for lost time, ٤ جَبَرَ مَا ضَيَّعَ مِنَ ٱلْوَقْتِ.

To make up to one, تَحَبَّبَ إِلَى – تَوَدَّدَ إِلَى.

Make, *n.* Form, appearance, صُورَة *pl.* صُوَر – هَيْئَة *pl.* هَيْئَات – ضَرْب – شَكْل – صِيغَة. Proportion, خِلْقَة – خَلْق. Manufacture, عَمَل – صُنْع – فَابْرِيكَة. Cut, fashion, زِيّ – كَسْم. A man of goodly —, رَجُلٌ حَسَنُ ٱلْخِلْقَةِ. Arrows of the same —, سِهَامٌ صِيغَةٌ. *See also* Manufacture, *n.*

Makebate, *n.* One who stirs up contention, مُفْتِن – مُفْسِد – ضَرَّابُ فِتَنٍ.

Make-peace, *n.* مُصْلِح – مُصْلِحٌ بَيْنَ – صَانِعُ ٱلسَّلَامِ.

Makeshift, *n.* سَدُّ مَسَدٍّ – بَدَل – بَاب – مَخْلَص.

Maker, *n.* صَانِع *pl.* صُنَّاع – مُصْطَنِع. A manufacturer, مُعَلِّم – صَاحِبُ مَعْمَلٍ. *See also* Creator, *n.*

Make-weight, *n.* رُجْحَانُ ٱلْمِيزَانِ – تَكْمِيلُ ٱلْوَزْنِ.

Making, *n.* The act of forming, عَمَل – صُنْع – فَعْل – صِنَاعَة. *See also* Make, *n.*

Malabathrum, *n.* The plant, سَاذَج.

Malaccia, *n.* A longing for clay, *etc.*, وَحَمَة – شَهْوَةُ ٱلطِّينِ.

Malachite, *n.* حَجَرٌ كَرِيمٌ أَخْضَرُ ٱللَّوْنِ يَتَوَلَّدُ فِي مَعْدِنِ ٱلصُّفْرِ.

Mal-administration, *n.* فَسَادُ ٱلْإِدَارَةِ – سُوءُ إِدَارَةٍ.

Maladroit, *a.* أَخْرَق. *See also* Awkward, Clumsy, *a.*

Malady, *n.* دَآء *pl.* أَدْوَآء – مَرَض *pl.* أَمْرَاض. *See also* Disease, *n.*

Mala fide, *ad.* بِٱلْخِيَانَةِ – خِيَانَةً.

Malaga, *n.* The wine of, ضَرْبٌ مِنَ ٱلْخَمْرِ مَصْنُوعٌ فِي إِيَالَةِ مَلْغَا.

Malapert, *a.* and *n.* *See* Impudent, Insolent, *a.*

Malapertness, *n.* *See* Impudence, Insolence, *n.*

Mal apropos, *ad.* فِي غَيْرِ وَقْتِهِ – فِي غَيْرِ مَحَلِّهِ.

Malaria, *n.* هَوَآءٌ وَخِيمٌ – وَبَال – وَبَلَة.

Malarious, *a.* مُتَوَخِّم – وَخَام – وَبِيل.

Mal-conformation, *n.* شَوْهَة – خِلْقَةٌ سَقَط.

Malcontent, *a.* } سَاخِطٌ عَلَى – غَيْرُ رَاضٍ عَنْ. Malcontents
Malcontent, *n.* } with the government, ٱلْغَيْرُ رُضَاةٍ عَنِ ٱلْحُكُومَةِ.
Malcontents, evil-doers, أَهْلُ ٱلشَّرِّ وَٱلْفَسَادِ.

Male, *a.* Belonging to the — sex, ذَكَر *pl.* ذُكْرَان and ذِكَارَة and ذُكُور. To make —, of the masculine gender, ذَكَّرَ; made masculine, مُذَكَّر.

Male, *n.* ذَكَر *pl.* ذِكَارَة and ذُكُور. The — of animals, especially a stallion, فَحْل *pl.* فِحَالَة and فُحُول.

Malediction, *n.* لَعْنَة *pl.* لِعَان and لَعَنَات – سَبّ – لَعْن – سُبَّة.

Malefactor, *n.* مُذْنِب *pl.* مُذْنِبُون – شِرِّير *pl.* أَشْرَار – مُجْرِم – خَبِيث.

Malevolence, *n.* إِحْنَة – غَلِيل – غِلّ – حَسِيكَة – حَنَق – سُخْمَة – ضِغْن – غُمُور – حِقْد – عَدَاوَة. *See also* Malice, *n.*

Malevolent, *a.* مُغِلّ – حَسِيك – حَنِق – ضَاغِن – غَوِيّ – مُسَخِّم – شِرِّير – حَقُود.

Malevolently, *ad.* بِحَسِيكَةٍ – بِحَنَقٍ – بِغِلٍّ – بِحِقْدٍ – بِضِغْنٍ.

Malfeasance, *n.* عَمَلٌ سُوءٌ – أَذِيَّة – شَرّ – سُوءُ عَمَلٍ.

Malformation, *n.* شَوْهَة – خِلْقَةٌ سَقَط.

Malic, *a.* Of apples, مِنَ ٱلتُّفَّاحِ. Malic acid, حُمُوضَةُ ٱلتُّفَّاحِ.

Malice, *n.* مُشَاحَنَة – غِمْر – إِحْنَة – حَسِيكَة – حَنَق – خَبَانَة – ضِغْن – حِقْد. To bear — in the heart, ء غَمِرَ. To bear — against, ء ضَغِنَ عَلَى – ء أَحِنَ عَلَى – تَسَخَّمَ عَلَى – تَحَقَّدَ عَلَى – تَحَقَّدَ عَلَى – ء حَقِدَ عَلَى. They bore mutual —, of many, تَضَاغَنُوا – تَحَاقَدُوا. To bear —, ء ضَغِنَ – ء غَلَّ صَدْرُهُ *aor.* يَغِلُّ. He bore — against me, غَمِرَ صَدْرُهُ عَلَيَّ. To treat with —, آحَنَ.

Malicious, *a.* حَسِيك – حَنِق – ضَاغِن – حَقُود – لَعِين *pl.* لُعَنَآء – شَقِيّ *pl.* أَشْقِيَآء – خَبِيث *pl.* خُبَثَآء – شِرِّير *pl.* أَشْرَار and شِرِّيرُون. Malicious words, أَقْوَالٌ خَبِيثَةٌ.

Maliciously, *ad.* تَحَقُّدًا – بِضِغْنٍ – بِغِمْرٍ – بِأَذِيَّةٍ – بِخَبَانَةٍ – بِرَدَآءَةٍ.

Maliciousness, *n.* *See* Malevolence, Malice, *n.*

Malign, *a.* سُوء – شَرّ – مُضِرّ – مُؤْذٍ.

Malign, *v.t.* ء حَكَرَ. *See also to* Defame, *v.t.*

Malignancy, *n.* Bitter hostility, خَبَانَة – حِقْد – رَدَآءَة – عَدَاوَة. Virulence, شِدَّة – قُوَّة. A noxious property, سَمّ – أَذِيَّة – رَدَآءَة.

Malignant, *a.* and *n.* Bad, malevolent, شَرّ – شِرِّير – دَنِس – شَقِيّ *pl.* أَشْقِيَآء – لَعِين – خَبِيث. Noxious, شَرّ – مُضِرّ – سُوء – مُؤْذٍ. *See also* Malicious, *a.*

Malignantly, *ad.* بِخَبَانَةٍ – شَرًّا – بِأَذِيَّةٍ – بِضِغْنٍ.

Maligner, *n.* حَكِر. *See also* Defamer, *n.*

Malignity, *n.* *See* Malignancy, *n.*

Malignly, *ad.* *See* Malignantly, *ad.*

Malinger, *v.i.* تَضَعَّفَ ـ تَمَارَضَ.

Malingerer, *n.* مُتَضَعِّف ـ مُتَمَارِض.

Malison, *n.* *See* Malediction, *n.*

Mall, *n.* A large mallet, مِرْزَبَّةٌ كَبِيرَةٌ ـ مِرْزَبَة *pl.* مَرَازِب. A place lined with trees, مُشَجَّرَة. A walk, مُتَنَزَّه.

Mall, *v.t.* To beat with a mall, دَقَّ-بِمِرْزَبَّةٍ ².

Mallard, *n.* A drake, بَطّ *pl.* بُطُوط.

Malleability, *n.* لِينَة ـ لَيَان ـ قَابِلِيَّةُ ٱلْمَطْلِ.

Malleable, *a.* لَيِّن ـ يُطْرَق ـ مِمَّا يُمْطَل. Malleable or soft iron, حَدِيدٌ أَنِيثٌ.

Malleate, *v.t.* طَرَقَ ² ـ مَطَلَ ².

Malleation, *n.* طَرْق ـ مَطْل.

Mallet, *n.* مِرْزَبَّة *pl.* مَرَازِب ـ مِطْرَقَة ـ دَقْمَاقٌ مِنْ خَشَبٍ. A — for driving pegs, مِيتَدَة; for loosening cotton together with the bow, مِنْدَف ـ مِحْرَن.

Mallow, *n.* } The plant, خُبَّاز ـ خُبَّازَة ـ خُبَيْزَة ـ مُلُوكِيَّة ـ
Mallows, } مُلُوخِيَّة. Marsh-mallows, خِطْمِيَّة ـ خِطْمِيّ ـ غِسْل.

Malmsey, *n.* ضَرْبٌ مِنَ ٱلْخَمْرِ.

Malpractice, *n.* شَرّ ـ فَسَاد ـ سُوءُ ٱلصَّنِيعِ.

Malt, *n.* شَعِيرٌ مَنْقُوعٌ لِصُنْعِ ٱلْبِيرَا.

Malt, *v.t.* أَعَدَّ ٱلشَّعِيرَ لِصُنْعِ ٱلْبِيرَا.

Malt, *v.i.* إِخْتَمَرَ ٱلشَّعِيرُ لِصُنْعِ ٱلْبِيرَا.

Malt-drink, *n.* }
Malt-liquor, } بِيرَا ـ بُوزَة.

Malt-house, *n.* مَعْمَلُ ٱلشَّعِيرِ لِلْبِيرَا.

Maltreat, *v.t.* أَسَاءَ إِلَى ـ أَقْبَحَ إِلَى ـ آذَى ـ ذَمَّمَ ـ جَافَى.

Maltreatment, *n.* سُوءُ مُعَامَلَةٍ ـ أَذِيَّة ـ جَفَاء.

Maltster, *n.* مُخَمِّرُ ٱلشَّعِيرِ لِلْبِيرَا.

Malum in se, *n.* شَرٌّ ذَاتِيّ ـ قَبِيحَةٌ بِٱلذَّاتِ.

Malum prohibitum, *n.* حَرَام ـ جَرِيمَة.

Malvaceous, *a.* مِنْ فَصِيلَةِ ٱلْخُبَّازَةِ.

Malversation, *n.* سَلّ ـ سَلْب ـ سَرِقَة ـ خِيَانَة.

Mam, Mamma, *n.* *See* Ma, Mother, *n.*

Mameluke, *n.* (More correctly, Mamlûk), *n.* مَمْلُوك *pl.* مَمَالِيك.

Mammal, *n.* حَيَوَانٌ مِنْ ذَوَاتِ ٱلثُّدِيِّ.

Mammalia, *n.* ذَوَاتُ ٱلثُّدِيِّ.

Mammalian, *a.* مُتَعَلِّقٌ بِذَوَاتِ ٱلثُّدِيِّ.

Mammalogy, *n.* العِلْمُ بِذَوَاتِ ٱلثُّدِيِّ.

Mammary, *a.* ثَدْيِيّ ـ مُتَعَلِّقٌ بِٱلثُّدِيِّ. The — glands, عُرُوقُ ٱلثُّدِيِّ.

Mammifer, *n.* *See* Mammal, *n.*

Mammiferous, *a.* حَيَوَانٌ مُرْضِعٌ ـ ذَاتُ ثُدِيٍّ.

Mammiform, *a.* فِي صُورَةِ ٱلثَّدْيِ.

Mammillary, *a.* Having pap-like protuberances, ذُو حُيُودٍ مِثْلَ ٱلثُّدِيِّ. *See also* Mammary, *a.*

Mammon, *n.* مَال ـ مَالُ ٱلدُّنْيَا.

Mammonist, *n.* مُحِبُّ ٱلْمَالِ ـ مُحِبُّ مَالِ ٱلدُّنْيَا.

Mammoth, *n.* حَيَوَانٌ مِنْ ذَوَاتِ ٱلْأَرْبَعِ كَبِيرٌ جِدًّا غَيْرُ مَوْجُودٍ ٱلْآنَ.

Mammoth, *a.* Very large, كَبِيرٌ جِدًّا ـ عَظِيمٌ لِلْغَايَةِ.

Man, *n.* A male of the human species, مَرْءٌ *pl.* رِجَال ـ إِنْسَان *coll.* نَاس ـ رَجُل *pl.* رِجَال *and* أَرْجَال. The human species; (*see* Mankind, *n.*) An individual, نَفَر *pl.* أَنْفَار ـ فَرْد *pl.* أَفْرَاد ـ شَخْص *pl.* أَشْخَاص. A manservant, خَدَّام ـ غُلَام. A husband, زَوْج *pl.* أَزْوَاج. A man, in draughts, فَصّ *pl.* فُصُوص ـ كَلْب *pl.* كِلَاب ـ حَجَرُ دَامَة *pl.* أَحْجَار; in chess, بَيْدَق *pl.* بَيَادِق. A brave man, بَطَل ـ جَذَع *pl.* جِذْعَان *vulg.* رَجَّال. A generous, noble, man, سَخِيّ ـ آدَمِيّ. He is my man, the one who suits me, هُوَ ٱلرَّجُلُ ٱلَّذِي يَصْلُحُ لِي ـ هُوَ ٱلَّذِي يَلِيقُ لِي. He is my man, that is, my debtor, or the one whom I have to deal with, هُوَ غَرِيمِي. He is my man, the one who does my business, هُوَ قَضَّاءُ أَشْغَالِي. He is the man for the work, هُوَ كُفُؤٌ لِلْعَمَلِ. He is the man for anything, هُوَ كُفُؤٌ لِكُلِّ شَيْءٍ ـ مَا يَشِذُّ عَلَيْهِ شَيْءٌ ². He is not the man to run away, لَيْسَ هُوَ مِنَ ٱلَّذِينَ يَهْرُبُونَ. He is not the man to pocket an affront, لَيْسَ هُوَ مِمَّنْ يَسْتَحْمِلُ ٱلْبَهْدَلَةَ. To behave like a man, تَفَحَّلَ. Quit you like men, كُونُوا رِجَالًا.

A full-grown man, بَالِغُ ٱلسِّنِّ ـ رَجُلٌ كَامِلُ ٱلسِّنِّ.

A man of letters, أَدِيب *pl.* أُدَبَاء ـ مِنْ أَصْحَابِ عِلْمِ ٱلْأَدَبِ ـ لَوْذَعِيّ.

A man of business, sharp and experienced in business, أَصْلَتِيّ ـ مُنْصَلِت.

A man of the law, فَقِيه *pl.* فُقَهَاء.

Between man and man, بَيْنَ ٱلرِّجَالِ ـ بَيْنَ ٱلنَّاسِ ـ بَيْنَ ٱلْأَوَادِمِ.

Every man, كُلُّ رَجُلٍ ـ كُلُّ إِنْسَانٍ; everybody, كُلُّ ٱلنَّاسِ ـ ٱلنَّاسُ أَجْمَعُ ـ كُلُّ أَحَدٍ ـ الكُلّ ـ كُلُّ وَاحِدٍ. Every man went out from him, خَرَجَ كُلُّ إِنْسَانٍ عَنْهُ ².

Fellow man, my fellow man, إِبْنُ جِنْسِي *pl.* أَبْنَاء.

Man and wife, زَوْجٌ وَزَوْجَةٌ.

Man's estate, حَالُ ٱلرُّجُولِيَّةِ ـ سِنُّ ٱلْبُلُوغِ.

Man-of-war, ship, أُسْطُول pl. أَسَاطِيل ـ جِفَان pl. جَفْنَة ـ بَارِجَة pl. بَوَارِجُ.

No man, لَيْسَ رَجُلٌ ـ لَيْسَ إِنْسَانٌ. There is no man with us, لَيْسَ إِنْسَانٌ مَعَنَا. Let no man, no one, leave his place, لَا يَخْرُجْ أَحَدٌ مِنْ مَكَانِهِ. Speak evil of no man, لَا تَطْعَنْ فِي أَحَدٍ.

Old man, the old man, old nature, ٱلْإِنْسَانُ ٱلْعَتِيقُ ـ ٱلطَّبِيعَةُ ٱلدَّنِسَةُ. One advanced in age, شَيْخ pl. شُيُوخ vulg. إِخْتِيَار pl. إِخْتِيَارِيَّة. The plant, شَيْبَة ـ مَامِيثَا ـ ذِقْنُ ٱلشَّيْخِ ـ أَفْسِنْتِين.

The Isle of Man, جَزِيرَةُ مَانِ ٱلْكَائِنَةُ بِٱلْقُرْبِ مِنْ جَزِيرَةِ أَنْكِلْتَرَا.

The man of the age, نَادِرُ ٱلزَّمَانِ ـ وَاحِدُ دَهْرِهِ.

To a man, all of them, بِأَسْرِهِمْ ـ قَاطِبَةً ـ أَجْمَعُ ـ كُلُّهُمْ.

You are no man! لَيْسَ أَنْتَ بِرَجُلٍ.

Man, v.t. To furnish with men, soldiers, جَهَّزَ بِٱلْعَسَاكِرِ. To man a ship with sailors, جَهَّزَ ٱلْمَرْكَبَ بِٱلْبَحْرِيَّةِ. To supply, as with means of defence, جَهَّزَ.

Manacle, n. قَيْدُ لِلْيَدِ ـ أَسْر pl. إِسَار ـ غُلّ pl. أَغْلَال ـ جَامِعَة pl. أَنْكَال ـ نِكْل pl. قُيُود.

Manacle, v.t. لَبَّسَ ٱلْأَنْكَالَ ـ قَيَّدَ يَدَيْهِ.

Manage, v.t. To carry on the concerns of, سَاسَ aor. يَسُوسُ ـ دَبَّرَ ـ بَاشَرَ. To keep under, ضَبَطَ ـ ـُ. To train, دَرَّبَ ـ مَرَّنَ; of a horse, رَاضَ aor. يَرُوضُ. To tame, طَبَّعَ ـ أَنَّسَ ـ أَقْمَعَ. To turn the mind of one from anything, أَدَارَ عَقْلَهُ عَنْ. To — a subject, بَاحَثَ عَنْ ـ فَاوَضَ ـ نَاضَلَ. To be economical, وَفَّرَ. To — one's affairs well, تَصَرَّفَ فِي أُمُورِهِ بِمُدَارَاةٍ وَتَدْبِيرٍ.

Manage, v.i. As one's own affairs, تَصَرَّفَ ـ دَبَّرَ أَمْرَهُ ـ تَدَبَّرَ أَمْرَهُ ـ أَجْرَى ـ سَلَكَ ـُ; vulg. إِصْطَفَلَ; طَفَّلَ أُمُورَهُ ـ فِي أُمُورِهِ. To act, مَشَى ـِ ـ سَعَى ـ فِعْلَهُ إِلَى. He manages very well, يُدَبِّرُ أُمُورَهُ بِتَدْبِيرٍ حَسَنٍ.

Manageable, a. Governable, يُدَبَّرُ (or يُتَدَبَّرُ) بِسُهُولَةٍ. Controllable, يُضْبَطُ ـ يُحْكَمُ ـ عَاجٌ ـ لَيِّنُ ٱلْإِنْعِطَافِ ـ مِذْعَان. Docile, tame, طَيِّع ـ طَوْع ـ ذَلُول ـ جَنِيب. That may be easily used, سَهْلُ ٱلْإِسْتِعْمَالِ. *See also* Handy, a.

Manageableness, n. Easiness of being directed, سُهُولَةُ ٱلتَّدْبِيرِ; of being controlled, سُهُولَةُ ٱلضَّبْطِ ـ إِذْعَان. Docility, ذُلُول ـ لَيَان ـ مُلَاءَمَة.

Management, n. Direction of affairs, سِيَاسَة ـ مُبَاشَرَة ـ تَدْبِير ـ إِدَارَة. Caution, attention, تَوَقٍّ ـ إِحْتِرَاس ـ مُدَارَاة. Artifice, تَحَيُّل ـ حِيلَة. To give the — of to, صَرَّفَ فِي; to have the — of, تَصَرَّفَ فِي; to commission, as an agent, أَجْرَى ـ جَرَّى. This requires great —, هٰذَا يَحْتَاجُ إِلَى غَايَةِ ٱلتَّوَقِّي.

Manager, n. A director, مُبَاشِر ـ مُدِير ـ مُدَبِّر ـ مُتَصَرِّف ـ عَامِل pl. عُمَّال. A frugal person, صَاحِبُ ـ قَتُور ـ مُقْتَصِد تَدْبِيرٍ وَمُدَارَاةٍ.

Managing, n. تَدْبِيرُ ٱلْأَشْغَالِ ـ سِيَاسَةُ ٱلْأُمُورِ. *See also* Management, n.

Managing, a. Directing, مُبَاشِر ـ مُدَبِّر ـ مُتَصَرِّف. Frugal, صَاحِبُ تَدْبِيرٍ وَمُدَارَاةٍ ـ مُقْتَصِد. A — director, أَحَدُ مُدِيرِي ٱلْإِدَارَةِ. *See also* Manager, n.

Managery, n. *See* Management, n.

Manatee, n. }
Manati, } بَقَرُ ٱلْبَحْرِ.

Mandamus, n. أَمْرٌ سَامٍ مِنْ مَحْكَمَةِ ٱلشَّرْعِ.

Mandarin, n. صَاحِبُ مَنْصِبٍ فِي بِلَادِ ٱلصِّينِ. A — orange, بُرْتُقَانَةٌ صِينِيَّةٌ ـ نَارَنْجٌ صِينِيٌّ.

Mandatary, n. }
Mandatory, } مُسْتَخْدَم ـ وَكِيل pl. وُكَلَاء ـ مَأْمُور ـ مُتَصَرِّف.

Mandate, n. أَمْر ـ وَصِيَّة pl. وَصَايَا ـ عَهْد pl. عُهُود ـ شُورَى. A royal —, خَطٌّ هُمَايُونِيٌّ ـ فِرْمَان ـ مَنْشُور.

Mandatory, a. آمِر ـ مُفَرِّض ـ مُصَرِّف ـ مُوَصٍّ.

Mandible, n. حَنَك pl. أَحْنَاك ـ مِنْقَار pl. مَنَاقِير ـ مِنْقَاف pl. مَنَاقِف.

Mandibular, a. مُتَعَلِّقٌ بِٱلْمِنْقَارِ.

Mandrake, n. أَبُو رُوحٍ ـ لُفَّاح ـ لُفَاحَة ـ بَيْرُوحٌ صَنَمِيٌّ ـ بَيْرُوح. The root of the —, لُفَّاح.

Mandrel, n. The — of a lathe, دَائِرَةُ ٱلْمِخْرَطِ.

Mandrill, n. A kind of ape, نَوْعٌ مِنَ ٱلْقُرُودِ ٱلْكَبِيرَةِ.

Manducate, v.t. مَضَغَ ـَـُ. *See also* to Chew, v.t.

Manducation, n. The act of chewing, مَضْغ ـ عَلْك.

Mane, n. As of a horse, عُرْف pl. أَعْرَاف ـ زُغْزُوعُ ٱلْفَرَسِ; the part of the neck where the — grows, مَعْرَفَة pl. مَعَارِف. The — of a lion or the movable feathers on the head of a bird, عُفْرَة. Having a long —, أَعْرَف. To clip the — of a horse, عَرَفَ ـِ ٱلْفَرَسَ.

Maned, a. ذُو عُفْرَةٍ ـ ذُو عُرْفٍ. *See also preceding article.*

Manege, n. Of horses, رِيَاض (or تَرْوِيض) ٱلْخَيْلِ ـ تَعْلِيمُ ٱلْخَيْلِ.

Manes, n. رُوحُ ٱلْمَيِّتِ pl. أَرْوَاحُ ٱلْمَوْتَى.

Manful, a. صِنْدِيد pl. صَنَادِيدُ ـ شَهْم ـ صَاحِبُ مُرُوَّةٍ ـ جَسُور.

Manfully, ad. بِمُرُوَّةٍ ـ شَجَاعَةً ـ بِجَسَارَةٍ vulg. كَرُجَّالٍ.

Manfulness, *n.* رُجولِيَّة ـ مُرُوءَة ـ إِقْدام.

Manganese, *n.* مَنْغَنِيس وَهُوَ ضَرْبٌ مِنَ ٱلْمَعْدِنِ صُلْبٌ وَسَرِيعُ ٱلْكَسْرِ.

Mange, *n.* جَرَب ـ حُصاص ـ طُلَيَّا ـ شَدًا ـ شَذًا. To have the —, جَرِبَ ـ. *See also under* Scab, *n.*

Mangel-wurzel, *n.* ضَرْبٌ مِنَ ٱلسَّلْجَمِ (*or* ٱللِّفْتِ).

Manger, *n.* مِذْوَد ـ مَعْلَف *pl.* مَعالِف ـ آدارِيّ *pl.* أَدارِيّ *pl.* مَذاوِد.

Manginess, *n.* حُصاص ـ حالُ ٱلْجَرَب.

Mangle, *v.t.* To tear in pieces, قَطَّعَ ـ خَمَّشَ; of wild beasts, اِفْتَرَسَ. To smooth with the mangle, ضَرَبَ ـ صَقَلَ بِٱلدُّولاب ـ بِٱلْجِنْدَرَة. His hand was mangled, تَأَشَّفَتْ يَدُهُ.

Mangle, *n.* جِنْدَرَة ـ دُولابُ ٱلصَّقْلِ ـ دُولاب صاقِل.

Mangler, *n.* One who cuts or tears in pieces, قَطّاع ـ مُفْتَرِس. One who uses a mangle, صَقّال بِٱلدُّولاب ـ ضَرّابُ جِنْدَرَة.

Mango, *n.* أَمْبا. The — tree, شَجَرَةُ ٱلأَمْبا.

Mangostan, *n.* }
Mangosteen, } فاكِهَةٌ هِنْدِيَّةٌ لَذِيذَةٌ جِدًّا.

Mangrove, *n.* The tree, اِسْمُ شَجَرَةٍ تَنْبُتُ فِي غِياضِ ٱلْهِنْدِ.

Mangy, *a.* مُجْرَب ـ أَجْرَب.

Man-hater, *n.* نَفُور ـ مُتَوَحِّش.

Man-hole, *n.* As of a drain, مَنْفَذٌ بِٱلْوَعَةٍ يَدْخُلُ فِيهِ رَجُل ـ مَنْفَذُ ٱلبالُوعَة.

Manhood, *n.* State of adult years in men, سِنُّ بُلُوغِ ٱلرَّجُلِ ـ بُلُوغُ ٱلْحُلُم. Manhood as opposed to womanhood, رُجولَة ـ رُجْلَة ـ رُجولِيَّة ـ رُجْلِيَّة. Virility, رُجْلِيَّة ـ نَهْمَة. Human nature, ناسُوت ـ إِنْسانِيَّة ـ بَشَرِيَّة. To attain to —, تَرَجَّلَ. *See also* Manfulness.

Mania, *n.* Madness, جُنُون ـ جِنَّة. A raging inclination, غَرام ـ وَلَع ـ سُوس ـ جُنُون ـ غَيْرَة. To have a — for, هَوِيَ ـ. He has a — for horses, لَهُ وَلَعٌ فِي ٱلْخَيْلِ.

Maniac, *a.* }
Maniacal, } *See* Mad, *a.*

Maniac, *n.* *See* Madman, *n.*

Manichean, *a.* مانَوِيّ. The — doctrines, الشَّنَوِيَّة ـ المانَوِيَّة.

Manichean, *n.* }
Manichee, } مِنْ أَصْحابِ مانِي ـ تابِعُ مانِي ـ مانَوِيّ ـ زِنْدِيق *pl.* زَنادِقَة.

Manicheism, *n.* الشَّنَوِيَّة ـ المانَوِيَّة.

Manifest, *a.* Evident, جَلِيّ ـ صُرَحاء *pl.* صَرِيح ـ بارِز ـ بادٍ ـ واضِح ـ مُبِين ـ بَيِّن ـ ظاهِر ـ مُسْتَبِين ـ عَلانِيّ. Notorious, مَشْهُور. To be —, evident, clear, تَبَيَّنَ ـ بانَ ـ تَجَلَّى ـ اِتَّضَحَ. To be —, notorious, اِشْتَهَرَ.

Manifest, *v.t.* To make apparent, جَلا ـ أَشْرَعَ ـ أَشْرَعَ ـ شَرَعَ ـ صَرَّحَ بِ ـ أَصْرَحَ ـ أَعْلَنَ ـ بَيَّنَ ـ أَوْضَحَ. To divulge, باحَ بِ. To display, تَبَدَّى ـ أَبْدَى ـ أَظْهَرَ. To be manifested, made apparent, صَرَحَ ـ أَظْهَرَ ـ اِعْتَلَنَ ـ عَلَنَ ـ اِتَّضَحَ ـ اِسْتَعْلَنَ ـ اِنْصَرَحَ. To — one's self, بانَ ـ ظَهَرَ ـ تَجَلَّى. He has not manifested anything to show that he is willing to..., لَمْ يَبْدُ مِنْهُ ما يَدُلُّ عَلَى أَنَّهُ يُرِيدُ أَن. The patience which the inhabitants have manifested, ما أَبْداهُ ٱلأَهْلُ مِنَ ٱلصَّبْرِ. The government is manifesting great care and diligence, الدَّوْلَةُ مُظْهِرَةٌ مَزِيدَ ٱلْهِمَّةِ وَٱلِاجْتِهادِ.

Manifest, *n.* An invoice of goods, قائِمَةُ ٱلْبَضائِعِ ـ قائِمَةُ ٱلْوَسْقِ.

Manifestation, *n.* The act of disclosing, making apparent, كَشْف ـ إِظْهار ـ إِيضاح ـ إِعْلان ـ تَصْرِيح ـ تَشْهِير. Appearance, تَجَلٍّ ـ ظُهُور ـ بَيان ـ صَراحَة.

Manifestly, *ad.* بِوُضُوحٍ ـ ظاهِرًا ـ عَلانِيَةً ـ سَرِحًا.

Manifestness, *n.* اِسْتِعْلان ـ عُلُون.

Manifesto, *n.* }
Manifest, } نَشْرَة ـ تَقْرِير ـ إِعْلان ـ مَنْشُور.

Manifold, *a.* Numerous, شَتَّى ـ ثَرِيّ. Diverse, مُتَنَوِّع. Multiplied, مُتَضاعِف. Complicated, مُشْتَبِك ـ مُلَبَّك ـ شَتّ ـ مُدَرَّج. How — are thy works! ما أَعْظَمَ أَعْمالَكَ. *See also under* Letter-writer, *n.*

Manifoldly, *ad.* بِتَضاعُف ـ تَنَوُّعًا.

Manifoldness, *n.* تَضاعُف ـ كَثْرَة ـ تَنَوُّع.

Manikin, *n.* A little man, قُصَيِّر ـ قَزَعَة ـ رُجَيْل. Something made up like a man, شَبِيهُ ٱلرَّجُلِ.

Manioc, *n.* The trees, شَجَرَةُ ٱلنَّشاءِ ٱلْمُسَمَّى تابِيُوكَة.

Maniple, *n.* A handful, حَفْنَة *pl.* حَفَنات ـ كَفّ *pl.* كُفُوف ـ جُمْعَة ـ قُبْضَة مِن. A band of soldiers, فِرْقَةُ عَسْكَرٍ. A scarf worn by Roman Catholic priests, كُمّ *pl.* أَكْمام.

Manipular, *a.* Pertaining to a hand, يَدِيّ ـ مُتَعَلِّقٌ بِٱلْيَدِ.

Manipulate, *v.t.* كَبَّسَ ـ دَعَكَ ـ كَمَزَ ـ عالَجَ. To —, as of medicines, عَجَنَ.

Manipulation, *n.* Manual operation, such as rubbing, rolling, *etc.*, صِناعَة ـ تَكْبِيس ـ دَعْك ـ كَمْز ـ مُعالَجَة. The — of medicines, عَجْنُ ٱلأَدْوِيَةِ.

Manipulator, *n.* One who rubs, presses with his hands, مُعالِج ـ مُكَبِّس ـ داعِك ـ كامِز.

Mankind, *n.* The human race, ٱلنَّاسُ ـ ٱلْبَشَرُ ـ جِنْسُ ٱلْبَشَرِ.
Mankind are of different sorts, and most of them are impure, (prov.) ٱلنَّاسُ أَجْنَاسٌ وَأَكْثَرُهُمْ أَنْجَاسٌ.

Manless, *a.* غَيْرُ مُجَهَّزٍ بِعَسَاكِرَ ـ خَالٍ مِنَ ٱلرِّجَالِ.

Manlike, *a.* *See* Manly, *a.*

Manliness, *n.* رُجُولِيَّةٌ ـ رُجُولَةٌ ـ إِقْدَامٌ ـ مُرُوَّةٌ ـ خُلُقٌ.

Manly, *a.* بَطَلٌ ـ صَاحِبُ مُرُوَّةٍ ـ صَاحِبُ إِقْدَامٍ ـ أَرْجَلُ ـ جَسُورٌ ـ صِنْدِيدٌ *pl.* صَنَادِيدُ. To affect to be —, تَفَحَّلَ.

Manna, *n.* The exudation from the حاج, a thorny tree, مَنٌّ ـ تَرَنْجَبِين ـ تِنْبِيل ـ تِنْبِير ـ مُغْفُور ـ مِغْفِير.

Manned, *a.* As with soldiers, مُجَهَّزٌ بِعَسَاكِرَ; with sailors, مُجَهَّزٌ بِبَحْرِيَّةٍ.

Manner, *n.* A custom, wont, عَادَةٌ *pl.* عَوَائِدُ ـ دَأْبٌ ـ سَمْتٌ. A mode, way, سُنَّةٌ *pl.* سُنَنٌ ـ طَرْقَةٌ *pl.* طُرَقٌ ـ أُسْلُوبٌ *pl.* أَسَالِيبُ ـ بَابٌ *pl.* أَبْوَابٌ ـ مِدَادٌ ـ طَرِيقَةٌ *pl.* طَرَائِقُ ـ وَجْهٌ *pl.* وُجُوهٌ ـ سِيَاقَةٌ ـ قَبِيلٌ ـ صُورَةٌ. A kind, نَوْعٌ *pl.* أَنْوَاعٌ ـ شَكْلٌ *pl.* أَشْكَالٌ ـ ضَرْبٌ *pl.* ضُرُوبٌ ـ جِنْسٌ *pl.* أَجْنَاسٌ. Order, نَسَقٌ ـ سِمْطٌ *pl.* سُمُوطٌ ـ تَرْتِيبٌ. Form, هَيْئَةٌ *pl.* هَيْآتٌ.
They built their houses in one —, style, بَنَوْا بُيُوتَهُمْ عَلَى مِدَادٍ وَاحِدٍ. It is his —, هٰذِهِ عَادَتُهُ. In this —, عَلَى هٰذَا ٱلْوَجْهِ.
What — of man is he? مَا هِيَ هَيْئَةُ ٱلرَّجُلِ. Such was the — of the king towards all, هٰكَذَا كَانَ أَمْرُ ٱلْمَلِكِ نَحْوَ ٱلْجَمِيعِ. In the usual —, عَلَى ٱلْوَجْهِ ٱلْمُعْتَادِ. Manners, way of acting, conduct, سُلُوكٌ ـ أَوْضَاعٌ ـ سِيرَةٌ ـ حَرَكَاتٌ ـ أَخْلَاقٌ ـ أَطْبَاعٌ ـ عَمَائِلُ ـ قِلَّةٌ. Good manners, لَطَافَةٌ ـ أَدَبٌ. Bad manners, سُوءُ أَدَبٍ ـ قِلَّةُ أَدَبٍ ـ نَظَاظَةٌ. Evil communications corrupt good manners, ٱلْمُعَاشَرَاتُ ٱلرَّدِيَّةُ تُفْسِدُ ٱلْأَخْلَاقَ ٱلْجَيِّدَةَ.
After a manner, بِوَجْهٍ. After a certain manner, بِوَجْهٍ مِنَ ٱلْوُجُوهِ.
In any manner, بِأَيِّ وَجْهٍ كَانَ ـ بِأَيِّ وَجْهٍ مِنَ ٱلْوُجُوهِ.
After the manner, حَسَبَ عَادَةٍ ـ كَ: After the manner of a man, مِثْلَ إِنْسَانٍ ـ كَإِنْسَانٍ. After the manner of an Indian, مِثْلَ ٱلْهُنُودِ. I speak after the manner of a man, أَتَكَلَّمُ كَإِنْسَانٍ.
After the most perfect manner, عَلَى أَكْمَلِ وَجْهٍ.
After the same manner, كَذٰلِكَ. After the same manner as, مِثْلَ.
As his manner, habit, was, حَسَبَ عَادَتِهِ. As the manner of some is, كَمَا لِقَوْمٍ عَادَةٌ.
In this manner, عَلَى هٰذَا ـ بِهٰذِهِ ٱلْمَنْزِلَةِ ـ عَلَى هٰذَا ٱلْمِنْوَالِ ـ هٰكَذَا ـ بِهٰذَا ٱلْقَبِيلِ ـ ٱلنَّسَقِ.

Mannerism, *n.* Affectation, تَأَنُّقٌ ـ صَنْعَةٌ ـ تَصَنُّعٌ ـ تَصَلُّفٌ.

Mannerist, *n.* An affected person, مُتَصَلِّفٌ ـ مُتَصَنِّعٌ ـ مُصَنِّعٌ ـ مُتَأَنِّقٌ.

Mannerly, *a.* مُؤَدَّبٌ ـ أَدِيبٌ ـ لَطِيفٌ ـ آدَمِيٌّ *pl.* أَوَادِمُ ـ ظَرِيفٌ; *from the Turkish*, شَلَبِيٌّ.

Mannerly, *ad.* بِلَطَافَةٍ ـ بِظَرَافَةٍ ـ بِأَدَبٍ.

Manners, *n.* *See under* Manner, *also* Deportment, *n.*

Mannish, *a.* Like a man, مِثْلَ ٱلرَّجُلِ ـ كَرَجُلٍ. *See also under* Masculine, *a.*

Manœuvre, *n.* As of troops, حَرَكَةُ عَسَاكِرَ *pl.* حَرَكَاتٌ ـ مَانُورَةٌ. A stratagem, خُدْعَةٌ ـ فَنٌّ *pl.* فُنُونٌ ـ حِيلَةٌ *pl.* حِيَلٌ ـ مَكِيدَةٌ *pl.* مَكَائِدُ ـ تَدْبِيرٌ; especially in war, خَدْعَةٌ. To practise manœuvres, stratagems, against, إِحْتَالَ عَلَى; in war, خَدَعَ ـ تَخَادَعَ.

Manœuvre, *v.i.* As of troops or ships, تَحَرَّكَ. The soldiers manœuvred, تَحَرَّكَتِ ٱلْعَسَاكِرُ. To act with address, to exercise stratagem, إِحْتَالَ ـ تَحَوَّلَ ـ تَحَيَّلَ. To endeavour, سَعَى ـ إِجْتَهَدَ ـ إِشْتَغَلَ.

Manœuvre, *v.t.* As of troops, حَرَّكَ (or دَبَّرَ) ٱلْعَسَاكِرَ.

Manœuverer, *n.* A stratagist, عَالِمٌ بِحَرَكَاتِ ٱلْعَسَاكِرِ. A schemer, خَدَّاعٌ ـ حَيَّالٌ ـ حُوَّلٌ قُلَّبٌ ـ حُوَّلٌ.

Manœuvering, *n.* Scheming, تَحَيُّلٌ ـ تَحَوُّلٌ. *See also* Manœuvre, *n.*

Man-of-war, *n.* *See under* Man, *n.*

Manor, *n.* زَعَامَةٌ ـ مُلْكٌ ـ اِلْتِزَامٌ. Lord of the —, زَعِيمٌ ـ صَاحِبُ ٱلزَّعَامَةِ.

Manor-house, *n.* مَسْكَنُ صَاحِبِ ٱلزَّعَامَةِ.

Manorial, *a.* مُخْتَصٌّ بِٱلزَّعَامَةِ ـ مُتَعَلِّقٌ بِٱلِٱلْتِزَامِ.

Manse, *n.* A parsonage, دَارٌ ـ بَيْتُ ٱلْقَسِّ ـ مَسْكَنُ ٱلْخُورِي ـ ٱلْخُورِي. *See also* Farm, *n.*

Mansion, *n.* A house of the great, مَنْزِلٌ ـ دِيَارٌ *pl.* دَارٌ لِلْأَعْيَانِ ـ أَكَابِرَ. A large house, مَنْزِلٌ وَسِيعٌ ـ قَصْرٌ. A dwelling, دَارٌ *pl.* دِيَارٌ ـ مَسْكَنٌ *pl.* مَسَاكِنُ ـ بَيْتٌ *pl.* بُيُوتٌ. The Mansions of the Moon, بُرُوجُ ٱلْقَمَرِ ـ نُجُومُ ٱلْأَنْوَاءِ (or ٱلْأَخْذِ). *See also* Manor-house, *n.*

Mansionary, *a.* سَاكِنٌ ـ مُقِيمٌ.

Manslaughter, *n.* قَتْلٌ بِغَيْرِ قَصْدٍ (or عَمْدٍ).

Man-slayer, *n.* قَاتِلٌ *pl.* قُتَّالٌ.

Man-stealer, *n.* سَالِبُ ٱلْبَشَرِ (or ٱلْأَوَادِمِ).

Man-stealing, *n.* سَلْبُ ٱلْبَشَرِ (or ٱلْأَوَادِمِ).

Mansuetude, *n.* لُطْفٌ ـ لَطَافَةٌ ـ حِلْمٌ ـ رِفْقٌ ـ مُلَاءَمَةٌ.

Mantel, n. } The ledge over a fire-place, رَفّ ـ رَفُّ ٱلْكَانُونِ ـ
Mantle, } كُنَّةُ ٱلْكَانُونِ ـ ٱلْمَوْقِدِ .

Mantelet, n. } A woman's cloak, ضَرْبٌ مِنَ ٱلْفَرَجِيَّةِ لِلنِّسَآءِ .
Mantlet, } A parapet, حَاجِز ـ سِتَارَة .

Mantilla, n. مِنْدِيل pl. مَنَادِيلُ .

Mantis, n. The insect, جَمَلُ ٱلْجَرَادِ .

Mantle, n. A cloak, رِدَآءٌ pl. أَرْدِيَة ـ بُرْنُس pl. بَرَانِسُ . A covering, حِجَاب ـ سِتَارَة ـ سُتْرَة . A — or scarf, طَرْحَة . He wrapped himself in his —, اِرْتَدَى (or تَرَدَّى) بِرِدَآئِهِ . See also Cloak, n.

Mantle, v.t. To cause to crimson, of the face, فَوَّرَ . See also to Cover, Disguise, Veil, v.t.

Mantle, v.i. To spread over, اِنْتَشَرَ عَلَى . To encompass, comprise, شَمِلَ ـ اِشْتَمَلَ عَلَى . To —, or wrap one's self up in his garment, اِشْتَمَلَ بِثَوْبِهِ . To foam, أَرْغَى ـ أَزْبَدَ . To diffuse itself, spread, rise up, فَارَ ـ ثَارَ aor. يَثُورُ . The blood mantled into his face, ثَارَ ٱلدَّمُ فِي وَجْهِهِ .

Mantle-piece, n. See Mantel, n.

Mantua-maker, n. خَيَّاطَةُ ٱلْفَسَاطِينِ ـ خَيَّاطَة .

Manual, a. مِنْ شُغْلِ ٱلْيَدِ ـ يَدَوِيّ . Manual exercise, of soldiers, تَمْرِين (or تَعْلِيمُ) ٱلسِّلَاحِ . Sign —, تَوْقِيع ـ إِمْضَآء .

Manual, n. كِتَابٌ صَغِيرٌ يُحْمَلُ فِي ٱلْيَدِ ـ مَجْمَعَة ـ رِسَالَة ـ دَسْتُور .

Manufactory, n. مَعْمَل pl. مَعَامِلُ ـ كَرْخَانَة pl. كَرَاخِينُ ـ فَابْرِيكَة .

Manufactural, a. مُتَعَلِّقٌ بِحَاصِلَاتِ ـ مَنُوطٌ بِٱلْمَصْنُوعَاتِ ٱلْمَعْمَلِ .

Manufacture, n. The act of manufacturing, مُعَالَجَة ـ صَنْع ـ عَمَل ; also from the Italian, فَابْرِيكَة . Anything manufactured, شَيْءٌ مَعْمُولٌ ـ صَنِيع . Manufactures, أَمْتِعَةٌ مَصْنُوعَةٌ ـ حَاصِلَاتٌ ـ صِنَاعِيَّةٌ ـ مَعْمُولَات ـ فَابْرِيكَات . Muskets bearing the mark of English —, مَكَاحِلُ بِعَلَامَةِ فَابْرِيكَاتٍ إِنْكِلِيزِيَّةٍ .

Manufacture, v.t. To make, عَالَجَ ـ صَنَعَ ـ اِصْطَنَعَ . To prepare, make, اِتَّخَذَ . He manufactured or wrought iron, عَالَجَ ٱلْحَدِيدَ . He manufactured beds, عَالَجَ فُرُشًا . See also to Invent, v.t.

Manufacturer, n. صِنَاعِيّ ـ صَانِع pl. صُنَّاع ـ فَابْرِيكَاتِيّ .

Manumission, n. إِطْلَاق ـ إِعْتَاق .

Manumit, v.t. فَكَّ ـ أَطْلَقَ ـ أَعْتَقَ . To be manumitted, عَتَقَ ـ اِنْفَكَّ ـ أُطْلِقَ . One manumitted, سَائِبَة ـ طَلِيق pl. طُلَقَآءُ ـ عَتِيق pl. عُتَقَآءُ .

Manurable, a. مِمَّا يُزَبَّلُ .

Manure, n. سَمَاد ـ دَمَال ـ دَبَال ـ زِبْل . See also Dung, a.

Manure, v.t. سَمَّدَ ـ دَمَلَ ـ زَبَلَ ـ زَبَّلَ . See also to Dung, v.t.

Manuring, n. دَمْل ـ دَمَلَان ـ زَبْل ـ زُبُول .

Manuscript, n. A book written with the hand, كِتَابٌ بِخَطِّ يَدٍ .

Manuscript, a. خَطُّ يَدٍ .

Many, a. عَدِيد ـ شَتَّى ـ كَثِير ـ مُتَعَدِّد . Many a time, كَثِيرًا مَا ـ شَتَّى ـ مِرَارًا . Respecting which (matter) there are — things to be said, ٱلَّذِي مِنْ جِهَتِهِ ٱلْكَلَامُ كَثِيرٌ .

A great or good many, كَثِيرُونَ ـ جَمٌّ ـ شَتَّى .

As many, قَدْر ـ مِقْدَار . As many as you find, كُلُّ مَنْ وَجَدْتُمُوهُ .

As many as desire, جَمِيعُ ٱلَّذِينَ يُرِيدُونَ . He will give him as many as he wants, يُعْطِيهِ قَدْرَ مَا يَحْتَاجُ .

Full many a ..., كَمْ مِنَ ٱلـ... .

How many? كَمْ . How many times? كَمْ مَرَّةً .

Too many, زَائِد ـ بِٱلزِّيَادَةِ ـ زَائِدٌ عَنِ ٱللُّزُومِ .

Many, n. شَتّ ـ كَثْرَة ـ ثَرْوَة ـ جَمّ . A multitude, نَهِير ـ ثَرِيّ .

Many-coloured, a. مُلَوَّن ـ كَثِيرُ ٱلْأَلْوَانِ .

Many-cornered, a. كَثِيرُ ٱلزَّوَايَا .

Many-flowered, a. كَثِيرُ ٱلْأَزْهَارِ .

Many-headed, a. كَثِيرُ ٱلرُّؤُوسِ .

Many-leaved, a. كَثِيرُ ٱلْأَوْرَاقِ .

Many-sided, a. كَثِيرُ ٱلْأَجْنَابِ .

Many-twinkling, a. كَثِيرُ ٱلتَّلَأْلُؤِ ـ مُتَلَأْلِئ .

Map, n. خَارِطَة pl. خَارِطَات ـ رُقْعَةٌ مَرْسُومَةٌ عَلَيْهَا صُورَةُ بِلَادٍ pl. رِقَاع .

Map, v.t. To delineate a country, رَسَمَ خَارِطَةً ـ رَسَمَ ٱلْبِلَادَ ـ رَسَمَ ٱلْبِلَادَ .

Maple, a. The tree, شَجَرَةُ ٱلْعَرَبِ ـ شَجَرَةُ ٱلْأَسْفَنْدَانِ .

Mapping, n. رَسْم ـ رَسْمُ ٱلْخَارِطَاتِ .

Mar, v.t. To injure, deface, أَفْسَدَ ـ فَسَخَ ـ ضَارَّ ـ أَضَرَّ ـ عَطَّلَ ـ أَعْطَبَ ـ خَسَّرَ ـ أَجْحَفَ بِ ـ ثَلَمَ . To — mirth, كَدَّرَ ٱلْفَرَحَ . To — beauty, شَوَّهَ ٱلْجَمَالَ . To — pride, أَهْبَطَ ٱلتَّكَبُّرَ . To — one's character; see to Defame, v.t. He who prefers the enjoyments of this life mars his enjoyment of the life to come, مَنْ آثَرَ ٱلدُّنْيَا أَجْحَفَ بِآخِرَتِهِ .

Mar, n. See Injury, n.

Marabout, n. (more correctly Marâbit) مُرَابِط pl. مُرَابِطَة .

Maranatha, a. "Anathema maranatha," مَلْعُونٌ عِنْدَ مَجِيءِ ٱلرَّبِّ .

Maraschino, *n.* ضَرْبٌ مِنَ ٱلْعَنْبَرِيِّ.

Marasmus, *n.* سُلال – سِلّ – نَشْفان – هُزال.

Maraud, *v.i.* أَغارَ عَلَى ٱلْبِلادِ لِلنَّهْبِ – 2 قَطَعَ ٱلطَّرِيقَ.

Marauder, *n.* حَرامِيٌّ – قُطّاع *pl.* قاطِعُ ٱلطَّرِيقِ – مَغاوِر *pl.* مِغْوار *pl.* حَرامِيَّة.

Maravedi, *n.* فَلْسٌ أَحْمَرُ – فَلْس.

Marble, *n.* مَرْمَر – رُخام. A slab of —, رُخامَة. A boy's playing —, أُكَر *pl.* أُكْرَة رُخام لِلَّعِبِ. A — or tablet with an inscription, مَرْقُوم – رَقِيم.

Marble, *a.* مِنْ رُخام – مِنْ مَرْمَر.

Marble, *v.t.* لَوَّنَ مِثْلَ ٱلْمَرْمَرِ.

Marble-edged, *a.* مُلَوَّنُ ٱلْأَشْفارِ كَالرُّخام.

Marbling, *n.* تَلْوِينُ ٱلشَّيْءِ بِلَوْنِ ٱلرُّخامِ.

Marcessent, *a.* Withering, مُضْمَحِلٌّ – ذابِل.

March, *n.* A movement of troops, سَيْرَةُ عَساكِرَ *pl.* سِيَر. A walk, مَشْيٌ – سَيْرَة. A journey, مَسِيرَة. A tune for soldiers to march by, لَحْنٌ (*or* نَوْبَةٌ) لِسِيرَةِ ٱلْعَسْكَرِ. A procession, رَكْبَة. Progress, رَوْجَة – إِفْلاح – تَقَدُّم – تَدْرِيج – نَجاح. A dead —, نَوْبَةُ ٱلْعَسْكَرِ عِنْدَ دَفْنِ ٱلْمَوْتَى. A forced —, سَيْرَةٌ حَثِيثَةٌ. To be on the —, كانَ فِي ٱلْمَسِيرِ. To steal a — upon, 2 سَبَقَ-إِلَى. He prevented the —, movements, of the troops, 2 مَنَعَ سِيَرَ ٱلْعَسْكَرِ.

March, *n.* The third month in the year, شَهْرُ آذارَ – آذار – شَهْرُ مارْش.

March, *v.i.* سارَ *aor.* يَسِيرُ – 2 ذَهَبَ – 2 مَشَى. To — back, 2 رَجَعَ – 2 عادَ. To — into, 2 دَخَلَ. To — off, set off, 2 أَخَذَ فِي – ٱنْطَلَقَ – إِرْتَحَلَ – ٱلْمَسِيرِ. To — off with, take away, 2 سارَ بِ – 2 مَضَى بِ – 2 ذَهَبَ بِ.

March, *v.t.* سَيَّرَ – ساقَ *aor.* يَسُوقُ – مَشَّى.

Marcher, *n.* A good walker, رَجِيل *pl.* رَجّالَة.

Marches, *n.* Borders, confines, حُدُود – تُخُوم.

Marching, *n.* مَسِير – مُرُور – سَيْر – رَحِيل.

Marchioness, *n.* إِمْرَأَةُ أَوْ أَرْمَلَةُ ٱلْأَمِيرِ ٱلْمُسَمَّى مارْكِيزْ – مارْكِيزَة.

Marcid, *a.* *See* Lean, Withered, *a.*

Marcidity, *n.* *See* Leanness, *n.*

Mare, *n.* فَرَسَة *pl.* فَرَسات – فَرَس *pl.* فُرُوس *and* أَفْراس. A breeding —, حِجْر *pl.* حُجُور.

Mare's-nest, *n.* بَيْضَةُ ٱلْعُقْرِ – ٱلْأَبْلَقُ ٱلْعَقُوقُ – بَيْضُ ٱلْأَنُوقِ – مُخُّ ٱلْبَعُوضَةِ. He sought a —, 2 طَلَبَ ٱلْعَقُوقَ. That was a —, كانَتْ بَيْضَةَ ٱلْعُقْرِ.

Mareshal, *n.* *See* Marshal, *n.*

Margarite, *n.* *See* Pearl, *n.*

Margin, *n.* A brink, as of a river, حَرْف *pl.* حُرُوف – حافَة – شَفِير – شُفْر *pl.* أَشْفار. An edge, end, طَرَف *pl.* أَطْراف – كَنَف *pl.* أَكْناف – شُفْر *pl.* أَشْفار. The — of a book, هامِش – حاشِيَة *pl.* حَواشِي. Excess, space, فَضْلَة – وَسْع. To write notes, as on the — of a book, عَلَّقَ – حَشَّى. *See also* Border, Brink, Edge, *n.*

Margin, *v.t.* To border, أَنارَ – نَيَّرَ – كَنَّفَ. *See also to* Border, *v.t.*

Marginal, *a.* In the margin (of a book), فِي ٱلْهامِشِ. Additional, مُلْحَق. A — note, حاشِيَة *pl.* حَواشِي. To write — notes on a book, أَضافَ ٱلْكِتابَ. *See also under* Margin, *n.*

Marginally, *ad.* فِي ٱلْهامِشِ.

Marginate, *a.* / Marginated, } Having a margin, (of a book), ذُو هامِشٍ – ذُو حاشِيَةٍ.

Margrave, *n.* مارْغَرِيف – شَرِيفٌ مِنْ أَهْلِ ٱلنَّمْسا.

Margraviate, *n.* مُلْكُ ٱلْمارْغَرِيفِ ٱلْمَذْكُورِ.

Margravine, *n.* مارْغَرِيفِين – إِمْرَأَةُ ٱلْمارْغَرِيفِ ٱلْمَذْكُورِ.

Marigenous, *a.* Produced in the sea, مَوْلُودٌ فِي ٱلْبَحْرِ – بَحْرِيٌّ.

Marigold, *n.* أُقْحُوان – قُحْوان.

Marine, *a.* بَحْرِيٌّ. Marine productions, مُوَلَّداتُ ٱلْبَحْرِ – ثَمَرَةُ ٱلْبَحْرِ. Marine forces, قُوَّةٌ بَحْرِيَّةٌ – قُوَّةٌ حَرْبِيَّةٌ بَحْرِيَّةٌ.

Marine, *n.* A soldier doing duty in a ship, عَسْكَرِيٌّ مِنَ ٱلْبَحْرِيَّةِ. Ships, مَراكِبُ – شُوَن. Mercantile —, مَراكِبُ تِجارِيَّةٌ. Minister of —, ناظِرُ ٱلْبَحْرِيَّةِ. Ministry of —, نَظارَةُ ٱلْبَحْرِيَّةِ.

Mariner, *n.* نُوتِيٌّ *pl.* نَواتِيُّ – صارٍ *pl.* صُرّاء – بَحْرِيٌّ *pl.* بَحْرِيَّة. The mariner's compass, بُوصْلَة – بَيْتُ ٱلْإِبْرَةِ. Master —, رَئِيسٌ بَحْرِيٌّ – ناخُوذاه *pl.* نَواخِذَة.

Marital, *a.* زَوْجِيٌّ. Marital rights, حُقُوقُ ٱلزَّوْجِ.

Maritime, *a.* Connected with the sea, بَحْرِيٌّ. Near the sea, ساحِلِيٌّ – سَواحِلِيٌّ – عَلَى شَطِّ ٱلْبَحْرِ. A — power, دَوْلَةٌ صاحِبَةُ مَراكِبَ – دَوْلَةٌ صاحِبَةُ دُونَنْما. The — powers, ٱلدُّوَلُ ٱلْبَحْرِيَّةُ. Maritime exploration to ..., كَشْفُ ٱلْمَراكِبِ عَن. A — expedition, مَسِيرَةُ سَفائِنَ.

Marjoram, *n.* Sweet —, the plant, غاغ – ٱلْمَرْزَنْجُوش – سَعْتَر. Wild —, سَمْسَق – حَبَقُ ٱلْفَتاةِ – عَنْقَز – حَبَقُ ٱلْفِيلِ – فُوذَنْج – نَصَف.

Mark, *n.* A sign, عَلامَة *coll.* عَلام *pl.* عَلامات – إِشارَة – رَسْم *pl.* رُسُوم – نِيشان *pl.* نَواشِين. An impression, stamp, as a trade-mark, دَمْغَة – نِيشان. A figure, line, price-mark, رَقْم: A price

— on a piece of cloth, رَقْمُ ٱلثَّوْبِ. An impression, trace, آيَة — عَلَامَة — رَسْم — رَشْم — آثار pl. أَثَر — عَلَامَة. A sign, token, إِشَارَة. Evidence, proof, شَاهِد pl. شَوَاهِد — بُرْهَان pl. بَرَاهِين. Design, object, مَقْصُود — غَرَض — نِيَّة. A degree, rank, دَرَجَة — رُتْبَة. A natural — on the body, شَامَة pl. شَامَات — عَلَامَة. Something to shoot at, نِيشَان — هَدَف — غَرَض. Something set up as a guide, مَعْلَم — إِشَارَة — صَدَح — عَلَم. A — instead of a regular signature, إِشَارَةٌ بِقَلَمٍ بَدَلَ إِمْضَاءٍ. A man of —, رَجُلٌ مَشْهُورٌ — رَجُلٌ مُعْتَبَرٌ. A —, or brand, on cattle, وِسَام — نَار. A — of infamy, عَيْب — عَار — فَضِيحَة. A — of friendship, عَلَامَةُ مَحَبَّةٍ. It bears the — of such a thing, عَلَيْهِ أَثَرُ كَذَا.

To be near the mark, truth, دَنَا مِنَ ٱلْحَقِّ [2]. I was near the —, nearly did it, كِدْتُ أَفْعَلُهُ. He was near the —, nearly hit it, كَادَ يُصِيبُهُ.

To be under the mark, wanting, كَانَ نَاقِصًا — إِنْتَقَصَ — نَقَصَ [2].

He was under the mark in his estimate, قَصَّرَ فِي حِسَابِهِ.

To go beyond the mark, to exceed, جَاوَزَ ٱلْحَدَّ — أَفْرَطَ.

To hit the mark, or butt, لَطَعَ ٱلنِّيشَانَ — أَصَابَ ٱلْهَدَفَ.

To hit the right point, أَصَابَ ٱلسَّدَادَ — أَصَابَ ٱلصَّوَابَ. *See also under to* Hit, *v.t.*

To set up a mark, صَمَدَ إِشَارَةً — نَصَبَ نَصِيبَةً — نَصَبَ عَلَامَةً [2].

To shoot at a mark, رَمَى فِي ٱلنِّيشَانِ — رَمَى فِي ٱلْغَرَضِ.

To overshoot the mark, butt, جَاوَزَ ٱلْغَرَضَ (or ٱلْهَدَفَ).

Mark, *v.t.* To draw a mark or sign upon, عَلَّمَ عَلَى — أَعْلَمَ عَلَى [2]; عَيَّنَ عَلَى — رَقَمَ [2]; especially the marking of goods with the price, or cloth, *etc.*, with lines or stripes, رَقَّمَ — رَقَمَ [2]. To put a trade or government — upon, دَمَغَ [2]. To indicate, عَيَّنَ. To leave a visible impression, trace, خَلَّى أَثَرًا — أَثَّرَ. To denote, testify, أَعْطَى شَاهِدًا — بَيَّنَ — أَعْلَنَ — أَظْهَرَ — أَبْدَى. To notice, observe, أَمْعَنَ ٱلنَّظَرَ فِي — لَاحَظَ — إِكْتَنَتَ إِلَى. To consider, meditate upon, إِعْتَبَرَ — تَأَمَّلَ فِي. Mark me, إِصْغَ إِلَيَّ. To — out, to draw, رَسَمَ [2]; to — out, as of a boundary, خَطَّطَ. To distinguish from others, مَيَّزَ — إِشْتَرَكَ. Mark (ye) the place, as with a —, أَعْلِمُوا ٱلْمَكَانَ. The commission intrusted with the duty of marking out (the limits) of the province, اللَّجْنَةُ ٱلْمَنُوطَةُ بِعُهْدَتِهَا تَخْطِيطُ تِلْكَ ٱلْوِلَايَةِ.

Mark, *v.i.* To make a mark, عَمِلَ إِشَارَةً — عَلَّمَ عَلَامَةً [2]. To note attentively, لَاحَظَ — إِنْتَبَهَ عَلَى — تَأَمَّلَ — خَلَّى أَثَرًا.

Marked, *a.* Having a mark upon it, مُعَيَّنٌ عَلَيْهِ — مَرْقُوم — مَرْسُوم; especially with a price, مَرْقُوم — مُرَقَّم. A — difference, فَرْقٌ مُبِينٌ.

To sell an article, marked with the price, is not allowable, لَا يَجُوزُ بَيْعُ ٱلشَّيْءِ بِرَقْمِهِ.

Marker, *n.* One who marks, رَاقِم — مُرَقِّم. One who places the stamp upon goods, دَمْغَجِي — وَاضِعُ ٱلدَّمْغَةِ. A book —, مَعْلَمُ كِتَابٍ pl. مَعَالِم.

Market, *n.* سُوق pl. أَسْوَاق. A dull —, سُوقٌ كَاسِدٌ (or كَاسِدَةٌ or أَكْسَدُ). Dullness of the —, كَسَاد. The — was active, رَاجَتِ ٱلسُّوقُ — قَامَتِ ٱلسُّوقُ [2]. The — was dull, كَسَدَتِ ٱلسُّوقُ.

Market, *v.i.* تَسَوَّقَ *vulg.* سَوَّقَ. The people marketed, trafficked, in the —, تَسَوَّقَ ٱلْقَوْمُ *vulg.* سَوَّقُوا.

Marketable, *a.* يُتَعَامَلُ بِهِ — يُبْتَاعُ — رَائِج.

Market-day, *n.* يَوْمُ سُوقٍ — سُوق.

Marketing, *n.* Going to market, تَسَوُّق. What is bought in the market, شِرًى pl. أَشْرِيَة — مُشْتَرًى. Selling in a market, سُوق.

Market-place, *n.* سُوق pl. أَسْوَاق.

Market-town, *n.* بَلْدَةٌ ذَاتُ سُوقٍ — سُوق.

Marking, *n.* عَلَم — رَقْم — كِتَابَة.

Marking-ink, *n.* حِبْرٌ رَاهِنٌ لِرَقْمِ ٱلثِّيَابِ.

Marking-iron, *n.* مِيسَم — لُوَيَا — مِكْوَاة pl. مَكَاوٍ.

Marksman, *n.* One who shoots with skill, أَرْمَى pl. أَرَامِي — نِشَانْجِي — قَوَّاس — هَدَّاف.

Marl, *n.* ضَرْبٌ مِنَ ٱلتُّرَابِ يُشْبِهُ ٱلطَّبَاشِيرَ.

Marl, *v.t.* To manure with —, سَمَّدَ ٱلْأَرْضَ بِٱلتُّرَابِ ٱلْمَذْكُورِ. To twist a small line round a rope, لَفَّ عَلَى — ٱلْمَرَسَ — لَبَسَ — فَتِيلًا [2] — فَتَلَ عَلَى — مَرَسًا.

Marlaceous, *a.* مِنْ جِنْسِ ٱلطَّبَاشِيرِ.

Marline, *n.* A small line for winding round cable, مَرَسُ تَوٍّ — فَتِيل — مَرَسُ فَتِيلٍ.

Marline-spike, *n.* بَرِيمَة — سِيخ — مِثْقَب.

Marly, *a.* مِنْ جِنْسِ ٱلطَّبَاشِيرِ.

Marmalade, *n.* مُرَبَّى ٱلْفَاكِهَةِ. Orange —, مُرَبَّى نَارِنْجٍ.

Marmoraceous *a.* }
Marmorean, } مِنْ رُخَامٍ — مِنْ مَرْمَرٍ — مَرْمَرِيّ.

Marmoset, *n.* نَوْعٌ مِنْ صِغَارِ ٱلْقِرْدِ.

Marocco, *n.* ٱلْمَرَاكِش.

Maronite, *n.* مَارُونِيّ pl. مَارُونِيَّة.

Maroon, *n.* لَقَبٌ لِلزُّنُوجِ ٱلْمَعْتُوقِينَ ٱلسَّاكِنِينَ فِي جِبَالِ جَزَائِرِ ٱلْهِنْدِ ٱلْغَرْبِيِّ.

Maroon, *v.t.* تَرَكَ فِي جَزِيرَةٍ قَفْرَةٍ قِصَاصًا لَهُ [2].

Maroon, *a.* أَكْلَف *fem.* كَلْفَآء *pl.* كُلْف ـ مُوَّر.

Marplot, *n.* مُفْسِد ـ خَبَّاص ـ عَوِق ـ مُبْرِم ـ عِوَق.

Marque, *n.* Letters of, بَرَآءَةٌ تُعْطَى لِمَرَاكِبِ ٱلتُّجَّارِ وَقْتَ ٱلْحَرْبِ ـ بَرَآءَةٌ مِنْ طَرَفِ دَوْلَتِهَا تُرَخِّصُ لَهَا فِي مُحَارَبَةِ مَرَاكِبِ ٱلْعَدُوِّ لِلْمُحَارَبَةِ.

Marquee, *n.* خَيْمَةٌ كَبِيرَةٌ ـ فُسْطَاط ـ وَطَاق *pl.* وَطَاقَات ـ مَضْرِب *pl.* مَضَارِب.

Marquis, *n.* مَرْكِيز ـ مَارْكُوِيس ـ أَمِير.

Marquisate, *n.* رُتْبَةُ ٱلْمَارْكُوِيسِ وَمَقَامُهُ.

Marriage, *n.* The act of marrying, نِكَاح ـ تَزْوِيج. The married state, نِكَاح ـ زَوَاج ـ زَوْجِيَّة ـ زِيجَة ; *vulg.* جِيزَة ـ جَازَة. The ceremony of marrying, نِكَاح ; (among Christians), تَكْلِيل. The — service, عَقْدُ ٱلنِّكَاحِ ـ رُتْبَةُ ٱلزِّيجَةِ. A — feast, wedding, وَلِيمَة ـ فَرَح ـ عُرْس. To prepare a — feast, أَعْرَسَ. A — license, رُقْعَةُ تَحْلِيلِ ٱلنِّكَاحِ. A — certificate, وَرَقَةُ شَهَادَةِ ٱلزَّوَاجِ. A — settlement; *See* Dower, *n.* A civil —, زَوَاجٌ مَدَنِيٌّ. To ask a woman in —, خَطَبَ ٱلْمَرْأَةَ ² ـ أَخْطَبَ ; the act of such asking, خِطْبَة ـ خَطْب. To ask a woman in — of such an one, خَطَبَ ٱلْمَرْأَةَ إِلَى فُلَانٍ ². To grant the request of —, أَنْكَحَ ـ أَخْطَبَ ـ خَطَبَ. A man who asks a woman in —, خُطْب ـ خَطِيب ـ خَاطِب ـ خِطْب. A woman asked in —, خُطْبَة ـ خَطِيبَة ـ خِطْبَة. Dissolution of —, فَسْخُ عَقْدِ ٱلنِّكَاحِ. The — tie, عِصْمَةُ ٱلنِّكَاحِ.

Marriageable, *a.* خَلِيقٌ لِلزِّيجَةِ *fem.* خَلِيقَةٌ ; of a female only, طَرُوقَة. To be —, free to marry, خَلَا مِنْ مَوَانِعِ ٱلنِّكَاحِ ².

Married, *a.* United in wedlock, مُتَأَهِّل ـ مُزَوَّج *fem.* مُزَوَّجَة ; *vulg.* مُجَوَّز *fem.* مُجَوَّزَة. The — state, زَوَاج ـ نِكَاح. A — man, زَوْج ـ مُزَوَّج ; a — woman, زَوْجَة ـ مُزَوَّجَة ـ مَنْكُوحَة. A newly — man, عَرِيس ; a newly — woman, عَرُوس. (Ordinary compliments addressed to a newly — man), مُبَارَك ; *Answer:* اللّٰهُ يُبَارِكُ فِيكَ. To a newly — pair, إِنْ شَآءَ ٱللّٰهُ تَتَهَنُّونَ وَتَتَوَفَّقُونَ وَتُرْزَقُونَ ٱلْمَالَ وَٱلْبَنِينَ. *See also* Conjugal, *a.*

Marrow, *n.* As of bones, مَخَاخَة ـ مُخّ ـ مُخُّ ٱلْعَظْمِ ـ نِقْيٌ ـ صَمِيم ـ مُخَاع ـ صُلَيْب ـ لُبّ ـ صَلَب ـ رِمٌّ ـ مُخّ ـ زُبْدَة ـ عَيْنَة. (*See also under* Best, *a.*). The best part, صَمِيم ـ مُخّ. The spinal —, مُخُّ ٱلصُّلْبِ ـ بِلَسِلَةِ ٱلظَّهْرِ. To take the — from a bone, تَمَخَّخَ ٱلْعَظْمَ (or صَلَبَ ²). Vegetable —, كُوسَاة *coll.* كُوسَا.

Marrowbone, *n.* A bone with marrow, عَظْمٌ مُرِمٌّ ـ نِقَآءَة. The bone of the knee, رُكْبَة *pl.* رُكَب. He went down on his marrow-bones, خَرَّ عَلَى رُكْبَتَيْهِ ².

Marrowfat, *n.* A delicious pea, جُلُبَّانٌ لَذِيذٌ ـ جُلُبَّانَةٌ لَذِيذَةٌ ـ بِسِلَّةٌ مُفْتَخَرَةٌ.

Marrowless, *a.* بِلَا مُخَاعٍ ـ بِدُونِ مُخٍّ.

Marrowy, *a.* Having marrow, ذُو مُخَاعٍ ـ مُرِمٌّ.

Marry, *v.t.* To join in wedlock, زَوَّجَ ـ زَوَّجَ ب ; *vulg.* جَوَّزَ. To take for a wife, (or husband by changing the suffix pronouns,) تَزَوَّجَ ب ـ تَزَوَّجَ ـ إِسْتَنْكَحَ ـ نَكَحَ ². He married his daughter to such an one, زَوَّجَ بِنْتَهُ ب (or مَعَ) فُلَانٍ. The priest married them, كَلَّلَهُمُ ٱلْقِسِّيسُ.

Mars, *n.* The god of war, إِلٰهُ ٱلْحَرْبِ ـ المَلِكُ ٱلْأَحْمَرُ. The planet, كَوْكَبُ ٱلْمِرِّيخِ.

Marsh, *n.* غَيْضَة *pl.* غِيَاض ـ أَجَمَة *pl.* أَجَمَات ـ غَمِقَة *pl.* غَمِقَات ـ بِرْكَة *pl.* بِرَك ـ بَطِيحَة *pl.* بَطَائِح. A salt —, سَبْخَة ـ سَبَخ.

Marshal, *n.* A lictor, man-at-arms, شُرْطِيّ *coll.* شُرْطَة ـ قَوَّاس *pl.* قَوَّاسَة. Head —, lictor, صَاحِبُ ٱلشُّرْطَةِ ـ قَوَّاس بَاشِي. A chief military commander, أَمِيرُ أُمَرَآءِ ٱلْعَسَاكِرِ ـ مُشِير ـ مَارِيشَال.

Marshal, *v.t.* As of an army, صَفَّ ٱلْعَسْكَرَ ² ـ صَفَّفَ. To be marshalled, إِصْطَفَّ.

Marshalled, *a.* مُصْطَفّ ـ مَصْفُوف.

Marshaller, *n.* مُصَفِّف.

Marshalling, *n.* تَصْفِيف ـ صَفّ.

Marshalsea, *n.* سِجْنٌ كَانَ قِدَمًا بِلَنْدَن.

Marshalship, *n.* The office of a marshal of the army, مُشِيرِيَّة ـ مَأْمُورِيَّةُ ٱلْمَارِيشَالِ.

Marsh-mallow, *n.* شَحْمَةُ ٱلْمَرْجِ ـ خَطْمِيّ. *See also* Mallow, *n.*

Marshy, *a.* أَبْطَح ـ غِيَاضِيّ ـ أَجَمِيّ ـ غَمِق.

Marsupial, *a.* }
Marsupiale, } (حَيَوَانٌ) ذُو جَيْبٍ فِي أَسْفَلِ بَدَنِهِ يَحْمِلُ فِيهِ صِغَارَهُ.
Marsupialia, *n.* }

Mart, *n.* *See* Market, *n.*

Martagon, *n.* نَوْعٌ مِنَ ٱلزَّنْبَقِ.

Martello-tower, *n.* بُرْجٌ مُحَصَّنٌ لِمُحَافَظَةِ ٱلسَّوَاحِلِ *pl.* أَبْرَاج.

Marten, *n.* A kind of weasel, فَنَك *pl.* أَفْنَاك ـ نَوْعٌ مِنَ ٱبْنِ عِرْسٍ. A stone —, سَمُّور.

Martial, *a.* Pertaining to war, military, حَرْبِيّ ـ جُنْدِيّ ـ عَسْكَرِيّ. Bellicose, مُحَارِب. Martial law, أَحْكَامُ ٱلْقَوَانِينِ ٱلْحَرْبِيَّةِ. To proclaim — law in a country, نَادَى بِحَالِ ٱلْمُحَاصَرَةِ فِي بَلَدٍ ـ أَعْلَنَ بِإِجْرَآءِ ٱلْأَحْكَامِ ٱلْحَرْبِيَّةِ فِي مَمْلَكَةٍ. A — appearance, هِيئَةٌ عَسكَرِيَّةٌ. A — nation, (حَرْبِيَّةٌ or) أُمَّةٌ عَسكَرِيَّةٌ. Martial equipage, أَثَاثٌ حَرْبِيَّةٌ. A — code, دُسْتُورُ ٱلْحَرْبِ — قَوَانِينُ حَرْبِيَّةٌ. Court —, دِيوَانُ حَرْبٍ. Under — law, تَحْتَ ٱلتَّحْرِيجَاتِ ٱلْعَسْكَرِيَّةِ.

Martin, n. The bird, خُطَّاف pl. خَطَاطِيفُ.

Martinet, n. ضَابِطٌ قَاسٍ — ضَابِطٌ مُؤَدِّبٌ — ضَابِطٌ مُدَقِّقٌ.

Martingal, n. / Martingale, } سَلَبَنْد — صَرِيمَة.

Martinmas, n. عِيدُ مَارِ مَرْتِينَ ٱلْوَاقِعُ فِي ١١ شَهْرِ نُوفَمْبَر.

Martlet, n. صُورَةُ عُصْفُورٍ فِي فَنِّ رَسْمِ ٱلْآرْمَا.

Martyr, n. One put to death in defence of any cause, شَهِيد pl. شُهَدَآء. A great sufferer from, مُتَأَلِّمٌ كَثِيرًا مِن — مُعَذَّبٌ بِ. To die a —, to be martyred, أُسْتُشْهِدَ — أُشْهِدَ.

Martyr, v.t. To put death as a —, قَتَلَ-شَهِيدًا. To torture, عَذَّبَ.

Martyrdom, n. مَوتُ شَهَادَةٍ — شَهَادَة. A place of —, مَشْهَد.

Martyrize, v.t. *See to* Martyr, v.t.

Martyrological, a. مُتَعَلِّقٌ بِتَرَاجِمِ (or سِيَرِ) ٱلشُّهَدَآءِ.

Martyrologist, n. مُتَرْجِمُ (or مُؤَلِّفُ) تَرَاجِمِ (or سِيَرِ) ٱلشُّهَدَآءِ.

Martyrology, n. تَارِيخُ ٱلشُّهَدَآءِ — تَذْكِرَةُ (or تَرْجَمَةُ) ٱلشُّهَدَآءِ. A book of (Christian) —, كِتَابُ سِنْكِسَارٍ.

Marum, n. The plant "old man," رَيْحَانٌ — حَبَقُ ٱلشُّيُوخِ. ٱلْمَرْوُ — ٱلشُّيُوخِ.

Marvel, n. غَرِيبَة — عَجِيبَة pl. عَجَائِبُ — مُعْجِزَة pl. مُعْجِزَات pl. غَرَائِبُ. The — of Peru, the flower so called, شَبُّ ٱللَّيْلِ. It is no — that..., لَيْسَ بِعَجِيبٍ أَن.

Marvel, v.i. إِنْذَهَلَ — أَخَذَهُ ٱلْعَجَبُ — تَعَجَّبَ — إِسْتَعْجَبَ.

Marvellous, a. عَجِيب — غَرِيب — بَدِيع. A — thing, عَجِيبَة pl. عَجَائِبُ — غَرِيبَة pl. غَرَائِبُ. What a — thing! يَا لِلْعَجَبِ.

Marvellously, a. عَجَبًا — بِنَوْعٍ عَجِيبٍ. He was helped —, عَجِبَتْ مُسَاعَدَتُهُ.

Mary, n. The name, مَرْيَم. The Virgin Mary, مَرْيَمُ ٱلْعَذْرَآءُ.

Masculine, a. In the — gender, مُذَكَّر. To put into the — gender, ذَكَّرَ; to be put into the — gender, تَذَكَّرَ. A — woman, إِمْرَأَةٌ فَحْلَةٌ — مُذَكَّرَة — مُذَكَّرَة. A — man, رَجُلٌ فَحِيلٌ. Masculine vigour, of a stallion, فُحُولَة — فَحْلَة.

Masculineness, n. فَحَالَة — فَحْلَة.

Mash, n. A mixture, مِزَاج — خَلِيط — تَخْلِيط — خِلْط. Bran and water, مَعْجُونُ نُخَالَةٍ — سَلِيخَةُ نُخَالَةٍ.

Mash, v.t. To bruise into a soft mass, دَهَكَ — عَفَسَ. To mix, خَلَطَ.

Mash-tub, n. مِعْجَن.

Mashy, a. مَعْجُون — مُعَفَّس.

Mask, n. A cover for the face, وَجْهٌ قُلْعَةٍ — وَجْهٌ عَارِيَّةٍ. A disguise, لِبْسُ تَنْكِيرٍ. A pretence, حِيلَة — دُولَاب — حُجَّة — كَيْد. One wearing a —, مُتَمَسْخِر — لَابِسُ وَجْهٍ عَارِيَّةٍ. Under the — of, تَحْتَ صُورَةٍ — كَأَنَّ — بِٱلتَّصَوُّرِ. To throw off the —, كَشَفَ — رَفَعَ عَنْ وَجْهِهِ — شَالَ بُرْقُعَ ٱلْحَيَآءِ — عَنْ وَجْهِهِ ٱلْغِمَآءَ — أَظْهَرَ ٱلْمُخْتَبِي — ٱلْغِمَآءَ.

Mask, v.t. To put on a mask, لَبَّسَ-وَجْهَ عَارِيَّةٍ. To cover under false appearances, to hide, سَتَّرَ — سَتَرَ. To conceal from view, حَجَبَ-عَنِ ٱلنَّظَرِ. To — one's proceedings, to use stratagem, تَحَيَّلَ. To — a battery, حَجَبَ ٱلطَّابِيَةَ — سَتَرَ ٱلطَّابِيَةَ. *See also to* Disguise, v.t.

Mask, v.i. To put a — on one's self, لَبِسَ وَجْهَ عَارِيَّةٍ. To disguise one's self, تَخَفَّى — تَنَكَّرَ. To — one's sentiments, تَسَتَّرَ.

Masker, n. مُتَمَسْخِر — لَابِسُ وَجْهٍ عَارِيَّةٍ.

Mason, n. فَاعِل pl. فُعُول — بَنَّآء pl. بَنَّاؤُونَ — مِعْمَار. *See also* Freemason, n.

Masonic, a. Belonging to the Freemasons, مُتَعَلِّقٌ — فِرْمَاسِيُونِيٌّ بِٱلْفِرْمَسِيُونِ.

Masonry, n. The occupation of a mason, شُغْلٌ — صِنَاعَةُ ٱلْبَنَّآءِ. Work done by a mason, عِمَارَة — بِنَايَة — بُنْيَان — بِنْيَة — ٱلْبَنَّآءِ — رَصْفُ ٱلْحِجَارَةِ.

Masora, n. تَأْلِيفٌ يَهُودِيٌّ فِي تَفْسِيرِ نُصُوصِ ٱلْكُتُبِ ٱلْمُنَزَّلَةِ ٱلْعِبْرَانِيَّةِ.

Masorite, n. مُؤَلِّفٌ يَهُودِيٌّ مِنْ مُفَسِّرِي نُصُوصِ ٱلْكُتُبِ ٱلْمُنَزَّلَةِ ٱلْعِبْرَانِيَّةِ.

Masquerade, n. An assembly wearing masks, جَمْلَة — مَسْخَرَة مِنَ ٱلْمُتَمَسْخِرِينَ. *See also* Disguise, n.

Masquerade, v.i. To assemble in masks, تَمَسْخَرُوا. *See also to* Mask, v.i.

Masquerader, n. مُتَمَسْخِر — لَابِسُ وَجْهٍ عَارِيَّةٍ.

Mass, n. A heap, جُمْلَة — كُومَة — هِدْفَة. The bulk, greater part, أَغْلَبُ — أَكْثَرُ — جُمْهُور — جُلٌّ — جُلَال. An assemblage, جَمْع — مَجْمُوع — جَمَاعَة. A slice, فِلْقَة — شَرِيحَة. A round —, كُتْلَة. A quantity, مِقْدَار. Many, عِدَّة — كَثِير. A large — of stone, صَخْرَة — صَمْدَة. Silver in —, فِضَّةٌ كُتْلَةٌ. In —,

بِٱلْكُلِّيَّةِ - بِٱلْجُمْلَةِ. He took the — of it, (جُلاَلَهُ or) أَخَذَ جُلَّهُ ². To become a —, heap, إِسْتَهْدَفَ. *See also* Heap, Lump, *n.*

Mass, *n.* The communion service in the Church of Rome, طَقْسُ ٱلْقُدَّاسِ - ٱلْقُدَّاسُ. To say —, قَدَّسَ. To hear —, حَضَرَ ٱلْقُدَّاسَ ². Low —, قُدَّاسٌ صَغِيرٌ; high —, قُدَّاسٌ حَبْرُوتٌ - قُدَّاسٌ كَبِيرٌ. To offer up a —, قَدَّمَ قُدَّاسًا.

Mass, *v.t.* To throw together, أَجْمَلَ - جَمَّعَ - ² جَمَعَ.

Mass-book, *n.* *See* Missal, *n.*

Massacre, *n.* مَقْتَلَةٌ - ذَبْحٌ - قَتْلٌ - قَتْلٌ عَامٌّ.

Massacre, *v.t.* قَتَّلَ - ذَبَّحَ - ² ذَبَحَ.

Massicot, *n.* }
Masticot, } ضَرْبٌ مِنَ ٱلدِّهَانِ.

Massiness, *n.* } The state of being massy, big, كُبْرٌ - جَسَامَةٌ - عِظَمٌ.
Massiveness, } Ponderousness, ثِقْلٌ - ثِقَلٌ. Solidity, مَتَانَةٌ - صَلَابَةٌ.

Massive, *a.* } Large, جَسِيمٌ - كَبِيرٌ - عَظِيمٌ. Solid, صَمِيمٌ -
Massy, } صَلِيبٌ - مَتِينٌ. Heavy, ثَقِيلٌ - وَزِينٌ. Solid, of masonry, رَصِيفٌ. Massive silver, فِضَّةٌ صَبٌّ.

Mass-meeting, *n.* جَوْقٌ - كَوْكَبَةٌ - غَمْرَةٌ - عُمُومَةٌ *pl.* عَمٌّ - جَمْعٌ أَجْوَاقٌ.

Mast, *n.* As of a ship, صَارِيَةٌ *pl.* صَوَارٍ - دَقَلٌ *pl.* أَدْقَالٌ. (*See also* Acorn, Nut, *n.*) Half-mast high, مَنْصُوبٌ نِصْفَ نَصْبَةٍ - مَنَكَّسٌ. To lower a flag half-mast high, خَنَّقَ ² (or خَفَضَ ²) ٱلْبَنْدِيرَةَ (يَعْنِي نَكَّسَهَا وَذَلِكَ عَلَامَةٌ لِلْحُزْنِ).

Masted, *a.* Having one mast, أَبُو صَارِيَةٍ - ذُو دَقَلٍ; having several masts, أَبُو صَوَارٍ - ذُو أَدْقَالٍ.

Master, *n.* One who directs, سَائِسٌ - مُدَبِّرٌ - ضَابِطُ ٱلزِّمَامِ - ضَابِطٌ *pl.* ضُبَّاطٌ - مُبَاشِرٌ. A lord, proprietor, سَيِّدٌ *pl.* سَادَةٌ - بَعْلٌ - صَاحِبٌ *pl.* أَصْحَابٌ - رَبٌّ *pl.* أَرْبَابٌ - مَوْلًى *pl.* مَوَالٍ. A teacher, مُعَلِّمٌ - مُدَرِّسٌ. Master, as of any trade, مُتَعَقِّدٌ - أُسْتَاذٌ *pl.* أَسَاتِيذُ; of any science, أُسْتَاذٌ - مَاهِرٌ فِي. One who overcomes, غَالِبٌ. A chief, principal, رَئِيسٌ *pl.* رُؤَسَاءُ - أَوَّلٌ - مُتَقَدِّمٌ. One uncontrolled, مُتَصَرِّفٌ - صَاحِبُ ٱلْٱخْتِيَارِ. Master of a ship, قُبْطَانٌ - رَئِيسُ مَرْكَبٍ - نَاخُوذَاةٌ *pl.* نَوَاخِذَةٌ. A title of young men, أَفَنْدِي - خَوَاجَةٌ. Master of the house, صَاحِبُ ٱلْبَيْتِ - صَاحِبٌ. Master of an inn, صَاحِبُ ٱلْمَنْزِلِ - لُوكَنْدَةٍ. Every one is — in his own house, كُلٌّ وَاحِدٍ فِي بَيْتِهِ سُلْطَانٌ. To be a — in, to be skilled, as in handicraft, تَعَقَّدَ فِي. To be — of the situation, قَبَضَ عَلَى ٱلتَّصَرُّفِ فِي ٱلْحَالِ - إِسْتَوْلَى عَلَى ٱلْمَوْقِعِ. To become — of, as of a trade, تَأَخَّذَ -

عِنْدَهُ مِنَ ٱلْ ... To possess, حَازَ ² - مَلَكَ ² - إِقْتَنَى. To obtain command over, إِسْتَوْلَى عَلَى.

Grand master, رَئِيسٌ أَعْظَمُ.

Head master, as of a school, رَائِيسُ ٱلْمُعَلِّمِينَ.

Master-at-arms, رَئِيسُ ٱلضَّبْطِيَّةِ - صَاحِبُ ٱلشُّرْطَةِ.

Master of Arts, مُجَازٌ (or مُدَرِّسُ) ٱلْعُلُومِ ٱلْأَدَبِيَّةِ.

Master of the Ceremonies, تَشْرِيفَاتْجِي.

Master of the Horse, أَمِيرُ ٱلْآخُورِ.

Master, *v.t.* To obtain, acquire, نَالَ ² - فَازَ بِ - إِسْتَحْوَذَ عَلَى - بَلَغَ ² - حَصَلَ عَلَى - حَظِيَ بِ. To obtain command over, إِسْتَوْلَى عَلَى. To learn, تَعَلَّمَ. To be master of, learned, in, يَعْلُو .aor عَلَا بِ. To conquer, حَاذَ ² - إِسْتَحْوَذَ عَلَى - تَمَهَّرَ فِي - أَنْجَحَ بِ - غَلَبَ. To hold in check, ضَبَطَ ² - أَوْقَفَ - حَاشَ ². To tame, أَنَّسَ - أَقْمَعَ - قَمَعَ. To be master of one's self, ضَبَطَ نَفْسَهُ ² - تَقَمَّعَ - تَمَاسَكَ. He mastered his affair, إِسْتَفْلَجَ (or إِسْتَفْلَجَ) بِأَمْرِهِ. He mastered the thing by knowledge, رَصَنَ ٱلشَّيْءَ مَعْرِفَةً.

Master-builder, *n.* رَائِيسُ ٱلْبَنَّائِينَ - مِعْمَارٌ.

Master-hand, *n.* مَاهِرٌ - مُعَلِّمٌ - أُسْتَاذٌ - مُتَعَقِّدٌ - عَبْقَرِيٌّ.

Master-key, *n.* A key that opens many locks, مِفْتَاحُ ٱلْأَبْوَابِ. A clue to difficulties, حَلُّ ٱلْمُشْكِلَاتِ.

Masterly, *a.* جَيِّدٌ - فَائِقٌ - حَاذِقٌ - مِفَنٌّ - صَنِيعٌ - مُتَعَقِّدٌ. To be —, as in handicraft, تَعَقَّدَ فِي.

Master-mind, *n.* عَقْلٌ بَارِعٌ.

Master-piece, *n.* مُلْحَةٌ *pl.* مُلَحٌ - شُغْلٌ أُسْتَاذٍ - شُغْلٌ بَارِعٌ.

Mastership, *n.* Superiority, رِئَاسَةٌ - تَقَدُّمٌ. The office of a master, teacher, وَظِيفَةُ ٱلْمُعَلِّمِ - مَنْصِبُ ٱلْمُعَلِّمِ. *See also* Mastery, *n.*

Master-stroke, *n.* إِصَابَةٌ - إِصَابَةُ أُسْتَاذٍ - سَدَادٌ.

Mastery, *n.* Dominion, تَسَلُّطٌ. Preëminence, فَضْلٌ - تَقَدُّمٌ. Control, ضَبْطٌ. Victory, إِسْتِحْوَاذٌ - غَلَبَةٌ - فَوْزٌ - ظَفَرٌ - نَصْرٌ. Eminent skill, تَعَقُّدٌ - بَرَاعَةٌ - بُرُوعٌ - مَهَارَةٌ. To strive for the —, جَاهَدَ. To get the — over, to overcome, إِسْتَحْوَذَ عَلَى - إِسْتَعْلَى عَلَى - يَعْلُو .aor عَلَا عَلَى - نَصَرَ عَلَى ² - تَغَلَّبَ عَلَى; to subdue, قَهَرَ ² - أَقْمَعَ; to surpass, excel, بَهَرَ ² - فَاقَ ². To have under one's control, authority, تَبَوَّأَ مِنْ: The man possesses the — over his wife, like as he possesses the same over his house, ٱلرَّجُلُ يَتَبَوَّأُ مِنْ أَهْلِهِ كَمَا يَتَبَوَّأُ مِنْ دَارِهِ. *See also under to* Master, *v.t.*, *and* Master, *n.*

Masthead, *n.* رَأْسُ ٱلصَّارِيَةِ - رَأْسُ ٱلدَّقَلِ - جَامُورٌ. To —, جَعَلَ ² عَلَى رَأْسِ ٱلصَّارِيَةِ قِصَاصًا لَهُ.

Mastic, *n.* }
Mastich, } عِلْكَة ـ المُصْطَكَا . A medicine made of —, دَوَآءٌ مُمَصْطَكٌ .

Masticable, *a.* عَالِكٌ ـ عَلِكٌ ـ يُمْضَغُ .

Masticate, *v.t.* ²لَاكَ ـ ²مَضَغَ ـ ²عَلَكَ .

Masticatory, *a.* مَاضِغٌ ـ عَالِكٌ .

Masticatory, *n.* عِلْكَة ـ لَوَاكٌ ـ مَضَاغٌ .

Masticot, *n.* *See* Massicot, *n.*

Mastiff, *n.* دِرْوَاس *pl.* دَرَاوِيس .

Mastitis, *n.* Inflammation of the breast, دَآءُ ٱلصَّدْرِ .

Mastless, *a.* Without a mast, مِنْ غَيْرِ دَقَلٍ ـ بِلَا صَارِيَةٍ .

Mastodon, *n.* حَيَوَانٌ يُشْبِهُ ٱلْفِيلَ غَيْرُ مَوْجُودٍ ٱلْآنَ .

Mastoid, *a.* عَلَى هَيْئَةِ حَلَمَةِ ٱلْبِزِّ ـ فِي شَكْلِ ٱلسَّعْدَانَةِ .

Masturbation, *n.* إِسْتِجْلَابُ ٱلذَّكَرِ ـ إِسْتِمْنَاءٌ . To practise —, ²طَرَقَ زَوْجَهُ ـ إِسْتَمْنَى .

Mat, *n.* Of straw or rushes, بَارِيَة ـ حَصِير (*vulg.* حَصِيرَة) *pl.* حُصُر . A long —, نَخّ *pl.* أَنْخَاخ . A — of wooden reeds, بَارِيّ *or* بُورِيّ *pl.* بَوَارِيّ . A maker of mats, حُصْرِيّ .

Mat, *v.t.* To cover with mats, غَطَّى بِحُصُرٍ . To spread mats over a floor, ²فَرَشَ بِحُصُرٍ . To press together into a mass, as the hair, *etc.*, شَعَّثَ . Matted, of hair, عَكِش ; to be matted, of hair, تَعَكَّشَ .

Mat, *v.i.* To become pressed into a mass, تَلَبَّدَ ـ ²غَبِيَ ـ تَشَعَّثَ .

Matador, *n.* A bull-fighter, مُقَاتِلُ ٱلثَّوْرِ .

Match, *n.* One who is equal to another, قِرْن ـ مَسَدّ ـ بَوَآءٌ *pl.* أَقْرَان ـ قَرِين *pl.* قُرَنَآء ـ مِثْل ـ مِثَال . That which suits or tallies with another, مُطَابِقَة ـ طِبْق ـ مُحَاذَاة ـ أَخ ـ أَخُو ـ أُخْت ـ مُقَابِل ـ قَبِيل ـ شِبْه ـ شَبِيه *pl.* أَشْبِهَة . A pair, زَوْجَان *pl.* أَزْوَاج ; they are a —, pair, هُمَا زَوْج ـ هُمَا زَوْجَان . A contest, مُسَابَقَة ـ سِبَاق . A game, لُعْبَة ـ دَسْت ـ دَوْر . A lucifer —, نُبَيْخَة ـ عُود كِبْرِيت ـ كِبْرِيتَة . Marriage, زَوَاج ـ زِيجَة .

A bad match, marriage, زَوَاجٌ مَشْؤُومٌ ـ زِيجَةٌ غَيْرُ مُنَاسِبَةٍ .

A good match, marriage, زِيجَةٌ مُنَاسِبَةٌ .

A love match, زِيجَةُ عِشْقٍ ـ زِيجَةٌ عَنْ حُبٍّ ـ زَوَاجٌ ٱخْتِيَارِيٌّ .

A quick match, فَتِيلٌ شَعَّالٌ .

A runaway match, زِيجَةُ فِرَارٍ ـ زِيجَةُ هَزِيمَةٍ .

A running match, مُرَاكَضَة ـ مُسَابَقَة .

A slow match, فَتِيلٌ خَامِدٌ .

A swimming match, مُسَابَحَة .

A wrestling match, مُصَارَعَة .

To be a match for, to equal, إِسْتَقْرَنَ ل ـ مَاثَلَ ـ حَاذَى ; to be equal to, capable of, كَانَ مُعِيدًا ل .

To meet one's match, لَقِيَ مَنْ حَاذَاهُ ـ ²لَقِيَ مَنْ قَعَدَ بِهِ .

Match, *v.t.* To pair, أَلَّفَ ـ زَوَّجَ شَيْئًا بِشَيْءٍ ـ زَوَّجَ إِلَى . To suit, طَابَقَ ـ وَفَّقَ ل ـ قَانَى . To marry, زَوَّجَ ب ـ زَوَّجَ . To equal, مَاثَلَ ـ عَادَلَ ـ حَاذَى ـ آزَرَ . She matched her in beauty, حَاذَتْهَا (*or* تَارَتْهَا) فِي ٱلْحُسْنِ . The thing matched the thing, آزَرَ ٱلشَّيْءُ ٱلشَّيْءَ . *See also to* Equal, *v.t.*

Match, *v.i.* To be equal in size, figure, *etc.* They two matched, تَوَافَقَا ـ تَمَاثَلَا ـ تَسَاوَيَا ـ تَحَاذَيَا . They matched together, of many, وَافَقَ بَعْضُهُمْ بَعْضًا . To marry, تَزَوَّجَ . To add something to of a like kind, ²جَمَعَ بَيْنَ وَبَيْنَ مِثْلِهِ ـ ²قَرَنَ بِمِثْلِهِ . *See also to* Resemble, *v.i.*

Matchless, *a.* فَائِق *pl.* فُوَقَآء ـ فَرِيد ـ وَحِيد ـ مَا لَهُ مَثِيل ـ مَا لَهُ نَظِير .

Matchlessly, *ad.* إِطْلَاقًا ـ مِنْ غَيْرِ تَشْبِيهٍ ـ بِلَا قِيَاسٍ .

Matchlessness, *n.* بَرَاعَة ـ فَضْل ـ نَيَافَة .

Match-lock, *n.* مِكْحَلَة فَتِيلَة *pl.* مَكَاحِل .

Match-maker, *n.* A maker of brimstone matches, صَانِعُ كِبْرِيتَات ـ كِبْرِيتَاجِي . One who effects marriages, مُجَاهِن *fem.* مُجَاهِنَة . A female professional —, خَاطِبَة ـ خَطَّابَة .

Match-making, *n.* The making of lucifers, صَنْعُ ٱلْكِبْرِيتَاتِ ; effecting marriages, خِطَابَة ـ تَجْهِنَة .

Mate, *n.* A husband, زَوْج ـ قَرِين ; wife, قَرِينَة ـ ذَاتُ قَرِينٍ ـ زَوْجَة . A companion, associate, حَرِيف *pl.* حُرَفَآء ـ إِلْف *pl.* آلَاف ـ رَفِيق *pl.* رُفَقَآء ـ صَاحِب *pl.* أَصْحَاب ـ قَرِين *pl.* قُرَنَآء . The second officer in a vessel, مُعَاوِن . Mate, in chess, شَاه مَات .

Mate, *v.t.* To join together, ²قَرَنَ بَيْنَ ـ أَقْرَنَ بَيْنَ ـ أَرْفَقَ ب . *See also to* Match, Checkmate, *v.t.*

Mateless, *a.* بِلَا صَاحِبٍ ـ بِدُونِ رَفِيقٍ .

Materia Medica, *n.* Medicines, أَدْوِيَة ; science of medicines, عِلْمُ ٱلْأَدْوِيَةِ .

Material, *a.* Consisting of matter, مَادِّيّ ـ هَيُولَانِيّ ـ جَوْهَرِيّ . Corporal, جِسْمَانِيّ ـ جِسْمِيّ . Important, جَوْهَرِيّ ـ مُهِمّ ـ أَهَمّ ـ أَلْزَم ـ ضَرُورِيّ ـ لَازِم . The seven — substances, ٱلْأَجْسَامُ ٱلسَّبْعَةُ . The — substances of different natures, ٱلْأَجْسَامُ ٱلْمُخْتَلِفَةُ ٱلطَّبَائِعِ . Not —, not necessary, غَيْرُ لَازِمٍ ـ غَيْرُ مُهِمٍّ ـ غَيْرُ ضَرُورِيٍّ . *See also* Important, Gross, *a.*

Material, *n.* The substance of which any thing is made, مَاهِيَّة . Materials, requisites, مَوَادّ ـ لَوَازِم ـ مُؤْنَة ـ أَجْزَآء . Raw materials, مَوَادُّ خَامٌ – مَاهِيَّاتٌ. Building materials, لَوَازِمُ لِلْبِنَاءِ; in a more general sense, كَرَسْتَة. Combustible materials, مَأْكُولُ ٱلنَّارِ – حَرَّاق. War materials, أَدَاةُ (or مُهِمَّاتُ) ٱلْحَرْبِ. Writing materials, أَدَاةُ ٱلْكِتَابَةِ. Materials, subjects, matter, مَوَادُّ – أَبْوَاب – مَوْضُوعَات – أَسْبَاب.

Materialism, *n.* مَذْهَبُ ٱلدَّهْرِيَّةِ – مَذْهَبُ – جَحْدُ ٱلْإِلٰهِيَّاتِ – إِلْحَاد – ٱلطَّبِيعِيِّينَ.

Materialist, *n.* دَهْرِيٌّ *pl.* دَهْرِيَّة – جَاحِدُ ٱلْإِلٰهِيَّاتِ – مِنْ أَهْلِ مَذْهَبِ ٱلطَّبِيعِيِّينَ – مُلْحِد.

Materiality, *n.* Material existence, هَيُولِيَّة – جِسْمِيَّة – مَادِّيَّة. Importance, مَهَمَّة – هِمَّة – لُزُوم – ضَرُورَة – ضَرُورِيَّة.

Materialize, *v.t.* To render corporeal, جَسَّمَ. To consider material as opposed to spiritual, أَعَدَّ-طَبِيعِيًّا – أَنْزَلَ-مَنْزِلَةَ ٱلطَّبِيعِيَّاتِ.

Materially, *ad.* As opposed to spiritually, هَيُولِيَّةً – جِسْمِيَّةً – جِسْمِيًّا. In an important manner, بِنَوْعٍ مُهِمٍّ – جَزِيلًا – جِدًّا.

Materialness, *n.* *See* Materiality, *n.*

Materiel, *n.* لَوَازِمُ. War —, مُهِمَّاتُ ٱلْحَرْبِ.

Maternal, *a.* أُمِّيٌّ – أُمَوِيٌّ – مَنُوطٌ بِٱلْأُمِّ. Maternal affection, مَحَبَّةُ ٱلْأُمِّ لِأَوْلَادِهَا. A — parent, أُمٌّ.

Maternally, *ad.* مِثْلَ ٱلْأُمِّ – أُمَوِيَّةً.

Maternity, *n.* أُمِّيَّة – أُمَوِيَّة.

Mathematic, *a.* } رِيَاضِيٌّ – هَنْدَسِيٌّ. Mathematical instru-
Mathematical, } ments, أَدَاةُ (or آلَاتُ) ٱلْهَنْدَسَةِ.

Mathematically, *ad.* حَسَبَ ٱلْقَوَاعِدِ ٱلرِّيَاضِيَّةِ – حَسَبَ قَوَاعِدِ ٱلْهَنْدَسَةِ.

Mathematician, *n.* عَالِمٌ بِٱلرِّيَاضِيَّاتِ – مُهَنْدِس – أَهْلُ هَنْدَسَةٍ.

Mathematics, *n.* ٱلْعُلُومُ ٱلرِّيَاضِيَّةُ – عِلْمُ ٱلْهَنْدَسَةِ.

Matins, *n.* صَلَاةُ ٱلضُّحَى – صَلَاةُ ٱلْفَجْرِ.

Matrice, *n.* The mould in which anything is cast, قَالِب *pl.* قَوَالِبُ – مِسْبَكَة; the female as opposed to the male mould, أُمٌّ *pl.* أُمَّهَات. Punches and matrices, أَبَّهَاتٌ وَأُمَّهَاتٌ. The place where any thing is found, مَلْقًى – مَوْجِد.

Matricidal, *a.* مُتَعَلِّقٌ بِقَتْلِ ٱلْأُمِّ.

Matricide, *n.* قَاتِلُ أُمِّهِ.

Matriculate, *v.t.* جَعَلَ- (or صَيَّرَ) مِنْ أَعْضَاءِ دَارِ ٱلْفُنُونِ رَسْمًا.

Matriculate, *v.i.* صَارَ مِنْ أَعْضَاءِ دَارِ ٱلْفُنُونِ رَسْمًا.

Matriculate, *n.* }
Matriculated, *a.* } مُجَاوِر – مِنْ أَعْضَاءِ دَارِ ٱلْفُنُونِ رَسْمًا.

Matriculation, *n.* إِنْضِمَامٌ رَسْمِيٌّ إِلَى أَعْضَاءِ دَارِ ٱلْفُنُونِ.

Matrimonial, *a.* مُخْتَصٌّ بِٱلزِّيجَةِ. A — alliance, زَوَاج.

Matrimonially, *ad.* بِٱلزَّوَاجِ – بِٱلزِّيجَةِ.

Matrimony, *n.* *See* Marriage, *n.*

Matrix, *n.* The womb, رَحِم *pl.* أَرْحَام – أُمُّ ٱلْأَوْلَادِ.

Matron, *n.* A middle-aged woman, نَصَف – مُسْلِف. A grave, good woman, إِمْرَأَةٌ صَالِحَةٌ. A female superintendent, مُدَبِّرَة – نَاظِرَة – مُبَاشِرَة.

Matronal, *a.* Of duties, those of a female superintendent, وَظِيفَةُ ٱلنَّاظِرَةِ.

Matronly, *a.* كَٱلنَّصَفِ – كَٱلْمُسْلِفِ.

Mattamore, *n.* مَطْمُورَة *pl.* مَطَامِيرُ.

Matted, *a.* Pressed together, of hair, *etc.*, مُتَلَبِّد.

Matter, *n.* The first principles of any material, هِيُولَى – هَيُولَى. Substance, جَوْهَر – مَادَّة *pl.* مَوَادُّ. Subject matter, مَوْضُوع – مَطْلَب – بَاب *pl.* أَبْوَاب – ٱلْمَبْحُوثُ فِيهِ – مَادَّة. A cause, claim, دَعْوَى *pl.* دَعَاوَى. An affair, أَمْر *pl.* أُمُور – مَصْلَحَة – مَادَّة – بَاب *pl.* أَبْوَاب – قَضِيَّة *pl.* قَضَايَا – قِصَّة *pl.* قِصَص. A — of fact, أَمْرٌ حَقِيقِيٌّ – أَمْرٌ مُحَقَّقٌ. Purulent —, pus, غُثّ – غَثِيث – غَثِيثَة – قَيْح – مِدَّة. Fluid — which collects in the corners of the eye, رَمَص – غَمَص; the same when it is dry, رَمَص. A small —, أَمْرٌ وَجِيزٌ; a great —, أَمْرٌ مُهِمٌّ – مَهَمَّة. To press — out of a wound, إِسْتَغَثَّ. Matters were in that state until he arrived, إِنْقَضَى ٱلْحَالُ إِلَى أَنْ وَصَلَ. What's the —? مَاذَا – مَا جَرَى – مَاذَا صَارَ *vulg.* أَيْش صَائِر. What's the — with you? مَا لَكَ – مَا بِكَ. Let us hear the conclusion of the whole —, فَلْنَسْمَعْ خِتَامَ ٱلْأَمْرِ كُلِّهِ. It makes no — to me, لَا فَرْقَ عِنْدِي. I do not wish to be a judge in these matters, لَسْتُ أَشَاءُ أَنْ أَكُونَ قَاضِيًا لِهٰذِهِ ٱلْأُمُورِ.
As to that matter, بِخُصُوصِ تِلْكَ ٱلْمَادَّةِ – نَظَرًا لِتِلْكَ ٱلْمَصْلَحَةِ.
In the matter of, بِخُصُوصِ – فِي مَادَّةِ – عَنْ.
The sum of the matter is, خِتَامُ ٱلْأَمْرِ هُوَ – ٱلْحَاصِلُ.
To come to the matter, تَصَدَّى لِلْأَمْرِ; (adverbially), وَٱلْحَاصِلُ.
To settle matters, أَصْلَحَ ٱلْأُمُورَ. To settle one's own matters, تَدَبَّرَ – دَبَّرَ أُمُورَهُ – طَفَّلَ أَمْرَهُ *vulg.* إِصْطَفَلَ (or this latter may be distorted from the root فَصَلَ).

Matter, *v.i.* To be of importance, لَزِمَ – هَمَّ. To form pus, غَثَّ – أَغَثَّ – أَمَدَّ. It matters not to me, لَا فَرْقَ عِنْدِي – مَا عَلَيَّ. It does not —, لَا بَأْسَ فِيهِ – مَا يُخَالِفُ. What does it — to you, مَا لَكَ وَذٰلِكَ *vulg.* أَيْش يَخُصُّكَ.

Matterless, *a.* Void of matter, substance, خَالٍ مِنَ ٱلْمَادَّةِ. Void of pus, خَالٍ مِنَ ٱلْمِدَّةِ.

Matter-of-fact, *a.* أَسَدٌّ ـ سَدِيد ـ سَلِيم ـ نَصُوح.

Mattery, *a.* *See* Purulent, *a.*

Matting, *n.* حَصِير ـ حُصُر. *See* Mat, *n.*

Mattock, *n.* مِعْوَل *pl.* مَعَاوِل.

Mattress, *n.* فِرَاش ـ طُمَّاحَة ـ طَرَّاحَة ٱلْفَرْشَة. A light —, such as is spread upon a couch frame, مَرْتَبَة *pl.* مَرَاتِب.

Maturant, *n.* دَوَآء مُنْضِج.

Maturate, *v.i.* Of a tumour, أَمَدَّ ـ أَغَثَّ ـ غَثَّ ـ غَذَّ ـ تَقَيَّح.

Maturate, *v.t.* Of a tumour, *etc.*, أَنْضَجَ.

Maturation, *n.* Suppuration, غُثِيث ـ غَذِيذَة.

Maturative, *a.* مُنْضِج.

Mature, *a.* Ripe, in a general sense, مُسْتَوٍ ـ أَدْرَكَ ـ بَالِغ. Perfect, تَامّ ـ كَامِل. Ripe, of fruits, يَانِع ـ نَضِيج ـ نَاضِج ـ طَيِّب. Of a mature age, بَالِغ ٱلرُّشْدِ ـ بَالِغ ٱلسِّنِّ ـ مُسْتَوٍ. Mature deliberation, مَشْوَرَة مُدَقَّقَة ـ تَأَمُّل كُلِّيّ. A man of — age, رَجُل كَامِل ٱلسِّنِّ; of — judgment, رَجُل عَاقِل ـ رَجُل رَزِين ـ رَجُل مُنَجَّذ.

Mature, *v.t.* To bring to perfection, أَتَمَّ ـ كَمَّلَ ـ أَبْلَغَ ـ بَلَّغَ. To ripen, أَنْضَجَ. To revolve, as in the mind, تَأَمَّلَ فِي.

Mature, *v.i.* To become ripe, إِسْتَوَى ـ نَضِجَ. To become perfect, تَكَمَّلَ ـ تَمَّ ـ تَكَمَّلَ. To become payable, حَلَّ مِيعَادُ ٱلدَّفْعِ ـ إِخْتَتَمَتِ ٱلْوَعْدَة.

Maturely, *ad.* With deliberation, بِٱنْتِبَاهٍ كُلِّيّ ـ بِتَأَمُّلٍ.

Maturescent, *a.* قَرِيب مِنَ ٱلِٱسْتِوَآءِ ـ عِنْدَ ٱلْبَلَاغِ ـ بَادِر.

Matureness, *n.* } State of being brought to perfection, بَلَاغ ـ
Maturity, } إِدْرَاك ـ بُلُوغ. Ripeness, as of fruits, إِسْتِوَآء ـ نُضْج; of age, بُلُوغ ـ سِنّ ٱلرُّشْدِ ـ أَشُدّ ـ رُشْد; of an affair, إِسْتِوَآء ـ إِسْتِحْكَام; of intellect, كَمَالُ ٱلْعَقْلِ. To attain to —, of fruits, أَنْضَجَ ـ نَضِجَ ـ بَدَرَ; of age, بَلَغَ أَشُدَّهُ ـ أَدْرَكَ; of any matter, إِسْتَحْكَمَ ـ إِسْتَوَى ـ أَدْرَكَ ـ بَلَغَ.

Matutinal, *a.* مُتَعَلِّق بِٱلصَّبَاحِ ـ مُخْتَصّ بِٱلضُّحَى.

Maudlin, *a.* Fuddled, سَكْرَان ـ مَسَّهُ سُكْر.

Maugre, *ad.* عَلَى رَغْمِ أَنْفِهِ ـ رَغْمًا عَن ـ غَصْبًا عَن.

Maul, *n.* *See* Mall, *n.*

Maul, *v.t.* نَكَى فِي ـ ضَرَبَ. They mauled him dreadfully, نَكَوا فِيهِ أَشَدَّ ٱلنِّكَايَةِ.

Maulstick, *n.* مَسْنَد يَدِ ٱلنَّقَّاشِ ـ سَنَدُ يَدِ ٱلنَّقَّاشِ.

Maund, *n.* The weight, مَنّ *pl.* أَمْنَان.

Maunder, *v.i.* *See to* Mutter, Grumble, *v.i.*

Maunday-Thursday, *n.* خَمِيسُ ٱلْعَهْدِ.

Mausolean, *a.* مُتَعَلِّق بِٱلتُّرَبِ.

Mausoleum, *n.* تُرْبَة *pl.* تُرَب ـ مَقَامٌ لِلْمَيِّتِ.

Mauve, *n.* The colour, مُوَر ـ لَوْن يَضْرِبُ إِلَى ٱلْأُرْجُوَانِ.

Mavis, *n.* *See* Thrush, *n.*

Maw, *n.* The stomach of a beast, كِرْش; of a bird, جِرِّيَّة ـ حَوْصَلَة ـ نَوْطَة.

Mawkish, *a.* بِلَا لَذَّةٍ ـ مَلِيخ ـ مَسِيخ ـ يُجْشَأُ عَنْهُ.

Mawkishness, *n.* عَدَمُ لَذَّةٍ ـ مَلَخ.

Maw-worm, *n.* دُودَة ـ صُغَار *coll.* دُود *pl.* دُودَان *and* دِيدَان.

Maxillar, *a.* } مُتَعَلِّق بِٱلْفَكِّ ـ فَكِّيّ.
Maxillary, }

Maxim, *n.* An established principle, قَاعِدَة *pl.* قَوَاعِد. To hold it as a —, إِتَّخَذَهُ قَاعِدَةً. *See also* Aphorism, Proverb, *n.*

Maximum, *n.* أَعْلَى دَرَجَةٍ ـ نِهَايَة ـ غَايَة. The — of the thermometer was . . . , أَعْلَى دَرَجَةِ مِيزَانِ ٱلْحَرَارَةِ كَانَتْ كَذَا.

Maximum, *a.* ٱلْأَعْظَمُ ـ ٱلْأَعْلَى.

May, *n.* The month of, شَهْرُ مَاي ـ أَيَّار. The hawthorn blossom, زَهْرُ ٱلْعِضَةِ ـ زَهْرُ شَجَرَةِ ٱلْعِضَاهِ.

May, *v. aux.* (*pret.*, Might), To be able, إِسْتَطَاعَ ـ قَدَرَ عَلَى ـ أَمْكَنَ. To be possible, مُمْكِن ـ يُمْكِن. As meaning perchance, رُبَّمَا ـ لَعَلَّ.

I may be happy, يُمْكِنُ أَنِّي أَسْعَدُ.

It may be so, رُبَّمَا يَكُونُ كَذَا.

It may be sufficient, لَعَلَّهُ كَافٍ.

May we not be forgiving? هَلَّا نَكُونُ مُسَامِحِينَ.

May he be my tutor? أَعَسَاهُ يَكُونُ مُدَرِّسِي.

May, *v.i.* To gather may, جَنَى زَهْرَ ٱلْعِضَاهِ.

May-bug, *n.* نَوْعٌ مِنَ ٱلْخُنْفُسِ.

May-day, *n.* رَأْسُ شَهْرِ مَاي.

Mayhap, *ad.* لَعَلَّ.

Mayor, *n.* أَمِينُ ٱلْمَدِينَةِ ـ رَئِيسُ أَعْيَانِ ٱلْبَلَدِ. Lord — of London, أَمِينُ مَدِينَةِ لَنْدَن.

Mayoralty, *n.* وَظِيفَةُ أَمِينِ ٱلْبَلَدِ ـ رِئَاسَةُ ٱلْأَعْيَانِ.

Mayoress, *n.* إِمْرَأَةُ أَمِينِ ٱلْبَلَدِ.

May-pole, *n.* نَصِيبَة يَرْقُصُونَ حَوْلَهَا فِي رَأْسِ شَهْرِ مَاي.

May-queen, *n.* جَارِيَة مُخْتَارَة يُكَلِّلُوهَا ٱلْمُعَيِّدُونَ عِنْدَ رَأْسِ شَهْرِ مَاي بِإِكْلِيلٍ مِنَ ٱلزَّهْرِ.

Mazarine, *n.* The colour, أَزْرَقُ غَامِق ـ أَزْرَق.

Maze, *n.* *See* Labyrinth, *n.*

Maze, *v.t.* حَيَّرَ ـ أَذْهَلَ ـ خَبَّلَ.

Mazy, *a.* *See* Labyrinthian, *a.*

M.C.S. (Member of the College of Surgeons), عِبَارَةٌ عَنْ مُجَازِ مَدْرَسَةِ ٱلْجِرَاحَةِ.

M.D. (Doctor of Medicine), عِبَارَةٌ عَنْ مُدَرِّسِ ـ مُجَازُ ٱلطِّبِّ ٱلطِّبِّ.

Me, *pr.* The objective case of I. To me, for me, لِأَجْلِي ـ لِي.

Mead, *n.* *See* Hydromel, *n.*

Mead, *n.* } **Meadow**, } رَوْضَة ـ رَبِيعَة ـ غُوطَالَة *pl.* رَوْض and رِيَاض and رِيضَان and رَوْضَات ـ مَرْج *pl.* مُرُوج.

Meager, *a.* } **Meagre**, } Lean, مُخْتَلٌّ ـ رَثِيث ـ رَثّ ـ غَثِيث ـ غَثّ ـ ضَعِيف ـ نَحِيف. Poor, destitute of richness, ضَعِيف ـ نَصِف ـ رَكِيك. Meagre language, كَلَامٌ غَثٌّ ـ كَلَامٌ رَثٌّ ـ رَكِيكٌ. Your speech is — and your arms worn out, حَدِيثُكُمْ غَثٌّ وَسِلَاحُكُمْ رَثٌّ. In speech there is that which is — and that which is vigorous, فِي ٱلْكَلَامِ ٱلْغَثُّ وَٱلسَّمِينُ. To be — in one's speech, أَغَثَّ فِي مَنْطِقِهِ (or فِي كَلَامِهِ). *See also* Barren, *a.*

Meagerly, *ad.* } **Meagrely**, } بِضَعْفٍ ـ بِخَلَلٍ ـ بِرَكَاكَةٍ.

Meagerness, *n.* } **Meagreness**, } Leanness, نَحَافَة ـ غَثَاثَة ـ خُلُول. Want of richness, قَصَف ـ دِقَّة ـ رَكَاكَة ـ غَثَاثَة ـ مَسْكَنَة ـ ضَعْف. *See also* Barrenness, *n.*

Meal, *n.* The substance of grain pounded to powder, طَحِين ـ دَقِيق. The food taken at one eating, أَكْل ـ أَكْلَة. To take a —, أَكَلَ أَكْلَةً [2]. He takes four meals a day, يَأْكُلُ فِي ٱلنَّهَارِ أَرْبَعَ وَقْعَاتٍ. I have made a hearty —, شَبِعْتُ ٱلْحَمْدُ لِلَّهِ.

Mealiness, *n.* لِيَانَة ـ لِينَة ـ طَحْن ـ دِقَّة.

Meal-time, *n.* سَاعَةُ ٱلْأَكْلِ ـ وَقْتُ ٱلْأَكْلِ.

Mealy, *a.* نَاعِم ـ لَيِّن ـ كَٱلطَّحِينِ ـ كَٱلدَّقِيقِ ـ أَدَقّ ـ دِقّ.

Mealy-mouthed, *a.* فَمٌ مَلِقٌ ـ مَلِق ـ فَمٌ مِشْغَبٌ ـ سَهْلُ ٱلْوَجْهِ.

Mean, *n.* The middle point, ٱلْوَسَطُ. A mean term, وَسَطٌ مُتَنَاسِبٌ. Intervening time, زَمَان ـ مُدَّة ـ غُضُون. An instrument, cause, وَاسِطَة ـ وَسِيلَة. *See also under* Means, *n.*

Mean, *a.* Despicable, base, رَذِيل ـ خَسِيس ـ سُفْلَانِيّ ـ خَزّ ـ حَقِير ـ أَشْقِيَاء *pl.* شَقِيّ ـ ذَلِيل ـ تَافِه. Poor, wretched, مَسَاكِين *pl.* مِسْكِين ـ رَقِيق ـ حَقِير ـ مِفْلَاق. Little, small, جُزْئِيّ ـ قَلِيل ـ تَافِه. Mean, paltry, things, دَقَائِقُ (or مَدَاقُّ) ٱلْأُمُور. Middle, مُتَوَسِّط ـ وَسَط. Coming between, وَاقِعٌ بَيْنَ ـ دَاخِلٌ بَيْنَ. *See also* Avaricious, Sordid, *a.*

Mean, *v.t.* To signify, عَنَى ـ ـ عَنَى بِ. To indicate, دَلَّ عَلَى ـ عَبَّرَ بِ or عَنْ [2]. To have in view, نَوَى ـ ـ عَمَدَ ـ قَصَدَ ـ ـ نَوَى أَنْ ـ تَعَمَّدَ ـ تَعَزَّمَ [2]. To — for, intend for, عَيَّنَ لِ ـ خَصَّصَ لِ. It means, namely, أَعْنِي or يَعْنِي. He meant me to understand by that . . . , أَرَادَنِي أَفْهَمُ بِذٰلِكَ كَذَا. What — you by this procession of yours? مَا هٰذِهِ ٱلزَّفَّةُ لَكُمْ. What do these things mean? مَا عَسَى أَنْ تَكُونَ هٰذِهِ.

Meander, *v.i.* تَفَتَّلَ ـ تَلَوَّى ـ تَضَوَّجَ.

Meandering, *a.* مُتَلَوٍّ ـ مُتَفَتِّل ـ مُتَضَوِّج.

Meaning, *n.* Signification, مَعْنِيَّة ـ مَعْنَاة ـ فَحْوَاء ـ فَحْوَى ـ مَحَطّ ـ مَضْمُون ـ عِبَارَات *pl.* عِبَارَة ـ مَعَانِي *pl.* مَعْنَى. The subject of a discourse, مُرَادُ ٱلْكَلَامِ ـ مَحَطُّ ٱلْكَلَامِ. A purpose, design, قَصْد ـ مَرَام ـ نِيَّة. An interpretation, تَأْوِيل. Having a double —, ذُو مَعْنَايَيْنِ. What is the — of this, مَا مَعْنَى هٰذَا. This and this are in — one, *i.e.*, have the same —, هٰذَا وَهٰذَا فِي ٱلْمَعْنَى وَاحِدٌ ـ هٰذَا فِي مَعْنَى هٰذَا. Of one and the same —, بِمَعْنًى وَاحِدٍ. If I do not know the —, إِنْ كُنْتُ لَا أَعْرِفُ ٱلْمَعْنَى (or قُوَّةَ ٱللُّغَةِ).

Meaningless, *a.* بِلَا مَعْنًى.

Meaningly, *ad.* بِمَرَامٍ ـ بِغَايَةٍ ـ بِمَعْنًى. Purposely, قَصْدًا ـ عَنْ قَصْدٍ.

Meanly, *ad.* Basely, بِخَسَاسَةٍ ـ بِرَذَالَةٍ. Poorly, wretchedly, بِمَسْكَنَةٍ ـ بِحَقَارَةٍ. In a small degree, جُزْئِيَّةً ـ قِلَّةً. Meanly clad, لَابِسٌ ثِيَابَ حَقَارَةٍ.

Meanness, *n.* Baseness, حَقَارَة ـ ذِلَّة ـ ذُلّ ـ خَسَاسَة. Poverty, paltriness, مَسْكَنَة ـ فَقْر ـ حَقَارَة ـ تَفَاهَة. Avarice, بُخْل ـ مَسَاكَة.

Means, *n.* An instrument, medium, وَاسِطَة ـ وَسَائِلُ *pl.* وَسِيلَة ـ وَسَائِط *pl.* طَرِيقَة ـ طَرَائِقُ *pl.* Wealth, ثَرْوَة ـ رِزْق ـ مَال. Livelihood, مَعَاش. Having small —, فَقِير ـ مُقِلّ ـ أَقَلّ. Having large —, غَنِيّ ـ صَاحِبُ مَالٍ. To take all — to . . . , عَمِلَ كُلَّ ٱلْوَسَائِطِ فِي كَذَا. They were a — to . . . , تَوَسَّطُوا فِي كَذَا. The only means I had was to go to him, مَا كَانَ فِي وُسْعِي إِلَّا ٱلذَّهَابُ إِلَيْهِ.

By all means, أَلْبَتَّةَ ـ عَلَى كُلِّ حَالٍ. I must by all means do so and so, يَنْبَغِي عَلَيَّ عَلَى كُلِّ حَالٍ أَنْ أَعْمَلَ كَذَا وَكَذَا.

By fair means, بِٱلطَّيِّبِ ـ بِوَسَائِطَ مُقْسِطَةٍ ـ طَوْعًا ـ بِصَلَاحٍ.

By foul means, قَهْرًا ـ عَنْوَةً ـ بِحِيلَةٍ.

By his means, عَلَى يَدِهِ ـ بِوَاسِطَتِهِ.

By no means, قَطْعًا ـ أَصْلًا ـ كَلَّا.

By some means or other, كَيْفَمَا كَانَ.

By what means, بِمَاذَا ـ كَيْفَ.

Lest by any means, لِئَلَّا.

To find the means, the money, تَكَلَّفَ بِٱلْمَصْرُوفِ ـ قَدَّمَ ٱلْمَصْرُوفَ.

To find the way, وَجَدَ طَرِيقَةً ـ تَدَبَّرَ *aor.* يَجِدُ.

To live on one's means, عَاشَ بِإِيرَادِهِ ـ عَاشَ مِنْ مَدْخُولِهِ.

Meantime, *ad.* / Meanwhile, } فِي أَثْنَاءِ ذٰلِكَ ـ فِي غُضُونِ ذٰلِكَ.

Measles, *n.* حَصْبَة ـ حَرْشَان ; in pork, جُذَام.

Measly, *a.* Covered with measles, مَحْصُوب ; of pork, مَجْذُوم.

Measurable, *a.* يُعَايَرُ ; of weight, extent, يُقَاسُ ; of capacity, يُكَالُ. Moderate, مُتَوَسِّط ـ مُقْتَصِد. Of small quantity, جُزْئِيٌّ.

Measurably, *ad.* مِنْ غَيْرِ إِفْرَاطٍ ـ بِٱلْقِيَاسِ.

Measure, *n.* Size, extent, مِقْدَار ـ قَدْر ـ قَدّ ـ إِمْتِدَاد ـ طَوْر. That which ascertains extent or weight, عِيَار ـ مِقْيَاس ـ قِيَاس ; of capacity, مِكْيَال ـ أَكْيَال *pl.* كَيْل. Weight, وَزْن. Extent of power or ability, إِقْتِدَار ـ طَاقَة ـ قُدْرَة ـ إِسْتِطَاعَة. Degree, rank, دَرَجَة ـ رُتْبَة. Measure, of music, وَزْن ـ إِيقَاع ; of poetry, بَحْر *pl.* بُحُور ـ وَزْنُ شِعْرٍ ـ أَعَارِيضُ *pl.* عَرُوض. A portion, حِصَّة ـ قِسْم ـ جُزْء *pl.* أَجْزَاء. Means to an end, وَسِيلَة *pl.* وَسَائِلُ ـ وَاسِطَة *pl.* وَسَائِطُ ـ تَدْبِير *pl.* تَدَابِيرُ. A stratum, طَبَقَة *pl.* طَبَقَات. Number, عَدَد. Good —, كَيْلٌ جَيِّدٌ. Measure piled up, كَيْلٌ مُعَرَّمٌ. Measure pressed down, كَيْلٌ مُلَبَّدٌ. Measure running over, كَيْلٌ فَائِضٌ. He exceeded his proper —, تَعَدَّى طَوْرَهُ ـ عَدَا طَوْرَهُ. One who gives short —, مُخْسِر ـ مُطَفِّف.

Beyond measure, إِلَى ٱلْغَايَةِ ـ فَوْقَ ٱلْحَدِّ. Beyond one's power, فَوْقَ ٱلطَّاقَةِ.

By measure, of capacity, بِٱلْكَيْلِ ; of weight, بِٱلْوَزْنِ ; of length, بِٱلْقِيَاسِ.

Coercive measures, تَدَابِيرُ جَبْرِيَّةٌ.

Common measure (mathematics), ٱلْمُشْتَرَكُ فِيهِ. Greatest common measure (mathematics), ٱلْمُشْتَرَكُ فِيهِ ٱلْأَخِيرُ.

Conservative measures, تَدَابِيرُ ٱحْتِيَاطِيَّةٌ.

Defensive measures, أَسْبَابُ دِفَاعٍ.

Disciplinary measures, تَدَابِيرُ تَهْذِيبِيَّةٌ.

Dry measures (of pulse), مِكْيَالُ ٱلْحُبُوبِ.

Energetic measures, تَدَابِيرُ قَوِيَّةٌ مُؤَثِّرَةٌ.

In a great measure, جِدًّا ـ كَثِيرًا. It was in a great measure owing to him, كَانَ هُوَ أَخَصَّ ٱلسَّبَبِ.

In measure, كِفَايَةً ـ بِٱلْحَقِّ ـ بِٱلْقِيَاسِ.

In some measure, عَلَى نَوْعٍ مَا ـ فِي وَجْهٍ مَا.

Legislative measures, تَدَابِيرُ تَنْظِيمِيَّةٌ.

Liberal measures, تَدَابِيرُ مُتَسَاهِلَةٌ.

Long measure, مِقْيَاسُ ٱلْمَسَاحَاتِ.

Measure of capacity, (of liquids), مِكْيَالُ ٱلْمَوَائِعِ.

Measure of weight, أَوْزَانُ ٱلْأَثْقَالِ.

Scant measure, إِيفَةٌ نَاقِصَةٌ.

To take a measure of, عَايَرَ ـ قَاسَ.

To take measures, دَبَّرَ تَدْبِيرًا ـ تَدَبَّرَ ـ إِتَّخَذَ أَسْبَابًا. He took proper measures to prevent such dangers, إِتَّخَذَ ٱلتَّدَابِيرَ ٱلنَّافِعَةَ لِحَسْمِ أَخْطَارٍ كَهٰذِهِ. He took all necessary measures, تَشَبَّثَ بِٱلْوَسَائِطِ ٱللَّازِمَةِ.

To take one's measure, أَخَذَ قِيَاسَهُ.

To take legal measures, اِلْتَجَأَ إِلَى ٱلشَّرْعِ ـ رَاجَعَ ٱلشَّرْعَ.

Measure, *v.t.* To ascertain extent or quantity, قَدَّرَ ـ عَايَرَ. To —, of long measure, قَاسَ ; of measure of capacity, كَالَ ـ كَيَّلَ ـ إِكْتَالَ. To —, or number, by conjecture, حَزَا ـ حَدَسَ ـ خَرَصَ ـ حَزَرَ ـ حَزَرَ ـ يَحْزُو *aor.* To — one thing by another, قَاسَ ـ عَلَى ـ قَاسَ ـ بِ. To make to measure, to proportion, قَدَّرَ ـ عَلَى ـ خَلَقَ ـ عَلَى. To — land, مَسَحَ ٱلْأَرْضَ ـ قَاسَ ٱلْأَرْضَ. To — one's language, وَزَنَ كَلَامَهُ ـ ضَبَطَ لَفْظَهُ ـ قَيَّدَ أَلْفَاظَهُ ـ يَزِنُ *aor.*

Measure, *v.i.* Of length, كَانَ طُولُهُ ; of capacity, كَانَ ٱتِّسَاعُهُ ; of extent, كَانَتْ مَسَاحَتُهُ ; of height, كَانَ ٱرْتِفَاعُهُ ; of number, quantity, كَانَ قَدْرُهُ ـ كَانَ مِقْدَارُهُ ; of bulk, size, كَانَ جِرْمُهُ.

Measured, *a.* Of weight or versification, مَوْزُون ; of capacity, مَكِيل ـ مَكْيُول. Equal, مُسَاوٍ. Uniform, عَلَى سِمَاطٍ ـ نَظِيرٌ لِ. Moderate, مُعْتَدِل ـ مُسَاوٍ ـ وَاحِد.

Measureless, *a.* لَا يُعَايَرُ ـ لَا يُقَاسُ. Boundless, غَيْرُ مَحْدُودٍ ـ بِلَا حَدّ. Vast, مُتَّسِع ـ وَاسِع.

Measurement, *n.* Of long measure, قِيَاس ; of measure of capacity, كِيَالَة ـ كَيْل ; of land, قِيَاس ـ مِسَاحَة. *See also* Mensuration, *n.*

Measurer, *n.* Of measures of capacity, كَيَّال ; of long measure, قَائِس ; of land, مَسَّاحُ ٱلْأَرْضِ ـ مَسَّاح.

Measuring-line, *n.* خَيْطُ (*or* حَبْلُ) ٱلْقِيَاسِ.

Measuring-rod, *n.* قَصَبَةُ ٱلْقِيَاسِ.

Meat, *n.* Food, قُوت ـ غِذَاء ـ طَعَام *pl.* أَطْعِمَة. Flesh for food, لَحْم ـ زَفَر. Provisions, ذَخِيرَة ـ مُؤْنَة. Dried —, flesh,

قَدِيد. Salt —, لَحْمٌ مُمَلَّحٌ. Forced —, حَشْوُ ٱللَّحْمِ. Hashed —, لَحْمٌ مَفْرُومٌ. Broken —, كِسَر. Roast —, لَحْمٌ مَشْوِيٌّ. Meats served up a second time, عُوَادَة. At —, at table, عَلَى ٱلسُّفْرَةِ. His — was bread and honey, كَانَ طَعَامُهُ خُبْزًا وَعَسَلًا. To sit at —, قَعَدَ عَلَى ٱلسُّفْرَةِ ε.

Meat-offering, n. تَقْدِمَة.

Meatus, n. The — of the vagina, السِّمَامُ ـ السَّمَّةُ. Meatus urinarius, المَبَالُ.

Mechanic, n. *See* Artisan, Mechanician, n.

Mechanic, a. / Mechanical, } Pertaining to machines, مُخْتَصٌّ بِٱلْآلَاتِ. Constructed according to the laws of mechanics, مُرَكَّبٌ حَسَبَ عِلْمِ ٱلْحَرَكَاتِ. Skilled in making machines, مَاهِرٌ فِي صُنْعِ ٱلْآلَاتِ. Pertaining to artisans, مُتَعَلِّقٌ بِٱلصُّنَّاعِ. Acting like a machine, without design or intelligence, مَثَلُهُ مَثَلُ ٱلْآلَةِ يَتَحَرَّكُ عَنْ غَيْرِ وَعْيٍ وَقَصْدٍ. Mechanical power, قُوَّةٌ آلِيَّةٌ. Mechanical powers, آلَاتُ جَرِّ ٱلْأَثْقَالِ.

Mechanically, ad. By the rules of mechanics, حَسَبَ قَوَاعِدِ فَنِّ ٱلْآلَاتِ. By mechanism, بِوَاسِطَةِ ٱلْآلَاتِ. Like a machine, كَٱلْآلَةِ. By force of habit, بِقُوَّةِ ٱلْعَادَةِ.

Mechanician, n. A maker of machines, صَانِعُ آلَاتٍ. One skilled in mechanics, أُسْتَاذُ ٱلْآلَاتِ pl. أَسَاتِيذُ.

Mechanics, n. مَعْرِفَةٌ ـ مَعْرِفَةُ ٱلْآلَاتِ ـ عِلْمُ تَرْكِيبِ ٱلْآلَاتِ ـ عِلْمُ ٱلْحِيَلِ ـ عِلْمُ جَرِّ ٱلْأَثْقَالِ ـ تَحْرِيكُ ٱلْأَثْقَالِ.

Mechanism, n. تَرْكِيب.

Machinist, n. *See* Mechanician, n.

Mechlin, n. The lace, ضَرْبٌ مِنَ ٱلتَّخْرِيمَةِ مُفْتَخَرٌ.

Meconium, n. *See* Opium, n.

Medal, n. قِطْع pl. قِطَاع or أَقْطُع or أَقْطَاع ـ شَخْص pl. شُخُوص ـ إِيقُونَة pl. إِيقُونَات; *vulg.* قُونَة pl. قُونَات ـ نِيشَانٌ فِي شَكْلِ ٱلسِّكَّةِ.

Medallist, n. One skilled in medals or coins, مَاهِرٌ فِي ٱلْمَسْكُوكَاتِ. One decorated with a medal, حَائِزُ نِيشَانِ شَرَفٍ ـ مُوَجَّهٌ بِنِيشَانِ شَرَفٍ.

Medallion, n. قِطْعٌ كَبِيرٌ ـ سِكَّةٌ كَبِيرَةٌ ـ إِيقُونَةٌ كَبِيرَةٌ.

Meddle, v.i. To meddle and muddle, شَابَ aor. يَشُوبُ: He meddles and muddles, يَشُوبُ وَيَرُوبُ. *See also to* Interfere, Intermeddle, v.i.

Meddler, n. / Meddlesome, a. } *See* Busybody, Intermeddler, n.

Meddlesomeness, n. / Meddling, } *See* Interference, Intermeddling, n.

Mediæval, a. مُتَعَلِّقٌ بِٱلْأَجْيَالِ ٱلْمُتَوَسِّطَةِ ـ مَنْسُوبٌ إِلَى ٱلْقُرُونِ ٱلْوُسْطَى.

Medial, a. وَسَط ـ أَوْسَطُ. Noting a mean average, بَيْنَ وَبَيْنَ.

Mediate, v.t. To interpose between, تَوَسَّطَ بَيْنَ. To — for, intercede for, تَشَفَّعَ فِي or ل. To — for one to another person, شَفَعَ ل-إِلَى ≤. To admit mediation on behalf of, شَفَّعَ-فِي ـ شَفَّعَ. He asked him to — with the queen, ε طَلَبَ مِنْهُ أَنْ يَتَوَسَّطَ لَدَى ٱلْمَلِكَةِ. *See also to* Intercede, v.i.; *to* Interpose, v.t.

Mediate, a. مُتَوَسِّط ـ بِوَاسِطَةٍ. A — cause, سَبَبُ ٱلسَّبَبِ ـ عِلَّةٌ مُتَوَسِّطَةٌ ـ وَاسِطَةٌ.

Mediately, ad. بِوَاسِطَةٍ. Instrumentally, بِآلَاتٍ ـ بِٱلْآلَاتِ.

Mediation, n. Interposition, وَسَاطَة ـ تَوَسُّط. Intercession, شَفَاعَة.

Mediator, n. An interposer, مِفْزَع ـ مُتَوَسِّط ـ وَسِيط; for reconciliation, مُصْلِح. An intercessor, شَفِيع pl. شُفَعَآء.

Mediatorial, a. مُتَعَلِّقٌ بِٱلتَّوْسِيطِ ـ مُتَعَلِّقٌ بِٱلشَّفِيعِ.

Mediatorship, n. Interposition, وَسَاطَة ـ تَوَسُّط. Mediation, شَفَاعَة.

Mediatrix, n. A female interposer, إِمْرَأَةٌ مُتَوَسِّطَةٌ; intercessor, إِمْرَأَةٌ شَفِيعَةٌ.

Medicable, a. *See* Curable, a.

Medical, a. حِكْمِيٌّ ـ طِبِّيٌّ. The — profession, occupation, حِرْفَةُ ٱلطِّبِّ; medical men generally, الأَطِبَّآء. Medical sciences, العُلُومُ ٱلطِّبِّيَّةُ. Medical studies, الدُّرُوسُ ٱلطِّبِّيَّةُ. Medical jurisprudence, الطِّبُّ ٱلْقَانُونِيُّ. A — institution, دَارُ ٱلْعُلُومِ ٱلطِّبِّيَّةِ. A — attendant, حَكِيم. Medical attendance, مُدَاوَاةُ ٱلْحَكِيمِ (or ٱلطَّبِيبِ) ـ مُعَالَجَاتُ ٱلْحَكِيمِ. Medical treatment, شِفَآء ـ طِبّ ـ مُعَالَجَة ـ مُعَالَجَات. By the advice of the — men, حَسَبَ مَشُورَةِ ٱلْأَطِبَّآءِ.

Medically, ad. طِبًّا. To treat —, دَاوَى.

Medicament, n. دَوَآء pl. أَدْوِيَة. A compound —, دَوَآءٌ مُرَكَّبٌ ـ أَقْرَابَاذِين ـ قَرَابَاذِين.

Medicaster, n. طَبِيبٌ دَجَّالٌ; *vulg.* حَكِيمٌ خَرَّاطٌ.

Medicate, v.t. To tincture with medicines, عَرَّقَ-دَوَآءً ـ خَلَطَ-بِٱلدَّوَآءِ ε. To heal with medicines, عَالَجَ-بِٱلدَّوَآءِ.

Medication, n. مُدَاوَاة ـ مُعَالَجَة.

Medicative, a. / Medicinal, } دَوَائِيّ ـ مُعَالِج ـ شَافٍ.

Medicinally, ad. Curatively, مُعَالَجَةً ـ مُدَاوَاةً ـ بِٱلدَّوَآءِ. In the shape of medicine, كَٱلدَّوَآءِ.

Medicine, *n.* A remedy, دَوَآءٌ *pl.* أَدْوِيَةٌ — عِلَاجٌ. The art of healing, عِلْمُ ٱلطِّبِّ. A — chest, صُنْدُوقُ أَدْوِيَةٍ.

Medicine, *v.t.* عَالَجَ — دَاوَى.

Medieval, *a.* *See* Mediæval, *a.*

Mediocre, *a.* وَسَطٌ — وَسْطَانِيٌّ. Very —, دُونٌ — أَدْنَى.

Mediocrity, *n.* A middle state, وَسَاطَةٌ. Smallness in degree, رَكَاكَةٌ — حَقَارَةٌ — تَفَاهَةٌ. Poorness, meanness, قِلَّةٌ — جُزْئِيَّةٌ — مَسْكَنَةٌ.

Meditate, *v.t.* and *i.* To ponder, contemplate, طَالَعَ — تَأَمَّلَ — أَبْرَمَ — [2] نَظَرَ فِي — طَالَعَ — تَأَمَّلَ فِي. To — upon, تَشَاوَرَ — لَهِجَ فِي — إِفْتَكَرَ فِي — تَفَكَّرَ فِي. To design, نَوَى — قَصَدَ [2].

Meditation, *n.* تَفَكُّرٌ — مُطَالَعَةٌ — إِبْرَامٌ — تَأَمُّلٌ — لَهَجٌ.

Meditative, *a.* مُطَالِعٌ — مُلَاحِظٌ — كَثِيرُ ٱلتَّأَمُّلِ.

Mediterranean, *a.* Enclosed by land, مُحَاطٌ بِٱلْبَرِّ. The — sea, بَحْرُ ٱلرُّومِ — ٱلْبَحْرُ ٱلْأَبْيَضُ — ٱلْبَحْرُ ٱلْمُتَوَسِّطُ.

Medium, *a.* أَوْسَطُ — وَسَطٌ.

Medium, *n.* A means, وَسِيلَةٌ طَرِيقَةٌ — وَاسِطَةٌ. An intermediary, مُتَوَسِّطٌ — وَاسِطَةٌ. The middle term of a syllogism, ٱلْحَدُّ ٱلْأَوْسَطُ. The space through which any thing moves, revolves, مَوْقِعٌ — دَائِرَةٌ — مَدَارٌ. A kind of printing paper, ضَرْبٌ مِنَ ٱلْوَرَقِ لِلطَّبْعِ. A circulating —, (monetary), مُعَامَلَةٌ مُتَدَاوِلَةٌ. To hold a — course, تَوَسَّطَ. A — course is the best, (prov.), خَيْرُ ٱلْأُمُورِ أَوْسَطُهَا.

Medlar, *n.* The fruit, ضَرْبٌ مِنَ ٱلزُّعْرُورِ — مُشْمُلَا.

Medley, *n.* خَبْصَةٌ — تَهَاوُشٌ — تَهَوُّشٌ — خَلِيطٌ — شَمَلٌ — أَشْوَابٌ. A —, of people, أَشَابَةٌ — أَشْوَابٌ; of a composition, تَلْفِيقَةٌ — مَجْمُوعٌ — جَمَاعَةٌ. *See also* Mixture, *n.*

Medullar, *a.* } مُخِّيٌّ — مُرِّيٌّ. The — cavities, ٱلسَّوَاعِدُ.
Medullary, }

Medusa, *n.* The sea-nettle, قُرَيْصُ ٱلْبَحْرِ.

Meed, *n.* Recompense, جَزَآءٌ — مُكَافَاةٌ — ثَوَابٌ — حَقٌّ — مُجَازَاةٌ. A good recompense, reward, فَوْزٌ — حُسْنُ ثَوَابٍ. Merit, إِسْتِحْقَاقٌ — إِسْتِيجَابٌ — إِسْتِئْهَالٌ.

Meek, *a.* Gentle, forbearing, وَدِيعٌ — سَلِيمٌ — حَلِيمٌ. Humble, مُتَوَاضِعٌ. Submissive, مُنْقَادٌ — مُطِيعٌ — طَائِعٌ. To be —, تَوَاضَعَ — [2] حَلُمَ.

Meeken, *v.t.* لَيَّنَ أَخْلَاقَهُ — لَيَّنَ — حَلَّمَ.

Meekly, *ad.* بِوَدَاعَةٍ — بِٱلتَّوَاضُعِ — بِحِلْمٍ — حِلْمًا.

Meekness, *n.* Gentleness, وَدَاعَةٌ — حِلْمٌ — تُؤَدَةٌ. Humility, خُضُوعٌ — تَوَاضُعٌ. Submissiveness, إِنْقِيَادٌ — إِطَاعَةٌ.

Meerschaum, *n.* ضَرْبٌ مِنَ ٱلطَّبَاشِيرِ خَفِيفٌ جِدًّا تُصْنَعُ مِنْهُ أَحْجَارُ ٱلْغَلَايِينِ.

Meet, *v.t.* To light on, encounter, لَقِيَ — [a] أَقْبَلَ عَلَى — إِلْتَقَى — تَلَقَّى — إِلْتَحَقَ بِ — أَصَابَ — صَادَفَ. To — with, as in company, إِجْتَمَعَ مَعَ. To — one with pleasure, بَشَّ لِ *aor.* يَبَشُّ — أَقْبَلَ عَلَى. To face, see, وَاجَهَ — قَابَلَ. To oppose, قَاوَمَ — تَعَرَّضَ لِ. To appoint to —, وَاعَدَ. To — danger, إِقْتَحَمَ ٱلْأَخْطَارَ. To — one's expenses, engagements, [2] قَامَ بِمَا عَلَيْهِ. He used effective measures to — the difficulty, إِسْتَعْمَلَ وَسَائِلَ فَعَّالَةً لِتَسْدِيدِ ٱلْمُشْكِلَةِ. Those who went out to — him, ٱلْخَارِجُونَ إِلَى لِقَائِهِ. He took the necessary means to — the circumstances, إِتَّخَذَ ٱلْوَسَائِلَ ٱللَّازِمَةَ لِتَدَارُكِ ٱلْحَالِ. It did not — with the approbation of the community, لَمْ يَقَعِ ٱلْأَمْرُ لَدَى ٱلْجُمْهُورِ مَوْقِعَ ٱلْإِسْتِحْسَانِ.

Meet, *v.i.* To assemble, of many, إِجْتَمَعُوا — إِنْتَدَوْا — إِلْتَمُّوا. To come in contact, to dash against, صَادَمَ. To join, وَلِيَ *aor.* يَلِي — قَارَبَ — إِتَّصَلَ بِ. The two mountains met or faced one another, تَصَادَفَا ٱلْجَبَلَانِ. They, the two, met one another half way, made mutual concessions, تَسَامَحَا. It did not — with his approval, مَا حَلَّ لَدَيْهِ مَحَلَّ ٱلْقَبُولِ. To be pleased at meeting with one, بَشَّ بِهِ [a].

Meet, *a.* *See* Fit, *a.*

Meeting, *n.* A lighting upon, encounter, تِلْقَآءٌ — لِقَآءٌ — مُقَابَلَةٌ — مُوَاجَهَةٌ. An interview, مُلَاقَاةٌ — إِقْبَالٌ — لُقًى. A contact, clash, لَطْمَةٌ — مُلَاطَمَةٌ — مُصَادَمَةٌ. An assembly, نَادٍ — لَجْنَةٌ — مُنْتَدَيَاتٌ *pl.* مُنْتَدِيَةٌ — مُنْتَدَيَاتٌ *pl.* مُنْتَدِيَةٌ. A — for conference, مَشْوَرَةٌ — شُورَى — جَمَاعَةٌ — إِجْتِمَاعٌ — مُؤْتَمَرٌ. A religious service, صَلَوَاتٌ. A place of —, where two or more things or persons meet, مُلْتَقًى. A — or confluence of waters, مُلْتَقَى ٱلْمِيَاهِ — مَصَبُّ ٱلْمِيَاهِ. Meetings of the heads of trade were called, إِنْتَدَتْ جَمْعِيَّاتٌ مِنْ أَرْبَابِ ٱلصَّنَائِعِ. An appointed place of —, مَوْعِدٌ — مِيعَادٌ *pl.* مَوَاعِدُ. The — was composed of the magnates, كَانَتِ ٱللَّجْنَةُ مُؤَلَّفَةً مِنَ ٱلْأَعْيَانِ. He ordered a —, أَمَرَ بِعَقْدِ لَجْنَةٍ. A — was got up, تَشَكَّلَتْ لَجْنَةٌ. A — was held, إِنْعَقَدَ مُؤْتَمَرٌ. There was a great — of the nobles, إِلْتَأَمَتْ جَمْعِيَّةٌ كَبِيرَةٌ مِنَ ٱلْأَشْرَافِ. To dissolve a —, [2] فَضَّ ٱللَّجْنَةَ.

Meeting-house, *n.* A place of meeting, مَجْمَعٌ. A place of worship, مَعْبَدٌ — مَسْجِدٌ — مُتَعَبَّدٌ *pl.* مَعَابِدُ.

Meetly, *ad.* *See* Fitly, *ad.*

Meetness, *n.* *See* Fitness, *n.*

Megalonyx, *n.* حَيَوَانٌ كَبِيرٌ مِنْ ذَوَاتِ ٱلْأَرْبَعِ لَا وُجُودَ لَهُ ٱلْآنَ.

Megalosaurus, *n.* حَيَوَانٌ كَبِيرٌ مِنْ جِنْسِ ٱلْوَرَلِ لَا وُجُودَ لَهُ ٱلْآنَ.

Megatherium, *n.* حَيَوَانٌ كَبِيرٌ مِنْ ذَوَاتِ ٱلْأَرْبَعِ لَا وُجُودَ لَهُ ٱلْآنَ.

Megrim, *n.* صُدَاع ـ شَقِيقَة.

Melancholic, *a.* } Depressed in spirits, مُكَدَّرُ ٱلْخَاطِرِ ـ كَئِيب.
Melancholy, } Causing depression, مُحْزِن. His face is always —, ظَلَّ وَجْهُهُ مُسْوَدًّا [2]. His face was —, إِسْوَدَّ وَجْهُهُ. *See also* Gloomy, *a.*

Melancholy, *n.* السَّوْدَآءُ ـ مَالَنْخُولِيَا. Heaviness of mind, كَآبَة ـ غَمٌّ ـ كَدَر. *See also* Gloom, *n.*

Melange, *n.* إِمْتِزَاج ـ إِخْتِلَاط ـ خَلْط. *See also* Medley, Mixture, *n.*

Melée, *n.* A scuffle, هَوْشَة ـ مَعْرَكَة ـ شَبْكَة.

Meliorate, *v.t.* *See to* Ameliorate, *v.t.*

Meliorate, *v.i.* *See to* Ameliorate, *v.i.*

Melioration, *n.* *See* Amelioration, *n.*

Melliferous, *a.* ذُو عَسَلٍ ـ عَسَلِيٌّ.

Mellification, *n.* تَعْسِيل ـ حَمْلُ ٱلْعَسَلِ.

Mellifluence, *n.* كِيَاسَة ـ حَلَاوَة ـ مَلَاحَة.

Mellifluent, *a.* } كَيِّس ـ حُلْوٌ ـ مَلِيح.
Mellifluous, }

Mellow, *a.* } Ripe, مُسْتَوٍ ـ نَاضِج. Soft, لَيِّن ـ نَاعِم ـ رَقِيق.
Mellowy, } A — voice, صَوْتٌ حُلْوٌ ـ صَوْتٌ رَخِيمٌ. Mellow wine, نَبِيذٌ لَذِيذٌ ـ سَلْسَل ـ سَلْسَال. To be —, ripe, أَنْضَجَ. To be —, soft, of the voice, رَقَّ [2] ـ رَخَمَ [2] ـ رَخُمَ.

Mellow, *v.t.* To ripen, طَيَّبَ ـ أَنْضَجَ. To make soft, لَيَّنَ ـ أَلْيَنَ. To — the voice, خَفَّضَ ٱلصَّوْتَ: She mellowed her voice, خَفَّضَتْ صَوْتَهَا.

Mellow, *v.i.* To become ripe, إِسْتَوَى ـ نَضَجَ ـ نَضِجَ. To be soft, تَلَيَّنَ ـ لَانَ. To become —, delicious, صَارَ لَذِيذًا.

Mellowness, *n.* Ripeness, إِسْتِوَآءٌ ـ نُضْج. Softness, لَيَان ـ لِينَة. Mellowness of the voice, رِقَّةُ صَوْتٍ ـ خَفْض.

Melocoton, *n.* A quince, سَفَرْجَل *pl.* سَفَارِجُ.

Melodious, *a.* *See* Harmonious, *a.*

Melodiously, *ad.* *See* Harmoniously, *ad.*

Melodiousness, *n.* *See* Harmony, *n.*

Melodist, *n.* *See* Harmonist, *n.*

Melodize, *v.t.* حَسَّنَ ـ صَيَّرَ مُطْرِبًا.

Melodrama, *n.* تَشَخُّص فِي مَرَاسِمِ ٱللَّعْبِ عَلَى إِنْغَامِ ٱلْمُوسِيقَى ـ سِيرَةٌ مُطْرِبَة.

Melodramatic, *a.* مَا نِيطَ بِٱلسِّيَرِ ٱلْمَذْكُورَة.

Melodramatist, *n.* مُؤَلِّفُ ٱلسِّيَرِ ٱلْمَذْكُورَة.

Melody, *n.* Harmony, أُلْفَةُ ٱلْأَصْوَاتِ ـ نَغَم ـ حَبْرَة ـ رَنِيم ـ نَغْمَة ـ رَنْمَة. A sweet tune, نَغْمَةٌ حَسَنَة ـ رَنْمَة ـ حُسْنُ ٱلْأَنْغَامِ ـ مَقَامَة. Instrumental or vocal music, سَمَاع. The voice of —, صَوْتُ ٱلتَّرَنُّمِ. To make —, تَرَنَّمَ.

Melon, *n.* عَبْدُ ٱللَّاوِي ـ حَرْش ـ قَاوُن; called in Syria, بِطِّيخٌ أَصْفَرُ ـ بِطِّيخٌ أَخْضَرُ ـ بِطِّيخ ـ فَجّ ـ دَابُوغ. Water —, بِطِّيخ; called in Syria, جَبَس; in Mesopotamia, شِمْزِيّ. A — field, pit, مَبْطَخَة.

Melt, *v.t.* To make liquid, ذَوَّبَ ـ أَذَابَ ـ أَمَاعَ ـ صَهَرَ ـ حَلَّ [2]; of grease, fat, ذَوَّبَ ـ سَيَّحَ. To — in a mould, صَاغَ *aor.* يَصُوغُ ـ سَبَكَ. To overpower with emotion, أَذَابَ قَلْبَهُ ـ لَيَّنَ قَلْبَهُ ـ حَنَّنَ قَلْبَهُ ـ نَجَعَ فِي. To dissipate, waste, أَزَالَ ـ أَذْهَبَ ـ ضَيَّعَ. To — to tears, أَجْرَى مِنْ عَيْنَيْهِ دُمُوعًا ـ بَكَّى.

Melt, *v.i.* To become liquid, تَحَلَّلَ ـ تَمَيَّعَ ـ مَاعَ ـ إِنْصَهَرَ ـ سَاحَ ـ تَذَوَّبَ ـ إِنْحَلَّ ـ ذَابَ [2]. To be softened, تَلَيَّنَ ـ رَقَّ قَلْبُهُ [2] ـ ذَابَ قَلْبُهُ [2]. To — or pass away, زَالَ ـ ذَابَ [2] *aor.* يَزُولُ. To — away, of the flesh, ذَبَلَ [2] ـ ذَهَبَ لَحْمُهُ. He was melted to tears, تَدَمَّعَ ـ أَجْرَى دُمُوعًا. It melted like wax, ذَابَ كَٱلشَّمْعِ [2].

Melter, *n.* سَبَّاك ـ مُفَرِّغ.

Melting, *n.* The act of melting, حَلّ ـ إِذَابَة ـ إِمَاعَة ـ صَهْر; of softening, تَلْيِين.

Meltingly, *ad.* تَدَمُّعًا ـ بِنَوْعٍ يُحَنِّنُ ٱلْقَلْبَ ـ تَلْيِينًا ـ تَحَنُّنًا.

Member, *n.* A limb of the body, عُضْوٌ *pl.* أَعْضَآءٌ. A clause, بَنْد *pl.* بُنُود ـ بَاب *pl.* أَبْوَاب ـ فَصْل *pl.* فُصُول. An individual of a society, corporation, عُضْوٌ *pl.* أَعْضَآء ـ مُؤَلَّفٌ مِنْ أَعْضَآءِ جَمْعِيَّةٍ. A — of parliament, مِنْ أَعْضَآءِ مَجْلِسِ ٱلشُّورَى. The members of the council, أَعْضَآءُ ٱلْمَجْلِسِ ـ أَرْبَابُ ٱلشُّورَى. A — of a trade corporation, عُضْو ـ مِنْ أَهْلِ حِرْفَةٍ. A joint —, عُضْوٌ مَعَ غَيْرِهِ ـ مُشْتَرِك. The members of a family, أَهْلُ ٱلْبَيْتِ ـ عِيَال. To become a — of, تَأَلَّفَ مِنْ ـ دَخَلَ فِي [2]. To make one a — of, أَلَّفَ مِنْ ـ أَدْخَلَ بَيْنَ.

Membership, *n.* عُضْوَة ـ مُشَارَكَة ـ شَرِكَة.

Membrane, *n.* حِجَاب *pl.* حُجُب ـ غِشَآءٌ *pl.* أَغْشِيَة ـ غِطَآء. The — which envelopes a child in the womb, مَشِيمَة ـ حُوَلَآء. The — of the brain, the *dura mater* and *pia mater*, أُمُّ ٱلرَّأْسِ ـ أُمُّ ٱلْمُخِّ. The — of the ribs, الْجِلْبُ.

Membraneous, Membranous, *a.* } غِشَائِيٌّ ـ ذُو حُجُب.
Membranaceous, Membraniferous, }

Memento, *n.* A hint, إِشَارَة ـ كِنَايَة ـ إِيمَآء. That which reminds, تَذْكَار ـ تَذْكِرَة ـ تَفْكِرَة.

Memoir, *n.* A memorandum, تَذْكِرَة. A biographical —, تَذْكِرَة. A sketch, pamphlet, رِسَالَة ـ بَيَان *pl.* رَسَائِلُ. *See also* Biography, *n.*

Memorabilia, *n.* مَذْكُورَات ـ وُقُوعَاتٌ غَرِيبَةٌ.

Memorable, *a.* Worthy of remembrance, مُسْتَحِقُّ ٱلذِّكْرِ ـ وَاجِبُ ٱلتَّذْكَارِ. Celebrated, مَذْكُور ـ شَهِير ـ مَشْهُور ـ مَوْصُوف ـ مَمْدُوح.

Memorably, *ad.* بِشُهْرَةٍ ـ إِشْهَارًا ـ بِنَوْعٍ يُذْكَرُ.

Memorandum, *n.* تَذْكِرَة ـ تَفْكِرَة. A list, جَدْوَل ـ عَلَم ـ سِيَاقَة ـ قَائِمَة. A — book, مَجْمَعَة ـ دَفْتَرُ تَفْكِرَةٍ ـ تَفْكِرَة ـ دُسْتُور. A — of expenses, وَرَقَةُ حِسَابٍ ـ عَلَمُ بَيَانِ ٱلدَّفْعِ. To make a — of, قَيَّدَ ـ دَوَّنَ.

Memorative, *a.* *See* Commemorative, *a.*

Memorial, *a.* لِلذِّكْرِ ـ مُذَكِّر ـ لِلتَّذْكَارِ.

Memorial, *n.* That which preserves remembrances, تَذْكِرَة ـ تَفْكِرَة ـ تَذْكَار. A written representation, petition, عَرْضُ حَالٍ. To present a — to such an one, قَدَّمَ عَرْضَ حَالٍ إِلَى فُلَانٍ. Any writing, كِتَابَة ـ تَقْرِير. He cut off their —, memory, from the earth, قَرَضَ ذِكْرَهُمْ مِنَ ٱلْأَرْضِ.

Memorialist, *n.* The writer of a memoir, مُؤَلِّفُ تَذْكِرَةٍ ـ مُؤَلِّفُ رِسَالَةٍ. One who presents a memorial, مُقَدِّمُ عَرْضِ حَالٍ.

Memorialize, *v.t.* To present a petition to, قَدَّمَ عَرْضَ حَالٍ إِلَى.

Memoriter, *ad.* غَيْبًا ـ عَلَى ظَهْرِ قَلْبِهِ.

Memorize, *v.t.* To record, حَرَّرَ ـ ²كَتَبَ ـ قَيَّدَ. To perpetuate the memory of, حَفِظَ ذِكْرَهُ ـ أَدَامَ ذِكْرَهُ.

Memory, *n.* The recollective faculty, ٱلْحِفْظُ ـ ٱلذَّاكِرَةُ ـ ٱلْحَافِظَةُ ـ حِفْظُ ٱلْقَلْبِ ـ ٱلْقُوَّةُ ٱلْحَافِظَةُ. Remembrance, the presence of a thing in the mind, ذِكْر. The time within which past events can be remembered, بَال ـ إِدْرَاك ـ ذِهْن ـ خَاطِر. Repute, ذِكْر ـ ذُكْر. Famous —, repute, شُهْرَة ـ صِيت. Having a good —, ذَكِير ـ ذَكِير ـ حَافِظ. Having a bad —, نَسْيَانُ ـ سَاهٍ. To the best of my —, عَلَى مَا فِي بَالِي. Within the — of man, فِي ذِكْرِ ٱلنَّاسِ. What is learnt in tender age becomes engraven on the —, [*lit.* is like cutting in stone]; but what is learnt in mature age is easily forgotten, [*lit.* is like writing on a clod], (*prov.*) العِلْمُ فِي ٱلصِّغَرِ مِثْلَ ٱلنَّقْشِ فِي ٱلْحَجَرِ وَٱلْعِلْمُ فِي ٱلْكِبَرِ مِثْلَ ٱلْخَطِّ فِي ٱلْمَدَرِ.

In memory of, لِذِكْرِ ـ تَذْكَارًا لِ.

From memory, by heart, عَلَى ظَهْرِ قَلْبِهِ ـ غَيْبًا.

Of blessed memory, سَعِيدُ ٱلذِّكْرِ ـ رَضِيَ ٱللّٰهُ عَنْهُ.

Of happy memory, طَابَ ثَرَاهُ ـ رَحْمَةُ ٱللّٰهِ عَلَيْهِ.

Of hateful memory, شَنِيعُ ٱلذِّكْرِ.

To commit to memory, تَعَلَّمَ ـ غَيْبًا ـ حَفِظَ.

To jog the memory of one, فَكَّرَ ـ فِي ـ أَذْكَرَ ـ ذَكَّرَ.

To jog one's own memory, تَفَكَّرَ ـ تَذَكَّرَ.

To make one to commit to memory, حَفَّظَ ـ أَحْفَظَ.

To obliterate from the memory, أَزَاحَ ـ مِنَ ٱلْبَالِ ـ أَزَالَ ـ مِنَ ٱلْبَالِ.

To recite from memory, حَكَى ـ غَيْبًا ـ حَدَّثَ بِهِ غَيْبًا ـ تَقَصَّصَ.

To slip or escape one's memory, ذَهَبَ عَلَى. It slipt my memory, ضَلَّ عَنِّي.

Menace, *v.t.* To threaten, رَعَبَ ـ هَدَّدَ ـ تَهَدَّدَ ـ تَدَرَّهَ ـ أَوْعَدَ ـ بِ ـ أَرْعَدَ ـ أَرْعَبَ. To show the probability of something happening, ²هَمَّ بِ. It menaced ruin, آلَ إِلَى ٱلْخَرَابِ *aor.* يَؤُولُ ـ أَشْرَفَ عَلَى ٱلْخَرَابِ. *See also to* Threaten, *v.t.*, and About, *ad.*

Menace, *n.* A threat, تَهْدِيد ـ وَعْد ـ رَعْب. To utter menaces, أَرْعَدَ وَأَبْرَقَ.

Menacer, *n.* مُهَدِّد ـ مُوعِدٌ بِ ـ مُرْعِب.

Menacing, *a.* Threatening, مُرْعِب ـ مُهَدِّد. Prognosticating, هَامٌّ بِ ـ مُوعِدٌ بِ.

Menage, *n.* }
Menagerie, } دَارُ ٱلسِّبَاعِ ـ مَحَلُّ ٱلْوُحُوشِ ٱلْغَرِيبَةِ.

Mend, *v.t.* In a general sense, to remedy, عَالَجَ. To —, as by joining broken parts, رَتَقَ. To repair, رَمَّ ـ رَمَّمَ *aor.* يَرُمُّ ـ أَصْلَحَ ـ صَلَّحَ. To —, as china, glass, *etc.*, قَانَ. To —, as clothes, صَلَّحَ ـ رَقَّعَ ـ رَفَا ـ رَفَا ـ لَقَطَ. To darn, رَفَا. To —, as of matters, ²جَبَرَ ـ ²سَدَّ ـ رَمْرَمَ. To — one's pace, أَسْرَعَ ـ إِسْتَعْجَلَ ـ طَارَ. To — a pen, بَرَى ٱلْقَلَمَ. To — matters, to make things worse, (adverbially,) وَأَشَرُّ مِنْ ذٰلِكَ. *See also to* Repair, Improve, *v.t.*

Mend, *v.i.* As in health, إِشْتَفَى ـ تَعَافَى. To become better, of things, or conditions, إِنْصَلَحَ ـ إِنْجَبَرَ ـ تَجَبَّرَ ـ إِجْتَبَرَ ـ تَرَوَّقَ ـ ²رَاقَ ـ إِسْتَتَبَّ ـ ²حَسُنَ. To —, of the weather, صَحَّتِ ٱلدُّنْيَا. *See also to* Amend, Improve, *v.i.*

Mendable, *a.* قَابِلٌ ـ يُرَمْرَمُ ـ يُرَمُّ ـ يُصْلَحُ ـ يُعَالَجُ ـ ٱلْإِسْتِتْبَابِ.

Mendacious, *a.* كَاذِب ـ كَذَّاب.

Mendacity, *n.* كِذْب.

Mender, *n.* A repairer generally, مُصَلِّح ـ مُعَالِج; of clothes, رَفَّاء ـ لَاقِط. A — of cracks, in bowls, *etc.*, شَعَّاب.

Mendicancy, *n.* State of beggary, مَسْكَنَة ـ عَالَة ـ فَاقَة. *See also* Beggary, *n.*

Mendicant, *n.* صَعْلُوك ـ طُلَّاب *pl.* طَالِب ـ شَحَّاذ. *See also* Beggar, *n.*

Mendicity, *n.* Begging, the life of a beggar, شَحْذ ـ شَحَّاذَة.

Mending, *n.* The act of repairing, تَسْوِيَة ـ إِصْلَاح ـ رَمْرَمَة ـ رَمّ; of clothes, تَرْقِيع ـ رَفَآء; of glass, china, *etc.*, قَيْن; of cracks, تَشْعِيب. Requiring —, مُتَصَلِّح ـ مُتَرَدِّم.

Menial, *a.* مُتَعَلِّق بِشُغْل ٱلْخُدَّام ـ حَقِير ـ أَدْنَى.

Menial, *n.* خَادِم *pl.* خَدَمَة *and* خُدَّام ـ أَجِير *pl.* أُجَرَآء ـ خَدَّام *pl.* خَدَّامُون.

Meninx, *n.* The — of the brain, أُمّ ٱلرَّأْس ـ ٱلسَّحَاءَة.

Meniscus, *n.* بِلَّوْرَة وَجْهُهَا مُقَعَّر وَقَفَاهَا مُحَدَّب.

Menses, *n.* / **Menstruation**, } عَادَات ٱلنِّسَآء ـ حَيْض ـ طَمْث. A single term of the —, حَيْضَة. A woman who has excessive —, مُسْتَحَاضَة. The days of the — of a woman, until the expiration of which, being a widow or divorced, she may not marry again, عِدَّة.

Menstrual, *a.* Of the menses, حَيْضِيّ. The — blood, دَم بَاحِر ـ مَحِيض ـ حِيَاض ـ دَم بَحْرَانِيّ. *See also* Monthly, *a.*

Menstruant, *a.* / **Menstruous**, } A — woman, حَائِض ـ طَامِث. Menstruous cloths, طَلِيَّة ـ لِجَام ـ حَشِيَّة ـ مَفَارِم ـ مَحِيضَة.

Menstruate, *v.i.* حَاضَت *aor.* تَحِيض. A woman that does not —, مَهْيَآء.

Menstruum, *n.* A dissolvent, مَآء مُحَلِّل ـ مُحَلِّل.

Mensurability, *n.* Capacity of being measured, قَابِلِيَّة ٱلْمِسَاحَة ـ قَابِلِيَّة ٱلْعِيَار.

Mensurable, *a.* مِمَّا يُعَايَر ـ مِمَّا يُقَاس ـ قَابِل ٱلْمِسَاحَة.

Mensuration, *n.* قِيَاس ـ مِسَاحَة. The art of —, عِلْم ٱلْمِسَاحَة.

Mental, *a.* Belonging to the mind, عَقْلِيّ ـ ذِهْنِيّ. Inward, بَاطِنِيّ ـ بَاطِن. Mental prayer, صَلَاة عَقْلِيَّة ـ صَلَاة بِٱلرُّوح.

Mentally, *ad.* Intellectually, عَقْلًا ـ ذِهْنًا. Inwardly, بَاطِنًا ـ سِرًّا ـ بِٱلرُّوح.

Mention, *n.* ذِكْر ـ ذِكْر بِٱللِّسَان ـ ذُكْر. Honourable —, ذِكْر بِٱلْجَمِيل (*or* بِخَيْر); unfavourable —, ذِكْر بِٱلْقَبِيح (*or* بِشَرّ). Successive —, تَرَادُف. To make — of, ذَكَرَ [2]. I will not make — of him, لَا أَذْكُرُهُ.

Mention, *v.t.* سَمَّى ـ ذَكَرَ بِٱللِّسَان ـ ذَكَرَ [2]. To — favourably, ذَكَرَ بِٱلْجَمِيل. Don't — him, لَا تَجِئْ بِذِكْرِهِ.

Mentionable, *a.* ذِكْرُهُ جَائِز ـ مِمَّا يُذْكَر.

Mentioned, *a.* مَذْكُور. The above —, ٱلْمَذْكُور آنِفًا. These above — things, هٰذِهِ ٱلْمَذْكُورَات. It was not —, لَمْ تَقَعْ عَلَيْهِ مُذَاكَرَة. Your sister was not —, أُخْتُكَ لَمْ تَكُنْ تُذْكَر. None of his actions shall be — against him, كُلّ أَفْعَالِهِ ٱلَّتِي فَعَلَهَا لَا تُذْكَر عَلَيْهِ. We mentioned before this, قَدْ أَسْلَفْنَا قَبْلَ هٰذَا.

Mentor, *n.* نَاصِح أَمِين ـ مُشِير صَادِق ـ مَاحِض نُصْح.

Mentorial, *a.* مُتَضَمِّن ٱلنَّصَائِح ـ نَاصِحِيّ.

Mephitic, *a.* / **Mephitical**, } مُقْتِل ـ مُضِرّ ـ كَثِير ٱلْوَخَم ـ زَنِخ ـ دَفِر ـ سَيِّئ.

Mephitis, *n.* / **Mephitism**, } أَذِيَّة ـ وَخَم ـ نَتْن ـ دَفَر.

Mercantile, *a.* تِجَارِيّ. Mercantile marine, ٱلْمَرَاكِب ٱلتِّجَارِيَّة.

Mercenarily, *ad.* مِنْ أَجْل ٱلرِّبْح ـ كَٱلْأَجِير ـ بِٱلْأُجْرَة.

Mercenary, *a.* Hired, مُسْتَأْجَر. Purchased, شَرِيّ. Greedy of gain, طَامِع فِي ٱلرِّبْح ـ طَامِع بِٱلرِّبْح.

Mercenary, *n.* مُكْرًى ـ أَجِير *pl.* أُجَرَآء ـ شَاكِرِيّ *pl.* شَاكِرِيَّة.

Mercer, *n.* بَيَّاع خُرْدَة ـ خُرْدَجِيّ *pl.* خُرْدَجِيَّة.

Mercery, *n.* خُرْدَة ـ أَسْبَاب ـ قُمَاش *pl.* أَقْمِشَة.

Merchandise, *n.* An article of —, مَتَاع *pl.* أَمْتِعَة ـ سِلْعَة *pl.* سِلَع ـ بِضَاعَة *pl.* بَضَائِع ـ سَبَب *pl.* أَسْبَاب. Trade, تِجَارَة ـ بَيْع وَشِرَآء. Foreign —, تِجَارَة أَجْنَبِيَّة ـ جَلَب *pl.* أَجْلَاب.

Merchandise, *v.i.* تَجَرَ [2] ـ اِتَّجَرَ ـ تَاجَرَ ـ بَاعَ وَٱشْتَرَى.

Merchant, *n.* تَاجِر *pl.* تُجَّار. A dealer, بَيَّاع *pl.* بَيَّاعَة *or* بَيَّاعُون ـ مُتَسَبِّب.

Merchantable, *a.* *See* Marketable, *a.*

Merchantman, *n.* سَفِينَة ٱلتِّجَارَة ـ مَرْكَب تُجَّار.

Merchant-tailor, *n.* بَيَّاع ٱلثِّيَاب ٱلْمَخْيُوطَة.

Merciful, *a.* رَفِيق ٱلْقَلْب ـ حَنَّان ـ رَحِيم. The Merciful (of God), ٱلْحَنَّان. The Pitiful, the Merciful, ٱلرَّحْمٰن ٱلرَّحِيم. To be — to, تَرَحَّمَ ـ رَحِمَ ـ تَسَمَّحَ بِ ـ تَحَنَّنَ عَلَى ـ حَنَّ عَلَى ـ تَرَحَّمَ عَلَى. God was — to such an one, اِرْتَاحَ ٱللّٰهُ لِفُلَان.

Mercifully, *ad.* بِتَرَحُّم ـ بِرَحْمَة ـ مَرْحَمَةً.

Mercifulness, *n.* مَرْحَمَة. *See also* Mercy, *n.*

Merciless, *a.* قَاسِي ٱلْقَلْب ـ قَاسٍ ـ عَسُوف ـ بِلَا رَحْمَة.

Mercilessly, *ad.* بِقَسَاوَة ـ بِعُنْف ـ بِلَا رَحْمَة.

Mercilessness, *n.* قَسَاوَة قَلْب ـ قَسَاوَة ـ عُنْف ـ عَدَم ٱلرَّحْمَة.

Mercurial, *a.* Belonging to quicksilver, مِنْ زِئْبَق ـ زِئْبَقِيّ. Full of vigour, خَفِيف ـ نَدْب ـ سَلِب ـ حَرِك.

Mercurialize, *v.t.* سَقَاهُ زِئْبَقًا.

Mercury, *n.* Quicksilver, زِئْبَق ـ زَاوُوق. The planet —, كَوْكَبُ ٱلْعُطَارِدِ. The two planets Venus and Mercury, السَّعْدَانِ. Sprightly qualities, سَوْرَة ـ خِفَّة ـ حُمَيَّا. *See also* Newspaper, *n.*

Mercy, *n.* Compassion, رَحْمَة ـ مَرَاحِمُ *pl.* مَرْحَمَة ـ رُحْم ـ مَغْفِرَة ـ غُفْرَان. Forgiveness, حَنِّيَّة *vulg.* ; حِنَّة ـ حَنَان. Goodness, providence, فَيْض ـ بَرَكَة ـ عِنَايَة. To have — on, تَرَحَّمَ عَلَى ـ رَحِمَ. To ask for —, طَلَبَ ٱلْأَمَانَ ـ إِسْتَرْحَمَ. The mercies of God, الْمَرَاحِمُ ٱلرَّبَّانِيَّة. May God have — on thee! رَحِمَكَ ٱللّٰهُ. Mercy! mercy! الْأَمَانُ ٱلْأَمَانُ.

Mercy-seat, *n.* The covering of the ark, غِطَآءُ تَابُوتِ ٱلشَّهَادَةِ. The throne of mercy, عَرْشُ ٱلرَّحْمَةِ لِحَضْرَةِ مُوسَى.

Mere, *a.* خَالِص ـ بَسِيط ـ مُجَرَّد ـ صَانِج ـ سُمَاق ـ أَقْحَاح *pl.* قُحّ. A — lie, كَذِبٌ خَالِصٌ ـ كَذِبٌ سُمَاقٌ. *See also under* Unmixed, Pure, *a.*

Merely, *ad.* لَا غَيْرَ ـ فَقَطْ.

Meretricious, *a.* False, borrowed, مُصَاغٌ (or مَصُوغٌ) بِٱلْكَذِبِ ـ مُمَوَّه ـ ذُو خِدَاعٍ ـ رَوْنَق ـ مُسْتَعَار. To adorn with — ornament, صَاغَ *aor.* يَصُوغُ ; of speech, صَاغَ ٱلْكَلَامَ ـ وَشَى *aor.* يَشِي. *See also* Whorish, *a.*

Meretriciously, *ad.* بِتَمْوِيهٍ ـ بِتَصَنُّعٍ ـ بِعَارِيَّةٍ ـ بِصَوْغٍ ـ بِوَشْيٍ. *See also* Whorishly, *ad.*

Meretriciousness, *n.* تَصَنُّع ـ صَوْغ ـ خِدَاعَة ـ وَشْي ـ شِيَة ـ تَمْوِيه. *See also* Whorishness, *n.*

Merge, *v.t.* To sink, settle, حَلَّ ـ خَلَّصَ. To extinguish, bring to an end, أَزَالَ ـ أَطْفَأَ. To — a thing into, to cause it to enter into, أَدْخَلَ ـ فِي ـ أَوْلَجَ ـ فِي. They merged their differences, of two, إِتَّفَقَا ـ تَصَالَحَا ; of many, إِتَّفَقُوا ـ تَصَالَحُوا. *See also to* Immerge, *v.t.*

Merge, *v.i.* To become extinguished, زَالَ ـ طَفِئَ. To — into, become, عَادَ إِلَى ـ حَصَلَ ـ أَصْبَحَ ـ يَؤُولُ *aor.* آلَ إِلَى ـ صَارَ. *See also to* Sink, *v.i.*

Meridian, *n.* The —, دَوَائِرُ *pl.* دَائِرَةُ نِصْفِ ٱلنَّهَارِ. The — line, خَطُّ ٱلشَّمَالِ وَٱلْجَنُوبِ ـ خُطُوط *pl.* خَطُّ نِصْفِ ٱلنَّهَارِ. Noon, إِرْتِفَاع ـ أَعْلَى ـ أَوْج. The highest summit, الظُّهْر ـ نِصْفُ ٱلنَّهَارِ. At the — of his glory, فِي أَوْجِ عِزِّهِ.
Brazen meridian, طَبْعُ (or شَكْلُ) دَائِرَةِ نِصْفِ ٱلنَّهَارِ مِنْ نُحَاسٍ. Magnetic meridian, خَطُّ ٱلشَّمَالِ وَٱلْجَنُوبِ حَسَبَ بَيَانِ ٱلْإِبْرَةِ ٱلْمَغْنَطِيسِيَّةِ.

Meridian, *a.* ظُهْرِيٌّ. Pertaining to the highest point, أَعْلَى. Extended from north to south, مِنَ ٱلشَّمَالِ إِلَى ٱلْجَنُوبِ.

Meridional, *a.* Having a southern aspect, مُشْرِفٌ عَلَى ـ جَنُوبِيٌّ ٱلْجَنُوبِ. Pertaining to the meridian, مُخْتَصٌّ بِٱلطُّولِ.

Meridionally, *ad.* طِبْقَ خَطِّ نِصْفِ ـ نَظَرًا لِخَطِّ نِصْفِ ٱلنَّهَارِ ٱلنَّهَارِ.

Merino, *n.* The stuff, مَرِينُوس ـ ضَرْبٌ مِنَ ٱلصُّوفِ ٱلنَّاعِمِ. Made of —, مِنْ مَرِينُوسٍ ـ مَرِينُوس.

Merit, *n.* Goodness entitling to reward, إِسْتِئْهَال ـ إِسْتِيجَاب ـ إِسْتِحْقَاق. Any performance which merits regard, فَضْل ـ قَدَم ـ فَخْر ـ فَضِيلَة. That which is earned, a recompense, مَثَابَة ـ أَجْر ـ ثَوَاب ـ مُكَافَاة. A man of —, رَجُلٌ فَاضِلٌ. To acquire — with God, إِكْتَسَبَ (or رَبِحَ) ٱلْأَجْرَ وَٱلثَّوَابَ عِنْدَ ٱللّٰهِ. To make a — of, إِفْتَخَرَ بِ. He wishes to vaunt his merits before you, يُرِيدُ يَرْمِي جَرِيدَهُ قُدَّامَكَ (*prov.* Literally, he wants to throw his jarid in your presence, *i.e.* to show how skilful he is). To make a — of necessity, إِتَّخَذَ ٱلضَّرُورَةَ فَضِيلَةً.

Merit, *v.t.* إِسْتَحَقَّ ـ إِسْتَوْجَبَ ـ إِسْتَأْهَلَ. To — above another, إِسْتَحَقَّ (or إِسْتَأْهَلَ) عَلَى غَيْرِهِ. He truly merits it, يَحِقُّ لَهُ. To — well of the state, to serve it well, نَفَعَ ٱلْمَمْلَكَةَ. *See also to* Deserve, *v.t.*

Merited, *a.* مُسْتَأْهِل ـ مُسْتَحِقّ.

Meritorious, *a.* Deserving praise, خَلِيقٌ ـ مُسْتَوْجِبُ ٱلثَّنَآءِ بِٱلثَّنَآءِ. Praised, مَبْرُور ـ مَحْمُود ـ مَمْدُوح. *See also* Praiseworthy, *a.*

Meritoriously, *ad.* بِٱسْتِيجَابٍ ـ بِٱسْتِحْقَاقٍ. *See also* Deservedly, *ad.*

Meritoriousness, *n.* *See* Merit, *n.*

Merlin, *n.* A species of hawk, نَوْعٌ مِنَ ٱلصَّقْرِ صَغِيرٌ.

Merlon, *n.* The part of a parapet, شُرَف *pl.* شُرْفَة *and* شُرُفَات.

Merops, *n.* The bird, وَرَاوِيرُ *pl.* وَرْوَارَة.

Mermaid, *n.* بِنْتُ ٱلْبَحْرِ ـ جِنِّيَّةُ ٱلْبَحْرِ.

Merrily, *ad.* بِسُرُورٍ ـ بِفَرَحٍ ـ تَكَيُّفًا ـ تَغَبُّطًا ـ بِطَرَبٍ ـ فَرِحًا ـ بِكَيْفٍ.

Merriment, *n.* طَرَب ـ سُرُور ـ نَعِيم ـ غِبْطَة ـ حُبُور ـ فَرَح ـ طِيبُ ٱلْقَلْبِ ـ تَكَيُّف ـ كَيْف.

Merry, *a.* طَرُوب ـ طَرِب ـ يَحْبُور ـ مَسْرُور ـ نَعِيم ـ مَغْبُوط ـ رَوِيّ ـ فَكِه ـ طَرِب ـ بَحْبُوح ـ مَبْسُوط ـ مِطْرَاب. To be —, فَرِحَ ـ تَغَبَّطَ ـ تَنَعَّمَ ـ طَابَ قَلْبُهُ ـ تَرَوَّى ـ إِرْتَوَى ـ يَرْوَى *aor.* رَوِيَ ـ أَطْرَبَ ـ حَبَّرَ ـ تَكَيَّفَ ـ إِسْتَسَرَّ ـ سُرَّ. To make one —, كَيَّفَ ـ أَطَابَ قَلْبَهُ ـ أَفْرَحَ ـ فَرَّحَ. They drank and were — with him, شَرِبُوا وَرَوُوا مَعَهُ. He sent the people away —,

صَرَفَ ٱلْقَوْمَ فارجين = . A — heart, قَلْبٌ طَيِّبٌ . A — set, حابور .

Merry-Andrew, *n.* مَسْخَرَة .

Merry-making, *n.* *See* Merriment, *n.*

Merry-thought, *n.* عَظْمٌ ذُو شُعْبَتَيْنِ فِي صَدْرِ ٱلطُّيُورِ .

Mesenteric, *a.* مُتَعَلِّقٌ بِٱلْهُشَّةِ .

Mesentery, *n.* هُوشَة ــ هُشَّة ــ غِشَاءُ ٱلْأَمْعَاءِ .

Mesh, *n.* عَيْن *pl.* عُيُون . Meshes, شَبَكَة .

Mesh, *v.t.* To catch with a net, صَادَ ـ بِٱلشَّبَكَةِ *aor.* يَصِيدُ .

Meshy, *a.* مُشَبَّكٌ .

Meslin, *n.* خَلِيطُ ٱلْحُبُوبِ .

Mesmeric, *a.* مُتَعَلِّقٌ بِٱلْجَاذِبِيَّةِ ٱلْمَغْنَطِيسِيَّةِ فِي ٱلْحَيَوَانَاتِ ــ مُخْتَصٌّ بِمَغْنَطِيسِيَّةِ ٱلْمُعَلِّمِ مَسْمَرَ .

Mesmerism, *n.* Animal magnetism, ٱلْجَاذِبِيَّةُ ٱلْمَغْنَطِيسِيَّةُ فِي ٱلْحَيَوَانَاتِ ــ مَغْنَطِيسِيَّةُ ٱلْمُعَلِّمِ مَسْمَرَ .

Mesmerist, *n.* عَامِلٌ بِٱلْجَاذِبِيَّةِ ٱلْمَغْنَطِيسِيَّةِ فِي ٱلْأَنْفُسِ .

Mesmerize, *v.t.* أَجْرَى فِي ـ ٱلْمَغْنَطِيسِيَّةَ .

Mesne, *a.* مُتَوَسِّطٌ ــ أَوْسَطُ .

Mesozoic, *a.* ٱلطَّبَقَةُ ٱلْوُسْطَى مِنْ طَبَقَاتِ أَحْجَارِ ٱلْأَرْضِ .

Mess, *n.* A dish or plate of any food, صَحْن *pl.* صُحُون . A portion, حِصَّة *pl.* حِصَص ــ قِسْمَة . A ration, رَاتِبٌ مِنَ ٱلْمَأْكُولِ . A medley, خَلِيطٌ ــ خَلْطٌ . A meal, أَكْلَة . A complication, difficulty, خَبْصَة ــ تَهَوُّش ــ شَوَاش ــ وَرْطَة ــ مُشْكِلَة ــ عَرَاقِيل . Filth, نَجَاسَة . Eating at one table, أَكْلٌ عَلَى ــ مُؤَاكَلَة ــ إِكَال ــ مَحَلُّ ٱلْأَكْلِ ــ مَأْكَل . ٱلْأَكْلُ سَوِيَّةً ــ مَائِدَةٌ وَاحِدَةٌ . A mess house, بَيْتُ ٱلْأَكْلِ . In a —, muddle, فِي حَيْرَةٍ وَفَشَلٍ . To belong to a —, كَانَ مِنْ جُلَسَاءِ ٱلْمَائِدَةِ . To be in a —, muddle, شَجَرَ ـ ² ــ تَشَوَّشَ ــ ٱشْتَبَكَ ــ تَلَوَّى . To make a —, litter, عَثْعَثَ ــ نَجَّسَ ــ أَدْرَنَ ; لَخْبَطَ ــ هَوَّشَ خَثْخَثَ ; to make filthy, نَجَّسَ ــ أَدْرَنَ . To make a — of any matter, عَثْعَثَ ــ خَثْخَثَ ــ شَوَّشَ ــ هَوَّشَ .

Mess, *v.i.* To eat with, أَكَلَ مَعَ ــ آكَلَ ² . They — together, يَأْكُلُونَ عَلَى مَائِدَةٍ وَاحِدَةٍ ــ يَأْكُلُونَ سَوِيَّةً ; (of Arabs who eat out of one dish it would be), يَأْكُلُونَ مِنْ قَصْعَةٍ وَاحِدَةٍ .

Mess, *v.t.* To supply with food, أَطْعَمَ . To supply with rations, وَزَّعَ ٱلرَّاتِبَ عَلَى . To dirty, لَوَّثَ ــ نَجَّسَ ــ أَدْرَنَ .

Message, *n.* كَلَام ــ رِسَالَة ــ أَلُوكَة . Intelligence, خَبَر . An order, مَأْمُورِيَّة ــ أَمْر . To communicate a — to, أَلَكَ ² ـ = ــ بَعَثَ (or أَرْسَلَ) كَلَامًا إِلَى = . They sent messages to one another, of many, تَرَاسَلُوا . He conveyed his —, إِسْتَأْلَكَ مَأْلُكَتَهُ ــ أَبْلَغَ رِسَالَتَهُ ــ إِسْتَأْلَكَهُ . To send a — by such an one, أَرْسَلَ كَلَامًا عَلَى يَدِ فُلَانٍ . To send on a —, سَرَّحَ ــ = سَرَحَ . I have a — from the governor to you, عِنْدِي كَلَامٌ مِنَ ٱلْحَاكِمِ إِلَيْكَ . When he heard this —, as he sat at meat, لَمَّا سَمِعَ هٰذَا ٱلْكَلَامَ وَهُوَ عَلَى ٱلسُّفْرَةِ (or ٱلْمَائِدَةِ) .

Messenger, *n.* سَاعٍ *pl.* سُعَاة ــ مُرْسَل ــ رَسُول *pl.* رُسُل *and* رُسَلَاءُ ــ مِرْسَال . A post —, بَرِيد . A —, one who carries messages or packets between one place and another, شَيَّال . To send a —, أَرْسَلَ رَسُولًا . To act as a — between, تَرَسَّلَ بَيْنَ ــ أَلَكَ بَيْنَ . Messenger, an angel, مَأْلَك . Fever is the — of death, ٱلْحُمَّى بَرِيدُ ٱلْمَوْتِ . A — came to the governor, جَاءَ رَسُولٌ إِلَى ٱلْحَاكِمِ = .

Messiah, *n.* The —, حَضْرَةُ ٱلْمَسِيحِ ــ ٱلْمَسِيحُ .

Messiahship, *n.* وَظِيفَةُ ٱلْمَسِيحِ .

Messianic, *a.* مَسِيحِيٌّ .

Messieurs, *n.*
Messrs., } أَفَنْدِيَّة ــ أَسْيَاد ــ سَادَة .

Messmate, *n.* At eating, شَرِيكُ ٱلْقَصْعَةِ ــ أَكِيل . A comrade, زَمِيل *pl.* زُمَلَاءُ ــ رَفِيق *pl.* أَرْفَاق ــ حَرِيف *pl.* حُرَفَاءُ .

Messuage, *n.* عَقَار *pl.* عَقَارَات .

Mestizo, *n.* مُوَلَّدٌ مِنْ أَبٍ أَسْبَانِيُولِيٍّ وَأُمٍّ هِنْدِيَّةٍ .

Met, *pret. of to* Meet, *v.t.*, *q.v.*

Metacarpal, *a.* مُتَعَلِّقٌ بِمُشْطِ ٱلْيَدِ ــ مُتَعَلِّقٌ بِٱلْوَظِيفِ .

Metacarpus, *n.* مُشْطُ ٱلْيَدِ ــ ٱلْوَظِيفُ .

Metachronism, *n.* تَأْخِيرُ ٱلتَّارِيخِ .

Metal, *n.* As iron, silver, *etc.*, مَعْدِن *pl.* مَعَادِن . Metal for roads, حَصًى . Metal cleared from dross, مَكِيب . *See also* Mineral, *n.*, *and* Mettle, *n.*

Metal, *v.t.* To lay, as of a road, with metal, رَصَفَ ـ بِٱلْحَصَى ² .

Metallic, *a.* Pertaining to metal, مَعْدِنِيٌّ . Metallic currency, نَقْد ــ سِكَّة .

Metalliferous, *a.* مُوَلِّدُ ٱلْمَعْدِنِ .

Metalliform, *a.* فِي هَيْئَةِ ٱلْمَعْدِنِ .

Metalline, *a.* مَعْدِنِيٌّ .

Metallist, *n.* A worker in metals, مُعَالِجُ ٱلْمَعَادِنِ . *See also* Metallurgist, *n.*

Metallization, *n.* تَصْيِيرُ ٱلشَّيْءِ مِثْلَ ٱلْمَعْدِنِ .

Metallize, *v.t.* صَيَّرَ (or صَنَعَ ـ =) مِثْلَ ٱلْمَعْدِنِ .

Metalloid, *n.* شِبْهُ ٱلْمَعْدِنِ .

Metalloidal, *a.* شَبِيهُ ٱلْمَعْدِنِ .

Metallurgic, *a.* مَا نِيطَ بِٱسْتِخْرَاجِ ٱلْمَعَادِنِ وَمُعَالَجَتِهَا .

Metallurgist, *n.* عالِمٌ ـ ماهِرٌ فِي صِناعةِ ٱسْتِخْراجِ ٱلْمَعادِنِ بِٱلْمَعادِنِ.

Metallurgy, *n.* صَنْعَةُ ٱسْتِخْراجِ ٱلْمَعادِنِ وَمُعالَجَتِها.

Metamorphic, *a.* ما دَلَّ عَلَى فاعِلِيَّةِ ٱلنّارِ فِي أَحْوالِ ٱلطَّبَقاتِ ٱلْأَرْضِيَّةِ ٱلْمَعْدِنِيَّةِ.

Metamorphism, *n.* أَحْوالُ ٱلطَّبَقاتِ ٱلْأَرْضِيَّةِ ٱلْمَعْدِنِيَّةِ مِنْ تَأْثِيرِ ٱلنّارِ فِيها.

Metamorphose, *v.t.* To transform into, حَوَّلَ ـ طَمَسَ ـ مَسَخَ ـ قَلَبَ, (the last word generally implies the being changed into something deformed). He metamorphosed him into a dog, قَلَبَهُ كَلْبًا; into a monkey, مَسَخَهُ قِرْدًا. She was metamorphosed into a serpent, تَحَوَّلَتْ حَيَّةً. To be metamorphosed, صارَ ـ إِنْقَلَبَ ـ تَحَوَّلَ ـ مُسِخَ ـ أُطْمِسَ. "O our Lord, — their possessions!" رَبَّنا ٱطْمِسْ عَلَى أَمْوالِهِمْ (*Kur.* x. 88.)

Metamorphosis, *n.* The act of, مَسْخ. Change of form, تَحَوُّلُ ٱلْهَيْئَةِ ـ إِنْبِدال ـ إِنْقِلاب ـ تَحَوُّل ـ تَقَلُّب ـ مُسُوخ *pl.* مَسْخ. One metamorphosed, مَسِيخ.

Metaphor, *n.* مَجاز ـ إِسْتِعارَة ـ أَمْثال *pl.* مَثَل ـ كِنايَة.

Metaphoric, *a.* / Metaphorical, مَجازِيّ ـ إِسْتِعارِيّ ـ مُسْتَعار.

Metaphorically, *ad.* مَجازًا ـ بِٱلْإِسْتِعارَةِ. To speak —, إِسْتَعارَ. To describe —, إِمْتَثَلَ ـ مَثَّلَ-بِ ـ كَنَى (or كَنا) بِ-عَن.

Metaphrase, *n.* تَرْجَمَةٌ حَرْفِيَّةٌ ـ تَرْجَمَةٌ لَفْظِيَّةٌ.

Metaphrastic, *a.* مُتَرْجَمٌ عِبارَةً بِعِبارَةٍ ـ لَفْظِيٌّ.

Metaphysic, *a.* / Metaphysical, إِلٰهِيٌّ ـ مُخْتَصٌّ بِٱلْمَعْقُولاتِ. Pertaining to the mind, فِكْرِيٌّ ـ عَقْلِيٌّ ـ نَظَرِيٌّ. Abstruse, غَوِيص.

Metaphysically, *ad.* إِلٰهِيَّةً ـ تَجْرِيدًا ـ عَقْلًا.

Metaphysician, *n.* عالِمٌ بِٱلْمَعْقُولاتِ ـ مُتَكَلِّم.

Metaphysics, *n.* عِلْمُ ـ الإِلٰهِيّاتُ ـ العِلْمُ ٱلْإِلٰهِيُّ ـ المَعْقُولاتُ ـ العالَمُ ٱلْإِلٰهِيُّ ـ عِلْمُ ٱلْحِكْمَةِ ـ ٱلْكَلام.

Metastasis, *n.* نُزُوحُ ٱلْأَمْراضِ.

Metatarsus, *n.* الوَظِيفُ ـ مُشْطُ ٱلرِّجْلِ.

Mete, *v.t.* *See to* Measure, *v.t.*

Metempsychosis, *n.* التَّقْمِيصُ ـ تَقَمُّصُ ٱلْأَرْواحِ ـ التَّناسُخُ.

Meteor, *n.* حَوادِثُ *pl.* حادِثٌ فِي ٱلْجَوِّ ـ شُهُب *pl.* شِهاب.

Meteors, النَّيازِكُ ـ الآثارُ ٱلسَّماوِيَّةُ.

Meteoric, *a.* مُتَعَلِّقٌ بِحَوادِثِ ٱلْجَوِّ ـ مُخْتَصٌّ بِٱلْآثارِ ٱلسَّماوِيَّةِ.

Meteorolite, *n.* / Meteorite, أَجْسامٌ صَلْدَةٌ *pl.* جِسْمٌ صَلْدٌ يَسْقُطُ مِنَ ٱلْجَوِّ ـ أَحْجار *pl.* حَجَرٌ ساقِطٌ مِنَ ٱلْجَوِّ.

Meteorological, *a.* مُخْتَصٌّ بِحَوادِثِ ٱلْجَوِّ.

Meteorologist, *n.* عالِمٌ بِعَلاماتِ ٱلسَّماءِ ـ عالِمٌ بِحَوادِثِ ٱلْجَوِّ.

Meteorology, *n.* عِلْمُ حَوادِثِ ٱلْجَوِّ ـ البَحْثُ عَنْ عَلاماتِ ٱلسَّماءِ.

Meteorous, *a.* يُشْبِهُ ٱلشِّهابَ.

Meter, *n.* / Metre, Measure, مِيزان ـ مِقْياس. Poetical —, نَظْم ـ مِيزانُ ٱلشِّعْرِ ـ أَوْزان *pl.* وَزْن ـ أَسْجاع *pl.* سَجْع ـ بُحُور *pl.* بَحْر. The French —, مِيتَر وَهُوَ قِياسٌ فَرَنْساوِيٌّ. To compose in —, سَجَّعَ ـ سَجَعَ ـ نَظَمَ.

Metheglin, *n.* *See* Hydromel, *n.*

Methinks, *v. imp.* البائِنُ لِي ـ عَلَى ظَنِّي.

Method, *n.* Orderly arrangement, نَظْم ـ ضَبْط ـ ضَباطَة ـ تَرْتِيب ـ نَسَق ـ نِظام ـ إِنْتِظام ـ سُمُوط *pl.* سِماط ـ قَواعِد *pl.* قاعِدَة. A way, manner, مِنْهاج ـ قاعِدَة ـ طَرِيقَة.

Methodic, *a.* / Methodical, نَسِيق ـ مُرَتَّب ـ مُنَسَّق ـ مُنْتَظِم ـ مَضْبُوط ـ حَسَبَ ٱلْقَواعِدِ. A — person, أَهْلُ ٱنْتِظام.

Methodically, *ad.* بِتَرْتِيبٍ ـ بِٱنْتِظامٍ ـ حَسَبَ ٱلْقَواعِدِ ـ عَلَى نَسَقٍ.

Methodism, *n.* The doctrines of the Methodists, مَذْهَبُ طائِفَةٍ مِنَ ٱلنَّصارَى ٱلْمُسَمّاةِ بِٱلْمِتُودِسْت.

Methodist, *n.* مِنْ أَصْحابِ ٱلشِّيعَةِ ٱلْمَذْكُورَةِ ٱلْمُدَّعِينَ بِصِحَّةِ ٱعْتِقادِهِمْ وَٱسْتِقامَةِ سُلُوكِهِمْ.

Methodistically, *ad.* Strictly, narrowly, بِنَسَقٍ ـ بِدِقَّةٍ ـ بِزُهْدٍ.

Methodize, *v.t.* رَتَّبَ ـ نَظَمَ ـ ضَبَطَ ـ نَسَّقَ. To be methodized, تَرَتَّبَ ـ إِنْتَظَمَ ـ إِتَّسَقَ ـ تَنَسَّقَ.

Methought, *v. imp.* عَلَى ما ظَنَنْتُ ـ بانَ لِي.

Methylic, *a.* / Methylated, مُقَطَّرٌ مِنَ ٱلْخَشَبِ. Methylated spirit, رُوحُ ٱلْعَرَقِ مَخْلُوطٌ بِماءٍ مُقَطَّرٍ مِنَ ٱلْخَشَبِ.

Metonymic, *a.* / Metonymical, كانٍ *pl.* كانُونَ *and* كُناة.

Metonymically, *ad.* بِكِنايَةٍ. To speak —, كَنا.

Metonymy, *n.* كِنايَة ـ تَلْوِيح ـ كُنًى *pl.* كُنْيَة. To describe by —, كَنَى (or كَنا) بِ-عَن. The science of metonymics, عِلْمُ ٱلْمَعانِي.

Metre, *n.* *See under* Meter, *n.*

Metrical, *a.* Measured, مَوْزُون. Consisting of verses, or of measured syllables, مَوْزُون ـ مُسَجَّع ـ مَنْظُوم.

Metrically, *ad.* عَلَى وَزْنٍ ـ وَزْنًا.

Metronome, *n.* آلَةٌ لِلْوَزْنِ.

Metronomy, *n.* وَزْنُ مُرُورِ ٱلزَّمانِ ـ وَزْنُ ٱلْأَوْقاتِ.

Metropolis, n. مِصْر pl. أَمْصَار — قَاعِدَة pl. قَوَاعِد — أُمّ ٱلْقُرَى — مَرْكَزُ ٱلسَّلْطَنَةِ — كُرْسِيُّ ٱلْمَمْلَكَةِ.

Metropolitan, a. Belonging to a metropolis, مُخْتَصّ بِمَرْكَزِ ٱلسَّلْطَنَةِ — مَدَنِيّ — مَدِينِيّ — مُخْتَصّ بِٱلْقَاعِدَةِ. Pertaining to a metropolitan, مَطْرَانِيّ — مُخْتَصّ بِٱلْمَطْرَانِ.

Metropolitan, n. مَطْرَان pl. مَطَارِنَة — مِتْرِيبُولِيت.

Mettle, n. شَوْكَة — مُرُوَّة حِدَّة — حُمَيَّا — ثَوْرَة. To put one on his —, حَرَّضَ — أَنْفَسَ.

Mettlesome, a. فَلْتَان — غَيْرَان — ذُو حِدَّةٍ — شَدِيدُ ٱلْحُمَيَّا. See also Spirited, Fiery, a.

Mettlesomeness, n. See Mettle, n.

Mew, n. The sea-bird, نَوْرَزَة. See also Coop, n.

Mew, v.a. To shut up, حَبَسَ. To inclose in a cage, حَطَّ فِي قَفَصٍ. To cast, as a skin, feathers, etc. أَنْسَلَ.

Mew, v.i. As of a cat, مَأَى — مَاغَ — نَغَمَ. To make a noise like a cat, أَمْوَأَ. To cast, as a skin, feathers, etc., نَسَلَ — أَنْسَلَ.

Mew, n. / Mewing, } As of a cat, مُوَاغ — مُوَّة — مُوَاء — مُوّ ٱلْقِطِّ. The act of casting off feathers or skin, إِنْسَال. Cast off feathers or skin, نُسَال.

Mewl, v.i. صَرَخَ. Mewling, n. صُرَاخ.

Mews, n. (إِصْطَبْلَات or) مَحَلّ أَصَاطِب — آخُور. The royal —, آخُورُ ٱلسُّلْطَانِ.

Mezereon, n. مَازَرْيُون — مَاذَرْيُون.

Mezzo-relievo, a. نِصْفُهُ بَارِزٌ.

Mezzo-tint, n. / Mezzo-tinto, } نُسْخَةٌ مَطْبُوعَةٌ مِنْ صَحِيفَةٍ نُحَاسِيَّةٍ طِبْقَ رَسْمٍ مَرْسُوم بِحِبْرٍ صِينِيّ.

Mezzo-voce, a. عِبَارَةٌ عَنْ صَوْتٍ خَفِيفٍ.

Miasma, n. بُخَارَاتٌ وَخِيمَةٌ — فَوَحَاتٌ رَدِيئَةٌ.

Miasmal, a. / Miasmatic, } وَخِيم — مُتَوَخِّم.

Mica, n. طَلْق — طَلْقٌ أَبْيَضُ.

Micaceous, a. مِنْ جِنْسِ ٱلطَّلْقِ.

Mice, n. pl. of Mouse, n., q.v.

Michaelmas, n. عِيدُ حَضْرَةِ (مَار or) مِيخَائِيل ٱلْوَاقِع فِي ٢٩ أَيْلُول.

Mickle, a. كَثِير.

Microcosm, n. عَالَمٌ صَغِيرٌ — عَالَمٌ مُخْتَصَرٌ.

Micrometer, n. مِقْيَاسُ ٱلْجُزْئِيَّاتِ.

Microscope, n. نَظَّارَةٌ تُكَبِّرُ ٱلْأَشْيَاءَ ٱلدَّقِيقَةَ.

Microscopic, a. / Microscopical, } Belonging to a microscope, مَا نِيطَ بِٱلنَّظَّارَةِ ٱلْمَذْكُورَةِ. Not apparent except through a microscope, مَا لَا يُرَى إِلَّا بِٱلنَّظَّارَةِ ٱلْمَذْكُورَةِ. Very small, جُزْئِيّ — صَغِيرٌ لِلْغَايَةِ.

Micturate, v.i. شَلْشَلَ بَوْلَهُ. See also under to Piddle, v.i.

Micturition, n. شَلْشَالُ ٱلْبَوْلِ — تَبَوُّل.

Mid, a. نَصْف — نِصْف.

Mid, n. See Midshipman, n.

Mid-course, n. Half-way, نِصْفُ ٱلطَّرِيقِ — نِصْفُ ٱلْمَسَافَةِ. A middle course, سَيْرٌ مُتَوَسِّطٌ — وَسَطُ ٱلطَّرِيقِ.

Mid-day, n. See Noon, n.

Middle, a. وُسْطَى — وَاسِط — مُتَوَسِّط — وَسْطَانِيّ. The — finger, ٱلْوُسْطَى. The — ages, ٱلْقُرُونُ ٱلْمُتَوَسِّطَةُ — ٱلْأَعْصَارُ ٱلْمُتَوَسِّطَةُ. A — term, وُسْطَى. To hold a — course, أَنْصَفَ — تَوَسَّطَ. A — course is the best, (prov.) خَيْرُ ٱلْأُمُورِ أَوْسَطُهَا.

Middle, n. The point equally remote from the extremes, جَوْز — حَاقّ — وَسَط. Centre, core, جَوْف — قَلْب pl. قِلَبَة. The waist, حَقْو — خَصْر. To cut through the —, to halve, شَطَرَ — شَطَّرَ. To bring into the —, وَسَّطَ. To attain the — of anything, نَصَّفَ — أَنْصَفَ.

Middle-age, n. عَوَان — نِصْف — نُصْف. To attain to —, نَصَفَ.

Middle-aged, a. نَصَف pl. نَصَفُونَ and أَنْصَاف. A — woman, مُسْلِف — نُصَيْف. Middle-aged women, نُصُف.

Middle-man, n. One who rents large tracts and lets them in small portions, مَنْ يَسْتَأْجِرُ ٱلْأَرَاضِي جُمْلَةً مِنْ صَاحِبِهَا ثُمَّ يُكْرِيهَا بُقْعَةً بُقْعَةً — أُخْرِين — ضَمَّانُ ٱلْأَرَاضِي — مُلْتَزِم. An agent, وَكِيل pl. وُكَلَاء. A broker, سِمْسَار pl. سَمَاسِرَة. The occupation of a —, إِلْتِزَام.

Middlemost, a. ٱلْأَوْسَطُ.

Middling, a. وَسَط — مُتَوَسِّط — وَسْطَانِيّ — مُقَارِب — بَيْنَ بَيْنَ. Of — stature, مُقْتَصِد.

Middlingly, ad. بَيْنَ بَيْنَ — عَلَى قَدْرٍ.

Middlings, n. Of flour, جَرِيش.

Middy, n. See Midshipman, n.

Midge, n. See Gnat, n.

Mid-heaven, n. وَسَطُ ٱلسَّمَاءِ.

Midland, a. وَاقِعٌ فِي أَوَاسِطِ ٱلْبِلَادِ — فِي دَاخِلِ ٱلْبِلَادِ.

Midleg, n. وَسَطُ ٱلسَّاقِ.

Mid-lent, n. وَسَطُ ٱلصِّيَامِ — وَسَطُ ٱلصَّوْمِ ٱلْكَبِيرِ.

Midmost, a. See Middlemost, a.

Midnight, n. وَسَطُ (or نِصْفُ) ٱللَّيْلِ. Just after —, بَعْدَ نِصْفِ

She arose at —, قَامَتْ فِي وَسَطِ ٱللَّيْلِ تَقْرِيبًا. He continued speaking till —, أَطَالَ ٱلْكَلَامَ إِلَى نِصْفِ ٱللَّيْلِ.

Midrib, *n.* Of a leaf, شُرْكٌ *pl.* الشِّرَاكُ ٱلْأَكْبَرُ فِي وَرَقَةٍ.

Midriff, *n.* حِجَابُ ٱلْكَبِدِ ـ حِجَابُ ٱلْقَلْبِ ـ النَّخِلُبُ ـ السِّبْرَآءُ.

Midship, *a.* مَا كَانَ فِي وَسَطِ ٱلْمَرْكَبِ.

Midshipman, *n.* مُلَازِمٌ ثَانٍ مِنَ ٱلْبَحْرِيَّةِ.

Midships, *ad.* Amidships, فِي وَسَطِ ٱلْمَرْكَبِ.

Midst, *n.* وَسَطٌ ـ وَسْطٌ ـ جَوْفٌ. In the — of a thing, فِي وَسَطِهِ; out of the —, مِنْ وَسَطِهِ. In the — of the people, وَسْطَ ٱلْقَوْمِ ـ فِي ٱلنَّاسِ. In the — of the affair, فِي أَثْنَآءِ ٱلْأَمْرِ. The door of the house was rent in the —, وَٱنْشَقَّ بَابُ ٱلدَّارِ مِنْ وَسَطِهِ. He went through the — of the city, عَبَرَ فِي وَسَطِ ٱلْمَدِينَةِ. Out of the — of the fire, مِنْ وَسْطِ ٱلنَّارِ. He went into the — of the people, دَخَلَ فِي وَسْطِ ٱلْقَوْمِ. *See also* Middle, *n.*

Mid-stream, *n.* وَسْطُ ٱلنَّهْرِ.

Midsummer, *n.* قَيْظٌ *pl.* أَقْيَاظٌ. Belonging to —, قَيْظِيٌّ.

Midway, *n.* نِصْفُ ٱلْمَسَافَةِ ـ نِصْفُ ٱلطَّرِيقِ.

Midwife, *n.* مُوَلِّدَةٌ ـ مُعْتَلِفَةٌ ـ قَبِيلٌ ـ قَبِيلَةٌ ـ قَابِلَةٌ *pl.* قَوَابِلُ ـ دَايَةٌ.

Midwifery, *n.* The office of a midwife, قِبَالَةٌ. The art of aiding childbirth, طِبُّ ٱلتَّوْلِيدِ.

Midwinter, *n.* نِصْفُ ٱلشِّتَآءِ.

Mien, *n.* مَنْظَرٌ ـ وَجْهٌ ـ وَضْعٌ ـ هِيئَةٌ ـ شَكْلٌ ـ سَمَامَةٌ. *See also under* Air, Face, *n.*

Miff, *n.* زَعَلٌ. He was in a — with him, زَعِلَ مِنْهُ.

Might, *v. aux.* (*pret. of* May), أَمْكَنَ لِ. I — have been rich, أَمْكَنَنِي أَنْ أَسْتَغْنِيَ ـ أَمْكَنَ لِي أَنْ أَسْتَغْنِيَ. They — have been early, لَعَلَّهُمْ يَتَبَكَّرُوا (or يَبْكُرُوا). They — be very prosperous, لَعَلَّهُمْ يَتَوَفَّقُونَ. You — be too hasty, لَعَلَّكَ شَدِيدُ ٱلْعَجَلَةِ.

Might, *n.* عِزٌّ ـ حَوْلٌ ـ حَيْلٌ ـ شِدَّةٌ ـ قُوَّةٌ ـ قُدْرَةٌ ـ بَطْشٌ ـ مَقْدِرَةٌ ـ شِدَّةٌ ـ سَوْرَةٌ ـ شَوْكَةٌ. Eminence, عِزٌّ. Vehemence, شِدَّةٌ ـ سَوْرَةٌ ـ شَوْكَةٌ. With — and main, بِكُلِّ ٱلْجُهْدِ. Above my —, فَوْقَ طَاقَتِي. *See also* Power, *n.*

Mightily, *ad.* بِحَيْلٍ ـ بِشِدَّةٍ ـ بِقُوَّةٍ ـ بِٱشْتِدَادٍ ـ عِزَّةً. Largely, جِدًّا. He cried out —, صَرَخَ بِصَوْتٍ عَظِيمٍ. It grew —, نَمَى بِشِدَّةٍ.

Mightiness, *n.* As a title; *See* Highness, *n.* *Also* Might, *n.*

Mighty, *a.* Eminent, glorious, عَزِيزٌ. Having great physical power, ذُو قُوَّةٍ ـ قَوِيٌّ ـ شَدِيدُ ٱلْبَطْشِ ـ قَدِيرٌ ـ قَادِرٌ. Great, large, عَظِيمٌ ـ كَبِيرٌ ـ جَزِيلٌ. Great in number, عَدِيدٌ ـ ثَرِيٌّ ـ شَدِيدٌ ـ مُجِيجٌ ـ ثَجٌّ ـ جَارِفٌ. Rushing with violence, شَتَّى. Important, great, مُهِمٌّ ـ عَظِيمٌ. A — king, مَلِكٌ أَعَزُّ. Mighty deeds, عَظَائِمُ. Mighty in deed, مُقْتَدِرٌ فِي ٱلْفِعْلِ. Mighty in speech, مُقْتَدِرٌ فِي ٱلْأَقْوَالِ. A — wind, رِيحٌ دَاعِبَةٌ. The Mighty, God, ٱلْأَكْبَرُ ـ ٱلْعَزِيزُ. To become —, عَزَّ. To make —, eminent, عَزَّزَ.

Mighty, *ad.* جِدًّا ـ كَثِيرًا.

Mignonette, *n.* فَاغِيَةٌ *vulg.* تَمْرَحِنَّا.

Migrate, *v.i.* إِنْتَقَلَ ـ تَنَقَّلَ; of birds, قَطَعَ قُطُوعًا. The birds migrated, ضَرَبَتِ ٱلطَّيْرُ.

Migrating, *n.* }
Migration, } نُقْلَةٌ *pl.* نُقَلٌ ـ إِنْتِقَالٌ; of birds, قُطُوعٌ or قِطَاعٌ (or قَطَاعٌ) ٱلطَّيْرِ.

Migratory, *a.* مُنْتَقِلٌ ـ نَاقِلٌ. A — body, قَوْمٌ سَافِرَةٌ ـ قَوْمٌ سَفْرٌ. Migratory birds, طَيْرٌ ضَوَارِبُ ـ قَوَاطِعُ ـ نَوَاقِلُ *as opposed to* أَوَابِدُ or non-migratory. *See also* Nomad, *n.*

Milch, *a.* حَلُوبٌ ـ حَلُوبَةٌ *pl.* حَلَائِبُ ـ حَلْبَانَةٌ. Milch animals, ذَوَاتُ ٱلدَّرِّ.

Mild, *a.* Soft, operating gently, لَيِّنٌ. Light, easy, خَفِيفٌ ـ لَيِّنُ ٱلْجَانِبِ ـ حَلِيمُ ٱلنَّفْسِ ـ وَدِيعٌ ـ حَلِيمٌ. Gentle, لَطِيفٌ. Not sharp, sweet, حُلْوٌ ـ عَذْبٌ ـ عَاذِبٌ. Slight, not heavy, قَلِيلٌ ـ خَفِيفٌ. Moderate, مُعْتَدِلٌ. Mild temperature, هَوَآءٌ مُعْتَدِلٌ. Mild speech, كَلَامٌ عَذْبٌ. A — aspect, mien, وَجْهٌ بَشُوشٌ. A — voice, صَوْتٌ رَقِيقٌ ـ صَوْتٌ خَفِضٌ ـ حَسَنٌ (or رَخِيمٌ).

Mildew, *n.* عُفُونَةٌ ـ يَرَقَانٌ.

Mildew, *v.t.* عَفَّنَ ـ ضَرَبَ يَرَقَانًا.

Mildew, *v.i.* تَعَفَّنَ ـ أُصِيبَ بِيَرَقَانٍ.

Mildewed, *a.* مُعَفَّنٌ ـ عَفِنٌ ـ مَيْرُوقٌ.

Mildly, *ad.* Not harshly, gently, بِلِينَةٍ ـ بِلَيَانٍ. With gentleness, softness, حِلْمًا ـ بِرِفْقٍ ـ بِلَطَافَةٍ. Without noise or tumult, مِنْ غَيْرِ ضَجَّةٍ ـ بِهُدُوٍّ. Delicately, بِلَطَافَةٍ ـ بِحِلْمٍ. Without precipitation, بِتَأَنٍّ ـ عَلَى مَهْلٍ ـ رُوَيْدًا. Moderately, بَيْنَ بَيْنَ ـ عَلَى قَدْرٍ. Laxly, بِرَخَاوَةٍ. To do a thing —, تَأَنَّى فِي ـ أَرْوَدَ فِي. He acted — towards him, أَرْوَدَهُ.

Mildness, *n.* Softness, gentleness, لُطْفٌ ـ لِينٌ ـ لِينَةٌ ـ لَيَانٌ; of disposition, لَطَافَةُ ٱلطَّبْعِ ـ رَأْفَةٌ ـ وَدَاعَةٌ ـ حِلْمٌ ـ لِينُ ٱلْجَانِبِ. Moderation, إِعْتِدَالٌ. Mildness of countenance, بَشَاشَةُ ٱلْوَجْهِ; of speech, عُذُوبَةُ ٱلْكَلَامِ; of the atmosphere, إِعْتِدَالُ ٱلْهَوَآءِ.

Mile, *n.* مِيلٌ *pl.* أَمْيَالٌ.

Mileage, *n.* مَكْسُ ٱلْمِيلِ.

Milestone, *n.* صُوَّةُ ٱلْمِيلِ *pl.* صُوًى — مَعْلَمُ ٱلْمِيلِ *pl.* مَعالِمُ ٱلْأَمْيالِ.

Miliary, *a.* A — fever, حَرارَةٌ ذاتُ حَصْبَةٍ مِثْلَ حَبِّ ٱلذُّرَةِ.

Milieu, *n.* La juste —, ٱلقَصْدُ.

Militant, *a.* مُجاهِد. The Church —, ٱلكَنِيسَةُ ٱلْمُجاهِدَةُ.

Militarily, *ad.* مِثْلَ ٱلعَسْكَرِ — جُنْدِيًّا.

Military, *a.* عَسْكَرِيٌّ — جُنْدِيٌّ — سَيْفِيٌّ. Warlike, حَرْبِيٌّ.

Military service, خِدْمَةٌ عَسْكَرِيَّةٌ. A — station, depôt, مَرْكَزُ عَسْكَرٍ — مَرْكَزُ طابُورٍ. A — man, عَسْكَرِيٌّ *pl.* عَساكِرُ. A — force, فَيْلَق — كَتِيبَة. Military ranks, ٱلرُّتَبُ ٱلعَسْكَرِيَّةُ.

Military, *n.* The body of soldiers, ٱلعَساكِرُ — ٱلجُنُودُ.

Militate, *v.i.* To — against, خالَفَ — ضادَّ.

Militia, *n.* عَسْكَرُ ٱلرَّدِيفِ — رَدِيفٌ عَسْكَرِيٌّ.

Militia-man, *n.* نَفَرٌ مِنَ ٱلرَّدِيفِ ٱلعَسْكَرِيِّ *pl.* أَنْفار.

Milk, *n.* حَلَب — حَلِيب — لَبَن. New —, حَلَب — رَمَث. New — into which cold water has been poured, شَنِين. Sour —, لَبَنٌ حامِضٌ — لَبَنٌ رائِبٌ — حَلِيبٌ مَرُوبٌ — ضَرِيب. Thickened or clotted —, خاثِر. The — of a pregnant woman, غَيْل; the first — drawn from a woman after childbirth, صِمْغَة. Milk of almonds, مُسْتَحْلَبُ ٱللَّوْزِ. To mix — with water, سَمَّرَ. To thicken, of —, أَخْثَرَ. Brought up on —, مَلْبُون — لَبِين. Skimmed —, مَخِيض. To have or give —, لَبِنَ ـَ — دَرَّتْ بِلَبَنِها ـِـُ.

Milk, *v.t.* حَلَبَ ـُـِ — إِسْتَحْلَبَ.

Milk-diet, *n.* فَرِيقَة — حُلْبَة — ضَرِيب.

Milker, *n.* حالِب *pl.* حَلَبَة — حَلُوب.

Milk-fever, *n.* حُمَّى ٱلْإِرْضاعِ.

Milkiness, *n.* خاصِّيَّةُ ٱللَّبَنِ.

Milking, *n.* حَلْب — حَلَبَة. A place of —, مَحْلَب.

Milk-jug, *n.* وِعاءُ ٱلْحَلِيبِ.

Milkmaid, *n.* حالِبَة *pl.* حالِبات — لَبّانَة.

Milkman, *n.* لَبّان.

Milkpail, *n.* عُلْبَة *pl.* عُلَب — مِلْبَن — مِحْلَب — مِعْلَق.

Milkpan, *n.* ماجُورُ ٱللَّبَنِ *pl.* مَواجِيرُ.

Milksop, *n.* أَخْرَق *pl.* خُرْق — أَبْلَهُ — جاهِل — طَرِيٌّ — جَبان.

Milk-tooth, *n.* راضِعَة *pl.* رَواضِعُ.

Milk-white, *a.* أَبْيَضُ كَٱللَّبَنِ.

Milkwoman, *n.* لَبّانَة.

Milkwort, *n.* لُوبانَةٌ مَغْرِبِيَّةٌ — فُرْفُور.

Milky, *a.* Yielding milk, لَبِنَة *fem.* لَبِن — لُبُون *pl.* لِبْن — ذاتُ لَبَنٍ. Made of milk, مُلَبَّن. Like milk, مِثْلُ ٱللَّبَنِ.

Milky-way, *n.* ٱلمَسْكَبَةُ — ٱلمَجَرَّةُ — ٱلحُبُكُ — ٱلشَّرَجُ — أُمُّ ٱلنُّجُومِ.

Mill, *n.* As for grinding, رَحًى *pl.* أَرْحاءٌ — طاحُون *pl.* طَواحِينُ. A — which is turned by a horse or mule, مَدار *pl.* مَدارات. A hand —, عَرِيبَة — رَحَى ٱلْيَدِ — جارُوشَة; a small — for grinding coarsely, مِجَشّ. A small — for pressing fruits, *etc.*, مِعْصَرَة *pl.* مَعاصِرُ. The building used for grinding, مِطْحَنَة *pl.* مَطاحِنُ. A machine, آلَة *pl.* آلات — دُولاب *pl.* دَوالِيبُ. The — round coin, زِنْجِير. A manufacture, صِناعَة. A manufactory, مَعْمَل. A — for stamping money, مِلْزَمَة. I turned the —, رَحَوْتُ ٱلرَّحَى.

Mill, *v.t.* To grind, as of corn, *etc.*, طَحَنَ ـَ. To turn a —, رَحَى *aor.* يَرْحُو. To stamp coin, ضَرَبَ ٱلسِّكَّةَ ـِ — سَكَّ ٱلدَّراهِمَ ـُ; to put an edge to coin, نَيَّرَ ٱلسِّكَّةَ — زَنْجَرَ ٱلسِّكَّةَ. To froth, as of chocolate, *etc.*, رَغَّى — أَرْغَى. To —, of cloth, قَصَرَ ـُ.

Mill-board, *n.* مُقَوًّى *pl.* مُقَوَّيات.

Mill-dam, *n.* سَدُّ ماءِ ٱلطّاحُونِ.

Milled, *n.* Of coin, سِكَّةٌ مُزَنْجَرَةٌ — سِكَّةٌ مُنَيَّرَةٌ; of cloth, مَقْصُور.

Millennarian, *a.* Consisting of a thousand years, أَلْفِيٌّ — مُتَضَمِّنٌ أَلْفَ عامٍ.

Millennarian, *n.*
Millennialist, } مِنْ أَهْلِ فِرْقَةٍ مِنَ ٱلنَّصارَى يَعْتَقِدُ أَصْحابُها رُجُوعَ ٱلْمَسِيحِ إِلَى ٱلْأَرْضِ ثانِيَةً لِيَمْلُكَ أَلْفَ عامٍ قَبْلَ يَوْمِ ٱلْبَعْثِ.

Millennarianism, *n.* إِعْتِقادُ ٱلْفِرْقَةِ ٱلْمَذْكُورَةِ.

Millennary, *n.* مُدَّةُ أَلْفِ سَنَةٍ.

Millennial, *a.* ما نِيطَ بِٱلْاِعْتِقادِ ٱلْمَذْكُورِ.

Millennium, *n.* مُدَّةُ أَلْفِ عامٍ بَنَى عَلَيْها ٱعْتِقادَهُمْ أَصْحابُ ٱلْفِرْقَةِ ٱلْمَذْكُورَةِ.

Millepede, *n.* دُوَيْبَّةٌ كَثِيرَةُ ٱلْأَرْجُلِ *vulg.* أَبُو سِتَّةٍ — أُمُّ أَرْبَعٍ وَأَرْبَعِينَ رِجْلًا.

Miller, *n.* طَحّان. The owner of a mill turned by animals, مَداراتِيّ.

Millesimal, *n.* A thousandth part, واحِدٌ مِنْ أَلْفٍ. Thousandth, ٱلْأَلْف.

Millet, *n.* The *holcus sorghum*, طَمّ — ذُرَة — ذُرَةٌ صَيْفِيٌّ — ذُرَةٌ بَيْضاءُ — حَبُّ ٱلشَّرانِقِ. A small kind of —, جاوَرْس — دُخْن.

Milliner, *n.* خَيّاطَةُ مَلْبُوسِ ٱلنِّساءِ — خَيّاطَة.

Millinery, *n.* أَمْتِعَةُ قِسْمِ ٱلنِّسْوانِ — مَلْبُوساتُ ٱلنِّساءِ.

Milling, *n.* Grinding, طَحْن — طِحانَة. Fulling, of cloth, قَصْر. Making a raised edge on coin, تَنْيِيرُ ٱلسِّكَّةِ — زَنْجَرَةُ ٱلسِّكَّةِ.

Million, *n.* مِئَةُ رِبْوَةٍ — أَلْفُ أَلْفٍ — مِلْيُون. Thousands of millions, أُلُوفُ رِبْوات.

Millionaire, *n.* غَنِيٌّ ـ مُدَرْهَم ـ أَتْرَب ـ مُثْرِب ـ مُقَنْطِر ـ أَتْرَب ـ تَرِب ـ صَاحِبُ آلَافٍ ـ لِلْغَايَةِ. To become a —, أَتْرَبَ ـ تَرِبَ.

Millionth, *n.* الأَلْفُ رِبْوَةٍ. A — part, وَاحِدٌ مِنْ أَلْفِ أَلْفٍ.

Mill-pond, *n.* بِرْكَةُ مَاءِ ٱلطَّاحُونِ.

Mill-race, *n.* مَجْرَى مَاءِ ٱلطَّاحُونِ.

Millstone, *n.* حَجَرُ طَاحُونٍ *pl.* أَحْجَار ـ رَحًى *pl.* أَرْحَاء ـ جِرْجَارَة ـ حِجَارَة. An upper —, مِرْدَاة; a lower —, ثُفَال ـ ثِفَال.

Mill-wright, *n.* A maker of mills, صَانِعُ ٱلطَّوَاحِينِ; of mill-stones, مُرْحٍ.

Milt, *n.* The spleen, طِحَال *pl.* طُحُل. The — of fish, مُخُّ ٱلسَّمَكِ.

Milter, *n.* الذَّكَرُ مِنَ ٱلسَّمَكِ.

Mime, *n.* A farce, لَعِبُ ٱلتَّقْلِيدِ *vulg.* لَعِبُ مَسْخَرَةٍ ـ مَسْخَرَة. An actor in a mime, مُتَشَخِّص ـ مُشَخِّص *vulg.* مُقَلِّد. A buffoon, هَزِل ـ هِزِّيل ـ مُضْحِك.

Mimetic, Mimetical, *a.* Mimic, } Imitating, مُتَشَخِّص ـ مُشَخِّص. Jocose, derisive, مَازِح ـ سُخَرَة ـ هِزِّيل ـ هَزْلِيٌّ.

Mimic, *n.* A personator, مُتَشَخِّص ـ مُشَخِّص. A buffoon, or one who ridicules, سُخَرَة ـ مَسْخَرَة ـ مُضْحِك.

Mimic, *v.t.* To personify, شَخَّصَ. To mock, ridicule, هَزِئَ ـ ب or سَخِرَ مِن ـ ب or مِن ـ ب *vulg.* قَلَّدَ.

Mimically, *ad.* As personifying, بِتَشْخِيصٍ ـ تَشَخُّصًا. Jocosely, مَزْحًا.

Mimicry, *n.* Personification, تَشْخِيص *vulg.* تَقْلِيد. Jocoseness, مُزَاحَة ـ مُزَاح ـ هَزْل.

Mimosa, *n.* The — *Nilotica*, السَّنْطُ ـ الصَّنْتُ.

Minacious, *a.* *See* Menacing, *a.*

Minaret, *n.* مِئْذَنَة ـ مَأْذَنَة ـ مَنَارَة *pl.* مَآذِنُ. The crier from the —, مُؤَذِّن ـ أَذِين. The call from the —, الأَذَانُ.

Minatory, *a.* *See* Menacing, *a.*

Mince, *v.t.* To cut up small, فَرَمَ ـ نَعَّمَ ـ فَرَمَ نَاعِمًا. To — one's words, قَطَّعَ كَلَامَهُ ـ تَأَنَّقَ فِي كَلَامِهِ. To palliate, سَتَرَ ـ دَارَى عَن ـ بِٱلْبَاطِلِ. Not to — matters with, to be unreserved with, إِنْبَسَطَ إِلَى.

Mince, *v.i.* To walk with affected nicety, خَطَرَ ـ تَمَشَّى ـ تَبَخْتَرَ ـ بَخْتَرَ ـ تَشَامَخَ ـ تَبَخْتَرَ. A mincing gait, بُخْتُرِيَّة. To speak with affectation, تَصَلَّفَ. To affect delicacy of manner, تَكَيَّسَ ـ تَظَرَّفَ.

Mince-meat, *n.* قِيمَة ـ لَحْمٌ مَفْرُومٌ ـ كُبَاب.

Mince-pie, *n.* سَنْبُوسَك.

Mincingly, *ad.* In small parts, كُبَابًا ـ تَكْبِيبًا. With affected delicacy, بِمُبَاهَاةٍ ـ بِتَكَيُّسٍ ـ بِتَظَرُّفٍ. One who walks —, بَخْتَرِيّ ـ بِخْتِير.

Mind, *n.* ضَمِير *pl.* ضَمَائِرُ. The heart, لُبّ *pl.* أَلْبَاب ـ قَلْب *pl.* قُلُوب. The intellect, intelligence, ذِهْن ـ ذِهْن ـ عَقْل. Thought, opinion, ظَنّ ـ رَأْي ـ فِكْر ـ ذَكَاء ـ فِطْنَة ـ فَهْم. Intention, مُرَاد ـ نِيَّة ـ مَرَام. Inclination, خَاطِر ـ مَيْل. Attention, بَال. Give me thy —, attention, أَعْطِنِي بَالَكَ. He had a — to the work, كَانَ لَهُ قَلْبٌ فِي ٱلْعَمَلِ. It was in my — to, نَوَيْتُ ب ـ كَانَ فِي قَلْبِي أَنْ. What never entered into my —, مَا لَمْ يَخْطُرْ بِبَالِي.

After one's mind, عَلَى كَيْفِهِ ـ عَلَى مُرَادِهِ ـ عَلَى خَاطِرِهِ.

A reprobate mind, ذِهْنٌ مَرْفُوضٌ.

Desire of the mind, رَغْبَةُ ٱلنَّفْسِ.

Grief of mind, غَمّ ـ مَرَارَةُ نَفْسٍ.

In one's right mind, سَالِمُ ٱلْعَقْلِ ـ عَاقِل.

Of doubtful mind, مُرِيب ـ مُتَقَلْقِل.

Of unsound mind, مَجْنُون ـ مُخْتَلُّ ٱلْعَقْلِ ـ مُخْتَلّ.

Presence of mind, جَرَاءَة ـ إِقْدَام ـ سُرْعَةُ عَقْلٍ.

Readiness of mind, خَاطِر ـ إِقْدَام ـ نَشَاط. With all readiness of mind, بِكُلِّ نَشَاطٍ.

Time out of mind, مِنْ زَمَانٍ مَنْسِيِّ ٱلذِّكْرِ ـ مِنَ ٱلْقَدِيمِ.

To one's mind, عَلَى خَاطِرِهِ ـ عَلَى مُرَادِهِ.

Turn of mind, خُلْق ـ خُلُق ـ طَبِيعَة ـ سُرْجُوجَة ـ سَجِيَّة ـ ضَرِيبَة.

To alter one's mind, عَدَلَ ـ رَجَعَ فِي رَأْيِهِ ـ أَحَالَ رَأْيَهُ (or أَضْرَبَ) عَنْ رَأْيِهِ.

To apply one's mind to, تَفَرَّسَ فِي ـ وَاظَبَ عَلَى ـ وَجَّهَ قَلْبَهُ إِلَى ـ شَبَكَ ٱلْعَقْلَ فِي.

To be easy in one's mind, إِرْتَاحَ بَالُهُ ـ إِطْمَأَنَّ خَاطِرُهُ.

To be fully persuaded in one's mind, تَيَقَّنَ فِي عَقْلِهِ.

To be of one mind with, وَافَقَ رَأْيَهُ. They were all of one mind about that, إِجْتَمَعَتْ آرَاؤُهُمْ عَلَى ذَلِكَ.

To be of sound mind, كَانَ سَالِمَ ٱلْعَقْلِ ـ تَعَقَّلَ ـ عَقَلَ.

To be out of one's mind, تَجَنَّنَ ـ جُنَّ ـ إِخْتَلَّ عَقْلُهُ.

To be uneasy in one's mind, إِضْطَرَبَ ـ تَقَلْقَلَ.

To bear in mind, أَضْمَرَ عَلَى ـ تَفَكَّرَ فِي ـ ذَكَرَ ـ تَذَكَّرَ.

To break one's mind to, كَشَفَ لِ ـ سِرَّهُ ـ بَيَّنَ لِ ـ مَا فِي خَاطِرِهِ ـ أَطْلَعَ ـ عَلَى سِرِّهِ.

To bring to the mind of one, أَذْكَرَ ـ ذَكَّرَ.

To call to mind, رَدَّدَ-فِي قَلْبِهِ ـ ² رَدَّ-فِي قَلْبِهِ ـ تَذَكَّرَ.

To change one's mind about, أَضْرَبَ عَن ـ ² عَدَلَ عَن.

To disburden one's mind to; *See* To break one's mind to; *supra.*

To enter one's mind, بَدَا لَهُ ـ ² خَطَرَ بِبَالِهِ ـ هَجَسَ فِي صَدْرِهِ *aor.* يَبْدُو. It had not entered the mind of any one, لَمْ يَخْطُرْ عَلَى بَالِ أَحَدٍ.

To find a thing to one's mind, إِسْتَطَابَ ـ إِسْتَحْسَنَ.

To float in one's mind, هَجَسَ فِي صَدْرِهِ.

To follow one's own mind, عَمِلَ ـ رَكِبَ رَأْيَهُ ـ إِقْتَدَى لِأَمْرِهِ عَلَى كَيْفِهِ.

To give one's mind to, مَارَسَ. *See also supra,* To apply one's mind to.

To go out of one's mind, to forget, ذَهَبَ عَلَيْهِ ـ ضَاعَ مِنْ بَالِهِ ـ نَسِيَ. To become crazy, إِسْتُجِنَّ ـ جُنَّ ـ إِخْتَلَّ عَقْلُهُ.

To have a mind to, وَشَكَ أَن ـ ² هَمَّ بِ ـ كَادَ ـ أَرَادَ *aor.* فِي خَاطِرِهِ أَن ـ يَوْشُكُ.

To have a great mind to, فِي غَايَةِ خَاطِرِهِ أَن ـ ² هَمَّ بِ-لِلْغَايَةِ.

To have a thing in one's mind, أَضْمَرَ عَلَى شَيْءٍ.

To have one's mind upon, إِهْتَمَّ بِ ـ تَفَكَّرَ فِي.

To know one's own mind, إِتَّقَنَ مَا فِي عَقْلِهِ.

To lose one's mind, طَارَ عَقْلُهُ. To lose one's presence of mind, جُنَّ ـ ضَيَّعَ الْمَعْقُولَ ـ ضَيَّعَ عَقْلَهُ ـ خَبِلَ.

To make up one's mind to, تَعَمَّدَ ـ جَمَعَ عَلَى ـ جَزَمَ عَلَى ـ أَزْمَعَ عَلَى.

To occur to one's mind; *See supra,* To enter into one's mind.

To put one in mind, أَذْكَرَ ـ ذَكَّرَ.

To recall to mind, إِسْتَذْكَرَ.

To set one's mind upon, وَضَعَ قَلْبَهُ عَلَى ـ ² هَمَّ بِ *aor.* يَضَعُ.

To satisfy one's mind, إِتَّقَنَ بِ ـ إِكْتَفَى بِ.

To speak one's mind, تَفَتَّحَ فِي الْكَلَامِ. To speak one's mind to, to be unreserved with, إِنْبَسَطَ إِلَى.

To turn one's mind from ... to, أَضْرَبَ عَن-إِلَى ـ انْتَكَثَ مِن-إِلَى.

To unbend one's mind from, إِسْتَرَاحَ مِن ـ تَفَرَّغَ مِن ـ تَفَصَّى مِن.

Mind, *v.t.* To attend to, obey, لَحَ إِلَى ـ إِنْصَتَ إِلَى ـ إِلْتَفَتَ إِلَى ـ سَمِعَ لِ. To think seriously about, to be mindful of, إِعْتَنَى بِ ـ إِهْتَمَّ بِ ـ تَفَكَّرَ فِي. To watch over, as at pasture, أَرْعَى. To watch, take care of, إِسْتَفْقَدَ ـ ² حَرَسَ ـ دَارَى. To heed, بَالَى بِ. He was minded to, أَرَادَ أَن ـ كَانَ فِي قَلْبِهِ أَن. I was minded to come to you, كُنْتُ أَشَاءُ أَنْ آتِيَ إِلَى عِنْدَكُمْ. I don't — him, لَا أُبَالِي بِهِ ـ مَا أَكْتَرِثُ لَهُ. Never mind! لَا تَنْزَعِجْ ـ لَا تَكْتَرِثْ. The soldiers did not — the orders of their officers, العَسَاكِرُ لَمْ تَطِعْ أَمْرَ ضُبَّاطِهَا.

Minded, *a.* مُهْتَمٌّ ـ مُتَفَكِّرٌ. Liberal —, وَاسِعُ ـ رَحِيبُ الصَّدْرِ الصَّدْرِ.

Mindful, *a.* Of the memory, ذَكِرٌ. To be — of one's affairs, رَعَيْتُ عَلَيْهِ ـ رَعَى أَمْرَهُ. I was — of the respect due to him, حُرْمَتَهُ. Mindful, regardful, رَصِينٌ. He is — of your want, هُوَ رَصِينٌ بِحَاجَتِكَ. To be — of one's self, تَحَفَّظَ.

Mindfully, *ad.* بِاعْتِنَاءٍ ـ اِهْتِمَامًا.

Mindfulness, *n.* مُرَاعَاةٌ ـ دَوَرَانُ بَالٍ ـ هِمَّةٌ ـ اِعْتِنَاءٌ ـ اِهْتِمَامٌ.

Mine, *pr.* لِي *vulg.* مَتَاعِي *or* بِتَاعِي. All that is — is thine, and what is thine is —, كُلُّ مَا هُوَ لِي فَهُوَ لَكَ وَمَا هُوَ لَكَ فَهُوَ لِي.

Mine, *n.* A place where minerals are dug, مَعْدِنٌ *pl.* مَعَادِنُ. A subterranean passage, لُغْمٌ *pl.* لُغُومٌ. To discover a —, of minerals, كَشَفَ عَنْ مَعْدِنٍ. To spring a —, طَيَّرَ اللُّغْمَ. To work a —, عَالَجَ الْمَعْدِنَ.

Mine, *v.t.* To dig a mine under..., ... حَفَرَ لُغْمًا تَحْتَ أَ... ـ لَغَمَ. To dig away, sap, نَبَشَ ـ ² نَقَبَ ـ حَفَرَ. To destroy slowly, أَزَالَ-تَدْرِيجًا.

Mine, *v.i.* *See to* Burrow, *v.t.*

Miner, *n.* As of mineral mines, مَعْدِنْجِي ـ مُعَدِّنٌ; of subterranean excavations, لُغْمْجِي ـ فَاعِلٌ فِي اللُّغْمِ. Military Sappers and Miners, عَسَاكِرُ الْخَنَادِقِ. *See also under* Pioneer, *n.*

Mineral, *n.* مَعْدِنٌ ـ رِكَازٌ *pl.* رِكْزَةٌ *or* رَكِيزَةٌ ـ سُيُوبٌ *pl.* سَيْبٌ *pl.* مَعَادِنُ ـ جِسْمٌ مَعْدِنِيٌّ *pl.* أَجْسَامٌ. Minerals, أَجْسَامٌ مَعْدِنِيَّاتٌ ـ جَمَادَاتٌ ـ مَعْدِنِيَّةٌ.

Mineral, *a.* مَعْدِنِيٌّ. Mineral waters, مِيَاهٌ مَعْدِنِيَّةٌ. Mineral substances, مُنْطَرِقَاتٌ.

Mineralist, *n.* *See* Mineralogist, *n.*

Mineralization, *n.* The impregnation with a mineral, إِدْخَالُ مَادَّةِ الْمَعَادِنِ فِي شَيْءٍ.

Mineralize, *v.t.* To impregnate with a mineral, أَدْخَلَ مَادَّةَ الْمَعَادِنِ فِي شَيْءٍ.

Mineralize, *v.i.* To look for minerals, فَتَّشَ عَنِ الْمَعَادِنِ (الرِّكَازِ *or* السُّيُوبِ *or*).

Mineralized, *a.* مَا كَانَ فِيهِ مَادَّةٌ ـ مَشْرُوبٌ مِنَ الْمَعَادِنِ مَعْدِنِيَّةٌ.

Mineralizer, *n.* The substance that mineralizes, الْمَادَّةُ الَّتِي تُصَيِّرُ الشَّيْءَ مَعْدِنًا.

Mineralogical, *a.* مَعْدِنِيٌّ ـ مُتَعَلِّقٌ بِالْمَعَادِنِ.

Mineralogist, *n.* مِنْ أَهْلِ عِلْمِ ٱلْمَعَادِنِ ـ عَالِمٌ بِٱلْمَعَادِنِ.

Mineralogy, *n.* عِلْمُ ٱلْمَعَادِنِ.

Minever, *n.* The fur, سِنْجَاب; the colour, سِنْجَابِيٌّ.

Mingle, *v.t.* خَلَطَ ـ خَلَّطَ ـ شَمَّطَ ـ مَزَجَ ـ بِ ـ مَشَجَ.

See also to Mix, *v.t.*

Mingle, *v.i.* To intermingle with, إِخْتَلَطَ ـ خَالَطَ ـ مَازَجَ.

Mingled, *a.* مَخْلُوط ـ مَمْزُوج ـ شَمِيط.

Mingler, *n.* خَالِط ـ مَازِج.

Mingling, *n.* إِخْتِلَاط ـ تَخْلِيط ـ مِزَاج ـ خَلْط ـ مَزْج.

Miniature, *n.* تَصْوِيرٌ رَفِيعٌ. In —, فِي صُورَةٍ صَغِيرَةٍ.

Miniature, *a.* رَفِيع ـ صَغِير.

Minikin, *a.* ظَرِيف ـ رَفِيع ـ صُغَيِّر.

Minikin, *n.* عَيْن ـ عَزِيز ـ مَحْبُوب.

Minim, *n.* A dwarf, حَنْبَس ـ هَبَنَّق. A note in music, عَلَامَةٌ فِي فَنِّ رَقْمِ ٱلْمُوسِيقَى. A drop, قَطْرَة *pl.* قَطَرَات.

Minimum, *n.* ٱلْمِقْدَارُ ٱلْأَدْنَى ـ أَدْنَى ـ أَقَلّ.

Mining, *a.* حَفَّار ـ مَعْدِنِيٌّ ـ مُتَعَلِّقٌ بِٱلْمَعَادِنِ ـ مُتَعَلِّقٌ بِٱلْحَفْرِ.

Mining, *n.* The working of mines, مُعَالَجَةُ ٱلْمَعَادِنِ; making military mines, حَفْرُ ٱللُّغُوم.

Minion, *n.* مُبَصْبِص ـ مُدَاهِن.

Minion-like, *a.* }
Miniously, } كَٱلْمُبَصْبِصِ ـ كَٱلْمُدَاهِنِ.

Minister, *n.* One who serves, خَادِم *pl.* خُدَّام. An agent, وَكِيل *pl.* وُكَلَاء ـ نَائِب *pl.* نُوَّاب. An ambassador or envoy, إِيلْجِي ـ سَفِير. One commissioned, مَأْمُور. A — of religion, among Muslims, إِمَام *pl.* أَئِمَّة ـ شَيْخ *pl.* مَشَايِخ. A Christian presbyter, قِسِّيس *pl.* قِسِّيس ـ قُسُس مِنَ ٱلْمِلَّةِ. A dissenting —, قِسِّيس مِنَ ٱلْمِلَّةِ ٱلْمُعْتَزِلَةِ عَنِ ٱلْكَنِيسَةِ ٱلْمَلَكِيَّةِ ٱلرَّسْمِيَّةِ. A chief officer in civil affairs, وَزِير *pl.* وُزَرَاء. To be (state) —, وَزَرَ *aor.* يَزِرُ. To be made or to act as (state) — to, تَوَزَّرَ ل. The Ministers, وُكَلَاءُ ٱلدَّوْلَةِ.

Prime Minister, ٱلْوَزِيرُ ـ صَدْرُ ٱلصُّدُورِ ـ ٱلْوَزِيرُ ٱلْأَعْظَمُ.

Minister of Commerce, وَزِيرُ ٱلتِّجَارَةِ.

Minister of Finance, وَزِيرُ ٱلْمَالِيَّةِ.

Minister of Foreign Affairs, وَزِيرُ ٱلْخَارِجِيَّةِ.

Minister of Home Affairs, وَزِيرُ ٱلدَّاخِلِيَّةِ.

Minister of Public Works, وَزِيرُ ٱلْمَنَافِعِ.

Minister of War, وَزِيرُ ٱلْحَرْبِيَّةِ.

Minister of Worship, وَزِيرُ ٱلْعِبَادَاتِ (or ٱلْأَدْيَانِ).

Minister, *v.t.* To — to, serve, خَدَمَ ². To supply, أَغَاثَ ـ أَمَدَّ ـ بِ ـ قَدَّمَ ل ـ أَعْطَى. *See also to* Administer, *v.t.*

Minister, *v.i.* To perform service in any office, خَدَمَ ب ² ـ عَمِلَ فِي ².

Ministerial, *a.* Official, رَسْمِيٌّ. Clerical, أَكْلِيرِيكِيٌّ ـ كَنَائِسِيٌّ. Pertaining to a state minister, مُتَعَلِّقٌ بِوَزِيرٍ. Ministerial (state) functions, مَأْمُورِيَّةُ وَزِيرٍ ـ وَزَارَة ـ وِزَارَة. A — partisan, مِنْ حِزْبِ ٱلْوُزَرَاءِ. A — party, حِزْبُ وُكَلَاءِ ٱلدَّوْلَةِ. A — crisis, حَالُ بُحْرَانٍ عِنْدَ وُزَرَاءِ ٱلدَّوْلَةِ. A — journal, صَحِيفَةٌ مُتَعَصِّبَةٌ لِلْوُزَرَاءِ.

Ministerially, *ad.* رَسْمِيًّا.

Ministrant, *a.* خَادِم ـ عَامِل *pl.* عُمَّال.

Ministration, *n.* إِجْرَاء ـ عَمَل ـ خِدْمَة.

Ministry, *n.* Office, مَأْمُورِيَّة ـ وَظِيفَة. Service, خِدْمَة. Agency, وَكَالَة. The ecclesiastical profession, ٱلْقُسُوسِيَّة. The office of a minister of state, وَزَارَة. The body of state ministers, وُزَرَاء (or وُكَلَاء) ٱلدَّوْلَةِ. To form a (state) —, شَكَّلَ هَيْئَةَ ٱلْوَزَارَةِ. A change of the (state) —, تَغْيِيرُ ٱلْوَزَارَةِ ـ تَبْدِيلُ ٱلْوُزَرَاءِ. The department of a state minister, نَظَارَة ـ وَزَارَة; *e.g.*, the Ministry of Foreign Affairs, وَزَارَة (or نَظَارَة) ٱلْخَارِجِيَّةِ. The present —, ٱلْوَزَارَةُ ٱلْحَالِيَّةُ.

Minium, *n.* سُلَاقُون.

Minnow, *n.* نَوْعٌ مِنْ صِغَارِ ٱلسَّمَكِ.

Minor, *a.* Less, أَصْغَرُ *fem.* صُغْرَى. Lower, أَسْفَلُ ـ أَحَطُّ ـ أَدْنَى. Light, خَفِيف. Small, صَغِير ـ وَجِيز. Of — importance, أَقَلُّ ضَرُورَةٍ. Asia Minor, أَنَاطُول ـ أَسِيَا ٱلصُّغْرَى. The — key, in music, ٱلطَّامَّةُ ٱلصُّغْرَى.

Minor, *n.* One under age, صَغِير *pl.* صِغَار *and* صُغَرَاء *fem.* صَغِيرَة *pl.* صِغَار *and* صَغَائِرُ ـ قَاصِر *pl.* قُصَّر. The — proportions of a syllogism, ٱلصُّغْرَى ـ ٱلْمُفْرَدَةُ ـ ٱلْمُفْرَدُ.

Minority, *n.* The state of being under age, صَبَاوَة ـ صُغْرَى ـ قُصْرُ ٱلْأَوْلَادِ. The smaller number, ٱلْأَقَلُّ. The opinion of the —, رَأْيُ ٱلْأَقَلِّ.

Minotaur, *n.* مَسْخٌ وَهْمِيٌّ نِصْفُهُ بَشَرٌ وَنِصْفُهُ ثَوْرٌ.

Minster, *n.* The church of a monastery, كَنِيسَةُ دَيْرٍ. *See also* Cathedral, *n.*

Minstrel, *n.* A singer, musician, مُزَمِّر ـ عَوَّاد ـ مُطْرِب. A poet, شَاعِر *pl.* شُعَرَاء.

Minstrelsy, *n.* تَرَنُّم ـ تَرْنِيم ـ نَوْبَة ـ غِنَاء. Poetry, شِعْر.

Mint, *n.* A place where coin is struck, دَارُ ٱلسِّكَّةِ ـ دَارُ ٱلضَّرْبِ. A manufactory, مَعْمَل. A source, مَعْدِن ـ مَنْبَع. A large amount, مَبْلَغٌ جَسِيم. The plant, نَعْنَاع ـ نَعْنَع. Water-mint,

حَبَقُ ٱلتِّمْسَاحِ ـ حَبَقُ ٱلْمَآءِ ـ ٱلْفُوتَنْجُ ٱلنَّهْرِيُّ . Master of the —, ناظِرُ دارِ ٱلسِّكَّةِ ـ ناظِرُ دارِ ٱلضَّرْبِ .

Mint, *v.t.* To coin money, ضَرَبَ ٱلسِّكَّةَ ـ سَكَّ ٱلدَّرَاهِمَ ـ ـُ . To invent, أَبْدَعَ ـ إِخْتَرَعَ .

Mintage, *n.* Coinage, ضَرْبُ سِكَّةٍ ـ ضَرْب . Duty for coining, حَقُّ ٱلضَّرْبِ .

Minuet, *n.* ضَرْبٌ مِنَ ٱلرَّقْصِ .

Minus, *ad.* Denoting subtraction, نَاقِص . Without, بِلا . With the exception of, ما عَدَا .

Minute, *n.* As of time, or of a circle, دَقِيقَةٌ *pl.* دَقَائِقُ . A summary note, as of proceedings, مَضْبَطَةٌ *pl.* مَضَابِطُ . A note, memorandum, تَذْكِرَة ـ تَذْكِرَة .

Minute, *v.t.* To note in few words, قَيَّدَ ـ ضَبَطَ ـ ـُ لَخَّصَ ـ خَطَّ .

Minute, *a.* Very small, جُزْئِيٌّ ـ دَقِيقٌ *pl.* دِقَاقٌ ـ رَفِيعٌ *pl.* رِفَاعٌ ـ رَقِيقٌ *pl.* رِقَاقٌ . Particular, exact, مُدَقِّقٌ ـ كَثِيرُ ٱلتَّدْقِيقِ . A — matter, أَمْرٌ زَهِيدٌ ـ تَفَاهَةٌ ـ شَيْءٌ وَجِيزٌ ـ شَيْءٌ دَنِيٌّ *pl.* أَشْيَآءُ دَنِيَّةٌ . A — quantity, قِرْطِيطَةٌ . To be or to become —, دَقَّ *aor.* يَدِقُّ ـ إِسْتَدَقَّ . *See also under* Small, *a.*

Minute-book, *n.* دَفْتَرُ مَضَابِطَ ـ دَفْتَرُ تَقْيِيدٍ ـ دُسْتُور .

Minute-glass, *n.* آلَةٌ مِنَ ٱلزُّجَاجِ فِيهَا رَمْلٌ تَصْلُحُ لِحِسَابِ ٱلدَّقَائِقِ *vulg.* رَمْلِيَّةُ ٱلدَّقَائِقِ .

Minute-gun, *n.* ضَرْبُ مِدْفَعٍ مَرَّةً فِي كُلِّ دَقِيقَةٍ عَلَامَةَ ٱلْخَطَرِ ـ ضَرْبُ مَدَافِعَ إِعْلَانًا بِٱلْخَطَرِ .

Minute-hand, *n.* عَقْرَبُ ٱلدَّقَائِقِ .

Minutely, *ad.* بِدِقَّةٍ ـ بِٱلتَّدْقِيقِ ـ بِرَفَاعَةٍ . To examine into —, أَغَارَ فِي .

Minuteness, *n.* نَزَارَة ـ دِقَّة ـ رَفَاعَة ـ رِقَّة .

Minutiæ, *n.* ٱلْأُمُورِ (دَقَائِقُ *or*) مَدَاقُّ ـ أَشْيَآءُ وَجِيزَةٌ ـ أُمُورٌ زَهِيدَةٌ ـ جُزْئِيَّات ـ تَفْصِيلَات .

Minx, *n.* A wanton girl, بِنْتٌ عَاهِرَةٌ ـ بِنْتٌ خَاسِرَةٌ .

Miocene, *a.* In geology, مَا نِيطَ بِٱلطَّبَقَةِ ٱلثَّالِثَةِ ٱلْوُسْطَى مِنْ طَبَقَاتِ ٱلْأَرْضِ .

Miracle, *n.* An act beyond the ordinary laws of nature, آيَةٌ *pl.* آيَات ـ مُعْجِزَةٌ *pl.* مُعْجِزَات . A prodigy, wonder, أُعْجُوبَةٌ *pl.* أَعَاجِيبُ ـ عَجِيبَةٌ *pl.* عَجَائِبُ .

Miraculous, *a.* Supernatural, آيَة ـ مِنْ عِنْدِ ٱللّٰهِ ـ فَوْقَ ٱلطَّبِيعَةِ ـ مِنْ سَمْتِ ٱلْمُعْجِزَةِ . Wonderful, عَجِيب ـ غَرِيب .

Miraculously, *ad.* By miracle, فِي سَمْتِ ٱلْمُعْجِزَةِ ـ بِنَوْعٍ يَفُوقُ ٱلطَّبِيعَةَ ـ مِنْ عِنْدِ ٱللّٰهِ . Wonderfully, عَجَبًا ـ بِنَوْعٍ عَجِيبٍ .

Mirage, *n.* آل ـ خَيْتَعُور ـ ٱلْخَيْدَعُ ـ عَسْعَاس ـ سَرَاب .

Mire, *n.* حَمْأَةٌ ـ غَمْقَةٌ ـ رَدَغَة ـ رَزَغَة ـ طِين . To fall into the —, إِرْتَدَغَ . *See also* Mud, *n.*

Mire, *v.t.* To soil with mire, لَوَّثَ ـ بِرَدَاغٍ . To fix in mire, غَمَسَ فِي ٱلرَّزَغِ ـ ـِ .

Mire, *v.i.* To sink in mire, غَاصَ فِي ٱلْحَمْأَةِ ـ ـُ إِنْغَمَسَ فِي ٱلرَّدَغِ . To stick in the mire, in a figurative sense, تَوَرَّطَ ـ إِرْتَبَكَ .

Mirificent, *a.* مُعْجِب .

Miriness, *n.* *See* Mire, *n.*

Mirror, *n.* A looking glass, سَجَنْجَل ـ مِرْآةٌ *pl.* مَرَاءٍ *and* مَرَايَا . He looked into the —, تَرَآءَى فِي ٱلْمِرْآةِ . To hold up a — to, أَرْأَى ـ ٱلْمِرْآةَ .

Mirror, *v.t.* To reflect, as in a mirror, رَدَّ ـ ـُ عَكَسَ ـ ـِ .

Mirth, *n.* طَرَب ـ غِبْطَة ـ حُبُور ـ سُرُور ـ فَرَح ـ إِنْبِسَاط ـ كَيْف .

Mirthful, *a.* مَغْبُوط ـ مَسْرُور ـ فَرْحَان ـ مَبْسُوط ـ بَجْبُوح . To be —, طَرِبَ ـ ـَ تَغَبَّطَ ـ إِغْتَبَطَ ـ إِنْبَسَطَ ـ تَبَجَّحَ ـ تَكَيَّفَ . *See also* Merry, *a.*

Mirthfully, *ad.* تَغَبُّطًا ـ بِسُرُورٍ ـ بِفَرَحٍ ـ بِٱنْبِسَاطٍ ـ بِطَرَبٍ ـ تَكَيُّفًا .

Mirthless, *a.* *See* Joyless, *a.*

Mirthlessness, *n.* *See* Joylessness, *n.*

Miry, *a.* رَادِغ ـ غَمِق ـ غَمِيق ـ وَحِل . A — place, رَدِغ ـ مَرْزَغ ـ غَمِقَة *pl.* غَمِقَات . To become —, أَرْزَغَ ـ رَدِغَ ـ ـَ أَرْدَغَ .

Mirza, *n.* مِيرْزَا .

Misacceptation, *n.* مَعْنًى مَغْلُوط ـ تَصْحِيفٌ فِي ٱلْمَعْنَى .

Misadventure, *n.* قَضَآءٌ ـ بَلَآءٌ ـ مُصِيبَةٌ .

Misanthrope, *n.* } Misanthropist, } مُتَوَحِّش ـ حُوشِيٌّ ـ وَحْشِيٌّ .

Misanthropic, *a.* } Misanthropical, } مُتَوَحِّش ـ حُوشِيٌّ ـ وَحْشِيٌّ ـ مُتَنَفِّر .

Misanthropy, *n.* حُوشِيَّة ـ وَحْشَة ـ نُفُور .

Misapplication, *n.* سُوءُ ٱسْتِعْمَالٍ ـ سُوءُ تَصَرُّفٍ .

Misapply, *v.t.* أَخْطَأَ فِي ٱسْتِعْمَالِ ٱلشَّيْءِ ـ غَلِطَ فِي تَصَرُّفِ ٱلْأَمْرِ ـ ـَ . *See also to* Mismanage, *to* Misinterpret, *to* Misuse, *v.t.*

Misapprehend, *v.t.* أَخْطَأَ فِي فَهْمِ (*or* إِدْرَاكِ) ٱلشَّيْءِ ـ غَلِطَ فِي ـ ـَ مَعْنَى ٱلشَّيْءِ .

Misapprehension, *n.* خَطَآءٌ ـ غَلَط ـ سَهْو .

Misappropriate, *v.t.* To pilfer, steal, إِخْتَلَسَ ـ سَرَقَ ـ ـِ .

Misappropriation, *n.* إِخْتِلَاس ـ سَرِق ـ سَرِقَة .

Misarrange, *v.t.* عَثْعَثَ ـ خَاحَثَ ـ لَبَّكَ ـ هَوَّشَ ـ لَخْبَطَ ـ خَبَّصَ .

Misbecome, *v.t.* مَا لَاقَ بِ ـ مَا لَبِقَ بِ.

Misbegotten, *a.* *See* Bastard, Illegitimate, *a.*

Misbehave, *v.i.* قَبُحَ ـ أَسَآءَ ـ تَصَرَّفَ بِقَبَاحَةٍ.

Misbehaviour, *n.* سُوْء أَدَبٍ ـ سِيرَةٌ رَدِيئَةٌ ـ سُوْءُ سُلُوكٍ ـ سُلُوكٌ رَدِئٌ.

Misbelief, *n.* سُوْءُ ٱعْتِقَادٍ ـ كُفْر.

Misbelieve, *v.i.* To be an unbeliever, كَفَرَ.

Misbestow, *v.t.* مَنَحَ ـ فِي غَيْرِ مَحَلِّهِ ـ أَعْطَى ـ مِنْ غَيْرِ حَقٍّ ـ ضَيَّعَ ٱلْإِحْسَانَ فِيهِ.

Miscalculate, *v.t.* أَخْطَأَ فِي ٱلْحِسَابِ ـ غَلِطَ فِي ٱلْحِسْبَةِ ـ غَلِطَ فِي.

Miscalculation, *n.* غَلَط ـ خَطَآء فِي ٱلْحِسَابِ.

Miscall, *v.t.* سَمَّى ـ بِٱلْغَلَطِ ـ غَلِطَ فِي ٱلتَّسْمِيَةِ ـ صَحَّفَ ـ صَحَّفَ عَلَى.

Miscarriage, *n.* Want of success, عَدَمُ نَجَاحٍ ـ خَيْبَة ـ فَشَل. A slip, lapse, fault, سِقَاط ـ سَقْطَة. Loss, خَسَارَة ـ خُسْرَان. Birth before the proper time, سُقْطُ ٱلْجَنِينِ ـ إِنْسِقَاط ـ طَرْح. The — of justice, عَدَمُ وَفَآءِ ٱلْحَقِّ.

Miscarry, *v.i.* Not to succeed, of a person, خَابَ *aor.* يَخِيبُ; of a thing, بَطَلَ ـ مَا صَحَّ. Not to arrive at its destination, مَا وَصَلَ ـ ضَاعَ ـ مَا بَلَغَ. To cast young, أَسْقَطَتِ ٱلْجَنِينَ ـ طَرَحَت.

Miscast, *v.t.* *See to* Miscalculate, *v.t.*

Miscellaneous, *a.* شَامِل ـ مُتَنَوِّع ـ مُتَلَوِّن ـ مُخْتَلِف ـ أَشْكَالٌ أَشْكَالٌ. A — collection, مَجْمُوعَة ـ مَجْمَعَة ـ جِمَاع.

Miscellaneously, *ad.* شَمْلًا ـ تَشْكِيلًا ـ إِلْتِقَاطًا.

Miscellaneousness, *n.* تَنَوُّع ـ شَمْل ـ تَلَوُّن ـ تَشْكِيل.

Miscellany, *n.* مَجْمَعَة ـ مَجْمُوعَة ـ جِمَاع.

Mischance, *n.* حَادِثَة *pl.* حَوَادِثُ ـ مُصِيبَة *pl.* مَصَائِبُ ـ قَضَآء ـ دَاهِيَة.

Mischarge, *n.* غَلَطٌ فِي ٱلْمُحَاسَبَةِ ـ خَطَآء فِي ٱلْحِسَابِ ـ تَقْيِيدُ غَلَطٍ.

Mischarge, *v.t.* ضَمَّ ـ إِلَى ٱلْحِسَابِ بِلَا حَقٍّ ـ حَسَبَ ـ لِ ـ مِنْ ـ غَيْرَ حَقٍّ ـ أَخْطَأَ فِي ٱلْحِسَابِ.

Mischief, *n.* Damage, injury, حَكْر ـ إِجْحَاف ـ ضُرّ ـ ضَرَر ـ مَضَرَّة. Loss, خَسَارَة. Evil, wrong doing, خَلَاعَة ـ سُوْء ـ شَرّ ـ أَذِيَّة ـ أَذًى. Discord, شَغْب ـ نِزَاع ـ فِتْنَة ـ فَسَاد. Trouble, difficulty, غَائِلَة *pl.* غَوَائِلُ ـ مُصِيبَة ـ فَسَاد. One ready for —, عَتِل. To do — to, to damage, ضَارَّ ـ أَضَرَّ ـ خَسَّرَ. To do —, فَعَلَ سُوْءًا ـ أَسَآءَ. To make —, stir up discord, among, شَغَّبَ وَقَّعَ ـ رَمَى ٱلْفِتْنَةَ بَيْنَ ـ أَلَّبَ بَيْنَ ـ عَلَى *or* بِ *or* فِي ـ هَيَّجَ ٱلْخِصَامَ بَيْنَ ـ بَيْنَ. To do — to, to harm, injure, حَكَرَ ـ أَجْحَفَ بِ ـ آذَى ـ شَارَّ ـ عَمِلَ بِ ـ شَرًّا. To practise — against, نَصَبَ عَلَى ـ شَرًّا ـ أَنْشَأَ عَلَى ـ شَرًّا. To fall into —, وَقَعَ بِشَرٍّ *aor.* يَقَعُ. To seek to do —, طَلَبَ ٱلشَّرَّ. To devise —, إِخْتَرَعَ ٱلشَّرَّ. Mischief befell him, صَادَفَهُ شَرٌّ. Prepared for —, مُتَأَهِّبٌ لِلشَّرِّ.

Mischief, *v.t.* To harm, *etc.*; *See preceding article.*

Mischief-maker, *n.* أَرَّاج ـ ذُو مَشَاغِبَ ـ شَغَّاب ـ مُشَغِّب ـ فَتَّان ـ مُفْسِد.

Mischief-making, *n.* أَرْش ـ شَغْب ـ تَشْغِيب ـ فِتَن ـ فِتْنَة ـ فَسَاد.

Mischievous, *a.* Harmful, ضَارّ ـ مُضِرّ. Doing what is disagreeable, annoying, حَكِر ـ أَذِي ـ أَذَوِيّ. Wicked, خَلِيع ـ خَبِيث ـ شِرِّير. Making mischief, discord, شَغَّاب ـ مُشَغِّب ـ ذُو مَشَاغِبَ ـ مُفْسِد. Mischievous things, مَفَاسِدُ. Mischievous persons, مُفْسِدُونَ. A — man, شَذَاةُ ٱلْخُلُقِ ـ سَيِّئُ ٱلْخُلُقِ. To entertain a — intention, تَفَكَّرَ بِمَكِيدَةٍ ـ تَخَيَّلَ شَرًّا. To be —, vicious, خَلُعَ.

Mischievously, *ad.* بِخَلَاعَةٍ ـ بِقَصْدِ سُوْءٍ ـ بِخَبَاثَةٍ ـ بِرَدَآءَةٍ ـ بِشَرٍّ.

Mischievousness, *n.* *See* Mischief, *n.*

Mischna, *n.* *See* Mishna, *n.*

Mischoose, *v.t.* أَخْطَأَ فِي ٱلْخِيرَةِ ـ إِخْتَارَ ـ بِٱلْخِلَافِ.

Mis-citation, *n.* *See* Misquotation, *n.*

Mis-cite, *v.t.* *See to* Misquote, *v.t.*

Mis-claim, *n.* طَلَبٌ مِنْ غَيْرِ حَقٍّ ـ إِدِّعَآءٌ بَاطِلٌ ـ دَعْوَةٌ بِلَا أَسَاسٍ.

Miscomputation, *n.* *See* Miscalculation, *n.*

Miscompute, *v.t.* *See to* Miscalculate, *v.t.*

Misconceit, *n.* } Misconception, } خَطَأٌ فِي ٱلْفَهْمِ ـ خَطَأٌ ـ غَلَطٌ.

Misconceive, *v.i.* أَخْطَأَ فِي فَهْمِ ٱلشَّيْءِ ـ إِلْتَبَسَ عَلَيْهِ فَهْمُ ٱلشَّيْءِ.

Misconduct, *n.* Wrong management, سُوْءُ تَدْبِيرٍ (*or* إِدَارَةٍ) ـ قِلَّةُ ضَبْطٍ ـ تَشْوِيش. *See also* Misbehaviour, *n.*

Misconduct, *v.t.* To manage badly, أَخْطَأَ فِي تَدْبِيرِ ٱلشَّيْءِ ـ شَوَّشَ ـ هَوَّشَ. *See also to* Misbehave, *v.i.*

Misconjecture, *n.* خَطَأٌ فِي ٱلظَّنِّ ـ غَلَطٌ فِي ٱلتَّخْمِينِ.

Misconjecture, *v.i.* أَخْطَأَ فِي ٱلظَّنِّ ـ غَلِطَ فِي ٱلتَّخْمِينِ.

Misconstruction, *n.* تَصْحِيف ـ تَحْرِيف ـ عَكْسُ ٱلْمَعْنَى.

Misconstrue, *v.t.* صَحَّفَ ـ حَرَّفَ ـ عَكَسَ ٱلْمَعْنَى.

Misconnt, *v.t.* To mistake in counting, غَلِطَ فِي ٱلْحِسَابِ ـ أَخْطَأَ فِي ٱلتَّعْدِيدِ. To estimate incorrectly, حَسَبَ ـ بِلَا دِقَّةٍ.

Miscount, *n.* خَطَأٌ ـ خَطَأٌ فِي ٱلتَّعْدِيدِ ـ غَلَطٌ فِي ٱلْحِسَابِ.

Miscreant, *n.* A vile wretch, مَهْتُوكٌ ـ فَاحِشٌ ـ خَبِيثٌ. *See also* Infidel, *n.*

Misdate, *v.t.* صَحَّفَ ٱلتَّارِيخَ ـ أَرَّخَ-غَلَطًا.

Misdate, *n.* غَلَطٌ فِي ٱلتَّارِيخِ ـ تَصْحِيفُ ٱلتَّارِيخِ.

Misdeed, *n.* ذَنْبٌ *pl.* ذُنُوبٌ ـ فِعْلٌ سُوءٌ ـ قَبَاحَةٌ *pl.* قَبَائِحُ ـ خَطِيئَةٌ *pl.* خَطَايَا ـ جُنَاحٌ.

Misdeem, *v.t.* غَلِطَ فِي-ظَنًّا ـ أَخْطَأَ فِي تَخْمِينِهِ إِيَّاهُ.

Misdemean, *v.t.* To — one's self; *See to* Misbehave, *v.i.*

Misdemeanour, *n.* ذَنْبٌ *pl.* ذُنُوبٌ ـ قَبَاحَةٌ ـ جُنَاحٌ.

Misdirect, *v.t.* To misconduct, أَخْطَأَ فِي تَدْبِيرِ ٱلشَّيْءِ ـ شَوَّشَ ـ هَوَّشَ. To — a letter, أَخْطَأَ فِي تَعْلِيقِ عِنْوَانِ ٱلْخَطِّ. To direct wrongly, أَرْشَدَ-غَلَطًا. To make to go astray, ضَلَّلَ.

Misdirection, *n.* Mismanagement, تَشْوِيشٌ ـ سُوءُ تَدْبِيرٍ (*or* إِدَارَةٍ). A wrong address, غَلَطٌ فِي ٱلْعِنْوَانِ. Wrong guidance, إِرْشَادٌ غَلَطٌ. Causing to go astray, إِغْوَاءٌ ـ تَضْلِيلٌ.

Misdo, *v.t.* To do badly, أَتَى بِبَشَاعَةٍ ـ أَفْسَدَ عَمَلَهُ ـ أَسَاءَ. To muddle, شَوَّشَ ـ هَوَّشَ ـ لَبَّكَ ـ خَمْخَمَ.

Misdo, *v.i.* أَفْسَدَ ـ أَقْبَحَ ـ أَسَاءَ فِي ٱلْعَمَلِ.

Misdoer, *n.* شِرِّيرٌ *pl.* أَشْرَارٌ ـ رَجُلٌ سُوءٌ ـ رَدِيءٌ *pl.* أَرْدِيَاءُ.

Misdoing, *n.* إِسَاءَةٌ ـ قَبَاحَةٌ ـ جُنَاحٌ ـ أَذِيَّةٌ ـ عَمَلٌ سُوءٌ.

Misdoubt, *v.t.* شَكَّ فِي *aor.* يَشُكُّ ـ أَرَابَ ـ ٱتَّهَمَ بِ ـ تَشَكَّكَ فِي.

Misdoubt, *n.* شَكٌّ ـ رِيبَةٌ ـ ٱتِّهَامٌ.

Misemploy, *v.t.* فَرَّطَ فِي ـ أَسَاءَ فِي ـ ٱنْتَهَكَ. He misemployed his time, ضَيَّعَ أَوْقَاتَهُ. He misemployed his talents, ضَيَّعَ فَضَائِلَهُ.

Misemployment, *n.* سُوءُ ٱسْتِعْمَالٍ ـ ٱنْتِهَاكٌ ـ إِسَاءَةٌ.

Mis-enter, *v.i.* أَخْطَأَ فِي تَقْيِيدِ ٱلشَّيْءِ ـ قَيَّدَ-(*or* دَوَّنَ-) غَلَطًا.

Mis-entry, *n.* غَلَطٌ فِي ٱلْقَيْدِ ـ خَطَأٌ فِي ٱلتَّقْيِيدِ.

Miser, *n.* بَخِيلٌ *pl.* بُخَلَاءُ ـ طَمَّاعٌ ـ طَامِعٌ ـ مَسَّاكٌ ـ شَحَّاحٌ ـ خَسِيسٌ. *See also* Avaricious, *a.*

Miserable, *a.* Unhappy, شَقِيٌّ ـ بَائِسٌ ـ مَشْؤُومٌ ـ نَحِسٌ ـ مِسْكِينٌ *pl.* مَسَاكِينُ ـ مَنْحُوسٌ. A — fellow, شَقِيٌّ لَقِيٌّ. Wicked, شِرِّيرٌ *pl.* أَشْرَارٌ ـ رَدِيءٌ *pl.* أَرْدِيَاءُ. Paltry, حَقِيرٌ ـ تَافِهٌ ـ زَهِيدٌ. Poor, فَقِيرٌ *pl.* فُقَرَاءُ ـ مِسْكِينٌ. Low, base, دَنِيءٌ ـ جُزْئِيٌّ ـ خَسِيسٌ ـ سَفِيلٌ ـ ذَلِيلٌ. To be —, unhappy, شَقِيَ ـ بَئِسَ ـ تَشَاءَمَ. In the most — condition, فِي أَسْوَإِ حَالٍ.

Miserably, *ad.* Unhappily, بِشَقَاوَةٍ ـ بِنَحْسٍ ـ نَحْسًا. Badly, رَدَاءَةً ـ بِرَدَاءَةٍ. In misery and wretchedness, فِي ٱلذُّلِّ وَٱلْمَسْكَنَةِ. *See also* Despicably, *ad.*

Miserly, *a.* *See* Miser, *n.* Avaricious, *a.*

Misery, *n.* Unhappiness, شَقَاوَةٌ ـ شَقَاءٌ ـ شَقًا ـ نَحْسٌ ـ نَحَاسَةٌ ـ نَهْسٌ. Indigence, ٱحْتِيَاجٌ كُلِّيٌّ ـ عَدَمٌ ـ حَوْبَةٌ ـ فَقْرٌ ـ مَسْكَنَةٌ ـ أَشَدُّ ٱلْعَازَةِ. Trouble, distress, مَشَقَّةٌ ـ أَذِيَّةٌ ـ ٱضْطِرَابٌ. To put one out of his —, to kill, أَمَاتَ.

Misfeasance, *n.* خَطَأٌ ـ خَطِيئَةٌ ـ تَعَدٍّ.

Misform, *v.t.* مَسَخَ ـ قَبَّحَ شَكْلَهُ ـ قَبَّحَ.

Misfortune, *n.* Ill-luck, سُوءُ بَخْتٍ ـ سُوءُ حَظٍّ. A disaster, كَرِيبَةٌ ـ حَوَادِثُ *pl.* حَادِثَةٌ ـ نَوَازِلُ *pl.* نَازِلَةٌ ـ نَوَائِبُ *pl.* نَائِبَةٌ ـ مَصَائِبُ *pl.* مُصِيبَةٌ ـ مُصَابَةٌ ـ بَوَائِقُ *pl.* بَائِقَةٌ ـ كَرَائِبُ *pl.* بَلَاءٌ ـ آفَاتٌ *pl.* آفَةٌ ـ شِقْوَةٌ. To fall into —, وَقَعَ فِي ٱلضِّيقِ ـ وَقَعَ فِي ٱلْبَلَاءِ ـ *aor.* يَقَعُ. To rejoice at the — of others, شَمِتَ.

Misgive, *v.t.* To fail in confidence, رَابَ *aor.* يَرِيبُ ـ أَرَابَ ـ ٱرْتَابَ فِي.

Misgiving, *n.* هَجْسٌ *pl.* هَوَاجِسُ ـ رِيبَةٌ ـ رَيْبٌ ـ ظِنَّةٌ ـ تُهْمَةٌ. To have — of, ٱتَّهَمَ بِ. It excited the misgivings of the people, أَثَارَ هَوَاجِسَ ٱلنَّاسِ.

Misgotten, *a.* مُكْتَسَبٌ بِٱلْحَرَامِ ـ حَرَامٌ.

Misgovern, *v.t.* أَسَاءَ فِي تَدْبِيرِهِ ٱ... ـ أَسَاءَ إِلَى-فِي ٱلسِّيَاسَةِ ـ أَفْسَدَ. He misgoverned the people, أَسَاءَ مُعَامَلَةَ ٱلرَّعِيَّةِ.

Misgovernment, *n.* فَسَادُ ٱلْحُكُومَةِ ـ خَلَلٌ بِٱلْإِدَارَةِ ـ سُوءُ إِدَارَةٍ.

Misguidance, *n.* إِغْوَاءٌ ـ إِضْلَالٌ ـ تَغْوِيَةٌ ـ تَشْوِيهٌ.

Misguide, *v.t.* ضَلَّلَ ـ تَوَّهَ. To suffer to be misguided, أَضَلَّ. O thou misguided one! يَا مُتَوَّهُ. Why does that misguided man act thus? مَا بَالُ ذَاكَ ٱلْمُتَوَّهِ يَفْعَلُ كَذَا.

Mishap, *n.* Ill chance, سُوءُ بَخْتٍ. A misfortune, مُصِيبَةٌ. *See also under* Mischance, Misfortune, *n.*

Mishmash, *n.* طَعَامٌ فَضِي ـ أَغْلَاثٌ.

Mishna, *n.* كِتَابُ أَحَادِيثِ ٱلْيَهُودِ.

Misimprove, *v.t.* أَسَاءَ فِي ٱسْتِعْمَالِهِ ٱلشَّيْءَ ـ تَقَصَّرَ بِ ـ غَفَلَ عَنْ ـ سَهَا عَنْ *aor.* يَسْهُو; as of an opportunity, أَفْلَتَ ٱلْفُرْصَةَ.

Misimprovement, *n.* سُوءُ ٱسْتِعْمَالٍ ـ ذُهُولٌ ـ غَبَاوَةٌ ـ تَسَاهُلٌ; as of an opportunity, فَوْتُ ٱلْفُرْصَةِ.

Misinform, *v.t.* أَفْهَمَ-غَلَطًا ـ أَشْعَرَ-بِخِلَافِ ٱلْحَقِّ ـ ضَلَّلَ.

Misinformation, *n.* خَبَرٌ غَلَطٌ ـ خَبَرٌ مُخَالِفٌ ـ ضَلَالَةٌ.

Misinformed, *a.* مُطَّلِعٌ عَلَى-غَلَطًا ـ صَاحِبُ خَبَرٍ غَيْرِ صَادِقٍ ـ فِي ضَلَالٍ.

Misinterpret, *v.t.* To explain erroneously, صَحَّفَ ـ حَرَّفَ ـ تَرْجَمَ-بِٱلْخِلَافِ.

Misinterpretation, *n.* تحريف ـ تصحيف ـ ترجمة مختلة ـ عكس المعنى.

Misinterpreted, *a.* محرف ـ مصحف ـ مترجم بالخلاف ـ معكوس المعنى.

Misjoin, *v.t.* أضاف بخرق ـ ـ خرق في إضافته إلى كذا.

Misjudge, *v.t.* غلط في ـ أخطأ بما ظن به ـ.

Misjudge, *v.i.* ـ ضل ـ ـ غلط ـ أخطأ.

Misjudged, *a.* Erroneously judged, مظنون ـ محكوم به غلطا ـ به غلطا.

Misjudgment, *n.* غرور ـ ضلال ـ غلط في الرأي ـ خطاء في الظن.

Mislaid, *a.* مفقود ـ ضال ـ ضائع. *See also* Misplaced, *a.*

Mislay, *v.t.* فقد ـ ـ ضيع ـ ـ ضل. *See also to* Misplace, *v.t.*

Misle, *v.i.* رش ع. It misled, أرشت السماء ـ رشت السماء.

Misle, *n.* Small rain, رشاش ـ رشة ـ رش.

Mislead, *v.t.* To cause to stray, err, ضيع ـ تيه ـ توه. To cause to fall into a mistake, أغلط ـ أزل ـ أسقط. To deceive, delude, جون ـ أخدع ـ زاوغ ـ أغوى. To be misled, deceived, انخدع. How greatly he is misled! ما أتيهه ـ ما أتوهه.

Misleader, *n.* *See* Deceiver, Deluder, *n.*

Misleading, *n.* A misguiding, ضل بتضلال ـ تشويه ـ تضليل ـ إغواء.

Misletoe, *n.* *See* Mistletoe, *n.*

Mislike, *v.t.* *See to* Dislike, *v.t.*

Misly, *a.* رش.

Mismanage, *v.a.* هوش ـ أساء في تدبير الأمر ـ خاخت ـ لبك ـ شوش.

Mismanagement, *n.* عدم ـ سوء تدبير ـ سوء إدارة ـ خاخة تدبير.

Mismanager, *n.* ملبك ـ شواش ـ هواش.

Mis-mark, *v.t.* أخطأ في عنوان الشيء ـ ـ غلط في رقم الشيء.

Mis-match, *v.t.* ـ قرن ب غلطا ـ أخطأ في تأليف الشيء.

Misname, *v.t.* أخطأ في تسمية الشيء ـ صحف على ـ صحف.

Misnomer, *n.* إسم غير مطابق ـ تصحيف ـ إسم غير مناسب.

Misogamist, *n.* كاره الزواج ـ شانئ الزيجة.

Misogamy, *n.* شناءة الزيجة ـ كراهة الزواج.

Mysogynist, *n.* كاره النساء.

Mysogyny, *n.* كراهة النساء.

Mis-opinion, *n.* ظن فاسد ـ رأي غلط.

Mispell, *v.t.* *See* Mis-spell, *v.t.*

Mispersuade, *v.t.* أضل ـ أخطأ في إقناعه.

Mispersuasion, *n.* إضلال ـ سوء استعطاف.

Misplace, *v.t.* To put in a wrong place, أخطأ في وضع الشيء ـ وضع في غير محله ـ ـ فقد. يضع .aor. To — one's affections, انخدع في وده. *See also* to Mislay, *v.t.*

Misplaced, *a.* موضوع في غير محله ـ مفقود. Misplaced affection, حب مغرور. *See also* Mislaid, *a.*

Misplead, *v.i.* أخطأ في التحجج.

Mispoint, *v.t.* ... ـ غلط في وضع النقط على ـ أخطأ في تعجيم ال...

Misprint, *v.t.* ... صحف في الطبع ـ أخطأ في طبع ال...

Misprint, *n.* غلط (or خطأ) في الطبع.

Misprinted, *a.* طبع غلط ـ مطبوع غلطا (or مغلوط).

Misprision, *n.* Neglect, سهو. Concealment, كتمان ـ تستر ـ تخبية.

Misprize, *v.t.* To value amiss, أخطأ في تسعير الشيء. To undervalue, إحتقر ـ إستقل سعر الشيء.

Mispronounce, *v.t.* صحف لفظة ـ أخطأ في تلفظ الكلمة.

Mispronounce, *v.i.* أخطأ في اللفظ.

Mispronunciation, *n.* تلفظ غلط ـ تصحيف اللفظ.

Misproportion, *n.* عدم مشاكلة ـ قلة مناسبة ـ عدم هندام.

Misquotation, *n.* نقل مغلوط ـ إقتباس غلط.

Misquote, *v.t.* ... أخطأ في اقتباس ال... ـ إقتبس من خطاء ـ ـ حكى عن غلطا.

Misreckon, *v.t.* *See to* Miscalculate, *v.t.*

Mis-reckoning, *n.* *See* Miscalculation, *n.*

Mis-relate, *v.t.* أخطأ بما حكى عن كذا ـ حرف الرواية.

Mis-remember, *v.t.* ... أخطأ في ذكر ال...

Misrepresent, *v.t.* لبس ـ يشي .aor وشى ـ صحف على ـ صحف.

Misrepresentation, *n.* تلبيس ـ تصحيف ـ وشي ـ شية.

Misrule, *n.* Mal-administration, سوء تدبير ـ سوء إدارة. Disorder, tumult, هرج مرج ـ فتن ـ فتنة ـ فساد ـ شواش ـ شغب.

Miss, *n.* An unmarried woman, بنت *pl.* بنات. The title —, ستي ـ ست.

Miss, *n.* A failure to hit, عدم إصابة ـ إخطاء. A failure to obtain, خيبة ـ قلة نجاح ـ عدم الحصول على الشيء. A —, of fire-arms, تكذيب. A loss, فقيد.

Miss, *v.t.* Not to hit, ـ ضاف عن ـ أخطأ ـ تخطأ ـ تخاطأ ـ أخطف. To fail of, قصر عن. Not to attain, ـ ضاف عن ما صح معه ـ ـ فقد ـ ما حصل على ـ ـ عدم. To let slip, أسقط ـ ع فات. To feel the absence of, إفتقد ـ ـ فقد. To — the way, أخطأ الطريق ـ ـ ع تاه ـ ـ ع طاح. The arrow missed him, أَخْطَأَهُ ٱلسَّهْمُ. The arrow missed the butt, ضَافَ ٱلسَّهْمُ عَنِ ٱلْهَدَفِ. The archer missed the butt, أَخْطَأَ ٱلرَّامِي ٱلْغَرَضَ. To — an opportunity, ضَيَّعَ (or أَفْلَتَ) ٱلْفُرْصَةَ. To — fire, كَذَّبَ; specially of a flint and steel, غَلَتَ ـ إِغْتَلَتَ. To — the road, ضَلَّ عَنِ ٱلطَّرِيقِ ـ ضَلَّ ٱلطَّرِيقَ. I missed the right road to the mosque, ضَلِلْتُ ٱلْمَسْجِدَ.

Miss, *v.i.* To fail to hit, تَطَوَّحَ ـ أَخْطَأَ. To be in want of, إِحْتَاجَ إِلَى ـ عَازَ ـ إِعْتَازَ. To feel the absence of, خَلَّ مِنْ ـ إِفْتَقَدَ. Not to succeed, خَابَ *aor.* يَخِيبُ. He died without being missed, مَاتَ غَيْرَ مَفْقُودٍ. The jewels were missed, تَفَقَّدَتِ ٱلْجَوَاهِرُ. To cause one to —, or to fail in finding, أَفْقَدَ. To seek after that which is missing, تَفَقَّدَ. He who seeks, (what is missing or wanting), will not find, مَنْ يَتَفَقَّدْهُ يَفْقِدْهُ. I missed such a thing, خَلِلْتُ مِنْ كَذَا. The camels missed the herbage, (and became lean in consequence), خَلَّ ٱلْبَعِيرُ مِنَ ٱلرَّبِيعِ.

Missal, *n.* كِتَابُ طَقْسِ ٱلْقُدَّاسِ ـ كِتَابُ ٱلْقُدَّاسِ.

Mis-send, *v.t.* أَخْطَأَ فِي إِرْسَالِهِ ٱلـ.... ـ أَرْسَلَ غَلَطًا.

Mis-sent, *a.* مَبْعُوثٌ إِلَى غَيْرِ مَحَلِّهِ ـ مُرْسَلٌ غَلَطًا.

Mis-serve, *v.t.* أَخَانَ ـ خَانَ *aor.* يَخُونُ ـ خَدَمَ بِخِيَانَةٍ.

Mis-shape, *v.t.* مَسَخَ ـ عَكَسَ ـ شَوَّهَ ـ قَبَّحَ.

Mis-shaped, *a.*
Mis-shapen, } بَشِعٌ ـ سَمِجٌ ـ مَمْسُوخٌ ـ قَبِيحٌ.

Missile, *n.* مِرْمَاةٌ *pl.* مَرَامٍ.

Missile, *a.* مَرْمِيٌّ *pl.* مَرَامٍ.

Missing, *a.* Not hitting, خَاطِئٌ *pl.* خَوَاطِئُ ـ صَائِفٌ عَنِ ٱلْغَرَضِ. Not to be found, مَفْقُودٌ ـ فَقِيدٌ. Absent, غَائِبٌ. Wanting, نَاقِصٌ.

Mission, *n.* A sending, إِرْسَالٌ. Persons sent, مَرَاسِيلُ. Service, خِدْمَةٌ. A charge committed to anybody by authority, مَأْمُورِيَّةٌ ـ وَفْدٌ.

A diplomatic mission, مَأْمُورِيَّةٌ سِفَارِيَّةٌ ـ سِفَارَةٌ.

An extraordinary mission, مَأْمُورِيَّةٌ فَوْقَ ٱلْعَادَةِ.

A government or official mission, مَأْمُورِيَّةٌ رَسْمِيَّةٌ ـ مَأْمُورِيَّةٌ مِنَ ٱلدَّوْلَةِ.

A secret mission, مَأْمُورِيَّةٌ خَفِيَّةٌ ـ وَفْدٌ خَفِيٌّ.

A special mission, مَأْمُورِيَّةٌ مَخْصُوصَةٌ ـ وَفْدٌ مَخْصُوصٌ.

A temporary mission, مَأْمُورِيَّةٌ وَقْتِيَّةٌ ـ وَفْدٌ وَقْتِيٌّ.

Mission, a station of missionaries, مَحَلُّ ٱلْمُرْسَلِينَ.

The head of a mission, رَئِيسُ ٱلْوَفْدِ (or ٱلْمَأْمُورِيَّةِ) ـ سَفِيرٌ.

The house of an embassy or mission, مَحَلُّ سِفَارَةٍ.

The members of a mission, أَعْضَاءُ سِفَارَةٍ.

Missionary, *n.* مُرْسَلٌ *pl.* مُرْسَلُونَ.

Missionary, *a.* مُخْتَصٌّ بِٱلْمُرْسَلِينَ ـ رَسُولِيٌّ.

Missive, *n.* A letter, مَكْتُوبٌ *pl.* مَكْتُوبَاتٌ ـ رِسَالَةٌ *pl.* رَسَائِلُ ـ رَقِيمٌ ـ تَحْرِيرٌ.

Mis-speak, *v.t.* *See to* Mispronounce, *v.i.*

Mis-speak, *v.i.* *See to* Mispronounce, *v.t.*

Mis-spell, *v.t.* أَخْطَأَ فِي كِتَابَةِ ٱلـ.... ـ أَخْطَأَ فِي تَهْجِيَةِ ٱلـ....

Mis-spelt, *a.* غَلَطُ ٱلْهِجَاءِ ـ هِجَاءٌ غَلَطٌ.

Mis-spend, *v.t.* أَتْلَفَ ـ ضَيَّعَ ـ صَرَفَ بَاطِلًا.

Mis-spent, *a.* مُتْلَفٌ ـ مُضَيَّعٌ ـ مَصْرُوفٌ بَاطِلًا.

Mis-state, *v.t.* *See to* Misrepresent, *v.t.*

Mis-statement, *n.* *See* Misrepresentation, *n.*

Mist, *n.* ضَبَابَةٌ ـ ضَبَابٌ. He has a — before his eye, فِي عَيْنِهِ ضَبَابَةٌ.

Mist, *v.t.* *See to* Becloud, *to* Dim, *v.t.*

Mist, *v.i.* To grow dim; *See under* Dim, *a.*

Mistakable, *a.* مِمَّا يُخْطَأُ فِيهِ ـ ٱلْغَلَطُ فِيهِ مُمْكِنٌ.

Mistake, *n.* An error, blunder, أُضْلُولَةٌ *pl.* أَضَالِيلُ ـ ضِلَّةٌ ـ ضُلٌّ ـ خَطَأٌ ـ زِلَّةٌ ـ سِقَاطٌ *pl.* أَسْقَاطٌ ـ سَهْوٌ ـ غَلْطَةٌ *pl.* غَلَطَاتٌ ـ غَلَطٌ. A — in writing or reading, تَصْحِيفٌ. It is a —, هُوَ سَهْوٌ. To make a —, زَلَّ زِلَّةً *aor.* يَزِلُّ ـ سَقَطَ ـ ضَلَّ ـ خَطِئَ ـ أَخْطَأَ ـ غَلِطَ. To attribute a — to, غَلَّطَ. To cause to make a —, أَسْقَطَ ـ أَغْلَطَ ـ تَسَقَّطَ. He spoke without making a single —, تَكَلَّمَ بِكَلَامٍ وَمَا سَقَطَ بِحَرْفٍ. One of the greatest mistakes, مِنْ أَسْوَإِ ٱلْغَلَطِ. Having mistakes, مُغَلَّطٌ ـ مَغْلُوطٌ ـ غَلَطٌ. A — occurred in the deed, وَقَعَ سَهْوٌ فِي ٱلْحُجَّةِ *aor.* يَقَعُ.

Mistake, *v.t.* To misunderstand, أَخْطَأَ فِي فَهْمِ ٱلـ.... To take wrongly, وَهِمَ فِي *aor.* يَوْهَمُ ـ غَلِطَ فِي ـ أَخْطَأَ فِي. To be deceived in, إِنْغَرَّ مِنْ ـ إِنْغَشَّ مِنْ ـ إِنْغَوَى مِنْ. I mistook him for his brother, ظَنَنْتُهُ أَخَاهُ ـ ظَنَنْتُ أَخَاهُ إِيَّاهُ. She mistook him for the porter, ظَنَّتْ أَنَّهُ ٱلْبَوَّابُ.

Mistaken, *a.* In error, ضَالٌّ ـ غَالِطٌ. Deceived, مَغْرُورٌ. Grossly —, مِغْلَاطٌ ـ ضِلِّيلٌ. A — idea, ضِلَّةٌ ـ رَأْيٌ غَلَطٌ ـ غُرُورٌ ـ ضَلَالٌ.

Mistakenly, *ad.* سَقَطًا ـ سَهْوًا ـ غَلَطًا ـ مِنْ زَلَّةٍ.

Mistaught, *a.* مُعَلَّمٌ سُوءًا ـ مَنْ سَاءَ تَعْلِيمُهُ ـ مُضَلَّلٌ.

Misteach, *v.t.* أَخْطَأَ فِي تَدْرِيسِ ٱلـ.... ـ أَسَاءَ فِي تَعْلِيمِ ٱلـ.... ـ ضَلَّلَ.

Mister, *n.* سَيِّدٌ ـ أَفَنْدِي. As the epithet of a merchant, خَوَاجَة (or خَوَاجَا); of an artisan, مُعَلِّم.

Misterm, *v.t.* صَحَّفَ ـ صَحَّفَ عَلَى.

Misthink, *v.t.* أَخْطَأَ بِمَا آرْتَأَى فِى ـ أَخْطَأَ بِمَا ظَنَّ بِ.

Mistily, *ad.* *See* Dimly, *ad.*

Mistime, *v.t.* To mistake as to time, أَخْطَأَ فِى ٱلْوَقْتِ. To do inopportunely, ـ أَتَى بِٱلشَّىْءِ فِى غَيْرِ وَقْتِهِ.

Mistimed, *a.* *See* Inopportune, *a.*

Mistiness, *n.* *See* Mist, Dimness, *n.*

Mistle, *v.i.* *See to* Misle, *v.i.*

Mistletoe, *n.* دَابُوق ـ دِبْق.

Mist-like, *a.* كَٱلضَّبَابِ.

Mistrain, *v.t.* ضَلَّلَ ـ أَسَآءَ تَأْدِيبَهُ ـ خَرِقَ فِى تَدْرِيبِ آ...

Mistranslate, *v.t.* صَحَّفَ تَرْجَمَةَ آ... ـ غَلِطَ فِى تَرْجَمَةِ آ.

Mistranslation, *n.* تَرْجَمَةٌ مُخَالِفَةٌ ـ تَصْحِيفٌ فِى ٱلتَّرْجَمَةِ.

Mistress, *n.* One who governs or teaches, خَانُم ـ مُعَلِّمَة ـ سَيِّدَة. A proprietress, صَاحِبَة. As a term of address, سِتّى ـ سِتّ ـ خَاتُون. A woman beloved, حَبِيبَة. A concubine, مَحْظِيَّة *pl.* مَحَاظِى ـ سُرِّيَّة *pl.* سَرَارِىُّ ـ حَظِيَّة. A woman who gives herself airs, مُتَصَلِّفَة.

Mistrust, *n.* عَدَمُ أَمْنِيَّة ـ وَسْوَسَة ـ شَكّ ـ تُهْمَة ـ ٱتِّهَام ـ هَجْس *pl.* هَوَاجِس. It excited their —, أَثَارَ هَوَاجِسَهُمْ.

Mistrust, *v.t.* شَكَّ فِى *aor.* يَشُكُّ ـ تَشَكَّكَ فِى ـ ٱتَّهَمَ بِ ـ ٱسْتَحْرَسَ مِن.

Mistrustful, *a.* عَدِيمُ ٱلْأَمْنِيَّةِ ـ مُوَسْوِس ـ مُسْتَحْرِس ـ مُتَوَهِّم.

Mistune, *v.t.* Of an instrument, أَسَآءَ لَحْنَ ٱلْآلَةِ; of a stringed instrument, أَسَآءَ شَدَّ أَوْتَارِ ٱلْآلَةِ.

Misty, *a.* مُضَبَّب ـ ضَبَاب. *See also* Cloudy, Dim, *a.*

Misunderstand, *v.t.* Not to understand correctly, أَخْطَأَ فِى فَهْمِ آ... ـ غَلِطَ فِى فَهْمِ آ... ـ مَا فَهِمَ بِضَبْطٍ (*or* حَقًّا). To take in a wrong sense, ـ فَهِمَ عَلَى سُوءٍ.

Misunderstanding, *n.* An error, غَلَط ـ خَطَأ ـ ٱلْخَطَأُ فِى فَهْمٍ. Want of agreement, discord, شِقَاق ـ نِزَاع ـ ٱرْتِبَاك ـ قَضِيَّة. Coolness, as of friendship, بُرُودَة. Without the least cause for —, بِدُونِ أَدْنَى سَبَبٍ لِلْخِلَافِ.

Misusage, *n.* Ill-treatment, سُوءُ ٱسْتِعْمَال ـ سُوءُ مُعَامَلَةٍ ـ ٱنْتِهَاك. Abuse, شَتْم ـ سَبّ ـ ذَمّ ـ عَرْبَدَة ـ بَذَاء. Harsh treatment, عَنَافَة ـ مُقَاهَرَة ـ إِعْنَاف ـ حَكْر. *See also* Ill-usage, *n.*

Misuse, *v.t.* To make a bad use of, to injure, damage, أَتْلَفَ ـ ضَيَّعَ. To use a thing improperly, ٱسْتَعْمَلَ بِغَيْرِ قَانُونٍ. To use awkwardly, خَرِقَ بِ. To mar, in a general sense, أَجْحَفَ ـ أَجْحَفَ بِ ـ جَحَفَ; of a blade, vase, *etc.*, to blunt, crack, damage, ـ ثَلَمَ. To use one badly, أَسَآءَ ـ أَسَآءَ ٱلْعَمَلَ بِ ـ تَعَدَّى عَلَى ـ عَدَا عَلَى ـ ضَامَ ـ هَتَكَ. To injure, wrong, To go to excess in any thing, أَفْرَطَ فِى ـ تَعَدَّى فِى ـ ٱعْتَدَى فِى. To abuse, contemn, عَرْبَدَ ـ شَتَمَ ـ ذَمَّ ـ بَذَأَ ـ تَهَاوَنَ بِ. To treat harshly, عَنِفَ عَلَى ـ قَاهَرَ ـ قَاسَحَ ـ حَكَرَ. *See also to* Ill-use, *v.t.*

Misuse, *n.* Bad use of any thing, سُوءُ ٱسْتِعْمَالٍ ـ ٱنْتِهَاك. Damage, marring, إِجْحَاف ـ جَحْف; as of a blade, and such like, ثَلْم. Awkward use of any thing, خُرْق.

Mis-used, *a.* Improperly used, مُسْتَعْمَلٌ بِخِلَافِ ـ مُسْتَعْمَل خَارِجًا عَنِ ٱلْحَقِّ. Ill-used, spoilt, مَعْدُوم. Not used, غَيْرُ مُسْتَعْمَلٍ. Ill-used, injured, ذُو جَوْرٍ.

Miswed, *v.t.* زَوَّجَ دُونَ مَقَامِهِ (*or* بِدُونِ مُنَاسَبَةٍ).

Miswrite, *v.t.* أَخْطَأَ فِى كِتَابَةِ آ... ـ صَحَّفَ ٱلْكِتَابَةَ.

Miswrought, *a.* رَدِىء ـ غَيْرُ مُهَنْدَمٍ ـ مُعَيَّب ـ مَمْسُوخُ ٱلْمُعَالَجَةِ.

Misyoke, *v.t.* *See to* Misjoin, Miswed, *v.t.*

Mite, *n.* A small insect, سُوسَة *coll.* سُوس ـ عُثَّة *pl.* عُثّ *and* عُثَث ـ دُوَيْبَّة. A small piece, a grain, حَبَّة. A small piece of money, فَلْس *pl.* فُلُوس.

Mitigable, *a.* قَابِلُ ٱلتَّلْيِينِ ـ مِمَّا يُلَيَّنُ ـ يُخَفَّفُ.

Mitigant, *a.* مُلَطِّف ـ مُخَفِّف ـ مُلَيِّن.

Mitigate, *v.t.* To soften, alleviate, خَفَّفَ ـ لَطَّفَ ـ لَيَّنَ. To lessen, قَلَّلَ ـ أَنْقَصَ ـ نَقَّصَ.

Mitigation, *n.* The act of alleviating, تَلْطِيف ـ تَلْيِين ـ تَخْفِيف; of diminishing, تَنْقِيص ـ تَقْلِيل. In — of, تَخْفِيفًا عَن.

Mitigative, *a.* } *See* Mitigant, *a.*
Mitigator, *n.* }

Mitrailleuse, *n.* مِدْفَعُ ٱلْمِتْرَالْيُوز.

Mitre, *n.* تَاجُ أُسْقُفٍ *pl.* تِيجَانُ. A bishopric, أُسْقُفِيَّة.

Mitre, *v.t.* لَبَّسَ تَاجًا ـ تَوَّجَ.

Mitred, *a.* مُتَوَّج.

Mitten, *n.* ضَرْبٌ مِنَ ٱلْكُفُوفِ.

Mittimus, *n.* A warrant of commitment to prison, أَمْرٌ بِحَبْسِ فُلَانٍ.

Mity, *a.* مُدَوِّد ـ مُسَوِّس.

Mix, *v.t.* To unite and blend together, ـ شَمَطَ ـ أَشَبَ ـ خَبَصَ ـ خَبَّصَ ـ خَلَّطَ ـ خَلَطَ ـ مَشَجَ ـ عَزَمَ ـ أَشْمَطَ. To stir, خَوَّضَ ـ ٱجْتَدَحَ ـ جَدَّحَ ـ جَدَحَ. To mix something into, ضَرَبَ بِ ـ مَزَجَ بِ ـ عَرَّقَ ـ خَشَبَ بِ. To — with, associate with, ٱسْتَصْحَبَ ـ عَاشَرَ ـ خَالَطَ. To — one's self up with, قَارَشَ ـ اِنْحَشَرَ فِي ـ تَدَاخَلَ فِي ـ ء لَحَصَ فِي. A thing to mix or stir with, مِخْوَضٌ ـ مِجْدَحٌ. To be mixed, اِخْتَلَطَ ـ اِخْتَبَصَ ـ تَأَشَّبَ. *See also to* Mingle, *v.t.*, *and under* Mixed, *a.*

Mix, *v.i.* خَالَطَ ـ مَازَجَ. *See also to* Mingle, *v.i.*

Mixable, *a.* مِمَّا يُمْتَزَجُ بِ ـ مِمَّا يُخْلَطُ.

Mixed, *a.* مَمْزُوجٌ ـ مَخْلُوطٌ ـ شَمِيطٌ ـ مَخْشُوبٌ ـ خَشِيبٌ; as with wine, *etc.*, مَمْزُوجٌ ـ مُعَرَّقٌ. A — multitude, جَمْعٌ لَفِيفٌ كَبِيرٌ ـ مُؤْتَشَبٌ. They were mixed up together, of combatants in a battle, تَعَاكَرُوا ـ اِعْتَكَرُوا. Such an one is of —, not pure, lineage, فُلَانٌ مُؤْتَشَبٌ.

Mixen, *n.* A dung heap, كُومَةُ زِبْلٍ. *See also* Dunghill, *n.*

Mixtilineal, *a.* }
Mixtilinear, } ذُو خُطُوطٍ مُسْتَقِيمَةٍ وَمُنْحَنِيَةٍ ـ مُخْتَلِطُ ٱلْأَضْلَاعِ.

Mixtion, *n.* The act of mixing, تَخْلِيطٌ ـ مَزْجٌ ـ خَلْطٌ ـ أَشْبٌ.

Mixture, *n.* The act of mixing, إِخْلَاطٌ ـ مَزْجٌ ـ تَخْلِيطٌ ـ خَلْطٌ. The state of being mixed, اِمْتِزَاجٌ ـ اِخْتِلَاطٌ. A compound, مِزَاجٌ ـ خَلِيطٌ ـ شَمِيطٌ. A — of texture, in cloth, تَفْنِينٌ. A —, a promiscuous multitude, أُشَابَةٌ. *See also* Medley, *n.*

Mizzen, *n.* The sail, شِرَاعُ ٱلصَّارِي ٱلَّذِي فِي مُؤَخَّرِ ٱلْمَرْكَبِ.

Mizzen-mast, *n.* ٱلصَّارِي ٱلَّذِي فِي مُؤَخَّرِ ٱلْمَرْكَبِ.

Mizzle, *v.i.* *See to* Misle, *v.t.*

Mnemonic, *a.* }
Mnemonical, } مُسَاعِدُ ٱلْقُوَّةِ ٱلذَّاكِرَةِ.

Mnemonics, *n.* عِلْمُ ٱلذِّكْرِ ـ عِلْمُ ٱلْحَافِظَةِ.

Moan, *v.i.* نَاحَ ـ يَئِنُّ *aor.* أَنَّ ـ تَأَلَّمَ ـ تَأَوَّهَ. To —, as a camel, ء ضَجَّ ـ ء أَطَّ; as the wind, ء حَنَّ. To — for; *see to* Bemoan, Lament, *v.t.*

Moan, *n.* حَنِينٌ ـ نَوْحٌ ـ أَوَّهٌ ـ أَنِينٌ ـ أَنَّةٌ; of a camel, أَطٌّ ـ ضَجِيجٌ ـ أَطِيطٌ; of the wind, حَنِينٌ.

Moaning, *a.* حَنِينٌ ـ أَنَّانٌ ـ آنٌّ.

Moat, *n.* خَنْدَقٌ *pl.* خَنَادِقُ. To make a — round, خَنْدَقَ ـ خَنْدَقَ حَوْلَ.

Moated, *a.* ذُو خَنْدَقٍ ـ مُخَنْدَقٌ.

Mob, *n.* A crowd, أَلْبٌ ـ إِلْبٌ ـ غَمْرَةٌ *pl.* غَمَرَاتٌ *and* غِمَارٌ ـ زَحْمَةٌ ـ اِزْدِحَامٌ مِنَ ٱلنَّاسِ ـ كَوْكَبَةٌ. The populace, ٱلْأَوْبَاشُ ـ مِنْ أَهْلِ ٱلسُّوقِ ـ أَسَافِلُ ٱلنَّاسِ ـ ٱلْأَسَافِلُ.

Mob, *v.t.* زَاحَمَتْهُ ٱلْأَوْبَاشُ ـ ء زَحَمَ أَهْلُ ٱلسُّوقِ ـ تَأَلَّبُوا عَلَى ـ زَاحَمَ ـ ء زَحَمَ.

Mob-cap, *n.* غِطَاءٌ لِلرَّأْسِ صَانِجٌ تَلْبَسُهُ ٱلنِّسَاءُ.

Mobile, *a.* *See* Versatile, *n.*

Mobility, *n.* Susceptibility of motion, حَرَكَةٌ ـ حَرَاكٌ. Quickness of motion, خِفَّةُ حَرَكَةٍ. The populace, ٱلْأَرَاذِلُ ـ ٱلْأَوْبَاشُ ـ ٱلْحَرَافِشُ. *See also* Fickleness, *n.*

Mobilize, *v.t.* As of troops, أَعَدَّ ٱلرَّدِيفَ ـ أَجْمَعَ ٱلْعَسَاكِرَ لِلْحَرْبِ لِلْحَرْبِ. The troops are still being mobilized, لَمْ تَزَلِ ٱلْعَسَاكِرُ تَنْتَقِلُ بِقَصْدِ ٱلتَّجَمُّعِ فِي مَحَلٍّ.

Moccasin, *n.* ضَرْبٌ مِنَ ٱلْجَوْرَبِ مِنْ جِلْدٍ.

Mock, *v.t.* To treat with scorn, تَسَخَّرَ ـ ء سَخِرَ مِنْ ـ فَلَحَ بِ ـ اِسْتَهْزَأَ بِ ـ تَهَزَّأَ بِ ـ ء ضَحِكَ عَلَى ـ تَهَاوَنَ بِ ـ مِنْ or بِ. To disappoint, خَيَّبَ ـ شَمَّتَ. To — at fear, ء ضَحِكَ مِنَ ٱلْخَوْفِ ـ ء سَخِرَ بِٱلْخَوْفِ.

Mock, *v.i.* اِسْتَهْزَأَ.

Mock, *a.* Not real, مُمَوَّهٌ ـ مَغْشُوشٌ ـ صِنَاعِيٌّ ـ كَذَّابٌ.

Mocker, *n.* سُخَرَةٌ ـ مُسْتَهْزِئٌ *pl.* مُسْتَهْزِئُونَ.

Mockery, *n.* The act of deriding, تَسَخُّرٌ ـ سُخْرِيَّةٌ ـ هُزُوٌ ـ تَهَاوُنٌ ـ اِسْتِهْزَاءٌ. An object of —, نَقُورَةٌ ـ مَسْخَرَةٌ ـ أُضْحُوكَةٌ. A disappointment, خَيْبَةٌ ـ فَشَلٌ ـ شَمَاتٌ. To make a — of; *See to* Mock, *v.t.*

Mocking, *n.* *See* Mockery.

Mocking-bird, *n.* طَائِرٌ يُحَاكِي مَا يَسْمَعُ مِنَ ٱلْأَصْوَاتِ.

Modal, *a.* عَرَضِيٌّ ـ حَالِيٌّ.

Modality, *n.* Form, كَيْفِيَّةٌ ـ حَالٌ. Accidental difference, عَرَضٌ.

Mode, *n.* Manner of existence or being كَيْفِيَّةٌ ـ حَالٌ *pl.* أَحْوَالٌ ـ شَكْلٌ. A way, manner, أُسْلُوبٌ *pl.* أَسَالِيبُ ـ مِنْوَالٌ ـ طَرِيقَةٌ *pl.* طَرَائِقُ ـ شَرِيَّةٌ ـ بَابٌ *pl.* أَبْوَابٌ ـ بَابَةٌ; as of a mould, cast, صِيغَةٌ ـ صِيَاغَةٌ. Mode of proceeding, قِدْيَةٌ. Custom, habit, عَادَةٌ. Particular manner of conjugating verbs, صِيغَةُ تَصْرِيفِ ٱلْأَفْعَالِ ـ صِيغَةٌ. *See also* Fashion, Gait, *n.*

Model, *n.* قَالِبٌ *pl.* قَوَالِبُ ـ طَبْعٌ ـ أُنْمُوذَجٌ ـ صَوْغٌ ـ قَاعِدَةٌ *pl.* قَوَاعِدُ ـ صُورَةٌ *pl.* صُوَرٌ ـ تِمْثَالٌ ـ قِدْوَةٌ. To take as a —, example, اِقْتَدَى بِ. On the — of..., عَلَى مِنْوَالِ كَذَا. Make it on this —, اِضْرِبْهُ عَلَى طَبْعِ هٰذَا. On the European —, عَلَى نَسَقِ أُورُبَا. *See also* Example, *n.*

Model, *v.t.* To fashion, shape, as in a mould, صَاغَ; as in drawing, صَوَّرَ; as in sculpture, نَقَّشَ. To make a model of in wax, ء عَمِلَ صُورَتَهُ مِنْ شَمْعٍ. To construct, put together, constitute, شَكَّلَ. *See also under to* Form, Delineate, *v.t.*

Modeller, *n.* A designer, painter, مُصَوِّرٌ; a sculptor, نَقَّاشٌ; a — in wax, صَانِعُ صُوَرٍ مِنْ شَمْعٍ.

Modelling, *n.* As in a mould, صِيَاغَةٌ; as in drawing, تَصْوِيرٌ; as in sculpture, نَقْشٌ; as of a body politic, تَشْكِيلٌ.

Moderate, *a.* Not excessive, مُتَوَسِّط ـ مُقْتَصِد ـ مُعْتَدِل ـ غَيْرُ مُفْرِط. Temperate, of the atmosphere, مُعْتَدِل. Moderate in disposition, حَلِيم ـ مُؤَدَّب ـ عَاقِل ـ زَهِيد. Light, little, قَلِيل ـ خَفِيف. His charge is very —, تَقَاضِيهِ مُقْتَصِدٌ. To be —, قَصَدَ ِ. To be — in, قَصَدَ فِي ـ ِ اِقْتَصَدَ فِي.

Moderate, *v.t.* To lessen, قَلَّلَ ـ خَفَّفَ ـ بَخَسَ َ. To lower, of a price, رَخَّصَ ـ أَهْبَطَ (or بَخَسَ َ) ٱلثَّمَنَ. To allay, لَيَّنَ ـ لَطَّفَ ـ سَكَّنَ. To repress, ضَبَطَ ُ ـ أَقْمَعَ ـ َ. To — one's passions, ضَبَطَ أَهْوَآءَ نَفْسِهِ ُ. To — one's desires, to be content, اِقْتَنَعَ.

Moderate, *v.i.* To become less violent, هَدَأَ َ ـ تَهَدَّأَ ـ سَكَنَ ُ ـ حَلُمَ ُ.

Moderately, *ad.* بِٱعْتِدَالٍ. Without excess, مِنْ غَيْرِ إِفْرَاطٍ. Wisely, بِعَقْلٍ ـ تَعَقُّلًا.

Moderateness, *n.* اِعْتِدَال ـ اِقْتِصَاد ـ إِنْصَاف. Justness, إِنْصَاف.

Moderation, *n.* The state of being moderate, اِعْتِدَال ـ اِقْتِصَاد ـ تَقْسِيط ـ تَقَلُّل. Forbearance, lenity, أَنَاة ـ تَحَمُّل ـ حِلْم. Rectitude, إِنْصَاف. Restraint of passions, اِمْتِلَاكُ ٱلنَّفْسِ ـ ضَبْطُ ٱلنَّفْسِ. With great —, forbearance, بِطُولِ ٱلْأَنَاةِ. To act with —, أَجْمَلَ ـ حَلُمَ ُ. To act with — in, قَسَّطَ فِي. To use with —, اِسْتَعْمَلَ بِعَقْلٍ. To speak with —, أَجْمَلَ فِي ٱلْكَلَامِ ـ تَكَلَّمَ بِلَطَافَةٍ. In —, بِٱعْتِدَالٍ ـ بِقَانُونٍ ـ بِعَقْلٍ ـ مِنْ غَيْرِ إِفْرَاطٍ.

Moderator, *n.* A president, صَدْر ـ رَأْس ـ نَظِيرَة. To act as —, تَصَدَّرَ. To make — over, صَدَّرَ فِي. An overseer, director, مُدَبِّر ـ ضَابِطُ ٱلزِّمَامِ ـ ضَابِط ـ نَاظِر.

Moderatorship, *n.* صَدَارَة ـ نِظَارَة.

Modern, *a.* مُتَأَخِّر ـ جَدِيد *pl.* جُدُد. The — or current language, ٱلْكَلَامُ (or ٱللِّسَانُ) ٱلدَّارِجُ. The moderns, as opposed to the ٱلْقُدَمَآءُ or ancients, ٱلْمُحْدَثُونَ ـ ٱلْمُتَأَخِّرُونَ ـ أَهْلُ ٱلزَّمَانِ.

Modernism, *n.* شِرْعَة جَدِيدَة ـ مِنْ بِنْيَةِ ٱلْمُتَأَخِّرِينَ.

Modernize, *v.t.* صَيَّرَ عَلَى طَرْزِ ٱلْمُتَأَخِّرِينَ ـ حَوَّلَ إِلَى طَرْزٍ جَدِيدٍ.

Modernized, *a.* مُحَوَّلٌ إِلَى طَرْزِ ٱلْمُتَأَخِّرِينَ.

Modernizer, *n.* مُجَدِّد ـ مُحَوِّلُ ٱلْقَدِيمِ إِلَى طَرْزٍ جَدِيدٍ.

Modernness, *n.* جِدَّة ـ جِدِّيَّة ـ حَدَاثَة.

Modest, *a.* Bashful, حَيِيّ *fem.* حَيِيَّة ـ خَفِر ـ خَجِل; of a woman, خَرِيدَة ـ خَفِرَة. Not forward, مُحْتَشِم ـ أَدِيب ـ مُؤَدَّب ـ مُتَّضِع ـ مُتَوَاضِع ـ بِأَدَبِهِ ـ مُحْتَشِم ـ نَفْسُهُ صَغِيرَة. Chaste, عَفِيف. Moderate, مُعْتَدِل ـ مُقْتَصِد. Small, of space, صَغِير; of numbers, قَلِيل. Modest apparel, لِبَاسُ ٱلْحِشْمَةِ. *See also* Bashful, *a.*

Modestly, *ad.* Bashfully, بِحَيَآءٍ ـ بِخَجَلٍ. Not boldly, بِحِشْمَةٍ ـ بِأَدَبٍ ـ بِٱتِّضَاعٍ.

Modesty, *n.* Bashfulness, حَيَآء ـ خَفَر ـ خَجْلَة ـ عَار. Chastity, عِفَّة. Unobtrusive deportment, حِشْمَة ـ أَدَب ـ تَوَاضُع. To act with —, لَزِمَ ٱلْأَدَبَ ـ قَعَدَ فِي أَدَبِهِ ُ ـ اِتَّضَاعَ. Modesty is the crown of virtue, (*prov.*) تَاجُ ٱلْمُرُوَّةِ ٱلتَّوَاضُعُ. Modesty is a part of faith, (*prov.*) ٱلْحَيَآءُ شُعْبَةٌ مِنَ ٱلْإِيمَانِ.

Modicum, *n.* قَلِيل مِن ـ حَبَّة ـ مِقْدَارٌ جُزْئِيٌّ ـ عِرْق. There is a — of acidity in it, فِيهِ عِرْقٌ مِنْ حُمُوضَةٍ.

Modifiable, *a.* يَتَبَدَّلُ ـ يَتَغَيَّرُ ـ قَابِلُ ٱلتَّعْدِيلِ.

Modification, *n.* The act of adjusting, تَعْدِيل; of altering, تَغْيِير ـ تَبْدِيل; of varying, تَخْرِيج ـ تَلْوِين; of lightening, تَخْفِيف ـ تَلْطِيف. A particular form or manner, كَيْفِيَّة ـ صُورَة ـ بِنْيَة ـ صَوْغ ـ ضَرْب.

Modify, *v.t.* To adjust, عَدَّلَ. To change, بَدَّلَ ـ غَيَّرَ ـ حَوَّلَ. To vary, خَرَّجَ ـ لَوَّنَ. To lighten, خَفَّفَ ـ لَطَّفَ. To restrain, حَصَرَ ُ ـ قَمَعَ َ.

Modish, *a.* *See* Fashionable, *a.*

Modishly, *ad.* *See* Fashionably, *ad.*

Modulate, *v.t.* طَرَّبَ ٱلصَّوْتَ ـ عَدَّلَ ٱلصَّوْتَ ـ رَجَّعَ (or رَنَّمَ) ـ صَوَّتَهُ ـ لَحَّنَ فِي صَوْتِهِ.

Modulation, *n.* The act of modulating the voice, تَطْرِيب ٱلصَّوْتِ ـ تَعْدِيلُ ٱلصَّوْتِ ـ تَلْحِينُ ٱلصَّوْتِ. Sounds modulated, melody, تَرْنِيم ـ لَحْن ـ تَرَنُّم.

Module, *n.* قِيَاس ـ صُورَة ـ قَدْر.

Mogador, *n.* مُقَادُور.

Mogul, *n.* كَبِيرُ ٱلْمُغْلِ ـ مَلِكُ ٱلْمُغْلِ.

Mohair, *n.* ضَرْبٌ مِنَ ٱلْبُشْتِ ـ ضَرْبٌ مِنْ أَقْمِشَةِ ٱلصُّوفِ.

Mohammed, *n.* *See* Muhammad, *n.*

Mohur, *n.* The coin, مُهْر ـ سِكَّةُ ٱلْمُهْرِ.

Moiety, *n.* نِصْف; *vulg.* نُصّ. *See also* Half, *n.*

Moire, *n.* A watered silk stuff, مُخَيَّر ـ كَرْمَسُوت ـ قُمَاش مِنْ حَرِيرٍ مُمَوَّجٍ.

Moil, *v.i.* *See* to Toil, *v.i.*

Moist, *a.* نَدِيٌّ ـ طَرِيٌّ ـ بَلٌّ ـ ثَرِيٌّ ـ رَطْب ـ رَطِيب ـ نَدْيَان ـ نَدِيٌّ. Moist sugar, سُكَّرٌ خَامٌ. A — atmosphere, هَوَآءٌ رَطْبٌ. To be —, طَرُوَ ُ ـ رَطُبَ ُ ـ نَدِيَ َ.

Moisten, *v.t.* بَلَّ ُ ـ أَنْدَى ـ طَرَّأَ ـ ثَرَّى ـ خَضَّلَ ـ أَخْضَلَ ـ رَطَّبَ ـ أَرْطَبَ. To be moistened, اِبْتَلَّ ـ اِنْتَدَى ـ نَدِيَ َ ـ تَسَقَّى.

Moistness, *n.* } بَلَل ـ عَرَق ـ ثَرَى ـ طَرَاوَة ـ خَضَل ـ نَدًى ـ
Moisture, } بِلَّة ـ نَدَاوَة ـ رُطُوبَة ـ بُلُولَة. A slight —, بِلَّة. To exude —, عَرِقَ. To be impregnated with —, تَرَطَّبَ ـ نَدِيَ. It lacked —, لَمْ تَكُنْ لَهُ رُطُوبَةٌ. *See also* Sap, *n.*

Molar, *n.* The tooth, ضِرْس ـ طَوَاحِن *pl.* طَاحِنَة ـ أَرْحَآء *pl.* رَحًا *pl.* أَضْرَاس. The molars, العَوَارِق.

Molar, *a.* }
Molary, } طَاحِن.

Molasses, *n.* دِبْس سُكَّر ـ عَسَل أَسْوَد ـ دِبْس.

Moldavia, *n.* بَغْدَان.

Mole, *n.* The animal, الفَارَةُ ٱلْعَمْيَآءُ ـ خِلْدَان *pl.* خُلْد. A natural spot on the body, شَامَة ـ خُوَيْل *dim.* خِيلَان *pl.* خَال *pl.* شَامَات *and* شَام. Marked with moles, أَشْيَم ـ مَشُوم ـ مَشِيم *fem.* شَيْمَآء ـ أَبُو شَامَاتٍ. A pier, رَصِيف. A construction of stones, رَصَّةُ أَحْجَارٍ ـ رَصَف. *See also* Mound, *n.*

Molecular, *a.* ذُو أَهْبَآء ـ جُزْئِيّ ـ هَبَائِيّ.

Molecule, *n.* هَبَآء *pl.* أَهْبَآء ـ جُزْء صَغِير *pl.* أَجْزَآء صِغَار.

Mole-eyed, *a.* Having small eyes, صَغِيرُ ٱلْعَيْنَيْنِ ـ أَخْفَش.

Mole-hill, *n.* جُحْرُ ٱلْخُلْدِ *pl.* جِحَرَة *and* أَجْحَار.

Molest, *v.t.* حَكَرَ ـ جَحَفَ ـ أَجْحَفَ بِ ـ آذَى ـ عَذَّبَ ـ أَضَرَّ ـ أَضْجَرَ ـ شَقَّ عَلَى ـ ضَاجَّ ـ مَلْمَلَ ـ حَرَّشَ ـ نَكَّدَ عَلَى ـ عَنَّفَ. *See also to* Vex, *v.t.*

Molestation, *n.* غَضَن ـ تَحْرِيش ـ إِجْحَاف ـ حَكَر ـ إِيذَآء ـ إِضْرَار ـ ضَجَر ـ مُضَاجَّة ـ ضِجَاج.

Mollah, *n.* (More correctly Mulla), مُلَّا *pl.* مَلَالِي.

Mollient. *See* Emollient.

Mollification, *n.* تَرْخِيَة ـ تَلْطِيف ـ تَلْيِين.

Mollifier, *n.* مُلَطِّف ـ مُلَيِّن.

Mollify, *v.t.* To soften, لَطَّفَ ـ لَيَّنَ ـ سَحَقَ. To assuage, أَهْدَأَ ـ هَدَّأَ ـ سَكَّنَ ـ. To appease, as of anger, طَيَّبَ خَاطِرَهُ ـ أَخْمَدَ غَضَبَهُ.

Mollifying, *a.* مُسَكِّن ـ مُلَيِّن ـ مُلَطِّف.

Mollusca, *n.* الحَيَوَانَاتُ ٱلْمَفْصِلِيَّةُ مِثْلَ ٱلدِّيدَانِ وَغَيْرِهَا.

Molluscous, *a.* مَا نِيطَ بِٱلْحَيَوَانَاتِ ٱلْمَفْصِلِيَّةِ كَٱلدِّيدَانِ وَغَيْرِهَا.

Mollusk, *n.* حَيَوَانٌ مِنْ قِسْمِ ٱلْحَيَوَانَاتِ ٱلْمَفْصِلِيَّةِ مِثْلَ ٱلدِّيدَانِ وَغَيْرِهَا.

Molten, *a.* مَصُوغ ـ مَسْبُوك.

Molybdenum, *n.* مُلِبْدِنُوم وَهُوَ ضَرْبٌ مِنَ ٱلْمَعَادِنِ.

Mome, *n.* *See* Dolt, *n.*

Moment, *n.* A minute portion of time, لَحْظَة ـ دَقِيقَة *pl.* دَقَائِق ـ لَحْظَةٌ مِنَ ٱلزَّمَانِ ـ نَفَس. Importance, consequence, عِظَم ـ عَظِيمَة ـ أَجْلَال *pl.* جَلَل. An affair of great —, ضَرُورَة ـ مُهِمَّة *pl.* عَظَائِم ـ أَمْرٌ مُهِمٌّ *pl.* أُمُورٌ مُهِمَّةٌ *or* مُهِمَّات. In a —, فِي لَحْظَةٍ مِنَ ٱلزَّمَانِ. In a —, now, immediately, السَّاعَةَ. Every moment after —, كُلَّ سَاعَةٍ ـ أَنْفَاسًا. The — has arrived, حَانَ ـ حَلَّ ٱلْوَقْتُ ـ ٱلْحِينُ. For a —, لِلَحْظَةٍ. A critical —, *un mauvais quart d'heure*, سَاعَةٌ سَوْءَآء. To consider of —, تَعَظَّمَ ـ اِسْتَعْظَمَ.

Momentarily, *ad.* Every moment, كُلَّ ـ أَنْفَاسًا ـ كُلَّ سَاعَةٍ لَحْظَةٍ. For a moment, لِلَحْظَةٍ.

Momentary, *a.* وَقْتِيّ ـ لِلَحْظَةٍ فَقَطْ ـ لِلَحْظَةٍ.

Momentous, *a.* (*see* Important, *a.*) A — affair, جَلَل *pl.* أَجْلَال ـ مُهِمَّة *pl.* مُهِمَّات.

Momentousness, *n.* *See* Importance, *n.*

Momentum, *n.* صَدْمَة ـ صِدَام.

Monacal, *a.* *See* Monastic, *a.*

Monachism, *n.* *See* Monasticism, *n.*

Monad, *n.* An animated atom, ذَرَّى حَيَّة ـ هَبَآءٌ ذُو حَيَاةٍ *pl.* أَهْبَآء. *See also* Atom, *n.*

Monarch, *n.* سُلْطَان *pl.* سَلَاطِين ـ مَلِك *pl.* مُلُوك.

Monarchic, *a.* }
Monarchical, } مُلُوكِيّ ـ سُلْطَانِيّ.

Monarchism, *n.* Principles of monarchy, أُصُولُ ٱلسَّلْطَنَةِ. Attachment to monarchy, تَعَصُّبٌ لِلسَّلْطَنَةِ.

Monarchist, *n.* مِنْ طَرَفِ ٱلسَّلْطَنَةِ ـ مُتَعَصِّبٌ لِلسَّلْطَنَةِ.

Monarchize, *v.i.* To play the monarch, تَصَنَّعَ ـ تَظَاهَرَ بِٱلسَّلْطَنَةِ كَأَنَّهُ سُلْطَانٌ.

Monarchize, *v.t.* To — over, to rule over, تَسَلَّطَ عَلَى. To convert into a monarchy, غَيَّرَ إِلَى أُصُولِ ـ حَوَّلَ إِلَى سَلْطَنَةٍ سَلْطَنَةٍ.

Monarchy, *n.* حُكُومَةٌ مُنْفَرِدَةٌ ـ دَوْلَةٌ مُنْفَرِدَةٌ ـ سَلْطَنَة. Hereditary —, مُلْكٌ تَلِيدٌ (*or* تِلَادٌ) ـ سَلْطَنَةٌ مُتَوَارَثَةٌ. A constitutional —, سَلْطَنَةٌ مُنْفَرِدَةٌ مُقَيَّدَةٌ ـ دَوْلَةٌ مَشْرُوطَةٌ. An elective —, دَوْلَةٌ مُنْفَرِدَةٌ مَبْنِيَّةٌ عَلَى أُصُولِ ٱلْاِنْتِخَابِ. *See also under* Government, *n.*

Monasterial, *a.* دَيْرِيّ ـ مُتَعَلِّقٌ بِدَيْرٍ.

Monastery, *n.* دَيْر *pl.* دُيُورَة. Head of a —, رَئِيسُ دَيْرٍ. A Muslim —, تَكِيَّة.

Monastic, *a.* }
Monastical, } رَهْبَانِيّ. Monastic life, الرَّهْبَنَة. The — orders, الرُّتَبُ ٱلرَّهْبَانِيَّةُ.

Monastic, *n.* *See* Monk, *n.*

Monastically, *ad.* كَالرُّهْبَانِ ـ مِثْلَ ٱلرَّاهِبِ.

Monasticism, *n.* رَهْبَنَة ـ رَهْبَانِيَّة.

Monday, *n.* يَوْمُ ٱلْاثْنَيْنِ ـ الإثْنَانِ.

Monetary, *a.* ما نِيطَ بِٱلدَّرَاهِمِ.

Money, *n.* Current coin, غُرُوش ـ نَقْد ـ فُلُوس ـ دَرَاهِمُ ـ مَال ـ ثَرْوَة. Wealth, property, مِصْرِيَّات ـ عُمْلَة ـ مُعَامَلَة. I have no —, ما مَعِي مِصْرِيَّاتٌ ـ ما عِنْدِي دَرَاهِمُ. A piece of —, a coin, سِكَّة *pl.* سِكَك.

Bad, base money, دَرَاهِمُ زَائِفَة ـ سِكَّة مَغْشُوشَة ـ مُعَامَلَة زَغَل.

Even money, المَبْلَغُ مَا عَدَا ٱلْكُسُورَ.

It is worth any money, يِسْوَى دُنْيَا *vulg.* يُسَاوِي دُنْيَا ـ لا يُثَمَّنُ.

Money in hand, دَرَاهِمُ تَحْتَ ٱلْيَدِ ـ دَرَاهِمُ حَاضِرَة.

Odd money, fractions, كُسُور.

Paper money, قَائِمَة *pl.* قَائِمَات ـ أَوْرَاق نَقْدِيَّة.

Pocket money, خَرْجِيَّة ٱلشَّبْرَقَة؛ *vulg.* خَرْج لِلْجَيْب.

Ready money, دَرَاهِمُ نَقْدِيَّة ـ نَقْد ـ نَضّ ـ عَيْن. Dealing in ready money, مُعَايَنَة. He obtained the amount from him in ready money, إِسْتَخْلَصَ ٱلْمَبْلَغَ مِنْهُ نَضًّا (*or* نَقْدًا).

To call in money, debt, طَلَبَ ٤ (*or* أَدْخَلَ) ٱلدُّيُونَ. To withdraw from circulation, رَفَعَ عَنِ ٱلتَّدَاوُلِ.

To give one the worth of ... in money, أَعْطَى ثَمَنَ ٱلشَّيْءِ نَقْدًا.

To have money about one, حَمَلَ مَعَ ٱلدَّرَاهِمَ ـ مَعَ دَرَاهِمُ.

To have money by one, عِنْدَ دَرَاهِمُ مَرْفُوعَة (*or* مُخَبَّأَة).

To make money, إِكْتَسَبَ دَرَاهِمَ ـ جَمَعَ دَرَاهِمَ ـ قَرَّشَ ـ أَنْفَلَ غُرُوشًا.

To put out money to interest, أَوْدَعَ ٱلدَّرَاهِمَ بِٱلْفَائِدَةِ ـ شَغَّلَ ٱلدَّرَاهِمَ.

To raise money, إِنْتَقَدَ ٱلْفُلُوسَ ـ حَصَّلَ دَرَاهِمَ ـ لَمَّ ٱلدَّرَاهِمَ ٤.

To sink or invest money in, أَوْدَعَ ٱلْمَالَ فِي ـ شَغَّلَ ٱلدَّرَاهِمَ فِي.

To throw away money, أَسْرَفَ ٱلْفُلُوسَ ـ أَتْلَفَ ٱلدَّرَاهِمَ.

To throw good money after bad, ضَيَّعَ ٱلنَّقْدَ فِي طَلَبِ ٱلْمَتْلُوفِ ـ رَمَى ٱلشَّعِيرَ خَلْفَ ٱلْمِخْلَاةِ (prov.) *literally*, he has thrown the barley after the nose-bag.

Money-changer, *n.* صَرَّاف ـ صَيَارِفَة *pl.* صَيْرَف *and* صَيْرَفِيّ.

Moneyed, *a.* عِنْدَهُ ثَرْوَة ـ غَنِيّ ـ صَاحِبُ مَالٍ ـ مُدَرْهَم ـ وَاسِعَة.

Moneyer, *n.* A coiner, ضَرَّابُ سِكَّةٍ.

Money-lender, *n.* مِدْيَان.

Moneyless, *a.* ما عِنْدَهُ دَرَاهِمُ ـ عَدِيمُ ٱلدَّرَاهِمِ ـ مُفْلِس. To be —, أَفْلَسَ.

Money-wort, *n.* The plant, خَوْخُ ٱلْمَاءِ.

Monger, *n.* بَيَّاع *pl.* بَيَّاعَة ـ مُتَسَبِّب.

Mongrel, *a.* *See* Hybrid, *a.*

Mongrel, *n.* *See* Hybrid, *n.*

Monition, *n.* نَصِيحَة *pl.* نَصَائِحُ ـ تَنْبِيه. *See also* Admonition, *n.*

Monitive, *a.* مُنَبِّه ـ نَاصِح.

Monitor, *n.* An adviser, نَاصِح *pl.* نُصَّاح ـ مُنْذِر. A — in a school, عَرِيف *pl.* عُرَفَاء ـ نَاظِر *pl.* نُظَّار ـ مُعَاوِنُ ٱلْمُعَلِّمِ. The — lizard, نَوْعٌ مِنَ ٱلْوَرَنِ زَعَمُوا أَنَّهُ يُنَبِّهُ ٱلتِّمْسَاحَ عَلَى ٱلْخَطَرِ. The armour-plated ship, بَارِجَة مُدَرَّعَة مِنْ طَرْزِ ٱلْمُرْنِيطُورِ.

Monitorial, *a.* Containing admonition, نَاصِح ـ تَنْبِيهِيّ. Pertaining to teachers, مُتَعَلِّق بِٱلْعُرَفَاءِ. The — system, قَاعِدَة ٱلْعُرَفَاءِ ـ ٱلتَّعْلِيمِ بِوَاسِطَةِ ٱلْعُرَفَاءِ تَحْتَ يَدِ ٱلْمُعَلِّمِ.

Monitorially, *ad.* In the way of counsel, عَلَى طَرِيقَةِ ٱلنَّصِيحَةِ.

Monitorship, *n.* عِرَافَة.

Monitory, *a.* نَاصِح ـ مُنْذِر ـ مُنَبِّه.

Monitress, *n.* As in a school, عَرِيفَة (*or* نَاظِرَة) فِي مَكْتَبٍ تَحْتَ يَدِ ٱلْمُعَلِّمِ أَوِ ٱلْمُعَلِّمَةِ.

Monk, *n.* رَاهِب *pl.* رُهْبَان *and* رَهَبَة. To become a —, تَرَهَّبَ.

Monkery, *n.* رَهْبَانِيَّة ـ رَهْبَنَة.

Monkey, *n.* The animal, قِرْد *pl.* قُرُود ـ سَعْدَان *pl.* سَعَادِينُ *vulg.* شَادِي. A mischievous person, شَيْطَان. A pile-driver, مِدَقّ ـ مِدَقَّة.

Monkhood, *n.* رَهْبَانِيَّة ـ رَهْبَنَة.

Monkish, *a.* رَهْبَانِيّ.

Monochromatic, *a.* مِنْ لَوْنٍ وَاحِدٍ ـ ذُو لَوْنٍ وَاحِدٍ.

Monochrome, *n.* صُورَة فِي لَوْنٍ وَاحِدٍ.

Monocotyledon, *n.* نَبَات ذُو أُذُنٍ وَاحِدَةٍ.

Monocular, *a.* } ذُو عَيْنٍ ـ عُورَان *and* عُور *pl.* عَوْرَاءُ *fem.* أَعْوَرُ وَاحِدَةٍ.
Monoculous, }

Monocule, *n.* دُوَيْبَّة ذَاتُ عَيْنٍ وَاحِدَةٍ.

Monodactylous, *a.* مَنْ فِي رِجْلِهِ أُصْبُعٌ وَاحِدَةٌ.

Monody, *n.* مَرْثِيَّة يَرْثِيهَا رَاوٍ وَاحِدٌ.

Monogamist, *n.* الزَّاهِدُ فِي كَثْرَةِ ـ المُقْتَصِرُ عَلَى زَوْجٍ وَاحِدٍ ـ ٱلزَّوْجَاتِ.

Monogamy, *n.* الزَّوَاجُ بِٱمْرَأَةٍ وَاحِدَةٍ.

Monogram, *n.* طُغْرَا ـ حُرُوف مُقَطَّعَة ـ مُوَصَّل.

Monograph, *n.* رِسَالَة فِي مَوْضُوعٍ وَاحِدٍ.

Monographic, *a.* } ما نِيطَ بِمُبَاحَثَةٍ فِي صَدَدٍ وَاحِدٍ.
Monographical, }

Monography, *n.* *See* Monograph, *n.*

Monolith, *n.* حَجَرٌ وَاحِدٌ ـ عَمُودٌ أَوْ أُسْطُوَانَةٌ مِنْ حَجَرٍ وَاحِدٍ ـ صَفِيحَةٌ مِنْ حَجَرٍ.

Monologue, *n.* كَلَامُ مَنْ يَتَكَلَّمُ وَحْدَهُ ـ كَلَامُ ٱلْمُشْتَرِكِ.

Monomania, *n.* ٱلْجُنُونُ بِمَا يَتَعَلَّقُ بِشَيْءٍ وَاحِدٍ فَقَطْ ـ خُلَاع.

Monomaniac, *a.* مَجْنُونٌ بِمَا يَؤُولُ إِلَى أَمْرٍ وَاحِدٍ فَقَطْ ـ ذُو خَيْلَع.

Monopetalous, *a.* (زَهْرٌ) ذُو وَرَقَةٍ وَاحِدَةٍ.

Monophysite, *n.* مَذْهَبُ ٱلْقَائِلِينَ بِقِيَامِ طَبِيعَتَيِ ٱلْمَسِيحِ فِي طَبِيعَةٍ وَاحِدَةٍ.

Monopolist, *n.* } مُلْتَزِم ـ صَاحِبُ ضَمَانٍ ـ صَاحِبُ ٱلْتِزَامٍ ـ
Monopolizer, } مُحْتَكِر ـ مُحَكِّر ـ صَاحِبُ يَدٍ وَاحِدَةٍ; called in Mesopotamia, صَاحِبُ مُقَاطَعَةٍ; in Egypt, حَوَّاطٌ عَلَى ٱلْبَضَائِعِ. A — of any thing, in a general sense, حَوَّاطٌ عَلَى.

Monopolize, *v.t.* To obtain possession of all goods, *etc.*, as for speculation, إِحْتَكَرَ (or حَكَّرَ) ٱلْبَضَائِعَ; in Egypt, حَوَّطَ عَلَى ٱلْبَضَائِعِ. *See also to* Engross, *v.t.*

Monopoly, *n.* إِحْتِصَارٌ ـ ٱلْتِزَام ـ إِحْتِكَار ـ ضَمَان ـ حُكْرَة ـ يَدٌ وَاحِدَةٌ ـ (or ٱلْحِصَارُ) ٱلْبَضَائِعِ; called also in Egypt, تَحْوِيطٌ عَلَى ٱلْبَضَائِعِ; in Mesopotamia, مُقَاطَعَة. To hold a —, ٱلْتَزَمَ ٱلْتِزَامًا ـ تَصَرَّفَ بِضَمَانٍ (or بِٱلْتِزَامٍ) ـ إِحْتَكَرَ ٱحْتِكَارًا. To give a — to, قَبَّضَهُ ضَمَانًا ـ أَعْطَاهُ ٱلْتِزَامًا ـ حَكَّرَهُ حُكْرَةً. By way of —, according to the rules of a —, عَلَى أُصُولٍ ـ عَلَى أُصُولِ ٱلْاِحْتِكَارِ ـ حَسَبَ أُصُولِ ٱلْحُكْرَةِ (or ٱلْمُقَاطَعَةِ) ـ ٱلضَّمَانِ.

Monospermous, *a.* وَحِيدُ ٱلْبَذْرِ.

Monostich, *n.* مِصْرَاع.

Monosyllable, *n.* سَبَبٌ وَاحِدٌ *pl.* أَسْبَاب ـ تَهْجِئَةٌ وَاحِدَةٌ.

Monotheism, *n.* ٱلتَّوْحِيدُ.

Monotheist, *n.* مُوَحِّد ـ مِنْ أَهْلِ ٱلتَّوْحِيدِ.

Monothelite, *n.* مَذْهَبُ ٱلْقَائِلِينَ بِقِيَامِ مَشِيئَتَيِ ٱلْمَسِيحِ فِي مَشِيئَةٍ وَاحِدَةٍ.

Monotone, *n.* لَحْنٌ وَاحِدٌ ـ سَوِيَّةُ (or سَوَاءُ) ٱلصَّوْتِ ـ طَامَّةٌ وَاحِدَةٌ.

Monotonous, *a.* Of sounds, عَلَى ـ جَعْجَاع ـ مُسْتَوِي ٱلصَّوْتِ طَامَّةٍ وَاحِدَةٍ. Uniformly dull, بَارِد ـ مُزَعِّل ـ تَافِه ـ مُمِلٌّ. *See also under* Dull, *a.*

Monotony, *n.* Want of variety, بُرَاد ـ بَرْد ـ مَلَالَة ـ تَفَاهَة. *See also* Dulness, *n.*

Mons Veneris, *n.* The —, ٱلشُّنَّة ـ العَانَة ـ الرَّكَبُ.

Monsieur, *n.* *See* Mister, *n.* (The Arabs write the word, مُسْيُو.)

Monsoon, *n.* مَوْسِمٌ *pl.* مَوَاسِمُ ـ مَوَاسِمُ أَرْيَاحٍ فِي بَحْرِ ٱلْهِنْدِ تَهُبُّ مُدَّةً مَعْلُومَةً.

Monster, *n.* An unnatural production, سَخْطَة. Something excessively ugly, مَسْخَة. One excessively wicked, شِرٌّ أَشْرَارٍ ـ خَبِيثُ أَخْبَثَ ـ ضِلُّ أَضْلَالٍ. A sea —, تِنِّين.

Monstrosity, *n.* } Quality of being monstrous, frightful, هَوْل.
Monstrousness, } Excessive wickedness, فَظَاعَة ـ شَنَاعَة. *See also* Horribleness, *n.*

Monstrous, *a.* Deviating from the natural form, مَمْسُوخ ـ مَهُول ـ مَسْخَة ـ سَخْطَة ـ خَارِجٌ عَنِ ٱلطَّبِيعَةِ. Horrible, مَهُول ـ هَائِل. Hateful, wicked, فَظِيع ـ شَنِيع. *See also under* Horrible, *a.*

Monstrously, *ad.* تَخْوِيفًا ـ بِهَوْلٍ ـ إِقْشِعْرَارًا. *See also* Horribly, *ad.*

Montanic, *a.* جَبَلِيٌّ.

Montenegro, *n.* The province, ٱلْجَبَلُ ٱلْأَسْوَدُ.

Month, *n.* شَهْرٌ *pl.* شُهُور *and* أَشْهُر. The beginning of the —, غُرَّةُ (or رَأْسُ) ٱلشَّهْرِ. The first ten days of the —, أَوَائِلُ ٱلشَّهْرِ; the ten days in the middle of the —, أَوَاسِطُ ٱلشَّهْرِ; the last ten days of the —, أَوَاخِرُ ٱلشَّهْرِ. The end of the —, سَلْخُ ٱلشَّهْرِ. A full —, شَهْرٌ كَرِيتٌ (or كَامِلٌ). A calendar —, شَهْرٌ رُومِيٌّ; a lunar —, شَهْرٌ قَمَرِيٌّ. This day —, عُقْبَ شَهْرٍ ـ مِنَ ٱلْيَوْمِ إِلَى شَهْرٍ. Until the end of the —, إِلَى غَايَةِ ٱلشَّهْرِ. For the space of a —, مُدَّةَ شَهْرٍ. To hire by the —, شَاهَرَ. To be a — old, or to reside in a place for a —, أَشْهَرَ.

Monthly, *a.* شَهْرِيٌّ. Monthly pay, wages, شَهْرِيَّة ـ مُشَاهَرَة.

Monthly, *ad.* مَرَّةً فِي كُلِّ شَهْرٍ ـ كُلَّ شَهْرٍ.

Monthly, *a.* A — publication, جَرِيدَةٌ تَصْدُرُ ـ جَرِيدَةٌ شَهْرِيَّةٌ مَرَّةً فِي كُلِّ شَهْرٍ.

Monument, *n.* A memorial, تَذْكَار ـ تَذْكِرَة. A building, بِنَاءٌ *pl.* أَبْنِيَة. A remain, monumental remains, أَثَر *pl.* آثَار ـ هَيْكَل *pl.* هَيَاكِل. A mark, sign, نِيشَان ـ عَلَامَة. A tomb, تُرْبَة *pl.* تُرَب ـ قَبْر *pl.* قُبُور. Celebrated monuments, remains, of works or buildings, آثَارٌ بَاهِرَةٌ.

Monumental, *a.* For remembrance, عَلَى ذِكْرٍ. Pertaining to a monument, building, مُتَعَلِّقٌ بِبِنَاءٍ. Pertaining to remains, مُتَعَلِّقٌ بِآثَارٍ. Pertaining to a tomb, مُتَعَلِّقٌ بِتُرْبَةٍ. Ancient — remains, آثَارٌ قَدِيمَةٌ.

Mood, *n.* Temper of mind, كَيْف ـ حَال ـ خَاطِر. Form, manner, هَيْئَة ـ مِنْوَال ـ صُورَة. Style of music, مَقَام. Tense, صِيغَة. To be in the — to, لَهُ خَاطِرٌ أَنْ ـ إِنْعَطَفَ إِلَى ـ أَخَالَ إِلَى. *See under* Conjunctive, Indicative, *etc., for moods of verbs.*

Moodily, *ad.* بِعُبُوسٍ ـ بِكَدَرٍ ـ بِشَرَشَةٍ.

Moody, *a.* Changeable, حَالَاتِيٌّ ـ مُتَلَوِّن ـ قَرَّار. *See also* Gloomy, *a.*

Moollah, *n.* *See under* Mollah, *n.*

Moon, *n.* قَمَر *pl.* أَقْمَار. The new —, هِلَال *pl.* أَهِلَّة *and* أَهَالِيل. The full —, بَدْر *pl.* بُدُور ـ قَمَرٌ فِي لَيْلَةِ تَمَامِهِ. To rise, of the —, هَلَّ ء. The disk of the —, قُرْصُ ٱلْقَمَرِ. A spot, as on the —, شَامَة *pl.* شَامَات; dark spots on the —, مَحْوٌ. The increase and wane of the —, زِيَادَةُ ضَوْءِ ٱلْقَمَرِ وَنُقْصَانُهُ. To become full, of the —, بَدَرَ ². To become a moon, of the crescent, أَقْمَرَ ٱلْهِلَالُ. *See also under* Phase, *n.*

Moon-beam, *n.* شُعَاعُ ٱلْقَمَرِ (شُعَاع *or*) شَعٌ *pl.* شِعَاع *and* أَشِعَّة.

Moon-blindness, رَمَدٌ قَمَرِيٌّ.

Moon-calf, *n.* *See* Dolt; *also* Monster, *n.*

Moonless, *n.* بِلَا قَمَرٍ. A — night, لَيْلَةٌ دَهْمَاءُ لَا قَمَرَ فِيهَا.

Moonlight, *n.* ضَوْءُ ٱلْقَمَرِ ـ ضِيَاءُ ٱلْقَمَرِ. A — night, لَيْلَةٌ قَمِرَةٌ ـ لَيْلَةٌ مُقْمِرَةٌ. To play or travel by —, أَقْمَرَ.

Moonshine, *n.* Show without substance, عَبَث ـ لَغْوٌ ـ تَفَاهَة ـ بَاطِل. *See also* Moonlight, *n.*

Moonshee, *n.* (From the Arabic مُنْشِئٌ) A writer, كَاتِب; a teacher, مُعَلِّم ـ مُدَرِّس.

Moonstruck, *a.* مَضْرُوبٌ بِٱلْقَمَرِ ـ مُصَابٌ بِٱلْقَمَرِ. *See also* Lunatic, *a.*

Moony, *a.* *See* Lunated, *a.*

Moor, *n.* A heath, قَاع *pl.* قِيعَان *and* أَقْوَاع ـ أُمٌّ دَرِينٍ ـ أَرْضٌ عَاقُول. An Arab of Africa, مَغْرِبِيٌّ *pl.* مَغَارِبَة. *See also* Fen, Marsh, *n.*

Moor, *v.t.* To secure by cables, رَبَطَ ². To — across the moorings of another ship, اِعْتَرَضَ مَرْسَةَ مَرْكَبٍ. To — alongside, رَبَطَ عِنْدَ ².

Moor, *v.i.* اِرْتَبَطَ.

Moorage, *n.* مَرْبَط ـ مِينَة ـ كَلًّا ـ مُكَلًّا ـ مَرْفَأ.

Moor-cock, Moor-fowl, *n.*, Moor-game, Moor-hen, } فَرْخُ ٱلْمَاءِ ـ دَجَاجَةُ ٱلْمَاءِ.

Moorland, *n.* *See* Moor, *n.*

Moorings, *n.* رِبَاط ـ مَرْسَة ـ سَلَبَة.

Moorish, *a.* *See* Marshy, Fenny, *a.*

Moorish, *a.* Pertaining to the Moors of Africa, مِنَ ٱلْمَرَاكِشِ.

Moose, *n.* نَوْعٌ مِنَ ٱلْإِيَّلِ كَبِيرٌ.

Moot, *v.t.* To raise a question, فَتَحَ بَحْثًا ء. To discuss, نَاضَلَ ـ تَكَلَّمَ فِي ـ بَحَثَ عَنْ ء ـ بَاحَثَ عَنْ ـ فَاوَضَ.

Moot, *n.*, Moot-case, Moot-point, } مُجَادَلَة ـ مَوْضُوعٌ فِيهِ نِزَاعٌ ـ مَسْأَلَة *pl.* مَسَائِل.

Mootable, *a.* مُشْكِل ـ فِيهِ خِلَاف ـ تَحْتَ ٱلْمُنَازَعَةِ.

Mop, *n.* نَشَّافَة.

Mop, *v.t.* To wipe with a mop, مَسَحَ بِٱلنَّشَّافَةِ ـ نَظَّفَ ـ مَسَحَ ء.

Mope, *v.i.* ضَانَى ـ ضَنِيَ ء ـ ضَاقَ صَدْرُهُ ء ـ مَلَّ ء ـ تَزَعَّلَ.

Mope, *v.t.* زَعَّلَ ـ أَمَلَّ ـ أَزْعَجَ ـ أَضْنَى ـ تَضَجَّرَ.

Mope, *n.* ضَنٍ ـ زَعْلَانُ ـ مَجْذُوب.

Moping, *a.*, Mopish, } ضَنٍ *fem.* ضَنِيَة ـ زَعْلَانُ ـ كَرِيب ـ مَلُول.

Mopishness, *n.* ضَنَاءَة ـ زَعَل ـ ضُجُور.

Moral, *a.* Pertaining to practice and manners, أَدَبِيٌّ. Upright, virtuous, صَالِح ـ مُسْتَقِيم ـ مَعْنَوِيٌّ ـ عَقْلِيٌّ. Metaphysical, The — Moral philosophy, عِلْمُ ٱلْأَخْلَاقِ ـ عِلْمُ ٱلْحِكْمَةِ ٱلْأَدَبِيَّةِ. The — law, سُنَّةُ ٱلْأَمْرِ وَٱلنَّهْيِ حَسَبَ ٱلدِّيَانَةِ وَٱلشَّرِيعَةِ. Moral sense, فُرْقَان ـ رُشْد. Moral instructions, تَعَالِيمُ أَدَبِيَّةٌ. What is the — condition of the people? مَا هِيَ حَالَةُ ٱلْمِلَّةِ فِيمَا يَخُصُّ ٱلْمَزَايَا ٱلْحَمِيدَةَ.

Moral, *n.* As of a fable, *etc.*, حِكْمَة ـ مَعْنًى ـ نَتِيجَةٌ عَقْلِيَّةٌ. The — of a parable, مَضْرِبُ مَثَلٍ ـ مَوْرِدُ مَثَلٍ. The — of the fable is this, مَثَلُ ٱلْخُرَافَةِ هٰذَا. A fable with a —, حَدِيث ـ مَضْرِب ـ مَثَل.

Moralist, *n.* One who teaches morality, مُعَلِّمُ عِلْمِ ٱلْأَدَبِ. A writer on morals, مُصَنِّفُ تَآلِيفَ أَدَبِيَّةٍ. A mere — man, أَدِيبٌ لَا غَيْرُ.

Morality, *n.* System of moral duties, عِلْمُ ٱلْأَخْلَاقِ. Character, manners, أَخْلَاق ـ سِيرَة. Quality, property, خَصْلَة ـ صِنْف ـ صِفَة ـ ذَات.

Moralize, *v.t.* To make moral, أَدَّبَ ـ صَحَّحَ ٱلْأَخْلَاقَ ـ خَرَّجَ. To make moral reflections on, وَعَظَ عَلَى *aor.* يَعِظُ.

Moralize, *v.i.* To make moral reflections, وَعَظَ *aor.* يَعِظُ. To write on moral subjects, صَنَّفَ تَآلِيفَ أَدَبِيَّةً.

Moralizer, *n.* *See* Moralist, *n.*

Moralizing, *n.* وَعْظ ـ مَوْعِظَة ـ عِظَة.

Morally, *ad.* Uprightly, بِٱسْتِقَامَةٍ. According to moral rules, عَقْلًا ـ بِٱلْعَقْلِ.

Morals, *n.* أَخْلَاق ـ سِيرَة. Having lax —, سَائِب ـ فَالِت ـ مُهَاوِد. A breach of —, ثَلْمُ ٱلْأَدَبِ. Good —, ٱلْمَزَايَا ٱلْحَمِيدَةُ.

Morass, *n.* *See* Marsh, *n.*

Morassy, *a.* *See* Marshy, *n.*

Moravian, *n.* One of the United Brethren, طَائِفَةٌ مِنَ ٱلنَّصَارَى تَعْتَصِمُ بِٱلِٱتِّحَادِ ٱلْأَخَوِيِّ.

Morbid, *a.* Not sound or healthy, عَلِيل ـ مُعَلّ ـ مَعْلُول ـ فَاسِد ـ مِمْرَاض ـ مَرِيض ـ سَقِم ـ سَقِيم . Unwholesome, وَبِيل . Morbid sensibility, حَسَاسٌ سَقِيمٌ ـ فَهْمٌ سَقِيمٌ . Morbid language, كَلَامٌ سَقِيمٌ .

Morbific, *a.* } Morbifical, } مُهْلِك ـ مُعِلّ ـ مُمْرِض ـ مُفْسِد ـ مُسْقِم .

Morbose, *a.* *See* Morbid, *a.*

Morceau, *n.* *See* Bit, Morsel, *n.*

Mordacious, *a.* عَضُوض ـ عَضَّاض . *See also* Sarcastic, *a.*

Mordacity, *n.* عِضَاض .

Mordant, *n.* A substance to fix colours, *etc.*, تَرْبِيَة ـ آهَار .

Mordant, *a.* Having the quality of fixing colours, مُرَبِّب .

Mordicant, *a.* *See* Biting, Acrid, *a.*

More, *n.* زِيَادَة ـ أَكْثَر ـ كُثْر .

More, *a.* As the comparative degree of Much, أَشَدّ ـ أَكْثَر ـ أَزْيَد ـ أَزْوَد . More angry, أَشَدّ غَضَبًا ; more detrimental, أَضَرّ ; more to be desired, أَشْهَى ; more black, blacker, أَشَدّ سَوَادًا ; more abundantly, أَكْثَر جِدًّا . To be more in number than, تَعَدَّى عَلَى ـ أَفْضَل عَن ـ نَيَّف عَلَى ـ أَنَاف عَلَى . Ten and more, عَشَرَة وَنَيِّف . It is not — than, لا يُزِيد عَلَى .

More, *ad.* To a greater degree, أَزْيَد ـ أَكْثَر . Again, further, أَيْضًا ـ بَعْدُ . More and more, زِيَادَة ـ أَكْثَر وَأَكْثَر . More than that, besides, ما عدا ذلِكَ ـ وَأَعْظَم مِنْ ذلِكَ . Neither more nor less, لا زَائِد وَلا نَاقِص ـ لا أَكْثَر وَلا أَقَلّ . He alone more than all other people, هُوَ وَحْدَهُ دُونَ سَائِرِ ٱلنَّاسِ . More or less, تَقْرِيبًا ـ زَائِدٌ أَوْ نَاقِصٌ . The more, كُلَّمَا . He set out more than two hours ago, سَافَرَ نَيِّف سَاعَتَيْنِ ـ سَافَرَ مُنْذُ أَكْثَر مِنْ سَاعَتَيْنِ . I have no more money, مَا بَقِي عِنْدِي دَرَاهِمُ . There is no more in it, مَا بَقِي فِيهِ ـ مَا فَضَلَ فِيهِ[2] . I saw him no more, مَا رَأَيْتُهُ بَعْدُ . He did not return to him any more, لَمْ يَرْجِعْ إِلَيْهِ أَيْضًا . He will not write any more until...., لا يَكْتُبُ بَعْدُ حَتَّى . I will not do the like any more, مَا أَفْعَلُ مِثْلَهُ بَعْدُ . He will not return any more to his house, لا يَرْجِعُ بَعْدُ إِلَى بَيْتِهِ . The more I love you, the less I am loved, كُلَّمَا أُحِبُّكُمْ أَكْثَرَ أُحَبُّ أَقَلَّ . The more they rooted them up, the more they grew, بِحَسْبِمَا ٱسْتَأْصَلُوهُمْ هٰكَذَا نَمُوا . Some gathered more, some less, مِنْهُمْ مَنْ أَكْثَرَ ٱلْجَمْعَ وَمِنْهُمْ مَنْ قَلَّلَ . Take with you one or two more, خُذْ مَعَكَ أَيْضًا وَاحِدًا أَوِ ٱثْنَيْنِ . I will extol him more and more, أَزِيدُ عَلَى تَعْظِيمِهِ .

Moreen, *n.* ثَوْبٌ مُشَجَّرٌ مِنْ صُوفٍ .

Moreover, *ad.* مِنْ دُونِ ذٰلِكَ ـ أَيْضًا ـ كَذٰلِكَ ـ مَا عَدَا ذٰلِكَ . *See also* Besides, *ad.*

Moresque, *a.* Arabic, عَرَبِيّ . Moorish, طَرْزٌ مَغْرِبِيّ ـ مَغْرِبِيّ .

Moresque, *n.* نَقْشٌ عَلَى طَرْزٍ مَغْرِبِيّ .

Morganatic, *a.* A — marriage, نِكَاحٌ يَقَعُ بَيْنَ ٱلْأُمَرَاءِ ٱلْمُتَسَاوِيِينَ وَبَيْنَ نِسَاءٍ دُونَهُمْ شَرَفًا وَرُتْبَةً يُشْتَرَطُ فِيهِ إِسْقَاطُ حَقِّهِنَّ وَحَقِّ أَوْلَادِهِنَّ مِنَ ٱلْإِرْثِ وَٱلْمُلْكِ شَرْعًا .

Moribund, *a.* and *n.* فِي حَالَةِ ٱلنَّزْعِ ـ مُشْرِفٌ عَلَى ٱلْمَوْتِ .

Morion, *n.* *See* Helmet, *n.*

Morisco, *n.* *See* Morris, *n.*

Mormon, *n.* } Mormonite, } مِنْ أَهْلِ ٱلْبِدْعَةِ ٱلْآتِي ذِكْرُهَا .

Mormonism, *n.* مَذْهَبٌ جَدِيدٌ ٱبْتَدَعَهُ يُوسُفُ إِسْمِيث فِي ٱلْبِلَادِ ٱلْمُتَّحِدَةِ بِأَمِيرِكَا ٱلشِّمَالِيَّةِ مُدَّعِيًا بِأَنَّ ٱللّٰهَ أَوْقَفَهُ عَلَى صَفَائِحَ ذَهَبِيَّةٍ كَانَتْ فِيهَا عَقَائِدُ ٱلْبَشَرِ ٱلْقُدَمَاءِ فَجَمَعَهَا إِلَى مُصْحَفٍ سَمَّاهُ بِكِتَابِ ٱلْمُورْمُون .

Morn, *n.* } Morning, } سَحَر ـ غُدُوّ ـ غَدَاة ـ غَدِيَة ـ غُدْوَة ـ صُبْح *pl.* أَصْبَاح . Morning tide, صَبَاح . A —, صُبْحِيَّة . The early —, ٱلْبُكْرَة ـ ٱلضَّحَاء[*] ـ ٱلضُّحَى . In the —, صُبْحًا ـ صَبَاحًا ـ مِنَ ٱلصُّبْحِ ـ عِنْدَ ٱلصَّبَاحِ ـ فِي ٱلصَّبَاحِ . Early in the —, عَلَى بُكْرَة ـ بَكِّير ـ تَبْكِيرَة ـ بَدْرِي . This —, ٱلْيَوْم عَلَى بُكْرَة ـ ٱلْيَوْمَ ٱلصُّبْحَ ـ هٰذِهِ ٱلصُّبْحِيَّةَ . Every —, كُلَّ يَوْمٍ ـ صَبَاحًا فَصَبَاحًا . Morning and evening, صَبَاحًا وَمَسَاءً ـ بُكْرَةً وَعَشِيَّةً ـ عَلَى بُكْرَة . In the — and evening, صَبَاحَ مَسَاءَ . On a certain —, ذَاتَ غَدَاةٍ . The middle of the —, from after day-break till noon, ضَحَاء ـ ضَحْو ـ ضَحْوَة ـ ضَحْوَةُ ٱلنَّهَارِ . To be or become —, أَصْبَحَ . To rise early in the —, بَكَّرَ ـ صَبَّحَ ـ سَحَّرَ[2] . To come in the —, غَدَا[2] ; he came in the — and left, غَدَا وَرَاحَ . I came to him early in the —, أَتَيْتُهُ بُكْرَةً . To bid good — to, or to go to one in the —, صَبَّحَ . Good — to you, نَعِمْتَ صَبَاحًا ـ أَنْعِمْ صَبَاحًا ـ صَبَاحُ ٱلْخَيْرِ . The — became advanced, إِرْتَفَعَتِ ٱلضُّحَى .

Morning, *a.* غَدِيّ ـ صُبْحِيّ . Morning sleep, صُبْحَة ـ صَبْحَة . A — draught, صَبُوح . A — meal, سَحُور ـ غَدَاء . To take a — meal, تَسَحَّرَ ـ تَصَبَّحَ ـ تَغَدَّى[2] ـ تَغَدَّى . The — star, نَجْمَةُ ٱلصَّبَاحِ . A — gown, سِتْرَةٌ لِلْبَيْتِ . A — watch, هَزِيعُ ٱلصُّبْحِ . The best — meals are those that are early, and the best evening meals are those thereof in which the food is seen before the invasion of night, (prov.) خَيْرُ ٱلْغَدَاءِ بَوَاكِرُهُ وَخَيْرُ ٱلْعَشَاءِ بَوَاصِرُهُ .

Morocco, *n.* The country, مَرَاكِش ; the leather, سَخْتِيَان .

Morone, *a.* *See* Maroon, *a.*

Morose, *a.* شَرِس ـ مَحْكَان ـ عَبَّاس ـ وَعِق ـ عَنِيف. Morose in countenance, شَتِيم. To be — towards, عَنَفَ عَلَى ـ أَعْنَفَ ـ. To look —, تَعَبَّسَ ـ تَقَطَّبَ.

Morosely, *ad.* بِخَشَانَةٍ ـ بِوَعَقَةٍ ـ بِعَنْفٍ ـ بِشَرَاسَةٍ.

Moroseness, *n.* فَظَاظَةٌ ـ خُشُونَةٌ ـ شَرَاسَةٌ ـ وَعْقَةٌ ـ عَنْفٌ.

Morphia, *n.* / **Morphine**, } مُرْفِين ـ خُلَاصَةُ ٱلْأَفْيُونِ.

Morra, *n.* The game, مُخَارَجَةٌ ـ مَخْرَبِيج ـ خَرَاج ـ خَرِيج.

Morris, *n.* / **Morris-dance**, } ضَرْبٌ مِنَ ٱلرَّقْصِ.

Morris-dancer, *n.* جَنْكِيٌّ ـ رَقَّاص.

Morrow, *n.* غَدْوٌ ـ غَد. To-morrow, بُكْرَةً ـ غَدًا. He was determined to depart on the —, كَانَ مُزْمِعًا أَنْ يَمْضِيَ فِي ٱلْغَدِ. *See also* To-morrow, *n.*

Morse, *n.* The walrus, عِجْلُ ٱلْبَحْرِ.

Morsel, *n.* A bite or mouthful, أُكْلَةٌ ـ لُقْمَةٌ *pl.* لُقَم ـ دُبْلَةٌ *pl.* دُبَل. A cut, slice, قِطْعَةٌ ـ شَقْفَةٌ *pl.* شُقَف; of meat, شَرِيحَةٌ ـ شَرَائِح. A — of bread, قِطْعَةُ خُبْزٍ *pl.* قِطَع ـ كِسْرَةُ عَيْشٍ; of meat, مُضْغَةٌ ـ شِنْشِنَةٌ. To make into morsels, gobbets, دَبَّلَ. To cut up into morsels, قَطَّعَ ـ جَزَّأَ ـ. To roll a — about in the mouth, لَجْلَجَ.

Mort, *n.* A tune sounded at the death of game, تَنْبِيقٌ عِنْدَ قَتْلِ ٱلصَّيْدِ.

Mortal, *a.* Subject to death, مَائِت ـ فَانٍ ـ يَمُوتُ. Deadly, قَاتِل ـ مُهْلِكٌ ـ مُوجِبُ ٱلْمَوْتِ. Human, بَشَرِيٌّ ـ إِنْسَانِيٌّ. Excessive, شَدِيد ـ كَثِير ـ كَبِير. A — sin, كَبِيرَةٌ *pl.* كَبَائِرُ. خَطِيئَةٌ مُمِيتَةٌ. Anything —, or destructive of life, غُول. A — disease, مُوتَان. A — enemy, عَدُوٌّ أَزْرَقُ. All men are —, كُلُّ نَفْسٍ ذَائِقَةُ ٱلْمَوْتِ. A — blow, ضَرْبَةٌ قَاتِلَةٌ.

Mortal, *n.* A man subject to death, إِنْسَان ـ إِنْسِيٌّ. Mortals, ٱلْبَشَرُ ـ ٱلْأَنَامُ.

Mortality, *n.* Subjection to death, ٱلْمَائِتُ. Death, مَوْت ـ وَفَاة. Destruction by death, هَلْك ـ هَلْكَاءُ ـ هَلَكَةٌ ـ وَبَآء. A great —, هَلَكَةٌ هَلْكَاءُ.

Mortally, *ad.* Fatally, لِحَدِّ ٱلْمَوْتِ ـ لِلْمَوْتِ. Greatly, شَدِيدًا ـ لِلْغَايَةِ. Mortally wounded, مَجْرُوحٌ جُرْحًا مُمِيتًا.

Mortar, *n.* As for building, of lime and sand, مِلَاط (called also in Egypt, خَافِقِيّ); of mud, طِين ـ مِلْطَم; of mud and straw, سَيَاع. A vessel in which substances are pounded, هَاوَن *pl.* هَوَاوِين. A piece of ordnance for throwing shells, هَاوَن *pl.* هَاوُونَات. To plaster with mortar composed of lime and sand, مَلَّطَ; with mud, طَيَّنَ ـ دَمَّمَ; with — made of straw and mud, سَيَّعَ.

Mortgage, *n.* The state of being pledged, رَهْن ـ رُهُون. A pledge, رَهْن *pl.* رِهَان ـ مَرْهُون ـ رَهِينَةٌ.

Mortgage, *v.t.* رَهَنَ ـ. He mortgaged the thing to him, رَهَنَهُ ٱلشَّيْءَ ـ رَهَنَ ٱلشَّيْءَ عِنْدَهُ. I mortgaged the goods for debt, رَهَنْتُ ٱلْمَتَاعَ بِٱلدَّيْنِ. *See also under to* Pledge, *v.t.*

Mortgaged, *a.* مَرْهُون ـ مَرْهُونٌ بِٱلدَّيْنِ ـ رَهِين.

Mortgage-deed, *n.* حُجَّةٌ رَهِينَةٌ ـ صَكُّ رَهْنٍ.

Mortgagee, *n.* صَاحِبُ ٱلرَّهْنِ ـ لَهُ حَقٌّ عَلَى ٱلرَّهِينَةِ ـ مُرْتَهِن مِن.

Mortgager, *n.* رَاهِن ـ رَاهِنٌ بِٱلدَّيْنِ.

Mortification, *n.* Gangrene, عُطْبَة ـ أُكَال ـ تَمْوِيت. Keeping in check, humiliation, قَمْع ـ إِمَاتَة. Chagrin, غَمّ ـ قَهْر ـ كَمَد ـ أَسَف. A cause of —, مُوجِبُ ٱلْقَهْرِ ـ مُورِثُ ٱلْغَمِّ. Self —, قَمْعُ ٱلنَّفْسِ ـ رِيَاضَةُ ٱلنَّفْسِ ـ قَمْعُ ٱلذَّاتِ. Mortifications, austerities, تَقَشُّف ـ زُهْد ـ زَهَادَة.

Mortify, *v.t.* To destroy the vital functions, مَوَّتَ ـ أَمَاتَ. To bring into subjection, keep in check, قَهَرَ ـ قَمَعَ ـ. To chagrin, أَضْجَرَ ـ فَجَّعَ ـ أَزْعَجَ ـ قَلَّقَ ـ أَغَمَّ. To humiliate, حَقَّرَ ـ أَهَانَ. To — one's self, قَهَرَ نَفْسَهُ ـ قَمَعَ ذَاتَهُ ـ.

Mortify, *v.i.* To gangrene, عَطِبَ ـ تَأَكَّلَ.

Mortifying, *a.* Humiliating, مُحَقِّر ـ مُهِين ـ مُذِلّ ـ مُخَيِّب.

Mortise, *n.* فَرْض *pl.* فِرَاض ـ حَزَّة *coll.* حَزّ.

Mortise, *v.t.* حَزَّ ـ فَرَضَ ـ.

Mortmain, *n.* An inalienable estate, أَمْوَالٌ مَوْقُوفَةٌ ـ وَقْف.

Mortuary, *n.* A bequest at death to a church, وَقْفٌ عِنْدَ ٱلْمَمَاتِ لِلْكَنِيسَةِ.

Mortuary, *a.* جَنَائِزِيٌّ ـ مُتَعَلِّقٌ بِٱلْجِنَازَةِ. A — chapel, مُصَلَّى ٱلْمَقْبَرَةِ.

Mosaic, *a.* / **Mosaical**, } Pertaining to Moses, مُوسَوِيٌّ. Composed of mosaic, زَوَاق ـ مُرَكَّبٌ مِنَ ٱلْأَحْجَارِ ٱلْمُلَوَّنَةِ ـ فُسَيْفِسَة.

Mosaic, *n.* زَوَاق ـ فُسَيْفِسَة.

Moses, *n.* حَضْرَةُ مُوسَى.

Moslem, *n.* *See* Muslim, *n.*

Mosque, *n.* A place of Muslim worship, مَسْجِد *pl.* مَسَاجِد. A congregational —, مَسْجِدٌ جَامِعٌ ـ جَامِع *pl.* جَوَامِعُ. The — of Makkah, مَسْجِدُ ٱلْحَرَامِ; the — of Jerusalem, مَسْجِدُ ٱلْأَقْصَى. The two mosques of Makkah and al-Madinah, ٱلْمَسْجِدَانِ.

Mosquito, *n.* *See* Musquito.

Moss, *n.* كُشْةُ ٱلْعَجُوزِ ـ شَيْبَةُ ٱلْعَجُوزِ ـ أُشْنَةٌ. Water —, طُحْلُب ـ غَلْفَق. Fine — on stones, لُزَيْقَة.

Moss-clad, *a.* / Moss-grown, } مُغطًى بِكُشْةِ ٱلْعَجُوزِ ـ عَلَيْهِ أُشْنَةٌ.

Mossiness, *n.* كَثْرَةُ ٱلْأُشْنَةِ.

Moss-land, *n.* مَغِيض ـ أَجَمَة.

Moss-trooper, *n.* *See* Bandit, Highwayman, *n.*

Mossy, *a.* عَلَيْهِ أُشْنَةٌ.

Most, *a.* جُلّ ـ أَجَلّ ـ أَعْظَم ـ أَشَدّ ـ ٱلْأَغْلَب ـ ٱلْأَكْثَر. Most men, أَغْلَبُ ٱلنَّاسِ. For the — part, فِي ٱلْأَغْلَبِ ـ غَالِبًا. Most of them were people of the town, جُلُّهُمْ مِنْ أَهْلِ ٱلْمَدِينَةِ. Most of their demands, جُلُّ مَطْلُوبِهِمْ.

Most, *n.* جُلال ـ جُلّ ـ أَكْثَر ـ أَغْلَب ـ مُعْظَم. He took the — of it, أَخَذَ جُلَّهُ ٤. To make the — of a thing, إِسْتَعْظَمَ ـ إِسْتَكْبَرَ.

Most, *ad.* أَكْثَر ـ بِالْأَكْثَرِ. Most loving, أَكْثَرُ حُبًّا. Especially, لا سِيَّمَا; they sorrowed — for his departure, تَأَسَّفُوا لا سِيَّمَا مِنْ سَفَرِهِ. At most, عَلَى ٱلْأَكْثَرِ. By two and two or at — by three and three, إِثْنَيْنِ ٱثْنَيْنِ أَوْ عَلَى ٱلْأَكْثَرِ ثَلٰثَةً ثَلٰثَةً.

Mostic, *n.* *See* Maulstick, *n.*

Mostly, *ad.* بِالْأَكْثَرِ ـ غَالِبًا ـ فِي ٱلْغَالِبِ.

Mote, *n.* هَبَآءَةٌ *pl.* أَهْبَآءٌ. A — in the eye, رَائِد ـ قَذًى ـ غُضَاب ـ عَوَاوِير *pl.* عُوَّار. A — in the sun, سِحْرَارَة. To fly about as a —, هَفَتَ ٢. His eye had a — cast into it, طَعِمَتْ عَيْنُهُ. I cast a — into his eye, أَطْعَمْتُ عَيْنَهُ قَذًى.

Moth, *n.* The insect, فَرَاشَة *coll.* فَرَاش. The winged —, فَرَاشُ ٱللَّيْلِ. The small insect that eats cloth, *etc.*, سُوس ـ سُوسَة ـ عُثّ ـ عُثَّة *pl.* عُثَث *and* عُثُوث. To erode as a —, عَثَّ ٤ ـ سَوَّسَ. To be attacked by —, سَاسَ *aor.* يَسُوسُ. To be eaten by —, تَسَوَّسَ.

Moth-eaten, *a.* مُسَوَّس.

Mother, *n.* أُمّ *pl.* أُمَّهَات ـ وَالِدَة. The cause of anything, سَبَب ـ أُمّ. (As an adjective): One's — country, وَطَن. The — country as regards a colony, أُمُّ ٱلْبِلَادِ. One's — tongue, لِسَانُ ٱلْوَطَنِ ـ لِسَانُ بَلَدِهِ. A — tongue from which another is derived, اللِّسَانُ ٱلْأَصْلِيُّ. The — or metropolitan church, الْكَنِيسَةُ ٱلْمَطْرَانِيَّةُ.

Mother, *v.i.* *See to* Concrete, *v.i.*

Mother, *v.t.* To take as her son, إِتَّخَذَتْهُ ٱبْنًا لَهَا; as a daughter, إِتَّخَذَتْهَا بِنْتًا لَهَا. *See also to* Adopt, *v.t.*

Mother Carey's Chicken, *n.* طَائِرٌ بَحْرِيٌّ يُرَى غَالِبًا وَقْتَ ٱلنَّوْءِ.

Motherhood, *n.* أُمِّيَّة.

Mother-in-law, *n.* Mother of a husband, حَمَاة ـ أُمُّ ٱلزَّوْجِ. The second wife of a father, إِمْرَأَةُ ٱلْأَبِ.

Motherless, *a.* بِلا أُمّ ـ عَجِيّ *fem.* عَجِيَّة.

Motherly, *a.* *See* Maternal, *a.*

Mother-of-pearl, *n.* صَدَف ـ صَدَفُ ٱلدُّرَّةِ ـ مَحَارَة *pl.* مَحَاوِر.

Mother-wit, *n.* ذِهْن ـ ذَكَآء ـ فَصَاحَة ـ عَقْل ـ سَلِيقِيَّة.

Mother-wort, *n.* فَرَاسِيُونُ ٱلْقَلْبِ.

Mothy, *a.* مَعْثُوث ـ مُسَوَّس.

Motion, *n.* A movement, حَرَكَة *pl.* حَرَكَات. The act of changing place, تَحْوِيل ـ نَقْل. Inward —, desire, هَوًى *pl.* أَهْوَآء ـ هَوِيَّة. Impulse, حَرَكَة ـ رَكْضَة. A proposition, ضَرِيبَة *pl.* ضَرَائِب ـ شَوْر ـ رَأْي ـ مَسْأَلَة ـ مَوْضُوع. An evacuation, مَجْلِس. An action, صَنِيعَة *pl.* صَنَائِع. Forward —, حَرَكَةٌ لِقُدَّامٍ ـ تَقَدُّم; backward —, حَرَكَةٌ لِوَرَآءٍ ـ تَأَخُّر ـ إِدْبَار ـ دُبُر ـ تَقَهْقُر. To be in —, تَحَرَّكَ ـ شَفَّ ٥. To put in —, حَرَّكَ. To put or propound a —, طَرَحَ مَسْأَلَةً ـ قَدَّمَ مَوْضُوعًا ـ قَدَّمَ ضَرِيبَةً ـ أَوْرَدَ مَوْضُوعًا ٢. To second a —, ظَاهَرَ ٱلضَّرِيبَةَ ـ سَانَدَ ٱلْمَوْضُوعَ. To carry a —, أَنْجَحَ ٱلضَّرِيبَةَ ـ فَازَ بِالْمَوْضُوعِ ٤. To make a — to, أَشَارَ إِلَى. This — was carried by 209 against 140 members, تَقَرَّرَتِ ٱلضَّرِيبَةُ بِمِائَتَيْ وَتِسْعَةِ أَصْوَاتٍ مِنَ ٱلْأَعْضَاءِ ضِدَّ ١٤٠ صَوْتًا.

Motion, *v.t.* and *i.* أَشَارَ إِلَى بِ. He motioned me to be seated, أَشَارَ إِلَيَّ بِالْجُلُوسِ.

Motionless, *a.* رَاكِد ـ سَاكِن ـ مُسْبِت ـ مُثْبِت ـ مُخْبِط ـ عَدِيمُ ٱلْحَرَكَةِ ـ جَامِد. To be —, سَبَتَ ٤ ـ أَسْبَتَ ـ رَكَدَ ٤ ـ أَرْكَدَ.

Motive, *a.* مُحَرِّكُ ٱلْحَرَكَاتِ ـ مُحَرِّك.

Motive, *n.* دَاعٍ *pl.* دُعَاة ـ بَاعِث ـ سَبَب *pl.* أَسْبَاب ـ مُوجِب. A good —, بَاعِثٌ حَسَنٌ; a bad —, بَاعِثٌ رَدِيءٌ. To adduce motives, إِحْتَجَّ بِحُجَجٍ ـ أَوْرَدَ أَسْبَابًا. There is no — for it, لا دَاعِ إِلَيْهِ.

Motivity, *n.* Power of producing motion, قُوَّةٌ مُحَرِّكَةٌ. The being influenced by motives, بَاعِث.

Motley, *a.* مَنْقُوش ـ مُشَكَّل ـ مُوَشًّى ـ مُدَبَّج ـ مُجَزَّع ـ مُخَرَّج ـ مُلَوَّن.

Motor, *n.* قُوَّةٌ مُحَرِّكَةٌ ـ مُحَرِّكُ ٱلْحَرَكَاتِ.

Mottled, *a.* *See* Motley, *n.*

Motto, *n.* An inscription, كِتَابَة. A saying, dictum, جُمْلَة ـ فَصْل ـ مَقَالَة *pl.* مَقَالَات ـ عِبَارَة ـ مَثَل *pl.* أَمْثَال. A —, as a distinguishing mark, عَلَامَة ـ سِمَة. He took it as his —, إِتَّخَذَهُ عَلَامَةً لَهُ. An engraving, نَقْش.

Mould, *n.* Soft earth, تُرَاب ـ أَرْضٌ طَيِّبَةُ ٱلتُّرْبَةِ. Mouldiness, تَعَفُّن ـ عَفَن. A form or matrix, قَوَالِب *pl.* قَالِب ـ سِبْكَة. Form, make, شَكْل ـ صِيغَة ـ ضَرْب ـ طَبْع. Shape, هَيْئَة *pl.* هَيْآت. Aggregate of form, of a man, *etc.*, حِلْيَة. Temperament, character, خَلِيقَة ـ خُلُق ـ طَبْع. A pattern, model, قَاعِدَة *pl.* قَوَاعِد ـ تِمْثَال ـ أُنْمُوذَج. Arrows of one —, سِهَامٌ صِيغَةٌ.

Mould, *v.t.* To cast in a mould, سَبَكَ ـ صَبَّ فِي قَالِبٍ. To fashion, صَاغَ *aor.* يَصُوغُ ـ جَبَلَ ـ فَطَرَ ـ ضَرَبَ. To train, طَبَّعَ ـ خَرَّجَ ـ دَرَّنَ. To make mouldy, عَفَّنَ. To cover with mould, earth, غَمَّ ـ تُرَابًا ـ تَرَّبَ. Mould it on this pattern, إِضْرِبْهُ عَلَى طَبْعِ هٰذَا.

Mould, *v.i.* To contract mould, تَعَفَّنَ ـ عَفِنَ.

Mouldable, *a.* يُسْبَكُ ـ قَابِلُ ٱلصِّيَاغَةِ ـ مِمَّا يُصَاغُ.

Moulder, *n.* سَبَّاك ـ صَائِغ.

Moulder, *v.i.* To decay, rot, رَمَّ *aor.* يَرِمُّ ـ بَلِيَ. To waste away, تَلِفَ ـ ذَهَبَ. To become dust, turn to dust, عَادَ إِلَى ٱلتُّرَابِ.

Moulder, *v.t.* To turn into dust, صَيَّرَ ـ تُرَابًا. To waste, أَذْهَبَ ـ أَتْلَفَ.

Mouldering, *n.* بَالٍ ـ رَامّ.

Mouldiness, *n.* تَعَفُّن ـ عُفُونَة.

Moulding, *n.* بَرْوَاز *vulg.* فَرْوَاز ـ خِرَاطَة. Moulding, tracery, on the inside and outside of buildings, specially those wrought on gypsum, الدَّوَاخِلُ وَٱلْخَوَارِجُ.

Mouldy, *a.* مُتَعَفِّن ـ مُعَفَّن. To become —, of bread, عَشَّشَ ٱلْخُبْزُ ـ عَكَّشَ ـ تَعَفَّنَ. To become —, through age, تَسَنَّهَ.

Moult, *v.i.* إِنْسَلَّ ـ نَسَلَ. Moulted feathers, *etc.*, نُسَال.

Moulting, *n.* The act of, إِنْسِلَال ـ نَسْل.

Mound, *n.* A bank in fortification, مَتَارِس *pl.* مِتْرَاس. A hillock, أَكَمَة *pl.* إِكَام ـ جُثْوَة ـ جُثًا *pl.* جُثْوَة ـ تَلّ *pl.* أَتْلَال. A — of stones, رَجِيمَة *pl.* رَجَائِم. A chain of sand mounds, سَلَاسِل. To raise a — against, أَقَامَ مِتْرَاسًا عَلَى.

Mound, *v.t.* To fortify with a mound, حَصَّنَ ـ بِمِتْرَاسٍ.

Mount, *n.* A panel or frame, as of paper, *etc.*, فَرَاوِز *pl.* فَرْوَاز ـ تَرْكِيب ـ دَائِرَة. *See also* Hill, Mound, Mountain, *n.*

Mount Ararat, جَبَلُ أَرَارَاتَ ـ جَبَلُ أَغْرِي.

Mount Carmel, جَبَلُ ٱلْكَرْمَلِ.

Mount Hermon, جَبَلُ ٱلشَّيْخِ.

Mount Hor, جَبَلُ هَارُونَ.

Mount Lebanon, جَبَلُ ٱلدُّرُوزِ ـ جَبَلُ لُبْنَانَ.

Mount of Olives, جَبَلُ ٱلزَّيْتُونِ.

Mount Olympus, جَبَلُ كَشِيشَ.

Mount Sinai, طُورُ سِينَا ـ جَبَلُ ٱلطُّورِ ـ جَبَلُ مُوسَى.

Mount, *v.t.* To lift on high, عَلَّى ـ رَفَعَ. To ascend, as a mountain, تَصَعَّدَ ـ صَعِدَ ـ طَلَعَ ـ تَشَرَّفَ عَلَى. To — a wall, تَسَوَّرَ. To place one's self, as on horseback, عَلَا *aor.* يَعْلُو ـ رَكِبَ. To — a horse from behind, شَذَّرَ ٱلْفَرَسَ ـ رَكِبَ عَلَى. To — another, provide with horse or carriage, رَكَّبَ عَلَى ـ رَكَّبَ. To set, as into a frame or a mount, رَكَّبَ ل ـ دائرة ـ فَرْوَزَ. To be furnished, as with guns, تَجَهَّزَ بِ ـ حَمَلَ. To place, as a gun on a carriage, رَكَّبَ ٱلْمِدْفَعَ عَلَى ٱلْجَرَّارِ. To — guard, تَوَلَّى ٱلنَّوْبَةَ. To — a throne, تَسَلْطَنَ ـ تَمَلَّكَ ـ جَلَسَ عَلَى ٱلْكُرْسِيِّ. He mounted the picture on pasteboard, رَكَّبَ ٱلصُّورَةَ عَلَى ٱلْمُقَوَّى. The guns were mounted against the town, كَانَتِ ٱلْمَدَافِعُ مُحَرَّرَةً عَلَى ٱلْبَلَدِ.

Mount, *v.i.* To rise, ascend, عَلَا *aor.* يَعْلُو ـ طَلَعَ ـ تَصَعَّدَ ـ صَعِدَ. To tower, عَلَا *aor.* يَعْلُو ـ إِرْتَفَعَ. To — up, as a price, غَلَا ـ إِزْدَادَ ثَمَنُهُ ـ زَادَ ثَمَنُهُ *aor.* يَزِيدُ ـ تَرَقَّى. To advance, تَقَدَّمَ. To attain, amount to, صَارَ مَبْلَغُهُ ـ بَلَغَ ـ لَحِقَ. To — up, as wine into the head سَارَ *aor.* يَسُورُ. To — a camel, رَكِبَ (*or* رَحَلَ) ٱلْبَعِيرَ. To — on horseback; *see preceding article.* The smoke mounted towards the sky, تَصَاعَدَ ٱلدُّخَانُ إِلَى ٱلسَّمَاءِ. The water mounted above the house, عَلَا ٱلْمَاءُ عَلَى ٱلْبَيْتِ. The fumes of the cup mounted to his head, سَارَتْ فِيهِ حُمَيَّا ٱلْكَأْسِ.

Mountain, *n.* طُور *pl.* أَطْوَار ـ جَبَل *pl.* جِبَال *or* أَجْبَال. The top, as of a —, قُرْن *pl.* قِرَان ـ فَرْعَة *pl.* فِرَاع ـ فَارِعَة ـ قُلَّة ـ رَأْس ـ قِمَّة. A chain of mountains, سِلْسِلَةٌ مِنَ ٱلْجِبَالِ. The — in labour brought forth a mouse, تَمَخَّضَتِ ٱلْجِبَالُ وَلَمْ تَلِدْ سِوَى فَارَةٍ.

Mountain, *a.* جَبَلِيّ.

Mountain-ash, *n.* شَجَرُ ٱلْغُبَيْرَاءِ.

Mountaineer, *n.* مِنْ أَهْلِ ٱلْجِبَالِ ـ سُكَّان *pl.* سَاكِنُ ٱلْجِبَالِ.

Mountainous, *a.* جَبَلِيّ ـ كَثِيرُ ٱلْجِبَالِ.

Mountebank, *n.* A quack doctor, طَبِيبٌ خَرَّاطٌ ـ طَبِيبٌ دَجَّالٌ. A buffoon, سُخْرَة ـ مَسْخَرَة ـ بَهْلَوَان.

Mounting, *n.* The act of ascending, صُعُود ـ طَلْع; of getting on horseback, رُكُوب. A setting, تَرْكِيب; as of jewels, تَرْصِيع ـ تَرْكِيب. A framing, فَرَاوِز *pl.* فَرْوَاز.

Mourn, *v.i.* شَجِنَ ـ نَاحَ ـ أَنَّ *aor.* يَئِنُّ ـ إِكْتَأَبَ ـ حَزِنَ ـ

تَحَزَّنَ ـ بَكَى ـ ٤. To cause to —, أَحْزَنَ ـ أَشْجَنَ. To — for; *see next article. See also to* Lament, *v.i.*

Mourn, *v.t.* نَاحَ عَلَى ـ ٤ بَكَى عَلَى ـ ٤ حَزِنَ عَلَى. To — for the dead, رَثَى ٱلْمَيِّتَ. *See also to* Lament, *v.t.*

Mourner, *n.* نَوَّاح ـ شاجن ـ حَزِين *pl.* حزان *and* حُزَنَآء. A — at a funeral, تابِعُ ٱلْجِنَازَةِ ـ تُبَّع *pl.* لاحِقُ ٱلْجِنَازَةِ *pl.* لاحِقُون. Chief mourner, صَدْرُ لاحِقِي ٱلْجِنَازَةِ. A professional female —, نَوَّاحَة. A company of female mourners, نِسآءٌ أَنْوَاحٌ.

Mournful, *a.* Sad, كَرِيب ـ حَزِين ـ مَكْرُوب. Causing sadness, مُحْزِن ـ مُكْرِب. *See also* Deplorable, Lamentable, *a.*

Mournfully, *ad.* بِنَوْعٍ مُحْزِنٍ ـ بِتَأَسُّفٍ ـ بِحُزْنٍ.

Mournfulness, *n.* غَمّ ـ حُزْن ـ كَآبَة ـ كَأْب ـ شَجَب.

Mourning, *n.* The act of sorrowing, نَوْحٌ وَبُكَآءٌ ـ حُزْن ـ تَأَسُّف. Dress of —, عَزَآء ـ حُزْنٌ عَلَى مَيِّتٍ. To put on —, لَبِسَ ٤ حَزِنَ عَلَى ـ ٤ لَبِسَ ثَوْبَ ٱلْحِدَادِ ـ ٤ لَبِسَ ثِيَابَ ٱلْعَزَآءِ ـ ٱلسَّوادَ. A house of —, بَيْتُ ٱلنَّوْحِ; a place of —, مَنَاحَة ـ مَعْزًى.

Mourning, *a.* Sorrowing, مَكْرُوب ـ كَرِيب ـ حَزِين. A — coach, عَرَبَةٌ تَسِيرُ فِي ٱلْجِنَازَةِ.

Mourning-dove, *n.* يَمَامَةٌ قَرْقَرَةٌ.

Mouse, *n.* فَار *fem.* فَارَة *pl.* فِيرَان. Abounding in mice, فَئِر.

Mouse, *v.i.* To catch mice, مَسَكَ (*or* إِصْطَادَ) ٱلْفِيرَانَ ٤.

Mouse-hole, *n.* جُحْرُ (*or* بَيْتُ) ٱلْفَارِ.

Mouser, *n.* صَيَّادُ ٱلْفِيرَانِ.

Mouse-trap, *n.* مَصْيَدَةٌ (*or* مِصْيَدَةٌ) لِلْفِيرَانِ.

Mouth, *n.* فَاه ـ فِيه ـ فَم ـ فِم ـ فُم *gen.* فم *acc.* فَا *or dual* فَمَانِ *or* فَمَوَانِ *pl.* أَفْوَاه; خَشْم ـ حَنَك *pl.* أَحْنَاك *vulg.* تُمّ. The angle or corner of the —, شِدْق *pl.* أَشْدَاق; the two corners of the —, ٱلسَّوَارَانِ. An entrance, door, بَاب ـ مَدْخَل. Mouth, as of a river, فَمُ نَهْرٍ ـ بُوغَاز ـ مَصَبّ ـ فِرَاض; of a valley, فُغْرَة. A voice, صَوْت. A principal speaker, ٱلْمُتَقَدِّمُ ـ ٱلْمُتَكَلِّمُ فِي ٱلْكَلَامِ. By word of mouth, لِسَانًا. Having a large —, أَفْوَه *fem.* فَوْهَآء. To talk with one — to —, شَافَهَ; the talking — to —, مُشَافَهَة. His — was near to my —, فُوهُ إِلَى فِيَّ. They say with their mouths what is not in their hearts, تَنْطِقُ شِفَاهُهُمْ بِمَا لَيْسَ فِي قُلُوبِهِمْ ـ يَقُولُونَ بِأَفْوَاهِهِمْ مَا لَيْسَ فِي قُلُوبِهِمْ. To be down in the mouth, إِنْكَسَرَ خَاطِرُهُ ـ إِنْقَطَعَ قَلْبُهُ ـ إِهْتَبَطَ. *See also* Dejected, *a.*

To be in every body's mouth, عَمَّ أَلْسُنَ ٱلنَّاسِ ٤. To open one's mouth, فَتَحَ فَاهُ ٤ ـ فَغَرَ ٤. To speak, تَكَلَّمَ ـ أَخَذَ فِي ٱلْكَلَامِ ٤. To make one to open his mouth, فَغَّرَ.

To seize with the mouth, أَزِمَ عَلَى ـ ٤ أَزَمَ ٤. To shut one's mouth, سَدَّ فَمَهُ ٤. To be silent, صَمَتَ ـ ٤ نَصَتَ ـ ٤ سَكَتَ ٤. To shut the mouth of another, to silence, أَصَمَّ ـ سَكَّتَ ـ أَفْحَمَ.

To make mouths, grimaces, تَلَوْلَقَ ـ ٤ كَشَرَ ـ إِخْتَلَجَ بِوَجْهِهِ. To make mouths at, تَلَوْلَقَ فِي ـ تَلَايَقَ فِي ـ كَشْرَلَ.

Mouth, *v.t.* To utter with a full affected voice, أَغْلَظَ ـ تَفَوَّهَ بِ ـ ٱلتَّطَقَ بِ. To reproach, insult, غَلَّظَ عَلَى ـ تَفَوَّهَ بِ ـ عَيَّرَ بِ ـ ٤ قَذَفَ بِ.

Mouth, *v.i.* To vociferate, ضَجَّ ـ ٤ صَيَّحَ ـ صَوَّتَ.

Mouthed, *a.* Having a mouth, ذُو فَمٍ. Hard mouthed, of a horse, حَاسِيُ ٱلْفَمِ ـ مَاكِنُ ٱلرَّأْسِ; tender —, لَيِّنُ ٱلْفَمِ.

Mouther, *n.* مُتَفَوِّه ـ مُغْلِظ ـ مِفَنّ.

Mouthful, *n.* لُقْمَة *pl.* لُقَم ـ زُخْمَة *pl.* زُخَم ـ دُبْلَة *pl.* دُبَل. To make into mouthfuls, دَبَّلَ. He gobbled a —, زَخِمَ زُخْمَةً ٤.

Mouthing, *n.* Affected utterance, تَغْلِيظ ـ تَفَوُّه ـ تَفَنُّن فِي ٱلْكَلَامِ ـ فِي ٱلْكَلَامِ.

Mouthless, *a.* بِلَا فَمٍ.

Mouth-piece, *n.* As of a musical instrument, قَصَبَة ـ صُلْبُوب; of a pipe, بُزّ *pl.* بِزَاز. A chief speaker, ٱلْمُتَقَدِّمُ فِي ـ ٱلْمُتَكَلِّمُ فِي ٱلْكَلَامِ. He is in many respects the — of the government, كَهُوَ فِي كَثِيرٍ مِنَ ٱلْأَحْوَالِ لِسَانُ ٱلدَّوْلَةِ.

Movable, *a.* مُتَنَقِّل ـ مُتَحَرِّك ـ جَرَّار. A — feast, عِيدٌ مُتَنَقِّلٌ *pl.* أَعْيَادٌ مُتَنَقِّلَةٌ. Movable property, مَالٌ مَنْقُولٌ. Movable troops, عَسْكَرٌ جَرَّارٌ. To render —, صَيَّرَ مُتَنَقِّلًا.

Movables, *n.* مَنْقُولَات.

Movably, *ad.* بِتَحَرُّكٍ ـ بِتَنَقُّلٍ.

Move, *v.t.* To put in motion, حَرَّكَ. To shake, زَعْزَعَ ـ قَلْقَلَ ـ هَزَّ ـ ٤ هَزْهَزَ ـ حَرَّكَ ـ رَجَّ ٤. To stir, خَوَّضَ. To remove, move from one place to another, حَوَّلَ ـ ٤ نَقَلَ. To induce, to excite to, حَثَّ ٤ عَلَى ـ حَرَّكَ إِلَى ـ ٤ حَمَلَ عَلَى ـ أَغْرَى عَلَى. To touch, affect, as the passions, أَثَّرَ فِي ـ ٤ هَاجَ ـ عَمِلَ فِي ـ حَرَّكَ ـ يَرُوعُ *aor.* رَاعَ ـ ٤ نَجَعَ فِي. To trouble, vex, أَزْعَجَ ـ قَلَّقَ ـ عَانَى ـ أَضْجَرَ. To excite, as tumult, أَهَاجَ ـ حَرَّكَ ـ قَوَّمَ. To — the tongue against, سَنَّ لِسَانَهُ عَلَى. To —, as of the tail, لَوَى بِ ٤. To —, make a move, as in chess, قَدَّمَ ضَرِيبَةً ـ طَرَحَ ٤. To —, as of a resolution, أَوْرَدَ مَوْضُوعًا ـ أَلْقَى (*or* أَطْرَحَ *or* قَدَّمَ) مَوْضُوعًا. It began to — him, إِبْتَدَأَ يُحَرِّكُهُ. In Him we live, and move, and have our being, بِهِ نَحْيَا وَنَتَحَرَّكُ وَنُوجَدُ. None of these things — me, لَسْتُ أَحْتَسِبُ

هٰذِهِ ٱلْأَشْيَآءَ بِشَيْءٍ. She moved him to ask the thing of her father, غَرَّتْهُ بِطَلَبِ ٱلشَّيْءِ مِنْ أَبِيهَا.

To move about, to swing to and fro, ذَبْذَبَ ـ رَدَّدَ; to move hither and thither, drag about, جَرَّ ـ حَوَّلَ ـ كَرْكَرَ ².

To move away, رَفَعَ ـ ; شَالَ بِ ـ ² أَبْعَدَ ـ ² نَقَلَ.

To move back, أَخَّرَ ـ أَخْلَفَ ـ أَدْبَرَ; to return to its place, رَدَّ إِلَى مَوْضِعِهِ ـ رَجَّعَ ².

To move down, سَفَّلَ ـ نَزَّلَ.

To move forward, قَدَّمَ; to bring nearer, قَرَّبَ ـ دَلَّى ـ أَدْنَى.

To move from; *See above* To move away.

To move in, سَلَكَ ـ جَوَّزَ ـ أَدْخَلَ.

To move off, أَبْعَدَ; to take away, رَفَعَ ـ شَالَ بِ ².

To move on, put forward, قَدَّمَ; to push forward, hasten, أَسْرَعَ ـ عَجَّلَ ـ أَعْجَلَ; to drive, سَاقَ ².

To move out, نَقَلَ ـ أَخْرَجَ ².

To move round, دَوَّرَ ـ أَدَارَ.

To move to and fro, to dangle, ذَبْذَبَ.

To move up, put higher up, رَفَعَ ـ عَلَّى. To bring nearer, قَرَّبَ ـ أَدْنَى.

Move, *v.i.* To stir, تَحَرَّكَ. To shake, تَزَعْزَعَ ـ اِهْتَزَّ ـ اِرْتَجَّ ـ تَقَلْقَلَ. To march, زَحَفَ. To sway to and fro, اِسْتَرْوَحَ ـ تَذَبْذَبَ ـ تَرَدَّدَ. The soldiers moved to some of the villages, زَحَفَ ٱلْعَسْكَرُ إِلَى بَعْضِ ٱلْقُرَى. He made them so that they could not —, جَعَلَهُمْ لَا يَسْتَطِيعُونَ حَرَاكًا.

To move about, to go hither and thither, تَكَرْكَرَ ـ تَرَدَّدَ. To shake about, تَدَرْدَرَ.

To move away, بَرِحَ مِنْ ـ تَبَعَّدَ ـ اِبْتَعَدَ ـ اِنْتَقَلَ.

To move back, أَدْبَرَ ـ تَقَهْقَرَ ـ تَأَخَّرَ ـ اِخْتَلَفَ.

To move down, هَبَطَ ² ـ نَزَلَ ـ اِنْحَدَرَ.

To move forward, تَقَدَّمَ; to approach nearer, دَنَا مِنْ ² ـ تَقَرَّبَ ـ اِقْتَرَبَ.

To move in, to enter, وَلَجَ *aor.* يَلِجُ ـ دَخَلَ ².

To move off, اِبْتَعَدَ ـ تَبَعَّدَ ـ تَجَنَّبَ ـ اِجْتَنَبَ.

To move on, تَدَرَّجَ ـ تَقَدَّمَ.

To move out, go outside, خَرَجَ ². To remove, as from a house, اِنْتَقَلَ.

To move round, دَارَ ² ـ اِسْتَدَارَ.

To move to and fro, to dangle, تَذَبْذَبَ.

To move up, upwards, صَعِدَ ـ تَصَعَّدَ ـ طَلَعَ ² ـ عَلَا *aor.* يَعْلُو; to approach nearer, دَنَا *aor.* يَدْنُو ـ تَقَرَّبَ ـ اِقْتَرَبَ.

To move up and down, as a swing, تَرَجَّحَ ـ اِرْتَجَّ.

Move, *n.* As in chess, طَرْح. An action, صَنِيعَة *pl.* صَنَائِعُ. To make a —, as in chess, طَرَحَ. *See also* Motion, Movement, *n.*

Moved, *adj.* and *part.*

To be moved, put in motion, تَحَرَّكَ; to be affected, تَأَثَّرَ; to be troubled, اِضْطَرَبَ; to be excited, ثَارَ ² ـ هَاجَ.

To be moved with anger, اِحْتَمَى غَضَبًا ـ اِسْتَغْضَبَ ـ اِغْتَاظَ.

To be moved with compassion for, تَشَفَّقَ عَلَى ـ تَحَنَّنَ عَلَى ـ تَرَحَّمَ عَلَى.

To be moved with envy against, غَارَ عَلَى ـ ضَغِنَ عَلَى ـ حَسَدَ عَلَى ² ـ بَغَى عَلَى.

To be moved with jealousy against, غَارَ عَلَى.

To be moved to tears, تَدَمَّعَ.

Movement, *n.* A motion, حَرَكَة *pl.* حَرَكَات. Excited action, تَحْرِيص ـ ثَوْر ـ تَرْوِيج ـ رَوَاج ـ اِسْتِفْزَاز. A strain in music, مَقَامَة ـ نَغْمَة. The wheel-work of a watch or clock, عُدَّةُ سَاعَةٍ ـ دَوَالِيبُ سَاعَةٍ. Movements, actions, صَنَائِعُ; efforts, مَسْعَاة ـ اِجْتِهَاد ـ جِدّ. The movements of an army, سَيْرُ ٱلْعَسْكَرِ ـ حَرَكَاتُ ٱلْعَسَاكِرِ. Large movements of soldiers, حَرَكَاتٌ جَسِيمَةٌ مِنَ ٱلْعَسَاكِرِ.

Mover, *n.* As of a proposition, مُورِدُ مَوْضُوعٍ ـ طَارِحُ مَسْأَلَةٍ ـ مُقَدِّمُ أُطْرُوحَةٍ.

Moving, *a.* Putting in motion, مُحَرِّك. Being in motion, مُتَحَرِّك. Not stable, as sand, هَابِط. Affecting, نَاجِع فِي ـ مُحَرِّكُ ٱلْقَلْبِ ـ مُحَنِّن ـ مُؤَثِّر.

Movingly, *ad.* Pathetically, بِنَوْعٍ يُرَقِّقُ ـ بِٱلتَّحَنُّنِ ـ مُجُوعًا ٱلْقَلْبَ.

Mow, *n.* جُزَاز ـ كُومَةُ تِبْنٍ ـ عُرْمَة *pl.* عُرَم حَشِيشٍ.

Mow, *v.t.* To cut grass, *etc.*, جَزَّ ² ـ اِجْتَزَّ ـ حَصَدَ ² ـ اِحْتَصَدَ ـ حَشَّ ². To — down, cut down, destroy, حَصَدَ ² ـ أَبَادَ ـ أَهْلَكَ. To —, to pile up, كَوَّمَ.

Mow, *v.i.* حَصَدَ ² ـ جَزَّ ² ـ حَشَّ حَشًّا.

Mower, *n.* حَاصِد *pl.* حَصَدَة *and* حُصَّاد ـ حَشَّاش ـ قَصَّال.

Mowing, *n.* حِصَاد ـ حَشّ ـ قَصْل. Mowing time, حِصَاد ـ زَمَنُ ٱلْحَشِّ.

Mown, *a.* مَحْشُوش ـ مَحْصُود. Mown grass, *etc.*, جُزَاز.

Moxa, *n.* كَيُّ ٱلْهِنْدِ ـ كَيُّ ٱلصِّينِ.

Mr., *n.* (Mister تَرْخِيمُ لَفْظَةِ). *See* Mister, *n.*

Mrs., *n.* (Mistress تَرْخِيمُ لَفْظَةِ). *See* Mistress, *n.*

MS., *n.* and *a.* *pl.* MSS., (Manuscript تَرْخِيمُ لَفْظَةِ). *See* Manuscript, *n.*

Much, *a.* Great in quantity, جَمٌّ ـ جَمِيمٌ ـ لَجٌّ ـ عِزٌّ ـ نَهِيرٌ ـ جَزِيلٌ ـ كَثِيرٌ. Long in duration, طَوِيلٌ. They are — the same, alike, هُمْ عَلَى سَوِيَّةٍ تَقْرِيبًا. He is — the same as he was, هُوَ عَلَى مَا كَانَ عَلَيْهِ تَقْرِيبًا. As —, مِثْلَ ـ قَدْرَ ـ مِقْدَارَ. As — as, بِقَدْرِ ـ عَلَى قَدْرِ. As — as possible, عَلَى قَدْرِ ٱلْإِمْكَانِ. As — as I can, عَلَى قَدْرِ طَاقَتِي. I can do as — as he can, أَقْدِرُ أَعْمَلُ مِثْلَهُ. I have as — money as you have, عِنْدِي مِثْلَمَا عِنْدَكَ مِنَ ٱلدَّرَاهِمِ. Twice as —, طَاقَانِ ـ الطَّاقُ مِثْلَيْنِ ـ المِثْلُ مِثْلَيْنِ بِقَدْرِهِ مَرَّتَانِ. Three times as —, ثَلَاثَةُ أَضْعَافٍ ـ ثَلَاثَ مَرَّاتٍ بِقَدْرِهِ. If I have taken any thing from you, I will restore to you ten times as —, إِنْ أَخَذْتُ مِنْكَ شَيْئًا فَأُعَوِّضُ عَلَيْكَ ٱلطَّاقَ عَشَرَةً.

How much? كَمْ; for how much? بِكَمْ. How much do you charge? كَمْ تَطْلُبُ.

Too much, زَائِدٌ ـ بِٱلزِّيَادَةِ.

To judge to be much, too much, إِسْتَكْثَرَ. He thought the price too much, إِسْتَكْثَرَ ٱلثَّمَنَ.

To make much of, عَزَّزَ ـ لِ *or* لَطَفَ بِ ـ ² لَطُفَ.

Much, *n.* / Muchness, كَمٌّ ـ كَمِّيَّةٌ ـ جَزْلٌ ـ جُبْلَةٌ ـ كَثِيرٌ ـ كَثْرَةٌ. To whom — is given from him — will be required, مَنْ أُعْطِيَ كَثِيرًا يُطْلَبُ مِنْهُ كَثِيرٌ.

Much, *ad.* كَثِيرًا ـ جَزِيلًا. *See also under* Much, *a.* *Also* Still, *ad.*

Mucilage, *n.* غِرَآءٌ ـ لَعَم ـ لُعَيْبَةٌ.

Mucilaginous, *a.* لَعَمِيٌّ ـ غِرَآئِيٌّ ـ ذُو لُعَيْبَةٍ.

Muck, *n.* Dung, زِبْلٌ ـ زُبَالَةٌ. To run a —, أَغَارَ يَمِينًا وَشِمَالًا لِلْفَتْكِ بِٱلنَّاسِ.

Muck-heap, *n.* / Muck-hill, مَزْبَلَةٌ.

Muckle, *a.* كَثِيرٌ ـ كَبِيرٌ.

Muck-worm, *n.* A worm in muck, دُودُ ٱلْمَزْبَلَةِ ـ شَحْمَةُ ٱلْأَرْضِ. A miser, بَخِيلٌ ـ خَسِيسٌ.

Mucky, *a.* *See* Filthy, *a.*

Mucous, *a.* بَلْغَمِيٌّ ـ خَمْلِيٌّ. The — membrane, غَاشِيَةُ ٱلْمَصَارِينِ ٱلْخَمْلِيَّةُ.

Muculent, *a.* *See* Mucilaginous, *n.*

Mucus, *n.* بَلْغَمٌ ـ مَادَّةٌ مُخَاطِيَّةٌ. Mucus from the nose; *see* Snot, *n.*

Mud, *n.* غَرْيَنٌ ـ سُوَاخٌ ـ وَحَلٌ *pl.* أَوْحَالٌ ـ طِينٌ. Black fetid —, حَمَأَةٌ. The — left by the overflowing of the Nile, طِينُ ٱلْإِبْلِيزِ. A piece of —, طِينَةٌ. To sink, be sunk, in the —, سَاخَ فِي ٱلْوَحَلِ *aor.* يَسُوخُ ـ تَسَوَّخَ. To stick, be stuck, in the —, وَحِلَ ـ ² تَوَحَّلَ. To plaster with —, طَيَّنَ. A — building, كِبْسٌ ـ بَيْتٌ مِنْ طِينٍ.

Mud, *v.t.* To make foul, as with mud, لَوَّثَ. To stick in the mud, أَوْحَلَ. To make turbid, أَعْكَرَ ـ عَكَّرَ ـ كَدَّرَ.

Muddied, *a.* Soiled with mud, مُلَوَّثٌ بِٱلطِّينِ ـ مُلَوَّثٌ. Made turbid, مُعَكَّرٌ ـ مُكَدَّرٌ. Confused in mind, مُرْتَبِكٌ ـ مُتَحَيِّرٌ.

Muddily, *ad.* Foully, بِدَرَنٍ ـ بِنَجَاسَةٍ ـ بِوَسَخٍ. With foul mixture, بِتَخْبِيصٍ.

Muddiness, *n.* State of being muddy, وَحَلٌ. Turbidity, كَدَرٌ ـ رَنَقٌ. Dirtiness, دَرَنٌ ـ وَسَخٌ ـ دَنَاسَةٌ. Muddiness of the mind, بَلَهٌ ـ بَلَاهَةٌ ـ غَبَاوَةُ ٱلْعَقْلِ.

Muddle, *v.t.* To make turbid, أَعْكَرَ ـ عَكَّرَ ـ كَدَّرَ. To make half drunk, سَكَّرَ ـ أَفْتَرَ. To stupefy, أَعْكَرَ. To confuse, make a mess of, حَاحَتَ ـ عَثْعَثَ ـ وَعَّرَ ـ شَوَّشَ ـ أَغْفَلَ ـ لَبَّكَ ـ خَبَّصَ ـ لَخْبَطَ. Especially of speech, غَثَّى ٱلْكَلَامَ ². To be muddled, confused, in a mess, تَهَوَّشَ ـ تَوَعَّرَ ـ إِرْتَبَكَ ـ تَشَوَّشَ ـ تَلَبَّكَ ـ إِلْتَبَكَ. To be half drunk, سَكِرَ ـ مَسَّهُ سُكْرٌ.

Muddle, *v.i.* To act confusedly, شَابَ *aor.* يَشُوبُ. He meddles and muddles, يَشُوبُ وَيَرُوبُ.

Muddle, *n.* A confused state, حَاحَتَةٌ ـ عَثْعَثَةٌ ـ إِرْتِبَاكٌ ـ فَضَا ـ شَوَاشٌ ـ شَجَرٌ ـ خَبْصَةٌ ـ لَخْبَطَةٌ ـ وَفَشَلٌ ـ حَيْرَةٌ. In a —, فِي حَيْرَةٍ وَفَشَلٍ. He left the affair in a —, تَرَكَ ٱلْأَمْرَ فَضَا ².

Muddler, *n.* هَكَّاكٌ ـ فَكَّاكٌ.

Muddy, *a.* Full of mud, طَانٍ ـ وَحِلٌ. A — place, مَوْحِلٌ. Muddy soil, أَرْضٌ طَانَةٌ. Turbid, رَنِقٌ ـ كَدِرٌ ـ كَدِيرٌ. To be —, رَنِقَ ـ تَرَنَّقَ ـ تَوَحَّلَ. To make —, dirty, أَوْحَلَ ـ لَوَّثَ ـ رَنَّقَ. To make —, turbid, أَعْكَرَ ـ عَكَّرَ ـ كَدَّرَ ـ أَدْرَنَ.

Muddy, *v.t.* *See to* Mud, *v.t.*

Muezzin, *n.* مُؤَذِّنٌ.

Muff, *n.* A fur for the hands, فَرْوَةٌ تَتَّخِذُهَا ٱلنِّسَآءُ لِإِدْفَاءِ أَيْدِيهِنَّ. *See also* Greenhorn, *n.*

Muffin, *n.* فَطِيرَةٌ *pl.* فَطَائِرُ.

Muffiner, *n.* For salt, مَمْلَحَةٌ ـ مَلَّاحَةٌ.

Muffle, *v.t.* To cover, conceal, خَمَّرَ ـ خَمَرَ ² ـ أَغْشَى عَلَى ـ سَتَرَ ² ـ أَخْفَى. To blindfold, عَصَبَ عَيْنَيْهِ. To deaden the sound of anything, خَفَّضَ (*or* أَخْفَى) صَوْتَهُ. To be muffled, of sound, خَفِيَ صَوْتُهُ ـ خَفَّضَ صَوْتُهُ ².

Muffled, *a.* Closely covered, مَخْمُورٌ ـ مُخَمَّرٌ ـ مَسْتُورٌ. Having the sound deadened, مَخْفُوضُ ٱلصَّوْتِ ـ خَفِيُّ ٱلصَّوْتِ.

Muffler, *n.* For the face, طَاقٌ ـ نَصِيفٌ ـ خِمَارٌ. To cover the face with a —, خَمَّرَ ـ أَخْمَرَ. To put on a —, on one's self, إِخْتَمَرَ.

Mufti, *n.* A Muslim jurisconsult, مُفْتٍ. Unofficial dress, المَلابِسُ ٱلْإِعْتِيادِيَّةُ.

Mug, *n.* بُلْبُلَة ـ كُوز *or* كُوزَة *pl.* أَكْوَاز ـ إِبْرِيق *pl.* أَبَارِيق.

Muggish, *a.* }
Muggy, } عَكّ ـ عَكِيك ـ وَخِم ـ مُغِمّ.

Mugwort, *n.* البِرِنْجَاسِفُ ـ حَبَقُ ٱلرَّاعِي.

Muhammad, *n.* مُحَمَّد.

Muhammadan, *n.* *See* Muslim, *n.*

Muhammadan, *a.* *See* Muslim, *a.*

Muhammadanism, *n.* *See* Islâm, *n.*

Mulatto, *n.* خِلاسِيّ ـ مُوَلَّد ـ نَغِيل.

Mulberry, *n.* The fruit, especially the white —, فِرْصَاد ـ تُوت *or* تُوث ـ تُوت بَلَدِيّ. The black —, تُوث حَامِض ـ تُوت شَامِيّ. A — tree, تُوثَة ـ تُوتَة ـ شَجَرَةُ ٱلتُّوت.

Mulct, *n.* غَرَام ـ غَرَامَة ـ جَرِيمَة. *See also* Fine, *n.*

Mulct, *v.t.* *See to* Fine, *v.t.*

Mule, *n.* The animal so called, بَغْل *pl.* أَبْغَال *and* بِغَال. A spinning jenny, دُولابُ ٱلْغَزْلِ.

Mule-spinner, *n.* مُدَوِّرُ دُولابِ ٱلْغَزْلِ *pl.* مُدَوِّرُون.

Muleteer, *n.* بَغَّال ـ مُكَارِي ـ قَاطِرْجِي.

Mulish, *a.* Stubborn, خَشِنُ ٱلْجَانِبِ ـ ضَرِس ـ مَارِد ـ مَرِيد ـ لا يَسْمَعُ ٱلنِّدَآءَ وَلا يَبْغِي ٱلْإِهْتِدَآءَ.

Mulishness, *n.* تَمَرُّد ـ شَكَاسَة ـ خَشَانَة ـ خُشُونَة.

Mull, *v.t.* To spice wine, تَابَلَ (*or* تَبَّلَ) ٱلْخَمْرَ ـ قَزَّحَ وَحَلَّى ٱلشَّرابَ. *See also to* Dispirit, Dull, *v.t.*

Mull, *n.* Fine muslin, شَاش نَاعِم.

Mullagatawny, *n.* حَسِيَّة مُفَلْفَلَة.

Mulled, *a.* Spiced and sweetened, مُتَبَّل وَمُحَلَّى.

Mullein, *n.* The plant, بُوصِير ـ لَبِيدَة بَيْضَآء.

Muller, *n.* وِصْقَلَة ـ مَلَسَة ـ مِسْحَق.

Mullet, *n.* بُورِي ـ بَارِي.

Mulligrubs, *n.* مَغْص. To have the —, مُغِصَ.

Mullion, *n.* قَائِمَة *pl.* قَوَائِم.

Mullioned, *a.* ذُو قَوَائِم.

Multangular, *a.* كَثِيرُ ٱلزَّوَايَا.

Multidendate, *a.* كَثِيرُ ٱلْأَسْنَانِ.

Multifarious, *a.* كَثِيرُ ٱلْأَجْنَاسِ ـ مُتَنَوِّع.

Multifariously, *ad.* In various ways, بِأَنْوَاعٍ وَطُرُقٍ كَثِيرَةٍ.

Multifariousness, *n.* كَثْرَة ـ تَنَوُّع.

Multifold, *a.* مُتَضَاعِف.

Multiform, *a.* كَثِيرُ ٱلْأَشْكَالِ ـ كَثِيرُ ٱلْأَنْوَاعِ ـ مُتَنَوِّع.

Multiformity, *n.* كَثْرَةُ ٱلْأَشْكَالِ ـ كَثْرَةُ ٱلْأَنْوَاعِ ـ تَنَوُّع.

Multilateral, *a.* كَثِيرُ ٱلْأَضْلاعِ ـ كَثِيرُ ٱلْأَجْنَابِ.

Multilinear, *a.* كَثِيرُ ٱلْخُطُوطِ.

Multilocular, *a.* Having many cells, كَثِيرُ ٱلْخَلايَا ـ كَثِيرُ ٱلْخِلالِ.

Multiloquence, *n.* بَقّ ـ بَقِيق ـ كَثْرَةُ كَلامٍ.

Multiparous, *a.* Bearing many at a birth, وَضْعُ أَجِنَّةٍ كَثِيرَةٍ فِي طَلْقَةٍ.

Multipartite, *a.* كَثِيرُ ٱلْأَجْزَآءِ.

Multiped, *n.* ذُو أَرْجُلٍ كَثِيرَةٍ ـ مِثْل حِمَارِ قَبَّانَ.

Multiple, *n.* ضِعْف ـ تَضْعِيف. The multiples of the thing, تَضَاعِيفُ ٱلشَّيْءِ. A common —, مُضَعَّف مُشْتَرَك.

Multiplex, *a.* مُتَضَاعِف. *See also* Manifold, *a.*

Multipliable, *n.* }
Multiplicable, } That may be increased, مِمَّا يُكَثَّرُ ـ قَابِلُ ٱلتَّكْثِيرِ. That may be multiplied by another number, يُضْرَبُ فِيهِ.

Multiplicand, *n.* المَضْرُوبُ.

Multiplicate, *a.* مُكَثَّر ـ مُتَنَوِّع ـ مُتَضَاعِف.

Multiplication, *n.* The act of increasing, تَكْثِير. The operation of — in arithmetic, ضَرْب ـ تَضْرِيب. A — table, جَدْوَلُ ٱلضَّرْبِ (*or* ٱلْكَرَّاتِ).

Multiplicator, *n.* المَضْرُوبُ فِيهِ.

Multiplicity, *n.* جَمّ ـ جُمُوم ـ كَثْرَة ـ تَنَوُّع.

Multiplier, *n.* One who increases any thing, مُكَثِّر. *See also* Multiplicator, *n.*

Multiply, *v.t.* To make more, ضَعَّفَ ـ أَكْثَرَ ـ كَثَّرَ ـ ٢ ذَرَأَ ـ ضَاعَفَ. To —, in arithmetic, ضَرَبَ كَذَا فِي كَذَا ـ ٢. He multiplied five by six, ضَرَبَ خَمْسَةً فِي سِتَّةٍ. Five multiplied by six is thirty, خَمْسَةٌ فِي سِتَّةٍ ثَلاثُون.

Multiply, *v.i.* ٤ جَمَّ ـ ٤ نَمَا ـ ٤ كَثُرَ ـ ٤ نَمَا ـ تَكَثَّرَ ـ تَكَاثَرَ.

Multisonous, *a.* كَثِيرُ ٱلْأَصْوَاتِ.

Multitude, *n.* An abundance, كَثْرَة ـ ثَرْوَة ـ وَفْرَة. A — of people, عُمُوم *pl.* عَمّ ـ جَمّ ـ عِدّ *pl.* أَعْدَاد ـ فَوْج *pl.* أَفْوَاج ـ جَمْع ـ قَوْم *pl.* أَقْوَام. The —, common people, العَامَّة ـ الشَّعْب.

Multitudinary, *a.* }
Multitudinous, } جَمّ ـ كَثِير ـ مُتَنَوِّع.

Multivalve, *a.* }
Multivalvular, } Of shells and such like, كَثِيرُ ٱلْقُشُورِ ـ كَثِيرُ ٱلْأَصْدَافِ.

Multum in parvo, *n.* شَيْءٌ صَغِيرُ ٱلْجِرْمِ كَثِيرُ ٱلنَّفْعِ (أَوِ ٱلْمِقْدَارِ).

Mum, *a.* Silent, سَاكِتٌ ـ صَامِتٌ. To be —, سَكَتَ ـ ² صَمَتَ ².

Mumble, *v.t.* or *i.* To bite or chew softly, هَمَسَ ـ دَرْدَرَ ـ نَقْنَقَ ـ بَرْبَرَ ـ فَطْفَطَ ـ اِهْتَمَسَ. To — words, مَغْمَغَ ـ ضَغْضَغَ. He mumbles his tongue in speaking, like as the horse moves about the tongue of the bit in his mouth, يَلُوكُ لِسَانَهُ فِي ٱلْكَلَامِ كَمَا يَعْلِكُ ٱلْفَرَسُ فَأْسَ ٱللِّجَامِ.

Mumbler, *n.* In speech, مُنَقْنِقٌ ـ مُهْتَمِسٌ ـ مُفَطْفِطٌ.

Mumbling, *n.* Of speech, بَرْبَرَةٌ ـ فَطْفَطَةٌ ـ هَسْهَسَةٌ ـ هَمْسٌ. The — of the tongue, rolling it about in the mouth, تَدْوِيمُ ٱللِّسَانِ.

Mummer, *n.* مَسْخَرَةٌ.

Mummery, *n.* مَلْعَبَةٌ ـ مَسْخَرَةٌ.

Mummification, *n.* The act of mummifying, اَلتَّحْوِيلُ إِلَى مُومِيَةٍ; the becoming a mummy, اَلِاسْتِحَالَةُ إِلَى مُومِيَةٍ.

Mummiform, *a.* كَٱلْمُومِيَةِ ـ بِهَيْئَةِ ٱلْمُومِيَةِ.

Mummify, *v.t.* صَيَّرَ كَٱلْمُومِيَةِ ـ صَيَّرَ مُومِيَةً. *See also to* Embalm, *v.t.*

Mummy, *n.* مُومِيَةٌ.

Mump, *v.t.* and *i.* *See to* Mumble, *v.t.* and *i.*

Mumper, *n.* *See* Beggar, *n.*

Mumpish, *a.* Cross, شَكِسٌ. Dull, down in the mouth, مَكْسُورُ ٱلْخَاطِرِ.

Mumps, *n.* The ailment, وَجَعُ ٱلسَّلَعِ ـ وَجَعُ ٱلْغُدَّةِ.

Munch, *v.t.* and *i.* عَلَكَ ² ـ لَاكَ ² ـ مَضَغَ ² ـ قَضِمَ ².

Muncher, *n.* عَالِكٌ ـ مَاضِغٌ ـ قَاضِمٌ.

Mundane, *a.* عَالَمِيٌّ ـ دُنْيَوِيٌّ.

Mundification, *n.* تَنْظِيفٌ ـ تَطْهِيرٌ.

Municipal, *a.* بَلَدِيٌّ. A — council, مَجْلِسُ دَائِرَةٍ بَلَدِيَّةٍ. Municipal order, regulations, نِظَامَاتٌ بَلَدِيَّةٌ. Municipal guards, حُرَّاسُ (*or* مُحَافِظَةُ) ٱلْبَلَدِ.

Municipality, *n.* أَهْلُ ٱلْإِدَارَةِ ٱلْبَلَدِيَّةِ ـ إِدَارَةٌ بَلَدِيَّةٌ.

Munificence, *n.* كَرَمٌ ـ خَيْرٌ ـ سَخَاوَةٌ ـ جُودٌ. *See also* Liberality, *n.*

Munificent, *a.* رَحِيبٌ ـ كَرِيمُ ٱلطَّبْعِ ـ جَوَادٌ ـ سَفَّاحٌ ـ غَيْدَاقٌ ـ ذُو خَيْرٍ ـ فَيَّاضٌ ـ فَائِضٌ ـ ٱلصَّدْرِ; most —, أَفْيَقُ. To be —, سَخَى ² ـ جَادَ ². *See also* Liberal, *a.*

Munificently, *ad.* بِسَخَاوَةٍ ـ بِكَرَمٍ ـ بِجُودٍ.

Muniment, *n.* A fortification, حِصَارٌ ـ اِسْتِحْكَامٌ ـ حِصْنٌ ـ قَلْعَةٌ. A deed by which claims are defended, صَكٌّ *pl.* صُكُوكٌ ـ حُجَّةٌ *pl.* حُجَجٌ.

Munition, *n.* A building, عِمَارَةٌ *pl.* عَمَائِرُ. Ammunition, provisions, ذَخِيرَةٌ *pl.* ذَخَائِرُ ـ مُؤْنَةٌ. Munitions of war, لَوَازِمُ ذَخَائِرَ حَرْبِيَّةٌ ـ حَرْبِيَّةٌ.

Mural, *a.* مُعَلَّقٌ فِي حَائِطٍ (*or* عَلَى حَائِطٍ) ـ مُتَعَلِّقٌ بِحَائِطٍ. A — aperture, طَاقٌ *pl.* طَاقَاتٌ ـ كُوَّةٌ *pl.* كُوَّاتٌ. A — tablet, مُعَلَّقَةٌ.

Murder, *n.* قَتِيلٌ ـ هَلَاكٌ. A — the perpetrator of which is unknown, قَتْلُ عِمِّيًّا. Self-murder, قَتْلُ ٱلذَّاتِ. To commit a —, قَتَلَ قَتِيلًا ².

Murder, *v.t.* قَتَلَ ² ـ ذَبَحَ ـ أَهْلَكَ ـ فَتَكَ بِ ². To be murdered, اِنْقَتَلَ ـ قُتِلَ. A murdered man, رَجُلٌ قَتِيلٌ; a murdered woman, اِمْرَأَةٌ قَتِيلٌ.

Murderer, *n.* فَاتِكٌ *pl.* فُتَّاكٌ ـ قَاتِلٌ *pl.* قُتَّالٌ.

Murderess, *n.* قَاتِلَةٌ *pl.* قَاتِلَاتٌ.

Murderous, *a.* Guilty of murder, or done with murder, فَاتِكٌ ـ قَاتِلٌ. A — weapon, سِلَاحٌ قَاتِلٌ. A — battle, حَرْبٌ ـ مَلْحَمَةٌ مُهْلِكَةٌ. Blood-thirsty, أَهْلُ ٱلدِّمَاءِ ـ ذُو دَمٍ. *See also* Bloody, *a.*

Murderously, *ad.* كَٱلْقَاتِلِ ـ فَتْكًا; cruelly, بِجَوْرٍ.

Muriate, *n.* *See* Hydrochlorate, *n.*

Muriatic acid, *n.* *See* Hydrochloric acid, *n.*

Murkily, *ad.* ظُلْمَةً ـ دُجْيَةً.

Murky, *a.* ثَقِيلٌ ـ عَاتِمٌ ـ مُظْلِمٌ ـ عَتِمٌ ـ أَكْدَرُ ـ كَدِرٌ.

Murmur, *v.i.* To grumble, مَرْمَرَ ـ دَمْدَمَ ـ تَذَمَّرَ. To — against, تَذَمَّرَ عَلَى. To —, as of wind, خَرَّ ² ـ عَزَفَ ². ـ; as of water, خَرْخَرَ ـ خَرَّ ² ـ خَرْخَرَ. To repine, complain, تَشَكَّى. The wind murmured, خَفَقَتِ ٱلرِّيحُ. *See also to* Mutter, *v.t.* and *i.*

Murmur, *n.* } A grumbling, دَمْدَمَةٌ ـ تَذَمُّرٌ. A —, as of water,
Murmuring, } خَرْخَرٌ ـ خَرْخَرَةٌ ـ خَرِيرٌ; of wind, هَزِيزٌ ـ حَفِيفٌ ـ عَزْفُ ٱلرِّيَاحِ ـ عَزِيفُ ٱلرِّيحِ.

Murmuring, *a.* Grumbling, مُدَمْدِمٌ ـ مُتَذَمِّرٌ. Of water, خَارٌّ ـ خَرَّارٌ. A — fountain, عَيْنٌ خَرَّارَةٌ.

Murmurer, *n.* مُتَشَكٍّ ـ مُدَمْدِمٌ ـ مُتَذَمِّرٌ.

Murrain, *n.* فَصْلُ ٱلْبَهَائِمِ ـ جَائِحَةٌ ـ وَبَاءٌ.

Muscadel, *n.* } The wine, ضَرْبٌ مِنَ ٱلْخَمْرِ لَذِيذٌ; the grape,
Muscadine, } ضَرْبٌ مِنَ ٱلْعِنَبِ لَذِيذٌ.

Muscat, *n.* }
Muscatel, } ضَرْبٌ مِنَ ٱلْكُمَّثْرَى.

Muscle, *n.* عَضَلَةٌ ـ عَضِيلَةٌ *pl.* عَضَلٌ *and* عَضَلَاتٌ.

Muscular, *a.* Sinewy, كَثِيرُ ٱلْعَضَلِ ـ عَضُلٌ ـ فَتِيرٌ. Vigorous, قَوِيٌّ ـ ضَلِيعٌ ـ صُلْبٌ ـ صَلِيبٌ.

Muscularity, *n.* The state of being sinewy, عَضَل. Vigour, جِدَّة ـ مُرُوَّة ـ صَلَابَة ـ جِدٌّ.

Muse, *n.* The goddess of poetry, إِلاهَةُ ٱلشِّعْرِ. An imaginary personage invoked by poets, مَعْبُودٌ وَهْمِيٌّ تَسْتَرْشِدُهُ ـ عَرُوسُ ٱلشِّعْرِ ٱلشُّعَرَآءُ. Deep thought, إِفْتِكَار ـ تَأَمُّل ـ تَفَكُّر. The Muses, ٱلْأَدَبُ ـ ٱلْفُنُونُ ٱللَّطِيفَةُ ـ بَنَاتُ ٱلْأَدَبِ.

Muse, *v.i.* To — upon, أَضْمَرَ عَلَى ـ تَأَمَّلَ ـ تَفَكَّرَ.

Museful, *a.* / Muser, *n.* } مُتَأَمِّل ـ مُتَفَكِّر.

Muses, *n.* *See under* Muse, *n.*

Museum, *n.* بَيْتُ ٱلتُّحَفِ ـ مَتْحَف ـ كَنْزُ ٱلتُّحَفِ.

Mush, *n.* عَصِيدَة.

Mushroom, *n.* فُطَارِى *pl.* فُطْر ـ عُشُّ ٱلْغُرَابِ ـ عَرَاهِينُ *pl.* عُرْهُون.

Music, *n.* ٱلْمُوسِيقَى ـ ٱللَّحْنُ ـ عَزْف ـ عَزِيف. Instrumental or vocal music, سَمَاع. Harmony, نَغَم ـ طَرَب ـ إِلْحَان ـ عِلْمُ ٱلْأَدْوَارِ ـ عِلْمُ ٱلتَّأْلِيفِ ـ أَلْفَةُ ٱلْأَصْوَاتِ. The science of —, فَنُّ ٱلْأَلْحَانِ ـ عِلْمُ ٱلْمُوسِيقَى. An air, song, مَقَامَات *pl.* مَقَامَة. A concert of voices and instruments, غِنَآء ـ آلَة ـ نَوْبَة. Music, such as is used in churches, سَمَاع. The — of the sphere, حَرَكَاتُ ٱلْأَفْلَاكِ.

Instrumental music, ٱللَّعْبُ بِٱلْمَعَازِفِ ـ ٱلْمَعَازِفُ.

Military music, مُوسِيقَى ٱلْعَسْكَرِ. Vocal music, غِنَآء. *See also under* Band, *n.*

Musical, *a.* Belonging to music, مُوسِيقِيٌّ ـ ما نِيطَ بِٱلْمُوسِيقَى. Harmonious, حَسَن ـ لَذِيذٌ لِلسَّمْعِ ـ مُطْرِب ـ ذُو نَغْمَةٍ. Fond of music, مُحِبُّ ٱلْمُوسِيقَى. Clever in music, مَاهِرٌ فِى ٱلْمُوسِيقَى. A — instrument, آلَةُ ٱلْمَلَاهِي ـ مَعَازِفُ *pl.* مِعْزَفَة ـ عَزْف *pl.* آلَاتٌ *pl.* آلَةُ ٱلْمُوسِيقَى ـ آلَات *pl.* آلَةُ ٱلطَّرَبِ ـ آلَات. Pulsatile — instruments, نَوْبَاتِيَّة ـ آلَاتِيَّة. A — company, a band, مَعَازِف. A — box, صَنْدُوقُ مُوسِيقَى. To play on a — instrument, عَزَفَ ـ.

Musically, *ad.* تَطْرِيبًا ـ بِإِلْحَانٍ ـ بِأَلْفَةِ ٱلْأَصْوَاتِ.

Music-book, *n.* كِتَابُ مُوسِيقَى.

Music-hall, *n.* مَرَاسِحُ *pl.* مَرْسَح ـ دَارُ ٱلْغِنَآءِ وَآلَاتِ ٱلطَّرَبِ.

Musician, *n.* A player on an instrument, عَازِف ـ آلَاتِيٌّ *pl.* آلَاتِيَّة ـ نَوْبَاتِيٌّ *pl.* نَوْبَاتِيَّة ـ مُوسِيقِيٌّ *pl.* مُوسِيقِيَّة. A female —, قِيَان *pl.* قَيْنَة ـ كَرَائِنُ *pl.* كَرِينَة. *See also* Singer, *n.*

Music-master, *n.* مُعَلِّمُ ٱلْمُوسِيقَى.

Music-stool, *n.* As for the piano, مَقْعَدُ ٱلْبِيَانُو.

Musing, *a.* مُتَأَمِّل ـ مُتَفَكِّر.

Musingly, *ad.* تَأَمُّلًا ـ تَفَكُّرًا ـ بِتَأَمُّلٍ ـ بِتَفَكُّرٍ.

Musk, *n.* The substance, مُسْك ـ مِسْك; the animal, غَزَالُ نَافِجَة ـ نُفْجَةُ مِسْكٍ ـ فَأْرَةُ ٱلْمِسْكِ ـ ٱلْمِسْكِ. A vesicle of —, فَأْرَةُ ٱلْمِسْكِ ـ. To perfume with —, مَسَّكَ. Perfumed with musk, مُسَكَّب ـ مُمَسَّك. A — rat, فَأْرَةُ ٱلْمِسْكِ.

Musk, *v.t.* مَسَّكَ.

Musket, *n.* بَارُودَة ـ بُنْدُقِيَّة *pl.* بَنَادِقُ ـ تُفَنْكَة *coll.* تُفَنْك ـ مِكْحَلَة *pl.* مَكَاحِلُ. Carrying a —, حَامِلُ بُنْدُقِيَّةٍ.

Musketeer, *n.* بُنْدُقْجِيَّة *pl.* بُنْدُقْجِيٌّ.

Musketoon, *n.* A musket of ancient make, زَنْبَلَك. *See also* Carbine, *n.*

Musketry, *n.* Muskets, مَكَاحِلُ ـ بَنَادِقُ. The fire of —, ضَرْبُ نَارٍ (*or* إِطْلَاقُ) ٱلْبَنَادِقِ ـ ٱلْبَنَادِقِ.

Musket-proof, *a.* لَا تَنْفُذُ فِيهِ رَصَاصَةُ ٱلْبُنْدُقِيَّةِ.

Musket-shot, *n.* The ball, رَصَاصَةُ بُنْدُقِيَّةٍ. The discharge of a musket, or the distance a — will carry, رَمْيَةُ بُنْدُقِيَّةٍ.

Muskiness, *n.* رَائِحَةُ ٱلْمِسْكِ.

Musky, *a.* مُمَسَّك ـ عَلَيْهِ رَائِحَةُ ٱلْمِسْكِ.

Muslim, *n.* مُسْلِمُونَ *pl.* مُسْلِم. The religion of the Muslims, ٱلْإِسْلَام. The Muslims, أَهْلُ ٱلْإِسْلَامِ ـ ٱلْمُسْلِمُونَ. To become a —, أَسْلَمَ ـ تَسَلَّمَ ـ تَمَسْلَمَ. To be called a —, تَمَسْلَمَ.

Muslim, *a.* إِسْلَامِيٌّ.

Muslin, *n.* شَاشَات *pl.* شَاش ـ مَوْصِلِيٌّ. Muslin-de-laine, شَاشٌ شَفَّاف ـ شَفّ ـ شِفّ ـ شَفِيف. Book —, شَالٌ فِرَنْجِيٌّ. A — curtain, نَامُوسِيَّة.

Muslinet, *n.* خَامٌ خَشِنٌ.

Musquito, *n.* بَعُوضَة *coll.* بَعُوض ـ بَقَّة *coll.* بَقّ ـ نَامُوسَة *coll.* نَامُوس.

Mussulman, *n.* and *a.* *See* Muslim.

Must, *aux. v.* To be obliged, أُضْطُرَّ إِلَى ـ أُلْزِمَ ـ حَلَّ عَلَى ـ ـ لَا مَحَالَةَ مِن ـ لَا بُدَّ مِن ـ حَقَّ عَلَى ـ. I — call upon him to-day, يَلْزَمُ أَنْ لَا بُدَّ أَنْ أَزُورَهُ ٱلْيَوْمَ. You — excuse me, تَعْذُرَنِى. You — have expected them, لَا بُدَّ وَٱنْتَظَرْتَهُمْ. We — speak the truth, يَجِبُ عَلَيْنَا أَنْ نَقُولَ ٱلْحَقَّ. She — be reproved, لَا بُدَّ مِنْ تَوْبِيخِهَا. It — be, لَا مَحَالَةَ مِنْهُ ـ لَا بُدَّ مِنْهُ. It — be so, لَا بُدَّ أَنْ يَكُونَ كَذَا.

Must, *v.i.* To grow mouldy, تَعَفَّنَ.

Must, *n.* سُلَاف.

Mustache, *n.* / Mustaches, / Mustachio, } شَنَبَات *pl.* شَنَب ـ شَوَارِبُ *pl.* شَارِب ـ سَبَلَة. The centre parting of the —, ٱلتُّومَةُ ـ ٱلْحُثْحُبَةُ. One whose — is beginning to grow, طَارٌّ. To clip, of the —, طَرَّ [2].

Mustachioed, *a.* أَبُو شَوَارِب ـ ذُو شَوَارِب .

Mustard, *n.* خَرْدَل . Mustard seed, خَرْدَل . A grain of — seed, حَبَّةُ خَرْدَلٍ . A mustard-pot, وِعَآءُ ٱلْخَرْدَلِ .

Mustee, *n.* } *See* Mestizo, *n.*
Mestee, }

Muster, *v.t.* To collect an army for review, جَمَعَ ٱلْعَسْكَرَ لِلْعَرْضِ . To collect, as an army, جَيَّشَ ـ ءِ جَمَعَ ـ جَمَّعَ ـ جَنَّدَ . To review troops, عَرَضَ ٱلْعَسَاكِرَ ءِ . To — up courage, تَجَرَّأَ ـ شَدَّ عَزْمَهُ ² ـ تَجَاسَرَ .

Muster, *v.i.* To collect together, إِجْتَمَعَ . To be reviewed, of an army, إِعْتَرَضَ ٱلْجَيْشُ .

Muster, *n.* A review, عِرْض . A collection, جَمْع ـ جَمَاعَة ـ جَمْعِيَّة ـ إِجْتِمَاع . A register of forces, دَفْتَرُ ٱلْعَسَاكِرِ .

Muster-master, *n.* As of troops, عَارِضُ ٱلْجَيْشِ .

Muster-roll, *n.* سِيَاقَةُ أَسَامِي .

Mustily, *ad.* تَعَفُّنًا ـ بِعُفُونَةٍ .

Mustiness, *n.* عُفُونَة . *See also* Mouldiness, *n.*

Musty, *a.* Old, عَتِيق . *See also* Mouldy, *a.*

Mutability, *n.* } Changeableness, قِلَّةُ قَرَارٍ ـ قِلَّةُ ثَبَاتٍ ـ تَلَوُّن ـ تَغَيُّر . Irresolution, تَرَدُّد ـ قِيلُولَة ـ سَفَه ـ طَيَشَان ـ عَدَمُ قَرَارٍ ـ طَيْش . *See also* Fickleness, *n.*
Mutableness, }

Mutable, *a.* Subject to change, عَدِيمُ ٱلْقَرَارِ ـ مُتَغَيِّر ـ مُغَيِّر . Irresolute, طَائِش ـ بِلَا عَزْمَةٍ وَعَزِيمَةٍ ـ قَرَّار ـ مُتَلَوِّن . *See also* Fickle, Irresolute, Inconstant, *a.*

Mutation, *n.* The act of changing, تَغْيِير ـ تَبْدِيل ـ تَحْوِيل . The being changed, تَغَيُّر ـ تَبَدُّل ـ تَحَوُّل .

Mutatis mutandis, *ad.* صَحَّ ٱلْقَوْلُ بِتَغْيِيرِ ٱلْأَحْوَالِ وَٱلْأَشْخَاصِ .

Mute, *a.* غَيْرُ نَاطِقٍ ـ صَامِت ـ أَخْرَس . To be —, صَمَتَ ² .

Mute, *n.* One who is silent, صَامِت ـ أَخْرَس . A mute letter, حَرْفٌ سَاكِتٌ ; the mute letters, ٱلْحُرُوفُ ٱلْمَهْمُوسَةُ . A utensil to deaden sound, آلَةٌ مُخَفِّضَةُ ٱلصَّوْتِ . A —, of a funeral, بَوَّابَةٌ *pl.* بَوَّابٌ يَقُومُ عَلَى بَابِ دَارِ مَيِّتٍ وَقْتَ جِنَازَتِهِ . Birds' dung, ذَرَاق ـ ذَرْق ـ شَخْط .

Mute, *v.i.* To dung, of birds, أَذْرَقَ ـ ذَرَقَ ² ; generally, to discharge from the bowels, سَكَّ ² ـ سَكَّ بِمَا فِي بَطْنِهِ ـ سَكَّ بِسَلْحِهِ ² .

Mutely, *ad.* بِسُكُوتٍ ـ بِصُمُوتٍ .

Muteness, *n.* سُكُوت ـ صُمْتَة ـ صُمَات ـ صُمُوت .

Mutilate, *v.t.* To cut off, as a limb, عَضَبَ ـ ءِ جَدَعَ ـ ءِ جَذَمَ ² . To cut off some part of, أَسْقَطَ مِن ـ ءِ قَطَعَ شَيْئًا مِن . To — the nose of, شَرَمَ ءِ . To be mutilated of the nose, شَرِمَ ءِ .

Mutilate, *a.* } مُجَذَّم ـ جَذِيم ـ أَجْذَم ـ أَجْدَع . Having the nose —, شَرِم . To be —, إِنْجَذَمَ .
Mutilated, }

Mutilation, *n.* The act of cutting off a limb, جَدْع ـ عَضْب ـ جَذْم .

Mutineer, *n.* } عَاصٍ *pl.* عُصَاة ـ مَفْتُون ـ مُفْتِن ـ شَغِب ـ عَصِيّ . *See also* Insurgent, *n.*
Mutinous, *a.* }

Mutiny, *n.* عِصْيَان ـ فِتْنَة ـ تَشْغِيب ـ شَغَب . To excite to —, أَفْتَنَ ـ شَغَّبَ . *See also* Insurrection, *n.*

Mutiny, *v.i.* قَامَ عَلَى ² ـ ءِ هَاشَ . To — against, عَصَى عَلَى ـ ءِ إِسْتَعْصَى عَلَى .

Mutter, *v.t.* To utter indistinctly, تَكَلَّمَ بِ ـ هَمْسًا . To utter, تَكَلَّمَ بِ .

Mutter, *v.i.* To speak indistinctly, إِهْتَمَسَ فِي كَلَامِهِ ـ فَرْتَنَ ـ طَأْطَأَ . To — to one's self, هَجَسَ فِي صَدْرِهِ ءِ . To rumble, as thunder, إِرْتَجَفَ ـ رَجَفَ ² . *See also to* Murmur, *v.i.*

Mutterer, *n.* هَامِس . *See also* Grumbler, Murmurer, *n.*

Muttering, *n.* هَمْس ـ إِهْتِمَاس . *See also* Grumble, Murmur, *n.*

Mutton, *n.* ضَأْنِيّ ـ لَحْمٌ ضَأْنِيٌّ ـ لَحْمُ ٱلضَّأْنِ .

Mutton-chop, *n.* شَرِيحَةُ لَحْمٍ ضَأْنِيٍّ ـ ضُلُوع *pl.* ضِلْعُ لَحْمِ ٱلضَّأْنِ .

Mutual, *a.* مُتَقَابِل ـ مِنَ ٱلطَّرَفَيْنِ ـ مُتَبَادِل . They have mutual love one for another, of many, يُحِبُّونَ بَعْضُهُمْ بَعْضًا ـ يَتَحَابُّونَ ـ يُحَابُّونَ . A — friend, حَبِيبُ ٱلطَّرَفَيْنِ . By — consent, بِرِضَآءِ ٱلطَّرَفَيْنِ . (The idea of mutuality is generally expressed by the sixth conjugation, thus:) they entertained — envy, they mutually envied one another, حَسَدُوا بَعْضُهُمْ بَعْضًا *for* تَحَاسَدُوا ; there was — hatred among them, أَبْغَضُوا بَعْضُهُمْ بَعْضًا *for* تَبَاغَضُوا .

Mutuality, *n.* تَقَابُل ـ مُقَابَلَة .

Mutually, *ad.* بِٱشْتِرَاكٍ ـ تَبَادُلًا . *See also under* Mutual, *a.*

Muzzle, *v.t.* كَمَّ ² ـ سَدَّمَ ـ ءِ عَكَمَ ـ ءِ كَعَمَ .

Muzzle, *n.* عِكَام ـ كِمَامَة ـ كِمَام ـ كِعَام . A — for a camel of netted rope, خُرْطُوم ـ خَطْم ـ حِجَام . A — for a kid to prevent its sucking, شِجَار ـ صَرِيم . The — of a cannon, فَمُ ٱلْمِدْفَعِ .

Muzzle-ring, *n.* دَائِرَةُ (*or* حَلْقَةُ) فَمِ ٱلْمِدْفَعِ .

Muzzy, *a.* *See* Bewildered, Absent, *a.*

My, *pron.* Expressed in Arabic by the pronoun ى after the noun, or by لِي ; and vulgarly by بِتَاعِي *or* مَالِي ; *e.g.* this is my book, هٰذَا كِتَابِي *or* هٰذَا ٱلْكِتَابُ لِي ; *vulg.* هٰذَا ٱلْكِتَابُ مَالِي *or* بِتَاعِي *i.e.* my property.

Mynheer, *n.* My lord, يَا سَيِّدِي .

Myography, *n.* عِلْمُ ٱلْبَحْثِ عَنِ ٱلْعَضَلِ (*or* ٱلْعَضَلَاتِ) .

Myologist, *n.* مُتَفَرِّغٌ لِعِلْمِ ٱلْعَضَلَاتِ .

Myology, *n.* *See* Myography, *n.*

Myope, *n.* One shortsighted, قَصِيرُ ٱلنَّظَرِ ـ أَخْفَش.

Myopy, *n.* قِصَرُ ٱلنَّظَرِ ـ خَفَش.

Myriad, *n.* Ten thousand or an immense number, رِبَاب ـ رِبَّة *pl.* رُبُوَة *pl.* أَرْبَآء *and* رُبْوَات.

Myrmidon, *n.* A ruffian, خَلِيع *pl.* خُلَعَآء.

Myrobalan, *n.* إِهْلِيلَجَة *coll.* إِهْلِيلَج ; yellow —, إِهْلِيلَج أَصْفَر ; chebulic —, إِهْلِيلَج كَابِلِيّ ; emblic —, إِهْلِيلَج أَمْلَج . *Myrobala bellerica*, بِلِيلَج.

Myrrh, *n.* مُرّ مَكَّة ـ صَبِر ـ مُرّ . To embalm in —, مَرَّر.

Myrtacious, *a.* ما نيط بِٱلرَّيْحَانِ ـ رَيْحَانِيّ.

Myrtle, *n.* رَيْحَان ـ هَدَس ـ آس ; called in Egypt, رَيْحَانُ ٱلْقُبُور.

Myrtle-berries, حَبُّ ٱلْآسِ ـ *vulg.* حُنْبُلاس.

Myself, *pron.* ذَاتِي ـ نَفْسِي . I speak of —, أَتَكَلَّمُ أَنَا عَنْ نَفْسِي . I also will come —, أَنَا أَيْضًا سَآتِي . I can do nothing by —, أَنَا لَا أَقْدِرُ أَنْ أَفْعَلَ شَيْئًا مِنْ نَفْسِي . I will go —, أَرُوحُ أَنَا بِذَاتِي.

Mystagogue, *n.* An interpreter of mysteries, مُفَسِّرُ ٱلْأَسْرَارِ.

Mysterious, *a.* Mystic, سِرِّيّ . Hidden, occult, بَاطِن ـ خَفِيّ . Strange, غَرِيب ـ عَجِيب ـ بَعِيد . Obscure, مُلْتَبِس . A — thing, something extraordinary, أَمْرٌ غَرِيبٌ ـ أَمْرٌ بَعِيدٌ.

Mysteriously, *ad.* Mystically, secretly, خِفْيَةً ـ سِرًّا . In a strange manner, بِنَوْعٍ غَرِيبٍ.

Mysteriousness, *n.* Obscurity, خَافِيَة . Strangeness, بُعْد ـ غَرَابَة ـ عَجَب . Perplexity, obscureness, اِلْتِبَاس.

Mystery, *n.* A profound secret, سِرّ *pl.* أَسْرَار *and* سَرَائِر . Something unknown respecting the future, غَيْب *pl.* غِيَاب *and* غُيُوب . A hidden or obscure thing, خَافِيَة ـ خَفَآء ـ خَفِيّ . A religious drama, رِوَايَةٌ مِنَ ٱلْمَصَاحِفِ تُشَخَّصُ فِي ٱلْمَرَاسِحِ . Mysteries, secret worship, عِبَادَةٌ خَفِيَّةٌ . The mysteries of the science of the Divine Essence, الحِكْمَةُ ٱلْمَسْكُوتُ عَنْهَا . The — was cleared up, بَرِحَ ٱلْخَفَآء . To make a — of, أَسَرَّ ـ خَبَّأَ ـ إِخْتَبَأَ.

Mystic, *a.* } Obscure, esoteric, بَاطِنِيّ ـ خَفِيّ ـ بَاطِن . Allegorical, رَمْزِيّ.
Mystical, }

Mystic, *n.* صُوفِيّ *pl.* صُوفِيَّة . To become a —, تَصَوَّفَ.

Mystically, *ad.* خِفْيَةً ـ بَاطِنًا ـ بِٱلرَّمْزِ ـ رَمْزًا.

Mysticalness, *n.* خَافِيَة ـ خَفَآء.

Mysticism, *n.* تَصَوُّف ـ مَذْهَبُ ٱلصُّوفِيَّةِ.

Mystification, *n.* The act of rendering mysterious, إِخْفَآء ـ تَطْبِيق ; of making obscure, enigmatical, تَعْمِيَة.

Mystify, *v.t.* To involve in mystery, أَخْفَى عَلَى ـ أَطْبَقَ عَلَى . To make obscure, enigmatical, عَمَّى ـ عَمَّى عَلَى ـ رَوَّجَ . He mystified his speech, رَوَّجَ كَلَامَهُ.

Myth, *n.* An ideal personage, إِسْمٌ مِنْ غَيْرِ جِسْمٍ ـ شَخْص خَيَالِيّ ـ خَيَال *pl.* أَخْيِلَة . A fiction, أُسْطُورَة *pl.* أَسَاطِير . *See also* Fable, *n.*

Mythic, *a.* } Ideal, خَيَالِيّ ; fabulous, أَسَاطِيرِيّ ـ خُرَافِيّ.
Mythical, } *See also* Fabulous, *a.*

Mythologic, *a.* } ما نيط بِأَسَاطِيرِ ٱلْجَاهِلِيَّةِ.
Mythological, }

Mythologist, *n.* عَالِم بِأَسَاطِيرِ ٱلْجَاهِلِيَّةِ.

Mythology, *n.* أَسَاطِيرُ ٱلْجَاهِلِيَّةِ ـ أَسَاطِيرُ سِيَرِ آلِهَةِ ٱلْوَثَنِيِّينَ.

N.

Nab, *v.t.* إِخْتَطَفَ ـ خَطَفَ ـ إِخْتَلَسَ .

Nabatheans, *n.* The — of Syria, الصَّرَاصِرَةُ .

Nabob, *n.* A deputy governor, نَائِبٌ *pl.* نُوَّابٌ . A rich man, غَنِيٌّ *pl.* أَغْنِيَاءُ .

Nacre, *n.* مَادَّةٌ لَامِعَةٌ مِنْ جِنْسِ ٱلصَّدَفِ .

Nacreous, *a.* لَامِعٌ كَٱلصَّدَفِ .

Nadir, *n.* النَّظِيرُ وَهُوَ مَا يُقَابِلُ سَمْتَ ـ النَّظِيرُ ـ نَظِيرُ ٱلسَّمْتِ ٱلرَّأْسِ .

Nag, *n.* دَابَّةٌ *pl.* دَوَابُّ ـ حَيَوَانٌ *pl.* حَيَوَانَاتٌ .

Naiad, *n.* عَرَائِسُ *pl.* عَرُوسُ ٱلْمِيَاهِ ـ إِلَاهَةُ ٱلْأَنْهَارِ .

Nail, *n.* As of the fingers or toes, ظُفْرٌ *pl.* أَظْفَارٌ *and* أَظَافِيرُ . The flesh round the nails, عِرَاقٌ (or حِتَارُ) ٱلظُّفْرِ ـ أُطْرَةٌ . The white spots that come on the nails, وَبْشٌ ـ فُوفٌ ـ وَبَسٌ . Having long nails, أَظْفَرُ ـ ظَفِرٌ ـ حُجُبٌ ـ نُمْنُمٌ ـ زُلْجِيرٌ . To tear out the — from the root, قَلَّفَ . To insert the nails into, عَلَّقَ أَظْفَارَهُ فِي ـ ظَفَّرَ فِي ـ أَظْفَرَ . To pare or cut the nails, قَصَّ ٱلْأَظَافِيرَ ـ بَرَى ٱلْأَظْفَارَ . Nail parings, بُرَايَةُ ٱلْأَظْفَارِ . A nail of iron, مِسْمَارٌ *pl.* مَسَامِيرُ . A dowel, دِسَارٌ *pl.* دُسُرٌ . He hit the right — on the head, أَصَابَ ٱلصَّوَابَ . To drive a — into, ضَرَبَ مِسْمَارًا فِي ـ دَسَرَ ٱلْمِسْمَارَ فِي . To hang on a —, عَلَّقَ عَلَى مِسْمَارٍ ـ أَوْفَاهُ . To pay one for down on the —, ٱلثَّمَنَ نَقْدًا .

Nail, *v.t.* To fasten with a nail, سَمَّرَ . To stud with nails, رَكَّبَ فِي مَسَامِيرَ .

Nail-brush, *n.* فُرْشَةُ ٱلْأَظَافِيرِ .

Nailer, *n.* A maker of nails, صَانِعُ ٱلْمَسَامِيرِ . A hitting of the right nail on the head, سَدَدٌ ـ سَدَادٌ .

Naive, *a.* سَاذِجٌ ـ بَسِيطٌ ـ سَلِيمٌ ـ نَصُوحٌ .

Naïveté, *n.* بَسَاطَةٌ ـ سَذَاجَةٌ .

Naked, *a.* Without clothes, عَارٍ *fem.* عَارِيَةٌ *pl.* عُرَاةٌ ـ عُرْيَانٌ ـ *vulg.* بِٱلزَّلْطِ ; made —, bared, مُعَرًّى . Bare, unadorned, بَسِيطٌ ـ سَاذِجٌ . Open, manifest, وَاضِحٌ ـ بَيِّنٌ ـ ظَاهِرٌ . Simple, mere, مُطْلَقٌ ـ مُجَرَّدٌ . Open, exposed, مَكْشُوفٌ . To be —, without clothes, عَرِيَ *aor.* يَعْرَى ـ تَعَرَّى ـ تَجَرَّدَ . To make one's self —, تَزَلَّطَ *vulg.* تَعَرَّى ـ مِنْ ثِيَابِهِ . To make —, bare, جَرَّدَ ـ مِنْ ثِيَابِهِ ـ أَعْرَى ـ مِنْ ـ عَرَّى *vulg.* زَلَّطَ . The truth is —, manifest, الْحَقُّ عَارٍ (or بَيِّنٌ) .

Nakedly, *ad.* Without covering, عُرْيَةً ـ عُرَاةً *vulg.* بِٱلزَّلْطِ . Openly, عَلَانِيَةً ـ عِيَانًا ـ بِصَرَاحَةٍ . Simply, merely, بَتَّةً ـ فَقَطْ ـ إِطْلَاقًا . Plainly, without adornment, بِسَذَاجَةٍ ـ بِبَسَاطَةٍ . Exposedly, عَلَى ٱلْمَكْشُوفِ ـ كَشْفًا .

Nakedness, *n.* Nudity, العُرْيُ ـ عُرْيَةٌ ـ عُرَاءٌ . The part of the body which modesty hides, عَوْرَةٌ . The part of the body which a female generally leaves unclad, المُعَرَّاةُ ـ الْجُرْدَةُ ـ الْمُجَرَّدُ . Want of adornment, بَسَاطَةٌ ـ سَذَاجَةٌ . A state of —, سَلْبَةٌ ـ حَالَةُ ٱلْعَرَاءِ . The — of the land, عَوْرَةُ ٱلْأَرْضِ .

Namby-pamby, *a.* مُتَأَنِّقٌ ـ قُطَارِيٌّ . *See also* Affected, *a.*

Name, *n.* إِسْمٌ *pl.* أَسْمَاءٌ *and* أَسَامٍ . Renown, صِيتٌ ـ شُهْرَةٌ ـ ذِكْرٌ ـ سِمْعٌ ـ إِسْمٌ . Remembrance, ذِكْرٌ ـ ذُكْرَةٌ . Appearance, ظَاهِرٌ . Title, as of a book, عُنْوَانٌ . What is your —? مَا ٱسْمُكَ ـ مَا ٱسْمُكَ بِٱلْخَيْرِ . In the —, on the part, of such an one, مِنْ طَرَفِ فُلَانٍ ـ مِنْ قِبَلِ فُلَانٍ ـ عَلَى ٱسْمِ فُلَانٍ . In the — of, as an adjuration, بِحُرْمَةِ كَذَا ـ بِحَقِّ كَذَا . In your —, عَلَى ٱسْمِكَ . In the — of God, the Pitiful, the Compassionate! بِسْمِ ٱللّٰهِ ٱلرَّحْمٰنِ ٱلرَّحِيمِ ; to pronounce this latter formula, بَسْمَلَ ; the pronunciation of the formula, بَسْمَلَةٌ .

Christian name, إِسْمُ ٱلْعِمَادِ ـ إِسْمٌ .

Family name, إِسْمُ ٱلْبَيْتِ ـ إِسْمُ ٱلْعِيَالِ .

Maiden name, إِسْمُ بَيْتِ ٱلْبِنْتِ قَبْلَ زَوَاجِهَا .

Proper name, عَلَمٌ *pl.* أَعْلَامٌ ـ إِسْمٌ خَاصٌّ .

To act in the name of one, أَجْرَى وَكَالَةً عَلَى ٱسْمِ فُلَانٍ .

To ask one his name, إِسْتَسْمَى .

To assume a name, إِتَّخَذَ ٱسْمًا .

To call one by name, دَعَى ـ بِٱسْمِهِ .

To call one names, لَقَّسَ ـ نَبَّزَ ـ نَبَزَ : They called one another names, of many, تَنَابَزُوا ـ تَلَاقَسُوا .

To give in or tell one's name to, قَالَ مَنْ هُوَ ـ عَرَّفَ ـ بِٱسْمِهِ .

To go by the name of, to be known as, عُرِفَ بِ : He who went by the name of the Great, المَعْرُوفُ بِٱلْكَبِيرِ .

To have a bad name, لَهُ صِيتٌ قَبِيحٌ .

To have a good name, لَهُ صِيتٌ حَسَنٌ .

To know by name only, عَرَفَ ـ بِٱلْإِسْمِ فَقَطْ .

To make one a name, جَعَلَ لَ ـ ٱسْمًا .

To mention by name, ذَكَرَ ـ بِٱسْمِهِ .

To take God's name in vain, إِتَّخَذَ ٱسْمَ ٱللّٰهِ بِٱلْبَاطِلِ .

Name, *v.t.* To give a name to, سَمَّى - سَمَّى-ب. To call by a name, دَعَا *aor.* يَدْعُو - دَعَا-ب. To mention, ذَكَرَ *aor.* جَآءَ بِذِكْرِهِ - يَجِيءُ. To — one to, to appoint to, عَيَّنَ-ل - خَصَّصَ-ل - قَلَّدَ-ب - سَمَّى. Don't — him, لَا تَجِئْ بِذِكْرِهِ. Don't — it, in reply to an excuse made for defect on the part of a giver or entertainer, خَيْرُكَ كَثِيرٌ.

Named, *a.* Called by a name, مُسَمًّى; mentioned, مَذْكُور. He is — 'Abdullah, إِسْمُهُ عَبْدُ ٱللّٰهِ.

Nameless, *a.* Having no name, مِنْ غَيْرِ ٱسْمٍ - مَا لَهُ ٱسْمٌ - بِلَا ٱسْمٍ. Unknown to fame, عَدِيمُ ٱلصِّيتِ - مَجْهُول - غَامِض. Who shall be —, whose name shall not be mentioned, ٱلَّذِي لَا يُسَمَّى ٱسْمُهُ.

Namely, *ad.* Particularly, خُصُوصًا. That is to say, وَهُوَ - أَعْنِي - يَعْنِي - مَعْنَى ٱلْكَلَامِ - مَعْنَاهُ - فَحْوَاهُ.

Namesake, *n.* سَمِيٌّ *pl.* سَمِيَّة - كَنِيٌّ *fem.* كَنِيَّة. He is a — of his, هُوَ كَنِيُّهُ.

Nankeen, *n.* قُمَاشُ ٱلْأَنْكِينَة.

Nap, *n.* A short sleep, نَوْم - نَوْمَة - ضَجْعَة. A midday —, قَيْلُولَة - تَقْيِيلَة. The — of cloth, خَمْل - زِغْبِر - زِئْبِر - غَفْر - خَمِيلَة. To have —, إِغْفَار.

Nap, *v.i.* To take a nap, نَامَ - ضَجَعَ. To — in the middle of the day, قَيَّلَ. To catch one napping, to come upon unawares, دَخَلَ عَلَى-بَغْتَةً - بَادَهَ. Days took away its freshness and shook off its nap, *i.e.*, it became old, ذَهَبَتِ ٱلْأَيَّامُ بِطَرَاوَتِهِ وَنَفَضَتْ زِئْبِرَهُ.

Nape, *n.* Of the neck, قَفًا *pl.* قُفِيٌّ - قَفْلَة - مَأْخَع - نُقْرَةُ ٱلرَّقَبَةِ.

Naphtha, *n.* نِفْط. Abounding in —, نَفَّاط.

Napkin, *n.* مِنْدِيل *pl.* مَنَادِيل - مَحْرَمَة *pl.* مَحَارِمُ.

Napless, *a.* Having no nap, بِلَا خَمِيلَةٍ - أَمْلَس.

Nappiness, *n.* Of cloth; *see* Nap, *n.*

Nappy, *a.* Of cloth, أَغْثَرُ *fem.* غَثْرَآءُ - مُزَأْبِر - ذُو خَمِيلَةٍ - مُخْمَل.

Narcissus, *n.* عَبْهَر - نِرْجِس. The yellow —, نِرْجِسٌ جَبَلِيٌّ.

Narcotic, *a.* مُرَقِّد - مُنَوِّم - مُخَدِّر.

Narcotic, *n.* مُخَدِّر *pl.* مُخَدِّرَات - دَوَآءٌ مُخَدِّرٌ.

Narcotine, *n.* جَوْهَرُ ٱلْأَفْيُونِ.

Narcotism, *n.* تَخْدِير.

Nard, *n.* نَارْدِين - نَرْدِين.

Narrate, *v.t.* حَدَّثَ ب - حَكَى. To — to, قَصَّ-عَلَى. We will narrate to thee the best of narratives, نَقُصُّ عَلَيْكَ أَحْسَنَ ٱلْقَصَصِ. To be narrated, إِقْتَصَّ. The story was narrated to him, إِقْتَصَّتْ لَهُ ٱلْقِصَّةُ. *See also to* Recite, *v.t.*

Narration, *n.* The act of narrating, تَحْدِيث - نَقْل - بَيَان. Description, وَصْف - بَيَان - تَعْرِيف. A recital, رِوَايَة - حَدِيث. An exposition, شَرْح. *See also* Narrative, *n.*

Narrative, *n.* A story, حَدِيث *pl.* أَحَادِيثُ - قِصَّة *pl.* قِصَص - رِوَايَة *pl.* رَوَايَا. *See also* Narration.

Narrative, *a.* رِوَائِيٌّ.

Narrator, *n.* مُحَدِّث - نَاقِل *pl.* نَقَلَة - رَاوٍ *pl.* رُوَاة - قَاصّ. A describer, وَاصِف.

Narrow, *a.* Of little breadth, ضَيِّق - أَضْيَق. Small, صَغِير. Restricted, مَحْصُور - مُخْتَصَر. Not liberal, niggardly, حَظِل - حَوْص - ذُو صَدْرٍ حَرِجٍ - حُرْقٌ. Narrow minded, بَخِيل - بَخِل - مَهْزُومُ ٱلصَّدْرِ - ٱلْحِمَارِ. Narrow circumstances, poverty, ضِيق - شِدَّة - عُسْرَة - عُسْر - ضِيقَة. A — road between mountains, مَأْزِم; (*see also* Pass, *n.*) To be —, of little breadth, ضَاقَ *aor.* يَضِيقُ - تَضَيَّقَ. To be in — circumstances, أَرَقَّ - صَارَ رَقِيقًا - أَقْتَرَ - أَعْسَرَ - ٱلْحَالِ. He had a — escape, نَجَا بِظُلُوفِ نَفْسِهِ. It was too — for him, ضَاقَ عَلَيْهِ - تَضَيَّقَ عَلَيْهِ. The cover was too — to cover one, ضَاقَ ٱلْغِطَآءُ عَنِ ٱلْإِلْحَافِ. The place was too — for us, ضَاقَ عَلَيْنَا ٱلْمَحَلُّ.

Narrow, *v.t.* To contract in breadth, أَضَاقَ - ضَيَّقَ. To draw into less compass, حَزَقَ. *See also to* Contract, *v.t.*

Narrow, *v.i.* To become less broad, ضَاقَ *aor.* - تَضَيَّقَ - حَرِجَ. أَحْصَرَ - يَضِيقُ. To contract in size, تَصَغَّرَ - إِقْتَلَّ حَزْمًا. *See also to* Contract, *v.i.*

Narrowing, *n.* The act of making less wide, تَضْيِيق. A narrow part, مَضِيق.

Narrowly, *ad.* In a contracted manner, عَلَى ٱلضِّيقِ. Closely, بِضَبْطٍ. Much, جِدًّا. Carefully, attentively, عَلَى - بِٱلتَّدْقِيقِ ٱلتَّدْقِيقِ. In detail, عَلَى كُلِّ وَجْهٍ. Nearly, تَقْرِيبًا. Barely, hardly, بِعُسْرٍ - كَرْهًا - صَعْبًا. To look — at, أَمْعَنَ ٱلنَّظَرَ فِي. To look — into, تَعَرَّفَ عَنْ - تَصَفَّحَ فِي. He — escaped, نَجَا بِظُلُوفِ نَفْسِهِ.

Narrowminded, *a.* مَهْزُومُ ٱلصَّدْرِ - حَوْصُ ٱلْحِمَارِ - ذُو حَرَجٍ. To be —, حَرِجَ صَدْرُهُ.

Narrowmindedness, *n.* هَزْمُ ٱلصَّدْرِ - صَدْرٌ حَرِجٌ.

Narrowness, *n.* Want of breadth, قِلَّةُ عُرْضٍ - ضِيق - حَرَج. Meanness, خَسَاسَة - دَنَآءَة. Narrowness of circumstances, ضِيق - فَقْر - عُسْر - جُحُود - جَحْد - ضِيقَة. Narrowness of mind; *see* Narrowmindedness, *n.*

Narrows, *n.* A narrow passage between hills, عَقَبَة - مَأْزِم. A narrow channel, بُوغَاز - زُقَاق - مَضِيق.

Narwal, *n.*
Narwhal, } The sea unicorn, كَرْكَدَنُّ ٱلْبَحْرِ.

Nasal, *a.* Belonging to the nose, أَنْفِيٌّ ــ ما نِيطَ بِٱلْأَنْفِ. Sounded through the nose, أَغَنُّ *fem.* غَنَّآءُ. A — sound, غُنَّةٌ ــ خَمْخَمَةٌ ــ خَنْخَنَةٌ. To speak with a — twang, أَغَنَّ ــ خَمْخَمَ ــ خَنْخَنَ ــ طَأْطَأَ. A — letter, حَرْفٌ أَغَنُّ ــ حَرْفُ غُنَّةٍ.

Nascent, *a.* آخِذٌ فِي ٱلطُّلُوعِ ــ طالِعٌ ــ نَاشٍ ــ نَامٍ.

Nasiform, *a.* بِصُورَةِ ٱلْأَنْفِ ــ كَٱلْأَنْفِ.

Nastily, *ad.* Dirtily, بِدَرَنٍ ــ بِدَنَاسَةٍ ــ قَذَرًا ــ أَفًّا ــ تَلَوُّثًا. Obscenely, بِٱلْفَحْشَاءِ ــ فُحْشًا ــ خَنًا. Meanly, بِدَنَآءَةٍ ــ بِرَذَالَةٍ ــ بِخَسَاسَةٍ.

Nastiness, *n.* Dirtiness, نَجَاسَةٌ ــ قَذَرٌ ــ رِجْسٌ ــ أُفٌّ ــ دَرَنٌ ــ وَسَخٌ ــ دَنَاسَةٌ. Obscenity, فَحَاشَةٌ ــ فِسْقٌ ــ قَذَعٌ ــ خَنَايَةٌ ــ خَنًا. Meanness, دَنَآءَةٌ ــ خَسَاسَةٌ ــ رَذَالَةٌ.

Nasturtium, *n.*
Nasturtion, } The plant, أَبُو خَاجِرٍ.

Nasty, *a.* Dirty, نَجِسٌ ــ دَنِسٌ ــ قَذِرٌ ــ رَجِسٌ ــ أَدْرَنُ ــ دَرِنٌ ــ وَسِخٌ. Obscene, فَاحِشٌ ــ بَذِيءٌ ــ خَنٍ ــ رَفَثٌ. Mean, رَذِيلٌ ــ خَسِيسٌ ــ دَنِيءٌ. Nasty, as of a day, the weather, *etc.*, رَدِيءٌ ــ بَشِعٌ ــ بَشِيعٌ ــ قَبِيحٌ; of a manner of eating, لَطِخٌ. Disagreeable, in a general sense, بَشِيعٌ ــ بَشِعٌ. *See also* Dirty, Foul, Obscene, Mean, *a.*

Natal, *a.* Relating to nativity, ما نِيطَ بِٱلْوِلَادَةِ. Natal day, مِيلَادٌ ــ مَوْلِدٌ. *See also* Native, *a.*

Natant, *a.* Swimming on the surface, عَوَّامٌ ــ طَائِفٌ ــ سَابِحٌ.

Natation, *n.* العَوْمُ ــ سِبَاحَةٌ.

Natatorial, *a.* Swimming or adapted to swim, عَوَّامٌ.

Natatory, *a.* سَبَّاحٌ ــ مُسْبِحٌ ــ مُعَوِّمٌ.

Nation, *n.* A distinct people, أُمَّةٌ *pl.* أُمَمٌ. A people, community, شَعْبٌ *pl.* شُعُوبٌ ــ قَوْمٌ *pl.* أَقْوَامٌ ــ طَائِفَةٌ *pl.* طَوَائِفُ. The people of a generation, جِيلٌ *pl.* أَجْيَالٌ.

National, *a.* Pertaining to a nation, وَطَنِيٌّ ــ ما نِيطَ بِٱلْأُمَّةِ. General, عُمُومِيٌّ. Attached to one's country, مُحِبُّ ٱلْوَطَنِ. What is their general — character? مَا هِيَ أَخْلَاقُهُمْ إِجْمَالًا. A — anthem or hymn, مَقَامَةُ ٱلْأُمَّةِ ــ أَنْغَامُ ٱلْأُمَّةِ.

National antipathies, مُنَافَرَاتُ ٱلْأُمَّةِ.

National bank, بَنْكُ ٱلْأُمَّةِ (or ٱلشَّعْبِ).

National flag, بَيْرَقُ ٱلدَّوْلَةِ.

National honour, عِرْضُ (or شَرَفُ) ٱلْأُمَّةِ وَنَامُوسُهَا.

National interests, مَنَافِعُ ٱلْأُمَّةِ.

National jealousy, رِقَابُ ٱلْقَوْمِ ــ مُرَاقَبَةٌ جِنْسِيَّةٌ ــ مُرَاقَبَةُ ٱلْأُمَّةِ.

National sentiment, أَفْكَارُ ٱلْأُمَّةِ.

National spirit, مُرُوءَةُ ٱلْأُمَّةِ ــ غَيْرَةُ ٱلْأُمَّةِ.

National representation, هَيْئَةُ وَكَالَةِ ٱلْأُمَّةِ.

National wealth, *n.* ثَرْوَةُ ٱلْأُمَّةِ.

Nationality, *n.* State of belonging to a nation, تَبَعِيَّةٌ: He is of French —, هُوَ فَرَنْسَاوِيٌّ ــ هُوَ مِنْ أُمَّةِ ٱلْفَرَنْسِيسِ. National character, أَخْلَاقُ ٱلْأُمَّةِ. Love of one's nation, حُبُّ ٱلْأُمَّةِ. The doctrine of —, ٱلتَّشْبِيَّةُ. With respect to their —, نَظَرًا لِجِنْسِيَّتِهِمْ.

Nationalize, *v.t.* To make general among a people, أَشْمَلَ (or عَمَّمَ) صَيَّرَ مُشَاعًا عِنْدَ ٱلْأُمَّةِ ــ ٱلْأُمَّةُ بِهِ. To imbue with a national spirit, عَرَّقَ فِيهِ ٱلْغَيْرَةَ ٱلْجِنْسِيَّةَ.

Native, *a.* Born with the being, خِلْقِيٌّ ــ ذَاتِيٌّ ــ جِبِلِّيٌّ ــ طَبِيعِيٌّ. Pertaining to the place of birth, وَطَنِيٌّ ــ مِنَ ٱلْوَطَنِ. Home, not foreign, دَاخِلِيٌّ ــ بَلَدِيٌّ. Born in, مَوْلُودٌ بِـ ــ اِبْنُ ــ مِنْ ــ نَاشِئٌ فِي ــ صَادِرٌ مِنْ ــ مِنْ; coming from, growing in, Native tongue, لُغَةُ ٱلْبِلَادِ: His — tongue, لُغَةُ بِلَادِهِ. Native productions, مَحْصُولَاتٌ بَلَدِيَّةٌ ــ مَحْصُولَاتُ ٱلْبَلَدِ. Native country, وَطَنٌ; his — country, وَطَنُهُ ــ مَسْقَطُ رَأْسِهِ. Native Indian troops, عَسَاكِرُ ٱلْهُنُودِ ٱلْأَهْلِيِّينَ. *See also* Natural, *a.*

Native, *n.* One born in a country, مِنْ أَهْلِ ــ اِبْنُ بِلَادٍ *pl.* أَوْلَادُ ٱلْبِلَادِ; the natives, أَوْلَادُ ٱلْبِلَادِ ــ أَهْلُ ٱلْبِلَادِ. A native product, مِنْ مَحْصُولَاتِ ٱلْبِلَادِ.

Natively, *ad.* By birth, أَصْلًا ــ مَوْلِدًا. *See also* Naturally, *ad.*

Nativeness, *n.* نَشْأَةٌ ــ تَوَلُّدٌ.

Nativity, *n.* Birth, مَوْلِدٌ ــ وِلَادَةٌ. Time or place of birth, مِيلَادٌ ــ مَوْلِدٌ. The feast of the —, عِيدُ ٱلْمِيلَادِ ــ المِيلَادُ. Horoscope of a —, طَالِعٌ ــ مَوْلِدٌ ــ نَجْمٌ. To cast a — for, كَشَفَ لَهُ ٱلنَّجْمَ.

Natural, *a.* Pertaining to the course of nature, طَبِيعِيٌّ. Innate, طَبِيعِيٌّ ــ خِلْقِيٌّ ــ جِبِلِّيٌّ ــ ذَاتِيٌّ ــ غَرِيزِيٌّ ــ فِطْرِيٌّ. Animal, حَيَوَانِيٌّ. Simple, unartificial, خِلْقِيٌّ ــ سَاذِجٌ. Frank, unaffected, مِنْ غَيْرِ تَصَنُّعٍ ــ بَسِيطٌ ــ سَلِيمٌ. Born out of wedlock, اِبْنُ حَرَامٍ *fem.* بِنْتٌ ــ اِبْنُ زِنَآءٍ *fem.* بِنْتٌ. Not revealed, طَبِيعِيٌّ غَيْرُ مُوحًى بِهِ مِنَ ٱللّٰهِ. A — disposition, فِطْرَةٌ *pl.* فِطَرٌ ــ سَجِيَّةٌ *pl.* سَجَايَا ــ خُلُقٌ ــ خِلْقَةٌ ــ خَلِيقَةٌ *pl.* أَخْلَاقٌ. Natural strength, virtue, essence, نَضَارَةٌ. Natural affection, حُنُوٌّ. A — body, جِسْمٌ حَيَوَانِيٌّ. Natural dispositions, مَزَايَا طَبِيعِيَّةٌ. Natural peculiarities, خَصَائِصُ طَبِيعِيَّةٌ. One's — face, وَجْهُ

— 2 ‑ فطس. To die a — death, that is, without disease, خِلْقَةً ‑ = طفس. The — man, الإِنْسَانُ ٱلطَّبِيعِيُّ. It is — to love one's kindred, مِنْ سَجِيَّةِ ٱلْإِنْسَانِ أَنْ ‑ حُبُّ ٱلْأَقَارِبِ مِنَ ٱلطَّبِيعَةِ. It is — that ..., هُوَ مِنْ مُقْتَضِيَاتِ ٱلطَّبِيعَةِ أَنْ. يُحِبَّ ٱلْأَقْرِبَاءَ. Is this — or artificial? هَلْ هٰذَا خِلْقَةٌ أَوْ صَنْعَةٌ. Not — but artificial, غَيْرُ طَبِيعِيٍّ بَلْ صِنَاعِيٌّ.

Natural fool, أَحْمَقُ ‑ أَحْمَقُ خِلْقَةً.

Natural hills, تِلَالٌ طَبِيعِيَّةٌ (or خِلْقَةً).

Natural history or science, عِلْمُ ٱلْمَوْجُودَاتِ ‑ العِلْمُ ٱلطَّبِيعِيُّ ‑ عِلْمُ ٱلْكَائِنَاتِ.

Natural philosophy, عِلْمُ ٱلْأَسْبَابِ ٱلطَّبِيعِيَّةِ وَنَتَائِجِهَا.

Natural theology, عِلْمُ ٱلْكَلَامِ فِيمَا يَخْتَصُّ بِٱلدَّلَائِلِ ٱلطَّبِيعِيَّةِ.

Natural, *n.* A born fool, أَحْمَقُ خِلْقَةً.

Naturalism, *n.* Mere state of nature, حَالُ ٱلطَّبِيعَةِ. The doctrine of those who deny supernatural agency, مَذْهَبُ مَذْهَبُ نَاكِرِي وَحْيِ ٱللّٰهِ ‑ مَذْهَبُ ٱلدَّهْرِيَّةِ ‑ ٱلطَّبِيعِيِّينَ إِلْحَادٌ ‑ وَمُعْتَزِلَةٌ.

Naturalist, *n.* مُتَفَرِّغٌ لِلْعُلُومِ ٱلطَّبِيعِيَّةِ.

Naturalization, *n.* ‑ اِنْضِمَامٌ فِي سِلْكِ ٱلتَّبَاعَةِ (or ٱلتَّبَعِيَّةِ) تَجْنِيسٌ ‑ اِسْتِجْنَاسٌ بِجِنْسِيَّةِ قَوْمٍ. Letters of —, بَرَاءَةُ ٱلْجِنْسِيَّةِ.

Naturalize, *v.t.* To confer on an alien the rights of citizenship, ‑ 2 ضَمَّ ‑ فِي سِلْكِ ٱلْجِنْسِيَّةِ ‑ أَدْخَلَ ٱلْأَجْنَبِيَّ فِي سِلْكِ ٱلتَّبَعِيَّةِ جَنَّسَ. To acclimate, عَوَّدَ ‑ عَلَى ٱلْهَوَاءِ. To accustom, عَوَّدَ. To be naturalized, accustomed to a thing, طُبِعَ (or جُبِلَ) عَلَى.

Naturally, *ad.* By nature, طَبْعًا. By an impulse or principle of nature, خِلْقَةً ‑ بِٱلطَّبِيعَةِ ‑ بِٱلطَّبْعِ. With simplicity, بِسَذَاجَةٍ ‑ بِبَسَاطَةٍ. What they understand —, مَا يَفْهَمُونَهُ بِٱلطَّبِيعَةِ. He is — of a generous disposition, هُوَ كَرِيمُ ٱلْخَلِيقَةِ. He is — frank, مِنْ طَبْعِهِ ٱلنُّصُوحُ. He is — generous, هُوَ مَطْبُوعٌ عَلَى ٱلْكَرَمِ.

Naturalness, *n.* The state of being produced by nature, ‑ فِطْرَةٌ خِلْقَةٌ. Conformity to nature, مُطَابَقَةُ ٱلطَّبِيعَةِ. Stamp, impress, طَابِعٌ. Language which bears the —, or stamp, of chasteness, كَلَامٌ عَلَيْهِ طَابِعُ ٱلْفَصَاحَةِ.

Nature, *n.* The universe and its belongings, الطَّبِيعَةُ. Natural constitution, ‑ شِيمَةٌ ‑ مَاهِيَّةٌ ‑ جِبِلَّةٌ ‑ فِطْرَةٌ ‑ خِلَّةٌ ‑ جِبِلَّةٌ ‑ خُلُقٌ ‑ ضَرِيبَةٌ ‑ طِيَّةٌ ‑ غَرِيزَةٌ. Disposition, خِلْقَةٌ ‑ طَبِيعَةٌ طَبِيعَةٌ ‑ طَبْعٌ ‑ سَجِيَّةٌ ‑ خَصَلَاتٌ *and* خِصَالٌ *pl.* خَصْلَةٌ. Sort, kind, شَكْلٌ ‑ نَوْعٌ. Natural inclination, طَبِيعَةٌ ‑ مَيْلٌ طَبِيعِيٌّ. Complexion, arrangement, تَرْكِيبٌ ‑ نَسَقٌ. Temperament, مِزَاجٌ.

Created things, المَوْجُودَاتُ ‑ الكَائِنَاتُ. Creation, ‑ الكَوْنُ الخَلِيقَةُ. Being, وُجُودٌ ‑ كَوْنٌ. A rule, principle, ‑ قَاعِدَةٌ دُسْتُورٌ. Providence, the Creator, البَارِئُ تَعَالَى ‑ الخَالِقُ. It is the — of the magnet to ..., مِنْ خَصَائِصِ ٱلْمَغْنَطِيسِ أَنْ. It is his — to ..., مِنْ طَبْعِهِ أَنْ. In a state of —, فِي حَالَةِ ٱلطَّبِيعَةِ. Nature orders us to honour father and mother, مِنْ نَامُوسِ ٱلطَّبِيعَةِ أَنْ نَحْتَرِمَ وَالِدَيْنَا. To follow the instincts of —, ‑ تَبِعَ ٱلْمَيْلَ ٱلطَّبِيعِيَّ ‑ طَاوَعَ ٱلطَّبِيعَةَ. It became second — to him, صَارَ ذٰلِكَ لَهُ خِلْقًا. To pay the debt of —, ‑ قَضَى نَحْبَهُ. To paint anything from nature, صَوَّرَ ‑ مِنَ ٱلْخِلْقَةِ.

Against nature, خِلَافُ ٱلطَّبِيعَةِ.

Animated nature, الحَيَوَانَاتُ.

By nature, خِلْقَةً ‑ بِٱلطَّبِيعَةِ ‑ طَبْعًا ‑ بِٱلطَّبْعِ.

Good nature, لُطْفٌ ‑ فَضْلٌ ‑ حِلْمُ ٱلطَّبْعِ. Ill nature, ‑ شَرَاسَةٌ رَدَاءَةُ ٱلطَّبْعِ.

Good natured, مُفْضِلٌ ‑ حَلِيمُ ٱلطَّبْعِ. Ill natured, ‑ شَرِسٌ رَدِيءُ ٱلطَّبْعِ.

Human nature, الطَّبِيعَةُ ‑ البَشَرِيَّةُ ‑ الإِنْسَانِيَّةُ ‑ النَّاسُوتُ ٱلْبَشَرِيَّةُ.

Inanimate nature, الجَمَادَاتُ.

The Divine nature, اللَّاهُوتُ.

Naught, *n.* Nothing, in the sense of there is —, لَا شَيْءَ. A cipher, صِفْرٌ. To set at —, ‑ 2 رَفَضَ ‑ اِسْتَقَلَّ ‑ اِسْتَهْزَأَ بِ. To bring to —, أَبَادَ ‑ أَهْلَكَ ‑ لَاشَى. To come to —, ‑ تَلَاشَى ضَاعَ ‑ يَضِيعُ *aor.* ‑ زَهَقَ ‑ تَطَوَّحَ ‑ حَبِطَ ‑ 2 زَالَ. His efforts have come to —, خَابَ سَعْيُهُ. *See also under* Nothing, *n.*

Naught, *a.* لَا طَائِلَ تَحْتَهُ ‑ رَدِيءٌ ‑ لَا فَائِدَةَ فِيهِ.

Naughtily, *ad.* Peevishly, بِشَكَاسَةٍ ‑ بِعَرْبَدَةٍ. Disobediently, بِقِلَّةِ طَاعَةٍ ‑ تَمَرُّدًا. Wickedly, شَرًّا ‑ بِرَدَاءَةٍ.

Naughtiness, *n.* Peevishness, شَكَاسَةٌ ‑ عَرْبَدَةٌ. Disobedience, قِلَّةُ طَاعَةٍ ‑ عُقُوقٌ. Wickedness, شَرٌّ ‑ رَدَاءَةٌ.

Naughty, *a.* Peevish, شَكِسٌ ‑ مُعَرْبِدٌ. Disobedient, ‑ عَاقٌّ مُعَانِدٌ ‑ قَلِيلُ ٱلطَّاعَةِ. Wicked, bad, رَدِيءٌ ‑ خَبِيثٌ.

Nausea, *n.* Sickness at the stomach, ‑ خُبْثُ (or خَبَاثَةُ) ٱلنَّفْسِ غَثَيَانُ ٱلنَّفْسِ ‑ جَيَشَانُ ٱلنَّفْسِ. Loathing, كَرَاهَةٌ ‑ كَرَاهِيَةٌ. To have —, ‑ غَثَتْ نَفْسُهُ ‑ 2 خَبُثَتْ (or تَخَبَّثَتْ) نَفْسُهُ تَجَيَّشَتْ (or جَاشَتْ) نَفْسُهُ ‑ لَعِبَتْ نَفْسُهُ.

Nauseate, *v.t.* To excite sickness at the stomach, خَبَّثَ ٱلنَّفْسَ *vulg.* لَعَّبَ (or دَوَّخَ) ٱلنَّفْسَ. To affect with disgust, ‑ كَرَّهَ ‑ إِلَى أَكْرَهَ ‑ إِلَى.

Nauseate, *v.i.* To loathe, إِسْتَكْرَهَ ـ كَرِهَ. He was nauseated at it, جَاشَتْ إِلَيْهِ نَفْسُهُ. The stomach is nauseated at it, تَجِيشُ إِلَيْهِ ٱلنَّفْسُ. *See also under* Nausea, *n.*

Nauseous, *a.* Causing sickness at the stomach, مُخَبِّثُ ٱلنَّفْسِ ـ مُقَلِّبُ ٱلنَّفْسِ ـ مُلَعِّبُ ٱلنَّفْسِ. Disgusting, كَرِيه ـ كَرِهٌ.

Nauseously, *ad.* كَرَاهِيَةً ـ بِكَرَاهَةٍ.

Nauseousness, *n.* كَرَاهِيَة ـ كَرَاهَة.

Nautical, *a.* بَحْرِيٌّ ـ مَا نِيطَ بِسَفَرِ ٱلْبَحْرِ. Nautical science, ٱلْمِلَاحَة ـ عِلْمُ ٱلْمِلَاحَةِ ـ ٱلْعُلُومُ ٱلْبَحْرِيَّة.

Nautilus, *n.* نَوْعٌ مِنَ ٱلصَّدَفِ جَمِيلٌ شَفَّافٌ يَعُومُ بِعَيْدَانٍ بَيْنٍ عَلَى وَجْهِ ٱلْبَحْرِ.

Naval, *a.* بَحْرِيٌّ. A — officer, ضَابِطُ ٱلْبَحْرِيَّةِ. Naval forces, قُوَّةٌ بَحْرِيَّةٌ ـ سَفَائِنُ وَعَسَاكِرُ بَحْرِيَّةٌ.

Nave, *n.* As of a church, صَحْنُ كَنِيسَةٍ; of a wheel, قُبُّ ٱلْعَجَلَةِ ـ مَرْكَزُ ٱلْبَكَرَةِ *pl.* قُبُوب.

Navel, *n.* سُرَّة *pl.* سُرَر ـ غَارَة. A protrusion of the —, بَجْرَة.

Navel-string, *n.* سُرٌّ *pl.* أَسِرَّة. To cut the —, سَرَّ [2]. The child's — was cut, سُرَّ ٱلصَّبِيُّ.

Navicular, *a.* Like a boat, بِشَكْلِ ٱلْقَارِبِ.

Navigable, *a.* يُسَافَرُ فِيهِ ـ تَجْرِي فِيهِ ٱلسُّفُنُ ـ حَامِلُ ٱلْمَرَاكِبِ ـ مَخْرُهُ مُمْكِنٌ.

Navigability, *n.* / Navigableness, إِمْكَانُ ٱلْإِبْحَارِ فِيهِ ـ إِمْكَانُ سَفَرِ ٱلْمَرَاكِبِ فِيهِ.

Navigate, *v.i.* As on the sea, مَخَرَ ـ أَبْحَرَ ـ أَقْلَعَ ـ سَافَرَ فِي ٱلْبَحْرِ ـ سَارَ فِي ٱلْبَحْرِ ـ أَبْحَرَ. To — on a river, (سَارَ or) فِي ٱلنَّهْرِ ـ سَافَرَ فِي ٱلنَّهْرِ.

Navigate, *v.t.* To manage a ship, سَيَّرَ (or ضَبَطَ [2]) ٱلْمَرْكَبَ ـ قَادَ ٱلسَّفِينَةَ [1]. *See also to* Navigate, *v.i.*

Navigation, *n.* The art of sailing over, إِبْحَار ـ مَخْر ـ مُخُور ـ مَسِيرَةُ ٱلسَّفَائِنِ فِي ٱلْبَحْرِ ـ سَفَرُ ٱلْمَرَاكِبِ فِي ٱلْبَحْرِ ـ إِقْلَاع. The management of a ship, تَدْبِيرُ ٱلْمَرْكَبِ ـ إِدَارَةُ مَرْكَبٍ. The art of —, عِلْمُ سَيْرِ ٱلسَّفَائِنِ ـ سِفَانَة ـ مَلَّاحِيَّة ـ مِلَاحَة. Aerial navigation, سَفَرُ ٱلْهَوَآءِ ـ ٱلسَّفَرُ فِي ٱلْهَوَآءِ. Perfect freedom of — on the river, حُرِّيَّةٌ تَامَّةٌ لِلسَّفَرِ فِي ٱلنَّهْرِ.

Navigator, *n.* One who navigates seas, رُبَّانِيٌّ ـ رُبَّان ـ مُسَافِرٌ فِي ٱلْبَحْرِ ـ قَطَّاعُ ٱلْبُحُورِ. One who directs the course of a ship, رُبَّانِيٌّ ـ رُبَّان ـ مُهَنْدِسُ ٱلسَّفِينَةِ ـ قَائِدُ ٱلْمَرْكَبِ *coll.* رُبَّانِيَّة.

Navy, *n.* A fleet of ships, سُفُن ـ أَسَاطِيلُ ـ شُون ـ دُونَنْمَا ـ مَرَاكِبُ. Officers and men of the —, بَحْرِيَّة. The naval service, ٱلْخِدْمَةُ ٱلْبَحْرِيَّةُ.

Nay, *n.* لَا. Let your yea be yea and your nay nay, لِيَكُنْ نَعَمُكُمْ نَعَمْ وَلَاكُمْ لَا.

Nay, *ad.* لَا. He will not say nay to thee, لَا يَرُدُّكَ. Don't say — to me, لَا تَرُدَّنِي.

Nazarene, *n.* An epithet applied to the early Christians, نَاصِرِيٌّ *pl.* نَاصِرِيُّونَ. An inhabitant of Nazareth, مِنْ أَهْلِ ٱلنَّاصِرَةِ.

Nazarite, *n.* نَذِيرٌ *pl.* نُذُر.

Naze, *n.* *See* Cliff, Headland, *n.*

N. B., إِشَارَةٌ إِلَى ٱلتَّنْبِيهِ.

N. E., إِشَارَةٌ إِلَى مَا بَيْنَ ٱلشَّمَالِ وَٱلشَّرْقِ.

Neap, *a.* Neap tide, جَزْرٌ تَمَامٌ ـ جَزْرٌ كَامِلٌ.

Neaped, *a.* Stranded, مُشَطَّط ـ مُبَلَّط.

Neapolitan, *a.* نَابُولِيتَانِيٌّ.

Neapolitan, *n.* نَابُولِيتَان *coll.* نَابُولِيتَانِيَّة.

Near, *a.* Close to, دَانٍ ـ دَنِيٌّ ـ مُقَارِب ـ قَرِيب ـ مِن قَرِيب. Intimate, خَاصٌّ ـ صَمِيمِيٌّ. Parsimonious, بَخِيل ـ خَسِيس. The left hand side, ٱلْيَسَارُ ـ ٱلْمُشْغَلِي. A — way, مَقْرَب. A — relation, قَرِيب *pl.* أَقْرِبَآء ـ نَسِيب *pl.* أَنْسِبَآء. A — friend, خِلٌّ ـ خَلِيل *pl.* أَخِلَّاء ـ حَبِيبٌ خَاصٌّ. Near of kin to, قَرِيبٌ إِلَى.

Near, *ad.* Within a little distance, دُون ـ عِنْدَ ـ قَرِيبٌ مِن; by the side of, جَنْبَ; in the presence of, بِحَضْرَةِ. Almost, nearly, تَقْرِيبًا ـ بِٱلتَّقْرِيبِ. Far and near, عَلَى ٱلْقُرْبِ وَٱلْبُعْدِ ـ مِنْ قَرِيبٍ وَمِنْ بَعِيدٍ. It is — midday, قَرُبَ ٱلظُّهْرُ [2] ـ ٱلظُّهْرَ. To be —, in relationship, نَاسَبَ ـ قَارَنَ ـ دَنَا مِن *aor.* قَرِيبٌ. To draw —, to approach, دَنَا مِن [2] ـ إِقْتَرَبَ ـ تَقَدَّمَ إِلَى *aor.* يَدْنُو. To be — arriving at a place, وَصَلَ إِلَى *aor.* يَصِلُ. To make or bring — to, قَرَّبَ إِلَى ـ أَدْنَى مِن. *See also to* Approach, *v.i.*

Nearer, *a.* دُون ـ أَقْرَبُ. This is — than that, هٰذَا دُونَ ذٰلِكَ ـ هٰذَا أَقْرَبُ مِنْ ذٰلِكَ. He is a kinsman — than I, هُوَ وَلِيٌّ أَقْرَبُ مِنِّي.

Nearest, *a.* ٱلْأَدْنَى ـ ٱلْأَقْرَبُ.

Nearly, *ad.* Almost, تَقْرِيبًا ـ بِٱلتَّقْرِيبِ. I — did it, كِدْتُ أَفْعَلُهُ ـ عَسَيْتُ أَنْ أَفْعَلَهُ. In a mean manner, بِخَسَاسَةٍ ـ بِبُخْلٍ. All but, إِلَّا قَلِيلًا. *See also under* Almost, *ad.*

Nearness, *n.* Propinquity, زُلْفَة ـ دَنَاوَة ـ قُرْب ـ قَرَابَة. Relationship, kindred, قُرْب ـ قَرَابَة ـ مَقْرَبَة ـ دَنَاوَة. Parsimony, بُخْل ـ خَسَاسَة.

Near-sighted, *a.* أَكْمَش ـ أَكْمَشُ ـ قَصِيرُ ٱلْبَصَرِ.

Nearsightedness, *n.* قِصَرُ ٱلْبَصَرِ.

Neat, *a.* Clean, نَظِيف ـ صَافٍ. Well arranged, مُرَتَّب ـ طَرِيف ـ كَيِّس ـ نُطَسَة ـ مَنْظُوم ـ مُنَظَّم. Trim, elegant, حَسَن ـ حُلْو ـ لَطِيف ـ مُحَبَّر. Chaste in style, of writing, مَضْبُوط. Unmixed, صَافٍ ـ خَالِص. Verily he is — and of goodly appearance, إِنَّهُ لَحَسَنُ ٱلْحِبْرِ وَٱلسِّبْرِ. *See also* Net, *a.*

Neat, *n.* Cattle of the bovine kind, بَقَر. A neat's foot, or hoof, ظِلْف بَقَرٍ.

Neatly, *ad.* Cleanly, بِنَظَافَةٍ. In good order, بِإِتْقَانٍ ـ بِكِيَاسَةٍ ـ بِطُلَاوَةٍ ـ بِٱنْتِظَامٍ ـ تَنَظُّمًا ـ بِتَرْتِيبٍ. Trimly, elegantly, بِلَطَافَةٍ ـ حَسَنًا ـ بِظَرَافَةٍ. With clearness, بِرَوْقٍ. Cleverly, بِمَهَارَةٍ ـ بِفَنٍّ.

Neatness, *n.* Cleanliness, نَظَافَة. Neat arrangement, إِتْقَان ـ طُلَاوَة ـ نِظَام ـ ٱنْتِظَام ـ تَرْتِيب. Trimness, elegancy, جَمَال ـ حُسْن ـ لَطَافَة ـ ظَرَافَة ـ كِيَاسَة. Neatness of style, ضَبْطُ ٱلْكَلَامِ ـ تَصْرِيحُ ٱلْكَلَامِ ـ حِبْرُ (*or* تَحْبِيرُ) ٱلْكَلَامِ.

Neb, *n.* *See* Beak, *of a bird, n.*

Nebula, *n.* A dark spot, especially in the moon, شَامَة *pl.* شَامَات ـ مَحْو. A dark spot either on sun or moon, شَامَة *pl.* شَامَات ـ ضَبَابَة. A cloud-like appearance among the stars, شَمْلٌ مِنَ ٱلْكَوَاكِبِ ٱلصِّغَارِ يُشْبِهُ ٱلضَّبَابَةَ. *See also* Film, *n.*

Nebular, *a.* مَا نِيطَ بِضَبَابَةِ ٱلنُّجُومِ.

Nebulosity, *n.* ضَبَابَة ـ ضَبَاب ـ لَطْخٌ مِنَ ٱلسَّحَابِ.

Nebulous, *a.* مُغَيِّم ـ ذُو ضَبَابٍ. Obscure, مُلْتَبِس. A — star, نَجْمَةٌ ذَاتُ ضَبَابَةٍ.

Necessarian, *n.* *See* Necessitarian, *n.*

Necessaries, *n.* إِحْتِيَاجَات ـ لَوَازِم.

Necessarily, *ad.* By necessity, عَنِ ٱضْطِرَارٍ ـ لَا مَرَدَّ لَهُ ـ عَلَى كُلِّ حَالٍ ـ مِنْ كُلِّ بُدٍّ. By all means, لَا مَحَالَةَ ـ بِٱلضَّرُورَةِ. As being necessary, right, obligatory, مِنَ ٱللَّازِمِ. It — results therefrom that …, يُسْتَلْزَمُ مِنْ ذَلِكَ أَنْ.

Necessariness, *n.* *See* Necessity, *n.*

Necessary, *a.* Requisite, لَازِم ـ ضَرُورِيٌّ. Indispensable, مُقْتَضَى ـ لَا بُدَّ مِنْهُ ـ مُطْلَقُ ٱلْوُجُوبِ. Right, proper, due, حَقّ ـ ضَرْبَةُ لَازِبٍ ـ لَازِم ـ لَا بُدَّ مِنْهُ ـ لَا يُرَدّ ـ وَاجِب. Inevitable, To be —, وَجَبَ *aor.* يَجِبُ ـ أَحْوَجَ ـ إِحْتَاجَ. To make —, وَجَّبَ عَلَى ـ لَزِمَ عَلَى ـ تَحَتَّمَ ـ أَوْجَبَ. To be — to, for, حَقَّ لِ. To declare to be —, إِسْتَوْجَبَ ـ وَجَّبَ. When it was found — to change the policy, لَمَّا وُجِدَ لُزُومٌ لِتَبْدِيلِ ٱلسِّيَاسَةِ. The — reforms, الإِصْطِلَاحَاتُ ٱللَّازِمُ إِجْرَاؤُهَا. The reforms which they shall deem — to be carried out, ٱلتَّعْدِيلَاتُ ٱلَّتِي يَرَوْنَ إِجْرَاءَهَا مِنَ ٱللَّازِمِ. It was —, the state of matters required, أَحْوَجَ ٱلْأَمْرُ. It was — that…, كَانَ يَجِبُ أَنْ. What was — for him, مَا ٱحْتَاجَ إِلَيْهِ. Necessary things, what is requisite, لَوَازِمُ ـ ضَرُورِيَّات; things that should be, وَاجِبَات; things wanting to be supplied, ضَرُورَات ـ إِحْتِيَاجَات ـ حَاجَات. Necessity called for it, أَحْوَجَتْ إِلَيْهِ ٱلضَّرُورَةُ.

Necessitarian, *n.* جَبْرِيٌّ *pl.* جَبْرِيَّة ـ مِنْ أَهْلِ مَذْهَبِ ٱلْجَبْرِ ـ مِنْ أَهْلِ ٱلْقَدَرِيَّةِ.

Necessitate, *v.t.* أَلْزَمَ إِلَى ـ أَحْوَجَ إِلَى ـ إِضْطَرَّ إِلَى. To be necessitated to, إِلْتَزَمَ بِ ـ أُلْزِمَ إِلَى ـ إِحْتَاجَ إِلَى ـ أُضْطُرَّ إِلَى. He was necessitated to do so, إِحْتَاجَ أَنْ يَفْعَلَ كَذَا.

Necessitous, *a.* مِسْكِين ـ فَقِير ـ مُحْتَاج ـ عَائِز ـ عَائِل.

Necessitousness, *n.* مَسْكَنَة ـ فَقْر ـ إِحْتِيَاج ـ عَدَم ـ عَوَز.

Necessity, *n.* Indispensableness, لُزُوم ـ إِقْتِضَاء ـ ضَرُورِيَّة ـ لَوَازِمُ ـ ضَرُورَة ـ لُزُومِيَّة. Force, جَبْر. Necessities, requirements, عِنْدَ ـ إِحْتِيَاجَات. Of —, بِٱلضَّرُورَةِ ـ ضَرُورَةً. In case of —, عِنْدَ ٱلِٱقْتِضَاءِ. Until — arises, إِلَى أَنْ تَمَسَّ ٱلضَّرُورَةُ. There is now no longer any —, لَمْ يَبْقَ ٱلْآنَ وُجُوبٌ. He recognized the —, إِعْتَرَفَ بِٱللُّزُومِ. Necessity impelled me to do such a thing, حَمَلَتْنِي ٱلضَّرُورَةُ عَلَى كَذَا ـ أُضْطُرِرْتُ إِلَى كَذَا. Necessity has no law, المَأْزِقَةُ لَا جَفَاوَةَ ـ الضَّرُورَاتُ تُبِيحُ ٱلْمَحْظُورَاتِ. Real —, إِحْتِيَاجٌ حَقِيقِيٌّ. As — may require, لِمَا تَقْتَضِيهِ ٱلْمَصْلَحَةُ. The necessities, requirements, of the situation called for that, مُقْتَضِيَاتُ ٱلْأَحْوَالِ أَحْوَجَتْ إِلَى ذَلِكَ. *See also* Need, *n.*

Neck, *n.* As of the body, جِيد *pl.* أَجْيَاد *and* جُيُود ـ عُنُق *pl.* أَعْنَاق ـ رَقَبَة *pl.* رِقَاب *and* رَقَب; of a bottle or vase, عُنُق ـ حُلْقُوم; of a musical instrument, صَعِيد; of land, لِسَان; of a shirt, or a similar garment, قَبَّة ـ جُرُبَّان. The part of the — where a necklace rests, جِيد *pl.* أَجْيَاد. Having a long —, أَعْنَق ـ بَتِع; of a camel, أَسْطَع. Having a long and well-made —, of a woman, عُطْبُول. A wry —, صَعَر; having a wry —, أَصْعَر. A stiff —, رَقَبَةٌ جَاسِيَةٌ. Neck and heels, بِطُولِهِ. The cord of the —, خَيْطُ ٱلرَّقَبَةِ ـ ٱلنُّخَاعُ. To seize by the —, عَنَّقَ: He seized him by the skin of his —, أَخَذَهُ بِطَوْقِ رَقَبَتِهِ. To stretch out the —, in looking at anything, تَطَالَّ. He fell on his — and kissed him, وَقَعَ عَلَى عُنُقِهِ وَقَبَّلَهُ *aor.* يَقَعُ. To break the — of one, كَسَرَ عُنُقَهُ. His — was broken and he died, إِنْكَسَرَتْ رَقَبَتُهُ وَمَاتَ. To wring the — of one, فَرْقَعَ. Neck or nothing! أَمَّا هَلَكَ أَمَّا مَلَكَ.

Neck-cloth, *n.* مِنْدِيلُ ٱلرَّقَبَةِ *pl.* مَنَادِيلُ.

Necked, *a.* بِهِ (لَهُ *or*) عُنُقٌ ـ ذُو رَقَبَةٍ.

Neckerchief, *n.* *See* Neckcloth, *n.*

Necklace, *n.* سِخَاب ـ عُلْطَةٌ ـ قَلَائِدُ *pl.* قِلَادَةٌ ـ مِخْنَقَةٌ ـ لَبَّةٌ ـ مِزْنَقَةٌ ـ عُقُود *pl.* عِقْدٌ ـ مُرْسَلَةٌ. A — of pearls, بُغْمَةٌ ـ أَطْوَاق *pl.* طَوْقٌ مِنْ ذَهَبٍ. A — of gold, عِقْدُ لُؤْلُؤٍ ـ حَبْلُ لُؤْلُؤٍ. A — of gold threads, (from the Persian,) گَرَادِينُ *pl.* گَرْدَان.

Necrological, *a.* مَا نِيطَ بِٱلْمَوْتَى.

Necrology, *n.* A register of deaths, دَفْتَرُ ٱلْأَمْوَاتِ; an account of the dead or deaths, قَائِمَةُ ٱلْمَوْتَى.

Necromancer, *n.* سَحَّار *pl.* سَاحِر.

Necromancy, *n.* سِحْر.

Necromantic, *a.* سَاحِر.

Necromantically, *ad.* بِٱلسِّحْرِ.

Necropolis, *n.* مَزَار ـ مَقْبَرَة. *See also* Burial-ground, *n.*

Nectar, *n.* The drink of the gods, الكَوْثَرُ ـ شَرَابُ ٱلْآلِهَةِ. Any exquisite beverage, رَحِيق ـ شَرَابُ سَلْسَبِيلٍ ـ سَلْسَبِيل.

Nectareal, Nectarean, *a.* Nectareous, } لَذِيذٌ لِلْغَايَةِ ـ كَٱلرَّحِيقِ ـ سَلْسَبِيلِيٌّ.

Nectarial, *a.* Pertaining to the nectary of a plant, مُخْتَصٌّ بِعَسَلِ ٱلْأَزْهَارِ.

Nectariferous, *a.* حَامِلُ ٱلْعَسَلِ.

Nectarine, *n.* ضَرْبٌ مِنَ ٱلْخَوْخِ.

Nectarine, *a.* لَذِيذ ـ لَذِيذٌ كَٱلسَّلْسَبِيلِ.

Nectarium, *n.* Nectary, } عَسَّالَةُ ٱلْأَزْهَارِ.

Nectarous, *a.* *See* Nectareal, *a.*

Need, *n.* Occasion for something, حَاجَة ـ أَرَب ـ إِرْب ـ إِحْتِيَازَات *pl.* إِحْتِيَاز ـ عَازَة ـ عَوَز ـ إِحْتِيَاج. The being without anything, عَدَم. A thing wanted, بُغْيَة ـ بَغِيَّة. Poverty, indigence, مَسْكَنَة ـ فَقْر ـ عَازَة ـ عَوَز ـ عَالَة ـ حَوْبَة. To be in —, to want, إِحْتَاجَ; to be in — of, إِحْتَاجَ إِلَى. To be in —, to be or become poor, إِفْتَقَرَ ـ إِحْتَاجَ. To feel the — of, فَقَدَ ـ ـ إِفْتَقَرَ إِلَى ـ تَفَقَّدَ. He is in — of nothing but…, مَا يُعْوِزُهُ مَا يَحْتَاجُ ـ مَا يُحْوِجُ ٱلْأَمْرَ إِلَى… There is no — to…, شَيْءٌ إِلَّا. مَا هُوَ لَازِمٌ أَنْ ـ ٱلْأَمْرَ إِلَى. To be in no — of, to be able to do without, إِسْتَغْنَى عَنْ ـ غَنِيَ عَنْ: You have no — of it (having already enough), أَنْتَ غَنِيٌّ عَنْهُ ـ مَا أَنْتَ مُفْتَقِرٌ إِلَيْهِ. I have — of nothing, كُفِيتُ وَوُقِيتُ. In case of —, عِنْدَ ٱلْإِقْتِضَاءِ. If — be, إِنْ كَانَ يَجِبُ ـ إِنْ لَزِمَ. There is no —, مَا يَلْزَمُ ـ مَا يَحْتَاجُ. *See also under* Necessity, Want, *n.*

Need, *v.t.* إِفْتَقَرَ إِلَى ـ إِحْتَاجَ إِلَى ـ إِحْتَاجَ ـ إِخْتَلَّ إِلَى ـ دَعَا إِلَى ـ إِفْتَقَرَ إِلَى. It needed, أَعَازَ. To cause to —, أَعْوَزَ *aor.* يَدْعُو. It needed to be repaired, دَعَا إِلَى إِصْلَاحِهِ. As though he needed anything, كَأَنَّهُ مُحْتَاجٌ إِلَى شَيْءٍ. I —, or have — of, them, أَنَا مُحْتَاجٌ إِلَيْهِمْ. I — you not, I have no — of you, لِيَ أَنْ أَسْتَغْنِيَ عَنْكَ ـ لَا حَاجَةَ لِي إِلَيْكَ.

Needer, *n.* A — of, مُحْتَاجٌ إِلَى. A — of the mercy of God, الفَقِيرُ إِلَى رَحْمَةِ ٱللّٰهِ.

Needful, *a.* ضَرُورِيٌّ ـ مُقْتَضًى ـ لَازِم ـ وَاجِب. Only one thing is —, الحَاجَةُ إِلَى وَاحِدٍ. Things — for the occasion, حَاجَاتُ ٱلْبَاعِثِ. It is more — for you to…, أَلْزَمُ لَكُمْ أَنْ. It was — that I should write to you, أُضْطُرِرْتُ أَنْ أَكْتُبَ إِلَيْكُمْ.

Needfully, *ad.* ضَرُورَةً ـ بِٱلضَّرُورَةِ.

Needily, *ad.* بِفَقْرٍ ـ بِعَوَزٍ ـ بِمَسْكَنَةٍ ـ بِٱحْتِيَاجٍ.

Neediness, *n.* مَسْكَنَة ـ فَقْر ـ عَازَة ـ عَوَز ـ إِحْتِيَاج.

Needle, *n.* For sewing, إِبَر *pl.* إِبْرَة ـ مِخْيَط ـ خِيَاط. The eye of a —, خُرْتٌ (*or*) خُرْتَةُ ٱلْإِبْرَةِ ـ سِمَام *pl.* سَمُّ ٱلْإِبْرَةِ. Narrower than the eye of a —, أَضْيَقُ مِنْ سَمِّ ٱلْإِبْرَةِ. A maker of needles, إِبَّار. A — case, مِئْبَر. A — gun, بَنَادِقُ *pl.* بُنْدُقِيَّةُ ٱلْإِبْرَةِ. A packing —, مَسَالّ *pl.* مِسَلَّة ـ شَرِيرَة. A magnetic —, إِبْرَةُ ٱلْبُوصْلَةِ. A dipping —, إِبْرَةُ ٱلْإِنْحِطَاطِ. To swallow a —, أَبِرَ. To thread a —, ضَمَّ ٱلْخَيْطَ فِي ـ عَبَّرَ (*or*) سَلَكَ ٱلْخَيْطَ فِي ٱلْإِبْرَةِ ٱلْإِبْرَةِ.

Needleful, *n.* فَتْلَةُ خَيْطٍ.

Needless, *a.* عَبَث ـ غَيْرُ ضَرُورِيٍّ ـ غَيْرُ لَازِمٍ ـ غَيْرُ مُحْتَاجٍ إِلَى. To render —, أَغْنَى عَنْ. It renders — thy doing so and so, يُغْنِي عَنْ أَنْ تَفْعَلَ كَذَا.

Needlessly, *ad.* بِلَا فَائِدَةٍ ـ مِنْ غَيْرِ لُزُومٍ ـ مِنْ غَيْرِ ٱحْتِيَاجٍ ـ سُدًى.

Needlessness, *n.* قِلَّةُ فَائِدَةٍ ـ عَدَمُ لُزُومٍ ـ عَدَمُ ٱحْتِيَاجٍ ـ عَدَمُ طَائِلٍ.

Needlework, *n.* مَشْغُولُ ٱلْإِبْرَةِ. Plain —, خِيَاطَة. Embroidery, تَطْرِيز.

Needs, *ad.* لَا بُدَّ مِنْ ـ ضَرُورَةً ـ بِٱلضَّرُورَةِ ـ لَا جَرَمَ. Such things must — be, لَا بُدَّ أَنْ تَكُونَ هٰذِهِ ٱلْأَشْيَاءُ. I must — go, أَنَا مُضْطَرٌّ إِلَى أَنْ أَذْهَبَ. We must — die, لَا بُدَّ أَنْ نَمُوتَ.

Needy, *a.* مِسْكِين ـ فَقِير ـ مُحْتَاج ـ عَائِل ـ عَائِز ـ عَوِز. To be or become —, إِفْتَقَرَ ـ أَعْدَمَ ـ أَعْوَزَ.

Ne'er, *ad.* *See* Never, *ad.*

Ne exeat, *n.* أَمْرٌ سَامٍ يَنْهِي ٱلْخُرُوجَ مِنَ ٱلْبَلَدِ.

Nefarious, *a.* فَظِيع – شَنِيع – قَبِيح – فَاجِر *pl.* فُجَّار – أَقْبَح – لَعِين. A — action, أَمْرٌ فَظِيعٌ – قَبَاحَة *pl.* قَبَائِح. *See also* Abominable, Detestable, *a.*

Nefariously, *n.* قَبَاحَةً – بِفَظَاعَةٍ – بِشَنَاعَةٍ – بِأَشَدِّ قَبَاحَةٍ.

Nefariousness, *n.* فُجُور – قَبَاحَة – فَظَاعَة – شَنَاعَة.

Negation, *n.* The act of denying, نَفْي – إِنْكَار; as in logic, سَلْب. The being absent, of a quality, *etc.*, عَدَم – عُدْم – عُدُم.

Negative, *a.* Implying denial or absence, مَنْفِيٌّ – نَفْيِيٌّ – سَلْبِيٌّ – إِنْكَارِيٌّ. A — sentence, كَلَامٌ مَنْفِيٌّ. A — proposition, نَفْي – إِنْكَار. A — particle, حَرْفُ نَفْيٍ. He answered him in the —, أَجَابَهُ بِٱلسَّلْبِ.

Negative, *n.* A proposition by which something is denied, نَفْي – إِنْكَار. A —, in photography, رَسْمٌ مَعْكُوسٌ. Having the power of negativing, صَاحِبُ ٱلنَّفْيِ. The word No, كَلِمَةُ لَا.

Negative, *v.t.* 2 رَدَّ – أَنْكَرَ – نَفَى – 2 نَفَا. He negatived the affair, 2 رَدَّ ٱلْأَمْرَ. He negatived to him the affair, رَدَّ عَلَيْهِ ٱلْأَمْرَ.

Negatively, *ad.* بِوَجْهِ ٱلرَّدِّ – بِإِنْكَارٍ – بِنَفْيٍ – سَلْبًا. Affirmatively and —, إِيجَابًا وَسَلْبًا – بِٱلسَّلْبِ وَبِٱلْإِيجَابِ.

Neglect, *v.t.* To be careless about, أَفْرَطَ فِي – 2 فَرَطَ فِي – غَبِيَ عَنْ – أَهْمَلَ – 2 غَفَلَ عَنْ – أَغْفَلَ – ذَهَلَ عَنْ – تَغَاضَى عَنْ. To omit, تَغَافَلَ عَنْ – 2 فَاتَ – 2 تَرَكَ. To come short in, تَقَصَّرَ بِ. To desert, leave to one's self, 2 خَذَلَ – خَذَلَ عَنْ – أَخْذَلَ – سَيَّبَ – 2 تَرَكَ. To disesteem, تَهَاوَنَ بِ. To lose, not to take advantage of, ضَيَّعَ. Not to take notice of, to ignore, جَهِلَ – أَضَاعَ. To cause to —, to be careless about, غَفَّلَ-عَنْ – أَذْهَلَ-عَنْ – أَغْفَلَ-عَنْ. To cause one to —, to stand aloof from, خَذَّلَ-عَنْ. He neglected to discharge the duties of his appointment, تَغَافَلَ عَنْ أَدَاءِ وَاجِبَاتِ مَأْمُورِيَّتِهِ. They neglected to inform him of it, ذَهَلُوا عَنْ إِخْبَارِهِ بِهِ. He altogether neglected the affair, جَعَلَ ٱلْأَمْرَ فِي ظَهْرِهِ. He neglected his family, أَضَاعَ (or أَخْذَلَ) عِيَالَهُ. He neglected the opportunity, ضَيَّعَ ٱلْفُرْصَةَ. They — business, يُهْمِلُونَ ٱلْأَشْغَالَ. To — one's self, تَهَاوَنَ بِنَفْسِهِ.

Neglect, *n.* Carelessness, inattention, إِهْمَال – غِرَّة – تَهَامُل – تَكَاهُل – تَسَاهُل – ذَهْل – ذُهُول – غَبْوَة – تَفْرِيط – غَفْلَة – غُفُول – خِذْلَان – خَذْل – قِلَّةُ ٱعْتِنَاءٍ – تَوَانٍ – خُذُول. Standing aloof from, نَسْو – نَسْوَة – قُصُور – سَهْو. Omission, forgetfulness, إِهْمَال. Contempt, تَهَاوُن. To fall into —, desuetude, أُلْغِيَ.

Neglected, *a.* Not attended to, مَذْهُولٌ عَنْهُ – مَغْفُولٌ عَنْهُ – مَذْهُولٌ عَنْهُ – مَتْرُوك. Cast off, despised, ضَائِع – مُهِين – مَتْرُوك – مُدَشَّر – مُعَطَّل – مُلْغًى. Disused, gone out of use, مُعَطَّل – مُلْغًى. A — family, عِيَالٌ ضُيَّعٌ.

Neglectful, *a.* طَسِيع – طَزِيع – كَاهِل – ذَاهِل – غَبِيّ – غَبِيٌّ – سَاهٍ – سَهْوَان – غَافِل – مُغَفَّل – غَفْلَان – مُتَكَاسِل. Neglectful of one's person, مُتَهَاوِنٌ بِنَفْسِهِ – مُتَقَشِّف. Made —, مُغَفَّل. To pretend to be —, تَغَافَلَ. To be —, غَبِيَ. *See also under to* Neglect, *v.t.*

Neglectfully, *ad.* بِغَيْرِ ٱعْتِنَاءٍ – سُدًى – غَفْلَةً – إِهْمَالًا.

Negligé, *n.* Of dress, تَخْفِيفَة. In —, مُتَخَفِّف.

Negligence, *n.* Carelessness; *see* Neglect, *n.*

Negligent, *a.* *See* Neglectful, *a.*

Negligently, *ad.* *See* Neglectfully, *ad.*

Negotiability, *n.* As of bills, *etc.*, سُلُوك – إِمْكَانُ ٱلتَّدَاوُلِ – مُدَاوَلَة.

Negotiable, *a.* As of bills, *etc.*, يُتَعَامَلُ بِهِ – مَاشٍ – سَالِك.

Negotiate, *v.t.* To treat with, عَامَلَ. To transfer by assignment, as bills of exchange, *etc.*, عَامَلَ فِي – دَاوَلَ. To — a treaty with, فَاوَضَ-فِي عَهْدٍ. To — for peace with, فَاوَضَ-فِي مُصَالَحَةٍ. To — with one and obtain his consent to, وَاطَى-عَلَى. To — together, and agree mutually to a compact, of many, تَعَاهَدُوا عَلَى. He would not — with any one respecting that matter except with the king himself, لَا يُفَاوِضُ فِي ذٰلِكَ إِلَّا ٱلْمَلِكَ نَفْسَهُ.

Negotiate, *v.i.* To carry on business, تَعَامَلَ. To carry on negotiations with a view to some arrangement, فَاوَضَ. To intervene in, تَوَسَّطَ فِي. The people — together in buying and selling with money, تَعَامَلَ ٱلنَّاسُ بِٱلدَّرَاهِمِ.

Negotiation, *n.* A trading, مُعَامَلَة – تَعَامُل. A discussion towards some arrangement, مُبَاحَثَة – مُذَاكَرَة – مُفَاوَضَة; in writing, مُكَاتَبَة; in personal colloquy, مُكَالَمَة. The — of a bill of exchange, مُدَاوَلَةُ حَوَالَةٍ. A resumption of negotiations, إِعَادَةُ ٱلْمُفَاوَضَةِ.

Negotiator, *n.* مُفَاوِض – مَأْمُور – مُعَامِلٌ مَأْمُورٌ – مُعَامِل.

Negress, *n.* A black woman, سَوْدَاءُ *pl.* سُودٌ. A — slave, جَارِيَةٌ سَوْدَاءُ *pl.* جَوَارٍ سُودٌ.

Negro, *n.* A black man, أَسْوَدُ *pl.* سُودَان. A — slave, عَبْدٌ أَسْوَدُ *pl.* عَبِيدٌ سُودٌ. The negroes, ٱلسُّودَانُ

Negroland, *n.* أَرْضُ ٱلسُّودَانِ.

Negus, *n.* شَرَابٌ يُصْنَعُ مِنْ خَمْرٍ وَمَاءٍ حَارٍّ وَسُكَّرٍ وَعَصِيرِ ٱللَّيْمُونِ.

Neigh, *v.i.* حَمْحَمَ – صَهَلَ – شَخَرَ. To — for fodder, إِسْتَعْلَفَ.

Neigh, *n.* حَمْحَمَة – صَهِيل – صُهَال – شَخِير. A — for fodder, إِسْتِعْلَاف.

Neighbour, *n.* جار ـ مُجَاوِر *pl.* جِوَار *and* جِيْرَان. A next door —, جارٌ مَكاسِرٌ. A familiar friend, خَلِيط *pl.* خُلَطَآء ـ مُخَالِط. To visit one's neighbours, or to be neighbourly with them, خَالَطَ (*or* عَاشَرَ) ٱلْجِيْرَانَ. Inquire for the neighbours before you take a house, and for the companions you will have before you undertake a journey, (*prov.*) أُطْلُبِ ٱلْجَارَ قَبْلَ ٱلدَّارِ وَٱلرَّفِيْقَ قَبْلَ ٱلطَّرِيقِ. To be or become one's —, جَاوَرَ.

Neighbour, *a.* *See* Neighbouring, *a.*

Neighbour, *v.t.* كَانَ قَرِيبًا مِن *or* إِلَى ـ جَاوَرَ. To border on, قَارَبَ ـ إِتَّصَلَ بِ ـ تَاخَمَ.

Neighbourhood, *n.* قُرْب ـ جِوَار ـ مُجَاوَرَة. A place, district, نَاحِيَة ـ جَانِب. Neighbours, الجِيرَان. To live in the — with, جَاوَرَ ـ سَاكَنَ.

Neighbouring, *a.* قَرِيبٌ مِن ـ مُجَاوِر. A — place, مَكانٌ مُجَاوِرٌ. The — towns, المُدُنُ ٱلْمُجَاوِرَةُ.

Neighbourly, *a.* أَلِيف ـ مِخْلاط ـ مُخَالِط ـ مُعَاشِر.

Neighbourly, *ad.* بِأُنْسٍ ـ بِمُعَاشَرَةٍ. *See* Sociably.

Neighing, *n.* *See* Neigh, *n.*

Neighing, *a.* صَهَّال.

Neither, *pr.* وَلَا. Neither this nor that, لا هٰذا وَلا ذَاكَ. Neither these nor those, لا هٰؤلاءِ وَلا أُولٰئِكَ. I — belong to you nor you to me, إِنِّي لَسْتُ مِنْكَ وَأَنْتَ لَسْتَ مِنِّي.

Neither, *conj.* وَلَا. Neither eat of it nor touch it, لا تَأْكُلْ مِنْهُ وَلا تَمَسَّهُ. Neither will I tell you, وَلا أَنا أَقُولُ لَكُمْ.

Nem. con., بِصَوْتٍ ـ بِٱلِٱتِّفَاقِ ـ عِبَارَةٌ عَن لَيْسَ مِن مُخَالِفٍ وَاحِدٍ.

Nemoral, *a.* Pertaining to a grove, ما نِيطَ بِغَابَةٍ.

Neological, *a.* Rationalistic, نَاكِرُ لُزُومِ وَحْيِ ٱللّٰهِ لِلْهُدَى ـ دَهْرِيٌّ ـ مُلْحِد.

Neologist, *n.* | Neologian, *n.* } A rationalist, مَنِ ٱعْتَقَدَ هُدًى دُونَ ٱلْوَحْيِ دَهْرِيٌّ ـ مُلْحِد ـ كَافِرٌ بِٱلْوَحْيِ ـ ٱلْمُنْزَلِ دَهْرِيٌّ *coll.* دَهْرِيَّة.

Neologize, *v.t.* عَلَّمَ بِكِفَايَةِ ٱلْعَقْلِ لِلْهُدَى بِدُونِ ٱلْوَحْيِ.

Neology, *n.* Rationalism, القَوْلُ بِكِفَايَةِ ٱلْعَقْلِ لِلْهُدَى بِدُونِ ٱلْوَحْيِ.

Neophyte, *n.* A proselyte, دَخِيل *pl.* دُخَلَاء. A novice, حَدِيثُ ٱلْإِيمَانِ ـ تِلْمِيذ *pl.* تَلامِيذُ.

Neoteric, *a.* New, recent, جَدِيد ـ مُسْتَطْرِف ـ حَدِيث ـ مُسْتَجِدّ.

Nepalism, *n.* Abstinence from intoxicating drinks, الإِنْقِطَاعُ عَنْ شُرْبِ ٱلْمُسْكِرَاتِ.

Nepenthe, *n.* A medicine that relieves pain, دَوَآء ـ سُلْوَان عِلَاجٌ مُهَدِّئ ـ مُخَفِّفُ ٱلْوَجَعِ.

Nephew, *n.* A brother's son, إِبْنُ أَخٍ *pl.* أَوْلَادُ أَخٍ; a sister's son, إِبْنُ أُخْتٍ *pl.* أَوْلَادُ أُخْتٍ.

Nephritic, *n.* A medicine for disease of the kidneys, دَوَآءٌ لِدَآءِ ٱلْكُلَى.

Nephritic, *a.* Pertaining to the kidneys, مُتَعَلِّقٌ بِٱلْكُلَى. Affected with gravel, مُحْصِيٌّ ـ بِهِ حَصَاةٌ.

Nephritis, *n.* إِلْتِهَابُ ٱلْكُلَى.

Nephrotomy, *n.* جِرَاحَةُ ٱلْحَصَى.

Nepotism, *n.* *See* Favouritism, *n.*

Ne plus ultra, *n.* بِدْع ـ شَيْءٌ فَائِقٌ.

Neptune, *n.* The god of the sea, إِسْمُ إِلٰهِ ٱلْبَحْرِ فِي ٱلْجَاهِلِيَّةِ. The planet —, سَيَّارَةُ نَبْتُونَ ـ نَجْمُ نَبْتُونَ.

Neptunian, *a.* Pertaining to the ocean, بَحْرِيٌّ ـ مُتَعَلِّقٌ بِٱلْبَحْرِ. The — theory, مَذْهَبُ ٱلْقَائِلِينَ أَنَّ أَصْلَ ٱلْكُرَةِ ٱلْأَرْضِيَّةِ كَانَ مَاءً قَبْلَ جُمُودِهَا.

Nereid, *n.* بِنْتُ ٱلْبَحْرِ *pl.* بَنَات.

Nerve, *n.* A sinew or tendon, عَقَبَة *coll.* عَقَب ـ عَصَبَة *coll.* عَصَب (*also*, improperly called, عِرْق *pl.* عُرُوق). Firmness, شَجَاعَة ـ جَسَارَة ـ مُرُوَّة ـ صَلَابَة ـ عَزْم ـ إِقْدَام. Strength, قُوَّة. To strain every —, بَذَلَ جُهْدَهُ.

Nerve, *v.t.* To invigorate, شَدَّدَ ـ شَجَّعَ. To — one's self, تَشَدَّدَ ـ تَشَجَّعَ.

Nerveless, *a.* Weak, ضَعِيف *pl.* ضُعَفَآء ـ خَامِل.

Nervine, *a.* مُقَوِّي (*or* مُشَدِّدُ) ٱلْعَصَبِ.

Nervine, *n.* دَوَآءٌ مُشَدِّدُ ٱلْعَصَبِ.

Nervous, *a.* Pertaining to the nerves, عَصَبِيٌّ. Full of nerves, كَثِيرُ ٱلْأَعْصَابِ. Strong in the nerves, شَدِيدُ ٱلْعَصَبِ ـ مَعْصُوب. Weak in the nerves, ضَعِيفُ ٱلْعَصَبِ. Easily agitated, fearful, مُفَزَّع ـ هَاعٌ لَاعٌ ـ خَوَّاف ـ مُوَسْوَس. Strong, of language, مُبَالِغ ـ مُحَذَّف ـ مُحَبَّر ـ مُؤَثِّر ـ شَدِيد; terse, مُبَالِغ. Powerful, قَدِير ـ قَوِيّ.

Nervously, *ad.* With vigour, بِإِقْدَامٍ ـ بِصَلَابَةٍ ـ بِعَزْمٍ. With agitation, timidity, بِوَسْوَاسٍ ـ بِٱضْطِرَابٍ.

Nervousness, *n.* Vigour, عَزْم ـ صَلَابَة ـ مُرُوَّة ـ إِقْدَام. Weakness, agitation of the nervous system, إِضْطِرَاب ـ مُخَاوَفَة ـ وَسْوَاس ـ خَفَقَان. Nervousness, or terseness of style, تَحْذِيف ـ ضَبْطُ ٱلْكَلَامِ ـ ٱلْكَلَام.

Nescience, *n.* عَدَمُ مَعْرِفَةٍ ـ جَهْل.

Nest, *n.* As of a bird, وَكْر or وَكْرَة *pl.* أَوْكَار *and* وُكُور — عُشّ *pl.* أَعْشَاش *and* عِشَاش. A — in a tree, عُشّ — عَرْش ; in a wall, مَوْكِنَة — مَوْكِن — وُكْنَة — أُوكُن *pl.* وُكُون *and* وُكُن ; in the ground, أُدْحِيّ *pl.* أَفَاحِيص ; specially of that of the ostrich, أُفْحُوص *pl.* أَدَاحٍ. The place where a hen broods upon its eggs to hatch them, مَحْضَن ; a shallow bowl used for that purpose, مَحْضَنَة *pl.* مَحَاضِن. An abode, مَأْوًى — مَكَان — مَنْزِل. A — of boxes, طَائِفَةٌ مِنْ حُقَقٍ تَسْلُكُ فِي بَعْضِهَا. To build a —, of a bird, رَصَّ ² ٱلطَّائِرُ عُشَّهُ — عَشَّشَ — أَعْشَشَ — اِتَّكَرَ. To keep to its —, عَشَّ ². To feather one's —, مَلَأَ ² جَيْبَهُ.

Nest-egg, *n.* بَيْضَةُ ٱلْمَحْضَنِ.

Nestle, *v.i.* To lie snug, as in a nest, وَكَرَ *aor.* يَكِرُ. To move about in one's seat, ضَرَبَ — تَمَوَّرَ.

Nestle, *v.t.* To cherish, رَبَّى — حَضَنَ ². To house, آوَى — سَكَّنَ — ضَيَّفَ. To — in the bosom, اِحْتَضَنَ — حَضَنَ ².

Nestling, *n.* فَرْخ *pl.* أَفْرَاخ.

Nestorian, *a.* and *n.* نَسْطُورِيّ.

Nestorianism, *n.* رَأْيُ نَسْطُورُس.

Net, *n.* An instrument of net-work for catching fish, شُبَّاك *pl.* شَبَابِيك — شِبَاك — شَبَكَة *pl.* شَبَك *and* شِبَاك — شَرَكَة. A fowler or hunter's —, كِفَّة *pl.* كِفَف — مِصْيَد *pl.* مَصَايِد — مِصْيَدَة. A snare, فَخّ *pl.* فُخُوخ. Net-work, نَسِيج — شَبَك — شَبَكَة. A cunning device, دَسِيسَة. A difficulty, وَرْطَة — عُسْرَة — مُشْكِلَة. Muslin, شَاش. To cast a net, أَلْقَى ٱلشَّبَكَةَ. To spread a —, نَشَرَ ² ٱلشَّبَكَةَ. To fall into one's own —, سَقَطَ ² فِي شُبَّاكِهِ.

Net, *a.* Clear of all charges and deductions, خَالِص. Net weight, وَزْنٌ خَالِصٌ. Net profit, رِبْحٌ خَالِصٌ — رِبْح — شِفّ.

Net, *v.t.* To make net-work of, شَبَّكَ. To gain in clear profit, رَبِحَ — اِسْتَشَفَّ. To give one in clear profit upon, رَابَحَ (*or* أَرْبَحَ) عَلَى. I netted or gave him a net profit on his commodity, رَابَحْتُهُ عَلَى بِضَاعَتِهِ — أَرْبَحْتُهُ عَلَى سِلْعَتِهِ.

Nether, *a.* Lower, أَدْنَى — دُون — أَسْفَل — أَحَطّ. A — part, أَسْفَل *pl.* أَسَافِل. A — millstone, رَحًى (the upper stone is called مِرْدَاة).

Nethermost, *a.* الأَقْصَى — السُّفْلَى *fem.* الأَسْفَل — الأَحَطّ *fem.* القُصْيَا.

Nett, *a.* *See* Net, *a.*

Netted, *a.* Reticulated, مُشَبَّك.

Netting, *n.* Net-work, شَبَكَة — شَبَك. A — of wicker, قَفَص ; of small threads, نَسِيج.

Netting-needle, *n.* مَكُّوك.

Nettle, *n.* The plant, قُرَّيْص — أَنْجُرَة — نَجَاع.

Nettle, *v.t.* نَكَى — أَوْغَرَ — جَفَا ² — جَرَحَ — نَقَرَ ² — لَسَعَ.

Nettled, *a.* مُنَكَّد — مُتَقَهِّر — مُصَدَّع.

Nettler, *n.* مُنَكِّد — مِطْعَان — مُصَدِّع.

Nettle-rash, *n.* مَرَاة — شَرَاة — نَمْل.

Net-work, *n.* *See* Netting, *n.*

Neuralgia, *n.* وَجَعُ ٱلْعَصَبِ.

Neuralgic, *a.* مُتَعَلِّقٌ بِوَجَعِ ٱلْعَصَبِ.

Neurologist, *n.* عَالِمٌ بِأَعْصَابِ ٱلْحَيَوَانَاتِ.

Neurology, *n.* العِلْمُ بِأَحْوَالِ ٱلأَعْصَابِ.

Neurotic, *a.* Seated in the nerves, كَائِنٌ فِي ٱلْعَصَبِ.

Neurotomy, *n.* جِرَاحَةُ ٱلْعَصَبِ.

Neuter, *a.* Not adhering to any party, غَيْرُ مُتَعَصِّبٍ لِعَصَبِيَّةٍ. Not adhering to one of two parties, لَا مَعَ — حَائِدٌ عَنِ ٱلطَّرَفَيْنِ — لَا مَعَ ذَاكَ وَلَا مَعَ هٰذَا. Of neither gender, لَا مُذَكَّرٌ وَلَا مُؤَنَّثٌ. A — verb, فِعْلٌ لَازِمٌ.

Neutral, *a.* Not adhering to any party, غَيْرُ مُتَعَصِّبٍ لِعَصَبِيَّةٍ مَّا. Not adhering to one of two parties, لَا مَعَ — حَائِدٌ عَنِ ٱلطَّرَفَيْنِ — لَا مَعَ ذَاكَ وَلَا مَعَ هٰذَا ; as between belligerent powers, حَائِدٌ عَنِ ٱلتَّعَصُّبِ لِدُوَلٍ مُتَحَارِبَةٍ أَوْ عَلَيْهَا. Neutral, of colour, أَخْسَبُ. A — tint, صِبْغٌ لَا يَغْلِبُ عَلَيْهِ لَوْنٌ مِنَ ٱلأَلْوَانِ — لَوْنٌ أَخْسَبُ. A — salt, مِلْحٌ لَا تَغْلِبُ عَلَيْهِ ٱلْحُمُوضَةُ وَلَا ٱلْحَرَافَةُ. A — territory, بِلَادٌ مُسْتَقِلَّةٌ بَيْنَ مَمْلَكَتَيْنِ. A — flag, بَيْرَقُ دَوْلَةٍ حَائِدَةٍ عَنِ ٱلدُّوَلِ ٱلْمُتَحَارِبَةِ. Neutral rights, حُقُوقُ ٱلْحَائِدِينَ عَنِ ٱلدُّوَلِ ٱلْمُتَحَارِبَةِ.

Neutral, *n.* As between belligerent powers, حَائِدٌ عَنِ ٱلدُّوَلِ ٱلْمُتَحَارِبَةِ ; as between two belligerent powers, حَائِدٌ عَنِ ٱلدَّوْلَتَيْنِ ٱلْمُتَحَارِبَتَيْنِ. As between two contending parties, litigants, حَائِدٌ عَنِ ٱلْخَصْمَيْنِ.

Neutrality, *n.* Non-adherence to any party, عَدَمُ ٱلْعَصَبِيَّةِ — الحِيَادُ عَنِ ٱلتَّعَصُّبِ — الاِعْتِزَالُ عَنِ ٱلْعَصَبِيَّةِ. The — of a nation between two belligerent powers, حِيَادُ ٱلأُمَّةِ عَنِ ٱلدَّوْلَتَيْنِ ٱلْمُتَحَارِبَتَيْنِ. To observe — between two belligerent powers, حَفِظَ ² ٱلْحِيَادَ (*or* بَقِيَ — رَاعَى) ٱلْحِيَادَ عَنِ ٱلدَّوْلَتَيْنِ ٱلْمُتَحَارِبَتَيْنِ عَلَى ٱلْحِيَادِ) عَنِ ٱلدَّوْلَتَيْنِ ٱلْمُتَحَارِبَتَيْنِ. To violate —, as between two belligerent powers, أَجْحَفَ (*or* أَخَلَّ) بِٱلْحِيَادِ عَنِ ٱلدَّوْلَتَيْنِ. The footing of —, قَانُونُ (*or* مَسْلَكُ) ٱلْحِيَادِ ٱلْمُتَحَارِبَتَيْنِ.

Neutralization, *n.* As of a territory, the making it neutral, independent, جَعْلُ ٱلْبِلَادِ مُسْتَقِلَّةً ; the being neutralized, of a territory, إِسْتِقْلَال (or إِسْتِبْدَاد) بِلَادٍ. The —, as of a salt, *etc.*, تَعْدِيل. The rendering null, إِبْطَال.

Neutralize, *v.t.* Of a territory, جَعَلَ ٱلْبِلَادَ مُسْتَقِلَّةً; of a salt, *etc.*, عَدَّلَ ـ عَادَلَ. To render null, أَبْطَلَ. To mitigate, لَطَّفَ.

Neutralized, *a.* As of territory, مُسْتَقِلٌّ. Reduced to a neutrality, as a salt, *etc.*, مُعَدَّل ـ مُعَادَل. Mitigated, مُلَطَّف. Rendered null, مُبْطَل.

Neutralizer, *n.* } That which neutralizes, مُعَادِل ـ مُعَدِّل;
Neutralizing, *a.* } which mitigates, مُلَطِّف; which renders null, مُبْطِل.

Neutrally, *ad.* Without taking sides, حِيَادًا ـ بِدُونِ عَصَبِيَّةٍ ـ عَلَى ٱلْحِيَادِ.

Never, *ad.* قَطُّ ـ أَبَدًا ـ أَصْلًا. Never hereafter, لَيْسَ مِنَ ٱلْآنَ وَصَاعِدًا. It was — so seen amongst us, لَمْ يَظْهَرْ قَطُّ مِثْلُ هٰذَا عِنْدَنَا. He answered him — a word, لَمْ يُجِبْهُ وَلَا عَنْ كِلْمَةٍ وَاحِدَةٍ. I — saw him, مَا رَأَيْتُهُ قَطُّ. I will — speak to him, لَا أُكَلِّمُهُ طَوَالَ ٱلدَّهْرِ. I have — done it, مَا فَعَلْتُهُ أَصْلًا. We had — seen him before, مَا كُنَّا نَرَاهُ أَصْلًا.

Nevertheless, *ad.* مَعَ ذٰلِكَ ـ مَعَ أَنَّ ـ لٰكِنْ. Nevertheless, for your sakes I will do it, لٰكِنْ مِنْ أَجْلِكُمْ أَفْعَلُهُ. Nevertheless, we ..., لٰكِنَّنَا. Nevertheless, he did it, وَمَعَ ذٰلِكَ قَدْ فَعَلَهُ.

New, *a.* جَدِيد *pl.* جُدُد *and* جُدَد ـ مُسْتَجِدٌّ. Recent, حَدِيث ـ حَادِث ـ مُسْتَجِدٌّ. Strange, غَرِيب ـ فَرِيٌّ. Newly invented, recently brought into use, بَدِيع. Fresh, طَرِيٌّ. A — thing, طَرِيف *pl.* طُرَف ـ حَدِيثَة *pl.* حَدِيثَات. A — word, expression, كَلَامٌ جَدِيدٌ ـ كَلَامٌ بَدِيعٌ. Brand —, جَدِيدٌ خَالِصٌ ـ بِجِدَّتِهِ. New, early, fruit, بَاكُورَة ـ بَكِيرَة. New to one, مُسْتَجِدٌّ لَهُ. New style, of the calendar, that used in the west, الحِسَابُ ٱلْغَرْبِيُّ. New year's day, نَوْرُوز ـ رَأْس (or أَوَّل) ٱلسَّنَةِ. To be new, as of a garment, جَدَّ ; to be —, recent, حَدَثَ. To make —, جَدَّدَ; to make —, originate, أَجَدَّ ـ إِسْتَجَدَّ ـ أَحْدَثَ ـ إِخْتَرَعَ. To consider new, إِسْتَجَدَّ ـ إِسْتَطْرَفَ.

New-born, *a.* Newly begotten, مَوْلُودٌ جَدِيدًا. Newly manifested, مُسْتَجِدٌّ.

New-comer, *n.* نَزِيل *pl.* نُزُل.

Newel, *n.* As of a staircase, عَقْدُ ٱلسَّلَالِم.

New-fangled, *a.* بَدِيع ـ بِدْع.

New-fashioned, *a.* As of dress, عَلَى زِيٍّ جَدِيدٍ; of make, عَلَى هَيْئَةٍ جَدِيدَةٍ.

Newish, *a.* جَدِيدٌ نَوْعًا ـ جَدِيدٌ بَعْضَ ٱلْجِدَّةِ.

Newly, *ad.* Lately, جَدِيدًا ـ جِدَّةً ـ حَدِيثًا ـ إِسْتِطْرَافًا. Again, بِهٰذَا ٱلْقُرْبِ ـ مِنْ مُدَّةٍ قَرِيبَةٍ ـ ثَانِيَةً ـ مِنْ جَدِيدٍ ـ ثَانِي مَرَّةٍ. Newly acquired property, طَرِيف ـ طَارِف. He was — appointed, تَعَيَّنَ حَدِيثًا.

New-model, *v.t.* صَوَّرَهُ (جَدَّدَ *or* أَجَدَّ *or*) إِسْتَجَدَّ.

Newness, *n.* جِدَّة. Recentness, حَدَاثَة. Innovation, بِدْعَة. Freshness, طَرَاوَة.

News, *n.* خَبَر *pl.* أَخْبَار ـ خَبَرِيَّة ـ خَبَرٌ. Good —, بِشَارَة ـ خَبَرٌ خَيْرٌ. Bad —, خَبَرُ سُوءٍ; sad —, أَخْبَارٌ مُكَدِّرَةٌ. Home —, أَخْبَارُ ٱلدَّاخِلِيَّةِ; foreign —, أَخْبَارُ ٱلْخَارِجِيَّةِ ـ ٱلْجَوَائِبُ. To ask for —, إِسْتَخْبَرَ ٱلْخَبَرَ ـ تَخَبَّرَ ـ تَخَبَّرَ ٱلْأَخْبَارَ. To ask — from one, تَخَبَّرَهُ ـ إِسْتَخْبَرَهُ. To spread —, أَشَاعَ خَبَرًا; the — was spread, شَاعَ ٱلْخَبَرُ *aor.* يَشِيعُ. The — is again circulated that ..., تَوَاتَرَتِ ٱلْأَخْبَارُ مَرَّةً أُخْرَى أَنْ. On the arrival of the —, عِنْدَ مَجِيءِ ٱلْخَبَرِ. News came to the governor, نَمَا (*or* وَصَلَ) ٱلْخَبَرُ إِلَى ٱلْحَاكِمِ. What is the —? مَا ٱلْخَبَرُ. No — is good —, مَا طَلَعَ خَبَرٌ مَا حَصَلَ ضَرَرٌ. No — has been received of him, مَا سُمِعَ عَنْهُ خَبَرٌ.

Newsmonger, *n.* مُتَعَاطِي ٱلْأَخْبَارِ ـ مُتَفَرِّغٌ لِلْأَخْبَارِ ـ حَوَادِثِيٌّ.

Newspaper, *n.* صَحِيفَةُ ٱلْأَخْبَارِ *pl.* صَحَائِف ـ جَرِيدَة *pl.* جَرَائِد ـ غَزِيتَة *pl.* غَزِيتَات ـ جُرْنَال *pl.* جُرْنَالَات. Editor of a —, مُنْشِئُ ـ صَاحِبُ جُرْنَالٍ ـ مُحَرِّرُ صَحِيفَةٍ ـ جَرِيدَةٍ. *See also under* Journal, *n.*

Newsvender, *n.* بَيَّاعُ ٱلْغَزِيتَاتِ ـ بَيَّاعُ ٱلْجَرَائِدِ.

Newt, *n.* وَرَلٌ صَغِيرٌ.

Newtonian, *a.* نِيُوتُنِيٌّ ـ عَلَى أُصُولِ فَلْسَفَةِ نِيُوتَن ٱلْإِنْكِلِيزِيِّ.

Newtonian, *n.* تَابِعُ فَلْسَفَةِ نِيُوتَن.

Next, *a.* Adjoining, وَلِيٌّ ـ مُتَّصِل. Next following, تَالٍ ـ قَادِم ـ آتٍ. Neighbouring, مُجَاوِر ـ قَرِيبٌ مِن. Second in rank, ثَانٍ. Next day, غَد; on the — day, فِي ٱلْغَدِ; till the evening of — day, إِلَى مَسَاءِ ٱلْغَدِ; the — day after the feast, فِي غَدِ ٱلْعِيدِ. Next year, السَّنَةُ ٱلْآتِيَةُ. Next Saturday, السَّبْتُ ٱلْقَادِمُ. Next, as in rank, to the king, ثَانِي ٱلْمَلِكِ. The —, neighbouring, villages, القُرَى ٱلْمُجَاوِرَةُ. The town next to the castle, المَدِينَةُ ٱلْقُرْبَى مِنَ ٱلْقَلْعَةِ. Next month I shall have been here three years, فِي ٱلشَّهْرِ ٱلْمُقْبِلِ يَكُونُ قَدْ مَضَى عَلَيَّ وَأَنَا هُنَا ثَلٰثُ سِنِينَ. In the — place, ثَانِيَةً ـ وَبَعْدُ. To be —, to follow, تَلَا. To be —, near to, إِقْتَرَبَ مِن.

Next, *ad.* That comes after, بَعْدُ. Firstly, أَوَّلًا. Then, ثُمَّ. A thing — to impossible, شَيْءٌ مُحَالٌ تَقْرِيبًا. I shall be — to thee, أَكُونُ لَكَ ثَانِيًا.

Nib, *n.* A point, سِنٌّ. Nib of a beak or of any thing pointed, سِنَان *pl.* أَسِنَّة. The — of a pen, سِنُّ قَلَمٍ ـ حَرْفُ قَلَمٍ.

Nib, *v.t.* As of a pen, بَرَى ٱلْقَلَمَ ـ. *See also under* Pen, *n.*

Nibbing, *n.* As of a pen, بَرْىُ ٱلْقَلَمِ. He made the — of the pen oblique, حَرَّفَ ٱلْقَلَمَ.

Nibble, *v.t.* To bite by little at a time, ضَغَمَ ـ مَغْمَغَ ـ تَطَعَّمَ ـ عَضْعَضَ ـ قَشْقَشَ ـ ضَغْضَغَ. To —, as sheep the grass, قَرَّطَ ـ قَرَّضَ ; as of birds, to peck, نَقَرَ ـ نَقَّرَ.

Nibble, *v.i.* To — at, to bite at; *see preceding article.* To —, or carp at, نَاقَدَ ـ قَرَضَ بِ ـ نَقَرَ ـ قَرَّطَ ـ قَرَّضَ.

Nibble, *n.* A little bite, ضَغْم ـ ضُغَامَة ـ تَطَعُّم ـ تَقَشِيش ـ ضَغْضَغَة.

Nibbler, *n.* One who bites a little at a time, ضَاغِم ـ قَشَّاش ـ مُتَطَعِّم ـ وَغْمَاغ. A carper, قَرَّاض ـ قَرَّاط ـ مُنَاقِر ـ مُنَاقِد ـ شَتِيم.

Nibbling, *a.* *See* Nibbler, *n.*

Nibbling, *n.* Biting in small bits, ضَغْم ـ مَغْمَغَة ـ ضَغْضَغَة. Carping, نَقْر ـ مُنَاقَدَة ـ قَرْض ـ شَتْم.

Nice, *a.* Fine, small, دَقِيق ـ رَفِيع. Agreeable, pleasing, of a person, حَلِيم ـ حَبَّذَا ـ لَطِيف ـ كَيِّس ـ أَنِيس ـ بَشُوش. Pleasant, of a place, نَزِيه ـ شَرِح ـ بَهِيج ; of a prospect, بَهِيج ـ فَرِح ـ مُبْهِج ـ شَهِيٌّ ; of a trip, excursion, حَبَّذَا ـ جَمِيل. Agreeable to the taste, لَذِيذ ـ طَيِّب ـ مُكَيِّف. Fragrant, عَذِق ـ شَمُوم ـ مُعَطَّر. Pretty, حَسَن ـ جَمِيل ـ حُلْوٌ. Sweet, حُلْوٌ. Clear, pleasant, صَافٍ ـ جَمِيل ـ بَدِيع. Exact, مُدَقِّق ـ مَضْبُوط. Dainty, squeamish, مُتَأَنِّق ـ نَفُور ـ مُتَنَعِّم ; dainty, of food, نَفِيس. Difficult, مُشْكِل. Nice in ..., as in an art, trade, *etc.* مُتَعَمِّد فِي. Nice, in dress, food, cleanliness, or speech, نُطَسَة ; to be —, in these respects, تَنَطَّسَ. To be —, exact, in one's language, دَقَّ فِي ٱلْكَلَامِ *aor.* يَدِقُّ. To be —, dainty, squeamish, تَجَوَّدَ ـ تَأَنَّقَ. To be —, as in an art, trade, *etc.*, تَعَمَّدَ فِي.

Nicely, *ad.* Well, حَسَنًا ـ جَيِّدًا. Accurately, بِدِقَّةٍ ـ عَلَى عَيْنٍ ـ بِضَبْطٍ ـ بِغَايَةِ ٱلْإِتْقَانِ ـ بِٱلتَّدْقِيقِ. Softly, kindly, بِلَطَافَةٍ ـ بِظَرَافَةٍ. Neatly, تَدْقِيقًا ـ بِدِقَّةٍ ـ بِطَلَاوَةٍ. With fragrance, بِعِطْرٍ ـ بِزَكَاءِ ٱلرَّائِحَةِ. (The verbs أَحْسَنَ and أَجْمَلَ may be used with the appropriate nouns to express doing any thing nicely; *e.g.* He acted nicely in the affair, أَجْمَلَ فِي ٱلْأَمْرِ ; he spake nicely, pleasantly, أَحْسَنَ فِي ٱلْقَوْلِ).

Nicene, *a.* نِيقَاوِيٌّ. The — creed, قَانُونُ ٱلْإِيمَانِ ٱلنِّيقَاوِيُّ.

Niceness, *n.* Fineness, smallness, رَقَاعَة ـ دِقَّة. Agreeableness, of a person, حِلْم ـ لَطَافَة ـ كِيَاسَة ـ بَشَاشَة ; of a place, نَزَاهَة ـ بَهْجَة ـ ٱنْشِرَاح. Tastiness, لَذَّة ـ طِيبَة. Fragrance, فَغْمَة ـ عِطْر ـ طِيب ـ رَائِحَة. Prettiness, طَلَاوَة ـ حُسْن ـ جَمَال. Sweetness, حَلَاوَة. Clearness, pleasantness, as of the weather, صَفَاوَة ـ بَدَاعَة ـ بَدُوع ـ جَمَال ـ رَوْنَق. Exactness, دِقَّة ـ ضَبْط. Daintiness, squeamishness, تَأَنُّق ـ تَجَوُّد. To affect —, to be squeamish, تَظَرَّفَ ـ تَأَنَّقَ ـ تَجَوَّدَ.

Nicety, *n.* Exact care, دِقَّة ـ ضَبْط. Fastidiousness, مَلَال ـ مَلَّة ـ ٱسْتِنْكَاف. Niceties, dainties, نَفَائِس ـ رَغَائِب ـ لَذَّات. Subtilties, دَقَائِقُ ٱلْأُمُورِ (or مَدَاقّ). To do to a —, دَقَّ فِي *aor.* يَدِقُّ. To cook something to a —, دَقَّ فِي طَبْخِهِ ـ أَحْسَنَ طَبْخَهُ. To a —, بِٱلتَّمَامِ ـ عَلَى ٱلْكَمَالِ ـ بِغَايَةِ ٱلْإِتْقَانِ.

Niche, *n.* طَاقَات *pl.* طَاق ـ بِهَاء *pl.* سَهْوَة ـ مِشْكَاة. A recess in a wall for shelves, رَفّ *pl.* رُفُوف. The — in a mosque indicating the direction of Mekkah, ٱلْمِحْرَاب.

Nick, *n.* In the — of time, فِي ٱلْحَزَّةِ ـ فِي وَقْتِ ٱلْحَاجَةِ ـ فِي ٱلْمُسْتَحَطِّ. I met him in the — of time, لَقِيتُهُ عَلَى حَزَّةٍ. Old Nick, ٱلشَّيْطَانُ. *See also* Notch, *n.*

Nick, *v.t.* To notch, حَزَّ ـ ٱحْتَزَّ. To do at a lucky time, فَعَلَ عَلَى حَزَّةٍ ـ. *See also to* Notch, *v.t.*

Nickel, *n.* نِكْل ـ مَعْدِنٌ أَبْيَضُ.

Nicknacks, *n.* مَدَاقُّ ٱلْأَشْيَاءِ ـ دَقَائِقُ ٱلْأَمْتِعَةِ.

Nickname, *n.* نَبَز *pl.* أَنْبَاز ـ قِزْيٌ ـ لَقَب *pl.* أَلْقَاب. They called one another nicknames, of many, تَدَاعَوْا بِٱلْأَلْقَابِ.

Nickname, *v.t.* نَبَزَ ـ لَقَّبَ. To be nicknamed, تَلَقَّبَ بِ.

Nicotine, *n.* رُوحُ ٱلدُّخَانِ.

Nictate, *v.i.* طَرَفَ بِعَيْنَيْهِ ـ غَمَزَ بِعَيْنَيْهِ ـ بَرَقَ بِعَيْنَيْهِ.

Nictation, *n.* طَرْفَةُ ٱلْعَيْنِ ـ غَمْزُ ٱلْعَيْنِ ـ بَرِيقُ ٱلْعَيْنِ.

Nidificate, *v.t.* ٱتَّكَرَ ـ أَعْشَشَ ـ عَشَّشَ.

Nidification, *n.* ٱتِّكَار ـ تَعْشِيش.

Nidus, *n.* A nest, عُشّ *pl.* عِشَاش. *See also* Cyst, *n.*

Niece, *n.* A brother's daughter, بِنْتُ أَخٍ *pl.* بَنَاتُ أَخٍ ; sister's daughter, بِنْتُ أُخْتٍ *pl.* بَنَاتُ أُخْتٍ.

Niggard, *n.* }
Niggard, *a.* } A miser or miserly, لَحِز ـ ضَنِين ـ نَكِد ـ جَحِد ـ شَحِيح ـ حَظِل ـ بَخِيل ـ قَذِر ـ خَسِيس.
Niggardly, *a.* } Very niggardly, شَدِيدُ ٱلْبُخْلِ. A — wealthy man, عَنْزٌ عَزُوزٌ لَهَا دَرٌّ جَمٌّ (*lit.* A she-goat narrow in the orifices of the teats that has much milk). To be a niggard, niggardly, عَسُرَ ـ جَحِدَ ـ بَخِلَ ـ يَشُحُّ *aor.* شَحَّ. To be — towards,

بَخِلَ عَلَى ,ـَ . To be — of, بَخُلَ بِ ,ـُ . To be —, as in giving, قَصَّرَ فِي . To charge one with being —, بَخَّلَ . To find one to be —, أَبْخَلَ .

Niggardliness, *n.* خَسَاسَة ـ جُحْد ـ بُخْل ـ شُحّ .

Niggardly, *ad.* بِخَسَاسَةٍ ـ كَالْبَخِيلِ ـ بِبُخْلٍ ـ بِشُحٍّ .

Nigh, *a.* *See* Near, *a.*

Nigh, *ad.* قَرِيبًا مِن . Nigh unto death, قَرِيبًا مِنَ ٱلْمَوْتِ . *See also* Near, *ad.*

Nighness, *n.* *See* Nearness, *n.*

Night, *n.* لَيْل *pl.* لَيَالٍ ـ لَيْلَة *pl.* لَيَالٍ *and* لَيَالِي . A cold and damp —, لَيْلَةٌ خَدِرَةٌ . A bright —, لَيْلَةٌ إِضْحِيَّةٌ ; a dark —, لَيْلَةٌ مُغْدِرَةٌ ـ لَيْلَةٌ ظَلْمَاءُ ـ لَيْلَةٌ دَأْدَاءٌ . To-night, اللَّيْلَةَ ; last —, فِي تِلْكَ ٱللَّيْلَةِ ـ لَيْلَتَئِذٍ ; in that —, لَيْلَةَ ٱلْبَارِحَةِ ـ ٱلْبَارِحَةَ ; to-morrow —, لَيْلَةَ غَدًا . I saw him to-night, رَأَيْتُهُ ٱللَّيْلَةَ ; I met him last —, لَقِيتُهُ ٱلْبَارِحَةَ ; I met him the — before last, لَقِيتُهُ ٱلْبَارِحَةَ ٱلْأُولَى . The — wore away, مَالَ ٱللَّيْلُ ,ـِ . Night overtook us, هَجَمَ عَلَيْنَا ٱللَّيْلُ ,ـُ . He died the same —, مَاتَ مِنْ لَيْلَتِهَا . Night is at hand, أَسْحَرَ ٱللَّيْلُ . Night and day, لَيْلَ وَنَهَارَ ; by — and by day, لَيْلًا وَنَهَارًا . At —, عِنْدَ ٱللَّيْلِ . Good — to you! لَيْلَتُكَ سَعِيدَةٌ ; (the courteous reply is, بِرُؤْيَاكُمْ). The — of the ceremony of conducting a bride to her husband, لَيْلَةُ ٱلدُّخْلَةِ . The Arabian Nights, كِتَابُ أَلْفِ لَيْلَةٍ وَلَيْلَةٍ . Night, obscurity, ظُلْمَة . Ignorance, جَهَالَة ـ جَهْل . To sit up at —, or to pass the —, بَيَّتَ ـ بَاتَ ,ـِ . To sit up at —, or to watch by —, سَهِرَ ,ـَ .

Nightcap, *n.* As for the head, تَخْفِيفَةُ ٱلرَّأْسِ ـ قَلَوْسَة . A last draught at night, غَبُوق .

Nightfall, *n.* عَشْوَة ـ عِشَاء ـ وَقْتُ ٱللَّيْلِ ـ ٱلعَتَمَة . He came to me at —, جَاءَ إِلَيَّ عَشِيَّةً . The prayer of —, صَلَاةُ ٱلْعِشَاءِ .

Nightgown, *n.* قَمِيصُ ٱللَّيْلِ .

Nighthawk, *n.* طَيْرُ ٱللَّيْلِ .

Nightingale, *n.* عَنْدَلِيب *pl.* عَنَادِلُ ـ صِفْرِد *pl.* صَفَارِدُ ـ بُلْبُل *pl.* بَلَابِل ـ هَزَار ـ أَبُو ٱلْمَلِيحِ .

Nightly, *a.* وَاقِعٌ فِي ٱللَّيْلِ ـ لَيْلِيٌّ . A — visitor, or anything coming at night, طَارِق . A — lodging-place, دِمَّة .

Nightly, *ad.* In the night, بِٱللَّيْلِ ـ لَيْلًا . Every night, فِي كُلِّ لَيْلَةٍ .

Nightman, *n.* مَشَاعِلِيٌّ ـ خَرَابَشِيٌّ ـ مُنَقٍّ ـ شَرَابَاتِيٌّ ـ نَزَّاح .

Nightmare, *n.* جَاثُوم ـ جُثَام ـ الزُّكَاب ـ كَابُوس ـ ضَاغُوط ـ حِمَارُ ٱللَّيْلِ . The — seized him, عَلَاهُ ٱلزُّكَابُ .

Nightshade, *n.* The plant, حَلْوَة مُرَّة ـ عِنَبُ ٱلذِّئْبِ ـ كَاكْنَج . The deadly —, حَشِيشَةُ ٱلْحِمَارِ . The creeping —, عِنَبُ ٱلثَّعْلَبِ .

Night-soil, *n.* أَوْسَاخ .

Night-time, *n.* *See* Nightfall, *n.*

Night-vision, *n.* A vision at night, رُؤَى ٱللَّيْلِ .

Night-waking, *n.* سَهَر .

Night-walker, *n.* One who strolls about at night, عَائِرُ ٱللَّيْلِ ـ دَوَّار (*or* عَيَّار) ٱللَّيْلِ . A somnambulist, مَنْ يَمْشِي وَهُوَ نَائِمٌ ـ مَاشٍ فِي نَوْمِهِ .

Night-watch, *n.* A night patrol, عَاسّ *pl.* عَسَس ـ عَسَّاس . A part or vigil of the night, هَزِيع *pl.* هُزَع .

Nigrescent, *a.* مُسْوَدٌّ ـ يَضْرِبُ إِلَى ٱلسَّوَادِ .

Nihilism, *n.* } Non-existence, العُدْم ـ العَدَم ـ العَدَمُ . The doctrine of
Nihility, } the modern Nihilists of Russia, مَذْهَبُ حِلْقَةٍ سِرِّيَّةٍ فِي بِلَادِ ٱلرُّوسِيَّةِ تَتَأَلَّفُ مِنْ قَوْمٍ يَتَأَلَّبُونَ عَلَى قَلْبِ ٱلدَّوْلَةِ ـ مَذْهَبُ ٱلْإِبَاحِيِّينَ .

Nihilist, *n.* مِنْ أَهْلِ ٱلْحِلْقَةِ ٱلْمَذْكُورَةِ .

Nile, *n.* The river, النِّيلُ ٱلْمُبَارَكُ ـ ٱلنِّيلُ . The — is rising, النِّيلُ أَخَذَ فِي ٱلزِّيَادَةِ .

Nill, *v.i.* To be unwilling, أَبَى *aor.* يَأْبَى .

Willy-nilly, *ad.* بِٱلطِّيبِ ـ بِٱلْغَصْبِ أَوْ بِٱلرِّضَاءِ ـ طَوْعًا أَوْ كَرْهًا أَوْ بِٱلْغَصْبِ .

Nilometer, *n.* That of the Nile, المِقْيَاس ـ مِقْيَاسُ ٱلنِّيلِ .

Nimble, *a.* شِمْلِيل ـ سَرِيع ـ حَرِك ـ نَشِط ـ نَدْب ـ أَلْوَب ـ شَاطِر ـ نَاشِط ـ نَبِيه ـ خَفِيف ـ فَزّ .

Nimble-fingered, handy with the fingers, *a.* صَنَاعُ ٱلْيَدَيْنِ .

Nimble-footed, *a.* شَجِعُ ٱلْقَوَائِمِ .

Nimbleness, *n.* شَمْلَلَة ـ سُرْعَة ـ مُرُوءَة ـ نَشَاط ـ خِفَّة ـ حِدَّة .

Nimbly, *ad.* بِشَمْلَلَةٍ ـ بِسُرْعَةٍ ـ بِنَشَاطٍ ـ بِخِفَّةٍ .

Nimbus, *n.* The circle of rays round the heads of saints, *etc.*, طُفَاوَة ـ هَالَة . A rain cloud, سَحَابٌ مَاطِرٌ .

Nincompoop, *n.* *See* Blockhead, *n.*

Nine, *n.* تِسْعَة *fem.* تِسْع . Nine men, تِسْعَةُ رِجَالٍ ; nine women, تِسْعُ نِسْوَةٍ . It is — o'clock, السَّاعَةُ تِسْعٌ . To make —, تَسَّعَ . A rope of — strands, مَتْسُوع .

Ninefold, *a.* تِسْعُ طَاقَاتٍ .

Ninepins, *n.* ضَرْبٌ مِنَ ٱللَّعِبِ .

Nine-holes, *n.* The old Arabic game of, المَدَاحِي ـ المَسَاوِي (the ball is called مِدْحَاة and each of the holes أُدْحِيَّة).

Nine-score, *a.* مِئَةٌ وَثَمَانُونَ.

Nineteen, *a.* تِسْعَ عَشَرَ *fem.* تِسْعَةَ عَشْرَةَ.

Nineteenth, *a.* التَّاسِعَ عَشَرَ *fem.* التَّاسِعَةَ عَشْرَةَ.

Ninetieth, *a.* التِّسْعُونَ.

Ninety, *a.* تِسْعُونَ.

Ninny, *n.* / Ninny-hammer, } أَرْقَعُ *fem.* رَقْعَاءُ. *See also* Fool, Greenhorn, Dolt, Dunce, *n.*

Ninth, *a.* تَاسِعٌ *fem.* تَاسِعَةٌ.

Ninth, *n.* تُسْعٌ — تُسُعٌ.

Niobium, *n.* نِيُوبِيُومُ وَهُوَ ضَرْبٌ مِنَ ٱلْمَعَادِنِ.

Nip, *v.t.* To pinch, قَرَصَ. To bite, عَضَّ. To break off, قَطَعَ — قَطَفَ — جَزَرَ — نَتَفَ. To blast, as herbage, شَوَّطَ — أَذْبَلَ — أَحْرَقَ — سَلَقَ. To — anything in the bud, destroy its beginnings, هَدَمَ أَوَائِلَهُ. To vex, قَرَصَ — أَضْجَرَ; with words, سَلَقَ بِٱلْكَلَامِ — لَذَعَ. The cold nipped the herbage, سَلَقَ ٱلْبَرْدُ ٱلنَّبَاتَ.

Nip, *n.* A pinch, قَرْصَةٌ. A bite, عَضَّةٌ. A blasting, سَلْقٌ — تَشْوِيطٌ — إِذْبَالٌ. A small quantity, لَطْخٌ — نُتْفَةٌ *pl.* نُتَفٌ — يَسِيرٌ; a small draught, مَصَّةٌ — مَصٌّ.

Nip-cat, *n.* The game, لَعْبُ ٱلْقُلَةِ (or ٱلْقُلَاتِ).

Nipper, *n.* A fore tooth, ثَنِيَّةٌ *pl.* ثَنَايَا. A pincher, biter, عَضَّاضٌ — قَرَّاصٌ.

Nippers, *n.* مِلْقَطٌ *pl.* مَلَاقِطُ — مِنْقَشٌ — مِنْقَاشٌ.

Nipping, *a.* Pinching, قَرَّاصٌ; biting, عَضَّاضٌ; blasting, سَالِقٌ — مُحْرِقٌ — مُذْبِلٌ. Cutting, tart, سَالِقٌ — حَادٌّ — لَاذِعٌ. Nipping cold, زَمْهَرِيرٌ.

Nippingly, *ad.* Tartly, بِحِدَّةٍ — بِغَضَبٍ — بِنِكَايَةٍ.

Nipple, *n.* حَلَمَةٌ *pl.* حَلَمَاتٌ — حَلَمَةُ ٱلثَّدْيِ — سَعْدَانَةٌ — قُرَادٌ. The — of a musket, حَلَمَةُ ٱلْبَارُودَةِ. The areola round the —, سَعْدَانَةُ ٱلثَّدْيِ.

Nisân, *n.* The month, شَهْرُ نِيسَانَ.

Nisi Prius, The Court of, إِسْمُ مَحْكَمَةٍ بِبِلَادِ ٱلْإِنْكِلِيزِ.

Nit, *n.* صُؤَابَةٌ *pl.* صِئْبَانٌ — صِيبَانَةٌ. Nits, أَعَاوِرُ — بَنَاتُ ٱلدُّرُوزِ — صِئْبَانٌ.

Nitrate, *n.* نِتْرَاتٌ — مِلْحٌ مُرَكَّبٌ مِنَ ٱلتِّيزَابِ وَأُسٍّ آخَرَ. Nitrate of potash, مِلْحُ ٱلْأُشْنَانِ. Nitrate of silver, نِتْرَاتُ ٱلْفِضَّةِ — حَجَرُ جَهَنَّمَ.

Nitre, *n.* نَطْرُونٌ — مِلْحُ بَارُودٍ — بَارُودٌ أَبْيَضُ.

Nitric, *a.* مَنْسُوبٌ تِيزَابٌ. Nitric acid, تِيزَابٌ خَالِصٌ.

Nitrify, *v.i.* صَارَ نَطْرُونًا — إِسْتَحَالَ إِلَى نَطْرُونٍ.

Nitrification, *n.* الْإِسْتِحَالَةُ إِلَى نَطْرُونٍ.

Nitrite, *n.* مِلْحٌ مُرَكَّبٌ مِنْ مَادَّةٍ مِنْ جِنْسِ ٱلتِّيزَابِ وَأُسٍّ آخَرَ.

Nitrogen, *n.* نِتْرُوجِين — مُوَلِّدُ ٱلنَّطْرُونِ — أُمُّ ٱلنَّطْرُونِ.

Nitrogenous, *a.* نِتْرُوجِينِيٌّ — مُوَلِّدُ ٱلنَّطْرُونِ.

Nitrous, *a.* / Nitry, } كَٱلْقِلْيِ — نَطْرُونِيٌّ — كَٱلنَّطْرُونِ.

Nitty, *a.* Full of nits, مَلْآنٌ مِنَ ٱلصِّئْبَانِ.

Niveous, *a.* Like snow, مِثْلُ ٱلثَّلْجِ — كَٱلثَّلْجِ.

N.N.E., (north-north-east), بَيْنَ ٱلشَّمَالِيِّ وَٱلشَّمَالِيِّ ٱلشَّرْقِيِّ.

N.N.W., (north-north-west), بَيْنَ ٱلشَّمَالِيِّ وَٱلشَّمَالِيِّ ٱلْغَرْبِيِّ.

Nizâm, *n.* The —, one of the sovereigns of India, حَضْرَةُ ٱلنِّظَامِ. The Turkish regular troops, عَسْكَرُ ٱلنِّظَامِ.

No, *a.* No one, لَا أَحَدَ — لَيْسَ أَحَدٌ. Not any, أَلْبَتَّةَ — أَصْلًا. In no place, أَصْلًا — لَيْسَ فِي مَوْضِعٍ مِنَ ٱلْمَوَاضِعِ. With no expense, بِلَا مَصْرُوفٍ أَصْلًا. No bread is given to them, لَيْسَ يُعْطَى لَهُمْ مِنَ ٱلْخُبْزِ. He had no sons, but daughters, لَمْ يَكُنْ لَهُ بَنُونَ بَلْ بَنَاتٌ. There was no day like that day either before or after, لَمْ يَكُنْ مِثْلُ ذٰلِكَ ٱلْيَوْمِ قَبْلَهُ وَلَا بَعْدَهُ. There was no king like Solomon, لَمْ يَكُنْ مَلِكٌ مِثْلَ سُلَيْمَانَ. He gave no answer, لَمْ يُجِبْ. No evil shall befall you, لَا يُلَاقِيكَ شَرٌّ. I have no husband, لَيْسَ لِي زَوْجٌ. We have no such custom, لَيْسَ لَنَا عَادَةٌ مِثْلُ هٰذِهِ. They have no need of a lamp, لَا يَحْتَاجُونَ إِلَى سِرَاجٍ. There had been no rain, لَمْ يَكُنْ مَطَرٌ. No, no one, (used as a negative particle,) قُلَّ: No man says so but Zaid, قُلَّ رَجُلٌ يَقُولُ ذٰلِكَ إِلَّا زَيْدٌ. No one like him was to be met with in past ages, لَا يُعْهَدُ لَهُ نَظِيرٌ فِي سَالِفِ ٱلدُّهُورِ.

No, *ad.* لَا. No, certainly not, كَلَّا. No, no, no, كَلَّا وَلَا وَلَا. No, not at all, never, أَصْلًا — قَطْعًا — قَطُّ. He said, no, قَالَ لَا. I will try them whether they know it or no, أَمْتَحِنُهُمْ أَيَعْرِفُونَهُ أَمْ لَا. I never met with anything like it, no not in the East, لَمْ أَجِدْ مِثْلَهُ وَلَا فِي ٱلْمَشْرِقِ. No, not one, وَلَا وَاحِدٌ.

No., *n.* (For Number), عِبَارَةٌ عَنْ عَدَدٍ أَوْ نُمْرَةٍ.

Noachian, *a.* مَنْسُوبٌ إِلَى حَضْرَةِ نُوحٍ.

Nob, *n.* *See* Head, *n.*

Nobilitate, *v.t.* *See to* Ennoble, *v.t.*

Nobility, *n.* Dignity of mind, نَبَالَةٌ — رِفْعَةٌ — كَرَامَةٌ — كَرَمٌ — نَجَابَةٌ — شُرْفَةٌ — شَرَفٌ — عُلُوٌّ. Distinction of family or rank, شَرَفٌ. The —, الْأَعْيَانُ — النُّبَلَاءُ — الشُّرَفَاءُ — الْأَرْكَانُ — نَوَاصِي ٱلنَّاسِ — الْأَكَابِرُ. A patent of —, بَرَاءَةُ ٱلتَّشْرِيفِ. Thy — is lofty and thy good fortune high, شَرَفُكَ تَامِكٌ وَإِقْبَالُكَ سَامِكٌ.

Noble, *a.* Dignified, excellent in worth, خَطِير ـ حُرّ *pl.* أَحْرَار ـ كَرِيم *pl.* كِرَام and كُرَمَآء ـ كُرَام *pl.* كُرَّمُونَ ـ أَصْل *pl.* أُصَلآء ـ كَرْم ـ نَبِيل *pl.* نِبَال ـ A — man, رَجُل كَرْم *pl.* رِجَال كَرْم ; a — woman, إِمْرَأَة كَرْم *pl.* نِسَآء كَرْم . Of high or ancient family, كَرِيم ـ شَرِيف *pl.* شُرَفَآء ـ نَجِيب *pl.* نُجَبَآء ـ أَصِيل *pl.* أُصَلآء ـ عَظِيمُ ٱلشَّأْنِ ـ سَنِيّ ـ فَخْم *pl.* فِخَام . High in rank, عَظِيمُ ٱلشَّأْنِ ـ سَنِيّ ـ فَخْم *pl.* فِخَام . Liberal, جَوَاد ـ سَخِيّ *pl.* أَسْخِيَآء ـ ذُو خَيْر ـ صَاحِبُ مُرُوَّة . Candid, سَلِيم ـ نَصُوح ـ صَارِح ـ صَادِق ـ Great, grand, عَظِيم ـ جَلِيل ـ فَاخِر ـ جَلِيّ . A — deed, مَكْرُمَة *pl.* مَكَارِم . To make —, شَرَّفَ ; to be made — by, تَشَرَّفَ بِ .

Noble, *n.* One of elevated rank, عَظِيمُ ٱلشَّأْنِ ـ فَخْم *pl.* فِخَام ـ سَنِيّ . The nobles; *see under* Nobility, *n.*

Nobleman, *n.* A man of high birth; *see under* Noble, *a.*

Nobleness, *n.* Worth, excellence, كَرَامَة ـ كَرَم ـ نُبْلَة . *See also* Nobility, *n.*

Noblesse, *n.* *See* The Nobility, *under* Nobility, *n.*

Nobly, *ad.* With dignity, بِرِفْعَة ـ كَٱلْحُرّ ـ بِكَرَامَة ـ بِنَجَابَة ـ بِنَبَالَة . With liberality, بِمُرُوَّة ـ بِسَخَاوَة ـ بِجُود . With splendour, بِبَهْجَة ـ بِفَخْر ـ بِجَلَال . Nobly born, كَرِيمُ ٱلْعُنْصُرِ ـ شَرِيفُ ٱلْأَصْلِ .

Nobody, *n.* لَيْسَ أَحَدٌ . Nobody is with us, لَيْسَ أَحَدٌ مَعَنَا . Nobody could enter, لَمْ يَكُنْ أَحَدٌ يَقْدِرُ أَنْ يَدْخُلَ . They saw — but..., لَمْ يَرَوْا أَحَدًا إِلَّا . We found — within, inside, لَمْ نَجِدْ فِي ٱلدَّاخِلِ أَحَدًا .

Nocent, *a.* *See* Hurtful, *a.*

Noctambulation, *n.* ٱلْمَشْيُ فِي ٱلنَّوْمِ .

Noctambulist, *n.* *See* Night-walker, *n.*

Noctum, *n.* An office of devotion at night, صَلَاةُ ٱللَّيْلِ ; for daybreak, صَلَاةُ ٱلْفَجْرِ .

Nocturnal, *a.* *See* Nightly, *a.*

Nocuous, *a.* *See* Hurtful, Injurious, *a.*

Nod, *v.t.* To bow, bend, ثَنَى ـ حَنَى . To shake, حَرَّكَ ـ هَزَّ ـ هَزْهَزَ . To — approbation, هَزَّ رَأْسَهُ ٱسْتِحْسَانًا . He nodded, bent, his head, نَكَسَ رَأْسَهُ .

Nod, *v.i.* To bow the head, نَكَسَ رَأْسَهُ . To — from drowsiness, نَاَن ـ خَفَقَ بِرَأْسِهِ ـ أَخْفَقَ ـ خَفَقَ . To flutter, خَفَقَ . To make a sign with the head, أَخْفَقَ بِرَأْسِهِ . To — to, make a sign to with the head, أَوْمَأَ إِلَى ـ بِرَأْسِهِ . To — to, to salute, سَلَّمَ عَلَى .

Nod, *n.* As in drowsiness, خَفْقَة . A movement, fluttering, حَرَكَة ـ خَفَقَان ـ خَفْق . A bow, obeisance, خُضُوع ـ سَلَام . A command, أَمْر . To beckon with a —, أَشَارَ إِلَى ـ بِرَأْسِهِ . To have at one's nod, كَانَ تَحْتَ أَمْرِهِ .

Nodding, *n.* As in drowsiness, نَوَدَان ـ نَوَاد ـ نَوْد ـ خُفُوق .

Nodding, *a.* Fluttering, quivering, خَفُوق ـ خَافِق . Moving the head in drowsiness, خَافِق . Nodding plumes, رِيش خَافِق .

Nodal, *a.* Belonging to the node of a plant, مُتَعَلِّق بِٱلْحَسَكِ (or بِٱلْعُقْدَة); to the intersection of the ecliptic, مُتَعَلِّق بِٱلْعُقْدَة . The — point, مَحَطُّ ٱلْعُقْدَة .

Nodated, *a.* *See* Knotty, *a.*

Nodder, *n.* One who nods in sleep, خَفُوق ـ خَافِق ـ نَائِد .

Noddle, *n.* *See* Head, *n.*

Node, *n.* As of a plant, عُقْدَة ـ حَسَكَة . A swelling in the bones, عُقْدَة *pl.* عُقَد . In astronomy, عُقْدَة . The ascending —, ٱلْعُقْدَةُ ٱلْفَوْقَانِيَّة ; the descending —, ٱلْعُقْدَةُ ٱلتَّحْتَانِيَّة .

Nodose, *a.*, Nodous, } *See* Knotty, *a.*

Nodosity, *n.* *See* Knottiness, *n.*

Nodular, *n.* كَٱلْعُقْدَة ـ دُبْلِيّ .

Nodule, *n.* دُبْلَة حَجَر *pl.* دُبَل ـ عُقْدَة *pl.* عُقَد .

Noggin, *n.* *See* Mug, Cup, *n.*

Noise, *n.* In a general sense, لَغَط *pl.* أَلْغَاط ـ صَوْت ـ حِسّ ـ ضَجَّة ـ ضَجِيج ـ زِيَاط . Clamour, صُرَاخ ـ صِيَاح ـ جَنَّات . Sound, صَوْت *pl.* أَصْوَات . A confused —, غَاغَة ـ رَجَّة ـ لَغَط ـ جَلَبَة ـ طَشَّة ـ غَوْشَة . A — of quarrelling, disturbance, ضَجَاج ـ فِتْنَة ـ غَوْشَة ـ مُقَاتَلَة . A — of rejoicing, صَوْتُ فَرَح ـ هُتَاف ; of wailing, صَوْتُ بُكَآء ـ بُكَآء . The — of the sea, عَجِيجُ ٱلْبَحْرِ ; of war, صَوْتُ ٱلْقِتَالِ ـ وَغَى ; of musical instruments, رَنَّة ; of coin, صَرِيرَة ; of machinery, or of the blazing of fire, زَمْزَمَة ; of arms, خَشْخَش ـ وَغَى ; of rustling feet, of fluttering wings, of rumbling wings, خَفْق ـ خَفَقَان ; of thunder or rain, مُجَلْجِل . Noise of dogs, هَرِير . Noise, report, صِيت ـ صَات ـ سُمْعَة . To make a noise, uproar, قَرْقَعَ ـ لَغَطَ ـ زَاطَ : They raised a —, of many, made a clamour, جَلَّبُوا ـ أَجْلَبُوا ـ جَلَبُوا . To make a — in the world, إِنْتَشَرَ صَوْتُهُ فِي ٱلنَّاسِ ـ صَارَ مَشْهُورًا فِي ٱلنَّاسِ . Don't make a —, أُسْكُتْ ـ لَا تَزِطْ . What means this —? مَا هُوَ هٰذَا ٱلصَّوْتُ .

Noise, *v.t.* To — abroad, أَذَاعَ ـ أَفْشَى ـ إِشْتَهَرَ ـ شَهَرَ . To be noised abroad, إِنْتَشَرَ ـ فَاضَ ـ فَشَا . When this was noised abroad, لَمَّا صَارَ هٰذَا ٱلصَّوْتُ .

Noiseless, *a.* Without noise, بِدُونِ — بِدُونِ زَيْطَةٍ — بِدُونِ حِسٍّ. Without clamour, بِدُونِ — بِدُونِ صِيَاحٍ (or جَلَبَةٍ) ضَجِيجٍ. Without sound, بِدُونِ صَوْتٍ. Silent, بِدُونِ صُرَاخٍ — حِتَاتٍ. صَامِت — سَاكُوت — صِمِّيت.

Noisily, *ad.* بِحِسٍّ — بِلَغَطٍ — بِضَجِيجٍ — بِزَيْطٍ. With clamour, بِصُرَاخٍ — بِصِيَاحٍ — بِحِتَاتٍ — بِجَلَبَةٍ.

Noisiness, *n.* *See* Noise, *n.*

Noisome, *a.* Hurtful, مُؤْذٍ — مُضِرٌّ — خَبِيث — رَدِيء. Offensive, stinking, وَسِخٌ — دَفِر — سَيِّئٌ. Dirty, filthy, دَرِن. *See also* Hurtful, *a.*

Noisomely, *ad.* Hurtfully, بِمَضَرَّةٍ — بِرَدَاءَةٍ. With ill odour, بِدَفَرَةٍ — بِنَتَانَةٍ. Filthily, بِدَرَنٍ.

Noisomeness, *n.* Hurtfulness, خُبْث — مَضَرَّة — رَدَاءَة. Offensiveness of smell, نَتَانَة — دَفَر — دَفَرَة. Filthiness, دَرَن. *See also* Hurtfulness, Injuriousness, *n.*

Noisy, *a.* مُقَرْقِع — زَائِط — لَغَّاط — لَاغِط — صَيِّت — صَائِت. Clamorous, ضَجُوج — صَارِخ — صَيَّاح — ضَاجّ. A — fellow, جِلِبَّان — رَجُلٌ صَاتٌ (or صَيِّتٌ). A — clamorous woman, جَلَبَّان — مُجَلِّبَة — جَلَّابَة.

Nole-cole, *n.* كُرُنْب.

Nolens-volens, بِٱلطَّيِّبِ أَوْ بِٱلْغَصْبِ — طَوْعًا أَوْ كَرْهًا — عَنْ كَرَاهِيَةٍ.

Nolle prosequi, عِبَارَةٌ عَنْ إِضْرَابِ ٱلْمُدَّعِي عَنْ دَعْوَاهُ رَسْمًا.

Nomad, *n.* نَاقِل *pl.* نَوَاقِل — أَهْلُ ٱلْبَدْوِ — أَهْلُ ٱلْوَبَرِ. Nomads and village- or town-residents, أَهْلُ ٱلْوَبَرِ وَأَهْلُ ٱلْمَدَرِ.

Nomadic, *a.* *See* Migratory, *a.*

Nomadism, *n.* إِنْتِقَال — نُقْلَة.

Nomadize, *v.i.* إِنْتَقَلَ — تَنَقَّلَ.

Nombles, *n.* أَحْشَاءُ ٱلظَّبْيِ.

Nom de Guerre, *n.* إِسْمٌ عَرَضِيٌّ. Nom de plume تَخَلُّص

Nomenclator, *n.* مُسَمِّي ٱلْأَسْمَاءِ — مُنَسِّقُ ٱلْأَسْمَاءِ.

Nomenclature, *n.* System of names, تَرْتِيبُ أَسْمَاءٍ — نَسَقُ أَسْمَاءٍ — سِيَاقَة — تَسْمِيَة.

Nominal, *a.* In name only, بِٱلِٱسْمِ فَقَطْ — بِٱللَّفْظِ فَقَطْ. Pertaining to a noun, إِسْمِيٌّ — سُمَوِيٌّ — سِمَاوِيٌّ. Reputed, إِعْتِبَارِيٌّ. A — list, سِيَاقَة — جَدْوَلُ (or دَفْتَرُ) أَسْمَاءٍ. Nominal value, قِيمَةٌ ٱعْتِبَارِيَّةٌ.

Nominally, *ad.* In name, بِٱلِٱسْمِ فَقَطْ — لَفْظًا — إِسْمًا. Reputedly, عَلَى مَا كَانَ يُظَنُّ — إِعْتِبَارًا.

Nominate, *v.t.* To name, سَمَّى. To appoint, جَعَلَ — أَقَامَ. وَجَّهَ — عَيَّنَ — قَلَّدَ. To propose, عَرَضَ. To be nominated, appointed, جُعِلَ — وُجِّهَ — تَعَيَّنَ.

Nomination, *n.* The act of naming, تَسْمِيَة; of appointing, تَعْيِين — تَوْجِيه — تَقْلِيد. The being nominated, تَقَلُّد — تَعَيُّن.

Nominative, *a.* Pertaining to the — case of nouns, مَرْفُوع. A word in the — case, لَفْظَةٌ مَرْفُوعَةٌ.

Nominative, *n.* The first case of nouns, ٱلرَّفْعُ — رَفْع.

Nominator, *n.* One who names or appoints, صَاحِبُ ٱلتَّسْمِيَةِ — مُوَجِّه — مُعَيِّن.

Nominee, *n.* مُوَجَّه — مُعَيَّن — مُسَمًّى — مُشَخَّص.

Non, أَدَاةُ نَفْيٍ.

Nonage, *n.* قِصَرُ ٱلْأَوْلَادِ — صَبَاوَة — صُغْرَى.

Nonagenarian, *n.* بَالِغٌ تِسْعِينَ سَنَةً.

Nonagesimal, *a.* Ninetieth, ٱلتِّسْعُونَ. Noting the highest point of the ecliptic above the horizon, أَعْلَى نُقْطَةٍ سَمْتِ ٱلشَّمْسِ عَنِ ٱلْأُفُقِ.

Non-appearance, *n.* عَدَمُ وُجُودٍ — عَدَمُ حُضُورٍ — عَدَمُ ظُهُورٍ — غَيْبَة — غِيَاب.

Non-approval, *n.* عَدَمُ ٱسْتِصْوَابٍ.

Non-attendance, *n.* Want of assiduity, عَدَمُ تَقَيُّدٍ — عَدَمُ مُبَاشَرَةٍ. *See also* Non-appearance, *n.*

Nonce, *n.* دَفْعَة — فُرْصَة. For the —, لِهٰذِهِ ٱلدَّفْعَةِ — لِهٰذِهِ ٱلْمَرَّةِ — لِلْحَاضِرِ.

Nonchalance, *n.* قِلَّةُ مُرُوَّةٍ — تَهَامُل — تَسَاهُل.

Non-commissioned, *a.* بِلَا بَرَاءَةٍ. A — officer, قَائِدُ ٱلْعَشَرَةِ — مِنْ دَرَجَةِ ٱلْأُونْ بَاشِي وَٱلْجَاوِيش.

Non-compliance, *n.* عَدَمُ رِضَاءٍ — عَدَمُ ٱسْتِجَابَةٍ — عَدَمُ إِيجَابٍ — إِبَاءٌ — إِبَاءَة — مُخَالَفَة — إِمْتِنَاع.

Non compos, a. / *Non compos mentis,* } أَبْلَهُ — مَجْنُون — فِي عَقْلِهِ هَبْتَةٌ — غَبِيٌّ.

Non-concurrence, *n.* عَدَمُ رِضَاءٍ — عَدَمُ قُبُولٍ — عَدَمُ مُوَافَقَةٍ — إِبَاءَة — إِمْتِنَاع.

Non-conductor, *n.* As of electricity, جِسْمٌ لَا يُشْرِكُ ٱلْكَهْرَبَائِيَّةَ.

Nonconforming, *a.* / Nonconformist, *n.* } Of religious dissent, غَيْرُ تَابِعٍ لِلْكَنِيسَةِ ٱلْمَلَكِيَّةِ — مُعْتَزِلٌ عَنِ ٱلْكَنِيسَةِ ٱلْمَلَكِيَّةِ. Not agreeing, غَيْرُ مُطَابِقٍ.

Nonconformity, *n.* Want of conformity, عَدَمُ مُطَابَقَةٍ. Of religious dissent, عَدَمُ مُتَابَعَةٍ لِلْكَنِيسَةِ ٱلْمَلَكِيَّةِ — إِعْتِزَالٌ عَنِ ٱلْكَنِيسَةِ ٱلْمَلَكِيَّةِ.

Non-contagious, *a.* غَيْرُ مُعْدٍ — غَيْرُ مُعْتَدٍ.

Non-content, *a.* and *n.* رَادٌّ عَلَى — غَيْرُ رَاضٍ بِ — آبٍ *pl.* آبُونَ *and* أُبَاة *and* أُبِيٌّ.

Non-delivery, *n.* عَدَمُ تَوْزِيعٍ ـ عَدَمُ تَسْلِيمٍ.

Nondescript, *a.* مَجْهُول ـ عَجِيب ـ غَرِيب ـ لا يُعْرَف.

Nondescript, *n.* غَرِيبَة ـ عَجِيبَة ـ شَيْءٌ غَرِيبٌ.

None, *a.* and *n.* No one, لَيْسَ أَحَدٌ ـ لا أَحَدٌ ; nothing, لا شَيْءَ. *The following examples will best convey how this word is rendered in Arabic:* None of those, لا وَاحِدٌ مِنْ أُولٰئِكَ. There is — here of that name, لَيْسَ أَحَدٌ هُنَا بِهٰذَا ٱلْاسْمِ. I have — of it, لَيْسَ لِي مِنْهُ. None of them shall return to his home, لا يَرْجِعُ أَحَدٌ مِنْهُمْ إِلَى وَطَنِهِ. He speaks to — of them but his brother, لا يُكَلِّمُ أَحَدًا مِنْهُمْ مَا عَدَا أَخَاهُ. I saw — of them but Zaid, لَمْ أَرَ مِنْهُمْ مَا عَدَا زَيْدًا. Let him give to him who has —, لِيُعْطِ مَنْ لَيْسَ لَهُ. He cared for — of those things, لَمْ يَهُمَّ شَيْءٌ مِنْ ذٰلِكَ. I looked for a man and found —, طَلَبْتُ رَجُلًا وَلَمْ أَجِدْ. I found — of them, لَمْ أَجِدْ أَحَدًا مِنْهُمْ.

Non-elect, *a.* and *n.* غَيْرُ مُخْتَصّ ـ غَيْرُ مُخْتَار ـ غَيْرُ مُنْتَخَب.

Non-electric, *a.* غَيْرُ كَهْرَبَائِيّ.

Nonentity, *n.* Non-existence, عَدَمُ وُجُودٍ ـ العَدَمُ. Of no consequence, of a person or thing, دُونَ ٱعْتِبَارٍ.

Nones, *n.* Of the ancient Roman calendar, عِبَارَةٌ عَنِ ٱلْيَوْمِ ٱلسَّابِعِ مِنْ شَهْرِ مَارِسَ وَمَايُو وَجُولَاي وَأُكْتُوبَرَ وَعَنِ ٱلْيَوْمِ ٱلْخَامِسِ مِنْ بَقِيَّةِ ٱلْأَشْهُرِ عِنْدَ ٱلرُّومَانِيِّينَ ٱلْقُدَمَاءِ.

Non-essential, *a.* مُلْحَق ـ غَيْرُ لَازِم ـ غَيْرُ جَوْهَرِيّ ـ غَيْرُ ضَرُورِيّ.

Non-essential, *n.* شَيْءٌ غَيْرُ جَوْهَرِيّ ـ شَيْءٌ غَيْرُ ضَرُورِيّ ـ شَيْءٌ مُلْحَق.

Non est inventus, عِبَارَةٌ عَنِ ٱلْمَفْقُودِ.

Nonesuch, *n.* شَخْص (or شَيْءٌ) فَائِق ـ شَيْءٌ لَيْسَ لَهُ مَثِيل.

Non-execution, *n.* عَدَمُ إِجْرَاءٍ ـ عَدَمُ ٱلْعَمَلِ بِ.

Non-existence, *n.* عَدَمُ وُجُودٍ ـ عَدَم. Existence and —, وُجُودٌ وَعَدَمٌ.

Non-existent, *a.* فَقِيد ـ غَيْرُ مَوْجُودٍ ـ مَعْدُوم ـ غَيْرُ كَائِنٍ.

Non-fulfilment, *n.* عَدَمُ إِيفَاءٍ ـ عَدَمُ وَفَاءٍ ـ عَدَمُ إِجْرَاءٍ.

Non-interference, *n.* عَدَمُ تَدَاخُل ـ حِيَاد.

Non-juring, *a.* }
Non-juror, *n.* } عِبَارَةٌ عَنْ قَوْمٍ أَبَوْا مُبَايَعَةَ ٱلدَّوْلَةِ ٱلْإِنْكِلِيزِيَّةِ عَقِبَ ٱعْتِزَالِ ٱلْمَلِكِ جِيمْسَ ٱلثَّانِي عَنْ دَسْتِ ٱلْمُلْكِ.

Non-observance, *n.* إِهْمَال ـ عَدَمُ حِفْظٍ ـ عَدَمُ مُرَاعَاةٍ ـ عَدَم تَرْك.

Non-official, *a.* *See* Unofficial, *a.*; *also under* Official, *a.*

Non-pareil, *n.* Something of unequalled excellence, شَيْءٌ فَائِقٌ ـ شَيْءٌ مَا لَهُ نَظِير. A kind of pear, ضَرْبٌ مِنَ ٱلْكُمَّثْرَى. A small printing type, ضَرْبٌ مِنَ ٱلْأَحْرُفِ ٱلصَّغِيرَةِ لِلطَّبْعِ.

Non-payment, *n.* عَدَمُ تَأْدِيَةٍ (or أَدَاءٍ) ـ عَدَمُ وَفَاءٍ ـ عَدَمُ جَزَاءٍ.

Non-performance, *n.* *See* Non-fulfilment, Non-execution, *n.*

Nonplus, *n.* حَيْرَان ـ تَحَيُّر ـ حَيْرَة ـ تِيه ـ تَيَهَان. Nonplussed, حَائِرٌ فِي أَمْرِهِ ـ مُتَحَيِّر ـ حَائِر ـ حَيْرَان. To be at a —, مُتَحَيِّر ـ إِسْتَحَار *aor.* يَحَارُ.

Nonplus, *v.t.* خَبَّلَ ـ حَيَّرَ ـ تَيَّهَ ـ تَوَّهَ.

Non-production, *n.* Of fruits, *etc.*, عَدَمُ حَمْلٍ ـ جَدْب ; of papers, *etc.*, عَدَمُ إِيرَادٍ ـ عَدَمُ إِظْهَارٍ ـ عَدَمُ بَيَانٍ.

Non-professional, *a.* Not belonging to any profession, لَيْسَ مِنْ أَهْلِ ٱلْحِرَفِ أَوِ ٱلْأَصْنَافِ. Not in the course of professional duty, خَارِجٌ عَنِ ٱلْمَطْلُوبِ ٱلرَّسْمِيِّ ـ خَارِجٌ عَنْ مُقْتَضَيَاتِ ٱلْوَظِيفَةِ.

Non-residence, *n.* عَدَمُ ٱلْإِقَامَةِ فِي مَحَلِّ ٱلْوَظِيفَةِ (or ٱلْمَنْصَبِ) ـ ٱلسُّكْنَى فِي مَحَلٍّ خَارِجَ ٱلْمَنْصَبِ (or ٱلشُّغْلِ).

Non-resident, *a.* غَيْرُ مُقِيمٍ فِي مَحَلِّ ٱلْوَظِيفَةِ (or ٱلْمَنْصَبِ) ـ سَاكِنٌ فِي مَحَلٍّ خَارِجَ ٱلْمَنْصَبِ (or ٱلشُّغْلِ).

Non-resistance, *n.* عَدَمُ مُدَافَعَةٍ ـ عَدَمُ دِفَاعٍ ـ عَدَمُ مُقَاوَمَةٍ.

Non-resistant, *a.* غَيْرُ دَافِعٍ ـ غَيْرُ مُقَاوِمٍ ـ غَيْرُ مُدَافِعٍ.

Nonsense, *n.* كَلَامٌ مِنْ غَيْرِ مَعْنًى ـ عَبَث ـ هُجْر ـ هَذَر ـ لَغْو ـ هَذَيَان ـ نَفْخٌ فِي ٱلْبُوقِ. To talk —, هَذَرَ ـ أَهْجَرَ ـ أَهْذَرَ. *See also* Absurdity, *n.*

Nonsensical, *a.* Talking nonsense, هَاذِر ـ هَاجِر. Without meaning, بِلَا مَعْنًى. A — fellow, رَجُلٌ فَسْخٌ ـ سَخِيف ـ فَسِيخ ـ عِبِّيث. *See also* Absurd, *a.*

Nonsensically, *ad.* عَنْ غَبَاوَةٍ ـ بِسَخَافَةٍ ـ بِهَذَيَانٍ.

Nonsensicalness, *n.* *See* Nonsense, *n.*

Non-sequitur, *n.* عِبَارَةٌ عَنِ ٱسْتِدْلَالٍ فَاسِدٍ مِنْ مُقَدِّمَاتِ ٱلْقِيَاسِ ـ نَتِيجَةٌ فَاسِدَةٌ.

Non-such, *n.* *See* Non-pareil, *n.*

Nonsuit, *n.* بُطْلَانُ دَعْوَى ٱلْمُدَّعِي.

Nonsuit, *v.t.* أَبْطَلَ دَعْوَى ٱلْمُدَّعِي. To be nonsuited, أُبْطِلَتْ دَعْوَى ٱلْمُدَّعِي.

Noodle, *n.* نُوْر ـ حِمَار ـ أَبْلَهُ ـ بَلِيد ـ أَحْمَقُ ـ أَخْرَقُ.

Nook, *n.* زَاوِيَة *pl.* زَوَايَا ـ قُرْنَة *pl.* قُرَانِي ـ مَضِيق *pl.* مَضَائِق. How many hidden things there are in the nooks and corners, كَمْ فِي ٱلزَّوَايَا مِنَ ٱلْخَبَايَا. *See also* Niche, *n.*

Noon, *n.* ٱلظُّهْرُ. It is —, صَارَ ٱلظُّهْرُ ـ ٱلظُّهْرُ أَذَّنَ.

Noonday, *n.* }
Noontide, } وَقْتُ ٱلظُّهْرِ ـ ٱلظُّهْرُ.

Noonday, *a.* }
Noontide, } عِنْدَ ٱلظُّهْرِ ـ ظُهْرِيٌّ. The — prayer, صَلَاةُ ٱلظُّهْرِ. Noonday heat, حَرُّ ٱلظُّهْرِ.

Nooning, *n.* A nap in the middle of the day, قَيْلُولَة ـ قائِلَة.

Noose, *n.* A running knot, عُقْدَة سالِكَة. A — for catching game, شَرَك ـ حِبالَة ـ خَنّاقَة; especially the lasso, جُرْزَة. A —, or loop, for securing animals by the neck, رَبْقَة ـ رِبْقَة; a rope having a number of such loops, رِبْق. A — or bow-string, for strangling, خِناق.

Noose, *v.t.* To catch with a noose, إِصْطادَ ـ بِخَنّاقَة (or بِحِبالَة); with the lasso, إِصْطادَهُ بِٱلْجُرْزَة. To tie in a noose or running knot, عَقَدَ ـ عُقْدَة سالِكَة ـ ;; into a noose or loop, جَعَلَ ـ حِبالَة (or رِبْقَة) ـ ;; into a bow-string, عَقَدَ ـ خِناقًا ـ.

Nopal, *n.* The prickly pear, الصَّبَيْر ـ التِّين ٱلشَّوْكِيّ.

Nor, *conj.* وَلا. Neither this nor that, لا هٰذا وَلا ذاكَ. I neither love nor fear him, لا أُحِبُّهُ وَلا أَخافُ مِنْهُ. Nor do I think that..., حَتَّى وَلا أَظُنُّ أَن.

Normal, *a.* Arranged in order, مَضْبُوط ـ مُنْتَظِم ـ مُنَسَّق. Regular, ordinary, إِعْتِيادِيّ ـ مُعْتاد. According to nature, عَلَى سِياقِ ٱلْفِطْرَة ـ مُطابِق ٱلطَّبِيعَة; according to rule, مُطابِق ٱلْقَواعِد ـ ٱلْقَواعِد. A — school, مَدْرَسَة ـ دار ٱلْمُعَلِّمِينَ لِلْمُعَلِّمِينَ.

Norman, *n.* مِنْ أَهْلِ نُورمَنْدا.

Normandy, *n.* النُّورمَنْدا (وَهِيَ وِلايَة مِنْ وِلاياتِ فَرَنْسا).

North, *n.* الشَّمال. The wind veered to the —, شَمَلَتِ ٱلرِّيحُ. Coming or blowing from the —, مَشْمُول.

North, *a.* / **Northern**, شَمالِيّ (called in Egypt, بَحْرِيّ; in Syria, سَماوِيّ). The — quarter, المَشْمَلَة ـ الشَّمال. A — wind, شَمال. The — wind, الرِّيح ٱلشَّمالِيَّة ـ الجِرْبِياء ـ الرِّيح ٱلشّامِيَّة.

North-east, *n.* The, بَيْنَ ٱلشَّمالِ وَٱلشَّرْق.

North-east, *a.* / **North-easterly**, شَمالِيّ شَرْقِيّ. A — wind, رِيح بَرّانِيَّة. They went in a — direction, أَشْمَلُوا وَشَرَّقُوا.

Northerly, *a.* شَمالِيّ ـ مِنَ ٱلشَّمال ـ نَحْوَ ٱلشَّمال.

Northerly, *ad.* إِلَى جِهَةِ ٱلشَّمال ـ شَمالًا. The wind blew —, هَبَّتِ ٱلرِّيحُ شَمالًا ـ أَشْمَلَتِ (or شَمَلَتِ) ٱلرِّيحُ.

Northern, *a.* See North, *a.*

Northernmost, *a.* فِي أَقْصَى ٱلشَّمال.

Northing, *n.* القَطْع نَحْوَ ٱلشَّمال ـ شُمُول.

Northman, *n.* مِنْ سُكّانِ ٱلْمِنْطَقَةِ ٱلشَّمالِيَّةِ وَهُمْ أَهْلُ دانِيمارْكا وَنُورُوِيجِيا.

Northward, *a.* / **Northwardly**, ضارِب إِلَى ٱلشَّمال ـ مَشْمَل ـ شَمالِيّ.

Northward, / **Northwardly**, *ad.* / **Northwards**, شَمالًا ـ مِنْ جِهَةِ ٱلشَّمال.

North-west, *n.* الشَّمالِيّ ٱلْغَرْبِيّ.

North-west, *a.* شَمالِيّ مُغَرِّب ـ شَمالِيّ غَرْبِيّ. A — wind, شَمالِيّ غَرْبِيّ ـ جِرْبِياء. The — passage, المَنْفَذ ٱلشَّمالِيّ ٱلْغَرْبِيّ.

North-westerly, *a.* نَحْوَ ٱلشَّمالِيّ ٱلْغَرْبِيّ.

North-western, *a.* مِنْ طَرَف ـ مُتَعَلِّق بِٱلشَّمالِيّ ٱلْغَرْبِيّ ٱلشَّمالِيّ ٱلْغَرْبِيّ.

Norway, *n.* بِلاد نُورُوِيجِيا.

Norwegian, *n.* مِنْ أَهْلِ نُورُوِيجِيا.

Norwegian, *a.* مِنْ نُورُوِيجِيا.

Nose, *n.* The — of the face, خَشْم ـ مَعْطِس ـ مُنْخُر pl. مَناخِر ـ مِنْخار pl. مَناخِير ـ أَنْف pl. آناف and أُنُوف. The end or prominent part of anything, خَشْم ـ أَنْف. The tip of the —, in a human being, (خَوْرَمَة (or رَوْثَة or أَرْنَبَة) ٱلْأَنْف; of a beast, مُخْرَة; of a pig, فِنْطِيسَة; of a camel, مَخْطِم. A sniffing of the —, سُدَّة ـ سُداد. The bridge of the —, وَتَرَة ٱلْأَنْف. The two sides of the —, مَرْتِيا ٱلْأَنْف. The lobule of the —, أَرْنَبَة (or جِشْرِمَة). One who speaks through the —, أَغَنّ. مَخْرِم ٱلْأَنْف ـ ٱلْأَنْف

Having an aquiline nose, أَقْنَى fem. قَنْواء.

Having a crooked nose, فِنْطِيس pl. فَناطِيس.

Having a flat nose, أَفْطَس fem. فَطْساء.

Having a long and large nose, أَخْطَم fem. خَطْماء ـ عُنّاب ـ أُنافِيّ.

Having a mutilated nose, أَشْرَم ـ أَسْلَت ـ أَخْرَم pl. شَرْماء pl. شُرْم.

Having a pug nose, أَذْلَف fem. ذَلْفاء pl. ذُلْف.

Having a receding or camoys nose, أَخْنَس fem. خَنْساء pl. خُنْس.

Having a red nose, أَنْكَع ـ قُفاعِيّ.

Having a turned-up nose, أَقْعَى fem. قَعْواء.

Having a wide or broad nose, أَفْطَس ـ أَفْطَأ ـ أَخْشَم.

To alight on or reach to the nose, أَنَفَ ـ ٤: The flies alighted on the noses of the camels, أُنِفَتِ ٱلْإِبِلُ.

To blow one's nose, مَخَطَ أَنْفَهُ ـ تَمَخَّطَ ـ مَخَطَ ـ ٤.

To break the nose of one, كَشَمَ أَنْفَهُ ـ هَشَمَ ـ ٤.

To cut off the nose of one, كَشَمَ ـ ٤ إِكْتَشَمَ أَنْفَهُ ـ خَرَمَ أَنْفَهُ ـ شَرَمَ ـ ٤.

To hit on the nose, أَنَفَ ـ ٤ ـ لَثَمَ ـ ٤ ـ رَثَمَ ـ ٤ ـ فَزَرَ ـ ٤.

To lead by the nose, at will, قادَ ـ مِنْ أُذْنِهِ ـ ٤.

To pick one's nose, إِمْتَخَطَ ـ مَخَطَ أَنْفَهُ.

To poke one's nose into, حَشَرَ حَالَهُ فِي ـ تَدَاخَلَ (or تَدَخَّلَ) فِي.
See also to Intermeddle, *v.i.*

To pour medicine into the nose of one, أَسْعَطَ.

To put one's nose out of joint, to supplant, أَسْقَطَ ـ تَعَقَّبَ ـ تَسَقَّطَ.

To run at the nose, أَصَابَهُ ٱلزُّكَامُ ـ زُكِمَ.

To turn up one's nose, to bear one's self haughtily, أَقْمَحَ بِأَنْفِهِ.

To turn up the nose at, خَنَتَ ـ يَهِزُّ *aor.* وَمَزَ بِأَنْفِهِ ـ أَنِفَ ل ـ بِأَنْفِهِ.

To wipe one's nose, مَسَحَ أَنْفَهُ. *See also* To blow one's nose; *supra.*

Nose, *v.t.* To scent, شَمَّمَ ـ شَمَّ ـ تَنَشَّى. To oppose to the face, قَاوَمَ ـ مُوَاجِهَةً ـ جَبَهَ. *See also* To lead by the nose, *under* Nose, *n.*

Nosebag, *n.* عَلِيقَة *pl.* عَلَائِق ـ مِخْلَاة *pl.* مَخَالٍ.

Nose-bleed, *n.* رُعَاف ـ نُزُول دَم مِنَ ٱلْأَنْف.

Nosegay, *n.* صُحْبَة زَهْر ـ رَبْطَة زَهْر ـ بَاقَة زَهْر.

Nose-halter, *n.* Such as is used for camels, زِمَام ـ خِطَام.

Noseless, *a.* بِلَا أَنْف. *See also* Having a mutilated nose, *under* Nose, *n.*

Nose-ring, *n.* خِزَام.

Nosle, *n.* A little nose, أُنَيْف. *See also* Nozzle.

Nosological, *a.* مَا نِيطَ بِتَعْرِيفِ ٱلْأَمْرَاضِ وَتَنْسِيقِهَا.

Nosologist, *n.* عَالِمٌ بِبَيَانِ ٱلْأَمْرَاضِ ـ مُنَسِّقُ ٱلْأَمْرَاضِ.

Nosology, *n.* Classification of disease, عِلْمُ تَنْسِيقِ ٱلْأَمْرَاضِ ـ سِيَاقَةُ (or بَيَانُ) ٱلْأَمْرَاضِ.

Nostalgia, *n.* مَرَضُ ٱلْحَنِينِ إِلَى ٱلْوَطَنِ. Having —, ٱبْتَلَى بِٱلْحَنِينِ إِلَى ٱلْوَطَنِ.

Nostril, *n.* مَنْخَر *pl.* مَنَاخِرُ (or مُنْخُر or مِنْخِر) مَنْخُور ـ *pl.* مَنَاخِيرُ. To inflate the nostrils, فَنْخَرَ. To have the nostrils inflated through anger, نَتَّ; such inflation of the nostrils, نَتِيت. The two dents of the nostrils, ٱلْأَشْهَرَانِ. The two orifices of the nostrils, مَنْفِذَا ٱلْأَنْف. Having wide inflated nostrils, مُنَفَّشُ ٱلْمَنَاخِرِ.

Nostrum, *n.* إِكْسِيرُ ٱلْجُهَّالِ ـ دَوَاءٌ دَجَّال.

Not, *ad.* لَا ـ مَا ـ لَيْسَ ـ لَنْ: (This latter negative particle is placed before a verb in the future tense; *e.g.* We will not believe you until we see him, لَنْ نُؤْمِنَ لَكَ حَتَّى نَرَاهُ. Is it not enough for you that I have come, أَلَنْ يَكْفِيَكُمْ أَنِّي جِئْتُ). لَمْ (this negative placed before the verb in the future tense gives it a preterite signification, *e.g.*, he did not eat, لَمْ يَأْكُلْ; he did not ride, لَمْ يَرْكَبْ). It is not, لَيْسَ: It is not good for him to be alone, لَيْسَ جَيِّدًا أَنْ يَكُونَ وَحْدَهُ. Do not approach this tree, لَا تَقْرَبُوا إِلَى هٰذِهِ ٱلشَّجَرَةِ. I do not know, مَا أَدْرِي. I found he had not any bread, مَا وَجَدْتُ عِنْدَهُ خُبْزًا. Zaid is not standing, مَا زَيْدٌ قَائِمًا. Not one man came to me, مَا جَاءَنِي مِنْ رَجُلٍ. Did not I? أَلَيْسَ (أَنَا). Will you not eat? أَلَا تَأْكُلُ. Will you not get up? أَمَا تَقُومُ. Do you not like? أَلَا تُحِبُّونَ. Is he in the house or not? أَفِي ٱلْبَيْتِ هُوَ أَمْ لَا. If not, on the other hand, وَإِلَّا ـ إِلَّا: if not, I will know, وَإِلَّا فَأَعْلَمُ. If not, tell me that I may know, وَإِلَّا فَأَخْبِرْنِي حَتَّى أَعْلَمَ. If he does not arrive, إِنْ لَمْ يَصِلْ. Not at all, بَتَّةً ـ قَطْعًا ـ أَصْلًا. Not but that..., وَلٰكِنْ ـ مَعَ مَا فِيهِ. Not only, لَيْسَ فَقَطْ. Whether we live or not, إِنْ عِشْنَا أَوْ مُتْنَا ـ إِنْ عِشْنَا أَمْ لَا. Whether he likes it or not, إِنْ عَجَبَهُ وَإِنْ مَا عَجَبَهُ.

Nota bene; عِبَارَةٌ عَنِ ٱلتَّنْبِيهِ.

Notable, *a.* Remarkable, rare, غَرِيب ـ عَجِيب ـ نَادِر. Conspicuous, مَشْهُور ـ شَهِير ـ جَلِيّ. Industrious, شَغَّال ـ كَدُود. A — man, رَجُلٌ شَهِيرٌ ـ ٱبْنُ جَلَاءٍ. To be —, conspicuous, ٱشْتَهَرَ; to make —, شَهَّرَ ـ شَهَرَ.

Notable, *n.* *See* Grandee, *n.*

Notableness, *n.* Remarkableness, rareness, عِزَّة ـ عِزّ ـ نُدُور. Conspicuousness, ٱشْتِهَار ـ شُهْرَة ـ جَلَاء. Industriousness, كَدّ ـ جُهْد ـ كَدْح.

Notably, *ad.* In a remarkable manner, بِنَوْعٍ غَرِيبٍ ـ عَجَبًا. Conspicuously, إِشْتِهَارًا ـ بِشُهْرَةٍ. Much, جِدًّا ـ جَزِيلًا ـ كَثِيرًا. Especially, خُصُوصًا.

Notarial, *a.* Done by a notary, مُقَيَّدٌ عِنْدَ ٱلْكَاتِبِ ٱلشَّرْعِيِّ.

Notary, *n.* / Notary public, } كَاتِبٌ شَرْعِيّ *pl.* كُتَّابٌ شَرْعِيُّونَ.

Notation, *n.* تَدْوِين ـ تَقْيِيد ـ رَقْم.

Notch, *n.* حُزُوز *pl.* حَزّ ـ فُلُول *pl.* فَلَل or فَلّ. A — in a stick measure, مَشْبَر *pl.* مَشَابِرُ; in a bow or arrow, مَحَزّ. Notchedness, تَحْزِيز.

Notch, *v.t.* اِحْتَزَّ ـ حَزَّزَ ـ حَزَّ ـ فَلَّلَ ـ فَلَّ ـ فَرَضَ. To be notched, تَحَزَّزَ ـ اِنْفَلَّ ـ تَفَلَّلَ. Notched, فَلِيل ـ أَفَلّ ـ مُتَحَزِّز.

Note, *n.* A mark, sign, وَسْم *pl.* وُسُوم ـ آيَة *pl.* آيَات ـ سِمَة ـ إِشَارَة ـ عَلَامَة *pl.* عَلَامَات. A memorandum, تَذْكِرَة ـ تَذْكِرَة. A diplomatic —, لَائِحَة. Comment, شَرْح ـ بَيَان ـ تَعْبِير. An obligation, draft, سَنَد ـ صُكُوك *pl.* صَكّ ـ تَمَسُّك. A — of expenses, a bill, تَشْرِيف ـ طُرُوس *pl.* طِرْس. A letter, عِلْم ـ قَائِمَة. A short writing, تَلْخِيص. A short letter, رُقْعَة *pl.* رِقَاع *and* رُقَع ـ. Accent, sound, صَوْت ـ حِسّ ـ مَقَامُ ٱلصَّوْتِ ـ مُودَّة. A musical —, نُقْطَةُ ٱلْغِنَاء ـ عَلَامَةُ ٱلْغِنَاء ـ شُهْرَة. Notability, إِعْتِبَار. A — of interrogation, عَلَامَةُ ٱلِٱسْتِفْهَامِ; of exclamation, عَلَامَةُ ٱلتَّعَجُّبِ. He handed him a — in which the government order was written, سَلَّمَهُ طِرْسًا كُتِبَ فِيهِ أَمْرُ ٱلدَّوْلَةِ.

A person of note, رَجُلٌ مَشْهُورٌ ـ وَجِيهٌ *pl.* وُجَهَاء ـ إِبْنُ جَلَاء ـ شَهِير.

Bank note, قَائِمَةٌ نَقْدِيَّةٌ *pl.* قَوَائِمُ ـ وَرَقَةٌ نَقْدِيَّةٌ.

Foot note, حَاشِيَةٌ فِي أَسْفَلِ ٱلصَّفْحَةِ.

Marginal note, حَاشِيَة *pl.* حَوَاشٍ ـ تَعْلِيقَة *pl.* تَعَالِيق.

Note of hand, Promissory note, } صَكّ *pl.* صُكُوك ـ تَمَسُّك *pl.* تَمَسُّكَات.

To issue bank notes, أَصْدَرَ قَوَائِمَ نَقْدِيَّةً.

To take note, to make a minute examination, غَاصَ عَلَى ـ دَقَّقَ ٱلْأَمْرَ.

To take notes of, to observe, لَاحَظَ ـ تَفَرَّسَ فِي in writing, أَدْرَجَ (or كَتَبَ or قَيَّدَ) عِبَارَاتٍ عَن.

To write notes on the margin of a book, حَشَّى.

Note, *v.t.* To observe, لَاحَظَ ـ أَشَافَ إِلَى ـ تَفَرَّسَ فِي ـ عَلَّمَ ـ نَظَرَ إِلَى. To — with particular care, دَقَّقَ. To mark, أَشَّرَ عَلَى ـ عَيَّنَ عَلَى ـ عَلَّى. To record, write, كَتَبَ. To note down, أَدْرَجَ ـ قَيَّدَ ـ كَتَبَ ـ دَوَّنَ. To — in a book, رَسَمَ ـ (or قَيَّدَ or كَتَبَ) فِي كِتَابٍ (or دَفْتَرٍ). Note (ye) that man, سِمُوا ذٰلِكَ ٱلرَّجُلَ.

Note-book, *n.* دُسْتُور ـ تَذْكِرَة ـ دَفْتَرُ تَذْكِرَةٍ ـ مَجْمَعَة.

Noted, *a.* مَشْهُور ـ مُشَاع. To be — for, إِشْتَهَرَ بِ.

Notedly, *ad.* Attentively, بِتَدْقِيقٍ ـ بِمُلَاحَظَةٍ. Specially, خَاصَّةً ـ بِٱلْأَخَصِّ ـ خُصُوصًا.

Notedness, *n.* صِيت ـ شُهْرَة ـ إِشْتِهَار.

Noteless, *a.* *See* Obscure, *a.*

Noter, *n.* One who makes notes, مُدْرِجٌ ـ مُقَيِّدُ ٱلْمُلَاحَظَاتِ ـ ٱلْعِبَارَاتِ. *See also* Annotator, *n.*

Nothing, *n.* لَا شَيْءَ. It is —, مَا هُوَ تَحْتَ ـ لَيْسَ هُوَ بِشَيْءٍ ـ خَبَرٍ. It is — to me, مَا لِي فِيهِ شَيْءٌ ـ لَا فَرْقَ عِنْدِي. There is — the matter with him, مَا بِهِ شَيْءٌ. For —, gratis, عَفْوًا ـ مَجَّانًا. For —, without cause, بِدُونِ عِلَّةٍ ـ مِنْ غَيْرِ سَبَبٍ. Have — to do with it, إِيَّاكَ وَذٰلِكَ ٱلْأَمْرَ ـ أَلْقِ بِهِ عَنْ يَدِكَ.

Nothing, with "but," إِلَّا with مَا: He is — but a fool, مَا هُوَ إِلَّا بِجَاهِلٍ. Good for —, of a person, قِشْبٌ خِشْبٌ. He has — in his hand, لَيْسَ فِي يَدِهِ شَيْءٌ. Do — to them, لَا تَفْعَلْ بِهِمْ شَيْئًا. He answered: Nothing, قَالَ لَا شَيْءَ. He answered —, لَمْ يُجِبْ بِشَيْءٍ. Answerest thou —, أَمَا تُجِيبُ بِشَيْءٍ. Nothing has been done for him, لَمْ يُعْمَلْ مَعَهُ شَيْءٌ. You shall want for —, لَا يُعْوِزُكُمْ شَيْءٌ. Nothing comes amiss to him, appears to be out of his line or sphere, مَا يَشِذُّ عَلَيْهِ شَيْءٌ. Do — rashly, لَا تَفْعَلُوا شَيْئًا ٱقْتِحَامًا. They spend their time in — else but to hear some new thing, لَا يَتَفَرَّغُونَ لِشَيْءٍ آخَرَ إِلَّا أَنْ يَسْمَعُوا شَيْئًا حَدِيثًا. Nothing but evil is designed by the spreading of that report, لَيْسَ ٱلْمُرَادُ مِنْ إِشَاعَةِ ذٰلِكَ ٱلْخَبَرِ سِوَى ٱلشَّرِّ. Having — to do, بَطَّال ـ فَارِغ. To think — of, إِسْتَحْقَرَ ـ إِسْتَقَلَّ.

Nothing, *ad.* In no degree, not at all, لَا بِوَجْهٍ مِنَ ـ أَصْلًا ـ قَطْعًا ـ بَتَّةً ـ ٱلْوُجُوهِ.

Nothingness, *n.* Non-existence, عَدَم. Little value or estimation, قِلَّةُ ٱعْتِبَارٍ ـ تَفَاهَة ـ تَفَه.

Notice, *n.* Observation, نَظَرٌ فِي ـ مُلَاحَظَة. Knowledge of, وُقُوفٌ عَلَى ـ أَخْبَارٌ بِ ـ خَبَرٌ بِ. Respectful treatment, حُسْنُ مُرَاعَاةٍ ـ حُسْنُ تَوَجُّهٍ ـ ٱلْتِفَاتٌ. An intimation, لَائِحَة ـ إِيمَاء ـ تَعْرِيف ـ تَنْبِيه ـ أَذَان ـ إِشَارَة. A notification, advertisement, إِشْعَار ـ إِعْلَام. A sketch, short account, تَلْخِيص. A biographical —, تَلْخِيصُ سِيرَةٍ ـ تَلْخِيصُ تَرْجَمَةٍ. A short notice of time, مُهْلَةٌ قَصِيرَةٌ. At short notice, فِي مُهْلَةٍ قَصِيرَةٍ. Worthy of —, مُسْتَحِقُّ ٱلذِّكْرِ. Notice to quit, إِنْذَارٌ بِٱلْإِخْلَاءِ. A — has been issued from the department, صَدَرَ إِشْعَارٌ مِنَ ٱلْإِدَارَةِ.

To attract notice, جَذَبَ نَظَرَ ٱلنَّاسِ ـ إِسْتَدْعَى ٱلِٱنْتِبَاهَ.

To bring one's self into notice, تَعَرَّضَ لِلْإِعْلَانِ ـ إِسْتَعْلَنَ ـ شَهَرَ نَفْسَهُ ـ نَفْسِهِ.

To cause notice to be given to, أَبْلَغَ ـ إِبْلَاغًا.

To draw one's notice to, فَاطَنَ ـ فِي.

To give notice of, أَخْبَرَ بِ ـ أَعْلَمَ بِ ـ أَشَاعَ بِ ـ أَعْلَنَ بِ.

To give notice to quit, أَنْذَرَ ـ بِإِخْلَاءِ ٱلدَّارِ.

To rise into notice, صَارَ مَشْهُورًا ـ إِكْتَسَبَ ٱلِٱعْتِبَارَ.

To take notice of, to observe, نَظَرَ ـ فَطَنَ لِ ـ لَاحَظَ ـ أَدْرَكَ ـ رَاعَى ـ إِمْتَثَلَ بِ إِلَى. To pay attention to, to obey, أَوْجَهَ ـ وَجَّهَ ـ رَاعَى عَلَى. To show attention to, to honour, فَطَنَ لَهُ ـ رَضِيَ عَن *aor.* يَرْضَى. He took notice of him or it, ضَرَبَ ـ

To take no notice of, to neglect, تَقَصَّرَ بِ ـ تَهَاوَنَ بِ ـ مَا ٱعْتَنَى فِي ـ إِبْتَذَلَ ـ إِسْتَقَلَّ عَن. Not to show respect to, مَا حَسِبَ لَهُ حِسَابًا.

Notice, *v.t.* To observe by the senses, لَحَظَ ـ نَظَرَ إِلَى. To pay attention to, to regard, اِمْتَثَلَ بِ ـ رَاعَى ـ اِلْتَفَتَ إِلَى ـ وَجَّهَ ـ اِعْتَبَرَ. To point out, أَشَّرَ. To treat with civilities, رَحَّبَ بِ ـ يَرْضَى *aor.* رَضِيَ عَن ـ وَدَّ ـ أَكْرَمَ ـ اِعْتَبَرَ. To observe intellectually, اِرْتَأَى ـ يَقِفُ *aor.* وَقَفَ عَلَى ـ أَدْرَكَ. What was noticed in his last work, ما ذُكِرَ فِي تَأْلِيفِهِ ٱلْأَخِيرِ. *See also under* Observation, *n.*

Noticeable, *a.* That may be observed, مِمَّا يُلَاحَظُ; that is worthy of observation, مُسْتَحِقُّ ٱلِاعْتِبَارِ ـ وَمِمَّا يُعْتَبَرُ.

Notification, *n.* تَبْلِيغ ـ إِعْلَام ـ إِشْعَار ـ تَنْبِيه ـ أَذَان ـ تَعْرِيف. A — was issued from the palace, صَدَرَ إِشْعَارٌ مِن ٱلسَّرَايَةِ.

Notify, *v.t.* To inform, to make known to, أَعْلَمَ ـ بِ ـ آذَنَ ـ بِ ـ أَبْلَغَ ـ بِ ـ بَلَّغَ ـ بِ ـ بَيَّنَ ـ لِ ـ خَبَّرَ ـ بِ ـ أَخْبَرَ ـ بِ. To publish, أَشْهَرَ ـ أَذَاعَ ـ نَشَرَ ـ أَشَاعَ بِ. To be notified, يَشِيعُ *aor.* شَاعَ ـ اِنْتَشَرَ ـ تَنَشَّرَ ـ اِسْتَعْلَنَ.

Notion, *n.* A conception, أَوْهَام *pl.* وَهْم ـ تَوَهُّم ـ تَصَوُّر. An opinion, آرَآء *pl.* رَأْي ـ ظُنُون *pl.* ظَنّ. A sentiment, إِشْعَار ـ حِسّ ـ هَوِيَّة ـ مَيْل. Knowledge, مَعْرِفَة ـ دِرَايَة. Inclination, قَصْد ـ نِيَّة. A design, قَصْد ـ نِيَّة. A confused —, knowledge, مَعْرِفَةٌ غَيْرُ مُحَقَّقَةٍ.

To entertain a high notion of one's self, أُعْجِبَ بِنَفْسِهِ. What a high notion he has of his own judgment! ما أَعْجَبَهُ بِرَأْيِهِ.

To have a notion or idea, ظَنَّ ـ تَخَيَّلَ ـ تَصَوَّرَ. To intend, أَرَادَ ـ تَعَمَّدَ ـ قَصَدَ ـ تَعَزَّمَ ـ تَنَوَّى.

To have no notion of, not to know, خَفِيَ عَن ـ جَهِلَ بِ ـ غَبِيَ عَن. To have no intention, لَمْ يَتَنَوَّ ـ لَمْ يَقْصِدْ ـ لَمْ يُضْمِرْ.

Notional, *a.* وَهْمِيّ ـ نَظَرِيّ ـ خَيَالِيّ.

Notionally, *ad.* بِٱلتَّصَوُّرِ ـ وَهْمًا ـ تَصَوُّرًا.

Notoriety, *n.* Publicity, مَشَاع ـ شُهْرَة ـ إِشْتِهَار ـ جِهَار. Fame, سِمْع ـ صِيت ـ سَمَاع. Ill fame, سِمْعٌ رَدِيٌّ ـ صِيتٌ قَبِيحٌ. A man of —, of fame, ذُو سَمَاعٍ ـ رَجُلٌ ذُو سِمْعٍ.

Notorious, *a.* Publicly known, جَلِيّ ـ ظَاهِر ـ وَاضِح ـ مُشَاع ـ مُسَمَّعٌ بِهِ ـ مَجْهُورٌ بِهِ ـ مَشْهُور ـ مَعْهُود. Notorious, in a bad sense, مَفْضُوحُ ٱلصِّيتِ ـ رَدِيءُ ٱلسُّمْعَةِ ـ مُشَهَّر. To be —, publicly known, إِشْتَهَرَ ـ تَجَلَّى; to make —, شَهَّرَ ـ شَهَرَ. To be —, in a bad sense, سُمِّعَ بِهِ; to make so —, سَمَّعَ بِهِ. He became —, إِشْتَهَرَ (or إِسْتَعْلَنَ or إِعْتَلَنَ). The thing became —, صَارَ شُهْرَةً ٱلْأَمْرُ. He became —, the common talk, among the people, تَسَامَعَ بِهِ ٱلنَّاسُ.

Notoriously, *ad.* Publicly, جِهَارًا ـ شُهْرَةً ـ إِشْتِهَارًا. Infamously, بِقَبَاحَةٍ ـ تَشْهِيرًا ـ بِفَضِيحَةٍ.

Notoriousness, *n.* *See* Notoriety, *n.*

Notwithstanding, *conj.* وَلٰكِنْ ـ مَعَ ـ مَعَ أَنْ ـ مَعَ ذٰلِكَ ـ وَلَوْ. Notwithstanding those obstacles, مَعَ وُجُودِ تِلْكَ ٱلْمَوَانِعِ. Do that —, that is, in spite of the seeming danger, or, in any case, إِفْعَلْ ذٰلِكَ عَلَى مَا خُيِّلَتْ (or عَلَى مَا شُبِّهَتْ).

Nought. *See* Naught, *n.* and *a.*

Noun, *n.* إِسْم *pl.* أَسْمَآء *and* أَسَامِيّ. An active or infinitive —, مَصْدَر *pl.* مَصَادِر. The governing of nouns in the genitive case, إِضَافَةُ ٱلِاسْمِ إِلَى ٱلِاسْمِ.

Abstract noun, إِسْمُ مَعْنًى.

Active participial noun, إِسْمُ ٱلْفَاعِلِ. Past participial noun, إِسْمُ ٱلْمَفْعُولِ.

Adverbial noun, إِسْمُ ٱلْفِعْلِ *pl.* أَسْمَآءُ ٱلْأَفْعَالِ.

Appellative noun, إِسْمُ عَيْنٍ.

Collective noun, إِسْمُ ٱلْكَثْرَةِ.

Diminutive noun, إِسْمُ مُصَغَّر.

Comparative noun, إِسْمُ ٱلتَّفْضِيلِ.

Generic noun, إِسْمُ ٱلْجِنْسِ.

Instrumental noun, إِسْمُ ٱلْآلَةِ.

Noun denoting one time or action, إِسْمُ ٱلْمَرَّةِ.

Noun denoting excess, إِسْمُ مُبَالَغَةٍ.

Noun of measures, of capacity, إِسْمُ ٱلْوِعَآءِ.

Noun of species, إِسْمُ ٱلنَّوْعِ.

Numerical noun, إِسْمُ ٱلْعَدَدِ.

Pronominal noun, إِسْمٌ مُضْمَرٌ.

Relative or Gentilic noun, إِسْمٌ مَنْصُوبٌ.

Nourish, *v.t.* To feed, أَطْعَمَ ـ قَاتَ ـ غَذَّى. To sustain, provide for, يَعُولُ *aor.* عَالَ ـ أَعْوَلَ. To bring up, رَبَّى. To cause to grow, أَنْمَى ـ نَمَّى. To entertain in the mind, أَضْمَرَ. To be nourished, fed, أُطْعِمَ ـ تَغَذَّى ـ اِغْتَذَى. To be nourished, brought up, تَرَبَّى. The rain nourishes it, اَلْمَطَرُ يُنَمِّيهِ. He was nourished by it, اِغْتَذَى بِهِ.

Nourisher, *n.* One who sustains, a provider, مُعِيل ـ عَائِل ـ رَازِق. One who brings up, مُرَبٍّ. *See also* Nourishment, *n.*

Nourishing, *a.* نَافِع ـ نَجُوع ـ مُشْبِع ـ غَاذٍ.

Nourishment, *n.* Food, أَكْل ـ طَعَام ـ قُوت ـ غِذَآء. The act of bringing up, تَرْبِيَة. That which sustains, causes to grow, رِزْق ـ قِيَام ـ قِوَام.

Novel, *a.* New, recent, بَدِيع ـ حَادِث ـ حَدِيث ـ جَدِيد. Strange, نادِر ـ غَرِيب A — thing; *see* Novelty, *n.*

Novel, *n.* أُحْدُوثَة ـ حِكَايَة *pl.* حِكَايَات ـ خُرَافَة *pl.* خُرَافَات. A pretty —, أُحْدُوثَة مَلِيحَة *pl.* أَحَادِيث.

Novelette, *n.* حِكَايَة (*or* خُرَافَة) قَصِيرَة.

Novelist, *n.* مُؤَلِّف ٱلْحِكَايَات.

Novelty, *n.* The freshness or first beginning of a thing, حِدْثَان ـ حَدَاثَة. Recentness, جِدَّة ـ حَدَاثَة. Something new, strange, غَرِيبَة *pl.* غَرَائِب ـ شَيْء جَدِيد ـ نَوَادِر *pl.* نَادِرَة. False opinions and novelties, آرَاء فَاسِدَة حَدِيثَة.

November, *n.* نُوفَمْبَر ـ تِشْرِينُ ٱلْآخِرُ (*or* ٱلثَّانِي).

Novice, *n.* A beginner, حَدِيث *pl.* أَحَادِيث. A learner, تِلْمِيذ *pl.* تَلَامِيذ. A greenhorn, جَذَع *pl.* جُذْعَان ـ مُجَدِّد ـ غَشِيم. A religious —, مُبْتَدِئ *pl.* مُبْتَدِئُون. He is a — in this affair, هُوَ فِي هٰذَا ٱلْأَمْرِ جَذَع.

Novitiate, *n.* The time of learning, مُدَّة ٱلتَّلْمَذَة. Novitiate for a monkish order, تَجْرِبَة فِي ٱلرَّهْبَنَة ـ تَجْرِبَة ٱلرَّهْبَنَة. *See also* Apprenticeship, *n.*

Nous, *n.* وِهْنَة. *See also* Mind, Intelligence, *n.*

Now, *ad.* حَالًا ـ ٱلْآنَ. Just now, تَوًّا ـ ٱلسَّاعَة. Now, therefore, فَٱلْآنَ. Every now and then, بَعْضَ ـ أَحْيَانًا ـ بُعَيْدَاتِ بَيْنٍ ـ تَارَةً ـ أَوْقَات. But just now, تَوًّا ـ لَيْسَ لَهُ زَمَان. Even now, ٱلْآنَ أَيْضًا. How now? مَا ذَا. Now, (as a connecting particle is often expressed by وَ *or* كَانَ; the latter when immediately referring to what precedes; *e.g.,*) Now, the man was a thief, وَكَانَ ٱلرَّجُلُ لِصًّا. Now or never! أَمَّا هٰلَكَ أَمَّا مَلَكَ.

Now, *n.* The present, ٱلْوَقْتُ ٱلْحَاضِرُ ـ ٱلْحَاضِرُ.

Nowadays, *ad.* فِي عَصْرِنَا هٰذَا ـ فِي هٰذِهِ ٱلْأَيَّامِ ـ فِي أَيَّامِنَا هٰذِهِ.

Noway, *ad.* } *See* Nowise, *ad.*
Noways, }

Nowhere, *ad.* لَيْسَ فِي مَكَانٍ ـ لَا فِي مَكَانٍ مِنَ ٱلْأَمْكِنَة. I went —, مَا ذَهَبْتُ إِلَى هُنَا أَوْ هُنَاكَ. It was — to be found, لَمْ يَجِدْ أَصْلًا ـ لَمْ يَجِدْ.

Nowise, *ad.* لَا ـ لَيْسَ بِوَجْهٍ مِنَ ٱلْوُجُوهِ ـ أَصْلًا ـ ٱلْبَتَّة. He shall in — lose his reward, لَا يُضِيعُ أَجْرَهُ. In no wise, no not at all, كَلَّا ـ ٱلْبَتَّة.

Noxious, *a.* *See* Harmful, Injurious, *a.*

Noxiously, *ad.* *See* Harmfully, Injuriously, *ad.*

Noxiousness, *n.* *See* Harmfulness, Injuriousness, *n.*

Noyau, *n.* ضَرْب مِنَ ٱلْعَنْبَرِيَّة.

Nozzle, *n.* The tip, end, خَشْم ـ مِنْقَار. A spout, مِيزَاب *pl.* مَآزِيب ـ صُنْبُور.

N.S. عِبَارَة عَنِ ٱلتَّارِيخِ ٱلْإِفْرِنْجِيّ دُونَ ٱلرُّومِيّ.

Nubile, *a.* *See* Marriageable, *a.*

Nubilous, *n.* *See* Cloudy, Gloomy, *a.*

Nuciferous, *a.* حَامِلُ ٱلْبُنْدُق.

Nucleiform, *a.* فِي شَكْلِ ٱلْبُنْدُق.

Nucleus, *n.* Principal or original mass, أَصْل ـ أُمّ ـ عُقْدَة ـ أَسَاس ـ مَرْكَز ـ بَدْء. A kernel, عَجْو ـ حَبّ ـ نَجْمَة. The — of a comet, جِرْمُ ٱلنَّجْمِ ذِي ٱلذَّنَب.

Nudation, *n.* تَعْرِيَة.

Nude, *a.* *See* Naked, *a.*

Nudge, *v.t.* قَصَفَ ـ دَفَعَ بِٱلْكُوع ; *vulg.* دَفَش. *See also to* Jog, *v.t.*

Nudge, *n.* قَصْف ـ دَفْع ; *vulg.* دَفْشَة. *See also* Jog, *n.*

Nudity, *n.* *See* Nakedness, *n.*

Nugatory, *a.* بَطَّال ـ بَاطِل ـ عَبَث. To render —, أَبْطَلَ ـ بَطَّلَ. *See also* Futile, *a.*

Nugget, *n.* A — of gold, شَذْرَة *pl.* شُذُور ـ تِبْر ـ نَدْرَة. *See also* Nodule, *n.*

Nuisance, *n.* Anything annoying or offensive, ضَجَر ـ زَعَج ـ أَذِيَّة ـ شِقَّة ـ عُطْبَة ـ شَنَاعَة. Anything disgusting, كَرَاهَة. Filth, ordure, رَدْن ـ وَسَخ ـ دَنَاسَة ـ نَجَاسَة ـ عَذِرَة ـ بَرَاز ـ قَذَر. Commit no nuisance here, ٱلْبُرُوزُ هُنَا مَمْنُوع.

Null, *a.* بَاطِل ـ لَا قُوَّةَ لَهُ ـ سَاقِط ـ حَابِط ـ بَطَّال. To be —, of no force, زَهَقَ ـ حَبِطَ ـ سَقَطَ ـ بَطَلَ. His work became —, was of no effect, حَبِطَ عَمَلُهُ. The law became —, بَطَلَ ٱلنَّامُوس.

Nullification, *n.* إِحْبَاط ـ إِسْقَاط ـ تَبْطِيل.

Nullifier, *n.* مُسْقِط ـ مُبَطِّل.

Nullify, *v.t.* أَحْبَطَ ـ أَسْقَطَ ـ أَبْطَلَ ـ بَطَّلَ. To —, as by an argument, أَدْحَضَ ـ ب.

Nullity, *n.* سَقْط ـ بُطْل ـ بُطُول. *See also* Nonentity, *n.*

Numb, *a.* Torpid, خَدِر ; from cold, مُكْتَزّ. To be —, torpid, خَدِرَ. To be —, as feeling like being pricked with "pins and needles," نَمِلَ.

Numb, *v.t.* *See to* Benumb, *v.t.*

Number, *n.* An assemblage of units, عِدَاد ـ عَدَد *pl.* أَعْدَاد. A —, such as affixed to an article in a list, نُمْرَة *pl.* نُمَر : to affix such numbers to anything, نَمَّرَ. No., as the contraction of —,

عدد ـ نُمَرَة *pl.* نُمَر. A quantity, عِدّة ـ مِقْدَار. Some, مِقْدَار ـ بَعْض. A party, body, جَمَاعَة ـ جَمْع ـ قَوْم. Number, in grammar, صِيغَة ـ العَدَد: the singular —, المُفْرَد; the plural —, الجَمْع. Verse, وَزْن. Poetry, شِعْر. A portion, part, جُزْء *pl.* أَجْزَآء. It is published in numbers, يَصْدُرُ أَجْزَآء ـ صُدُورُهُ جُزْءًا جُزْءًا. We have read in one of the numbers of that paper, قَدْ قَرَأْنَا فِي أَحَدِ أَعْدَادِ تِلْكَ ٱلْجَرِيدَةِ.

A great number, عِدَّة ـ كَثِير ـ وَفْرَة ـ وُفُور ـ فَوْج *pl.* أَفْوَاج.

A small number, عِدَّةٌ يَسِيرَةٌ ـ قَلَائِل *pl.* قَلِيل.

Among the number, بَيْنَ ـ مِنْ جُمْلَةِ. He was among the number (of them), كَانَ مِنْ جُمْلَتِهِمْ.

Cardinal number, إِسْمُ عَدَدٍ.

Even number, زَكًا ـ زَوْج *pl.* أَزْوَاج.

Few in number, قَلِيلُونَ عَدَدًا.

Fractional number, كَسْر *pl.* كُسُورَات.

Golden number, العَدَدُ ٱلذَّهَبِيُّ وَهُوَ عِبَارَةٌ عَنْ عَدَدٍ يَدُلُّ عَلَى رَأْسِ ٱلسَّنَةِ ٱلقَمَرِيَّةِ.

Many in number, شَتَّى ـ عِدَّة ـ كَثِيرُونَ عَدَدًا.

Mixed number, عَدَدٌ مُخْتَلِطٌ.

Odd number, فَرْد *pl.* أَفْرَاد.

Ordinal number, إِسْمٌ مُشْتَقٌّ مِنَ ٱلعَدَدِ.

Round number, عَدَدٌ تَامٌّ ـ عَدَدٌ بِلَا كُسُورٍ.

Whole number, عَدَدٌ صَحِيحٌ.

Without a number, بِلَا نُمْرَةٍ ـ غَيْرُ مُرَقَّمٍ.

Without number, numberless, بِلَا عَدَدٍ ـ لَا يُحْصَى ـ لَا يُعَدُّ.

Number, *v.t.* To count, reckon, حَسَبَ ³ ـ أَحْصَى ـ عَدَّ ³ ـ عَدَّدَ. To be numbered, إِعْتَدَّ. To affix a number to, رَقَمَ ³ ـ نَمَّرَ ـ خَطَّ ٱلنُّمْرَ عَلَى ³. A thing included in a number or numbering, مُعْتَدٌّ بِهِ. He was numbered with us, كَانَ مَعْدُودًا بَيْنَنَا. He was numbered among the slain, أُحْصِيَ مَعَ ٱلقَتْلَى. *See also to* Reckon, *v.t.*

Numberer, *n.* مُعَدِّد ـ حَاسِب.

Numberless, *n.* بِلَا عَدَدٍ ـ لَا يُعَدُّ ـ لَا يُحْصَى.

Numbers, *n.* The fourth book of the Pentateuch, سِفْرُ العَدَدِ.

Numbness, *n.* Torpidity, خُدْرَة ـ خَدَر; from cold, كُزَاز.

Numerable, *a.* يُعْتَدُّ ـ مِمَّا يُحْصَى.

Numeral, *n.* عدد *pl.* أَعْدَاد ـ رَقْم *pl.* أَرْقَام. What Europeans call "Arabic numerals," الأَرْقَامُ ٱلهِنْدِيَّةُ.

Numeral, *a.* عَدَدِيٌّ.

Numerally, *ad.* حَسَبَ ٱلعَدَدِ ـ بِٱلعَدَدِ ـ إِحْصَآءً.

Numerate, *v.t.* *See to* Number, *v.t.*

Numeration, *n.* The act of numbering, عَدٌّ ـ تَعْدَاد ـ حِسَاب. In arithmetic, قَاعِدَةُ حِسَابِ ٱلأَعْدَادِ لَفْظًا.

Numerator, *n.* One who numbers, مُعَدِّد ـ حَاسِب. *In fractions,* بَسْط ـ صُورَةُ ٱلكَسْرِ ـ البَسِيطُ.

Numeric, *a.} Numerical,* مَا نِيطَ بِٱلأَعْدَادِ ـ عَدَدِيٌّ.

Numerically, *ad.* عَدَدًا ـ مِنْ جِهَةِ ٱلعَدَدِ.

Numerous, *a.* كَثِير ـ وَافِر ـ عَدِيد ـ مُتَعَدِّد ـ شَتَّى ـ ثَرٌّ. To be —, تَكَاثَرَ ـ كَثُرَ ³ ـ تَوَافَرَ.

Numerously, *ad.* عَدِيدًا ـ مِنْ كَثِيرِينَ. The meeting was — attended, كَثِيرُونَ حَضَرُوا ٱلمَجْلِسَ.

Numerousness, *n.* كَثْرَة ـ عِدَّة ـ ثَرْوَة ـ وَفْرَة.

Numismatic, *a.* مَا نِيطَ بِٱلمَسْكُوكَاتِ ـ مُخْتَصٌّ بِٱلمَسْكُوكَاتِ ٱلقَدِيمَةِ.

Numismatics, *n.* فَنُّ تَشْخِيصِ ٱلمَسْكُوكَاتِ.

Numismatologist, *n.* مَاهِرٌ فِي فَنِّ تَشْخِيصِ ٱلمَسْكُوكَاتِ.

Numismatology, *n.* *See* Numismatics, *n.*

Nummular, *a.} Nummary,* *See* Numismatic, *a.*

Nummulite, *n.* صَدَفٌ مُتَحَجِّرٌ بِصُورَةِ ٱلسِّكَّةِ.

Numskull, *n.* *See* Blockhead, Dolt, *n.*

Nun, *n.* رَاهِبَة *pl.* رَاهِبَات.

Nuncio, *n.* A papal —, قَاصِدٌ رَسُولِيٌّ ـ سَفِيرُ ٱلبَابَا.

Nuncupation, *n.* تَسْمِيَة.

Nuncupative, *a.} Nuncupatory,* Verbal, شِفَاهِيٌّ ـ لَفْظِيٌّ. Nominal, إِسْمِيٌّ.

Nunnation, *n.* The Arabic declension, التَّنْوِينُ.

Nunnery, *n.* دَيْرُ ٱلرَّاهِبَاتِ.

Nuptial, *a.* عُرْسِيٌّ ـ زِيجِيٌّ.

Nuptials, *n.* Marriage, تَزْوِيج ـ نِكَاح ـ زِيجَة. Marriage festivities, فَرَح ـ عُرْس.

Nurse, *n.* A woman who has the care of a child, a dry-nurse, دَايَة *pl.* دَايَات ـ حَاضِنَة. One who suckles a child, a wet-nurse, مُرْضِعَة. One who nurses the sick, مُطَلٍّ ٱلمَرْضَى *fem.* مُطَلِّيَة ـ خَادِمُ ٱلمَرْضَى *fem.* خَادِمَة. To put out to —, أَرْضَعَ عِنْدَ غَيْرِ أُمِّهِ ـ أَرْضَعَ عِنْدَ مُرْضِعَةٍ.

Nurse, *v.t.* To tend, as of a child, حَضَنَ ³. To suckle, أَرْضَعَ ـ رَضَّعَ. To —, or tend the sick, خَدَمَ ٱلمَرْضَى ³ ـ طَلَّى ٱلمَرْضَى ـ عَالَ ³ (or دَارَى) ٱلمَرْضَى. To —, cherish, support, countenance,

ظَهَرَ عَلَى - ظَاهَرَ - رَاعَى - دَارَى. To —, encourage, شَيَّعَ - شَجَّعَ - جَرَّأَ. To manage with economy, نَفِسَ بِ² - تَقَنَّى - وَفَّرَ فِي. To dandle, fondle, دَلَّلَ - رَفَّهَ. To — one's self up, تَرَفَّهَ - رَفَّهَ نَفْسَهُ.

Nursery, *n.* A room for children, حُجْرَةٌ لِلْأَوْلَادِ - بَيْتُ ٱلْأَوْلَادِ. A — for young trees, مَشْتَل - شَجَرِيَّة - مَغْرِس *pl.* مَغَارِسُ. A place where anything is fostered, مَنْشَأٌ. A school, مَدْرَسَة *pl.* مَدَارِسُ. A — plant, شَتْلَة *pl.* شَتْلَات.

Nursery-garden, *n.* شَجَرِيَّة - مَغْرِس - مَشْتَل.

Nursery-governess, *n.* مُعَلِّمَةُ ٱلْأَوْلَادِ ٱلصِّغَارِ.

Nursery-maid, *n.* خَادِمَةُ ٱلْأَوْلَادِ - دَايَة *pl.* دَايَات.

Nursery-man, *n.* بُسْتَانِيُّ ٱلْمَغْرِسِ (*or* ٱلْمَشْتَلِ).

Nurseling, *n.* Of a child at the breast, رَضِيع *pl.* رُضَعَاءُ; of a plant, فَرْخ شَجَرَة *pl.* فِرَاخ - شَتْلَة *pl.* شَتْلَات.

Nurture, *n.* تَرْبِيَة. *See also* Nourishment, *n.*

Nurture, *v.t.* To foster, أَنْشَأَ - نَشَّأَ. To be nurtured, fostered, إِنْتَشَأَ. *See also to* Nourish, *v.t.*

Nut, *n.* A filbert, جِلَّوْزَة - جِلَّوْز *coll.* فُنْدُقَة *coll.* فُنْدُق *pl.* فَنَادِقُ - بُنْدُقَة *coll.* بُنْدُق *pl.* بَنَادِقُ. A walnut, جَوْزَة *coll.* جَوْز *pl.* جَوْزَات. An almond, لَوْزَة *coll.* لَوْز *pl.* لَوْزَات. The nut of a screw, زِرُّ ٱلْبُرْغِيِّ *pl.* أَزْرَار. To crack nuts, كَسَرَ ٱلْبُنْدُقَ. A hard nut to crack, a difficulty, مِحْنَة - مُشْكِلَة - صُعُوبَة - مَعْسَرَة. To give one a hard nut to crack, أَوْحَلَ - أَوْرَطَ فِي وَرْطَةٍ. To be nuts to crack to, to rejoice at, تَغَبَّطَ مِنْ - إِنْبَسَطَ مِنْ.

Nut, *v.i.* قَطَفَ (*or* جَنَى) ٱلْبُنْدُقَ.

Nutant, *a.* *See* Nodding, *a.*

Nutation, *n.* اِهْتِزَازُ ٱلْأَرْضِ - خَطَرَانُ ٱلْأَرْضِ عَلَى مَرْكَزِهَا.

Nut-brown, *a.* أَكْلَفُ *fem.* كَلْفَاءُ *pl.* كُلْف.

Nutcracker, *n.* / Nutcracks, } آلَةٌ لِكَسْرِ ٱلْجَوْزِ *vulg.* كَاسُورَة.

Nut-gall, *n.* عَفْصَة *coll.* عَفْص.

Nut-shell, *n.* As of filberts, قِشْرَةُ ٱلْبُنْدُقِ *coll.* قُشُور.

Nutmeg, *n.* جَوْزُ ٱلطِّيبِ - جَوْزُ بَوَّا.

Nutrient, *a.* *See* Nourishing, *a.*

Nutriment, *n.* *See* Nourishment, *n.*

Nutrimental, *a.* *See* Nourishing, *a.*

Nutrition, *n.* *See* Nourishment, *n.*

Nutritious, *a.* / Nutritive, } *See* Nourishing, *a.*

Nutritiveness, *n.* / Nutriture, } *See* Nourishment, *n.*

Nutting, *n.* Gathering nuts, قَطْفُ ٱلْبُنْدُقِ.

Nux-vomica, *n.* جَوْزُ ٱلْقَيْءِ.

Nuzzle, *v.t.* خَضَنَ².

Nuzzle, *v.i.* To burrow in the mud, بَحَثَ ٱلطِّينَ بِٱلْفِنْطِيسَةِ.

Nyctalopia, *n.* خَفَش. Having —, أَخْفَشُ *fem.* خَفْشَاءُ *pl.* خُفْش.

Nylghau, *n.* نَوْعٌ مِنَ ٱلْبَقَرِ يُوجَدُ فِي جِبَالِ ٱلْهِنْدِ.

N.W. (North-west), عِبَارَةٌ عَنِ ٱلشَّمَالِيِّ ٱلْغَرْبِيِّ.

Nymph, *n.* A goddess of the streams, جِنِّيَّةُ ٱلْمَاءِ. A beautiful lady, حَوَارِيَّة *pl.* حَوَارِيَّات. *See also* Chrysalis, *n.*

Nympha, *n.* The — of the clitoris, عُرْوَة. The nymphæ, الْعُرْوَتَانِ.

Nymphean, *a.* مُتَعَلِّقٌ بِٱلْجِنِّيَّاتِ.

Nymph-like, *a.* / Nymphly, } مِثْلَ ٱلْحَوَارِيَّاتِ - مِثْلَ ٱلْجِنِّيَّاتِ.

Nymphomania, *n.* عِلَّةُ ٱلْجِمَاعِ - جِنَّةُ (*or* دَاءُ) ٱلْعِشْقِ.

O.

O! *interj.* (As a vocative particle, in the sense of) O there! soho! or, holla! أَى — أَيَا — أَى ; *e.g.*, O Zaid, draw near! (أَيَا *or*) أَى زَيْدُ قَرِّبْ. (As a particle of invocation,) يَا. O God! يَا أَللّٰهُ ; O man! يَا أَيُّهَا ٱلرَّجُلُ. *See also under* Oh!

O'. *a.* تَرْخِيمُ لَفْظَةِ ٱبْنٍ أَوْ مِنْ آلِ فُلَانٍ ; *e.g.* O'Donnell, مَعْنَاهُ ٱبْنُ أَوْ مِنْ آلِ دُوْنَل.

Oaf, *n.* A changeling, وَضِيعَةٌ. *See also* Dunce, Dolt, *n.*

Oafish, *a.* *See* Stupid, Doltish, *a.*

Oak, *n.* بَلُّوط ; the tree, شَجَرَةُ ٱلْبَلُّوطِ. The evergreen oak, سِنْدِيَان (called in Syria, ٱلدَّوَامُ) ; the tree, شَجَرَةُ ٱلسِّنْدِيَانِ. Ground —, بَلُّوطُ ٱلْأَرْضِ. The gall —, ٱلْبَلُّوطُ ٱلْعَفْصِيُّ. The cork —, ٱلْبَلُّوطُ ٱلْفَلِّينِيُّ.

Oak, *a.*
Oaken, } مِنْ سِنْدِيَانٍ — مِنْ بَلُّوطٍ.

Oak-apple, *n.* The round —, سِنْدِيَان — سِنْدِجَان ; the oblong, مَلُّول.

Oakling, *n.* شَتْلَةُ ٱلسِّنْدِيَانِ — شُجَيْرَةُ ٱلسِّنْدِيَانِ.

Oakum, *n.* نُسَر — نَبْخَة — نَبْخَة — نُبَيْخَة (from the Italian,) أُصْطُبَّة.

Oaky, *a.* Hard like oak, hard, صُلْب — مَتِين — مَتِينٌ كَٱلسِّنْدِيَانِ.

Oar, *n.* مِجْدَاف *pl.* مَجَادِيف — مِقْذَاف *pl.* مَقَاذِيف.

Oar, *v.i.* } جَدَفَ — قَذَفَ ـ. He oared the boat, جَدَفَ ـ
Oar, *v.t.* } قَذَفَ بِٱلسَّفِينَةِ — ٱلْقَارِبَ ـ. *See also to* Row, *v.t.*

Oarsman, *n.* قَذَّاف — قَاذِف — نُوتِيّ *pl.* نَوَاتِيّ.

Oasis, *n.* وَادٍ *pl.* أَوْدَاء and أَوْدَاة and أَوْدِيَة.

Oast, *n.* A kiln to dry hops, فُرْنٌ لِتَجْفِيفِ حَشِيشَةِ ٱلدِّينَارِ.

Oat, Oats, *n.* شُوفَان — خُرْطَان — هُرْطُمَان. Wild —, شُوفَانٌ بَرِّيٌّ. To sow one's wild —, (فَرَغَ مِنْ شَبِيبَتِهِ (*or* غَمْرَتِهِ.

Oat-cake, *n.* رَغِيفٌ مِنْ شُوفَانٍ.

Oaten, *n.* مِنْ شُوفَانٍ.

Oath, *n.* عَهْد — قَسَم *pl.* أَقْسَام — قَسَامَة — قَسِيمَة — شَهَادَة — يَمِين *pl.* أَيْمُن *or* أَيْمَان — حَلْفَة — حَلْف. A false —, يَمِينٌ زُورٌ. Blasphemous swearing, سَبٌّ — تَجْدِيف. A volley of oaths, ضَرْبُ سَبٍّ. Oaths of allegiance, أَيْمَانُ ٱلْبَيْعَةِ.

To administer an oath, حَلَّفَ — أَحْلَفَ.

To break an oath, حَنِثَ فِي يَمِينِهِ ـ.

To call upon one to take an oath, ٱسْتَحْلَفَ — ٱسْتَقْسَمَ.

To swear or take an oath, حَلَفَ — أَقْسَمَ — حَلَفَ حَلْفَةً يَمِينًا. *See also to* Swear.

Oatmeal, *n.* دَقِيقُ ٱلشُّوفَانِ.

Obduracy, *n.* تَمَرُّد — وَعْقَة — قَسَاوَة — عِنَاد — شَكَاسَة.

Obdurate, *a.* مُرَدَاءُ *pl.* مَرِيد — مَرَدَة *pl.* مَارِد — خَشِنُ ٱلْجَانِبِ — شَكِس *pl.* شُكْس — وَعْق. To be —, عَانَدَ — شَكِسَ ـ.

Obdurately, *ad.* تَمَرُّدًا — بِعِنَادٍ — مُعَانَدَةً — بِشَكَاسَةٍ.

Obdurateness, *n.* *See* Obduracy, *n.*

Obedience, *n.* Submission, خُضُوع — طَاعَة — إِطَاعَة — إِذْعَان. Compliance with a command, إِسْتِجَابَة — إِمْتِثَال — مُمَاثَلَة — إِسْتِجَابَةٌ لِ — إِذْعَان — إِئْتِمَار. In — to, in compliance with, إِطَاعَةً لِ — حَسَبَ — إِذْعَانًا لِ. To demand one's —, إِسْتَطَاعَ. To reduce to —, طَوَّعَ. To render — to, إِنْقَادَ لِ. To place one's self under the — of, أَدْخَلَ تَحْتَ طَاعَتِهِ.

Obedient, *a.* Submissive to authority, مُذْعِن — أَخْضَعُ — خَاضِع — طَائِع — مُطِيع. Yielding compliance with commands, سَامِعٌ لِ — سَمِيع *pl.* سُمَعَاءُ — مِنْقَاد — وَدِيع. To be — to, أَذْعَنَ لِ — أَطَاعَ.

Obediently, *ad.* بِإِذْعَانٍ — بِٱنْقِيَادٍ — طَوْعًا — سَمْعًا وَطَاعَةً.

Obeisance, *n.* سُجُود — خُضُوع. To do — to, سَجَدَ لِ ـ — ضَرَبَ لَهُ تَمَنِّيًا — خَضَعَ لِ ـ.

Obeisant, *a.* سَاجِد — خَاضِع.

Obelisk, *n.* مِسَلَّة — عَمُودٌ عَلَى هَيْئَةِ مِسَلَّةٍ.

Obese, *a.* ضَخْم — ضَخْم — شَحِيم — شَخِيص — سَمِين. To be —, شَحُمَ — سَمِنَ — ضَخُمَ ـ.

Obeseness, *n.*
Obesity, } نُعُومَة — بَدَانَة — ضَخَامَة — سِمَن.

Obey, *v.t.* To submit to, يَطِيعُ *or* يَطُوعُ *aor.* طَاعَ لِ — أَطَاعَ — أَذْعَنَ لِ — قَامَ بِأَمْرِهِ — إِنْطَاعَ لِ. To comply with commands, إِسْتَجَابَ لِ — أَصْغَى إِلَى — إِمْتَثَلَ — أَذْعَنَ لِ — سَمِعَ لِ — إِنْقَادَ لِ. To yield to, إِئْتَمَرَ — إِسْتَسْلَمَ لِ — أَسْلَمَ لِ. He obeyed his own instinct, إِئْتَمَرَ رَأْيَ نَفْسِهِ. Why did you not — him? لِمَاذَا مَا تَسْمَعُ لِصَوْتِهِ.

Obfuscate, *v.t.* To confuse, تَيَّهَ — حَيَّرَ — كَدَّرَ. *See also to* Darken, Obscure, *v.t.*

Obfuscation, *n.* The act of confusing, تَكْدِير – تَحْيِير – تَشْوِيه ; the being confused, confounded, كَدَر – حَيْرَة . The act of darkening, veiling, إِكْتِتَام – حَجْب . The being dark, غَتْم – ظُلْمَة – غَتَمَة .

Obit, *n.* *See* Decease, *n.*

Obiter, *ad.* *See* Incidentally, *ad.*

Obituary, *n.* A register of deaths, دَفْتَر (*or* جَدْوَل) ٱلْأَمْوَات .

Obituary, *a.* ما نِيطَ بِٱلْمَوْتَى .

Object, *n.* A thing, شَيْءٌ *pl.* أَشْيَآءُ – حَاجَة *pl.* حَاجَات . A subject matter, مَوْضُوع . An aim, design, قَصْد – مَرَام – سَعْي – مُرَاد – طَوِيَّة – خُطَّة – غَرَض *pl.* أَغْرَاض – مَقْصُود . A mark to aim at, نِيشَان – هَدَف . The subject of any sentiment or action, مَظْهَر . The — of royal favour, مَظْهَرُ ٱلْأَلْطَافِ ٱلْمُلُوكِيَّةِ . An — of pity, مِمَّا يُرْثَى لِحَالِهِ – مَظْهَرُ ٱلرَّحْمَةِ . An — of love, مَعْشُوق – مَحْبُوب . An — of merchandise, سِلْعَة *pl.* سِلَع – بِضَاعَة *pl.* بَضَائِعُ – مَتَاع *pl.* أَمْتِعَة . An — of ridicule, مَضْحَكَة . *In grammar*, that which follows the transitive verb, ٱلْمَفْعُولُ بِهِ . Money is no — to him, لَيْسَ لَهُ غَرَضٌ بِٱلدَّرَاهِمِ – ما يُبَالِي بِٱلدَّرَاهِمِ – يَسْتَغْنِي عَنِ ٱلدَّرَاهِمِ .

Object, *v.t.* To oppose, إِعْتَرَضَ عَلَى – إِمْتَنَعَ عَلَى .

Object, *v.i.* To object to, to offer opposition to, تَعَرَّضَ لِ – عَرَضَ لِ ـِ – إِعْتَرَضَ لِ – عَارَضَ – خَالَفَ – ضَادَدَ . To — to, as in a reply, رَدَّ عَلَى 2 . He objected to the thing, رَدَّ ٱلْأَمْرَ 2 – عَارَضَ فِي ٱلْأَمْرِ . I objected to his words, *i.e.*, in reply to them, رَدَدْتُ قَوْلَهُ . If you do not —, إِنْ شِئْتَ – إِذَا ٱسْتَحْسَنَ لَكَ .

Objection, *n.* The act of opposing, تَعَرُّض – إِعْتِرَاض . Adverse reason, إِعْتِرَاض *pl.* إِعْتِرَاضَات . A groundless —, إِعْتِرَاضٌ بَاطِلٌ . An unanswerable —, إِعْتِرَاضٌ لا مَرَدَّ لَهُ – إِعْتِرَاضٌ قَاطِعٌ . There is no — to that, لَيْسَ فِي ذٰلِكَ مَانِعٌ .

To anticipate an objection, إِنْتَظَرَ ٱلْإِعْتِرَاضَ .

To have no objection, رَضِيَ بِ ـَ – لَمْ يَعْتَرِضْ عَلَى ٱلشَّيْءِ .

To make an objection, تَعَرَّضَ – إِعْتَرَضَ ٱعْتِرَاضًا .

To meet or answer an objection, رَدَّ ٱلْإِعْتِرَاضَ 2 .

To raise or start an objection, قَدَّمَ (*or* أَعْرَضَ *or* نَصَبَ 2) ٱلْإِعْتِرَاضَ – إِعْتَرَضَ ٱعْتِرَاضًا .

To remove an objection, رَفَعَ ـَ (*or* أَزَالَ) ٱلْإِعْتِرَاضَ .

To urge an objection, إِعْتَرَضَ ٱعْتِرَاضًا بِٱلْحَاحٍ .

Objectionable, *a.* Against which objections may be raised, مِمَّا يُعْتَرَضُ عَلَيْهِ . Reprehensible, مِمَّا يُلَامُ – ذَمِيم – مَلَام . Inadmissible, غَيْرُ مَقْبُولٍ – لا يُقْبَلُ .

Objective, *a.* External to the mind, خَارِجٌ عَنِ ٱلْعَقْلِ – خَارِجِيٌّ . What is —, ٱلْخَارِجُ . Objective things, ٱلْأُمُورُ ٱلْخَارِجِيَّةُ . The — case, as made such by a verb, ٱلْمَفْعُولُ ; by a preposition, ٱلْمَجْرُورُ .

Objectively, *ad.* By way of objection, إِعْتِرَاضًا . In the manner or state of an object, خَارِجًا عَنِ ٱلْعَقْلِ .

Objectiveness, Objectivity, *n.* } The being external to the mind, حَالُ وُجُودِ ٱلشَّيْءِ خَارِجًا عَنِ ٱلْعَقْلِ .

Objectless, *a.* عَبَث – بِدُونِ مَقْصُودٍ – بِدُونِ مَرَامٍ .

Objector, *n.* مُعْتَرِض – مُعَانِد .

Objurgate, *v.t.* To chide, scold, تَعَيَّبَ – عَاتَبَ – سَخِطَ عَلَى ـَ – وَبَّخَ – عَلَى .

Objurgation, *n.* تَوْبِيخ – أُعْتُوبَة – عِتَاب – سُخْطَة .

Objurgatory, *a.* تَوْبِيخِيّ – عَتَّاب – سَاخِط .

Oblate, *a.* Flattened at both ends or sides, مُسَطَّحُ ٱلطَّرَفَيْنِ – مُصَفَّحُ ٱلطَّرَفَيْنِ .

Oblateness, *n.* تَسْطِيحُ ٱلطَّرَفَيْنِ – سَطْحُ ٱلصَّفْحَتَيْنِ .

Oblation, *n.* The act of offering, تَقْرِيب . An offering, تَقْدِمَة – قُرْبَان *pl.* قَرَابِينُ . A sacrifice, ذَبِيحَة *pl.* ذَبَائِحُ – أُضْحِيَّة . *See also* Gift, Offering, *n.*

Obligation, *n.* The binding force of a promise, contract, *etc.*, ضَرُورَة – وَاجِبَة *pl.* وَاجِبَات . Any act by which one binds himself, عَهْد *pl.* عُهُود – عُهْدَة – ذِمَّة *pl.* ذِمَام – حِمَال – حَمَالَة . A written bond, صَكّ *pl.* صُكُوك – تَمَسُّك – سَنَد *pl.* سَنَدَات . Coercion, إِضْطِرَار – جَبْر – إِلْزَام . The duty imposed by civilities received, مِنَّة *pl.* مِنَن – مِنَّتِي . A religious —, duty, فَرْض *pl.* فُرُوض – فَرِيضَة *pl.* فَرَائِضُ . To discharge one's religious obligations, فَرَّضَ . To be free, as of an —, حَلَّ مِنْ ـِ . To free from an —, جَعَلَ فِي حَلٍّ مِنْ قِبَلِهِ ـَ . To be under —, for civilities received, حَمَلَ مِنَّتِي ـِ – كَانَ تَحْتَ ٱلْمِنَّتِي . The obligations which I am under to you, إِحْسَانُكَ عَلَيَّ – مِنَّتُكَ عَلَيَّ – أَفْضَالُكُمُ ٱلَّتِي عَمَّتْ عَلَيَّ . I am under the greatest obligations to him, أَنَا غَرِيقٌ فِي بَحْرِ جُودِهِ وَأَلْطَافِهِ . I am under obligation, obliged, to you, أَنَا مَدْيُونٌ لِمَعْرُوفِكَ ; *colloquial*, أَنَا مَمْنُونٌ لَكَ – أَنَا تَحْتَ مَمْنُونِيَّتِكَ .

Obligatory, *a.* لَازِم – ضَرُورِيّ . To be —, حَقَّ 2 – وَجَبَ *aor.* يَجِبُ . To be — on, حَقَّ عَلَى ـِ – وَجَبَ عَلَى *aor.* يَجِبُ – حَلَّ عَلَى ـِ . A thing made —, مُفْتَرَض – مَفْرُوض – وَاجِب *pl.* وَاجِبَات – فَرِيضَة *pl.* فَرَائِضُ . The debt was — on him, حَلَّ عَلَيْهِ ٱلدَّيْنُ ـِ . The — statutes of God, عَزَائِمُ ٱللّٰهِ . Obligatory religious duties, فَرَائِضُ – سُنَنُ ٱلْهُدَى .

Oblige, *v.t.* To compel, أَكْرَهَ ـ أَلْزَمَ ـ = غَصَبَ ـ اِلْتَحَصَ ـ اِضْطَرَّ-إِلَى ـ أَجْبَرَ ـ اِسْتَكْرَهَ. To constrain, impel, move, حَمَّلَ- (or = حَمَلَ-) عَلَى ـ أَلْجَأَ-إِلَى. To impose, as a duty, upon, أَلْزَمَ-بِ ـ أَوْجَبَ-عَلَى. To do a favour to, = مَنَّ عَلَى ـ أَنْعَمَ عَلَى ـ عَمِلَ مَعَهُ مَعْرُوفًا (or خَيْرًا). To be obliged, compelled, constrained to, أُلْزِمَ بِ ـ لَزِمَ عَلَى ـ أُضْطُرَّ إِلَى. I shall be much obliged to you for it, أَكُونُ لَكَ فِي غَايَةِ ٱلْاِمْتِنَانِ لِأَجْلِ ذٰلِكَ. You would — us very much, لَكُنْتَ تَجْعَلُنَا لَكَ مَمْنُونِينَ جِدًّا. I was obliged to go, أُضْطُرِرْتُ إِلَى ٱلرَّوَاحِ. They obliged him to do it, غَصَبُوهُ عَلَى ذٰلِكَ. The duty of his office obliges him to this, هٰذا بِمُقْتَضَى وَظِيفَتِهِ. They were obliged to return, أُضْطُرُّوا إِلَى ٱلرُّجُوعِ.

Obliged, *a.* Constrained, مَجْبُورٌ ـ مَلْزُومٌ ـ مُضْطَرٌّ. Favoured, مُنْعَمٌ عَلَيْهِ ـ مُحْسَنٌ إِلَيْهِ.

Obliging, *a.* عَمِيمُ ٱلْإِحْسَانِ ـ لَطِيفٌ ـ خَيِّرٌ ـ صَاحِبُ مَعْرُوفٍ ـ مِنْعَامٌ ـ صَاحِبُ مُرُوَّةٍ.

Obligingly, *ad.* خَيْرًا ـ بِمَعْرُوفٍ ـ بِإِنْعَامٍ ـ بِلُطْفٍ.

Obligingness, *n.* مَعْرُوفٌ ـ كَرَمٌ ـ لُطْفٌ.

Oblique, *a.* Deviating from a right line, زَائِغٌ ـ مُتَعَرِّضٌ ـ مُنْحَرِفٌ ـ مَائِلٌ ـ غَيْرُ مُسْتَقِيمٍ. To be —, ² زَاغَ ـ تَعَرَّضَ ـ اِنْحَرَفَ. To make —, حَرَّفَ ـ أَزَاغَ. A noun being or being put into the — case, مَجْرُورٌ or مَنْصُوبٌ. An — or equivocal phrase, مِعْرَاضٌ ـ تَوْرِيَةٌ. An — or side wind, رِيحٌ مُشَارِكٌ ـ نَكْبَاءُ. An — look, glance, نَظَرٌ عَنْ جَانِبٍ ـ نَظَرٌ عَنْ عُرْضٍ.

Obliquely, *ad.* بِٱنْحِرَافٍ ـ اِنْحِرَافًا ـ بِعِوَجٍ ـ عُرْضًا. To speak —, ambiguously, equivocally, عَرَّضَ. To go or walk —, out of the right course, تَعَرَّضَ ـ تَعَوَّجَ ـ ² زَاغَ : he walks —, going from side to side in his course, يَتَعَرَّضُ فِي سَيْرِهِ. To look at anything —, نَظَرَ إِلَى-عَنْ عُرْضٍ (or عَنْ جَانِبٍ).

Obliqueness, *n.* } Indirectness, اِعْوِجَاجٌ ـ تَعَرُّضٌ ـ عِوَجٌ ـ
Obliquity, } مَيْلٌ ـ تَمَايُلٌ ـ اِنْحِرَافٌ. Deviation from moral rectitude, زَلَّةٌ ـ طُغْيَانٌ ـ ضَلَالٌ ـ عَدَمُ ٱسْتِقَامَةٍ. There is no — in him, لَا عِوَجَ فِيهِ.

Obliterate, *v.t.* ² = طَلَسَ ـ كَحَّصَ ـ = كَحَصَ ـ = طَمَسَ ـ ² مَحَا ـ أَزَالَ ـ طَلَّسَ. To be obliterated, تَطَلَّسَ ـ اِمَّحَى. *See also to* Erase, *v.t.*

Obliterated, *a.* مَمْحُوٌّ ـ مَدْرُوسٌ ـ مُنْدَرِسٌ ـ مُطَلَّسٌ. A written paper of which the writing has been —, طِلْسٌ ـ طِرْسٌ. Obliterated, as the impression on a coin, مُسَيَّفٌ.

Obliteration, *n.* إِزَالَةٌ ـ كَحْصٌ ـ تَطْلِيسٌ ـ مَحْوٌ.

Oblivion, *n.* نِسْيٌ ـ نِسَاوَةٌ ـ نِسْيَانٌ. To fall into —, = نَسِيَ. To consign to —, = جَعَلَ مَنْسِيًّا ـ أَنْسَى ـ أَدْرَجَ-فِي طَيِّ ٱلنِّسْيَانِ ـ أَغْرَقَ-فِي بَحْرِ ٱلنِّسْيَانِ. Consigned to —, مُفْرَطٌ.

Oblivious, *a.* غَبِينٌ ـ نَاسٍ ـ نَسْيَانُ. To be —, = غَبِنَ فِي ـ = نَسِيَ ـ = غَبِنَ. *See also* Forgetful, *a.*

Oblong, *a.* مُطَاوِلٌ ـ مُسْتَطِيلٌ. To be —, اِسْتَطَالَ. To make —, أَزَّجَ. An — room or structure, أَزَجٌ *pl.* آزَاجٌ *and* آزُجٌ. An — piece of cloth, شُقَّةٌ *pl.* شُقَقٌ ـ سَبِيبَةٌ مُسْتَطِيلَةٌ ـ بَصِيرَةٌ. An — book, سَفِينَةٌ. Not every round thing is a walnut, nor every — thing a plantain, (*prov.*) لَا كُلُّ مُدَوَّرٍ جَوْزٌ وَلَا كُلُّ مُسْتَطِيلٍ مَوْزٌ.

Oblongish, *a.* يَضْرِبُ إِلَى ٱلْاِسْتِطَالَةِ.

Oblongly, *ad.* عَلَى هَيْئَةٍ مُسْتَطِيلَةٍ.

Oblongness, *n.* اِسْتِطَالَةٌ.

Obloquy, *n.* Censorious speech, لَوْمٌ ـ شَتْمٌ ـ طَعْنٌ ـ تُهَمَةٌ ـ تَقْبِيحٌ ـ مَلَامٌ. He cast — upon him, ² نَمَّ ـ = ² طَعَنَ فِيهِ. To bring into —, ² = جَلَبَ عَلَى-ٱلْقَبَاحَةَ ـ قَبَّحَ. *See also* Disgrace, *n.*

Obnoxious, *a.* Exposed or subject to, مُعَرَّضٌ (or مَعْرُوضٌ) لِ. Deserving of, مُسْتَوْجِبٌ. Reprehensible, ذَمِيمٌ ـ مُلِيمٌ. Odious, كَرِيهٌ ـ قَبِيحٌ ـ مَقْبُوحٌ. To be —, exposed, to, تَعَرَّضَ لِ. To deserve, اِسْتَوْجَبَ. They became — to the anger of God, ² حَلَّ عَلَيْهِمْ غَضَبُ ٱللّٰهِ.

Obnoxiously, *ad.* In a state of liability, بِتَعَرُّضٍ ـ تَعَرُّضًا لِ. Reprehensibly, بِمَذَمَّةٍ ـ مَلَامًا. Odiously, كَرَاهَةً ـ قَبْحًا ـ قَبَاحَةً.

Obnoxiousness, *n.* Liability to, مَعْرُوضٌ ـ تَعَرُّضٌ لِ. Offensiveness, كَرَاهَةٌ ـ مَذَمَّةٌ ـ قَبَاحَةٌ.

Oboe, *n.* *See* Hautboy, *n.*

Obolus, *n.* فَلْسٌ *pl.* فُلُوسٌ ـ پَارَةٌ *pl.* پَارَاتٌ.

Obovate, *a.* مَا كَانَ تَعَرُّهُ بِشَكْلِ ٱلْبَيْضَةِ.

Obscene, *a.* مُفْحِشٌ ـ أَعْوَرُ ـ رَفَثٌ ـ خَنٍ ـ بَذِيءٌ ـ بَذِيٌّ ـ فَاحِشٌ ـ فَاسِقٌ. Obscene in speech, بَذِيءُ ٱللِّسَانِ. Obscene speech, كَلَامٌ خَنٍ. An — book, كِتَابٌ ذَمِيمٌ ـ كِتَابٌ أَعْوَرُ *pl.* كُتُبٌ عُوْرٌ ـ مِنْ سَقَطِ ٱلْكُتُبِ. An — woman, عَاهِرَةٌ ـ فَاحِشَةٌ.

Obscenely, *ad.* بِفَحْشَاءَ ـ بِرَفَثٍ ـ فُحْشًا ـ خَنًا. To act —, تَفَاحَشَ ـ أَفْسَدَ ـ ² فَسَقَ ـ أَبْذَى ـ يَبْذَى *aor.* بَذِيَ. To speak —, تَفَحَّشَ فِي ٱلْكَلَامِ ـ = بَذِيَ فِي ٱلْكَلَامِ.

Obsceneness, *n.* } فَاحِشَةٌ ـ خَنَايَةٌ ـ فُحْشٌ ـ رَفَثٌ ـ قَذَعٌ ـ
Obscenity, } عَارٌ ـ عَيْبٌ. An obscenity, عَارٌ ـ عَوْرَاءُ ـ سَقَطٌ ـ فَاحِشَةٌ.

Obscuration, n. The act of darkening, تَغْتِيم ـ إِقْتِتَام ; the being dark, ظُلْمَة ـ قَتَمَة. The act of making abstruse, difficult, تَعْقِيد ـ إِبْهَام ـ تَشْبِيه.

Obscure, a. Destitute of light, قَاتِم pl. قَوَاتِمُ ـ أَقْتَمُ ـ مُظْلِم. Secret, hidden, خَفِيٌّ. Unknown, مَجْهُول. Abstruse, difficult, مُلْتَبِس ـ غَامِض ـ مُعَقَّد ـ مُشْكِل ـ مُشْتَبِه ـ غَلِق ـ مُعَمًّى ـ مُغْلَق ـ مُبْهَم. Of — birth, مَجْهُولُ ٱلنَّسَبِ ـ مَغْمُور. Not known to fame, of a thing, غَمِيس ـ مَغْمُول ; of a person, سَاقِطٌ ـ خَامِل ـ غَامِض ـ لَاقِطٌ مَاقِطٌ. An — question, مَسْأَلَةٌ غَامِضَةٌ. To be —, abstruse, to one, إِشْتَبَهَ عَلَى ـ عَمِيَ عَلَى ـ إِلْتَبَسَ بِ. To make —, غَمَّضَ.

Obscure, v.t. To darken, أَظْلَمَ ـ إِقْتَتَمَ. To make abstruse, difficult, عَقَّدَ ـ غَمَّضَ ـ عَمَّى ; to make — to, عَمَّى-عَلَى ـ شَبَّهَ-عَلَى ـ أَبْهَمَ-عَلَى ـ لَبَّسَ-عَلَى. Insanity obscured his intellect, أَطْبَقَ عَلَيْهِ ٱلْجُنُونُ. He obscured the meaning of the verse, عَمَّى مَعْنَى ٱلْبَيْتِ. He obscured his meaning, made it enigmatical, عَمَّى مُرَادَهُ.

Obscurely, ad. Not brightly, ظُلْمَةً ـ عَتَمَةً. In an obscure manner, إِبْهَامًا ـ بِٱلْتِبَاسٍ ـ شُبْهَةً ـ إِشْتِبَاهًا. In a poor unknown manner, عَلَى ٱلْمَجْهُولِ ـ خُمُولًا. Privately, سِرًّا ـ خِفْيَةً. Hintingly, غَمْزًا ـ رَمْزًا ـ بِإِلْمَاءٍ.

Obscureness, n. / Obscurity, } Want of light, عَتَمَة ـ ظُلْمَة. Abstruseness, إِلْتِبَاس ـ تَعْقِيد ـ شُبْهَة ـ عَمَايَة ـ إِشْتِبَاه. Humble state, خُمُول. The not being much known, خَفَاء ـ خُمُول. Free from —, clear, لَا عُثْرَ فِيهِ ـ لَا غُبَارَ عَلَيْهِ.

Obsequies, n. جِنَازَة pl. جَنَائِزُ. To perform the funeral — of, جَنَّزَ.

Obsequious, a. لَيِّنُ ٱلْجَانِبِ ـ خَافِضُ ٱلْجَنَاحِ ـ طَائِع ـ طَيِّع ـ مُتَوَاضِع. To be —, تَوَاضَعَ ـ خَفَضَ ٱلْجَنَاحَ ـ طَاوَعَ. To make —, خَفَّضَ ـ طَوَّعَ.

Obsequiously, ad. بِتَوَاضُعٍ ـ بِلِينَةِ ٱلْجَانِبِ ـ بِخَفْضِ ٱلْجَنَاحِ ـ بِمُطَاوَعَةٍ.

Obsequiousness, n. تَوَاضُع ـ لِينَةُ ٱلْجَانِبِ ـ خَفْضُ ٱلْجَنَاحِ ـ مُطَاوَعَة.

Observable, a. That may be observed or noticed, مِمَّا يُلَاحَظُ ـ يُدْرِكُهُ ٱلنَّظَرُ ـ مِمَّا يُرَى. Worthy of notice, مُسْتَحِقُّ ٱلْمُلَاحَظَةِ. It is — in summer, يُرَى (or يَبِينُ or يَظْهَرُ) فِي ٱلصَّيْفِ.

Observably, ad. بِنَوْعٍ يَجْلُبُ ٱلنَّظَرَ ـ تَبْيِينًا ـ تَظَاهُرًا.

Observance, n. Performance, قَضَاء ـ إِيفَاء ـ إِجْرَاء. Strict regard to, مُرَاعَاة ـ رِعَايَة. Compliance, obedience, إِمْتِثَال ـ إِذْعَان ـ إِسْتِجَابَة ـ مُمَاثَلَة. A custom, ceremony, عَادَة pl. عَادَات ـ رَسْم pl. رُسُوم ـ قَانُون pl. قَوَانِينُ. Observance of rights, مُرَاعَاةُ ٱلْحُقُوقِ. *See also* Observation, n.

Observanda, n. أَشْيَاءُ مُسْتَحِقَّةُ ٱلْمُلَاحَظَةِ.

Observant, a. Taking notice, مُلَاحِظ ـ صَاحِبُ مُلَاحَظَةٍ ـ صَاحِبُ نَظَرٍ. Mindful, attentive, مُرَاعٍ ـ رَاعٍ عَلَى ـ مُعْتَنٍ بِ ـ حَافِظ ـ قَائِمٌ فِي. Obeying, مُمْتَثِل ـ مُذْعِن ـ مُطِيع. Observant of the laws, مُرَاعٍ لِلشَّرَائِعِ.

Observation, n. The act of fixing the attention on any thing, مُلَاحَظَة ـ نَظَرٌ فِي ـ تَفَرُّسٌ فِي. Expression of what is observed, note, remark, تَعْبِير ـ بَيَان ـ قَوْل ـ شَرْح. A viewing of the heavenly bodies, and such like, رَقْب ـ رُقُوب ـ مُرَاقَبَة ـ رَصْد ـ تَرَصُّد ; one such —, رَقْبَة ـ رَقَابَة ـ رَصْدَة. Control, inspection, نَظَارَة ـ مُبَاشَرَة. A party of —, شَيِّقَة. He took an astronomical —, رَصَدَ [2] رَصْدًا فَلَكِيًّا.

To come or fall under one's observation, تَعَرَّضَ لِ ـ وَقَعَ فِي نَظَرِهِ.

To draw one's observation to, جَلَبَ [2] نَظَرَهُ إِلَى ـ فَاطَنَ-فِي ـ نَبَّهَ-عَلَى.

To escape one's observation, فَاتَ [2] نَظَرَهُ ـ سَهَا [2] عَنْ.

To make an observation, remark, أَفَادَ ـ عَبَّرَ عَنْ ـ قَالَ aor. يَقُولُ.

To take an observation, رَقَبَ [2] ـ إِرْتَقَبَ ـ رَصَدَ [2] ـ إِرْتَصَدَ.

Observatory, n. An elevated place for observation, مَرْبَأَة ـ مَطْلَعَة. An — for astronomical purposes, مَرْصَدُ ٱلْكَوَاكِبِ ـ دَارُ ٱلرَّصْدِ.

Observe, v.t. To behold with attention, تَعَرَّضَ لِ ـ نَظَرَ [2] إِلَى ـ دَقَّ [2] ٱلنَّظَرَ إِلَى. To consider with attention, وَقَفَ عَلَى aor. يَقِفُ ـ نَظَرَ [2] فِي ـ إِسْتَشَفَّ ـ أَمْعَنَ ٱلنَّظَرَ فِي ـ فَطِنَ [2] لِ or إِلَى ـ لَاحَظَ ـ or بِ. To utter or express, أَفَادَ ـ قَالَ aor. يَقُولُ. To observe, as of the stars, رَقَبَ [2] ـ إِرْتَقَبَ ـ إِرْتَصَدَ ـ رَصَدَ [2]. To keep to in practice, حَفِظَ ـ رَاعَى. To comply with, إِمْتَثَلَ بِ ـ أَذْعَنَ لِ ـ إِئْتَمَرَ ـ سَمِعَ ـ إِسْتَجَابَ لِ. To —, as of a promise, أَوْفَى بِ ـ أَمْسَكَ بِ. He that observeth the wind shall not sow, and he that regardeth the clouds shall not reap, مَنْ يَرْصُدِ ٱلرِّيحَ لَا يَزْرَعُ وَمَنْ يُرَاقِبِ ٱلسُّحُبَ لَا يَحْصُدُ. He sees many things but does not observe them, يَنْظُرُ إِلَى أَشْيَاءَ كَثِيرَةٍ وَلَا يُلَاحِظُهَا. Observed, executed, carried out, مَرْعِيٌّ. The treaty shall continue to be observed, or shall continue in force, تَبْقَى ٱلْمُعَاهَدَةُ مَرْعِيَّةَ ٱلْإِجْرَاءِ.

Observer, n. One who looks on, نَاظِر pl. نُظَّارَة ـ شَاهِد pl. شُهُود ـ

— صَاحِبُ نَظَرٍ One who takes notice, مُتَفَرِّجُونَ pl. مُتَفَرِّج. One who watches, looks out, as at the stars, رَاقِبٌ — رَاصِدٌ فَاطِنٌ. One who keeps, fulfils, صَاحِبُ وَفَاءٍ — رَاعٍ عَلَى — مُرَاعٍ — حَافِظٌ.

Observing, *a.* *See* Observant, *a.*

Observingly, *ad.* *See* Attentively, *ad.*

Obsession, *n.* The act of besieging, مُحَاوَطَةٌ — مُحَاصَرَةٌ — حَصْرٌ.

Obsidian, *n.* ضَرْبٌ مِنَ ٱلْحَجَرِ ٱلْمَعْدِنِيِّ أَسْوَدُ ٱللَّوْنِ.

Obsidional, *a.* مُتَعَلِّقٌ بِٱلْمُحَاصَرَةِ.

Obsolescence, *n.* نَهْرٌ — زَوَالٌ — إِشْرَافٌ عَلَى عَدَمِ ٱلِٱسْتِعْمَالِ لِلِٱضْمِحْلَالِ.

Obsolescent, *a.* مَائِلٌ إِلَى عَدَمِ ٱلِٱسْتِعْمَالِ — زَائِلٌ.

Obsolete, *a.* — هَامِدٌ — سَاقِطٌ عَنِ ٱلِٱسْتِعْمَالِ — مُفْرَطٌ — مَهْجُورٌ مُلْغًى — غَيْرُ مُسْتَعْمَلٍ. Given up, abandoned, مَتْرُوكٌ. Obsolete, of words, مُهْمَلٌ — مَهْجُورٌ — مُمَاتٌ. To become —, — أَفْرَطَ — أُلْغِيَ — أُهْمِلَ — [2] سَقَطَ عَنِ ٱلِٱسْتِعْمَالِ ; of words, أُهْمِلَ. That law has been —, ذٰلِكَ ٱلْقَانُونُ قَدْ أُلْغِيَ. Although the treaty is now regarded as —, it has not been formally abrogated, وَإِنْ كَانَتِ ٱلْمُعَاهَدَةُ تُحْسَبُ ٱلْآنَ مُلْغَاةً إِلَّا أَنَّهَا مَا أُبْطِلَتْ رَسْمًا.

Obsoleteness, *n.* — سُقُوطٌ عَنِ ٱلِٱسْتِعْمَالِ — تَرْكٌ — عَدَمُ ٱلِٱسْتِعْمَالِ إِلْغَاءٌ.

Obstacle, *n.* — عَائِقٌ — أَسْدَادٌ pl. سَدٌّ — حَاجِزٌ — عَارِضٌ — عُرْضَةٌ pl. عُوَّقٌ — مَانِعٌ pl. مَوَانِعُ. There is no — in the way of it, لَيْسَ دُونَهُ مَانِعٌ — لَيْسَ دُونَهُ شَيْءٌ. An — was raised between them, ضُرِبَ بَيْنَهُمْ سَدٌّ. *See also under* Objection, *n. to* Object, *v.t.* To throw an obstacle in the way of, — عَوَّقَ — أَعَاقَ — [2] سَدَّ عَلَى تَعَرَّضَ لِ.

To meet, repel, an obstacle, إِنْتَصَرَ عَلَى ٱلْمَانِعِ.

To meet with an obstacle, صَادَفَهُ مَانِعٌ — [2] عَرَضَهُ عَارِضٌ.

To raise an obstacle, to interfere, تَعَرَّضَ. To raise an obstacle to one, تَعَرَّضَ لَهُ.

To surmount an obstacle, أَنْجَحَ بِٱلْعَائِقَةِ — غَلَبَ عَلَى ٱلْمَانِعِ.

Obstetric, *a.* مَا نِيطَ بِفَنِّ ٱلْقِبَالَةِ.

Obstetrician, *n.* طَبِيبٌ — طَبِيبٌ قَبِيلٌ — مِنْ أَهْلِ فَنِّ ٱلْقِبَالَةِ مُوَلِّدٌ.

Obstetrics, *n.* فَنُّ ٱلْقِبَالَةِ.

Obstinacy, *n.* — مُشَاحَنَةٌ — مُكَابَرَةٌ — تَمَرُّدٌ — كُنُودٌ — مُرُودٌ — عِنَادٌ قَوْمَةٌ عَلَى — مُعَانَدَةٌ. *See also* Stubbornness, *n.*

Obstinate, *a.* — مُتَمَرِّدٌ — عَنِيدٌ — كَنُودٌ — مُكَابِرٌ — خَشِنُ ٱلْجَانِبِ لَا يَسْمَعُ ٱلنِّدَاءَ وَلَا يَبْغِي ٱلِٱهْتِدَاءَ — جَافِي ٱلطَّبْعِ — مُعَانِدٌ — مَارِدٌ. To make —, قَسَّى. To be —, أَعْنَدَ — عَنَدَ — [2] مَرَدَ — عَانَدَ. *See also* Stubborn, *a.*

Obstinately, *ad.* بِمُعَانَدَةٍ — بِعِنَادٍ — تَمَرُّدًا — مُعَانَدَةً. To act —, أَعْنَدَ — عَانَدَ.

Obstipation, *n.* *See* Costiveness, *n.*

Obstreperous, *a.* *See* Clamorous, Noisy, *a.*

Obstreperousness, *n.* *See* Clamour, Noise, *n.*

Obstreperously, *ad.* *See* Clamorously, Noisily, *ad.*

Obstriction, *n.* *See* Obligation, *n.*

Obstruct, *v.t.* To stop up, as a way or passage, [2] سَدَّ. To hinder by obstacles, — [2] حَجَبَ — عَزَرَ عَنْ — عَوَّقَ عَنْ — [2] كَفَّ عَنْ مَنَعَ — أَوْقَفَ — أَمْسَكَ — أَسَدَّ عَنْ. To intervene, to be in the way, حَالَ aor. يَحُولُ — إِعْتَرَضَ. The river obstructed us, preventing communication, [2] حَالَ ٱلنَّهْرُ بَيْنَنَا. An impediment, or an intruder, obstructed me, عَاقَنِي عَاقٍ — عَاقَنِي عَائِقٌ. To be obstructed, blocked up, إِشْتَدَّ — إِنْسَدَّ ; to be debarred, prevented, تَمَنَّعَ — تَثَبَّطَ عَنْ — إِحْتَجَبَ — تَعَوَّقَ — أَعْتَرَضَ. To be obstructed, as a road by crossing people, مُزْدَحِفٌ — إِنْسَدَّ.

Obstructed, *a.* Blocked up, مَسْدُودٌ ; as by a concourse of people, مُزْدَحِفٌ. Debarred, مَمْنُوعٌ — مُتَمَنِّعٌ — مُحْتَجِبٌ.

Obstructor, *n.* — مَانِعٌ — عُوَّقٌ pl. عَائِقٌ — عَيَّقٌ — عَيْقٌ — عُوَقٌ مَنَّاعٌ — مُسَدِّدٌ.

Obstruction, *n.* A stoppage, أَسْدَادٌ pl. سَدٌّ. An impediment, عَوَائِقُ pl. عَائِقَةٌ — حَاجِزٌ — عُرْضَةٌ — عَوَارِضُ pl. عَارِضٌ. An — from crossing crowds, مُنَاغَفَةٌ. Some intervening object to prevent communication, حَوَائِلُ pl. حَائِلٌ. An —, in the nose, *etc.*, سُدَدٌ pl. سُدَّةٌ — سُدَادٌ. For the removal of obstructions, لِإِزَالَةِ ٱلْمَوَانِعِ. Without their meeting with any —, بِدُونِ أَنْ يُصَادِفُوا مَانِعًا. *See also under* Obstacle, Impediment, *n.*

Obstructive, *a.* Hindering, preventing, عَائِقٌ — مَنَّاعٌ — مَنُوعٌ عَوَائِقُ pl. — عَوَّاقٌ. An — person, عَيِّقٌ — عَوِقٌ. *See also* Obstructor, *n.*

Obstructively, *ad.* تَعَرُّضًا — إِعَاقَةً — إِعْتِرَاضًا — تَمَنُّعًا — بِمُمَانَعَةٍ.

Obstruent, *a.* *See* Obstructive, *a.*

Obstruent, *n.* *See* Obstruction, *n.*

Obtain, *v.t.* — أَدْرَكَ بِ — إِقْتَنَى — أَحْرَزَ — [2] قَنِيَ — إِغْتَنَمَ — [2] نَالَ — حَصَّلَ — إِحْتَظَى بِ — [2] حَازَ — [2] فَازَ بِ — أَدْرَكَ [2] حَصَلَ عَلَى. To — leave from, إِسْتَأْذَنَ مِنْ. He obtained the object of his desire, إِحْتَظَى — [2] بَلَغَ (or [2] نَالَ) مَقْصُودَهُ حَصَّلَ مَطْلُوبَهُ — بِٱلْمَطْلُوبِ. To —, to arrive at a result,

حَصَلَ عَلَى [2]. He has now obtained, attained, the rank of Wazir, وَقَدْ أَحْرَزَ ٱلْيَوْمَ رُتْبَةَ ٱلْوِزَارَةِ. To endeavour to —, to aim at, صَمَدَ إِلَى [2]. *See also to* Attain, *v.t.*

Obtain, *v.i.* To be in force or fashion, جَرَى – صَارَ جَارِيًا – إِسْتَحْكَمَ – صَارَ عَادَةً – إِسْتَقَامَ.

Obtainable, *a.* That may be obtained, يُحَصَّلُ – تَحْصِيلُهُ مُمْكِنٌ; that may be found, مَوْجُود – مِمَّا يَجِدُ.

Obtest, *v.t.* *See to* Beseech, *v.t.*

Obtainment, *n.* إِدْرَاكٌ – إِغْتِنَام – تَحْصِيل – إِسْتِحْصَال – نَوَال – حَوْز. *See also* Attainment.

Obtrude, *v.t.* and *i.* *See to* Intrude, *v.t.* and *i.*

Obtruder, *n.* *See* Intruder, *n.*

Obtruncate, *v.t.* *See to* Amputate, Dismember, *v.t.*

Obtrusion, *n.* *See* Intrusion, *n.*

Obtrusive, *a.* *See* Intrusive, *a.*

Obtrusively, *ad.* *See* Intrusively, *ad.*

Obtuse, *a.* Not sharp, جَبَل – كَهَام – كَلِيل – فَنْقَاس. Applied to an angle, مُنْفَرِج. Dull, stupid, أَخْرَق – أَبْلَهُ – ثَقِيل – بَلِيد. Dull, of a sound, خَفِيض – ثَقِيل. An — angle, زَاوِيَةٌ مُنْفَرِجَةٌ. Obtuse angled, مُنْفَرِجُ ٱلزَّوَايَا.

Obtuseness, *n.* Bluntness, كَلٌّ – غِلَاظَةُ ٱلْحَدِّ. Dullness, of sound, ثِقَل – خَفْض. Stupidity, خُرْق – خُرْق – بَلَادَة – حَمَاقَة – بَلَهَ. Obtuseness, as of an angle, إِنْفِرَاج.

Obumbrate, *v.t.* *See to* Shade, Darken, *v.t.*

Obumbration, *n.* إِقْتِتَام – تَظْلِيل.

Obverse, *a.* مَا كَانَ أَعْلَاهُ أَعْرَضَ مِنْ أَسْفَلِهِ.

Obverse, *n.* The face of a coin opposed to the reverse, ٱلْوَجْهُ ٱلثَّانِي. On the reverse of the coin, عَلَى أَحَدِ وَجْهَيِ ٱلسِّكَّةِ, and on the obverse, وَعَلَى ٱلْوَجْهِ ٱلثَّانِي.

Obvert, *v.t.* دَوَّرَ – مُقَابِلَ ٱلشَّيْءِ [2].

Obviate, *v.t.* To repel, avert, رَدَّ [2] – أَرْتَدَ – دَفَعَ. To oppose, قَاوَمَ – عَارَضَ – ضَادَّ. To remove, as difficulties, سَهَّلَ – أَذْهَبَ – رَفَعَ.

Obvious, *a.* عَيَان – وَاضِح – ظَاهِر – مُبِين – صَرِيح – جَلِيّ. An — truth, حَقٌّ مُبِينٌ; an — fact, أَمْرٌ ظَاهِرٌ. To be —, إِتَّضَحَ – تَجَلَّى. To make —, أَوْضَحَ – بَيَّنَ – صَرَّحَ.

Obviously, *ad.* صَرَاحَةً – إِيضَاحًا – عِيَانًا – بِبَيَانٍ.

Obviousness, *n.* وُضُوح – إِيضَاح – صَرَاحَة – بَيَان.

Occasion, *n.* A casual exigency, an opportunity, فُرْصَة *pl.* فُرَص. A cause, سَبَب *pl.* أَسْبَاب; a means, وَسِيلَة *pl.* وَسَائِل. A motive, بَاعِث. A particular time, يَوْم – وَقْت – مَوْقِت. Need, لُزُوم – إِحْتِيَاج – إِقْتِضَاء. A time, once, خَطْرَة – نَوْبَة – مَرَّة – خَطْرَة *pl.* مِرَار. On that —, when, عِنْدَ – عِنْدَمَا. On one —, مَرَّةً: I only met him on one —, مَا لَقِيتُهُ إِلَّا خَطْرَةً. On all occasions, دَائِمًا. On the first —, فِي أَوَّلِ فُرْصَةٍ. There is no —, need, for it, مَا يَحْتَاجُ إِلَيْهِ – لَا حَاجَةَ لَهُ. As — requires, فِي عَلَى مُقْتَضَى ٱلْفُرْصَةِ – وَقْتِ ٱلْحَاجَةِ. What is the — for that? لِمَاذَا – مَا ٱلْبَاعِثُ عَلَى ذَٰلِكَ. Until —, need, shall require, إِلَى أَنْ تَمَسَّ إِلَيْهِ ٱلضَّرُورَةُ.

To avail one's self of, or to seize or embrace an occasion, إِفْتَرَصَ – ٱلْفُرْصَةَ (or إِغْتَنَمَ) إِنْتَهَزَ ٱلْفُرْصَةَ.

To find an occasion, صَادَفَ ٱلْفُرْصَةَ – وَجَدَ فُرْصَةً *aor.* يَجِدُ. To find an occasion against, as in order to traduce, وَقَعَ بِ *aor.* يَقَعُ. Do as thou shalt find occasion, opportunity, إِفْعَلْ حَسْبَمَا تَجِدُهُ يَدُكَ. To give one an occasion, opportunity, for ..., أَعْطَى فُرْصَةً لِ. To cause, give rise to, جَعَلَ: By this you have given your enemies occasion to rejoice, بِهٰذَا جَعَلْتَ أَعْدَاءَكَ يَفْرَحُونَ.

To have occasion, need, for, إِخْتَلَّ إِلَى – إِحْتَاجَ إِلَى – إِضْطَرَّ إِلَى – إِعْتَازَ.

To look for an occasion, إِسْتَفْرَصَ ٱلْفُرْصَةَ – تَرَصَّدَ ٱغْتِنَامَ ٱلْفُرْصَةِ.

To lose an occasion, ضَيَّعَ ٱلْفُرْصَةَ – فَرَّطَ فِي ٱلْفُرْصَةِ – فَوَّتَ ٱلْفُرْصَةَ – فَاتَتْهُ ٱلْفُرْصَةُ.

To seek an occasion, cause, طَلَبَ عِلَّةً [2]: They sought an occasion against him, طَلَبُوا عِلَّةً يَجِدُونَهَا عَلَيْهِ.

To shun an occasion, إِمْتَنَعَ عَنِ ٱلْفُرْصَةِ – إِحْتَرَزَ عَنِ ٱلْفُرْصَةِ – إِجْتَنَبَ ٱلْفُرْصَةَ.

To use as an occasion for, إِتَّخَذَ فُرْصَةً لِ.

Occasion, *v.t.* To cause, سَبَّبَ – صَارَ سَبَبًا لِ; to —, as a result, أَعْقَبَ. It occasioned misunderstandings and difficulties, صَارَ دَاعِيًا إِلَى ٱلْإِرْتِبَاكِ وَٱلْمَصَائِبِ. It occasioned him repentance, أَعْقَبَهُ نَدَمًا. He partook of a repast which occasioned him sickness, أَكَلَ أَكْلَةً أَعْقَبَتْهُ سَقَمًا.

Occasional, *a.* Occurring at times, وَاقِعٌ ذَاتَ ٱلْمِرَارِ. Incidental, عَارِضِيٌّ – إِتِّفَاقِيٌّ. As occasion may require, إِقْتِضَائِيٌّ – عَلَى مُقْتَضَى ٱلْفُرْصَةِ. *See also next article.*

Occasionally, *ad.* ذَاتَ – بُعَيْدَاتِ بَيْنٍ – خَطْرَةً بَعْدَ خَطْرَةٍ – إِتِّفَاقًا – فِي ٱلْفَرْطِ – ٱلْمِرَارِ.

Occident, *n.* ٱلْمَغْرِبُ – ٱلْغَرْبُ.

Occidental, *a.* مَغْرِبِيٌّ – غَرْبِيٌّ.

Occipital, *a.* قَفَائِيٌّ ـ مُتَعَلِّقٌ بِٱلْقَفْلَةِ.

Occiput, *n.* قَفْلَة ـ قَفًا *pl.* أَقْفَآء *and* أَقْفِيَة.

Occult, *a.* خَفِيٌّ ـ مَكْتُوم. The — sciences, عُلُومُ ٱلْعَرَّافِينَ ـ الْعُلُومُ ٱلسِّرِّيَّة ـ الْكِهَانَة.

Occultation, *n.* خُسُوف ـ خَسْف.

Occulted, *a.* مَخْسُوف.

Occultness, *n.* خَفَآء ـ كُتُوم ـ كَتْم.

Occupancy, *n.* Holding and dwelling in a place, مُبَآءَة ـ تَبَوُّءٌ ـ إِسْتِبَآءَة ـ إِقَامَةٌ ب ـ سُكْنَى. Seizing, holding possession, حَوْز ـ ضَبْط ـ تَصَرُّف ـ تَمَلُّك.

Occupant, *n.* } One who holds, dwells in, and keeps possession
Occupier, } of a place, مُسْتَبِيءٌ ـ مُتَبَوِّئٌ. One who holds, keeps, صَاحِب ـ مَالِك ـ ضَابِط ـ حَائِز. One who disposes of, discharges any office, مُتَصَرِّفٌ ب. A dweller, مُقِيمٌ ب ـ سَاكِن *pl.* سُكَّان. The place became destitute of its occupants, خَلَا ٱلْمَكَانُ مِنْ أَهْلِهِ ².

Occupation, *n.* Taking and dwelling in or occupying, تَبَوُّؤٌ ـ إِسْتِبَآء. A seizing, holding, keeping, حَوْز ـ إِسْتِمْلَاك ـ إِتِّخَاذ ـ أَخْذَة ـ ضَبْط. A using, تَصَرُّف. Residence, إِقَامَة ـ سُكْنَى. That which engages the attention, مَشْغَلَة ـ أُشْغُولَة ـ هَمٌّ ـ إِهْتِمَام. Avocation, employment, حِرْفَة ـ شُغْل ـ صِنَاعَة ـ مَشْغَلَة ـ وَظِيفَة ـ صَنْعَة. Military —, تَبَوُّءٌ. What is your —? مَا صِنَاعَتُكَ. To be without —, بَطَلَ ² ـ عَطَلَ ² ـ تَعَطَّلَ. To change one's — from ... to ..., إِنْتَكَ مِنْ-إِلَى.

Occupy, *v.t.* To take and keep in possession, تَبَوَّأَ ـ إِسْتَبَآءَ. To seize, hold, حَازَ ² ـ أَخَذَ ² ـ إِتَّخَذَ ـ مَلَكَ ـ ضَبَطَ ². To inhabit, أَقَامَ فِي ـ سَكَنَ ². To employ, إِسْتَخْدَمَ ـ شَغَّلَ; to employ one in, شَغَلَ-ب ـ أَشْغَلَ-ب. To — one by drawing off his attention from something, شَاغَلَ-عَن. To take up, to fill, as room, إِسْتَوْعَبَ ـ وَسِعَ *aor.* يَسَعُ. To —, as of a town, كَبَسَ. To busy one's self in, تَعَاطَى ـ خَاضَ فِي ² ـ تَصَرَّفَ ب ـ إِشْتَغَلَ ب. To be occupied, to be held as a place of abode, by, تُبُوِّئَ مِن; to be inhabited, سُكِنَ ². To be occupied in, تَصَرَّفَ فِي ـ سَعَى فِي *aor.* يَسْعَى. It occupied the place of, حَلَّ مَحَلَّ. It occupied all his time, إِسْتَوْعَبَ جَمِيعَ أَوْقَاتِهِ. The council was occupied about that, وَقَعَتْ فِي ٱلْمَجْلِسِ ٱلْمُذَاكَرَةُ عَلَى ذٰلِكَ. He occupied or interested himself about it, إِهْتَمَّ بِهِ. The provinces which the Germans occupied they still continue to occupy, ٱلْأَقَالِيمُ ٱلَّتِي تَبَوَّأَهَا ٱلْجِرْمَانِيُّونَ لَا يَزَالُونَ مُتَبَوِّئِينَ بِهَا.

An occupied island, occupied militarily, جَزِيرَةٌ مُتَبَوَّأَةٌ مِنَ ٱلْعَسَاكِرِ.

Occupied, busy, مَشْغُول ـ مُشْتَغِل.

Occur, *v.i.* To happen, وَقَعَ *aor.* يَقَعُ ـ جَآءَ *aor.* يَجِيءُ ـ جَرَى ـ تَعَرَّضَ ـ حَصَلَ ². To — or happen to one, عَهِدَ ل ـ عَرَضَ ل ـ تَعَرَّضَ ل. To — to one's mind, بَدَا ل *aor.* يَبْدُو ـ خَطَرَ بِبَالِهِ ² ـ عَنَّ ب ـ هَجَسَ فِي صَدْرِهِ. It occurred to my mind, خَطَرَ بِبَالِي ² ـ هَجَسَ فِي صَدْرِي ـ بَدَا لِي. Nothing like it occurred to him before, لَمْ يَعْهَدْ لَهُ مِثَالٌ. *See also to* Happen, *v.i.*

Occurrence, *n.* وُقُوع ـ كَائِنَة *pl.* كَائِنَات ـ عَارِض *pl.* أَعْرَاض ـ وَاقِعَة *pl.* وَقَائِع ـ حَادِثَة *pl.* حَوَادِث ـ مَا جَرَى. An unexpected —, بَدِيهَة ـ بَدَاهَة ـ بُدَاهَة.

Ocean, *n.* بَحْرٌ مُحِيطٌ ـ قَامُوس *pl.* قَوَامِيس ـ أُوقِيَانُوس. The ocean, الْبَحْرُ ٱلْمُحِيطُ ـ الْمُحِيطُ; The Indian —, بَحْرُ ٱلْهِنْدِ.

Ocean, *a.* }
Oceanic, } بَحْرِيٌّ ـ مُتَعَلِّقٌ بِٱلْبَحْرِ ٱلْمُحِيطِ.

Oceania, *n.* جَزَائِرُ ٱلْبَحْرِ ٱلْمُحِيطِ ٱلشَّرْقِيِّ.

Ocelot, *n.* A panther of South America, نَوْعٌ مِنَ ٱلنَّمِرِ مَوْلُودُ أَمِيرِكَا ٱلْجَنُوبِيَّةِ.

Ochre, *n.* أَزْنَكَان ـ ضَرْبٌ مِنَ ٱلطِّينِ. Red —, مَغْرَة ـ مَغَرَة.

Ochreous, *a.* كَٱلْأَزْنَكَانِ ـ أَزْنَكَانِيّ. Of a colour, like red ochre, أَمْغَرُ ـ مَغِر.

O'clock, *ad.* سَاعَة. What — is it? كَمِ ٱلسَّاعَةُ. It is four —, السَّاعَةُ أَرْبَعَةٌ.

Octagon, *n.* مُثَمَّن.

Octagonal, *a.* مُثَمَّن. To make —, ثَمَّنَ.

Octahedron, *n.* ذُو ثَمَانِيَةِ سُطُوحٍ مُتَسَاوِيَةٍ.

Octangular, *a.* مُثَمَّنٌ ـ مُثَمَّنُ ٱلزَّوَايَا.

Octave, *n.* As in music, الْبُعْدُ ٱلْكُلِّيُّ. The —, or eighth day after a festival, الْيَوْمُ ٱلثَّامِنُ بَعْدَ عِيدٍ; the eight days of a festival, ثَمَانِيَةُ أَيَّامِ عِيدٍ.

Octavo, *a.* Of the size of a book, فِي قِطْعِ ٱلثُّمْنِ. Royal —, قِطْعٌ وَزِيرِيٌّ.

Octennial, *a.* Coming once in eight years, وَاقِعٌ مَرَّةً فِي كُلِّ ثَمَانِي سِنِينَ; lasting eight years, مُسْتَدِيمٌ ثَمَانِي سَنَوَاتٍ.

Octennially, *ad.* مَرَّةً فِي كُلِّ ثَمَانِي سِنِينَ.

October, *n.* تِشْرِينُ ٱلْأَوَّلُ ـ شَهْرُ أُكْتُوبَر.

Octo-decimo, *a.* فِي قِطْعِ ٱلثُّمْنِ ٱلْعَاشِرِ.

Octogenarian, *n.* إِبْنُ ثَمَانِينَ سَنَةً.

Octo-syllabic, *a.* مُثَمَّنُ ٱلْهِجَآءِ.

Octroi, n. ضَرائِبُ (or عَوائِدُ) ٱلْبَلَدِ.

Octuple, *a.* ثَمانِيَةُ أَضْعافٍ,

Ocular, *a.* Connected with the sight, مُتَعَلِّقٌ بِٱلْعَيْنِ (or ٱلْبَصَرِ) — بَصَرِيٌّ. To give — proof to, to show, أَظْهَرَ-لِ عِيانًا — أَشْهَدَ-عَلَى — أَرْأَى-لِ — أَرْأَى. An — witness, شاهِدٌ — ناظِرٌ pl. نُظّارٌ.

Ocularly, *ad.* مُعايَنَةً — عِيانًا.

Oculist, *n.* طَبِيبُ ٱلْعُيُونِ.

Odalisque, *n.* مَحْظِيَّةُ ٱلسُّلْطانِ pl. مَحاظِي.

Odd, *a.* Uneven in number, فَرْدٌ pl. فِرادٌ — مُفْرَدٌ. Over and above, زائِدٌ — فاضِلٌ — باقٍ. Strange, بِمَكانٍ — مِنَ ٱلْبُعْدِ — بِلا قاعِدَةٍ — خارِجٌ عَنِ — شاذٌّ. Uncommon, أَغْرَبُ — غَرِيبٌ — مُسْتَغْرَبٌ — غَرِيبٌ — غَيْرُ مُعْتادٍ — (or فَوْقَ) ٱلْعادَةِ. An — or uncommon word, كَلِمَةٌ فاذَّةٌ (or شاذَّةٌ). Cast aside, trifling, ساقِطٌ — مِنَ ٱلتَّرِكاتِ.

At odd times, بُعَيْداتٍ بَيْنَ — فِي ٱلْفَرْطِ — إِتِّفاقًا. To consider —, strange, إِسْتَغْرَبَ. *See also* Even, *a.*, Pair, *n.*

An odd book, كِتابٌ صِنْوٌ; one of two volumes, أَحَدُ مُجَلَّدَيْنِ.

An odd glove, كَفٌّ صِنْوٌ.

An odd number, عَدَدٌ مُفْرَدٌ — فَرْدٌ عَدَدِيٌّ.

An odd or peculiar man, رَجُلٌ مُلْتَوٍ — مَجْنُونٌ — فِي عَقْلِهِ هَبْتَةٌ.

An odd or strange thing, غَرِيبَةٌ pl. غَرائِبُ.

Odd or even, of two things, فاذّانِ أَوْ تَوْءَمانِ; *in a general way*, فَرْدٌ أَوْ زَوْجٌ — وِتْرٌ أَوْ شَفْعٌ — زَكًا أَوْ خَسًا.

The odd piastres, فَضْلَةُ ٱلْغُرُوشِ — ٱلْغُرُوشُ ٱلْكُسُورُ.

Thirty pounds odd, ثَلاثُونَ لِيرَةً وَكُسُورٌ.

Oddity, *n.* Singularity, غَرابَةٌ. A strange thing, عَجِيبَةٌ pl. عَجائِبُ — غَرِيبَةٌ pl. غَرائِبُ. An odd man, رَجُلٌ مُلْتَوٍ — مَجْنُونٌ — أَخِيذٌ — رَجُلٌ فِي عَقْلِهِ هَبْتَةٌ — رَجُلٌ غَرِيبٌ. An old —, of a man, رَجُلٌ غَرِيبٌ.

Oddly, *ad.* Unevenly, فَرْدًا — بِدُونِ مُفاوَضَةٍ. Strangely, بِصُورَةٍ غَرِيبَةٍ — بِنَوْعٍ غَرِيبٍ — بِوَجْهٍ عَجِيبٍ — عَجَبًا. Oddly enough I did not know him, وَمِنَ ٱلْعَجَبِ أَنِّي ما عَرَفْتُهُ.

Odd-man, *n.* One who does jobs, رَقّابَةٌ — رَجُلٌ وَغْدٌ.

Oddness, *n.* The being of an odd number, فَرْدٌ. *See also* Oddity, *n.*

Odds, *n.* Inequality, فَرْقٌ — عَدَمُ مُساواةٍ — عَدَمُ ٱقْتِرانٍ. Excess, كَثْرَةٌ — زِيادَةٌ — فَرْطٌ. Advantage, مَنْفَعَةٌ — نَفْعٌ. Odds and ends, شِقَقٌ — حِصَصٌ — قِطَعٌ — أَقْمِشَةٌ — تَرِكاتٌ. To pick up — and ends, لَقَّطَ — قَمَّشَ. At —, at variance, بَيْنَهُمْ مُشاجَرَةٌ — بَيْنَهُمْ نِزاعٌ. Without —, بِٱلْمُفاوَضَةِ — بِٱلسَّوِيَّةِ. What's the odds? ما ٱلْفَرْقُ — ما يَفْرُقُ — ما يَضُرُّ. It makes no —, لا بَأْسَ فِيهِ — ما يُخالِفُ.

To be at odds, variance, of many, إِخْتَلَفُوا — تَنازَعُوا — تَشاجَرُوا.

To give odds to, as in play, أَفانَ — زَوَّدَ-عَلَى.

To have the odds against one, to contend with a larger number, قاتَلَ (or خاصَمَ) مَنْ هُوَ أَقْوَى مِنْهُ. The odds, luck, are against me, ٱلنَّصِيبُ عَلَيَّ.

To lay the odds, to wager with, راهَنَ-عَلَى.

To set at odds, أَرَّثَ بَيْنَ — أَرَّشَ بَيْنَ — وَقَّعَ بَيْنَ — رَمَى — أَلْقَى ٱلْفِتْنَةَ بَيْنَ.

Ode, *n.* غَزَلٌ — قَصِيدَةٌ pl. قَصائِدُ.

Odeon, *n.* ضَرْبٌ مِنَ ٱلتِّياتْرُو أَوْ مَحَلٌّ لِلْإِمْتِحانِ.

Odious, *a.* كَرِيهٌ — مَكْرُوهٌ — قَبِيحٌ pl. قِباحٌ — مَبْغُوضٌ — مَنْفُورٌ — بَغِيضٌ — مَبْغُوضٌ. To be —, قَبُحَ. To render —, بَغَّضَ.

Odiously, *ad.* قُبْحًا — قَباحَةً — بِنَوْعٍ كَرِيهٍ — كَراهِيَةً.

Odiousness, *n.* قَباحَةٌ — قُبْحٌ — كَراهِيَةٌ — كُرْهٌ.

Odium, *n.* عَيْبٌ — عارٌ — سُبَّةٌ — خِزْيَةٌ. To bring — upon, أَخْزَى — خَزِيَ. To fall into —, خَزِيَ aor. يَخْزَى. Odium theologicum, نَفْسانِيَّةُ ٱللّاهُوتِيِّينَ.

Odometer, *n.* مِقْياسٌ يُوضَعُ فِي عَرَبَةٍ يُقاسُ بِهِ سَيْرُها.

Odontalgia, *n.* داءُ (or وَجَعُ) ٱلْأَسْنانِ.

Odontalgic, *a.* مُتَعَلِّقٌ بِداءِ ٱلْأَسْنانِ.

Odontalgic, *n.* عِلاجٌ لِداءِ ٱلْأَسْنانِ.

Odontoid, *a.* بِهَيْئَةِ ٱلسِّنِّ.

Odoriferous, *a.* Fragrant, أَرِجٌ — عَطِرٌ — ذَكِيُّ ٱلرّائِحَةِ — طَيِّبُ ٱلرّائِحَةِ. To be —, عَطِرَ — طابَتْ رائِحَتُهُ aor. تَطِيبُ.

Odoriferous substances, مَجْمَرٌ — أَطْيابٌ — عُطُورٌ — عِطارَةٌ.

Odoriferousness, *n.* *See* Fragance, *n.*

Odorous, *a.* *See* Odoriferous, *a.*

Odorously, *ad.* بِعِطْرٍ — بِذَكاءِ ٱلرّائِحَةِ.

Odour, *n.* A smell, رائِحَةٌ pl. رَوائِحُ — فَوْحَةٌ pl. فَوَحاتٌ — نَشْوَةٌ. A sweet —, نَفْحَةٌ — أَطْيابٌ pl. طِيبٌ — رائِحَةٌ طَيِّبَةٌ — رائِحَةٌ ذَكِيَّةٌ. A fetid —, رائِحَةٌ مُنْتِنَةٌ — رائِحَةٌ وَخْشَةٌ. To perceive an —, راحَ — أَراحَ — أَرْوَحَ — إِسْتَراحَ — إِسْتَرْوَحَ — شَمَّ.

Oesophagus, *n.* مَرِيءٌ — مَبْلَعٌ — مَسْرَطٌ — حَلْقٌ — بُلْعُومٌ.

O'er, *prep.* *See* Over, *prep.*

Of, *prep.* From, out of, مِنْ. God hath created every animal of water [*i.e.* of seminal fluid]; and of them is such that goeth on his belly, and of them is such that goeth upon two legs, and of them is such that goeth upon four, (Kurân, xxiv. 44), ٱللّٰهُ خَلَقَ كُلَّ دابَّةٍ مِنْ ماءٍ فَمِنْهُمْ مَنْ يَمْشِي عَلَى بَطْنِهِ وَمِنْهُمْ مَنْ يَمْشِي عَلَى رِجْلَيْنِ وَمِنْهُمْ مَنْ يَمْشِي عَلَى أَرْبَعٍ. Man is

composed of soul and body, الإِنْسَانُ مُرَكَّبٌ مِنْ نَفْسٍ وَجَسَدٍ.
One of them, وَاحِدٌ مِنْهُم ـ أَحَدُهُم. Not one of; (*See* None).
Of, as indicative of the genitive case, is expressed as follows:—
A son of a king, إِبْنُ مَلِكٍ. A son of the king, إِبْنٌ لِلْمَلِكِ.
The son of the king, إِبْنُ ٱلْمَلِكِ. The servant of a merchant, خَدَّامُ تَاجِرٍ. A servant of the merchant, خَدَّامٌ لِلتَّاجِرِ. Of, proceeding from, مِن ـ مُنْبَثِقٌ مِن ـ مُشْتَقٌّ مِن. Of, as indicating belonging to, is expressed thus: A man of Egypt, an Egyptian, (مِنْ أَهْلِ مِصْرَ (or) مِصْرِيٌّ; a man of the pen, مِنْ أَهْلِ ٱلْقَلَمِ. As signifying possessing, thus: a man of wealth, صَاحِبُ مَالٍ; a man of prudence, صَاحِبُ فِطْنَةٍ. Of late, بِهٰذَا ٱلْقُرْبِ.

Off, *a.* The farthest, الأَقْصَى ـ الأَبْعَدُ ـ الأَنْزَحُ. The off side, اليَمِينُ ـ الطَّرَفُ ٱلأَيْمَنُ.

Off, *ad.* Of distance, far, بَعِيدٌ. Off, as indicating separation, مُنْفَصِلٌ ـ مُنْقَلِعٌ ـ مَقْلُوعٌ. Off, at an end, تَمَّ ـ إِنْتَهَى. Near to, قَرِيبٌ مِن. At large, مُطْلَقُ ٱلْعِنَانِ ـ سُدًى. A mile off, بُعْدَ مِيلٍ. The fever is off, إِنْقَطَعَتِ ٱلسُّخُونَةُ ـ إِرْتَفَعَتِ ٱلْحُمَّى. The affair is off, إِنْفَضَّ ٱلأَمْرُ ـ مَا صَحَّ ٱلأَمْرُ. The marriage is off, إِنْفَسَخَتِ ٱلْخِطْبَةُ. The ship is off the port, المَرْكَبُ قِبَالَ السَّفِينَةُ دُونَ ٱلْمِينَةِ ـ ٱلْمِينَةِ. Badly off, poor, عَائِلٌ ـ عَائِزٌ ـ فَقِيرٌ ـ مِسْكِينٌ; badly off for, مُحْتَاجٌ إِلَى. Well off, صَاحِبُ جِدَّةٍ ـ غَنِيٌّ *pl.* أَغْنِيَاءُ ـ صَاحِبُ ثَرْوَةٍ ـ وَجِيهٌ. Off and on, now and then, خَطْرَةً بَعْدَ خَطْرَةٍ ـ بُعَيْدَاتٍ بَيْنَ; nearing and distancing, إِسْتِقْرَابًا وَٱسْتِبْعَادًا; coming and going, تَرَدُّدًا. To be off, go away, ذَهَبَ ـ سَارَ *aor.* يَسِيرُ: I am off, أَنَا رَائِحٌ ـ أَنَا ذَاهِبٌ. To be off one's food, to have no appetite, كَانَ بِلَا ٱشْتِهَاءٍ لِلأَكْلِ. To be off any thing, be released from it, تَخَلَّى مِن. (*For the word "off" when joined to a verb, as to* Cut off, *to* Fall off, *see the verbs*).

Off, *int.* Off with you! be off! إِنْقَلِعْ ـ إِذْهَبْ. Be off from me! إِنْقَلِعْ عَنِّي ـ إِلَيْكَ عَنِّي. Off with him! خُذُوهُ.

Offal, *n.* Refuse meat, entrails, أَكَارِعُ ـ حَشًا ـ سَقَطُ ٱلذَّبِيحِ وَأَحْشَاءُ ٱلْبَهَائِمِ. Refuse, rubbish, خُشَارَةٌ ـ لُقَاطَةٌ ـ قَشِيشٌ. *See also* Refuse, *n.*

Offence, *n.* A transgression, crime, fault, جُرْمٌ ـ جَرِيمَةٌ ـ ذَنْبٌ ـ جِنَايَةٌ ـ سَيِّئَةٌ *pl.* سَيِّئَاتٌ ـ أَسَاءَةٌ ـ مَسَاءَةٌ ـ تَفَاوُتٌ ـ خَطِيئَةٌ *pl.* خَطَايَا ـ قَبَاحَةٌ ـ ذَنُوبٌ *pl.* A slip, عَثْرَةٌ. A cause of stumbling, عَثْرَةٌ *pl.* عَثَرَاتٌ. A short-coming, تَقْصِيرٌ ـ قُصْرَةٌ. An injury, insult, إِنْتِهَاكٌ ـ مَشْتَمَةٌ ـ مَذَمَّةٌ ـ ضَرَرٌ ـ أَذِيَّةٌ ـ عَيْبَةٌ (or) نَقْصٌ فِي حَقِّ وَاحِدٍ ـ جُرْحٌ ـ مَسَبَّةٌ ـ إِنْفِعَالٌ. A trespass, تَعَدٍّ ـ هُجُومٌ. No offence! إِعْذِرْنِي ـ عَنْ إِذْنِكَ.
Weapons of —, أَسْلِحَةُ ٱلدِّفَاعِ ـ آلَاتُ ٱلْحَرْبِ وَٱلضَّرْبِ.
To commit an offence; *see to* Offend, *v.t.*
To give offence, أَسَاءَ ـ أَفْسَدَ.
To give offence to, عَابَ فِي ـ أَسَاءَ إِلَى *or* عَلَى *or* ل *or* ب ـ أَهَانَ ـ أَضْجَرَ ـ أَغَمَّ ـ آذَى ـ كَسَرَ خَاطِرَهُ ـ حَقَّهُ.
To take offence at, أَخَذَ ـ إِنْقَهَرَ مِن ـ إِغْتَاظَ مِن ـ إِنْغَمَّ مِن عَلَى خَاطِرِهِ مِن.

Offenceless, *a. See* Innocent, Harmless, *a.*

Offend, *v.t.* To displease, كَدَّرَ عَلَى ـ أَغَاظَ ـ أَغَمَّ ـ فَرَطَ عَلَى; with words or bad language, سَلَقَ ـ بِٱلْكَلَامِ. To disgust, أَكْرَهَ ـ صَدَّعَ ـ آذَى ـ شَقَّ عَلَى ـ أَضْجَرَ. To annoy, قَرَّفَ ـ أَقْرَفَ. To wrong, insult, حَكَرَ ـ جَنَى عَلَى ـ جَانَى. To cause to stumble, عَثَّرَ ـ عَثَّرَ ـ أَعْثَرَ. To — one's dignity, إِنْتَهَكَ. To be offended, disgusted, at, كَرِهَ ـ شَنِعَ ب. (To be offended at, displeased with; *see* To take Offence, *under preceding article.*)
To offend, sin, against, أَسَاءَ إِلَى ـ أَذْنَبَ إِلَى ـ أَخْطَأَ إِلَى.

Offend, *v.i.* To transgress, أَخْطَأَ ـ أَثِمَ ـ أَفْسَدَ ـ أَسَاءَ. To do what is unseemly, قَبُحَ.

Offender, *n.* A transgressor, مُجْرِمٌ ـ خُطَاةٌ *pl.* خَاطِئٌ ـ جَانٍ ـ مُذْنِبٌ. One guilty of an outrage, صَاحِبُ ـ عَائِبٌ ـ حَاكِرٌ قَبِيحَةٍ. An old or inveterate —, خَطَّاءٌ.

Offended, *a.* Displeased, مُكَدَّرُ ٱلْخَاطِرِ ـ مُنْغَمٌّ ـ مُغْتَاظٌ ـ مَحْكُورٌ.
The — party, المَعْدُوُّ (or المَعْدِيُّ) عَلَيْهِ ـ المَجْرُوحُ ـ المُسَاءُ إِلَيْهِ.

Offending, *a.* Making angry, مُكَدِّرٌ عَلَى ـ مُغِمٌّ ـ نَارِطٌ عَلَى.
Causing to stumble, مُعَثِّرٌ ـ مُعْثِرٌ. Sinning, مُذْنِبٌ ـ خَاطِئٌ.
The — party, البَادِئُ بِٱلشَّرِّ ـ المُعْتَدِي ـ المُتَعَدِّي.

Offensive, *a.* Causing displeasure, مُغْضِبٌ ـ مُغِيظٌ ـ جَانٍ ـ شَاقٌّ عَلَى ـ مُضْجِرٌ ـ مُكَدِّرٌ. Disgusting, كَرِيهٌ ـ نَافِرٌ ـ مُقْرِفٌ. Injurious, سَيِّئٌ ـ مُضْجِرٌ ـ مُصَدِّعٌ. Annoying, مُؤْذٍ ـ مُضِرٌّ. Foul, سَيِّئٌ.
An — smell, رَائِحَةٌ مُتَقَرِّزَةٌ ـ رَائِحَةٌ كَرِيهَةٌ. Offensive weapons, أَسْلِحَةُ ٱلدِّفَاعِ ـ آلَاتُ ٱلْحَرْبِ وَٱلضَّرْبِ. An alliance — and defensive, مُعَاهَدَةٌ عَلَى ٱلْهُجُومِ وَٱلدِّفَاعِ. To be —, disgusting, to, كَرِهَ عِنْدَهُ ـ قَبُحَ عِنْدَهُ ـ فَتَحَ ٱلْمُخَاصَمَةَ. To take the —, حَرَّكَ ٱلشَّرَّ ـ طَلَبَ ٱلشَّرَّ ـ بَدَأَ بِٱلشَّرِّ.

Offensively, *ad.* In a disgusting manner, بِكَرَاهَةٍ ـ إِقْتِيَاتًا ـ إِشْمِئْزَازًا. Injuriously, بِأَذِيَّةٍ ـ بِمَضَرَّةٍ ـ جِنَايَةً. With annoyance, بِتَصَدُّعٍ ـ بِتَصْدِيعٍ. With ill intent, بِأَسَاءَةٍ. With trespass, بِبَغْيٍ ـ بِتَجَاوُزٍ ـ إِجْحَافًا ـ إِفْرَاطًا. To act — towards, فَرَطَ عَلَى (or أَفْرَطَ).

Offensiveness, *n.* The quality that disgusts, كَرَاهَة ـ كَرَاهِيَة ـ قَبَاحَة ـ إِشْمِئْزَاز ـ شَمَز. The quality which injures, مَضَرَّة ـ أَذِيَّة. The quality which annoys, إِزْعَاج. Obscenity, رَفَث ـ فُحْش ـ فَحَاشَة ـ خَنَايَة ـ قَذَع.

Offer, *v.t.* To present to for refusal or acceptance, ـ عَرَضَ-ل ـ عَرَضَ بِ-ل ـ *or* عَلَى ـ قَدَّمَ-ل. To — to, as of a present, قَدَّمَ ل-هَدِيَّةً ـ هَدَى. To —, as a sacrifice, ذَبَحَ ـ قَدَّمَ قُرْبَانًا ـ ذَبِيحَةً. To — for sale, عَرَضَ-لِلْبَيْعِ. To — one's self to, أَعْرَضَ ذَاتَهُ ل ـ قَدَّمَ نَفْسَهُ ل ـ إِنْتَدَبَ ل. To — to, as a proposition, طَرَحَ-عَلَى ـ عَرَضَ عَلَى-كَذَا. To —, give, أَعْطَى: He offered him money, قَدَّمَ لَهُ دَرَاهِمَ. How much do you — for this book? كَمْ تُعْطِي فِي هٰذَا ٱلْكِتَابِ. He offered himself to their favour, تَعَرَّضَ لِمَعْرُوفِهِمْ. To — violence to, جَارَ عَلَى *aor.* يَجُورُ ـ أَعْنَفَ ـ شَدَّدَ عَلَى. To — prayers, قَدَّمَ ٱلصَّلَوَاتِ. To be offered, تَقَدَّمَ.

Offer, *v.i.* To present itself, إِعْتَرَضَ ـ أَعْرَضَ ـ عَرَضَ: The thing offered itself to him, was present to him, or was in his power, أَعْرَضَ (*or* تَعَرَّضَ) لَهُ ٱلشَّيْءُ. A better opportunity will not — to you, لَمْ تَلْقَ ـ لَمْ تَعْرِضْ لَكَ فُرْصَةٌ أَحْسَنُ مِنْ هٰذِهِ ـ فُرْصَةٌ أَحْسَنَ مِنْ هٰذِهِ. To essay, كَادَ ـ سَعَى. He offered, attempted, to land, سَعَى أَنْ يَنْزِلَ إِلَى ٱلْبَرِّ.

Offer, *n.* A proposal, عُرُوض ـ إِعْرَاض. An attempt, جِدٌّ ـ سَعْي. A price bid, إِعْرَاضُ سِعْرٍ. To close with an —, قَبِلَ ٱلْإِعْرَاضَ ـ إِرْتَضَى بِٱلْمَعْرُوضِ ـ إِتَّفَقَ عَلَى ٱلْعُرُوضِ.

Offerable, *a.* مِمَّا يُقَدَّمُ.

Offerer, *n.* One who offers, مُقَدِّم ـ عَارِض; one who offers a price, مُعْرِضُ سِعْرٍ; one who bids above another, مُزَوِّد; an —, as of sacrifice, مُقَرِّب.

Offering, *n.* Any thing presented, تَقْدِمَة *pl.* تَقْدِمَات. A present, هَدِيَّة *pl.* هَدَايَا ـ تُحْفَة *pl.* تُحَف ـ لَطَف. An — or present which one brings to his family after absence from them, عُرَاضَة. A sacrifice, ذَبِيحَة *pl.* ذَبَائِحُ ـ قُرْبَان *pl.* قَرَابِينُ ـ تَقْرِبَة ـ تَقْدِمَة.

A heave offering, رَفِيعَة.

A peace offering, ذَبِيحَةُ سَلَامَةٍ.

A sin offering, ذَبِيحَةُ خَطِيئَةٍ:

A thank offering, ذَبِيحَةُ شُكْرٍ.

Offertory, *n.* The alms collected, as in a church, إِهْدَاءُ ٱلصَّدَقَاتِ ـ حَسَنَة.

Off-hand, *a.* Without premeditation, مُبْتَدِهٌ ـ مُرْتَجِل. Rude, غَلِيظ ـ جَافٍ ـ فَظٌّ. The — side, اليَمِينُ ـ الطَّرَفُ ٱلْأَيْمَنُ.

Off-hand, *ad.* Impromptu, عَلَى ٱلْبَدِيهَةِ ـ بِٱرْتِجَالٍ. Anything done —, بَدِيهَة ـ بُدَاهَة. He made the speech —, إِبْتَدَهَ ٱلْخُطْبَةَ.

Office, *n.* Employment, occupation, حِرْفَة *pl.* حِرَف ـ صَنْعَة ـ شُغْل ـ خِدْمَة ـ مَأْمُورِيَّة. An appointment, مَنْصَب *pl.* مَنَاصِبُ ـ وَظِيفَة *pl.* وَظَائِف ـ مَأْمُورِيَّة. A set — or task, رَاتِبَة *pl.* رَوَاتِبُ. A place of business, مَوْضِعُ إِدَارَةٍ ـ مَحْرِف ـ قَلَم *pl.* أَقْلَام ـ مَكْتَب. A kitchen, مَطْبَخ. A pantry, كِلَار ـ بَيْتُ ٱلْمُؤْنَةِ ـ ٱلْأَكْلِ. Offices, out-houses, حَيِّز (*or* حَوْز) ٱلدَّارِ. (*See also* Outbuilding, *n.*) A formulary of religious service, طَقْس *pl.* طُقُوس ـ خِدْمَة. An act, treatment, مُعَامَلَة ـ فِعْل *pl.* أَفْعَال ـ عَمَل *pl.* أَعْمَال. Rank, station, رُتْبَة *pl.* رُتَب ـ مَرْتَبَة *pl.* مَرَاتِبُ.

Good offices, kindly acts, مُعَاوَنَة ـ جَمِيل ـ أَنْعَام ـ مَعْرُوف:

To do good offices to, أَحْسَنَ إِلَى ـ مَنَّ عَلَى ـ أَوْلَى-مَعْرُوفًا.

Ill offices, سُوءٌ ـ أَذِيَّة ـ أَذَاة: to do ill offices to, آذَى ـ أَسَاءَ إِلَى.

Holding the office of ..., المُوَظَّفُ بِوَظِيفَةِ ٱلـ.

To appoint to an office, أَقَامَ-فِي (*or* وَجَّهَ-إِلَى) مَنْصَبٍ ـ عَيَّنَ-لِوَظِيفَةٍ ـ قَلَّدَ-مَنْصَبًا.

To come into office, شَرَعَ فِي وَظِيفَتِهِ ـ دَخَلَ فِي مَأْمُورِيَّتِهِ.

To do the office or duty of ..., قَامَ ـ قَامَ عَلَى خِدْمَةِ ٱلـ... ; to hold the place of, قَامَ مَكَانَ ـ حَلَّ مَحَلَّ بِوَظِيفَةِ ٱلـ....

To restore to office, رَدَّ-إِلَى مَقَامِهِ (*or* وَظِيفَتِهِ).

To retire from office, تَرَكَ ٱلْوَظِيفَةَ ـ تَقَعَّدَ عَنِ ٱلْوَظِيفَةِ. To ask to —, إِسْتَعْفَى مِنَ ٱلْخِدْمَةِ.

Office-bearer, *n.* مُتَوَظِّف ـ مَأْمُور *pl.* مَأْمُورُونَ ـ صَاحِبُ وَظِيفَةٍ.

Office-bearers, officials, أُولُوا ٱلْمَنَاصِبِ.

Office-keeper, *n.* حَارِسُ ٱلْمَكْتَبِ (*or* بَيْتِ ٱلْإِدَارَةِ).

Officer, *n.* One who holds any office, صَاحِبُ وَظِيفَةٍ *pl.* أَصْحَاب ـ مَأْمُور *pl.* مَأْمُورُونَ ـ مُوَظَّف. A military —, ضَابِطُ ٱلْعَسْكَرِ *pl.* ضُبَّاط; a naval —, ضَابِطُ ٱلْبَحْرِيَّةِ. Employed as an —, official, مُتَوَظِّف. (In 'Omân an — of an irregular corps is called عَقِيد).

Field-officer, ضَابِطٌ رُتْبَتُهُ فَوْقَ رُتْبَةِ أُوبَيْنِ ٱلْآلَى.

Flag-officer, بَاشَا ٱلْبَحْرِيَّةِ.

General-officer, بَاشَا ٱلْعَسْكَرِ.

Non-commissioned officer, مِنْ دَرَجَةِ قَائِدِ ٱلْعَشَرَةِ (*or* ٱلْأُون بَاشِي).

Staff-officer, ضَابِطٌ مِنْ أَرْكَانِ ٱلْحَرْبِ.

Warrant officer, ضَابِطٌ دُونَ رُتْبَةِ قَائِدِ ٱلْمِئَةِ (*or* ٱلْيُوز بَاشِي).

Officer, *v.t.* عَيَّنَ لِ-مِنَ ٱلضُّبَّاطِ. The ship was officered by ..., كَانَتْ ضُبَّاطُ ٱلْمَرْكَبِ مِنْ كَذَا.

Official, *n.* *See under* Office-bearer, *n.*

Official, *a.* رَسْمِيٌّ. An — demand, communication, إِسْتِعْلَامٌ رَسْمِيٌّ.

Charged with an office, مُتَوَظِّف . An — character, صِفَةٌ رَسْمِيَّةٌ . Official correspondence, مُرَاسَلَاتٌ (or مُكَاتَبَاتٌ) ــ مُحَرَّرَاتٌ رَسْمِيَّةٌ رَسْمِيَّةٌ . An — dispatch, قِطْعَةُ تَحْرِيرَاتٍ رَسْمِيَّةٍ . An — journal, جَرِيدَةٌ رَسْمِيَّةٌ . Non-official, having no office, غَيْرُ مُتَوَظِّفٍ . The government has received no — information, لَمْ يَصِلْ إِلَى ٱلدَّوْلَةِ خَبَرٌ رَسْمِيٌّ .

Officially, *ad.* عَلَى وَجْهٍ رَسْمِيٍّ ــ رَسْمًا .

Officiate, *v.i.* To perform the duties of…, قَامَ بِخِدْمَةِ ٱلْ… ــ ² قَامَ بِوَظِيفَةِ ٱلْ… ². To act in the place of one, حَلَّ مَحَلَّهُ ــ ² قَامَ مَكَانَهُ ² ــ . To serve, as in a church, خَدَمَ ².

Officinal, *a.* مِنَ ٱلدَّكَاكِينِ ــ مِنَ ٱلْحَوَانِيتِ .

Officious, *a.* Meddlesome, عِرْنِض ــ مِشْيَاح ــ تَيَّاح ــ تَيَّحَان ــ مُتَكَلِّف ــ فُضُولِيٌّ . Not official, غَيْرُ رَسْمِيٍّ . Approaching to what is official, مُشَبَّهٌ بِٱلرَّسْمِيِّ . The — or semi-official journal, ٱلْجَرِيدَةُ ٱلشَّبِيهَةُ بِٱلرَّسْمِيَّةِ . To be —, to intermeddle, عَرَّضَ ــ قَارَشَ ــ تَدَاخَلَ ــ تَعَرَّضَ .

Officiously, *ad.* In a meddling manner, بِمُدَاخَلَةٍ ــ كَٱلْمِشْيَاحِ ــ بِتَعَرُّضٍ ــ بِفُضُولٍ . Not officially, عَلَى وَجْهٍ غَيْرِ رَسْمِيٍّ . Semi-officially, بِشُبْهَةٍ رَسْمِيَّةٍ .

Officiousness, *n.* Meddlesomeness, فُضُول ــ مُدَاخَلَة ــ تَعَرُّض ــ مُقَارَشَة ــ تَدَاخُل .

Offing, *n.* The open (sea), ٱلْعَمِيقُ ــ ٱلْوَاسِعُ . In the —, دُونَ ٱلْمِينَةِ ــ فِي ٱلْوَاسِعِ .

Offscouring, *n.* Offscum, } Refuse matter, دَنَاسَة ــ نَجَاسَة ــ وَسَخ . The — of the people, ٱلسَّفَلَة .

Offset, *n.* A shoot or sprout, عُسْلُوج or عُسْلُج *pl.* عَسَالِيجُ ــ ظَاهِرَة ــ ظَهْر ــ صَعْدَة . A plateau, فَرْع *pl.* فُرُوع ــ فِرَاخ *pl.* فَرْخ ــ سَطْح *pl.* سُطُوح . Something set against another as a compensation, مُقَابَلَة ــ مُعَاوَضَة ــ مُعَارَضَة .

Offset, *v.t.* قَابَلَ ــ أَعَاضَ ــ عَوَّضَ ــ عَرَّضَ ــ عَارَضَ-بِ .

Offshoot, *n.* Branch, as of a tree, river, *etc.*, شُعْبَة *pl.* شُعَب .

Offspring, *n.* A child or children, وَلَد *pl.* أَوْلَاد ــ اِبْن *pl.* أَبْنَاء . Descendants, زَرْع ــ نَسْل *pl.* أَنْسَال ــ ذُرِّيَّة ــ آل . Production, نَشَاءَة ــ حَاصِل ــ تَوْلِيد . To die leaving —, أَعْقَبَ ; to die leaving no —, مَاتَ عَنْ غَيْرِ أَوْلَادٍ ².

Oft, *adv.* Often, Oftentimes, Ofttimes, } طَالَمَا ــ كَثِيرًا مَا ــ مِرَارًا ــ أَكْثَرَ ــ ذَاتَ ٱلْمِرَارِ مِرَارًا كَثِيرَةً . As often as, كُلَّمَا ــ مَهْمَا . How often? كَمْ مَرَّةٍ . Not often, رُبَّمَا ــ قَلَّمَا ــ غِبًّا فِي ٱلنَّادِرِ . He did it often, كَثُرَ ذٰلِكَ مِنْهُ ². He often comes to me, يَتَرَدَّدُ عَلَيَّ مِرَارًا . He often manifests his personal opinions other than they really are, كَثِيرًا مَا يُظْهِرُ أَفْكَارَهُ ٱلشَّخْصِيَّةَ عَلَى غَيْرِ مَا هِيَ عَلَيْهِ .

Ogle, *v.t.* نَظَرَ إِلَى-مُعَارَضَةً (or عَنْ عُرْضٍ) ² ــ لَحَظَ ــ غَمَزَ-بِٱلْعَيْنِ ; *vulg.* بَصَّ ل ; especially of a woman towards a man, هَجَلَتْ بِهِ ². To — with the eyes, (*v.i.*) رَأْرَأَ بِعَيْنَيْهِ .

Ogler, *n.* غَامِز ــ نَاظِرٌ عَنْ عُرْضٍ ; of a woman to a man, هَاجِلَة .

Ogling, *n.* غَمْز ــ بَصْبَصَة ــ ٱلنَّظَرُ عَنْ عُرْضٍ ; of a woman a man, هَجْل .

Ogre, *n.* غُول *pl.* غِيلَان ــ عِفْرِيت *pl.* عَفَارِيتُ .

Ogress, *n.* جِنِّيَّة ــ عِفْرِيتَة .

Oh! *int.* آه ــ أَوَّهْ ــ يَهْ . Oh that…! يَا لَيْتَ ــ لَيْتَ . Oh that I…! يَا لَيْتَنِي ; oh that thou…! يَا لَيْتَكَ (and so through the other pronouns). Oh, how fine! يَا هَيَّ ; oh, how pleasant, how good! يَا حَبَّذَا .

Oil, *n.* An unctuous substance, دُهْن *pl.* أَدْهَان *and* دِهَان . Olive oil, زَيْت ــ سَلِيط (the latter in al-Yáman is applied to sesame oil). Sesame oil, شِيرَج ــ شَيْرَج ــ سِيرَج ــ سَلِيط . Linseed oil, دُهْنُ ٱلْكَتَّانِ . Castor oil, زَيْتُ ٱلْخِرْوَعِ . An oil bottle or can, مُدْهُن *pl.* مَدَاهِنُ ــ مُدْهُنَة . An oil-press, مَدْهَنَة . A large oil jar made of skin, دَبَّة *pl.* دِبَاب . A seller of oil, زَيَّات . Holy oil, chrism, مَيْرُون .

Oil, *v.t.* زَاتَ *aor.* يَزِيتُ ــ دَهَنَ ² . To oil one's self, اِدَّهَنَ ــ اِزْدَاتَ .

Oil-bag, *n.* لَوْزَةُ ٱلدُّهْنِ .

Oil-cake, *n.* مَعْجُونُ ٱلسِّمْسِمِ .

Oil-colour, *n.* صِبَاغٌ (or لَوْنٌ) بِزَيْتٍ .

Oilcloth, *n.* بِسَاطٌ مُشَمَّعٌ .

Oiliness, *n.* دَسَم ــ دُسُوم .

Oilman, *n.* A seller of oil, زَيَّات .

Oilshop, *n.* دُكَّانُ ٱلزَّيَّاتِ .

Oilskin, *n.* مُشَمَّع .

Oily, *a.* دَهِن ــ مُدْهَان ــ دَسِم .

Ointment, *n.* دُهْن *pl.* أَدْهَان ــ مَرْهَم *pl.* مَرَاهِمُ ــ دِهَان . A box for ointments, قُرْز .

Okra, *n.* The vegetable, بَامِيَة .

Old, *a.* Aged, مُسِنٌّ *fem.* مُسِنَّة ــ طَاعِنٌ فِي ٱلسِّنِّ ــ كَبِير *fem.* كَبِيرَة ــ كَبِيرٌ فِي ٱلْعُمْرِ ــ مُتَقَدِّمٌ فِي ٱلْعُمْرِ ــ شَيْخ *pl.* شُيُوخ . To be or become old, أَسَنَّ ــ طَعَنَ فِي ٱلسِّنِّ ² ــ شَاخَ ــ اِشْتَسَنَ ــ تَشَيَّخَ ــ عَجِزَ . To be too old to, عَجِزَ عَنْ . To be older than, كَبَرَ-بِ ² ــ كَبِرَ : he was one year older than him, كَبَرَهُ بِسَنَةٍ .

How old are you? كَمْ لَكَ مِنَ ٱلْعُمْرِ. He is older than you, هُوَ أَكْبَرُ مِنْكَ فِي ٱلْعُمْرِ. You old fool! يَا شَيْبَةَ ٱلْعَارِ. Old, ancient, عَادِيٌّ — قَدِيمٌ — عَتِيقٌ pl. عُتَقَاءُ — عَاتِقٌ pl. عَوَاتِقُ. From old time, مِنْ سَالِفِ ٱلدَّهْرِ. To be of old, قَدُمَ ². To become old, of a thing, عَتُقَ ² — عَتَقَ ². Old wine, (رَاحٌ or) خَمْرٌ عَتِيقٌ. It was kept till it became old, عُتِّقَتْ زَمَانًا. Old, of food, سَنِهٌ. Old, worn out, خَلِيعٌ — حَشِيفٌ — رَثٌّ — أَرَثُّ — رِثَّةٌ — بَالٍ — عَتِيقٌ. Old or paltry chattels, articles of furniture, etc., رَثٌّ — رِثَّةٌ — رِثَّةُ ٱلْمَتَاعِ. To become old, worn out, أَرَثَّ — رَثَّ ² — عَتُقَ ². Old, obsolete, مُلْغًى — هَامِدٌ — غَبِيرٌ — مُسْتَعْمَلٌ. An old man who begets a child in his old age, مُصِيفٌ. Of old, مِنْ سَالِفِ ٱلدَّهْرِ — مِنَ ٱلْقَدِيمِ. Two months old, عُمْرُهُ شَهْرَيْنِ. An old worn-out garment, خَلِيعٌ: He dresses him in his old clothes, يَكْسُوهُ مِنْ خَلِيعِهِ.

Old clothes, ثِيَابٌ رَثِيثَةٌ — حَشِيفٌ — خُلْقَانٌ — أَخْلَاقٌ — ثِيَابٌ مُسْتَعْمَلَةٌ.

Old-clothes man, بَيَّاعُ ٱلثِّيَابِ ٱلْمُسْتَعْمَلَةِ — سَقَطِيٌّ — خُلْقَانِيٌّ — بَيَّاعُ ٱلثِّيَابِ ٱلْبَالِيَةِ.

Old-clothes market, سُوقُ ٱلسَّقَطِيَّةِ — سُوقُ ٱلثِّيَابِ ٱلْمُسْتَعْمَلَةِ.

Old man, شَائِبٌ — شَيِّبٌ — عَجَائِزُ pl. عَجُوزٌ — رَجُلٌ بَدَنٌ; vulg. إِخْتِيَارٌ pl. إِخْتِيَارِيَّةٌ.

Old woman, عُتَّةٌ — عَجُوزَةٌ pl. عَجَائِزُ.

Old style, of chronological reckoning, ٱلْحِسَابُ ٱلرُّومِيُّ — ٱلْحِسَابُ ٱلْفِرَنْجِيُّ.

Old age, n. شَيْبَةٌ — شَيْخُوخَةٌ — شُيُوخِيَّةٌ. A good —, شَيْبَةٌ صَالِحَةٌ.

Old bachelor, n. مُتَعَزِّبٌ زَمَانًا — مُدْمِنُ ٱلْعُزُوبَةِ.

Olden, a. عَتِيقٌ — قَدِيمٌ. In olden time, فِي ٱلزَّمَانِ ٱلْقَدِيمِ. From olden time, مِنَ ٱلْقَدِيمِ.

Old-fashioned, a. In shape, etc., عَلَى طَرْزٍ عَتِيقٍ — مُعَتَّقٌ — عَلَى هَيْئَةٍ قَدِيمَةٍ. Like old people, مِثْلَ ٱلشُّيُوخِ — مِثْلَ ٱلْعَجَائِزِ — مُعَجَّزٌ fem. مُعَجَّزَةٌ.

Oldish, a. مُشْرِفٌ عَلَى ٱلشُّيُوخِيَّةِ.

Old maid, n. تَرِيكَةٌ — نَقْلَةٌ.

Oldness, n. Old age; see above under Old. Antiquity, عِتْقٌ — عَتَاقَةٌ.

Oleaginous, a. مُدْهَانٌ — دَهِنٌ — زَيْتِيٌّ.

Oleaginousness, n. صِفَةٌ دَهِنَةٌ — دُسُومَةٌ.

Oleander, n. ٱلدِّفْلَى — سَمُّ ٱلْحِمَارِ.

Oleaster, n. The wild olive tree, زَيْتُونَةٌ بَرِّيَّةٌ — عُتْمٌ or أُتْمٌ.

Oleometer, n. مِيزَانُ ٱلْأَدْهَانِ.

Olfactory, a. مِشَمٌّ. The — nerves, ٱلْعُرُوقُ ٱلشَّامَّةُ — عُرُوقُ ٱلشَّمِّ.

Olibanum, n., Oliban, n. } كُنْدُرٌ — لُبَانٌ — كُشْكٌ or كُنْدُرٌ.

Oligarchal, a., Oligarchical, } مُتَعَلِّقٌ بِحُكُومَةِ ٱلْخَوَاصِّ.

Oligarchy, n. حُكُومَةُ ٱلْخَوَاصِّ.

Olio, n. See Medley, n.

Olivaceous, a. Of colour, زَيْتُونِيُّ ٱللَّوْنِ — زَيْتُونِيٌّ.

Olive, n. The fruit, زَيْتُونَةٌ coll. زَيْتُونٌ; the tree, زَيْتُونٌ — زَيْتُونَةٌ — شَجَرَةُ ٱلزَّيْتُونِ. An olive-yard, زَيْتُونٌ. A wild — tree, زَيْتُونَةٌ بَرِّيَّةٌ — عُتْمٌ or أُتْمٌ.

Olive-branch, n. غُصْنُ زَيْتُونٍ pl. أَغْصَانٌ. An emblem of peace, عِبَارَةٌ عَنِ ٱلصُّلْحِ. To hold out the — to, بَادَرَ بِٱلْمُصَالَحَةِ. A child, وَلَدٌ pl. أَوْلَادٌ.

Olla-podrida, n. The dish so called, يَخْنَةٌ. See also Medley, n.

Omega, n. آخِرُ حَرْفِ ٱلْهِجَاءِ فِي ٱللُّغَةِ ٱلْيُونَانِيَّةِ.

Omelet, n. عُجَّةٌ — عُجَّةُ بَيْضٍ.

Omen, n. A good or bad —, but more frequently the latter, طَائِرٌ — طَيْرٌ — طِيَرَةٌ; a good or bad —, but more generally the former, فَأْلٌ pl. فُؤُولٌ and أَفْؤُلٌ. A good —, فَأْلٌ مُبَارَكٌ — بَشَارَةٌ — خَيْرٌ; a bad —, طَيْرٌ نَحْسٌ. Birds of ill —, طَيْرُ ٱلشِّمَالِ. See also Augury, n., to Augur, v.

Omentum, n. ثَرْبٌ pl. ثُرُوبٌ.

Omer, n. The Hebrew measure, عُمْرٌ وَهُوَ كَيْلٌ عِنْدَ بَنِي إِسْرَائِيلَ.

Ominous, a. Foreboding ill, مُوعِدٌ بِٱلشَّرِّ — مُشِيرٌ بِٱلنَّحْسِ; foreboding good, مُوعِدٌ بِٱلْخَيْرِ — مُبَشِّرٌ بِٱلْحَظِّ.

Ominously, ad. Of ill, تَوَعُّدًا بِٱلشَّرِّ — إِنْذَارًا بِٱلنَّحْسِ; of good, إِنْذَارًا بِٱلْخَيْرِ — إِسْتِبْشَارًا بِٱلْحَظِّ.

Ominousness, n. تَوَعُّدٌ — تَهَدُّدٌ — مَوْعِدٌ — هَمٌّ بِ — خَطَرٌ — عَلَامَةُ ٱلْوُقُوعِ.

Omissible, a. مِمَّا يُتْرَكُ — مِمَّا يُحْذَفُ.

Omission, n. Failure to do, neglect, إِهْمَالٌ — تَرْكٌ — غُفُولٌ. A leaving out, حَذْفٌ — إِسْقَاطٌ — ضَرْبٌ عَنْ — فَوَاتٌ — تَرْكٌ. A shortcoming, قُصُورٌ. The sin of —, تَرْكُ ٱلْوَاجِبِ. To make an —; see to Omit, v.t.

Omissive, a. حَاذِفٌ — مُسْقِطٌ — ضَارِبٌ عَنْ — فَائِتٌ.

Omit, v.t. To — intentionally, أَسْقَطَ — حَذَفَ ² — إِحْتَذَفَ — تَرَكَ ² — ضَرَبَ عَنْ ² — فَاتَ ²; unintentionally, سَهَا عَنْ aor. يَسْهُو — غَفَلَ عَنْ ² — نَسِيَ ². To come short in, تَقَصَّرَ بِ. To —, as in a reckoning, أَوْهَمَ ب ; he omitted so much in the account, أَوْهَمَ كذا مِنَ ٱلْحِسَاب . We have omitted to mention, قَدْ فَاتَنَا أَنْ نَذْكُرَ .

Omnibus, *n.* أُمْنِيبُوس ـ عَرَبِيَّة كِرْوَةٍ لِلْجُمْهُور . The — Company has ceased running its carriages because all its horses have been taken for military service, قَدْ عُطِّلَتْ شِرْكَةُ ٱلْأُمْنِيبُوسِ لِأَنَّ خَيْلَهَا أُخِذَتْ لِلْخِدْمَةِ ٱلْعَسْكَرِيَّةِ .

Omnifarious, *a.* مُتَنَوِّع .

Omnific, *a.* خَلَّاق .

Omniform, *a.* مِنْ كُلِّ شَكْلٍ ـ مُتَنَوِّع .

Omnipotence, *n.* / Omnipotency, } قُدْرَةٌ مُطْلَقَةٌ ـ قُدْرَةٌ كُلِّيَّةٌ .

Omnipotent, *a.* قَهَّار ـ ضَابِطُ ٱلْكُلِّ ـ قَادِرٌ عَلَى كُلِّ شَيْءٍ . The Omnipotent (God), القَهَّار .

Omnipotently, *ad.* بِقُدْرَةٍ مُطْلَقَةٍ ـ بِقُدْرَةٍ كُلِّيَّةٍ .

Omnipresence, *n.* تَنَزُّهٌ عَنِ ٱلْمَكَانِ ـ حُضُورٌ مُطْلَقٌ .

Omnipresent, *a.* مُنَزَّهٌ عَنِ ٱلْمَكَانِ ـ حَاضِرٌ فِي كُلِّ مَكَانٍ .

Omniscience, *n.* / Omnisciency, } مَعْرِفَةٌ مُطْلَقَةٌ ـ عِلْمُ ٱلْغَيْبِ ـ عِلْمٌ مُطْلَقٌ . The — of God, عِلْمُ ـ مَعْرِفَةُ ٱللّٰهِ ٱلْكُلِّيَّةُ ٱللّٰهِ ٱلْمُطْلَقُ .

Omniscient, *a.* عَالِمٌ مُطْلَقٌ ـ عَالِمٌ بِٱلْغَيْبِ . The Omniscient (God), العَلَّامُ ـ العَالِمُ ـ العَلِيمُ .

Omnisciently, *ad.* بِعِلْمٍ مُطْلَقٍ .

Omnium, *n.* An aggregate of the public stocks, ضَمِيمَةُ إِيرَادِ ٱلْخَزْنَةِ .

Omnium-gatherum, *n.* مَجْمُوعَة ـ مَجْمَعَة .

Omnivorous, *a.* آكِلُ كُلِّ ٱلْمَأْكُولَاتِ .

Omoplate, *n.* لَوْحُ ٱلْكَتِفِ .

Omphalic, *a.* Pertaining to the navel, مُتَعَلِّقٌ بِٱلسُّرَّةِ .

On, *prep.* upon, فَوْقَ ـ عَلَى ـ فِي . By, near, قَرِيبٌ ـ عِنْدَ مِنْ . At the time of, وَقْتَ ـ عِنْدَ . On, by, as of swearing, حَقَّ ـ عَلَى . The paper is on the table, الوَرَقَةُ عَلَى ٱلسُّفْرَةِ . Baghdâd on the Tigris, بَغْدَادُ عِنْدَ (*or* عَلَى) ٱلدِّجْلَةِ . On my honour! عَلَى ذِمَّتِي . On the arrival of my brother, عِنْدَ وُصُولِ أَخِي . To play on an instrument, ضَرَبَ ٱلْآلَةَ . On Monday next, فِي يَوْمِ ٱلْاِثْنَيْنِ ٱلْآتِي .

On a sudden, بَغْتَةً ـ عَلَى ٱلْفَوْرِ .

On fire, مُلْتَهِب ـ مُشْتَعِل ـ شَاعِل .

On the alert, مُتَيَقِّظ ـ صَاحٍ ـ فَائِق .

On the way, فِي ٱلطَّرِيقِ .

On the wing, طَائِر .

On, *ad.* Towards, إِلَى ـ نَحْوَ . Onwards, لِقُدَّام ـ مُتَقَدِّمًا ـ إِلَى قُدَّام . In succession, عَلَى ٱلتَّوَالِي . Adhering, بِمُلَازَمَةٍ ـ تَمَسُّكًا بِ ـ بِدُونِ ٱنْفِصَالٍ . Happening, going on, جَارٍ ـ وَاقِع . Far on in the night, عِنْدَ تَنَاهِي ٱللَّيْلِ . Sleep on now, نَمِ ٱلْآنَ ـ ظَلَّ نَائِمًا . Say on, تَكَلَّمْ .

And so on, وَهَلُمَّ جَرًّا ـ وَمِثَالُ ذٰلِكَ ـ إِلَى آخِرِهِ .

Come on! تَعَالَ ـ أَيْ ـ هَلُمَّ . Come on, Zaid! أَيْ زَيْدُ أَقْبِلْ .

Go on! advance, تَقَدَّمْ ـ رَوِّجْ ; Go on! continue, ظِلَّ ـ إِظْلِلْ .

On and off, with interruptions, بُعَيْدَاتٍ بَيْنٍ ـ بِتَعْطِيلٍ ـ بِٱنْقِطَاعٍ .

On and on, هَلُمَّ جَرًّا .

For the adverb "On" when suffixed to a verb, as *to* "Carry on," *to* "Lay on," *etc.*, see under the verbs).

Onager, *n.* The wild ass, حِمَارٌ وَحْشِيٌّ ـ يَحْمُور .

Onanism, *n.* إِسْتِمْنَاء . A woman given to —, سَحَّاقَة .

Once, *ad.* One time, طَرْقَةً ـ مَرَّات *pl.* مَرَّةً ـ زَنَّةً *and* مِرَار فِي وَقْتٍ ـ وَقْتًا مَا . At one time, كَرَّةً ـ خَطْرَةً ـ ذَاتَ مَرَّةٍ ـ تَارَةً . Formerly, قَبْلًا ـ فِي ٱلسَّابِقِ ـ سَابِقًا ـ مِنَ ٱلْأَوْقَاتِ . Once, upon a morning, or, one morning, ذَاتَ صَبَاحٍ ; upon an evening, ذَاتَ مَسَاءٍ ; upon a day, ذَاتَ يَوْمٍ . Once or twice, طَرْقًا أَوْ طَرْقَتَيْنِ ـ بِٱلْمَرَّةِ ـ مَرَّةً ـ هَبَّةً . All at once, مَرَّةً أَوْ مَرَّتَيْنِ . At once, now, فِي ٱلْحَالِ ـ السَّاعَةَ ـ حَالًا . This once only, هٰذِهِ ٱلْمَرَّةَ فَقَطْ . Once more, مَرَّةً ثَانِيَةً ـ مَرَّةً أَيْضًا . I met him once or twice, لَقِيتُهُ مَرَّةً أَوْ مَرَّتَيْنِ . They sent to him once and again, أَرْسَلُوا إِلَيْهِ مَرَّةً وَمَرَّتَيْنِ . To settle a matter at —, out of hand, تَنَجَّزَ (*or* تَنَضَّضَ) ٱلْحَاجَةَ .

On dit, *n.* قَوْل *pl.* أَقْوَال ـ تَوَاتُر ـ كَلَامُ ٱلنَّاسِ .

One, *a.* أَحَد ـ أَفْرَد ـ فَرْد ـ وِتْر *pl.* فَرْدَة *fem.* أَفْرَاد *pl.* إِحْدَى *fem.* ; *pl. masc.* أُحْدَان *and* آحَاد *pl. fem.* إِحَد ـ وَاحِد *pl.* وُحْدَان *fem.* إِحْدَى *and* وَاحِدَة . Single, only, فَرِيد ـ فَرْد . One of two, طَاقَة ـ فَرْد . Say: He is God, one (God), قُلْ هُوَ ٱللّٰهُ أَحَدٌ . Take thou one of the three (females), خُذْ إِحْدَى ٱلثَّلَاثِ . One of these days, فِي بَعْضِ هٰذِهِ ٱلْأَيَّامِ . One night, on a certain night, ذَاتَ لَيْلَةٍ . All one, the same, لَا فَرْقَ فِيهِمْ ـ عَلَى ٱلسَّوِيَّةِ . Such an one, فُلَان . It is all one to me, لَا فَرْقَ عِنْدِي . Ten to one, of a bet, عَشَرَةٌ عَلَى وَاحِدٍ ـ قِبَالَ وَاحِدٍ . They came one by one, جَاؤُوا فُرَادَى . To bring forth one at a time, of a ewe, أَفَذَّتْ ; a ewe that so brings forth, أَفَذُّ . To make (into) one, وَحَّدَ ; to be made (into) one, تَوَحَّدَ . To be all to one, كَانَ وَحِيدًا ـ كَانَ فَرِيدًا عِنْدَهُ . To make one (of a party), صَارَ جَلِيسًا مَعَهُمْ (*or* جَلِيسَهُمْ) عِنْدَهُ .

At one, in accord, of many, مُتَّحِدُونَ ـ مُتَّفِقُونَ .

One after another, وَاحِدٌ بَعْدَ وَاحِدٍ. She brought forth three sons one after another, *i.e.* without any girls between them, وَلَدَتْ ثَلَاثَةً بَنِينَ عَلَى سَاقٍ وَاحِدٍ. Three children were born to him one after another, وُلِدَ لَهُ ثَلَاثَةُ أَوْلَادٍ سَاقًا عَلَى سَاقٍ.

One and all, without exception, جُمْلَةً ـ بِأَسْرِهِمْ ـ طُرًّا ـ قَاطِبَةً ـ بَتَّةً.

One and the same, هُوَ هُوَ عَيْنًا ـ هُوَ بِعَيْنِهِ ـ هُوَ هُوَ.

One by one, فُرَادًا ـ فُرَادَى ـ إِنْفِرَادًا ـ وَاحِدًا وَاحِدًا ـ أُحَادَ. They came —, جَاؤُوا فُرَادًا (or أُحَادَ). I counted them one by one, عَدَدْتُهُمْ إِفْرَادًا وِحَادًا ـ عَدَدْتُهُمْ أَفْرَادًا.

One with another, سَوَآءً ـ مَعًا ـ هٰذَا وَهٰذَاكَ.

One, *n.* A person, individual, نَفَرٌ ـ بَعْضٌ ـ أَحَدٌ ـ شَخْصٌ *pl.* أَنْفَارٌ. (One, in the indefinite sense in which it is used in English, in connexion with a verb, is variously expressed in Arabic, but usually the intransitive or participial form of the verb is adopted, *e.g.*,) One sees that, وَمِنَ ٱلْبَائِنِ أَنْ ـ يَبِينُ أَنْ; one knows that, وَمِنَ ٱلْمَعْلُومِ أَنْ. One says, *or* some say, يَقُولُ ٱلْبَعْضُ; one asserts, *or* some assert, that, يَدَّعِي ٱلْبَعْضُ أَنْ.

One thing, شَيْءٌ وَاحِدٌ. But one thing is wanting, الحَاجَةُ إِلَى وَاحِدٍ. From one upwards, مِنْ وَاحِدٍ فَصَاعِدًا.

Any one, أَيُّ مَنْ كَانَ ـ كُلُّ مَنْ كَانَ ـ كَائِنٌ مَنْ كَانَ.

Each one of them, كُلُّ وَاحِدٍ مِنْهُمْ ـ كُلُّ وَاحِدٍ مِنْهُمْ ـ كُلٌّ مِنْهُمْ بِمُفْرَدِهِ.

Every one, كُلُّ مَنْ ـ الكُلُّ ـ كُلُّ وَاحِدٍ. Every one of you, كُلُّكُمْ; Every one of them, كُلُّهُمْ.

No one, لَا أَحَدَ. There is no one in the house, لَا أَحَدَ فِي ٱلدَّارِ.

Not one, وَلَا وَاحِدٌ. There remained not one, لَمْ يَبْقَ وَاحِدٌ.

One another, (*in accus.*) بَعْضُهُمْ بَعْضًا: Love one another, أَحِبُّوا بَعْضُكُمْ بَعْضًا.

One's self, ذَاتٌ ـ نَفْسٌ. His own self, هُوَ نَفْسُهُ.

One-eyed, *a.* أَعْوَرُ *fem.* عَوْرَآءُ *pl.* عُورٌ.

Oneirocritic, *a.* }
Oneirocritical, } Pertaining to the interpretation of dreams, مُتَعَلِّقٌ بِتَعْبِيرِ ٱلرُّؤْيَا.

Oneiromancy, *n.* تَعْبِيرُ ٱلرُّؤْيَا.

Oneness, *n.* وَحْدَانِيَّةٌ ـ وَحْدَةٌ.

Onerous, *a.* ثَقِيلٌ. To be — to, ثَقُلَ عَلَى ². To make — to, ثَقَّلَ- (or أَثْقَلَ-) عَلَى.

One's self, *n.* ذَاتٌ ـ نَفْسٌ. Beside —, طَائِرٌ ـ غَائِبُ ٱلْعَقْلِ ـ مِثْلُ ٱلْمَذْعُورِ ـ ٱلْعَقْلِ. By —, مُنْفَرِدٌ ـ وَحْدَهُ. To be beside —, إِخْتَلَّ. To come to —, أَفَاقَ ـ رَجَعَ إِلَى نَفْسِهِ.

To take care of —, تَحَرَّسَ ـ تَحَفَّظَ ـ وَفَّرَ نَفْسَهُ ـ سَاسَ نَفْسَهُ ² ـ إِعْتَنَى بِنَفْسِهِ.

One-sided, *a.* Having one side, ذُو جَنْبٍ وَاحِدٍ. Looking at one side only, مُشْرِفٌ عَلَى طَرَفٍ وَاحِدٍ فَقَطْ. Prejudiced, غَيْرُ ذِي عَصَبِيَّةٍ ـ مُنْصِفٍ.

One-sidedness, *n.* The having one side, وَحْدَةُ ٱلْجَانِبِ. Prejudice, want of justice, عَصَبِيَّةٌ ـ عَدَمُ إِنْصَافٍ. *See also* Bias, *n.*

Onion, *n.* بَصَلَةٌ *coll.* بَصَلٌ. A wild —, بَصَلُ ٱلزِّيزِ ـ بَلْبُوسٌ ـ بَصَلٌ بَرِّيٌّ ـ بَصَلُ ٱلذِّئْبِ. A stew of meat and onions, بَصَلِيَّةٌ.

Only, *a.* Single, لَا غَيْرُ ـ وَحِيدٌ ـ فَرِيدٌ. Thou only, (*masc.*), أَنْتَ وَحْدَكَ; (*fem.*) أَنْتِ وَحْدَكِ; he only, هُوَ وَحْدَهُ; she only, هِيَ وَحْدَهَا, *etc.* I have only one, عِنْدِي وَاحِدٌ لَا غَيْرُ; I took only ten, قَبَضْتُ عَشَرَةً لَا غَيْرُ. He had an only daughter, كَانَ لَهُ بِنْتٌ وَحِيدَةٌ. The only son of his mother, and she was a widow, إِبْنٌ وَحِيدٌ لِأُمِّهِ وَهِيَ أَرْمَلَةٌ. Thou alone art the Lord God only, or the only God, أَنْتَ أَنْتَ ٱلرَّبُّ ٱلْإِلٰهُ وَحْدَكَ. To God the only wise, لِلّٰهِ ٱلْحَكِيمِ وَحْدَهُ. Against Thee only have I sinned, إِلَيْكَ وَحْدَكَ أَخْطَأْتُ. *See also* Alone, *a.*

Only, *ad.* Merely, without more, فَقَطْ ـ لَا غَيْرُ. But, on the other hand, وَأَمَّا. You have only this, مَا عِنْدَكَ إِلَّا هٰذَا فَقَطْ. Only, but, as regards this man, وَأَمَّا مِنْ طَرَفِ هٰذَا ٱلرَّجُلِ. Not this only, but that also, لَيْسَ هٰذَا فَقَطْ بَلْ ذَاكَ أَيْضًا.

Onomasticon, *n.* كِتَابُ ٱللُّغَةِ ـ مِصْبَاحُ ٱلْكَلِمَاتِ.

Onomatopœia, *n.* تَأْتَأَةٌ. To use —, (literally to reiterate the ت in speaking), تَأْتَأَ. One who so speaks, تَأْتَاءٌ.

Onset, *n.* }
Onslaught, } An assault, هَجْمَةٌ ـ هُجُومٌ ـ بَطْشٌ ـ شَدَّةٌ ـ كَبَّةٌ ـ حَمْلَةٌ. To make an — upon, بَطَشَ عَلَى ² ـ هَجَمَ عَلَى ² ـ شَدَّ عَلَى ². A beginning, شُرُوعٌ. *See also* Assault, Charge, *n.*

Ontological, *a.* مَا نِيطَ بِعِلْمِ تَجْرِيدِ ٱلْمَوْجُودَاتِ.

Ontology, *n.* عِلْمُ تَجْرِيدِ ٱلْمَوْجُودَاتِ ـ عِلْمُ تَجْرِيدِ ٱلْوُجُودِ.

Onus, *n.* The burden, الحِمْلُ. An obligation, وُجُوبٌ ـ لُزُومٌ. The *onus probandi* is with you, لُزُومُ ٱلْإِثْبَاتِ (or ٱلْبُرْهَانِ) عِنْدَكَ.

Onward, *ad.* }
Onwards, } إِلَى قُدَّامٍ ـ لِقُدَّامٍ ـ تَقَدُّمًا. *See also* Forward, *a.* and *ad.*

Onward, *a.* Going forward, progressive, مُتَرَوِّجٌ ـ مُتَقَدِّمٌ. An — or progressive course, تَرَقٍّ ـ إِفْلَاحٌ ـ تَقَدُّمٌ ـ رَوَاجٌ.

Onyx, *n.* جَزْعٌ ـ جِزْعٌ; one — stone, جَزْعَةٌ ـ جِزْعَةٌ.

Oolite, *n.* حَجَرُ ٱلْجِيرِ فِي هَيْئَةِ ٱلشُّعْفُرِ (or ٱلْبَطَارِخِ) طَبْعًا.

Oolitic, *a.* كَٱلْحَجَرِ ٱلْجِيْرِ ٱلَّذِى فِى هَيْئَةِ ٱلشُّعْفُرِ (or ٱلْبَطَارِخِ) طَبْعًا.

Ooze, *n.* What oozes out, رَشْحَان ـ فَزِيز ـ نَضِيض ـ نُتُوع ـ رَشْح. *See also* Slime, *n.*

Ooze, *v.i.* To flow gently, as from pores, نَضَّ ـ فَزَّ ـ نَتَعَ ـ ٢ ـ تَرَشَّحَ ـ رَشَحَ. To make to —, رَشَّحَ.

Oozy, *a.* *See* Muddy, Slimy, *a.*

Opacity, *n.* Want of transparency, عَدَمُ شَفَفٍ ـ كَثَافَة ـ لَمًى. Cloudiness, ظُلْمَة ـ سُحَابَة ـ تَغَيُّم. *See also* Turbidity, *n.*

Opacous, *a.* غَيْرُ شَفَّافٍ ـ كَثِيف ـ لَمْيَاءُ *fem.* أَلْمَى. To be —, لَمِىَ. *See also* Thick, Turbid, *a.*

Opal, *n.* عَيْنُ ٱلشَّمْسِ ـ عَيْنُ ٱلْهِرِّ.

Opalescence, *n.* بَرِيقُ ٱلْمَعَادِنِ.

Opalescent, *a.* بَرَّاقٌ كَعَيْنِ ٱلْهِرِّ.

Opaline, *a.* شَبِيهٌ بِعَيْنِ ٱلشَّمْسِ.

Opaque, *a.* *See* Opacous, *a.*

Opaqueness, *n.* *See* Opacity, *n.*

Ope, *v.t.* / Open, } To unclose, as of a door, *etc.*, فَجَا ٢ ـ إِسْتَفْتَحَ ـ إِفْتَتَحَ ـ فَتَّحَ ـ أَشْرَعَ ـ فَتَحَ. To —, crack, as of a nut, *etc.*, كَسَرَ. To unbar, فَكَّ ٢. To unloose, untie, حَلَّ ٢. To slit, شَقَّ ٢ ـ بَزَّلَ. To —, or cut, of a wound, بَطَّ ٢. To —, as of the ground, to dig, حَفَرَ ٢. To unfold, spread out, شَرَحَ ـ فَرَشَ ٢ ـ بَسَطَ ـ شَرَّحَ. To —, explain, شَرَحَ ـ صَرَّحَ بِ ـ أَصْرَحَ. To — or show to, أَرَاى ـ بَيَّنَ ـ لِ ـ عَرَضَ ـ لِ ـ أَظْهَرَ ـ لِ *vulg.* وَرَّى. To —, as of a seal, فَضَّ ٢ ـ فَكَّ ٢. To reveal, كَشَفَ ـ كَشَّفَ ـ أَجْهَرَ. To —, as to the air, sun, *etc.*, نَشَرَ ٢. To — with, as of a discourse, شَرَحَ ـ إِسْتَفْتَحَ بِ ـ إِفْتَتَحَ بِ. To — one's heart to, شَرَحَ صَدْرَهُ لِ. To —, as of a bottle, شَالَ ٱلسِّدَادَ ـ سَلَّكَ ٢. To be or become open, unclosed, إِنْفَتَحَ ـ تَفَتَّحَ; to be unbarred, إِنْفَكَّ ـ إِنْفَكَّ; to be unloosed, untied, إِنْحَلَّ; to be slit, إِنْشَقَّ ـ تَبَزَّلَ; to be unfolded, spread out, إِنْشَرَحَ ـ إِنْبَسَطَ ـ تَبَسَّطَ; to be opened out, revealed, made manifest, إِنْصَرَحَ ـ إِجْتَهَرَ ـ صَرَحَ ـ إِنْكَشَفَ; to be opened out, exposed, as to the sun, *etc.*, إِنْتَشَرَ ـ تَنَشَّرَ; to be opened, dug, حُفِرَ. To ask to be opened, إِسْتَفْتَحَ; to ask to be dug, إِسْتَحْفَرَ. It is time for the river, or rivulet, to be opened, dug, cleared, إِسْتَحْفَرَ ٱلنَّهْرُ.

Open, *v.i.* As of a flower, تَفَتَّحَ ـ تَفَغَّمَ ـ فَغَمَ ٢ ـ فَغَرَ. To begin, شَرَعَ فِى ـ إِبْتَدَأَ فِى ـ إِبْتَدَأَ. To —, of speaking, تَفَتَّحَ فِى ٱلْكَلَامِ. To — out, expand, إِتَّسَعَ ـ تَمَدَّدَ ـ إِمْتَدَّ. To split, تَفَزَّرَ ـ إِنْشَقَّ. To — out one's heart, disclose one's secrets to, أَطْلَعَ عَلَى سِرِّهِ ـ كَشَفَ لِ سِرَّهُ. To — out to the view, ظَهَرَ ـ تَظَاهَرَ. To — at par, of stock, إِنْفَتَحَ مَزَادُ ٱلْأَسْهَامِ بِٱلْقِيمَةِ ٱلْأَصْلِيَّةِ. To —, fly —, as of a door, إِنْفَجَى. The doors — towards the mosque, ٱلْأَبْوَابُ شَارِعَةٌ إِلَى ٱلْمَسْجِدِ.

Open, *a.* Not shut, فَتْح ـ مَفْتُوح. Not barred, مَفْكُوك. Not tied, مَحْلُول ـ مَفْكُوك. Not sealed, مَفْضُوض ـ مَفْكُوك. Not closed up, uncorked, غَيْرُ مَخْتُوم ـ مَفْتُوح ـ مُسَلَّك. Open, dug, مَحْفُور ـ مَفْتُوح ـ مَفْتُوح ـ مَسْدُود. Manifest, بَارِح ـ ظَاهِر ـ مُبَيَّن ـ بَيِّن ـ بَائِن. Open or exposed to, مُعَارِضٌ لِ. Not stopped or corked, لَيْسَ عَلَيْهِ سِدَادٌ ـ مَفْتُوح; an — vessel, أَنَاءٌ مَفْتُوحٌ. Not defended, غَيْرُ مُسْتَحْكَمٍ (or مُحَصَّنٍ). Plain, level, سَطْح ـ سَهْل ـ بَسِيط ـ مُنْبَسِط. Airy, ذُو نَفَسٍ. Frank, جَلِىّ ـ مُخْلِص ـ سَلِيم ـ صَافٍ ـ صَفِىّ. Patent, apparent, عَيَان ـ مُتَوَضِّح ـ مُتَّضِح ـ صَرِيح ـ عَلَانِىّ. Made plain, مُتَّضِح. Wide —, مَفْتُوح ـ خَالِص. Open to discussion, فِيهِ مُنَازَعَةٌ ـ غَيْرُ مُثْبَتٍ. Open war, حَرْبٌ مَشْهُورَةٌ ـ ٱلْحَرْبُ ٱلْعَوَانُ. Of an — countenance, طَلِيقُ ٱلْوَجْهِ; of an — temper, مَشْرُوحُ ٱلصَّدْرِ. In the — air, عَلَى وَجْهِ ٱلْهَوَاءِ ـ فِى ٱلْفَضَاءِ. An — place, فَتَق ـ شَارِع ـ بَرَاح ـ فَضَاءٌ; an — valley, بُقْعَة. An — rebuke, تَوْبِيخٌ ظَاهِرٌ. To be —, exposed, to, تَعَرَّضَ لِ (*see also under to* Expose, *v.t.*). To be — to, unreserved with, صَارَحَ ـ إِنْبَسَطَ إِلَى. To be — to, as to an offer, إِسْتَعَدَّ لِلْمَعْرُوضِ ـ تَوَجَّزَ ٱلْعُرُوضَ. To lay one's self — to, إِسْتَهْدَفَ لِ. To put to — shame, شَهَرَ ـ إِشْتَهَرَ.

Opener, *n.* One who opens, فَتَّاح; one who begins, is first, أَوَّل. An interpreter, commentator, مُعَبِّر ـ مُفَسِّر. The Opener *or* Conqueror, one of the names of God, ٱلْفَتَّاحُ.

Open-handed, *a.* سَخِىّ ـ طَلْقُ ٱلْيَدَيْنِ ـ وِهْدَاءٌ. *See also* Liberal, *a.*

Open-hearted, *a.* مَشْرُوحُ ٱلصَّدْرِ ـ لَهْمُوم. *See also* Frank, *a.*

Opening, *n.* An aperture, نَقْب ـ شَقّ ـ فَتْحَة; an — for light, سَهْوَة *pl.* سِهَاءٌ; a mural —, كُوَّة ـ طَاقَة *pl.* طَاقَات. A breach, نُقْبَة ـ فُرْجَة ـ ثُغْرَة ـ ثَغْر. A chink, خَلَّة *coll.* خَلّ. A beginning, فَوَاتِح *pl.* فَاتِحَة ـ بَدْو. An — in a garment, as for the neck, arms, *etc.*, جُيُوب *pl.* جَيْب. An — in the clouds, بُرْصَة. An exordium, مَطْلَع. An interstice, فَجْوَة *pl.* فُجَج. A way, بَاب ـ طَرِيق ـ سَبِيل. A means, وَسِيلَة ـ وَاسِطَة. The — or first exhibition of anything, إِفْتِتَاح. An opportunity, فُرْصَة. An — or chance of success, مَحَلٌّ لِ ـ مَطْمَع ـ بَاب. He has the — of it every morning, عَلَيْهِ فَاتِحَةُ كُلِّ صَبَاحٍ. The — of the exhibition, إِفْتِتَاحُ ٱلْمَعْرِضِ. *See also* Breach, *n.*

Opening, *a.* First, أَوَّل *fem.* أُولَى. That opens, يَنْفَتِحُ. Opening upon, overlooking, شارِعٌ فِي *or* عَلَى.

Openly, *ad.* بَرَاحًا ـ صَرَاحَةً ـ صَرْحَةً ـ ضَاحِيَةً ـ صَرْحَةً بَرْحَةً ـ بِٱلْمَكْشُوفِ ـ جَهْرًا ـ عَلَانِيَةً ـ جَهْرَةً ـ جِهَارًا ـ عِيَانًا. To act —, كَاشَفَ ـ صَارَحَ ـ جَاهَرَ ـ صَافَى. To act — with, جَاهَرَ ـ أَعْلَنَ. I acted — with him in the matter, جَاهَرْتُهُ (*or* عَالَنْتُهُ) بِٱلْأَمْرِ. He walked — among them, مَشَى بَيْنَهُمْ عَلَانِيَةً. No one spoke — about him, لَمْ يَكُنْ أَحَدٌ يَتَكَلَّمُ عَنْهُ جِهَارًا. He spake the words —, قَالَ ٱلْقَوْلَ عَلَانِيَةً [2]. Not — but in secret, لَا ظَاهِرًا بَلْ فِي ٱلْخَفَاءِ. He told us, or he did the thing to us, —, جَاءَنَا بِٱلْأَمْرِ بَرَاحًا.

Open-work, *n.* Of wood and such like, شُغْلٌ مَنْقُورٌ. *See also* Embroidery, *and* Tracery, *n.*

Openness, *n.* As of a situation, بَحْبُوحَة ـ فُضُوٌّ ـ فَضَاءٌ ـ نَفَس. Frankness, مُجَاهَرَة ـ مُعَالَنَة ـ صَرَاحَة ـ مُصَافَاة ـ صِدْق. Publicity, مُعَالَنَة. Unconstrainedness, إِنْشِرَاح ـ طَلْق.

Opera, *n.* تَأْلِيفُ غِنَاءٍ لِلتِّيَاتْرُو. *See also* Opera-house.

Opera-glass, *n.* نَظَّارَةٌ لِلتِّيَاتْرُو ـ نَظَّارَةٌ صَغِيرَةٌ.

Opera-house, *n.* أُوبَرَا ـ تِيَاتْرُو ٱلْغِنَاءِ وَٱلْمَعَازِفِ.

Operant, *n.* *See* Operator.

Operate, *v.i.* To exert power, إِشْتَغَلَ. To perform a surgical operation, إِجْتَرَحَ جِرَاحَةً. To take effect, أَنْفَذَ ـ نَفَذَ. To operate or take effect upon, أَثَّرَ فِي ـ عَمِلَ فِي ـ فَعَلَ فِي. To be operated upon, to receive an impression, تَأَثَّرَ. To be operated upon, as by a surgeon, عُمِلَتْ فِيهِ صِنَاعَةُ ٱلْجِرَاحَةِ. To — in the stocks, تَعَاطَى شُغْلَ ٱلْبُورْسِ. To —, as of troops, تَحَرَّكَ ـ تَبَرَّزَ.

Operate, *v.t.* To do, effect, أَحْدَثَ ـ فَعَلَ ـ جَاءَ بِ ـ صَنَعَ.

Operatic, *a.* } مُخْتَصٌّ بِٱلْأُوبَرَا ـ مُتَعَلِّقٌ بِٱلتِّيَاتْرُو.
Operatical, }

Operation, *n.* An action, فِعْل *pl.* أَفْعَال ـ عَمَل *pl.* أَعْمَال. An effect, تَأْثِير ـ مَجُوع. Calculation, حِسَاب. An —, as of an army, حَرَكَة *pl.* حَرَكَات ـ تَبَرُّز. A surgical —, عَمَلٌ مِنْ صِنَاعَةِ ٱلْجِرَاحِيِّ. A mercantile —, مِنْ مُبَاشَرَاتِ ٱلتِّجَارَةِ. To carry into —, أَجْرَى ـ فِعْلًا. They determined to carry the law into —, عَزَمُوا عَلَى إِجْرَاءِ ٱلْقَانُونِ فِعْلًا. *See also* Action, *n.*

Operative, *a.* Belonging to action, عَمَلِيٌّ. Acting, producing an effect, مُؤَثِّر ـ عَمَّال ـ عَامِل ـ نَفِيذ ـ نَفَّاذ ـ نَافِذ. The — classes, أَهْلُ ٱلصَّنَائِعِ ـ ٱلصُّنَّاعُ.

Operative, *n.* صَانِع *pl.* صُنَّاع ـ فَاعِل *pl.* فَعَلَة ـ صَنَائِعِيٌّ.

Operator, *n.* عَامِل *pl.* عُمَّال. A surgical —, جَرَائِحِيٌّ.

Operculum, *n.* غِطَاء *pl.* أَغْطِيَة ـ طَبَق *pl.* أَطْبَاق.

Operose, *a.* *See* Laborious, Troublesome, *a.*

Ophicleide, *n.* ضَرْبٌ مِنَ ٱلْبُوقِ كَبِيرٌ.

Ophidian, *a.* مَا نِيطَ بِٱلْحَيَّاتِ.

Ophiological, *a.* مُتَعَلِّقٌ بِٱلْبَحْثِ عَنْ طَبَائِعِ ٱلْحَيَّاتِ.

Ophiologist, *n.* عَالِمٌ بِطَبَائِعِ ٱلْحَيَّاتِ ـ مِنْ أَهْلِ ٱلْبَحْثِ عَنْ طَبَائِعِ ٱلْحَيَّاتِ.

Ophiology, *n.* عِلْمُ ٱلْبَحْثِ عَنْ طَبَائِعِ ٱلْحَيَّاتِ.

Ophiomancy, *n.* ٱلتَّطَيُّرُ (*or* ٱلتَّفَوُّلُ) مِنَ ٱلْحَيَّاتِ.

Ophthalmic, *a.* مُتَعَلِّقٌ بِٱلْعُيُونِ. Ophthalmic treatment, طِبُّ (*or* مُعَالَجَةُ) ٱلْعُيُونِ.

Ophthalmotology, *n.* أُصُولُ مُعَالَجَةِ ٱلْعُيُونِ.

Ophthalmy, *n.* رَمَدَة ـ رَمَد ـ سَاهِك ـ أُخُذ. He has —, (in one eye,) رَمِدَتْ عَيْنُهُ ـ بِعَيْنِهِ سَاهِكٌ. To have —, رَمِدَ ـ هَاجَتْ عَيْنُهُ ـ إِرْمَدَّ ـ أَرْمَدَ.

Opiate, *n.* A medicine containing opium, مَعْجُونُ ٱلْأَفْيُونِ *pl.* مَعَاجِين. Something quieting, شَيْءٌ مُسَكِّنٌ ـ سُلْوَان.

Opine, *v.i.* تَوَهَّمَ ـ ظَنَّ [2]. *See also* To have an opinion, *under* Opinion, *n.*

Opiniative, *a.* Stiff in his opinions, مُؤْتَمِرٌ رَأْيِهِ ـ مُعْجَبٌ بِرَأْيِهِ ـ فِيهِ مُنَازَعَةٌ ـ رَائِيٌّ; of a man or woman, فُوَيْت. Not proved, غَيْرُ مُحَقَّقٍ. To be —, opiniated, تَعَجَّبَ فِي رَأْيِهِ ـ عَانَدَ ـ مُعَانِد.

Opinion, *n.* Judgment formed by the mind, idea, conjecture, وَهْم *pl.* أَوْهَام ـ تَخْمِين ـ قِيَاس ـ حَدْس ـ خَمْن ـ خَرْص ـ رَأْي *pl.* آرَاء ـ ذِهْن ـ ظَنّ *pl.* ظُنُون ـ زَعْمَة ـ تَصَوُّر. A belief, creed, إِعْتِقَاد *pl.* إِعْتِقَادَات ـ مَذْهَب *pl.* مَذَاهِب. A statement, قَوْل ـ مَقَالَة ـ إِفَادَة. A legal —, فَتْوَى. A correct —, رَأْيٌ صَوَابٌ. An — different from one previously held, بَدَاءٌ. Public —, ٱلْأَذْعَانُ ٱلْعُمُومِيُّ ـ ٱلْآرَاءُ ٱلْعُمُومِيَّةُ ـ أَفْكَارُ ٱلْعَامَّةِ ـ رَأْيُ ٱلشَّعْبِ. One who follows the prevailing opinion without troubling himself to find out what is best, رَهْمَانُ ـ رَهُوم. The — of the majority, رَأْيُ ٱلْأَكْثَرِ; of the minority, رَأْيُ ٱلْأَقَلِّ. In accordance with public —, مُلَاحِقُ (*or* مُوَافِقُ) ٱلْآرَاءِ ٱلْعُمُومِيَّةِ. The predominant —, ٱلْآرَاءُ ٱلْغَالِبَةُ. A private —, رَأْيٌ ذَاتِيٌّ ـ ظَنٌّ مَخْصُوصٌ. A decided —, ظَنٌّ مُقَرَّرٌ ـ رَأْيٌ مُثَبَّتٌ. A man of manifold opinions, ذُو بَدَوَاتٍ. According to my —, حَسَبَ رَأْيِي ـ عَلَى ظَنِّي. I formed a bad — of him, أَسَأْتُ بِهِ ظَنًّا; I formed a good — of him, أَحْسَنْتُ بِهِ ظَنًّا. We are of — that a congress must be convened, إِرْتَأَيْنَا أَنَّهُ لَا بُدَّ مِنْ تَشْكِيلِ لَجْنَةٍ. This, in my —, is more excellent than this, هٰذَا عِنْدِى أَفْضَلُ مِنْ هٰذَا. This statement, in my —, is correct, هٰذَا ٱلْقَوْلُ عِنْدِى صَوَابٌ. It is the prevailing — that he will return, غُلِبَ عَلَى ٱلظَّنِّ أَنَّهُ سَيَعُودُ. I cannot give my — on this particular subject, لَا يُمْكِنُنِي أَنْ أُبْدِيَ رَأْيِي فِي هٰذَا ٱلصَّدَدِ.

To agree in opinion with one, وَافَقَ رَأْيَهُ.

To follow or embrace the opinion of one, تَبِعَ رَأْيَهُ ـ أَرْيَهُ.

To follow one's own opinion, to act independently, إِسْتَبَدَّ بِرَأْيِهِ.

To form or have an opinion, to think, judge, خَرَصَ ـ حَدَسَ ـ رَأَى aor. يَرَى ـ ظَنَّ ـ تَوَهَّمَ ـ زَعَمَ ـ تَخَيَّلَ ـ خَمَّنَ ـ إِرْتَآءَ. To form an opinion of, ظَنَّ فِي ـ خَرَصَ فِي ـ إِرْتَآءَ فِي ـ خَمَّنَ. To submit something to one for his opinion, إِسْتَفْتَى.

To put forth one's opinion, بَيَّنَ (or أَعْلَنَ) بِرَأْيِهِ.

To yield to the opinion of one, أَذْعَنَ (or سَلَّمَ) لِرَأْيِهِ.

Opinionated, *a.* *See* Opiniative. To be —, تَعَجَّبَ فِي رَأْيِهِ ـ تَعَانَدَ ـ عَانَدَ ـ عَنَدَ فِي رَأْيِهِ.

Opinionatively, *ad.* بِعِنَادٍ ـ بِعُجْبِ ٱلرَّأْيِ ـ بِعُجْبٍ.

Opinionativeness, *n.* مُعَانَدَةٌ ـ عِنَادٌ ـ عُجْبُ ٱلرَّأْيِ ـ عُجْبٌ.

Opinioned, *a.* / Opinionist, *n.* } *See* Opiniative, *a.*

Opium, *n.* أَفْيُونٌ. An — eater, أَفْيُونِيٌّ.

Opodeldoc, *n.* مَرْهَمٌ مُرَكَّبٌ مِنْ كَافُورٍ وَصَابُونٍ.

Opossum, *n.* نَوْعٌ مِنَ ٱلْحَيَوَانَاتِ يُوجَدُ فِي أَمِيرِكَا.

Oppidan, *n.* An inhabitant of a town, مِنْ ـ مِنْ أَهْلِ ٱلْحَضَرِ أَهْلِ مَدِينَةٍ.

Opponent, *n.* / Opponent, *a.* } خَصْمٌ *pl.* خُصُومٌ ـ مُخَاصِمٌ ـ مُعَارِضٌ ـ مُقَاوِمٌ ـ خَصِيمٌ *pl.* خُصَمَآءُ ـ مُعَانِدٌ. *See also* Adverse, *a.*, Adversary, *n.*

Opportune, *a.* فِي مَحَلِّهِ ـ فِي وَقْتِهِ ـ مُوَافِقٌ. Should the time be —, إِذَا طَاوَعَ ٱلْوَقْتُ.

Opportunely, *ad.* مُوَافَقَةً ـ بِوَقْتِهِ ـ لِلْوَقْتِ.

Opportuneness, *n.* مُنَاسَبَةٌ ـ وَفْقٌ ـ مُوَافَقَةٌ.

Opportunity, *n.* فُرْصَةٌ *pl.* فُرَصٌ ـ نُهْزَةٌ. To lose an —, فَاتَ (or أَفْلَتَ) ٱلْفُرْصَةَ ـ فَرَّطَ فِي ٱلْفُرْصَةِ ـ ضَيَّعَ ٱلْفُرْصَةَ. To watch for an —, تَرَبَّصَ ٱلْفُرْصَةَ. To seize an —, إِفْتَرَصَ ٱلْفُرْصَةَ ـ إِغْتَنَمَ (or إِنْتَهَزَ) ٱلْفُرْصَةَ. As soon as they saw the —, أَوَّلَ مَا تَسَنَّحَ لَهُمُ ٱلْفُرْصَةُ. How many opportunities they had! مَا أَكْثَرَهُمْ مِنَ ٱلْفُرَصِ. After the — had passed away, بَعْدَ فَوَاتِ ٱلْفُرْصَةِ. When the — offered, عِنْدَ سُنُوحِ ٱلْفُرْصَةِ. *See also* Occasion, *n.*

Oppose, *v.t.* To act against, عَارَضَ ـ قَاوَمَ ـ ضَادَّ ـ ضَارَّ ـ آرَى ـ إِمْتَنَعَ ـ إِعْتَرَضَ عَلَى ـ دَافَعَ. To resist, إِعْتَرَضَ عَلَى. To hinder, حَجَزَ ـ حَجَبَ ـ عَكَسَ ـ عَنْ ـ صَدَّدَ ـ أَصَدَّ ـ مَنَعَ. To oppose, in litigation, نَاقَدَ ـ نَازَعَ ـ شَاجَرَ. To put anything opposite to another, أَقْبَلَ ـ عَلَى. To —, as differing from, خَالَفَ. To stop, stop up, سَدَّدَ ـ سَدَّ. They opposed one another, of many, تَخَالَفُوا ـ تَعَانَدُوا ـ تَعَارَضُوا. They are determined to oppose, resist, أَصَرُّوا عَلَى ٱلدِّفَاعِ.

Oppose, *v.i.* To hinder, thwart, إِعْتَرَضَ ـ ضَادَّ ـ حَجَزَ. The thing opposed, presented, an obstacle, إِعْتَرَضَ ٱلشَّيْءُ. To be opposed in, prevented from, إِعْتَرَضَ عَنْ.

Opposer, *n.* One who acts in opposition, مُضَادٌّ ـ مُضَارٌّ ـ مُعَازٌ ـ مُقَاوِمٌ. One who resists, مُعْتَرِضٌ عَلَى ـ مُدَافِعٌ. A hinderer, مُمَانِعٌ ـ مُصِدٌّ ـ عِرِّيضٌ. An —, in litigation, مُنَازِعٌ ـ مُشَاجِرٌ مُنَاقِدٌ. *See also* Opponent, *n.*

Opposing, *a.* Acting against, مُقَاوِمٌ ـ مُعْرِضٌ. (*See also* Opponent, *n.*) Opposing forces, قُوَّاتٌ مُتَدَافِعَةٌ ـ قُوَّاتٌ مُدَافِعَةٌ.

Opposite, *a.* Contrary in position, حِذَآءَ ـ مَا يُحَاذِي ـ صَدَدَ ـ مُقَابِلٌ لِ ـ مُتَقَابِلٌ ـ حِيَالَ ـ نَظِيرٌ ـ بِلِقَاءِ ـ مُجَابَآءَ. Adverse, repugnant, خِلَافٌ ـ ضِدِّيدٌ ـ ضِدٌّ *pl.* أَضْدَادٌ ـ حِيَالَ ـ مُعْتَرِضٌ ـ مُقَاوِمٌ. His house is — to mine, دَارُهُ بِلِقَاءِ دَارِي ـ مَنْزِلُهُ مُقَابِلُ مَنْزِلِي. He went on the — side of the road to him, عَارَضَهُ فِي ٱلسَّيْرِ. They look or face — to one another, of many, يَتَنَاظَرُوا. To be — to, lay over against, a place, عَارَضَ ـ حَاذَى ـ آزَى ـ قَابَلَ. To be — to, in meaning, *etc.*, خَالَفَ ـ قَابَلَ. *See also* Contradictory, *a.*

Opposite, *n.* That which is contrary, ضِدٌّ *pl.* أَضْدَادٌ ـ خِلَافٌ ـ ضِدِّيدَةٌ ـ حِيَالٌ ـ إِخْتِلَافٌ. The — to your sayings, حِيَالُ كَلِمَتِكَ. To say the — of what one means, عَكَّسَ.

Oppositely, *ad.* Adversely, مُخَالَفَةً ـ إِعْتِرَاضًا ـ مُضَادَّةً. In front of, before, فِي مُقَابَلَةٍ ـ قِبَالَ.

Oppositeness, *n.* The being before, in face of, مُحَاذَاةٌ ـ مُوَازَاةٌ ـ مُوَاجَهَةٌ ـ مُقَابَلَةٌ ـ لِقَاءٌ.

Opposition, *n.* The act of opposing, acting against, مُضَارَّةٌ ـ إِعْتِرَاضٌ ـ مُعَارَضَةٌ ـ مُقَاوَمَةٌ ـ مُعَانَدَةٌ ـ عِنَادٌ ـ مُضَادَّةٌ. Contrariety, مُخَالَفَةٌ ـ مُعَارَضَةٌ ـ مُضَادَّةٌ ـ مُعَاكَسَةٌ. Opposition in litigation, مُشَاجَرَةٌ ـ مُجَادَلَةٌ ـ مُنَازَعَةٌ ـ مُخَاصَمَةٌ. Contrariety, as of meaning, مُخَالَفَةٌ ـ مُقَابَلَةٌ. Opposition, in astronomy, إِسْتِقْبَالٌ ـ مُقَابَلَةٌ. The collective body of opposers, the — party, أَصْحَابُ ٱلْمُخَالَفَةِ ـ ٱلْمُخَالِفُونَ ـ ٱلضِّدُّ ـ حِزْبُ ٱلْمُخَالِفِينَ: A member of the —, عُضْوٌ مِنْ أَعْضَآءِ ـ مِنْ أَصْحَابِ ٱلْمُخَالِفِينَ

ٱلْمُخَالِفِينَ. He offered him —, تَعَرَّضَ لَهُ. In — to him, إِضْدَادًا لَهُ ـ تَعَرُّضًا لَهُ. There was a great meeting of the —, اِلْتَأَمَتْ جَمْعِيَّةٌ كَبِيرَةٌ مِنَ ٱلْمُخَالِفِينَ لِرَأْيِ ٱلدَّوْلَةِ. *See also* Oppositiveness, *n.*

Oppositionist, *n.* مِنْ حِزْبِ ٱلْمُخَالِفِينَ ـ مُعْتَرِضٌ ـ مُعَانِدٌ.

Oppress, *v.t.* To treat with harshness, tyrannize over, ضَايَقَ ـ أَشَرَّ إِلَى ـ قَاهَرَ ـ ٢ بَغَى عَلَى ـ تَعَدَّى عَلَى ـ ٢ ظَلَمَ. To persecute, اِضْطَهَدَ. To defraud, ٢ غَبَنَ. To put to a hard task without payment, سَخَّرَ. To — in mind, ضَايَقَ ـ أَضْجَرَ. They oppressed one another, of many, تَبَاغَوْا.

Oppression, *n.* The act of oppressing, tyrannizing, ظُلْمٌ ـ بَغَاءٌ ـ قَهْرٌ ـ جَوْرٌ ـ مُضَايَقَةٌ. The state of being tyrannized over, ضَجَرٌ ـ حَصْرٌ ـ ضِيقٌ ـ مَشَقَّةٌ ـ ضِيقَةٌ. Oppression of spirits, ضِيقَةٌ ـ ضِيقٌ ـ ضَجْرَةٌ. To charge with —, ظَلَّمَ ـ جَوَّرَ. To complain of the — of one, تَظَلَّمَ مِنْ. *See also* Severity, Harshness, Depression, *n.*

Oppressive, *a.* Tyrannical, unjust, بَاغٍ ـ ظَلَّامٌ ـ ظَالِمٌ ـ جَائِرٌ ـ مُضَايِقٌ ـ شَاقٌّ. Heavy, ثَقِيلٌ. Depressing, مُكْرِبٌ ـ مُضْجِرٌ.

Oppressively, *ad.* With tyranny, بِظُلْمٍ ـ بِٱعْتِسَافٍ ـ بِجَوْرٍ ـ بِقَهْرٍ. Heavily, بِضِيقَةٍ ـ بِثِقْلٍ.

Oppressiveness, *n.* *See* Oppression.

Oppressor, *n.* بَاغٍ *pl.* بُغَاةٌ ـ قَهَّارٌ ـ ظَالِمٌ ـ ظَلَّامٌ ـ مِنْ أَهْلِ ٱلظُّلْمِ ـ شِرِّيرٌ ـ مُضَايِقٌ.

Opprobrious, *a.* خَبِيثٌ ـ قَبِيحٌ ـ فَضِيحٌ ـ فَضُوحٌ ـ خَزٍ. *See also* Disgraceful, Infamous, *a.*

Opprobriously, *ad.* ذِلَّةً ـ بِٱلْعَارِ ـ قَبْحًا ـ قَبَاحَةً.

Opprobriousness, *n.* }
Opprobrium, } عَارٌ ـ فَضَاحَةٌ ـ قَبَاحَةٌ ـ خُبْثٌ ـ خَبَاثَةٌ ـ ذِلَّةٌ ـ عَيْبٌ ـ عَوْرَةٌ. *See also* Disgrace, *n.*

Oppugn, *v.t.* To resist, oppose, اِعْتَرَضَ عَلَى ـ عَانَدَ ـ دَافَعَ ـ قَاوَمَ. *See also to* Oppose, *v.t.*

Oppugnancy, *n.* مُخَالَفَةٌ ـ اِعْتِرَاضٌ ـ مُقَاوَمَةٌ ـ مُعَانَدَةٌ ـ مُدَافَعَةٌ. *See also* Opposition, *n.*

Oppugnant, *a.* }
Oppugner, *n.* } مُعَانِدٌ ـ مُخَالِفٌ ـ مُدَافِعٌ ـ مُقَاوِمٌ. *See also* Opponent, Opposer, *n.*

Optative, *a.* Expressive of desire, مُتَمَنٍّ. The — mood, صِيغَةُ ٱلتَّمَنِّي.

Optic, *a.* }
Optical, } Pertaining to vision, بَصَرِيٌّ ـ نَظَرِيٌّ. Relating to optics, مَا نِيطَ بِعِلْمِ ٱلنُّورِ وَٱلْبَصَرِ. Optical instruments, آلَاتٌ نَظَرِيَّةٌ. An — delusion, مَنْظَرٌ وَهْمِيٌّ ـ اِنْخِدَاعُ ٱلْبَصَرِ. The — nerve, organ of sight, ٱلْجَارِحَةُ.

Optician, *n.* One skilled in optics, أُسْتَاذٌ فِي مَعْرِفَةِ ٱلنُّورِ وَٱلْبَصَرِ. A maker of optical instruments, صَانِعُ آلَاتِ ٱلْبَصَرِ.

Optics, *n.* عِلْمُ ٱلنُّورِ وَٱلْبَصَرِ ـ مَعْرِفَةٌ بِٱلنُّورِ وَٱلْبَصَرِ.

Optimacy, *n.* }
Optimates, } The —, ٱلْأَشْرَافُ ـ ٱلْأَعْيَانُ.

Optime, *n.* عِبَارَةٌ عَنِ ٱلتِّلْمِيذِ ٱلَّذِي يَفُوزُ بِٱلدَّرَجَةِ ٱلثَّانِيَةِ مِنَ ٱلشَّرَفِ فِي مَدْرَسَةِ كَمْبْرِيج.

Optimism, *n.* The doctrine of —, رَأْيُ ٱلْمُسْتَصْوِبِينَ كُلَّ شَيْءٍ ـ اِسْتِحْسَانٌ كُلِّيٌّ (or مُطْلَقٌ) ـ صَالِحًا كَانَ أَوْ طَالِحًا.

Optimist, *n.* مُسْتَحْسِنُ كُلِّ شَيْءٍ ـ مِنْ أَهْلِ ٱلرَّأْيِ ٱلْمَذْكُورِ ـ حَمَّادٌ. *See also preceding article.*

Option, *n.* اِخْتِيَارٌ ـ خِيرَةٌ ـ خِيَارٌ ـ وُدٌّ. It was by my —, كَانَ بِوُدِّي. You have the —, أَنْتَ بِٱلْخِيَارِ.

Optional, *a.* اِخْتِيَارِيٌّ.

Optionally, *ad.* بِٱلِاخْتِيَارِ ـ اِخْتِيَارًا.

Opulence, *n.* حَظٌّ ـ مَالٌ ـ غِنًى ـ جَاهٌ ـ ثَرْوَةٌ.

Opulent, *a.* وَسِيعُ ٱلْمَالِ ـ حَظِيظٌ ـ وَجِيهٌ ـ غَنِيٌّ ـ غَانٍ.

Opulently, *ad.* بِثَرْوَةٍ ـ بِجَاهٍ.

Opuscule, *n.* رِسَالَةٌ *pl.* رَسَائِلُ ـ كُرَّاسَةٌ.

Or, *n.* In heraldry, عِبَارَةٌ عَنِ ٱلْأَجْزَاءِ ٱلْمُمَوَّهَةِ بِٱلذَّهَبِ فِي ٱلْأَرْمَا.

Or, *conj.* أَوْ ـ أَمْ ـ وَإِلَّا ـ أَمَّا. Either this or that, هٰذَا أَوْ ذَاكَ. Do this or I will beat you, اِفْعَلْ هٰذَا وَإِلَّا فَأَضْرِبُكَ. *See also* Either, *conj.*

Oracle, *n.* The place of a pagan deity, مِحْرَابُ ٱلصَّنَمِ. The pretended declaration of a pagan deity, كَلَامُ كِهَانَةِ ٱلصَّنَمِ. The oracles of God, كَلَامُ ٱللّٰهِ. An opinion deemed infallible, رَأْيٌ مُعْتَبَرٌ بِٱعْتِبَارٍ كُلِّيٍّ ـ رَأْيٌ يُعَوَّلُ عَلَيْهِ ـ بِمَنْزِلَةِ ٱلْعِصْمَةِ. A wise man, عَلَّامٌ.

Oracle, *v.i.* To utter oracles, (of pagan worship), كَهَنَ ـ ٤. To utter wise sayings, تَكَلَّمَ بِكَلَامِ ٱلْحُكَمَاءِ.

Oracular, *a.* }
Oraculous, } Uttering oracles, كَاهِنٌ *pl.* كَهَنَةٌ ـ مُتَكَهِّنٌ. Authoritative, قَاطِعٌ ـ شَافٍ ـ فَاصِلٌ. Ambiguous, مُشْتَبِهٌ ـ مُلْتَبِسٌ.

Oracularly, *ad.* }
Oraculously, } بِكِهَانَةٍ ـ تَكَهُّنًا. Authoritatively, فَصْلًا ـ بَتَّةً. Ambiguously, بِٱلْتِبَاسٍ ـ تَعْمِيَةً ـ إِبْهَامًا.

Oraculousness, *n.* The state of being oraculous, صِفَةُ ٱلتَّكَهُّنِ (or ٱلْكِهَانَةِ); of being authoritative, فَصْلٌ ـ حُكْمٌ ـ شِفَاءٌ ـ بَتٌّ.

Oraison, *n.* *See* Orison, *n.*

Oral, *a.* مِنَ ٱلْفَمِ ـ فَمِيٌّ ـ شَفَاهِيٌّ.

Orally, *ad.* مِنَ ٱلْفَمِ ـ بِٱلْمُشَافَهَةِ ـ شَفَاهًا.

Orange, *n.* بُرْدُقَان *coll.* بُرْدُقَانَة ـ بُرْتُقَان *coll.* بُرْتُقَانَة ـ نَارَنْج.

Orangeade, *n.* شَرَابٌ مِنْ عَصِيرِ ٱلْبُرْدُقَانِ.

Orangeat, *n.* مُرَبَّى ٱلْبُرْدُقَانِ.

Orangery, *n.* مَغْرِس *pl.* مَغَارِس (*or*) مَحَلُّ ٱلْبُرْدُقَانِ.

Orang-outang, *n.* نَوْعٌ مِنَ ٱلْقُرُودِ أَشْبَهُ شَيْءٍ بِٱلْإِنْسَانِ.

Oration, *n.* مَقَالَة ـ خُطْبَة ـ كَلَام. To make an —, أَلْقَى مَقَالَةً. To make an — to, خَطَبَ [2]. He began to make an — to them, جَعَلَ يُخَاطِبُهُمْ.

Orator, *n.* مُتَكَلِّم ـ خَطِيب ـ حَاذِقٌ بِٱلْكَلَامِ ـ كَلَامَانِيٌّ.

Oratorial, *a.* | Oratorical, } بَلِيغ ـ مِصْقَع ـ مِنْطِيق ـ فَصِيح ـ خُطَبِيٌّ. Of great — power, طَلْقٌ ذَلْقٌ.

Oratorically, *ad.* | Oratorially, } بِبَلَاغَةٍ ـ بِبَيَانٍ ـ بِفَصَاحَةٍ.

Oratorio, *n.* A religious composition set to music, أُنْشُودَةٌ دِينِيَّةٌ مَنْظُومَةٌ عَلَى عَزْفِ ٱلْمَعَازِفِ وَٱلْغِنَاءِ. *See also* Oratory, *n.*

Oratory, *n.* مَسْجِد *pl.* مَسَاجِد ـ مُصَلًّى ـ مِحْرَاب.

Oratory, *n.* بَلَاغَة ـ فَصَاحَة ـ بَيَان. Natural —, كَلَامٌ سَلِيقِيٌّ.

Orb, *n.* The celestial orbs, الفَلَكُ. The sun's —, disc, فِنَاءُ (*or*) فَاثُورُ ٱلشَّمْسِ. *See also* Globe, *n.*

Orb, *v.t.* To form into a circle, صَيَّرَ مُدَوَّرًا ـ أَدَارَ ـ دَوَّرَ.

Orbate, *a.* *See* Bereaved, *a.*

Orbed, *a.* | Orbicular, } مُدَوَّر ـ مُسْتَدِير ـ مُدَحْرَج.

Orbicularly, *ad.* بِٱسْتِدَارَةٍ ـ اِسْتِدَارَةً.

Orbiculate, *a.* *See* Orbicular, *a.*

Orbit, *n.* A path round the centre, سَيْر ـ دَوْرَة ـ دَائِرَة ـ دَوْر. The — of the eye, حِجَاج *pl.* حَجَاجُ ٱلْعَيْنِ ـ وَقْبُ ٱلْعَيْنِ ـ بَيْتُ ٱلْعَيْنِ.

Orbital, *a.* Pertaining to the pathway of the planets, *etc.*, مُتَعَلِّقٌ بِدَوَرَانِ ٱلْكَوَاكِبِ; to the orbit of the eye, مَا يُنِيطُ بِحِجَاجِ (*or*) وَقْبِ ٱلْعَيْنِ.

Orchard, *n.* فِرْدَوْس *pl.* فَرَادِيس ـ جَنَّة ـ بُسْتَان *pl.* بَسَاتِين ـ حَدِيقَة *pl.* حَدَائِق.

Orchardist, *n.* بُسْتَانِيٌّ ـ غَيْطَانِيٌّ ـ جَنَانِيٌّ.

Orchestra, *n.* The place of the musicians, مَكَانُ ٱلْعَازِفِينَ. The body of musicians, النَّوْبَاتِيَّة ـ النَّوْبَة.

Orchestral, *a.* Connected with the place of the musicians, مَنُوطٌ بِمَقَامِ ٱلْعَازِفِينَ; connected with the body of musicians, مُتَعَلِّقٌ بِٱلنَّوْبَاتِيَّةِ.

Orchidaceous, *a.* | Orchideous, } مِنْ جِنْسِ نَبَاتِ ٱلسَّحْلَبِ.

Orchilla, *n.* Moss, أُشْنَة. *See also under* Wars, *n.*

Orchis, *n.* نَبَاتُ ٱلسَّحْلَبِ.

Orchitis, *n.* دَاءُ ٱلْخُصَى. Having —, خَصِي.

Ordain, *v.t.* To appoint, عَيَّنَ ـ عَمِلَ ـ أَقَامَ ـ جَعَلَ. To prescribe, as laws, أَفْرَضَ ـ فَرَضَ ـ آمَرَ فِي. To settle, determine, قَضَى ـ بَتَّ ـ حَكَمَ بِ ـ حَتَمَ. To decree, أَتَاحَ ـ كَتَبَ [2]. To direct, command, أَوْصَى بِ. To confer holy orders upon, رَسَمَ [2] ـ أَعْطَى دَرَجَةً مِنْ دَرَجَاتِ ٱلْإِكْلِيرُسِ. To be ordained, decreed, to, كُتِبَ لِ ـ يَتُوحُ *aor.* تَاحَ لِ ـ أُتِيحَ لِ. To be ordained, admitted to holy orders, اِرْتَسَمَ. He fell into a place of destruction and God ordained one to save him, وَقَعَ فِي مَهْلَكَةٍ فَأَتَاحَ ٱللّٰهُ لَهُ رَجُلًا مَنْ أَنْقَذَهُ.

Ordained, *a.* Appointed, مُعَيَّن ـ مُقَام. Prescribed, مَفْرُوض. Determined, مُنْقَضِيٌّ ـ مَحْتُوم. Decreed, مُتَاح. Admitted to holy orders, مُرْتَسِم. Ordained to eternal life, مُعَيَّنٌ لِلْحَيٰوةِ ٱلْأَبَدِيَّةِ.

Ordainer, *n.* One who decrees, مُتِيح ـ كَاتِب. One who prescribes, as laws, فَارِض ـ مُفْرِض. One who confers holy orders, رَاسِم.

Ordaining, *n.* | Ordainment, } The act of appointing, تَعْيِين ـ إِقَامَة ـ نَصْب. Investing with holy orders, رَسْم. Decreeing, حَتْم ـ تَقْرِير ـ حُكْم ـ قَضَاء.

Ordeal, *n.* Trial, examination, اِمْتِحَان ـ مِحْنَة *pl.* مِحَن. A severe affliction, بَلِيَّة ـ مُصِيبَة. To undergo an —, test, أَمْتُحِنَ; to undergo an —, affliction, أُبْتُلِيَ; *vulg.* اِبْتَلَى.

Order, *n.* Methodical arrangement, سِيَاقَة ـ نَسَق ـ سِلْك ـ سِمَاط ـ نَظْم ـ نِظَام ـ تَرْتِيب: they are in one —, هُمْ عَلَى سِيَاقَةٍ وَاحِدَةٍ (*or*) سِمَاطٍ وَاحِدٍ. Established mode, أُصُول ـ رَسْم ـ قَانُون. A mandate, أَمْر *pl.* أَوَامِر ـ مَنْشُور *pl.* مَنَاشِير ـ وَصِيَّة *pl.* وَصَايَا ـ حُكْم *pl.* أَحْكَام. Discipline, سِيَاسَة ـ ضَبْط ـ تَرْتِيب ـ قَاعِدَة ـ نَظْم. An honorary decoration, نِيشَانُ ٱفْتِخَارٍ ـ نِيشَان *pl.* نَوَاشِين. A note, memo., تَذْكِرَة *pl.* تَذَاكِر. A class, kind, طَبَقَة *pl.* طَبَقَات ـ صِنْف *pl.* أَصْنَاف. Dignity, position, قِيَام ـ مَقَام. A degree, rank, دَرَجَة *pl.* دَرَجَات ـ مَرْتَبَة ـ رُتْبَة *pl.* رُتَب. A class, division, قِسْم *pl.* أَقْسَام. An order, rite, طَقْس *pl.* طُقُوس. Holy orders, دَرَجَاتُ ٱلْإِكْلِيرُسِ ـ دَرَجَاتُ ٱلْكَهَنُوتِ. A method, way, طَرِيقَة ـ طَرْز. A rank, row, صَفّ *pl.* صُفُوف. A body, company, جَمَاعَة ـ طَائِفَة *pl.* طَوَائِف. A religious order, confraternity, جَمَاعَة ـ أَخَوِيَّة. An — of architecture, قَاعِدَةُ ٱلْبِنَاءِ

A concatenation, سِلْسِلَة *pl.* سَلَاسِل. A money —, cheque, وَرَقَة حَوَالَة *pl.* أَوْرَاق — تَحْوِيل. *pl.* قَوَاعِد — طِرَاز (*or* طَرْز) ٱلْبِنَاء. Orders of men, طَبَقَاتُ ٱلنَّاسِ. The higher orders, ٱلْخَوَاصّ — ٱلْأَغْنِيَاء — ٱلْأَكَابِر — ٱلرُّؤَسَاء; the lower orders, أَطْرَافُ ٱلنَّاسِ — ٱلْعَوَامّ — عَوَامُّ ٱلنَّاسِ — أَسَافِلُ ٱلنَّاسِ. Public —, ٱلْأَمْنُ ٱلْعُمُومِيّ — ٱلْعُمُومِيّ. Standing orders, أَوَامِرُ وَتَنْبِيهَاتٌ جَارِيَةٌ دَائِمًا. Order of the day, in military matters, أَمْرٌ لِلْيَوْم — تَنْبِيهُ ٱلنَّهَار — أَمْرٌ يَوْمِيّ; mode of proceeding for the day, ٱلسِّمَاطُ لِلنَّهَار — ٱلْمَوْضُوعُ لِلنَّهَار — مَوْضُوعُ ٱلْبَحْثِ لِلنَّهَار. In alphabetical —, مُرَتَّبٌ عَلَى تَرْتِيبِ حُرُوفِ ٱلْهِجَاء. In apple-pie —, فِي غَايَةِ — فِي أَصَحِّ ٱلتَّرْتِيب — ٱلنِّظَام (*or* ٱلْإِتْقَان). Out of —, damaged, مَعْيُوب — مُكَسَّر — سَاقِط; out of the regular course, خَارِجٌ عَنِ — خَارِجٌ عَنِ ٱلْقَانُونِ — خَارِجٌ عَنِ ٱلْأُصُولِ — ٱلْقَدِيمَة. Made to —, مُوَصًّى بِهِ. In — that ..., لِكَيْ — كَيْ — عَلَى أَنْ — بِقَصْدِ. Till further orders, إِلَى مَا شَاءَ ٱللهُ — إِلَى أَنْ يَصْدُرَ أَمْرٌ جَدِيد. Payable to —, يُدْفَعُ بِٱلتَّحْوِيلِ. He wore the — of the Majīdiyyah, كَانَ مُتَقَلِّدًا بِنِيشَانِ ٱلْمَجِيدِيَّة. The — of the Majīdiyyah was presented to ..., أُحْسِنَ بِٱلنِّشَانِ ٱلْمَجِيدِيِّ إِلَى فُلَانٍ. Order! order! أُسْكُتْ — بِسْكِتَة. We had ordered our affairs beforehand, قَدْ أَخَذْنَا أَمْرَنَا مِنْ قَبْلُ.

To arrange in orders, نَسَّقَ — صَفَّفَ-صُفُوفًا; to be arranged in orders, إِنْتَسَقَ — تَنَسَّقَ — إِصْطَفَّ صُفُوفًا.

To be at one's orders, كَانَ — كَانَ تَحْتَ يَدِهِ — كَانَ تَحْتَ أَمْرِهِ — فِي طَاعَتِهِ.

To call to order, silence, أَوْعَزَ إِلَى-بِٱلسُّكُوتِ.

To give an order, command, أَصْدَرَ أَمْرًا. To give an order, commission, as to a tradesman, وَصَّى-عَلَى أَنْ — وَصَّى-بِ.

To give one an order upon, حَوَّلَ-عَلَى.

To keep in order, in check, دَارَى: He ought certainly to keep his people in —, لَا بُدَّ لَهُ مِنْ مُدَارَاةِ قَوْمِهِ.

To make payable to the order of ..., جَعَلَ دَفْعَهُ بِٱلتَّحْوِيلِ إِلَى فُلَانٍ.

To put or set in order, سَاسَ *aor.* يَسُوسُ — ضَبَطَ — نَظَمَ — رَتَّبَ — مَهَّدَ — نَظَّمَ. To arrange, as the scattered leaves of a book, طَبَّقَ. To arrange, as an affair, دَبَّرَ. To mend, repair, عَالَجَ — سَوَّى.

To put out of order, لَخْبَطَ — خَبَّطَ — هَوَّشَ — شَوَّشَ — لَبَّكَ. *See also to* Damage, *v.t.*

To take an order for a thing from one, أَخَذَ وَصِيَّةً مِنْ-بِ.

To take holy orders, إِرْتَسَمَ بِدَرَجَاتِ ٱلْإِكْلِيرُسِ.

Order, *v.t.* To enjoin, charge, عَهِدَ إِلَى-بِ — عَهِدَ إِلَى-بِأَمْرٍ — أَوْعَزَ إِلَى — أَمَرَ بِ — أَمَرَ — أَشَارَ عَلَى-بِ. To give a commission for, وَصَّى بِ. To put in —, دَبَّرَ — رَتَّبَ — نَظَمَ — سَاسَ *aor.* يَسُوسُ. To arrange in —, نَسَّقَ; to arrange in orders, صَفَّفَ. To decree, ثَبَّتَ — حَتَمَ — قَضَى. He ordered, decided, that ..., قَضَى أَنْ. He ordered a signet ring to be made for himself, وَصَّى بِخَاتِمٍ لِنَفْسِهِ — أَضْرَبَ لِنَفْسِهِ خَاتِمًا. *See also to* Ordain, *v.t.*

Ordered, *a.* Arranged, نَسِيق — مُرَتَّب — مُنَظَّم — مَنْظُوم. Arranged in orders, مُصَفَّف.

Orderer, *n.* One who enjoins, مُشِير — آمِر — إِزَاء. One who puts in order, مُنَظِّم — مُدَبِّر — سَائِس — مُرَتِّب.

Ordering, *n.* The act of putting in order, نَظْم — ضَبْط — سِيَاسَة; of repairing, مُعَالَجَة — تَسْوِيَة.

Orderless, *a.* مُتَهَوِّش — مُلَتْبِك — غَيْرُ مُرَتَّب — بِلَا تَرْتِيب — مُتَشَوِّش.

Orderliness, *n.* Regularity, حُسْنُ — إِنْتِظَام — نِظَام — نَسَق — ضَبْط — تَرْتِيب. Good conduct, حُسْنُ ٱلسِّيرَة — حُسْنُ سُلُوك. Quietude, رَاحَة — هُدُوّ — سَكِينَة.

Orderly, *a.* Observant of method, أَهْلُ سِيَاسَةٍ — أَهْلُ ضَبْطٍ. Arranged in good order, مُنَسَّق — نَسِيق — مَضْبُوط — مُدَقَّق — مُنَظَّم — مَنْظُوم. Not unruly, مُرْتَاح — هَادٍ — سَاكِت. An — officer, ضَابِطُ ٱلنَّوْبَةِ ٱلْيَوْمِيّ. Orderly-book, دُسْتُور (*or* كِتَاب) ٱلتَّنْبِيهَاتِ.

Orderly, *n.* As of a private soldier, نَفَرٌ نَوْبَتْجِي; of a corporal, أُونْ بَاشِي نَوْبَتْجِي; of a serjeant, جَاوُش نَوْبَتْجِي.

Orderly, *ad.* According to rule, حَسَبَ ٱلْقَوَانِينِ; in good order, بِٱنْتِظَامٍ — بِضَبْطٍ — بِنِظَامٍ; without unruliness, بِسَكِينَةٍ — بِهُدُوّ.

Orders, *n.* *See under* Order, *n.*

Ordinal, *a.* Noting order, عِبَارَةٌ عَنِ ٱلنَّسَقِ. An — number, عَدَدٌ تَرْتِيبِيّ — إِسْمُ عَدَدٍ عَلَى وَزْنِ ٱلْفَاعِلِ.

Ordinal, *n.* A book of rites, كِتَابُ ٱلطُّقُوس; of the rites of ordination, كِتَابُ طُقُوسِ ٱلرِّسَامَةِ.

Ordinance, *n.* A rule, order, regulation, حُكْم *pl.* أَحْكَام — قَانُون *pl.* قَوَانِين — حُكُومَة *pl.* حُكُومَات — تَرْتِيب — قَاعِدَة *pl.* قَوَاعِد. A decree, حَتْم *pl.* حُتُوم — قَضَاء *pl.* أَقْضِيَة. A law, سُنَّة *pl.* سُنَن — شَرِيعَة *pl.* شَرَائِع. A prescribed religious —, فَرْض *pl.* فُرُوض — فَرِيضَة *pl.* فَرَائِض. A restrictive —, حَدّ *pl.* حُدُود. The ordinances of God, فَرَائِضُ ٱللهِ. *See also* Order, *n.*

Ordinarily, *ad.* عَلَى ٱلْعَادَةِ — بِٱلْعَادَةِ — عَلَى ٱلْأَغْلَبِ — إِعْتِيَادًا — بِٱلْأَكْثَرِ. He rises — before day-break, مِنْ عَادَتِهِ أَنْ يَقُومَ قَبْلَ ٱلْفَجْرِ — أَكْثَرُ عَادَتِهِ أَنْ يَقُومَ قَبْلَ ٱلضَّوْءِ.

Ordinary, *a.* Usual, إعْتِيَادِيٌّ ـ مُعْتَاد. Common, inferior, دُوْن. *See also* Common, *a.*

Ordinary, *n.* A bishop, أُسْقُف *pl.* أَسَاقِفَة. The — of a prison, قِسِّيس ٱلْمَحْبُوسِينَ ـ قِسِّيس ٱلسِّجْنِ. A chaplain in — to the queen, قِسِّيس عَادِيٌّ لَدَى حَضْرَةِ ٱلْمَلِكَةِ. A public eating-house, دُكَّان طَبَّاخ. A place where ships are laid up, مَحَلّ ٱلْمَرَاكِبِ ٱلْمُعَطَّلَةِ مِنَ ٱلشُّغْلِ.

Ordinate, *a.* *See* Orderly, *a.*

Ordinate, *n.* Of a line, خَطّ تَرْتِيب.

Ordinately, *ad.* *See* Orderly, *ad.*

Ordination, *n.* The act of ordaining, appointing, إِقَامَة ـ تَعْيِين ـ عَمَل ـ جَعْل; of conferring holy orders, تَقْلِيد ٱلْإِكْلِيرُسِ ـ رَسْم ـ رَسَامَة.

Ordinative, *a.* / Ordinator, *n.* } مُنَظِّم ـ مُنَسِّق ـ مُرَتِّب ـ مُعَيِّن ـ مُقِيم ـ مُثَبِّت.

Ordnance, *n.* Guns, artillery, أَطْوَاب ـ مَدَافِع. Heavy —, مَدَافِع كِبَار. A piece of —, طُوْب ـ مِدْفَع. The — department, نَظَارَةُ ٱلطُّوبْخَانَةِ. Master-General of the — department, مُشِيرُ ٱلطُّوبْخَانَةِ.

Ordure, *n.* خَرَاءَة ـ بَرَاز ـ غَائِط ـ دَبَال ـ دَمَان. Human —, عَذِرَة ـ عَائِر. *See also* Dung, Excrement, *n.*

Ore, *n.* Any metal, مَعْدِن *pl.* مَعَادِنُ. Native ore, تِبْر (this word is mostly applied to gold ore), مَعْدِنٌ خَامٌ ـ جَوْهَر.

Organ, *n.* The wind instrument, أَرْغُنُون ـ أَرْغُن. A member, as of the body, عُضْو *pl.* أَعْضَاء. An instrument of action or motion, آلَة *pl.* آلَات. An — as of one of the senses, جَارِحَة *pl.* جَوَارِح; the — of sight, الجَارِحَةُ ٱلنَّاظِرَةُ. According to the jurisconsults faith is the action of the heart alone, or of the tongue alone, or of both combined, and that either separately or in conjunction with all the other organs, الإِيمَانُ عِنْدَ ٱلْفُقَهَاءِ هُوَ فِعْلُ ٱلْقَلْبِ فَقَطْ أَوِ ٱللِّسَانِ فَقَطْ أَوْ فِعْلُهُمَا جَمِيعًا وَذٰلِكَ وَحْدَهُمَا أَوْ مَعَ سَائِرِ ٱلْجَوَارِحِ. The organs of generation, آلَاتُ (or أَعْضَاءُ) ٱلتَّنَاسُلِ ـ العُسَيْلَتَانِ. The male (generative) organ, آلَةُ ٱلذَّكَرِ; the female —, آلَةُ ٱلْأُنْثَى. Organ or speaker of a party, المُتَكَلِّمُ. A medium, وَاسِطَة. He was the — of communication, كَانَ هُوَ وَاسِطَةَ ٱلْمُخَالَطَةِ. The organs of public authority, the authorities, المَأْمُورُونَ ـ مَأْمُورُونَ ٱلدَّوْلَةِ. An official —, newspaper, جَرِيدَةٌ رَسْمِيَّةٌ. (For the organs of smell, sight, *etc.*, *see under* Sense, *n.*)

Organ-builder, *n.* صَانِعُ ٱلْأَرَاغِنِ.

Organic, *a.* / Organical, } Consisting of organs, ذُو أَعْضَاءٍ ـ مُرَكَّبٌ مِنْ أَعْضَاءٍ. Produced by the organs, مَا أَنْتَجَتْهُ ٱلْأَعْضَاءُ. Referring to the natural organs, مُتَعَلِّقٌ بِالْأَعْضَاءِ ٱلطَّبِيعِيَّةِ. Acting, عَامِل ـ فَاعِل. An — body, co-partnership, مُشَارَكَة ـ شِرْكَة ـ هَيْئَةُ ٱلشِّرْكَةِ; a body having organs, جِسْمٌ ذُو أَعْضَاءٍ. An — law, دُسْتُور *pl.* دَسَاتِيرُ ـ نِظَامٌ أَسَاسِيٌّ *pl.* نِظَامَاتٌ أَسَاسِيَّةٌ. Organic remains, آثَارُ ٱلْأَجْسَامِ ذَاتِ ٱلْأَعْضَاءِ. An — body, the principles of which are unknown, جِسْمٌ نَامٍ.

Organism, *n.* تَرْكِيبُ أَعْضَاءٍ ـ تَرْكِيب.

Organist, *n.* ضَارِبُ ٱلْأَرْغُنِ.

Organization, *n.* The act of organizing, ضَبْط ـ تَعْقِيد ـ تَنْسِيق ـ تَنْظِيم ـ تَرْتِيب ـ تَرْكِيب ـ ضِبَاطَة. Structure, arrangement of parts, مَاهِيَّة ـ تَرْكِيب ـ تَرْتِيب ـ نِظَام ـ نَسَق.

Organize, *v.t.* رَكَّبَ ـ نَظَّمَ ـ عَقَّدَ ـ رَتَّبَ ـ نَسَّقَ. To be organized, تَرَكَّبَ ـ إِنْعَقَدَ ـ تَنَسَّقَ ـ إِنْتَسَقَ.

Organized, *a.* مُرَكَّب ـ مُنْعَقِد ـ مُرَتَّب ـ مُتَّسِق ـ مُنَسَّق ـ مُنَظَّم.

Organizer, *n.* مُؤَسِّس. The organizers of that meeting, مُؤَسِّسُو تِلْكَ ٱلْجَمْعِيَّةِ.

Organ-loft, *n.* مَحَلُّ ٱلْأَرْغُنِ.

Organography, *n.* شَرْحُ أَعْضَاءِ ٱلْبَشَرِ وَٱلْحَيَوَانَاتِ وَٱلنَّبَاتَاتِ.

Organology, *n.* عِلْمُ ٱلْبَحْثِ عَنْ أَعْضَاءِ ٱلْبَشَرِ وَٱلْحَيَوَانَاتِ وَٱلنَّبَاتَاتِ.

Organon, *n.* / Organum, } قَاعِدَة ـ نَسَق.

Organzine, *n.* حَرِيرٌ مُزْدَوِجُ ٱلْبَرْمِ.

Orgasm, *n.* شِدَّة ـ حُمَيًّا ـ هَيَجَان.

Orgeat, *n.* مُسْتَحْلَبُ ٱللَّوْزِ وَٱلْبُزُورِ ٱلْمُبَرِّدَةِ.

Orgies, *n.* Drunken revelry, إِدْمَانُ ٱلْخَمْرِ وَٱلْبَطَرِ وَٱلْمُنَادَمَاتِ ـ بَطَرٌ وَسُكْرٌ.

Oriel, *n.* / Oriol, } The window so called, طَاقَةٌ مُدَوَّرَةٌ.

Orient, *a.* Rising, as of the sun, مُشْرِق. Bright, shining, بَارِق ـ لَامِع ـ مُتَلَأْلِئ. Eastern, شَرْقِيٌّ.

Orient, *n.* الشَّرْقُ ـ المَشْرِقُ.

Oriental, *a.* Eastern, شَرْقِيٌّ ـ مَشْرِقِيٌّ. The — countries, states, الأَقْطَارُ ٱلشَّرْقِيَّةُ ـ أَرْضُ ٱلْمَشْرِقِ ـ بِلَادُ ٱلشَّرْقِ.

Oriental, *n.* مِنْ أَهْلِ ٱلشَّرْقِ ـ مَشْرِقِيٌّ ـ شَرْقِيٌّ. The orientals, الشَّرْقِيُّونَ ـ أَهْلُ ٱلشَّرْقِ.

Orientalism, *n.* لُغَةٌ شَرْقِيَّةٌ ـ عِبَارَةٌ شَرْقِيَّةٌ.

Orientalist, *n.* مِنَ ٱلْمُتَضَلِّعِينَ بِاللُّغَاتِ ٱلشَّرْقِيَّةِ وَآدَابِهَا.

Orifice, *n.* A mouth, opening, نَفَذ *pl.* أَنْفَاذ ـ فَم *pl.* أَفْوَاه.

The — of the stomach, فَمُ ٱلْمِعْدَةِ ; of the womb, مَهْبِلٌ pl. مَهَابِلُ. The orifices of the body, ٱلنَّوَافِذُ ـ ٱلْمَخَارِقُ ـ ٱلْمَسَامِعُ. *See also* Mouth, Perforation, *n.*

Oriflamme, *n.* رَايَةٌ سُلْطَانِيَّةٌ.

Origan, *n.* } *See* Marjoram, *n.*
Origanum, }

Origin, *n.* Natural state, أَصْلٌ ـ عِكْرٌ. The beginning of a thing, بَدْءٌ ـ أَوَّلٌ ـ ٱبْتِدَآءٌ. Source, مَنْبَعٌ ـ مَبْدَأٌ ـ جِذْمٌ ـ نَسَبٌ ـ مَحْتِدٌ. Stock, lineage, أَصْلٌ pl. أُصُولٌ ـ نِصَابٌ ـ مَصْدَرٌ ـ عُنْصُرٌ ـ نَسْلٌ ـ آلٌ. Root, derivation, as of words, عِرْقٌ pl. عُرُوقٌ ـ صِيغَةٌ ـ نِسْبَةٌ. Of good —, of a person, كَرِيمُ ٱلْأَصْلِ (or ٱلْعِكْرِ). To go back to the —, عَادَ إِلَى ٱلْأَصْلِ. To derive one's (own) — from, ٱنْتَسَبَ إِلَى. *See also* Lineage, Birth, *n.*

Original, *a.* Preceding all others, أَوَّلٌ fem. أُولَى. Foundational, أَصْلِيٌّ. Natural, طَبِيعِيٌّ ـ جِبِلِّيٌّ ـ ذَاتِيٌّ. Novel, بَدِيعٌ ـ مُخْتَرَعٌ ـ حَدِيثٌ. Quaint, queer, غَرِيبٌ: of make, غَرِيبُ ٱلشَّكْلِ ; of disposition, غَرِيبُ ٱلطَّبْعِ. Original sin, ٱلْخَطِيئَةُ ٱلْأَصْلِيَّةُ. An — document, copy, نُسْخَةٌ أَصْلِيَّةٌ ـ سَنَدٌ أَصْلِيٌّ. The — text, عَيْنُ ٱلنَّصِّ ـ ٱلْمَتْنُ ٱلْأَصْلِيُّ. An — article, as in a newspaper, مَقَالَةٌ ٱلْمُنْشِئِ ـ نُبْذَةٌ أَصْلِيَّةٌ. The — copy, ٱلنُّسْخَةُ ٱلْأَصْلِيَّةُ ـ نُسْخَةُ ٱلْأَصْلِ. An — man, a man of genius, صَاحِبُ فِطْنَةٍ ـ ذَكِيٌّ ـ ذَهِينٌ ـ ذُو قَرِيحَةٍ. Original or natural speech, كَلَامٌ سَلِيقِيٌّ.

Original, *n.* First, source, أَصْلٌ ـ مَصْدَرٌ ـ أُمٌّ ـ مَنْبَعٌ ـ أَوَّلٌ. An —, as opposed to a copy, أَصْلٌ pl. أُصُولٌ. A quaint man, غَرِيبُ ٱلطَّبْعِ ـ رُجَيْلٌ غَرِيبٌ. To compare the copy with its original, قَابَلَ ٱلصُّورَةَ عَلَى أَصْلِهَا.

Originality, *n.* Quality of being original, أَصْلِيَّةٌ. Genius, إِدْرَاكٌ ـ فِطْنَةٌ ـ ذَكَاوَةٌ ـ ذِهْنٌ. Originality in speech, سَلِيقِيَّةٌ. He speaks with —, فِي كَلَامِهِ سَلِيقِيَّةٌ ـ يَتَكَلَّمُ بِٱلسَّلِيقِيَّةِ. Quaintness, نُكْتَةٌ ـ غَرَابَةٌ.

Originally, *ad.* فِي ٱلْأَصْلِ ـ مِنَ ٱلْأَصْلِ ـ فِي ٱلْأَوَّلِ ـ ٱبْتِدَآءً ـ أَوَّلًا.

Originate, *v.t.* To cause to be, أَوْجَدَ. To produce what is new, أَبْدَعَ ـ ٱخْتَرَعَ ـ أَحْدَثَ ـ ٱسْتَجَدَّ ـ أَجَدَّ ـ فَطَرَ ـ ٱفْتَطَرَ ـ ٱقْتَرَحَ.

Originate, *v.i.* تَبَدَّأَ ـ أَنْشَأَ مِن ـ بَدَأَ ـ حَدَثَ. A fault originated with or in him or it, حَدَثَ بِهِ عَيْبٌ.

Origination, *n.* ٱقْتِرَاحٌ ـ إِيجَادٌ ـ ٱخْتِرَاعٌ ـ إِحْدَاثٌ ـ فَطْرٌ ـ فِطْرَةٌ.

Originator, *n.* مُبْدِعٌ ـ بَادِعٌ ـ مُخْتَرِعٌ ـ مُوجِدٌ ـ فَاطِرٌ ـ مُقْتَرِحٌ.

Oriole, *n.* طَائِرٌ مِنَ ٱلطُّيُورِ ٱلصَّافِرَةِ.

Orion, *n.* The constellation, ٱلْجَبَّارُ ـ ٱلْجَوْزَآءُ.

Orison, *n.* طَلْبَةٌ pl. طَلَبَاتٌ ـ صَلَاةٌ pl. صَلَوَاتٌ.

Orlop, *n.* The deck so called, ٱلْأَنْبَارُ ٱلتَّحْتَانِيُّ ـ كَرْدُون.

Ormolu, *n.* صُفْرٌ ـ صُفْرٌ مُشَبَّهٌ بِٱلذَّهَبِ ـ صُفْرٌ مُمَوَّهٌ بِٱلذَّهَبِ ـ مُزَوَّقٌ بِٱلذَّهَبِ.

Ornament, *n.* حَلْيٌ pl. حُلِيٌّ ـ حِلْيَةٌ pl. حُلًى and حِلْيَةٌ ـ حَلِيَّةٌ ـ زِينَةٌ pl. زِيَنٌ ; of colours, variegation, دِيبَاجٌ. A silver —, وَضَحٌ pl. أَوْضَاحٌ. A grace, زِينٌ pl. أَزْيَانٌ. Embellishment of the person, such as tattooing, *etc.*, or decoration of ceilings, زَوَاقٌ. Ornament, or embellishments, in a general sense, تَزَاوِيقُ. *See also* Decoration, Embellishment, *n.*

Ornament, *v.t.* زَوَّقَ ـ زَخْرَفَ ـ زَيَّنَ. To — one's self, تَزَيَّنَ ـ تَزَخْرَفَ ـ تَزَيَّقَ ـ تَزَوَّقَ. To —, as with colours, دَبَّجَ.

Ornamental, *a.* مُزَخْرِفٌ ـ مُزَيِّنٌ ـ زَخْرَفَةٌ ـ زَوَاقٌ ـ زِينَةٌ ; of colours, مُدَبِّجٌ.

Ornamentally, *ad.* تَزْوِيقًا ـ زَخْرَفَةً ـ بِزِينَةٍ ـ زِينَةً.

Ornamentation, *n.* The act of, تَزْيِينٌ ـ زَخْرَفَةٌ ـ تَزْوِيقٌ. Self —, تَزَيُّنٌ ـ تَزَوُّقٌ ; as with colours, تَدْبِيجٌ. *See also* Ornament, *n.*

Ornamented, *a.* مُزَوَّقٌ ـ مُزَخْرَفٌ ـ مُتَزَيِّنٌ ـ مُزَيَّنٌ. Set, as with jewels, مُرَصَّعٌ ; as with colours, مُدَبَّجٌ. *See also* Ornate, *a.*

Ornate, *a.* Of speech, مُزَوَّقٌ ـ مُفَنَّنٌ. His speech was —, رَقَّ ـ زَوَّقَ ٱلْكَلَامَ ـ ٱفْتَنَّ فِي ٱلْكَلَامِ ـ كَلَامُهُ. *See also* Ornamented, *a.*

Ornately, *ad.* Of speech, بِزَوَاقٍ ـ بِتَزْوِيقٍ ـ تَفَنُّنًا.

Ornateness, *n.* Of speech, زَوَاقٌ ـ تَزْوِيقٌ. *See also* Ornament, *n.*

Ornithological, *a.* مَا نِيطَ بِعِلْمِ طَبَائِعِ ٱلطُّيُورِ ـ مُخْتَصٌّ بِٱلطُّيُورِ.

Ornithologist, *n.* حَاذِقٌ فِي عِلْمِ طَبَائِعِ ٱلطُّيُورِ.

Ornithology, *n.* عِلْمُ ٱلْبَحْثِ عَنْ طَبَائِعِ ٱلطُّيُورِ.

Ornithomancy, *n.* فَتْحُ ٱلْفَالِ بِٱلطُّيُورِ ـ ٱلتَّفَوُّلُ بِٱلطُّيُورِ.

Ornithorhynchus, *n.* حَيَوَانٌ غَرِيبُ ٱلصُّورَةِ وُجُودُهُ فِي نَوَاحِي فَلَمَنْكَ ٱلْجَدِيدَةِ ذُو مِنْقَارٍ وَأَصَابِعَ مَضْمُومَةٍ إِلَى بَعْضِهَا بِغِشَآءٍ مِثْلَ أَصَابِعِ ٱلْبَطِّ.

Orological, *a.* مُتَعَلِّقٌ بِعِلْمِ ٱلْبَحْثِ عَنْ فِطْرَةِ ٱلْجِبَالِ.

Orologist, *n.* مَاهِرٌ فِي عِلْمِ فِطْرَةِ ٱلْجِبَالِ.

Orology, *n.* عِلْمُ ٱلْبَحْثِ عَنْ مَاهِيَّةِ ٱلْجِبَالِ.

Orphan, *n.* One bereft of both parents, يَتِيمٌ ـ لُطْمٌ pl. لَطِيمٌ fem. يَتِيمَةٌ pl. m. أَيْتَامٌ and يَتَامَى and يَتَمَةٌ and مَيْتَمَةٌ. (The last word is also used of children who have lost only one parent). One who has lost the mother, عَجِيٌّ fem. عَجِيَّةٌ. To be left an —, يَتِمَ aor. يَيْتَمُ. To make an —, يَتَّمَ.

Orphan, *a.* يَتِيمٌ.

Orphanage, n. } State of being an orphan, يُتْم ـ يَتْم . Orphan-
Orphanism, } age, a home for orphans, مَأْوَى ـ دَارُ ٱلْيَتَامَى ٱلْيَتَامَى.

Orphaned, a. مُيَتَّم ـ يَتِيم.

Orphean, a. } مُتَعَلِّقٌ بِٱلشَّاعِرِ Orpheus, (أُنْظُرِ ٱلْكَلِمَةَ ٱلْآتِيَةَ).
Orphic, }

Orpheus, n. إِسْمُ شَاعِرٍ وَهُوَ مَشْهُورٌ بِٱلْمُوسِيقَى وَٱلْغِنَاءِ عِنْدَ ٱلْيُونَانِيِّينَ ٱلْقُدَمَاءِ.

Orpiment, n. رَهْجٌ أَصْفَرُ ـ زِرْنِيخ.

Orrery, n. آلَةٌ يُكْشَفُ بِهَا دَوَرَانُ ٱلسَّيَّارَاتِ.

Orris, n. ايرسا. Orris-root, عِرْقُ ٱلطِّيبِ ـ ايرسا.

Ort, n. *See* Fragment, Refuse, n.

Orthodox, a. Following the right way, belief, مِنْ أَهْلِ ـ رَاشِد ٱلسُّنَّةِ ـ سُنِّيٌّ ـ أَرْثُوذُكْسِيٌّ. Conformable to the right belief, حَقٌّ ـ مُوَافِقُ ٱلدِّينِ ٱلْحَقِّ ـ مُوَافِقُ سُنَّةِ أَهْلِ ٱلْكِتَابِ سُنَّةُ ٱلْهُدَى. True, صَحِيح ـ لَا رَيْبَ فِيهِ ـ رَشَاد. Orthodox belief, To be —, إِسْتَرْشَدَ ـ ² رَشَدَ. To account or declare to be —, رَشَّدَ.

Orthodoxly, ad. عَلَى عَقَائِدِ ٱلدِّينِ ٱلْحَقِّ ـ بِرَشَادٍ ـ رَشَادًا.

Orthodoxness, n. } صِحَّةُ ٱلْعَقَائِدِ ـ مُطَابَقَةُ سُنَّةِ ٱلْهُدَى ـ رَشَاد ـ
Orthodoxy, } أَرْثُوذُكْسِيَّة. The orthodox creed, ٱلْقَيِّمَةُ ـ سُنَّةُ ٱلْهُدَى. The body of the orthodox, جَمَاعَةُ ـ ٱلْجَمَاعَةُ ٱلرَّاشِدِينَ.

Orthoepist, n. فَصِيحُ ٱلنُّطْقِ ـ مُحْكِمُ ٱللَّفْظِ ـ جَيِّدُ ٱلتَّلَفُّظِ.

Orthoepy, n. دِقَّةُ (or صِحَّةُ) ٱلتَّلَفُّظِ.

Orthographer, n. } حَاذِقٌ فِي عِلْمِ وَضْعِ ٱلْخَطِّ ـ مِنْ أَهْلِ ٱلْإِمْلَاءِ.
Orthographist, }

Orthographic, a. } مُتَعَلِّقٌ بِعِلْمِ وَضْعِ ـ مَنُوطٌ بِضَبْطِ ٱلْأَسْمَاءِ
Orthographical, } مُخْتَصٌّ بِصِحَّةِ ٱلْإِمْلَاءِ ـ ٱلْخَطّ.

Orthographically, ad. بِإِتْقَانٍ ـ بِصِحَّةِ ٱلْإِمْلَاءِ ـ بِضَبْطِ ٱلْأَسْمَاءِ ٱلتَّهْجِيَةِ. To write —, (v.t.) كَتَبَهُ عَلَى ـ ² كَتَبَهُ بِصِحَّةِ ٱلْإِمْلَاءِ ٱلْوَضْعِ.

Orthography, n. عِلْمُ وَضْعِ ٱلْخَطِّ ـ ضَبْطُ ٱلْكِتَابَةِ ـ ضَبْطُ ٱلْأَسْمَاءِ ـ إِتْقَانٌ فِي ٱلتَّهْجِيَةِ ـ إِمْلَاء.

Orthopedist, n. مُعَالِجُ ٱعْوِجَاجِ ٱلْأَرْجُلِ.

Orthopedy, n. مُعَالَجَةُ ٱعْوِجَاجِ ٱلْأَرْجُلِ.

Ortive, a. *See* Orient, a.

Ortolan, n. أَرْتُولَان وَهُوَ طَائِرٌ صَغِيرٌ لَذِيذُ ٱللَّحْمِ.

Oryx, n. يَحْمُور ـ نَوْعٌ مِنَ ٱلظِّبَاءِ يُوجَدُ فِي أَفْرِيقِيَّةَ ٱلْجَنُوبِيَّةِ.

Os, n. *See* Bone, n.

Oscillate, v.i. To vibrate, إِرْتَجَّ ـ إِهْتَزَّ ـ تَرَجْرَجَ ـ إِرْتَجَحَ ـ رَجْرَجَ ـ ² رَجَّ. To cause to —, تَرَجْرَجَ ـ ² رَقَصَ.

Oscillation, n. رَقْص ـ إِهْتِزَاز ـ رَجْرَجَة ـ هَزْهَزَة ـ إِرْتِجَاج.

Oscillatory, a. رَقْصِيٌّ ـ مُرْتَجٌّ ـ مُتَرَجْرِج ـ مُتَرَجِّح.

Os coccygis, n. ٱلْعُقْدَةُ ـ ٱلْعُصْعُصُ ـ ٱلثَّعْلَبَةُ.

Osculation, n. A kissing, بَوْس ـ تَقْبِيل ـ قُبْلَة. The contact of a curve with its circle, مُمَاسَّةُ ٱلْقَوْسِ بِدَائِرَتِهِ.

Osculatory, n. A tablet of a saint made to be kissed, لَوْحَةٌ عَلَيْهَا صُورَةٌ لِلتَّبَرُّكِ بِهَا.

Osier, n. A reed or cane for making baskets, خُوص ـ خَيْزُرَان ـ حَطَبُ ٱلْحِنَّا. The *Salix Egyptiaca,* صَفْصَاف ـ خِلَاف (*vulg.* خَلَاف).

Osiered, a. مُحَاطٌ بِصَفْصَافٍ.

Osmazome, n. خُلَاصَةُ ٱللِّيفِ.

Osmium, n. أُسْمِيُوم وَهُوَ ضَرْبٌ مِنَ ٱلْمَعَادِنِ.

Ospray, n. عُقَاب *pl.* عِقْبَان.

Osseous, a. عِظَامِيٌّ ـ عَظْمِيٌّ.

Ossicle, n. عُظَيْم ـ عَظْمٌ صَغِيرٌ ـ عُشَّاق *pl.* عَاشِق.

Ossiferous, a. مُنْشِئُ ٱلْعَظْمِ.

Ossific, a. مُحَوِّلٌ إِلَى عَظْمٍ.

Ossification, n. إِسْتِحَالَةٌ (or تَحَوُّلٌ) إِلَى عَظْمٍ.

Ossifrage, n. نِسْرُ ٱلْبَحْرِ.

Ossify, v.t. حَوَّلَ إِلَى عَظْمٍ ـ صَيَّرَ (or أَصَارَ) عَظْمًا.

Ossify, v.i. إِسْتَحَالَ ـ إِسْتَحَالَ (or تَحَوَّلَ) إِلَى عَظْمٍ ـ صَارَ عَظْمًا عَظْمًا.

Ossiverous, a. آكِلُ ٱلْعِظَامِ.

Ossuary, n. *See* Charnel-house, n.

Ostensibility, n. بَيَان ـ تَظَاهُر ـ ظُهُور.

Ostensible, a. Seeming, حَسَبَ ٱلرُّؤْيَةِ ـ مُتَشَبِّهٌ بِ ـ مُتَظَاهِر. Not real, مُلْتَبِس ـ مُزَيَّف ـ مُمَوَّه ـ زَغَل ـ مُرْهَق. Declared, avowed, مُتَّضِح ـ مُبَيَّن ـ وَاضِح. *See also* Apparent, a.

Ostensibly, ad. Colourably, لِعُيُونِ ٱلنَّاسِ ـ بِٱلصُّورَةِ ـ فِي ٱلظَّاهِرِ. Openly, جِهَارًا ـ عَلَانِيَةً. *See also* Colourably, Apparently, ad.

Ostensive, a. مُبَيِّن ـ مُظْهِر ـ مُعْلِن.

Ostentation, n. Boasting, تَفَاخُر ـ تَكَبُّر ـ تَعَظُّم. Ambitious display, إِفْتِخَار ـ مُبَاهَاة. The — of a woman who displays her finery, تَبَرُّج.

Ostentatious, a. Boasting, مُفْتَخِر ـ مُتَعَظِّم ـ مُتَكَبِّر. Making an ambitious display, فَخُور ـ مُبَاهٍ. To be — of, إِفْتَخَرَ بِ. To be —, of a woman who displays her charms, تَبَرَّجَتْ.

Ostentatiously, *ad.* بِمُبَاهَاةٍ ـ بِٱفْتِخَارٍ ـ بِتَعَظُّمٍ ـ بِتَكَبُّرٍ ; of a woman, بِتَبَرُّجٍ.

Ostentatiousness, *n.* *See* Ostentation, *n.*

Osteogeny, *n.* تَكَوُّنُ ٱلْعِظَامِ.

Osteological, *a.* مَنُوطٌ بِعِلْمِ ٱلْبَحْثِ عَنْ تَرْكِيبِ ٱلْعِظَامِ ـ مُتَعَلِّقٌ بِشَرْحِ ٱلْعِظَامِ.

Osteologer, *n.* }
Osteologist, } مَاهِرٌ فِي عِلْمِ تَرْكِيبِ ٱلْعِظَامِ.

Osteology, *n.* The science of animal bones, فَنُّ ٱلْبَحْثِ عَنْ تَرْكِيبِ ٱلْعِظَامِ. The system of animal bones, مَاهِيَّةُ ٱلْعِظَامِ.

Ostler, *n.* *See* Groom, *n.*

Ostracism, *n.* Expulsion, نَفْيٌ ـ إِخْرَاجٌ ـ تَخْرِيجٌ ـ طَرْدٌ.

Ostracize, *v.t.* To expel, نَفَا ² ـ طَرَدَ ـ أَخْرَجَ. To be ostracized, ٱنْطَرَدَ ـ إِطَّرَدَ.

Ostrich, *n.* نَعَامَةٌ *coll.* نَعَامٌ *pl.* نَعَائِمُ. A female —, أُمُّ ٱلْبَيْضِ. The male —, ظَلِيمٌ *pl.* ظِلْمَانٌ *and* أَظْلِمَةٌ. Ostrich feathers, رِيشُ نَعَامٍ ـ خَمِيلَةٌ ـ خَمَالَةٌ. An — egg, تُومَةٌ *pl.* تُومٌ ـ بَيْضَةُ نَعَامٍ *coll.* بَيْضٌ.

Otalgia, *n.* دَآءُ ٱلْأُذُنِ.

Other, *a.* and *n.* آخَرُ *fem.* أُخْرَى *pl. masc.*, آخَرُونَ *and* أُخَرُ *pl. fem.* أُخْرَيَاتٌ *and* أُخَرُ ـ غَيْرٌ. The one and the —, الْوَاحِدُ وَٱلْآخَرُ ـ الْإِثْنَانِ ـ كِلَيْهِمَا ـ هٰذَا وَهٰذَاكَ. Other than me, غَيْرِي ـ أَحَدٌ غَيْرِي. No —, لَا غَيْرُ. The — day, ذٰلِكَ ٱلْيَوْمَ. The —, الثَّانِي ـ الْآخَرُ. Other than, سِوَى ـ دُونَ: Other than he, سِوَاهُ. I saw — than thee, رَأَيْتُ سِوَاكَ. Other than thou came to me, جَاءَنِي غَيْرُكَ ـ جَاءَنِي سِوَاكَ. None — than thou came to me, مَا جَاءَنِي سِوَاكَ. The men came and others, جَآؤُا ٱلرِّجَالُ وَغَيْرُهُمْ. I have one and no —, عِنْدِي وَاحِدٌ لَا غَيْرُ. No —, except, nothing more than, إِلَّا: you are no — than human beings like ourselves, مَا أَنْتُمْ إِلَّا بَشَرٌ مِثْلُنَا. This is none — than he himself, مَا هٰذَا إِلَّا هُوَ بِنَفْسِهِ. He is like — men, هُوَ كَوَاحِدٍ مِنَ ٱلنَّاسِ. He who came to me the — day, الَّذِي جَآءَ إِلَيَّ ذٰلِكَ ٱلْيَوْمَ. There is no — like him here, لَيْسَ أَحَدٌ سِوَاهُ هُنَا. His hand was restored whole like the —, عَادَتْ يَدُهُ صَحِيحَةً كَٱلْأُخْرَى. He is not like — men, لَيْسَ هُوَ مِثْلَ بَاقِي ٱلنَّاسِ. What do ye more than others? مَاذَا ـ أَيَّ فَضْلٍ تَصْنَعُونَ. And many — things, وَأَشْيَآءُ أُخَرُ كَثِيرَةٌ. تَفْعَلُونَ أَكْثَرَ مِنْ غَيْرِكُمْ. We trust to the information of others, نَعْتَمِدُ عَلَى أَخْبَارِ ٱلْغَيْرِ. *See also* Another, *a.*

Otherwise, *ad.* In a different manner, فِي نَوْعٍ ـ فِي غَيْرِ مِنْوَالٍ آخَرَ. Lest, لِئَلَّا. If not, مَاذَا وَإِلَّا ـ وَإِلَّا. Contrary, بِٱلْخِلَافِ ـ بِٱلضِّدِّ. Should he say —, إِنْ قَالَ بِٱلْخِلَافِ. He must do it, — we will inform his father, لَا بُدَّ أَنْ يَفْعَلَهُ وَإِلَّا سَنُخْبِرُ أَبَاهُ. How could it be — when the boy was never taught? كَيْفَ لَا وَٱلصَّبِيُّ مَا تَعَلَّمَ قَطُّ.

Otium cum dignitate, *n.* رَاحَةٌ بِوَقَارٍ ـ إِسْتِرَاحَةٌ وَرَفَاهِيَةٌ ـ رَاحَةٌ وَرَفَاهٌ.

Ottar, *n.* (Correctly 'Itr), عِطْرٌ. Ottar of roses, عِطْرٌ ـ عِطْرُ ٱلْوَرْدِ.

Otter, *n.* The animal, كَلْبُ ٱلْمَآءِ ـ ثَعْلَبُ ٱلْمَآءِ ـ قُنْدُسٌ.

Ottoman, *a.* عُثْمَانِيٌّ. The — empire, الدَّوْلَةُ ٱلْعُثْمَانِيَّةُ ـ الدَّوْلَةُ ٱلْعَلِيَّةُ ٱلْعُثْمَانِيَّةُ.

Ottoman, *n.* عُثْمَانِيٌّ *pl.* عُثْمَانِيَّةٌ *or* عُثْمَانِيُّونَ.

Ouch, *n.* فَصٌّ *pl.* فُصُوصٌ.

Ought, *n.* *See* Aught, *n.*

Ought, *v.i.* وَجَبَ *aor.* يَجِبُ ـ اِنْبَغَى ـ حَقَّ *aor.* يَحِقُّ ـ لَزِمَ ـ ². I — to write, يَنْبَغِي لِي أَنْ أَكْتُبَ. It — to be so, كَانَ يَنْبَغِي أَنْ يَكُونَ كَذَا. Ought it not to have been so? أَلَيْسَ كَانَ يَجِبُ أَنْ يَصِيرَ هٰكَذَا. Ought they not to be punished? أَمَا يَسْتَحِقُّونَ ٱلْعُقُوبَةَ. What — he to do? مَاذَا يَنْبَغِي لَهُ أَنْ يَفْعَلَ. Why — he to do so? لِمَاذَا يَجِبُ عَلَيْهِ أَنْ يَفْعَلَ هٰكَذَا. I think he — to be rewarded, عَلَى ظَنِّي أَنَّهُ يَسْتَحِقُّ ٱلْمُكَافَاةَ. They — not to have done so, مَا كَانَ يَنْبَغِي لَهُمْ أَنْ يَعْمَلُوا هٰكَذَا. He — to have been here, كَانَ يَنْبَغِي أَنْ يَحْضُرَ هُنَا. These things — not to be done, هٰذِهِ ٱلْأَعْمَالُ لَا تُعْمَلُ. These things — not to be so, لَا يَصْلُحُ أَنْ تَكُونَ هٰذِهِ ٱلْأُمُورُ هٰكَذَا. They say things that they — not, يَتَكَلَّمُونَ بِمَا لَا يَجِبُ. You — to do this, عَلَيْكَ أَنْ تَفْعَلَ هٰذَا.

Ounce, *n.* Of weight or measure, وُقِيَّةٌ ـ أَوَاقِي *pl.* وَاقِيَةٌ *pl.* أَوَاقٍ *and* أُوقِيَّةٌ *and* وُقِيٌّ.

Ounce, *n.* The animal, نَوْعٌ مِنَ ٱلنَّمِرِ صَغِيرٌ ـ شُنَارَى.

Our, *pron.* Belonging to us, (expressed in Arabic by the postposition of the plural pronoun, *e.g.*,) our house, بَيْتُنَا ; our right, حَقُّنَا.

Ourang-outang, *n.* *See* Orang-outang, *n.*

Ouranography, *n.* عِلْمُ تَعْرِيفِ هَيْئَةِ ٱلسَّمَآءِ.

Ourology, *n.* }
Ouroscopy, } الْإِسْتِدْلَالُ عَلَى ٱلْأَمْرَاضِ مِنْ هَيْئَةِ ـ تَفْسِرَةٍ ـ قَشْرِ ٱلْبَوْلِ.

Ours, *pron.* Belonging to us, لَنَا. Ours, our things, مَتَاعُنَا. (The vulgar word for expressing "Ours" is بِتَاعْنَا *or* مَالُنَا). What he has carried off from the house is ours, مَا سَلَبَهُ مِنَ ٱلْبَيْتِ فَهُوَ لَنَا. What is theirs and what is ours, الَّذِي لَهُمْ وَٱلَّذِي لَنَا. Ours, meaning our set, party, حِزْبُنَا ـ جَمَاعَتُنَا.

Ourself, *pron.* نَحْنُ.

Ourselves, *pron.* نَحْنُ ـ أَنْفُسُنَا. We —, نَحْنُ أَنْفُسُنَا. We relied on —, إِتَّكَلْنَا عَلَى أَنْفُسِنَا.

Ousel, *n.* The bird, نَوْعٌ مِنَ ٱلشُّحْرُورِ *pl.* شَحَارِيرُ.

Oust, *v.t.* أَخْرَجَ ـ ² طَرَدَ ـ ² نَفَى.

Out, *ad.* (Frequently used adjectively), Outside, فِي ٱلْخَارِجِ ـ بَرًّا ـ خَارِجًا. Out of, from out of, مِنْ : He went out of the door, ² خَرَجَ مِنَ ٱلْبَابِ. He is out of town, هُوَ خَارِجَ ٱلْمَدِينَةِ ـ هُوَ فِي خارجِ ٱلْبَلَدِ (*vulg.* هُوَ بَرَّاةَ ٱلْبَلَدِ). To be out, not in, ² غَابَ عَنْ ـ ² خَرَجَ ـ كَانَ خَارِجًا. To be out of, not to have more of, ما بَقِيَ عِنْدَهُ مِنْ ـ مَا فَضَلَ لَهُ مِنْ. Out, in the sense of :—

Expired, كامِل : The time was out, ² كَمَلَ ٱلْوَقْتُ.

Extinguished, مُطْفِئٌ : The fire is out, طَفِئَتْ (*or* اِنْطَفَأَتْ) ٱلنَّارُ.

Finished, expended, بائد ـ نافِد : The wine is out, ² نَفِدَ ٱلْخَمْرُ ـ ² فَرَغَ ٱلشَّرَابُ.

Loud, جَهُور : Speak out, تَكَلَّمْ جَهِيرًا.

Mistaken, غَالِط : I am out in my reckoning, غَلِطْتُ فِي ٱلْحِسَابِ.

Omitted, مَوْهُوم ـ مَتْرُوك ـ مَحْذُوف : It is out of the account, لَيْسَ هُوَ فِي ٱلْحِسَابِ.

On the march, in the field, مَبْرُوز ـ فِي ٱلْمِيدَانِ : The soldiers are out, العَسْكَرُ فِي ٱلْمِيدَانِ.

Published, made known, مَشْهُور ـ مُشْتَهَر : The thing is out, إِشْتَهَرَ ٱلْأَمْرُ.

Unemployed, بَطَّال ـ مُعَطَّل : He is out of work, هُوَ مُعَطَّلٌ.

Out and out, (*ad.*) بَتَّةً ـ بِٱلتَّمَامِ ـ بِٱلْكُلِّيَّةِ ـ فِي كُلِّ وَجْهٍ ـ كُلِّيًّا ـ بِٱلْمَرَّةِ.

Out at elbow, مُرَقَّع ـ رَثُّ ٱلثِّيَابِ.

Out at heel, مُنْخَرِقُ ٱلنَّعْلِ.

Out of breath, مُنْبَهِر ـ بَهِير.

Out of cash, مُفْلِس.

Out of countenance, out of heart, فَشِل ـ مُخْتَبِل ـ مُخَبَّل ـ مَخْيُوب ـ مُتَحَيِّر.

Out of danger, لَيْسَ عَلَيْهِ خَطَرٌ ـ سَلِيم.

Out of fashion, become old, مُعَتَّق. Not like the fashion of the day, لَيْسَ عَلَى زِيِّ ٱلْيَوْمِ.

Out of hand, quickly, عَلَى ٱلْفَوْرِ ـ بِسُرْعَةٍ. To settle a matter out of hand, تَنْجُزُ (*or* تَنْتَقِضُ) ٱلْحَاجَةُ.

Out of office, بِلا مَنْصِبٍ ـ خَارِجٌ عَنِ ٱلْوَظِيفَةِ ـ مَعْزُول.

Out of order, against rule, خِلَافَ ٱلْقَانُونِ. *See also under* Order, *n.*

Out of patience, مَعْدُومُ ٱلصَّبْرِ ـ عائِلُ ٱلصَّبْرِ.

Out of print, as of a book, نَفِقَتْ سُوقُهُ ـ إِنْبَاعَ بِأَسْرِهِ.

Out of reach, لَا وُصُولَ إِلَيْهِ ـ لَا يُدْرَكُ.

Out of season, not in its proper time, خَارِجٌ عَنْ وَقْتِهِ ـ فِي غَيْرِ مَحَلِّهِ ; of fruits and such like, لَيْسَ فِي إِبَّانِهِ.

Out of sight, بَعِيدٌ عَنِ ٱلْأَعْيُنِ ـ بَعِيدٌ عَنِ ٱلنَّظَرِ.

Out of sorts, not well in health, مُخْتَلّ ـ مَرِيض ـ سَقِيم ـ عَلِيلُ ٱلْمِزَاجِ.

Out of spirits, مَخْيُوب ـ كَئِيب ـ حَزِين ـ مَكْرُوب.

Out of time, of music, خَارِجٌ عَنِ ٱلْوَزْنِ ـ لَحْنٌ مَغْلُوطٌ.

Time out of mind, قَبْلَ ٱلدُّهُورِ ـ مِنَ ٱلْقَدِيمِ.

(For the verbs to which "Out" is suffixed, *e.g.*, *to* Cast out, *to* Drive out, see the verbs).

Out, *int.* Out upon him! أُفٍّ لَهُ وَتُفٍّ ـ أُفَّةً لَهُ ـ أُفًّا لَهُ ـ أُفًّا وَتُفًّا لَهُ. Out with it! tell it! تَكَلَّمْ ـ أَفْرِزْ ـ قُلْ. Out with him! أُطْرُدْهُ ـ أَخْرِجْهُ ـ خُذْهُ خُذْهُ.

Out, *v.t.* *See to* Oust, *v.t.*

Outact, *v.t.* To exceed, بَالَغَ فِي ـ ² زَادَ عَلَى. To excel, ² فَاقَ ـ ² نَافَ عَلَى ـ عَلَى.

Outbalance, *v.t.* To outweigh, ² رَجَحَ ; to make to —, رَجَّحَ. To surpass in, بَرَزَ عَلَى ـ ² فَاقَ ـ فِي ـ ² رَجَحَ ـ فِي. *See also to* Outweigh, *v.t.*

Outbid, *v.t.* زَايَدَ : One of them outbade the other, زَايَدَ أَحَدُهُمْ عَلَى ٱلْآخَرِ. They outbade one another for the horse, تَزَايَدُوا عَلَى ٱلْفَرَسِ. They outbid one another (of many) in the price, تَزَايَدُوا فِي ٱلثَّمَنِ.

Outbid, *n.* مُزَايَدَة.

Outbidder, *n.* مُزَايِد.

Outbound, *a.* مُسَافِرٌ إِلَى ٱلْخَارِجِ ـ مُتَغَرِّب ـ مُسَافِرٌ إِلَى ٱلْغُرْبَةِ.

Outbrave, *v.t.* To embolden one's self against, تَجَاسَرَ عَلَى ; they outbraved each other, of many, تَجَاسَرُوا. To exceed in splendour, ² فَاقَ ـ فِي ٱلْبَهْجَةِ.

Outbrazen, *v.t.* ² زَادَ وَقَاحَةً عَلَى ـ رَاجَحَ ـ فِي ٱلْوَقَاحَةِ ـ ² غَلَبَ عَلَى ـ فِي ٱلسَّفَاهَةِ.

Outbreak, *n.* } هَيَجَان ـ ثَوْرَة ـ سَوْرَة. An — of passion, سَوْرَةُ
Outbreaking, } ٱلْغَضَبِ ; an — of measles, ثُؤُورُ (*or* ثَوَرَانُ) ٱلْحَصْبَةِ.

See also Insurrection, *n.*

Outbuilding, *n.* حَوْزَةُ ٱلدَّارِ ـ حَوْزَة. Outbuildings, مَرَافِقُ ـ حَيِّزُ ٱلدَّارِ ـ (*or* مَنَافِعُ *or* نَوَاحِي) ٱلدَّارِ.

Outburst, *n.* *See* Outbreak, *n.*

Outcast, *a.* } Driven out, مُطَرَّد ـ مَرْفُوض ـ مَطْرُود ـ طَرِيح.
Outcast, *n.* } An exile, نَفِيٌّ. An — from society, خَلِيع ـ خَلِيعٌ ـ مَرْفُوضٌ مِن ٱلنَّاسِ ـ مَطْرُودٌ مِنَ ٱلْمُعَاشَرَةِ ـ مَخْلُوعُ ٱلنَّاسِ.

Outclimb, *v.t.* فَاقَ ـ فِي ٱلتَّسَوُّرِ ـ رَجَحَ عَلَى ـ تَسَلُّقًا.

Outcome, *n.* ثَمَرَة ـ نَتِيجَة ـ مَحْصُول ـ مَخَارِجُ ـ حَاصِل.

Outcrop, *v.i.* (In geology), شَخَصَ عَلَى سَطْحِ ٱلْأَرْضِ.

Outcrop, *n.* As of a stratum, بُرُوزُ طَبَقَةٍ مِنْ طَبَقَاتِ ٱلْأَرْضِ.

Outcry, *n.* صَرْخَة ـ صِيَاح ـ صُرَاخ ـ ضَجَاج ـ ضَجَّة. To make an —, صَرَخَ ـ ضَجَّ. To raise an —, أَثَارَ ضَجِيجًا ـ هَيَّجَ صُرَاخًا.

Outdare, *v.t.* أَنَافَ عَلَى ـ جَسَارَةً ـ تَجَاسَرَ عَلَى.

Outdo, *v.t.* To surpass, بَرَزَ عَلَى ـ أَنَافَ عَلَى ـ بَرَعَ. *See also to* Excel, *v.t.*

Outdoing, *n.* تَفَوُّت ـ إِنَافَة ـ مُجَاوَزَة.

Outdone, *a.* مُفَازٌ بِهِ ـ مَقْهُور ـ مَغْلُوب.

Outdoor, *a.* خَارِجٌ عَنِ ٱلْبَيْتِ. Outdoor exercise, رِيَاضَةُ ٱلْجِسْمِ خَارِجَ ٱلْبَيْتِ.

Outdoors, *ad.* بَرًّا ـ فِي ٱلْفَضَاءِ ـ مِنْ خَارِجِ ٱلْبَيْتِ.

Outer, *a.* بَرَّانِيٌّ ـ خَارِجِيٌّ ـ خَارِج. *See also under* Inner, *a.*

Outermost, *a.* ٱلْأَبْعَدُ ـ ٱلْأَقْصَى.

Outface, *v.t.* To outstare, أَبْهَرَ (or أَقْمَعَ) بِٱلنَّظَرِ. *See also to* Brave, *v.t.*

Outfall, *n.* A fall, as of water, إِنْصِبَاب ـ صَبِيب. An embouchure, as of a river, مَصَبّ ـ فِرَاض ـ فَم. *See also* Outcome, *n.*

Outfit, *n.* Provision for a journey, زَاد; to provide such an outfit for one's self, تَزَوَّدَ; for another, زَوَّدَ. Equipment, جِهَاز ـ لَوَازِمُ ـ تَعْمِير. Money for outfit, خَرْجُ (or مَصْرَفُ) ٱلْجِهَازِ.

Outflank, *v.t.* طَرَّفَ ـ سَارَ عَلَى جَانِبِهِ.

Outflow, *n.* *See* Outfall, *n.*

Outfly, *v.t.* سَبَقَ ـ فِي ٱلطَّيْرُورَةِ.

Outfool, *v.t.* زَادَ حَمَاقَةً عَلَى ـ رَجَحَ عَلَى ـ فِي ٱلْحَمَاقَةِ.

Outfrown, *v.t.* سَطَا بِ ـ تَعَبُّسًا ـ أَقْمَعَ ـ بِتَقَطُّبِ وَجْهِهِ. *See also to* Brave, Defy, *v.t.*

Outgeneral, *v.t.* زَادَ سِيَاسَةً عَلَى ـ فَاقَ ـ فِي سِيَاسَةِ ٱلْعَسْكَرِ ـ تَغَلَّبَ عَلَى.

Outgive, *v.t.* فَاقَ ـ كَرَمًا ـ زَادَ إِنْعَامًا عَلَى.

Outgo, *v.t.* To outstrip, سَبَقَ ـ فَارَطَ. To excel, surpass, بَرَعَ ـ بَرَزَ عَلَى ـ أَنَافَ عَلَى.

Outgoing, *n.* The act of going out, بُرُوز ـ خُرُوج. Expense, كُلْفَة ـ خَرْج ـ نَفَقَة. The state of going out, مَخْرَج *pl.* مَخَارِجُ ـ مَطْلَع *pl.* مَطَالِعُ. The utmost border, حَدّ *pl.* حُدُود ـ أَقْصَى. The outgoings, expenditure, مَصَارِيفُ.

Outgrow, *v.t.* To surpass in growth, زَادَ (or إِزْدَادَ عَلَى) نَشَاءَةً. To grow too large for, كَبُرَ عَلَى; of length, طَالَ عَلَى.

Out-Herod, *v.t.* To exceed in cruelty, زَادَ ـ زَادَ عَنْفًا عَلَى ـ بَالَغَ فِي ـ أَفْرَطَ فِي ـ عَلَى ـ فِي ٱلْقَسَاوَةِ. To overact a part, بَالَغَ فِي.

Outhouse, *n.* *See* Outbuilding, *n.*

Outlandish, *a.* Foreign, بَرَّانِيٌّ ـ غَرِيب ـ أَجْنَبِيٌّ. Rude, جَافٍ ـ فَظّ ـ غَلِيظ ـ خَشِن.

Outlast, *v.t.* To exceed in duration, فَاقَ ـ فِي ـ زَادَ دَوَامًا عَلَى ٱلدَّوَامِ. To last longer than, دَامَ (or إِسْتَدَامَ) أَكْثَرَ مِن. To survive, عَاشَ بَعْدَهُ ـ بَقِيَ بَعْدَهُ.

Outlaw, *n.* خَلِيع ـ طَرِيد ـ مَحْكُومٌ عَلَيْهِ بِٱلنَّفْيِ.

Outlaw, *v.t.* حَكَمَ عَلَى ـ بِٱلطَّرْدِ ـ حَكَمَ عَلَى ـ بِٱلنَّفْيِ.

Outlawry, *n.* ٱلْحُكْمُ بِٱلنَّفْيِ ـ ٱلْحُكْمُ بِٱلطَّرْدِ.

Outlay, *n.* خَرْج ـ مَصْرُوف ـ نَفَقَة. *See also* Expense, *n.*

Outleap, *v.t.* نَطَّ أَبْعَدَ مِن ـ أَنَافَ عَلَى ـ فِي ٱلْقَفْزِ ـ جَازَهُ نَطًّا.

Outlet, *n.* مَخْرَج *pl.* مَخَارِجُ ـ مَنْفِذ *pl.* مَنَافِذُ ـ بَاب *pl.* أَبْوَاب. An — for water, in a trough, tank, *etc.*, مَثْعَب *pl.* مَثَاعِبُ.

Outline, *n.* An exterior line of a figure, دَوَار ـ دَائِرَة ـ رَسْم. Shape, هَيْئَة *pl.* هَيْآت. A rough sketch, مُسَوَّدَة. An abridgment, مُجْمَل ـ مُخْتَصَر.

Outline, *v.t.* To draw رَسَمَ دَائِرَةَ ٱلشَّيْءِ ـ رَسَمَ. To give an abridgment of, أَوْجَزَ ـ أَشَّرَ. To sketch without filling up, حَشَا *aor.* يَحْشُو.

Outlive, *v.t.* To survive, عَاشَ بَعْدَهُ ـ بَقِيَ بَعْدَهُ. To live down, عَاقَبَ. The old men who outlived the plague, ٱلشُّيُوخُ ٱلَّذِينَ ٱسْتَحْيَاهُمُ ٱلطَّاعُونُ. *See also to* Outlast, *v.t.*

Outlook, *v.t.* To look over, to command, رَمَى ـ أَشْرَفَ عَلَى ـ عَلَى. *See also to* Outface, *v.t.*

Outlook, *n.* A view, مُعَايَنَة ـ مَنْظَرَة ـ مَنْظَر. Expectation, إِنْتِظَار ـ مُنْيَة ـ مَأْمُول. The future, ٱلْمُسْتَقْبَلُ.

Outlying, *a.* Being at a distance, فِي ٱلْأَطْرَافِ ـ بَعِيد. Neighbouring, مُتَّصِل ـ مُتَجَاوِر. The — provinces, ٱلْأَقَالِيمُ ٱلْمُتَجَاوِرَةُ.

Out-manœuvre, *v.t.* *See to* Outgeneral, *v.t.*

Outmarch, *v.t.* سَبَقَ ـ سَبَقَ ـ فِي ٱلْمَسِيرِ.

Outmeasure, *v.t.* إِزْدَادَ عَلَى ـ مِقْدَارًا ـ فَاقَ ـ ٱمْتِدَادًا.

Outmost, *a.* فِي ٱلْأَطْرَافِ ـ ٱلْأَبْعَدُ ـ ٱلْأَقْصَى. The — parts, ٱلْأَقَاصِي.

Outnumber, *v.t.* كَانَ أَكْثَرَ مِن ـ كَثَرَ عَدَدًا ـ أَنَافَ عَلَى عَدَدًا.

Outnumbered, *a.* مُتَعَدِّد. They outnumbered them by ten thousand, أَنَافُوا عَلَيْهِم عَشَرَةَ آلَافٍ.

Outpace, *v.t.* *See to* Outgo, Outmarch, *v.t.*

Outparish, *n.* أَبْرَشِيَّةٌ بَرَّانِيَّةٌ.

Outport, *n.* مِينَةٌ فِي ٱلْخَارِجِ.

Outpost, *n.* مَحَلُّ سُلَافِ ٱلْعَسْكَرِ ـ مُقَدَّمَة ـ مُقَدِّمَة.

Outpour, *v.t.* صَبَّ ـ سَكَبَ ـ أَجَشَّ.

Outpour, *v.i.* إِنْبَجَسَ ـ إِنْصَبَّ ـ تَدَفَّقَ.

Outpouring, *n.* إِنْصِبَاب; an — of rain, مَطَرٌ عِزٌّ ـ نَضَّاح ـ غَيْثٌ مِدْرَارٌ.

Outrage, *v.t.* To insult, نَقَصَ فِي عِرْضِهِ ـ فَضَحَ ـ شَتَمَ ـ بَهْدَلَ. To do despite to, أَسَاءَ إِلَى. To treat harshly, أَعْنَفَ ـ عَاسَرَ ـ قَرَفَ عَلَى.

Outrage, *n.* An insult, بَهْدَلَة ـ إِهَانَة ـ إِنْتِهَاكُ ٱلْحُرْمَةِ ـ نَقْصٌ فِي ٱلْعِرْضِ. An atrocity, قَبِيحَة *pl.* قَبَائِحُ ـ فَظَاعَة ـ جَائِفَة ـ شَنَاعَة ـ فَاحِشَة *pl.* فَوَاحِشُ ـ أَفْعَالٌ فَظِيعَةٌ *pl.* فِعْلٌ فَظِيعٌ. They committed outrages too hateful to mention, فَعَلُوا فَظَائِعَ يَقْبُحُ ذِكْرُهَا. The outrages committed by the soldiery upon the inhabitants of the town, ٱلْفَظَائِعُ ٱلَّتِي ٱرْتَكَبَهَا ٱلْعَسْكَرُ وَأَسَاءُوا بِهَا إِلَى أَهْلِ ٱلْبَلَدِ.

Outraged, *a.* Insulted, مُبَهْدَل ـ مَفْضُوح ـ مَشْتُوم. Treated harshly, مُعَاسَر ـ مَقْرُوفٌ عَلَيْهِ ـ مُعْنَف.

Outrageous, *a.* Insulting, مُفْضِح ـ مُنْتَهِك ـ مُهِين ـ شَتَّام ـ مُبَهْدِل. Atrocious, فَظِيع ـ جَائِف ـ قَبِيح ـ شَنِيع.

Outrageously, *ad.* With atrocity, بِقَبَاحَةٍ ـ بِشَنَاعَةٍ. Excessively, لِلْغَايَةِ ـ بِإِفْرَاطٍ.

Outrageousness, *n.* *See* Enormity, Atrocity, *n.*

Outré, *a.* مُفْرَط. *See also* Extravagant, *a.*

Outride, *v.t.* To ride faster than one, سَبَقَ فِي ٱلرُّكُوبِ.

Outride, *v.i.* تَرَدَّدَ رَاكِبًا ـ دَارَ رَاكِبًا.

Outrider, *n.* A summoner, مُخْضِر ـ مُنَادٍ. A riding attendant, رَكِيبٌ مِنَ ٱلْخَدَّامِينَ.

Outrigger, *n.* سَارِيَةٌ فِي جَانِبِ ٱلْمَرْكَبِ; *from the Italian,* مَتَافُورَة.

Outright, *ad.* At once, عَلَى ٱلْفَوْرِ ـ حَالًا. Entirely, جَمْعَاءَ ـ بِٱلتَّمَامِ ـ كَافَّةً ـ جُمْلَةً ـ بَتَّةً ـ كَتْعَاءَ. I bought the house —, إِشْتَرَيْتُ ٱلدَّارَ جَمْعَاءَ كَتْعَاءَ.

Outrival, *v.t.* فَاضَلَ.

Outrun, *v.t.* To surpass in running, سَبَقَ ـ فَاتَ. To exceed, to be immoderate in, أَفْرَطَ فِي. He outran his income, صَرَفَ أَكْثَرَ مِنْ مَدْخُولِهِ.

Outsail, *v.t.* سَبَقَ ـ سَبَقَ ٱلسَّفِينَةَ مَحْرًا.

Outsell, *v.t.* To sell more than, بَاعَ أَكْثَرَ مِن ـ زَادَ ٱلْبَيْعَ عَلَى. To gain a higher price than, أَفْضَلَ ـ أَدْرَكَ ثَمَنًا أَوْفَرَ مِنْ فُلَانٍ فِي تِجَارَتِهِ أَكْثَرَ مِنْ فُلَانٍ.

Outset, *n.* إِفْتِتَاح ـ أَوَّل ـ شُرُوع ـ إِبْتِدَاء ـ بُدَاءَة.

Outshine, *v.t.* To excel in brightness, فَاقَ فِي ـ زَادَ رَوْنَقًا عَلَى ٱلضِّيَاءِ. *See also to* Excel, *v.t.*

Outside, *n.* The outward part, ٱلْخَارِجُ. Superficial appearance, ٱلظَّاهِرُ. The utmost, ٱلْغَايَةُ ـ ٱلنِّهَايَةُ; the most, ٱلْأَكْثَرُ ـ ٱلْأَغْلَبُ. At the —, بِٱلْكَثِيرِ ـ بِٱلْأَكْثَرِ.

Outside, *a.* بَرَّانِيّ ـ خَارِج. On the —, without, بَرًّا ـ فِي ٱلْخَارِجِ.

Outside, *ad.* بَرًّا ـ فِي ٱلْخَارِجِ. I sat —, جَلَسْتُ بَرًّا. I went — the house, خَرَجْتُ بَرًّا.

Outskirt, *n.* Extremity, طَرَف ـ حَدّ. The — of a town, ضَاحِيَةُ مَدِينَةٍ *pl.* ضَوَاحِي.

Outspoken, *a.* مُتَكَلِّم ـ مُصَارِحٌ فِي ٱلْكَلَامِ ـ نَاصِحٌ فِي ٱلْكَلَامِ ـ غَيْرُ كَتُوم ـ بِصَرَاحَةٍ. To be —, frank, unreserved, with, إِنْبَسَطَ إِلَى.

Outspread, *v.t.* To spread open, نَشَرَ ـ فَرَشَ ـ بَسَطَ. To extend, مَدَّ ـ نَدَحَ. *See also to* Spread, *v.t.*

Outspread, *v.i.* To spread open, إِفْتَرَشَ ـ إِنْبَسَطَ. To extend, إِمْتَدَحَ ـ تَمَدَّحَ ـ إِمْتَدَّ. *See also to* Spread, *v.i.*

Outspreading, *a.* مُمْتَدّ ـ مُفْرِش. Branching, مُتَشَعِّب.

Outstanding, *a.* Not collected, غَيْرُ مَجْمُوعٍ ـ غَيْرُ مَلْمُومٍ. Not reaped, زَرْع ـ غَيْرُ مَحْصُودٍ. Not paid, لَمْ يُوفَ ـ غَيْرُ مَدْفُوعٍ.

Outstanding debts, دَيْنٌ بَاقٍ ـ مَطْلُوبَات ـ مَطْلُوب.

Outstare, *v.t.* *See to* Outface, *v.t.*

Out-street, *n.* زُقَاقٌ فِي خَارِجِ ٱلْبَلَدِ ـ سِكَّةٌ فِي ضَاحِيَةِ ٱلْمَدِينَةِ.

Outstretch, *v.t.* To extend far, بَسَطَ ـ مَدَّدَ ـ نَدَحَ بَعِيدًا. To expand, مَدَّ ـ وَسَّعَ ـ مَطَّ. *See also to* Expand, Extend, *v.t.*

Outstretched, *a.* Extended, مُنْبَسِط ـ مُمْتَدّ. Expanded, مُمْتَدّ ـ مُتَّسِع ـ مُمْتَطّ. With an — arm, بِذِرَاعٍ رَفِيعَةٍ. With — or open arms, of a welcome, بِٱسْتِقْبَالٍ ـ بِيَدٍ مُمْتَدَّةٍ ـ بِتَرَحُّبٍ.

Outstride, *v.t.* إِخْتَطَى ـ تَخَطَّى ـ فَاقَ فَسْحًا.

Outstrip, *v.t.* To surpass, excel, أَنَافَ عَلَى ـ بَرَعَ ـ بَرَزَ عَلَى. To outrun, سَبَقَ. I outstripped him, سَبَقْتُهُ ـ أَتْلَيْتُهُ. To outstrip, of a horse coming in first in a race, سَبَقَ ٱلْفَرَسُ فِي ٱلْحَلْبَةِ. To endeavour to outstrip, فَارَطَ ـ بَارَى.

Out-swear, *v.t.* Of profane swearing, أَنَافَ عَلَى فِي ٱلتَّجْدِيفِ.

To belie the oath of another, كَذَّبَ يَمِينَ فُلَانٍ. To exceed in cursing, زَادَ سَبًّا عَلَى ـ أَنَافَ عَلَى ـ فِي ٱلسَّبِّ.

Out-talk, *v.t.* فَاقَ ـ فِي ٱلْقِيلِ وَٱلْقَالِ ـ أَنْمَعَ ـ بِٱلنُّطْقِ.

Out-value, *v.t.* زَادَ ـ ثَمَنًا ـ فَاضَلَ ـ سِعْرًا.

Outvie, *v.t.* غَلَبَ ـ فَاضَلَ ـ فَفَضَلَهُ.

Out-villain, *v.t.* فَاقَ ـ فِي ٱلْخَبَاثَةِ ـ زَادَ خُبْثًا عَلَى

Outvote, *v.t.* حَازَ آرَآءً أَكْثَرَ مِن ـ حَصَّلَ آرَآءَ أَكْثَرَ مِن ـ غَلَبَ ـ بِرَأْيِ ٱلْأَكْثَرِينَ.

Outwalk, *v.t.* سَبَقَ ـ فِي ٱلْمَسِيرِ ـ بَرَزَ عَلَى ـ فِي ٱلْمَشْيِ.

Outwall, *n.* حَائِطٌ بَرَّانِيٌّ ـ سُورٌ خَارِجٌ.

Outward, *a.* Outer, on the outside, بَرَّانِيٌّ ـ خَارِجِيٌّ ـ فِي ٱلْخَارِجِ. Corporeal, جَسَدِيٌّ. Outward appearance, مَنْظَرٌ. The — man, ٱلْإِنْسَانُ ٱلْخَارِجُ. Outward adornment, زِينَةٌ خَارِجَةٌ.

Outward, *n.* بَرَّاةٌ ـ خَارِجٌ ـ مَنْظَرٌ ـ حَضْرَةٌ.

Outward, *ad.* Toward the outside, towards foreign ports, إِلَى ٱلْخَارِجِ ـ إِلَى ٱلْغُرْبَةِ. *See also* Out-bound, *a.*

Outwardly, *ad.* In appearance, فِي ٱلْخَارِجِ ـ ظَاهِرًا ـ فِي ٱلظَّاهِرِ. These buildings appear — beautiful, هٰذِهِ ٱلْأَبْنِيَةُ تَظْهَرُ مِنْ خَارِجٍ جَمِيلَةً.

Out-watch, *v.t.* Of watchfulness, زَادَ يَقْظَةً عَلَى ـ فَاقَ ـ سَهَرًا.

Outwear, *v.t.* *See to* Outlast, *v.t.*

Outweigh, *v.t.* تَرَجَّحَ عَلَى ـ رَجَحَ عَلَى. One of the scales outweighed the other, رَجَحَتْ إِحْدَى ٱلْكِفَّتَيْنِ عَلَى ٱلْأُخْرَى. One of his two speeches outweighed the other, رَجَحَ أَحَدُ قَوْلَيْهِ عَلَى ٱلْآخَرِ. *See also to* Outbalance, *v.t.*

Outwit, *v.t.* To surpass in cunning, خَاتَلَ ـ خَتَلَ ـ آرَبَ ـ بَرَزَ عَلَى ـ فِي ٱلْخِدَاعِ ـ فَاقَ ـ حِيلَةً ـ دَاهَى ـ رَاوَغَ. To overreach, deceive, آرَبَ ـ إِحْتَالَ عَلَى ـ غَدَرَ بِ. To endeavour to —, آرَبَ. The act of endeavouring to —, مُؤَارَبَةٌ.

Outwork, *n.* إِسْتِحْكَامٌ خَارِجِيٌّ *pl.* إِسْتِحْكَامَاتٌ خَارِجِيَّةٌ ـ مِتْرَاسٌ بَرَّانِيٌّ *pl.* مَتَارِيسُ بَرَّانِيَّةٌ.

Outwork, *v.t.* فَاقَ ـ فِي ٱلْعَمَلِ ـ زَادَ ـ كَدًّا عَلَى ـ سَعَى أَكْثَرَ مِن *aor.* يَسْعَى.

Oval, *a.* بَيْضِيٌّ. *See also* Elliptic, *a.*

Oval, *n.* بَيْضِيٌّ ـ فِي شَكْلِ بَيْضَةٍ. *See also* Ellipse, *n.*

Ovarious, *a.* حَاوِي ٱلْبَيْضِ.

Ovarium, *n.* }
Ovary, } مَحَلُّ ٱلْبَيْضِ فِي بَطْنِ ٱلْأُنْثَى.

Ovate, *a.* إِهْلِيلَجِيٌّ ـ بَيْضِيٌّ ـ فِي شَكْلِ ٱلْبَيْضِ.

Ovation, *n.* تَرْحَابٌ ـ تَرْحِيبٌ ـ إِقْبَالٌ ـ مَوْكِبٌ.

Oven, *n.* فُرْنٌ *pl.* أَفْرَانٌ. A clay —, تَنُّورٌ *pl.* تَنَانِيرُ. An — for bread, مَخْبَزٌ. An — in the ground, سَاجُورٌ. The keeper of an —, فَرَّانٌ. An — rake, مِسْجَرَةٌ. Fuel for an —, سَجُورٌ.

Over, *prep.* and *ad.* Above, فَوْقَ ـ عَلَى. Across, قَاطِعٌ ـ عِبْرَ ـ ذَاتَ ٱلصَّوْبِ. More than, أَكْثَرَ مِن. Ended, تَمَّ. Above, beyond, reaching above, مِنْ عَلَى. Upon, فِي ـ عَلَى. Altogether, بِٱلْكُلِّ ـ بِأَسْرِهِ ـ قَاطِبَةً ـ طُرًّا ـ بَتَّةً. Too much, بِٱلزِّيَادَةِ ـ زِيَادَةً.

Over-difficult, صَعْبٌ بِٱلزِّيَادَةِ.

All over, finished, أُكْمِلَ ـ إِنْقَضَى ـ تَمَّ. Everywhere, فِي كُلِّ مَكَانٍ ـ بِٱلْكُلِّ ـ بَتَّةً ـ إِتْمَامًا ـ طُرًّا. Wholly, عُمُومًا ـ أَيْنَمَا كَانَ.

He was black all over, كَانَ كُلُّهُ أَسْوَدَ.

Not over and above, لَا بِزِيَادَةٍ ـ لَا بِكَثِيرٍ.

Over again, ثَانِي مَرَّةٍ ـ أَيْضًا ـ تَكْرِرَةً ـ تَكْرَارًا ـ مِنْ جَدِيدٍ. To do over again, ثَنَّى ـ كَرَّرَ.

Over against, قِبَالَ ـ حِيَالَ ـ بِحِذَآءِ. He sat — him, جَلَسَ بِحِذَائِهِ. My house is — his house, دَارِي حِذَآءَ دَارِهِ.

Over and above, more than, زِيَادَةً عَلَى ; remaining over, فَاضِلٌ. Besides that, دُونَ ذٰلِكَ ـ وَمَعَ ذٰلِكَ. Over and above all this, وَمَعَ هٰذَا كُلِّهِ. To be over and above, more than was required, شَفَّ.

Over and over, again and again, مَرَّةً عَنْ مَرَّةٍ ـ مِرَارًا ـ مِرَارٍ ـ جُمْلَةَ مِرَارٍ. Round and round, of rolling, دَحْرَجَةً عَنْ دَحْرَجَةٍ ـ تَكَرْكُبَةً عَنْ تَكَرْكُبَةٍ. From top to bottom, مِنْ فَوْقُ إِلَى أَسْفَلَ. Always, عَلَى ٱلدَّوَامِ ـ مِنْ غَيْرِ ٱنْقِطَاعٍ ـ دَائِمًا.

To be over, finished, إِنْقَضَى ـ تَمَّ. To exist no longer, زَالَ ـ بَلَغَ أَمَدَهُ ـ إِنْقَضَى بِتَمَامِهِ ـ قَدْ أُكْمِلَ عُدِمَ. It is all over, The winter is over, إِنْقَضَى ٱلشِّتَآءُ. To be over and above, to be redundant, شَفَّ : It was over and above (what was required) about an ell, شَفَّ نَحْوًا مِنْ ذِرَاعٍ.

To be all over, to cover, غَطَا عَلَى ـ غَطَى عَلَى ـ إِغْتَمَرَ ـ إِغْتَطَى (or تَغَطَّى) بِ. The small-pox was all over his body, إِنْتَشَرَ ٱلْجُدَرِيُّ فِي كُلِّ جِلْدِهِ.

To be all over with, قَضَى أَمْرَهُ. It is all over with him, there is no hope of his cure, لَا مَطْمَعَ فِي بُرْئِهِ.

To be almost over, finished, تَمَّ تَقْرِيبًا ـ كَادَ أَنْ يَتِمَّ.

To be almost over with, to approach ruin, loss of fortune, أَشْرَفَ عَلَى ٱلْإِفْلَاسِ ـ عَلَى ٱلتَّلَفِ ; to be on the verge of death, أَشْرَفَ عَلَى ٱلْمَوْتِ.

To have something over, فَضَلَ لِ. To have nothing over, لَمْ يَفْضُلْ لِ.

To remain over and above, فَضَلَ ².

(For other verbs with the suffix "over," *e.g., to* Bring over, *to* Carry over, see under the verbs.)

Over, *a.* Upper, outward, بَرَّانِيٌّ — فَوْقَانِيٌّ.

Overabound, *v.i.* زَادَ ² — تَكَاثَرَ — تَوَافَرَ — يَفِرُ *aor.* وَفَرَ.

Overact, *v.t.* To perform to excess, أَفْرَطَ فِي — بَالَغَ فِي. He overacted his part in the play, theatrical representation, بَالَغَ فِي تَقْلِيدِهِ (or فِي تَشْخِيصِهِ).

Overact, *v.i.* To do something supererogatory, أَنْفَلَ — تَنَفَّلَ — تَطَوَّعَ بِ.

Overalls, *n.* سَرَاوِيلُ *pl.* سِرْوَال.

Over-anxious, *a.* مِقْلَاقٌ لِلْغَايَةِ — زَائِدُ ٱلْإِهْتِمَامِ — مُهْتَمٌّ بِٱلزِّيَادَةِ. He was —, طَمَا بِهِ هَمٌّ وَخَوْفٌ ².

Overarch, *v.t.* *See to* Arch, *v.t.*

Overawe, *v.t.* To restrain by awe, خَشَّى — هَوَّلَ بِ *or* عَلَى. To intimidate, خَوَّفَ — أَدْهَشَ — هَيَّبَ.

Overbalance, *v.t.* *See to* Outbalance, Outweigh, *v.t.*

Overbalance, *n.* Excess of weight or value, رَجْحَان — رُجُوح. Surplus, excess, فَضْل — مُبَالَغَة — نَيِّف — فَرْط — زِيَادَة.

Overbear, *v.t.* To subdue, سَطَا بِ — إِقْتَرَّ عَلَى — أَقْمَعَ *aor.* يَسْطُو — قَهَرَ ².

Overbearing, *a.* مُتَكَبِّر — جَائِر — بَطِر — غِطْرِيس. To behave in an — manner, بَطِرَ ². *See also* Imperious, Insolent, *n.*

Overbid, *v.t.* تَزَايَدَ — زَايَدَ. *See also to* Outbid, *v.t.*

Overboard, *ad.* فِي ٱلْبَحْرِ. To throw —, رَمَى ² (or طَرَحَ ²) فِي ٱلْبَحْرِ. To throw one's self —, رَمَى ² (or أَلْقَى) نَفْسَهُ فِي ٱلْبَحْرِ. To fall —, وَقَعَ فِي ٱلْبَحْرِ *aor.* يَقَعُ.

Overburden, *v.t.* To load to excess, حَمَّلَ فَوْقَ طَاقَتِهِ — ثَقَّلَ عَلَى. To — one's self with, ثَقَّلَ نَفْسَهُ بِ — تَحَمَّلَ بِ فَوْقَ طَاقَتِهِ.

Overburdened, *a.* مُثَقَّل — مُحَمَّلٌ فَوْقَ طَاقَتِهِ. Overburdened with business, غَارِقٌ فِي ٱلْأَشْغَالِ.

Overcast, *v.t.* To darken, أَظْلَمَ عَلَى. To sew over, شَلَّ ². To compute at too high a rate, بَالَغَ فِي ٱلْجُمْلَةِ.

Overcast, *a.* Cloudy, مُظْلِم — مُعْتِم — مُغَيِّم. Overcast with sorrow, غَارِقٌ فِي ٱلْهُمُومِ — مُصَابٌ بِٱلْغَمِّ.

Overcautious, *a.* حَرِيص — مُفْرِطٌ فِي ٱلْإِحْتِيَاطِ — زَائِدُ ٱلْحَذَرِ لِلْغَايَةِ.

Overcharge, *v.t.* To charge too much, أَغْلَى — غَالَى فِي ٱلطَّلَبِ بِٱلثَّمَنِ. To crowd too much, أَفْرَطَ فِي حَشْرِهِ (or فِي تَكْبِيسِهِ). To load, as of fire-arms, too much, أَفْرَطَ فِي تَعْمِيرِ (or فِي تَذْخِيرِ) ...ٱ. *See also to* Overburden, *v.t.*

Overcharge, *n.* An overburden, ثِقْلٌ زَائِدٌ — حِمْلٌ فَوْقَ ٱلطَّاقَةِ. A charge, price asked, over what is proper, طَلَبٌ — مُغَالَاةٌ — غِلَاءٌ زَائِدٌ. An excessive charge, as of fire-arms, تَعْمِيرَةٌ زَائِدَةٌ.

Overcloud, *v.t.* أَظْلَمَ عَلَى. *See also to* Cloud, *v.t.*

Overcome, *v.t.* To get the better of, to vanquish, إِسْتَعَزَّ بِ — تَغَلَّبَ عَلَى — تَسَلَّطَ عَلَى — إِسْتَوْلَى عَلَى — قَهَرَ ² — أَفْلَجَ عَلَى — أَلْجَمَ بِ — غَلَبَ ² — غَلَبَ عَلَى ². To —, as in argument, عَزَّ فِي ٱلْخِطَابِ ² — عَزْعَزَ — بَرَّزَ عَلَى — عَزَّ ². To surpass, excel, فَضَلَ عَلَى ² — بَهَرَ ². To — in litigation, حَاجَّ — حَجَّ ². To —, as a disease or misfortune, فَقَعَ ². To be —, vanquished, إِنْغَلَبَ — تَغَلَّبَ. To be —, as by a disease or misfortune, إِسْتَعَزَّ بِهِ — أُسْتُثْقِلَ مَرَضًا (or مُصِيبَةً). He was — by sleep, إِسْتَعَزَّ بِهِ ٱلنَّوْمُ — أُسْتُثْقِلَ نَوْمًا. He was — by the disease, إِسْتَعَزَّ بِهِ ٱلْمَرَضُ. He was — by his feelings, إِسْتَعَزَّ بِرَوْعِهِ. They were —, as of an army, كَانَتِ ٱلدَّائِرَةُ عَلَيْهِمْ. The moon in its brightness overcame the light of the stars, بَهَرَ ٱلْقَمَرُ ٱلنُّجُومَ ². He overcame the thing by knowledge, رَصَنَ ٱلشَّيْءَ مَعْرِفَةً. He strove to — me and I overcame him, عَازَّنِي فَعَزَزْتُهُ. I contended with him for superiority, in excellence, and I overcame him, فَاضَلْتُهُ فَفَضَلْتُهُ.

Over-confident, *a.* *See* Headstrong, *a.*

Overdo, *v.t.* To cook too much, طَبَخَ ² بِٱلزِّيَادَةِ — أَفْرَطَ فِي طَبْخِهِ; to be overdone, cooked too much, هَرِئَ ² — هَرَى — تَهَرَّى. To do to excess, of anything, أَفْرَطَ فِي. *See also to* Outdo, Overact, *v.t.*

Overdone, *a.* Over-cooked, مَطْبُوخٌ لِلْغَايَةِ — هَارِئ — مُتَهَرِّئ.

Overdose, *n.* أَخْذَةٌ مِنَ ٱلدَّوَاءِ مُفْرِطَةٌ. He took an —, أَفْرَطَ فِي ٱتِّخَاذِ ٱلدَّوَاءِ.

Overdraw, *v.t.* Of money, by cheques on one's banker, بَعَثَ ² صَكَّ حَوَالَةٍ إِلَى صَرَّافِهِ بِمَبْلَغٍ يُنِيفُ عَلَى دَرَاهِمِهِ ٱلْمَوْضُوعَةِ عِنْدَهُ.

Overdress, *v.t.* Of one's self, أَفْرَطَ فِي ٱلتَّزَيُّنِ — بَالَغَ فِي ٱلزِّينَةِ. An overdressed woman, (*colloq.*) إِمْرَأَةٌ مُشَنْتِفَةٌ — إِمْرَأَةٌ صَائِرَةٌ خُصْلَةً وَعُنْقُودًا.

Overdrive, *v.t.* سَاقَ ² فَوْقَ طَاقَتِهِ — إِسْتَكَدَّ.

Overdue, *a.* فَاتَ ² وَقْتُهُ (or وَعْدُهُ).

Over-eager, *a.* مُتَهَوِّر — كَثِيرُ ٱلرَّغْبَةِ — كَثِيرُ ٱلْحُمَيَّا — زَائِدُ ٱلْغَيْرَةِ.

Over-eagerness, *n.* كَثْرَةُ ٱلْغَيْرَةِ — فَرْطُ ٱلْحُمَيَّا — زِيَادَةُ ٱلرَّغْبَةِ — تَهَوُّر.

Overeat, *v.i.* أَفْرَطَ فِي ٱلْأَكْلِ — تَخِمَ فِي ٱلْأَكْلِ ².

Overestimate, *v.t.* To value at too high a price, أَغْلَى — أَغْلَى

أَسْعَرَ-(or سَعَّرَ-)فَوْقَ ثَمَنِهِ – قِيمَتَهُ. To judge too highly of, أَفْرَطَ فِي ٱسْتِحْسَانِهِ ٱلشَّيْءَ – فَضَّلَ. To judge too highly of the power of, أَفْرَطَ فِي تَقْدِيرِ قُوَّتِهِ. To think too highly of one's self, تَعَجَّبَ فِي نَفْسِهِ.

Overeye, *v.t.* To observe, لَاحَظَ – نَظَرَ إِلَى. To superintend, سَايَسَ – بَاشَرَ – نَظَرَ إِلَى.

Overfar, *ad.* بِبُعْدٍ مَدِيدٍ – بِأَبْعَدِ مَسَافَةٍ.

Overfatigue, *v.t.* أَكَلَّ – أَعْيَا-لِلْغَايَةِ – أَتْعَبَ-كَثِيرًا.

Overfatigue, *n.* كَلَال – كَلّ – فَرْطُ ٱلتَّعَبِ – كَثْرَةُ ٱلْإِعْيَاءِ.

Overfeed, *v.t.* أَفْرَطَ فِي تَطْعِيمِهِ; of cattle, أَفْرَطَ فِي إِعْلَافِهِ.

Overflow, *v.t.* To spread over, as water, غَطَا – غَمَرَ – أَفَاضَ – غَشَّى. To cause to overflow, أَطَافَ – أَفَاضَ. To cover, to fill, مَلَّأَ – مَلَأَ – غَطَّى – غَشَّى. The flood overflowed me, غَمَرَنِي ٱلسَّيْلُ. It overflowed the bridge, طَمَا عَلَى ٱلْجِسْرِ. He caused the water to overflow the land, أَفَاضَ ٱلْمِيَاهَ عَلَى ٱلْأَرْضِ. *See also to* Inundate, *v.t.*

Overflow, *v.i.* طَمَا – إِنْغَمَرَ – غَطَا عَلَى – فَاضَ – أَفَاضَ *aor.* يَطْمُو – طَمَى *aor.* يَطْمِي. The wine press overflows with wine, تَفِيضُ ٱلْمَعْصَرَةُ خَمْرًا. The river overflowed, فَاضَ ٱلنَّهْرُ. The vessel overflowed with its contents, فَاضَ ٱلْإِنَاءُ بِمَا فِيهِ.

Overflow, *n.* } A running over, inundation, غِمَار *pl.* غَمْر – غَمِير
Overflowing, } *and* غُمُور – فَيْض – طُمُوّ – فَيَضَانُ ٱلْمِيَاهِ.
Abundance, وَفْرَة – فَيَضَان – ثَرْوَة – كَثْرَة.

Overflowing, *a.* طَامٍ – فَائِض – غَامِر. Overflowing water, مَاءٌ طَامٍ. An — flood, carrying away everything, سَيْلٌ جَارِفٌ.

Over-fond, *a.* زَائِدُ ٱلْوُدِّ – مُتَدَلِّل.

Overgrow, *v.t.* To cover, as herbage, كَسَا – غَطَّى – غَشَّى. To grow beyond, أَنْمَى دُونَ ٱلْ... – نَمَى عَلَى. To rise above, أَشْرَفَ عَلَى – إِسْتَعْلَى عَلَى. *See also to* Outgrow, *v.t.*

Overgrow, *v.i.* To grow beyond the proper size, نَمَا فَوْقَ ٱلْعَادَةِ – ٱلْحَدِّ – أَنْمَى فَوْقَ ٱلْحَدِّ – نَمَى بِإِفْرَاطٍ. To be covered, clad with, تَعَطَّفَ – إِكْتَسَى بِ.

Overgrown, *a.* As with herbage, مُغَطًّى بِ – مُغَشًّى بِ – مُعَطَّفٌ بِ. Grown beyond the proper size, مُفْرِطُ ٱلنُّمُوِّ – مُبَالِغٌ فِي ٱلنَّمَاءِ. The valleys were — with wheat, تَعَطَّفَتِ ٱلْأَوْدِيَةُ بُرًّا.

Overgrowth, *n.* Excessive growth, خِصْب – نُمُوٌّ مُفْرِطٌ. *See also* Exuberance, *n.*

Overhang, *v.t.* To project over, أَشْرَفَ عَلَى. To be suspended over, تَعَلَّقَ بِ. To threaten, هَمَّ بِ – أَوْعَدَ بِ.

Overhanging, *a.* Projecting over, مُشْرِفٌ عَلَى – نَاشِعٌ عَلَى. Having an overhanging upper lip, أَغْسَرُ – كَابِس.

Overharden, *v.t.* To make too hard, شَدَّدَ صَلَابَتَهُ – أَفْرَطَ فِي تَصْلِيبِهِ. To temper too highly, سَقَى-بِٱلزِّيَادَةِ – أَفْرَطَ فِي سَقْيِهِ *aor.* يَسْقِي.

Overhaste, *n.* عَجَلَةٌ مُفْرِطَةٌ – إِسْتِعْجَالٌ زَائِدٌ – فَرْطُ ٱلسُّرْعَةِ.

Overhastiness, *n.* تَهَوُّر – بَادِرَةٌ زَائِدَةٌ – جَزَعٌ زَائِدٌ – فَرْطُ ٱلتَّهَوُّرِ – قِلَّةُ صَبْرٍ.

Overhasty, *a.* قَلِيلُ – سَرِيعُ ٱلطَّيْشِ – هَيِّر – طَائِش – مُتَهَوِّر ٱلصَّبْرِ.

Overhaul, *v.t.* To examine, فَتَّشَ – تَحَرَّى فِي – تَصَفَّحَ – تَفَحَّصَ. To overtake, أَدْرَكَ – أَلْحَقَ – لَحِقَ. To gain upon, سَابَقَ.

Overhead, *ad.* مِنْ فَوْقٍ – فَوْقَ – عَلَى. In the zenith, فِي سَمْتِ ٱلرَّأْسِ. In the sky, heaven, فِي ٱلسَّمَاءِ – فِي ٱلْجَوِّ.

Overhear, *v.t.* سَمِعَ-(or تَسَمَّعَ-)ٱتِّفَاقًا – إِسْتَمَعَ عَلَى. He overheard him while he was riding, إِسْتَمَعَ عَلَيْهِ وَهُوَ رَاكِبٌ.

Overheat, *v.t.* أَفْرَطَ فِي تَسْخِينِهِ; with clothing, كَثَّرَ دِفَاءَهُ. To — one's self, إِحْتَمَى – حَمِيَ.

Overissue, *n.* As of notes, فَرْطُ إِخْرَاجِ (or إِصْدَارِ) ٱلْقَوَائِمِ.

Overlabour, *v.t.* To work too hard, شَغَّلَ-فَوْقَ طَاقَتِهِ – إِسْتَكَدَّهُ. To take too much pains with, دَقَّقَ فِي – أَفْرَطَ فِي كَدِّهِ.

Overlaboured, *a.* *See* Elaborate, *a.*

Overlade, *v.t.* *See to* Overburden, *v.t.*

Overlaid, *a.* Covered with, as of a surface, مَطْلِيٌّ بِ – مُغَشًّى بِ – مُمَوَّهٌ بِ. Lain or slept upon, مُضْطَجَعٌ (or مُضْجَعٌ) عَلَيْهِ.

Overland, *a.* مِنَ ٱلْبَرِّ – بَرِّيٌّ – بِٱلْبَرِّ. The — route, طَرِيقُ ٱلْبَرِّ. They traversed the — route, سَافَرُوا بَرًّا – مَرُّوا عَلَى طَرِيقِ ٱلْبَرِّ.

Overland, *ad.* بِٱلْبَرِّ – بَرًّا.

Over-large, *a.* مُفْرِطُ ٱلْكِبَرِ – كَبِير.

Overlay, *v.t.* To cover, spread over, as of a surface, with, طَلَى-بِ – طَلَا-بِ – غَشَّى-بِ. To lie upon, إِضْطَجَعَ عَلَى. To — one another of many, تَرَاكَبُوا; as feathers, إِطَّرَقُوا. To be on the surface of, عَلَا *aor.* يَعْلُو.

Overlay, *v.i.* To be superincumbent, إِرْتَكَبَ.

Overlaying, *n.* A covering over the surface, طَلْيَة – طَلْيٌ – تَغْشِيَة – غِشْيٌ.

Overleap, *v.t.* *See to* Outleap, *v.t.*

Over-leather, *n.* وَجْهُ ٱلنَّعْلِ *pl.* وُجُوه.

Overlie, *v.t.* To lie over or upon, تَرَكَّبَ عَلَى – إِضْطَجَعَ عَلَى – إِطَّرَقَ عَلَى. *See also to* Overlay, *v.t.*

Overlive, *v.i.* To live too well, أَفْرَطَ فِي ٱلْمَعِيشَةِ – رَفُهَ عَيْشُهُ – عَاشَ مُتَرَفِّهًا.

Overlive, *v.t.* *See to* Outlive, *v.t.*

Overload, *v.t.* *See to* Overburden, *v.t.*

Overlook, *v.t.* To command from a higher place, اِطَّلَعَ عَلَى ـ أَشْرَفَ عَلَى. To view from a higher place, اِطَّلَعَ عَلَى ـ أَشْرَفَ عَلَى ـ شَارَفَ. To — the road, شَرَعَ. To —, as the faults of another, صَفَحَ عَن ـ تَغَمَّدَ ـ غَمَّدَ ـ تَجَاوَزَ. To forgive, عَفَا عَن aor. يَعْفُو. To superintend, نَظَرَ إِلَى ـ سَامَحَ ـ عَن ـ سَايَسَ ـ بَاشَرَ. To omit, as from an account, أَوْهَمَ. To omit, generally, أَسْقَطَ ـ عَدَى عَن ـ ضَلَّ عَنِّي. I overlooked it, ضَلَّ عَنِّي. He is inclined to — several clauses in the treaty, يَمِيلُ أَنْ يَعْدُوَ عَنْ بَعْضِ أَبْوَابٍ فِي ٱلْمُعَاهَدَةِ. He overlooked the people, had a view of them, أَجْبَأَ (or) أَشْرَفَ عَلَى ٱلْقَوْمِ.

Overlooking, *a.* Commanding, مُطَّلِعٌ عَلَى ـ مُشْرِفٌ عَلَى. Overlooking the road, شَارِعٌ *fem.* شَارِعَةٌ *pl.* شُرُوعٌ.

Overlooker, *n.* *See* Looker-on, *n.*

Overmast, *v.t.* أَفْرَطَ فِي تَرْكِيبِ ٱلصَّوَارِي فِي ٱلسَّفِينَةِ.

Overmasted, *a.* An — ship, سَفِينَةٌ زَائِدَةُ ٱلصَّوَارِي.

Overmatch, *v.t.* As in strength, قَوِيَ عَلَى; in numbers, أَنَافَ ـ كَثُرَ ـ عَلَى ـ عَدَدًا. To be overmatched, in strength, اِقْتَوَى عَلَى; in number, تَعَدَّنَ عَلَى.

Overmatch, *n.* Stronger than, أَقْدَرُ مِن ـ أَقْوَى مِن.

Over-measure, *n.* As of quantity, مِقْدَارٌ زَائِدٌ; of long measure, مِقْيَاسٌ زَائِدٌ; of measure of capacity, مِكْيَالٌ زَائِدٌ.

Overmodest, *a.* كَثِيرُ ٱلْحَيَاءِ ـ مُفْرِطُ ٱلْحَيَاءِ.

Overmost, *a.* ٱلَّذِي فَوْقَ ٱلْكُلِّ ـ ٱلْأَعْلَى.

Overmuch, *a.* زَائِدٌ ـ مُفْرِطٌ. Overmuch sorrow, حُزْنٌ مُفْرِطٌ. Lest you should be swallowed up with — sorrow, لِئَلَّا تُبْتَلَعُوا مِنَ ٱلْحُزْنِ ٱلْمُفْرِطِ.

Overmuch, *n.* كَثْرَةٌ ـ زِيَادَةٌ ـ فَرْطٌ.

Overmuch, *ad.* كَثِيرًا ـ بِٱلزِّيَادَةِ. Be not righteous —, لَا تَكُنْ بَارًّا كَثِيرًا.

Overnight, *ad.* The previous night, لَيْلَةَ أَمْسِ ـ ٱللَّيْلَةَ ٱلْبَارِحَةَ.

Overpass, *v.t.* To pass over, عَبَرَ. To go beyond, جَاوَزَ ـ تَجَاوَزَ. To omit, عَدَا عن aor. يَعْدُو ـ أَسْقَطَ. To neglect, سَهَا عَن aor. يَسْهُو ـ أَغْفَلَ ـ تَغَفَّلَ عَن. To leave out, as from an account, أَوْهَمَ. *See also to* Exceed, Excel, *v.t.*

Overpassionate, *a.* كَثِيرُ ٱلْغَضَبِ ـ غَضُوبٌ لِلْغَايَةِ.

Overpast, *a.* Passed away, مُعْتَبَرٌ. Until these troubles are —, إِلَى أَنْ تَعْبُرَ هٰذِهِ ٱلْمَصَائِبُ.

Over-patient, *a.* صَبُورٌ لِلْغَايَةِ ـ كَثِيرُ ٱلصَّبْرِ ـ صَبَّارٌ.

Over-pay, *v.t.* To pay one too much, وَفَّاهُ فَوْقَ حَقِّهِ; to purchase dearly, اِشْتَرَى بِٱلْغَالِي. To recompense too largely, جَزَى بِإِفْرَاطٍ ـ أَفْرَطَ فِي جَزَائِهِ. I overpaid him the debt, جَزَيْتُهُ أَكْثَرَ مِنَ ٱلدَّيْنِ.

Overpeer, *v.t.* *See to* Overlook, *v.t.*

Overpeering, *a.* مُشْرِفٌ ـ حَابٍ ـ حَبِيٌّ. An — mountain, جَبَلٌ حَابٍ. Overpeering sands, showing their breadth, رَمْلٌ حَابٍ.

Overpeople, *v.t.* أَفْرَطَ فِي تَعْمِيرِهِ ٱ... كَثَّرَ فِي ٱلنَّاسِ.

Overpersuade, *v.t.* أَقْنَعَ ـ أَفْرَطَ فِي إِلْحَاحِهِ عَلَى ـ حَاوَلَ ـ أَلْجَأَ بِ. To be overpersuaded by, اِرْتَضَى كُرْهًا.

Overplus, *n.* What is over, فُضُولٌ ـ فَضْلٌ ـ فَرْطٌ ـ زِيَادَةٌ; what is left, بَقِيَّةٌ. The — of the revenue after paying expenses, ٱلزَّائِدُ مِنَ ٱلْإِيرَادِ بَعْدَ أَدَاءِ ٱلْمَصَارِيفِ. The — of revenue over expenditure, ٱلزَّائِدُ مِنَ ٱلْإِيرَادِ عَلَى ٱلْمَصْرُوفِ.

Overpoise, *v.t.* *See to* Outbalance, Outweigh, *v.t.*

Overpoise, *n.* *See* Overbalance, *n.*

Overpower, *v.t.* To bear down by force, سَطَا بِ ـ اِعْتَزَّ عَلَى aor. يَسْطُو ـ اِسْتَعْلَى عَلَى ـ قَوِيَ عَلَى. To —, as a misfortune, فَقَعَ; as a disease, اِسْتَعَزَّ عَلَى. To prostrate, throw on the ground, جَعَفَ. To be overpowered by, in a general sense, أَسْتَعِزُّ بِ. *See also to* Overcome, *v.t.*

Overpowering, *a.* Distressing, مُهْلِكٌ ـ مُتْعِبٌ ـ عَزِيزٌ. Irresistible, لَا يُقَاوَمُ ـ عِزٌّ. Applied to a torrent, جُحَافٌ ـ جُعَافٌ ـ جَاعِفٌ.

Overpress, *v.t.* To bear upon with force, شَدَّ عَلَى. To follow closely, لَاحَقَ ـ تَتَبَّعَ. To importune for, to constrain, صَادَرَ عَلَى ـ لَجَّ عَلَى. To compel, اِضْطَرَّ إِلَى ـ اِسْتَكْرَهَ. *See also to* Overdrive, Overpower, Overwhelm, *v.t.*

Overprize, *v.t.* بَالَغَ فِي عِزِّ ٱلشَّيْءِ ـ أَفْرَطَ فِي ٱعْتِبَارِ ٱلشَّيْءِ ـ زَادَ فِي ٱعْتِبَارِ ٱلشَّيْءِ.

Overrate, *v.t.* *See to* Over-estimate, *v.t.*

Overreach, *v.t.* To go beyond, جَاوَزَ ـ سَبَقَ. To come up to, لَحِقَ بِ ـ لَحِقَ. To rise above, عَلَا عَلَى ـ أَشْرَفَ عَلَى aor. يَعْلُو ـ اِسْتَعْلَى عَلَى. To deceive by artifice, اِحْتَالَ عَلَى ـ غَبَنَ ـ غَبَنَ فِي ـ مَكَرَ بِ ـ غَدَرَ بِ. To cheat, deceive, غَشَّ ـ جَوَّنَ ـ خَدَعَ. To — one's self, stretch one's self too much;. *see under* Overstretch, *v.t.*

Overreaching, *n.* The act of cheating, غَدْرٌ ـ مَكْرٌ ـ غَبْنٌ ـ غِشٌّ ـ جَوْنٌ. The act of asking too much for a thing, طَمَاعِيَةٌ.

Over-ready, *a.* Too prompt, كَثِيرُ ٱلْفَوْرِ ـ زَائِدُ ٱلسُّرْعَةِ ـ مُفْرِطُ ٱلْخِفَّةِ.

Override, *v.* To ride beyond the strength of, ـَ رَكِبَ فَوْقَ طَاقَتِهِ. *See also to* Overrule, *v.t.*

Over-ripe, *a.* مُسْتَوٍ بِٱلزِّيَادَةِ ـ زَائِدُ ٱلنُّضْجِ.

Over-ripen, *v.t.* Of fruit, أَفْرَطَ فِي إِنْضَاجِ ٱلْأَثْمَارِ.

Over-ripen, *v.i.* إِسْتَوَى بِٱلزِّيَادَةِ ـ ـَ نَضِجَ بِٱلزِّيَادَةِ.

Overrule, *v.t.* To control, check, ـَ مَنَعَ ـ حَاسَرَ ـ ـَ قَمَعَ. To object to, إِعْتَرَضَ عَلَى ـ إِعْتَرَضَ عَلَى. To overpower, إِسْتَعْلَى عَلَى ـ ـَ قَوِيَ عَلَى. To overrule, do away with, بَطَّلَ ـ ²أَكَلَ: This tradition overrules the other traditions, هٰذَا ٱلْحَدِيثُ يَأْكُلُ ٱلْأَحَادِيثَ ٱلْأُخَرَ.

Overruling, *a.* Directing, controlling, سَائِس ـ حَاكِم ـ ضَابِط ـ مُدَبِّر ـ مُتَسَلِّطٌ عَلَى. Checking, restraining, قَامِع ـ مَانِع ـ مَنَّاع ـ حَاسِر.

Overrun, *v.t.* To outrun, ²فَاتَ ـ ²سَبَقَ. To exceed, أَفْرَطَ فِي ـ جَاوَزَ فِي. To overgrow, to cover, as herbage, غَشَّى ـ غَطَّى. To infest, ²غَزَا ـ ـَ إِمْتَلَأَ مِن. To ravage, تَوَغَّلَ فِي ـ ²غَارَ عَلَى ـ ²دَاسَ عَلَى ـ إِسْتَوْلَى عَلَى. To tread under foot, ²دَاسَ ـ كَبَسَ ـ ـَ دَعَسَ. To overrun, of lines, حَوَّلَ ٱلْأَسْطُرَ. *See also to* Infest, *v.t.*

Overrun, *v.t.* *See to* Overflow, *v.i.*

Oversea, *a.* بَرَّانِيٌّ ـ أَجْنَبِيٌّ ـ مِنْ عِبْرِ ٱلْبَحْرِ.

Oversee, *v.t.* To superintend, ²نَظَرَ إِلَى ـ بَاشَرَ ـ سَايَسَ. *See also to* Inspect, *v.t.*

Overseer, *n.* نَقِيب ـ مُبَاشِر ـ نُظَّار .pl نَاظِر ـ وُكَلَاءُ .pl وَكِيلٌ عَلَى ـ نُقَبَاءُ .pl. *See also* Inspector, *n.*

Overset, *v.t.* *See to* Overturn, *v.t.*

Overshade, *v.t.* } To throw a shade over, ظَلَّلَ ـ فَيَّأَ. To be
Overshadow, } overshadowed, تَظَلَّلَ ـ تَفَيَّأَ. To shelter, آوَى. To protect, shield, جَوَّبَ عَلَى ـ ـِ عَصَمَ ـ ـِ خَفَرَ ـ ²حَمَى.

Overshadowing, *a.* Throwing a shade, مُظَلِّل. Protecting, عَاصِم ـ خَافِر ـ حَامٍ.

Overshoe, *n.* جُرْمُوق .pl جَرَامِيق.

Overshoot, *v.t.* To shoot beyond the mark, ـِ رَمَى دُونَ ٱلْهَدَفِ ـ جَاوَزَ ٱلنِّيشَانَ ـ فَصَاعِدًا. To go too far in, to exceed in, بَالَغَ فِي ـ أَفْرَطَ فِي ـ جَاوَزَ فِي.

Overshoot, *v.i.* To fly above, عَلَا .aor يَعْلُو ـ عَلَا عَلَى .aor يَعْلُو.

Overshot, *a.* An — wheel, دُولَاب .pl دَوَالِيب ـ نَاعُورَة .pl نَوَاعِير.

Oversight, *n.* Inspection, superintendence, نَظَارَة ـ رُؤْيَة ـ إِدَارَة ـ مُنَاظَرَة ـ سِيَاسَة ـ مُبَاشَرَة : having the — of, ...مُدِيرُ ٱلْ ـ مُوَكَّلٌ عَلَى ـ مُتَكَلِّفٌ بِٱلنَّظَرِ فِي. A failing to notice, omission, خَطَاء ـ قُصُور ـ سَهْوَة ـ سَهْو.

Overskip, *v.t.* *See to* Overleap, *v.t.*

Oversleep, *v.i.* To — one's self, إِسْتَثْقَلَ نَوْمًا ـ ²سَبَخَ ـ تَأَخَّرَ فِي ٱلنَّوْمِ.

Oversoon, *ad.* بِدَارًا ـ بَدْرًا ـ قَبْلَ ٱلْوَقْتِ.

Overspent, *a.* Wearied outright, تَعِبٌ لِلْغَايَةِ ـ مُكَلّ.

Overspread, *v.t.* To cover over, عَلَا .aor يَعْلُو ـ غَطَا .aor يَغْطُو ـ غَشَّى. To —, as the night covering any thing, غَطَّى عَلَى. To comprehend, involve, إِرْتَكَبَ ـ تَضَمَّنَ. To scatter over, ²رَشَّ عَلَى ـ ²فَرَشَ عَلَى. To overspread wholly, ²عَمَّ: the disease overspread them, عَمَّهُمُ ٱلْمَرَضُ. His face was —, flushed, with beauty, ²دَمَّ وَجْهُهُ حُسْنًا. *See also to* Outspread, Overrun, *v.t.*

Overspread, *v.i.* To be scattered over, تَنَشَّرَ عَلَى ـ إِنْتَشَرَ عَلَى ـ تَرَشَّشَ عَلَى ـ إِفْتَرَشَ عَلَى ـ ـِ شَعَّ فِي. To —, as a tree, أَغْطَى. To branch out, إِنْشَعَبَ ـ تَشَعَّبَ: all the country was overspread by them, تَشَعَّبَ مِنْهُمْ كُلُّ ٱلْبِلَادِ.

Overspreading, *a.* As of a tree, light, *etc.*, مُتَشَعِّب ـ مُشِعّ ـ مُغَطّ ـ شَارِق.

Overstate, *v.t.* أَفْرَطَ فِي ٱلتَّعْبِيرِ ـ بَالَغَ فِي ٱلْإِفَادَةِ.

Overstep, *v.t.* تَجَاوَزَ ـ جَاوَزَ.

Overstock, *v.t.* To fill too full, أَطَافَ ـ أَفَاضَ. To supply with more than is wanted, ـَ شَحَنَ بِٱلزِّيَادَةِ ـ وَفَّرَ ـ ²سَدَّ ـ كَثَّرَ.

Overstock, *n.* وَفْرَة ـ وَفْر ـ زِيَادَة ـ كَثْرَة ـ فُضُول ـ فَرْط ـ شَحْنٌ زَائِد.

Overstocked, *a.* شَاحِن ـ مُفْعَم ـ مَوْفُور ـ فَاضِل ـ مُفْرَط ـ مَشْحُون.

Overstore, *v.t.* *See to* Overstock, *v.t.*

Overstrain, *v.t.* To stretch to excess, ²مَدَّ (or ²مَطَّ) بِٱلزِّيَادَةِ ـ وَسَّعَ بِٱلزِّيَادَةِ. To push too far, to wrest, put a wrong construction upon, حَرَّفَ ـ تَعَسَّفَ فِي. To — one's self, make too great efforts, أَفْرَطَ فِي ٱلْإِجْتِهَادِ ـ تَقَصَّى ـ تَصَلَّبَ ـ أَفْرَطَ فِي ٱلْكَدِّ. To — one's self in stretching, تَشَنَّجَ.

Overswell, *v.t.* To rise above. *See to* Overflow, Overreach, *v.t.*

Overt, *a.* وَاضِح ـ ظَاهِر ـ مُبِين ـ جَلِيّ ـ عَالِن.

Overtake, *v.t.* To come up with, أَلْحَقَ ـ أَدْرَكَ ـ ـَ لَحِقَ. To come upon suddenly, ²غَالَ ـ ـَ بَدَهَ ـ بَادَهَ. To —, as a misfortune, أُصِيبَ بِ ـ ـِ نَزَلَ بِ. I walked till I overtook him,

مَشِيتُ حَتَّى أَدْرَكَنْهُ . Distress overtook me, أَدْرَكَنِي ٱلْجَهْدُ . A calamity overtook him, غَالَتْهُ غُوْلٌ . Punishment overtook them, حَلَّ بِهِمِ ٱلْعَذَابُ . They overtook one another, of many, تَدَارَكُوا . He pursued after such an one but did not overtake him, طَلَبَ فُلَانًا وَمَا شَقَّ غُبَارَهُ .

Overtask, *v.t.* بَهَرَ ‒ أَفْرَطَ فِي كَدِّهِ ‒ شَدَّدَ عَلَى‒بِٱلشُّغْلِ .

Overtax, *v.t.* To tax to excess, كَثَّرَ ٱلْجِزْيَةَ ‒ أَفْرَطَ عَلَى‒ٱلْوَضَائِعَ عَلَى . *See also to* Overtask, *v.t.*

Overthrow, *v.t.* To throw down, to prostrate, ‒ جَعَبَ ‒ جَعَفَ ‒ كَبَّ ‒ أَكَبَّ ‒ هَدَّ ‒ هَدَّمَ . To pull down, raze, هَدَّ . To defeat, غَلَبَ عَلَى ‒ قَهَرَ ‒ هَزَمَ ‒ كَسَرَ ‒ أَنْجَحَ بِ . To be overthrown, thrown down, إِنْجَعَبَ ‒ إِنْجَعَفَ ‒ إِنْكَبَّ . To be overthrown, razed, إِنْهَدَّ ‒ إِنْهَدَمَ ‒ تَهَدَّمَ . To be overthrown, defeated, إِنْهَزَمَ ‒ إِنْكَسَرَ . *See also to* Overturn, *v.t.*

Overthrow, *n.* The being prostrated, إِنْجِعَاب ‒ إِنْكِبَاب . The being razed, إِنْهِدَام ‒ تَهَدُّم . *See also* Defeat, *n.*

Overthwart, *a.* مُعْتَرِض ‒ مَعْكُوس .

Overtime, *n.* Time of labour beyond the stated time, شُغْلٌ فَوْقَ ٱلْوَقْتِ ٱلْمَحْدُودِ .

Overtire, *v.t.* *See to* Overfatigue, *v.t.*

Overtly, *ad.* عَلَانِيَةً ‒ صَرَاحَةً ‒ جَهْرَةً . *See also* Openly, *ad.*

Overtop, *v.t.* } As in height, ‒ يَعْلُو *aor.* عَلَا عَلَى ‒ أَشْرَفَ عَلَى
Overtower, } إِسْتَعْلَى عَلَى . In superiority, بَرَعَ . It overtopped what was around it, أَشْرَفَ عَلَى مَا حَوْلَهُ . It overtopped the bridge, طَمَى فَوْقَ ٱلْجِسْرِ .

Overtrade, *v.i.* To trade beyond one's capital, ‒ تَجَرَ فَوْقَ طَاقَتِهِ إِتَّجَرَ فَوْقَ رَأْسِ مَالِهِ .

Overture, *n.* A proposal, opening, تَخْيِير ‒ عَرْض ‒ مَعْرُوض *pl.* مَعْرُوضَات ‒ قَوْل ‒ فَتْحُ بَابٍ . A commencement, opening, إِفْتِتَاح ‒ فَاتِحَة . To make overtures, أَجْرَى ٱلْمَعْرُوضَاتِ . To make overtures to, فَاتَحَ ‒ عَرَضَ عَلَى‒ٱلْمَعْرُوضَاتِ .

Overturn, *v.t.* To turn upside down, ‒ جَعَبَ ‒ جَعَّبَ جَعَفَ ‒ قَلَبَ ‒ نَكَسَ ‒ خَرَّبَ . To destroy, دَمَّرَ ‒ أَبَادَ . *See also to* Demolish, Overthrow, *v.t.*; *also under* Upside-down, *a.*

Over-value, *v.t.* *See to* Overestimate, Overprize, *v.t.*

Overweening, *a.* ‒ زَخِيف ‒ مُعْجَب ‒ مُتَعَجِّبٌ فِي نَفْسِهِ مُفْتَخِر .

Overweeningly, *ad.* بِتَعَجُّبٍ ‒ زَخْفًا .

Overweigh, *v.t.* *See to* Outbalance, Outweigh, *v.t.*

Overweight, *n.* رُجُوح ‒ تَرْجِيح ‒ رَجْحَان ‒ وَزْنٌ زَائِدٌ .

Overwhelm, *v.t.* To surround, إِشْتَمَلَ عَلَى ‒ أَشْمَلَ . To immerse, أَغْرَقَ ‒ غَمَّرَ ‒ غَمَرَ . To sweep away, جَرَفَ ‒ جَرَّفَ . He overwhelmed them with kindness, أَشْمَلَهُمْ ‒ غَمَّرَهُمْ بِٱلْإِحْسَانِ خَيْرًا . *See also to* Overbear, Overcome, *v.t.*

Overwhelming, *a.* *See* Overpowering, *a.*

Overwhelmingly, *ad.* إِشْمَالًا ‒ إِغْرَاقًا ‒ جَرْفَةً ‒ لِلْغَايَةِ .

Overwise, *a.* مُتَعَجِّب . *See also* Conceited, *a.*

Overwork, *v.t.* *See to* Overlabour, Overtask, *v.t.*

Over-wrought, *a.* *See* Elaborate, *a.*

Over-zeal, *n.* ‒ كَثْرَةُ ٱلْغَيْرَةِ ‒ فَرْطُ ٱلْحَرَارَةِ ‒ تَعَصُّب ‒ حَمَاسَة تَحَمُّس .

Over-zealous, *a.* ‒ زَائِدُ ٱلْغَيْرَةِ ‒ مُفْرِطُ ٱلْحَرَارَةِ ‒ كَثِيرُ ٱلْغَيْرَةِ أَحْمَس ‒ مُتَحَمِّس .

Ovicular, *a.* بَيْضِيٌّ ‒ مُخْتَصٌّ بِٱلْبَيْضِ .

Ovine, *a.* Pertaining to sheep, ضَانِيٌّ ‒ مُخْتَصٌّ بِٱلْغَنَمِ .

Oviparous, *a.* بَيُوض ‒ بَيَّاضَة ‒ بَيِّضُ ٱلْبَيْضِ ‒ وَاضِعَةُ ٱلْبَيْضِ .

Oviform, }
Ovoid, *a.* } فِي هَيْئَةِ ٱلْبَيْضَةِ ‒ بِشَكْلِ ٱلْبَيْضَةِ . *See also* Elliptical, *a.*
Ovoidal, }

Ovum, *n.* An egg, بَيْضَة *coll.* بَيْض *pl.* بَيْضَات .

Owe, *v.t.* To owe or be in debt to, مَدْيُونٌ لِ ‒ عَلَيْهِ لِ ‒ عَلَيْهِ دَيْنٌ لِ ‒ عِنْدَهُ لِ ‒ فِي ذِمَّتِهِ إِلَى . He owes a debt, عَلَيْهِ دَيْنٌ . Muhammad owes 'Aly one hundred piastres, مُحَمَّدٌ مَدْيُونٌ لِعَلِيٍّ بِمِئَةِ غِرْشٍ ‒ مُحَمَّدٌ عَلَيْهِ لِعَلِيٍّ مِئَةُ غِرْشٍ . Nâsir owes me fifty purses, نَاصِرٌ مَدْيُونٌ لِي بِخَمْسِينَ ‒ لِي عَلَى نَاصِرٍ خَمْسُونَ كِيسًا كِيسًا . You owe me, لِي عَلَيْكَ . He owes you, لَكَ عَلَيْهِ دَيْنٌ . A debt is owed to him, لَهُ دَيْنٌ . Owe no one anything, لَا تَكُنْ مَدْيُونًا لِأَحَدٍ بِشَيْءٍ . Pay what you owe me, أَوْفِنِي مَا لِي عَلَيْكَ . I will pay what he owes, أَنَا أُوفِي مَا عَلَيْهِ مِنَ ٱلدَّيْنِ . I acknowledge that I owe to the bearer of this note the sum of one thousand liras, عِنْدِي وَفِي ذِمَّتِي إِلَى نَاقِلِ هٰذِهِ ٱلْوَرَقَةِ مَبْلَغُ أَلْفِ لِيرَةٍ .

Owe, *v.t.* To be bound by obligation, ‒ لَزِمَ عَلَى ‒ إِلْتَزَمَ بِ أَلْزَمَ بِ . To owe as a duty, ‒ حَقَّ عَلَى ‒ يَجِبُ *aor.* وَجَبَ عَلَى حَلَّ عَلَى . He owes his success to his brother, كَانَ أَخُوهُ سَبَبَ نَجَاحِهِ ‒ نَجَاحُهُ مِنْ فَضْلِ أَخِيهِ . This is all owing to you, هٰذَا كُلُّهُ مِنْكَ . This is all owing to your kindness, هٰذَا كُلُّهُ مِنْ فَضْلِكَ وَإِحْسَانِكَ . *See also under* Obligation, *n.*

Owing, *a.* Due, obligatory, مَطْلُوب ‒ ضَرُورِيٌّ ‒ حَقٌّ . A sum owing to, مَبْلَغٌ مُسْتَحِقٌّ لِ ‒ دَيْنٌ لِ .

Owl, *n.* أَبْوَام *pl.* بُومَة ‒ بُوم ‒ هَامَات *pl.* هَامَة . The screech —, صُوعٌ .

Owlet, *n.* فَرْخُ ٱلْبُوم *pl.* فِرَاخ.

Owlish, *a.* مِثْلَ ٱلْبُوم.

Owl-light, *n.* *See* Nightfall, *n.*

Owl-like, *a.* بُوم — بُومِيٌّ — مِثْلَ ٱلْبُوم.

Own, *a.* خَاصَّة — لِ — مَا هُوَ لِنَفْسِهِ — مَا هُوَ لَهُ ; *vulg.* بِتَاع *fem.* بِتَاعَة — مَتَاع *fem.* مَتَاعَة — مَال ; (and as a simple pronoun with the proper pronominal suffix attached, *e.g.*) This is my own book, هٰذَا ٱلْكِتَابُ مَالِي — هٰذَا كِتَابِي — هٰذَا ٱلْكِتَابُ لِي. May I not do what I like with my own? أَمَا يَحِلُّ لِي أَنْ أَفْعَلَ مَا أُرِيدُ بِمَالِي. He is not his own, مَا هُوَ لِنَفْسِهِ. You are not your own, لَسْتُمْ لِأَنْفُسِكُمْ. Own, one's own people, set, خَاصَّة. One's own family, أَهْل — عَايِلَة. One's own followers, أَتْبَاع. The King's Own (regiment,) ٱلْكَتِيبَةُ ٱلْهُمَايُونِيَّةُ ٱلْخَاصَّة.

Own, *v.t.* To be the proprietor of, to possess, مَلَكَ — حَوَى — حَازَ. To admit, acknowledge, قَبِلَ — أَقَرَّ بِ — سَلَّمَ بِ — أَجَابَ إِلَى. To own, as of a fault, أَقَرَّ بِ — إِعْتَرَفَ بِ.

Owner, *n.* رَبٌّ *pl.* أَرْبَاب — مَالِك — صَاحِب *pl.* أَصْحَاب — ذُو *pl.* ذَوُو ; *fem.* ذَاتُ *pl.* ذَوَاتُ — وَلِيٌّ *pl.* أَوْلِيَآء ; *fem.* وَلِيَّة *pl.* وَلِيَّات.

Ownership, *n.* مِلْكَة — مُلْكَة — مَلَكَة — مَلَاكَة.

Ox, *n.* ثَوْر *pl.* ثِيرَان — بَقَرَة *pl.* بَقَرَات *or* بَقَر *or* بُقَّار — بَقَر *pl.* أَبْقَار *and* أَبْقُر.

Oxalic acid, *n.* حَامِضُ ٱلْحُمَّيْضِ.

Ox-eye, *n.* The plant, بَهَارُ ٱلْبَرِّ — خَسْوَة — عَرَارَة — عَيْنُ ٱلْبَقَرِ.

Ox-gall, *n.* صَفْرَآء (*or* مَرَارَةُ) ٱلْبَقَرِ.

Ox-goad, *n.* مِنْسَاسُ ٱلْبَقَرِ *pl.* مَنَاسِيس. *See also* Goad, *n.*

Ox-herd, *n.* بَقَّار — رَاعِي ٱلْبَقَرِ *pl.* رُعَاة.

Oxide, *n.* مِلْحٌ مُرَكَّبٌ مِنْ أَصْلِ ٱلْحَوَامِضِ وَأُسٍّ آخَرَ — أُكْسِيد.

Oxidate, *v.t.* / Oxidize, } صَيَّرَ مِلْحًا مُرَكَّبًا مِنْ أَصْلِ ٱلْحَوَامِضِ وَأُسٍّ آخَرَ — أَكْسَدَ. To be oxidized, تَأَكْسَدَ.

Oxidation, *n.* مُرَكَّبٌ مِنْ أَصْلِ ٱلْحَوَامِضِ وَأُسٍّ آخَرَ — إِكْسَاد.

Oxygen, *n.* أَصْلُ ٱلْحَوَامِضِ — أُمُّ ٱلْحُمُوضَةِ — مُوَلِّدُ ٱلْحُمُوضَةِ — أُكْسِيجِين وَهُوَ مَادَّةٌ تَدْخُلُ فِي تَرْكِيبِ ٱلْهَوَآءِ وَتَنْفَعُ لِلْاِحْتِرَاقِ وَتَنَفُّسِ ٱلْحَيَوَانَاتِ ذَوَاتِ ٱلدَّمِ ٱلْأَحْمَرِ.

Oxygenate, *v.t.* / Oxygenize, } جَعَلَ فِيهِ ٱلْأُكْسِيجِين.

Oxygenation, *n.* تَرْكِيبٌ بِٱلْأُكْسِيجِين.

Oxygenous, *a.* مِنْ أَصْلِ ٱلْحَوَامِضِ — مُتَعَلِّقٌ بِأُمِّ ٱلْحُمُوضَةِ — أُكْسِيجِينِيٌّ.

Oxy-hydrogen, *n.* بُورِيٌّ يُسْتَعْمَلُ لِتَوْلِيدِ ٱلْحَرَارَةِ بِإِحْمَاءِ ٱلْأُكْسِيجِينِ وَٱلْهِيدْرُوجِينِ مَعًا.

Oxymel, *n.* سِكَنْجَبِين.

Oxytone, *a.* Having an acute sound, جَهُورُ ٱلصَّوْتِ.

Oxytone, *n.* صَوْتٌ جَهُورٌ.

Oyer, *n.* إِسْتِمَاع. Court of Oyer and Terminer, مَحْكَمَةٌ لِاسْتِمَاعِ ٱلدَّعَاوِي وَفَصْلِهَا.

Oyez, *int.* ٱلسُّكُوتُ — ٱلسَّكْتَة.

Oyster, *n.* حَيَوَانٌ صَدَفِيٌّ *pl.* حَيَوَانَات — مَحَارَة *coll.* مَحَارٌ *pl.* مَحَاوِرُ — أُسْتَرِيدِيَا.

Oyster-bed, *n.* مَحَلُّ ٱلْمَحَارِ.

Oyster-fisher, *n.* صَيَّادُ ٱلْمَحَارِ.

Oyster-fishery, *n.* مَصِيدُ ٱلْمَحَارِ.

Oyster-man, *n.* بَيَّاعُ ٱلْمَحَارِ.

Oyster-shell, *n.* مَحَارَة *coll.* مَحَارٌ *pl.* مَحَاوِرُ — صَدَف *pl.* أَصْدَاف.

Oz., *n.* عِبَارَةٌ عَنْ لَفْظَةِ Ounce وَهِيَ ٱلْأُوقِيَّةُ.

Ozone, *n.* حَالَةٌ مِنْ حَالَاتِ ٱلْأُكْسِيجِينِ ٱلْمَوْجُودِ فِي ٱلْهَوَآءِ — أُزُون.

P.

P. *or* p., (The contraction for "page,") تَرْخِيمُ لَفْظَةِ صَحِيفَةٍ. Pp. تَرْخِيمُ لَفْظَةِ صَحِيفَتَيْنِ أَوْ أَكْثَر. مِثَالُ ذٰلِكَ p. 8. مَعْنَاهُ ٱلصَّحِيفَةُ ٱلثَّامِنَةُ

P.M., (The contraction for *post meridiem*,) تَرْخِيمُ لَفْظَتَي بَعْدَ ٱلظُّهْرِ مِثَالُ ذٰلِكَ 5·30 p.m. مَعْنَاهُ ٱلسَّاعَةُ ٱلْخَامِسَةُ وَنِصْفٌ بَعْدَ ٱلظُّهْرِ.

Pabular, *a.* } يُقْتَاتُ بِهِ ـ قُوتِيٌّ ـ مَأْكُول.
Pabulous, }

Pabulum, *n.* Food, مَعَاش ـ غِذَآء ـ قُوت; for cattle, عَلِيق. Fuel, وَقِيد.

Pace, *n.* A step, خَطْوَة *pl.* خَطَوَات. The space between the two feet in walking, خُطْوَة *pl.* خُطُوات. Manner of walking, سَيْر ـ مِشْوَار ـ مِشْيَة. I took one —, خَطَوْتُ خَطْوَةً وَاحِدَةً. A quick —, مَشْيٌ رَوْجَة ـ مُوَاشَكَة ـ وِشَاك ـ سُرْعَة. A slow —, بِطَآء ـ بُطَآءَة ـ عَلَى رُوَيْد: at a slow —, بِبِطَآءٍ ـ رُوَيْدًا ـ عَلَى مَهَلٍ. He has a good —, إِنَّهُ لَحَسَنُ ٱلسَّيْرِ ـ هُوَ وَشِيكٌ. A horse having a good —, فَرَسٌ حَسَنُ ٱلسَّيْرِ ـ حِصَانٌ حَسَنُ ٱلْمِشْوَارِ; a horse having a slow —, فَرَسٌ قَطُوفٌ. As often as the porters of the load advanced six paces, كُلَّمَا خَطَا حَامِلُو ٱلْحِمْلِ سِتَّ خَطَوَاتٍ.

To go at a good pace, هَرْوَلَ ـ أَنَاجَ ـ أَوْنَصَ ـ وَاشَكَ ـ أَوْشَكَ.

He went at a good or quick pace, سَارَ سَيْرًا شَدِيدًا ـ. Going at a quick —, مُوَاشِكٌ.

To hurry one's own pace, خَفَّ رِجْلَهُ ـ إِسْتَعْجَلَ ـ أَسْرَعَ ـ.

To keep pace with, جَارَى ـ سَايَرَ.

To mend one's pace; *see* To hurry one's pace; *supra.*

To put one through his paces, أَخْطَى.

To slacken one's pace, إِسْتَرْخَى فِي ـ تَرَاخَى ـ تَمَهَّلَ فِي ٱلسَّيْرِ ٱلْمَشْيِ.

Pace, *v.i.* To step, walk, سَارَ ـ يَخْطُو *aor.* خَطَا ـ إِخْتَطَى *aor.* مَشَى ـ يَسِيرُ ـ.

Pace, *v.t.* To measure by pacing, قَاسَ ـ خَطْوًا ـ. To — over or beyond, تَخَطَّى. To go pace by pace over, تَخَطَّى. To make another to —, أَخْطَى.

Paced, *a.* Having a particular pace, ذُو مِشْوَارٍ ـ لَهُ مَسِيرٌ: quick-paced, سَرِيعُ ٱلْمَسِيرِ; heavy-paced, ثَقِيلُ ٱلْمَسِيرِ.

Pacer, *n.* A fast walker, مَشَّآء ـ رَجِيل ـ رَاجِل ـ وَسَّاع.

Pacha, *n.* *See* Pâsha, *n.*

Pachydermata, *n.* حَيَوَانَاتٌ مِنْ ذَوَاتِ ٱلْحَوَافِرِ وَجِلْدٍ مُسْتَغْلِجٍ.

Pachydermatous, *a.* ذُو جِلْدٍ خَشِنٍ ـ ذُو جِلْدٍ مُسْتَغْلِجٍ.

Pacific, *a.* Peace-making, مُصَالِح ـ مُسَالِم ـ صَانِعُ ٱلسَّلَامِ. Peaceable, quiet, مُسْتَرِيح ـ مُطْمَئِنٌّ ـ هَادٍ. Peace-loving, مُحِبُّ ٱلصُّلْحِ. Pacific assurances, تَأْمِينَاتٌ مُسَالِمَةٌ. *See also the next article.*

Pacific, *n.* The — Ocean, ٱلْبَحْرُ ٱلْمُحِيطُ ٱلشَّرْقِيُّ.

Pacification, *n.* The act of making peace, إِصْلَاح; re-establishment of peace, concord, مُصَالَحَة. The —, as of a country, تَرْفِيَةُ ٱلْأَحْوَالِ ـ تَصْلِيحُ ٱلْأَحْوَالِ. System of —, أُصُولُ ٱلتَّسْكِينِ.

Pacificator, *n.* One who makes peace, مُصْلِح ـ صَانِعُ ٱلسَّلَامِ. One who restores order, رَافِي ٱلْأَحْوَالِ ـ مُصْلِحُ ٱلْأَحْوَالِ.

Pacificatory, *a.* *See* Pacific, *a.*

Pacifier, *n.* مُسَكِّن ـ مُلَطِّف ـ رَافٍ.

Pacify, *v.t.* *See to* Appease, *v.t.* His anger was pacified, سَكَنَ غَضَبُهُ [2].

Pacing, *a.* Measuring by steps, قَائِسٌ خَطْوًا. *See also* Ambling, *a.*

Pacing, *n.* The act of measuring by steps, ٱلْقِيَاسُ خَطْوًا. *See also* Amble, *n.*

Pack, *n.* A bundle, صُرَّة *pl.* صُرَر. A load, حِمْل ـ حَمْلَة. A set, assortment, طَقْم ـ طَائِفَة. A set, crew, party, جُمْلَة ـ حِزْب ـ. A mass, كُبْشَة ـ هِدْفَة ـ كُومَة ـ كُوم. طَائِفَة. A — of cards, شَدَّةُ وَرَقٍ. A —, as of hounds, كُلَيْب. *See also under* Package, *n.*

Pack, *v.t.* To press together closely, كَبَسَ ـ رَصَّ [2]. To make into a bundle, صَرَّ [2]. To put, as into boxes, عَبَّأَ ـ عَبَا. To —, stuff up, as with cotton, *etc.*, لَبَّدَ. To —, as one vessel into another, أَسْلَكَ ـ (سَلَكَ [2] *or*) فِي. To select deceitfully, إِنْتَخَبَ ـ (إِنْتَدَبَ *or*). To — a jury, إِنْتَخَبَ ٱلْوُكَلَآءَ بِمَكْرٍ ٱلْمُسْتَحْلَفِينَ بِحِيلَةٍ. I packed the things in the box, عَبَّأْتُ ٱلْأَمْتِعَةَ فِي ٱلصُّنْدُوقِ.

To pack off, prepare and send away, أَنْفَذَ ـ نَفَّذَ ـ شَيَّعَ. To dismiss, discharge, دَشَرَ ـ طَرَدَ [2] ـ نَفَى [2].

Pack, *v.i.* To be easy of being packed, سَهُلَتْ [2] (تَسَهَّلَتْ *or*) تَعْبِئَتُهُ. To — off, to go away in haste, إِنْطَلَقَ بِسُرْعَةٍ ـ أَوْشَكَ ـ إِرْتَحَلَ عَاجِلًا.

Package, *n.* A bundle, ضِبارَة ـ صُرَّة *pl.* صُرَر ـ رِزْمَة *pl.* رِزَم ـ حُزْمَة *pl.* حُزَم . A — of books or writings, (إِضْبارَة or) إِضْمامَة مِنَ ٱلْكُتُبِ . A bale, شَدَّة *pl.* شَدّات ـ فَرْدَة *pl.* فَرْدات. To make up into a —, ضَمَّرَ ـ ضَمَّرَ ـ صَرَّ ². A charge for package, كُلْفَة (or حَقُّ) ٱلشَّغْبِيَة. *See also under* Bale, Packet, Parcel, *n.*

Packer, *n.* حَزّام ـ مُعَبِّي ـ حَزّامُ ٱلْبِضائِعِ.

Packet, *n.* A small bundle, رَبِيط *pl.* أَرْبِطَة ـ صُرَّة *pl.* صُرَر. A paper —, رِزْمَة *pl.* رِزَم. A — of clothes, بُقْجَة (or صُرَّة) حَوائِج. A — of matches, ضَمِيمَة كِبْرِيت. A — of letters, إِضْمامَة (or مُغَلَّف or رِزْمَة) مَكاتِيب. A —, any small bundle tied together, as of flowers, *etc.*, باقَة ـ رَبْطَة. A packet-boat or ship, مَرْكَب بُوسْطَة ـ سَفِينَةُ ٱلْبَرِيدِ.

Packet-boat, *n.*
Packet-ship, } *See under* Packet, *n.*

Pack-horse, *n.* بِرْذَوْن *pl.* بَراذِين ـ دابَّة *pl.* دَوابّ (the latter applies as well to mules and asses of burden).

Packing, *n.* The act of packing, تَعْبِئَة; cording, حَزْم; close packing, رَصّ ـ كَبْس; the stuff used in —, مُشاقَة ـ حَشْو. To send one —, to dismiss, طَرَدَ ـ دَشَّرَ ².

Packing-case, *n.* صَنْدُوق *pl.* صَنادِيق (or صُنْدُوق).

Packing-case maker, *n.* صانِعُ ٱلصَّنادِيقِ ـ صَنْدُوقْجِي.

Packing-cloth, *n.* خامُ ٱلْحَزْمِ.

Packing-needle, *n.* مِسَلَّة *pl.* مَسالّ.

Pack-saddle, *n.* For a camel, رَحْل *pl.* رِحال ـ شاغِر *pl.* شَواغِر ـ كُور *pl.* أَكْوار. A small — for a camel, حَداجَة. A stuffed — for a mule or ass, بَرْذَعَة *pl.* بَراذِع ـ حِلْس *pl.* حُلُوس. A — made of wood only, سَمَر. A maker of pack-saddles, بَراذِعِيّ *pl.* بَراذِعِيَّة.

Pack-thread, *n.* مَرَس ـ سِلْك.

Pack-wax, *n.* غُرْضُوفُ ٱلرَّقَبَةِ.

Pact, *n.*
Paction, } مُشارَطَة ـ مُعاهَدَة ـ عَهْد ـ قَوْل.

Pactional, *a.* مُتَعَلِّق بِٱلْعَهْدِ ـ عَهْدِيّ.

Pad, *n.* A small cushion, وِسادَة *pl.* وَسائِد; a pad wound round anything, لِوايَا. A stuffed lining, بِطانَة ـ حَشْو ـ بِدان. A —, such as is placed under a saddle, رِفادَة ـ جَدِيدَة. A low soft saddle, أَكاف *pl.* آكِفَة and أُكُف ـ بَرْذَعَة *pl.* بَراذِع. A highwayman, قَطّاعُ ٱلطَّرِيقِ. An easy paced horse, رَهْوان.

Pad, *v.i.* To amble, رَهْوَن ـ هَرْوَل. To rob on foot, قَطَعَ ٱلطَّرِيقَ ².

Pad, *v.t.* To stuff, حَشَا *aor.* يَحْشُو; to line, بَطَّنَ. To imbue with a mordant, شَرَّبَ ـ تَرْبِيَة مِنَ ٱلْغِراءِ. To —, as of writing, حَشَا *aor.* يَحْشُو.

Padded, *a.* Stuffed, مَحْشِيّ; lined, مُبَطَّن.

Padder, *n.* قاطِعُ ٱلطَّرِيقِ. *See also* Highwayman, *n.*

Padding, *n.* Stuffing, حَشْو *pl.* مَحاشِي; lining, بِطانَة. A mordant, غِراء ـ آهار ـ تَرْبِيَة. Redundant matter, speech, لَغْو ـ حَشْو.

Paddle, *v.i.* To play in water, لَعِبَ فِي ٱلْماءِ ـ تَبَحْبَحَ فِي ٱلْماءِ ². To row, قَدَفَ بِٱلْمِقْداف ـ جَدَفَ (or جَذَفَ) بِٱلْمِجْداف ².

Paddle, *v.t.* To propel with an oar, جَدَفَ ـ جَذَفَ ².

Paddle, *n.* A small oar, مِقْداف *pl.* مَقادِيف. A blade or small spade, وَتَد *pl.* أَوْتاد. The board or float of a paddle-wheel, لَوْحَة (or تَخْتَة) ٱلدُّولابِ.

Paddle-box, *n.* طَبَقُ دُولابِ ٱلْباخِرَةِ.

Paddle-wheel, *n.* دُولابُ ٱلْباخِرَةِ *pl.* دَوالِيب.

Paddock, *n.* A plot of ground, بُقْعَة *pl.* بِقاع ـ مَشارَة ـ طَبَقَة. *See also* Frog, Toad, *n.*

Paddy, *n.* Rice in the husk, رُزّ (or أَرُزّ) فِي قِشْرِهِ. The cant name for an Irishman, لَقَبٌ لِأَهْلِ إِيرْلانْد.

Padisha, *n.* (More correctly, Pâdshâh), پادْشاه.

Padlock, *n.* قُفْل *pl.* أَقْفال ـ قُفْلٌ صَغِير.

Padlock, *v.t.* شَدَّ بِٱلْقُفْلِ ².

Pæan, *n.* A song of triumph, نَشِيد ـ تَسْبِحَة ـ نَشِيدُ ٱلظَّفَرِ.

Pagan, *n.* An idolater, وَثَنِيّ ـ عابِدُ ٱلْأَوْثانِ *pl.* عُبّاد; a polytheist, مُشْرِك *pl.* مُشْرِكُون. An infidel, كافِر *pl.* كُفّار and كافِرُون.

Pagan, *a.* وَثَنِيّ. A — temple, مَسْجِدٌ وَثَنِيّ ـ مَسْجِدُ عُبّادِ ٱلْأَوْثانِ ـ بَيْتُ صَنَمٍ (called in Egypt, as designating the ancient temples there, بَرْبَة *pl.* بَرابِي).

Paganism, *n.* Idolatry, عِبادَةُ ٱلْأَوْثانِ ـ عِبادَةُ ٱلْأَصْنامِ. Polytheism, ٱلشِّرْك. The time of —, or ignorance, before Islâm, ٱلْجاهِلِيَّة.

Paganize, *v.t.* To make like pagans, صَيَّرَ كَعُبّادِ ٱلْأَصْنامِ. To convert to paganism, رَدَّ إِلَى عِبادَةِ ٱلْأَصْنامِ ².

Paganized, *a.* مُرْتَدّ إِلَى حالِ ٱلْوَثَنِيِّينَ.

Page, *n.* As of a book, صَفْحَة *pl.* صَفَحات ـ صَحِيفَة *pl.* صَحائِف ـ وَجْه *pl.* وُجُوه and أَوْجُه. A — with double columns, صَفْحَة ذاتُ جَدْوَلَيْنِ. The — of history, ٱلتّارِيخ ـ ٱلتَّوارِيخ. A boy attendant, غُلام *pl.* غِلْمان.

Page, *v.t.* رَقَمَ عَدَدَ ٱلصَّحائِفِ ـ أَصْحَفَ ².

Pageant, n. إِحْتِفَال ـ فُرْجَة ـ زِينَة ـ مَوْكِب.

Pageantry, n. إِحْتِفَال ـ فَخْر ـ رَنَآء ـ بَهَآء.

Paging, n. تَرْقِيمُ ٱلصَّحَائِفِ ـ إِصْحَاف.

Pagoda, n. A heathen temple, بَيْتُ صَنَم ـ بَرْبَة pl. بَرَابِي. An Indian gold coin, سِكَّةُ ذَهَبٍ هِنْدِيَّةٌ.

Paid, part. See to Pay, v.t.

Pail, n. سَطْل pl. سُطُول. See also Bucket, n.

Pailfull, n. مِلْءُ سَطْلٍ.

Paillasse, n. طَرَّاحَةُ تِبْنٍ.

Pain, n. Physical —, أَلَم pl. آلام ـ وَجَع pl. أَوْجَاع. Distress, trouble, أَذِيَّة ـ عَذَاب ـ حُزْن ـ غَمّ ـ إِضْطِرَاب ـ عَنَآء ـ هَمّ. Penalty, punishment, مُجَازَاة ـ عَذَاب ـ عِقَاب ـ عُقُوبَة. For, from, or through —, مِنَ ٱلْوَجَعِ: he bit his tongue through —, عَضَّ عَلَى لِسَانِهِ مِنَ ٱلْوَجَعِ. The — of childbirth, مَخَاض. On or under — of, تَحْتَ حُكْمِ ـ بِوَبَالِ: on — of death, تَحْتَ بِوَبَالِ ٱلرَّأْسِ ـ ٱلْحُكْمِ بِٱلْهَلَاكِ. He had a — in his belly, ءأَلِمَ بَطْنُهُ; in his head, أَلِمَ رَأْسُهُ ـ يُوجِعُ رَأْسُهُ ـ يُوجِعُهُ رَأْسُهُ. See also Distress, Ache, n.

To be in pain, أَلِمَ ـ ءوَجِعَ aor. يَجِعُ ـ أَشْكَى. His foot pained him, يَشْتَكِي رِجْلَهُ.

To be seized with pain, أَخَذَ ٱلْوَجَعُ [2]. They were seized with pain, أَخَذَهُمُ ٱلْوَجَعُ. (For "Pains," see below).

To complain of pain, تَفَجَّعَ ـ تَوَجَّعَ ـ تَأَلَّمَ. He complained of a pain in one of his members, تَشَكَّى عُضْوًا مِنْ أَعْضَائِهِ ـ [2]شَكَا عُضْوًا.

To feel all over one, إِمْتَلَأَ وَجَعًا.

To give one physical pain, آلَمَ ـ أَوْجَعَ. To distress, أَضْجَرَ ـ [2]غَمَّ ـ [2]شَقَّ عَلَى ـ كَدَّرَ ـ إِسْتَصْعَبَ (or أَصْعَبَ) عَلَى. The matter gave him pain, إِسْتَصْعَبَ عَلَيْهِ ٱلْأَمْرُ.

Pain, v.t. To give physical pain to, آلَمَ ـ أَوْجَعَ. To make uneasy in mind, فَجَّعَ ـ أَحْزَنَ ـ [2]غَمَّ. To vex, فَجَّعَ ـ أَضْجَرَ ـ أَزْعَجَ. It pains me that..., لَهْفِي عَلَى أَنْ. I am pained at my very heart, تُوجِعُنِي صَمِيمُ قَلْبِي. See also to Distress, Afflict, v.t.

Painful, a. Of physical pain, أَلِيم ـ مُؤْلِم ـ وَجِيع ـ مُوجِع. Distressing, مُحْزِن ـ شَاقّ ـ مُضْجِر ـ فَاجِع. A — death, مَوْتٌ فَاجِعٌ. Most —, distressing, أَفْجَعُ. See also Distressing, Afflictive, a.

Painfully, ad. With pain, بِأَلَمٍ ـ بِوَجَعٍ. Laboriously, جَهْدًا ـ بِكَدٍّ ـ بِكُلِّ دِقَّةٍ ـ بِتَعَبٍ. Distressingly, بِمَشَقَّةٍ ـ بِصُعُوبَةٍ ـ بِضَجَرٍ.

Painfulness, n. كَدّ ـ تَعَب. See also Pain, n.

Painim, n. See Pagan, n.

Painless, a. بِدُونِ أَلَمٍ ـ بِلَا وَجَعٍ.

Pains, n. Effort, care, activity, كَدّ ـ سَعْي ـ عَنَآء ـ حِرْص ـ إِعْتِنَآء ـ جِدّ ـ جُهْد ـ إِجْتِهَاد ـ تَعَب. With all —, care, بِكُلِّ دِقَّةٍ وَٱعْتِنَآءٍ. Pains and penalties, مُجَازَاتٌ مُخْتَلِفَةٌ. For one's —, جَزَآءً لَهُ. To be at — to, تَكَلَّفَ بِ ـ ءتَعِبَ فِي ـ أَتْعَبَ نَفْسَهُ فِي ـ تَعَذَّبَ فِي. To take — in, [2]جَدَّ فِي ـ [2]كَدَّ فِي ـ [2]بَذَلَ جُهْدَهُ فِي ـ =دَقَّ فِي ـ دَقَّقَ فِي.

Painstaking, a. كَدُود ـ مُدَاقّ ـ سُعَاوِقٌ ـ جَادّ ـ مُجِدّ ـ مُتَكَلِّف ـ مُلَازِم ـ صَبِير.

Painstaking, n. جِدّ ـ كَدّ ـ سَعْي ـ إِجْتِهَاد.

Paint, v.t. To cover with paint, دَهَنَ [2]. To variegate with colours, نَمْنَمَ ـ نَقَّشَ ـ دَبَّجَ ـ وَشَّى. To draw, as pictures, صَوَّرَ. To — letters, adorn writing, نَمَّقَ. To describe, وَصَفَ aor. يَصِفُ. To — the eyebrows, خَطَّطَ ٱلْحَوَاجِبَ. To — or dye with henna, حَنَّأَ. To — with antimony, كَحَّلَ: She painted her eyes with antimony, تَكَحَّلَتْ ـ كَحَّلَتْ بِٱلْإِثْمِدِ عَيْنَيْهَا. He painted his nails with henna, حَنَّأَ أَظَافِيرَهُ. To — one's self with henna, تَحَنَّأَ.

Paint, v.i. To practise painting, drawing, صَوَّرَ ـ [2]رَسَمَ ـ تَعَطَّى (or تَعَاطَى) ٱلتَّصْوِيرَ.

Paint, n. Substance used in painting, دِهَان. A colour, لَوْن pl. أَلْوَان ـ صِبَاغ. Paint for the face, rouge, حُمْرَة ـ حُسْنُ يُوسُفَ ـ إِسْفِيدَاج.

Painter, n. One who paints, decorates, as houses, etc. وَاشٍ ـ دَهَّان ـ زَوَّاق ـ نَقَّاش. An artist, —, مُصَوِّر ـ مُصَوِّرَاتِيّ. A rope to fasten a boat, حَبْلُ ٱلْفَلُوكَةِ ـ مَرَسَةُ ٱلْقَارِبِ. A describer, وَاصِف.

Painting, n. Laying on colours, of houses, etc., دَهْن ـ دَهْنَة ـ تَزْوِيق ـ تَدْبِيج ـ تَنْقِيش. Drawing, the art of painting, فَنُّ ٱلتَّصْوِيرِ. A picture, تَصْوِير pl. تَصَاوِير ـ صُورَة pl. صُوَر.

Pair, n. A brace, زَوْج or زَوْجَان pl. أَزْوَاج ـ إِثْنَان. One of a —, صِنْو. A —, of pigeons, زَوْجَانِ مِنْ حَمَامٍ ـ زَوْجَا حَمَامٍ. A — of sandals, زَوْجَا نِعَالٍ. They are a —, هُمَا زَوْجَانِ ـ هُمَا زَوْجٌ. A husband and wife, زَوْجٌ وَزَوْجَةٌ ـ أَعْرَاس.

Pair, v.t. To couple one thing with another, زَوَّجَ بِ ـ زَوَّجَ إِلَى. To join in couples, زَوَّجَ. He paired them, males and females,

زَوَّجَهُمْ ذُكْرَانًا وَإِنَاثًا. To be paired, زُوِّجَ: And when the souls shall be paired, (in Paradise), *i.e.* united to their fellows, (*Kur.* lxxxi. 7), وَإِذَا ٱلنُّفُوسُ زُوِّجَتْ.

Pair, *v.i.* As of birds, *etc.* زَاوَجَ ـ اِزْدَوَجَ: The birds paired, اِزْدَوَجَتِ ٱلطَّيْرُ. To depart in pairs, اِنْطَلَقُوا أَزْوَاجًا. To — off, as members of parliament on absence from a vote, اِتَّفَقُوا أَزْوَاجًا مِنْ فِرْقَتَى حِزْبِ ٱلْمَجْلِسِ عَلَى ٱلْغِيَابِ عَنْ إِعْطَاءِ ٱلرَّأْيِ فِي مَسْأَلَةٍ مَّا.

Palace, *n.* سَرَايَة ـ قُصُور *pl.* قَصْر ـ مَجَادِل *pl.* مِجْدَل. Officers of the —, خَدَمُ ٱلْقَصْرِ ; *from the Turkish,* أَنْدَرُونْ هُمَايُونْ.

Paladin, *n.* *See* Knight-errant, *n.*

Palanquin, *n.* ضَرْبٌ مِنَ ٱلتَّخْتِ رَوَان.

Palatable, *a.* لَذِيذ ـ ذُو طَعْمٍ.

Palatableness, *n.* لَذَّة ـ طَعْم.

Palatably, *ad.* بِلَذَّةٍ ـ بِطَعْمٍ.

Palatal, *a.* Belonging to the palate, حَنَكِيٌّ ـ مُتَعَلِّقٌ بِٱلْحَنَكِ. Uttered by aid of the palate, نَطْعِيٌّ.

Palatal, *n.* A palatal letter, حُرُوف نَطْعِيَّة *pl.* حَرْف نَطْعِيٌّ.

Palate, *n.* The roof of the mouth, نَطْع ـ مَحَاوِر *pl.* مَحَارَة *pl.* أَنْطَاع ـ أَحْنَاك *pl.* حَنَك ـ سَقْفُ ٱلْفَمِ. Taste, relish, طَعْم ـ مَذَاق. The thin bone of the —, غَار.

Palatial, *a.* سُلْطَانِيٌّ ـ بَهِيٌّ ـ جَلِيل ـ فَاخِر ـ كَٱلْقَصْرِ.

Palatinate, *n.* The province of a palatine, وِلَايَة ـ حُكْمَدَارِيَّة مَالِكِ حُكْمَدَارِيَّةٍ.

Palatine, *a.* حَائِزُ ٱلْإِمْتِيَازَاتِ ٱلسُّلْطَانِيَّةِ.

Palatine, *n.* One invested with royal privileges, حَائِزُ ٱلْإِمْتِيَازَاتِ ٱلسُّلْطَانِيَّةِ ـ مَالِكُ حُقُوقِ حُكْمَدَارِيَّةٍ.

Palaver, *n.* Talk, كَلَام ـ مُكَالَمَة ـ قِيلٌ وَقَال ـ لَغْوٌ. Flattery, تَمْلِيق.

Palaver, *v.t.* مَلَّقَ ـ رَاوَغَ ـ حَاوَلَ.

Pale, *a.* As of a colour, light, مَفْتُوحُ ٱللَّوْنِ ـ مَفْتُوح ـ خَفِيف ; of the face, مُصْفَرٌّ ـ أَصْفَرُ ٱلْوَجْهِ. Of a dingy ash colour, as applied, *e.g.*, to a horse, فَرَسٌ أَخْضَرُ. To become —, in the face, اِصْفَرَّ وَجْهُهُ. Every face turned —, تَحَوَّلَ كُلُّ وَجْهٍ إِلَى صُفْرَةٍ.

Pale, *n.* A stake, أَوْتَاد *pl.* وَتَد ـ خَوَازِيقُ *pl.* خَازُوق. An inclosure, حَيِّز ـ حَدِيقَة ـ جُدَيْر ـ جِدَار ـ حَوْزَة. A sphere, circle, دَائِرَة. The bosom, حِضْن. One without the pale, خَارِجِيٌّ *pl.* خَوَارِجُ.

Pale, *v.t.* To inclose with pales, أَحَاطَ بِأَوْتَادٍ. *See also to* Empale, *v.t.*

Pale, *v.i.* To become pale, اِصْفَرَّ.

Pale-faced, *a.* أَصْفَرُ ٱلْوَجْهِ. Haggard in look, شَاحِبُ ٱللَّوْنِ.

Paleness, *n.* As of colour, سَوَاد ـ خُضْرَة ; of the face, صُفْرَة ـ صَفْرَنَة ـ اِصْفِرَار.

Paleographer, *n.* مَاهِرٌ (*or* خَارِقٌ) فِي فَنِّ قِرَاءَةِ ٱلْكِتَابَةِ وَٱلْأَقْلَامِ ٱلْقَدِيمَةِ.

Paleographic, *a.* } Paleographical, } مَا نِيطَ بِفَنِّ قِرَاءَةِ ٱلْكِتَابَةِ وَٱلْأَقْلَامِ ٱلْقَدِيمَةِ.

Paleography, *n.* The ancient manner of writing, ٱلْخَطُّ ٱلْقَدِيمُ ـ أَقْلَامُ ٱلْقُدَمَاءِ. The study and art of explaining ancient writings, ٱلْبَحْثُ عَنْ أَقْلَامِ ٱلْأَقْدَمِينَ وَفَكُّهَا.

Paleological, *a.* مُتَعَلِّقٌ بِٱلْبَحْثِ عَنْ أَحْوَالِ ٱلْأَقْدَمِينَ.

Paleologist, *n.* خَارِقٌ فِي أَحْوَالِ ٱلْقُدَمَاءِ وَكُلِّمَا يَتَعَلَّقُ بِهِمْ.

Paleology, *n.* ٱلْبَحْثُ عَنْ أَحْوَالِ ٱلْأَقْدَمِينَ وَكُلِّمَا يَتَعَلَّقُ بِهِمْ.

Paleosaurus, *n.* نَوْعٌ مِنَ ٱلضَّبِّ غَيْرُ مَوْجُودٍ ٱلْآنَ.

Paleontological, *a.* مَا نِيطَ بِفَنِّ ٱلْمُتَحَجِّرَاتِ مِنَ ٱلْحَيَوَانَاتِ وَٱلنَّبَاتَاتِ ٱلْمَعْدُومَةِ (*or* ٱلْبَائِدَةِ).

Paleontologist, *n.* مُدَرِّسُ فَنِّ ٱلْمُتَحَجِّرَاتِ مِنَ ٱلْحَيَوَانَاتِ وَٱلنَّبَاتَاتِ ٱلْمَعْدُومَةِ (*or* ٱلْبَائِدَةِ).

Paleontology, *n.* فَنُّ ٱلْمُتَحَجِّرَاتِ مِنَ ٱلْحَيَوَانَاتِ وَٱلنَّبَاتَاتِ ٱلْغَيْرِ مَوْجُودَةٍ ٱلْآنَ.

Paleotherium, *n.* نَوْعٌ مِنْ ذَوَاتِ ٱلْأَرْبَعِ جَسِيمٌ جِدًّا يُشْبِهُ ٱلْخِنْزِيرَ قَدْ بَادَ ٱلْآنَ.

Paleozoic, *a.* Denoting the lowest fossil-bearing strata, عِبَارَةٌ عَنِ ٱلطَّبَقَاتِ مِنَ ٱلْأَرْضِ ٱلسُّفْلَى تُوجَدُ فِيهَا ٱلْمُتَحَجِّرَاتُ. Denoting the lowest forms of life, عِبَارَةٌ عَنِ ٱلدَّرَجَاتِ ٱلسُّفْلَى مِنَ ٱلْحَيَوَانَاتِ.

Palestra, *n.* A place for wrestling, مَصْرَع ـ رِيَاضَة ـ مَعْرَك.

Palestrian, *a.* } Palestric, } مُخْتَصٌّ بِٱلْمُصَارَعَةِ ـ مُتَعَلِّقٌ بِٱلْمُرَاوَغَةِ.

Paletot, *n.* جُبَب *pl.* جُبَّة.

Palette, *n.* *See* Pallet, *n.*

Palfrey, *n.* A horse for state, حِصَانٌ لِلزِّينَةِ ـ فَرَسٌ لِلْاِحْتِفَالِ.

Palilogy, *n.* The repetition of a word, تَرْجِيعُ (*or* تَكْرَارُ) ٱلْكَلِمَةِ.

Palimpsest, *n.* أَطْلَاس *pl.* طِلْس ـ أَطْرَاس *pl.* طِرْس.

Palindrome, *n.* مَقْلُوبُ ٱلْكُلِّ ـ مَقْلُوبٌ مُسْتَوٍ.

Paling, *n.* A board, أَلْوَاح *pl.* لَوْح. A fence, إِحَاطَة ـ جِدَار ـ جُدْرَان *pl.* جِدَار ـ حِجْر.

Palingenesia, *n.* تَنَاسُخ ـ تَجْدِيدُ ٱلْخِلْقَةِ.

Palinode, *n.* تَكْذِيب ـ تَغْيِيرُ ٱلْكَلَامِ ـ إِنْكَار.

Palisade, *n.* A fortification of stakes, حَسِيكَةٌ ـ دَائِرَةُ أَوْتَادٍ ـ رَصُّ خَوَازِيقَ. A — to keep off cattle, سِلْغَاف.

Palisade, *v.t.* أَحَاطَ بِأَوْتَادٍ لِلتَّحْصِينِ ـ أَحَاطَ بِحَسِيكَةٍ.

Palish, *n.* As of the face, يَضْرِبُ إِلَى ٱلِٱصْفِرَارِ. Verging to light, of colour, أَبْيَضُ كَابٍ.

Pall, *n.* A robe of state, خِلْعَةٌ *pl.* خِلَعٌ ـ فَرَّاجَةٌ رَسْمِيَّةٌ. A covering for a coffin, غِطَآءٌ (مِنْ قَطِيفَةٍ أَوْ جُوخٍ) لِلتَّابُوتِ. The —, as of a wheel, ضَابِطَةٌ.

Pall, *v.i.* To become insipid, مَلُخَ. To pall upon, قَزَّ عَنْ ـ شَبِعَ مِنْهُ ـ كَرِهَ عِنْدَهُ ـ تَقَزَّزَ مِنْ.

Pall, *v.t.* To cloak, cover, كَفَّرَ عَلَى ـ كَفَرَ ـ غَطَا ـ غَطَّى.

Palladium, *n.* An effective defence, protection, حِرْز ـ حَارِس ـ مَرْكَزُ ٱلْأَمْنِ ـ مَأْمَن ـ حَامٍ. A kind of metal, بَلَادِيُوم وَهُوَ ضَرْبٌ مِنَ ٱلْمَعَادِنِ.

Pallas, *n.* The Grecian goddess of wisdom, إِلَاهَةُ ٱلْحِكْمَةِ عِنْدَ ٱلْيُونَانِ ٱلْأَقْدَمِينَ. The small planet so called, إِسْمُ سَيَّارَةٍ صَغِيرَةٍ مَا بَيْنَ ٱلْمِرِّيخِ وَٱلْمُشْتَرِي.

Pall-bearer, *n.* مَاسِكُ غِطَاءِ ٱلتَّابُوتِ عِنْدَ دَفْنِ ٱلْمَيِّتِ.

Pallet, *n.* Of a painter, صَحْنُ (or لَوْحَةُ) ٱلْأَلْوَانِ. A small miserable bed, مَنَامٌ حَقِيرٌ ـ حَصِيرَة (literally, a mat).

Palliasse, *n.* طَرَّاحَةُ تِبْنٍ.

Palliate, *v.t.* To cover with excuses, to excuse, سَتَرَ ـ أَعْذَرَ ـ دَارَى عَنْ. To soften, خَفَّفَ ـ أَقَلَّ. To appease, سَكَّنَ ـ هَدَّأَ.

Palliation, *n.* As of an offence, سَتْر ـ عُذْر. The act of softening, quieting, تَخْفِيف ـ تَسْكِين ـ إِهْدَآء.

Palliative, *a.* Excusing, مُعْذِر ـ مُعَذِّر. Lessening, quieting, مُخَفِّف ـ مُسَكِّن ـ مُهْدِئ.

Palliative, *n.* That which excuses, مَعْذِرَة ـ عُذْر; that which lessens, alleviates, تَسْكِين ـ تَخْفِيف ـ تَقْلِيل ـ إِهْدَآء.

Pallid, *a.* *See* Pale, *a.*

Pallidness, *n.* *See* Paleness, *n.*

Pallium, *n.* As of bishops, طَيْلَسَانُ ٱلْمَطَارِنَةِ.

Pall-mall, *n.* The game, لَعِبُ ٱلصَّوْلَجَانِ.

Pallor, *n.* *See* Paleness, *n.*

Palm, *n.* The tree, نَخْلَة ـ نَخْل *pl.* نَخِيل. The male —, فُحَّال ـ فَحْل. A green — branch, شَطْبَة *pl.* شَطَائِب; a dry — branch, with its leaves, سَعَفَة *pl.* سَعَفَات ـ سَعَف *pl.* سُعُوف; a — branch stripped of its leaves, عَسِيب *pl.* عُسُب ـ عَسَائِب ـ جَرِيدَة *pl.* جَرَائِد. The Theban —, دَوْمَة ـ دَوْم; the fruit of the same, مُقْل. The — of the hand, صَفْحُ ٱلْكَفِّ ـ فَقْحَة *pl.* فِقَاح ـ فَقَاحَة ـ كَفّ ـ بَطْنُ (or رَاحَةُ) ٱلْكَفِّ. To smite with the palms of the hand, لَطَمَ. To spread out the palms of the hands in supplication to, أَفْضَى بِيَدَيْهِ إِلَى; the putting the two palms of the hands together in prayer, ٱلتَّطْبِيق. The lines in the palms of the hands, أَسَارِيرُ.

Palm, the measure, فِتْر ـ شِبْر *pl.* أَشْبَار. To carry off the —, to obtain the victory, حَازَ قَصَبَ ٱلسَّبْقِ ـ حَازَ قَصَبَ ٱلرِّهَانِ ـ فَاقَ.

Palm, *v.t.* To conceal in the hand, خَبَأَ فِي كَفِّهِ. To impose something on one, غَشَّ فِي ـ إِحْتَالَ عَلَى فِي.

Palma-Christi, *n.* The plant, خِرْوَع ـ شَجَرُ حَبِّ ٱلْمُلُوكِ.

Palmate, *a.* / Palmated, } Having the shape of the hand, بِشَكْلِ ٱلْكَفِّ ـ فِي هَيْئَةِ ٱلرَّاحَةِ (or رَاحَةِ ٱلْكَفِّ). Web-footed, ذُو غِشَآءٍ بَيْنَ ٱلْأَصَابِعِ.

Palmer, *n.* A pilgrim to Jerusalem, مُقْدِسِيّ *pl.* مَقَادِسَة.

Palmerworm, *n.* يُسْرُوع ـ أُسْرُوع *pl.* أَسَارِيع.

Palmetto, *n.* نَخْلَةٌ صَغِيرَةٌ بَرِّيَّةٌ.

Palmiferous, *a.* حَامِلُ ٱلنَّخِيلِ.

Palmified, *a.* *See* Web-footed, *a.*

Palmister, *n.* قَائِف ـ ضَرَّابُ سِيمِيَا ـ مَاهِرٌ بِعِلْمِ ٱلْأَسَارِيرِ.

Palmistry, *n.* عِلْمُ ٱلْكَفِّ ـ عِلْمُ ٱلسِّيمِيَا ـ عِلْمُ ٱلْقِيَافَةِ.

Palm-oil, *n.* زَيْتٌ يُقْطَرُ مِنْ ضَرْبٍ مِنَ ٱلنَّخْلِ.

Palm-Sunday, *n.* يَوْمُ ٱلسَّبَاسِبِ ـ أَحَدُ ٱلشَّعَانِينِ.

Palmy, *n.* Abounding in palms, كَثِيرُ ٱلنَّخْلِ. Flourishing, فَالِح ـ نَاجِح; happy, سَعِيد ـ مَسْعُود ـ حَظِيظ.

Palpability, *n.* / Palpableness, } The being perceptible to the touch, ٱلْإِحْسَاسُ بِٱلشَّيْءِ ـ مَحْسُوس ـ ٱلْإِحْسَاسُ بِٱللَّمْسِ. Obviousness, وُضُوح ـ بَيَان.

Palpable, *a.* That may be felt by the touch, مَحْسُوسٌ بِٱللَّمْسِ; a — thing, مَحْسُوس *pl.* مَحْسُوسَات. Obvious, عِيَان ـ وَاضِح. To be —, obvious, إِتَّضَحَ; to make —, أَوْضَحَ.

Palpably, *ad.* So as to be perceived by the touch, يُشْعَرُ بِٱللَّمْسِ. Obviously, عَرْضَ عَيْنٍ ـ عِيَانًا ـ بِجَلَآءٍ ـ صُرَاحًا.

Palpebal, *a.* Pertaining to the eye-brows, مُتَعَلِّقٌ بِٱلْحَوَاجِبِ.

Palpebrous, *a.* Having large eye-brows, أَزَجّ ـ طَوِيلُ ٱلْحَاجِبَيْنِ.

Palpi, *n.* The — of insects, قُرُونٌ لَامِسَةٌ ـ مَلَامِس.

Palpiform, *a.* بِشَكْلِ ٱلْقُرُونِ ٱللَّامِسَةِ ـ بِشَكْلِ قُرُونِ ٱلْحَشَرَاتِ.

Palpitate, *v.i.* خَفَقَ ـ رَجَفَ ـ إِرْتَجَفَ. To cause to —, أَرْجَفَ.

Palpitation, *n.* خَفَقَان ـ رَجْف ـ رَجَفَان. Palpitation of the heart, رَجْفَةُ (or خفقانُ) ٱلْقَلْبِ. Palpitation through hunger, لَجَاجَة.

Palsical, a. } Having the palsy, مَفْلُوج; impotent, powerless,
Palsied, } عَاجِز.

Palsy, n. عُطْل ــ القَالِجُ ــ خَبَل ــ خَبَل. To have the —, فُلِجَ ــ خَبِلَ. To pretend to have the —, تَفَالَجَ.

Palsy, v.t. To strike with palsy, رَمَى-بِٱلفَالِجِ. To destroy action or energy, عَطَّلَ ــ أَعْجَزَ-عَن ــ إِخْتَبَلَ ــ خَبَلَ.

Palter, v.t. See to Balk, v.t.

Palter, v.i. To fiddle-faddle, لَعِبَ ــ تَلَعَّبَ ــ عَبِثَ ــ بَطَّلَ. See under to Fiddle, v.i.

Palterer, n. لَعَّاب ــ عِبِّيث ــ عَابِث ــ مُبْرِم ــ بَطَّال ــ مُتَبَطِّل.

Paltriness, n. دَنَاءَة ــ نَذَارَة ــ تَفَاهَة ــ حَقَارَة ــ ذُلّ ــ ذِلَّة.

Paltry, a. Mean, مَسْكِين ــ سَاقِط ــ دَنِيّ ــ دَنِيء ــ حَقِير ــ تَافِه ــ ذَلِيل ــ سَفِيل. A — thing, جُلّى pl. أَجْلَال ــ جُلَل pl. جَلَل.

Paltry, of goods or furniture, سَقَط ــ رِثَّة. Paltry things, مَدَاقّ (or دَقَائِق) ٱلْأُمُورِ. To be —, تَفِهَ ــ تَفُهَ. To be — in giving, أَتْفَهَ فِي عَطَائِهِ. He sought after — things, دَنَّى تَدْنِيَةً دَنَّى فِي ٱلْأُمُورِ.

Paludal, a. See Marshy, a.

Paly, a. See Pale, a.

Pampas, n. The prairies of South America, جُهُدُ (or صَحَارِيُّ) أَمِيرِكَا ٱلْجَنُوبِيَّةِ.

Pamper, v.t. To glut, أَشْبَعَ ــ أَنْصَحَ. To spoil with indulgence, فَتَّقَ ــ فَانَقَ. To be pampered, or to lead a pampered life, تَنَعَّمَ مُتَرَفِّهًا ــ تَفَانَقَ. A pampered life, عَيْش مُفَانِق.

Pamphlet, n. كُرَّاسَة pl. كَرَارِيس and كُرَّاس ــ كُتَيِّب pl. كُتَيِّبَات ــ رِسَالَة pl. رَسَائِل.

Pamphleteer, n. كَاتِبُ ٱلرَّسَائِلِ ــ مُؤَلِّفُ ٱلرَّسَائِلِ.

Pamphleteering, n. تَأْلِيفُ ٱلرَّسَائِلِ وَتَبْرِيزُهَا ــ تَأْلِيفُ ٱلرَّسَائِلِ.

Pan, n. As for cooking in, طِنْجِرَة pl. طَنَاجِرُ ــ مَاجُور pl. مَوَاجِيرُ. (See also Frying-pan). The —, as of a gun-lock, بَيْتُ ٱلذَّخِيرَةِ ــ مُكْحِلَةُ ٱلذَّخِيرَةِ ــ جُرْن ــ فَالِيَة. The — or chamber of a breech-loader, جُعْبَة. The — of the knee, الدَّاغِصَة.

Panacea, n. دَوَاءٌ عَامٌّ.

Panada, n. ثَرِيد ــ فَتَّةُ خُبْزٍ.

Pancake, n. عُجَّة pl. عُجَج ــ رُقَاق pl. رِقَاق ــ زَنْكَلَة pl. زَنَاكِل.

Pancreas, n. لَوْزَةُ ٱلْمِعْدَةِ ــ لَوْزَة.

Pancreatic, a. مُتَعَلِّق بِلَوْزَةِ ٱلْمِعْدَةِ.

Pandean-pipes, n. ضَرْبٌ مِنَ ٱلْأَرْغُنِ ــ ضَرْبٌ مِنَ ٱلْمِزْمَارِ.

Pandect, n. The pandects of Justinian, مَجَلَّةُ ٱلْقَوَانِينِ لِلرُّومَانِيِّينَ ٱلْقُدَمَاءِ مَنْسُوبَةٌ إِلَى ٱلْقَيْصَرِ يُوسْطِينِيَانُوس. A digest of laws, مَجْمَعُ قَوَانِينَ وَفَتَاوَى.

Pandemonium, n. مَجْمَعُ شَيَاطِينَ ــ دِيوَانُ إِبْلِيسَ.

Pander, n. A pimp, دَيُّوث ــ مُعَرِّص; a — to one's own wife, دَيُّوث ــ مُمْذٍ.

Pander, v.i. To play the pimp, تَدَيَّثَ; to one's own wife, أَمْذَى ــ مَاذَى. To — or to minister to the lusts of, سَايَرَ (or رَاعَى-) فِي ٱلْخُبْثِ.

Panderism, n. إِمْذَاءٌ ــ تَدَيُّث.

Pandit, n. عَالِمٌ مِنَ ٱلْبَرَاهِمَةِ ــ عَالِمٌ هِنْدِيٌّ.

Pandora's box, n. Figuratively, the source of all evils, مَنْبَعُ جَمِيعِ ٱلْبَلَايَا.

Pane, n. As of glass, لَوْحُ زُجَاجٍ pl. أَلْوَاح. A square compartment, مُرَبَّعَة. Small panes of talc used in the roof of baths, etc., مَضَاوِي.

Paned, n. As with glass, مُرَكَّبٌ بِأَلْوَاحٍ مِنَ ٱلزُّجَاجِ. Variegated, مُخَلَّب ــ مُدَبَّج. In squares, ذُو بُيُوتٍ مُرَبَّعَةٍ.

Panegyric, n. See Eulogy, n.

Panegyric, a. } See Eulogistic, a.
Panegyrical, }

Panegyrize, v.t. See to Eulogize, v.t.

Panel, As of a door, فَرْوَاز pl. فَرَاوِيز. A board, wainscot, لَوْح pl. أَلْوَاح ــ فَرْوَاز pl. فَرَاوِيز. A list of jurymen, سِيَاقَةُ (or دَفْتَرُ) أَسَامِي ٱلْوُكَلَاءِ ٱلْمُسْتَحْلَفِينَ. The whole jury, ٱلْوُكَلَاءُ ٱلْمُسْتَحْلَفُونَ ــ أَهْلُ ٱلْجُورِي ــ جُمْلَة. See also Jury, n.

Panel, v.t. To form with panels, جَعَلَ-عَلَى هَيْئَةِ ٱلْفَرَاوِيزِ. See also to Empanel, v.t.

Panelled, a. Formed with panels, عَلَى هَيْئَةِ ٱلْفَرَاوِيزِ.

Pang, n. A pain, أَلَم pl. آلَام ــ غُصَّة ــ غَمّ pl. غُمُوم. The pangs of death, نَزْعُ ٱلْمَوْتِ ــ نَزْع ــ سِيَاق ــ غَمَرَاتُ ٱلْمَوْتِ. The pangs of childbirth, مَخَاض. To give one a —, غَمَّ ــ أَغَصَّ.

Pangolin, n. See Ant-eater, n.

Panic, n. A sudden fright, commotion, هَوْل ــ رَوْعَة ــ دَهْشَة ــ وَكْرَة. To strike with —, رَوَّعَ ــ أَدْهَشَ. To be struck with —, تَرَوَّعَ ــ ارْتَاعَ ــ دَهِشَ.

Panic, }
Panicum, n. } جَلِيل ــ ثُمَام.
Panic-grass, }

Panicle, n. طَلْعَة coll. طَلْع.

Panicled, a. }
Paniculate, } ذُو طَلْعٍ مُزْهِرٍ.

Panic-struck, a. مَرْعُوب ـ مُوَهَّر ـ مُرْتَاع ـ مَدْهُوش.

Pannade, n. *See* Curvet, n.

Pannel, n. A rustic saddle, بَرْذَعَة pl. بَرَاذِعَة ـ حِلْس pl. حُلُوس.

Pannier, n. A wicker basket, قُفَّة pl. قُفَف ـ سَلَّة pl. سَلَل ـ زِنْبِيل pl. زَنَابِيل. A — to be carried on camels, *etc.*, مِحَارَة (*vulg.* مَحَارَة) pl. مَحَائِر and مَحَارَات ـ مِحَفَّة. A woman's —, bustle, حَشِيَّة.

Panoplied, a. شَوِكُ ٱلسِّلَاحِ ـ شَاكُّ ٱلسِّلَاحِ ـ مُسَلَّحٌ بِٱلتَّكْمِيلِ.

Panoply, n. سِلَاحٌ كَامِلٌ.

Panorama, n. A wide view, مَنْظَرٌ عَامٌّ ـ مَنْظَرٌ وَسِيعٌ. A circular painting, صُورَةٌ مُسْتَدِيرَةٌ. A drawing with an extensive view, رَسْمٌ وَسِيعُ ٱلْمَنْظَرِ.

Panoramic, a. مُسْتَدِير ـ وَسِيعُ ٱلْمَنْظَرِ.

Pansy, n. زَهْرَةُ ٱلثَّالُوثِ تُشْبِهُ ٱلْبَنَفْسَجَ.

Pant, v.i. To beat rapidly, breathe heavily, بُهِرَ ـ نَهِجَ ـ نَهَجَ ـ ضَبَحَ ـ اِبْتَهَرَ ـ لَهَثَ ـ لَهِدَ. To make to pant, بَهَرَ. The horses panted, ضَبَحَتِ ٱلْخَيْلُ. My heart panted, was perplexed, تَاهَ قَلْبِي. To — after, long for, إِشْتَاقَ إِلَى. *See also* to Palpitate, v.i.

Pant, n. فُوَاق ـ أُنُوح ـ لَهْث ـ إِبْتِهَار ـ نَهَج ـ ضَبْح.

Pantagraph, n. آلَةٌ لِتَكْبِيرِ ٱلْخَارِطَاتِ وَغَيْرِهَا أَوْ لِتَصْغِيرِهَا.

Pantaloon, n. *See* Buffoon, n.

Pantaloons, n. Trousers, بَنْطَلُون ـ شِرْوَال ـ أَلْبِسَة pl. لِبَاس.

Pantechnicon, n. مَحَلُّ ٱلتَّفَرُّجِ ـ مَعْرِضُ جَمِيعِ ٱلصِّنَاعَاتِ عَلَى جَمِيعِ ٱلصَّنَائِعِ.

Pantheism, n. مَذْهَبُ ٱلشِّرْكِ ـ مَذْهَبُ عَبَدَةِ جَمِيعِ ٱلْآلِهَةِ.

Pantheist, n. مُشْرِك ـ مِنْ أَهْلِ مَذْهَبِ عَبَدَةِ جَمِيعِ ٱلْآلِهَةِ ـ مُشْرِكِيّ.

Pantheistic, a. }
Pantheistical, } مُشْرِكِيّ ـ مَنُوطٌ بِمَذْهَبِ عَبَدَةِ جَمِيعِ ٱلْآلِهَةِ.

Pantheon, n. A temple for all the gods, مَعْبَدٌ لِجَمِيعِ ٱلْمَعْبُودَاتِ. All the gods, ٱلْمَعَابِيدُ كَافَّةً. A place for curiosities, *etc.*, مَحَلُّ ٱلْغَرَائِبِ ـ مَحَلُّ ٱلتُّحَفِ.

Panther, n. نَمِر pl. نُمُر ـ كَنْعَم ـ بَبْر pl. بُبُور; the male cub of the —, فِزْر *fem.* فِزْرَة or فَزَارَة.

Panting, a. بَهِير ـ مُبْتَهِر; as with dread, خَشْيَان.

Panting, n. نَهَج ـ أُنُوح. *See also* Pant, n.

Pantofle, n. بَابُوجَة ـ بَابُوج pl. بَوَابِيج.

Pantomime, n. One that imitates by mute action, لَعَّابٌ بِٱلْإِيمَاءِ. Representation by dumb show, مَسْخَرَة ـ لَعْبُ ٱلْوَمَاءِ.

Pantomimic, a. }
Pantomimical, } مَسْخَرَاتِيّ ـ مِنْ طِرَازِ لَعِبِ ٱلْإِيمَاءِ.

Pantomimist, n. مَسْخَرَاتِيّ ـ لَعَّابٌ بِٱلْإِيمَاءِ.

Pantry, n. بَيْتُ ٱلْمُؤْنَةِ ـ كِلَار.

Pap, n. A nipple, حَلَمَةُ ٱلثَّدْيِ pl. حَلَمَات ـ قُرَاد. The breast of a female, ثَدْي *du.* ثَدْيَانِ pl. ثُدِيّ. Soft food, سَوِيق ـ حَرِيرَة ـ فِيرَة ـ فَرِيقَة. Pulp, لُبّ ـ شَحْمَة ـ شَحْم.

Papa, n. أَب ـ بَابَا. To call one —, بَأْبَأَ. *See also* Father, n.

Papacy, n. ٱلْبَابَاوِيَّة.

Papal, a. بَابَاوِيّ.

Papalize, v.t. صَيَّرَ مِنْ مَذْهَبِ ٱلْبَابَا ـ صَيَّرَ مِنْ أَهْلِ ٱلْبَابَا.

Papalize, v.i. ذَهَبَ مَذْهَبَ ٱلْبَابَا.

Papaverous, a. مِنْ جِنْسِ ٱلْخَشْخَاشِ.

Papaw, n. ضَرْبٌ مِنَ ٱلْفَاكِهَةِ.

Paper, n. كَاغَد ـ كَاغَذ ـ قِرْطَاس pl. قَرَاطِيس ـ وَرَق pl. أَوْرَاق. A piece of —, قِطْعَةُ وَرَقٍ ـ وَرَقَة ـ طَلْحِيَّة. A newspaper, غَزِيتَة pl. غَزِيتَات ـ وَرَقَةُ أَخْبَارٍ ـ جَرِيدَة pl. جَرَائِدُ. Any written instrument, سَطْر ـ كِتَابَة pl. كِتَابَات ـ صَحِيفَة pl. صَحَائِف. A legal —, سِجِلّ pl. سِجِلَّات ـ صَكّ pl. صُكُوك ـ حُجَّة pl. حُجَج.

Money paper, قَائِمَةٌ نَقْدِيَّةٌ pl. قَوَائِمُ نَقْدِيَّةٌ.

Paper for walls, *etc.*, وَرَقٌ لِلْحِيطَانِ ـ وَرَقُ سِجَافٍ.

To commit to paper, سَطَّرَ فِي قِرْطَاسٍ ـ كَتَبَ فِي وَرَقَةٍ.

To make paper, وَرَّقَ.

To put pen to paper, حَرَّرَ ـ سَطَّرَ ـ كَتَبَ.

To put the hair in paper, جَعَّدَ ٱلشَّعْرَ بِفَتْلِ ٱلْوَرَقِ عَلَيْهِ.

To subscribe to a paper, إِشْتَرَكَ فِي جَرِيدَةٍ.

Blotting paper, وَرَقٌ مُنَشِّفٌ ـ وَرَقُ ٱلتَّنْشِيفِ.

Brown or coarse paper, وَرَقٌ خَشِنٌ.

Drawing paper, وَرَقُ ٱلرَّسْمِ.

Glazed paper, وَرَقٌ مَصْقُولٌ.

Note paper, وَرَقُ ٱلرِّقَاعِ.

Oiled paper, وَرَقٌ مَدْهُونٌ.

Silver or tissue paper, وَرَقٌ قَزٌّ.

Very thin paper, وَرَقٌ رَقِيقٌ ـ وَرَقٌ جِنْوِي (*i.e.* Genoa paper.)

Waste paper, سَقَطُ ٱلْوَرَقِ ـ وَرَقٌ بَوَارٌ.

Paper, a. Made of paper, مِنْ وَرَقٍ. Thin, slight, سَخِيف ـ رَقِيق ـ دَقِيق.

Paper, v.t. To cover with paper, غَطَّى بِٱلْوَرَقِ. To roll up in paper, لَفَّ - فِي وَرَقٍ [2]. To —, as of walls, *etc.*, فَرَشَ - بِٱلْوَرَقِ [2] — لَزَقَ ٱلْوَرَقَ فِي ٱل....

Paper-hanger, *n.* مُزَوِّقٌ — مُلَزِّقُ ٱلْوَرَقِ عَلَى ٱلْحِيطَانِ.

Paper-hangings, *n.* وَرَقٌ لِلْحِيطَانِ — وَرَقُ ٱلتَّزْوِيقِ — وَرَقٌ سِجَافٌ.

Paper-maker, *n.* وَرَّاقٌ — مُوَرِّقٌ.

Paper-making, *n.* صِنَاعَةُ ٱلْوَرَقِ — تَوْرِيقٌ.

Paper-mill, *n.* مَعْمَلُ ٱلْوَرَقِ.

Paper-seller, *n.* كَاغَدِيٌّ — وَرَّاقٌ.

Paper-stainer, *n.* مُلَوِّنُ (or مُشَكِّلُ or مُنَقِّشُ) ٱلْوَرَقِ.

Paphian, *a.* Pertaining to the rites of Venus, مُتَعَلِّقٌ بِعِبَادَةِ ٱلزُّهَرَةِ.

Papier-maché, *n.* ضَرْبٌ مِنَ ٱلْمُقَوَّى.

Papilionaceous, *a.* Bearing a flower resembling the butterfly, حَامِلُ أَزْهَارٍ تُشْبِهُ هَيْئَةَ ٱلْفَرَاشِ. Resembling a butterfly, فِي شَكْلِ ٱلْفَرَاشِ.

Papilla, *n.* A small nipple, حَلَمَةٌ صَغِيرَةٌ جِدًّا. The termination of nerves, سَعْدَانُ ٱلْعَصَبِ.

Papillary, *a.* / Papillous, } Resembling nipples, يُشْبِهُ ٱلْحَلَمَاتِ. Covered with papillæ, ذُو سَعْدَانَاتٍ.

Papillote, *n.* A curl paper, وَرَقٌ لِتَجْعِيدِ ٱلشَّعْرِ.

Papist, *n.* مِنْ أَهْلِ مَذْهَبِ ٱلْبَابَا — بَابَاوِيٌّ.

Papistic, *a.* / Papistical, } بَابَاوِيٌّ.

Papistry, *n.* بَابَاوِيَّةٌ.

Pappous, *a.* ذُو جَوَالِحَ — أَبُو جَالِحَةٍ. *See also* Downy, *a.*

Pappus, *n.* جَوَالِحُ — جَالِحَةٌ.

Pappy, *a.* Like pap, مِثْلَ ٱللُّبِّ — كَٱلْفَرِيقَةِ — مِثْلَ ٱلسَّوِيقِ. Soft, succulent, رَطِيبٌ — سَهْوَقٌ — خَاضِلٌ.

Papulæ, *n.* *See* Pimple, *pl.*, *n.*

Papulose, *a.* / Papulous, } Covered with little vesicles, مَمْلُوٌّ مِنْ مَجَالٍ — ذُو سُلَاقٍ (or خُرَاجٍ). *See also* Pimply, *a.*

Papyrus, *n.* سَقِيٌّ — قَصَبُ ٱلْبَرْدِيِّ — فَيْلَكُونُ — غَرْيَفٌ — كَوْلَانٌ — بَرْدِيٌّ. The cotton of the —, قُطْنُ ٱلْبَرْدِيِّ.

Par, *n.* Equality, مُسَاوَاةٌ. One who is equal to another, كُفْوٌ — نَظِيرٌ — كُفُوٌّ — كُفُؤٌ — كِفَآءٌ. On a par, مُسَاوٍ: They two are on a par, هُمَا عَلَى سَوِيَّةٍ. At par, of stocks, مُعَادِلُ ٱلْقِيمَةِ ٱلْأَصْلِيَّةِ — رَأْسٌ بِرَأْسٍ. He has no —, equal, لَا كِفَآءَ لَهُ.

Para, *n.* بَارَةٌ — مَصَارِي *pl.* مِصْرِيَّةٌ — فُلُوس *pl.* فَلْس.

Parable, *n.* تَشْبِيهٌ *pl.* تَشْبِيهَاتٌ — مَثَلٌ *pl.* أَمْثَالٌ. To speak in parables, تَكَلَّمَ بِأَمْثَالٍ. To propound a —, ضَرَبَ مَثَلًا [2]. He made him or it the subject of a —, or example, ضَرَبَ بِهِ مَثَلًا [2].

Parabola, *n.* قَطْعٌ مُكَافِئٌ.

Parabolic, *a.* / Parabolical, } Expressed by parable, بِٱلْمَثَلِ — تَشْبِيهِيٌّ. In the form of a parabola, فِي شَكْلِ ٱلْقَطْعِ ٱلْمُكَافِئِ.

Parabolically, *ad.* By way of parable, تَمْثِيلًا — تَشْبِيهًا. In the form of a parabola, فِي شَكْلِ ٱلْقَطْعِ ٱلْمُكَافِئِ. To describe —, by parable, اِمْتَثَلَ — مَثَّلَ - بِ.

Paraboliform, *a.* فِي شَكْلِ ٱلْقَطْعِ ٱلْمُكَافِئِ.

Paraboloid, *n.* مُجَسَّمٌ مُكَافِئٌ — قَطْعٌ مُكَافِئٌ مُجَسَّمٌ.

Paracentric, *a.* غَيْرُ صَادِقٍ (or شَاذٌّ عَنِ) ٱلِٱسْتِدَارَةِ.

Parachute, *n.* آلَةٌ فِي شَكْلِ شَمْسِيَّةٍ كَبِيرَةٍ.

Paraclete, *n.* The —, ٱلرُّوحُ ٱلْقُدُسُ — ٱلْمُعَزِّي — ٱلْفَارَقْلِيطُ.

Parade, *n.* Pompous exhibition, طَنْطَنَةٌ — مُبَاهَاةٌ — مُفَاخَرَةٌ — وَكْبَةٌ — مَوْكِبٌ — اِفْتِخَارٌ — اِحْتِفَالٌ. Military display, a review, كَشْفٌ عَلَى ٱلْعَسَاكِرِ — عَرْضُ ٱلْجُنْدِ. (*See also under* Show, *n.*) Place of review, مَيْدَانُ تَعْلِيمِ ٱلْعَسْكَرِ — مَحَلُّ عَرْضِ ٱلْجُنْدِ. To make a — of, to boast of, اِفْتَخَرَ بِ — تَبَاهَى بِ.

Parade, *v.t.* To make a show of, exhibit, أَظْهَرَ — أَشْهَرَ. To — troops, كَشَفَ عَلَى ٱلْعَسْكَرِ [2] — عَرَضَ ٱلْجَيْشَ [2]. To show off, as a horse, by riding him to and fro, شَوَّرَ — أَشَارَ — شَارَ [2].

Parade, *v.i.* As of troops, عُرِضَ ٱلْعَسْكَرُ — اِعْتَرَضَ ٱلْجَيْشُ. The soldiers paraded on the parade-ground, اِعْتَرَضَ ٱلْجَيْشُ فِي مَيْدَانِ ٱلتَّمْرِينِ.

Paradigm, *n.* وَزْن *pl.* أَوْزَان — مِيزَان. Paradigmata, أَمْثِلَةٌ — سِيَاقَةٌ — جَدْوَلِيَّةٌ.

Paradigmatic, *a.* Exemplary, أَمْثَلُ *fem.* مُثْلَى *pl.* أَمَاثِلُ.

Paradigmatic, *n.* رَاوِي تَرَاجِمِ أَصْحَابِ ٱلْفَضَائِلِ عِبْرَةً لِمَنْ يَعْتَبِرُ.

Parading, *n.* The act of making a show, مُبَاهَاةٌ — إِظْهَارٌ — إِشْهَارٌ. Review of troops, عَرْضُ ٱلْعَسَاكِرِ.

Paradise, *n.* فِرْدَوْس *pl.* فَرَادِيسُ — ٱلْجَنَّةُ *pl.* ٱلْجَنَّاتُ — دَارُ ٱلنَّعِيمِ — جَنَّةُ ٱلْخُلْدِ — دَارُ ٱلْخُلْدِ — دَارُ ٱلسَّلَامِ. The — of Eden, جَنَّةُ عَدْنٍ. A bird of —, طَيْرُ ٱلْجَنَّةِ — (*Persian*, هُمَا). Paradise lost, ٱلْفِرْدَوْسُ ٱلْمَفْقُودُ.

Paradisiacal, *a.* مُتَعَلِّقٌ بِٱلْفِرْدَوْسِ — مَنْسُوبٌ إِلَى ٱلْجَنَّةِ — مِنْ جَنَّةِ ٱلْخُلْدِ.

Paradox, *n.* A proposition seemingly absurd yet true, تَنَاقُضٌ وَهْمِيٌّ. An enigma, لُغْز *pl.* أَلْغَاز. A dissentient state or condition, بِدْعَةٌ.

Paradoxical, *a.* Seemingly absurd yet true, مُحَالٌ مَوْهُومٌ. Dissentient, مِنْ صِيغَةِ ٱلْبِدْعَةِ. Enigmatical, مُحْتَوٍ عَلَى لُغْزٍ — مُعَمًّى.

Paradoxically, *ad.* بِطِرَازٍ مُحَالٍ مَوْهُومٍ — لُغْزًا.

Paraffine, *n.* زَيْتُ ٱلْقَطْرَانِ.

Paragon, *n.* أُنْمُوذَج ـ قِدْوَة ـ أَمْثَلُ.

Paragon, *v.i.* مَاثَلَ ـ شَابَهَ ـ أَشْبَهَ.

Paragon, *v.t.* مَثَّلَ-ب ـ شَبَّهَ-ب.

Paragram, *n.* تَجْنِيس.

Paragraph, *n.* آيَة *pl.* آيَات ـ فَصْل *pl.* فُصُول ـ عِبَارَة *pl.* عِبَارَات ـ بَنْد *pl.* بُنُود. The — mark, عَلامَةٌ تَدُلُّ عَلَى فَصْلٍ جَدِيدٍ (وَهِيَ ¶).

Paragraph, *v.t.* To write paragraphs, حَرَّرَ ـ كَتَبَ ٱلْفُصُولَ ٱلْبُنُودَ. To put into paragraphs, جَعَلَ-فُصُولاً (or بُنُوداً).

Paragraphic, *a.* }
Paragraphical, } مُرَتَّبٌ عَلَى فُصُولٍ ـ بُنُودٌ بُنُودٌ.

Paraleipsis, *n.* }
Paralipsis, } فَوَات ـ حَذْف.

Parallactic, *a.* مُتَعَلِّقٌ بِٱخْتِلافِ مَنْظَرِ ٱلْكَوَاكِبِ.

Parallax, *n.* إِخْتِلافُ مَنْظَرِ ٱلْكَوَاكِبِ ـ إِخْتِلافُ ٱلْمَنْظَرِ.

Parallel, *a.* Equidistant, مُتَوَازٍ ـ مُوَازٍ. Resembling, مُشَابِه ـ مُمَاثِل ـ نَظِير.

Parallel, *n.* A — line, خَطٌّ مُتَوَازٍ *pl.* خُطُوطٌ مُتَوَازِيَة. Resemblance, مُشَابَهَة. Conformity, مُوَافَقَة ـ مُقَابَلَة. Comparison, تَشْبِيه. A —, or entrenchment, in an approach to attack, خَطٌّ ٱلِاسْتِحْكَام (or مَوْقِع). They seized their first parallel, إِسْتَوَلَوْا عَلَى أَوَّلِ خَطِّ ٱسْتِحْكَامَاتِهِمْ.

Parallel, *v.t.* To preserve the same direction, وَازَى. To be equal to, in weight, تَوَازَنَ ـ وَازَنَ. To resemble, شَابَهَ. To correspond to, وَافَقَ ـ قَابَلَ. To liken to, إِقْتَاسَ ـ شَبَّهَ-ب ـ عَارَضَ-ب. *See also to* Compare, *v.t.*

Parallelism, *n.* The state of being parallel, مُوَازَاة ـ تَوَازٍ ـ مُوَازَاة; resemblance, مُشَابَهَة.

Parallelogram, *n.* مُتَوَازِي ٱلْأَضْلاعِ. A rectangular —, مُسْتَطِيل. An oblique —, شَبِيهٌ بِٱلْمُعَيَّنِ.

Parallelogrammic, *a.* }
Parallelogrammical, } مُتَوَازِي ٱلْأَضْلاعِ.

Parallelopiped, *n.* } مُتَوَازِي ٱلسُّطُوحِ. A rectangular —,
Parallelopipedon, } مُتَوَازِي ٱلْمُسْتَطِيلاتِ.

Paralogism, *n.* }
Paralogy, } قِيَاسٌ فَاسِدٌ.

Paralysis, *n.* فَالِج ـ عُطْل. *See also* Palsy, *n.*

Paralytic, *a.* }
Paralytical, } مَفْلُوج. *See also* Palsied, *a.*

Paralytic, *n.* مَفْلُوج. *See also* Palsied, *a.*

Paralyze, *v.t.* *See to* Palsy, *v.t.*

Paralyzed, *a.* *See* Palsied, *a.*

Paralyzing, *a.* Destroying function, مُعَطِّل ـ مُعْجِز ـ مُخْتَبِل ـ مُضَيِّق ـ مُخْمِد.

Paramount, *a.* Superior, chief, principal, أَعْظَم ـ أَكْبَر ـ أَعْلَى ـ أَفْضَل. Paramount or ruling over, مُتَسَلِّطٌ عَلَى. *See also* Dominant, *a.*

Paramount, *n.* سُلْطَان ـ مُتَسَلِّط. *See also* Sovereign, *n.*

Paramour, *n.* A lover, عَاشِق *fem.* عَاشِقَة. A mistress, courtesan, سِرِّيَّة *pl.* سَرَارِيّ ـ مَحْظِيَّة *pl.* مَحَاظِي.

Paranymph, *n.* *See* Brideman, *n.*

Parapet, *n.* As of a rampart, دَائِرُ ٱلسُّورِ ـ سِتَارَة; as of a bridge, *etc.* حَاجِز *pl.* حَوَاجِز; of a roof, سُتْرَة.

Paraphernia, *n.* } The goods of a wife beyond her dower, صَدَاق ـ
Paraphernalia, } مَالُ ٱلزَّوْجَةِ. Appendages, تَعَلُّقَات ـ تَابِعَة. Ornaments, زِينَة ـ حِلْيَة. A fit, an outfit, جِهَاز ـ تَجْهِيز.

Paraphernal, *a.* جِهَازِيّ ـ مُتَعَلِّقٌ بِٱلتَّجْهِيزِ.

Paraphrase, *n.* شَرْح ـ تَفْسِير ـ إِيضَاح ـ تَعْبِير ـ تَأْوِيل.

Paraphrase, *v.t.* عَبَّرَ ـ أَوْضَحَ ـ فَسَّرَ ـ شَرَحَ ـ تَأَوَّلَ.

Paraphrast, *n.* مُعَبِّر ـ مُؤَوِّل ـ مُتَأَوِّل ـ مُفَسِّر ـ شَارِح *pl.* شُرَّاح.

Paraphrastic, *a.* }
Paraphrastical, } تَشْرِيحِيّ ـ مُوَضِّح ـ تَأْوِيلِيّ.

Paraphrastically, *ad.* تَشْرِيحًا ـ بِٱلتَّأْوِيلِ ـ بِٱلتَّشْرِيحِ.

Paraplegia, *n.* }
Paraplegy, } فَالِجُ أَسْفَلِ ٱلْبَدَنِ.

Paraquet, *n.* }
Paraquito, } بَبَغَا صَغِيرَة.

Parasang, *n.* فَرْسَخ *pl.* فَرَاسِخ.

Parascene, *n.* } بَيْتُ لُبْسِ ٱللَّاعِبِينَ فِي ٱلتِّيَاتْرُو عِنْدَ ٱلرُّومَانِيِّينَ
Parascenium, } ٱلْأَقْدَمِينَ.

Paraselene, *n.* A circle round the moon, هَالَة *pl.* هَالات ـ دَارَة ـ دَوَّارَةُ ٱلْقَمَرِ ـ ٱلْقَمَرِ. A mock moon, قَمَرٌ كَاذِبٌ.

Parasite, *n.* A hanger-on, طُفَيْلِيّ *pl.* طُفَيْلِيَّة ـ لَقْلُوق *pl.* لَقَالِيق ـ كَشُوثُ ٱلشَّجَرِ; a whispering —, دَسِيس ـ دَاسُوس.

Parasite, of a plant, عُلَّيْق ـ كَشُوث ـ كُشُوث ـ شَكِير *pl.* شُكُر.

He is a —, فُلانٌ كَشُوثُ ٱلشَّجَرِ. A parasitical insect, دُوَيْبَةٌ عَلُوقَةٌ. *See also* Sycophant, *n.*

Parasitic, *a.* | Parasitical, | Like a parasite, sycophant, مِثْلَ ـ مِثْلَ ٱلطُّفَيْلِيِّ ـ مِنْ ـ مِنْ جِنْسِ ٱلشُّكْرِ ٱللَّقْلُوقِ . Of plants, جِنْسِ ٱلْكَشُوثِ .

Parasol, *n.* شَمْسِيَّةٌ صَغِيرَةٌ ـ مِظَلَّةٌ .

Parboil, *v.t.* To boil partly, سَلَقَ ـ نَشَفَ ـ سَلَقَ بَعْضَ ٱلسَّلْقِ ـ سَلْقٍ .

Parcel, *n.* A quantity, مِقْدَار . A number, جُمْلَةٌ ـ عَدَدٌ . A bundle, صُرَّةٌ *pl.* صُرَر ـ حُزْمَةٌ *pl.* حُزَم ـ ضِبَارَةٌ *pl.* ضَبَائِر . A portion, حِصَّةٌ *pl.* حِصَص . A — of land, بُقْعَةٌ ـ قِطْعَةٌ مِنَ ٱلْأَرْضِ *pl.* بِقَاع . A — of books, إِضْمَامَةٌ (*or*) إِضْبَارَةٌ مِنَ ٱلْكُتُبِ . A pack, دَسْت *pl.* دُسُوت . A party, قَوْم *pl.* أَقْوَام ـ طَائِفَةٌ *pl.* طَوَائِف . To be part and — of, كَانَ مِن ـ كَانَ جُزْءًا مِن . To make up in a —, صَرَّ²; of books, ضَبَرَ ـ ضَبَّرَ . *See also* Bundle, Pack, Packet, Set, *n.*

Parcel, *v.t.* To divide into portions, قَطَّعَ ـ جَزَّأَ ـ جَزَأَ . To divide, distribute, فَرَّقَ ـ قَسَّمَ ـ وَزَّعَ . To — a rope, لَفَّ² شَيَّدَ ٱلْحَبْلَ ـ تَشْيِيدًا عَلَى ٱلْحَبْلِ .

Parcenary, *n.* Coheirship, شِرْكَةٌ فِي ٱلْإِرْثِ .

Parcener, *n.* A coheir, شَرِيكٌ فِي ٱلْإِرْثِ .

Parch, *v.t.* To scorch, of the sun, سَقَرَ² . To nip, blast, سَلَقَ² ـ شَوَّطَ ـ أَحْرَقَ . To —, by not watering, أَعْطَشَ . To dry, يَبَّسَ ـ جَفَّفَ . Parched corn, فَرِيك . Parched land, حَرَّةٌ ـ سَبَخَةٌ ـ مَعْطَشَةٌ .

Parch, *v.i.* To be scorched, as by the sun, سُقِرَ . To be nipped, blasted, سُلِقَ ـ إِحْتَرَقَ . To be thirsty from want of water, عَطِشَ . To be dried up, إِتَّبَسَ ـ تَجَفَّفَ .

Parchedness, *n.* Dryness from want of water, عَطَش ـ مَعْطَش . The being dried up, يُبُوسَةٌ ـ جُفُوف ـ يُبْس ـ تَجَفُّف .

Parchment, *n.* رَقّ *pl.* رُقُوق ـ رَقُّ ٱلْغَزَالِ . A — maker, صَانِعُ رَقِّ ٱلْغَزَالِ .

Pard, *n.* *See* Leopard, *n.*

Pardon, *v.t.* صَفَحَ عَن ـ عَفَا عَن² ـ تَرَحَّمَ عَلَى ـ رَحِمَ ـ غَفَرَ لَ ـ سَمَحَ لَهُ بِ . To excuse, make allowances for, سَامَحَ ـ عَذَرَ ـ عَذَرَ فِي ـ سَامَحَ بِ . Pardon me, ٱلْعَفْوَ ـ سَامِحْنِي ـ لَا تُؤَاخِذْنِي . *See also to* Forgive, *v.t.*

Pardon, *n.* Forgiveness, مُسَامَحَةٌ ـ عَفْوٌ ـ صَفْح ـ رَحْمَةٌ . A certificate of pardon, تَذْكِرَةُ ٱلْعَفْوِ . Remission of sins, مَغْفِرَةٌ ـ غُفْرَان . He proclaimed a general —, amnesty, for ..., أَعْلَنَ ٱلْعَفْوَ ٱلْعَامَّ عَن . To beg —, إِسْتَغْفَرَ ـ إِعْتَذَرَ . I ask your —, by your leave, بِدُسْتُورِكَ ـ ٱلْعَفْوَ ـ عَنْ إِذْنِكَ . I ask — for having troubled you, سَامِحْنِي ـ كَلَّفْتُ خَاطِرَكَ بِإِزْعَاجِ ٱلْخَاطِرِ . (The ordinary reply to these courteous speeches is, وَاجِبٌ عَلَيَّ). *See also* Forgiveness, *n.*

Pardonable, *a.* حَلَّ ـ مِمَّا يُعْفَى عَنْهُ ـ حَلُّ ٱلْعَفْوِ ـ يُغْفَرُ ٱلْمُسَامَحَةِ . *See also* Excusable, *a.*

Pardoner, *n.* | Pardoning, *a.* | غَفُور ـ رَحْمٰن ـ غَافِر ـ مُعْفٍ . *See also* Forgiving, *a.*

Pare, *v.t.* To peel, قَشَّرَ ـ قَشَرَ² ـ جَلَفَ² . To abrade, scrape or rub off, سَحَلَ ـ جَلَفَ² . To —, as of leather, حَمَرَ²; of the nails, قَصَّ² (*or*) بَرَى ٱلْأَظْفَارَ ; of a pen, بَرَى ٱلْقَلَمَ . To — down, lessen, قَلَّلَ ـ أَنْقَصَ ـ نَقَّصَ .

Paregoric, *a.* مُخَفِّفُ ٱلْوَجَعِ ـ مُسَكِّنُ ٱلْوَجَعِ ـ سُلْوَان .

Parent, *n.* Father, وَالِد ; mother, وَالِدَةٌ ; father and mother, the two parents, ٱلْوَالِدَانِ ـ أَبَوَانِ ـ أَبَانِ . A cause, عِلَّةٌ ـ سَبَب ـ بَاعِث . A source, مَنْبَع ـ مَصْدَر ـ مَطْلَع . They are his parents, father and mother, هُمَا أَبَوَاهُ . I saw his parents, his father and mother, رَأَيْتُ أَبَوَيْهِ .

Parentage, *n.* نَسَب ـ نَسْل ـ أَصْل ـ بَدَن . *See also* Birth, Descent, Extraction, *n.*

Parental, *a.* مُتَعَلِّقٌ بِٱلْوَالِدَيْنِ ـ وَالِدِيٌّ . Paternal, أَبَوِيٌّ ; maternal, أُمِّيٌّ .

Parentally, *adv.* مِثْلَ ٱلْوَالِدَيْنِ ـ كَٱلْوَالِدَيْنِ ـ كَٱلْأَبَوَيْنِ .

Parenthesis, *n.* A parenthetical sentence, جُمْلَةٌ مُعْتَرِضَةٌ ـ جُمْلَةٌ دَاخِلَةٌ فِي جُمْلَةٍ أُخْرَى ـ إِعْتِرَاض ـ حَشْوٌ . The brackets of a —, ( ) هِلَالَانِ يُسَوِّرَانِ جُمْلَةً مُعْتَرِضَةً عَلَى هٰذِهِ ٱلصِّفَةِ .

Parenthetical, *a.* عِبَارَةٌ عَنْ جُمْلَةٍ مُعْتَرِضَةٍ ـ مُعْتَرِض .

Parenthetically, *ad.* بِٱعْتِرَاضٍ ـ إِعْتِرَاضًا . The clause intervened —, إِعْتَرَضَتِ ٱلْجُمْلَةُ .

Parenticide, *n.* The killer of father or mother, قَاتِلُ أَبِيهِ أَوْ أُمِّهِ . The murder of a father or mother, قَتْلُ أَبِيهِ أَوْ أُمِّهِ . *See also* Matricide, Parricide, *n.*

Parentless, *a.* بِلَا وَالِدَيْنِ . *See also* Orphan, *a.*

Parer, *n.* One who pares, جَالِف ـ حَامِر . An instrument for paring leather, *etc.*, مِحْمَر ـ مِجْلَفَةٌ .

Parget, *n.* تَلْبِيس . Parget mixed with straw, شِيَاع . *See also* Plaster, *n.*

Parget, *v.t.* لَبَّسَ ـ شَيَّعَ . *See also to* Plaster, *v.t.*

Pargeter, *n.* جَبَّاس ـ مُلَبِّس . *See also* Plasterer, *n.*

Parhelion, *n.* شَمْسٌ كَاذِبَةٌ .

Pariah, *n.* لَقَبُ أَحْقَرِ طَائِفَةٍ مِنْ طَوَائِفِ ٱلْهِنْدِ .

Parian, *a.* مَنْسُوبٌ إِلَى جَزِيرَةِ بَارُهْ ٱلْكَائِنَةِ فِي ٱلْبَحْرِ ٱلْأَبْيَضِ.

Parian, *n.* A composition in imitation of marble, حَجَرٌ مَطْبُوخٌ يُشْبِهُ ٱلرُّخَامَ.

Parietal, *a.* Pertaining to the walls of a building, مُتَعَلِّقٌ بِحِيطَانِ ٱلْبِنَاءِ. A — bone, صَفِيحَةٌ *pl.* صَفَائِحُ. The — bones, including the frontal and occipital, ٱلصَّفَائِحُ — ٱلْقَبَائِلُ.

Paring, *n.* A rind, peel, قِشْرَةٌ. Something scraped or rubbed off, قُرَاضَةٌ — قُصَاصَةٌ. Parings, قُرَاضَةٌ — بُرَايَةٌ — بُرَوَةٌ; nail parings, قُسَيْطٌ. A small piece, حِتَّةٌ *pl.* حِتَتٌ. A knife for paring, مِبْرَاةٌ; *See also under* Parer, *n.*

Pari passu, ad. مُسَاوَاةً — بِٱلسَّوِيَّةِ.

Parish, *n.* The district of a cure, أَبْرَشِيَّةُ ٱلْخُورِي. A district, quarter, مَحَلٌّ *pl.* مَحَلَّاتٌ — حَارَةٌ *pl.* حَارَاتٌ.

Parishioner, *n.* One belonging to a parish, church, cure, مِنْ أَبْنَاءِ رَعِيَّةِ ٱلْخُورِي; belonging to a district, مِنْ أَهْلِ — مِنَ ٱلْمَحَلِّ ٱبْنُ ٱلْحَارَةِ — ٱلْمَحَلِّ.

Parisian, *a.* مِنْ بَارِيسَ.

Parisian, *n.* مِنْ أَهْلِ بَارِيسَ.

Parity, *n.* Likeness in condition, degree, *etc.*, مُسَاوَاةٌ — مُشَابَهَةٌ — تَسَاوٍ. By a — of reasoning, بِذَاتِ ٱلْقِيَاسِ.

Park, *n.* An inclosure of lands, بُسْتَانٌ — حَدَائِقُ *pl.* حَدِيقَةٌ *pl.* بَسَاتِينُ. A — of artillery, مَجْمَعُ ٱلْمَدَافِعِ.

Park, *v.t.* To make into a park, صَيَّرَ حَدِيقَةً. To — artillery, جَعَلَ ٱلْمَدَافِعَ فِي مَحَلٍّ مَخْصُوصٍ.

Parker, *n.* A keeper of a park, حَارِسُ (*or* نَاظِرُ) ٱلْحَدِيقَةِ.

Parlance, *n.* كَلَامٌ — حَدِيثٌ — مُكَالَمَةٌ — مُحَاوَرَةٌ.

Parley, *v.i.* To confer together, فَاوَضَ (of many, تَفَاوَضُوا). To treat about, they had a parley about, تَحَدَّثُوا فِي — تَفَاوَضُوا فِي — تَدَاوَلُوا عَنْ.

Parley, *n.* مُكَالَمَةٌ — مُفَاوَضَةٌ — مُدَاوَلَةٌ — ٱئْتِمَارٌ.

Parliament, *n.* دِيوَانُ أُمَرَاءِ ٱلشَّعْبِ وَوُكَلَائِهِ — مَجْلِسُ ٱلشُّورَى — مَجْلِسُ ٱلْبَارْلِمَنْتُو — مَجْلِسُ ٱلْأُمَّةِ. The Upper House of —, مَجْلِسُ أُمَرَاءِ ٱلْأُمَّةِ; the Lower House of —, مَجْلِسُ وُكَلَاءِ ٱلْأُمَّةِ. A member of —, مِنْ أَعْضَاءِ مَجْلِسِ ٱلشُّورَى. To convoke —, أَمَرَ بِٱجْتِمَاعِ مَجْلِسِ ٱلشُّورَى [2]. To elect a new —, جَدَّدَ مَجْلِسَ ٱلشُّورَى; election of a new —, تَجْدِيدُ مَجْلِسِ ٱلشُّورَى.

Parliamentary, *a.* Belonging to parliament, مُتَعَلِّقٌ بِمَجْلِسِ ٱلشُّورَى. Enacted by parliament, مَحْكُومٌ بِهِ مِنْ مَجْلِسِ ٱلشُّورَى. According to the usages of parliament, حَسَبَ قَوَانِينِ مَجْلِسِ ٱلشُّورَى.

Parlour, *n.* A room for conversation and sitting, بَيْتُ ٱلْقُعُودِ — دِيوَانٌ — مَقْعَدٌ. A small room, غُرْفَةٌ *pl.* غُرَفٌ — عِلِّيَّةٌ *pl.* عَلَالِيُّ.

Parnassian, *a.* مَا نِيطَ بِجَبَلِ بَرْنَسُوسَ ٱلْمُسَمَّى ٱلْآنَ بِجَبَلِ لِيَاكُورَةَ. *See also the next article.*

Parnassus, *n.* جَبَلُ بَرْنَسُوسَ ٱلْمُسَمَّى ٱلْآنَ بِجَبَلِ لِيَاكُورَةَ ٱلْكَائِنُ فِي بِلَادِ ٱلرُّومِ مَشْهُورٌ عِنْدَ ٱلْيُونَانِ بِعِبَادَةِ إِلٰهَةِ ٱلشِّعْرِ وَٱلْعَزْفِ.

Parochial, *a.* Belonging to a cure, مَا نِيطَ بِرَعِيَّةِ ٱلْخُورِي. Belonging to a district, مَحَلِّيٌّ — مُتَعَلِّقٌ بِٱلْمَحَلِّ (*or* ٱلْحَارَةِ).

Parochially, *ad.* According to the cure, حَسَبَ مَحَطِّ ٱلْخُورِي; by the district, حَسَبَ ٱلْمَحَلِّ.

Parodist, *n.* قَلَّابُ (*or* مُحَرِّفُ) كَلَامِ ٱلْجِدِّ إِلَى هَزْلٍ.

Parody, *n.* قَلْبُ (*or* تَحْرِيفُ) كَلَامِ ٱلْجِدِّ إِلَى هَزْلٍ.

Parody, *v.t.* قَلَّبَ (*or* حَرَّفَ) كَلَامَ ٱلْجِدِّ هَزْلًا.

Parol, *a.* / Parole, } *See* Oral, *a.*

Parol, *n.* / Parole, } A statement, إِفَادَةٌ — تَقْرِيرٌ. A watchword, شِعَارٌ — سِرُّ ٱللَّيْلِ. A pledge by a prisoner released, عَهْدُ ٱلْمَعْتُوقِ بِٱلِٱسْتِسْلَامِ ثَانِيَةً عِنْدَ ٱلِٱقْتِضَاءِ. To release on —, أَعْتَقَ بِشَرْطِ ٱلِٱسْتِسْلَامِ ثَانِيَةً عِنْدَ ٱلِٱقْتِضَاءِ. To be on —, إِنْعَتَقَ بِشَرْطِ ٱلِٱسْتِسْلَامِ ثَانِيَةً عِنْدَ ٱلِٱقْتِضَاءِ.

Paranomasia, *n.* تَجْنِيسٌ.

Paroquet, *n.* *See* Paraquet, *n.*

Parotid, *a.* A — gland, بِنْتُ ٱلْأُذُنِ *pl.* بَنَاتٌ. A tumour of the — gland, نَزْلَةٌ فِي بَنَاتِ ٱلْأُذُنِ.

Paroxysm, *n.* شِدَّةُ مَرَضٍ — دَوْرٌ — بُرَحَاءُ — وُرُودٌ — مُعَاوَدَةٌ — عُرَوَاءُ. The — has seized him, أَصَابَتْهُ ٱلْبُرَحَاءُ.

Paroxysmal, *n.* Coming in paroxysms, بِٱلدَّوْرِ — وَاقِعٌ بُرَحَاءَ بُرَحَاءَ.

Parquetry, *n.* زَوَاقٌ — تَعْبِيقٌ — تَرْصِيعٌ — فُسَيْفِسَةٌ.

Parrel, *n.* As for a mast, حِفَاظُ ٱلسَّارِيَةِ.

Parricidal, *a.* قَاتِلُ ٱلْوَالِدَيْنِ — مَا نِيطَ بِقَتْلِ ٱلْوَالِدَيْنِ.

Parricide, *n.* *See* Parenticide, *n.*

Parrot, *n.* بَبَّغَاءُ — بَبْغَاءُ (*vulg.* بَبْغَان *and* دُرَّة).

Parry, *v.t.* To ward off, أَجْنَبَ — جَنَّبَ — جَنَبَ [2]. To repel, to rebut, دَفَعَ — دَسَعَ. To turn aside from, as from a blow or misfortune, أَبْطَلَ ٱلضَّرْبَةَ — صَرَفَ عَنْهُ ٱلضَّرْبَةَ — وَقَى *aor.* يَقِي. To avoid, إِجْتَنَبَ — حَادَ عَنْ — تَوَقَّفَ عَنْ.

Parry, *v.i.* *See to* Fence, *v.i.*

Parse, *v.t.* أَعْرَبَ.

Parsee, *n.* عَابِدُ ٱلنَّارِ مِنْ سُكَّانِ ٱلْهِنْدِ *pl.* عُبَّادٌ — فَارِسِيٌّ *pl.* فَارِسِيَّةٌ.

Parseeism, *n.* مَذْهَبُ عَبَدَةِ ٱلنَّارِ بِٱلْهِنْدِ — مَذْهَبُ ٱلْفَارِسِيَّةِ.

Parsimonious, *a.* مُتَحَرِّق ـ قَرِط ـ شَحِيح ـ قَتُور ـ حَظِل ـ بَخِيل ـ مَسِيك. To be —, شَحَّ *aor.* يَشِحُّ. To be — towards, قَتَرَ عَلَى ². *See also* Niggardly, Miserly, *a.*

Parsimoniously, *ad.* بِبُخْلٍ ـ بِمَسَاكَةٍ ـ بِشُحٍّ ـ بِقَتْرٍ.

Parsimoniousness, *n.* }
Parsimony, } مَسَاكَة ـ شُحَّة ـ شُحّ ـ قَتْر ـ حِظْلَان ـ بُخْل ـ حَرَق. *See also* Niggardliness, Avarice, Economy, *n.*

Parsing, *n.* إِعْرَاب.

Parsley, *n.* بَقْدُونِس ـ مَقْدُونِس.

Parsnep, *n.* }
Parsnip, } نَوْعٌ مِنَ ٱلْجَزَرِ ٱلْأَبْيَضِ; (called in Barbary جَعْدَة *or* سَفْرَانِيَّة; and in Turkish, يبان هاوجى.)

Parson, *n.* The priest of a parish, خُورِي *pl.* خَوَارِنَة. A clergyman, قَسّ *or* قِسِّيس *pl.* قُسَّان *and* قِسِّيسُون.

Parsonage, *n.* بَيْتُ ٱلْخُورِي.

Part, *n.* A piece, جُزْءٌ *pl.* أَجْزَاءٌ ـ شُعْبَة *pl.* شُعَب ـ حِتَّة *pl.* حِتَت. A portion, division, قِسْم ـ قِسْمَة ـ نَصِيب ـ حِصَّة *pl.* حِصَص. A chapter, part of a book, جُزْءٌ *pl.* أَجْزَاءٌ ـ فَصْل *pl.* فُصُول. A duty, مَا هُوَ عَلَى ـ ٱلْوَاجِبُ عَلَى. Direction, situation, نَاحِيَة ـ صَوْب ـ نَاحِيَة ـ طَرَف ـ مَوْقِع. Place, district, مَحَلّ ـ جِرْبَة ـ نَاحِيَة ـ طَرَف ـ مَوْقِع. Place, district, مَحَلّ ـ جِرْنَة *pl.* نَوَاحِي ـ جَنْب *pl.* أَجْنَاب. An office, calling, وَظِيفَة ـ عَلَاقَة. A share, حِصَّة. Some, بَعْض. A side, party, جَانِب ـ طَرَف ـ صَوْب ـ حِزْب *pl.* أَحْزَاب. Parts, pieces, فَنَص. Parts, abilities, شَمَائِل ـ مَنَاقِب ـ فَضَائِل. Consisting of many parts, كَثِيرُ ٱلْأَجْزَاءِ. Divided into parts, مُجَزَّأٌ. Part by —, شَيْئًا فَشَيْئًا. You have no — with me in the matter, لَيْسَ لَكَ مَعِي نَصِيبٌ فِي ٱلْأَمْرِ. A — of them were with the soldiers and a — in the city, كَانَ بَعْضُهُمْ مَعَ ٱلْعَسْكَرِ وَبَعْضُهُمْ فِي ٱلْمَدِينَةِ. You have neither — nor lot in this matter, nothing to do with it, لَيْسَ لَكَ دَعْوَى وَلَا طَلَبَة فِي هٰذَا ٱلْأَمْرِ. The secret parts, ٱلْعَوْرَةُ.

Aliquant parts, كَسْرٌ أَصَمّ.

Aliquot parts, كَسْرٌ صَحِيحٌ.

A person of parts, لَوْذَعِيٌّ ـ صَاحِبُ شَمَائِل فَضَائِل.

Component parts, ٱلْأَجْزَاءُ ٱلْمُرَكَّبَةُ.

Foreign parts, ٱلنَّوَاحِي ٱلْبَرَّانِيَّةُ ـ ٱلْمَمَالِكُ ٱلْأَجْنَبِيَّةُ.

For my part, مِنْ جِهَتِي ـ مِنْ قِبَلِي ـ مِنْ طَرَفِي.

For the most part, غَالِبًا ـ بِٱلْأَكْثَرِ ـ فِي ٱلْأَغْلَبِ.

In part, بَعْض ـ عَلَى جِهَةٍ. We know in part, نَعْلَمُ بَعْضَ ٱلْعِلْمِ.

In parts, جُزْءًا جُزْءًا. It is published in parts, صُدُورُهُ كُرَّاسَةً كُرَّاسَةً ـ نَشْرُهُ جُزْءًا جُزْءًا.

In good part, بِٱسْتِحْسَانٍ ـ بِطِيبِ خَاطِرٍ.

In bad or ill part, تَقْبِيحًا ـ تَنْكِيسًا ـ بِتَقْبِيحٍ ـ بِمُخَالَفَةٍ.

In the lowest part of the earth, فِي أَسَافِلِ ٱلْأَرْضِ.

On the part of, مِنْ جِهَةِ ـ مِنْ قِبَلِ ـ مِنْ طَرَفِ.

Part and parcel of, مِنْ ـ قِسْمٌ مِنْ ـ جُزْءٌ مِنْ.

Part of speech, قِسْمٌ مِنَ ٱلْكَلَامِ *pl.* أَقْسَام ـ كَلِمَة *pl.* كَلِمَات.

Uttermost parts of the earth, أَقَاصِي ٱلْأَرْضِ.

To act, perform, or play a part, as in a play, drama, كَانَ مِنْ لُعَّابِ تَشَخَّصَ مَعَ لُعَّابِ ٱلسِّيرِ فِي ٱلتِّيَاتْرُو ـ ٱلتَّشْخِيصِ فِي ٱلتِّيَاتْرُو.

To play a part in any undertaking, عَمِلَ فِي ـ ٱشْتَرَكَ فِي ².

To pretend, تَصَنَّعَ بِ ـ تَظَاهَرَ بِ.

To be or form a part of, كَانَ مِنْ جُمْلَةِ ـ كَانَ جُزْءًا مِنْ ـ كَانَ مِنْ ـ كَانَ دَاخِلًا فِي.

To do one's part, جَاءَ بِمَا ـ أَقَامَ بِمَا عَلَيْهِ ـ قَضَى مَا عَلَيْهِ ـ وَجَبَ عَلَيْهِ.

To take a part in, share in, ٱشْتَرَكَ فِي. To take a portion of, أَخَذَ حِصَّةً مِنْ ².

To take a part of, أَخَذَ مِنْ ² ـ أَخَذَ حِصَّةً مِنْ ².

To take the part of, حَامَى عَنْ ـ شَدَّ مَعَ ² ـ تَعَصَّبَ لِ ـ أَعَانَ عَلَى.

To take part with, share with, ٱشْتَرَكَ مَعَ ـ شَارَكَ ـ حَاصَصَ.

To alternate with, أَعْقَبَ ـ عَاقَبَ.

Part, *v.t.* To divide, قَسَمَ ²; to — into different pieces, قَسَّمَ ـ وَزَّعَ عَلَى ـ قَسَمَ بَيْنَ ـ جَزَّأَ ـ جَزَأَ ² ـ قَطَّعَ. To divide amongst, وَزَّعَ ـ فَرَّقَ عَلَى ـ قَسَمَ بَيْنَ. To — or separate from, فَارَقَ ـ فَصَلَ مِنْ ـ فَرَّقَ عَلَى. To —, as of the legs, أَفْجَّ. To — with, give up, سَيَّبَ ـ أَطْلَقَ ـ تَخَلَّى عَنْ ـ فَاتَ ². To — a cable, قَطَعَ ² (*or* شَقَّ ²) ٱللَّبَانَ. There is not one to — them, لَيْسَ مَنْ يَفْصِلُ بَيْنَهُمْ. *See also to* Divide, *v.t.*

Part, *v.i.* To divide, ٱنْقَسَمَ. To separate, ٱنْفَصَلَ ـ ٱفْتَرَقَ. To be distributed, to distribute itself, ٱنْشَعَبَ ـ تَشَعَّبَ ـ تَوَزَّعَ. To — into pieces, ٱنْفَلَجَ ـ تَفَلَّقَ ـ ٱنْفَلَقَ. To be parted or disunited from, ٱنْفَضَّ مِنْ. The ship parted asunder, تَخَلَّعَتِ (*or* تَفَكَّكَتِ) ٱلسَّفِينَةُ.

Partake, *v.i.* To share with in, شَارَكَ فِي ـ شَرِكَ فِي ². To cause to — in, أَشْرَكَ فِي ـ أَحْصَصَ فِي ـ حَاصَصَ فِي. To take of, أَخَذَ مِنْ ² ـ تَنَاوَلَ مِنْ ـ ٱتَّخَذَ مِنْ. To eat of, أَكَلَ مِنْ ².

Partaker, *n.* A sharer, مُشَارِك ـ شَرِيك *pl.* شُرَكَاءُ. An accomplice, رَفِيقٌ فِي ـ شَرِيكٌ فِي.

Partaking, *n.* مُشَارَكَة ـ شِرْكَة.

Parted, *a.* Separated, مُنْفَصِل ; divided, distributed, مُتَوَزِّع ; parted asunder, split, مَشْقُوق ـ مُنْفَلِق ـ مُتَخَلِّع ; shared, مُشْتَرَك فِيهِ . From there the river was parted into four heads, وَمِنْ هُنَاكَ يَنْقَسِمُ ٱلنَّهْرُ فَيَصِيرُ أَرْبَعَةَ رُؤُوسٍ .

Parterre, *n.* A flower garden, رَوْضَة *pl.* رِيَاض ـ بُسْتَان *pl.* بَسَاتِين . The pit of a theatre, أَرْضُ ٱلْمَرْسَح ـ صَحْنُ ٱلتِّيَاتْرُو .

Partial, *a.* Including a part only, جُزْئِيّ ـ مُحْتَوٍ عَلَى بَعْضٍ فَقَطْ ـ غَيْرُ شَامِلٍ ـ غَيْرُ عَامٍّ ـ غَيْرُ عُمُومِيّ . Biassed, صَاحِبُ غَرَضٍ ـ غَيْرُ مُنْصِف ـ مُوَالِس . Partial to, liking, مُحِبّ ـ مُوِدٌّ إِلَى ; well inclined to, مُسْتَعْطِفٌ إِلَى . To be — towards, حَابَى ـ أَخْطَأَ عَلَى : You have been —, acted with partiality, in the law, حَابَيْتُمْ فِي ٱلشَّرِيعَةِ . To be — to, to like, أَحَبَّ ـ وَدَّ ; to be favourably disposed to, إِسْتَعْطَفَ إِلَى ـ تَعَطَّفَ عَلَى ـ لَوِيَ عَلَى .
See also under to Like, to Favour, *v.t.*

Partiality, *n.* Undue bias, غَرَض ـ مُرَاعَاةُ ٱلْخَوَاطِرِ ـ مُحَابَاة ـ مُوَالَسَة . Do nothing with —, لَا تَعْمَلْ شَيْئًا بِمُحَابَاةٍ . Predilection for, مَيْلٌ إِلَى ـ إِنْعِطَافٌ إِلَى . Taste, love, for, وُدٌّ إِلَى .
See also Liking, *n.*

Partially, *ad.* With bias, بِغَرَضٍ ـ بِمُرَاعَاةِ ٱلْخَوَاطِرِ ـ بِمُحَابَاةٍ ـ بِمُوَالَسَةٍ . In part only, بَعْضَ ـ بِوَجْهٍ فَقَطْ ـ جُزْءًا : We know it —, in part only, نَعْلَمُهُ بَعْضَ ٱلْعِلْمِ فَقَطْ . It is only — clean, هُوَ نَظِيفٌ بَعْضَ ٱلنَّظَافَةِ فَقَطْ .

Partibility, *n.* Susceptibility of severance, قَابِلِيَّةُ ٱلِٱنْفِصَالِ ; of division, قَابِلِيَّةُ ٱلِٱنْقِسَامِ .

Partible, *a.* That may be severed, مِمَّا يَنْفَصِلُ ـ مِمَّا يَفْتَرِقُ ; that may be divided, يَنْقَسِمُ .

Participable, *a.* مِمَّا يُشْتَرَكُ فِيهِ .

Participant, *a.* and *n.* مُشَارِك ـ شَارِك .

Participate, *v.i.* He participated with him in it, شَرِكَهُ فِيهِ ـ شَارَكَهُ فِيهِ . They all participated in it, إِشْتَرَكُوا فِيهِ جُمْلَةً . *See also to* Partake, *v.i.*

Participation, *n.* إِشْتِرَاك ـ مُشَارَكَة ـ شِرْكَة .

Participator, *n.* *See* Partaker, *n.*

Participial, *a.* Having the nature of a participle, مِنْ صِيغَةِ ٱسْمِ ٱلْفَاعِلِ أَوِ ٱسْمِ ٱلْمَفْعُولِ . Formed from a participle, مُشْتَقٌّ مِنِ ٱسْمِ فَاعِلٍ أَوِ ٱسْمِ مَفْعُولٍ .

Participially, *ad.* فِي صِيغَةِ ٱسْمِ ٱلْفَاعِلِ أَوِ ٱسْمِ ٱلْمَفْعُولِ .

Participle, *n.* An active —, إِسْمُ فَاعِلٍ ; a passive —, إِسْمُ مَفْعُولٍ .

Particle, *n.* A minute portion, هُشَامَة ـ ذَرَّى ـ جِثَّة *pl.* جِثَث ; particles, دُقَاقَة ـ دُقَاق ; of gold or silver, تِبْر ; fragments, رُفَات ـ كُسَار . In grammar, أَدَاة *pl.* أَدَوَات ـ حَرْفُ مَعْنًى *pl.* حُرُوف . A compensative or conditional —, حَرْفُ جَزَاءٍ ـ حَرْفُ شَرْطٍ . An adjunctive —, حَرْفُ عَاطِف ـ حَرْفُ عَطْفٍ . A vocative —, نِدَاء .

Parti-coloured, *a.* *See* Party-coloured, *a.*

Particular, *a.* Distinct, special, مَخْصُوص ـ خَاصّ *pl.* خَوَاصّ ; particular to one, مُخْتَصّ بِهِ ـ مَخْصُوص لَهُ ـ مُخَصَّص لَهُ . Remarkable, غَرِيب ـ نَادِر ـ عَجِيب . Minute, exact, مُدَقِّق ـ كَثِيرُ ٱلتَّدْقِيقِ . To be —, exact, in, دَقَّ فِي ـ إِسْتَدَقَّ فِي . To be — about, as one's dress, *etc.*, تَأَنَّقَ فِي ـ بَالَغَ فِي . There is nothing — in his book, لَيْسَ فِي تَأْلِيفِهِ شَيْءٌ غَرِيبٌ . To be —, special, to one, تَخَصَّصَ بِ ـ إِخْتَصَّ بِ .

Particular, *n.* A point or circumstance, خُصُوص ـ أَمْر *pl.* أُمُور ـ مَادَّة *pl.* مَوَادّ ـ بَاب *pl.* أَبْوَاب ـ حَادِثَة *pl.* حَوَادِث ; particulars, details, أَحْوَال ـ أَغْرَاض ـ تَفْصِيلَات . A — person, شَخْص *pl.* أَشْخَاص . A — thing or friend, خَاصَّة ; a — little friend, خُوَيْصَّة . In this —, فِي هٰذَا ٱلْخُصُوصِ .

Particularity, *n.* Something peculiar, خَاصَّة . A particular property, خَاصَّة ـ خَاصِّيَّة *pl.* خَاصِّيَّات *and* خَصَائِص . Detail, تَفْصِيل ـ شَرْحٌ بِٱلتَّفْصِيلِ . Exactness, دِقَّة .

Particularization, *n.* The act of denoting specially, تَخْصِيص . Noticing in detail, ذِكْرٌ بِٱلتَّفْصِيلِ .

Particularize, *v.t.* To individuate, distinguish, عَيَّنَ ـ خَصَّصَ . To be rendered particular, special, (of a thing), تَخَصَّصَ ; of a person, إِخْتَصَّ ـ تَخَصَّصَ . To detail, فَصَّلَ ـ شَرَحَ شَرْحًا مُفَصَّلًا . *See also to* Detail, *v.t.*

Particularize, *v.i.* To be exact, دَقَّ ـ إِسْتَدَقَّ .

Particularly, *ad.* Specially, خَاصَّةً ـ خُصُوصًا ـ بِٱلْأَخَصِّ ; in detail, شَيْئًا فَشَيْئًا ـ بِٱلتَّفْصِيلِ ; extremely, لِلْغَايَةِ ـ بِزِيَادَةٍ . To mention —, عَيَّنَ ; to be mentioned —, تَعَيَّنَ .

Parting, *n.* A separation, مُفَارَقَة . An adieu, farewell, وِدَاع . A division, إِنْقِسَام . A breaking, قَطْع ـ كَسْر . The place of —, as of the hair, مَفْرِق .

Parting, *a.* Given at parting, مَوْهُوبٌ عِنْدَ ٱلْوِدَاعِ . Declining, زَائِل . A — gift, هَدِيَّةُ ٱلْوِدَاعِ . The — day, ٱلنَّهَارُ ٱلزَّائِلُ .

Partisan, *n.* A party-man, مُتَعَصِّب . One of a party, مِنْ حِزْبٍ ـ مِنْ حِلْفَةٍ ـ حِلْف *pl.* أَحْلَاف ـ حَلِيف *pl.* حُلَفَاءُ ـ مِنْ جَمَاعَةٍ . An adherent, تَابِع *pl.* تُبَّاع . A — for, مُتَعَصِّب لِ *or* مَعَ ; a — against, مُتَعَصِّبٌ عَلَى . *See also* Halbert, *n.*

Partisan, *a.* Irregular, of warfare, مُحَارَبَةٌ غَيْرُ نِظَامِيَّةٍ ; of insurgent warfare, قِتَالُ فِتْنَةٍ .

Partisanship, *n.* حِلْفَة ـ حِلْف : In favour of, عَصَبِيَّةٌ ل ـ تَعَصُّبٌ ل ; against, عَصَبِيَّةٌ عَلَى ـ تَعَصُّبٌ عَلَى . A banding together, تَشَعُّب .

Partite, *a.* مَفْصُول ـ مُنْفَصِل ـ مُنْقَسِم .

Partition, *n.* The act of dividing, تَقْسِيم ـ قَسْم ـ تَجْزِئَة ; a division, قِسْم *pl.* أَقْسَام ـ قِسْمَة . The act of distributing, تَوْزِيع . A portion, حِصَّة *pl.* حِصَص . A place of parting, joining, مَفْرَق ـ مَوْصَل . A — wall, حَاجِز *pl.* حَوَاجِز . It formed a — between the two, حَجَزَ بَيْنَهُمَا [2] . Any — between two objects, بَرْزَخ *pl.* بَرَازِخ . *See also* Compartment, *n.*

Partition, *v.t.* To divide into shares, قَسَّمَ ـ أَحْصَصَ . To — off, put a partition between, حَجَزَ بَيْنَ [2] .

Partitive, *a.* قِسْمِيٌّ .

Partitively, *ad.* تَوْزِيعًا ـ بِٱلتَّقْسِيمِ ـ بِٱلتَّوْزِيعِ .

Partlet, *n.* *See* Hen, *n.*

Partly, *ad.* In part, بَعْض ـ جُزْءًا ـ عَلَى جِهَةٍ . Partly red, — white, مِنْهُ أَسْوَدُ مِنْهُ أَبْيَضُ . I — believe it, أُصَدِّقُهُ بَعْضَ ٱلتَّصْدِيقِ .

Partner, *n.* As in business, شَرِيك *pl.* شُرَكَآءُ . A sharer, as in land, شَقِيص : he is — or sharer with me, هُوَ شَقِيصِي . An associate, or husband, قَرِين *pl.* قُرَنَآءُ ; *fem.* قَرِينَة *pl.* قَرَائِنُ . A companion, رَفِيق *pl.* رُفَقَآءُ *fem.* رَفِيقَة *pl.* رَفَائِقُ ـ صَاحِب *pl.* أَصْحَاب *fem.* صَاحِبَة *pl.* صَوَاحِبُ *and* صَاحِبَات . A — at play, لُعْبَة ـ خَلِيع . A managing —, شَرِيكٌ مُدِيرٌ ـ شَرِيكُ ٱلْإِدَارَةِ . A sleeping —, مُضَارِب . One who associates a — with God, مُشْرِكٌ ـ مُشْرِكِيٌّ . To take as a — in, شَارَكَ ـ فِي .

Partnership, *n.* As in business, إِشْتِرَاك ـ مُشَارَكَة ـ شِرْكَة . Partnership in one particular thing exclusive of the rest, شِرْكَةُ ٱلْعِنَانِ . To be in — with, شَارَكَ . Partnership, an association, صُحْبَة ; to be in — with, to associate one's self with, إِصْطَحَبَ ـ صَاحَبَ .

Partridge, *n.* حَجَل *pl.* حِجْلَان ـ قَبْجَة *coll.* قَبْج . A young —, سُلَكَة *coll.* سُلَك *pl.* سِلْكَان ـ سُلَح *pl.* سِلْحَان . A ground —, قَطَاة *coll.* قَطًا *pl.* قَطَوَات . The Greek —, شُنَّار .

Parturient, *a.* وَالِدَة ـ وَاضِعَة .

Parturition, *n.* وِلَادَة ـ تَوْلِيد .

Party, *n.* A faction, عُصْبَة ـ تَشَعُّب ـ عَصَبِيَّة ـ حِلْف ـ سِرْب *pl.* فِرْقَة *pl.* فِرَق ـ أَحْزَاب *pl.* حِزْب ـ عُصَب ـ زُمْرَة ـ أَسْرَاب . A society, جَمَاعَة ـ شِرْذِمَة ـ جَمْع . A set, فِرْقَة ـ طَائِفَة *pl.* طَوَائِفُ . A side, جَانِب ـ طَرَف . A collected body, شَمْل ـ جَمْع ـ فَرِيق ـ عُنُق *pl.* أَعْنَاق . A —, as of soldiers, فِرْقَة *pl.* فِرَق ; of horsemen, كَتِيبَة *pl.* كَتَائِبُ . A — to a suit, a claimant, مُدَّعٍ ; a defendant, مُدَّعًى عَلَيْهِ . An individual, شَخْص *pl.* أَشْخَاص . An accomplice, رَفِيقٌ فِي *pl.* رُفَقَآءُ . A party or body broken up, separated, قَوْمٌ شَتٌّ . The people came in successive parties, جَآءَ ٱلْقَوْمُ عُنُقًا عُنُقًا [3] .

A belligerent party, طَرَفٌ مُتَحَارِبٌ .

A contracting party, طَرَفٌ مُتَعَاهِدٌ .

A dinner party, مَأْدُبَة ـ وَلِيمَة ـ ضِيَافَة .

An evening party, ضِيَافَةٌ (or مَأْدُبَةٌ) لَيْلِيَّةٌ .

An interested party, له نَائِبٌ فِي ـ لَهُ عَلَاقَةٌ فِي .

A musical party, مَعْشَرُ مُغَنِّينَ وَمُزَمِّرِينَ ـ نَوْبَة .

A party man; *See* Partisan, *n.*

The head of a party, رَأْس ـ رَأْسُ ٱلْعُصْبَةِ ـ مَاسِكُ ٱلْعِنَانِ ٱلْحِزْبِ .

To be a party to, to approve of, إِرْتَضَى بِ . To take part in, إِشْتَرَكَ فِي . To be an accomplice in, with, رَافَقَ ـ عَلَى .

To be one of a party, حَازَبَ ـ كَانَ مِنَ ٱلْحِزْبِ .

To form a party of many, تَحَزَّبُوا ـ حَازَبُوا .

To join a party, إِتَّحَدَ مَعَ ـ حَازَبَ .

To lead a party, كَانَ رَئِيسَ ٱلْعُصْبَةِ ـ تَرَأَّسَ عَلَى ٱلْحِزْبِ .

Party-coloured, *a.* مُشَكَّل ـ مُلَوَّن ـ مُخَلَّب ـ مُدَبَّج ـ مَنْقُوش .

Party-spirit, *n.* عَصَبِيَّة .

Party-wall, *n.* حَاجِز *pl.* حَوَاجِزُ .

Parvenu, *n.* رَجُلٌ طَرِفٌ فِي نَسَبِهِ ـ نَشَأَة ـ مُحْدَث .

Pas, *n.* A step, خَطْوَة . Right of precedence, قُدُوم ـ تَقَدُّم .

Paschal, *a.* مُتَعَلِّقٌ بِٱلْفِصْحِ ـ فِصْحِيٌّ .

Pâsha, *n.* بَاشَا *pl.* بَاشَاوَات .

Pâshâlik, *n.* بَاشَاوِيَّة ـ سَنَاجِق *pl.* سِنْجَق ـ إِيَالَة .

Pasquinade, *n.* هَجْو ـ هِجَآء ـ نَقْرَى .

Pasquinade, *v.t.* نَقَرَ [2] ـ هَجَا [2] .

Pass, *v.t.* To cross, as a river, road, mountains, جَازَ [2] ـ عَبَرَ [2] ـ قَطَعَ ـ قَطَّعَ ; to make to —, cross, cross over, نَفَذَ [3] ـ عَبَّرَ ـ أَجَازَ ـ أَنْفَذَ . To pass, to hand, hand to, نَاوَلَ ـ إِلَى . To pass to go by, فَاتَ عَلَى [2] or مِن ـ مَرَقَ مِن [2] ـ مَرَّ بِ [2] ـ جَازَ عَلَى [2] ـ عَدَّى مِن . To pass, let pass, أَجَازَ ـ جَازَ [2] . To approve, as of accounts, قَبِلَ وَصَدَّقَ ـ إِسْتَصْحَ [3] . To pass, as after an examination, أَجَازَ . To pass, to make current, أَجَازَ ـ جَوَّزَ [2] ـ رَوَّجَ ; to change, of money, for, صَرَفَ ـ بِ [3] . To go beyond, سَبَقَ [2] ـ أَنْفَذَ ـ أَنْهَى ; to pass a limit, جَاوَزَ ٱلْحَدَّ ـ فَاتَ [2] . To transmit,

— حَوَّلَ — شَيَّعَ — نَفَذَ — أَوْفَدَ-إِلَى — وَفَدَ. To transport, move, نَقَلَ ². To pass, as of time, قَضَى ♪: He passed five years in prison, مَضَتْ عَلَيْهِ خَمْسُ سِنِينَ وَهُوَ فِي ٱلْحَبْسِ. To surpass, أَنَافَ عَلَى — بَرَّزَ عَلَى — ² فَاقَ. To pass, or pass over a thing, not to mention, or to refer to slightly, ² ذَكَرَ بِلَطَافَةٍ — أَضْرَبَ عَنْ. To appear to be blind to, to pass over, — أَغْمَضَ عَنْ — غَمَّضَ عَنْ — أَغْضَى عَنْ — ² سَكَتَ عَنْ. إِغْتَمَضَ عَنْ. To omit, to be silent about, فَوَّتَ — ♪ سَمَحَ ل-عَنْ — تَجَاوَزَ عَنْ — ♪ صَفَحَ ل. فَاتَ ². To forgive,

(*For the forms to* Pass judgment, censure, compliments, *etc.*, *see to* Judge, Censure, Compliment, *etc.*).

To bring to pass, تَمَّمَ — أَتَمَّ — أَكْمَلَ. To be brought to pass, ♪ صَارَ — ² حَصَلَ — ² حَدَثَ.

To pass a law or edict, سَنَّنَ سُنَّةً. To pass, as a resolution, act of parliament, bill, *etc.*, أَجَازَ.

To pass by, go by, عَدَّى مِن — ² مَرَّ ب — ² جَازَ عَلَى. Not to make much of, to refer to slightly, to omit, to pardon; *see under to* Pass, *v.t.*

To pass for, be estimated as, قِيلَ عَنْهُ أَن — إِشْتَهَرَ ب.

To pass in, دَخَّلَ — أَدْخَلَ — جَوَّزَ — أَجَازَ.

To pass on, to forward, transmit, — أَوْصَلَ-إِلَى — أَوْفَدَ-إِلَى — ذَهَّبَ — أَجَازَ — أَنْفَذَ. To make to go on, through, شَيَّعَ-إِلَى — أَذْهَبَ.

To pass over, to act exclusively of, تَفَوَّتَ عَلَى: He passed him over in respect of his property, تَفَوَّتَ عَلَيْهِ فِي مَالِهِ. To cross over, to omit, be silent about, to pardon; *See under to* Pass, *v.t.*

To pass round, يَدُورُ aor. دَارَ — دَوَّرَ — أَدَارَ.

To pass something off for, as coin, ♪ صَرَفَ-ب — جَوَّزَ-ب. To show something as, أَظْهَرَ-ب. To pass one's self off for, إِدَّعَى ب — تَظَاهَرَ ب — تَصَلَّفَ ب: He passed himself off as some great man, إِدَّعَى بِأَنَّهُ رَجُلٌ عَظِيمٌ.

To pass through, as through a country, *etc.*, — قَطَعَ — عَبَّرَ — تَخَلَّلَ — أَمَرَّ — عَدَّى — جَاوَزَ-ب. To pass through, as through a sieve, صَفَّى; as through a needle, أَسْلَكَ — سَلَكَ. *See also to* Penetrate, *v.t.*

Pass, *v.i.* To go, go along, move, سَارَ — ² مَرَّ — ♪ ذَهَبَ aor. يَسِيرُ — إِنْتَقَلَ — ♪ مَشَى — ² سَلَكَ ٱلطَّرِيقَ. To transpire, as of time, مَضَى ♪ — ² مَرَّ — حَالَ aor. يَحُولُ: the year passed over him, حَالَ عَلَيْهِ ٱلْحَوْلُ; years have passed over them, مَرَّتْ عَلَيْهِمِ ٱلسِّنُونَ. To —, be current, ² سَلَكَ: the Spanish dollar passes for 21 piastres, الرِّيَالُ أَبُو مِدْفَعٍ يَسْلُكُ بِأَحَدٍ وَعِشْرِينَ غِرْشًا; the sovereign passes for 100 piastres, اللِّيرَةُ سَالِكَةٌ بِمِئَةِ غِرْشٍ.

To come to pass, ² حَدَثَ — صَارَ — كَانَ — ♪ جَرَى.

To pass along, as a road; *see to* Pass, *v.i.*, *first sentence.*

To pass away, ² زَالَ — ² عَبَرَ — ♪ فَنِيَ — ² دَرَجَ; to fade, — ² ذَبَلَ — ♪ فَنِيَ. To pass away from, ² عَبَرَ عَن — ² خَلَا. To pass, as an opportunity, *etc.*, ² فَاتَ. The thing passed away from him, was neglected by him, فَاتَهُ ٱلْأَمْرُ. Grief passed away from him, خَلَاهُ ٱلْحُزْنُ. Generation after generation passed away, ² دَرَجَ قَرْنٌ بَعْدَ قَرْنٍ. The people passed away, perished, ² دَرَجَ — إِنْدَرَجُوا — ٱلْقَوْمُ.

To pass by, go along, as on a road, — ² مَرَّ — ² سَلَكَ ٱلطَّرِيقَ — إِجْتَازَ ب.

To pass into, enter into, ² دَخَلَ فِي — ♪ دَخَلَ — ♪ خَشَّ فِي. To become, آلَ إِلَى aor. يَؤُولُ — صَارَ — تَحَوَّلَ إِلَى.

To pass off, clear off, as clouds, *etc.*, ♪ صَحَّ — تَرَوَّقَ — ² رَاقَ. To come to an end, ♪ تَمَّ — إِنْتَهَى. The evening passed off admirably, إِنْتَهَتِ ٱللَّيْلَةُ عَلَى أَكْمَلِ حَظٍّ وَسُرُورٍ.

To pass on, ² مَرَّ — ² رَاحَ إِلَى حَالِ سَبِيلِهِ.

To pass out, ² طَلَعَ بَرًّا — ² خَرَجَ مِن.

To pass over, as of water, ♪ سَالَ عَلَى — ♪ سَاحَ عَلَى; as of time, أَتَى عَلَى: a year passed over him, أَتَى عَلَيْهِ حَوْلٌ. They allowed no one to pass over, لَمْ يَدَعُوا أَحَدًا يَعْبُرُ.

To wish to pass over, إِسْتَعْبَرَ — أَرَادَ ٱلْعُبُورَ.

Pass, *n.* A defile, بُوغَاز — مَضِيق — خَانِق — مَأْزِم. A mountain —, عَقَبَة — مَنَاقِب *pl.* مَنْقَب — فَيْف — فَيْفَة. A passage, place of passage, مَجَاز — سِيرَة — مَمَرّ — مَعْبَر. A road, سِكَّة — طَرِيق. A permit to pass, تَذْكِرَةُ جَوَازٍ — جَوَاز. A state, condition, — حَال — حَالَة. A difficulty, وَرْطَة — مُعْضِلَة — صُعُوبَة. A thrust — دَسْر — صِنَاعَة — كُنْز — مُعَالَجَة. طَعْنَة — صَدْمَة — دَرْأَة. Manipulation,

Passable, *a.* That may be passed, نَافِذ — سَالِك — يُعْبَرُ مِنْهُ — يَنْسَلِكُ — يُسْلَكُ — العُبُورُ مِنْهُ مُمْكِن. Popular, received, جَائِز — دَارِج. Tolerable, middling, عَلَى قَدِّهِ — مُتَوَسِّط — مُقَارِب — بَيْنَ بَيْنَ — لَيْسَ بِرَدِيءٍ. To make a road —, طَرَّقَ ٱلطَّرِيقَ. To make a way — to or by, طَرَّقَ ل. *See also* Navigable, *a.*

Passably, *ad.* بَيْنَ بَيْنَ — عَلَى قَدِّهِ.

Passado, *n.* A thrust, طَعْنَة — صَدْمَة — دَرْأَة — دَسْر.

Passage, *n.* The act of crossing, passing over, — عُبُور — مُرُور — سُلُوك. The place of passage, مَقْطَع — مَمَرّ — مَسْلَك — مَجَاز — طَرِيق — سِكَّة. A road, مَخَاضَة — مَعْبَر; a ford, مَعْبَر

مَقْطَع. An encounter, conflict, وَقْعَة pl. وَقَعَات — مُضَارَبَة — مُصَارَعَة. A hall, corridor, دِهْلِيز pl. دَهَالِيز; a covered way, سَابَاط pl. سَوَابِيطُ. A journey, سِيرَة pl. سِيَر — سَفَر pl. أَسْفَار; time occupied in the same, مُدَّةُ ٱلسَّفَرِ. An action, صَنِيعَة pl. صَنَائِعُ. A —, as for fluids, مَجْرًى pl. مَجَارٍ — مَمَرٌّ. Access to, دُخُولٌ إِلَى — وُصُولٌ إِلَى. Passage of a bill or law, إِجَازَة. Part of a book or writing, بَنْد pl. بُنُود — عِبَارَة pl. عِبَارَات. A bird of —, a migratory bird, طَيْرٌ قَاطِعٌ pl. قَوَاطِعُ; a wayfarer, عَابِرُ سَبِيلٍ pl. عَابِرُوا سَبِيلٍ or عُبَّارُ سَبِيلٍ. To take a — in, to sail in, سَافَرَ فِي; to secure a berth in, أَخَذَ مَحَلًّا فِي ². To force a —, vent, as for water, etc., فَجَّرَ — بَجَّسَ. To force a —, vent, for itself, تَفَجَّرَ — اِنْبَجَسَ — اِنْفَجَرَ. To make a —, road, for, to make it passable by, طَرَّقَ لِ. To ask one for a —, as through his territories, اِسْتَطْرَقَ. He refused them — through his borders, أَبَى أَنْ يَسْمَحَ لَهُمْ بِٱلْمُرُورِ فِي تُخُومِهِ. *See also* Quotation, *n.*

Passage-money, *n.* مَصْرُوفُ ٱلسِّكَّةِ — حَقُّ ٱلطَّرِيقِ — مَصْرُوفُ ٱلسَّفَرِ.

Pass-book, *n.* A book of purchases on credit, دَفْتَرُ أَشْرِيَةٍ بِٱلدَّيْنِ. A book of entries, دَفْتَرُ تَقْيِيدٍ.

Passed, *a.* } Gone by, زَائِلٌ — مُتَبَرِّحٌ — مَاضٍ. Crossed, مَعْبُور.
Past, } Enacted, مُجَاز — مَشْرُوع. Accepted, مَقْبُول.

A — man, one who has passed an examination, مُجَاز. All our days are — away, كُلُّ أَيَّامِنَا قَدِ ٱنْقَضَتْ.

Passenger, *n.* One that passes along a road, عَابِرُ سَبِيلٍ pl. عَابِرُوا سَبِيلٍ or عُبَّارُ سَبِيلٍ — اِبْنُ ٱلسَّبِيلِ — مُسَافِر pl. مُسَافِرُونَ. A foot —, مَاشٍ pl. مُشَاة — رَاجِل pl. رَجَّالَة — زَلَمَة pl. زِلَام. A sea —, رَاكِبُ ٱلْبَحْرِ pl. رُكَّاب. The passengers and others on board a ship, رُكَّابُ ٱلسَّفِينَةِ.

Passer-by, *n.* عَابِرٌ — عَابِرُ ٱلطَّرِيقِ — مَارٌّ — وَارِدٌ.

Passibility, *n.* قَابِلِيَّةُ ٱلْآلَامِ.

Passible, *a.* قَابِلُ ٱلْآلَامِ.

Passim, *ad.* طُرًّا — بِٱلتَّمَامِ — من أَوَّلِهِ إِلَى آخِرِهِ.

Passing, *n.* *See* Passage, *n.*

Passing, *a.* Crossing, عَابِرٌ — مَارٌّ. Passing away, زَائِلٌ — فَانٍ.

Passing, *ad.* Very, كَثِيرًا — بِٱلزِّيَادَةِ. Passing strange, غَرِيبٌ لِلْغَايَةِ.

Passing-bell, *n.* *See* Knell, *n.*

Passion, *n.* That which is suffered, أَلَم — تَأَلُّم — عَذَاب. Emotion of love, desire, هَوًى pl. أَهْوَآء — هَوِيَّة; strong desire, love, غَرَام — عِشْق; ecstacy, وَجْد. Ardour, zeal, غَيْرَة — مُرُوَّة — إِقْدَام. Vehemence of anger, سَوْرَةُ ٱلْغَضَبِ — حُمَيًّا; anger, حَنَق — غَيْظ — غَضَب. A fit of —, غَضْبَة. Passion is the stumbling-block of judgment, (prov.) آفَةُ ٱلرَّأْيِ ٱلْهَوَى. Resist — and you will be guided aright, (prov.) خَالِفْ هَوَاكَ تُرْشَدُ. Passion is an idol, (prov.) الْهَوَى إِلٰهٌ مَعْبُودٌ. He who is led by his — is lost, (prov.) مَنْ تَبِعَ هَوَاهُ هَلَكَ. In a —, angry, غَضْبَانُ — غَضُوب — ثَائِر. He is a man of like passions with ourselves, هُوَ إِنْسَانٌ تَحْتَ ٱلْآلَامِ مِثْلَنَا. *See also* Emotion, *n.*

To be in a passion, اِسْتَغْضَبَ — ء غَضِبَ — اِنْغَاظَ — اِغْتَاظَ.

To excite one's passion, love, for, أَغْرَمَ بِ — أَوْلَعَ بِ.

To fly into a passion, ثَارَ غَضَبًا — اِحْتَمَى غَضَبًا — تَغَضَّبَ aor. ء هَاجَ غَيْظًا — يَثُورُ.

To give way to one's passions, أَعْطَى ٱلنَّفْسَ هَوَاهَا — ء تَبِعَ هَوَاهُ — ² سَلَكَ بِحَسَبِ هَوَاهُ.

To have a passion for, to like exceedingly, ء رَغِبَ فِي — ء هَوِيَ — تَوَلَّعَ بِ — اِرْتَغَبَ فِي. To love much, be smitten with, تَوَلَّعَ بِحُبِّ فُلَانٍ — أُغْرِمَ بِ — أُولِعَ بِ.

To lull the passions of one, سَكَّنَ غَيْظَهُ — هَدَّأَ غَضَبَهُ.

To move the passions, يَرُوعُ — رَاعَ aor. — أَثَّرَ فِي — ² هَيَّجَ فِي — ء هَاجَ حَرَّكَ ٱلْأَهْوَآءَ.

To put one into a passion, أَغْضَبَ — غَاضَبَ — أَغَاظَ — ء غَاظَ أَثَارَ غَضَبَهُ — أَسْخَطَ.

To wreak one's passion on, أَفَاضَ رِجْزَهُ — ² صَبَّ عَلَى سَخْطَهُ ² سَكَبَ غَضَبَهُ عَلَى — عَلَى.

Passionate, *a.* Impassioned, مُغْرَم — مُهَيَّج — مُحَرَّض — عَذُوْر. Irascible, غَضُوب — ثَائِر — سَرِيعُ ٱلْغَضَبِ. Sharp, piercing, حَادٌّ.

Passionately, *ad.* With passion, بِحُمَيًّا — بِحِدَّةٍ — بِشِدَّةٍ بِغَرَامٍ — بِوُلُوعٍ. Passionately fond of, مُغْرَمٌ بِ.

Passionateness, *n.* Sharpness, quickness, شِدَّة — حِدَّة — حُمَيًّا. *See also* Passion, Anger, *n.*

Passion-flower, *n.* زَهْرَةُ ٱلْآلَامِ.

Passionless, *a.* Without passion, عَدِيمُ ٱلْحِدَّةِ — خَالِي ٱلْحُمَيَّا. Calm, مُطْمَئِنٌّ — رَزِين — رَصِين — سَاكِن.

Passion-week, *n.* جُمْعَةُ ٱلْآلَامِ.

Passive, *a.* Not acting, غَيْرُ عَامِلٍ — غَيْرُ فَاعِلٍ. Receiving impressions from without, مُتَأَثِّرٌ بِهِ. Not resisting, غَيْرُ مُقَاوِمٍ. A — verb, فِعْلٌ مَجْهُولٌ. A — participle, اِسْمُ ٱلْمَفْعُولِ.

Passively, *ad.* Without resistance, بِدُونِ مُقَاوَمَةٍ; without contention, struggle, مِنْ غَيْرِ مُعَانَاةٍ ; resignedly, بِٱسْتِسْلَامٍ. Patiently, بِصَبْرٍ ـ تَصَبُّرًا ـ بِتَصَبُّرٍ.

Passiveness, *n.* The quality of receiving impressions, ٱنْفِعَال ـ قَابِلِيَّةُ ٱلتَّأَثُّرِ. Resignation, تَسْلِيم ـ ٱسْتِسْلَام ـ صَبْر. The being passive, as of a verb, حَالُ ٱلْمَجْهُولِ.

Passivity, *n.* رَكَانَة ـ رُكُون ـ سَكْنَة ـ سُكُون.

Pass-key, *n.* مِفْتَاحُ ٱلْأَبْوَابِ.

Passless, *a.* ٱلْعُبُورُ مِنْهُ مُحَالٌ ـ لَا يُجَازُ بِهِ ـ غَيْرُ سَالِكٍ ـ غَيْرُ نَافِذٍ.

Passover, *n.* عِيدُ ٱلْفِصْحِ ـ ٱلْفِصْحُ.

Passport, *n.* جَوَاز ـ تَذْكِرَةُ ٱلسَّفَرِ ـ بَاسَابُورْط *pl.* بَاسَابُورْطَات. A — signed by the consul, تَذْكِرَةُ ٱلسَّفَرِ بِإِمْضَاءِ ٱلْقُنْصُلِ.

Pass-word, *n.* شِعَار ـ سِرُّ ٱللَّيْلِ.

Past, *n.* The time past, مَا سَلَفَ مِنَ ٱلزَّمَانِ ـ ٱلسَّالِفُ ـ ٱلزَّمَانُ ٱلْمَاضِي ـ ٱلسَّابِقُ.

Past, *a.* The — tense, صِيغَةُ ٱلْمَاضِي. In times —, فِي ٱلْأَجْيَالِ ٱلْمَاضِيَةِ. The Past, the Present, and the Future, as applied to verbs, ٱلْمَعْهُودُ وَٱلْمَشْهُودُ وَٱلْمَوْعُودُ. *See also* Passed, Last, *a.*

Past, *prep.* Beyond, بَعِيدٌ عَنْ ـ أَبْعَدُ مِن ـ فَوْقَ ـ دُونَ ـ وَرَآءَ ـ مِن وَرَآءِ. More than, أَكْثَرُ مِن. Without, بِلَا. Past the boundary, وَرَآءَ ٱلْحَدِّ. Past shame, فَاقِدُ ٱلْحَيَآءِ. Past a doubt, لَا رَيْبَ ـ بِلَا شَكٍّ ـ بِلَا رَيْبٍ. When he was a little — the top of the hill, لَمَّا عَبَرَ قَلِيلًا عَنِ ٱلْقِمَّةِ. It is — one o'clock, أَذَّنَتِ ٱلسَّاعَةُ ٱلْوَاحِدَةُ. It is ten minutes — five, ٱلسَّاعَةُ خَمْسَةٌ وَعَشَرَ دَقَائِقَ. Past finding out, بَعِيدٌ عَنِ ٱلْفَحْصِ.

Paste, *n.* Dough, عَجِين ـ عَجِينَة ـ خَمِيرَة. Flour — for sticking, غِرَآءٌ ـ غِرَآءٌ مِنَ ٱلدَّقِيقِ. A compost, electuary, مَعْجُون. Artificial —, مُصَنَّع ـ مُمَوَّهٌ : paste diamonds, أَلْمَاسٌ مُصَنَّعٌ. The substance in which minerals are imbedded, طِين.

Paste, *v.t.* To cement with paste, لَزَقَ (ـ) *or* لَصَقَ ـ غَرَا ٤ بِٱلْغِرَآءِ. To — up, as on a wall, لَزَقَ فِي ٱلْحَائِطِ بِغِرَآءٍ ـ عَلَّقَ فِي ٱلْحَائِطِ.

Pasteboard, *n.* For rolling paste, طُلْم. A species of thick paper, مُقَوًّى ـ كُرْتُونٌ أَيْ لَوْحٌ مِنَ ٱلْوَرَقِ تُشَدُّ بِهِ ٱلْكُتُبُ *pl.* كَرَاتِينُ.

Pasted, *a.* Cemented with flour paste, مُلَصَّقٌ بِغِرَآءِ ٱلدَّقِيقِ ـ مَغْرُوٌّ.

Pastel, *n.* The plant, نُوَّرَة ـ نُوَّر ـ عِظْلِم ـ وَسْمَة *or* وَسِمَة.

Pastern, *n.* مَعْقِم *pl.* مَعَاقِم ـ مُخْتَبِل ـ وَظِيفَة ـ وَظِيف *pl.* أَوْظِفَة *or* وُظُف ـ عُرْقُوب.

Pastille, *n.* قُرْصَة *pl.* قُرَص ـ حَبّ *pl.* حُبُوب.

Pastime, *n.* لَهْوٌ ـ بَحْبَحَة ـ تَنَزُّه ـ ٱنْشِرَاح ـ نَفَس ـ كَيْفِيَّة.

Pastor, *n.* A shepherd, رَاعٍ *pl.* رُعَاة. A minister, clergyman, خُورِي *pl.* خَوَارِنَة ـ قِسِّيس *pl.* قِسِّيسُون *or* قُسُس ـ خَادِم *pl.* خُدَّام.

Pastoral, *a.* Connected with shepherds, مُتَعَلِّقٌ بِٱلرُّعَاةِ. Rural, رِيفِيّ ـ مُتَعَلِّقٌ بِٱلرِّيفِ. Clerical, كَنَائِسِيّ ـ أَكْلِيرِيكِيّ.

Pastoral, *n.* A poem on rural affairs, قَصِيدَةٌ فِي ٱلرُّعَاةِ ـ قَصِيدَةٌ فِي ٱلْفِلَاحَةِ. A clerical edict, مَنْشُور *pl.* مَنَاشِيرُ.

Pastorale, *n.* غِنَآءٌ حَنَّانٌ ـ مَقَامٌ حَنُونٌ.

Pastorate, *n.* The office of a pastor, minister, خِدْمَة ـ خُورْنَة ـ وَظِيفَةُ ٱلْخُورِي.

Pastorly, *a.* } كَمَا يَلِيقُ بِٱلْقِسِّيسِ ـ كَٱلرَّاعِي.
Pastor-like, }

Pastorship, *n.* Ministry, خِدْمَة ـ خُورْنَة.

Pastry, *n.* فَطِيرَة *pl.* فَطَائِرُ.

Pastry-cook, *n.* فَطَائِرِيّ *pl.* فَطَائِرِيَّة ; called in Egypt, فَطَاطِرِيّ *and* خَاوِرْجِيّ.

Pasturage, *n.* } The business of grazing cattle, رَعْي ـ رِعْيَة.
Pasture, } Land for pasturing, أَرْضٌ مُرْبِعَةٌ ـ مَرْعًى ـ مَرْعَاة ـ مَرْتَع ـ مُخْصِب. Dry —, حَشِيش. Abounding in —, عَشِب. Cattle pasturing, رَعِيَّة. To send, as of a horse, to —, أَمْذَى ـ = مَذَى.

Pasture, *v.i.* To feed, as cattle, رَعَى *aor.* يَرْعَى ـ ٱرْتَعَى ـ تَرَعَّى. The cattle pastured, (ٱرْتَعَتْ *or*) رَعَتِ ٱلْمَاشِيَةُ.

Pasture, *v.t.* أَرْعَى : He pastured the cattle, أَرْعَى ٱلْمَاشِيَةَ.

Pasty, *a.* Like dough, عَجِين ـ نِيءٌ ـ مِثْلُ ٱلْعَجِينِ. *See also* Doughy, *a.*

Pasty, *n.* فَطِيرٌ مَحْشُوٌّ بِلَحْمٍ.

Pat, *a.* Ready, *à propos*, بِٱلصَّوَابِ ـ سَدَادًا ـ فِي مَحَلِّهِ ـ مُتَوَكِّد ـ حَاضِر. He is pat with his answer, هُوَ حَاضِرٌ بِٱلْجَوَابِ ـ يُصِيبُ ٱلسَّدَادَ. He is pat, in speech or action, هُوَ حَاضِرُ ٱلْحُجَّةِ.

Pat, *ad.* تَوَكُّدًا ـ بِٱلصَّوَابِ ـ فِي مَحَلِّهِ ـ عَلَى ٱلسَّدَادِ.

Pat, *v.t.* To tap, طَبْطَبَ لِ ـ ٤ ـ = خَفَقَ. To pat on the back, figuratively, to approve of what one has done, صَوَّبَ.

Pat, *n.* A tap, خَفْق ـ طَبْطَبَة. A pat, mould, قَالِب *pl.* قَوَالِب.

Patch, *n.* As of a garment, رُقْعَة *pl.* رُقَع *and* رِقَاع. A rag, خِرْقَة *pl.* خِرَق. A black — for ornament, عَلَط ـ عَلْطَة ـ لَغْطَة. A — of ground, بُقْعَة *pl.* بِقَاع ـ قِطْعَةُ أَرْضٍ. His skin became one — of the small-pox, صَارَ جِلْدُهُ غَضْبَةً وَاحِدَةً مِنَ ٱلْجُدَرِيِّ.

Patch, *v.t.* To put a — on, رَقَعَ ـ = رَقَّعَ. To repair hurriedly,

عَثَمَ - اِعْتَثَمَ - عاجِلاً ‏(رَمَّ .aor يَرُمُّ or رَمَّمَ or) ‏- رَمْرَمَ. To stop up holes, and, generally, to — up, رَقَّعَ.

Patched, *a.* رَقِيعٌ - مَرْقُوعٌ. A — garment, مُتَرَدَّمٌ - مُرَقَّعٌ.

Patcher, *n.* رَقَّآءٌ *fem.* رَقَّايَةٌ. *See also* Botcher, *n.*

Patchwork, *n.* A garment or piece patched all over, رَدِيمٌ - تَرْقِيعٌ - مُرَقَّعٌ - مُرَدَّمٌ. Work clumsily put together, شُغْلٌ - شُغْلٌ خَشِنٌ - تَرْكِيبٌ بِلا مُنَاسَبَةٍ - عَلَى عَثَمٍ. A medley, applied also to a literary composition, تَلْفِيقَةٌ. It was a — destined to be torn, كانَ تَرْقِيعًا يُعاقِبُهُ خَرْقٌ.

Pate, *n.* هَامَةٌ - رَأْسٌ.

Patella, *n.* *See* Knee-pan, *n.*

Patelliform, *a.* In the form of a dish, فِى شَكْلِ ٱلصَّحْنِ.

Paten, *n.* } A plate for the bread in the Holy Communion,
Patin, } صِينِيَّةُ ٱلْكَأْسِ - بِيلاس. Chalice and paten, كَأْسٌ وَبِيلاس.

Patent, *a.* Open, obvious, عَيَانٌ - ظَاهِرٌ - جَلِيٌّ - مَحْضٌ - وَاضِحٌ. Letters —, أَمْرٌ نامَه سَاوِى - بَرَآءَةٌ - مَنَاشِيرُ *pl.* مَنْشُورٌ - فِرْمَانٌ. To be —, أَوْضَحَ - صَرَّحَ - اِتَّضَحَ - تَجَلَّى; to make —, أَشْهَرَ - بَيَّنَ. He was condemned for a — crime against the government, قُضِىَ عَلَيْهِ لِجُرْمٍ جَلِيٍّ ضِدَّ ٱلدَّوْلَةِ.

Patent, *n.* In a general sense, بَرَآءَةٌ *pl.* بَرَآآتٌ. A — of privileges, such as is given to a college or corporation, *etc.*, تَقْرِيرٌ *pl.* تَقَارِيرُ. A — of honour, تَشْرِيفٌ *pl.* تَشْرِيفَاتٌ. A —, as accorded to an inventor, بَرَآءَةٌ تَحْصُرُ بَعْضًا مِنَ ٱلِامْتِيَازَاتِ فِى مَا بِاسْتِنْبَاطِهِ - تَقْرِيرٌ - بَرَآءَةٌ - مُبْتَدِعٍ ٱخْتِرَاعًا. To grant a —, letters —, to, أَنْعَمَ عَلَى - بِبَرَآءَةٍ. To give a —, for invention, *etc.*, to, قَرَّرَ - أَعْطَى - تَقْرِيرًا. To infringe a —, اِتَّخَذَ ٱمْتِيَازَاتِ - اِفْتَرَى عَلَى بَرَآءَةٍ كَذِبًا - بَرَآءَةَ ٱلْغَيْرِ زُورًا.

Patent, *a.* Belonging to patents, مَا نِيطَ - مُتَعَلِّقٌ بِٱلتَّقَارِيرِ - بِٱلْبَرَآآتِ. Patent office, قَلَمُ ٱلتَّقَارِيرِ - قَلَمُ ٱلْبَرَآآتِ.

Patent, *v.t.* To grant a — to for, أَعْطَى - تَقْرِيرًا (or بَرَآءَةً) عَلَى - قَرَّرَ - لِ. To take out a — for, اِتَّخَذَ عَلَى - تَقْرِيرًا (or بَرَآءَةً).

Patented, *a.* مُقَيَّدٌ فِى قَلَمِ - مُقَرَّرٌ بِبَرَآءَةٍ - مُعْطًى عَلَيْهِ تَقْرِيرٌ - ٱلْبَرَآآتِ.

Patentee, *n.* بَرَآءتْلِى - صَاحِبُ ٱمْتِيَازٍ - صَاحِبُ بَرَآءَةٍ.

Paternal, *a.* On the father's side, مِنْ جِهَةِ - مِنْ طَرَفِ ٱلْأَبِ. Fatherly, ٱلْوَالِدِ - وَالِدِىٌّ - أَبَوِىٌّ. Hereditary, مُتَوَارَثٌ - إِرْثِىٌّ. Kind, شَفُوقٌ - حَنَّانٌ.

Paternally, *ad.* Like a father, مِثْلَ ٱلْأَبِ. Kindly, شَفَقَةً - بِحِنَّةٍ.

Paternity, *n.* أَبُوِيَّةٌ - أُبُوَّةٌ.

Pater noster, n. صَلاةُ أَبَانَا ٱلَّذِى - ٱلصَّلاةُ ٱلرَّبَّانِيَّةُ.

Path, *n.* A road, track, جُدَّةٌ - جَادَّةٌ *pl.* جَوَادُّ - سَبِيلٌ *pl.* سُبُلٌ - سَبِيلَةٌ - طُرُقٌ *pl.* طَرِيقٌ - مَسَالِكُ *pl.* مَسْلَكٌ - سِرَاطٌ - صِرَاطٌ. Course, as of action, سِيرَةٌ - جَادَّةٌ. The right —, جَادَّةُ ٱلصَّوَابِ: He is on the right —, هُوَ عَلَى ٱلْجَادَّةِ; he is on the —, the main —, of truth, هُوَ عَلَى جَادَّةِ ٱلْحَقِّ. To walk in a certain —, سَلَكَ ᵘ. To take a certain —, course, سَلَكَ - أَسْلَكَ - فِى - سَلَكَ ᵘ - فِى - مَسْلَكًا (or سِيرَةً). To put one on a —,

Pathetic, *n.* The — style, رِقَّةُ ٱلنَّصِّ - حِنَّةُ ٱلْكَلامِ.

Pathetic, *a.* }
Pathetical, } مُحَرِّكُ ٱلشَّفَقَةِ - مُرِقُّ ٱلْقَلْبِ - مُحَنِّنٌ.

Pathetically, *ad.* بِتَحَنُّنٍ - بِشَفَقَةٍ - بِحِنَّةٍ.

Patheticalness, *n.* رِقَّةٌ - حَنِيَّةٌ - حَنَانٌ - حِنَّةٌ.

Pathognomonic, *a.* *See* Characteristic, *a.*

Pathologic, *a.* }
Pathological, } مُتَعَلِّقٌ بِتَعْرِيفِ ٱلْأَمْرَاضِ - نِطَاسِىٌّ.

Pathologically, *ad.* حَسَبَ قَوَاعِدِ تَشْخِيصِ ٱلْأَمْرَاضِ - نُطْسَةً.

Pathologist, *n.* عَالِمٌ - نَاطِسُ ٱلْأَمْرَاضِ - نِطَاسِىٌّ - نِطِّيسٌ بِٱلْأَمْرَاضِ.

Pathology, *n.* عِلْمُ طَبَائِعِ - فَنُّ تَعْرِيفِ ٱلْأَمْرَاضِ - نُطْسَةٌ ٱلْأَمْرَاضِ وَٱخْتِلافَاتِهَا وَأَسْبَابِهَا وَإِشَارَاتِهَا.

Pathos, *n.* تَحَنُّنٌ - رِقَّةٌ - حَرَارَةٌ - حِنَّةٌ.

Pathway, *n.* A pavement, مَمْشًى. *See also* Path, *n.*

Patience, *n.* طُولُ رُوحٍ - صَبْرٌ - اِصْطِبَارٌ - أَنَاةٌ - تَأَنٍّ. Patience under loss, عَزَآءٌ - عِزْوَةٌ. To have —, or to be patient, صَبَرَ ᶦ - طَوَّلَ بَالَهُ - تَأَسَّى - تَعَزَّى - تَأَنَّى - تَصَبَّرَ - اِصْطَبَرَ. To have —, or to be patient, under, صَبَرَ ᶦ - تَعَزَّى عَن - تَصَبَّرَ عَن. To have —, or to be patient, with, اِسْتَأْنَى بِ - تَأَنَّى فِى - عَلَى - أَصْبَرَ - عَزَّى. To beg one to have —, to be patient, صَابَرَ. To lose —, ضَيَّعَ - عَدِمَ ٱلْمُصْطَبَرَ - عَدِمَ ٱلصَّبْرَ ᶦ - صَبَّرَ - عَلَى ٱلصَّبْرِ. To constrain one's self to have —, تَصَبَّرَ. To take —, or consolation, by reflecting on some person or thing, تَأَسَّى بِ - تَعَزَّى بِ. To enjoin to — under the loss of something, سَلَّى - عَن - عَزَّى - عَن. He waited with —, or patiently, or was patient in the affair, تَأَنَّى فِى ٱلْأَمْرِ. Patience was had with him for a year, أُسْتُؤْنِىَ بِهِ حَوْلاً. I waited with — for the food, اِسْتَأْنَيْتُ فِى ٱلطَّعَامِ. I waited with —, or patiently, for you until I have no — left, تَأَنَّيْتُكَ حَتَّى لا أَنَاةَ بِى. (The following are Arabic proverbs: The best kind of — is the constraining one's self to be patient, أَفْضَلُ ٱلصَّبْرِ ٱلتَّصَبُّرُ. He who is patient gains the day, attains his end, مَنْ صَبَرَ نَالَ ـ فِي ٱلصَّبْرِ إِدْرَاكُ ٱلْمَرَامِ ـ مَنْ صَبَرَ ظَفِرَ ـ (مَنْ تَأَنَّى أَدْرَكَ مَا تَمَنَّى). *See also* Endurance, *n.*

Patient, *a.* صَابِر ـ عَزِيّ ـ عَزٍ ـ صَبِير *pl.* صُبَرَآء ـ صَبَّار ـ صَبُور ـ أَبُو صَبْرٍ. To be —; *see under preceding article*; *also* Enduring, *a.*

Patiently, *ad.* بِطُولِ رُوحٍ ـ بِأَنَاةٍ ـ صَبْرًا ـ بِصَبْرٍ. Very —, بِطُولِ ٱلْأَنَاةِ. That which you could not bear —, مَا لَمْ تَسْتَطِعْ عَلَيْهِ صَبْرًا. I waited — for him, إِنْتِظَارًا ٱنْتَظَرْتُهُ. Having waited — he at length received the promised reward, إِذْ تَأَنَّى نَالَ ٱلْمَوْعِدَ. *See also under* Patience.

Patly, *ad.* *See* Pat, *ad.*

Patness, *n.* سَدَاد ـ عِتَادَة ـ صَوَاب.

Patois, *n.* لَغْوَة ـ لَغْوٌ.

Patriarch, *n.* As of the Old Testament, رَئِيسُ ٱلْآبَآءِ *pl.* رُؤَسَآءُ ٱلْآبَآءِ. The head of a Christian church, بَطْرِيَرْكُ or بَطْرَكُ *pl.* بَطَارِكَة and بَطَارِيكُ. An elder, شَيْخ *pl.* شُيُوخ.

Patriarchal, *a.* As of the Old Testament patriarchs, مُتَعَلِّقٌ بِرُؤَسَآءِ ٱلْآبَآءِ. Connected with the headship of a Christian church, بَطْرِيَرْكِيّ ـ بَطْرَكِيّ.

Patriarchate, *n.* The dignity of a Christian patriarch, بَطْرَكِيَّة. The residence of a patriarch, بَطْرَكْخَانَة ـ مَحَلُّ ٱلْبَطْرَكِ.

Patrician, *a.* Of noble family or state, أَصِيل ـ نَبِيل *pl.* نُبَال ـ شَرِيف *pl.* شُرَفَآء ـ كَرِيم *pl.* كِرَام ـ أُصَل *pl.*

Patrician, *n.* رِجَالُ كَرَمٍ *pl.* رَجُلُ كَرَمٍ ـ نَجِيب *pl.* نُجَبَآء. *See also under* Noble, *n.*

Patrimonial, *a.* مُتَوَارِث ـ إِرْثِيّ ـ مَوْرُوث.

Patrimonially, *ad.* وِرَاثَةً ـ بِٱلْإِرْثِ.

Patrimony, *n.* An estate derived from a father or parentage, مِيرَاث ـ مُخَلَّفَاتُ ٱلْوَالِدَيْنِ ـ مَالُ ٱلْوَالِدَيْنِ ـ مَالُ ٱلْأَبِ. A church estate, مُلْكُ ٱلْكَنِيسَةِ.

Patriot, *n.* مُحِبُّ ٱلْوَطَنِ ـ مُعِزُّ وَطَنِهِ ـ مُحِبُّ مَأْلَفِهِ *pl.* مُحِبُّو ٱلْوَطَنِ ـ مُتَعَصِّبٌ لِلْوَطَنِ ـ صَاحِبُ غَيْرَةٍ عَلَى وَطَنِهِ.

Patriotic, *a.* مُخْتَصٌّ بِإِعْزَازِ ٱلْوَطَنِ ـ مُتَعَلِّقٌ بِحُبِّ ٱلْوَطَنِ ـ مُتَعَلِّقٌ بِحُبِّ ٱلْمَأْلَفِ.

Patriotism, *n.* إِعْزَازُ ٱلْوَطَنِ ـ غَيْرَةٌ عَلَى ٱلْوَطَنِ ـ حُبُّ ٱلْوَطَنِ.

Patrol, *n.* طَوْف ـ طَائِف ـ عَسَس ـ عَسَس *pl.* عَاسّ ـ خَفَر ـ قَوْل.

Patrol, *v.i.* To go the rounds, طَافَ [2] ـ إِعْتَسَّ ـ عَسَّ [2].

Patrol, *v.t.* To patrol around, إِعْتَسَّ عَلَى ـ عَسَّ عَلَى [2] ـ طَافَ حَوْلَ [2].

Patron, *n.* One who countenances or protects a person or cause, حَامٍ ـ وَلِيُّ ٱلنِّعَمِ ـ وَلِيّ ـ ظَهِير ـ ظِهْرَة ـ مُعْتَمَد ـ عُمْدَة. Patron of a benefice, وَلِيُّ ٱلْأَبْرَشِيَّةِ. A — saint, قِدِّيسٌ حَامٍ. The — of a party, عِمَادُ (or سَنَدُ) ٱلْقَوْمِ.

Patronage, *n.* Support, countenance, عِنَايَة ـ إِلْتِفَات ـ تَوَجُّه ـ صِيَانَة ـ حِمَايَة ـ ظَهْر ـ مُظَاهَرَة. Guardianship, حِمَايَة. Right of presenting to a benefice, حَقُّ ٱلتَّوْلِيَةِ عَلَى أَبْرَشِيَّةٍ.

Patroness, *n.* In a general sense, حَامِيَة ـ وَلِيَّةُ ٱلنِّعَمِ. Patroness of a living, benefice, وَلِيَّةُ ٱلْأَبْرَشِيَّةِ.

Patronize, *v.t.* To support, uphold, شَدَّدَ ـ أَيَّدَ ـ سَنَّدَ ـ ظَاهَرَ ـ ظَهَرَ عَلَى [2] ـ أَصْلَحَ إِلَى.

Patronizer, *n.* مُسَنِّد ـ مُؤَيِّد ـ حَمَاة *pl.* حَامٍ ـ ظَهْر ـ مُظَاهِر. *See also* Patron, *n.*

Patronizing, *a.* Protecting, defending, مُتَوَجِّه ـ حَامٍ ـ ظَهِير. Assuming, مُتَكَبِّر ـ مُتَفَضِّلٌ عَلَى.

Patronymic, *n.* كُنْيَةٌ تُبَيِّنُ ٱلنَّسَبَ ـ أَنْسَاب *pl.* نَسَب.

Patten, *n.* The base, as of a column, عِمَاد *pl.* عَمَد ـ عُمْدَة ـ قَوَاعِدُ *pl.* قَاعِدَة. Pattens for the feet, قَبْقَاب.

Patter, *v.i.* خَفَقَ [2] ـ : The rain pattered, خَفَقَ ٱلْمَطَرُ. The feet pattered on the ground, خَفَقَتِ ٱلْأَقْدَامُ عَلَى ٱلْأَرْضِ.

Pattering, *n.* خَفْق ـ خَفِيق. The sound of the — of feet, خَفْقُ ٱلْأَقْدَامِ.

Pattern, *n.* An example for imitation, قِدْوَة ـ أُدْمَة. A model, أُنْمُوذَج ـ قَوَاعِدُ *pl.* قَاعِدَة ـ ضَرْب ـ صِيغَة ـ صَوْغ. A specimen, as of cloth, *etc.*, مَسْطَرَة ـ نَمُونَة ـ عَيْنِيَّة ـ عَيِّنَة. According to this —, مِثْلَ هٰذَا ـ عَلَى هٰذَا ٱلشَّكْلِ. Make it on this —, إِضْرِبْهُ عَلَى طَبْعِ هٰذَا. He is a — to them, هُوَ أُدْمَةٌ لَهُمْ. To follow the — of, إِقْتَدَى بِ. *See also* Example, Model, *n.*

Pattern, *v.t.* To copy, to follow, تَبِعَ أَثَرَهُ [2] ـ إِقْتَدَى بِ ـ تَمَثَّلَ بِ ـ إِتَّبَعَ.

Patty, *n.* فُطَيْرَة ـ سَنْبُوسَك.

Patty-pan, *n.* قَالِبُ ٱلْفُطَيْرَةِ ـ قَوَالِبُ *pl.* قَالِبُ ٱلسَّنْبُوسَكِ.

Paucity, *n.* قِلَّة ـ قُلّ.

Paul, *n.* The name, بُولُس. The apostle Paul, بُولُسُ ٱلرَّسُولُ.

Pauline, *a.* مَنْسُوبٌ إِلَى ـ بُولُسِيّ ـ مُتَعَلِّقٌ بِبُولُسَ ٱلرَّسُولِ ـ بُولُسَ ٱلرَّسُولِ.

Paunch, *n.* بُطُون *pl.* بَطْن ـ كِرْش.

Paunch, *v.t.* *See to* Embowel, *v.t.*

Pauper, *n.* فَقِير *pl.* فُقَرَآء ـ مِسْكِين *pl.* مَسَاكِين ـ صُعْلُوك *pl.* صَعَالِيك.

Pauperism, *n.* مَسْكَنَة ــ فَقْر ــ فَقْرَة.

Pauperization, *n.* إِفْقَار.

Pauperize, *v.t.* أَفْقَرَ ــ صَعْلَكَ. To become pauperized, إِفْتَقَرَ ــ تَصَعْلَكَ.

Pause, *n.* Cessation of action, تَوَقُّف ــ رَكْزَة ــ حَطَّة. A — of silence, سَكْتَة. A — for a reader to stop, مَقْطَع ــ وَقْف *pl.* مَقَاطِع. A mark of cessation, عَلَامَة ٱلْوَقْف.

Pause, *v.i.* To cease, تَوَقَّفَ ــ تَأَيَّا. To — upon, as on a word or syllable, وَقَفَ عَلَى *aor.* يَقِفُ. To —, to act with deliberation, إِسْتَدَامَ: He paused, acted deliberately, in the matter, تَأَيَّا فِي ٱلْأَمْرِ ــ إِسْتَدَامَ ٱلْأَمْرَ. *See also to* Hesitate, *v.i.*

Pauser, *n.* One who deliberates, حَرِيص ــ مُحْتَرِز ــ مُتَنَبِّه.

Pave, *v.t.* As with slabs, بَلَّطَ. To — with, فَرَشَ-بِ ــ ². فَرَّشَ-بِ. To — or prepare the way for, أَعَدَّ-لِ ــ أَجْمَعَ لِ. He paved some of the streets, رَصَفَ بَعْضَ ٱلْأَزِقَّةِ بِٱلْبَلَاطِ ².

Paved, *a.* Paved with, مَفْرُوش بِ; paved with slabs, مُبَلَّط.

Pavement, *n.* The act of paving, تَبْلِيط ــ فَرْش. A layer of flat stones, بَلَاط ــ فَرْش. A footpath —, مَمْشًى.

Paver,
Pavier, *n.* } مُبَلِّط.
Pavior,

Pavilion, *n.* A tent, خَيْمَة *pl.* خِيَم *and* خِيَام ــ مِظَلَّة ــ وِطَاق. A building or structure with a dome, قُبَّة *pl.* قِبَاب. A — on top of a house, جَوْسَق *pl.* جَوَاسِق. A — of wood, طَارِمَة.

Pavilion, *v.t.* To furnish with tent, خَيَّمَ لِ. To shelter, آوَى ــ أَظَلَّ.

Paving, *n.* The act of laying a pavement, تَبْلِيط ــ فَرْش. *See also* Pavement, *n.*

Paw, *n.* The foot of a beast, قَائِمَة *pl.* قَوَائِم ــ رِجْل *pl.* أَرْجُل; a hand, كَفّ *pl.* كُفُوف. He walked or went on his two paws, مَشَى عَلَى رَاحَتَيْهِ.

Paw, *v.t.* As a horse the ground, خَبَطَ ــ تَخَبَّطَ ــ إِخْتَبَطَ ــ بَحَثَ ــ ² نَبَشَ ــ نَبَّشَ. To scrape, scrape up, دَبَكَ ــ ² هَمَزَ ــ إِبْتَحَثَ. To handle roughly, خَرَقَ بِٱلشَّيْءِ ².

Paw, *v.i.* To scrape with the foot, as a horse, *etc.*, خَبَطَ ــ خَبَطَ (*or* تَخَبَّطَ) بِرِجْلِهِ ــ تَخَبَّطَ.

Pawed, *a.* Having paws, ذُو قَوَائِم ــ ذُو أَرْجُلٍ.

Pawl, *n.* حَاجِز.

Pawn, *n.* A pledge, رَهْن *pl.* رِهَان *and* رُهُون *and* رُهُن. A — in chess, بَيْدَق *pl.* بَيَادِق. To take a —, pledge, from, إِرْتَهَنَ-مِن. To demand a — from, إِسْتَرْهَنَ.

Pawn, *v.t.* To give in pawn, رَهَنَ ــ أَرْهَنَ: He pawned the thing to him, رَهَنَهُ (*or* رَهَنَهُ) ٱلشَّيْءَ ــ أَرْهَنَهُ ــ رَهَنَهُ عِنْدَهُ.

Pawnbroker, *n.* سَلَّاف بِرُهُونٍ ــ مُرْتَهِن.

Pawnbroking, *n.* التَّسْلِيف بِرُهُونٍ.

Pawner, *n.* مُرْهِن ــ رَاهِن.

Pax-wax, *n.* *See* Pack-wax, *n.*

Pay, *v.t.* To discharge, as a debt, أَدَّى ــ وَفَى ٱلدَّيْنَ *aor.* يَفِي ــ أَوْفَى ــ أَدَّى ٱلدَّيْنَ ــ جَزَى ٱلدَّيْنَ ــ قَضَى ٱلدَّيْنَ. To discharge as a duty, وَفَى *aor.* يَفِي ــ أَوْفَى ــ قَامَ بِ ــ ² كَمَّلَ. To requite, قَابَلَ ــ أَعَاضَ ــ عَوَّضَ ــ جَزَى. To pay, as a price, أَدَّى ــ دَفَعَ. To besmear with, طَلَى-بِ ــ ² دَهَنَ-بِ. I paid the debt, أَوْفَيْتُ (*or* جَزَيْتُ) ٱلدَّيْنَ. I paid him his due, أَوْفَيْتُهُ حَقَّهُ ــ جَزَيْتُهُ حَقَّهُ. I have not been paid, مَا قَبَضْتُ حَقِّي. I will pay you, that is, pay you out, punish you for this, خُذْ مِنِّي مَا يَجِيكَ ــ أَنَا سَأُقَابِلُكَ عَلَى هٰذَا. The bearer of the letter is paid, prepaid, حَامِلُ ٱلرِّسَالَةِ خَالِصُ ٱلْأُجْرَةِ. He promises to pay the amount in the course of 15 months, يَتَعَهَّدُ بِأَدَاءِ ٱلْمَبْلَغِ فِي ظَرْفِ خَمْسَةَ عَشَرَ شَهْرًا. The yearly amount which he is bound to pay, ٱلْمُرَتَّبُ ٱلسَّنَوِيُّ ٱلَّذِي يَجِبُ عَلَيْهِ إِيفَاؤُهُ. Pay to-day, trust to-morrow, عَاجِلٌ بِعَاجِلٍ ــ يَدٌ بِيَدٍ ــ نَاجِزٌ بِنَاجِزٍ. *See also to* Careen, *v.t.*

To pay at once, or to pay one promptly, زَكَأَ ــ ² نَقَدَ لِ ــ دَفَعَ لَهُ ٱلْمَبْلَغَ نَقْدًا.

To pay at sight, دَفَعَ-حَالًا ــ دَفَعَ-فِي ٱلسَّاعَةِ.

To pay away, to expend, صَرَفَ ــ أَنْفَقَ ــ أَخْرَجَ.

To pay back, to repay, أَعَاضَ ــ عَوَّضَ ــ رَجَّعَ-لِ.

To pay for, to give price of, دَفَعَ ثَمَنَ ٱلشَّيْءِ. To pay dear for, إِشْتَرَى-بِٱلْغَالِي. To pay through the nose for, إِشْتَرَى-بِثَمَنٍ مُفْرِطٍ ــ إِنْغَشَّ فِي ٱلسِّعْرِ. To pay for, to expiate, كَفَّرَ عَن. To pay for one, أَدَّى عَنْهُ.

To pay in advance, دَفَعَ-سَلَفًا.

To pay off, settle with and discharge, أَوْفَى حَقَّهُ وَرَخَّصَهُ. To requite, جَزَى ــ عَوَّضَ. To reward, punish, قَابَلَ-عَلَى ــ جَازَى ــ عَاقَبَ.

To pay one for the loss of his time, عَوَّضَ عُطْلَتَهُ.

To pay one in his own coin, قَابَلَ-بِمِثْلِ مَا صَنَعَ ــ عَامَلَ-بِمُعَامَلَتِهِ.

To pay out; *see above under* To pay away. To pay out, as of a cable, أَرْخَى ــ سَيَّبَ.

To pay one's addresses to, to court, تَوَدَّدَ إِلَى.

To pay one a compliment; *see to* Compliment, *v.t.*

To pay one's respects to, سَلَّمَ عَلَى.

Pay, *v.i.* To recompense, خَلَّصَ : This does not pay me, هٰذَا مَا يُخَلِّصُنِي.

Pay, *n.* Wages, salary, مَعَاش ـ جُعْل ـ عُلُوفَة ـ مَاهِيَّة ـ وَظِيفَة. Pay, allowance, as of soldiers, stated pay, رَاتِب *pl.* رَوَاتِب ـ عُلُوفَة *pl.* عَلَائِف ـ جَامَكِيَّة *pl.* جَمَكِيَّات ـ جُومَك *pl.* جَوَامِك. To be in the pay of one, كَانَ أَجِيرًا ـ أُوجِرَ عِنْدَهُ ـ كَانَ فِي خِدْمَتِهِ ـ عِنْدَهُ.

Daily pay, يَوْمِيَّة.

Extra pay, مَعَاش ضَمّ.

Full pay, مَعَاش عَادِيّ ـ مَعَاش مُسْتَوْفٍ.

Half pay, نِصْفُ جَامَكِيَّةٍ ـ نِصْفُ مَعَاشٍ. Retired half pay, مَعَاشُ ٱلتَّقَاعُدِ.

Monthly pay, شَهْرِيَّة.

Yearly pay, سَنَوِيَّة.

Payable, *a.* To be paid, يُدْفَعُ ـ يُؤَدَّى. Payable by, due by, مَطْلُوبٌ مِنْ ـ مَدْيُونٌ بِ. Falling due, مُسْتَحِقٌّ : the debt payable, الدَّيْنُ ٱلْمُسْتَحِقُّ. To make — to, جَعَلَ ـَ تَأْدِيَتَهُ لِ ـ حَوَّلَ دَفْعَهُ إِلَى.

Pay-bill, *n.* تَذْكِرَةُ ٱلْمَعَاشِ.

Pay-day, *n.* يَوْمُ دَفْعِ ٱلْمَعَاشِ.

Payee, *n.* قَابِضُ ٱلْمَبْلَغِ ـ الْمُؤَدَّى إِلَيْهِ.

Payer, *n.* دَافِع. One who pays promptly, دَفَّاع.

Paymaster, *n.* In the navy or army, ضَابِطُ ٱلْمَعَاشَاتِ ـ مَأْمُورُ ٱلْمَعَاشَاتِ; *from the Turkish*, سَرْكِي أَمِينِي. Paymaster-General, مَأْمُورُ ٱلْمَعَاشَاتِ كَافَّةً.

Payment, *n.* The act of paying, دَفْع ـ دَفْعَة ـ أَدَآء ـ تَأْدِيَة.

Payment, as of debts, وَفَآء ـ أَدَآء ـ إِيفَآء ـ جَزَآء. Ready —, نَقْد. Compensation, مُجَازَاة ـ مُكَافَاة. Wages, مَعَاش ـ جَزَآء ـ عُلُوفَة. The time for the — of the debt, أَجَلُ ٱسْتِحْقَاقِ ٱلدَّيْنِ.

Payment on account, جَانِبٌ مِنَ ٱلْمَبْلَغِ. To receive — in advance, تَسَلَّفَ. To demand —, إِقْتَضَى ـ طَلَبَ ٱلدَّفْعَ 2. He ordered the — of the debt, أَمَرَ بِإِيفَآءِ ٱلدَّيْنِ 2. To suspend —, وَقَّفَ ٱلدَّفْعَ. To stop —, بَطَّلَ ٱلدَّفْعَ. To resume —, عَادَ 2 إِلَى ٱلدَّفْعِ.

Paynim, *n.* *See* Pagan, *n.*

Pay-office, *n.* مَكْتَبُ دَفْعِ ٱلْمَعَاشَاتِ; *from the Turkish*, سَرْكِي.

Pay-table, *n.* سِيَاقَة (*or* جَدْوَلُ) ٱلْمَعَاشَاتِ.

Pea, *n.* The common pea, جُلُبَّان ـ بِسِلَّة. Chick-pea, حِمِّص; roasted chick-peas, قَضَامَة. The sweet pea, جُلُبَّانٌ مُعَطَّرٌ. Everlasting pea, جُلُبَّانُ ٱلْأَعْرَابِ.

Peace, *n.* A state of quiet, هُدُوّ ـ سِلْم ـ هُدْنَة. Calm, repose, رَاحَة. State of not being at war, صُلْح ـ هُدْنَة ـ صَلَاح. Reconciliation, مُصَالَحَة ـ صَلَاح. Peace of mind, إِطْمِئْنَانُ ٱلْبَالِ ـ مُسَالَمَة ـ وِفَاق ـ إِتِّحَاد ـ إِتِّفَاق. Accord, رَاحَةُ بَالٍ ـ تَسْلِيَة. Silence, سُكُوت ـ رَوَاقَة. Rest, رَاحَة ـ سُكُون ـ عَدَمُ ٱخْتِلَالٍ. The continuance of —, دَوَامُ (*or* إِدَامَةُ) ٱلسِّلْمِ. Peace be to you! السَّلَامُ عَلَيْكَ. Be at — one with another, سَالِمُوا بَعْضُكُمْ بَعْضًا.

I wished to prevent anything which might disturb the general —, tranquillity, أَرَدْتُ مَنْعَ مَا يُخِلُّ بِٱلرَّاحَةِ ٱلْعُمُومِيَّةِ.

A definitive peace, الصُّلْحُ ـ مُصَالَحَةٌ كَامِلَةٌ ـ مُصَالَحَةٌ قَطْعِيَّةٌ ٱلْقَطْعِيُّ.

A general peace, صُلْحٌ عُمُومِيٌّ ـ مُصَالَحَةٌ عُمُومِيَّةٌ ـ سِلْمٌ عَامٌّ.

A perpetual peace, صُلْحٌ أَبَدِيٌّ ـ مُصَالَحَةٌ مُؤَبَّدَةٌ.

A preliminary peace, مُقَدِّمَاتُ ٱلصُّلْحِ.

A separate peace, مُصَالَحَةٌ مُنْفَرِدَةٌ.

A shameful or dishonourable peace, صُلْحٌ خِزْيٌ ـ صُلْحٌ فَاحِشٌ.

A sure peace, مُصَالَحَةٌ قَوِيَّةٌ. An uncertain peace, صُلْحٌ بِلَا دَوَامٍ.

A treaty of peace, مُعَاهَدَةُ ٱلصُّلْحِ.

Attempts or crimes against the public peace, جِنَايَاتٌ عَلَى ٱلرَّاحَةِ ٱلْعَامَّةِ ـ التَّعَدِّي عَلَى سِلْمِ ٱلْجُمْهُورِ.

On a peace footing, عَلَى هَيْئَةِ ٱلصُّلْحِ. To put an army on a peace footing, جَعَلَ ـَ ٱلْعَسْكَرَ عَلَى هَيْئَةِ ٱلصُّلْحِ.

Peace at any price, السِّلْمُ عَلَى أَيِّ وَجْهٍ كَانَ.

To be at peace, in a state of calm, إِطْمَأَنَّ ـ سَكَنَ 2 ـ إِسْتَقَرَّ ـ إِسْتَكَنَّ. To be in safety, سَلِمَ ـَ. To die, تُوُفِّيَ ـ إِنْتَقَلَ إِلَى رَحْمَةِ ٱللّٰهِ.

To conclude a peace, عَقَدَ ـِ مُصَالَحَةً ـ أَجْرَى مُصَالَحَةً. To conclude a peace with, عَقَدَ ـِ مُصَالَحَةً مَعَ.

To hold one's peace, سَكَتَ 2 ـ نَصَتَ ـِ ـ أَنْصَتَ. To hold one's peace about, أَغْضَى عَلَى.

To keep the peace, حَفِظَ ـَ ٱلصُّلْحَ ـ رَاعَى ٱلصُّلْحَ.

To make peace, to become at peace, إِسْتَسْلَمَ. The two made peace, تَصَالَحَا ـ إِصْطَلَحَا.

To make one's peace with, سَالَمَ ـ صَالَحَ ـ تَصَالَحَ مَعَ.

To negotiate a peace with, ذَاكَرَ فِي ٱلصُّلْحِ ـ ذَاكَرَ فِي مُعَاهَدَةِ ٱلصُّلْحِ.

To ratify a peace, صَدَّقَ ٱلصُّلْحَ ـ عَقَدَ ٱلْمُصَالَحَةَ.

To trouble the peace, كَدَّرَ ٱلسِّلْمَ ـ أَخَلَّ بِٱلصُّلْحِ ـ قَلَّقَ ٱلصُّلْحَ.

Peace! *int.* صَهْ ـ السَّكْتَةَ .

Peaceable, *a.* At rest, unruffled, رَائِق ـ قَرَّار ـ سَاجٍ ـ مُطْمَئِنٌّ ـ مِنْ غَيْرِ أَكْدَارٍ . Disposed to peace, مُسَالِمٌ *pl.* مُسَالِمُونَ . A — land, أَرْضٌ مُسْتَرِيحَةٌ . Peaceful measure, وَسَائِطُ سِلْمِيَّةٌ . A — habitation, مَسْكَنُ ٱلسَّلَامِ . A — life, حَيوٰةٌ مُطْمَئِنَّةٌ . These people are — with us, هٰؤُلَاءِ ٱلْقَوْمُ مُسَالِمُونَ لَنَا . *See also* Calm, *a.*

Peaceableness, *n.* The state of being peaceable, مُسَالَمَةٌ . Tranquillity, as of mind, رَاحَةُ بَالٍ ـ رَاحَة ـ طُمَأْنِينَة ـ إِطْمِئْنَان . Quietness, هُدُون ـ سَكِينَة ـ سُكُون . *See also* Calmness, *n.*

Peaceably, *ad.* With a disposition to peace, بِمُسَالَمَةٍ ـ صُلْحًا . Without disturbance, بِسَلَامٍ . To speak — to, كَلَّمَ بِسَلَامٍ ـ كَلَّمَ بِٱلسَّلَامِ . To come — to, جَآءَ بِسَلَامٍ إِلَى . To live — with, سَالَمَ : Live — with all men, سَالِمُوا جَمِيعَ ٱلنَّاسِ .

Peace-breaker, *n.* مُقْلِقُ ٱلنَّاسِ ـ مُتَعَدٍّ عَلَى ٱلسِّلْمِ .

Peaceful, *a.* *See* Peaceable, Calm, Tranquil, *a.*

Peacefully, *ad.* *See* Peaceably, *ad.*

Peacefulness, *n.* *See* Peaceableness, *n.*

Peaceless, *n.* بِلَا ٱطْمِئْنَانٍ ـ مُقْلَق ـ غَيْرُ مُرْتَاحٍ ـ بِلَا رَاحَةٍ .

Peace-maker, *n.* مُفَرِّع ـ صَانِعُ ٱلسَّلَامِ *pl.* صَانِعُو ٱلسَّلَامِ ـ مُصْلِحُ بَيْنَ ـ مُصْلِح ـ مُصَالِح .

Peace-offering, *n.* A sacrifice of peace, ذَبِيحَةُ سَلَامٍ *pl.* ذَبَائِحُ . A present to secure peace, reconciliation, هَدِيَّةُ ٱلْمُصَالَحَةِ .

Peach, *n.* The fruit, فِرْسِيك ـ دُرَّاق ـ خَوْخَة *coll.* خَوْخ . A — tree, شَجَرَةُ ٱلدُّرَّاقِ ـ خَوْخَة .

Peach, *v.i.* To tell, to blab, فَشَّ [2] . To — upon, أَفْشَى بِ ـ سَمَّعَ بِ ـ أَشْهَرَ .

Peachick, *n.* The young of the peacock, فَرْخُ ٱلطَّاوُوسِ *pl.* فِرَاخٌ *and* أَفْرَاخٌ .

Peach-colour, *n.* لَوْنُ زَهْرَةِ ٱلْخَوْخِ ـ لَوْنُ ٱلدُّرَّاقِ .

Peacock, *n.* ٱلصَّرَّاخُ ـ طَاوُوس *pl.* طَوَاوِيسُ *and* أَطْوَاس . A small —, طُوَيْس . She, a woman, adorned herself like a —, تَطَوَّسَتْ .

Peahen, *n.* طَاوُوسَة *pl.* طَاوُوسَات .

Pea-jacket, *n.* قَبُوط .

Peak, *n.* The slender summit of a mountain, شِمْرَاخٌ *pl.* شَمَارِيخُ ـ أَنْفُ جَبَلٍ ـ قُلَل *pl.* قُلَّة ـ ضِرْس *pl.* أَضْرَاس ـ بُرْعُوم *pl.* بَرَاعِيمُ ـ أَنْف *pl.* آنَاف . A point, extremity, حَدٌّ ـ طَرَف . A shade, as of a cap, ظُلَّة ـ ظُلَيْلَة .

Peaked, *a.* *See* Pointed, *a.*

Peakish, *a.* هَزِيل ـ شَاحِب . To be or to look —, شَحَبَ [2] ـ هَزَلَ [2] .

Peal, *n.* A succession of sounds, تَتَابُعٌ ـ ٱرْتِجَازُ ٱلْأَصْوَاتِ ـ طَنْطَنَة ـ طَنِين ـ ٱلْأَصْوَات . A — of thunder, ٱرْتِجَازُ ٱلرَّعْدِ . A pealing of bells, طَنْطَنَةُ (or طَنِينُ) ٱلْأَجْرَاسِ ; a set of bells, طَائِفَةُ (or طَقْمُ) أَجْرَاسٍ .

Peal, *v.t.* To sound, دَقَّ [2] ـ أَصَاتَ ـ صَوَّتَ . To — bells, دَقَّ ٱلْأَجْرَاسَ ـ دَقَّ ٱلْأَجْرَاسَ بِنَغْمَةٍ [2] ; of small bells, جَلْجَلَ ٱلْجَلَاجِلَ .

Peal, *v.i.* To utter a succession of sounds, ٱرْتَجَزَ ـ تَرَجَّزَ . To resound, صَلَّ ـ صَلْصَلَ [2] . The thunder pealed, ٱرْتَجَزَ ٱلرَّعْدُ . The bells pealed, دَقَّتِ (or ٱرْتَجَزَتِ) ٱلْأَجْرَاسُ .

Pealing, *a.* مُصَلْصِل ـ مُتَرَجِّز ـ مُرْتَجِز .

Pean, *n.* *See* Pæan, *n.*

Pea-nut, *n.* *See* Ground-nut, *n.*

Pear, *n.* كُمَّثْرَاة *coll.* كُمَّثْرَى *or* كُمَّثْرَة *pl.* كُمَّثْرَيَات ـ إِنْجَاص . A small —, كُمَيْمِثْرَة ـ كُمَيْثِرَة . A pear tree, شَجَرَةُ ٱلْإِنْجَاصِ ٱلْكُمَّثْرَى .

Pearl, *n.* The — or a large — in its shell, عَقِيلَة ـ عَقِيلَةُ ٱلْبَحْرِ . An ordinary —, لُؤْلُؤ *pl.* دُرَّات *or* دُرَر *pl.* دُرّ ـ سَفَانَة ـ لَآلِئ . A large —, or a bead fashioned like a —, تُومَة *pl.* تُوَم . A false —, لُؤْلُؤ كَذَّاب . A string of pearls, سِمْطُ لُؤْلُؤٍ . A head-dress of pearls, شَبَّالَةُ لُؤْلُؤٍ . A seller of pearls, لَأْلَاء .

Pearl, *v.t.* To stud with pearls, رَصَّعَ بِلُؤْلُؤٍ .

Pearlash, *n.* أُشْنَان مُكَرَّر ـ أُشْنَان ـ قِلْي .

Pearled, *a.* Set with pearls, مُرَصَّع بِلُؤْلُؤٍ .

Pearl-bank, *n.* مَغَاصُ ٱللُّؤْلُؤِ .

Pearl-fishery, *n.* مَغَاصُ ٱللُّؤْلُؤِ . This is a —, هٰذَا مَغَاصُ ٱللُّؤْلُؤِ .

Pearl-oyster, *n.* أُمُّ تُومَةٍ .

Pearl-powder, *n.* إِسْفِيدَاج ـ حُسْنُ يُوسُفَ .

Pearl-shell, *n.* صَدَف *pl.* أَصْدَاف .

Pearly, *a.* Like pearl, لُؤْلُؤِيٌّ . Of a pearl colour, لُؤْلُوَانٌ . *See also* Clear, Transparent, *n.*

Peasant, *n.* فَلَّاح *pl.* فَلَّاحُونَ .

Peasantry, *n.* ٱلْفَلَّاحُونَ ـ فَلَّاحُونَ .

Peascod, *n.* } قِشْرُ ٱلْبِسِلَّةِ ـ قِشْرُ ٱلْجُلُبَّانِ .
Peashell, }

Pease, *n.* *See plurals of nouns under* Pea.

Peat, *n.* لِبْدَةٌ طَبِيعِيَّةٌ تُجْبَلُ مِنْ جُذُورِ ٱلشَّجَرِ تَصْلُحُ لِلْوَقُودِ .

Peat-moss, *n.* بَطِيحَةٌ ذَاتُ ٱللِّبْدَةِ ٱلْمَذْكُورَةِ آنِفًا .

Pebble, *n.* } A round small stone, حَصَاة *pl.* حَصَيَات *and*
Pebble-stone, } حَصًى ـ جَمْرَة *pl.* جِمَار . Pebbles, generally,

حَصًى ـ حَصْبَآءٌ ـ رَضْرَاض ـ رَضْرَض. Rock crystal, حَجَرُ ٱلْبِلَّوْرِ ـ مِلْحُ ٱلْقَاقِ. A place or land abounding with pebbles, أَرْض حَصِيَّةٌ ـ مَحْصَاةٌ. To strew with pebbles, حَصَّبَ. To pelt with pebbles, حَصَبَ ـِ ـُ. They pelted one another with pebbles, of many, تَحَاصَبُوا.

Pebbled, *a.* | Pebbly, *a.* حَصَوِيٌّ. A — river, نَهْرٌ حَصَوِيٌّ ـ نَهْرٌ ذُو رَضْرَاضٍ. *See also under* Pebble, *n.*

Peccability, *n.* تَعَرُّضٌ لِلْخَطِيئَةِ ـ إِمْكَانُ ٱلْخَطَآءِ ـ مَيْلٌ إِلَى ٱلشَّرِّ.

Peccable, *a.* مُتَعَرِّضٌ لِلْخَطِيئَةِ ـ قَابِلُ ٱلْخَطَآءِ.

Peccadillo, *n.* زَلَّةٌ ـ صَغِيرَةٌ *pl.* صَغِيرَات *and* صَغَائِرُ. Peccadillos, مُحَقَّرَات ـ صَغَائِرُ.

Peccant, *a.* Guilty of transgression, مُذْنِب ـ خَاطِئٌ. Morbid, corrupt, فَاسِد. Peccant humours, أَخْلَاطٌ فَاسِدَةٌ.

Peccary, *n.* نَوْعٌ مِنَ ٱلْخَنَازِيرِ يُوجَدُ فِي أَمِيرِيكَا.

Peccavi, *int.* أَخْطَأْتُ.

Peck, *n.* A kind of measure, ضَرْبٌ مِنَ ٱلْمِكْيَالِ. A quantity, حُمْلَةٌ ـ مِقْدَار. A set; *see* Pack, *n.*

Peck, *v.t.* As with the beak, نَقَرَ ـُ ـ نَقَّرَ. To — up, لَقَطَ ـُ ـ اِلْتَقَطَ ـ تَلَقَّطَ.

Pecker, *n.* نَقَّار. *See also* Woodpecker, *n.*

Pecten, *n.* A membrane in the eye of birds, غِشَآءٌ فِي عُيُونِ ٱلطُّيُورِ. *See also* Clam, *n.*

Pectinal, *a.* فِي شَكْلِ ٱلْمُشْطِ.

Pectinal, *n.* سَمَكَةٌ ذَاتُ عِظَامٍ تُشْبِهُ أَسْنَانَ ٱلْمُشْطِ.

Pectoral, *a.* Relating to the breast, مُتَعَلِّقٌ بِٱلصَّدْرِ ـ صَدْرِيٌّ. Good for the chest, نَافِعٌ لِلصَّدْرِ.

Pectoral, *a.* A breastplate, دِرْع ـ صَدْرِيَّةٌ. A medicine for the chest, دَوَآءٌ لِلصَّدْرِ.

Peculate, *v.t.* سَرَقَ ـِ ـ أَسَلَّ ـ إِخْتَلَسَ ـ زُورًا.

Peculation, *n.* سَرِقَة ـ إِخْتِلَاس بِٱلزُّورِ.

Peculator, *n.* سَارِق ـ سَلَّابَة ـ رَجُلٌ مُسِلٌّ.

Peculiar, *a.* Special, خَاصٌّ ـ مَخْصُوص. Quaint, غَرِيب ـ عَجِيب. A — attribute, خَوَاصٌّ ـ خُجْرِيٌّ ـ حُجْرِيٌّ ـ خَاصَّة *pl.* خَوَاصّ ـ خَاصِّيَّة *pl.* خَصَائِصُ. *See also* Particular, *a.*

Peculiar, *n.* As of property, مُلْكٌ مَخْصُوص ـ مُلْكٌ خَاصٌّ.

Peculiarity, *n.* A peculiar property, خُصُوصِيَّة ـ خَاصَّة ـ شَأْن. Quaintness, غَرَابَة. It is one of the peculiarities of the present age, مِنْ خَصَائِصِ هٰذَا ٱلْعَصْرِ.

Peculiarize, *v.t.* *See to* Particularize.

Peculiarly, *ad.* Particularly, specially, خَاصَّةً ـ خُصُوصًا ـ بِٱلْأَخَصِّ. In a singular manner, عَجَبًا ـ بِنَوْعٍ غَرِيب ـ بِنَوْعٍ عَجِيب.

Pecuniarily, *ad.* مِمَّا يُنَاطُ بِٱلنُّقُودِ ـ فِيمَا يَخْتَصُّ بِٱلدَّرَاهِمِ.

Pecuniary, *a.* مُخْتَصٌّ بِٱلدَّرَاهِمِ. A — consideration, عِوَضُ فُلُوسٍ. A — payment, دَفْعُ نَقْدٍ.

Pedagogic, *n.* مَا نِيطَ بِتَعْلِيمِ ٱلصِّغَارِ.

Pedagogism, *n.* تَعْلِيمُ ٱلصِّغَارِ.

Pedagogue, *n.* مُعَلِّمُ ٱلصِّغَارِ ـ مُعَلِّمُ كُتَّاب.

Pedal, *a.* رِجْلِيٌّ ـ مُخْتَصٌّ بِٱلرِّجْلِ.

Pedal, *n.* As of an organ, أُنْبُوبٌ مِنْ أَنَابِيبِ ٱلْأَرْغُنِ. An instrument for modulating sound, آلَةٌ مُعَدِّلَةٌ ـ آلَةٌ مُطْرِبَةٌ. A base, قَاعِدَة *pl.* قَوَاعِدُ ـ كُرْسِيٌّ.

Pedant, *n.* نَحْوِيٌّ *pl.* نُحَاة ـ مُتَظَرِّفٌ بِٱلْعِلْمِ ـ صَلِف *pl.* صُلَفَآءُ (the latter in ridicule).

Pedantic, *a.* | Pedantical, مِفَنٌّ ـ صَلِف *pl.* صُلَفَآءُ ـ مُتَبَاهٍ بِٱلْعِلْمِ ـ مُتَصَنِّعٌ بِٱلْعِلْمِ. To be —; *see to* Pedantize, *v.t.*

Pedantically, *ad.* تَظَرُّفًا بِٱلْعِلْمِ ـ تَصَنُّعًا بِٱلْعِلْمِ ـ بِزَخِيف ـ تَعَجْرُفًا.

Pedantize, *v.i.* تَكَلَّفَ ٱلصَّلَفَ ـ تَصَنَّعَ بِٱلْعِلْمِ ـ تَصَلَّفَ ـ تَعَجْرَفَ ـ تَظَرَّفَ بِٱلْعِلْمِ.

Pedantry, *n.* تَعَجْرُف ـ تَظَرُّف (or تَصَنُّع or تَصَلُّف) بِٱلْعِلْمِ.

Peddle, *v.i.* To trifle, عَبِثَ ـَ ـ تَهَابَلَ ـ طَرَّزَ. To travel and retail goods, دَارَ يَبِيعُ ـُ ـ دَارَ يَتَسَبَّبُ بِ.

Peddler, *n.* A hawker, عِتَّاش ـ ٱلَّذِي يَطُوفُ فِي ٱلْقُرَى لِيَبِيعَ ٱلْأَشْيَآءَ. A trifler, طَرَّاز ـ مُتَهَابِل.

Peddlery, *n.* Peddler's wares, خُرْدَة ـ أَسْبَاب ـ خُرْدَةُ ٱلْعِتَّاشِ.

Peddling, *n.* The going about selling small wares, شُغْلُ ٱلْعِتَّاشِ ـ ٱلطَّوَفَانُ فِي ٱلْقُرَى لِبَيْعِ ٱلْأَشْيَآءِ.

Pedestal, *n.* كُرْسِيٌّ *pl.* كَرَاسِيُّ ـ قَاعِدَة *pl.* قَوَاعِدُ ـ عُمْدَة ـ عِمَاد ـ عِمَاد. *See also* Base, *n.*

Pedestrial, *a.* مُخْتَصٌّ بِٱلرِّجْلِ ـ رِجْلِيٌّ.

Pedestrian, *n.* رَجِيل ـ مُشَاة ـ مَاشٍ *pl.* رُجَّال *and* رَجَّالَة ـ رَاجِل *pl.* رُجَّال *and* رَجَّالَة. A — tour, طَوَافٌ رَجْلًا ـ سَفَرٌ مَشْيًا.

Pedestrian, *a.* *See* Pedestrian, *n.*

Pedestrianism, *n.* Walking, سِيرَة ـ سَيْر ـ تَرَجُّل ـ رُجْلَة. Walking for a wager, مُرَاكَضَة ـ مُرَاجَلَة.

Pedestrianize, *v.i.* مَارَسَ ٱلْمَشْيَ ـ سَعَى ـَ فِي ٱلْمَشْيِ ـ تَرَجَّلَ.

Pedigree, *n.* سِلْسِلَة ـ ذُرِّيَّة ـ أَنْسَاب *pl.* نَسَب ـ مَجْل *pl.* سَلَاسِلُ. They stated their —, بَيَّنُوا نَسْلَهُمْ. Without —, بِلَا نَسَب. *See also* Genealogy, Lineage, *n.*

Pediment, *n.* An ornamental crowning of the front of a building, قَوْصَرَة ـ أَفْرِيز *pl.* أَفَارِيز .

Pedo-baptism, *n.* القَوْلُ بِجَوَازِ مَعْمُودِيَّةِ ٱلْأَطْفَالِ ـ مَعْمُودِيَّةِ ٱلْأَطْفَالِ .

Pedo-baptist, *n.* قَائِلٌ بِجَوَازِ مَعْمُودِيَّةِ ٱلْأَطْفَالِ .

Peduncle, *n.* The stalk of a plant, سَاق ـ شِمْرَاخ *pl.* شَمَارِيخ *pl.* سُوق and سُؤُوق ; the — of a date bunch, عِثْكَال *pl.* عَثَاكِيل .

Pedunculate, *a.* ذُو شَمَارِيخ ـ ذو عَثَاكِيل ـ مُشَمْرَخ ـ مُعَثْكَل .

Peek, *v.i.* *See to* Peep, *v.i.*

Peel, *v.t.* To take off the rind, حَمَرَ ² ـ حَمَّرَ ـ جَرَّكَ ـ جَلَفَ ² ـ قَشَرَ ² ـ قَشَّرَ . To strip, as a bark, حَسَرَ ² ـ شَذَّبَ ; as flesh from a bone, عَرَمَ ² ـ تَعَرَّمَ . To be peeled, of a rind, إِنْقَشَرَ . *See also to* Flay, Plunder, *v.t.*

Peel, *v.i.* To lose the rind, تَقَشَّرَ . To — off, as the hair, إِنْجَرَدَ ـ إِنْحَمَرَ ـ تَحَسَّرَ .

Peel, *n.* Rind, قِشْر ـ قِشْرَة *pl.* قُشُور . Bark, as of a tree, لِحَاءَة ـ لِحَادَة ـ قِشْر ـ مَجَب . A baker's shovel, مِسْجَرَة . Having a —, rind, قَشِر ; having no —, أَقْشَر *fem.* قَشْرَآء .

Peeled, *a.* Stripped of rind, مُقَشَّر ـ مَقْشُور ـ مَحْمُور ـ جَلِيف . Despoiled, plundered, مُنْتَهَب ـ مُسْتَلَب ـ مَسْلُوب .

Peeler, *n.* One who takes off the rind, مُقَشِّر . A plunderer, نَهَّاب ـ نَهَّابَة *pl.* نَاهِب .

Peep, *v.i.* To dawn, إِنْفَجَرَ ٱلصُّبْحُ ـ أَفْصَحَ ٱلصُّبْحُ . To —, as through a crevice, لَاصَ ² . To appear, ظَهَرَ ـ بَانَ ـ . To — or look at, نَظَرَ إِلَى ـ تَطَلَّعَ إِلَى . To — in at, to pay a flying visit to, فَاتَ عَلَى ² ـ شَقَّ عَلَى ² . To — out, as out of a door, تَطَلَّعَ إِلَى ٱلْخَارِجِ . To chirp like a chicken, صَاحَ ـ زَقْزَقَ .

Peep, *n.* The first appearance, dawn, طُلُوع ـ مَبْرَق . A look, as through a crevice, نَظْرَة إِلَى ـ مُلَاوَصَة ـ لَوْص . A looking at, تَطَلُّع إِلَى . To take a sly — at, سَارَقَ ٱلنَّظَرَ إِلَى .

Peep-hole, *n.* نُقْبَة لِلَّوْصِ .

Peeper, *n.* One who peeps, مُلَاوِص ـ لَائِص . A chicken, فَرُّوج *pl.* فَرَارِيج . An eye, عَيْن *pl.* عُيُون .

Peer, *n.* An equal, نَظِير ـ قُرَنَآء *pl.* قَرِين ـ أَقْرَان *pl.* قِرْن *pl.* نُظَرَآء ـ مَثِيل ـ . A companion, صَاحِب *pl.* أَصْحَاب ـ رَفِيق *pl.* رُفَقَآء . A nobleman, عَيْن *pl.* أَعْيَان ـ شَرِيف *pl.* شُرَفَآء or أَشْرَاف ـ أَمِير *pl.* أُمَرَآء ـ أَصِيل *pl.* أُصَلَآء .

Peer, *v.i.* To come in sight, بَدَا *aor.* يَبْدُو ـ تَبَدَّى ـ نَدَرَ ² ـ ظَهَرَ ـ تَظَاهَرَ ـ تَبَيَّنَ . To —, by contracting the eyelids, أَغْضَى (or غَضَّى) طَرْفَهُ . To — over, أَشْرَفَ عَلَى ـ تَطَلَّعَ عَلَى . *See also to* Peep, *v.i.*

Peerage, *n.* The dignity of a peer, رُتْبَةُ ٱلْأَمِيرِ ـ رُتْبَةُ ٱلْأَعْيَانِ . The body of peers, الأَعْيَانُ ـ الأَشْرَافُ ـ الأُمَرَآءُ ٱلْأُصُلُ ـ مَعْشَرُ ٱلْأُمَرَآءِ .

Peeress, *n.* The consort of a peer, إِمْرَأَةُ أَمِيرٍ ـ قَرِينَةُ أَمِيرٍ ـ حَلِيلَةُ أَمِيرٍ . A — in her own right, أَمِيرَةٌ أَصِيلَةٌ .

Peerless, *a.* بِلَا نَظِيرٍ ـ لَا مِثَالَ لَهُ ـ فَائِق *pl.* فُوَقَآء . *See also* Incomparable, *a.*

Peerlessly, *ad.* بِنَوْعٍ لَا مِثَالَ لَهُ ـ بِنَوْعٍ فَائِقٍ .

Peerlessness, *n.* فَضْلٌ لَا نَظِيرَ لَهُ ـ نَادِرَة ـ فَوَقَان ـ فَوَاق .

Peevish, *a.* قَتِب ـ نَكِد ـ عَارِم ـ شَكِس ـ شَرِس ـ وَعِق ـ عَفِش . To be —, تَنَكَّدَ ـ شَرِسَ ـ شَكِسَ ـ وَعِقَ *aor.* يَعِقُ . *See also* Fretful, *a.*

Peevishly, *ad.* بِشَرَاسَةٍ ـ بِشَكَاسَةٍ ـ بِوَعَقَةٍ .

Peevishness, *n.* شَرَاسَة ـ شَكَاسَة ـ وَعَقَة .

Peg, *n.* A stake, شِجَاج ـ وَتَد *pl.* أَوْتَاد . A peg or pin of iron, سَكّ *pl.* سِكَاك ; a peg, pivot, of iron or wood, مِرْوَد *pl.* مَرَاوِد . A dowel, دِسَار *pl.* دُسُر . A small peg of wood, عُصْفُور *pl.* عَصَافِير ; of iron, مِسْمَارٌ صَغِيرٌ *pl.* مَسَامِير . A peg in a wall, مِلْوَى *pl.* مَلَاوِي . The peg of a musical instrument, عِيَار *pl.* عَيْر . An attempt, سَعْي . A turn, دَوْر . A draught, شَرْبَة . There is not so much as a peg, anything, in the house, مَا بِٱلدَّارِ شِجَاجٌ . To take one down a peg, خَفَضَ ـ وَضَعَ ـ أَخْضَعَ . To have a peg at, to attempt, سَعَى فِي ـ جَرَّبَ . To drink of, شَرِبَ مِن ـ شَرِبَ شَرْبَةً مِن . To take a turn with somebody else, عَاقَبَ .

Peg, *v.t.* To fasten with pegs, stakes, أَوْتَدَ ـ وَتَّدَ . To drive small wooden pegs into, رَكَّبَ بِعَصَافِيرَ ـ سَمَّرَ بِعَصَافِيرَ .

Pegasus, *n.* The constellation, الفَرَسُ ٱلْأَعْظَمُ . The fabulous horse so named, فَرَسٌ ذُو جَنَاحَيْنِ مَشْهُورٌ فِي أَسَاطِيرِ ٱلْيُونَانِيِّينَ ٱلْقُدَمَآءِ .

Pegged, *a.* Fastened with pegs, stakes, مُوَتَّد ـ مُحْكَمٌ بِأَوْتَادٍ . Having small pegs driven into it, مُرَصَّعٌ أَصَافِيرَ .

Pegtop, *n.* خُذْرُوف ـ خَرَّارَة .

Pekoe, *n.* A kind of tea, ضَرْبٌ مِنَ ٱلشَّايِ أَسْوَدُ .

Pelagian, *n.*
Pelagian, *a.* } تَابِعُ بِلَاجِيُوسَ ـ بِلَاجِيُوسِيٌّ .

Pelagic, *a.* Of the sea, بَحْرِيٌّ .

Pelargonium, *n.* جِنْسٌ مِنَ ٱلنَّبَاتَاتِ يُشْبِهُ إِبْرَةَ ٱلرَّاعِي .

Pelerine, *n.* As of a woman's dress, فَرْوَة *pl.* فِرَآء .

Pelf, *n.* مَال ـ مَكْسَب .

Pelican, *n.* رَخَم *pl.* رَخَمَة ـ حَمَلُ ٱلْبَحْرِ ـ سَقَّآء.

Pelisse, *n.* فُسْتَان.

Pell, *n.* A roll, طُومَار *pl.* طَوَامِيرُ.

Pellet, *n.* For a bow, بُنْدُقَة *coll.* بَنَادِقُ ـ جُلاهِقَة *coll.* جُلاهِق. A bow for shooting pellets, قَوْسُ ٱلْبُنْدُقِ ـ قَوْسُ ٱلْجُلاهِقِ. A small ball or mass, كُرَة *pl.* كُرَر ـ حَبَّة *coll.* حَبّ. To make into pellets, small balls, حَبَّبَ.

Pellicle, *n.* A thin skin or film, ذُوَايَة ـ غِلَاف *pl.* غُلُف ـ قُوف *pl.* أَقْوَاف ـ غِلَالَة. The — of an egg, غِرْقِئٌ ـ قَيْقَة ـ خِرْشَآء; of a date-stone, سِيَرَآء.

Pellmell, *ad.* بَدَدْ بَدَدْ ـ بَدَادِ بَدَادِ ـ بَدَدًا بَدَدًا ـ شِذَرَ مِذَرَ ـ خَلْطَةً بَلْطَةً ـ خِلْطًا مِلْطًا ـ شَتَاتَ شَتَاتَ. The people were dispersed —, تَفَرَّقَ ٱلْقَوْمُ بَدَادِ.

Pellucid, *a.* Clear, صَافٍ ـ صَفِيٌّ *pl.* أَصْفِيَآء. Transparent, شَفَّاف. To be —, clear, صَفَا *aor.* يَصْفُو ـ أَصْفَحَ. *See also* Clear, Limpid, *a.*

Pellucidness, *n.* Clearness, صَفَآء ـ صُفُوّ. Transparency, شَفِيف ـ شَفَف.

Pelt, *n.* The skin of a beast, جِلْد *pl.* جُلُود. A throw, رَجْم ـ رَمْيَة ـ ضَرْبَة ـ ضَرْب.

Pelt, *v.t.* To throw, رَمَى ; to throw at, as with stones, رَجَمَ ـ حَصَبَ. They pelted one another with stones, of many, تَرَاجَمُوا بِٱلْحِجَارَةِ.

Pelting, *n.* رَمْيٌ ـ رُجُوم ـ رَجْم.

Pelting, *a.* As of rain, pattering, شَدِيد ـ خَافِق.

Peltry, *n.* Skins of animals, جُلُود ; furs, فِرَآء ـ فَرْوَات.

Pelvic, *n.* ما نِيطَ بِغَوْرِ ٱلْجَوْفِ ٱلْأَسْفَلِ.

Pelvis, *n.* الحَوْضُ ـ غَوْرُ ٱلْجَوْفِ ٱلْأَسْفَلِ.

Pemmican, *n.* Meat cut and dried in the sun to be used in travelling, قَدِيد ـ وَشِيق ـ *from the Turkish,* بَسْطُرْمَا.

Pen, *n.* As for writing, قَلَم *pl.* أَقْلَام. A quill, رِيشَة *coll.* رِيش ; a quill pen, قَلَمُ رِيشٍ. A pen for cattle, زَرِيبَة ـ أَسِيدَة ـ أَسِدَة *pl.* زَرَائِبُ ـ حَظِيرَة *pl.* حَظَائِرُ. To make or mend a pen, بَرَى ٱلْقَلَمَ.

Pen, *v.t.* To write, سَطَرَ ـ كَتَبَ ـ حَرَّرَ. To shut cattle in a pen, حَظَرَ ـ حَظَرَ عَلَى ـ زَرَبَ ـ أَزْرَبَ. To confine, حَصَرَ ـ حَبَسَ. To lock up, قَفَلَ عَلَى.

Penal, *a.* قِصَاصِيٌّ ـ حَدِّيٌّ ـ جَزَائِيٌّ. A — code, دُسْتُورُ ٱلْجَزَآءِ ـ قَوَانِينُ جَزَائِيَّة. Penal procedure, أُصُولُ ٱلْمُحَاكَمَةِ ٱلْجَزَائِيَّةِ. A — clause, شَرْطٌ جِنَائِيٌّ ـ شَرْطٌ جَزَائِيٌّ. *See also* Criminal, *a.*

Penally, *ad.* فِي صُورَةِ ٱلْجَزَآءِ.

Penalty, *n.* Punishment, حَدّ *pl.* حُدُود ـ قِصَاص ـ جَزَآء ـ مُجَازَاة. A fine, غَرَام ـ غَرَامَة ـ جَرِيمَة. One who inflicts a —, حَدَّاد. The extreme — of the law, قَتْل ـ صَلْب ـ قِصَاصُ ٱلْمَوْتِ.

Penance, *n.* As imposed by a priest, كَفَّارَة ـ قَانُون. To impose — upon, عَمِلَ (or فَرَضَ) عَلَى ـ قَانُونًا. To perform the — inflicted, وَفَى *aor.* يَفِي ٱلْقَانُونَ. By way of —, عَلَى مِنْوَالِ ٱلْقَانُونِ.

Penates, *n.* Household gods of the ancient Romans, مَعَابِدُ ٱلدَّارِ عِنْدَ ٱلرُّومَانِيِّينَ ٱلْأَقْدَمِينَ.

Pen-case, *n.* مِقْلَمَة.

Pence, *n.* Plural of Penny, بِنْس (*sing.* سِكَّةُ ٱلْبِنِي). Money, small money, فُلُوسٌ صِغَارٌ ـ ٱلْخُرْدَةُ مِنَ ٱلدَّرَاهِمِ ـ مِصْرِيَّات.

Penchant, n. See Inclination, *n.*

Pencil, *n.* A lead —, قَلَمُ رَصَاصٍ. A small brush for painting, رِيش ـ قَلَمُ شَعْرٍ *pl.* أَقْلَام. A collection of rays, مَرْكَزُ شُعَاعٍ. The art of painting, فَنُّ ٱلرَّسْمِ ـ فَنُّ ٱلتَّصْوِيرِ.

Pencil, *v.t.* To draw, رَسَمَ ـ صَوَّرَ. To draw, as of lines, خَطَّطَ. *See also to* Sketch, *v.t.*

Pencil-case, *n.* غِلَافُ ٱلْقَلَمِ.

Pencilled, *a.* Drawn, مَرْسُوم ـ مُصَوَّر. Having pencilled eye-brows, أَزَجّ *fem.* زَجَّآء *pl.* زُجّ.

Pencilling, *n.* The art of drawing, فَنُّ ٱلرَّسْمِ ـ فَنُّ ٱلتَّصْوِيرِ. A drawing, رَسْم *pl.* رُسُوم ـ تَصْوِير *pl.* تَصَاوِيرُ. *See also* Sketch, *n.*

Pendant, *n.* Any small article suspended, عِلَاق ; as of an earring, شَنْف *pl.* شُنُوف ـ قُرْط *pl.* قُرُوط ; of a necklace, مِعْلَاق *pl.* مَعَالِيقُ. A ship's —, طَرَّادَة ـ فَلَانْدَرَة. A broad —, بَيْرَق *pl.* بَيَارِقُ. Something corresponding to another, نَظِير ـ مُقَابِل ـ أَخٌ ـ أَخُو. *See also* Pennon, *n.*

Pendence, *n.* A slope, صَبَب ـ حُضُور.

Pendency, *n.* Suspense, hesitation, تَوَقُّف ـ تَأَخُّر ـ تَضَرُّب ـ تَمَخْطُر.

Pendent, *a.* Suspended, مُنَاط ـ مُتَسَمِّط ـ مُعَلَّق. Pendent, of the hair, مُتَسَدِّل. Jutting over, بَارِز ـ مُشْرِف. To be —, suspended, تَعَلَّقَ. To be — from, عَلِقَ بِ ـ تَعَلَّقَ بِ ـ إِعْتَلَقَ بِ.

Pendente lite, ad. مُدَّةَ رُؤْيَةِ ٱلدَّعْوَى.

Pending, *a.* Undecided, غَيْرُ مَفْصُولٍ ـ مُعَلَّق. The case is —, ٱلدَّعْوَى مُعَلَّقَة.

Pending, *prep.* During, فِي مُدَّةِ ـ طُولَ ـ بِطُولِ.

Pendulous, *a.* Hanging loose, سَاقِط ـ نَوِس ـ أَجْنَف ـ خَرِيع ـ

— أَغْضَف Flabby, مُسْتَرْخٍ — مُرْخٍ — مُدَنْدِل — مُنْسَدِل خَطِل. To be —, hanging loose, يَرْخَى aor. رَخِيَ — اِسْتَرْخَى. To be —, flabby, خَطِلَ ـ. Having — ears, أَغْضَف — أَخْطَل pl. خُطْل.

Pendulousness, n. } State of hanging loose, نَوَسَان — نَوْس —
Pendulosity, } اِسْتِرْخَاء. Flabbiness, غَضَف خَطَل.

Pendulum, n. A clock, سَاعَة. The —, as of a clock, رَقَّاص. To move to and fro like a —, نَاسَ ـ — تَذَبْذَبَ — تَنَوَّحَ.

Penetrability, n. Susceptibility of entrance, قَابِلِيَّة ٱلدُّخُولِ فِيهِ; as by water, قَابِلِيَّة ٱلتَّطَرُّقِ إِلَيْهِ; of being pierced, قَابِلِيَّة ٱلنُّفُوذِ فِيهِ; of being acted upon, قَابِلِيَّة ٱلتَّأْثِيرِ فِيهِ; of being discovered, قَابِلِيَّة إِدْرَاكِهِ — قَابِلِيَّة ٱلْوُقُوفِ عَلَيْهِ; of being entered into, as a country, forest, etc., قَابِلِيَّة ٱلْوُغُولِ فِيهِ (or ٱلتَّطَرُّقِ إِلَيْهِ).

Penetrable, a. That may be entered, يُدْخَلُ فِيهِ; that may be pierced, يُنْفَذُ فِيهِ; as by water, يَتَطَرَّقُ إِلَيْهِ; that may be acted upon, يُؤَثِّرُ فِيهِ; that may be discovered, known, يُفْهَمُ — يُدْرَكُ — مُدْرَك — يُكْشَفُ عَنْهُ; that may be entered, as a country, forest, etc. يُوغَلُ فِيهِ — يَتَطَرَّقُ إِلَيْهِ.

Penetralia, n. Hidden or deep parts of any thing, عَمَائِق; secret places, أَمَاكِنُ مُسْتَتِرَة — مَخَابِئ; secrets, أَسْرَار — سَرَائِر.

Penetrate, v.t. To pierce, pierce through, مَضَى ـ — خَرَقَ ـ — قَطَعَ فِي ـ — أَنْفَذَ — نَفَذَ ـ — تَخَلَّلَ — خَسَقَ ـ — خَرَقَ ـ نَقَبَ. To bore, دَخَلَ ـ. To enter, خَشَّ فِي ـ. To — into, as into a country, غَسَّ فِي ـ — غَمَضَ فِي ـ — شَقَّ ـ — تَخَلَّلَ — تَطَرَّقَ إِلَى. To — into, to find a way into, as damp, etc., تَطَرَّقَ إِلَى: Wet cannot penetrate into it, لَا يَتَطَرَّقُ إِلَيْهِ ٱلْبَلَلُ. To —, as troops into a country, وَغَلَ فِي aor. يَغِلُ. To —, as into a desert, طَعَنَ فِي ـ — خَشَّ فِي ـ. To affect, make an impression upon, أَثَّرَ فِي — قَطَعَ فِي ـ. To look into, to scrutinize, تَصَفَّحَ — تَفَحَّصَ — تَبَحَّرَ فِي. To go deeply into a thing, as a study, اِطَّلَعَ عَلَى — يَقِفُ aor. وَقَفَ عَلَى ٱلسِّرِّ. To — or discover a secret, تَجَوَّنَ فِي — عَرَفَ ٱلسِّرَّ ـ — اِطَّلَعَ عَلَى ٱلسِّرِّ. To cause to penetrate, أَمْضَى — أَنْفَذَ; as oil into the hair, etc., غَلَّ ـ. To be penetrated, pierced, تَخَلَّلَ ٱلْقَلْبَ. It penetrated the heart, تَخَرَّقَ — اِنْخَرَقَ — نُفِذَ.
See also to Pierce, v.t.

Penetrating, a. Making way into, piercing, نَافِذ — خَارِق — ثَاقِب. Effective, مُؤَثِّر — شَخْشَخَان. Sharp, cutting, صَارِم pl. صَوَارِمُ. Sharp, discerning, مَعِيّ — ثَاقِب — حَاذِق بَاذِق — فَاطِن — نَبِيه — ذَهِين — حَاذِق. Penetrating, of a wind, وَخْشِيَّة — زَمْهَرِير.

Penetration, n. The act of piercing, نَفَاذ — نُفُوذ; of entering, دُخُول — وُغُول; of affecting, تَأْثِير; of going far into a country, وُغُول; penetrative power, as of a sword, هَبَّة; acuteness of intellect, نَبَاهَة — ذَكَاء — حَذْق عَقْل — فِطْنَة — وِهْنَة.

Penetrative, a. Penetrative power, نَفْذ — هَبَّة. Penetrative genius, عَاقِلَة نَظَرِيَّة.

Penguin, n. نَوْعٌ مِنْ طُيُورِ ٱلْبَحْرِ.

Peninsula, n. جَزِيرَة — شَبَهُ (or شِبْهُ) ٱلْجَزِيرَةِ pl. جَزَائِرُ — بَرْزَخ pl. بَرَازِخُ. The — of Arabia, جَزِيرَةُ ٱلْعَرَبِ. The —, meaning that of Spain and Portugal, جَزِيرَةُ (or بِحَيْجَزِيرَة) إِسْبَانِيَا وَبُورْتُوقَال.

Peninsular, a. Relating to a peninsula, مُتَعَلِّق بِجَزِيرَةٍ (or بِبَرْزَخٍ); like a peninsula, مِثْلَ ٱلْبَحَيْجَزِيرَة (or ٱلْجَزِيرَة). The — war, ٱلْحَرْبُ فِي جَزِيرَتَي إِسْبَانِيَا وَبُورْتُوقَال.

Penis, n. زُبّ pl. أَزْبَاب — ذُنْذُب — جُوْقَان — عَوْف — أَيْر pl. آيَار and أُيُور — ذَكَر pl. ذُكُور. Having a large —, أَيَارِيّ. A weak —, حَوْقَلَة. The corona of the glans penis, ٱلْحَوْق.

Penitence, n. } نَدَامَة — تَوْبَة. See also Repentance, n.
Penitency, }

Penitent, a. } تَائِب — نُدَّام pl. نِدَام and نَدْمَان. To be —,
Penitent, n. } تَابَ ـ — رَجَعَ عَنِ ٱلذَّنْبِ ـ. See also Repentant, a., and to Repent, v.i.

Penitential, a. مُتَعَلِّق بِٱلتَّوْبَةِ. The seven penitential psalms, سَبْعَة مَزَامِيرِ ٱلتَّوْبَةِ.

Penitential, n. A book directing penance, كِتَاب مُرْشِدُ ٱلتَّائِبِينَ — كِتَاب مُرْشِد لِلتَّوْبَةِ.

Penitentiary, a. Relating to penance, مُتَعَلِّق بِٱلتَّوْبَةِ. Relating to a penitentiary, مَا نِيطَ بِسِجْنِ ٱلتَّأْدِيبِ. A — offence, ذَنْب مُسْتَحِقّ ٱلْحَبْسِ فِي سِجْنِ ٱلتَّأْدِيبِ.

Penitentiary, n. One who prescribes rules of penance, وَاضِع قَانُونِ ٱلتَّوْبَةِ. One that does penance, تَحْتَ ٱلْقَانُونِ. A house of correction, حَبْس لِلتَّأْدِيبِ — حَبْس لِلتَّهْذِيبِ.

Penitently, ad. بِٱلتَّوْبَةِ — بِنَدَامَةٍ — نَدَامَةً.

Penknife, n. مِبْرَاة — مِطْوَى (vulg. مَطْوَى) pl. مَطَاوٍ; from the Turkish, قَلَم تَرَاش.

Penman, n. One who writes a good hand, خَطَّاط pl. خَطَّاطُونَ. A writer, author, كَاتِب pl. كُتَّاب — مُؤَلِّف pl. مُؤَلِّفُونَ — مُصَنِّف.

Penmanship, n. The art of writing, كِتَابَة — خَطّ. See also Caligraphy, n.

Pennant, n. } Such as is borne on a spear, أُمُّ ٱلرُّمْحِ — عَذَب —
Pennon, } عَذَبَة pl. عَذَبَات. See also Pendant, n.

Pennate, *a.* / Pennated, } Winged, ذُو أَجْنِحَةٍ. Having several leaflets, ذُو وُرَيْقَاتٍ.

Penniform, *a.* In the form of a quill, فِي هَيْئَةِ رِيشَةٍ.

Penniless, *a.* مُفْلِس.

Penny, *n.* An English —, پَنِي وَهُوَ سِكَّةٌ إِنْكِلِيزِيَّةٌ تُسَاوِي عِشْرِينَ پَارَة *pl.* پَنْس. A small sum, فَلْس. He has not got a —, مَا عِنْدَهُ فَلْسٌ. To turn a —, رَبِحَ ـ كَسَبَ.

Penny-a-liner, *n.* كَاتِبُ سَطْرٍ بِفَلْسٍ وَهُوَ عِبَارَةٌ عَنْ مُكَاتِبِ الْجَرَائِدِ الَّذِي يَأْخُذُ ثَمَنًا حَقِيرًا حَقَّ مُكَاتَبَتِهِ.

Penny-royal, *n.* The plant, صَعْتَرُ ٱلْفَرَسِ ـ حَبَق ـ فُوتَنْج ـ غَاغ.

Penny-weight, *n.* وَزْنٌ إِنْكِلِيزِيٌّ قَدْرُهُ أَرْبَعٌ وَعِشْرُونَ شَعِيرَةً.

Penny-wise, *a.* مُوَفِّرُ ٱلْبَارَاتِ ـ مُقْتَصِدُ ٱلْخُرْدَةِ مِنَ ٱلدَّرَاهِمِ.

Penny-wise and pounds foolish, مُقْتَصِدُ ٱلْبَارَاتِ مُبَذِّرُ ٱللِّيرَاتِ.

Pennywort, *n.* The plant, قَصْعَةُ ٱلْمَاءِ.

Pennyworth, *n.* / Pen'orth, } بِپَنِي ـ شِرَى پَنِي. Buy ten — of bread, إِشْتَرِي خُبْزًا بِعَشَرَةِ پَنْسٍ. *See under* Penny, *n.*

Pensile, *a.* مُعَلَّق. To make a building —, that is, supported on a stage above the ground, عَلَّقَ ٱلْبِنَاءَ.

Pension, *n.* An allowance for past services, رَاتِب *or* رَاتِبَة *pl.* رَوَاتِبُ ـ مَعَاش ـ جَامَكِيَّة *pl.* جَوَامِكُ. A retiring —, مَعَاشُ (*or* رَاتِبُ) ٱلتَّقَاعُدِ. A — or annuity office, (قَلَمُ (*or* مَكْتَبُ ٱلرَّوَاتِبِ; *from the Turkish,* رُوزْنَامْجِيَّة. A yearly pension, رَاتِبٌ سَنَوِيٌّ.

Pension, *v.t.* عَيَّنَ لـ-مَعَاشًا ـ عَيَّنَ لـ-رَاتِبًا. To — off, to pay and discharge, عَيَّنَ لـ-مَعَاشًا وَرَخَّصَهُ.

Pensionary, *a.* رَاتِبِيٌّ.

Pensionary, *n.* / Pensioner, } One who receives a pension, صَاحِبُ رَاتِبٍ *pl.* أَصْحَابُ ٱلرَّوَاتِبِ. One who receives a retiring pension, صَاحِبُ رَاتِبِ ٱلتَّقَاعُدِ. One who receives alms, إِبْنُ ٱلصَّدَقَةِ. One who pays for lodgings and board, دَافِعُ حَقِّ ٱلْأَكْلِ وَٱلسُّكْنَى. *See also* Dependent, *n.*

Chelsea pensioner, عِبَارَةٌ عَنْ عَسْكَرِيٍّ مُتَقَاعِدٍ.

Gentleman pensioner, عِبَارَةٌ عَنْ مَقَامٍ يُشْبِهُ ٱلْقَبُوأَغَاسِي.

Greenwich pensioner, عِبَارَةٌ عَنْ بَحْرِيٍّ مُتَقَاعِدٍ.

Pensive, *a.* Reflective, مُتَفَكِّر ـ فَكُور ـ فَكِير ـ مُتَأَمِّل. Sad, كَرِيب ـ شَجِب. To be —, sad, شَجِبَ ـ إِكْتَرَبَ.

Pensively, *ad.* With thoughtfulness, تَفَكُّرًا; sadly, بِشَجَبٍ ـ بِضِيقٍ.

Pensiveness, *n.* Thoughtfulness, تَأَمُّل ـ فِكْر ـ تَفَكُّر. Sadness, ضِيق ـ هَمّ ـ شَجَب ـ كَآب.

Penstock, *n.* حَاجِز ـ سَدّ.

Pent, *a.* Closely confined, مَحْصُور. To be pent up, إِنْحَصَرَ.

Pentachord, *n.* آلَةُ ٱلطَّرَبِ ذَاتُ خَمْسَةِ أَوْتَارٍ.

Pentagon, *n.* مُخَمَّس. To make into a —, خَمَّسَ.

Pentagonal, *a.* ذُو خَمْسِ زَوَايَا ـ مُخَمَّسُ ٱلزَّوَايَا.

Pentagraph, *n.* *See* Pantagraph, *n.*

Pentahedron, *n.* مُخَمَّسٌ مُجَسَّمٌ.

Pentameter, *n.* مِصْرَاعٌ ذُو خَمْسَةِ تَفَاعِيلَ.

Pentangular, *a.* ذُو خَمْسِ زَوَايَا.

Pentastich, *n.* شِعْرٌ مُخَمَّسٌ ـ مُخَمَّس.

Pentastyle, *n.* بِنَاءٌ عَلَى خَمْسَةِ صُفُوفٍ مِنَ ٱلْأَعْمِدَةِ.

Pentateuch, *n.* تَوْرَاةُ مُوسَى ـ ٱلتَّوْرَاةُ.

Pentecost, *n.* Of the Jews, عِيدُ ٱلْخَمْسِينَ; of the Christians, عِيدُ حُلُولِ ٱلرُّوحِ ٱلْقُدُسِ ـ عِيدُ ٱلْعَنْصَرَةِ ـ عِيدُ ٱلْمَوْقِفِ.

Pentecostal, *a.* مُتَعَلِّقٌ بِعِيدِ ٱلْعَنْصَرَةِ.

Pent-house, *n.* مِظَلَّة ـ كُوخ *pl.* أَكْوَاخ.

Pent-roof, *n.* سَقْفٌ هَبُوطٌ ـ جَمَلُون.

Penult, *n.* / Penultima, } The last syllable but one in a word, الْهِجَاءُ ٱلْوَاقِعُ مَا قَبْلَ آخِرِ ٱلْكَلِمَةِ.

Penultimate, *a.* وَاقِعٌ قَبْلَ ٱلْأَخِيرِ.

Penumbra, *n.* The — in an eclipse, (بَدْءُ ٱلظِّلِّ (*or* ظِلٌّ خَفِيفٌ عِنْدَ ٱلْكُسُوفِ.

Penurious, *a.* يَدُهُ مَاسِكَةٌ ـ بَخِيل ـ خَسِيس ـ شَحِيح. To be —, شَحَّ *aor.* يَشِحُّ ـ بَخِلَ. *See also* Avaricious, Niggardly, *a.*

Penuriously, *ad.* بِشُحٍّ ـ بِخَسَاسَةٍ ـ بِبُخْلٍ.

Penuriousness, *n.* شُحّ ـ مَسَاك ـ مَسَاكَة ـ خَسَاسَة ـ بُخْل.

Penury, *n.* إِحْتِيَاجٌ كُلِّيٌّ ـ فَقْر ـ فَقْرُ حَالٍ ـ قِلَّة ـ حَوْبَة ـ عَدَم.

Pen-wiper, *n.* قُرَّاعَة.

Peon, *n.* شُرْطِيٌّ *pl.* شُرْطَة ـ قَوَّاس *pl.* قَوَّاسَة.

Peony, *n.* عُودُ ٱلصَّلِيبِ ـ فَاوُنِيَا.

People, *n.* A body of individuals, نَاس ـ خَلْق ـ شَعْب ـ عَالَم ـ أُنَاس. A tribe, company, قَبِيلَة *pl.* قَبَائِل ـ قَوْم *pl.* أَقْوَام ـ أَهْلُ بِلَادٍ. أُمَّة *pl.* أُمَم ـ طَائِفَة *pl.* طَوَائِفُ. The — of a country, رَعِيَّة *pl.* رَعَايَا. The — of a state, subjects, جِيل *pl.* أَجْيَال. The — of a generation, جِيل *pl.* أَجْيَال. The —, populace, ٱلْخَلْقُ ـ ٱلشَّعْبُ. The common —, أَطْرَافُ ٱلنَّاسِ ـ عُرْضُ ٱلنَّاسِ ـ ٱلْأَسَافِلُ. A crowd of mixed —, وَبْش *pl.* أَوْبَاش. The higher and lower orders of the —, ٱلْخَوَاصُّ وَٱلْعَامُّ.

People, *v.t.* عَمَرَ ـ أَعْمَرَ: He peopled the land, عَمَرَ ٱلْأَرْضَ. To be or become peopled, عَمَرَ: the land was peopled, عَمَرَتِ ٱلْأَرْضُ.

Peopled, *a.* مَعْمُور — آهِل. A well-peopled land, عُمْرَان — بِلَادٌ ذُو عِمَارَةٍ — بِلَادٌ عَامِرَةٌ — أَرْضٌ عَامِرَةٌ. Thinly peopled, قَلِيلُ ٱلْأَهْلِ — قَلِيلُ ٱلْعِمَارَةِ.

Pepper, *n.* فِلْفِل — فُلْفُل — بَهَار. Long —, دَارُ ٱلْفِلْفِلِ — عِرْقُ ٱلذَّهَبِ — فِلْفِل طَوِيل.

Pepper, *v.t.* To sprinkle with pepper, فَلْفَلَ. To season with pepper, حَيَّقَ بِفِلْفِلٍ. To throw or pelt at, رَمَى بِـ =. *See to* Pelt, *v.t.*

Pepper-box, *n.* حُقَّةُ ٱلْفِلْفِلِ — وِعَاءُ ٱلْفُلْفُلِ.

Pepper-corn, *n.* حَبُّ ٱلْفِلْفِلِ *pl.* حُبُوب.

Peppered, *a.* Sprinkled with pepper, مُفَلْفَل. Pelted at, مَرْمِيٌّ عَلَيْهِ.

Peppering, *n.* As with pepper, رَشٌّ بِفِلْفِلٍ; a pelting, as with stones, رَجْم — رُجُوم.

Peppermint, *n.* نَعْنَعٌ (or نَعْنَاعٌ) رُوحِيٌّ. Peppermint drops, حَبُّ ٱلنَّعْنَاعِ بِسُكَّر.

Peppery, *a.* Hot, pungent, حَاذِق — أُجَاج — حَرِيف — حَامِز — حَادّ. *See also* Irascible, *a.*

Pepsin, *n.* مَادَّةٌ مَوْجُودَةٌ فِي مَعِدَةِ ٱلْحَيَوَانَاتِ تُيَسِّرُ ٱلْهَضْمَ.

Peptic, *a.* Promoting digestion, نَافِعٌ لِلْهَضْمِ — هَضَّام — هَاضُوم.

Peradventure, *ad.* لَعَلَّ — عَسَى. *See also* Perhaps, *ad.*

Perambulate, *v.t.* To walk round, حَفَّ بِـ = — طَافَ حَوْلَ ² — دَارَ ². To walk through, عَارَ فِي = — عَالَ فِي = — بَرَمَ ².

Perambulation, *n.* The act of walking round, طَوَاف — دَوْر; of walking through, عَيْل — عُيُول — بَرْم. A journey, سَيْر — سِيَاحَة.

Perambulator, *n.* An instrument to measure distance, آلَةٌ لِلْقِيَاسِ. A — for children, عَرَبِيَّةٌ (or نَقَّالَةٌ) لِلْأَوْلَادِ.

Per annum, *ad.* By the year, بِٱلسَّنَةِ.

Perceivable, *a.* That may be apprehended by the senses, يُدْرَكُ بِٱلْحَوَاسِّ. Perceivable to the mind, يُدْرَكُ بِٱلْعَقْلِ — مِمَّا يُشْعَرُ بِهِ; to the sight, يُدْرَكُ بِٱلْبَصَرِ — مِمَّا يُعَايَنُ; to the touch, مِمَّا يُدْرَكُ بِٱللَّمْسِ. It is not — by the sight, لَا يُدْرِكُهُ ٱلنَّظَرُ.

Perceivably, *ad.* So as to be perceived by the senses, بِهَيْئَةٍ تُدْرِكُهَا ٱلْحَوَاسُّ. Openly, visibly, عَلَانِيَةً — بَيَانًا — عِيَانًا.

Perceive, *v.t.* To receive by way of impression on the mind, to understand, أَدْرَكَ — أَحَسَّ — شَعَرَ بِـ = — وَجَدَ *aor.* يَجِدُ. To — with the eye, عَايَنَ — أَحَسَّ بِٱلْعَيْنِ. To — an odour, أَرَاحَ — شَمَّ ² — ٱسْتَرْوَحَ — ٱسْتَرَاحَ — أَرْوَحَ. To — with the mind, فَطِنَ = — بَصُرَ بِـ ² — أَبْصَرَ. To cause to —, أَشْعَرَ بِـ — بَصَّرَ بِـ.

Perceived, *a.* مُدْرَك — مَحْسُوس. Things perceived by the senses, مَحْسُوسَات.

Per cent, *ad.* فِي ٱلْمِئَةِ — بِٱلْمِئَةِ.

Per-centage, *n.* As on goods, *etc.*, حَقٌّ (or مَعْلُومٌ) فِي ٱلْمِئَةِ.

Perceptible, *a.* As by the senses, حِسِّيٌّ. *See also* Perceivable, *a.*

Perceptibly, *ad.* *See* Perceivably, *ad.*

Perception, *n.* The act of perceiving, feeling, إِحْسَاس — حِسٌّ. Discernment, comprehension, حَسَاس — شِعْر — فِطْنَة — بَصَر — بَصِيرَة — نَظَر — إِدْرَاك. An idea, رَأْيٌ *pl.* آرَاء. Intuitive —, بَدِيهَة. To have a mental — of, ٱسْتَبْصَرَ — حَسَّ بِـ ² — أَحَسَّ بِـ. The — of an odour, ٱسْتِرْوَاح — إِرْوَاح — شَمّ. Having strong —, كَثِيرُ ٱلْإِدْرَاكِ — دَرَّاك — حَسَّاس دَرَّاك.

Perceptive, *a.* بَصِير — مُدْرِك — فَاطِن. The — faculty, ٱلْقُوَّةُ ٱلْمُدْرِكَةُ.

Perch, *n.* The fish, نَوْعٌ مِنْ سَمَكِ ٱلْأَنْهُرِ. The measure, قِيَاسٌ إِنْكِلِيزِيٌّ. A rod, staff, قَضِيب *pl.* قُضْبَان. A roost for fowls, مَحَلٌّ (or عُودُ) جُثُومِ ٱلطُّيُورِ — مَجْثَم.

Perch, *v.i.* To light on, as a bird on a tree, *etc.*, جَثَمَ عَلَى = ². To alight on, sit on, حَطَّ عَلَى ² — حَلَّ عَلَى ².

Perch, *v.t.* To place on a perch, جَثَّمَ. To place upon, أَقَامَ عَلَى — نَصَبَ عَلَى ².

Perchance, *ad.* *See* Perhaps, *ad.*

Percipience, *n.* *See* Perception, *n.*

Percipient, *a.* *See* Perceptive, *a.*

Percolate, *v.i.* *See to* Filter, *to* Leak, *v.i.*

Percolate, *v.t.* *See to* Filter, *v.t.*

Percolation, *n.* تَصْفِيَة — تَرْوِيق — بَزْل.

Percolator, *n.* مِصْفَاة — مِشْخَل — مِبْزَل — رَاوُوق; *vulg.* مِصْفِيَّة.

Percuss, *v.t.* صَادَمَ — طَرَقَ ².

Percussion, *n.* The act of striking, طَرْق — صَدْم. A shock, collision, مُصَادَمَة — صَدْمَة.

Percussion-cap, *n.* كُبْسُول *pl.* كُبْسُولَات. (The *Muhitu-'l-Muhiti*, under "كبسل," gives the following definition of the word: الكُبْسُولُ هَنَةٌ شِبْهُ قُمْعٍ فِيهَا مَادَّةٌ تَحْتَرِقُ عِنْدَ الضَّغْطِ تُسْتَخْدَمُ فِي اطلاقِ البَوَارِيدِ وَنَحْوِهَا).

Percussion-lock, *n.* دِيكُ بَارُودَةٍ مُكَبْسَلَةٍ.

Percussive, *a.* مُصَادِم — طَارِق.

Percutient, *n.* مِطْرَقَة.

Per diem, *ad.* كُلَّ يَوْمٍ — بِٱلْيَوْمِ — يَوْمًا.

Perdition, *n.* Destruction, ruin, تَلَف — دَمَار — عَطَب — هَلَكَة — هُلْك. Ruin of the soul, هَلَاكُ ٱلنَّفْسِ — خُسْرَانُ ٱلْآخِرَةِ. He went to —, خَسِرَ ٱلْآخِرَةَ =. *See also* Destruction, *n.*

Perdu, *ad.* } Lost, تَلَفًا ـ هَلَكَةً. In a state of concealment,
Perdue, } فِي حَالِ ٱلْخَفَآءِ ـ إِحْتِجَابًا ـ إِكْتِتَامًا ـ تَكَمُّنًا ـ تَطَفُّشًا.

Perdu, *n.* One placed in ambush, كَمِينٌ *pl.* كُمَنَآءُ.

Perdu, *a.* Abandoned, مَهْجُورٌ ـ مَتْرُوكٌ. Desperate, قَانِطٌ ـ بَؤُوسٌ ـ مِنْ غَيْرِ رَجَآءٍ.

Peregrinate, *v.i.* To go about, سَاحَ ـ جَالَ *aor.* يَجُولُ ـ جَوَّلَ ـ إِجْتَالَ. To — in, through, قَطَرَ فِي ² ـ عَارَ فِي ـ عَالَ فِي ـ طَوَى ـ قَطَعَ ـ تَمَطَّرَ فِي ـ مَطَرَ فِي ² ـ نَاصَ فِي ² ـ جَالَ فِي ٱلْبِلَادِ.

Peregrination, *n.* جَوَلَانٌ ـ جَوْلَانٌ ـ تَجْوَالٌ ـ جِيلَانٌ ـ مُطُورٌ ـ عَيْلٌ ـ سَفَرٌ ـ عَيْرٌ.

Peregrinator, *n.* سَيَّاحٌ ـ جَوَّالَةٌ ـ جَوَّالٌ.

Peregrine, *a.* Foreign, خَارِجِيٌّ ـ أَجْنَبِيٌّ.

Peremptorily, *ad.* Absolutely, قَطْعًا ـ إِطْلَاقًا. Positively, أَلْبَتَّةَ ـ بَتَّةً ـ تَحْكِمًا ـ حُكْمًا.

Peremptoriness, *n.* Positiveness, فَيْصَلٌ ـ فَصْلٌ ـ تَحَكُّمٌ ـ بَتَّةٌ. Dogmatism, تَعَانُدٌ ـ عِنَادٌ ـ تَكَبُّرٌ ـ غُرُورٌ ـ تِيهٌ. To act with —, dogmatism, تَاهَ *aor.* يَتِيهُ.

Peremptory, *a.* Precluding debate, قَطْعِيٌّ ـ شَافٍ ـ مُبِتٌّ ـ فَاصِلٌ ـ قَطْعِيٌّ ـ قَاطِعٌ ـ بَتَّاتٌ. Positive, مُفْحِمٌ ـ مُقْنِعٌ ـ تَاهٌ ـ تَيَّاهٌ ـ مُتَحَكِّمٌ ـ فَيْصَلٌ. Absolute, مُطْلَقٌ. Dogmatical, مُتَكَبِّرٌ ـ مُتَجَبِّرٌ.

Perennial, *a.* Lasting, مُسْتَدِيمٌ ـ رَاهِنٌ ـ مَاكِدٌ. Perpetual, قَيُّومٌ ـ ثَابِتٌ ـ دَائِمٌ. Perennial, of plants, أُعْرُوَانٌ. A — stream, جَدْوَلٌ مُطَّرِدٌ.

Perennially, *ad.* بِٱسْتِمْرَارٍ ـ دَائِمًا ـ بِدَوَامٍ.

Perennity, *n.* عَدَمُ زَوَالٍ ـ دَوَامٌ ـ إِسْتِمْرَارٌ.

Per fas et nefas, *ad.* فِي ٱلْخَيْرِ وَفِي ٱلشَّرِّ.

Perfect, *a.* Complete, كَامِلٌ ـ تَامٌّ ـ تَمَامٌ. Whole, صَحِيحٌ ـ سَالِمٌ ـ بِلَا نُقْصَانٍ. Sufficient, وَافٍ ـ كَافٍ. Perfect in make, خَلِيقٌ ـ مُخَلَّقٌ. Firm, sound, compact, مُرْصَنٌ ـ رَصِينٌ. Of full weight, *etc.*, of a coin, قَائِمٌ. Done, completed, مَقْضِيٌّ ـ مُكَمَّلٌ. Perfect, accomplished, good, كَامِلٌ ـ فَاضِلٌ ـ بَارِعٌ ـ ذُو كَمَالٍ. The perfect tense, الْفِعْلُ ٱلْمَاضِي. A — man, رَجُلٌ مُكَمَّلٌ. In the most — way, فِي غَايَةِ ٱلْإِتْقَانِ ـ عَلَى أَكْمَلِ وَجْهٍ.

Perfect, *v.t.* To make perfect, أَكْمَلَ ـ كَمَّلَ; of a thing, to make complete, رَصَنَ ². To accomplish, finish, أَتَمَّ ـ قَضَى ـ أَنْفَذَ ـ تَمَّمَ. To — one's self, تَكَمَّلَ. To be —, as in skill, تَمَهَّرَ ـ مَهَرَ ² ـ بَرَعَ ². He perfected himself in the art, تَمَهَّرَ (*or* تَفَرَّسَ) فِي ٱلْفَنِّ.

Perfected, *a.* Made perfect, مُكَمَّلٌ; completed, مُتَمَّمٌ ـ مَقْضِيٌّ.

Perfectibility, *n.* قَابِلِيَّةُ ٱلْكَمَالِ.

Perfectible, *a.* قَابِلُ ٱلْكَمَالِ ـ وَمِمَّا يُكَمَّلُ.

Perfection, *n.* Completeness, كَمَالٌ. Integrity, absence of defect, صِحَّةٌ ـ سَلْمٌ ـ سِلْمٌ. Completion, تَمَامَةٌ ـ تَمَامٌ; the act of completing, إِتْمَامٌ. An accomplishment, فَضِيلَةٌ *pl.* فَضَائِلُ. Excellent skill, knowledge, *etc.*, بَرَاعَةٌ. To —, *as an adverb*, عَلَى أَكْمَلِ وَجْهٍ ـ فِي نِهَايَةِ ٱلْكَمَالِ ـ بِٱلْكَمَالِ ـ عَلَى ٱلْإِعْلَاءِ.

Perfectionism, *n.* مَذْهَبُ ٱلْقَائِلِينَ أَنَّ بُلُوغَ ٱلْكَمَالِ مُمْكِنٌ حَتَّى فِي هٰذَا ٱلْعَالَمِ.

Perfectionist, *n.* مِنْ أَهْلِ مَذْهَبِ ٱلْقَائِلِينَ أَنَّ بُلُوغَ ٱلْكَمَالِ مُمْكِنٌ حَتَّى فِي هٰذَا ٱلْعَالَمِ.

Perfective, *a.* مُكَمِّلٌ.

Perfectively, *ad.* بِبَرَاعَةٍ ـ بِتَكْمِيلٍ ـ تَكْمِيلًا.

Perfectly, *ad.* In a perfect manner, عَلَى ٱلتَّمَامِ وَٱلْكَمَالِ ـ بِكَمَالٍ ـ فِي غَايَةِ ٱلْإِتْقَانِ ـ فِي غَايَةِ ٱلْكَمَالِ. Wholly, entirely, كُلِّيًّا ـ بَتَّةً ـ بِٱلتَّمَامِ ـ إِتْمَامًا ـ بِأَسْرِهِ ـ طُرًّا. In every way, عَلَى كُلِّ وَجْهٍ. He explained it to him more —, شَرَحَهُ لَهُ بِأَكْثَرِ تَدْقِيقٍ. He became — whole, healthy, نَالَ ٱلشِّفَآءَ. You know — well, أَنْتُمْ تَعْلَمُونَ بِٱلتَّحْقِيقِ.

Perfectness, *n.* Consummate excellence, نِهَايَةُ ٱلْكَمَالِ ـ غَايَةُ ٱلْكَمَالِ ـ ٱلْفَضْلِ. Accurate skill, نِهَايَةُ ٱلذِّهْنِ غَايَةُ ٱلذَّكَآءِ ـ بَرَاعَةٌ. *See also* Perfection, *n.*

Perficient, *n.* *See* Performer, *n.*

Perfidious, *a.* خَائِنٌ ـ غَدَّارٌ ـ غِدِّيرٌ ـ خَتِيرٌ ـ خَتَّارٌ ـ خَاتِرٌ ـ خَوَّانٌ.

Perfidiously, *ad.* بِخِيَانَةٍ ـ بِغَدْرٍ ـ بِخَتْرٍ. To act —, خَانَ ² ـ خَتَرَ ² ـ غَادَرَ ـ غَدَرَ بِ ². To act — towards, عَلَى *or* غَدَرَ.

Perfidiousness, *n.* } نَكْثُ ٱلْعَهْدِ ـ خِيَانَةٌ ـ غَدْرٌ ـ خَوْنٌ ـ خَتْرٌ.
Perfidy, }

Perforate, *v.t.* خَرَمَ ـ خَرَتَ ² ـ خَزَمَ ² ـ خَرَقَ ² ـ نَقَبَ ² ـ خَرَزَ ² ـ ثَقَبَ ² ـ جَابَ *aor.* يَجُوبُ. To —, as of beads, *etc.*, قَصَّ ² ـ عَيَّنَ.

Perforated, *a.* مَخْرُوتٌ ـ مَثْقُوبٌ ـ مَخْزُومٌ; as of beads, مُعَيَّنٌ ـ مَقْصُوصٌ. To be perforated, إِنْثَقَبَ ـ تَخَرَّقَ. A — pearl, دُرٌّ مُثَقَّبٌ.

Perforation, *n.* The act of, خَرْزٌ ـ خَرْقٌ ـ خَزْمٌ ـ ثَقْبٌ. A hole bored, خَرْقٌ *pl.* خُرُوقٌ ـ نَقْبٌ ـ ثُقْبَةٌ ـ ثُقْبٌ. A small —, as that in a bead, in the ear, or the eye of a needle, *etc.*, خُرْتٌ ـ خَرْقٌ ـ خُرْتَةٌ.

Perforative, *a.* نَفَّاذ – خَرَّاز – نَقَّاب – خَرَّاق – خَرَّام – ثَقَّاب.

Perforator, *n.* A boring instrument, مِنْقَب – مِجْوَاب – مِثْقَب.

Perform, *v.t.* To do, صَنَعَ – عَمِلَ – جَآءَ بِ *aor.* يَجِيءُ. To execute, carry out, أَمْضَى – أَجْرَى – أَنْفَذَ – تَفَتَّكَ بِ. To accomplish, تَمَّمَ – أَتَمَّ – أَجَازَ – أَحْكَمَ. To effect, to overcome a thing, تَمَكَّنَ (*or* إِسْتَمْكَنَ) مِنَ ٱلْأَمْرِ. In a general sense, to —, pay, fulfil, أَدَّى. I know not how to — it, لَمْ أَجِدْ كَيْفَ أَفْعَلُهُ. He performed, fulfilled, his oath, أَبَتَّ يَمِينَهُ. To discharge, as a promise, duty, *etc.*, وَفَى بِ *aor.* يَفِي – أَبَتَّ – بَتَّ – أَوْفَى بِ. To —, as on a musical instrument, ضَرَبَ. *See also to* Accomplish, Execute, *v.t.*

Perform, *v.i.* To act a part in a play, لَعِبَ – تَشَخَّصَ. To — on an instrument, دَقَّ بِٱلْآلَةِ – ضَرَبَ ٱلْآلَةَ – عَزَفَ.

Performable, *a.* *See* Practicable, *a.*

Performance, *n.* The act of doing, صُنْع – عَمَل; of carrying out, executing, إِمْضَآء – إِجْرَآء – إِنْفَاذ – نَفَاذ; of accomplishing, تَتْمِيم – إِتْمَام – إِجَازَة – إِحْكَام; of discharging, as a promise, duty, *etc.*, إِيفَآء – وَفَآء – أَدَآء. That which is done, فِعْل *pl.* أَفْعَال – عَمَل *pl.* أَعْمَال – صَنِيعَة *pl.* صَنَائِع – قَضِيَّة *pl.* قَضَايَا. A musical —, نَوْبَة – ضَرْبُ آلَاتِ ٱلطَّرَبِ – عَزْف – عَزِيف. A theatrical —, لَعِبُ رِوَايَةٍ – لَعِبُ ٱلتِّيَاتْرُو – لَعِبُ ٱلتَّقْلِيدِ (*or* ٱلتَّشْخِيصِ) – يُشَخِّصُهُ أَهْلُ ٱلتِّيَاتْرُو (*or* ٱلْمَرْسَحِ ٱلْعَامِّ). A literary —, تَصْنِيف – تَأْلِيف.

Performer, *n.* An actor, عَامِل *pl.* عُمَّال – صَانِع *pl.* صُنَّاع – فَاعِل *pl.* فَعَلَة. A —, as of a promise, وَافٍ بِ. A musical —, آلَاتِيّ *pl.* آلَاتِيَّة – نَوْبَاتِيّ *pl.* نَوْبَاتِيَّة – عَازِف. A theatrical —, مُتَشَخِّص (*or* لَعِيبٌ) فِي ٱلتِّيَاتْرُو – لَعِيب.

Perfume, *n.* A sweet scent, عَرْفَة – شَمِيم – نَفْحَة – رَائِحَة *pl.* رَوَائِح – رِيحَة. A substance emitting —, عِطْر *pl.* عُطُور – طِيب *pl.* أَطْيَاب – بَخُور. Perfumes, scents, شَمَامَات – مَشَامّ. A small case for perfumes, *etc.*, عَتِيدَة *pl.* عَتَائِد. Perfumes used in burial, حَنُوط. To emit a —, عَرِفَ. To make much use of perfumes, عَرِفَ.

Perfume, *v.t.* عَطَّرَ – طَيَّبَ – فَوَّحَ – أَرَّجَ. To —, as of oil, *etc.*, by putting perfume into it, رَوَّحَ – طَرَّى. To — in order to expel bad air, بَخَّرَ. To — one's self, تَعَطَّرَ – تَبَخَّرَ: she perfumed herself, تَعَطَّرَتْ. To — clothes or dress, كَبَّى.

Perfumed, *a.* مُطَيَّب – مُبَخَّر – مُطَرًّى – مُعَطَّر – أَرِج – مُرَوَّح – مَشْمُوم.

Perfumer, *n.* One who sells perfumes, عَطَّار *pl.* عَطَّارُون – صَيْقَبَانِيّ. A man or woman who perfumes himself or herself, مِعْطَار – مِعْطِير – مِعْطَارَة.

Perfumery, *n.* عِطَارَة.

Perfunctorily, *ad.* رَسْمًا فَقَط – بِوَفَآءِ ٱلصُّورَةِ وَلٰكِنْ بِغَيْرِ ٱهْتِمَام.

Perfunctory, *a.* رَسْمِيّ فَقَط – وَافٍ ٱلصُّورَةَ وَلٰكِنْ بِغَيْرِ ٱهْتِمَام.

Perhaps, *ad.* يُمْكِن – رُبَّمَا – عَسَى – لَعَلَّ – عَلَّ. Perhaps I, لَعَلِّي – لَعَلَّنِي; perhaps thou, لَعَلَّكَ; perhaps he, لَعَلَّهُ; perhaps she, لَعَلَّهَا, *etc.* Perhaps I may do it, عَلِّي أَفْعَلُهُ; perhaps I shall do it, لَعَلَّنِي أَفْعَلُهُ. Perhaps he may see you, عَسَى أَنْ يَرَاكَ. Perhaps they may do it, عَسَى أَنْ يَفْعَلُوهُ.

Peri, *n.* (Persian), پری.

Pericardian, *a.* مُتَعَلِّق بِشَغَافِ ٱلْقَلْبِ.

Pericarditis, *n.* شُغَاف.

Pericardium, *n.* The envelope of the heart, شَغَاف – غَاشِيَة *pl.* غَوَاشٍ – قِنْع *pl.* قُنُع – غِلَاف – جِرَابُ ٱلْقَلْبِ.

Pericarp, *n.* خَرِيطَة *pl.* خَرَائِط – سِنْف *pl.* سِنَفَة – قِشْرُ ٱلثَّمَرِ.

Pericranium, *n.* سِمْحَاق *pl.* سَمَاحِيق (which means also a wound in the —).

Perigee, *n.* }
Perigeum, } ٱلْحَضِيض – حَضِيضُ ٱلْأَرْضِ – أَقْرَبُ مَوْضِعِ ٱلسَّيَّارَاتِ مِنَ ٱلْأَرْضِ.

Perihelion, *n.* }
Perihelium, } حَضِيض شَمْسِيّ – أَقْرَبُ مَوْضِعِ ٱلسَّيَّارَاتِ مِنَ ٱلشَّمْسِ.

Peril, *n.* خَطَر *pl.* أَخْطَار – مُخَاطَرَة – تَهْلُكَة – غَرَر – مَهْلَكَة *pl.* مَهَالِك – مَعْطَب *pl.* مَعَاطِب. Perils of the sea, أَخْطَارُ ٱلْبَحْرِ; perils of the desert, أَخْطَارُ ٱلْبَرِّيَّةِ. He is in great —, هُوَ عَلَى خَطَرٍ عَظِيمٍ. At the — of his life, بِخَطَرِ ٱلرَّأْسِ – بِخَطَرِ نَفْسِهِ. At your —, وَأَنْتَ ٱلضَّامِنُ – وَأَنْتَ ٱلْمُطَالَبُ بِهِ.

Peril, *v.t.* عَرَّضَ عَلَى ٱلْخَطَرِ – خَاطَرَ بِ. He perilled his life, أَخْطَرَ بِنَفْسِهِ. *See also to* Endanger, Hazard, *v.t.*

Peril, *v.i.* To be in danger, كَانَ فِي خَطَرٍ. To — one's self, خَاطَرَ (*or* أَخْطَرَ) بِنَفْسِهِ.

Perilous, *a.* مُخْطِر – ذُو خَطَرٍ. A — undertaking, قُحْمَة. Perilous times, أَزْمِنَة صَعْبَة.

Perilously, *ad.* بِمُخَاطَرَةٍ – بِخَطَرٍ.

Perilousness, *n.* *See* Peril, *n.*

Perimeter, *n.* شَكْل – مُحِيط.

Perinæum, *n.* The —, ٱلشَّرْجُ – ٱلْعِجَانُ – ٱلْعَضْرَطُ – مَا بَيْنَ ٱلثَّرِّ وَٱلْفَرِّ.

Period, *n.* A round of time, circle of years, دَوْر *pl.* أَدْوَار – دَهْر

pl. دُهُور — عَصْر pl. أَعْصَار. Time, وَقْت — حِين — زَمَان. An indefinite — of time, مُدَّة. A short — of time, رُوبَةٌ مِنَ ٱلزَّمَانِ — بُرْهَةٌ مِنَ ٱلزَّمَانِ — بُرْهَة — تَوَّة — سَاعَة. An appointed time, term, أَمَد pl. آمَاد. Time of recurrence, as of a fever, *etc.*, دَوْر pl. أَدْوَار — بُرَحَآء — وُرُود. Time, the season for anything, أَوَان pl. آوِنَة — إِبَّان. A sentence, paragraph, جُمْلَة — عِبَارَة — بَنْد pl. بُنُود. A dot to denote completion of a sentence, نُقْطَةٌ تَدُلُّ عَلَى كَمَالِ ٱلْجُمْلَةِ. He or it reached his or its utmost —, or term, بَلَغَ أَمَدَهُ. He assigned to him or it a fixed —, or limit, ضَرَبَ لَهُ أَمَدًا. A rounded —, sentence, عِبَارَةٌ مُتْقَنَةٌ.

Periodic, *a.* } Denoting a period, ذُو أَمَدٍ — وَقْتِيّ — مُوَقَّت.
Periodical, } Recurring at intervals, دَائِر — دَوْرِيّ. A — fever, حُمَّى دَائِرَة.

Periodical, *n.* Of a publication, جَرِيدَةٌ مُوَقَّتَةٌ — جَرِيدَةٌ تَبْرُزُ (or تَصْدُرُ) فِي أَوْقَاتٍ مَعْلُومَةٍ.

Periodically, *ad.* فِي وَقْتٍ مُوَقَّتٍ — بِٱلدَّوْرِ — فِي أَوْقَاتٍ مَعْلُومَةٍ — لِوَقْتِهِ.

Periodicity, *n.* دَوَرَان — وُقُوعٌ بِٱلتَّوَالِي فِي أَوْقَاتٍ مَعْلُومَةٍ — مَدَار.

Periosteum, *n.* قِشْرُ (or غِشَآءُ) ٱلْعَظْمِ — سِمْحَاق pl. سَمَاحِيق.

Peripatetic, *a.* Walking, walking round, طَائِف — مَاشٍ. Pertaining to Aristotle's philosophy, مُتَعَلِّقٌ بِحِكْمَةِ أَرِسْطُو. The — philosophy, فَلْسَفَةُ أَرِسْطَاطَالِيسَ — مَذْهَبُ أَرِسْطُو.

Peripatetic, *n.* A walker, مَشَّآء. A follower of Aristotle, تَابِعُ حِكْمَةِ أَرِسْطَاطَالِيسَ. The Peripatetics, ٱلْمَشَّاؤُونَ أَصْحَابُ أَرِسْطَاطَالِيسَ.

Peripheral, *a.* مَا نِيطَ بِمُحِيطِ شَكْلٍ هَنْدَسِيٍّ.

Periphery, *n.* دَائِرَة — مُحِيطُ ٱلْجِسْمِ ٱلْهَنْدَسِيِّ.

Periphrase, *n.* } دَوْرَةٌ فِي ٱلْكَلَامِ — تَسَلْسُل — مَحَاشٍ pl. حَشْو.
Periphrasis, }

Periphrase, *v.i.* To use circumlocution, دَارَ² — سَلْسَلَ ٱلْحَدِيثَ فِي ٱلْكَلَامِ.

Periphrastic, *a.* } دَوَّارِيّ — مُتَسَلْسِل.
Periphrastical, }

Periphrastically, *ad.* بِٱلدَّوْرَةِ فِي ٱلْكَلَامِ — بِٱلتَّسَلْسُلِ.

Peripneumonic, *a.* مُتَعَلِّقٌ بِدَآءِ ٱلرِّئَةِ.

Peripneumony, *n.* ذَاتُ ٱلرِّئَةِ.

Peripteral, *a.* Having columns on all sides, مُدَار — مُدَارُ أَعْمِدَةٍ — ذُو ٱلْعِمَادِ — أَسَاطِين.

Peripterous, *a.* Feathered on all sides, مُدَارُ رِيشٍ.

Periscian, *n.* مِنْ أَهْلِ مِنْطَقَةِ ٱلْجُمُودِ حَيْثُ ظِلُّ ٱلشَّخْصِ مُدَّةَ ٱلنَّهَارِ يَدُورُ حَوْلَهُ بِٱلتَّدْرِيجِ نَحْوَ جَمِيعِ ٱلْجِهَاتِ. Periscii, *pl.* أَهْلُ ٱلْمِنْطَقَةِ ٱلْمَذْكُورَةِ.

Periscope, *n.* *See* Panorama, *n.*

Periscopic, *a.* *See* Panoramic, *n.*

Perish, *v.i.* To come to naught, عَدِمَ — طَاحَ aor. يَطُوحُ and يَطِيحُ — ضَاعَ aor. يَضِيعُ. To cause to — or come to naught, تَوَفَّى — فَاظَ² — ضَيَّعَ — طَوَّحَ بِ — أَعْدَمَ — طَوَّحَ. To die, مَاتَ². To — by water, غَرِقَ — إِسْتَغْرَقَ. To — with hunger, هَلَكَ جُوعًا. To be destroyed, دَمَرَ² — إِمْتَحَقَ — تَبَرَ — هَلَكَ — حَبِطَ — تَلِفَ — فَنِيَ — ضَلَّ — ضَاعَ — بَادَ. To cause to —, to be destroyed, دَمَّرَ عَلَى — أَتْلَفَ — دَمَّرَ — أَبَادَ — أَهْلَكَ. He perished in the waters, مَاتَ² فِي ٱلْمِيَاهِ. My hope is perished, بَادَ رَجَائِي. His memorial has perished, بَادَ ذِكْرُهُ. The harvest has perished, تَلِفَ ٱلْحَصِيدُ. Mayest thou perish! بَعِدْتَ. *See also to* Decay, Fade, *v.i.*

Perishable, *a.* زَاهِق — فَانٍ — زَائِل — ضَائِع — هَالِك — بَالٍ; of property, تَوٍ — تَاوٍ. The — things of this world, عَرَضُ ٱلدُّنْيَا — حُطَامُ ٱلدُّنْيَا.

Perishableness, *n.* فَنَآء — تَوًى.

Perished, *a.* هَالِك — حَابِط. Perished with cold, مُكَنَّز — هَالِكٌ بِٱلْبَرْدِ. Perished with hunger, هَالِكٌ جُوعًا. The wheat is —, قَدْ تَلِفَ ٱلْقَمْحُ.

Perishing, *a.* ضَائِع — تَلْفَان — تَلِف.

Perispheric, *a.* *See* Spherical, *a.*

Peristaltic, *a.* Spiral, لَوْلَبِيّ. The — motion of the bowels, حَرَكَةٌ لَوْلَبِيَّةٌ فِي ٱلْمَصَارِينِ.

Peristrephic, *a.* Revolving, مُسْتَدِير — دَائِر.

Peristyle, *n.* رِوَاق pl. أَرْوِقَة.

Peritoneum, *n.* صِفَاق.

Periwig, *n.* شَعْرٌ عَارِيَّةٌ.

Periwinkle, *n.* The plant, عُشْبَةٌ أَوْرَاقُهَا تُشْبِهُ أَوْرَاقَ ٱلْغَارِ. The sea snail, حَلَزُونُ ٱلْبَحْرِ.

Perjure, *v.t.* To take a false oath, to — one's self, حَنِثَ — خَانَ² ٱلْعَهْدَ — حَلَفَ زُورًا — فِي يَمِينِهِ. To make to —, أَحْنَثَ — فِي يَمِينِهِ.

Perjured, *a.* } خَائِنُ ٱلْعَهْدِ — حَالِفٌ بِٱلزُّورِ — مُحْنِث — حَانِث.
Perjurer, *n.* }

Perjury, *n.* خِيَانَةُ ٱلْعَهْدِ — يَمِينُ زُورٍ — حِنْث. To pronounce guilty of —, جَعَلَ — حَانِثًا — حَنَّثَ.

Perk, *a.* Smart, نَشِيط ـ خَفِيف. Mincing, مُتَظَرِّف ـ مُتَكَيِّس.

Perk, *v.i.* تَكَيَّس ـ تَظَرَّف ـ تَشَامَخ.

Permanence, *n.* } **Permanency,** } Fixedness, ثُبُوت ـ ثَبَات ـ اِسْتِمْرَار ـ اِسْتِقْرَار ـ بَقَآء ـ مُدَاوَمَة ـ دَوَام. Continuance, subsistence, جَرَيَان ـ رُهُون.

Permanent, *a.* Lasting, مُسْتَمِرّ ـ مُسْتَقِرّ ـ ثَابِت ـ بَاقٍ ـ دَائِم. Subsisting, going on, رَاهِن ـ جَارٍ. Permanent food, طَعَام رَاهِن. Continuous, جَارٍ. A — supply of wine, خَمْر رَاهِنَة. A — state, that is, remaining to the present, حَالَة رَاهِنَة. A — charitable bequest, صَدَقَة جَارِيَة. To be —, fixed, ثَبَتَ ـ اِسْتَمَرَّ ـ اِسْتَقَرَّ; to be —, to continue, رَهَنَ. To make —, أَرْهَنَ ـ قَرَّرَ ـ أَثْبَتَ.

Permanently, *ad.* اِسْتِمْرَارًا ـ اِسْتِقْرَارًا ـ عَلَى ٱلدَّوَام. The thing belongs to you —, شَفَّ لَكَ ٱلشَّيْء.

Permeability, *n.* تَطَرُّق ـ قَابِلِيَّة ٱلنَّفَاذ فِيهِ.

Permeable, *a.* That may be passed through, يَتَطَرَّق إِلَيْهِ ـ مِمَّا يُقْطَع فِيهِ ـ قَابِل ٱلنَّفَاذ فِيهِ.

Permeate, *v.i.* To go through, قَطَعَ فِي. To spread through, over, عَمَّ. To find a way into, of water, *etc.*, تَطَرَّقَ إِلَى. Wet cannot — it, لَا يَتَطَرَّق إِلَيْهِ ٱلْبَلَل.

Permeation, *n.* The act of passing through the pores, نَفَاذ مِن ٱلْمَسَام ـ نَفَاذ ـ قَطْع; of spreading over, through, عُمُوم.

Permissible, *a.* جَائِز ـ مَأْذُون ـ طِلْق ـ مُبَاح ـ مُسَوَّغ. It is — to you, هُوَ لَكَ طِلْقًا. The thing was —, جَازَ ٱلشَّيْء. The doing of the thing was — to him, سَاغَ لَهُ مَا فَعِلَ. The doing of the thing was —, سَاغَ فِعْلُ ٱلشَّيْء. If that is not — to individuals, إِذَا لَمْ يَسَعْ ذَلِكَ فِي أَفْرَاد ٱلنَّاس.

Permission, *n.* إِذْن ـ دُسْتُور ـ رُخْصَة *pl.* رُخَصَات ـ إِجَازَة. To ask —, اِسْتَأْذَنَ ـ اِسْتَجَازَ. To take —, تَرَخَّصَ. The royal — as granted by diploma, تَسْوِيغ. By your —, or leave, عَنْ إِذْنِكَ ـ بِدُسْتُورِكَ. I say this by —, أَقُولُ هٰذَا عَلَى سَبِيلِ ٱلْإِذْن.

Permissive, *a.* مُجَوِّز ـ مُجِيز ـ مُسَوِّغ.

Permissively, *ad.* بِٱلْإِذْن ـ بِٱلرُّخْصَة ـ بِٱلْإِجَازَة.

Permit, *v.t.* To allow, أَطْلَقَ لِ ـ اِتَّسَعَ لِ ـ سَوَّغَ لِ ـ فَسَحَ لِ ـ أَذِنَ لِ ـ فِي ـ رَخَّصَ لِ ـ فِي. To let alone, خَلَّى. Permit me to . . . , دَعْنِي أَنْ ـ أَسْمَحْ لِي بِكَذَا. He will not — that . . . , لَا يُبِيح أَنْ. It is not permitted to him to . . . , لَا مَسُوغ لَهُ أَنْ. If the Lord —, إِنْ أَذِنَ ٱلرَّبّ.

Permit, *n.* جَوَاز ـ تَذْكِرَة (*or* وَرَقَة) إِجَازَة ـ فَسْح ـ إِجَازَة ـ إِذْن.

Permittance, *n.* *See* Permission, *n.*

Permutable, *a.* مُتَبَادِل ـ مُبَادِل.

Permutation, *n.* مُبَادَلَة ـ تَبَادُل.

Pernicious, *a.* رَدِيء ـ مُؤْذٍ ـ مُضِرّ ـ مُهْلِك ـ مُفْسِد. Pernicious ways, تَهْلُوكَات. *See also* Harmful, Noxious, *a.*

Perniciously, *ad.* بِمَسَآءَة ـ بِمَضَرَّة ـ بِضَرَر.

Perniciousness, *n.* مُضَاجَّة ـ مَسَآءَة ـ مَضَرَّة ـ ضَرَر.

Peroration, *n.* خَاتِمَة كَلَام ـ خَاتِمَة.

Peroxide, *n.* حُمَّض أَخِير.

Perpendicle, *n.* A plumb line, شَاقُول.

Perpendicular, *a.* عَمُود ـ قَائِم ـ مُسْتَقِيم ـ مُنْتَصِب. A — line, خَطّ قَائِم (*or* مُسْتَقِيم) ـ عَمُود *pl.* عُمُد. The two — supports, القَائِمَتَان.

Perpendicular, *n.* قَائِم *pl.* قَوَائِم ـ عَمُود *pl.* عُمُد.

Perpendicularity, *n.* نَصِيبَة ـ قِيَام ـ اِنْتِصَاب.

Perpendicularly, *ad.* صُعُدًا ـ قِيَامًا ـ عَمُودِيًّا ـ اِنْتِصَابًا ـ اِنْتِصَابًا.

Perpetrate, *v.t.* To do, فَعَلَ ـ صَنَعَ. To commit, as a crime, اِرْتَكَبَ ـ اِقْتَرَفَ ـ جَرَّ جَرِيرَة عَلَى *or* إِلَى. To — a crime against, جَانَى ـ جَنَى عَلَى.

Perpetration, *n.* The act of doing, صُنْع ـ فِعْل. Execution, carrying out, إِجْرَآء. Commission, as of a crime, اِقْتِرَاف ـ اِرْتِكَاب.

Perpetual, *a.* دَائِم ـ لَا ٱنْقِطَاعَ لَهُ ـ بَاقٍ ـ مُؤَبَّد ـ قَيُّوم ـ مُخَلَّد ـ لَا يَزَال. A — possession, مُلْك. A — decree, فَرِيضَة أَبَدِيَّة. To be —, اِسْتَدَامَ ـ دَامَ. Perpetual motion, دَوْر دَائِم.

Perpetually, *ad.* بِلَا فُتُور ـ دَائِمًا ـ إِلَى ٱلْأَبَد ـ عَلَى ٱلدَّوَام ـ بِلَا ٱنْقِطَاع.

Perpetuate, *v.t.* خَلَّدَ ـ أَدَامَ ـ أَبْقَى ـ بَقَّى ـ أَبَّدَ. To — itself, تَخَلَّدَ ـ بَقِيَ *aor.* يَبْقَى.

Perpetuation, *n.* تَأْبِيد ـ تَخْلِيد ـ إِدَامَة ـ إِبْقَآء.

Perpetuity, *n.* دَوَام ـ قَرَار ـ اِسْتِقْرَار ـ بَقَآء ـ اِسْتِمْرَار.

Perplex, *v.t.* To make intricate, عَقَّدَ ـ شَبَّكَ ـ شَوَّشَ ـ لَبَّكَ ـ خَبَصَ ـ لَخْبَطَ. To distract the mind, puzzle, دَهَّشَ ـ أَدْهَشَ ـ تَوَّهَ ـ تَيَّهَ ـ أَحَمَّ ـ قَلَّقَ ـ أَضْجَرَ ـ حَيَّرَ. To — through shame, خَجَّلَ ـ أَخْجَلَ. To be perplexed, confused, made intricate, تَشَوَّشَ ـ تَلَبَّكَ ـ اِلْتَبَكَ ـ تَشَبَّكَ ـ تَلَخْبَطَ. To be perplexed, puzzled, ضَلَّ ـ تَاهَ ـ تَاهَ ـ اِضْطَرَبَ ـ أُحِمَّ ـ كَدِرَ ـ اِسْتَحَارَ ـ دَهِشَ ـ دَجِرَ ـ تَحَيَّرَ. To be perplexed, through shame, خَجِلَ.

Perplexed, *a.* Intricate, مُشَبَّك ـ مُلْتَبِس ـ مُلْتَبِك ـ

ـ مُضطَرِب ـ مُتَوَّه . Confounded, puzzled, مُعَقَّد ـ مُشَوَّس
ـ خَجِل . مُتَحَيِّر . Perplexed through shame, مُتَحَيِّر ـ حَيْرَان ـ مُحْتَار
خَجْلَان . Their affairs became — to them, إِخْتَلَطَ عَلَيْهِمْ أَمْرُهُمْ.

Perplexedly, *ad.* With intricacy, بِتَعْقِيدٍ ـ بِتَشْوِيشٍ ـ بِٱلْتِبَاكٍ ; with mental confusion, بِٱضْطِرَابٍ ـ بِحَيْرَةٍ ـ تَحَيُّرًا .

Perplexing, *a.* Puzzling, مُشَبِّك ـ مُشْكِل ـ مُلْبِك ـ قَلِق . Dubious, obscure, مُبْهَم ـ مُغَمَّس ـ عَمِيس ـ عَمُوس .

Perplexity, *n.* State of intricacy, تَشْوِيش ـ شَبْك ـ اِلْتِبَاك ـ . State of mental confusion, حَيْرَة وَفَشَل ـ خَبْص ـ لَخْبَطَة ـ لَبْكَة ـ خَبْلَة ـ دَجْر ـ حَيْرَة ـ تِيه ـ تَوْه ـ ضِلَّة ـ دَكْش ـ قَلَق . Perplexity of speech, تَعْقِيد ; obscurity of speech, اِلْتِبَاس . A difficulty, وَرْطَة ـ بَلْشَة ـ صُعُوبَة . In a state of —, فِي حَيْرَةٍ . He fell into — about the thing, وَقَعَ فِي مَهْجُوسٍ مِنَ ٱلْأَمْرِ وَفَشَلٍ .

Perquisite, *n.* عَائِدَة *pl.* عَائِدَات *and* عَوَائِد .

Perquisition, *n.* تَفْتِيش ـ فَحْص ـ تَفَحُّص .

Perry, *n.* شَرَابُ عَصِيرِ ٱلْإِجَاصِ ـ شَرَابُ ٱلْكُمَّثْرَى .

Persecute, *v.t.* To harass, injure, اِضْطَهَدَ ـ تَعَدَّى عَلَى ـ جَنَى عَلَى ـ جَارَ عَلَى *aor.* يَجُورُ ـ عَاكَسَ ـ أَجْحَفَ بِ ـ أَمَلَّ ـ أَزْعَجَ ـ أَقْلَقَ ـ أَضْجَرَ . To vex, torment, أَظْلَمَ ـ زَكَّشَ ـ أَتْعَبَ .

Persecution, *n.* The act of persecuting, harassing, اِضْطِهَاد ـ جَوْرٌ عَلَى ـ تَعَدٍّ عَلَى ; of vexing, tormenting, إِضْجَار ـ إِقْلَاق ـ تَزْهِيق ـ إِزْعَاج . The state of being persecuted, harassed, اِضْطِهَاد ـ ظُلْم ; of being tormented, اِضْطِرَاب ـ ضَجَر ـ ضُجْرَة ـ زَعَج .

Persecutor, *n.* ظَالِم ـ مُضْطَهِد .

Perseverance, *n.* إِصْرَار ـ اِسْتِمْرَار ـ مُلَازَمَة ـ لُزُوم ـ مُوَاظَبَة ـ إِدْمَان ـ مُدَاوَمَة ـ عَزِيمَة ـ مُرَابَطَة .

Persevere, *v.i.* To continue steadfast in, أَزَمَ عَلَى ـ أَدْمَنَ ـ أَلَظَّ بِ *or* فِي ـ أَقَامَ فِي ـ بَارَكَ عَلَى ـ تَعَشَّقَ بِ ـ عَسِقَ بِ ـ وَاظَبَ عَلَى ـ أَدْمَنَ عَلَى ـ اِعْتَزَمَ فِي ـ مَرَنَ عَلَى ـ عَاقَرَ فِي ـ أَصَرَّ ـ لَاطَ فِي ـ أَصَرَّ عَلَى ـ لَازَمَ ـ لَزِمَ بِ ـ مَرَنَ عَلَى ـ لَمْ يَبْرَحْ ـ دَاوَمَ عَلَى ـ اِسْتَمَرَّ فِي . To continue to do, ظَلَّ ـ لَمْ يَزَلْ . To —, as in search of, or in searching out, تَتَبَّعَ .

Persevering, *a.* مُدَاوِم ـ مُقِيم فِي ـ مُصِرّ عَلَى ـ مُبْتَرِك عَلَى ـ مُوَاظِب عَلَى ـ مُدْمِن ـ مُبَارِك عَلَى ـ مُسْتَمِرّ عَلَى ـ عَلَى . *See also* Assiduous, *a.*

Perseveringly, *ad.* بِعَزِيمَةٍ ـ بِمُوَاظَبَةٍ ـ بِمُدَاوَمَةٍ ـ بِإِدْمَانٍ ـ بِلُزُومٍ .

Persia, *n.* بِلَادُ فَارِسَ ـ بِلَادُ ٱلْعَجَمِ ـ ٱلْعَجَمُ ـ عَجَمِسْتَان ـ إِيرَان .

Persian, *a.* عَجَمِيّ ـ إِيرَانِيّ . The — language, ٱلْفَارِسِيَّة ـ ٱلْفَارِسِيّ . A — wheel, نَاعُورَة *pl.* نَوَاعِير .

Persian, *n.* عَجَمِيّ *pl.* أَعْجَام *coll.* عَجَم ـ فَارِسِيّ *pl.* فُرْس .

Persiflage, *n.* هُجْو .

Persist, *v.i.* To continue firm in, أَصَرَّ عَلَى ـ نَسَكَ فِي ـ لَجَّ فِي ـ وَاظَبَ عَلَى ـ دَاوَمَ عَلَى ـ ثَبَتَ فِي ـ ثَبَتَ فِي . He persisted in drinking wine, تَخَلَّعَ فِي ٱلْخَمْرِ . He persisted in this conduct, دَاوَمَ عَلَى هٰذَا ٱلْعَمَلِ . *See also to* Persevere, *v.t.*

Persistence, *n.} Persistency, } Fixedness, perseverance, نُسُوك ـ إِصْرَار ـ مُوَاظَبَة ـ إِدْمَان ـ ثُبُوت ـ ثَبَات . *See also* Obstinacy, *n.*

Persistent, *a.} Persisting, } مُوَاظِب عَلَى ـ مُدْمِن ـ مُصِرّ عَلَى . *See also* Persevering, *a.*

Persistingly, *ad.* بِإِصْرَارٍ ـ بِإِدْمَانٍ ـ بِثَبَاتٍ . To do a thing —; *see under to* Persist, *v.i.*

Person, *n.* An individual, male or female, نَفَر *pl.* أَنْفَار ـ شَخْص *pl.* أَشْخَاص *and* شُخُوص *and* شِخَاص ـ ظَلَم *pl.* ظُلُوم ـ إِنْسَان *pl.* نَاس *or* أُنَاس . Many persons, نَاس ـ أُنَاس . A man, مَرْء ; a woman, اِمْرَأَة *pl.* نِسَاء *and* نِسْوَان ; a young —, meaning a young woman, بِنْت *pl.* بَنَات . One's self, نَفْس ـ ذَات : it was he in —, himself, كَانَ هُوَ ذَاتَهُ ـ كَانَ هُوَ بِذَاتِهِ . Some —, بَعْض ـ أَحَد . The body or corporeal man, حَوْبَاء ـ أُقْنُوم *pl.* أَقَانِيم ـ شَخْص *pl.* أَشْخَاص . Exterior appearance, شَكْل ـ صُورَة ـ هَيْئَة ـ سَمَامَة . A distinction in the Trinity, أُقْنُوم *pl.* أَقَانِيم : God is One in three persons, اللّٰهُ وَاحِدٌ فِي ثَلٰثَةِ أَقَانِيمَ . Person, *in grammar*, ٱلضَّمِيرُ ; the first — singular, ٱلْمُتَكَلِّمُ ; the first — plural, جَمْعُ ٱلْمُتَكَلِّمِ ; the second —, ٱلْمُخَاطَبُ ; the third —, ٱلْغَائِبُ . In —, شَخْصًا ـ ذَاتًا ـ بِٱلذَّاتِ . To have respect, undue deference, for persons, نَظَرَ إِلَى وُجُوهِ ٱلنَّاسِ .

Personable, *n.* Of good appearance, هَيِّئ ـ حَسَنُ ٱلْحِبْرِ وَٱلسِّبْرِ ـ مَلِيح ـ كَيِّس ـ جَمِيل ـ صَاحِبُ جَمَالٍ ـ حَسَنُ ٱلسَّمَامَةِ ـ عَلِيّ *pl.* مِلَاح .

Personage, *n.* A distinguished person, عَالِي ـ مِنْ عِلْيَةِ ٱلنَّاسِ ـ مِنَ ٱلْعِلِّيِّينَ ـ مِنْ عِلْيَةِ ٱلنَّاسِ ـ ٱلْكَعْب . *See also* Person, *n.*

Personal, *a.* Belonging to or denoting a person, ذَاتِيّ ـ شَخْصِيّ ـ مُتَعَلِّق ـ مُخْتَصّ لِ . Exterior, denoting outward appearance, ظَاهِر ـ خَارِج ـ بِٱلسَّمَامَةِ . Reproaching, لَائِم *pl.* لُوَّم *and* لُوَّام ـ ذَامّ ـ لُومَة ـ لَيِّم . He was not assured of his — safety, كَانَ غَيْرَ مُطْمَئِنٍّ عَلَى حَالِهِ . In his — character, فِي أَوْصَافِهِ ٱلشَّخْصِيَّةِ . Matters not —, ٱلْأُمُورُ غَيْرُ ٱلشَّخْصِيَّةِ . To be —, as against one,

عَيَّنَ عَلَيْهِ. To be — to, to make invidious remarks on, لَدَّ بِ ـ تَكَلَّمَ ـ عَيَّبَ ـ ‌ِ ٢ طَعَنَ فِي ـ بِٱلْقَوْلِ ـ ‌ِ حَكَرَ ـ إِحْتَكَرَ ـ قَوْلًا فِي حَقِّهِ.

Personal accomplishments, ٱلْمَحَاسِنُ ٱلذَّاتِيَّةُ.

Personal appearance, مَنْظَرٌ ـ طَلْعَةٌ ـ سَمَامَةٌ.

Personal identity, وَحْدَةُ ٱلشَّخْصِ ـ ذَاتُ ٱلشَّخْصِ.

Personal pronoun, إِسْمٌ مُضْمَرٌ ـ ضَمِيرٌ.

Personal, as distinct from real, property, مَنْقُولَاتٌ ـ مَالٌ مَنْقُولٌ.

Personal remarks, إِفَادَاتٌ لَوْمِيَّةٌ ـ تَعْيِيبٌ.

Personal verb, فِعْلٌ يَتَضَمَّنُ صِيغَةَ ٱلْمُتَكَلِّمِ وَٱلْمُخَاطَبِ وَٱلْغَائِبِ.

Personality, *n.* Individuality, وَحْدَةٌ ـ وَحْدَانِيَّةٌ ـ أَحَدِيَّةٌ ٱلشَّخْصِ. A disparaging remark on another, حَكْرٌ ـ إِحْتِكَارٌ ـ لَوْمٌ ـ لَأْمَةٌ ـ عَيْبَةٌ ـ تَعْيِيبٌ. To give a — to, to individualize, وَحَّدَ ـ شَخَّصَ ـ عَيَّنَ.

Personally, *ad.* In person, شَخْصًا ـ ذَاتًا. Individually, إِفْرَادًا. The orders were communicated to all the agents —, صَارَ تَسْلِيمُ ٱلْأَوَامِرِ إِلَى جَمِيعِ ٱلْوُكَلَاءِ إِفْرَادًا.

Personalty, *n.* مَنْقُولَاتٌ ـ مَالٌ مَنْقُولٌ.

Personate, *v.t.* تَشَخَّصَ بِ ـ تَمَثَّلَ بِ ـ تَشَبَّهَ بِ.

Personation, *n.* تَقْلِيدٌ ـ تَشَخُّصٌ بِ ـ تَشَبُّهٌ بِ.

Personator, *n.* مُتَشَخِّصٌ بِ ـ مُتَشَبِّهٌ بِ.

Personification, *n.* *See* Impersonation, *n.*

Personify, *v.t.* *See to* Impersonate, *v.t.*

Personnel, *n.* ذَات. The — of the army staff, ذَاتُ ٱلْأَرْكَانِ ٱلْحَرْبِيَّةِ. The — of the army, ذَاتُ ٱلْعَسَاكِرِ. The — of an embassy, ذَاتُ ٱلسِّفَارَةِ.

Perspective, *a.* مُتَعَلِّقٌ بِعِلْمِ ٱلْمَنَاظِرِ.

Perspective, *n.* The art of, عِلْمٌ يُعْرَفُ بِهِ كَيْفِيَّةُ ـ عِلْمُ ٱلْمَنَاظِرِ عِلْمُ تَصْوِيرِ ـ مِقْدَارِ ٱلْأَشْيَاءِ بِسَبَبِ قُرْبِهَا وَبُعْدِهَا عَنْ نَظَرِ ٱلنَّاظِرِ ـ ٱلْأَشْيَاءِ حَسْبَمَا تَرَاهَا ٱلْعَيْنُ. A —, or view from afar, مُنَاظَرَةٌ ـ ٱلنَّظَرُ مِنَ ٱلْجَانِبَيْنِ فِي ٱلشَّبَهِ بَيْنَ ـ طَلَلٌ ـ نَظْرَةٌ مِنْ بَعِيدٍ هٰذَاكَ يَمْنَعُ ٱلشَّيْئَيْنِ إِظْهَارًا لِلصَّوَابِ. That impedes the —, مَنَاظِرُ هَوَائِيَّةٌ ٱلنَّظَرَ. Linear —, مَنَاظِرُ طُولِيَّةٌ. Aerial —, مَنَاظِرُ هَوَائِيَّةٌ. A glass through which objects are viewed, دُورْبِينٌ ـ نَظَّارَةٌ.

Perspectively, *ad.* حَسَبَ ـ حَسْبَ قَوَاعِدِ عِلْمِ ٱلْمَنَاظِرِ ٱلطَّلَلِ.

Perspicacious, *a.* Discerning, مُبْصِرٌ ـ حَاذِقٌ ـ فَطِينٌ ـ فَاطِنٌ ـ بَصِيرٌ. To be —, ‌ِ حَذِقَ ـ ٢ بَصُرَ ـ ‌ِ فَطِنَ.

Perspicaciousness, *n.* }
Perspicacity, } فِطْنَةٌ ـ بَصَارَةٌ ـ حَذَاقَةٌ ـ حِذَاقٌ ـ بَيَانٌ ـ فَصَاحَةٌ ـ شَهَامَةٌ. To speak with —, تَفَصَّحَ ـ ٢ فَصُحَ.

Perspicuity, *n.* رَوْقٌ ـ تَصْرِيحٌ ـ بَيَانٌ ـ فَصَاحَةٌ ـ وُضُوحٌ.

Perspicuity of style, تَصْرِيحُ ٱلْكَلَامِ ـ فَصَاحَةٌ.

Perspicuous, *a.* Clear, مُبِينٌ ـ بَيِّنٌ ـ صَرِيحٌ ـ مُخَلَّصٌ ـ وَاضِحٌ; in speech, فَصِيحٌ ـ فَتِيقُ ٱللِّسَانِ. To be —, ٢ صَرُحَ ـ وَضَحَ *aor.* يَضِحُ. To make —, صَرَّحَ بِ ـ أَوْضَحَ ـ وَضَّحَ.

Perspicuously, *ad.* بَيَانًا ـ وُضُوحًا ـ بِصَرَاحَةٍ. To speak —, تَفَصَّحَ. To affect to speak —, أَفْصَحَ ـ ٢ فَصُحَ.

Perspicuousness, *n.* رَوْقٌ ـ بَيَانٌ ـ وُضُوحٌ. *See also* Perspicuity, *n.*

Perspiration, *n.* Sweat, عَرَقٌ ـ رَشِيحٌ ـ رَشْحٌ; *vulg.* بُوَاخ. The — of the armpits, groin, *etc.*, صُنَانٌ ـ صِنَّةٌ ـ صُمَاحٌ. The disagreeable smell of —, سُهُوكَةٌ ـ سَهَكَةٌ; having that smell, سَهِكٌ. To smell of —, ‌ِ سَهِكَ. The — of fever, ٱلرُّحَضَاءُ. Drops of —, فَرَاشٌ. Moist with —, لَثِقٌ. To be moist with —, of clothes, ‌ِ لَثِيَ; to make moist with —, أَلْثَى. A cloth or cap to catch the —, عَرَّاقَةٌ. Bathed in one's —, غَارِقٌ فِي عَرَقِهِ.

Perspirative, *a.* }
Perspiratory, } عَارِقٌ ـ رَاشِحٌ.

Perspire, *v.i.* To sweat, تَرَشَّحَ عَرَقًا ـ أَرْشَحَ عَرَقًا ـ ‌ِ رَشَحَ ـ ‌ِ عَرِقَ. To make to —, عَرَّقَ.

Perspire, *v.t.* To emit through the pores of the skin, أَنْفَذَ مِنَ ٱلْمَسَامِّ.

Persuadable, *a.* *See* Persuasible, *a.*

Persuade, *v.t.* To satisfy, convince, أَقْنَعَ; to be persuaded, convinced, إِقْتَنَعَ ـ قَنِعَ. To —, to cause to believe, أَثْبَتَ عِنْدَهُ ـ ‌ِ قَطَعَ عَقْلَ أَنْ ـ حَقَّقَ لِ. To be persuaded, to believe fully, إِتَّقَنَ ـ يَثِقُ وَثِقَ *aor.* ـ صَدَّقَ ـ إِعْتَقَدَ: I am persuaded that, إِنِّي مُتَيَقِّنٌ أَنْ ـ إِنِّي مُوقِنٌ أَنْ; I am persuaded as regards them, أَنَا مُوقِنٌ مِنْ جِهَتِهِمْ; let every one be persuaded in his own mind, فَلْيَتَيَقَّنْ كُلُّ وَاحِدٍ فِي عَقْلِهِ. To —, to entice, in a bad sense, إِسْتَعْطَفَ ـ دَارَى ـ رَاوَغَ ـ رَاوَدَ ـ ‌ِ غَوَى. To —, to wheedle, دَارَى ـ رَاوَغَ ـ رَاوَدَ. To —, to make to lean towards one's opinions, أَمَالَ إِلَى رَأْيِهِ. To —, to stir up, ٢ حَثَّ عَلَى ـ أَحَثَّ ـ ٢ حَثَّ ـ حَرَّضَ. To —, lead one to do a thing, ‌ِ حَمَلَ عَلَى ـ أَرْضَى بِ. To be persuaded by, to listen to, أَصْغَى إِلَى: I was nearly persuaded to become a soldier, بِقَلِيلٍ أُقْنِعْتُ أَنْ أَصِيرَ عَسْكَرِيًّا. We will — him and secure you, نَحْنُ نَسْتَعْطِفُهُ وَنَجْعَلُكُمْ مُطْمَئِنِّينَ. He persuaded, convinced, all who were present, أَقْنَعَ جَمِيعَ ٱلْحَاضِرِينَ.

Persuader, *n.* One who convinces, مُقْنِعٌ; who entices, غَاوٍ; who allures, wheedles, مُسْتَعْطِفٌ ـ مُدَارٍ; who incites, دَاعٍ ـ

مُحَرِّكٌ ـ مُحَرِّض. An adviser, نَاصِح. One who excites to emulation, مُرَغِّب.

Persuasibility, *n.* } لِينَةُ ٱلْأَعْطَافِ ـ قابِلِيَّةُ ٱلْقُنُوع.
Persuasibleness, }

Persuasible, *a.* يُقْطَعُ عَقْلُهُ ـ إِقْنَاعُهُ مُمْكِنٌ ـ قابِلُ ٱلْقُنُوع.

Persuasion, *n.* The act of persuading, convincing, إِقْنَاع; of making to believe, قَطْعُ ٱلْعَقْلِ ـ إِثْبَاتٌ; of causing to incline towards, إِمَالَةٌ إِلَى ـ إِسْتِعْطَاف; of enticing, deceiving, إِغْوَآء; of wheedling, إِسْتِعْطَاف ـ مُرَاوَغَة ـ مُرَاوَدَة ـ مُدَارَاة; of inciting, تَحْرِيكٌ ـ تَحْرِيضٌ ـ حَثٌّ. Belief, تَصْدِيق ـ إِعْتِقَاد ـ إِتْقَان. Opinion, رَأْي *pl.* آرَآء. A creed, مَذْهَب *pl.* مَذَاهِب ـ دِين *pl.* أَدْيَان ـ إِيمَان.

Persuasive, *a.* Convincing, مُقْنِع ـ قَاطِعُ ٱلْعَقْلِ ـ مُسْتَعْطِف. Wheedling, مُرَاوِغ ـ مُرَاوِد.

Persuasively, *ad.* إِقْنَاعًا ـ بِوَجْهٍ مُقْنِعٍ ـ بِٱسْتِعْطَافٍ ـ بِمُدَارَاةٍ.

Persuasiveness, *n.* قُوَّةٌ مُقْنِعَةٌ ـ عَاطِفَة ـ إِنْعِطَاف.

Pert, *a.* Forward, saucy, قَلِيلُ ٱلْحَيَآءِ ـ وَقِيح ـ صَفِيقُ ٱلْوَجْهِ. To be —, وَقُحَ *aor.* يَوْقُحُ. To be — to, تَوَقَّحَ عَلَى. *See also* Impudent, *a.*

Pertain, *v.i.* (*See to* Appertain, *v.i.*) It pertaineth not to you to interfere in this matter, لَيْسَ لَكَ أَنْ تُخَالِطَ هٰذَا ٱلْأَمْرَ. In what pertaineth to the conscience, فِي مَا لِلضَّمِيرِ.

Pertinacious, *a.* Holding with obstinacy, لَا يَسْمَعُ ٱلنِّدَآءَ وَلَا يَنْبَغِي ـ مُصِرٌّ عَلَى ـ شَدِيدُ ٱلتَّمَسُّكِ بِ ـ ذَيْمُرِيٌّ ـ دَيْمُرِيٌّ ـ ٱلْإِعْتِدَآء. Pertinacious in litigation, أَلَدّ *pl.* لُدّ *and* لِدَاد ـ لَجُوج. To be —, to hold to pertinaciously, أَصَرَّ عَلَى. To be —, litigious, لَجَّ ٢; to be —, litigious with, لَدَّ ٤. *See also* Obstinate, *a.*

Pertinaciously, *ad.* بِلَجَاجَةٍ ـ بِإِصْرَارٍ.

Pertinaciousness, *n.* } شِدَّةُ ٱلتَّمَسُّكِ بِ ـ لَجَاجَة ـ إِصْرَارٌ عَلَى; in litigation, لَدّ.
Pertinacity, }

Pertinence, *n.* } Appropriateness, مُطَابَقَة ـ مُوَافَقَة ـ مُنَاسَبَة ـ مَصْلَحَة; of speech, سَدَد ـ سَدَاد ـ سُدُود.
Pertinency, }

Pertinent, *a.* فِي مَحَلِّهِ ـ لَائِق ـ مُوَافِق ـ مُنَاسِب; of speech, سَدِيد. A — speech or remark, سِدّ. To be — to, نَاسَبَ ـ وَافَقَ. To be — in one's speech, سَدَّ ـ أَسَدَّ.

Pertinently, *ad.* Appropriately, كَمَا ـ كَمَا يَجِبُ ـ بِمُنَاسَبَةٍ; of speech, بِسُدُودٍ ـ صَوَابًا ـ سَدَدًا ـ سَدَادًا ـ يَنْبَغِي. He speaks —, يُسِدُّ فِي ٱلْقَوْلِ.

Pertly, *ad.* بِقِلَّةِ حَيَآءٍ ـ بِوَقَاحَةٍ. *See also* Impudently, *ad.*

Pertness, *n.* قِلَّةُ حَيَآءٍ ـ وَقَاحَة. *See also* Impudence, *n.*

Perturb, *v.t.* } *See to* Agitate, Disturb, *v.t.*
Perturbate, }

Perturbation, *n.* *See* Agitation, Disturbance, *n.*

Pertusion, *n.* The act of punching, boring, ثَقْب ـ خَرْم ـ خَزْم. A small hole bored, خَرْق *pl.* خُرُوق ـ ثُقْبَة ـ خُرْتَة.

Peruke, *n.* *See* Periwig, *n.*

Perusal, *n.* The act of reading, قِرَآءَة ـ مُطَالَعَة ـ تِلَاوَة. Examination, study, مُلَاحَظَة ـ دِرَاسَة.

Peruse, *v.t.* To read, طَالَعَ ـ قَرَأَ بِ ـ قَرَأَ ـ تَلَا. To examine, study, لَحَظَ ـ دَرَسَ. He perused the book, عَبَّرَ ٱلْكِتَابَ.

Peruser, *n.* قَارِئٌ *pl.* قَارِئُونَ *and* قُرَّآء *and* قَرَأَة ـ مُطَالِع ـ مُدَارِس.

Peruvian, *a.* مُتَعَلِّقٌ بِمَمْلَكَةِ بِرُو فِي أَمِيرِكَا ٱلْجَنُوبِيَّةِ. Peruvian bark, قِشْرُ شَجَرَةِ ٱلْقِينَا قِينَا.

Pervade, *v.t.* To enter, pass through, قَطَعَ فِي ـ دَخَلَ. To —, so as to rise above, command, rule over, عَلَا (*or* إِسْتَعْلَى) ـ عَلَا ـ إِسْتَوْلَى عَلَى ـ عَلَى. To be in all parts, affect all, شَمِلَ ـ عَمَّ ـ إِسْتَوْعَبَ. To infect, خَامَرَ ـ خَالَطَ. To —, as a scent, عَمَّ ـ تَنَشَّمَ بِ ـ أَفْعَمَ ـ أَفْعَمَ ـ فَاحَ ـ فَاجَ ـ فَارَ. To act upon, إِشْتَغَلَ بِ ـ نَجَعَ فِي ـ فَعَلَ فِي ـ أَثَّرَ فِي. To infest, خَالَطَ ـ خَامَرَ: the disease pervaded him, خَالَطَهُ (*or* خَامَرَهُ) ٱلدَّآء. Great anxiety pervaded his heart, خَالَطَ قَلْبَهُ هَمٌّ عَظِيمٌ. The rain pervaded the land, was general, عَمَّ ٱلْمَطَرُ ٱلْأَرْضَ. The disease pervaded all, شَمِلَهُمْ (*or* عَمَّهُمْ) ٱلْمَرَضُ. To cause to —, to make general, عَمَّمَ.

Pervading, *a.* مُسْتَوْلٍ ـ مُسْتَوْعِب ـ مُعَمّ ـ شَامِل.

Pervasion, *n.* The act of pervading, عُمُوم ـ شَمْل ـ شُمُول ـ إِسْتِيعَاب ـ إِسْتِيلَآء.

Pervasive, *a.* عَامٌّ نَوْعًا ـ شَامِلٌ نَوْعًا.

Perverse, *a.* شَكِس ـ شَرِس ـ مُلْتَوٍ ـ عَارِم ـ عَرِم ـ ضَرِس ـ صَعْب *pl.* صِعَاب. A — thing, فَسَاد. A — heart, person, مُلْتَوِي ٱلْقَلْبِ. A — tongue, مُتَقَلِّبُ ٱللِّسَانِ. A — generation, جِيلٌ مُلْتَوٍ. To be —, or to act perversely, عَرَمَ ـ عَرُمَ ـ تَلَوَّى ـ شَكِسَ ـ شَرِسَ. *See also* Obstinate, *a.*

Perversely, *ad.* بِشَرَاسَةٍ ـ بِشَكَاسَةٍ ـ بِعَرَامَةٍ ـ عُرَامًا ـ تَمَرُّدًا. To act — towards, شَارَسَ ـ شَاكَسَ ـ إِفْتَرَى عَلَى ـ عَانَدَ.

Perverseness, *n.* } شَرَاسَة ـ شَكَاسَة ـ عَرَم ـ عُرَام ـ عَرَامَة ـ عِنَاد. *See also* Obstinacy, *n.*
Perversity, }

Perversion, *n.* The act of leading astray, إِضْلَال ـ تَضْلَال; the being led astray, ضَلَّ ـ ضَلَالَة ـ ضَلَال. Perversion of meaning, تَحْرِيف ـ عَكْس ـ تَصْحِيف. Apostacy, اِرْتِدَاد.

Pervert, *v.t.* To lead astray, ضَلَّلَ ـ أَضَلَّ ـ أَفْسَدَ. To —, wrest, as of meaning, صَحَّفَ ـ حَرَّفَ ـ عَكَسَ ـِ. To corrupt, أَفْسَدَ. To —, as of the judgment or opinion, فَسَخَ ـَ. To —, as of a judgment, حَرَّفَ ـ عَكَسَ ـِ ـ عَوَّجَ. To —, or turn one aside, from, لَوَى عن ـِ. To be perverted, led astray, فَسَدَ ـ أَفْسَدَ ـ ضَلَّ ـِ. To be perverted, of a meaning, تَصَحَّفَ ـ اِنْعَكَسَ. To be perverted from, to apostatize from, اِرْتَدَّ عن. He, a judge, perverted judgment, عَالَ فِي ٱلْحُكْمِ ـُ.

Pervert, *n.* One led astray, ضَالّ *pl.* ضَالُّونَ ـ ضَلُول ـ ضِلِّيل ـ مُضَلَّل; an apostate, مُرْتَدّ.

Perverted, *a.* Led astray, ضَالّ ـ ضِلِّيل ـ مُضَلَّل. Wrested, of language, مَعْكُوس ـ مُصَحَّف ـ مُنْعَكِس. Perverted in intellect, مَأْفُون ـ مَأْفُوك.

Perverter, *n.* One who leads astray, مُفْسِد ـ مُضِلّ; who perverts meaning, مُصَحِّف.

Pervertible, *a.* That may be led astray, يُفْسَدُ ـ يُضَلُّ. That may be wrested, of language, مِمَّا يُعْكَسُ ـ يُصَحَّفُ.

Pervious, *a.* That may be penetrated, مُمْكِنٌ النُّفُوذُ إِلَيْهِ ـ مُمْكِنٌ الدُّخُولُ فِيهِ ـ يُتَطَرَّقُ إِلَيْهِ. That may be comprehended, يُدْرَكُ ـ مُدْرَك.

Perviousness, *n.* State of being subject to penetration, قَابِلِيَّةُ ٱلنُّفُوذِ إِلَيْهِ ـ قَابِلِيَّةُ ٱلتَّطَرُّقِ إِلَيْهِ; state of being comprehensible, قَابِلِيَّةُ ٱلْإِدْرَاكِ.

Pessary, *n.* صُوفَة.

Pessimist, *n.* ذَمَّام ـ مُذَمِّمُ كُلِّ شَيْءٍ.

Pest, *n.* A pestilence, هَيْضَة ـ وَبَأ ـ طَاعُون. Anything noxious, مُضْجِر ـ ضَرَر ـ مَضَرَّة. One who troubles, vexes, أَذِيّ ـ آذٍ ـ مُضْجِر. Annoyance, أَذَاة ـ أَذِيَّة.

Pester, *v.t.* To torment, vex, آذَى ـ عَجَّزَ ـ أَضْجَرَ ـ كَدَّ ـُ ـ أَكَدَّ.

Pest-house, *n.* دَارٌ لِلْمَطْعُونِينَ.

Pestiferous, *a.* *See* Noxious, Malignant, *a.*

Pestilence, *n.* The disease of the plague, هَيْضَة ـ مُوتَان ـ دَبْل ـ طَاعُون ـ وَبَأ *pl.* أَوْبَآء. Corruption, as of morals, فَسَاد. Anything troublesome, إِيذَآء ـ أَذًى ـ أَذِيَّة. To prevail, as of a —, وَبِئَ *aor.* يَيْبَأُ ـ أَوْبَأَ. He was attacked by the —, أَصَابَتْهُ ٱلْهَيْضَة.

Pestilent, *a.* Noxious, مُفْسِد ـ مُضِرّ. Stirring up contention, مُهَيِّجُ ٱلْفِتْنَةِ ـ مُفْسِد ـ مُفْتِن. Vexatious, آذٍ ـ أَذِيّ. *See also* Pestilential, *a.*

Pestilential, *a.* Tending to produce plague, مُوَلِّد (*or* مُنْشِئ) ٱلْوَبَآء. A — land, a land smitten with pestilence, أَرْض وَبِئَة ـ أَرْض مُوبِئَة. *See also* Pestilent, *a.*

Pestilently, *ad.* Vexatiously, بِأَذِيَّةٍ ـ بِرَدَاءَةٍ. Destructively, تَهْلُكَةً ـ مَهْلَكَةً.

Pestle, *n.* مِجْاز ـ مِدَقَّة ـ يَدُ ٱلْهَاوَنِ وَٱلْجُرْنِ.

Pet, *n.* A favourite, مُدَلَّل ـ مَحْبُوب ـ عَزِيز. A fit of peevishness, زَعَج ـ ضَجَر ـ حُمَيَّا ـ طَلْعَةُ خُلُقٍ. To be in a —, تَضَجَّرَ ـ اِنْزَعَجَ.

Pet, *v.t.* To fondle, دَلَّلَ ـ لَاطَفَ.

Petal, *n.* وَرَقَةُ زَهْرٍ *pl.* أَوْرَاق.

Petaled, *a.* / Petalous, ذُو أَوْرَاقٍ ـ زَهْرٌ وَرِق.

Petard, *n.* صَارُوخ بَارُودٍ *pl.* صَوَارِيخ ـ فَوْشِيق *pl.* فَوَاشِيق. To fire a — at, أَطْلَقَ ٱلصَّارُوخَ عَلَى.

Peterel, *n.* طَيْرٌ بَحْرِيّ ـ طَيْرُ ٱلنَّوْءِ.

Peter's-pence, *n.* فَلْسُ بُطْرُسَ وَهُوَ عِبَارَةٌ عَنْ إِيرَادِ ٱلْبَابَا مِنْ جَمِيعِ ٱلطَّوَائِفِ ٱلْكَاثُولِيكِيَّةِ عَلَى وَجْهِ ٱلْأَرْضِ.

Petiolar, *a.* / Petiolary, Growing on a petiole, نَاشٍ عَلَى شِمْرَاخٍ (*or* سَاقٍ).

Petiole, *n.* A leaf stalk, شِمْرَاخُ وَرَقَةٍ *pl.* شَمَارِيخ ـ سَاقُ وَرَقَةٍ *pl.* سُوُوق.

Petioled, *a.* / Petiolate, ذُو شِمْرَاخٍ ـ ذُو سَاقٍ.

Petition, *n.* A formal request, prayer, دُعَآء ـ سُؤْلَة *pl.* سُؤْلَات ـ اِلْتِمَاس ـ رَجَآء. Intercession, شَفَاعَة. A memorial, عَرِيضَة ـ عَرْض *pl.* أَعْرَاض ـ رُقْعَة ـ عَرْضُ حَالٍ. Petitions, grievances, اِقْتِرَاحَات. God grant thy —, ٱللّٰهُ يُعْطِيكَ سُؤْلَكَ. I have one small — to make to you, أَسْأَلُكَ سُؤَالًا وَاحِدًا صَغِيرًا. To make — to in behalf of, شَفَعَ ـَ لِ ـ إِلَى.

Petition, *v.t.* To make request to, طَلَبَ إِلَى ـ اِلْتَمَسَ مِن ـ دَعَا ـُ ـ تَرَجَّى ـ تَرَجَّى مِن. To present a — to, قَدَّمَ عَرْضَ حَالٍ إِلَى.

Petitioner, *n.* One who requests, begs, رَغُوب ـ رَاغِبٌ إِلَى. One who presents a petition, مُتَرَجٍّ ـ صَاحِبُ عَرْضِ حَالٍ ـ صَاحِبُ رُقْعَةٍ.

Petit-maitre, *n.* *See* Fop, *n.*

Petitioning, *n.* *See* Petition, *n.*

Petitio principii, *n.* دَوْر ـ حَاصِلُ ٱلْمَحْصُولِ.

Petrel, *n.* *See* Peterel, *n.*

Petrifaction, *n.* The act of petrifying, صَيْرُورَةُ ٱلشَّىْءِ حَجَرًا ـ تَحْجِير . That which is converted into stone, إِسْتَحْجَار ـ تَحَجُّر .

Petrifactive, *a.* مُحَوِّلُ ٱلشَّىْءِ إِلَى حَجَرٍ ـ جَاعِلُ ٱلشَّىْءِ حَجَرًا .

Petrification, *n.* The process of petrifying, إِسْتَحْجَار ـ تَحَجُّر .

Petrified, *a.* Changed into stone, مُسْتَحْجِر ـ مُتَحَجِّر . Petrified through fear, مَدْهُوش ـ مَعْقُور .

Petrify, *v.t.* To convert into stone, صَيَّرَ حَجَرًا . To — through fear, دَهَّشَ ـ أَدْهَشَ ـ أَعْقَرَ .

Petrify, *v.i.* To become stone, إِسْتَحْجَرَ ـ تَحَجَّرَ ـ صَارَ حَجَرًا . To be petrified through fear, دَهِشَ ـ عَقِرَ .

Petrifying, *a.* Converting into stone, مُحَوِّلُ ٱلشَّىْءِ إِلَى حَجَرٍ ـ جَاعِلُ ٱلشَّىْءِ حَجَرًا . Fixing in amazement, مُدْهِش ـ مُعْقِر .

Petroleum, *n.* بَتْرُول ـ نِفْط . A — spring, نَفَّاطَة ـ نَفَّاط ـ عَيْنُ ٱلْبَتْرُولِ *pl.* عُيُون ـ نَفَّاط .

Petronel, *n.* بَارُودَة ـ طَبَنْجَة .

Petrous, *a.* Like stone, كَٱلْحَجَرِ .

Petted, *a.* مُلَاطَف ـ مُدَلَّل .

Petticoat, *n.* فُسْتَانٌ تَحْتَانِيٌّ . Petticoat government, تَسَلُّطُ ٱلْمَرْأَةِ عَلَى زَوْجِهَا .

Pettifogger, *n.* خَسِيس ـ تَفِهٌ ـ تَافِهٌ ـ حُوَّلٌ قُلَّبٌ ; a pettifogging lawyer, وَكِيلٌ سُفْلِيٌّ .

Pettifogging, *a.* تَفِهٌ ـ تَافِهٌ ـ دَنِيءٌ ـ خَسِيس .

Pettifogging, *n.* دَنَآءَة ـ تَفَاهَة ـ خَسَائِس .

Pettiness, *n.* Smallness, meanness, خَسَاسَة ـ دَنَآءَة ـ حَقَارَة ـ تَفَاهَة . *See also* Paltriness, *n.*

Pettish, *a.* Fractious, نَكِد ـ شَكِس ـ وَعِق ـ شَرِس ـ شَرِيس . To be —, شَرِسَ ـ شَكِسَ ـ وَعِقَ .

Pettishly, *ad.* بِوَعَقَةٍ ـ بِشَكَاسَةٍ .

Pettishness, *n.* شَرَاسَة ـ شَكَاسَة ـ وَعَقَة .

Pettitoes, *n.* The feet of pigs, أَرْجُلُ ٱلْخِنْزِيرِ .

Petto, *n.* The breast, ٱلصَّدْر . *In petto*, مَكْتُومٌ فِي ٱلصَّدْرِ .

Petty, *a.* Inconsiderable, طَفِيف ـ صَغِير ـ جُزْئِيٌّ ـ زَهِيد ـ دَنِيءٌ ـ تَافِه ـ قَلِيل . A — dealer, خُرْدَجِي . Petty expenses, نَفَقَاتٌ مُتَفَرِّقَةٌ . Petty wares, خُرْدَة ـ دَقَائِقُ ٱلْأَمْتِعَةِ . *See also* Peddlery, Pedlar, *n.*

Petulance, *n.* / Petulancy, حِدَّةُ مِزَاجٍ ـ حِدَّةُ طَبْعٍ ـ بَطَر ـ شَكَاسَة ـ شَرَاسَة ـ تَمَرُّد .

Petulant, *a.* حَادُّ ٱلْمِزَاجِ ـ مُتَمَرِّد ـ بَطِر ـ شَكِس ـ شَرِس . To be —, شَرِسَ ـ شَكِسَ ـ وَعِقَ . To be — towards, شَارَسَ ـ شَاكَسَ ـ عَرَمَ عَلَى .

Petulantly, *ad.* تَمَرُّدًا ـ بِبَطَرٍ ـ بِشَكَاسَةٍ ـ بِشَرَاسَةٍ .

Petunia, *n.* The flower, ضَرْبٌ مِنَ ٱلْأَزْهَارِ .

Pew, *n.* مَحْفِلٌ خَاصٌّ فِي كَنِيسَةٍ .

Pewit, *n.* / Pewet, ٱلشَّاتُوِيتُ ـ ٱلشَّبَّاحُ .

Pewter, *n.* The metal, قَصْدِير ـ قَلْعِيٌّ . A — vessel, قَصْدِيرَة . Utensils of pewter, *etc.*, أَمْتِعَةٌ مِنْ قَصْدِيرٍ ـ قَصْدِيرَات .

Pewterer, *n.* رَصَّاص ـ مُعَالِجُ ٱلْقَصْدِيرِ .

Phaeton, *n.* An open carriage, عَرَبِيَّةٌ بِلَا سِتْرٍ ـ عَرَبِيَّةٌ مَكْشُوفَةٌ ـ كَرُّوصَةٌ مَفْتُوحَةٌ .

Phalangal, *a.* / Phalangial, مُتَعَلِّقٌ بِعُقَدِ ٱلْأَصَابِعِ .

Phalanges, *n.* عُقَلُ ٱلْأَصَابِعِ *sing.* عُقْلَة ـ عُقَدُ ٱلْأَصَابِعِ *sing.* عُقْدَة ـ ٱلْأَعْظَامُ ٱلسُّلَامِيَاتُ ـ ٱلسُّلَامِيَات *sing.* سُلَامَى .

Phalangium, *n.* The genus of insects so called, ٱلرُّتَيْلَى .

Phalangium, *n.* The plant, زَهْرُ ٱلْعَنْكَبُوتِ ـ ٱلرُّتَيْلَى .

Phalanx, *n.* As of soldiers, كُرْدُوسَة *pl.* كَرَادِيس . A compact body of men, عِصَابَة ـ عُصْبَة .

Phanerogamous, *a.* ذُو أَزْهَارٍ فِيهَا آلَاتٌ مُذَكَّرَةٌ وَمُؤَنَّثَةٌ .

Phantasm, *n.* An imaginary form, طَيْف ـ خَيَال ـ طَيْف ـ خَيَالٌ . A vain imagination, خَيَالٌ بَاطِلٌ ـ وَهْمِيَّة *pl.* وَهْمِيَّات . Phantasms, suspicions, هَوَاجِس . *See also* Phantom, *n.*

Phantasmagoria, *n.* / Phantasmagory, *See* Magic-lantern, *under* Lantern, *n.*

Phantastic, *a.* *See* Fantastic, *a.*

Phantasy, *n.* *See* Fantasy, Fancy, *n.*

Phantom, *n.* A spectre, أَخْيِلَة *pl.* خَيَال ـ أَزْوَال *pl.* زَوْل . The — of a dream, أَطْوَاف *pl.* طَوْف ـ طَائِف ـ طَيْفُ خَيَالٍ ـ طَيْف .

Pharaoh, *n.* Name of the Kings of Egypt, فَرَاعِنَة *pl.* فِرْعَوْنُ .

Pharaonic, *a.* مُتَعَلِّقٌ بِٱلْفَرَاعِنَةِ ـ فِرْعَوْنِيٌّ .

Pharisaic, *a.* / Pharisaical, Hypocritical, مُدَاهِن ـ مُرَآئِيٌّ ـ مُنَافِق .

Pharisaically, *ad.* Hypocritically, بِنِفَاقٍ ـ بِمُنَافَقَةٍ ـ بِمُرَآءٍ .

Pharisaism, *n.* The doctrines of the Pharisees, مَذْهَبُ ٱلْفَرِّيسِيِّينَ . Hypocrisy, مُدَاهَنَة ـ نِفَاق ـ رِئَآء ـ مُرَايَاة . *See also* Fanaticism, *n.*

Pharisean, *a.* مُتَعَلِّقٌ بِٱلْفَرِّيسِيِّينَ ـ فَرِّيسِيٌّ .

Pharisee, *n.* فَرِّيسِيٌّ *pl.* فَرِّيسِيُّونَ . A hypocrite, مُنَافِق ـ مُرَآءٍ ـ مُدَاهِن . To play the —, دَاهَنَ ـ نَفَّقَ . *See also* Fanatic, *n.*

Pharmaceutic, *a.* / Pharmaceutical, مُخْتَصٌّ بِتَرْكِيبِ ٱلْأَدْوِيَةِ .

Pharmaceutics, *n.* فنّ تركيب الأدوية.

Pharmaceutist, *n.* }
Pharmacist, } مركّب (*or* صانع) الأدوية.

Pharmacologist, *n.* حاذق (*or* ماهر) في فنّ تركيب الأدوية.

Pharmacology, *n.* فنّ تركيب الأدوية ـ فنّ الأدوية.

Pharmacopœia, *n.* مجمعة الأدوية ـ كتاب الأدوية.

Pharmacy, *n.* The preparation of medicines, تركيب الأدوية. The business of an apothecary, صناعة الصيادلة.

Pharos, *n.* *See* Lighthouse, *n.*

Pharyngeal, *a.* متعلّق بفم الحنجرة.

Pharyngitis, *n.* التهاب فم الحنجرة ـ داء فم الحنجرة.

Pharyngotomy, *n.* شقّ فم الحنجرة.

Pharynx, *n.* فم الحنجرة ـ فم الحنجور.

Phase, *n.* As of the moon, تبدّل *pl.* تبدّلات ـ وجه *pl.* وجوه ـ رؤية *pl.* رؤى ; of the first quarter of the moon, غرّة *pl.* غرر. Appearance, condition, وجه ـ شكل ـ حال *pl.* أحوال ـ هيئة ـ فنّ. To assume different phases, تلوّن ـ تغوّل. The question continues to assume different phases, المسألة لم تزل تنتقل من حال إلى حال. The question has entered into a new —, دخلت المسألة في عهد جديد. Every one who has studied the varying phases of the Eastern Question during the late years, كلّ من تأمّل كيفيّة انقلاب المسألة الشرقيّة في هذه السنين الأخيرة. Life has two phases, العيش فنّان.

Pheasant, *n.* لوم ـ ضريس ـ طيهوج *pl.* طياهيج ـ ديك برّيّ *pl.* ديوك برّيّة ـ تدرج ـ تذرج ـ قيجة *pl.* قيجات.

Phenix, *n.* العنقاء ـ سمندر ـ سمندل.

Phenomenal, *a.* عارض ـ واقع ـ ظاهريّ ـ حدثيّ.

Phenomenally, *ad.* حداثةً ـ بالظاهر ـ عرضًا ـ هيئةً.

Phenomenon, *n.* Some new occurrence, حدث ـ حادث ـ حادثة *pl.* حوادث. Anything remarkable, نادرة *pl.* نوادر ـ غريبة *pl.* غرائب ـ عجيبة *pl.* عجائب.

Phial, *n.* قرّان ـ قارورة *pl.* قوارير ـ قنّينة *pl.* قناني.

Phial, *v.t.* عبّأ في قارورة.

Philander, *v.i.* دلّ *aor.* يدلّ ـ تدلّل.

Philanthropic, *a.* }
Philanthropical, } متعلّق ـ محبّ البشر ـ خيّر ـ خيريّ ـ شفيق ـ بحبّ البشر.

Philanthropically, *ad.* بحبّ البشر ـ خيرًا ـ حبًّا بالإنسانيّة ـ بخير ـ بشفقة.

Philanthropist, *n.* خيريّ ـ خيّر *pl.* أخيار *fem.* خيّرة *pl.* خيّرات ـ محبّ البشر.

Philanthropy, *n.* خير ـ شفقة ـ خير ـ حبّ البشر.

Philharmonic, *n.* محبّ الألحان ـ متعلّق بحبّ النغم. A — hall, مرسح الموسيقى.

Philibeg, *n.* فستان يلبسه أهل أسقوتلاند.

Phil-hellenist, *n.* محبّ أهل الروم.

Philippic, *n.* شتم ـ طعنان ـ قدح ـ رسالة قدح.

Philippize, *v.i.* استعمل الطعن ـ استعمل القدح.

Philistine, *n.* An inhabitant of Palestine, فلسطينيّ *pl.* فلسطينيّون.

Philologic, *a.* }
Philological, } متعلّق بعلم اللغة.

Philologically, *ad.* نظرًا لقواعد علم اللغة.

Philologist, *n.* أهل اللغة ـ أديب *pl.* أدباء.

Philology, *n.* علم الأدبيّات ـ علم اللغة ـ علم الأدب.

Philomel, Philomela, *n.* *See* Nightingale.

Philoprogenitiveness, *n.* حبّ الذرّيّة.

Philosopher, *n.* A devotee to science, فيلسوف ـ حكيم *pl.* حكماء ـ فلسفيّ *pl.* فلاسفة. One who takes trials calmly, متأنّ ـ متصبّر ـ عز. The philosopher's stone, حجر الكيميا ـ إكسير ـ الحجر المكرّم.

Philosophic, *a.* } Connected with philosophy, فلسفيّ ـ حكميّ ـ
Philosophical, } متعلّق بالفلسفة. Calm, وقور. To be —, calm, توقّر ـ اتّقر.

Philosophically, *ad.* According to philosophy, على طرز الفلسفة ـ بفلسفة. Calmly, بوقار ـ بعزاء ـ اطمئنانًا.

Philosophism, *n.* فلسفة كاذبة ـ تصوّف.

Philosophist, *n.* فيلسوف كاذب ـ صوفيّ.

Philosophize, *v.i.* تفلسف. *See also to* Reason, *v.i.*

Philosophy, *n.* فلسفة ـ الرياضيّات ـ علم الحكمة. Natural —, علم الحكمة الطبيعيّة. Moral —, علم الأخلاق.

Philostorgy, *n.* حبّ النسب.

Philotechnic, *a.* محبّ الفنون.

Philtre, *n.* معجون للعشق ـ شربة أخذة.

Philtre, *v.t.* شرّب شربة أخذة ـ أطعم معجونًا للعشق.

Phiz, *n.* *See* Face, *n.*

Phlebotomist, *n.* حجّام ـ فصّاد.

Phlebotomize, *v.t.* فصد ـِ.

Phlebotomy, *n.* الفصد ـ الفصاد.

Phlegm, *n.* Animal fluid from the chest, *etc.*, خراشيّ ـ نخامة ـ بلغم ـ قشيعة ـ قشاعة. Coldness, indifference, تساهل ـ تكاسل ـ فتور ـ برودة. To void —, تنخّم ـ نخم ـَ ـ ألقى الخراشيّ.

Phlegmatic, *a.* Abounding with phlegm, بَلْغَمِيٌّ. Cold, indifferent, فَاتِر ـ بَارِد ـ مُتَسَاهِل ـ مُتَكَاسِل ـ فُطَارِيٌّ.

Phlegmatically, *ad.* Coldly, heavily, بِفُتُور ـ بِبُرُودَةٍ ـ بِتَكَاسُلٍ.

Phlegmon, *n.* جِبْن *pl.* حُبُون ـ دُبَيْلَة ـ دُمَّل *pl.* دَمَامِيلُ ـ خُرَاج.

Phleam, *n.* *See* Fleam, *n.*

Phlogiston, *n.* *See* Caloric, *n.*

Phlogosis, *n.* *See* Inflammation, *n.*

Phoca, *n.* The seal, عِجْلُ ٱلْبَحْرِ.

Phœbus, *n.* *See* Sun, *n.*

Phœnix, *n.* *See* Phenix, *n.*

Phonetic, *a.* Vocal, مُتَعَلِّقٌ بِٱلصَّوْتِ ـ حِسِّيٌّ ـ لَفْظِيٌّ. Written as pronounced, مَا كُتِبَ طِبْقَ ٱللَّفْظِ.

Phonetics, *n.* / Phonics, } The science of sounds, عِلْمُ ٱلْأَصْوَاتِ.

Phonographic, *a.* / Phonographical, } شَارِحُ ٱلْأَصْوَاتِ ٱلْمَلْفُوظَةِ.

Phonography, *n.* / Phonology, } عِلْمُ ٱلْأَصْوَاتِ ٱلْمَلْفُوظَةِ.

Phosphate, *n.* مِلْحٌ فُصْفُورِيٌّ أَخِيرٌ.

Phosphite, *n.* مِلْحٌ فُصْفُورِيٌّ أَوَّلُ.

Phosphor, *n.* The morning star, كَوْكَبُ ٱلْفَجْرِ.

Phosphorate, *v.t.* فَصْفَرَ ـ رَكَّبَ ـ (*or* شَرَّبَ ـ) فُصْفُورًا.

Phosphorated, *a.* مُفَصْفَر ـ مُرَكَّب (*or* مَشْرُوب) فُصْفُورٍ.

Phosphorescence, *v.i.* أَضَاءَ كَٱلْفُصْفُورِ.

Phosphorescence, *n.* ضِيَاءٌ كَلَمَعَانِ ٱلْفُصْفُورِ ـ ضِيَاءٌ فُصْفُورِيٌّ.

Phosphoric, *a.* مِنَ ٱلْفُصْفُورِ ـ فُصْفُورِيٌّ. Phosphoric acid, حَامِضُ ٱلْفُصْفُورِ ٱلْأَخِيرِ.

Phosphorous, *a.* فُصْفُورِيٌّ. Phosphorous acid, حَامِضٌ فُصْفُورِيٌّ أَوَّلُ.

Phosphorus, *n.* فُسْفُور ـ فُصْفُورَة ـ فُصْفُور. *See also* Phosphor, *n.*

Phosphuret, *n.* مُرَكَّبُ ٱلْفُصْفُورِ.

Phosphuretted, *a.* مُفَصْفَر ـ مُرَكَّبُ فُصْفُورٍ.

Photogenic, *a.* Producing light, مُضِيءٌ. Of taking pictures by the sun's rays, مَا نِيطَ بِٱلتَّصْوِيرِ بِوَاسِطَةِ ٱلنُّورِ.

Photogeny, *n.* ٱلتَّصْوِيرُ بِوَاسِطَةِ ٱلنُّورِ.

Photograph, *n.* صُورَةٌ فُوتُوغْرَافِ ـ صُورَةٌ مُصَوَّرَةٌ بِوَاسِطَةِ ٱلنُّورِ.

Photographer, *n.* فُوتُوغْرَافْجِي.

Photographic, *a.* / Photographical, } فُوتُوغْرَاف ـ مُتَعَلِّقٌ بِٱلتَّصْوِيرِ بِوَاسِطَةِ ٱلنُّورِ.

Photography, *n.* صَنْعَةُ ٱلْفُوتُوغْرَاف ـ صَنْعَةُ ٱلتَّصْوِيرِ بِوَاسِطَةِ ٱلنُّورِ.

Photologic, *a.* / Photological, } مُتَعَلِّقٌ بِٱلنُّورِ وَٱلْبَحْثِ عَنْهُ.

Photology, *n.* عِلْمٌ يُبْحَثُ فِيهِ عَنِ ٱلنُّورِ.

Photometer, *n.* مِيزَانُ ٱلنُّورِ.

Photometry, *n.* عِلْمُ تَحْقِيقِ دَرَجَاتِ ٱلنُّورِ.

Phrase, *n.* A short sentence, جُمْلَة *pl.* جُمَل ـ عِبَارَة *pl.* عِبَارَات ـ بَنْد *pl.* بُنُود. A technical or conventional —, إِصْطِلَاح *pl.* إِصْطِلَاحَات. Phrase by —, كُلُّ جُمْلَةٍ بِمُفْرَدِهَا.

Phrase, *v.t.* To name or style, سَمَّى ـ دَعَا *aor.* يَدْعُو. To express, لَفَظَ بِ ـ [2] نَطَقَ بِ.

Phrase-book, *n.* دُسْتُورُ ٱلْإِصْطِلَاحَاتِ ـ كِتَابُ جُمَلٍ وَٱصْطِلَاحَاتٍ.

Phraseologic, *a.* مِنْ صِفَةِ ٱلْعِبَارَةِ ـ إِصْطِلَاحِيٌّ.

Phraseology, *n.* A mode of speech, عِبَارَة ـ إِصْطِلَاح ـ فَنّ. He has a good —, هُوَ حَسَنُ ٱلْعِبَارَةِ. *See also* Diction, *n.*

Phrenetic, *a.* *See* Frantic, Frenzied, *a.*

Phrenitis, *n.* Inflammation of the brain, ٱلْتِهَابُ ٱلدِّمَاغِ ـ سِرْسَام. *See also* Frenzy, Madness, *n.*

Phrenological, *a.* Relating to the science of the mind, مُتَعَلِّقٌ بِعِلْمِ ٱلضَّمِيرِ وَخَوَاصِّهِ. The same, as supposed to be connected with the organs of the brain, مُتَعَلِّقٌ بِعِلْمِ قِيَافَةِ ٱلدِّمَاغِ.

Phrenologist, *n.* One versed in the science of the mind, حَاذِقٌ فِي عِلْمِ ٱلضَّمِيرِ وَخَوَاصِّهِ. The same, as supposed to be connected with the organs of the brain, أَهْلُ عِلْمِ قِيَافَةِ ٱلدِّمَاغِ.

Phrenology, *n.* Science of the mind and its properties, عِلْمُ ٱلضَّمِيرِ وَخَوَاصِّهِ. The science of the mind as supposed to be connected with the organs of the brain, عِلْمُ قِيَافَةِ ٱلدِّمَاغِ.

Phrensy, *n.* *See* Frenzy, *n.*

Phthisic, *n.* ضِيقُ ٱلصَّدْرِ ـ ضِيقُ ٱلنَّفَسِ.

Phthisical, *a.* مَسْلُول ـ مُصَابٌ بِضِيقِ ٱلنَّفَسِ. *See also* Consumptive.

Phthisis, *n.* *See* Consumption, *n.*

Philacter, *n.* / Philactery, } A bandage for the head, عِصَابَة *pl.* عَصَائِب. A spell, charm, عُوذَة *pl.* عُوَذ ـ تَعْوِيذ *pl.* تَعَاوِيذ ـ مَعَاذَة *pl.* مَعَاذَات.

Physic, *n.* The art of healing, عِلْمُ ٱلطِّبِّ ـ ٱلطِّبّ. Medicine, دَوَاء ـ عِلَاج. A cathartic, شَرْبَة ـ دَوَاءٌ مُسْهِل ـ مُسْهِل. To practise —, تَعَاطَى ٱلطِّبَّ ـ تَطَبَّبَ.

Physic, *v.t.* To treat medicinally, دَاوَى ـ شَفَى ـ عَالَجَ. To give a purge to, شَرَّبَ شَرْبَةً ـ [2] سَقَى مُسْهِلًا.

Physical, *a.* Pertaining to nature, طَبِيعِيٌّ. Bodily, بَدَنِيٌّ ـ جِسْمِيٌّ. Medicinal, طِبِّيٌّ.

Physical constitution, خِلْقَة ـ بِنْيَة بَدَنِيَّة.

Physical education, رِيَاضَة جِسْمِيَّة ـ تَرْبِيَة بَدَنِيَّة.

Physical force, غَضْب ـ جُبُور ـ زُور ـ جَبْر ـ حَوْل ـ حِيلَة.

Physical superiority, إِسْتِعْلَاء فِي ٱلْقُوَّة ـ زُور.

Physically, *ad.* According to nature, حَسَبَ ٱلطَّبِيعَةِ ـ طَبْعًا. Bodily, بَدَنًا ـ جِسْمًا. Medicinally, طِبًّا.

Physician, *n.* طَبِيب ـ مُتَطَبِّب ـ نِطِّيس ـ نِطَاسِيّ *pl.* أَطِبَّاء ـ حَكِيم *pl.* حُكَمَاء.

Physics, *n.* الحِكْمَة ٱلطَّبِيعِيَّة ـ عِلْمُ ٱلطَّبِيعِيَّاتِ.

Physiognomic, *a.* / Physiognomical, } ما نِيطَ بِعِلْمِ ٱلْفِرَاسَةِ ـ مُتَعَلِّقٌ بِعِلْمِ ٱلْقِيَافَةِ.

Physiognomics, *n.* عِلْمُ ٱلْفِرَاسَةِ.

Physiognomist, *n.* مِنْ أَهْلِ عِلْمِ ٱلْفِرَاسَةِ ـ أَقْوَف ـ قَافَة *pl.* قَائِف.

Physiognomy, *n.* The science of, عِلْمٌ ـ عِلْمُ ٱلْفِرَاسَةِ ـ ٱلْفِرَاسَةِ ٱلْقِيَافَةِ. Countenance, وَجْه ـ سِيمَا ـ طَلْعَة ـ مُحَيًّا. To judge one from the —, تَفَرَّسَ فِي.

Physiography, *n.* عِلْمُ ٱلْمَوْجُودَاتِ ٱلطَّبِيعِيَّةِ.

Physiologic, *a.* / Physiological, } Pertaining to physiology, مُتَعَلِّقٌ بِعِلْمِ تَرْكِيبِ ٱلطَّبَائِعِ. Natural, animal, طَبِيعِيٌّ ـ جِبِلِّيٌّ ـ جِسْمِيٌّ ـ حَيَوَانِيٌّ ـ بَدَنِيٌّ.

Physiologically, *ad.* According to physiology, نَظَرًا لِعِلْمِ ٱلْبَحْثِ عَنِ ٱلْحَيَاةِ ٱلْبَدَنِيَّةِ. Physically, naturally, بَدَنًا ـ جِسْمًا ـ طَبْعًا.

Physiologist, *n.* عَالِمٌ بِتَرْكِيبِ ٱلطَّبَائِعِ.

Physiology, *n.* The science of the functions of animals and plants, عِلْمُ ٱلْحَيَوَانِ وَٱلنَّبَاتِ وَخَوَاصِّهَا. The science of animal life, عِلْمُ ٱلْبَحْثِ عَنِ ٱلْحَيَاةِ ٱلْحَيَوَانِيَّةِ.

Phytography, *n.* / Phytology, } عِلْمُ ٱلْبَحْثِ عَنِ مَاهِيَّةِ ـ عِلْمُ ٱلنَّبَاتِ ٱلنَّبَاتِ.

Phytologist, *n.* مِنْ أَهْلِ عِلْمِ ٱلنَّبَاتِ.

Piacular, *a.* / Piaculous, } إِسْتِغْفَارِيٌّ ـ تَكْفِيرِيٌّ. *See also* Expiatory, *a.*

Pia Mater, *n.* أُمُّ ٱلدِّمَاغِ ـ أُمُّ ٱلرَّأْسِ.

Pianissimo, *ad.* بِغَايَةِ ٱلْخَفْضِ.

Pianist, *n.* أُسْتَاذُ ٱلْبِيَانُو.

Pianiste, *n.* مُعَلِّمَةُ ٱلْبِيَانُو.

Piano, *ad.* بِخَفْضٍ.

Piano, *n.* / Pianoforte, } بِيَانُو.

Piastre, *n.* Of Egypt or Turkey, قِرْش ـ غُرُوش *pl.* غِرْش *pl.* قُرُوش. A dollar, رِيَال *pl.* رِيَالَات. *See also* Dollar, *n.*

Piazza, *n.* A portico, قَيْسَارِيَّة. A court, square, سَاحَة *pl.* سَاحَات.

Pibroch, *n.* نَغْمَة مُحَرِّضَة يَعْزِفُ بِهَا أَهْلُ إِسْكُوتْلَانْد عَلَى ٱلْقِرْبَةِ.

Pic, *n.* The Eastern measure of about 25 inches, ذِرَاعٌ بَلَدِيٌّ *pl.* أَذْرُع.

Pica, *n.* Of type, طَرْزٌ مِنَ ٱلْحُرُوفِ لِلطَّبْعِ.

Picadoor, *n.* A bull-fighter, مُقَاتِلُ ٱلثَّوْرِ.

Picaroon, *n.* *See* Pirate, *n.*

Pick, *n.* The tool, مِعْوَل *pl.* مَعَاوِلُ ـ صَاقُور. Choice, إِخْتِيَار. The best of any thing, صَمِيم ـ عَقِيلَة ـ غُرَّة.

Pick, *v.t.* As with a pickaxe, نَقَرَ ² ـ عَزَقَ ² ـ حَفَرَ ـِ ـ نَكَشَ ² ـِ. To —, as a bone, عَرَقَ ² ـ تَعَرَّقَ ـ لَاكَ ² ـ قَرَضَ ² ـ عَرْدَشَ. To gather, as of fruit, خَرَفَ ² ـ جَنَى ـِ ـ إِجْتَنَى; of flowers, قَطَفَ ـِ ـ قَطَّفَ. To — the nose, مَخَطَ (or) أَنْفَهُ إِمْتَخَطَ. To — the teeth, خَلَّلَ أَسْنَانَهُ ـ سَوَّكَ أَسْنَانَهُ ـ سَاكَ ² أَسْنَانَهُ. To — the ears, نَكَشَ ² ـِ أُذُنَيْهِ. To —, or feather, of a bird, نَتَفَ ـِ ـ نَتَّفَ. To — a pocket, طَرَّ ² ٱلْجَيْبَ ـ سَرَقَ مِنَ ٱلْجَيْبِ ـِ. To — from a pocket, زَبَقَ ² ـِ ـ طَرَّ ² مِنَ ٱلْجَيْبِ. To — a lock, فَشَّ ² ٱلْقُفْلَ ـ فَتَحَ ٱلْقُفْلَ بِٱلْكُلَّابَةِ ـَ ـ ٱلْقُفْلَ. To —, to clear from impurities, نَقَّى.

To pick off, take off, رَفَعَ ـَ ـ شَالَ ² ـِ ب. To hit by taking special aim, أَصَابَ ـ عَمْدًا.

To pick out, to select, إِنْتَخَبَ ـ إِخْتَارَ. To choose from among others, as the good from the bad, أَنْقَى ـ تَنَقَّى ـ نَقَّى. To draw out, as a thorn, *etc.*, إِنْتَقَشَ ـ نَقَشَ ². To pick out, of the eyes, فَوَّرَ.

To pick up, as from the ground, لَقَطَ ² ـ إِلْتَقَطَ ـ تَنَاوَلَ ـ إِكْتَسَبَ ـ حَصَّلَ ـ فَازَ ² ب. To obtain, acquire, شَالَ ² ـِ ب. To pick up here and there, تَلَقَّطَ. To pick up, to find, وَجَدَ *aor.* يَجِدُ.

To pick a quarrel with, طَلَبَ ² ـ يَقَعُ *aor.* وَقَعَ ب ـ تَعَرَّضَ ل عِلَّةً عَلَى.

To pick holes in one's coat, to criticise, censure, نَقَرَ ² ـ أَدْغَلَ ـ نَعَى ـَ عَلَى ـ فَضَحَ ـَ.

Pick, *v.i.* To eat daintily, تَنَقَّقَ فِي ٱلْأَكْلِ ـ قَشَّشَ. To — up, to gain strength, صَحَّ ـِ ـ إِسْتَصَحَّ ـ تَجَبَّرَ ـ إِسْتَشْفَى.

Pickaxe, *n.* فَأْس ـ مِعْدُور ـ مَعَاوِلُ *pl.* مِعْوَل ـ صَاقُور ـ مِعْدَن *pl.* فُؤُوس. A small —, مِنْكَاش.

Pickback, *ad.* عَلَى ٱلظَّهْرِ.

Picked, *a.* } Pointed, sharp, حَادٌّ ـ مُؤَنَّف ـ مُحَدَّد. Picked
Piked, } up, as from the ground, مَلْقُوط. The picked men of an army, شُرْطَة.

Pickerel, *n.* The fish, نَوْعُ صَغِيرٍ مِنَ سَمَكِ ٱلْأَنْهُرِ.

Picket, A sharp stake, خَازُوق *pl.* خَوَازِيق. Picket, as of an advancing army, طَلِيعَة. A small guard, بَعْضُ خُفَرَآء *vulg.* غَفَر. A body of men kept ready accoutred, بَعْضُ أَنْفَارٍ مُتَأَهِّبَةٍ.

Picket, *v.t.* To drive a stake into, خَوْزَقَ. To post a picket guard, أَقَامَ خَفَرًا (*or* غَفَرًا).

Picking, *n.* The act of plucking, of fruit, جَنْي ـ جِنَايَة; of flowers, قَطْف; what is plucked, of fruit, مَجْنِي; of flowers, بَاقَة ـ قِطْف. Choice from among others, نُقَايَة; what is chosen, نُقَاة. Pickings, stray pieces picked up, litter, قُصَاصَة ـ تَفَارِيق. Accidental gains, لُقَاط.

Pickle, *n.* Brine for pickling, مَآءُ ٱلْمِلْحِ; *from the Italian,* سَلَامُورَة ـ سَلَامُول. Any vegetable pickled, قِطْنِيَّة (*or* قُطْنِيَّة) مُخَلَّلَة *pl.* قَطَانِيُّ مُخَلَّلَة ـ *vulg.* كَبِيس. An awkward state, وَرْطَة ـ حَالُ سُوْءٍ ـ عَرَاقِيل ـ اِلْتِبَاك. Seasoning, تَابِل.

Pickle, *v.t.* To preserve in brine, مَلَّحَ; in vinegar, خَلَّلَ. To season, تَبَّلَ.

Pickling, *n.* In brine, تَمْلِيح; in vinegar, تَخْلِيل; with seasoning, تَتْبِيل.

Picklock, *n.* A person who opens locks, فَشَّاشُ ٱلْأَقْفَالِ ـ زَابِق. A tool to pick locks, مُكَلِّبُ ٱلْأَقْفَالِ ـ كُلَّابٌ لِلْأَقْفَال.

Picnic, *n.* ضِيَافَة ـ ضِيَافَةٌ رِيفِيَّةٌ خَرَجُها بِٱلشَّرِاكَةِ (*or* بِدَادَة) رِيفِيَّة.

Pickpocket, *n.* } طَرَّار. To be a —, to steal from the pocket,
Pickpurse, } طَرَّ ـ مِنَ ٱلْجَيْبِ. *See* Cutpurse, *n.*

Pickthank, *n.* An officious fellow, فُضُولِيٌّ ـ عِرِّيض. A whispering parasite, دَاسُوس ـ دَسِيس.

Picktooth, *n.* خِلَالَة *pl.* خِلَالَات. What the — brings away, خُلَالَة.

Pictorial, *a.* Drawn, painted, مَنْقُوش ـ مُصَوَّر ـ مَرْسُوم. Illustrated by pictures, مُدَبَّج (*or* مُزَيَّن) بِٱلتَّصَاوِيرِ ـ مُوَشَّحٌ بِٱلصُّوَرِ. Descriptive, وَصْفِيّ.

Pictorially, *ad.* بِٱلتَّصَاوِيرِ.

Picture, *n.* A representation by drawing, نَقْش *pl.* نُقُوش ـ تَصْوِير *pl.* تَصَاوِير. صُورَة *pl.* صُوَر ـ تِمْثَال *pl.* تَمَاثِيل. Representation, description, وَصْف ـ بَيَان. Resemblance, شِبْه ـ مُشَابَهَة.

Anything pretty, تُحْفَة *pl.* تُحَف ـ نَضْرَة ـ بَهْجَة; a picture of surpassing beauty, صُورَةٌ ذَاتُ بَهْجَةٍ غَالِبَةٍ. Form, shape, شَكْل ـ هَيْئَة. He is the — of his father, يُشَابِهُ وَالِدَهُ. *See also* Likeness, *n.*

Picture, *v.t.* To draw, صَوَّرَ ـ رَسَمَ ـ نَقَشَ. To describe, وَصَفَ *aor.* يَصِفُ ـ صَوَّرَ. To — to one's self تَمَثَّلَ ـ تَصَوَّرَ ـ تَخَيَّلَ.

Pictured, *a.* Drawn, مُصَوَّر ـ مَنْقُوش ـ مَرْسُوم. Pictured to the mind, مُتَخَيَّل ـ مُتَصَوَّر ـ مُتَمَثَّل.

Picturesque, *a.* بَهِيج *the fem. epithet is,* بَهِيجَة ـ بَهِيٌّ ـ مِبْهَاج ـ نَاضِر.

Picturesquely, *ad.* نَضْرَة ـ بِبَهَآءٍ ـ بِبَهْجَةٍ.

Picturesqueness, *n.* نَضْرَة ـ بَهَآء ـ بَهْجَة.

Piddle, *v.i.* To feed daintily, نَقَّشَ ـ تَنَقَّقَ فِي ٱلْأَكْلِ. To make water by dribblets, شَلْشَلَ بَوْلَهُ ـ شَغَّى. *See also to* Trifle, *v.i.*

Piddler, *n.* One who eats daintily, مُنَقِّش ـ مُتَنَقِّق فِي ٱلْأَكْلِ. *See also* Trifler, *n.*

Pie, *n.* As of fruit, مَحْشُوٌّ بِفَاكِهَةٍ ـ فَطِيرٌ مَحْشِيٌّ بِفَاكِهَةٍ; of meat, فَطِيرٌ مَحْشِيٌّ بِلَحْمٍ. Printer's pie, تَخْلِيطٌ مِنَ ٱلْأَحْرُفِ. *See also* Magpie, *n.*

Piebald, *a.* أَبْلَق *fem.* بَلْقَآء *pl.* بُلْق.

Piece, *n.* A bit of anything, قِطْعَة *pl.* قِطَع ـ شِقْص *pl.* شِقَاص ـ شِقَّة *pl.* شِقَق ـ شَقَفَة *pl.* شَقَفَات ـ جُزْء *pl.* أَجْزَآء ـ جِثَّة *pl.* جِثَث ـ حَبَّة. A slice, شَرِيحَة ـ فِلْذَة ـ شَرْحَة. A small —, A — of cloth put on to another, a patch, رُقْعَة; a rag, خِرْقَة. A — of land, قُطْعَة *pl.* قُطَع ـ قِطْعَةُ حَقْلٍ ـ دَبْرَة ـ مَشَارَة ـ بُقْعَة *pl.* بِقَاع. A — of money, قِطْعَةٌ سِكَّةٍ *pl.* قِطَع. A — of bread, كِسْرَة خُبْزٍ *pl.* كِسَر ـ قُشَام ـ قُصَاص ـ قُصَص ـ كِسْفَة. A fragment, شَقَفَة *pl.* شَقَفَات ـ شُتَامَة ـ كِسَر. A —, that is, a whole —, as of cloth, ثَوْب *pl.* ثِيَاب ـ طَاقَة *pl.* طَاقَات ـ مَقْطَعُ قُمَاشٍ. A theatrical —, رِوَايَةٌ (or سِيرَةٌ) يُشَخِّصُهَا أَهْلُ ٱلتِّيَاتْرُو *pl.* مَقَاطِيع (*or* ٱلْمَرْسَحِ ٱلْعَامِّ). A —, literary composition, تَأْلِيف *pl.* تَآلِيفَات ـ تَصْنِيف. A model, as for coin, قِطْعَةُ ٱلسِّكَّةِ ـ قِطْعَة. A — of water, بِرْكَة *pl.* بِرَك ـ بُحَيْرَة ـ مُسْتَنْقَعُ مَآءٍ ـ نَامَة. A — of ordnance, مِدْفَع *pl.* مَدَافِع. A — joined to another, وُصْلَة *pl.* وُصْلَات. A — of business, a circumstance, أَمْر *pl.* أُمُور ـ قَضِيَّة *pl.* قَضَايَا. An act, فِعْل ـ عَمَل; a — of benevolence, مَعْرُوف; a — of impudence, وَقَاحَة. Piece by —, قِطْعَةً قِطْعَةً ـ شَيْئًا فَشَيْئًا. A-piece, الْوَاحِد: they cost so much apiece, بَلَغَ ثَمَنُ كُلِّ مِنْهَا كَذَا. In pieces, broken to pieces, مُرَضْرَض ـ مُكَسَّر ـ مَهْدُوم. In pieces or parts, جُزْءًا جُزْءًا. The other —, part, ٱلْقِسْمُ ٱلثَّانِي. To break into (small) pieces, to crush, *v.t.* كَسَّرَ ـ حَطَّمَ ـ رَضَّ ـ رَضْرَضَ ـ سَحَقَ. To destroy, pull down, هَدَمَ.

To break into pieces, *v.i.* تَكَسَّرَ ـ إِرْتَضَّ ـ تَرَضَّضَ.

To fall to pieces, تَحَطَّمَ ـ إِنْحَطَمَ ـ حَطِمَ.

To fly to pieces, تَطَايَرَ ـ تَفَقَّعَ ـ إِنْصَدَعَ ـ تَصَدَّعَ.

To hew in pieces, قَطَّعَ.

To pull to pieces, to tear, شَرَطَ ـ مَزَّقَ. To unsew, take to pieces, فَكَّكَ ـ فَكَّ ـ فَتَّقَ ـ فَتَقَ. To pluck asunder, loosen, as of cotton, فَتَّقَ. To rend, disjoin, unstitch, فَتَّكَ.

To be pulled to pieces, unsewn, إِنْفَتَقَ ـ تَفَتَّقَ. To be pulled to pieces, torn, تَمَزَّقَ. To criticise, vilify, نَقَدَ ـ هَتَكَ ـ تَوَرَّكَ عَلَى.

To tear in pieces, as a wild beast, إِفْتَرَسَ.

Piece, *v.t.* To enlarge by adding a piece, وَصَلَ ـ بِ *aor.* يَصِلُ.

To patch, رَقَّعَ.

Piece, *v.i.* تَوَصَّلَ بِ ـ إِتَّصَلَ بِ.

Pieceless, *a.* *See* Entire, *a.*

Piecemeal, *a.* Separate, مُنْفَرِدٌ ـ مُتَجَرِّدٌ ـ مُفَصَّلٌ ـ مُنْفَصِلٌ.

Piecemeal, *ad.* قِطْعَةً قِطْعَةً ـ شَيْئًا فَشَيْئًا.

Piecer, *n.* *See* Patcher, *n.*

Pied, *a.* *See* Particoloured, Speckled, Piebald, *a.*

Pier, *n.* The support of an arch, صُدْغُ قَنْطَرَةٍ *pl.* أَصْدَاغٌ. A support, stand, عُمْدَةٌ *pl.* عُمَدٌ ـ عِمَادٌ ـ دِعَامَةٌ. The space between two windows, مَا بَيْنَ طَاقَتَيْنِ. A mound or mole to break the force of water, رَصَفٌ ـ رَصَفَةٌ. A quay, jetty, رَصِيفٌ ـ إِسْكَلَةٌ (in the Persian Gulf called a بُلْط).

Pierage, *n.* مَكْسُ ٱلْإِسْكَلَةِ.

Pierce, *v.t.* To enter, دَخَلَ ـ جَازَ فِي ـ أَنْفَذَ ـ نَفَذَ. To make a hole in, ثَقَبَ ـ خَرَمَ ـ نَقَبَ. To —, as with a spear, arrow, sword, خَزَقَ ـ شَجَرَ ـ بِ ـ لَهَزَ ـ سَنَّ ـ رَشَقَ ـ طَعَنَ ـ بِ. To —, as with a needle or a sting, غَرَزَ ـ بِ. To — with the tongue, لَسَعَ ـ لِسَانًا. To touch the affections, رَاعَ *aor.* يَرُوعُ : حَرَّكَ ـ نَجَعَ فِي ـ هَاجَ. To —, to open, فَتَحَ. To be pierced, bored, إِنْثَقَبَ ـ إِنْخَرَمَ; to be pierced, as with a sword, *etc.*, طُعِنَ ـ إِنْخَزَقَ. Pierced with arrows, مَرْشُوقٌ بِٱلسِّهَامِ. *See also to* Penetrate, Perforate, Move, *v.t.*

Pierceable, *a.* *See* Penetrable, *a.*

Piercer, *n.* The tool, مِثْقَبٌ ـ خِلَالٌ ـ مِبْزَلٌ ـ مِجْوَابٌ.

Piercing, *a.* *See* Keen, *a.*

Piercingly, *ad.* *See* Keenly, *ad.*

Piercingness, *n.* *See* Keenness, *n.*

Pier-glass, *n.* مِرْآةٌ كَبِيرَةٌ بَيْنَ طَاقَتَيْنِ.

Pietism, *n.* تَصَوُّفٌ. *See also under* Fanaticism, *n.*

Pietist, *n.* صُوفِيٌّ *pl.* صُوفِيُّونَ *and* صُوفِيَّةٌ. *See also* Fanatic *and* Devotee, *n.*

Piety, *n.* وَرَعٌ ـ دِيَانَةٌ ـ دِينٌ ـ تَزَهُّدٌ ـ زُهْدٌ ـ صَلَاحٌ ـ حِكْمَةٌ ـ تَقْوَى ـ وُرُوعٌ. Filial —, بِرُّ ٱلْوَالِدَيْنِ. To practise —, تَزَهَّدَ ـ وَرِعَ *aor.* يَرِعُ ـ إِتَّقَى.

Pig, *n.* The animal, خِنْزِيرٌ *pl.* خَنَازِيرُ; a young —, خِنَّوْصٌ *pl.* خَنَانِيصُ. A mass, as of metal, سَبِيكَةٌ *pl.* سَبَائِكُ.

Pig, *v.t.* or *i.* To litter, of a pig, خَلَّفَتِ (or وَضَعَتِ) ٱلْخِنْزِيرَةُ.

To pig together, تَعَايَشُوا مِثْلَ ٱلْخَنَازِيرِ.

Pigeon, *n.* يَمَامَةٌ *coll.* يَمَامٌ *pl.* يَمَامَاتٌ ـ حَمَامٌ *pl.* حَمَائِمُ ـ حَمَامَةٌ *pl.* حَمَامَاتٌ. A ring —, حَمَامٌ مُطَوَّقٌ; a tumbling —, حَمَامٌ مَرْعَشٌ; a — with feathered legs, حَمَامَةٌ مُسَرْوَلَةٌ. The carrier —, حَمَامُ ٱلزَّاجِلِ; carrier pigeons, مَنَاسِيبُ.

Pigeon-breasted, *a.* أَزْوَرُ *fem.* زَوْرَآءُ *pl.* زُورٌ ـ مُتَقَاعِسٌ ـ قَعِسٌ ـ أَبْزَى ـ زُوْرٌ.

Pigeon-hearted, *a.* خَوَّافٌ ـ مُخَيَّبٌ ـ فَشِيلٌ ـ خَشِلٌ فَشِلٌ.

Pigeon-hole, *n.* A small aperture to let in light, سَهْوَةٌ *pl.* سِهَآءٌ. A division in a case, بَيْتٌ *pl.* بُيُوتٌ. A place where things are put and neglected, زَاوِيَةُ ٱلْإِهْمَالِ *pl.* زَوَايَا.

Pigeon-house, *n.* بَيْتُ حَمَامٍ. A pigeon-turret, بُرْجُ حَمَامٍ *pl.* بُرُوجٌ.

Pig-eyed, *a.* أَخْفَشُ *fem.* خَفْشَآءُ *pl.* خُفْشٌ.

Piggery, *n.* مَحَلُّ ٱلْخَنَازِيرِ.

Piggin, *n.* *See* Dipper, *n.*

Pig-headed, *a.* *See* Obstinate, *a.*

Pig-headedness, *n.* *See* Obstinacy, *n.*

Pig-iron, *n.* سَبِيكَةُ حَدِيدٍ.

Pig-lead, *n.* سَبِيكَةُ رَصَاصٍ.

Pigmean, *a.* *See* Dwarf, Dwarfish, *a.*

Pigment, *n.* صِبْغَةٌ ـ صِبْغٌ *pl.* أَصْبَاغٌ ـ نِقْشٌ. Red —, عَقَارٌ ـ زُنْجُفْرٌ. *See also* Paint, Cosmetic, *n.*

Pigmental, *a.* مَا نِيطَ بِٱلْأَصْبَاغِ.

Pigmy, *n.* *See* Dwarf, *n.*

Pig-nut, *n.* *See* Ground-nut, *n.*

Pigsty, *n.* مَحَلُّ ٱلْخَنَازِيرِ ـ زَرِيبَةُ ٱلْخَنَازِيرِ.

Pigtail, *n.* The tail of a pig, عُصْعُصُ ٱلْخِنْزِيرِ. The tail or end of anything, ذَيْلٌ *pl.* أَذْيَالٌ. A roll of tobacco, لِفَافٌ مِنْ وَرَقِ ٱلتَّبْغِ.

Pike, *n.* A spear, حَرْبَةٌ *pl.* حِرَابٌ ـ مِطْرَدٌ *pl.* مَطَارِدُ ـ خِشْتٌ *pl.* خُشُوتٌ. The fish, سَمَكُ ٱلْكَرَاكِيِّ.

Piked, *a.* Acuminated, حُدَّاد ـ مُوَتَّل ـ مُؤَنَّف.

Pikeman, *n.* حَامِلُ حَرْبَةٍ *pl.* حَمَلَةُ ٱلْحِرَابِ.

Pikestaff, *n.* قَنَاةُ ٱلْحَرْبَةِ *pl.* قَنًا *and* قَنَوَات.

Pilaster, *n.* عِضَادَة *pl.* عِضَادَات ـ عَمُودٌ مُرَبَّعٌ *pl.* عُمُدٌ مُرَبَّعَةٌ.

Pilastered, *a.* ذُو عِضَادَاتٍ ـ ذُو عُمُدٍ مُرَبَّعَةٍ.

Pilau, *n.* رُزٌّ مُفَلْفَل.

Pilchard, *n.* سَرْدِينَة ـ راى.

Pile, *n.* A mass, كُومَة *pl.* أَكْوَام ـ كُدْس ـ كُدَاسَة. An edifice, عِمَارَة *pl.* عَمَائِرُ ـ بَنِيَّة *pl.* بَنَايَا. A lofty building, عِمَادَة *coll.* عِمَاد. A stake, وَتَد *pl.* أَوْتَاد. A —, as of muskets, حُزْمَة. Pile of cloth, *etc.*; (*see* Nap). A — of stones, أَكَمَة *pl.* أَكَمَات ـ رَجْمَة ـ رِجَام *pl.* رُجَم. A funeral —, كُومَةُ حَطَبٍ لِإِحْرَاقِ ٱلْجُثَّةِ. A galvanic —, بَطَّارِيَّةٌ غَلْوَانِيَّةٌ.

Pile, *v.t.* To heap up, كَوَّمَ ـ كَدَّسَ ـ كَرَّسَ ـ رَكَمَ [2]. To raise on piles, أَوْتَدَ ـ وَتَّدَ. To drive piles, نَصَبَ عَلَى أَوْتَادٍ [2]. To be piled together, تَرَاكَمَ ـ اِرْتَكَمَ ـ تَرَكَّبَ بَعْضُهُ عَلَى بَعْضٍ ـ تَكَوَّمَ.

Piled, *a.* Heaped together, مُتَكَوِّم ـ مُتَرَاكِم. Piled, as muskets, مُتَحَزِّم. Supported on piles, مَنْصُوبٌ عَلَى أَوْتَادٍ. Having nap, مُخَمَّل ـ مُزَأْبَر. Long-piled, having a long pile, of cloth, *etc.*, أَغْثَر.

Pile-driver, *n.* } آلَةٌ لِدَقِّ ٱلْأَوْتَادِ ـ طَبْطَابَة.
Pile-engine, }

Piles, *n.* The disease; *see* Hemorrhoids, *n.*

Pilfer, *v.t.* اِخْتَلَسَ ـ أَسَلَّ ـ اِسْتَرَقَ ـ تَسَرَّقَ.

Pilfered, *a.* مَسْرُوق ـ مُخْتَلَس ـ مَسْلُوب.

Pilferer, *n.* سَارِق *pl.* سَرَقَة *and* سُرَّاق ـ سَلَّال ـ سَالّ.

Pilfering, *n.* تَتَبُّعُ ٱلسَّرِقَةِ ـ سَرِقَة ـ إِسْلَال ـ اِخْتِلَاس ـ الغَشّ الدُّون.

Pill-garlick, *n.* } صُعْلُوك *pl.* صَعَالِيك ـ مِسْكِين.
Pilled-garlick, }

Pilgrim, *n.* A visitor to any sacred place, زَائِر *pl.* زُوَّار *fem.* زَائِرَة *pl.* زَائِرَات. A — to Jerusalem, مَقْدِسِيّ *pl.* مَقَادِسَة; to Mekkah, حَاجّ *pl.* حُجَّاج *fem.* حَاجَّة *pl.* حَاجَّات. A —, in the Scriptural sense of a sojourner, stranger, غَرِيب *pl.* غُرَبَآء.

Pilgrimage, *n.* A visit to some holy shrine, زِيَارَة; to perform such, زَارَ [2]. The — to Jerusalem, زِيَارَةُ ٱلْقُدْسِ; to perform such, تَقَدَّسَ. The — to Mekkah, حِجَّة ـ حِجّ ـ حَجّ; to perform such, حَجَّ [2] ـ اِحْتَجَّ ـ حَجَّ ٱلْبَيْتَ: they performed the — to Mekkah, حَجُّوا مَكَّةَ. He made a vow to perform five pilgrimages, نَذَرَ خَمْسَ حِجَجٍ [2]. The body of pilgrims, الحَاجّ ـ الحَجِيج. By the — of God! as an oath, وَحَجَّةِ ٱللّٰهِ. Pilgrimage, in the Scriptural sense, غُرْبَة.

Piliferous, *a.* } Bearing hair, حَامِلُ (*or*) نَابِتُ شَعْرٍ. Hairy,
Piligerous, } شَعْرَانِيّ ـ شَعِر.

Pill, *n.* حَبَّة ـ حَبّ *pl.* حُبُوب. To make into pills, حَبَّبَ. To gild the pill, of something disagreeable, حَلَّى; to swallow the —, something unpleasant, بَلِعَ ٱلْمُرَّ. It was a bitter — for him to swallow, كَانَ شَجًا فِي حَلْقِهِ.

Pillage, *n.* The act of pillaging, نَهْب ـ سَلْب. What is pillaged, نُهْبَة ـ نَهْب ـ سَلَب. *See also* Booty, *n.*

Pillage, *v.t.* اِنْتَهَبَ ـ سَلَبَ [2] ـ نَهَبَ [2]. To allow to be pillaged, أَنْهَبَ. Their houses were pillaged, نُهِبَتْ بُيُوتُهُمْ.

Pillager, *n.* نَاهِب *pl.* نَهَّاب ـ نَهَّابَة *pl.* نَهَّابَة ـ سَلَّاب *pl.* سَلَّابَة.

Pillaged, *a.* مَسْلُوب ـ سَلِيب.

Pillar, *n.* A column, عَمُود *pl. of pauc.*, أَعْمِدَة *of mult.*, عُمُد. The base of anything, قَاعِدَة *pl.* قَوَاعِد. عُمْدَة *pl.* عُمَد ـ عِمَاد. A support of stone, عِضَادَة. A stay or support of anything or person, عُمْدَة ـ عِمَاد ـ عَمِيد. A monument, بِنَآء *pl.* أَبْنِيَة. An iron —, عَمُودٌ حَدِيدٌ. The pillars of state, أَرْكَانُ ٱلدَّوْلَةِ. To support on pillars, عَمَّدَ ـ جَعَلَ عَلَى أَعْمِدَةٍ; to be so supported, تَعَمَّدَ.

Pillared, *a.* Like a pillar, مِثْلَ ٱلْعَمُودِ. Supported on pillars, مُسْنَدٌ عَلَى أَعْمِدَةٍ. Having pillars, ذُو ٱلْعِمَادِ.

Pillau, *n.* *See* Pilau, *n.*

Pillion, *n.* A saddle for a woman (on a camel), مِحَفَّة ـ حِدَاج ـ هَوْدَج. To ride —, *i.e.* behind another, اِسْتَرْدَفَ; one who so rides, زَمِيل.

Pillory, *n.* (The nearest approach to this in Arabic is the جِنَاك with which the neck of a captive is bound, preventing him from turning his head; or the حِمَار, literally, donkey, consisting of a triangle of wood to which he is tied for punishment.)

Pillory, *v.t.* To put into a pillory, رَكَّبَ ٱلْحِمَارَ ـ لَبَّسَ ٱلْجِنَاكَ. To expose a criminal to public disgrace, أَعْرَضَ ٱلْمُذْنِبَ لِلنَّاسِ ـ جَرَّسَ بِٱلْمُذْنِبِ.

Pillow, *n.* وِسَادَة *pl.* وُسُد *and* وَسَائِد ـ مِصْدَغَة ـ مِنْبَذَة ـ مِخَدَّة *pl.* مَخَدَّات.

Pillow, *v.t.* وَسَّدَ ـ وَسَّدَ بِمَخَدَّاتٍ. To be pillowed, تَوَسَّدَ ـ اِتَّكَى عَلَى ٱلْمَخَدَّاتِ.

Pillow-case, *n.* غِطَآءُ مِخَدَّةٍ *pl.* أَغْطِيَة ـ وَجْهُ مِخَدَّةٍ.

Pillowed, *a.* Supported by pillows, مُوَسَّدٌ عَلَى ٱلْمِخَدَّاتِ.

Pilose, *a.*
Pilous, } *See* Hairy, Downy, *a.*

Pilosity, *n.* *See* Hairiness, *n.*

Pilot, *n.* As of a ship, رُبَّان – رُبَّانِيٌّ *pl.* رُبَّانِيَّة – مُسْتَعْمِل – مُسْتَعْمِلُ مَرْكَب ; *Turkish*, قَلاغُوز. *See also* Guide, *n.*

Pilot, *v.t.* To — a ship, كَانَ رُبَّانَ ٱلْمَرْكَبِ – دَبَّرَ ٱلْمَرْكَبَ – كَانَ مُسْتَعْمِلَ ٱلْمَرْكَبِ. *See also to* Guide.

Pilotage, *n.* The pay of a pilot, أُجْرَةُ ٱلرُّبَّانِ – أُجْرَةُ ٱلْمُسْتَعْمِلِ.

Pilot-boat, *n.* قَارِبُ ٱلرُّبَّانِ – قَارِبُ ٱلْمُسْتَعْمِلِ.

Pilot-fish, *n.* نَوْعٌ مِنْ سَمَكِ ٱلْبَحْرِ.

Piloting, *n.* تَدْبِيرُ ٱلرُّبَّانِ – تَدْبِيرُ ٱلْمُسْتَعْمِلِ.

Pimento, *n.* بَهَار. *See also* Allspice, *n.*

Pimp, *n.* *See* Pander, *n.*

Pimp, *v.i.* *See to* Pander, *v.i.*

Pimpernel, *n.*
Pimpinel, } The plant, مَرِيجَانَة – أَنَاغَالِيس.

Pimple, *n.* ظَبْظَاب – بَثْر *pl.* بُثُور – دُمَّلَة *pl.* دَمَامِل – حَبٌّ *pl.* حُبُوب. Pimples, pustules, سُلَاق – خُرَاج. To be affected with pimples, إِنْسَلَقَ. To break out in pimples, بَثِرَ – تَبَثَّرَ – تَحَبَّبَ. To make to break out into pimples, بَثَّرَ. Our mouths broke out into pimples, سُلِقَتْ أَفْوَاهُنَا.

Pimpled, *a.*
Pimply, } مُبَثَّر – كَثِيرُ ٱلْبُثُورِ – مُدَمَّل – ذُو خُرَاجٍ.

Pin, *n.* With which one pins a garment, *etc.*, خِلَال *pl.* أَخِلَّة – دَبُّوس *pl.* دَبَابِيس – إِبْرَة *pl.* إِبَر – دَبَابِيس. An iron —, سَكّ *pl.* سِكَاك *and* سُكُوك. A peg, عَيْر *pl.* عِيَار. A dowel, دِسَار *pl.* دُسُر. A rivet, عِرْزَان *pl.* أَعْرِزَة. A hair —, مِشْقَاة – مِدْرَاة. The — of a pulley, مِحْوَر – سَفُّود. A pivot, مَدَار; the — or pivot of a door, عَقِب *pl.* أَعْقَاب. The pin or peg, as of a musical instrument, مِلْوَى *pl.* مَلَاوِي. A small ornament, مَصَاغ – جَوْهَرَة. To have the feeling of "pins and needles," نَمِلَ. Not to care a pin for, إِسْتَحْقَرَ – إِسْتَقَلَّ. He does not care a pin, مَا يُبَالِي ٱلْبَتَّةَ. *See also* Peg, *n.*

Pin, *v.t.* To fasten with a common pin, خَلَّ (or شَكَّ) – أَحْكَمَ بِدَبُّوسٍ. To fix, رَكَزَ – رَكَّزَ – أَرْسَخَ – أَحْكَمَ. To seize, ضَبَطَ – قَبَضَ – بَطَشَ بِ. To pin one down to, to oblige, to ..., أَلْزَمَ بِ ; to bind one hand and foot, so as to render him helpless to move in a matter, غَلَّ يَدَهُ عَنْ. To pin, to nail, سَمَّرَ. *See also to* Peg, *v.t.*

Pinafore, *n.* نِقَاض. *See also* Apron, *n.*

Pincase, *n.* بَيْتٌ لِلدَّبَابِيسِ – ظَرْف *pl.* ظُرُوف دَبَابِيس.

Pincers, *n.* كَلْبَتَانِ – كُلَّابَة – كَمَّاشَة. A blacksmith's —, قِرْزِل – كَلْبَتَانِ. Small — for pulling out hairs, مِلْقَط.

Pinch, *v.t.* To squeeze with the fingers, نَتَشَ – مَرَزَ – مَرَّزَ – قَرَصَ. To gripe, compress, حَزَقَ. To stint, to grudge, ضَيَّقَ عَلَى – نَفِسَ عَلَى. To — with the nails, قَطَفَ – قَطَّفَ. To hurt, to give pain to, آلَمَ – أَوْجَعَ. To behave hardly to, ضَغَطَ عَلَى – آذَى – قَاسَى – أَسَاءَ إِلَى. It (the shoe) pinched him, حَزَقَ رِجْلَهُ – ضَغَطَ رِجْلَهُ. To be pinched, contracted, shrivelled, تَقَلَّصَ – تَقَبَّضَ – انْقَبَضَ. Pinched with a tight boot, حَازِق. No counsel is possible to one who is pinched with a tight boot, (*prov.*) لَا رَأْيَ لِحَازِقٍ. *See also to* Nip, *v.t.*

Pinch, *v.i.* To be hard, distressing, صَعُبَ – عَسُرَ – تَعَسَّرَ. To be sparing, اِقْتَصَدَ – تَقَشَّفَ. To be straitened, تَضَايَقَ – تَضَيَّقَ.

Pinch, *n.* A squeeze with the fingers, قَرْص – قَرْصَة. A compression, ضَغْط – حَزْق. A — with the nails, قَطْف. What can be taken up by the fingers, قُبْصَة – قَبْصَة – قَبِيصَة – قُرْزَة – نُتْفَة *pl.* نُتَف. Pinch, difficulty, straits, ضُغْطَة – ضِيق – مُضَايَقَة – عُسْر. At a —, عِنْدَ ٱلِاضْطِرَارِ – عِنْدَ ٱلضَّرُورَةِ. A —, as of snuff, شَمَّة – تَنْشِيقَة.

Pinched, *a.* *See under to* Pinch, *v.t.*

Pinchbeck, *n.* The metal, مَعْدِنٌ خَلِيطُ ٱلصُّفْرِ وَٱلْخَارْصِينِي (or ٱلتُّوتِيَاءِ).

Pinchers, *n.* كُلَّاب *pl.* كَلَالِيب.

Pinching, *n.* *See* Pinch, *n.*

Pincushion, *n.* مِغْرَزُ ٱلدَّبَابِيسِ وَٱلْإِبَرِ.

Pine, *n.* The tree, أَرْز *coll.* أَرْزَة – صَنَوْبَر – شَجَرَةُ ٱلصَّنَوْبَرِ ; a — cone, صَنَوْبَر – جَوْزُ ٱلصَّنَوْبَرِ. The ground —, عَرْصَف. The gum of the — tree, عِلْك *pl.* عُلُوك.

Pine, *v.i.* To grow emaciated, هَزِلَ – اِخْتَلَّ جِسْمُهُ – ذَابَ جِسْمُهُ. To languish, اِكْتَرَبَ – تَعَنَّى. To —, as under a passion, ضَنِيَ – اِنْسَقَمَ. To — for, to bemoan, حَزِنَ عَلَى – تَحَسَّرَ عَلَى ; to long for, نَافَسَ فِي – تَنَافَسَ فِي – جَادَ إِلَى *aor.* يَجُودُ – اِشْتَاقَ إِلَى – حَنَّ إِلَى.

Pine-apple, *a.* أَنَانَاس – عَيْنُ ٱلنَّاسِ.

Pine-barren, *n.* حِرْشُ صَنَوْبَرٍ.

Pinery, *n.* Of pine-apples, صِوَانُ ٱلْأَنَانَاسِ.

Pinhole, *n.* خَرْقُ دَبُّوسٍ.

Pining, *n.* The act of wasting away, هَزْل – اِخْتِلَال ; of languishing, تَعَنٍّ — إِكْتِرَاب ; of longing for, جَوًى إِلَى — إِشْتِيَاقٌ إِلَى — حَنِينٌ إِلَى.

Pinion, *n.* The end of the wing, طَرَفُ ٱلْجَنَاحِ — كَتِف *pl.* أَكْتَاف. A wing, جَنَاح *pl.* أَجْنِحَة. A feather, رِيشَة *coll.* رِيش. The — of a wheel, جَنَاحُ عَجَلَةٍ. Fetters for the arms, صِفَاد — قَيْد *pl.* قُيُود.

Pinion, *v.t.* To tie the wings, رَبَطَ ٱلْأَجْنِحَةَ [2]. To cut the wing, قَصَّ ٱلْأَكْنَافَ [2]. To — the arms, قَيَّدَ — قَيَّدَ ٱلْأَعْضَادَ.

Pinioned, *a.* Having the wings cut, مَقْصُوصُ ٱلْأَجْنَاحِ. Having wings, ذُو أَجْنَاحٍ. Shackled, مَرْبُوط — مُقَيَّد.

Pink, *n.* The flower, قَرَنْفُل. A rose colour, لَوْنٌ وَرْدِيٌّ. The — of perfection, عَيْنُ ٱلْكَمَالِ — صَاحِبُ كَمَالٍ.

Pink, *v.t.* To work with eyelet holes, عَيَّنَ.

Pinked, *a.* With eyelet holes, مُعَيَّن.

Pinking, *n.* تَعْيِين.

Pin-maker, *n.* صَانِعُ ٱلدَّبَابِيسِ *pl.* صُنَّاع.

Pin-money, *n.* رَاتِبٌ لِنَفَقَةِ ٱلنِّسَاءِ.

Pinnace, *n.* A small vessel, مَرْكَبٌ صَغِيرٌ. The — of a man-of-war, فَلُوكَة.

Pinnacle, *v.t.* To furnish with pinnacles, شَرَّفَ.

Pinnacle, *n.* A turret, شُرْفَة *pl.* شُرَف *and* شُرُفَات — شُرَّفَة. A summit, قُلَّة *pl.* قُلَل — قِمَّة *pl.* قِمَم — شَعَفَة *pl.* شُعُوف *and* شِعَاف.

Pinnacled, *a.* Turreted, ذُو شُرَفٍ — شَرْفَآء.

Pinnate, *a.* }
Pinnated, } ذُو وُرَيْقَاتٍ عَلَى ٱلْجَانِبَيْنِ.

Pinner, *n.* *See* Pin-maker, *n.*

Pint, *n.* بَيْنت وَهُوَ مِكْيَالُ ٱلْمَوَائِعِ يَسَعُ ١٤٥ دِرْهَمًا — ثُمْنُ ٱلْكَالَن. *See under* Gallon, *n.*

Pintail, *n.* } An iron pin, سَكّ *pl.* سِكَاك *and* سُكُوك. The
Pintle, } hooks on which a rudder hangs, حَلَقُ ٱلدَّفَّةِ.

Piny, *a.* Abounding in pines, كَثِيرُ ٱلصَّنَوْبَرِ.

Pioneer, *n.* As of an army, بَلْطَجِي *pl.* بَلْطَجِيَّة. Pioneers, ٱلْبَلْطَجِيَّة وَأَهْلُ ٱلْأَلْغَامِ. One who prepares the way for others, مُسَلِّكُ ٱلطُّرُقِ.

Pioneer, *v.t.* هَيَّأَ ٱلطَّرِيقَ — سَلَّكَ ٱلطُّرُقَ.

Pious, *a.* صَالِح *pl.* صُلَحَآء — قَانِت — مُتَّقٍ — وَرِع — وَرِيع — تَقِيّ *pl.* أَتْقِيَآء — مُتَدَيِّن — دَيِّن — رَبَّانِيّ.

Piously, *ad.* بِتَقْوَى — بِوَرَعٍ — بِوُرُوعٍ — تَدَيُّنًا.

Pious-minded, *a.* تَقَوِيّ.

Pip, *n.* A seed, as of an orange, *etc*, عَجَم *pl.* أَعْجَام — عَجَمَة *pl.* عَجَمَات. A disease in birds, دَآءٌ يَحْصُلُ لِلْعَصَافِيرِ. A — in cards, نُقْطَة *pl.* نُقَط — فَصّ *pl.* فُصُوص.

Pip, *v.i.* *See to* Chirp, *v.i.*

Pipe, *n.* A tube, أُنْبُوب *pl.* أَنَابِيبُ — قَصَبَة *coll.* قَصَب. The — which conveys the water from a roof, إِرْدَبَّة — بَرْبَخ ; an ordinary — for conveying water, سَرَب. A musical —, نَاي — مِزْمَار — شَبَّابَة — مِنْ قَصَبٍ. A whistle, صَفَّارَة. A — for smoking having a long stem, شُبُك *pl.* شُبُكَات — دَوَايَة — عُود *pl.* عِيدَان — قَصَبَة *pl.* قَصَبَات — غَلْيُون *pl.* غَلَايِينُ. A water — for smoking, made of glass, شِيشَة *pl.* شِيَش ; made of a cocoa-nut, نَارْجِيلَة *pl.* نَرَاجِيلُ — أَرْجِيلَة *pl.* أَرَاجِيلُ. The voice, ٱلصَّوْتُ. A cask, دَنّ *pl.* دِنَان. A whiff, as of a —, نَفَس *pl.* أَنْفَاس. The — does not go, being stopped up, ٱلْغَلْيُونُ مَا يَشْتَغِلُ (*or* مَا يَتَنَفَّسُ). Iron pipes, أَنَابِيبُ مِنْ حَدِيدٍ.

Pipe, *v.t.* and *i.* To play on a pipe, زَمَّرَ. To whistle or pipe as a bird, صَفَّرَ. *See also to* Whistle, *v.t.*

Pipeclay, *n.* طَبَاشِير. Tailor's —, طَبَاشِيرُ ٱلْخَيَّاطِ.

Pipeclay, *v.t.* طَلَا بِٱلطَّبَاشِيرِ *aor.* يَطْلُو.

Piped, *a.* Formed with a tube, ذُو أُنْبُوبٍ — مُلَوْلَب.

Piper, *n.* A player on a pipe, زَمَّار *fem.* زَامِرَة.

Piperin, *n.* رُوحُ ٱلْفِلْفِلِ.

Piping, *a.* Making a piping noise, صَفَّار — زَامِر — صَافِر. Feeble, ضَعِيف. Burning, مُحْرِق : piping hot, حَارٌّ لِلْغَايَةِ — أَجَّاج.

Piping, *n.* Whistling, تَصْفِير — صَفِير. Playing on a pipe, زَمْر — زَمِير. The —, as of a dress, شَرِيط — زِيقَة. Tubing, مَتَاعُ ٱلْأَنَابِيبِ — أَنَابِيبُ.

Pipkin, *n.* بُرْمَة *pl.* بُرَم — جَرَّة *pl.* جِرَر.

Pippin, *n.* ضَرْبٌ مِنَ ٱلتُّفَّاحِ.

Piquancy, *n.* Pungency, حَرَارَة — حِدَّة. Attractiveness, طَلَاوَة — لَطَافَة — مَلَاحَة. Sharpness, severity, حِدَّة — جَفَآء — قَسَاوَة — سَلَاطَة.

Piquant, *a.* Pungent, أُجَاج — حَرِيف — قَارِص — حَادّ. Sarcastic, سَلِيط. Pleasing, حَبَّذَا — لَطِيف. Offensive, جَارِح — مُؤْلِم — نَاقِر — نَاكِث فِي.

Piquantly, *ad.* Sharply, tartly, بِحِدَّةٍ ; sarcastically, بِسَلَاطَةٍ. Attractively, بِطَلَاوَةٍ — بِلَطَافَةٍ — بِمَلَاحَةٍ.

Pique, *n.* Slight offence taken, تَظَلُّم — شَكْوَى — إِشْتِكَآء — إِسْتِآء. A difference, misunderstanding, إِرْتِبَاك — شِقَاق. Spite, حِقْد — حَنَق.

Pique, *v.t.* To excite, أَنْهَضَ. To nettle, لَسَعَ — نَقَرَ [2] — أَوْغَرَ —

To — one as to his honour, أَثَارَ فِي رَأْسِهِ ٱلنَّخْوَةَ ـ نَخَّى ـ جَرَّحَ. He was piqued in his honour, ثَارَتْ فِي رَأْسِهِ ٱلنَّخْوَةُ. To — one's self, إِدَّعَى ـ تَصَلَّفَ ـ صَلِفَ.

Piquet, *n.* ضَرْبٌ مِنْ لَعْبِ ٱلْوَرَقِ.

Piracy, *n.* On the seas, قَطْعُ ـ إِصَابَةُ ٱلْبَحْرِ ـ ضَرْبُ ٱلْمَرَاكِبِ ـ لُصُوصِيَّةٌ فِي ٱلْبَحْرِ ـ ٱلْبَحْرِ. Piracy of literature, إِنْتِحَالُ ٱلْمُؤَلَّفَاتِ بِدُونِ إِذْنِ ٱلْمُؤَلِّفِ. *See also* Plagiarism, *n.*

Pirate, *n.* On the seas, قَاطِعُ ـ ضَرَّابَةٌ *pl.* ضَرَّابُ ٱلْمَرَاكِبِ ـ قَرَاصِنَةٌ *pl.* قُرْصَانٌ ـ لُصُوصٌ *pl.* لِصٌّ فِي ٱلْبَحْرِ ـ ٱلْبَحْرِ. One who appropriates the literature of others, مُنْتَحِلُ ٱلْمُؤَلَّفَاتِ بِدُونِ إِذْنِ مُؤَلِّفِيهَا. *See also* Plagiarist, *n.*

Pirate, *v.t.* To appropriate without permission, إِنْتَحَلَ ـ بِدُونِ إِذْنٍ ـ إِخْتَلَسَ. *See also to* Plagiarize, *v.t.*

Pirate, *v.i.* To rob on the sea, أَصَابَ ـ تَلَصَّصَ عَلَى ٱلْبَحْرِ ـ قَرْصَنَ ـ ضَرَبَ ٱلْمَرَاكِبَ ـ قَطَعَ ٱلْبَحْرَ ـ ٱلْبَحْرَ.

Piratical, *a.* مُقَرْصِنٌ ـ ضَارِبُ ٱلْمَرَاكِبِ ـ قَاطِعُ ٱلْبَحْرِ.

Piratically, *ad.* عَلَى سَبِيلِ ٱلْقَرْصَنَةِ ـ عَلَى سَبِيلِ قُطَّاعِ ٱلْبَحْرِ.

Pirating, *a.* *See* Piracy, *n.*

Pirogue, *n.* بَلَمٌ مَصْنُوعٌ مِنْ جِذْلِ شَجَرَةٍ.

Pirouette, *n.* لَفَّةٌ ـ بَرْمَةٌ ـ دَوْرَةٌ ـ حَلْقَةٌ. To make a —, فَتَلَ ـ بَرَمَ ـ دَارَ حَلْقًا.

Piscatorial, *a.* مُتَعَلِّقٌ بِصَيْدِ ٱلسَّمَكِ.

Piscatory, *a.* سَمَكِيٌّ ـ مُتَعَلِّقٌ بِٱلسَّمَكِ.

Pisces, *n.* The constellation, السَّمَكَةُ ـ الحُوتُ. Piscis Australis, الحُوتُ ٱلْجَنُوبِيُّ.

Pisciculture, *n.* تَرْبِيَةُ ٱلسَّمَكِ.

Piscivorous, *a.* مُقْتَاتٌ بِٱلسَّمَكِ ـ آكِلُ ٱلسَّمَكِ.

Piscina, *n.* A sacred washing vessel, مِهْرَاسٌ.

Pish! *int.* أُفٍّ وَتُفٍّ ـ أُفٍّ.

Pish, *v.i.* تَأَفَّفَ ـ يَؤُفُّ *aor.* أَفَّ. To — or say — to one, تَأَفَّفَ بِهِ ـ أَفَّفَ بِهِ ـ أَفَّفَهُ.

Pismire, *n.* The insect; *see* Ant, *n.*

Piss, *v.i.* شَخَّ ـ بَالَ ـ غَاصَ. To — here and there, as a camel, شَقَّحَ ـ أَشْغَرَ. To — as a dog, holding up the leg, شَغَرَ. A place to —, a urinal, مَغَاصٌ *pl.* مَغَائِصُ.

Piss, *n.* شَخٌّ ـ بَوْلٌ ـ غَاصٌ.

Pissabed, *n.* شَخَّاخٌ فِي فِرَاشِهِ ـ مِغْغَاصٌ.

Pistachio, *n.* فُسْتُقٌ ـ الحَبَّةُ ٱلْخَضْرَاءُ. Of a — colour, فُسْتُقِيٌّ ـ لَوْنُ ٱلْفُسْتُقِ.

Pistil, *n.* آلَةُ ٱلْأُنْثَى فِي ٱلنَّبَاتِ.

Pistol, *n.* طَبَنْجَةٌ *pl.* طَبَنْجَاتٌ ـ بَارُودَةٌ *pl.* بَارُودَاتٌ ـ فَرْدٌ *pl.* فُرُودٌ. A pair of pistols, زَوْجُ طَبَنْجَاتٍ.

Pistol, *v.t.* ضَرَبَ ـ طَبَنْجَةً.

Pistole, *n.* سِكَّةُ ذَهَبٍ إِسْبَانِيُولِيَّةٌ.

Piston, *n.* مِكْبَاسٌ ـ مِكْبَاسُ ٱلطُّولُنْبَةِ وَغَيْرِهَا.

Piston-rod, *n.* يَدُ ٱلْمِكْبَاسِ.

Pit, *n.* A cavity in the earth, حُفْرَةٌ *pl.* حُفَرٌ. A hollow, جَوْبَةٌ *pl.* جَوْبَاتٌ ـ وَقْرَةٌ *pl.* وَقَرَاتٌ *and* وُقُورٌ. A mine, مَعْدِنٌ *pl.* مَعَادِنُ. A grave, قَبْرٌ *pl.* قُبُورٌ. A dimple; (*see* Dimple, *n.*) The pit or hollow at the top of the chest between the two collar-bones, ثُغْرَةٌ. A mark, as of the small-pox, *etc.*, أَثَرٌ ـ رَشْمٌ *pl.* رُشُومٌ ـ عَلَامَةٌ *pl.* عَلَامَاتٌ ـ آثَارٌ *pl.* The pit of a theatre, أَرْضُ ٱلْمَلْعَبِ (*or* ٱلتِّيَاتِرُو *or* ٱلْمَرْسَحِ). A pit for fighting, مَصْرَاعٌ ـ مَعْرَكٌ. A pit for taking game; (*see* Pitfall, *n.*) The bottomless pit, hell, جَهَنَّمُ ـ الهَاوِيَةُ. To dig a pit, حَفَرَ حُفْرَةً.

Pit, *v.t.* To hollow, قَوَّرَ. To mark, leave a mark, خَلَّى ـ أَثَّرَ أَثَرًا. To pit one against another, قَابَلَ ـ بِ ـ قَاوَمَ ـ بِ.

Pitapat, *ad.* بِخَفَقَانٍ ـ خَفْقًا. His heart went —, خَفَقَ قَلْبُهُ.

Pitch, *n.* The resin, زِفْتٌ ـ قِيرٌ ـ قَارٌ. Burgundy —, لُبَانٌ شَامِيٌّ. The head-plunge of a ship, غَتٌّ ـ غَطٌّ. A cast, throw, طَرْحَةٌ ـ رَمْيَةٌ. A degree, دَرَجَةٌ ـ رُتْبَةٌ. Size, مِقْدَارٌ ـ قَدْرٌ. Bearing, aspect, مَنْظَرٌ ـ ظَاهِرٌ ـ هَيْئَةٌ. The highest point, degree, حَدٌّ ـ تَمَامٌ ـ غَايَةٌ ـ أَعْلَى دَرَجَةٍ. Inclination, صَغًا ـ مَيْلٌ ـ حُدُورٌ ـ ٱلْحِدَارُ ـ إِنْحِطَاطٌ. Elevation, عُلُوٌّ ـ إِرْتِفَاعٌ. Pitch of the voice, مَقَامُ ٱلصَّوْتِ ـ صَوْتٌ. To rise to a high —, إِرْتَفَعَ ـ طَمَّ ـ يَعْلُو *aor.* عَلَا ـ تَعَالَى. Pitch dark, ظَلِمٌ: a — dark night, لَيْلَةٌ ظَلْمَاءُ.

Pitch, *v.t.* To smear with —, قَيَّرَ ـ زَفَّتَ. To throw, طَرَحَ ـ رَمَى ـ أَرْمَى. To set up, أَقَامَ ـ نَصَبَ ـ صَمَدَ. To — a tent, ضَرَبَ خَيْمَةً. To —, cast down, أَوْقَعَ. To give the key-note, أَعْطَى طَبَقَةَ ٱلنَّغَمِ. He smeared it inside and outside with —, طَلَى مِنْ دَاخِلٍ وَخَارِجٍ بِٱلْقَارِ.

Pitch, *v.i.* To rest from flight, as a bird, قَعَدَ ـ جَثَمَ. To —, as a ship, غَطَسَ ـ غَاصَ ـ إِغْتَطَّ. To —, to put up at a place, نَزَلَ فِي ـ ضَرَبَ فِي. To —, from ... to, رَمَى ـ مِنْ ... إِلَى. To — on, to select, نَقَّى ـ إِخْتَارَ. To — into, as into an affair, أَخَاضَ ـ يَخُوضُ *aor.* خَاضَ فِي ٱلْأَمْرِ. To — into, to scold, عَاتَبَ ـ سَخِطَ عَلَى. To — into, to eat, أَكَلَ مِنْ.

Pitched, *a.* Smeared with pitch, مُزَفَّتٌ ـ مُقَيَّرٌ. Set up, مَنْصُوبٌ ـ مُقِيمٌ ـ مَصْمُودٌ; of tents, مَضْرُوبٌ. Put in array,

— A. مَطْرُوح ـ مُلْقَى. Thrown, مُجْهَز ـ مُرَتَّب ـ مُصَفَّف battle, مُحَارَبَةُ مَيْدَانٍ ـ وَاقِعَةٌ مُصَفَّفَةٌ ـ حَرْبٌ مُصَفَّفَةٌ.

Pitcher, *n.* One who pitches anything, رَامٍ ـ طَارِح. An earthen vessel with a spout, شَرْبَة ـ مِشْرَبَة ـ كُوزَة *pl.* كِيزَان ـ أَبَارِيقُ *pl.* إِبْرِيق. A vessel that pitches, سَفِينَةٌ غَطَّاسَةٌ. An empty pitcher, جَرَّةٌ فَارِغَةٌ *pl.* جِرَارٌ فَارِغَةٌ.

Pitchfork, *n.* مُصَبَّع.

Pitchiness, *n.* *See* Blackness, Darkness, *n.*

Pitching, *n.* As of a ship, غَطْس ـ مَغَاصّ ـ إِغْتِطَاط.

Pitching, *a.* Sloping, مُنْصَبّ ـ مُنْحَدِر ـ هَبُوط.

Pitch-pipe, *n.* مِيزَانُ ٱلنَّغَم.

Pitchy, *a.* Like pitch, مِثْلَ ٱلزِّفْت. Smeared with pitch, مُزَفَّت. *See also* Dark, Black, *a.*

Pit-coal, *a.* فَحْمٌ مَعْدِنِيٌّ ـ فَحْمٌ أَرْضِيٌّ.

Piteous, *a.* Lamentable, يُرْثَى لَهُ ـ كَئِيب ـ مُحْزِن ـ حَزِين. Compassionate, شَفِيق ـ رَؤُوف ـ حَنِين. Miserable, لَئِيم ـ نَحِس ـ مَشْؤُوم ـ شَقِيّ. To be —, compassionate, to, رَثَى ل ـ رَقَّ ل. To be in — circumstances, أَضَاقَ ـ رَقَّتْ حَالُهُ ـ ضَاقَ عَلَيْهِ مَعَاشُهُ.

Piteously, *ad.* In a way to excite pity, بِنَوْع ـ بِنَوْعٍ مُحْزِنٍ يُرْثَى لَهُ.

Piteousness, *n.* Sadness, هَمّ ـ حُزْن. Compassion, شَفَقَة ـ تَرَحُّم. Wretchedness, foolishness, ضُعْف ـ رَثِيثَة ـ رَثَّة.

Pitfall, *n.* A pit for taking game, مِغْوَاة ـ أُغْوِيَّة ـ أُخْذَة ـ عَاثُور.

Pith, *n.* As of plants, قِلْبَة *pl.* قَلْب ـ جُمَّار ـ لُبُوب *pl.* لُبّ; the — of the palm or date tree, شَحْمَةُ ٱلنَّخْلَةِ ـ شَحْمُ ٱلنَّخْلِ. Vigour, force, قُوَّة ـ فَاضِلَة ـ دِقَّة ـ جِدَّة. Gist, substance, فَصّ ـ مَضْمُون ـ لُبّ ـ خُلَاصَة ـ زُبْدَة ـ جَوْهَر.

Pithily, *ad.* With energy, تَأْثِيرًا ـ سَدَادًا ـ بِجِدَّةٍ. *See also* Concisely, *ad.*

Pithiness, *n.* Energy, قُوَّة ـ تَأْثِير ـ جِدَّة. Conciseness, إِقْتِصَار ـ إِيجَاز.

Pithy, *a.* Having pith, ذُو جُمَّارٍ ـ ذُو لُبٍّ. Sharp, critical, قَدْحِيّ ـ هَجْوِيّ. To the point, أَسَدّ ـ سَدِيد. *See also* Concise, *a.*

Pitiable, *a.* *See* Piteous, *a.*

Pitiably, *ad.* *See* Piteously, *ad.*

Pitiful, *a.* Full of pity, شَفِيق ـ مُشْفِق ـ شَفُوق ـ رَحِيم ـ رَقِيقُ ٱلْقَلْبِ ـ رَؤُوف. Contemptible, مِسْكِين ـ حَقِير ـ رَذِيل. Small, يَسِير ـ قَلِيل ـ جُزْئِيّ ـ زَهِيد. To be — towards, تَحَنَّنَ عَلَى ـ حَنَّ عَلَى ـ تَرَحَّمَ عَلَى ـ رَؤُفَ ب[2]. *See also* Pitiable, *a.*

Pitifully, *ad.* With pity, بِشَفَقَةٍ ـ بِحَنَانٍ ـ بِرَأْفَةٍ ـ رَحْمَةً. Meanly, بِحَقَارَةٍ ـ بِرَذَالَةٍ. Poorly, in a careless manner, بِرَكَاكَةٍ ـ حَقَارَةً ـ بِرَثَاثَةٍ ـ بِغَيْرِ ٱعْتِنَاءٍ.

Pitifulness, *n.* Tenderness, compassion, حَنِيَّة ـ رِقَّةُ قَلْبٍ ـ رَأْفَة. Meanness, wretchedness, حَقَارَة ـ رَثِيثَة ـ رَثَّة.

Pitiless, *a.* قَاسِي ٱلْقَلْبِ ـ قَاسٍ ـ بِلَا حَنِيَّةٍ ـ عَدِيمُ ٱلشَّفَقَةِ. To be — towards, قَاهَرَ ـ عَاسَرَ ـ أَعْنَفَ. Severe, شَدِيد. Pitiless cold, زَمْهَرِير. A — storm, نَوْءٌ شَدِيدٌ.

Pitilessly, *ad.* بِلَا تَرَحُّمٍ ـ مِنْ غَيْرِ رَحْمَةٍ.

Pitilessness, *n.* Want of pity, عَدَمُ ٱلشَّفَقَةِ ـ عَدَمُ ٱلرَّحْمَةِ. Severity, شِدَّة ـ جِدَّة.

Pitman, *n.* One who works in a mine, مَعْدِنْجِي ـ مُعَدِّن. The lower sawyer, مَاسِكُ أَسْفَلِ ٱلْمِنْشَارِ.

Pitsaw, *n.* مِنْشَارٌ مُزْدَوِجٌ ـ مِنْشَارٌ يَنْشُرُ بِهِ رَجُلَانِ.

Pittance, *n.* قِلّ ـ شَيْءٌ جُزْئِيّ ـ كَفَاف.

Pitted, *a.* Marked with hollows, as of small-pox, بِهِ رَسْمٌ آ... ـ ذُو جُوَبَاتٍ. Having pits or hollows, مَجْدُور ـ بِهِ أَثَرٌ آ...

Pitted against, مُقَاوِمٌ ب ـ مُقَابِلٌ ب.

Pituitary, *a.* بَلْغَمِيّ.

Pituitous, *a.* مِثْلَ ٱلْبَلْغَمِ.

Pity, *n.* Compassion, شَفَق ـ تَرَحُّم ـ رُحْم ـ رَأْفَة ـ حَنَان ـ رِقَّةُ قَلْبٍ ـ شَفَقَة. Something to be regretted, حَسْرَة ـ خَسَارَة. To take — upon, تَحَنَّنَ عَلَى ـ تَرَحَّمَ عَلَى. To excite one to — another, حَنَّنَ ـ عَلَى. To ask for —, إِسْتَرْحَمَ. For pity's sake, out of —, تَرَحُّمًا ـ رَحْمَةً. What a pity! يَا خَسَارَةُ ـ يَا حَسْرَةُ.

Pity, *v.t.* رَحِمَ ـ تَرَحَّمَ عَلَى ـ رَؤُفَ ب[2] ـ حَنَّ عَلَى ـ تَحَنَّنَ عَلَى ـ أَشْفَقَ عَلَى ـ رَقَّ ل ـ قَلْبُهُ.

Pivot, *n.* That on which anything turns, مَدَار; the — of a door, the top of which turns in a socket in the lintel, and the bottom in the threshold, صَائِر (the lintel is called سَاكِف and the pivot which enters into the threshold, عَقِب *pl.* أَعْقَاب. The centre of a circle, مَرْكَز). A principal agent, رَأْس ـ أَسَاس ـ مَدَار.

Pix, *n.* حُقَّةُ ٱلْقُرْبَانِ ٱلْمُقَدَّسِ.

Pixy, *n.* *See* Fairy, *n.*

Placability, *n.* } رَأْفَة ـ لَيَان.
Placableness, }

Placable, *a.* رَؤُوف ـ لَيِّنُ ٱلْقَلْبِ.

Placard, *n.* إِعْلَانٌ مُعَلَّقٌ فِي حَائِطٍ *pl.* إِعْلَانَات.

Placard, *v.t.* To post up placards, عَلَّقَ إِعْلَانَاتٍ عَلَى حَائِطٍ.

Placate, *v.t.* طَيَّبَ نَفْسَهُ ـ صَالَحَ. *See also to* Appease, *v.t.*

Place, *n.* Space, فُسْحَة ـ مَطَارِح *pl.* مَطْرَح ـ مَضْرَب. A spot, particular —, مَوْضِع ـ أَمَاكِن *pl.* مَكَان ـ مَحَلَّات *pl.* مَحَلّ *pl.* مَوَاضِع. A — of abode, مَسْكَن ـ مَقَام. A — from which anything is taken, where it is found, مَأْخَذ: the place from whence birds are taken, مَأْخَذُ ٱلطَّيْرِ. A — where anything takes place, situation, مَوْقِع. Direction, نَوَاحِي *pl.* نَاحِيَة ـ جِهَة. An appointment, خِدْمَة ـ مَأْمُورِيَّة ـ مَنْصِب ـ وَظَائِف *pl.* وَظِيفَة. Place, a town, village, *etc.*, مَحَلّ. Country, بِلَاد. A strong or fortified —, مَحَلّ مُسْتَحْكَم ـ حِصْن ـ قَلْعَة. A substitute, بَدَل. The — of a joining, مَوْصِل. A — of meeting, rendezvous, مِيعَاد ـ مَوَاعِد *pl.* مَوْعِد. The — of one departed, خَلَّة (*see under* Gap, *n.*). Place, mention, ذِكْرَة ـ ذِكْر. The first — in an assembly, presidency, ٱلصَّدْر. If I were in your —, لَوْ كُنْتُ فِي مَوْضِعِكَ. In the — of, مَكَان. In his —, stead, مَكَانَهُ ـ بَدَلَهُ. He has a — in history, ذُكِرَ فِي ٱلتَّوَارِيخ. He was appointed in the — of such an one, تَعَيَّنَ بَدَلَ فُلَانٍ.

In the first place, firstly, أَوَّلًا.

In the next place, ثُمَّ ـ وَبَعْدَهُ.

In the second place, ثَانِيَة.

Out of place, inopportune, فِي غَيْرِ مَحَلِّهِ ـ غَيْرُ سَائِغ. Unemployed, قَاعِد ـ بَطَّال ـ مُعَطَّل.

To give a place to, to appoint, قَعَّدَ ـ عَيَّنَ ـ وَظَّفَ.

To give place, room, to, وَسَّعَ لِ ـ ٢ فَسَحَ (or أَفْسَحَ or تَفَسَّحَ) لَهُ ـ أَذْعَنَ لِ ـ أَعْطَى مَكَانًا. To concede to, to be obedient to, أَذْعَنَ لِ.

To give something to one in the place of, أَعْوَضَ ـ عَوَّضَ.

To hold a place, an appointment, حَازَ وَظِيفَةً ـ ٢ قَامَ فِي مَنْصِبٍ *aor.* يَحُوزُ. To keep possession of, as a fortress, حَافَظَ.

To hold the first place in, تَقَدَّمَ فِي ـ تَصَدَّرَ فِي.

To put one in the first place in, قَدَّمَ فِي ـ صَدَّرَ فِي.

To take place, to occur, حَدَثَ ٢ ـ وَقَعَ *aor.* يَقَعُ ـ إِتَّفَقَ ـ ٢ حَصَلَ ـ ٢ جَرَى. To appear, ٢ بَانَ ـ ٢ ظَهَرَ.

To take a place, a situation, إِتَّخَذَ خِدْمَةً. To capture, ٢ فَتَحَ ـ إِسْتَوْلَى عَلَى ـ ٢ ضَبَطَ.

To take the place of, ٢ قَامَ مَقَامَهُ ـ ٢ حَلَّ مَحَلَّهُ. He took his place, ٢ قَامَ بَدَلًا عَنْهُ.

Place, *v.t.* To put in a particular spot, وَضَعَ ـ ٢ جَعَلَ فِي *aor.* يَضَعُ ـ ٢ حَطَّ. To arrange, رَتَّبَ ـ نَظَّمَ ـ نَسَّقَ. To put into a situation, قَعَّدَ. To set up, ٢ نَصَبَ ـ ٢ صَمَدَ. To — one over, as a watch, *etc.* أَوْقَفَ عَلَى. *See also to* Put, Set, *v.t.*

Placed, *a.* Set, fixed, مَرْكُوز ـ مَنْصُوب ـ مَوْضُوع. Placed on one another, مُرَكَّب ـ مُنَصَّب. Set up, مَصْمُود.

Placeman, *n.* صَاحِبُ مَنْصِبٍ ـ مَأْمُورُونَ *pl.* مَأْمُور ـ أَصْحَابُ *pl.* مَنَاصِب. *See also* Functionary, *n.*

Placenta, *n.* قِطْعَةٌ مِنَ ٱلْمَشِيمَةِ ـ سَلَى.

Placer, *n.* One who places, وَاضِع; one who appoints, مُعَيِّن.

Placid, *a.* Untroubled, رَزِين ـ سَاكِن ـ مُطْمَئِنّ. Gentle, سَلِيم ـ حَلِيم. To be —, untroubled, إِطْمَأَنَّ ـ ٢ رَزُنَ ـ تَرَزَّنَ. *See also* Calm, *a.*

Placidity, *n.* / Placidness, } Serenity, رَزَانَة ـ إِطْمِئْنَان ـ طُمَأْنِينَة. Gentleness, لِينَة ـ وَدَاعَة ـ حِلْم. *See also* Calmness, *n.*

Placidly, *a.* بِرَزَانَةٍ ـ بِٱطْمِئْنَانٍ. *See also* Calmly, *ad.*

Placing, *n.* The act of putting, وَضْع; of fixing, رَكْز ـ إِثْبَات ـ تَقْرِير; of appointing, تَقْعِيد ـ تَعْيِين.

Plagiarism, *n.* The act of purloining another's writings, تَنَحُّل ـ سَرِقَة ـ سَرِق ـ إِنْتِحَال. An accidental —, تَوَارُد.

Plagiarist, *n.* سَرَّاق ـ مُنْتَحِل ـ مُتَنَحِّل.

Plagiarize, *v.t.* ٢ سَرَقَ كَلَامَ ٱلْغَيْرِ ـ إِنْتَحَلَ ـ تَنَحَّلَ.

Plagiary, *n.* *See* Plagiarist, *n.*

Plague, *n.* The disease, طَاعُون ـ أَوْبَاء *pl.* وَبَاء ـ شَوْكَة ـ هَيْضَة; (called also in Egypt, كُبَّة.) An epidemical disease, جَارِف. A disaster, بَلَاء ـ مُصِيبَة ـ أَذِيَّة ـ ضَجَر. Anything troublesome, أَذِيَّة ـ ضَجَر. To have the —, طُعِنَ; having the —, مَطْعُون. To be a — to, عَنَّى ـ تَعَنَّى ـ أَضْجَرَ ـ آذَى. *See also under* Pest, *n.*

Plague-spot, *n.* A bane, آفَة *pl.* آفَات. The — of affectation in manners is self-conceit; that of science is forgetfulness, (prov.), آفَةُ ٱلظَّرْفِ ٱلصَّلَفُ وَآفَةُ ٱلْعِلْمِ ٱلنِّسْيَانُ. The — of speech is lying; of science forgetfulness, (prov.), آفَةُ ٱلْحَدِيثِ ٱلْكَذِبُ وَآفَةُ ٱلْعِلْمِ ٱلنِّسْيَانُ. There is a — in everything, but science has many plague-spots, (prov.), لِكُلِّ شَيْءٍ آفَةٌ وَلِلْعِلْمِ آفَاتٌ.

Plague, *v.t.* To vex, annoy, ٢ كَدَّ ـ أَضْجَرَ ـ فَجَعَ ـ أَزْعَجَ ـ عَنَّى ـ آذَى.

Plaguily, *ad.* إِضْجَارًا ـ بِأَذِيَّةٍ ـ إِزْعَاجًا.

Plaguy, *a.* Vexatious, مُزْعِج ـ أَذِيّ ـ آذٍ ـ مُضْجِر ـ فَاجِع. Much, كَثِيرًا ـ لِلْغَايَةِ.

Plaice, *n.* نَوْعٌ مِنَ ٱلسَّمَكِ.

Plaid, *n.* رِدَاء (or إِزَار) يَلْبِسُهُ أَهْلُ إِسْكُتْلَنْد.

Plain, *a.* Level, مُسْتَوٍ ـ مُسَطَّح ـ سَهِل ـ سَهْل. Void of ornament, سَاذِج ـ مَا لَا نَقْشَ فِيهِ ; *vulg.* سَادَه. Artless, مُخْلِص ـ سَلِيم ـ نَاصِح ـ صَادِق ـ بَسِيط ـ سَلِيم ـ سَاذَج. Candid,

مَجْهُورٌ بِهِ ـ مُسْتَبْصَر ـ ظَاهِر ـ مَحْض ـ صَافٍ. Clear, obvious, بَيِّن ـ سَهْل ـ هَيِّن ـ أَهْوَن. Ugly, بَشِع ـ صَرِيح ـ وَاضِح. Easy, قَبِيح ـ وَحْش. To be plain, clear, إِنْتَضَحَ ـ صَرَّحَ ـ إِنْصَرَحَ; to make —, clear, أَصْرَحَ ـ صَرَّحَ بِ; to be —, evident, بَانَ ـ أَشْرَعَ ـ شَرَّعَ ـ تَبَيَّنَ ـ تَجَلَّى ـ إِسْتَبَانَ. To make —, evident, بَيَّنَ. To make —, smooth, easy, سَهَّلَ. To be —, frank, with, صَارَحَ ـ إِنْبَسَطَ إِلَى. The — truth, الحَقُّ ٱلْخَالِصُ. In — English, *i.e.*, in — words, بِلا مُحَاوَلَةٍ. Plain clothes, مَلابِسُ آلْتِيَادِيَّةٌ. A — or right path, صِرَاطٌ مُسْتَقِيمٌ.

Plain, *n.* Level ground, قَاعٌ *pl.* قِيعَان ـ صَاعٌ *pl.* أَصْوَاع ـ صَاعَة ـ سَهْل *pl.* سُهُول ـ بُقْعَة. A desert plain, دَشْت. An extensive —, صَحْرَآء *pl.* صَحَارَى ـ فَضَآء. *See also under* Field, *n.*

Plain, *v.t.* سَهَّلَ. *See also to* Level, *v.t.*

Plain, *ad.* Simply, distinctly, بَيَانًا ـ بِوُضُوحٍ ـ بِصَرَاحَةٍ ـ عَلَانِيَةً.

Plain-dealing, *n.* مُبَاسَطَة ـ إِسْتِقَامَة ـ مُنَاصَحَة ـ مُصَارَحَة.

Plain-dealing, *a.* مُبَاسِط ـ مُسْتَقِيم ـ نَاصِح ـ مُصَارِح.

Plain-hearted, *a.* سَلِيم ـ نَاصِح ـ سَلِيمُ ٱلْقَلْبِ.

Plainly, *ad.* Sincerely, بِإِخْلَاصٍ ـ نُصُوحًا ـ سِلْمًا. Clearly, openly, عَلَانِيَةً ـ بِصَرَاحَةٍ ـ جَهْرًا ـ جِهَارًا ـ جَهْرَةً. Without ornament, بِسَذَاجَةٍ. Tell us —, قُلْ لَنَا جَهْرًا. He told them —, قَالَ لَهُمْ عَلَانِيَةً.

Plainness, *n.* Levelness, إِسْتِوَآء ـ سُهُولَة. Clearness, وُضُوح ـ صَرَاحَة. Easiness, سُهُولَة ـ هَيْنَة. Ugliness, بَشَاعَة ـ سَمَاجَة ـ قَبَاحَة. Artlessness, إِخْلَاص ـ نُصُوح ـ بَسَاطَة. Simplicity, سَذَاجَة. Plainness of speech, مُجَاهَرَة فِي ٱلْكَلَامِ.

Plain-spoken, *a.* Speaking with sincerity, مُنْبَسِط ـ نَاصِح فِي ٱلْكَلَامِ ـ صَادِق. To be — with, إِنْبَسَطَ إِلَى.

Plaint, *n.* An audible expression of sorrow, أَنِين ـ أُنَان ـ حَنِين. Lamentation, نَوْح ـ نِيَاح ـ نَحِيب. *See also* Complaint, *n.*

Plaintful, *a.* أَنَّان ـ أُنَان ـ آنّ ـ حَنِين.

Plaintiff, *n.* مُدَّعٍ. Plaintiff and defendant, المُدَّعِي وَٱلْمُدَّعَى عَلَيْهِ.

Plaintive, *a.* Sad, mournful, حَنَّان ـ حَزِين ـ مُحْزِن ـ كَئِيب. A — sound, رَنَّة ـ رَنِين. To emit — sounds, رَنَّ *aor.* يَرِنُّ ـ حَنَّ. The lute emitted — sounds, حَنَّ ٱلْعُودُ. *See also* Plaintful, *a.*

Plaintively, *ad.* بِأَنِينٍ ـ بِحَنِينٍ ـ أَنَانًا.

Plaintiveness, *n.* أَنَّان ـ أُنَان ـ رَنِين ـ رَنَّة.

Plait, *n.* A fold, غَضْن ـ طِيَّة *pl.* أَطْوَآء ـ ثَنْيَة. A —, as of straw, *etc.*, دَسْج ـ ضَفِيرَة ـ سَفِيفَة ـ عِقَاص. A — of hair, جَمِيرَة ـ ضَفِيرَة *pl.* ضَفَائِر ـ ضُفُور *pl.* ضَفْر.

Plait, *v.t.* To weave with the fingers, as mats, *etc.*, سَفَّ ـ ضَفَرَ. To — the hair, ٱلشَّعْرَ (جَمَّرَ or عَقَصَ or) ضَفَرَ ـ أَسَفَّ ضَفْرُ ٱلشَّعْرِ.

Plaited, *a.* Folded, مَثْنِيّ; of straw and such like, سَفِيف; of the hair, مَضْفُور ـ ضَفِير.

Plan, *n.* Anything devised, a project, قَصْد ـ نِيَّة *pl.* نِيَّات ـ مَرَام. The drawn representation of anything, رَسْم *pl.* رُسُوم. A chart, خَارِطَة *pl.* خَارِطَات. A move, cast, طَرْح. Method, تَرْتِيب ـ تَدْبِير. Order, طَرِيقَة ـ قِدْيَة ـ مِدَاد ـ مِنْهَاج. System, سِيَاقَة ـ أُصُول ـ نَسَق ـ مِنْهَاج. A well-devised plan, scheme, سِدَاد. *See also* Course, Scheme, Contrivance, *n.*

Plan, *v.t.* To delineate, رَسَمَ ـ صَوَّرَ. To form in design, قَصَدَ ـ تَصَوَّرَ. I planned the building, رَسَمْتُ ٱلْبِنَآءَ. *See also to* Contrive, *v.t.*

Planch, *v.t.* *See to* Plank, *v.t.*

Planching, *n.* *See* Planking, *n.*

Plane, *n.* A level surface, سَطْح مُسْتَوٍ ـ سَطْح *pl.* سُطُوح ـ مُسَطَّح. The joiner's tool, فَارَة ـ رَنْدَج. The tree so called, دُلْب ـ صِنَار, *called in Syria*, حَوْر. An inclined —, سَطْح مَائِل.

Plane, *a.* Level, مُسَطَّح. *See also* Level, Smooth, *a.*

Plane, *v.t.* As with a plane, مَسَحَ بِٱلْفَارَةِ ـ رَنْدَجَ. To make smooth, سَهَّلَ ـ مَلَّسَ. To work anything with carpenter's tools, نَجَرَ.

Planed, *a.* Made smooth, مُسَهَّل; planed with a plane, مَمْسُوح بِٱلْفَارَةِ ـ مُرَنْدَج.

Planet, *n.* سَيَّارَة *pl.* سَيَّارَات. The five primary planets, ٱلسَّيَّارَاتُ ـ ٱلسَّيَّارَةُ; (The planets are sometimes styled, الجَوَارِي ٱلْكُنَّسُ.) *See also under* Star, *n.*

Planetarium, *n.* *See* Orrery, *n.*

Planetary, *a.* Pertaining to planets, مُتَعَلِّق بِٱلسَّيَّارَاتِ. The — system, نَسَقُ ٱلسَّيَّارَاتِ.

Planet-struck, *a.* Blasted by a planet, (مَضْرُوب or) مُصَاب بِسَيَّارَةٍ.

Planimetry, *n.* عِلْمُ قِيَاسِ ٱلسُّطُوحِ ـ مِسَاحَةُ ٱلْمُسَطَّحَاتِ ٱلْمُسْتَوِيَةِ.

Planisphere, *n.* رَسْمُ ٱلْكُرَةِ مُسَطَّحًا.

Plank, *n.* A board, دَفّ *pl.* دُفُوف ـ دَفَّة ـ لَوْح *pl.* أَلْوَاح. Any broad piece, board, or plate, صُفَّاحَة or صَفِيحَة *pl.* صَفَائِح.

A — in the interior of a ship, طائق *pl.* طَوَائِق; of a deck, سَقِيفَة *pl.* سَقائف.

Plank, *v.t.* تَخَّتَ — ² فَرَشَ-بِأَلْوَاح. *See also to* Board, *v.t.*

Planking, *n.* The act of, تَخْتِيت — فَرْش بِأَلْوَاح. Boards laid down, as on a roof or ceiling, تُخُوت — أَلْوَاح — دُفُوف.

Planner, *n.* A delineator, رَاسِم — رَسَّام. An arranger, مُدَبِّر — مُرَتِّب. *See also* Contriver, *n.*

Plano-concave, *a.* مُسَطَّح مِنْ ناحِيَةٍ وَمُتَقَعِّر مِنَ ٱلْأُخْرَى.

Plano-convex, *a.* مُسَطَّح مِنْ ناحِيَةٍ وَمُحَدَّب مِنَ ٱلْأُخْرَى.

Plant, *n.* A herb, tree, *etc.*, عُشْبَة *coll.* عُشْب *pl.* أَعْشَاب — نَبَاتَة *coll.* نَبَات *pl.* نَبَاتَات — غَرْس *pl.* أَغْرَاس *and* غِرَاس. A tender —, فَرْخ *pl.* فُرُوخ. A — for transplanting, شَتْلَة *pl.* شَتْلَات. The stock or utensils of a business, أَدَوَات — طَقْم. To grow as a —, ² نَبَتَ — أَنْبَتَ.

Plant, *v.t.* As of herbs, *etc.*, ² = غَرَسَ — نَبَّتَ — أَغْرَسَ; of seeds, ² = زَرَعَ. To set up, ² أَقَامَ — نَصَّبَ — ² نَصَبَ — صَمَدَ. To fix, to stick, as into the ground, ² رَكَزَ. To rear, as of plants, نَبَّتَ — رَبَّى. To —, as a colony, سَكَّنَ — اِسْتَعْمَرَ-فِي — أَعْمَرَ. To — one's self in a place, وَطَّنَ — اِتَّطَنَ.

Plant, *v.i.* = زَرَعَ زَرْعًا — = غَرَسَ غَرْسًا.

Plantain, *n.* مَوْزَة *coll.* مَوْز. The — tree, شَجَرُ ٱلْمَوْزِ — طَلْح.

Plantation, *n.* The act of planting, زَرْع — غَرْس. A place planted with trees, *etc.*, زَرَاعَة — مَغَارِس *pl.* مَغْرِس — زَرْعَة — غِرْس (called on the east coast of Africa a شَامْبا.) *See also* Colony, *n.*

Planted, *a.* مَغْرُوس; set up, مَنْصُوب — مَصْمُود; fixed, as into the ground, رَكِيز — مَرْكُوز; furnished with inhabitants, مُسْتَعْمَر — مُعْمَر.

Planter, *n.* One who plants, as trees, *etc.*, غَارِس — زَرَّاع *pl.* غُرَّاس — غارِسُون. One who owns plantations, صاحِبُ مَغَارِس. A founder, أَصْل — مُبْدِع — مُنْشِئ. A propagator, نَاشِر.

Plantership, *n.* The business of an owner of plantations, شُغْل صَاحِبِ ٱلْمَغَارِسِ.

Planticle, *n.* شَتْلَة — فُرُوخ *pl.* فَرْخُ ٱلنَّبَاتِ.

Plantigrade, *a.* مَنْ يَمْشِي عَلَى بَطْنِ ٱلرَّاحَةِ.

Planting, *n.* The act of, زَرْع — غَرْس. The time for —, غِرَاس.

Plash, *n.* A puddle of water, مُسْتَنْقَعُ مَاءٍ — مَنَاقِع *pl.* مَنْقَعُ مَاءٍ.

Plash, *v.i.* To dabble, as in water, تَخَضْخَضَ — تَمَرَّغَ — تَبَرْبَطَ.

Plashing, *n.* The act of sprinkling colours, as on walls, *etc.*, رَشّ تَطْرِيشُ ٱلْأَلْوَانِ — ٱلْأَلْوَانِ.

Plashy, *a.* Of land abounding in puddles, أَرْض سَوَّاخَى.

Plaster, *n.* As for walls, سَارُوج — صُوَاح — شَارُوق — دِمَام — جَصّ — جِبْس — جِير — جَصّ — قَرْمَد — شِيد. Gypsum, جِبْس. A — for a wound, *etc.*, لَزْقَة — مَرْهَم *pl.* مَرَاهِم — ضِمَاد — ضِمَادَة — لَزُوق — لَصْقَة — لَزُوق.

Plaster, *v.t.* As of walls, *etc.*, ² دَمَّ — دَمَّمَ — شَانَ — = طَيَّنَ — قَرْمَدَ — جَيَّرَ; with gypsum, جَصَّصَ. To —, as a wound, مَرْهَمَ — يَضَعُ *aor.* وَضَعَ لَزْقَةً عَلَى.

Plasterer, *n.* طَيَّان — جَيَّار.

Plastered, *a.* As of a wall, مُدَمَّم — مُطَيَّن — مُقَرْمَد — مَشِيد.

Plastering, *n.* The act of plastering walls, *etc.*, دَمّ — تَدْمِيم — تَجْبِيس — شَيْد — تَطْيِين.

Plastic, *a.* Giving form, فاطِر — جابِل — مُشَكِّل — مُصَوِّر. Capable of being moulded, قَابِلُ ٱلْجَبْلِ — مِمَّا يُجْبَلُ — مِمَّا يُفْطَرُ. Easy, soft, لَيِّن. Plastic clay, طِينُ ٱلْإِبْلِيزِ.

Plasticity, *n.* Capacity of being moulded, قابِلِيَّةُ ٱلْجَبْلِ — قابِلِيَّةُ ٱلْفَطْرِ. Softness, elasticity, لِينَة — لَيَان.

Plastron, *n.* رِفَادَةٌ لِلصَّدْرِ.

Plat, *v.t.* To interweave, حَيَّكَ — = ² نَسَجَ — ² سَفَّ. *See also to* Plait, *v.t.*

Plat, *n.* Platted work, حِيَاكَة — نَسْج — سَفِيف. A — of ground; *see* Plot, *n.*

Plate, *n.* A flat thin piece, as of metal, صَفِيحَة *pl.* صَفَائِح; a slab, as of metal, *etc.*, طابَق *pl.* طَوَابِق — لَوْح *pl.* أَلْوَاح. Wrought silver, فِضَّة — مَصَاغ فِضَّة. A shallow vessel, طَبَق *pl.* أَطْبَاق — صَحْن *pl.* صُحُون — أَجْر *pl.* أَنَاجِر — زَبْدِيَّة *pl.* زَبَادِي. A — to print from, لَوْحَة لِلطَّبْع — قالِب; an impression from a —, صُورَة *pl.* صُوَر. A prize at races, خَطَر مِنْ فِضَّةٍ يُعْطَى لِمَنْ يُحْرِزُ قَصَبَ ٱلسَّبَاقِ. A — for supporting rafter, عَارِضَة *pl.* عَوَارِض. A clamp, ضَبَّة: he put a —, clamp, upon the door, ضَبَّبَ ٱلْبَابَ. Silver —, utensils of silver, آنِيَةُ ٱلْفِضَّةِ. Gold —, utensils of gold, آنِيَةُ ٱلذَّهَبِ. A copper plate, لَوْحُ صُفْرٍ. Copper-plate, drawn on copper, مَرْسُوم عَلَى لَوْحٍ مِنَ ٱلصُّفْرِ. Plate glass, بِلَّوْر.

Plate, *v.t.* To cover with some metal, ² طَلَا-ب — مَوَّهَ-ب — لَبَّسَ-ب. To — with silver, فَضَّضَ — مَوَّهَ-بِفِضَّةٍ; with gold, ذَهَّبَ — مَوَّهَ-بِٱلذَّهَبِ. To put plates, of any metal, upon, لَبَّسَ-صَفَائِح. To beat into plates, ² مَطَلَ-(صَيَّرَ- *or*)- دَرَّعَ صَفَائِح. Armour-plated, مُدَرَّع.

Plateau, *n.* A table-land ظَهْر — ظَهْرَة — صَعْدَة — صَعِيد — سَطْح *pl.* سُطُوح. *See also* Epergne, *n.*

Plated, *a.* As with any metal, مُلَبَّس ب — مُطْلَى ب — مُمَوَّه ب. Silver —, مُفَضَّض; gold —, مُذَهَّب.

Plateful, *n.* مِلْءُ صَحْنٍ.

Plate glass, *n.* *See under* Glass, Plate, *n.*

Platen, *n.* Of a printing press, مَكْبَس.

Platform, *n.* A level plan, رَسْمٌ مُسَطَّحٌ. A boarding of planks, فَرْشٌ مُتَخَّتٌ ـ فَرْشٌ مِنْ أَلْوَاحٍ (*or* دُفُوفٍ). A raised platform, دِكَّةٌ *pl.* دِكَكٌ; the raised — in a mosque, مَحْفِلٌ. Platform, in the sense of doctrine, قَاعِدَةٌ ـ مَذْهَبٌ ـ كُرْسِيٌّ.

Platina, *n.* }
Platinum, } بَلَاطِين ـ ذَهَبٌ أَبْيَضُ.

Plating, *n.* The act of overlaying with a metal, تَلْبِيس ـ طَلْيٌ ـ تَمْوِيه.

Platitude, *n.* هَاجِرَةٌ *pl.* هَاجِرَات ـ سَمَاجَة ـ تَفَاهَة.

Plato, *n.* إِفْلَاطُونُ.

Platonic, *a.* Relating to Plato, إِفْلَاطُونِيٌّ. Refined, pure, طَاهِر ـ خَالِص ـ مَحْض. Undefined, abstract, إِسْمٌ بِلَا مُسَمًّى.
Platonic love, عِشْقٌ عَقْلِيٌّ ـ عِشْقٌ بِغَيْرِ شَهْوَةٍ.

Platonism, *n.* مَذْهَبُ إِفْلَاطُونَ ٱلْحَكِيمِ.

Platonist, *n.* إِفْلَاطُونِيٌّ ـ مِنْ جَمَاعَةِ إِفْلَاطُونَ.

Platoon, *n.* صَرَّةُ عَسْكَرٍ. Platoon exercises, تَمْرِينُ (*or* تَعْلِيمُ) صَرَّةٍ مِنَ ٱلْعَسْكَرِ. Platoon firing, إِطْلَاقُ ٱلْبَنَادِقِ صَرَّةً صَرَّةً.

Platter, *n.* قَصْعَةٌ *pl.* قِصَاعٌ *and* قِصَعٌ *and* قَصَعَاتٌ ـ كَأْسٌ *pl.* كُؤُوسٌ *and* كَأْسَاتٌ.

Platting, *n.* Slips, as of straw, platted together, نَسْج ـ سَفِيف ـ حِيَاكَة.

Plaudit, *n.* Praise, ثَنَاءٌ ـ مَدْحٌ ـ إِسْتِحْسَان; with the hands, تَصْفِيق ـ تَصْفِيح.

Plauditory, *a.* مُثْنٍ عَلَى ـ مَادِح ـ مُسْتَحْسِن.

Plausibility, *n.* } The semblance of propriety, إِظْهَارُ ٱلْوَاجِبِ ـ
Plausibleness, } تَظَاهُرٌ بِٱلْجَمِيلِ (*or* ٱلصَّوَاب) ـ (*or* ٱلصَّوَاب).
Shakiness, unsoundness, خَلَل ـ خِلَال. A pretext, عِلَّة ـ إِعْتِلَال.
Skilful address, مُزَاوَلَة.

Plausible, *a.* Seeming appropriate, مُتَظَاهِرٌ ـ مُظْهِرُ ٱلْوَاجِبِ بِٱلْجَمِيلِ. Of skilful address, سَهْلُ ٱلْوَجْهِ ـ مُزَاوِل. Excusatory, deceitful, غَرُور ـ مُغْتَلٌّ. Having defects, incoherent, خَائِل ـ خَالٌّ ـ مُخْتَلٌّ. A — excuse, حُجَّةٌ ـ رُوَيْغَة ـ مَحِيلَة ـ مَعْذِرَةٌ.

Plausibly, *ad.* With seeming propriety, بِصُورَةِ ٱلْمُنَاسَبَةِ ـ تَظَاهُرًا بِٱلصَّوَابِ (*or* بِٱلْجَمِيلِ). With address, مُزَاوَلَةً ـ بِتَصَنُّعٍ. With an excuse, بِحُجَّةٍ ـ بِعِلَّةٍ. To act —, to affect, تَظَاهَرَ بِ; as of excellence, goodness, تَحَاسَنَ ـ تَظَرَّفَ ـ تَجَمَّلَ. To act with address, زَاوَلَ. He acted — in the matter, أَظْهَرَ ٱلصَّوَابَ فِي ٱلْأَمْرِ ـ تَظَاهَرَ بِٱلْجَمِيلِ فِي ٱلْأَمْرِ.

Play, *v.t.* and *i.* To sport, لَعِبَ. To trifle, لَعِبَ ـ لَعَّبَ ـ بَطِرَ ـ إِنْخَلَعَ ـ دَعَبَ ـ تَلَاعَبَ ـ تَلَعَّبَ. To gamble, لَعِبَ ٱلْقِمَارَ. To —, to work or act freely, إِشْتَغَلَ. To act, move, تَحَرَّكَ. To perform, as an actor, شَخَّصَ فِي ٱلْمَرْسَحِ ـ لَعِبَ فِي ٱلتِّيَاتْرُو ـ ٱلْعَامِّ. To —, as a fountain, بَجَسَ ـ تَبَجَّسَ ـ إِنْبَجَسَ ـ إِشْتَغَلَ. To —, as on a musical instrument, عَزَفَ ـ ضَرَبَ ـ دَقَّ بِٱلْآلَةِ. To — the tambourine, نَقَرَ عَلَى ٱلدُّفِّ. To —, to put in action, عَالَجَ ـ شَغَّلَ ـ مَشَّى. They played together, of many, لَعِبُوا جُمْلَةً ـ لَعِبُوا سَوِيَّةً; they joked together, تَدَاعَبُوا. Some of the Arab girls were playing outside the door, كَانَ بَعْضُ بَنَاتِ ٱلْعَرَبِ يَلْعَبْنَ خَارِجَ ٱلْبَابِ.

To play away, as of money, to spend in gaming, ضَيَّعَ بِٱلْقِمَارِ.

To play fair, عَدِلَ فِي ٱللَّعِبِ.

To play for love, لَعِبَ لِلتَّسَلِّي فَقَطْ.

To play high, for high stakes, لَعِبَ لِرَهْنٍ جَزِيلٍ.

To play into one's hands, give one the advantage, أَفَادَ ـ مَنَحَ ـ أَرْبَحَ ـ كَسَّبَ.

To play off, to perform, عَمِلَ ـ صَنَعَ ـ جَاءَ بِ *aor.* يَجِيءُ. To play one thing off against another, عَارَضَ ـ بِ ـ بَارَى ـ بِ ـ قَابَلَ ـ بِ.

To play on, to shine on, لَأْلَأَ عَلَى ـ تَلَأْلَأَ عَلَى ـ إِرْتَفَّ عَلَى.

To play on, to discharge upon, as guns, water from an engine, *etc.*, أَطْلَقَ ـ عَلَى ـ ضَرَبَ عَلَى ـ بِ.

To play one a trick, joke, لَعِبَ عَلَى ـ أُلْعُوبَةً ـ ضَحِكَ عَلَى. To practise a fraud upon, لَعِبَ عَلَى ـ دُولَابًا ـ مَكَرَ بِ.

To play one false, خَدَعَ ـ جَوَّنَ ـ غَرَّ ـ خَانَ *aor.* يَخُونُ.

To play one's last stake, قَمَرَ مَا بَقِيَ عِنْدَهُ.

To play the amiable, تَظَرَّفَ ـ تَظَارَفَ ـ تَلَطَّفَ.

To play the fool, حَمُقَ ـ حَمِقَ.

To play the man, تَجَلَّدَ ـ تَشَدَّدَ.

To play the whore, زَانَتْ ـ بَاغَتْ: She plays the whore, تُزَانِي ـ تُبَاغِي.

To play tricks, to trifle, لَعِبَ ـ لَعَّبَ ـ عَبِثَ ـ دَاعَبَ.
To play tricks with, to adulterate, غَشَّ; especially of coin, (colloquial,) زَغَلَ.

To play with, make sport of, تَهَزَّأَ بِ ـ تَسَخَّرَ بِ ـ إِسْتَهْزَأَ بِ. To dawdle, trifle, with anything, تَلَهَّى بِ ـ لَهَا بِ ـ عَبِثَ بِ ـ لَعِبَ بِ. To play or dally with, as with a woman, غَازَلَ ـ هَانَغَ.

Play, *n.* Free action, وُسْع — طَلَاق — إِنْطِلَاق — سُهُولَة ; space for action, مَضْرَب — مَيْدَان — فُسْحَة — سَعَة . Sport, لَهْو — لَعِب . Fun, jest, هَزَالَة — هَزْل — مُزَاح . Gambling, خَلَاعَة — قِمَار — لَعِب . A game, لُعْبَة : Whose — is it? whose turn is it to play? لِمَنِ ٱللُّعْبَة . Action, movement, فِعْل — حَرَكَة . Manner of acting, conduct, مُعَامَلَة — سُلُوك . The theatre, ٱلتِّيَاتْرُو — ٱلْمَرْسَح ٱلْعَامّ . A drama, سِيرَة تَتَشَخَّص فِي ٱلتِّيَاتْرُو . Play, dalliance, as with a woman, مُهَانَغَة — مُغَازَلَة . A spectacle, exhibition, مَنْظَر — فُرْجَة . A design, مَرَام — قَصْد — نِيَّة . An opportunity, فُرْصَة — مَعْرِض . A — upon words, تَصْحِيف . Not desirous of —, عَزُوف عَنِ ٱللَّهْو .

Fair play, play without cheating, لَعِب عَدْل ; justice, سَوَآء — نَصَف مِنَ ٱلْجِهَتَيْنِ — شَرْع — قِسْط — إِنْصَاف .

Foul play, treachery, غَدْر — خِيَانَة . An outrage, شَنَاعَة — جَائِفَة — فَظَاعَة . Murder, قَتْل .

Full of play or fun, أُلْعُبَان — لَعُوب — مُلَاعِب — هَزِل .

To be play to one, easy, تَسَهَّلَ ل — تَيَسَّرَ ل .

To bring or call into play, أَعْرَضَ — جَآءَ بِ *aor.* يَجِيء — إِسْتَعْمَلَ .

To give play to, أَطْلَقَ — أَجْرَى — أَعْطَى مَيْدَانًا .

To give one fair play, عَدَلَ عَلَى — أَقْسَطَ عَلَى .

To have free or full play, أَطْلَقَ — جَرَى جِرْيَة ٱلطَّلُوق — تَطَلَّقَ — إِنْطَلَقَ . To expatiate, تَفَسَّحَ .

To make a thing one's play, تَلَاهَى بِ — عَبِثَ بِ — تَسَلَّى بِ .

Play-bill, *n.* جَدْوَل (or سِيَاقَة) لَعِب ٱلتِّيَاتْرُو (or ٱلْمَرْسَح) .

Play-book, *n.* كُرَّاسَة لَعِب ٱلتِّيَاتْرُو (or ٱلْمَرْسَح) .

Player, *n.* One who plays, sports, لِعَب — مُلَاعِب — لَعِبِيّ . A gamester, خَلِيع — لُعَيْب — قِمَارَاتِيّ . A — on a musical instrument, عَازِف *pl.* عَازِفُون — نَوْبَاتِيّ *pl.* نَوْبَاتِيَّة — آلَاتِيّ *pl.* آلَاتِيَّة . One who teaches to play, sport, لَعَّاب .

Playful, *a.* Full of play, frolic, أُلْعُبَان — لَعُوب — لَعِب — مُلَاعِب — لَعْبَان — هَزِل — دُعْبُوب — خَلَاعِيّ — بَطِر . Jocose, witty, of a man, مُلْهٍ .

Playfully, *ad.* هَزْلًا — بِهَزْل — مَزْحًا — بِدُعَابَة — لَهْوًا .

Playfulness, *n.* ٱلْخِلَاع — هَزْل — دُعَابَة .

Playground, *n.* مَلْهَى — مَلْعَب — مَلْعَبَة — مَيْدَان ٱللَّعِب .

Playhouse, *n.* *See* Theatre, *n.*

Playgoer, *n.* مُتَرَدِّد إِلَى ٱلتِّيَاتْرُو (or ٱلْمَرْسَح) .

Playing, *n.* Performing, عَمَل ; pretending, تَصَنُّع ; playing on an instrument, نَدْف — ضَرْب — لَعِب عَلَى ; theatrical acting, لَعِب فِي ٱلتِّيَاتْرُو — تَشَخُّص فِي ٱلْمَرْسَح .

Playmate, *n.* رَفِيق فِي ٱللَّعِب *pl.* رُفَقَآء .

Playsome, *a.* *See* Playful, *a.*

Plaything, *n.* أُلْهُوَّة — أُلْهِيَّة — لَهْو — لُعْبَة *pl.* لُعَب . Something to divert one, مَلْهًى *pl.* مَلَاهٍ . Something given to children to play with and keep them quiet, عُلَالَة . A —, as applied to a woman, لَهْو — لَهْوَة .

Playwright, *n.* *See* Dramatist, *n.*

Plea, *n.* What is alleged in defence or justification, حُجَّة *pl.* حُجَج — عِلَّة *pl.* عِلَل — مُحَاكَمَة — مُرَافَعَة — دَعْوَى *pl.* دَعَاوَى . To adduce as a —, إِحْتَجَّ بِ — إِعْتَلَّ بِ . To adduce a — against one, إِحْتَجَّ عَلَى - بِحُجَّة — إِعْتَلَّ عَلَى - بِعِلَّة . He urged or he established his plea, أَدْلَى بِحُجَّتِهِ . Pleas, apologies, مَعَاذِر .

Plead, *v.i.* As in a lawsuit, حَاجَّ . To supplicate earnestly, إِبْتَهَلَ — تَضَرَّعَ . To — for, to, تَشَفَّعَ إِلَى - فِي or بِ . He pleaded, was pertinacious in litigation, and won the day, لَجَّ فَحَجَّ . To adduce arguments, *etc.*; *see under* Plea, *n.*

Plead, *v.t.* To urge a plea, argument, أَدْلَى بِحُجَّة . To — or litigate with, حَاجَّ — نَازَعَ — خَاصَمَ . To — or allege things against, لَفَّ عَلَى - كَذَا . To — for, protect, defend, قَاتَلَ عَن — حَامَى عَن . They pleaded together, of many, تَحَاجُّوا . *See also to* Allege, *v.t.*

Pleadable, *a.* That may be alleged in defence, مِمَّا يُحْتَجّ بِهِ — مِمَّا يُتَعَلَّل بِهِ — ٱلْإِحْتِجَاج بِهِ جَائِز .

Pleader, *n.* One who pleads for, defends, مُحَامٍ عَن — وَكِيل — صَاحِب ٱلدَّعْوَى . An interceder, شَافِع — شَفِيع .

Pleading, *n.* Advocacy, مُحَامَاة — مُحَاجَّة — حِجَاج — بَيَان . Intercession, شَفْعَة — شَفَاعَة .

Pleasant, *a.* Delightful, affording gratification, مُشْتَهًى — شَهِيّ — لَطِيف *pl.* لِطَاف and لُطَفَآء . Pleasant, of a place, *etc.*, حَسَن — نَعِيم — أَنِيق — نَزِيه — بَهِيج ; of a wind, day, or night, رَيِّح ; of personal appearance, جُهَيْر — جَهِر — حَسَن ٱلْحِبْر وَٱلسِّبْر ; of a person, بَشَّاش — هَشّ بَشّ — كَيِّس — أَنِيس — لَطِيف — بَشُوش . Lively, رَوَّاح — مُطْرِب — مُفْرِح . Sweet, حُلْو . A — place, نُزْه — مُتَنَزَّه . Pleasant things, مُشْتَهَيَات . To speak — words, to talk pleasantly, أَطَابَ قَوْلًا . To lead a — life, نَعِمَ — تَنَعَّمَ . To consider —, إِسْتَطَابَ . To be or to seem — to, حَلَا ل . To be — with one, sociable towards him, حَلِيَ بِعَيْنِهِ . To meet one in a —, cheerful, manner, أَقْبَلَ عَلَى — بَشْبَشَ بِ — بَشَّ ل . I have never seen one more — than he is to the meeter, *i.e.* to meet with, مَا رَأَيْتُ أَبَشَّ مِنْهُ بِٱلْمُلَاقِي . This is more — to me than that, هٰذا أَشْهَى إِلَيَّ مِنْ ذٰلِكَ . How — it is! ما أَطْيَبَهُ . *See also* Agreeable, *a.*

Pleasantly, *ad.* لَطافَةً ـ بِلُطْفٍ ـ بَشًّا ـ نَغْمَةً ـ طَلاوَةً ـ بَبَشاشَةٍ ـ بِأُنْسٍ ـ بِحَلاوَةٍ . *See also* Agreeably, *ad.*

Pleasantness, *n.* حَلاوَة ـ طُلاوَة ـ نَغْمَة ـ لَطافَة ـ حُسْن ـ كِياسَة ـ بَشاشَة ظَرافَة ; of a place, نَزْه ـ بَهْجَة ; agreeableness, أُنْس .

Pleasantry, *n.* Jocoseness, هَزْل ـ مَزْح ـ دُعابَة ـ شِماعَة ـ هُزالَة ـ مُمازَحَة . To use —, دَعَبَ ـ مَزَحَ ـ مَزَّة ـ شَمَعَ .

Please, *v.i.* and *t.* To content, satisfy, أَرْضَى ـ أَقْنَعَ . To gratify, أَعْجَبَ ـ سَرَّ ـ أَبْهَجَ ـ وَاتَّ . I pleased him, سُؤْتُهُ . To be pleased, satisfied with, رَضِيَ عَن *aor.* يَرْضَى ـ عُجِبَ إِلَى . To be pleased, gratified with, اِسْتَلَذَّ ـ طابَتْ بِهِ نَفْسُهُ ـ أُعْجِبَ بِ ـ إِنْبَسَطَ بِ . To be pleased with one's self, أُعْجِبَ بِنَفْسِهِ . To be pleased to . . ., اِسْتَحْسَنَ أَنْ ـ أَرادَ ـ يَشاءُ *aor.* شاءَ أَنْ : it pleased him to . . ., صَلُحَ فِي عَيْنِهِ أَنْ . It pleased me, راقَنِي . He pleased me, شاءَنِي . He was pleased with him or it, أُعْجِبَ بِهِ ـ طابَتْ بِهِ نَفْسُهُ . He cannot — everybody, لا يُمْكِنُهُ أَنْ يُرْضِي جَمِيعَ ٱلنَّاسِ . Will you — to sit next to me? إِنْ شاءَ خاطِرُكَ تَجْلِسُ بِٱلْقُرْبِ مِنِّي . It did not — me, ما أُعْجِبْتُ بِهِ ـ ما راقَنِي ـ ما أَعْجَبَنِي . Do what you —, اِعْمَلْ عَلَى ـ شَأْنَكَ وَمَا تُرِيدُ ـ هَواكَ . He shall do what I —, يَعْمَلُ ما سُرِرْتُ بِهِ . If God pleases, إِنْ شاءَ ٱللّٰهُ . If you —, have the kindness, مِنْ فَضْلِكَ . I did it to — you, فَعَلْتُهُ إِكْرامًا لِخاطِرِكَ (*or* كَرَمًا لَكَ) . I left him to do as he pleased, خَلَّيْتُهُ وَسَوْمَهُ . *See also to* Gratify, *v.t.*

Pleased, *a.* Satisfied, راضٍ *pl.* رُضاةٌ ـ رَضِيٌّ . Gratified, مَسْرُور ـ مَحْظُوظ . To be mutually —, of many, تَراضَوْا . *See also under to* Please, *v.t.*

Pleasing, *a.* مَقْبُول ـ جَمِيل ـ حُلْوٌ ـ سارٌّ ـ حَسَن ـ حَسِين ـ عَلَى وَفْقٍ . To consider or esteem as —, اِسْتَلَذَّ ـ اِسْتَحْلَى .

Pleasing, *n.* قُبُول ـ رِضًى .

Pleasingly, *ad.* بِلَطافَةٍ ـ بِطَلاوَةٍ .

Pleasingness, *n.* Of aspect, جُهْر ـ جُهُورَة ـ جَهارَة . Beauty, طُلاوَة ـ لَطافَة .

Pleasurable, *a.* لَذِيذ *pl.* لِذاذ *and* لُدٌّ ـ سارٌّ .

Pleasurably, *ad.* بِحَظٍّ ـ بِسُرُورٍ ـ بِلَذَّةٍ .

Pleasure, *n.* Gratification of the senses or mind, ذَوْق ـ رَوْق ـ حَظٌّ ـ لَذَّة ـ حَظٌّ ـ تَلَذُّذ . Contentment, satisfaction, سُرُور ـ بَحْبَحَة ـ لَذَّة ـ تَسَلٍّ . An amusement, رِضْوان ـ رِضًى ـ إِنْبِساط . Will, خاطِر ـ أَمْر ـ وُدٌّ ـ اِخْتِيار ـ مُراد ـ مَشِيئَة . Delight, jollity, إِبْتِهاج ـ كَيْف ـ عَيْش وَعِشْرَة . Pleasures, لَذّات ـ تَنَعُّم .

It was my — that it should be so, بُودِّي أَنْ يَكُونَ كَذا . It gave him great —, حَصَلَ عِنْدَهُ مِنْ ذٰلِكَ كَمالُ ٱلسُّرُورِ . He did it for his —, amusement, عَمِلَ ذٰلِكَ حَتَّى يَتَسَلَّى بِهِ . It gives me great — to serve you, ما عِنْدَنا نَقْلَةٌ بِكُلَّما يَخُصُّكُمْ . If it is your —, إِنْ كانَ لَكَ خاطِرٌ . What is your —? ماذا تَشْتَهِي ـ ما مُرادُكَ ـ ماذا تُرِيدُ . I have much — in stating, مِنْ حُسْنِ حَظِّي أَنْ أَقُولَ .

At pleasure, as he pleases, كَيْفَما ـ حَسَبَ رِضاهُ ـ حَسَبَ إِرادَتِهِ يَشاءُ . Anyhow, كَيْفَما ٱتَّفَقَ . *See also under* Favour, *n.*

During pleasure, مُدَّةَ ـ مُدَّةَ حُسْنِ ٱلرِّضاءِ ـ مُدَّةَ ٱلإِسْتِصْوابِ ٱلإِسْتِحْسانِ . For an indefinite period, إِلَى ما شاءَ ٱللّٰهُ .

For pleasure, gratification, لِلْكَيْفِ ـ لِلإِنْبِساطِ ـ لِلتَّسَلِّي لِلإِبْتِهاجِ .

To do the pleasure of one, قَضَى حاجَتَهُ ـ عَمِلَ مَرْضاتَهُ ـ اِمْتَثَلَ مُرادَهُ .

To derive pleasure from, اِسْتَمْتَعَ بِ .

To do one a pleasure, kindness, أَصْلَحَ إِلَى ـ عَمِلَ مَعَهُ مَعْرُوفًا .

To esteem it a pleasure, أَحَظَّ مِنْ ـ اِبْتَهَجَ بِ ـ تَعَزَّزَ بِ .

To experience, feel, or have pleasure, اِبْتَهَجَ ـ بَهِجَ ـ سُرَّ ـ راقَ اِنْبَسَطَ .

To indulge in pleasure, اِنْهَمَكَ فِي ـ تَعاطَى ٱللَّذّاتِ ـ تَنَعَّمَ ٱلتَّنَعُّمِ .

To take pleasure in, تَكَيَّفَ بِ ـ اِنْبَسَطَ مِنْ ـ اِبْتَهَجَ بِ ـ سُرَّ بِ .

Pleasure, *v.t.* *See to* Gratify, *v.t.*

Pleasure-ground, *n.* رَوْضَة *pl.* رِياض ـ بُسْتان *pl.* بَساتِينُ .

Plebeian, *n.* }
Plebeian, *a.* } مِنَ ٱلْعَوامِّ ـ مِنَ ٱلسَّفَلَةِ ـ سُفْلِيٌّ ـ عامِّيٌّ ـ عُمِّيٌّ . Plebeians, persons in a low condition, سُفْلِيُّون .

The plebeians, commonalty, العامَّة .

Plebeianism, *n.* سَفال . Plebeian manners, أَوْضاعُ ٱلسَّفَلَةِ .

Plebiscite, *n.* دَعْوَةُ عُمُومِ ٱلأُمَّةِ .

Plectrum, *n.* As of a musical instrument, مِضْراب . *See also* Uvula, *n.*

Pledge, *n.* A pawn, رَهْن *pl.* رُهُون *and* رُهْن ـ رَهِينَة . A guarantee, قَبالَة ـ كَفالَة ـ ضَمان . A promise, عَهْد ـ وَعْدَة . An earnest, عُرْبُون ـ مُسْكان . A toast, تَحِيَّةٌ عِنْدَ شُرْبِ ٱلْمُدامِ . To give in —, رَهَنَ ـ أَرْهَنَ (أَوْ غَيْرِهِ) حُبَّةً بِأَحَدٍ . To redeem a —, pawn, اِفْتَكَّ (*or* فَكَّ) ٱلرَّهْنَ ; one who redeems a —, pawn, فَكّاكُ رَهْنٍ . My hand is a — to thee, يَدِي لَكَ رَهْنٌ . The country will become a — to, or, under the influence of, the government of Russia, ٱلْبِلادُ تَصِيرُ رَهِينَةَ حُكُومَةِ ٱلرُّوسِيّا . *See also* Pawn, Hostage, *n.*

Pledge, *v.t.* To give in pawn, أَرْهَنَ ـ ـَ رَهَنَ. To promise, وَعَدَ بِ *aor.* يَعِدُ ـ أَوْعَدَ. To guarantee, ضَمِنَ ـ ـُ كَفَلَ بِ ـ تَكَفَّلَ بِ. To drink to one's health, شَرِبَ بِسِرِّهِ ـ ـَ شَرِبَ مَحَبَّةً فِيهِ. To — one's self, تَعَهَّدَ.

Pledged, *a.* Pawned, مَرْهُون. Promised, bound, مُتَعَهِّد ـ مَوْعُود ـ مُلْتَزِم.

Pledgee, *n.* One to whom a pawn is given, مُرْتَهِن.

Pledger, *n.* One who pawns, مُرْهِن ـ رَاهِن.

Pledget, *n.* نُسَالَة ـ ضِمَادَة ـ ضِمَاد. To put a — on a wound, ضَمَدَ (or غَمَلَ ‎²) ٱلْجُرْحَ ‎².

Pleiads, *n.* / Pleiades, } The constellation, الثُّرَيَّا.

Pleiocene, *n.* الطَّبَقَةُ ٱلْأَحْدَثُ مِنَ ٱلطَّبَقَاتِ ٱلثَّلَاثِ ٱلْكُبْرَى مِنَ ٱلْأَرْضِ.

Plenarily, *ad.* *See* Fully, *ad.*

Plenariness, *n.* *See* Plenitude, *n.*

Plenary, *a.* Entire, full, كَامِل ـ كُلِّيّ ـ عَامّ. To invest with — powers in, صَرَّفَ فِي; to have — powers in, تَصَرَّفَ فِي. Having — power, صَاحِبُ ٱلْعَقْدِ وَٱلْحَلِّ. Plenary indulgence, سَمَاحٌ كُلِّيّ.

Plenipotence, *n.* قُدْرَةٌ كُلِّيَّةٌ ـ قُوَّةٌ مُطْلَقَةٌ ـ إِسْتِقْلَال.

Plenipotentiary, *n.* مُرَخَّص ـ مُتَصَرِّف ـ مُسَيْطِر ـ مُسَطِّر. A minister —, إِيلْچِي (or سَفِيرٌ) مُرَخَّصٌ.

Plenitude, *n.* Fullness, إِمْتِلَآء ـ فَيْض ـ مِلْءٌ. Completeness, تَمَام ـ كُلِّيَّة ـ كَمَال.

Plenteous, *a.* *See* Plentiful, *a.*

Plenteously, *ad.* *See* Plentifully, *ad.*

Plenteousness, *n.* *See* Plentifulness, *n.*

Plentiful, *a.* Adequate to every purpose, وَافٍ ـ كَافٍ ـ وَفِيّ. Fruitful, of soil, مُخْصِب ـ خَصِيب. A — year, سَنَةٌ شَبِيعَةٌ. A — harvest, حَصَادٌ كَثِيرٌ. A — rain, مَطَرٌ غَزِيرٌ. Abundant, كَثِير ـ غَفِير ـ غَزِير ـ عَمِيم ـ فَيَّاض ـ جَمّ. Of a life, easy, غَضِر. To be —, كَثُرَ ـ ـِ فَاضَ ـ ‎² غَزُرَ ‎². *See also* Abundant, Copious, *n.*

Plentifully, *ad.* بِكَثْرَةٍ ـ غَزَارَةً. To bring forth —, of soil, أَخْصَبَ. *See also* Abundantly, Copiously, *ad.*

Plentifulness, *n.* / Plenty, } كَثْرَة ـ فَرْط ـ جُمُوم ـ فَيْض ـ غَزَارَة ـ وَفْرَة ـ بَرَكَة. *See also* Abundance, Copiousness, *n.*

Pleonasm, *n.* لَفْظٌ زَائِدٌ ـ كَلَامٌ زَائِدٌ ـ حَشْوٌ قَبِيحٌ ـ حَشْوٌ *pl.* مَحَاشٍ.

Pleonastic, *a.* / Pleonastical, } مُتَضَمِّنُ مَحَاشٍ ـ زَائِد.

Pleonastically, *ad.* بِٱلزِّيَادَةِ ـ بِمَحَاشٍ.

Plesiosaurus, *n.* نَوْعٌ مِنَ ٱلتِّمْسَاحِ غَيْرُ مَوْجُودٍ ٱلْآنَ.

Plethora, *n.* كَثْرَة ـ فُضُول ـ إِمْتِلَآء. *See also* Excess, *n.*

Pleura, *n.* غِشَآءُ ٱلصَّدْرِ وَٱلرِّئَةِ مِنْ دَاخِلٍ.

Pleurisy, *n.* / Pleuritis, } ذَاتُ ـ ذَاتُ ٱلْجَنْبِ ـ مُوم ـ بِرْسَام ـ بِلْسَام ـ شَوْصَة ـ ٱلدَّفّ.

Pleuritic, *a.* / Pleuritical, } مُبَرْسَم ـ بِرْسَامِيّ.

Pleurodyne, *n.* كَشْح. To have —, كُشِحَ. Having —, مَكْشُوح.

Plexiform, *a.* مُشَبَّك.

Plexus, *n.* شِبَاك ـ جِسْمٌ مُشَبَّكٌ.

Pliability, / Pliableness, *n.* / Pliancy, } Flexibility, قَابِلِيَّةُ ٱلْعَوَجِ ـ سُرْعَةُ ٱلتَّعَوُّجِ ـ لَيِّن ـ رُطُوبَة ـ لَيَان. Pliancy of disposition, سَدَاجَة ـ لَيَانُ ٱلْجَانِبِ ـ دَمَاثَة ـ مُسَايَرَة ـ رُطُوبَةُ ٱلْخُلُقِ. *See also* Flexibility, *n.*

Pliable, *a.* / Pliant, } Flexible, لَيِّن ـ رَطِيب ـ مُنْحَنٍ ـ سَهْلُ ٱلْعُطُوفِ ـ سَهْو ـ سَمْح. A — bow, قَوْسٌ سَمْحَةٌ. Pliant in disposition, سَاذَج ـ لَيِّنُ ٱلْإِنْعِطَافِ ـ لَيِّنُ ٱلْأَعْطَافِ. Manageable, تَاجّ ـ مِذْعَان. Easy, سَمْح. To be —, flexible, رَطُبَ ‎² ـ لَانَ. To make —, لَيَّنَ ـ رَطَّبَ. To be —, easy, submissive, أَسْمَحَ ـ سَامَحَ. *See also* Flexible, *a.*

Pliantly, *ad.* With flexibility, بِرُطُوبَةٍ ـ بِلَيَانٍ. With pliancy of disposition, بِسَمَاحَةٍ ـ بِلَيَانِ ٱلْجَانِبِ ـ بِدَمَاثَةٍ.

Pliantness, *n.* *See under* Pliability, *n.*

Plicate, *a.* / Plicated, } مَطْوِيّ ـ ذُو مَطَاوٍ (or أَطْوَآء) ـ ذُو أَثْنَآء.

Plicature, *n.* / Plication, } ثَنِيّ *pl.* أَثْنَآء ـ طَيّ *pl.* مَطَاوٍ *and* أَطْوَآء. An original —, رَاحَة.

Pliers, *n.* كَلَّابَة ـ كَلْبَتَانِ ـ مِلْقَط. Tweezers, مِنْتَاش ـ مِنْقَاش ـ مِنْتَاف.

Plight, *v.t.* To pledge, عَهِدَ ـ ـَ ضَمِنَ ـ رَهَنَ ـ ـَ. I — you my troth, أُقَرِّرُ لَكَ عَهْدِي.

Plight, *n.* Plighting, pledging, عِهْدَان. Condition, state, حَال ـ حَالَة. A sorry —, حَالٌ سُوءٌ ـ حَالٌ يُرْثَى لَهُ. In a most wretched —, فِي أَسْوَإِ حَالٍ. They are all in the same —, هُمْ عَلَى حَالٍ (or بِسَاطٍ) وَاحِدٍ. *See also under* Condition, *n.*

Plighted, *a.* *See* Pledged, *a.*

Plinth, *n.* عُمْدَة ـ كُرْسِيّ ـ كُرْسِيُّ عَمُودٍ.

Pliocene, *a.* مَا نِيطَ بِٱلطَّبَقَةِ ٱلْمُسْتَجِدَّةِ مِنَ ٱلطَّبَقَاتِ ٱلثَّلَاثِ ٱلْكُبْرَى مِنَ ٱلْأَرْضِ.

Plod, *v.i.* To do anything slowly, أَرْوَدَ فِي. To give close application to, أَجَدَّ فِي ـ وَاظَبَ عَلَى ـ 2 = جَدَّ فِي. He plodded on his way, 2 = جَدَّ فِي ٱلسَّيْرِ.

Plodding, *n.* Doing anything slowly, رُوَيْد ـ مَرْوَد ـ رُوْد. Close attention, مُوَاظَبَة ـ جِدّ.

Plodding, *a.* Acting leisurely, ذُو رُوَيْدٍ. Diligent, مُوَاظِب ـ مُجْتَهِد ـ ذُو جِدّ.

Plot, *n.* A small piece of ground, بُقْعَة ـ أَعْرَاس *pl.* عَرْصَة *pl.* قِطْعَةٌ مِنَ ٱلْأَرْضِ ـ حَقْلَة ـ طَبَقَة ـ مَشَارَة ـ بِقَاع. The plan of a — of ground, خَارِطَة (*or*) رَسْم عَرْصَةٍ. The —, as of a play, تَأْوِيل ـ مَضْمُون. A stratagem, حِيلَة *pl.* حِيَل ـ دُوْلَاب. A conspiracy, فَسَاد ـ مُحَالَفَةٌ خَفِيَّةٌ ـ مُرَابَطَة ـ مُعَاهَدَة; a — against, إِحْتِيَالٌ عَلَى ـ تَعَصُّبٌ عَلَى. *See also* Conspiracy, *n.*

Plot, *v.t.* To make a plan of, صَوَّرَ ـ 2 رَسَمَ. To contrive, أَحْدَثَ ـ إِخْتَرَعَ. To project, = قَصَدَ ـ تَصَوَّرَ. To — against, أَطْرَقَ فُلَانًا ـ تَعَصَّبَ عَلَى ـ تَفَكَّرَ بِٱلشَّرِّ عَلَى ـ إِحْتَالَ عَلَى ـ لِفُلَانٍ.

Plot, *v.i.* To — against, أَطْرَقَ لِ: Such an one plotted against such an one, أَطْرَقَ فُلَانٌ لِفُلَانٍ. To conspire together, of many, تَرَابَطُوا ـ إِتَّفَقُوا. To — together against, إِحْتَالُوا عَلَى ـ تَعَصَّبُوا عَلَى.

Plotter, *n.* *See* Schemer, *n.*

Plotting, *n.* Projecting, قَصْد ـ تَصَوُّر. Delineating, تَصْوِير ـ رَسْم. Conspiring for evil, إِحْتِيَالٌ عَلَى ـ فَسَاد ـ مُرَابَطَةٌ فِي شَرٍّ.

Plough, *n.* حَرْث ـ مِحْرَاث *pl.* مَحَارِيث ـ فَدَّان *pl.* فَدَادِين. The handle of a —, لِسَانُ ٱلْفَدَّانِ ـ مِقْوَم.

Plough, *v.t.* = 2 حَرَثَ ـ 2 = فَلَحَ (*or*) فَلَحَ ٱلْأَرْضَ. To — the sea, of a ship, 2 = شَجَّ ـ = مَخَرَ.

Plough, *v.i.* إِشْتَغَلَ بِٱلْفَدَّانِ ـ إِسْتَعْمَلَ ٱلْمِحْرَاثَ ـ إِحْتَرَثَ.

Ploughable, *a.* That may be ploughed, مِمَّا يُحْرَثُ ـ مِمَّا يُفْلَحُ ـ مُحْرَث.

Ploughboy, *a.* سَائِقُ ثِيرَانِ ٱلْمِحْرَاثِ.

Ploughed, *a.* Turned up by the plough, حَرْث ـ أَرْضٌ مُثَارَةٌ ـ مَحْرُوث. Ploughed, as the sea by a ship, مَشْجُوج ـ مَمْخُور. Ploughed land ready for sowing, حَرْث ـ فِلْحَان ـ أَعْرَاف.

Ploughing, *n.* The act of turning up the soil with a plough, فَلْحُ ٱلْأَرْضِ ـ فَلَاحَة ـ حِرَاثَة ـ حَرْث. Ploughing the waters, شَجّ ـ مَخْر. A bull for —, فَدَّان *pl.* فَدَادِين.

Plough-land, *n.* أَرْضٌ مُثَارَةٌ ـ أَرْضٌ مَحْرُوثَةٌ.

Ploughman, *n.* فَلَّاح ـ حَرَّاث.

Ploughshare, *n.* عِيَان *pl.* عُيُن ـ عُقَاب ـ سِنَّة ـ سِكَّة *pl.* سِكَك ـ مِحْرَاث ـ نَوْرَج *pl.* نَوَارِج. A maker of ploughshares, سَكَّاك.

Pluck, *v.t.* As of flowers, قَطَّفَ ـ = قَطَفَ; of fruit, produce, إِجْتَنَى ـ = جَنَى ـ إِخْتَرَفَ ـ 2 خَرَفَ; of feathers, = نَتَفَ ـ نَتَّفَ. To be plucked, of flowers, *etc.*, إِقْتَطَفَ; of feathers, إِنْتَتَفَ. To —, turn back, as from an examination, 2 رَدَّ.

To pluck asunder, to separate, = قَطَعَ ـ = فَصَلَ ـ مِن ـ أَشَذَّ ـ 2 شَذَّ بَيْنَ.

To pluck away, to snatch, إِخْتَطَفَ ـ = خَطِفَ ـ 2 نَتَرَ ـ إِعْتَنَفَ.

To pluck out, أَقْلَعَ ـ قَلَّعَ ـ = قَلَعَ. To —, as of hairs, with tweezers, = نَتَفَ ـ = نَتَخَ. To pluck out the eye; *see under* Eye, *n.*

To pluck up, as by the roots, إِسْتَأْصَلَ ـ إِجْتَثَّ ـ 2 جَثَّ.

To be plucked up, إِنْجَثَّ. *See also to* Eradicate, *v.t.*

To pluck up courage, شَدَّدَ عَزْمَهُ ـ تَجَاسَرَ ـ تَجَرَّأَ ـ إِجْتَرَأَ.

Pluck, *n.* The heart, liver, and lights of an animal, جَوْف ـ مِعْلَاق. Courage, شَجَاعَة ـ جُرْأَة ـ جَسَارَة ـ مُرُوَّة.

Plucked, *a.* Of feathers, مُنَتَّف ـ مَنْتُوف. Gathered, of flowers, مَقْطُوف; of fruits, جَنَاة ـ جَنِيّ ـ جَنًى ـ خَرِيف. Turned back, as from an examination, مَرْدُود.

Plucky, *a.* عَزُوم ـ جَسُور ـ مِقْدَام ـ صَاحِبُ مُرُوَّةٍ.

Plug, *n.* سِدَادَة ـ سِدَاد ـ أُسْكُوبَة ـ إِسْكَابَة ـ صِمَام.

Plug, *v.t.* 2 صَمَّ ـ 2 سَدَّ. To be plugged, إِسْتَدَّ ـ إِنْسَدَّ.

Plugging, *n.* سَدّ ـ صَمّ.

Plum, *n.* The fruit, بُرْقُوق (*vulg.* برقوق) ـ إِجَّاص ـ خَوْخ; called in Syria, عَيْنُ بَقَرٍ. A small kind of plum, قَلْبُ ٱلطَّيْرِ. Dry plums, إِجَّاصٌ مُجَفَّفٌ.

Plumage, *n.* رِيش *pl.* رِيَاش.

Plumb, *n.* A mason's, شَقُول ـ شَاقُول ـ زِيج.

Plumb, *a.* Perpendicular, straight, عَدِل ـ عَمُود.

Plumb, *v.t.* To adjust by a plumb line, 2 شَقَلَ ـ عَدَّلَ ـ بِٱلشَّاقُولِ.

To sound, = قَاسَ بِٱلْبَلَدِ ـ = قَاسَ. To stop up, 2 سَدَّ.

Plumbaginous, *a.* مِثْلُ ٱلْأُسْرُبِّ.

Plumbago, *n.* أُسْرُبّ ـ أُسْرُب.

Plumbean, *a.* } Of lead, مِنْ رَصَاصٍ ـ رَصَاصِيّ. *See also* Dull, *a.*
Plumbeous, }

Plumber, *n.* رَصَّاص.

Plumbery, *n.* Work done by a plumber, شُغْلُ ٱلرَّصَّاصِ. A place where lead is worked, مَعْمَلُ رَصَاصٍ.

Plumbing, *n.* The act of working in lead, شُغْلُ رَصَاصٍ.

Plumb-line, *n.* خَيْطُ ٱلشَّاقُولِ.

Plumb-rule, *n.* جَدْوَلُ ٱلشَّاقُولِ.

Plum-cake, *n.* قُرْصٌ مَحْشِيٌّ بِزَبِيبٍ.

Plum-pudding, *n.* ضَرْبٌ مِنَ ٱلزَّرْدَى بِزَبِيبٍ.

Plume, *n.* A feather, رِيشَةٌ *coll.* رِيشٌ. An ornamental jewelled sprig, رِيشَةٌ. Honour, glory, فَخْر ـ شَرَف ـ اِفْتِخَار.

Plume, *v.t.* To pluck feathers, نَتَّفَ. To adorn with feathers, زَيَّنَ-بِرِيشٍ. To — itself, of a bird, نَشْنَشَ. To — or pride one's self on anything, اِفْتَخَرَ بِ ـ اِعْتَزَّ بِ.

Plumeless, *a.* بِلَا رِيشٍ.

Plumiped, *n.* مُرَيَّشُ ٱلْأَرْجُلِ ـ مُسَرْوَلٌ بِرِيشٍ.

Plummet, *n.* A piece of lead for sounding, بَلَد. An instrument to show the perpendicular, مِطْمَار. A pencil of lead, قَلَمُ رَصَاصٍ ـ رَصَاصَةٌ.

Plumose, *a.* } Having feathers, مُرَيَّش ـ ذُو رِيشٍ; resembling
Plumous, } feathers, رِيشِيٌّ ـ مِثْلَ ٱلرِّيشِ. Having feathers on the sides, ذُو رِيشٍ عَلَى ٱلْجَوَانِبِ.

Plump, *a.* Fat and full, لَبِيخ ـ خَدْل ـ كِنَاز *pl.* كُنُز ـ سَمِين ـ ضَخْم ـ أَضْخَمُ ـ مُرَبْرَب; especially in the arms and legs, of a woman, خَدَلَّجَة; in the fore-arms, also of a woman, جَسْرَةُ ٱلسَّوَاعِدِ. Corpulent, شَخِيص. Downright, مَحْض ـ صَافٍ ـ مُطْلَق ـ خَالِص. A woman — in the shanks, خَدَالَةُ ٱلسَّاقِ. *See also* Frank, *a.*

Plump, *v.t* To fatten, سَمَّنَ ـ صَيَّرَ-ضَخْمًا. To swell, dilate, أَغْلَظَ ـ وَرَّمَ. To — a vote, أَعْطَى رَأْيَهُ فِي ٱلِانْتِخَابِ إِلَى طَالِبٍ وَاحِدٍ.

Plump, *v.i.* To become plump, سَمِنَ ـ 2 خَدُلَ ـ 2 ضَخُمَ. To swell, dilate, وَرِمَ *aor.* يَرِمُ ـ 2 غَلُظَ.

Plump, *ad.* At once, بِٱلْمَرَّةِ ـ كَبَّةً. Heavily, بِثِقَلٍ.

Plumper, *n.* An unqualified lie, كَذِبٌ سُمَاقٌ. An exclusive vote, إِعْطَاءُ ٱلرَّأْيِ فِي ٱلِانْتِخَابِ إِلَى طَالِبٍ وَاحِدٍ.

Plumply, *ad.* Fully, without reserve, بِصَرَاحَةٍ ـ بِوُضُوحٍ ـ إِطْلَاقًا ـ بَتَّةً.

Plumpness, *n.* ضِخَم ـ خَدَالَة ـ خُدُولَة ـ سَمَانَة.

Plumule, *n.* As of a plant, أَصْلُ سَاقِ ٱلشَّجَرَةِ.

Plumy, *a.* ذُو رِيشٍ ـ مُزَيَّنٌ بِرِيشٍ.

Plunder, *n.* سَلَب ـ نَهْب. Booty, خُلْسَة ـ خَلِيسَة ـ نُهْبَة ـ غَنِيمَة. *See also under* Booty, *n.*

Plunder, *v.t.* سَلَبَ 2 ـ حَرَبَ 2 ـ نَهَبَ 2 ـ اِنْتَهَبَ. To permit to —, أَنْهَبَ. Their houses were plundered, اِنْتَهَبَتْ بُيُوتُهُمْ.

Plunderer, *n.* نَاهِب *pl.* نِهَاب ـ نَهَّاب. A — on the road, قَاطِعُ ٱلطَّرِيقِ *pl.* قُطَّاع; as in war, غَزَّاء.

Plunderer, *n.* حَرْب ـ سَلْب ـ نَهْب; on the road, إِصَابَةُ ٱلطُّرُقَاتِ. A — expedition, غَزْوَة ـ مَغْزَاة. To send on a — expedition, أَغْزَى ـ غَزَّى.

Plunge, *v.t.* and *i.* To thrust something into a liquid, 2 غَطَّ-فِي ـ غَطَسَ-فِي ـ أَقْمَشَ-فِي ـ 2 قَمَشَ-فِي ـ غَمَسَ-فِي. To be plunged in, as into water, اِنْغَمَسَ فِي ـ اِغْتَمَسَ فِي ـ اِنْغَطَّ فِي ـ اِنْقَمَشَ فِي ـ غَطَسَ. To drive into any state, اِضْطَرَّ-إِلَى ـ غَرَّقَ-فِي ـ رَمَى-فِي *aor.* يَرْمِي: He plunged him into a sea of troubles, غَرَّقَهُ فِي بَحْرِ ٱلْآلَامِ. To — one's self into water, to dive, اِنْغَطَّ فِي ـ غَطَسَ فِي ـ 2 غَاصَ فِي. To — one's self into any business, اِنْغَمَرَ فِي ـ اِنْهَمَكَ فِي ـ غَرِقَ فِي ـ عَسَمَ بِ ـ اِغْتَمَرَ فِي ـ خَاضَ فِي ٱلْأَمْرِ *aor.* يَخُوضُ; of a conflict, غَامَسَ (or غَامَرَ) فِي. He plunged into vain discourse, خَاضَ *aor.* يَخُوضُ ٱلْبَاطِلَ. To — into war, غَشِيَ ٱلْحَرْبَ. To —, as a bird, from the air towards the ground, 2 زَفَّ زَفِيفًا. They were plunged into a war, تَهَوَّرُوا فِي حَرْبٍ.

Plunge, *v.i.* As of a horse, وَثَبَ *aor.* يَثِبُ.

Plunge, *n.* A thrusting into a liquid, غَمْس ـ غَطْس. A plunging of one's self, as into water, غِيَاص ـ غِيَاصَة ـ اِنْغِطَاط. A —, as of a horse, وَثْب ـ وِثَاب.

Plunger, *n.* As of a horse, *etc.*, وَثَّاب. The cylinder of a pump, مَكْبَسُ ٱلطُّلُمْبَةِ.

Plunging, *a.* Rushing, driving headlong, مُتَهَوِّر ـ هَيِّر ـ سَادِر; of a horse, *etc.*, وَثَّاب; a — horse, فَرَسٌ وَثَبِيٌّ; a — camel, نَاقَةٌ وَثَبِيٌّ. A — fire, إِطْلَاقُ ٱلْمَدَافِعِ مِنْ عِلْوَةٍ إِلَى تَحْتُ.

Pluperfect, *a.* The — tense, صِيغَةُ ٱلْمَاضِي ٱلْأَسْبَقِ.

Plural, *n.* ٱلْجَمْعُ. Perfect —, جَمْعٌ سَالِمٌ ـ جَمْعٌ صَحِيحٌ. Plural of paucity, جَمْعُ قِلَّةٍ; of multitude, جَمْعُ كَثْرَةٍ; plural of a —, جَمْعُ جَمْعٍ.

Pluralist, *n.* خُورِي مُتَمَتِّعٌ بِإِيرَادِ قُرًى مُتَعَدِّدَةٍ.

Plurality, *n.* تَعَدُّد ـ جِمَاع ـ كَثْرَة. Belief in a — of gods, or attributing — to the Godhead, شِرْك. To ascribe — to God, to associate any person with Him, أَشْرَكَ بِٱللهِ.

Plus, *ad.* أَيْضًا ـ عِبَارَةٌ عَنِ ٱلزِّيَادَةِ. Three — six, ثَلَاثَةٌ وَزِدْ عَلَى ذٰلِكَ سِتَّةً.

Plush, *n.* ضَرْبٌ خَشِنٌ مِنَ ٱلْقَطِيفَةِ ٱلدُّونِ.

Pluto, *n.* إِسْمُ إِلٰهِ جَهَنَّمَ عِنْدَ ٱلرُّومَانِيِّينَ فِي عَصْرِ ٱلْجَاهِلِيَّةِ.

Plutonian, *n.* } مِنْ أَهْلِ رَأْيِ ٱلْقَائِلِينَ أَنَّ ٱلْجِبَالَ تَرَاكَمَتْ مِنْ
Plutonist, } فَاعِلِيَّةِ ٱلنَّارِ.

Plutonic, *a.* Of — rocks, عِبَارَةٌ عَنِ ٱلصُّخُورِ ٱلنَّارِيَّةِ ٱلْمَطْمُورَةِ فِي ٱلْأَرْضِ.

Pluvial, *a.* } مَطَرِيٌّ ـ مُتَعَلِّقٌ بِٱلْمَطَرِ.
Pluvious, }

Pluviameter, *n.* } مِقْيَاسُ هَطْلِ ٱلْمَطَرِ ـ مِيزَانُ ٱلْمَطَرِ.
Pluviometer, }

Ply, *v.t.* To try to ..., to endeavour to ..., سَعَى إِلَى *aor.* يَسْعَى ـ جَرَّبَ. To pull, pull at, جَرَّ ². To practise anything with diligence, جَدَّ فِي ² ـ اِجْتَهَدَ فِي ـ لَزِمَ ². To employ, اِسْتَعْمَلَ ـ أَعْمَلَ. To keep at work, as of a machine, شَغَّلَ ـ عَالَجَ. To importune, أَلَحَّ عَلَى ـ لَجَّ عَلَى ² ـ أَكَدَّ ـ أَلَتَّ عَلَى. To — one with, as arguments, *etc.*, so as to influence him, صَانَعَ ـ بِ ـ أَدَرَّ. To do anything to one again and again, عَلَّ ²: The beater plied the beaten with continued strokes, عَلَّ ٱلضَّارِبُ ٱلْمَضْرُوبَ. He plied the oar, جَذَفَ بِٱلْمِجْدَافِ ².

Ply, *v.i.* To busy one's self, to strive, كَدَّ ² ـ تَعَنَّى ـ اِجْتَهَدَ ـ تَعَمَّلَ. To try to make progress against the wind, سَعَى ضِدَّ ٱلرِّيحِ *aor.* يَسْعَى. To go to and fro, تَرَدَّدَ.

Ply, *n.* *See* Fold, Plait, Bias, *n.*

Plying, *n.* An endeavour, اِجْتِهَادٌ ـ جِدٌّ ـ سَعْيٌ. Use, using, اِسْتِعْمَالٌ ـ إِعْمَالٌ. Keeping at work, تَشْغِيلٌ ـ مُعَالَجَةٌ. Importunity, إِلْحَاحٌ ـ لَجَاجَةٌ ـ مُحَاجَاةٌ. Plying, as with arguments, مُصَانَعَةٌ; as with an oar, جَذْفٌ ـ جَذْفٌ.

Pneumatic, *a.* } Pertaining to air, مُتَعَلِّقٌ بِٱلْهَوَآءِ ـ هَوَائِيٌّ
Pneumatical, } وَٱلرِّيحِ. Moved by air, يُحَرِّكُهُ ٱلْهَوَآءُ ـ هَوَائِيٌّ.

Pneumatics, *n.* } عِلْمُ ٱلْهَوَآءِ وَحَرَكَاتِهِ وَكَذٰلِكَ عِلْمُ ٱلْأَرْوَاحِ
Pneumatology, } وَٱلْكَائِنَاتِ ٱلرُّوحِيَّةِ.

Pneumonia, *n.* } ذَاتُ ٱلرِّئَةِ.
Pneumony, }

Pneumonic, *a.* Pertaining to the lungs, مُتَعَلِّقٌ بِٱلرِّئَةِ. A —, a medicine for the lungs, دَوَآءٌ نَافِعٌ لِلرِّئَةِ.

Pneumonitis, *n.* *See* Pneumonia, *n.*

Poach, *v.t.* To boil slightly, سَلَقَ ² ـ سَلَقَ ـ نَصَّفَ سَلْقٍ. To steal game, سَرَقَ ² (*or* اِسْتَرَقَ) ٱلصَّيْدَ. To leave marks on soft ground, أَثَّرَ فِي ٱلرَّخَّةِ. To —, of literature, تَسَرَّقَ: He poached my poetry, bit by bit, تَسَرَّقَ شِعْرِي.

Poach, *v.i.* To be trodden with deep tracks, تَأَثَّرَتِ ٱلرَّخَّةُ.

Poached, *a.* Slightly boiled, مَسْلُوقٌ ـ مَسْلُوقٌ نَصْفَ سَلْقٍ.

Poached land, trodden with tracks, أَرْضٌ مُتَأَثِّرَةٌ.

Poacher, *n.* Of game, سَارِقُ ٱلصَّيْدِ *pl.* سَرَقَةٌ *and* سُرَّاقٌ.

Poaching, *n.* Of game, سَرِقَةُ ٱلصَّيْدِ; of literature, تَسَرُّقٌ.

Poachy, *a.* Soft, muddy, of land, رَخَّةٌ ـ أَرْضٌ رَخَاخٌ.

Pock, *n.* Of the small-pox, حَبَّةُ ٱلْجُدَرِيِّ.

Pocket, *n.* As of a garment, جَيْبٌ *pl.* جُيُوبٌ ـ جُيَيْبَةٌ *pl.* جَيْبٌ. A breast —, عُبٌّ ـ جُيَيْبَةُ ٱلْعُبِّ ـ سَيَّالَةٌ. Out of his own —, at his own expense, مِنْ كِيسِهِ ـ مِنْ جَيْبِهِ. To be in — by, to gain, رَبِحَ مِنْ ² ـ اِكْتَسَبَ مِنْ. To be out of —, to have no money, أَفْلَسَ. To be out of — by, خَسِرَ مِنْ ². To pick a —, سَرَقَ مِنَ ٱلْجَيْبِ ². To spare one's —, وَفَّرَ جُيَيْبَهُ.

Pocket, *v.t.* To put into the —, حَطَّ فِي ٱلْجَيْبِ. To steal, سَرَقَ ² ـ اِسْتَرَقَ. To —, an affront, اِحْتَمَلَ (*or* تَجَرَّعَ *or* ² جَرَعَ) ٱلْإِهَانَةَ.

Pocket-book, *n.* خَرِيطَةٌ *pl.* خَرَائِطُ ـ كُتَيِّبٌ يُحْمَلُ فِي ٱلْجَيْبِ.

Pocket-money, *n.* فُلُوسٌ لِلْجَيْبِ ـ مَبْلَغٌ لِلتَّنَزُّهِ; *vulg.* شِبْرِقَةٌ.

Pock-marked, *a.* مَنْقُورٌ بِٱلْجُدَرِيِّ; in the face, مَجْدُورُ ٱلْوَجْهِ.

Pocky, *a.* Infected with small-pox, مُجَدَّرٌ ـ مُصَابٌ بِٱلْجُدَرِيِّ.

Pod, *n.* عُلْفَةٌ *coll.* عُلَّفٌ ـ خَرِيطَةٌ *pl.* خَرَائِطُ ـ غِمَادٌ *pl.* أَغْمَادٌ.

Podagric, *a.* } *See* Gouty, *a.*
Podagrical, }

Podex, *n.* ٱلسَّافِلَةُ ـ دُبُرٌ ـ مِجْعَرٌ ـ اِسْتٌ.

Podgy, *a.* ضَخْمٌ ـ مُرَبْرَبٌ ـ مُؤَنَّفٌ.

Poem, *n.* شِعْرٌ *pl.* أَشْعَارٌ. A short —, قَصِيدَةٌ *pl.* قَصَائِدُ. A — in praise of women, مَغْزَلٌ ـ غَزَلٌ. A current or popular —, قَافِيَةٌ شَرُودٌ. Unfamiliar rhymes or poems, أَوَابِدُ ـ قَوَافٍ شَوَارِدُ.

Poesy, *n.* *See* Poetry, *n.*

Poet, *n.* شَاعِرٌ *pl.* شُعَرَآءُ. A great or famous —, شَاعِرٌ مُفْلِقٌ: *the gradations downwards are these,* 2. شَاعِرٌ; 3. شُوَيْعِرٌ; 4. شُعْرُورٌ; 5. مُتَشَاعِرٌ. To be a —, or to poetize, شَعَرَ ². To affect to be a —, or poetry, تَشَاعَرَ.

Poetaster, *n.* شُعْرُورٌ.

Poetess, *n.* شَاعِرَةٌ.

Poetic, *a.* } شِعْرِيٌّ. Written in verse, مَنْظُومٌ. To speak in —
Poetical, } language, قَالَ شِعْرًا ² ـ شَعَرَ ². Very —, أَشْعَرُ.

One who affects to be —, مُتَشَاعِرٌ.

Poetically, *ad.* تَنْظِيمًا ـ نَظْمًا ـ عَلَى طَرْزِ ٱلشُّعَرَآءِ.

Poetize, *v.i.* شَعَرَ ² شَعُرَ ـ .

Poet-laureate, *n.* شَاعِرُ ٱلْمَلِكِ.

Poetry, *n.* شِعْر *pl.* أَشْعَار. A piece of poetry, a poem, قَصِيدَة *pl.* قَصَائِد ـ نَشِيد *pl.* أَنْشَاد. A collection of —, or the collected poems of a particular poet, دِيوَان *pl.* دَوَاوِينُ. I spoke in — to, شَعَرْتُ ل. Had he known his deficiency he would not have attempted to speak —, لَوْ شَعَرَ بِنَقْصِهِ لَمَا شَعَرَ.

Poignancy, *n.* شِدَّة ـ حِدَّة.

Poignant, *a.* شَدِيد ـ حَادٌّ.

Poignantly, *ad.* بِشِدَّةٍ ـ بِحِدَّةٍ.

Point, *n.* A headland, cape, طَنَف *pl.* طُنُوف ـ رَأْس *pl.* رُؤُوس. Point, as of a knife, beak, *etc.*, سِنَان *pl.* أَسِنَّة; as of a spear, نَصْل *pl.* نِصَال *and* أَنْصُل; as of a pen, سِنَّة *pl.* سِنَن. An edge, شَفَا ـ حَدٌّ ـ شُفْر. An engraver's tool, قَلَم ـ مِنْقَاش. An aim, غَرَض ـ مِنْهَاج ـ مُرَاد ـ مَقْصَد ـ نِيَّة. A situation, position, مَحَلّ ـ مَوْقِع ـ مَوْضِع ـ جِهَة ـ طَرَف. Condition, حَال ـ حَالَة. A — on which anything turns, مَدَار *pl.* مَدَارَات. Subject matter, مَحَطّ ـ مَوْضُوع. A question, مَسْأَلَة. A degree, دَرَجَة ـ مَرْتَبَة ـ رُتْبَة. Point, as of time, وَقْت ـ زَمَان ـ سَاعَة ـ دَقِيقَة. A dot, نُقْطَة *pl.* نُقَط *and* نِقَاط. A period, مَحَطّ. A vowel-point, حَرَكَة *pl.* حَرَكَات. A — of the compass, جِهَة *pl.* جِهَات. Point, meaning, force, مَعْنًى ـ قُوَّة ـ سِدَاد. A point, as of a railway, مِفْتَاح. Good points, مَحَاسِن ـ شَمَائِل.

At the point of death, مُشْرِف عَلَى ٱلْمَوْتِ ـ عَلَى شَفَا ٱلْمَوْتِ.

In all points, فِي كُلِّ ٱلْوُجُوهِ ـ فِي كُلِّ شَيْءٍ.

In point of, with regard to, نَظَرًا إِلَى ـ بِخُصُوصِ.

In point of fact, حَقِيقَةً ـ الحَقِيقَةَ.

Not to the point, غَيْرُ سَدِيدٍ ـ غَيْرُ مُسِدٍّ.

The four cardinal points of the compass, الجِهَاتُ ٱلْأَرْبَعُ ٱلْأَصْلِيَّةُ.

To the point, سَدَادًا ـ سَدَدًا.

To be on the point of, doing, *etc.*, شَفَرَ عَلَى ـ كَانَ عَلَى بَنَاتِ ٱلْأَمْرِ ـ أَشْرَفَ عَلَى ـ أَشْفَى عَلَى ـ كَادَ ـ هَمَّ ب ²: He is on the point of accomplishing his affair, هُوَ عَلَى شَرَفٍ مِنْ قَضَاءِ حَاجَتِهِ.

To be to the point, سَدَّ *aor.* يَسِدُّ ـ إِسْتَدَّ ـ تَسَدَّدَ.

To come to the point, أَسَدَّ ـ سَدَّدَ: He comes to the point in what he said, يُسِدُّ فِي ٱلْقَوْلِ.

To gain one's point, نَالَ (or ² بَلَغَ) مُرَادَهُ ـ أَنْجَحَ بِمَرَامِهِ.

To make it a point to, اِخْتَصَّ أَن ـ إِسْتَوْجَبَ أَن.

To stretch a point, عَمِلَ فَوْقَ ٱلطَّاقَةِ ـ إِسْتَلْزَمَ.

Point, *v.t.* and *int.* To sharpen to a point, أَسَلَّ ـ نَسَّلَ ـ أَنْصَلَ ـ أَحَدَّ ـ حَدَّدَ ـ سَنَّ ² ـ أَسَنَّ. To be pointed, sharpened, اِحْتَدَّ ـ إِنْسَنَّ. To put dots on, as of letters, رَقَشَ ² ـ رَقَّشَ ـ نَقَطَ ² ـ نَقَّطَ. To be dotted, نُقِطَ. To put the vowel points to letters, شَكَلَ ² ـ أَشْكَلَ ـ أَعْجَمَ ـ عَجَّمَ. To have the vowel points affixed, أُعْجِمَ. To —, as of a spear or sword, at, شَرَعَ ² ـ شَرَّعَ (or شَرَّعَ ـ or أَشْرَعَ ـ) قِبَلَهُ (or نَحْوَهُ). (*See also to* Aim, *v.t.*) To fill interstices with mortar, عَقَدَ ٱلْخِلَالَ بِٱلْجِصِّ ـ. To —, to shift, as of sails, حَوَّلَ.

To point anything towards, وَجَّهَ إِلَى ـ صَوَّبَ إِلَى. To be pointed towards, تَوَجَّهَ إِلَى ـ تَصَوَّبَ إِلَى.

To point at, to indicate, أَشَارَ إِلَى ـ أَشَّرَ إِلَى. To point the finger at, in contumely, صَبَّعَ ب ـ.

To point one to, to advise, أَشَارَ عَلَى ب ـ نَصَحَ ـ نَصَحَ ل ـ.

To point out, to make known, indicate, أَشَارَ ب ـ دَلَّ إِلَى ² ـ أَظْهَرَ: He pointed it out to him, نَصَّهُ عَلَيْهِ ². To intimate, as by motions of the face, to hint at, *etc.*, رَمَزَ إِلَى ² ـ وَغَزَ إِلَى ـ أَوْمَى إِلَى ـ عَبَّرَ عَن or ب.

Point-blank, *a.* Horizontal, أُفُقِيٌّ ـ بَسِيط ـ عَدِل. Point-blank range, تَشْرِيع (or مَنْزِل) عَدِل.

Point-d'appui, *n.* مَرْكَز *pl.* مَرَاكِز ـ مَغْرِز.

Pointed, *a.* Having an acute point, مُؤَسَّل ـ مُؤَنَّف ـ مُذَبَّب. Sharp edged, حَادٌّ ـ حُدَّان. Marked with diacritical points, مُنَقَّط ـ مَنْقُوط; with vowel points, مُعْجَم. Aimed at, مُشَرَّع ـ شَارِع. To the point, of a speech, سَدِيد. Sharp, of a speech, حَادٌّ ـ جَارِح ـ عَضْب; pointed in speech, عَضْبُ ٱللِّسَانِ. Singling out, مُخَصِّص ـ مُعَيِّن. A — ear, أُذُنٌ مُؤَسَّلَةٌ. *See also* Piquant, *a.*

Pointedly, *ad.* As singling out, تَخْصِيصًا ـ تَعْيِينًا. Exactly, directly, عَيْنًا ـ أَكِيدًا ـ تَصْرِيحًا وَبَيَانًا.

Pointedness, *n.* Aim, as of a remark, speech, أَمَد ـ مَقْصُود ـ مُرَاد. Sharpness, حِدَّة. *See also* Point, *n.*

Pointer, *n.* A thing that points the way, عَلَم *pl.* أَعْلَام ـ مَعْلَم ـ إِشَارَة. The —, as of a clock, *etc.*, عَقْرَب *pl.* عَقَارِب. A — dog, ضِرْو or ضَرِيّ *pl.* أَضْرٍ *and* ضِرَاء.

Point-lace, *n.* شَبِيكَة *vulg.* تَخْرِيمَة.

Pointless, *a.* Having no point, بِلَا نَصْلٍ ـ بِلَا سِنَانٍ. Blunt, كَلِيل ـ كَهَام ـ بَارِد. Meaningless, بِلَا مَعْنًى ـ جِبِل.

Pointsman, *n.* As on a railway, مَاسِكُ ٱلْمِفْتَاحِ.

Poise, *n.* Weight, ثِقْل ـ ثَقَالَة. Balance, equilibrium, مُوَازَنَة.

Poise, *v.t.* To weigh, وَزَنَ *aor.* يَزِنُ. To balance, وَازَنَ. To — itself in the air, of a bird, صَفَّ ². *See also to* Balance, *v.t.*

Poison, *n.* قِشْب *pl.* أَقْشَاب — سَمٌّ or سِمٌّ *pl.* سِمَام *and* سُمُوم. Mortal —, سَمٌّ قَاتِلٌ — ذُعَاف — سَمٌّ ذِيفَانٌ — سَمٌّ ذُعَافٌ. Venom, حُمَة. An instantaneous —, سَمٌّ سَاعَةٍ. To die of —, مَاتَ مَسْمُومًا. The — crept into his veins, دَبَّ ٱلسَّمُّ فِي عُرُوقِهِ ₂. The — crept into him, سَرَى فِيهِ ٱلسَّمُّ ₂.

Poison, *v.t.* To infect with poison, سَقَى سَمًّا — سَمَّمَ — سَمَّ ² ₂. To corrupt, أَفْسَدَ. To deprave, خَسَّرَ — أَخْبَثَ — أَخْرَبَ. To turn one against, كَرَّهَ إِلَى.

Poisoned, *a.* Killed by or containing poison, مَسْمُوم.

Poisoner, *n.* سَامٌ.

Poisonous, *a.* سَامٌّ; of any animal, سَامَّة. Corrupting, مُفْسِد — مُخْبِث. *See also under* Obscene, *a.*

Poisonously, *ad.* بِسَمٍّ.

Poisonousness, *n.* *See* Poison, *n.*

Poke, *n.* A pocket, جَيْب *pl.* جُيُوب. A small bag, جِرَاب — كِيس. A push, thrust, صَدْمَة — دَفْعَة — دَفْع — دَسْع. He bought a pig in a —, شَرَى شَيْئًا بِدُونِ أَنْ يَرَاهُ.

Poke, *v.t.* To push, thrust, دَفَرَ ² — صَدَمَ ₂ — دَفَعَ ₂ — دَسَعَ ₂. To — with a pointed instrument, طَعَنَ ² — نَخَزَ ₂ — ضَغَطَ ² دَفَشَ ². To —, as a fire, حَرَّكَ — حَشَّ ². To — out, قَلَعَ — أَخْرَجَ — أَبْرَزَ.

Poke, *v.i.* *See to* Grope, *v.i.*

To poke about a place, تَرَدَّدَ إِلَى — ٱلْتَزَمَ — إِخْتَلَفَ إِلَى.

To poke about for, فَتَّشَ عَلَى — تَلَمَّسَ: He is poking about with some object in view, هُوَ يَحُومُ حَوْلَ غَرَضٍ لَهُ.

To poke one's nose into, حَشَرَ حَالَهُ ² ₂ — تَدَخَّلَ فِي — تَدَاخَلَ فِي — قَارَشَ فِي: He pokes his nose into other people's affairs, يَتَدَخَّلُ فِي أُمُورِ غَيْرِهِ.

Poke, *n.* }
Poke-weed, } عِنَبُ ٱلثَّعْلَبِ — عِنَبُ ٱلذِّئْبِ.

Poker, *n.* For stirring a fire, مِحْرَاك — مِحَشَّة — مِحَشّ.

Poking, *n.* Poking about a place, تَرَدُّد — ٱلْتِزَام — إِخْتِلَاف. *See also* Poke, Interference, *n.*

Polacre, *n.* }
Polacca, } شَخْتُور — فَلُوكَة.

Poland, *n.* بُلُونِيَا — بُولَانْد — ٱللَّهِسْتَانُ.

Polar, *a.* مُتَعَلِّقٌ بِٱلْقُطْبِ — قُطْبِيٌّ; near the pole, قَرِيبٌ مِنَ ٱلْقُطْبِ. The — circle, دَائِرَةُ ٱلْقُطْبِ — مَدَارُ ٱلْقُطْبِ. The — star, ٱلْقُطْبُ — ٱلْكَوْكَبُ ٱلشَّمَالِيُّ. A — bear, دُبٌّ كَبِيرٌ أَبْيَضُ مِنْ أَطْرَافِ ٱلْبَحْرِ ٱلْمُجَمَّدِ. The pole star of the age, قُطْبُ ٱلزَّمَانِ.

Polarity, *n.* State of a body as having two poles, ذَاتُ قُطْبَيْنِ. Quality of pointing to the pole, شَأْنُ (or خَاصَّةُ) ٱلتَّوَجُّهِ نَحْوَ ٱلْقُطْبِ.

Polarization, *n.* The act of giving polarity to, ٱلتَّوْجِيهُ نَحْوَ ٱلْقُطْبِ. *See also* Polarity, *n.*

Polarize, *v.t.* سَقَاهُ مَا يُوَجِّهُهُ نَحْوَ ٱلْقُطْبِ ₂.

Polarized, *a.* مُسْقِيٌّ مَا يُوَجِّهُهُ نَحْوَ ٱلْقُطْبِ.

Pole, *n.* Of the heavens, قُطْب *pl.* قُطُوب *and* أَقْطَاب *and* قِطَاب. A long and slender piece of timber, عَصًا طَوِيلَةٌ — عَتَلَة — رَايَة — قَضِيب *pl.* قُضْبَان. A rafter, جِسْر *pl.* أَجْسُر *and* جُسُور. A prop, support, دِعَام or دِعَامَة *pl.* دَعَائِمُ — عُمْدَة — عَمُود *pl.* عُمُد. A mast, دَقَل *pl.* أَدْقَال — صَارِيَة *pl.* صَوَارِي. A — for propelling boats, مِدْرًا *vulg.* مِدْرًا — مُرْدِيٌّ — خَيْزُرَان — سَيْب *pl.* سُيُوب. A — to hang clothes on, غِدَان. The — of a rope-dancer, مِيزَانُ ٱلرَّقَّاصِ. Pole of a carriage, عَتَلَةُ ٱلْعَرَبَةِ. A shoulder —, one on which things are carried, عَتَلَة; one who carries such a pole, عَتَّال. A — for measuring, قَصَبَةُ ٱلْقِيَاسِ. A tent —, مِسْطَح *pl.* مَسَاطِحُ — سِطَاح — أُسْطُوَان *pl.* أَسَاطِينُ — عَمُود *pl.* عُمُد — عِمَاد *pl.* عُمُد: To put up a tent-pole, شَجَرَ ². We are poles asunder, أَنْتَ فِي وَادٍ وَنَحْنُ فِي وَادٍ. Pole, a native of Poland, لَهِيٌّ *pl.* مِنْ أَهْلِ لَهِسْتَانَ — لَهِيَّة. To be under bare poles, كَانَ بِلَا قُلُوع.

The north pole, قُطْبُ ٱلشَّمَالِ — ٱلْقُطْبُ ٱلشَّمَالِيُّ. The north celestial pole, فَلَكُ ٱلسَّمَاءِ.

The south pole, قُطْبُ ٱلْجَنُوبِ — ٱلْقُطْبُ ٱلْجَنُوبِيُّ.

The magnetic pole, ٱلشَّمَالُ حَسَبَ ٱلْإِبْرَةِ ٱلْمَغْنَطِيسِيَّةِ.

Pole, *v.t.* To drive a boat by poling, مَرَدَ ². To furnish with poles, دَعَمَ ₂ — أَعْمَدَ — عَمَدَ ₂.

Pole-axe, *n.* *See* Battle-axe, *n.*

Pole-star, *n.* كَوْكَبٌ قُطْبِيٌّ — كَوْكَبُ ٱلْقُطْبِ. A guide, هَادٍ — دَلِيل — مُرْشِد. *See also under* Polar, *a.*

Pole-cat, *n.* *See* Skunk, *n.*

Polemic, *n.* }
Polemical, *a.* } لَدٌّ *pl.* أَلَدُّ *and* لِدَاد — لَاذٌّ — مُجَادِل — مُبَاحِث — مِغْلَاق — مُعَارِض. A polemic, one vehement in altercation, رَجُلٌ مِغْلَاقٌ — رَجُلٌ ذُو مِغْلَاقٍ.

Polemics, *n.* مُجَادَلَة — مُبَاحَثَة — مُعَارَضَة.

Police, *n.* ضَبْطِيَّة — ضَابِطِيَّة — ٱلشُّرَطُ — ٱلشُّرْطَةُ; *also in modern parlance,* بُولِيس — بُولِيس (or ضَابِطِيَّة) مِنَ ٱلْخَيَّالَةِ. Mounted —, Native —, ضَابِطِيَّةٌ أَهْلِيَّةٌ — شُرْطَةٌ أَهْلِيَّةٌ. Reform of the —, تَنْظِيمُ أَحْوَالِ ٱلضَّابِطِيَّةِ (or ٱلشُّرْطَةِ or ٱلْبُولِيسِ).

Police court, مَحْكَمَةُ ٱلضَّابِطِيَّةِ (or ٱلشُّرْطَةِ) — مَحْكَمَةُ ٱلْبُولِيسِ.

Police inspector, مُفَتِّشُ ٱلْبُولِيسِ ـ مُفَتِّشُ ٱلضَّابِطِيَّةِ (or ٱلشُّرْطَةِ).

Police officer, مَأْمُورُ ٱلضَّابِطِيَّةِ (or ٱلشُّرْطَةِ) ـ صاحِبُ ٱلشُّرْطَةِ *pl.* مَأْمُورُونَ ـ مَأْمُورُ ٱلْبُولِيسِ.

Police spy, جاسُوسُ ٱلضَّابِطِيَّةِ (or ٱلشُّرْطَةِ) *pl.* جَواسِيسُ.

Police station, مَرْكَزُ ـ مَحَلُّ (or مَرْكَزُ) ٱلضَّابِطِيَّةِ (or ٱلشُّرْطَةِ) ٱلْبُولِيسِ.

Policeman, *n.* ضابِطِيٌّ ـ شُرَطَةٌ *or* شُرَط *pl.* شُرَطِيٌّ *or* شُرْطِيٌّ *pl.* ضابِطِيَّةٌ ـ قَوَّاسٌ *pl.* قَوَّاسُ ٱلضَّابِطِيَّةِ ـ نَفَرٌ مِنَ ٱلْبُولِيسِ *pl.* أَنْفار. A — in plain clothes, مَأْمُورٌ مِنَ ٱلضَّابِطِيَّةِ خَفِيٌّ ـ شُرْطِيٌّ مُنَكَّرٌ نَفَرٌ مِنَ ٱلْبُولِيسِ مُنَكَّرٌ *pl.* أَنْفار.

Policy, *n.* A system of government, تَدْبِيرُ أُمُورٍ ـ سِياسَةٌ ـ حُكُومَةٌ فَنُّ ٱلْبُولِيتِيكَةِ ـ مَمْلَكَةٌ. Prudence in management, عَقْلٌ وَبَصِيرَةٌ ـ فِدْيَةٌ ـ سِيرَةٌ ـ مِنْوال. A course, procedure, تَدْبِيرٌ ـ فَنٌّ طَرِيقَةٌ ـ سُلُوكٌ. A — of insurance, سَنَدُ سِكُورْتا. A change of — calls for a change in the Government, تَغْيِيرُ ٱلْحُكْمِ يَسْتَلْزِمُ تَغْيِيرَ ٱلْحُكُومَةِ.

An adventurous policy, سِياسَةٌ (or بُولِيتِيكَةٌ) هَوائِيَّةٌ (or جِرالِيَّةٌ).

An aggressive policy, بُولِيتِيكَةٌ مُتَجاوِزَةٌ.

A retrograde policy, سِياسَةٌ (or بُولِيتِيكَةٌ) مُوجِبَةُ ٱلتَّأَخُّرِ.

Bad policy, سِياسَةٌ مُتَهَوِّرَةٌ ـ سِياسَةٌ غافِلَةٌ.

Good policy, سِياسَةٌ مُسْتَحْكَمَةٌ.

Foreign policy of a Government, سِياسَةُ ٱلدَّوْلَةِ ٱلْخارِجِيَّةُ.

Home policy of a Government, سِياسَةُ ٱلدَّوْلَةِ ٱلدَّاخِلِيَّةُ.

To establish a policy, قامَ بِسِياسَةٍ ـ [2] اِتَّخَذَ سِياسَةً.

Polish, *a.* Belonging to Poland, مِنْ بُولانْدا ـ مِنْ لَهِسْتان ـ لَهِيٌّ. The — language, لِسانُ أَهْلِ بُولانْد ـ لِسانُ لَهِسْتان ـ لِسانُ ٱللَّهِيَّةِ.

Polish, *v.t.* To make smooth, to give a gloss to, خَشَبَ ـ [2] جَلا ـ صَقَلَ [2]. To smear with a polish, [2] طَلا بِتَرْبِيَةٍ ـ [2] دَهَنَ بِدِهانٍ. To refine in manners, أَنَّسَ ـ أَدَّبَ. To — off, finish, تَمَّمَ ـ أَكْمَلَ ـ أَنْهَى. To —, as of speech, تَوَبَّلَ (or قَزَّحَ or بَزَّرَ) ٱلْكَلامَ.

Polish, *n.* Gloss, جَلاءٌ ـ صِقال ـ صَقْلٌ. A substance to polish with, تَرْبِيَةٌ ـ دِهان. Elegance, طَلاوَةٌ ـ إِناقَةٌ ـ ظَرافَةٌ; of style, language, حَبْر ـ تَحْبِير ـ فَصاحَةٌ وَبَلاغَةٌ ـ مَلاحَةٌ.

Polishable, *a.* قابِلُ ٱلصِّقالِ ـ يُصْقَلُ.

Polished, *a.* Made smooth, مَصْقُول ـ صَقِيل. Elegant in manners, كَيِّسٌ ـ ظَرِيفٌ ـ مُؤَدَّبٌ ـ أَدِيبٌ ـ صاحِبُ طَلاوَةٍ. Polished language, كَلامٌ بَلِيغٌ ـ كَلامٌ فَصِيحٌ ـ كَلامٌ مُحَبَّرٌ. He was — in speech, أَظْرَفَ فِي ٱلْعِبارَةِ. To be — in manners, speech, *etc.*, [2] ظَرُفَ. To affect to be —, تَظَرَّفَ. To become —, refined, إِسْتَأْدَبَ ـ تَأَدَّبَ.

Polisher, *n.* One who polishes, صَقَّال. A — of arms, هالِكِيٌّ ـ صَيْقَل; of brazen vessels, جَرّاد. A polishing tool, مَلَسَةٌ ـ سَفَن; a shell for polishing paper, مِصْقَلَةٌ.

Polishing, *n.* The act of giving a gloss, جَلاءٌ ـ صَقْل; of refining, as of manners, تَأْنِيس ـ تَأْدِيب.

Polite, *a.* Refined, well-bred, خَلِيق ـ أَدِيب *pl.* أُدَباءُ ـ كَيِّس ـ لَطِيف ـ أَهْلُ لَطافَةٍ ـ ذُو أَدَبٍ ـ مُتَأَدِّب. Polite literature, عِلْمُ ٱلْأَدَبِ ـ كُتُبٌ أَدَبِيَّةٌ. To be —, إِسْتَأْدَبَ ـ كانَ ذا أَدَبٍ ـ تَأَدَّبَ ـ [2] أَدُبَ. The people are very —, ٱلْقَوْمُ أَهْلُ لَطافَةٍ لِلْغايَةِ. To make —, to instruct in politeness, أَدَّبَ.

Politely, *ad.* بِكِياسَةٍ ـ بِظَرافَةٍ ـ بِلَطافَةٍ ـ بِأَدَبٍ ـ تَأَدُّبًا ـ بِرِعايَةٍ. To act — to, تَلاطَفَ ل ـ تَلَطَّفَ ل.

Politeness, *n.* تَأَدُّب ـ كِياسَة ـ ظَرافَة ـ لَطافَة ـ أَدَب ـ رِعايَة. To affect —, تَكَيَّسَ ـ تَظَرَّفَ.

Politesse, *n.* تَظَرُّف.

Politic, *a.* Sagacious, ذَهِن ـ أَرِيب *pl.* أُرَباءُ ـ أَرِب ـ كَيِّس ـ بَصِير. Suitable, well adapted, مُوافِقٌ ـ خَلِيقٌ ب. To be —, to act with sagacity, تَكَيَّسَ ـ [2] كاسَ ـ [2] أَرُبَ ـ [2] أَرِبَ ـ [2] ذَهِنَ ـ كانَ بَصِيرًا: He was — in the matter, أَرِبَ بِٱلشَّيْءِ. The body —, ٱلْجُمْهُورُ ـ ٱلْأُمَّةُ.

Political, *a.* Relating to public measures, سِياسِيٌّ ـ حُكُومِيٌّ ـ دُوَلِيٌّ ـ مَلَكِيٌّ. A — party, clique, فِرْقَةٌ مِنْ أَهْلِ ٱلسِّياسَةِ ـ حِزْبٌ بُولِيتِيكِيٌّ. This circumstance may be considered as a grave — question, هٰذِهِ ٱلْحادِثَةُ تُعَدُّ مِنَ ٱلْمَسائِلِ ٱلسِّياسِيَّةِ ٱلْخَطِيرَةِ.

Political application, study, مُمارَسَةٌ سِياسِيَّةٌ.

Political circles, ٱلدَّوائِرُ (or ٱلْمَحافِلُ) ٱلسِّياسِيَّةُ.

Political combinations, تَدابِيرُ ٱلْبُولِيتِيكَةِ ـ تَدابِيرُ سِياسِيَّةٌ.

Political complications, difficulties, عَراقِيلُ ـ غَوائِلُ سِياسِيَّةٌ ٱلسِّياسَةِ.

Political economy, عِلْمُ ٱلْبُولِيتِيكَةِ ـ عِلْمُ ٱلسِّياسَةِ.

Political equilibrium, مُوازَنَةٌ مَلَكِيَّةٌ ـ مُوازَنَةٌ دُوَلِيَّةٌ.

Political influence, نُفُوذٌ سِياسِيٌّ ـ اِعْتِبارٌ دُوَلِيٌّ.

Political interests, مَنافِعُ دُوَلِيَّةٌ ـ مَنافِعُ مَلَكِيَّةٌ.

Political intrigues, دَسائِسُ ٱلسِّياسَةِ (or ٱلْبُولِيتِيكَةِ).

Political laws, نِظاماتٌ دُوَلِيَّةٌ ـ قَوانِينُ مَلَكِيَّةٌ.

Political liberty, حُرِّيَّةٌ مَلَكِيَّةٌ.

Political measures, تَدابِيرُ سِياسِيَّةٌ.

Political negotiations, مُذاكَراتٌ سِياسِيَّةٌ.

Political programme, بَيانُ ٱلْبُولِيتِيكَةِ ـ سِياقَةٌ (or بَيانُ) ٱلسِّياسَةِ.

Political relations, مُعامَلاتُ ٱلبُولِيتِيكَةِ ـ مُعامَلاتٌ سِياسِيَّةٌ.

Political struggles, (ٱلبُولِيتِيكَةِ *or*) اِنْقِلابُ أَحْوالِ ٱلسِّياسَةِ.

Politically, *ad.* حَسَبَ أُصُولِ ـ بِٱلبُولِيتِيكَةِ ـ بِحَسَبِ ٱلسِّياسَةِ ٱلبُولِيتِيكَةِ. This province will be — subject to the Sultan, هٰذِهِ ٱلوِلايَةُ تَكُونُ تابِعَةً ٱلسُّلْطانِ تابِعِيَّةً سِياسِيَّةً.

Politician, *n.* أَهْلُ سِياسَةٍ. One versed in politics, حاذِقٌ بِعِلْمِ ٱلسِّياسَةِ *pl.* حُذَّاق ـ بُولِيتِيكِيٌّ. Politicians, أَرْبابُ ٱلسِّياسَةِ. What seems most probable to politicians, ٱلأَرْجَحُ عِنْدَ أَرْبابِ ٱلسِّياسَةِ.

Politics, *n.* The public affairs of a country, أُمُورُ ٱلدَّوْلَةِ. System of government, تَدابِيرُ دَوْلَةٍ ـ أُصُولُ سِياسَةٍ. The science of government, بُولِيتِيكَةٌ ـ عِلْمُ تَدْبِيرِ دَوْلَةٍ ـ عِلْمُ ٱلسِّياسَةِ.

Polity, *n.* Structure of a government, أُصُولُ دَوْلَةٍ ـ نَسَقُ دَوْلَةٍ.

Polka, *n.* ضَرْبٌ مِنَ ٱلرَّقْصِ.

Poll, *n.* The head, رَأْس; the back of the head, قَفًا *pl.* قِفِيٌّ *and* قُفِيٌّ. A register of heads, names, دَفْتَرُ أَسامِي. A list of electors, جَدْوَلُ مُنْتَخِبِينَ. Election, اِنْتِخاب. To go to the —, offer one's self for election, عَرَضَ نَفْسَهُ لِلاِنْتِخابِ.

Poll, *v.t.* To receive votes at an election, نالَ أَصْواتًا فِي ٱلاِنْتِخابِ. To inscribe one's name on the poll, قَيَّدَ ٱسْمَهُ فِي جَدْوَلِ ٱلمُنْتَخِبِينَ. To lop, شَذَّبَ. To — or cut off the hair, قَصَّ ٱلشَّعْرَ.

Pollard, *n.* A tree with the head lopped, شَجَرَةٌ مُشَذَّبَةُ ٱلفَرْعِ. A mixture of bran and meal, خَلِيطُ نُخالَةٍ وَطَحِينٍ. The fish so called, ضَرْبٌ مِنَ ٱلسَّمَكِ ـ شِيلان *pl.* شال.

Pollard, *v.t.* *See to* Lop, *v.t.*

Pollen, *n.* The fecundating dust of flowers, لَقاح ـ كُش ـ جُشّ ـ جُشَر; of palm flowers, مَأْبَر ـ أَبُور ـ مِئْبَر ـ مَأْبِر.

Poller, *n.* One who lops trees, مُشَذِّبُ ٱلأَشْجارِ. One who registers votes, مُقَيِّدُ أَسامِي ٱلمُنْتَخِبِينَ. One who has a vote, مُنْتَخِب.

Polling, *n.* Getting votes for an election, تَحْصِيلُ ٱلآراءِ لِلاِنْتِخابِ.

Polling-booth, *n.* مَوْضِعُ إِعْطاءِ آراءِ ٱلمُنْتَخِبِينَ.

Poll-tax, *n.* *See under* Capitation, *n.*

Pollute, *v.t.* To profane, دَنَّسَ ـ نَجَّسَ. To make foul, أَدْرَنَ ـ لَوَّثَ ـ نَجَّسَ ـ دَسَّمَ ـ وَسَّخَ. To ravish, هَتَكَ. To be polluted, profaned, تَدَنَّسَ ـ تَنَجَّسَ; to be polluted, made dirty, دَرِنَ ـ دَنِسَ ـ تَدَنَّسَ ـ تَلَوَّثَ ـ تَدَسَّمَ. *See also to* Corrupt, *to* Defile, *v.t.*

Polluted, *a.* Defiled, مُدَنَّس ـ مُنَجَّس. Dirtied, مُلَوَّث ـ مُوَسَّخ.

Polluter, *n.* One who pollutes, مُدَنِّس ـ مُنَجِّس. One who pollutes himself, مُتَدَنِّس ـ مُتَنَجِّس.

Pollution, *n.* The act of defiling, تَدْرِين ـ تَدْنِيس ـ تَنْجِيس; the state of being defiled, دَرَن ـ دَنَس ـ دَناسَة. Self-pollution; *see* Masturbation, *n.*

Polonaise, *n.* A kind of dress, ضَرْبٌ مِنَ ٱلجُبَّةِ. A kind of dance, ضَرْبٌ مِنَ ٱلرَّقْصِ.

Poltroon, *n.* نَجِيب. *See also* Coward, *n.*

Poltroonery, *n.* *See* Cowardice, *n.*

Polyandria, *n. pl.* أَزْهارٌ ذاتُ عِشْرِينَ آلَةً وَنَيِّفٍ مِنْ آلاتِ ٱلذُّكُورِ.

Polyandrian, *a.* عِبارَةٌ عَنِ ٱلأَزْهارِ ٱلمَذْكُورَةِ.

Polyanthus, *n.* نَباتٌ ذُو أَزْهارٍ شَتَّى ـ نَباتٌ ذُو أَزْهارٍ فِي هَيْئَةِ ٱلعَناقِيدِ.

Polygamist, *n.* One who takes more wives than one, مُتَزَوِّجٌ أَكْثَرَ مِنِ ٱمْرَأَةٍ واحِدَةٍ. One who vindicates polygamy, مَنْ يَسْتَحْسِنُ ٱلزَّواجَ بِأَكْثَرَ مِنِ ٱمْرَأَةٍ واحِدَةٍ.

Polygamy, *n.* كَثْرَةُ ٱلزَّوْجاتِ ـ ٱلتَّزَوُّجُ بِأَكْثَرَ مِنِ ٱمْرَأَةٍ واحِدَةٍ.

Polyglot, *a.* مُتَضَمِّنٌ جُمْلَةَ أَلْسُنٍ.

Polyglot, *n.* تَأْلِيفٌ فِي جُمْلَةِ أَلْسُنٍ.

Polygon, *n.* كَثِيرُ ٱلأَضْلاعِ. A regular —, شَكْلٌ مُنْتَظِمٌ.

Polygonal, *a.* ذُو أَضْلاعٍ كَثِيرَةٍ.

Polygonum, *n.* عَصا ٱلرّاعِي.

Polygraph, *n.* آلَةٌ مُضَعِّفَةُ ٱلكِتابَةِ.

Polygynia, *n. pl.* أَزْهارٌ ذَواتُ آلاتِ إِناثٍ شَتَّى.

Polygynous, *a.* عِبارَةٌ عَنِ ٱلأَزْهارِ ذَواتِ آلاتِ إِناثٍ شَتَّى.

Polyhedral, *a.* كَثِيرُ ٱلسُّطُوحِ.

Polyhedron, *n.* جِسْمٌ ذُو سُطُوحٍ شَتَّى.

Polymathy, *n.* مَعارِفُ مُتَنَوِّعَةٌ.

Polymorphous, *a.* ذُو أَشْكالٍ شَتَّى ـ ذُو هَيْئاتٍ شَتَّى.

Polynesia, *n.* مَجْمُوعُ ٱلجَزائِرِ ٱلواقِعَةِ فِي ٱلبَحْرِ ٱلمُحِيطِ ٱلشَّرْقِيِّ ـ بُولِينِيسِيا.

Polynesian, *a.* مِنْ بُولِينِيسِيا ـ ما نِيطَ بِٱلجَزائِرِ ٱلمَذْكُورَةِ.

Polynominal, *a.* كَثِيرُ ٱلأَسامِي ـ ذُو أَسْماءٍ شَتَّى.

Polype, *n.* حَيَوانٌ يُشْبِهُ ٱلنَّباتَ.

Polypetalous, *a.* عِبارَةٌ عَنِ ٱلأَزْهارِ ذَواتِ وُرَيْقاتٍ شَتَّى.

Polyphonous, *a.* كَثِيرُ ٱلأَصْواتِ.

Polypody, *n.* The plant, أَضْراسُ ٱلكَلْبِ ـ بَسْفايِج.

Polypous, *a.* Having many feet, ذُو سِيقانٍ كَثِيرَةٍ. Having the nature of a tumour, مِنْ جِنْسِ ٱلدُّبَيْلَةِ ٱلمُتَشَعِّبَةِ (of a small tumour it would be, (.وِنْ جِنْسِ ٱلْبَثْرَةِ ٱلْمُتَشَعِّبَةِ) *In common parlance,* .وِنْ جِنْسِ ٱللَّحْمِ ٱلزَّائِدِ

Polypus, *n.* Something that has many feet, .ذُو سِيقَانٍ كَثِيرَةٍ The tumour so called; a large one would be, دُبَيْلَةٌ مُتَشَعِّبَةٌ; a small one, .بَثْرَةٌ مُتَشَعِّبَةٌ For a fleshy excrescence the common word is, .لَحْمٌ زَائِدٌ

Polysyllabic, *a.* } **Polysyllabical**, } عِبَارَةٌ عَنْ كَلِمَةٍ ذَاتِ هِجَاءَاتٍ شَتَّى (أَوْ أَكْثَرَ .وِنْ ثَلَاثَةٍ)

Polysyllable, *n.* .كَلِمَةٌ مُرَكَّبَةٌ مِنْ ثَلَاثِ تَهْجِيَاتٍ فَصَاعِدًا

Polytechnic, *a.* .مُتَعَلِّقٌ بِفُنُونٍ وَصَنَائِعَ شَتَّى A — institution, .مَحَلُّ ٱلْفُنُونِ وَٱلصَّنَائِعِ

Polytheism, *n.* .الشِّرْكُ

Polytheist, *n.* } **Polytheistical**, *a.* } .مُشْرِكٌ – مُشْرِكِيٌّ *pl.* مُشْرِكُونَ

Pomace, *n.* .عُصَارَةُ (*or* كُبِيس) ٱلتُّفَّاحِ

Pomaceous, *a.* .مِثْلَ عُصَارَةِ (*or* كُبِيسِ) ٱلتُّفَّاحِ

Pomade, *n.* } **Pomatum**, } .دِهَانٌ – دُهْنٌ

Pomatum, *v.t.* .دَهَنَ-بِدِهَانٍ [2]

Pomegranate, *n.* رُمَّانَةٌ *coll.* رُمَّانٌ *pl.* .رُمَّانَاتٌ The outer skin of the —, قِرْفٌ – قِرْفَةٌ *pl.* قِرَفٌ; the fine inner skin of the —, .شَحْمَةُ ٱلرُّمَّانِ The flower of the —, .جُلَّنَارٌ

Pomiferous, *a.* .حَامِلُ ٱلتُّفَّاحِ (وَنَظِيرِ ٱلتُّفَّاحِ فِي ٱلشَّكْلِ)

Pommel, *n.* A knob, عُجْرَةٌ *pl.* .عُجَرٌ The — of a sword, – تُومَةٌ رُمَّانَةٌ – قَبَائِعُ *pl.* قَبِيعَةٌ; of a saddle, قَرَبُوسٌ حِنْوُ ٱلسَّرْجِ *pl.* قَرَابِيسُ; the fore and aft pommels of a saddle, .الْقَرَبُوسَانِ

Pommel, *v.t.* .قَتَلَ-قَتْلَةً [2] – رَزَعَ – ضَرَبَ – يَكُزُ *aor.* وَكَزَ

Pommeled, *a.* Having knobs, .ذُو عُجَرٍ Having a pommel, of a sword, ذُو رُمَّانَةٍ; of a saddle, .ذُو قَرَبُوسٍ

Pommeling, *n.* The act of thrashing, .رَزْعَةٌ – قَتْلٌ – ضَرْبٌ

Pommelion, *n.* Of a cannon, .عُجْرَةُ ٱلْمِدْفَعِ

Pomological, *a.* .مُتَعَلِّقٌ بِفَنِّ تَرْبِيَةِ ٱلنَّبَاتِ

Pomologist, *n.* .حَاذِقٌ فِي تَرْبِيَةِ ٱلنَّبَاتِ

Pomology, *n.* .فَنُّ تَرْبِيَةِ ٱلنَّبَاتِ

Pomp, *n.* Show, ceremony, – طَنْطَنَةٌ – تَبْجِيلٌ – إِحْتِفَالٌ .مَوْكِبٌ – وَكْبَةٌ – إِحْتِشَامٌ – زِينَةٌ – بَهَاءٌ – حَشْمَةٌ Grandeur, .عَظَمَةٌ – عِزٌّ – فَخْرٌ The pomps and vanities of the world, .زَخَارِفُ وَأَبَاطِيلُ ٱلْعَالَمِ

Pompion, *n.* *See* Pumpkin.

Pomposity, *n.* } **Pompousness**, } Ostentatiousness, – عَظَمَةٌ – مُبَاهَاةٌ – إِفْتِخَارٌ Boasting, – رُفَاعَةٌ – تَعَظُّمٌ – نَفْخٌ – تَنَفُّخٌ .تَفَاخُرٌ *See also* Pomp, *n.*

Pompous, *a.* Ostentatious, .فَخُورٌ – مُبَاهٍ Boasting, – مُتَعَظِّمٌ .إِحْتِفَالِيٌّ – بَهِيٌّ – بَاهٍ – مُطَنْطَنٌ Grand, – مُفَاخِرٌ – مُتَكَبِّرٌ .عَظِيمٌ

Pompously, *ad.* With show, – بِإِحْتِفَالٍ – بِطَنْطَنَةٍ – بِمَوْكِبٍ .بِإِحْتِشَامٍ Ostentatiously, .بِإِفْتِخَارٍ – بِمُبَاهَاةٍ Boastingly, .بِتَكَبُّرٍ – تَعَظُّمًا

Pond, *n.* – بَقْعَةٌ – مَنْقَعٌ – غَدِيرٌ *pl.* غُدْرَانٌ *and* أَغْدِرَةٌ – .بِرْكَةٌ *pl.* بِرَكٌ – مُسْتَنْقَعُ مَاءٍ

Ponder, *v.t.* To think upon closely, – تَأَمَّلَ فِي – تَفَكَّرَ فِي – أَبْرَمَ .تَبَصَّرَ – [2] نَظَرَ فِي – أَضْمَرَ عَلَى To weigh, وَزَنَ *aor.* .يَزِنُ To order with care, مَهَّدَ: Ponder thy paths, .مَهِّدْ خَطَوَاتِكَ

Ponder, *v.i.* إِفْتَكَرَ – تَشَاوَرَ – تَأَمَّلَ – تَفَكَّرَ: He pondered them in his heart, .تَفَكَّرَ بِهَا فِي قَلْبِهِ

Ponderability, *n.* .قَابِلِيَّةُ ٱلْوَزْنِ

Ponderable, *a.* .مِمَّا يُوزَنُ – قَابِلُ ٱلْوَزْنِ

Ponderingly, *ad.* .بِتَأَمُّلٍ – تَفَكُّرًا

Ponderous, *a.* Heavy, .ثَقِيلٌ – رَزِينٌ Weighty, important, .عَظِيمٌ – مُهِمٌّ – بَارِعٌ

Poniard, *n.* خَنْجَرٌ *pl.* .خَنَاجِرُ

Poniard, *v.t.* .ضَرَبَ-خَنْجَرًا [2]

Pontage, *n.* .رَسْمُ عُبُورِ ٱلْجِسْرِ

Pontiff, *n.* A high priest, رَئِيسُ كَهَنَةٍ *pl.* .رُؤَسَاءُ – حَبْرٌ أَعْظَمُ The Sovereign —, the Pope, .حَضْرَةُ ٱلْبَابَا

Pontifical, *a.* .حَبْرِيٌّ – مُتَعَلِّقٌ بِرُؤَسَاءِ ٱلْكَهَنَةِ

Pontifical, *n.* .كِتَابُ طُقُوسٍ كَنَائِسِيَّةٍ

Pontificals, *n.* The full dress of a bishop, مَلَابِسُ ٱلْمَطْرَانِ ٱلرَّسْمِيَّةُ (*or* ٱلْإِحْتِفَالِيَّةُ).

Pontificate, *n.* The dignity of a high priest, مَقَامُ (*or* رُتْبَةُ) .حَبْرَةٌ – رَئِيسُ ٱلْكَهَنَةِ The reign of a pontiff, رِئَاسَةُ رَئِيسِ .كَهَنَةٍ

Pontoon, *n.* .جِسْرٌ عَوَّامٌ – ذَاتُ ٱلرَّفِيفِ *See also* Lighter, *n.*

Pony, *n.* .حِصَانٌ صَغِيرٌ – قُلْهُزَمٌ *or* قَلْهُزَمٌ

Poodle, *n.* .كَلْبٌ صَغِيرٌ – كُلَيْبٌ

Pool, *n.* A — of water, غَدِيرٌ *pl.* .غُدْرَانٌ A — for retaining water, إِخَاذٌ *pl.* .أُخُذٌ The stakes played for at cards, الرِّهَانُ .فِي لَعِبِ ٱلْقِمَارِ *See also* Pond, *n.*

Poop, *n.* Of a ship, .قَصْرُ ٱلْمَرْكَبِ

Poop, *v.t.* To strike on the poop, لَطَمَ قَصَرَ ٱلْمَرْكَبِ ـَ.

Pooped, *a.* Having a poop, ذُو قَصَرٍ. Struck on the poop, مَلْطُومُ ٱلْقَصَرِ.

Poor, *a.* صُعْلُوكٌ *pl.* صَعَالِيكُ ـ عَائِلٌ *pl.* عَالَةٌ *and* عُيَّلٌ *and* عَيْلَى ـ مُعْتَرٌّ ـ مِسْكِينٌ *pl.* مَسَاكِينُ ـ فَقِيرٌ *pl.* فُقَرَآءُ. Needy, مُحْتَاجٌ ـ مُعْوِزٌ ـ عَوِزٌ ـ عَائِزٌ. Mean, حَقِيرٌ ـ رَقِيقٌ. Spiritless, رَكِيكٌ ـ قَصِفٌ ـ حَشِلٌ فَشِلٌ ـ حَشِلٌ فَشِلٌ. Weak, untrustworthy, ضَعِيفٌ *pl.* ضُعَفَآءُ. Poor, of soil, أَرْضٌ ـ أَسِيفَةٌ ـ أَسَافَةٌ. Poor in spirit, مِسْكِينٌ بِٱلرُّوحِ. أَرْضٌ رَكِيكَةٌ ـ عَجْفَآءُ (*See also* Inferior, *a.*) Poor, of a language, ضَيِّقٌ ـ رَقِيقٌ; of language, رَكِيكٌ. How — he is! مَا أَفْقَرَهُ. Truly, he is very —, إِنَّهُ لَعَوِزٌ لَوِزٌ. Poorer than Job, أَفْقَرُ مِنْ وَحٍّ. To be or to become —, needy, فَقُرَ ـ أَعَالَ ـ عَالَ *aor.* يَعِيلُ ـ تَصَعْلَكَ ـ أَعْوَزَ ـ عَوِزَ ـِ ـ أَفْتَقَرَ ـ أَعْدَمَ ـ تَفَاقَرَ ـ إِفْتَقَرَ. To make —, reduce to poverty, أَفْقَرَ ـ أَعْدَمَ.

Poor-house, *n.* دَارٌ لِلْفُقَرَآءِ.

Poor-laws, *n.* ٱلْقَوَانِينُ ٱلْمَرْسُومَةُ لِإِعَانَةِ ٱلْفُقَرَآءِ.

Poorly, *a.* Indisposed, ضَعِيفٌ *pl.* ضُعَفَآءُ ـ مَشْكُوٌّ ـ شَاكٍ ـ عَلِيلٌ. To be —, شَكَا *aor.* يَشْكُو ـ عَلَّ ـِ.

Poorly, *ad.* In a mean manner, بِمَسْكَنَةٍ ـ حَقَارَةً. In a small degree, قَلِيلًا ـ جُزْءًا ـ جُزْئِيَّةً ـ بِقِلَّةٍ مَعْرِفَةٍ ـ بِقِلَّةِ صَنْعَةٍ. Clumsily, بِخُرْقٍ. *See also under* Slightly, *ad.*, Meanly, *ad.*

Poorness, *n.* As of soil, language, material, *etc.*, رَكَاكَةٌ ـ أَسَافَةٌ ـ رِقَّةٌ ـ رِكَّةٌ. Want of copiousness in a language, ضَيِّقَةُ لُغَةٍ.

Poor-rate, *n.* رَسْمٌ لِلْفُقَرَآءِ ـ مَخَالِيفُ *pl.* مِخْلَافٌ. The — prescribed by the Kurân, ٱلزَّكَاةُ. A collector of poor-rates, مُصَدِّقٌ.

Poor-spirited, *a.* إِجْفِيلٌ ـ قَصِفٌ ـ حَقِيرٌ ـ حَشِلٌ فَشِلٌ ـ جَبَانٌ.

Pop, *n.* A sharp sound or report, فَقْعَةٌ ـ فَقْعٌ ـ طَقْطَقَةٌ ـ نَوْرَةٌ. An effervescing drink, مَشْرُوبٌ فَوَّارٌ. To take a pop at, أَطْلَقَ عَلَى.

Pop, *ad.* Unexpectedly, بَغْتَةً ـ عَلَى ٱلْفَوْرِ ـ عَلَى غِرَارٍ ـ عَلَى غَفْلَةٍ.

Pop, *v.t.* To make to emit a sharp sound, فَقَّعَ. To let off, discharge, أَطْلَقَ. To pop or thrust anything into, دَسَّ ـُ فِي ـ أَخْرَجَ ـ بِسُرْعَةٍ. To pop one off, شَمَّرَ. To pop one out of, أَهْجَمَ ـ أَفْلَتَ ـ مِنْ ـ مِنْ. To pop the question, make a sudden proposal of marriage, أَطْلَقَ بِٱلْخِطْبَةِ. To pop upon one or happen to one, suddenly, بَدَهَ ـَ ـ بَغَتَ ـَ ـ بَاغَتَ.

Pop, *v.i.* To make a sudden sharp noise, طَقْطَقَ ـ فَقَعَ ـَ ـُ. To glide swiftly along, زَلَّ *aor.* يَزِلُّ. To pop one's self into, أِنْدَسَّ فِي. To pop in suddenly, هَجَمَ ـُ. To pop off, إِنْسَلَّ. To pop to do anything, تَشَمَّرَ لِ ـ أَسْرَعَ ـ تَأَتَّى لِ. To pop, to hasten to do anything, أَسْرَعَ فِي.

Pope, *n.* ٱلْبَابَا.

Popedom, *n.* مَنْصِبُ ٱلْبَابَا ـ ٱلْبَابَاوِيَّةُ.

Popery, *n.* مَذْهَبُ ٱلْبَابَا ـ ٱلْبَابَاوِيَّةُ.

Pope's-eye, *n.* إِسْمُ غُدَّةٍ فِي وَسَطِ ٱلْفَخْذِ.

Pope's-head, *n.* مِكْنَسَةٌ طَوِيلَةٌ.

Popgun, *n.* بُنْدُقِيَّةٌ هَوَائِيَّةٌ لِلْأَوْلَادِ.

Popinjay, *n.* A parrot, بَبْغَا (*vulg.* بَبْغَان). A woodpecker, صُرَدٌ. A fop, مُتَظَرِّفٌ ـ أُطَيْرٌ. A scarecrow, خَيَالٌ.

Popish, *a.* بَابَاوِيٌّ.

Popishly, *ad.* بِٱلْمَيْلِ إِلَى ٱلْبَابَاوِيَّةِ.

Poplar, *n.* حَوْرٌ ـ دُلْبٌ (the name of the genus; but حَوْرٌ indicates rather the white —). The black —, ٱلْحَوْرُ ٱلْأَسْوَدُ; the Italian —, ٱلْحَوْرُ ٱلرُّومِيُّ.

Poplin, *n.* خَزٌّ ـ نَسِيجُ صُوفٍ وَحَرِيرٍ.

Poppy, *n.* خَشْخَاشٌ. The garden —, ٱلْخَشْخَاشُ ٱلْبُسْتَانِيُّ. The wild Egyptian —, ٱلْخَشْخَاشُ ٱلْمَنْثُورُ. The horned —, ٱلْخَشْخَاشُ ٱلْمُقَرَّنُ. The spottling —, ٱلْخَشْخَاشُ ٱلزَّبَدِيُّ.

Populace, *n.* The lower people, أَسَافِلُ ٱلنَّاسِ ـ ٱلسَّفِلَةُ ـ ٱلْجُعَيْدِيَّةُ ـ ٱلْحَوَشُ ـ ٱلْهَمَجُ ـ ٱلْأَوْبَاشُ. *See also under* People, *n.*

Popular, *a.* Prevailing among the people, رَائِجٌ بَيْنَ ٱلنَّاسِ ـ جَارٍ بَيْنَ ٱلْخَلْقِ ـ مَشْهُورٌ عِنْدَ ٱلنَّاسِ. Pleasing to the people, مَقْبُولٌ عَامَّةً ـ مَقْبُولٌ عِنْدَ ٱلنَّاسِ. General, belonging to the people, عَامٌّ ـ عُمُومِيٌّ ـ مُخْتَصٌّ بِٱلْعَوَامِّ. Vulgar, عَامِّيٌّ; the — language, ٱللِّسَانُ ٱلْمُتَدَاوَلُ. The — sciences, ٱلْمَعَارِفُ ٱلْعُمُومِيَّةُ. To be —, general among the people, رَاجَ بَيْنَ ٱلنَّاسِ *aor.* يَرُوجُ. To be pleasing to the people, رَضِيَ عَنِ ٱلنَّاسِ *aor.* يَرْضَى ـ قُبِلَ مِنَ ٱلْجُمْهُورِ.

Popularity, *n.* State of having the popular favour, قَبُولُ ٱلشَّعْبِ ـ مُسَايَرَةُ ٱلشَّعْبِ ـ ٱلْقَبُولُ عِنْدَ ٱلشَّعْبِ. Renown, reputation, بِهِ ـ صِيتٌ بَيْنَ ٱلشَّعْبِ.

Popularize, *v.t.* To make the use of common among the people, عَمَّمَ ـ (أَجْرَى ـ *or* رَوَّجَ ـ *or*) بَيْنَ ٱلنَّاسِ. To make acceptable to the people, جَعَلَ ـَ مَقْبُولًا عِنْدَ ٱلشَّعْبِ. To be popularized, regarded with general favour, تَبَشْبَشَ بِهِ ٱلنَّاسُ طُرًّا.

Popularly, *ad.* Generally, عَامَّةً ـ مَا بَيْنَ ٱلنَّاسِ ـ عِنْدَ ٱلْجُمْهُورِ.

Populate, *v.i.* To breed, as of people, to increase, عَمَرَ ـ ٢ عَمِرَ ـ ٢ نَمَى ـ تَكَاثَرَ ـ أَنْمَى. The land became populated, عَمِرَتِ ٱلْأَرْضُ.

Populate, *v.t.* ٢ عَمَرَ ـ أَعْمَرَ ـ عَمَّرَ بِٱلسُّكَّانِ.

Populated, *a.* آهِل ـ مَأْهُول ـ مُعَمَّر ـ مَعْمُور ـ مَسْكُون.

Population, *n.* The act of peopling, تَعْمِير ـ إِعْمَار ـ عَمْر. The inhabitants of a country, أَهْل ـ سُكَّان ـ أَهَالٍ.

Populous, *a.* عَامِرٌ بِٱلشَّعْبِ ـ كَثِيرُ ٱلسُّكَّانِ ـ مَعْمُور. More —, أَكْثَرُ عُمْرَانًا. A — nation, أُمَّةٌ كَبِيرَةٌ.

Populously, *ad.* عُمْرَانًا ـ بِكَثْرَةِ ٱلسُّكَّانِ.

Populousness, *n.* كَثْرَةُ أَهَالٍ ـ كَثْرَةُ سُكَّانٍ ـ عُمْرَان.

Porcelain, *n.* and *a.* صِينِيٌّ ـ فَرْفُورِيٌّ ـ فَغْفُورِيٌّ.

Porch, *n.* صُفَّةٌ *pl.* صُفَف ـ كُنَّةٌ *pl.* كُنَّات ـ قَيْسَارِيَّة ـ سُدَّة ـ سَقِيفَة ـ رِوَاق ـ دِهْلِيز *pl.* دَهَالِيزُ ـ إِيوَان *pl.* أَوَاوِينُ. The house has five porches, لِلْبَيْتِ خَمْسَةُ أَرْوِقَةٍ. *See also* Portico, *n.*

Porcine, *a.* مِثْلَ ٱلْخِنْزِيرِ ـ مُتَعَلِّقٌ بِٱلْخَنَازِيرِ.

Porcupine, *n.* قُنْفُذ *pl.* قَنَافِذُ.

Pore, *n.* As of the skin, *etc.*, مَسَمٌّ *pl.* مَسَامُّ ـ مَنْفَذ *pl.* مَنَافِذُ. The pores of the body, مَسَامُّ ٱلْجَسَدِ (*or* ٱلْبَدَنِ).

Pore, *v.i.* To pore over, to study, وَاظَبَ عَلَى ـ ٥ عَقَلَ ـ طَالَعَ ٱلدَّرْسَ. To fix the eyes upon, تَطَلَّعَ إِلَى.

Porgy, *a.* *See* Podgy, *a.*

Pork, *n.* لَحْمُ خِنْزِيرٍ ـ لَحْمُ ٱلْخِنْزِيرِ.

Porker, *n.* / Porkling, } فَرْخُ خِنْزِيرٍ ـ خِنَّوص *pl.* خَنَانِيصُ.

Porosity, *n.* / Porousness, } ذَاتُ ٱلْمَسَامِّ.

Porous, *a.* ذُو مَسَامَّ.

Porphyraceous, / Porphyritic, *a.* } صَوَّانٌ بِرْفِيرِيٌّ ; called in Egypt, سُمَاقِيٌّ.

Porphyry, *n.* صَوَّانُ ٱلْبِرْفِيرِ ; called in Egypt, بِرْفِيرِيٌّ.

Porpoise, *n.* دِرْفِيل ـ خِنْزِيرُ ٱلْبَحْرِ ـ سَمَكُ يُونُسَ.

Porridge, *n.* عَصِيدَة.

Porringer, *n.* قَصْعَة *pl.* قِصَاع *and* قَصَعَات ـ قُصَيْعَة.

Port, *n.* A harbour, بَنْدَر *pl.* بَنَادِرُ ـ مِينَا *pl.* مَوَانٍ ـ مِينَة *pl.* مِينَات ـ مَرْسًى ـ إِسْكِلَة *pl.* أَسَاكِلُ. An opening in a ship's side for a gun, كُوَّةٌ لِلْمِدْفَعِ فِي جِدَارِ ٱلسَّفِينَةِ *pl.* كُوَّات ـ مَزْغَل *pl.* مَزَاغِلُ مَرْكَبٍ ; the lid for a —, سَدٌّ (*or* غِطَآءٌ) لِلْكُوَّةِ ٱلْمَذْكُورَةِ *pl.* سِدَاد. The larboard side of a ship, ٱلْجَانِبُ ٱلْأَيْسَرُ مِنَ ٱلْمَرْكَبِ. Bearing, mien, سِمْت ـ أَوْضَاع ـ حَرَكَات. Manner of walk, مِشْيَة. A kind of wine, ضَرْبٌ مِنَ ٱلْخَمْرِ ٱلْمُسَمَّى پُورْت.

Port, *v.t.* As of a musket, عَدَّلَ. To put to the —, larboard, صَلَّحَ. Port! (*or* Larboard!) صَلِّحْ.

Portability, *n.* قَابِلِيَّةُ ٱلنَّقْلِ ـ خِفَّةٌ لِلْحَمْلِ ـ خِفَّة.

Portable, *a.* نَقْلِيٌّ ـ خَفِيفٌ لِلْحَمْلِ ـ خَفِيف ـ خِفٌّ. To be —, كَانَ خِفًّا ـ ٥ خَفَّ لِلْحَمْلِ. A — bedstead, سَرِيرٌ نَقْلِيٌّ.

Portage, *n.* The act of carrying, حَمْل ـ حُمْلَان ـ نَقْل ـ شَيْل. Price of carriage, حَمْل ـ حُمْلَان ـ حَقُّ ٱلْحَمْلِ. A carrying place between two ports, مَوْصِل ـ مَحَطٌّ (*or* مَوْصِلٌ) بَيْنَ بَنْدَرَيْنِ.

Portal, *n.* A gate, بَاب *pl.* أَبْوَاب. An arched gateway, طَاق *pl.* أَطْوَاق. An entrance, مَنْفَذ ـ مَدْخَل. A large door, رَتَج ـ رِتَاج *pl.* رَتَائِجُ. *See also under* Porch, *n.*

Port-crayon, *n.* مُسْكَةُ ٱلْقَلَمِ.

Portcullis, *n.* مِشْرَسُ بَابِ ٱلْقَلْعَةِ.

Porte, *n.* The Sublime Porte, ٱلْبَابُ ٱلْعَالِي. The Ottoman Porte, ٱلدَّوْلَةُ ٱلْعَلِيَّةُ ـ ٱلدَّوْلَةُ ٱلْعُثْمَانِيَّةُ.

Porte-monnaie, *n.* *See* Purse, *n.*

Portend, *v.t.* ٢ دَلَّ عَلَى ـ ٢ هَمَّ بِ ـ أَوْعَدَ بِ ـ أَرْعَدَ.

Portent, *n.* An ill omen, إِشَارَةُ سُوءٍ ـ عَلَامَةُ شَرٍّ ـ إِرْعَاد. *See also* Sign, *n.*

Portentous, *a.* Foreboding, هَامٌّ بِ ـ مُوعِدٌ بِ ـ وَاعِدٌ بِ. Monstrous, frightful, مُدْهِش ـ مُهِيب ـ فَظِيع ـ مُشِيرٌ بِ. *See also* Menacing, Ominous, *a.*

Portentously, *ad.* مَهْمَهَةً ـ إِرْعَادًا ـ تَبْشِيرًا.

Porter, *n.* A doorkeeper, بَوَّاب *pl.* بَوَّابَة. A carrier, حَمَّال *pl.* حَمَّالَة ـ شَيَّال *pl.* شَيَّالَة ; one who carries burdens on a pole, عَتَّال *pl.* عَتَّالَة. The drink so called, بِيرَةٌ سَوْدَآءُ ـ مِزْر.

Porterage, *n.* The business of a porter, carrier, شِيَالَة ـ حِمَالَة. Hire paid to a porter; *See under* Portage, *n.*

Portfire, *n.* فَتِيلَةٌ كِيمَاوِيَّةٌ (called in the Turkish army, مَاهْتَاب ـ مَاهْتَابُ ٱلْمِدْفَعِ).

Portfolio, *n.* For holding papers, مِحْفَظَة *pl.* مَحَافِظُ ـ ضَمَامَة ـ جُزْدَان. The office of an administration, مَنْصِبُ إِدَارَةٍ.

Porthole, *n.* طَاق *pl.* طَاقَات (*or* كُوَّةٌ) لِلْمِدْفَعِ فِي جَنْبِ مَرْكَبٍ (called as follows in the Turkish and Egyptian navies, مَزْغَلُ مَرْكَبٍ *pl.* مَزَاغِلُ ـ لُومْبَار ـ بَنْجَرَة *pl.* بَنَاجِرُ).

Portico, *n.* A gallery, رِوَاق *pl.* أَرْوِقَة ـ صُفَّة *pl.* صُفَف ـ قَيْسَارِيَّة ـ سَقِيفَة *and* رُوُق. A small — over a door, كُنَّة *pl.* كُنَّات.

Portion, *n.* A separate part, قِطْعَة *pl.* قِطَع ـ شُعْبَة *pl.* شُعَب ـ جَانِب ـ قِسْم *pl.* أَقْسَام ـ جُزْء *pl.* أَجْزَاء. A part, number, some, بَعْض ـ حِزْب *pl.* أَحْزَاب ـ عِدَّة. A —, as of a book, a paragraph, آيَة *pl.* آيَات . A part assigned, سَهْم ـ سُهْمَان *pl.* سُهْمَة *pl.* رَاتِبَة, قِسْم ـ أَقْسَام *pl.* حِصَّة ـ حِصَص *pl.* . A ration, allowance, أَسْهَام *pl.* رَاتِب ـ رَوَاتِب . Lot, fortune, نَصِيب ـ قِسْمَة . Portion of an inheritance, حِصَّة مِيرَاث . A marriage —; (*see* Dower, *n.*) To become the — of one, حَصَّ ²: My — of the property was so much, حَصَّنِي مِنَ ٱلْمَالِ كَذَا . I divided the thing with him, each taking his —, حَاصَصْتُهُ ٱلشَّيْءَ . I gave him his —, أَحْصَصْتُهُ . I gave the men their —, أَحْصَصْتُ ٱلْقَوْمَ . This province shall bear a — of the Ottoman debt, هٰذِهِ ٱلْوِلَايَةُ سَتَحْمِلُ جَانِبًا مِنَ ٱلدَّيْنِ ٱلْعُثْمَانِيِّ .

Portion, *v.t.* To divide into pieces, قَسَّمَ ـ ٢ جَزَّأَ . To — among, أَنْصَبَ ـ أَحْصَصَ . To give a portion to, فَرَّقَ ـ عَلَى ـ قَسَّمَ ـ بَيْنَ . They (namely creditors) portioned the property among themselves in portions or shares, تَحَاصُّوا ـ حَاصُّوا . *See also to* Dower, *v.t.*

Portionless, *a.* Having no portion, مِنْ غَيْرِ حِصَّةٍ . *See also* Dowerless, *a.*

Portliness, *n.* Dignity of mien, هَيْبَة ـ رَزَانَة . Bulkiness of person, ضَخَامَة ـ بَدَانَة . *See also* Corpulence, *n.*

Portly, *a.* Of dignified mien, مُهِيب ـ مَهُوب ـ رَزِين . Corpulent, جَسِيم ـ بَدِين ـ ضَخْم ـ أَضْخَم ـ بَدَنِيّ .

Portmanteau, *n.* جِرَاب *pl.* جُرُبَات ـ عَيْبَة *pl.* عِيَاب *and* عَيْبَات .

Portrait, *n.* / Portraiture, *n.* } Likeness, شَبِيه . A painted likeness, صُورَة *pl.* صُوَر ـ تَصْوِير *pl.* تَصَاوِير . A description, وَصْف *pl.* أَوْصَاف ـ بَيَان ـ تَعْرِيف .

Portrait-painter, *n.* رَسَّامُ ٱلتَّصَاوِيرِ ـ رَسَّام .

Portrait-painting, *n.* رَسْمُ ٱلتَّصَاوِيرِ ـ رَسْم .

Portray, *v.t.* To draw, paint, صَوَّرَ ـ ² رَسَمَ . To describe, وَصَفَ *aor.* يَصِفُ ـ ٢ شَرَحَ . To be portrayed, described, إِتَّصَفَ ـ تَوَصَّفَ .

Portrayal, *n.* *See* Portrait, Portraiture, *n.*

Portreeve, *n.* / Portreve, } مَأْمُورُ ٱلْبَنْدَرِ ـ شَاهُ بَنْدَرٍ .

Port-town, *n.* بَنْدَر *pl.* بَنَادِر .

Portugal, *n.* بِلَادُ بُرْتُقَال .

Portuguese, *a.* مِنْ بُرْتُقَال . The — language, لِسَانُ أَهْلِ بُرْتُقَال .

Portuguese, *n.* مِنْ أَهْلِ بُرْتُقَال .

Pory, *a.* *See* Porous, *a.*

Pose, *v.t.* To puzzle, حَيَّرَ ـ ٢ بَهَتَ ـ خَبَّلَ ـ أَدْهَشَ . To place in a posture, أَقْعَدَ ـ قَعَّدَ . To be posed, puzzled, ٢ خَبِلَ ـ بُهِتَ ـ تَحَيَّرَ ـ إِنْدَهَشَ .

Pose, *n.* *See* Posture, *n.*

Poser, *n.* One who puzzles, مُحَيِّر ـ مُخَبِّل ـ مُدْهِش . Something that puzzles, مَطْلَب وَعْر ـ صُعُوبَة ـ مُعْضِلَة .

Position, *n.* The state of being placed, مَوْضِع *pl.* مَوَاضِع ـ مَطْرَح *pl.* مَطَارِح ـ مَحَلّ *pl.* مَحَلَّات ـ مَقَام *pl.* مَقَامَات . Manner of standing or position, مَقَام ـ وَضْع ـ قِيَام . The situation which anything occupies or where anything takes place, مَوْقِع . Position occupied, as by an army, مَحَطَّة ـ مَرْكَز *pl.* مَرَاكِز . State, as of affairs, حَالَة ـ حَال . Office, مَنْصِب *pl.* مَنَاصِب . A principle laid down, a subject, مَحَطّ ـ مَوْضُوع . An assertion, قَوْل ـ قَضِيَّة ـ إِدِّعَاء . A —, in arithmetic, قَاعِدَة مُعَادِلَة . A false —, حَالَة مُتَنَاقِضَة ـ حَالُ ٱلتَّنَاقُضِ ـ حَالُ ٱلْمُضَادَّةِ .

To be in a position to, to be able to . . . , أَطَاقَ عَلَى ـ أَمْكَنَ ـ أَن ـ إِسْتَطَاعَ عَلَى ـ كَانَ مُعِدًّا ل .

To be in a false position, كَانَ فِي حَالَةٍ ـ كَانَ فِي حَالِ ٱلتَّنَاقُضِ ٱلْمُضَادَّةِ .

To draw, as an enemy, from a position, by a feigned retreat, إِسْتَطْرَدَ لَهُ .

To occupy a position, situation, حَلَّ ² مَحَلَّ كَذَا . To occupy the position of . . . , as of another, حَلَّ ² مَحَلَّهُ ـ قَامَ مَقَامَهُ . To hold an office, حَازَ مَنْصِبًا *aor.* يَحُوزُ ـ كَانَ فِي مَنْصِبٍ .

To put one in a position to, to enable one to effect, أَمْكَنَ ـ مِن (مَكَّنَ ـ *or*).

To take up a (military) position, إِرْتَكَزَ فِي ـ إِسْتَبَاءَ ـ تَبَوَّأَ . To take up a position, to assert, إِدَّعَى بِ ـ أَكَّدَ .

Positive, *a.* Unconditional, absolute, مُطْلَق ـ قَطْعِيّ ـ بَتّ . Certain, مُثْبَت ـ حَقّ ـ أَكِيد . Not negative, إِيجَابِيّ ـ وَضْعِيّ ـ صَحِيح ـ لَا رَيْبَ فِيهِ ـ مُوجِب . Direct, complete, شَافٍ . True, حَقِيق ـ حَقِيقِيّ . Real, حَقِيقِيّ . A — answer, جَوَاب شَافٍ . Positive orders, أَوَامِرُ قَطْعِيَّة . Dogmatical, مُتَجَبِّر ـ تَائِه ـ تَيَّاه . To be —, certain of, كَانَ عَلَى يَقِينٍ مِن ـ إِسْتَثْبَتَ ـ ² حَقَّ . He had — information of it, كَانَ عِلْمُهُ بِهِ يَقِينًا . *See also* Peremptory, *a.*

Positive, *n.* As of a photograph plate, رَسْم عَدِل .

Positively, *ad.* Absolutely, إِطْلَاقًا ـ قَطْعًا ـ بَتَّة . Not negatively, إِيجَابًا . Actually, فِي ٱلْوَاقِعِ ـ فِعْلًا . Certainly, حَقًّا ـ يَقِينًا ـ بِلَا رَيْبٍ ـ حَقِيقَةً . *See also* Dogmatically, Peremptorily, *ad.*

Positiveness, *n.* Undoubting assurance, إِتْقَان ـ إِسْتِثْبَات . Certainty, ثُبُوت ـ صِحَّة ـ حَقِيقَة . Reality of existence, وُجُود ـ حَقِيقَةُ ٱلْوُجُودِ . *See also* Dogmatism, *n.*

Positivism, *n.* رَأْيُ ٱلْقَائِلِينَ أَنَّ حِكْمَةَ ٱلدَّهْرِ جَدِيدَةٌ بِأَنْ . مَذْهَبُ ٱلدَّهْرِيَّةِ ـ نَحِلُّ مَحَلَّ ٱلدِّينِ

Posse, *n.* Power, قُوَّة ـ مُكْنَة. In posse, فِي ٱلْإِمْكَانِ.

Posse comitatus, *n.* قَوْمٌ مِنْ أَهْلِ مَحَلٍّ تَسْتَنْجِدُهُمُ ٱلْحُكُومَةُ فِي أَمْرٍ مَّا.

Possess, *v.t.* To hold, have, أَحْرَزَ ـ اِقْتَنَى ـ مَلَكَ ـ عِنْدَ ـ حَازَ ـ اِحْتَوَى عَلَى ـ حَوَى ـ كَانَ لِ. To seize, اِسْتَوْلَى عَلَى. To have dominion over, تَحَاوَى ـ ضَبَطَ ـ قَبَضَ. To hold or occupy by force, as of a passion, تَسَلَّطَ عَلَى ـ تَحَكَّمَ فِي. اِسْتَوْلَى عَلَى ـ اِقْتَنَى. To —, or be master of, one's self, مَلَكَ نَفْسَهُ. I — wealth, عِنْدِي مَالٌ. *See also to* Have, *v.t.*

Possessed, *a.* As by another, مَمْلُوك. Possessed of, having, being master of, ذُو ـ مَالِك ـ حَوِيٌّ ـ حَائِز* (*See end of paragraph.*) ـ صَاحِب *fem.* صَاحِبَة. Possessed of wealth, أَخُو ـ أَخُو ٱلْخَيْرِ ;صَاحِبُ مَالٍ ـ غَنِيٌّ ـ ٱلْغِنَى ;possessed of goodness, صَاحِبُ خَيْرٍ ـ خَيِّر. Possessed, as by an evil spirit, madness, *etc.*, بِهِ خُطْف ـ مَخْبُول ـ خَبَل ـ مُصَاب ـ مُشْجَع ـ مُخَبَّل ـ سَعِر ـ مَجْنُون ـ مَلْبُوس. To be —, mad, جُنَّ ; to cause to be —, خَبَّلَ ـ اِخْتَبَلَ.

* The word ذُو is declined thus:—

Masc. singular.	*Dual, masc.*	*Plural, masc.*
ذُو *nom.* ذَا *acc.* ذِي *gen.*	ذَوَا *nom.* ذَوَيْ *acc.* and *gen.*	ذَوُو *nom.* ذَوِي *acc.* and *gen.*
Fem. sing.	*Dual, fem.*	*Plural, fem.*
ذَاتُ *nom.* ذَاتَ *acc.* ذَاتِ *gen.*	ذَوَاتَا *nom.* ذَوَاتَيْ *acc.* and *gen.*	ذَوَاتُ *nom.* ذَوَاتِ *acc.* and *gen.*

Possession, *n.* The act of holding, مُلْك ـ ضَبْط ـ تَمَلُّك ـ حَوْز ـ مَلَكَة ـ تَصَرُّف. Possessions, wealth, رِزْق *pl.* أَرْزَاق ـ مَال ـ أَمْلَاك *pl.* مُلْك. The state of being under some occult power, madness, جُنُون ـ جِنَّة ـ خَبْطَة ـ سُعْر. To take — of, أَمْلَكَ ـ قَبَضَ ـ ضَبَطَ ـ تَمَلَّكَ. To give — of to, قَبَضَ ـ مَلَّكَ. To gain — over by force, تَغَلَّبَ عَلَى. The lands which have come into their —, ٱلْأَرَاضِي ٱلَّتِي دَخَلَتْ فِي حَوْزِهِمْ.

Possessive, *a.* عِبَارَة عَنِ ٱلتَّمَلُّكِ. The — case, اِسْمٌ مَجْرُورٌ ـ ٱلْمُضَافُ إِلَيْهِ. A — pronoun, ضَمِيرٌ مَجْرُورٌ.

Possessor, *n.* مَالِك ـ أَرْبَاب *pl.* رَبّ ـ مَوَالِي *pl.* مَوْلًى ـ ذُو ـ أَصْحَاب *pl.* صَاحِب ـ مُتَصَرِّف ـ قَابِض ـ ضَابِط. (*See the note * under* Possessed, *a.*)

Posset, *n.* شَرَابٌ مِنْ مَزْيجِ ٱلْحَلِيبِ وَٱلْخَمْرِ وَمَا جَرَى مَجْرَاهُمَا.

Possibility, *n.* إِمْكَان ـ أَمْرٌ نَاصٌّ. There is no — that…, لَيْسَ مِنَ ٱلْمُمْكِنِ أَنْ. Possibilities, things possible, مُمْكِنَات.

Possible, *a.* That may be, مُمْكِن ـ نَاصٌّ. That is within power, مُسْتَطَاع. Supposable, admissible, مُحْتَمَل. A — thing, أَنَصّ ـ نَصّ ـ أَمْرٌ نَاصٌّ (or مُمْكِنٌ). To be —, that may be, اِسْتَطَاعَ ;كَانَ مُمْكِنًا ; to be —, within the power of one, هُوَ فِي حَيِّزِ ٱلْإِمْكَانِ. To be —, admissible, اِحْتَمَلَ. It is — that…, إِنْ أَمْكَنَ ـ لَوْ أَمْكَنَ ـ إِذَا أَمْكَنَ. If —, يُمْكِنُ أَنْ ـ أَنْ إِنْ كَانَ مُمْكِنًا. It is not — that…, لَا يُمْكِنُ أَنْ. If it is — for him, إِذَا أَمْكَنَهُ. If it had been — you would have done so, لَوْ أَمْكَنَ لَفَعَلْتُمْ كَذَا. Everything is — with God, عِنْدَ ٱللّٰهِ كُلُّ شَيْءٍ مُسْتَطَاعٌ. It is —, supposable, that…, مِنَ ٱلْمُحْتَمَلِ أَنْ. Is it —! يَا لَلْعَجَبِ ـ يَا سَلَامُ.

Possibly, *ad.* يُمْكِنُ ـ رُبَّمَا ـ عَسَى ـ لَعَلَّ. Not —, مُحَال ـ قَطْعًا ـ غَيْرُ مُمْكِنٍ. *See also under* Perhaps, *ad.*

Post, *n.* A special messenger going post-haste, or any beast carrying such a messenger, بَرِيد *pl.* بُرُد (this word has now been supplanted by the Arabicized word بُوسْطَة.) A — office, مَحَلّ ٱلْبُوسْطَةِ. Letters of or for the —, مَكَاتِيبُ بُوسْطَةٍ. An office, employment, مَنْصَب ـ مَأْمُورِيَّة ـ خِدْمَة. A military —, مَحَطٌّ عَسْكَرِيٌّ ـ مَرْكَزُ عَسَاكِرَ. The place of an appointment, office, مَحَلٌّ ـ مَكَان ـ مَوْضِع. A place, spot, مَحَلُّ مَأْمُورِيَّةٍ. An advanced —, of an army, مُرَابَطَة. Any timber and such like stuck up, نَصِيبَة ـ عَلَم. A piece of timber set up, قَائِمَة *pl.* قَوَائِمُ ـ صَارٍ *pl.* صَوَارٍ ـ خَشَبَة. A finger —, مَعْلَم ـ صَدَح ـ عَلَم *pl.* أَعْلَام. A rubbing or scratching —, for animals, جِذْل *pl.* أَجْذَال. A winning —, غَايَة. *See also under* Position, *n.*

Post, *v.t.* To station, lodge, أَقَامَ ـ بَوَّأَ ـ مَنْزِلًا ـ أَبَاءَ مَنْزِلًا ـ أَنْزَلَ ـ نَزَّلَ ; to place, جَعَلَ ـ وَضَعَ *aor.* يَضَعُ. To —, as a letter, جَعَلَ فِي ٱلْبُوسْطَةِ. To stick or paste on to, عَلَّقَ عَلَى ـ أَلْزَقَ بِ. To — one up, to publish his disgrace, جَرَّسَ بِ ـ شَهَّرَ. To transfer to a ledger, حَوَّلَ إِلَى دَفْتَرٍ. To be well posted up in, to know well, تَدَرَّبَ بِ ـ اِحْتَوَى عَلَى عِلْمًا ـ اِحْتَوَى عِلْمًا. أَدْرَكَهُ حَقَّ ٱلْإِدْرَاكِ. To post, to send one as a post or speedy messenger, أَبْرَدَ بَرِيدًا ـ أَبْرَدَ ـ بَرَّدَ.

Post, *v.i.* To travel post, سَافَرَ مَنْزِلًا. To hasten, أَسْرَعَ ـ بَادَرَ. *See also under to* Hasten, *v.i.*

Postage, *n.* Money paid for letters, *etc.* by post, أُجْرَةُ ٱلْبُوسْطَةِ.

Postage-card, *n.* قِرْطَاسٌ مُخَابَرَةٍ إِعْلَانِيَّةٍ *pl.* قَرَاطِيسُ.

Postage-stamp, *n.* طَابِعُ ٱلْبُوسْطَةِ *pl.* طَوَابِعُ.

Postage- or Post-paid, *a.* خَالِصُ أُجْرَةِ ٱلْبُوسْطَةِ. Post-paid letters, مَكَاتِيبُ بِضَمِّ أُجْرَةِ ٱلْبُوسْطَةِ.

Postal, *a.* مُتَعَلِّقٌ بِٱلْبُوسْطَةِ. The — department, إِدَارَةُ ٱلْبُوسْطَةِ. Postal arrangements, تَدَابِيرُ (*or* تَرَاتِيبُ) ٱلْبُوسْطَةِ. The — treaty, ٱلْمُعَاهَدَةُ ٱلْبُوسْطِيَّةُ.

Postbill, *n.* جَدْوَلُ (*or* تَقْوِيمُ) مَكَاتِيبِ ٱلْبُوسْطَةِ.

Postboy, *n.* Of post-horses, سَاعِي دَوَابٍّ ـ سَاعِي دَوَابِّ ٱلْبَرِيدِ ٱلْمَنْزِلِ; *from the Turkish,* صُورِيجِي *pl.* صُورِيجِيَّة; of a post-house, غُلَامُ ٱلْمَنْزِلِ.

Postchaise, *n.* عَرَبِيَّةُ بُوسْطَةٍ ـ عَرَبَةُ ٱلْمَنْزِلِ.

Post-classical, *a.* مُحْدَثٌ. A — author, مُؤَلِّفٌ مُحْدَثٌ ـ مُؤَلِّفٌ مُوَلَّدٌ.

Post-communion, *n.* The — office, خَاتِمَةُ طَقْسِ ٱلْقُدَّاسِ.

Post-date, *v.t.* أَرَّخَ ـ عُقْبَ ٱلتَّارِيخِ ٱلصَّحِيحِ. Post-dated, مُؤَرَّخٌ عُقْبَ ٱلتَّارِيخِ ٱلصَّحِيحِ.

Post-date, *n.* تَارِيخٌ مُتَأَخِّرٌ ـ تَارِيخٌ عُقْبَ ٱلتَّارِيخِ ٱلصَّحِيحِ.

Postdiluvial, *a.* }
Postdiluvian, } عُقْبَ طُوفَانِ حَضْرَةِ نُوحٍ.

Postdiluvian, *n.* كُلُّ مَا وُجِدَ عُقْبَ طُوفَانِ حَضْرَةِ نُوحٍ.

Poster, *n.* A courier, بَرِيدٌ *pl.* بُرُدٌ. A large bill for posting up, إِعْلَانٌ كَبِيرٌ لِلتَّعْلِيقِ عَلَى ٱلْحِيطَانِ.

Posterior, *a.* Later, مُتَأَخِّرٌ ـ مُتَخَلِّفٌ ـ مُعَقِّبٌ ـ عَاقِبٌ. To be — to, تَخَلَّفَ ـ أَعْقَبَ ـ عَقَّبَ ـ عَاقَبَ ـ [2] عَقَبَ.

Posteriority, *n.* تَخَلُّفٌ ـ عَاقِبَةٌ ـ عُقْبَةٌ ـ إِعْقَابٌ.

Posteriorly, *ad.* عَاقِبَةً ـ عُقْبَةً ـ بَعْدُ.

Posteriors, *n.* أَدْبَارٌ *pl.* دُبُرٌ ـ أَرْدَافٌ. Having large —, رَجَّاحٌ ـ رَاجِحٌ ـ نَتُّ ٱلْحَقِيبَةِ; of a woman, أَعْجَزُ. Having no —, of a woman, رَسْحَاءُ ـ زَلَّاءُ. *See also* Buttocks, *n.*

Posterity, *n.* Offspring remaining after the father, بَقِيَّةٌ ـ عَاقِبَةٌ ـ عَقْبٌ ـ عَقِبٌ. Offspring, أَوْلَادٌ ـ ذُرِّيَّةٌ. Those that come after their parents, خُلَفَاءُ.

Postern, *n.* A back door, بَابٌ سِرِّيٌّ ـ بَابٌ وَرَّانِيٌّ. The — of a fort, بُوَيْبَةٌ خَفِيَّةٌ فِي قَلْعَةٍ.

Post-fix, *v.t.* To add at the end, أَضَافَ ـ إِلَى ـ أَلْحَقَ ـ بِ وَصَلَ ـ بِ *aor.* يَصِلُ.

Post-haste, *n.* غَايَةُ ٱلسُّرْعَةِ ـ مُبَادَرَةٌ.

Post-haste, *ad.* عَلَى ٱلْفَوْرِ ـ عَلَى ٱلْعَجَلَةِ ـ بِغَايَةِ ٱلسُّرْعَةِ ـ مُبَادَرَةً.

Post-horse, *n.* دَابَّةُ بُوسْطَةٍ ـ دَوَابُّ *pl.* دَابَّةُ مَنْزِلٍ ـ بُرُدٌ *pl.* بَرِيدٌ.

Post-house, *n.* مَنْزِلُ خَانَةٍ ـ مَنْزِلٌ ـ بَرِيدٌ. *See also* Post-office, *n.*

Posthumous, *a.* Born after a father's death, مَوْلُودٌ يَتِيمًا. A — work, تَأْلِيفٌ مَبْرُوزٌ عُقْبَ وَفَاةِ ٱلْمُؤَلِّفِ ـ عُقْبَةٌ ـ عَقْبٌ.

Posthumously, *ad.* بَعْدَ وَفَاةِ صَاحِبِهِ.

Postil, *n.* *See* Marginal-note, *under* Marginal, *a.*

Postillion, *n.* سَائِقُ ٱلْخَيْلِ *pl.* سَاقَةٌ ـ سُورِيجِي *pl.* سُورِيجِيَّةٌ.

Posting, *n.* Transferring of accounts to a ledger, تَقْيِيدُ ٱلْحِسَابَاتِ فِي دَفْتَرٍ. Travelling post, ٱلسَّفَرُ مَعَ ٱلْبَرِيدِ ـ ٱلسَّفَرُ مَعَ ٱلْبُوسْطَةِ.

Post-man, *n.* بُسْطَجِي *pl.* بُسْطَجِيَّةٌ.

Post-mark, *n.* دَمْغَةُ ٱلْبُوسْطَةِ.

Post-master, *n.* One who has charge of a post-house, صَاحِبُ ٱلْبَرِيدِ ـ مَنْزِلْجِي; of a post-office, مُدِيرُ بَيْتِ ٱلْبُوسْطَةِ. Post-master General, مُدِيرُ عُمُومِ ٱلْبُوسْطَةِ.

Post-meridian, *a.* and *ad.* بَعْدَ ٱلظُّهْرِ ـ عُقْبَ ٱلظُّهْرِ.

Post-mortem, *ad.* عُقْبَ ٱلْمَوْتِ. A — examination, تَشْرِيحُ ٱلْجُثَّةِ لِتَحْقِيقِ أَسْبَابِ ٱلْمَوْتِ.

Post-note, *n.* قَائِمَةٌ نَقْدِيَّةٌ يُدْفَعُ مَبْلَغُهَا بِوَقْتٍ مُعَيَّنٍ.

Post-obit, *n.* صَكُّ وَعْدٍ بِدَفْعِ ٱلْمَبْلَغِ ٱلْمَرْهُونِ عُقْبَ وَفَاةِ ٱلرَّاهِنِ.

Post-office, *n.* بَيْتُ (*or* مَحَلُّ) ٱلْبُوسْطَةِ. A general —, بُوسْطَةٌ عُمُومِيَّةٌ. A district —, بُوسْطَةٌ مَحَلِّيَّةٌ.

Post-paid, *a.* *See under* Postage, *n.*

Postpone, *v.t.* To defer to another time, سَوَّفَ ـ أَنَّى ـ آنَى ـ تَأَخَّرَ إِلَى ـ أَبْقَى ـ إِلَى ـ حَذَفَ ـ إِلَى ـ أَخَّرَ. To be postponed to, أُبْقِيَ إِلَى ـ إِحْتَذَفَ إِلَى. *See also to* Defer, *v.t.*

Postponement, *n.* The act of, تَأْخِيرٌ ـ إِيْنَاءٌ ـ تَسْوِيفٌ. To grant one a —, delay, أَجَّلَ. To ask one for a —, إِسْتَأْجَلَ ـ تَأَجَّلَ. *See also* Delay, *n.*

Post-positive, *a.* مُعَلَّقٌ بِ ـ مَوْصُولٌ بِ ـ مُضَافٌ إِلَى.

Postscript, *n.* حَوَاشٍ *pl.* حَاشِيَةٌ ـ مُلْحِقَةٌ ـ تَعْلِيقَاتٌ *pl.* تَعْلِيقَةٌ. (The Arabs generally place the word صح as we do P. S., before a postscript.)

Post-town, *n.* بَلْدَةُ بُوسْطَةٍ ـ بَلْدَةٌ حَاوِيَةٌ بُوسْطَةً.

Postulant, *n.* طَالِبٌ *pl.* طُلَّابٌ.

Postulate, *n.* مَوْضُوعٌ.

Postulate, *v.t.* To solicit, لَجَّ فِي طَلَبِهِ إِيَّاهُ ـ [2] طَلَبَ. To assume, to take for granted, إِتَّخَذَ ـ صَادِقًا (*or* مُسَلَّمًا).

Postulation, *n.* The act of entreating, إِلْتِمَاسٌ ـ إِقْتِرَاحٌ ـ طَلَبٌ; of propounding, عَرْضٌ ـ وَضْعٌ ـ تَخْمِينٌ.

Postulatory, *a.* Without proof, supposed, غَيْرُ مُبَرْهَنٍ ـ مُخَمَّنٌ ـ مَفْرُوضٌ ـ فَقَطْ.

Posture, *n.* Attitude, قِعْدَةٌ ـ وَضْعٌ *pl.* أَوْضَاعٌ ـ هَيْئَةٌ *pl.* هَيْآتٌ.

State, condition, حَالَةٌ ـ حَال ـ هَيْئَات *pl.* هَيْأَةٌ *or* هَيْئَةٌ. Disposition, bearing, طَوْرٌ وَحَرَكَةٌ ـ طَوْرٌ وَشُورَةٌ ـ مَيْل. *See also* Position, *n.*

Posture, *v.t.* أَقْعَدَ ـ قَعَّدَ.

Posture-master, *n.* مُعَلِّمُ ٱلْقِعْدَةِ.

Posy, *n.* A device on a ring, رَسْمُ ٱلْخَاتِمِ. *See also* Nosegay, *n.*

Pot, *n.* A vessel for holding drinkable liquids, مِشْرَبَةٌ *pl.* مَشَارِبُ. A — full, مِلْءُ مِشْرَبَةٍ. A cooking —, بُرْمَةٌ *pl.* بِرَام ـ قِدْرٌ *pl.* قُدُور ـ طَابَقٌ *pl.* طَوَابِقُ ـ تَسَاخِينُ ـ مَرَاجِلُ : cooking-pots, تَسَاخِينُ. To go to —, to be ruined, هَلَكَ ; to become bankrupt, أَفْلَسَ. *See also* Chamber-pot, *n.*

Pot, *v.t.* To put into pots, جَعَلَ فِي أَوْعِيَةٍ ـ أَوْعَى. To put into flower-pots, جَعَلَ (or غَرَسَ) فِي أَقْحَافِ ٱلزَّهْرِ. To preserve or season with spices, تَبَّلَ ـ تَوْبَلَ.

Pot-pourri, *n.* خَبْصَة ـ مَخْلُوطَة ـ خَلِيط.

Potable, *a.* شَرُوب ـ مِمَّا يُشْرَبُ.

Potable, *n.* شَرَاب *pl.* أَشْرِبَة ـ شَرُوب ـ مَشْرَب ـ شَرِيب.

Potableness, *n.* صِفَةُ ٱلشَّرُوبِ.

Potash, *n.* مِلْحُ ٱلْقِلْيِ ـ قِلْيٌ ـ أُشْنَان.

Potassa, *n.* بُوتَاس.

Potassium, *n.* بُوتَاسِيُوم.

Potation, *n.* A drinking, شُرْب ; a single —, شَرْبَة ; a drinking together, مُنَادَمَة ـ مُشَارَبَة.

Potato, *n.* بَطَاطَا *coll.* بَطَاطَة ـ قُلْقَاسٌ فِرِنْجِيٌّ ـ كَمْأَةٌ فِرِنْجِيَّةٌ.

Potatory, *a.* مُتَعَلِّقٌ بِٱلشُّرْبِ.

Pot-bellied, *a.* حَبَنْبَل ـ بَاجِر ـ أَبْجَر ـ أَعْجَر ـ أَكْبَدُ ـ ضَبْعَان ـ أَبُو كِرْشٍ ـ بَطِين. To be —, بَجِرَ.

Pot-belly, *n.* كِرْش ـ بَجَر ـ بُجْر.

Potboy, *n.* غُلَامُ حَانُوتٍ *pl.* غِلْمَان ـ صَبِيُّ خَمَّارَةٍ.

Pot-companion, *n.* شَرِيب *pl.* شُرُب ـ نَدِيم *pl.* نُدَمَاءُ ـ نَدْمَان *pl.* نِدَام.

Poteen, *n.* عَرَقُ إِيرْلَانْد.

Potency, *n.* فِعْل ـ تَأْثِير ـ قُوَّة ـ شِدَّة ـ بَأْس ـ عِزَّة ـ عِزٌّ. *See also* Power, Strength, *n.*

Potent, *a.* مُؤَثِّر ـ شَدِيد ـ قَوِيٌّ. *See also* Cogent, Powerful, Strong, *a.*

Potentate, *n.* عَزِيز *pl.* عِزَاز ـ حَاكِم *pl.* حُكَّام ـ سُلْطَان *pl.* سَلَاطِينُ ـ مَلِك *pl.* مُلُوك.

Potential, *a.* Having power, ذُو قُوَّةٍ ـ قَوِيٌّ ـ مُقْتَدِر. Existing in possibility, مُمْكِن ـ مُحْتَمَل ـ مُقْتَدِر. The — mood, ٱلْفِعْلُ ٱلْمُمْكِنُ.

Potentiality, *n.* إِمْكَان ـ اِحْتِمَال ـ اِقْتِدَار ـ عِزَّة ـ عِزٌّ.

Potentially, *ad.* In possibility, بِٱلْإِمْكَانِ ـ بِٱلِٱحْتِمَالِ.

Potently, *ad.* بِتَأْثِيرٍ ـ بِقُوَّةٍ ـ بِشِدَّةٍ. *See also* Powerfully, *ad.*

Pot-hanger, *n.* *See* Pot-hook.

Pother, *n.* *See* Bustle, *n.*

Pother, *v.t.* *See to* Bother, *v.t. and to* Bustle, *v.i.*

Pot-herb, *n.* تَابِل *pl.* تَوَابِلُ ـ بَقْل *pl.* بُقُول. Pot-herbs, بَقْلَة ـ خُضَار.

Pot-hook, *n.* عِلَاقَة *pl.* عَلَائِقُ ـ مِعْلَاقُ ٱلدَّسْتِ *pl.* مَعَالِيقُ. A scrawling letter, حَرْفٌ مُخَرْبَشٌ. Pot-hooks and hangers, خَطٌّ مُخَرْبَشٌ ـ مُشَبَّكٌ (or شَابِكٌ). To make pot-hooks, to scrawl letters, خَرْبَشَ.

Pot-house, *n.* خَمَّارَة ـ حَانُوت.

Potion, *n.* شَرْبَة *pl.* شَرَبَات.

Potluck, *n.* عُجَالَة. To take — with one, أَكَلَ ٱلْعُجَالَةَ ـ أَكَلَ مَعَهُ ٱلْعُجَالَةَ.

Potsherd, *n.* كِسْرَةٌ مِنَ ٱلْخَزَفِ ـ شَقْفَة ـ شُقْفَة.

Potshot, *n.* As at a bird with a musket, رَمْيَةٌ بِٱلْبَارُودَةِ فِي طَيْرٍ جَاثِمٍ. To take such a —, رَمَى ٱلطَّيْرَ ٱلْجَاثِمَ بِٱلْبَارُودَةِ.

Pottage, *n.* سَوِيق ـ فَتِيت ـ سَلِيقَة ـ طَبِيخُ عَدَسٍ.

Potted, *a.* Placed in pots, مَحْطُوطٌ فِي أَوْعِيَةٍ (or أَقْحَافٍ) ; placed in flower-pots, مَحْطُوطٌ (or مَغْرُوسٌ) فِي أَقْحَافِ ٱلزَّهْرِ. Preserved with spices, مُتَبَّل.

Potter, *n.* فَخَّارِيٌّ ـ جَرَّار ـ خَزَّاف.

Potter, *v.i.* طَرْزَ ـ عَبِثَ.

Potter's-clay, *n.* طِينُ ٱلْأَبْلِيزِ.

Pottery, *n.* فَخَّار ـ خَزَف. The art of —, فِخَارَة ـ جِرَارَة. A seller of —, فَخَرَانِيٌّ ـ فَاخُورِيٌّ.

Pottle, *n.* A measure of four pints, كَيْلٌ إِنْكِلِيزِيٌّ يَسَعُ ٥٠١ دِرْهَمًا ـ كَيْلُ أَرْبَعَةِ أَرْطَالٍ ـ مِنَ ٱلْمَوَائِعِ. A flagon, قُمْقُم ـ قَانُور. *See also* Jar, Pot, *n.*

Pot-valiant, *a.* مُشَجَّعٌ مِنَ ٱلْمُدَامِ.

Pouch, *n.* A pocket, جَيْب *pl.* جُيُوب. A fowler's —, خَرِيطَةُ ٱلصَّيَّادِ. The — or crop of a bird, حَوْصَلَة. A bag, كِيس *pl.* أَكْيَاس. A receptacle, ظَرْف *pl.* ظُرُوف. A soldier's —, بَيْتُ ٱلْفِشَكِ ; *in Turkish,* پَلَاسْقَة.

Pouch, *v.t.* To drink, of a bird, نَغَبَ. *See also to* Pocket, *v.t.*

Pouched, *a.* *See* Marsupial, *a.*

Poult, *n.* فَرُّوج *pl.* فَرَارِيجُ ـ فَرْخ *pl.* أَفْرَاخ *and* فِرَاخ. *See also* Chicken, *n.*

Poulterer, *n.* بَيَّاعُ دَجَاجٍ.

Poultice, *n.* لَبْخَة ـ لَبِخَة ـ ضِمَاد.

Poultice, *v.t.* جَعَلَ لَبْخَةً عَلَى ـ ضَمَّدَ بِضِمَادٍ.

Poulticed, *a.* عَلَيْهِ لَبْخَة ـ مُضَمَّدٌ بِضِمَادٍ.

Poultry, *n.* طُيُور ـ دَجَاج.

Poultry-yard, *n.* صِيَرَةُ ٱلدَّجَاجِ.

Pounce, *n.* The claw of a bird of prey, مِخْلَب *pl.* مَخَالِب. Pounce powder, رُشَاشُ ٱلسَّنْدَرُوسِ.

Pounce, *v.t.* To sprinkle with pounce, (ذَرَّ or رَمَّلَ or رَشَّ) بِٱلسَّنْدَرُوسِ.

Pounce, *v.i.* To pounce upon, as of a bird, خَاتَ ـ إِخْتَاتَ ـ إِخْتَاتَ: The hawk pounced on the bird, (تَخَوَّتَ or إِخْتَاتَ) ٱلصَّقْرُ ٱلطَّيْرَ.

Pounce-box, *n.* حُقَّةُ مِرَشَّةِ ٱلسَّنْدَرُوسِ.

Pouncet-box, *n.* مِبْخَرَة ـ حُقَّةُ ٱلرَّوَائِحِ ٱلذَّكِيَّةِ.

Pound, *n.* Of weight, رِطْل *pl.* أَرْطَال: (the Arab and Syrian رِطْل contains twelve أَوَاقِي, or ounces, of forty دَرَاهِم each, so that the رِطْل weighs 480 *dirhams*). A —, or a piece of twenty shillings, لِيرَة *pl.* لِيرَات. An inclosure for stray cattle, زَرِيبَةٌ لِلسَّائِبَاتِ.

Pound, *v.t.* To bruise, crush, دَقَّ ـ جَرَشَ ـ أَجَشَّ ـ جَشَّ ـ سَحَقَ ـ هَرَسَ. To beat, to drub, ضَرَبَ ـ وَكَزَ *aor.* يَكِزُ ـ سَلَخَ. *See also to* Impound, *v.t.*

Poundage, *n.* ضَرِيبَةٌ عَلَى ٱللِّيرَةِ.

Pounder, *n.* A pestle, مِدَقَّة ـ مِنْجَاز. One who pounds, دَقَّاق ـ جَرَّاش ـ سَحَّاق. The designation of anything by pounds' weight, ذُو أَرْطَالٍ كَذَا *fem.* ذَاتُ. A 48-pounder gun, مِدْفَعُ عِيَارِهِ ثَمَانِيَة وَأَرْبَعُونَ يَعْنِي يُطْلِقُ كُلَّةً ثِقْلُهَا ٤٨ رِطْلًا.

Pounding, *n.* The act of, جَشّ ـ جَرْش ـ دَقّ. A beating, رَشّ. *See also* Hiding, *n.*

Pour, *v.t.* كَبَّ ـ فَضَّ ـ صَبَّ ـ سَكَبَ. To — upon, صَبَّ عَلَى ـ فَرَّغَ عَلَى ـ قَرَّ عَلَى ـ أَفَاضَ عَلَى. To —, as of water, upon, to irrigate, سَقَى *aor.* يَسْقِي ـ أَسْقَى. To —, as of water, into anything, سَقَى *aor.* يَسْقِي: I poured water into the water-skin, سَقَيْتُ ٱلْقِرْبَةَ. To be poured out, إِنْفَضَّ ـ إِنْصَبَّ ـ إِنْسَكَبَ ـ إِنْكَبَّ. To — out for one's self, إِصْطَبَّ: I poured out a cup for myself, إِصْطَبَبْتُ لِنَفْسِي قَدَحًا.

Pour, *v.i.* To issue forth in a stream, to flow, صَبَّ ـ إِنْصَبَّ ـ دَرَّ ـ تَدَفَّقَ ـ تَصَبَّبَ ـ إِنْبَجَسَ ـ إِنْفَجَرَ ـ تَفَجَّرَ. To — down, as of rain, عَزَّ ـ صَابَ *aor.* يَصُوبُ ـ إِنْصَابَ ـ تَصَوَّبَ: The sky poured down rain, دَرَّتِ ٱلسَّمَاءُ بِٱلْمَطَرِ. The clouds — with rain, ٱلسَّحَابُ يَنْبَجِسُ بِٱلْمَطَرِ. It pours, rains heavily, تَدِرُّ ـ عَزَّ ٱلْمَطَرُ. The enemy poured upon them suddenly, إِنْفَجَرَ عَلَيْهِمُ ٱلْعَدُوُّ.

Pouring, *a.* As of rain, مُنْصَبّ ـ عِزّ ـ صَائِب. A — rain, مُنْفَجِر ـ مُنْبَجِس. Gushing, مَطَرٌ نَدَّاخٌ ـ مَطَرٌ عِزٌّ.

Pout, *n.* A fit of sullenness, with grimacing, بُسُول ـ بَسَالَة. A pouting of the lips, تَبْوِيز ـ تَجَهُّم ـ تَعَبُّس. A kind of fish, نَوْعٌ مِنَ ٱلسَّمَكِ. A kind of bird, نَوْعٌ مِنَ ٱلطَّيْرِ.

Pout, *v.i.* To be sullen, شَكِسَ ـ شَرِسَ ـ وَحُمَ. To — with the lips, to grimace, تَعَبَّسَ ـ تَبَرْطَمَ ـ بَوَّزَ ـ تَجَهَّمَ.

Pouter, *n.* A — pigeon, حَمَامٌ أَقْعَس.

Poverty, *n.* Want, indigence, فَاقَة ـ عَيْلَة ـ عَالَة ـ حَوْبَة ـ فَقْر ـ مَسْكَنَة ـ عَوَز ـ ضِيقَة ـ عَدَم. Poverty-struck, مُصَاب بِٱلْفَقْرِ ـ مُحْتَاج. To be in —, إِحْتَاجَ. To plead —, as an excuse, تَعَذَّرَ ٱلْفَقْرَ ـ إِعْتَذَرَ ٱلْمَسْكَنَةَ. To allege one's —, ذَكَرَ فَقْرَهُ. To come to —, إِفْتَقَرَ. *See also* Poorness, *and under* Poor, *a.*

Powder, *n.* A dry substance in minute particles, سَفُوف ـ سُفَّة ـ دَقِيق ـ تُرَاب. A medicinal —, سَفُوف ـ سُفَّة. Powder for placing on a wound, ذَرُور; for the eyes, دَقُوق. Gunpowder, بَارُود. To grind to —, طَحَنَ حَتَّى صَارَ غُبَارًا ـ سَحَقَ. To take a —, إِسْتَفَّ. To throw — into one's eyes, in a figurative sense, أَعْمَى ـ عَمَّى.

Powder, *v.t.* To sprinkle, as of a powder, upon, ذَرَّبَ; as of dust, غَبَّرَ. To put powder on a wound, أَسَفَّ ٱلْجُرْحَ دَوَاءً. To grind to powder; *see under preceding article.*

Powder-flask, *n.* }
Powder-horn, } وِعَاءٌ لِلْبَارُودِ ـ مُذَخِّرُ ٱلْبَارُودِ ـ مُذَخِّر.

Powder-mill, *n.* مَعْمَلُ بَارُودٍ.

Powdery, *a.* مِثْلَ ٱلْغُبَارِ (or ٱلتُّرَاب or ٱلسُّفَّة).

Power, *n.* The faculty of doing, حَيْل ـ حَوْل ـ قِبَل ـ طَوْل ـ قُوَّة ـ مُكْنَة ـ إِطَاقَة ـ إِسْتِطَاعَة ـ طَاقَة ـ ذِرَاع ـ ذَرْع ـ بَاع. Might, majesty, جَلَال ـ عَظَمَة ـ رِفْعَة ـ عِزّ. Authority, وُسْع ـ إِقْتِدَار ـ سُلْطَان ـ سُلْطَة ـ حُكُومَة ـ حُكْم ـ سَعَة. Faculty, delegated powers, وَكَالَة ـ تَفْوِيض ـ رُخْصَة. Possession, حَوْز ـ يَد ـ مُلْك. Force, شِدَّة. Efficacy, تَأَثُّر ـ تَأْثِير; effect, إِنْفِعَال. One having —, ذُو قُوَّةٍ; a ruler, حَاكِم *pl.* حُكَّام. A government, دَوْلَة *pl.* دُوَل. Right, privilege, حَقّ *pl.* حُقُوق ـ إِمْتِيَاز *pl.* إِمْتِيَازَات. Influence, نُفُوذ ـ تَأْثِير ـ عَمَلٌ فِي.

Excellency of —, فَضْلُ ٱلْعِزِّ. I have no — to do it, مَا لِي بِهِ قِبَلٌ — مَا أَقْدِرُ أَفْعَلُهُ — لَا أَسَعُ ذٰلِكَ — لَا طَاقَةَ لِي بِهِ. I have no — to walk, لَا أَسْتَطِيعُ أَمْشِي — مَا أَقْدِرُ أَمْشِي. He has no — to rise, لَا يُمْكِنُهُ ٱلنُّهُوضُ. There is nothing in our —, لَيْسَ شَيْءٌ فِي طَاقَةِ يَدِنَا. He has no — to help, لَيْسَ لَهُ قُوَّةٌ لِلْمُسَاعَدَةِ. He lost the —, زَالَتْ عَنْهُ ٱلْقُوَّةُ. He has — over, لَهُ سُلْطَانٌ عَلَى. They hoped to get — over them, إِنْتَظَرُوا أَنْ يَتَسَلَّطُوا عَلَيْهِمْ. Was it not in your —? أَلَمْ يَكُنْ فِي سُلْطَانِكَ (*or* طَاقَتِكَ)؟ It is in my —, فِي قُدْرَةِ يَدِي. It is not in my —, لَيْسَ فِي وُسْعِي. Powers, abilities, شَمَائِلُ — إِدْرَاكٌ — مَنَاقِبُ. The friendly powers, الدُّوَلُ ٱلْمُتَحَابَّةُ. There is no strength nor — but in, or through, God, the High, the Great, لَا حَوْلَ وَلَا قُوَّةَ إِلَّا بِٱللّٰهِ ٱلْعَلِيِّ ٱلْعَظِيمِ. *See also* Ability, Authority.

Absolute power, حُكُومَةٌ مُطْلَقَةٌ — قُوَّةٌ مُسْتَقِلَّةٌ.

Abuse of power, سُوءُ ٱلِٱسْتِعْمَالِ فِي نُفُوذٍ مَأْمُورِيَّةٍ.

Administrative power, or powers, إِدَارَةٌ مُلْكِيَّةٌ — حُكُومَةٌ.

Coercive power, قُوَّةٌ جَبْرِيَّةٌ.

Discretionary power, سَعَةٌ ٱخْتِيَارِيَّةٌ.

Excess of power, as in an office, تَجَاوُزُ ٱلْمَأْمُورِيَّةِ.

Executive power, حُكُومَةٌ إِجْرَائِيَّةٌ.

Full powers, رُخْصَةٌ تَامَّةٌ — سَعَةٌ كَامِلَةٌ. A document giving full powers, رُخْصَةٌ نَامَه — *from the Turkish* بَرَاءَةُ ٱلرُّخْصَةِ ٱلْكَامِلَةِ.

Governmental power, قُوَّةٌ سِيَاسِيَّةٌ — أَمْرٌ سِيَاسِيٌّ.

Horse power, قُوَّةٌ تُوَازِي قُوَّةَ ٱلْحِصَانِ. A steamer of 500 —, بَاخِرَةٌ قُوَّتُهَا تُوَازِي قُوَّةَ ٥٠٠ حِصَانًا.

Judiciary power, حَقُّ ٱلْمُحَاكَمَاتِ — قُوَّةُ ٱلْمُحَاكَمَةِ.

Legislative power, حَقُّ وَضْعِ ٱلْقَوَانِينِ.

Legitimate power, قُوَّةٌ قَانُونِيَّةٌ.

Legitimation of powers, رُؤْيَةُ بَرَاءَةِ ٱلرُّخْصَةِ وَتَحْقِيقُهَا.

Limited power, سَعَةٌ مَحْدُودَةٌ — رُخْصَةٌ مُنْحَصِرَةٌ.

Power of attorney, صَكٌّ (*or* بَرَاءَةُ) ٱلْوَكَالَةِ.

Power of life and death, سُلْطَانٌ عَلَى قَتْلِ ٱلْمُجْرِمِينَ وَٱلْعَفْوِ عَنْهُمْ.

To the utmost of one's power, عَلَى قَدْرِ ٱلطَّاقَةِ — مَهْمَا أَمْكَنَ لَهُ — عَلَى قَدْرِ ٱلْإِمْكَانِ.

Animal power or powers, القُوَّةُ ٱلطَّبِيعِيَّةُ (*or* ٱلْحَيَوَانِيَّةُ).

Discerning or discriminating powers, القُوَّةُ ٱلنَّظَرِيَّةُ.

Human powers, القُوَّةُ ٱلْإِنْسَانِيَّةُ.

Imaginative powers, القُوَّةُ ٱلْوَهْمِيَّةُ.

Intellectual powers, القُوَّةُ ٱلْعَاقِلَةُ — القُوَّةُ ٱلْعَقْلِيَّةُ.

Letters giving powers, مُحَرَّرَاتٌ مُرَخِّصَةٌ.

Motive powers, القُوَّةُ ٱلْبَاعِثَةُ.

Natural powers, as of growth, *etc*, القُوَّةُ ٱلطَّبِيعِيَّةُ.

Operative or effective powers, القُوَّةُ ٱلْفَاعِلَةُ — القُوَّةُ ٱلْعَمَلِيَّةُ.

Reasoning powers, القُوَّةُ ٱلْعَاقِلَةُ — القُوَّةُ ٱلنَّاطِقَةُ.

Reflecting powers, القُوَّةُ ٱلْفِكْرِيَّةُ.

Retentive powers, القُوَّةُ ٱلْحَافِظَةُ.

Spiritual power, حُكُومَةٌ رُوحِيَّةٌ.

Temporal power, حُكُومَةٌ دُنْيَوِيَّةٌ.

To act in virtue of powers, ٢ عَمِلَ بِحَسَبِ ٱلرُّخْصَةِ.

To break or abolish one's power, أَبْطَلَ قُوَّتَهُ — أَفْرَغَ قُوَّتَهُ.

To come into power, as ministers, *etc.* إِنْتَصَبَ فِي ٱلْإِدَارَةِ — يَصِلُ *aor.* وَصَلَ إِلَى ٱلنِّظَارَةِ.

To employ all one's power, ٤ بَذَلَ — ٢ صَرَفَ مَا لَهُ مِنَ ٱلِٱقْتِدَارِ — كُلَّ جُهْدِهِ.

To exceed one's power, تَجَاوَزَ حَدَّ ٱلْمَأْمُورِيَّةِ.

To exercise power, أَجْرَى — تَسَلَّطَ — ٤ سَلَطَ — ٢ عَمِلَ بِسُلْطَانِ ٱلْحُكُومَةِ. To exercise power over, تَسَلَّطَ عَلَى.

To give power to, to strengthen, شَيَّدَ. To give authority to, إِتَّسَعَ لِ — صَرَّفَ-فِي — رَخَّصَ-فِي — مَكَّنَ — أَعْطَى-قُوَّةً.

To give power to over, as of authority, إِتَّسَعَ — سَلَّطَ-عَلَى — صَرَّفَ-فِي — لِ-عَلَى. To enable one to effect anything, أَمْكَنَ- (*or* مَكَّنَ-) مِن.

To have power, to be able, ٤ قَدَرَ — إِقْتَدَرَ — إِسْتَطَاعَ — أَمْكَنَ — فِيهِ أَنْ.

To have no power to...., مَا قَدَرَ عَلَى — مَا ٱسْتَطَاعَ عَلَى — مَا أَمْكَنَهُ — لَيْسَ لَهُ سُلْطَانٌ أَنْ.

To have power with one, ٤ قَدَرَ عِنْدَهُ — كَانَ لَهُ نُفُوذٌ عِنْدَهُ. What power he has with the Amir! مَا أَمْكَنَهُ عِنْدَ ٱلْأَمِيرِ.

To have full powers, ٤ حَازَ رُخْصَةً كَامِلَةً.

To usurp power, ٢ غَصَبَ ٱلْحُكُومَةَ.

Powerful, *a.* Mighty, puissant, عَزِيزٌ — أَعَزُّ — صَاحِبُ قُوَّةٍ — قَهَّارٌ — قَوِيُّ ٱلِٱقْتِدَارِ — قَدِيرٌ — قَادِرٌ — وَٱقْتِدَارٍ. Strong, قَوِيٌّ. Efficacious, فَعَّالٌ — مُؤَثِّرٌ. Robust, قَوِيٌّ — ظَهِيرٌ — عَفِيٌّ — مُتَعَافٍ. A — medicine, دَوَاءٌ فَعَّالٌ. A — army, جَيْشٌ عَظِيمٌ. A — smell, فَائِحَةٌ. The All-powerful, God, القَادِرُ — القَهَّارُ — القَاهِرُ.

To be or to become —, ٢ عَزَّ — تَعَزَّزَ.

Powerfully, *ad.* Mightily, بِعِزٍّ — عِزَّةً — بِقُوَّةٍ — بِشِدَّةٍ. With effect, تَأْثِيرًا — بِتَأْثِيرٍ. With strength, بِحَيْلٍ. In a great degree, wholly, طُرًّا — جِدًّا — بِٱلْكُلِّيَّةِ — بَتَّةً.

Powerfulness, *n.* *See* Power, *n.*

Powerless, *a.* ضَعِيف *pl.* ضُعَفَآء ـ عَاجِز ـ قَاصِرُ ٱلْيَدِ ـ لَا قُوَّةَ لَهُ . To be — to, عَجِزَ عَن . He is —, that is, has no longer any power to order or forbid, هُوَ عَدِيمُ ٱلْأَمْرِ وَٱلنَّهْيِ .

Power-loom, *n.* نَوْل تُشَغِّلُهُ قُوَّةٌ آلِيَّةٌ .

Power-press, *n.* مَطْبَعَةٌ تُشَغِّلُهَا قُوَّةٌ آلِيَّةٌ .

Pox, *n.* The syphilitic —, مَرَضٌ فِرَنْجِيٌّ ـ بَلَآءٌ ـ حَبٌّ فِرَنْجِيٌّ .

Praam, *n.* *See* Lighter, *n.*

Practicability, *n.* / Practicableness, } قَابِلِيَّة ـ إِمْكَان ـ إِمْكَانُ ٱلْإِجْرَآءِ . The — of a road, مَقْدِرَةٌ بِٱلسُّلُوكِ فِيهِ ـ إِمْكَانُ ٱلسُّلُوكِ فِيهِ . The — of carrying anything up, مَقْدِرَةٌ بِتَصْعِيدِ ٱلشَّيْءِ فِيهِ ـ إِمْكَانُ تَصْعِيدِ ٱلشَّيْءِ فِيهِ .

Practicable, *a.* Feasible, نَاضٌّ ـ إِجْرَآؤُهُ مُمْكِنٌ ـ حُصُولُهُ مُمْكِنٌ ـ مِمَّا يُصْنَعُ ـ مُمْكِنٌ ـ يَسِيرٌ . A — thing, أَمْرٌ نَاضٌّ (*or* مُمْكِنٌ) . A — road, دَرْبٌ (*or* طَرِيقٌ) سَالِكٌ . A — breach, ثُغْرَةٌ يُمْكِنُ ٱلدُّخُولُ مِنْهَا . To be — to, تَأَتَّى لِ ـ أَنَضَّ لِ . *See also* Easy, *a.*

Practical, *a.* As opposed to theoretical, عَمَلِيٌّ ـ رِيَاضِيٌّ ـ إِسْتِعْمَالِيٌّ . One who works much, عَمَّال ـ فَعُول . Experienced, مُدَرَّب ـ مُنَجَّد ـ مُلَقَّح . A — man, a good man of business, رَجُلٌ أَتِيٌّ .

Practically, *ad.* In practice, فِي ٱلْعَمَلِ . By experience, بِٱلتَّجْرِبَةِ ـ بِوَجْهِ ٱلْإِمْتِحَانِ . In reality, فِي ٱلْحَقِيقَةِ ـ حَقًّا .

Practice, *n.* Customary use, مُمَارَزَة ـ مُمَارَسَة ـ تَمَرُّنٌ عَلَى ـ إِدْمَان . Action, use, عَمَل ـ إِسْتِعْمَال ; carrying into use, إِجْرَآءٌ فِعْلًا . Mode of action, قِدْيَة . Experience, خِبْرَة ـ تَجْرِبَة . Custom, عَادَة *pl.* عَوَائِد . Exercise, as of a profession, تَعَاطٍ ـ عَمَل ـ عَمَلِيَّات : medical —, عَمَلِيَّاتٌ طِبِّيَّةٌ ـ مُمَارَسَة ـ تَعَاطِي ٱلطِّبِّ . The — of virtue, مُمَارَسَةُ ٱلْفَضَائِلِ . Pious practices, رُسُومُ ٱلدِّينِ ـ إِجْرَآءُ ٱلْعِبَادَةِ . Given to covetous practices, مُنْهَمِكٌ فِي ٱلطَّمَعِ . Sharp —, غَبْن ـ غَدْر ـ حِيلَة ـ إِحْتِيَال ـ مَكْر . *See also* Exercise, *n.*

Practise, *v.t.* and *i.* To perform certain arts customarily, مَارَسَ ـ عَمِلَ ـ تَمَرَّنَ عَلَى . To carry out into practice, أَجْرَى فِعْلًا . To — medicine, تَعَاطَى (*or* تَعَطَّى) ٱلطِّبَّ . To — evil against, أَنْشَأَ عَلَى ٱلشَّرَّ . To — upon, to deceive, مَكَرَ بِ . To — one's self in, مَارَزَ . To use, employ, إِسْتَعْمَلَ . To be practised, expert, in, أَرِبَ بِ . *See also to* Exercise, *v.t.*

Practised, *a.* *See* Experienced, *a.*

Practitioner, *n.* One engaged in any art or profession, مُتَعَاطٍ ـ مُتَعَاطٍ ـ عَامِل *pl.* عُمَّال ـ مُمَارِس . A legal —, وَكِيلُ ٱلدَّعَاوِي ـ مِنْ أَهْلِ ٱلشَّرْعِ . A medical —, طَبِيب *pl.* أَطِبَّآء ـ حَكِيم *pl.* حُكَمَآء .

Pragmatic, *a.* / Pragmatical, } *See* Meddling, Dictatorial, *a.*

Prairie, *n.* صَحْرَآء ـ دَسْت ـ دَشْت .

Prairie-dog, *n.* كَلْبٌ مِنْ كِلَابِ صَحَارِ أَمِيرِكَا .

Praise, *n.* Commendation, the act of praising, of man, إِثْنَآء ـ تَثْنِيَة ـ تَحْمِيد *pl.* تَحَامِيدُ ـ تَمْجِيد *pl.* تَمَاجِيدُ ; of God, تَسْبِيح ـ ذِكْر ـ تَكْبِير . A tribute of gratitude, مَجْد ـ ثَنَآء ـ مَدْح ـ شُكْر . Extravagant —, إِطْرَآء ـ تَفْرِيط ـ تَقْرِيظ . It will lessen his —, يُقَصِّرُ ٱلثَّنَآءَ عَنْهُ . Praise be to God! (or, rather, Praise belongs unto God!) ٱلْحَمْدُ لِلّٰهِ ـ لِلّٰهِ ٱلْحَمْدُ ـ حَمْدٌ لِلّٰهِ ـ سُبْحَانَ ٱللّٰهِ . To God be the — for what you have done, لِلّٰهِ دَرُّكَ .

Praise, *v.t.* As applied to God, ذَكَرَ ـ سَبَّحَ ـ شَكَرَ . To commend, مَدَحَ ـ مَدَّحَ ـ زَكَّى ـ حَمِدَ عَلَى ـ شَكَرَ لِ ـ حَمَدَ ـ أَثْنَى عَلَى ـ ذَكَرَ بِٱلْجَمِيلِ . To extol, فَخَّمَ ـ كَبَّرَ ـ فَضَّلَ ـ عَظَّمَ . To — extravagantly, أَطْرَأَ ـ قَرَّظَ ـ فَرَّطَ ـ نَوَّهَ بِ . To — one's self, تَمَدَّحَ ـ تَحَمَّدَ . To — one over another, فَخَّرَ عَلَى ـ أَفْخَرَ عَلَى . To — one for, to ascribe praiseworthy qualities to, وَصَفَ بِ *aor.* يَصِفُ : he praised him for his justice, وَصَفَهُ بِٱلْعَدْلِ . To be praised, تَمَدَّحَ .

Praised, *a.* Of God, مَذْكُور ; of man, *etc.*, مُثْنًى عَلَيْهِ ـ مُحَمَّد ـ حَمِيد ـ حَمُود ـ مَمْدُوح ـ مُمَدَّح .

Praiser, *n.* A — of God, شَاكِرُ رَبِّهِ ـ سَبُّوح ; of man, مَادِح ـ مَدَّاح ـ وَصَّاف .

Praiseworthily, *ad.* بِمِنْوَالٍ خَلِيقٍ ـ بِأُسْلُوبٍ خَلِيقٍ بِٱلثَّنَآءِ ـ تَمْدِيحًا ـ بِٱلْمَدْحِ .

Praiseworthiness, *n.* مَحْمَدَة ـ أُمْدُوحَة ـ حُسْن ـ خَيْر ـ فَضْل .

Praiseworthy, *a.* مَبْرُور ـ مَدِيح *pl.* مَدَائِح ـ مَجِيد ـ خَلِيق ـ خَلِيقٌ بِٱلثَّنَآءِ ـ بِٱلْمَدْحِ . A — act, مَحْمَدَة ـ مَدْحَة . Praiseworthy qualities, مَحَامِدُ ـ مَحَاسِنُ . Praiseworthy efforts, ٱلْمَسَاعِي ٱلْمَبْرُورَةُ .

Prance, *v.i.* As of a horse, قَفَزَ ـ شَبَّ .

Prance, *n.* قَفْزَة ـ شَبِيب .

Prancer, *n.* / Prancing, *a.* } Of a horse, قَافِز ـ قَفَّاز ـ شَابٌّ .

Prank, *v.t.* زَيَّنَ ـ حَلَّى .

Prank, *n.* *See* Caper, *n.*

Prate, *v.i.* هَذَرَ ـ زَحْلَفَ فِي ٱلْكَلَامِ ـ أَنْشَرَ ٱلْقَوْلَ . *See also to* Chatter, *v.i.*

Prate, *n.* هَذَر ـ تَهْذَار . *See also* Chatter, *n.*

Prater, *n.* }
Prating, *a.* } هَذَّار ـ هَاذِر ـ غَبِيُّ ٱلشَّفَتَيْنِ. *See also* Chatterer, *n.*

Pratique, *n.* Licence for intercourse after quarantine, إِنْقِضَآءُ مُدَّةِ ٱلْكَوَارَنْتِينَا; *from the Italian*, بَرَاتِيكَة. To admit to —, أَعْطَى ٱلْبَرَاتِيكَة ـ أَعْطَى بَرَآءَةَ ٱلصِّحَّةِ. *See also* Quarantine, *n.*

Prattle, *v.i.* As of a child, طَمْطَمَ. *See also to* Chatter, *v.i.*

Prattle, *n.* Children's talk, طَمْطَمَةُ ٱلْأَوْلَادِ. *See also* Chatter, *n.*

Prattler, *n.* مُطَمْطِم. *See also* Chatterer, *n.*

Pravity, *n.* *See* Depravity, *n.*

Prawn, *n.* جَرَادٌ بَحْرِيٌّ coll. جَرَاد *or* جَرَادَةُ ٱلْبَحْرِ كَبِيرَةٌ.

Praxis, *n.* Use, إِسْتِعْمَال. An example to teach practice, عِبْرَةٌ لِمَنْ يَعْتَبِرُ.

Pray, *v.t.* To entreat, beg, ask, سَأَلَ *aor.* يَسْأَلُ ـ طَلَبَ إِلَى ـ ². I — you, أَتَرَجَّاكَ ـ أَلْتَمِسُ إِلَيْكَ. تَرَجَّى ـ اِلْتَمَسَ مِن To — for, to God, دَعَا ٱللّٰهَ لِ ـ صَلَّى ٱللّٰهَ عَلَى *aor.* يَدْعُو. To — to God against, دَعَا ٱللّٰهَ عَلَى. To — God, تَضَرَّعَ إِلَى ـ صَلَّى ٱللّٰهَ ٱللّٰهِ.

Pray, *v.i.* To be engaged in prayer, صَلَّى. To say prayers, أَدَّى ٱلصَّلَاةَ.

Prayer, *n.* A single prayer, as to God, دَعْوَة ـ صَلَاة. Prayer, as to God, صَلَاة *pl.* صَلَوَات ـ دُعَآء ـ سُبْحَة ـ طَلَبَة ـ تَضَرُّع. A request, entreaty, رَجَآء ـ سُؤَال ـ طَلَبَة. To say the morning —, صَلَّى ٱلصُّبْحَ; the noonday —, صَلَّى ٱلظُّهْرَ. To be earnest in —, تَضَرَّعَ ـ اِبْتَهَلَ. A place of —, مُصَلًّى. He spent the whole night in —, قَضَى ٱللَّيْلَ كُلَّهُ فِي ٱلصَّلَاةِ.

Prayer-book, *n.* كِتَابُ صَلَوَاتٍ.

Prayerful, *a.* مُتَدَيِّن ـ دَيِّن ـ مُمَارِسُ ٱلصَّلَاةِ ـ مُصَلٍّ.

Prayerfully, *ad.* Entreatingly, بِٱبْتِهَالٍ ـ بِتَضَرُّعٍ; with continued prayer, بِمُمَارَسَةِ ٱلصَّلَاةِ.

Prayerless, *a.* غَيْرُ مُصَلٍّ ـ تَارِكُ ٱلصَّلَاةِ.

Prayerlessness, *n.* تَرْكُ ٱلصَّلَاةِ.

Preach, *v.t.* كَرَزَ بِ ـ كَرَزَ: he preached the Gospel, نَادَى كَرَزَ بِٱلْإِنْجِيلِ ـ بِبِشَارَةِ ٱلْإِنْجِيلِ. To — to, خَطَبَ ² خَطَبَ. To — about to, خَاطَبَ ـ كَرَزَ لِ ـ عَلَى ـ خَاطَبَ بِ. To — up, extol, كَبَّرَ ـ عَظَّمَ ـ فَخَّرَ. To — down, نَادَى بِ depreciate, اِسْتَقَلَّ ـ اِسْتَحْقَرَ.

Preach, *v.i.* خَطَبَ ² كَرَزَ ـ وَعَظَ *aor.* يَعِظُ. To — to one about, to admonish, وَعَظَ عَلَى. To be preached, announced, بُشِّرَ ـ مَوْعُوظٌ بِهِ.

Preached, *a.* Announced, مُبَشَّرٌ بِهِ; inculcated, كُرِزَ بِهِ.

Preacher, *n.* خَطِيب *pl.* خُطَبَآءُ ـ كَارِز *pl.* كَارِزُونَ ـ وَاعِظ *pl.* وُعَّاظ.

Preachership, *n.* مَنْصِبُ (*or* رُتْبَةُ) ٱلْوَاعِظِ.

Preaching, *n.* كِرَازَة ـ عِظَة ـ وَعْظ ـ خُطْبَة.

Preachment, *n.* *See* Sermon, *n.*

Pre-acquaintance, *n.* Foreknowledge, عِلْمٌ سَابِقٌ; prior friendship, أُلْفَةٌ سَابِقَةٌ. His —, previous knowledge, عِلْمُهُ ٱلسَّابِقُ.

Pre-acquainted, *a.* Knowing previously, عَارِفٌ بِ (*or* مُطَّلِعٌ عَلَى) سَبْقًا.

Pre-adamite, *n.* One who lived before Adam, مَنْ عَاشَ قَبْلَ حَضْرَةِ آدَمَ. One who believes that persons existed before Adam, قَائِلٌ بِوُجُودِ ٱلنَّاسِ قَبْلَ آدَمَ.

Pre-admonish, *v.t.* سَبَقَ فَنَصَحَهُ ـ ² سَبَقَ فَنَبَّهَهُ.

Pre-admonition, *n.* تَنْبِيهٌ سَابِقٌ ـ نَصِيحَةٌ سَابِقَةٌ ـ نُصْحٌ سَابِقٌ.

Preamble, *n.* دِيبَاجَة ـ مُقَدِّمَة ـ طَالِعَة.

Preamble, *v.t.* قَدَّمَ بِدِيبَاجَةٍ.

Preambulatory, *a.* سَابِق ـ مُتَقَدِّم.

Prebend, *n.* رَاتِبُ قِسِّيسٍ (*or* شَيْخٍ) كَنِيسَةٍ مَطْرَانِيَّةٍ أَوْ مَدْرَسِيَّةٍ.

Prebendal, *a.* مَا نِيطَ بِٱلْمَذْكُورِ آنِفًا.

Prebendary, *n.* صَاحِبُ رَاتِبٍ مِنْ كَنِيسَةٍ مَطْرَانِيَّةٍ أَوْ مَدْرَسِيَّةٍ.

Precarious, *a.* مُعَلَّق ـ غَيْرُ مُقَرَّرٍ ـ غَيْرُ ثَابِتٍ ـ غَيْرُ يَقِينِيٍّ. A — situation, حَالٌ بِلَا دَوَامٍ وَعَدِيمُ ٱلثَّبَاتِ.

Precariously, *n.* مِنْ غَيْرِ قَرَارٍ ـ بِلَا يَقِينٍ ـ مِنْ غَيْرِ ثَبَاتٍ.

Precariousness, *n.* عَدَمُ قَرَارٍ ـ قِلَّةُ ثَبَاتٍ ـ عَدَمُ يَقِينٍ.

Precative, *a.* }
Precatory, } مُتَرَجٍّ ـ مُتَضَرِّع ـ تَضَرُّعِيّ.

Precaution, *n.* حَذَر ـ حِذْر ـ مَحْذُورَة ـ حَزْم ـ اِحْتِيَاط ـ اِحْتِذَار ـ اِنْتِبَاه. To take —, حَذِرَ ـ تَحَزَّمَ ـ اِحْتَذَرَ ـ اِحْتَاطَ. To take — against, اِحْتَاطَ مِن ـ اِحْتَذَرَ مِن ـ حَاذَرَ ـ اِحْتَرَزَ مِن ـ حَذِرَ مِن ـ تَدَرَّكَ مِن. He took his —, أَخَذَ حِذْرَهُ ². Precaution is useless against destiny, (*prov.*) لَا يَنْفَعُ حِذْرٌ مِنْ قَدَرٍ. By way of —, عَلَى سَبِيلِ ٱلِاحْتِيَاطِ. It led him to take the necessary precautions, أَخْرَجَهُ إِلَى أَخْذِ ٱلْحِذْرِ ٱللَّازِمِ.

Precaution, *v.t.* حَذَّرَهُ ـ ² سَبَقَ فَحَذَّرَهُ. To — against, حَذَّرَ مِن.

Precautional, *a.* }
Precautionary, } ذُو حِذْرٍ ـ حَذَرِيّ ـ اِحْتِذَارِيّ ـ اِحْتِيَاطِيّ ـ تَحَفُّظِيّ ـ مِنْ قَبِيلِ ٱلِاحْتِيَاطِ (*or* ٱلتَّحَذُّرِ).

Precautious, *a.* حَاذِر ـ أَحْذَر ـ حَذِر ـ مُسْتَحِيط ـ مُحْتَذِر ـ مُتَحَزِّم ـ أَحْزَم.

Precede, *v.t.* To take the precedence of, فَاتَ ² ـ سَبَقَ ـ ². To go before, of locality, بَكَّرَ ـ قَدَمَ ² ـ تَقَدَّمَ عَلَى ـ سَابَقَ

تَقَدَّمَ ـ ٤ ـ سَبَقَ ; of time, تَقْدَمَ ـ ٤ ـ سَبَقَ . To make to —, ـ ٤ قَدَّمَ. To —, in an intransitive sense, قَدَّمَ ـ سَلَّفَ ـ بَكَّرَ ٤ سَلَفَ. He preceded his companions, بَكَّرَ عَلَى أَصْحَابِهِ. The thing preceded me, فَاتَنِي ٱلْأَمْرُ.

Precedence, *n.* } As in rank, قُدْمِيَّة ـ رِجْل ـ سَابِقَة ـ تَصَدُّر ـ
Precedency, } مَسْبُوقِيَّة ـ سَابِقِيَّة ـ تَقَدُّم ـ قَدَم ; of locality, تَقَدُّم ـ سَبْق ; of time, سُلُوف ـ قِدَم ـ سَبْق . He has the — in this matter, لَهُ سَابِقَةٌ فِي هٰذَا ٱلْأَمْرِ. The — belongs to me, الرِّجْلُ لِي. Those having the —, going before, السَّابِقَاتُ سَبْقًا (Kurân, lxxix. 4.) To give one the — over, قَدَّمَ-عَلَى.

Precedent, *a.* سَلِيف ـ سَالِف ـ مُتَقَدِّم ـ سَابِق. Such as have gone before, preceding generations, سَلِيف ـ سَلَف ـ سُلُوف. That was in the time of —, or preceding, peoples and preceding generations, كَانَ ذٰلِكَ فِي ٱلْأُمَمِ ٱلسَّالِفَةِ وَٱلْقُرُونِ ٱلسَّوَالِفِ.

Precedent, *n.* قَبِيل (or مِثَال or مَثَل) سَابِق ـ سَابِقَة. To serve as a —, صَلُحَ لِقَبِيلٍ ـ ٤ قَامَ بِمَقَامِ مِثَالٍ ـ ٤. Without —, عَدِيمُ ٱلْأَمْثَالِ. To consult precedents, رَاجَعَ ٱلْأَمْثَالَ ٱلسَّابِقَةَ. An action that has had no —, بِكْر ـ بَاكُورَة.

Precedented, *a.* سَبَقَ لَهُ سَابِقَةٌ ـ ٤ ـ سَبَقَ لَهُ مِثَالٌ.

Precedently, *ad.* سَبْقًا ـ مُتَقَدِّمًا ـ أَوَّلًا.

Preceding, *a.* *See* Precedent, *a.*

Precentor, *n.* مُقَدَّمُ ٱلْمُغَنِّينَ.

Precentorship, *n.* وَظِيفَةُ مُقَدَّمِ ٱلْمُغَنِّينَ.

Precept, *n.* A rule, order, رَسْم ـ وَصَايَا *pl.* وَصِيَّة ـ سُنَن *pl.* سُنَّة ـ رُسُوم *pl.* قَاعِدَة *pl.* قَوَاعِدُ. An order, أَمْر ـ حُكْم. Advice, نَصِيحَة. An obligatory religious —, فَرْض ـ فَرَائِضُ *pl.* فَرِيضَة *pl.* فُرُوض.

Preceptor, *n.* A teacher, مُدَرِّس ـ مُعَلِّم. One who gives precepts, مُوَصٍّ.

Preceptorial, *a.* مَا نِيطَ بِٱلْمُدَرِّسِ ـ تَعْلِيمِيٌّ.

Preceptory, *a.* مُوَصٍّ.

Preceptress, *n.* مُدَرِّسَة ـ مُعَلِّمَة.

Precession, *n.* إِسْتِقْبَال. The — of the equinoxes, إِسْتِقْبَالُ نُقْطَتَيِ ٱلْإِعْتِدَالَيْنِ.

Precinct, *n.* A limit, حَدّ *pl.* حُدُود. A district, نَاحِيَة *pl.* نَوَاحِي ـ دِيَار ـ مَحَلّ *pl.* مَحَلَّات. A surrounding, the surroundings, دَائِر ـ جِوَار ـ إِحَاطَة.

Precious, *a.* Of great price or value, فَاخِر ـ ثَمِين ـ سَنِيّ ـ نَفِيس ـ مُثْمِن ـ ذُو قِيمَةٍ. Much esteemed, أَعَزّ ـ عَزِيز. A — thing, مُتْحَفَة ; precious or rare things, تُحَف. More — than gold, أَعَزُّ مِنَ ٱلذَّهَبِ. The — metals, ٱلْمَعَادِنُ ٱلثَّمِينَةُ مِثْلَ ٱلذَّهَبِ وَٱلْفِضَّةِ. A — stone, فَرِيدَة *pl.* فَرَائِدُ ; (*see also* Jewel, *n.*). How — is thy love to me! مَا أَكْرَمَ حُبَّكَ عِنْدِي. To be —, estecmed, rare, عَزَّ ـ ٢. To be — to one, كَانَ عَزِيزًا عِنْدَهُ ـ كَرِيمًا عِنْدَهُ. Precious, (ironically), رَدِيء ـ خَبِيث ـ بَطَّال.

Preciously, *ad.* Of price, نَفَاسَةً ـ بِثَمَنٍ عَظِيمٍ. With esteem, بِعِزٍّ. Badly, بِخَبَاثَةٍ ـ بِرَدَاءَةٍ.

Preciousness, *n.* Costliness, قِيمَةٌ وَافِرَةٌ ـ خَطَر ـ نَفَاسَة. Rarity, esteem, عِزّ ـ عِزَّة.

Precipice, *n.* مَوْرِط ـ مَسْقِط ـ أَلْهَاب *pl.* لِهْب ـ حَدَر ـ وِرَاط *pl.* وَرْطَة. We descended a difficult —, هَبَطْنَا فِي حَدُورٍ صَعْبَةٍ.

Precipitance, *n.* } Excessive haste, إِسْتِعْجَالٌ زَائِدٌ ـ عَجَلَةٌ زَائِدَةٌ.
Precipitancy, } Rashness, عَدَمُ تَأَمُّلٍ ـ بَطْش ـ بَادِرَة ـ تَهَوُّر.

Precipitant, *a.* مُتَهَوِّر ـ عَجَالَى *pl.* عَجْلَى *fem.* عِجَال *pl.* عَجْلَانُ ـ طَائِش ـ هَيِّر.

Precipitant, *n.* مُهَبِّط ـ مُرَسِّب.

Precipitantly, *ad.* بِطَيْشٍ ـ بِتَهَوُّرٍ ـ عَلَى ٱلْعَجَلِ ـ عَلَى أَوْفَاضٍ. To speak —, تَكَلَّمَ فِرَاطًا ـ بِلَا تَأَمُّلٍ.

Precipitate, *n.* رَاسِب.

Precipitate, *v.t.* To throw headlong, ٤ هَبَطَ ـ ٢ طَرَحَ-إِلَى أَسْفَلَ ـ أَرْمَى بِ-فِي ـ أَسْقَطَ-فِي ـ وَرَّطَ-فِي ـ أَوْرَطَ-فِي. To throw into, أَهْبَطَ. To hasten, أَعْجَلَ ـ يَسُوقُ *aor.* سَاقَ ـ أَسْرَعَ. أَهْبَطَ-فِي. To throw for solution, رَسَّبَ. To — one's self, تَسَاقَطَ ـ إِهْتَبَطَ إِلَى أَسْفَلَ. To — one's self upon, إِنْطَبَقَ عَلَى ـ إِنْقَضَّ عَلَى ـ تَسَاقَطَ عَلَى ـ رَمَى نَفْسَهُ عَلَى ـ إِنْحَذَفَ عَلَى ـ ٢. To — one's self into, as into any affair or danger, عَسَمَ بِ ـ ٢ : He precipitated himself into the affair, عَسَمَ فِي ٱلْأَمْرِ ـ ٢. He precipitated himself into the midst of the people, عَسَمَ بِنَفْسِهِ وَسَطَ ٱلْقَوْمِ. To — one's self into, as into a well, *etc.*, إِنْحَذَفَ فِي ـ تَوَرَّطَ فِي ـ أَرْمَى نَفْسَهُ فِي. To be precipitated, of a solution, تَرَسَّبَ.

Precipitate, *a.* Hasty, زَائِدُ ٱلْعَجَلَةِ ـ كَثِيرُ ٱلسُّرْعَةِ. Rash, مُتَهَوِّر ـ هَيِّر ـ مِغْشَم. A — retreat, رُجُوع ـ رَجْعَةٌ قَهْقَرِيَّةٌ ـ رَجْعَةٌ بِٱلْعَجَلَةِ ـ شِذَرَ مِذَرَ.

Precipitation, *n.* The act of throwing for solution, تَرْسِيب ; of throwing down to the bottom, إِهْبَاطٌ إِلَى أَسْفَلَ ; of throwing into, تَوْرِيطٌ فِي ـ إِسْقَاطٌ فِي ; of precipitating one's self, تَسَاقُط ـ إِهْتِبَاط ; of precipitating one's self rashly into any matter, عَسْمٌ بِنَفْسِهِ. *See also* Precipitance, *n.*

Precipitately, *ad.* *See* Precipitantly, *ad.*

Precipitator, *n.* One who hastens, سَائِق ـ مُعَجِّل. One who precipitates a solution, مُرَسِّب.

Precipitous, *a.* Very steep, ذُو مَزْلَقٍ ـ كَالْجُرْف ـ مُنْحَدِر. A — place, أُحْدُور ـ حَدَر ـ حادُور ـ مُنْحَدَر. *See also* Precipitate, *a.*

Precipitously, *ad.* With steep descent, بِحُدُورٍ كُلِّيّ. *See also* Precipitantly, *ad.*

Precipitousness, *n.* Steepness of descent, حُدُورٌ كُلِّيّ ـ جُرْف. *See also* Precipitance, *n.*

Precise, *a.* Having definite limits, مَقْطُوع ـ مَحْدُود ـ مُحَدَّد ـ مَضْبُوط ـ مُدَقَّق ـ مُعَيَّن ـ مُحَكَّم. Correct, صَحِيح. Exact, مَضْبُوط ـ مُدَقَّق. Over-nice, scrupulous, مُتَأَنِّق ـ مُدَقِّق ـ مُتَنَوِّق ـ مُتَجَوِّد. To be —, exact, دَقَّ *aor.* يَدِقُّ. To be — with, دَاقَّ: he was — with him in the accounts, دَاقَّهُ فِي الْحِسَابِ; he was — with him in the affair, دَاقَّهُ فِي الْأَمْرِ. To be —, nice, scrupulous, تَأَنَّق ـ تَجَوَّد.

Precisely, *ad.* Correctly, exactly, بِالضَّبْطِ ـ بِإِحْكَامٍ ـ بِالتَّحْقِيقِ. Perfectly, عَلَى عَيْنٍ ـ بِكَمَالٍ ـ فِي غَايَةِ الْإِتْقَانِ. With over-niceness, بِتَأَنُّقٍ ـ بِتَجَوُّدٍ ـ بِتَنَوُّقٍ ـ تَجَوُّدًا.

Preciseness, *n.* } Correctness, تَحْكِيم ـ ضَبْط ـ صِحَّة. Concise-
Precision, } ness, إِيجَاز. Strict conformity, تَدْقِيق ـ دِقَّة. Over-nicety, scrupulousness, تَنَوُّق ـ تَجَوُّد ـ تَأَنُّق. With great — and care, بِغَايَةِ الدِّقَّةِ وَالْاعْتِنَاءِ ـ بِغَايَةِ الْإِتْقَانِ.

Precisian, *n.* مُتَجَوِّد ـ مُتَنَوِّق ـ مُتَأَنِّق. *See also* Fanatic, *n.*

Precisianism, *n.* تَجَوُّد ـ تَنَوُّق ـ تَأَنُّق. *See also* Fanaticism, *n.*

Preclude, *v.t.* عَوَّقَ-عَن ـ أَعَاقَ-عَن ـ يَعُوقُ *aor.* عَاقَ-عَن ـ حَجَبَ-عَن ². To be precluded from, إِحْتَجَبَ ـ تَعَوَّقَ عَن ـ إِمْتَنَعَ عَن ـ تَحَجَّبَ عَن ـ عَن. Brothers of a deceased person — the mother from receiving the third of the inheritance, إِخْوَةُ الْمَيِّتِ يَحْجُبُونَ الْأُمَّ عَنِ الثُّلُثِ. *See also to* Prevent, *v.t.*

Preclusion, *n.* The act of, حَجْب ـ إِعَاقَة ـ تَعْوِيق ـ عَوْق. The state of being precluded, إِحْتِجَاب ـ تَحَجُّب ـ تَعَوُّق ـ مَنْع ـ إِمْتِنَاع.

Preclusive, *a.* حَائِل ـ مَانِع ـ مُعَوِّق ـ حَاجِب.

Preclusively, *ad.* إِعَاقَةً ـ عَوْقًا ـ حَجْبًا ـ بِإِعَاقَةٍ.

Precocious, *a.* Ripe before the natural time, بَدْرِيّ *pl.* بَدَارَى ـ قَبْلَ الْإِبَّانِ ـ عَاجِل ـ بَكِير ـ بَاكِر. A — child, وَلَدٌ بَكْرٌ (or مُبَادِرٌ); a — girl, بِنْتٌ مُبَادِرَةٌ (or بَكِيرَةٌ).

Precocity, *n.* } تَبْدِير ـ بَدْر ـ مُبَادَرَة.
Precociousness, }

Precociously, *ad.* تَبْدِيرًا ـ مُبَادَرَةً ـ بِتَبْدِيرٍ ـ بِمُبَادَرَةٍ.

Precogitate, *v.t.* إِطَّلَعَ عَلَى-سَبْقًا ـ ² سَبَقَ تَتَأَمَّلَهُ.

Precognition, *n.* إِطِّلَاعٌ عَلَى-سَبْقًا ـ عِلْمٌ سَابِقٌ.

Preconceive, *v.t.* سَبَقَ فَأَضْمَرَهُ ـ ² سَبَقَ فَتَصَوَّرَهُ. He preconceived the thing, ² سَبَقَ ذِهْنُهُ إِلَى الشَّيْءِ.

Preconception, *n.* ظَنٌّ سَابِقٌ ـ تَصَوُّرٌ سَابِقٌ.

Preconcert, *v.t.* سَبَقَ فَرَتَّبَهُ ـ ² سَبَقَ فَاخْتَرَعَهُ. They preconcerted it together, سَبَقُوا فَتَشَاوَرُوا فِي الْأَمْرِ.

Preconcerted, *a.* مُتَشَاوَرٌ عَلَيْهِ سَبْقًا ـ مُرَتَّبٌ سَبْقًا.

Precontract, *n.* شَرْطٌ سَابِقٌ ـ مُوَاطَاةٌ سَابِقَةٌ ـ إِرْتِبَاطٌ سَابِقٌ.

Precursor, *n.* A harbinger, مُبَشِّر ـ بَشِير. A prognostic, بُشْرَى ـ عَلَامَةٌ سَابِقَةٌ ـ دَلِيل.

Precursory, *a.* مُؤْذِنٌ بِ ـ مُسْتَدِلٌّ بِ-سَبْقًا ـ مُبَشِّر.

Predaceous, *a.* Living by plunder, مَعَاشُهُ مِنَ النَّهْبِ ـ يَعْتَاشُ بِالسَّلْبِ.

Predal, *a.* نَهَّاب ـ مُتَعَلِّقٌ بِالنَّهْبِ. Predal animals, ذَوَاتُ الصَّيْدِ.

Predatorily, *ad.* نَهْبًا ـ بِالنَّهْبِ ـ مِثْلَ النَّهَّابِ.

Predatory, *a.* نَهَّاب ـ نَاهِب ـ مُسْتَلِب ـ سَالِب.

Predecease, *v.t.* ² مَاتَ قَبْلَهُ.

Predecessor, *n.* سَالِف ـ الَّذِي قَبْلَهُ *pl.* أَسْلَاف. Predecessors, سُلْفَة ـ سَلِيف ـ سَلَف.

Predesign, *v.t.* تَعَمَّدَهُ سَبْقًا ـ ² سَبَقَ فَقَصَدَهُ.

Predesigned, *a.* سَابِقُ الْعَمْدِ ـ مُتَنَوًّى سَبْقًا ـ مُتَعَمَّدٌ سَبْقًا.

Predestinarian, *n.* مُؤْمِنٌ بِالْقَضَاءِ وَالْقَدَرِ ـ قَدَرِيَّة *pl.* قَدَرِيّ.

Predestinarianism, *n.* إِعْتِقَادُ الْقَدَرِيَّةِ.

Predestinate, *a.* } مُقَدَّر ـ مُعَيَّنٌ سَبْقًا.
Predestinated, }

Predestinate, *v.t.* } ² سَبَقَ فَعَيَّنَهُ. To —, or decree, what must
Predestine, } happen to one, قَدَّرَ-عَلَى. To — something for one's good, قَدَّرَ-لِ.

Predestination, *n.* قَدَر ـ قَضَاء ـ قَضَاءٌ وَقَدَر ـ تَعْيِينٌ سَابِقٌ. The doctrine of —, الْقَضَاءُ وَالْقَدَرُ ـ قَدَر.

Predestinator, *n.* مُقَدِّر.

Predeterminate, *a.* مُقْضًى بِهِ سَبْقًا ـ مَحْتُومٌ بِهِ سَبْقًا ـ مَفْصُولٌ سَبْقًا.

Predetermination, *n.* عَزْمٌ سَابِقٌ ـ قَضَاءٌ سَابِقٌ ـ حَتْمٌ سَابِقٌ.

Predetermine, *v.t.* ² سَبَقَ ـ ² سَبَقَ فَحَتَمَ بِ ـ ² سَبَقَ فَحَتَمَهُ ـ فَفَصَلَهُ.

Predial, *a.* مُتَعَلِّقٌ بِالْأَرَاضِي وَالْأَمْلَاكِ. A — or real estate, عِقَار ـ مُلْك ـ عُقَد *pl.* عُقْدَة.

Predicability, *n.* إِمْكَانُ النِّسْبَةِ إِلَيْهِ ـ إِمْكَانُ الْإِسْنَادِ إِلَيْهِ.

Predicable, *a.* مِمَّا يُسْنَدُ إِلَى ـ يُقَالُ عن ـ يُنْسَبُ إِلَى.

Predicament, *n.* A series or order, نِظَام ـ رُتْبَة ـ سِيَاقَة. State, condition, حَال ـ حَالَة. Unfortunate condition, حَالَةٌ يُرْثَى لَهَا ـ بَلِيَّة ـ حَالُ سُوءٍ ـ وَرْطَة. What has placed you in this —, ما طَرَحَكَ هٰذَا ٱلْمَطْرَحَ.

Predicate, *v.t.* To affirm one thing as the predicate of another, أَسْنَدَ-إِلَى. *See also to* Affirm, *v.t.*

Predicate, *n.* مَحْمُول ـ خَبَر ـ مُسْنَد. The —, ٱلْمُسْنَدُ إِلَيْهِ. The subject and —, ٱلْمُسْنَدُ وَٱلْمُسْنَدُ إِلَيْهِ.

Predication, *n.* إِسْنَاد. *See also* Affirmation, *n.*

Predicatory, *a.* *See* Affirmative, Positive, *a.*

Predict, *v.t.* نَبَّأَ بِ ـ تَنَبَّأَ بِ ـ أَوْعَدَ ـ وَعَدَ بِ *aor.* يَعِدُ. To — to, أَنْبَأَ-بِ.

Predicted, *a.* مُتَنَبَّأٌ بِهِ ـ مُنَبَّأٌ بِهِ ـ مُوْعَدٌ بِهِ.

Prediction, *n.* إِنْبَاء ـ إِخْبَارٌ بِٱلْمُسْتَقْبِلِ ـ مَوْعِد *pl.* مَوَاعِد ـ بِٱلْغَيْبِ. Predictions about public affairs, مَلَاحِمُ.

Predilection, *n.* شَوْق ـ عَطْف ـ خَاطِر ـ مَيْل ـ أَهْوَاء *pl.* هَوًى. To have a — for, مَالَ إِلَى ـ لَوَى عَلَى ـ تَشَوَّقَ إِلَى. *See also under to* Incline, *v.i.*

Predispose, *v.t.* To arrange beforehand, سَبَقَ ـ سَبَقَ فَرَتَّبَهُ. To cause to be favourably inclined to, عَطَفَ-عَلَى ـ فَأَعَدَّهُ. To be predisposed to, as to a disease, كَانَ لَهُ سَابِقَةٌ لِ ـ رَغِبَ-فِي.

Predisposition, *n.* Pre-arrangement, تَرْتِيبٌ سَابِقٌ. Preparation for, إِسْتِعْدَادٌ لِ. Predisposition, as to disease, سَابِقَة. *See also* Predilection, *n.*

Predominance, *n.* } Ascendency, إِسْتِيلَاء ـ إِسْتِعْلَاء ـ طُمُوم.
Predominancy, } General prevalence, عُمُوم ـ شَمْلُ ٱلْجَمَاعَةِ.

Superiority, command, تَغَلُّب ـ تَسَلُّط. The government always objected to the — of Persia over Herât, الدَّوْلَةُ كَانَتْ دَائِمًا تُعَارِضُ ٱسْتِيلَاءَ إِيرَانَ عَلَى هَرَاة.

Predominant, *a.* Ruling, أَغْلَب ـ ضَابِط ـ مُتَسَلِّط ـ مُسْتَوْلٍ. Generally prevailing, مُطِمّ ـ عَامّ ـ شَامِلُ ٱلْجَمَاعَةِ ـ غَالِب. A — calamity, دَاهِيَةٌ شَامِلَةٌ ـ طَامَّة. Generosity was — in him, غَلَبَ عَلَيْهِ ٱلْكَرَمُ.

Predominantly, *ad.* إِشْتِمَالًا ـ عُمُومًا ـ بِٱسْتِعْلَاءٍ ـ طُمُومًا.

Predominate, *v.i.* To be superior, in the ascendant, كَانَ غَالِبًا ـ كَانَ مُتَسَلِّطًا. To rise to a high pitch and overcome, طَمَّ. To be general, عَمَّ. To — over, to be in the ascendant and to overcome, غَلَبَ عَلَى ـ قَوِيَ عَلَى ـ طَمَّ عَلَى ـ عَلَا *aor.* يَعْلُو ـ إِسْتَعْلَى عَلَى. A calamity that predominates over other calamities, دَاهِيَةٌ تَطُمُّ عَلَى ٱلدَّوَاهِي.

Pre-elect, *v.t.* سَبَقَ فَٱخْتَارَهُ ـ سَبَقَ فَٱصْطَفَاهُ ـ سَبَقَ فَٱجْتَبَاهُ.

Pre-election, *n.* إِخْتِيَارٌ سَابِقٌ ـ إِصْطِفَاءٌ سَابِقٌ ـ إِجْتِبَاءٌ سَابِقٌ.

Pre-eminence, *n.* عِزَّة ـ عِزّ ـ بَرَاعَة ـ قُدْمِيَّة ـ تَقَدُّم ـ إِسْتِعْلَاء ـ فَضِيلَة ـ تَفَوُّق. Pre-eminence in rank or position, تَقَدُّم ـ تَصَدُّر ـ تَقَدُّمٌ عَلَى. To have the — over, عَزَّ عَلَى ـ إِعْتَلَى ـ إِسْتَعْلَى عَلَى. To get the — over, فَازَ بِ.

Pre-eminent, *a.* عَزِيز ـ بَارِع ـ فَائِق *pl.* فُوَقَاء ـ أَفْضَل ـ أَعْظَم ـ رَفِيعُ ٱلْحَسَبِ ـ مُرْتَفِعُ ٱلشَّأْنِ. Pre-eminent in dignity, أَوَّل ـ وَٱلْقَدْرِ. Pre-eminent in learning, عَلَّام ـ فَاضِل ـ فَضِيلُ ٱلْعِلْمِ. The Pre-eminent (God), الظَّاهِرُ. To be —, بَرَعَ.

Pre-eminently, *ad.* عِزَّةً ـ فَائِقٍ ـ بِوَجْهٍ ـ لِلْغَايَةِ ـ أَصْلًا ـ بِٱلزِّيَادَةِ ـ بِبَرَاعَةٍ.

Pre-emption, *n.* The right of, الشُّفْعَة. He made a demand upon him respecting that which was sold, for the right of —, شَفَعَ إِلَيْهِ فِي مَا بَاعَ; and, he admitted to him his right of —, فَشَفَّعَهُ.

Preen, *v.t.* To clean and adjust the feathers, of a bird, نَشْنَشَ.

Pre-engage, *v.t.* سَبَقَ ـ سَبَقَ فَٱرْتَبَطَهُ ـ سَبَقَ فَٱرْتَبَطَ مَعَ فَعَاهَدَهُ.

Pre-engaged, *a.* مُعَاهَدٌ سَبْقًا ـ مُرْتَبِطٌ سَبْقًا.

Pre-engagement, *n.* مُعَاهَدَةٌ سَابِقَةٌ ـ إِرْتِبَاطٌ سَابِقٌ.

Pre-establish, *v.t.* أَحْكَمَ-سَبْقًا ـ قَرَّرَ-سَبْقًا ـ سَبَقَ فَقَرَّرَهُ.

Pre-establishment, *n.* إِحْكَامٌ سَابِقٌ ـ تَقْرِيرٌ سَابِقٌ.

Pre-exist, *v.i.* وُجِدَ مِنْ قَبْلُ ـ سَبَقَ فَكَانَ.

Pre-existence, *n.* سَابِقُ ٱلْوُجُودِ ـ كَوْنٌ سَابِقٌ.

Pre-existent, *a.* } كَائِنٌ مِنْ قَبْلُ ـ مَوْجُودٌ مِنْ قَبْلُ ـ كَائِنٌ سَبْقًا.
Pre-existing, }

Preface, *n.* مُقَدِّمَة ـ طَالِعَة ـ دِيبَاجَة.

Preface, *v.i.* To introduce by preliminary remarks, فَتَحَ ـ سَبَقَ فَطَرَحَ بَعْضَ إِفَادَاتٍ ـ أَفَادَ بِٱفْتِتَاحٍ ـ ٱفْتِتَاحًا.

Preface, *v.t.* To put a preface to, قَدَّمَ-بِدِيبَاجَةٍ ـ صَدَّرَ. To introduce by preliminary remarks, فَتَحَ-بِٱفْتِتَاحٍ.

Prefatory, *a.* مُتَقَدِّم ـ أَوَّلِيّ ـ إِفْتِتَاحِيّ.

Prefect, *n.* شَيْخُ ٱلْقُرَى ـ نُقَبَاء *pl.* نَقِيب ـ قَادَة *pl.* قَائِد *pl.* مَشَايِخ.

Prefectship, *n.* } إِدَارَةُ (or وَظِيفَةُ) شَيْخِ ٱلْقُرَى ـ قِيَادَة ـ نِقَابَة.
Prefecture, }

Prefer, *v.t.* To esteem before others, آثَرَ-عَلَى ـ أَشْفَقَ-عَلَى ـ إِسْتَحْسَنَ ـ فَضَّلَ-عَلَى ـ إِسْتَحَبَّ-عَلَى. To hold to be preferable, فَضَّلَ-عَلَى ـ رَجَّحَ ـ حَسِبَ-أَفْضَلَ مِنْ. To distinguish, to choose by preference, إختارَ-دُونَ ـ إختارَ ـ إِنْتَقَى ـ مَيَّزَ-مِن ـ ٥ مازَ غَيْرِهِ. To raise, as in rank, رَفَّعَ ـ رَقَّى ـ قَدَّمَ. To present to, قَدَّمَ-لِ ـ ٥ عَرَضَ لِ or عَلَى. I would —, أَحَبَّ عَلَيَّ. I preferred this above that, أَشْفَقْتُ هٰذا عَلَى ذاكَ. I preferred some of my children above some, أَشْفَقْتُ بَعْضَ وَلَدِي عَلَى بَعْضٍ. He preferred to do such a thing, آثَرَ أَنْ يَفْعَلَ كَذا. He prefers actions to words, يُفَضِّلُ ٱلْعَمَلَ عَلَى ٱلْقَوْلِ. I — such an one to myself, آثَرْتُ فُلانًا عَلَى نَفْسِي. I (prefer) death rather than disgrace, المَنِيَّةَ لا الدَّنِيَّةَ. He preferred a complaint against him to the Governor, رافَعَهُ إِلَى ٱلْحاكِمِ. *See also under to* Choose, *v.t.*

Preferable, *a.* أَخْيَرُ ـ أَوْلَى ـ مُرَجَّحٌ ـ أَرْجَحُ. It is — that..., الأَوْلَى أَنْ. Happiness is — to riches, الغِبْطَةُ مُفَضَّلَةٌ عَلَى ٱلْغِنَى. This is the — of the two, هٰذا أَكْثَرُ ٱلاثْنَيْنِ فَضْلًا. That which is —, الأَرْجَحُ.

Preferably, *ad.* دُونَ غَيْرِهِ ـ بِٱلتَّرْجِيحِ ـ بِٱلتَّفْضِيلِ ـ بِإِيثارٍ.

Preference, *n.* Estimating over others, تَرْجِيحٌ ـ إِيثارٌ ـ أُثْرَةٌ ـ إِخْتِيارٌ ـ خِيارٌ ـ إِقْتِراحٌ. Choice, إِسْتِحْبابٌ ـ إِسْتِحْسانٌ ـ تَفْضِيلٌ. By —, choice, إِخْتِيارًا ـ بِٱلْخِيارِ. To give the — to, رَجَّحَ ـ فَضَّلَ-عَلَى. To have the —, choice, هُوَ بِٱلْخِيارِ (or بِٱلْمُخْتارِ). To be preferred to, فُضِّلَ عَلَى. I hold him in —, لَهُ عِنْدِي أُثْرَةٌ. He has a — in the estimation of the Amîr, هُوَ ذُو أُثْرَةٍ عِنْدَ ٱلأَمِيرِ. Preference shares, أَسْهامٌ مُمْتازَةٌ.

Preferment, *n.* The act of advancing to a higher office, تَرْقِيَةٌ ـ أَرْفَعُ ـ أَعْلَى مَنْصِبٍ. Superior place or office, تَرْفِيعُ ٱلرُّتْبَةِ وَظِيفَةٌ.

Prefiguration, *n.* رَمْزٌ سابِقٌ ـ تَمْثِيلٌ سابِقٌ ـ تَمْثِيلُ بِ-سَبْقًا مِثالُ ٱلآتِي.

Prefigurative, *a.* ما هُوَ مِثالُ ٱلآتِي ـ مُمَثِّلٌ بِ-سَبْقًا.

Prefigure, *v.t.* دَلَّ عَلَى ٱلآتِي بِٱلرَّمْزِ ـ ٤ سَبَقَ فَرَمَزَ إِلَى.

Prefix, *v.t.* To fix or appoint beforehand, ٤ سَبَقَ فَعَيَّنَهُ ـ عَيَّنَ-سَبْقًا. To place at the beginning, ٤ دَخَلَ بِ; to be prefixed, ٤ دَخَلَ عَلَى.

Prefix, *n.* كَلِمَةٌ (or أَداةٌ) تُصَدِّرُ كَلِمَةً أُخْرَى.

Preformative, *n.* لَفْظَةٌ ٱبْتِدائِيَّةٌ.

Pregnable, *a.* ضَبْطُهُ مُمْكِنٌ ـ فَتْحُهُ مُمْكِنٌ.

Pregnancy, *n.* The state of being with young, حَبَلٌ ـ حَمْلٌ. The time of —, مَحْبَلٌ. Fertility, غَزارَةٌ ـ إِثْمارٌ. Inventive power, إِخْتِراعٌ ـ قُوَّةٌ مُبْدِعَةٌ.

Pregnant, *n.* Being with young, حُبْلَى ـ حامِلَةٌ ـ حامِلٌ *pl.* حَبالَى. To be full of, to abound in, ٤ طَمَّ بِ ـ ٥ طَفَحَ بِ. To be or become —, إِسْتَحْبَلَتْ ـ حَمَلَتْ ـ حَبِلَتْ. To make —, صَيَّرَ-حامِلَةً ـ أَحْبَلَ.

Pregnantly, *ad.* As with fertility, طَفُوحًا ـ بِطُمُومٍ ـ بِطُفُوحٍ.

Prehensile, *a.}* Prehensory, } جَدِيرٌ بِٱلْخَطْفِ ـ خَلِيقٌ بِٱلتَّضْبِيبِ.

Prehension, *n.* ضَبٌّ ـ إِضْبابٌ ـ إِخْتِطافٌ ـ خَطْفٌ.

Prejudge, *v.t.* To judge before the facts are fully known, تَهافَتَ عَلَى ٱلْحُكْمِ فِي ـ ٤ حَكَمَ فِي-قَبْلَ ٱلْفَحْصِ ـ ٤ سَبَقَ فَحَكَمَ فِي.

Prejudgment, *n.* قَضْلٌ سابِقٌ ـ حُكْمٌ سابِقٌ.

Prejudicate, *v.t.* To decide against beforehand, ٤ سَبَقَ فَحَكَمَ عَلَى ـ ٤ حَكَمَ عَلَى-قَبْلَ ٱلْفَحْصِ.

Prejudication, *n.* حُكْمٌ عَلَى-بِلا فَحْصٍ ـ حُكْمٌ سابِقٌ عَلَى.

Prejudicative, *a.* حاكِمٌ عَلَى-بِلا فَحْصٍ ـ حاكِمٌ عَلَى-سَبْقًا.

Prejudice, *n.* A judgment or opinion formed beforehand, ظَنٌّ سابِقٌ ـ قِياسٌ سابِقٌ; a judgment from analogy, حُكْمٌ قِياسِيٌّ ـ حُكْمٌ ٱعْتِبارِيٌّ. A —, as indicative of a motive, غَرَضٌ *pl.* أَغْراضٌ ـ عِلَّةٌ غائِيَّةٌ. An opinion formed without examination, ظَنٌّ بِلا فَحْصٍ. Suspicion, ظِنَّةٌ. A — in favour of, عُلْقَةٌ ـ عَلاقَةٌ ـ ظَنٌّ سُوءٍ فِي ـ خُصُومَةٌ ـ تَنَفُّرٌ; a — unfavourable to, حُسْنُ ظَنٍّ فِي. Party spirit, in favour of, تَعَصُّبٌ لِ; against, تَعَصُّبٌ عَلَى. A mere opinion, وَهْمٌ *pl.* أَوْهامٌ. Injury or wrong of any kind, مَضَرَّةٌ ـ ضَرَرٌ ـ ضَيْمٌ. To his —, مَضَرَّةٌ لَهُ. Without — to the rights of such an one, بِدُونِ إِخْلالٍ (or إِجْحافٍ) بِحُقُوقِ فُلانٍ. He is the object of my —, suspicion, هُوَ ظِنَّتِي.

Prejudice, *v.t.* To damage, injure, أَضَرَّ ـ ٤ ضَرَّ ـ ٤ ضَرَّبَ ـ أَجْحَفَ بِ ـ ضارَّ ـ إِسْتَضامَ ـ يَضِيمُ *aor.* ضامَ. *See also to* Bias, *v.t.*

Prejudiced, *a.* Having a party spirit, in favour of, مُتَعَصِّبٌ لِ; against, مُتَعَصِّبٌ عَلَى. Prejudiced through interest, صاحِبُ غَرَضٍ. Prejudiced in favour of, مُتَعَلِّقٌ بِ ـ مُحْسِنُ ٱلظَّنِّ فِي; against, لَقِنَ عَنْ. I was — against him, had a bad opinion of him, سُؤْتُ بِهِ ظَنًّا ـ أَسَأْتُ بِهِ ٱلظَّنَّ. I was — in his favour, had a good opinion of him, أَحْسَنْتُ بِهِ ظَنًّا.

Prejudicial, *a.* مُؤْذٍ ـ ضارٌّ ـ مُضِرٌّ ـ ضامَّةٌ *pl.* ضائِمٌ ـ مُجْحِفٌ بِ.

Prejudicially, *ad.* بِإِجْحافٍ ـ بِضَرَرٍ ـ ضَرَرًا ـ مَضَرَّةً.

Prelacy, *n.* الأَسْقُفِيَّةُ ـ المَطْرَنَةُ.

Prelate, *n.* أُسْقُفٌ ـ مِطْرانٌ *pl.* مَطارِنَةٌ ـ رَئِيسُ كَنِيسَةٍ *pl.* أَساقِفَةٌ.

Prelatic, *a.}* Prelatical, } مُتَعَلِّقٌ بِٱلْمَطارِنَةِ وَٱلأَساقِفَةِ ـ أُسْقُفِيٌّ ـ مِطْرانِيٌّ.

Prelatism, *n.* *See* Prelacy, *n.*

Prelatist, *n.* مِنْ طَرَفِ ٱلْأَسَاقِفَةِ ـ مُتَعَصِّبٌ لِلْمَطَارِنَةِ.

Prelect, *v.t.* قَرَأَ دَرْسًا فِي مَحْفِلٍ.

Prelection, *n.* دَرْسٌ عَامٌّ.

Prelector, *n.* مُدَرِّسٌ عَامٌّ.

Prelibation, *n.* *See* Foretaste, *n.*

Preliminarily, *ad.* فِي ٱلْأَوَّلِ ـ ٱفْتِتَاحًا ـ بِوَجْهِ ٱلِٱفْتِتَاحِ ـ أَوَّلًا.

Preliminary, *a.* مُتَقَدِّمٌ ـ ٱفْتِتَاحِيٌّ ـ أَوَّلِيٌّ. Preliminary matter, articles, *etc.*, مَوَادُّ مُتَقَدِّمَةٌ.

Preliminary, *n.* مُقَدَّمَةٌ *pl.* مُقَدَّمَاتٌ ـ تَقْدِمَةٌ ـ فَاتِحَةٌ *pl.* فَوَاتِحُ. The preliminaries of peace, مُقَدَّمَاتُ ٱلصُّلْحِ.

Prelude, *n.* Of music, *etc.*, ٱفْتِتَاحٌ ـ بَدْءٌ ـ فَاتِحَةٌ ـ مَطْلَعٌ ـ مُقَدَّمَةٌ. A sign, indication, عَلَامَةٌ ـ إِشَارَةٌ ـ دَلِيلٌ.

Prelude, *v.t.* To introduce, begin with, بَدَأَ بِ ـ ٱبْتَدَأَ بِ ـ قَدَّمَ بِ ـ ٱفْتَتَحَ ـ ٱفْتَتَحَ بِ.

Prelude, *v.i.* تَبَدَّأَ ـ قَامَ بِمَقَامِ مُقَدَّمَةٍ.

Prelusive, *a.* } مُتَقَدِّمٌ ـ بَدِيءٌ ـ ٱفْتِتَاحِيٌّ.
Prelusory, }

Premature, *a.* Ripe too soon, مُسْتَوٍ قَبْلَ ـ نَاضِجٌ قَبْلَ ٱلْإِبَّانِ ـ عَاجِلٌ ـ أَعْجَلُ ـ أَسْبَقُ وَقْتِهِ ـ أَعْجَلُ عَنْ وَقْتِهِ. Too early, أَوَانِهِ. Out of season, خَارِجٌ عَنْ وَقْتِهِ ـ فِي غَيْرِ أَوَانِهِ. Happening before its time, وَاقِعٌ (or بَالِغٌ) قَبْلَ ٱلْأَوَانِ. Doing before the proper time, مِعْجَالٌ ـ مُعْجِلٌ ـ مُعْجِلُ ٱلشَّيْءِ عَنْ وَقْتِهِ. A — birth, وِلَادَةٌ قَبْلَ ٱلْأَوَانِ ـ مَوْتٌ فِي عَيْنِ ٱلْكَمَالِ ـ ٱخْتِضَارٌ. A — death, مَوْتٌ فِي ٱلشَّبَابِ. To be —, to do a thing prematurely, أَعْجَلَ ٱلشَّيْءَ عَنْ وَقْتِهِ.

Prematurely, *ad.* قَبْلَ وَقْتِهِ ـ قَبْلَ ٱلْأَوَانِ. To bring forth —, أَعْجَلَتْ ـ أَعْجَلَتْ وَلَدَهَا. To die —, ٱخْتُضِرَ (*i.e.* he died in a green age. Young men used to say to an old man: أَجْزَرْتَ يَا شَيْخُ Thou hast attained to the time for dying, *lit.* for being cut; and he replied: أَيْ بَنِيَّ وَتُخْتَضَرُونَ, *i.e.* O my sons, and ye shall be cut off prematurely, or, in your youth.)

Prematureness, *n.* } عَجَلٌ ـ عَجَلَةٌ ـ سُرْعَةٌ ـ مُبَادَرَةٌ ـ بُلُوغٌ
Prematurity, } وُقُوعٌ قَبْلَ ٱلْأَوَانِ ـ قَبْلَ ٱلْأَوَانِ.

Premeditate, *v.t.* To think of, care for, beforehand, سَبَقَ ² ٱعْتَنَى بِ ـ مِنْ قَبْلُ ـ وَتَفَكَّرَ فِي. To design beforehand, سَبَقَ ² فَتَعَمَّدَهُ ـ مِنْ قَبْلُ ـ (or قَصَدَ =) ـ ٱعْتَمَدَ.

Premeditate, *v.i.* ٱعْتَنَى مِنْ قَبْلُ ـ تَأَمَّلَ مِنْ قَبْلُ ـ سَبَقَ وَتَفَكَّرَ.

Premeditated, *a.* Previously designed or contrived, مَقْصُودٌ سَبْقًا ـ مُتَعَمَّدٌ سَبْقًا ـ قَصْدِيٌّ ـ عَمْدِيٌّ. A — crime, جُنَاحٌ عَمْدِيٌّ.

Premeditately, *ad.* Designedly, عَمْدًا ـ قَصْدًا.

Premeditation, *n.* Previous consideration, تَفَكُّرٌ ـ تَأَمُّلٌ سَابِقٌ مِنْ قَبْلُ. Previous intent, design, قَصْدٌ ـ إِعْتِمَادٌ ـ تَعَمُّدٌ ـ عَمْدٌ ـ عُمْدَةٌ. To answer one without —, hastily, بَدَهَ. To speak without —, impromptu, ٱبْتَدَهَ ٱلْخُطْبَةَ. The faculty of speaking without —, بَدِيهَةٌ ـ ٱرْتِجَالٌ فِي ٱلْكَلَامِ.

Premier, *a.* أَوَّلُ *pl.* أَوَّلُونَ *fem.* أُولَى ـ أَصْلٌ ـ مُتَقَدِّمٌ.

Premier, *n.* The first minister of state, صَدْرٌ ـ ٱلصَّدْرُ ٱلْأَعْظَمُ ـ كَبِيرُ ٱلْوُزَرَاءِ ـ ٱلصُّدُورُ.

Premiership, *n.* صَدَارَةٌ ـ ٱلصَّدَارَةُ ٱلْعُظْمَى.

Premise, *n.* A first or antecedent proposition, مُقَدَّمَةٌ.

Premise, *v.t.* To lay down beforehand, سَبَقَ ² فَعَرَضَهُ ـ سَبَقَ ² فَطَرَحَ عَلَى ـ كَذَا ـ عَرَضَ = سَبْقًا.

Premise, *v.i.* أَوْرَدَ مُقَدِّمَةً ـ فَتَحَ ٱفْتِتَاحًا ـ قَدَّمَ مُقَدَّمَاتٍ.

Premises, *n.* The two first propositions of a syllogism, ٱلْمُقَدَّمَتَانِ. Premises, things previously mentioned, مُقَدَّمَاتٌ مَذْكُورَةٌ آنِفًا. Houses, lands, *etc.*, بُيُوتٌ ـ أَبْنِيَةٌ وَمُتَعَلِّقَاتُهَا ـ وَعَقَارٌ وَمَا يَتَعَلَّقُ بِهَا.

Premium, *n.* A prize won by success, جَزَاءٌ ـ ثَوَابُ ٱلْفَوْزِ ـ ٱلنَّجَاحِ. A douceur, حُلْوَانٌ. Amount paid for insurance, أُجْرَةُ سِكُورْتَا. Premium, of loans, shares, *etc.*, فَضْلَةٌ ـ تَمَتُّعٌ ـ عَلَى إِكْرَامِيَّةٍ ـ بِتَمَتُّعٍ ـ بِفَضْلَةٍ : at a —, إِكْرَامِيَّةٌ.

Premonish, *v.t.* نَبَّهَ ـ سَبْقًا ـ سَبَقَ ² = فَحَذَّرَهُ ـ سَبَقَ ² = فَنَصَحَهُ.

Premonishment, *n.* } تَنْبِيهٌ سَابِقٌ ـ عِبْرَةٌ سَابِقَةٌ ـ نَصَاحَةٌ سَابِقَةٌ.
Premonition, }

Premonitory, *a.* حَذِيرٌ ـ سَابِقُ ٱلتَّنْبِيهِ.

Premunire, *n.* قَوْلٌ أَوْ فِعْلٌ يَلْحَقُ إِهَانَةً بِٱلْمَلِكِ أَوْ بِٱلْمَجْلِسِ.

Premunition, *n.* إِحْتِيَاطٌ سَابِقٌ ـ إِحْتِرَازٌ سَابِقٌ.

Prenomen, *n.* إِسْمٌ *pl.* أَسَامٍ *and* أَسْمَاءٌ *and* أَسَامِيٌّ.

Prenominate, *v.t.* سَبَقَ فَسَمَّاهُ.

Prentice, *n.* *See* Apprentice, *n.*

Preoccupancy, *n.* Previous residence, سُكْنَى ـ مُبَاءَةٌ سَابِقَةٌ. Previous holding, possessing, ضَبْطٌ سَابِقٌ ـ تَصَرُّفٌ سَابِقٌ ـ سَابِقَةٌ ـ تَمَلُّكٌ سَابِقٌ.

Preoccupation, *n.* As of the mind, إِنْشِغَالٌ ـ غَيْبَةُ بَالٍ ـ غَيْبَةٌ ـ شُغْلُ ٱلْبَالِ ـ ٱلْبَالِ. *See also* Pre-occupancy, *n.*

Preoccupied, *a.* Occupied previously, مُسْتَبَاءٌ سَبْقًا ـ مُبَوَّأٌ سَبْقًا ـ مُسْكَنٌ سَبْقًا. Having the mind previously engaged, غَالِبُ ٱلْبَالِ ـ مَشْغُولُ ٱلْبَالِ.

Preoccupate, *v.t.* } To reside in previously, سَبَقَ ² فَتَبَاءَ بِ ـ =
Preoccupy, } سَبَقَ فَتَبَوَّأَ بِ. To hold previously, سَبَقَ ² =

To prepared, غَيَّبَ ـ أَغْفَلَ . سَبَقَ فَتَصَرَّفَ بِ ـ فَضَبَطَهُ . To be preoccupied, to have the mind distracted by, شَغَلَ بَالَهُ ـ أُشْغِلَ بَالُهُ بِ ـ شُغِلَ بِ .

Pre-ordain, *v.t.* عَيَّنَ-سَبْقًا ـ سَبَقَ فَعَيَّنَهُ ـ سَبَقَ فَأَعَدَّهُ .

Pre-ordinance, *n.* حُكْمٌ سَابِقٌ ـ قَضَآءٌ سَابِقٌ .

Pre-ordination, *n.* إِعْدَادٌ سَابِقٌ ـ تَعْيِينٌ سَابِقٌ .

Pre-ordained, *a.* مَحْكُومٌ بِهِ سَبْقًا ـ مُعَيَّنٌ سَبْقًا .

Prepaid, *a.* دَافِعُ ٱلْأُجْرَةِ . Prepaid, as of postage, خَالِصُ بِضَمِّ أُجْرَةِ ٱلْبُوسْطَةِ ـ ٱلْأُجْرَةِ .

Preparation, *n.* The act of making ready, إِجْمَاعٌ ـ إِعْدَادٌ ـ إِخْضَارٌ ـ تَهْيِئَةٌ ـ إِيهَابٌ ـ إِعْدَادٌ ـ إِسْتِعْدَادٌ . The state of being prepared, إِسْتِعْدَادٌ ـ تَعَدُّدٌ . The act of fitting up, تَجْهِيزٌ ; of arranging, ordering, تَدْبِيرٌ ـ تَرْتِيبٌ ; of mixing, compounding, تَرْكِيبٌ . Anything compounded, such as medicines, *etc.*, مَعْجُونٌ ـ تَرْكِيبٌ . Parts of animals preserved for anatomical purposes, أَعْضَآءٌ مِنَ ٱلْحَيَوَانَاتِ مَحْفُوظَةٌ لِإِفَادَةِ عِلْمِ ٱلتَّشْرِيحِ . Preparations, arrangements made, إِسْتِعْدَادَاتٌ ـ تَدْبِيرٌ ـ تَدَابِيرُ ـ جِهَازٌ . To make preparations for, أَعَدَّ لِ ـ هَيَّأَ لِ . This is a — for, points to, هٰذَا يَجُوجُ إِلَى . A thing prepared, ready at hand, عَتِيدٌ *pl.* عَتَائِدُ ـ عَتَدٌ . The preparations which he made, ٱلْإِسْتِعْدَادَاتُ ٱلَّتِي ٱسْتَعَدَّ بِهَا . Government is increasing its preparations, ٱلْحُكُومَةُ تَزِيدُ فِي ٱسْتِعْدَادَاتِهَا وَتَجْهِيزَاتِهَا . In order that the Government may be in a state, or on a footing, of — for what may happen in Europe, حَتَّى تَكُونَ ٱلدَّوْلَةُ عَلَى قَدَمِ ٱلْإِسْتِعْدَادِ لِمَا عَسَى أَنْ يَطْرَأَ فِي أُورُبَّا .

Military preparations, تَجْهِيزَاتٌ عَسْكَرِيَّةٌ .

Naval preparations, تَجْهِيزَاتٌ بَحْرِيَّةٌ .

Warlike preparations, تَحْضِيرَاتٌ (or تَجْهِيزَاتٌ) حَرْبِيَّةٌ .

Preparative, *a.* Of arrangement, إِسْتِعْدَادِيٌّ ; inceptive, إِبْتِدَائِيٌّ .

Preparative, *n.* تَدْبِيرُ *pl.* تَدَابِيرُ لِ ـ عَتِيدٌ *pl.* عُتُدٌ ـ إِسْتِعْدَادٌ .

Preparatory, *a.* إِسْتِعْدَادِيٌّ ـ مُعْتَدٌّ ـ مُعْتَدٌ ـ إِبْتِدَائِيٌّ . A — school, مَكْتَبٌ ٱسْتِعْدَادِيٌّ *pl.* مَكَاتِبُ ٱسْتِعْدَادِيَّةٌ .

Prepare, *v.t.* To make ready, أَعَدَّ ـ أَعْتَدَ ـ أَحْضَرَ ـ أَجْمَعَ ـ هَيَّأَ . To equip, جَهَّزَ ـ أَهَّبَ ـ عَبَأَ ـ عَبَّأَ . To — anything for, إِسْتَعَدَّ لِ ـ إِعْتَدَّ لِ ـ أَعَدَّ لِ ـ جَعَلَ لِ . To — one's self for, تَأَهَّبَ لِ ـ تَحَضَّرَ لِ ـ إِسْتَعَدَّ لِ ـ أَعَدَّ لِ ـ تَهَيَّأَ لِ ـ تَشَمَّرَ لِ ; especially for departure, or for a journey, أَبَّ لِ . To — or accoutre one's self for, تَأَدَّى (or آدَى) لِلْأَمْرِ . To — something as a means to, هَيَّأَ لِ ـ سَبَّبَ لِ ـ إِتَّخَذَ لِ . To —, to make, manufacture, صَنَعَ ـ إِتَّخَذَ . To —, in the sense of to appoint, ordain, أَتَاحَ : He prepared, against him, an envious tongue, أَتَاحَ لَهُ لِسَانًا حَسُودًا . He fell into a place of destruction and God prepared one to save him, وَقَعَ فِي مَهْلَكَةٍ فَأَتَاحَ ٱللّٰهُ لَهُ مَنْ أَنْقَذَهُ . That they may — to meet at ..., أَنْ يَتَهَيَّأُوا لِلْإِجْتِمَاعِ فِي . The Government is still preparing steamers, مَا بَرِحَتِ ٱلدَّوْلَةُ عَلَى تَجْهِيزِ ٱلْبَوَاخِرِ . Prepare your work, هَيِّئْ عَمَلَكَ .

Prepared, *a.* Made ready, مُسْتَعَدٌّ ـ مُعَدٌّ ـ مُعْتَدٌ ـ مُعْتَدٌّ ـ مُتَوَكَّدٌ . To be prepared, عَتُدَ ـ أَعَدَّ ـ إِعْتَدَّ ـ تَعَدَّدَ ـ إِسْتَعَدَّ ـ حَاضِرٌ ـ تَهَيَّأَ . Prepared, made up, as of medicines, *etc.* مَعْمُولٌ ـ مُرَكَّبٌ ـ مَعْجُونٌ . Prepared for, ready to, عَتِيدٌ لِ . Fit for, جَدِيرٌ أَنْ ـ خَلِيقٌ بِ . He was — to jump, إِسْتَوَى لِلْوَثْبَةِ . He was — to set about the work, تَشَمَّرَ (أَشْمَرَ or تَشَذَّرَ or) لِلْأَمْرِ . To be —, appointed, ordained, تَاحَ *aor.* يَتِيحُ : He fell into a place of destruction and a man was prepared, appointed, to save him, وَقَعَ فِي مَهْلَكَةٍ وَتَاحَ لَهُ رَجُلٌ فَأَنْقَذَهُ . *See also under* Ready, *a.*

Preparer, *n.* مُعِدٌّ ـ مُهَيِّئٌ .

Prepay, *v.t.* دَفَعَ ٱلْأُجْرَةَ إِلَى ـ سَلَّفَ ـ سَبَقَ فَدَفَعَ ٱلْأُجْرَةَ إِلَى . To —, as postage letters, ضَمَّ أُجْرَةَ ٱلْبُوسْطَةِ . To pay for in advance, سَلَّفَ فِي كَذَا ـ أَسْلَفَ فِي كَذَا .

Prepayment, *n.* دَفْعُ ٱلْأُجْرَةِ سَلَفًا ـ سَلَفٌ ـ سَلَمٌ . Prepayment of postage, ضَمُّ أُجْرَةِ ٱلْبُوسْطَةِ .

Prepense, *a.* *See* Premeditated, *a.*

Preponderance, *n.* } Of weight, تَرْجِيحٌ ـ رُجْحَانٌ ـ رُجُوحٌ ; of
Preponderancy, } power, غَلَبَةٌ ـ تَرْجِيحٌ ـ عِزَّةٌ ; of numbers, نَيِّفٌ ـ كَثْرَةٌ .

Preponderate, *v.i.* Of weight, رَجَحَ ; of a scale, عَالَ . To have the ascendency, to prevail, طَمَّ ـ عَزَّ ـ إِفْتَرَّ ـ إِبْتَزَّ ـ كَانَ غَالِبًا . To — in number, كَثُرَ عَدَدًا . To — over, نَافَ عَلَى ; as in numbers, نَافَ عَلَى-عَدَدًا .

Preponderating, *a.* Of weight, رَاجِحٌ ـ وَازِنٌ . Prevailing most, غَالِبٌ .

Preposition, *n.* حَرْفُ جَرٍّ *pl.* حُرُوفُ جَرٍّ ـ أَدَاةُ جَرٍّ *pl.* أَدَوَاتٌ .

Prepositions, حُرُوفُ ٱلْإِضَافَةِ (or ٱلْخَفْضِ) .

Prepossess, *v.t.* *See to* Prejudice, *v.t.*

Prepossessed, *a.* *See* Prejudiced, *a.*

Prepossessing, *a.* *See* Attractive, *a.*

Prepossession, *n.* *See* Preoccupance *and* Prejudice; *also* Bent, Bias, *n.*

Preposterous, *a.* Upside-down, مَعْكُوسٌ ـ مَنْكُوسٌ . Absurd,

– مُحَالٌ بِهِ – مُحَال. Out of the question, سَفْسَاف – عِبْث
– مَنْكُوسَة. A — birth, مَنْكُوس *fem.* مُخَالِفٌ لِلْعَقْلِ – مُسْتَحِيل

Preposterously, *ad.* بِوَجْهٍ يُخَالِفُ ٱلْعَقْلَ – بِسَخَافَةٍ.

Preposterousness, *n.* حَمَاقَة – غَبَاوَة – عَبَث – سَخَافَة. *See also* Absurdity, *n.*

Prepuce, *n.* غُرْلَة – خِتَان – غِمَامَة – قُلْفَة – غُذْرَة: having a —, أَغْلَف – أَغْرَل – أَقْلَف. The — of the clitoris, بَظْر – بُظَارَة – بَظِير. To cut off the —, أَغْذَف.

Prerequisite, *a.* ضَرُورِيٌّ – مُحْتَاجٌ إِلَى – أَلْزَمُ – لَازِم.

Prerequisite, *n.* ضَرُورَة – حَاجَة *pl.* حَاجَات – مُلَازَمَة.

Prerogative, *n.* إِمْتِيَاز – حَقّ. Prerogatives, as meaning special rights, إِمْتِيَازَاتٌ وَخَصَائِص. Prerogative Court, مَحْكَمَةٌ خَاصَّةٌ لِفَصْلِ ٱلدَّعَاوَى ٱلْمُتَعَلِّقَةِ بِٱلْمِيرَاثِ. Prerogative office, إِدَارَةُ قَلَمِ ٱلْوِصَايَةِ وَصُكُوكِ ٱلْمَوَارِيثِ.

Presage, *n.* *See* Omen, *n.*

Presage, *v.t.* وَعَدَ بِ *aor.* يَعِدُ. *See also to* Predict, *v.t.*

Presbyter, *n.* An elder of the church, شَيْخُ ٱلْكَنِيسَةِ *pl.* شُيُوخ – قُسُّس *or* قِسِّيس *pl.* قِسِّيسُون *or* قُسُوس – قَسّ *pl.* مَشَايِخ *or*.

Presbyterian, *a.* مُتَعَلِّقٌ بِٱلْمَذْهَبِ ٱلْمُسَمَّى بِرَسْبِتِيرِيَانِسْم. *See* Presbyterianism, *n.*

Presbyterian, *n.* مِنْ أَهْلِ ٱلْمَذْهَبِ ٱلْمُسَمَّى بِرَسْبِتِيرِيَانِسْم. *See* Presbyterianism, *n.*

Presbyterianism, *n.* مَذْهَبُ جَمَاعَةٍ (*or* طَائِفَةٍ) مِنَ ٱلنَّصَارَى يَقُولُونَ أَنَّ رُتْبَةَ ٱلرِّئَاسَةِ وَإِدَارَةَ ٱلْكَنِيسَةِ فِي يَدِ ٱلْمَشَايِخِ (أَيِ ٱلْقُسُوسِ) عَلَى سَوِيَّةٍ.

Presbytery, *n.* جَمَاعَةُ مَشَايِخَ (أَيْ قُسُوسٍ) يَتَوَلَّوْنَ أُمُورَ ٱلطَّائِفَةِ ٱلْمَذْكُورَةِ.

Prescience, *n.* Foreknowledge, عِلْمُ ٱلْمُسْتَقْبِلِ – عِلْمُ ٱلْغَيْبِ – عِلْمٌ سَابِقٌ. Prudence, foresight, بَصِيرَة – رُشْد – فِرَاسَة.

Prescient, *a.* Foreknowing, عَالِمُ ٱلْغَيْبِ. Prudent, having foresight, صَاحِبُ بَصِيرَةٍ – مُتَنَبِّه – حَازِم.

Prescribe, *v.t.* To ordain, as of a law, فَرَضَ – سَنَّ – شَرَعَ – أَفْرَضَ. To — to, أَفْرَضَ-عَلَى – فَرَضَ-عَلَى – رَسَمَ لِ-كَذَا – أَوْجَبَ لِ-كَذَا – شَرَعَ لِ-كَذَا – أَوْصَى-بِ. To order, command, أَمَرَ – أَوْعَزَ فِي *or* إِلَى *or* بِ – أَمَرَ بِ. To lay down, as of a rule, *etc.*, وَضَعَ *aor.* يَضَعُ. To —, as a physician, وَصَفَ *aor.* يَصِفُ: to — for, وَصَفَ لِ-كَذَا. To — bounds, حَدَّدَ. To —, to appoint to, عَيَّنَ-لِ. To be prescribed, ordained, set, وُضِعَ – شُرِعَ – فُرِضَ.

Prescript, *n.* *See* Ordinance, Precept, *n.*

Prescription, *n.* The act of prescribing, ordaining, شُرُوع – سَنّ – فَرْض. A rule, precept, وَصِيَّة *pl.* وَصَايَا – سُنَّة. A medical —, تَذْكِرَةُ عِلَاجِيَّةٍ – صِفَةُ ٱلدَّوَاءِ. Claim by long use, حَقُّ ٱلتَّصَرُّفِ فِي شَيْءٍ بِمُرُورِ ٱلزَّمَانِ عَلَيْهِ (*or* مِنْ فَوَاتِ ٱلْمِيعَادِ). To acquire by —, مَلَكَ وَتَصَرَّفَ فِي-بِمُرُورِ ٱلزَّمَانِ عَلَيْهِ (*or* مِنْ فَوَاتِ ٱلْمِيعَادِ). To be annulled by right of —, سَقَطَ ٱلْحَقُّ (*or* ٱلتَّصَرُّفُ فِي شَيْءٍ) بِمُرُورِ ٱلزَّمَانِ عَلَيْهِ (*or* مِنْ فَوَاتِ ٱلْمِيعَادِ). He sought a medical — for his pain, إِسْتَطَبَّ لِوَجَعِهِ. To ask one for a medical —, إِسْتَوْصَفَ.

Prescriptive, *a.* مُرَتَّبٌ عَلَى مُرُورِ ٱلزَّمَانِ (*or* فَوَاتِ ٱلْمِيعَادِ) – مُؤَسَّسٌ عَلَى ٱلتَّصَرُّفِ بِهِ مِنَ ٱلْقَدِيمِ.

Presence, *n.* The state of being present, حُضُور – حَضْرَة. Existence, كَوْن – وُجُود. Air, demeanour, وَضْع – سِمَامَة – هَيْئَة – مَنْظَر. Presence, the object of resort, as, the — of such an one, meaning his dignity, جَنَابُ فُلَانٍ – حَضْرَةُ فُلَانٍ (the former being of higher import.) In the — of, بِحَضْرَةِ – بِحُضُورِ – بِمَرْأَى – أَمَامَ – قُدَّامَ. Presence of mind, سُرْعَةُ عَقْلٍ – عَارِضَة – عَارِض – قَلْبُهُ حَاضِرٌ – شَدِيدُ ٱلْعَارِضَةِ: One who has — of mind, إِقْدَام – مِقْدَام. A — chamber, دِيوَانُ (*or* مَحْضَرُ) ٱلسُّلْطَانِ. He turned from his —, تَحَوَّلَ مِنْ أَمَامِهِ. To demand the — of, إِسْتَحْضَرَ.

Present, *a.* Not absent, حَاضِر – مُحْتَضِر. Looking on, شَاهِد *pl.* شُهُود. Present, seated, جَالِس. Existing, as being in, forming a part of, anything, مَوْجُود. At hand, مُعْتَد – عَتِيد. To be —, not absent, حَضَرَ – تَحَضَّرَ – إِحْتَضَرَ. To be —, to exist, وُجِدَ. To cause to be —, أَحْضَرَ – أَشْهَدَ – آتَى. To be —, as a looker on, to witness, شَاهَدَ – شَهِدَ عَلَى – حَاضَرَ. He was — at, or with him, or he attended or came to him, إِحْتَضَرَهُ – حَضَرَهُ – تَحَضَّرَهُ. I was — at, attended, the court of the judge, حَضَرْتُ مَجْلِسَ ٱلْقَاضِي. He was — at, attended, a lecture, حَضَرَ دَرْسًا. A banquet at which 400 persons were —, مَأْدُبَةٌ حَضَرَهَا ٤٠٠ نَفَرٍ. The — state of affairs in Europe, ٱلْأَحْوَالُ ٱلْحَاضِرَةُ فِي أُورُبَّا. Such a thing was — to my mind, حَضَرَنِي كَذَا. He numbered the people —, عَدَّ ٱلشَّعْبَ ٱلْمَوْجُودَ. There was — at that time, كَانَ حَاضِرًا فِي ذَٰلِكَ ٱلْوَقْتِ. I have spoken to you being — with you, كَلَّمْتُكُمْ وَأَنَا عِنْدَكُمْ. All the shaikhs were —, حَضَرَ جَمِيعُ ٱلْمَشَايِخِ. Be — here at noon, أُحْضُرْ أَنْتَ هُنَا عِنْدَ ٱلظُّهْرِ. It did not prevent the people of the town from being —, لَمْ يَعُقْ أَهْلَ ٱلْمَدِينَةِ عَنِ ٱلْحُضُورِ. Whether we be — or absent, *i.e.*, at home or abroad, مُسْتَوْطِنُونَ كُنَّا أَوْ مُتَغَرِّبُونَ. The — tense, فِعْلُ ٱلْحَالِ. At —, ذَا ٱلْوَقْتَ – ٱلْآنَ – ٱلْحَالَ – ٱلسَّاعَةَ. For the —,

لِلْوَقْتِ ٱلْحَاضِرِ ـ لِلْحَالِ. The — day, هٰذَا ٱلْيَوْمُ. Up to the — day, إِلَى يَوْمِنَا هٰذَا ـ إِلَى هٰذَا ٱلْيَوْمِ.

Present, *n.* A gift, عَطَا *pl.* أَعْطِيَة ـ عَطِيَّة *pl.* عَطَايَا ـ تَقْدِمَة *pl.* تَقْدِمَات ـ مَوْهِبَة *pl.* مَوَاهِب ـ هَدِيَّة *pl.* هَدَايَا. A rare —, تُحْفَة *pl.* تُحَف. A — which one brings home to his family, عُرَاضَة. A — made to a bride by the bridegroom the morning after marriage, صَبَاحِيَّة. A — for bringing news, حُذْيَا ـ بِشَارَة; to workmen, مُصَانَعَة. Present, the — time, ٱلْحَال ـ ٱلْوَقْتُ ٱلْحَاضِرُ. Presents, an official decree, proclamation, سَنَد ـ خَطّ ـ مَنْشُور: Know all by these presents, لِيَعْلَمْ كُلُّ وَاقِفٍ عَلَى هٰذَا ٱلْمَنْشُورِ. To make a — to, وَهَبَ لِ ـ مَوْهِبَة ـ هَدَى ـ هَدِيَّة *aor.* يَهَبُ ـ أَعْطَى ـ عَطِيَّة.

Present, *v.t.* To set or place, as before a superior, أَوْقَفَ ـ أَمَامَهُ. To —, as an offering, قَرَّبَ ـ قَدَّمَ. To offer, expose, propose, عَرَضَ ². To —, as prayers, قَدَّمَ صَلَوَاتٍ. To — to an office, وَجَّهَ ـ أَلِي مَنْصَب. To — arms, رَفَعَ ٱلسَّلَامَ ـ أَجْرَى ٱلسَّلَامَ ـ سَلَّمَ. To — to, introduce to, قَدَّمَ ـ لِ ـ أَبْرَزَ ـ إِلَى. To bring before, to submit to, عَرَضَ ـ عَلَى ـ رَفَعَ ـ إِلَى ². To give to, as a present, هَدَى ـ أَتْحَفَ ـ بِ ـ أَعْطَى ـ يَهَبُ *aor.* وَهَبَ لِ. To — one with, مَثَلَ بَيْنَ ². To — to view, أَظْهَرَ. To — one's self to one, حَضَرَ قُدَّامَهُ ـ يَقِفُ *aor.* وَقَفَ عِنْدَهُ (*or* أَمَامَهُ) ـ يَدَيْهِ ². To — itself, as of an opportunity, *etc.*, وُجِدَ ـ تَمَثَّلَ بَيْنَ يَدَيْهِ. وَقَعَ *aor.* يَقَعُ ـ إِتَّفَقَ: Should the occasion — itself, إِذَا ٱتَّفَقَتْ ٱلْفُرْصَةُ ـ إِذَا ٱتَّفَقَ ٱلْوَقْتُ. He presented, or addressed, himself to obtain their favour, تَعَرَّضَ (*or* إِعْتَرَضَ) لِمَعْرُوفِهِمْ. *See also under to* Introduce, *v.t.*

Presentable, *a.* That may be presented, مِمَّا يُقَدَّمُ ـ مِمَّا يُعْرَضُ. Fit to be introduced, حَرِيٌّ أَنْ يُبْرَزَ ـ خَلِيقٌ لِلْإِبْرَازِ ـ جَدِيرٌ بِٱلْإِبْرَازِ. In a — state, حُشْمِيٌّ ـ فِي حَالِ ٱللِّيَاقَةِ.

Presentation, *n.* The act of presenting, عَرْض ـ تَقْدِيم; of presenting, as to an office, appointment, تَوْجِيه ـ تَوْظِيف ـ تَنْصِيب ـ إِقَامَة: the right of — to, حَقُّ ٱلتَّوْجِيهِ إِلَى. The act of presenting, of gifts, وَهْب ـ إِعْطَاء ـ تَهْدِيَة; of introducing, إِبْرَاز. Presentation at court, تَعْرِيفٌ بِحَضْرَةِ ٱلْمَلِكِ ـ إِبْرَازٌ رَسْمِيٌّ. A — copy, نُسْخَةٌ هَدِيَّةٌ. *See also under* Introduction, *n.*

Presentee, *n.* One who is presented to an appointment, مُوَجَّهٌ إِلَى ـ مُنْعَمٌ عَلَى ـ بِ ـ مُعَيَّنٌ إِلَى.

Presenter, *n.* One who presents to an appointment, مُوَجِّهٌ إِلَى ـ مِنْعَام ـ مُعَيِّنٌ إِلَى. A giver, مُعْطٍ.

Presentient, *a.* شَاعِرٌ بِ ـ مِنْ قَبْلُ ـ مُحِسٌّ بِ ـ سَبْقًا.

Presentiment, *n.* مُكَاشَفَة ـ حَاسَّةٌ سَابِقَةٌ ـ حَسٌّ سَابِقٌ. To have a — of, سَبَقَ فَحَسَّ بِ ². I had some vague presentiments, حَدَّثَتْنِي نَفْسِي بِأَشْيَاءَ مَا أَرَى لَهَا أَصْلًا.

Presently, *ad.* Directly, immediately, ٱلسَّاعَةَ ـ فِي ٱلْحَالِ ـ حَالًا ـ ٱلْآنَ. Shortly, تَوًّا ـ أَوَّلَ سَاعَةٍ ـ عَنْ قَرِيبٍ.

Presentment, *n.* The act of accusation, تُهَمَة ـ إِتِّهَام. *See also* Presentation, *n.*

Preservable, *a.* جَدِيرٌ بِٱلْمُحَافَظَةِ ـ حِفْظُهُ مُمْكِنٌ.

Preservation, *n.* The act of preserving, as from injury, *etc.*, صِيَانَة ـ مُحَافَظَة ـ حِفْظ ـ حِرْس ـ تَحْرِيز ـ حِرَاسَة ـ خِفَارَة. Preservation in life, إِبْقَاء ـ بُقْيَا. Preservation of fruits with sugar, تَرْبِيَةُ ٱلْفَاكِهَةِ بِسُكَّرٍ; with spices, تَبْل ـ تَتْبِيل. Self —, تَصَاوُن ـ تَحَفُّظ. In a good state of —, فِي حَالٍ ـ فِي حَالِ ٱلصِّحَّةِ ـ ٱلْكَمَالِ ـ مَصُون ـ بِلَا عَيْبٍ ـ بِلَا عَوَارٍ.

Preservative, *a.*
Preservatory, } صَائِن ـ مُحَافِظ ـ حَافِظ ـ مُوَقٍّ.

Preservative, *n.* حِرْز ـ حِفْظ.

Preserve, *v.t.* To take care of, صَانَ ـ إِحْتَفَظَ بِ ـ حَفِظَ ² *aor.* يَصُونُ. To —, to guard, protect, خَفَرَ ـ تَخَفَّرَ بِ ² ـ حَامَى ـ حَمَى ² ـ عَصَمَ ـ مِنْ ² ـ حَرَزَ ـ حَرَّزَ ـ أَحْرَزَ ـ حَرَسَ ². To —, as from danger, يَقِي *aor.* وَقَى ـ مِنْ ـ وَقَّى ـ مِنْ. To — alive, continue in existence, أَبْقَى ـ عَمَّرَ ـ حَيَّى. To —, as fruits, with sugar, رَبَّى ـ بِسُكَّرٍ; as with spices, تَبَّلَ; as with salt, مَلَّحَ. To — one's self, إِحْتَرَزَ ـ تَحَرَّسَ ـ تَصَاوَنَ ـ تَصَوَّنَ ـ تَحَفَّظَ. To be preserved, to be in safety, حَرُزَ ². He preserved his honour, صَانَ عِرْضَهُ ². He preserved him scot free from ..., عَصَمَهُ مِنْ ². He preserved the honour of his companion, حَفِظَ حُرْمَةَ صَاحِبِهِ ². May God — you! أَبْقَاكَ ٱللّٰهُ. God preserved him, أَبْقَاهُ ٱللّٰهُ. *See also to* Keep, *v.t.*

Preserve, *n.* As of fruit, مُرَبَّى *pl.* مُرَبَّات; preserves, confections, made with honey or sugar, مُرَبَّيَات. A — for game, حِكْرٌ (*or* حَاكُورَةٌ) لِلصَّيْدِ ـ مَحَلٌّ لِحِفْظِ ٱلصَّيْدِ.

Preserved, *a.* Guarded, protected, مَحْرُوس ـ مَصُون ـ مَحْفُوظ. Preserved, as with sugar, مُرَبَّب; with spices, مُتَبَّل; with salt, مُمَلَّح. The preserved city, ٱلْمَدِينَةُ ٱلْمَحْرُوسَةُ.

Preserver, *n.* One who guards, protects, مُحَافِظ ـ حَافِظ ـ خَفِير ـ مُحَام ـ حَارِس. One who preserves fruits, صَانِعُ ٱلْمُرَبَّبَاتِ (*or* ٱلْمُرَبَّيَاتِ). The Preserver, (God,) ٱلْحَفِيظُ. *See also* Life-preserver, *n.*

Preside, *v.i.* To be in or to take the first place, تَقَدَّمَ ـ قَدَمَ ٤ ـ . To — over, to have the direction of, دَبَّرَ ـ قَادَ ٤ ـ تَصَدَّرَ ـ تَوَلَّى . ساسَ ـ قَامَ بِ ٤ . The court over the proceedings of which the Sultan presides in person, المَحْكَمَةُ ٱلَّتِي يَتَوَلَّى ٱلسُّلْطَانُ بِنَفْسِهِ أَحْكَامَهَا .

Presidency, *n.* Occupation of the first place, صَدَارَةٌ ـ صَدْر ـ تَصَدُّر . Superintendency, نَظَارَةٌ ـ رِئَاسَةٌ . The office of president, مَقَامُ (or وَظِيفَةُ) ٱلرِّئَاسَةِ ـ صَدَارَةٌ . The term of a president's office, أَمَدُ ٱلرِّئَاسَةِ (or ٱلصَّدَارَةِ) . To give the — to in, صَدَّرَ ـ فِي . To take the —, تَصَدَّرَ .

President, *n.* A — of the people, صَدْرُ ٱلْقَوْمِ . A presiding officer, رَئِيسٌ ـ مُدِيرٌ . The — of the United States of America, رَئِيسُ جُمْهُورِيَّةِ أَمِيرِيكَا ٱلْمُتَّحِدَةِ .

Presidential, *a.* مُتَعَلِّقٌ بِٱلرِّئَاسَةِ ـ مُتَعَلِّقٌ بِٱلصَّدَارَةِ . The — chair, كُرْسِيُّ ٱلصَّدَارَةِ .

Presidentship, *n.* The office of president, term of a president's office; *see under* Presidency, *n.*

Presidial, *a.* }
Presidiary, } مَا نِيطَ بِٱلشِّحْنَةِ ـ مُتَعَلِّقٌ بِٱلْمُحَافَظَةِ .

Presignify, *v.t.* دَلَّ عَلَى ـ سَبْقًا ـ سَبَقَ فَدَلَّ عَلَى ٤ ـ .

Press, *v.t.* As with a press, to press down with force, ضَغَطَ ـ كَبَسَ عَلَى ـ عَصَدَ ـ لَبَّدَ . To squeeze, of fruits, *etc.*, إِعْتَصَرَ ـ عَصَرَ . To — and rub, to shampoo, دَلَكَ ـ دَلَّكَ ٤ ـ دَعَكَ . To pack close together, as of goods, عَبَأَ ـ عَبَّأَ . To hurry, to urge on, عَجَّلَ ـ سَاقَ ٤ ـ إِسْتَفَزَّ . To urge with importunity, لَزَّ ـ حَثَّ عَلَى ـ أَلَحَّ عَلَى ٤ . To —, as of grapes, in a wine-press, نَطَلَ . To — upon, to push against, دَافَعَ ـ دَسَرَ ٤ ـ . To —, as a creditor a debtor, لَأَطَ عَلَى ـ زَحَمَ ـ ضَغَطَ . To —, to straiten, ضَيَّقَ عَلَى ـ ضَاغَطَ ; to — with words, or arguments, ضَايَقَ ـ بِكَلَامٍ . To — one for, to demand anything of one, إِقْتَرَحَ عَلَى فُلَانٍ كَذَا (أَوْ بِكَذَا) . To — one with a difficult thing, أَرْهَقَ ـ عُسْرًا ـ أَرْهَقَ . To — upon, as men in battle, شَدَّ عَلَى ٤ . To — upon, as trouble, *etc.*, إِشْتَدَّ عَلَى . To — to the bosom, ضَمَّ ـ إِلَى صَدْرِهِ ٤ . To — towards, to aim or follow after, سَعَى إِلَى ـ . To —, or force one's self to, إِغْتَصَبَ نَفْسَهُ إِلَى . To be pressed in spirit, تَضَيَّقَ ـ تَضَيَّقَ بِٱلرُّوحِ ـ انْحَصَرَ بِٱلرُّوحِ . To — or throng upon, إِصْطَمَّ عَلَى . The people pressed together upon him, تَزَاحَمُوا عَلَيْهِ ـ إِصْطَمَّ ٱلنَّاسُ عَلَيْهِ . To — into service, سَخَرَ ـ سَخَّرَ ـ إِصْطَرَّ ـ إِلَى ـ أَلْزَمَ ـ بِ ـ جَبَرَ ـ عَلَى ٤ . To force, The people pressed, thronged, me, دَافَعُونِي ـ زَحَمَنِي ٱلنَّاسُ . The people approach, against, crowded, one another, تَزَاحَمُوا ـ تَضَايَقُوا ـ زَحَمَ ٱلنَّاسُ بَعْضُهُمْ بَعْضًا ـ تَضَاغَطُوا . To —, to continue to attack, شَدَّ عَلَى . to straiten, لَزَّ ٤ ـ ضَيَّقَ عَلَى .

Press, *v.i.* To approach, as time, تَسَرَّعَ ـ سَرُعَ ٤ ـ تَعَجَّلَ . To approach, أَشْرَفَ ـ . as to incommode, أَضْرَبَ . To be imminent, يُوشِكُ ٱلْوَقْتُ ـ يُوشِكُ ـ أَوْشَكَ : Time presses, *aor.* وَشُكَ .

Press, *n.* As for grapes, olives, *etc.* مِعْصَرَةٌ ـ مِعْصَارٌ . A printing —, مَطْبَعَةٌ . A —, for squeezing or pressing anything, مِكْبَسٌ *pl.* مَكَابِسُ ـ مِلْزَمٌ . Press, the art of printing, صَنْعَةُ ٱلطَّبْعِ ; the newspapers, publications, الْمَطْبُوعَاتُ ـ الْجَرَائِدُ . A — for clothes, خِزَانَةُ (or خِزَانَةُ) ٱلْمَلْبُوسِ ـ أَصْوِنَةٌ *pl.* صِوَانٌ . A throng, إِزْدِحَامٌ ـ زَحْمٌ . A crowding, pushing, دَسْرٌ ـ ضَغْطٌ ـ زَحْمَةٌ . A straitening, مُضَايَقَةٌ ـ تَضْيِيقٌ ـ ضِيقٌ . Urgency, importance, ضَرُورِيَّةٌ ـ ضَرُورَةٌ ـ لُزُومٌ . A pressure, multiplicity, كَثْرَةٌ ـ زِيَادَةٌ ـ فَرْطٌ ـ إِفْرَاطٌ . The forcing of men into service, سُخْرَةٌ ـ تَسْخِيرٌ . A — of sail, طِمٌّ مِنَ ٱلْقُلُوعِ . Liberty of the —, إِمْتِيَازَاتُ ٱلطَّبْعِ ـ إِسْتِقْلَالُ ٱلْمَطْبُوعَاتِ . A smoothing or glazing —, مِكْبَسُ ٱلصَّقْلِ . A steam —, آلَةُ ٱلْبُخَارِ لِلْكَبْسِ . It is in the —, being printed, قَدْ شُرِعَ فِي طَبْعِهِ . Press laws or regulations, رُسُومَاتُ ٱلْمَطْبُوعَاتِ .

Pressed, *a.* Pressed down with force, مَكْبُوسٌ . Squeezed, عَصِيرٌ ـ عُصَارَةٌ . Pressed or expressed juice, عَصِيرٌ ـ مَعْصُورٌ ـ عُصَارٌ . Pressed to the bosom, مَضْمُومٌ إِلَى ٱلصَّدْرِ . Hurried, مُسْتَعْجَلٌ . Pressed, glazed, مُصَقَّلٌ ـ مَصْقُولٌ . One pressed into a service, سُخْرَةٌ ـ سُخَرَةٌ *pl.* سُخْرِيٌّ . If you are not — for time, إِنْ كَانَ لَكَ مُهْلَةٌ ـ إِنْ تَيَسَّرَ لَكَ . *See also under to* Press, *v.t.* and *i.*

Presser, *n.* As of grapes, *etc.*, مُعْتَصِرٌ ـ عَصَّارٌ . A — in a bath, one who kneads the bathers, دَلَّاكٌ ـ دَعَّاكٌ . One who works a press, other than a printing-press, مُكَبِّسٌ .

Press-gang, *n.* زُمْرَةٌ ـ زُمْرَةٌ مُسَخِّرِينَ (فِي ٱلْعَسْكَرِيَّةِ أَوِ ٱلْبَحْرِيَّةِ) مُسَخِّرِينَ .

Pressing, *a.* Urgent, important, لَازِمٌ ـ ضَرُورِيٌّ ـ مُهِمٌّ . Importunate, لَجُوجٌ ـ مُلِحٌّ ـ مُلِثٌّ ـ مُشَدِّدٌ . Distressing, مُضَيِّقٌ ـ مُضْجِرٌ ـ مُضِيقٌ . A — want, حَاجَةٌ ـ لُزُومٌ ٱلزَمُ ـ حَاجَةٌ مُبِينَةٌ . A — letter, مَكْتُوبٌ مُشَدِّدٌ . A — petition, prayer, رَجَاءٌ كُلِّيٌّ ـ إِقْتِرَاحٌ كُلِّيَّةٌ . A steam — engine, آلَةُ ٱلْبُخَارِ ـ مِكْبَسُ بُخَارٍ لِلْكَبْسِ .

Pressingly, *ad.* With force, بِشِدَّةٍ كُلِّيَّةٍ . Urgently, بِإِلْحَاحٍ ـ إِقْتِرَاحًا ـ بِلَجَاجَةٍ

Press-man, *n.* Of a printing press, طَبَّاع ـ شَاغِلُ ٱلْمَطْبَعَةِ.

Press-money, *n.* أُجْرَةُ ٱلْمُسَخَّرِ (فِي ٱلْعَسْكَرِيَّةِ أَوِ ٱلْبَحْرِيَّةِ).

Pressure, *n.* The act of pressing, pressing down, كَبْس; of squeezing, عَصْر ـ إِعْتِصَار ـ ضَغْط ـ تَدْعِيك; of shampooing, تَدْلِيك; of bearing upon, constraining, قَهْر ـ إِضْطِرَار ـ تَضْيِيق; of urging, إِلْحَاف ـ إِلْثَاث ـ لَجَاجَة. A multiplicity, إِفْرَاط ـ كَثْرَة ـ فَرْط. A weight, ثِقْل. Force, شِدَّة. A state of —, difficulty, مُضَايَقَة ـ ضِيق ـ إِعْسَار ـ ضُغْطَة ـ وَرْطَة. A — of business, كَثْرَةُ أَشْغَالٍ. High —, كَبْسٌ أَشَدُّ مِنْ كَبْسِ ٱلْهَوَآءِ. Low —, كَبْسٌ مُسَاوٍ لِكَبْسِ ٱلْهَوَآءِ. To bring — to bear upon, to influence, أَجْرَى ٱلنُّفُوذَ فِي ـ أَلَحَّ عَلَى ـ أَنْهَضَ عَلَى: He saw the necessity of bringing — to bear upon the government, رَأَى لُزُومَ ٱلْإِلْحَاحِ عَلَى ٱلدَّوْلَةِ.

Prestige, *n.* شُهْرَة ـ حُسْنٌ سَابِقٌ.

Presto, *ad.* In music, عِبَارَةٌ عَنِ ٱسْتِعْجَالِ ٱلنَّغْمَةِ فِي ٱلْمُوسِيقَى. Quickly, عَلَى ٱلْعَجَلِ.

Presumable, *a.* مِمَّا يُحْتَمَلُ ـ يُتَصَوَّرُ ـ مِمَّا يُظَنُّ ـ مِمَّا يُخَمَّنُ. It is —, يُحْتَمَلُ.

Presumably, *ad.* حَدْسًا ـ إِحْتِمَالًا ـ تَخْمِينًا ـ بِٱلتَّخْمِينِ.

Presume, *v.t.* and *i.* To conjecture, قَالَهُ رَجْمًا ـ ٤رَجَمَ بِٱلظَّنِّ ـ قَطَعَ عَقْلُهُ أَنْ ـ خَمَّنَ ـ ٤حَدَسَ ـ تَخَيَّلَ ـ ٤ظَنَّ ـ إِحْتَمَلَ; of a thing unknown, ٤رَجَمَ بِٱلْغَيْبِ.

Presume, *v.i.* To venture without permission, تَجَاسَرَ ـ تَجَرَّأَ. To act beyond bounds, أَفْرَطَ ـ تَجَاوَزَ. The man who shall — to speak in my name, ٱلرَّجُلُ ٱلَّذِي يَطْغِي فَيَتَكَلَّمُ بِٱسْمِي. They presumed to go to the top of the hill, تَجَبَّرُوا وَصَعِدُوا إِلَى رَأْسِ ٱلْجَبَلِ.

Presumer, *n.*
Presuming, *a.* } *See* Presumptuous, *a.*

Presumption, *n.* A supposition, ظَنّ ـ وَهْم ـ زُعْم ـ رَجْمٌ بِٱلظَّنِّ ـ رَجْمٌ بِٱلْغَيْبِ; of a thing unknown, تَخْمِين ـ قِيَاس ـ تَصَوُّر. Arrogance, boldness, بَطَر ـ أَنَانِيَّة ـ جَسَارَة ـ تَجَاسُر ـ بَغْي ـ تَغَطْرُف ـ تَجَبُّر ـ تَكَبُّر ـ طُغْيَان. Self —, self-conceit, رَهَق ـ تِيه ـ غُرُور ـ خُيَلَآء ـ إِعْجَابٌ بِنَفْسِهِ ـ بَغْي ـ تَصَلُّف.

Presumptive, *a.* Assumed, presumed, مَظْنُون ـ مُتَصَوَّر ـ مُتَخَيَّل ـ مُحْتَمَل. Presumptive evidence, دَلَائِلُ جُزْئِيَّةٌ قَرِيبَةٌ. Heir —, ٱلْمَظْنُونُ بِهِ أَنْ تَقَعَ لَهُ ٱلْوِرَاثَةُ; to a crown, ٱلْوَارِثُ ٱلْأَقْرَبُ ـ وَلِيُّ ٱلْعَهْدِ.

Presumptively, *ad.* بِٱلتَّصَوُّرِ ـ بِٱلتَّخْمِينِ ـ بِٱلظَّنِّ ـ إِحْتِمَالًا.

Presumptuous, *a.* جَسُور ـ بَاغٍ ـ صَلِف ـ رَهِق ـ ذُو خُيَلَآءَ ـ تَيَّاه ـ مُتَغَطْرِف ـ صَاحِبُ غُرُورٍ ـ مُدَّعٍ ـ مُتَكَبِّر ـ مُعْجَبٌ بِنَفْسِهِ.

Presumptuously, *ad.* بِغُرُورٍ ـ بِطُغْيَانٍ ـ بِتِيهٍ ـ بِخُيَلَآءَ. To act —, تَغَطْرَفَ ـ غَطْرَفَ ـ تَكَبَّرَ ـ تَجَبَّرَ ـ ٢بَغَى ـ ٢طَغَى ـ ٢تَاهَ ـ ٤بَطِرَ ـ تَصَلَّفَ.

Presumptuousness, *n.* Arrogance; *see under* Presumption, *n.*

Presupposal, *n.*
Presupposition, } A previous supposal, حَدْسٌ أَوَّلُ ـ ظَنٌّ سَابِقٌ ـ رَجْمٌ بِٱلظَّنِّ ـ مَفْرُوضٌ سَابِقٌ. A conjecture, رَجْمٌ بِٱلظَّنِّ.

Presuppose, *v.t.* ٢فَرَضَ فِي سَبْقًا ـ ٢سَبَقَ فَفَرَضَهُ. *See also to* Presume, *v.t.*

Pretence, *n.* A show of what is not real, عِضَة *pl.* عِضُون ـ تَظَاهُر ـ تَمْوِيه ـ تَصَنُّع. A holding out of something feigned, إِدِّعَآء ـ شَوَائِبُ *pl.* شَائِبَة ـ عِلَّة *pl.* عِلَل ـ تَعِلَّة. A claim, زَعْم. For a —, لِعِلَّةٍ. Whether in — or truth, سَوَآءٌ كَانَ بِعِلَّةٍ أَوْ بِحَقٍّ. By false pretences, بَاطِلًا. There is not in it the least —, show, or claim, to ownership, لَيْسَ فِيهِ شَائِبَةُ مُلْكٍ ـ لَيْسَ فِيهِ عُلْقَةٌ وَلَا شُبْهَةُ مُلْكٍ.

Pretend, *v.t.* and *i.* To simulate, أَظْهَرَ ـ تَظَاهَرَ بِ. To arrogate to one's self more than is due, ٤صَلِفَ ـ تَصَلَّفَ. To make a pretence, claim, to, إِدَّعَى بِ. To affirm, ٢زَعَمَ: He pretended that it was so, ٢زَعَمَ أَنَّهُ كَذَا. The Hánafis pretended, said, asserted, زَعَمَتِ ٱلْحَنَفِيَّةُ. To — illness, تَمَارَضَ. To — ignorance, تَجَاهَلَ. To — to be elegant, well-bred, *etc.* تَكَيَّسَ ـ تَظَرَّفَ ـ تَظَارَفَ. (The sixth form of the verb offers many similar instances of the idea conveyed by the verb to Pretend). *See also to* Affect, Feign, *v.t.*

Pretended, *a.* Counterfeit, not real, زَغَل ـ مُمَوَّه ـ مُفْتَرًى ـ مُلَبَّس. Seeming, مُتَشَبِّهٌ بِ ـ مُتَظَاهِرٌ بِ. *See also* Hypocritical, *a.*

Pretender, *n.* A claimant, مُدَّعٍ. A claimant without right, مُدَّعٍ بِغَيْرِ ٱسْتِحْقَاقٍ. A boaster, مُتَشَبِّع. One who seeks after anything, a candidate, طَالِب *pl.* طُلَّاب.

Pretension, *n.* A claim, إِدِّعَآء ـ طَلَب ـ مَطْلُوب ـ مُطَالَبَة. On the — that . . . , بِٱلدَّعْوَى أَنْ. *See also* Pretence, *n.*

Pretentious, *a.* صَلِف ـ بَالِغٌ فِي ٱلْإِدِّعَآءِ. *See also* Presumptuous, *a.*

Preterimperfect, *a.* The — tense, صِيغَةُ ٱلْمَاضِي ٱلْغَيْرِ ٱلتَّامِّ.

Preterit, *a.*
Preterite, } The — tense, صِيغَةُ ٱلْمَاضِي ـ ٱلْمَاضِي ـ ٱلْفِعْلُ ٱلْمَاضِي.

Preternatural, *a.* Different from what is natural, خِلَافُ ٱلطَّبِيعَةِ ـ فَوْقَ ٱلطَّبِيعَةِ. Wonderful, عَجِيب. Spiritual, رُوحِيٌّ.

Preterperfect, *a.* The — tense, صِيغَةُ ٱلْفِعْلِ ٱلْمَاضِي.

Preterpluperfect, *a.* The — tense, صِيغَةُ ٱلْفِعْلِ ٱلْمَاضِي ٱلْأَسْبَقِ.

Pretext, *n.* حُجَّةٌ ـ عِلَّةٌ ـ حِيلَةٌ. A false —, عِضَةٌ *pl.* عِضُونَ ـ حُجَّةٌ بَارِدَةٌ ـ حُجَّةٌ بَاطِلَةٌ. Under a —, بِحُجَّةٍ. To adduce a —, إِعْتَلَّ ـ إِحْتَجَّ. He adduced a — for it, إِعْتَلَّ عَلَيْهِ بِحُجَّةٍ. He cannot use it as a —, لَا يُمْكِنُهُ ٱلتَّعَلُّلُ بِهِ. *See also under* Pretence, *n.*

Pretipify, *v.t.* *See to* Prefigure, *v.t.*

Pretor, *n.* إِسْمُ ٱلْقَاضِي عِنْدَ ٱلرُّومَانِيِّينَ ٱلْأَوَّلِينَ.

Pretorial, *a.*
Pretorian, } مُتَعَلِّقٌ بِٱلْقَاضِي عِنْدَ ٱلرُّومَانِيِّينَ ٱلْأَوَّلِينَ.

Pretorship, *n.* وَظِيفَةُ ٱلْقَاضِي عِنْدَ ٱلرُّومَانِيِّينَ ٱلْأَوَّلِينَ.

Prettily, *ad.* بِطَلَاوَةٍ ـ بِحَلَاوَةٍ ـ بِظَرَافَةٍ ـ بِلَطَافَةٍ ـ بِمَلَاحَةٍ.

Prettiness, *n.* حَلَاوَةٌ ـ جَمَالٌ ـ مَلَاحَةٌ ـ صَبَاحَةٌ ـ نُضُورٌ ـ نَضْرٌ ـ طَلَاوَةٌ.

Pretty, *a.* نَضِيرٌ ـ نَاضِرٌ ـ صُبْحَانٌ ـ صَبِيحٌ ـ مِلَاحٌ *pl.* مَلِيحٌ ـ حُلْوٌ ـ ظَرِيفٌ ـ لَطِيفٌ ـ حَبَّذَا ـ جَمِيلٌ. You are a — fellow! (in satire), مَا شَآءَ ٱللّٰهُ عَلَيْكَ. A — trick, piece of deception, دُولَابٌ ـ خَدْعَةٌ ـ حِيلَةٌ. To be —, صَبُحَ ².

Pretty, *ad.* Somewhat, نَوْعًا مَّا. He is — well, صِحَّتُهُ مُعْتَدِلَةٌ ـ مِزَاجُهُ مُعْتَدِلٌ.

Prevail, *v.i.* To be strong, in the ascendency, عَزَّ ـ إِعْتَزَّ ـ غَلَبَ ـ قَوِيَ. To grow large, become great, عَظُمَ ². To be general, عَمَّ ² ـ إِشْتَمَلَ عَلَى. To rise to a high pitch, as water, *etc.*, طَمَّ ². To — against, قَدَرَ عَلَى ² ـ قَدُمَ عَلَى ² ـ قَوِيَ عَلَى ـ غَلَبَ ـ تَسَلَّطَ عَلَى ـ إِعْتَزَّ عَلَى *or* بِ ـ إِسْتَطَالَ عَلَى. To — upon, to induce, أَغْرَى ـ بِ ـ إِضْطَرَّ ـ إِلَى ـ غَلَبَ عَلَى ـ حَمَلَ ـ عَلَى. To cause one to —, غَلَّبَ ـ عَلَى ـ غَلَّبَ. The matter prevailed, had the ascendency, طَمَّ ٱلْأَمْرُ ². The cholera prevails there, ٱلْهَيْضَةُ مُنْتَشِرَةٌ هُنَاكَ. He could — nothing, لَا يَنْفَعُ شَيْئًا; you will not — at all, لَا تَنْفَعُونَ شَيْئًا. Their voices prevailed, قَوِيَتْ أَصْوَاتُهُمْ. The famine prevailed among them, إِشْتَدَّ ٱلْجُوعُ عَلَيْهِمْ. *See also to* Predominate, *to* Persuade, *v.t.*

Prevailing, *a.*
Prevalent, } General, غَالِبٌ ـ عَامٌّ ـ مُشْتَمِلٌ ـ شَامِلٌ. Current, جَارٍ ـ غَالِبٌ ـ رَائِجٌ. The most — wind has been the south-west, كَانَتْ ٱلرِّيحُ ٱلْجَنُوبِيَّةُ ٱلشَّرْقِيَّةُ هِيَ ٱلْغَالِبَةَ. The most — disease, ٱلدَّآءُ ٱلْأَغْلَبُ. The — distress, ٱلضَّنْكُ ٱلْحَاصِلُ ٱلْآنَ.

Prevalence, *n.*
Prevalency, } Superiority, إِسْتِعْلَآءٌ ـ إِعْتِزَازٌ ـ إِسْتِيلَآءٌ ـ غَلَبَةٌ. Predominancy, رَوَاجٌ ـ شَمَلٌ ـ عُمُومٌ ـ كَثْرَةٌ ـ غَلَبَةٌ ـ طُمُومٌ.

Prevalently, *ad.* غَلَبَةً ـ عُمُومًا ـ بِٱسْتِيلَآءٍ.

Prevaricate, *v.i.* صَاغَ زُورًا ² ـ حَاوَلَ ـ تَحَيَّلَ ـ تَحَوَّلَ ـ إِحْتَالَ. He prevaricated in the matter, تَحَوَّلَ (*or* إِحْتَالَ) فِي ٱلْأَمْرِ.

Prevarication, *n.* حِيلَةٌ *pl.* حِيَلٌ ـ مَحِيلَةٌ ـ مَحَالَةٌ ـ تَحَوُّلٌ ـ صَوْغُ ٱللِّسَانِ ـ مُحَاوَلَةٌ.

Prevaricator, *n.* صَوَّاغٌ ـ صَيِّغٌ ـ مُحْتَالٌ ـ حَوَلِيٌّ ـ حُوَّلٌ.

Prevenient, *a.* سَابِقٌ ـ أَسْلَفُ. More — than the thoughts, (prov.) أَسْبَقُ مِنَ ٱلْأَفْكَارِ.

Prevent, *v.t.* To hinder, حَجَبَ ² ـ عَزَرَ ² ـ عَزَّرَ ـ عَن ـ عَفَّقَ ـ عَن ـ أَخْرَقَ ـ عَن ـ ثَبَّتَ ـ عَن ² ـ حَجَزَ ² ـ حَدَّ ـ عَن ـ دَارَ ـ عَن ـ حَبَسَ ـ خَزَلَ ـ عَن ² ـ حَصَرَ ² ـ يَهُقُ *aor.* وَهَقَ ـ عَن ـ عَوَّقَ ـ عَاقَ ـ عَن ² ـ مَنَعَ ـ أَمْسَكَ ـ يَدُورُ *aor.* To go before, تَمَسَّكَ ـ تَثَبَّطَ ـ إِحْتَجَبَ ـ أَسْبَقَ ـ أَسْلَفَ. To be prevented, إِحْتَجَبَ. He prevented its introduction into Syria, مَنَعَ دُخُولَهُ إِلَى سُورِيَّةَ. They were the cause of preventing the evils arising therefrom, كَانُوا سَبَبًا فِي حَسْمِ ٱلْمَضَرَّاتِ ٱلنَّاشِئَةِ مِنْ ذٰلِكَ. He was prevented from going to his house, إِعْتَرَضَ عَنْ بَيْتِهِ. There is nothing to — the meeting of the congress, إِجْتِمَاعُ ٱلْمُؤْتَمَرِ لَا مَانِعَ مِنْهُ. There is nothing to —, مَا مِنْ مَانِعٍ. One who is prevented or prohibited, مَحْجُورٌ عَلَيْهِ. *See also to* Hinder, *v.t.*

Preventable, *a.* مَنْعُهُ مُمْكِنٌ ـ يُحْصَرُ ـ مِمَّا يُحْجَزُ.

Preventative, *n.* حِجَازَةٌ ـ مَانِعٌ: As a — against insurrection, دَفْعًا لِلْفِتْنَةِ.

Preventer, *n.* مَانِعٌ ـ عَوَّاقٌ ـ عَائِقٌ.

Prevention, *n.* Hindrance, حِجَازَةٌ ـ حَصْرٌ ـ حَجْبٌ ـ ذِيَادٌ ـ مَنْعٌ ـ قَصْرٌ عَن ـ تَشْبِيطٌ ـ حَدٌّ ـ عَزْرٌ ـ حَجْزٌ. *See also* Anticipation, *n.*

Preventive, *a.* مَانِعٌ ـ مُحْزِقٌ ـ حَاصِرٌ ـ حَاجِزٌ ـ عَائِقٌ. Preventive service, the coast-guard to prevent smuggling, خِدْمَةُ حُرَّاسِ ٱلْكُمْرُكِ بَرًّا وَبَحْرًا عَلَى ٱلسَّوَاحِلِ.

Preventive, *n.* مَانِعٌ ـ مَقْطَعَةٌ ـ مَحْسَمَةٌ ـ حَاجِزٌ.

Previous, *a.* سَالِفٌ ـ سَلِيفٌ ـ سَابِقٌ ـ مُتَقَدِّمٌ ـ أَوَّلُ. The — question, ٱلْمَسْأَلَةُ ٱلسَّابِقَةُ. To be — to, تَقَدَّمَ ـ سَبَقَ ².

Previously, *ad.* سَبْقًا ـ تَقَدُّمًا ـ أَوَّلًا.

Prevision, *n.* *See* Prescience, *n.*

Prey, *n.* Booty, خَلِيسَةٌ ـ غَنِيمَةٌ ـ غَنَائِمُ ـ سَلَبٌ. Game, صَيْدٌ. The — of a wild beast, فَرِيسَةٌ. A beast of —, سَبُعٌ *pl.* سِبَاعٌ. A bird or beast of —, جَارِحَةٌ *pl.* جَوَارِحُ. Beasts or birds of —, ذَوَاتُ ٱلصَّيْدِ. To seize its —, of a wild beast, إِفْتَرَسَ. To be a — to, إِسْتَعْزَبَ ـ أَسْتَثْقِلَ. He was a — to disease, إِسْتَوْلَى عَلَيْهِ ٱلْمَرَضُ ـ مَرِضًا. *See also under to* Overcome, *v.t.*

Prey, *v.i.* To seize on, as game, صَادَ *aor.* يَصِيدُ: The hawk preys, *i.e.*, seizes, game, الصَّقْرُ يَصِيدُ. To — on, to devour, as a wild beast, إِفْتَرَسَ; to plunder, نَهَبَ – سَلَبَ. To — on, to corrode, أَكَلَ – قَرَضَ – سَرَفَ. To — on, to cause to pine away, أَضْنَى – أَسْقَمَ – تَعَنَّى – عَنَّى – شَفَّ – شَفْشَفَ: Grief preyed on his mind, إِسْتَوْلَى عَلَيْهِ ٱلْغَمُّ.

Priapism, *n.* The disease, مُوَالَاةُ ٱنْتِصَابِ ٱلذَّكَرِ بِوَجَعٍ شَدِيدٍ – دَآءُ ٱلْإِنْتِصَابِ.

Price, *n.* قِيمَةٌ *pl.* قِيَمٌ – ثَمَنٌ *pl.* أَثْمَانٌ – سِعْرٌ *pl.* أَسْعَارٌ. Estimation, قِيمَةٌ – إِعْتِبَارٌ. The — of blood, دِيَةٌ *pl.* دِيَاتٌ. Recompense, reward, pay, جَزَآءٌ – حُلْوَانٌ. To ask one the — of a thing, إِسْتَامَ عَلَى ٱلشَّيْءِ: He asked the — of the article, إِسْتَامَ بِٱلسِّلْعَةِ. To fetch a —, إِبْتَاعَ عَلَى. To keep up a —, أَثْبَتَ ٱلثَّمَنَ – قَامَ بِٱلثَّمَنِ. To lower a —, أَنْقَصَ – أَرْخَصَ. To offer a —, عَرَضَ قِيمَةً – إِسْتَبَاعَ. أَهْبَطَ ٱلثَّمَنَ – مِنَ ٱلسِّعْرِ. To sell under —, بَاعَ دُونَ ٱلثَّمَنِ – بَاعَ بِأَرْخَصِ ثَمَنٍ. To set a — upon the head of one, وَضَعَ عَلَى *aor.* يَضَعُ. What is the — of this per ell? بِكَمْ ذِرَاعُ هٰذَا. At what — will you sell me this book? بِكَمْ تَبِيعُنِي هٰذَا ٱلْكِتَابَ. Everything has its —, كُلُّ شَيْءٍ يُحْرِزُ ثَمَنَهُ. At any —, بِأَيِّ سِعْرٍ كَانَ – بِقَدْرِ مَا يَكُونُ. Peace at any —, ٱلسِّلْمُ عَلَى أَيِّ وَجْهٍ كَانَ. Without —, gratis, مَجَّانًا – بِلَا ثَمَنٍ. Of great —, ثَمِينٌ – كَثِيرُ ٱلثَّمَنِ. Beyond all —, لَا يُثَمَّنُ – لَا ثَمَنَ لَهُ. *See also under* Sale, *n.*

Cost price, رَأْسُ ٱلْمَالِ – ثَمَنُ رَأْسِ ٱلْمَالِ – ٱلسِّعْرُ ٱلْأَصْلِيُّ. I will sell it to you at cost price, أَبِيعُهُ لَكَ بِٱلثَّمَنِ ٱلَّذِي وَاقِفٌ بِهِ عَلَيَّ.

Current price, ٱلسِّعْرُ ٱلرَّائِجُ – ٱلسِّعْرُ ٱلْجَارِي – ٱلسِّعْرُ ٱلْحَاضِرُ.

Exorbitant price, ثَمَنٌ زَائِدٌ – ثَمَنٌ وَافِرٌ – سِعْرٌ مُتَجَاوِزٌ.

Fair or moderate price, ثَمَنٌ مُتَوَسِّطٌ – ثَمَنٌ مُنْصِفٌ.

Fixed price, سِعْرٌ مَعْلُومٌ – سِعْرٌ مَقْطُوعٌ.

Price current, a schedule of prices, سِيَاقَةُ (or جَدْوَلُ) أَسْعَارٍ.

Price, *v.t.* To set a value upon, ثَمَّنَ. To mention the — of, سَامَ بِ: He stated the price of the commodity, سَامَ بِٱلسِّلْعَةِ. *See also under to* Value, *v.t.*

Priced, *a.* High-priced, غَالٍ – غَلِيٌّ. Low-priced, رَخِيصٌ.

Priceless, *a.* لَا يُثَمَّنُ – لَا ثَمَنَ لَهُ.

Prick, *v.t.* As with a needle, *etc.*, نَخَزَ بِ – نَخَسَ بِ – غَرَزَ بِ – شَكَّ بِ – نَكَزَ بِ; as with a thorn or spear, شَصَرَ. To mark out by puncture, نَقَّطَ. To — or point sewing work or embroidery, ضَرَّبَ. To affect with sharp pain, أَوْجَعَ – جَرَحَ. To erect, نَصَّبَ. A thorn pricked him, شَصَرَتْهُ شَوْكَةٌ. He pricked him with a spear, شَصَرَهُ بِرُمْحٍ. A needle has pricked me, شَكَّتْنِي إِبْرَةٌ. To — a horse, as with spurs, وَكَزَ ٱلْحِصَانَ *aor.* يَكِزُ. To — up the ears, نَشَرَ (or نَصَّبَ) ٱلْأُذُنَيْنِ: He came pricking up his ears, جَآءَ نَاشِرًا أُذُنَيْهِ. He pricked him, wounded him slightly, with the sword, نَفَحَ بِٱلسَّيْفِ. He was pricked to the heart, نُخِسَ (or إِنْنَخَسَ) فِي قَلْبِهِ.

Prick, *v.i.* As does a needle, شَكَّ – غَرَزَ – نَخَزَ – نَخَسَ; as a thorn, شَصَرَ.

Prick, *n.* As by a needle, *etc.*, شَكَّةٌ – نَخْزَةٌ – نَكْزَةٌ – غَرْزَةٌ; as by a thorn, شَصِيرٌ. It is hard for thee to kick against pricks, صَعْبٌ عَلَيْكَ أَنْ تَرْفُسَ مَنَاخِسَ.

Pricker, *n.* مِنْقَاشٌ – مِنْخَسٌ.

Pricking, *a.* Painful, مُؤْلِمٌ. A — pain, أَلَمٌ – وَجَعٌ نَاخِسٌ شَاكٌّ.

Pricking, *n.* The sensation of, شَكٌّ – نَكْزٌ – غَرْزٌ – نَخْزٌ.

Prickle, *n.* شَوْكَةٌ *coll.* شَوْكٌ.

Prickliness, *n.* شَوْكٌ (or مِلْءُ) كَثْرَةُ.

Prickly, *a.* شَائِكٌ – شَاكٌ – شَوِكٌ. A — tree, شَجَرَةٌ مُشِيكَةٌ – شَجَرَةٌ شَوِكَةٌ. Prickly trees, شَجَرٌ شَائِكٌ.

Prickly-heat, *n.* حَصَفٌ.

Prickly-pear, *n.* تِينٌ هِنْدِيٌّ – تِينٌ شَوْكِيٌّ – تِينٌ فِرِنْجِيٌّ – صُبَيْرٌ *coll.* صُبَيْرَةٌ.

Pride, *n.* Inordinate self-esteem, insolent exultation, عُظْمٌ – كِبْرِيَآءُ – عُتُوٌّ – تَعَظُّمٌ – إِسْتِكْبَارٌ – تَكَبُّرٌ. Pride of wealth, بَطَرٌ. Self-respect, عِزَّةُ ٱلنَّفْسِ. Self-conceit, عُجْبٌ – تَصَلُّفٌ. Pomp, تَبْجِيلٌ – زِينَةٌ – إِخْتِيَالٌ – مَوْكِبٌ – فَخْرٌ – بَهَآءٌ – غُرُورٌ. To take — in, تَعَزَّزَ بِ – إِعْتَزَّ بِ. To humble one's —, وَضَّعَ – كَسَرَ نَفْسَهُ – أَخْضَعَ. London pride, the plant, إِسْمُ فَصِيلَةٍ مِنَ ٱلنَّبَاتِ.

Pride, *v.i.* To pride one's self, to affect proud airs, بَطِرَ – إِسْتَكْبَرَ – تَكَبَّرَ. To boast, إِفْتَخَرَ. To — one's self upon, إِفْتَخَرَ بِ – تَعَزَّزَ بِ – إِعْتَزَّ بِ. *See also to* Boast, *v.i.*

Prier, *n.* دَسِيسٌ – مُتَفَتِّشٌ – مُتَجَسِّسٌ.

Priest, *n.* كَاهِنٌ *pl.* كَهَنَةٌ – قَسٌّ *pl.* قُسُوسٌ – قِسِّيسٌ *pl.* قُسَّانٌ and قِسِّيسُونَ. To be ordained a —, إِرْتَسَمَ كَاهِنًا.

Priestcraft, *n.* حِيَلُ ٱلْقُسَّانِ (أَوِ ٱلْأَئِمَّةِ) – دَسَائِسُ ٱلْقُسَّانِ.

Priestess, *n.* كَاهِنَةٌ *pl.* كَاهِنَاتٌ.

Priesthood, *n.* ٱلْكَهَنُوتُ – ٱلْقُسُوسِيَّةُ. The order of the —, دَرَجَةُ ٱلْكَهَنُوتِ.

Priest-like, *a.* / Priestly, } شَبِيهُ ٱلْقَسِّ ـ مِثْلَ ٱلْقِسِّيسِ ـ كَاهِنِيٌّ ـ كَهُنُوتِيٌّ.

Priest-ridden, *a.* تَحْتَ سَطْوَةِ ٱلْقُسَّانِ ـ تَحْتَ سُلْطَةِ ٱلْقُسَّانِ (أَوِ ٱلْأَئِمَّةِ).

Prig, *n.* A conceited fellow, مُعْجَبٌ بِنَفْسِهِ ـ مُتَصَلِّفٌ. A thief, سَرَّاقٌ ـ مُخْتَلِسٌ.

Prig, *v.t.* *See to* Filch, *v.t.*

Priggish, *a.* Conceited, مُتَصَلِّفٌ ـ زَاحِفٌ ـ مُتَكَبِّرٌ ـ مُتَعَظِّمٌ ـ مُعْجَبٌ بِنَفْسِهِ. Affected, مُتَأَنِّقٌ ـ مُتَظَرِّفٌ ـ مُصَانِعٌ ـ مُتَشَبِّعٌ. Pert, saucy, وَقِحٌ ـ سَفِيهٌ.

Prim, *a.* Affecting great nicety, مُتَظَرِّفٌ ـ مُتَجَوِّدٌ ـ مُتَأَنِّقٌ. Formal, reserved, طِرِّيقٌ ـ بَارِدٌ. To be —, reserved, أَطْرَقَ.

Prim, *v.t.* زَخْرَفَ ـ زَيَّنَ.

Primacy, *n.* Supremacy, رِئَاسَةٌ ـ إِسْتِيلَاءٌ ـ صَدَارَةٌ ـ تَقَدُّمٌ. The dignity of an archbishop, مَنْصَبُ رَئِيسِ ٱلْأَسَاقِفَةِ.

Prima donna, *n.* أَوَّلُ مُغَنِّيَةٍ فِي تِيَاتْرُو ٱلْإِيطَالِيَانِيِّينَ.

Prima facie, ad. أَوَّلَ وَهْلَةٍ.

Primage, *n.* إِنْعَامٌ مَحْسُوبٌ عَلَى ٱلْوَسْقِ يُعْطَى لِرَئِيسِ ٱلْمَرْكَبِ وَٱلْبَحْرِيَّةِ.

Primarily, *ad.* أَوَّلًا ـ أَوَّلَ بَابٍ ـ فِي ٱلْأَصْلِ.

Primary, *a.* First, original, أَوَّلُ ـ أَوَّلِيٌّ ـ أَصْلِيٌّ ـ أَسَاسِيٌّ. Elementary, مُخْتَصٌّ بِٱلْأُصُولِ وَٱلْقَوَاعِدِ. Preparatory, إِبْتِدَائِيٌّ. Primary instruction, تَعْلِيمٌ ٱبْتِدَائِيٌّ. Primary schools, مَكَاتِبُ ٱبْتِدَائِيَّةٌ. A — rock, صَخْرٌ أَصْلِيٌّ خَالٍ مِنْ نَبَاتٍ مُتَحَجِّرٍ أَوْ غَيْرِهِ.

Primate, *a.* Head, chief, كَبِيرٌ ـ رَئِيسٌ. An archbishop, رَئِيسُ أَسَاقِفَةٍ. Primate of all England, رَئِيسُ أَسَاقِفَةِ كَنِيسَةِ ٱلْإِنْكِلِيزِ ٱلْمَلَكِيَّةِ.

Primateship, *n.* Headship, رِئَاسَةٌ ـ صَدَارَةٌ. The office of an archbishop, مَنْصَبُ رَئِيسِ أَسَاقِفَةٍ.

Primatial, *a.* / Primatical, } مَنْسُوبٌ إِلَى ٱلصَّدَارَةِ ـ مُتَعَلِّقٌ بِٱلرِّئَاسَةِ.

Prime, *a.* First, أَوَّلُ. Original, أَصْلِيٌّ. Of the highest value, أَثْمَنُ. Highest, best, أَعْلَى ـ أَحْسَنُ ـ أَفْضَلُ ـ أَفْخَرُ. A — number, عَدَدٌ أَصَمُّ. A — joint, شِلْوَةٌ فَاخِرَةٌ ـ أَطْيَبُ شَرْحَةٍ مِنَ ٱللَّحْمِ. *For* Prime Minister, Prime cost, *See* Premier *and under* Price, *n.*

Prime, *n.* The dawn, morning, صَبَاحٌ ـ فَجْرٌ ـ شَقُّ ٱلْفَجْرِ. The best of anything, عَيْنَةٌ ـ صَمِيمٌ ـ صَفْوَةٌ. The first or first beauty of anything, عُنْفُوَانٌ: He is in the — of youth, هُوَ فِي عُنْفُوَانِ شَبَابِهِ ـ هُوَ فِي جِنِّ شَبَابِهِ. One in the — of life, قَارِحٌ *pl.* قَوَارِحُ. A — number, عَدَدٌ أَصَمُّ ـ عَدَدٌ أَصْلِيٌّ.

Prime, *v.t.* Of a gun, ذَخَّرَ. To lay the first coat of paint, صَبَغَ ـ أَوَّلَ صَبْغَةٍ ـ دَهَنَ ـ أَوَّلَ دَهْنَةٍ. To lay a train of gunpowder, أَعَدَّ فَتِيلَةَ بَارُودٍ. To post up, instruct, دَرَّبَ ـ عَلَّمَ.

Primer, *n.* An elementary book, كِتَابُ أُصُولٍ ـ مَدْخَلُ ٱلْعُلُومِ ٱلْقِرَاءَةِ.

Primeval, *a.* أَوَّلُ ـ أَقْدَمُ ـ قَدِيمٌ ـ أَصْلِيٌّ. Primeval creation, الفِطَحْلُ ـ الفِطْرَةُ.

Priming, *n.* As of a gun, ذَخِيرَةٌ. First colour laid in painting, أَوَّلُ صَبْغَةٍ ـ أَوَّلُ دَهْنَةٍ ـ أَوَّلُ دِمَامٍ. Acceleration of the tides, سُرْعَةُ ٱلْمَدِّ وَٱلْجَزْرِ. The hot water which goes from the boilers into the cylinders, الْمَاءُ ٱلْغَالِي ٱلَّذِي يَخْرُجُ مِنْ قُدُورِ ٱلْبَاخِرَةِ وَيَدْخُلُ فِي ٱلدَّوَالِيبِ.

Primitial, *a.* بَاكُورٌ ـ بَكُورٌ ـ بَكِيرٌ.

Primitive, *a.* Pertaining to early times, قَدِيمٌ *pl.* قُدَمَاءُ ـ مُقَدَّمٌ ـ سَابِقٌ. Original, أَصْلِيٌّ. Simple, بَسِيطٌ ـ سَاذَجٌ *or* سَاذِجٌ.

Primitively, *ad.* فِي ٱلْأَوَّلِ ـ أَوَّلًا ـ فِي ٱلْبَدْءِ ـ فِي ٱلْأَصْلِ ـ إِبْتِدَاءً.

Primitiveness, *n.* Originality, أَوَّلِيَّةٌ ـ أَصْلِيَّةٌ. Simplicity, بَسَاطَةٌ ـ سَذَاجَةٌ.

Primness, *n.* Affecting great nicety, تَظَرُّفٌ ـ تَجَوُّدٌ ـ تَأَنُّقٌ. Formality, reserve, إِطْرَاقٌ ـ بُرُودَةٌ. Preciseness, دِقَّةٌ. *See also* Nicety, Neatness, *n.*

Primogenitor, *n.* الْأَبُ ٱلْأَوَّلُ.

Primogeniture, *n.* كِبَرُ ٱلسِّنِّ ـ بَكُورِيَّةٌ. The rights of —, حُقُوقُ ٱلْوَلَدِ ٱلْبِكْرِ ـ حُقُوقُ (*or* إِمْتِيَازَاتُ) ٱلْبَكُورِيَّةِ.

Primordial, *a.* أَوَّلُ ـ أَصْلِيٌّ ـ مُتَقَدِّمٌ. Primordial creation, الفِطَحْلُ ـ الفِطْرَةُ.

Primrose, *n.* آذَانُ ٱلدُّبِّ ـ زَهْرُ ٱلرَّبِيعِ.

Primus, *n.* أَوَّلُ ـ رَئِيسٌ ـ صَدْرٌ.

Prince, *n.* A king's son, إِبْنُ مَلِكٍ *pl.* بَنُو مَلِكٍ ـ نَجْلُ مَلِكٍ *pl.* أَنْجَالٌ ـ بِرِنْس. A sovereign, ruler, مَلِكٌ *pl.* مُلُوكٌ ـ سُلْطَانٌ ـ حَاكِمٌ *pl.* حُكَّامٌ. The title given to European grandees, بِرِنْس. A liberal man, صَاحِبُ سَخَاوَةٍ. The Prince of Wales, أَمِيرٌ *pl.* أُمَرَاءُ ـ خِدِيو ـ خُدَيْوِيٌّ ـ لَقَبُ وَلِيٍّ ـ بِرِنْس أُفْ وِيلْسْ عَهْدِ ٱلدَّوْلَةِ ٱلْبِرِيطَانِيَّةِ وَوَارِثُ ٱلْمُلْكِ.

Princedom, *n.* رُتْبَةُ (أَوْ حُكُومَةُ) ٱلْبِرِنْس.

Princelike, *a.* / Princely, } Like a prince, مِثْلَ ـ مِثْلَ مَلِكٍ ـ مُلُوكِيٌّ ٱلْمُلُوكِ. Grand, magnificent, بَهِيٌّ ـ جَلِيٌّ ـ فَاخِرٌ ـ جَلِيلٌ ـ عَظِيمٌ. Liberal, سَخِيٌّ ـ جَوَادٌ.

Princeliness, *n.* Magnificence, عَظَمَةٌ ـ جَلَالٌ ـ عِزٌّ ـ سَلْطَنَةٌ ـ بَهَاءٌ. Liberality, سَخَاوَةٌ ـ جُودٌ.

Prince's-feather, *n.* The plant, أَبُو بَرُوخِيْس.

Princess, *n.* A king's daughter, بِنْتُ مَلِكٍ *pl.* بَنَات — بِرِنْسِيسَة. A female sovereign, سُلْطَانَة — مَلِكَة. The consort of a prince, إِمْرَأَةُ بِرِنْس.

Principal, *a.* Highest in rank, *etc.*, أَعْظَمُ — أَكْبَرُ — أَقْدَمُ — رَئِيس. Most essential, important, أَكْبَرُ — أَهَمُّ — أَخَصُّ. The — reason is that..., أَكْبَرُ ٱلْأَسْبَابِ هُوَ أَن. Supper is my — meal, رَكِّي عَلَى ٱلْعَشَاء. The — works are completed, أَخَصُّ ٱلْأَشْغَالِ تَمَّتْ.

Principal, *n.* Head, head man, مُسَيْطِر — زَعِيم *pl.* زُعَمَآء — رَئِيس — كَبِير — ضَابِط — مُدِير — مُتَقَدِّم — صَاحِب. A chief instructor, أَوَّلُ مُعَلِّمٍ — أَوَّلُ مُدَرِّسٍ. The — in a crime, *etc.*, أَصْلُ ٱلْجِنَاح — أَسَاسُ ٱلشَّرِّ. A — or capital sum, رَأْسُ ٱلْمَالِ. A — man, grandee, مَشْهُور *pl.* مَشَاهِيرُ — كَبِير *pl.* أَكَابِرُ — عَيْن *pl.* أَعْيَان. The — writer, رَئِيسُ ٱلْكَتَبَة.

Principality, *n.* Sovereignty, حُكُومَة — مَمْلَكَة — سَلْطَنَة. A prince's domain, سَلْطَنَة إِمَارَة. The principalities of Moldavia and Wallachia, المَمْلَكَتَانِ. The — of Servia, إِمَارَةُ سَرْبِسْتَان.

Principally, *ad.* بِالْأَكْثَرِ — خُصُوصًا — بِالْأَخَصِّ — خَاصَّةً.

Principia, *n.* مَبَادِئُ — أُصُول — مَبْدَأ.

Principle, *n.* Something primary or fundamental, إِسْطَقِس *pl.* إِسْطَقِسَات — مَبْدَأ *pl.* مَبَادِئُ — بَدَآءَة *pl.* بَدَآءَة — أَسَاس *pl.* آسَاس and إِسَاس — أَصْل *pl.* أُصُول. That from which anything springs, a source, origin, مَبْدَأ — مَنْشَأ — مَأْخَذ — مَنْبَع — أَصْل. The vital —, الرُّوحُ — النَّفْسُ. An operative cause, سَبَب *pl.* أَسْبَاب — سَبَبٌ أَصْلِيٌّ — أَصْلُ سَبَبٍ. Root, essence, matter, عُنْصُر — جَوْهَر — مَادَّة. Belief, إِعْتِقَاد — مَذْهَب. A rule, maxim, قَاعِدَة *pl.* قَوَاعِدُ — قَانُون *pl.* قَوَانِينُ. To establish certain principles, إِتَّخَذَ أُصُولًا. To act on —, رَشَدَ [2] — أَقْسَطَ — رَشَدَ أَمْرَهُ [2] — سَلَكَ بِٱلْقَانُونِ [2]. To act up to one's principles, عَمِلَ بِقَوَاعِدِهِ — سَلَكَ حَسَبَ قَوَاعِدِهِ [2] — طَابَقَ قَوَاعِدَهُ فِعْلًا — إِمْتَثَلَ قَوَاعِدَهُ — إِمْتِثَالًا بِٱلْقَوَاعِدِ — ذِمَّةً — بِٱلْقِسْطِ. On principle, بِالرَّشَادِ — بِالصَّوَابِ.

A man of no principle, رَجُلُ سَوْءٍ — عَدِيمُ ٱلْإِسْتِقَامَة.

A man of principle, صَاحِبُ ٱسْتِقَامَةٍ — زَكِيٌّ *pl.* أَزْكِيَآء — صَادِق.

Fixed principles, قَوَاعِدُ مَقْطُوعَة — أُصُولٌ مَضْبُوطَة.

Fundamental principles, قَوَاعِدُ أَسَاسِيَّة.

General principles, قَوَاعِدُ عُمُومِيَّة.

National principles, قَوَاعِدُ ٱلْأُمَّةِ.

Political principles, قَوَاعِدُ سِيَاسِيَّة — قَوَاعِدُ بُولِيتِيكِيَّة.

Sound principles, قَوَاعِدُ صَحِيحَة — قَوَاعِدُ حَقِيقِيَّة — أَرْكَانٌ رَكِينَة.

The evil principle, مَنْبَعُ ٱلشَّرِّ وَٱلْفَسَادِ — الشَّيْطَانُ.

Principled, *a.* Of good and bad principles; *see the last two entries.*

Print, *v.t.* As with types, طَبَعَ [2]. To stamp, as cloth, بَصَمَ [2]. To be printed, as with types, طُبِعَ; as on cloth, إِنْبَصَمَ. To —, as marks, on the body of men or animals, وَسَمَ *aor.* يَسِمُ; to make marks on one's own person, إِتَّسَمَ.

Print, *n.* Printed matter, طَبْع. A stamp on cloth, بَصْم — بَصْمَة. A mark made by pressure, أَثَر *pl.* آثَار. A mark made on the body, وَسْم *pl.* وُسُوم. The impression of a seal, خَتْم. A footprint, أَثَرُ ٱلْأَقْدَامِ *pl.* آثَار. A mould, قَالِب *pl.* قَوَالِبُ. A cast, سَبِيكَة. A newspaper, جَرِيدَة *pl.* جَرَائِدُ — جُورْنَال *pl.* جُورْنَالَات. An engraving, picture, نَقْش *pl.* نُقُوش — تَصْوِير *pl.* تَصَاوِيرُ — صُورَة *pl.* صُوَر. Calico —, شِيتٌ هِنْدِيٌّ — شِيتٌ يَمَنِيٌّ. In —, printed, مَطْبُوع; copies still to be had, يُجَدُ مِنْهُ. Out of —, نُسَخُهُ فَرَغَتْ — لَمْ يُجَدْ مِنْهُ بَعْدُ — إِنْبَاعَ كُلُّهُ. To appear in —, to — one's work, طَبَعَ تَالِيفَهُ.

Printer, *n.* As of books, طَبَّاع — مَطْبَعْجِي.

Printing, *n.* The art of, صِنَاعَةُ ٱلطَّبْعِ. Matter printed, طَبْع — مَطْبُوعَات. Letter-press —, طَبْعُ حُرُوف. Copper-plate —, الطَّبْعُ مِنَ أَلْوَاحِ ٱلنُّحَاسِ. Lithographic —, الطَّبْعُ مِنَ ٱلْحَجَرِ.

Printing-ink, *n.* دُهْنُ لِلطَّبْعِ — حِبْرُ ٱلطَّبْعِ.

Printing-machine, *n.* دُولَابُ ٱلطَّبْعِ.

Printing-office, *n.* دَارُ ٱلطِّبَاعَةِ — مَطْبَعَة — مَطْبَع.

Printing-press, *n.* مَطْبَع — مَطْبَعَة *pl.* مَطَابِعُ.

Prior, *a.* *See* Antecedent, Previous, Preceding, *a.*

Prior, *n.* A superior, head, شَيْخ *pl.* شُيُوخ — رَئِيس *pl.* رُؤَسَآء.

Prior of a monastery, رَئِيسُ دَيْرٍ.

Priorate, *n.* رِئَاسَة — رِئَاسَةُ دَيْرٍ.

Prioress, *n.* رَئِيسَةُ دَيْرٍ.

Priority, *n.* Antecedence, سَابِقَة — سَلَف — سُلُوف — تَقَدُّم. *See also* Precedence, Preference, *n.*

Priori. *See A priori.*

Priory, *n.* دَيْر *pl.* دُيُورَة.

Prism, *n.* مَنْشُور *pl.* مَنَاشِيرُ.

Prismatic, *a.* مَنْشُورِيٌّ. Prismatic colours, أَلْوَانٌ مَنْشُورِيَّة.

Prismoid, *n.* جِسْمٌ عَلَى هَيْئَةِ ٱلْمَنْشُورِ.

Prison, *n.* سِجْن *pl.* سُجُون — مَحْبِس *pl.* مَحَابِسُ — حَبْس *pl.* حُبُوس. A subterranean —, مُطْبِق. The keeper of a —, سَجَّان.

To cast into —, أَلْقَى-فِي ٱلسِّجْنِ. To loose from —, حَلَّ-مِنَ ² ٱلسِّجْنِ.

Prison, *v.t.* *See to* Imprison, *v.t.*

Prisoner, *n.* One under arrest, سَجِين *pl.* سُجَنَآء – مَسْجُون – مَحْبُوس. To take —, captive, أَسَرَ ². *See also* Captive, *n.*

Prison-house, *n.* *See* Prison, *n.*

Pristine, *a.* أَصْلِيّ – قَدِيم – أَوَّل.

Privacy, *n.* The being alone, retirement, خَلَآء – خُلُوّ – جَنْبَة – وَحْشَة – خَلْوَة – عُزْلَة. Secrecy, خَفَآء – سِرّ – خَافِيَة. Solitude, خَلْوَة – وَحْدَة. A place of —, خَلَآء – مَعْزِل. To retire into —, خَلَا *aor.* يَخْلُو – أَخْلَى – أَخْلَى بِنَفْسِهِ (*or* أَخْلَى) خَلَا.

Private, *a.* Peculiar to one's self or to a joint number, خَاصّ ل – مَخْصُوص ل – مُخَصَّص ل – مُخْتَصّ ب. Sequestered from company, مُجْتَنِب – مُنْفَرِد – عَلَى حِدَةٍ – مُسْتَخْلٍ. Secret, not publicly known, سِرِّيّ – مَكْنُون – خَفِيّ – مَسْتُور. Not invested with office, عُمُومِيّ – عَامّ – غَيْرُ مُقَلَّدٍ بِوَظِيفَةٍ – بِلَا وَظِيفَةٍ. Personal, ذَاتِيّ. A — chamber, خَلْوَة. A man easy in — conference, رَجُل سَهْلُ ٱلْخَلْوَةِ. Private aims, ٱلْمَقَاصِدُ ٱلذَّاتِيَّةُ ٱلْخَاصَّة. Private life, living in retirement from the public service, عِيشَةُ ٱلْقَاعِدِ عَنْ خِدْمَةِ ٱلدَّوْلَةِ; association with friends, مُعَاشَرَة – عِيشَةُ ٱلصُّدْقَانِ – ٱلْأَحْبَاب. Be alone with me that I may speak to you in —, أَخْلِ مَعِي حَتَّى أُكَلِّمَكَ. He was in — with the governor, خَلَا ² (*or* أَخْلَى *or* إِسْتَخْلَى) بِٱلْحَاكِمِ. He asked a — interview with the wazir, إِسْتَخْلَى ٱلْوَزِيرَ. Keep — in the matter, أَخْلِ إِلَيْكَ بِٱلْأَمْرِ. He was alone or in — with him, أَخْلَى بِهِ – إِسْتَخْلَى بِهِ. The — parts, ٱلشَّوَار. A — soldier; *see below.*

Private, *n.* A private soldier, نَفَر مِنَ ٱلْعَسْكَرِ *pl.* أَنْفَار.

Privateer, *n.* The ship, سَفِينَة مُخْتَصَّة بِأَفْرَادٍ أَوْ بِشِرْكَةٍ مُرَخَّصَة مِنَ ٱلدَّوْلَةِ فِي سَلْبِ (*or* تَخَطُّفِ) سُفُنِ ٱلْعَدُوّ.

Privateer, *v.i.* سَارَ فِي سَفِينَةٍ مِنَ ٱلسُّفُنِ ٱلْمَذْكُورَةِ لِسَلْبِ ² سُفُنِ ٱلْعَدُوّ. He has prepared vessels to — on English ships, جَهَّزَ ٱلسُّفُنَ ٱلْمَذْكُورَةَ لِسَلْبِ ٱلسُّفُنِ ٱلْإِنْكِلِيزِيَّةِ.

Privateering, *n.* سَيْرُ ٱلسُّفُنِ ٱلْمَذْكُورَةِ لِسَلْبِ سُفُنِ ٱلْعَدُوّ. The treaty made at Paris declared against —, ٱلْمُعَاهَدَةُ ٱلَّتِي ٱنْعَقَدَتْ فِي بَارِيسَ قَدْ صُرِّحَ فِيهَا بِٱلنَّهْيِ عَنِ ٱسْتِعْمَالِ ٱلسُّفُنِ ٱلْمَذْكُورَةِ.

Privately, *ad.* In retirement, فِي جَنْبَةٍ – فِي خَلْوَةٍ – فِي عُزْلَةٍ – فِي مَعْزِلٍ. Alone, apart, إِنْفِرَادًا. Secretly, خُفْيَةً – عَلَى خَفَآءٍ – سِرًّا. Privately and openly, سِرًّا وَجَهْرًا – سِرًّا وَعَلَانِيَةً. They came to him —, تَقَدَّمُوا إِلَيْهِ عَلَى ٱنْفِرَادٍ. He took him aside —, تَنَحَّى بِهِ مُنْفَرِدًا.

Privateness, *n.* *See* Privacy, *n.*

Privation, *n.* The act of depriving, إِعْدَام – حَرْم – رَفْع عَن – تَجْرِيد; the being deprived, حِرْمَة – عَدَم – سَلْب – حِرْمَان. Want, عَوَز – إِحْتِيَاج – حَاجَة – عَدَم.

Privative, *a.* Causing privation or loss, مُعْدِم – سَالِب – حَارِم. Negative, نَفْيِيّ.

Privative, *a.* A — word or particle, أَدَاةُ ٱلنَّفْيِ – حَرْفُ نَفْيٍ.

Privet, *n.* فَغْو – فَاغِيَة. *See also* Henna, *n.*

Privilege, *n.* A peculiar advantage, خَاصَّة *pl.* خَصَائِص – إِمْتِيَاز *pl.* إِمْتِيَازَات. A benefit, نِعْمَة. Immunity, إِعْفَآء – مُعَافَاة – بَرَآءَة. Special permission, رُخْصَة – إِذْن مَخْصُوص. Enjoyment of a —, تَمَتُّع وَٱنْتِفَاع بِٱلْإِمْتِيَازِ. An exclusive —, إِمْتِيَاز مُنْحَصِر بِشَخْصٍ مَخْصُوصٍ. Consular privileges, خَصَائِص وَٱمْتِيَازَات مُخْتَصَّة بِٱلْقَنَاصِلِ. The document conveying a —, مَنْشُور *pl.* مَنَاشِير – بَرَآءَة. The privileges which all the subjects of foreign powers enjoy at present, ٱلْإِمْتِيَازَاتُ ٱلشَّامِلَةُ ٱلْآنَ رَعَايَا ٱلدُّوَلِ ٱلْأَجْنَبِيَّةِ. Whilst they continued excluded from all privileges, مَا دَامُوا مَحْرُومِينَ مِنْ جَمِيعِ ٱلْإِمْتِيَازَاتِ.

Privilege, *v.t.* To grant a privilege to, أَحْسَنَ إِلَى-بِٱمْتِيَازٍ – أَعْطَى-ٱمْتِيَازًا. To give permission to, رَخَّصَ-فِي. To exempt from, أَعْفَى-مِن.

Privileged, *a.* Having privileges, ذُو – صَاحِبُ خَصَائِصَ – ٱمْتِيَازَاتٍ – حَائِزُ ٱمْتِيَازَاتٍ. Exempted from, مُعْفًى مِن. Permitted, مُرَخَّص – مُرَخَّص عَلَى وَجْهٍ مَخْصُوصٍ.

Privily, *ad.* عَلَى خَفَآءٍ – خُفْيَةً – سِرًّا. *See also* Privately, *ad.*

Privities, *n.* The private parts; *see under* Private, *a.*

Privity, *n.* عِلْم ب – إِطِّلَاع ب – خَبَر وَٱتِّفَاق ب.

Privy, *a.* Not public, مَخْفِيّ – خَفِيّ – مَسْتُور – مَكْتُوم. Privately knowing, مُطَّلِع عَلَى – خَبِير ب – سِرًّا. Admitted to secrets of state, مَوْضِعُ أَسْرَارِ ٱلْحُكُومَةِ. His wife was — to it, إِمْرَأَتُهُ لَهَا خَبَرُ ذٰلِكَ.

Privy Chamber, خَلْوَةُ أَرْبَابِ ٱلسِّيَاسَةِ.

Privy Council, مَجْلِسُ أَحْكَامِ ٱلدَّوْلَةِ.

Privy Councillor, أَحَدُ أَعْضَآءِ مَجْلِسِ أَحْكَامِ ٱلدَّوْلَةِ.

Privy purse, ٱلْإِيرَادُ ٱلْهُمَايُونِيُّ ٱلْخَاصّ.

Privy Seal, *n.* Of the Privy Council, مُهْرُ مَجْلِسِ أَرْبَابِ ٱلسِّيَاسَةِ. The holder of the —, مُهْرْدَار (*or* أَمِينُ مُهْرٍ) مَجْلِسِ أَرْبَابِ ٱلسِّيَاسَةِ.

Privy, *n.* A necessary, مَخْرَأَة – مَبْرَز – مَجَاز – مُتَوَضَّأ – خَلَآء – مُسْتَرَاح – بَيْتُ ٱلْمَآءِ – بَيْتُ ٱلْفَرَاغِ – مَخْرَج – مَحَشّ – كَنِيف *pl.* كُنُف.

Prize, n. What is taken from an enemy in war, غَنِيمَة pl. غَنَائِم — مُكَافَاة — جِعَالَة. Anything gained in rivalry, خَلِيسَة — خُلْسَة — نَصِيب — نَصِيبٌ رَابِحٌ — رَبَح. A — drawn in a lottery, مُجَازَاة — سَفِينَة — مَرْكَبٌ خَلِيسٌ. A ship taken as a —, رَابِحٌ فِي ٱلْقُرْعَةِ. A good and lawful —, غَنِيمَةٌ حَلَالٌ — ٱلْغَنِيمَة.

To offer a prize, عَرَضَ مُكَافَأَةً — وَعَدَ بِجِعَالَةٍ aor. يَعِدُ.

To obtain or win a prize, إِغْتَنَمَ ٱلْمُكَافَأَةَ — فَازَ بِٱلْجِعَالَةِ.

To draw a prize, as from a lottery, إِكْتَسَبَ نَصِيبًا رَابِحًا.

Prize, v.t. To set value upon, to esteem, رَغِبَ فِي — أَعَزَّ — إِعْتَبَرَ. To set a value upon, as of goods, ثَمَّنَ — قَدَّرَ. *See also to* Esteem, Estimate, v.t.

Prize-fighter, n. مُعَارِكٌ عَلَى جِعَالَةٍ.

Prize-fighting, n. مُعَارَكَةٌ عَلَى ٱلْجِعَالَةِ.

Prize-money, n. نَصِيبُ ٱلْعَسَاكِرِ (أَوِ ٱلْبَحْرِيَّةِ) مِنْ غَنَائِمِ (or خُلْسَةِ) ٱلْعَدُوِّ.

Pro or Con, For or against, مَعَ أَوْ عَلَى: For him or against him, مَا لَهُ وَعَلَيْهِ — مَعَهُ أَوْ عَلَيْهِ. The pros and cons of anything, مَا لَهُ وَعَلَيْهِ.

Proa, n. ضَرْبٌ مِنَ ٱلْقَوَارِبِ تُسْتَعْمَلُ فِي ٱلْبَحْرِ ٱلْمُحِيطِ ٱلشَّرْقِيِّ.

Probability, n. An appearance of truth, تَخْمِين — إِحْتِمَال — قُرْبٌ لِلْعَقْلِ. Anything that has the appearance of truth, مُحْتَمَل. There is no — that..., لَا يُحْتَمَلُ أَنْ. The probabilities of the situation, مَظْنُونُ ٱلْمَوْقِعِ — قَرَائِنُ ٱلْحَالِ. The present probabilities of the case indicate that, ..., قَرَائِنُ ٱلْحَالِ ٱلْآنَ تَدُلُّ عَلَى أَنْ. *See also* Likelihood, Credibility, Chance, n.

Probable, a. Likely to be, or to be true, قَرِيبٌ — مُحْتَمَل — مِنَ ٱلْمُحْتَمَلِ — ٱلْإِحْتِمَالِ. More —, أَقْرَبُ. It is not — that..., لَمْ يَكُنْ مِنَ ٱلْمُمْكِنِ أَنْ. But it is more — that..., لٰكِنْ أَقْرَبُ مِنْ ذٰلِكَ أَنْ. It is, or what is, deemed most —, أَقْرَبُ مَا يَخْطُرُ. It is most — that..., ٱلْغَالِبُ عَلَى ٱلظَّنِّ — بِٱلْبَالِ أَنْ. What is most —, what occurs first to the mind, ٱلْمُتَبَادِرُ إِلَى ٱلذِّهْنِ. *See also* Likely, a.

Probably, ad. بِٱلتَّخْمِينِ — عَلَى ٱلتَّخْمِينِ — بِٱلْإِحْتِمَالِ — عَسَى — ٱللّٰهُ أَعْلَمُ — تَخْمِينًا.

Probang, n. مِسْبَارٌ لِلْحَلْقِ — مَجَسٌّ لِلْمَبْلَعِ — لَوْلَبٌ لِلْبُلْعُومِ.

Probate, n. Of a will, تَقْيِيدُ ٱلْوَصِيَّةِ وَإِثْبَاتُهَا رَسْمًا. To take out — of a will, أَثْبَتَ صِحَّةَ ٱلْوَصِيَّةِ رَسْمًا.

Probation, n. Trial, تَجْرِبَة — إِمْتِحَان. Moral trial, فِتْنَة — تَجْرِيب. The act of proving, إِثْبَات. *See also* Noviciate, n.

Probational, a. }
Probationary, } إِمْتِحَانِيّ — لِلتَّجْرِبَةِ — لِلْإِمْتِحَانِ.

Probationer, n. مُرِيد — طَالِبٌ تَحْتَ ٱلْإِمْتِحَانِ pl. طُلَّاب and طَلَبَة.

Probative, a. }
Probatory, } مُبَرْهِن — مُحَقِّق — مُثْبِت.

Probe, n. مِسْبَار — سِبَار — مِغْرَاف — مِيل pl. أَمْيَال — مِحْجَاج.

But for the — the depth of the wound would not be known, (prov.) لَوْلَا ٱلْمِسْبَارُ مَا عُرِفَ غَوْرُ ٱلْجُرْحِ.

Probe, v.t. As with a probe, حَجَّ [2] — سَبَرَ — حَجَّ — بِمِيلٍ [2]. To — a thing to the bottom, تَقَعَّرَ فِي. *See also to* Investigate, Scrutinize, v.t.

Probity, n. أَمَانَة — عَدَالَة — صَلَاح — صَدَاقَة — إِسْتِقَامَة.

Problem, n. A question for solution, مَسْأَلَة pl. مَسَائِل. A mathematical —, مَسْأَلَةٌ رِيَاضِيَّةٌ. A difficulty, مُشْكِلَة. An enigma, أُحْجِيَّة — حُجْوَى.

Problematical, a. مُحْتَمَل — مُخَيِّل — مُرْتَابٌ فِيهِ — مُشْتَبِه — ذُو رِيبَةٍ — ٱلشَّكّ.

Problematically, ad. بِرِيبَةٍ — بِشَكٍّ — إِشْتِبَاهًا.

Proboscis, n. Of an elephant, خُرْطُومُ ٱلْفِيلِ — مِلْمَلَة. A —, or snout, خُرْطُوم — خُرْطُم pl. خَرَاطِيم.

Procedure, n. Course of action, conduct, مَسْلَك — قِدَّيَة — سِيَاقَة. Mode of —, أَوْضَاعٌ وَحَرَكَاتٌ — سِيرَة — أَعْمَال — سُلُوك. His — towards me was most kind, عَامَلَنِي بِٱلْمَعْرُوفِ وَٱلْجَمِيلِ. Mode of — in a court of justice, أُصُولُ ٱلْمُرَافَعَةِ — أُصُولُ ٱلْمُحَاكَمَاتِ.

Civil procedure, أُصُولُ ٱلْمُحَاكَمَاتِ ٱلْحُقُوقِيَّةِ.

Criminal procedure, أُصُولُ ٱلْمُحَاكَمَاتِ ٱلْجِنَائِيَّةِ.

Legal forms of procedure, ٱلْأُصُولُ ٱلْقَانُونِيَّةُ.

Proceed, v.i. To go, go on, سَارَ aor. يَسِيرُ — مَرَّ [2] — ذَهَبَ — مَشَى — إِنْسَلَكَ. To move, remove, إِنْتَقَلَ. To take a course, نَهَجَ مَنْهَجًا — سَلَكَ سُلُوكًا [2]. To make progress, مَشَى — تَدَرَّجَ — تَقَدَّمَ — يَرُوجُ aor. رَاجَ — أَخَذَ فِي [2]. To — to, to begin, بَاشَرَ — بَادَرَ إِلَى — إِبْتَدَأَ فِي — شَرَعَ فِي. To — from, to spring out of, صَدَرَ عَنْ [2]; to — from, as of the Divine nature, إِنْبَعَثَ مِنْ — إِنْبَثَقَ مِنْ. To — against, as in a court of law, رَافَعَ — إِلَى — ٱدَّعَى عَلَى — فِي ٱلْمَحْكَمَةِ — حَاكَمَ — إِلَى ٱلْحَاكِمِ ٱلْحَاكِمِ. To cause to — from, أَصْدَرَ — عَنْ. He proceeded and said, عَادَ فَقَالَ [2]. He proceeded and seized the woman also, عَادَ فَقَبَضَ عَلَى ٱلْإِمْرَأَةِ أَيْضًا. They shall — no further, لَا يَتَقَدَّمُونَ أَكْثَرَ. The words proceeded out of his mouth, خَرَجَتِ ٱلْكَلِمَاتُ مِنْ فَمِهِ. He proceeded on his way, إِنْطَلَقَ إِلَى حَالِ سَبِيلِهِ. Let us — to business, نَشْرَعُ فِي ٱلشُّغْلِ.

Proceeding, *n.* An action, عَمَل *pl.* أَعْمَال ـ قَضِيَّة *pl.* قَضَايَا. Conduct, treatment, مُعَامَلَة ـ سِيرَة ـ دَأْب. A course, way, مَنْهَج ـ مِدَاد ـ طَرِيقَة. Their mode of — is to..., مِنْ دَأْبِهِمْ أَنْ.

Proceedings, conduct, actions, حَرَكَات ـ أَوْضَاع ـ أَفْعَال ـ أَعْمَال. Doings, a course of measures, تَدَابِير ـ قَضَايَا. Official proceedings, تَدَابِير (or) قَضَايَا رَسْمِيَّة. Summary proceedings at law, مُحَاكَمَة مُسْتَعْجَلَة ـ عَلَى وَجْهِ ٱلْإِجْمَالِ. Legal proceedings, مُحَاكَمَة ـ دَعْوَى. To take legal — against; *See* To Proceed against, *under to* Proceed, *v.i.*

Proceeds, *n.* حَاصِل ـ مَحْصُول ـ حَصِيلَة *pl.* حَصَائِل ـ مُحَصَّل ـ مَحْصُولَات. Net —, مَحْصُول خَالِص. Amount, مَبْلَغ.

Process, *n.* A moving or operation, حَرَكَة *pl.* حَرَكَات ـ عَمَل *pl.* أَعْمَال. A way, mode, manner, سِمَاط ـ مَنْهَج ـ قِدِّيَّة ـ طَرِيقَة ـ بَاب مِنَ ٱلْأَبْوَاب. Methodical arrangement, سِيَاقَة ـ تَنْسِيق ـ نِظَام ـ ضِبَاطَة. Concatenation, تَسَلْسُل ـ سِلْسِلَة. A series of changes in growth, تَبَدُّلَات طَبِيعِيَّة. The projecting part of a bone, سِيس *pl.* سَنَاسِن ـ زَائِدَة *pl.* زَوَائِد. A summons to appear, أَمْر شَرْعِيّ بِٱلْحُضُور. A chemical —, صَنْعَة ـ تَأْثِير كِيمَاوِيّ ـ كِيمَاوِيَّة. In — of time, لَمَّا طَالَ ٱلزَّمَان ـ مِنْ بَعْدِ أَيَّام. To be in —, كَانَ يَصِير ; *vulg.* عَمَّال يصير. To serve a — upon, نَاوَلَ أَمْرًا شَرْعِيًّا بِٱلْحُضُور.

Procession, *n.* A train of persons, مَحْفِل ـ مَوْكِب ـ زَفَّة. A religious — conducted by priests, دَوْرَة ـ دَوَرَان ـ زِيَاح *pl.* زِيَاحَات. A bridal —, زَفَّة. A — round anything, طَوَاف. Emanation, صُدُور. The — of the Holy Spirit, إِنْبِثَاق ٱلرُّوح ٱلْقُدُس. A funeral —, مَوْكِب يُشَيِّع ٱلْجِنَازَة. *See also* Proceeding, *n.*

Processional, *a.* / **Processionary**, } Pertaining to a procession, مُتَعَلِّق بِمَوْكِب ; consisting in procession, وَاكِب. A — chant, تَرْتِيل يُرَتَّل عِنْدَ ٱلزِّيَاح.

Procès-verbal, *n.* مَضْبَطَة *pl.* مَضَابِط. To draw up a —, نَظَّمَ مَضْبَطَة.

Proclaim, *v.t.* To publish, أَذَّنَ بِ ـ نَادَى بِ ـ أَذَاعَ بِ ـ بَثَّ ٱلْخَبَر ـ أَشْهَرَ ـ أَعْلَنَ بِ. To make known, أَذَاعَ ـ أَشْهَرَ. To declare, affirm, أَكَّدَ ـ شَهِدَ ـ أَثْبَتَ. It shall be proclaimed, يُنَادَى بِهِ. They proclaimed a fast, نَادَوْا بِصَوْم.

Proclaimer, *n.* مُنَادٍ.

Proclamation, *n.* A solemn publication, أَذَان ـ مُنَادَاة. The act of making public, إِشْهَار. A notice, تَنْبِيه ـ إِعْلَان. A written proclamation, edict, مَنْشُور ـ فِرْمَان. He made a — throughout the land, أَطْلَقَ نِدَاءً فِي ٱلْبِلَاد.

Proclivity, *n.* *See* Inclination, *n.*

Proconsul, *n.* قَائِم مَقَام ٱلْقُنْصُلِ فِي أَيَّامِ حُكُومَةِ ٱلْقَنَاصِلِ عِنْدَ ٱلرُّومَانِيِّينَ ٱلْأَقْدَمِين.

Proconsular, *a.* مُتَعَلِّق بِقَائِم مَقَام ٱلْقُنْصُلِ ٱلْمَذْكُورِ.

Proconsulate, *n.* / **Proconsulship**, } وَظِيفَة قَائِم مَقَام ٱلْقُنْصُلِ ٱلْمَذْكُورِ.

Procrastinate, *v.i.* تَوَانَى عَن ـ أَنِيَ ـ تَرَاخَى ـ جَارَ ـ تَأَخَّرَ ـ تَطَاوَلَ. *See also to* Delay, *v.i.*

Procrastination, *n.* تَطَاوُل ـ تَأَخُّر ـ تَأْخِير ـ فَتْرَة ـ عَاقَة. *See also* Delay, *n.*

Procrastinator, *n.* مُتَطَاوِل ـ مُعَقِّب ـ مُؤَخِّر ـ وَقَّاف. One who puts off paying his debts, مَطُول.

Procreant, *a.* بَاعِث ـ مُورِث ـ مُوَلِّد.

Procreate, *v.t.* To generate, produce, أَنْشَأَ ـ أَنْتَجَ ـ نَتَجَ ـ أَحْدَثَ. To — children, وَلَدَ ـ نَتَجَ ذُرِّيَّة *aor.* يَلِدُ. *See also to* Beget, *v.t.*

Procreation, *n.* The act of generating, producing, نَتْج ـ تَوْلِيد ـ إِصْدَار ـ إِحْدَاث ـ نِتَاج ; of producing young, تَوْلِيد.

Procreative, *a.* Generating, producing, مُحْدِث ـ مُنْتِج ـ نَاتِج ـ مُصْدِر ; of young, مُوَلِّد.

Procreator, *n.* وَالِد ـ مُوَلِّد.

Proctor, *n.* An attorney, وَكِيل دَعْوَى فِي مَحْكَمَةِ ٱلْمِيرَاث. An officer in a university, مُدِير فِي مَدْرَسَةِ ٱلْفُنُون.

Proctorship, *n.* وَظِيفَة ٱلْمُدِير فِي دَارِ ٱلْفُنُون.

Procumbent, *a.* Lying down, مُنْسَطِح ـ مُنْبَطِح ـ مُتَمَدِّد ـ نَائِم. Trailing, مُنْسَدِل ـ مُنْسَحِب.

Procurable, *a.* الْحُصُول عَلَيْهِ مُمْكِن ـ مِمَّا يُدْرَك ـ مِمَّا يُحَصَّل ـ مَوْجُود ـ يُوجَد مِنْهُ. *See also* Obtainable.

Procuration, *n.* The act of procuring, تَوْزُّب ـ إِدْرَاك ـ تَحْصِيل. Management, إِدَارَة ـ تَدْبِير. Agency, وَكَالَة.

Procurator, *n.* One who manages for another, نَائِب *pl.* نُوَّاب ـ وَكِيل *pl.* وُكَلَاء.

Procure, *v.t.* To get, obtain, اِقْتَنَى ـ أَدْرَكَ ـ فَازَ بِ ـ حَازَ ـ نَالَ ـ حَصَّلَ ـ حَصَلَ عَلَى. To bring about, as of an effect, أَنْتَجَ ـ أَحْدَثَ ـ سَبَّبَ ـ أَوْجَبَ. *See also to* Acquire, Get, Obtain, *v.t.*

Procurement, *n.* The act of procuring, إِدْرَاك ـ حَوْز ـ تَوْزُّب ـ تَحْصِيل. Causing to be effected, نَتْج ـ إِنْتَاج ـ إِحْدَاث ـ إِيجَاب.

Procurer, *n.* One who procures, حَائِز ـ مُدْرِك ـ مُحَصِّل. *See also* Pander, *n.*

Procuress, *n.* *See* Bawd, *n.*

Procyon, *n.* The star, الغُمَيْصَآءُ.

Prod, *n.* A goad, مِنْخَاس ـ مِنْخَز. An awl, مِخْرَاز ـ مِخْرَز.

Prodigal, *a.* Given to lavish expenditure, مُضَيِّع ـ مِضْيَاع ـ سَفَّاح ـ مُبَذِّرٌ مَالِهِ ـ مُتْلِفٌ لِمَالِهِ ـ مُسْرِف. Munificent, كَرِيمُ الخَيْرِ ـ جَوَاد. To be —, wasteful, أَسْرَفَ فِي مَالِهِ; to be munificent, سَخِيَ. To be — in, بَالَغَ فِي ـ أَفْرَطَ فِي.

Prodigal, *n.* مُبَذِّرُ مَالِهِ ـ مُسْرِف ـ مُضَيِّع. The prodigal son, in the Gospel, الوَلَدُ الشَّاطِرُ ـ الاِبْنُ الضَّالُّ.

Prodigality, *n.* Lavish expenditure, تَبْذِير ـ إِسْرَاف ـ سَرَف ـ إِفْرَاطٌ فِي المَالِ ـ المَالِ. Munificence, كَرَم ـ جُود ـ سَخَاوَة.

Prodigally, *ad.* Wastefully, تَبْذِيرًا ـ بِإِسْرَافٍ. Munificently, بِسَخَاوَةٍ ـ بِكَرَمٍ ـ بِجُودٍ.

Prodigious, *a.* Very great, جَسِيم ـ كَبِير ـ عَظِيم. Wonderful, غَرِيب ـ عَجِيب. *See also* Huge, Marvellous, *a.*

Prodigiously, *ad.* In a wonderful manner, بِنَوْعٍ عَجِيبٍ. Greatly, لِلْغَايَةِ ـ كَثِيرًا ـ جِدًّا.

Prodigiousness, *n.* Wonderfulness, غَرَابَة. Greatness, عِظَم ـ جَسَامَة ـ كِبَر ـ عَظَامَة.

Prodigy, *n.* A miracle, مُعْجِزَة. Anything wonderful, غَرِيبَة *pl.* غَرَائِب ـ أُعْجُوبَة *pl.* أَعَاجِيب ـ عَجِيبَة *pl.* عَجَائِب. A sign, portent, آيَة *pl.* آيَات. *See also* Monster, *n.*

Produce, *v.t.* To bring forward, جَآءَ بِ ـ قَدَّمَ ـ أَوْرَدَ *aor.* يَجِيءُ. To offer to view, exhibit, أَرَاى (*vulg.* وَرَّى) ـ فَرَّجَ ـ أَظْهَرَ. To bring into being, فَطَرَ ـ إِنْفَطَرَ ـ أَحْدَثَ ـ أَنْشَأَ. To beget, of young, وَلَدَ ـ وَلَّدَ ـ أَوْلَدَ ـ خَلَّفَ ـ أَنْتَجَ ـ نَتَجَ *aor.* يَلِدُ. To occasion, سَبَّبَ ـ صَارَ سَبَبًا لِ. To bring forth, as fruit, حَمَلَ ـ أَثْمَرَ ـ أَغَلَّ. To — fruit every alternate year, عَاوَمَ ـ عَوَّمَ. To —, as of a book, to write one, صَنَّفَ ـ أَلَّفَ ـ أَنْشَأَ. Produce your cause, قَدِّمُوا دَعْوَاكُمْ.

Produce, *n.* That which is brought forth, حَمْل ـ حَاصِل ـ مَحْصُول; as of grain, غَلَّة. Amount, مَبْلَغ. A result, نَتِيجَة. An emolument, عَائِدَة.

Producer, *n.* A maker, originator, مُنْشِئ ـ فَاطِر. The Producer, God, الفَاطِرُ. *See also* Grower, *n.*

Producible, *a.* That may be brought forward, مِمَّا يُورَدُ ـ مِمَّا يُقَدَّمُ. That may be done, مِمَّا يُعْمَلُ. That may be brought into being, مِمَّا يُحْدَثُ ـ مِمَّا يُنْتَجُ ـ مِمَّا يُنْشَأُ. That may be found, مَوْجُود.

Product, *n.* *In arithmetic*, حَاصِلُ الضَّرْبِ. *See also* Produce, *n.*

Production, *n.* The act of producing, of bringing into being, إِنْتَاج ـ إِبْرَاز ـ إِصْدَار ـ إِنْشَآء ـ إِحْدَاث ـ فَطْر ـ إِنْفِطَار ـ تَوْلِيد. What is produced, brought forth, حَاصِل ـ مَحْصُول ـ ثَمَرَة. A literary —, إِنْشَآء ـ تَأْلِيف ـ تَصْنِيف. The productions of the country, مَحْصُولَاتُ البِلَادِ. Productions imported from a foreign country, الأَصْنَافُ الوَارِدَةُ مِنَ البُلْدَانِ الأَجْنَبِيَّةِ. Productions of art, إِنْشَآءُ الصَّنَائِعِ; of nature, المُوَلَّدَاتُ. *See also* Produce, *n.*

Productive, *a.* مُوَلِّد ـ مُنْبِت ـ مُثْمِر. Fruitful, خَصِيب; especially of grain, مُغِلّ. Causing, مُسَبِّب ـ بَاعِث ـ مُوجِب. Productive soil, أَرْضٌ كُرُمٌ ـ كَرَم. The land was —, أَرْضَتِ الأَرْضُ. *See also* Creation, Efficient, *a.*

Productiveness, *n.* خِصْب ـ بَرَكَة. *See also* Fruitfulness, *n.*

Proem, *n.* مُقَدِّمَة. An ornate —, دِيبَاجَة. To write a — to a book, صَدَّرَ كِتَابًا.

Profanation, *n.* The act of profaning, تَدْنِيس. Profaneness, دَنَاسَة ـ نِفَاق ـ عَدَمُ حُرْمَةٍ. Misuse, خَسَارَة ـ إِنْتِهَاك ـ سُوءُ اسْتِعْمَالٍ.

Profane, *a.* Irreverent, عَدِيمُ الحُرْمَةِ ـ مُسْتَبَاح. Impious, wicked, طَالِح ـ دَنِس ـ مُنَافِق ـ نَجِس. Secular, عَادِيّ ـ مُخْتَصٌّ بِأُمُورِ الدُّنْيَا ـ دُنْيَاوِيّ.

Profane, *v.t.* دَنَّسَ ـ نَقَضَ حُرْمَتَهُ ـ نَجَّسَ.

Profanely, *ad.* Irreverently, wickedly, بِعَدَمِ حُرْمَةٍ ـ بِنِفَاقٍ.

Profaneness, *n.*
Profanity, } إِلْحَاد ـ نِفَاق ـ دَنَاسَة ـ نَقْضُ الحُرْمَةِ. To act with — in, أَلْحَدَ فِي.

Profaner, *n.* مُدَنِّس ـ نَاقِضُ الحُرْمَةِ ـ مُنَافِق ـ مُلْحِد.

Profess, *v.t.* To declare, صَرَّحَ بِ ـ صَارَحَ بِ. To make a show of, أَوْرَدَ ـ أَبْدَى ـ تَظَاهَرَ بِ ـ أَظْهَرَ. To acknowledge, confess, أَقَرَّ ـ إِسْتَقَرَّ ـ إِعْتَرَفَ. To —, as of a religion, creed, تَعَاهَدَ بِ ـ ذَهَبَ مَذْهَبَ ال... ـ تَبِعَ. To —, as of a trade or profession, تَعَطَّى ـ تَعَاطَى ـ عَمِلَ حِرْفَةَ ال... To — medicine, physic, تَطَبَّبَ ـ تَعَاطَى الطِّبَّ. To lay claim to, إِدَّعَى بِ. They — themselves to be wise, يَزْعُمُونَ أَنَّهُمْ حُكَمَآءُ. They — to know it, but in practice they deny it, يَعْتَرِفُونَ بِأَنَّهُمْ يَعْرِفُونَهُ وَلٰكِنَّهُمْ بِالأَعْمَالِ يُنْكِرُونَهُ.

Professedly, *ad.* Avowedly, إِقْرَارًا ـ إِعْتِرَافًا. By word of mouth, لِسَانًا.

Profession, *n.* Open declaration, إِيضَاح ـ إِعْتِرَاف ـ إِقْرَار ـ شَهَادَة. Any business followed, a trade, صَنْعَة ـ حِرْفَة. A collective body of persons engaged in a calling, أَهْلُ حِرْفَةٍ ـ صِنْف

pl. أَصْنَاف. A — of faith, creed, عَقِيدَة *pl.* عَقَائِد ـ كَلِمَةُ شَهَادَةٍ. To change from one —, belief, to another, اِنْتَكَثَ مِنْ دِينٍ إِلَى دِينٍ آخَرَ.

Professional, *a.* مُتَعَلِّقٌ بِٱلْحِرْفَةِ. Professional services, as of a physician, خِدْمَةٌ طِبِّيَّةٌ; as of a lawyer, خِدْمَةٌ شَرْعِيَّةٌ.

Professionally, *ad.* By profession, occupation, حِرْفَةً. Professionally, as a physician, كَطَبِيبٍ; as a lawyer, كَفَقِيهٍ. I attended him —, as a physician, طَبَّبْتُهُ [2].

Professor, *n.* One who makes a formal profession, مُعْتَرِف. A public teacher, مَشَايِخ *pl.* شَيْخ ـ أُسْتَاذ ـ مُدَرِّس ـ مُعَلِّم.

Professional, *a.* مُخْتَصٌّ بِٱلْمُعَلِّمِ ـ مُتَعَلِّقٌ بِٱلْمُدَرِّسِ.

Professorship, *n.* مَنْصَبُ ٱلْمُعَلِّمِ ـ وَظِيفَةُ ٱلْمُدَرِّسِ.

Proffer, *v.t.* *See to* Offer, *v.t.*

Proffer, *n.* *See* Offer, *n.*

Proficience, *n.* } Progress, advancement, تَقَدُّم ـ اِرْتِقَاء ـ تَرَقٍّ.
Proficiency, } Mental acquirements, learning, مَعْلُومَات ـ بُلُوغُ ٱلْعُلُومِ ـ بَرَاعَة ـ عِلْم ـ مَهَارَة. Perfection, كَمَال. Priority, precedence, سَابِقَة. To acquire —, تَمَهَّرَ. He attained the utmost — in science, بَلَغَ فِي ٱلْعِلْمِ ٱلْمَبَالِغَ [2].

Proficient, *a.* كَامِل ـ أَهْلُ ٱرْتِقَاء ـ مَاهِر ـ بَارِع ـ عَبْقَرِيٌّ ـ حَاذِق ـ لَوْذَعِيٌّ ـ عَلَّام. To be — in, مَهَرَ فِي *or* ب ـ [2] بَرَعَ فِي.

Proficiently, *ad.* بِبَرَاعَةٍ ـ بِكَمَالٍ ـ بِمَهَارَةٍ ـ بِٱرْتِقَاء.

Profile, *n.* A side view, مُعَايَنَةٌ عَرْضٍ ـ طَلْعَةُ جَانِبٍ. *See also* Outline, *n.*

Profit, *n.* As in trade, رِبْح ـ رَبَاح ـ شَفّ. A return, عَائِدَة ـ فَائِدَة. Advantage, utility, خَيْر ـ مَنْفَعَة ـ نَفْع ـ طَائِل. Net result, حَاصِل ـ ثَمَرَة. Income, مَدْخُول ـ دَخْل. Net — of money, فَوَاضِلُ ٱلْمَالِ. Profit made by servants, as on purchases, *etc.*, نَصِيبَة. To derive — from, as in trade, اِرْتَجَعَ مِنْ ـ أَفْضَلَ فِي ـ رَبِحَ فِي ـ اِسْتَشَفَّ فِي ـ شَفَّ فِي. To derive —, advantage, from, اِسْتَفَادَ مِنْ ـ اِنْتَفَعَ ب. To enjoy the — of, تَمَتَّعَ ب. He sold his camels and obtained a good — on them, بَاعَ إِبِلَهُ فَٱرْتَجَعَ مِنْهَا رِجْعَةً صَالِحَةً. This will not bring you any —, return, هٰذَا لَا يَأْتِي عَلَيْكَ بِفَائِدَةٍ ـ هٰذَا لَا يَرُدُّ عَلَيْكَ. There is no —, advantage, in it, لَيْسَ لَهُ ثَمَرَةٌ ـ لَا طَائِلَ تَحْتَهُ ـ لَيْسَ بِهِ مَنْفَعَةٌ. It will turn to his —, يَعُودُ إِلَيْهِ بِٱلنَّفْعِ. I say this for your —, هٰذَا أَقُولُهُ لِخَيْرِكُمْ.

Profit, *v.t.* To advance the interests of one, أَفَادَهُ ـ أَصْلَحَ إِلَيْهِ ـ نَفَعَهُ. To make to —, أَكْسَبَ ـ كَسَّبَ; as in trade, أَرْبَحَ. This will not — you, مَا يُجْدِي عَنْكَ هٰذَا.

Profit, *v.i.* To gain in trade, أَفْضَلَ فِي ٱلتِّجَارَةِ ـ رَبِحَ ـ اِكْتَسَبَ فِي ٱلتِّجَارَةِ ـ اِسْتَشَفَّ فِي ٱلتِّجَارَةِ. To derive advantage, اِسْتَفَادَ ـ اِنْتَفَعَ. To improve, أَفْلَحَ ـ تَرَقَّى ـ اِكْتَسَبَ. To — by an opportunity, اِغْتَنَمَ ٱلْفُرْصَةَ ـ تَقَدَّمَ ٱلْفُرْصَةَ. There is no doubt but that he will — by this matter, لَا شَكَّ أَنَّهُ سَيَسْتَفِيدُ مِنْ هٰذَا ٱلْأَمْرِ.

Profitable, *a.* Yielding gain, فِيهِ مَكْسَبٌ ـ رَبِيح ـ رَابِح. Advantageous, كَثِيرُ ٱلْفَوَائِدِ ـ مُفِيد ـ نَافِع ـ خَيْرِيٌّ. Profitable traffic, تِجَارَةٌ رَابِحَةٌ ـ مَتْجَرٌ رَبِيحٌ ـ مَتْجَرٌ رَابِحٌ.

Profitably, *ad.* With gain, بِمَكْسَبٍ ـ بِٱلرِّبْحِ ـ بِٱلرَّبَاحِ ـ شَفًّا. With advantage, بِتَمَتُّعٍ ـ بِمَنْفَعَةٍ ـ بِإِفَادَةٍ.

Profitless, *a.* بَاطِل ـ عَدِيمُ ٱلْخَيْرِ ـ بِلَا فَائِدَةٍ ـ غَيْرُ نَافِعٍ ـ لَا طَائِلَ تَحْتَهُ.

Profligacy, *n.* فَسَاد ـ فُجُور ـ خَلَاعَة ـ فِسْق ـ خَسَارَة ـ خَسَار.

Profligate, *a.* } أَشْرَار *pl.* شِرِّيرٌ خَاسِرٌ ـ خَاسِر ـ فَاجِر ـ فَاسِق ـ
Profligate, *n.* } خَلِيع. To lead a — life, خَلَعَ عِذَارَهُ ـ غَمَطَ ـ تَفَاحَشَ فِي ٱلسِّيرَةِ ـ [2] خَلُعَ.

Pro forma, رَسْمًا ـ لِمُرَاعَاةِ ٱلْعَادَةِ.

Profound, *a.* Deep, عَمِيق ـ قَعِير. Dug deep, نَقِير. Intellectually deep, learned, مُتَبَحِّرٌ فِي ٱلْعُلُومِ ـ عَالِمٌ مُتَبَحِّرٌ ـ خَارِق. Secret, مَخْفِيٌّ ـ خَفِيٌّ ـ مَكْتُوم. Thorough, كَامِل ـ كُلِّيّ ـ مُكَمَّل. *See also* Deep, *a.*

Profound, *n.* *See* Abyss, Ocean, *n.*

Profoundly, *ad.* *See* Deeply, *ad.*

Profoundness, *n.* } *See* Depth, *n.*
Profundity, }

Profuse, *a.* Prodigal, lavish, فَاضِل ـ مُفْرِط ـ مُبَذِّر ـ مُسْرِف. Abundant, فَاضِل ـ فَيَّاض. Profuse in speech, فَصِيح ـ بَلِيغ. To be — in speech, بَالَغَ فِي ـ سَبَحَ فِي ٱلْكَلَامِ ـ سَابَ فِي ٱلْكَلِمِ ـ اِنْفَجَرَ (or) تَفَجَّرَ بِٱلْكَرَمِ ٱلْكَلَامِ. He was — in his liberality, *See also* Lavish, Prodigal, Exuberant, *a.*

Profusely, *ad.* Lavishly, بِإِسْرَافٍ ـ إِفْرَاطًا ـ تَبْذِيرًا ـ بِإِفْرَاطٍ. With exuberance, لِلْغَايَةِ ـ كَثِيرًا ـ بِوَفْرَةٍ.

Profuseness, *n.* Prodigality, waste, إِفْرَاط ـ إِسْرَاف ـ تَبْذِير ـ بَعْزَقَة ـ تَفْرِيط. *See also* Lavishness, Prodigality, *n.*

Profusion, *n.* Great abundance, فُضُول ـ فَيْض ـ كَثْرَة ـ وَفْرَة ـ بَرَكَة. *See also* Profuseness, *n.*

Prog, *n.* Victuals picked up here and there, طَعَامٌ قُمَاشٍ ـ قَشّ ـ مَطَاعِمُ لُقَاطٍ. One who picks up victuals here and there, قَشَّاش ـ مُلْقِطُ ٱلْمَطَاعِمِ.

Progenitor, *n.* سَلَف *pl.* أَسْلَاف — جِدّ *pl.* أَجْدَاد.

Progeny, *n.* نَسْل *pl.* أَنْسَال — آل — ذُرِّيَّة — أَوْلَادٌ وَأَحْفَادٌ — أَوْلَاد. *See also* Offspring, Race, *n.*

Prognathous, *a.* كَابِسُ ٱلْأَفْكَاكِ — بَارِزُ ٱلْأَفْكَاكِ.

Prognosis, *n.* As of a disease, ٱلْاِسْتِدْلَالُ بِٱلْعَلَامَاتِ ٱلْحَاضِرَةِ عَلَى نَتَائِجِ ٱلْعِلَّةِ — تَشْخِيصُ ٱلْأَمْرَاضِ. To take the — of a disease, شَخَّصَ ٱلْمَرَضَ.

Prognostic, *n.* عَلَامَة — دِلَالَة — عَلَامَةٌ دَالَّةٌ — مَوْعِد *pl.* مَوَاعِد. *See also* Foreboding, *n.*

Prognostic, *a.* دَالٌّ عَلَى — مَوْعِدٌ بِ — مُشِيرٌ بِ. *See also* Foreboding, Foreshowing, *a.*

Prognosticate, *v.t.* دَلَّ عَلَى — نَبَّأَ بِ — أَوْعَدَ — وَعَدَ بِ *aor.* يَعِدُ — تَنَبَّأَ بِ — يَدُلُّ *aor.* *See also to* Foretell, Predict, Presage, Threaten, *v.t.*

Prognostication, *n.* The act of, وَعْد — مَوْعِدَة — تَنَبُّؤ. A foretoken, دِلَالَة — إِشَارَة — إِشَارَةٌ سَابِقَةٌ — خَبَر.

Prognosticator, *n.* عَرَّاف — مُخَبِّر — نَبِيٌّ *pl.* أَنْبِيَاءُ.

Programme, *n.* سِيَاقَة — بَيَان — لَائِحَة — تَعْرِيف — تَعْرِيفٌ — مُخْتَصَر — تَقْوِيم.

Progress, *n.* A course or moving forward, قُدُوم — سِيرَة — تَقَدُّم — تَقَدُّم — مَسِيرَة — إِسْتِدْرَاج — تَدْرِيج — رَوَاج. Leisurely progress, إِرْوَاد — رُود — زَحْف — زُحُوف. Passage from place to place, جَوَلَان. Advance in business or knowledge, إِفْلَاح — رَوَاج — نَجَاح — تَرَقٍّ — تَقَدُّم. Increase, اِزْدِيَاد — زِيَادَة. A triumphant —, سَيْرُ ٱلْمُظَفَّرِ ٱلْمَنْصُورِ. We are not making —, مَا نَحْنُ بِمُنْجِحِينَ. The matter is making —, ٱلْأَمْرُ سَالِكٌ مَسْلَكَ ٱلتَّقَدُّمِ. The glorious — of the age, ٱلتَّقَدُّمَاتُ ٱلْجَلِيلَةُ ٱلْعَصْرِيَّةُ. To make —; *see to* Progress. *See also* Advance, *n.*

Progress, *v.i.* To move forward, دَرَجَ [2] — تَدَرَّجَ — تَقَدَّمَ. To — leisurely, أَرْوَدَ — زَحَفَ. To — rapidly, of an affair, وَشُكَ *aor.* يَوْشُكُ — وَشُكَ. To make improvement, اِزْدَادَ فِي ٱلنَّجَاحِ — سَارَ فِي سَبِيلِ ٱلنَّجَاحِ. To — in science, تَرَقَّى فِي ٱلْعِلْمِ. To make to —, سَيَّرَ فِي سَبِيلِ ٱلنَّجَاحِ. The work begins to —, أَخَذَ ٱلْعَمَلُ فِي ٱلنَّجَاحِ [2].

Progression, *n.* Movement, حَرَكَة; movement forward, تَدَرُّج — تَقَدُّم. Arithmetical —, تَسَلْسُلُ ٱلْجَمْعِ وَٱلطَّرْحِ. Geometrical —, تَسَلْسُلُ ٱلضَّرْبِ وَٱلْقِسْمَةِ. Unbroken —, مُتَابَعَة. Progression and retrocession, ٱلتَّقَدُّمُ وَٱلتَّأَخُّرُ. *See also* Progress, *n.*

Progressional, *a.* إِسْتِدْرَاجِيّ.

Progressive, *a.* تَدْرِيجِيّ — مُتَقَدِّم — مُتَزَايِدٌ بِٱلتَّدْرِيجِ.

Progressively, *ad.* بِٱلتَّدْرِيجِ — تَدْرِيجًا — إِسْتِدْرَاجًا.

Progressiveness, *n.* تَدْرِيج — تَرْوِيج — تَقَدُّم — إِسْتِدْرَاج.

Pro hac vice, مُخْتَصٌّ بِهٰذَا ٱلصَّدَدِ — خُصُوصًا.

Prohibit, *v.t.* To interdict, forbid, حَرَّمَ — زَجَرَ عَن [2] — حَرَّجَ — مَنَعَ ٱلنَّاسَ عَن — حَظَرَ — حَظَرَ عَلَى [2]. To — or forbid to, عَصَرَ — حَرَّمَ عَلَى — حَرَّجَ عَلَى. To keep one from, to prevent, اِعْتَصَرَ — حَجَرَ عَن [2] — نَهَى عَن. To —, by speech or reproof, زَجَرَ [2]. To be prohibited, حُرِمَ; to be prohibited to, حُرِمَ عَلَى. Power to order and to —, ٱلْأَمْرُ وَٱلنَّهْيُ. He (the judge) prohibited him from wasting his property, حَجَرَ [2] — حَجَرَ عَلَيْهِ عَلَيْهِ فِي مَالِهِ.

Prohibited, *a.* Prevented, مَمْنُوع — مَحْجُور. Forbidden, مَحْظُور — حَرَام — حِجْر — حَاجُور — مَحْجُور — مَحْرُوم — مُحَرَّم. Anything —, حَرَام — حِرْمَة. Prohibited things, مَنَاهِي. Prohibited trade, تِجَارَةٌ مَمْنُوعَةٌ. The — degrees, of marriage, دَرَجَاتُ ٱلْقَرَابَةِ ٱلَّتِي لَا يَحِلُّ فِيهَا ٱلزَّوَاجُ. One who is —, as from using his property as he pleases, مَحْجُورٌ عَلَيْهِ. This is —, unlawful, to you, هٰذَا حِجْرٌ عَلَيْكَ.

Prohibition, *n.* The act of interdicting, حَرَم — حَظْر — حُرْمَة *pl.* حُرَم — زَجْر — حَرَج — تَحْرِيج — نُهْيَة *pl.* نُهًا — نَهْي. Prevention, مَنْع — إِمْتِنَاع — مُمَانَعَة. The Divine prohibitions, حُرُمَاتُ ٱللّٰهِ. A legal —, مُمَانَعَةٌ قَانُونِيَّةٌ.

Prohibitionist, *n.* As of a foreign trade, مُعِيقٌ (or) مُعَوِّقُ ٱلتِّجَارَةِ ٱلْأَجْنَبِيَّةِ.

Prohibitive, *a.* }
Prohibitory, } مَنَّاع — تَحْرِيجِيّ — مُعَوِّق. Prohibitive measures, مُعَامَلَةٌ زَجْرِيَّةٌ — مُعَامَلَةٌ ٱلْحِصَارِيَّةُ. A — system, أُصُولٌ زَجْرِيَّةٌ — أُصُولُ ٱلْحِصَارِيَّةِ.

Project, *v.t.* To throw out, throw, رَمَى — طَرَحَ — أَلْقَى. To plan, draw, رَسَمَ [2] — صَوَّرَ. To design, intend, قَصَدَ — هَمَّ بِ [2] — تَنَوَّى — تَعَمَّدَ. To conceive, تَخَيَّلَ — تَصَوَّرَ.

Project, *v.i.* To jut out, نَتَأَ — أَشْرَفَ — بَرَزَ [2].

Project, *n.* A design, قَصْد — نِيَّة — مُرَاد — مَرَام — مَطْلَب. Delineation, رَسْم — تَصْوِير.

Projectile, *a.* طَارِح — رَامٍ — مُلْقٍ. A — weapon, مِرْمَاة *pl.* مَرَامٍ.

Projecting, *a.* نَاتِئ — نَاتٍ — بَارِز — مُشْرِف — نَاشِع.

Projectile, *n.* جِسْمٌ مَرْمِيٌّ — جِرْمٌ مَحْذُوف — مِرْمَاة *pl.* مَرَام.

Projection, *n.* The act of throwing, رَمْي — طَرْح — إِلْقَاء. A part jutting out, طَنَف *pl.* طُنُوف — خَرْم — بُرُوز. A plan, delineation, رَسْم — شَكْل. *See also* Project, *n.*

Projector, *n.* One who plans or delineates, مُصَوِّر ـ رَسَّام . A contriver, مُبْتَدِع ـ بَادِع ـ مُخْتَرِع ـ مُبْدِع .

Projet, n. See Draft, *n.*

Prolapse, *n.*
Prolapsion, } نُزُول ـ سُقُوط .

Prolate, *a.* Enlarged at the poles, of a sphere, كُرَةٌ مُسْتَطِيلَةُ ٱلْقُطْبَيْنِ .

Prolegomena, *n.* مُقَدِّمَات .

Prolepsis, *n.* Anticipation of objections, إِسْتِدْرَاكُ ٱلِاعْتِرَاضِ . Dating an event before the actual time, تَارِيخٌ ـ سَبْقٌ فِي ٱلتَّارِيخِ قَبْلَ ٱلْوَقْتِ .

Proletariat, *n.* The poorer classes, ٱلْفُقَرَآءُ ـ ٱلصَّعَالِيكُ ـ ٱلْأَوْبَاشُ .

Prolific, *a.*
Prolifical, } Fruitful, مُثْمِر ـ ثَمْرَآء ـ خَصِيب ; of a woman, نَثُور ـ إِمْرَأَةٌ نَثُورٌ ـ إِمْرَأَةٌ نَفُوضٌ ـ نَسُولَة . To be — in herbage, غَنِيَ بِعُشْبٍ .

Prolix, *a.* مُطَوَّل ـ نَفِس ـ مُفَصَّل ـ مُطِيل ـ مُبَالِغ . To be —, أَطَالَ ٱلْكَلَامَ ـ بَالَغَ فِي ٱلْكَلَامِ ـ سَابَ فِي ٱلْكَلَامِ . A — book, كِتَابٌ نَفِسٌ .

Prolixity, *n.*
Prolixness, } إِطَالَةُ ٱلْكَلَامِ ـ تَطْوِيلُ ٱلْكَلَامِ ـ مُبَالَغَة .

Prolixly, *ad.* بِٱلْقِيلِ ـ بِإِطَالَةِ ٱلْكَلَامِ ـ بِتَفْصِيلٍ ـ بِمُبَالَغَةٍ وَٱلْقَالِ .

Prolocutor, *n.* رَئِيسُ مَجْلِسِ قُسُوسٍ ـ صَدْرُ قَوْمِ ٱلْإِكْلِيرُسِ .

Prologue, *n.* خُطْبَة ـ مُقَدِّمَة ـ فَاتِحَة .

Prologue, *v.t.* أَفَادَ بِٱلْإِفْتِتَاحِ ـ فَتَحَ بِٱلْإِفْتِتَاحِ ـ قَدَّمَ بِفَاتِحَةٍ .

Prolong, *v.t.* To lengthen in space, طَوَّلَ ـ مَدَّ ; in time, طَوَّلَ ـ أَطَالَ ـ مَدَّ . To —, as of life, طَوَّلَ ـ أَبْقَى . To — time, as to a debtor to pay, مَاطَلَ ـ مَطَلَ بِ ـ مَدَّ . To — the voice, أَبَدَّ نَظْرَةً . To — a look, مَدَّ (or طَرَّنَ) ٱلصَّوْتَ . To delay, عَوَّقَ . To be prolonged, lengthened, طَالَ *aor.* يَطُولُ ـ إِسْتَطَالَ ـ تَطَاوَلَ . He prolonged the time of the assembly, أَطَالَ ٱلْمَجْلِسَ . The council was prolonged, طَالَ ٱلْمَجْلِسُ . The consultation of the council on that matter was prolonged, طَالَتِ ٱلْمُذَاكَرَةُ فِي ٱلْمَجْلِسِ عَلَى ذٰلِكَ . Their life was prolonged, تَطَاوَلَ عَلَيْهِمُ ٱلْعُمْرُ . May God — your days! ٱللّٰهُ يُطَوِّلُ ٱللّٰهُ يَمُدُّ فِي أَيَّامِكَ ـ عُمْرَكَ .

Prolongation, *n.* The act of, إِطَالَة ـ تَطْوِيل ـ مَدّ ـ تَمْدِيد . The being prolonged, إِمْتِدَاد ـ مَدٌّ . Time of delay, مُهْلَة . Postponement, إِمْهَال ـ تَأْخِير .

Promenade, *n.* A walk for amusement or exercise, رِيَاضَة ـ شَمُّ ٱلْهَوَآءِ ـ دَوْرَة ـ مَسِيرَة ـ سَيْر . A place for walking, مَسِيْر ـ مُنْتَزَه ـ مُنْتَزَهَة ـ مُنْتَزَه . To go out for a —, خَرَجَ ـ خَرَجَ يَتَبَسَّطُ ـ يَتَمَشَّى . We have taken a —, دُرْنَا دَوْرَةً .

Promenade, *v.t.* دَارَ فِي ـ تَمَشَّى فِي ـ جَوَّلَ ـ يَجُولُ *aor.* جَالَ فِي .

Promenade, *v.i.* شَمَّ ٱلْهَوَآءَ ـ تَسَيَّرَ ـ تَبَحْبَحَ ـ تَمَشَّى ـ تَنَزَّهَ .

Prominence, *n.*
Prominency, } An elevation, تَعَلٍّ ـ إِرْتِفَاع . A jutting out, بُرُوز ـ نُشُوز ـ حَدَب *pl.* حِدَاب . Conspicuousness, شَرَف ـ إِشْتِهَار ـ سُمْعَة ـ جِهَار ـ جَهْر . A — in a mountain, أَنْفُ جَبَلٍ ـ مَخْرِمُ جَبَلٍ ـ خَرْم . To bring into —, إِشْتَهَرَ ـ شَهَّرَ ـ شَهَرَ . *See also* Protuberance, *n.*

Prominent, *a.* Elevated, مُتَعَلٍّ ـ مُرْتَفِع . Projecting, كَابِس ـ مُشْرِف ـ نَاشِع ـ نَاتِئٌ ـ نَاتٍ . Conspicuous, جَلِيٌّ ـ مَجْهُورٌ بِهِ ـ مَشْهُور ـ شَهِير . Important, chief, أَهَمّ ـ مُهِمٌّ . To be —, to jut out, أَشْرَفَ ـ بَرَزَ ـ نَتَأَ ; to be conspicuous, تَجَلَّى ـ جَهَرَ ـ إِشْتَهَرَ . A — eye, عَيْنٌ ظَاهِرَةٌ . *See also* Protuberant, *a.*

Prominently, *ad.* Standing out, إِشْرَافًا ـ بِبُرُوزٍ ـ بِنُشُوزٍ . Conspicuously, بِجَلَآءٍ ـ بَيَانًا ـ شُهْرَةً ـ إِشْتِهَارًا ـ جَهْرًا .

Promiscuous, *a.* Confounded together, of people, مُؤْتَشِب ـ مُتَشَاوِش ـ مُتَهَاوِش . Indiscriminate, بِدُونِ فَرْقٍ ـ سَوَآءٌ ـ بِلَا تَمْيِيزٍ . General, common, عَامٌّ . A — multitude, لَفِيف ـ أَشَائِبُ *pl.* أُشَابَة .

Promiscuously, *ad.* Confusedly, بِلَا تَمْيِيزٍ ـ بِتَشَوُّشٍ ـ بِتَهَوُّشٍ ـ سَوَآءً . To be mixed together —, of people, تَأَشَّبُوا . To mix together —, أَشَبَ .

Promiscuousness, *n.* Confusion, تَشَوُّش ـ تَهَوُّش ـ تَأَشُّب ـ لِفَافَة ـ لَفِيفَة ـ عَدَمُ تَمْيِيزٍ .

Promise, *n.* عَهْد *pl.* عُهُود ـ وَعْدَة ـ وَعْد *pl.* وُعُود ـ مَوْعُود *pl.* مَوَاعِيد . The time during which a — holds, or the place of a —, a trysting-place, rendezvous, مَوْعِد *pl.* مَوَاعِدُ ـ مِيعَاد . A written obligation, تَمَسُّك . A youth of —, شَبَابٌ يُتَرَقَّبُ مِنْهُ ٱلْخَيْرُ . This — could not be kept, هٰذَا ٱلْوَعْدُ كَانَ دُونَ تَرَوٍّ .

A breach of promise, نَقْضُ ٱلْعَهْدِ ـ إِخْلَافُ ٱلْوَعْدِ .

A breach of promise of marriage, نَقْضُ وَعْدِ ٱلزِّيجَةِ .

An express promise, وَعْدٌ صَرِيحٌ .

An implied promise, وَعْدٌ مُضْمَرٌ ـ وَعْدٌ مُقَدَّرٌ .

The Land of Promise, أَرْضُ ٱلْمِيعَادِ (or ٱلْمَوْعِدِ) ـ أَرْضُ كَنْعَانَ .

To break a promise, خَانَ ٱلْعَهْدَ ـ خَالَفَ ٱلْوَعْدَ ـ أَخْلَفَ ٱلْوَعْدَ .

To break a promise to one, أَخْلَفَهُ مَا وَعَدَهُ .

To fulfil or keep a promise, كَمَّلَ ـ ² قَامَ بِٱلْوَعْدِ ـ ² عَهِدَ ٱلْوَعْدَ ـ وَفَى ٱلْوَعْدَ ـ ٱلْوَعْدَ *aor.* يَفِي. To keep one's promise to, ² عَهِدَ لِ. To make a promise, ² عَهِدَ ـ يَعِدُ *aor.* وَعَدَ.

Promise, *v.t.* عَاهَدَ-عَلَى ـ أَوْعَدَ ـ يَعِدُ *aor.* وَعَدَ-بِ ـ ² عَهِدَ ـ أَعْطَى-عَهْدًا. To portend, أَوْعَدَ. To — one's self, to hope, تَرَقَّبَ ـ تَمَنَّى. They promised one another, of many, تَوَاعَدُوا.

Promisee, *n.* الْمَوْعُودُ لَهُ.

Promiser, *n.* مُتَعَهِّد ـ وَاعِد.

Promising, *a.* Hopeful, لا يَضِيعُ (*or* يَخِيبُ) ٱلرَّجَآءُ فِيهِ.

Promissorily, *ad.* بِسِيَاقَةِ ٱلْوَعْدِ ـ عَلَى وَجْهِ ٱلْوَعْدِ.

Promissory, *n.* مُتَضَمِّنٌ ٱلْوَعْدِ ـ عِدِيٌّ ـ عِدَوِيٌّ. A — note, تَحْوِيل ـ تَمَسُّك.

Promontory, *n.* خَزْم ـ شَنَاخ ـ حَرْف ـ طُنُوف *pl.* طَنَف ـ رَأْس *pl.* رُؤُوس. *See also* Cape, *n.*

Promote, *v.t.* As in rank, رَفَعَ رُتْبَتَهُ ـ ² رَفَعَ دَرَجَتَهُ ـ رَقَّى; to — in rank by degrees, إِسْتَدْرَجَ ـ دَرَّجَ. To contribute to the advancement of, أَنْجَحَ ـ رَوَّجَ ـ قَدَّمَ ـ أَنْجَدَ. To stir up, حَرَّكَ. To render easy, سَهَّلَ ـ مَهَّدَ. To increase, ² زَادَ. Virtue promotes happiness, الفَضِيلَةُ تَزِيدُ ٱلْغِبْطَةَ. It might — his welfare, رُبَّمَا يُزِيدُ خَيْرَهُ. He was promoted to . . . , تَرَقَّى إِلَى.

Promoter, *n.* مُؤَيِّد ـ ظِهْرَة ـ ظَهِير ـ مُرَوِّج.

Promotion, *n.* The act of promoting, in rank, رَفْعٌ فِي ٱلدَّرَجَةِ; of advancing, encouraging, مُظَاهَرَة ـ إِنْجَاد ـ تَرْوِيج ـ تَرْقِيَة. The being promoted, in rank, إِرْتِفَاعٌ فِي ٱلدَّرَجَةِ. Advancement, تَقْدِيم ـ تَنْجِيح ـ تَرَقٍّ ـ تَقَدُّم.

Promotive, *a.* مُرَقٍّ ـ مُقَدِّم ـ مُؤَيِّد ـ مُرَوِّج. Augmentative, مُزِيد.

Prompt, *a.* نَدْب *pl.* نُدُوب *and* نُدَبَآء ـ مِنْدَبِي ـ وَجْز ـ مُسْتَعِدٌّ ـ خَفِيف ـ سَرِيع ـ وَشِيك. Prompt payment, نَقْد. Prompt in speech, طَقْطُوق. Prompt to reply, ذُو بَدِيهَةٍ ـ مِبْدَهٌ ـ وَجْز ـ حَاضِرُ ٱلْجَوَابِ ـ نَقِل. To be —, ready, quick, ² نَدَبَ ـ يَوْشُكُ *aor.* وَشُكَ ـ تَوَجَّزَ ـ يَجِزُ *aor.* وَجَزَ.

Prompt, *v.t.* To excite to action, ² حَثَّ-عَلَى ـ إِسْتَفَزَّ ـ رَوَّجَ ـ هَيَّجَ ـ أَنْهَضَ. To assist a speaker when at a loss, عَلَّمَ ـ ذَكَّرَ ـ لَقَّنَ ـ ² فَتَحَ عَلَى. To suggest to the mind, أَلْهَمَ ـ حَدَّثَ-بِ ـ أَخْطَرَ-بِٱلْبَالِ. To ask to be prompted, إِسْتَفْتَحَ.

Prompter, *n.* One who incites, مُرَوِّج ـ مُهَيِّج. One who reminds a speaker, مُلَقِّن. An adviser, وَاعِظ ـ نَاصِح.

Promptitude, *n.* }
Promptness, } سُرْعَة ـ خِفَّة ـ وَشَاكَة ـ وَشْك ـ سَرَاح ـ إِسْتِعْدَاد; in speech, طَقْطَقَة.

Promptly, *ad.* Readily, بِٱلْعَجَلِ ـ بِسُرْعَةٍ ـ بِوَشَاكَةٍ ـ وَشْكًا. Immediately, حَالًا ـ عَلَى ٱلْفَوْرِ.

Promulgate, *v.t.* أَشَاعَ بِ ـ ² شَاعَ بِ ـ أَشْهَرَ ـ ² شَهَرَ ـ أَصْدَرَ. To be promulgated, يَشِيعُ *aor.* شَاعَ ـ إِشْتَهَرَ.

Promulgation, *n.* The act of, إِشَاعَة ـ إِشْهَار ـ شَهْر. A publication, notice, إِشْتِهَار ـ إِعْلَان.

Promulgator, *n.* مُشِيع ـ مُشْتَهِر.

Prone, *a.* *See under* Apt, Inclined, Disposed, *a.*

Proneness, *n.* *See* Aptness, Inclination, *n.*

Prong, *n.* شُعْبَة *pl.* شُعَب: Stick the meat on the prongs of the fork or skewer, إِغْرِزِ ٱللَّحْمَ فِي شُعَبِ ٱلسَّفُّودِ.

Pronged, *a.* ذُو شُعَب.

Pronominal, *a.* مِنْ جِنْسِ ٱلضَّمِيرِ ـ مُتَعَلِّقٌ بِٱلضَّمِيرِ.

Pronominally, *ad.* فِي حَالِ ٱلضَّمِيرِ ـ كَضَمِيرٍ.

Pronoun, *n.* ضَمِير *pl.* ضَمَائِرُ ـ إِسْمٌ مُضْمَرٌ ـ مُضْمَر *pl.* مُضْمَرَات.

Demonstrative pronoun, إِسْمُ إِشَارَةٍ ـ إِسْمُ ٱلْإِشَارَةِ.

Indefinite pronoun, إِسْمٌ مُبْهَمٌ.

Personal pronoun, ضَمِيرٌ شَخْصِيٌّ.

Possessive pronoun, ضَمِيرٌ مَجْرُورٌ.

Relative pronoun, إِسْمٌ مَوْصُولٌ.

Pronounce, *v.t.* To utter, ² لَفَظَ ـ ² نَطَقَ بِ ـ تَفَوَّهَ بِ ـ عَبَّرَ عَنْ ـ تَلَفَّظَ بِ ـ تَلَفَّظَ ـ ² لَفَظَ بِ. To recite, ² تَلَا ـ ² قَرَأَ. To say, يَقُولُ *aor.* قَالَ. To declare formally, أَثْبَتَ ـ ² نَطَقَ بِٱلْقَضَاءِ ـ ² حَكَمَ شِفَاهًا بِ. To — sentence, بَيَّنَ.

Pronounceable, *a.* مِمَّا يُنْطَقُ بِهِ ـ يُتَلَفَّظُ.

Pronunciation, *n.* تَلَفُّظ ـ لَفْظ ـ نُطْق. Words difficult of —, تَنَافُر.

Proof, *n.* A test, إِمْتِحَان ـ تَجْرِبَة ـ خِبْرَة. That which furnishes evidence, حُجَّة *pl.* حُجَج ـ دَلِيل *pl.* دَلَائِل ـ بَيِّنَة ـ بَيَان ـ بُرْهَان *pl.* بَرَاهِين. Evidence, testimony, شَهَادَة ـ إِسْنَاد *pl.* أَسَانِيدُ. Strength of spirits, عِيَار ـ عِبَارَةٌ عَنْ قُوَّةِ رُوحِ ٱلْعَرَقِ. An impression for correction, نُسْخَةٌ لِلتَّصْحِيحِ ـ تَجْرِبَة. A clear or decided —, بُرْهَانٌ قَاطِعٌ ـ بَيِّنَة. The — of that is. . . , وَٱلدَّلِيلُ عَلَى ذٰلِكَ هُوَ ـ وَٱلشَّاهِدُ عَلَى ذٰلِكَ هُوَ. Not requiring —, غَنِيٌّ عَنِ ٱلْبَيَانِ. By many proofs, بِبَرَاهِينَ كَثِيرَةٍ. To give — of, to show, أَبْدَى ـ أَظْهَرَ ـ بَيَّنَ. To adduce —, ² أَتَى بِبَيِّنَاتٍ ـ قَدَّمَ ٱلْبَرَاهِينَ. To put to the —, إِمْتَحَنَ ـ جَرَّبَ ـ إِحْتَجَّ ـ إِحْتَجَّ.

Proof, *a.* Proof against, لا يَفْعَلُ فِيهِ ٱ . . . ـ لا يُؤَثِّرُ فِيهِ ٱ . . . ـ لا تُؤَثِّرُ فِيهِ ـ مَعْصُومٌ مِنَ ٱ . . . ـ لا يَنْفُذُ فِيهِ ٱ . . . Bomb-proof,

أَلْقُشْبُرَةُ. Water-proof, لا يَتَطَرَّقُ إِلَيْهِ ٱلْمَآءُ. Proof against conviction, لا يَقْبَلُ ٱلْحُجَّةَ ـ لا يَبْكُتُ بِٱلْحُجَّةِ.

Proofless, *a.* بِلا إِثْبَاتٍ ـ لَيْسَ لَهُ حُجَّةٌ ـ عَدِيمُ ٱلدَّلِيلِ.

Prop, *n.* A stay, support, pillar, دِعَامَةٌ *pl.* دَعَائِمُ ـ دِعَمٌ *pl.* دِعَمٌ ـ عُمْدَةٌ *pl.* أَعْمِدَةٌ ـ عِمَادٌ ـ إِيَادٌ ـ سَنَدٌ *pl.* أَسْنَادٌ ـ مِسْنَدٌ *pl.* مَسَانِدُ. A — of a tree, زَفَرٌ. A — of the people, عِمَادُ ٱلْقَوْمِ. *See also* Support, Stay, *n.*

Prop, *v.t.* دَعَمَ ـ عَمَدَ ـ أَعْمَدَ ـ رَدَأَ ـ أَرْدَأَ ـ سَنَدَ ـ أَسْنَدَ. To aid, back, شَيَّعَ ـ أَيَّدَ ـ ظَاهَرَ. He propped himself upon a staff, إِدَّعَمَ عَلَى عَصًا. He propped himself upon the palms of his hands, إِدَّعَمَ عَلَى رَاحَتَيْهِ. I propped myself upon him, إِعْتَمَدْتُ عَلَيْهِ.

Propagable, *a.* That may be propagated, by generation, مِمَّا يُوَلَّدُ مِنْهُ ـ مِمَّا يَنْمَى. That may be multiplied, مِمَّا يَنْمَى ـ مِمَّا يُكَثَّرُ مِنْهُ ـ قَابِلُ ٱلتَّكْثِيرِ. That may pass from one to another, as a disease, مُعْدٍ ـ مُعْتَدٍ ـ مِمَّا يَتَفَشَّى بِ. That may be spread abroad, يَنْتَشِرُ ـ مِمَّا يُشَاعُ بِهِ ـ مِمَّا يَفْشَى.

Propaganda, *n.* The — of Rome, مَجْمَعٌ فِي رُومِيَّةَ مُخْتَصٌّ بِٱنْتِشَارِ مَذْهَبِ ٱلْبَابَا.

Propagandism, *n.* سَعْيٌ وَغَيْرَةٌ عَلَى ٱنْتِشَارِ ٱلْآرَآءِ وَٱلْمَذَاهِبِ.

Propagandist, *n.* صَاحِبُ غَيْرَةٍ عَلَى ٱنْتِشَارِ ٱلْآرَآءِ وَٱلْمَذَاهِبِ.

Propagate, *v.t.* To multiply by generation, رَبَّى ـ وَلَّدَ ـ أَنْمَى. To multiply, نَمَّى ـ كَثَّرَ. To cause to go from one to another, of a disease, أَعْدَى. To give currency to, to publish, شَاعَ بِ ـ أَشَاعَ بِ ـ أَذَاعَ بِ ـ نَشَرَ ـ إِشْتَهَرَ ـ شَهَرَ. To spread, أَنْشَأَ. To teach, عَلَّمَ ـ لَقَّنَ. To give birth to, to originate, أَوْجَدَ ـ أَحْدَثَ. To be propagated, as a disease, تَفَشَّى بِ ـ فَشَا. To be propagated, multiplied, as of sheep, *etc.*, نَمَا. To be propagated, spread abroad, شَاعَ ـ إِنْتَشَرَ.

Propagate, *v.i.* To have young or issue, وَلَدَ *aor.* يَلِدُ ـ حَمَلَ. To multiply, نَمَا ـ نَمَى ـ كَثُرَ ـ تَكَاثَرَ ـ ثَرَا.

Propagation, *n.* The act of generation, وِلَادَةٌ ـ تَوْلِيدٌ ـ إِنْسَالٌ; of spreading, publishing, إِذَاعَةٌ ـ إِنْتِشَارٌ ـ إِشَاعَةٌ ـ نَشْرٌ; of teaching, تَعْلِيمٌ ـ تَلْقِينٌ; of multiplying, إِنْمَآءٌ ـ تَكْثِيرٌ; of rearing, تَرْبِيَةٌ. The — of a disease, إِعْدَآءُ ٱلدَّآءِ.

Propagator, *n.* One who publishes, مُشِيعٌ ـ نَاشِرٌ; who teaches, مُعَلِّمٌ ـ مُلَقِّنٌ; who rears, مُرَبٍّ; who generates, مُوَلِّدٌ ـ وَالِدٌ; who multiplies, مُكَثِّرٌ.

Propel, *v.t.* To drive, أَزْجَى فِي *or* لِ ـ دَسَعَ ـ دَرَأَ ـ دَسَرَ ـ أَطْرَدَ ـ دَفَعَ ـ سَوَّقَ ـ سَاقَ. To — a thing before one, قَادَ; from behind, to drive, سَاقَ. To be propelled, إِنْدَفَعَ ـ تَسَوَّقَ ـ إِطَّرَدَ.

Propeller, *n.* مِدْرَأٌ ـ دَافِعٌ ـ سَوَّاقٌ ـ طَرَّادٌ ـ دَاسِرٌ. A screw —, of a steamer, مِدْرَأُ ٱلْبَاخِرَةِ.

Propense, *a.* *See* Inclined, Disposed, *a.*

Propension, *n.* } Inclination, مَيَلَانٌ ـ مَيْلٌ. Bent of mind,
Propensity, } مَيْلٌ ـ مَيَلَانٌ ـ طَيَّةٌ ـ شَوْقٌ. To show a — for, تَشَوَّقَ. *See also under* Inclination, Disposition, *n.*

Proper, *a.* One's own, مُخْتَصٌّ بِ ـ مَخْصُوصٌ ـ خَاصٌّ لِ ـ ذَاتِيٌّ. Suited to, مَحَلٌّ لِ ـ خَلِيقٌ لِ ـ جَدِيرٌ بِ *or* لِ. Correct, fit, مُوَافِقٌ ـ مُنَاسِبٌ ـ لَائِقٌ. Correct, right, مَضْبُوطٌ ـ جَمِيلٌ ـ تَامٌّ ـ مُلَائِمٌ ـ سَوِيٌّ ـ زَيْنٌ ـ مِلَاحٌ *pl.* مَلِيحٌ ـ مُحْكَمٌ ـ صَحِيحٌ ـ صَوَابٌ. Real, أَصْلِيٌّ ـ حَقِيقِيٌّ. A — name, إِسْمٌ خَاصٌّ. A — speech, قَوْلٌ صَوَابٌ. One's own — house, دَارُهُ ـ بَيْتُهُ ـ دَارٌ خَاصَّةٌ بِهِ. In their own — tongue, فِي لُغَتِهِمْ. The — element of any creature, مَكَانٌ ـ مَوْضِعٌ. It would be more — for him to …, أَوْلَى بِهِ أَنْ. It is — that you should do it, لا يَلِيقُ بِكَ بِٱلْأَحْرَى أَنْ تَفْعَلَهُ. It is not — for you to say so, لا يَلِيقُ بِكَ أَنْ تَقُولَ كَذَا. It is not — for me to …, لا يَسْمَحُ لِي أَنْ. To deem —, إِسْتَصْوَبَ ـ إِسْتَحْسَنَ.

Properly, *ad.* Fitly, كَمَا يَجِبُ ـ بِلِيَاقَةٍ ـ مُنَاسَبَةً. Exactly, correctly, بِٱلصَّوَابِ ـ بِٱلتَّحْكِيمِ ـ بِضَبْطٍ ـ بِغَايَةِ ٱلْإِتْقَانِ. Properly dressed, مُهَنْدَمُ ٱللِّبَاسِ ـ نَقِيُّ ٱلثِّيَابِ.

Property, *n.* A peculiar quality, خَاصِّيَّةٌ ـ خَاصَّةٌ *pl.* خَوَاصُّ ـ كَيْفِيَّةٌ مَخْصُوصَةٌ ـ خَصِيصَةٌ *pl.* خَصَائِصُ. The —, as of any stones or minerals, شَأْنٌ *pl.* شُؤُونٌ. An essential —, ذَاتِيَّةٌ. A quality, disposition, خَصْلَةٌ *pl.* خِصَالٌ ـ شِيمَةٌ *pl.* شِيَمٌ ـ صِفَةٌ ـ خُلَّةٌ ـ صِنْفٌ. Ownership, حَقٌّ بِ ـ إِسْتِمْلَاكٌ ـ تَمَلُّكٌ. Possessions, goods, wealth, عِلَاقَةٌ ـ مُلْكٌ *pl.* أَمْلَاكٌ ـ رِزْقٌ *pl.* أَرْزَاقٌ ـ مَالٌ *pl.* أَمْوَالٌ ـ مَتَاعٌ. Absolute —, مُلْكٌ مُطْلَقٌ. Fundamental —, أَمْلَاكٌ. Real —, عَقَارٌ ـ عَقَارٌ وَضِيَاعٌ ـ عِكْرٌ. Government —, مِيرِيَّةٌ. Foundational —, أَمْلَاكٌ مَوْقُوفَةٌ. Newly acquired —, طَرِيفٌ. Property which is bound up and not available, مَالٌ رَتَجٌ. Property, landed estate, عُقْدَةٌ *pl.* عُقَدٌ. Literary —, مَالُ ٱلتَّآلِيفَاتِ ـ تَصَرُّفٌ مَعْنَوِيٌّ ـ مَعْنَوِيَّةٌ. Possessing much —, ثَرْوَةٌ ـ صَاحِبُ ثَرْوَةٍ ـ مُعْفِرٌ ـ ثَرِيٌّ. To have or take the sole — in anything, إِسْتَبَدَّ بِٱلْمَالِ ـ تَفَرَّدَ بِٱلْمَالِ. To make over — to another, to put him in possession of it, أَمْلَكَ ـ مَلَّكَ: To come into one's —, تَصَرَّفَ بِمَالِهِ.

Prophecy, *n.* نُبُوَّةٌ ـ نِبَاوَةٌ. *See also* Prediction, *n.*

Prophesy, *v.t.* نَبَّأَ ب ـ نَبَّأَ ـ أَنْبَأَ ب. To — to of ..., نَبَّأَ-ب. To exercise the office of a prophet, تَنَبَّأَ.

Prophesy, *v.i.* أَخْبَرَ بِٱلْغَيْبِ ـ تَنَبَّأَ.

Prophet, *n.* نَبِيٌّ *pl.* أَنْبِيَآءُ. A false —, نَبِيٌّ كَذَّابٌ *pl.* أَنْبِيَآءُ كَذَبَةٌ. No one is a — in his own country, (prov.) العَالِمُ فِي أَرْضِ مِيلَادِهِ مِثْلَ ٱلذَّهَبِ فِي مَعْدِنِهِ: *Literally*, the learned man in his own country is like gold in the mine.

Prophetess, *n.* نَبِيَّةٌ.

Prophetic, *a.* } Prophetical, } مُخْتَصٌّ بِٱلنَّبِيِّ ـ نَبَوِيٌّ.

Prophetically, *ad.* إِنْبَآءً ب ـ تَنْبِئَةً ـ بِوَجْهِ ٱلنُّبُوَّةِ.

Prophylactic, *n.* دَوَآءٌ لِحِفْظِ ٱلصِّحَّةِ ـ عِلَاجٌ مُوَقٍّ ٱلصِّحَّةِ.

Propinquity, *n.* دَنَاوَةٌ ـ قَرَابَةٌ ـ قُرْبٌ.

Propitiable, *a.* Appeasable, يُسَكَّنُ غَضَبُهُ. That may be made propitious, favourable to, يُوَفَّقُ ل ـ يُعَطَّفُ عَلَى.

Propitiate, *v.t.* To render one favourable, إِسْتَعْطَفَ. To conciliate, وَفَّقَ ـ صَالَحَ ـ أَصْلَحَ. To pacify, لَثَّمَ ـ أَهْدَأَ. To gain over, رَبِحَ ـ إِسْتَمْلَكَ.

Propitiation, *n.* The act of making favourable, إِسْتِعْطَاف; of appeasing, تَسْكِين ـ إِهْدَآء; of reconciling, مُصَالَحَة ـ تَوْفِيق ـ إِصْلَاح. An atonement, كَفَّارَةٌ. To offer a —, قَدَّمَ كَفَّارَةً.

Propitiator, *n.* One who appeases, مُسَكِّنُ ٱلْغَضَبِ ـ مُهْدِئٌ; one who conciliates, مُصَالِح ـ مُوَفِّق; one who offers an atonement, مُقَدِّمُ كَفَّارَةٍ.

Propitiatory, *a.* Making favourable, مُسْتَعْطِف; appeasing, مُسَكِّن ـ مُهْدِئٌ; reconciling, مُصَالِح ـ مُوَفِّق; atoning, مُكَفِّرٌ عن ـ مُفْدِئٌ ـ جَازٍ.

Propitiatory, *n.* The mercy seat, عَرْشُ ٱلرَّحْمَةِ. The lid of the ark of the covenant, غِطَآءُ تَابُوتِ ٱلْعَهْدِ.

Propitious, *a.* Kindly disposed, gracious, كَرِيم ـ مَنَّان ـ لَطِيف. Ready to forgive, غَفُور ـ غَفَّار. Favourable to success, مُعَاوِن ـ مُسَاعِد. Favourable, مُوَافِق ـ مُوَفِّق. May God be — to thee! نَعِمَ ٱللّٰهُ بِكَ. May God be — to our design! وَفَّقَ ٱللّٰهُ أَمْرَنَا ـ ٱللّٰهُ يُسَاعِدُنَا عَلَى نَيْلِ ٱلْمُرَادِ. A — time, وَقْتٌ مُوَافِقٌ. Look upon me with a — eye, أُنْظُرْ إِلَيَّ بِعَيْنِ ٱللُّطْفِ.

Propitiously, *ad.* بِتَوْفِيقٍ ـ بِلُطْفٍ ـ بِمُوَافَقَةٍ.

Propitiousness, *n.* مُوَافَقَة ـ لُطْف ـ تَوْفِيق ـ مُسَاعَدَة.

Proplasm, *n.* *See* Mould, *n.*

Propolis, *n.* مَادَّةٌ لَزِجَةٌ تَسُدُّ بِهَا ٱلنَّحْلُ خِلَالَ ٱلْقَفِيرِ.

Proponent, *n.* *See* Proposer, *n.*

Proportion, *n.* Adaptation of one thing to another, تَنَاسُب ـ مُنَاسَبَة ـ مُطَابَقَة ـ مُمَاثَلَة. Symmetry, shape, خَلْق ـ خِلْقَة ـ هِنْدَام. Of perfect proportions, of a man, خَلْقٌ غَمْرٌ. A share, portion, حِصَّة ـ مِقْدَارٌ مُنَاسِبٌ. Size, capacity, سَعَة. A man perfect in —, رَجُلٌ تَامُّ ٱلْخَلْقِ. In — to, عَلَى قَدْرِ ـ بِٱلنِّسْبَةِ إِلَى. Having the proportions of an elephant, فِي تَقَاطِيعِ ٱلْفِيلِ. Mathematical —, نِسْبَة ـ مُعَادَلَة. Rule of —, in arithmetic, قَاعِدَةُ ٱلْأَرْبَعَةِ ٱلْمُتَنَاسِبَةِ. Arithmetical —, تَنَاسُبٌ عَدَدِيٌّ. Geometrical —, تَنَاسُبٌ هَنْدَسِيٌّ.

Proportion, *v.t.* To measure to or for, قَدَّرَ-عَلَى ـ [2] خَلَقَ-ل ـ قَاسَ-عَلَى ـ نَاسَبَ-ل. To make symmetrical, هَنْدَمَ ـ عَدَّلَ. To be proportioned to, نَاسَبَ. Proportion your expenses to your income, عَلَى قَدْرِ بِسَاطِكَ ٱمْدُدْ رِجْلَيْكَ *lit.* Stretch your legs according to the length of your carpet; (prov.).

Proportionable, *a.* That may be proportioned, يُتَنَاسَبُ. Suitable, مُنَاسِب.

Proportionably, *ad.* مُنَاسَبَةً ـ بِٱلْمُنَاسَبَةِ ـ بِٱلتَّنَاسُبِ.

Proportional, *a.* } مُنَاسِب ـ مُتَنَاسِب ـ مُعْتَدِل ـ مُهَنْدَم.
Proportioned, } Well —, مُعْتَدِل ـ مُتَنَاسِبُ ٱلْبِنْيَةِ. Ill —, غَيْرُ مُعْتَدِلٍ ـ غَيْرُ مُهَنْدَمٍ.

Proportional, *n.* A proportional quantity, مُتَنَاسِب. A mean —, مُتَنَاسِبٌ وَسَطٌ.

Proportionality, *n.* تَنَاسُب ـ مُنَاسَبَة.

Proportionally, *ad.* بِٱلتَّنَاسُبِ ـ بِٱلْمُنَاسَبَةِ ـ بِهِنْدَامٍ.

Proportionate, *a.* مُتَنَاسِب.

Proportionate, *v.t.* *See to* Proportion, *v.t.*

Proportionately, *ad.* بِمُنَاسَبَةٍ ـ بِهِنْدَامٍ ـ بِٱعْتِدَالٍ.

Proportioned, *a.* *See under* Proportional, *a.*

Proportionless, *a.* بِلَا مُنَاسَبَةٍ ـ مِنْ غَيْرِ هِنْدَامٍ.

Proposal, *n.* An offer, تَخْيِير ـ عَرْض ـ مَعْرُوض ـ قَوْل. A prospectus, بَيَان ـ سِيَاقَة. A design, قَصْد ـ نِيَّة ـ مَطْلَب. A — of marriage, خَطْب ـ خِطْبَة. *See also under* Overture, *n.*

Propose, *v.t.* To offer, put forward, خَيَّرَ ـ عَرَضَ ـ طَرَحَ ـ قَدَّمَ. He proposed the thing to him, عَرَضَ عَلَيْهِ ٱلشَّيْءَ. To — marriage to, خَطَبَ ـ أَخْطَبَ ـ [2] عَرَضَ عَلَى-ٱلزَّوَاجِ. He proposed the question to him, طَرَحَ عَلَيْهِ ٱلْمَسْأَلَةَ. *See also to* Purpose, *v.i.*

Proposer, *n.* One who makes a proposition, طَارِحُ مَسْأَلَةٍ ـ مُقَدِّمُ مَسْأَلَةٍ ـ مُبَلِّغُ ٱلْمَعْرُوضِ.

Proposition, *n.* Something set forth, مَوْضُوع ـ قَضِيَّة *pl.* قَضَايَا.

A query, demand, مَطْلَب ـ مَسْأَلَة *pl.* مَسَائِل. A prelude, مُقَدِّمَة. An admissible —, مَطْلَب مَقْبُول. The subject of a —, المُسْنَد ; the second —, or predicate, المُسْنَد إِلَيْهِ.

Propositional, *a.* مُحْتَوٍ عَلَى ـ مُتَضَمِّن مَسْأَلَة ـ مُتَعَلِّق بِقَضِيَّة ـ مَوْضُوع.

Propound, *v.t.* عَرَضَ ـ طَرَحَ ـ قَدَّمَ : He propounded a proverb, ضَرَبَ مَثَلًا.

Propounder, *n.* As of a proverb, ضَارِب مَثَل. *See also* Proposer, *n.*

Proprietary, *n.* A possessor in his own right, صَاحِب مَال ـ صَاحِب ـ صَاحِب مُلْك.

Proprietary, *a.* مُتَعَلِّق بِالْمُلْك. A — right, حَقّ صَاحِب ـ حَقّ بِالْمُلْك ـ الْمُلْك.

Proprietor, *n.* رَبّ *pl.* أَرْبَاب ـ مَوْلَى *pl.* مَوَالٍ ـ صَاحِب *pl.* أَصْحَاب ـ صَاحِب المَال. A large landed —, مُعْقِر.

Proprietorship, *n.* حَقّ ب ـ حَقّ ـ مُلْك ـ حَقّ الْمُلْك.

Proprietress, *n.* مَوْلَاة ـ صَاحِبَة ـ صَاحِبَة المَال.

Propriety, *n.* Appropriateness, لِيَاقَة ـ مُنَاسَبَة ; fitness, جَدَارَة ـ مُوَافَقَة. Accuracy, دِقَّة ـ صِحَّة ـ ضَبْط. Decorum, المُتَوَجِّب ـ الوَاجِب ـ أَرْكَان الآدَاب ـ أَدَب ـ تَهْذِيب. Propriety of speech, ضَبْط الكَلَام ـ الكَلَام. To observe the proprieties, قَعَدَ فِي أَدَبِهِ ـ حَفِظَ النَّامُوس. Contrary to —, ضِدّ الأَدَب ـ مُخَالِف الأَدَب.

Propugn, *v.t.* *See to* Defend, *v.t.*

Propugner, *n.* *See* Defender, *n.*

Propulsion, *n.* طَرْح ـ سَوْق ـ دَفْع ـ دَسْع ـ دَسْر.

Propulsive, *a.* طَارِح ـ سَائِق ـ دَافِع ـ دَاسِع ـ دَاسِر.

Propylon, *n.* *See* Porch, Portico, *n.*

Pro rata, *ad.* عَلَى قَدْر قِسْط الحِسَاب.

Pro re nata, *ad.* حَسَب الاِقْتِضَاء.

Prorogation, *n.* As of parliament, *etc.*, تَأْخِير ـ تَعْطِيل ـ تَعْطِيل مُوَقَّت. *See also* Delay, Adjournment, *n.*

Prorogue, *v.t.* As of parliament, *etc.*, أَخَّرَ ـ سَوَّفَ ـ إِلَى ـ حَذَفَ ـ عَطَّلَ ـ لِوَقْت ـ غَيْر وَقْت.

Proruption, *n.* *See* Eruption, *n.*

Prosaic, *a.* Consisting of prose, مَنْثُور ـ نَثْر ـ نَثْرِيّ. Dull, uninteresting, تَافِه ـ مُزَعِّل ـ مُمِلّ ـ سَقِيطَة ـ مُنَفِّر.

Prosaist, *n.* A writer of prose, مُؤَلِّف نَثْر.

Proscenium, *n.* صَدْر مَلْعَب التِّيَاتْرُو (or المَرْسَح).

Proscribe, *v.t.* To outlaw, حَكَمَ عَلَى ـ بِالطَّرْد ـ حَكَمَ عَلَى ـ بِالنَّفْي. To condemn, أَوْقَعَ عَلَى ـ ب. To cast off, renounce, reject one, خَلَعَ. To declare unlawful, حَرَّمَ. To prevent, مَنَعَ. To put an end to, to suspend, أَبْطَلَ. To doom to death, أَمَرَ بِقَتْلِهِ. To expel, طَرَدَ.

Proscriber, *n.* مُبْطِل ـ طَارِد ـ مَانِع ـ حَارِم.

Proscription, *n.* Condemning to exile, حُكْم بِالطَّرْد ـ أَمْر بِالنَّفْي. Rejection, حِرْمَان ـ حَرْم ـ طَرْد ـ خَلْع. Dooming to death, حُكْم بِالمَوْت. Suspension, putting an end to, إِبْطَال.

Proscriptive, خَالِع ـ حَارِم ـ طَارِد ـ مُحَرِّم ـ مُبْطِل ـ مَانِع ـ حَاكِم عَلَى.

Prose, *n.* مَنْثُور ـ نَثْر.

Prose, *a.* مَنْثُور.

Prose, *v.i.* نَثَرَ الكَلَام ـ بَالَغَ فِي الكَلَام ـ سَابَ فِي الكَلِم.

Prosecute, *v.t.* To follow after with a view to accomplish, جَدَّ فِي طَلَب الشَّيْء ـ تَتَبَّعَ ـ تَطَلَّبَ ـ طَلَبَ ـ لَحِقَ ـ اِجْتَهَدَ فِي تَحْصِيل الشَّيْء. To persist in efforts, وَاظَبَ ـ أَدْمَنَ عَلَى ـ أَقَامَ فِي ـ بَارَكَ عَلَى ـ لَزِمَ ب ـ أَصَرَّ عَلَى. To carry on, أَجْرَى ـ سَاقَ *aor.* يَسُوق. To seek to obtain from one by legal process, اِرْتَجَعَ عَلَى ـ فِي الشَّرْع ـ رَجَعَ بِهِ عَلَى كَذَا ـ صَادَرَ ـ عَلَى كَذَا ـ اِدَّعَى عَلَى ـ فِي الشَّرْع. To accuse of a crime, جَنَى عَلَى ـ جَانَى عَلَى ـ تَجَنَّى عَلَى. To —, as for debt, طَالَبَ. He prosecuted him before the judge, حَاكَمَهُ إِلَى الحَاكِم. I prosecuted the man for my due, تَبِعْتُ (or تَابَعْتُ) الرَّجُل بِحَقِّي. *See also under to* Try, *v.t.*

Prosecution, *n.* The act or process of endeavouring to attain, اِرْتِجَاع ـ تَطَلُّب ـ تَتَبُّع ـ جِدّ فِي الطَّلَب ـ جَهْد ـ مُجَاهَدَة ـ اِجْتِهَاد. Endeavour, مَسْعَاة ـ مَسْعًى. Perseverance, مُوَاظَبَة ـ إِدْمَان ـ مُلَازَمَة ـ اِسْتِمْرَار. A legal —, إِقَامَة دَعْوَى ـ مُصَادَرَة ـ مُطَالَبَة شَرْعِيَّة ـ طَلَب إِلَى الشَّرِيعَة ـ مُدَاعَاة قُدَّام الشَّرْع.

Prosecutor, *n.* A plaintiff, مُشْتَكٍ ـ شَاكٍ ـ مُدَّعٍ. A public —, مَأْمُور بِالمُحَاكَمَات الشَّرْعِيَّة. One who carries on, perseveres in, مُدْمِن عَلَى ـ سَائِق ـ مُوَاظِب عَلَى ـ مُصِرّ عَلَى.

Proselyte, *n.* دَخِيل *pl.* دُخَلَاء ـ غِرْس *pl.* أَغْرَاس. To become a — to, دَخَلَ فِي. To gain a —, كَسَبَ دَخِيلًا. *See also* Convert, *n.*

Proselyte, *v.t.* هَدَى ـ إِلَى ـ رَدَّ ـ إِلَى ـ رَجَّعَ ـ إِلَى ـ قَلَبَ إِيمَانَهُ ـ جَلَبَ ـ إِلَى دِين.

Proselytism, *n.* غَيْرَة فِي جَلْب النَّاس إِلَى مَذْهَب مَا.

Proser, *n.* A writer of prose, مُؤَلِّف النَّثْر. A tedious person, سَائِب فِي الحَدِيث ـ نَيْثُرَان ـ نَثِر ; in talk, مُمِلّ ـ شَاقّ.

Prosing, *n.* تَطْوِيل فِي الكَلَام ـ مُبَالَغَة. *See also* Prolixity, *n.*

Prosodial, *a.* } مُتَعَلِّق بِعِلْم العَرُوض ـ عَرُوضِيّ.
Prosodical, }

Prosodian, *n.* }
Prosodist, } مِنْ أَهْلِ عِلْمِ ٱلْعَرُوضِ ـ عَرُوضِيٌّ.

Prosody, *n.* عِلْمُ ٱلْعَرُوضِ ـ عَرُوض.

Prosopopœia, *n.* The figure representing things as persons, نَوْعٌ مِنَ ٱلْبَدِيعِ يَتَّخِذُ بِهِ ٱلْخَطِيبُ شَيْئًا غَيْرَ نَاطِقٍ بِمَنْزِلَةِ نَاطِقٍ; of absent persons introduced as speaking, إِسْتِحْضَارُ شَخْصٍ غَائِبٍ مُتَكَلِّمًا.

Prospect, *n.* A view, مَنْظَرَة ـ مَنْظَر ـ مَطْمَح. Position of the front of a building, وَجْه. A picture, صُورَة ـ رَسْم. Expectation, تَرَصُّد ـ تَرَقُّب ـ إِنْتِظَار ـ مُنْيَة ـ مَأْمُول; ground of expectation, مَأْمُول. A delightful —, مَنْظَرٌ بَهِيجٌ. He has no — of attaining his object, لَا أَمَلَ لَهُ بِنَوَالِ آرَابِهِ. He has no prospects, لَيْسَ لَهُ بَابٌ. In prospect, expected, مُنْتَظَر ـ مُتَرَقَّب. The house had a southern —, كَانَ وَجْهُ ٱلْبَيْتِ نَحْوَ ٱلْجَنُوبِ.

Prospective, *a.* At a distance, فِي ٱلْبُعْدِ ـ بَعِيد. Future, فِي ٱلْمُسْتَقْبَلِ ـ قَابِل. Hoped for, مُنْتَظَر ـ مَأْمُول.

Prospective, *n.* مَنْظَرٌ مُمْتَدٌّ طُولًا وَعَرْضًا.

Prospectively, *ad.* إِنْتِظَارًا ـ فِي ٱلْمُسْتَقْبِلِ.

Prospectus, *n.* جَدْوَلُ بَيَانٍ ـ وَرَقَةُ تَعْرِيفٍ ـ بَيَان ـ سِيَاقَة ـ إِعْلَان.

Prosper, *v.i.* To be or to become successful, to thrive, سَعِدَ ـ نَجَحَ ـ إِسْتَفْلَحَ ـ أَفْلَحَ ـ تَوَفَّقَ ـ أَنْجَحَ ـ سُعِدَ. This shall not —, هٰذَا لَا يَنْجَحُ. I wish you to —, أَرُومُ أَنْ تَكُونَ نَاجِحًا. To grow, نَمَا ـ نَمَى.

Prosper, *v.t.* أَنْجَحَ ـ وَفَّقَ ـ يَسَّرَ لِ ـ أَسْعَدَ: God prospered him, أَنْجَحَهُ ٱللّٰهُ.

Prosperity, *n.* Success, نَجَاح ـ إِقْبَال ـ صَلَاح ـ خَيْر ـ فَلَاح ـ غِبْطَة ـ غَضَارَة ـ تَوْفِيق. Happiness, comfort, رَفَاهِيَة ـ رَفَاهَة ـ مَفْلَحَة ـ سَعَادَة ـ عِزّ ـ نِعْمَة ـ نُعْم ـ طُمَأْنِينَة. A cause of —, مَفْلَحَة. Good condition, رَفَاهِيَة ـ رَخَاء ـ رِخْوَة. Abundance, بَرَكَة. The general —, الْخَيْرُ ٱلْعُمُومِيُّ. Enjoying great peace and —, فِي غَايَةِ ٱلرَّاحَةِ وَٱلرَّفَاهِيَةِ (*or* ٱلرَّفَاهَةِ). In — and in adversity, فِي حَالَتَي ٱلرَّخَاءِ وَٱلشِّدَّةِ. They ended their days in —, قَضَوا أَيَّامَهُمْ بِٱلْخَيْرِ. *See also* Affluence, Welfare, *n.*

Prosperous, *a.* Successful, مُنْجِح *pl.* مَنَاجِح ـ نَجِيح ـ نَاجِح ـ مُقْبِل ـ مُوَفَّق ـ مُفْلِح. Fortunate, بَخِيت. In easy circumstances, مُتَرَفِّه ـ رَفْهَان ـ رَافِه. A — life, عَيْشٌ رَفِيهٌ. Happy, مَسْعُود ـ غَضِر ـ سَعْد. A — or affluent man, رَجُلٌ غَضِيرٌ. He is in a most — state, هُوَ فِي أَرْفَهِ حَالٍ ـ مَغْضُور ـ ٱلنَّاصِيَةِ. A — people, قَوْمٌ أَفْلَحٌ. إِنَّهُ لَفِي غَضْرَاءِ عَيْشٍ. God made his way —, أَنْجَحَ ٱللّٰهُ طَرِيقَهُ.

Prosperously, *ad.* بِإِقْبَالٍ ـ بِنَجَاحٍ ـ بِتَوْفِيقٍ ـ غَضَارَةً; of a life, بِرَفَاهِيَةٍ ـ تَرَفُّهًا ـ طُمَأْنِينَةً.

Prosperousness, *n.* *See* Prosperity, *n.*

Prostate, *n.* The — gland, عُقْدَةُ ٱلْمَثَانَةِ.

Prosternation, *n.* *See* Depression, *n.*

Prostitute, *v.t.* To give up to lewdness, عَرَّضَ عَلَى ـ دَنَّسَ ـ تَسَقَّطَ عَلَى ٱلْفَاحِشَةِ. To debase, رَذَّلَ. To — one's self to...., تَرَذَّلَ لِ. She prostituted her daughter, عَرَّضَتْ عَلَى بِنْتِهَا. She prostituted herself for hire, آجَرَتْ نَفْسَهَا.

Prostitute, *a.* آجِرَةُ نَفْسِهَا *fem.* آجِرُ نَفْسِهِ.

Prostitute, *n.* A lewd woman, a whore, سَوْقَة ـ سَرَارِيّ *pl.* سِرِّيَّة ـ قُحْبَة *pl.* قِحَاب ـ فَاعِلَة.

Prostitution, *n.* Common lewdness, فُحْش ـ فِسْق ـ فُجُور ـ قُحْبَة. The act of setting one's self up for sale for lewd purposes, تَرَذَّلَ لِ ـ تَسَقَّطَ عَلَى; of degrading one's self to, تَعَرُّض لِلْفَاحِشَةِ.

Prostitutor, *n.* Of one's self, مُتَفَاحِش ـ مُتَرَذِّل.

Prostrate, *a.* Lying at length, مُتَبَطِّح ـ مُنْبَطِح. Flat, سَطِيح ـ مُسَطَّح. In the posture of humility, خُضُوع ـ خَاضِع; of prayer, سَاجِد ـ رَاكِع. Thrown down, مَسْدُوح ـ سَدِيح ـ صَرِيع. Worn out with fatigue, *etc.*, مَهْدُوم ـ مَهْدُود. To fall —, إِنْسَطَحَ ـ خَرَّ ـ إِنْسَدَحَ. To fall — in worship, خَرَّ سَاجِدًا ـ سَجَدَ.

Prostrate, *v.t.* To throw down, جَفَأَ ـ جَفَأَ بِهِ ـ أَجْفَأَ بِهِ ـ حَفَلَ ـ سَطَحَ ـ كَبَتَ ـ فَطَأَ بِهِ ـ أَكَبَّ ـ كَبَّ ـ سَطَرَ ـ صَرَعَ ـ أَخْبَطَ ـ أَوْقَعَ ـ أَهْبَطَ ـ هَبَطَ ـ سَدَحَ. To — one's self, as in prayer, خَرَّ سَاجِدًا ـ رَكَعَ ـ سَجَدَ. To —, or humble one's self to, خَضَعَ لِ ـ تَضَعْضَعَ لِ. To —, of strength, to tire, أَكَلَّ ـ هَبَطَ ـ بَرَى. To be prostrated, as in strength, إِنْهَبَطَ ـ كَلَّ.

Prostration, *n.* The act of throwing down, كَبّ ـ صَرْع ـ هَبْط ـ إِجْفَال ـ إِنْصِرَاع ـ هُبُوط; of falling down, جَفْل. Prostration in worship, سُجُود ـ رُكُوع ـ خُرُور. A single — in worship, رَكْعَة ـ مَصْرُوع.

Prostyle, *n.* رِوَاق ـ صَفُّ أَعْمِدَةٍ فِي مُقَدَّمِ بِنْيَةٍ *pl.* أَرْوِقَة.

Prosy, *a.* Dull, مُمِلّ ـ مُعْجِز ـ تَافِه; prolix, مُطَوِّلٌ فِي ٱلْكَلَامِ ـ سَائِبٌ فِي ٱلْكَلِمِ ـ مُبَالِغ.

Pro tanto, ad. أَوَّلُ مَرْتَبَةٍ ـ أَوَّل دَرَجَةٍ.

Protean, *a.* Changing shape readily, يَتَّخِذُ أَشْكَالًا شَتَّى ـ مِثْلَ ٱلْحِرْبَاءِ ـ مِثْلَ أَبُو ٱلْحِيَلِ ـ مُتَلَوِّن.

Protect, *v.t.* To secure from injury, to keep safely, وَقَى *aor.* يَقِي — أَذَمَّ — حَفِظَ — إِحْتَفَظَ بِ — عَصَمَ — خَفَرَ — حَامَى — حَمَى. To — against, to save from, أَنْقَذَ مِن — أَسْلَمَ مِن — سَلَّمَ مِن. To — against attack, أَجَارَ — حَصَّنَ. To patronize, support, عَاوَنَ — رَوَّجَ — ظَاهَرَ — شَيَّعَ — صَانَ عَن. To — one's self, إِحْتَمَى. He had no power to — them, ضَاقَ بِهِمْ ذَرْعًا. *See also to* Defend, *v.t.*

Protected, *a.* مَصُون — مَصْوُون; as against attack, حَصِين — مَحْفُوظ.

Protection, *n.* The act of protection, وِقَايَة — إِجَارَة — صِيَانَة — مُحَافَظَة — خُفَارَة — حِمَايَة — صَوْن. A place of —, a refuge, مَلْجَأ — مَلَاذ. A protector, حَامٍ — حَافِظ — خَفِير. A safe conduct, تَذْكِرَة أَمَان. Aid, support, ظَهْر — عَوْن — مُظَاهَرَة — مُعَاوَنَة. Safety, أَمْن. A promise of —, ذِمَّة — أَمَان. The — of rights, صَوْن ٱلْحُقُوق. For the — of government, as a precautionary measure, لِٱحْتِيَاطِ ٱلدَّوْلَة. To ask — of, إِسْتَجَارَ بِ. To seek — from God, against, تَعَوَّذَ (or يَعُوذُ *aor.* عَاذَ) بِٱللّٰهِ عَن or مِن. To seek —, to screen one's self, through, إِحْتَجَرَ بِ. To seek — from, إِحْتَجَرَ مِن. He entered within the pale of his —, دَخَلَ فِي أَمَانِهِ. O God, I seek Thy — against the devil, أَللّٰهُمَّ أَنِّي أَعُوذُ بِكَ مِنَ ٱلشَّيْطَانِ. Protection of home industry by increased duty on foreign goods, تَرْوِيجُ ٱلْأَمْتِعَةِ ٱلْبَلَدِيَّةِ بِوَاسِطَةِ وَضْعِ ٱلرُّسُومِ عَلَى ٱلْأَمْتِعَةِ ٱلْخَارِجِيَّةِ. For the — of . . . , لِوِقَايَةِ كَذَا.

Protectionist, *n.* جَادٌّ بِتَرْوِيجِ ٱلْأَمْتِعَةِ ٱلْبَلَدِيَّةِ بِوَاسِطَةِ وَضْعِ ٱلرُّسُومِ عَلَى ٱلْأَمْتِعَةِ ٱلْخَارِجِيَّةِ.

Protective, *a.* Defensive, حَامٍ — مُحَامٍ — صَائِن. Protective duties, رُسُومٌ مَضْرُوبَةٌ عَلَى ٱلْبَضَائِعِ ٱلْخَارِجِيَّةِ لِتَرْوِيجِ ٱلْبَضَائِعِ ٱلْبَلَدِيَّةِ.

Protector, *n.* One who protects, حَامٍ *pl.* حُمَاة — مُحَامٍ — حَافِظ. Supporter, مُعَاوِن — مُرَوِّج — ظَهِير. One holding the place of the sovereign, نَائِبُ ٱلسَّلْطَنَةِ.

Protectorate, *n.* Protection, حِمَايَة. Government by a Protector, نِيَابَة سَلْطَنَة.

Protectorship, *n.* Protection, حِمَايَة. Office of a Protector, وَظِيفَة نَائِبِ ٱلسَّلْطَنَةِ — نِيَابَة سَلْطَنَة.

Protectress, *n.* مُحَامِيَة — حَامِيَة.

Protegé, *n.* One under protection, مَحْمِيّ — تَحْتَ ٱلْحِمَايَةِ — فِي مُظَاهَرَةِ فُلَانٍ.

Pro tempore, ad. وَقْتًا — لِلْوَقْتِ — لِلْحَالِ.

Protest, *v.i.* To affirm solemnly, شَهِدَ عَلَى — أَقْسَمَ أَن — أَكَّدَ — حَلَفَ عَلَى. To — against, أَقَامَ ٱلْحُجَّةَ عَلَى — أَقَرَّ بِخِلَافِ ٱلشَّيْءِ — إِتَّخَذَ — أَقَامَ ٱلْحُجَّةَ. To make a protest, قَامَ عَلَى (or ٱلدَّعْوَى) — عَمِلَ (or بَرُوتِسْتُو).

Protest, *v.t.* To — a bill of exchange, رَجَّعَ حَوَالَةً عَلَى ٱلضَّامِنِ. To declare solemnly, أَكَّدَ.

Protest, *n.* A solemn declaration, تَأْكِيد — شَهَادَة — حَلْف عَلَى إِقَامَةُ ٱلدَّعْوَى — إِقْرَارٌ بِٱلْخِلَافِ — مُنَاقَضَة. A — against, شَيْءٌ عَلَى — بَرُوتِسْتُو *pl.* بَرُوتِسْتَات. The — of a bill of exchange, رُجُوعُ حَوَالَةٍ عَلَى ٱلضَّامِنِ.

Protestant, *a.*
Protestant, *n.* } بَرُوتِسْتَان — بَرُوتِسْتَانْت.

Protestantism, *n.* مَذْهَبُ ٱلْبَرُوتِسْتَانْت.

Protestation, *n.* *See* Protest, *n.*

Protester, *n.* صَاحِبُ بَرُوتِسْتُو — مُنَاقِض.

Proteus, *n.* أَبُو ٱلْحِيَلِ.

Prothonotary, *n.* *See* Protonotary, *n.*

Protocol, *n.* مَضْبَطَة.

Proto-martyr, *n.* رَئِيسُ ٱلشُّهَدَاءِ.

Protonotary, *n.* أَمِينُ ٱلسِّجِلَّاتِ.

Protoplast, *n.* أَوَّلُ ٱلْمَصْنُوعَاتِ — ٱلْفِطَحْل.

Prototype, *n.* أَصْل — أَوَّل أُنْمُوذَج.

Protozoa, *n.* دُوَيْبَّات — نُغَل.

Protract, *v.t.* To lengthen, أَطَالَ — طَوَّلَ. To delay, لَبَّثَ — أَخَّرَ — عَوَّقَ — أَعَاقَ — عَقَّبَ. To defer, put off, أَبْقَى — حَذَفَ إِلَى غَيْرِ وَقْتٍ. To draw out, جَذَبَ.

Protracted, *a.* مُزْمِن — زَمِن — مُتَرَاخٍ. The affair became —, تَرَاخَى ٱلْأَمْرُ. A — disease, ضَمَن. Affected with a — disease, مُزْمَن — مَضْمُون — ضَمِن.

Protracter, *n.* مُعَقِّب — عَائِق — مُطَوِّل.

Protraction, *n.* The act of lengthening out, مَدّ — تَطْوِيل. Delay, تَوَانٍ — تَرَاخٍ — تَأْخِير. Laying down measures, تَرْسِيم — مِسَاحَة. The — of war, تَشَذُّر.

Protractive, *a.* *See* Dilatory, *a.*

Protractor, *n.* A — for measuring, مِقْيَاس.

Protrude, *v.t.* To thrust out, let fall, أَنْتَشَعَ — نَشَعَ — أَدْلَعَ — دَلَعَ — مَدَّ — خَشَفَ بِ: He protruded his tongue, دَلَعَ لِسَانَهُ; his leg, بَسَطَ رِجْلَهُ.

Protrude, *v.i.* To stick out, be protuberant, بَزَا — بَزَى — أَنْتَأَ — نَتَأَ. His tongue protruded, إِنْدَلَعَ (or إِدَّلَعَ) لِسَانُهُ.

Protrusion, *n.* The act of pushing out or forward, إِبْزَاء —

ـ دَلَع ـ مَدّ ـ نَشْع ـ اِنْتِشاع. The state of being protruded, اِمْتِداد ـ اِنْدِلاع.

Protrusive, *a.* دافِع ـ ناشِع ـ دالِع.

Protuberance, *n.* A swelling out, حَيْدَة ـ عَيْر *pl.* أَعْيار ـ بَرْزا ـ نَتْأ ـ نُتُوّ ـ حِدْب ـ عُجْرَة. A — in a badly set joint, عُقْدَة. His arm was badly set so that there was produced a — in the bone, جُبِرَتْ يَدُهُ عَلَى عُقْدَةٍ. *See also* Knob, Tumour, *n.*

Protuberant, *a.* دالِع ـ أَحْدَب ـ ناتِئ. His belly became —, اِنْدَلَعَ بَطْنُهُ. Having a — back or belly, أَبْزَى. The girl's breast became —, شاكَ ثَدْيُ ٱلْجارِيَةِ.

Protuberate, *v.i.* اِنْدَلَعَ ـ نَتَأَ ـ بَرَزَ.

Proud, *a.* Haughty, مَغْرُور ـ مُعْجِب ـ تائِه ـ مَزْهُوّ ـ مَنْخُوّ ـ مُتَعَجْرِف. Superb, grand, مُتَكَبِّر ـ نافِخ ـ مُفْتَخِر ـ شامِخ ـ عَظِيم ـ بَهِيّ ـ فاخِر ـ جَلِيل ـ جَلِيّ. To be —, أَعَزَّ ـ اِسْتَكْبَرَ ـ تَكابَرَ ـ تَكَبَّرَ ـ شَمَخَ بِأَنْفِهِ. Proud flesh, غَثِيثَة ـ لَحْمٌ مُعَفَّن.

Proudly, *ad.* بِنَفْخٍ ـ بِٱفْتِخارٍ ـ تَكَبُّرًا ـ بِٱلتَّكَبُّرِ. To behave —, تَكَبَّرَ ـ تَفَجَّسَ. To talk —, تَكَبَّرَ فِي ٱلْكَلامِ. To deal — with, بَغَى عَلَى. *See also* Haughtily, *ad.*

Provable, *a.* إِثْباتُهُ مُمْكِن ـ مِمّا يُثْبَتُ.

Prove, *v.t.* As by testimony or argument, أَثْبَتَ ـ حَقَّقَ ـ بَرْهَنَ ـ بَيَّنَ. To try, جَرَّبَ. To know by experience, اِخْتَبَرَ. To tempt, أَفْتَنَ ـ فَتَنَ. To examine into, to test, مَحَنَ ـ اِمْتَحَنَ. To be proved, established, تَحَقَّقَ: it was proved against him, أُثْبِتَ عَلَيْهِ. He said this to — him, قالَ هٰذا لِيَمْتَحِنَهُ. This proves that ..., هٰذا يَدُلُّ عَلَى أَن.

Provender, *n.* عَلِيق ـ عَلَف. To feed with —, عَلَفَ ـ أَعْلَفَ. Fed with —, مَعْلُوف ـ عَلُوفَة ـ عَلِيف.

Proverb, *n.* مَثَل *pl.* أَمْثال. To use a —, ضَرَبَ مَثَلًا. To use as a —, تَمَثَّلَ بِ. To be used as a —, اِمْتَثَلَ بِ. The Book of Proverbs, سِفْرُ ٱلْأَمْثالِ ـ سِفْرُ أَمْثالِ سُلَيْمانَ.

Proverbial, *a.* يُضْرَبُ بِهِ ٱلْمَثَلُ.

Proverbialism, *n.* *See* Proverb, *n.*

Proverbialist, *n.* One who uses proverbs, ضارِبُ ٱلْأَمْثالِ; one who writes proverbs, مُؤَلِّفُ ٱلْأَمْثالِ.

Proverbially, *ad.* مِثْلَ ٱلْمَثَلِ ـ بِنَوْعِ ٱلْمَثَلِ ـ بِٱلْمَثَلِ.

Provide, *v.t.* To prepare, get ready, أَعَدَّ ـ اِعْتَدَّ ـ أَعْدَدَ; to make ready for, أَعَدَّ ل. To supply with, زَوَّدَ ب ـ أَمَدَّ ب ـ قَدَّمَ ل ـ مِن ـ جَهَّزَ ب. To — for, take care of, اِعْتَنَى بِ; to — with subsistence, رَزَقَ. To —, for one's family, أَعالَ ـ عالَ ـ كَدَشَ ل. To —, as against an emergency, اِحْتَكَرَ. He provided himself for the affair, اِسْتَعَدَّ لِلْأَمْرِ. He provided himself with a letter from the governor to the ambassador, تَزَوَّدَ مِنَ ٱلْحاكِمِ كِتابًا إِلَى ٱلسَّفِيرِ. God provided for him, رَزَقَهُ ٱللّٰهُ. Provide yourselves with ..., أَنْظِرُوا لَكُمْ كَذا ـ اِعْمَلُوا لَكُمْ كَذا.

Provided, *conj.* Provided that, بِشَرْطِ أَن.

Providence, *n.* Timely care, preparation, مُحاسَبَة ـ اِحْتِكار ـ بَصِيرَة ـ اِحْتِياط ـ حِسابُ ٱلْعَواقِبِ. Arrangement, تَدْبِير. The course of —, the superintendence over the course of events, الحِكْمَةُ ٱلْإِلٰهِيَّةُ ـ الحِكْمَةُ ٱلرَّبّانِيَّةُ ـ المَقْفِيَّةُ ٱلعَلِيَّةُ. The — of God, His care, العِنايَةُ ٱلْإِلٰهِيَّةُ. A good —, fortunate circumstance, تَوْفِيق. God the Provider, حَضْرَةُ ٱلرَّزّاقِ ـ البارِئُ تَعالَى.

Provident, *a.* صاحِبُ ٱحْتِياطٍ ـ مُحْتَكِر ـ مُدَبِّر ـ ضابِط ـ صاحِبُ نَظَرٍ فِي ٱلْعَواقِبِ ـ حَسِيب ـ حَرِيص.

Providential, *a.* مِمّا يُنْسَبُ إِلَى ٱلْعِنايَةِ ـ مَقامُ ٱلْعِنايَةِ ٱلْإِلٰهِيَّةِ ٱلرَّبّانِيَّةِ. A — escape, نَجاةٌ بِقَدَرِ ٱللّٰهِ.

Providentially, *ad.* بِقَدَرِ ٱللّٰهِ ـ مِنَ ٱللّٰهِ ـ بِٱلْعِنايَةِ ٱلْإِلٰهِيَّةِ ـ بِتَوْفِيقِ ٱلْمَقْفِيَّةِ ٱلْإِلٰهِيَّةِ.

Providently, *ad.* بِٱلنَّظَرِ فِي ٱلْعَواقِبِ ـ بِٱحْتِياطٍ ـ بِٱحْتِكارٍ.

Provider, *n.* رَزّاق. The lion's —, the animal so called, البَرِيد ـ الفُرانِق. *See also* Purveyor, *n.*

Province, *n.* إِقْلِيم *pl.* أَقالِيم ـ وِلايَة *pl.* وِلايات. The central provinces, الأَقالِيمُ ٱلْوُسْطَى. Business, office, مَأْمُورِيَّة ـ وَظِيفَة ـ شُغْل ـ عَلاقَة. The north-west provinces, الأَقالِيمُ ٱلشَّمالِيَّةُ ٱلْغَرْبِيَّةُ. The jurisdiction over a —, إِيالَة ـ وِلْيَة *pl.* وَلايا ـ حُكْمَدار ـ وِلاة. The governor of a —, مُتَوَلٍّ ـ والٍ *pl.* وُلاة ـ حُكْمَدارِيَّة. To place one over a —, وَلَّى ـ وِلايَة. It is not my — to ..., ما يَتَعَلَّقُ بِي أَن ـ لَيْسَ شُغْلِي أَن. The matter belongs to the — of the medical men, المَرْجِعُ إِلَى ٱلْأَطِبّاءِ. Appertaining to the —, department, of the sciences, مُناطٌ بِنَظارَةِ ٱلْمَعارِفِ.

Provincial, *a.* Belonging to a province, مِنَ ـ ما نِيطَ بِوِلايَةٍ ـ مِنَ ٱلْإِيالَةِ ـ الوِلايَةِ. *See also* Rude, *a.*

Provincial, *n.* مِنْ سُكّانِ ٱلرِّيفِ ـ مِنْ أَهْلِ إِيالَةٍ. A general overseer, ناظِرٌ عُمُومِيّ ـ مُسَيْطِر; of a religious body, رَئِيسُ ٱلْأَقْلِيمِ.

Provincialism, *n.* لُغَةُ أَهْلِ ٱلْوِلاياتِ *pl.* لُغات.

Provision, *n.* The act of making ready, تَعْداد ـ إِعْداد ـ اِعْتِداد ـ اِسْتِعْداد. What is made ready, حاضِر ـ تَدْبِير ـ عُدَّة. Provisions, food, مَأْكَلَة ـ طَعام ـ ذَخِيرَة ـ زاد ـ مُؤْنَة ـ بُرْزَة. Provisions for a journey, زَوادَة ـ زاد. Provision, such as God sends, رِزْق pl. أَرْزَاق . A stipulation, شَرْط pl. شُرُوط ـ شَرِيطَة : One of its provisions is ..., مِنْ شَأْنِهِ أَن . The expenses of their provisions, مَصَارِيفُ مُؤْنَتِهِمْ . Provisions of war, لَوَازِمُ حَرْبِيَّةٌ ـ مُهِمَّاتُ ٱلْحَرْبِ . To take in a stock of provisions for a journey, تَزَوَّدَ ; to furnish with such, زَوَّدَ . The provisions lasted all the distance, ٱلْمِيرَةُ ٱسْتَدَامَتْ طُولَ ٱلْمَسَافَةِ . To make — for, to set one up, رَتَّبَ لِ-كَذَا ـ قَامَ عَلَى ع ـ أَعْطَاهُ مَنْصَبًا ـ نَصَّبَ . *See also under to* Provide, *v.t.*

Provision, *v.t.* جَهَّزَ ـ زَوَّدَ .

Provisional, *a.* Temporary, مُوَقَّتٌ ـ وَقْتِيٌّ . Conditional, شَرْطِيٌّ .

Provisionally, *ad.* وَقْتًا ـ لِلْوَقْتِ .

Provisioned, *a.* مُجَهَّزٌ بِٱللَّوَازِمِ ـ مُجَهَّزٌ بِٱلذَّخَائِرِ وَٱلْمُؤْنَةِ .

Proviso, *n.* شَرْط pl. شُرُوط . With a — that ..., بِشَرْطِ أَن .

Provocation, *n.* The act of exciting, إِخْتِرَاش ـ تَحْرِيش ـ حَشّ ـ جَلْب ـ تَحْرِيك . Provocation to anger, إِغْضَاب . To give — to, حَشَّ ع ـ إِخْتَرَشَ ـ حَرَّكَ ـ أَغْضَبَ .

Provocative, *a.* جَالِب ـ مُحَرِّك ـ مُخْتَرِش ـ حَاشّ .

Provocative, *n.* سَبَب ـ مُوجِب .

Provoke, *v.t.* To excite, حَشَّ ع ـ إِخْتَرَشَ ـ جَلَبَ ع ـ دَعَى-إِلَى ـ أَثَارَ ـ هَيَّجَ ـ حَرَّضَ . To — to anger, آسَفَ ـ أَغْضَبَ ـ أَغَاظَ ـ أَسْخَطَ . To — war, حَشَّ ٱلْحَرْبَ ع . To — to jealousy, أَغَارَ . To be provoked, إِحْتَدَّ ـ ثَارَ aor. يَثُورُ ـ تَثَوَّرَ ـ هَاجَ . To be provoked with, against, one, إِحْتَدَّ عَلَيْهِ ـ حَدَّ عَلَيْهِ . Not easily provoked, لَا يَحْتَدُّ . He was provoked by them, تَحَدَّدَ بِهِمْ ـ تَحَرَّشَ بِهِمْ .

Provoker, *n.* مُوجِب ـ مُحَرِّض ـ مُحَرِّك ـ مُخْتَرِش ـ مُحِشّ .

Provoking, *a.* Irritating, مُغِيظ ـ مُغْضِب ـ مُخْتَرِش . Captious, مُلْتَوٍ . Vexatious, مُضْجِر ـ فَاجِع .

Provokingly, *ad.* حَشًّا ـ إِخْتِرَاشًا ـ تَحْرِيشًا ـ بِتَحْرِيشٍ .

Provost, *n.* ضَابِط ـ مُدِير . Provost of a college, نَاظِرُ دَارِ ٱلْفُنُونِ ـ رَئِيسُ مَدْرَسَةٍ .

Provost-marshal, *n.* كَبِيرُ مَأْمُورِي ٱلضَّبْطِيَّةِ (or ٱلشُّرْطَةِ) .

Provostship, *n.* نَظَارَة ـ وَظِيفَةُ ٱلْمُدِيرِ .

Prow, *n.* مُقَدَّمُ ٱلْمَرْكَبِ ـ صَدْرُ ٱلسَّفِينَةِ ـ مَرْكَحَة .

Prowess, *n.* شَجَاعَة ـ مُرُوءَة ـ بَطْش ـ أَزْل . *See also* Bravery, *n.*

Prowl, *v.i.* To roam about, يَعِيرُ aor. عَارَ ـ تَرَدَّدَ ـ إِخْتَلَفَ . To —, of a beast, عَسْعَسَ ـ تَعَسْعَسَ ـ إِعْتَسَّ . To — by night, عَسَّ ع ـ إِعْتَسَّ .

Prowling, *a.* عَائِر ـ عَيَّار . Prowling animals, such as foxes, wolves, *etc.*, كَجَارِس .

Proximate, *a.* أَقْرَب ـ قَرِيب . The — cause, as of a disease, وَاصِلَة . Proximate value, قُرَابَة .

Proximately, *ad.* تَقْرِيبًا ـ بِٱلتَّقْرِيبِ Immediately, حَالًا .

Proximity, *n.* قُرْب ـ جِوَار ـ زُلْفَة . Of relationship, قَرَابَة .

Proximo, *n.* Of a month, ٱلشَّهْرُ ٱلْآتِي .

Proxy, *n.* Agency of a substitute, وَكَالَة . A substitute, وَكِيل pl. وُكَلَاءُ . A writing authorizing a substitute, صَكُّ وَكَالَةٍ .

Proxyship, *n.* وَكَالَة .

Prude, *n.* إِمْرَأَةٌ مُتَصَنِّعَةٌ ـ إِمْرَأَةٌ مُتَحَذْلِقَةٌ ـ إِمْرَأَةٌ مُتَكَيِّسَةٌ بِفَرْطِ ٱلْحَيَاءِ .

Prudence, *n.* رُشْد ـ حِكْمَة ـ جَوْل ـ حَزْم ـ نَاهِيَة ـ كِيَاسَة ـ فِطْنَة ـ إِحْتِيَاط ـ إِنْتِبَاه ـ بَصِيرَة ـ عَقْل . To act with —, إِحْتَذَرَ ـ تَحَزَّمَ .

Prudent, *a.* كَيِّس pl. كَيِّسَة ـ لَبِيب pl. أَلِبَّاءُ ـ حَازِم ـ مَنْهَاة ـ صَاحِبُ رَأْيٍ وَتَدْبِيرٍ ـ فَاطِن ـ فَطِين ـ عَاقِل .

Prudential, *a.* إِحْتِذَارِيٌّ ـ إِحْتِيَاطِيٌّ . For — considerations, لِأَجْلِ ٱلْإِحْتِيَاطِ ـ لِأَجْلِ أَسْبَابٍ ٱحْتِذَارِيَّةٍ .

Prudently, *ad.* إِحْتِيَاطًا ـ بِفِطْنَةٍ ـ بِٱحْتِيَاطٍ ـ بِحَزْمٍ ـ بِعَقْلٍ . To act —, عَقَلَ ع .

Prudery, *n.* مُصَانَعَة ـ تَصَنُّع بِإِفْرَاطِ ٱلْعِفَّةِ ـ تَظَاهُر بِإِفْرَاطِ ٱلْحَيَاءِ .

Prudish, *a.* مُتَأَنِّق ـ مُتَصَنِّع ـ مُتَحَذْلِق ـ مُتَكَيِّس .

Prune, *n.* إِجَّاص *coll.* إِجَّاصَة ; called in Syria, خَوْخ *coll.* خَوْخَة .

Prune, *v.t.* As of trees, *etc.*, قَضَبَ ـ شَذَّبَ ـ قَلَّمَ ـ كَسَحَ ٱلْأَشْجَارَ To erase, cut out, as from a writing, أَزَالَ ـ نَقَّحَ .

Prunella, *n.* } ضَرْبٌ مِنَ ٱلْقُمَاشِ مِنْ صُوفٍ .
Prunello, }

Pruner, *n.* شَذَّاب ـ مُشَذِّب ـ كَسَّاح .

Pruning, *n.* قَضْب ـ تَشْذِيب ـ تَقْلِيم ـ كَسْحُ ٱلْأَشْجَارِ .

Pruning-knife, } مِخْطَب ـ مِشْذَب ـ مِجْنَاث ـ عَتَلَة ـ شَفْرَة .
Pruning-hook, *n.* }
Pruning-shears, }

Prurience, *n.* } Great desire, شَوْق ـ هُوِيَّة . Sensuality, رَفَث ـ غُلْمَة ـ شَهْوَة .
Pruriency, }

Prurient, *a.* Libidinous, شَهْوَانِيٌّ ـ نَفْسَانِيٌّ ـ هَوِس ـ غَلِم ـ فَاسِق .

Prurigo, *n.* أُكَال .

Prussia, *n.* مَمْلَكَةُ بُرُوسِيَا .

Prussian, *a.* مِنْ بُرُوسِيَا .

Prussian, *n.* مِنْ أَهْلِ بُرُوسِيَا .

Prussiate, *n.* مِلْحٌ بُرُوسِيٌّ .

Prussic, *a.* Prussic acid, حامِضٌ بُرُوسِيٌّ.

Pry, *v.t.* To spy into, تَجَسَّسَ — لَوَّصَ; to scrutinize, اِسْتَشَفَّ — تَعَرَّضَ فِي — تَداخَلَ فِي. To intermeddle with, تَصَفَّحَ — تَفَحَّصَ.

Pry, *v.t.* To lift with a lever, (بِمُخْلٍ *or*) أَشالَ بِعَتَلَةٍ.

Prying, *a.* عِرِّيضٌ — مُتَفَحِّصٌ — مُتَجَسِّسٌ — مُلاوِصٌ.

Prying, *n.* تَجَسُّسٌ — تَفَحُّصٌ — مُلاوَصَةٌ — لَوْصٌ.

Psalm, *n.* مَزْمُورٌ *pl.* مَزامِيرُ. The Psalms of David, الزَّبُورُ — مَزامِيرُ داوُدَ.

Psalmist, *n.* A writer of psalms, مُؤَلِّفٌ — صاحِبُ مَزامِيرَ. The — David, داوُدُ النَّبِيُّ — حَضْرَةُ داوُدَ — مَزامِيرَ.

Psalmodical, *a.* مُناطٌ بِالتَّرْتِيلِ — مُتَعَلِّقٌ بِمَزامِيرَ.

Psalmodist, *n.* زَمّارُ المَزامِيرِ — مُرَتِّلُ مَزامِيرَ.

Psalmody, *n.* تَرْتِيلٌ — تَزْمِيرُ المَزامِيرِ.

Psalter, *n.* كِتابُ مَزامِيرَ.

Psaltery, *n.* سِنْطِيرٌ — قانُونٌ.

Pseudo, *a.* كَذّابٌ.

Pseudo-apostle, *n.* رَسُولٌ كَذّابٌ *pl.* رُسُلٌ كَذَبَةٌ.

Pseudology, *n.* كِتابَةٌ كاذِبَةٌ.

Pseudonymous, *a.* حامِلُ اسْمٍ غَيْرِ اسْمِهِ — لَهُ اسْمٌ كَذّابٌ — الحَقِيقِيِّ.

Pseudo-philosopher, *n.* فَيْلَسُوفٌ كَذّابٌ.

Pseudo-philosophy, *n.* فَلْسَفَةٌ كاذِبَةٌ.

Pseudo-prophet, *n.* نَبِيٌّ كَذّابٌ *pl.* أَنْبِياءُ كَذَبَةٌ.

Pshaw, *int.* بَهْ بَهْ — بَهْ — أُفٍّ.

Psiltaceous, *a.* مِنْ جِنْسِ البَبْغا.

Psora, *n.* *See* Itch, *n.*

Psychical, *a.* مُخْتَصٌّ بِالنَّفْسِ وَما يَتَعَلَّقُ بِها.

Psychologic, *a.* } Psychological, } مُخْتَصٌّ بِعِلْمِ البَحْثِ عَنِ الرُّوحِ وَما يَتَعَلَّقُ بِها.

Psychologically, *ad.* نَظَرًا لِعِلْمِ البَحْثِ عَنِ الرُّوحِ الحَيَوانِيَّةِ (البَشَرِيَّةِ *or*) وَما يَتَعَلَّقُ بِها.

Psychologist, *n.* مِنْ أَهْلِ عِلْمِ البَحْثِ عَنِ الرُّوحِ الإِنْسانِيَّةِ (الحَيَوانِيَّةِ *or*).

Psychology, *n.* عِلْمٌ يُبْحَثُ فِيهِ عَنِ الرُّوحِ الإِنْسانِيَّةِ (الحَيَوانِيَّةِ *or*) وَما يَتَعَلَّقُ بِهِما.

Ptarmigan, *n.* طَيْرٌ مِنْ جِنْسِ القَطا.

Ptisan, *n.* مَشْرُوبٌ مُبَرِّدٌ.

Ptolemaic, *a.* مَنْسُوبٌ إِلَى بَطْلِيمُوسَ.

Ptolemy, *n.* بَطْلِيمُوسُ.

Ptyalism, *n.* كَثْرَةُ لُعابٍ — كَثْرَةُ رِيقٍ.

Puberal, *a.* حُلُمِيٌّ — مُتَعَلِّقٌ بِالبُلُوغِ (بِالحُلُمِ *or*).

Puberty, *n.* حَدُّ البُلُوغِ — حُلُمٌ — بَلاغٌ — بُلُوغٌ. He attained to —, بَلَغَ الحُلُمَ — احْتَلَمَ — ² حَلَمَ.

Pubescence, *n.* State of puberty, حَدُّ البُلُوغِ — حُلُمٌ. The down on plants, زُغابَةُ النَّباتِ.

Pubescent, *a.* Arrived at puberty, حاصِلُ البُلُوغِ — لاحِقُ الحُلُمِ. *See also* Downy, *a.*

Public, *a.* Pertaining to a nation or community, عُمُومِيٌّ — عامٌّ — شَعْبِيٌّ — جُمْهُورِيٌّ — مُخْتَصٌّ بِالأُمَّةِ. Manifest, open, عَيانٌ — مَعْلُومٌ عِنْدَ الجُمْهُورِ — مَشْهُورٌ — مُشاعٌ — شائِعٌ — عَلانِيٌّ. Belonging to the state, مُخْتَصٌّ بِالدَّوْلَةِ — مِيرِيٌّ. To make —, أَشْهَرَ — أَعْلَنَ بِ. He made him a — example, شَهَّرَهُ. To be made —, اِشْتَهَرَ — اِجْتَهَرَ — يَشِيعُ *aor.* شاعَ — ² شَهَرَ — اِسْتَعْلَنَ. In —, عَلانِيَةً — قُدّامَ النّاسِ — عَلَى مَلَإِ النّاسِ. (*See also* Apparent, *a.*)

The public authorities, أَرْبابُ المَناصِبِ — المَأْمُورِيَّةُ.

Public baths, حَمّاماتٌ عُمُومِيَّةٌ.

Public buildings, أَبْنِيَةٌ مِيرِيَّةٌ.

Public business, أَشْغالٌ مِيرِيَّةٌ — خُطُوبٌ مِيرِيَّةٌ.

Public debate, مُذاكَراتٌ وَمُباحَثاتٌ عَلانِيَةٌ.

Public debt, دُيُونُ الدَّوْلَةِ — دُيُونٌ مِيرِيَّةٌ.

Public domain, أَمْلاكٌ (أَراضِي *or*) مِيرِيَّةٌ.

Public establishment, تَأْسِيسَةٌ مِيرِيَّةٌ *pl.* تَأْسِيساتٌ.

Public functionary, مَأْمُورٌ — صاحِبُ مَنْصِبٍ *pl.* أَصْحابُ المَناصِبِ.

Public interests, المَصالِحُ العُمُومِيَّةُ — مَنافِعُ (فَوائِدُ *or*) الأُمَّةِ. Injurious to the public interests, مُضِرٌّ بِالمَصالِحِ العُمُومِيَّةِ.

Public law, حُقُوقُ الأُمَّةِ.

Public morals, الآدابُ العُمُومِيَّةُ.

Public opinion, هَواجِسُ النّاسِ — الأَفْكارُ العُمُومِيَّةُ — أَفْكارُ العامَّةِ.

Public order, سِياسَةٌ عُمُومِيَّةٌ — سِياسَةُ الأُمَّةِ — ضَبْطٌ عُمُومِيٌّ.

Public places, مَحَلّاتٌ عامَّةٌ.

Public revenue, حاصِلاتٌ مِيرِيَّةٌ — وارِداتٌ مِيرِيَّةٌ.

Public safety, أَمْنٌ عُمُومِيٌّ.

Public sentiment, خَواطِرُ النّاسِ (الأُمَّةِ *or*).

Public welfare, خَيْرُ النّاسِ عُمُومًا.

Public woman; *See* Prostitute, *n.*

Public works, المَنافِعُ المِيرِيَّةُ. The department of public works, النّافِعَةُ.

Public worship, عِبادَةٌ جُمْهُورِيَّةٌ — عِبادَةُ الجُمْهُورِ.

Public, *n.* The body of the people, النَّاسُ ـ الجُمْهُورُ ـ العَامُّ ـ الأُمَّةُ.

Publican, *n.* A collector of tolls, مُحَصِّل ـ مَاكِس ـ عَشَّار. The keeper of a public house, صَاحِبُ خَمَّارَةٍ ـ صَاحِبُ حَانُوتٍ.

Publication, *n.* The act of publishing, making known, تَشْهِير ـ إِعْلَانٌ بِ ـ إِذَاعَةٌ بِ ـ إِشْهَار. The being published, made known, إِشْتِهَار ـ إِسْتِعْلَان. The act of publishing a book, تَبْرِيزُ كِتَابٍ ـ طَبْعُ كِتَابٍ وَنَشْرُهُ. A printed and published book, كِتَابٌ مَطْبُوعٌ وَمُبَرَّزٌ (or مَنْشُورٌ) ـ مَطْبُوعَة pl. مَطْبُوعَات. Publications, مَنْشُورَات ـ إِشْهَارَات. *See also* Disclosure, *n.*

Public-house, *n.* حَانُوت pl. حَوَانِيتُ ـ خَمَّارَة pl. خَمَامِيرُ.

Publicist, *n.* فَقِيه pl. فُقَهَآءُ ـ شَرْعِيٌّ.

Publicity, *n.* عَلَانِيَة ـ شُهْرَة ـ إِنْتِشَار ـ إِشْتِهَار ـ شُيُوع.

Publicly, *ad.* عَلَانِيَةً ـ قُدَّامَ ٱلنَّاسِ ـ جَهْرًا ـ عَلَى مَلَأٍ ٱلنَّاسِ. He taught them —, عَلَّمَهُمْ جَهْرًا.

Public-minded, *a.* } خَيِّر ـ رَاغِبٌ فِي مَنَافِعِ ٱلْعَامَّةِ.
Public-spirited, }

Publish, *v.t.* To make known, to spread abroad, نَشَرَ ² ـ أَشَاعَ بِ ـ أَعْلَنَ بِ ـ نَادَى بِ ـ أَذَاعَ بِ ـ أَذَاعَ ـ يُشِيعُ aor. شَاعَ بِ. To put into circulation, to issue, بَرَّزَ ـ أَصْدَرَ. To — a book, نَشَرَ كِتَابًا ² ـ طَبَعَ كِتَابًا وَنَشَرَهُ ـ أَبْرَزَ (or بَرَّزَ) كِتَابًا. To be published, made known, إِنْتَشَرَ ـ تَنَشَّرَ ـ يَشِيعُ aor. شَاعَ ـ يَذِيعُ aor. ذَاعَ ـ إِسْتَعْلَنَ. To be published, of a book, أَبْرَزَ (or بَرَّزَ) طُبِعَ ٱلْكِتَابُ وَٱنْتَشَرَ ـ ٱلْكِتَابُ. A published book, one issued and in circulation, كِتَابٌ مَطْبُوعٌ وَمُبَرَّزٌ (or مَنْشُورٌ). They published it in the telegraphic news, أَشَاعُوهُ فِي خَبَرِ ٱلتِّلِغْرَافِ. It is published (comes out) every Tuesday and Friday, يَصْدُرُ فِي يَوْمَيِ ٱلثُّلَثَآءِ وَٱلْجُمْعَةِ مِنْ كُلِّ أُسْبُوعٍ. It was published in the *al-Jawâib*, إِنْدَرَجَ فِي جَرِيدَةِ ٱلْجَوَائِبِ. Published or circulating journals or prints, صَحَائِفُ نَشْرِيَّةٌ. Published by Kegan, Paul and Co., London, نُشِرَ عَلَى يَدِ شِرْكَةِ كِيغَنْ پَاوُل فِي لَنْدَن.

Publisher, *n.* One who makes known, مُذِيع ـ مُشِيع ـ مُنَادٍ. One who publishes books, مُبَرِّزُ ٱلْكُتُبِ ـ نَاشِرُ ٱلْكُتُبِ; a seller of books, كُتُبِيٌّ.

Puce, *a.* Of the colour, مُوَر.

Puck, *n.* *See* Demon, *n.*

Pucker, *v.t.* شَنَّجَ ـ غَضَّنَ. To be puckered, تَغَضَّنَ. A puckered tunic, قَبَآءٌ مُشَنَّجٌ. Puckered, مُتَغَضِّن ـ مُشَنَّج. *See also to* Crease, *v.t.*

Pucker, *n.* غَضْن pl. غُضُون ـ تَشَنُّج ـ تَشْنِيج. *See also* Crease, *n.*

Pudder, *n.* *See* Bustle, Tumult, *n.*

Pudding, *n.* بُودِينَة ـ قَالُون ـ نَوْعٌ مِنَ ٱلْحَلْوَآءِ ـ زَرْدَى. Black —, مَحْشِيٌّ مِنْ دَمٍ وَدُهْنٍ. Hasty —, عَصِيدَة.

Pudding-stone, *n.* حَجَرٌ مُكَوَّنٌ مِنَ ٱلْحَصَى.

Puddle, *n.* A — of water, فَشَّة coll. فَشّ pl. فِشَاش ـ مَنْقَع pl. مُسْتَنْقَعُ مَآءٍ ـ مَنَاقِعُ. A kind of mortar, مِلَاط.

Puddle, *v.t.* To make foul, عَكَّرَ ـ نَجَّسَ ـ كَدَّرَ. To close with puddle, mortar, مَلَّطَ ـ سَدَّ بِمِلَاطٍ ². To — iron, حَوَّلَ ٱلْحَدِيدَ ٱلْمَسْبُوكَ إِلَى حَدِيدٍ مَطْرُوقٍ.

Puddler, *n.* A — of iron, مُحَوِّلُ ٱلْحَدِيدِ ٱلْمَسْبُوكِ إِلَى حَدِيدٍ مَطْرُوقٍ.

Puddling, *n.* As with mortar, تَمْلِيط. The — of iron, تَحْوِيلُ ٱلْحَدِيدِ ٱلْمَسْبُوكِ إِلَى حَدِيدٍ مَطْرُوقٍ.

Puddly, *a.* ذُو مَنَاقِعَ. Puddly soil, أَرْضٌ سُوَاخَى. The soil became —, صَارَتِ ٱلْأَرْضُ سُوَّاخًا.

Pudency, *n.* } *See* Modesty, *n.*
Pudicity, }

Pudendum, *n.* Of a man, أَيْر ـ حَيَآء ـ جِفْش ـ شَوَار; of a boy, زُبّ; of a woman, بِرٌّ pl. كُسّ ـ هَنٌ ـ جِهَاز ـ كَعْثَب ـ فَرْج ـ الأَجَبُّ ـ مَشْرَح ـ جُحْر ـ أَسْرَار; common to both sexes, فَرْج pl. فُرُوج ـ عَوْرَة pl. عَوْرَات. Having the — exposed, أَفْرَجُ. The — of a he-camel, مِقْلَم; of a horse, جُرْدَان; of an ass, غُرْمُول; of a he-goat, قَضِيب; of a dog, عُقْدَة; of the ضَبّ or *lacerta caudiverbera*, نَزْك; of the male fly, مَتْك. The — of all female cloven-hoofed animals, حَيَآء; of all female solid-hoofed animals, ظَبْيَة.

Puerile, *a.* Belonging to children, صُغَارِيّ ـ طِفْلِيّ ـ صِبَائِيّ. *See also under* Childish, Frivolous, *a.*

Puerileness, *n.* } Boyhoodness, صَبْوَة ـ صَبَآء. *See also* Childish-
Puerility, } ness, Frivolity, *n.*

Puerperal, *a.* مَا نِيطَ بِٱلْوِلَادَةِ ـ مُتَعَلِّقٌ بِٱلنِّفَاسِ. Puerperal fever, حُمَّةُ ٱلْوِلَادَةِ ـ حُمَّةُ ٱلنِّفَاسِ.

Puff, *n.* A breath, whiff, نَفْخَة ـ نَفَس pl. أَنْفَاس. A blast of wind, هَبَّةُ رِيحٍ ـ نَسَمَة ـ رِيحَة ـ عَصْفَة. A — of smoke, دَخْنَة. A powder —, وِرْشَة ـ مِذَرَّة ـ مِذَرَّةُ حُسْنِ يُوسُفَ. A — in a woman's garments, تَكْمِيش. A —, of pastry, فَطِيرَة pl. فَطَائِرُ. An exaggerated commendation, تَقْرِيظ ـ تَقْرِيض ـ إِطْرَآء ـ تَنْفِيخ ـ مَدْحٌ زَائِدٌ.

Puff, *v.t.* To drive with a blast of wind, نَفَخَ ـ نَفَخَ بِ ². To swell, نَفَخَ فِي ـ دَاجَ ². To praise with exaggeration, نَوَّهَ بِ ـ

نَفَخَ ـ بَالَغَ فِي مَدِيحِهِ ـ قَرَّضَ ـ قَرَّظَ ـ أَطْرَأَ . To — up with pride, صَيَّرَ مُنْتَفِخًا . To be puffed up, إِنْتَفَخَ . To be puffed out, نَتَأَ ـ. To — at, in scorn, نَفَثَ فِي ـ.

Puff, *v.i.* As air with the mouth, تَنَفَّسَ . To breathe with vehemence, to pant, زَحَرَ ـ أَنَحَّ ـ نَفَخَ ـ لَهَدَ ـ نَهَجَ ـ.

Puffer, *n.* One who puffs, blows, نَفَّاخ ـ مُتَنَفِّس . *See also* Boaster, *n.*

Puffiness, *n.* Turgidity, وَرَم ـ إِنْتِفَاخ ـ نُتُوء ـ نَتَأ .

Puffing, *n.* A short breathing, زَحِير ـ زُحُور ـ لَهَد ـ نَهَج .

Extravagant praise; *see under* Puff, *n.*

Puffy, *a.* Swollen, وَارِم ـ مُنْتَفِخ ـ نَاتِئ . *See also* Bombastic, *a.*

Pug, *n.* / Pug-dog, } كَلْبٌ صَغِيرٌ ـ كُلَيْب .

Pug-nose, *n.* أَنْفٌ أَذْلَف .

Pug-nosed, *a.* أَذْلَف *fem.* ذَلْفَاء *pl.* ذُلْف .

Pugilism, *n.* مُضَارَبَةٌ بِٱلْكَفِّ ـ مُلَاكَمَة .

Pugilist, *n.* مُلَاكِم ـ لَاكِم ـ ضَارِبُ كَفٍّ .

Pugilistic, *a.* مُتَعَلِّقٌ بِٱلْمُلَاكَمَةِ .

Pugnacious, *a.* أَلَدّ *pl.* لُدّ *and* لِدَاد ـ مُتَهَوِّشٌ لِلْقِتَالِ ـ مُتَمَرِّد ـ مَارِد ـ شَرِس ـ وَمُتَحَمِّسٌ لِلنِّزَالِ .

Pugnacity, *n.* لَدّ ـ شَرَاسَة ـ شَكَاسَة ـ مُرُود .

Puisne, *a.* Inferior, second, دُون ـ ثَانٍ . A — judge, قَاضٍ ثَانٍ .

Puissance, *n.* *See* Power, Strength, Valour, *n.*

Puissant, *a.* *See* Powerful, Brave, *n.*

Puke, *v.i.* إِسْتَفْرَغَ ـ دَسَعَ ـ قَذَفَ ـ.

Puke, *n.* *See* Emetic, *n.*

Puking, *n.* إِسْتِفْرَاغ ـ دَسْعَة .

Pule, *v.i.* بَكَى ـ يَئِنّ *aor.* أَنَّ ـ تَأَوَّهَ ـ.

Pull, *v.t.* To drag, draw, جَذَبَ ـ سَحَبَ ـ جَرَّ ـ خَلَجَ ـ.

To be pulled, dragged, إِنْجَذَبَ ـ إِنْسَحَبَ ـ إِنْجَرَّ . To pull fruit; *See under to* Pluck, *v.t.*

To pull about, to maul, نَكَأَ فِي ـ.

To pull apart, to separate, فَارَقَ ـ فَكَّكَ ـ جَزَّنَ ـ شَدَّ ـ.

To pull away, to disengage, أَعْتَقَ ـ فَكَّ ـ.

To pull back, جَذَبَ إِلَى وَرَاءٍ ـ.

To pull down, to demolish, أَخْرَبَ ـ هَدَّ ـ هَدَمَ ـ ضَعْضَعَ .

To make to come down, أَنْزَلَ . To abase, أَخْضَعَ ـ وَضَعَ ـ أَخْزَى .

To pull in, to make to enter, أَدْخَلَ ـ أَخَشَّ . To contract, ضَيَّقَ ـ قَصَّرَ .

To pull in pieces, to tear, مَزَّقَ ; to dissunder, dissolve, فَسَخَ ـ; to criticize, تَعَقَّبَ عَلَى .

To pull off, to draw aside, جَنَّبَ . To take off, as garments, شَلَحَ ـ قَلَعَ ـ خَلَعَ ـ.

To pull one's ears, *i.e.* the ears of another, أَذَّنَ .

To pull out, as from a pit, نَشَلَ ـ أَنْقَذَ مِن ـ. To extract, أَخْرَجَ ـ سَلَّ ـ. To release, save, خَلَّصَ ـ أَعْتَقَ . To draw out, as a fish from the sea, إِصْطَادَ ; as a spear from a wound, إِخْتَلَجَ ـ خَلَجَ .

To pull up, drag up, سَحَبَ إِلَى فَوْقُ ـ رَفَعَ ـ. To bring to a standstill, أَوْقَفَ ـ وَقَّفَ . To call to account, حَاسَبَ ـ طَالَبَ .

To pull one through, to enable him to effect, overcome, مَكَّنَ مِن ـ أَمْكَنَ مِن . To pull one through a sickness, شَفَى مِن مَرَضِهِ ـ.

See also under to Drag, *v.t.*

Pull, *v.i.* To row, جَذَفَ ـ قَذَفَ ـ. To pull up, come to a standstill, وَقَفَ *aor.* يَقِفُ ; to curtail one's expenses, قَلَّلَ مَصْرُوفَهُ .

He pulled through the affair, overcame it, تَمَكَّنَ مِنَ ٱلْأَمْرِ . He pulled through his sickness, أَفَاقَ مِن مَرَضِهِ .

Pull, *n.* The act of drawing, جَذْب ـ سَحْب ـ جَرّ ; of plucking, as of fruit, قَطْف . A row, قَذْف . A —, as at a pipe, نَفَس .

To have a —, to row, قَذَفَ ـ. To have a —, as at a pipe, شَرِبَ نَفَسًا ـ.

Pullback, *n.* مَانِع *pl.* مَوَانِع ـ عَائِق *pl.* عَوَائِق .

Puller, *n.* One that pulls, جَارّ ـ جَاذِب ـ سَاحِب . A rower, قَذَّاف .

Pullet, *n.* فَرُّوج *pl.* فَرَارِيج ـ فَرْخ *pl.* أَفْرَاخ ـ فَلُّوس *pl.* فَلَالِيس .

See also Chicken, *n.*

Pulley, *n.* عَلَق *pl.* أَعْلَاق ـ قَعْو *pl.* قُعِيّ ـ بَكَرَة *pl.* بَكَر *and* بَكَرَات ; an iron —, خُطَّاف . The apparatus by which a — is suspended, عَلَق .

Pullulate, *v.i.* *See to* Bud, Germinate, *v.i.*

Pulmonic, *a.* / Pulmonary, } مُخْتَصّ بِٱلرِّئَةِ ـ سَحْرِيّ . A — disease, ذَاتُ وَارِيَة ـ وَرًى ـ ٱلرِّئَةِ .

Pulmonic, *n.* A medicine for diseases of the lungs, دَوَاءٌ لِلرِّئَةِ .

One affected with pulmonary disease, مُصَابٌ بِذَاتِ ٱلرِّئَةِ .

Pulp, *n.* The soft part of fruit, لُبّ ـ شَحْمَة ـ شَحْم . A soft mass, عَجِين . The — of the colocynth, شَحْمَةُ ٱلْحَنْظَلِ . *See also* Marrow, *n.*

Pulp, *v.t.* To deprive of pulp, جَرَّدَ مِنَ ٱلشَّحْمَةِ .

Pulpit, *n.* مِنْبَر *pl.* مَنَابِرُ.

Pulpous, *a.* / Pulpy, } ذُو لُبٍّ ـ شَحِيم. Like a soft mass, كَٱلْعَجِينِ. Fat, full, فَعْم. To be —, fat, full, فَعُمَ [2].

Pulsate, *v.i.* نَبَضَ ـ فَارَ ـ دَرَّ [2] ـ دَرَّ [2]: The artery pulsated, دَرَّ ٱلْعِرْقُ [2]. *See also to* Throb, *v.i.*

Pulsatile, *a.* لِلدَّقِّ ـ يَنْدَقُّ. Pulsatile instruments, مَعَازِفُ *sing.* عَزْف.

Pulsation, *n.* As of the arteries, ضَرْبُ ٱلنَّبْضِ ـ دُرُور ـ فَوَرَان. *See also* Throb, *n.*

Pulsative, *a.* / Pulsatory, } ضَارِب ـ فَائِر ـ دَارّ ـ خَالِج.

Pulse, *n.* A beating of the arteries, نَبْض ـ نَبَض; one stroke of the —, نَبْضَة. Leguminous plants, their seeds, قُطْنِيَّة ـ مَاشّ *pl.* قَطَانِيُّ ـ حُبُوبَات. To feel the —, جَسَّ ٱلنَّبْضَ [2]. *See also* Oscillation, *n.*

Pulsific, *a.* مُحَرِّكُ ٱلنَّبْضِ.

Pulverable, *a.* يَنْدَقُّ ـ قَابِلُ ٱلسَّحْقِ ـ مِمَّا يُسْحَقُ.

Pulverization, *n.* دَقّ ـ سَحْن ـ سَحْق.

Pulverize, *v.t.* دَقَّقَ ـ سَحَقَ ـ سَحَنَ. To be pulverized, اِنْسَحَقَ ـ اِنْدَقَّ.

Pulverulence, *n.* غَبَرَة ـ اِعْتِفَار ـ تَعَفُّر.

Pulverulent, *a.* مُغَبَّر ـ مُعَفَّر.

Puma, *n.* نَوْعٌ مِنَ ٱلْجَوَارِحِ يُشْبِهُ ٱلْقِطَّ ٱلْبَرِّيَّ.

Pumice, *n.* / Pumice-stone, } خُرْفُش ـ شَوَّافَة ـ نِشَاف *and* نَشْف *pl.* نَشْفَة ـ رَغْوَةُ ٱلْبَحْرِ.

Pummel, *n.* *See* Pommel, *n.*

Pump, *n.* For drawing water, طُلُمْبَة ـ تُرُمْبَة. A light shoe, مَدَاس ـ تَاسُومَةٌ خَفِيفَةٌ.

Pump, *v.t.* To raise water with a pump, رَفَعَ ٱلْمَاءَ بِٱلتُّرُمْبَةِ ـ نَزَحَ ٱلْمَاءَ بِٱلطُّلُمْبَةِ. To draw out by artful examination, سَبَرَ [2] ـ تَجَسَّسَ.

Pump-brake, *n.* فِعَالُ ٱلتُّرُمْبَةِ ـ مِقْبَضُ ٱلطُّلُمْبَةِ.

Pumper, *n.* *See* Fireman, *n.*

Pumpion, *n.* / Pumpkin, } The plant, قَرْعَة *coll.* قَرْع.

Pun, *n.* تَوْرِيَة ـ تَعْرِيض ـ مِعْرَاض ـ نُكْتَة *pl.* نُكَت.

Pun, *v.i.* تَكَلَّمَ بِٱلنُّكَتِ ـ عَرَّضَ.

Punch, *n.* A tool for making holes, مِثْقَب ـ مِخْوَاب. The male driver, tool, أَب *pl.* آبَاء ـ أُبَّهَات. The drink so called, شَرْبَةٌ ـ شَرْبَةُ ٱلْبُونْج ـ مِنْ عَرَقٍ وَمَاءٍ وَسُكَّرٍ وَلَيْمُونٍ. A buffoon, سُخْرَة ـ مَسْخَرَة. A thrust, blow, لَطْشَة ـ دَفْعَة ـ ضَرْبَة ـ دَسْرَة. Punch and Judy, مَلْهًى مُضْحِكٌ يُؤَلَّفُ مِنْ صُنْدُوقٍ مَضْمُودٍ عَلَى أَرْبَعِ قَوَائِمَ لَهُ كُوَّةٌ مَفْتُوحَةٌ فِي أَعْلَاهُ يَحْمِلُهُ ٱللَّاعِبُ عَلَى ظَهْرِهِ وَيَطُوفُ بِهِ ٱلشَّوَارِعَ ثُمَّ يَضَعُهُ فِي ٱلْأَزِقَّةِ وَيَتَوَارَى عَنِ ٱلْعَيْنِ فِي أَسْفَلِهِ ثُمَّ يُخْرِجُ تِمْثَالَيْنِ مِنْ خَشَبٍ فِي هَيْئَةِ رَجُلٍ وَٱمْرَأَةٍ عَلَيْهِمَا مَلَابِسُ سُخْرِيَّةٍ وَيَجْعَلُهُمَا تَارَةً يَرْقُصَانِ وَأُخْرَى يَتَحَابَّانِ وَآوِنَةً يَتَدَلَّلَانِ وَأُخْرَى يَتَضَارَبَانِ ثُمَّ يَتَعَانَقَانِ وَكُلُّ هٰذَا يُجْرِيهِ ٱللَّاعِبُ وَهُوَ يُحَاكِي ٱلتِّمْثَالَيْنِ بِصَوْتٍ مُصْطَنَعٍ كَمَنْ يَنْطِقُ بِٱلْكَلَامِ مِنْ بَاطِنِهِ. (The Turks have a somewhat similar show, which is generally very indecent, called by them, (كَرَا كُوز وَعِيوَاز *or* عَوَض).

Punch, *v.t.* To perforate, خَرَمَ ـ نَقَبَ [2] ـ ثَقَبَ [2]. To beat, ضَرَبَ; to thrust, دَفَعَ ـ دَسَرَ [2].

Punch-bowl, *n.* طَاسٌ لِلْبُونْج. *See* Punch, *n.*

Puncheon, *n.* A tool for stamping, سِكَّة ـ أَبُ ٱلسِّكَّةِ. The cask, بَرْمِيلٌ يَسَعُ ١٢٠ غَالِنًا. *See* Gallon, *n.*

Puncher, *n.* One who uses a punch, مُثَقِّب ـ ثَقَّاب. A tool, the punch; *See* Punch, *n.*

Punchinello, *n.* A Buffoon; *see under* Punch, *n.*

Punchy, *a.* مَجْمُوع ـ مُكَتَّل.

Punctate, *a.* / Punctated, } Dotted, مُنَقَّط. Acuminated, مُؤَنَّف ـ مُؤَسَّل ـ حُدَّان.

Punctilio, *n.* A nice point in ceremony, مِنْ مَدَاقِّ ٱلتَّكَالِيفِ ـ مِنْ دَقَائِقِ ٱلتَّشْرِيفَاتِ.

Punctilious, *a.* As in ceremony, مُتَجَوِّد ـ مُدَقِّقٌ فِي ٱلتَّكَالِيفِ ـ مُتَنَوِّق ـ فِي ٱلتَّشْرِيفَاتِ. *See also* Ceremonious, Precise, *a.*

Punctiliously, *ad.* بِمُبَالَغَةِ ٱلدِّقَّةِ ـ بِتَجَوُّدٍ ـ بِتَنَوُّقٍ.

Punctiliousness, *n.* As in ceremonial, ٱلتَّدَاقُّ فِي ٱلتَّكَالِيفِ *See also* Preciseness, *n.*

Punctual, *a.* Precise in observing time, رَاعِي ـ رَاعِي ٱلْمِيعَادِ ـ مُدَقِّقٌ فِي مُرَاعَاةِ ٱلْعَهْدِ ـ ٱلْعَهْدِ. Happening in its proper time, وَاقِعٌ فِي وَقْتِهِ. *See also* Precise, *a.*

Punctuality, *n.* As in observing time, مُرَاعَاةُ ٱلْمِيعَادِ. *See also* Preciseness, *n.*

Punctually, *ad.* As to time, فِي سَاعَتِهِ ـ فِي وَقْتِهِ. *See also* Precisely, *ad.*

Punctuate, *v.t.* As with stops, وَضَعَ ل ـ عَلَامَاتِ *aor.* يَضَعُ ـ قَسَّمَ ٱلْمَكْتُوبَ بِإِشَارَاتِ ٱلْوَقْفِ ـ جَعَلَ فِي ٱلْهِجَاءِ ـ ٱلْوَقْفِ.

Punctuated, مَنْقُوط.

Punctuation, *n.* As with stops, تَرْكِيبُ ٱلْمَكْتُوبِ بِعَلَامَاتِ ٱلْهِجَاءِ ـ تَقْسِيمُ ٱلْعِبَارَاتِ بِإِشَارَاتِ ٱلْوَقْفِ.

Puncture, *n.* نَخْزَة ـ شَكَّة ـ غَرْز ـ نَكْز .

Puncture, *v.t.* ² شَكَّ ـ ² نَخَزَ ـ = غَرَّزَ ـ ² نَكَزَ .

Pundit, *n.* عَالِمٌ مِنَ ٱلْبَرَاهِمَةِ *pl.* عَالِمُونَ .

Pungency, *n.* Sharpness, حَرَاقَة ـ حَرَارَة ـ حُثُومَة ـ حَمَازَة ـ حِدَّة . Sarcasm, سَلَاطَة .

Pungent, *a.* Sharp to the taste, حِرِّيف ـ أُجَاج ـ حَاذِق ـ ذَفِر ـ حَادّ ; of a smell, ذَكِيّ : a — smell, رَائِحَةٌ ذَكِيَّةٌ . Sarcastic, سَلِيط .

Punic, *a.* Belonging to Carthage, مَنْسُوبٌ إِلَى قَرْطَاجَنَّةَ ٱلْقَدِيمَةِ ٱلَّتِي حَلَّتْ مَحَلَّهَا ٱلْآنَ مَدِينَةُ تُونِسَ . Punic faith, غَدْر ـ خِيَانَة .

Puniness, *n.* Littleness, صُغْر ; meanness, حَقَارَة ـ تَفَاهَة ; weakness, هُزَال ـ ضُعْف .

Punish, *v.t.* عَاقَبَ ـ تَعَقَّبَ ـ قَاصَّ ـ عَذَّبَ . To — with death, عَاقَبَ (or تَعَقَّبَ) بِٱلْمَوْتِ . He shall surely be punished, لَا بُدَّ أَنْ يُعَاقَبَ . He punished him for his offence, عَاقَبَهُ بِذَنْبِهِ . If ye —, then — ye with the like of that with which ye have been punished, وَإِنْ عَاقَبْتُمْ فَعَاقِبُوا بِمِثْلِ مَا عُوقِبْتُمْ بِهِ (Kur. xvi. 127.) To be punished, عُذِّبَ ـ عُوقِبَ .

Punishable, *a.* مُسْتَحِقُّ ٱلْقِصَاصِ ـ يُقَاصَصُ ـ يُعَاقَبُ .

Punishment, *n.* عُقُوبَة ـ مُعَاقَبَة ـ عِقَاب ـ قِصَاص ـ عَذَاب . Punishment overtook them, حَلَّ بِهِمِ ٱلْعَذَابُ = . The threatened — of God, أَمْرُ ٱللّٰهِ . He carried out the —, أَجْرَى ٱلْعِقَابَ . And their Lord made — to fall upon them universally, فَدَمْدَمَ عَلَيْهِمْ رَبُّهُمْ (Kur. xci. 14.) ـ أَطْبَقَ رَبُّهُمْ عَلَيْهِمِ ٱلْعَذَابَ .

Punitive, *a.* }
Punitory, } حَدِّيّ ـ قِصَاصِيّ ـ عَذَابِيّ . *See also* Penal, *a.*

Punk, *n.* Decayed wood, touchwood, صُوفَان . A lewd woman, شَرْمُوطَة ـ قَحْبَة ـ عَاهِرَة .

Punka, *n.* مِرْوَحَةٌ كَبِيرَةٌ .

Punning, *n.* ٱلتَّكَلُّمُ بِٱلنُّكَتِ ـ تَعْرِيض .

Punster, *n.* مُتَكَلِّمٌ بِٱلنُّكَتِ ـ مُعَرِّض .

Punt, *n.* قَارِبٌ صَغِيرٌ ذُو قَعْرٍ مُسَطَّحٍ called in the Persian Gulf, بَلَم .

Puny, *a.* Little, صُغَيِّر ; mean, حَقِير ـ تَافِهٌ ; weak, هَزِل ـ ضَعِيف . A — infant, مَوْدُون .

Pup, *n.* جِرْو *pl.* جِرَاءٌ .

Pup, *v.i.* وَلَدَتْ ـ أَجْرَتْ .

Pupa, *n.* *See* Chrysalis, *n.*

Pupil, *n.* A ward, قَاصِر *pl.* قُصَّر ـ يَتِيم *pl.* أَيْتَام . A scholar, learner, تِلْمِيذ *pl.* تَلَامِيذُ . The — of the eye, فَصُّ ٱلْعَيْنِ ـ بُؤْبُؤُ ٱلْعَيْنِ ـ حَدَقَةُ ٱلْعَيْنِ ـ إِنْسَانُ ٱلْعَيْنِ .

Pupillage, *n.* State of being a ward, حَالُ ٱلْقَاصِرِ ; of being a scholar, حَالُ ٱلتَّلْمَذَةِ . Minority, صَبْوَة .

Puppet, *n.* A small doll, بِنْت *pl.* بَنَات ـ لُعْبَة ـ عَرُوسَة . A person under the control of another, آلَة *pl.* آلَات .

Puppet-show, *n.* تَمَاثِيلُ يَتَّخِذُهَا ٱلصِّبْيَانُ لِلَّعِبِ .

Puppy, *n.* A mean conceited fellow, مُتَصَلِّف ـ جَعْدُ ٱلْقَفَا ـ جُعَيْدِيّ ـ سَفِيه ـ غُنْدَر *vulg.* غَنْدُور . *See also* Pup, *n.*

Puppyism, *n.* سَفَاهَة ـ سَفَه ـ تَأَنُّق ـ تَصَلُّف .

Pur, *v.i.* ² خَرَّ ـ خَرْخَرَ .

Pur, *n.* خَرِير ـ خُرُور .

Purblind, *a.* أَخْفَش *fem.* خَفْشَاءُ ـ قَصِيرُ ٱلنَّظَرِ .

Purblindness, *n.* خَفَش .

Purchasable, *a.* مِمَّا يُشْتَرَى ـ شِرَاؤُهُ مُمْكِن ; with money, يُشْتَرَى بِٱلدَّرَاهِمِ .

Purchase, *v.t.* To buy, شَرَى = ـ اِشْتَرَى ـ اِبْتَاعَ . To make purchases, تَسَوَّقَ ـ تَبَضَّعَ . *See also to* Buy, *v.t.*

Purchase, *n.* The act of buying, اِشْتِرَاء ـ شِرًى ـ شِرَاء . A thing purchased, شِرًى *pl.* أَشْرِيَة ـ مُشْتَرًى ـ شِرَايَة ـ شِرْوَة .

Purchaser, *n.* مُشْتَرٍ ـ شَارٍ *pl.* ² شُرَاة ـ مُبْتَاع . A customer, زَبُون *pl.* زَبَائِنُ .

Pure, *a.* Clear, limpid, صَافٍ ـ قَرَاح ـ قَرِيح ; to be —, limpid, صَفَا *aor.* يَصْفُو ; to become —, تَصَفَّى . Unmixed, بَحْت ـ صِرْف ـ مَحْض ـ صَرِيح ـ خَالِص ـ صُرَاح ـ نَصُوح ـ قُحّ *pl.* أَقْحَاح ـ سَادِج ـ سُمَاق : a — lie, كَذِبٌ سُمَاقٌ . Pure, of colour, نَاصِع ; pure white, نَاصِعُ ٱلْبَيَاضِ ; pure yellow, أَصْفَرُ نَاصِعٌ . Clean, free from dirt, *etc.*, نَقِيّ *pl.* نِقَاء *and* ² أَنْقِيَاء . Clean of heart, holy, زَكِيّ ـ مُخْلِص ـ صَادِق ـ طَاهِر . Correct, in style, مُحَبَّر ـ مَضْبُوط . Pure gold, ذَهَبٌ خَالِصٌ . A — intention, نِيَّةٌ خَالِصَةٌ ـ نِيَّةٌ صَافِيَةٌ . To be —, unsullied, نَقِيَ = . To be —, of pure descent, صَرُحَ ² . To be —, exempt, from, ² خَلَا مِن ـ طَهُرَ مِن ² .

Purely, *ad.* Without admixture, بِصَرَاحَةٍ ; without guilt, بِزَكَاةٍ ـ بِطَهَارَةٍ ; merely, فَقَطْ ـ تَجْرِيدًا ; completely, بِٱلْكُلِّيَّةِ ـ بَتَّةً ـ طُرًّا . I did it — for fun, فَعَلْتُهُ لِلَّهْوِ فَقَطْ .

Pureness, *n.* *See* Purity, *n.*

Purgation, *n.* The act of cleansing, تَطْهِير . Purgation of the conscience, تَبْرِئَةُ ٱلذِّمَّةِ . The act of purging, تَسْهِيل .

Purgative, *a.* Cleansing, مُطَهِّر . Purging, مُسْهِل .

Purgative, *n.* جُلَّاب ـ دَوَاءٌ مُسْهِلٌ ـ مُسْهِل .

Purgatory, *n.* ٱلْمَطْهَرُ .

Purge, *v.t.* To cleanse, طَهَّرَ . To — the conscience, طَهَّرَ ٱلضَّمِيرَ .

To clear from accusation, بَرَّأَ ـ أَبْرَأَ . To — the bowels, ـ أَمْشَى أَسْهَلَ ٱلْبَطْنَ . To —, or justify, one's self, بَرَّرَ نَفْسَهُ . To take a purge, شَرِبَ شَرْبَةً ـ أَخَذَ شَرْبَةً .

Purging, *n.* Evacuation by stool, تَسْهِيلُ ٱلْبَطْنِ .

Purification, *n.* The act of purifying, cleansing, تَطْهِير ; of making clear, تَصْفِيَة ; of justifying, تَبْرِير ـ تَبْرِئَة . A washing, cleansing, غُسْل . The being clear from accusation, زَكَاة . A place of —, مَطْهَرَة . To make a — for, صَنَعَ تَطْهِيرًا لِ .

Purificative, *a.* }
Purificatory, } مُصَفٍّ ـ مُطَهِّر .

Purified, *a.* Cleansed, صَافٍ ـ مُصَفًّى ـ مُطَهَّر . Purified silver, فِضَّةٌ مُصَفَّاة . To be —, to be or become pure, صَفَا ـ خَلَصَ .

Purifier, *n.* مُصَفٍّ ـ مُطَهِّر . A — of metals, سَبَّاك ; of silver from the stone of the mine, مُحَصِّل .

Purify, *v.t.* To make pure, clean, ـ خَلَّصَ ـ أَصْفَى ـ صَفَّى ـ طَهَّرَ أَخْلَصَ . To make pure, to free from blame, to justify, زَكَّى . To —, cleanse, one's self, تَطَهَّرَ ـ اِطَّهَّرَ ; to justify one's self, تَبَرَّرَ ـ تَزَكَّى . To — metals from the minerals, حَصَّلَ .

Purist, *n.* A — in language, ـ مُتَصَفِّحٌ فِي ٱلْكَلَامِ ـ مُدَقِّقٌ فِي ٱللُّغَةِ مُحَبِّرٌ فِي ٱللُّغَةِ .

Puritan, *n.* مُتَحَمِّس ـ مُدَّعٍ بِٱلرَّشَادِ ـ مُتَصَوِّف .

Puritanic, *a.* } Devoted to religion, or affecting much devotion,
Puritanical, } ـ مُتَحَمِّس ـ مُدَّعٍ بِٱلرَّشَادِ ـ مُتَصَوِّف أَحْمَس .

Puritanically, *ad.* بِٱلتَّحَمُّسِ ـ بِٱلتَّصَوُّفِ .

Puritanism, *n.* تَحَمُّس ـ الِادِّعَآءُ بِٱلرَّشَادِ ـ تَصَوُّف .

Purity, *n.* Freedom from extraneous matter, ـ خَلَاص ـ خُلُوص خَالِصَة ـ نَقَاوَة . Clearness, صَفَاوَة ـ صَفَآء ـ صُفُوٌّ ـ نَقَاوَة . Moral purity, نَقَاوَة ـ عِصْمَة ـ عِفَّة . زَكَاة ـ طَهَارَة . Chastity, innocence, Correctness, ضَبْط ـ دِقَّة . Purity of intention, ـ بَرَآءَةُ ذِمَّةٍ تَحْبِيرُ ٱلْكَلَامِ . ـ صَفَآءُ ٱلنِّيَّةِ ـ خُلُوصُ ٱلنِّيَّةِ . Purity of style, ضَبْطُ (or دِقَّةُ) ٱللُّغَةِ ; of lineage, قَلْبَة .

Purl, *n.* A border, سِجَاف ; a border of lace, سِجَافٌ مِنْ شَبِيكَةٍ . Spiced beer, بِيرَةٌ مُتَبَّلَةٌ (or مُطَيَّبَةٌ) . *See also* Purling, *n.* and under *Beer*, *n.*

Purl, *v.i.* To murmur, of water, خَرْخَرَ ـ خَرَّ .

Purlieu, *n.* صَدَد ـ جِوَار ـ أَطْرَاف ـ حُدُود .

Purling, *n.* خَرْخَر ـ خَرْخَرَة ـ خَرِير .

Purling, *a.* خَرَّار ـ خَارّ .

Purloin, *v.t.* ـ سَلَّ ـ مِنْ ـ اِسْتَلَبَ ـ سَلَبَ ـ أَلْمَى بِ اِخْتَلَسَ ـ أَسَلَّ ـ سَرَقَ . *See also to* Plagiarize, *v.t.*

Purloiner, *n.* سَارِق ـ سَلَّابَة ـ سَالِب ـ مُخْتَلِس . *See also* Plagiarist, *n.*

Purloining, *n.* سِرْقَة ـ سَلَّابَة ـ سَلْب ـ إِلْمَآء .

Purple, *a.* فِرْفِيرِيٌّ ـ قِرْمِزِيٌّ ـ أَحْمَرُ قَانٍ ـ أُرْجُوَانِيٌّ .

Purple, *n.* فِرْفِير ـ لَوْنٌ قِرْمِز ـ أُرْجُوَان .

Purplish, *a.* يَضْرِبُ إِلَى لَوْنِ ٱلْقِرْمِزِ ـ يَضْرِبُ إِلَى ٱلْأُرْجُوَانِ .

Purport, *n.* إِفَادَة ـ غَرَض ـ مَضْمُون ـ مَعْنًى ـ فَحْوَى .

Purport, *v.t.* دَلَّ عَلَى ـ عَنَى بِ ـ أَفَادَ . The letter purports to have been written by the governor, ٱلظَّاهِرُ أَنَّ ٱلْخَطَّ كَتَبَهُ ٱلْحَاكِمُ .

Purpose, *n.* An object to be accomplished, غَرَض ـ قَصْد *pl.* غَايَة ـ مُطَالَعَة ـ مَقْصُود ـ مُرَاد ـ مَرَام ـ أَغْرَاض . An intention, قَصْد ـ عَمْدَة ـ عَمْد ـ عَزِيمَة ـ نَوًى ـ نِيَّة . I understood your —, فَهِمْتُ غَرَضَكَ .

A fixed purpose, عَزِيمَة ـ صَرِيمَة .

Foreign to the purpose, خَارِجَ ٱلْمَوْضُوعِ ـ خَارِجَ ٱلسَّدَدِ .

On purpose, عَمْدًا ـ قَصْدًا ـ عَمْدَ عَيْنٍ .

To no purpose, بِلَا طَائِلٍ ـ سُدًى ـ بِلَا فَائِدَةٍ ـ عَبَثًا ـ بَاطِلًا .

To some purpose, إِفَادَةً ـ بِنَفْعٍ مَا .

To the purpose, فِي مَحَلِّهِ ـ سَدِيدًا .

To what purpose ? لِأَيِّ شَيْءٍ ـ لِأَيِّ مَقْصُودٍ ـ لِمَاذَا .

To answer no purpose, ـ كَانَ غَيْرَ طَائِلٍ ـ مَا صَدَرَتْ مِنْهُ إِفَادَةٌ لَيْسَ هُوَ بِطَائِلٍ .

To answer one's purpose, أَفَادَ ـ لَاقَ بِمَقْصُودِهِ ـ وَافَقَ مَرَامَهُ .

To be at cross purposes, of many, اِخْتَلَفُوا ـ تَخَالَفُوا فِي ٱلْمَقْصُودِ فِي ٱلْأَمْرِ .

To come to the purpose, سَدَّدَ ـ أَسَدَّ .

To defeat one's own purposes, ـ خَيَّبَ مَقْصُودَهُ ـ خَيَّبَ نَفْسَهُ عَكَسَ أَمْرَهُ .

To gain one's purpose, ـ حَصَّلَ ٱلْمَطْلُوبَ ـ نَالَ ٱلْمَقْصُودَ حَظِيَ بِٱلْمَقْصُودِ .

Purpose, *v.t.* To intend, ـ تَعَزَّمَ عَلَى ـ عَزَمَ عَلَى ـ صَمَّدَ اِعْتَمَدَ ـ هَمَّ بِ ـ قَصَدَ ـ تَعَمَّدَ ـ تَنَوَّى ـ نَوَى أَنْ . To decide on, أَزْمَعَ عَلَى ـ أَجْمَعَ عَلَى . They purposed, decided on, the thing, اِيتَمَرُوا بِٱلْأَمْرِ .

Purposeless, *a.* ـ بَاطِل ـ خَالٍ عَنِ ٱلْمَقْصُودِ ـ بِدُونِ مَرَامٍ بِدُونِ طَائِلٍ .

Purposely, *ad.* قَصْدًا ـ عَمْدًا .

Purr, *v.i.* *See to* Pur, *v.i.*

Purring, *n.* *See* Pur, *n.*

Purse, *n.* A bag for money, صُرَّة *pl.* صُرَر ـ عِفَاص ـ سَلَف *pl.*

أَكْيَاس .pl كِيس — سُلُوف. A sum of money laid by, دَرَاهِمُ صَرِيرَةٌ. A sum of 500 piastres, كِيس .pl أَكْيَاس. A prize at a race, خَطَرٌ — سِبَاق. A long —, wealth, غَنَاءٌ — ثَرْوَة; having a long —, بَيْتٌ — الْخَزِينَةُ. The public —, صَاحِبُ مَالٍ — غَنِيٌّ — مُدَرْهَم — الْمَالِ. You cannot make a silk — out of a swine's ear, لا تُقْتَنَى مِنْ كَلْبٍ سُوءٍ جِرْوًا (prov. *Literally*, You will not get a whelp out of a bad dog). To draw the strings, as of a —, أَشْرَجَ. To tie up, as of a —, صَرَّ.

Purse, *v.t.* To put into a purse, كَيَّسَ — يَضَعُ .aor وَضَعَ في كِيس. To wrinkle, غَضَّنَ — شَنَّجَ. To — the mouth, شَنَّجَ فَمَهُ.

Purse-pride, *n.* غُرُورُ الْمَالِ — تَعَظُّمُ الْغَنَاءِ.

Purse-proud, *a.* مُتَعَظِّمٌ بِغَنَائِهِ — مَغْرُورٌ بِالْمَالِ.

Purser, *n.* Of a ship, مُحَاسِبٌ بَحْرِيٌّ.

Pursership, *n.* وَظِيفَةُ الْمُحَاسِبِ.

Pursiness, *n.* State of being contracted, تَشَنُّج; of being swollen, اِنْتِفَاخ — وَرَم — تَوَرُّم. Shortness of breath, ضَيْقُ نَفَسٍ.

Purslain, *n.* الرِّجْلَة — كُفّ — بَقْلَة — الْبَقْلَةُ الْحَمْقَاءُ — فَرْفَخ.

Pursuable, *a.* التَّتَبُّعُ — الإِجْرَاءُ بِهِ مُمْكِنٌ — التَّعْقِيبُ بِهِ مُمْكِنٌ — مِمَّا يُتَّخَذُ — فِيهِ مُمْكِنٌ.

Pursuance, *n.* A following, prosecution, مُدَاوَمَة — تَتَبُّع — دَوَامٌ عَلَى — سَعْي — نَهْج — مُوَاظَبَة. Accordance, مُمَاثَلَة — حَسَبَ — اِمْتِثَالاً بِ — تَطْبِيقًا لِ — مُطَابَقَة — اِمْتِثَال. In — of, مُطَابَقَة.

Pursuant, *a.* مُمَاثِل — مُطَابِق.

Pursue, *v.t.* To follow after in order to overtake, لَحِقَ — جَدَّ فِي طَلَبِهِ — تَبِعَ — طَرَدَ — سَعَى وَرَاءَهُ. To follow with perseverance, تَطَلَّبَ — طَلَبَ — تَتَبَّعَ — نَهَجَ — اِسْتَمَرَّ عَلَى. To —, as a course of conduct, ذَهَبَ — سَمَتَ — سَلَكَ مَذْهَبًا. He pursued a course, سَلَكَ طَرِيقًا. He pursued a good course, ذَهَبَ مَذْهَبًا حَسَنًا. He pursued the course of such an one, ذَهَبَ مَذْهَبَ فُلَانٍ. He pursued a course which severely injured him, سَلَكَ سُلُوكًا أَضَرَّهُ كُلَّ الضَّرَرِ. To cause one to — a course, أَسْلَكَ فِي — سَلَكَ فِي. *See also to* Prosecute, *v.t.*

Pursuer, *n.* One who runs after another, طَارِد — سُعَاة .pl سَاعٍ — طُرَّاد .pl. One who strives after anything, طُلَّاب .pl طَالِب. *See also* Prosecutor, *n.*

Pursuit, *n.* A running after, سَعْيٌ وَرَاءَ الشَّيْءِ — مُطَارَدَة — تَعْقِيب. Endeavour, جُهْد — مُجَاهَدَة — جِدّ — طَلَب — سَعْي. Occupation, وَظِيفَة — مَشْغَلَة — شُغْل — سَعَاة. An object of aim, أَغْرَاض .pl غَرَض.

Pursuivant, *n.* مُعَاوِنُ الْمُنَادِي.

Pursy, *a.* Inflated, وَارِم — مُنْتَفِخ — نَاتِئ. Short-breathed, ضَيِّقُ النَّفَسِ.

Purtenance, *n.* The pluck of an animal, أَمْعَاءٌ — جَوْف. *See also* Appurtenance, *n.*

Purulence, *n.* }
Purulency, } قَيْح — مِدَّة — غِثِيث — غَثِيثَة — قَصِيص. To clear a wound of —, اِسْتَغَثَّ الْجُرْحَ. *See also* Matter, *n.*

Purulent, *a.* ذُو غَثِيثٍ — مُقَيِّح — قَائِح. To be —, قَصَّ — قَاحَ — أَغَثَّ — غَثَّ.

Purvey, *v.t.* جَهَّزَ لِ — قَدَّمَ الْمُؤْنَةَ لِ — مَانَ. *See also to* Provision, *v.t.*

Purveyance, *n.* Procurement of supplies, تَقْدِيمُ الْمُؤْنَةِ — مَأْن — تَقْدِيمُ الزَّادِ. *See also* Provision, *n.*

Purveyor, *n.* مُوَّان — مُتَسَوِّق — كلارجي — كرارجي.

Purview, *n.* Scope, غَرَض — مَضْمُون — مَعْنَى — سَدَد — فَحْوَى. *See also under* Drift, *n.*

Pus, *n.* مِدَّة — قَيْح — غَثِيث — غَثّ.

Push, *v.t.* To press against with force, صَكَمَ — دَسَعَ — ضَغَطَ — دَفَرَ — دَفَشَ — دَفَعَ — يَسْطُو .aor سَطَا بِ — دَسَرَ. To drive, سَوَّقَ. To — one, as in a crowd, زَحَمَ — زَاحَمَ. To —, as into a corner, ضَيَّقَ عَلَى — قَصَفَ. To —, as with the horns, نَاطَحَ — نَطَحَ. To —, drive back, as of an enemy, دَرَأَ — اِرْتَدَّ — رَدَّ — رَجَعَ إِلَى وَرَاءٍ — لَزَّ — دَفَعَ — صَرَفَ. To attack, هَجَمَ عَلَى. To importune, أَلَحَّ عَلَى. To urge, حَرَّضَ. To be pushed, اِنْدَفَعَ — اِنْضَغَطَ — اِنْدَسَعَ. To push one's self against, اِنْضَغَطَ إِلَى — صَدَمَ. He pushed the matter too far, بَالَغَ فِي الْأَمْرِ — زَادَ وَكَثَّرَ فِي الْأَمْرِ. He pushed his cruelty to such an extent that..., بَلَغَتْ بِهِ الْقَسَاوَةُ إِلَى هٰذَا الْحَدِّ أَنْ.

The people pushed me, زَحَمَنِي النَّاسُ.

To push about, رَفَشَ — خَبَطَ — رَضْرَضَ — طَرَدَ.

To push an advantage, بَالَغَ فِي الْغَلَبَةِ.

To push an objection, أَصَرَّ عَلَى الِاعْتِرَاضِ.

To push away, أَبْعَدَ — طَرَدَ — دَفَعَ — رَدَّ.

To push back, رَدَّدَ — رَدَّ — رَجَعَ إِلَى وَرَاءٍ — لَزَّ — دَرَأَ — صَرَفَ.

To push or throw down, أَهْبَطَ — أَوْقَعَ — صَرَعَ.

To push forward, قَدَّمَ. To cause to progress, أَنْجَحَ — نَجَّحَ — رَوَّجَ — اِسْتَنْجَحَ.

To push or thrust in, أَدْخَلَ — دَسَرَ; to squeeze in, كَبَسَ; to make to penetrate, نَفَذَ — أَخَشَّ.

To push on, drive, سَوَّقَ — ـُ سَاقَ. To make to advance, قَدَّمَ. To make to progress, نَجَّجَ — أَنْجَجَ — رَوَّجَ.

To push one's self forward, to advance, to try to progress, سَعَى ـَ — تَرَوَّجَ — نَجَّجَ ـَ — تَقَدَّمَ. *See also to* Intrude, *v.t.*

To push out, expel, طَرَدَ ـُ — أَخْرَجَ.

Push, *v.i.* To push on, to advance, make progress, تَقَدَّمَ — تَرَوَّجَ — سَعَى ـَ. To push off, اِنْقَلَعَ — تَبَاعَدَ — اِسْتَبْعَدَ.

Push, *n.* A thrust, move, دَسْر — صَكْمَة — زَحْمَة — سَطْوَة — دَرْأَة — صَدْمَة — دَفْع — دَفْعَة — مُدَافَعَة. An impulse, مُسَاوَرَة. An exigency, ضَرُورَة — اِقْتِضَاء — لُزُوم. At a —, عِنْدَ ٱلِاقْتِضَاءِ — عِنْدَ ٱلضَّرُورَةِ.

Pushed, *a.* Thrust, مَدْسُور — مَضْغُوط — مَدْسُوع — مَصْكُوم — مُنْدَفِع — مَدْفُوش. To be —, to be in straits, تَضَيَّقَ عَلَيْهِ — اِنْحَصَرَ عَلَيْهِ. Pushed, in straits, مَحْصُور.

Pushing, *a.* Enterprising, مُرَوِّج — نَدِب — مِنْدَبِي — جَسُور. *See also* Intrusive, *n.*

Pusillanimity, *n.* فَشَل — نَخَب — جَبَانَة — جُبْن — جَبَانَة. *See also* Cowardice, *n.*

Pusillanimous, *a.* خَشْلٌ فَشْلٌ — فَشِيل — نَخِيب — جَبَان. *See also* Cowardly, *a.*

Puss, *n.*
Pussy, } قُطَيْط — دِرْص — اِبْنُ ٱلسِّنَّوْرِ.

Pussiness, *n.* *See* Pursiness, *n.*

Pussy, *a.* *See* Pursy, *a.*

Pustulate, *v.i.* تَنَقَّطَ — نَفِطَ ـَ — بَثِرَ ـَ — بَثَرَ ـُ — تَبَثَّرَ.

Pustule, *n.* نَفْطَة — نِفْطَة — نَافِطَة — بَثْرَة *coll.* بَثْر *pl.* بَثَرَات — صِمْغَة — عَدَسَة — دُمَّل *pl.* دَمَامِيل *and* دَمَامِل. A — on the face, غُدَّة. A — on the lips after a fever, عُقْبُول *pl.* عَقَابِيل. The — broke, عَزَّتِ ٱلْقَرْحَةُ ـِ. A — broke out upon him and he squeezed it, خَرَجَتْ بِهِ بَثْرَةٌ فَعَصَرَهَا. *See also under* Pimple, *n.*

Pustulous, *a.* نَافِط — مَنْفُوط — نَفِيط — مُتَبَثِّر — ذُو بَثَرَاتٍ — ذُو دَمَامِل.

Put, *v.t.* To lay or place, جَعَلَ ـَ — وَضَعَ *aor.* يَضَعُ — حَطَّ ـُ. To put a case, as, "for example," مَثَلًا. To put, as a key into its lock, جَعَلَ ـَ (*or* رَكَّبَ) ٱلْمِفْتَاحَ فِي ٱلْقُفْلِ. To put everything in its place, رَتَّبَ (*or* رَكَّنَ) كُلَّ شَيْءٍ فِي مَوْضِعِهِ. To put one's hand to a thing, to begin, شَرَعَ ـَ فِي.

To put about, to make to circulate, رَوَّجَ. To trouble, annoy, أَضْجَرَ — قَلَّقَ — كَلَّفَ — أَزْعَجَ. To make to turn round, أَجَالَ — دَوَّرَ-بِهِ.

To put aside, at a distance, جَنَّبَ — أَبْعَدَ; to be put aside, اِبْتَعَدَ — تَجَنَّبَ. To lay up, take care of, رَفَعَ ـَ — حَفِظَ ـَ — أَبْقَى. To give up, to abandon, تَخَلَّى عَنْ — تَرَكَ ـُ — سَيَّبَ.

To put away, to dismiss, أَذْهَبَ — طَرَدَ ـُ — نَفَى — دَشَّرَ. To put in a place of security, حَفِظَ ـَ — رَفَعَ ـَ — خَبَّأَ. To put out of hand, رَفَعَ ـَ — تَفَرَّغَ مِنْهُ. To abandon, abjure, تَرَكَ ـُ — رَفَضَ ـِ ـُ. To divorce, أَطْلَقَ — طَلَّقَ.

To put back, behind, أَدْبَرَ — أَخَّرَ — رَجَّعَ-إِلَى وَرَاءٍ. To put back into its place, رَدَّ ـُ — رَجَّعَ-إِلَى مَوْضِعِهِ — أَعَادَ-إِلَى مَكَانِهِ.

To put, or lay before, to submit to, وَجَّهَ-إِلَى — عَرَضَ-عَلَى ـِ.

To put by, lay up, ذَخَرَ ـَ — اِدَّخَرَ — خَبَّأَ — رَفَعَ ـَ — حَفِظَ ـَ.

To place by the side of one, جَعَلَ-إِلَى جَانِبِهِ ـَ.

To put down, out of hand, وَضَعَ *aor.* يَضَعُ — حَطَّ ـُ. To humiliate, أَذَلَّ — ذَلَّلَ — أَخْضَعَ — خَفَضَ ـِ — كَسَرَ نَفْسَهُ ـِ. To forbid, مَنَعَ ـَ — نَهَى ـَ — حَرَّمَ. To suppress, أَبْطَلَ. To quell, crush, قَمَعَ ـَ — ضَبَطَ ـُ ـِ. To lower, نَزَّلَ — أَنْزَلَ — وَطَّى. To put to silence, سَكَّتَ — أَسْكَتَ — قَطَعَ بِ — قَطَعَ لِسَانَهُ ـَ. To confute, نَاقَضَ — غَلَّطَ — رَدَّ عَلَى ـُ. To write down, كَتَبَ ـُ — قَيَّدَ — رَقَمَ ـُ. To put down as, to reckon as, نَزَّلَ-مَنْزِلَةَ كَذَا.

To put forth, outside, أَخْرَجَ. To extend, as the hand, *etc.*, مَدَّ ـُ. To put, set forth, to propose, عَرَضَ ـِ — طَرَحَ ـَ — قَدَّمَ. To publish, أَبْرَزَ — بَرَّزَ — نَشَرَ ـُ. To put forth, as a tree its leaves, وَرَقَ *aor.* يَرِقُ — وَرَّقَ — أَخْرَجَ ٱلْأَوْرَاقَ — نَبَّتَ ٱلْأَوْرَاقَ.

To put forward, advance, قَدَّمَ. To set forth, propose; *see under preceding sentence.*

To put in, within, أَدْخَلَ — دَخَّلَ — أَخَشَّ. To push in, دَسَرَ ـُ — دَسَّسَ — دَسَّ ـُ. To insert, أَدْرَجَ — دَرَّجَ. To make to penetrate, سَلَّكَ — نَفَذَ ـِ. To put in, as a claim, عَرَضَ — قَدَّمَ — اِدَّعَى بِ.

To put in an appearance, حَضَرَ ـُ — اِحْتَضَرَ.

To put in fear, خَوَّفَ — أَرْعَبَ — أَدْهَشَ — فَزَّعَ — أَفْزَعَ.

To put in mind, فَكَّرَ — ذَكَّرَ — أَنْبَهَ — نَبَّهَ.

To put in practice, أَجْرَى-فِعْلًا — اِسْتَعْمَلَ.

To put into one's hand, سَلَّمَ-إِلَى. To hand to, نَاوَلَ-لِ.

To put into one's power, to enable, أَمْكَنَ — قَدَّرَ-عَلَى — مَكَّنَ. To deliver up to, سَلَّمَ-إِلَى.

To put into port, طَلَبَ ٱلْمِينَا ـُ — دَخَلَ ٱلْمِينَا ـُ.

To put off, as clothes, نَزَعَ ـِ ... رَفَعَ ـَ عَنْ-ٱلـ — خَلَعَ ـَ — شَلَحَ ـَ — جَرَّدَ-مِنْ; to put off, as clothes, from one's self, اِنْجَرَدَ (*or* تَجَرَّدَ) مِنْ — خَلَعَ ـَ-عَنْ بَدَنِهِ — شَلَحَ ـَ ثِيَابَهُ. To defer,

أَخَّرَ — أَمْهَلَ — أَبْقَى - إِلَى — جَارَّ — آنَى — عَوَّقَ . To put off with promises, سَوَّفَ — ع مَطَلَ . To put off the payment of a debt, مَاتَنَ . To put off a creditor, جَارَّ . To turn from, ـِ عَدَلَ - عَن .

To put on, to place upon, وَضَعَ - عَلَى *aor.* يَضَعُ . To put on, as garments, تَكَسَّى بِ — ـَ لَبِسَ . To adopt, اِتَّخَذَ . To manifest, affect, تَصَنَّعَ — أَظْهَرَ — تَظَاهَرَ بِ . Put on, affected, مُمَوَّهٌ — مُتَصَنَّعٌ .

To put one off the scent, جَوَّنَ — تَيَّهَ — ضَيَّعَ .

To put one on his guard against, حَذَّرَ - مِن — أَنْذَرَ - بِ — نَبَّهَ - عَلَى .

To put one's hand to, وَضَعَ يَدَهُ عَلَى *aor.* يَضَعُ . To lay hold of, تَمَاسَكَ بِ — أَمْسَكَ بِ . To begin, ـَ شَرَعَ فِي . To sign, أَمْضَى — عَلَّمَ عَلَى — وَقَّعَ عَلَى .

To put one to it, to oblige, اِضْطَرَّ - إِلَى — أَلْزَمَ - بِ . To be put to it, to be obliged, اُضْطُرَّ إِلَى — اِلْتَزَمَ بِ .

To put one up to a thing, عَلَّمَ .

To put out, outside, أَخْرَجَ . To stretch out, as the hand, ع مَدَّ — ع بَسَطَ . To drive out, expel, ع طَرَدَ — أَخْرَجَ . To extinguish, as a candle, أَطْفَأَ ; as a fire, أَهْمَدَ — أَخْبَى . To cause to cease, أَبْطَلَ — أَزَالَ — أَبَادَ . To derange, disconcert, حَيَّرَ — وَعَّرَ — قَلْقَلَ — أَعْقَلَ — ـِ خَبَلَ . To put out, as efforts, ـَ سَعَى — اِجْتَهَدَ . To put out to interest, ع حَطَّ ٱلدَّرَاهِمَ بِٱلْفَائِدَةِ — شَغَّلَ فُلُوسَهُ . To put out, to take out, ـَ قَلَعَ . To put out the eyes, ـَ قَلَعَ ٱلْأَعْيُنَ .

To put upon, place upon, وَضَعَ - عَلَى *aor.* يَضَعُ — ـَ جَعَلَ - عَلَى . To place one thing upon another, رَكَّبَ - عَلَى . To be hard upon, ـِ ظَلَمَ — ع شَدَّ عَلَى — عَاسَرَ — عَسَّرَ عَلَى — قَاهَرَ — ضَايَقَ . To be put upon, treated harshly, ظُلِمَ — ضُيِّقَ عَلَى .

To put over, upon, وَضَعَ - عَلَى *aor.* يَضَعُ . To cover with, ع غَطَّا - بِ — لَبَّسَ - بِ — غَطَّى - بِ . To put one in command over, وَلَّى - بِ — رَأَّسَ - عَلَى .

To put to, as a question, ـِ عَرَضَ عَلَى - سُؤَالاً — ـَ سَأَلَ ; as horses to a carriage, ـِ رَبَطَ - فِي — ع كَدَنَ - فِي — عَلَّقَ - فِي . To add to, وَصَّلَ - بِ — ـِ زَادَ - فِي — أَضَافَ - إِلَى . To expose to, عَرَّضَ - عَلَى .

To put to death, ع قَتَلَ — ع أَمَرَ بِقَتْلِهِ .

To put to paper, ع كَتَبَ — حَرَّرَ .

To put to the sword, ـِ عَرَضَ - عَلَى ٱلسَّيْفِ .

To put to the torture, عَذَّبَ .

To put to trial, to try, test, اِمْتَحَنَ — جَرَّبَ . To try before a judge, حَاكَمَ .

To put together, collect together, ـَ جَمَعَ — ع لَمَّ . To arrange, أَصْلَحَ — رَمَّمَ — أَحْكَمَ — نَظَّمَ — رَتَّبَ — نَسَّقَ . To repair, رَمَّمَ ; as of glass, *etc.*, ـِ قَانَ ; as stones, in order, ع رَصَفَ .

To put up, on high, ـَ رَفَعَ — عَلَّى . To set up, as of a post, *etc.*, ـَ رَفَعَ — أَقَامَ — ع نَصَبَ — ع صَمَدَ . To put aside, lay by, ـَ حَفِظَ — خَبَّأَ . To pack, as in boxes, ـَ عَبَأَ — عَبَّأَ ; as in a parcel, ع صَرَّ .

To put up, as a prayer, قَدَّمَ صَلَوٰةً — قَدَّمَ دُعَآءً . To put up, of a sword, ع رَدَّ ٱلسَّيْفَ إِلَى غِلَافِهِ — غَلَّفَ ٱلسَّيْفَ . To give lodgings to, أَضَافَ — أَنْزَلَ — آوَى — بَوَّأَ . To make known, أَعْلَنَ .

To put up to auction, ـَ طَرَحَ - فِي — ع حَطَّ - فِي ٱلْمَزَادِ — ـِ بَاعَ - بِٱلْمَزَادِ . To put up for sale, ـِ عَرَضَ - عَلَى ٱلْبَيْعِ — ٱلْمَزَادِ .

To put upon, of expense, duty, *etc.*, كَلَّفَ - بِ .

Put, *v.i.*

To put about, as of a ship, ع دَارَ — جَالَ *aor.* يَجُولُ — اِنْجَالَ — اِجْتَالَ .

To put back, as of a ship, *etc.*, ـِ رَجَعَ — عَادَ إِلَى *aor.* يَعُودُ .

To put into harbour, ع دَخَلَ ٱلْمِينَةَ (*or* ٱلْمِينَآءَ) .

To put off, to sail, start, سَارَ *aor.* يَسِيرُ — ـَ ذَهَبَ — أَقْلَعَ — سَافَرَ — سَافَرَ .

To put to sea ; *See* To put off, *supra.*

To put up at a place, ـِ نَزَلَ بِ — ع حَلَّ بِ . *See also to* Lodge, *v.i.*

To put up for a place, to be a candidate for, ع طَلَبَ .

To put up with a thing, تَصَبَّرَ عَلَى — اِحْتَمَلَ .

Put, *n.* A strait, difficulty, ضِيقَةٌ — ضَيِّقَةٌ — شِدَّةٌ .

Putative, *a.* مَحْسُوبٌ — مَظْنُونٌ . A — son, عَلِيتٌ — مُعْتَلِيتٌ .

Put-off, *n.* A shift, evasion, حُجَّةٌ — مُحَاوَلَةٌ — حِيلَةٌ — رُوَيْغَةٌ .

Putrefaction, *n.* The process of —, تَعَفُّنٌ — عُفُونَةٌ . Anything putrified, شَيْءٌ مُتَعَفِّنٌ .

Putrefactive, *a.* مُعَفِّنٌ .

Putrefied, *a.* مُتَعَفِّنٌ — مَعْفُونٌ — مُعَفَّنٌ — عَفِنٌ . To consider —, أَعْفَنَ .

Putrefy, *v.t.* عَفَّنَ — ـِ عَفَنَ .

Putrefy, *v.i.* تَعَفَّنَ — ـَ عَفِنَ . *See also under* Putrid, *a.*

Putrescence, *n.* *See* Putrefaction, *n.*

Putrescent, *a.* مُتَعَفِّنٌ .

Putrescible, *a.* قَابِلُ ٱلْعُفُونَةِ — مِمَّا يَتَعَفَّنُ .

Putrid, *a.* مُتَعَفِّنٌ — مَعْفُونٌ — مُعَفَّنٌ — عَفِنٌ ; of water, آسِنٌ .

A — fever, حُمَّى عَفِنِيَّةٌ. To become —, تَعَفَّنَ ـ ٤ عَفِنَ; of water, أَسَنَ ٢ ـ أَجَنَ ٢. *See also under to* Spoil, *v.i.*

Putridity, *n.* / Putridness, } عُفُونَة; of water, أَجُون ـ أَسَن.

Putty, *n.* غِرَآءٌ لِلزُّجَاجِ ـ مَعْجُونٌ لِتَرْكِيبِ ٱلزُّجَاجِ.

Putty, *v.t.* سَدَّ ٢ ـ بِٱلْغِرَآءِ.

Puzzle, *v.t.* حَيَّرَ ـ دَهَّشَ ـ أَدْهَشَ ـ تَشَوَّشَ عَلَى ـ تَوَّهَ ـ خَبَّلَ. To be puzzled, تَحَيَّرَ ـ إِسْتَحَارَ ـ ضَلَّ ـ تَاهَ ٢ ـ دَجَرَ. The affair puzzled him, تَشَوَّشَ عَلَيْهِ ٱلْأَمْرُ.

Puzzle, *n.* A cause of embarrassment, حَيْرَة ـ مُشْكِلَة ـ صُعُوبَة ـ ضِلَّة. A game to try ingenuity, لَعِبٌ مُشْكِلٌ.

Puzzler, *n.* One who puzzles, مُحَيِّر ـ مُخَبِّل ـ مُدْهِش. A cause of embarrassment; *see preceding article.*

Puzzling, *a.* مُشْكِل ـ عَسِير ـ صَعْب ـ مُحَيِّر ـ مُخَبِّل ـ مُدْهِش.

Puzzolana, *n.* ضَرْبٌ مِنَ ٱلْمِلَاطِ لَايَنْفِذُ فِيهِ ٱلْمَآءُ *called in Egypt,* خَرَاسَانِيٌّ.

Pygmy, *a.* *See* Dwarfish, Dwarf, *a.*

Pyloric, *a.* مُتَعَلِّقٌ بِفَمِ ٱلْمِعْدَةِ ٱلتَّحْتَانِيِّ.

Pylorus, *n.* فَمُ ٱلْمِعْدَةِ ٱلتَّحْتَانِيُّ.

Pyramid, *n.* The figure, هَرَم *pl.* أَهْرَام *and* هِرَام. The pyramids of Egypt, هِرَامُ (*or* أَهْرَامُ) مِصْرَ. A regular —, هَرَمٌ مُنْتَظِمٌ.

Pyramidal, *a.* / Pyramidic, } بِشَكْلِ ٱلْهَرَمِ ـ مِثْلَ ٱلْهَرَمِ.

Pyre, *n.* كُومَةُ حَطَبٍ لِإِحْرَاقِ ٱلْجُثَثِ.

Pyrexia, *n.* عِلَّةُ ٱلْحُمَّى.

Pyriform, *a.* بِشَكْلِ ٱلْكُمَّثْرَى.

Pyrites, *n.* ضَرْبٌ مِنَ ٱلْمَعَادِنِ ـ حَجَرُ نَارٍ.

Pyritic, / Pyritical, *a.* / Pyritous, } مِثْلَ مَعْدِنِ حَجَرِ ٱلنَّارِ ـ مُتَعَلِّقٌ بِحَجَرِ ٱلنَّارِ.

Pyro-acetic acid, *n.* حُمُوضَةُ ٱلْخَلِّ مُسْتَخْرَجَةٌ بِوَاسِطَةِ ٱلنَّارِ.

Pyrolatry, *n.* عِبَادَةُ ٱلنَّارِ.

Pyroligneous, *a.* / Pyrolignic, } مُسْتَخْرَجٌ مِنَ ٱلْحَطَبِ بِوَاسِطَةِ ٱلنَّارِ. Pyroligneous acid, حُمُوضَةٌ مُقَطَّرَةٌ مِنَ ٱلْحَطَبِ بِوَاسِطَةِ ٱلنَّار.

Pyrologist, *n.* عَالِمٌ بِكَيْفِيَّاتِ ٱلنَّارِ وَمَا يَتَعَلَّقُ بِهَا.

Pyrology, *n.* عِلْمٌ يُبْحَثُ فِيهِ عَنْ كَيْفِيَّاتِ ٱلنَّارِ وَمَا يَتَعَلَّقُ بِهَا.

Pyromancy, *n.* ٱلتَّفَأُّلُ بِوَاسِطَةِ ٱلنَّارِ.

Pyrometer, *n.* مِيزَانُ ٱلنَّارِ.

Pyrophorus, *n.* فُسْفُور ـ مَادَّةٌ تَلْتَهِبُ إِذَا عُرِضَتْ لِلْهَوَآءِ.

Pyrotechnic, *a.* / Pyrotechnical, } مُتَعَلِّقٌ بِأَلْعَابِ ٱلْبَارُودِ وَصِنَاعَتِهَا.

Pyrotechnics, *n.* / Pyrotechny, } صِنَاعَةُ أَلْعَابِ ٱلْبَارُودِ.

Pyrotechnist, *n.* صَانِعُ أَلْعَابِ ٱلْبَارُودِ.

Pyrrhic, *a.* The — dance, ضَرْبٌ مِنَ ٱلرَّقْصِ عِنْدَ ٱلْيُونَانِيِّينَ.

Pyrrhonism, *n.* The doctrine of doubt, مَذْهَبُ أَهْلِ ٱلشَّكِّ.

Pyrrhonist, *n.* مِنْ أَهْلِ ٱلشَّكِّ.

Pythagorean, *n.* مِنْ أَهْلِ رَأْيِ فِيثَاغُورَسِ ٱلْحَكِيمِ.

Pythagorism, *n.* مَذْهَبُ فِيثَاغُورَسِ ٱلْحَكِيمِ.

Pythoness, *n.* *See* Soothsayer, *n.*

Pyx, *n.* / Pyxes, } A box for holding the consecrated host, حُقَّةُ ٱلْقُرْبَانِ ـ بَيْتُ ٱلْقُرْبَانِ ـ ٱلْمُقَدَّسِ. A box for testing coin, حُقَّةٌ لِعِيَارِ ٱلْمَسْكُوكَاتِ.

Q.

Quack, *v.i.* To — like a duck, بَطْبَطَ . To boast, إِفْتَخَرَ ـ تَفَخَّرَ ـ طَنَّبَ فِي حَالِهِ .

Quack, *n.* As of a duck, بَطْبَطَة . A charlatan, empiric, كَذَّاب ـ *vulg.* فَشَّار ـ خَرَّاط .

Quack, *a.* غَاشّ ـ كَذَّاب . Quack medicine, دَوَآءٌ غَاشّ ـ دَوَآءُ ٱلْغَشْمَآءِ ـ دَوَآءٌ غَيْرُ مُرَكَّبٍ عَلَى قَوَاعِدِ ٱلطِّبِّ .

Quackery, حِكْمَةٌ كَاذِبَةٌ ـ تَعَاطِي حِرْفَةٍ أَوْ صَنْعَةٍ بِدُونِ ٱتْقَانٍ ـ *vulg.* خَرْط .

Quadragesima, *n.* صَوْمُ ٱلْأَرْبَعِينَ ـ ٱلصَّوْمُ ٱلْكَبِيرُ .

Quadragesimal, *a.* أَرْبَعِينِيٌّ ـ مُتَعَلِّقٌ بِٱلصَّوْمِ ٱلْكَبِيرِ .

Quadrangle, *n.* A figure of four equal angles, شَكْلٌ مُرَبَّعٌ ـ ذُو أَرْبَعَةِ أَضْلَاعٍ . The inner court of a house, فُسْحَة ـ صَحْن ـ حَوْش *pl.* أَحْوَاش .

Quadrangular, *a.* ذُو أَرْبَعِ زَوَايَا .

Quadrant, *n.* The fourth part, رُبْع *pl.* أَرْبَاع . The fourth part of a circle, رُبْعُ دَائِرَةٍ . Ninety degrees, تِسْعُونَ دَرَجَةً . An instrument for taking altitudes, مِزْوَلَة . Quadrant of altitude, جَدْوَلُ ٱلِٱرْتِفَاعِ .

Quadrantal, *a.* مُتَعَلِّقٌ بِٱلرُّبْعِ . A — triangle, مُثَلَّثٌ تَامُّ ٱلضُّلُوعِ .

Quadrate, *a.* Square, مُرَبَّع . Having four parallel sides, قَائِمُ ٱلزَّوَايَا .

Quadrate, *n.* جِسْمٌ مُرَبَّعٌ .

Quadrate, *v.i.* To be accommodated to, to square with, طَابَقَ ـ نَاسَبَ ـ وَافَقَ .

Quadratic, *a.* مُرَبَّعِيٌّ . Quadratic equation, مُعَادَلَةُ ٱلدَّرَجَةِ ٱلثَّانِيَةِ .

Quadrature, *n.* تَرْبِيع .

Quadrennial, *a.* Happening once in four years, وَاقِعٌ مَرَّةً فِي أَرْبَعِ سِنِينَ .

Quadrennially, *ad.* مَرَّةً فِي أَرْبَعِ سِنِينَ .

Quadrilateral, *a.* ذُو أَرْبَعَةِ ضُلُوعٍ .

Quadrilateral, *n.* مُرَبَّع ـ جِسْمٌ ذُو أَرْبَعَةِ ضُلُوعٍ .

Quadriliteral, *a.* رُبَاعِيٌّ ; quasi-quadriliteral, مُلْحَقٌ بِٱلرُّبَاعِيِّ .

Quadriliteral, *n.* ذُو أَرْبَعَةِ أَحْرُفٍ ـ رُبَاعِيٌّ .

Quadrille, *n.* ضَرْبٌ مِنَ ٱلرَّقْصِ .

Quadrinomial, *a.* ذُو أَرْبَعَةِ حُدُودٍ .

Quadripartite, *a.* مُنْقَسِمٌ إِلَى أَرْبَعَةِ أَقْسَامٍ . A — international treaty, مُعَاهَدَةٌ بَيْنَ أَرْبَعِ دُوَلٍ .

Quadrisyllable, *n.* كَلِمَةٌ مُرَكَّبَةٌ مِنْ أَرْبَعَةِ أَجْزَآءٍ .

Quadroon, *n.* اِبْنُ (*or* بِنْتُ) أَبٍ أَبْيَضَ وَأُمٍّ خِلَاسِيَّةٍ أَيِ ٱمْرَأَةٍ بَيْنَ أَبَوَيْنِ أَبْيَضَ وَأَسْوَدَ .

Quadruman, *n.* }
Quadrumana, *n. pl.* } حَيَوَانٌ ذُو أَرْبَعِ أَيَادٍ .

Quadrumanous, *a.* ذُو أَرْبَعِ أَيَادٍ .

Quadruped, *n.* بَهِيمَة *pl.* بَهَائِمُ ـ مَاشِيَة *pl.* مَوَاشٍ ـ ذُو ٱلْأَرْبَعِ ـ ذُو أَرْبَعِ قَوَائِمَ ـ ذَوَاتُ ٱلْأَرْبَعِ *pl.* .

Quadruple, *a.* ذُو أَرْبَعَةِ أَضْعَافٍ ـ أَرْبَعَةُ أَضْعَافٍ .

Quadruple, *n.* أَرْبَعَةُ أَضْعَافٍ .

Quadruple, *v.t.* ضَاعَفَ أَرْبَعَ مِرَارٍ .

Quadruple, *v.i.* تَضَاعَفَ أَرْبَعَ مِرَارٍ .

Quadruplicate, *a.* Four times repeated, مُكَرَّرٌ أَرْبَعَ كَرَّاتٍ . *See also* Quadruple, *a.*

Quadruplicate, *v.t.* كَرَّرَ أَرْبَعَ كَرَّاتٍ . *See also to* Quadruple, *v.t.*

Quadruplication, *n.* تَكْرِيرُ أَرْبَعِ كَرَّاتٍ .

Quære, *int.* مَسْأَلَة ـ فَكَيْفَ ـ كَيْفَ ـ يَا تَرَى .

Quaff, *v.t.* To drink up all, إِلْتَمَعَ ـ ‹ قَمَعَ . *See also to* Drink, *v.t.*

Quag, *n.* }
Quagmire, } وَيْغَاس ـ رَخَاخِيٌّ *pl.* رَخَآءٌ .

Quaggy, *a.* أَوْعَس ـ رَخِيخ ـ رَخْرَخ .

Quail, *n.* The bird, سُمَانَى *coll.* سُمَان *pl.* سُمَانَات ـ سَلْوَاة *pl.* سَلْوَى *and* سَلْوَات .

Quail, *v.i.* To shrink from, ‹ جَبَأَ عَنْ ـ ‹ فَشِلَ عَنْ . To languish, تَخَفَّضَ ـ اِنْكَسَرَ قَلْبُهُ ـ اِهْتَبَطَ ـ ‹ فَشِلَ .

Quail, *v.t.* *See to* Depress, *v.t.*

Quaint, *a.* خَارِجٌ عَنِ ـ بَدِيع ـ غَرِيب ـ مِنْ جِنْسِ ٱلتُّحَفِ ٱلْعَادَةِ . A — thing or saying, نَادِرَة *pl.* نَوَادِرُ .

Quaintly, *ad.* بِوَجْهٍ غَرِيبٍ ـ بِصُورَةٍ غَرِيبَةٍ ـ عَجَبًا .

Quaintness, *n.* عَجَب ـ غَرَابَة ـ بَدَاعَة ـ نُدُور .

Quake, *v.i.* اِرْتَعَشَ ـ اِرْتَجَّ ـ اِخْتَلَجَ ـ ‹ رَجَفَ ـ ‹ رَعَشَ .

اِرْتَعَدَ . To cause to —, رَجَّ ² – أَرْجَفَ – أَرْعَدَ . The earth quaked, رَجَفَتِ ٱلْأَرْضُ .

Quake, n. } Quaking, n. } رُعَاش – اِرْتِعَاش – رَجْرَجَة – رَعْش – رِعْدَة .

Quaker, n. مِنْ أَهْلِ طَائِفَةٍ مِنَ ٱلنَّصَارَى يُؤْمِنُونَ بِٱلْوَحْيِ ٱلْخَاصِّ فِي أُمُورِ ٱلدِّينِ وَٱلْحَيَاةِ .

Quakerism, n. مَذْهَبُ ٱلنَّصَارَى ٱلْمُؤْمِنِينَ بِٱلْوَحْيِ ٱلْخَاصِّ فِي أُمُورِ ٱلدِّينِ وَٱلسُّلُوكِ .

Quaking, a. رَجْرَاج – رَجْرَج – مُرْتَعِش – رَعِش .

Qualifiable, a. That may be modified, قَابِل – مِمَّا يُعَدَّلُ ٱلتَّعْدِيلِ . That may be lightened, مِمَّا يُخَفَّفُ .

Qualification, n. Modification, تَخْفِيف – تَعْدِيل . Fitness, اِسْتِقْرَان – صَلَاحِيَة – صَلَاح – أَهْلِيَّة – جَدَارَة – خَلَاقَة . Restriction, شَرْط – قَيْد . The act of describing, وَصْف . An accomplishment, فَضِيلَة – بَرَاعَة pl. فَضَائِلُ ; accomplishments, شَمَائِلُ . *See also under* Quality, n.

Qualified, a. Moderated, مُعَدَّل ; softened, مُلَطَّف – مُخَفَّف . Fitted, أَهْل – خَلِيق – جَدِير . Qualified for, مُتَرَشِّح ل – كُفْؤ ل – قَادِر عَلَى – كَافٍ ل – خَلِيق ل – جَدِير ب – أَهْل ل . A qualified person, مَخْلَقَة – مَحْرَاة – مَجْدَرَة . He is — for (doing)..., هُوَ جَدِير ب – إِنَّهُ لَمَجْدَرَةٌ أَن . Restricted, مَحْدُود – مَحْصُور – مَحْبُوس . In a — sense, فِي مَعْنًى مَحْدُودٍ . To be —, fit to ..., خَلُقَ ل ² – جَدُرَ أَن ² . To deem —, أَهَّلَ .

Qualify, v.t. To make fit for, أَهَّلَ ل – جَدَّرَ ب – صَيَّرَ مُسْتَحِقًّا أَن . To moderate, لَطَّفَ – خَفَّفَ – عَدَّلَ . To enable, authorize, رَخَّصَ فِي – قَدَّرَ عَلَى – أَمْكَنَ مِن . To permit, أَذِنَ ل – ب – فِي or اِتَّسَعَ ل ² . To restrict, حَبَسَ – حَدَّدَ .

Qualitative, a. مُخْتَصٌّ بِٱلْكَيْفِيَّةِ . Qualitative analysis, تَحْقِيقُ ٱلْكَيْفِيَّاتِ .

Quality, n. That which belongs to a body, مَاهِيَّة – كَيْفِيَّة – حَال – صِفَة pl. صِفَات – شَأْن pl. شُؤُون . Nature, طَبْع . Character, صِفَة pl. صِفَات – خَصْلَة pl. خِصَال and خَصَلَات – خَلَّة . Disposition, طَبِيعَة – ضَرِيبَة – خَلِيقَة – مَشْرَب – شِيمَة pl. شِيَم . A kind, نَوْع pl. أَنْوَاع – صِنْف pl. أَصْنَاف – جِنْس pl. أَجْنَاس . Station, rank, شَأْن – دَرَجَة – مَرْتَبَة – مَنْزِلَة – رُتْبَة . A natural —, صِفَةٌ خِلْقِيَّةٌ ; an acquired —, صِفَةٌ ٱخْتِيَارِيَّةٌ ; an accidental —, صِفَةٌ عَرَضِيَّةٌ – عَرَض pl. أَعْرَاض ; an essential —, ذَاتِيَّة . Good (moral) qualities, مَحَاسِنُ – مَحَامِدُ – خَيْرَات – أَوْصَاف حَمِيدَة . A bad moral —, خَبِيثَة pl. خَبَائِثُ ; bad moral qualities, أَخْلَاق رَدِيَّة – أَوْصَاف رَدِيَّة . Endowed with good qualities, مَوْصُوفٌ بِأَوْصَافٍ حَمِيدَةٍ وَخِصَالٍ مَجِيدَةٍ – حَسَنُ ٱلشَّمَائِلِ لَطِيفُ ٱلْخَصَائِلِ . Of a good quality, جَيِّدُ ٱلصِّنْفِ ; of a good —, texture, جَيِّدُ ٱلنَّسْجِ . He took him in the — of secretary, أَخَذَهُ بِمَقَامِ كَاتِبٍ . In my — of..., مِنْ حَيْثُ أَنِّي . In the — of an adviser not of deciding, فِي صِفَةِ مُشَاوِرٍ لَا فِي صِفَةِ حُكْمٍ . Merchandise of the first —, بِضَاعَةٌ خَارِقَةٌ – بِضَاعَةٌ مِنَ ٱلْعَالِ – مِنَ ٱلْخَوَاصِّ . A man of —, صَاحِبُ حَسَبٍ وَنَسَبٍ – رَجُلٌ كَبِيرٌ – صَاحِبُ رُتْبَةٍ . The quality, persons of rank, أَصْحَابُ حَسَبٍ وَنَسَبٍ – ٱلْخَوَاصُّ – ٱلْأَكَابِرُ . Quality and quantity, ٱلْكَيْفِيَّةُ وَٱلْكَمِّيَّةُ .

Qualm, n. Nausea, غَثَيَان – خَبَاثَةُ ٱلنَّفْسِ . A — of conscience, شَكّ . To have qualms of conscience, تَشَكَّكَ .

Qualmish, a. Affected with nausea, خَبِيثُ ٱلنَّفْسِ .

Qualmishness, n. *See* Qualm, n.

Quandary, n. صُعُوبَة – مُعْضِلَة – حَيْرَة – وَرْطَة . In a —, فِي حَيْرَةٍ وَفَشَلٍ . To be in a —, تَوَرَّطَ فِي وَرْطَةٍ . To throw one's self into a —, اِسْتَوْرَطَ فِي وَرْطَةٍ .

Quantity, n. That property of anything which may be increased or diminished, قَدْر – كَمّ – كَمِّيَّة . An indefinite extent, قَدّ – مِقْدَار – قَدْر – حَسَب – طَوْر . Measure, as in versification, مِيزَان – أَوْزَان pl. وَزْن . A small —, جُزْء pl. جُزْعَة – نُضَيِّض – جُزْعَة pl. نُتْفَة – نُتَف – قَلِيل – قِلَّة – قِرْطِيطَة – عُلْصَة – جُزَيْعَة . A large —, كَثْرَة – جُبْلَة .

Quarantine, n. مُدَّةُ أَرْبَعِينَ يَوْمًا أَوْ أَقَلَّ مِنْ ذٰلِكَ تُمْنَعُ فِيهَا ٱلْمَرَاكِبُ أَوِ ٱلرُّكَّابُ أَوِ ٱلْأَمْتِعَةُ مِنَ ٱلِاخْتِلَاطِ بِٱلْغَيْرِ خَوْفًا مِنَ ٱلطَّاعُونِ وَغَيْرِهِ مِنَ ٱلْأَمْرَاضِ – كُورَنْتِينَا . To impose — upon, رَسَمَ ² ٱلْكُورَنْتِينَا عَلَى . Orders have been issued imposing — on all arrivals from thence, صَدَرَ ² أَمْرٌ بِوَضْعِ ٱلْكُورَنْتِينَا عَلَى مَنْ قَدِمَ مِنْ هُنَاكَ . He has ordered ten days' — on the vessels arriving at Egyptian ports, رَسَمَ ² بِٱلْكُورَنْتِينَا مُدَّةَ عَشَرَةِ أَيَّامٍ عَلَى ٱلسُّفُنِ ٱلَّتِي تَرِدُ إِلَى مَرَاسِي مِصْرَ . To be in —, كَرْتَنَ . A — board, دِيوَانُ ٱلصِّحَّةِ .

Quarrel, n. A breach of friendship, شِقَاق – خِلَاف – صَرِيمَة – تَنَاجُز . A cause of difference, صُرْم – شَجْر – شُجُور . A dispute, غَاغَا – خِنَاق – مُنَازَعَة – نِزَاع – مُشَاجَرَة . A noisy —, brawl, غَوْشَة – فِتْنَة – قِتَال . An arrow with a square head, نُشَّابَةٌ مُرَبَّعَةُ ٱلنَّصْلِ . A diamond pane of glass, لَوْحُ زُجَاجٍ شَكْلَ ٱلْمُعَيَّنِ . The matter was a cause of — between them, شَجَرَ ² ٱلْأَمْرُ بَيْنَهُمْ . Respecting their —, or cause of difference, فِيمَا شَجَرَ بَيْنَهُمْ . Avoid the — which has arisen among my companions, إِيَّاكُمْ وَمَا

شَجَرَ بَيْنَ أَصْحَابِى. A groundless —, مُنَازَعَةٌ لا أَصْلَ لَهَا وَلا فَصْلَ. To seek a — against one, تَعَرَّضَ لَهُ — وَقَعَ بِهِ aor. يَقَعُ.

Quarrel, *v.i.* To dispute, contend, تَنَازَعَ — تَشَاجَرَ — تَنَاجَزَ — تَخَالَفَ. They quarrelled amongst themselves, of many, إِشْتَجَرُوا — تَنَاجَزُوا — تَعَالَجُوا. To — with, شَاجَرَ — نَازَعَ — خَاصَمَ.

Quarreller, *n.* *See* Quarrelsome, *a.*

Quarrelling, *n.* *See* Quarrel, *n.*

Quarrelsome, *a.* أَلَدُّ *pl.* لُدٌّ *and* لِدَاد — مَرِث — شَكِس — شَرِس — شَرِيس. To be —, مَرِثَ — شَكِسَ — شَرِسَ. *See also under* Pugnacious, *a.*

Quarrelsomeness, *n.* لَدٌّ — مَرَث — شَكَاسَة — شَرَاسَة.

Quarrier, *n.* *See* Quarry-man, *n.*

Quarry, *n.* A stone mine, مَحْجَر *pl.* مَحَاجِر — مَعْدِنُ حَجَرٍ *pl.* مَعَادِنُ. Game, صَيْد.

Quarry, *v.t.* To take stones from a quarry, قَطَعَ الْحِجَارَةَ مِنَ الْمَعْدِنِ — عَالَجَ مَعْدِنَ الْحَجَرِ. *See also to* Mine, *v.t.*

Quarrying, *n.* قَطْعُ الْحَجَرِ مِنْ مَعْدِنِ الْحَجَرِ — مُعَالَجَةُ مَعْدِنِ.

Quarry-man, *n.* مُعَدِّنُ الْحَجَرِ — قَطَّاعُ الْحَجَرِ فِى مَعْدِنٍ.

Quart, *n.* The fourth of a gallon, كُوَارْت وَهُوَ مِكْيَالُ الْمَوَائِعِ رُبْعُ الْكَالَن — يَسَعُ ٢٨٠ دِرْهَمًا. *See under* Gallon, *n.*

Quartan, *a.* Denoting a fourth, عِبَارَةٌ عَنِ الرُّبْعِ. Occurring every fourth day, وَاقِعٌ مَرَّةً فِى أَرْبَعَةِ أَيَّامٍ. A — fever, حُمَّى الرِّبْعِ.

Quarter, *n.* A fourth part, رُبْع *pl.* أَرْبَاع. A limb of a slaughtered animal, بَدَن *pl.* أَبْدَان. The weight called a —, 28lbs., وَزْنٌ نَحْوَ ٢٨ رِطْلًا. A —, or eight bushels, مِكْيَالٌ نَحْوَ ١٠ أَمْدَادٍ. Point, direction, جِهَة *pl.* جِهَات — طَرَف *pl.* أَطْرَاف — نَاحِيَة *pl.* نَوَاحِى — صَوْب. A region, district, ثُغْرَة *pl.* ثُغَر — نَاحِيَة *pl.* نَوَاحِى — أَقْلِيم *pl.* أَقَالِيم — دِيَار — بِلَاد — حَوَالِى — أَطْرَاف. A continent, قَارَّة. A —, as of a town, حَارَة *pl.* حَارَات — مَحَلَّة *pl.* مَحَلَّات; a — outside the town walls, ضَاحِيَة *pl.* ضَوَاحٍ. Quarter of the wind, that from which it blows, مَرَاد الرِّيحِ. The hind part of a ship, مُؤَخَّرُ الْمَرْكَبِ. A quarter, three months, رُبْعُ سَنَةٍ — ثَلَثَةُ أَشْهُرٍ. A — of the moon, رُبْعُ مَسِيرِ الْقَمَرِ. Mercy shown by a conqueror, ذِمَّة — أَمَان. Quarter, as of a boot, جَانِب *pl.* جَوَانِب. Quarters, lodgings, مَنْزِل — سُكْنَى — مَحَلّ — مَبِيت. Soldiers' quarters, مَنْزِلُ الْعَسْكَرِ — قُشْلَة. Winter quarters, مَشْتًا. In different quarters, places, فِى جِهَاتٍ مُتَفَرِّقَةٍ. The nations which are in the four quarters of the earth, الْأُمَمُ الَّتِى فِى أَرْبَعَةِ أَقْطَارِ الْأَرْضِ. They used to come to him from every —, كَانُوا يَأْتُونَ إِلَيْهِ مِنْ كُلِّ نَاحِيَةٍ.

A fore quarter of lamb, رُبْعُ الْخَارُوفِ مِنْ طَرَفِ الْكَتِفِ.

A hind quarter of lamb, رُبْعُ الْخَارُوفِ مِنْ طَرَفِ الرِّجْلِ.

To ask for quarter, إِسْتَأْمَنَ — طَلَبَ الْأَمَانَ.

To beat to quarters, دَقَّ بِالْإِسْتِحْضَارِ.

To beat up one's quarters, زَارَ aor. يَزُورُ — طَلَبَ مَنْزِلَهُ.

To change one's quarters, تَحَوَّلَ.

To come to close quarters, as in battle, of many, قَامُوا عَلَى سَاقٍ.

To give quarter, آمَنَ — أَعْطَى الْأَمَانَ.

Quarter, *v.t.* To divide into four parts, قَسَمَ أَرْبَعَةَ أَجْزَاءٍ. To give quarters to, أَنْزَلَ — سَكَّنَ — بَوَّأَ — آوَى.

Quarter, *v.i.* *See to* Lodge, *v.i.*

Quarter-day, *n.* أَمَدُ ثَلَاثَةِ أَشْهُرٍ *pl.* آمَاد.

Quarter-deck, *n.* دِيوَانُ مُؤَخَّرِ الْمَرْكَبِ — سُلُوقِيَّةُ الرُّبَّانِ; *from the Italian*, كَمَرِيَّة — كَمْرَتَّة.

Quartering, *n.* Division into four parts, تَقْسِيمٌ إِلَى أَرْبَعَةِ أَجْزَاءٍ. The act of lodging, إِيوَاء — تَبْوِئَة — تَسْكِين. A station, مَنْزِل — مَحَطّ — مَحَطَّة — مَقَام. Division of a shield, in heraldry, تَرْسِيمُ عَلَامَاتِ النَّسَبِ فِى صُورَةِ الْأَرْمَا. A —, or station, of soldiers, مُعَسْكَر.

Quarterly, *a.* وَاقِعٌ مَرَّةً فِى ثَلَاثَةِ أَشْهُرٍ.

Quarterly, *ad.* كُلَّ ثَلَاثَةِ أَشْهُرٍ.

Quarterly, *n.* Of a book, جَرِيدَةٌ تَصْدُرُ مَرَّةً فِى ثَلَاثَةِ أَشْهُرٍ.

Quarter-master, *n.* Of a military force, ضَابِطٌ مَأْمُورٌ بِتَبْوِئَةِ الْعَسَاكِرِ; of a ship, بَحْرِىٌّ مَأْمُورٌ بِحِفْظِ الْبُوصَلَةِ وَالْبَيَارِقِ وَمَا أَشْبَهَهَا.

Quarter-Master General, كَبِيرُ الضُّبَّاطِ الْمَأْمُورِينَ بِتَبْوِئَةِ الْعَسْكَرِ — مُدِيرُ النُّزُلِ.

Quartern, *n.* A fourth part of a pint, مِكْيَالٌ يَسَعُ نَحْوَ ٣٥ دِرْهَمًا.

Quartern-loaf, *n.* رَغِيفٌ وَزْنُهُ رِطْلَانِ *pl.* رُغْفَان *and* رُغُف.

Quarter-sessions, *n.* مَحْكَمَةٌ تُقَامُ فِى الْأَيَالَاتِ مَرَّةً فِى ثَلَاثَةِ أَشْهُرٍ.

Quarter-staff, *n.* دَبُّوس — تَقْصِيرَة.

Quartet, *n.* / Quartette, } A stanza of four lines, رُبَاعِىٌّ. A piece of music for four voices or instruments, مَقَامَةٌ مُرَتَّبَةٌ لِأَرْبَعَةِ نَوْبَاتِيَّةٍ أَوْ أَرْبَعَةِ مُغَنِّينَ.

Quarto, *a.* فِى قَطْعَةِ الرُّبْعِ — فِى الرُّبْعِ. A book in —, كِتَابٌ فِى قَطْعَةِ الرُّبْعِ — كِتَابٌ مُرَبَّعُ الشَّكْلِ.

Quartz, *n.* مَرْوَة *coll.* مَرْو — صَوَّان.

Quartziferous, *a.* مِنَ الصَّوَّانِ — ذُو صَوَّانٍ.

Quartzose, *a.* صَوَّانِىٌّ — مِثْلُ الصَّوَّانِ.

Quash, *v.t.* To crush, أَجَشَّ ـ دَقَّ ² ـ سَحَقَ ² ـ هَرَسَ ². To destroy, annul, أَبْطَلَ ـ فَسَخَ ². To beat down, دَكَّ ² ـ هَدَّ ². To extinguish, أَطْفَأَ.

Quasi, *prefix.* As if, كَأَنَّ. Almost, تَقْرِيبًا. *As an adjective*, like to, approaching to, مُلْحَقٌ بِ. A — sound verb, فِعْلٌ مِثَالٌ.

Quasi-passive, مُطَاوِعٌ.

Quassia, *n.* شَجَرَةٌ قِشْرُهَا مُرٌّ كَالْقِينَا قِينَا.

Quaternion, *n.* As of soldiers, رَابِعٌ مِنَ ٱلْعَسْكَرِ.

Quatrain, *n.* رُبَاعِيٌّ.

Quaver, *v.i.* Of the voice, رَجَّعَ صَوْتَهُ ـ تَرَنَّمَ.

Quaver, *n.* Of the voice, تَطْرِيبٌ ـ تَرْجِيعٌ (*or* تَطْرِيبُ) ٱلصَّوْتِ ـ ٱلتَّدَعِّي ـ تَرَنُّمٌ. The musical note, إِشَارَةٌ فِي كِتَابَةِ ٱلْمُوسِيقَى.

Quavering, *n.* *See* Quaver, *n.*

Quay, *n.* رَصِيفٌ ـ رَصَفٌ ـ إِسْكَلَةٌ.

Quayage, *n.* أُجْرَةُ ٱلرَّصِيفِ ـ حَقُّ ٱلْإِسْكَلَةِ.

Queachy, *a.* *See* Quaggy, *a.*

Quean, *n.* سَلِيطَةٌ ـ سِلْقَةٌ ـ عَاهِرَةٌ.

Queasiness, *n.* *See* Nausea, *n.*

Queasy, *a.* Having nausea, خَابِثُ ٱلنَّفْسِ.

Queen, *n.* سُلْطَانَةٌ ـ مَلِكَةٌ. Queen, at chess, فِرْزَانٌ *pl.* فَرَازِينُ. To become a — at chess, تَفَرْزَنَ.

Queen bee, أُمُّ ٱلنَّحْلِ. The king bee, يَعْسُوبٌ.

Queen Consort, زَوْجَةُ سُلْطَانٍ ـ زَوْجَةُ مَلِكٍ.

Queen Dowager, أَرْمَلَةُ سُلْطَانٍ ـ أَرْمَلَةُ مَلِكٍ.

Queen Mother, وَالِدَةُ سُلْطَانٍ ـ وَالِدَةُ مَلِكٍ.

Queen Regent, مَلِكَةٌ نَائِبَةٌ.

Queenlike, *a.*
Queenly, *ad.* } مِثْلَ ٱلْمُلُوكِ ـ مِثْلَ ٱلْمَلِكَةِ.

Queen's-metal, *n.* مَعْدِنٌ أَبْيَضُ.

Queen-post, *n.* قَائِمَةٌ ـ عُمْدَةُ ٱلرَّوَافِدِ.

Queer, *a.* Not feeling well, عَلِيلٌ ـ شَاكٍ ـ مَشْكُوٌّ. *See also* Odd, Quaint, Strange, *a.*

Queerly, *ad.* *See* Oddly, Quaintly, *ad.*

Queerness, *n.* *See* Oddity, Quaintness, *n.*

Quell, *v.t.* To still, أَسْكَتَ ـ سَكَّتَ ـ أَهْدَأَ ـ هَدَّأَ ـ سَكَّنَ. To overpower, reduce, أَخْضَعَ ـ قَمَعَ ². To put out, extinguish, as a rebellion, أَطْفَأَ ـ قَمَعَ ².

Queller, *n.* One who subdues, غَالِبٌ ـ قَهَّارٌ ـ قَاهِرٌ.

Quench, *v.t.* To extinguish, أَطْفَأَ ـ أَهْمَدَ ـ أَبَاخَ. To — thirst, كَسَرَ ٱلظَّمَأَ ². To be quenched, extinguished, طَفِئَ ² ـ اِنْطَفَأَ ـ هَمَدَ ².

Quenchable, *a.* That may be extinguished, مِمَّا يُطْفَأُ; that may be put down, quieted, مِمَّا يُهْمَدُ.

Quenchless, *a.* لَا يُطْفَأُ.

Quenchlessness, *n.* عَدَمُ ٱلْإِطْفَاءِ.

Querimonious, *a.* *See* Querulous, *a.*

Querimoniously, *ad.* *See* Querulously, *ad.*

Querimoniousness, *n.* *See* Querulousness, *n.*

Querist, *n.* سَائِلٌ *pl.* سَأَلَةٌ *and* سُؤَّالٌ.

Querl, *v.t.* To twirl, فَتَلَ ² ـ دَوَّرَ.

Quern, *n.* رَحَى ٱلْيَدِ ـ غَرِيبَةٌ.

Querulous, *a.* مُتَذَمِّرٌ ـ مُدَمْدِمٌ ـ مُتَنَاجِلٌ ـ شَاكٍ ـ شَكِيٌّ.

Querulously, *ad.* بِتَذَمُّرٍ ـ بِدَمْدَمَةٍ ـ بِتَشَكٍّ.

Querulousness, *n.* تَذَمُّرٌ ـ دَمْدَمَةٌ ـ تَشَكٍّ.

Query, *v.t.* سَأَلَ *aor.* يَسْأَلُ ـ اِسْتَخْبَرَ مِنْ ـ اِسْتَفْهَمَ.

Query, *v.i.* سَأَلَ مَسَائِلَ *aor.* يَسْأَلُ.

Query, *n.* مَسْأَلَةٌ *pl.* مَسَائِلُ. *See also* Question, *n.*

Quest, *n.* طَلَبٌ ـ تَفْتِيشٌ. To go in — of, سَارَ فِي تَفْتِيشِهِ ² ـ اِنْطَلَقَ فِي طَلَبِهِ ـ سَارَ فِي نَشْدِهِ ².

Question, *n.* The act of asking, سُؤَالٌ ـ اِسْتِفْهَامٌ ـ اِسْتِخْبَارٌ. That which is asked, مَسْأَلَةٌ *pl.* مَسَائِلُ ـ سُؤَالٌ *pl.* سُؤَالَاتٌ. A subject of debate, مَسْأَلَةٌ ـ صَدَدٌ ـ مَادَّةٌ *pl.* مَوَادُّ ـ مَطْلَبٌ ـ مَوْضُوعٌ ـ مَبْحَثٌ ـ مَا نَحْنُ فِيهِ ـ كَلَامٌ. Responsibility, مَسْئُولِيَّةٌ. A doubt, إِشْكَالٌ ـ رَيْبٌ ـ شُبْهَةٌ ـ اِشْتِبَاهٌ. A dispute, controversy, نِزَاعٌ ـ مُنَازَعَةٌ. A vexed —, عُقْلَةٌ مِنَ ٱلْعُقَلِ. An affair, مَصْلَحَةٌ. A — put, proposed, أُطْرُوحَةٌ. Difficult questions, غَوَامِضُ ٱلْمَسَائِلِ. A political —, مَسْأَلَةٌ سِيَاسِيَّةٌ. Let us return to the —, نَرْجِعُ إِلَى مَا نَحْنُ فِيهِ ـ نَرْجِعُ إِلَى مَا نَحْنُ بِصَدَدِهِ ـ فِي أَيِّ شَيْءٍ ٱلْكَلَامُ ـ مِنَ ٱلْكَلَامِ. What is the — ? مَاذَا ٱلْمَطْلَبُ ـ مَاذَا هُوَ صَدَدُ ٱلْكَلَامِ. Most of the questions connected with this matter, جُلُّ ٱلْمَسَائِلِ ٱلْمُتَعَلِّقَةِ بِهٰذَا ٱلْأَمْرِ. The — is to know whether…, ٱلْمُرَادُ لِكَيْ نَعْرِفَ إِنْ. I put the — to him, طَرَحْتُ عَلَيْهِ ٱلْمَسْأَلَةَ. I put forward a contradiction or contrariety in the —, طَرَحْتُ ٱلْخِلَافَ فِي ٱلْمَسْأَلَةِ. Out of the —, debate, خَارِجٌ عَنِ ٱلْكَلَامِ. He laid himself open to —, عَرَّضَ نَفْسَهُ ² لِلْمَسْئُولِيَّةِ. This is one of the questions which…, هٰذِهِ ٱلْمَسْأَلَةُ مِنْ ضِمْنِ ٱلْمَسَائِلِ ٱلَّتِي. It is out of the —, مُحَالٌ. There can be no —, doubt, about it, لَا شُبْهَةَ فِيهِ ٱلْبَتَّةَ. Beyond all question, مِنْ غَيْرِ شَكٍّ ـ بِلَا شَكٍّ ـ لَا وَهْمَ. Fair question, سُؤَالٌ جَائِزٌ ـ مَسْأَلَةٌ جَائِزَةٌ. In question, debate, مَبْحُوثٌ عَنْهُ. In dispute, فِيهِ مُنَازِعٌ.

Leading question, مَسْأَلَةٌ يَعْرِضُهَا ٱلسَّائِلُ عَلَى مُخَاطِبِهِ بِقَصْدِ تَفْرِيطِهِ فِي جَوَابٍ يُلَائِمُ غَرَضَهُ — مَسْأَلَةٌ ٱسْتِنْطَاقِيَّةٌ.

The Eastern Question, المَسْأَلَةُ ٱلشَّرْقِيَّةُ.

Unfair question, مَسْأَلَةٌ غَيْرُ جَائِزَةٍ — سُؤَالٌ غَيْرُ جَائِزٍ.

To beg the question, فَرَضَ — قَدَّرَ ٱلْمَجْهُولَ — حَصَّلَ ٱلْمَحْصُولَ ٱلْمَبْحُوثَ عَنْهُ.

To call in question, to doubt, deny, تَمَارَى فِي — أَنْكَرَ — نَكِرَ — اِخْتَلَجَ.

To call to question, حَاكَمَ: We shall certainly be called to question for this matter, لَا بُدَّ مِنْ أَنْ نُحَاكَمَ مِنْ أَجْلِ هٰذَا ٱلْأَمْرِ.

To put a question, طَرَحَ سُؤَالًا — عَرَضَ مَسْأَلَةً.

To solve a question, فَكَّ ٱلْمُشْكِلَةَ — حَلَّ ٱلْمَسْأَلَةَ.

To state a question, وَضَعَ مَسْأَلَةً — بَيَّنَ مَسْأَلَةً — أَوْرَدَ مَسْأَلَةً aor. يَضَعُ.

Question, *v.t.* To interrogate, سَأَلَ-عَنْ aor. يَسْأَلُ — اِسْتَفْهَمَ مِنْ. To — or interrogate judicially, اِسْتَنْطَقَ. To hold a colloquy with, حَاوَرَ — جَاوَبَ. To express doubt of, أَنْكَرَ — تَشَكَّكَ فِي — شَكَّ فِي. To try with questions, اِمْتَحَنَ-بِمَسَائِلَ. To dispute, نَازَعَ — نَاظَرَ فِي.

Question, *v.i.* To ask a question, سَأَلَ مَسْأَلَةً aor. يَسْأَلُ — سَأَلَ aor. يَسْأَلُ. He persisted in questioning, لَجَّ بِٱلسُّؤَالِ. They questioned among themselves, سَأَلَ بَعْضُهُمْ بَعْضًا. When he was questioned about his act, لَمَّا سُئِلَ عَنْ فِعْلِهِ.

Questionable, *a.* Contestable, مَشْكُوكٌ — عَقِيمٌ — فِيهِ مَنَازِعُ — إِنْكَارُهُ مُمْكِنٌ — فِيهِ خِلَافٌ. Suspicious, مُشْتَبِهٌ.

Questionableness, *n.* شُبْهَةٌ.

Questionably, *ad.* بِصُورَةٍ يُشَكُّ فِيهَا.

Questioner, *n.* سَائِلٌ *pl.* سَأَلَةٌ *and* سُؤَّالٌ.

Questioning, *n.* The state of being questioned, مَسْئُولِيَّةٌ; the act of interrogating judicially, اِسْتِنْطَاقٌ.

Questionist, *n.* رَجُلٌ سُؤَلَةٌ — سَأَّالٌ.

Questionless, *a.* لَا شَكَّ فِيهِ — مُسَلَّمٌ.

Questor, *n.* دَفْتَرْدَارٌ عِنْدَ ٱلرُّومَانِيِّينَ ٱلْأَقْدَمِينَ.

Questorship, *n.* مَنْصِبُ ٱلدَّفْتَرْدَارِ عِنْدَ ٱلرُّومَانِيِّينَ ٱلْأَقْدَمِينَ.

Qui vive? inter. مَنْ — مَنْ هُوَ. To be on the —, تَيَقَّظَ — اِنْتَبَهَ.

Quib, *n.* قَارِصَةٌ *pl.* قَوَارِصُ — سَلَاطَةٌ.

Quibble, *n.* كَلَامٌ بَاطِلٌ — مُحَاوَلَةٌ — رُوَيْغَةٌ — تَحَيُّلٌ. *See also* Equivocation, *n.*

Quibble, *v.i.* اِحْتَالَ. *See also to* Equivocate, *v.i.*

Quibbler, *n.* رَوَّاغٌ — صَيِّغٌ — حِيَلِيٌّ.

Quick, *a.* Living, حَيٌّ *pl.* أَحْيَاءٌ. Speedy, سَرِيعٌ — آزِفٌ *pl.* سُرْعَانٌ *fem.* سَرِيعَةٌ *pl.* سِرَاعٌ — عَجُولٌ — عَجِلٌ. Nimble, prompt, خَفِيفٌ — نَشِطٌ — طِرْفُ ٱلْعِنَانِ — وَجْزٌ — سَلِبٌ — حَثِيثٌ. Active, بُلْبُلٌ. نَدْبٌ *pl.* نُدُوبٌ; quick and elegant, of a man or boy, بُلْبُلٌ.

Quick in gait, خَفِيفٌ ذَفِيفٌ — ذَفِيفٌ — وَشِيكٌ. Quick to apprehend, سَرِيعُ ٱلْحِفْظِ; to punish, سَرِيعُ ٱلْعِقَابِ. Quick at answering, بَدِيهِيُّ ٱلِٱرْتِجَالِ فِي ٱلْأَجْوِبَةِ. Acute in mind, خَفِيفٌ عَاقِلٌ — سَرِيعُ ٱلْعَقْلِ — ذَكِيٌّ — فَهِيمٌ — خَفِيفُ ٱلرُّوحِ — ٱلْقَلْبِ. Quick with child, حَامِلَةٌ. The — and the dead, ٱلْأَحْيَاءُ وَٱلْأَمْوَاتُ. To be —, to make haste, أَسْرَعَ — سَرُعَ. To be —, prompt, تَوَجَّزَ — يَجُزُ aor. وَجَزَ — يَوْشُكُ aor. وَشُكَ. Quick! Quick! ٱلسَّرْعَ ٱلسَّرْعَ.

Quick, *n.* Living flesh, لَحْمٌ حَيٌّ. To cut to the —, قَطَعَ فِي ٱلْعَظْمِ. To pierce to the —, to wound the heart, جَرَحَ قَلْبَهُ — جَرَحَ فِي ٱلْعَظْمِ — جُرِحَ قَلْبُهُ; to be so pierced, جُرِحَ — فِي قَلْبِهِ.

Quicken, *v.t.* To increase the speed of, عَجَّلَ — رَوَّجَ — نَكَّظَ. To actuate, sharpen, اِسْتَهَمَّ-عَلَى — حَرَّضَ-عَلَى — أَنْهَضَ — اِسْتَفَزَّ. To — the intellect, فَتَحَ عَيْنَهُ — شَحَذَ ٱلذِّهْنَ — فَطَّنَ. To make alive, أَحْيَى; as from the dead, بَعَثَ. He quickened his pace, أَسْرَعَ فِي مَشْيِهِ. *See also to* Hasten, *v.t.*

Quicken, *v.i.* To become alive, حَيِيَ *or* حَيَّ aor. يَحْيَا *or* يَحَيُّ.

To be quick, speedy; *See under* Quick, *a.*

Quickener, *a.* } Causing haste, مُنَكِّظٌ — مُسْتَوْفِضٌ — مُوفِضٌ —
Quickening, } مُرَوِّجٌ — مُنْهِضٌ — مُسْتَفِزٌّ — مُعَجِّلٌ. Inciting, مُحَرِّضٌ. Giving life, بَاعِثٌ — مُحْيِي.

Quickening, *n.* The act of hastening, تَنْكِيظٌ — إِعْجَالٌ — تَعْجِيلٌ; of inciting, تَحْرِيكٌ — تَرْوِيجٌ — تَحْرِيضٌ — اِسْتِفْزَازٌ; of living life, إِحْيَاءٌ.

Quick-eyed, *a.* Of the eyes, حَادُّ ٱلْبَصَرِ — حَدِيدُ ٱلنَّظَرِ. *See also* Acute, Hawk-eyed, *a.*

Quicklime, *n.* كِلْسٌ — كِلْسٌ غَيْرُ مُطْفِيٍّ.

Quickly, *ad.* عَلَى ٱلْفَوْرِ — بِسُرْعَةٍ — سَرِيعًا — عَلَى ٱلْعَجَلِ — وَشَاكَةً — أَوْشَكَ — بِٱلْعَجَلِ. To do anything —, خَفَّ فِي عَمَلِهِ; to walk —, خَفَّ فِي سَيْرِهِ — وَاشَكَ. Send — and tell him, أَرْسِلُوا عَاجِلًا وَأَخْبِرُوهُ. Come down —, أَسْرِعْ وَٱنْزِلْ.

Quick-match, *n.* فَتِيلَةٌ — فَتِيلٌ.

Quickness, *n.* State of acting rapidly, رَوْجَةٌ — سُرْعَةٌ. Sprightliness, وَجْزٌ — نَشَاطٌ — خِفَّةٌ. Quickness of the understanding, ذَكَاوَةٌ — ذَكَاءٌ. *See also* Activity, *n.*

Quicksand, *n.* مِيعَاس – أَوْعَس *pl.* أَوَاعِس . To walk on a —, أَوْعَس .

Quick-scented, *a.* حَادُّ ٱلشَّامَّةِ – حَدِيدُ ٱلشَّمِّ .

Quick-set, *a.* نَابِت – مَغْرُوس – غَرْس .

Quick-set, *n.* Of a hedge, سِيَاجٌ مَغْرُوسٌ – وَشِيعٌ غَرْسٌ .

Quick-sighted, *a.* *See* Quick-eyed, Hawk-eyed, *a.*

Quick-sightedness, *n.* حِدَّةُ ٱلنَّظَرِ – حَذَاقَةُ ٱلْبَصَرِ .

Quicksilver, *n.* زِئْبَق – زَاوُوق – مِدْقَس – فَرَّار . To wash with —, زَوَّق . Washed with —, مُزَوَّق .

Quick-witted, *a.* حَاذِق – خَفِيفُ ٱلْقَلْبِ – فَطِين – ذَكِيٌّ .

Quid, *n.* *See* Chew, *n.*

Quiddity, *n.* Essence, ذَاتِيَّة – مَاهِيَّة . A subtlety, حِيلَة *pl.* حِيَل – مَكْر . Quiddities, مَوَاكِر . *See also* Nicety, *n.*

Quiddle, *v.i.* *See to* Trifle, *v.t.*

Quiddler, *n.* *See* Trifler, *n.*

Quidnunc, *n.* مِشْيَاح – عِرْيَض – مُتَفَرِّغٌ لِلسُّؤَالِ عَنِ ٱلْخَبَرِ – سَأَّال .

Quid pro quo, n. مُقَابَلَة – مُقَابِل – بَدَل .

Quiesce, *v.i.* To be silent, صَمَتَ [2] – نَصَتَ = – أَنْصَتَ . To be mute, of a letter, سَكَنَ [2] . To be still, at rest, إِطْمَأَنَّ – إِسْتَكَنَّ .

Quiescence, *n.* Silence, سُكُوت – صَمْت . Quiescence, as of a letter, سُكُون – سَكْنَة . Rest, repose, طُمَأْنِينَة – إِطْمِئْنَان – رَاحَة .

Quiescent, *a.* Resting, in repose, مُطْمَئِنٌّ – مُرْتَاح . Quiescent, of a letter, سَاكِن ; made —, مَجْزُوم – مُسَكَّن . To make a letter —, جَزَمَ ٱلْحَرْفَ = – سَكَّنَ . The — letters, الْحُرُوفُ ٱلْمُصْمَتَةُ .

Quiescently, *ad.* بِٱلسَّكِينَةِ – بِٱلسُّكُونِ .

Quiet, *a.* In a state of rest, سَاكِن *pl.* سُكَّان – قَرَّار – سَاجٍ . Silent, سَاكِت – صَامِت . Undisturbed, at repose, مُطْمَئِنٌّ . Calm, as of the sea, رَاكِن . Sedate, رَكِين – رَزِين . Mild, gentle, وَدِيع : a — beast, دَابَّةٌ سَمِحَةٌ . To be —, at rest, إِسْتَكَنَّ – إِرْتَاحَ . To be —, tranquil, at peace, إِطْمَأَنَّ . To be —, calm, as of the sea, سَجَا [2] . To be —, sedate, تَرَكَّنَ – رَكُنَ [2] . To lead a — life, قَضَى = حَيٰوةً مُطْمَئِنَّةً هَادِئَةً . You ought to be —, يَنْبَغِي أَنْ تَكُونُوا هَادِئِينَ . Be quiet, still, إِهْدَأْ . To be —, to keep silence, سَكَتَ [2] – صَمَتَ [2] . To be —, silent, about, أَغْضَى عَلَى . *See also* Calm, *a.*

Quiet, *n.* Rest, رَاحَة – هُدُوٌّ . Silence, سُكُوت – صَمْت . Freedom from disturbance, طُمَأْنِينَة – إِطْمِئْنَان . Quiet of mind, رَاحَةُ بَالٍ – إِطْمِئْنَانُ بَالٍ .

Quiet, *v.t.* To reduce to a state of rest, هَدَّأَ – = هَدَنَ – طَامَنَ – أَهْدَأَ – سَكَّنَ . To re-assure, إِسْتَقَرَّ – أَقَرَّ – خَفَّضَ . To — one's mind, رَيَّحَ بَالَهُ . To silence, سَكَّتَ – أَسْكَتَ – صَمَّتَ . To — one's self, إِرْتَاحَ فِكْرُهُ – إِطْمَأَنَّ – سَكَّتَ نَفْسَهُ – هَدَّأَ نَفْسَهُ . To —, as one's fears, رَفَا *aor.* يَرْفُو : I quieted the man, رَفَوْتُ ٱلرَّجُلَ .

Quietism, *n.* مَذْهَبُ ٱلْقَائِلِينَ أَنَّ كَمَالَ ٱلدِّينِ قَائِمٌ فِي ٱطْمِئْنَانِ ٱلْبَالِ وَٱلتَّأَمُّلِ فِي ٱلْبَارِئِ تَعَالَى – تَصَوُّف .

Quietist, *n.* صُوفِيّ – مِنْ أَهْلِ ٱلْمَذْهَبِ ٱلْمَذْكُورِ *pl.* صُوفِيَّة .

Quietistic, *a.* مُتَعَلِّقٌ بِٱلْمَذْهَبِ ٱلْمَذْكُورِ آنِفًا .

Quietly, *ad.* In a tranquil manner, بِهُدُوٍّ . Secretly, سِرًّا . Silently, بِسُكُوتٍ . With serenity, calmness, بِوَقَارٍ – بِرَزَانَةٍ . Mildly, حِلْمًا . Slowly, رُوَيْدًا – عَلَى مَهْلٍ .

Quietude, *n.*
Quietness, } *See* Quiet, *n.*

Quietus, *n.* That which produces quiet, مُورِثُ ٱلسُّكُوتِ . A soothing draft, سُلْوَان ; as for children, صُمْتَة . To give one his —, to reduce to silence, قَطَعَ لِسَانَهُ = ; to kill, قَتَلَ [2] .

Quill, *n.* The entire — of a feather, صُفَّار . A feather, رِيشَة *coll.* رِيش *pl.* أَرْيَاش . A porcupine's —, قَلَمُ ٱلْقُنْفُذِ *pl.* أَقْلَام . A weaver's —, قَلَم . A writing —, قَلَمُ رِيشٍ . A writer, كَاتِب – مُؤَلِّف .

Quill, *v.t.* To plait, سَفَّ [2] – أَسَفَّ – رَمَلَ [2] – أَرْمَلَ – ثَنَّى – شَرَطَ [2] = .

Quill-driver, *n.* كَاتِب – مُؤَلِّف .

Quill-driving, *n.* كِتَابَة – تَأْلِيف .

Quilling, *n.* تَثْنِيَة – شَرْط – رَمْل – سَفّ .

Quilt, *n.* لِحَاف *pl.* لُحُف .

Quilt, *v.t.* ضَرَّبَ .

Quilted, *a.* مُضَرَّب .

Quilting, *n.* تَضْرِيب .

Quince, *n.* سَفَرْجَل *pl.* سَفَارِجُ . A — tree, شَجَرَةُ ٱلسَّفَرْجَلِ . Quince marmalade, مَيْبَة .

Quinia, *n.*
Quinine, } قِينَا – قِينِينَا . Sulphate of —, صُلْفَاتُو .

Quinquagesima, *n.* اَلْيَوْمُ ٱلْخَمْسُونَ قَبْلَ ٱلصَّوْمِ ٱلْكَبِيرِ . Quinquagesima Sunday, الْأَحَدُ ٱلْمُسَمَّى ٱلْخَمْسِينَ .

Quinquangular, *a.* *See* Pentangular, *a.*

Quinqueliteral, *a.* ذُو خَمْسَةِ أَحْرُفٍ – خُمَاسِيٌّ .

Quinquennial, *a.* وَاقِعٌ مَرَّةً فِي خَمْسِ سِنِينَ .

Quinquepartite, *a.* Divided into five parts, مُقَسَّمٌ إِلَى خَمْسَةِ أَجْزَاءٍ . A — international treaty, مُعَاهَدَةٌ بَيْنَ خَمْسِ دُوَلٍ .

Quinsy, *n.* خَنَانِيق – خُنَّاق – خُنَاق – فِيلَةُ ٱلْحُلْقُومِ .

Quint, *n.* خَمْسَةٌ مُتَداوِلَةٌ.

Quintain, *n.* قائِمَةُ ٱلْغَرَضِ ـ خَشَبَةُ ٱلْهَدَفِ.

Quintal, *n.* قِنْطار *pl.* قَناطِير.

Quintessence, *n.* The virtue or best part, جَوْهَر ـ خُلاصَة ـ زُبْدَة ـ ذات. *See also* Essence, *n.*

Quintuple, *a.* خَمْسَةُ أَضْعاف.

Quintuple, *v.t.* ضاعَفَ-خَمَّسَ مَرّات.

Quintuple, *v.i.* تَضاعَفَ خَمْسَ مَرّات.

Quip, *n.* هَزْوٌ ـ مِزاح ـ لَطِيفَة *pl.* لَطائِف.

Quire, *n.* Of paper, دَسْتَة وَرَق ـ دَسْت مِنَ ٱلْوَرَقِ *pl.* دَسْتات.

Quirk, *n.* لَطِيفَة *pl.* لَطائِف ـ تُحْفَة. *See also* Quibble, *n.*

Quit, *v.t.* To leave, as a place, زالَ مِن ـ بَرِحَ ـ طَلَعَ مِن. To give up, to separate from, تَرَكَ ـ تَخَلَّى عَن ـ فاتَ. To —, as a fever, أَقْلَعَ عَن. To secede from, إِعْتَزَلَ عَن ـ تَعَزَّلَ عَن. To — or prepare one's self for, تَشَمَّرَ لِ. To abandon, go abroad from, هَجَرَ. He did not — his place, ما بَرِحَ مَكانَهُ. The fever quitted him, إِخْطَفَتْهُ ٱلْحُمَّى. The disease quitted him, زالَ عَنْهُ ٱلْمَرَضُ ـ إِرْتَفَعَ عَنْهُ ٱلْمَرَضُ. He quitted the service, تَجَرَّدَ مِنَ ٱلْخِدْمَةِ. Quit you like men, كُونُوا رِجالاً ـ تَشَدَّدُوا وَكُونُوا رِجالاً. *See also under* Notice, *n.*; *also to* Abandon, Leave, *v.t.*

Quit, *a.* As of a responsibility, خَلِيٌّ مِن ـ خَلٌّ مِن; as of a fault, بَرِيٌّ مِن. Released from, مُعْتَقٌ مِن ـ مُتَخَلِّصٌ مِن. I am — of you, أَنا مِنْكَ خَلاء ـ أَنا خَلِيٌّ مِنْكَ. He became — of his debt, خَرَجَ مِن دَيْنِهِ. I am — of this matter, أَنا خَلِيٌّ مِنْ هٰذا ٱلْأَمْرِ. He was or became — of the affair, عَرِيَ مِنَ ٱلْأَمْرِ. He is not, or does not become, — of this affair, ما يَعْرَى مِنْ هٰذا ٱلْأَمْرِ. Quit of grief, خالٍ مِنَ ٱلْغَمِّ.

Quite, *ad.* بِٱلْكُلِّيَّةِ ـ جُمْلَةً ـ بِٱلتَّمامِ ـ طُرّاً ـ تَماماً ـ تَكْمِيلاً ـ بَتَّةً. He stripped him — naked, أَعْراهُ تَعْرِيَةً.

Quit-rent, *n.* إِجارَةٌ مُؤَجَّلَةٌ.

Quits, *ad.* رَأْسٌ بِرَأْسٍ ـ عَلَى سَوِيَّةٍ. To cry —, قالَ رَأْسٌ بِرَأْسٍ. To be — with, لا لِأَحَدٍ مِنْهُمْ شَيْءٌ عَلَى ٱلْآخَرِ. *See also under* Quit, *a.*

Quittance, *n.* A discharge or receipt of a debt, غِلاق ـ خَلاص ـ وُصُول ـ تَبْرِئَة ـ خَلاص ـ وَرَقَةُ. *See also* Recompense, *n.*

Quiver, *n.* For arrows, جَفِير ـ جَشِير ـ جُعْبَة *pl.* كُنّات ـ كِنانَة ـ إِبْنَةُ حَوْب ـ قَرَن *pl.* أَقْران ـ جَعْبَة *pl.* جِعاب.

Quiver, *v.i.* خَفَقَ ـ خَطَرَ ـ رَعَشَ ـ إِرْتَعَشَ ـ إِرْتَعَدَ ـ إِرْتَجَّ. My lips quivered, رَجَفَتْ شَفَتايَ. The sword quivered, عَرِصَ ٱلسَّيْفُ. His skin quivered, إِقْشَعَرَّ جِلْدُهُ. To make to —, رَجَّ ـ أَرْعَدَ ـ أَرْعَشَ.

Quivering, *a.* خَطّار ـ راجِف. A — sound, خَفِيف. Of a fleshy part, رَضْراض: quivering buttocks, كَفَلٌ رَضْراضٌ.

Quivering, *n.* خَطَران ـ عَرَص ـ خَفَقان ـ خُلُوج.

Quixotic, *a.* حَمُوقَة ـ مُتَهَوِّر ـ سائِب ـ خَيالِيٌّ ـ طالِبُ ٱلْخَيالِ.

Quixotism, *n.* تَهَوُّر ـ أُحْمُوقَة ـ جُنُون ـ طَلَبُ ٱلْخَيالِ.

Quiz, *v.t.* To ridicule, ضَحِكَ عَلَى ـ سَخِرَ مِن ـ تَسَخَّرَ مِن ـ تَضَحَّكَ عَلَى. To — through a glass, بَصْبَصَ ـ لَحَظَ-بِٱلنَّظّارَةِ عَلَى-بِٱلنَّظّارَةِ. *See also to* Puzzle, *v.t.*

Quiz, *n.* A riddle, لُغْز *pl.* أَلْغاز ـ أُحْجِيَّة. A puzzle, مُشْكِلَة. A wag, ضَحّاك ـ مُسْتَهْزِئٌ بِٱلنّاسِ.

Quizzical, *a.* *See* Funny, *a.*

Quizzing, *n.* The act of making a fool of, ضَحِكٌ عَلَى ـ سَخَرٌ ـ هَزْوٌ ـ مُضاحَكَة. Looking at through a glass, لَحْظٌ إِلَى ـ مِن أَحَدٍ بِٱلنَّظّارَةِ.

Quizzing-glass, *n.* نَظّارَةٌ صَغِيرَةٌ.

Quoif, *n.* *See* Coif, *n.*

Quoin, *n.* A corner, قُرْنَة *pl.* قَرانِي. A wedge, سَفِينَة *coll.* سَفِين *pl.* سَفائِن *or* سُفُن ـ شَرْخ *pl.* شُرُوخ.

Quoit, *n.* وَطْنَةٌ حَدِيدٍ. The game of quoits, لَعِبُ طَتٍّ ـ لَعِبُ ٱلطَّتِّ ـ ٱلْحَدِيدِ.

Quondam, *a.* سابِق.

Quorum, *n.* A special commission of justices, مَحْكَمَةٌ نِظامِيَّةٌ مَخْصُوصَةٌ. A sufficient number for doing business, عَدَدٌ كافٍ مِن أَعْضاءِ مَجْلِسٍ لِإِجْراءِ ٱلْأُمُورِ.

Quota, *n.* حِصَّة *pl.* حِصَص.

Quotable, *a.* مِمّا يُقْتَبَسُ ـ إِقْتِباسُهُ جائِزٌ (*or* مُمْكِنٌ).

Quotation, *n.* A passage cited, إِقْتِباس. A —, as an authority, إِسْناد *pl.* أَسانِيدُ. A specified price of commodities, سِعْر ـ أَسْعار ـ فِئات.

Quote, *v.t.* To cite from, إِقْتَبَسَ مِن ـ نَقَلَ عَن. To — as an authority for, أَسْنَدَ-إِلَى. To — from the speech of another, حَكَى عَن. To — instances from, نَقَلَ مِن ـ إِمْتَثَلَ مِن. To name the price of any commodity, ذَكَرَ أَسْعارَ ٱلسِّلْعَةِ.

Quoth, *v.i.* Quoth I, قُلْتُ; quoth he, قالَ; quoth she, قالَتْ.

Quotidian, *a.* يَوْمِيٌّ.

Quotidian, *n.* A — fever, حُمَّى واظِبَةٌ.

Quotient, *n.* خارِجُ ٱلْقِسْمَةِ ـ حاصِلُ ٱلتَّقْسِيمِ ـ حاصِل.

Quo Warranto, *ad.* سِجِلٌّ يَحْتَوِي ٱلسُّؤالَ عَنْ أَيِّ سُلْطانٍ جَرَى ما هُوَ كَذا وَكَذا.

R.

Rabbet, *v.t.* عَشَّقَ (ٱلْخَشَبَ) – عَشَّقَ فِي بَعْضِهِ.

Rabbet, *n.* تَعْشِيقُ ٱلْخَشَبِ – تَعْشِيق.

Rabbet-plane, *n.* رَنْدَةُ ٱلتَّعْشِيقِ.

Rabbi, *n.* }
Rabbin, } رَبَّانِيٌّ – خَاخَام *pl.* خَوَاخِيمُ.

Rabbinic, *a.* }
Rabbinical, } مُتَعَلِّق بِٱلتَّلْمُودِ – خَاخَامِيٌّ – رَبَّانِيٌّ.

Rabbinist, *n.* تَلْمُودِيٌّ *pl.* تَلْمُودِيُّونَ *or* تَلْمُودِيَّة.

Rabbit, *n.* أَرْنَب *pl.* أَرَانِبُ – أَرْنَبٌ بَلَدِيٌّ. *See also* Rarebit, *n.*

Rabble, *n.* أَسَافِلُ ٱلنَّاسِ – أَوْبَاش – سَفِلَة – سُقَاطُ ٱلنَّاسِ.

Rabid, *a.* Mad, furious, مُصَاب – مُتَهَوِّر – مَجْنُون; as applied to animals, أَثْوَلُ; to dogs, كَلِب *pl.* كَلْبَى.

Rabidly, *ad.* Furiously, بِتَهَوُّرٍ – بِجُنُونٍ; as of a dog, بِكَلَابٍ.

Rabidness, *n.* Furiousness, madness, تَهَوُّر – جُنُون; in animals, ثَوَل *fem.* ثَوْلَاءُ *pl.* ثُوْل; in a dog, كَلَاب.

Raccoon, *n.* حَيَوَانٌ مَوْجُودٌ فِي أَمِيرِكَا يُشْبِهُ ٱلثُّفَةَ وَهُوَ عَنَاقُ ٱلْأَرْضِ.

Race, *n.* The continued stock of descendants, عُنْصُر *pl.* عَنَاصِرُ – نَسْل *pl.* أَنْسَال – آل – سِلْسِلَة – أَصْل. Offspring, descendants, ذُرِّيَّة – أَوْلَاد. Origin, make, shape, ضَرْب – صِيغَة. A people, شَعْب *pl.* شُعُوب – أُمَّة *pl.* أُمَم. Kind, صِنْف *pl.* أَصْنَاف – نَوْع *pl.* أَنْوَاع – جِنْس *pl.* أَجْنَاس. Race, kind, in the abstract, جِنْسِيَّة : unity of —, وَحْدَةُ ٱلْجِنْسِيَّةِ – وَحْدَةُ ٱلْأَهْلِيَّةِ. Strength of taste, جِدَّة. A course, as of a struggle, جِهَاد – سَعْيٌ. A run, running, رَكْض. A course, life, طَرِيقَة – سِيرَة. A contest in running, ضَمَّة – سِبَاق – مُسَابَقَة – مُجَارَاة. A water-course, قَنَاة – مَجْرَى ٱلْمَاء – سَاقِيَة. One of noble —, شَرِيف – كَرِيمُ ٱلْعُنْصُرِ – ٱلْأَصْلِ; of a horse, كُحَيْل *pl.* كُحْلَان – حِصَانٌ أَصِيلٌ. A man of mixed —, رَجُل خِلْطٌ مِلْطٌ. To run a — with, جَارَى – رَاكَضَ. To compete with one in a —, سَابَقَ. To start horses in a —, سَبَّقَ ٱلْخَيْلَ. A wager laid between persons in a —, سَبَق *pl.* أَسْبَاق – سُبْقَة.

Race, *v.i.* To run swiftly, أَفَجَّ – رَكَضَ ² – جَرَى ².

Race, *v.t.* To contend in running with, جَارَى – رَاكَضَ – سَابَقَ.

He tied up the mare to prepare her for his racing her, اِرْتَبَطَ ٱلْفَرَسَ لِيُغَالِقَ عَلَيْهَا.

Race-course, *n.* مِضْمَار – مَيْدَان – مَيْدَانُ ٱلْمُسَابَقَةِ.

Race-ginger, *n.* زَنْجَبِيل غَيْرُ مَدْقُوقٍ – عِرْقُ ٱلزَّنْجَبِيلِ.

Racehorse, *n.* جَوَاد – جَوْد *pl.* جِيَاد – حِصَانٌ لِلْمُسَابَقَةِ *pl.* حُصُن – حِصَانٌ سَبَقٌ – ضَامِر. One who trains racehorses, مُضَمِّر.

Raceme, *n.* عِذْق *pl.* أَعْذَاق – عُرْجُون *pl.* عَرَاجِينُ – عُنْقُود *pl.* عَنَاقِيدُ. A —, as of dates, كِبَاسَة *pl.* كَبَائِسُ.

Racemous, *a.* }
Racemose, } ذُو أَعْذَاقٍ – ذُو عَرَاجِينَ – ذُو عَنَاقِيدَ.

Racer, *n.* A runner, رَاكِض – رَكُوض. *See also* Racehorse, *n.*

Races, *n.* A race, ضَمَّة – سِبَاق – مُسَابَقَة.

Rachitis, *n.* *See* Rickets, *n.*

Raciness, *n.* Of liquors, ذَكَاء – ذَكَاوَة. Freshness, of style, نُدُور – نَدْر – جِدَّة – ذَكَاء.

Rack, *n.* An instrument of torture, آلَةُ ٱلتَّعْذِيبِ – ٱلْعَذْرَاء *pl.* عَذَارَى. A wooden horse for torture, حِمَار. Torture, عَذَاب. A frame on which things are laid, قَاعِدَة – مَقَام – رَفّ *pl.* رُفُوف. A — for cattle's fodder, مَعْلَف *pl.* مَعَالِفُ. To be on the —, in torture, difficulty, كَانَ فِي عَذَابٍ. To go to — and ruin, هَلَكَ ² ⁊. To put to the —; *see to* Rack, *v.t.*

Rack, *v.t.* To torture, عَذَّبَ. To clear, as of wine, صَفَّى. To decant, فَرَّغَ مِنْ أَنَاءٍ إِلَى أَنَاءٍ. To — one's own brains, تَبَرَّمَ – تَضَجَّرَ – شَغَّلَ بَالَهُ.

Racker, *n.* مُعَذِّب.

Racket, *n.* A noise, لَغْط – هَوْشَة – هَيْشَة – غَوْشَة – جَلَبَة – زَيْطَة – ضَجِيج – حِسٌّ; *vulg.* كَرْكَبَة. An instrument to strike a ball with, صَوْلَجَان *pl.* صَوَالِجَة. To make a —, noise, لَغَطَ ² – صَوَّتَ – ضَجَّ ² – زَاطَ ⁊.

Rackety, *a.* *See* Noisy, *a.*

Racking, *a.* Painful, أَلِيم – وَجِيع – مُوجِع.

Rack-rent, *n.* كِرَاءٌ وَافٍ.

Rack-renter, *n.* مُسْتَأْجِرٌ بِكِرَاءٍ وَافٍ.

Racy, *a.* Of liquors, ذَكِيٌّ; of style, حَدِيد – حَادٌّ – ذَكِيٌّ – نَادِر.

Radial, *a.* Pertaining to the fore-arm, مُتَعَلِّقٌ بِٱلسَّاعِدِ.

Raddle, *v.t.* عَقَّدَ. *See also to* Interweave, *v.t.*

Raddle, *n.* *See* Hedge, *n.*

Radiance, *n.* / Radiancy, } Glitter, glare, لَمَعَان ـ رَوْنَق ـ بَهَآءٌ. Light, splendour, نُور ـ ضِيَآءٌ ـ جَلَآءٌ. Radiance, as of the countenance, تَبَسُّم ـ بَشَاشَة. *See also* Brightness, *n.*

Radiant, *a.* Emitting rays, مُشِعُّ ٱلشُّعَاعِ ـ لَامِع. Bright, shining, جَلِيٌّ ـ مُنِير ـ نَيِّر ـ سَاطِع ـ دُرِّيٌّ. Smiling, مُتَبَسِّم. To be —, لَمَعَ ـ تَجَلَّى ـ سَطَعَ ـ شَعْشَعَ. His face was —, أَشْرَقَ وَجْهُهُ.

Radiant, *n.* A point from which light emanates, مَرْكَزٌ ـ مَنَار ـ مَشْرِقُ ٱلنُّورِ ـ مَرْكَزُ ٱلْأَشِعَّةِ ـ ٱلنُّورِ.

Radiantly, *ad.* Brightly, بِجَلَآءٍ ـ بِرَوْنَقٍ ـ بِبَهَآءٍ. Smilingly, تَبَسُّمًا ـ بِبَشَاشَةٍ.

Radiata, *n.* نَوْعٌ مِنَ ٱلْحَيَوَانَاتِ ذَاتِ أَعْضَآءٍ مُرَتَّبَةٍ حَوْلَ مَرْكَزٍ كَٱلشُّعَاعِ.

Radiate, *v.t.* To emit rays from a point or surface, نَشَرَ ٱلشُّعَاعَ [2] أَشَعَّ ٱلشُّعَاعَ مِنْ مَرْكَزٍ ـ مِنْ مَرْكَزٍ. To emit, throw off, from a point, أَشَعَّ ـ نَشَرَ مِنْ مَرْكَزٍ [2]. To shed brightness on, نَوَّرَ ـ أَضَآءَ ـ أَنَارَ.

Radiate, *v.i.* To issue in rays from a point, شَعَّ ٱلشُّعَاعُ مِنْ ـ إِنْتَشَرَ ٱلشُّعَاعُ مِنْ مَرْكَزٍ ـ مَرْكَزٍ. To shine, sparkle, إِشْتَنَارَ ـ تَلَأْلَأَ ـ لَأْلَأَ ـ لَمَحَ ـ تَنَوَّرَ.

Radiate, *a.* As of a flower, مُشَعْشَع.

Radiated, *a.* Adorned with rays of light, مُنَوَّرٌ بِشُعَاعِ نُورٍ ـ مُشَعْشَع.

Radiating, *a.* Emitting rays of light, مُشِعُّ ٱلشُّعَاعِ; of heat, مُشِعُّ ٱلْحَرَارَةِ.

Radiation, *n.* Emission of light, إِشْعَاعُ ٱلشُّعَاعِ, of heat, إِشْعَاعُ ٱلْحَرَارَةِ. Shooting, of rays, *etc.*, from a centre, إِشْعَاعٌ مِنْ مَرْكَزٍ.

Radiator, *n.* نَاشِرُ ٱلشُّعَاعِ ـ مُشِعُّ ٱلشُّعَاعِ.

Radical, *a.* Pertaining to the root, أَصْلِيٌّ ـ جِذْرِيٌّ. Implanted by nature, طَبِيعِيٌّ ـ جِبِلِّيٌّ ـ ذَاتِيٌّ ـ خِلْقِيٌّ. Fundamental, أَسَاسِيٌّ ـ أَصْلِيٌّ. Entire, perfect, كُلِّيٌّ ـ تَامٌّ. A — defect, أَصْلُ ٱلْعَيْبِ ـ عَيْبٌ أَصْلِيٌّ. A — cure, شِفَآءٌ تَامٌّ. Radical measures, تَدَابِيرُ أَسَاسِيَّةٌ. The — party, أَصْحَابُ ٱلْإِنْقِلَابِ. He has a —, or hereditary, disposition to generosity, لَهُ عِرْقٌ فِي ٱلْكَرَمِ. A — or hereditary disposition, عِرْق *pl.* أَعْرَاق. The — disposition is wont to enter, *i.e.*, is hereditary, ٱلْعِرْقُ دَسَّاسٌ.

Radical, *n.* The root of a word, an infinitive noun, مَصْدَر. An underived word, لَفْظَةٌ أَصْلِيَّةٌ ـ كَلِمَةٌ أَصْلِيَّةٌ ـ كَلِمَةٌ غَيْرُ مُشْتَقَّةٍ. The element of a substance, عُنْصُر *pl.* عَنَاصِرُ. A word of three radicals, radical letters, ثُلَاثِيٌّ; of four, رُبَاعِيٌّ; of five, خُمَاسِيٌّ. A —, in politics, مُتَعَصِّبٌ لِٱسْتِئْصَالِ قَوَانِينِ ٱلدَّوْلَةِ ٱلْقَدِيمَةِ ـ صَاحِبُ ٱلْإِنْقِلَابِ ـ مِنْ دَأْبِهِ ٱسْتِئْصَالُ مَبَادِئِ ٱلسِّيَاسَةِ ٱلْأَصْلِيَّةِ *pl.* أَصْحَاب. The Radicals, ذَوُو ٱلْإِنْقِلَابِ.

Radicalism, *n.* مَذْهَبُ ٱلَّذِينَ يَوَدُّونَ ٱسْتِئْصَالَ ٱلْمَبَادِئِ ٱلْأَصْلِيَّةِ ـ أُصُولُ ٱلْإِنْقِلَابِ ـ أَفْكَارُ ٱلْإِنْقِلَابِ.

Radically, *ad.* Originally, أَصْلًا ـ مِنَ ٱلْأَصْلِ; from the root or foundation, مِنَ ٱلْأَسَاسِ; thoroughly, بِٱلتَّمَامِ ـ تَمَامًا ـ حَتْمًا ـ بَتَّةً.

Radicalness, *n.* The state of being radical, أَصْلِيَّةٌ; of being innate, فِطْرَة ـ خِلْقَة ـ جِبِلَّة.

Radicle, *n.* The origin of a root, أَصْلُ ٱلْعِرْقِ ـ جِذْمُ ٱلْعِرْقِ ـ مَنْبَتُ ٱلْعِرْقِ. A fine or small root, شُعْبَةُ ٱلْعِرْقِ ـ شُكْر *pl.* شُكَيْر ـ شُعَب *pl.* شِرْش *pl.* شُرُوش.

Radish, *n.* فُجْلَة ـ حِلَّب *coll.* فُجْل *or* فُجْل. A seller of radishes, فَجَّال.

Radius, *n.* In geometry, نِصْفُ قُطْرٍ. The exterior bone of the fore arm, ٱلْأَعْلَى مِنَ ٱلزَّنْدَيْنِ ـ ٱلزَّنْدُ ٱلْأَعْلَى.

Radix, *n.* *See* Radical, *n.*; *also* Root, *n.*

Raff, *n.* Sweepings, كُنَاسَة ـ زُبَالَة ـ سُبَاطَة. *See also* Rabble, *n.*

Raffle, *n.* As with dice, مُقَارَعَةٌ بِٱلْكِعَابِ.

Raffle, *v.i.* As with dice, إِقْتَرَعَ عَلَى ـ بِمُقَارَعَةٍ فِي لَعْبِ ٱلْكِعَابِ. To — or cast lots for, إِقْتَرَعَ عَلَى.

Raffle, *v.t.* As with dice, حَطَّ ـ فِي مُقَارَعَةٍ لَعْبِ ٱلْكِعَابِ [2]. To submit to be cast lots for, جَعَلَ ـ فِي ٱلْمُقَارَعَةِ.

Raft, *n.* رَمَث *pl.* أَرْمَاث ـ كَلَك *pl.* أَكْلَاك. A small —, طَوْف *pl.* أَطْوَاف ـ عَامَة.

Raft, *v.t.* نَقَلَ ـ عَلَى رَمَثٍ (*or* كَلَكٍ) [2].

Rafter, *n.* A large —, عَارِض *or* عَارِضَة *pl.* عَوَارِض ـ خَشَبَة *pl.* خَشَبَات. A — of a roof, جِسْر (*or* جَسْر) *pl.* جُسُور. The rafters of a house, ٱلرَّوَافِدُ; the smaller rafters of a ceiling, ٱلسَّقَائِفُ.

Raftered, *a.* عَلَى عَوَارِض.

Rafting, *n.* Carriage by a raft, ٱلنَّقْلُ عَلَى كَلَكٍ (*or* رَمَثٍ).

Raftsman, *n.* كَلَّاك ـ جَاذِفُ ٱلرَّمَثِ ـ كَلَكْجِي.

Rag, *n.* A tattered cloth, رِثَّة *pl.* رِثَث ـ جُدَّة *pl.* جُدَد ـ جَرْدَة ـ شَرْطُوطَة ـ خِلْقَة *pl.* خِلَق ـ خِرْقَة *pl.* خِرَق ـ قَزَعَة ـ قِزَاع. Old and worn-out garments, حَشِيف. A kind of silicious stone, ضَرْبٌ مِنْ حَجَرِ ٱلصَّوَّانِ. In rags, tattered, مُمَزَّق; shabby, خَلَقِيٌّ; patched, مُرَقَّع. Clad in rags, مُتَحَشِّف ـ خَلَقِيٌّ. To boil to rags, أَهْذَى - أَهْرَأَ - هَرَّأَ - ء هَرَأَ ; to be so boiled, تَهَرَّأَ - ء هَرِئَ . He does not possess a —, ما عِنْدَهُ قَزَعَةٌ .

Ragamuffin, *n.* فَلَاتِيٌّ - جُعَيْدِيٌّ - خَسِيس .

Rage, *n.* Violent anger, غَضَب - غَيْظ - خَنَق - خَشْم . Vehemence, حِدَّة - حُمَيَّا - تَهَوُّر - هَيَجَان . Eagerness, passion, zeal, حَمِيَّة - رَغْبَة - غَيْرَة . To be in a —, اِغْتَاظَ - ء غَضِبَ - ء حَنِقَ . To put in a —, أَغَاظَ - غَيَّظَ . To have a — for, أُولِعَ بِ - ء رَغِبَ . It is all the —, النَّاسُ - ٤ سَلَبَ عُقُولَ ٱلنَّاسِ صَارَ كَٱلْمَجْنُونِ بَيْنَ ٱلنَّاسِ - مُولَعُونَ بِهِ . Choking — boiled in his bosom, ء جَاشَتِ ٱلْغُصَّةُ فِي صَدْرِهِ . *See also* Fury, *n.*

Rage, *v.i.* To be in a fury, passion, ء غَضِبَ - ء حَنِقَ - اِغْتَاظَ . To be moved violently, اِرْتَجَّ - ء هَاجَ - اِهْتَاجَ . To boil over, with rage, or as the sea, جَاشَ *aor.* يَجِيشُ ; of the sea, waves, تَمَوَّجَ - ٤ خَبَّ ٱلْبَحْرُ . His bosom raged, with anger, ء جَاشَ صَدْرُهُ . War raged between them, جَاشَتِ ٱلْحَرْبُ بَيْنَهُمْ . The plague rages in the town, عَمَّهُمُ ٱلطَّاعُونُ فِي ٱلْبَلَدِ . *See also under* Furious, *a.*

Ragged, *a.* Old and worn out, رَثِيث - رَثٌّ - خَشِيف . Torn into fragments, مُقَطَّع - مُمَزَّقٌ إِرَبًا . Covered with rags, مُتَخَشِّف . A — school, مَكْتَبٌ لِأَوْلَادِ أَفْقَرِ ٱلنَّاسِ .

Raggedness, *n.* State of being ragged, هِيئَةٌ - رَثَاثَةٌ - رُثُوثَةٌ رَثَّةٌ . The being clad in rags, تَخَشُّف .

Raging, *a.* Enraged, greatly angered, مُحْنَق - خَنِق - خَنِيق - سَاخِط . Vehemently agitated, هَائِج - مُرْتَجّ . Billowy, stormy, مُتَمَوِّج - زَخَّار - زَاخِر .

Raging, *n.* Violent anger, جَنَان - خَنَق - سَخَط . Violence, rushing, حُمَيَّا - هَيَجَان - هِيَاج . Impetuosity, تَهَوُّر . Raging, as of the sea, تَمَوُّج - زُخُور - زَخْر .

Ragman, *n.* A collector of rags, عُتَقِيٌّ *pl.* عُتَقِيَّة ; a seller of rags and damaged articles, سَقَطِيٌّ - سَقَّاط - خُلْقَانِيٌّ .

Ragout, *n.* طَعَامٌ بِبَهَارٍ *pl.* يَخْنَة - أَطْعِمَة .

Rags, *n.* Old worn-out garments, رِثَّة - رَثٌّ .

Rag-stone, *n.* *See under* Rag, *n.*

Rag-wheel, *n.* دُولَابٌ مُسَنَّنٌ .

Rag-work, *n.* *See* Rubble, *n.*

Ragusa, *n.* The town, رَاغُوسَا .

Raid, *n.* *See* Incursion, *n.*

Raider, *n.* مُغَاوِر *pl.* مَغَاوِيرُ . A body of mounted raiders, خَيْلٌ مُغِيرَةٌ .

Rail, *n.* A paling, جِدَارٌ مِنْ خَشَبٍ - قَوَائِمُ مَصْفُوفَةٌ . A bar, قَضِيب *pl.* قُضْبَان ; a bar of iron, مُحْل - حَدِيدَة *pl.* أَمْحَال . A balustrade, دَرَابْزُون *or* دَرَابْزِين *pl.* دَرَابْزُونَات . A — to rail anything off with, حَاجِز . The — of a ship, دَرَابْزِين . A bar, as of a railroad, قَضِيب *pl.* قُضْبَان . The bird, دُرَّاج . To run off the —, ٤ زَلَقَ عَنِ ٱلسِّكَّةِ .

Rail, *v.t.* To enclose with wooden rails, ٤ جَدَرَ بِجِدَارٍ مِنْ خَشَبٍ . To — off, as by a rail, ٤ حَجَزَ بِحَاجِزٍ .

Rail, *v.i.* To — at, ء عَضَبَ - عَيَّرَ - اِسْتَهْزَأَ بِ - جَدَفَ عَلَى .

Railer, *n.* A scoffer, عَضَّاب - مُعَيِّر - شَتَّام - مُجَدِّف .

Railing, *a.* مُسْتَهْزِئٌ - عُيَبَة - عَيَّاب - مُفْتَرٍ .

Railing, *n.* Scoffing, عَضْب - تَعْيِيب - تَعْيِير - اِسْتِهْزَاء - اِفْتِرَاء . A barricade, دَرَابْزِين - حَاجِز . Rails, as for a railway, قُضْبَان .

Railingly, *ad.* بِٱفْتِرَاءٍ - بِٱسْتِهْزَاءٍ - تَعْيِيرًا .

Raillery, *n.* *See* Pleasantry, *n.*

Railroad, *n.* } Railway, } سِكَّةُ حَدِيدٍ *pl.* سِكَك . A — train, قِطَار *pl.* قُطُر *and* قِطَارَات . A — station, مَوْقِف (*or* مَحَطَّة) سِكَّةِ ٱلْحَدِيدِ . A — platform, رَصِيفُ سِكَّةِ ٱلْحَدِيدِ . A — receipt, بُولِيصَة *pl.* بَوَالِص (*or* وُصُول *or* رَجْعَة) سِكَّةِ ٱلْحَدِيدِ . A — ticket, تَذْكِرَةُ سِكَّةِ ٱلْحَدِيدِ *pl.* تَذَاكِر . To lay down a —, ٤ مَدَّ سِكَّةَ حَدِيدٍ . For laying down a —, لِمَدِّ سِكَّةِ حَدِيدٍ .

Raiment, *n.* ثِيَاب - أَلْبِسَة - مَلْبُوس - لِبَاس . *See also* Clothing, Dress, *n.*

Rain, *n.* مَطَر - غَيْث *pl.* أَمْطَار . Continual —, أُسْكُوب - سَكْب . Continual light —, هَطَلَان . Light —, a shower, نَضِيضَة *pl.* رَشَّة - رَشٌّ - طَشٌّ - نَضَائِضُ . Heavy —, نَوْءٌ - مَطَرٌ عِزٌّ *pl.* مَطَرٌ جَوْدٌ - جَوْدٌ - أَنْوَاءٌ . A general —, غَيْثٌ مُغِيثٌ . Early —, بَاكُورَة - بَكُور - بَدْرِيٌّ . The early and the latter —, ٱلْمَطَرُ ٱلْمُبَكِّرُ وَٱلْمُتَأَخِّرُ . To send —, (of God), ء غَاثَ . To fall, as — on the ground, صَابَ - ء غَاثَ *aor.* يَصُوبُ : The — fell upon or caught him, أَصَابَهُ ٱلْمَطَرُ . To ask for —, اِسْتَمْطَرَ . It threatens —, هَمَّتِ ٱلسَّمَاءُ بِٱلْمَطَرِ . The — fell upon the land, ء غَاثَ ٱلْغَيْثُ ٱلْأَرْضَ . The — became intense, heavy, اِعْتَكَرَ ٱلْمَطَرُ .

Rain, *v.i.* أَمْطَرَ - أَمْطَرَتِ ٱلسَّمَاءُ . To — continuously, تَصَوَّبَ ٱلْمَطَرُ - ء هَطَلَ ٱلْمَطَرُ . To cause to —, أَمْطَرَ . To — upon, ء غَاثَ - أَمْطَرَ عَلَى . Rained upon, مَغْيُوث - مَغِيث . It rains, تُمْطِرُ . It threatens to rain, هَمَّتِ ٱلدُّنْيَا بِٱلْمَطَرِ . The land was rained upon, غِيثَتِ ٱلْأَرْضُ . It rained in torrents that day, هَطَلَتِ ٱلْأَمْطَارُ فِي ذٰلِكَ ٱلْيَوْمِ . They experienced — for two days, أَصَابَهُمُ ٱلْمَطَرُ مُدَّةَ يَوْمَيْنِ . A prayer for —, صَلَاةُ ٱلِاسْتِسْقَاءِ .

To pray for —, إِسْتَسْقَى. He went to the mosque to offer the prayer for —, سَارَ إِلَى ٱلْجَامِعِ لِتِلَاوَةِ صَلَاةِ ٱلْإِسْتِسْقَاءِ.

Rainbow, *n.* قَوْسُ قُزَحَ ـ نَدْأَةٌ ـ قُسْطَانَةٌ.

Rainbow, *a.* مِنْ أَلْوَانِ قَوْسِ قُزَحَ.

Rain-gauge, *n.* مِيزَانُ ٱلْمَطَرِ.

Raininess, *n.* أَمْطَار ـ تَمَطُّر ـ هَطْلَان.

Rainy, *a.* مَاطِر ـ مَطِر ـ غَيِّث ـ مُمْطِر. The — season, إِبَّانُ ٱلْمَطَرِ.

Raise, *v.t.* To lift up, as on high, رَفَعَ ـ عَلَّى. To lift, شَالَ بِ *aor.* يَشُولُ ـ أَشَالَ ; *vulg.* شَالَ *aor.* يَشِيلُ : I raised the stone, شَلْتُ ٱلْحَجَرَةَ ـ أَشَلْتُ ٱلْحَجَرَةَ ; *vulg.* شَلْتُ بِٱلْحَجَرَةِ ; the scorpion raised its tail, شَالَتِ ٱلْعَقْرَبُ بِذَنَبِهَا ; he raised his arm or hand, شَالَ بِيَدِهِ. To — or pick up, as from the ground, لَقَطَ ـ اِلْتَقَطَ ـ شَالَ بِ ـ شَالَ. To set up, صَمَدَ ـ نَصَبَ ـ نَصَّبَ ـ أَقَامَ ـ قَوَّمَ ; to be so raised, تَنَصَّبَ ـ اِنْتَصَبَ ـ قَوَّمَ. To build, بَنَى ـ شَيَّدَ ـ عَمَرَ ـ عَمَّرَ. To establish, found, set on foot, أَسَّسَ ـ أَنْشَأَ ـ أَوْجَدَ. To evoke, occasion, اِسْتَجْلَبَ ـ سَبَّبَ ـ أَوْرَثَ. To —, as a spirit, to bring up, أَصْعَدَ ـ أَحْضَرَ. To elevate in dignity, سَنَّى ـ عَزَّزَ ـ رَقَّى ـ عَظَّمَ ـ شَرَّفَ ـ رَفَعَ شَأْنَهُ. To grow, cultivate, رَبَّى ـ زَرَعَ. To incite, أَنْهَضَ ـ حَرَّضَ ـ هَيَّجَ ـ حَثَّ ; to incite to rebellion, أَفْتَنَ ـ اِفْتَتَنَ ـ أَفْسَدَ. To increase, زَادَ ـ زَيَّدَ : to — in price, أَغْلَى ٱلثَّمَنَ ـ عَلَّى ٱلثَّمَنَ. To spread, disseminate, as a report, بَثَّ خَبَرًا ـ أَشَاعَ بِخَبَرٍ. To — in spirits, شَجَّعَ ـ رَوَّجَ ـ شَيَّعَ. To strengthen, قَوَّى ـ أَيَّدَ ـ شَدَّدَ. To — or levy soldiers, جَيَّشَ ـ جَمَعَ عَسَاكِرَ ـ لَمَّ عَسَاكِرَ. To — a siege, رَفَعَ ٱلْحِصَارَ. To — money, حَصَّلَ ٱلدَّرَاهِمَ ـ اِنْتَقَدَ ٱلْفُلُوسَ ـ حَوَّشَ ٱلْفُلُوسَ. To — from the dead, بَعَثَ ـ أَقَامَ مِنَ ٱلْأَمْوَاتِ. To — or stir up against, أَقَامَ عَلَى ٱلْ... ـ هَيَّجَ عَلَى ٱلْ.... To — up, as a pile of stone, *etc.*, كَوَّمَ. To — up strife, هَيَّجَ ٱلْخُصُومَةَ. To — up the head to look at anything, أَطْلَعَ رَأْسَهُ ـ تَطَلَّعَ. To — the eyes towards, طَمَحَ بِبَصَرِهِ إِلَى ـ طَمَحَ ٱلْبَصَرَ إِلَى. In raised characters, أَجْرَامًا.

Raiser, *n.* One who builds, مُعَمِّر ; one who establishes, مُوجِد ـ مُؤَسِّس ـ مُنْشِئ ; who grows, cultivates, مُرَبٍّ ـ زَارِع ; who stirs up, مُحَرِّض ـ مُهَيِّج. *See also* Incendiary, *a.*

Raisin, *n.* زَبِيبَة *coll.* زَبِيب.

Raising, *n.* The act of raising on high, رَفْع ; of lifting, شَوْل ـ شَيْل ـ إِشَالَة ; of setting up, صَمْد ـ نَصْب ـ إِقَامَة ; of picking up, اِلْتِقَاط ; of building, تَعْمِير ـ تَشْيِيد ; of establishing, founding, إِيجَاد ـ إِنْشَاء ـ تَأْسِيس ; of bringing up, causing to appear, إِصْعَاد ـ إِحْضَار ; of elevating in dignity, تَعْزِيز ـ تَرْقِيَة ـ رَفْع مَقَام (or شَأْن) ـ تَشْرِيف ; of growing, cultivating, تَرْبِيَة ـ زَرْع ـ زِرَاعَة ; of inciting, تَهْيِيج ـ تَحْرِيض ; of inciting to rebellion, إِفْسَاد ـ إِفْتَان ; of increasing, تَزْيِيد ـ زَوْد ; of raising a price, إِغْلَاء ٱلثَّمَنِ ; of disseminating, بَثّ ـ إِشَاعَة ـ نَشْر ; of encouraging, تَشْجِيع ـ تَرْوِيج ـ تَشْيِيع ; of strengthening, تَأْيِيد ـ تَشْدِيد ; of levying soldiers, تَجْيِيش ـ لَمّ ٱلْعَسَاكِرِ ـ جَمْع ٱلْعَسَاكِرِ ; of raising a siege, رَفْعُ ٱلْحِصَارِ ; of raising money, تَحْصِيلُ ٱلدَّرَاهِمِ ; of raising from the dead, بَعْث ـ إِقَامَة مِنَ ٱلْأَمْوَاتِ ; of piling together, تَكْوِيم ; of raising up against, إِقَامَة عَلَى.

Raisonné, *a.* مَشْرُوح ـ عَلَى طَرِيقِ ٱلْإِسْتِيضَاحِ.

Rajah, *n.* رَاجَاه ـ حُكْمُدَار ـ اِسْمُ ٱلْوَالِي عِنْدَ أَهْلِ ٱلْهِنْدِ.

Rajahship, *n.* حُكْمُدَارِيَّة ـ مَقَامُ ٱلْوَالِي عِنْدَ أَهْلِ ٱلْهِنْدِ ـ رُتْبَةُ ٱلرَّاجَاه ـ هِنْدِيَّة.

Rake, *n.* A — to collect hay or to rake the ground with, مِدَمَّة ـ مِجْرَفَة ـ جُرَّافَة. A dissipated fellow, خَلِيع *pl.* خُلَعَاءُ ـ فَاسِق *pl.* فَسَقَة *and* فُسَّاق. *See also* Libertine, *n.*

Rake, *v.t.* To collect or clear away with a rake, جَرَفَ ـ بِٱلْمِجْرَفَةِ ـ جَرَفَ. To fire in the direction of the length of anything, أَطْلَقَ ٱلنَّارَ عَلَى طُولِ ٱلطَّرَفِ ـ أَطْلَقَ ٱلنَّارَ عَلَى ـ تَطْرِيفًا. To — out, أَخْرَجَ ; to — out, as a fire, أَخْمَدَ. To — together, to collect, قَمَّشَ ـ حَبَّشَ ـ حَشَّ ـ جَمَعَ ـ لَمَّ. To — up, to search for, فَتَّشَ عَن ـ حَشَّ. To stir, as a fire, *etc.*, حَرَّثَ ـ أَضْرَمَ. *See also* to Scratch, *v.t.*

Rake, *v.i.* To use the rake, اِسْتَعْمَلَ ٱلْمِجْرَفَةَ. To search minutely, فَتَّشَ ـ تَفَحَّصَ ـ تَنَقَّرَ ـ تَجَسَّسَ. To lead a dissolute life, اِنْهَمَكَ فِي ـ فَحُشَ ـ اِنْغَرَطَ ـ غَمَطَ ـ خَلُعَ ٱللَّذَّاتِ.

Raker, *n.* One who uses a rake, جَرَّاف.

Raking, *n.* The act of using a rake, جَرْف ـ جَرْفَة. The quantity raked, ٱلْمَجْرُوف.

Raking, *a.* A — fire, إِطْلَاق ٱلنَّارِ عَلَى طُولِ ٱلطَّرَفِ ـ إِطْلَاق ٱلنَّارِ تَطْرِيفًا.

Rakish, *a.* Dissolute, خَلِيع ـ فَاجِر *pl.* فُجَّار ـ فَلَاتِيّ ـ فَاسِق. Inclined backwards, مَائِل إِلَى وَرَاءِ.

Rakishness, *n.* خَلَاعَة ـ فُجُور ـ فِسْق ـ فَلْت ـ فِسْق وَفَسَاد.

Rally, *n.* The act of collecting disordered troops, ضَمّ ٱلشَّارِدِينَ ـ لَمّ ٱلشَّتْرِ. A collection, مَجْمَع ـ جَمَاعَة

ـ دُعابَة. The exercise of satirical merriment, لَمَّة ـ ضَمَّة ـ جَمْع ـ مُمازَحَة ـ مَزْح ـ مِزاح ـ مَزْه.

Rally, *v.t.* To banter, دَاعَبَ ـ مَازَهَ ـ مَازَحَ. To collect together the dispersed, لَمَّ ٱلنَّشْرَ ـ ضَمَّ ٱلشَّارِدِينَ ـ ² ضَمَّ. *See also to* Banter, Ridicule, *v.t.*

Rally, *v.i.* To use pleasantry, ـ دَعَبَ ـ دَعِبَ ـ شَمَعَ ـ هَذِرَ ـ هَزَلَ ـ مَزَهَ ـ مَزَحَ. To assemble together, of the dispersed, إِنْضَمُّوا إِلَى بَعْضِهِمْ بَعْضٍ ـ إِنْضَمَّ ٱلشَّارِدُونَ. To — to one, of many, حَشَدُوا لَهُ ². To grow better, get into better order, تَجَبَّرَ ـ إِسْتَصْلَحَ ـ إِنْصَلَحَ ـ صَحَّ ـ إِسْتَتَبَّ. A rallying point, مَضَمٌّ ـ مَوْضِعُ ٱلْإِنْضِمَامِ. The order given to soldiers to rally, أَمْرٌ بِٱلْإِلْتِئَامِ.

Ram, *n.* A male sheep, كَبْش *pl.* كِبَاش. A battering —, مَنْجَنِيق *pl.* مَنَاجِق ـ مَجَانِيق. A — for raising water, طُلُومْبَة ـ طُرُمْبَة. The sign of the zodiac, بُرْجُ ٱلْحَمَلِ ـ ٱلْحَمَلُ. A drive, as with a ramrod, دَكَّة. A steel ram on the prow of a ship, آلَةٌ لِلنَّطْحِ مِنْ حَدِيدٍ فِي مُرَجَّحِ ٱلسَّفِينَةِ. A ship armed with a ram, سَفِينَةٌ نَطَّاحَةٌ.

Ram, *v.t.* As with a ramrod, دَكَّ ². To cram, ـ شَحَنَ ـ حَشَا ² ـ كَبَسَ. To — close together, رَصَّ ² ـ رَصَّصَ.

Ramadhân, *n.* رَمَضَان.

Ramble, *n.* A wandering to and fro, عِيَار. A trip, jaunt, شَمُّ هَوَآءٍ ـ سَيْرٌ لِلتَّنَزُّهِ ـ تَفْسِيح ـ سَفْرَة ـ سِيَاحَة. To take a —, تَفَسَّحَ.

Ramble, *v.i.* To wander about, سَاحَ ـ طَاحَ ². To — about in countries, عَارَ فِي ٱلْبِلَادِ ـ عَالَ فِي ٱلْبِلَادِ ² ـ طَوَى ٱلْبِلَادَ. To — in the mind, طَاشَ. To — in talk, سَابَ فِي ٱلْمَنْطِقِ (*or* فِي ٱلْكَلَامِ) ـ أَهْتَرَ ـ أَهْذَرَ.

Rambler, *n.* One who roams about, سَيَّاح ـ عَائِر ـ عَيَّار. A — in talk, سَائِبٌ فِي ٱلْكَلَامِ ـ مُهْتِر.

Rambling, *a.* Roaming, سَائِح ـ عَائِر; of speech, ٱلشُّيُوبُ فِي ٱلْكَلَامِ ـ هَيْذَار ـ هَذَّار ـ هَذِر. Restless, of a man, جُرْجُجَة وُلَجَة ـ فِي رَأْسِهِ نُعَرَة. Skill in speech is more eloquent (or effectual) than — words, إِنَّ ٱلْحِيلَةَ بِٱلْمَنْطِقِ أَبْلَغُ مِنَ ٱلشُّيُوبِ فِي ٱلْكَلَامِ.

Rambling, *n.* *See* Ramble, *n.*

Ramification, *n.* A branching, تَشْعِيب ـ تَشَعُّب ـ تَفَرُّع. A branch, division or sub-division, فَرْع *pl.* فُرُوع ـ شُعْبَة *pl.* شُعَب. A question having many ramifications, مَسْأَلَةٌ كَثِيرَةُ ٱلشُّعَبِ.

Ramify, *v.i.* تَفَرَّعَ ـ إِنْشَعَبَ ـ تَشَعَّبَ ـ شَعَّبَ.

Rammed, *a.* مَرْصُوص ـ مَكْبُوس ـ مَدْكُوك.

Rammer, *n.* An instrument for driving, مِيْطَدَة ـ مِدَكٌّ. A — of a gun, مِدَكُّ ٱلْمِدْفَعِ; *from the Turkish,* تُومَار.

Rammish, *a.* Strong-scented, تَفِل.

Ramose, *a.* / Ramous, } كَثِيرُ ٱلْفُرُوعِ ـ كَثِيرُ ٱلْأَغْصَانِ ـ مُتَشَعِّب.

Ramp, *v.i.* *See to* Frisk, Leap, Romp, *v.i.*

Ramp, *n.* A slope for ascending or descending, ـ نَزْلَة ـ طَلْعَة ـ مَهْبَط. *See also* Romp, *n.*

Rampancy, *n.* Exuberance of growth, تَكْثِيَة ـ كَثَأ. Exuberance, تَجَاوُز ـ كَثْرَة ـ وُفُور ـ بَذَارَة. Excessive prevalence, ـ شُمُول ـ تَعْمِيم ـ عُمُوم ـ شَمَل. Extravagance of conduct, طُغْيَان. Predominance, إِسْتِيلَآء ـ غَلَبَة. *See also* Wantonness, *n.*

Rampant, *a.* Exuberant in growth, أَخْصَب. Exuberant, excessive, مُفْرِط ـ مُتَجَاوِز ـ مُتَوَافِر. Extravagant in conduct, immoderate, طَاغِيَة. Predominating, شَامِلُ ٱلْجَمَاعَةِ ـ مُطِمّ ـ عَامّ. A lion —, سَبْعٌ رَابِضٌ عَلَى عَجْزِهِ وَيَدَاهُ مَرْفُوعَتَانِ. To be —, to predominate, عَمَّ ².

Rampantly, *ad.* Excessively, ـ فَوْقَ ٱلْحَدِّ ـ بِإِفْرَاطٍ ـ فَرْطًا لِلْغَايَةِ. With precipitation, بِتَهَوُّرٍ ـ تَهَوُّرًا. *See also* Rashly, *ad.*, Predominantly, *ad.*

Rampart, *n.* مِتْرَاس ـ أَسْوَار *pl.* سُور ـ إِسْتِحْكَام *pl.* إِسْتِحْكَامَات *pl.* مَتَارِيس ـ سَدّ *pl.* أَسْدَاد.

Ramrod, *n.* مِدَكّ *pl.* مِدَكَّات ـ شِيش *pl.* شِيَاس; *from the Turkish* تُومَار.

Rancid, *a.* زَنِخ ـ سَنِخ. To be —, تَسَنَّخَ ـ زَنِخَ ـ سَنِخَ.

Rancidity, *n.* / Rancidness, } زَنَاخَة ـ سَنَاخَة ـ سَنَخ ـ زَنَخ.

Rancorous, *a.* ـ دَحِل ـ ضَاغِن ـ ضَغِن ـ مُسَخِّم ـ حَسِيك غَبِيّ ـ كَاشِح ـ حَقُود ـ مُغِلّ.

Rancorously, *ad.* بِغَبَاوَةٍ ـ بِحَسَكٍ ـ بِحِقْدٍ ـ بِغِلٍّ.

Rancour, *n.* ـ حِقْد ـ غِلّ ـ سُخْمَة ـ ضِغْن ـ غِبْر ـ إِحْنَة كَشَاحَة ـ غَلِيل ـ غَبَاوَة ـ حَسَك ـ حَقِيدَة. To bear — against, تَسَخَّمَ عَلَى ـ ضَغِنَ عَلَى ـ تَحَقَّدَ عَلَى ـ حَقَدَ عَلَى ـ أَحِنَ عَلَى. To entertain —, غَلَّ صَدْرُهُ *aor.* يَغِلُّ. They entertained mutual —, of many, تَحَاقَدُوا. He entertained — in his heart, أَضَبَّ ـ غَبِرَ عَلَى غِلٍّ فِي قَلْبِهِ. To treat with —, آحِنَ.

Random, *a.* Chance, إِتِّفَاقِيّ ـ عَارِضِيّ. Without design, غَيْرُ مُتَعَمَّدٍ. A — arrow hit him, أَصَابَهُ سَهْمٌ عَرَضٍ. Random speech, ٱلشُّيُوبُ فِي ٱلْكَلَامِ.

Random, *n.* Want of direction, إِعْتِسَاف ـ سَيَبَان. Conjecture, حَدْس. A thing done at —, فَلْتَة. To do a thing at —, خَبَطَ خَبْطَ عَشْوَآءَ ـ 2. To act at —, إِعْتَسَفَ (or) تَعَسَّفَ فِي ٱلْأَمْرِ. He travelled the road at —, عَسَفَ ٱلطَّرِيقَ ـ 2 إِعْتَسَفَ. To roam at — through a land, سَكَّ فِي ٱلْأَرْضِ 2. They go at —, يَمْشُونَ ٱلرَّكَّبَات. He goes at —, يَرْكَبُ رَأْسَهُ. He fired a shot at —, ضَرَبَ غَيْرَ مُتَعَمِّدٍ ـ 2. To stray at —, سَابَ ـ 2 عَارَ aor. يَعِيرُ. To talk at —, سَابَ فِي ٱلْكَلِمِ ـ 2 إِفْتَلَتَ ٱلْكَلَامَ ـ هَلَجَ 2. He said it at —, قَالَهُ بِٱلْحَدْسِ. He ran at —, in a headlong manner, إِسْتَنَّ (or) تَسَنَّنَ) فِي عَدْوِهِ (or) جِرِّيَتِهِ).

Rane, *n.* *See* Reindeer, *n.*

Rang. *See to* Ring, *v.t.*

Range, *n.* A row, صَفٌّ *pl.* صُفُوف ـ طَوْر *pl.* أَطْوَار. A wandering excursion, سَيْر ـ عِيَار ـ سِيَاحَة. Extent, مَدَار ـ إِمْتِدَاد. Compass, إِسْتِدَار ـ دَائِرَة. Scope, فُسْحَة ـ مَدًى; of time, أَمَد ـ مُدَّة. A step of a ladder, عَتَبَة *pl.* عَتَبَات ـ دَرَجَة *pl.* دَرَجَات. Power, طَاقَة ـ مُكْنَة. A cooking —, مَوْقِدَةٌ ـ (طَوْر (or) طَقْم) طَوَابِق. A — of mountains, سِلْسِلَةُ جِبَالٍ. Within — of the eye, فِي مَدَى ٱلْبَصَرِ. *See also* Class, Series, *n.*

Range, *v.t.* To place in order, رَتَّبَ ـ نَظَّمَ ـ نَسَّقَ. To put in a row, صَفَّفَ ـ صَفَّ 2. To dispose in classes, series, نَسَّقَ. To traverse, طَافَ فِي 2 ـ عَالَ فِي 2 ـ عَارَ فِي 2.

Range, *v.i.* To roam, طَافَ aor. يَطُوفُ ـ سَاحَ aor. يَسِيحُ ـ دَارَ 2. To —, as along a coast, سَافَرَ بِٱلْقُرْبِ مِنَ ٱلسَّوَاحِلِ ـ 2 شَطَأَ. To — up alongside of, جَانَبَ.

Ranger, *n.* A keeper, as of a forest, نَاظِرُ حِرْشٍ ـ أَمِينُ غَابَةٍ. A dog, كَلْب *pl.* كِلَاب. *See also* Roamer, *n.*

Rangership, *n.* أَمَانَةُ غَابَةٍ ـ وَظِيفَةُ أَمِينِ ٱلْغَابَةِ.

Ranging, *a.* Roaring, ثَائِر.

Rank, *n.* A row, صَفٌّ *pl.* صُفُوف. A —, as of people, سِمَاط *pl.* أَسْمِطَة. A series, order, نَسَق ـ نِظَام ـ نَظْم ـ سِيَاقَة. Degree, position, dignity, رُتْبَة *pl.* رُتَب ـ مَقَام ـ دَرَجَة ـ قِيَام ـ مَرْتَبَة *pl.* مَرَاتِبُ ـ جَاه. Eminence, عِزّ ـ عِزَّة ـ عَلَآء ـ مَعْلَاة. A man of —, كَرِيم *pl.* كِرَام ـ شَرِيف *pl.* شُرَفَآءُ ـ عَزِيز ـ رُتْبَةٌ عَالِيَةٌ ـ عَلِيُّ ٱلشَّأْنِ ـ نَبِيل *pl.* نُبَال ـ كِرَام. The heavenly ranks, ٱلصَّافَاتُ ٱلسَّمَوِيَّةُ ـ ٱلصَّافَاتُ. Ranks, soldiers, عَسْكَر; private soldiers, أَفْرَادٌ مِنَ ٱلْعَسَاكِرِ ـ نَفَرَات ـ أَنْفَار. Rank and file, أَفْرَاد ـ نَفَرَات ـ أَنْفَار. In ranks, صَفِيفٌ. Holding the — of..., حَائِزٌ رُتْبَةَ ٱلـ... In the first —, فِي أَوَّلِ صَفٍّ. In the —, footing, of the European governments, فِي مَصَافِّ ٱلدُّوَلِ ٱلْأُورُبَاوِيَّةِ.

To break the ranks, نَفَضَ ٱلصُّفُوفَ 2: They broke their (own) ranks and ran, فَشِلُوا وَٱنْهَزَمُوا.

To draw up in a rank, صَفَّفَ ـ صَفَّ 2. To be so drawn up, of many, تَرَاصُّوا ـ إِصْطَفُّوا.

To be in the ranks, كَانَ مِنْ أَنْفَارِ ٱلْعَسْكَرِ.

To reduce to the ranks, حَطَّهُ إِلَى مَنْزِلَةِ ٱلنَّفَرِ 2.

To take rank with, تَرَتَّبَ عَلَى مَرْتَبَةِ فُلَانٍ.

To take rank after, تَرَتَّبَ دُونَ فُلَانٍ ـ كَانَ دُونَ فُلَانٍ.

To take rank before, تَقَدَّمَ عَلَى.

Rank, *a.* Strong-scented, حَادُّ ٱلرَّائِحَةِ ـ تَفِل; a — smell, حَرْوَة. Strong, شَدِيد ـ حَادّ ـ حَدِيد. Luxuriant, of vegetation, أَخْصَبُ ـ كَاثٍ 2. High-tasted, حَادُّ ٱلذَّوْقِ ـ حَاذِق ـ أُجَاج. Rancid, سَنِخ ـ زَنِخ. Extreme, آخِرٌ ـ أَشَدُّ ـ أَعْظَمُ. Destructive, قَاتِل ـ مُهْلِك. Coarse, غَلِيظ. Rank poison, سَمٌّ قَاتِلٌ. Fat, full, سَمِين ـ فَعِم. To be —, fat, full, فَعُمَ 2.

Rank, *v.t.* To put into a rank or row, صَفَّفَ. To estimate, نَزَّلَ مَنْزِلَةَ كَذَا ـ عَدَّ 2 ـ حَسِبَ 2. To put into a rank, dignity, أَعْطَى رُتْبَةً ـ عَيَّنَ لِـ رُتْبَةً ـ وَجَّهَ إِلَى مَرْتَبَةٍ. I ranked him with the common people, نَزَّلْتُهُ مَنْزِلَةَ ٱلْعَوَامِّ.

Rank, *v.i.* To be in a rank, dignity, كَانَ فِي رُتْبَةٍ. To be ranged, إِصْطَفَّ. He ranks with a general, رُتْبَتُهُ رُتْبَةُ ٱلْأَمِيرِ.

Rankle, *v.i.* To be inflamed, إِلْتَهَبَ. To bear rancour, غَلَّ صَدْرُهُ aor. يَغِلُّ. To fester, تَقَرَّحَ ـ تَقَيَّحَ.

Rankling, *n.* The becoming inflamed, إِلْتِهَاب. Active irritation, إِلْتِهَاب ـ إِغَاظَة. *See also* Rancour, *n.*

Rankly, *ad.* Strongly, بِشِدَّةٍ ـ بِحِدَّةٍ. Excessively, بِإِفْرَاطٍ ـ فَوْقَ ٱلْحَدِّ ـ وَفْرَةً ـ بِبَذَارَةٍ ـ لِلْغَايَةِ. Luxuriantly, بِكَثَآءٍ ـ بِتَكَثُّفٍ. With a strong smell, سَنَخَة. To smell —, سَنِخَ 2.

Rankness, *n.* Of smell, زَنَخ ـ سَنَخ ـ حَرَاقَة ـ حُمُوضَة ـ حِدَّة; of vegetation, تَكَثُّفَة ـ كَثَآء. Coarseness, غِلَظ. Exuberance, وُفُور ـ كَثْرَة ـ بَذَارَة ـ فُضُول ـ إِفْرَاط ـ وَفْرَة.

Ransack, *v.t.* To search narrowly, نَبَّشَ ـ فَتَّشَ. To plunder, نَهَبَ 2 ـ سَلَبَ 2.

Ransacking, *n.* The act of searching, تَنْبِيش ـ تَفْتِيش; of plundering, سَلْب ـ نَهْب.

Ransom, *n.* The price paid for redeeming, فِدَآء ـ فَدًى ـ فِدًى ـ فِدْيَة. To give a —, دَفَعَ فِدَآءً 2. To take a — for, أَخَذَ فِدَآءً لِـ. I am your —, جُعِلْتُ فِدَاكَ. He accepted from him the — of the captive, أَفْدَاهُ ٱلْأَسِيرَ.

Ransom, *v.t.* To free by paying a ransom, فَدَى 2 ـ إِفْتَدَى بِهِ.

فَادَى. To be ransomed, أُفْتُدِيَ. To be ransomed with, أُفْتُدِيَ بِ. To deliver, rescue, سَلَّمَ ـ خَلَّصَ ـ فَكَّ ـ 2 نَقَذَ ـ 2 إِسْتَنْقَذَ. To — one's self, إِفْتَدَى: He ransomed himself from him with such a thing, إِفْتَدَى مِنْهُ بِكَذَا. *See also* to Redeem, *v.t.*

Ransomer, *n.* فَادٍ; a deliverer, مُخَلِّص.

Ransomless, *a.* Not to be ransomed, لَا يُفْدَى. Not having a ransom, لَا فِدَآءَ لَهُ.

Rant, *n.* لَغْوٌ ـ هَذْرٌ ـ هَذَيَان ـ هِتْر ـ هِتْرٌ هَاتِرٌ ـ هَتْرَمَة ـ كَثْرَةُ كَلَامٍ ـ كَلَامٌ بَاطِلٌ.

Rant, *v.i.* 2 لَغَا ـ هَذَى ـ 2 هَذَرَ ـ هَتَرَ ـ أَهْتَرَ ـ هَتْرَمَ ـ دَرْدَشَ ـ كَثَّرَ ٱلْكَلَامَ.

Ranter, *n.* هَاتِر ـ مُهَتْرِم ـ هَذَّار ـ هَاذٍ. The sect of Ranters, إِسْمُ شِيعَةٍ مِنَ ٱلنَّصَارَى.

Ranting, *a.* مُهَتَّر ـ بَاطِل ـ هُذْرَة.

Ranting, *n.* *See* Rant, *n.*

Rantipole, *a.* مَجْنُون ـ مُتَهَوِّر.

Ranunculus, *n.* شَقِيقٌ نُعْمَانِيٌّ.

Rap, *v.t.* To strike, لَاكَمَ ـ 2 لَكَمَ ـ 2 ضَرَبَ. To — with the hand, لَطَمَ ـ (2 طَرَقَ or) بِكَفِّهِ. To — at a door, 2 طَرَقَ ٱلْبَابَ ـ 2 دَقَّ ٱلْبَابَ. To seize and bear away, 2 سَلَبَ.

Rap, *n.* A blow, مُلَاكَمَة ـ ضَرْبَة; as at a door, طَرْق ـ دَقّ.

Rapacious, *a.* Given to plunder, سَلَّاب. Voracious, مُتَلَعِّس. Greedy of prey, خَاطِف *pl.* خُطَّاف ـ جَارِح *pl.* جَوَارِحُ; of a dog, عَقُور. A — animal, سَبُع *pl.* سِبَاع.

Rapaciously, *ad.* Ravenously, تَلَعُّسًا ـ بِحِرْصٍ; by rapine, forcibly, إِخْتِطَافًا ـ بِخَطْفٍ ـ قَهْرًا.

Rapaciousness, *n.* } Disposition to plunder, سَلَبُوت ـ سَلَّابَة.
Rapacity, } Voraciousness, حِرْص ـ قَرَم. Violence, قَهْر.

Rape, *n.* A seizing by violence, إِخْتِطَاف ـ خَطْف ـ سَلْب. Carnal knowledge by force, هَتْكُ آمْرَأَةٍ ـ غَصْبُ نَفْسِ ٱلِٱمْرَأَةِ ـ إِغْتِصَابُ آمْرَأَةٍ. Something carried away, سَلِيب ـ نَهِيب. The plant, نَبَاتٌ مِنْ فَصِيلَةِ ٱلشَّلْجَمِ يُسْتَخْرَجُ مِنْ بِزْرِهِ ٱلزَّيْتُ. To commit a — upon a woman, إِبْتَارَ ـ هَتَكَ ـ قَهَرَ ـ ضَاجَعَ غَصْبًا.

Rapid, *a.* Quick, مُوَاشِك ـ وَشِيك ـ سَرِيع ـ طَيَّار; of a torrent or stream, قُحَاف ـ قُعَاف ـ سَيَّال. *See also* Quick, Swift, Fleet, *a.*

Rapidity, *n.* } وِشَاك ـ وُشْك ـ سُرْعَة. *See also* Quickness,
Rapidness, } Swiftness, *n.*

Rapidly, *ad.* وِشَاكًا ـ وَشْكًا ـ بِسُرْعَةٍ. To move —, وَجَزَ *aor.* يَجِزُ ـ وَشُكَ ـ وَاشَكَ ـ أَوْشَكَ ـ 2 سَرُعَ ـ أَسْرَعَ. *See also* Quickly, Swiftly, *ad.*

Rapids, *n.* As of a river, طَيَّار.

Rapier, *n.* نَصْل *pl.* نِصَال *and* أَنْصَال ـ بَالَة ـ مِغْوَل ـ مِشْمَل ـ سِيخ ـ سَيْف.

Rapine, *n.* نَهْب ـ نُهْبَة ـ إِنْتِهَاب. *See also* Plunder, Pillage, *n.*

Rapparee, *n.* قَاطِعُ ٱلطَّرِيقِ *pl.* قُطَّاع.

Rappee, *n.* A kind of snuff, ضَرْبٌ مِنَ ـ ضَرْبٌ مِنَ ٱلْأَنْفِيَّةِ ٱلنَّشُوقِ.

Rapper, *n.* One who raps, ضَارِب ـ طَارِق. The knocker of a door, مِطْرَقَة ـ مِطْرَقَةُ بَابٍ.

Rapt, *a.* Transported in ecstacy, مُتَوَجِّدٌ بِهِ ـ فِي حَالِ ٱلْوَجْدِ ـ مُسْطُول.

Rapture, *n.* Ecstasy, وَجْد ـ حَالُ ٱلْوِجْدَانِ. Extreme joy, غَايَةُ ٱلسُّرُورِ ـ فَرْطُ ٱلْحَظِّ. To be in a —, ecstasy, تَوَجَّدَ بِهِ ـ إِنْسَلَبَ قَلْبُهُ بِٱلْفَرَحِ ـ كَانَ فِي غَايَةِ ٱلسُّرُورِ ـ إِنْسَطَلَ. To be in raptures, *See also* Ecstasy, *n. and to* Enravish, *v.t.*

Raptured, *a.* With delight, فِي غَايَةِ ٱلسُّرُورِ ـ مُنْسَلِبُ ٱلْقَلْبِ بِٱلْفَرَحِ.

Rapturous, *a.* مُسْلِبُ ٱلْعَقْلِ ـ مُسْلِبُ ٱلْقَلْبِ ـ مُذْهِل. *See also* Ecstatic, *a.*

Rapturously, *ad.* بِفَرْطِ ٱلسُّرُورِ ـ بِغَايَةِ ٱلْحَظِّ. *See also* Ecstatically, *ad.*

Rara avis, *n.* A rare, uncommon, bird, طَيْرٌ نَادِرٌ ـ طَيْرٌ غَرِيبٌ. An unusual person, فَرِيدُ ٱلْعَصْرِ ـ نَادِرَةُ ٱلزَّمَانِ.

Rare, *a.* Seldom found, قَلِيلُ ٱلْوُجُودِ; seldom occurring, قَلِيلُ ٱلْوُقُوعِ. Out of the common, نَادِر. Special, as of a friend, ضِنٌّ. Strange, غَرِيب ـ عَجِيب. Precious, عَزِيز. Underdone, as of meat, نِيءٌ. Rare, of the atmosphere, مُتَخَلِّل. A — thing, 2 عَزَّ. A — or nice bit, طَيِّبَة. To become —, نَادِرَة *pl.* نَوَادِرُ.

Rare-bit, *n.* Welsh rabbit, قِطْعَةُ خُبْزٍ بِجُبْنٍ مَشْوِيٌّ.

Raree-show, *n.* فُرْجَةٌ جَرَّارَةٌ.

Rarefaction, *n.* Of the air, (لَطَافَة or) لَطْف or تَخَلُّلُ ٱلْهَوَآءِ.

Rarefiable, *a.* مِمَّا يَتَخَلَّلُ ـ قَابِلُ ٱلتَّخَلُّلِ ـ مِمَّا يَلْطُفُ.

Rarefied, *a.* مُتَخَلِّل ـ مُلَطَّف.

Rarefy, *v.t.* لَطَّفَ ـ صَيَّرَ مُتَخَلِّلًا.

Rarely, *ad.* بِنَدْرَةٍ ـ فِي ٱلنَّادِرِ ـ فِي ٱلْقَلِيلِ.

Rareness, *n.* } Infrequent occurrence, قِلَّةُ وُقُوعٍ; the being
Rarity, } seldom found, قِلَّةُ وُجُودٍ. Uncommonness, نَدْرَة. Preciousness, عِزّ ـ عِزَّة ـ عَزَازَة. A rare thing, طُرْفَة *pl.*

A strange thing, طُرْفَة — تُرَف .pl تُحْفَة — تُحَف .pl نَادِرَة — نَوَادِرُ .pl عَجِيبَة — عَجَائِبُ .pl غَرِيبَة — غَرَائِبُ. Rarities, تُحَف.

Rascal, *n.* Rascalion, } خُلَعَآءُ .pl خَلِيعٌ — خَاسِرٌ — خَبِيثٌ — قِبَاحٌ .pl قَبِيحٌ.

Rascality, *n.* خَلَاعَة — خَبَاثَة — قَبَاحَة — خَسَار — خَسَارَة.

Rascally, *a.* قَبِيحٌ — خَبِيثٌ — ذَلِيلٌ. To act in a — manner, خَلُعَ ² — أَقْبَحَ.

Rase, *v.t.* ضَعْضَعَ — نَسَفَ — إِنْتَسَفَ — هَدَمَ — دَكَّ ².

Rash, *a.* Precipitate, هَيِّر — مُتَهَوِّر — مُتَهَالِك. Heedless, أَبْلَهُ — قَلِيلُ ٱلِاعْتِنَآءِ. Not caring for what he says or does, مَاجِن. A — undertaking, قُحَم .pl قُحْمَة. *See also* Precipitate, *a.*

Rash, *n.* An eruption, طَفْحَة — خُرُوج.

Rasher, *n.* A slice, شَرْحَة — شَرِيحَة — شِقَّة .pl شِقَق — قِطْعَة .pl قِطَع.

Rashly, *ad.* اِقْتِحَامًا — بِتَهَوُّرٍ. Do nothing —, لَا تَفْعَلُوا شَيْئًا اِقْتِحَامًا. To do a thing —, عَسَفَ فِي ٱلْأَمْرِ — تَعَسَّفَ — إِعْتَسَفَ. *See also* Precipitantly, *ad.*

Rashness, *n.* إِعْتِسَاف — تَهَوُّر. *See also* Heedlessness, Precipitancy, *n.*

Rasp, *n.* سَفَن — مِحَكَّة. A foot —, such as is used in baths, حَجَرٌ — دَلُوك — نَشَّاف .pl نَشَفَة — نِسَاف and نُسَف .pl نَسْفَة ٱلْحَمَّامِ.

Rasp, *v.t.* حَكَّ ² — حَكَّ بِٱلْمِحَكَّةِ ².

Raspberry, *n.* عُلَّيْقٌ — تُوتُ ٱلْعُلَّيْقِ. A — bush, عُلَّيْقَى.

Rat, *n.* فَأْر .pl فِيرَان: a field —, جُرَذ .pl جِرْذَان vulg. جردون .pl جرادين. To smell a —, شَكَّ فِي ٱلْأَمْرِ ² — تَشَكَّكَ فِي ٱلْأَمْرِ. To abound in rats, فَئِرَ aor. يَفْأَرُ. A place abounding in rats, فَئِر — مَفْأَرَة.

Rat, *v.i.* To desert one's party, خَانَ حِزْبَهُ ² — اِرْتَدَّ عَنْ حِزْبِهِ.

Ratable, *a.* عَلَيْهِ — عَلَيْهِ تَكَالِيفُ — مِمَّا تُوضَعُ عَلَيْهِ ٱلضَّرَائِبُ. دَفْعُ ضَرِيبَةٍ.

Ratably, *ad.* بِحِصَّتِهِ — بِٱلْحِصَّةِ.

Ratafia, *n.* عَنْبَرِيٌّ.

Ratan, *n.* The cane so called, خَيْزُرَان. A walking stick of —, عَصَا خَيْزُرَانٍ.

Rat-catcher, *n.* صَيَّادُ ٱلْفِيرَانِ.

Ratchet, *n.* سِنٌّ لِضَبْطِ ٱلدُّولَابِ.

Ratchet-wheel, *n.* دُولَابٌ مُسَنَّنٌ.

Rate, *n.* Degree of value, or price, حِسَاب. Standard price, سِعْر .pl أَسْعَار. Speed, going, مَشْي — سِيرَة — سَيْر — جَرَيَان. A tax, ضَرِيبَة .pl ضَرَائِبُ — تَكْلِيف .pl تَكَالِيف — رَسْم .pl رُسُوم. A ration, وَظِيفَة .pl وَظَائِف — رَاتِبَة .pl رَوَاتِبُ. Poor-rate, مِخْلَاف .pl مَخَالِيف; a collector of poor-rates, مُصَدِّق. An order or class, as of ships, صِنْف .pl أَصْنَاف — دَرَجَة .pl دَرَجَات. Rate of money, سِعْرُ ٱلْمُعَامَلَةِ. To impose rates, taxes, upon, ضَرَبَ = أَلْقَى ٱلتَّكَالِيفَ عَلَى — عَلَى ضَرَائِبَ.

At a daily rate, كُلَّ يَوْمٍ بِيَوْمِهِ.

At any rate, in any case, عَلَى كُلِّ حَالٍ — مَهْمَا — كَيْفَمَا كَانَ — عَلَى أَيِّ وَجْهٍ كَانَ — يَحْصُلُ.

At that rate, عَلَى هٰذَا ٱلطَّرْزِ — عَلَى هٰذَا ٱلْحَالِ — حَسَبَ ذٰلِكَ.

At the rate of, بِسِعْرِ كَذَا.

At a dear rate, بِسِعْرٍ غَالٍ — غَالٍ.

At a furious rate, هِيَاجًا — بِتَهَوُّرٍ — بِجُنُونٍ.

At a great rate, speedily, وَشْكًا — بِسُرْعَةٍ — سَرْعًا.

First-rate, of the best quality, أَعْلَى مَا يَكُونُ — أَحْسَنُ مَا يَكُونُ. Of the first class, مِنَ ٱلصِّنْفِ ٱلْأَوَّلِ.

Second rate, of an inferior quality, دُون. Of the second class, مِنَ ٱلصِّنْفِ ٱلثَّانِي.

Rate, *v.t.* To set a value upon, حَسَبَ ثَمَنَهُ — ثَمَّنَ — سَعَّرَ ². To apportion taxes to, عَيَّنَ لِـ ٱلتَّكَالِيفَ — قَطَعَ عَلَى ٱلضَّرَائِبَ — قَدَّرَ عَلَى ٱلرُّسُومَ. To rank, to put down as, حَسِبَ = = — حَقَّقَ ٱلْمَسَافَةَ — خَمَّنَ ٱلْمَسَافَةَ. To — a distance, نَزَّلَ مَنْزِلَةَ ٱ... To —, as of a ship, *etc.*, أَدْخَلَ فِي = = — حَسِبَ فِي ٱلصِّنْفِ ٱ... To scold, عَاتَبَ — عَتَبَ عَلَى ² — سَخِطَ عَلَى = ٱلدَّرَجَةِ ٱ... صَعِدَ بِ — وَنَزَلَ — شَتَمَ ².

Rate, *v.i.* To be set or considered in a class, حُسِبَ فِي ٱلصِّنْفِ ٱ... — ٱ... كَانَ مِنَ ٱلصِّنْفِ. To be in a rank, dignity, كَانَ فِي رُتْبَةِ ٱ...

Rather, *ad.* أَعْظَمُ — أَحْسَنُ — أَخْيَرُ — خَيْرٌ — بَلْ — فَضْلًا — بِٱلْحَرِى. I think it — better for you, لَعَمْرِى خَيْرٌ لَكَ. Rather than that..., قَبْلَ أَنْ — أَحْرَى مِنْ أَنْ. He should or ought — to..., أَوْلَى بِهِ أَنْ. How much —, كَمْ بِٱلْحَرِى. Death — than slavery, ٱلْمَوْتُ خَيْرٌ مِنَ ٱلْأَسْرِ — ٱلْمَوْتُ وَلَا ٱلْأَسْرُ. (I prefer) death — than dishonour, ٱلْمَنِيَّةُ لَا ٱلدَّنِيَّةُ. I would — die than..., عِنْدِى ٱلْمَوْتُ أَحْسَنُ مِنْ أَنْ. I admire your virtue — than your knowledge, أَنَا مُتَعَجِّبٌ مِنْ فَضْلِكَ دُونَ عِلْمِكَ. Rather, it may be said, ٱلْأَحْرَى أَنْ يُقَالَ. He derived no benefit from it but — grew worse, لَمْ يَنْتَفِعْ شَيْئًا مِنْ ذٰلِكَ بَلْ صَارَ إِلَى حَالٍ أَرْدَأَ. I pray that you would — do this, أَوَدُّ لَوْ تَفْعَلُوا هٰذَا.

Rather, as expressing the degree of a quality, نَوْعًا ـ بَعْض : He is — tall, هُوَ طَوِيلٌ بَعْضَ ٱلطُّولِ ـ هُوَ طَوِيلٌ نَوْعًا . He is — handsome, هُوَ جَمِيلٌ نَوْعًا . *See also under to* Prefer, *v.t.*

Ratification, *n.* Approval, رِضًى ب ; signature of approval, تَجْدِيدُ ٱلْإِمْضَاءِ ـ إِمْضَاءٌ بِٱلْقَبُولِ . Ratification, as of a treaty, تَصْدِيق . The deed containing the —, صَكُّ ٱلتَّصْدِيقِ . To exchange ratifications (of two parties), تَبَادَلَا ٱلتَّصْدِيقَ . An exchange of ratifications, مُبَادَلَةُ ٱلتَّصْدِيقِ . Subject to —, مُحْتَاجٌ إِلَى ٱلتَّصْدِيقِ ـ مَوْقُوفٌ عَلَى ٱلتَّصْدِيقِ .

Ratifier, *n.* مُمْضٍ عَلَى ـ مُصَدِّق ـ مُعَقِّد .

Ratify, *v.t.* رَضِيَ ب ـ أَمْضَى ـ بِٱلرِّضَاءِ ـ عَقَّدَ ـ عَقَدَ ـ صَدَّقَ . He ratified the treaty, صَدَّقَ ٱلْمُعَاهَدَةَ ـ عَقَدَ ٱلْعَهْدَ . He ratified the sale, عَقَدَ ٱلْبَيْعَ . He ratified the sale with him, ضَرَبَ عَلَى يَدِهِ .

Rating, *n.* Valuation, تَثْمِين ـ تَسْعِير . The act of rating in a class, إِدْخَالٌ فِي صَنْف . A class, رُتْبَة . A scolding, عِتَاب ـ مُعَاتَبَة ـ سُخْطَة ـ شَتْم .

Ratio, *n.* حِسَاب ـ نِسْبَة . *See also under* Rate, *n.*

Ratiocination, *n.* إِسْتِدْلَال ـ قِيَاس .

Ration, *n.* A fixed provision, رَاتِبَة ـ رَاتِب *pl.* رَوَاتِب . Soldiers' rations, رَاتِبُ مَعَاشِ ٱلْعَسْكَرِ ـ عُلُوفَة ـ عَلَفَة . To serve out rations, وَزَّعَ ٱلرَّوَاتِبَ .

Rational, *a.* Endowed with reason, نَاطِق ; the — soul, ٱلرُّوحُ ٱلنَّفْسُ ٱلنَّاطِقَةُ ـ ٱلْإِنْسَانِيُّ . *See also* Reasonable, *a.*

Rationale, *n.* Theoretical explanation, تَفْصِيلَاتُ ٱلْحِكْمَةِ ـ حِكْمَة . A detailed exposition, بَيَانٌ مُفَصَّلٌ .

Rationalism, *n.* مَذْهَبٌ ـ مَذْهَبُ أَصْحَابِ ٱلرَّأْيِ دُونَ ٱلْوَحْيِ ـ إِنْكَارُ ٱلْوَحْيِ ـ ٱلدَّهْرِيَّةُ .

Rationalist, *n.* مِنْ أَهْلِ مَذْهَبِ أَصْحَابِ ٱلرَّأْيِ دُونَ ٱلْوَحْيِ ـ نَاكِرُ ٱلْوَحْيِ ـ دَهْرِيٌّ .

Rationalistic, *a.* }
Rationalistical, } مُطَابِقٌ مَذْهَبِ أَصْحَابِ ٱلرَّأْيِ دُونَ ٱلْوَحْيِ ـ دَهْرِيٌّ .

Rationalistically, *ad.* بِمُطَابَقَةِ مَذْهَبِ أَصْحَابِ ٱلرَّأْيِ دُونَ ٱلْوَحْيِ ـ حَسَبَ قَوْلِ ٱلدَّهْرِيَّةِ .

Rationality, *n.* The power of reasoning, عَاقِلَة . *See also* Reasonableness, *n.*

Rationally, *ad.* *See* Reasonably, *ad.*

Rationalness, *n.* صَوَاب ـ حَقٌّ ـ مُنَاسَبَة ـ مَعْقُول .

Ratline, *n.* }
Ratling, } حَبْلُ سُلَّمِ ٱلدَّقَلِ .

Ratsbane, *n.* طَعْمُ ٱلْفَأْرِ ـ سَمُّ ٱلْفَأْرِ .

Rat's-tail, *n.* The saw, مِنْشَارٌ فِي شَكْلِ ذَنَبِ ٱلْفَأْرِ .

Rattan, *n.* *See* Ratan, *n.*

Rattle, *v.i.* To make a sharp noise, صَلَّ *aor.* يَصِلُّ ـ صَلْصَلَ ـ طَنْطَنَ ـ طَنَّ ـ رَنَّ ـ تَخَشْخَشَ . To — off, to do quickly, خَفَّ فِي ـ أَسْرَعَ فِي . The arrows rattled against him, صَلَّ عَلَيْهِ ٱلسِّهَامُ . *See also to* Clatter, *v.i.*

Rattle, *v.t.* خَشْخَشَ ـ أَطَنَّ ـ رَنَّنَ . *See also to* Scold, *v.t.*

Rattle, *n.* A succession of sharp sounds, طَقْطَقَة ـ قَرْقَعَة ـ شَخْشَخَة ـ خَشْخَشَة . The —, or rattling, of carriage wheels, صَوْتُ رِعْشَةِ (or رَجَّةِ) بَكَرِ ٱلْعَرَبَاتِ . A child's —, شُخْشِيخَة . The death —, تَنَازُع ـ تَقَعْقُع ـ حَشْرَجَة ـ غَرْغَرَة : to have the death —, حَشْرَجَ ـ تَغَرْغَرَ ـ غَرْغَرَ .

Rattle-headed, *a.* رَأْسٌ فَارِغٌ ـ مَطْيُور ـ طَائِش ـ أَثْوَلُ .

Rattles, *n.* *See* Croup, *n.*

Rattlesnake, *n.* حَيَّةٌ ذَاتُ ٱلْأَجْرَاسِ ـ ثُعْبَانٌ أَبُو جَرَسٍ .

Rattletrap, *n.* سَقَط ـ شَيْءٌ بَطَّالٌ ـ جَرِين ـ جَارِن .

Rattling, *a.* Making sharp sounds, طَقْطَاق ـ مُطَقْطِق ـ مُقَرْقِع ـ مُطِنٌّ ـ مُخَشْخِش . A — tongue, لِسَانٌ طَلِقٌ . A — wind, رِيحٌ قَاصِفٌ . A — pace, رَوْجَة ـ سُرْعَة ـ وِشَاك .

Rattling, *n.* *See* Rattle, *n.*

Raucity, *n.* *See* Hoarseness, *n.*

Raucous, *a.* *See* Hoarse, *a.*

Ravage, *v.t.* To lay waste, أَخْرَبَ ـ خَرَّبَ ـ جَعَلَ خَرَابًا . To plunder, نَهَبَ . To make incursions upon, غَارَ عَلَى ـ غَزَا .

Ravage, *n.* }
Ravages, } خَسَارَة ـ خَرَاب ـ تَخْرِيب ـ هَدْم .

Ravager, *n.* مُهْلِك ـ مُخَرِّب ـ خَرَّاب .

Rave, *v.i.* To be delirious, to utter nonsense in delirium, أَفْنَدَ ـ جُنَّ ـ طَاشَ ـ هَذَرَ ـ أَهْتَرَ . *See also to* Rage, *v.i.*

Ravel, *v.t.* To entangle, عَقَّدَ ـ عَقَدَ ـ شَبَّكَ . To — out, نَسَلَ . To be ravelled, entangled, إِنْعَقَدَ ـ تَشَبَّكَ . *See also to* Entangle, *v.t.*

Ravelin, *n.* إِسْتِحْكَامٌ فِي شَكْلِ ٱلزَّاوِيَةِ .

Ravellings, *n.* سُقَاطَة .

Raven, *n.* غُرَاب ـ شَاحِب *pl.* غِرْبَان .

Raven, *n.* Plunder, pillage, نَهِيب ـ سَلِيب .

Raven, *v.t.* To eat voraciously, هَرَسَ ـ شَرِسَ ـ زَقَمَ . *See to* Devour, *v.t.*

Raven, *v.i.* To be voracious, هَرِسَ ـ كَانَ حَرِيصًا .

Ravening, *n.* Eagerness for plunder, سَلَابَة ـ سَلَبُوت.

Ravenous, *a.* مُفْتَرِس ـ جَارِح ـ أَكُول ـ حَرِيص ـ مُتَلَعِّس. A — bird, طَيْرٌ كَاسِرٌ *pl.* كَوَاسِرُ ـ كَاسِر. A — wild beast, وَحْشٌ مُفْتَرِس.

Ravenously, *n.* بِشَرَهٍ ـ بِقَرَمٍ ـ حِرْصًا ـ بِحِرْصٍ ـ إِلْهَافًا.

Ravenousness, *n.* إِلْهَاف ـ شَرَهٌ ـ حِرْص ـ قَرَم.

Ravine, *n.* خَانِق ـ جَوْف *pl.* أَجْوَاف ـ جَوْبَة *pl.* جُوَب and جَوْبَات.

Raving, *a.* مَجْنُون ـ مَسْعُور ـ طَائِش ـ مُفْنِد.

Ravish, *v.t.* To seize and carry away, خَطَفَ ² ـ سَلَبَ ². To transport with delight, فَتَنَ ² ـ إِسْتَهْوَى. (*See also to* Enrapture, *v.t.*) To force a woman to carnal embrace, غَصَبَهَا ² (or إِغْتَصَبَهَا) نَفْسَهَا. *See also under* Rape, *n.*

Ravished, *a.* Snatched away by force, مَخْطُوف ـ مَسْلُوب. Delighted to ecstacy, مَحْظُوظٌ لِلْغَايَةِ ـ مَسْرُورٌ لِلْغَايَةِ. Forced to carnal embrace, of a female, مُنْهَتِكَة ـ مَقْهُورَة.

Ravisher, *n.* One who enraptures, سَلَّابُ ٱلْقُلُوبِ. One who forces a woman, هَاتِكُ ٱمْرَأَةٍ.

Ravishing, *a.* *See* Delightful, *a.*

Ravishment, *n.* *See* Rapture, *n.*

Raw, *a.* Not altered from its natural state; also, unbleached, untanned, unrefined, خَامٌ. Uncooked or half cooked, مُعَلْهَص ـ نِيءٌ. Bare of skin and flesh, عَرِق ـ عُرَاق. Not ripe, غَيْرُ مُسْتَوٍ ـ فِجّ. Unadulterated, خَالِص ـ صَافٍ ـ صَرِيح ـ مَحْض. Inexperienced, غِرّ ـ غَرِير ـ غُمْر ـ أَخْرَقُ ـ خَرِق ـ زَبَّانٌ *pl.* زَبُون *pl.* أَغِرَّة ـ غَشِيم *pl.* غُشَمَآء. Excoriated, قَلِيلُ ٱلْخِبْرَةِ ـ غَيْرُ مُدَرَّب ـ مُنْسَلِق ـ مَسْحُوج ـ سَحِيج. Moist and cold, نَدِيٌّ وَبَارِدٌ. A raw place, a gall, سَلِيقَة ـ إِنْسِحَاج ـ عُقْرَة.

Raw-boned, *a.* قَضِيف ـ نَحِيف. A — person, شَخْت ـ شَخِيت ـ مَمْصُوص.

Raw-head, *n.* تَخْوِيفَة ـ غُول ـ اللَّعِينُ ـ خَيَال.

Rawish, *a.* Rather uncooked, نِيءٌ نَوْعًا.

Raw-hide, *n.* كِرْبَاج ـ سَوْط.

Rawly, *ad.* Unskilfully, بِلَا مَعْرِفَةٍ ـ بِلَا حِرْفَةٍ ـ بِخُرْقٍ; without experience, بِغَبَاوَةٍ ـ بِلَا خِبْرَةٍ.

Rawness, *n.* Unskilfulness, قِلَّةُ صَنْعَةٍ ـ قِلَّةُ مَعْرِفَةٍ ـ خُرْق. Inexperience, قِلَّةُ خِبْرَةٍ. The being raw, uncooked, نُيُوءٌ; the being unripe, فَجَاجَة; the being excoriated, إِنْسِلَاق ـ إِنْسِحَاج. Rawness, as of the atmosphere, نَدَاوَةٌ وَبُرُودَةٌ.

Ray, *n.* Of the sun, شُعَاعَة *coll.* شُعَاع *pl.* أَشِعَّة and شِعَاع and شُعُع.

A gleam, لَمْعَة ـ لَمْع ـ بُرْقَان ـ سَطْع ـ رَفَّة ـ رَفٌّ. Intellectual light, نُورُ ٱلْعِلْمِ وَٱلْفُرْقَانِ. A — of hope, ذَرَّةٌ مِنَ ٱلْأَمَلِ. Lustre, رَوْنَق ـ جَلَاءٌ. A —, as of a flower, شُعَاع ـ شَعٌّ. The cartilage of a fish's fin, غُرْضُوفُ جَنَاحِ ٱلسَّمَكِ. The fish so called, ضَرْبٌ مِنَ ٱلسَّمَكِ. To break through the clouds, as of the rays of the sun, فَتَقَ.

Ray, *v.t.* To streak, قَلَّمَ ـ خَطَّطَ.

Rayless, *a.* ظُلْمَانِيٌّ ـ بِلَا نُورٍ ـ بِلَا شُعَاعٍ.

Raze, *v.t.* *See to* Rase, Demolish, *v.t.*

Razee, *n.* Of a ship, مَرْكَبٌ مَجْزُومٌ ـ سَفِينَةٌ جَرِيمَةٌ.

Razee, *v.t.* Of a ship, جَرَمَ ٱلْمَرْكَبَ ².

Razor, *n.* مُوسَى or مُوسٰى *pl.* مَوَاسِي ـ مُوسُ ٱلْحِلَاقَةِ *pl.* أَمْوَاس. To shave with a —, مَاسَ ².

Razor-strop, *n.* جِلْدٌ لِشَبْرَقَةِ ٱلْأَمْوَاسِ. *See also under* Strap, *n.*

Rasure, *n.* *See* Erasure, *n.*

Razzia, *n.* *See* Incursion, *n.*

Reabsorb, *v.t.* To absorb again, تَشَرَّبَ أَيْضًا ـ عَادَ فَتَشَرَّبَهُ *aor.* يَعُودُ ـ عَادَ فَقَدِمَهُ ـ قَدِمَ أَيْضًا ².

Reabsorption, *n.* تَشَرُّبُ ٱلشَّيْءِ ثَانِيَةً.

Reaccess, *n.* دُخُول ثَانٍ ـ وُرُود.

Reach, *v.t.* To — out, extend, مَدَّ ². To extend to, بَلَغَ ² ـ بَلَغَ إِلَى ² ـ وَصَلَ إِلَى *aor.* يَصِلُ. To — after, to persevere in searching for or out, تَتَبَّعَ. To attain, to arrive at, بَلَغَ ² ـ أَدْرَكَ ـ أَصَابَ ـ وَفَدَ عَلَى *aor.* يَفِدُ ـ إِنْتَهَى إِلَى ـ أَقْبَلَ عَلَى ـ أَفْضَى إِلَى ـ وَرَدَ إِلَى *aor.* يَرِدُ ـ وَصَلَ إِلَى *aor.* يَصِلُ. To endeavour to —, obtain, صَمَدَ إِلَى ². To overtake, لَحِقَ ² ـ أَلْحَقَ ـ لَحِقَ بِ ². أَدْرَكَ. To —, as a letter, نَفَذَ إِلَى ² ـ تَأَدَّى إِلَى: the letter reached him, وَرَدَ عَلَيْهِ ٱلْكِتَابُ ـ تَأَدَّى إِلَيْهِ ٱلْخَطُّ. To hand to, نَاوَلَ. To touch, مَسَّ ². To hit, as from a distance, أَصَابَ. Reach hither thy hand, هَاتِ بِيَدِكَ. This road reaches to, هٰذَا ٱلطَّرِيقُ يَدْفَعُ (or يُفْضِي) إِلَى. The top of it reached to the sky, عُلُوُّهُ (or رَأْسُهُ) بَلَغَ إِلَى ٱلسَّمَآءِ. As far as the eye reaches, قَدْرَ مَدَى ٱلْبَصَرِ. The news reached him, أَنْهَى إِلَيْهِ ٱلْخَبَرُ. What has reached our knowledge, مَا ٱتَّصَلَ بِعِلْمِنَا.

Reach, *v.i.* To be extended, إِمْتَدَّ. To penetrate, كَانَ نَافِذًا. To cause to —, to transmit, أَنْفَذَ ـ أَدَّى. *See also to* Retch, *v.i.*

Reach, *n.* Extent, distance, مَسَافَة ـ إِمْتِدَاد. Power, capacity, طَاقَة ـ قُدْرَة ـ مَنْزِلَة ـ مُكْنَة. Effort, إِجْتِهَاد ـ جِدّ ـ سَعْي. Range, مَدًى. A stratagem, فَنٌّ *pl.* فُنُون ـ حِيلَة *pl.* حِيَل ـ دَوْلَاب. The — of a river, مَسِيلُ مَآءِ ٱلنَّهْرِ. Beyond reach, as of the eye, خارِجٌ عَنْ مَدَى ٱلْبَصَرِ ; unattainable, ٱلبُلُوغُ إِلَيْهِ لا يُدرَكُ ـ تَحْصِيلُهُ غَيْرُ مُمْكِنٍ ـ غَيْرُ مُمْكِنٍ. Beyond seizure, حَيْثُ لا يُقْبَضُ بِهِ (or عَلَيْهِ). To be beyond reach, unattainable, عالَ عَن aor. يَعِيلُ : The thing was beyond my —, عالَنِي ٱلشَّيْءُ. The thing was beyond —, عَزَّ (or تَعَزَّزَ) ٱلشَّيْءُ. He is beyond —, not to be coped with, ما يُطاقُ. Within —, at hand, قَرِيبٌ ـ حاضِرٌ ـ عَتِيدٌ. To be within one's —, power, أَطاقَ عَلَى ـ كانَ قادِرًا عَلَى. It is within my —, power, فِي قُدْرَةِ يَدِي. *See also* Retch, *n.*

React, *v.i.* To return an impulse or impression, رَدَّ ٱلتَّأْثِيرَ ـ رَجَعَ ٱلتَّأْثِيرَ. To act reciprocally in opposition, of many, تَصادَمُوا ـ تَضادُّوا ـ تَدافَعُوا.

React, *v.t.* فَعَلَ-أَيْضًا ـ أَعادَ ـ كَرَّرَ ـ ثَنَّى. To — upon, أَثَّرَ فِي-أَيْضًا.

Reaction, *n.* Action in opposition, مُضادَّةٌ ـ مُراجَعَةٌ ـ مُدافَعَةٌ. A return to, رَجْعَةٌ إِلَى. Reciprocation, مُقابَلَةٌ ـ رَدُّ عَمَلٍ. Political —, تَجْدِيدُ ٱلْأَحْوالِ ـ إِسْتِرْجاعُ ٱلْأَحْوالِ ٱلسّابِقَةِ. The party of —, حِزْبُ ٱلْأَحْوالِ ـ أَصْحابُ تَجْدِيدِ ٱلْأَحْوالِ ٱلسّابِقَةِ.

Reactionary, *a.* مُقابِلٌ ـ مُراجِعٌ ـ مُضادٌّ ـ مُدافِعٌ. Reactionary opinion, as in politics, مَيَلانٌ ـ أَفْكارُ ٱلْأَحْوالِ ٱلسّابِقَةِ إِلَى أَفْكارِ ٱلْأَحْوالِ ٱلسّابِقَةِ.

Reactive, *a.* مُقابِلٌ ـ مُراجِعٌ ـ مُدافِعٌ.

Reactively, *ad.* بِٱلْمُقابَلَةِ ـ بِٱلْمُراجَعَةِ ـ بِٱلْمُدافَعَةِ.

Reactiveness, *n.* *See* Reaction, *n.*

Read, *v.t.* As of a book, قَرَأَ ب ـ قَرَأَ. To — or recite, تَلا. To peruse, study, طالَعَ ـ دَرَسَ. To — with another, قارَأَ. To — with, take lessons from, قَرَأَ عَلَى. To give one something to —, أَقْرَأَ. To — over to, تَلا-عَلَى. To — backwards, نَكَسَ. To read a book through carefully, عَبَرَ ٱلْكِتابَ. To —, as of one's thoughts, عَرَفَ ـ إِطَّلَعَ عَلَى ـ كَشَفَ. How — you? What do you understand from the passage? كَيْفَ تَقْرَأُ ٱلْعِبارَةَ ـ كَيْفَ تُفَسِّرُ ٱلْعِبارَةَ. He has only to — the letter written by the Amir to the Shâh of Persia, ما عَلَيْهِ إِلَّا أَنْ يَقْرَأَ ٱلرَّقِيمَ ٱلَّذِى كَتَبَهُ ٱلْأَمِيرُ إِلَى شاهِ ٱلْعَجَمِ.

Read, *v.i.* To perform the act of reading, قَرَأَ. To study, دَرَسَ. To appear in reading, as a passage, كانَ مَكْتُوبًا : So the passage reads, هٰكَذا هُوَ مَكْتُوبٌ ـ هٰكَذا فِي ٱلْعِبارَةِ.

Read, *a.* Versed in books, مُدارِسٌ ـ مُدَرِّسُ ٱلْكُتُبِ.

Readable, *a.* That may be read, يُقْرَأُ ـ مِمّا يُقْرَأُ. Pleasant to read, لَطِيفُ ٱلْقِراءَةِ ـ قِراءَتُهُ تُسَلِّي.

Reader, *n.* قارِئٌ *pl.* قارِئُونَ *and* قُرّاءٌ *and* قَرَأَةٌ. One who reads much, قَرّاءٌ *pl.* قَرّاؤُونَ ـ مُدارِسٌ. A —, or lecturer, مُدَرِّسٌ ـ مُعَلِّمٌ. An assiduous — of the Kurân, مُتَقَرِّئٌ. A —, as one who reads in a mosque, إِمامٌ *pl.* أَئِمَّةٌ. A corrector of the press, مُحَرِّرٌ (or مُصَلِّحُ) أَوْراقِ ٱلْمَطْبَعَةِ.

Readership, *n.* The office of a reader, as in a university, وَظِيفَةُ ٱلْمُدَرِّسِ ; of a reader in a mosque, إِمامَةٌ.

Readily, *ad.* Quickly, فِي ٱلْحالِ ـ بِمُبادَرَةٍ ـ بِٱلْعَجَلِ ـ وَشاكَةً ـ حالًا. Willingly, بِسْمِ ٱللّٰهِ ـ عَلَى ٱلرَّأْسِ وَٱلْعَيْنِ ـ تَكَرُّمًا.

Readiness, *n.* The state of being ready, عَتادَةٌ ـ عَتِيدٌ ـ إِسْتِعْدادٌ. Promptitude, سَراحٌ ـ خِفَّةٌ ـ سُرْعَةٌ ـ نَشاطٌ. Willingness, سُرُورٌ ـ نَشاطٌ ـ نَشاطُ ٱلْإِرادَةِ. Facility, سُهُولَةٌ. Readiness of speech, فَيَضانُ ٱلْكَلامِ ـ طَقْطَقَةٌ. *See also* Promptitude, *n.*

Reading, *n.* The act of, قَرْأٌ ـ قُرْآنٌ ـ قِراءَةٌ ـ تِلاوَةٌ. Study, مُطالَعَةٌ ـ دَرْسٌ. Manner of interpretation, تَفْسِيرٌ. Variation of copies, رِوايَةٌ أُخْرَى ـ فَرْقُ نُسَخٍ. A gloss, مَعْنًى ـ بَيانٌ ـ تَعْبِيرٌ ـ شَرْحٌ. *See also* Lecture, *n.*

Reading-room, *n.* بَيْتٌ لِلْقِراءَةِ.

Readjust, *v.t.* صَلَّحَ ـ أَعادَ نَظْمَهُ ـ نَظَّمَ-أَيْضًا.

Readjustment, *n.* تَصْلِيحٌ ـ تَنْظِيمٌ ثانِيَةً.

Readmission, *n.* إِدْخالٌ ثانٍ ـ إِدْخالٌ ثانِيَةً.

Readmit, *v.t.* أَدْخَلَ-ثانِيَ مَرَّةٍ ـ عادَ فَأَدْخَلَهُ ـ أَدْخَلَ-أَيْضًا.

Ready, *a.* Prompt, نَدِبٌ *pl.* نُدُوبٌ ـ نَشِطٌ ـ وَشِيكٌ ـ وَجِزٌ ـ مُسْتَعِدٌّ ـ مُتَوَكِّدٌ. Prompt to reply, ذُو بَدِيهَةٍ ـ مِبْدَهٌ. Quick, سَرِيعٌ. Ready, prepared, حاضِرٌ ـ مُسْتَعِدٌّ. Ready at hand, عَتِيدٌ ـ حاضِرٌ. Acute of understanding, ذَكِيٌّ ـ ذُو ٱلْبَيانِ. Disposed, willing, مُنْعَطِفٌ إِلَى ـ بِٱخْتِيارِ ٱلْخاطِرِ ـ مُبادِرٌ. Short, easy, هَيِّنٌ ـ وَجِيزٌ. Having presence of mind, تَلِبٌ ـ شَدِيدُ ٱلْعارِضَةِ. A — writer, كاتِبٌ ماهِرٌ. A — answer, جَوابٌ حاضِرٌ. Ready at answering, سَرِيعُ ٱلْجَوابِ ـ نَقِلٌ. Ready in judging of circumstances, حاضِرُ ٱلْحُكْمِ فِي ٱلْأَحْوالِ. Ready money, نَضٌّ ـ دَراهِمُ نَقْدٌ ـ عَيْنٌ. The readiest way, ٱلطَّرِيقُ ٱلْأَوْجَزُ. Very —, to do good or evil, مِسْراعٌ. Ready or prepared for, عَتِيدٌ لِ. He obtained the amount from him in — money, إِسْتَخْلَصَ ٱلْمَبْلَغَ مِنْهُ نَضًّا (or نَقْدًا).

Ready armed, مُسَلَّحٌ.

Ready at hand, as of time, مُهَيَّأٌ.

Ready to battle, مُسْتَعِدٌّ لِلْوَغَى (or لِلْقِتالِ).

Ready, about, to die, مُشْرِفٌ عَلَى ٱلْمَوْتِ ـ مُسَلِّمُ ٱلرُّوحِ.

Ready to fall, as of a wall, مُنْقَضٌّ.

Ready to forgive, غَفُور.

Ready to perish, تَالِهٌ.

Ready to vanish away, قَرِيبٌ مِنَ ٱلِاضْمِحْلَالِ.

To be ready, prompt, brisk, تَوَجَّزَ ـ يَجِزُ .aor وَجِزَ ـ أَوْشَكَ. To be ready, prepared, of things, عَتُدَ ². He was ready to, was on the point of, he wished to..., أَرَادَ ـ تَهَيَّأَ لِ ـ ² هَمَّ بِ. He or it was ready, prepared, حَضَرَ ². To make ready, عَبَّأَ ـ أَحْضَرَ ـ أَعَدَّ ـ ² عَبَأَ. He is ready with his answer, هُوَ حَاضِرٌ بِٱلْجَوَابِ. He was ready a year ago, كَانَ مُسْتَعِدًّا مُنْذُ ٱلْعَامِ ٱلْمَاضِي. I am ready to go with you, أَنَا مُسْتَعِدٌّ أَنْ أَمْضِيَ مَعَكَ. *See also* Prompt, *a.*; *also to* Prepare, *v.t.*

Ready-made, *a.* حَاضِر. A warehouse for — clothes, دُكَّانُ ٱلثِّيَابِ ٱلْمُخَيَّطَةِ.

Re-affirm, *v.t.* أَعَادَ ٱلْ... ـ كَرَّرَ ٱلْ....

Re-affirmance, *n.* إِعَادَةُ ٱلْ... ـ تَكْرِيرُ ٱلْ....

Re-agent, *n.* مِعْيَار.

Real, *a.* Having a positive existence, أَصْل ـ أَصِيل ـ جِسْمِيٌّ. Genuine, حَقَّانِيٌّ ـ حَقِيقِيٌّ ـ صَحِيحٌ .pl صِحَاحٌ ـ صَرِيحٌ. Pure, صَافٍ ـ خَالِصٌ ـ مَحْض. Living, حَيٌّ. The — thing, the thing itself, عَيْنُ ٱلشَّيْءِ. Standing as a fact, holding good, ثَابِت ـ ثَبِيت. The — state of the case, حَقِيقَةُ ٱلْحَالِ. He advised him to look into the — state of the case, ² نَصَحَهُ أَنْ يَطَّلِعَ عَلَى حَقِيقَةِ ٱلْحَالِ. Real estate, أَمْلَاكٌ وَعَقَارٌ. Real, material, جِسْمِيٌّ: real benefits, مَصَالِحُ جِسْمِيَّةٌ. Real presence in the holy Eucharist, حُلُولُ ٱلْحَضْرَةِ ٱلْإِلٰهِيَّةِ فِي ٱلْقُرْبَانِ.

Real, *n.* *See* Rial, *n.*

Realgar, *n.* طَعْمُ ٱلْفَارِ مُكَلَّس ـ رَهَجٌ أَحْمَرُ ـ زِرْنِيخٌ أَحْمَرُ.

Realism, *n.* The doctrine of, مَذْهَبُ طَائِفَةٍ مِنَ ٱلْفَلَاسِفَةِ يَقُولُونَ بِحَقِيقَةِ ٱلتَّجْرِيدِ.

Realist, *n.* فَيْلَسُوفٌ مِنْ أَهْلِ ٱلْمَذْهَبِ ٱلْمَذْكُورِ.

Realistic, *a.* مَا نِيطَ بِٱلْمَذْهَبِ ٱلْمَذْكُورِ.

Reality, *n.* Actual existence, شَيْءٌ وَاقِعٌ بِهِ. Subsistency, substantiality, ثُبُوت ـ ثَبَات. The being intrinsic, genuine, صِحَّة ـ حَقِيقَة. A real thing, أَمْرٌ حَقِيقِيٌّ. Essence, جَوْهَر ـ ذَات. In —, in fact, حَقِيقَةً ـ فِي ٱلْحَقِيقَةِ; but in —, in fact, the matter is so, إِلَّا أَنَّ ٱلْوَاقِعَ كَذَا. The —, or fact, is the very opposite of that, ٱلْوَاقِعُ عَكْسُ ذٰلِكَ.

Realizable, *a.* That may be brought home to one's self, مِمَّا يَتَحَقَّقُ; that may be experienced, مِمَّا يُذَاقُ; that may be accomplished, مِمَّا يُقْضَى ـ مِمَّا يُنْفَذُ; that may be gained, acquired, مِمَّا يُقْتَنَى ـ مِمَّا يُكْسَبُ ـ مِمَّا يُحَصَّلُ; that may be turned into money, صَرْفُهُ بِٱلنَّقْدِ مُمْكِنٌ.

Realization, *n.* The act of bringing home to the mind, تَحْقِيق; of perception, إِحْسَاس ـ حِسّ ـ فِطْن; of holding good, being sound, valid, ثُبُوت ـ ثَبَات; of attaining, إِبْلَاغ ـ بُلُوغ; of acquiring, إِكْتِسَاب ـ تَحْصِيل; of turning into money, صَرْف (or تَبْدِيل) بِٱلنَّقْدِ.

Realize, *v.t.* To bring home to one's own case, to experience, ² ذَاقَ ـ حَقَّقَ ـ اِطَّلَعَ عَلَى ـ بِٱلتَّجْرِبَةِ ـ ² فَطِنَ بِ ـ تَعَقَّلَ ـ جَرَّبَ ـ أَحَسَّ. To bring into act, to accomplish, أَجْرَى ـ أَنْجَزَ ـ أَجْرَى ـ فِعْلًا. To render tangible or real, حَقَّقَ ـ ثَبَّتَ ـ صَحَّحَ. To treat as real, أَصَحَّ. To acquire, حَصَّلَ ـ ³ قَنَى. To convert into money, بَدَّلَ ـ بِٱلنَّقْدِ ـ ³ صَرَفَ ـ بِٱلنَّقْدِ. To receive, ³ قَبَضَ. The bank undertakes to — all drafts, ٱلْبَنْكُ يَقْبِضُ سَائِرَ ٱلْحِوَالَاتِ.

Really, *ad.* In truth, فِي ٱلْحَقِيقَةِ ـ حَقِيقَةً ـ جَيْرِ. Actually, فِي ٱلْوَاقِعِ. Doubtless, لَا شَكَّ ـ لَا جَرَمَ.

Realm, *n.* مَمْلَكَة .pl مَمَالِكُ ـ دَوْلَة .pl دُوَل.

Ream, *n.* As of paper, رِزْمَةُ وَرَقٍ .pl رِزَم ـ مَاعُونُ وَرَقٍ .pl مَوَاعِين.

Reanimate, *v.t.* To restore to life, ³ بَعَثَ ـ أَحْيَى. To revive the spirits of, قَوَّى قَلْبَهُ ـ ³ بَعَثَ. To rouse, حَرَّضَ ـ أَنْهَضَ ـ نَشَّطَ ـ رَوَّجَ.

Reanimation, *n.* The act of restoring to life, إِحْيَاء ـ بَعْث; of reviving the spirits, تَقْوِيَةُ ٱلْقَلْبِ ـ بَعْث; of rousing, animating, تَنْشِيط ـ تَرْوِيج ـ تَحْرِيض ـ إِنْهَاض.

Re-annex, *v.t.* To reunite, ² عَادَ فَأَلْحَقَ ـ بِ ـ أَضَافَ ـ إِلَى ـ ثَانِيَةً. To seize upon again, as territory, ² عَادَ فَحَازَهُ ـ ² حَازَ ـ ثَانِيَةً.

Re-annexation, *n.* The act of reuniting, إِضَافَةٌ ثَانِيَةٌ ـ تَضْمِيم. Seizure again, of territory, حَوْزٌ ثَانٍ.

Reap, *v.t.* To cut with a sickle, ³ حَصَدَ. To — or enjoy the fruits of, تَمَتَّعَ بِ. To gather, of fruits, ³ جَنَى ـ اِجْتَنَى. To obtain, حَصَّلَ ـ ³ قَنَى ـ اِقْتَنَى. Reaped, what is reaped, حَصِيد. Reaped grain, حَبُّ ٱلْحَصِيدِ.

Reaper, *n.* حَاصِد .pl حُصَّاد ـ حَصَّاد.

Reaping, *n.* The act of cutting with a sickle, حِصَاد ـ حَصِيدَة.

Reaping-hook, *n.* مَحَشّ ـ مِشْوَل ـ مِفْصَل ـ مِخْلَب ـ مِنْجَل ـ مِحْصَد.

Re-apparel, *v.t.* عَادَ فَلَبِسَهُ ـ أَلْبَسَ-ثَانِيَةً.

Re-appear, *v.i.* تَبَيَّنَ ثَانِيَةً ـ ظَهَرَ ثَانِيَةً.

Re-appearance, *n.* بَيَانٌ ثَانٍ ـ ظُهُورٌ ثَانٍ.

Re-apply, *v.t.* To place upon a second time, وَضَعَ-عَلَى-ثَانِيَةً ـ جَعَلَ-ثَانِيَةً ـ صَمَدَ-ثَانِيَةً. To have recourse to a second time, عَادَ فَالْتَجَأَ إِلَى ـ قَصَدَ-ثَانِيَةً.

Re-appoint, *v.t.* عَادَ فَأَقَامَهُ ـ قَلَّدَ-ثَانِيَةً ـ عَيَّنَ-ثَانِيَةً. To leave one, as in his office, أَبْقَى.

Re-appointment, *n.* إِعَادَةُ إِقَامَةٍ ـ تَقْلِيدٌ ثَانٍ ـ تَعْيِينٌ ثَانٍ. The act of leaving one in his office, إِبْقَاءٌ.

Re-apportion, *v.t.* عَادَ فَقَسَمَهُ ـ قَطَعَ-عَلَى-ثَانِيَةً ـ قَسَّمَ-ثَانِيَةً.

Re-apportionment, *n.* إِعَادَةُ تَفْرِيقٍ ـ تَخْصِيصٌ ثَانٍ ـ تَقْسِيمٌ ثَانٍ.

Rear, *n.* The part behind, مُؤَخَّر ـ وَرَاءٌ. A — or rearing, as of a horse, تَقَنْطُر ـ شُبُوب ـ شَبِيب ـ شِبَاب. In the — of me, خَلْفِي ـ وَرَائِي; of him, خَلْفَهُ. The — of an army, مُؤَخَّرُ الْجَيْشِ. To bring up the — of an army, تَسَاوَقَتِ الْعَسْكَرُ ـ كَانُوا فِي سَوْقَةِ الْجَيْشِ. To go to the —, to satisfy a want of nature, بَرَزَ.

Rear, *a.* مُؤَخَّر.

Rear, *v.t.* To raise, set up, صَمَدَ ـ نَصَبَ ـ أَقَامَ. To —, as after a fall, رَفَعَ ـ قَيَّمَ ـ شَالَ بِ ـ أَشَالَ. To foster, رَبَّى ـ حَضَنَ. To grow, cultivate, sow, رَبَّى ـ زَرَعَ. To establish, أَنْشَأَ ـ أَوْجَدَ. To erect, build, بَنَّى ـ بَنَى ـ عَمَّرَ.

Rear, *v.i.* As of a horse, تَقَنْطَرَ ـ شَبَّ.

Rear-admiral, *n.* أَمِيرُ الْبَحْرِ مِنَ الدَّرَجَةِ الثَّانِيَةِ; *from the Turkish,* ريالة باشا.

Rear-guard, *n.* أَوَاخِرُ الْجَيْشِ ـ مُؤَخَّرُ الْعَسْكَرِ ـ سَاقَةٌ.

Rear-mouse, *n.* The common bat, خُفَّاش ـ وَطْوَاط *pl.* وَطَاوِط *pl.* خَفَافِيش.

Rear-rank, *n.* الصَّفُّ الثَّانِي ـ الصَّفُّ الْمُؤَخَّرُ.

Rearward, *n.* *See* Rearguard, *n.*

Re-ascend, *v.i.* عَادَ فَصَعِدَ ـ صَعِدَ ثَانِيَةً.

Re-ascension, *n.* إِعَادَةُ صُعُودٍ ـ صُعُودٌ ثَانٍ.

Re-ascent, *n.* *See* Acclivity, *n.*

Reason, *n.* The reasoning faculty, الْعِلْمُ ـ اللُّبُّ ـ الْحِجْرُ ـ الْعَقْلُ. The right employment of —, good sense, integrity, wisdom, عَدَالَة ـ رُشْد ـ إِنْصَاف ـ صَوَاب ـ تَعَقُّل ـ عَقْل. That which is right, proper, just, حَقّ ـ صَوَاب. A cause, motive, عِلَّة ـ بَوَاعِث *pl.* بَاعِث ـ دَوَاعِي *pl.* دَاعٍ ـ أَسْبَاب *pl.* سَبَب *pl.* عِلَل. A fundamental cause, سَبَبٌ أَصْلِيٌّ. Wisdom of arrangement or order, حِكْمَة. Argument, proof, شَاهِد *pl.* شَوَاهِد ـ دَلِيل *pl.* أَدِلَّة ـ بُرْهَان *pl.* بَرَاهِين ـ حُجَّة *pl.* حُجَج. Agreeable to —, طِبْقَ الْعَقْلِ ـ مُوَافِقُ الْعَقْلِ وَالْإِنْصَافِ. In —, truly, بِالْحَقِّ ـ الْحَقَّ ـ حَقًّا. Bring forth your reasons, أَخْبِرُوا حُجَجَكُمْ. I have given ear to your reasons, أَصْغَيْتُ إِلَى حُجَجِكُمْ. Bring what reasons you please, إِحْتَجَّ بِمَا شِئْتَ. By — of, on account of, بِسَبَبِ ـ مِنْ أَجْلِ; by — of sorrow, مِنَ الْحُزْنِ ـ مِنْ. For what —? لِمَاذَا ـ لِأَيِّ سَبَبٍ. For that —, مِنْ ثَمَّ ـ لِذَلِكَ ـ أَجْلِ ذَلِكَ. One has — to say that ..., صَدَقَ ـ قَدْ صَدَقَ الَّذِي قَالَ ـ الْمَثَلُ أَنْ. With greater —, how much more, كَمْ بِالْأَكْثَرِ ـ مِنْ بَابِ أَوْلَى ـ كَمْ بِالْحَرِي. Reason would that I ..., لَكُنْتُ بِالْحَقِّ أَنْ. To lose one's —, to go mad, جُنَّ; to be in a state of perplexity, to lose one's self, طَاشَ ـ غَابَ عَنِ الرُّشْدِ ـ ضَيَّعَ الْمَعْقُولَ ـ ضَيَّعَ عَقْلَهُ. To regain one's reason, صَحَا ـ فَاقَ عَلَى عَقْلِهِ ـ رَجَعَ إِلَى عَقْلِهِ.

Reason, *v.i.* To use the faculty of reason, to be intelligent, تَعَقَّلَ ـ عَقَلَ. To make use of the reason, intellect, تَعَقَّلَ ـ صَرَفَ ذِهْنَهُ. To infer, draw conclusion, إِسْتَدَلَّ ـ إِسْتَنْتَجَ. To — with one's self, تَفَكَّرَ ـ تَدَبَّرَ. To — with another, to argue with, حَاجَّ. To — with, to hold a colloquy with, حَاوَرَ ـ جَاوَبَ. To —, to adduce reasons, arguments, إِحْتَجَّ بِحُجَجٍ. To — or dispute with one about, نَاظَرَ-فِي. To — or talk about, تَكَلَّمَ عَنْ. He reasoned against his adversary with a strong plea, إِحْتَجَّ عَلَى خَصْمِهِ بِحُجَّةٍ شَهْبَاءَ. He used to —, adduce reasons, with them, كَانَ يُحَاجِجُهُمْ. Let us — together, هَلُمَّا نَتَحَاجَجُ. The people began to — among themselves about ..., إِبْتَدَأَ الْقَوْمُ يُفَكِّرُونَ فِي. Whilst they (two) reasoned, discussed together, فِيمَا هُمَا يَتَحَاوَرَانِ.

Reason, *v.t.* To — one into a thing, to convince, حَجَّ ـ أَقْنَعَ ـ قَطَعَ عَقْلَهُ. To — one out of a thing, أَلْزَمَ-بِتَرْكِ ـ حَجَّ-عَنِ-الْأَمْرِ.

Reasonable, *a.* Endowed with reason, ذُو عَقْلٍ ـ عَاقِل ـ نَاطِق. Pertaining to the reason, عَقْلِيٌّ. What is agreeable to reason, مِنَ الْعَقْلِ ـ حَقٌّ ـ مُوَافِقُ الْعَقْلِ ـ مَعْقُول. Intelligent, making use of his reason, مُتَعَقِّل ـ مُتَبَصِّر. Right, proper, أَهْلُ إِنْصَافٍ ـ صَائِب ـ سَدِيد. Just, equitable, of a person, مُنْصِف. Moderate, مُتَوَسِّط ـ مُعْتَدِل ـ مُنْصِف. More —, more in accordance with what is wise, أَوْفَرُ حِكْمَةً. A — price, ثَمَنٌ مُنَاسِبٌ ـ ثَمَنٌ مُعْتَدِلٌ. It is — that ..., حَقٌّ أَنْ ـ مِنَ الْمَعْقُولِ أَنْ. It is not — that ..., لَيْسَ بِعَدْلٍ أَنْ.

لَيْسَ بِحَقٍّ أَنْ . To be — with, to treat fairly, لا حَقَّ أَن — أَنْصَفَ .

Reasonableness, *n.* Agreeableness to reason, مَعْقُول — سَداد — حَقٌّ — صَواب . Fitness, propriety, مُناسَبَة — لِياقَة . Moderation, إِنْصاف — إِعْتِدال .

Reasonably, *ad.* In accordance with reason, بِٱلْمَعْقُولِ — بِعَقْلٍ — حَقًّا — بِلِياقَةٍ — مُناسَبَةً . بِٱلْحَقِّ وَٱلْإِنْصافِ . Fitly, properly, Moderately, بِقانُونٍ — بِٱعْتِدالٍ — بِإِنْصافٍ . To act —, justly, أَنْصَفَ — أَقْسَطَ ; rationally, تَعَقَّلَ ; with moderation, عَدَلَ .

Reasoner, *n.* مُبَرْهِن مُحاجٌّ . A litigator, مُحَاجّ .

Reasoning, *n.* The exercise of the faculty of reason, تَعَقُّل . An argument, حُجَّة . Thought, reflection, فِكْر . Disquisition, مُباحَثَة .

Re-assemble, *v.t.* جَمَعَ ثانِيَةً — عادَ فَلَمَّ — حَشَدَ ثانِيَةً .

Re-assemble, *v.i.* إِجْتَمَعَ ثانِيَةً — اِلْتَمَّ ثانِيَةً — إِحْتَشَدَ (or تَحَشَّدَ) أَيْضًا .

Re-assert, *v.t.* To affirm again, كَرَّرَ — عادَ فَأَكَّدَ . To claim again, عادَ فَٱدَّعَى ب .

Re-assertion, *n.* Re-affirmation, تَكْرار — إِعادَةُ تَأْكِيدٍ ; as of rights, إِعادَةُ إِدِّعاء .

Re-assign, *v.t.* To appoint again, جَعَلَ ثانِيَةً — عَيَّنَ ثانِيَةً ; as a lease, حَوَّلَ .

Re-assignment, *n.* As of a lease, حَوالَة — تَحْوِيل .

Re-assume, *v.t.* To take again, ضَبَطَ ثانِيَةً — عادَ فَٱتَّخَذَهُ ; as a debt, responsibility, تَكَفَّلَ ب ثانِيَةً . *See also to* Resume, *v.t.*

Re-assumption, *n.* The act of taking again, إِعادَةُ — ضَبْطٌ ثانٍ أَخْذٍ (or ٱتِّخاذٍ) .

Re-assurance, *n.* Repeated assurance, تَكْرار — تَأْكِيد . The act of giving confidence, إِسْتِقْرار — إِقْرار — تَأْمِين . A second insurance against loss, as in an insurance company, تَكْرارُ ٱلتَّأْمِينِ (or ٱلسِّكُورْتا) .

Re-assure, *v.t.* To assure again, أَمَّنَ ثانِيَةً . To restore courage to, أَمَّنَ — عادَ فَٱسْتَقَرَّهُ — أَقَرَّ ثانِيَةً . To insure again, in an insurance office, ضَمَّنَ ثانِيَةً فِي سِكُورْتا . He was re-assured, quieted, thereby, قَرَّ بِهِ عَيْنًا . The intelligence from India is not re-assuring, الأَخْبارُ ٱلْوارِدَةُ مِنَ ٱلْهِنْدِ غَيْرُ سارَّةٍ .

Re-attachment, *n.* Of affection, مَحَبَّةٌ ثانِيَةٌ — تَعَلُّقٌ ثانٍ — وُدٌّ جَدِيدٌ .

Rebaptism, *n.* مَعْمُودِيَّةٌ ثانِيَةٌ — عِمادٌ ثانٍ .

Rebaptize, *v.t.* عَمَّدَ ثانِيَةً . To be rebaptized, إِعْتَمَدَ ثانِيَةً .

Rebate, *v.t.* To blunt, ثَلَمَ — ثَلَّمَ — أَعْدَمَ ٱلْحَدَّ . To abate from, بَخَسَ — أَنْقَصَ — نَقَّصَ — أَبانَ . To lower, as of a price, حَطَّ مِن — أَسْقَطَ .

Rebate, *n.* / Rebatement, *n.* The act of abatement, تَقْلِيل — تَنْقِيص . What is taken away from, سَماح — ٱلْمَحْسُومُ مِن — هِبَة ; of price, هَبْط . Discount, إِسْقاط .

Rebate, *n.* *See* Rabbet, *n.*

Rebel, *a.* *See* Rebellious, *a.*

Rebel, *n.* مارِد *pl.* مَرَدَة — باغٍ *pl.* بُغاة *and* بُغْيان *and* بُغّاء — عاصٍ *pl.* عُصاة — خارِجٌ عَن *pl.* خَوارِجُ عَن — مُفْتِن .

Rebel, *v.i.* To —, تَمَرَّدَ — شَقَّ ٱلْعَصا — خَرَجَ عَن — عَصَى against, عَصَى — عَصَى عَلَى — لَوَى عَن — تَمَرَّدَ عَلَى — خَرَجَ عَلَى . خَرَجَ عَنْ أَمْرِهِ . To excite, to rebel, أَفْتَنَ — إِفْتَتَنَ .

Rebellion, *n.* خُرُوجٌ عَلَى فُلانٍ — خُرُوجٌ عَنْ أَمْرِ فُلانٍ — طُغْيان — عِصْيان — عَصًى — مَعْصاة — فِتْنَة — تَمَرُّد . When the — broke out, لَمَّا أَثارَتِ ٱلْفِتْنَةُ . To put down a —, أَطْفَأَ ٱلْفِتْنَةَ . *See also* Disobedience, *n.*

Rebellious, *a.* مارِد — مَفْتُون — مُفْتِن — باغٍ *pl.* بُغاة — عاصٍ *pl.* عُصاة — مَرِيد *pl.* مُرَداء — عاصٍ *pl.* عُصاة . A stubborn and — son, إِبْنٌ مُعانِدٌ وَمارِدٌ — إِبْنٌ عَقُوق .

Rebelliously, *ad.* بِعِصْيانٍ — تَمَرُّدًا — بِعَدَمِ إِطاعَةٍ .

Rebelliousness, *n.* عِصْيان — عِناد — تَمَرُّد .

Rebound, *v.i.* To fly or spring back, تَقَهْقَرَ — تَحَرَّفَ — إِنْحَرَفَ — رَجَعَ — نَطَّ إِلَى وَراءٍ . *See also to* Resound, *v.i.*

Rebound, *n.* قَهْقَرَة — رُجُوع — نَطٌّ إِلَى وَراءٍ — تَقَهْقُر — إِنْحِراف .

Rebuff, *n.* A beating back, رَدٌّ — دَفْع . A defeat, frustration, تَخْيِيب — عَناق — عَناقَة . A refusal, عَدَمُ رِضاءٍ — عَدَمُ قُبُولٍ . A bad reception, مُلاقاةٌ سَيِّئَةٌ .

Rebuff, *v.t.* To drive back, رَدَّ — دَفَعَ . To refuse, to send away disappointed, خَيَّبَ — رَدَّ خائِبًا .

Rebuild, *v.t.* عَمَّرَ ثانِيَةً — عَمَّرَ — جَدَّدَ ٱلْبِناءَ . Its rebuilding shall not be permissible, لا تَسُوغُ إِعادَةُ بِنائِهِ . To be rebuilt, put in order, إِسْتَتَبَّ .

Rebukable, *a.* Deserving rebuke, مُسْتَحِقُّ ٱلتَّوْبِيخِ .

Rebuke, *v.t.* To repress, إِنْتَهَرَ . To reprehend, chide, زَجَرَ — عاتَبَ — وَبَّخَ . To — sharply, زَجَرَ بِصَرامَةٍ . To stand rebuked, إِنْزَجَرَ .

Rebuke, *n.* The act of repressing, إِنْتِهار . Reproof, زَجْر — تَوْبِيخ — عِتاب . Open —, تَوْبِيخٌ ظاهِرٌ . I have suffered —, إِحْتَمَلْتُ ٱلْعارَ .

Rebukeful, *a.* مُوَبِّخ — زاجِر .

Rebuker, *n.* مُوَبِّخ ـ زَجَّار ـ زَاجِر.

Rebukingly, *ad.* بِتَوْبِيخٍ ـ بِزَجْرٍ.

Re-burial, *n.* إِعَادَةُ دَفْنِهِ ـ دَفْنٌ ثَانٍ.

Re-bury, *v.t.* ² عَادَ فَدَفَنَهُ ـ ² دَفَنَ ثَانِيَةً.

Rebus, *n.* ضَرْبٌ مِنَ ٱلْمُعَمَّى ـ مُعَمًّى.

Rebut, *v.t.* ـ دَفَعَ ـ ² رَدَّ : I rebutted the saying, دَفَعْتُ ٱلْقَوْلَ ـ رَدَدْتُ ٱلْكَلَامَ. I rebutted him, saying in reply to him, رَدَدْتُ عَلَيْهِ قَوْلَهُ. There is no good in a saying rebutted and reiterated, لَا خَيْرَ فِي قَوْلٍ مَرْدُودٍ وَمُرَدَّدٍ.

Recalcitration, *n.* A kicking behind, رَفْسَةٌ إِلَى خَلْفٍ. Resistance, rebellion, عَدَمُ ٱنْقِيَادٍ ـ تَمَرُّد.

Recall, *v.t.* To summon again, ² عَادَ فَنَادَاهُ ـ إِسْتَدْعَى ثَانِيَةً. To revoke, ² نَقَضَ ـ فَسَخَ ـ ² أَبْطَلَ ـ ² رَجَعَ فِي. To call back, as from an appointment, ² أَمَرَ بِٱلرُّجُوعِ. To make to come back, ² رَدَّ ـ رَجَّعَ ـ أَعَادَ. To — one's word, ² رَجَعَ عَنْ كَلَامِهِ. To — to the mind of any one, فَكَّرَ ـ نَبَّهَ ـ ذَكَّرَ. To — to one's own mind, ² فَاقَ عَلَى ـ إِدَّكَرَ ـ إِذَّكَرَ ـ تَنَبَّهَ عَلَى. To — to life, ² بَعَثَ ـ أَحْيَى. He recalled the gift, إِسْتَرَدَّ ٱلْهِبَةَ. I — this to mind, أَرُدُّ هٰذَا فِي قَلْبِي.

Recall, *n.* A calling back, رَدٌّ ـ تَرْجِيعٌ ـ إِعَادَةٌ ـ إِسْتِرْدَاد. An order to return, أَمْرٌ بِٱلرُّجُوعِ. Revocation, فَسْخٌ ـ رُجُوعٌ فِي ـ إِبْطَال ـ نَقْض. A going back, as from one's word, promise, رُجُوعٌ عَنْ.

Recant, *v.t.* To retract, ² رَجَعَ فِي ـ أَنْكَرَ ـ ² نَكَرَ ـ إِسْتَرَدَّ. To apostatize from, إِرْتَدَّ عَنْ ـ أَضْرَبَ عَنْ.

Recantation, *n.* Retraction, رُجُوعٌ فِي ـ إِسْتِرْدَاد ـ إِنْكَار. Apostacy, إِرْتِدَاد ـ إِضْرَابٌ عَنْ.

Recapacitate, *v.t.* ² عَادَ فَقَدَّرَ عَلَى ـ مَكَّنَ ثَانِيَةً.

Recapitulate, *v.t.* To repeat in a summary manner, أَجْمَلَ ـ ² ذَكَرَ إِجْمَالًا مَا قَدْ شُرِحَ مُفَصَّلًا. To reiterate, repeat, كَرَّرَ ـ أَعَادَ. To recapitulate, (adverbially,) حَاصِلُ ٱلْكَلَامِ ـ ٱلْحَاصِلُ.

Recapitulation, *n.* The act of giving a summary, إِجْمَال ـ تَكْرَارُ ٱلْكَلَامِ عَلَى سَبِيلِ ٱلْإِجْمَالِ. A summary, مُخْتَصَر ـ مُوجَز ـ مُجْمَل.

Recapitulatory, *a.* إِجْمَالِيٌّ ـ مُجْمِل.

Recaption, *n.* As of booty, إِسْتِرْدَادُ غَنِيمَةٍ ـ إِعَادَةُ مَغْنَمٍ.

Recaptor, *n.* مُسْتَرِدُّ غَنِيمَةٍ.

Recapture, *n.* غَنِيمَةٌ مُسْتَرَدَّةٌ.

Recapture, *v.t.* إِسْتَرَدَّ ٱلْغَنِيمَةَ ـ إِسْتَرَدَّ.

Recast, *v.t.* To cast or mould again, ² عَادَ ـ ² سَبَكَ ثَانِيَةً ـ فَسَبَكَهُ. To remodel, غَيَّرَ ـ غَيَّرَ صُورَتَهُ ـ ² صَاغَ ثَانِيَةً. To add up again, عَادَ فَجَمَعَهُ ـ أَجْمَلَ ثَانِيَةً.

Recede, *v.i.* To move or fall back, تَرَاجَعَ ـ ² عَاجَ ـ تَقَهْقَرَ. To — from, to fall back from, تَرَاجَعَ عَنْ ـ تَنَحَّى عَنْ ـ تَرَاكَ. To — from, to desist from, ² كَفَّ عَنْ ـ ² جَبَأَ عَنْ ـ تَرَاكَ عَنْ ـ تَوَقَّفَ عَلَى. The eye recedes or recoils from him, تَعْلُو عَنْهُ ٱلْعَيْنُ. He receded from the compact, ² حَالَ عَنِ ٱلْعَهْدِ. Having a receding forehead, أَكْبَس. *See also to* Retire, *v.i.*

Receipt, *n.* The act of receiving, تَسَلُّم ـ أَخْذ ـ تَنَاوُل ـ قَبْض ـ إِتِّخَاذ. That which is received, مَقْبُوض ـ مَأْخُوذ. A place of receiving, مَكَانُ (or مَحَلُّ) ٱلْأَخْذِ ـ مَأْخَذ; (*see also under* Office, *n.*) A writing acknowledging —, وُصُول ـ وُرُود *pl.* وُصُولَات ـ رُجْعَة. A direction for making anything, وَصْفَة ـ صِفَة. A — in full, وَرَقَةُ خَلَاصٍ ـ تَبْرِئَة ـ خَلَاص ـ غَلَاق. Acknowledgment to one of —, as of a letter, تَعْرِيفٌ بِوُصُولٍ. To acknowledge receipt to, عَرَّفَ بِٱلْوُصُولِ. On — of,... عِنْدَ وُصُولِ ٱلْ... To demand a —, ² طَلَبَ وُصُولًا. To give a — for; *see below to* Receipt.

Receipt, *v.t.* To give a writing acknowledging that something has been received, عَلَّمَ عَلَى ـ عَلَّمَ عَلَى وَرَقَةٍ لِبَيَانِ وُصُولِ ٱلْ... وَرَقَةٍ بِقَبْضِ ٱلْ...

Receivable, *a.* That may be received, قُبُولُهُ جَائِزٌ. That should be received, قُبُولُهُ لَازِمٌ. Payable to, مِمَّا يُدْفَعُ لِ. Receivable from, due by, مَطْلُوبٌ مِنْ.

Receive, *v.t.* To take what is offered, تَسَلَّمَ ـ ² أَخَذَ ـ ² قَبِلَ. To acquire, ² نَالَ. To admit, concede, سَلَّمَ بِ ـ ² قَبِلَ. To admit, give entrance to, أَدْخَلَ ـ طَرَّقَ لِ ـ أَجَابَ إِلَى. To —, as money, *etc.*, ² أَخَذَ ـ ² قَبَضَ. To —, bear, put up with, ² صَبَرَ عَلَى ـ تَحَمَّلَ. To —, a letter, وَصَلَهُ مَكْتُوبٌ *aor.* يَصِلُ ـ وَرَدَ عَلَيْهِ مَكْتُوبٌ *aor.* يَرِدُ ـ وَفَدَ عَلَى كِتَابٌ *aor.* يَفِدُ. To —, accost, or treat with, تَلَقَّى بِ ـ لَاقَى ـ إِسْتَقْبَلَ بِ. To welcome, إِحْتَفَلَ بِ ـ أَقْبَلَ عَلَى ـ تَرَحَّبَ. To —, to happen to, أَصَابَ ـ ² نَزَلَ بِ. To entertain, as a guest, أَوْلَمَ ـ أَوَى ـ ضَيَّفَ. To give refuge to, آوَى. To approve of, ² رَضِيَ بِ. To be susceptible of, ² قَبِلَ. To — from, as a tradition, ² أَخَذَ عَنْ. To — anything back, إِسْتَعَادَ. He was received with honour and respect, قُوبِلَ بِٱلْإِكْرَامِ وَٱلْجَلَالِ. He received us gladly, ² قَبِلَنَا بِفَرَحٍ. What we ask we receive, مَهْمَا سَأَلْنَا نَنَالُ. Every man received a piastre, أَخَذُوا غِرْشًا غِرْشًا. Destined to —, مَزْمَعٌ أَنْ يَقْبَلَ. To — stolen goods, خَبَّأَ ٱلْمَالَ ٱلْمَسْرُوقَ. The Wazir did not — him, لَمْ يَحْتَفِلْ بِهِ ٱلْوَزِيرُ.

To receive a beating, أَكَلَ قَتْلَةً ـ أَكَلَ ضَرْبَةً ².

To receive an affront, تَبَهْدَلَ ـ صَارَتْ لَهُ بَهْدَلَةٌ.

To receive forgiveness, نَالَ غُفْرَانًا ².

To receive one's sight, أَبْصَرَتَا عَيْنَاهُ ـ أَبْصَرَ.

To receive a recompense, نَالَ جَزَآءً ².

To receive a wound, جُرِحَ ـ جُرِحَ ².

To receive the sacrament, eucharist, تَنَاوَلَ ٱلْقُرْبَانَ.

Receiver, *n.* One who receives, مُتَسَلِّم ـ آخِذ ـ نَائِل ـ مُتَنَاوِل ـ قَابِل. One who is charged to receive, as rents, *etc.*, مُلْتَزِم ـ دَفْتَرْدَار ـ مُحَصِّل ـ مُسْتَوْفٍ. Any vessel to hold liquids, *etc.*, مُخَبَّئ ـ مَأْخَذ. A — of stolen goods, خَابِئُ ٱلْمَالِ ٱلْمَسْرُوقِ ـ ٱلسَّرِقَةِ. The — of a letter, مُتَسَلِّمُ (or) نَائِلُ ٱلْمَكْتُوبِ.

Receiving-house, *n.* An office, مَكْتَب ـ مَكَان ـ مَحَلّ ـ مَخْرَف.

Recency, *n.* Newness of origin, جِدَّة ـ حَدَاثَة. Lateness in occurrence, حَدَاثَةُ وُقُوعٍ.

Recension, *n.* Enumeration, حِسَاب ـ تِعْدَاد ـ إِحْصَآء. Examination, بَحْث. Review, تَصَفُّح.

Recent, *a.* Late, as of origin, غَضّ ـ طَرِيف ـ حَدِيث *pl.* وُقُوعُهُ ـ حُدُوثُهُ مِنْ قَرِيبٍ. Not long past, جَدِيد ـ غِضَاض ـ بِهٰذَا ٱلْقُرْبِ. A — thing, novelty, حَدَث ـ طُرْف طَرِيف *pl.* *pl.* أَحْدَاث. To be —, new, of late origin, حَدَثَ ². *See also* Novel, *a.*

Recently, *n.* مِنْ قَرِيبٍ ـ جِدَّةً ـ إِسْتِحْدَاثًا.

Recentness, *n.* *See* Recency, Newness, Lateness, *n.*

Receptacle, *n.* A vessel for receiving anything, وِعَآء *pl.* أَوْعِيَة *and* أَوْعِيَة ـ إِنَآء *pl.* آنِيَة. A place for the same, مَأْخَذ ـ مَحَلّ. A — for travelling provisions, تَأْمُورَة ـ تَأْمُور. A case, as for scissors, *etc.*, ظَرْف *pl.* ظُرُوف. A sheath, غِلَاف *pl.* غُلُف. A — for sweepings, مَزْبَلَة. *See also* Refuge, *n.*

Receptacular, *a.* مِنَ ٱلْوِعَآءِ. A — noun, إِسْمُ وِعَآءٍ.

Reception, *n.* Receipt, إِتِّخَاذ ـ قُبُول ـ تَنَاوُل. Mode of receiving, صُورَةُ قُبُولٍ ـ مُلَاقَاة ـ قُبُول. Treatment, مُعَامَلَة. Welcome, تَرَحُّب ـ إِقْبَال. Reception, as of persons, إِسْتِقْبَال. Style of reception, إِنْزَال ـ مُنْزَل. He accorded me a happy —, أَنْزَلَنِي مُنْزَلًا مُبَارَكًا. They accorded him a most favourable —, لَاقَوْهُ بِأَحْسَنِ مُلَاقَاةٍ ـ أَكْرَمُوا قُدُومَهُ. An official —, زِيَارَةٌ رَسْمِيَّةٌ. An official — room, دَائِرَةُ ٱلتَّشْرِيفَاتِ. A — room, دِيوَان. To hold an official —, إِسْتَقْبَلَ زِيَارَةً رَسْمِيَّةً. *See also* Receipt, *n.*

Receptive, *a.* مُتَّخِذ ـ قَابِل ـ مُتَنَاوِل.

Recess, *n.* A withdrawing or moving back, تَبَاعُد ـ بَرَاح ـ تَقَهْقُرٌ إِلَى وَرَآءٍ ـ تَرَاءٍ ـ تَرَاجُع. Suspension, as of business, فَضَاوَة ـ فَرَاغ ـ تَعْطِيل ـ تَقَاعُد. Leisure, the being disengaged, فَرَاغ. A retirement or private abode, مَعْزِل. An alcove, رَفّ ـ سِدِلّى *pl.* رُفُوف ـ قُبَّة *pl.* قُبَب. The recesses of the mind, ٱلْبَاطِن. During the —, suspension of business, مُدَّةَ ـ مُدَّةَ ٱلتَّعْطِيلِ ٱلتَّقَاعُدِ. Lay open the recesses of thy mind and thou wilt know thy vices and thy faults, (*prov.*) إِفْتَحْ صُرَّتَكَ تَعْلَمْ عُجَرَكَ.

Recession, *n.* A withdrawing, retreating, رُجُوع ـ إِنْصِرَاف عَنْ. A —, as from a claim, تَسْلِيم ـ جَبَآء عَنْ ـ رُجُوع فِي ـ تَرَاءٍ عَنْ.

Recharge, *v.t.* To charge or attack again, حَمَلَ عَلَى ـ ثَانِيَةً ² ـ عَادَ فَهَجَمَ عَلَيْهِ ².

Recharter, *n.* As of a ship, مُكَارَاة ـ كِرْوَةُ مَرْكَبٍ مُسْتَجِدَّةٍ ـ مَرْكَب جَدِيدَة.

Recharter, *v.t.* Of a ship, إِسْتَكْرَى ٱلْمَرْكَبَ ثَانِيَةً ـ عَادَ ² فَٱسْتَكْرَى ٱلْمَرْكَبَ.

Recherché, *a.* تُحْفَة ـ عَزِيز ـ مَطْلُوب ـ نَفِيس *pl.* تُحَف.

Rechoose, *v.t.* عَادَ فَٱقْتَرَحَهُ ـ إِخْتَارَ ـ ثَانِيَةً ².

Recipe, *n.* *See under* Prescription, *n.*

Recipiency, *n.* مُنَاوَلَة ـ أَخْذ ـ إِتِّخَاذ ـ قُبُول.

Recipient, *n.* مُتَسَلِّم ـ مُتَّخِذ ـ قَابِل ـ نَائِل.

Reciprocal, *a.* Acting in turn, مُتَنَاوِب; acting in return, مُتَبَادِل ـ مُتَرَاءٍ. Mutual, shared in by another, مُشْتَرَك. Reciprocal, mutually repelling, مُتَدَافِع; mutually attracting, مُتَجَاذِب. Reciprocal love, صَفَآء. Reciprocal treatment, مُعَامَلَةٌ مُتَبَادِلَةٌ. A — guarantee, كَفَالَةٌ مُتَبَادِلَةٌ. *See also* Mutual, *a.*

Reciprocal, *n.* In mathematics, عَدَدٌ مَقْلُوبٌ ـ مَقْلُوب.

Reciprocally, *ad.* بِٱلْمُقَابَلَةِ. *See also* Alternately, Mutually, *ad.*

Reciprocalness, *n.* } تَقَابُل ـ مُقَابَلَة.
Reciprocality,

Reciprocate, *v.t.* قَابَلَ ـ أَعَاضَ ـ عَوَّضَ ـ رَدَّدَ ـ رَجَّعَ ـ قَابَلَ ـ بِ.

Reciprocate, *v.i.* *See to* Alternate, *v.i.*

Reciprocation, *n.* مُفَاوَضَة ـ تَرْجِيع ـ مُعَاوَضَة ـ مُقَابَلَة. *See also* Alternation, *n.*

Reciprocity, *n.* مُقَابَلَة ـ مُقَابَلَةٌ بِٱلْمِثْلِ. The principle of —, أُصُولُ ٱلْمُقَابَلَةِ بِٱلْمِثْلِ. Perfect —, in action, مُعَامَلَةٌ مُتَقَابِلَةٌ تَامَّةٌ. They made a treaty of —, تَعَاقَدُوا بِٱلْمُقَابَلَةِ.

Recision, *n.* إِسْقَاط ـ قَطْع ـ حَذْف.

Recital, *n.* The act of reading, قِرَآءَة ـ تِلَاوَة. A narrative or enumeration of facts, *etc.*, إِفَادَة ـ حِكَايَة ـ رِوَايَة ـ قِصَّة ـ ذِكْر ـ نَقْل. An address, خِطَاب. *See also under* Account, *n.*

Recitation, *n.* Repetition, تَكْرِير ـ تَكْرَار ـ تَثْنِيَة. Rehearsal, of what was said or written by another, نَقْل ـ حِكَايَة عَن.

Recitative, *a.* مُتَوَاتِرُ ٱلْكَلَامِ ـ مِثْلَ ٱلْقِرَآءَةِ ـ نَاقِل.

Recitative, *n.* غِنَآءٌ غَيْرُ مَوْزُونٍ.

Recite, *v.t.* To narrate, يَرْوِي *aor.* رَوَى ـ ٢ نَقَلَ ـ ٢ ذَكَرَ. To —, or rehearse, the words of another, حَكَى ـ تَرَوَّى. To read over, ٢ تَلَا. To —, as a quotation, to quote, أَوْرَدَ. To — or rehearse the whole, خَتَمَ. Recite thou the ode, أَنْشِدِ ٱلْقَصِيدَةَ. He recited the whole of the Kurân, خَتَمَ ٱلْقُرْآنَ. *See also to* Recapitulate, *v.t.*

Recite, *v.i.* As of lessons, ٢ تَلَا ٱلدَّرْسَ; as an exhortation, ٢ خَطَبَ خُطْبَةً.

Reciter, *n.* نَاقِل *pl.* نَقَلَة ـ رَاوٍ *pl.* رُوَاة.

Reckless, *a.* مُتَغَفِّل ـ هَيِّر ـ لَا هَمَام ـ مُغَامِر ـ مُغْمَّر ـ خَرِيم ـ مُتَهَوِّر ـ مُتَهَامِل. To be —, تَهَوَّرَ.

Recklessly, *ad.* تَغَفُّلًا ـ تَهَوُّرًا ـ بِتَهَوُّرٍ ـ بِتَهَامُلٍ. To plunge — into, غَامَرَ فِي ـ غَامَسَ فِي. To attack one —, غَامَرَ.

Recklessness, *n.* تَهَوُّر ـ تَغَافُل ـ تَهَامُل ـ غَمْرَة.

Reckon, *v.t.* To number, ٢ حَسَبَ ـ عَدَّ ـ أَحْصَى. To form an account or estimate of, to estimate, إِعْتَبَرَ ـ أَعَدَّ ـ حَسِبَ ـ نَزَّلَ مَنْزِلَةَ كَذَا. To — one's self, حَسِبَ نَفْسَهُ. To — upon, to expect, إِنْتَظَرَ ـ تَرَقَّبَ ـ إِحْتَسَبَ. To — with, حَاسَبَ. To — to, ٢ حَسَبَ لِ ـ كَذَا. To be reckoned, counted, إِعْتَدَّ. To —, add up, جَمَّعَ ـ أَجْمَلَ. It is not reckoned in the statement of account, estimate, لَمْ يُوجَدْ لَهُ تَقْيِيدٌ فِي ٱلْمَضْبَطَةِ ـ لَمْ يَجْرِ لَهُ قَيْدٌ فِي ٱلْمَضْبَطَةِ. Reckoned from the date of the signature of this treaty, إِعْتِبَارًا مِنْ يَوْمِ ٱلتَّوْقِيعِ عَلَى هٰذِهِ ٱلْمُعَاهَدَةِ. When he began to —, لَمَّا ٱبْتَدَأَ فِي ٱلْمُحَاسَبَةِ.

Reckon, *v.i.* ٢ حَسَبَ. I — that …, أَحْسُبُ أَنْ. To — with, حَاسَبَ.

Reckoned, *a.* Counted, مَعْدُود; taken into account, مَحْسُوب.

Reckoner, *n.* حَاسِب *pl.* حُسَّاب ـ حَسِيب ـ حِسَابْجِي. A ready —, the book so called, جَدْوَلُ مُسَهِّلِ ٱلْحِسَابَاتِ ـ دُسْتُورُ لِلْحِسَابَاتِ.

Reckoning, *n.* Enumeration, إِحْصَآء ـ حِسَاب ـ تِعْدَاد. An account, bill, حِسَاب. Reckoning with one, مُحَاسَبَة. Reckoning or counting with the fingers, حِسَابُ عَقْدِ ٱلْأَصَابِعِ. The day of —, يَوْمُ ٱلْحِسَابِ. Dead-reckoning, of a ship's course, حِسَابُ سَيْرِ ٱلْمَرْكَبِ حَسَبَ ٱلْبُوصْلَةِ وَٱلْبَلْدِ (*or* ٱلْبَرْكِيتَةِ).

Reclaim, *v.t.* To claim to have restored, as from another, ٢ طَالَبَ ـ طَالَبَ بِ. To call from error, هَذَّبَ ـ أَصْلَحَ ـ رَدَّ عَنِ ٱلْمَحَارِمِ ـ تَوَّبَ ـ أَنَابَ. To —, as from a wild state, أَنَّسَ. To — land from the sea, نَحَّى (*or* نَشَّفَ) جَانِبًا مِنْ أَرْضٍ. I reclaimed more than 50 acres of land, نَحَّيْتُ (*or* نَشَّفْتُ) أَكْثَرَ مِنْ خَمْسِينَ فَدَّانًا مِنْ أَرْضِ ٱلْبَحْرِ.

Reclaimable, *a.* That may be claimed, demanded, مِمَّا يُطَالَبُ بِهِ ـ طَلَبُهُ جَائِز; that may be reformed, مِمَّا يُهَذَّبُ ـ مِمَّا يُصْلَحُ ـ رَدُّهُ عَنِ ٱلْمَحَارِمِ مُمْكِنٌ. Reclaimable land, as from the sea, جَانِبٌ مِنْ أَرْضِ ٱلْبَحْرِ مَجْدَرَةٌ أَنْ تَصِيرَ يَبَسًا.

Reclaimant, *n.* مُدَّعٍ ـ مُطَالِب ـ طَالِب.

Reclamation, *n.* A demand, طَلَبَة ـ مُطَالَبَة ـ إِشْتِكَآء ـ شِكَايَة ـ إِدِّعَآء. Reformation, تَهْذِيب ـ تَثْوِيب ـ إِصْلَاح ـ إِسْتِتَابَة; the bringing from a wild state, تَأْنِيس; the recovery of land, as from the sea, تَنْحِيَة (*or* تَنْشِيف) جَانِبٍ مِنَ ٱلْأَرْضِ مِنَ ٱلْبَحْرِ.

Reclinate, *a.* Bent down, مُلْتَوٍ ـ مُنْحَنٍ ـ مَعْطُوف.

Reclination, *n.* إِنْحِنَآء ـ إِنْضِجَاع ـ إِتِّكَآء.

Recline, *v.i.* To lean back or to one side, تَنَحَّى ـ إِنْتَحَى ـ إِتَّكَى. To lie on the side, ضَجَعَ ـ تَضَجَّعَ ـ إِضْجَعَ. To take repose, إِسْتَرَاحَ. *See also to* Lean, *to* Incline, *v.t.* and *int.*

Reclining, *a.* مَائِل. A — chair, كُرْسِيٌّ لِلْإِضْطِجَاعِ ـ مُضْطَجَع. A — position, مَيْل ـ إِنْضِجَاع ـ ضَجْع.

Reclose, *v.t.* To stop up again, ٢ سَدَّ ثَانِيَةً. To shut again, ٢ عَادَ نَغْلَقَهُ ـ غَلَّقَ ثَانِيَةً.

Recluse, *a.* مُتَوَحِّد ـ مُنْعَزِلٌ عَنِ ٱلنَّاسِ. To live a — life, تَزَهَّدَ.

Recluse, *n.* سَائِح *pl.* سَائِحُون ـ زَاهِد *pl.* زُهَّاد ـ مُتَوَحِّد; a Christian —, حَبِيس *pl.* حُبَسَآء; one who keeps at home, حَبِيس ـ مُلَازِمُ دَارِهِ.

Reclusely, *ad.* كَٱلزَّاهِدِ ـ تَوَحُّدًا ـ فِي ٱلْعُزْلَةِ.

Recluseness, *n.* } وَحْشَة ـ تَزَهُّد ـ عُزْلَة.
Reclusion, }

Reclusive, *a.* بِهِ عُزْلَةٌ.

Recoction, *n.* إِعَادَةُ طَبْخٍ ـ طَبْخٌ ثَانٍ.

Recognition, *n.* The act of knowing, مَعْرِفَة ـ عِرْفَان. Avowal, مُرَاعَاة ـ تَسْلِيم ـ إِعْتِرَاف ـ إِقْرَار. Avowal of benefits received, عِرْفَانُ ٱلْجَمِيلِ ـ شُكْرُ ٱلْجَمِيلِ. A recompense, مُجَازَاة ـ أَجْر ـ مُكَافَأَة. Recognition of belligerency, إِعْتِرَافٌ بِٱلْمُحَارَبَةِ; of independence, إِقْرَارٌ بِٱسْتِقْلَالِ دَوْلَةٍ. In — of, in reward of, مُكَافَأَةً لِ. In token of —, عَلَامَةَ ٱلْمَعْرِفَةِ. *See also* Acknowledgment, *n.*

Recognizable, *a.* That may be known, مِمَّا يُعْرَفُ ـ يُعْرَفُ ـ مَعْرُوف.

Recognizance, *n.* A bond of record, صَكُّ ٱلْكَفَالَةِ ـ صَكُّ ٱلتَّعَهُّدِ ـ كَفَالَةٌ رَسْمِيَّةٌ ـ وَرَقَةُ كَفَالَةٍ.

Recognize, *v.t.* To know, عَرَفَ ـ. To perceive, experience, ٱسْتَقْرَبَ ـ أَقَرَّ بِ ـ عَرَفَ ـ عَلِمَ بِ. To acknowledge, admit, سَلَّمَ بِ ـ قَبِلَ ـ ٱعْتَرَفَ. To acknowledge formally, to be obedient to, أَذْعَنَ لِ ـ قَبِلَ. To avow, as an obligation, to be thankful for, رَاعَى ٱلْجَمِيلَ ـ عَرَفَ. To recompense, قَابَلَ ـ عَرَفَ ـ كَافَى. To — as a belligerent, ٱعْتَرَفَ مُحَارِبًا. In the manner recognized by the state, بِٱلْكَيْفِيَّةِ ٱلْمُتَعَارَفَةِ بِٱلْمَمْلَكَةِ. They do not — the distinction between the commander and the commanded, لَا يَعْرِفُونَ ٱلنِّسْبَةَ بَيْنَ ٱلرَّئِيسِ وَٱلْمَرْؤُوسِ. Recognized internationally, مُعْتَرَفٌ بِهِ بَيْنَ ٱلْأُمَمِ. Recognized or admitted by..., مُسَلَّمٌ مِنْ. Recognized by all, مُسَلَّمٌ عِنْدَ ٱلْجَمِيعِ. They did not the least thing against the rules acted upon in civilized towns, or against the rights generally recognized by the powers, لَمْ يَفْعَلُوا أَدْنَى شَيْءٍ مُغَايِرٍ لِلْقَوَانِينِ ٱلْعُمُومِيَّةِ ٱلْمَعْمُولِ بِهَا فِي ٱلْمُدُنِ ٱلْمُتَمَدِّنَةِ أَوِ ٱلْحُقُوقِ ٱلْمُتَعَارَفَةِ بَيْنَ ٱلدُّوَلِ.

Recognizee, *n.* مُتَسَلِّمُ ٱلتَّعَهُّدِ ـ مُتَسَلِّمُ ٱلْكَفَالَةِ ٱلرَّسْمِيَّةِ.

Recognizor, *n.* مُتَعَهِّدٌ رَسْمًا ـ مُتَكَفِّلٌ رَسْمًا.

Recoil, *v.i.* To move or start back, تَرَاجَعَ ـ تَقَهْقَرَ ـ تَرَاجَعَ. To return upon, as evil on the perpetrator, رَجَعَ عَلَى ـ عَادَ عَلَى ـ حَلَّ عَلَى ـ رَجَعَ عَلَى رَأْسِهِ. To shrink from, جَفَا عَنْ ـ تَجَافَى عَنْ ـ جَبَأَ عَنْ. He recoiled from it, was disgusted at it, ٱسْتَكْرَهَهُ ـ كَرِهَهُ. My eyes recoiled from the thing, جَبَأَتْ عَيْنِي عَنِ ٱلشَّيْءِ. *See also to* Recede, *to* Rebound, *v.t.*

Recoil, *n.* A starting back; *see* Rebound, *n.*

Recoiling, *n.* *See* Recession, *n.*

Recoin, *v.t.* عَادَ فَضَرَبَ ٱلسِّكَّةَ ـ ضَرَبَ ٱلسِّكَّةَ ثَانِيَةً.

Recoinage, *n.* The act of recoining, إِعَادَةُ ضَرْبِ ٱلسِّكَّةِ. New coin, سِكَّةٌ جَدِيدَةٌ.

Re-collect, *v.t.* To collect again, عَادَ فَلَمَّهُ ـ جَمَعَ ثَانِيَةً.

Recollect, *v.t.* To recall or call to mind, تَذَكَّرَ ـ ذَكَرَ ـ تَنَبَّهَ عَلَى ـ ٱسْتَذْكَرَ. To seek to —, ٱسْتَذْكَرَ. To cause another to —, ذَكَّرَ. I don't — it, ضَلَّ عَنِّي. I remembered the thing after forgetting it, تَذَكَّرْتُهُ ـ ذَكَرْتُ ٱلشَّيْءَ بَعْدَ ٱلنِّسْيَانِ. He tied a thread upon his finger to — thereby the thing that he wanted, رَبَطَ فِي أُصْبُعِهِ خَيْطًا يَسْتَذْكِرُ بِهِ حَاجَتَهُ. He recollected, was mindful of, his claim, ذَكَرَ حَقَّهُ.

Recollection, *n.* The act of recollecting, ٱسْتِذْكَار ـ تَذَكُّر. Memory, ذُكْرَة ـ ذِكْرَة ـ ذِكْر. A cogitation, خَاطِر: To the best of my —, عَلَى مَا فِي بَالِي ـ عَلَى مَا فِي خَاطِرِي. *See also* Memory, Mind, *n.*

Re-colonize, *v.t.* عَادَ فَٱسْتَوْطَنَهُ ـ عَمَّرَ ثَانِيَةً.

Recolour, *v.t.* عَادَ فَزَوَّقَهُ ـ صَبَغَ ثَانِيَةً.

Re-combine, *v.t.* To collect again, جَمَعَ ثَانِيَةً ـ ضَمَّ ثَانِيَةً. To arrange again, رَتَّبَ ثَانِيَةً.

Recommence, *v.t.* عَادَ فَشَرَعَ فِيهِ ـ ٱسْتَأْنَفَ ثَانِيَةً ـ ٱسْتَأْنَفَ ـ بَدَأَ مِنْ جَدِيدٍ ـ أَعَادَ. We have recommenced sending, ٱسْتَأْنَفْنَا ٱلْإِرْسَالَ. He was ready to — the war, كَانَ مُسْتَعِدًّا لِٱسْتِئْنَافِ ٱلْحَرْبِ.

Recommencement, *n.* إِعَادَة ـ شُرُوعٌ جَدِيدٌ ـ بَدَاءَةٌ ثَانِيَةٌ ـ ٱسْتِئْنَاف ـ ٱفْتِتَاحٌ ثَانٍ.

Recommend, *v.t.* To commend to another, to his care, *etc.*, وَصَّى عَلَى ـ وَصَّى فِي. To describe as desirable, good, *etc*, أَثْنَى عَلَى ـ وَصَفَ بِٱلْجَمِيلِ ـ يَصِفُ *aor.* وَصَفَ ـ مَدَحَ ـ ذَكَرَ بِٱلْجَمِيلِ. To — to, confide or make over to, ٱسْتَوْدَعَ إِلَى ـ سَلَّمَ إِلَى. I have recommended you to him, وَصَّيْتُهُ فِيكَ ـ وَصَّيْتُهُ عَلَيْكَ. He is recommended by so-and-so, هُوَ مُوَصًّى فِيهِ مِنْ فُلَانٍ. I — him to your care, attention, ٱعْتَنُوا بِهِ ـ أَلْقُوا نَظَرَكُمْ عَلَيْهِ ـ أَجْعَلُوا نَظَرَكُمْ عَلَيْهِ. I can — this dish to you, كُلْ مِنْ هٰذَا ٱلطَّبِيخِ فَإِنَّهُ طَيِّبٌ. Can you — me to any shop where I can buy hardware? أَتَقْدِرُ أَنْ تَدُلَّنِي عَلَى دُكَّانٍ سَقَطِيٍّ أَشْتَرِي مِنْهُ خُرْدَةً. *See also to* Commend, *v.t.*

Recommendable, *a.* Worthy of praise, حَمِيد ـ مَدِيح.

Recommendation, *n.* A — to one's care, attention, *etc.*, وَصِيَّة ـ تَوْصِيَة. The act of praising, ذِكْرٌ بِٱلْجَمِيلِ ـ مَدْح ـ ثَنَاء. That which commends to favour, فَضِيلَة ـ مَدَارُ ٱلِٱسْتِحْسَانِ. A letter of —, مَكْتُوبُ تَوْصِيَةٍ.

Recommendatory, *a.* Commending to care, *etc*, مُوَصٍّ ـ ذُو تَوْصِيَةٍ.

Recommission, *v.t.* As of a ship, *etc.*, عَادَ فَجَهَّزَ وَأَعَدَّ لِأَمْرٍ مَخْصُوصٍ; of an official, عَادَ فَوَظَّفَ ثَانِيَةً ـ جَدَّدَ وَظِيفَتَهُ ـ تَوَجَّهَهُ إِلَى.

Recommission, *n.* As of a ship, إِعَادَةُ تَجْهِيزِ ٱلْمَرْكَبِ لِأَمْرٍ مَخْصُوصٍ.

Recommit, *v.t.* To commit again, as of a crime, عَادَ فَٱقْتَرَفَ (*or* عَادَ فَٱرْتَكَبَ) ٱلذَّنْبَ. To — to prison, حَبَسَ ثَانِيَةً. To refer a thing again to, عَادَ فَحَوَّلَ إِلَى ـ حَوَّلَ إِلَى ثَانِيَةً. To — to memory, عَادَ فَحَفِظَ غَيْبًا.

Recommitment, *n.* } As of a crime, اِرْتِكَابُ ذَنْبٍ ـ اِقْتِرَافٌ ثَانٍ
Recommittal, } ثَانِيَةٌ ـ سَجْنٌ ثَانٍ ; re-imprisonment, إِعَادَةُ حَبْسٍ ; re-reference, تَحْوِيلٌ ثَانٍ ـ تَحْوِيل ; recommittal to memory, إِعَادَةُ حِفْظٍ غَيْبًا.

Recompense, *n.* جَزَآءٌ ـ كِفَآءٌ ـ مَثُوبَةٌ ـ عِوَضٌ ـ مُفَاوَضَةٌ ـ حُسْنُ ثَوَابٍ ـ ثَوَابٌ ـ مُكَافَأَةٌ ـ مَجْزَاةٌ ـ جَازِيَةٌ. A good —, حُسْنُ ثَوَابٍ. A — by way of punishment, مُعَاقَبَةٌ. Did he not expect any —? أَلَمْ يَتَرَقَّبْ عِوَضًا.

Recompense, *v.t.* To reward, جَزَى ـ أَثَابَ ـ ثَوَّبَ ـ كَافَى ـ بِٱلْخَيْرِ ـ جَازَى. To requite, give instead of, عَوَّضَ. To make up to by something equivalent, قَابَلَ ـ بِ ـ كَافَى ـ عَلَى ـ تَقَابَلَ ـ بِ ـ أَفَاضَ. To punish, عَاقَبَ.

Recompose, *v.t.* To arrange again, عَادَ فَرَتَّبَهُ ـ رَتَّبَ ـ ثَانِيَةً. To put together again, رَكَّبَ ـ ثَانِيَةً. To rewrite, أَلَّفَ ـ ثَانِيَةً. To quiet again, عَادَ فَسَكَّنَهُ ـ أَهْدَأَ ـ ثَانِيَةً.

Reconcilable, *a.* Capable of adjustment, المُوَافَقَةُ بَيْنَ ـ مُمْكِنَةٌ ـ قَابِلُ ٱلْمُوَافَقَةِ ـ يَتَّفِقُ مَعَ كَذَا ; capable of renewal of friendship, يَقْبَلُ ٱلْمُصَالَحَةَ ـ يَتَصَالَحُ.

Reconcilably, *ad.* With congruity, بِمُوَافَقَةٍ ـ بِٱتِّفَاقٍ ; with renewal of friendship, بِمُصَالَحَةٍ.

Reconcilableness, *n.* Capacity of adjustment, قَابِلِيَّةُ ٱلِٱتِّفَاقِ ; of renewal of friendship, قَابِلِيَّةُ ٱلْإِصْلَاحِ بَيْنَ ـ قَابِلِيَّةُ ٱلْمُصَالَحَةِ.

Reconcile, *v.t.* To make consistent with or between, صَحَّحَ بَيْنَ ـ وَفَّقَ بَيْنَ ـ سَاوَى بَيْنَ ـ سَوَّى بَيْنَ. To bring to acquiescence, أَقَرَّ ـ تَوَخَّى رِضَاهُ ـ أَرْضَى. To reform, amend, of circumstances, لَأَمَ ـ رَتَقَ ٱلْفَتْقَ : he closed up the breach, or reconciled the circumstances between them, رَتَقَ ـ أَدَمَ (or آدَمَ) بَيْنَهُمْ ـ فَتْقَهُمْ. To conciliate, صَالَحَ. To pacify, أَهْدَأَ ـ لَثَّمَ. To — between, to effect a reconciliation between, صَحَّحَ بَيْنَ ـ لَأَمَ بَيْنَ ـ وَفَّقَ بَيْنَ ـ صَالَحَ بَيْنَ ـ جَمَعَ بَيْنَ. To —, to make one to bear patiently, صَبَّرَ ـ عَلَى ـ أَصْبَرَ. The two were mutually reconciled, تَصَالَحَا ـ تَسَالَمَا ; of more than two, تَصَالَحُوا ـ تَسَالَمُوا. To be reconciled to a thing, to bear it patiently, تَصَبَّرَ ـ صَبَرَ عَلَى ـ تَعَذَّرَ ـ اِسْتَصْلَحَ ـ إِلَى ذِمَّتِهِ ـ اِصْطَبَرَ. To — to one's conscience, اِعْتَذَرَ. He became reconciled to him, صَالَحَهُ. *See also to* Conciliate, *v.t.*

Reconcilement, *n.* } Agreement, أُلْفَةٌ ـ وِفَاقٌ ـ مُوَافَقَةٌ ـ وَفْقٌ.
Reconciliation, } The act of reconciling parties, إِصْلَاحٌ ـ لَأْمٌ بَيْنَ ـ إِسْدَآءٌ بَيْنَ ـ جَمْعٌ بَيْنَ. A renewal of friendship, مُصَالَحَةٌ ـ مُسَالَمَةٌ ـ صُلْحٌ ـ سِلْمٌ ـ مُلَاءَمَةٌ. A —, atonement, كَفَّارَةٌ. He effected a — between the two, أَسْدَى بَيْنَهُمَا ـ أَصْلَحَ بَيْنَهُمَا. He determined on a —, قَدْ أَفْضَى إِلَى ٱلْمُسَالَمَةِ. To offer a —, propitiation, for, قَدَّمَ كَفَّارَةً عَنْ. *See also* Conciliation, *n.*

Reconciler, *n.* مُسَالِمٌ ـ مُصَالِحٌ. *See also* Mediator, *n.*

Reconciliatory, *a.* ذُو مُسَالَمَةٍ ـ مُحِبٌّ عَلَى ٱلْمُصَالَحَةِ.

Recondite, *a.* مُغْلَقٌ ـ دَقِيقٌ ـ دِقٌّ ـ خَفِيٌّ ـ غَامِضٌ. To make, غَمَّضَ. To be —, غَمُضَ. *See also* Abstruse, *a.*

Reconduct, *v.t.* عَادَ فَرَافَقَ ـ إِلَى ـ أَوْصَلَ ـ ثَانِيَةً ـ شَيَّعَ ـ مِنْ ـ جَدِيدٍ.

Reconnoissance, *n.* The examination of a tract of country, كَشْفٌ ـ طِلْعٌ ـ مُعَايَنَةٌ ; for military purpose, طِلْعٌ. A reconnoitring party, كُشَّافٌ ; as of soldiers, طَلِيعَةٌ ـ كُشَّافٌ ـ دَيْدَبَانٌ.

Reconnoitre, *v.t.* كَشَفَ ـ اِطَّلَعَ عَلَى ـ دَيْدَبَ : he reconnoitred the enemy, اِطَّلَعَ طِلْعَ ٱلْعَدُوِّ.

Reconquer, *v.t.* رَدَّ ـ إِلَى حُكُومَةِ آلِ... (or فُلَانٍ) ـ مَلَكَ ـ ثَانِيَةً ـ فَتَحَ ـ ثَانِيَةً.

Reconquest, *n.* إِعَادَةُ فَتْحٍ ـ فَتْحٌ ثَانٍ.

Reconsider, *v.t.* رَجَعَ إِلَى ـ اِطَّلَعَ عَلَى ـ ثَانِيَةً ـ طَالَعَ ـ ثَانِيَةً ـ عَادَ فَأَضْمَرَ عَلَى ـ رَجَعَ إِلَى تَأَمُّلِهِ.

Reconsideration, *n.* مُطَالَعَةٌ ثَانِيَةٌ ـ إِعَادَةُ نَظَرٍ فِي ـ بَحْثٌ جَدِيدٌ.

Reconstruct, *v.t.* To rebuild, عَمَّرَ ـ ثَانِيَةً ـ عَمَّرَ ـ مِنْ جَدِيدٍ ; to re-arrange, عَادَ فَنَظَّمَهُ ـ رَتَّبَ ـ ثَانِيَةً. To become reconstructed, rightly disposed, اِسْتَتَبَّ. Reconstructed, put in good order, مُسْتَتِبٌّ.

Reconstruction, *n.* The act of building again, إِعَادَةُ بِنَآءٍ ; of being restored to a right state, اِسْتِتْبَابٌ.

Reconvey, *v.t.* To carry back, عَادَ فَجَآءَ بِ ـ نَقَلَ ـ ثَانِيَةً. To return, give back to, رَدَّ ـ إِلَى ـ رَجَّعَ ـ إِلَى. To transfer again, حَوَّلَ ـ ثَانِيَةً. To — across, عَبَّرَ ـ ثَانِيَةً.

Record, *v.t.* To write down, كَتَبَ. To register, دَوَّنَ ـ قَيَّدَ ـ فِي دَفْتَرٍ ـ كَتَبَ ـ فِي دَفْتَرٍ. To narrate, حَدَّثَ بِ ـ حَدَّثَ ـ ذَكَرَ. To — or inscribe with a date, أَرَّخَ : he recorded the date of the voucher, أَرَّخَ ٱلْبَيِّنَةَ. To place as a record, memorial, جَعَلَ ـ لِتَذْكِيرٍ. The recording angels, الحَفَظَةُ.

Record, *n.* A writing, كِتَابَةٌ. A written paper of a contract or a judicial —, سِجِلٌّ ـ مَحْضَرٌ ـ صَكٌّ *pl.* صُكُوكٌ *and* صِكَاكٌ *pl.* سِجِلَّاتٌ. A —, as of one's life, سِيرَةٌ *pl.* سِيَرٌ. Anything written in a book or writing, قَيْدٌ ـ دَرْجٌ مَكْتُوبٌ. A book for keeping records, دَفْتَرُ ٱلْقَيْدِ ـ دِيوَان. Records, books or papers recording events, سِفْرُ تَذْكَارِ ٱلْأَيَّامِ ـ سِفْرُ أَخْبَارٍ. A witness, شَهَادَة. I call God to —, أَسْتَشْهِدُ ٱللّٰهَ. I call heaven and earth to — against you, أُشْهِدُ عَلَيْكُمُ ٱلسَّمَآءَ وَٱلْأَرْضَ. A court of —, دِيوَانُ ٱلسِّجِلَّاتِ. A keeper of records, وَرَّاق.

Recorder, *n.* One who records, as in a register, مُقَيِّد ـ مُدَوِّن; one who registers judicial records, مُقَيِّدُ ٱلسِّجِلَّاتِ. A judical officer, مَأْمُورٌ بِٱلْقَضَآءِ.

Recordership, *n.* Of records, وَظِيفَةُ ٱلْمُقَيِّدِ; of the official, وَظِيفَةُ ٱلْمَأْمُورِ بِٱلْقَضَآءِ.

Recount, *v.t.* To enumerate, عَدَّدَ ـ عَدَّ [2]. To relate, رَوَى *aor.* يَرْوِي ـ حَكَى [3] ـ ذَكَرَ [2] ـ حَدَّثَ ـ نَقَلَ [2]. To describe, وَصَفَ *aor.* يَصِفُ ـ بَيَّنَ ـ شَرَحَ [3].

Recourse, *n.* Application or going to, رُجُوعٌ إِلَى ـ صَمْدٌ إِلَى; as for assistance, إِسْتِمْدَاد ـ إِسْتِعَانَة ـ إِلْتِجَآءٌ إِلَى; as an expedient, إِلْتِبَاط. Recourse to action in law, مَرْجِع. To have — to, إِلْتَجَأَ إِلَى ـ وَقَعَ عَلَى *aor.* يَقَعُ ـ صَمَدَ إِلَى [2]; to have frequent recourse to, صَمَّدَ إِلَى. To have — to for assistance, إِسْتَعَانَ ـ إِسْتَمَدَّ; as an expedient, إِلْتَبَطَ إِلَى. He has —, at law, against so-and-so, لَهُ مَرْجِعٌ عَلَى فُلَانٍ. *See also under to* Repair, *v.i.*

Recover, *v.t.* To regain what was lost, إِسْتَرَدَّ ـ رَدَّ [2] ـ إِسْتَعَادَ. To seize or regain possession of, أَخَذَ ثَانِيَةً ـ عَادَ فَضَبَطَهُ [2]. To get again, حَصَّلَ ثَانِيَةً ـ عَادَ فَحَصَّلَهُ [2] ـ عَادَ فَمَلَكَهُ [2]. To attain, overtake, دَارَكَ. To — one from sickness, (or أَقَامَ) شَفَى [3] ـ أَشْفَى ـ أَفَاقَ مِنَ ٱلْمَرَضِ ـ صَحَّحَ ـ (or أَبْرَأَ) مِنَ ٱلْمَرَضِ. To repair, أَصْلَحَ ـ جَبَرَ [2] ـ جَبَّرَ. To —, as a debt from the effects of a debtor, إِنْتَصَرَ مِنْ مَالِ ٱلْمَدْيُونِ. To —, to get possession of, حَازَ [2] ـ إِتَّخَذَ. To —, to refresh, أَرَاحَ: he recovered, refreshed, his camel, أَرَاحَ بَعِيرَهُ. To —, as land from the sea, *etc.* (*see under to* Reclaim, *v.t.*) Why have you not recovered it during this time? لِمَا مَا تَسْتَرِدُّهَا فِي هٰذِهِ ٱلْمُدَّةِ. He went to — his authority near the hills, خَرَجَ [2] يُرِيدُ ٱسْتِرْجَاعَ سُلْطَتِهِ بِجِوَارِ ٱلْجِبَالِ. To — one's former condition, تَجَبَّرَ ـ إِنْجَبَرَ. They recovered themselves out of the difficulty, إِنْتَصَرُوا عَلَى ٱلْمُشْكِلَةِ. I recovered him from his embarrassment, broken fortune, جَبَرْتُهُ. To — one's own spirits, تَبَلَّجَ ـ إِنْتَعَشَ. *See also to* Revive, *v.t.*

Recover, *v.i.* To regain health, صَحَّ مِنَ ٱلْمَرَضِ [2] ـ بَرِئَ [3] ـ أَفَاقَ ـ شُفِيَ ـ إِسْتَفَاقَ ـ نَقَهَ مِنْ مَرَضِهِ [3]. To regain one's former condition after loss, *etc.*, تَجَبَّرَ ـ إِنْجَبَرَ. He had recovered his health, قَدْ شُوفِيَ (or أُشْفِيَ). To —, as at law, إِنْتَصَرَ.

Recoverable, *a.* That may be regained after having been lost, مِمَّا يُسْتَرَدُّ ـ مِمَّا يُسْتَعَادُ; that may be taken again, مِمَّا يُعَادُ ضَبْطُهُ ـ مِمَّا يُؤْخَذُ ثَانِيَةً; that may be reacquired, مِمَّا يُحَصَّلُ ثَانِيَةً; that may be cured, يُشْفَى ـ يُبْرَأُ. Recoverable, as a debt from the assets of a debtor, مِمَّا يُنْتَصَرُ مِنْ مَالِ ٱلْمَدْيُونِ. *See also* Reclaimable, *n.*

Recovery, *n.* As of what was lost, رَدّ ـ إِسْتِرْدَاد ـ إِسْتِعَاد. Seizure again, إِعَادَةُ أَخْذٍ ـ ضَبْطٌ ثَانٍ. Restoration to health, إِتِّجَاهٌ إِلَى ٱلصِّحَّةِ ـ تَعْدِيلُ ٱلْمِزَاجِ ـ صِحَّة ـ نُقُوه ـ شَفَآء; to good order, إِسْتِتْبَاب. Restoration of broken fortune, *etc.*, جُبُور ـ تَجَبُّر ـ تَصْلِيح. Recovery of money from assets of debtor, إِنْتِصَار مِنْ مَالِ ٱلْمَدْيُونِ. The act of obtaining, حَوْز ـ تَحْصِيل. *See also* Reclamation, *n.*

Recreancy, *n.* Cowardice, meanness, جَبَانَة ـ خَسَاسَة ـ دَنَآءَة. Perfidy, غَدْر ـ خِيَانَة. *See also* Cowardice, *n.*

Recreant, *a.* } سَاقِط ـ جَبَان ـ دَنِيّ ـ مُدَنّ. To be —, دَنِيَ
Recreant, *n.* } *aor.* يَدْنَى ـ جَبُنَ [2]. *See also under* False, Cowardly, *a.*

Recreate, *v.t.* To create anew, جَدَّدَ ـ فَطَرَ [2] (or خَلَقَ [2]) ثَانِيَةً. To refresh, نَفَّسَ ـ أَرَاحَ. To delight, أَنْزَهَ ـ أَبْهَجَ ـ شَرَحَ [3] ـ بَسَطَ [2] خَاطِرَهُ. To —, refresh, one's self, تَنَفَّسَ ـ إِرْتَاحَ ـ إِسْتَرَاحَ; to delight one's self, to be delighted, تَنَزَّهَ ـ تَفَكَّهَ ـ إِبْتَهَجَ ـ إِنْشَرَحَ خَاطِرُهُ.

Recreation, *n.* A forming anew, إِعَادَةُ خِلْقَةٍ ـ فَطْرٌ ثَانٍ ـ تَجْدِيد. Refreshment, as after toil, نَفَس ـ رَاحَة ـ تَنَفُّس. Amusement, diversion, تَنَزُّه ـ مُفَاكَهَة. Amusements, sports, مَلَاهِي. *See also* Diversion, *n.*

Recreative, *a.* Tending to give relief, rest, مُنَفِّس ـ مُرِيح. Amusing, diverting, مُطْرِب ـ مُفَرِّح ـ مُبْهِج ـ فَكِه.

Recrement, *n.* *See* Dross, *n.*

Recremental, *a.* *See* Drossy, *a.*

Recriminate, *v.t.* or *i.* رَادَّهُ ـ سَابَّ ـ رَاجَعَهُ ٱلْقَوْلَ ـ سَابَعَ ـ تَعَايَرُوا ـ تَعَايَبُوا ـ ٱلتُّهْمَةَ. They recriminated one another, تَعَايَرُوا ـ تَعَايَبُوا ـ تَسَابُّوا; of two persons, تَعَايَرَا ـ تَسَابَّا ـ تَعَايَبَا.

Recrimination, *n.* مُعَاتَبَة ـ مُشَاتَمَة ـ مُسَابَّة ـ سِبَاع.

Recriminative, *a.* } مُسَابِع ـ سَبّ ـ سِبّ ـ مُنْتَشِب ـ
Recriminator, *n.* } مُعَاتِب ـ مُتَاهِم.
Recriminatory, *a.* }

Recross, *v.t.* عَبَرَ ثَانِيَةً [2] ـ عَادَ فَعَبَرَهُ [2].

Recrudescence, *n.* Return to soreness, عَرَب ـ غَبَر ـ غَفَر ـ غَادٌّ ـ إِعَادَةٌ إِلَى ٱلْإِنْسِحَاجِ ـ رُجُوعٌ إِلَى ٱلْإِنْسِلَاقِ.

Recrudescent, *a.* Growing raw or sore again, مُعِيدٌ إِلَى ـ غَبِر ٱلْإِنْسِحَاج. A — wound, جُرْحٌ غَبِرٌ. To be —, غَبِرَ ـ غَفَرَ.

Recruit, *v.t.* To repair, صَحَّحَ ـ أَصْلَحَ. To retrieve, to restore, as one's losses, *etc.*, جَبَرَ ـ جَبَّرَ ـ إِجْتَبَرَ. To fill up the ranks of soldiers, لَمَّ (*or* جَمَعَ) عَسَاكِرَ جُدُدًا لِتَكْمِيلِ ٱلْعَدَدِ. To — or to become better in health, طَابَ ـ إِسْتَعْدَلَ مِزَاجُهُ ـ رَاقَ مِزَاجُهُ ـ تَوَجَّهَ إِلَى ٱلْعَافِيَةِ ـ إِسْتَرَاحَ. *See also to Enlist, Levy, v.t.*

Recruit, *n.* A newly enlisted soldier, عَسْكَرِيٌّ جَدِيدٌ *pl.* عَسَاكِرُ جُدُدٌ. A supply of anything, مَدَد ـ إِمْدَاد.

Recruiter, *n.* Of soldiers, مِلَمٌّ (*or* لَمَّامُ) ٱلْعَسَاكِرِ لِتَكْمِيلِ ٱلْعَدَدِ ـ جَمَّاعُ عَسْكَرٍ.

Recruiting, *n.* }
Recruitment, } Of health, صِحَّة ـ مُعَافَاة ـ إِسْتِعْدَالُ ٱلْمِزَاجِ. The act of affording supplies, being supplied, مَدَد ـ إِمْدَاد. The — of soldiers, لَمُّ (*or* جَمْعُ) ٱلْعَسَاكِرِ لِتَكْمِيلِ ٱلْعَدَدِ. A recruiting sergeant, قَائِدُ عَشَرَةٍ (*or* اون باشي) جَمَّاعُ عَسَاكِرَ جُدُدٍ.

Recrystallization, *n.* تَكْرَارُ ٱلتَّبَلْوُرِ ـ تَبَلْوُرٌ ثَانٍ.

Recrystallize, *v.t.* صَيَّرَ مِثْلَ حَجَرِ ٱلْبِلَّوْرِ ثَانِيَةً. To become recrystallized, تَبَلْوَرَ ثَانِيَةً.

Rectangle, *n.* مُسْتَطِيل.

Rectangular, *a.* قَائِمُ ٱلزَّاوِيَةِ. The side of a — triangle, ضِلْع *pl.* أَضْلَاع.

Rectifiable, *a.* يُعَدَّلُ ـ تَصْحِيحُهُ مُمْكِنٌ ـ قَابِلُ ٱلتَّسْوِيَةِ ـ إِسْتِتْبَابُهُ مُمْكِنٌ ـ مِمَّا يُعَالَجُ ـ مِمَّا يُصْلَحُ.

Rectification, *n.* The act of correcting, تَحْرِير ـ تَصْحِيح ـ تَصْلِيح ـ تَعْدِيل ـ إِصْلَاح; by way of supplement, إِسْتِدْرَاك; of refining, تَصْفِيَة. Rectification of liquors, تَكْرَار ـ تَكْرِير. Rectification, in geometry, تَقْوِيم. The act of repairing, تَرْمِيم ـ رَمْرَمَة. A — of boundaries, تَعْدِيلُ ٱلتُّخُومِ. The being rectified, put into good order, إِسْتِتْبَاب.

Rectified, *a.* Corrected, مُحَرَّر ـ مُصَحَّح ـ مُعَدَّل ـ مُصَلَّح; repaired, مُرَمْرَم; put into good order, مُسْتَتِبّ; refined, مُصَفًّى. of spirits, liquors, مُكَرَّر. To be —, corrected, made straight, إِنْصَلَحَ ـ إِعْتَدَلَ ـ تَعَدَّلَ ـ إِسْتَتَبَّ.

Rectifier, *n.* A corrector, مُحَرِّر ـ مُصَلِّح ـ مُصَحِّح ـ مُعَدِّل ـ مُعَالِج.

Rectify, *v.t.* To make right, correct, حَرَّرَ ـ قَوَّمَ ـ سَدَّدَ ـ أَطَابَ ـ أَصْلَحَ ـ سَوَّى ـ عَالَجَ. To repair, رَمَّ ـ رَمَّمَ ـ رَمْرَمَ. To — of liquors, spirits, كَرَّرَ. To — a frontier, عَدَّلَ ٱلْحُدُودَ. To —, trim, of language, فَنَّقَ. To — one's conduct, هَذَّبَ سِيرَتَهُ ـ ثَقَّفَ سِيرَتَهُ. To —, by way of emendation, to supplement, in that sense, إِسْتَدْرَكَ عَلَى: I rectified, by way of emendation, or by supplying what was defective in his speech, إِسْتَدْرَكْتُ عَلَيْهِ قَوْلَهُ.

Rectilineal, *a.* }
Rectilinear, } مُسْتَقِيمُ ٱلْخُطُوطِ ـ مُسْتَقِيمُ ٱلْأَضْلَاعِ.

Rectitude, *n.* سَدَد ـ سَوِيَّة ـ سَوَآء ـ صَوَاب ـ صَلَاح ـ صِحَّة ـ إِسْتِقَامَة. *See also* Uprightness.

Rector, *n.* A ruler, administrator, سَائِس ـ مُدَبِّر ـ مُدِير. The minister of a parish, خُورِي *pl.* خَوَارِنَة. Head, as of a college, رَئِيس *pl.* رُؤَسَآء.

Rectorate, *n.* }
Rectorship, } The office of an administrator, وَظِيفَةُ ٱلْمُدِيرِ ـ مُدِيرِيَّة; of a head, رِئَاسَة; of a parish priest, وَظِيفَةُ ٱلْخُورِي.

Rectorial, *a.* Belonging to a rector, minister of a parish, مُخْتَصّ ـ مُتَعَلِّق بِٱلْخُورِي; to a director, head, مُتَعَلِّق بِٱلرَّئِيسِ ـ بِٱلْمُدِيرِ.

Rectory, *n.* The living of a rector, أَبْرَشِيَّةُ ٱلْخُورِي; the house of a rector, مَنْزِلُ (*or* بَيْتُ) ٱلْخُورِي.

Rectum, *n.* Of a human being, سُرْم ـ مَحْشَاة ـ ٱلْمِعَى ٱلْمُسْتَقِيمُ; of a beast, خَوَّارَة ـ خَوْرَان ـ مَبْعَر.

Recumbence, *n.* }
Recumbency, } إِتِّكَآء ـ ضَجْع ـ ضُجُوع ـ إِضْجَاع ـ إِضْطِجَاع.

Recumbent, *a.* مُتَّكِئ ـ مُضْطَجِع ـ ضَاجِع ـ مُضَّجِع.

Recuperative, *a.* }
Recuperatory, } مُعِيد ـ مُصِحّ ـ مُعَالِج ـ مُصَحِّح ـ مُعَدِّل.

Recur, *v.i.* To return to the mind, رَجَعَ إِلَى ٱلْبَالِ ـ خَطَرَ ـ عَادَ فَخَطَرَ عَلَى ٱلْبَالِ ـ بِٱلْبَالِ ثَانِيَةً. To occur again, عَادَ فَجَرَى. To — or have recourse to, صَمَدَ إِلَى ـ إِلْتَجَأَ إِلَى ـ إِنْبَسَطَ إِلَى. To — to anything time after time, صَمَدَ إِلَى ـ تَفَقَّدَ ـ تَعَهَّدَ ـ تَعَاهَدَ. We shall — to this subject, نَعُودُ إِلَى هٰذَا ٱلْمَوْضُوعِ.

Recurrence, *n.* }
Recurrency, } تَكْرَارُ ٱلْوُقُوعِ ـ تَكِرَّة ـ تَكَرُّر.

Recurrent, *a.* مُكَرَّرُ ٱلْوُقُوعِ. Oft-recurring, مُتَوَاتِر.

Recurvate, *a.* أَحْجَنُ *fem.* حَجْنَآءُ *pl.* حُجْنٌ.

Recurvation, *n.* }
Recurvity, } تَحَجُّن.

Recurvi-rostral, *a.* مَقْلُوبُ ٱلْمِنْقَارِ إِلَى فَوْقُ.

Recurvous, *a.* Bent backwards, أَخْجَنُ ـ مُنْحَنٍ إِلَى وَرَآءٍ .

Recusancy, *n.* *See* Nonconformity, *n.*

Recusant, *n.* *See* Nonconformist, *n.*

Red, *a.* أَحْمَرُ *fem.* حَمْرَآءُ *pl.* حُمْرٌ. Bright —, أَحْمَرُ نَاضِرٌ. Red clothes, ثِيَابٌ حُمْرٌ. To become —, إِحْمَرَّ ـ إِحْمَارَّ. To dye —, or to write with red ink, حَمَّرَ. He became alternately — and pale, جَعَلَ يَحْمَارُّ مَرَّةً وَيَصْفَارُّ أُخْرَى ².

Redan, *n.* طَابِيَةٌ كَبِيرَةٌ .

Red-book, *n.* A register of all persons in the service of the state, دُسْتُورُ (or دَفْتَرُ قَيْدِ) مَأْمُورِي ٱلدَّوْلَةِ .

Redbreast, *n.* عُصْفُورٌ أَحْمَرُ ٱلصَّدْرِ .

Red-chalk, *n.* طَبَاشِيرُ أَحْمَرُ .

Redcoat, *n.* *See* Soldier, *n.*

Redden, *v.t.* To make red, حَمَّرَ. To make to blush خَجَّلَ ـ خَشَّمَ .

Redden, *v.i.* To become red, إِحْمَرَّ ـ إِحْمَارَّ. To blush, خَجِلَ ² ـ قُلِبَ أَحْمَرَ ـ ² فَارَ وَجْهُهُ ـ إِسْتَحْيَى .

Reddish, *a.* أَحْمَرَانِيٌّ ـ مُحْمَرٌّ ـ يَضْرِبُ إِلَى ٱلْحُمْرَةِ .

Reddishness, *n.* ضَرْبٌ إِلَى ٱلْحُمْرَةِ .

Reddition, *n* Surrender, return, تَسْلِيمٌ ـ رَدٌّ .

Redeem, *v.t.* To purchase back, فَدَى ². To —, as a pledge, فَكَّ ² ـ إِفْتَكَّ. To save, deliver, خَلَّصَ ـ إِسْتَنْقَذَ; to set at liberty, أَعْتَقَ ـ أَطْلَقَ. To — one with, فَدَى ب ²; to — one from, فَدَى مِن ². To — one's self, فَدَى نَفْسَهُ ـ إِفْتَدَى ². To — one's promise, وَفَى بِٱلْوَعْدِ ـ قَامَ ² بِٱلْوَعْدِ ـ كَمَّلَ وَعْدَهُ *aor.* يَفِي. He redeemed him from slavery, فَدَاهُ مِنَ ٱلْأَسْرِ. *See also to* Ransom, *v.t.*

Redeemable, *a.* That may be purchased back, فِدَاهُ ـ يُفْدَى; that may be redeemed, as a pledge, يَنْفَكُّ ـ يُفَكُّ ـ مُمْكِنٌ; that may be saved, خَلَاصُهُ مُمْكِنٌ ـ مِمَّا يُخَلَّصُ ـ مِمَّا يُسْتَنْقَذُ .

Redeemableness, *n.* The state of being redeemable, purchased back, إِمْكَانُ ـ إِمْكَانُ ٱلْفِدَى; as of a pledge, إِمْكَانُ ٱلْفَكِّ ٱلْإِسْتِرْجَاعِ .

Redeemed, *a.* Purchased back, مَفْدِيٌّ ـ فِدَآءٌ ـ مَفْدِيٌّ; of a pledge, مَفْكُوكٌ. The —, أَهْلُ ٱلْخَلَاصِ. To be redeemed, فُدِيَ .

Redeemer, *n.* مُخَلِّصٌ ـ فَادٍ. The Redeemer, ٱلْمُخَلِّصُ .

Redeeming, *a.* Tending to repair, make up for, مُسِدٌّ ـ جَابِرٌ .

Re-deliver, *v.t.* To liberate again, خَلَّصَ ثَانِيَةً ـ أَطْلَقَ ثَانِيَةً ـ أَعَادَ فَكَّهُ. To re-distribute, عَادَ ² فَسَلَّمَ آل.... ـ وَزَّعَ ثَانِيَةً. *See also to* Repay, *v.t.*

Re-deliverance, *n.* A second act of liberation, إِطْلَاقٌ ثَانٍ ـ إِعَادَةُ تَخْلِيصٍ; the being delivered a second time, خَلَاصٌ ثَانٍ .

Redelivery, *n.* A second delivery, distribution, تَوْزِيعٌ ثَانٍ. A delivering back, رَدٌّ .

Redemand, *v.t.* طَلَبَ ² ثَانِيَةً ـ إِسْتَرْجَعَ ـ إِسْتَرَدَّ .

Redemandable, *a.* يُطْلَبُ ثَانِيَةً ـ مِمَّا يُسْتَرْجَعُ ـ مِمَّا يُسْتَرَدُّ .

Redemption, *n.* Repurchase of what is taken, seized, فِدًى ـ فِدَآءٌ ـ فِدًى; of a pledge, فُكُوكٌ ـ فَكٌّ. Deliverance, خَلَاصٌ ـ إِسْتِنْقَاذٌ ـ إِسْتِخْلَاصٌ. Redemption of a debt, إِفْتِدَآءُ دَيْنٍ. The price paid for —, فِدْيَةٌ ـ فِدَآءٌ ـ فِدًى ـ فَدًى .

Redemptioner, *n.* فَادِي نَفْسِهِ ـ مُفْتَدٍ .

Redemptive, *a.* فَادٍ .

Redemptory, *a.* مَدْفُوعٌ لِلْفِدَآءِ .

Red-hot, *a.* مُحْمًى ـ حَامٍ .

Redintegrate, *v.t.* أَصْلَحَ. To be redintegrated, إِنْصَلَحَ ـ إِسْتَتَبَّ .

Redintegration, *n.* The act of, إِصْلَاحٌ; of being redintegrated, إِسْتِتْبَابٌ ـ إِنْصِلَاحٌ .

Redisburse, *v.t.* *See to* Repay, Refund, *v.t.*

Redistribute, *v.t.* قَسَّمَ ثَانِيَةً ـ عَادَ ² فَوَزَّعَهُ .

Redistribution, *n.* تَقْسِيمٌ ثَانٍ ـ إِعَادَةُ تَوْزِيعٍ .

Red-lead, *n.* سَلَاقُونُ .

Red-letter day, *n.* One of the great festival days, عِبَارَةٌ عَنْ عِيدٍ مِنَ ٱلْأَعْيَادِ ٱلْكِبَارِ. A fortunate day, يَوْمٌ مُبَارَكٌ ـ يَوْمٌ بَخِيتٌ .

Redness, *n.* إِحْمِرَارٌ ـ حُمْرَةٌ. Redness of the sky before and after sunset, نُورُ ٱلشَّفَقِ ـ نَائِرَةٌ .

Redolence, *n.* } رَائِحَةٌ ذَكِيَّةٌ ـ رَائِحَةٌ ـ عِطْرٌ ـ نَفْحَةٌ ـ فَوْغَةٌ
Redolency, } (or طَيِّبَةٌ).

Redolent, *a.* Redolent of, مُعْرِفٌ ب ـ مُتَنَسِّمٌ ب. To be — of, عَرِفَ ² ب .

Redouble, *v.t.* To double or fold again, عَادَ فَثَنَّاهُ ـ طَبَّقَ ثَانِيَةً. To make twice twofold, ضَعَّفَ ثَانِيَةً ـ ضَاعَفَ. To increase, reiterate, أَزَادَ ـ كَثَّرَ. To — one's efforts, تَصَلَّبَ فِي ـ تَشَدَّدَ ل .

Redouble, *v.i.* To become twice as much, تَضَاعَفَ .

Redoubt, *n.* طَابِيَةٌ *pl.* طَوَابِي ـ حِصْنٌ *pl.* حُصُونٌ .

Redoubtable, *a.* *See* Formidable, *a.*

Redound, *v.i.* To — to, to proceed in consequence of an effect, سَبَّبَ ـ يَؤُولُ *aor.* آلَ إِلَى ـ أَوْجَبَ ـ إِسْتَجْلَبَ. To conduce to, آلَ إِلَى. To increase, زَادَ ل ². To fall back upon, عَادَ ² إِلَى ـ عَدَّى إِلَى. This redounds to his credit, إِزْدَادَ بِذٰلِكَ شَرَفًا .

Redraw, *v.t.* To make a second draft of, عَمِلَ تَسْوِيدًا ثَانِيًا مِنْهُ ; to draw again, صَوَّرَ-ثَانِيَةً.

Redress, *v.t.* To set right, عَدَّلَ ـ أَصْلَحَ ـ صَحَّحَ ـ قَوَّمَ. To remedy, عَالَجَ ـ جَبَرَ [2]. To deliver, as of the oppressed, from wrong, أَغَاثَ ٱلْمَظْلُومِينَ ـ خَلَّصَ حُقُوقَ ٱلْمَظْلُومِينَ ـ أَنْصَفَ ـ سَدَّ ٱلشِّكَايَةَ [2].

Redress, *n.* A remedy, مُعَالَجَة ـ جُبُور ـ جَبْر. A remedy for wrong, or for oppression, إِغَاثَة ـ سِدَادُ ٱلشِّكَايَةِ ـ تَخْلِيصُ حَقٍّ ـ إِنْصَاف ـ ٱلْمَظْلُومِينَ.

Redresser, *n.* Of grievances, مُغِيثُ ٱلْمَظْلُومِينَ ـ مُسِدُّ ٱلشِّكَايَةِ ـ مُنْصِف.

Redressible, *a.* That may be remedied, مِمَّا يُجْتَبَرُ ـ مِمَّا يُعَالَجُ ـ مِمَّا يُجْبَرُ ; that may be relieved, as grievances, مِمَّا يَنْسَدُّ ـ مِمَّا يُنْصَفُ ـ مِمَّا يُسَاعَفُ ـ يَسْتَدُّ.

Redressive, *a.* Remedial, مُجَبِّر ـ مُعَالِج ; of wrongs, مُسِدٌّ ـ مُخَلِّص مِن ـ مُبَطِّل.

Redressless, *a.* Having no remedy, بِلَا مُعَالَجَةٍ ـ لَا عِلَاجَ لَهُ ; as from wrong, لَا إِسْعَافَ لَهُ ـ لَا يَنْسَدُّ ـ لَا مَسَدَّ لَهُ.

Reduce, *v.t.* To bring back again رَدَّ [2] : he reduced the thing to its original shape, رَدَّ ٱلشَّيْءَ إِلَى أَصْلِهِ [2]. To diminish in size, قَصَّرَ ـ أَوْجَزَ ; in numbers, قَلَّلَ ـ أَقَلَّ ; in length, صَغَّرَ ـ أَصْغَرَ ; in width, ضَيَّقَ ; as in price, to abate, أَنْقَصَ ـ نَقَّصَ. To lighten, خَفَّفَ. To —, as a copy into a smaller scale, رَدَّ-إِلَى صُورَةٍ صُغْرَى ـ صَغَّرَ ٱلرَّسْمَ [2] : he reduced the fourth to a fifth part, رَدَّ ٱلرُّبْعَ خُمْسًا [2]. To —, as a bone, joint, جَبَرَ [2] ـ رَدَّ ـ جَبَّرَ [2]. To bring into subjection, قَهَرَ ـ أَقْمَعَ ـ قَمَعَ ـ ضَبَطَ [2] ـ جَعَلَ-تَحْتَ ٱلطَّاعَةِ. To capture, take, فَتَحَ ـ أَجْحَفَ بِ ـ تَمَلَّكَ-قَهْرًا ـ غَلَبَ عَلَى. To impair, injure, أَجْحَفَ بِ. To degrade, حَطَّ-عَن [2] ـ عَزَلَ ـ أَسْقَطَ ـ أَسْقَطَ ـ أَضَرَّ. *See also under* Rank, *n.*

To reduce to, constrain to, أَلْزَمَ-بِ ـ جَبَرَ [2] ـ اِضْطَرَّ-عَلَى ـ حَوَّلَ-إِلَى ـ أَحْوَجَ-إِلَى ـ أَلْجَأَ-إِلَى. To make or convert into, حَوَّلَ-إِلَى ـ أَعَادَ ـ صَيَّرَ ـ جَعَلَ. To restrain to or within, حَصَرَ-فِي [2].

To reduce to order, good arrangement, نَظَّمَ ـ رَتَّبَ ; to good discipline, سَاسَ *aor.* يَسُوسُ ـ قَامَ بِ [2] ـ دَبَّرَ. To be reduced to good order, اِسْتَتَبَّ.

To reduce to poverty, أَفْقَرَ ـ أَعْدَمَ.

To reduce to reason, هَدَى-إِلَى ٱلصَّوَابِ ـ أَقْنَعَ ـ ضَبَطَ [2].

To reduce to silence, سَكَّتَ ـ قَطَعَ بِ ـ قَطَعَ لِسَانَهُ ; as by an argument, رَمَى-بِسُكَاتَةٍ وَصُمَاتَةٍ ـ قَطَعَ-بِٱلْحُجَّةِ.

To reduce to straits, ضَيَّقَ عَلَى ـ عَسَّرَ عَلَى.

To be reduced, made less, صَغُرَ ; in numbers, قَلَّلَ ; in length, قَصَّرَ ; in width, ضُيِّقَ ; in price, نَقَصَ ـ أُسْقِطَ ; in weight, خُفِّفَ ; in quantity, آلَ *aor.* يَؤُولُ : It was cooked till it was reduced to a third, طُبِخَ حَتَّى آلَ إِلَى ٱلثُّلْثِ. To be reduced to good order, اِسْتَتَبَّ.

To be reduced to, to be obliged to, أُضْطُرَّ إِلَى ـ أُلْجِئَ إِلَى. To be in reduced circumstances, ضَاقَ عَلَيْهِ مَعَاشُهُ ـ أَعْسَرَ ـ اِفْتَقَرَ ـ كَانَ فِي ضِيقَةٍ. To be reduced or brought to, آلَ *aor.* يَؤُولُ : The case became reduced to this, آلَ ٱلْأَمْرُ إِلَى كَذَا.

Reducible, *a.* That may be brought back, مِمَّا يُرَدُّ ; that may be lessened in size, مِمَّا يُصَغَّرُ ; in numbers, مِمَّا يُقَلَّلُ ; in length, مِمَّا يُقَصَّرُ ; in price, مِمَّا يُنْقَصُ ـ مِمَّا يُرَخَّصُ ; that may be made into, مِمَّا يُصَيَّرُ. It is — to such a meaning, يَرْجِعُ إِلَى مَعْنَى كَذَا.

Reduction, *n.* The act of bringing back, as to a former condition, رَدٌّ إِلَى ; the being so brought back, اِرْتِدَاد. The act of — in size, تَصْغِير ; in numbers, تَقْلِيل ـ إِقْلَال ; in length, إِيجَاز ـ تَقْصِير ; in width, تَضْيِيق ; in price, تَنْقِيص ـ تَرْخِيص ـ إِسْقَاط ; in weight, تَخْفِيف. Reduction, as of a copy into a smaller size, تَصْغِيرُ ٱلرَّسْمِ. Reduction, as of a joint, جَبْر ـ رَدٌّ ـ تَجْبِير. The act of bringing into subjection, إِقْمَاع ـ قَمْع ـ غَلَبَة عَلَى ـ قَهْر ; of capturing, تَمَلُّكٌ قَهْرًا ـ ضَبْط ـ فَتْح ; of degrading, إِسْقَاط ـ عَزْل ـ تَعْزِيل ; of obliging, constraining, إِلْزَام ـ إِلْجَاء ـ اِضْطِرَار ـ جَبْر ـ جُبُور ; of turning or making into, إِعَادَة ـ تَحْوِيل ـ تَصْيِير ـ جَعْل ـ رَدٌّ إِلَى ـ تَأْوِيل. Reduction to order, تَنْظِيم ـ تَرْتِيب ; to poverty, إِعْدَام ; to silence, تَسْكِيت ـ قَطْعُ لِسَانٍ ; to straits, تَضْيِيقٌ عَلَى ـ تَعْسِيرٌ عَلَى. The rule of reduction, in arithmetic, قَاعِدَةُ حِسَابِ ٱلتَّحْوِيلِ ; of fractions by a common divisor, الحَطّ ; in algebra, المُعَادَلَة.

Redundance, *n.* } Redundancy, } فَضْل ـ بَذَارَة ـ طُفُوح ـ شِفّ ـ شَفِيف ـ زِيَادَة ـ كَثْرَة ـ فَرْط ; of words, كَلَامٌ زَائِدٌ ـ فَوْضَلَة. There is a — in this over this, لِهٰذَا عَلَى هٰذَا شِفٌّ. *See also* Exuberance, *n.*

Redundant, *a.* زَائِد ـ فَاضِل ـ مُوَفَّر ـ طَافِح ـ مُسْتَدْرَك ; of words, زَائِد. To be —, زَادَ ـ أَنَافَ عَلَى ـ فَضَلَ ـ شَفَّ ـ تَفَوْضَلَ ـ كَانَ زَائِدًا. He said what was —, قَالَ قَوْلًا شِفًّا.

Redundantly, *ad.* فَرْطًا ـ مَعَ ٱلزِّيَادَةِ ـ كِفَايَةً وَزِيَادَةً ـ زِيَادَةً.

Reduplicate, *v.t.* ضَعَّفَ ـ ضَاعَفَ. *See also to* Double, *v.t.*

Reduplication, *n.* إِضَافَة ـ تَضْعِيف ـ مُضَاعَفَة.

Re-echo, *v.t.* رَدَّ ٱلصَّدَى [2] ـ أَصْدَى-ثَانِيَةً.

Re-echo, *v.i.* أَعَادَ ٱلصَّدَى.

Re-echo, *n.* رَدُّ ٱلصَّدَى.

Reed, *n.* The plant, قَصَبَة *coll.* قَصَب; a long —, غَابَة *coll.* غَاب. A musical pipe, شَبَّابَةٌ مِنْ قَصَبٍ ـ زَمَّارَة ـ مِزْمَار ـ نَاى. A measuring —, قَصَبَةُ ٱلْقِيَاسِ. The bark of a —, لِيطَة ـ لِيط. A player on a —, زَمَّار, *fem.* زَمَّارَة. *See also* Arrow, Pen, *n.*

Reeden, *a.* قَصَبِيّ ـ مِنْ قَصَب.

Re-edification, *n.* تَجْدِيد ـ إِعَادَةُ تَعْمِيرٍ ـ تَعْمِيرٌ ثَانٍ. The being re-edified, brought into order, إِسْتِتْبَاب.

Re-edify, *v.t.* عَادَ فَعَمَّرَهُ ـ عَمَّرَ ثَانِيَةً. To be re-edified, brought into order, إِسْتَتَبَّ.

Reedy, *a.* مِقْصَاب. Reedy land, أَرْضٌ مَقْصَبَةٌ. A — place, غَرِيف ـ غَيْضَة.

Reef, *v.t.* Of a sail, لَمَّ ٱلْقِلْعَ (or ٱلشِّرَاعَ). To single —, لَمَّ ٱلْقِلْعَ طَاقًا. To double —, لَمَّ ٱلْقِلْعَ طَاقَيْنِ. To close —, لَمَّ جَمِيعَ ٱلطَّاقَاتِ.

Reef, *n.* Of a sail, طَاقٌ مِنَ ٱلشِّرَاعِ ـ ثِنْيٌ مِنَ ٱلْقِلْعِ *pl.* أَثْنَاء ـ *pl.* طَاقَات. The loop (of a sail,) زَنْد *pl.* زُنُود; the cord for reefing, عُرْوَة *pl.* عُرًى *vulg.* عَرَاوِى. A cluster of rocks near the surface of water, شِعْب ـ زِرْبَة ـ زَرْبَة ـ جُهْن ـ أَتَانُ ٱلضَّحْلِ *pl.* شِعَاب.

Reefy, *a.* ذُو شِعَاب.

Reek, *n.* فَوْحَة ـ بُخَار.

Reek, *v.i.* فَاحَ مِنْهُ بُخَار ـ فَاحَتْ مِنْهُ فَوْحَات.

Reeky, *a.* Blackened, as with smoke, مُسَخَّم ـ مُسَوَّد ـ مُدَخَّن. *See also under* Foul, *a.*

Reel, *n.* To wind thread, *etc.*, upon, مِسْلَكَة ـ مِطْوًى. A stagger, إِرْتِنَاح ـ تَمَاوُج. A kind of dance, ضَرْبٌ مِنَ ٱلرَّقْصِ.

Reel, *v.t.* To wind, لَفَّ عَلَى ٱلْمِسْلَكَةِ ـ سَلَّكَ.

Reel, *v.i.* To totter in walking, تَفَرَّكَ ـ سَعْسَعَ; like a drunken man, إِرْتَنَحَ ـ تَرَنَّحَ ـ تَمَيَّحَ ـ كَعْتَرَ فِى مَشْيِهِ. He or it reeled and staggered, صَارَ يَمِيلُ مَيْلَ ٱلْعَرُوسِ أَوْ مَنْ دَامَتْ عَلَيْهِ ٱلْمُدَامُ كُؤُوسًا. To go round, دَارَ ـ فَتَلَ ـ بَرِمَ. My head reeled, دَاخَ رَأْسِى *aor.* يَدُوخُ.

Re-elect, *v.t.* عَادَ فَٱنْتَخَبَهُ ـ إِنْتَخَبَ ثَانِيَةً.

Re-election, *n.* إِعَادَةُ ٱلْإِنْتِخَابِ ـ إِنْتِخَابٌ ثَانٍ; one re-elected again, مُنْتَخَبٌ ثَانِيَةً.

Re-eligibility, *n.* صَلَاحِيَّةٌ لِلْإِنْتِخَابِ ـ لِيَاقَةٌ بِٱلنُّخْبَةِ ثَانِيَةً ثَانِيَةً.

Re-eligible, *a.* أَهْلٌ لِلْإِنْتِخَابِ ثَانِيَةً ـ أَهْلٌ لِلنُّخْبَةِ ثَانِيَةً.

Reeling, *n.* The act of winding, تَسْلِيك ـ تَلْفِيف; of staggering, تَفَرُّك ـ سَعْسَعَة ـ سَعْسَع; like a drunken man, تَرَنُّح ـ تَمَيُّح.

Re-embark, *v.t.* نَزَّلَ فِى ٱلسَّفِينَةِ ثَانِيَةً ـ رَكَّبَ ٱلْمَرْكَبَ ثَانِيَةً.

Re-embark, *v.i.* عَادَ فَنَزَلَ إِلَى ـ رَكِبَ ٱلْمَرْكَبَ ثَانِيَةً ٱلْمَرْكَبِ.

Re-embarkation, *n.* The act of putting on board ship again, تَنْزِيلٌ إِلَى ٱلْمَرْكَبِ ثَانِيَةً; going on board ship again, رُكُوب إِعَادَةُ نُزُولٍ إِلَى ٱلْمَرْكَبِ ـ ٱلْمَرْكَبِ ثَانِيَةً.

Re-embody, *v.t.* To collect together again in a body, جَمَّعَ ثَانِيَةً; to re-inclose, أَدْرَجَ ثَانِيَةً ـ عَادَ فَدَرَّجَهُ; to unite again, as in a mass, عَادَ فَجَمَّعَ فِى.

Reeming, *n.* فَتْحُ خُرُوزِ ٱلسَّفِينَةِ لِأَجْلِ ٱلْجَلْفَطَةِ (or ٱلْقَلْفَطَةِ).

Re-enact, *v.t.* وَضَعَ قَانُونًا ثَانِيَةً ـ عَادَ فَحَكَمَ بِ ـ سَنَّ ثَانِيَةً *aor.* يَضَعُ.

Re-enactment, *n.* إِشْتِرَاعٌ ثَانٍ ـ إِعَادَةُ وَضْعٍ ـ إِعَادَةُ شَرْعٍ.

Re-enforce, *v.t.* To put into force again, عَادَ ـ أَجْرَى ثَانِيَةً فَقَضَى بِ. To strengthen with fresh troops, أَمَدَّ بِعَسْكَرٍ.

Re-enforce, *n.* The — of a cannon, أَشَدُّ جِرْمِ ٱلْمِدْفَعِ.

Re-enforcement, *n.* The act of putting into force again, إِجْرَاء إِعَادَةُ إِجْرَاءٍ ـ ثَانٍ; of strengthening, as with fresh troops, إِمْدَاد; the soldiers sent for that purpose, مَدَدٌ مِنَ ٱلْعَسْكَرِ. To ask for a —, إِسْتَمَدَّ.

Re-engage, *v.t.* To engage again to work, إِسْتَخْدَمَ ثَانِيَةً. To mix one up with anything a second time, شَبَّكَ ثَانِيَةً. To hire again, عَادَ فَٱسْتَأْجَرَ... ـ عَادَ فَأَكْرَى... To promise again, عَادَ فَتَعَهَّدَ بِكَذَا. To encounter, fight, again, عَادَ فَبَارَزَ... ـ قَاتَلَ ثَانِيَةً.

Re-engagement, *n.* The act of taking into service again, إِسْتِخْدَامٌ ثَانٍ; of hiring again, إِعَادَةُ إِكْرَاءٍ ـ إِسْتِئْجَارٌ ثَانٍ; of promising again, إِعَادَةُ تَعَهُّدٍ; of fighting again, مُقَاتَلَة ـ مُبَارَزَةٌ ثَانِيَةً مُحَارَبَةٌ ثَانِيَةً ـ ثَانِيَةً.

Re-enlist, *v.t.* As of soldiers, عَادَ فَقَيَّدَ فِى ـ جَنَّدَ ثَانِيَةً دَفْتَرِ ٱلْعَسْكَرِ.

Re-enlist, *v.i.* Of soldiers, عَادَ فَدَخَلَ فِى ٱلْعَسْكَرِ ـ تَجَنَّدَ ثَانِيَةً.

Re-enlistment, *n.* The act of, إِعَادَةُ تَقْيِيدٍ فِى ـ تَجْنِيدٌ ثَانٍ ٱلْعَسْكَرِ; of being re-enlisted, دُخُولٌ فِى ٱلْعَسْكَرِ ثَانِيَةً ـ تَجَنُّدٌ ثَانٍ.

Re-enter, *v.t.* عَادَ فَدَخَلَ فِى ـ دَخَلَ ثَانِيَةً.

Re-entering, *a.* Of an angle, دَاخِلِيّ. A — angle, of a fortification, زَاوِيَةٌ دَاخِلِيَّةٌ مِنَ ٱلْإِسْتِحْكَامِ.

Re-entrance, *n.* إعادةُ دُخولٍ ـ دُخولٌ ثانٍ.

Reermouse, *n.* *See* Bat, the animal, *n.*

Re-establish, *v.t.* To confirm or prove again, أثبتَ-ثانيةً; to set on foot again, أقامَ-ثانيةً ـ أنشأ-ثانيةً; to put into place, office, again, أعادَ-إلى خِدمَتِهِ ـ رَجَّعَ-إلى مَنصِبِهِ; to reform, put in order, again, عَدَّلَ ـ أصلَحَ. To renew, جَدَّدَ. To be re-established, put into order, إستتبَّ. *See also to* Re-enact, *v.t.*

Re-establishment, *n.* The act of confirming anew, إثباتٌ ثانٍ; of setting on foot again, إقامةٌ ثانيةٌ ـ تعقيدٌ ثانٍ; of restoring to order, تعديلٌ ـ إصلاحٌ; the being restored to health, شَفى. The being put into order again, إستتباب.

Reeve, *n.* وَكيلٌ *pl.* وُكلاءُ.

Reeve, *v.t.* سَلَكَ ² ـ أسلَكَ.

Re-examination, *n.* Re-inquiry, بحثٌ ثانٍ; reconsideration, إعادةُ تأمُّلٍ ـ إطِّلاعٌ ثانٍ. The act of trying again, إمتحانٌ ثانٍ. On —, reconsideration, مِن بعدِ إعادةِ المُطالعةِ.

Re-examine, *v.t.* To inquire into again, بحثَ في-ثانيةً; to consider again, إطَّلعَ على-ثانيةً; to test again, إمتحنَ-ثانيةً; to try again, as of weights, *etc.*, عادَ فاعتبرهُ ² ـ عَيَّرَ-ثانيةً.

Re-export, *v.t.* To export imports, أرسلَ البضائعَ المُجتلَبةَ إلى الخارجِ.

Re-export, *n.* Any commodity exported again, بضائعُ مُجتلَبةٌ مرسولةٌ إلى الخارجِ ثانيةً.

Re-exportation, *n.* إرسالُ البضائعِ المُجتلَبةِ إلى الخارجِ.

Refashion, *v.t.* شَكَّلَ-ثانيةً ـ صَوَّرَ-ثانيةً.

Refection, *n.* لُقمةٌ.

Refective, *a.* مُنفِّس ـ مُريِّح ـ مُحيِي.

Refectory, *n.* مأكَل ـ بيتُ الأكلِ ـ مَحَلُّ المائدةِ.

Refel, *v.t.* *See to* Refute, *v.t.*

Refer, *v.t.* and *i.* To send one to, as for information, *etc.*, وَجَّهَ-إلى ـ أوَّلَ-إلى ـ آلَ-إلى *aor.* يؤولُ ـ رَدَّ-على ² ـ أرسلَ-إلى ـ بعثَ-إلى ـ أحالَ-على ـ حَوَّلَ-على. To —, as of a matter, to, عرضَ-على ـ أوردَ-على. To guide or point out to, دَلَّ-على ². To — anything, as to a judge or other authority, for adjudication, رافعَ-إلى. To — to, to support by reference to, أسندَ-إلى ـ رفعَ-إلى. To ascribe to, نَسَبَ-إلى ²; to ascribe to, as laying the blame upon, حَمَلَ-على. To defer, to postpone something till...., أخَّرَ-إلى ـ أبقى-إلى. To — to, to have relation with, تعلَّقَ ب. To allude to, to be in allusion to, كَنَى عن ² ـ أشارَ-إلى ـ عَنَى ب. He referred the choice to him, فَوَّضَهُ بالإختيارِ ـ فوَّضَ إليهِ الإختيارَ. Every difficult matter is referred to him, كُلُّ مُشكِلةٍ تُرَدُّ عليهِ. The affair between them was referred to the governor, أُحيلتِ الدعوى ما بينهم إلى الحاكمِ. He referred his complaint to ..., أبلغَ شكواهُ إلى. I referred the matter to the Sultan, رفعتُ الأمرَ إلى السُّلطانِ. He referred him for payment to, أحالَ-على; he was referred for payment to, إحتالَ على-بدفعِ المَبلغِ. He referred the tradition to such a source, رفعَ الحديثَ إلى كذا. Whoso is referred (for the payment of a debt,) to a solvent man, let him accept the reference, مَن أُتبِعَ على مَليٍّ فليَتبَعْ. The correspondent referred to, المُكاتِبُ المومأُ إليهِ.

Referable, *a.* That may be brought before, ascribed to, يُرفَعُ إلى; that may be ascribed or attributed to, يَرجِعُ إلى ـ ينتسبُ إلى. That may be charged against, laid at the door of, يُحمَلُ على. It is — to such a thing, يَرجِعُ إلى كذا.

Referee, *n.* وَكيلٌ عُرفيٌّ ـ فيصليٌّ ـ فيصل. *See also* Arbiter, *n.*

Reference, *n.* The act of referring, as to a person, تأويلٌ ـ ترجيعٌ ـ رُجوعٌ ـ رَدٌّ. Information, إستفهام ـ بيان ـ خبر. Recommendation, توجيهٌ. A person referred to as recommending, المُوصَّى ب ـ صاحِبُ التوجيهِ. Relation with, تعلُّق مع ـ علاقةٌ مع. Allusion, عبارةٌ ـ إيماءٌ ـ إشارةٌ ـ رمزٌ ـ كنايةٌ. Reference, as to an authority for confirmation, إسنادٌ إلى ـ رفعٌ إلى. A mark alluding to a foot-note, إشارةٌ *pl.* إشاراتٌ. With reference to, إعتبارًا بكذا ـ بخصوصِ كذا ـ مِن جهةِ كذا. On reference to, عِندَ المُراجعةِ إلى ـ بعدَ الرفعِ إلى ـ باعتبارِ كذا. To give one a — to, وجَّهَ-إلى. To accept a — from a debtor to another for payment, تبِعَ.

Referential, *a.* يَرجِعُ إلى ـ مُشيرٌ إلى.

Referrible, *a.* *See* Referable, *a.*

Refine, *v.t.* To clear from impurities, كَرَّرَ ـ أخلصَ ـ خلَّصَ; of metals, مَحَّصَ. To clarify, صفَّى. To —, as by picking out what is inferior, نقَّى ـ نقَّحَ. To improve in accuracy, حرَّرَ ـ ضَبَطَ ². To make fine, thin, slender, أدقَّ ـ دقَّقَ. To —, as in manners, هذَّبَ ـ أدَّبَ. To — in style, language, حَبَرَ ² ـ نقَّحَ ـ حرَّرَ ـ حبَّرَ. To make elegant, ظرَّفَ ـ وشَّى.

Refine, *v.i.* To become clear, تصفَّى. To become thin, fine, دَقَّ *aor.* يَدِقُّ ـ إستدقَّ. To be subtile or nice in speech, دقَّ في كلامِهِ. To — on, to outvie, فاضَلَ.

Refined, *a.* Free from impurities, مُصفًّى ـ خالِص ـ مُخلَّص ـ

— مُكرَّر. Fine, high, thin, رَفِيع — دَقِيق. Elegant, لَطِيف — ظَرِيف — كَيِّس. Subtile, nice, abstruse, مُدَقِّق — دِقّ.

Refinedly, *ad.* With affected nicety, بِتَأَنُّق — تَظَرُّفًا — تَجَوُّدًا.

Refinement, *n.* The act of freeing from impurities, تَخْلِيص — تَصْفِيَة — تَكْرَار — تَكْرِير; of metals, تَمْحِيص. The state of being so refined, خَلَاص — خَالِصَة — صِفْوَة — صَفَآء. Polish of language, ضَبْط (or تَحْبِير) ٱلْكَلَام — دِقَّة فِي ٱلْكَلَام. Moral —, طَهَارَة — زَكَاة. Polish of manners, كَمَال — لَطَافَة — ظَرَافَة — كِيَاسَة. Excess of —, تَظَرُّف — تَجَوُّد. To affect —, زَوَّدَ تَدْقِيق — زَوَّدَ دِقَّة — رَفَاعَة.

Refiner, *n.* As of metals, مُمَحِّص. A clarifier, مُصَفٍّ. A —, as of sugar, spirits, *etc.*, مُكَرِّر. A — in style, مُحَبِّر — مُدَقِّق. A — of silver, مُمَحِّص ٱلْفِضَّة.

Refinery, *n.* مَعْمَل — مَعْمَل ٱلتَّكْرَار. A sugar —, مَعْمَل سُكَّر.

Refit, *v.t.* To put in order, to repair, set up, قَوَّمَ — أَصْلَحَ. To — a ship, عَمَّرَ ٱلْمَرْكَب بِمَا ٱحْتَاجَ إِلَيْهِ — جَهَّزَ ٱلْمَرْكَب وَأَعَدَّهُ.

Refit, *v.i.* Of a ship, تَجَهَّزَ ٱلْمَرْكَب بِمَا ٱحْتَاجَ إِلَيْهِ.

Refitment, *n.* A second fitting out, تَجْهِيز ثَانٍ; the being fitted out again, جِهَاز ثَانٍ — تَجَهُّز ثَانٍ.

Reflect, *v.t.* As of light, عَكَسَ. To throw back, رَدَّ — دَفَعَ.

Reflect, *v.i.* As of light, اِنْعَكَسَ. To be thrown back, اِرْتَدَّ. To — upon, to consider attentively, نَظَرَ فِي — طَالَعَ عَلَى — تَفَكَّرَ فِي — تَأَمَّلَ — أَضْمَرَ عَلَى. To censure, reproach, criticize, لَامَ — ذَمَّ — عَيَّرَ — عَيَّبَ — تَهَكَّمَ — عَابَ — نَدَّدَ بِ. To — or bring blame upon, جَلَبَ ٱلْعَارَ عَلَى — أَوْجَبَ ٱلْعَارَ عَلَى — أَخْجَلَ.

Reflected, *a.* As of light, مَعْكُوس — مُنْعَكِس. To be —, اِنْعَكَسَ.

Reflectible, *a.* قَابِل ٱلِٱنْعِكَاس.

Reflecting, *n.* Throwing back, دَافِع — رَادّ; of light, عَاكِس. Thoughtful, مُتَفَكِّر — فَكِّير — مُفْتَكِر — رَزِين.

Reflectingly, *ad.* Thoughtfully, تَفَكُّرًا — بِمُلَاحَظَة — بِتَفَكُّر.

Reflection, *n.* The act of reflecting light, عَكْس; the being reflected, اِنْعِكَاس; the — from a mirror, صُورَة مُنْعَكِسَة — خَيَال. Operation of the mind, thought, مُلَاحَظَة — إِتْقَان — مُرَادَّة فِكْر — تَأَمُّل — تَفَكُّر; reflections, تَأَمُّلَات. Censure, criticism, اِخْتِكَار — تَعْيِير — تَعْيِيب — مَذَمَّة — مَلَام — لَوْم — تَهَكُّم. Result of — or thought, إِفَادَة.

Reflective, *a.* Throwing back, دَافِع — رَادّ — مُرِدّ. Considering things past, مُفْتَكِر بِٱلْقَدِيم — رَادّ ٱلْغَائِب.

Reflector, *n.* آلَة عَاكِسَة ٱلنُّور أَوِ ٱلْحَرَارَة.

Reflex, *a.* مَعْكُوس — مُرْتَدّ.

Reflexibility, *n.* قَابِلِيَّة ٱلِٱنْعِكَاس (or ٱلِٱعْتِكَاس).

Reflexible, *a.* قَابِل ٱلِٱنْعِكَاس — يَنْعَكِس — مِمَّا يَنْعَكِس.

Reflexive, *a.* Having reference to the past, مُتَعَلِّق بِمَا مَضَى — ذَاكِر ٱلْمَاضِي.

Reflexively, *ad.* In a backward direction, إِلَى خَلْف — إِلَى وَرَآء — تَرْدَادًا. With a regard to censure, بِوَجْه ٱللَّوْم — بِطَرِيقَة ٱلْمَلَام — اِخْتِكَارًا.

Reflorescence, *n.* إِعَادَة تَزْهِير — تَزْهِير ثَانٍ.

Refluence, *n.* }
Refluency, } جَزْر — رُجُوع — اِرْتِدَاد.

Refluent, *a.* جَازِر — رَاجِع — مُرْتَدّ.

Reflux, *n.* جَزْر — رُجُوع — اِرْتِدَاد.

Refoment, *v.t.* To apply a fomentation again, عَادَ فَكَمَّدَ ٱلـ... To excite anew, عَادَ فَأَضْرَمَ ٱلـ... — قَوَّمَ ثَانِيَة — هَبَّلَ ثَانِيَة — عَادَ فَهَيَّجَ ٱلـ...

Reform, *v.t.* To bring back to its former state, اِسْتَعَادَ إِلَى مَا — رَجَّعَ إِلَى مَا كَانَ عَلَيْهِ — كَانَ عَلَيْهِ. To renew, جَدَّدَ. To remodel, شَكَّلَ ثَانِيَة — صَاغَ ثَانِيَة — صَوَّرَ ثَانِيَة. To correct, put in better order, رَتَّبَ — نَظَّمَ — صَحَّحَ — أَصْلَحَ — رَتَقَ. To —, as the manners of, mode of living, نَظَّمَ سِيرَة فُلَان — هَذَّبَ — ثَقَّفَ — ثَقَّفَ أَخْلَاق فُلَان. To —, as soldiers into another line, صَفَّفَ — عَادَ فَصَفَّفَ ٱلْعَسْكَر — ٱلْعَسْكَر ثَانِيَة. To be reformed, of arrangements, اِسْتَتَبَّ.

Reform, *v.i.* As one in his manners, mode of living, صَلَحَ — تَهَذَّبَ — تَثَقَّفَ — اِسْتَصْلَحَ. To form again, as of soldiers into a line, or in proper order, اِنْتَظَمُوا — تَنَظَّمُوا ثَانِيَة — تَصَافُّوا ثَانِيَة.

Reform, *n.* }
Reformation, } The act of forming anew, تَشْكِيل ثَانٍ — صِيَاغَة ثَانِيَة; of changing for the better, إِصْلَاح — تَصْحِيح — تَعْدِيل — تَقْوِيم — رَتْق; in manners, mode of living, تَنْظِيم سِيرَة — تَهْذِيب — تَثْقِيف; the being so reformed, اِنْصِلَاح ٱلسِّيرَة — تَثَقُّف — تَهَذُّب — اِنْصِلَاح — اِسْتِتْبَاب. Reformation or cutting down of expenses, تَنْقِيص — تَقْتِير. Reforms, generally, إِصْلَاحَات. The Reformation, of the church, إِصْلَاح ٱلْكَنِيسَة ٱلْمَسِيحِيَّة عَلَى قَاعِدَة ٱلْكُتُب ٱلْمُقَدَّسَة — ٱلْإِصْلَاح ٱلْكَنَائِسِيّ ٱلْمَعْرُوف. The promised reforms, ٱلْإِصْلَاحَات ٱلْمَوْعُودَة. The — of the military arrangements, تَنْظِيم ٱلْأَحْوَال ٱلْعَسْكَرِيَّة. The government does not care for the — of affairs, ٱلدَّوْلَة غَيْر مُبَالِيَة بِإِصْلَاح ٱلْحَال.

Reformative, *a.* } Forming again, مُجَدِّد — مُشَكِّل ثَانِيَة.
Reformatory, } Tending to produce reformation, مُصْلِح — مُثَقِّف — مُهَذِّب.

Reformatory, *n.* A — for children, بَيْتُ ٱلْإِصْلَاحِ (or) مَصْلَحٌ لِلْأَوْلَادِ.

Reformed, *a.* Changed in form, renewed, مُقَلَّبُ ٱلشَّكْلِ — مُجَدَّدُ ٱلصُّورَةِ — مُجَدَّد. One who has been reformed, مُثَقَّف — مُهَذَّب. The — religion, مَذْهَبُ أَهْلِ ٱلْإِصْلَاحِ; protestantism, مَذْهَبُ ٱلْبُرُوتِسْتَانْت.

Reformer, *n.* مُصْلِحُ ٱلْأُمُورِ — مُصْلِح.

Reformist, *n.* دَاعٍ لِلْإِصْلَاحِ — مُسَاعِدُ ٱلْإِصْلَاحِ.

Refract, *v.t.* Of rays, light, عَكَسَ شُعَاعَ ٱلنُّورِ وَكَسَرَهَا.

Refracted, *a.* Of rays, مَعْكُوسُ ٱلشُّعَاعِ.

Refracting, *a.* عَاكِسُ ٱلشُّعَاعِ وَمُحَرِّفُهَا.

Refraction, *n.* اِنْعِطَافُ ٱلشُّعَاعِ — اِنْعِطَافُ ٱلشُّعَاعِ وَتَحْرِيفُهَا.

Refractive, *a.* عَاطِفُ ٱلشُّعَاعِ.

Refractorily, *ad.* بِجُمُوحٍ — بِشَكَاسَةٍ — تَمَرُّدًا — مُعَانَدَةً.

Refractoriness, *n.* شَكَاسَة — جُمُوح — عُرْضِيَّة — وَعْقَة — شَمَاسَة — عِنَاد — تَمَرُّد.

Refractory, *a.* شَكِس *pl.* شُكُس — شَمُوس — ضَرِس — خَشِن — وَعْق — صَعْب — عُرْضِيٌّ — جَامِح — فَرَطِيٌّ — جَمُوح — ٱلْجَانِبِ — لَا يَسْمَعُ ٱلنِّدَاءَ وَلَا يَبْغِي ٱلِٱقْتِدَاءَ — مُتَمَرِّد — عَنِيد. A — horse, فَرَسٌ شَرُودٌ. To be —, شَكِسَ — وَعُقَ *aor.* يَعْقُ — عَنِدَ — شَرَدَ [2] — عَانَدَ. To make —, شَرَّدَ.

Refragable, *a.* *See* Refutable, *a.*

Refrain, *v.t.* To hold back, حَجَزَ عَن [2] — حَصَرَ عَن [2] — مَنَعَ عَن — أَوْقَفَ عَن — تَمَنَّعَ مِن — كَفَّ عَن [2] — أَبْدَ عَن. *See also to* Prevent, *v.t.*

Refrain, *v.i.* To abstain from, اِحْتَجَزَ — أَزَمَ عَن — جَبَأَ عَن — ضَرَبَ عَن — اِمْتَنَعَ عَن — اِجْتَنَبَ مِن — كَفَّ عَن [2] — عَن — اِنْفَصَلَ عَن. To constrain one's self, as from complaining, تَجَلَّدَ. He could not — himself, لَمْ يَسْتَطِعْ يَضْبِطُ نَفْسَهُ. They refrained from talking, أَمْسَكُوا عَنِ ٱلْكَلَامِ. I will not — my mouth, لَمْ أَمْنَعْ فَمِي. He refrained his tongue from ..., كَفَّ لِسَانَهُ [2] عَنْ كَذَا.

Refrain, *n.* As of a song, مَرَدُّ ٱلْغِنَاءِ — مَرَدّ.

Refrangibility, *n.* قَابِلِيَّةُ ٱلشُّعَاعِ لِلِٱنْحِرَافِ — قَابِلِيَّةُ ٱلِٱنْعِطَافِ.

Refrangible, *a.* قَابِلُ ٱلِٱنْكِسَارِ وَٱلِٱنْحِرَافِ — قَابِلُ ٱلِٱنْعِطَافِ.

Refresh, *v.t.* To make cool, بَرَّدَ — رَطَّبَ — طَرَّى. To give rest to, أَحْيَى — رَدَّ نَفْسَهُ [2] — نَفَّسَ — رَيَّحَ — أَرَاحَ. To animate, أَكَلَ — قَاتَ [2] — رَبَّقَ ٱلْقُوتَ — رَوَّجَ — حَضَّضَ. To — with food, To improve, أَصْلَحَ — صَلَّحَ. To —, cool, one's self, تَبَرَّدَ. To — one's self, as after toil, اِسْتَرَاحَ — اِرْتَاحَ — تَنَفَّسَ; as with food, تَقَوَّتَ بِ.

Refreshed, *a.* Rested, مُتَنَفِّس — مُرْتَاح. To be —, enlivened, freed from care, تَفَرَّجَ — فَرِجَ.

Refreshing, *a.* Cooling, مُبَرِّد — مُرَطِّب. Giving rest, مُرِيح — مُنَفِّس. Enlivening, مُنْبَسِط — سَارّ — مُفْرِح — مُفَرِّج. Refreshing drinks or medicines, مُبَرِّدَات.

Refreshment, *n.* The act of making cool, تَبْرِيد — تَرْطِيب; of giving rest, as after toil, تَنْفِيس — إِرَاحَة; as with food, تَرْبِيق — قِيَاتَة — قُوت; of enlivening, تَفْكِيه — مَسَرَّة. Relief after toil, *etc.*, رَغْرَغَة — تَرَغْرُغ — رُوَيْحَة — رَوَاحَة — رَاحَة. Food, قُوت — أَكْل. Refreshments, meats and drinks, مَأْكُولَاتٌ وَمَشْرُوبَاتٌ. A place of —, for eating, مَأْكَل; for drinking, مَشْرَب. A — room, مَطْعَم. *See also* Recreation, *n.*

Refrigerant, *a.* مُبَرِّد — مُرَطِّب.

Refrigerant, *n.* A cooling drink, شَرْبَةٌ مُبَرِّدَةٌ. Cooling drinks, مُبَرِّدَات.

Refrigerate, *v.t.* طَرَّى — بَرَّدَ — رَطَّبَ.

Refrigeration, *n.* تَبْرِيد.

Refrigerative, *a.* مُبَرِّد.

Refrigerator, *n.* آلَةٌ لِلتَّبْرِيدِ.

Refuge, *n.* A place of —, مَفَرّ — مَنْجَاة — عِيَاذ — عَوْذ — مَعَاذ — مَلْجَأ — مَأْوًى — مُعْتَصَر — مَهْرَب. A resort, remedy, عِلَاج. A pretext, loophole, مَنْفَذ — عِلَّة — حُجَّة. A protector, ظَهِير — حَامٍ. A city of —, مَدِينَةُ مَلْجَأٍ *pl.* مُدُنُ مَلْجَأٍ. A fort of —, مَعْقِل *pl.* مَعَاقِل.

To afford a refuge to, أَوَى — آوَى; as of God, أَعَاذَ — عَوَّذَ.

To flee for refuge to, أَوَى إِلَى *aor.* يَأْوِي — (or) أَوَى تَأَوَّى إِلَى — اِلْتَجَأَ إِلَى — اِحْتَمَى إِلَى — يَعُوذُ *aor.* عَاذَ بِ. I flee for refuge to God against ..., أَعُوذُ بِٱللّٰهِ مِنْ كَذَا. I flee for refuge to God, meaning, May God protect me, أَعُوذُ بِٱللّٰهِ مَعَاذًا — مَعَاذَ ٱللّٰهِ.

Refugee, *n.* مُهَاجِر *pl.* مُهَاجِرُون — مُلْتَجِئٌ.

Refulgence, *n.* } بَرِيق — لَمَعَان — جَلَاء — رَوْنَق.
Refulgency, }

Refulgent, *a.* بَارِق — بَرَّاق — لَامِع — مُتَلَأْلِئ — مُنِير — نَيِّر.

To be —, أَبْرَقَ — بَرَقَ [2] — تَلَأْلَأَ.

Refulgently, *ad.* بِجَلَاءٍ — بِتَلَأْلُؤٍ — بِبَرَقَانٍ.

Refund, *v.t.* To restore, رَدَّ [2]. *See also to* Repay, Reimburse, *v.t.*

Refunding, *n.* The act of restoring, رَدّ. *See also* Repayment, Reimbursement, *n.*

Refusable, *a.* مِمَّا يُؤْبَى — عَدَمُ ٱلْقُبُولِ بِهِ مُمْكِنٌ.

Refusal, *n.* Denial, as of a request, إِعْدَام — إِعْرَاض عَن — رَدّ —

— عَدَمُ رِضَآءٍ — إِبَآءٌ — إِبَآءٌ رَدٌّ. Rejection, رَفْض. Declining to do, — إِمْتِنَاعٌ عَن — عَدَمُ قُبُولٍ. Option, إِخْتِيَار — خِيَرَة. To give one the first — of a thing, خَيَّرَ أَوَّلًا بِٱلْقُبُولِ وَبِٱلرَّدِّ. To have the first — of a thing, تَخَيَّرَ أَوَّلًا بِٱلْقُبُولِ وَبِٱلرَّدِّ. To meet with a —, رَجَعَ بِٱلْخَيْبَةِ.

Refuse, *v.t.* To deny, as a request, — عَزَّ — رَدَّ — أَعْدَمَ — عَارَضَ عَن. To decline to do, أَبَى — إِمْتَنَعَ *aor.* رَدَّ عَلَى — يَأْبَى. To reject, رَفَضَ. He refused to let me go, أَبَى أَنْ يَسْمَحَ لِي بِٱلذَّهَابِ. He used to —, decline, fresh-meat, كَانَ يَأْبَى ٱللَّحْمَ. He refused, or refrained from, drinking water, أَبَى مِنْ شُرْبِ ٱلْمَآءِ. He refused him his consent to the thing, or, objected to it, or disapproved of it, رَدَّ عَلَى — ٱلْأَمْرَ — رَادَّهُ ٱلشَّيْءَ — أَبَاهُ ٱلشَّيْءَ — تَأَبَّى عَلَيْهِ. He refused him, was unyielding to him, تَأَبَّى عَلَيْهِ. To make one to —, forbear, dislike anything, to turn one against, آبَى — ٱلشَّيْءَ *e.g.* I made him to — it, آبَيْتُهُ إِيَّاهُ. He refused or disappointed him, رَدَّهُ خَائِبًا. He refused to know me, أَبَى أَنْ يَعْرِفَنِي. He refused to be called his son, أَبَى أَنْ يُدْعَى ٱبْنَهُ.

Refuse, *n.* بُوَار — دُشَار — سُقَاطَة — نُفْيَة — خُشَارَة — نُفَايَة. The — of the people, رُذَالَةُ ٱلنَّاسِ — ٱلسِّفْلَة. The — of wheat, نُفَايَةُ ٱلْقَمْحِ.

Refuser, *n.* One who declines, أَبْيَان — أَبِيٌّ — آبٍ; who rejects, رَافِض.

Refutable, *a.* تَبْطِيلُهُ — وَمِمَّا يُنْتَقَض — نَقْضُهُ مُمْكِنٌ — يُرَدُّ عَلَيْهِ مُمْكِنٌ.

Refutation, *n.* The act of refuting, إِبْطَال — نَقْض — رَدٌّ عَلَى; disproof, تَنَاقُض — مُنَاقَضَة. The — of a man's witness, تَجْرِيحُ ٱلشَّاهِدِ.

Refutatory, *a.* مُنَاقِض — جَارِح.

Refute, *v.t.* أَبْطَلَ قَوْلَهُ — نَقَضَ كَلَامَهُ — نَاقَضَ — رَدَّ عَلَى — غَلَّطَ فِي كَلَامِهِ. To —, or annul, as the testimony of a witness, جَرَّحَ ٱلرَّجُلَ — جَرَحَ ٱلشَّاهِدَ. He refuted him with an argument, دَفَعَهُ بِحُجَّةٍ. Refuted, مَرْدُود.

Regain, *v.t.* To recover what was lost, رَدَّ — إِسْتَرَدَّ — إِسْتَعَادَ. To obtain possession of again, عَادَ فَحَصَّلَهُ — فَازَ بِ — ثَانِيَةً. To attain, أَدْرَكَ. *See also under to* Recover, *v.t.*

Regal, *a.* *See* Royal, Kingly, *a.*

Regale, *n.* *See* Banquet, *n.*

Regale, *v.t.* As with a feast, إِتَّخَذَ مَأْدُبَةً لِ — أَضَافَ — أَوْلَمَ. To afford pleasure to, أَطْرَبَ — شَرَحَ صَدْرَهُ — طَيَّبَ نَفْسَهُ. He has regaled us with this piece of news, أَتْحَفَنَا بِهٰذَا ٱلْخَبَرِ. *See also to* Gratify, *v.i.*

Regale, *v.i.* To fare sumptuously, تَنَعَّمَ مُتْرَفًا.

Regalement, *n.* The act of regaling, as with a feast, إِيْلَام — ضِيَافَة — وَلِيمَة — مَأْدُبَة — أَدْب — أَدَب — إِضَافَة. A banquet, *See also* Entertainment, Qualification, *n.*

Regalia, *n.* Ensigns of royalty, تَزْيِينَاتُ ٱلْمَلِكِ ٱلرَّسْمِيَّةُ. The privileges of a king, إِمْتِيَازَاتُ ٱلْمَلِكِ وَخَصَائِصُهُ. Royal patrimony granted to a church, وَقْفٌ مُلُوكِيٌّ إِلَى كَنِيسَةٍ.

Regality, *n.* *See* Kingship, *n.*

Regally, *a.* *See* Kingly, *a.*

Regard, *v.t.* To look at, تَطَلَّعَ — نَظَرَ إِلَى — تَشَوَّفَ لِ. To attend to, to heed, — نَظَرَ إِلَى — أَصْغَى إِلَى — طَلَّعَ فِي — إِلَى — كَرَّمَ — وَدَّ. To esteem, بَالَى بِ — يَعِي *aor.* وَعَى عَلَى — رَاعَى — نَزَّلَ مَنْزِلَةَ كَذَا. To estimate, إِعْتَبَرَ — أَكْرَمَ — عَدَّ — حَسِبَ. To care for, إِعْتَنَى بِ — إِهْتَمَّ بِ. To notice with favour, خَصَّ — يَرْضَى *aor.* رَضِيَ عَن. To concern, have respect to, — لَحَظَ — إِلْتَفَتَ إِلَى — عَنَى. To observe, remark, consider, تَأَمَّلَ — تَطَلَّعَ إِلَى. To have regard to one's entreaties, to pity, رَاعَى — فِي — أَشْفَقَ عَلَى — تَرَحَّمَ عَلَى. To — in the heart, أَضْمَرَ عَلَى — قَلْبِهِ. To — persons, قَبِلَ ٱلْوُجُوهَ — نَظَرَ إِلَى ٱلْوُجُوهِ. They used to —, or follow him, كَانُوا يَتَّبِعُونَهُ. As regards..., — بِخُصُوصِ — وَفِيمَا يَخُصُّ كَذَا — نَظَرًا لِ — كَذَا.

Regard, *n.* Attention of the mind, إِلْتِفَات — نَظَر — مُلَاحَظَة. Respect, consideration, — إِلْتِفَات — إِعْتِبَار — مَحْسَبَة — حِسَاب — دَوَرَانُ بَالٍ. Heedfulness, إِصْغَآء — مُرَاعَاة — إِحْتِرَام — إِكْرَام — إِهْتِمَام. Relation, تَعَلُّق — نِسْبَة. Aspect, as of a thing or matter, وَجْه — بَاب. Regard is had in it (word or speech) to such a thing, رُوعِيَ فِيهِ كَذَا.

In that regard, مِنْ قِبَلِ ذٰلِكَ.

In regard to ..., — نَظَرًا إِلَى كَذَا — بِخُصُوصِ كَذَا — مِنْ قِبَلِ كَذَا — إِعْتِبَارًا بِكَذَا — بِٱعْتِبَارِ كَذَا.

No regard is due to it, لَا عِبْرَةَ بِهِ. Have no regard to him, لَا تَلْتَفِتْ لِقَتِهِ (or إِلَيْهِ)

Out of regard for, إِكْرَامًا لِ: I do this out of regard for you, أَفْعَلُ هٰذَا كَرَامَةً لَكَ.

To pay regard to, to listen to, سَمِعَ. I will pay no regard to it or him, لَا أُلْقِي إِلَيْهِ بَالًا. *See also under to* Regard, *v.t.*

To send one's best regards to, بَعَثَ سَلَامًا مَخْصُوصًا إِلَى.

To send one's regards to, بَعَثَ سَلَامًا إِلَى — بَعَثَ يُسَلِّمُ عَلَى.

Regardable, *a.* *See* Noticeable, *a.*

Regarder, *n.* Of persons, مُرَاعِي ٱلْوُجُوهِ – قَابِلُ ٱلْوُجُوهِ – مُحَابِي وُجُوهٍ.

Regardful, *a.* *See* Mindful, *a.*

Regardless, *a.* Inattentive, قَلِيلُ ٱلِٱلْتِفَاتِ – غَافِلٌ – سَهْوَانُ – سَاهٍ. Indifferent, غَيْرُ مُبَالٍ – عَدِيمُ ٱلْمُبَالَاةِ – مُتَسَاهِلٌ – مُتَكَاسِلٌ. *See also* Careless, *a.*

Regardlessly, *ad.* بِدُونِ – بِتَكَاسُلٍ – بِقِلَّةِ ٱلْتِفَاتٍ – بِتَوَانٍ مُبَالَاةٍ. *See also* Carelessly, *ad.*

Regardlessness, *n.* Inattention, قِلَّةُ ٱلْتِفَاتٍ – تَوَانٍ – تَغَافُلٌ. Indifference, عَدَمُ ٱلِٱعْتِنَاءِ – بُرُودَةٌ – فُتُورٌ – تَكَاسُلٌ – تَسَاهُلٌ. *See also* Carelessness, Heedlessness, *n.*

Regather, *v.t.* To collect again, 2 عَادَ فَجَمَّعَهُ – 2 لَمَّ-ثَانِيَةً. To pluck again, as of grapes, = قَطَفَ-ثَانِيَةً – 2 عَادَ-فَقَطَفَهُ; of fruits, إِجْتَنَى-ثَانِيَةً – 2 عَادَ فَجَنَى ٱلْ...

Regatta, *n.* مُسَابَقَةُ قَوَارِبَ.

Regency, *n.* Government by a regent, نِيَابَةُ سَلْطَنَةٍ. Men intrusted with vicarious government, مَأْمُورُوا نِيَابَةِ سَلْطَنَةٍ. The time of a —, وَقْتُ نِيَابَةِ سَلْطَنَةٍ. The district under a —, وِلَايَةُ نَائِبِ ٱلسُّلْطَانِ.

Regeneracy, *n.* } The state of having repented, حَالَةُ ٱلتَّوْبَةِ –
Regenerateness, } حَالُ ٱلصَّلَاحِ وَٱلْهُدَى – تَتْوِبَةٌ.

Regenerate, *v.t.* To reform, هَذَّبَ – ثَقَّفَ – أَصْلَحَ. To implant holiness in the heart, = هَدَى-إِلَى – = غَرَسَ ٱلتَّقْوَى فِي ٱلْقَلْبِ = ٱلتَّقْوَى. To renew, جَدَّدَ.

Regenerate, *a.* } In nature, مُثَقَّفُ ٱلطَّبْعِ. Having holiness
Regenerated, } implanted in the heart, غَرِيقُ ٱلتَّقْوَى – مُجَدَّدُ ٱلطَّبِيعَةِ بِنِعْمَةِ ٱللّٰهِ.

Regeneration, *n.* The act of reforming, تَثْقِيفٌ – إِصْلَاحٌ – تَهْذِيبٌ; of renewing the heart, غَرْسُ ٱلتَّقْوَى فِي ٱلْقَلْبِ – هُدًى إِلَى ٱلتَّقْوَى; of renewing, تَجْدِيدٌ. The being regenerated, brought back to order, إِسْتِتْبَابٌ.

Regenerative, *a.* } Tending to reform, مُهَذِّبٌ – مُثَقِّفٌ. Re-
Regeneratory, } newing, مُجَدِّدٌ.

Regent, *n.* One who governs vicariously, نَائِبُ سُلْطَانٍ – نَائِبُ سَلْطَنَةٍ.

Regentship, *n.* وَظِيفَةُ ٱلنَّائِبِ – صِفَةُ ٱلنَّائِبِ.

Regicide, *n.* قَاتِلُ سُلْطَانٍ – قَاتِلُ مَلِكٍ.

Regime, *n.* حُكُومَةٌ – حُكْمٌ – أُصُولٌ.

Regimen, *n.* Regulation of diet, رِيَاضَةٌ – تَدْبِيرُ ٱلْأَكْلِ – حِمْيَةٌ. Any remedy, عِلَاجٌ. That part of grammar which regulates the government of words: of verbs, الفَاعِلُ وَٱلْمَفْعُولُ; of prepositions, الجَارُّ وَٱلْمَجْرُورُ. The — of a verb, المَفْعُولُ; of a preposition, المَجْرُورُ. Regimen, order, arrangement, system, أُصُولٌ – نَسَقٌ – نِظَامٌ.

Regiment, *n.* *pl.* طَابُورٌ – أَلَايٌ *pl.* أَلَايَاتٌ – كَتِيبَةٌ *pl.* كَتَائِبُ – *pl.* طَوَابِيرُ.

Regimental, *a.* طَابُورِيٌّ – مِنْ طَابُورٍ – مُتَعَلِّقٌ بِٱلْأَلَايِ.

Regimentals, *n.* أَلْبِسَةُ ٱلْعَسْكَرِ ٱلرَّسْمِيَّةُ.

Region, *n.* *pl.* قُطْرٌ – أَطْرَافٌ *pl.* طَرَفٌ – حَوَاضِرُ *pl.* حَضْرَةٌ – أَقَالِيمُ *pl.* أَقْلِيمٌ – بُلْدَانٌ *pl.* بِلَادٌ – نَوَاحِي *pl.* نَاحِيَةٌ – أَقْطَارٌ حَوَالَى.

Register, *n.* A book for registering, دِيوَانٌ – جَرِيدَةٌ – دُسْتُورٌ – دَفْتَرٌ *pl.* دَفَاتِرُ. A record, سِجِلٌّ *pl.* سِجِلَّاتٌ. A — of a ship, بَاتَنْتَةُ مَرْكَبٍ – تَقْرِيرٌ يُعْطَى لِسَفِينَةٍ مِنْ طَرَفِ ٱلْحُكُومَةِ. A contrivance wherewith to register or regulate anything, آلَةٌ مِيزَانٌ – آلَةُ ٱلتَّصْلِيحِ – ٱلتَّسْوِيَةِ. A church —, of marriages, births, and deaths, دَفْتَرُ ٱلْكَنِيسَةِ وَهُوَ مَا تُسَجَّلُ فِيهِ أَسْمَاءُ ٱلْمُعَمَّدِينَ وَٱلْمُتَزَوِّجِينَ وَٱلْمَدْفُونِينَ. The —, as of a letter, تَقْيِيدٌ. *See also* List, *n.*

Register, *v.t.* To enter in a register, سَجَّلَ – قَيَّدَ-فِي دَفْتَرٍ – دَوَّنَ. To — a letter, قَيَّدَ ٱلْمَكْتُوبَ.

Registered, *a.* مُقَيَّدٌ – مُسَجَّلٌ – مُدَوَّنٌ; of a letter, مُقَيَّدٌ.

Registrar, *n.* مُقَيِّدُ ٱلدَّفْتَرِ – كَاتِبُ ٱلسِّجِلَّاتِ – مِنْ أَهْلِ ٱلدِّيوَانِ – دَفْتَرْدَارٌ – أَمِينُ ٱلدَّفْتَرِ.

Registrarship, *n.* وَظِيفَةُ مُقَيِّدِ ٱلدَّفْتَرِ – خِدْمَةُ أَمِينِ ٱلدَّفْتَرِ – دَفْتَرْدَارِيَّةٌ.

Registration, *n.* تَقْيِيدٌ فِي دَفْتَرٍ – تَسْجِيلٌ – تَدْوِينٌ; of a letter. تَقْيِيدُ مَكْتُوبٍ.

Registry, *n.* A registering, تَقْيِيدٌ فِي دَفْتَرٍ – تَسْجِيلٌ – تَدْوِينٌ. What is entered into a register, المُقَيَّدُ – المُدْرَجُ – المُدَوَّنُ. A place where a register is kept, دَائِرَةُ ٱلتَّقْيِيدِ – مَحَلُّ ٱلتَّقْيِيدِ – دَفْتَرْدَارِيَّةٌ.

Regius Professor, *n.* مُدَرِّسُ فَنٍّ أَوْ عِلْمٍ مَعَاشُهُ مَوْقُوفٌ مِنْ طَرَفِ ٱلسُّلْطَانِ أَوِ ٱلدَّوْلَةِ.

Regnant, *a.* (بِٱلْمُلْكِ *or*) القَائِمُ بِٱلْحُكُومَةِ. Queen —, مَلِكَةٌ قَائِمَةٌ بِٱلْمُلْكِ مِنْ ذَاتِهَا بِٱلْإِرْثِ وَٱلِٱسْتِحْقَاقِ.

Regorge, *v.t.* To eject from the stomach, إِسْتَفْرَغَ. To swallow again, 2 عَادَ فَبَلِعَهُ – تَلَهَّمَ-ثَانِيَةً.

Regrant, *v.t.* To return to a former owner, 2 رَدَّ-إِلَى صَاحِبِهِ أَعْطَى-لِصَاحِبِهِ ثَانِيَةً – ٱلْأَوَّلِ.

Regrate, *v.t.* Of stones, قَشَطَ ـ ءَ كَشَطَ.

Regrating, *v.t.* Of stones, قَشْط ـ كَشْط.

Regress, *n.* رَدّ ـ رُجُوع ـ عَوْد.

Regress, *v.i.* رَدَّ ـ ءَ رَجَعَ ـ ² عَادَ.

Regression, *n.* *See* Regress, *n.*

Regressive, *a.* رَادّ ـ رَاجِع ـ عَائِد.

Regret, *n.* Sorrow, لَهْف ـ تَلَهُّف ـ أَسَف ـ تَأَسُّف ـ تَنَدُّم ـ نَدَامَة ـ نَدَم ـ تَحَسُّر ـ حَسْرَة. Repentance, تَنَدُّم ـ نَدَامَة ـ نَدَم. With —, repugnance, مِنْ غَيْرِ خَاطِرٍ. With —, sorrow, أَسَفًا. To my —, عَلَى حَسْرَتِي. Oh my — for it or him! يَا حَسْرَتَا عَلَيْهِ. Your absence has caused us —, أَوْحَشْتَنَا.

Regret, *v.t.* To be sorry for, تَلَهَّفَ عَلَى ـ ءَ لَهِفَ عَلَى ـ تَأَسَّفَ عَلَى ـ ءَ أَسِفَ عَلَى ـ تَحَسَّرَ عَلَى ـ ءَ حَسِرَ عَلَى. To repent of, تَنَدَّمَ عَلَى ـ ءَ نَدِمَ عَلَى. We — to learn what is stated in some of the journals, قَدْ غَمَّنَا مَا ذُكِرَ فِي بَعْضِ ٱلْجَرَائِدِ. It is to be regretted that ..., هُوَ مِمَّا يُوجِبُ ٱلْأَسَفَ أَنْ. They showed the excess of their —, أَظْهَرُوا فَرْطَ أَسَفِهِمْ.

Regret, *v.i.* تَأَسَّفَ ـ ءَ أَسِفَ. I — that ...., لَهْفِي عَلَى أَنْ.

Regretful, *a.* Affected with regret, مُتَأَسِّف; causing regret, مُوجِبُ ٱلتَّأَسُّفِ; deserving —, مُسْتَحِقُّ ٱلْأَسَفِ.

Regular, *a.* In a continuous course, without interruption, مُطَّرِد. Analogical, قِيَاسِيّ. Disposed in — order, رَصِيف ـ نَسِيق. Measured, مَقِيس. According to rule, عَلَى ٱلْقَانُونِ ـ عَلَى ٱلْقَاعِدَةِ. Well arranged, orderly, مُرَتَّب ـ مَضْبُوط ـ مَضْبُوط ـ مَنْظُوم ـ مُنْتَظِم. Systematized, مُنَسَّق. Punctual, exact, مَضْبُوط ـ مُدَقَّق ـ مُحْكَم. Regular, of monks, مِنَ ٱلرَّهْبَانِيَّةِ ـ رَهْبَانِيّ. Regular soldiers, عَسْكَرُ ٱلنِّظَامِ. His teeth are —, أَسْنَانُهُ رَصِيفَةٌ (*or* مُرْتَصِفَةٌ).

Regular, *n.* A monk, رَاهِب *pl.* رُهْبَان; a regular soldier, عَسْكَرِيُّ ٱلنِّظَامِ. A — verb, فِعْلٌ قِيَاسِيٌّ ـ فِعْلٌ سَالِمٌ. *See also under* Orderly, *a.*

Regularity, *n.* Uninterrupted course, اِطِّرَاد. The being arranged in order, as layers of stones, *etc.*, رَصَف. Correct intermeasurement, قِيَاس. Strict observance of rule, نِظَام ـ مُحَافَظَةُ ٱلْقَوَانِينِ. The being in accordance with rule, مُطَابَقَةُ ٱلْقَاعِدَةِ ـ مُوَافَقَةُ ٱلْقَوَانِينِ. Order, good arrangement, نِظَام ـ تَرْتِيب ـ هِنْدَام ـ اِنْتِظَام. Exactness, دِقَّة ـ ضَبْط ـ تَحْكِيم. With —; *see* Regularly. *See also* Order, Punctuality, *n.*

Regularly, *ad.* In an uninterrupted course, بِٱطِّرَادٍ. According to rule, measure, عَلَى ٱلْقِيَاسِ. According to rule, order, حَسَبَ ٱلْقَوَانِينِ ـ بِٱلْقَاعِدَةِ. Exactly, فِي غَايَةِ ٱلْإِتْقَانِ ـ عَلَى وَجْهِ ٱلتَّدْقِيقِ. According to system, بِٱلنَّسَقِ ـ بِضَبْطٍ ـ بِدِقَّةٍ. Wholly, بِٱلتَّمَامِ ـ بِٱلْكُلِّيَّةِ ـ طُرًّا ـ قَاطِبَةً.

Regulate, *v.t.* To adjust, سَوَّى ـ عَدَّلَ. To make accurate, عَدَّلَ ـ دَقَّقَ ـ ضَبَّطَ. To put in order, دَبَّرَ ـ رَتَّبَ ـ نَظَّمَ. To —, as the affairs of a state, سَاسَ *aor.* يَسُوسُ ـ قَامَ بِ ـ دَبَّرَ. *See also to* Order, *v.t.*

Regulation, *n.* The act of adjusting, تَسْوِيَة ـ تَعْدِيل; of making accurate, تَضْبِيط ـ تَدْقِيق; of putting in order, تَرْتِيب ـ تَنْظِيم ـ تَدْبِير ـ تَعْدِيل; of regulating, as of the affairs of a state, تَدْبِير ـ سِيَاسَة ـ إِقَامَة بِ. A rule, order, قَاعِدَة *pl.* قَوَاعِدُ ـ ضَابِطَة *pl.* ضَوَابِطُ ـ قَانُون *pl.* قَوَانِينُ. Regulations, orders, نِظَامَات.

Regulation, *a.* حَسَبَ ٱلنِّظَامِ ٱلْمُعَيَّنِ ـ حَسَبَ ٱلنِّظَامِ. Official, رَسْمِيّ.

Regulative, *a.* مُحَكِّم ـ مُرَتِّب ـ مُنَظِّم.

Regulator, *n.* One who regulates, مُنَظِّم ـ نَاظِم ـ ضَابِط ـ إِزَاءٌ; of the affairs of a state, مُقِيمٌ بِ ـ مُدَبِّر ـ سَائِس. Anything which produces order, مُوجِبُ ٱلنِّظَامِ. Any instrument for regulating, مِيزَان ـ آلَةُ ٱلتَّعْدِيلِ.

Regulus, *n.* Pure metal, مَعْدِنٌ مُصَفًّى. The large star in *Leo*, قَلْبُ ٱلْأَسَدِ.

Regurgitate, *v.t.* To make to well, spring up, بَجَّسَ ـ ءَ ² بَجَسَ.

Regurgitate, *v.t.* تَبَجَّسَ ـ اِنْبَجَسَ.

Regurgitation, *n.* تَبَجُّس ـ اِنْبِجَاس.

Rehabilitate, *v.t.* جَدَّدَ ـ رَجَّعَ إِلَى مَا كَانَ عَلَيْهِ ـ قَيَّمَ. To be rehabilitated, اِسْتَتَبَّ.

Rehabilitation, *n.* The act of, تَرْجِيعُ ٱلشَّيْءِ ـ تَقْيِيم ـ تَجْدِيد إِلَى مَا كَانَ عَلَيْهِ; the being rehabilitated, اِسْتِتْبَاب.

Rehear, *v.t.* اِسْتَمَعَ ثَانِيَةً. He reheard the case, ² عَادَ فَٱسْتَمَعَ ٱلدَّعْوَى.

Rehearsal, *n.* A recital, شَرْح ـ بَيَان ـ نَقْل ـ قَصّ ـ رِوَايَة ـ إِفَادَة. Rehearsal by heart, عَرْض. Rehearsal, as at a school, تَعْلِيم ـ رِيَاضَةُ ٱلْأَوْلَادِ ـ تَقْوِيَةُ ٱلْأَوْلَادِ; as of a theatrical piece, عَرْضُ ٱلتَّشْخِيصِ فِي ٱلتِّيَاتْرُو لِأَجْلِ ٱلْاِمْتِحَانِ.

Rehearse, *v.t.* To state, narrate, detail, ² نَقَلَ ـ تَكَلَّمَ بِ ـ ءَ شَرَحَ ـ بَيَّنَ ـ ءَ حَكَى ـ رَوَى *aor.* يَرْوِي. To repeat, ثَنَّى; to — in praise of, أَثْنَى عَلَى خَيْرًا; in dispraise of, أَثْنَى عَلَى شَرًّا. To — in the hearing of, to — to, وَضَعَ فِي مَسَامِعِ ...ٱ *aor.* يَضَعُ ـ سَمَّعَ. To — or compose verses, ءَ قَرَضَ. To — from the speech or writings of another, ءَ حَكَى عَنْ ـ ² نَقَلَ عَنْ ـ

تَقَصَّصَ عَنْ. To — from memory, عَرَضَ ـ تَقَصَّصَ. I rehearsed the book from memory, عَرَضْتُ ٱلْكِتَابَ. He began to — the matter to him, consecutively, اِبْتَدَأَ يَشْرَحُ لَهُ ٱلْأَمْرَ بِٱلتَّتَابُعِ.

Reign, *v.i.* كَانَ فِي مُلْكٍ ـ مَلَكَ. To — over, مَلَكَ عَلَى ـ تَرَأَّسَ عَلَى ـ تَسَلَّطَ عَلَى.

Reign, *n.* Sovereignty, dominion, حُكُومَة ـ سَلْطَنَة ـ مُلْك ـ دَوْلَة. Period of rule, أَيَّامُ سَلْطَنَةٍ. Period, time, وَقْت ـ عَصْر ـ زَمَان ـ أَيَّام. Period of success, أَيَّامُ نُفُوذٍ ـ أَيَّامُ ٱلتَّغَلُّبِ; of use, أَيَّامُ ٱسْتِعْمَالٍ; of predominance, أَيَّامُ ٱسْتِعْلَاءٍ. His — came to an end, اِنْقَضَتْ دَوْلَتُهُ.

Reigning, *n.* Holding present sovereignty, جَالِسٌ حَالًا ـ مَالِكٌ حَالًا. *See also under* Prevailing, *a.*

Re-illume, *v.t.* / **Re-illuminate**, } Of light, أَنَارَ-ثَانِيَةً; of the mind, عَادَ فَفَطَّنَهُ; as with lamps, عَادَ فَأَوْقَدَ ٱلْ...; of books, نَقَشَ-ثَانِيَةً ـ عَادَ فَزَوَّقَ ٱلْكِتَابَ.

Reimport, *v.t.* جَلَبَ ٱلْبَضَائِعَ ٱلْخَارِجَةَ ثَانِيَةً.

Reimportation, *n.* جَلْبُ ٱلْبَضَائِعِ ٱلْخَارِجَةِ ثَانِيَةً.

Reimburse, *v.t.* To replace, as in a treasury, خَزَنَ-ثَانِيَةً ـ رَدَّ-إِلَى ٱلْخَزِينَةِ. To repair by repayment, أَعَاضَ ـ أَوْفَى ـ كَافَى-بِ ـ عَوَّضَ.

Reimbursement, *n.* The act of refunding, إِعَادَة ـ إِيفَاء ـ مُكَافَاة ـ تَعْوِيض.

Reimburser, *n.* مُكَافٍ ـ مُعَوِّض ـ مُوَفٍّ.

Rein, *n.* As of a bridle, عِنَان *pl.* أَعِنَّة; the reins, ٱلدِّزْكِين. The nose — of a camel, زِمَام *pl.* أَزِمَّة. Rein, government, or that by which anything is restrained, قِيَاد ـ زِمَام. The reins of the administration of the country, زِمَامُ تَدْبِيرِ ٱلْبِلَادِ.
To let go the rein, to slacken the reins, مَلَأَ ـ أَطْلَقَ ٱلْعِنَانَ: He gave the reins to his beast, مَلَأَ عِنَانَ دَابَّتِهِ. To take the reins, as of government, أَخَذَ ٱلزِّمَامَ.

Rein, *v.t.* To guide by reins, قَادَ-بِٱلْعِنَانِ. *See also to* Restrain, *v.t.*

Reindeer, *n.* نَوْعٌ مِنَ ٱلْإِيَّلِ وُجُودُهُ فِي ٱلْأَقْطَارِ ٱلشَّمَالِيَّةِ يَجُرُّ ٱلْعَرَبَاتِ عَلَى ٱلثَّلْجِ.

Reinforce, *v.t.* *See* Re-enforce, *v.t.*

Reinforcement, *n.* *See* Re-enforcement, *n.*

Reinless, *a.* Without reins, بِلَا عِنَانٍ; without restraint, بِلَا ضَابِطَةٍ ـ مِنْ غَيْرِ ضَبْطٍ ـ طَلْقَ ٱلْعِنَانِ.

Reinlist, *v.t.* and *int.* *See to* Re-enlist, *v.t.*

Reins, *n.* The kidneys or lower part of the back, ٱلصُّلْبُ ـ ٱلْكُلَى. The inward parts, the heart, ٱلْقَلْبُ ـ ٱلدَّاخِلُ ـ ٱلْجَوْفُ.

Re-insert, *v.t.* To put in again, أَدْخَلَ-ثَانِيَةً; to thread again, عَادَ فَسَلَكَهُ ـ سَلَكَ-ثَانِيَةً; to insert again, as into a paper, writing, أَدْرَجَ-ثَانِيَةً.

Re-insertion, *n.* The act of putting in again, إِدْخَالٌ ثَانٍ ـ إِعَادَةُ إِدْخَالٍ; of threading again, تَسْلِيكٌ ثَانٍ; of inserting again, as into a column, paper, إِدْرَاجٌ ثَانٍ.

Re-inspire, *v.t.* *See to* Revive, *v.t.*

Re-instal, *v.t.* As into an office, أَجْلَسَ-فِي مَنْصِبٍ ثَانِيَةً ـ عَادَ فَوَجَّهَ-إِلَى مَأْمُورِيَّةٍ.

Re-instalment, *n.* إِعَادَةُ تَجْلِيسٍ فِي ـ إِجْلَاسٌ ثَانٍ فِي مَنْصِبٍ ـ مَأْمُورِيَّةٍ.

Re-instate, *v.t.* رَجَّعَ ـ صَرَّفَ-ثَانِيَةً.

Re-instatement, *n.* The act of, تَرْجِيعٌ ـ إِعَادَةُ تَصْرِيفٍ; the being reinstated, إِعَادَةُ تَصَرُّفٍ ـ تَصَرُّفٌ ثَانٍ.

Re-insurance, *n.* A second insurance; *see under* Re-assurance, *n.*

Re-insure, *v.t.* To insure again; *see under to* Re-assure, *v.t.*

Re-issue, *v.t.* To issue or distribute again, وَزَّعَ-ثَانِيَةً; to promulgate again, أَصْدَرَ-ثَانِيَةً; to publish again, as of a book, نَشَرَ-ثَانِيَةً ـ بَرَّزَ-ثَانِيَةً.

Reissue, *n.* The act of distributing again, إِعَادَةُ تَوْزِيعٍ; of promulgating again, إِصْدَارٌ ثَانٍ; of publishing again, as a book, تَبْرِيزٌ ثَانٍ ـ نَشْرٌ ثَانٍ. What is distributed again, ٱلْمُوَزَّعُ ثَانِيَةً; what is promulgated again, ٱلْمُذَاعُ ثَانِيَةً; what is published again, of a book, طَبْعٌ ثَانٍ ـ بُرُوزٌ ثَانٍ.

Reiterate, *v.t.* أَعَادَ ـ كَرَّرَ ـ ثَنَّى ـ رَدَّدَ. *See also to* Repeat, *v.t.*

Reiteration, *n.* إِعَادَة ـ تَكْرِير ـ تَكْرَار ـ تَثْنِيَة ـ تَرْدِيد. *See also* Repetition, *n.*

Reject, *v.t.* As of an offer, رَدَّ ـ رَدَّ عَلَى ـ أَعْرَضَ عَنْ. To cast off, رَفَضَ. To repudiate, renounce, خَلَعَ. To dismiss, دَشَّرَ *vulg.* نَفَى ـ طَرَدَ. To —, as of a claim, أَسْقَطَ. To — the testimony of a witness, جَرَحَ ٱلشَّاهِدَ. To —, as what is true, عَانَدَ ـ عَنَدَ. To abhor, أَنِفَ مِنْ ـ اِسْتَقْبَحَ. To cast away as useless, رَمَى بِ ـ طَرَحَ *aor.* يَرْمِي. Can I — such clear evidence, أَأَنِفُ مِنْ مِثْلِ هٰذِهِ ٱلْحُجَّةِ ٱلْبَيِّنَةِ. Do not — his proposal, لَا تُعْرِضْ عَنْ عَرْضِهِ.

Rejectable, *a.* That may be rejected, مِمَّا يُرْفَضُ; that may be dismissed, مِمَّا يُطْرَدُ; that may be set aside, as a claim, مِمَّا يُجْرَحُ. *See also* Refusable, *a.*

Rejected, *a.* Returned, مَرْدُود; cast off, مَرْفُوض; repudiated, renounced, as by his family, *etc.*, مَخْلُوع ـ خَلِيع. Rejected as bad, of coin, *etc.*, بَهْرَج . A — son, إِبْنٌ نَفِيٌّ ـ خَلِيعٌ . A — saying, قَوْلٌ مُطَّرَحٌ . To be —, cast off, إِطَّرَحَ .

Rejecter, *n.* A refuser, آبٍ ; one who casts off, a non-conformist, رَافِض *pl.* رُفَّاض .

Rejection, *n.* The act of refusing, رِدَّة ـ رَدٌّ ـ عَدَمُ قُبُولٍ ; of casting off, رَفْض ; of repudiating, خَلْع ; of sending off, dismissal, طَرْد ; of not receiving the evidence of, جَرْح ; of contesting what is true, عِنَاد ـ مُعَانَدَة ; of abhorring, إِسْتِقْبَاح ـ أَنَف مِن .

Rejoice, *v.i.* To experience joy, ـ فَرِحَ ـ سُرَّ ـ إِبْتَهَجَ ـ بَهِجَ ـ سُرَّ بِ ـ إِبْتَهَجَ بِ . To — in or at, إِنْشَرَحَ صَدْرُهُ ـ شَرِحَ خَاطِرُهُ ـ شَرِحَ خَاطِرُهُ بِ ـ إِسْتَبْهَجَ بِ ـ تَبَجَّحَ بِ ـ فَرِحَ بِ . To manifest joy, أَظْهَرَ ٱلسُّرُور . He rejoiced in my company, تَبَجَّحَ بِصُحْبَتِي . To —, as at the distress of an enemy, شَمِتَ بِ .

Rejoice, *v.t.* بَسَطَ ـ شَرَحَ خَاطِرَهُ ـ أَبْهَجَ ـ أَفْرَحَ ـ سَرَّ . It rejoiced the sight, أَبْهَجَ ٱلنَّظَرَ . What rejoices her rejoices me, يَبْسُطُنِي مَا يَبْسُطُهَا . It rejoiced me, (*vulg.*) أَبْسَطَنِي .

Rejoicing, *n.* The experiencing of joy, حَظٌّ ـ سُرُور ـ فَرَح ـ شَرْحُ خَاطِرٍ ـ بَهْجَة ; the subject of joy, فُرْحَة ـ مَسَرَّة . Public rejoicings, مَوَاسِمُ ـ مَرَاسِمُ فَرَحٍ .

Rejoin, *v.t.* To join again, جَمَعَ بَيْنَ ـ ثَانِيَةً ـ وَاصَلَ ـ ثَانِيَةً ـ أَلْحَمَ ـ بِ ـ ثَانِيَةً ـ عَادَ فَٱلْتَحَقَ ـ بِ . To overtake, لَحِقَ ـ أَلْحَقَ . To meet again, عَادَ فَٱجْتَمَعَ بِ ـ تَلَقَّى ـ ثَانِيَةً .

Rejoin, *v.i.* To come together again, عَادَ ـ إِلْتَصَقَ ثَانِيَةً ـ فَٱلْتَحَمَ . To answer, reply, أَجَابَ ـ رَدَّ جَوَابًا ـ جَاوَبَ ـ رَدَّ عَلَى .

Rejoinder, *n.* رَجْعَة ـ جَوَاب ـ عَقِب .

Rejoint, *v.t.* To reunite joints, وَصَلَ ٱلْمَفَاصِلَ ثَانِيَةً *aor.* يَصِلُ . To cut up again into joints, عَضَّى ـ ثَانِيَةً . To fill up old joints of stone with plaster, عَقَدَ ٱلْخِلَالَ بِٱلْجِصِّ ثَانِيَةً .

Rejointing, *n.* As with mortar, عَقْدُ ٱلْخِلَالِ بِٱلْجِصِّ .

Rejudge, *v.t.* To decide upon again, قَطَعَ ـ حَكَمَ فِي ـ ثَانِيَةً . To consider again, عَادَ فَتَأَمَّلَ فِي ـ ثَانِيَةً .

Rejuvenate, *v.t.*
Rejuvenize, } جَدَّدَ شَبَابَهُ .

Rejuvenescence, *n.* رُجُوعٌ إِلَى ٱلشَّبَابِ .

Rekindle, *v.t.* Of a fire, شَعَّلَ ٱلنَّارَ ثَانِيَةً ـ عَادَ فَأَضْرَمَ ٱلنَّارَ ـ أَلْهَبَ ـ ثَانِيَةً ـ عَادَ فَعَلَّقَ ٱلنَّارَ . To inflame or exasperate again, عَادَ فَأَنْهَضَهُ . To rouse again, اعَادَ إِضْرَامَهُ . To —, of war, عَادَ فَأَثَارَ ٱلْحَرْبَ .

Reland, *v.t.* رَدَّ ـ إِلَى ٱلْبَرِّ ـ نَزَلَ ـ مِنَ ٱلْمَرْكَبِ ثَانِيَةً .

Relapse, *v.i.* To fall back into, عَادَ فَسَقَطَ فِي ـ سَقَطَ فِي ـ ثَانِيَةً ـ عَادَ فَسَقَطَ فِي ٱلضَّلَالِ ـ عَادَ فَوَقَعَ فِي . To —, as into error, إِرْتَدَّ عَنِ ٱلرَّشَادِ ـ ضَلَّ ثَانِيَةً . To fall back from convalescence, تَنَكَّسَ فِي ـ إِنْتَكَسَ ـ نُكِسَ ـ هَاضَ ـ ٱلْمَرَضُ ـ غُفِرَ ـ غَفِرَ مَرَضٍ . To cause a relapse, as into a disease, نَكَسَ .

Relapse, *n.* A falling back into, رُجُوعٌ إِلَى ـ إِعَادَةُ سُقُوطٍ فِي ; as into error, إِعَادَةُ سُقُوطٍ فِي ٱلضَّلَالِ ـ إِرْتِدَادٌ عَنِ ٱلرَّشَدِ ; of a disease, نُكَاس ـ هَيْضَة ـ نُكْسَة ـ نُكْس ـ غَفْر .

Relate, *v.t.* To narrate, حَدَّثَ ـ حَكَى ـ ذَكَرَ ـ نَقَلَ ـ حَكَى ـ نَقَلَ عَن ـ رَوَى ـ أَخْبَرَ . To —, as quoted from another, عَن . I related the speech as from him, حَكَيْتُ عَنْهُ ٱلْكَلَامَ . To ally by connexion or kindred, نَسَبَ ـ إِلَى ـ قَرَنَ ـ بِ . To — something as done by another, نَقَلَ مِن . He related his adventures, or tale, to me, قَصَّ ـ حَكَى لِي مَا قَدْ جَرَى لَهُ . We will — to you the best of stories, نَقُصُّ عَلَيْكَ أَحْسَنَ ٱلْقِصَصِ . He related to me a narrative from such an one, حَدَّثَنِي عَنْ فُلَانٍ حَدِيثًا . To be related, narrated, ذُكِرَ ـ رُوِيَ ـ نُقِلَ . To be related to, connected with, إِقْتَرَنَ بِ ـ قَرُبَ مِن ـ كَانَ قَرِيبًا لِ ; تَعَلَّقَ بِ ـ إِنْتَسَبَ إِلَى ; of kindred, قَرَنَ . It has been related of him, *i.e.* as heard from or stated by another, رُوِيَ عَنْهُ . It is related, or, it reads, thus, رُوِيَ كَذَا . It relates to so and so, يَعُودُ عَلَى كَذَا . Relating to, in an adverbial sense, بِنَاءً عَلَى .

Relate, *v.i.* *See under* To be related *in the foregoing article.*

Relater, *n.* رَاوٍ ـ قَاصٌّ .

Related, *a.* Narrated, مَسْرُود ـ مَنْقُول ـ مَرْوِيّ . Connected with, مُتَعَلِّق بِ ـ مُقْتَرِن بِ ; as by kindred, مُقَرَّب بِٱلْأَهْلِيَّةِ ـ قَرِيب *pl.* أَقَارِب ـ نَسِيب *pl.* نَسَائِب .

Relation, *n.* A narration, نَقْل ـ قِصَّة *pl.* قِصَص ـ حِكَايَة *pl.* حِكَايَات ـ رِوَايَة *pl.* رِوَايَا ـ أَحَادِيث *pl.* حَدِيث ـ إِفَادَة ـ بَيَان . Connexion, عَلَاقَة ـ نِسْبَة ـ تَعَلُّق ; friendly relations, عَلَاقَة وِدَادِيَّة . Relationship, قَرَابَة ـ مَقْرَبَة ـ دَنَاوَة ـ صِهْر . Relations, kinsfolk, عَشِيرَة ـ أَقْرِبَاء . A relative, kinsman, قَرِيب *pl.* أَقْرِبَاء ـ أَنْسِبَاء *pl.* نَسِيب . A — on the wife's side, خَتَن *pl.* أَخْتَان ; on the husband's side, حَمٌ ـ حَمًا *pl.* أَحْمَاء . Relations on either side, أَصْهَار . A near —, relative, خَاتٌّ *pl.* خَوَاتٌّ ـ صِهْر *pl.* أَصْهَار ـ قَرِيبُ ٱلْقَرَابَةِ مِن . He is my —, هُوَ قَرِيبِي ـ هُوَ نَسِيبِي . In — to, in comparison with, بِٱلْإِضَافَةِ إِلَى ـ بِٱلنِّسْبَةِ إِلَى . With regard to; *see under* Regard, *n.*

Relational, *a.* مُنْتَسِب إِلَى ـ إِقْتِرَانِيّ ـ مُتَعَلِّق ـ مُقْتَرِن .

Relationship, *n.* *See* Relation, *n.*

Relative, *a.* Connected by inter-relation, وَاقِعَةٌ بَيْنَهُمْ نِسْبَةٌ ـ مُتَعَلِّقٌ بِ ـ دَائِر ـ مُتَنَاسِب ـ مُتَضَايِف. Respecting, مُخْتَصٌّ بِ. Denoting inter-relation, مُشْتَرَك. Not absolute, restricted, مُقَيَّد. Relative rights, مَا يَحِقُّ عَلَى ٱلْوَاحِدِ لِلْآخَرِ. Relative duties, مَا يَجِبُ عَلَى ٱلْوَاحِدِ لِلْآخَرِ. Relative, in grammar, مَوْصُول. A — noun or adjective, (مَوْصُول *or*) اِسْمٌ مَنْسُوبٌ *pl.* (مَوْصُولَةٌ *or*) أَسْمَاءٌ مَنْسُوبَةٌ. *See also under* Correlative, *a.*

Relative, *n.* That which has relation to something else, مَنْسُوب. *See also under* Relation, *n.*, Relative, *a.*

Relatively, *ad.* In comparison to, نِسْبَةً إِلَى ـ بِٱلنِّسْبَةِ إِلَى. With respect to, بِخُصُوصِ كَذَا ـ فِيمَا يَخُصُّ كَذَا.

Relativeness, *n.* حَالُ ٱلْمَنْسُوب.

Relax, *v.t.* To make less tense, رَاخَى ـ أَرْخَى. To make less rigorous, لَيَّنَ ـ خَفَّفَ ـ سَهَّلَ. To — the bowels, أَطْلَقَ ٱلْبَطْنَ ـ أَسْهَلَ ٱلْبَطْنَ. To weaken, أَضْعَفَ. To diminish, قَلَّلَ. To — one's efforts, إِسْتَرْخَى فِي سَعْيِهِ ـ تَرَاخَى فِي هِمَّتِهِ. To — one's hold, to let go, سَيَّبَ ـ أَطْلَقَ بِ.

Relax, *v.i.* To become less tense, رَخِيَ *aor.* إِسْتَرْخَى ـ يَرْخَى. To become less rigorous, تَلَيَّنَ ـ ـَـ لَانَ ـ ـُـ خَفَّ; of a wind, ـَـ هَدَأَ ـ ²سَكَنَ ـ ـِـ كَلَّ. To — one's self, to take relaxation, إِسْتَرَاحَ ـ تَنَفَّسَ.

Relaxation, *n.* The act of making less tense, مُرَاخَاة ـ إِرْخَاءٌ; of making less rigorous, severe, تَخْفِيف ـ تَلْيِين ـ تَسْهِيل; of relaxing the bowels, تَلْيِينُ ٱلْبَطْنِ ـ إِسْهَالُ ٱلْبَطْنِ. The state of being less tense, إِرْتِخَاءٌ ـ رَخَاوَة; of being less rigorous, لِينَة ـ سُهُولَة; of the bowels being relaxed, لِينَةُ ٱلْبَطْنِ; the becoming less interested in, إِسْتِرْخَاءٌ فِي ـ تَرَاخٍ فِي. Weakness, ضُعْف ـ عَجْز. Relaxation of the mind, تَنَفُّس ـ رَاحَةُ ٱلْبَالِ. He requires — from political duties for a time in order that he may be able to return to his post, يَحْتَاجُ إِلَى ٱعْتِزَالِ ٱلْمَصَالِحِ ٱلسِّيَاسِيَّةِ مُدَّةً لِيُمْكِنَهُ أَنْ يَعُودَ إِلَى وَظِيفَتِهِ. *See also* Recreation, *n.*

Relaxed, *a.* Slackened, مُرَاخًى ـ مُرْخًى; of the bowels, مُسْهَلُ ٱلْبَطْنِ; weakened, مَنْهُوكُ ٱلْقُوَّةِ.

Relaxing, *a.* Weakening, مُضْعِف; purgative, مُلَيِّنُ ٱلْبَطْنِ.

Relay, *n.* Of horses, تَغْيِيرُ خَيْلٍ ـ إِبْدَالُ (تَبْدِيلُ *or*) خَيْلٍ.

Relay, *v.t.* To lay or place again, ²حَطَّ ثَانِيَةً ـ ـَـ جَعَلَ ثَانِيَةً. To spread again, as of a carpet, ²بَسَطَ ثَانِيَةً; as with a colour, *etc.*, طَلَّى ثَانِيَةً.

Release, *v.t.* As from confinement, سَيَّبَ ـ أَطْلَقَ. To suffer to escape, to let go, أَفْلَتَ. To free from obligation or penalty, ـَـ رَفَعَ عَنْ ـ مَا عَلَيْهِ ـ أَبْرَأَ. To free one, generally, from anything, خَلَّصَ مِنْ ـ سَلَّمَ مِنْ ـ أَنْقَذَ مِنْ. To — one's conscience of, أَبْرَأَ ذِمَّتَهُ مِنْ. To —, of property, to put it into a good state and to take possession of it, أَعْتَقَ ٱلْمَالَ. To —, to let one alone to do as he pleases, خَلَّى سَبِيلَهُ ـ خَلَّى. He released him of his shackles, ـَـ خَلَعَ قَيْدَهُ. To — a slave, أَعْتَقَ عَبْدًا. We shall be released from our promise, نَكُونُ فِي حَلٍّ مِنْ وَعْدِنَا. You are released from this matter, irresponsible for it, أَنْتَ طِلْقٌ مِنْ هٰذَا ٱلْأَمْرِ. *See also to* Free, Discharge, Acquit, *v.t.*

Release, *n.* Liberation from restraint, imprisonment, *etc.*, خَلَاص ـ عِتْق ـ إِطْلَاق ـ إِطْلَاقٌ مِنَ ٱلْحَبْسِ; from penalty or obligation, إِبْرَاءٌ; freedom from anything, خَلَاصٌ مِنْ; the leaving one free to do as he pleases, تَخْلِيَة. *See also* Quittance, *n.*

Releasement, *n.* *See* Release, *n.*

Relegate, *v.t.* *See to* Banish, Exile, *v.t.*

Relegation, *n.* *See* Exile, Banishment, *n.*

Relent, *v.i.* ـِـ رَقَّ قَلْبُهُ ـ ـِـ لَانَ. To — towards, تَرَحَّمَ عَلَى ـ تَرَقَّقَ لِ ـ ـِـ رَقَّ لِ ـ تَحَنَّنَ عَلَى.

Relentless, *a.* أَلَدُّ *pl.* لُدٌّ *and* لِدَاد ـ لَا يُلَيَّنُ ـ لَا يَعْفُو ـ بِلَا حِنَّةٍ ـ بِلَا رَحْمَةٍ. *See also* Merciless, *a.*

Relentlessly, *ad.* بِلَدَدٍ ـ بِعَدَمِ رَحْمَةٍ ـ بِعَدَمِ حِنَّةٍ.

Relentlessness, *n.* لَدَدٌ ـ عَدَمُ ٱللِّينَةِ ـ عَدَمُ حِنَّةٍ ـ عَدَمُ رَحْمَةٍ.

Relessee, *n.* ٱلْمُبْرَأُ.

Relessor, *n.* ٱلْمُبْرِئُ.

Relevance, *n.* } مَصْلَحَة ـ مُوَافَقَة ـ مُنَاسَبَة. *See also* Pertinence,
Relevancy, } Applicability, *n.*

Relevant, *a.* لَائِق ـ مُوَافِق ـ مُنَاسِب. Every escaped word is —, (prov.) لِكُلِّ سَاقِطَةٍ لَاقِطَةٌ. *See also* Pertinent, Applicable, *a.*

Reliability, *n.* } ثِقَة ـ تَعْوِيل ـ مُعَوَّل.
Reliableness, }

Reliable, *a.* (بِهِ *or*) مِمَّا يُوثَقُ بِهِ ـ مِمَّا يُعَوَّلُ عَلَيْهِ. A — man, عَلَيْهِ ٱلْمُعَوَّلُ ـ أَخُو ثِقَةٍ ـ ثِقَة ـ مُعَوَّل. Reliable historians, ثِقَاتُ ٱلْمُؤَرِّخِينَ.

Reliance, *n.* إِتِّكَاءٌ ـ ثِقَة ـ وَثِيقَة ـ تَوَكُّل ـ إِتِّكَال ـ تَعْوِيل ـ إِعْتِمَاد. Ground of —, مُعْتَمَد. There is no — to be placed in him, لَا ٱعْتِمَادَ عَلَيْهِ ـ مَا عَلَى فُلَانٍ مُعْتَمَدٌ. He is my —, هُوَ عِوَلِي.

Reliant, *n.* Self-reliant, مُتَوَثِّق. To be —, وَثِقَ *aor.* يَوْثَقُ ـ تَوَثَّقَ.

Relic, *n.* A — in a general sense, حُشَاشَة ـ حُشَاش. That which remains after decay or loss, رَسْم *pl.* رُسُوم ـ بَقِيَّة *pl.* بَقَايَا. Relic, as of a saint, ذَخِيرَة *pl.* ذَخَائِر. There remained not of the sun save a departing relic, مَا بَقِيَ مِنَ ٱلشَّمْسِ إِلَّا حُشَاشَةٌ نَازِعٌ. *See also under* Remains, *n.*

Relict, *n.* A widow, أَرْمَلَة *pl.* أَرَامِل.

Relied, *part. of* Rely. To be relied on, ثِقَة ـ مِمَّا يُعْتَمَدُ عَلَيْهِ ـ عَلَيْهِ ٱلْمُعَوَّل *pl.* ثُقَات.

Relief, *n.* The act generally, of removing or relieving from, تَرْوِيح عَن ـ رَفْع ـ دَفْع; that which so removes or relieves, مِرْفَع ـ مِدْفَع ـ إِرَاحَة. Removal of evil, دَفْعُ ٱلشَّرِّ; of disease, دَفْعُ ٱلْمَرَضِ. The act of lightening from, as from a burden, تَخْفِيف عَن; of mitigation, as of pain, *etc.*, تَخْفِيف: relief of pain, تَخْفِيفُ ٱلْوَجَعِ ـ تَهْدِئَةُ ٱلْوَجَعِ; of anxiety, تَفْرِيجُ ٱلْهَمِّ. Escape or deliverance from anything, فَرَج ـ تَفَرُّج; the act of affording such deliverance, تَفْرِيج. Comfort, the being comforted, عَزَآء ـ تَسَلٍّ; the act of affording comfort, تَسْلِيَة ـ تَعْزِيَة. Assistance, in a general sense, عَضْد ـ عَوْن ـ مُعَاوَنَة ـ مُسَاعَفَة ـ إِسْعَاف. A remedy, إِصْلَاح ـ مُعَالَجَة ـ عِلَاج. Relief, as from a post or appointment, إِعْفَآء مِن ـ حَلّ مِن. Reparation, خَلَاص حَقٍّ ـ إِيفَآء حَقٍّ ـ وَفَآء ٱلْحَقِّ. The act of relieving, as a sentry, تَغْيِيرُ ٱلنَّوْبَتْجِي ـ إِبْدَالُ ٱلْخَفَرِ (*vulg.* ٱلْغَفَرِ); the sentry relieving, بَدِيل ـ ٱلنَّوْبَتْجِي ٱلْجَدِيد ـ ٱلْخَفَرُ (*vulg.* ٱلْغَفَرُ) ٱلْجَدِيدُ. A military relief, ٱلْبَدَلُ ٱلْعَسْكَرِيُّ. A subvention, as in money, إِسْعَاف. Something to be of service, شَيْءٌ لِغَرَضٍ مُفِيدٍ. Giving to the poor, charity, حَسَنَة ـ صَدَقَة. Reinforcement, as of soldiers, نَجْدَة ـ مَدَد. The act of relieving, as soldiers from a station, تَحْوِيلُ نَوْبَةِ ٱلْعَسْكَرِ ـ تَبْدِيلُ نَوْبَةٍ; the relieving party, نَوْبَةٌ بَدَلٌ ـ نَوْبَةٌ جَدِيدَةٌ. The prominence of a figure beyond the plane, as in sculpture; the act of giving such relief, تَجْسِيم; of being so relieved, تَجَسُّم. The prominence or light which one thing receives from another, بُرُوز ـ جَهَارَة. *See also* Release, Redress, *n.*

Bass-relief; *See* Basso-relievo, *n.*

High-relief; *See* Alto-relievo, *n.*

In-door relief, ٱلْإِسْعَافُ ٱلْمُعْطَى لِلْمُقِيمِينَ فِي دَارِ ٱلْمَسَاكِينِ.

Out-door relief, ٱلْإِسْعَافُ ٱلْمُعْطَى لِلْفُقَرَآءِ ٱلْمُقِيمِينَ خَارِجَ دَارِ ٱلْمَسَاكِينِ.

Parish relief, إِسْعَافٌ مِنَ ٱلْمَحَلَّةِ ـ إِسْعَافٌ مِنَ ٱلْأَبْرَشِيَّةِ.

To afford or give relief; *see to* Relieve, *v.t.*

To bring into relief, prominence, أَجْهَرَ ـ جَهْرَب ـ أَجْهَرَ ب.

To find relief, rest, ease, from, إِسْتَرَاحَ مِن.

To flee to for, or to ask relief, aid, of, إِسْتَعَانَ ـ إِسْتَعَانَ ب; to ask one to aid in rebutting anything, removing it, إِسْتَدْفَعَ.

Relievable, *a.* That may be removed from one, that he may be relieved of, يُدْفَعُ عَن ـ يُرْفَعُ عَن. That may be helped, assisted, يُسْعَفُ ـ مِمَّا يُسْعَفُ ـ قَابِلُ ٱلتَّخْفِيفِ. That may be mitigated, مِمَّا يُخَفَّفُ. *See also under* Redressible, *a.*

Relieve, *v.t.* To — one, as of a burden, *etc.*, رَفَعَ عَن-كَذَا. To —, as by warding off, دَفَعَ عَن-كَذَا ـ خَفَّفَ عَن-كَذَا. To mitigate, as a pain, أَرَاحَ ـ خَفَّفَ ـ سَكَّنَ ـ هَدَّأَ. To —, as from a difficulty, to get one free of any trouble, نَقَّذَ (*or* نَقَذَ) مِن ـ خَلَّصَ-مِن ـ فَرَجَ عَن-كَذَا ـ فَرَّجَ عَن-كَذَا. To comfort, عَزَّى ـ سَلَّى. To help, assist, عَضَدَ ـ سَاعَدَ ـ أَغَاثَ ـ عَزَّرَ ـ أَعَانَ; to — or help one against another, عَاضَدَ ـ أَعَانَ-عَلَى ـ نَصَرَ-عَلَى; to — or help one with, أَغَاثَ-ب. To remedy, أَصْلَحَ ـ عَالَجَ. To —, as from a post or appointment, أَعْفَى-مِن ـ حَلَّ-مِن. To —, as the soul, mind, رَدَّ نَفْسَهُ. To send something by way of relief, help, أَرْسَلَ شَيْئًا فِي سَبِيلِ ٱلْإِسْعَافِ. To —, as sentries, corps, *etc.*, بَدَّلَ ـ غَيَّرَ. To —, to send relief or reinforcements to, أَمَدَّ. To — or do justice to, أَنْصَفَ. To —, to take a turn after another, عَاقَبَ: they relieved one another, alternated, of many, تَعَاقَبُوا ـ تَدَاوَلُوا ـ سَعَوْا بِٱلدَّوْرِ. To give rest to, أَرَاحَ ـ نَفَّسَ. To give relief to, as in sculpture, جَسَّمَ. To give prominence to, أَجْهَرَ ـ أَجْهَرَ ب. To beautify, as by contrast, حَسَّنَ ـ جَمَّلَ. He was relieved from his appointment, عُفِيَ مِنْ مَأْمُورِيَّتِهِ. He was relieved of it, comforted for the loss of, تَسَلَّى عَنْهُ.

Reliever, *n.* عَضُد ـ عَاضِد ـ مُسَاعِد ـ مُعِين ـ مُعَاوِن ـ عَوْن *pl.* أَعْوَان.

Relievo, *n.* Prominence of a figure above the plane; *see under* Relief, *n.*

Religion, *n.* A system of religious faith, دِين *pl.* أَدْيَان ـ إِيمَان. Piety, دِيَانَة ـ تَقْوَى ـ خَلَاق. Devotion, عِبَادَة. Fidelity, أَمَانَة. A creed, persuasion, doctrine, مِلَّة *pl.* مِلَل ـ مَذْهَب *pl.* مَذَاهِب. The Christian —, ٱلنَّصْرَانِيَّة ـ ٱلدِّيَانَةُ ٱلنَّصْرَانِيَّةُ. The Muslim —, ٱلْإِسْلَام. The Jewish —, ٱلدِّيَانَةُ ٱلْيَهُودِيَّةُ. An easy —, مِلَّةٌ سَمْحَةٌ. He has no —, لَا دِينَ لَهُ. For the sake of, or in the interests of —, فِي سَبِيلِ ٱللّٰهِ. He forsook his —, خَرَجَ مِنْ دِينِهِ. He conformed to their —, دَانَ بِدِينِهِمْ.

He conformed to the Muslim —, دَانَ بِٱلْإِسْلَامِ ـ ٤. Their religions shall be respected, تَكُونُ مَذَاهِبُهُمْ مَرْعِيَّةً.

Religionism, *n.* Fanaticism, party spirit, تَعَصُّب. *See also* Fanaticism, *n.*

Religionist, *n.* مُتَعَصِّب. *See also* Fanatic, *n.*

Religious, *a.* Pertaining to religion, مُتَعَلِّق بِٱلدِّينِ ـ دِينِيٌّ; to a sect, مُتَعَلِّق بِمِلَّةٍ ـ مَذْهَبِيٌّ. Devoted to religion, devout, مُخْتَصّ ـ مُتَّقٍ ـ مُتَعَبِّد ـ دَيِّن. Connected with — worship, دَائِرٌ بِٱلدِّيَانَةِ ـ بِٱلْعِبَادَةِ. Exact, مَضْبُوط ـ مُدَقِّق. Engaged by vows to a — life, ناذِر *pl.* نُذَّار ـ رَاهِب *pl.* رُهْبَان. A — ceremonial, مَنْسَك *pl.* مَنَاسِك. Obligatory — duties, سُنَنُ ٱلْهُدَى. Supererogatory — duties, سُنَنُ ٱلزَّوَائِدِ. Religious belief, الإِيمَانُ. Religious freedom, حُرِّيَّةُ ٱلدِّيَانَةِ. The — law of God, الشَّرِيعَةُ ـ ٱلدِّينُ. To devote one's self to — duties, تَعَبَّدَ ـ ٤ نَسَكَ ـ ٤ أَبَلَ. A — order, أُخْوِيَّةٌ (or جَمَاعَةٌ) دِينِيَّةٌ. A — house, monastery, دَيْر *pl.* دُيُورَة. Religious feelings, الإِحْسَاسَاتُ ٱلدِّينِيَّةُ. Difference in religious belief and creeds, الاِخْتِلَافُ فِي ٱلْمَذَاهِبِ وَٱلِاعْتِقَادَاتِ. He devoted himself to — worship, تَجَرَّدَ لِلْعِبَادَةِ. *See also* Pious, *a.*

Religious, *n.* One devoted to religious exercises, أَبِيل *pl.* آبَال. A monk, أَبِيل *pl.* آبَال ـ رَاهِب *pl.* رُهْبَان; a nun, رَاهِبَة *pl.* رَاهِبَات. A darwish, دَرْوِيش *pl.* دَرَاوِيش.

Religiously, *ad.* In a religious manner, بِتَقْوَى ـ بِدِيَانَةٍ ـ بِدِينٍ. Scrupulously, بِصَدَاقَةٍ كَامِلَةٍ ـ بِتَدْقِيقٍ ـ بِضَبْطٍ.

Religiousness, *n.* دِيَانَة.

Relinquish, *v.t.* To withdraw from, أَحْجَزَ عَن ـ أَجْفَرَ ـ اِعْتَزَلَ عَن ـ تَعَزَّلَ عَن ـ تَنَحَّى عَن ـ ٤ رَفَعَ عَن. To secede from, ـ ٤ خَلَعَ ـ سَيَّبَ ـ ٤ تَرَكَ. To abandon, give up, اِسْتَعْفَى ـ تَجَرَّدَ مِن. To forego, ـ ٤ فَاتَ ـ سَيَّبَ. To —, as an appointment, To cease from, to restrain one's self from, ٤ كَفَّ عَن. To give up claim to, ٤ نَزَلَ عَنْ دَعْوَتِهِ. To give up, as an idea of doing anything, ٤ عَفَّ عَن. They relinquished the war, رَفَعُوا ٱلْحَرْبَ.

Relinquisher, *n.* One who withdraws from, رَافِع ـ مُتَنَحٍّ عَن ـ تَارِك عَن; a seceder, مُعْتَزِل; one who abandons, gives up, مُسَيِّب; who restrains himself from, كَافّ عَن; who gives up a claim, نَازِل عَنْ دَعْوَتِهِ.

Relinquishment, *n.* The act of withdrawing from, ـ أَحْجَاز عَن ـ تَنَحٍّ عَن; of seceding from, تَعَزُّل عَن ـ اِعْتِزَال عَن; of abandoning, تَسْيِيب ـ مُتَارَكَة ـ تَرْك; of giving up, as an appointment, اِسْتِعْفَاء ـ تَجَرُّد مِن; of desisting from, كَفّ عَن; of giving up a claim, نُزُول عَنْ دَعْوَى; as the notion of doing anything, ـ عَفّ ـ عَفَاف ـ اِسْتِعْفَاف.

Reliquary, *n.* أُنْبُوبَة ـ صُنْدُوق ذَخَائِرِ ٱلْقِدِّيسِينَ.

Relique, *n.* *See* Relic, *n.*

Reliquiæ, *n.* As of bones, رِمَام ـ رِمَم. Remains, in a general sense, بَقَايَا.

Relish, *n.* An agreeable flavour, لَذَّة ـ طَعْم. The faculty of perceiving taste, ذَوْق. Desire, appetite, ـ نَفْس ـ اِشْتِهَاء ـ شَوْق. Discernment, تَمْيِيز. Inclination for a thing, مَيْل. Something taken to increase appetite, لُهْنَة ـ لُهْجَة ـ مُرِّيّ *vulg.* مُرِيّ. It has no —, of food, مَا لَهُ لَذَّةٌ ـ مَا لَهُ طَعْمٌ. What is lean has no —, لَيْسَ لِلْغَثِّ طَعْمٌ. Taste, and you will have —, تَطَعَّمْ تَطْعَمْ.

Relish, *v.t.* To like the taste of, as of food, اِسْتَلَذَّ ـ ٤ طَعِمَ. To enjoy, ـ تَنَعَّمَ ـ تَمَتَّعَ ب. To approve of, ـ اِسْتَصْوَبَ اِسْتَحْسَنَ. To be pleased with, أَعْجَبَ ٱلشَّيْءُ. To be inclined to, ٤ مَالَ إِلَى.

Relish, *v.i.* To have a pleasant taste, ٤ لَذَّ ـ كَانَ لَذِيذًا.

Relishable, *a.* لَذِيذ ـ مِمَّا يُتَلَذَّذُ بِهِ ـ ذُو لَذَّةٍ.

Reluctance, *n.* } قِلَّة ـ قِلَّةُ رِضَاءٍ ـ قِلَّةُ إِرَادَةٍ ـ اِسْتِمْسَاك
Reluctancy, } تَكَرُّه ـ قِلَّةُ خَاطِرٍ ـ رَغْبَة. With —, بِقِلَّةِ خَاطِرٍ ـ بِقِلَّةِ إِرَادَةٍ ـ عَلَى تَكَرُّهٍ ـ بِٱسْتِمْسَاكٍ. *See also* Repugnance, *n.*

Reluctant, *a.* ـ قَلِيلُ ٱلرِّضَاءِ ـ مُتَرَدِّد ـ مُتَضَرِّب ـ مُتَمَاسِك قَلِيلُ ٱلْإِرَادَةِ. A — consent, رِضَاءٌ بِٱضْطِرَارٍ ـ إِجَابَةٌ عَنْ كَرَاهِيَةٍ. To be —, to hesitate, اِخْتَارَ ـ تَضَرَّبَ ـ تَرَدَّدَ ـ تَوَقَّفَ. *See also* Repugnant, *a.*

Reluctantly, *ad.* بِقِلَّةٍ ـ بِقِلَّةِ إِرَادَةٍ ـ بِٱسْتِمْسَاكٍ ـ بِتَكَرُّهٍ خَاطِرٍ.

Relume, *v.t.* }
Relumine, } *See to* Re-illumine, *v.t.*

Rely, *v.i.* To rely upon, to trust in, ـ اِسْتَكْفَى ب ـ ٤ خَلَا عَلَى تَحَمَّلَ ب ـ ٤ رَكَنَ إِلَى ـ تَوَكَّلَ عَلَى ـ اِتَّكَلَ عَلَى ـ عَوَّلَ ب *or* صَدَّقَ بِ ـ اِعْتَمَدَ عَلَى ـ عَلَى; to believe, وَثِقَ ب *aor.* يَثِقُ ـ *or* ب *or* عَلَى.

Remain, *v.i.* To abide in a place, ـ ٤ مَكَثَ ـ ٤ لَطِيَ ب ـ ٤ تَعَدَ ـ اِسْتَقَامَ ـ أَقَامَ ـ أَحَالَ ب ـ ٤ ثَوَى ـ اِسْتَقَرَّ ـ ٤ بَاتَ تَبَقَّى ـ ٤ بَقِيَ مِن ـ ٤ سَكَنَ. To be left, as a remainder, ٤ فَضَلَ مِن. To endure, continue, last, اِسْتَمَرَّ ـ بَقِيَ ـ ٤. To continue, as in action, to continue doing, ظَلَّ *aor.* يَظَلُّ ـ اِسْتَمَرَّ ـ بَقِيَ ـ ٤

vulg. تَمّ ع. To suffer to —, to let live, أَبْقَى. He or it remained in the same state, بَقِيَ عَلَى حَالِهِ ع. To cause or let remain, to keep, أَبْقَى. Let none of it — until the morning, لا تُبْقُوا مِنْهُ إِلَى ٱلصَّبَاحِ. So much remained of it, فَضَلَ (or بَقِيَ) مِنْهُ كَذا ع. Remain in your place, أُقْعُدْ فِي مَكَانِكَ ـ اِلْزَمْ مَكَانَكَ. I remained alone, بَقِيتُ أَنَا وَحْدِي. No strength remained in me, لَمْ تَبْقَ فِيَّ قُوَّةٌ. They remained in the house eating and drinking, أَقَامُوا فِي ٱلْبَيْتِ آكِلِينَ وَشَارِبِينَ. He remained speechless, بَقِيَ صَامِتًا ع. There is nothing remaining in it, مَا فِيهِ بُلَالَةٌ وَلَا عُلَالَةٌ. To — at home, to keep to the house; *see under* House, *n.*

Remainder, *n.* What remains over and above, عُلَالَةٌ ـ نُضَاضَةٌ ـ بُلَالَةٌ ـ فَضْل *pl.* فُضُول ـ فَضْلَةٌ *pl.* فَضَل ـ تُلَاوَة ـ بَقِيَّة *pl.* بَقَايَا and بَقِيَّات. Residue, سَائِر. Remainder, fractions, قُصُور. Remainder, in law, عَوْدَةٌ إِلَى ـ رُجُوعٌ إِلَى. When will you bring me the — of the amount? مَتَى تُؤَدِّينِي ٱلْعُلَالَةَ (or بَقِيَّةَ ٱلْمَبْلَغِ). In remainder, reversible, بِٱلْعَوْدَةِ ـ بِٱلرُّجُوعِ.

Remaining, *a.* } Continuing, بَاقٍ; over and above, فَاضِل; staying in a place,
Remanent, } مُقِيم ـ عَاكِف ـ ثَاوٍ; abiding, مُسْتَقِرّ. He left none of them —, as in a battle, لَمْ يُبْقِ شَارِدًا.

Remains, *n.* What is left; (*see under* Remainder, *n.*) Mortal —, تُرَاب ـ جِنَازَة ـ جَسَدٌ مَيِّتٌ. The (last) — of the spirit, or of life, in a sick or wounded man, حُشَاشَة ـ حُشَاش. There was not left of manliness save a last —, or relic, wavering in the entrails of one at the point of death, مَا بَقِيَ مِنَ ٱلْمُرُوَّةِ إِلَّا حُشَاشَةٌ تَتَرَدَّدُ فِي أَحْشَاءِ مُحْتَضِرٍ.

Remake, *v.t.* فَطَرَ ـ مِنْ ـ جَدَّدَ ـ عَادَ فَعَمِلَهُ ع ـ عَمِلَ ـ ثَانِيَةً ع جَدِيدٍ.

Remand, *v.t.* To send or call back, رَدَّ ع ـ رَجَّعَ ـ أَعَادَ ـ اِسْتَرْجَعَ ـ اِسْتَعَادَ. To refer one to another person, وَجَّهَ ـ إِلَى ـ حَوَّلَ ـ عَلَى. To order a case to be referred to such an one, أَمَرَ ع بِرَفْعِ ٱلدَّعْوَى إِلَى فُلَانٍ. To — a prisoner, أَمَرَ بِرَدِّ ٱلْمَحْبُوسِ إِلَى ٱلْحَبْسِ لِأَجْلِ تَكْمِيلِ ٱلتَّحْقِيقَاتِ عَنْ جُرْمِهِ.

Remand, *n.* As of a prisoner by a judge or magistrate, أَمْرٌ بِرَدِّ ٱلْمَحْبُوسِ إِلَى ٱلْحَبْسِ لِأَجْلِ تَكْمِيلِ ٱلتَّحْقِيقَاتِ عَنْ ذَنْبِهِ.

Remanence, *n.* ثُبُوت ـ ثَبَات.

Remark, *n.* تَنَبُّه ـ إِفَادَة *pl.* إِفَادَات ـ مُلَاحَظَة *pl.* مُلَاحَظَات. To make a —, أَفَادَ ـ قَالَ *aor.* يَقُولُ. To make a — about, عَبَّرَ عَنْ. To make (disparaging) remarks on, ذَمَّ ع ـ ذَلَّ ع ـ عَيَّبَ. Here several remarks may be made, هُنَا مُلَاحَظَةٌ مِنْ عِدَّةِ أَوْجُهٍ. *See also* Observation, Notice, *n.*

Remark, *v.t.* To notice, by the senses, نَظَرَ إِلَى ع ـ لَاحَظَ ـ أَشَافَ إِلَى. To consider with attention, وَقَفَ عَلَى *aor.* يَقِفُ ـ لَاحَظَ ـ فَطِنَ إِلَى ع ـ اِسْتَشَفَّ. To distinguish, مَيَّزَ.

Remarkable, *a.* Worthy of remark, جَدِيرٌ بِٱلْمُلَاحَظَةِ. Extraordinary, نَادِر ـ غَرِيب ـ عَجِيب. Eminent, note-worthy, بَدِيع ـ مَشْهُور. To be — for, اِشْتَهَرَ بِ.

Remarkableness, *n.* The quality of deserving particular notice, صِفَةٌ تَسْتَدْعِي ٱلِٱنْتِبَاهَ. Strangeness, نَدَارَة ـ غَرَابَة.

Remarkably, *ad.* In a way deserving of notice, بِنَوْعٍ يَسْتَحِقُّ ٱلِٱعْتِبَارَ. Unusually, بِصُورَةٍ عَجِيبَةٍ ـ فَوْقَ ٱلْعَادَةِ. Exceedingly, لِلْغَايَةِ ـ جِدًّا ـ كَثِيرًا.

Remarker, *n.* مُفِيد ـ مُلَاحِظ.

Remarry, *v.i.* عَادَ فَتَزَوَّجَ ع ـ تَزَوَّجَ ثَانِيَةً.

Remast, *v.t.* رَكَّبَ لِ ـ أَدْقَالًا ثَانِيَةً.

Remediable, *a.* That may be remedied, قَابِلُ ٱلْعِلَاجِ ـ مِمَّا يُعَالَجُ ـ مِمَّا يُصْلَحُ ـ جَبْرُهُ مُمْكِنٌ; that may be cured, مِمَّا يُشْفَى; that may be repaired, or treated medically, مِمَّا يُدَاوَى.

Remediably, *ad.* بِصُورَةٍ قَابِلَةٍ ٱلْعِلَاجَ.

Remedial, *a.* شِفَائِيّ ـ طِبِّيّ ـ عِلَاجِيّ ـ شَافٍ ـ مُصْلِح ـ جَابِر.

Remediless, *a.* *See* Incurable, *a.*

Remedy, *n.* شِفَاءٌ ع *pl.* أَشْفِيَة ـ دَوَاءٌ *pl.* أَدْوِيَة ـ إِصْلَاح ـ مُعَالَجَة ـ عِلَاج. To prescribe a —, وَصَفَ دَوَاءً ـ أَشْفَى *aor.* يَصِفُ. God made honey to be his —, أَشْفَاهُ ٱللّٰهُ عَسَلًا. I gave the thing to thee as a —, أَشْفَيْتُكَ ٱلشَّيْءَ ع.

Remedy, *v.t.* جَبَرَ ع ـ جَبَّرَ ـ أَشْفَى ـ عَالَجَ ـ أَصْلَحَ ـ دَاوَى. To — a difficulty, اِسْتَدْرَكَ ٱلضَّرَرَ.

Remember, *v.t.* To bear in mind, تَنَبَّهَ عَلَى ـ اِسْتَذْكَرَ ـ تَذَكَّرَ ـ ذَكَرَ ع. To try to —, اِسْتَذْكَرَ. To cause to —, ذَكَّرَ ـ أَذْكَرَ.

Remembrance, *n.* The power of remembering, ذِكْر ـ ذُكْر ـ ذِكْرَة ـ ذُكْرَة. Mind, خَاطِر ـ ذِهْن. The presence of a thing in the mind, ذِكْرٌ بِٱلْقَلْبِ. Place thou him or it in thy —, اِجْعَلْهُ مِنْكَ عَلَى ذِكْرٍ. He did not cease to be in my —, مَا زَالَ مِنِّي عَلَى ذُكْرٍ. You are in my —, أَنْتَ مِنِّي عَلَى ذُكْرٍ. To bring to one's —, ذَكَّرَ ـ أَذْكَرَ. To give one's remembrances to, سَلَّمَ عَلَى. In —, تَذْكَارًا. *See also under* Mind, Memory, *n.*

Remembrancer, *n.* That which reminds or recalls to remembrance, تَذْكِرَة ـ تَذْكَار ـ تَفْكِرَة. The — of a court, *etc.*, أَمِينُ ٱلدَّفَاتِرِ.

Remind, *v.t.* نَبَّهَ ـ ذَكَّرَ ـ فَكَّرَ. To be reminded of, تَنَبَّهَ عَلَى. To be reminded, admonished, as by passing events, اِعْتَبَرَ: He was reminded, warned, by what had passed, اِعْتَبَرَ بِمَا مَضَى.

Reminder, *n.* تَنْبِيه ـ تَذْكار.

Remington rifle, *n.* بُنْدُقِيَّةٌ مُسَدَّسَةٌ مَنْسُوبَةٌ إِلَى رِيمِنْطُون.

Reminiscence, *n.* *See* Memory, *n.*

Remise, *v.t.* To grant back, رَدَّ ² ـ عادَ-إِلَى; to give up, سَلَّمَ; to quit, vacate, فَرَّغَ.

Remiss, *a.* Careless, مُتَغافِل ـ غافِل ـ غابِن ـ مُسْتَرْخٍ ـ مُتَراخٍ; not vigorous, cold, فاتِر. To be —, careless in, إِنْفَشَّ عَن ـ قَصَّرَ فِي ـ تَراخَى فِي ـ إِسْتَرْخَى فِي ـ أَخَلَّ ب ـ غَبِنَ فِي; to be without interest in, تَفَتَّرَ عَن ـ فَتَرَ عَن ². To make —, uninterested in, فَتَّرَ-عَن. *See also under* Careless, Inattentive, Negligent, *a.*

Remissible, *a.* That may be pardoned, حَلُّ ٱلْعَفْوِ ـ يُغْفَرُ ـ مِمَّا يُصْفَحُ عَنْهُ ـ مِمَّا يُعْفَى عَنْهُ ـ مَغْفُور.

Remission, *n.* Diminution of intensity, abatement, تَخْفِيف ـ تَنْزِيل ـ تَقْلِيل ـ تَنْقِيص; of a disease, paroxysm, مُهاوَدَة. Pardon, غُفْران ـ مَغْفِرَة ـ مُعافاة ـ عَفْوٌ.

Remissly, *ad.* بِفُتُورٍ ـ بِإِهْمالٍ ـ بِتَراخٍ.

Remissness, *n.* تَقْصِير ـ قُصُور ـ إِهْمال ـ إِسْتِرْخاء ـ تَراخٍ. *See also* Inattention, Negligence, *n.*

Remit, *v.t.* To send back, رَدَّ ² ـ رَجَّعَ ـ أَعادَ ـ أَوَّلَ-إِلَى. To deliver over to, سَلَّمَ-إِلَى. To send to, أَوْفَدَ-إِلَى *or* عَلَى ـ نَفَّذَ- (or أَنْفَذَ-) إِلَى ـ أَرْسَلَ-إِلَى. To refer one to, حَوَّلَ-عَلَى. To lighten, diminish in intensity, خَفَّفَ. To —, as part of a punishment to, فَتَّرَ عَنْهُ ٱلْقِصاص. To pardon, تَجاوَزَ عَن ـ سامَحَ-ب ـ غَفَرَ-ل ـ عَفا عَن *aor.* يَعْفُو. To —, as of a debt, to, أَعْفَى-عَن ـ سَمَحَ لَهُ ب ـ فاتَ لَهُ ٱلدَّيْن ².

Remit, *v.i.* To abate in violence, هَدَأَ ـ قَلَّ ـ إِرْتَخَى ـ نَقَصَ ². To become less, as a pain, خَفَّ. To cool in ardour, تَرَخَّصَ فِي ـ تَفَتَّرَ ـ فَتَرَ ² ـ تَرَخَّى ـ إِرْتَخَى; as in any affair, تَرَخَّصَ فِي. The heat remitted, رَقَدَ ٱلْحَرُّ ². The cold remitted, فَتَرَ ٱلْبَرْدُ ². *See also to* Abate, Relax, *v.i.*

Remitment, *n.* The act of remitting to custody, رَدٌّ إِلَى ٱلْحَبْسِ ـ إِعادَةٌ إِلَى ٱلسِّجْنِ. Forgiveness, عَفْوٌ ـ عُفُوٌّ ـ مُعافاة. Abatement, as of a debt, سِماح ـ سَماح ـ مُسامَحَة.

Remittal, *n.* Surrender, تَسْلِيم. *See also* Remission, *n.*

Remittance, *n.* The act of transmitting money, إِرْسالُ ٱلدَّراهِمِ ـ تَسْلِيمُ ٱلدَّراهِمِ; a sum remitted, دَراهِمُ مُرْسُولَةٌ (or مَوْفُوضَة).

Remittent, *a.* مُطْبِق. A — fever, حُمَّى مُطْبِقَةٌ ـ حُمَّى لازِمَةٌ ـ حُمَّى دائِمَةٌ.

Remnant, *n.* بَقِيَّة *pl.* بَقايا ـ خَلْف ـ غُدْرَة *pl.* غُدْرات ـ حاصِل; as of a piece of cloth, فَضْلَة *pl.* فِضال *and* فَضَلات. In him is a — of disease, بِهِ غادِرٌ مِنْ مَرَضٍ.

Remodel, *v.t.* جَدَّدَ ـ نَسَّقَ-ثانِيَةً ـ صَوَّرَ-ثانِيَةً ـ شَكَّلَ-ثانِيَةً ـ نَسَقَهُ.

Remould, *v.t.* To recast, سَبَكَ-ثانِيَةً ² ـ صاغَ-ثانِيَةً ² ـ عادَ ² فَصاغَهُ.

Remonstrance, *n.* تَنْذِير ـ إِنْذار ـ شَكْوٌ ـ شَكْوَى ـ إِعْتِراض. Remonstrances, مَعْرُوضات ـ إِخْطارات. To make remonstrances, أَجْرَى ٱلْمَعْرُوضاتِ ـ أَجْرَى ٱلْإِخْطاراتِ. *See also* Expostulation, *n.*

Remonstrant, *a.* مُعْتَرِض ـ شَكِيٌّ ـ شاكٍ ـ مُنَبِّه ـ مُنْذِر.

Remonstrate, *v.i.* أَجْرَى ٱلْإِخْطاراتِ ـ أَجْرَى ٱلْمَعْرُوضاتِ. To — against, إِمْتَنَعَ عَلَى ـ إِعْتَرَضَ عَلَى. *See also under to* Expostulate, *v.i.*

Remorse, *n.* لَسْعُ ٱلذِّمَّةِ ـ نَخْزُ ٱلضَّمِيرِ ـ أَكْلُ ٱلسَّرِيرَةِ. He has no —, ما يَنْخِزُهُ ضَمِيرُهُ ـ ما تَلْعَسُهُ ذِمَّتُهُ. *See also* Compunction, *n.*

Remorseful, *a.* Full of remorse, لاسِعُ ٱلذِّمَّةِ ـ آكِلُ ٱلسَّرِيرَةِ ـ مُنْخَزُ ٱلضَّمِيرِ. *See also* Compassionate, *a.*

Remorsefully, *ad.* بِنَخْزِ ٱلْقَلْبِ ـ بِلَسْعِ ٱلذِّمَّةِ. *See also* Compassionately, *ad.*

Remorseless, *a.* Unpitying, قاسِي ـ قاسِح ـ عَسُوف ـ بِلا رَحْمَةٍ ـ بِلا حِنَّةٍ ـ ٱلْقَلْبِ.

Remorselessly, *ad.* بِقَساوَةِ قَلْبٍ ـ بِقَساوَةٍ ـ بِعَنْفٍ ـ بِلا رَحْمَةٍ ـ بِلا حِنَّةٍ.

Remorselessness, *n.* قَساوَة ـ قَساوَة ـ عَنْف ـ عَدَمُ ٱلرَّحْمَةِ ـ عَدَمُ ٱلْحِنَّةِ ـ قَلْب.

Remote, *a.* In place, بَعِيد ـ أَقْصاء ـ أَقْصاء *pl.* قاصٍ ـ أَقْصاء *pl.* قَصِيٌّ; in place, time, or quantity, باعِد ـ بُعاد ـ بَعِيد. Slight, inconsiderate, زَهِيد ـ تافِهٌ ـ جُزْئِيٌّ. Most —, of place, أَقْصَى: most — places, ends, أَقاصِي. To be — from, تَقَصَّى عَن ـ أَبْعَدَ عَن ـ تَباعَدَ عَن. To be —, in a general sense, بَعُدَ ². *See also under* Distant, Foreign, Improbable, *a.*

Remotely, *ad.* At a distance, فِي ٱلْبُعْدِ ـ بُعْدَةً. Slightly, قِلَّةً ـ جُزْءًا ـ خِفَّةً. *See also* Distantly, Improbably, *ad.*

Remoteness, *n.* State of being distant, of place, غُرْبَة ـ غُرْب ـ بُعْدَة ـ بُعْد ـ قَصًى ـ قَصاء; of being unlikely, بُعْد. Slightness, جُزْئِيَّة ـ قِلَّة. *See also* Distance, Improbability, *n.*

Remount, *v.t.* To ascend again, عادَ ² فَٱرْتَقاهُ ـ صَعِدَ-ثانِيَةً. To put one on horseback again, عادَ ² فَرَكَّبَ-عَلَى ٱلْفَرَسِ ـ رَكَّبَ عَلَى ٱلدّابَّةِ ثانِيَةً. To set again, رَكَّبَ-ثانِيَةً.

Remount, *v.i.* To ascend again, عَادَ فَٱرْتَقَى ـ عَادَ فَصَعِدَ. To get on horseback again, عَادَ فَرَكِبَ ـ رَكِبَ ٱلْفَرَسَ ثَانِيَةً ٱلدَّابَّةَ.

Removability, *n.* Capacity of being removed, as from one place to another, قَابِلِيَّةُ ٱلنَّقْلِ ـ إِمْكَانُ ٱلتَّحْوِيلِ; of being displaced from office, قَابِلُ ٱلْعَزْلِ.

Removable, *a.* As from one place to another, تَحْوِيلُهُ مُمْكِنٌ ـ مِمَّا يَنْتَقِلُ; that may be dispelled, إِذْهَابُهُ مُمْكِنٌ ـ مِمَّا يُذْهَبُ; that may be displaced from office, يُعْزَلُ ـ تَحْتَ ٱلْعَزْلِ.

Removal, *n.* The act of putting an end to or putting away, إِزَاحَةٌ ـ تَقْلِيعٌ ـ قَلْعَةٌ ـ قَلْعٌ ـ إِذْهَابٌ ـ دَفْعٌ ـ صَرْفٌ ـ رَفْعٌ; of changing one's abode, تَعْزِيلٌ ـ عَزْلٌ ـ تَحْوِيلٌ ـ حَوْلٌ; the state of such change, عُزْلَةٌ ـ حِوَلٌ. The act of moving anything from off a place, *etc.*, ـ إِنْتِقَالٌ ـ رَفْعٌ ـ نَقْلٌ; of being so removed, تَنَقُّلٌ ـ رَفْعٌ; to a distance, إِبْتِعَادٌ. The act of removing from office, تَنْزِيعٌ ـ تَعْزِيلٌ ـ عَزْلٌ; of being so removed, عُزْلَةٌ. Removal, departure, إِبْعَادٌ ـ ذِهَابٌ ـ رَحِيلٌ ـ رَحْلٌ. The act of casting off, طَرْدٌ. Removal of one's self from anything, تَعَزُّلٌ عُزْلَةٌ عَنْ ـ عَنْ. Death, مَوْتٌ.

Remove, *v.t.* To take away, put an end to, ـ رَفَعَ ـ أَزَالَ ـ أَزَاحَ أَذْهَبَ. To move, as from a place, *etc.*, ـ نَقَلَ ـ حَوَّلَ ـ بَدَّ قَلَعَ. To — or move aside or to a distance, ـ حَادَ بِ ـ جَنَّبَ أَشْذَى ـ مِن. To — or separate one, as from another, أَبْعَدَ ـ أَحَادَ. To be removed, as from a place, تَنَقَّلَ ـ إِنْتَقَلَ ـ تَحَوَّلَ; to a distance or aside, تَبَاعَدَ ـ أُحِيدَ بِهِ ـ تَجَنَّبَ ـ إِجْتَنَبَ. To — one from a place or office, ـ نَزَعَ ـ مِن ـ عَزَلَ ـ عَن ـ عَزَلَ ـ عَن ـ حَوَّلَ ـ هَادَ نَحَّى عَن ـ خَلَعَ ـ ٱ...; especially from a place, خُلِعَ ـ أَنْخَلَعَ عَن قُلِعَ ـ عَن; to be removed, as from office, نُزِعَ عَن ـ عُزِلَ عَن. To — one's self from, to go aside or to separate from, إِجْتَنَبَ ـ تَعَزَّلَ عَن ـ إِعْتَزَلَ عَن ـ إِعْتَزَلَ ـ تَعَزَّلَ. To —, to cast off, drive away, expel, طَرَدَ. To —, as anything which conceals, to uncover, reveal, كَشَفَ عَن.

Remove, *v.i.* To change place, تَحَوَّلَ ـ حَالَ. To go away from, أَقْلَعَ عَن ـ رَحَلَ (or إِرْتَحَلَ or تَرَحَّلَ) عَن ـ إِنْفَكَّ عَن ـ إِنْطَلَقَ مِن ـ ذَهَبَ مِن. To — to a distance, غَرَبَ إِبْتَعَدَ ـ تَبَاعَدَ ـ تَغَرَّبَ. To — to one side, إِجْتَنَبَ. He removed from his place, حَالَ مِنْ مَكَانِهِ. Remove from me; be off! أُغْرُبْ عَنِّي.

Remove, *n.* A step in the scale of gradation, دَرَجَةٌ *pl.* دَرَجَاتٌ ـ رُتْبَةٌ *pl.* رُتَبٌ. A move, حَرَكَةٌ. Distance, بُعَادٌ ـ بُعْدٌ. Degree of kindred and affinity, دَرَجَةُ ٱلْقَرَابَةِ وَٱلنَّسَبِ. A — of dishes, طَائِفَةٌ مِنَ ٱلْأَطْعِمَةِ.

Removed, *a.* Displaced, مَعْزُولٌ; carried away, مَنْقُولٌ; driven away, مَطْرُودٌ; uncovered, مَكْشُوفٌ عَنْهُ. First-cousin (uncle's son) removed, إِبْنُ عَمٍّ فِي أَوْلَى دَرَجَةِ ٱلْقَرَابَةِ; of an aunt's son, إِبْنُ خَالَةٍ فِي أَوْلَى دَرَجَةِ ٱلْقَرَابَةِ.

Remover, *n.* مُعَزِّلٌ ـ نَاقِلٌ ـ مُحَوِّلٌ.

Remunerable, *a.* مِمَّا يُجَازَى ـ مِمَّا يُكَافَى.

Remunerate, *v.t.* *See to* Compensate, Recompense, *v.t.*

Remuneration, *n.* *See* Compensation, Recompense, *n.*

Remunerative, *a.* / Remuneratory, } Tending to recompense, مُجَازٍ ـ جَازٍ ـ مُكَافٍ. *See also* Profitable, *a.*

Renal, *a.* Pertaining to the kidneys, مُتَعَلِّقٌ بِٱلْكُلْوَاتِ ـ كُلَائِيٌّ.

Renard, *n.* *See* Fox, *n.*

Renascence, *n.* / Renascency, } A new growth, نَشْأَةٌ جَدِيدَةٌ. A new appearance, occurrence, ظُهُورٌ ـ حُدُوثٌ ثَانٍ بَدْءٌ ـ حُدُوثٌ ثَانٍ ـ ثَانٍ.

Renascent, *a.* Growing again, نَاشٍ ثَانِيَةً. Occurring again, بَادٍ ثَانِيَةً ـ حَادِثٌ ثَانِيَةً.

Rencounter, *n.* *See* Encounter, *n.*

Rencounter, *v.t.* *See to* Encounter, *v.t.*

Rend, *v.t.* To tear, مَزَّقَ ـ مَزَقَ ـ خَرَقَ ـ فَتَقَ ـ شَرَمَ. To split, شَقَّ ـ فَلَجَ ـ نَضَّ. To — as of a wild beast, إِفْتَرَسَ. To — away from, to deprive of, خَطِفَ ـ عَن. To lacerate, wound, جَرَّحَ ـ جَرَحَ ـ كَلَمَ ـ عَرَّى ـ عَن. To be rent or torn, تَفَتَّقَ ـ تَمَزَّقَ ـ إِنْشَرَمَ ـ تَشَرَّمَ; to be split, إِنْشَقَّ. *See also to* Tear, Split, *v.t.*

Render, *v.t.* To return, رَجَعَ ـ رَدَّ ـ أَوَّلَ ـ إِلَى. To recompense, requite, جَازَى ـ عَوَّضَ ـ عَنْ كَذَا. To give, أَعْطَى. To deliver, make over, سَلَّمَ. To make or cause to be, صَيَّرَ ـ أَوَّلَ. To boil or melt down, ذَوَّبَ ـ صَيَّرَ ذَائِبًا أَعَادَ. To give to one for use or profit, أَفَادَ. To — into, to translate into, نَقَلَ ـ إِلَى تَرْجَمَ ـ إِلَى. To — justice to, عَدَلَ فِي ٱلْأَمْرِ ـ أَنْصَفَ. To — thanks to, تَشَكَّرَ لِ ـ شَكَرَ لِ. To — or present an account, قَدَّمَ عَرَضَ ٱلْحِسَابَ ـ حِسَابًا. He shall — to every man according to his work, يَرُدُّ عَلَى كُلِّ إِنْسَانٍ مِثْلَ عَمَلِهِ. Render to no man evil for evil, لَا يُجَازِ أَحَدٌ أَحَدًا عَنْ شَرٍّ بِشَرٍّ.

Renderable, *a.* That may be rendered, returned, مِمَّا يُرَدُّ; that may be given, مِمَّا يُعْطَى; that may be given up, مِمَّا يُسَلَّمُ; that may be made into, مِمَّا يَتَصَيَّرُ ـ مِمَّا يُؤَوَّلُ إِلَى; that may be boiled down, مِمَّا يُذَوَّبُ; that may be translated into, مِمَّا يُنْقَلُ إِلَى.

Rendering, *n.* Explanation, تَفْسِير ـ تَأْوِيل.

Rendezvous, *n.* As of troops, مَضَمّ. An appointed place of meeting, مَوْعِد ـ مِيعَاد ـ مَعْهَد ـ مُلْتَقَى. To appoint a —, وَاعَدَ. They, of many, appointed a — at the castle, تَوَاعَدُوا إِلَى ٱلْقَلْعَةِ. The — is in the garden, ٱلْمَوْعِدُ فِي ٱلْبُسْتَانِ.

Rendezvous, *v.t.* As of troops, ضَمَّ-إِلَى.

Rendezvous, *v.i.* إِنْضَمُّوا إِلَى.

Rendition, *n.* The act of giving up, تَسْلِيم; of translating, تَرْجَمَة ـ نَقْل.

Renegade, *n.* } مُرْتَدّ. *See also* Apostate, *n.*
Renegado, }

Renerve, *v.t.* ² عَادَ فَشَجَّعَهُ ـ شَدَّدَ-ثَانِيَةً ـ شَجَّعَ-ثَانِيَةً. To — one's self, ² عَادَ فَتَشَدَّدَ ـ تَشَجَّعَ ثَانِيَةً.

Renew, *v.t.* To make new, جَدَّدَ. To restore to a good state, أَصْلَحَ ـ صَحَّحَ; as of pictures, colours, *etc.*, جَنْدَرَ. To begin anew, ـ بَدَأَ بِ-مِنْ جَدِيدٍ ـ إِسْتَأْنَفَ ـ ² عَادَ فَاسْتَأْنَفَ إِبْتَدَأَ بِ-مِنْ جَدِيدٍ. To confirm, ثَبَّتَ ـ أَكَّدَ. To make vigorous, ـ ثَنَّى ـ كَرَّرَ قَوَّى ـ شَدَّدَ ـ شَجَّعَ. To repeat a thing, أَعَادَ. To —, as one's acquaintance with, تَفَقَّدَ ـ تَعَاهَدَ ـ تَعَهَّدَ. To — a conversation, ² عَادَ فَعَقَدَ ٱلْمُحَاوَرَةَ. To — one's affection, أَعَادَ عَقْدَ ٱلْمَحَبَّةِ. He renewed his zeal, إِزْدَادَ غَيْرَةً. The war will not be renewed till next month, لَا تُسْتَأْنَفُ ٱلْحَرْبُ إِلَّا فِي ٱلشَّهْرِ ٱلْآتِي. *See also to* Repair, Rebuild, Re-establish, Revive, Restore, Repeat, *v.t.*

Renewable, *a.* That may be made new, قَابِلٌ ـ مِمَّا يَتَجَدَّدُ ـ وِمِمَّا يُثَبَّتُ ـ مِمَّا يُؤَكَّدُ ٱلتَّجْدِيدَ; that may be confirmed again, تَثْبِيتُهُ جَائِزٌ.

Renewal, *n.* The act of making new, تَجْدِيد; as of colours, ـ جَنْدَرَة; the being made new, تَجَدُّد. Repetition, تَكْرِير ـ إِعَادَة; تَكْرَار; the being repeated, تَكَرُّر ـ مُعَاوَدَة ـ عَوْد. The act of rebuilding, تَعْمِير; the state of being rebuilt, عُمْرَان. The act of putting in order, strengthening, تَشْيِيد ـ تَحْكِيم ـ تَأْيِيد; the being so put in order, strengthened, تَشَيُّد ـ تَأَيُّد ـ تَحَكُّم. A recurrence, إِسْتِنْجَاد ـ وُقُوعٌ ثَانٍ. For the — of our friendly relations, لِتَجْدِيدِ عَلَاقَتِنَا ٱلْوِدَادِيَّةِ. Renewal of negotiations, إِعَادَةُ ٱلْمُفَاوَضَاتِ.

Renewed, *a.* Made new, مُجَدَّد; as of colours, مُجَنْدَر; repeated, مُكَرَّر; put in order, repaired, مُشَيَّد ـ مُحَكَّم ـ مُصْلَح ـ مُسْتَتِبّ; re-occurring, مُسْتَجِدّ.

Renewedly, *ad.* Again, repeatedly, تَكْرَارًا ـ أَيْضًا ـ ثَانِيَةً.

Renewer, *n.* مُجَدِّد; as of colours, paintings, *etc.*, مُجَنْدِر.

Renewing, *n.* *See* Renewal, *n.*

Renewing, *a.* مُجَدِّد.

Reniform, *a.* فِي شَكْلِ ٱلْكُلْوَاتِ ـ بِهَيْئَةِ ٱلْكُلْوَاتِ.

Renitence, *n.* } Resistance to pressure, صَلَابَة ـ دَفْعَة. *See also*
Renitency, } Reluctance, *n.*

Renitent, *a.* Resisting, as pressure, دَافِع. *See also* Reluctant, *a.*

Rennet, *n.* ضُون ـ مِنْفَحَة ـ إِنْفَحَة ـ يَتْن.

Renounce, *v.t.* To deny, disavow, ـ جَحَدَ ـ أَنْكَرَ ـ نَكِرَ كَذَّبَ. To reject, رَفَضَ ². To disown, رَفَضَ ². To cast off, so as not to be answerable for, خَلَعَ: Verily we have renounced, cast off, such an one, إِنَّا قَدْ خَلَعْنَا فُلَانًا. One so cast off, ـ خَلِيع مَخْلُوع. To be so renounced, cast off, خَلَعَ ². To turn off, طَرَدَ ـ نَفَى ². To —, as of a claim, نَزَلَ عَنْ. *See also to* Disown, Disclaim, Deny, Reject, *v.t.*

Renouncement, *n.* *See* Renunciation, *n.*

Renovate, *v.t.* *See to* Renew, *v.t.*

Renovation, *n.* *See* Renewal, *n.*

Renovator, *n.* *See* Renewer, *n.*

Renown, *n.* صِيت ـ صِيتَة ـ إِسْم ـ ذِكْر ـ سِمْع. A man of —, ذُو ٱسْمٍ *pl.* ذَوُو ٱسْمٍ. To acquire —, أَصَاتَ ـ إِشْتَهَرَ: The age resounded with his —, إِنْصَاتَ بِهِ ٱلزَّمَانُ. *See also* Glory, Fame, Reputation, *n.*

Renowned, *a.* ـ مَشْهُور ـ جَلِيل ـ ذُو ٱسْمٍ *pl.* ذَوُو ٱسْمٍ ـ مَذْكُور صَاحِبُ شُهْرَةٍ. *See also* Famous, *a.*

Renownedly, *ad.* شُهْرَةً ـ بِجَلَالٍ ـ بِشُهْرَةٍ.

Renownless, *a.* مَجْهُول ـ غَيْرُ مَذْكُورٍ ـ بِلَا ٱسْمٍ.

Rent, *part. of to* Rend, *v.t.*

Rent, *n.* A tear, مَزْقَة ـ تَمْزِيق ـ غُرُور *pl.* غَرّ ـ تَشْرِيم ـ شَرْم. A crack, split, شَقّ *pl.* شُقُوق. A — in a garment, مَفْتَق. Rents, tears, فِزَر. *See also* Fissure, Rupture, Breach, *n.*

Rent, *v.t.* and *i.* *See under to* Hire, *v.t.*

Rent, *n.* *See* Hire, *n.*

Rental, *n.* } A schedule of rent, بِيَانَة ـ جَرِيدَةُ ٱلْعُمَالَةِ
Rent-roll, } (جَدْوَلُ *or*) ٱلْكِرَاءِ.

Renter, *n.* *See* Hirer, *n.*

Renter, *v.t.* To fine-draw, رَفَا.

Renunciation, *n.* Denial, إِسْتِنْكَار ـ إِنْكَار. Rejection, رَفْض. Casting off, طَرْد ـ خَلْع. Relinquishment, تَرْك ـ نُزُول عَنْ.

Re-open, *v.t.* ² عَادَ فَأَشْرَعَهُ ـ أَعَادَ فَتْحَهُ ـ فَتَحَ-ثَانِيَةً.

Re-open, *v.i.* To open again, تَفَتَّحَ ثَانِيَةً; to begin again, عَادَ فَٱبْتَدَأَ ² — اِبْتَدَأَ ثَانِيَةً.

Re-ordain, *v.t.* To prescribe again, as laws, سَنَّ-ثَانِيَةً ² — عَادَ فَأَمَرَ بِ ² — أَفْرَضَ-ثَانِيَةً. To readmit to holy orders, عَادَ فَرَسَمَهُ ² — رَسَمَ-ثَانِيَةً.

Reordination, *n.* The act of enacting again, إِفْرَاضٌ ثَانٍ — إِعَادَةُ تَثْنِيَةُ فَرْضٍ (or ٱشْتِرَاعٍ); of readmitting to holy orders, رَسَامَةٌ ثَانِيَةٌ — رَسْمٌ ثَانٍ — ٱلرِّسَامَةُ; the being so readmitted, اِرْتِسَامٌ جَدِيدٌ — اِرْتِسَامٌ ثَانٍ.

Reorganization, *n.* The act of, تَرْتِيبٌ ثَانٍ — تَنْسِيقٌ ثَانٍ — تَنْظِيمٌ; the being organized anew, نِظَامٌ — نِظَامٌ ثَانٍ — نَسَقٌ ثَانٍ — اِسْتِتْبَابٌ.

Reorganize, *v.t.* رَتَّبَ-ثَانِيَةً ² — عَادَ فَنَسَّقَهُ — نَسَّقَ-ثَانِيَةً — نَظَّمَ — نَظَّمَ-ثَانِيَةً.

Repack, *v.t.* As into boxes, عَادَ فَعَبَّأَهُ ² — عَبَّأَ-ثَانِيَةً; as into bundles, عَادَ فَصَرَّهُ ² — صَرَّ-ثَانِيَةً.

Repair, *v.t.* To restore to a sound state, عَمَّرَ — صَحَّحَ — أَصْلَحَ. To make repairs to, رَمَّمَ — رَمْرَمَ ² — رَمَّ; especially of a musical instrument, and such like, لَأَمَ ²; to be repaired, in this sense, اِلْتَأَمَ. To —, as with gypsum, *etc.*, دَمَّمَ. To —, of a difficulty, *etc.*, سَدَّ ²; as a breach between friends, *etc.*, لَثَّمَ. To —, as of glass, قَانَ ² — رَتَقَ ² — عَالَجَ — صَحَّحَ. To remedy, جَبَرَ ². To mend, amend, morally, هَذَّبَ. To —, as of a man's broken fortune, جَبَّرَ ² — جَبَرَ ² — تَجَبَّرَ; to have one's fortune repaired, اِجْتَبَرَ. To be repaired, stopt up, remedied, اِنْسَدَّ — اِسْتَتَبَّ; to have repairs made to it, تَرَمَّمَ — تَرَمْرَمَ.

Repair, *v.i.* To go to, تَعَمَّدَ — قَصَدَ ² — صَمَدَ ² — صَمَدَ إِلَى; as to a place of refuge, أَوَى إِلَى *aor.* يَأْوِي. To — to frequently, تَرَدَّدَ إِلَى — اِخْتَلَفَ إِلَى — صَمَدَ إِلَى. He repaired to him in his exigencies, صَمَدَ إِلَيْهِ فِي حَوَائِجِهِ ². He repaired to the mountain (for refuge), آوَى إِلَى ٱلْجَبَلِ.

Repair, *n.* Restoration to a sound state, of buildings and such like, تَرْمِيمٌ — مَرَمَّةٌ — تَعْمِيرٌ — اِسْتِتْبَابٌ; restoration, in a general sense, إِصْلَاحٌ — تَصْحِيحٌ — رَتْقٌ — اِسْتِتْبَابٌ. A remedy, عِلَاجٌ — مُعَالَجَةٌ; as of broken fortune, تَجْبِيرٌ — جُبُورٌ. Repairs, مَرَمَّةٌ — تَعْمِيرَاتٌ. Repair, the act of going too frequently, تَصْمِيدٌ إِلَى — تَرَدُّدٌ إِلَى. A place of —, haunt, مَعْهَدٌ — مَأْوًى — مَأْلَفٌ.

To be in good repair, of a building, عَمَرَ ² — كَانَ فِي عِمَارَةٍ — كَانَ عُمْرَانًا; in a general sense صَلَحَ ² — كَانَ مَرْمُومًا — اِسْتَتَبَّ — كَانَ فِي حَالِ ٱلصَّلَاحِ.

To be out of repair, To require repairs, } اِحْتَاجَ إِلَى ٱلتَّعْمِيرِ — اِحْتَاجَ إِلَى ٱلْمَرَمَّةِ — دَعَا إِلَى إِصْلَاحِهِ ² — اِسْتَرَمَّ.

To be under repair, كَانَ تَحْتَ ٱلْمَرَمَّةِ.

Repairable, *a.* **Reparable**, } That may be repaired, as a building, مَرَمَّةٌ — قَابِلُ ٱلْعُمْرَانِ — قَابِلُ ٱلْمَرَمَّةِ — مُمْكِنَةٌ; specially of glass and such like, (مِمَّا يُقَانُ or يُشْعَبُ); that may be soldered, مِمَّا يُلْحَمُ; that may be remedied, مِمَّا يُعَالَجُ; that may be stopped, averted, prevented, يَسْتَدُّ — يَنْسَدُّ — مِمَّا يُسَدُّ; as a breach of friendship, مِمَّا يُلْثَمُ; as a broken fortune, مِمَّا يَتَجَبَّرُ — يَنْجَبِرُ.

Repairer, *n.* One who mends, مُرَمِّمٌ; who repairs, مُصْلِحٌ; as by cementing, دَمَّامٌ; who restores, as a broken fortune, or who sets bones, *etc.*, جَابِرٌ; who removes difficulties, مُسِدٌّ. A repairer of bowls, and such like, شَعَّابٌ.

Repairing, *n.* The art of, such as cracks, *etc.*, شِعَابَةٌ.

Reparation, *n.* Amends, وَفَاءٌ — تَعْوِيضٌ — مُكَافَأَةٌ — مُجَازَاةٌ. To make — to for, جَازَى-عَنْ — كَافَى-عَنْ — خَلَاصُ حَقٍّ — حَقٌّ. To make —, أَعَاضَ-عَنْ — أَفَاضَ-عَنْ ² سَدَّ ٱلْخَسَارَةَ. *See also* Repair, *n.*

Reparative, *a.* مُعَالِجٌ — مُسِدٌّ — جَابِرٌ — مُصْلِحٌ.

Reparative, *n.* دَوَاءٌ — عِلَاجٌ.

Repartee, *n.* جَوَابٌ — سُكَاتٌ — سُكَاتَةٌ. He gave him a —, رَمَاهُ بِسُكَاتَةٍ.

Repass, *v.t.* To pass or cross over again, عَادَ ² — عَبَرَ-ثَانِيَةً ² عَادَ فَنَفَذَ ٱلْ... — فَقَطَعَ ٱلْ....

Repass, *v.i.* عَادَ فَسَلَكَ ² — جَازَ ثَانِيَةً ².

Repast, *n.* أَكْلَةٌ — أَكْلٌ. A banquet, ضِيَافَةٌ — مَأْدُبَةٌ. To make a —, أَكَلَ ². To give a —, banquet, اِتَّخَذَ مَأْدُبَةً. To invite to a —, أَدَبَ-عَلَى مَأْدُبَةٍ — آدَبَ ² — أَدَبَ. When the — was over, لَمَّا ٱنْتَهَى ٱلطَّعَامُ.

Repay, *v.t.* وَفَى *aor.* يَفِي — أَوْفَى — جَزَى ² — جَازَى — كَافَى — أَعَاضَ. I repaid him the debt, جَزَيْتُهُ ٱلدَّيْنَ. To — or requite one with, جَزَى-بِ ² — جَازَى-بِ — كَافَى-بِ.

Repayable, *a.* That is to be repaid, يُرَدُّ دَفْعُ ٱلْمَبْلَغِ — يُرْجَعُ.

Repayment, *n.* رَدٌّ وَتَأْدِيَةٌ. Requital, جَزَاءٌ — وَفَاءٌ — مُجَازَاةٌ.

Repeal, *n.* The act of abrogation, إِبْطَالٌ — فَسْخٌ — نَسْخٌ — نَقْضٌ; the being abrogated, بُطْلَانٌ — اِنْفِسَاخٌ — تَنَاقُضٌ.

Repeal, *v.t.* أَبْطَلَ ² — فَسَخَ ² — نَسَخَ ² — نَقَضَ ². To be repealed, أُبْطِلَ — اِنْفَسَخَ — تَنَاقَضَ. *See also to* Abrogate, *v.t.*

Repealable, *a.* مِمَّا يُنْقَضُ — مِمَّا يُنْسَخُ — فَسْخُهُ مُمْكِنٌ — إِبْطَالُهُ مُمْكِنٌ.

Repealer, *n.* مُبْطِل ـ نَاسِخ ـ نَاقِض.

Repeat, *v.t.* To say again, أَعَادَ ـ كَرَّرَ. To do again, ثَنَّى ـ كَرَّرَ ـ أَعَادَ ـ عَادَ ² ـ رَدَّدَ ـ رَجَّعَ ـ عَقَّبَ. To — from memory, تَقَصَّصَ. To ask one to —, as a speech, narrative, عَكَّ ²: I asked him to — the story, عَكَكْتُهُ ٱلْحَدِيثَ. I ceased not to — the speech to him until he was angry, مَا زِلْتُ أَعُكُّهُ (or أُرَدِّدُ عَلَيْهِ) بِٱلْقَوْلِ حَتَّى غَضِبَ. He repeated the affair to me until he wearied me, عَكَّنِي بِٱلْأَمْرِ. He repeated, or rehearsed, to them the oath, creed, رَدَّ عَلَيْهِمِ ٱلْإِيمَانَ ². He began, or did it once, and then repeated it, بَدَأَ ثُمَّ أَعَادَ. He repeated his efforts, or made repeated efforts, in the affair, تَرَدَّدَ ـ عَقَّبَ فِي ٱلْأَمْرِ ـ فِي ٱلْأَمْرِ. *See also to* Recite, Rehearse, *v.t.*

Repeat, *v.i.* To use repetitions, كَرَّرَ ٱلْكَلَامَ ـ لَجْلَجَ.

Repeated, *a.* Said over and over again, مَقُول; done over and over again, مُكَرَّر; happening repeatedly, وَاقِعٌ تَكْرَارًا. Oft-repeated, of a story, tradition, *etc.*, مُتَوَاتِر.

Repeatedly, *ad.* جُمْلَةَ مِرَارٍ ـ تَكْرَارًا ـ مِرَارًا ـ مَرَّةً عَنْ مَرَّةٍ. To befall one —, تَعَاهَدَ ـ تَعَهَّدَ. He asked him the question —, عَاوَدَهُ بِٱلْمَسْأَلَةِ. The fever returned to him —, عَاوَدَتْهُ ٱلْحُمَّى.

Repeater, *n.* One who repeats words, speeches, *etc.*, عَيَّادُ ٱلْكَلَامِ. A — watch, سَاعَةٌ تَدُقُّ ٱلسَّاعَاتِ. *See also* Reciter, *n.*

Repeating, *a.* Saying or doing again, مُعِيد ـ مُكَرِّر ـ مُثَنٍّ. Copying, مُقَلِّد.

Repel, *v.t.* To drive back, دَرَأَ ـ رَدَّ ² ـ دَفَعَ. To drive away, ذَادَ *aor.* يَذُودُ ـ رَفَضَ ² ـ طَرَدَ ². To — from, in the sense of defending, ذَبَّ عَنْ ². To — from, in the sense of preventing, averting, حَدَّ عَنْ ² ـ ذَادَ عَنْ: May God — the mischief of such an one from us, حَدَّ ٱللَّهُ عَنَّا شَرَّ فُلَانٍ. To endeavour to —, رَادَّ ـ دَارَأَ ـ عَاضَبَ. The government is able to — any attack upon it from without, ٱلدَّوْلَةُ قَادِرَةٌ عَلَى أَنْ تَدْفَعَ عَنْهَا أَيَّ هُجُومٍ يَأْتِي عَلَيْهَا مِنَ ٱلْخَارِجِ.

Repellency, *n.* قُوَّةٌ دَافِعَةٌ.

Repellent, *n.* مِدْفَع.

Repellent, *a.* دَافِع; in a medical sense, مُحَوِّل.

Repent, *v.i.* تَابَ ² ـ نَدِمَ. To — towards, to, تَابَ إِلَى. To — for, رَجَعَ عَنْ ـ تَنَدَّمَ عَلَى. You will — when repentance will be of no avail, تَنْدَمُ حَيْثُ لَا يَنْفَعُكَ ٱلنَّدَمُ. He repented of the sin, crime, رَجَعَ عَنِ ٱلذَّنْبِ. God repented towards him, تَابَ ٱللَّهُ عَلَيْهِ ².

Repent, *a.* Creeping, of a plant, أَثِيث ـ مُفَرَّش ـ دَغِل.

Repentance, *n.* تَوْبَة ـ نَدَامَة ـ تَوْب. To call to —, اِسْتِتَابٌ. It occasioned him —, أَعْقَبَهُ نَدَمًا. That which occasions —, that of which one repents, مَنْدَمَة. *See also* Penitence, *n.*

Repentant, *a.*
Repenter, *n.* } تَائِب ـ تَوَّاب ـ نَدْمَان *pl.* نِدَام *and* نُدَّام.

Repeople, *v.t.* أَعْمَرَ ـ عَمَرَ ثَانِيَةً ² ـ عَادَ فَأَعْمَرَهُ ². The land was repeopled, عُمِرَتِ ٱلْبِلَادُ ثَانِيَةً.

Repercuss, *v.t.* رَدَّ ـ رَجَّعَ ².

Repercussion, *n.* The act of driving back, رَدّ ـ تَرْجِيع. Reverberation, عَكْس ـ رَدّ ـ صَلْصَلَة.

Repercussive, *a.* Driving back, مُرَجِّع ـ دَافِع. Causing to reverberate, مُصَلْصِل.

Repertory, *n.* A miscellany, collection, مَجْمَع. A repository, magazine, مَخْزَن *pl.* مَخَازِن ـ كَنْز *pl.* كُنُوز.

Repetition, *n.* The act of repeating, تَرْجِيع ـ تَثْنِيَة ـ ثِنْي ـ إِعَادَة ـ عِيَاد ـ تَكْرَة ـ تَكْرَار ـ تَكْرِير. The — of a thing time after time, مُعَاوَدَة. The — of the act a second time, اِسْتِئْنَاف. The — of a benefit, the conferring it twice or thrice, ٱلْعَمَلُ مَرَّةً أُخْرَى. The — of a benefit, مَثْنَى ٱلْأَيَادِي. The useless — of words in discourse, لَجْلَجَة. Useless repetitions of words, تَكْرِيرُ ٱلْكَلَامِ بَاطِلًا. He used frequent repetitions in his speech, لَجْلَجَ فِي ٱلْحَدِيثِ. Repetition is useless, (prov.) لَيْسَ فِي ٱلْإِعَادَةِ إِفَادَةٌ.

Repetitional, *a.*
Repetitious, } مُتَوَاتِر.

Repine, *v.i.* مَرْمَرَ ـ تَذَمَّرَ ـ تَضَجَّرَ ـ تَظَلَّمَ. *See also to* Murmur, *v.i.*

Repiner, *n.*
Repining, *a.* } مُتَذَمِّر ـ مُتَضَجِّر ـ مُتَظَلِّم.

Repining, *n.* تَذَمُّر ـ تَضَجُّر ـ تَظَلُّم.

Repiningly, *ad.* بِتَذَمُّرٍ ـ تَضَجُّرًا ـ تَظَلُّمًا.

Replace, *v.t.* To return to its place, رَدَّ إِلَى ² ـ أَعَادَ إِلَى مَكَانِهِ ـ مَوْضِعِهِ. To compensate to, عَوَّضَ. To —, as coming after, يَجِيءُ ² *aor.* جَاءَ بَعْدَهُ ـ أَعْقَبَ. To supply the place of one, to supersede, قَامَ مَقَامَهُ ² ـ خَلَفَ ². To — a thing, to compensate for, to meet the case or exigency of, سَدَّ مَسَدَّ كَذَا ². If any one can be found to — his services, إِنْ وُجِدَ مَنْ يَسُدُّ مَسَدَّهُ فِي خِدْمَتِهِ. He replaced him in doing the work, نَابَ عَنْهُ فِي عَمَلِ ٱلشَّيْءِ ² ـ قَامَ مَقَامَهُ ². To —, as a joint, limb, جَبَّرَ ـ جَبَرَ ².

Replacement, *n.* The act of returning, as a thing to its place, رَدّ ـ إِعَادَة; the being so replaced, عَوْد ـ رُجُوع ـ اِرْتِدَاد. The act of compensating, تَعْوِيض; what is given as compensation, عِوَض. The act of replacing, as coming after, عَقْب ـ إِعْقَاب; that which so replaces, عَقِيب. Something which provides for a case, exigency, سَدٌّ مَسَدٌّ. The act of superseding, إِقَامَةٌ مَقَام; the person superseding, قَائِمٌ مَقَام. The act of replacing a joint, جَبْر ـ تَجْبِير; the state of being so replaced, تَجَبُّر ـ ٱلْجِبَار.

Replant, *v.t.* Of herbs, *etc.*, غَرَسَ-ثَانِيَةً ـ. To set up again, نَصَبَ-) ² or) صَمَدَ- ² ثَانِيَةً.

Replantable, *n.* Of herbs, *etc.*, مِمَّا يُغْرَسُ ثَانِيَةً.

Replantation, *n.* The act of, of herbs, *etc.*, إِعَادَةُ ـ غَرْسٍ ثَانٍ; إِغْرَاس; what is replanted, غِرْسٌ ثَانٍ. The act of setting up again, إِعَادَةُ نَصْبٍ.

Replenish, *v.t.* To fill up again, أَمْلَأَ-ثَانِيَةً. To fill up, ـ نَعَمَ ـ طَمَّ ² ـ مَلَأَ ـ ¹. To supply what is wanting, سَدَّ مَسَدَّ كَذَا ². أَشْبَعَ. To be replenished, filled, إِمْتَلَأَ. *See also to* Fill, *v.t.*

Replenish, *v.i.* To recover former fullness, إِمْتَلَأَ ثَانِيَةً ـ إِمْتَلَأَ.

Replete, *a.* Full, مَلْآنُ ـ مُمْتَلِئٌ ـ مَمْلُوٌّ ـ مَشْحُون ـ غَامِر; *fem.* مَلْآنَةُ *pl.* مِلَاءٌ. To be —, with food, بَطِنَ ². Replete with food, مَبْطُون. Stuffed, مَحْشُوٌّ ـ مَحْشِيٌّ. *See also under* Full, *a.*

Repletion, *n.* فَيْض ـ فِعَامَة ـ إِمْتِلَاء ـ مِلْأ. Repletion with food, بِطْنَة. Repletion of the stomach, كِظَّة. Repletion banishes intelligence, (prov.) البِطْنَةُ تُذْهِبُ ٱلْفِطْنَةَ. *See also* Fullness, *n.*

Repletive, *a.* مُمْلِئٌ ـ مُفْعِم.

Repleviable, *a.* المُصَادَرَةُ بِٱسْتِرْدَادِهِ جَائِزَةٌ.

Replevin, *n.* مُصَادَرَةٌ بِٱلِٱسْتِرْدَادِ.

Replevy, *v.t.* صَادَرَ-عَلَى ٱسْتِرْدَادِهِ.

Replicate, *a.* Folded back, مَطْوِيٌّ إِلَى وَرَآءٍ.

Replication, *n.* The rejoinder of a plaintiff, رَدُّ ٱلْمُدَّعِي عَلَى حُجَّةِ ٱلْمُدَّعَى عَلَيْهِ. *See also* Rejoinder, *n.*

Reply, *v.i.* لَبَّى ـ أَجَابَ ـ أَحَارَ. To — to, أَجَابَ ـ رَدَّ عَلَى ـ إِسْتَجَابَ ². To —, to return one answer for answer, to bandy words with, جَاوَبَ. He replied to his letter, رَدَّ عَلَيْهِ ². To — to a letter, رَدَّ جَوَابَ ² رَدَّ عَلَيْهِ جَوَابَ مَكْتُوبِهِ ـ جَوَابًا ². He forbore to —, سَكَتَ عَنِ ٱلْجَوَابِ ². المَكْتُوب.

Reply, *n.* جَوَاب ـ رَدّ ـ رَجْعَة. A satisfactory —, جَوَابٌ شَافٍ. I say in — to you, أَقُولُ مُجِيبًا لَكَ.

Repolish, *v.t.* جَلَا-ثَانِيَةً ² ـ عَادَ فَصَقَلَهُ ².

Report, *v.t.* To give an account of, أَخْبَرَ ـ نَقَلَ عَن-كَذَا ² حَكَى ـ ذَكَرَ ² ـ رَوَى *aor.* يَرْوِي عَن-كَذَا ـ عَن-كَذَا. To send to, as a report, أَنْهَى-إِلَى. To — to, tell, inform of, أَخْبَرَ-بِ ـ سَمَّعَ ـ بَلَّغَ ـ خَبَّرَ-بِ. To — to, make a complaint against, إِشْتَكَى عَلَى. To spread abroad, أَشَاعَ بِ. To —, as from another person or authority, نَقَلَ عَن-كَذَا ². To — to government officially, أَفَادَ ٱلدَّوْلَةَ رَسْمًا. To be reported, spread abroad, شَاعَ ـ. A communication has been received from the Amir reporting that ..., وَرَدَ خِطَابٌ مِنَ ٱلْأَمِيرِ يَتَضَمَّنُ أَن *aor.* يَرِدُ. It is reported among the people, قَدْ سُمِعَ (or شَاعَ) بَيْنَ ٱلنَّاسِ. It is commonly reported that ..., يُسْمَعُ قَطْعًا أَن. As we are maliciously reported, كَمَا يُفْتَرَى عَلَيْنَا. He was well reported of, كَانَ مَشْهُودًا لَهُ. The news received from India reports that..., الأَخْبَارُ ٱلْوَارِدَةُ مِنَ ٱلْهِنْدِ تُفِيدُ أَن. It is reported respecting the place, رُوِيَ عَنِ ٱلْمَكَانِ. *See also to* Describe, *v.t.*

Report, *v.i.* To make a statement of facts, أَفَادَ.

Report, *n.* An official statement, إِفَادَةٌ رَسْمِيَّةٌ ـ إِنْهَآء. A statement, تَقْرِير ـ نَقْل ـ بَيَان ـ عَرْض. Information, عِلْم ـ امْرٌ شَتٌّ ـ مُسْتَفَاضٌ فِيهِ ـ مُسْتَفِيض. Rumour, خَبَر ـ نَبَأ ـ سِمْع ـ ذِكْر ـ قَوْل ـ سِمْعَة ـ صَات ـ أَمْرٌ شَتَاتٌ. Reputation, صِيت. The noise of a gun, حِسّ (or صَوْتُ) ـ فَقْعُ ٱلْمِدْفَعِ. A false —, خَبَرٌ كَاذِبٌ; false reports, أَرَاجِيفُ. A malicious —, نَمِيمَة ـ خَبَرٌ خَبِيثٌ. They spread an evil — of the country, أَشَاعُوا مَذَمَّةَ ٱلْأَرْضِ. It is only a —, مَا هُوَ إِلَّا حَدِيثٌ. There is no truth in the — that ..., لَا صِحَّةَ لِمَا شَاعَ أَن. The — will reach the governor, يَبْلُغُ ٱلْخَبَرُ إِلَى ٱلْوَالِي. This — was current among them, شَاعَ هٰذَا ٱلْقَوْلُ عِنْدَهُمْ. Men of honest —, رِجَالٌ مَشْهُودٌ لَهُمْ.

Reported, *a.* Current, spread abroad, مُشَاع.

Reporter, *n.* One who makes reports, نَاقِل *pl.* نَقَلَة. A writer, كَاتِب *pl.* كَتَبَة. A quick writer, سَرِيعُ ٱلْكِتَابَةِ. One who gives or writes news, مُكَاتِب ـ مُخْبِر. A faithful or correct —, كَاتِبٌ ثِقَةٌ.

Reporting, *n.* The act of giving reports of, نَقْل. Correspondence, مُكَاتَبَة.

Reposal, *n.* *See* Repose, *n.*

Repose, *v.t.* To lay quietly or at rest, سَكَّنَ ـ رَيَّحَ. To place, وَضَعَ *aor.* يَضَعُ ـ حَطَّ ² ـ جَعَلَ ـ. To — confidence in, إِتَّكَلَ عَلَى ـ إِسْتَكْفَى بِ ـ إِعْتَمَدَ عَلَى. *See also under to* Rely, *v.i.*

Repose, *v.i.* To rest, إِسْتَرَاحَ. To sleep, نَامَ ـ. To recline, ضَجَعَ ـ إِضْطَجَعَ ـ إِضَّجَعَ.

Repose, *n.* Rest, رَاحَة ـ إِسْتِرَاحَة ـ إِرْتِيَاح. Quiet, هُدُوّ ـ

قَرَار — عَدَمُ حَرَكَةٍ — سُكُون. Tranquillity, security, أَمْنِيَّة — اِطْمِئْنَان. Sleep, نَوْم. In repose, at rest, مُسْتَرِيح. A place of —, مَضْجَع.

Reposit, *v.t.* To lay up in, ذَخَرَ-فِي ـ. *See also to* Deposit, *v.t.*

Reposition, *n.* رَفْع — وَضْع — تَوْضِيع.

Repository, *n.* مَخْزَن *pl.* مَخَازِن — كَنْز *pl.* كُنُوز — أَنْبَار *pl.* أَنَابَارَات — صِوَان. A vessel to contain anything, وِعَاء *pl.* أَوْعِيَة.

Repossess, *v.t.* To hold or have again, عَادَ — مَلَكَ-ثَانِيَةً. To — one's self of, رَجَعَ فِي — اِرْتَجَعَ — اِسْتَرْجَعَ — فَاقْتَنَاهُ. He repossessed himself of his gift, رَجَعَ فِي هِبَتِهِ — اِسْتَرَدَّ.

Repossession, *n.* The act of, إِعَادَةُ ٱقْتِنَاءٍ — مُلْكٌ ثَانٍ. The act of repossessing one's self to, اِسْتِرْدَاد — اِسْتِرْجَاع. The state of being repossessed, إِعَادَةُ ضَبْطٍ — تَمَلُّكٌ ثَانٍ.

Reprehend, *v.t.* ثَلَبَ — عَتَبَ — عَاتَبَ — ذَمَّ. *See also to* Blame, Chide, *v.t.*

Reprehender, *n.* *See* Reprehensive, *a.*

Reprehensible, *a.* مُسْتَحِقٌّ — عَلَيْهِ مَلَامَةٌ — يُلَامُ — مُلِيم — مُسْتَحِقُّ ٱلتَّوْبِيخِ — ٱلْمَلَامَةِ. *See also* Culpable, *a.*

Reprehensibleness, *n.* لَوْمَة — ذَمَّة — مَلَامَة.

Reprehensibly, *ad.* ذَمَّةً — لَوْمَةً — مَلَامَةً.

Reprehension, *n.* تَوْبِيخ — عِتَاب — ذَمّ — ثَلْب. *See also* Censure, Blame, *n.*

Reprehensive, *a.}*
Reprehensory, } مُعَزِّر — ثَالِب — مُوَبِّخ — مُذِمّ — مُعَاتِب.

Represent, *v.t.* To show or exhibit, أَرْأَى *vulg.* وَرَّى — عَرَضَ-عَلَى — تَشَخَّصَ بِ — تَمَثَّلَ بِ — تَشَبَّهَ بِ. To personate, فَرَّجَ — قَدَّمَ-لِ. To draw, depict, رَسَمَ — صَوَّرَ — نَقَشَ. To describe, شَرَحَ — عَبَّرَ عَنْ — فَسَّرَ — وَصَفَ *aor.* يَصِفُ. To stand in the place of, of a person, قَامَ مَقَامَهُ — حَلَّ مَحَلَّهُ — نَابَ عَنْ; of a thing, سَدَّ عَنْ. To be the figure of, كَانَ صُورَةَ ٱلشَّيْءِ. To — to, to make known to, خَبَّرَ-بِ — سَمَّعَ — أَفَادَ — بَلَّغَ. To bring to the notice of, to present to, عَرَضَ-عَلَى. To — to one's self, to one's own mind, تَخَيَّلَ-فِي عَقْلِهِ — تَصَوَّرَ-فِي عَقْلِهِ. To —, as on a stage, in a theatre, لَعِبَ-تَقْلِيدًا (*or* شَخَّصَ-) فِي ٱلتِّيَاتْرُو. This represents, stands for, is expressive of, means so and so, مَعْنَاهُ كَذَا — هٰذَا يُعَبِّرُ عَنْ كَذَا — هٰذَا عِبَارَةٌ عَنْ كَذَا. Another represented or spoke for him, عَبَّرَ عَنْهُ غَيْرُهُ. I represented, or spoke for, such an one, عَبَّرْتُ عَنْ فُلَانٍ. *See also to* Report, *v.t.*

Representable, *a.* That may be described, مِمَّا — مِمَّا يُوصَفُ — قَابِلُ ٱلْبَيَانِ — يُبَيَّنُ; that may be drawn, depicted, مِمَّا يَتَصَوَّرُ.

Representation, *n.* The act of exhibiting, عَرْض — تَوْرِيَة — تَقْدِيم; of drawing, delineating, نَقْش — تَصْوِير — تَرْسِيم; what is represented, a picture, صُورَة — تَصْوِير — تِمْثَال — رَسْم — شَكْل. The act of describing شَرْح — تَعْبِير — تَفْسِير — وَصْف. A statement, تَقْرِير — إِفَادَة — إِنْهَاء. The business of acting as the substitute of another, نِيَابَة — وَكَالَة. Exhibition by imitative actions, تَشْخِيص — تَقْلِيد — تَشَخُّص. A — on a theatrical stage, لَعْبُ تَقْلِيدٍ فِي ٱلتِّيَاتْرُو — فِي ٱلْمَرْسَحِ. A representative body, وُكَلَاء — نُوَّاب. He submitted a detailed —, قَدَّمَ تَقْرِيرًا مُفَصَّلًا.

Representative, *a.* Exhibiting likeness, مُمَاثِل. Standing in the place of, قَائِمٌ مَقَامَ كَذَا. Descriptive, signifying, مُعَبِّرٌ عَنْ. Bearing the authority of another, بِمَنْزِلَةِ ٱلنَّائِبِ — نَائِب — مُوَكَّل.

Representative government, حُكُومَةٌ مَبْنِيَّةٌ عَلَى — حُكُومَةٌ شُورِيَّةٌ — حُكُومَةٌ ٱنْتِخَابِيَّةٌ — أُصُولُ ٱلْإِنْتِخَابِ. A — assembly, مَجْلِس — مَجْلِسُ وُكَلَاءِ ٱلْأُمَّةِ — مُنْتَخَبِي ٱلْأُمَّةِ. A — character, form, صِفَةُ وَكَالَةٍ.

Representative, *n.* That which is present in place of another, a substitute, قَائِمٌ مَقَامٍ — بَدَل. Bearing the authority of another, نَائِب *pl.* نُوَّاب — وَكِيل *pl.* وُكَلَاء. *See also* Deputy, Delegate, *n.*

Representatively, *ad.* As exhibiting a likeness, مُمَاثَلَةً; as bearing the authority of another, وَكَالَةً; as signifying, meaning, تَعْبِيرًا عَنْ.

Representment, *n.* *See* Representation, *n.*

Repress, *v.t.* زَجَرَ — قَهَرَ — ضَبَطَ — قَمَعَ — حَكَمَ — أَحْكَمَ — مَنَعَ. *See also to* Check, Restrain, *v.t.*

Repression, *n.* مَنْع — ضَبْط — زَجْر — تَحْكِيم. *See also* Check, *n.*

Repressive, *a.* مَانِع — ضَابِط — زَاجِر — مُحَكِّم.

Repressively, *ad.* ضَبْطًا — زَجْرًا — تَحْكِيمًا.

Reprieve, *v.t.* To respite for a time, أَمْهَلَ — طَوَّلَ لِ. To — after sentence of death, أَخَّرَ ٱلْقَتْلَ — أَمْهَلَهُ ٱلْقَتْلَ إِلَى مُدَّةٍ — إِلَى مُدَّةٍ.

Reprieve, *n.* Delay of the punishment of death, تَأْخِيرُ ٱلْقَتْلِ — إِمْهَالُ ٱلْقَتْلِ. Interval of ease or relief, مُهْلَةُ تَنَفُّسٍ — مُدَّةُ رَاحَةٍ.

Reprimand, *n.* نَهْرَة — تَوْبِيخ — عِتَاب. *See also* Reproof, *n.*

Reprimand, *v.t.* وَبَّخَ — عَاتَبَ — عَتَبَ عَلَى — نَهَرَ عَلَى.

Reprint, *v.t.* To print again, طَبَعَ-ثَانِيَةً. To print another edition, طَبَعَ طَبْعَةً ثَانِيَةً.

Reprint, *n.* طَبْعَةٌ ثَانِيَةٌ — طَبْعٌ ثَانٍ.

Reprisal, *n.* From an enemy, أَخْذُ ٱلْمُقَابَلَةِ بِٱلْمِثْلِ مِنَ ٱلْعَدُوِّ;

in a more general sense, مُعَامَلَةٌ مُتَقَابِلَةٌ ٱنْتِقَامِيَّةٌ. The taking vengeance, أَخْذُ ثَارٍ. The right of —, قَاعِدَةُ ٱلْمُقَابَلَةِ بِٱلْمِثْلِ. To make use of —, أَجْرَى ٱلْمُقَابَلَةَ بِٱلْمِثْلِ ـ أَجْرَى ٱلِٱنْتِقَامَ بِمُقَابَلَةِ ٱلْمِثْلِ.

Reproach, *v.t.* To censure severely, ثَلَبَ ـ قَذَفَ بِ ـ ثَرَّبَ ـ طَعَنَ فِي ـ شَتَمَ ـ تَعَيَّبَ ـ عَابَ *aor.* يَعِيبُ ـ عَيَّبَ ـ عَيَّرَ بِ ـ قَذَفَ ـ قَدَحَ. To — one's self for, عَتَبَ عَلَى نَفْسِهِ بِ ـ لَامَ نَفْسَهُ عَلَى. He reproached him with something bad, رَمَاهُ بِٱلْقَبِيحِ. They reproached one another, of many, تَعَايَبُوا ـ تَشَاتَمُوا.

Reproach, *n.* Opprobrious censure, ثَلْب ـ قَذْف ـ شَتِيمَة ـ شَتْم ـ تَعْيِيب ـ قَدْح. Shame, infamy, عَار ـ عَيْب ـ ذُلّ ـ رَذَالَة. One who is a —, مَطْرُود ـ مَقْبُوح ـ عَار. He became a — to them, صَارَ عَارًا عِنْدَهُمْ. To fall into —, سَقَطَ فِي ٱلتَّعْيِيرِ. To bring — upon, جَلَبَ عَارًا عَلَى.

Reproachable, *a.* يُثْلَبُ ـ مِمَّا يُعَابُ ـ يُعَابُ ـ مُسْتَحِقّ ٱلتَّعْيِيبِ ـ مُلِيم.

Reproachably, *ad.* بِطَرِيقَةٍ تَسْتَحِقُّ ٱلتَّعْيِيبَ.

Reproachful, *a.* شَتَّام ـ ثَالِب ـ قَادِح ـ طَاعِنٌ فِي ـ قَاذِف ـ مُعَيِّب.

Reproachfully, *ad.* Opprobriously, بِشَتْمٍ ـ ثَلْبًا ـ قَدْحًا ـ قَذْفًا ـ بِٱلتَّعْيِيبِ. Bringing reproach on, بِٱسْتِجْلَابِ ٱلْعَارِ عَلَى.

Reprobate, *n.* One rejected, cast off, مَخْلُوع ـ خَلِيع ـ مَرْفُوض *pl.* مَرْفُوضُونَ. An abandoned wretch, رَذِيل نَذْل ـ فَحَّاش ـ مَلْعُون.

Reprobate, *a.* Rejected, خَلِيع ـ مَرْفُوض. Abandoned, شَقِيّ ـ شَنِيع ـ غَاوٍ ـ غَوِيّ ـ مَخْذُول ـ مَتْرُوك. Corrupted, مَرْذُول ـ ضَالّ. Reprobate silver, فِضَّةٌ مَرْفُوضَةٌ. A — mind, ذِهْنٌ مَرْفُوضٌ. To be —, renounced, cast off, خُلِعَ.

Reprobate, *v.t.* To reject, رَفَضَ ـ خَلَعَ. To detest, كَرِهَ ـ شَنَأَ ـ رَفَضَ ـ قَبَّحَ ـ قَذَفَ.

Reprobateness, *n.* The being reprobate, rejected, غَيّ ـ خِذْلَان ـ خَلَاعَة; the being lost to virtue, ضَلّ ـ ضَلَالَة ـ هَلَاك ـ غَيّ ـ خِلَاعَة.

Reprobater, *n.* خَاذِل ـ رَافِض.

Reprobation, *n.* The act of rejecting, خِذْلَان ـ خَذْل ـ رَفْض ـ خَلْع; of detesting, تَقْبِيح ـ كَرَاهَة ـ قَذْف ـ رَفْض. The being reprobate, lost to virtue; *see* Reprobateness, *n.*

Reproduce, *v.t.* To bring forward again, أَوْرَدَ ثَانِيَةً ـ عَادَ فَقَدَّمَهُ. To offer to view a second time, أَرْأَى ثَانِيَةً *vulg.* وَرَّى ـ أَظْهَرَ ثَانِيَةً. To bring into being again, أَحْدَثَ ثَانِيَةً ـ أَوْلَدَ ثَانِيَةً ـ أَعَادَ إِيجَادَهُ. To bring forth again, of young, وَلَدَتْ ثَانِيَةً ـ خَلَّفَتْ; of trees, أَثْمَرَ ثَانِيَةً ـ عَادَ فَحَمَلَ. To re-write, of a book, أَلَّفَ ثَانِيَةً ـ أَنْشَأَ ثَانِيَةً. To re-insert, as in a journal, أَدْرَجَ ثَانِيَةً. *See also to* Repeat, *v.t.*

Reproducer, *n.* مُعِيد ـ مُكَرِّر ـ مُخَلِّف.

Reproduction, *n.* The act of bringing forward again, إِيرَادٌ ثَانٍ ـ إِعَادَةُ تَقْدِيمٍ; the being so brought forward, وُرُودٌ ثَانٍ ـ تَقْدِمَةٌ ثَانِيَةٌ. The act of bringing into being again, إِحْدَاثٌ ثَانٍ; the being so brought, حُدُوثٌ ثَانٍ. The offering to view a second time, إِرَاءَةٌ ثَانِيَةٌ ـ إِعَادَةُ عَرْضٍ; a second exposure to view, ظُهُورٌ ثَانٍ ـ إِعَادَةُ إِعْرَاضٍ. The act of generating, تَوْلِيد ـ تَخْلِيف; what is generated, وِلَادَة ـ خَلْف. The act of recomposing, as a book, إِنْشَاءٌ ثَانٍ ـ تَأْلِيفٌ ثَانٍ; a work reproduced, نَشْأَةٌ ثَانِيَةٌ ـ نُسْخَةٌ جَدِيدَةٌ. The reinsertion of anything, as in a journal, إِدْرَاجٌ ثَانٍ; what is so reinserted, مَدْرُوجٌ ثَانِيَةً.

Reproductive, *a.* Tending to reproduction, مُخَلِّف ـ مُوَلِّد. Causing again, مُوجِبٌ ثَانِيَةً ـ مُسَبِّبٌ ثَانِيَةً. Yielding profit, مُثْمِر ـ مُكْسِب ـ خَيْرِيّ ـ مُفِيد ـ نَافِع. Useful and — works, ٱلْأَعْمَالُ (or ٱلْأَشْغَالُ) ٱلنَّافِعَةُ ٱلَّتِي تَعُودُ بِٱلْعَائِدَةِ ٱلصَّالِحَةِ.

Repromulgate, *v.t.* أَصْدَرَ ثَانِيَةً ـ عَادَ فَأَشَاعَ بِ ـ أَشْهَرَ ثَانِيَةً. *See also to* Re-enact, *v.t.*

Reproof, *n.* تَوْبِيخ ـ عِتَاب. To despise —, رَذَلَ ٱلتَّوْبِيخَ. To regard —, لَاحَظَ ٱلتَّوْبِيخَ. *See also* Censure, Reprehension, *n.*

Reprovable, *a.* *See* Reprehensible, Blamable, *a.*

Reprovableness, *n.* *See* Reprehensibleness, Culpability, *n.*

Reprovably, *ad.* *See* Reprehensibly, *ad.*

Reprove, *v.t.* وَبَّخَ ـ عَاتَبَ ـ شَتَمَ ـ ٱنْتَهَرَ. *See also to* Reprehend, Reprimand, *v.t.*

Reprover, *n.* مُوَبِّخ ـ مُعَاتِب.

Reptation, *n.* دَبّ ـ مَدَبّ.

Reptile, *a.* Creeping, دَبَب ـ دَبِيب. Vile, base, رَذِيل ـ دَنِيء ـ خَسِيس.

Reptile, *n.* A creeping animal, شِقْذَة *pl.* شِقْذَان ـ كَامَّة *pl.* هَوَامّ ـ دِبَّة ـ دَبِيب *pl.* دَوَابّ: the reptiles of the earth, خَشَاشُ ٱلْأَرْضِ ـ هَوَامُّ ٱلْأَرْضِ. A noxious —, حَنَش *pl.* أَحْنَاش. A vile person, دَنِيء ـ خَبِيث ـ خَسِيس.

Reptilian, *a.* Belonging to reptiles, مُتَعَلِّق ـ مُخْتَصّ بِٱلدَّوَابِّ بِٱلْهَوَامِّ.

Republic, *n.* A commonwealth, جُمْهُور; government by the election of the citizens, حُكُومَةٌ جُمْهُورِيَّةٌ ـ جُمْهُورِيَّة ـ جُمْهُور.

The — of letters, sciences, ٱلمَعارِف; of the learned, جُمْهُورُ أَرْبَابُ ٱلعُلُومِ وَٱلفُنُونِ ـ ٱلآدَاب. President of the —, رَئِيسُ ٱلجُمْهُورِيَّة.

Republican, *a.* جُمْهُورِيّ. A — government, حُكُومَةٌ جُمْهُورِيَّةٌ. Republican tendencies, ٱلمَيَلَانُ إِلَى ٱلحُكُومَةِ ٱلجُمْهُورِيَّةِ. France has finally adopted the — form of government, فَرَنْسَةُ ٱسْتَقَرَّتْ عَلَى ٱلحُكُومَةِ ٱلجُمْهُورِيَّةِ.

Republican, *n.* One of a republic, تَابِعُ جُمْهُورٍ *pl.* تُبَّع ـ مِنْ أَهْلِ جُمْهُورٍ. One who prefers a republic, مُتَعَصِّبٌ لِلْحُكُومَةِ ـ مِنْ طَرَفِ ٱلجُمْهُورِ ـ ٱلجُمْهُورِيَّةِ.

Republicanism, *n.* System of republican government, جُمْهُورِيَّةٌ ـ أُصُولُ ٱلجُمْهُورِيَّةِ; attachment to republican forms of government, غَيْرَةٌ جُمْهُورِيَّةٌ ـ تَعَصُّبٌ لِلْجُمْهُورِيَّةِ.

Republicanize, *v.t.* To convert into a republic, صَيَّرَ جُمْهُورِيَّةً ـ صَيَّرَ عَلَى أُصُولِ ٱلجُمْهُورِيَّةِ. To bring over to republicanism, جَذَبَ إِلَى ٱلجُمْهُورِيَّةِ.

Republication, *n.* The act of repromulgating, إِعَادَةُ نَشْرٍ ـ إِشَاعَةٌ ثَانِيَةٌ ـ إِشْهَارٌ ثَانٍ ـ إِصْدَارٌ ثَانٍ; what is repromulgated, إِشْتِهَارٌ ثَانٍ ـ إِشْتِغَالٌ ثَانٍ ـ صُدُورٌ ثَانٍ. The act of republishing a book, إِعَادَةُ طَبْعِ كِتَابٍ وَنَشْرِهِ ـ تَبْرِيزُ كِتَابٍ ثَانِيَةً; a reprint, تَأْلِيفٌ مَطْبُوعٌ ثَانِيَةً ـ طَبْعٌ ثَانٍ.

Republish, *v.t.* As of a book, طَبَعَ وَنَشَرَ ـ بَرَّزَ كِتَابًا ثَانِيَةً ـ كِتَابًا ثَانِيَةً. *See also to* Repromulgate, *v.t.*

Repudiable, *a.* That may be rejected, مِمَّا يُنْكَرُ ـ مِمَّا يُرْفَضُ.

Repudiate, *v.t.* To deny, disown, نَكِرَ ـ رَفَضَ ـ أَنْكَرَ. To — a debt, أَنْكَرَ ٱلدَّيْنَ. To cast off, so as not to be answerable for one, خَلَعَ. To be so repudiated, خُلِعَ. One so repudiated خَلِيعٌ ـ مَخْلُوعٌ ـ خَوْلَعٌ. *See also to* Divorce, *v.t.*

Repudiation, *n.* The act of denying, disowning, رَفْضٌ ـ إِنْكَارٌ; of casting off, خَلْعٌ. The being so disowned, خُذْلَانٌ خَلَاعَةٌ. *See also* Divorce, *n.*

Repudiator, *n.* رَافِضٌ ـ مُنْكِرٌ.

Repugn, *v.t.* *See to* Oppose, Resist, *v.t.*

Repugnance, *n.* } Contrariety, مُخَالَفَةٌ ـ مُضَادَّةٌ ـ تَضَادٌّ. Aver-
Repugnancy, } sion, إِعْتِيَافٌ ـ كَرَاهَةٌ ـ تَنَفُّرٌ ـ إِسْتِكْرَاهٌ. To have a — towards, كَرِهَ ـ إِسْتَكْرَهَ ـ نَفَرَ قَلْبُهُ مِنْ. With —, بِغَيْرِ رِضًى ـ بِتَنَفُّرٍ ـ كُرْهًا. *See also* Reluctance, *n.*

Repugnant, *a.* The being opposed to, ضِدٌّ ـ مُخَالِفٌ ـ مُضَادٌّ. The being so as to cause dislike in one, كَرِيهٌ ـ مَنْفُورٌ ـ مُسْتَكْرَهٌ. To be —, contrary, to, خَالَفَ ـ ضَادَّ. To be mutually repugnant, of many, تَدَافَعُوا. The being mutually —, contradictory, مُتَدَافِعٌ. To be — to; *See* To have a repugance for, *in the next preceding article.* *See also* Reluctant, *a.*

Repugnantly, *ad.* With opposition, بِمُخَالَفَةٍ ـ بِمُضَادَّةٍ; with mutual repugnance, contrariety, بِتَدَافُعٍ; with aversion, كُرْهًا ـ بِعَدَمِ رِضًى ـ بِتَنَفُّرٍ. *See also* Reluctantly, *ad.*

Repulse, *n.* A check, the being driven back, تَدَفُّعٌ ـ إِنْدِفَاعٌ ـ تَدَافُعٌ ـ دَفْعَةٌ. To meet with a repulse, تَدَافَعَ ـ تَدَفَّعَ ـ إِنْدَفَعَ. *See also under* Refusal, Denial, *n.*

Repulse, *v.t.* دَفَعَ ـ رَدَّ. *See also to* Repel, *v.t.*

Repulsion, *n.* The act of repelling, رَدٌّ ـ دَفْعٌ; the being repulsed, تَدَافُعٌ ـ تَدَفُّعٌ ـ إِنْدِفَاعٌ. Mutual —, تَدَافُعٌ.

Repulsive, *a.* Propelling, دَافِعٌ ـ رَادٌّ; mutually —, مُتَدَافِعٌ. Forbidding, ugly, قَبِيحٌ ـ مُقْرِفٌ ـ كَرِهٌ ـ كَرِيهٌ ـ سَمِجٌ ـ سَمِيجٌ. *See also under* Hideous.

Repulsively, *ad.* *See* Repugnantly, *ad.*

Repulsiveness, *n.* Ugliness, سَمَاجَةٌ ـ كَرَاهِيَةٌ ـ كَرَاهَةٌ ـ رَدَاءَةٌ ـ قَبَاحَةٌ. *See also* Hideousness, *n.*

Repulsory, *a.* *See* Repugnant, Repellent, *a.*

Repurchase, *v.t.* إِشْتَرَى ثَانِيَةً.

Repurchase, *n.* شِرًى جَدِيدٌ.

Repurchasing, *n.* إِشْتِرَاءٌ ثَانٍ ـ شِرَاءٌ جَدِيدٌ.

Reputable, *a.* Of good repute, مُعْتَبَرٌ ـ مُكَرَّمٌ ـ مَشْهُودٌ لَهُ. Creditable, حَسَنٌ ـ مَدِيحٌ ـ مُعْتَبَرٌ ـ حَمِيدٌ. صَاحِبُ عِرْضٍ.

Reputableness, *n.* Consistency with honour, مُطَابَقَةُ ٱلعِرْضِ ـ صَلَاحٌ.

Reputably, *ad.* With honour, بِٱعْتِبَارٍ ـ بِإِكْرَامٍ. Creditably, حَسَنًا ـ مِدْحَةً ـ حَمْدًا.

Reputation, *n.* } A good name, صِيتٌ ـ سِمْعٌ ـ إِسْمٌ ـ جَانِبٌ ـ
Repute, } نَامُوسٌ ـ إِعْتِبَارٌ ـ صِيتَةٌ ـ ذِكْرٌ. Reputation by report, شُهْرَةٌ. His — spread among the people, إِشْتَهَرَ صِيتُهُ فِي ٱلنَّاسِ. For the sake of your —, لِأَجْلِ حُسْنِ سِمْعَتِكَ. To injure the — of one, ثَلَمَ ـ خَرَقَ نَامُوسَهُ ـ حَكَرَ ـ إِحْتَكَرَ صِيتَهُ. His — has been blasted, إِنْثَلَمَ صِيتُهُ. He has the — of being an upright man, هُوَ مَشْهُورٌ بِٱلِٱسْتِقَامَةِ. To hold in —, كَرَّمَ.

Reputative, *a.* *See* Putative.

Repute, *v.t.* To hold in estimation, إِعْتَبَرَ ـ كَرَّمَ. To reckon, account, حَسِبَ ـ عَدَّ. To estimate, consider in the rank of, نَزَّلَ مَنْزِلَةَ كَذَا.

Reputed, *a.* *See* Putative, *a.*

Reputeless, *a.* مَجْهُول ـ مَا لَهُ صِيتٌ.

Request, *n.* An asking, سُؤَال ـ مَسْأَلَة ـ طَلَبَة. A thing asked for, مُرَاد ـ إِرَادَة. A desire, wish, مَطْلُوب ـ مَسْأَلَة. A prayer, اِلْتِمَاس ـ تَمَنٍّ. I ask a — of you, أَطْلُبُ مِنْكَ طَلَبَة. Requests, أَدْعِيَة. To make known one's — to, عَرَّفَهُ (or أَعْلَمَهُ) بِطَلَبَاتِهِ. In —, sought after, مَطْلُوب. In —, current, رَائِج. He acceded to his —, أَجَابَ إِلَى ـ أَجَابَهُ إِلَى مَا طَلَبَ ـ طَلَبِهِ. *See also* Desire, Demand, *n.*

Request, *v.t.* To ask, تَطَلَّبَ ـ طَلَبَ ². To solicit of, اِقْتَرَحَ عَلَى ـ كَذَا. To — of, طَلَبَ ـ مِن; to — or ask of, سَأَلَ ـ مِن. To —, to call for, as a thing to be brought, دَعَا بِ ². To beg, أَمَلَ ـ تَمَنَّى ². To hope for, اِلْتَمَسَ ـ تَرَجَّى ـ طَلَبَ إِلَى ². To do as requested by so-and-so, فَعَلَ كَقَوْلِ فُلَانٍ. It is requested that ..., الْمَرْجُو أَنْ. *See also under to* Desire, *v.t.*

Requiem, *n.* صَلَوٰةٌ لِأَجْلِ أَرْوَاحِ الْمَوْتَى ـ دُعَاءٌ لِأَجْلِ الْمَوْتَى.

Requirable, *a.* That may be asked for, مِمَّا يُسْتَدْعَى; which may be wanted, مِمَّا يُحْتَاجُ إِلَيْهِ.

Require, *v.t.* To demand, request, طَلَبَ ²; to — something of, طَلَبَ ـ مِن ². To — the presence of, to call, summon, دَعَا ² ـ اِسْتَدْعَى. To — from, as in conformity to some order, اِفْتَرَضَ عَلَى ـ كَذَا. To make necessary, اِقْتَضَى ـ اِسْتَلْزَمَ. To need, حَاجَ إِلَى aor. يَحُوجُ ـ اِحْتَاجَ إِلَى ـ تَحَوَّجَ إِلَى. Such an one was required, اُحْتِيجَ إِلَى فُلَانٍ. I — such a thing, لِي حَاجَةٌ إِلَى كَذَا. Why do you — it? مَا حَاجَتُكَ إِلَيْهِ. A matter not requiring explanation, أَمْرٌ غَنِيٌّ عَنِ الْبَيَانِ. All that you — of me I will do it for you, كُلُّ مَا تَتَمَنَّاهُ مِنِّي أَفْعَلُهُ لَكَ. It required repair, دَعَا إِلَى إِصْلَاحِهِ ـ اِحْتَاجَ إِلَى التَّرْمِيمِ ². As the case may —, لِمَا تَقْتَضِيهِ الْمَصْلَحَة. *See also to* Demand, *v.t.*

Requirement, *n.* اِحْتِيَاج ـ حَاجَة ـ طَلِبَة. It is not suitable according to the requirements of the present age, هُوَ غَيْرُ مُنَاسِبٍ لِمَا تَقْتَضِيهِ الْحَالَةُ فِي هٰذَا الْعَصْرِ. According to the requirements of the case, عَلَى حَسَبِ مُقْتَضِيَاتِ الْحَالِ.

Requisite, *a.* Necessary, ضَرُورِيّ ـ مُقْتَضَى ـ لَازِم ـ مُسْتَلْزَم. Proper, fit, مُنَاسِب ـ وَاجِب ـ لَائِق. To make —, necessary, أَلْزَمَ ـ أَوْجَبَ. To be — for one, on account of his office, *etc.*, لَزِمَ; to be —, fit, proper, اِنْبَغَى ـ حَقَّ ². It was —, fit, that ..., كَانَ يَنْبَغِي أَنْ. Requisites, لَوَازِم. *See also* Necessary, *a.* and *n.*

Requisiteness, *n.* حَاجَة ـ اِحْتِيَاج ـ حَوْج ـ ضَرُورَة ـ ضَرُورِيَّة.

Requisition, *n.* The act of demanding, طَلَب; a demand, طَلَبَة.

Requisitive, *a.* مُسْتَدْعٍ ـ طَالِب.

Requital, *n.* عِوَض ـ مُكَافَاة ـ مُجَازَاة ـ جَزَاء. A good —, reward, ثَوَاب ـ مَثُوبَة ـ تَثْوِبَة. In —, مُقَابَلَةً ـ مُكَافَاةً. The day of —, judgment, يَوْمُ الدِّينِ. The Lord of the day of —, مَالِكُ يَوْمِ الدِّينِ.

Requite, *v.t.* To repay, either good or evil, أَعَاضَ ـ عَوَّضَ ـ أَعْقَبَ ـ بِ. To reward, with good, عَرَفَ ـ كَافَى ـ جَازَى ـ كَافَى ـ بِالْخَيْرِ ـ ثَوَّبَ. To judge, دَانَ. He requited him for his obedience, عَاقَبَهُ بِطَاعَتِهِ. As thou requitest (judgest) so shalt thou be requited, كَمَا تَدِينُ تُدَانُ. May God — you! جَزَاكَ اللّٰهُ خَيْرًا. God will requite, recompense, الْأَجْرُ عِنْدَ اللّٰهِ ـ الْعِوَضُ عَلَى اللّٰهِ. To be requited, تَكَافَى ـ تَجَازَى.

Rere, *a.* Of meat: *see under* Raw, *a.*

Rearward, *n.* *See* Rearguard, *n.*

Resail, *v.t.* عَادَ فَسَافَرَ ـ عَادَ فَأَقْلَعَ ـ أَقْلَعَ ثَانِيَةً ².

Resale, *n.* بَيْعٌ ثَانٍ.

Rescind, *v.t.* *See to* Repeal, *v.t.*

Rescission, *n.* The act of repealing, نَقْض ـ إِبْطَال ـ نَسْخ ـ فَسْخ.

Rescissory, *a.* مُبْطِل ـ مُفْسِخ.

Rescript, *n.* فِرْمَان ـ مَنْشُور ـ خَطٌّ شَرِيفٌ ـ أَمْرٌ جَلِيلٌ.

Rescription, *n.* مُجَاوَبَة ـ جَوَاب.

Rescue, *v.t.* To save, liberate, protect, خَفَرَ ـ خَفَرَ بِ ² ـ خَلَّصَ ـ أَسْلَمَ ـ سَلَّمَ ـ تَخَفَّرَ بِ ـ خَفَّرَ. To —, as from difficulties, أَفْرَجَ ـ مِن ـ فَرَّجَ ـ مِن ـ نَقَذَ ـ (or نَقِّذَ) مِن ².

Rescue, *n.* تَخْلِيص ـ خَلَاص ـ خِفَارَة ـ خُفَارَة ـ خُفْرَة; from difficulties, the act of, تَفْرِيج ـ إِفْرَاج ـ إِنْقَاذ; the being so rescued, فَرَج.

Rescuer, *n.* مُخَلِّص ـ خَفِير ـ نَاقِذ.

Research, *n.* *See* Investigation, *n.*

Research, *v.t.* *See to* Investigate, *v.t.*

Reseat, *v.t.* أَقْعَدَ ـ ثَانِيَةً ـ أَجْلَسَ ـ ثَانِيَةً. To be reseated, عَادَ فَجَلَسَ ـ قَعَدَ ثَانِيَةً ².

Reseize, *v.t.* عَادَ فَضَبَطَهُ ـ قَبَضَ بِ ـ ثَانِيَةً ـ ضَبَطَ ـ ثَانِيَةً ².

Reseizure, *n.* ضَبْطٌ ثَانٍ.

Resell, *v.t.* أَعَادَ بَيْعَهُ ـ بَاعَ ـ ثَانِيَةً. To be resold, اِبْتَاعَ ثَانِيَةً.

Resemblance, *n.* The state of being like, مُمَاثَلَة ـ مُقَارَبَة ـ مُشَابَهَة ـ شَبَه ـ مُشَاكَلَة ـ شَاكِلَة ـ لَمْحَة ـ تَشَابُه ـ مُنَاظَرَة ـ تَمْثِيل. Something similar, an image, مِثْل ـ شَكْل *pl.* أَشْكَال ـ

صُورَة . A perfect —, the being exactly like, عَيْن . There is a — between the two, بَيْنَهُمَا شَبَهٌ . The cows seem to us to have a — to one another, إِنَّ ٱلْبَقَرَ تَشَابَهَ عَلَيْنَا . There is in him a — to him or it, بِهِ شُبْهَةٌ لَهُ . *See also* Likeness, *n.*

Resemble, *v.t.* تَشَاكَلَ ـ شَاكَلَ ـ مَاثَلَ ـ حَاكَى ـ قَارَبَ ـ نَاظَرَ ـ تَمَثَّلَ بِ ـ أَشْبَهَ ـ شَابَهَ ـ ضَاهَى . To make one's self to —, تَمَثَّلَ بِ . He resembled his mother, تَشَبَّهَ بِ (or تَقَيَّلَ or تَأَسَّنَ or تَأَسَّلَ or شَابَهَ) أُمَّهُ . What is the thing like, and to what shall I resemble it? مَاذَا يُشْبِهُ ٱلشَّيْءُ وَبِمَاذَا أُشَبِّهُهُ . Day succeeds day and yet they do not resemble one another, مَا يَمْضِي يَوْمٌ وَيَجِيءُ مِثْلُهُ . I resembled him, or it, حَاكَيْتُهُ ـ حَكَيْتُهُ : He resembles the sun in beauty, يَحْكِي ٱلشَّمْسَ حُسْنًا . To make to —, مَثَّلَ ـ بِ ـ شَبَّهَ ـ بِ . To make one's self to —, to imitate, to assume a likeness to one, تَشَبَّهَ بِهِ . They resembled each other, of many, تَشَابَهُوا .

Resembling, *part.* and *n.* مُتَشَابِه ـ أَشْكَلُ ـ مُمَاثِل ـ مَثِيل .

Resent, *v.t.* To take ill, إِسْتَآءَ ـ إِسْتَصْعَبَ عَلَى ـ ٱلشَّيْءَ ـ إِسْتَقْبَحَ ٱلشَّيْءَ ـ لِلشَّيْءِ . To be angry at, إِغْتَاظَ مِنْ . To take as an injury, أَذِيَ بِ ـ تَأَذَّى بِ ـ تَظَلَّمَ مِنْ .

Resentful, *a.* Resentive, } أَنْطَوَى صَدْرُهُ عَلَى ٱلْبَغْضَآءِ ـ غَالُّ ٱلصَّدْرِ ـ ثَنَى صَدْرَهُ عَلَى ٱلْبَغْضَآءِ . Easily irritated, سَرِيعُ ٱلْغَضَبِ . *See also* Irascible, *a.*

Resentment, *n.* غَيْظ ـ غِلّ . To entertain —, غَلَّ صَدْرُهُ ـ ثَنَى صَدْرَهُ . To stifle —, كَظَمَ ٱلْغَيْظَ ـ أَخْفَى (or كَتَمَ) ٱلْغَيْظَ .

Reservation, *n.* The act of reserving or keeping back, إِبْقَآء ـ تَخْبِئَة ; what is kept back, مُخَبَّأ ـ بَقِيَّة ـ مُسْتَبْقَى . The act of excepting, إِسْتِثْنَآء ; what is excepted, مُسْتَخْرَج ـ مُسْتَثْنَى ـ شَاذّ . Mental —, إِضْمَارُ ٱلضَّمِيرِ ـ كَتْمُ ٱلنِّيَّةِ . *See also under* Reserved, *a.*

Reservatory, *n.* *See* Depository, Repository, *n.*

Reserve, *n.* That which is kept back from present use, ذُخْر ـ ذَخِيرَة *pl.* ذَخَائِر . Something kept back from disclosure, خَفَآء ـ خَبِيئَة *pl.* خَبَايَا . The habit of keeping one's thoughts to one's self, إِخْتِفَآء ـ إِطْرَاق ـ إِخْتِفَآء وَقِلَّة مُبَالَغَةٍ . Circumspection, caution, تَحَفُّظ ـ إِحْتِيَاط ـ مُحَاسَبَة . A corps of —, عَسْكَرٌ مُذَخَّرٌ ـ عَسَاكِرُ ٱحْتِيَاطِيَّة . A corps of —, stationed in the rear of a column, فِئَة *pl.* فِئَات *and* فِئُون . The — force of a country, عَسْكَرُ ٱلرَّدِيفِ ـ ٱلرَّدِيف ـ عَسَاكِرُ مُسْتَحْفَظَة . To call out the reserves, جَمَعَ ٱلرَّدِيفَ .

Under reserve, تَحْتَ ٱلشَّرْطِ .

Under the sole reserve, تَحْتَ ٱلشَّرْطِ ٱلْوَاحِدِ .

With reserve, حَصْرًا وَقَصْرًا ; without reserve, exception, بِدُونِ ـ مِنْ غَيْرِ إِبْقَآءٍ ـ ٱسْتِثْنَآءٍ .

To speak with reserve, تَحَرَّزَ (or تَحَفَّظَ) ـ تَكَلَّمَ بِٱلْحَذَرِ وَٱلِٱحْتِيَاطِ فِي ٱلْكَلَامِ .

To speak without reserve, إِنْبَسَطَ (or تَفَتَّحَ) فِي ٱلْكَلَامِ .

Reserve, *v.t.* To retain in store, صَانَ ـ إِدَّخَرَ ـ ذَخَرَ ـ خَلَّى بِ ـ خَبَّأَ . To keep, حَفِظَ . To keep, in the sense of leaving, suffering to remain, أَبْقَى . To exclude, except, إِسْتَثْنَى . To — for one's self, ذَخَرَ ـ لِنَفْسِهِ : He reserved for himself a good story, ذَخَرَ لِنَفْسِهِ حَدِيثًا حَسَنًا . He reserved some of his strength, ذَخَرَ مِنْ قُوَّتِهِ . He reserved his men to fight the soldiers of…, خَبَّأَ قَوْمَهُ لِقِتَالِ عَسَاكِرِ فُلَانٍ . To — one's rights, حَافَظَ عَلَى حُقُوقِهِ . I have reserved it for myself, أَبْقَيْتُهُ لِنَفْسِي .

Reserved, *a.* Kept, secured, مَحْفُوظ ـ مُذَّخَر ـ مَصُون . Left, مَا فَضَلَ ـ مُسْتَبْقَى . Backward, as in conversation and manner, كَثِيرُ ٱلْإِطْرَاقِ ـ مِطْرَاق ـ كَتُوم ـ طِرِّيق . Cautious, wary, مُحْتَرِز ـ حِرِّيس ـ عَاقِل . Reserved or kept for judgment, مَحْرُوسٌ لِلْقَضَآءِ . To whom is — the punishment, مَنْ قَدْ حُفِظَ لَهُ ٱلْقِصَاصُ . A — clause, reservation, شَرِيطَةٌ ٱحْتِيَاطِيَّةٌ ـ شَرْط *pl.* شُرُوط ـ قَيْد *pl.* قُيُود . A — attitude, حَالُ ٱلِٱحْتِيَاطِ . Reserved language, كَلَامٌ ٱحْتِيَاطِيٌّ . Reserved forces, ٱلرَّدِيفُ وَٱلْعَسَاكِرُ ٱلْمُسْتَحْفَظَة . In a — manner, تَحَفُّظًا ـ إِحْتِرَازًا ـ بِمُحَافَظَةٍ ـ بِٱحْتِيَاطٍ ـ بِإِطْرَاقٍ . All claims —, سَائِرِ ٱلدَّعَاوَى . It is a characteristic of him to be —, مِنْ شِيمَتِهِ ٱلِٱخْتِفَآءُ وَقِلَّةُ ٱلْمُبَالَغَةِ . To be — in manner, تَوَقَّرَ ـ تَرَزَّنَ .

Reservedly, *ad.* بِٱخْتِفَآءٍ ـ بِإِطْرَاقٍ ; cautiously, بِٱحْتِيَاطٍ ـ تَحَرُّزًا ـ إِحْتِرَازًا ـ بِتَحَذُّرٍ .

Reservedness, *n.* إِحْتِيَاط ـ تَحَفُّظ ـ تَكَتُّم ـ إِطْرَاق . *See also* Reserve, *n.*

Reservoir, *n.* حَوْض *pl.* أَحْوَاض *and* حِيَاض ـ مَصْنَعَة *pl.* مَصَانِعُ ـ صِهْرِيج *pl.* صَهَارِيجُ ـ سَاقِيَة *pl.* سَوَاقِي .

Reset, *v.t.* As of a plant, عَادَ فَغَرَسَهُ ـ غَرَسَ ـ ثَانِيَةً ; of a stone, jewel, عَادَ فَرَصَّعَهُ ـ رَصَّعَ ـ ثَانِيَةً ; of a bone, جَبَرَ ـ ثَانِيَةً ـ عَادَ فَجَبَرَهُ .

Resettle, *v.t.* To establish again, قَرَّرَ ـ ثَانِيَةً . To fix or bind again, رَبَطَ ـ ثَانِيَةً . To settle in a place again, أَسْكَنَ ـ ثَانِيَةً ـ عَادَ فَٱسْتَعْمَرَ ـ فِي . To —, as a dispute between, لَأَمَ بَيْنَ ـ ثَانِيَةً . *See also to* Repeople, *v.t.*

Resettle, *v.i.* As in a place, ع عادَ فنَزَلَ بِ ـ أقامَ فِي ـ ثانِيَةً ـ ع عادَ فَسَكَنَ ٱلْمَحَلَّ.

Resettlement, *n.* The act of establishing anew, إِعادَةُ ـ تَقْرِيرٌ ثانٍ ـ تَقْرارٌ; the being so established, قَرارٌ ثانٍ. The act of resettling, as in a country, إِعْمارٌ ثانٍ ـ اِسْتِعْمارٌ ثانٍ ـ تَسْكِينٌ ثانٍ; the being so resettled, إِقامَةٌ ثانِيَةٌ ـ سُكْنَى ثانِيَةٌ. The act of resettling, as of a dispute, لَأْمٌ ثانٍ بَيْنَ ٱلْخُصَماءِ; the being so resettled, مُلاءَمَةٌ ثانِيَةٌ بَيْنَ ٱلْخُصَماءِ.

Reship, *v.t.* *See to* Re-embark, *v.t.*

Reshipment, *n.* *See* Re-embarkation, *n.*

Reside, *v.i.* To dwell in, ع قَطَنَ بِ ـ أَحالَ بِ ـ وَطَنَ بِ ـ ع سَكَنَ ـ ع = عَمَرَ ـ = عَمَرَ بِ ـ أَقامَ بِ. *aor.* يَطِنُ. Those who wish to — out of the town, الَّذِينَ يُرِيدُونَ ٱلسُّكْنَى خارِجًا عَنِ ٱلْمَدِينَةِ. *See also to* Abide, Dwell, *v.i.*

Residence, *n.* Continuance of dwelling, قُطُون ـ مُتُونٌ بِ ـ إِقامَةٌ ـ ظَلَّةٌ. A place of abode, مَقام ـ دار *pl.* دِيار ـ مَحَلٌّ ـ بَيْت ـ مَسْكَن *pl.* مَساكِنُ ـ مَحَلَّة *pl.* مَحَلَّات ـ مَقْعَد *pl.* مَقاعِد *pl.* بُيُوت. *See also* Dwelling, House, *n.*

Residency, *n.* The office of a Resident, وَظِيفَةُ وَكِيلِ ٱلدَّوْلَةِ (or ٱلْمُتَصَرِّفِ) ـ سِفارَة; the house of a Resident, دارُ (or مَحَلُّ) وَكِيلِ ٱلدَّوْلَةِ (or ٱلْمُتَصَرِّفِ). The British —, دارُ ٱلْمُتَصَرِّفِ ٱلْإِنْكِلِيزِيِّ.

Resident, *a.* مُقِيم ـ ساكِن ـ قاطِن. Resident ambassador, سَفِيرٌ (or إِيلْچِيٌّ) مُقِيمٌ.

Resident, *n.* ساكِن *pl.* سُكّان ـ قاطِن *pl.* قاطِنُونَ *and* قَطِينٌ *and* قُطّان *and* قاطِنَة. The — and the wayfarer, المُقِيمُ وَٱلْمُسافِرُ. *See also* Inhabitant, *n.*

Resident, *n.* A public minister at a foreign court, وَكِيلُ ٱلدَّوْلَةِ ـ مُتَصَرِّف ـ سَفِير *pl.* سُفَراءُ. The British —, المُتَصَرِّفُ ٱلْإِنْكِلِيزِيُّ.

Residential, *a.* *See* Resident, *a.*

Residentiary, *n.* Of an ecclesiastic, قِسِّيس مُقِيمٌ.

Residual, *a.* فاضِل ـ باقٍ.

Residuary, *a.* مُتَعَلِّقٌ بِٱلْبَقِيَّةِ. *See also under* Legatee, *n.*

Residue, *n.* *See* Remainder, *n.*

Residuum, *n.* ثُفْل ـ بَقِيَّة ـ ثافِل.

Resign, *v.t.* To give up, quit, ع تَرَكَ ـ سَيَّبَ. To cease to do, ع كَفَّ عَنْ. To give up, as of an office, اِسْتَعْفَى ـ تَخَلَّى عَنْ. To — one's self to, أَسْلَمَ نَفْسَهُ لِ ـ اِسْتَسْلَمَ لِ ـ = صَبَرَ عَلَى ـ تَصَبَّرَ عَلَى. He resigned himself to the will of God, سَلَّمَ أَمْرَهُ لِلّٰهِ ـ تَوَكَّلَ عَلَى ٱللّٰهِ. He resigned his right, ع تَرَكَ ـ = نَزَلَ عَنْ حَقِّهِ ـ حَقَّهُ. The ministers who had resigned will retain their places, الوُزَراءُ ٱلَّذِينَ ٱسْتَعْفَوْا يَبْقَوْنَ فِي مَناصِبِهِمْ.

Resign, *v.t.* To sign again, ع عادَ فَوَقَّعَ عَلَى ـ ع عادَ فَأَمْضاهُ.

Resignation, *n.* The act of giving up, تَرْك ـ تَسْيِيب; of ceasing or abstaining from, كَفّ عَنْ; of resigning an office, اِسْتِعْفاءٌ. Submission, patience, إِسْلام ـ تَسْلِيم ـ صَبْر.

Resigned, *a.* مُتَصَبِّر ـ مُصْطَبِر ـ صابِر ـ صَبُور. To be —, تَصَبَّرَ ـ اِصْطَبَرَ.

Resignedly, *ad.* بِتَسْلِيمٍ ـ صَبْرًا ـ بِتَصَبُّرٍ ـ تَصَبُّرًا.

Resile, *v.i.* تَدَفَّعَ ـ اِنْدَفَعَ. *See also to* Recoil, *v.i.*

Resilience, *n.* }
Resiliency, } دِفاع. *See also* Recoil, *n.*

Resilient, *a.* مُتَدَفِّع ـ مُتَدافِع.

Resilition, *n.* دِفاع.

Resin, *n.* صُعْرُور ـ صَمْغ ـ لَثًى; especially of the pine, راتِينَج. The — used for fiddle-bows, صَمْغُ ٱلْبُطْمِ.

Resin, *v.t.* To rub the strings with fiddler's resin, ع مَسَحَ ٱلْأَوْتارَ بِٱلصَّمْغِ.

Resiniferous, *a.* حامِلُ ٱللَّثَى; especially of the pine, حامِلُ ٱلرّاتِينَجِ.

Resinous, *a.* ذُو صَمْغٍ ـ لَثِيث; especially of the pine, راتِيناجِيٌّ ـ ذُو راتِينَجٍ.

Resist, *v.t.* To stand against, قاوَمَ. To act in opposition to, ضادَّ ـ اِعْتَرَضَ ـ اِمْتَنَعَ ـ خالَفَ. They resisted one another, of many, تَضادُّوا ـ تَدافَعُوا. He could not — him, لَمْ يَقْدِرْ أَنْ يُقاوِمَهُ. Who resists his will? مَنْ يُقاوِمُ مَشِيئَتَهُ. To —, as in an argument, جاوَبَ ـ شاجَرَ. To —, to bear with, اِحْتَمَلَ ـ تَحَمَّلَ ـ = صَبَرَ عَلَى. To —, as the effects of the weather, *etc.*, أَصْبَرَ عَلَى ـ ...ٱل لا يُؤَثِّرُ فِيهِ (or لا يَنْفُذُهُ): a vessel which resists fire, إِناءٌ صابِرٌ عَلَى ٱلنّارِ.

Resistance, *n.* The act of resisting, مُقاوَمَة ـ دِفاع; of hindering, preventing, مُمانَعَة ـ مُعاناة; of opposing, مُخالَفَة ـ مُضادَّة. The quality of not yielding to a force, عِزَّة ـ عِزّ ـ صَلابَة ـ صَبْرٌ عَلَى. Mutual —, تَدافُع ـ مُدافَعَة. *See also* Imperiousness, *n.*

Resistant, *a.* مُقاوِم ـ دافِع. Mutually —, مُتَدافِع. Resisting, irresistible, عَزِيز ـ أَعَزّ.

Resistibility, *n.* إِمْكانُ ٱلْمُقاوَمَةِ. *See also* Resistance, *n.*

Resistible, *a.* That may be resisted, يُقاوَمُ ـ مِمّا يُقاوَمُ; that may be borne, مِمّا يُحْتَمَلُ.

Resistive, *a.* *See* Resistant, *a.*

Resistless, *a*. Not resistible, لا يُقَاوَمُ ـ عَزِيزٌ ـ صُلْبُ ٱلْمَعْجَمِ; not bearable, لا يُحْتَمَلُ. *See also* Irresistible, *a*.

Resistlessness, *n*. The quality of being irresistible, عِزَّةٌ ـ عِزٌّ; of not being bearable, عَدَمُ إِمْكَانِ ٱلتَّحَمُّلِ ـ عَدَمُ إِمْكَانِ ٱلْمُقَاوَمَةِ.

Resoluble, *a*. *See* Resolvable, *a*.

Resolute, *a*. صِنْدِيدٌ ـ عَزُومٌ ـ عَزِيزُ ٱلرُّوحِ ـ صُلْبُ ٱلْمَعْجَمِ *pl.* صَنَادِيدُ ـ مُسْتَوْثِقٌ ـ رَسِيٌّ ـ صَاحِبُ حَزْمٍ. To be —, رَسَا *aor.* يَرْسُو ـ تَرَسَّى. To be — in, صَلُبَ فِي ـ اِشْتَدَّ فِي. *See also* Determined, *a*.

Resolutely, *ad*. بِثَبَاتٍ ـ بِحَزْمٍ ـ بِعَزْمٍ ـ عَمْدًا ـ بِصَلَابَةٍ.

Resoluteness, *n*. Determination, وَثَاقَةٌ ـ عَزِيمَةٌ ـ رَوْقَةٌ ـ صَلَابَةٌ ـ إِقْدَامٌ ـ ثَبَاتُ ٱلْقَلْبِ ـ شِدَّةُ عَزْمٍ ـ حَزْمٌ ـ جَوْلٌ; boldness, مُرُوءَةٌ ـ شَجَاعَةٌ ـ زَمَامٌ. *See also* Determination, *n*.

Resolution, *n*. The act or process of resolving something difficult, تَخْرِيجٌ ـ حَلٌّ; of a compound, تَحْلِيلٌ ـ حَلٌّ; the state of being resolved, اِنْحِلَالٌ. A fixed purpose, قَصْدٌ ـ نِيَّةٌ. Firmness of mind, قُوَّةُ عَزْمٍ ـ رُسُوخٌ ـ قَرَارٌ ـ ثَبَاتٌ. Resolution, as of a tumour, تَحْلِيلٌ ـ حَلٌّ. A formal declaration passed by a public body, اِئْتِمَارٌ ـ حَتْمٌ *pl.* حُتُومٌ. Annulment, إِبْطَالٌ ـ فَسْخٌ. *See also* Resoluteness, Firmness, *n*.

Resolvable, *a*. حَلُّهُ مُمْكِنٌ ـ مِمَّا يَنْحَلُّ ـ يَنْحَلُّ.

Resolve, *v.t.* To separate things combined, حَلَّلَ ـ حَلَّ [2]. To disentangle, as a difficulty, حَلَّ ٱلْمُشْكِلَةَ [2] ـ خَرَّجَ. To decide, to determine, فَصَلَ ـ أَنْهَى ـ بَتَّ [2] ـ فَتَحَ. To analyze, ذَوَّبَ ـ أَذَابَ ـ مَاثَ. To dissolve, اِسْتَخْرَجَ ٱلْأُصُولَ ـ حَلَّ [2]. To — something into, تَأَوَّلَ إِلَى ـ أَوَّلَ إِلَى. He resolved upon the thing, أَنْبَرَ عَلَى ٱلْأَمْرِ [2]. It was resolved that ..., قَرَّ ٱلرَّأْيُ عَلَى أَنْ. To — itself into, آلَ إِلَى ـ صَارَ ـ عَادَ [2] ـ اِسْتَحَالَ إِلَى *aor.* يَؤُولُ. *See also to* Decide, Determine, *v.t.*

Resolve, *v.i.* To determine on, اِعْتَمَدَ عَلَى ـ تَعَمَّدَ ـ عَمَدَ ـ عَزَمَ عَلَى ـ أَزْمَعَ عَلَى ـ أَصَرَّ عَلَى ـ أَجْمَعَ عَلَى. To purpose, أَضْرَبْتُ عَلَى ـ اِعْتَزَمَ عَلَى ـ تَعَزَّمَ عَلَى. I resolved on the thing, ٱلشَّيْءِ. They resolved (after consultation) on the affair, passed resolutions upon it, تَآمَرُوا عَلَى ٱلْأَمْرِ ـ اِئْتَمَرُوا عَلَى ٱلْأَمْرِ. They resolved unitedly on the matter, agreed to the thing, اِتَّفَقَ ـ أَجْمَعُوا عَلَى ٱلْأَمْرِ ـ رَأْيُهُمْ عَلَى ٱلْأَمْرِ. I am resolved what to do, قَدْ عَلِمْتُ مَاذَا أَفْعَلُ. *See also under to* Decide, Determine, *v.t.*

Resolve, *n*. *See* Resolution, Determination, *n*.

Resolvedness, *n*. *See* Resoluteness, *n*.

Resolvent, *n*. مُحَلِّلٌ ـ حَالٌّ.

Resonance, *n*. صَوْتٌ ـ رَنَّةٌ ـ صَلِيلٌ.

Resonant, *a*. رَنَّانٌ ـ مِصْوَاتٌ.

Resorb, *v.t.* *See to* Absorb, *v.t.*

Resorbent, *a*. *See* Absorbent, *a*.

Resort, *v.i.* To — to, to frequent, آلَفَ ـ أَلِفَ *aor.* يُؤَالِفُ ـ اِجْتَمَعَ إِلَى ـ لَقِيَ ـ تَرَدَّدَ إِلَى ـ تَعَهَّدَ ـ يَأْوِي *aor.* أَوَى إِلَى. The people resorted to him, اِجْتَمَعَ إِلَيْهِ ٱلْقَوْمُ. He often resorted thither with his friends, كَانَ يَجْتَمِعُ هُنَاكَ كَثِيرًا مَعَ أَصْحَابِهِ. Where the people always resort, حَيْثُ يَجْتَمِعُ ٱلْقَوْمُ دَائِمًا. *See also under* Recourse, *n*.

Resort, *n*. The act of frequenting, أُوِيٌّ ـ مُؤَالَفَةٌ ـ إِلْفٌ ـ تَرَدُّدٌ. A place of —, مُلْتَقًى ـ مَأْوًى ـ مَعْهَدٌ ـ مَأْلَفٌ. In the last —, نِهَايَةَ ٱلْأَمْرِ. *See also under* Recourse, Rendezvous, *n*.

Resound, *v.t.* To make to ring or twang, of a bow, *etc.*, رَنَّنَ; of a bell or a piece of iron, صَلَّ ـ صَلْصَلَ. To make to sound, أَصَاتَ ـ صَوَّتَ. To spread the fame of, أَشْهَرَ صِيتَهُ ـ أَشْهَرَ.

Resound, *v.i.* As of a bow, أَرَنَّ ـ رَنَّ; as a bell or a piece of iron when struck, صَلْصَلَ ـ صَلَّ. To sound, reverberate, صَاتَ *aor.* يَصُوتُ. The age resounded with his fame, اِنْصَاتَ بِهِ ٱلزَّمَانُ ـ اِنْتَشَرَ صَوْتُهُ فِي ٱلنَّاسِ.

Resounding, *a*. صَائِتٌ ـ مِصْلَالٌ.

Resource, *n*. A remedy, عِلَاجٌ ـ مُعَالَجَةٌ. A source of aid or support, مُسْتَعَانٌ ـ مَرْجِعٌ. An expedient, اِلْتِبَاطٌ. A stratagem, حِيلَةٌ *pl.* حِيَلٌ ـ دُولَابٌ. Resources, wealth, money, مَالٌ ـ وُسْعٌ; means, openings, أَبْوَابٌ. Resources, as of a country, مَصَادِرُ (or يَنَابِيعُ) ٱلثَّرْوَةِ وَٱلْقُدْرَةِ. Great resources, يَنَابِيعُ كَثِيرَةٌ ٱلْفَوَائِدِ; innumerable resources, يَنَابِيعُ ٱلثَّرْوَةِ لا تُعَدُّ. Resources, revenue, وَارِدَاتٌ: ordinary —, وَارِدَاتٌ عَادِيَّةٌ; extraordinary —, وَارِدَاتٌ فَوْقَ ٱلْعَادَةِ. *See also under* Recourse, *n*.

Respect, *v.t.* To have respect to, نَظَرَ إِلَى. To listen to, اِلْتَفَتَ إِلَى ـ سَمِعَ. To embolden, keep in countenance, رَفَعَ وَجْهَهُ. To have relation to, عَنَى ـ خَصَّ [2]. To revere, honour, اِحْتَرَمَ ـ أَكْرَمَ ـ كَرَّمَ ـ فَخَّمَ ـ وَقَّرَ ـ أَعَزَّ. To — one's self, أَكْرَمَ نَفْسَهُ: He who does not — himself will not be respected by others, (prov.) مَنْ لا يُكْرِمْ نَفْسَهُ لا يُكْرِمْهُ غَيْرُهُ. To — persons, اِحْتَرَمَ ـ عَزَّ ـ تَوَقَّرَ ـ قَبِلَ ٱلْوُجُوهَ. To be respected, honoured, As respects their relations with one another, بِنِسْبَةِ بَعْضِهِمْ إِلَى بَعْضٍ. *See also to* Regard, *v.t.*

Respect, *n*. The act of respecting, honouring, تَوْجِيهٌ ـ تَفْخِيمٌ ـ حُرْمَةٌ ـ تَهْشِيمٌ ـ تَوْقِيرٌ ـ إِعْزَازٌ ـ تَكْرِيمٌ. Esteem shown, تَفْخِيمٌ

إِحْتِرَام ـ إِعْتِبَار ـ تَوَقُّر ـ كَرَامَة. Respect of persons, favouritism, مُحَابَاة. Reference, relation, خُصُوص ـ بَاب ـ جِهَة ـ صَوْب. To send one's respects to, سَلَّمَ عَلَى. To show — to, حَشَمَ لَهُ عَلَى كَرَامَةً. I have a great — for him, أَوْجَهَ ـ وَجَّهَ ـ تَهَشَّمَ. With — to, in regard of, فِي ـ مِنْ قِبَلِ كَذَا ـ بِنَآءً عَلَى ـ نَظَرًا إِلَى ـ مِنْ جِهَةِ كَذَا. With — to such, بِاعْتِبَارِ كَذَا ـ إِعْتِبَارًا ـ بِكَذَا. Considered in one —, بِاعْتِبَارٍ وَاحِدٍ ـ مِنْ جِهَةٍ وَاحِدَةٍ. In every —, بَتَّةً ـ قَطْعًا ـ مِنْ كُلِّ ٱلْوُجُوهِ ـ مِنْ بَابٍ وَاحِدٍ بِٱلْكُلِّيَّةِ. Out of — for him, مُرَاعَاةً لِخَاطِرِهِ. *See also under* Regard, *n.*

Respectability, *n.* The quality of deserving respect, of rank, position, *etc.*, إِعْتِبَار ـ عِزَّة ـ عِزّ ـ رِفْعَة. Propriety, decency, لِيَاقَة ـ مُنَاسَبَة ـ مُتَوَجِّب ـ أَدَب ـ حِشْمَة. Good character, أَدَب ـ حِشْمَة ـ مَهَابَة ـ إِحْتِشَام. *See also under* Credit, Decency, Propriety, *n.*

Respectable, *a.* Worthy of respect, respectable, حَشِيم ـ مُوَقَّر ـ مُحْتَرَم ـ مُكَرَّم ـ مُعْتَبَر ـ وُجَهَآء *pl.* وَجِيه ـ مُحْتَشَم. Proper, مُنَاسِب ـ لَائِق. Laudable, creditable, حَمِيد ـ مَدِيح. Moderate, كَافٍ ـ مُقْتَصِد ـ مُتَوَسِّط. A — حَسِين ـ مُعْتَبَر livelihood, مَعِيشَةٌ حَسَنَةٌ.

Respectableness, *n.* *See* Respectability, *n.*

Respectably, *ad.* So as to deserve respect, مَدْحًا ـ مَحْمَدَةً ـ حَسَنًا. Passably, بَيْنَ بَيْنَ ـ عَلَى قَدْرِهِ.

Respecter, *n.* One who respects, مُكَرِّم. A — of persons; *See under* Regarder, *n.*

Respectful, *a.* Of a person, مُؤَدَّب ـ أَدِيب ـ مُعَزِّز ـ هَيَّابَان ـ مُرْعٍ ـ رَاعٍ ـ لَائِق ـ مُحْتَرِم ـ صَاحِبُ ٱلْتِفَاتٍ; of an action, مُتَضَمِّنُ رِعَايَةٍ. Respectful to, مُعَزِّز لِ.

Respectfully, *ad.* بِإِكْرَامٍ ـ بِأَدَبٍ ـ بِتَوْقِيرٍ ـ بِٱحْتِرَامٍ.

Respecting, *ad.* عَنْ ـ مِنْ قِبَلِ كَذَا ـ فِي ـ مِنْ جِهَةِ كَذَا. Respecting me, عَنِّي; respecting thee, عَنْكَ; respecting which, عَمَّا. *See also under* Respect, *n.*

Respective, *a.* Having relation to, إِقْتِرَانِيّ ـ مُقْتَرِنٌ بِ ـ مُخْتَصّ بِ ـ مُنْتَسِب لِ ـ مُتَعَلِّق بِ. Particular, مَخْصُوص. Each, كُلّ ـ كُلٌّ مِنْ ـ كُلّ وَاحِدٍ. Their — مُخْتَصّ بِكُلِّ وَاحِدٍ claims, دَعَاوَى كُلٍّ مِنْهُمْ; their — claims upon or against one another, دَعَاوَى كُلٍّ مِنْهُمْ عَلَى ـ دَعَاوَى كُلِّ وَاحِدٍ عَلَى ٱلْآخَرِ. He gave to every man according to his — ability, أَعْطَى لِكُلِّ وَاحِدٍ عَلَى قَدْرِ طَاقَتِهِ صَاحِبِهِ.

Respectively, *ad.* Relatively, نِسْبَةً إِلَى ـ بِٱلنِّسْبَةِ إِلَى. As relating to each, عِبَارَةً عَنْ كُلِّ وَاحِدٍ. They — submitted a petition, قَدَّمَ كُلُّ وَاحِدٍ عَرْضَ حَالٍ.

Respirable, *a.* مِمَّا يَتَنَفَّسُ ـ يَتَنَسَّمُ.

Respiration, *n.* تَنَفُّس ـ نَسَمَة ـ نَفَس. *See also* Breathing, *n.*

Respirator, *n.* آلَةٌ لِصِيَانَةِ ٱلتَّنَفُّسِ.

Respiratory, *a.* مُتَعَلِّقٌ بِٱلتَّنَفُّسِ ـ تَنَفُّسِيّ.

Respire, *v.i.* To breathe, تَنَسَّمَ ـ تَنَفَّسَ ـ [2]أَخَذَ نَفَسًا. *See also under to* Breathe.

Respire, *v.t.* *See to* Exhale, *v.t.*

Respite, *n.* Temporary suspension or delay, مُهْلَة ـ فُوَاق. Respite, as from work, تَنَفُّس. Solace, فَرَج. Grant us seven days' —, أَتْرُكْنَا سَبْعَةَ أَيَّامٍ. He gave him a — from punishment, أَخَّرَ عَنْهُ ٱلْعَذَابَ. He granted them a —, delay, أَمْهَلَهُمْ رُوَيْدًا. When he saw there was —, a chance of escape, لَمَّا رَأَى أَنَّهُ قَدْ حَصَلَ ٱلْفَرَجُ. *See also under* Reprieve, *n.*

Respite, *v.t.* To grant a respite, delay, to, أَمْهَلَ ـ طَوَّلَ لِ ـ تَمَهَّلَ عَلَى. *See also under to* Reprieve, *v.t.*

Resplendence, *n.* } جَلَآء ـ بَرِيق ـ لَمَعَان ـ رَوْنَق ـ تَلَأْلُأ ـ
Resplendency, } بَهْجَة ـ ضِيَآء ـ نُور.

Resplendent, *a.* بَهِيّ ـ مُتَلَأْلِئ ـ مُضِيء ـ لَامِع ـ دُرِّيّ ـ بَارِق ـ سَاطِعُ ٱلنُّورِ. To be — لَمَعَ ـ [2]بَهُجَ ـ تَلَأْلَأَ ـ لَأْلَأَ.

Resplendently, *ad.* بِلَمَعَانٍ ـ بِجَلَآءٍ ـ بِبَهْجَةٍ ـ بِتَلَأْلُؤٍ ـ تَلَأْلُؤًا.

Respond, *v.i.* To answer, أَجَابَ ـ [2]رَدَّ جَوَابًا. To — to, رَدَّ لِ ـ جَوَابًا ـ أَجَابَ ـ جَاوَبَ ـ إِسْتَجَابَ إِلَى. To —, correspond to, suit, وَافَقَ ـ طَابَقَ. To — to, to agree to, consent, قَبِلَ ـ إِرْتَضَى بِ ـ أَجَابَ إِلَى. To — for, to be answerable for, تَكَفَّلَ بِ. *See also to* Reply, Correspond, *v.i.*

Respond, *n.* تَسْبِيحٌ يُتْلَى فِي خِلَالِ ٱلصَّلَاةِ.

Respondent, *a.* مُنَاسِب ـ مُطَابِق ـ مُوَافِق.

Respondent, *n.* One who answers in a suit, the defendant, ٱلْمُدَّعَى عَلَيْهِ; one who responds in a disputation, مُجَاوِب.

Responsal, *n.* } A reply, جَوَاب. The being in correspondence,
Response, } agreement, إِجَابَة ـ مُوَافَقَة ـ مُطَابَقَة.

Responsibility, *n.* } The being liable to be called to account,
Responsibleness, } مَسْئُولِيَّة ـ مُطَالَبَة. Liability to pay, ضَمَان ـ ذِمَّة. To acquit of —, أَحَلَّ ـ حَلَّلَ ـ أَعْهَدَ مِنْ; to acquit one's self of —, تَحَلَّلَ. To undertake the — of, إِلْتَزَمَ بِ ـ تَحَمَّلَ بِ. Free of —, خَلِيٌّ مِنْ ـ فُرَاحِيٌّ مِنْ ـ فُرْحَان مِنْ. Ministerial —, مَسْئُولِيَّةُ ٱلْوُزَرَآءِ. Personal —, ٱلْمَسْئُولِيَّةُ مَسْئُولِيَّةٌ شَخْصِيَّةٌ. The entire —, ٱلْمَسْئُولِيَّةُ كَافَّةً. To assume the — of the matter, إِتَّخَذَ مَسْئُولِيَّةَ ٱلْأَمْرِ. Under the — of his office, تَحْتَ مَسْئُولِيَّةِ وَظِيفَتِهِ. The — for this neglect rests

with the government, ٱلْمَسْئُولِيَّةُ عَنْ هٰذَا ٱلتَّهَامُلِ تَعُودُ عَلَى ٱلْحُكُومَةِ. To decline all —, ٢ أَبَى ٱلْمَسْئُولِيَّةَ بَتَّةً. He cleared himself of the — of whatever might result from the affair, تَبَرَّأَ مِنَ ٱلْمَسْئُولِيَّةِ عَمَّا عَسَى أَنْ يَحْصُلَ مِنَ ٱلْمَصْلَحَةِ. I hold thee clear of — for his running away, أَنَا أُعْفِيكَ مِنْ إِبَاقِهِ.

Responsible, *a.* Liable to be called to account, مُطَالَبٌ بِ — مَسْئُولٌ عَنْ or بِ — تَحْتَ ٱلْمَسْئُولِيَّةِ. A — editor, مُدِيرُ جَرِيدَةٍ مَسْئُولٌ. To make —, place under responsibility, صَيَّرَ — تَحْتَ ٱلْمَسْئُولِيَّةِ. Responsible, as a guarantee, ضَامِنٌ — زَعِيمٌ *pl.* ضُمَنَاءُ — كَفِيلٌ *pl.* كُفَلَاءُ. To be — for, ٢ ضَمِنَ ٱلشَّيْءَ — تَضَمَّنَ — تَحَمَّلَ بِ — اِلْتَزَمَ بِ. To be — to for, ٢ ضَمِنَ لِ — كَذَا — تَكَفَّلَ لِ — بِ. To make one —, ضَمَّنَ. I am — for such a thing, أَنَا بِهِ زَعِيمٌ — فِي ضَمَانِي (or ذِمَّتِي) كَذَا. You are — if anything happens, ٱلْمَطْلُوبُ مِنْكَ إِذَا جَرَى شَيْءٌ. You will be — before God, تَكُونُ أَنْتَ ٱلْمُطَالَبُ بِهِ عِنْدَ ٱللّٰهِ. He would be — for that, مَسْئُولِيَّةُ ذٰلِكَ تَكُونُ عَلَيْهِ. He alone is — for it, هُوَ وَحْدَهُ مَسْئُولٌ عَنْهُ. I held him — for the crime, أَلْزَمْتُ ٱلذَّنْبَ إِيَّاهُ — رَكَّكْتُ ٱلذَّنْبَ فِي عُنُقِهِ.

Responsive, *a.* عَلَى طَرْزِ (or طَرِيقَةِ) ٱلْجَوَابِ. A — particle, حَرْفُ جَوَابٍ. *See also* Corresponding, *a.*

Responsively, *ad.* بِٱلْمُجَاوَبَةِ.

Responsory, *a.* مُتَضَمِّنُ جَوَابٍ.

Rest, *n.* Cessation of motion, عَدَمُ حَرَكَةٍ — سُكُونٌ — قَرَارٌ. Repose, cessation from action, اِسْتِرَاحَةٌ — رَاحَةٌ — اِسْتِقْرَارٌ — قَرَارٌ — اِرْتِيَاحٌ. Relief, as from pain, رَاحَةٌ — رَوَاحَةٌ — رَوْحَةٌ. Quiet, tranquillity, سُكُونٌ — هُدُوٌّ — اِطْمِئْنَانٌ — طُمَأْنِينَةٌ — عَدَمُ ٱضْطِرَابٍ. Cessation, intermission, كُفُوفٌ — تَوَقُّفٌ. Recreation, تَنَفُّسٌ. Rest of mind, رَاحَةُ (or اِطْمِئْنَانُ) ٱلْبَالِ. Something to — on, عَمَدٌ — سَنَدٌ — مُسْنَدٌ. A stop, وَقْفٌ. Sleep, رُقُودٌ — نَوْمٌ. A place of —, quiet, مُسْتَرَاحٌ — مَسْكَنُ ٱلسَّلَامِ; a place to lie down in to sleep, مَرْقَدٌ — مَرْبَضٌ. A place, مَحَلٌّ. Eternal —, happiness, سَعَادَةٌ أَبَدِيَّةٌ. Rest, remainder, فَاضِلٌ — بَقِيَّةٌ — بَاقٍ — سَائِرٌ. At —, at ease, or dead, مُسْتَرِيحٌ; sitting, قَاعِدٌ; sleeping, رَاقِدٌ — نَائِمٌ. *See also under* Ease, Repose, *n.*

To be at rest, without motion, ٢ هَدَأَ — ٤ سَكَنَ — اِسْتَقَرَّ. To be at ease, as after toil, اِرْتَاحَ — اِسْتَرَاحَ. To sleep, ٢ نَامَ — ٤ رَقَدَ.

To be tranquil, secure, اِطْمَأَنَّ — اِسْتَكَنَّ.

To disturb one's rest, tranquillity, أَقْلَقَ — أَزْعَجَ — كَدَّرَ عَلَى.

To find rest from, اِسْتَرَاحَ مِنْ.

To go to one's rest, to die, أَرَاحَ: He went to his rest and so gave rest (to others from him,) أَرَاحَ فَأَرَاحَ.

To have a rest, اِسْتَرَاحَ — اِرْتَاحَ. To have a rest from, تَرَوَّحَ عَنْ.

To lose one's rest, to toss about from want of sleep, تَقَرَّعَ — ٢ عَلِزَ — اِنْقَرَعَ.

To place in rest, of a spear, قَوَّمَ سِنَانَ ٱلرُّمْحِ.

To retire to rest, sleep, ٤ رَاحَ يَنَامُ.

To set at rest, to decide, ٢ ٤ بَتَّ. To be set at rest, decided, بُتَّ — اِسْتَقَرَّ عَلَيْهِ ٱلرَّأْيُ.

Rest, *v.i.* To cease from action or motion, اِسْتَقَرَّ — ٢ قَرَّ — ٤ سَكَنَ. To take —, اِسْتَرَاحَ — أَرَاحَ. To be at —, in tranquillity, اِطْمَأَنَّ. To be unruffled, تَهَدَّأَ — ٢ هَدَأَ. To lie down, to sleep, ٢ نَامَ — اِضْطَجَعَ — ٢ ضَجَعَ. To —, or stay one's self against, اِسْتَنَدَ إِلَى — ٤ سَنَدَ إِلَى — اِدَّعَمَ عَلَى — تَمَكَّنَ عَلَى. To abide, اِسْتَقَرَّ — اِسْتَقَامَ. It rests with, as for decision, *etc.*, يُحَالُ عَلَى. To alight, as birds, upon, ٢ نَزَلَ — يَقَعُ *aor.* وَقَعَ عَلَى — ٤ ٢ جَثَمَ عَلَى. To — or descend upon, ٤ حَلَّ عَلَى. He could not —, be quiet or quieted, لَا يَسْتَطِيعُ أَنْ يَهْدَأَ. He rests not, that is, continues, day or night, لَا يَزَالُ نَهَارًا وَلَيْلًا. They — in their beds, يَسْتَرِيحُونَ فِي مَضَاجِعِهِمْ. He rested and gave rest (to others), أَرَاحَ فَأَرَاحَ. *See also under to* Repose, *v.i.*

Rest, *v.t.* To give rest to, رَيَّحَ — رَوَّحَ — أَرَاحَ. To quiet, هَدَّأَ — أَهْدَأَ. To place, as on a support, سَانَدَ — إِلَى — أَسْنَدَ — إِلَى — ٢ دَعَمَ — عَلَى.

Restaurant, *n.* مَوْضِعُ طَعَامٍ *pl.* مَوَاضِعُ — مَطْعَمٌ — مَأْكَلٌ.

Restaurateur, *n.* صَاحِبُ ٱلْمَطْعَمِ (or مَحَلِّ ٱلْأَكْلِ) — صَاحِبُ مَوْضِعِ ٱلطَّعَامِ — ٱلْمَأْكَلِ.

Rest-harrow, *n.* The plant, عَجْرَمَةٌ.

Restiff, *a.* *See* Restive, *a.*

Restiffness, *n.* *See* Restiveness, *n.*

Resting-place, *n.* A place of rest, مَضْجَعٌ — مَبَاءَةٌ — مَوْضِعُ قَرَارٍ. A burial-place, تُرْبَةٌ — مَرْقَدٌ. A basis, مَرْكَزٌ — مَغْرَزٌ.

Restitution, *n.* The act of restoring, giving back, رَجْعٌ — رَدٌّ — رِجَاعٌ. Surrender, تَسْلِيمٌ. The act of making good, of damage, *etc.*, تَضْمِينُ ضَرَرٍ — تَضْمِينٌ. To make — to, to guarantee, ضَمَّنَ — ضَمَّنَ — ٱلْخَسَارَةَ.

Restive, *a.* As of a horse, *etc.*, حَرُونٌ — طَمُوحٌ — مُحَرَّمُ ٱلظَّهْرِ *pl.* حُرُنٌ — شَامِسٌ *pl.* شُمُوسٌ — شَمُسٌ. To be —, ٤ حَرَنَ. *See also* Obstinate, Stubborn, *a.*

Restiveness, *n.* As of a horse, حُرُونٌ — حِرَانٌ — شَمَاسَةٌ. *See also* Obstinacy, *n.*

Restless, *a.* Void of rest, مُتَمَلْمِل ـ مُتَقَلْقِل ـ عَدِيمُ ٱلرَّاحَةِ. Unquiet, of a man, خَرُوجٌ وَلُوجٌ ـ خَرَّاجٌ لَجَّاجٌ ـ رَجُلٌ خُرَجَةٌ وُلَجَةٌ ـ طائش ـ أَفْزَاز *pl.* فَزٌّ ـ فِي رَأْسِهِ نُعَرَة. Restless, as from want of sleep, عَلِز. Restless, from activity, نَمِل. Disquieted, قَلِق ـ مَشْغُولُ ٱلْفِكْرِ ـ مُضْطَرِب ـ مِقْلَاق. A — woman, a gad-about, تَمَحَّش ـ إِمْرَأَةٌ نَمْلَى ـ سَيَّارَة; from activity, إِمْرَأَةٌ نَمْلَى. To be —, unquiet, طَاشَ ـ فَزَّ ـ تَمَحَّسَ. To be — from want of sleep, أَرِقَ ـ بَاتَ يَتَقَرَّعُ ـ عَلِزَ. To be —, disquieted, قَلِقَ ـ إِضْطَرَبَ. *See also* Turbulent, *a.*

Restlessly, *ad.* Without rest, quiet, بِلَا رَاحَةٍ ـ بِلَا قَرَارٍ; unquietly, بِطَيَشَانٍ ـ بِطَيْشٍ ـ بِفَزَازَةٍ; with disquietude, بِٱضْطِرَابٍ ـ بِهَمٍّ ـ بِقَلَقٍ. *See also* Turbulently, *ad.*

Restlessness, *n.* A state of motion, حَرَكَة; the being in a state of unrest, عَدَمُ رَاحَةٍ ـ عَدَمُ قَرَارٍ ـ عَدَمُ سُكُونٍ. Unquietness, of a man, طَيَشَان ـ طَيْش ـ فَزَازَة. Restlessness from want of sleep, تَقَرُّع ـ عَلَز. Disquietude, قَلْقَلَة ـ إِضْطِرَاب; of mind, وَسْوَاس ـ هَمّ ـ قَلَق ـ إِضْطِرَاب.

Restorable, *a.* That may be returned, رَدُّهُ مُمْكِنٌ ـ مِمَّا يُرَدُّ; that may be renewed, مِمَّا يُحْدَثُ ـ يُجَدَّدُ; as of a painting, مِمَّا يُعَادُ إِلَى قَابِلُ ٱلْجَنْدَرَةِ; that may be remedied, مِمَّا يُعَالَجُ ـ مِمَّا يُصْلَحُ ـ مِمَّا يُجْبَرُ. *See also* Recoverable, *a.*

Restoration, *n.* The act of returning, replacing, رَجْع ـ رُجُوع ـ إِسْتِرْجَاع ـ إِعَادَة ـ إِرْدَاد ـ رَدّ. Renewal, تَجْدِيد ـ إِحْدَاث. The act of repairing, rebuilding, تَعْمِير ـ رَمْرَمَة; of correcting, putting in order, إِصْلَاح ـ تَسْوِيَة ـ تَصْحِيح; as of a writing which had been obliterated, تَطْرِيس; of colours, pictures, and such like, جَنْدَرَة; of making good, تَضْمِينُ ضَرَرٍ ـ تَضْمِين; of setting up again, إِقَامَة; of remedying, putting in better circumstances, or reconciling, تَجْبِير. Generally, the act of rectifying, repairing, putting in order, تَجْدِيد ـ تَنْظِيم ـ تَسْوِيَة ـ تَعْمِير ـ تَصْحِيح ـ إِصْلَاح; of being so rectified, صَلَاح ـ إِسْتِتْبَاب. *See also under* Recovery, Re-establishment, Reparation, Restitution, *n.*

Restorative, *a.* مُقَوٍّ ـ شَافٍ.

Restorative, *n.* Of a medicine, عِلَاجٌ مُقَوٍّ ـ دَوَاءٌ شَافٍ.

Restore, *v.t.* To give or bring back, or to return to, رَدَّ ـ عَلَى ـ رَدَّ ـ إِلَى ـ رَجَعَ ـ إِلَى ـ رَجَّعَ ـ إِلَى ـ أَعَادَ ـ إِلَى; as to an office, رَجَعَ ـ إِلَى. To make good to, to supply, as in the place of something, خَلَفَ ـ أَخْلَفَ عَلَى ـ كَذَا ـ عَلَى ـ كَذَا. To —, as writing which had been obliterated, طَرَّسَ; of colours, pictures, *etc.*, جَنْدَرَ. To —, as of a waste place, عَمَّرَ ـ عَمَرَ ٱلْخَرَابَ. To —, in the sense of rectifying, repairing, putting in order, جَدَّدَ ـ سَوَّى ـ عَدَّلَ ـ عَمَّرَ ـ نَظَّمَ ـ أَصْلَحَ ـ صَحَّحَ ـ أَحْدَثَ. To remedy, recover, عَالَجَ ـ عَافَى ـ شَفَى. To — to life, أَحْيَى. To —, as from bad circumstances to good, or as a joint, جَبَرَ ـ جَبَّرَ. To set up again, establish, أَقَامَ ـ قَوَّمَ. May God —, make good, to thee (what thou hast lost!) خَلَفَ (or أَخْلَفَ) ٱللّٰهُ عَلَيْكَ خَيْرًا. Which it is intended to —, ٱلْمُرَادُ إِحْدَاثُهُ. To be restored, of health, إِسْتَفَاقَ (or أَفَاقَ) مِنَ ٱلْمَرَضِ. He shall — the lands which were formerly in their possession, يُعِيدُ ٱلْأَرَاضِي ٱلَّتِي كَانَتْ سَابِقًا فِي حَوْزِهِمْ. To be restored, restorated, put on a good footing, إِنْصَلَحَ ـ إِسْتَتَبَّ. *See also to* Recover, Re-establish, Repair, *v.t.*

Re-store, *v.t.* To store anew, دَخَرَ ـ ثَانِيَةً ـ كَنَزَ ـ ثَانِيَةً ـ عَادَ فَذَخَرَهُ.

Restorer, *n.* مُصْلِح; as of pictures, *etc.*, مُجَنْدِر. The Restorer, (God), ٱلْجَبَّارُ ـ ٱلْمُعِيدُ.

Restrain, *v.t.* To — from, عَكَفَ ـ عَنْ ـ عَكَّ ـ عَنْ ـ وَهَقَ ـ عَنْ ـ قَفَعَ ـ عَنْ ـ أَقْدَعَ ـ عَنْ ـ كَبَحَ ـ عَنْ ـ قَدَعَ ـ عَنْ ـ حَبَسَ ـ عَنْ ـ حَجَزَ ـ عَنْ ـ حَجَرَ ـ عَنْ ـ نَبَّرَ ـ عَنْ ـ يَعُوقُ *aor.* عَوَّقَ ـ عَنْ ـ مَنَعَ ـ عَنْ ـ أَمْسَكَ ـ عَنْ. To —, check, as a horse, تَقَفَّعَ ـ جَبَأَ ـ حَكَمَ ـ حَكَّمَ. To — one's self, إِسْتَمْسَكَ عَنْ ـ كَفَّ عَنْ ـ تَحَبَّسَ عَنْ ـ حَبَسَ نَفْسَهُ عَنْ ـ تَقَبَّضَ عَنْ. To be restrained, إِنْقَفَعَ. To — anger, كَظَمَ. He restrained his hand from him, قَبَضَ يَدَهُ عَنْهُ. He restrained his anger, إِبْتَلَعَ رِيقَهُ.

Restrainable, *a.* مِمَّا يُضْبَطُ ـ مِمَّا يُحْكَمُ ـ مِمَّا يُحْجَزُ ـ كَبْحُهُ مُمْكِنٌ ـ إِمْسَاكُهُ مُمْكِنٌ ـ مِمَّا يُمْتَنَعُ.

Restrainer, *n.* A withholder, حَابِس ـ كَابِح ـ مَانِع ـ ضَابِط. A mediator, وَزَعَ.

Restraint, *n.* The act of restraining, إِمْسَاك ـ وَهْق ـ حِجَارَة ـ ضَرُورَة ـ إِضْطِرَار ـ زَجْر ـ جَبْر ـ مَنْع. Obligation, constraint, إِلْتِزَام. Confinement, حَبْس ـ قَيْد. To throw off —, قَلَعَ عِذَارَهُ. Under no —, خَلِيعُ ٱلْعِذَارِ. He is still under —, لَمْ يَزَلْ تَحْتَ ٱلْحَصْرِ.

Restrict, *v.t.* To — from, حَصَرَ ـ عَنْ ـ حَدَّدَ ـ عَنْ ـ حَدَّ ـ عَنْ. To — to, حَبَسَ ـ عَلَى ـ قَصَرَ ـ عَلَى. To —, as the signification of a word, حَدَّدَ ـ حَدَّ. To — one's self to, خَلَا عَلَى. To — one's self, حَبَسَ نَفْسَهُ ـ إِقْتَصَرَ عَلَى. He restricted the property to him (by will or otherwise), حَبَسَ ٱلْمُلْكَ عَلَيْهِ. He restricted himself to certain dishes, خَلَا عَلَى بَعْضِ ٱلطَّعَامِ.

He restricted himself to living on milk and eggs, 2 خلا عَلَى ٱللَّبَنِ وَٱلْبَيْضِ. The number will be restricted to ten, يَنْتَهِي ٱلْعَدَدُ إِلَى عَشَرَةٍ.

Restricted, *a.* مُنْحَصِر ـ مَحْدُود ـ مَحْصُور.

Restriction, *n.* The act of restricting, حَصْر ـ حَبْس ـ تَبْر ـ تَحْدِيد; the state of being restricted, حَالُ ٱلْحَصْرِ ـ ٱنْحِصَار. A —, condition, قَيْد *pl.* قُيُود ـ شَرْط *pl.* شُرُوط ـ قَيْدٌ وَشَرْطٌ. Restrictions, قُيُودَات ـ تَقْيِيدَات ـ تَحْدِيدَات. Without —, بِلَا قَيْدٍ وَشَرْطٍ ـ بِدُونِ قَيْدٍ. To attach a — to, = 2 رَبَطَ ـ بِقَيْدٍ وَشَرْطٍ ـ = 2 حَصَرَ ـ بِبَعْضِ تَقْيِيدَاتٍ.

Restrictive, *a.* ٱنْحِصَارِيّ ـ تَحْدِيدِيّ. Restrictive clauses, شُرُوطٌ تَحْدِيدِيَّةٌ ـ شُرُوطٌ ٱنْحِصَارِيَّةٌ ـ قُيُودٌ تَحْدِيدِيَّةٌ.

Restrictively, *ad.* حَصْرًا ـ بِٱلتَّحْدِيدِ ـ بِٱنْحِصَارٍ.

Restringe, *v.t.* *See to* Contract, to Restrict, *v.t.*

Restringency, *n.* *See* Astringency, *n.*

Restringent, *a.* قَابِض ـ مُقَبِّض. *See also* Astringent, *a.*

Restringent, *n.* دَوَآءٌ قَابِضٌ. *See also* Astringent, *n.*

Resty, *a.* *See* Restive, *a.*

Result, *v.i.* To arise or spring from, أَنْتَجَ مِنْ ـ = نَتَجَ مِنْ ـ تَأَتَّى مِنْ ـ 2 حَصَلَ مِنْ ـ أَعْقَبَ ـ يَجِيءُ *aor.* جَآءَ مِنْ. To — in, to necessitate, سَبَّبَ ـ أَنْتَجَ ـ إِسْتَلْزَمَ. To — in, to be the consequence of, آلَ إِلَى *aor.* يَؤُولُ: The blow resulted in destroying life, آلَتِ ٱلضَّرْبَةُ إِلَى ٱلنَّفْسِ. The affair resulted in war, آلَ ٱلْأَمْرُ إِلَى ٱلْحَرْبِ. It results that ..., ٱلنَّتِيجَةُ أَنْ. He ate of a repast which resulted in his sickness, 2 أَكَلَ أَكْلَةً أَعْقَبَتْهُ سَقَمًا. A bad effect has resulted therefrom, 2 حَصَلَ مِنْ ذٰلِكَ سُوءُ تَأْثِيرٍ.

Result, *n.* حَاصِل ـ نَتَائِج *pl.* نَتِيجَة ـ عُقْبَة ـ عَوَاقِب *pl.* عَاقِبَة ـ مَحْصُول ـ مُتَحَصَّل. These results cannot be denied, هٰذِهِ ٱلْعَوَاقِبُ لَا يُمْكِنُ جَحْدُهَا. The — of it is not known yet, لَا يُعْرَفُ لَهُ نَتِيجَةٌ بَعْدُ. The efforts of the Wazīr continue to be barren of —, لَمْ تَزَلْ مَسَاعِي ٱلْوَزِيرِ بِدُونِ نَتِيجَةٍ. To consider, weigh, the results, تَرَتَّبَ عَلَى ٱلْعَوَاقِبِ ـ تَعَقَّبَ ٱلْعَوَاقِبَ. *See also under* Consequence, *n.*

Resultant, *a.* حَاصِل ـ نَاتِج.

Resultant, *n.* حَصِيلَة ـ حَاصِل ـ نَتِيجَة.

Resumable, *a.* That may be taken back, مِمَّا يُؤْخَذُ ـ مِمَّا يُسْتَرَدُّ. That may be taken up again, continued, مِمَّا يُؤْخَذُ ثَانِيَةً ـ ثَانِيَةً ٱلرُّجُوعُ إِلَيْهِ مُمْكِنٌ ـ مِمَّا يُسْرَدُ.

Résumé, *n.* خُلَاصَة ـ إِيجَاز ـ وَجْز.

Resume, *v.t.* To take back, 2 عَادَ تَأَخَذَهُ ـ 2 أَخَذَ ثَانِيَةً ـ إِسْتَرَدَّ. To begin again, as after interruption, = سَرَدَ ـ 2 سَرَدَ: He resumed the narrative, 2 سَرَدَ ٱلْحَدِيثَ. Let us resume our discourse, نَرْجِعُ إِلَى مَا كُنَّا فِي صَدَدِهِ ـ لِنَرْجِعْ إِلَى سِيَاقِ ٱلْكَلَامِ. To —, to sum up, (adverbially,) خُلَاصَةُ ٱلْكَلَامِ ـ ٱلْحَاصِلُ.

Resummon, *v.t.* إِسْتَدْعَى ثَانِيَةً ـ 2 طَلَبَ ثَانِيَةً ـ أَحْضَرَ ثَانِيَةً.

Resumption, *n.* A taking again, إِسْتِرْدَاد ـ أَخْذٌ ثَانٍ; of a discourse, رَجْعَة ـ تَسْرِيد ـ سَرْد.

Resumptive, *a.* ضَابِطٌ ثَانِيَةً ـ آخِذٌ ثَانِيَةً ـ مُسْتَرِدٌّ.

Resupinate, *a.* *See* Inverted, *a.*

Resupine, *a.* Lying on the back, نَائِمٌ عَلَى ظَهْرِهِ ـ مُسْتَلْقٍ.

Resurrection, *n.* As from the dead, بَعْث ـ نُشُور ـ نَشْر ـ إِنْبِعَاث ـ قِيَامَة. The day of —, ٱلسَّاعَةُ ٱلْكُبْرَى ـ ٱلرَّقَّة ـ يَوْمُ ٱلْقِيَامَةِ ـ يَوْمُ ٱلْبَعْثِ ـ يَوْمُ ٱلْجَمْعِ ـ ٱلسَّاعَةُ.

Resurrectionist, *n.* } A digger up of corpses, نَبَّاشُ ٱلْجُثَثِ ـ
Resurrection-man, } نَبَّاش.

Resurvey, *v.t.* 2 عَادَ تَكَشَّفَ عَنْهُ وَمَسَحَهُ ـ تَصَفَّحَ ثَانِيَةً.

Resuscitate, *v.t.* As from death, أَحْيَى ـ = بَعَثَ ـ أَنْشَرَ ـ 2 نَشَرَ. To reanimate, inspirit, قَوَّى ـ رَوَّجَ ـ أَنْفَسَ ـ حَضَّضَ ـ أَعَاشَ. *See also to* Animate, *v.t.*

Resuscitation, *n.* The act of reviving, as from death, إِنْشَار ـ إِعَاشَة ـ إِحْيَآء ـ بَعْث; the being so revived, إِنْبِعَاث ـ نَشْر ـ حَيَاة ـ قِيَامَة. *See also* Animation, *n.*

Resuscitation, *a.* مُحْيِي ـ بَاعِث. *See also* Animating, *a.*

Resuscitator, *n.* The, of God, ٱلْمُعِيدُ.

Retail, *n.* The sale of commodities in small quantities, تَسَبُّب ـ ٱلْبَيْعُ بِٱلْمُفَرَّقِ (*or* بِٱلتَّقْطِيعِ).

Retail, *v.t.* To sell in small quantities, = بَاعَ ـ تَسَبَّبَ بِ بِٱلتَّقْطِيعِ (*or* بِٱلتَّفْرِيقِ). To tell again, 2 نَقَلَ وَأَشَاعَهُ. He retails hardware, يَتَسَبَّبُ بِٱلْخُرْدَةِ. He retails, sells in retail, يَبِيعُ بِٱلتَّقْطِيعِ.

Retailer, *n.* قَطَّاع ـ مُتَسَبِّب.

Retailing, *n.* *See* Retail, *n.*

Retain, *v.t.* To hold in possession, إِحْتَوَى عَلَى ـ أَضَبَّ عَلَى ـ 2 حَازَ ـ = حَبَسَ ـ = ضَبَطَ عَلَى ـ 2 ضَبَطَ ـ = مَسَكَ بِ. To —, so as to prevent escape, = حَبَسَ ـ إِحْتَقَنَ ـ = 2 حَقَنَ. To —, to keep by one, with one, = مَسَكَ عِنْدَهُ ـ أَبْقَى عِنْدَهُ. To — in one's service, أَبْقَى فِي ٱلْخِدْمَةِ ـ = حَفِظَ عِنْدَهُ. To detain, عَوَّقَ. To — one, as a guest or otherwise, (-نَشَّطَ *or*) 2 كَفَّ ـ أَلْزَمَ أَنْ يَمْكُثَ ـ عَنِ ٱلذَّهَابِ. To — in mind, = حَفِظَ ـ

— مُسِكٌ — إِنْضَبَطَ. To be retained, أَبْقَى-فِي قَلْبِهِ — يَعِي aor. وَعَى. Do you still — your opinion? هَلْ أَنْتَ مُتَمَسِّكٌ بَعْدُ بِرَأْيِكَ . حُبِسَ. *See also to* Keep, *v.t.*

Retainer, *n.* One who retains, ضَابِطٌ — مَاسِكٌ. A dependent, follower, تَابِعٌ *pl.* تُبَّعٌ — مُلَازِمٌ — خَدَّامٌ. Retainers, retinue, خَدَمٌ وَحَشَمٌ — دَائِرَةٌ.

Retake, *v.t.* To — forcibly, إِسْتَرْجَعَ-عَنْوَةً. *See also to* Resume, *v.t.*

Retairing, *a.* A — wall, فَصِيلٌ *pl.* فُصْلَانٌ.

Retaliate, *v.t.* قَابَلَ-بِٱلْمِثْلِ — قَاصَّ. They retaliated upon one another, of two persons, تَقَاصَّ. *See also to* Requite, *v.t.*

Retaliate, *v.i.* قَابَلَ ٱلْمِثْلَ بِٱلْمِثْلِ.

Retaliation, *n.* مُقَابَلَةٌ بِٱلْمِثْلِ — قِصَاصٌ — مُقَاصَّةٌ; of murder, ثَأْرٌ. *See also* Requital, *n.*

Retaliative, *a.* / Retaliatory, } مُقَابِلٌ بِٱلْمِثْلِ — قِصَاصِيٌّ.

Retard, *v.t.* To keep back, تَعَوَّقَ — عَوَّقَ — ثَبَّطَ-عَنْ — بَطَّأَ — أَعَاقَ. To delay, أَخَّرَ. To be retarded, تَعَوَّقَ — تَثَبَّطَ. *See also to* Delay, Hinder, *v.t.*

Retardation, *n.* / Retardment, } تَأْخِيرٌ — إِعَاقَةٌ — تَعْوِيقٌ — إِبْطَاءٌ.

Retarder, *n.* مُؤَخِّرٌ — مُعَوِّقٌ.

Retch, *v.i.* جَاشَتْ نَفْسُهُ *aor.* تَجِيشُ.

Retell, *v.t.* *See to* Repeat, *v.t.*

Retention, *n.* The act of retaining, ضَبْطٌ — إِمْسَاكٌ — حَوْزٌ — قَبْضٌ — ضَبَاطَةٌ. Retention of urine, إِحْتِبَاسُ ٱلْبَوْلِ — عُسْرُ ٱلْبَوْلِ فِي ٱلْمَثَانَةِ. *See also* Retentiveness, *n.*

Retentive, *a.* Having the power of holding, ضَابِطٌ — حَافِظٌ — حَابِسٌ; of memory, عَدِيمُ ٱلنِّسْيَانِ — ذَكِيرٌ — ذِكِرٌ. The — faculty, ٱلْقُوَّةُ ٱلْحَافِظَةُ. A man of — memory, رَجُلٌ حُفَظَةٌ.

Retentiveness, *n.* As of memory, حَافِظَةٌ — حِفْظُ ٱلذِّكْرِ — حِفْظٌ — عَدَمُ ٱلنِّسْيَانِ.

Reticle, *n.* *See* Reticule, *n.*

Reticular, Reticulate, / Reticulated, Retiform, } مُشَبَّكٌ. To make —, شَبَّكَ; to be —, تَشَبَّكَ — إِنْشَبَكَ.

Reticulation, *n.* The act of, تَشْبِيكٌ — شَبْكٌ; the being reticulated, إِنْشِبَاكٌ — تَشَبُّكٌ.

Reticule, *n.* كِيسٌ *pl.* أَكْيَاسٌ — جِرَابٌ *pl.* جُرُبٌ.

Retina, *n.* أَلْيَافُ ٱلْعَيْنِ ٱلْمُشَبَّكَةُ (*or* ٱلْمُتَشَبِّكَةُ).

Retinoid, *a.* مِنْ جِنْسِ ٱلرَّاتِينَجِ.

Retinue, *n.* دَائِرَةٌ — ٱلْزَامٌ — حَشَمٌ — خَدَمٌ وَحَشَمٌ — مَوْكِبٌ.

Retire, *v.i.* To recede, retrograde, أَخَّرَ أُخْرًا — تَأَخَّرَ — تَرَاجَعَ — تَنَحَّى عَنْ — إِعْتَزَلَ عَنْ. To —, as from a place, تَرَدَّدَ — تَرَادَّ — تَغَيَّبَ عَنْ — غَابَ عَنْ — طَلَعَ عَنْ — إِنْكَفَّ عَنْ. To —, retreat, from, كَرْكَرَ عَنْ — تَقَهْقَرَ عَنْ — قَهْقَرَ عَنْ. To — from by a feigned retreat, to draw off the enemy from a position, إِسْتَطْرَدَ لَهُ. To —, to go aside from, أَعْرَى — إِنْصَرَفَ عَنْ — إِجْتَنَبَ مِنْ. To —, of the sea, جَزَرَ — حَسَرَ — إِنْحَسَرَ. To —, to desist, from, أَضْرَبَ عَنْ — صَدَفَ عَنْ — كَفَّ عَنْ. To —, secede, from, إِعْتَزَلَ عَنْ — شَرَدَ عَنْ — شَذَّ عَنْ. To — from, to resign, تَقَاعَدَ عَنْ — إِعْتَزَلَ عَنْ — تَعَزَّلَ عَنْ. To —, as to a mosque, *etc.*, for devotion, إِعْتَكَفَ. They retired, were beaten, as troops, إِنْغَلَبُوا — إِنْكَسَرُوا. They retired in excellent order, إِنْصَرَفُوا فِي غَايَةِ ٱلتَّرْتِيبِ وَٱلْإِنْتِظَامِ. Eat thou that from which the sea retires, and leave what floats upon it, كُلْ مَا حَسَرَ عَنْهُ ٱلْبَحْرُ وَدَعْ مَا طَفَا عَلَيْهِ. I retired, withdrew, as to a distance, إِجْتَنَبْتُ — أَعْرَيْتُ. He retired from the people, خَلَصَ مِنَ ٱلْقَوْمِ. To cause one to —, to withdraw him, أَبَدَّ. Retire from me! أَخِّرْ عَنِّي. *See also to* Withdraw, *v.i.*

Retire, *v.t.* إِسْتَرَدَّ — إِسْتَرْجَعَ — رَجَّعَ — أَبَدَّ.

Retired, *a.* Withdrawn, مُسْتَرَدٌّ — مُسْتَرْجَعٌ — مُرَجَّعٌ. Secluded, مُبْتَعِدٌ — مُجْتَنِبٌ — مُنْفَرِدٌ — مُسْتَخْلٍ. On the — list, مِنَ ٱلْمُتَقَاعِدِينَ. To live a — life, خَلَا — قَرْصَعَ *aor.* يَخْلُو. A — man, one who retires into himself, رَجُلٌ مُنْقَبِضٌ فِي ذَاتِهِ; one who retires to a place for devotion, مُعْتَكِفٌ. He placed them on — pay, جَعَلَ لَهُمْ رَاتِبَ ٱلتَّقَاعُدِ.

Retiredly, *ad.* فِي ٱلْخُلُوِّ — فِي عُزْلَةٍ — إِجْتِنَابًا — إِنْفِرَادًا.

Retiredness, *n.* عُزْلَةٌ — وَحْشَةٌ — خَلْوَةٌ.

Retirement, *n.* The act of withdrawing, taking back, تَرْجِيعٌ — إِسْتِرْدَادٌ; of receding, تَرَدُّدٌ — تَرَادٌّ — تَرَاجُعٌ; of retiring from a place, غِيَابٌ — طُلُوعٌ — إِعْتِزَالٌ; of retreating, كَرْكَرَةٌ — قَهْقَرَةٌ; of going back, as of the sea, جَزْرٌ — حَسْرٌ — إِنْحِسَارٌ; of desisting from, ضَرْبٌ عَنْ — كَفٌّ عَنْ — صَدَافٌ عَنْ; of seceding from, شُذُوذٌ عَنْ — إِعْتِزَالٌ عَنْ — صُدُوفٌ عَنْ; of resigning, إِسْتِعْفَاءٌ — تَقَاعُدٌ — تَعَزُّلٌ — إِعْتِزَالٌ; of going to reside in a place for devotion, إِعْتِكَافٌ. Seclusion, جَنْبَةٌ — خُلُوٌّ — عُزْلَةٌ. A place of —, مَعْزَلٌ; for devotion, مُعْتَكَفٌ. Retirement is a mode of devotion, (prov.) ٱلْعُزْلَةُ عِبَادَةٌ.

Retiring, *a.* A — or retired allowance, رَاتِبُ ٱلْمُتَقَاعِدِينَ — رَاتِبُ ٱلتَّقَاعُدِ. *See also* Modest, *a.*

Retort, *n.* A sharp answer, رَدّ ـ بُكَات ـ بُكَاتَة; an answer, جَوَاب ـ مُجَاوَبَة. The vessel used in chemistry, أَنْبِيق *pl.* أَنَابِيق ـ أَنْبك *pl.* أَنَابِك.

Retort, *v.t.* and *i.* To answer one with a retort, رَمَاهُ بِسُكَاتَةٍ. To return, answer, عَادَ ـ جَاوَبَ ـ رَدَّ عَلَى. To turn against one, as of an argument, أَدَارَ ـ عَلَى.

Retorter, *n.* مُجَاوِب ـ رَام بِسُكَاتَةٍ.

Retoss, *v.t.* عَادَ فَطَرَحَهُ ـ رَمَى ـ ثَانِيَةً.

Retouch, *v.t.* To touch again, عَادَ فَلَمَسَهُ ـ مَسَّ ـ ثَانِيَةً. To improve, repair, صَلَّحَ ـ رَمَّمَ ـ أَصْلَحَ ـ حَرَّرَ; as of writing, رَاجَعَ ـ حَرَّرَ; as of colours, or a painting, جَنْدَرَ. Retouched, of any writing or drawing, مُجَنْدَر ـ مَرْجُوع ـ مُحَرَّر.

Retrace, *v.t.* To delineate anew, عَادَ فَرَسَمَهُ ـ رَسَمَ ـ ثَانِيَةً. To trace back, as one's origin, رَجَعَ ـ إِلَى. To — one's steps, عَقَّبَ. They retraced their steps, اِرْتَدُّوا عَلَى آثَارِهِمْ قَصَصًا. To go back, to recur to, رَجَعَ فِي.

Retract, *v.t.* To take back again, اِسْتَرَدَّ ـ اِسْتَرْجَعَ ـ رَجَعَ فِي. To disavow, deny, أَنْكَرَ ـ نَكِرَ. To recall, as a declaration, رَجَعَ عَن ـ رَجَعَ فِي ـ ضَرَبَ عَن. *See also to* Recant, *v.t.*

Retractable, *a.* مِمَّا يُنْكَرُ ـ الرُّجُوعُ فِيهِ مُمْكِنٌ ـ مِمَّا يُضْرَبُ عَنْهُ.

Retractation, *n.* إِنْكَار ـ ضَرْبٌ عَن ـ رُجُوعٌ عَن ـ رَجْعٌ فِي. *See also* Recantation.

Retractible, *a.* } Retractile, } مِمَّا يُسْتَرَدُّ. *See also* Contractile, *a.*

Retraction, *n.* اِسْتِرْجَاع ـ اِسْتِرْدَاد. *See also* Retractation, *n.*

Retractive, *a.* مُسْتَرِدّ ـ مُسْتَرْجِع.

Retread, *v.t.* عَبَرَ ـ ثَانِيَةً ـ عَادَ فَدَاسَهُ ـ دَاسَ ـ ثَانِيَةً ـ رَجَعَ فِي ـ عَادَ فَعَبَرَهُ. *See also to* Retrace, *v.t.*

Retreat, *n.* The act of retiring, as from an enemy, كَرْكَرَة ـ قَهْقَرَان ـ قَهْقَرَة; through cowardice, خَيْمُومَة. A place of retirement, مَعْزَل; for devotional purposes, مُعْتَكَف. A shelter, asylum, مَلْجَأ ـ مَأْمَن ـ مَعَاذ ـ مَفِرّ ـ مَفَرّ ـ وِفْرّ ـ مَلَاذ *pl.* مَلَاجِئ. To beat a —, to cut and run, وَلَّى هَارِبًا. To make a feigned — in order to draw an enemy from a position, اِسْتَطْرَدَ لَهُ. *See also under* Retirement, *n.*

Retreat, *v.i.* As from an enemy, تَقَهْقَرَ ـ قَهْقَرَ ـ كَرْكَرَ. To go back by degrees, تَرَاجَعَ ـ تَرَادَّ ـ تَرَدَّدَ ـ تَأَخَّرَ. To — from, through cowardice, خَامَ عَن. *See also to* Retire, *v.i.*

Retrench, *v.t.* To cut off, قَطَعَ ـ أَزَالَ. To lessen, as of expenses, *etc.*, قَلَّلَ ـ أَسْقَطَ مِن ـ نَزَّلَ ـ قَصَّرَ ـ اِقْتَصَدَ فِي. *See also to* Intrench, *v.t.*

Retrenchment, *n.* The act of cutting off, قَطْع ـ إِزَالَة; of lessening, إِسْقَاط ـ تَقْصِير ـ تَقْلِيل; as of expenses, اِقْتِصَاد. Financial retrenchments, تَنْقِيحَاتٌ مَالِيَّةٌ. *See also* Intrenchment, *n.*

Retribute, *v.t.* جَازَى ـ كَافَى. *See also to* Repay, Recompense, *v.t.*

Retribution, *n.* مُعَاقَبَة ـ عِقَاب ـ عِيَاض ـ تَعْوِيض ـ عِوَض ـ مُجَازَاة ـ مُكَافَاة. *See also* Recompense, *n.*

Retributive, *a.* } Retributory, } مُعَاقِب ـ مُجَاز ـ مُكَافِئ ـ تَقْسِيمِيّ. Retributive justice, قِسْمَةُ الْحَقِّ.

Retrievable, *a.* That may be repaired, مِمَّا ـ يَنْسَدُّ ـ يُسَدُّ ـ مِمَّا يُعَالَجُ ـ يُجْبَرُ; that may be recovered, مِمَّا يُسْتَعَادُ ـ مِمَّا يُرَدُّ. *See also* Repairable, Restorable, Recoverable, *a.*

Retrievableness, *n.* إِمْكَان ـ إِمْكَانُ التَّجْبِيرِ ـ إِمْكَانُ الْمُعَالَجَةِ ـ اِنْسِدَاد ـ الْاِسْتِرْدَادِ.

Retrievably, *ad.* بِصُورَةٍ ـ بِإِمْكَانِ الْمُعَالَجَةِ ـ بِإِمْكَانِ التَّجْبِيرِ ـ قَابِلَةٍ الْاِنْسِدَادِ.

Retrieval, *n.* } Retrievement, } *See* Recovery, Reparation, Restoration, *n.*

Retrieve, *v.t.* To repair, جَبَّرَ ـ جَبَرَ ـ أَصْلَحَ. To restore, as from loss or injury, جَبَرَ ـ دَاوَى ـ عَالَجَ ـ أَخْلَفَ عَلَى. To —, as a loss, سَدَّ الْخَسَارَةَ. He retrieved his character, مَحَا عَنْهُ الْعَارَ. *See also to* Restore, Repair, Recover, *v.t.*

Retriever, *n.* The dog, كَلْبٌ مُعَلَّمٌ عَلَى الصَّيْدِ.

Retroact, *v.i.* On what precedes, اِشْتَمَلَ عَلَى السَّابِقِ; to act in return, رَدَّ الْفَاعِلِيَّةَ.

Retroaction, *n.* As on what precedes, اِشْتِمَالٌ عَلَى السَّابِقِ; action in return, رَدُّ الْفَاعِلِيَّةِ.

Retroactive, *a.* As on the preceding, مُشْتَمِلٌ عَلَى السَّابِقِ; reacting in return, رَادُّ الْفَاعِلِيَّةِ.

Retroactively, *ad.* As on what precedes, اِشْتِمَالًا عَلَى السَّابِقِ; as operating in return, رَدًّا.

Retrocede, *v.t.* To grant back, رَجَّعَ ـ رَجَعَ ـ رَدَّ.

Retrocession, *n.* The act of going back, كَرْكَرَة ـ قَهْقَرَة ـ رُجُوع; of giving back, تَرْجِيع ـ رَدّ.

Retroflex, *a.* مُخْتَلِفُ الْاِنْعِطَافِ.

Retrogradation, *n.* *See* Retrogression, *n.*

Retrograde, *a.* Going backward, رَاجِعٌ إِلَى ـ مُتَقَهْقِر ـ مُكَرْكِر ـ مُنْقَلِب ـ وَرَاء. Retrograde ideas, أَفْكَارٌ عَتِيقَةٌ ـ أَفْكَارٌ سَابِقَةٌ. Retrograde policy, سِيَاسَةٌ مَائِلَةٌ إِلَى الْأَفْكَارِ السَّابِقَةِ.

Retrograde, *v.i.* To go backwards, تقهقر إلى وراء ـ تقهقر ـ كركر ـ انقلب. To decline from, عال في or عن ـ ع. He retrograded, in morals, went back to his former evil ways, عاد إلى عكره ع. *See also to* Decline, *v.i.*

Retrogression, *n.* The act of going backwards, قهقرة ـ كركرة ـ رجعة ـ رجوع ـ انقلاب ـ تقهقر.

Retrogressive, *a.* *See* Retrograde, *a.*

Retropulsive, *a.* متراجع ـ دافع إلى وراء.

Retrospect, *n.* ملاحظة الأمور ـ عطف النظر إلى السابق. To take a — of, لحظ ـ ع عطف النظر إلى السابق ـ السابقة ـ الأمور السابقة.

Retrospection, *n.* ملاحظة الأمور السابقة.

Retrospective, *a.* متعلق بما قد مضى ـ ملاحظ الأمور السابقة. *See also* Retroactive, *a.*

Retrospectively, *ad.* بملاحظة السابق ـ بالنظر إلى ما قد مضى.

Retrovert, *v.t.* To turn back, رد ع ـ رجع.

Return, *v.i.* To come back to, رجع ـ ع قدم من ـ أدبر إلى ـ إلى ـ عاد إلى ـ يعود *aor.* آل إلى ـ يؤول *aor.* To —, as a disease, نكس ع. To come back upon, as a result, أعقب. He returned to health, رجع إلى الصحة ع. To cause to —, ردد ـ رجع. To oblige to —, اضطر إلى الرجوع. To — upon, to — to attack, رجع على ع. When he returns, لما يرجع ـ عند رجوعه. *See also to* Repent, *v.i.*

Return, *v.t.* To give back, رجع ـ ع رجع ـ أعاد ـ رد على ع ـ رد ع. To repay, كافى ـ أعاض ـ عوض. To — an answer, رد جوابا. To — a visit, رد الزيارة. He returned evil for good, قابل الجميل بالقبيح. To —, as of a member to parliament, انتخب لمجلس الشورى. To ask one to — anything, or to get it returned, استرجع ـ استرد. *See also to* Restore, *v.t.*

Return, *n.* The act of coming or going back, عود ـ رجوع ـ رجعة ـ عودة ـ معاد. Restoration, إعادة. Something given as an equivalent, مقابلة ـ مجازاة ـ عوض. Return, as of a fever or disease, نكس ـ نكاس. Return, in the sense of profit, عائدة ـ فائدة ـ ربح ـ رجعة ـ استرجاع. Repetition, إعادة ـ تكرير ـ تكرار. A list, إعلام ـ جدول ـ تقويم ـ سياقة. Election, انتخاب. In — for, في مقابلة كذا ـ مقابلة. This will give you no —, هذا ما يرد عليك. The returns, incomings, revenue, الواردات. They demand the —, restoration, of the Muslims to their country, طلبوا إعادة المسلمين إلى بلادهم. *See also* Statement, Report, *n.*

Returnable, *a.* That may be returned, مما يرد; that should be returned, رده لازم; that may be elected, مما ينتخب.

Reunion, *n.* As after separation, وصل بعد الفراق. A gathering, جمعية ـ اجتماع. The act of joining, ضم إلى ـ وصل ـ توصيل; the being joined, انضمام إلى ـ اتصال ـ وصلة. Agreement, reconciliation, مصالحة ـ اتفاق.

Reunite, *v.t.* As after separation, وصل بعد الافتراق. To assemble together, جمع ـ ع لم ع. To join to something else, ضم إلى ـ وصل ب. To reconcile, صالح بين ـ وفق. *See also to* Join, *v.t.*

Reunite, *v.i.* As of people, التموا ـ اجتمعوا; of flesh, a wound, *etc.*, ضم ع ـ قطب.

Reveal, *v.t.* To lay open, to disclose, كشف ـ ع أعلن ـ أفشى ـ كشف. To — to, بشر ب ـ أعلن ب ـ أفضى إلى ب ـ أعلن ل. To explain, expound, شرح ع. To divulge, make public, أباح ـ بث ع ـ أجهر ـ أذاع ب ـ أذاع ـ نادى ب. To suggest, inspire, as in a supernatural manner, أوحى; so to — to, وحى ب ـ وحى إلى ـ يحي *aor.* وحى (الله) في قلبه. To be revealed, disclosed, تكشف ـ انكشف ـ استعلن. To be revealed, divulged, تفشى ـ فشا ع ـ اجتهر ـ ذاع ع. He revealed his thoughts with the greatest frankness, أفصح عن أفكاره بغاية الإخلاص.

Revealer, *n.* مبشر ـ كشاف ـ معلن ـ مفش. A — of secrets, كاشف الأسرار.

Revealed, *a.* Made known, معلن ـ مستعلن ـ مفشى. Supernaturally —, موحى ب ـ موحى ب. Ready to be —, مستعد أن يعلن.

Reveille, *n.* هتاف البوق (أو دق الطبل) لإيقاظ العسكر في الصبح ـ دق التنبيه.

Revel, *v.i.* To enjoy one self, تنفس ـ تبحبح ـ أشر ع ـ مرح ع ـ بطر في ع. To carouse, نادم ـ تمتع باللذات ـ بطر ع ـ المنادمات.

Revel, *n.* Excessive rejoicing or exultation, بطر ـ مرح ـ أشر. Sensual enjoyment, تمتع باللذات. A carousal, منادمة. Revellings, بطر ـ منادمات.

Revelation, *n.* The act of disclosing, تكشيف ـ كشف ـ إعلان; the being disclosed, استعلان; what is disclosed, إعلان *pl.* إعلانات. Anything supernaturally revealed, وحي *pl.* وحي ـ تنزيل ـ إلهام. The Book of Revelations, سفر الرؤيا.

Reveller, *n.* عياش ـ ندماء *pl.* نديم ـ أشران ـ أشر ـ بطر.

Revel-rout, *n.* *See* Revel, *n.*

Revelry, *n.* Enjoyment, تَلَذُّذ ـ تَنَفُّس ـ تَمَتُّع . *See also* Revel, *n.*

Revendicate, *v.t.* إِسْتَدْعَى بِرَدِّهِ ـ إِسْتَرَدَّ . *See also to* Reclaim, *v.t.*

Revendication, *n.* طَلَبُ بِالرَّدِّ ـ إِسْتِرْدَاد ـ إِسْتِدْعَاءُ بِالرَّدِّ .

Revenge, *n.* نَقِمَات *pl.* نَقْمَة ـ إِنْتِقَام ـ ثَأْر ـ أَخْذُ ٱلثَّأْرِ . Blood —, تَارَات *pl.* ثَأْرَة ـ ثَأْر ـ ذَحْل . He took his — of him, أَخَذَ مِنْهُ ٱلْقِصَاصَ [2]. To take one's — upon, for, مَثَّلَ إِنْتَقَمَ مِنْ-عَلَى ـ نَقَمَ مِنْ-عَلَى ـ مِنْ-عَلَى . To take — for another, خَلَّصَ لَهُ حَقَّهُ ـ خَلَّصَ لَهُ ثَأْرَهُ ـ أَخَذَ لَهُ ثَأْرَهُ [2]. Out of —, إِنْتِقَامًا . Revenge is not a crime, (prov.) أَخْذُ ٱلثَّأْرِ مَا هُوَ عَارٌ .

Revenge, *v.t.* إِنْتَقَمَ ; of blood, ثَأَرَ بِ ـ ثَأَرَ . To — one's self, إِنْتَقَمَ لِنَفْسِهِ . To be revenged, إِنْتَقَمَ ; of blood, ثُئِرَ . *See also under* Revenge, *n.*, *also to* Avenge, *v.t.*

Revengeful, *a.* حَرِيصٌ عَلَى أَخْذِ ٱلثَّأْرِ ـ حَقُود ـ ضَغِن ـ طَالِبُ ٱلْإِنْتِقَامِ ـ حَسِكٌ . *See also* Rancorous, *a.*

Revengefully, *ad.* إِنْتِقَامًا ـ بِغَبَاوَة ـ بِحَسَكٍ ـ بِحِقْدٍ ـ بِضِغْنٍ .

Revengefulness, *n.* حَقِيدَة ـ حَسَكٌ ـ طَلَبُ ٱلْإِنْتِقَامِ ـ ضِغْن ـ حِقْد . *See also* Rancour, *n.*

Revenger, *n.* مُنْتَقِم . *See also* Avenger, *n.*

Revenue, *n.* مَدْخُول ـ مَحْصُول ـ إِيرَاد ـ دَخْل . The public —, الحَاصِلَاتُ ٱلْمِيرِيَّة ـ الوَارِدَاتُ ٱلْمِيرِيَّة ـ إِيرَادُ ٱلدَّوْلَةِ . The — is short of the expenditure, الدَّخْلُ يَنْقُصُ عَنِ ٱلْخَرْجِ . A — cutter, سَفِينَةٌ حَافِظَةٌ ٱلْكُمْرُكَ . Revenue officer, مَأْمُورٌ أَمِينٌ ـ مُحَصِّل . A collector of —, دَيْدَبَان ـ ٱلِاحْتِسَابِ ٱلْإِيرَادَاتِ .

Reverberant, *a.* *See* Resounding, *a.*

Reverberate, *v.t.* To send or beat back, as light or heat, عَكَسَ ـ رَدَّ [2]. *See also to* Resound, *v.t.*

Reverberate, *v.i.* إِرْتَدَّ ـ إِنْعَكَسَ . *See also to* Resound, *v.i.*

Reverberation, *n.* The act of returning, of light or heat, رَدٌّ ـ عَكْس ; the being so reverberated, إِرْتِدَاد ـ إِنْعِكَاس . *See also* Resonance, *n.*

Reverberatory, *a.* As of sound, رَنَّان ـ مِصْوَات .

Revere, *v.t.* As applied to persons, إِحْتَرَمَ ـ أَكْرَمَ ـ كَرَّمَ ـ وَقَّرَ ; in a sense implying awe, يَخْشَى *aor.* خَشِيَ مِن ـ جَبَأَ عَن ; as applied to God, تَهَيَّبَ ـ إِهْتَابَ ـ هَابَ . To be revered, respected, تَكَرَّمَ ـ تَوَقَّرَ . *See also under to* Fear, *v.t.*

Revered, *a.* Respected, مُوَقَّر ـ مُحْتَرَم ـ مُكَرَّم ; with awe, مُعْتَزّ ـ مَهُوب . *See also* Fearful, *a.*

Reverence, *n.* Respect, إِكْرَام ـ إِحْتِرَام ـ تَوَقُّر . Veneration, مَهَابَة ـ هَيْبَة ـ رَجَب ـ حُرْمَة ـ خِشْيَان ـ خَشْيَة . A bow in —, خُشُوع ـ خُضُوع . As a title applied to clergymen, مُحْتَرَم ـ ذُو فَضِيلَةٍ ـ ذُو ٱحْتِرَامٍ .

Reverence, *v.t.* *See to* Revere, *v.t.*

Reverend, *a.* To be held in awe, fearful, مَهُوب . Regarded with reverence, مُحْتَشَم ـ حَشِيم . As a title given to the clergy, *etc.*, Reverend, المُحْتَرَم .

Most Reverend, الكُلِّيُّ ٱلْإِكْرَامِ .

Right Reverend, الجَزِيلُ ٱلْإِحْتِرَامِ .

Very Reverend, الكَثِيرُ ٱلْإِحْتِرَامِ .

Reverent, *a.* } **Reverential**, } خَاشٍ *fem.* خَشْيَانُ ـ ذُو هَيْبَةٍ ـ مُتَهَيِّب ـ خُضُوع ـ خَاضِع ـ خَشْيَانَة *and* خَشْيَا .

Reverentially, *ad.* بِحُرْمَةٍ ـ بِتَوْقِيرٍ ـ بِٱحْتِرَامٍ .

Reverently, *ad.* بِخُضُوعٍ ـ بِخِشْيَانٍ ـ تَهَيُّبًا .

Reverer, *n.* *See* Reverent, *a.*

Reverie, *n.* } **Revery**, } إِفْتِكَار ـ فِكْر . Deep in a —, غَارِقٌ فِي بَحْرِ ٱلْأَفْكَارِ .

Reversal, *n.* As of a judgment, تَبْطِيل ـ فَسْخٌ وَإِبْطَال .

Reverse, *v.t.* To change from one position to the opposite, قَلَبَ ـ عَكَسَ ـ أَرْكَسَ ـ رَكَسَ [2]. To annul, فَسَخَ ـ نَسَخَ ـ نَقَضَ [2] ـ أَبْطَلَ . He reversed the order of its parts, رَدَّ بَعْضَهُ [2]. He reversed the order of the affair or case, رَدَّ ٱلْأَمْرَ ـ رَدَّ ٱلشَّيْءَ [2] عَلَى بَعْضٍ ـ ٱلْأَمْرَ عَلَى بَعْضٍ . I will not — it, لَا أَرُدُّهُ . He reversed it, made the last part of it to be first, رَدَّ أَوَّلَهُ عَلَى آخِرِهِ [2]. I cannot — it, لَا أَقْدِرُ أَنْ أَرُدَّهُ .

Reverse, *n.* A change or vicissitude, تَقَلُّبَة ـ صُرُوف *pl.* صَرْف ـ تَحْوِيل ـ عَوَاقِب *pl.* عَاقِبَة ـ تَقَلُّبَات *pl.* A — of fortune, دَبْرَة ـ مُصِيبَة ـ دَوَائِر *pl.* دَائِرَة ـ آفَات *pl.* آفَة ـ دَاهِيَة ـ دَوْرَة ـ مَصَائِب *pl.* The contrary, opposite, إِرْتِكَاس ـ ضِدٌّ ـ عَكْس ـ قَلْب . A — side, عَوَارِض *pl.* عَارِضَة . Reverse, as of a coin, medal, قَفًا ـ قَفَاء . Reverses befell them, دَارَتْ عَلَيْهِمِ ٱلدَّوَائِرُ . He met with a —, misfortune, أَصَابَتْهُ مُصِيبَةٌ ; with a defeat, إِنْكَسَرَ . *See also* Vicissitude, *n.*

Reverse, *a.* *See* Reversed.

Reversed, *a.* As to position, مُرْتَكِس ـ مَعْكُوس ـ مُنْعَكِس ـ مَقْلُوب . Reversed or reverted language, كَلَامٌ مَعْكُوسٌ . To be —, إِنْعَكَسَ ـ إِرْتَكَسَ . The state has become —, إِنْعَكَسَ ٱلْحَالُ . Not to be —, لَا يُرَدُّ .

Reversely, *ad.* بِٱلْمَقْلُوبِ ـ بِٱلْقَلْبِ ـ بِٱلْعَكْسِ .

Reversible, *a.* That may be reverted, as to position, مِمَّا يَرْتَكِسُ — مِمَّا يَنْعَكِسُ — مِمَّا يَنْقَلِبُ. That may be annulled, مِمَّا يُرَدُّ — مِمَّا يَنْسَخُ — مِمَّا يَبْطُلُ.

Reversion, *n.* As of an estate, عَوْدَةٌ إِلَى — رُجُوعٌ إِلَى — رُجُوعٌ إِلَى — التَّصَرُّفُ بِهِ — الْإِنْتِقَالُ — رُجُوعٌ وَٱنْتِقَالٌ. By right of —, بِحَقِّ ٱلرَّجْعَةِ.

Reversionary, *a.* عَائِدٌ إِلَى — رَاجِعٌ إِلَى — مِمَّا يَنْتَقِلُ إِلَى.

Reversioner, *n.* صَاحِبُ ٱلرُّجُوعِ وَٱلْإِنْتِقَالِ.

Revert, *v.i.* To — or return to, عَادَ إِلَى ² — عَاوَدَ — رَجَعَ إِلَى ـ ـ — اِرْتَدَّ إِلَى — اِرْتَدَّ عَنْ — رَجَعَ عَنْ ـ ـ. To — from, اِنْصَرَفَ عَنْ — آلَ عَنْ *aor.* يَؤُولُ. To — to, as property, رَجَعَ وَٱنْتَقَلَ إِلَى ـ ـ. The eye reverts from him on account of his ugliness, يَرْتَدُّ ٱلْبَصَرُ عَنْهُ مِنْ قُبْحِهِ. He reverted frequently to conversation with him, عَاوَدَهُ ٱلْكَلَامَ — رَاجَعَهُ ٱلْكَلَامَ. He reverted frequently to the question in talking with him, عَاوَدَهُ بِٱلْمَسْأَلَةِ. *See also to* Resume, Return, *v.i.*

Revertible, *a.* مِمَّا يُرْجَعُ وَيَنْتَقِلُ.

Revertive, *a.* عَاكِسٌ — مُقَلِّبٌ.

Revest, *v.t.* *See to* Reinvest, *v.t.*

Revetment, *n.* تَطْبِيقٌ بِحَجَرٍ — تَأْزِيرٌ بِحَجَرٍ. To line with a —, طَبَّقَ بِحَجَرٍ — أَزَّرَ بِحَجَرٍ.

Revibrate, *v.t.* *See to* Resound, Reverberate, *v.t.*

Revictual, *v.t.* عَادَ فَزَوَّدَهُ — زَوَّدَ (or) مَوَّنَ ثَانِيَةً.

Review, *v.t.* To take a retrospect of, نَظَرَ فِي سِيَاقِ ٱلْأَمْرِ ـ ـ. To consider again, عَادَ فِي ². To —, as troops, عَرَضَ ـ ـ (or) اِعْتَرَضَ ٱلْجُنْدَ. To re-examine, as of a book, تَصَفَّحَ. The army was reviewed, اِعْتَرَضَ ٱلْجُنْدُ. The army was reviewed before him, عُرِضَتْ عَلَيْهِ ٱلْعَسَاكِرُ.

Review, *n.* A retrospect, النَّظَرُ إِلَى ٱلْمَاضِي. Reconsideration of anything, رُجُوعٌ إِلَى. Inspection, كَشْفٌ — تَفْتِيشٌ — تَصَفُّحٌ. A — of troops, عَرْضُ ٱلْجُنْدِ — سَرْدُ ٱلْعَسَاكِرِ. A —, as of a book and such like, تَصَفُّحٌ *pl.* تَصَفُّحَاتٌ.

Reviewer, *n.* As of troops, عَارِضُ ٱلْجَيْشِ; of a book, *etc.*, مُتَصَفِّحٌ.

Revile, *v.t.* لَقَسَ ² — عَضَبَ ـ ـ — سَافَهَ — طَلَّى — أَزْرَفَ بِ — قَرَفَ عَلَى ـ ـ — رَجَمَ بِٱلْقَوْلِ ² — شَتَمَ ² — سَبَّ ².

Reviler, *n.* رَجِيمٌ — مُسَبِّبٌ — شَتَّامٌ — شَتِيمٌ.

Reviling, *n.* تَطْلِيَةٌ — عُضُوبَةٌ — سَبٌّ — شَتْمٌ — شَتِيمَةٌ. Mutual revilings, تَسَابٌّ — مُشَاتَمَةٌ.

Revindicate, *v.t.* *See to* Revendicate, Reclaim, *v.t.*

Revisal, *n.* *See* Revision, *n.*

Revise, *v.t.* To look over with care, تَصَفَّحَ. To correct, حَرَّرَ — صَلَّحَ — صَحَّحَ — نَقَّحَ. *See also under to* Review, *v.t.*

Revise, *n.* As of a printed sheet, نُسْخَةٌ لِلتَّصْحِيحِ — تَجْرِبَةٌ — مُسَوَّدَةٌ.

Reviser, *n.* مُحَرِّرٌ — مُتَصَفِّحٌ — مُصَحِّحٌ — مُصَلِّحٌ — مُصْلِحُ ٱلْغَلَطِ.

Revision, *n.* The act of revising, looking over again, تَصَفُّحٌ; of correcting, تَحْرِيرٌ — تَصْحِيحٌ — تَصْلِيحٌ — إِصْلَاحُ ٱلْغَلَطِ; of proving, تَحْقِيقٌ; of an account, رُؤْيَةُ حِسَابٍ.

Revisional, *a.* } مُتَعَلِّقٌ بِٱلتَّصْحِيحِ — تَحْقِيقِيٌّ — تَصْحِيحِيٌّ.
Revisionary, }

Revisit, *v.t.* أَعَادَ ² — عَادَ — تَعَهَّدَ ثَانِيَةً — زَارَ ثَانِيَةً *aor.* يَزُورُ.

Revisitation, *n.* عِيَادَةٌ — عَوْدَةٌ — زِيَارَةٌ ثَانِيَةٌ.

Revival, *n.* A return to life, عَوْدَةٌ إِلَى ٱلْحَيَاةِ — إِنْتِعَاشٌ; recovery, تَعْدِيلٌ — تَجَبُّرٌ — تَصْلِيحٌ; as after fatigue, إِرَاحَةٌ — إِسْتِرَاحَةٌ; as of trade, رَوَاجٌ. Prosperity, advancement, فَلَاحٌ — نَجَاحٌ. A — of religion, نَشْرُ ٱلدِّينِ — قِيَامُ ٱلدِّينِ مِنْ جَدِيدٍ.

Revivalist, *n.* In religion, نَاشِرُ ٱلدِّينِ — مُحْيِي ٱلدِّينِ.

Revive, *v.t.* To restore to life, بَعَثَ ـ ـ — عَيَّشَ — أَعَاشَ — أَحْيَى. To recover from a state of depression, حَايَى — أَحْيَى — بَعَثَ ـ ـ — قَوَّى; as of trade, رَوَّجَ. To give rest to, أَرَاحَ. To rouse, أَنْهَضَ — نَشَّطَ — حَرَّضَ.

Revive, *v.i.* To return to life, رَجَعَ إِلَى ٱلْحَيَاةِ ـ ـ — عَاشَ *aor.* يَعِيشُ — اِنْتَعَشَ. To recover from a state of depression, حَيَّ *aor.* يَحْيَا (or) يَحِيُّ — اِنْتَهَضَ — هَاجَ ـ ـ — اِشْتَدَّ. To —, as herbage, نَشَرَ ². His spirit revived, عَاشَتْ رُوحُهُ — رَجَعَتْ نَفْسُهُ. Will the government take advantage of this opportunity to — a second time, هَلْ تَغْتَنِمُ ٱلدَّوْلَةُ مِنْ هٰذِهِ ٱلْفُرْصَةِ وَتَنْتَعِشُ مَرَّةً أُخْرَى.

Reviver, *n.* One who restores to life, مُحْيِي. *See also* Restorer, *n.*

Revivification, *n.* *See* Reanimation, *n.*

Revivify, *v.t.* *See to* Revive, Reanimate, *v.t.*

Revivescence, *n.* *See* Revival, *n.*

Revivor, *n.* رَجْعَةٌ — الرُّجُوعُ إِلَى دَعْوَى.

Revocable, *a.* That may be recalled, يُسْتَرَدُّ; that may be repealed, مِمَّا يُنْقَضُ — مِمَّا يُنْسَخُ — إِبْطَالُهُ مُمْكِنٌ.

Revocableness, *n.* قَابِلِيَّةُ ٱلْإِسْتِرْدَادِ — قَابِلِيَّةُ ٱلْإِبْطَالِ.

Revocation, *n.* The act of repealing, نَسْخٌ — فَسْخٌ — نَقْضٌ — إِبْطَالٌ. *See also under* Recantation, *n.*

Revocatory, *a.* نَاقِضٌ — نَاسِخٌ — مُبْطِلٌ.

Revoke, *v.t.* To recall, اِرْتَدَّ — اِسْتَرَدَّ — رَجَعَ فِي ـ ـ. To retract, نَكِرَ ـ ـ — أَنْكَرَ. To annul, repeal, نَقَضَ ـ ـ ² — نَسَخَ ـ ـ — فَسَخَ ـ ـ — أَبْطَلَ. *See also to* Abrogate, *v.t.*

Revolt, *v.i.* To — or rebel against, قَامَ عَلَى ـ ٤ عَصَى عَلَى ـ ٣ عَاصَى. To cause to — against, قَوَّمَ-عَلَى. *See also to* Rebel, *v.i.*

Revolt, *v.t.* To do violence to, بَغَى عَلَى ـ ٣ حَكَرَ ـ إِحْتَكَرَ ـ. To disgust, cause to abhor, كَرَّهَ ـ أَسَامَ ـ أَبْرَمَ ـ أَقْنَفَ. قَرَّفَ ـ أَقْرَفَ.

Revolt, *n.* Rebellion, قَوْمَة ـ خُرُوجٌ عَنِ ٱلطَّاعَةِ ـ عِصْيَان ـ فَسَاد. A general —, قَوْمَةٌ عُمُومِيَّةٌ ـ عِصْيَانٌ عَامٌّ. In a state of —, فِي حَالِ ٱلْعِصْيَانِ. The head of a —, رَأْسُ ٱلْفِتْنَةِ ـ رَئِيسُ ٱلْفَسَادِ. The spirit of —, رُوحُ ٱلْعِصْيَانِ. To excite a —, هَيَّجَ ٱلْفَسَادَ. To appease a —, سَكَّنَ ٱلْفَسَادَ. *See also* Rebellion, *n.*

Revolter, *n.* *See* Rebel, *n.*

Revolting, *a.* Given to revolt, rebel, مَرِيد ـ مُتَمَرِّد ـ مَطْبُوعٌ ـ مَطْبُوعٌ عَلَى ٱلْفَسَادِ ـ عَلَى ٱلشَّرِّ. Ugly, disgusting, كَرِه ـ كَرِيه ـ بَشِيع. He has a — countenance, هُوَ بَشِعُ ٱلْمَنْظَرِ.

Revoluble, *a.* يَدُور ـ يَفْتِل.

Revolute, *a.* مُنْقَلِبٌ إِلَى وَرَآءٍ.

Revolution, *n.* A rolling or moving round, دَوْر *pl.* أَدْوَار ـ دَوَرَان. Course, as of time, دَوَرَان ـ مُرُور. Change, إِنْقِلَاب ـ تَقَلُّب ـ تَبَدُّل ـ تَحَوُّل ـ تَغْيِير. A disordered state of affairs, of government, *etc.*, إِخْتِلَال. A political —, إِنْقِلَابُ ٱلْأَحْوَالِ ٱلسِّيَاسِيَّةِ. A moral —, تَبْدِيلُ ٱلْآرَآءِ وَٱلْاِعْتِقَادَاتِ ـ تَقَلُّبُ. A social —, تَبَدُّلٌ أَوْ تَقَلُّبُ ٱلْأَخْلَاقِ وَٱلْعَادَاتِ ٱلْأَفْكَارِ وَٱلْآرَآءِ. *See also* Rebellion, Revolt, *n.*

Revolutionary, *a.* Tending to produce revolt, مُسْتَفْسِد ـ مُوجِبُ ٱلْعِصْيَانِ; tending to produce change, مُوجِبُ ٱلْاِنْقِلَابِ وَٱلتَّبْدِيلِ. A — movement, حَرَكَةُ ٱلْعِصْيَانِ ـ حَرَكَةُ ٱلْفَسَادِ. Revolutionary opinions, أَفْكَارٌ ٱخْتِلَالِيَّةٌ ـ أَفْكَارُ فَسَادٍ. A — government, إِدَارَةُ عُصَاةٍ.

Revolutioner, *n.* } مِنْ أَصْحَابِ ٱلْفَسَادِ ـ سَاعٍ بِٱلْفَسَادِ ـ مِنْ
Revolutionist, } أَهْلِ ٱلْاِخْتِلَالِ ـ مِنْ أَرْبَابِ ٱلْعِصْيَانِ. *See also* Rebel, *n.*

Revolutionize, *v.t.* To effect an entire change, بَدَّلَ ـ غَيَّرَ ـ قَلَّبَ. To excite to rebel, حَرَّضَ-(or هَيَّجَ-) عَلَى ٱلْفَسَادِ. To upset, vitiate, أَضَلَّ ـ أَفْسَدَ.

Revolve, *v.i.* To turn or roll round, دَارَ *aor.* يَدُورُ ـ إِسْتَدَارَ ـ أَدَارَ. To —, of time, حَالَ ٤; of a person, جَالَ *aor.* يَجُولُ ـ جَوَّلَ ـ إِجْتَالَ. It revolved in his mind, هَجَسَ فِي صَدْرِهِ ٣. The firmament revolved on its axis, دَارَ ٱلْفَلَكُ فِي مَدَارِهِ.

Revolve, *v.t.* دَوَّرَ ـ أَدَارَ ـ دَارَ بِ ٤ ـ أَدَارَ بِ ـ دَوَّرَ بِ ـ إِسْتَدَارَ بِ ـ أَجَالَ ـ أَجَالَ بِ. To — something in the mind, أَجَالَ ٱلْفِكْرَ فِي.

Revolvency, *n.* دَوَرَان.

Revolver, *n.* A — pistol, طَبَنْجَةٌ دَوَّارَةٌ ـ طَبَنْجَةٌ مُسَدَّسَةٌ *pl.* طَبَنْجَات.

Revolving, *a.* دَوَّار ـ دَوَّارِيٌّ. A — gun, مِدْفَعٌ يَدُورُ عَلَى مِحْوَرِهِ.

Revulsion, *n.* مُضَادَّة ـ تَحْوِيل ـ تَبْدِيلُ حَالٍ.

Revulsive, *a.* مُضَادّ ـ مُحَوِّل ـ مُبَدِّلُ ٱلْحَالِ.

Reward, *v.t.* To give to in return, either good or evil, عَوَّضَ ـ عَوَّضَ عَلَى ـ قَابَلَ-بِ ـ أَفَاضَ ـ كَافَى. To give in token of merit or approbation, ثَوَّبَ ـ أَثَابَ ـ جَزَى ـ ٣ جَازَى. They rewarded evil for good, جَازُوا عَنِ ٱلْخَيْرِ شَرًّا ـ كَافَى-بِٱلْخَيْرِ. They rewarded him double, جَازُوهُ ضِعْفًا. May God reward thee! جَازَاكَ ٱللّٰهُ. *See also to* Recompense, to Repay, *v.t.*

Reward, *n.* Whether good or evil, عِوَض. A recompense for good, جَزَآء ـ ثَوَاب ـ مَثُوبَة. Pay, hire, أَجْر ـ أُجْرَة. They have received their reward, قَدِ ٱسْتَوْفَوْا أَجْرَهُمْ. He shall receive a — according to his work, سَيَأْخُذُ أُجْرَتَهُ بِحَسَبِ تَعَبِهِ. He shall not lose his —, لَا يُضِيعُ أَجْرَهُ. For —, the sake of —, لِأَجْلِ أُجْرَةٍ. How excellent a reward! نِعْمَ ٱلثَّوَابُ.

Rewardable, *a.* مِمَّا يُجَازَى ـ يُكَافَى.

Rewarder, *n.* مُجَازٍ ـ ثَوَّاب.

Rewardless, *a.* بِدُونِ جَزَآءٍ ـ مِنْ غَيْرِ ثَوَابٍ.

Rewrite, *v.t.* ٤ عَادَ فَكَتَبَهُ ـ كَتَبَ-ثَانِيَةً.

Rex, *n.* *See* King, *n.*

Reynard, *n.* *See* Fox, *n.*

Rhapsodic, *a.* } مِنْ غَيْرِ تَتَابُعٍ ـ مِهْذَار ـ سَائِب. Rhapsodical
Rhapsodical, } talk, عَسْطَلَة ـ هُرَآء ـ مَنْطِقٌ.

Rhapsodist, *n.* هَرَّآء ـ سَائِبٌ فِي ٱلْكَلَامِ ـ مِهْذَار.

Rhapsodize, *v.i.* ٣ ٤ هَذَرَ فِي ٱلْكَلَامِ ـ أَهْرَأَ فِي ٱلْحَدِيثِ ـ سَابَ فِي ٱلْكَلَامِ *aor.* يَسِيبُ ـ سَابَ فِي مَنْطِقِهِ ٣.

Rhapsody, *n.* سَيَبَانٌ فِي ٱلْكَلَامِ ـ هَذَر ـ تَهْذَار ـ إِهْرَآء ـ لَغْو ـ تَخْيِيل.

Rhatany, *n.* The root, ضَرْبٌ مِنَ ٱلْعُرُوقِ ٱلْعَفِصَةِ.

Rhenish, *a.* مِنْ نَهْرِ ٱلرِّينِ.

Rhetoric, *n.* The science of, عِلْمُ ٱلْفَصَاحَةِ ـ عِلْمُ ٱلْكَلَامِ ـ عِلْمُ ٱلْبَيَانِ. *See also* Persuasiveness, *n.*

Rhetorical, *a.* Oratorical, خُطَبِيٌّ ـ فَصِيح ـ مِنْطِيق ـ مِصْقَع; belonging to rhetoric, مُتَعَلِّقٌ بِعِلْمِ ٱلْفَصَاحَةِ ـ بَلِيغ. A — speaker, خَطِيبٌ مِصْقَعٌ.

Rhetorically, *ad.* تَفَصُّحًا ـ بِفَصَاحَةٍ ـ بِبَيَانٍ ـ بِبَلَاغَةٍ. To speak —, تَفَصَّحَ.

Rhetorician, *n.* خَطِيبٌ مِصْقَعٌ ـ فَصِيحٌ ـ مِنْ أَهْلِ عِلْمِ ٱلْفَصَاحَةِ.

Rheum, *n.* رَشْحٌ ـ نَزْلَةٌ ـ زُكَام ـ زُكْمَةٌ. To have the —, أُرِضَ ـ بِهِ نَزْلَةٌ ـ زُكِمَ. *See also under* Cold, *n.*

Rheumatic, *a.* Pertaining to rheumatism, حُضَارِيٌّ; affected with rheumatism, مُصَابٌ بِٱلْحُضَارِ.

Rheumatism, *n.* حُضَار ـ وَجَعُ ٱلْمَفَاصِلِ. Suffering from —, مُبْتَلًى بِأَمْرَاضٍ عَصَبِيَّةٍ.

Rheumy, *a.* مُتَرَشِّحٌ ـ بِهِ زُكَامٌ.

Rhino, *n.* مِصْرِيَّات ـ فُلُوس ـ دَرَاهِمُ.

Rhinocerial, *a.* مُتَعَلِّقٌ بِٱلْكَرْكَدَّنِ.

Rhinoceros, *n.* كَرْكَدَّن ـ مِرْمِيس *vulg.* كَرْكَدَان.

Rhinoplastic, *a.* مُتَعَلِّقٌ بِشَكْلِ ٱلْأَنْفِ. The — operation, تَشْكِيلُ أَنْفٍ بِصِنَاعَةِ ٱلْجَرَّاحِ.

Rhizoma, *n.* أُرُومَةٌ.

Rhodium, *n.* ضَرْبٌ مِنَ ٱلْمَعَادِنِ شَدِيدُ ٱلصَّلَابَةِ.

Rhododendron, *n.* الدِّفْلَى.

Rhomb, *n.* }
Rhombus, } مُعَيَّن.

Rhombic, *a.* فِي شَكْلِ ٱلْمُعَيَّنِ.

Rhomboid, *a.* شَبِيهٌ بِٱلْمُعَيَّنِ.

Rhomboidal, *a.* فِي شَكْلِ ٱلْمُعَيَّنِ.

Rhubarb, *n.* The medicinal, رَاوَنْد ـ رِيوَنْد. China —, رَاوَنْدٌ صِينِيٌّ; a coarser kind is called, رَاوَنْدٌ خُرَاسَانِيٌّ; bastard —, رَاوَنْدٌ ذَكَرٌ. The garden —, رِبَاس ـ أَشْقِين (both these words are Turkish; the latter is pronounced أَشْخِين by the Arabs of Mesopotamia).

Rhumb, *n.* A — on the compass-card, عَلَامَةُ جِهَةٍ مِنْ جِهَاتِ ٱلْهَوَآءِ فِي وَرَقَةِ ٱلْبُوصَلَةِ (*or* بَيْتِ ٱلْإِبْرَةِ).

Rhyme, *n.* Correspondence of sounds in the ends or other parts of verses, قَافِيَةٌ *pl.* قَوَافٍ. A harmonical succession of sounds in verses, speech, *etc.*, سَجْعٌ *pl.* أَسْجَاع *and* أَسَاجِيعُ ـ أُسْجُوعَةٌ ـ كَلَامٌ مُسَجَّعٌ. A — or rhyming letter, رَوِيٌّ. Metre, وَزْن *pl.* أَوْزَان. Without — or reason, بِلَا سَبَبٍ أَصْلًا. Prose in —, سَجْع ـ كَلَامٌ مُسَجَّعٌ. To speak or write in —, سَجَعَ ـ ـَ سَجَّعَ.

Rhyme, *v.i.* To accord in sound, جَآءَ عَلَى ٱلْقَافِيَةِ ـَ; to make rhyming verses, سَجَعَ ـ ـَ سَجَّعَ.

Rhyme, *v.t.* سَجَّعَ ـ سَجَعَ ـَ.

Rhymer, *n.* }
Rhymist, } سَاجِع ـ سَجَّاع *See also* Poet, Poetaster, *n.*
Rhymster, }

Rhythm, *n.* }
Rhythmus, } وَزْن *pl.* أَوْزَان.

Rhythmical, *a.* مَوْزُون ـ مُسَجَّع.

Rhythmically, *ad.* بِوَزْنٍ ـ تَسْجِيعًا.

Rial, *n.* رِيَالٌ ٱسْمُ لِسِكَّةٍ إِسْبَانِيَّةٍ.

Rib, *n.* One of the side bones in animals, ضِلَع *pl.* ضُلُوع *and* أَضْلَاع *and* أَضْلُع ـ ضِلَعَة. The ribs of the breast below the paps, جَوَانِحُ *pl.* جَانِحَة ـ (*sing.* بَانِيَة) بَوَانٍ; those between the paps and the collar-bone, تَرَائِبُ *pl.* تَرِيبَة. A — of the back, or true rib, ضِلْعٌ صَحِيحٌ. A false —, ضِلْعٌ كَاذِبٌ. The cartilage of the ribs, شُرْسُوف *pl.* شَرَاسِيفُ. The broadest — in the chest, الزُّخْبَى. The two ribs next the armpit, الزُّخْبَيَانِ. Rib, as of a ship's side, ضِلَع *pl.* ضُلُوع. Any ridge for strengthening, عُمْدَة ـ سَنَد ـ مِشَدٌّ. Rib, as of a leaf, عَيْر *pl.* أَعْيَار; as of a moulding, خَطٌّ ـ خَرْط; as on the back of a book, حِبَاكَة; as on cloth, ضِلَع *pl.* أَضْلَاع. A wife, زَوْجَة ـ إِمْرَأَة. Having strong ribs, robust, ضَلِيع Having the ribs broken, مَضْلُوع.

Rib, *v.t.* ضَلَّعَ ـ خَطَّطَ ـ قَلَّمَ.

Ribald, *n.* بَذِيٌّ ـ فَاحِش ـ فَاسِق.

Ribald, *a.* بَذِيٌّ ـ خَنٍ ـ مُفْحِش ـ فَاحِش. To use — language, خَنِيَ فِي مَنْطِقِهِ *aor.* يَخْنَى.

Ribaldry, *n.* خَنًا ـ رَفَث ـ فُحْش ـ فَوَاحِشُ.

Ribbed, *a.* As of cloth, *etc.*, مُضَلَّع ـ مُخَطَّط ـ مُقَلَّم.

Ribbon, *n.* شَرِيط *pl.* أَشْرِطَة ـ رِبَان. (Ribbons; *See* Reins, *n.*) To go to ribbons, تَمَزَّقَ ـ تَقَطَّعَ. To tear to ribbons, مَزَّقَ ـ قَطَّعَ.

Ribboned, *a.* مُزَيَّنٌ بِشَرِيطٍ (*or* بِرِبَانٍ).

Rice, *n.* أُرْزٌ ـ رُزٌّ. A — merchant, رَزَّاز. Rice milk, رُزٌّ بِحَلِيبٍ.

Rice-paper, *n.* وَرَقٌ مِنْ رُزٍّ.

Rich, *a.* Possessing much property, ذُو غِنًى ـ ذُو طَوْلٍ فِي مَالِهِ ـ صَاحِبُ مَالٍ ـ حَظِيٌّ ـ مُطْرِب ـ مُدْرَهِم ـ مُثْرٍ ـ وَسَعَة ـ غَنِيٌّ *pl.* أَغْنِيَآء ـ صَاحِبُ ثَرْوَةٍ. Fertile, خَصِيب ـ غَزِير ـ مُثْمِر; rich soil, أَرْضٌ سَمِينَةٌ. Abundant, جَمٌّ ـ فَائِض ـ غَفِير ـ غَزِير. Valuable, precious, عَزِيز ـ مُثْمِن ـ كَثِير. Superb, beautiful, جَمِيل ـ بَهِيج ـ فَاخِر ـ بَاهٍ. Delicious, of taste, لَذِيذ; of smell, عَطِر ـ شَمُوم ـ عَذِق. Rich in virtues, كَثِيرُ ٱلْفَضَائِلِ. Copious, as of a language, وَاسِع. Full, abounding in, غَلِيل ـ غِلٌّ. Rich, as of food, دَسِم; food of a — flavour, طَعَامٌ مُعَرَّف ـ فَائِض. The rich, الْأَغْنِيَآءُ. To be —, opulent, غَنِيَ ـ ـَ تَغَنَّى ـ قَرَّشَ ـ إِقْتَرَشَ.

Riches, *n.* Wealth, opulence, غِنًى — أَمْوَال — مَال — وُجْد — دَوْلَة — رِزْق. Abundance, كَثْرَة — جَمٌّ — فَيْض.

Richly, *ad.* With riches, بِدَوْلَةٍ — بِوُجْدٍ; splendidly, بِفَخْرٍ — بِجَلَالٍ — بِبَهْجَةٍ; abundantly, كَثِيرًا — بِكَثْرَةٍ — بِوُفُورٍ; in every way, مِنْ كُلِّ وَجْهٍ — مِنْ كُلِّ جَانِبٍ.

Richness, *n.* Opulence, غَنَآءٌ — غِنًى — مَغْنًى — غُنْيَان. Fertility, خِصْب — إِثْمَار — بَرَكَة. Abundance, فَرْط — فَيْض — كَثْرَة — وُفُور. Magnificence, بَهْجَة — فَخْر. Deliciousness, لَذَّة. Copiousness, as of language, سَعَة — وُسْع. Richness, as of food, دَسَم — وَدَك. Preciousness, ثَمَانَة — نَفَاسَة. Beauty, طَلَاوَة — ظَرَافَة — مَلَاحَة — صَبَاحَة — جَمَال.

Rick, *n.* عَرَمَة *pl.* عَرَم — كَوْمَة *pl.* أَكْوَام.

Rickets, *n.* زَمَانَة — كُسَاحَة — كَسَح *vulg.* كُسَاح.

Rickety, *a.* Affected with rickets, مُكَسَّح. Weak, ضَعِيف; from disease, مَنْهُوك — نَهِيك; in mind, أَخْرَق — سَخِيف. Liable to decay, فَانٍ — وَانٍ. Tumble-down, مُتَضَعْضِع. Unsound, غَيْرُ مُحْكَمٍ — بَاطِل — عَائِب — سَقِيم — رَكِيك.

Ricochet, *n.* قَفْزُ ٱلْكُلَّةِ عَلَى ٱلْأَرْضِ.

Ricochet, *v.a.* قَفَّزَ ٱلْكُلَّةَ عَلَى ٱلْأَرْضِ.

Ricochet, *v.i.* تَقَفَّزَتِ ٱلْكُلَّةُ عَلَى ٱلْأَرْضِ.

Rid, *v.t.* To free from, أَسْلَمَ-مِنْ — سَلَّمَ-مِنْ — أَنْقَذَ-مِنْ. To expel from, أَخْرَجَ-مِنْ. To save from, خَلَّصَ-مِنْ — نَجَّى-مِنْ. To destroy, annihilate, from, أَبَادَ-مِنْ — أَزَالَ-عَنْ — أَنْقَذَ-مِنْ. Get rid of it out of your hands, أَلْقِ بِهِ عَنْ يَدِكَ. To ask one to rid him of anything, طَلَبَ إِلَى-أَنْ يُنْقِذَهُ مِنْ.

Riddance, *n.* Deliverance, خَلَاص — نَجَاة — نَقْذ. The act of driving away, clearing away, إِخْرَاج — إِزَالَة — إِبَادَة. It is a good — for you, نَجَاةٌ لَكَ. A good — of bad rubbish, نَقْذٌ مِنَ ٱلْبَاطِلِ.

Riddle, *n.* A sieve, غِرْبَال *pl.* غَرَابِيل. A puzzling question, صُعُوبَة — ضِلَّة — مُشْكِلَة. An enigma, أُحْجِيَّة — لُغْز *pl.* أَلْغَاز — مُعَمًّى. The propounding of a riddle, مُحَاجَاة — مُدَاعَاة. To propound a — to, حَاجَى — دَاعَى: I propounded a — to him, دَاعَيْتُهُ.

Riddle, *v.t.* As with a sieve, غَرْبَلَ. To perforate, خَرَبَ — خَبْرَقَ — خَرْبَقَ. To solve, حَلَّ. To be riddled, with holes, إِسْتَخْرَبَ; of a tree, *etc.*, under corrosion, أُخْرِبَ — تَخَرَّبَ. He was riddled with wounds, أُثْخِنَ بِٱلْجِرَاحَاتِ.

Riddle, *v.i.* To speak enigmatically, عَرَّضَ.

Ride, *v.i.* and *t.* As on horseback or in a carriage, عَلَا *aor.* يَعْلِي — رَكِبَ — رَكِبَ عَلَى; as on a camel, رَحَلَ — اِرْتَحَلَ. To make to —, as on a horse, *etc.*, رَكَّبَ — أَرْكَبَ. To assign one, as a horse, to —, أَرْكَبَ. To ask one to assign him an animal to — upon, إِسْتَرْكَبَ. To become fit to —, of a colt, أَرْكَبَ. To — behind another, *i.e.* on the same beast, رَدِفَ; to make one so to —, أَرْدَفَ — اِرْتَدَفَ; to ask one to let him so —, إِسْتَرْدَفَ. To —, float, … طَفَا فَوْقَ ٱلْ… — عَامَ عَلَى ٱلْ…; as a bird in the air, رَفْرَفَ. To — at anchor, رَسَا عَلَى ٱلْأَنْجَرِ; to — at single anchor, رَسَا عَلَى أَنْجَرٍ وَاحِدٍ. To — easy, of a ship, تَرَسَّى ٱلْمَرْكَبُ بِسُهُولَةٍ; to — hard, صَعُبَ ٱلْإِرْسَآءُ. To — out a storm, of a ship, تَرَسَّتِ ٱلسَّفِينَةُ فِي ٱلنَّوْءِ. To —, to overlay, رَكِبَ. To — the high horse, شَمَخَ أَنْفُهُ — تَكَبَّرَ — تَعَظَّمَ. This is the horse on which I have ridden for years, هٰذَا ٱلْحِصَانُ ٱلَّذِي رَكِبْتُ عَلَيْهِ مُنْذُ سِنِينَ.

Ride, *n.* A single riding, رَكْبَة. A mode of riding, رِكْبَة. To take a —, as on a horse, *etc.*, تَبَحْبَحَ رَاكِبًا — تَسَيَّرَ رَاكِبًا.

Rider, *n.* As of a horse, *etc.*, رَاكِب *pl.* رُكَّاب *and* رُكْبَان. A good —, أَفْرَس; a bad —, كِفْل *pl.* أَكْفَال. A fellow —, رَكِيب. A hard —, رَاكِبٌ عَنِيفٌ. A company of riders, رَكْبَة. One who rides behind another, رَدِيف — زَمِيل *pl.* رَدَافَى *and* رِدَاف. A supplement, as to a set of rules, *etc.*, إِضَافَة — ذَيْل.

Ridge, *n.* As of the backbone, سِلْسِلَةُ ٱلظَّهْرِ. A protuberance, حَيْد *pl.* حُيُود. Ridge of a mountain, حَرْف *pl.* حُرُوف — رَأْس *pl.* رُؤُوس — شُوشَة. An abrupt —, as of the banks of a stream, جُرُف *pl.* أَجْرَاف. Ridge, of a channel in a sword blade, عَمُود *pl.* عُمُد — شُطْبَة *pl.* شُطَب. Anything prominent in the body or elsewhere, عَيْر *pl.* أَعْيَار. Ridge of a roof, or a ridged roof, جَمَالُون. Ridge, of a furrow, تَلَم *pl.* أَتْلَام.

Ridge, *v.t.* خَطَّطَ — خَطَّ — خَدَّ. *See also to* Wrinkle, *v.t.*

Ridgy, *a.* ذُو حِدَابٍ — ذُو أَعْيَارٍ — ذُو جُرُوفٍ — ذُو شُطَبٍ.

Ridicule, *n.* سُخْر — سَخَر — هُزْؤ — هُجُوّ — هِجَاء — تَقْلِيح — نِقَاسَة. An object of —, سُخْرَة — سُخْرِيّ — هُزْأَة. They made him an object of —, إِتَّخَذُوهُ سُخْرِيًّا.

Ridicule, *v.t.* خَنَّثَ — فَلَحَ بِ — نَقَسَ — لَقَسَ — سَخِرَ مِنْ — إِسْتَهْزَأَ بِ — تَهَزَّأَ بِ — هَزَأَ بِ — شَمَعَ بِ — ضَحِكَ عَلَى — شَانَعَ — تَسَخَّرَ بِ *or* مِنْ.

Ridiculer, *n.* هُزْأَة — سُخْرَة — مَسْخَرَة.

Ridiculous, *a.* ضُحْكَة — سُخْرَة — مَسْخَرَة — سُخْرِيَّة. Anything —, شَيْءٌ مُضْحِكٌ — أُضْحُوكَة. Ridiculous things, مُضْحِكَات — مَسَاخِر.

Ridiculously, *ad.* سُخْرًا ـ سُخْرَةً.

Ridiculousness, *n.* مَسْخَرَة. *See also* Ridicule, *n.*

Riding, *n.* The act of one who rides, رُكُوب; a mode of, رِكْبَة.

Riding, *n.* One of the three divisions of Yorkshire, قَسْمٌ مِنَ ٱلْأَقْسَامِ ٱلثَّلَاثَةِ مِنْ إِيَالَةِ يُورْك فِي بِلَادِ ٱلْإِنْكِلِيزِ.

Riding, *a.* مَا نِيطَ بِٱلرُّكُوبِ.

Riding-coat, *n.* بُنُش (or بِنِش) ٱلسَّفَرِ.

Riding-habit, *n.* فُسْتَانُ ٱلرُّكُوبِ.

Riding-hood, *n.* قَرَاجَةُ ٱلرُّكُوبِ.

Riding-school, *n.* مَكَانٌ لِتَعْلِيمِ ٱلرُّكُوبِ.

Riding-whip, *n.* كِرْبَاج ـ سَوْط.

Rife, *a.* رَائِج ـ غَالِب ـ عَامّ ـ شَائِع ـ شَامِل. To be —, عَمَّ ² ـ شَمِلَ ـ رَاجَ *aor.* يَرُوجُ. Generally known, مُشَاع.

Rifely, *ad.* شُمُولًا ـ عُمُومًا ـ فِي ٱلْغَالِبِ ـ بِٱشْتِهَارٍ.

Rifeness, *n.* غَلَبَة ـ رَوَاج ـ شَمْل ـ عُمُوم.

Riffraff, *n.* Of the people, سَفِلَة. *See also* Refuse, *n.*

Rifle, *n.* (مُضَلَّعَة or مُثَمَّنَة or) بَارُودَةٌ مُسَدَّسَةٌ; *vulg.* شَشْخَانَة *pl.* شَشْخَانَات.

Rifle, *v.t.* To pillage, سَلَبَ ـ نَهَبَ ² ـ شَلَّحَ ². To make into a rifle, صَيَّرَ ـ شَشْخَنَ ـ ضَلَّعَ (or سَدَّسَ or ثَمَّنَ) ٱلْبَارُودَةَ شَشْخَانَةً. To — graves, إِخْتَفَى ـ نَبَشَ ².

Rifleman, *n.* حَامِلُ شَشْخَانَةٍ ـ حَامِلُ بَارُودَةٍ مُسَدَّسَةٍ.

Rifle-pit, *n.* غَيْبٌ لِلْمُحَاصِرِينَ *pl.* غُيُوب.

Rifler, *n.* نَاهِب *pl.* نُهَّاب ـ نَهَّابَة ـ سَلَّاب *pl.* سَلَّابَة. A — of graves, مُخْتَفٍ ـ نَبَّاش.

Rift, *n.* *See* Cleft, Fissure, *n.*

Rift, *v.t.* شَقَّ ² ـ شَجَّ ـ فَلَقَ ـ فَلَعَ. *See also* to Split, *v.t.*

Rift, *v.i.* إِنْشَقَّ ـ إِنْفَتَحَ ـ إِنْفَلَعَ. *See also* to Split, *v.i.*

Rifty, *a.* ذُو فُلُوجٍ ـ ذُو عَوْرَاتٍ ـ ذُو شُرُومٍ ـ مُعْوِر ـ عَوِر.

Rig, *v.t.* To fit with rigging, رَكَّبَ لِ-حِبَالًا. To dress, لَبَّسَ. To rig out, to adorn, زَيَّنَ ـ زَخْرَفَ. To — or fit out, جَهَّزَ. To — the market, رَوَّجَ ٱلسُّوقَ بِحِيلَةٍ.

Rig, *n.* Manner of being rigged, of a ship, طَرْزُ حِبَالٍ. Accoutrement, أَثَاث ـ جِهَاز. Dress, costume, زِيّ ـ لِبْس. A romp, wanton, إِمْرَأَةٌ فَحْلَةٌ ـ عَاهِرَة. To run a rig, لَعِبَ ـ لَعِبَ عَلَى-مَلْعُوبًا. To run one a rig, لَعِبَ عَلَى مَلْعُوبًا ـ تَحَارَفَ عَلَى ـ إِحْتَالَ عَلَى ـ نَصَبَ عَلَى-حِيلَةً ².

Rigadoon, *n.* ضَرْبٌ مِنَ ٱلرَّقْصِ.

Rigation, *n.* *See* Irrigation, *n.*

Rigel, *n.* The star upon the left foot of Orion, رِجْلُ ٱلْجَبَّارِ ـ رِجْلُ ٱلْجَوْزَآءِ ٱلْيُسْرَى; that on the right foot is called, رِجْلُ ٱلْجَوْزَآءِ ٱلْيُمْنَى.

Rigger, *n.* As of a ship, رَكَّابُ حِبَالٍ.

Rigging, *n.* Of a ship, حِبَال. Accoutrements, implements, أَثَاث ـ جِهَاز. Dress, costume, زِيّ ـ مَلْبُوس ـ أَلْبِسَة.

Right, *a.* Straight, as in a line, مُسْتَوٍ ـ عَدِل ـ مُسْتَقِيم. Direct, سَدِيد. Erect, وَاقِف ـ قَائِم ـ مُقَوَّم ـ مَصْمُود. Equitable, just, مُسْتَقِيم ـ حَقّ ـ صَوَاب ـ سَدَاد ـ قَصْد. Real, true, حَقَّانِيّ. Not erroneous, صَحِيح ـ مَضْبُوط. Proper, fit, لَائِق ـ كَمَا يَلِيقُ ـ مُنَاسِب. The — hand, ٱلْيَمِينُ ـ ٱلْيَدُ ٱلْيُمْنَى ـ ٱلْمَيْمَنَة. On or to the —, يَمِينًا. Right and left, يَمِينًا وَشِمَالًا. The — side, ٱلْيَمِينُ ـ ٱلْيَامِنُ ـ ٱلْيَمَنُ. Right against, مُقَابِل. Right well, يَقِينًا. He is — in what he says, قَالَ سَدَادًا ـ أَنَّهُ لَيُسِيدُ فِي ٱلْقَوْلِ. Right or wrong, I will do it, صَوَابًا كَانَ أَوْ غَيْرَ صَوَابٍ سَأَفْعَلُهُ. He hits the — thing, يُصِيبُ ٱلسَّدَادَ. He is following a — course, هُوَ عَلَى سَدَادٍ. His affair is going all —, أَمْرُهُ يَجْرِي عَلَى ٱلسَّدَادِ. All right! go on, رَوِّجْ. We were — in what we said, قَدْ صَدَقْنَا فِي قَوْلِنَا. Thou shalt do what is —, تَصْنَعُ ٱلْحَقَّ. Thou hast done —, عَمِلْتَ ٱلْحَقَّ. I will give you what is —, أُعْطِيكُمْ مَا يَحِقُّ لَكُمْ. To be —, just, حَقَّ ² ـ سَدَّ. To become —, in its place, تَعَدَّلَ. To make —, straight, equitable, عَدَّلَ. To do —, سَدَّدَ ـ أَسَدَّ. To find all —, لَقِيَ كُلَّ شَيْءٍ عَلَى ضَبْطٍ. To go to the —, يَمَّنَ ـ تَيَامَنَ. To go the — way to work, عَرَفَ كَيْفَ يَعْمَلُ ـ إِتَّقَنَ بِٱلْمَصْلَحَةِ. To consider —, to approve, إِسْتَحْسَنَ ـ إِسْتَصْوَبَ. To pronounce to be —, صَوَّبَ. To sit on the —, يَمَنَ *aor.* يَيْمِنُ. *See also* Direct, *a.*

Right angle, زَاوِيَةٌ قَائِمَةٌ.

Right angled, قَائِمُ ٱلزَّوَايَةِ.

Right ascension, مَطْلَعٌ ٱسْتِوَائِيّ.

Right-hand man, مَأْمُون ـ أَمَان ـ أَمِين.

Right line, خَطٌّ مُسْتَقِيم.

Right side of cloth, وَجْهُ ٱلْجُوخِ.

Right, *ad.* Justly, بِٱلْعَدْلِ ـ صَوَابًا. Very, كَثِيرًا. Right Honourable, مَزِيدُ ٱلْإِكْرَامِ. *See also* Directly, *ad.*

Right, *n.* Rectitude, justice, إِسْتِقَامَة ـ صَلَاح ـ إِنْصَاف ـ صَوَاب. Propriety, fitness, لِيَاقَة ـ مُنَاسَبَة. Just claim, حَقّ *pl.* حُقُوق. Power, prerogative, سُلْطَان ـ قُدْرَة ـ قُوَّة ـ إِقْتِدَار. A privilege, immunity, بَرَآءَة ـ إِمْتِيَاز *pl.* إِمْتِيَازَات. Reserved rights, حُقُوقٌ مَحْفُوظَةٌ; unreserved rights, حُقُوقٌ غَيْرُ مَحْفُوظَةٍ. Right procedure, رَشَاد. The — is mine, ٱلْحَقُّ بِيَدِي.

The — is against you, الحَقُّ عَلَيْكَ. You are in the —, الحَقُّ مَعَكَ. This is my —, هٰذا حَقِّي. Without —, مِنْ غَيْرِ حَقٍّ. He has the — of primogeniture, لَهُ حَقُّ ٱلْبَكُورِيَّةِ. I have more — to it than you, أَنَا أَحَقُّ مِنْكَ بِهِ. They have no —, power, to . . . , لا سُلْطانَ لَهُمْ أَنْ. To give or carry out the —, أَجْرَى ٱلقَضَآءَ. To maintain the —, أَقامَ ٱلحَقَّ. To put or set to rights, عَدَّلَ ـ نَظَّمَ ـ أَصْلَحَ ـ قَوَّمَ. To be put to rights, إِسْتَتَبَّ.

Right, *v.t.* To do justice to, أَعْطَى حَقَّهُ ـ أَجْرَى حَقَّهُ ـ أَنْصَفَ ـ بَيَّضَ وَجْهَهُ ـ خَلَّصَ حَقَّهُ. To put into a — position, عَدَّلَ. To make straight, قَوَّمَ ـ عَدَّلَ ـ ثَقَّفَ.

Right, *v.i.* To come into a right position, تَعَدَّلَ.

Righteous, *a.* Good, upright, صَالِح ـ عَادِل ـ مُسْتَقِيم *pl.* صُلَحَآءُ ـ صِدِّيق ـ صَادِق. Pious, بَرّ ـ بَارّ ـ تَقِيّ ـ زَكِيّ *pl.* أَزْكِيَآءُ. To be —, pious, بَرَّ ـ أَبَرَّ *aor.* يَبَرُّ. He was — in his saying, بَرَّ فِي قَوْلِهِ.

Righteously, *ad.* بِصَدَاقَةٍ ـ بِصَلاحٍ ـ بِٱلْإِنْصَافِ ـ بِحَقٍّ ـ حَقًّا.

Righteousness, *n.* Integrity, uprightness, عَدَالَة ـ إِسْتِقَامَة ـ صَدَاقَة ـ صَلاح. Piety, بِرّ ـ زَكَاة ـ تَقْوَى. To behave with — towards, بَارَّ.

Rightful, *a.* *See* Legitimate, *a.*

Rightfully, *ad.* حَسَبَ ٱلحَقِّ ـ بِحَقٍّ ـ حَقًّا ـ صَوَابًا ـ سَدَادًا. *See also* Legitimately, *ad.*

Rightfulness, *n.* حَقّ. *See also* Legitimacy, Right, *n.*

Right-hand, *n.* *See under* Right, *a.*

Rightly, *ad.* With right, بِحَقٍّ ـ حَقًّا. Correctly, صَوَابًا ـ سَدَادًا ـ بِضَبْطٍ. Properly, بِلِيَاقَةٍ ـ مُنَاسَبَةً. You have decided —, حَكَمْتَ بِٱلصَّوَابِ. He spoke —, justly, تَكَلَّمَ بِٱلْإِسْتِقَامَةِ.

Rightness, *n.* *See* Right, Rectitude, *n.*

Rigid, *a.* Difficult to bend, stiff, شَدِيد ـ كَزّ ـ صُلْب ـ جَاسِئ ـ مَتِين. Harsh, فَظّ ـ عَنِيف ـ شَاقّ. Strict, exact, مُدَقِّق. Rigid in religion, حَمِس ـ حَمِس ـ مُتَحَمِّس *pl.* حُمْس أَحْمَس. Opiniated, مُعْجَب بِرَأْيِهِ ـ مُعَانِد ـ مُتَعَصِّب. A — forehead, جَبْهَة حَشْبَآء. A man having a — forehead, أَخْشَبُ ٱلْجَبْهَةِ. To be —, stiff, as with cold, *etc.*, جَسَا ـ كَزَّ. To be —, stiff, hard, صَلُبَ; to make —, صَلَّبَ. To be —, as in the observance of religion, تَحَمَّسَ ـ حَمِسَ. To be —, harsh, towards, عَسَّرَ عَلَى ـ عَاسَرَ ـ شَدَّدَ عَلَى. To be strict, exact, دَاقَّ ـ تَجَوَّدَ. His joints became —, جَسَأَتْ مَفَاصِلُهُ. A beast having — legs, دَابَّة جَاسِئَةُ ٱلقَوَائِمِ. *See also* Hard, Inflexible, *a.*

Rigidity, *n.* } As from cold, كُزَاز. Stiffness, جَاسِئَآء ـ جُسْأَة.
Rigidness, } Hardness, solidity, مَتَانَة ـ صَلابَة. Strictness, غَايَةُ ٱلدِّقَّةِ ـ تَدْقِيق. Rigidity in religion, حَمَاسَة ـ حَمَس. Harshness, فَظَاظَة ـ شِدَّة ـ عُنْف. Obstinacy, مُعَانَدَة ـ عِنَاد ـ تَمَرُّد.

Rigidly, *ad.* Strictly, بِتَدْقِيقٍ; as in religous matters, تَحَمُّسًا ـ بِحَمَاسَةٍ. Harshly, بِفَظَاظَةٍ ـ بِعُنْفٍ. Strongly, severely, شَدِيدًا ـ بِشِدَّةٍ. Carefully, بِمُرَاعَاةٍ ـ بِٱعْتِنَآءٍ. To act — towards, عَاسَرَ عَلَى ـ أَعْنَفَ ـ عَنُفَ ب or عَلَى.

Rigmarole, *n.* جَمْهَرَة ـ لَغْو ـ غَذْمَرَة ـ طَفَانِين: He gave a — account of the affair, غَذْمَرَ ٱلخَبَرَ ـ جَمْهَرَ عَلَى ٱلخَبَرِ.

Rigour, *n.* Severity, شِدَّة. The — of winter, شِدَّةُ ٱلشِّتَآءِ. The rigours of war, غَمْرَةُ ٱلحَرْبِ *See also* Rigidity, Harshness, *n.*

Rigorous, *a.* Severe, شَدِيد. *See also* Rigid, Harsh, *a.*

Rigorously, *ad.* Severely, بِشِدَّةٍ ـ شَدِيدًا. *See also* Rigidly, Harshly, *ad.*

Rigorousness, *n.* شِدَّة. *See also* Rigidity, Harshness, *n.*

Rill, *n.* جَدْوَل *pl.* جَدَاوِلُ ـ سَاقِيَة *pl.* سَوَاقِي ـ مَجْرَى مَآءٍ *pl.* مَجَارِي.

Rill, *v.i.* *See to* Meander, *v.i.*

Rim, *n.* حِتَار *pl.* حُتُر ـ حَافِيَة. A round —, دَائِرَة. *See also* Border, *n.*

Rime, *n.* جَلِيد ـ سَقِيع ـ سَقِيط ـ صَرِيد.

Rimose, *a.* }
Rimous, } مَفْرُوج ـ مُفَقَّع ـ مُشَقَّق.

Rimosity, *n.* فَرْجَة ـ تَفَقُّع ـ تَشَقُّق.

Rimple, *n.* حِبَاك *pl.* حُبُك ـ حَبِيكَة *pl.* حَبَائِكُ ـ غَضْن *pl.* غُضُون. The rimples of the hair, حُبُكُ ٱلشَّعْرِ. Hair having rimples, wavy, curly, شَعْر أَحْجَنُ (or مُعَقَّف).

Rimple, *v.t.* حَبَّكَ ـ غَضَّنَ. Rimpled, shrivelled, مُتَكَسِّر.

Rimpling, *n.* Undulation, تَمَوُّج ـ تَمَاوُج.

Rimy, *a.* *See* Frosty, *a.*

Rind, *n.* As of a tree, جَب ـ قِشْرَة ـ قِشْر *pl.* قُشُور; of a fruit, قِشْرَة ـ قِشْر *pl.* قُشُور. A husk, غِمْد *pl.* غُمُود and أَغْمَاد. *See also* Bark, Husk, *n.*

Ring, *n.* A circle, دَائِرَة *pl.* دَوَائِرُ. A hoop, circle, حَلْقَة *pl.* حَلَقَات or حِلَقَات or حَلَق. A — of gold or silver, or a small — attached to women's ornaments, خُرْص *pl.* خِرْصَان. A — for the finger, with a stone set in it, خَاتِم *pl.* خَوَاتِمُ; without a stone, مَحْبَس *pl.* مَحَابِسُ. Rings for the ancles, such as are worn by women, خَلْخَال *pl.* خَلاخِيلُ ـ حِجْل *pl.* أَحْجَال and حُجُول. A — such as is worn in the nose, خِزَام. A — to shoot at, دَرِيئَة ـ وَتِيرَة . A — of people, حَلْقَة ـ مَحْضَر ـ جَمْعِيَّة . The iron — of a gate or door, زَرْفِين ـ حَمَامَة ـ حَلْقَة . An iron — to which anything is hung, كُلَّب *pl.* كَلَالِيب . The — of a sword-scabbard, بَكَرَة *pl.* بَكَرَات ـ كُلَّب *pl.* كِلَاب . The rows of rings in a coat of mail, حُبُكُ دِرْعٍ . A — for the neck, طَوْق *pl.* أَطْوَاق ـ طَارَة ـ جُلْجُلَة . Ring, as of a bell, قَرْع ـ صَلْصَلَة ـ دَقّ ـ طَنِين . In rings, *ad.* حِلَاقًا .

Ring, *v.t.* To cause to sound, دَقَّ [2] ـ قَرَعَ ـ طَنَّنَ ـ طَنَّ . To — the praises of, كَبَّرَ ـ أَثْنَى عَلَى ـ أَطْرَأَ ـ نَوَّهَ بِ . To — the changes on; *see to* Repeat, *v.t.*

Ring, *v.i.* To resound, رَنَّ ـ صَلَّ *aor.* يَصِلُّ ـ صَلْصَلَ ـ تَصَلْصَلَ . To —, as a bell, دَقَّ [2] . The lute rang, حَنَّ ٱلْعُودُ ـ ٱصْطَفَقَ ٱلْعُودُ . The bells rang, دَقَّتِ ٱلْأَجْرَاسُ . *See also to* Tingle, *v.i.*

Ringing, *n.* As of a bell, قَرْع ـ دَقّ ـ صَلْصَلَة . A tinkling, صَلِيل . A resounding, as of the strings of a lute, حَنِين . A —, as in the ears, طَنِين .

Ring-bolt, *n.* حَلْقَة *pl.* حَلْقَات .

Ring-dove, *n.* حَمَامَةٌ ذَاتُ ٱلطَّوْقِ ـ حَمَامَةٌ مُطَوَّقَةٌ .

Ringer, *n.* Of bells, قَارِع (*or* دَقَّاق) ٱلْأَجْرَاسِ .

Ring-fence, *n.* إِحَاطَةٌ مُتَّصِلَةٌ .

Ring-finger, *n.* ٱلْبِنْصِرُ .

Ringing, *a.* As of pottery, *etc.*, when struck, صَلَّال .

Ringleader, *n.* زُعَمَاءُ *pl.* زَعِيمٌ ـ زِمَامُ ٱلْأَمْرِ ـ رَأْس ـ مِقْدَام .

Ringlet, *n.* A small ring, حَلْقَةٌ صَغِيرَةٌ ـ حُلَيْقَة . *See also* Curl, *n.*

Ringstreak, *n.* طَوْق ـ خَطٌّ . The two ringstreaks on collared doves, ٱلْخُطَّتَانِ ـ ٱلطَّوْقَانِ

Ringstreaked, *a.* مُخَطَّط .

Ringworm, *n.* حَصَف ـ قَوَابِيُّ *pl.* قُوبَاء .

Rinse, *v.t.* مَضْمَضَ ـ شَطَفَ [2] شَطَفَ : He rinsed his mouth, مَضْمَضَ فَمَهُ ـ فَمَهُ .

Rinse, *n.* شَطْف ـ شَطْفَة . To give anything a rinse; *see to* Rinse, *v.t.*

Rinser, *n.* شَاطِف ـ مِضْمَاض .

Riot, *n.* Noisy festivity, مُنَادَمَة ـ دِعَارَة ـ خَلَاعَة ـ بَطَر . Dissipation, إِسْرَاف ـ إِبَادَة ـ إِفْرَاط . Sedition, فَسَاد ـ قَوْمَة ـ فِتْنَة . A seditious meeting, تَأَلُّب . Uproar, a row, شَغَب ـ هَوْشَة ـ هَيْشَة ـ غَوْغَاء . To quell a —, سَكَّنَ ٱلْفِتْنَةَ . To meet together for a —, of many, تَأَلَّبُوا . To run —, into debauchery, رَكَضَ إِلَى فَيْضِ ٱلْخَلَاعَةِ [2] ; to be unrestrained, سَابَ فِي سِيرَتِهِ *aor.* يَسِيبُ ـ كَانَ سَائِبًا فِي سِيرَتِهِ . To excite to —, أَلَّبَ ـ

شَغَبَ ـ شَغَبَ فِي ـ شَغَبَ عَلَى . Without giving rise to —, بِدُونِ حُدُوثِ شَغَبٍ . *See also* Disturbance, *n.*

Riot, *v.i.* To make an uproar, حَرَّشَ ـ شَغَبَ شَغْبًا ; قَوَّمَ غَوْغَاءَ ; of many, تَأَلَّبُوا . *See also to* Revel, *v.i.*

Riot-act, *n.* قَانُونٌ ضِدُّ ٱلشَّغَبِ ـ شَرِيعَةٌ نَاهِيَةُ ٱلْفِتَنِ .

Rioter, *n.* One who stirs up mischief, فَتَّان ـ ذُو مَشَاغِبَ ـ مُفْتِن . *See also* Reveller, *n.*

Riotous, *a.* Marked with riot, noisy, مُشْغِب ـ شَغِب ـ ذُو مَشَاغِبَ . Licentious, loose, فَلْتَان ـ مُسْرِف ـ سَائِب ـ فَرْطِيّ . Riotous living, عَيْشٌ مُسْرِفٌ . A companion of — men, صَاحِبُ ٱلْمُسْرِفِينَ .

Riotously, *ad.* Tumultuously, بِتَشْغِيبٍ ـ بِشَغَبٍ ـ شَغْبًا ـ بِغَوْغَاءَ ; with excess, بِخَلَاعَةٍ ـ بِفَرْطٍ ـ بِإِفْرَاطٍ ـ إِسْرَافًا .

Riotousness, *n.* State of being seditious, حَالَةٌ ـ حَالَةُ ٱلشَّغَبِ ـ فَسَاد ـ ٱلْفِتْنَةِ ; of being intemperate, فُرْط ـ إِفْرَاط ـ فَرْط ـ فَلَت . Licentiousness, فِسْق ـ خَلَاعَة ـ دِعَارَة ـ دَعَارَة .

Rip, *v.t.* To tear by splitting, شَقَّ [2] . To —, as the belly, فَتَحَ ـ شَقَّ [2] ـ بَقَرَ ـ بَعَجَ . To unsew, فَتَقَ [2] ـ فَتَّقَ . To open, فَتَحَ ; to re-open, عَادَ فَفَتَحَهُ [2] . To rip off, قَطَعَ . To be ripped, split, إِنْشَقَّ ; of the belly, إِنْبَعَجَ ; of sewing, تَفَتَّقَ ـ إِنْفَتَقَ . They ripped up the women with child, شَقُّوا ٱلْحَوَامِلَ . *See also to* Tear, *v.t.*

Rip, *n.* A rent, split, شَقّ *pl.* شُقُوق . A — in the belly, إِنْبِعَاج . An unsewing, فَتْق ـ فَتْقَة . A tear, rent, خَرْقَة ـ مَزْقَة .

Riparian, *a.* مُتَعَلِّقٌ بِٱلشَّطِّ ـ شَاطِئِيّ .

Ripe, *a.* Of fruit, نَاضِج ـ نَضِيج ـ يَانِع ـ مُسْتَوٍ . Of a boil, مُنْتَهٍ ـ مُقْرِن . Ready for, حَاضِرٌ لِ ـ مُسْتَعِدٌّ لِ . Hastening to, مُبَادِرٌ إِلَى . Of — age, بَالِغُ ٱلسِّنِّ ـ كَامِلُ ٱلسِّنِّ . Of — judgment, بَازِل ـ رَزِين . Opportune, مُوَافِق ـ فِي وَقْتِهِ ـ فِي مَحَلِّهِ . First ripe fruits, بَاكُورَة ـ بَاكُورَةُ ٱلْفَاكِهَةِ . The harvest is —, ٱلْحَصِيدُ قَدْ نَضِجَ . The grapes are —, ٱلْعِنَبُ قَدْ نَضِجَ . *See also* Mature, *a.*

Ripely, *ad.* With deliberation, بِتَأَمُّلٍ ـ بِٱنْتِبَاهٍ كُلِّيّ . Opportunely, فِي مَحَلِّهِ ـ فِي وَقْتِهِ .

Ripen, *v.t.* To make ripe, أَنْضَجَ . To bring to perfection, بَلَّغَ ـ أَبْلَغَ ـ أَتَمَّ ـ كَمَّلَ .

Ripen, *v.i.* To grow ripe, بَدَرَ [2] ـ نَضِجَ ـ نَضَجَ ـ إِسْتَوَى . To become perfect, تَكَمَّلَ ـ تَمَّ . To attain to, أَدْرَكَ . To —, as a boil, أَقْرَنَ ـ أَنْهَى ـ حَانَ ٱنْفِجَارُهُ .

Ripeness, *n.* The state of being ripe, تَنْضِيج ـ نُضْج ـ إِسْتِوَاء . Ripeness of age, رُشْد ـ أَشُدّ ـ سِنُّ ٱلرُّشْدِ ; of intellect, بُزُول ـ

رَزَانَة ـ بُزْل ـ كَمَالُ ٱلْعَقْلِ. Full growth, بُلُوغ ـ بَلَاغ. Perfection, كَمَال. *See also* Maturity, *n.*

Ripening, *a.* Becoming ripe, نَضِيج.

Ripper, *n.* A splitter, شَقَّاق ـ مُشَقِّق. A — of the belly, مُبَعِّج. One who unsews, فَتَّاق ـ مُفَتِّق.

Ripping, *n.* *See* Rip, *n.*

Ripple, *v.t.* إِسْتَدْرَجَ ـ ² نَسَجَ. To be rippled, إِنْتَسَجَ. The wind rippled the pebbles, إِسْتَدْرَجَتِ ٱلرِّيحُ ٱلْحَصَا.

Ripple, *v.i.* إِنْتَسَجَ ـ ² عَسَلَ.

Ripple, *n.* As on the water, عَسَلَان ـ عَسَل; ripples, on the water, حَبَكُ ٱلْمَآءِ ـ دَرَجُ ٱلْمَآءِ ـ حِبَابُ ٱلْمَآءِ ـ حَبَبُ ٱلْمَآءِ ـ حِبَاكُ ٱلْمَآءِ. The wind left ripples upon the sand, دَرَجَتِ ٱلرِّيحُ. *See also* Comb, *n.*

Rippling, *n.* حِبَاب ـ تَكَسُّر. *See also* Ripple, *n.*

Rippiy, *a.* مُتَكَسِّر ـ مُتَسَلْسِل ـ مُسَلْسِل ـ مُحَبَّك.

Rise, *v.i.* As from a seat, قَامَ ² ـ إِنْتَهَضَ ـ نَهَضَ: he rose from his place, نَهَضَ عَنْ مَكَانِهِ; he rose to do something, نَهَضَ لِلْأَمْرِ. To —, as the sun or moon, بَزَقَ ² ـ بَزَغَ ² ـ بَزَغَتِ ٱلشَّمْسُ ـ طَلَعَ ² ـ أَشْرَقَ ـ شَرَقَ ²: the sun rose, أَشْرَقَتِ ٱلشَّمْسُ. To —, of water, طَمَا ٱلْمَآءُ ²; of clouds, نَشَصَ ٱلْغَيْمُ ²; of the day, مَتَعَ ٱلنَّهَارُ; of a sound, نَقَعَ ٱلصَّوْتُ; of a bird, to soar, حَلَّقَ ٱلطَّيْرُ. To —, spread, diffuse itself, إِطَّلَعَ ـ طَلَعَ ² ـ سَطَعَ: the odour of the musk rose to my nose, سَطَعَتْنِي رَائِحَةُ ٱلْمِسْكِ. To —, ascend, صَعِدَ ـ طَلَعَ ² ـ إِصْطَعَدَ ـ تَصَعَّدَ. To —, as a pimple or such like on the skin, نَتَأَ. To —, as from sleep, إِسْتَيْقَظَ مِنَ ـ إِنْتَبَهَ ـ قَامَ مِنَ ٱلنَّوْمِ ² ـ ٱلنَّوْم. To —, as into view, نَبَعَ ب ـ ² بَرَزَ ـ تَبَيَّنَ ـ بَيَّنَ ـ ظَهَرَ. To —, as from a fall, قَامَ ² ـ نَهَضَ. To —, as a river, طَمَا *aor.* يَطْمُو. To —, to spring from, as of a liquid, إِنْبَجَسَ مِن ـ ² نَبَعَ مِن. To — or proceed from, جَآءَ مِن *aor.* يَجِيءُ ـ نَتَجَ مِن ـ ² صَدَرَ عَن. To —, as in price, صَعِدَ ٱلثَّمَنُ ـ إِزْدَادَ ٱلثَّمَنُ ـ إِرْتَفَعَ ٱلسِّعْرُ. To —, as after a misfortune, تَجَبَّرَ. To —, as in dignity, عَلَا ² ـ تَرَقَّى فِي ٱلشَّرَفِ. To — by degrees in, تَدَرَّجَ فِي. To — in the mind, خَطَرَ بِٱلْبَالِ (or عَلَى ٱلْبَالِ). To —, as from the dead, إِنْبَعَثَ ـ قَامَ مِنْ بَيْنِ ٱلْأَمْوَاتِ ². To —, as in rebellion, عَصَى ـ تَمَرَّدَ ـ شَقَّ ٱلْعَصَا ². To —, to break up, as of an assembly, إِنْفَضَّ. To — to, to regain, حَصَّلَ ثَانِيَةً ـ أَدْرَكَ. To — up against, قَامَ عَلَى ² ـ خَرَجَ عَلَى ² ـ شَغَبَ عَلَى ـ لَوَى عَن. The wind rose, صَارَتِ ٱلرِّيحُ تَهُبُّ. To — above, to overcome, عَلَا ب ـ فَاضَلَ ـ بَهَرَ ـ غَلَبَ عَلَى ـ أَنْجَحَ ب; to excel, عَلَا *aor.* يَعْلُو. To — or jut out, بَرَزَ ². To — early, بَكَرَ ² ـ بَكَّرَ ـ أَبْكَرَ.

Rise, *n.* The act of rising, قَوْمَة ـ قِيَام ـ قَوْم ـ نُهُوض. Ascension, طُلُوع ـ صُعُود. A source, نَبْع. Appearance, ظُهُور. Rise, as in price, إِرْتِفَاع. The act of occurring, وُقُوع ـ حُدُوث. Increase, تَزَايُد. Advance, تَقَدُّم ـ تَرْقِيَة ـ تَرَقٍّ ـ تَدَرُّج. Commencement, إِبْتِدَآء ـ شُرُوع. An ascent, as of a hill, مِعْرَاج ـ طُلُوع ـ طَلْعَة ـ عُلْوَة ـ رُقِيَّة. To be on the —, as a river, طَمَا *aor.* يَطْمُو ـ صَارَ فِي ٱلطُّمُوِّ; as of a price, صَارَ فِي ـ إِرْتَفَعَ ٱلْإِرْتِفَاعِ; as in price, صَارَ فِي ٱلتَّزَايُدِ ـ تَزَايَدَ. To give — to, to occasion, أَوْرَثَ ـ سَبَّبَ ـ أَنْتَجَ. To take its —, spring, from, نَبَعَ مِن ² ـ تَبَدَّأَ ـ حَدَثَ ²; to originate, نَشَأَ. *See also* Rising, *n.*

Riser, *n.* One who rises, قَائِم ـ نَاهِض. The — of a stair, لَوْحُ ٱلدَّرَجَةِ ـ صَفِيحَةُ ٱلدَّرَجَةِ. An early —, مُبَكِّر. A late —, نَوَّام.

Risibility, *n.* The power of laughing, ٱلْقُوَّةُ ٱلضَّاحِكَةُ. Proneness to laugh, قَرِيحَةُ ٱلضَّحِكِ.

Risible, *a.* Having the power of laughing, بِهِ قُوَّةُ ٱلضَّحِكِ ـ ضَاحِك. Adapted to excite laughter, مُضْحِك.

Risibly, *ad.* بِضَحِكٍ ـ بِنَوْعٍ مُضْحِكٍ.

Rising, *n.* Ascension, طُلُوع ـ صُعُود. Standing up, نَهْض ـ قِيَام. A —, as a pustule, *etc.*, نُتُوّ ـ نَتْأ. An insurrection, طِغْيَان ـ عِصْيَان ـ هَرْج ـ فِتْنَة. Rising, as of a council, *etc.*, رَفْع ـ إِنْفِضَاض; as from death, إِنْبِعَاث ـ قِيَامَة ـ قِيَامَةٌ مِنْ بَيْنِ ٱلْأَمْوَاتِ. A place of —, مَشْرِق ـ مَطْلَع. The — of the morning star, ٱلشَّرِيقَة ـ ٱلشَّرْقَة ـ ٱلشَّارِق ـ مَطْلَعُ ٱلْفَجْرِ. The sun-rising, Towards the sun —, نَحْوَ شُرُوقِ ٱلشَّمْسِ. *See also* Rise, *n.*

Risk, *n.* Danger, خَطَر *pl.* أَخْطَار ـ مُخَاطَرَة ـ تَهْلُكَة ـ غَرَر. Chance, بَخْت. He is in great —, هُوَ عَلَى خَطَرٍ عَظِيمٍ. At the — of his life, بِخَطَرِ نَفْسِهِ. At your —, وَأَنْتَ ٱلضَّامِنُ ـ وَأَنْتَ ٱلْمُطَالَبُ بِهِ. To expose to —, خَاطَرَ بِ ـ عَرَّضَ عَلَى ٱلْخَطَرِ. *See also* Peril, Danger, Hazard, *n.*

Risk, *v.t.* To expose to risk; *see under preceding article.* To — one's self, خَاطَرَ بِنَفْسِهِ ـ أَخْطَرَ بِنَفْسِهِ. *See also under to* Endanger, Peril, Hazard, *v.t.*

Risky, *a.* *See* Perilous, Hazardous, *a.*

Rite, *n.* As of religion, فَرِيضَة *pl.* فَرَائِض ـ رَسْم *pl.* رُسُوم ـ طَقْس *pl.* طُقُوس. People belonging to a —, مِلَّة *pl.* مِلَل ـ مَذْهَب. Rites, such as are observed in mosques, *etc.*, مَنَاسِك.

Ritual, *a.* Belonging to rites, مُتَعَلِّقٌ بِٱلطُّقُوسِ.

Ritual, *n.* كِتَابُ طُقُوسٍ (*or*) مَنَاسِكُ. The — of the pilgrimage to Makkah, that is, all the ceremonies connected therewith, شَعَائِرُ (*or* مَنَاسِكُ) ٱلْحَجِّ.

Ritualism, *n.* A system of rites, تَرْتِيبُ ٱلطُّقُوسِ ـ نَسَقُ ٱلرُّسُومِ. Excessive attachment to ritual, تَعَصُّبٌ لِلطُّقُوسِ.

Ritualist, *n.* One skilled in ritual, مَاهِرٌ فِي ـ مُعَلِّمُ ٱلرُّسُومِ ٱلطُّقُوسِ (*or* ٱلْمَنَاسِكِ). One excessively attached to ritual, مُتَمَسِّكٌ بِٱلطُّقُوسِ.

Ritually, *ad.* بِمُقْتَضَى ٱلرُّسُومِ (*or* ٱلْمَنَاسِكِ) ـ حَسَبَ ٱلطُّقُوسِ.

Rival, *n.* } مُفَاضِلٌ ـ مُنَافِسٌ ـ مُغَايِرٌ ـ مُخَايِرٌ ـ مُعَارِضٌ ـ
Rival, *a.* } مُبَارٍ ـ غَابِطٌ لِ. He has disposed of all rivals, رَدَّ جَمِيعَ ٱلطُّلَّابِ 2. *See also* Emulator, *n.* Emulative, *a.*

Rival, *v.t.* Of good, خَايَرَ; in a general sense, بَارَى ـ نَافَسَ ـ عَارَضَ. They rivalled one another, of many, تَبَاهُوا ـ تَفَاخَرُوا ـ تَجَادَلُوا ـ تَرَابَعُوا. *See also to* Emulate, *v.t.* to Compete, *v.i.*

Rivalry, *n.* مُعَارَضَةٌ ـ مُبَارَاةٌ ـ مُخَايَرَةٌ. *See also* Emulation, Competition, *n.*

Rive, *v.t.* شَقَّ 2. *See also to* Cleave, Split, *v.t.*

Rive, *v.i.* تَشَقَّقَ ـ إِنْشَقَّ. *See also to* Split, *v.i.*

Rivel, *v.t.* *See to* Contract, Shrivel, *v.t.*

River, *n.* نَهْرٌ *pl.* أَنْهَارٌ *and* نُهُورٌ *and* أَنْهُرٌ *and* نُهُرٌ. A large —, شَطٌّ *pl.* شُطُوطٌ. A passage to a —, شَرِيعَةٌ *pl.* شَطٌّ ـ شُطُوطٌ. A bend or cut in a — from which water is taken, فُرْضَةٌ. The mouth of a —, فَمُ نَهْرٍ ـ فِرَاضُ نَهْرٍ. The — Nile, بَحْرُ ٱلنِّيلِ. To walk, as by a —, شَطَأَ ـ. The — divided itself into branches, تَشَعَّبَ (*or* إِنْشَعَبَ) ٱلنَّهْرُ.

River, *a.* عِنْدَ نَهْرٍ ـ نَهْرِيٌّ.

River-horse, *n.* *See* Hippopotamus, *n.*

Rivet, *v.t.* To fasten with rivets, سَمَّرَ ـ بِشَعَائِرَ ـ أَحْكَمَ ـ بِأَغْرِنَةٍ ـ أَحْكَمَ ـ ضَبَطَ 2 ـ أَحْكَمَ ـ بِبَرَاغِيَّ ـ سَمَّرَ ـ بِمَسَامِيرَ. To fasten, شَدَّ ـ وَكَّدَ 2. To be riveted, attached, to, تَعَلَّقَ بِ; to be absorbed in, إِسْتَغْرَقَ فِي.

Rivet, *n.* شَعِيرَةٌ *pl.* شَعَائِرُ ـ عِرَانٌ *pl.* أَغْرِنَةٌ ـ مِسْمَارٌ *pl.* مَسَامِيرُ ـ بُرْغِيٌّ *pl.* بَرَاغِيُّ.

Rivulet, *n.* سَرِيٌّ *pl.* أَسْرِيَةٌ ـ سَيْلٌ *pl.* سُيُولٌ ـ جَدْوَلٌ *pl.* جَدَاوِلُ ـ فَلَجٌ *pl.* فُلُوجٌ ـ مَجْرَى مَآءٍ *pl.* مَجَارِي. A — for irrigation, سَاقِيَةٌ *pl.* سَوَاقِي.

Rix-dollar, *n.* سِكَّةٌ مِنْ فِضَّةٍ ثَمَنُهَا من ١٨ إِلَى ٢٥ غِرْشًا.

Roach, *n.* ضَرْبٌ مِنْ سَمَكِ ٱلْأَنْهَارِ.

Road, *n.* شَرًى *pl.* أَشْرَآءٌ ـ سَبِيلَةٌ ـ سَبِيلٌ *pl.* سُبُلٌ ـ دَرْبٌ *pl.* دُرُوبٌ ـ طَرِيقَةٌ *pl.* طَرِيقَاتٌ ـ طُرُقٌ *pl.* طَرِيقٌ. A way, passage, مَجَازٌ ـ دَرْبٌ ـ بَابٌ. A beaten —, طَرِيقٌ مُسْتَتِبٌّ ـ دَرْبٌ طَرِيقٌ. A carriage —, طَرِيقٌ لِلْعَرَبَاتِ. A high road, دَرْبٌ سُلْطَانِيٌّ ـ شَوَارِعُ *pl.* شَارِعٌ ـ وَارِدَةٌ. A branch —, or a separate or straggling —, تُرَّهَةٌ *pl.* تُرَّهَاتٌ ـ مَطْرَبٌ *pl.* مَطَارِبُ ـ مَطْرَبَةٌ. A mountain —, عَقَبَةٌ *pl.* عِقَابٌ. A — between two mountains, فَيْفَاةٌ ـ فَيْفٌ. The beaten track of a —, مَطْرَبَةٌ. The branches of a — that vary and lead in every direction, بَنَاتُ ٱلطَّرِيقِ. A metalled —, سِكَّةٌ مَرْصُوفَةٌ بِحَصًى. To beat a —, make it smooth or passable, طَرَّقَ ٱلطَّرِيقَ. To make a — for, to make it passable for, طَرَّقَ لِ. To stop a —, سَدَّ ٱلطَّرِيقَ 2. To intercept a —, by plundering thereon, قَطَعَ ٱلطَّرِيقَ ـ. To take to the —, become a highwayman, أَصَابَ ٱلطَّرِيقَ. Road, a course, way, manner, طَرِيقَةٌ. Road, for shipping; *see next article. See also* Way, *n.*

Roadstead, *n.* فُرْضَةٌ *pl.* فُرَضٌ ـ مَرْسًى *pl.* مَرَاسِي ـ مَوْرِدَةٌ.

Roadster, *n.* A vessel anchored in a bay, سَفِينَةٌ رَاسِيَةٌ فِي خَلِيجٍ. A horse for travelling, بِرْذَوْنٌ *pl.* بَرَاذِينُ ـ كَدِيشٌ *pl.* كُدُشٌ *and* أَكَادِيشُ.

Roam, *v.t.* عَارَ *aor.* يَعِيرُ ـ عَالَ ـ سَاحَ *aor.* يَسِيحُ. To — over, سَكَّ فِي ٱلْأَرْضِ 2 ـ عَارَ فِي ـ عَالَ فِي. To — at random in a land, To send to —, of cattle, سَرَّحَ ـ أَسْرَحَ.

Roamer, *n.* } سَيَّاحٌ ـ عَيَّارٌ ـ عَائِرٌ. Restless, خُرَجَةٌ وُلَجَةٌ.
Roaming, *a.* } Roaming peoples, نَوَاقِلُ.

Roan, *a.* أَشْقَرُ ـ صِنَابِيٌّ *fem.* شَقْرَآءُ *pl.* شُقْرٌ. *See also* Bay, *a.*

Roan, *n.* جِلْدٌ شَبِيهٌ ٱلسِّخْتِيَانِ مِنْ جُلُودِ ٱلْغَنَمِ.

Roar, *v.i.* To make a loud noise, صَوَّتَ ـ أَصَاتَ ـ صَاحَ ـ صَيَّحَ. To —, as a lion or camel, هَدَرَ ـ نَهَتَ ـ. To —, grumble aloud, to growl, زَأَرَ ـ تَزَأَّرَ ـ أَزْأَرَ. To —, as the wind, قَصَفَ ـ; as the sea, also of a multitude of people, لَجِبَ ـ. The sea roars, عَجَّ ٱلْبَحْرُ; the lion roared, هَرَّ ٱلْأَسَدُ ـ; the thunder roared, رَعَدَ ٱلرَّعْدُ 2 ـ. To — with laughter, قَرْقَرَ ـ قَهْقَهَ. Roars of laughter, قَهْقَهَةٌ.

Roar, *n.* } A loud noise, صِيَاحٌ ـ صَوْتٌ; as of a lion or camel,
Roaring, } نَهِيتٌ ـ نُهَاتٌ ـ تَهْدَارٌ ـ هَدِيرٌ ـ هَدْرٌ. A grumbling, growling, زَئِيرٌ ـ زَأْرٌ. A —, as of the wind or thunder, قَصْفٌ ـ رَعْدٌ; as of the sea or a multitude of people, لَجَبٌ.

Roaring, *a.* Of clamour, صَيَّاحٌ; of a lion or camel, *etc.*, هَادِرٌ ـ نَهَّاتٌ ـ مُنْهِتٌ; of the wind, قَاصِفٌ; of thunder, رَاعِدٌ; of the sea or a number of people, لَجِبٌ. A — sea, بَحْرٌ ذُو لَجَبٍ. A — lion, أَسَدٌ مُزَمْجِرٌ.

Roarer, *n.* مُزَجِّر ـ صَيَّاح. *See also under* Roaring, *a.*

Roast, *v.t.* أَشْوَى ـ شَوَّى ـ شَوَى ـِ. To be roasted, إِشْتَوَى ـ إِنْشَوَى. To — on stones or in an earth-oven, حَنَذَ ـِ. To —, as coffee and such like, حَمَّرَ. To —, scorch, as the sun, حَنَذَ ـِ ـ حَرَقَ ـِ. *See also to* Scold, *v.t.*, *and to* Scorch, *v.t.*

Roast, *n.* } Cooked by the fire, مَشْوِيٌّ ـ شِوَآءٌ ـ شَوِيٌّ. Small
Roasted, *a.* } pieces of roast meat, كَبَاب. A piece of — meat, شِوَآءٌ; the same, cooked on the stones or in an earth-oven, حَنِيذ ـ حَنَذ. A seller of — meat, شَوَّآءٌ.

Roaster, *n.* One who roasts, شَوَّآءٌ. A place for roasting, مَشْوَى. A pig for roasting, خِنُّوصٌ لِلشِّوَآءِ.

Roasting, *n.* The act of, شَيٌّ; on stones or in an earth-oven, حَنَذ.

Roasting, *a.* For roasting, لِلشَّيِّ.

Rob, *v.t.* To take feloniously, نَشَلَ ـُ ـ سَرَقَ ـِ ـ إِسْتَرَقَ. To take by force, إِسْتَلَبَ ـ سَلَبَ ـُ ـ خَطِفَ ـَ ـ خَلَسَ ـِ ـ خَلَّسَ. To deprive of, خَطِفَ ـَ عن ـ عَرَّى عن ـ شَلَّحَ ـ أَعْدَمَ. To be robbed, bereft, of, to lose, ثَكِلَ ـَ. Robbed or bereft of, ثَكُول ـ مُثْكَل ـ مَثْكُول. I have been robbed of my reputation, سُرِقَتْ عِرْضِي. A bear robbed of its whelps, دُبَّةٌ ثَكُولٌ.

Rob, *v.i.* إِسْتَعْمَلَ ٱلسَّرِقَةَ (*or* ٱلسَّرِقَةَ) ـ صَارَ سَارِقًا.

Rob, *n.* مَعْجُون ـ رُبٌّ.

Robber, *n.* سَارِق *pl.* سُرَّاق ـ لِصّ *pl.* لُصُوص ـ نَشَّال ـ *vulg.* حَرَامِيّ *pl.* حَرَامِيَّة. A highway —, ٱبْنُ ٱلطَّرِيقِ ـ ٱبْنُ ٱللَّيْلِ. *See also* Highwayman, *n.*

Robbery, *n.* The act of robbing, سَرِق ـ لَصَص ـ لَصَاص ـ سَرِيقَة ـ سَرِقَة ـ لُصُوصِيَّة; something stolen, حَرَام ـ سَرِقَة ـ خَلِيسَة ـ خُلْسَة. He did not consider it a —, لَمْ يَحْسِبْهُ خُلْسَةً.

Robe, *n.* A kind of loose dress, either for men or women, جُبَّة; for a woman, مِنْتَانَة; for a man, مُصَبَّغَة ـ قُفْطَان. A — of honour, خِلْعَة *pl.* خِلَع. An official dress, لِبَاسٌ رَسْمِيٌّ. Gentlemen of the long —, lawyers, أَهْلُ ٱلشَّرْعِ. He divested himself of the — which he had on, خَلَعَ ٱلْجُبَّةَ ٱلَّتِي عَلَيْهِ. He arrayed him in a splendid —, أَلْبَسَهُ حُلَّةً فَاخِرَةً.

Robe, *v.t.* To put one on a robe, لَبَّسَ. To — one with a robe of honour, خَلَعَ عَلَى ـ خَلَعَ عَلَى ـ خِلْعَةً. To — one's self, تَلَبَّسَ بِ ـ لَبِسَ ـَ.

Robin, *n.* }
Robin-redbreast, } عُصْفُورٌ أَحْمَرُ ٱلصَّدْرِ.

Roborant, *a.* مُقَوٍّ.

Roborant, *n.* دَوَآءٌ مُقَوٍّ.

Robust, *a.* قَوِيٌّ *pl.* أَقْوِيَآءُ ـ عَفِيٌّ ـ صَلِيع ـ صَلْب ـ صُلْب ـ شَدِيد *pl.* شِدَاد. To be —, ضَلُعَ ـُ ـ صَلُبَ ـُ.

Robustly, *ad.* بِقُوَّةٍ ـ بِصَلَابَةٍ.

Robustness, *n.* قُوَّة ـ عَافِيَة ـ ضَلَاعَة ـ بَطْش ـ صَلَابَة.

Roc, *n.* }
Rock, } The bird, طَيْرُ ٱلرُّخِّ ـ ٱلرُّخُّ.

Roche-alum, *n.* }
Rock-alum, } شَبٌّ ـ حَجَرُ ٱلشَّبِّ.

Rochet, *n.* كَتُّونَة.

Rock, *n.* صَخْر *or* صَخَر *pl.* صُخُور; a single —, صَخْرَة. A piece or lump of —, or such a — rising out of shallow water, جَلْمَد *pl.* جَلَامِد ـ جُلْمُود *pl.* جَلَامِيد. A great round —, جَلْهَة. A sunken —, أَتَانُ ٱلضَّحْلِ. A large piece of — that falls from a mountain, ٱبْنُ ٱلطَّوْدِ. A hard and smooth —, صَخْرَةٌ صَمَّآءُ. Smooth, slippery rocks, صُفُوح. A —, rocking, تَذَبْذُب ـ هَزَّة ـ هَزْهَزَة. The — of Gibraltar, جَبَلُ طَارِق. Rock, sweetmeat, حَلَاوَة ـ مُلَبَّس. In the clefts of the rock, فِي مَحَاجِئِ ٱلصَّخْرِ. They rolled him down from the rocks, دَحْرَجُوهُ عَنِ ٱلصُّخُورِ.

Rock, *v.t.* To swing to and fro, ذَبْذَبَ. To shake, هَزَّ ـُ ـ هَزْهَزَ ـ ذَبْذَبَ. To —, as a cradle, هَزْهَزَ ـ هَزَّزَ.

Rock, *v.i.* To swing to and fro, تَذَبْذَبَ ـ تَرَجَّحَ ـ إِرْتَجَّ. To shake, تَهَزْهَزَ ـ إِهْتَزَّ ـ تَهَزَّزَ. *See also to* Reel, *v.i.*

Rock-bound, *a.* مُصْخِر ـ صَخِر ـ مُحَاطٌ بِصُخُورٍ.

Rock-crystal, *n.* حَجَرُ ٱلْبِلَّوْرِ.

Rocker, *n.* One that rocks, مُهَزِّز ـ مُذَبْذِب. Rocker, the wood —, as of a cradle, مَرْجِيحَة.

Rocket, *n.* شِهَابٌ ٱلْبَارُودِ *pl.* شُهُب ـ صَارُوخ *pl.* صَوَارِيخ ـ أَبُو قُصَيْبَة.

Rocket, *n.* The plant, جَرْجِير.

Rock-fish, *n.* سَمَكُ ٱلصُّخُورِ.

Rockiness, *n.* كَثْرَةُ صُخُورٍ ـ صَخَرَات. Ruggedness, وَعْر ـ وُعُور.

Rocking-chair, *n.* كُرْسِيٌّ مَرْجِيحَةٍ.

Rock-oil, *n.* نِفْط ـ بَطْرَالُون ـ بِتْرُول.

Rock-salt, *n.* مِلْحٌ حَجَرِيّ.

Rock-work, *n.* تَرْكِيبُ صُخُورٍ ـ تَرْكِيبُ حَصًى.

Rocky, *a.* Full of rocks, صَخِر ـ مُصْخِر. Rugged, وَعِر *pl.* أَوْعَار ـ وَاعِر. Hard, صُلْب ـ صَلِيب ـ صَلِيد ـ مَتِين.

Rod, *n.* A stick, staff, قَضِيب *pl.* قُضْبَان ـ عَصًا *pl.* عِصِيّ. A switch, twig, branch, عُسْلُوج *pl.* عَسَالِيج ـ خُصْلَة ـ غُصْنَة ـ قَضِيب *pl.* قُضْبَان. A — for punishment, مِقْرَعَة ـ عَصَب ـ

سَوْط. A — for beating cotton, *etc.*, مِطْرَقَة ـ مِطْرَق. A fishing —, قَصَبَةُ ٱلصَّيْدِ. A sceptre, قَضِيبُ ٱلْمُلْكِ. Chastisement, تَعْزِير ـ تَوْبِيخ. A —, the measure, قِيَاسٌ طُولُهُ نَحْوَ ١١ قَدَمًا. To beat with a —, for punishment, ضَرَبَ بِسَوْطٍ ـ جَلَدَ ٣ ـ قَضَبَ ٣. To have a — in pickle for, أَضْمَرَ عِقَابَهُ: I have a — in pickle for you, خُذْ مِنِّي مَا يَجِيكَ.

Rodent, *a.* قَرَّاض ـ عَارِق ـ لَاكّ.

Rodentia, *n.* الحَيَوَانَاتُ ٱلْقَرَّاضَة.

Rodomontade, *n.* فُشَار ـ هَذَيَان ـ لَغْو ـ عَذْمَرَة.

Rodomontadist, *n.* فَشَّار ـ هَذَّاء.

Roe, *n.* The female of the hart, ظَبْيَة ـ أُنْثَى ٱلْأَيِّلِ *pl.* ظِبَاء *and* ظَبْيَات. A wild —, ظَبْيَة بَرِّيَّة. The — of a fish, بَطَارِخ. Soft —, مُخُّ ٱلسَّمَكِ.

Roebuck, *n.* ظَبْي *pl.* أَظْبٍ *and* ظُبِيّ *and* ظِبَاء.

Rogation, *n.* Supplication, اِبْتِهَال. Rogation Sunday, أَحَدُ ٱلِٱبْتِهَالِ. Rogation week, أُسْبُوعُ ٱلِٱبْتِهَالِ. The three — days, أَيَّامُ ٱلِٱبْتِهَالِ ٱلثَّلَاثَة.

Rogue, *n.* A scoundrel, قَبِيح *pl.* قِبَاح ـ شَقِيّ *pl.* أَشْقِيَاء ـ خَلِيع ـ خَدَّاع ـ مَكَّار ـ مُحْتَال. Playfully mischievous, شَيْطَان ـ مُسْخِر ـ مُهَرِّج ـ لَعُوب. *See also* Knave, *n.*

Roguery, *n.* Knavery, خِيَانَة ـ خَلَاعَة ـ خِدَاع ـ مَكْر ـ قَبَاحَة. Mischievousness, pleasantry, شَيْطَنَة ـ مَزْح ـ هَذَر.

Rogue's-yarn, *n.* جُمْلَةٌ مَصْبُوغَةٌ مُجَدَّلَةٌ فِي أَحْبَالِ ٱلْمَرَاكِبِ ٱلْمِيرِيَّةِ وِقَايَةً عَنِ ٱلسَّرِقَةِ.

Roguish, *a.* Knavish, خَدَّاع ـ شَقِيّ ـ مَكَّار ـ غَدَّار ـ غَابِن. Waggish, mischievous, لَعُوب ـ شَيْطَان ـ بَطِر ـ مُهَرِّج ـ مُسْخِر.

Roguishly, *ad.* Knavishly, بِخِيَانَةٍ ـ بِخِدَاعٍ ـ بِمَكْرٍ. Playfully, mischievously, بِشَيْطَنَةٍ ـ أُلْعُوبَةً ـ هَزْلًا.

Roguishness, *n.* Knavery, نَصْب ـ خِدَاع ـ غَبْن ـ غَدْر ـ مَكْر. Waggishness, mischievousness, تَهْرِيجَة ـ مَزْح ـ هَذَر ـ بَطَر ـ شَيْطَنَة.

Roil, *v.t.* *See to* Muddle, *to* Vex, *v.t.*

Roisterer, *n.* فَشَّار *vulg.* ـ مُتَهَوِّر ـ عَجَّاج.

Roland, *n.* The name, رُولَنْد. A — for an Oliver, مُقَابَلَةٌ بِٱلْمِثْلِ. To give one a — for an Oliver, قَابَلَ بِٱلْمِثْلِ.

Roll, *v.t.* As of a stone, *etc.*, دَحْرَجَ ـ ٣ حَدَرَ ٢; to be rolled, تَدَحْرَجَ. To roll down, دَهْدَهَ ـ زَحْلَفَ ـ خَرَّ ٢ ـ زَحْلَقَ; to be rolled down, تَدَهْدَهَ ـ تَدَأْدَأَ ـ تَزَحْلَفَ ـ تَدَحْرَجَ ـ تَزَحْلَقَ. To —, as paste, خَلَجَ ٣ ٢. To turn round, revolve, أَدَارَ ـ دَوَّرَ. To wind, لَفَّ ٢ ـ سَلَّكَ; to be wound, اِلْتَفَّ.

To — up, as into a roll, طَمَّرَ. To — up, to wrap, in a general sense, أَدْرَجَ ـ دَرَّجَ; to be so rolled up, اِنْدَرَجَ. To — in the dust, عَفَّرَ فِي ٱلتُّرَابِ ـ مَرَّغَ فِي ٱلتُّرَابِ. To — one's self in the dust, تَلَبَّثَ فِي ٱلتُّرَابِ ـ تَعَفَّرَ فِي ٱلتُّرَابِ ـ تَمَرَّغَ فِي ٱلتُّرَابِ. To — anything about in the mouth, لَجْلَجَ ـ هَرْمَزَ. To — one's self about, تَقَالَبَ. To — into a ball, كَبَّبَ. To —, as the ground with a roller, دَلَكَ ٢ بِمِحْدَلَةٍ. To — out, as into plates, صَفَّحَ. They rolled away the stones from the place, دَحْرَجُوا ٱلْحَجَرَ عَنِ ٱلْمَكَانِ.

Roll, *v.i.* As of a ball on a plane, تَدَحْرَجَ ـ تَدَأْدَأَ. To revolve, دَارَ ٢ ـ اِسْتَدَارَ. To —, as the sea, مَاجَ ٢ ـ تَمَوَّجَ ـ اِعْتَلَجَ. To —, as a ship, تَخَبَّطَ ـ تَقَلَّبَ. To —, as thunder, جَلَبَ ٣ ٢ ـ رَعَدَ ٣ ٢ ـ أَرْعَدَ; of thunder, the clouds, a mill, *etc.*, أَزَّ ٢. To sound, as a drum, *etc.*, صَلَّ ٣ ـ صَلْصَلَ ـ صَوَّتَ ـ أَصَاتَ. To wind, اِلْتَفَّ. To — down, تَدَأْدَأَ ـ تَدَهْدَهَ ـ تَزَحْلَفَ ـ تَزَحْلَقَ ـ تَدَحْرَجَ. To — on, as time, حَالَ *aor.* يَحُولُ ـ مَضَى ٣ ـ مَرَّ ٢. To — on, to follow one another, تَتَابَعَ. His eye rolled about, دَوَّمَتْ عَيْنُهُ. The wine intoxicated the drinker so that it made him — about, دَوَّمَتِ ٱلْخَمْرُ شَارِبَهَا. The sun rolled about in the sky, as if it were spinning, or as though it were motionless, دَوَّمَتِ ٱلشَّمْسُ ـ دَوَّمَتِ ٱلشَّمْسُ فِي كَبِدِ ٱلسَّمَاءِ. *See also under to* Reel, *v.i.*

Roll, *n.* The act of rolling, as on a plane, تَدَأْدُؤ ـ دَحْرَجَة; the state of being rolled, تَدَحْرُج ـ دِحْرَاج. A turn, دَوْر ـ دَوْرَة. A —, a tumble, هُبُوط ـ هَبْط ـ وَقْع ـ وُقُوع. A paper or document made up into a —, طُومَار *pl.* طَوَامِير. A packet, مِلَفّ ـ صُرَّة *pl.* صُرَر; a paper — or packet, رِزْمَة *pl.* رِزَم ـ وَرَقَة ـ قِرْطَاس. A list, as of names, سِيَاقَة ـ جَدْوَل ـ دَفْتَر. The —, as of a drum, *etc.*, دَرْج ـ صَوْت ـ تَتَابُعُ أَصْوَاتٍ ـ رَنَّة. A book, volume, سِفْر *pl.* أَسْفَار. A —, as of the sea, مَوْج ـ تَمَوُّج; of a ship, تَقَلُّب ـ تَخَبُّط ـ اِضْطِرَابُ ٱلْمَرْكَبِ. A —, as of bread, قُرْص *pl.* أَقْرَاص. A — on the ground, as with a roller, for smoothing, دَلْكٌ بِمِحْدَلَةٍ. A — in the dust, تَمَرُّغٌ فِي ٱلتُّرَابِ ـ تَعَفُّر. A —, as of thunder, رَعْد ـ إِرْعَاد; of thunder, or of the noise of water, of a mill, *etc.*, أَزِيز: The rolling of the thunder terrified me, هَالَنِي أَزِيزُ ٱلرَّعْدِ. Rolls, archives, بَيْتُ ٱلْأَسْفَارِ ـ الْقُيُودُ ـ الْقُيُودَاتُ. A keeper of the rolls, وَرَّاق.

Master of the Rolls, صَدْرُ مَحْكَمَةٍ عَالِيَةٍ فِي مَدِينَةِ لَنْدَن.

Roll-call, *n.* اِسْتِدْعَاءُ كُلِّ جُنْدِيٍّ بِٱسْمِهِ.

Rolls-Court, مَحْكَمَةٌ عَالِيَةٌ فِي مَدِينَةِ لَنْدَن.

Roller, *n.* A cylinder, أُسْطُوَانَة ـ سَارِيَة *pl.* أَسَاطِينُ *and* أُسْطُوَانَات ـ عَامُود *pl.* أَعْمِدَة. A — for levelling the ground, مِحْدَلَة. A wrapper, مِلَفّ ـ مِجَلَّة ـ جِلال *pl.* جُلّ. A bandage, compress, رِفَادَة *pl.* رَفَائِدُ ـ عِصَابَة *pl.* عَصَائِبُ. A —, for pastry, شُوْبَك *pl.* شَوَابِكُ ـ شُوْبَق ـ مِحْلَاج ـ مِحْوَر. A —, or rolling stone, for rolling clods, رَحًى *pl.* أَرْحَآء. A baker's —, أُسْطُوَانَة ـ شُوْبَق ـ كَرِيب. A — for drawing out, as into plates, آلَةُ التَّرْقِيقِ ـ مِصْفَحَة. A rolling beast, دَابَّةٌ مِرْغَاغَةٌ. A rolling pigeon, مُرَعِّش وَهُوَ نَوْعٌ مِنَ الْحَمَامِ. A rolling ship, سَفِينَةٌ مَرْكَبٌ مُتَقَلِّبٌ ـ مُتَخَبِّطَةٌ. Roller, a heavy wave, آذِيٌّ *pl.* أَوَاذِيُّ; rollers, waves, أَوَاذِيُّ ـ حَبَابُ الْمَوْجِ.

Rollick, *v.i.* تَغَطْرَسَ ـ تَخَطَّلَ ـ تَعَيَّلَ.

Rollicking, *a.* مُتَغَطْرِس ـ مَيَّاح ـ فَيَّاد ـ عَيَّال.

Rolling, *n.* *See* Roll, *n.*

Rolling, *a.* As on a plane, مُتَدَأْدِئ ـ مُدَحْرَج; as of thunder, رَاعِد ـ مُجَلِّب; as of a ship, مُتَقَلِّب. *See also under* Roller, *n.*

Rolling-pin, *n.* For paste, شُوْبَك ـ فَيْلَكُون ـ مِحْلَاج ـ مِحْوَر *pl.* شَوَابِكُ.

Rolling-press, *n.* مَكْبَس ـ مِلْزَمَةُ التَّرْقِيقِ ـ مِلْزَمُ التَّصْفِيحِ ذُو أَسَاطِين *pl.* مَكَابِسُ.

Rolling-stock, *n.* *See under* Stock, *n.*

Roly-poly, *n.* The pudding, ضَرْبٌ مِنَ الْحَلْوَى فِي شَكْلِ الْأُسْطُوَانَةِ مَحْشُوٌّ بِمُرَبَّى.

Romaic, *a.* رُومِيٌّ. The — language, لِسَانُ الرُّومِ.

Roman, *a.* رُومَانِيٌّ. Roman Catholic, بَابَاوِيٌّ ـ لَاتِينِيٌّ. A — nose, أَنْفٌ أَقْنَى ـ أَنْفٌ قُعْبٌ.

Roman, *n.* A native of Rome, مِنْ أَهْلِ رُومِيَّةَ.

Romance, *n.* A fabulous tale, خُرَافَة *pl.* خُرَافَات ـ حِكَايَة *pl.* حِكَايَات ـ قِصَّةٌ اخْتِرَاعِيَّةٌ. A lie, كَاذِبَة ـ كَذِب. The dialect so called, لُغَةٌ كَانَتْ مُسْتَعْمَلَةً قَدِيمًا فِي جَنُوبِ فَرَنْسَا.

Romance, *v.i.* To write fictions, أَلَّفَ ـ صَنَّفَ الْخُرَافَاتِ الْحِكَايَاتِ. To tell stories, قَصَّ الْقِصَصَ ـ حَكَى حِكَايَاتٍ. *See also to* Lie, *v.i.*

Romancer, *n.* قَصَّاص ـ مُصَنِّفُ الْخُرَافَاتِ.

Romanesque, *a.* Fabulous, خُرَافِيٌّ ـ خَيَالِيٌّ ـ أَسَاطِيرِيٌّ ـ مِنْ قَبِيلِ الْأَسَاطِيرِ.

Romanism, *n.* مَذْهَبُ الْبَابَاوِيَّةِ ـ عَقَائِدُ الْكَنِيسَةِ اللَّاتِينِيَّةِ.

Romanist, *n.* بَابَاوِيٌّ *pl.* بَابَاوِيَّة ـ تَابِعُ الْكَنِيسَةِ اللَّاتِينِيَّةِ.

Romanize, *v.t.* صَيَّرَ بَابَاوِيًّا ـ قَلَبَ إِلَى الْمَذْهَبِ اللَّاتِينِيِّ.

Romanize, *v.i.* صَارَ بَابَاوِيًّا ـ تَدَيَّنَ بِالدِّينِ اللَّاتِينِيِّ.

Romantic, *a.* Fanciful, خَيَالِيٌّ ـ أَسَاطِيرِيٌّ ـ مِنْ قَبِيلِ الْأَسَاطِيرِ. Sentimental, مُرَقِّقُ الْقَلْبِ. Wild, بَرِّيٌّ ـ وَحْشِيٌّ.

Romantically, *ad.* Fancifully, تَخَيُّلًا ـ تَخَيِّيًا. In a wild situation, فِي مَحَلِّ الْوَحْشَةِ ـ فِي وَحْشَةٍ ـ وَحْشَةً. Extravagantly, بِخَبَلِ عَقْلٍ ـ بِفَرْطٍ ـ إِفْرَاطًا.

Romanticism, *n.* تَخَيُّل.

Romanticness, *n.* Wildness, وَحْشَة ـ حَالُ الْوَحْشَةِ ـ صَحْرَآء. Extravagance, folly, حُمْق ـ حَمَاقَة ـ خَلَلُ الْعَقْلِ (*or* خَبَلُ) ـ جُنُون.

Rome, *n.* رُومِيَّة.

Romish, *a.* Of Rome, رُومَانِيٌّ. Roman Catholic, بَابَاوِيٌّ ـ لَاتِينِيٌّ.

Romist, *n.* *See* Romanist, *n.*

Romp, *n.* A boisterous girl, بِنْتٌ فَرْتَعٌ ـ صَبِيَّةٌ بَلْهَآءُ ـ بِنْتٌ فَخِلَة. Frolic, تَلَعُّب.

Romp, *v.i.* تَصَبَّى ـ تَصَابَى ـ مَزَحَ ـ لَعِبَ ـ تَصَعْرَنَ ـ تَوَلْدَنَ.

Rompish, *a.* مُتَصَبٍّ ـ مُتَصَابٍ ـ لَعْبَانُ ـ لَعَّاب.

Rompishness, *n.* تَصَبٍّ ـ تَصَابٍ ـ تَلَعُّب.

Rondeau, *n.* }
Rondo, } A poem in three couplets, قَصِيدَةٌ مُثَلَّثَةُ الْأَبْيَاتِ. A piece of music in three strains, مَقَامَةٌ ذَاتُ ثَلَاثِ نَغَمَاتٍ.

Rood, *n.* A crucifix, صُورَةُ الْمَصْلُوبِ. The fourth of an acre, رُبْعُ فَدَّانٍ.

Roof, *n.* The upper covering of a building, سَقْف *pl.* سُقُوف ـ سَطْح *pl.* سُطُوح. The materials of a —, غَمًى ـ غِمَآء. A vaulted —, عَقْد *pl.* عُقُود ـ قُبَّة *pl.* قُبَب *and* أَقْبَاب. A ridged —, جَمَالُون *pl.* جَمَالِين. A projecting —, جَنَاح. The — of a carriage, سَطْحُ الْعَرَبَانَةِ. The — of the mouth, حَنَك *pl.* أَحْنَاك: his tongue clave to the — of his mouth, لَصِقَ لِسَانُهُ بِحَنَكِهِ. Without a — to cover his head, لَيْسَ لَهُ أَيْنَ يُسْنِدُ رَأْسَهُ.

Roof, *v.t.* To cover with a roof, سَقَفَ ـ سَقَّفَ. To — with a vault, عَقَّدَ ـ قَبَّبَ. To lodge, آوَى ـ بَوَّأَ ـ أَنْزَلَ.

Roofing, *n.* The act of, تَسْقِيف. Materials for —, غِمَآء ـ غَمًى ـ مَوَادُّ التَّسْقِيفِ.

Roofless, *a.* Without a roof, مِن غَيْرِ سَطْحٍ ـ بِدُونِ سَقْفٍ. Without shelter, مِن غَيْرِ مَأْوًى ـ بِدُونِ مَنْزِلٍ. *See also* Homeless, *a.*

Roofy, *a.* مُسَقَّف ـ كَثِيرُ السُّقُوفِ.

Rook, *n.* The bird, زَاغ *pl.* زِيغَان. The — at chess, الرُّخّ. A cheat, مَكَّار ـ غَدَّار ـ مُزَوِّر.

Rook, *v.t.* *See to* Cheat, Defraud, *v.t.*

Rookery, *n.* For rooks, مَحَلُّ ٱلزِّيغَانِ. A low place, مَحَلٌّ سَفِيلٌ.

Rooky, *a.* كَثِيرُ ٱلزِّيغَانِ.

Room, *n.* Space, سَعَة — مَحَلّ — فُسْحَة — مَكَان — مَوْضِع — مَطْرَح. An apartment, حُجْرَة *pl.* حُجَر — بَيْت *pl.* بُيُوت — *vulg.* أُوضَة *pl.* أُوَض. A — on the ground floor, سَهْوَة *pl.* سِهَآء. A — in a house other than an upper —, عَرْصَة *pl.* أَعْرَاص *and* عَرَصَات. Rooms, *n.* In the sense of a hall or office of a literary society, نَدْوَةُ ٱلْجَمَاعَةِ. To make — for, أَرْحَبَ ل — فَرَّجَ ل — فَسَحَ ل — تَفَسَّحَ ل — وَسَّعَ ل. To take up —, اِسْتَوْعَبَ — وَسِعَ *aor.* يَسَعُ. So that there was no — for it, حَتَّى لَمْ يَعُدْ يَسَعُهُ. There was no — for him in the house, لَمْ يَكُنْ لَهُ مَوْضِعٌ فِي ٱلْمَنْزِلِ. I have no — to collect my books together, لَيْسَ لِي مَوْضِعٌ أَجْمَعُ فِيهِ كُتُبِي. There is — yet, يُوجَدُ أَيْضًا مَكَانٌ. Is there — in the house for us to pass the night, هَلْ فِي ٱلْبَيْتِ مَكَانٌ لِنَبِيتَ. In the — of, مَحَلَّ — مَكَانَ: in his —, مَكَانَهُ; in their —, مَكَانَهُمْ. He placed him in the —, place, of his father, جَعَلَهُ مَكَانَ أَبِيهِ. He was placed in the — of his father, جُعِلَ فِي مَكَانِ أَبِيهِ. To set in the — of ..., جَعَلَ مَكَانَ فُلَانٍ. Make room! أَرْحِبْ.

Ball-room, مَحَلُّ ٱلرَّقْصِ — بَيْتُ ٱلزِّفَافِ — صَالُونُ ٱلْبَالُو.

Bed-room, مَنَامَة — بَيْتُ ٱلنَّوْمِ — خَلْوَةُ ٱلرُّقَادِ.

Dining-room, مَأْكَل — بَيْتُ ٱلْأَكْلِ.

Drawing-room, بَيْتُ ٱلْمُسَافِرِينَ — صَالُون.

Sitting-room, بَيْتُ ٱلْقُعُودِ — مَقْعَد — أُوضَةُ ٱلدِّيوَانِ.

State-room, قَاعَة — دِيوَان; of a ship, طَارِمَة — مَقْعَد.

Student's room, as in a college, رِوَاق *pl.* أَرْوِقَة.

Underground room, مَطْمُورَة — سِرْدَاب *pl.* سَرَادِيب.

Upper room, عِلِّيَّة *pl.* عَلَالِيّ — غُرْفَة — حُجْرَة فَوْقَانِيَّة.

Waiting room, بَيْتُ ٱلْإِنْتِظَارِ.

Roomfull, *n.* بَيْتٌ مَشْحُونٌ — حُجْرَةٌ مُمْتَلِئَةٌ.

Roominess, *n.* فُسْحَة — رُحْب — سَعَة.

Roomy, *a.* رَحْب — رَحِيب — فَسِيح — وَاسِع — وَسِيع. To be —, فَسَحَ — رَحُبَ — وَسِعَ *aor.* يَسَعُ — اِتَّسَعَ.

Roost, *n.* As for fowl, مَجْثَم — مَحَلُّ (*or* عُود) جُثُومِ ٱلطُّيُورِ. To go to —; *see next article.*

Roost, *v.i.* As of a fowl, جَثَمَ ٱلطَّيْرُ لِلنَّوْمِ — قَعَدَ عَلَى ٱلْمَجْثَمِ.

Rooster, *n.* A cock, دِيك *pl.* دُيُوك — أَبُو يَقْظَانَ.

Root, *n.* Of a tree, جِذْر *or* جَذْر *pl.* جُذُور — عِرْق *pl.* عُرُوق — أَصْل *pl.* أُصُول — جُرْثُومَة *pl.* جَرَاثِيم; a slender —, شِرْش *pl.* شُرُوش. A source, origin, جِذْم *pl.* أَجْذَام — أَصْل *pl.* أُصُول — مَصْدَر — مَنْشَأ — مَبْدَأ — مَنْبَع; specially of lineage, جُرْثُومَة — عُنْصُر — مَنْصِب. A cause, سَبَب. A square —, شَيْء *pl.* أَشْيَآء — ضِلْع *pl.* أَضْلَاع — جَذْر *pl.* جُذُور — جَذْرٌ مُرَبَّعٌ. A cube —, جَذْرٌ مُكَعَّبٌ. Having a —, عَرِيق. Root, as of a word, the infinitive noun, ٱلْمَصْدَرُ. The —, as of the tongue, عَكَدَة — عَلْصَمَة; of the ear, مَغْد; of a tooth, جِذْم — سِنْخ; of the tail, عَجْب; especially of a bird's tail, زِمِكَّى. The trees struck their roots into the ground, ضَرَبَ ٱلشَّجَرُ بِعُرُوقِهِ فِي ٱلْأَرْضِ — أَعْرَقَ ٱلشَّجَرُ. Root and branch, أَصْلًا وَفَرْعًا. To pull up by the roots, as of vegetables, weeds, *etc.*, اِجْتَفَّ — اِجْتَفَأَ. To take —, to Root out or up; *see the next two articles.*

Root, *v.i.* To take root, تَأَصَّلَ — اِسْتَأْصَلَ — أَعْرَقَ. To be rooted, grounded, in, أَصُلَ: He was well rooted in it, أَصُلَهُ عِلْمًا — قَتَلَهُ عِلْمًا. Rooted in knowledge, رَاسِخٌ فِي ٱلْعِلْمِ. To —, as a swine with the nose, حَفَرَ ٱلْأَرْضَ — نَبَشَ ٱلْأَرْضَ بِٱلْبُوزِ بِفِنْطِيسَتِهِ.

Root, *v.t.* To plant deeply, firmly, أَصَّلَ. To make to have a foundation, to fix firmly, أَثَّلَ — أَرْسَخَ — أَصَّلَ. To — out, اِسْتَأْصَلَ — قَلَعَ ٱلْأَصْلَ — أَجَثَّ — جَثَّ. *See also under to* Eradicate, *v.t.*

Rooted, *a.* Having a root, ذُو أَصْلٍ — أَصِيل — عَرِيق. Fixed, firm, أَصِيل — مُؤَصَّل — رَاسِخ. Rooted and grounded in knowledge, مُتَأَصِّلٌ وَمُتَأَسِّسٌ فِي ٱلْعِلْمِ. *See also under* to Root, *v.i.* *also under* Grounded, *a.*

Rootedly, *ad.* تَأَصُّلًا — تَأَسُّسًا — بِرُسُوخٍ.

Rootlet, *n.* شِرْش *pl.* شُرُوش. *See also* Radicle, *n.*

Rooty, *a.* كَثِيرُ ٱلْجُذُورِ.

Rope, *n.* A large cord, رَسَن *pl.* رُسُن — جَرِير *pl.* أَجِرَّة — مَرَس *pl.* مَرَسَة *and* أَمْرَاس — حَبْل *pl.* أَحْبَال. A slender —, حَبْلٌ دَقِيقٌ. A — of three strands, حَبْلٌ مَثْلُوثٌ; of six, مَسْدُوس; of seven or more, مَسْبُوع. A leading —, مِقْوَد. A well-rope, حَبْلُ ٱلدَّلْوِ — رِشَآء *pl.* أَرْشِيَة — تِرْشَآء. A twisted —, قَلِيذ — مَقْلُوذ. A — made of twisted hair or leather, جَدِيل *pl.* جُدُل. A tent-rope, طُنُب *pl.* أَطْنَاب. Any — to tie with, رِبَاط — مِرْبَط. A looped — to ascend palm-trees, حَابُول — مِصْعَاد — كَرّ — طَوْق. Ropes of sails, كَرّ *pl.* كُرُور. To let down by a —, دَلَّى بِحَبْلٍ. He pulled up the bucket with a —, أَدْلَى ٱلدَّلْوَ بِحَبْلٍ. Rope, a line of things connected, تَسَلْسُل — سِلْسِلَة.

Rope, *v.i.* As of viscous matter, تَمَطَّطَ — تَسَعَّبَ.

Rope-dancer, *n.* بَهْلَوَان *pl.* بَهَالْوِين.

Rope-dancing, *n.* بَهْلَوَانِيَّة.

Rope-maker, *n.* حَبَّال.

Rope-making, *n.* حَبَّالَة.

Ropery, *n.* / Rope-walk, } مَعْمَلُ ٱلْأَحْبَالِ ـ حَبَّالَة.

Rope-yarn, *n.* تِيِيل.

Ropiness, *n.* تَمَطُّط ـ تَسَعُّب.

Ropy, *a.* Viscid, مُتَمَطِّط ـ مُتَسَعِّب.

Roquelaur, *n.* بُرْنُس *pl.* برانِس ـ مَشْلَح *pl.* مَشَالِح.

Roral, *a.* *See* Dewy, *a.*

Rorqual, *n.* ضَرْبٌ مِنَ ٱلْحُوتِ ـ ضَرْبٌ مِنَ ٱلْبَالِ.

Rosaceous, *a.* مِثْلَ ـ وَرْدِيّ.

Rosary, *n.* Where roses grow, بِسْتَانُ وَرْدٍ. A string of beads such as is used by Muslims, مِسْبَحَة ـ سُبْحَة; by Christians, وَرْدِيَّة.

Rose, *n.* وَرْدَة *coll.* وَرْد *pl.* وُرُود. Under the —, under pretext, بِحُجَّة; secretly, عَلَى خَفَآء ـ خُفْيَةً. To do things under the —, ـ فَعَلَ-خُفْيَةً.

Carnation rose, وَرْدٌ نَصِيبِيّ.

Damask rose, وَرْدٌ جُورِيّ.

Dog-rose, نِسْرِين.

Double or Cluster rose, (مُطَبَّق *or*) وَرْدٌ مُضَاعَف.

Ottar or Otto of Roses, عِطْرُ ٱلْوَرْدِ.

Peony rose, وَرْدُ ٱلْحَمِيرِ.

Rose water, مَآءُ وَرْدٍ.

Wild or Meadow rose, وَرْدٌ جَبَلِيّ.

Roseate, *a.* Of a rose colour, وَرْدِيّ ـ وَرْد *fem.* وَرْدَة. Blooming, blossoming, مُنَوِّر; cheerful, سَارّ ـ فَارِح ـ طَرِب ـ يَحْبُور. A — evening sky, عَشِيَّةٌ وَرْدَة.

Rose-bay, *n.* الدِّفْلَى.

Rose-diamond, *n.* أَلْمَاسٌ وَرْدِيّ.

Rosemary, *n.* عَبَيْثُرَان ـ إِكْلِيلُ ٱلْجَبَلِ ـ حَصَى لِبَانٍ أَخْضَر.

Rosette, *n.* عُقْدَةٌ فِي هَيْئَةِ ٱلْوَرْدِ ـ عُقْدَة.

Rose-window, *n.* طَاقَةٌ فِي شَكْلِ ٱلْوَرْدِ ـ كُوَّةٌ مُدَوَّرَة.

Rosewood, *n.* بَقَّمٌ قُبْرُصِيّ.

Rosicrucian, *a.* إِسْمٌ لِطَائِفَةٍ مِنَ ٱلْكِيمَاوِيِّينَ ٱلنِّمْسَاوِيِّينَ ذَوِي خُيَلَاءَ قَدِ ٱدَّعُوا مُنْذُ قَرْنَيْنِ بِكَمَالِ ٱلْفُنُونِ.

Rosin, *n.* *See* Resin, *n.*

Rosin, *v.t.* *See to* Resin, *v.t.*

Rosiness, *n.* تَوَرُّد; of complexion, شُقْرَة. *See also* Ruddiness, *n.*

Rosiny, *a.* *See* Resinous.

Roster, *n.* جَدْوَل *pl.* جَدَاوِلُ ـ دَفْتَر *pl.* دَفَاتِرُ ـ بِيَاقَة.

Rostral, *a.* Resembling a beak, بِشَكْلِ ٱلْمِنْقَارِ; like the beak of a ship, بِشَكْلِ مِنْطَحِ ٱلْمَرْكَبِ.

Rostrate, *a.* Having a beak, ذُو مِنْقَارٍ.

Rostrated, *a.* Having a beak, ذُو مِنْقَارٍ; of a ship, ذُو مِنْطَحٍ.

Rostriform, *a.* بِشَكْلِ ٱلْمِنْقَارِ.

Rostrum, *n.* A beak, مِنْقَار ـ مِنْقَاف. A platform for orators, مِنْبَر *pl.* مَنَابِرُ ـ كُرْسِيّ.

Rosy, *a.* Like a rose, مِثْلَ ٱلْوَرْدِ ـ وَرْدَة *fem.* وَرْد ـ وَرْدِيّ. Dyed of a — colour, مُوَرَّد. Blooming, cheerful, فَارِح ـ طَرِب ـ سَارّ. Blushing, خَجِل. *See also* Ruddy, *a.*

Rot, *v.i.* In a general sense, فَسَدَ [2] ـ إِسْتَفْسَدَ. Of eggs and nuts, مَذِرَ ـ تَمَذَّرَ ـ أَنِخَ [2]; of meat, عَفِنَ ـ تَعَفَّنَ ـ ; of wood, نَخِرَ ـ سَوَّسَ ـ تَسَوَّسَ ـ أَسَاسَ; of a tooth, سَوَّسَ ـ أَسَاسَ; of the bone, أَرَمَّ ـ بَلِيَ ـ رَمَّ *aor.* يَرِمُّ; of a water-skin, تَعَيَّنَ; of fruits, تَعَفَّنَ; of a rope, عَفِنَ ـ تَعَفَّنَ ـ رَمَّ *aor.* يَرِمُّ; of clothes, رَمَّ *aor.* يَرِمُّ.

Rot, *v.t.* Of eggs or nuts, أَمْذَرَ; of meat, أَنْخَ ـ عَفَّنَ; of wood, or a tooth, سَوَّسَ; of the bones, or of clothes, أَبْلَى ـ بَلَّى.

Rot, *n.* Putrefaction, تَعَفُّن ـ عُفُونَة ـ إِسْتِفْسَاد. The — in sheep, مُوَتَان ـ فَصْلُ ٱلْغَنَمِ.

Rota, *n.* The — of Rome, إِسْمٌ لِمَجْمَعٍ بِرُومِيَّةَ مُؤَلَّفٍ مِنِ ٱثْنَيْ عَشَرَ أُسْقُفًا.

Rotary, *a.* دَوَّار ـ دَوَّارِيّ. Rotary or rotatory dust, جَوْلَان.

Rotate, *v.i.* دَارَ *aor.* يَدُورُ ـ إِسْتَدَارَ ـ أَدَارَ.

Rotate, *v.t.* دَوَّرَ ـ أَدَارَ.

Rotation, *n.* The act of turning on itself, إِدَارَة ـ دَوَرَان ـ دَوْر. By —, بِٱلدَّوْرِ ـ بِٱلنَّوْبَةِ. *See also under* Turn, *n.*

Rotative, *a.* / Rotatory, } *See* Rotary, *a.*

Rote, *n.* Frequent repetition of words, تَكْرُرُ ٱلْكَلَامِ. To learn by —, حَفِظَ-عَلَى ظَهْرِ قَلْبِهِ ـ حَفِظَ-غَيْبًا. To repeat by —, حَكَى-عَلَى ظَهْرِ قَلْبِهِ ـ تَقَصَّصَ.

Rotten, *a.* As of eggs, or nuts, مَذِر; of meat, عَفِن ـ نَخَّان; of wood, مَعْفُون; of the bones, clothes, rope, *etc.*, رِمَام ـ رَمِيم; of the teeth, مُسَوَّس ـ كَفُوف; of fruits, نَخِر ـ نَاخِر ـ مُتَسَوِّس. Unsound, سَاقِط ـ نَاقِص ـ سَقِط ـ فَاسِد. Rotten garments, مَلَابِسُ بَالِيَة ـ مُعَفَّن.

Rottenness, *n.* As of eggs or nuts, تَمَذُّر; of meat, عُفُونَة — مُخُوخ; of the bones, clothes, rope, *etc.*, رِمَّ; of wood, نَخِيرَة — سُوس; of the teeth, تَسَوُّس — سُوس; of fruits, عُفُونَة. Unsoundness, نُقْصَان — سَقَط — فَسَاد.

Rotten-stone, *n.* حَجَرُ طَرَابُلُس — خُرَاسَان — سُنْبَاذَج.

Rotund, *a.* Round and flat, مُقَرَّص. Spherical, كُرِيّ — كُرَوِيّ — مُدَوَّر — مُسْتَدِير. Fat, stout, جَسِيم — ضَخْم — ضَخَام. To be —, stout, ضَخُمَ ².

Rotunda, *n.* }
Rotundo, } قُبَّة *pl.* قُبَب — بِنَآءُ مُدَوَّر — بَيْتٌ مُدَوَّر.

Rotundifolious, *a.* ذُو أَوْرَاقٍ مُدَوَّرَة.

Rotundity, *n.* Roundness, تَدْوِيرَة — إِسْتِدَارَة; sphericity, كُرَوِيَّة — كُرَة. Fatness, stoutness, جَسَامَة — ضَخْم — ضَخَامَة.

Rouble, *n.* إِسْمُ سِكَّةٍ مِنْ فِضَّةٍ فِي ٱلرُّوسِيَا.

Roué, *n.* *See* Debauchee, *n.*

Rouge, *n.* طِلَآءٌ تُحَمِّرُ بِهِ ٱلْمَرْأَةُ وَجْهَهَا — كُلْگُون — دِمَام — حُمْرَة.

Rouge, *v.t.* دَهَنَ بِحُمْرَةٍ ² (*or* بِكُلْگُون *or* بِدِمَام). She rouged her cheeks, دَهَنَتْ خَدَّيْهَا بِحُمْرَة.

Rouge, *v.i.* إِسْتَعْمَلَ ٱلْحُمْرَة.

Rough, *a.* Of the skin, or new coin, notched, or coarse, أَحْرَش *fem.* حَرْشَآءُ ² *pl.* حُرْش. Burly, hardy, coarse, خَشِب — خَشِيب — أَخْشَب. Rough to the feel, خَشِن — حَرِش — شَرِس; especially of a new garment, أَشْوَك *fem.* شَوْكَآءُ ²; of cloth, قَاسِح. Rough, of temper, غَلِيظ — خَشِن — عَنِيف — جَافٍ — أَفَظّ — أَشْرَس; of sound, أَجَشّ *fem.* جَشَّآء — أَبَحّ *fem.* بَحَّآءُ ² *and* بَحَّة *pl.* بُحّ; to the taste, فَظّ — عَزِيز — عَزّ; in manners, حَادّ — حِرِّيف; of the weather, مُقْشَعِرّ; of a wind, عَاصِف; of a road, وَعِر. Violent, difficult, عَزِيز — صَعْب — شَدِيد. Rude, stupid, أَخْرَق — خَرِق. Rough-hewn and not yet trimmed, خَشِيبٌ لَمْ يُنَقَّح. Raw, unwrought, خَام. Approximate, قَرِيب — تَقْرِيبًا. To be or become —, hard, tough, callous, جَسَأَ ³: his hand became —, جَسَأَتْ يَدُهُ; the ground became —, hard, جَسِئَتِ ٱلْأَرْضُ. To fashion a thing in the —, خَشَبَ ³. To be —, as of the sea, مَاجَ ². To be —, cruel, harsh, قَسَحَ ³ — فَظَّ ³. To be hard, coarse, خَشُنَ ² — غَلُظَ ³. Rough ground, أَرْضٌ خَشْبَآء; rough places, عَرَاقِيب. A — guess, حَدْس — حَدْسُ ٱلظَّنّ — تَخْمِين. A — cloth or wrapper, مُلَآءَةٌ خَشْنَآءُ ². A — edge, as of cloth, هُدْب — هُدَّاب — شَرَارِيب. The — edge of appetite, شِدَّةُ ٱلْإِشْتِهَآء. He lived a — life, عَاشَ عَيْشًا خَشِنًا ³ — إِخْشَوْشَبَ فِي عَيْشِهِ. *See also* Harsh, Rugged, *a.*

Rough, *n.* A base fellow, سُفْلِيّ. The roughs, ٱلْأَوْبَاش.

Rough, *v.i.* To lead a rough life; *see under preceding article.* To bear, إِحْتَمَلَ — تَعَزَّى — تَصَبَّرَ.

Rough-cast, *v.t.* خَشَبَ ³.

Rough-cast, *a.* خَشِيب — مَخْشُوب.

Rough-draught, *n.* مُسَوَّدَة — تَسْوِيد.

Rough-draw, *v.t.* سَوَّدَ.

Roughen, *v.i.* To become rough, تَخَشَّنَ — غَلُظَ ³. *See also under* Rough, *a.*

Roughen, *v.t.* خَشَّنَ — غَلَّظَ.

Rough-hew, *v.t.* خَشَبَ ³.

Rough-hewn, *a.* خَشِيب — مَخْشُوب.

Roughly, *ad.* Rudely, coarsely, بِخُرْقٍ — بِخُشُونَةٍ — بِغِلَاظَةٍ. Harshly, بِشَرَاسَةٍ — بِعُنْفٍ — بِجَفَآءٍ — بِقَسْرٍ. Roughly, to the ear, بِجُشَّةٍ — بِصَرِيفَةٍ — بِبُحَّةٍ; to the taste, بِحَرَافَةٍ — بِحَرَارَةٍ. To treat —, خَاشَنَ — أَعْنَفَ — قَاهَرَ — غَلُظَ عَلَى — عَاسَرَ. To speak — to, تَكَلَّمَ مَعَ بِجَفَآءٍ. He took the thing —, أَعْنَفَ ٱلشَّيْءَ ². He did a thing —, in an unstudied manner, جَآءَ بِٱلْمَخْشُوبِ. To live —, إِخْشَوْشَنَ — تَخَشَّنَ. To guess —, حَدَسَ ³ — خَمَّنَ ². *See also* Harshly, *ad.*

Roughness, *n.* Thickness, coarseness, خُشُونَة — خَشَانَة — غِلَظ — غِلَاظَة; of temper, جَفَآء — عُنْف — مُظَاظَة; of weather, شِدَّة; of wind, عَصْف; of the voice, بُحَّة — جُشَّة — صَرِيف; of the sea, مَوْج — تَمَوُّج; to the taste, حَرَافَة — حَرَارَة; to the touch, قَسَاحَة; of a road, وَعْر — وُعُور; of the intellect, خُرْق. Callosity, as of the hands, also ruggedness, جُسُوءٌ — جَسْأ. To have the feeling of roughness, as after shaving, شَوَّكَ. *See also* Harshness, Ruggedness, *n.*

Rough-rider, *n.* مُرَوِّضُ ٱلْخَيْلِ — مُطَبِّعُ ٱلْخَيْلِ.

Roughshod, *a.* مُبَيْطَر (*or* مُنَعَّل) وِقَايَةً عَنِ ٱلزَّلَقِ عَلَى ٱلثَّلْجِ (*or* ٱلْجَلِيدِ). To ride — over one, قَسَرَ ³ — هَوَّرَ — أَقْهَرَ — قَهَرَ ³ — إِقْتَسَرَ عَلَى — عَلَى.

Rouleau, *n.* A —, as of money, قِرْطَاس *pl.* قَرَاطِيس. *See also* Roll, *n.*

Roumania, *n.* Consisting of Wallachia and Moldavia, رُومَانِيَا أَيِ ٱلْأَفْلَاقُ وَبُغْدَانُ.

Round, *a.* Circular, مُدَوَّر — مُسْتَدِير. Flat and —, مُقَرَّص. Spherical, كُرِيّ — كُرَوِيّ. Cylindrical, مُدَمْلَج — عَامُودِيّ — فِي شَكْلِ ٱلْأُسْطُوَانَةِ. Round with an opening in the centre, as a crown, *etc.*, مُجَوَّف — حَلْقَة. Round, made —, like a ball, مُكَبَّب — مُكَبْكَب — مُكَبْتَل — مُدَعْبَل. Large, عَظِيم: A —

sum, مَبْلَغٌ عَظِيمٌ . Quick, سَرِيعٌ ـ حَثِيثٌ ـ خَفِيفٌ : A — trot, رَتْكٌ خَفِيفٌ . Fat, stout, سَمِينٌ ـ شَحِيمٌ ـ فَعْمٌ ـ ضَخْمٌ . Frank, نَاصِحٌ ـ سَلِيمٌ . Severe, عَنِيفٌ ـ صَارِمٌ ـ قَاسٍ ـ شَدِيدٌ . A — number, عَدَدٌ تَامٌّ بِدُونِ كُسُورٍ . A — game, لُعْبَةٌ مُسْتَدِيرَةٌ ـ لَعْبُ ٱلدَّائِرَةِ .

Round, *n.* A circle, دَوَائِرُ *pl.* دَائِرَةٌ ـ أَدْوَارٌ *pl.* دَوْرٌ . A ring, حَلْقَةٌ *pl.* حِلَقٌ . A hoop, حِتَارٌ *pl.* حُتُرٌ . A sphere, كُرَةٌ *pl.* كُرَاتٌ . A turn, دَوْرٌ *pl.* أَدْوَارٌ ـ نَوْبَةٌ *pl.* نَوْبَاتٌ . A twist, دَوْرٌ *pl.* أَدْوَارٌ ـ لَفٌّ *pl.* لُفُوفٌ ـ فَتْلٌ ـ فَتْلَةٌ . A walk, سَيْرٌ ـ سَيْرَةٌ ـ دَوْرَةٌ ـ شَمُّ ٱلْهَوَآءِ . The rundle of a ladder, دَرَجَةُ سُلَّمٍ *pl.* دَرَجَاتٌ . A successive or periodical visitation, دَوْرَةٌ . A single assault, دَوْرٌ ـ هَجْمَةٌ . A charge of ammunition, تَعْمِيرَةٌ (عَمَارُ *or*) بَارُودٍ *pl.* تَعْمِيرَاتٌ . A volley, of guns, إِطْلَاقُ مَدَافِعَ . A — of applause, هُتَافٌ بِٱلثَّنَآءِ (*or* بِٱلْقَبُولِ) . A — of beef, كُتْلَةٌ مِنْ لَحْمِ بَقَرٍ . Rounds, patrol, عَاسٌّ *pl.* عَسَسٌ ـ عَسَسٌ ـ طَائِفٌ ـ قَوْلٌ : to go the rounds, to patrol, عَسَّ ـ إِعْتَسَّ ـ طَافَ ع ـ طَافَ ٱلْقَوْلُ ع . To go the — of, دَارَ ع . To take a —; *see to* Promenade, *v.i.*

Round, *v.t.* To make circular, أَدَارَ ـ دَوَّرَ ـ صَعْرَرَ . To make — and flat, قَرَّصَ . To make into a sphere, صَيَّرَ كُرَةً ـ دَوَّرَ . To cut —, قَصَّ مُسْتَدِيرًا ع . To go — a place, سَافَرَ ـ دَارَ حَوْلَ ٱلْمَحَلِّ ع ـ طَافَ حَوْلَ ٱلْمَكَانِ ع ـ عَدَّى حَوْلَ ٱلْمَكَانِ . To walk —, طَيَّفَ . To —, as of a period, sentence, فَصَّحَ فِي ـ بَلَغَ فِي ٱلْعِبَارَةِ ع ٱلْجُمْلَةِ . To —, or make —, by rubbing in the hands, كَمَزَ . To —, to make into balls, حَبَّبَ ـ كَبَّبَ .

Round, *v.i.* To become round, إِسْتَدَارَ . To become —, comely, حَسُنَ ع ـ جَمُلَ ع . To go —, دَارَ حَوْلَ ٱلْمَحَلِّ ع . The moon rounded, became full, إِسْتَدَارَ ٱلْقَمَرُ .

Round, *ad.* or *prep.* About, near, حَوْلَ ـ عِنْدَ ـ جَنْبَ . On all sides, مِنْ كُلِّ جَانِبٍ ـ حَوَالَيْ . All —, on all sides, مِنْ كُلِّ جَانِبٍ ; by turns, بِٱلدَّوْرِ ; one after another, عُرْفًا عُرْفًا ـ وَاحِدًا بَعْدَ وَاحِدٍ ; consecutively, بِٱلتَّتَابُعِ ; all together, طُرًّا ـ بِأَسْرِهِمْ ـ بَتَّةً ـ كَافَّةً ـ جُمْلَةً .

To come round, (or sail round,) to double, سَافَرَ ـ دَارَ حَوْلَ ٱ... ع حَوْلَ ٱ... . To go or walk round, تَطَوَّفَ ـ طَافَ حَوْلَ ٱ... ع حَوْلَ ٱ... . To come to terms with, to be reconciled with, صَالَحَ ; to agree with, رَاضَى ـ وَافَقَ . To come to one's senses, أَفَاقَ ـ أَصْحَى ; to improve in health, بَرِئَ ـ شَفِيَ ـ أَفَاقَ ـ صَحَّ مِنَ ٱلْمَرَضِ . The days come round in their turn, دَارَتِ ٱلْأَيَّامُ .

To get or go round, إِسْتَدَارَ ـ دَارَ ع . To go round, to circulate among, دَارَ بَيْنَ ع : the cup went round, دَارَتْ بَيْنَهُمُ ٱلْكَأْسُ . To get one round, bring to his senses, أَصْحَى ; to recover, صَحَّ ـ شَفِيَ ـ أَشْفَى ـ أَقَامَ . To circumvent, cheat, رَاوَغَ ـ دَاوَرَ ـ غَشَّ ع ـ خَدَعَ ـ خَدَعَ ـ آرَبَ بِ ـ آرَبَ ـ خَتَلَ ع ـ إِحْتَالَ عَلَى .

To go round with, in company with, دَارَ مَعَهُ ع ; to go round with, as in vertigo, دَارَ بِهِ ع .

To go round and round, إِسْتَدَارَ ـ دَارَ ع : it went round on its axis, دَارَ فِي مَدَارِهِ ع .

To hand or pass round, طَافَ عَلَيْهِمْ بِٱلشَّيْءِ ع ـ دَارَ بِ ع .

To make to go round, أَدَارَ بِ ـ دَوَّرَ بِ ـ دَارَ بِ ع ـ دَوَّرَ .

To wind round, لَفَّ ع ـ أَدَارَ : he wound the turban round his head, أَدَارَ ٱلْعِمَامَةَ عَلَى رَأْسِهِ .

Roundabout, *a.* Indirect, دَوَّارِيٌّ ـ مُعَرَّضٌ . Ambiguous, مُشْتَبِهٌ ـ مُلْتَبِسٌ . A — question, تَوْرِيَةٌ ـ مِعْرَاضٌ . A — road, عَوْجَةٌ ـ دَوْرَةٌ ـ لَفَّةٌ .

Roundabout, *n.* A whirligig, دَوَّارَةٌ .

Roundelay, *n.* *See* Rondo, *n.*

Roundhouse, *n.* A prison, حَبْسٌ ـ مَحْبَسٌ . A —, as of a ship, قُبَّةٌ فِي شَكْلِ ٱلْخَيْمَةِ عَلَى سَطْحِ ٱلسَّفِينَةِ ـ قُبَّةٌ مُسْتَدِيرَةٌ .

Roundish, *a.* يَضْرِبُ إِلَى ٱلِٱسْتِدَارَةِ ـ مُدَوَّرٌ نَوْعًا .

Roundishness, *n.* إِسْتِدَارَةٌ ـ صِفَةُ ٱلِٱسْتِدَارَةِ .

Roundlet, *n.* حَلْقَةٌ ـ دَائِرَةٌ صَغِيرَةٌ .

Roundly, *ad.* In a round form, إِسْتِدَارَةً . Openly, بِبَسَاطَةٍ ـ بِصَرَاحَةٍ ـ مِنْ غَيْرِ لَفٍّ . Frankly, نَصِيحَةً ـ صَدَاقَةً . Severely, بِشِدَّةٍ ـ بِصَرَامَةٍ .

Roundness, *n.* Circularity, تَدْوِيرٌ ـ إِسْتِدَارَةٌ . Sphericity, كُرَةٌ ـ صِفَةُ ٱلْكُرَةِ . Roundness with flatness, تَقْرِيصٌ ـ قَرْصٌ . Roundness, as of a scroll or cylinder, إِسْتِدَارَةُ ٱلْعَمُودِ ـ دَمْلَجَةٌ . إِسْتِدَارَةُ ٱلْأُسْطُوَانَةِ . Roundness, as of periods, language, فَصَاحَةٌ ـ بَلَاغَةٌ . Openness, frankness, صَفَآءٌ ـ خُلُوصٌ ـ نُصُوحٌ . Plumpness, ضَخَامَةٌ ـ سَمَانَةٌ ـ خَدَالَةٌ ـ ضَخْمٌ .

Round-ridge, *v.t.* *See to* Ridge, *v.t.*

Round-robin, *n.* عَرْضٌ يُوَقِّعُ أَسَامِيَهُمْ عَلَيْهِ أَصْحَابُ ٱلِٱقْتِرَاحِ ـ عَرْضٌ مَحْضَرٌ ـ عَلَى دَائِرَةٍ حَتَّى لَا يُعْرَفَ مَنْ مِنْهُمُ ٱلزَّعِيمُ .

Rounds, *n.* *See under* Round, *n.*

Round-tower, *n.* بُرْجٌ مُسْتَدِيرٌ ـ بُرُوجٌ *pl.* بُرْجٌ بِشَكْلِ ٱلْعَمُودِ .

Roup, *n.* *See* Auction, *n.*

Rouse, *v.t.* To awaken, صَحَّى ـ أَيْقَظَ ـ يَقَّظَ . To excite, stir up, إِسْتَفَزَّ ـ حَرَّضَ ـ هَيَّجَ ـ أَنْهَضَ ـ حَضَّضَ ـ بَعَثَ . To be roused, as to do anything, فَارَ ع ـ تَهَيَّجَ ـ إِهْتَاجَ ـ إِنْبَعَثَ .

Rouser, *n.* مُسْتَفِزٌّ ـ مُحَرِّضٌ ـ مُنْهِض ـ هَيَّاج.

Rout, *n.* As of an army, كَسْرَة ـ دائرة ـ هَزِيمَة ـ شَرْد. A mob, الأَوْباش ـ أَهْلُ ٱلسُّوقِ. A feast, banquet, ضِيافَة ـ مَأْدُبَة. A dance, رَقْص.

Rout, *v.t.* As of an army, to defeat, كَسَرَ ـ هَزَمَ ـ شَرَّدَ. To be routed, كانَتِ ٱلدَّائِرَةُ عَلَيْهِمْ ـ شَرَدَ ـ إنْكَسَرَ ـ إنْهَزَمَ.

Route, *n.* The course or way travelled, مَذْهَب ـ مَدْرَج ـ مَسْلَك. A way, road, دَرْب *pl.* دُرُوب ـ سَرْب *pl.* سُرُوب ـ طَرِيق *pl.* طُرُق. *En route,* فِي ٱلطَّرِيقِ. *En route* for, مُسافِرٌ إلَى. He took the — to . . . , سَلَكَ ٱلطَّرِيقَ إِلَى كَذا.

Routine, *n.* Round or course of business, طَرْز ـ شَأْن ـ طَوْر ـ عادَة ـ طَرِيقَة. Method, أُسْلُوب ـ مَدان ـ قِدْيَة. Stated order, تَرْتِيب ـ سِياقَة ـ رَسْم ـ أُصُول.

Rove, *v.i.* *See to* Roam, *v.i.*

Rove, *v.t.* To draw, as through an eye, أَسْلَكَ ـ فِي ـ سَلَكَ ـ فِي.

Rover, *n.* *See* Roamer, *n.*

Roving, *a.* *See* Roaming, *a.*

Row, *n.* A line of persons or things, سَطْر مُصْطَفّ ـ شِكَّة ـ صَفّ *pl.* صُفُوف; a line, streak, سَطْر *pl.* سُطُور ـ طُرْقَة *pl.* طُرَق. A —, as of houses, ساق ـ طَوْر *pl.* أَطْوار; of grape-vines, سُرْبَة *pl.* سُرَب; of stones, ساف *pl.* سافات ـ سافَة ـ سُورَة; the same in a wall, مِدْماك *pl.* مَدامِيك ـ عَرَق. A —, series, ساق ـ نَسَق ـ سِياقَة. A —, as of beads on a string, عَرْقَة. To place in a —, صَفَّ ـ صَفَّفَ; to be placed in a —, إصْطَفَّ; placed in a —, مُصْطَفّ ـ مُسَلْسَل. In a —, شِكاكًا ـ سِكاكًا. Tents, or houses, placed in a —, شِكاك: They pitched their tents in one —, ضَرَبُوا بُيُوتَهُمْ شِكاكًا (or سِكاكًا). They built their houses in one —, بَنَوا بُيُوتَهُمْ عَلَى ساقٍ واحِدٍ.

Row, *n.* A disturbance, شَغَب ـ غَيْشَرَة ـ هَوْشَة *pl.* هَوْشات ـ شَغَب ـ غَوْشَة ـ لَجَاجٌ وَصَخَب ـ هَيْشَة. To make or kick up a —, غَوَّشَ ـ حَرَّشَ ـ تَهَيَّجَ ـ صَخِبَ ـ شَغَبًا: They kicked up a —, of many, تَصاخَبُوا ـ إصْطَخَبُوا. *See also* Disturbance, *n.*

Row, *v.t.* To impel with oars, قَذَفَ ـ جَذَفَ; *vulg.* قَدَّفَ. They all — in the same boat, are in the same plight, هُمْ عَلَى حالٍ (or بِساطٍ) واحِدٍ.

Rowdy, *n.* صَخِب ـ صَخَّاب ـ صَخُوب *pl.* صُخُب ـ صَخْبانُ *pl.* صُخْبان.

Rowel, *n.* As of a spur, شَوْكَةُ ٱلْمِهْمازِ ـ شَوْكَة. *See also* Seton, *n.*

Rower, *n.* جاذِف ـ قاذِف ـ نُوتِيّ *pl.* نَواتِيّ; *vulg.* قَدَّاف.

Rowing, *n.* جَذْف ـ قَذْف. A — match, مُسابَقَةُ ٱلْقَوارِبِ.

Rowlock, *n.* Of an oar, بَيْتُ ٱلْمِجْداف ـ بَيْتُ ٱلْمِقْذافِ.

Royal, *a.* Pertaining to a king, مَلَكِيّ ـ سُلْطانِيّ ـ مُلُوكِيّ. Becoming a king, مِثْلَ مَلِكٍ ـ مِثْلَ ٱلْمُلُوكِ ـ مُلُوكِيّ ـ شاهانِيّ ـ هُمايُونِيّ. Belonging to government, مِيرِيّ. Royal, of paper, قِطْعَةٌ وَزِيرِيَّةٌ. A — regiment, طابُورٌ (or آلاي) خاصّ. The — troops, العَساكِرُ ٱلشَّاهانِيَّةُ. Royal dainties, لَذَّاتُ مُلُوكٍ.

Royal, *n.* The sail, قُنْتَرَة بابافِنْقُو. One of a — regiment, نَفَرٌ مِنَ ٱلطَّابُورِ ٱلْخاصِّ.

Royalism, *n.* تَعَصُّبٌ لِلْمَلِكِ ـ مَحَبَّةٌ لِلْمَلِكِ.

Royalist, *n.* مِنَ ٱلْحِزْبِ ٱلْمَلَكِيِّ ـ مِنْ حِزْبِ ٱلْمَلِكِ.

Royalist, *a.* مَلَكِيّ. The — party, الحِزْبُ ٱلْمَلَكِيُّ.

Royalize, *v.t.* صَيَّرَ ـ مِنَ ٱلْحِزْبِ ٱلْمَلَكِيِّ ـ شَرَّبَ ـ حُبَّ ٱلْمَلِكِ.

Royally, *ad.* مِثْلَ ٱلْمُلُوكِ.

Royalties, *n.* Emblems of royalty, زِيناتُ ٱلْمَلِكِ ٱلرَّسْمِيَّةُ. Privileges of a king, إمْتِيازاتُ ٱلْمَلِكِ وَخَصائِصُهُ.

Royalty, *n.* The state of a king, مُلْك ـ مَلَكُوت ـ مَمْلَكَة. A tax to be paid for certain privileges, جائِزَة.

Roysterer, *n.* *See* Roisterer, *n.*

Rub, *v.t.* To move over a surface with pressure, عَرَكَ ـ مَعَكَ ـ دَعَكَ ـ فَرَكَ ـ دَلَكَ; to rub well, دَلَّكَ. To rub, as men do those who frequent the bath, كَبَّسَ ـ دَلَّكَ; to rub one's self, in that way, تَدَلَّكَ. To rub, or injure, as of the skin, عَفَسَ. To rub, as in washing clothes, مَعَكَ ـ دَعَكَ. To apply frequent frictions, فَرَّكَ ـ مَرَّخَ. To bruise or pound, سَحَكَ ـ سَهَكَ. To rub, as in the hands, فَرَكَ. To rub, in order to alleviate pain, مَرَخَ. To rub one's self against anything, إحْتَكَّ بِ ـ تَمَرَّسَ بِ. To wipe, مَسَحَ. To polish, صَقَلَ.

To rub away, حَتَّ.

To rub down, to clean, مَسَحَ. To curry, as of a horse, فَرْجَنَ (or حَسَّ) ٱلْحِصانَ.

To rub in, as oil into the hair, *etc.,* غَلَّ ـ فِي.

To rub off, as of the skin, سَحا ـ إسْتَحَى. To rub off old scores, سَدَّ ٱلْحِسابَ.

To rub out, to erase, حَتَّ ـ مَحا ـ أَطْمَلَ ـ طَمَسَ ـ طَرْمَسَ ـ طَلَسَ.

To rub up, to furbish, polish, صَقَلَ ـ جَلا. To rouse, إسْتَفَزَّ ـ حَضَّضَ ـ حَضَّ ـ هَيَّجَ ـ حَرَّضَ ـ أَنْهَضَ. To rub up, as of colours or a painting, جَنْدَرَ. *See also to* Retouch, *v.t.*

Rub, *v.i.* To chafe, gall, عَقَرَ ـ جَرَشَ. To rub on, to persevere, أَصَرَّ عَلَى ـ ظَلَّ ـ لازَمَ ـ أَضْمَرَ.

Rub, *n.* The act of rubbing, a friction, دَلْك ـ دَعْك ـ حَكّ ـ تَدْلِيك; as between the fingers, تَفْرِيك ـ فَرْك. A — or rubbing off, as of the skin, سَحْج ـ إِسْتِحَاءٌ ـ مَعْس. A — or rubbing or colliding together, of two or more bodies, مُحَاكَّة ـ تَلاطُم. A wipe, مَسْحَة. A polish, جِلاءٌ ـ صَقْل. A difficulty, صُعُوبَة ـ مُشْكِلَة ـ مُعْضِلَة ـ وَرْطَة. A sarcasm, سَلاطَة ـ قارِصَة ـ نَقْر. To give one a —, or rubeke, قَرَصَ ب ـ نَقَرَ ـ سَخِطَ عَلَى.

Rubber, *n.* A — of the bath, the man who rubs, دَلَّاك. A burnisher, مِسْحَل. A —, to rub paints, *etc.*, with, مِسْحَنَة; for rubbing paints, *etc.*, upon, مَداك ـ صَلايَة ـ قُسْطُنَاس. A whetstone, مِسَنّ ـ مِسْحَنَة. *See also* India-rubber, *n.*

Rubbing, *n.* A copy taken by rubbing, صُورَةٌ مَأْخُوذَةٌ بِٱلدَّلْك. *See also* Rub, *n.*

Rubbing-post, *n.* الجِذْلُ ٱلْمُحَكَّك ـ حِكاك.

Rubbish, *n.* Sweepings, زُبَالَة ـ كُنَاسَة ـ قُشَاش ـ قَشِيش; such as is borne by a torrent, غُثَاءٌ ـ غُثَّاءٌ. Refuse matter, بَوار ـ تَبْوِيزَة ـ دُشار ـ نَفِيَّة ـ نُفايَة ـ خُشارَة. A heap of stones mixed with earth, *etc.*, fallen from a building, دَبْش ـ رَدْم. Old —, عُتَاقَة; specially old furniture, رِثَّةُ ٱلْمَتاع ـ رِثَّة ـ رَثّ. Trash, foolish sayings, بَطّالات. A worthless thing, شَيْءٌ بَطّال ـ تَفاهَة. Paltry goods, سَقَطُ ٱلْمَتاع.

Rubble, *n.* Of dust and stones, أَثْلَب; of bricks and pottery, أَعْقاب ـ عُقاب.

Rubefacient, *a.* مُوَرِّد ـ مُحَمِّر.

Rubescent, *a.* مُحْمَرّ.

Rubican, *a.* Of the colour, صِنابِيّ. *See also* Bay, Sorrel, *a.*

Rubicon, *n.* To pass the —, خاطَرَ ـ رَمَى ٱلْغَمْد ـ إِسْتَحْمَطَ بِنَفْسِهِ إِطْلاقًا.

Rubicund, *a.* أَحْمَرُ نَوْعًا.

Rubied, *a.* Red, as a ruby, مِنْ لَوْنِ ٱلْيَاقُوت ـ يَاقُوتِيّ. Studded with rubies, مُرَصَّعٌ بِٱلْيَواقِيت.

Rubific, *a.* مُحَمِّر ـ مُوَرِّد.

Rubification, *n.* تَحْمِير ـ تَوْرِيد.

Rubigo, *n.* *See* Mildew, *n.*

Rubric, *a.* Red, أَحْمَر.

Rubric, *n.* حَاشِيَة *pl.* حَواشِي ـ تَنْبِيه *pl.* تَنْبِيهات.

Rubrical, *a.* مُتَعَلِّقٌ بِٱلْحَواشِي ـ تَنْبِيهِيّ.

Ruby, *n.* يَاقُوت *pl.* يَواقِيت.

Ruby, *a.* أَحْمَر ـ قِرْمِزِيّ ـ يَاقُوتِيّ.

Ruby, *v.t.* حَمَّرَ ـ وَرَّدَ ـ صَيَّرَ بِلَوْنِ ٱلْيَاقُوت.

Ruck, *n.* *See* Wrinkle, *n.*

Ruck, *v.t.* *See to* Wrinkle, *v.t.*

Rucks, *v.i.* *See to* Wrinkle, *v.i.*

Ructation, *n.* *See* Eructation, *n.*

Rud, *n.* Redness, حُمْرَة. *See also* Ochre, *n.*

Ruddel, *n.* تُرابٌ أَحْمَر ـ مَغْرَة.

Rudder, *n.* As of a ship, سُكّان ـ دَفَّة ـ كَوْثَل.

Ruddiness, *n.* حُمْرَة ـ شُقْرَة.

Ruddy, *a.* أَقْرَف ـ قِرْفِيّ ـ أَحْمَرُ قُرّاص ـ فُقاع *fem.* قَرْفاءُ ـ حُمْر *pl.* حَمْراءُ *fem.* أَحْمَر ـ شُقْر *pl.* شَقْراءُ *fem.* أَشْقَر ـ قُرْف *pl.* He was —, and of a fair countenance, كانَ أَشْقَرَ وَحَسَنَ ٱلْمَنْظَر.

Rude, *a.* Uncivil, بِلا أَدَب ـ غَلِيظ ـ فَظّ ـ عُتُلّ. Brutal, قاسٍ ـ جافٍ. Rude in speech, عامِّيٌّ فِي ٱلْكَلام. Inelegant, rough, أَخْرَق ـ هَمَج *coll.* هَمَجَة ـ خَشِن ـ غَلِيظ ـ سَمِيج. Uncivilized, أُمِّيّ ـ حُوشِيّ ـ جافٍ. Impudent, وَقِيح ـ سَفِيه. Ignorant, غُشَماءُ *pl.* غَشِيم ـ جُهّال *pl.* جاهِل. Rough, of wind, قاصِف; of weather, مُقْشَعِرّ. Severe, شَدِيد ـ فَظِيع. Rude ignorance, جَهْلٌ فَظِيع. He is very —, coarse, uncivil, إِنَّهُ لَفَظٌّ بَظٌّ. He who lives in the desert becomes —, (prov.) مَنْ بَدا جَفا. *See also under* Rough, Barbarous, *a.*

Rudely, *ad.* Uncivilly, بِعَدَمِ ٱلْأَدَب ـ بِغَلاظَة ـ بِفَظاظَة. Brutally, cruelly, بِقَساوَة ـ بِجَفاء ـ بِقَساحَة. Roughly, inelegantly, بِغَلاظَة ـ بِخُشُونَة. Impudently, بِوَقاحَة ـ بِسَفاهَة. Ignorantly, بِغَشَم ـ بِجَهْل ـ بِدُونِ مَعْرِفَة ـ بِخُرْقَة. To speak — to, غَلَّظَ ل ـ سَفَّهَ مَع ـ فِي ٱلْكَلام. To treat —, harshly, قاسَحَ. To behave — towards, غَلَّظَ عَلَى. To do anything —, not well, clumsily, خَشَبَ. To speak or utter words —, without refinement, خَشَبَ ٱلْكَلام.

Rudeness, *n.* Incivility, قِلَّةُ أَدَب ـ غِلاظَة ـ فَظاظَة. Inelegance, غِلاظَة ـ غِلْظَة ـ خُشُونَة. Roughness, خُرْق ـ خُرْقَة. Harshness, cruelty, قَساوَة ـ جَفاءٌ ـ قَساحَة. Impudence, سَفاهَة ـ وَقاحَة. Ignorance, غَشَم ـ جَهْل ـ خُرْقَة. The being uncivilized, حُوشِيَّة ـ خُشُونَة ـ جَفاءٌ. Roughness, as of weather, شِدَّة; as of wind, قَصْف. *See also* Roughness, Barbarism, *n.*

Rudiment, *n.* First element of anything, مَبْدَأ *pl.* مَبادِئ ـ أَصْل *pl.* أُصُول ـ أَصْلٌ وَمَبْدَأ *pl.* أُصُولٌ وَمَبادِئ. The rudiments of a science, مَبادِئُ عِلْم. *See also* Element, *n.*

Rudiment, *v.t.* أَفادَ ٱلْأُصُول ـ عَلَّمَ ٱلْمَبادِئ.

Rudimental, *a.* }
Rudimentary, } مُخْتَصٌّ بِٱلْأُصُول ـ مُخْتَصٌّ بِٱلْمَبادِئ. *See also* Elementary, *a.*

Rue, *n.* The herb, سَذاب ـ خُفْت ـ فَيْجَن. Wild —, حَرْمَل.

Rue, *v.t.* To deplore, تَأَسَّفَ عَلَى ـ تَنَدَّمَ عَلَى ـ نَدِمَ عَلَى. To make to —, آسَفَ ـ أَنْدَمَ.

Rueful, *a.* مَغْمُوم ـ حَزِين ـ كَئِيب ـ مَكْرُوب ـ كَرِيب ـ مُضْطَرِب.

Ruefully, *ad.* اِضْطِرَابًا ـ بِغَمّ ـ بِحُزْن ـ بِشَجَب.

Ruefulness, *n.* اِضْطِرَاب ـ غَمّ ـ حُزْن ـ شَجَب ـ كَآبَة.

Ruff, *n.* For the neck, طَوْقٌ مِنَ ٱلْكَشْكَشِ تَضَعُهُ ٱلْمَرْأَةُ حَوْلَ رَقَبَتِهَا. A kind of ringed bird, نَوْعٌ مِنَ ٱلطُّيُورِ ٱلْمُطَوَّقَةِ. A kind of river fish, نَوْعٌ مِنْ سَمَكِ ٱلنُّهُورِ. The — of a drum, دَقُّ ٱلطَّبْلِ.

Ruff, *v.t.* *See to* Ruffle, *v.t.*

Ruffian, *n.* خَبِيث *pl.* خِبَاث ـ خَلِيع ـ مُخَالِع. *See also* Bandit, Brigand, *n.*

Ruffian, *a.*
Ruffianish,
Ruffianlike,
Ruffianly,
} Of a person, خَبِيث *pl.* خِبَاث ـ خَلِيع *pl.* خُلَعَاء; of a thing or action, جَائِف ـ شَنِيع ـ فَظِيع ـ قَبِيح.

Ruffianism, *n.* خَلَاعَة ـ فَظَاعَة ـ جَائِفَة ـ عِنْف ـ خَبَاثَة.

Ruffle, *v.t.* To furnish with ruffles, رَكَّبَ ٱلْكَشْكَشَ عَلَى. To —, as a bird its feathers, نَفَشَ [2]. To wrinkle, خَدَّ [2] ـ ثَنَى ـ غَضَّنَ ـ شَنَّجَ. To vex, قَلَّقَ ـ زَعَجَ ـ أَكَدَّ ـ أَزْعَجَ ـ أَضْجَرَ. To make turbid, سَجَّسَ ـ كَدَّرَ. To be ruffled, flurried, قَلِقَ ـ تَضَجَّرَ ـ اِضْطَرَبَ ـ خَفَّ. *See also to* Flurry, *v.t.*, and *to* Rumple, *v t.*

Ruffle, *v.i.* To grow turbid, تَكَدَّرَ ـ كَدِرَ ـ سَجِسَ. To —, as of the feathers of a bird, تَجَفَّلَ ـ تَنَفَّشَ; in anger, تَطَوَّسَ. Of the wind, تَسَفَّهَ. *See also to* Flutter, *v.i.*

Ruffle, *n.* Agitation, اِضْطِرَاب ـ ضَجَاج ـ زَعَج ـ حَيْرَة. Ruffle, of a drum, تَطْبِيلُ ٱلسَّلَامِ ـ طَبْلُ ٱلسَّلَامِ; to beat a — on the drum, طَبَّلَ (or طَبَلَ [2]) ٱلسَّلَامَ. A — for the neck; *see* Ruff, *n.*

Rufous, *a.* أَشْقَرُ *fem.* شَقْرَاءُ *pl.* شُقْر.

Rug, *n.* زِرْبِيٌّ *pl.* زَرَابِيُّ; for praying upon, سَجَّادَة. *See also* Coverlid, *n.*

Rugate, *a.* مُشَنَّج ـ مُتَغَضِّن ـ مُتَخَدِّد ـ مُخَدَّد.

Rugged, *a.* Rough, uneven, شَرِس *fem.* شَرْسَاءُ *pl.* شُرْس ـ أَخْشَنُ ـ خُشْن ـ خَشِن *pl.* خَشِب ـ خَشِيب ـ أَخْشَبُ. Rocky, stony, وَعْر *pl.* أَوْعَار ـ وَعِير ـ وَاعِر. A — and devious road, ثَنِيَّة ـ عَقَبَة. A — place, مَكَانٌ شَرْس. Rugged land, أَرْضٌ شَرْسَاءُ ـ شَرَاس. To ascend a — place, اِقْتَحَمَ ٱلْعَقَبَةَ. *See also* Rough, *a.*

Ruggedly, *ad.* *See* Roughly, Rudely, *ad.*

Ruggedness, *n.* Unevenness, خُشُونَة ـ خَشَب. Rockiness, وُعُور ـ وَعْر.

Rugose, *a.*
Rugous,
} مُتَغَضِّن ـ مُغَضَّن. *See also* Rugate, *a.*

Rugosity, *n.* تَشَنُّج ـ تَغَضُّن ـ تَغْضِين.

Ruin, *n.* The being destroyed, خَرَاب; the act of destroying, إِخْرَاب ـ تَخْرِيب. A ruined place, خَرِبَة *pl.* خَرِب *and* خَرَائِب *and* خِرْبَات ـ خِرْبَة *pl.* خِرَب; old ruins, خَرِبٌ عَادِيٌّ. Perdition, هَلَاك ـ هَلَكَة ـ مَحَاق. Want, waste, need, إِخْلَال ـ إِفْلَاس ـ تَلَف ـ إِخْتِلَال ـ خَلَل. The loss of fortune, إِفْلَاس ـ تَلَف. Ruin of character, إِخْلَالُ ٱلْعِرْضِ. A cause of —, destruction, بَاعِثٌ عَلَى ٱلْخَرَابِ; of perdition, بَاعِثٌ عَلَى ٱلْهَلَاكِ; of loss of fortune, بَاعِثٌ عَلَى ٱلْإِفْلَاسِ ـ بَاعِثٌ عَلَى ٱلتَّلَفِ. In ruins, خَرَاب. The road to —, دَرْبُ ٱلْهَلَاكِ. To be one's —, to ruin, أَهْلَكَ ـ أَتْلَفَ. To fall into —, صَارَ خَرَابًا ـ تَخَرَّبَ ـ خَرِبَ ـ تَضَعْضَعَ. To run to —, perdition, أَسْرَعَ إِلَى ٱلْهَلَاكِ. It will be your —, يَكُونُ لَكَ مَهْلَكَةً. Its preservation from —, حِفْظُهُ (or صِيَانَتُهُ عَنِ) مِنَ ٱلتَّلَفِ.

Ruin, *v.t.* To reduce to ruins, خَرَّبَ ـ أَخْرَبَ ـ ضَعْضَعَ. To demolish, هَدَمَ. To cause loss to, أَضَاعَ ـ أَتْلَفَ ـ أَعْدَمَ ـ ضَيَّعَ. To bring to perdition, هَلَّكَ ـ طَوَّحَ بِ ـ طَوَّحَ ـ أَطَاحَ ـ أَهْلَكَ. To make poor or wretched, أَفْقَرَ ـ أَلْوَى بِ ـ أَعْدَمَ ـ أَعْدَمَ ـ خَرَّبَ بَيْتَهُ. To make bankrupt, صَيَّرَ مُفْلِسًا. To be ruined, هَلِكَ.

Ruination, *n.* Subversion, overthrow, تَخْرِيب ـ خَرَاب. *See also* Ruin, *n.*

Ruinous, *a.* In a state of ruin, خَرِبَة *pl.* خَرَاب ـ مُتَضَعْضِع; a — heap, رَجْمَةُ رَدْمٍ. Destructive, مُتْلِف ـ مُعْدِم ـ مُفْقِد ـ مُهْلِك. *See also* Pernicious, Destructive, *a.*

Ruinously, *ad.* بِوَجْهٍ مُعْدِمٍ ـ بِنَوْعٍ مُتْلِفٍ.

Ruinousness, *n.* خَرَاب ـ إِعْدَام ـ هَلَكَة.

Rulable, *a.* That may be ruled over, ضَبْطُهُ ـ إِدَارَتُهُ مُمْكِنَةٌ ـ مُمْكِنٌ. According to rule, مُوَافِقُ ٱلْقَوَاعِدِ. Declared to be according to rule, مُفْتًى بِهِ.

Rule, *n.* Government, رِئَاسَة ـ سِيَادَة ـ حُكُومَة ـ حُكْم ـ مُلْك ـ سِيَاسَة. A precept, law, ضَابِطَة *pl.* ضَوَابِطُ ـ قَانُون *pl.* قَوَانِينُ ـ عَادَة *pl.* قَاعِدَة *pl.* قَوَاعِدُ ـ سُنَّة *pl.* سُنَن. A custom, habit, عَادَة *pl.* عَوَائِدُ ـ قَانُون *pl.* قَوَانِينُ. Good order, نِظَام. A principle, as of a science, قَانُون *pl.* قَوَانِينُ ـ قَاعِدَة *pl.* قَوَاعِدُ. A model, قِدْوَة ـ عِمْدَة. A — or directory of procedure, دُسْتُورُ ٱلْعَمَلِ.

Style, manner, طَرِيقَة — دَأْب. An instrument to draw lines with, مِسْطَرَة. A flat — of brass, such as is used in printing, صَفِيحَة *pl.* صَفَائِح. According to —, حَسَبَ ٱلْقَانُونِ. I make it a — to..., جَعَلْتُ عَلَى نَفْسِي قَانُونًا أَن. To have or obtain the — over, تَسَلَّطَ عَلَى — ² حَكَمَ عَلَى. To give the — over, حَكَّمَ عَلَى — سَلَّطَ عَلَى. The Rule of Three, قَاعِدَةُ ٱلْأَرْبَعَةِ ٱلْمُتَنَاسِبَةِ *See also under* Ruler, *n.*

Rule, *v.i.* To have power or command, ⁓ مَلَكَ — تَسَلَّطَ. To — over, ⁓ مَلَكَ عَلَى — تَسَلَّطَ عَلَى — ² حَكَمَ عَلَى. To govern, direct, ⁓ رَعَى. To direct, keep in order, نَظَّمَ — دَبَّرَ — ² سَاسَ — ² قَادَ. To decide, ⁓ فَصَلَ — ⁓ جَزَمَ بِ — ⁓ قَطَعَ — ² بَتَّ. It was ruled that..., إِسْتَقَرَّتِ ٱلْقَاعِدَةُ أَن. They ruled that..., إِلْتَمَرُوا عَلَى أَن. The government ruled that..., ⁓ قَرَّرَ رَأْيُ ٱلدَّوْلَةِ عَلَى أَن.

Ruler, *n.* One who bears rule, حَاكِم *pl.* حُكَّام — مَلِك *pl.* مُلُوك; a — by the authority of God, قَائِمٌ بِأَمْرِ ٱللّٰهِ. A governor, ضَابِط *pl.* ضُبَّاط — مَأْمُور *pl.* مَأْمُورُون — وَالٍ *pl.* وُلَاة. A — to rule lines with, مِسْطَرَة — مِخَطّ. A wooden —, مِخْطَاط. A — for hitting on the fingers, مِقْفَعَة.

Ruling, *a.* Bearing rule, مُتَسَلِّط — حَاكِم — مُسْتَوْلٍ. Predominant, غَالِب.

Ruling, *n.* قَضَآء — فَصْل — حُكْم. *See also* Decision, *n.*

Rum, *n.* The spirit, عَرَقُ ٱلرُّومِ — رُوم.

Rum, *a.* *See* Odd, Queer, *a.*

Rumble, *n.* As of a carriage, مَقْعَدُ مُؤَخَّرِ ٱلْعَرَبَانَةِ.

Rumble, *v.i.* As of the belly, تَخَرْخَرَ; of water, ² خَرَّ; of thunder, ⁓ رَعَدَ — أَرْجَفَ — ² رَجَفَ; of any rumbling sound, فَرْفَرَ — ⁓ صَرَّ. The thunder rumbled, ² رَجَفَ ٱلرَّعْدُ.

Rumbling, *n.* As of the belly, تَخَرْخُر; of water, خَرِير; of thunder, رُعُود — رُجُوف — رَجِيف — رَجَفَان — رَجْف; of any — sound, صَرِير — فَرْفَرَة.

Rumbling, *a.* As of the belly, مُتَخَرْخِر; of water, خَارّ; of thunder, رَاعِد — رَجَّاف — رَاجِف; of any — sound, صَارّ — فَرْفَار.

Rumen, *n.* *See* Cud, *n.*

Ruminant, *a.* مُشْتَرّ — مُجْتَرّ.

Ruminant, *n.* حَيَوَانٌ مُشْتَرّ — حَيَوَانٌ مُجْتَرّ.

Ruminantia, *n.* ٱلْحَيَوَانَاتُ ٱلْمُجْتَرَّة.

Ruminate, *v.i.* To chew the cud, إِشْتَرَّ — إِجْتَرَّ — أَفَاضَ. To meditate, muse, تَأَمَّلَ — تَفَكَّرَ. To — upon, تَأَمَّلَ فِي — تَفَكَّرَ فِي.

Rumination, *n.* The act of chewing the cud, إِجْتِرَار — إِشْتِرَار. Meditation, تَفَكُّر — تَأَمُّل.

Rummage, *n.* تَقْلِيب — نَبْش — تَفْتِيش.

Rummage, *v.t.* قَلَّبَ — ² نَبَشَ — فَتَّشَ.

Rummer, *n.* قَدَحٌ كَبِير.

Rumour, *n.* خَبَر *pl.* أَخْبَار. False and mischievous rumours, أَرَاجِيف. He heard a —, ⁓ سَمِعَ خَبَرًا. This — went forth, ² خَرَجَ هٰذَا ٱلْخَبَرُ. *See also* Report, *n.*

Rumour, *v.t.* أَشَاعَ خَبَرَهُ. *See also to* Report, *v.i.*

Rump, *n.* The buttocks, دُبُر *pl.* أَدْبَار. The rump bone, عُكْدَة; of a bird, زِمِكَّآء — زِمِكَّى. A — steak, شَرِيحُ لَحْمٍ مِنْ دُبُرِ ٱلْبَقَرِ. A — of beef, لَحْمُ عَجُزِ ٱلْبَقَرِ.

Rumple, *v.t.* رَضْرَضَ — ² رَضَّ.

Rumple, *v.i.* تَرَضْرَضَ — إِرْتَضَّ.

Rumpled, *a.* مُتَرَضْرِض — مُرْتَضّ.

Rumpus, *n.* شَغَب — غَوْشَة — هَوْشَة — لَجَاجٌ وَصَخَبٌ — غَيْشَرَة.

Run, *v.i.* To move with rapidity, وَفَضَ *aor.* يَفِضُ — إِسْتَوْفَضَ — ⁓ جَرَى — ² رَكَضَ — ⁓ سَعَى — إِرْقَدَّ — إِرْمَدَّ — أَوْفَضَ — أَوْكَشَ. To run quickly, ⁓ طَارَ. To run furiously, أَغَارَ. To make haste, أَسْرَعَ — ² سَرَبَ. To flow, سَالَ *aor.* يَسِيلُ — سَابَ *aor.* يَسِيبُ — سَاحَ *aor.* يَسِيحُ — ⁓ جَرَى. To run, as of a sore, أَغَذَّ — ⁓ غَذَّ — ⁓ فَصَّ — ⁓ فَزَّ — ⁓ نَجَّ — أَغَثَّ — ⁓ غَثَّ. To run, as one colour into another, تَشَرَّبَ. To pass away, as time, *etc.*, حَالَ *aor.* يَحُولُ — ² مَرَّ — ⁓ مَضَى — ⁓ بَرِحَ. To extend, إِمْتَدَّ. To —, as of a candle, ⁓ سَالَ — ² نَطَفَ. To leak, وَكَفَ *aor.* يَكِفُ — أَوْكَفَ — ⁓ سَرَبَ. To trickle, ⁓ نَضَّ. To ply, ² رَاحَ مِنْ كَذَا إِلَى: the steamer still runs between Alexandria and Bairût, لَا زَالَتِ ٱلْبَاخِرَةُ تَتَرَدَّدُ بَيْنَ إِسْكَنْدَرِيَّةَ وَبَيْرُوتَ. To run, as of a controversy, ⁓ جَرَى: a dispute ran, or ran on, respecting, ⁓ جَرَى ٱلْخِلَافُ فِي كَذَا. To be in use, ⁓ جَرَى — أُسْتُعْمِلَ. To —, of tears, ⁓ ذَرَفَ ٱلدَّمْعُ: his eyes ran with tears, ذَرَفَتْ عُيُونُهُ. So the story runs, هٰكَذَا ٱلْقِصَّةُ — هٰكَذَا ٱلْخَبَرُ. To make to run, أَجْرَى — رَكَّضَ. To make to — or flow, أَجْرَى — أَسَالَ. Let me run, دَعْنِي أَجْرِ.

To run about, to walk, ⁓ مَشَى. To run hither and thither, ² تَرَدَّدَ — ² دَارَ. The water ran about the place, ⁓ جَرَى ٱلْمَآءُ حَوْلَ ٱلْمَكَانِ.

To run after, behind, ² رَكَضَ خَلْفَهُ. To follow, ⁓ تَبِعَ — لَحِقَ — ² خَلَفَ. To seek, فَتَّشَ عَنْ — فَتَّشَ.

To run aground, as of a ship, شَطَّ; (also as an active verb), they ran the ship aground, شَطَّطُوا ٱلسَّفِينَةَ.

To run against, to collide with, صَدَمَ ـ أَصَابَ ـ صَادَمَ ـ سَلَقَ. To meet, encounter, اِلْتَقَى مَعَ ـ اِلْتَقَى.

To run a race, رَكَضَ فِي ٱلْمَيْدَانِ (or ٱلْمُسَابَقَةِ). To run a race with, جَارَى ـ رَاكَضَ.

To run at, to attack, حَمَلَ ـ هَجَمَ عَلَى ـ يَسْطُو .aor سَطَا بِ ـ تَسَاقَطَ عَلَى. To precipitate one's self against, اِنْقَضَّ عَلَى ـ اِرْتَمَى عَلَى ـ عَلَى.

To run a risk, خَاطَرَ بِنَفْسِهِ ـ تَعَرَّضَ لِ : He ran the risk of being killed, تَعَرَّضَ لِلْقَتْلِ.

To run at random, اِسْتَنَّ (or تَسَنَّنَ) فِي جَرْيَتِهِ.

To run away, to flee, اِنْفَلَّ ـ اِنْهَزَمَ ـ وَلَّى هَارِبًا ـ جَفَلَ ـ فَرَّ ـ نَجَا مِنْ ـ هَرَبَ مِنْ. To run away from, هَرَبَ مِنْ. To lose itself, تَطَوَّحَ ـ يَطُوحُ .aor طَاحَ. To disappear, غَابَ. To become expended, ذَهَبَ ـ تَصَرَّفَ ـ ضَاعَ.

To run away with, in company with, وَلَّى مَعَ ـ اِنْهَزَمَ مَعَ. To run away with, to seize, carry off, اِنْفَلَ ـ مَضَى بِ ـ خَطِفَ. To run away with an idea, رَأَى رَأْيًا ـ اِتَّخَذَ رَأْيًا ـ اِرْتَأَى رَأْيًا ـ يَرَى .aor

To run back, اِنْصَرَفَ رَاكِضًا ـ رَجَعَ رَاكِضًا ـ رَكَضَ رَاجِعًا.

To run before, رَكَضَ أَمَامَ ٱلشَّيْءِ.

To run counter to, خَالَفَ ـ عَارَضَ ـ قَاوَمَ ـ ضَادَّ.

To run down, as a hill, stairs, *etc.*, هَبَطَ ـ رَكَضَ نَازِلًا ـ سَرَبَ مُنْحَدِرًا ـ اِنْحَدَرَ رَاكِضًا ـ رَاكِضًا. To flow down, حَدَرَ ـ اِنْحَدَرَ. To stop, as a watch, *etc.*, وَقَفَ .aor يَقِفُ.

To run for, as a prize, رَكَضَ لِيَنَالَ ٱلْجِعَالَةَ.

To run for one's life, هَرَبَ ٱبْتِغَاءَ ٱلنَّجَاةِ ـ فَازَ.

To run foul of; *see* To run against.

To run high, of prices, اِرْتَفَعَ; as a party spirit, اِشْتَدَّ ـ اِشْتَدَّ تَعَصُّبًا.

To run in, to enter in haste, دَخَلَ رَاكِضًا ـ خَشَّ فِي رَاكِضًا.

To run in the blood, كَانَ مِنْ خِلْقَتِهِ ـ كَانَ مِنْ طَبْعِهِ. It runs in his blood, as of an hereditary disposition, كَانَ مِنْ عِرْقِهِ.

To run in vain, خَابَ ـ يَخِيبُ .aor سَعَى بَاطِلًا.

To run into, to become, عَادَ إِلَى ـ أَصْبَحَ ـ يَؤُولُ .aor آلَ إِلَى ـ صَارَ. To empty itself into, اِنْصَبَّ فِي ـ تَصَبَّبَ فِي ـ اِنْسَكَبَ فِي. To cast one's self into, اِنْدَفَعَ إِلَى. To be pierced with, دَخَلَ فِيهِ ـ أَنْفَذَهُ ـ جَازَ فِيهِ; as a spear, غَمَضَ فِي ـ صَدَمَ. To dash itself against, صَدَمَ ـ سَلَقَ. To run into error, زَلَّ ـ تَاهَ ـ ضَلَّ. To run into vice, دَعِرَ ـ اِنْهَمَكَ فِي ٱللَّذَّاتِ ـ أَخْبَثَ ـ خَبُثَ ـ تَدَعَّرَ.

To run mad, جُنَّ ـ تَجَنَّنَ ـ خَبِلَ.

To run off, to escape; (*see* To run away.) To run off, as off a line, زَلَقَ عَنْ ـ زَاغَ عَنْ ـ زَلَّ عَنْ ـ اِنْحَدَرَ عَنْ.

To run on, to continue, ظَلَّ ـ لَمْ يَزَلْ ـ اِسْتَمَرَّ عَلَى ـ أَدْمَنَ عَلَى.

To run on, as on an axis, دَارَ .aor يَدُورُ ـ اِسْتَدَارَ; as on wheels, مَشَى عَلَى ـ تَدَحْرَجَ عَلَى. To run on, as the mind on a subject, دَارَ حَوْلَ ٱلْأَمْرِ ـ أَضْمَرَ فِي ضَمِيرِهِ ـ يَقِفُ .aor وَقَفَ عَلَى.

To run out, as from a place, أَسْرَعَ فَخَرَجَ ـ خَرَجَ رَاكِضًا. To leak, سَرِبَ ـ وَكَفَ ـ يَكِفُ .aor وَكَفَ. To become expended, ذَهَبَ ـ تَصَرَّفَ. To run out of, to have no more of, مَا فَضَلَ لَهُ مِنْ ـ مَا بَقِيَ عِنْدَهُ مِنْ.

To run over, to overflow, فَاضَ ـ يَطْمُو .aor طَمَا ـ اِنْغَمَرَ. To drive over, سَاقَ عَلَى. To roam over, عَارَ فِي ـ عَالَ فِي. To look over, peruse, قَرَأَ ـ طَالَعَ. To ascend above, اِرْتَفَعَ فَوْقَ كَذَا.

To run or flow softly, slowly, نَضَّ.

To run to meet one, رَكَضَ لِلِقَائِهِ.

To run the gauntlet, تَعَزَّرَ ـ عَنْتَرَ. *See also under* Gauntlet, *n.*

To run the way of, to keep, observe, حَفِظَ ـ رَعَى. To conduct one's self, as after an example, اِحْتَذَى ـ اِحْتَذَى بِ ـ اِقْتَدَى بِ ـ تَمَثَّلَ بِ.

To run through, to leak, سَرِبَ ـ يَكِفُ .aor وَكَفَ. To dissipate, spend, أَبَادَ ـ أَتْلَفَ ـ أَسْرَفَ. To pervade, عَمَّ ـ جَرَى فِي ـ سَرَى فِي. To roam over; *see* To run over. To pierce; *see* To run into.

To run to, to become, عَادَ إِلَى ـ أَصْبَحَ ـ يَؤُولُ .aor آلَ إِلَى ـ صَارَ. To apply to, to have recourse to, قَصَدَ ـ صَمَدَ ـ وَقَعَ عَلَى ـ اِلْتَجَأَ إِلَى ـ اِلْتَبَطَ إِلَى; as for help, قَصَدَ إِلَى ـ يَقَعُ .aor. To run to excess, رَكَضَ إِلَى ٱلْفَيْضِ.

To run to and fro, طَوَّفَ ـ طَافَ ـ جَالَ ـ تَرَدَّدَ ـ دَارَ.

To run to excess, أَفْرَطَ; to run to excess in, اِنْهَمَكَ فِي ـ أَفْرَطَ فِي.

To run up a hill, *etc.*, صَعِدَ ٱلْجَبَلَ ـ صَعِدَ عَلَى ٱلْجَبَلِ رَاكِضًا ـ رَاكِضًا. To run up, as an account, أَجْرَى حِسَابًا.

To run up to, as in meeting, رَكَضَ إِلَى ـ أَسْرَعَ إِلَى لِقَائِهِ. To amount to, صَارَ مَبْلَغُهُ ـ بَلَغَ.

To run with, رَكَضَ مَعَ.

Run, *v.t.* To drive, سَاقَ ـ سَوَّقَ. To chase, طَارَدَ ـ رَوَّحَ ـ تَصَيَّدَ ـ قَنَصَ ـ طَرَدَ ـ لَاحَقَ; to chase, as game, قَنَصَ ـ تَصَيَّدَ. To push, أَرْكَضَ ـ رَكَّضَ. To make to —, دَفَعَ ـ يَسْطُو .aor سَطَا بِ. To force, أَغْصَبَ ـ أَلْزَمَ ـ اِضْطَرَّ إِلَى. To thrust, صَدَمَ. To melt, حَلَّ ² ـ ذَوَّبَ ـ أَذَابَ ـ أَمَاعَ. To form, as in a mould, صَبَّ ² ـ فِي قَالِبٍ. To —, of sewing, غَرَزَ ². To escape the custom house with goods, هَرَّبَ ـ مِنَ ٱلْكُمْرُكِ. To run, as a course, سَارَ سِيْرَةً ². To run one's horse in a race, أَطْلَقَ خَيْلَهُ فِي ٱلْحَلْبَةِ.

To run back, رَدَّ ² ـ رَجَعَ.

To run down, as of a ship, *etc.*, خَبَطَ ² ـ خَبَّطَ. To silence, صَمَّتَ ـ سَكَّتَ ـ أَسْكَتَ. To depreciate, حَكَرَ ² ـ إِحْتَكَرَ ـ إِسْتَقَلَّ ـ هَتَكَ ² ـ إِسْتَحْقَرَ ـ عَيَّبَ ـ عَيَّرَبَ ـ فَضَحَ ². To haul down, نَزَّلَ ـ أَنْزَلَ.

To run hard, عَسَّرَ عَلَى ـ ضَايَقَ ـ ضَيَّقَ عَلَى.

To run in, to make to enter, أَخَشَّ ـ أَدْخَلَ.

To run into, to pierce, دَخَلَ ـ فِي ـ أَدْخَلَ ـ فِي ـ أَنْفَذَ; as with a sword, أَغْمَضَ ـ فِي. To pass through, as a thread, rope, *etc.*, أَسْلَكَ ـ فِي ـ سَلَكَ ² ـ فِي. To run one into expenses, جَعَلَ ـ يَصْرِفُ ².

To run out, to make to go out hastily, طَرَدَ ² ـ أَخْرَجَ ـ رَاكِضًا.
To prolong, أَطَالَ ـ طَوَّلَ. To expend, make an end of, أَكَلَ ² ـ تَمَّمَ ـ أَتَمَّ ـ أَسْرَفَ. To extend, to stretch out, مَدَّ ² ـ بَسَطَ ² ـ نَتَحَ ² ـ جَذَبَ ². To expend, spend, أَصْرَفَ.
To waste, أَبَادَ ـ أَتْلَفَ ـ أَسْرَفَ.

To run over, to peruse, قَرَأَ ² ـ إِطَّلَعَ عَلَى. To narrate, حَدَّثَ ـ حَكَى ² ـ حَدَّثَ بِ. To pass one over, عَبَّرَ ـ مِن عَلَى *or* عَبَّرَ.

To run through, to pierce; (*see* To run into.) To be general among, شَمَلَ ² ـ عَمَّ ².

To run up, as a flag, نَشَرَ ² ـ رَفَعَ ²; as a price, زَيَّدَ ـ عَلَى ـ رَفَعَ ² ـ أَزَانَ; as a building, to build up slightly, عَمَّ ـ إِغْتَمَّ:
He ran up the building, عَمَّ ٱلْبِنَاءَ ².

Run, *n.* The act of running, رَكْضٌ ـ جَرَيَانٌ ـ جَرْيٌ; style of running, جِرْيَةٌ; a single heat, شَرَفٌ *pl.* أَشْرَافٌ. The act of flowing, جَرَيَانٌ ـ سَيَلَانٌ ـ سَيْلٌ. Distance, مَسَافَةٌ ـ مِشْوَارٌ ـ مَسِيرَةٌ. Concatenation, as of events, *etc.*, تَوَالٍ ـ تَتَالٍ ـ تَسَلْسُلٌ. General reception, قُبُولٌ عَامٌّ. A walk, outing, سِيرَةٌ ـ تَمَشٍّ ـ مِشْوَارٌ. A voyage, سَفَرٌ; on the sea, سَفَرٌ ـ قُلْعَةٌ. An attack, هُجُومٌ. Fashion, custom, عَادَةٌ. A pasture, مَرْعَاةٌ ـ مَرْعًى. Run, as on a bank for money, مُطَالَبَةٌ مُتَوَالِيَةٌ ـ مُجَارَاةٌ إِلَى ـ تَرَاكُضٌ إِلَى.
A — of good luck, نَصِيبٌ خَيْرٌ ـ حَظٌّ مُتَتَابِعٌ ـ دَهْرٌ مُوَافِقٌ. A — of bad luck, نَحْسٌ مُتَتَابِعٌ ـ دَهْرٌ مُخَالِفٌ ـ دَبْرَةٌ لِمُدَّةٍ مَا.
In the long —, فِي نِهَايَةِ ٱلْأَمْرِ ـ عَاقِبَةً. *See also* Course, *n.*

To have its run, to be current among, سَارَ فِي ². To be prevalent among, عَمَّ فِي ². To run its time, حَالَ حَوْلُهُ *aor.* يَحُولُ ـ جَرَى مَجْرَاهُ ² ـ لَحِقَ أَجَلَهُ ².

To have one's run, as of luck, حَظَّ حَظَّهُ ².

To have the run of, to be free of, تَرَخَّصَ فِي.

To take or have a run, walk, تَمَشَّى ـ سَارَ مِشْوَارًا ² ـ تَسَيَّرَ ـ دَارَ دَوْرَةً ².

Runagate, *n.* An apostate, مُرْتَدٌّ ـ رَافِضِيٌّ *pl.* رُفَّاضٌ ـ كَافِرٌ *pl.* كُفَّارٌ. A vagabond, صِلِّيلٌ ـ هَامِلٌ *pl.* هَوَامِلُ. *See also* Runaway, *n.*

Runaway, *a.* } A fugitive, فَرٌّ *pl. masc.* فَرَرَةٌ *pl. fem.* فُرُورٌ ـ
Runaway, *n.* } شَارِدٌ *pl.* شُرَّدٌ ـ هَارِبٌ. *See also* Deserter, *n.*

Rundle, *n.* As of a ladder, دَرَجَةُ سُلَّمٍ *pl.* دَرَجَاتٌ.

Rundlet, *n.* } بَرْمِيلٌ *pl.* بَرَاوِيلُ.
Runlet, }

Rune, *n.* حَرْفٌ مِنَ ٱلْحُرُوفِ ٱلْمُسْتَعْمَلَةِ فِي قَدِيمِ ٱلزَّمَانِ فِي شَمَالِ أُورُبَا.

Runic, *a.* ٱلْكِتَابَةُ ٱلْمُسْتَعْمَلَةُ فِي قَدِيمِ ٱلزَّمَانِ عِنْدَ أَهَالِي أُورُبَا ٱلشَّمَالِيَّةِ.

Runlet, *n.* } *See* Brook, *n.*
Runnel, }

Runner, *n.* One who runs, رَاكِضٌ *pl.* رُكَّاضٌ *and* رَاكِضُونَ; a swift —, رَكُوضٌ ـ رَكَّاضَةٌ ـ مِجْرَآءٌ. A messenger, رَسُولٌ ـ مُرْسَلٌ ـ قَاصِدٌ *pl.* قُصَّادٌ ـ سُعَاةٌ *pl.* سَاعٍ. A creeper-plant, عُشْبَةٌ ـ عُشْبٌ ـ أُرَيْتٌ ـ نَبَاتٌ مُفَرَّشٌ ـ دَغَلٌ. A running ring, حَلْقَةٌ سَلَّاكَةٌ. An agent of the police, مَأْمُورُ ٱلضَّبْطِيَّةِ. A timber for sliding anything upon, زُحْلُوقَةٌ مِنْ خَشَبٍ ـ مَسْلَكٌ مِنْ خَشَبٍ.
A scarlet runner, لُوبِيَةٌ مُوَرَّدَةٌ.

Runnet, *n.* *See* Rennet, *n.*

Running, *n.* A flowing, جَرَيَانٌ ـ سَيَلَانٌ ـ نَزْزٌ. Suppuration, عَثِيثٌ ـ غَذِيذَةٌ. Running, of sewing, غُرْزَةٌ. A —, of a sore, نَزِيزٌ; of the nose, ذَنِينٌ ـ ذُنَانٌ. *See also* Run, *n.*

Running, *a.* As on the legs, جَارٍ ـ رَاكِضٌ. Flowing, ثَعْبٌ ـ جَارٍ ـ سَرِبٌ ـ سَائِلٌ. Following, consecutive, مُتَوَالٍ. A — knot, عُقْدَةٌ سَالِكَةٌ. Running over, فَائِضٌ ـ سَدِيمٌ. A — fight, مُضَارَبَةٌ بَيْنَ ٱلطَّارِدِينَ وَٱلْهَارِبِينَ. A — fire, إِطْلَاقُ نَارٍ مُتَوَالٍ. A — sore, غَاذٌّ. A — account, حِسَابٌ جَارٍ: the bank opens running accounts, ٱلْبَنْكُ يَفْتَحُ حِسَابَاتٍ جَارِيَةً. Running rigging, حِبَالٌ سَالِكَةٌ.

Runt, *n.* An animal below the usual size of the species, حَيَوَانٌ مَسْخُوطٌ ـ مَسْخُوطٌ.

Rupee, *n.* رُوبِيَّةٌ *pl.* رُوبِيَّاتٌ.

Rupture, *n.* A breakage, كَسْر ـ كَسْرَة; the place of a —, كَسْرَة. A — between persons, صُرْم ـ صَرْم ـ شِقَاق ـ قَطِيعَة. A —, as of amicable relations, قَطْعُ عَلَاقَةٍ ـ بُرُودَة. A — of the peace, فَسْخُ ٱلصُّلْحِ ـ نَقْضُ ٱلصُّلْحِ. An open —, قَطْعُ عَلَاقَةٍ عَلَانِيَّة. A complete —, قَطْعُ عَلَاقَةٍ بَتَّة. The — of negotiations, قَطْعُ ٱلْمُذَاكَرَاتِ. To come to a —, وَقَعَ ـ aor. يَقَعُ ـ فَسْخٌ بَيْنَهُمْ ـ وَقَعَتْ بَيْنَهُمْ ـ ٱنْقَطَعُوا عَنْ بَعْضِهِمْ ـ بَيْنَهُمْ فَسْخُ ٱلْعَلَاقَةِ. To lead to a —, أَفْضَى إِلَى قَطْعِ عَلَاقَةٍ. To cause a — between, فَتَقَ ² بَتَّ ٱلْعَلَاقَةَ بَيْنَ ـ بَيْنَ. *See also* Hernia, *n.*

Rupture, *v.t.* To break, cut, burst, كَسَرَ ـ قَطَعَ ـ ² بَتَّ ـ فَتَقَ ² ـ فَضَخَ ـ صَرَمَ ـ صَدَعَ. To — one's self, إِنْفَتَقَ. To be ruptured, broken, إِنْفَضَخَ. Ruptured, having hernia; *see under* Hernia, *n.*

Rural, *a.* Belonging to the country, سَوَادِيٌّ ـ مُتَعَلِّقٌ بِٱلسَّوَادِ ـ خَلَاوِيٌّ ـ رِيفِيٌّ ـ مُخْتَصٌّ بِٱلرَّسَاتِيقِ. A — district, سَوَاد *pl.* أَسْوِدَة *and* أَسَاوِد ـ رَزْدَاق *pl.* رَزَادِيق ـ رُسْتَاق *pl.* رَسَاتِيق ـ رِيف *pl.* أَرْيَاف. A — dean, رَئِيسُ ٱلْإِكْلِيرُوسِ فِي مَحَلٍّ مِنَ ٱلرِّيفِ. *See also under* Dean, *n.*

Ruralist, *n.* رِيفِيٌّ ـ مُتَرَيِّف ـ مِنْ أَهْلِ ٱلرِّيفِ.

Ruralize, *v.i.* رَافَ *aor.* يَرِيفُ ـ تَرَيَّفَ.

Rurally, *a.* تَرَيُّفًا.

Ruralness, *n.* رِيف ـ تَرَيُّف.

Ruse, *n.* حِيلَة *pl.* حِيَل ـ دُولَاب *pl.* دَوَالِيب ـ خِدْعَة ـ دَسِيسَة *pl.* دَسَائِس. *Ruse de guerre*, خِدْعَةُ ٱلْحَرْبِ.

Rush, *n.* A pushing or pushing forward with haste, a dash, قَصْفَة ـ وَثْبَة ـ سَطْوَة ـ كَبَّة ـ ٱلْتِحَام ـ ثَارَة ـ زَحْف ـ ٱزْدِحَام. A —, as of water, هَدِير ـ عُجُوج ـ عَجِيج; as of wind, هُبُوب. A — into the head, as of wine, *etc.*, حُمَيَّا ـ سَوْرَة. The plant, سِمَار ـ بَرْدِيَّة *coll.* بَرْدِيٌّ ـ أَسَل ـ حَلْفَاء ـ قَشُّ ٱلْحُصْرِ ـ دَيْس. Not to care a — for, إِسْتَقَلَّ بَتَّة. It is not worth a —, لَا يُسَاوِي فَلْسًا.

Rush, *v.i.* To pass or move with vehemence, ثَارَ *aor.* يَثُورُ ـ وَثَبَ *aor.* يَثِبُ ـ تَوَثَّبَ. To —, as water, هَاجَ ـ تَثَوَّرَ ـ ثَجَّ ـ إِنْبَجَسَ; as wind, هَبَّ ². To —, as into the head, سَارَ *aor.* يَسُورُ ـ ثَارَ *aor.* يَثُورُ. To — to do anything, طَارَ إِلَى ـ وَثَبَ إِلَى. To — upon, سَطَا بِ *aor.* يَسْطُو ـ وَثَبَ *aor.* يَثِبُ ـ إِنْطَبَقَ عَلَى ـ طَفَّ عَلَى ² ـ تَفَلَّتَ إِلَى; to attack, حَمَلَ عَلَى ـ هَجَمَ عَلَى.

Rushiness, *n.* State of abounding with rushes, كَثْرَةُ سِمَارٍ ـ كَثْرَةُ أَسَلٍ.

Rushing, *a.* Moving with vehemence, هَائِج ـ ثَائِر; of water, بَجِيس ـ ضَجِيج: rushing water, مَاءٌ بَجِيسٌ. A — noise, صَوْتٌ رَاعِدٌ. A — wind, رِيحٌ هَبُوبٌ.

Rush-light, *n.* فَتِيلَة.

Rushy, *a.* كَثِيرُ ٱلْبَرْدِيِّ ـ كَثِيرُ ٱلْأَسَلِ ـ كَثِيرُ ٱلسِّمَارِ.

Russ, *a.* *See* Russian, *n.*

Russet, *a.* Of the colour, أَمْغَر ـ أَشْقَر *fem.* شَقْرَاء *pl.* شُقْر ـ أَصْدَأ *fem.* صَدْآء.

Russet, *n.* } The colour, مَغَر ـ شُقْرَة. A — apple, تُفَّاحَة
Russeting, } سَمْرَاء.

Russia, *n.* مَمْلَكَةُ ٱلرُّوسِيَّا ـ بِلَادُ ٱلْمُسْكُوبِ ـ رُوسِيَا.

Russian, *a.* مِنَ ٱلرُّوسِيَّا ـ مُسْكُوبِيٌّ. The — language, لِسَانُ ٱلْمُسْكُوبِ ـ رُوسِيَا.

Russian, *n.* مُسْكُوبِيٌّ *pl.* مُسْكُوبِيَّة ـ مِنْ أَهْلِ ٱلرُّوسِيَّا *pl.* أَهْلُ ٱلرُّوسِيَّا.

Russophilist, *n.* مُتَعَصِّبٌ لِلْمُسْكُوبِ ـ مِنْ طَرَفِ ٱلْمُسْكُوبِ.

Russophobist, *n.* ضِدُّ ٱلْمُسْكُوبِ.

Rust, *n.* Oxide of a metal, صَدًى ـ صَدَآء ـ سَهَكَة. Effect of dampness, عَفَن ـ عُفُونَة. To remove —, صَدَّأَ.

Rust, *v.i.* To become rusty, صَدِئَ ـ. To become impaired, ضَعُفَ ² ـ تَضَعَّفَ.

Rust, *v.t.* To make rusty, صَدَّأَ. To impair, أَسْقَطَ ـ أَضْعَفَ.

Rustic, *a.* Pertaining to the country, رِيفِيٌّ; (*see also* Rural.) Rude, unpolished, حُوشِيٌّ ـ خَشِن ـ غَلِيظ ـ أَخْرَق. Simple, سَاذِج ـ سَلِيم ـ غَشِيم. *See also* Rough, Rude, *a.*

Rustic, *n.* A peasant, فَلَّاح *pl.* فَلَّاحُون ـ خَلَاوِيٌّ *pl.* خَلَاوِيَّة ـ مِنْ أَهْلِ ٱلسَّوَادِ.

Rustical, *a.* *See* Rural, *a.*

Rustically, *ad.* Clownishly, rudely, بِخُرْقَةٍ ـ بِغَلَاظَةٍ ـ بِخُشُونَةٍ ـ مِثْلَ ٱلْفَلَّاحِ.

Rusticalness, *n.* Want of refinement, حُوشِيَّة ـ خُرْق ـ خُرْقَة ـ خُشُونَة ـ غَشْم ـ غِلَاظَة.

Rusticate, *v.i.* *See to* Ruralize, *v.i.*

Rusticate, *v.t.* To oblige to reside in the country, أَلْزَمَ ٱلرِّيفَ. To banish from a college for a time, طَرَدَ ² مِنْ مَدْرَسَةٍ إِلَى حِينٍ.

Rustication, *n.* Residence in the country, تَرَيُّف. The act of banishing from a college for a time, طَرْدٌ مِنْ مَدْرَسَةٍ إِلَى حِينٍ; the being so banished, نَفْيٌ مِنْ مَدْرَسَةٍ لِمُدَّةٍ.

Rusticity, *n.* Rustic manners, أَطْبَاعٌ رِيفِيَّةٌ ـ أَوْضَاعُ أَهْلِ ٱلرِّيفِ. Rudeness, absence of refinement, غِلَاظَة ـ غِلَظ ـ خُرْق ـ خُرْقَة ـ خُشُونَة ـ غَشْم. Simplicity, سَذَاجَة ـ بَسَاطَة ـ إِخْلَاص.

Rustiness, *n.* State of being rusty, سَدًى — حَالُ ٱلصَّدَآءِ ; of being unused, عَدَمُ ٱسْتِعْمَالٍ ; of being coated with extraneous damp matter, تَعَفُّنٌ .

Rustle, *v.i.* خَفَقَ ² — تَخَشْخَشَ — هَشْهَسَ — خَرَّ ². To —, as a viper in motion, كَشَّ ² — كَشْكَشَ . The wind rustled, خَفَقَتِ ٱلرِّيحُ . *See also under to* Quiver, *v.i.*

Rustle, *n.* }
Rustling, } خَرِيرٌ — خَرْخَرَةٌ — خَشْخَشَةٌ — هَشْهَشَةٌ ; as of a viper in motion, كَشْكَشَةٌ — كَشِيشٌ ; as of an arrow through the air, نَمِيمَةٌ .

Rustling, *a.* مُتَخَشْخِشٌ — مُهَسْهِسٌ — خَارٌّ . A — noise, خَفِيقٌ .

Rusty, *a.* Covered with rust, أَصْدَأُ *fem.* صَدْآءُ ; covered with foul extraneous matter, مُتَعَفِّنٌ . Impaired, as by inaction. مُتَضَعِّفٌ — مُضَعَّفٌ . Not quick, بَطِيءٌ — كَاهِلٌ — مُهْمِلٌ . A body of troops having — arms, كَتِيبَةٌ صَدْآءُ . *See also* Morose, *a.*

Rut, *v.i.* To be in rut, of animals, حَاوَلَ ٱلْجِمَاعَ — طَالَبَ . The being in rut, حَائِلٌ — طَالِبٌ . The rutting season, زَمَنُ ٱلتَّعْشِيرِ .

Rut, *n.* As of a wheel, أُخْدُودٌ *pl.* أَخَادِيدُ — خُدَّةٌ *pl.* خُدَدٌ .

Rut, *v.t.* As of a wheel, خَدَّ ² .

Ruth, *n.* Pity, compassion, حَنَانٌ — رَأْفَةٌ — شَفَقَةٌ — رِقَّةُ قَلْبٍ .

Ruthless, *a.* عَدِيمُ ٱلشَّفَقَةِ — قَاسٍ — بِلَا حِنَّةٍ — قَاسِي ٱلْقَلْبِ .

Ruthlessly, *ad.* بِلَا تَرَحُّمٍ — مِنْ غَيْرِ رَحْمَةٍ — قَسَاوَةً .

Ruthlessness, *n.* عَدَمُ ٱلرَّحْمَةِ — عَدَمُ ٱلشَّفَقَةِ — قَسَاوَةُ قَلْبٍ .

Rutilant, *a.* دُرِّيٌّ — نَيِّرٌ — مُنِيرٌ — لَامِعٌ — بَرِيقٌ — بَرَّاقٌ .

Rutilate, *v.i.* تَلَأْلَأَ — لَمَعَ ² — أَضَاءَ — تَنَوَّرَ — اِسْتَنَارَ — بَرَقَ ² — أَبْرَقَ .

Ruttish, *a.* *See* Lascivious, *a.*

Rutty, *a.* Abounding in ruts, كَثِيرُ ٱلْأَخَادِيدِ .

Ryder, *n.* As of a bill, *etc.* *See* Rider, *n.*

Rye, *n.* The grain, قَطَانِيٌّ ; *from the Turkish*, جَاوْدَار . Spurred rye ; *see* Ergot, *n.*

Ryno, *n.* دَرَاهِمُ — فُلُوسٌ — مَضْرُوبَاتٌ . Ready —, دَرَاهِمُ نَقْدِيَّةٌ .

Ryot, *n.* A renter of land in India, مُلْتَزِمٌ مِنْ أَهْلِ ٱلْهِنْدِ *pl.* مُلْتَزِمُونَ . A peasant, فَلَّاحٌ *pl.* فَلَّاحُونَ .

S.

S. As a contraction for "South," كِنَايَةٌ عَنْ لَفْظَةِ ٱلْجَنُوبِ .

Sabaism, *n.* *See* Sabianism, *n.*

Sabaoth, *n.* جُنُودٌ — جُمُوعٌ .

Sabbatarian, *a.* Pertaining to the Sabbath, Sunday, مَا نِيطَ بِيَوْمِ ٱلْأَحَدِ ; to the strict observance of the Sabbath, مَا نِيطَ بِٱلتَّعَصُّبِ لِحِفْظِ يَوْمِ ٱلْأَحَدِ وَتَقْدِيسِهِ .

Sabbatarian, *n.* مُتَعَصِّبٌ لِحِفْظِ يَوْمِ ٱلْأَحَدِ وَتَقْدِيسِهِ .

Sabbatarianism, *n.* ٱلتَّعَصُّبُ لِحِفْظِ يَوْمِ ٱلْأَحَدِ وَتَقْدِيسِهِ .

Sabbath, *n.* The sabbath of the Jews, ٱلسَّبْتُ — يَوْمُ ٱلسَّبْتِ . Sunday, يَوْمُ ٱلْأَحَدِ .

Sabbath-breaker, *n.* Of Saturday, نَاقِضُ ٱلسَّبْتِ ; of Sunday, نَاقِضُ ٱلْأَحَدِ .

Sabbath-breaking, *n.* Of Saturday, نَقْضُ ٱلسَّبْتِ ; of Sunday, نَقْضُ ٱلْأَحَدِ .

Sabbatic, *a.* }
Sabbatical, } Pertaining to the Sabbath, مَا نِيطَ بِٱلسَّبْتِ (أَوْ بِٱلْأَحَدِ) . Denoting rest from labour, عِبَارَةٌ عَنِ ٱلْعُطْلَةِ (*or* ٱلرَّاحَةِ) .

Sabian, *n.* صَابِئٌ *pl.* صَابِئُونَ . The Sabians, ٱلصَّابِئَةُ — ٱلصَّابِئُونَ .

Sabianism, *n.* ٱلصَّابِئَةُ — ٱلصَّبْوَةُ .

Sable, *n.* The animal, سَمُّورٌ *pl.* سَمَامِيرُ . Any garment made of —, سَمُّورٌ *pl.* سَمَامِيرُ .

Sable, *a.* Black, أَسْوَدُ *fem.* سَوْدَاءُ *pl.* سُودٌ . Dark, أَغْتَمُ — ظَلِمٌ . Belonging to mourning, مَا نِيطَ بِٱلْحِدَادِ .

Sabre, *n.* سَيْفٌ *pl.* سُيُوفٌ .

Sabre, *v.t.* ضَرَبَ بِسَيْفٍ ² — خَذَبَ ² — عَرَضَ لِلسَّيْفِ ² .

Sabretach, *n.* }
Sabretash, } خَرِيطَةُ ٱلْأَسْوَارِ .

Sabulosity, *n.* Sandiness, grittiness, صِفَةُ ٱلرَّمْلِ ; *vulg.* رَمْلِيَّةٌ .

Sabulous, *a.* Sandy, gritty, رَمْلِيٌّ — مُرَمَّلٌ — حَصِبٌ .

Sac, *n.* *See* Sack, *n.*

Saccade, *n.* نَخْعَةٌ — طَعْنَةٌ .

Sacchariferous, *a.* حَامِلُ ٱلسُّكَّرِ .

Saccharify, *v.t.* صَيَّرَ سُكَّرًا .

Saccharine, *a.* سُكَّرِيٌّ .

Saccharometer, *n.* مِيزَانٌ تُعْرَفُ بِهِ كَمِّيَّةُ ٱلسُّكَّرِ ٱلْمَوْجُودِ فِي ٱلْأَجْسَامِ .

Sacerdotal, *a.* مَا نِيطَ بِٱلْكَاهِنِ ـ كَهَنُوتِيٌّ . A — character, priesthood, كَهَنُوت .

Sacerdotally, *ad.* عَلَى أُسْلُوبِ ٱلْكَهَنُوتِ ـ كَٱلْكَاهِنِ .

Sachel, *n.* A bag, كِيس *pl.* أَكْيَاس ; a small — for books, *etc.*, خَرِيطَة *pl.* خَرَائِطُ .

Sachem, *n.* شَيْخُ قَبِيلَةٍ مِنَ ٱلْقَبَائِلِ ٱلْأَصْلِيَّةِ فِي أَمِيرِكَا *pl.* شُيُوخ .

Sack, *n.* A large bag, جُوَالِق *pl.* جَوَالِيقُ (*or* جُوَالَق) *and* جَوَالِقُ ; for straw, غِرَارَة *pl.* غَرَائِرُ ; a hair — for ditto, خَيْشَة *pl.* خِيَش ; for grain or flour, عِدْل *pl.* أَعْدَال ـ زَكِيبَة *pl.* زَكَائِبُ ـ تِلِّيس *pl.* تَلَالِيسُ ـ شِكَارَة *pl.* شَكَائِرُ . A — or bag for travelling, خُرْج *pl.* أَخْرَاج . The measure of three bushels, قَدْرُ ثَلَاثَةِ مِدَادٍ . A kind of wine, ضَرْبٌ مِنَ ٱلْخَمْرِ . Pillage, نَهْب . *See also* Pillage, Plunder, *n.*

Sack, *v.t.* To put into sacks, عَبَّأَ ـ فِي جَوَالِقَ . To plunder, نَهَبَ 2 . *See also to* Pillage, Plunder, *v.t.*

Sackage, *n.* نَهْب ـ سَلْب .

Sackbut, *n.* رَبَاب .

Sackcloth, *n.* } **Sacking**, } مِسْح *pl.* مُسُوح *and* أَمْسَاح ـ قُمَاشٌ لِلْغَرَائِرِ . Sacking of a bedstead, قُمَاشُ ٱلسَّرِيرِ . Clothed in —, لَابِسٌ مُسُوحًا . *See also* Plunder, *n.*

Sacker, *n.* A plunderer, نَاهِب *pl.* نُهَّاب ـ نَهَّاب .

Sackful, *n.* مِلْءُ جُوَالِقٍ .

Sacrament, *n.* A —, as of the Church, سِرّ *pl.* أَسْرَار . The Holy Eucharist, ٱلْعَشَاءُ ٱلرَّبَّانِيُّ ـ سِرُّ ٱلْقُدَّاسِ . To administer a —, خَدَمَ سِرًّا 2 ; to administer a — to, مَنَحَ ـ سِرًّا . To receive a —, اِقْتَبَلَ سِرًّا . To administer the Holy Eucharist to, نَاوَلَ ـ ٱلْقُرْبَانَ . To administer the Holy Eucharist, قَدَّسَ . *See also* Oath, *n.*

Sacramental, *a.* مُتَعَلِّقٌ بِٱلْأَسْرَارِ ـ سِرِّيّ .

Sacramentally, *ad.* عَلَى أُسْلُوبِ خِدْمَةِ ٱلْأَسْرَارِ ـ حَسَبَ ٱلْأَسْرَارِ .

Sacramentary, *a.* } **Sacramentarian**, } *See* Sacramental, *a.*

Sacred, *a.* Interdicted from common use, مُحَرَّم ـ حَرَام . Inviolable, مَحْجُور ـ حِجْر . Holy, مُحَرَّم ـ مُقَدَّس . Special, مَخْصُوص ـ خَاصّ . Made sacred, as by ordination, مَرْسُوم ; by anointing, مَمْسُوح . Sacred, as to religious purposes, مُخْتَصٌّ بِٱلدِّينِ وَٱلْعِبَادَةِ . The — or holy House of God, namely, the al-Ka'abah, ٱلْبَيْتُ ٱلْحَرَامُ . The — temple at Makkah, ٱلْحَرَمُ ـ حَرَمُ ٱللّٰهِ ـ حَرَمُ رَسُولِ ٱللّٰهِ ـ ٱلْمُحَرَّمُ . The two — Places, of al-Madinah and Makkah, ٱلْحَرَمَانِ . The Sacred Writings, ٱلْكُتُبُ ٱلْمُقَدَّسَةُ . To pronounce to be —, حَرَّمَ . To sanctify, قَدَّسَ .

Sacredly, *ad.* Inviolably, بِحُرْمَةٍ ; holily, بِقُدْسٍ ; religiously, بِنُسْكٍ ـ بِدِيَانَةٍ ; faithfully, بِوَفَاءٍ .

Sacredness, *n.* Inviolability, حُرْمَة ـ حُرُمَة ـ حُرَمَة ; holiness, قُدْس ـ طَهَارَة .

Sacrific, *a.* مَا يُسْتَعْمَلُ فِي تَقْرِيبِ ٱلذَّبَائِحِ .

Sacrificant, *n.* *See* Sacrificer, *n.*

Sacrificatory, *a.* Offering sacrifice, ذَابِح ـ مُقَرِّبُ ٱلذَّبَائِحِ . Connected with sacrifice, مَا نِيطَ بِتَقْرِيبِ ٱلذَّبَائِحِ .

Sacrifice, *n.* The act of offering a —, تَقْرِيبُ قُرْبَانٍ ـ عَرْض . An offering, as to God, for a religious purpose, ذَبِيحَة ـ قُرْبَان . قُرْبَان *pl.* قَرَابِينُ ـ ذَبِيحَة *pl.* ذَبَائِحُ ـ ذِبْح ـ نُسُك . An offering, تَقْدِمَة ـ عَرِيضَة . A victim for —, قَتِيل ـ نَسِيكَة *pl.* نَسَائِكُ ـ ذَبِيحَة *pl.* ذَبَائِحُ ـ أُضْحِيَّة *pl.* أَضَاحِيّ ـ ضَحِيَّة *pl.* ضَحَايَا . Loss, خَسَارَة *pl.* خَسَائِرُ . The act of relinquishing anything, as for another, تَرْكُ شَيْءٍ ـ فَوَات ـ تَنَازُلٌ عَنْ شَيْءٍ حُبًّا بِأَحَدٍ . A burnt —, وُقُود . The rites of —, مَنَاسِكُ . Human sacrifices, ضَحَايَا بَشَرِيَّةٌ . To offer —, قَرَّبَ ٱلْقُرْبَانَ ; to offer — to, قَرَّبَ لِ قُرْبَانًا . To fall a — to, هَلَكَ فِي 2 . I am your —, your redemption, *i.e.*, I will sacrifice myself for you, جُعِلْتُ فِدَاكَ ـ أَنَا قُرْبَانُكَ ـ أَنَا فِدَاكَ .

Sacrifice, *v.i.* قَرَّبَ ذَبَائِحَ ـ قَدَّمَ قَرَابِينَ .

Sacrifice, *v.t.* To offer sacrifice to, قَرَّبَ ٱلْقَرَابِينَ لِ ـ قَرَّبَ لِ . To immolate, ذَبَحَ 2 ـ ضَحَّى بِ . To make a sacrificial victim of, جَعَلَ ـ ضَحِيَّةً (*or* أُضْحِيَّةً) 2 . He sacrificed a sheep, ضَحَّى ـ ضَحَّى بِشَاةٍ . To —, immolate, a human being, ضَحَّى بِبَشَرٍ . To — anything for the sake of another, فَاتَ شَيْئًا 2 (*or* عَدَّى عَنْ شَيْءٍ) حُبًّا بِأَحَدٍ *or* حَرَمَ نَفْسَهُ شَيْئًا 2 . To —, to give up, as a friend, *etc.*, تَرَكَ 2 ـ تَخَلَّى عَنْ ـ فَاتَ 2 . To — one's self for, فَدَى ـ بِنَفْسِهِ ـ أَهْلَكَ نَفْسَهُ لِأَجْلِ كَذَا . To lose, خَسِرَ 2 .

Sacrificer, *n.* One who immolates, ذَابِح ; the priest who offers a sacrifice, كَاهِن *pl.* كَهَنَة .

Sacrilege, *n.* Profanation of sacred things, تَدْنِيس (*or* نَقْض) ٱلْمَحْرُومَاتِ (*or* ٱلْحُرُومَاتِ) . Plunder of temples, إِسْتِبَاحَة (*or* سَرْق) ٱلْهَيَاكِلِ . Uttering what is unseemly or doing what is wrong respecting sacred things, تَجْدِيف ـ هَتْكُ ٱلْمَحْرُومَاتِ . To commit —, سَرَقَ ٱلْهَيَاكِلَ 2 .

Sacrilegious, *a.* Of a person, نَاقِضُ ٱلْمَحْرُومَاتِ (*or* ٱلْحُرُومَاتِ) ـ هَتَّاكُ ٱلْمَحْرُومَاتِ . Impious, مُجَدِّف . A — robber, سَارِقُ ٱلْهَيَاكِلِ .

Sacrilegiously, *ad.* تَجْدِيفًا ـ بِهَتْكِ ٱلْمَحْرُومَاتِ .

Sacrilegiousness, *n.* نَقْضٌ (*or* خَلَلٌ) ـ هَتْكٌ (*or* نَقْضُ) ٱلْحُرْمَةِ فِي حُرْمَةِ ٱلدِّينِ.

Sacrist, *n.* نَاسِخُ ٱلتَّرَاتِيلِ وَحَافِظُ كُتُبِ ٱلْكَنِيسَةِ.

Sacristan, *n.* خَادِمُ ٱلْكَنِيسَةِ ـ قَنْدَلَفْتٌ *pl.* قَنْدَلَفْتِيَّةٌ.

Sacristy, *n.* بَيْتُ ٱلْخِدْمَةِ ـ خِزَانَةُ ٱلْبَدَلَاتِ.

Sad, *a.* Afflicted, sorrowful, شَجِبٌ ـ شَاجِبٌ ـ مُغْتَمٌّ ـ مَحْزُونٌ ـ حَزِينٌ ـ كَئِيبٌ ـ مَغْمُومٌ. Saddening, grievous, مُغِمٌّ ـ مُحْزِنٌ ـ مُؤْلِمٌ ـ شَاقٌّ ـ كَرِيبٌ ـ فَاجِعٌ. Sad of countenance, مُكْمَدُ ٱلْوَجْهِ. Vexatious, صَعْبٌ ـ مُكَدِّرٌ ـ مُغِمٌّ. Bad, vicious, شَقِيٌّ ـ دَنِيٌّ ـ خَبِيثٌ ـ شِرِّيرٌ ـ شَنِيعٌ. He went away —, مَضَى حَزِينًا. To make —; *see to* Sadden, *v.t.* To be —, شَجِبَ ـ حَزِنَ ـ إِكْتَرَبَ ـ تَأَسَّفَ ـ كَئِبَ. *See also* Melancholic, *a. and to* Grieve, *v.i.*

Sadden, *v.t.* شَجَّبَ ـ أَغَمَّ ـ أَهَمَّ ـ أَكْرَبَ ـ أَكْأَبَ ـ ضَيَّقَ ـ كَسَرَ خَاطِرَهُ ـ أَحْزَنَ.

Saddle, *n.* سَرْجٌ *pl.* سُرُوجٌ; for a camel, رَحْلٌ *pl.* رِحَالٌ *and* أَرْحَالٌ; for an ass or mule, a pack-saddle, بَرْذَعَةٌ *pl.* بَرَاذِعُ ـ جِلَالٌ *pl.* جِلَالٌ. A side-saddle, سَرْجٌ لِلنِّسَاءِ ـ سَرْجٌ لِلْحَرِيمِ. A — of mutton, لَحْمُ ظَهْرِ غَنَمٍ. The seat of a —, بَحْرُ ٱلسَّرْجِ. The back of a —, آخِرَةُ ٱلسَّرْجِ. Unsteady in the —, أَمْيَلُ ـ قُلْعَةٌ ـ قَلَّاعٌ. To be in the —, to have an appointment, كَانَ فِي مَنْصِبٍ ـ أَجْرَى مَأْمُورِيَّةً ـ حَفِظَ مَأْمُورِيَّةً. To put one on a —, to mount, رَكَّبَ.

Saddle, *v.t.* To put a saddle on a horse, *etc.*, سَرَجَ ـ سَرَّجَ ـ أَسْرَجَ ـ شَدَّ ٱلدَّابَّةَ; on a camel, رَحَلَ ٱلْبَعِيرَ. To — on to, to add to, أَضَافَ إِلَى. To — one with, كَلَّفَ بِ; to be saddled with, تَكَلَّفَ بِ. To be saddled, of a horse, *etc.*, تَسَرَّجَ. To keep constantly to the —, to be constantly riding, أَشْبَطَ عَلَى رِكَابِهِ. Saddle ye the horse for me, شُدُّوا لِي عَلَى ٱلْحِصَانِ.

Saddle-back, *ad.* عَلَى ٱلسَّرْجِ.

Saddle-bag, *n.* خُرْجٌ *pl.* خِرَجَةٌ; a pair of —, خُرْجَانِ.

Saddle-bow, *n.* حَفٌّ ـ قَرَبُوسٌ *pl.* قَرَابِيسُ.

Saddle-cloth, *n.* One to cover the saddle, طَرَّاحَةٌ ـ مِفْرَشَةٌ ـ رَخْتٌ; one to put under the saddle, لِبْدٌ *pl.* لُبُودٌ.

Saddle-cushion, *n.* غَرَقٌ.

Saddle-girth, *n.* حُزُمٌ *pl.* حِزَامٌ ـ ضَفِيرٌ ـ وَضِينٌ ـ وَلَمٌ; a — going round the chest, سِنَافٌ *pl.* سُنُفٌ.

Saddle-maker, *n.* *See* Sadler, *n.*

Saddled, *a.* As with a saddle, مُسَرَّجٌ. Saddled with, مُكَلَّفٌ بِ.

Sadler, *n.* سَرَّاجٌ ـ سُرُوجِيٌّ; of packsaddles, بَرْذَعَانِيٌّ.

Saddle-room, *n.* بَيْتُ ٱلسُّرُوجِ.

Saddlery, *n.* A sadler's materials, أَثَاثُ ٱلسَّرَّاجِ; the trade of, سِرَاجَةٌ.

Saddle-tree, *n.* مِشْجَبٌ (*or* خَشَبَةُ) ٱلسَّرْجِ.

Sadducee, *n.* صَدُوقِيٌّ *pl.* صَدُوقِيُّونَ.

Sadly, *ad.* Sorrowfully, بِشَجَبٍ ـ بِغَمٍّ ـ بِحُزْنٍ. Unhappily, بِنَحْسٍ. Badly, بِشَاعَةٍ ـ بِرَدَاءَةٍ. Why look you so — to-day? لِمَاذَا وَجْهُكَ مُكْمَدٌ ٱلْيَوْمَ.

Sadness, *n.* Heaviness of heart, غَمٌّ ـ هَمٌّ ـ شَجَبٌ ـ كَآبَةٌ ـ حُزْنٌ. Unhappiness, شَقَاوَةٌ ـ شَقًا ـ نَحْسٌ. Grievousness, ضِيقٌ ـ صُعُوبَةٌ ـ أَلَمٌ ـ مَشَقَّةٌ ـ كَرْبٌ.

Sáfar, *n.* The Muslim month, صَفَرٌ. The two Sáfars, ٱلصَّفَرَانِ.

Safe, *a.* Free from danger or harm, سَلِيمٌ ـ آمِنٌ ـ أَمِينٌ; safe from, سَالِمٌ مِنْ. In safe custody, مَحْفُوظٌ ـ مَصُونٌ ـ مَحْرُوسٌ. To be trusted, مُعْتَقَدٌ ـ أَمِينٌ. Tried, مُجَرَّبٌ. This is the safest way, هٰذَا ٱلطَّرِيقُ ٱلْأَسْلَمُ. To be —, أَمِنَ ـ سَلِمَ; to be — from, أَمِنَ مِنْ ـ سَلِمَ مِنْ. To feel —, اِطْمَأَنَّ. To make —, أَسْلَمَ ـ سَلَّمَ ـ آمَنَ ـ وَكَّدَ ـ أَوْكَدَ. Safe and sound, سَالِمٌ آمِنٌ. Is the lad — ? أَسَالِمٌ لِلْفَتَى. He received him —, قَبِلَهُ سَالِمًا.

Safe, *n.* A place for keeping things safe, of food, كِلَار; of other things, money, *etc.*, خَزْنَةٌ ـ خِزَانَةٌ; for clothes, صُوَانٌ ـ صِوَانٌ ـ مَصَانٌ ـ صَوَانٌ. A — to protect food from ants, نَمْلِيَّةٌ.

Safe-conduct, *n.* A passport, صَكٌّ ـ وَرَقَةُ أَمَانٍ ـ أَمَانٌ ـ تَلَاءٌ ٱلْمُسَافِرِ. *See also* Escort, *n.*

Safeguard, *n.* صَوْنٌ ـ صِيَانَةٌ ـ حِمَايَةٌ ـ حِفْظٌ ـ أَمَانٌ ـ ذِمَّةٌ; of a person, حَافِظٌ ـ حَامٍ.

Safe-keeping, *n.* حِفْظٌ; safe custody, صِيَانَةٌ.

Safely, *ad.* In a manner to secure from danger, بِأَمْنٍ وَأَمَانٍ ـ بِأَمْنِيَّةٍ; carefully, بِحِرْسٍ; in close custody, بِضَبْطٍ. He led them —, هَدَاهُمْ آمِنِينَ. He dwelt —, سَكَنَ آمِنًا. He trusts — in him, يَثِقُ بِهِ. He kept them —, حَرَسَهُمْ بِضَبْطٍ.

Safeness, *n.* أَمْنِيَّةٌ.

Safety, *n.* Freedom from danger or loss, صَوْنٌ ـ حِفْظٌ ـ أَمَانٌ ـ سَلَامٌ ـ سَلَامَةٌ ـ أَمْنِيَّةٌ ـ أَمْنٌ وَأَمَانٌ. Safety, escape from danger, سَلَامَةٌ ـ خَوْجٌ ـ نَجَاةٌ ـ سَلَامٌ ـ فَوْزٌ. Safe custody, حِرَاسَةٌ ـ ضَبْطٌ ـ صَوْنٌ ـ صِيَانَةٌ. A place of —, مَأْمَنٌ. The public —, ٱلسَّلَامَةُ ٱلْجُمْهُورِيَّةُ. You are in —, أَنْتَ فِي أَمْنٍ. Distrust is the parent of —, (prov.) الِاسْتِخْوَانُ يُوَلِّدُ ٱلْأَمَانَ ـ مَنْ خَافَ نَجَا. A — lamp, فَانُوسُ ٱلْأَمْنِيَّةِ. A — valve, غِشَاءُ (*or* حَاجِزُ) ٱلْأَمْنِيَّةِ.

They found the house shut with all —, وَجَدُوا ٱلْبَيْتَ مُغْلَقًا بِكُلِّ حِرْصٍ. Safety to you! May you be safe! حَوْجًا لَكَ.

Safflower, *n.* عُصْفُر – إِخْرِيض – قُرْطُم – قِرْطِم – شُوْرَان. To dye with —, عَصْفَرَ; to be so dyed, تَعَصْفَرَ.

Saffron, *n.* رَادِن – جَادِيّ – جَسَد – عُمَار – غُمْر – رَزْنَب – زَعْفَرَان. Indian —, كُرْكُم – وَرْس.

Safety-lamp, Safety-valve, } *See under* Safety, *n.*

Sag, *v.i.* مَالَ – اِجْتَنَحَ – اِنْعَطَفَ.

Sag, *v.t.* عَطَفَ – أَمَالَ – صَوَّبَ.

Saga, *n.* أَسَاطِيرُ أَهَالِي شَمَالِ أُورُبَّا ٱلْأَقْدَمِينَ وَقِصَصُهُمْ.

Sagacious, *a.* Wise, discerning, لَبِيب – ذَهِيّ – أَرِب *pl.* أَلِبَّاء – ذَكِيّ *pl.* أَذْكِيَاء – ذَهِن – فَطِن – أَهْلُ فَرَاسَةٍ. Quick of scent, حَاذِقُ ٱلشَّمِّ. To be —, فَطِنَ – ذَهِنَ – أَرِبَ. To make —, فَطَّنَ – أَرَّبَ. To affect to be —, تَأَرَّبَ.

Sagaciously, *ad.* بِفِطْنَةٍ – بِفَرَاسَةٍ – بِذَكَاءٍ – بِدَهَاءٍ – بِإِرْبٍ – بِذِهْنٍ – بِفَنٍّ.

Sagaciousness, *n.* Sagacity, } فَرَاسَة – فِطْنَة – فَنّ – ذَكَاء – دَهَاء – إِرْب – ذَهْن – ذِهْن.

Sage, *a.* حَكِيم *pl.* حُكَمَاء – فَطِين – فَاطِن – فَطِن *pl.* فُطُون *or* فُطُن.

Sage, *n.* A wise man, حَكِيم *pl.* حُكَمَاء. The herb, مَرْيَمِيَّة – قُوَيْسَة – قُوَيْسَةُ ٱلْعَيْنِ – سَالِبِيَّة – ٱلنَّعْمَة.

Sagely, *ad.* بِفِطْنَةٍ – حِكْمَةً.

Sageness, *n.* فِطْنَة – حِكْمَة.

Sagittarius, *n.* The sign of the Zodiac, ٱلْقَوْسُ – ٱلرَّامِي.

Sago, *n.* ضَرْبٌ مِنَ ٱلْحَبِّ مَصْنُوعٌ مِنْ لُبِّ (*or* شَحْمِ) نَخْلِ ٱلْهِنْدِ.

Sa'īd, *n.* سَعِيد. Port —, بُورْتُ سَعِيد.

Sail, *n.* As of a ship, جُلّ *pl.* جُلُول – قِلَاعَة – قِلْع *pl.* قِلَاع *and* قُلُوع – شِرَاع *pl.* شُرُع *and* أَشْرِعَة. A ship, سَفِينَة *pl.* سَفَائِنُ – مَرْكَب *pl.* مَرَاكِبُ. An excursion in a vessel, سِيْرَةٌ فِي ٱلْبَحْرِ – مِشْوَارٌ فِي ٱلْبَحْرِ. Having sails, مُقَلَّع; having sails set, (of a ship, مُشْرَع (مَرْكَب – مُنْشَأَة *pl.* مُنْشَآت: (of a ship, سَفِينَة) – مَرْفُوعُ ٱلْقُلُوعِ. To put sails to, شَرَّعَ. To hoist —, أَقْلَعَ – رَفَعَ (*or* فَتَحَ) ٱلْقُلُوعَ. To take in —, لَمَّ ٱلْقُلُوعَ. To strike —, أَنْزَلَ (*or* نَزَّلَ) ٱلْقُلُوعَ. They could not spread the —, لَمْ يَقْدِرُوا أَنْ يَنْشُرُوا ٱلْقِلْعَ.

Sail, *v.i.* سَارَ *aor.* يَسِيرُ – أَقْلَعَ – بَحَّرَ – أَبْحَرَ – مَخَرَ. To — about, as a bird in the air, تَكَرْكَرَ. To — from, سَافَرَ مِن. The English fleet will shortly sail up ٱلْإِنْكِلِيزِ لَا تَلْبَثُ أَنْ تَمْخَرَ إِلَى هُنَا. He found a ship that was sailing to Egypt, وَجَدَ *aor.* يَجِدُ سَفِينَةً عَابِرَةً إِلَى مِصْرَ.

Sail, *v.t.* To manage a vessel, أَسَارَ ٱلسَّفِينَةَ – سَيَّرَ ٱلْمَرْكَبَ – دَبَّرَ ٱلْمَرْكَبَ. To — or pass over, of a ship, أَبْحَرَ فِي – سَافَرَ فِي. *See also to* Navigate, *v.t.* and *i.*

Sailable, *a.* *See* Navigable, *a.*

Sail-cloth, *n.* قُمَاشُ ٱلْقُلُوعِ.

Sailing, *a.* Having sails, مُشَرَّع. A — ship, مَرْكَبٌ مُقَلَّعٌ – سَفِينَةٌ شِرَاعِيَّةٌ – مَرْكَبُ شِرَاعٍ.

Sailing, *n.* The act of, مَخْر – إِبْحَار – إِقْلَاع – سَيْر. Sailing had become dangerous, صَارَ ٱلسَّفَرُ فِي ٱلْبَحْرِ خَطِرًا. *See also* Navigation, *n.*

Sailing-master, *n.* مُهَنْدِسُ ٱلْمَرْكَبِ – مُسَيِّرُ ٱلْمَرْكَبِ.

Sail-loft, *n.* مَعْمَلُ ٱلْقُلُوعِ.

Sail-maker, *n.* صَانِعُ قُلُوعٍ.

Sailor, *n.* صَارٍ *pl.* صُرَّاء – صَرَارِيّ *pl.* صَرَارِيُّون – مَلَّاح – نُوتِيّ *pl.* نَوَاتِيّ – بَحْرِيّ *pl.* بَحْرِيَّة.

Sailor-like, *a.* مِثْلَ ٱلْبَحْرِيَّةِ.

Sail-room, *n.* أَنْبَارُ ٱلْقُلُوعِ.

Sainfoin, *n.* The plant, نَبَاتٌ مِنْ جِنْسِ ٱلْقُرْطِ (*or* ٱلْبِرْسِيمِ).

Saint, *n.* As among Muslims, وَلِيّ *pl.* أَوْلِيَاء; among Christians, قِدِّيس *pl.* قِدِّيسُون; the word used denominately by the latter is مَار *or* قِدِّيس, *e.g.*, Saint Peter, ٱلْقِدِّيسُ بُطْرُسُ: *or* مَار بُطْرُس; among Muslims the equivalent word is, حَضْرَة. A holy person, بَارّ *pl.* أَبْرَار – طَاهِر *pl.* أَطْهَار. The saints in heaven, أَصْحَابُ ٱلْجَنَّةِ. All Saints' Day, عِيدُ جَمِيعِ ٱلْقِدِّيسِينَ – عِيدُ ٱلْقِدِّيسِينَ. Saint Anthony's fire, حُمْرَة. Saint Vitus's Dance, عِلَّةُ تَشَنُّجِ ٱلْمَفَاصِلِ.

Saint, *v.t.* *See to* Canonize, *v.t.*

Sainted, *a.* Holy, مُقَدَّس – [illegible] – قِدِّيس – طَاهِر. Referring to one departed, dead, مَغْفُور – مَرْحُوم.

Saint-like, *a.* Saintly, } طَاهِر – قِدِّيس – [illegible].

Saintship, *n.* طَهَارَة – قَدَاسَة.

Sake, *n.* Cause, سَبَب. Reason, motive [illegible] – بَاعِث – مُوجِب. Regard, خَاطِر. Design, قَصْد – نِيَّة. Love, حُبّ – [illegible].

For the — of, out of love for one, حُبًّا بِهِ – [illegible] – [illegible] ; out of regard for me, لِخَاطِرِي – [illegible] ... of one, بِسَبَبِهِ. For God's —, لِأَجْلِ ٱللّٰهِ – [illegible] حُبًّا. For man's —, لِأَجْلِ ٱلْإِنْسَانِ. [illegible]

مِنْ شَأْنِ ـ كَرَمًا لِي ـ كَرَمًا لِخَاطِرِي ـ مِنْ أَجْلِي ـ جَرَاى ـ مِنْ جَرَاكَ ـ مِنْ جَنْلِكَ ـ لِأَجْلِكَ ـ خَاطِرِي. For your —, كَرَمًا لِخَاطِرِكَ. For the — of one person a thousand are served, (prov.) كَرَمًا لِعَيْنٍ تُكْرَمُ أَلْفُ عَيْنٍ. For the — of, with mercenary motives, طَمَعًا فِي.

Sal, *n.* مِلْح *pl.* أَمْلَاح.

Sal-ammoniac, *n.* مِلْحُ ٱلنَّشَادِرِ ـ نُشَادِر.

Salacious, *n.* *See* Lustful, Lewd, Obscene, *a.*

Salaciously, *ad.* *See* Lewdly, Obscenely, *ad.*

Salaciousness, *n.* } *See* Lustfulness, Lewdness, Obscenity, *n.*
Salacity, }

Salad, *n.* طَعَامٌ يُعْمَلُ مِنَ ٱلْخُضَرِ ٱلْمُقَطَّعَةِ مُتَبَّلًا بِٱلْخَلِّ وَٱلْمِلْحِ ـ سَلَطَة ـ سَلَاطَة.

Salâm, *n.* سَلَام.

Salamander, *n.* A species of lizard, أُعْجَايَة ـ سَمَنْدَر ـ سَمَيْدَر. An animal fabled to live in fire, حَيَوَانٌ وَهْمِيٌّ زَعَمَ ٱلْقُدَمَآءُ أَنَّهُ يَعِيشُ فِي وَسَطِ ٱلنَّارِ.

Salamandrine, *a.* Like a salamander, مِثْلَ ٱلسَّمَنْدَرِ. Enduring fire, يَعِيشُ فِي ٱلنَّارِ ـ يَحْتَمِلُ ٱلنَّارَ.

Salary, *n.* وَظِيفَة *pl.* وَظَائِف ـ عُلُوفَة ـ خِدْمَة ـ رَاتِب ـ رَوَاتِب ـ مَعَاش; *from the Turkish,* جَامَكِيَّة *pl.* جَوَامِك. A daily —, يَوْمِيَّة; a monthly —, شَهْرِيَّة; a yearly —, سَنَوِيَّة. *See also* Stipend, *n.*

Sale, *n.* The act of selling, بَيْع. Mode of selling, بِيعَة. Power of sale, حَقُّ ٱلْبَيْعِ ـ بَيْع. Trade, سَوْم ـ أَخْذٌ وَعَطَآءٌ. A market, سُوق. Currency, رَوَاج. A bill of —, صَكّ ـ عُهْدَة ٱلْبَيْعِ. For —, لِلْبَيْعِ. A public —, auction, مَزَاد. A private —, بَيْعٌ خَاصٌّ ـ بَيْعٌ عَلَى حِدَةٍ. Sale without reserve, بَيْعٌ مُطْلَقٌ ـ بَيْعٌ بِلَا ٱسْتِثْنَآءٍ. To offer or put up for —, عَرَضَ لِلْبَيْعِ. To offer for — at a price, سَامَ ـ ٱسْتَامَ: he offered the commodity for — at a price, سَامَ ٱلسِّلْعَةَ (or بِٱلسِّلْعَةِ). I offered my commodity for — to such an one at such a price, سُمْتُ (or سَاوَمْتُ) فُلَانًا سِلْعَتِي. To bid against one in a —, ٱسْتَامَ عَلَى: he bid against me in the — of the article, ٱسْتَامَ عَلَيَّ ٱلسِّلْعَةَ. An article having a good —, شَيْءٌ نَافِقٌ ـ سِلْعَةٌ; having a dull —, شَيْءٌ كَاسِدٌ; تُبَاعُ بِسُهُولَةٍ.

Saleable, *a.* That may be sold, يُبَاعُ ـ يَنْبَاعُ; having a ready sale, رَائِج.

Saleableness, *n.* إِمْكَانُ ٱلْبَيْعِ; readiness of sale, رَوَاج.

Salebrous, *a.* *See* Rough, Rugged, *a.*

Salep, *n.* سَحْلَب.

Saleratus, *n.* مِلْحُ ٱلْقِلْيِ.

Salesman, *n.* One who finds sale for the goods of others, دَلَّال ـ بَيَّاع ـ شَرَّآء ـ وَكِيل *pl.* وُكَلَآء. A — in a warehouse, مُسْتَخْدَمٌ فِي مَخْزَنٍ.

Sal gem, *n.* مِلْحٌ مَخْتُوم ـ مِلْحٌ أَنْدَرَانِيٌّ; *vulg.* مِلْحٌ أَنْدَرَانِيٌّ ـ مِلْحٌ مَعْدِنِيٌّ.

Salic, *a.* عِبَارَةٌ عَنْ شَرِيعَةٍ تَمْنَعُ ٱلنِّسَآءَ عَنِ ٱلْجُلُوسِ عَلَى تَخْتِ ٱلْمَمْلَكَةِ.

Salicine, *n.* ضَرْبٌ مِنَ ٱلْمِلْحِ يُسْتَخْرَجُ مِنَ ٱلصَّفْصَافِ.

Salient, *a.* Shooting forth, بَارِز. Prominent, important, مُهِمّ. Outward, خَارِجِيّ. A — angle, زَاوِيَةٌ خَارِجِيَّةٌ (or بَارِزَةٌ). *See also* Prominent, *a.*

Saliently, *ad.* *See* Prominently, *ad.*

Saliferous, *a.* مَوْجُودٌ فِيهِ مَعْدِنُ ٱلْمِلْحِ طَبْعًا.

Salifiable, *a.* مَا يُسْتَخْرَجُ مِنْهُ مِلْحٌ بِٱلتَّرْكِيبِ مَعَ حُمُوضَةٍ أَوْ غَيْرِهَا ـ قَابِلُ ٱلتَّمْلِيحِ.

Salification, *n.* The act of, تَرْكِيبٌ وَتَمْلِيحٌ.

Salify, *v.t.* صَيَّرَ مِلْحًا بِٱلتَّرْكِيبِ مَعَ حُمُوضَةٍ أَوْ غَيْرِهَا ـ رَكَّبَهُ مَعَ حُمُوضَةٍ وَمَلَّحَهُ.

Saline, *a.* فِيهِ مِلْحٌ ـ مَالِح. Saltish, brackish, مَلِيح. A saline draught, شَرْبَةٌ سَهْلَةٌ (or مُسْهِلَةٌ) مِنَ ٱلْمُلُوحَاتِ.

Saliva, *n.* رِيق ـ لُعَاب ـ بُصَاق ـ بُزَاق ـ رُضَاب.

Salivary, *a.* رِيقِيّ.

Salivate, *v.t.* أَحْدَثَ فِي كَثْرَةَ ٱللُّعَابِ.

Salivation, *n.* كَثْرَةُ ٱلرِّيقِ ـ كَثْرَةُ ٱللُّعَابِ.

Salix, *n.* } The willow, ٱلصَّفْصَاف.
Sallow, *n.* }

Sallow, *a.* Pale, أَصْفَرُ *fem.* صَفْرَآءُ *pl.* صُفْر ـ مُصْفَارّ. *See also* Pale, *a.*

Sallowness, *n.* ٱصْفِيرَار ٱصْفِرَار.

Sally, *n* A springing or rushing forth, سَطْوَة ـ ٱقْتِحَام ـ ثَارَة ـ فُصُول ـ بُذَارَة ـ زَحْف. An attack, هُجُوم ـ حَمْل. Exuberance, كَثْرَة ـ وَفْرَة. A — of wit, نُكْتَةٌ لَطِيفَةٌ *pl.* نُكَت ـ ظَرِيفَة *pl.* ظَرَائِف. The sallies, follies, of youth, ٱلشَّبِيبَة.

Sally, *v.i.* *See to* Rush, *v.i.*

Sally-port, *n.* Of a fortification, بَابُ ٱلْهُجُومِ ـ بَابُ ٱلْخُرُوجِ; of a fire ship, بَابٌ لِلْفِرَارِ مِنْ حَرَّاقَةٍ.

Salmagundi, *n.* A medley, mixture, طَعَامٌ ـ مَخْلُوطَة ـ خَبِيصَة مِنْ أَنْوَاعٍ شَتَّى.

Salmon, *n.* صُومُونٌ وَهُوَ سَمَكٌ بَحْرِيٌّ ـ حُوتُ سُلَيْمَانَ .

Salmon-trout, *n.* سَمَكُ أَرْيُوانٍ كَبِيرٌ (in Turkish, الا بالغى).

Saloon, *n.* سالُون ـ بَيْتُ ٱلْقُعُودِ ـ دِيوَان ـ مَقْعَد .

Salsify, *n.* The plant, قُعْبُول ـ قُعْبَارُون .

Salsuginous, *a.* مَالِحٌ نَوْعًا ـ مَالِح ـ مَلِيح .

Salt, *n.* مِلْحٌ *pl.* مِلْحٌ *and* مِلَاح . Common —, مِلْحُ ٱلْعَادَةِ ـ مِلْحُ ٱلْعَامَّةِ . Mineral —, مِلْحٌ أَنْدَرَانِيٌّ *vulg.* مِلْحٌ دَرَانِيٌّ . Sea —, مِلْحُ ٱلْبَحْرِ . Wit, humour, نُكْتَة ـ ظَرَافَة ـ لَطَافَة ـ فَكَاهَة . He is not worth his —, لا يُسَاوِي فَتَّةً (*lit.* He is not worth a crumbled piece of camel's dung.)

Salt, *v.t.* مَلَّحَ ـ أَمْلَحَ ـ ــِ مَلَحَ .

Salt, *v.i.* رَبَّى ٱلْمِلْحَ .

Salt, *a.* Of the flavour, مَالِح . Salted, مُمَلَّح .

Saltless, *a.* بِلَا مِلْح . *See also* Insipid, *a.*

Saltant, *a.* / Saltatory, } نَطَّاط ـ قَافِز ـ نَطٌّ .

Saltation, *n.* قَفْزٌ ـ قَفْز ـ نَطٌّ .

Salt-cellar, *n.* مَلَّاحَة ـ مَمْلَحَة ـ وِعَاءُ ٱلْمِلْحِ .

Salter, *n.* One who salts, مَلَّاح ; who sells salt, بَيَّاعُ مِلْحٍ .

Salt-duty, *n.* ضَرِيبَةٌ عَلَى ٱلْمِلْحِ ـ مِيرِي ٱلْمِلْحِ .

Salted, *a.* مُمَلَّح ـ مُمَلَّح ـ مَمْلُوح . Salted meat, or fish, مَلُوحَة *pl.* مَلُوحَات ـ مَمْلُوحَة *pl.* مَمْلُوحَات .

Saltern, *n.* مَلَّاحَة .

Saltigrade, *a.* نَاطٌّ طَبْعًا ـ قَافِزٌ طَبْعًا .

Saltish, *a.* مَالِحٌ نَوْعًا ـ مَلِيح .

Salt-lake, *n.* بُحَيْرَةُ مَاءٍ مَالِحٍ .

Salt-marsh, *n.* مَلَّاحَة .

Salt-meat, *n.* لَحْمٌ مُمَلَّحٌ .

Salt-mine, *n.* مَعْدِنُ مِلْحٍ .

Saltness, *n.* مُلُوحَة ـ مَلَّاحَة . To lose —, صَارَ بِلَا مُلُوحَةٍ ـِ .

Salt-pan, *n.* / Salt-pit, } مَلَّاحَة .

Saltpetre, *n.* مِلْحُ ٱلْبَارُودِ ـ بُورَق .

Salt-rheum, *n.* *See* Herpes, *n.*

Salt-spring, *n.* يَنْبُوعُ مَاءٍ مَالِحٍ .

Salts, *n.* *See* Epsom-salts, *n.*

Salt-water, *n.* مَاءٌ مَالِحٌ .

Salt-works, *n.* مَعْمَلُ مِلْحٍ .

Salty, *a.* مَالِحٌ نَوْعًا ـ مَالِح .

Salubrious, *a.* نَزِهٌ *pl.* نِزَاه *and* نُزَهَاءُ ـ نَزِيه ـ شَافٍ ـ سَلِيم . *See also* Healthy, Wholesome, *a.*

Salubriously, *ad.* بِمُعَافَاةٍ ـ بِسَلَامَةٍ .

Salubriousness, *n.* / Salubrity, } سَلَامَة ـ نُزْهَة ; of climate, إِعْتِدَالُ هَوَاءٍ . *See also* Healthiness, Wholesomeness, *n.*

Salutarily, *ad.* إِفَادَةً وَسَلَامَةً .

Salutariness, *n.* مَنْفَعَة ـ نَفْع ـ فَائِدَة . *See also* Healthfulness, Wholesomeness, *n.*

Salutary, *a.* Conducive to health, طَيِّبٌ لِلصِّحَّةِ ـ شَافٍ . Useful, نَافِع ـ مُفِيد . *See also* Beneficial, *a.*

Salutation, *n.* تَحِيَّة ـ تَسْلِيم ـ سَلَام . He returned him the —, رَدَّ عَلَيْهِ ٱلسَّلَامَ [2].

Salute, *v.t.* To greet, سَلَّمَ عَلَى ـ حَيَّى . To kiss, بَاسَ ـ قَبَّلَ *aor.* يَبُوسُ . To —, with arms, رَفَعَ سَلَامًا لِ ـَ . To —, with guns, أَطْلَقَ ٱلْمَدَافِعَ إِكْرَامًا لِ . They saluted him as king, or successor to a king, حَيَّوْهُ بِٱلْمُلْكِ ـ سَلَّمُوا عَلَيْهِ بِٱلْخِلَافَةِ ـ بَايَعُوهُ بِٱلسَّلْطَنَةِ . They came to the island to — the king, أَقْبَلُوا إِلَى ٱلْجَزِيرَةِ لِيُسَلِّمُوا عَلَى ٱلْمَلِكِ . Our friends — you, يُسَلِّمُ عَلَيْكَ ٱلْأَحِبَّاءُ .

Salute, *n.* A salutation, تَسْلِيم ـ سَلَام ـ تَحِيَّة ; with arms, رَفْعُ سَلَامٍ ; with guns, إِطْلَاقُ ٱلْمَدَافِعِ لِلْإِكْرَامِ . The military —, سَلَامُ ٱلْعَسْكَرِ . A — of 21 guns will be fired in honour of the king, يُطْلَقُ ٢١ مِدْفَعًا إِكْرَامًا لِلْمَلِكِ . A salute was fired to announce it, أُطْلِقَتِ ٱلْمَدَافِعُ تَبْشِيرًا بِهِ . A kiss, بَوْسَة ـ قُبْلَة .

Salutiferous, *a.* شَافٍ .

Salvable, *a.* مِمَّا يُخَلَّصُ ـ مِمَّا يَنْجَا .

Salvage, *n.* أُجْرَةُ ٱلْخَلَاصِ ـ أُجْرَةُ نَجَاةِ مَرْكَبٍ أَوْ وَسْقِهِ مِنَ ٱلْخَطَرِ (or ٱلتَّخْلِيصِ).

Salvation, *n.* The act of saving, تَخْلِيص ـ نَجَاة ; the being saved, خَلَاص . The means of —, وَسِيلَةُ ٱلنَّجَاةِ ـ وَسِيلَةُ ٱلْخَلَاصِ . Forgiveness, مَغْفِرَة ـ غُفْرَان . Eternal —, خَلَاصٌ أَبَدِيٌّ .

Salve, *n.* طِلَاءٌ ـ مَرْهَم *pl.* مَرَاهِمُ ـ دُهْن *pl.* دِهَان . There is a — for every sore, (prov.) مَا مِنْ مَرَضٍ إِلَّا وَلَهُ خُطْفٌ . *See also* Remedy, *n.*

Salve, *v.t.* As with a salve, طَلَى ـ بِ ـ دَهَنَ [2] ـِ . To palliate, دَارَى عَنْ ـ أَعْذَرَ ـ سَتَرَ [2] .

Salver, *n.* طَبَق *pl.* أَطْبَاق ـ فَانُور *vulg.* صِينِيَّة *pl.* صَوَانِيُّ .

Salvo, *n.* An exception, إِسْتِثْنَاءٌ . An excuse, عُذْر . A — of guns, إِطْلَاقُ مَدَافِعَ .

Sal-volatile, *n.* رُوحُ ٱلنُّشَادِرِ .

Salvor, *n.* As of a ship, مُخَلِّصُ مَرْكَبٍ.

Samaria, *n.* السَّامِرَةُ. Samaria now called Nâbulus, السَّامِرَةُ ٱلْمَعْرُوفَةُ ٱلْآنَ بِنَابُلُسَ.

Samaritan, *n.* / Samaritan, *a.* } سَامِرِيٌّ *pl.* سَامِرِيُّونَ *and* سَامِرَةٌ.

Same, *a.* Identical, هُوَ — عَيْن — وَاحِد — فَرْد — ذَات. As designating any particular thing referred to, ٱلْمَذْكُورُ. As standing for a relative pronoun, ٱلَّذِي *pl.* ٱلَّذِينَ *fem.* ٱلَّتِي *pl.* ٱللَّاتِي. As standing for a person, نَفْس *pl.* أَنْفُس — شَخْص *pl.* أَشْخَاص. You are the —, أَنْتَ هُوَ — أَنْتَ أَنْتَ. From the rising of the sun until the going down of the —, مِنْ مَشْرِقِ ٱلشَّمْسِ إِلَى مَغْرِبِهَا. Let these — (men) say, لِيَقُلْ هٰؤُلَاءِ أَنْفُسُهُمْ. On that — day, فِي ذٰلِكَ ٱلْيَوْمِ. That — man, ذَاتُ ٱلرَّجُلِ. It or he is the —, هُوَ هُوَ عَيْنًا — هُوَ هُوَ بِعَيْنِهِ. He went out the — day, خَرَجَ فِي يَوْمِهِ. Of the — kind, مِنْ جِنْسٍ وَاحِدٍ. They are of the — colour, لَوْنُهُمْ وَاحِدٌ. That — night, فِي تِلْكَ ٱللَّيْلَةِ بِعَيْنِهَا. It is the — to me whether you stand or sit, سَوَآءٌ عَلَيَّ قُمْتَ أَوْ قَعَدْتَ. Much the —, as usual, كَٱلْعَادَةِ. Much the —, alike, of many things or persons, شِبَاه — أَمْثَال. To be the — with, or to do the — as, مَاثَلَ. *See also* Identical, Like, *a.*

Sameness, *n.* Identity, سَوَآء — عَيْن — عَيَان. Likeness, مُمَاثَلَة. Correspondence, مُقَارَنَة — مُطَابَقَة — مُوَافَقَة. *See also under* Insipidity, *n.*

Samian, *a.* Of Samos, سِيسَامِيٌّ — مِنْ سِيسَام. Samian earth, طِينٌ مَخْتُومٌ.

Samos, *n.* سِيسَامُ.

Samphire, *n.* رَازْيَانَجٌ بَحْرِيٌّ — شُمْرَةٌ بَحْرِيَّةٌ.

Sample, *v.t.* To take samples of, أَخَذَ مَسَاطِرَ مِن [2].

Sample, *n.* عَيِّنَة *pl.* عَيِّنَات — عَرُوضَة — شَكْل *pl.* أَشْكَال — نَمُونَة *pl.* نَمُونَات — مَسْطَرَة *pl.* مَسَاطِر — عَيِّنِيَّة. Samples of stuffs, مَسَاطِرُ ٱلْقُمَاشِ — أَشْكَالُ ٱلْقُمَاشِ. A — of wheat, عَيِّنَةُ حِنْطَةٍ.

Sampler, *n.* قِطْعَةُ حِنْفَاصٍ لِتَعْلِيمِ ٱلطِّرَازِ عَلَيْهَا.

Sanability, *n.* إِمْكَانُ ٱلشِّفَآءِ.

Sanable, *a.* يُشْفَى — مِمَّا يُشْفَى.

Sanation, *n.* إِبْرَآء — شِفَآء.

Sanative, *a.* مُبْرِئٌ — شَافٍ.

Sanativeness, *n.* حِفْظُ ٱلصِّحَّةِ — قُوَّةٌ مُبْرِئَةٌ.

Sanatory, *a.* حَافِظُ ٱلصِّحَّةِ — شَافٍ.

Sanctification, *n.* The act of sanctifying, تَقْدِيس; the being sanctified, holiness, قَدَاسَة.

Sanctifier, *n.* مُقَدِّس.

Sanctify, *v.t.* قَدَّسَ — طَهَّرَ. *See also to* Consecrate, *v.t.*

Sanctimonious, *a.* مُتَخَلِّقٌ بِٱلطَّهَارَةِ — مُتَشَبِّعٌ بِٱلتَّقْوَى — مُتَصَنِّعٌ بِٱلْقَدَاسَةِ — مُتَصَوِّف — مُنَافِق *pl.* مُنَافِقُونَ.

Sanctimoniously, *ad.* تَخَلُّقًا بِٱلطَّهَارَةِ — تَشَبُّعًا بِٱلتَّقْوَى — تَصَنُّعًا بِٱلْقَدَاسَةِ — بِنِفَاقٍ.

Sanctimoniousness, *n.* / Sanctimony, } ٱلتَّخَلُّقُ بِٱلطَّهَارَةِ — ٱلتَّشَبُّعُ بِٱلتَّقْوَى — ٱلتَّصَنُّعُ بِٱلْقَدَاسَةِ — نِفَاق.

Sanction, *n.* Ratification, تَثْبِيت — تَقْرِير. Permission, allowance, إِسْتِصْوَاب — إِذْن — نَظَر — رُخْصَة — إِبَاحَة — تَجْوِيز. Legal —, مُكَافَاةٌ قَانُونِيَّةٌ. Penal —, مُكَافَاةٌ جَزَائِيَّةٌ. Official —, تَصْدِيقٌ رَسْمِيٌّ.

Sanction, *v.t.* To ratify, ثَبَّتَ — أَثْبَتَ. To permit, allow, إِسْتَصْوَبَ — أَجَازَ — جَوَّزَ — إِسْتَبَاحَ — أَبَاحَ. The letters sanctioning his being ambassador of France at the Sublime Porte, ٱلْمُحَرَّرَاتُ ٱلْمُؤْذِنَةُ بِكَوْنِهِ سَفِيرًا لِدَوْلَةِ فَرَانْسَا لَدَى ٱلْبَابِ ٱلْعَالِي.

Sanctity, *n.* / Sanctitude, } قَدَاسَة — طَهَارَة. *See also* Sacredness, *n.*

Sanctuary, *n.* A sacred place, حَرَم *pl.* أَحْرَام — قُدْس *pl.* أَقْدَاس. A temple, هَيْكَل *pl.* هَيَاكِل. A place of worship, مَسْجِد *pl.* مَسَاجِد — مَعْبَد. A place of refuge, مَلَاذ — مَلْجَأ — مَغَار. The —, or place in a church where the altar stands, بَيْتُ ٱلْمَقْدِسِ — ٱلْهَيْكَلُ. A place where the pursued is beyond the power of the pursuer, مَأْمَنٌ (or مَحَلٌّ أَمِينٌ) إِذَا ٱلْتَجَأَ إِلَيْهِ مُجْرِمٌ أَوْ شَارِدٌ لَا يُبَاحُ لِلطَّارِدِ أَوْ لِلْمُدَّعِي أَنْ يَدْخُلَهُ. To take —, إِلْتَجَأَ إِلَى مَأْمَنٍ لَا يُبَاحُ لِمُقْتَحِمٍ أَنْ يَدْخُلَهُ. To have a right of —, of a place, حَازَ ٱلْمَكَانُ حَقًّا فِي حِمَايَةِ مَنْ يَلْتَجِئُ إِلَيْهِ مِنَ ٱلْمُجْرِمِينَ وَٱلْهَارِبِينَ بِدُونِ أَنْ يُسْمَحَ لِأَحَدٍ أَنْ يَقْبِضَ عَلَيْهِ [2].

Sanctum, *n.* A small private room, حُجْرَة *pl.* حُجَر — خَلْوَة.

Sanctum Sanctorum, *n.* قُدْسُ ٱلْأَقْدَاسِ.

Sand, *n.* رَمْل *pl.* رِمَال. Fine or pure sand, رَمْلَةٌ حُرَّةٌ — رَمْلٌ نَاعِمٌ. A grain of —, حَبَّةُ رَمْلٍ. A tract or collection of —, رَمْلَة — حَبْلٌ مِنَ ٱلرَّمْلِ. A heap of —, زُخْفُ رَمْلٍ — كُومَةُ رَمْلٍ. They were as numerous as the —, كَانُوا كَثِيرِينَ كَٱلرَّمْلِ.

Sand, *v.t.* رَشَّ عَلَى ٱلرَّمْلَ — رَمَّلَ [2].

Sandal, *n.* غِرْفَة *pl.* غِرَف — حِذَآء *pl.* أَحْذِيَة. A thong of a —, شِسْع — شِرَاك. A maker of sandals, حَذَّآء. *See also* Slipper, *n.*

Sandal, *n.* }
Sandal-wood, } صَنْدَل.

Sandarack, *n.* سِنْدَرُوس ـ سِنْدَلُوس.

Sand-bag, *n.* جُوَالِقُ رَمْلٍ لِلْمِتْرَاسِ *pl.* جَوَالِيق.

Sand-box, *n.* حُقَّةٌ (*or* مِرَشَّةٌ) لِلرَّمْلِ ; *vulg.* رَمْلِيَّة ـ مِرْمَلَة.

Sand-coloured, *a.* رَمْلِيُّ ٱللَّوْنِ.

Sanders, *n.* The wood, ضَرْبٌ مِنَ ٱلْبَقَّمِ. *See also* Sandal-wood, *n.*

Sandever, *n.* }
Sandiver, } رِغْوَةُ ٱلْبِلَّوْرِ.

Sand-fly, *n.* بَرْغَشَة *coll.* بَرْغَش *pl.* بَرَاغِيش.

Sandiness, *n.* The quality of being sandy, صِفَةُ ٱلرَّمْلِ.

Sandish, *a.* مِثْلَ ٱلرَّمْلِ. *See also* Gritty, *a.*

Sand-paper, *n.* أَوْرَاقُ ٱلصَّقْلِ ـ أَوْرَاقٌ مُرَمَّلَةٌ لِلصَّقْلِ.

Sand-piper, *n.* عُصْفُورُ ٱلرَّمْلِ *pl.* عَصَافِيرُ.

Sand-pit, *n.* رَمْلَة.

Sandstone, *n.* حَجَرُ ٱلْبَلَاطِ ـ حَجَرُ ٱلرَّمْلِ.

Sandwich, *n.* شَرِيحَةُ لَحْمٍ ـ بُزْمَاوَرْد *vulg.* ضَرْبٌ مِنَ ٱلزُّمَاوَرْدِ مُطَبَّقَةٌ بَيْنَ قِطْعَتَيْنِ مِنَ ٱلْخُبْزِ.

Sandy, *a.* كَثِيرُ ٱلرَّمْلِ ـ رَمْلِيٌّ. Sandy, of colour, أَشْقَرُ *fem.* شَقْرَاءُ *pl.* شُقْر. Mixed with sand, مُرَمَّل. To become —, to have sand upon it, أَرْمَلَ.

Sane, *a.* In mind, سَالِمُ ٱلْعَقْلِ ; in health, سَالِم ـ مُتَعَافٍ ـ صَحِيح ـ سَالِمُ ٱلصِّحَّةِ. Whole, سَالِم ـ سَلِيم.

Saneness, *n.* As of mind, سَلَامَةُ عَقْلٍ ; of health, صِحَّة ـ عَافِيَة ـ سَلَامَةُ صِحَّةٍ. Wholeness, صِحَّة ـ سَلَامَة.

Sangaree, *n.* شَرْبَةُ نَبِيذٍ بِسُكَّرٍ.

Sang-froid, *n.* عَدَمُ فَشَلٍ ـ عَدَمُ ٱضْطِرَابٍ ـ رَوَاقَة ـ رَزَانَة ـ حَزْم ـ جَرَاءَة. A man having —, جَرِيءٌ ـ حَازِم ـ حَزِيم ـ بِحَزْمٍ ـ بِسُكُونِ ٱلْبَالِ ـ بِرَوَاقَةٍ ـ بِرَزَانَةٍ. With —, قَلْبُهُ حَاضِرٌ بِجَرَاءَةٍ.

Sanguiferous, *a.* مُوَلِّدُ ٱلدَّمِ. A — vessel, مَجْرَى ٱلدَّمِ.

Sanguification, *n.* تَوْلِيدُ ٱلدَّمِ.

Sanguify, *v.t.* وَلَّدَ ٱلدَّمَ.

Sanguinary, *a.* Attended with bloodshed, قَتُول ـ قَتْل ـ ذُو ٱلدِّمَاءِ. A — man, سَفَّاكُ ٱلدِّمَاءِ. *See also under* Bloody, *a.*

Sanguine, *a.* Abounding with blood, كَثِيرُ ٱلدَّمِ ـ دَمَوِيٌّ. Of the colour of blood, دَمِيٌّ ـ قِرْمِزِيٌّ. Ardent, حَامٍ ـ كَثِيرُ ٱلْحَرَارَةِ. Confident, كَثِيرُ ٱلْعَوَلِ ـ كَثِيرُ ٱلثِّقَةِ. Sanguine about, مُتَلَهِّفٌ إِلَى.

Sanguinely, *ad.* Ardently, بِحَرَارَةٍ ـ بِرَغْبَةٍ ; confidently, عَلَى ثِقَةٍ.

Sanguineness, *n.* Fullness of blood, كَثْرَةُ ٱلدَّمِ. Ardour, حَرَارَة ـ رَغْبَة. Confidence, وُثُوق ـ ثِقَة ـ طُمَأْنِينَة ـ تَلَهُّف.

Sanguineous, *a.* مِثْلَ ٱلدَّمِ.

Sanguinivorous, *a.* آكِلُ ٱلدَّمِ.

Sanhedrim, *n.* مَجْلِسُ ٱلْيَهُودِ.

Sanies, *n.* مِدَّة ـ قَيْح ـ غَثِيث ـ غَثّ.

Sanious, *a.* ذُو غَثِيثٍ ـ مُقَيِّح ـ قَاثِح.

Sanitarium, *n.* مَحَلٌّ شَافٍ ـ مَحَلٌّ لِلشِّفَاءِ.

Sanitary, *a.* صِحِّيّ ـ شَافٍ. The — Board, المَجْلِسَةُ ٱلصِّحِّيَّةُ. Sanitary regulation, نِظَامَاتٌ صِحِّيَّةٌ. Sanitary measures, تَدَابِيرُ صِحِّيَّة ـ مُعَامَلَاتٌ صِحِّيَّةٌ. The — authorities, المَأْمُورِيَّةُ ٱلصِّحِّيَّةُ. A — cordon, حَدٌّ لِلْمُحَافَظَةِ.

Sanity, *n.* *See* Saneness, *n.*

Sank, *pret. of to* Sink, *q.v.*

Sans, *prep.* مِنْ غَيْرِ كَذَا ـ بِلَا.

Sanscrit, *n.* لِسَانُ ٱلْهِنْدِ ٱلْقَدِيمُ.

Sans-culottes, *n.* مُتَحَشِّف ـ بِلَا سِرْوَالٍ.

Sans-souci, *a.* *See* Careless, Indifferent, *a.*

Santon, *n.* رَبِيط *or* رَابِط *pl.* مُرَابِطَة ـ دَرْوِيش *pl.* دَرَاوِيش.

Sap, *n.* Of a tree, صَبِيب ـ لَبَن *pl.* أَلْبَان ـ رَشْحَةُ شَجَرٍ. A trench for undermining, خَنْدَق *pl.* خَنَادِق ـ لَغْم *pl.* لُغُوم.

Sap, *v.t.* To undermine, حَفَرَ لُغْمًا تَحْتَهُ ـ ٢. To subvert, destroy, هَدَمَ ـ ٢ هَدَمَ ٱلْأَسَاسَ ـ ٢ خَرَّبَ.

Sapid, *a.* لَذِيذ. *See also* Savoury, *a.*

Sapidity, *n.* }
Sapidness, } طَعْم ـ لَذَّة. *See also* Savour, *n.*

Sapience, *n.* دِرَايَة ـ فِطْنَة ـ عَقْل.

Sapient, *a.* عَارِف ـ فَاطِن ـ عَاقِل.

Sapless, *a.* بِلَا لَبَنٍ ـ عَدِيمُ ٱلصَّبِيبِ.

Sapling, *n.* شُجَيْرَة *pl.* شُجَيْرَات ـ شَتْلَة *pl.* شَتَلَات.

Saponaceous, *a.* صَابُونِيٌّ.

Saponification, *n.* التَّحْوِيلُ إِلَى صَابُونٍ.

Saponify, *v.t.* صَيَّرَ صَابُونًا ـ حَوَّلَ إِلَى صَابُونٍ.

Sapor, *n.* *See* Taste, *n.*

Saporific, *a.* مُذَوِّق ـ مُسَبِّبُ ٱلذَّوْقِ.

Sapper, *n.* عَسْكَرِيُّ ٱلْخَنَادِقِ *pl.* عَسَاكِرُ ; from the Persian, طَبَرْدَار *pl.* طَبَرْدَارِيَّة.

Sapphire, *n.* يَاقُوتٌ أَزْرَقُ ـ صَفِير *pl.* صُفْرَاء ـ الأَكْحَل.

Sapphirine, *a.* مِنَ ٱلصَّفِيرِ ـ مِثْلَ ٱلصَّفِيرِ.

Sappiness, *n.* رُطُوبَة. *See also* Sap, *n.*

Sappy, *a.* Full of sap, ذُو صَبِيبٍ ـ نَغْدٌ مَغْدٌ. To become —, تَسَقَّى. *See also* Juicy, *a.*

Sapwood, *n.* خَشَبٌ طَرِيٌّ يُشْبِهُ ٱلصُّوفَانَ يُوجَدُ بَيْنَ قِشْرِ ٱلشَّجَرِ وَٱلْخَشَبِ ٱلصُّلْبِ.

Saraband, *n.* ضَرْبٌ مِنَ ٱلرَّقْصِ.

Saracen, *n.* شَرْقِيٌّ *pl.* شَرْقِيُّونَ — عَرَبِيٌّ *coll.* ٱلْعَرَبُ. The Saracens, ٱلْعَرَبُ.

Saracenic, *a.* عَرَبِيٌّ — شَرْقِيٌّ.

Sarcasm, *n.* تَهَكُّمٌ — سَلَاطَةٌ — نَقْرَى ; sarcasms, نَوَاقِرُ. An object of —, أُهْكُومَةٌ. To launch a — against, تَهَكَّمَ — رَمَى بِسَلَاطَةٍ — نَقَرَ.

Sarcastic, *a.* / Sarcastical, } نَاقِرٌ — سَلِيطٌ — تَهَكُّمِيٌّ.

Sarcastically, *ad.* بِتَهَكُّمٍ — بِسَلَاطَةٍ — نَقْرًا.

Sarcenet, *n.* سُنْدُسٌ — قَزٌّ — إِبْرِيسَمٌ سَخِيفٌ.

Sarcology, *n.* عِلْمٌ يُبْحَثُ فِيهِ عَنِ ٱللُّحُومِ.

Sarcophagous, *a.* آكِلُ ٱللَّحْمِ.

Sarcophagus, *n.* قَبْرٌ مِنْ حَجَرٍ — قَبْرٌ *pl.* قُبُورٌ.

Sarcophagy, *n.* أَكْلُ ٱللَّحْمِ.

Sarcotic, *a.* مُوَلِّدُ ٱللَّحْمِ.

Sarculation, *n.* As with a rake, جَرْفٌ — جَرْفٌ بِمِجْرَفَةٍ.

Sardine, *n.* سَرْدِينَةٌ *coll.* سَرْدِين.

Sardinia, *n.* جَزِيرَةُ سَرْدِينِيَا.

Sardinian, *a.* مِنْ سَرْدِينِيَا.

Sardinian, *n.* مِنْ أَهْلِ سَرْدِينِيَا.

Sardonian, *a.* / Sardonic, } مُزَمْهِرٌ — صَفْرَاوِيٌّ. A — laugh, ٱزْمِهْرَار — ضَحِكٌ صَفْرَاوِيٌّ.

Sardonyx, *n.* جَزْعٌ عَقِيقِيٌّ.

Sarsaparilla, *n.* سَبَارِينَا ; called in commerce, حَشِيشَةُ ٱلْمَحْمُودِيَّةِ.

Sasafras, *n.* سَاسَفْرَاس.

Sash, *n.* As for the waist, حِزَامٌ *pl.* أَحْزِمَةٌ *and* حِزَامَاتٌ — زُنَّارٌ *pl.* زَنَانِيرُ. An embroidered or jewelled —, such as is worn by Eastern ladies, حِيَاصَةٌ — حِزَامٌ. Sash, of a window, فَرْوَازُ ٱلطَّاقَةِ (*or* فَلْقَةٌ).

Satan, *n.* ٱللَّعِينُ — إِبْلِيسُ — ٱلشَّيْطَانُ.

Satanic, *a.* / Satanical, } شَيْطَانِيٌّ.

Satanically, *ad.* بِشَيْطَنَةٍ — شَنَاعَةً — بِكَمَالِ ٱلْخُبْثِ.

Satchel, *n.* *See* Sachel.

Sate, *v.t.* أَنْصَحَ — أَشْبَعَ — شَبَّعَ. *See also to* Satisfy, *v.t.*

Sateless, *a.* لَا يُشْبَعُ.

Satellite, *n.* A small planet revolving round a larger one, تَابِعَةٌ — سَيَّارَةٌ صَغِيرَةٌ تَدُورُ حَوْلَ أُخْرَى أَكْبَرَ مِنْهَا — تَوَابِعُ *pl.* An attendant, help, تَابِعٌ *pl.* أَتْبَاعٌ — عَوْنٌ *pl.* أَعْوَانٌ. An obsequious attendant, مُدَاهِنٌ — مُبَصْبِصٌ.

Satiable, *a.* يُشْبَعُ — مِمَّا يُشْبَعُ.

Satiate, *a.* شَبْعَانُ *fem.* شَبْعَانَةٌ *pl. masc.* شَبَاعَى *and* شِبَاعٌ.

Satiate, *v.t.* To fill to satiety, أَنْصَحَ — أَشْبَعَ — شَبَّعَ. To gratify, content, أَرْضَى — أَقْنَعَ. Anything that satiates, شِبَعٌ — شُبْعٌ : The cake (of bread) satiates me, ٱلرَّغِيفُ شِبْعِي. Satiating food, طَعَامٌ طُعْمٌ.

Satiation, *n.* The act of filling to satiety, إِشْبَاعٌ ; the being so filled, شِبَعٌ. *See also* Gratification, *n.*

Satiety, *n.* شِبَعٌ — شَبَاعَةٌ.

Satin, *n.* أَطْلَسٌ *pl.* طُلْسٌ.

Satinet, *n.* جِنْفَاص *or* جِنْفِيص.

Satin-wood, *n.* خَشَبٌ نَاعِمٌ كَٱلْأَطْلَسِ.

Satire, *n.* فِرْيَةٌ — إِفْرَاءٌ — هِجَاءٌ — هَجْوٌ — أُهْجِيَّةٌ. To compose a —, أَهْجَى. A writer of satires, هَاجِيٌّ. Scurrilous satires, ٱلْأَهَاجِي.

Satiric, *a.* / Satirical, } هَجْوِيٌّ. A — speech, قَارِصَةٌ *pl.* قَوَارِصُ.

Satirically, *ad.* بِإِفْرَاءٍ — بِنَوْعِ ٱلْهَجْوِ — هِجَاءً.

Satirist, *n.* هَاجِيٌّ.

Satirize, *v.t.* فَرَى — أَفْرَى — هَجَا — نَقَرَ — أَنْشَدَ بِ. They satirized one another, of many, تَهَاجَوا — ٱهْتَاجَوا.

Satisfaction, *n.* Contentment, رِضًى — مَرْضَاةٌ — قَنَاعَةٌ — رَاحَةُ بَالٍ — خَاطِرٌ — وَدٌّ. Pleasure, gratification, حُبُورٌ — بَهْجَةٌ — سُرُورٌ — ٱنْبِسَاطٌ. The act of satisfying, إِقْنَاعٌ — إِرْضَاءٌ. Compensation, أَجْرٌ — جَزَاءٌ — مُكَافَاةٌ — ثَوَابٌ — عِوَضٌ — تَضْمِينٌ. The act of repairing an injury or offence, إِصْلَاحُ ٱلْعَمَلِ ٱلْقَبِيحِ — تَعْوِيضُ ٱلضَّرَرِ. It is a cause of the greatest —, أَبْهَجُ مَا تُسَرُّ بِهِ ٱلنُّفُوسُ (*or* ٱلْإِهَانَةِ). "One soul shall not at all make — for another," لَا تَجْزِي نَفْسٌ عَنْ نَفْسٍ شَيْئًا (Kur. ii. 45).

To demand satisfaction from, طَلَبَ حَقَّهُ مِنْ — طَلَبَ ٱلْحَقَّ مِنْ.

To find satisfaction in, تَشَفَّى بِ.

To get or obtain satisfaction from, خَلَّصَ حَقَّهُ مِنْ — أَخَذَ ٱلْحَقَّ مِنْ — ٱنْتَصَرَ مِنْ.

To give satisfaction to, to content, please, أَرْضَى — رَضَّى. To make reparation to, to compensate for, كَافَى عَنْ — جَازَى عَنْ — أَعَاضَ عَنْ. To give satisfaction to, as for an offence, injury, كَافَى عَمَّا صَدَرَ مِنَ ٱلنَّقْصِ فِي حَقِّهِ — وَفَى *aor.* يَفِي (*or* أَوْفَى) لِ

أَعْطَاهُ حَقَّهُ. To try to give satisfaction to, to content, please, إِسْتَرْضَى ـ تَرَضَّى.

Satisfactorily, *ad.* In a satisfactory manner, عَلَى أَحْسَنِ مِنْوَالٍ ـ عَلَى وَفْقِهِ. Agreeably to one, إِقْنَاعًا ـ كِفَايَةً ـ عَلَى سَبِيلِ ٱلتَّرْضِيَةِ. Satisfactorily to the will of the nation, عَلَى مُرَادِ ٱلْأُمَّةِ. On satisfactory grounds, عَلَى أُصُولٍ مُرْضِيَةٍ.

Satisfactoriness, *n.* كِفَايَة ـ وَفْق.

Satisfactory, *a.* Contenting, pleasing, سَارّ ـ كَافٍ ـ مُرْضٍ; as of intelligence, *etc.*, meaning, generally —, مِمَّا يَشْرَحُ ٱلصُّدُورَ ـ وَيُحَقِّقُ ٱلْمَأْمُولَ. A — proof, بُرْهَانٌ مُقْنِعٌ. To the point, سَدِيد. A — answer, جَوَابٌ شَافٍ. A — result, نَتِيجَةٌ مُرْضِيَةٌ. Satisfactory reasons, أَسْبَابٌ كَافِيَةٌ (or سَدِيدَةٌ). Satisfactory assurances, تَأْمِينَاتٌ مُرْضِيَةٌ. Satisfactory explanations, إِيضَاحَاتٌ مُرْضِيَةٌ. The matter continues to be —, مَا زَالَ ٱلْأَمْرُ عَلَى وَفْقِ ٱلْمَرَامِ. This matter was not deemed — by the other governments, هٰذَا ٱلْأَمْرُ لَمْ يَقَعْ لَدَى بَقِيَّةِ ٱلدُّوَلِ مَوْقِعَ ٱلْقَبُولِ.

Satisfiable, *a.* إِقْنَاعُهُ مُمْكِنٌ.

Satisfied, *part.* and *a.* As with food, شَبْعَانُ. Contented, pleased, رَاضٍ ـ رَضِيٌّ *pl.* رُضَاة ـ سَلِيٌّ ـ مُسْتَغْنٍ ـ *vulg.* مَبْسُوط. Self-satisfied, مُعْجَبٌ بِنَفْسِهِ. To be — with, رَضِيَ عَن ـ إِكْتَفَى ب ـ إِقْتَنَعَ ب ـ قَنِعَ ب ـ غَنِيَ ب ـ جَزَأَ ب *aor.* يَرْضَى.

Satisfy, *v.t.* As with food, أَشْبَعَ ـ شَبَّعَ. To content, أَجْزَأَ ـ أَرْضَى ـ نَشَّعَ ـ أَقَرَّ ـ جَزَأَ. To convince, أَقْنَعَ. To —, as a claim, أَوْفَى ـ وَفَّى ـ كَفَى ـ أَجْزَأَ. To — one's wishes, قَضَى مُرَادَهُ ـ شَفَى قَلْبَهُ مِن. To — one's vengeance upon, إِنْتَقَمَ مِن. To pretend to be satisfied, of food, تَشَبَّعَ. The eye is not satisfied with seeing, العَيْنُ لَا تَشْبَعُ مِنَ ٱلنَّظَرِ. He satisfied his desire to see his family, بَلَّ شَوْقَهُ مِنْ أَهْلِهِ. He satisfied himself that..., إِقْتَنَعَ أَن. He was not satisfied with his colloquy with the Wazir, لَمْ يَقْتَنِعْ بِمُحَاوَرَةِ ٱلْوَزِيرِ. Satisfying food, طَعَامٌ طَعِمٌ.

Satisfy, *v.i.* To feed to the full, شَبِعَ ـ شَبَّعَ.

Satrap, *n.* مَرْزُبَان *pl.* مَرَازِبَة.

Satrapy, *n.* مَرْزُبَة.

Saturable, *a.* يُشْرَب ـ مِمَّا يُرَوَّغُ ـ مِمَّا يُشْبَعُ.

Saturant, *a.* مُشْرِب ـ مُرَوِّغ ـ مُشْبِع.

Saturate, *v.t.* أَشْبَعَ ـ أَشْرَبَ ـ رَوَّغَ. To be saturated, شَرِقَ ـ تَشَرَّبَ ـ أُشْبِعَ ـ أُشْرِبَ. Saturated with, مُشْبَعٌ مِن. The garment was saturated with (the dye of) saffron, شَرِقَ ٱلثَّوْبُ بِٱلْجَادِيّ.

Saturation, *n.* The act of saturating, إِشْبَاع ـ إِشْرَاب ـ تَرْوِيغ; the being saturated, تَشَرُّب ـ تِشْرَاب ـ شَرْب ـ شَرَق.

Saturday, *n.* يَوْمُ ٱلسَّبْتِ ـ ٱلسَّبْتُ. Holy —, that before Easter Sunday, سَبْتُ ٱلنُّورِ.

Saturn, *n.* The planet, ٱلزُّحَلُ. The heathen deity, مَعْبُودٌ مِنْ مَعَابِيدِ ٱلْوَثَنِيِّينَ ٱلْقُدَمَاءِ ـ سَاطُورْن.

Saturnalia, *a.* The festivities in honour of Saturn, عِيدُ ٱلْمَعْبُودِ ٱلْمَذْكُورِ. Riot, debauchery, فِسْق وَفَسَاد ـ دَعَارَة ـ خَلَاعَة.

Saturnalian, *a.* Pertaining to the festival of Saturn, مُتَعَلِّقٌ بِعِيدِ ٱلْمَعْبُودِ سَاطُورْن. Loose, dissolute, فَاسِق ـ خَلِيع ـ فُجَّار ـ فَلَاتِيّ.

Saturnian, *a.* Pertaining to Saturn, مُتَعَلِّقٌ بِٱلْمَعْبُودِ سَاطُورْن. Happy, مَغْبُوط ـ حَظِيظ ـ سَعِيد ـ حَبُور.

Saturnine, *a.* Heavy, dull, ظَلِيم ـ ثَقِيل ـ شَاقّ.

Saturnist, *n.* فَظّ ـ مُتَعَبِّس ـ عَبِس.

Satyr, *n.* The fabulous monster, نَسْنَاس *pl.* نَسَانِيس. The — of Scripture, مَعَزُ ٱلْوَحْشِ.

Satyric, *a.* مُتَعَلِّقٌ بِٱلنَّسْنَاسِ.

Sauce, *n.* Of food, طَرْطُور ـ مَرَقَة. Impudence, وَقَاحَة ـ وَقْح ـ سَفَاهَة.

Sauce, *v.t.* To put sauce upon, صَبَّ ـ جَعَلَ عَلَى ـ طَرْطُورًا عَلَى ـ مَرَقَةً.

Sauce-boat, *n.* إِنَاءُ ٱلطَّرْطُورِ ـ سُكُرُّجَة.

Sauce-box, *n.* وَقِيح *fem.* وَقِيحَة ـ سَفِيه *fem.* سَفِيهَة.

Saucepan, *n.* طِنْجِير *pl.* طَنَاجِير; *vulg.* طَنْجَرَة *pl.* طَنَاجِر. A small —, مِسْخَنَة.

Saucer, *n.* ظَرْف ـ سُكُرُّجَة *pl.* ظُرُوف.

Saucily, *ad.* بِوَقَاحَةٍ ـ بِسَفَاهَةٍ.

Sauciness, *n.* قِلَّةُ حَيَاءٍ ـ وَقَاحَة ـ سَفَاهَة.

Saucy, *a.* قَلِيلُ ٱلْحَيَاءِ ـ وَقِيح ـ سَفِيه.

Sauer-kraut, *n.* كُرُنْبِيَّة مُمَلَّحَة ـ كُرُنْب مُمَلَّح.

Saunter, *v.i.* تَوَقَّفَ ـ تَحَوَّسَ ـ تَحَوَّزَ. *See also to* Loiter, *v.t.*

Saunterer, *n.* مُتَوَانٍ ـ مُتَوَقِّف ـ مُتَحَوِّس ـ مُتَحَوِّز. *See also* Loiterer, *n.*

Sauria, *a.* عِبَارَةٌ عَنْ طَائِفَةٍ مِنَ ٱلْحَيَوَانَاتِ كَٱلتِّمْسَاحِ وَٱلْكَرْكَدَنِّ وَٱلْوَرَلِ إِلَخْ.

Saurian, *a.* مُتَعَلِّقٌ بِٱلطَّائِفَةِ مِنَ ٱلْحَيَوَانَاتِ ٱلْمَذْكُورَةِ آنِفًا.

Sausage, *n.* طَعَامٌ يُعْمَلُ مِنْ لَحْمٍ وَشَحْمٍ مَحْشُوَّيْنِ فِي مُصْرَانٍ ـ مَقَانِق; *from the Turkish,* مُنْبَار *pl.* مَنَابِير ـ سُجُق ـ ٱلْغَنَمِ وَغَيْرِهِ.

Savable, *a.* حِفْظُهُ مُمْكِنٌ ـ خَلَاصُهُ مُمْكِنٌ.

Savage, *a.* Pertaining to the woods, بَرِّيٌّ. Wild, untamed, وَحْشِيٌّ ـ حُوشِيٌّ. Rude, untutored, خَشِن ـ جَافٍ ـ هَمَجَة ـ غَلِيظ. Cruel, ظَالِم ـ جَافٍ ـ جَائِر ـ عَنِيف. Ferocious, كَاسِر ـ ضَرِيٌّ ـ أَضَرّ ـ حُدَاد.

Savage, *n.* One uncivilized, in his native state, وَحْشِيٌّ ـ مُتَوَحِّش. A cruel person, ظَالِم ـ جَافٍ ـ جَائِر. The savages, barbarians, الْهَمَج ـ الْمُتَوَحِّشُون.

Savagely, *ad.* Cruelly, بِفَرْعَنَةٍ ـ بِجَفَآءٍ ـ بِعُنْفٍ ـ عَنْفًا. Ferociously, بِغَشْمَرَةٍ ـ بِضَرَاوَةٍ. In the manner of a savage, مِثْلَ ٱلْوَحْشِ ـ بِتَوَحُّشٍ.

Savageness, *n.* An untamed or barbarous state, وَحْشَة ـ تَوَحُّش ـ وَحْشِيَّة. Rudeness, خُشْنَة ـ غِلَاظَة ـ فَظَاظَة. Cruelty, جَفَآء ـ جَوْر ـ ظُلْم ـ عُنْف ـ قَسَاحَة. Ferociousness, ضَرَاوَة ـ غَشْمَرِيَّة.

Savagism, *n.* حَالُ ٱلْوَحْشَةِ.

Savanna, *n.* صَاع *pl.* أَصْوَاع ـ بُقْعَة *pl.* بِقَاع.

Savant, *n.* عَالِم *pl.* عُلَمَآء ـ حَكِيم *pl.* حُكَمَآء ـ مُتَفَنِّن ـ لَوْذَعِيٌّ.

Save, *v.t.* As from danger, *etc.*, خَلَّصَ-مِن ـ سَلَّمَ-مِن ـ أَنْقَذَ-مِن ـ نَقَذَ-مِن ـ نَجَّى-مِن. To protect, rescue, خَفَرَ ـ خَفَرَ-بِ ـ خَفَّرَ ـ تَخَفَّرَ-بِ ـ حَفِظَ ـ صَانَ. To — from, to prevent from, مَنَعَ-عَن. To —, not to waste, قَتَّرَ ـ تَقَنَّى ـ أَبْقَى; *vulg.* وَفَّرَ. To lay by, to hoard, ذَخَرَ ـ إِدَّخَرَ. To — bloodshed, حَقَنَ سَفْكَ ٱلدِّمَآءِ. To spare, excuse, عَفَا عَن *aor.* يَعْفُو. To let live, إِسْتَحْيَى. To — one's self, نَجَا ـ إِنْسَلَّ ـ نَقِذَ; to escape, نَقَذَ مِن ـ تَخَلَّصَ ـ خَلَصَ مِن ـ إِنْهَزَمَ; to betake one's self to a place of refuge, إِحْتَمَى إِلَى ـ إِلْتَجَأَ إِلَى; to provide against, حَرَسَ ـ إِحْتَرَسَ مِن. To — appearances, دَارَى (or حَفِظَ) ٱلنَّامُوسَ ٱلظَّاهِرَ. May God bless and — him! صَلَّى ٱللّٰهُ عَلَيْهِ وَسَلَّمَ. God — the Queen, لِتَحْيَ ٱلْمَلِكَةُ.

Save, *v.i.* To — expense, to be frugal, إِقْتَصَدَ ـ تَقَنَّى.

Save, *conj.* Except, إِلَّا ـ مَا عَدَا. None stood up — Zaid, مَا قَامَ إِلَّا زَيْدٌ.

Save-all, *n.* For candles, آلَةٌ تُؤْخَذُ لِإِيقَادِ عُقْبِ ٱلشُّمُوعِ.

Saver, *n.* An economist, مُقْتَصِد ـ مُقَتِّر; *vulg.* مُوَفِّر.

Savin, *n.* أَبْهَل.

Saving, *a.* Frugal, مُقْتَصِد ـ مُقَتِّر ـ مُتَقَنٍّ; *vulg.* مُوَفِّر. *See also* Exceptional, *a.*

Saving, *n.* Something saved, ذَخِيرَة *pl.* ذَخَائِر; *vulg.* تَصْمِيد ـ تَوْفِير. An exception, reservation, مُسْتَثْنَى ـ مُسْتَخْرَج ـ شَاذّ.

Savingly, *ad.* So as to be saved, delivered, فِي سَبِيلِ ٱلنَّجَاةِ (or ٱلْخَلَاصِ). Economically, بِٱلِٱقْتِصَادِ ـ بِٱلتَّقْتِيرِ ـ بِتَقَنٍّ; *vulg.* بِٱلتَّصْمِيدِ ـ بِٱلتَّوْفِيرِ.

Savingness, *n.* Frugality, إِقْتِصَاد ـ تَقْتِير ـ تَقَنٍّ; *vulg.* تَوْفِير ـ تَصْمِيد.

Savings-bank, *n.* صَنْدُوقُ ٱلِٱدِّخَارِ ـ صَنْدُوقُ ٱلْأَمْنِيَّةِ.

Saviour, *n.* A liberator, خَفِير ـ مُخَلِّص. The Saviour of the world, مُخَلِّصُ ٱلْعَالَمِ. Jesus Christ our Saviour, سَيِّدُنَا يَسُوعُ ٱلْمَسِيحُ مُخَلِّصُنَا.

Savorily, *ad.* بِلَذَّةٍ ـ تَلَذُّذًا.

Savoriness, *n.* } Of taste, لَذَّة ـ طَعْم; of smell, نَعْمَة ـ بَنَّة ـ

Savour, } رَائِحَة ـ رَائِحَة. A sweet —, رَائِحَةُ سُرُورٍ ـ طَيِّبَة. A stinking —, نَتْن ـ دَفَر. To lose its —, فَسَدَ.

Savour, *v.i.* To have a particular taste, كَانَ طَعْمُهُ كَطَعْمِ ٱلْ...; to have a particular smell, كَانَتْ رَائِحَتُهُ كَرَائِحَةِ ٱلْ.... To partake of the nature of, لَهُ رَائِحَةُ كَذَا ـ أَشْبَهَ. To concern, إِهْتَمَّ بِ. *See also to* Smell, *v.i.*

Savour, *v.t.* To relish, like, إِسْتَلَذَّ ـ ذَاقَ ـ تَلَذَّذَ بِ. To — with, طَيَّبَ-بِ ـ تَبَّلَ-بِ ـ تَوْبَلَ-بِ.

Savourless, *a.* Of food, بِلَا لَذَّةٍ ـ مَلِيخ; of scent, لَا رَائِحَةَ لَهُ. *See also* Insipid, *a.*

Savourly, *a.* *See* Savoury, *a.*

Savourly, *ad.* بِلَذَّةٍ ـ تَلَذُّذًا.

Savoury, *a.* To the taste, لَذِيذ; of smell, طَيِّب. To be —, of taste, لَذَّ ـ كَانَ لَذِيذًا; of smell, طَابَ *aor.* يَطِيبُ. To make —, طَيَّبَ.

Savoy, *n.* The country, بِلَادُ سَاوُويَا.

Savoy, *n.* A kind of cabbage, ضَرْبٌ مِنَ ٱلْكُرُنْبِ.

Savoyard, *n.* مِنْ أَهْلِ سَاوُويَا.

Saw, *n.* The tool, مِقَدّ ـ مِنْشَار *pl.* مَنَاشِير. A saying, proverb, قَوْل *pl.* أَقْوَال ـ ضَرْبُ مَثَلٍ ـ مَثَل *pl.* أَمْثَال.

Saw, *v.i.* To work with a saw, إِشْتَغَلَ بِٱلْمِنْشَارِ. To be sawed, نُشِرَ.

Saw, *v.t.* نَشَرَ ـ قَطَعَ-بِمِنْشَارٍ.

Sawer, *n.* *See* Sawyer, *n.*

Saw-bones, *n.* جَرَّاح.

Sawdust, *n.* نُشَارَة.

Saw-fish, *n.* سَمَكُ أَبِي مِنْشَارٍ.

Saw-mill, *n.* مَحَلُّ ٱلنَّشْرِ ـ دُولَابٌ لِلنَّشْرِ.

Saw-pit, *n.* خَنْدَقٌ لِلنَّشْرِ فِيهِ.

Saw-wort, *n.* The plant, صَعْتَر ــ زَعْتَر.

Saw-wrest, *n.* آلَةٌ لِتَنْظِيمِ أَسْنَانِ ٱلْمِنْشَارِ.

Sawyer, *n.* نَشَّار *pl.* نَشَّارُونَ *and* نَشَّارَة.

Saxifrage, *n.* مِرَضَّةُ ٱلْحَصَى.

Saxifragous, *a.* مُرَضِّضُ ٱلْحَصَى.

Saxon, *a.* سَكْسُونِيٌّ.

Saxon, *n.* سَكْسُونِيٌّ *pl.* سَكْسُونِيُّونَ ــ سَكْسُونَ ــ مِنْ أَهْلِ سَكْسُونَ.

Saxony, *n.* بِلَادُ سَكْسُونَ.

Say, *v.t.* To speak, حَكَى ــ ‌ تَكَلَّمَ ــ قَالَ *aor.* يَقُولُ. To utter, أَفَادَ. نَطَقَ بِ ــ لَفَظَ بِ ــ تَفَوَّهَ بِ ــ فَاهَ. To state, أَفَادَ. To declare, أَكَّدَ ــ قَرَّرَ ــ بَيَّنَ. To testify, شَهِدَ. To say again, to repeat, كَرَّرَ ــ أَعَادَ. To say on, to continue saying, وَاظَبَ عَلَى ٱلْقَوْلِ ــ لَمْ يَزَلْ قَائِلًا. To begin to say, بَدَأَ يَقُولُ. To say to, قَالَ إِلَى *or* ل. To say something about, قَالَ عَن *or* فِي. To say something against, تَقَوَّلَ عَلَى. To ask one to say, قَوَّلَ. I will never say that I am he, لَنْ أَقُولَ قَطُّ بِأَنِّي هُوَ. Say what you please, تَكَلَّمْ بِمَا أَحْبَبْتَ ــ قُلْ مَا شِئْتَ. What do you say? مَاذَا تَقُولُ ــ لَبَّيْكَ. We do not say that it is necessary, لَمْ نَقُلْ أَنَّهُ وَاجِبٌ. I have heard it said that ..., سَمِعْتُ أَن ــ سَمِعْتُ مَنْ يَقُولُ أَن. The poet is right when he says, مَا أَحْسَنَ ٱلشَّاعِرُ إِذْ قَالَ. It suffices me to say, حَسْبِي أَنْ أَقُولَ. We have many things to say about that, لَنَا كَلَامٌ كَثِيرٌ فِي ذٰلِكَ. Well said on your part! نِعْمَ مَا قُلْتَ ــ سَلِّمْ فَمَكَ ٱلصِّدْقِ (*vulg.* تُمَّكَ). That is to say, أَيْ ــ مَعْنَاهُ ــ أَعْنِي ــ يَعْنِي. I dare say, لَعَلَّ ــ تَخْمِينًا ــ يُمْكِنُ. He said his lesson, قَرَأَ دَرْسَهُ. There is no saying, مَجْهُولٌ ــ لَيْسَ هُوَ مِنَ ٱلْمَعْلُومِ. He will not say thee nay, لَا يَرُدُّكَ. It may be said, يُمْكِنُ أَنْ يُقَالَ.

Say, *n.* *See* Saying, *n.*

Saying, *n.* A speech, قَوْل *pl.* أَقْوَال ــ مَقَالَة ــ قِيل. An adage, مَثَل *pl.* أَمْثَال ــ ضَرْبُ مَثَلٍ. A witty —, لَطِيفَة ــ ظَرِيفَة. Dark sayings, أَلْغَاز. The — pleased me well, حَسُنَ ٱلْكَلَامُ لَدَيَّ.

Sayyid, *n.* سَيِّد *pl.* سَادَة.

Scab, *n.* The incrustation over a sore, قُوبَة ــ قُوبَاء ــ قِرْفَة ــ قِشْرَةُ ٱلْجُرْحِ ــ خَشْكَة ــ جُلْب *pl.* جُلْبَة. A disease in sheep, جَرَبُ ٱلْغَنَمِ ــ طُلَيَّا. The mange, شَذًا ــ شَذَا. To remove a —, قَرَفَ. To have the — removed, تَقَرَّفَ. To have the —, جَرِبَ ــ عَرَّ.

Scab, *v.i.* جَلَبَ ــ أَجْلَبَ.

Scabbard, *n.* خِلَّة *pl.* خِلَل *and* خِلَال ــ جَفْن *pl.* جُفُون ــ غِلَاف *pl.* غُلُف ــ غِمْد *pl.* أَغْمَاد ــ قِرَاب *pl.* قُرُب ــ بَيْت.

Scabbard, *v.t.* غَلَّفَ ــ أَغْمَدَ. *See also to* Sheathe, *v.t.*

Scabbiness, *n.* جَرَب ــ قُوبَاء ــ جُلْبَة.

Scabby, *a.* Having scabs, ذُو جُلَب. Having the mange, أَعَرّ ــ عَرُور ــ جَرِب ــ أَجْرَب ــ مُصَابٌ بِحُصَامٍ; of a camel, عَارّ. Mean, خَسِيس ــ رَذِيل ــ حَقِير.

Scabious, *a.* ذُو جُلَب ــ أَجْرَب *fem.* جَرْبَاءُ *pl.* جُرْب ــ جَرْبَان *fem.* جَرِبَة *pl.* جَرْبَى.

Scabrous, *a.* أَحْرَش. *See also* Rough, Rugged, *a.*

Scabrousness, *n.* حَرَش. *See also* Roughness, Ruggedness, *n.*

Scaffold, *n.* A temporary stage for workmen, صِقَالَة ــ تَخْشِيبَة. A —, as for spectators, مَحْفِل *pl.* مَحَافِل ــ مَسْطَبَةٌ مِنْ أَلْوَاحٍ *pl.* مَسَاطِب ــ دَكَّة *pl.* دِكَك ــ تَخْت *pl.* تُخُوت. A gallows, مِشْنَقَة. A —, or block, for decapitation, وَضَمٌ لِقَطْعِ ٱلرُّؤُوسِ عَلَيْهِ.

Scaffold, *v.t.* نَصَبَ ــ رَكَّبَ ل ــ صِقَالَةً ــ رَكَّبَ ل ــ تَخْشِيبَةً ٱلصِّقَالَاتِ فِي (*or* حَوْلَ) كَذَا.

Scaffolding, *n.* نَصْبُ صِقَالَاتٍ ــ صِقَالَات.

Scagliola, *n.* مَعْجُونٌ مُلَوَّنٌ يُشْبِهُ ٱلْمَرْمَرَ.

Scalable, *a.* مِمَّا يُتَسَوَّرُ عَلَيْهِ بِٱلسَّلَالِمِ ــ مِمَّا يُتَسَلَّقُ إِلَيْهِ.

Scalade, *n.* *See* Escalade, *n.*

Scald, *n.* A burning with hot liquid, سُمُوط ــ سَمِيط. Scurf on the head, تَبْرِيَة ــ حَزَاز.

Scald, *v.t.* As with boiling water, سَمَطَ. To — off, as the hair from a sheep, *etc.*, سَلَقَ ــ سَمَطَ. To put into boiling water, غَمَسَ ــ فِي ٱلْمَاءِ ٱلْحَارِّ.

Scald-head, *n.* قَرَع ــ حَزَاز.

Scalding, *a.* سَامِط.

Scale, *n.* The dish of a balance, كِفَّة ــ كَفَّة ــ قَصْعَة *pl.* قِصَع *dual* كِفَّتَانِ. A balance, مِيزَان *pl.* مَوَازِين. A —, of a fish, فَلْس *pl.* فُلُوس ــ قِشْرَة *pl.* قِشْر; scales of fish, حَرْشَف. Something resembling scales, شَيْءٌ كَأَنَّهُ قُشُورٌ. A standard of weight or measure, عِيَار ــ مِعْيَار. Any separable laminæ, صَفِيحَة ــ طَبَقَة *pl.* صَفَائِحُ ــ قِشْرَة *pl.* قِشْر. A ladder, سُلَّم *pl.* سَلَالِمُ. Any graduated —, مِقْيَاس ــ قِيَاس. An order, degree, رُتْبَة *pl.* رُتَب. The (social) —, فَانُور ــ بَسْط ــ بِسَاط ــ أَصْنَافُ ٱلنَّاسِ ــ مَرَاتِبُ. A thin plate, صَفِيحَة *pl.* صَفَائِحُ. To turn the —, to preponderate, رَجَحَ ــ تَرَجَّحَ ــ أَمَالَ ٱلْمِيزَانَ: One of the two scales outweighed the other, رَجَحَتْ إِحْدَى ٱلْكِفَّتَيْنِ عَلَى ٱلْأُخْرَى. They are on the same (social) —, هُمْ عَلَى فَانُورٍ وَاحِدٍ. Having scales, of fish; *see* Scaly, *ad.*

Scale, *v.t.* To scrape off scales, نَقَّى فُلُوس ــ نَقَّى ٱلْفُلُوسَ

قَشَّرَ ـ ٱلسَّمَكَ ; as of layers, بَصَّلَ . To — a wall by ladders, تَسَوَّرَ ٱلْحَائِطَ بِسَلَالِمَ ـ تَسَلَّقَ ٱلْجِدَارَ بِسَلَالِمَ .

Scale, *v.i.* To come off in thin layers, قَشَّرَ ـ تَقَشَّرَ .

Scaleless, *a.* بِلَا فُلُوسٍ ـ بِلَا قِشْرٍ ; of fish, بِلَا حَرْشَفٍ .

Scalene, *n.* مُخْتَلِفُ ٱلْأَضْلَاعِ .

Scaliness, *n.* فُلُوس ـ حَرْشَف .

Scaling-ladder, *n.* سُلَّمٌ لِلتَّسَوُّرِ ـ سُلَّمُ ٱلتَّسَلُّقِ .

Scall, *n.* On the head, قَرَع . *See also* Leprosy, *n.*

Scallion, *n.* كُرَّاث ـ كَرَّاث .

Scallop, *n.* The shell, ضَرْبٌ مِنَ ٱلْوَدَعِ ـ مَحَارَةٌ . The scalloping of an edge, قُرُونُ (or تَسْنِينُ) ٱلْحَاشِيَةِ .

Scallop, *v.t.* Of a border, سَنَّنَ ـ جَعَلَ ـ فِي شَكْلِ ٱلْقُرُونِ .

Scalloped, *a.* Formed into scallops, مُقَرَّن ـ مُسَنَّن . A — border, حَاشِيَةٌ قَرْنَاءُ (or مُقَرَّنَةٌ) .

Scalp, *n.* The skin of the top of the head, جِلْدُ هَامَةِ ٱلرَّأْسِ ـ فَرْوَةُ ٱلرَّأْسِ .

Scalp, *v.t.* سَلَخَ جِلْدَ هَامَةِ ٱلرَّأْسِ .

Scalpel, *n.* مِبْضَع ـ مِشْرَاط ـ مَشَارِطُ *pl.* مِشْرَطَة or وِشْرَطَة ـ لَزِيمَة .

Scaly, *a.* Having scales, أَبُو فُلُوسٍ ـ ذُو حَرْشَفٍ ; having coats, as an onion, مُتَبَصِّل . Laminated, ذُو صَفَائِحَ . Mean, حَقِير ـ رَذِيل ـ دَنِيءٌ .

Scammony, *n.* سَقَمُونِيَا .

Scamp, *n.* مَخْلُوع ـ خَلِيع ـ خَوْلَع .

Scamper, *v.i.* To run quickly, رَكَضَ ـ ارْتَدَّ ـ أَوْفَضَ ـ هَفَّ . To — off or away, وَلَّى هَارِبًا ـ فَرَّ .

Scan, *v.t.* To examine closely, دَقَّقَ فِي ـ تَصَفَّحَ فِي ـ تَفَرَّسَ فِي . To look at closely, أَمْعَنَ ٱلنَّظَرَ فِي . To glance at, لَمَحَ إِلَى ـ أَلْمَحَ إِلَى . To —, as a verse of poetry, قَطَّعَ .

Scandal, *n.* A cause of offence, شَكٌّ ـ عَيْب ـ عَثْرَة . Reproachful aspersion, بُهْتَان ـ اِفْتِرَاء ـ نَمَائِمُ *pl.* نَمِيمَة ـ حَكْر ـ رَذَالَة ـ عَار ـ عَيْب ـ تَعْيِيب ـ عَيْبَة . Opprobrium, disgrace, رَذَالَة ـ عَار ـ عَيْب . The noise made by a —, جُرْسَة .

Scandal, *v.t.* To treat opprobriously, to defame, هَتَكَ ـ حَكَرَ ـ عَيَّرَ ـ أَعْثَرَ ـ نَمَّ ـ هَشَّرَ . *See also* to Defame, *v.t.*

Scandalize, *v.t.* To offend, to give cause of offence to, أَشَكَّ ـ عَثَّرَ . To be scandalized or vexed at, اِغْتَاظَ مِن . *See also* to Scandal, *v.t.*

Scandalous, *a.* Causing offence, جَالِبُ ـ مُخْزٍ ـ مُشَكِّكٌ ٱلشَّكِّ . Defamatory, قَذْفِيٌّ ـ نَمٌّ ـ اِفْتِرَائِيٌّ ـ فَضُوح ـ نَمِيمِيٌّ . Shameful, دَنِيءٌ ـ ذَلِيل ـ قَبِيح ـ خَزٍ .

Scandalously, *ad.* Disgracefully, بِٱلْعَارِ ـ قَبْحًا ـ ذِلَّةً . Basely, بِرَذَالَةٍ . With aspersion, بِٱفْتِرَاءٍ ـ بِنَمِيمَةٍ ـ بِبُهْتَانٍ ـ حَكْرًا .

Scandalousness, *n.* رَذَالَة ـ عَار ـ عَيْب . *See also* Scandal, *n.*

Scandalum Magnum, *n.* اَلِٱفْتِرَاءُ عَلَى أَرْبَابِ ٱلْمَنَاصِبِ .

Scandent, *a.* *See* Climbing, *a.*

Scanning, *n.* Close examination, تَدْقِيق ـ تَصَفُّح ـ تَفَرُّس . Close inspection, إِمْعَانُ ٱلنَّظَرِ . The act of resolving a verse into its component feet, تَفْعِيل ـ تَقْطِيعُ مِصْرَاعٍ ـ تَقْطِيع .

Scant, *v.t.* To limit, حَدَّدَ . To straiten, ضَيَّقَ عَلَى ـ ضَيَّقَ . To restrain from, أَمْسَكَ عَن ـ كَفَّ عَن ـ عَكَّ عَن ـ مَنَعَ عَن .

Scant, *a.* Wanting, نَاقِص . Light of weight, خَفِيف . Scant measure, of length, قِيَاسٌ نَاقِصٌ ; of capacity, كَيْلٌ نَاقِصٌ . *See also* Scanty, *a.*

Scantily, *ad.* بِقِلَّةٍ ـ بِضِيقٍ ـ بِنُقْصَانٍ . *See also* Poorly, *ad.*

Scantiness, *n.* Deficiency, قِلَّة ـ نُقْصَان ; in width, ضِيق ; in length, قِصَر . Littleness, جُزْئِيَّة . *See also* Poorness, Poverty, *n.*

Scantle, *v.t.* To divide into thin pieces, قَطَّعَ صَفَائِحَ . To shiver, كَسَّرَ ـ هَدَّمَ .

Scantle, *v.i.* To be deficient, اِنْتَقَصَ ـ نَقَصَ ـ قَلَّ . To fail, قَصَّرَ عَن ـ قَصَرَ عَن .

Scantling, *n.* A pattern, مِسْطَرَة ـ نَمُونَة ـ شَكْل . A small quantity, قَلِيل ـ نُتَف *pl.* نُتْفَة ـ جُزَيْئَة ـ جَزْء *pl.* جُزْعَة . A narrow piece of timber for roofing; *see* Lath, *n.*

Scantly, *ad.* *See* Scantily, *ad.*

Scantness, *n.* *See* Scantiness, *n.*

Scanty, *a.* Narrow, ضَيِّق . Scanty in length, قَصِير . Light, خَفِيف . Deficient, قَلِيل ـ نَاقِص . Little, جُزْئِيٌّ . A — dress, ثَوْبٌ عَاجِزٌ . To be —, narrow, ضَاقَ *aor.* يَضِيقُ . To be —, in length, قَصُرَ ; in weight, خَفَّ . To be —, defective, نَقَصَ .

Scape, *n.* Of a tree, سَاق *pl.* سِيقَان ـ جِذْلٌ مِنَ ٱلْعِرْقِ *pl.* أَجْذَال ـ شُرُوش *pl.* شِرْش .

Scape-goat, *n.* Of the Israelites, اِسْمُ ٱلتَّيْسِ ٱلَّذِي كَانَ ٱلْإِسْرَائِيلُونَ يُسَرِّحُونَهُ فِي ٱلْبَرِّيَّةِ كَفَّارَةً عَنْ ذُنُوبِ ٱلشَّعْبِ . One made to bear the evil deserts of another, اَلْقَائِمُ بِٱلْكَفَّارَةِ عَنِ ٱلْغَيْرِ .

Scapegrace, *n.* مَخْلُوع ـ مَعْكُوس ـ خَلِيع ـ فَلَاتَان *pl.* فِلْتَان .

Scapement, *n.* *See* Escapement, *n.*

Scaphoid, *a.* *See* Hollow, *a.*

Scapula, *n.* عَظْمُ ٱلْكَتِفِ ـ لَوْحُ ٱلْكَتِفِ *pl.* أَلْوَاح .

Scapular, *a.* كَتِفِيٌّ ـ مُتَعَلِّقٌ بِلَوْحِ ٱلْكَتِفِ .

Scapular, *n.*
Scapulary, } حَمَائِلُ.

Scar, *n.* A mark of a wound, أَثَر – أُثْر – عَلَب *pl.* عُلُوب – آثار *pl.* أَثَرُ ٱلْجُرْحِ – عَذِير – عَذِيرَة – عَاذِر – قُطُوف *pl.* قَطْف. A blemish, عَيْب *pl.* عُيُوب – عُوَار.

Scar, *v.t.* قَطَّفَ – قَطَفَ. A —, or wale, from a rod, حَبْر – حَبَار – جِبَار – حَبَر. The wound left scars (in the flesh), حَبِرَ ٱلْجُرْحُ. There were scars of the beating on his skin, بِجِلْدِهِ حَبَارُ ٱلضَّرْبِ.

Scaramouch, *n.* مَسْخَرَاتِيّ – مُهَرِّج.

Scarce, *a.* Not plentiful, قَلِيل. Seldom found, قَلِيلُ ٱلْوُجُودِ; seldom occurring, قَلِيلُ ٱلْوُقُوعِ. Uncommon, نَادِر. To be or become —, not plentiful, قَلَّ. To be or to become —, rare, عَزَّ. To make one's self —, to run away, فَرَّ – وَلَّى; to abscond, إِكْتَمَنَ. *See also* Rare, *a.*

Scarce, *ad.*
Scarcely, } Scantily, بِقِلَّةٍ. Hardly, تَقْرِيبًا. With difficulty, بِٱلْجَهْدِ. He — restrained the people from . . ., كَفَّ ٱلْجُمُوعَ بِٱلْجَهْدِ عَنْ أَنْ. He had — gone when his father entered, لَمْ يَذْهَبْ إِلَّا قَدْ دَخَلَ أَبُوهُ. He — knows how to read Arabic, بِٱلْجَهْدِ يَعْرِفُ أَنْ يَقْرَأَ ٱلْعَرَبِيَّةَ. He has — entered, تَوًّا دَخَلَ. He had — pronounced these words when the assembly rose up against him, مَا لَفَظَ بِهٰذَا ٱلْكَلَامِ إِلَّا قَدْ قَامَتِ ٱلْجَمَاعَةُ عَلَيْهِ. *See also* Barely, Hardly, *ad.*

Scarceness, *n.*
Scarcity, } Dearth, قَحْط. Smallness of quantity, قِلَّة. Want, poverty, فَاقَة – عَجْز – فَقْر. Infrequent occurrence, قِلَّةُ وُقُوعٍ. The being seldom found, عَزَازَة – عِزّ – عِزَّة – قِلَّةُ وُجُودٍ. Preciousness, عِزّ.

Scare, *n.* تَخْوِيفَة – مَحْذُور.

Scare, *v.t.* To terrify, أَفْزَعَ – هَوَّلَ – خَوَّفَ – أَرْهَبَ. To —, of game, حَاشَ *aor.* يَحُوشُ – أَحَاشَ. To — away, زَعَقَ بِ – جَفَّلَ – أَجْفَلَ – طَيَّرَ. To be scared away, جَفَلَ – أَجْفَلَ – تَجَفَّلَ. To —, by throwing one into a difficulty, وَقَّعَ فِي مَحْذُورٍ.

Scare-crow, *n.* تَخْوِيفَة – خَيَال.

Scarf, *n.* For the shoulders, طَيْلَسَان *pl.* طَيَالِسَة – طَرْحَة – رِدَاء *pl.* أَرْدِيَة – رِدَاء – مِرْدَاة; for the waist, وِشَاح *pl.* وُشُح and أَوْشِحَة. To put on a —, for the shoulders, لَبِسَ ٱلرِّدَاءَ; to put such a — on one, لَبَّسَ ٱلرِّدَاءَ. To put a — round one's own waist, تَوَشَّحَ – تَوَشَّحَ بِٱلْوِشَاحِ; to put it on another, وَشَّحَ – وَشَّحَ بِٱلْوِشَاحِ.

Scarf, *v.t.* To join pieces of timber at the ends, وَاصَلَ أَطْرَافَ ٱلْأَلْوَاحِ.

Scarfing, *n.* مُوَاصَلَةُ أَطْرَافِ ٱلْأَلْوَاحِ.

Scarf-skin, *n.* *See* Epidermis, *n.*

Scarification, *n.* تَشْرِيط – شَرْط.

Scarifier, *n.* The instrument, مِشْرَاط. The operator, شَارِط.

Scarify, *v.t.* شَرَّطَ – شَرَطَ – بَزَغَ. To — the flesh behind the ears, شَطَبَ – شَطَّبَ ٱلْآذَانَ.

Scarlatina, *n.* حُمَّى حَصْبِيَّة خَفِيفَة.

Scarlatinous, *a.* مَا نِيطَ بِٱلْحُمَّى ٱلْحَصْبِيَّةِ. *See also* Scarlet, *a.*

Scarlet, *n.* A scarlet colour, لَوْنٌ قِرْمِزِيّ. Scarlet cloth, جُوخٌ قِرْمِزِيّ.

Scarlet, *a.* قِرْمِزِيّ.

Scarlet-bean, *n.*
Scarlet-runner, } لُوبِيَة مُوَرَّدَة.

Scarlet-fever, *n.* حُمَّى حَصْبِيَّة.

Scarp, *n.* حُدُورُ ٱلْخَنْدَقِ – حُدُورُ ٱلْخَنْدَقِ مِنْ طَرَفِ ٱلْقَلْعَةِ ٱلْجُوَّانِيّ.

Scarp, *v.t.* صَيَّرَ حُدُورًا. To cut into a perpendicular, قَطَعَ فِي هَيْئَةِ ٱلْجُرْفِ.

Scath, *n.* *See* Damage, *n.*

Scath, *v.t.* *See to* Damage, *v.t.*

Scathful, *a.* Injurious, ضَارّ – مُؤْذٍ – مُضِرّ.

Scatheless, *a.* سَالِم – بِدُونِ مَضَرَّةٍ. One who comes off — from a pestilence, قُرْحَان.

Scatter, *v.t.* To disperse, فَضَّ – ذَرَّ – بَذَرَ – بَذَّرَ – مَذَرَ – شَتَّتَ – أَشَذَّ – بَدَّدَ. To dissipate, أَزَالَ – شَذَّبَ: He scattered, dissipated, the property, شَذَّبَ ٱلْمَالَ. To waste, أَتْلَفَ – أَسْرَفَ – أَبَادَ. To —, as seed, أَذْرَى – بَذَرَ. To strew, فَرَشَ. To put to flight, شَرَّدَ – هَزَمَ – أَنْفَرَ – نَفَّرَ. To — among, فَرَّقَ بَيْنَ كَذَا. To — about, بَعْزَقَ – فَرَّقَ – بَذَّرَ. He scattered his urine, شَعَّ بَوْلَهُ. To be scattered; *see next article.*

Scattered, *a.* Dispersed, شَتّ – شَتِيت – شَتُوت – مُنْتَشِر – مُتَنَشِّر – مُشَتَّت – مُفْتَرِق. Scattered, as leaves from trees, *etc.*, تَحَاتّ. Put to flight, مُنْهَزِم. The —, or dispersed, of a people, *etc.*, شُذَّانُ ٱلنَّاسِ. They came —, in a state of dispersion, جَاؤُوا أَشْتَاتًا (or مُتَفَرِّقِينَ). To be —, dispersed, زَعْبَقَ – بَعْزَقَ – تَنَفَّضَ – إِنْفَضَّ – إِنْتَشَرَ – تَنَشَّرَ – شَذَّ – تَشَتَّتَ – تَشَذَّرَ. To be —, put to flight, إِنْهَزَمَ. To be —, as leaves, *etc.*, falling one after the other, تَنَاثَرَ – تَحَاتَّ – إِنْحَتَّ. The leaves were —, تَحَاتَّ ٱلْوَرَقُ. They were all — through the villages, تَشَتَّتَ ٱلْجَمِيعُ فِي ٱلْكُوَرِ.

Scatter-brain, *n.* مَجْنُون ـ مَلْطُوش ـ طَائِش ـ أَطْيَرُ ـ خَرِيم.

Scatteringly, *ad.* Pall-mall, شَتَاتًا ـ شَذَرَ مَذَرَ.

Scatterings, *n.* شَتَات ـ أَشْيَآء شَتَّى ـ تَفْرِيق ـ بَعْزَقَة ـ زَغْبَقَة.

Scavenger, *n.* زَبَّال *pl.* زَبَّالَة; of the street, كَنَّاسُ ٱلْوَحَلِ.

Scene, *n.* The stage of a theatre, ٱلْمَرْسَحُ (or) مَحْفِلُ ـ دَكَّة ـ مَلْعَب ـ مَلْعَبُ ٱلتِّيَاتْرُو. The series of actions exhibited, مَوْضُوعُ ٱللُّعْبَةِ ـ فُصُولُ ٱللُّعْبَةِ. A part of a play, فَصْل مِنَ ٱللُّعْبَةِ *pl.* فُصُول. A spectacle, مَنَاظِرُ *pl.* مَنْظَرَة ـ مَنْظَر ـ مَرْأًى. A place of occurrence, مَحَلّ ـ مَحَلُّ ٱلْوُقُوعِ ـ مَوْقِع. A drawing, رَسْم *pl.* رُسُوم. Exhibition of strong feelings between persons, اِشْتِبَاك ـ وَقْعَة. A row, disturbance, نِزَاع ـ غَوْغَآء ـ شَغْب. A sylvan —, مَنْظَرٌ رِيفِيٌّ. To lay the — at the castle, جَعَلَ ٱلْمَوْقِعَ عِنْدَ ٱلْقَلْعَةِ.

Scenery, *n.* Of a view, مَنْظَرَة ـ مَنْظَر ـ مَرْأًى; of a theatre, أَشْكَالُ ٱلْمَنَاظِرِ فِي ٱلتِّيَاتْرُو ـ المَنَاظِرُ فِي ٱلتِّيَاتْرُو. Beautiful —, مَنَاظِرُ بَهِيجَة.

Scenic, *a.* } Appertaining to scenery, مُتَعَلِّقٌ بِٱلْمَنَاظِرِ; to
Scenical, } beautiful scenery, مَنْظَرَانِيٌّ ـ مَنْظَرِيٌّ; to theatrical exhibitions, مُتَعَلِّقٌ بِأَلْعَابِ ٱلتِّيَاتْرُو.

Scenographic, *a.* } *See* Perspective, *a.*
Scenographical, }

Scenography, *n.* *See* Perspective, *n.*

Scent, *n.* The power of smelling, القُوَّة ـ سَامَّة ـ شَمّ ـ نَشَا ـ ٱلشَّامَّة. A smell, odour, رَائِحَة ـ نَشْر ـ رَيًّا ـ فَغْمَة ـ نَشْوَة *pl.* رَوَائِح. A remnant of anything, an idea of, شَذًا ـ عِرْق. A sweet —, طِيب ـ فَغْمَةٌ طَيِّبَةٌ ـ عِطْر *pl.* عُطُور. Sweet scents, عُطُور ـ شَمَامَات ـ مَشَامّ. Scent, trace, أَثَر *pl.* آثَار. To have a good —, to smell from afar, شَمَّ مِنْ بَعِيدٍ. To follow the — of, تَقَفَّرَ ـ اِقْتَفَى أَثَرَهُ. To lose the — of, ضَاعَ أَثَرَهُ. To put on the right —, قَبَّضَ ٱلْأَثَرَ; to direct aright, أَرْشَدَ. To put on the wrong —, أَغْلَطَ ٱلْأَثَرَ; to deceive, ضَلَّلَ ـ أَضَلَّ ـ اغْوَى. Its — will not change, لَا تَتَغَيَّرُ رَائِحَتُهُ. *See also* Odour, Smell, *n.*

Scent, *v.t.* To perceive by the nose, نَشَا ـ تَنَشَّى ـ اِنْتَشَى ـ شَمَّمَ ـ شَمَّ ـ اِشْتَمَّ. To give a scent to, أَشَمَّ. To perfume, عَطَّرَ ـ يَطِيب *aor.* طَابَ ـ أَطَابَ ـ طَيَّبَ. To be scented, perfumed, تَعَطَّرَ ـ تَطَيَّبَ. To — out, to find out, كَشَفَ عَنْ ـ ظَهَرَ عَلَى; to search for sharply, جَسَّ ـ تَجَسَّسَ. *See also* to Perfume, to Smell, *v.t.*

Scent-bottle, *n.* بَالَة *coll.* بَال ـ قَارُورَةُ ٱلْعِطْرِ (or ٱلْأَطْيَابِ).

Scent-box, *n.* حُقَّة *coll.* حُقّ *pl.* حُقَق ـ حُقَّةُ ٱلْعُطُورِ (or ٱلْأَطْيَابِ).

Scentful, *a.* *See* Odorous, *a.*

Scentless, *a.* لَا رَائِحَةَ لَهُ.

Sceptic, *n.* مُرْتَاب *pl.* مُرْتَابُونَ ـ مِنْ أَهْلِ ٱلشُّكُوكِ ـ دَهْرِيّ.

Sceptic, *a.* } Of a person, مُرْتَاب ـ دَهْرِيّ; of a writing,
Sceptical, } مُرِيب ـ رَائِب. To be or to become —, اِرْتَابَ.

Sceptically, *ad.* اِرْتِيَابًا ـ بِشَكٍّ ـ بِرِيبَةٍ ـ كَٱلدَّهْرِيِّ.

Scepticism, *n.* رِيبَة ـ مَذْهَبُ أَهْلِ ٱلشُّكُوكِ ـ رَأْيُ ٱلدَّهْرِيَّةِ.

Sceptre, *n.* مِخْصَرَة *pl.* مَخَاصِرُ ـ قَضِيبُ ٱلْمُلْكِ.

Sceptred, *a.* حَامِلُ قَضِيبِ ٱلْمُلْكِ.

Sceptreless, *a.* مُعَرًّى مِنْ قَضِيبِ ٱلْمُلْكِ.

Schedule, *n.* A paper, account, وَرَقَة *pl.* أَوْرَاق ـ قَائِمَة ـ عِلْم. A list, inventory, سِيَاقَة ـ فِهْرِس *pl.* فَهَارِس ـ جَدْوَل *pl.* جَدَاوِل ـ دَفْتَرُ أَسَامٍ *pl.* دَفَاتِرُ ـ بَيَان.

Schedule, *v.t.* فَهْرَسَ ـ رَتَّبَ فِي جَدْوَلٍ ـ نَسَّقَ ـ نَسَّقَ فِي سِيَاقَةٍ.

Schematism, *n.* هَيْآت.

Schematist, *n.* *See* Schemer, *n.*

Scheme, *n.* Arrangement, order, تَرْتِيب ـ سِمَاط ـ نِظَام. System, فَنّ ـ مِنْهَاج ـ نَسَق ـ أُصُول. Delineation, رَسْم *pl.* رُسُوم. A method, طَرْز ـ قِدْيَة ـ مِدَاد ـ طَرِيقَة. A project, اِخْتِرَاع ـ قَصْد ـ نِيَّة ـ مَرَام ـ غَايَة. A well-devised —, بِدَاد. A wild —, مَرَامٌ خَيَالِيٌّ.

Scheme, *v.t.* To plan, contrive, اِخْتَرَعَ ـ أَبْدَعَ ـ دَبَّرَ.

Scheme, *v.i.* To form plans, تَصَوَّرَ ـ تَخَيَّلَ. To act as a trickster, عَمِلَ حِيلَةً ـ تَحَوَّلَ ـ اِحْتَالَ.

Schemer, *n.* A projector, مُبْتَدِع ـ مُخْتَرِع ـ مُبْدِع. A trickster, قُلَّب ـ حُوَّل ـ صَاحِبُ حِيَلٍ ـ حَيَّال ـ خَدَّاع. Schemers, أَرْبَابُ ٱلْغَايَاتِ.

Schism, *n.* اِعْتِزَال ـ اِنْشِقَاق ـ شِقَاق ـ اِفْتِرَاق.

Schismatic, *a.* } مُتَعَلِّقٌ بِٱلْخَوَارِجِ ـ رَافِضِيّ. Tending to
Schismatical, } schism, مُوَلِّدُ ٱلِانْشِقَاقِ.

Schismatic, *n.* شَارٍ *pl.* شُرَاة ـ مُعْتَزِل *pl.* مُعْتَزِلَة ـ خَارِجِيّ *pl.* خَوَارِج ـ رَافِضِيّ *pl.* رَوَافِض ـ مُشَاقِق.

Schist, *n.* حَجَرٌ مُرَكَّبُ صَفَائِحَ صَفَائِحَ ـ حَجَرٌ مُصَفَّحٌ.

Schistose, *a.* } مُرَكَّبُ صَفَائِحَ.
Schistous, }

Scholar, *n.* One who learns of a teacher, طَالِبُ عِلْمٍ *pl.* طُلَّاب — تِلْمِيذ *pl.* تَلَامِيذ — مُتَعَلِّم . A — at a college, مُجَاوِر *pl.* مُجَاوِرُون . A boy that goes to school, وَلَدُ ٱلْكُتَّابِ *pl.* أَوْلَاد ; of a girl, بِنْتُ ٱلْكُتَّابِ *pl.* بَنَات . A learned man, عَالِم *pl.* عُلَمَاء — لَوْذَعِيّ — مِنْ أَهْلِ ٱلْعِلْمِ — عَلَّامَة — تِعْلَامَة . An elegant —, أَدِيب *pl.* أُدَبَاء .

Scholar-like, *a.* and *ad.* / Scholarly, } مِثْلَ أَصْحَابِ ٱلْعِلْمِ — مِثْلَ ٱلْعَالِمِينَ — بِسَعَةِ ٱلْعِلْمِ .

Scholarship, *n.* Erudition, سَعَةُ ٱلْعِلْمِ — فَنّ — عِرْفَان — مُدَارَسَة .

A foundation for the support of a scholar, رَاتِبُ مُجَاوِرٍ .

Scholastic, *a.* / Scholastical, } Pertaining to a school, مَدْرَسِيّ — مَكْتَبِيّ — مُتَعَلِّقٌ بِٱلْمَكْتَبِ ; to learning, مَا نِيطَ بِٱلْعُلُومِ وَٱلْفُنُونِ — بِٱلْعِلْمِ ; to teaching, مَا نِيطَ بِٱلتَّعْلِيمِ ; to scholasticism, مَا نِيطَ بِحِكْمَةِ ٱلْأَوَّلِينَ . A — year, سَنَةٌ مَدْرَسِيَّةٌ .

Scholastic, *n.* One who adheres to the subtleties of the schools, مُتَعَصِّبٌ لِحِكْمَةِ ٱلْأَوَّلِينَ .

Scholastically, *ad.* مِثْلَ ٱلْحُكَمَاءِ ٱلْأَوَّلِينَ .

Scholasticism, *n.* أُصُولُ حِكْمَةِ ٱلْأَوَّلِينَ .

Scholiast, *n.* A commentator, شَارِح *pl.* شَارِحُونَ . A writer of glosses, مُعَلِّقُ حَوَاشٍ .

Scholium, *pl.* Scholia, *n.* حَاشِيَة *pl.* حَوَاشٍ .

School, *n.* A place of education, مَكْتَب *pl.* مَكَاتِبُ — كُتَّاب *pl.* كَتَاتِيبُ — مَدْرَسَة *pl.* مَدَارِسُ . A system of doctrine, مَذْهَب *pl.* مَذَاهِبُ ; those belonging to a system, أَهْلُ مَذْهَبٍ — جَمَاعَة — فِرْقَةٌ مَذْهَبِيَّةٌ — مَذْهَب . A —, of the ancients, schoolmen, أَهْلُ ٱلْحِكْمَةِ ٱلْقَدِيمَةِ .

Boarding school, مَكْتَبٌ تَسْكُنُ فِيهَا ٱلتَّلَامِيذُ وَتَقْتَاتُ *pl.* مَكَاتِبُ .

Charity school, مَكْتَبٌ لِلْفُقَرَاءِ *pl.* مَكَاتِبُ .

Commercial school, مَكْتَبٌ لِلتِّجَارَةِ *pl.* مَكَاتِبُ تِجَارِيَّةٌ .

Day school, مَكْتَبٌ يَوْمِيٌّ *pl.* مَكَاتِبُ نَهَارِيَّةٌ .

Elementary or Preparatory school, مَكْتَبٌ ٱبْتِدَائِيٌّ *pl.* مَكَاتِبُ — مَكْتَبٌ ٱسْتِعْدَادِيٌّ *pl.* مَكَاتِبُ ٱسْتِعْدَادِيَّةٌ — ٱبْتِدَائِيَّةٌ .

Engineering school, مَكْتَبٌ لِلْهَنْدَسَةِ *pl.* مَكَاتِبُ .

Free school, مَكْتَبٌ مَجَّانِيٌّ *pl.* مَكَاتِبُ مَجَّانِيَّةٌ .

Grammar school, مَكْتَبُ ٱلْأُصُولِ — مَكْتَبٌ رِشْدِيٌّ .

Medical school, مَكْتَبٌ لِلطِّبِّ *pl.* مَكَاتِبُ طِبِّيَّةٌ .

Military school, مَكْتَبٌ لِلْعَسْكَرِ *pl.* مَكَاتِبُ عَسْكَرِيَّةٌ .

Native school, مَكْتَبٌ أَهْلِيٌّ *pl.* مَكَاتِبُ أَهْلِيَّةٌ .

Night school, مَكْتَبٌ لَيْلِيٌّ .

School of Agriculture, مَكْتَبٌ لِلزِّرَاعَةِ *pl.* مَكَاتِبُ .

School of Trades, مَكْتَبٌ لِلصَّنَائِعِ *pl.* مَكَاتِبُ .

School of Midwifery, مَكْتَبٌ لِلْقَوَابِلِ *pl.* مَكَاتِبُ .

Veterinary school, مَكْتَبٌ لِلْبَيْطَرَةِ *pl.* مَكَاتِبُ .

To be at school, كَانَ فِي مَكْتَبٍ .

To keep a school, فَاتِحُ مَكْتَبٍ .

To put to school, جَعَلَ فِي مَكْتَبٍ .

School, *v.t.* To teach, instruct, دَرَّسَ — عَلَّمَ . To train, هَذَّبَ — خَرَّجَ — دَرَّبَ .

School-boy, *n.* وَلَدُ ٱلْكُتَّابِ *pl.* أَوْلَاد .

School-dame, *n.* مُعَلِّمَةُ مَكْتَبٍ .

School-fellow, *n.* رَفِيقٌ فِي ٱلْمَكْتَبِ *pl.* رُفَقَاءُ and أَرْفَاق .

School-house, *n.* مَكْتَب *pl.* مَكَاتِبُ — كُتَّاب — مَدْرَسَة *pl.* مَدَارِسُ .

Schooling, *n.* Instruction, تَعْلِيم — تَدْرِيس . Training, تَهْذِيب — تَمْرِين — تَدْرِيب . A reprimand, تَوْبِيخ — عِتَاب .

Schoolman, *n.* مِنْ أَهْلِ ٱلْحِكْمَةِ ٱلْقَدِيمَةِ . *See also* Scholastic, *n.*

Schoolmaster, *n.* مُعَلِّمُ مَكْتَبٍ *pl.* مُعَلِّمُونَ — صَاحِبُ مَكْتَبٍ ; called in Egypt, فَقِيه *pl.* فُقَهَاءُ .

Schoolmate, *n.* *See* Schoolfellow, *n.*

Schoolmistress, *n.* مُعَلِّمَةُ مَكْتَبٍ *pl.* مُعَلِّمَات .

Schooner, *n.* مَرْكَبٌ بِقِلْعَيْنِ — أَشْقُونَة .

Sciatic, *a.* مُتَعَلِّقٌ بِٱلنَّسَا — مَا نِيطَ بِعِرْقِ ٱلنَّسَا .

Sciatica, *n.* عِرْقُ ٱلنَّسَا .

Science, *n.* عِلْم *pl.* عُلُوم — فَنّ *pl.* فُنُون . A seeker of —, رَائِد *pl.* رُوَّاد — طَالِبُ ٱلْعِلْمِ *pl.* طُلَّاب .

Scientific, *a.* / Scientifical, } عِلْمِيّ — مُتَعَلِّقٌ بِٱلْعُلُومِ وَٱلْفُنُونِ . A — man, عَالِم *pl.* عُلَمَاءُ — عَلَّامَة *pl.* عَلَّام . Scientific men, أَهْلُ ٱلْحِكْمَةِ .

Scientifically, *ad.* عِلْمًا — حَسَبَ ٱلْقَوَاعِدِ ٱلْعِلْمِيَّةِ .

Scilicet, *ad.* وَهُوَ — مَعْنَاهُ — أَعْنِي — يَعْنِي .

Scintillant, *a.* مُتَلَأْلِئ — نَيِّر — مُنِير — لَامِع — بَرَّاق .

Scintillate, *v.i.* تَلَأْلَأَ — ٱسْتَنَارَ — تَنَوَّرَ — لَمَعَ — بَرَقَ — أَشَعَّ .

Scintillation, *n.* تَلَأْلُؤ — ٱسْتِنَارَة — تَنَوُّر — بَرْق — لَمَعَان — بَرَقَان .

Scio, *n.* The island, سَاقِس .

Sciolism, *n.* عِلْمٌ خَفِيف — قِلَّةُ عِلْمٍ .

Sciolist, *n.* عُوَيْرِف — قَلِيلُ ٱلْعِلْمِ .

Sciomancy, *n.* ٱلتَّفَاؤُلُ بِوَاسِطَةِ ٱلْخَيَالِ .

Scion, *n.* A shoot of a tree, عُسْلُج or عُسْلُوج *pl.* عَسَالِيجُ — فَرْع *pl.* فُرُوع . A graft, تَطْعِيم — غُرْز *pl.* غُرُوز . A child, descendant, ٱبْن *pl.* بَنُونَ and أَبْنَاءُ .

Scire facias, *n.* إِعْلَامٌ مِنَ ٱلْمَحْكَمَةِ لِلْمُدَّعَى عَلَيْهِ لِيُقَدِّمَ حُجَّتَهُ عَلَى مَا حُكِمَ عَلَيْهِ بِهِ مِنَ ٱلشَّرْعِ.

Scirocco, *n.* رِيحٌ جَنُوبِيَّةٌ شَرْقِيَّةٌ ; *from the Italian,* رِيحٌ شُلُوكٌ.

Scirrhosity, *n.* Induration of the glands, تَعَقُّدٌ ـ جَرَذ ـ جُرَذ ٱللَّوْزَاتِ.

Scirrhous, *a.* مُتَعَقِّد ـ ذُو جَرَذٍ. The wound or ulcer became —, جَرِذَتِ ٱلْقَرْحَةُ.

Scirrhus, *n.* وَرَمٌ مُتَعَقِّدٌ ـ جَرَذ ـ غُدَّة.

Scissible, *a.* / Scissile, } مِمَّا يُقْطَعُ ـ قَطْعُهُ مُمْكِنٌ.

Scission, *n.* The act of cutting, شَقّ ـ قَطْع ; the being cut, اِنْقِطَاع.

Scissors, *n.* مِقْرَاض *pl.* مَقَارِيض ـ مِقَصّ *pl.* مِقَصَّات.

Scissure, *n.* شَقّ *pl.* شُقُوق ـ فِلْذَة *pl.* فِلَذ ـ شَرِيحَة *pl.* شَرَائِحُ.

Sclavonian, *a.* / Sclavonic, } مُتَعَلِّقٌ بِٱلصِّرْبِ ـ صِرْبِيٌّ.

Sclerotic, *a.* شَدِيد ـ صُلْب.

Sclerotic, *n.* The outer coat of the eye, شَحْمَة ـ غَضَنُ ٱلْعَيْنِ ٱلْعَيْنِ.

Scobiform, *a.* فِي هَيْئَةِ ٱلْبُرَادَةِ ـ فِي هَيْئَةِ ٱلنُّشَارَةِ.

Scobs, *n.* Raspings, بُرَادَة. *See also* Dross, *n.*

Scoff, *v.i.* To — at, اِسْتَهْزَأَ بِ ـ ضَحِكَ مِن *or* بِ ـ خَنَتَ ـ سَخِرَ مِن *or* بِ ـ هَزِئَ مِن. *See also to* Mock, Gibe, *v.i.* and *t.*

Scoff, *n.* نَقَرَى ـ سَخَر *or* سُخْر ـ اِسْتِهْزَاء ـ مَسْخَرَة.

Scoffer, *n.* مُسْتَهْزِئٌ *pl.* مُسْتَهْزِئُونَ ـ سُخَرَة.

Scoffingly, *ad.* بِسُخْرٍ ـ بِٱسْتِهْزَاءٍ.

Scold, *v.i.* To brawl, تَسَخَّطَ ـ كَثَّرَ ٱلْعِيَاطَ ـ صَوَّتَ.

Scold, *v.t.* To chide, to rate, سَخِطَ عَلَى ـ عَتَبَ عَلَى *or* بِ ـ بَهْدَلَ ـ عَزَّرَ ـ زَجَرَ ـ تَعَتَّبَ عَلَى ـ عَاتَبَ.

Scold, *n.* زَجَّار ـ عَتَّاب. A female —, سَلِيطَة ـ سِلْقَة *pl.* سِلْقَان.

Scolding, *n.* مُعَاتَبَة ـ مَعْتَبَة ـ سُخْطَة ـ عَتَبَان ـ عَتْب.

Scollop, *n.* *See* Scallop, *n.*

Scollop, *v.t.* *See to* Scallop, *v.t.*

Sconce, *n.* A candlestick, شَمْعَدَان ـ مَنَارَة ; a hanging candlestick, ثُرَيَّا.

Scoop, *n.* A large ladle, مِغْرَفَة ـ مِنْقَر *pl.* مَنَاقِيرُ ـ خَاشُوقَة. A sweeping stroke, جَفْل ـ جُفُول ـ ضَرْبَة. A hollow, حُفْنَة. The quantity taken up by the two hands, حَفْنَة.

Scoop, *v.t.* To cut into a hollow, نَقَرَ فِي ـ حَفَرَ ـ قَعَّرَ ـ جَوَّفَ. To — out, to ladle, صَبَّ بِمِغْرَفَةٍ. To — out, with the two hands, حَفَنَ.

Scoop-net, *n.* مِجْرَف ; *vulg.* جَرَّافَة.

Scope, *n.* Extent of view, اِمْتِدَادُ ٱلْبَصَرِ. Range, compass, مَدًى. Limit of intellectual view, إِحَاطَةُ ٱلْعَقْلِ. Space, place, مَضْرَب ـ سَعَة ـ مَحَلّ ـ مَكَان ـ مَحَطّ. Room for action, فُسْحَة. Design, aim, فَحْوَى ـ مَقْصُود ـ مَقْصَد *pl.* مَقَاصِد ـ غَرَض *pl.* أَغْرَاض ـ مَرَام ـ نِيَّة. Power, قُدْرَة ـ طَاقَة ـ مُكْنَة. Liberty, license, إِجَازَة ـ رُخْصَة. Field, arena, مَيْدَان. Time, space, مُدَّة ـ فُسْحَة. To give — to, أَرْخَى لِ ـ أَطْلَقَ لِ ـ فَسَحَ لِ : Give him ample — for his judgment, discretion, *etc.*, أَرْخِ لَهُ ٱلْحَبْلَ. Within the — of the plenipotentiaries' powers, فِي وُسْعِ ٱلْمُرَخَّصِينَ.

Scorbutic, *a.* فَاسِدُ ٱلدَّمِ ـ مَفْسُودُ ٱلدَّمِ.

Scorch, *v.t.* Of fire, أَحْرَقَ ; of the sun, صَمَدَ ـ سَقَرَ ـ أَحْرَقَ. To —, in cooking, شَيَّطَ ـ أَشَاطَ. To be scorched, as by fire, اِحْتَرَقَ; of anything cooked, شَاطَ *aor.* يَشِيطُ ـ تَشَيَّطَ. The fire scorched him, سَقَرَتْهُ ٱلنَّارُ; the sun scorched him, سَقَرَتْهُ ٱلشَّمْسُ. The sun scorched his face, صَمَدَتِ ٱلشَّمْسُ وَجْهَهُ. To be scorched or dried up, جَفَّ *aor.* يَجِفُّ ـ تَجَفَّفَ.

Scorching, *a.* Of fire, حِرَاق ـ حُرَاق ـ مُحْرِق ; of the sun, سَاقِر. A — day, نَهَارٌ مُسْمَقِرٌّ. Scorching heat, سَقْر. Burning, blazing, لَهْبَانُ *fem.* لَهْبَى *pl.* لِهَاب ـ وَهِيج ـ وَهَّاج.

Score, *n.* A line, خَطّ *pl.* خُطُوط ـ سَطْر *pl.* سُطُور. A notch, فَلّ *pl.* فِلَال *and* فُلُول ـ حَزّ *pl.* حُزُوز. A — in a stick measure, مَشْبَر *pl.* مَشَابِرُ. A mark, sign, عَلَامَة *pl.* عِلَام *and* عَلَامَات ـ إِشَارَة ـ نِيشَان *pl.* نَوَاشِينُ. A list, سِيَاقَة. An account, حِسَاب *pl.* حِسَابَات. Expense, cost, مَصْرَف ـ مَصْرُوف ـ نَفَقَة. Debt, دَيْن. A head, subject, مَادَّة ـ مَوْضُوع ـ أَمْر ـ فَصْل. A —, in music, تَرَاكِيبُ ٱلْمُوسِيقَى. A motive, دَاعٍ *pl.* دُعَاة ـ بَاعِث ـ سَبَب *pl.* أَسْبَاب. Twenty, عِشْرُون. On the —, or subject, of ..., فِي مَادَّةِ كَذَا ـ عَنْ مَوْضُوعِ كَذَا. To wipe off old scores, of debt, أَوْفَى مَا عَلَيْهِ مِنَ ٱلدَّيْنِ.

Score, *v.t.* To notch, حَزَى ـ حَزَّزَ ـ فَلَّ. To mark upon, أَعْلَمَ عَلَى ـ عَيَّنَ عَلَى ـ رَقَّمَ عَلَى. To take, as an account, حَسَبَ ; to — against, حَسَبَ عَلَى. To draw lines on, خَطَّطَ ـ سَطَّرَ. To form for music, رَكَّبَ (*or* رَتَّبَ) لِلْمُوسِيقَى. To — out, to trace, design, رَسَمَ.

Scorer, *n.* *See* Marker, *n.*

Scoria, *n.* رَغْوَةُ ٱلْمَعَادِنِ ـ تُوبَال. Detritus, جُفَاء. *See also* Dross, *n.*

Scoriaceous, *a.* مِثْلَ رَغْوَةِ ٱلْمَعَادِنِ ـ كَٱلتُّوبَالِ. *See also* Drossy, *a.*

Scorification, *n.* تَصْفِيَةُ ٱلْمَعَادِنِ مِنَ ٱلْخَبَثِ.

Scoriform, *a.* فِي هَيْئَةِ خَبَثِ ٱلْمَعَادِنِ.

Scorify, *v.t.* صَفَّى ٱلْمَعَادِنَ مِنَ ٱلْخَبَثِ.

Scoring, *n.* Of music, تَرْكِيبُ لِلْمُوسِيقَى. A whipping, جَلْد ـ ضَرْبٌ بِسَوْطٍ. *See also* Score, *n.*

Scorious, *a.* Scoriaceous, *a.*

Scorn, *n.* Contempt, إِسْتِخْفَاف ـ أَنَفَة ـ إِسْتِهْزَآء ـ إِهَانَة ـ إِحْتِقَار; the subject of —, سُخْرَة ـ هُزْأَة ـ عَار. The being above doing anything derogatory, أَنَفَة ـ حَمِيَّة. He was the — of his neighbours, صَارَ عَارًا عِنْدَ ٱلْجِيرَانِ. He made him the — of the people, جَعَلَهُ عَارًا عِنْدَ ٱلْأُمَّةِ. To laugh to —, إِسْتَهْزَأَ بِ. To excite to —, آنَفَ.

Scorn, *v.t.* To contemn أَهَانَ ـ إِسْتَخَفَّ بِ ـ إِحْتَقَرَ ـ قَانَحَ. To be above, شَرُفَ ـ حَمِيَ مِن ـ حَمِيَ عَن ـ أَنِفَ مِن ـ إِسْتَحَى مِن ـ عَن. His soul scorned the thing, شَرُفَتْ نَفْسُهُ عَنِ ٱلشَّيْءِ. *See also to* Disdain, *v.t.*

Scorner, *n.* مُهِين ـ مُسْتَحْقِر ـ مُسْتَهْزِئٌ *pl.* مُسْتَهْزِئُونَ.

Scornful, *a.* مُهِين ـ أَنُوف ـ أَنِف ـ حَمِيُّ ٱلْأَنْفِ ـ مُتَعَزِّز ـ مُسْتَخِفٌّ بِ.

Scornfully, *ad.* إِسْتِحْقَارًا ـ بِٱسْتِحْقَارٍ ـ بِٱسْتِهْزَآءٍ ـ بِهَوَانٍ ـ بِتَعَزُّزٍ.

Scornfulness, *n.* عِزَّة ـ عِزٌّ. *See also* Scorn, *n.*

Scorpion, *n.* عَقْرَب *pl.* عَقَارِبُ. The claw of the —, زُبَانَى ٱلْعَقْرَبِ; the two claws, زُبَانَيَا ٱلْعَقْرَبِ. The sting (instrument) of a —, شَوْكَةُ ٱلْعَقْرَبِ. The constellation, العَقْرَبُ; the stars composing the constellation, البُرْق. The — stung him, لَدَغَتْهُ ٱلْعَقْرَبُ. A place abounding in scorpions, مَكَانٌ مُعَقْرِبٌ.

Scorpion-grass, *n.* ذَنَبُ ٱلْعَقْرَبِ.

Scortatory, *a.* *See* Lewd, Obscene, *a.*

Scot, *v.t.* To stop, to wedge, حَجَزَ ـ ضَبَطَ.

Scot, *n.* A share, حِصَّة. *See also* Scotchman, *n.*

Scotch, *a.* مِنْ أَهْلِ إِسْكُتْلَنْد ـ مِنْ إِسْكُتْلَنْد. The — fiddle; *see* Itch, *n.*

Scotch, *n.* A slight incision, فَلٌّ *pl.* فِلَال.

Scotch, *v.t.* To cut with slight incisions, فَلَّ ـ حَزَّ ـ إِحْتَزَّ ـ شَقَّ. To wound slightly, خَمَشَ ـ جَرَحَ.

Scotch-collops, *n.* لَحْمُ عِجْلٍ مَفْرُومٌ.

Scotchman, *n.* مِنْ أَهْلِ إِسْكُتْلَنْد

Scot-free, *a.* Excused from payment, مُعَاف. Safe and sound, سَالِمٌ آمِنٌ ـ بِلَا أَدْنَى مَضَرَّةٍ.

Scotland, *n.* إِسْكُتْلَنْد ـ بِلَادُ إِسْكُتْلَنْد.

Scotticism, *n.* لُغَةُ أَهْلِ إِسْكُتْلَنْد.

Scottish, *a.* *See* Scotch, *a.*

Scoundrel, *n.* قَلَطِيٌّ ـ قُلَّاط ـ قَبِيح *pl.* قِبَاح ـ خَبِيث ـ خَلِيع ـ شِرِّير *pl.* أَشْرَار ـ لَعِين. O you scoundrels! يَا آلَ غُدَرَ. To act as a —, أَقْبَحَ.

Scoundrel, *a.* شِرِّير ـ رَذِيل ـ غُدَر ـ دَنِيٌّ ـ خَبِيث.

Scoundrelism, *n.* رَذَالَة ـ فَضَاحَة ـ خَلَاعَة ـ خَبَاثَة.

Scour, *v.t.* To clean by rubbing, صَقَلَ ـ نَظَّفَ ـ جَلَى. To wash, غَسَلَ. To — from grease, أَزَالَ ٱلدُّهْنَ عَنْهُ. To purge, أَسْهَلَ ٱلْبَطْنَ ـ أَمْشَى. To overrun, roam over, عَالَ فِي ـ غَزَا ـ أَغَارَ عَلَى ـ عَارَ فِي. To range over in order to attack, إِسْتَوْلَى عَلَى. To — or brush along, to walk quickly, أَوْشَكَ ـ هَفَّ ـ خَفَّ فِي ٱلسَّيْرِ ـ وَاشَكَ. He scoured the forest, جَسَّ ٱلْغَابَةَ ـ دَارَ فِي ٱلْحِرْشِ ـ فَتَّشَ فِي ٱلْحِرْشِ. *See also to* Range, *v.t.*

Scour, *n.* } A rubbing, cleaning, صِقَال ـ تَنْظِيف ـ جِلَآء

Scouring, } صَقْل.

Scourer, *n.* A polisher, صَقَّال ـ صَيْقَل ـ جَالٍ; a washer, غَسَّال.

Scourge, *n.* A whip, سَوْط *pl.* سِيَاط *and* أَسْوَاط ـ مِقْرَعَة ـ دِرَّة *pl.* دِرَر. An infliction, misfortune, دَاهِيَة ـ مُصِيبَة ـ بَلَآء ـ آفَة.

Scourge, *v.t.* As with a whip, سَوَّطَ ـ يَسُوطُ *aor.* سَاطَ ـ جَلَدَ ـ ضَرَبَ سَوْطًا. To punish, عَاقَبَ ـ قَاصَصَ. To chastise, correct, وَبَّخَ ـ عَزَّرَ.

Scourger, *n.* جَلَّاد ـ سَوَّاط ـ شُرْطِيٌّ.

Scout, *n.* As of an army, رَبِيئَة *pl.* رَبَايَا ـ رَقِيب *pl.* رُقَبَآء ـ رَائِدُ ٱلْعَسْكَرِ *pl.* رُوَّاد; a party of scouts, نَفِيضَة *pl.* نَفَائِض ـ طَلِيعَة ـ شَيِّقَة. A — or servant of a college, خَادِمُ مَدْرَسَةٍ.

Scout, *v.i.* To act as a scout, إِرْتَبَأَ ـ رَبَأَ: He scouted for the party, إِرْتَبَأَ ٱلْقَوْمَ ـ رَبَأَ ٱلْقَوْمَ. To — or sneer at, نَقَرَ ـ إِسْتَحْقَرَ.

Scout, *v.t.* To treat with disdain, حَكَرَ ـ إِسْتَحْقَرَ ـ أَهَانَ ـ إِسْتَخَفَّ ـ قَانَحَ.

Scovel, *n.* مِكْنَسَةٌ لِلْفُرْنِ.

Scow, *n.* زَوْرَق *pl.* زَوَارِق ـ شَخْتُور *pl.* شَخَاتِير.

Scow, *v.t.* عَبَّرَ فِي زَوْرَقٍ.

Scowl, *v.i.* شَتَمَ ـ بَسَرَ ـ عَبَسَ ـ تَعَبَّسَ ـ جَهَمَ ـ تَقَطَّبَ ـ أَظْلَمَ ـ عَتَمَ ـ تَدَجَّى. To lower, look gloomy, عَبَسَ وَجْهُهُ. To — at, جَهَمَ ـ جَهِمَ ـ تَجَهَّمَ ـ تَجَهَّمَ لِ. *See also to* Frown, *v.i.*

Scowl, *n.* بَسَالَة ـ بُسُول ـ جُهُومَة ـ بُسُور ـ عَبْس ـ عُبُوس ـ قَطْب.

Scowling, *a.* مُعَبِّس ـ عَابِس . *See also* Frowning, *a.*

Scowlingly, *ad.* عَبْسًا ـ بِجَبِينٍ مُعَبِّسٍ ـ بِوَجْهٍ مُقَطِّبٍ .

Scrabble, *v.t.* and *i.* *See to* Scribble.

Scrabbler, *n.* *See* Scribbler, *n.*

Scrag, *n.* Something lean and rough, شَيْءٌ شَخْتٌ أَخْرَشُ .

Scragged, *a.* / Scraggy, } Rough, rugged, أَخْرَشُ *fem.* خَرْشَآء *pl.* خُرْشٌ ـ وَعِيرٌ ـ وَعِرٌ ـ أَخْشَبُ . Lean, emaciated, شَخْتٌ ـ نَحِيفٌ ـ مَهْزُولٌ ـ مُخْتَلٌّ . To be —, lean, slender, شَخُتَ [2]. *See also* Rough, Rugged, *a.*

Scraggedness, *n.* / Scragginess, } Roughness, ruggedness, خُشُونَة ـ خَشَب ـ وُعُور . Emaciation, نَحَافَة ـ خَسَف ـ شُخُوتَة ـ هُزَال .

Scraggily, *ad.* With roughness, بِخُشُونَةٍ ـ بِخَشَبٍ ; with leanness, بِنَحَافَةٍ ـ بِشُخُوتَةٍ .

Scramble, *v.i.* To strive, attempt, سَعَى *aor.* يَسْعَى ـ تَعَنَّى ـ تَعَمَّلَ . To — for, أَصَرَّ عَلَى ـ اِجْتَهَدَ فِي ـ هَمَّ بِ [2]. To — up, تَسَوَّرَ ـ تَسَلَّقَ .

Scramble, *n.* / Scrambling, } Eager competition, مُجَاهَدَة ـ تَعَنٍّ ـ تَعَمُّل ـ سَعْي ـ مُخَايَرَة ـ مُسَامَاة ـ مُبَارَاة . A climbing up, تَسَوُّر ـ تَسَلُّق . *See also* Scuffle, Dispute, Contention, *n.*

Scrambler, *n.* A competitor, مُبَارٍ ـ مُفَاضِل ـ مُنَافِس ـ مُغَايِر . A climber, مُتَسَوِّر ـ مُتَسَلِّق .

Scranch, *v.t.* To grind between the teeth, صَلْقَمَ ـ قَضِمَ ـ مَضَغَ ـ لَاكَ [2] [2].

Scrap, *n.* A little piece, حِتَّة *pl.* حِتَت . A fragment, جُزْءٌ *pl.* أَجْزَآء ـ قِطْعَةٌ صَغِيرَةٌ *pl.* قِطَع . A — of food, كِسْرَة ـ عُلَاس . A small residue, فَضْلَة ـ بَقِيَّة *pl.* بَقَايَا ـ فَضْل ـ فُضَالَة . Scraps, fragments of victuals, *etc.*, كِسَر . To live on scraps, قَشَّ [2]. I have not eaten a —, مَا أَكَلْتُ عُلَاسًا .

Scrap-book, *n.* مُجَلَّدٌ يُجْتَمَعُ فِيهِ ٱلتَّصَاوِيرُ وَغَيْرُهَا ـ مُجَلَّدٌ يَحْتَوِي عَلَى تَصَاوِيرَ وَغَيْرِهَا .

Scrape, *v.t.* To rub off, as with the hand or a stone, *etc.*, حَتَّ [2] ـ جَلَفَ [2]. To rub, grate, or chafe, جَرَشَ [2] ـ قَشَرَ [2] ـ حَكَّ [2]. To wipe, مَسَحَ ـ مَشَحَ . To — off, as a rind or outer surface, سَفَنَ ـ قَشَرَ ـ قَشَطَ . To be scraped off, تَحَاتَّ ـ اِنْحَتَّ . To scrape acquaintance with, تَعَرَّفَ إِلَى ـ تَعَارَفَ مَعَ .

To scrape one's self with . . . , اِحْتَكَّ بِ .

To scrape together, to amass, حَبَّشَ ـ قَمَّشَ ـ لَقَطَ ـ هَبَّشَ ـ جَمَعَ .

To scrape one's shoes, مَسَحَ نِعَالَهُ .

To scrape up, as a fowl the ground, بَحَثَ ; to dig up, as out of the ground, نَبَشَ [2].

Scrape, *n.* A rubbing, حَتٌّ ـ جَلْف ; a grating, chafing, جَرْش ـ قَشْر ـ حَكٌّ ; a rubbing off of the rind, قَشْط ; a wiping, مَسْح . A thin coating, طَلْي ـ طَلْيَة . A difficulty, مَعْسَرَة ـ مُشْكِلَة ـ مِحْنَة ـ صُعُوبَة ـ وَرْطَة . Scrapes, difficulties, عَرَاقِيل .

To draw into a scrape, رَمَى فِي بَلِيَّةٍ ـ رَمَى فِي ٱلْاِرْتِبَاكِ (or) وَرْطَةٍ .

To get one's self into a scrape, اِرْتَبَكَ فِي أَمْرٍ ـ وَقَعَ فِي بَلِيَّةٍ *aor.* يَقَعُ .

To get one's self out of a scrape, سَلِمَ مِنَ ـ تَفَرَّجَ مِنَ ٱلْاِرْتِبَاكِ ٱلْآفَةِ . He has no chance of getting himself out of this scrape, لَيْسَ لَهُ وَجْهٌ لِلتَّخَلُّصِ مِنْ هٰذَا ٱلْاِرْتِبَاكِ .

To get one out of a scrape, أَفْرَجَ ـ (or فَرَّجَ ـ) مِنَ ٱلْاِرْتِبَاكِ ـ سَلَّمَ ـ مِنَ ٱلْآفَةِ .

Scraper, *n.* An instrument for scraping, مِقْشَط *pl.* مَقَاشِط ـ مِحَكَّة ـ جَارُوف . An awkward fiddler, نَقَّار ـ رَبَابِيٌّ أَخْرَقُ .

See also Miser, *n.*

Scraping, *n.* A paring, cutting, جُرَاشَة ـ حُكَاكَة . What is scraped together, كُومَة ـ كُبْشَة ـ لَمَّة . What is scraped off, جُلَيْف . Awkward play on a fiddle, ٱلْخُرْقُ فِي ضَرْبِ ٱلرَّبَابِ .

See also Scrape, *n.*

Scratch, *v.t.* To rub or tear the surface of, to chafe, جَرَشَ [2] ـ جَرَّشَ ـ حَكَّ [2] ـ قَشَرَ . To — with the nails, أَرَشَ [2] ـ خَدَشَ ـ خَدَّشَ ـ خَمَشَ ـ خَمَّشَ . To — the ground like a fowl, بَحَثَ فِي ٱلْأَرْضِ . To — out, to erase, طَمَسَ [2] ـ مَحَا ـ حَكَّكَ ـ تَمَرَّسَ ـ طَرْمَسَ ـ طَلَسَ ـ نَسَخَ . To — one's self, تَمَرَّسَ ; to — one's self against, اِحْتَكَّ بِ . He scratched his head with a comb, دَرَى رَأْسَهُ . The woman scratched, or wounded, the skin of her face with her nail, خَمَشَتِ ٱلْمَرْأَةُ وَجْهَهَا بِظُفْرِهَا . To —, or spirtle, as a pen the ink, رَشَّشَ .

Scratch, *v.i.* Of a pen, تَرَشَّشَ ٱلْقَلَمُ . *See also under to* Scratch, *v.t.*

Scratch, *n.* As with the nails, خَدْش ـ أَرْش ـ تَأْرِيش ـ حَكٌّ ـ خُمُوش ـ خَمْش *pl.* خُمُوش ـ خُدُوش . A laceration, تَخْمِيش . A slight wound, جُرْحٌ خَفِيفٌ ـ خُمَاشَة . Severity, as of a contest, اِشْتِدَاد ـ شِدَّة . To come to the —, أَوْفَى بِٱلْأَمْرِ ـ ٱلْمُجْز . To bring to the —, أَلْجَأَ ـ إِلَى ٱلْأَمْرِ ـ أَلْزَمَ ـ بِٱلشَّيْءِ .

Scratcher, *n.* One who scratches, خَمَّاش ـ خَدَّاش . *See also* Scraper, *n.*

Scratch-post, *n.* حِكَاك .

Scrawl, *v.t.* To draw clumsily, رَسَمَ - بِخُرْبَقَةٍ ²; to write clumsily, كَتَبَ - بِخُرْبَقَةٍ ². To write or draw awkwardly, كَتَبَ - بِخَطٍّ ² خَرْبَشَ - خَرْمَشَ - مُشْتَبِكٌ. To make a rough draft of, سَوَّدَ.

Scrawl, *v.i.* شَبَّكَ ٱلْخَطَّ - تَشَبَّكَ فِي خَطِّهِ.

Scrawl, *n.* خَطٌّ مُخَرْبَشٌ (*or* مُخَرْمَشٌ) - خَطٌّ مُشْتَبِكٌ.

Scrawler, *n.* خَطَّاطٌ غَشِيمٌ - كَاتِبٌ مُخَرْبِشٌ - مُشَبِّكُ ٱلْخَطِّ.

Screak, *v.t.* To make a shrill noise, زَعَقَ ₌ - صَرَّ ₌. *See also to* Creak, *v.i.*

Screak, *n.* صَرِيرٌ - زَعْقٌ.

Scream, *v.i.* صَرَخَ ² ₌ - أَعْوَلَ - إِعْتَوَلَ - صَرَّ ₌ - صَيَّحَ - زَعَقَ ₌. To —, as a vulture or hawk, صَرْصَرَ. He screamed in his talk, تَلَهْيَعَ فِي حَدِيثِهِ.

To scream, *v.t.* زَأَطَ ₌.

Scream, *n.* صَرْخَةٌ - صَرِيرٌ - عَوِيلٌ - عَوْلٌ *pl.* أَعْوَالٌ - زِئَاطٌ - صِيَاحٌ - عِيَاطٌ - صُرَاخٌ.

Screamer, *n.* صَيَّاحٌ - عَيَّاطٌ - صَرَّاخٌ.

Screech, *v.i.* *See to* Scream, *v.i.*

Screech, *n.* *See* Scream, *n.*

Screech-owl, *n.* قُطْرُبٌ *pl.* قَطَارِبُ - بُومَةٌ *coll.* بُومٌ.

Screed, *n.* خِرَاطَةٌ.

Screen, *v.t.* As with a screen, سَتَرَ ² ₌. To — off, to put a partition between, حَجَزَ بَيْنَ ². To — from, to defend from, سَتَرَ - مِن ² ₌ - دَارَى عَن - حَفِظَ - مِن ₌ - خَفَرَ - مِن ² ₌ - حَمَى - مِن ₌. To —, as the faults of another, تَغَمَّدَ - غَمَّدَ. To hide, خَبَأَ ₌ - أَخْفَى. To sift through a —, غَرْبَلَ. To — one's self by means of, إِحْتَجَزَ بِ; to — one's self from, إِحْتَجَزَ مِن.

Screen, *n.* A curtain, veil, covert, or anything by which one is protected, سِتْرٌ *pl.* سُتُورٌ *and* سُتُرٌ - سِتَارَةٌ - سُتْرَةٌ. A fire —, حَائِلٌ دُونَ ٱلنَّارِ - حَاجِزٌ عَنِ ٱلنَّارِ. A partition, حَاجِزٌ *pl.* حَوَاجِزُ. A folding —, سِتْرٌ ذُو مَصَارِيعَ. A fold of a —, مِصْرَاعُ سِتْرٍ. A riddle, sieve, غِرْبَالٌ *pl.* غَرَابِيلُ.

Screw, *n.* لَوْلَبٌ *pl.* لَوَالِبُ - بُرْغِيٌّ *pl.* بَرَاغِيُّ. A large —, as for a press, مِلْوَى. There is a — loose in the matter, لَا بُدَّ مِنْ خَلَلٍ فِي ٱلْأَمْرِ. *See also* Miser, *n.*

Screw, *v.t.* To fasten with screws, أَحْكَمَ - (*or* ضَبَطَ ² ₌) - بِبَرَاغِيَّ. To turn a screw, لَوَى ٱلْبُرْغِيَّ ₌. To — up one's courage, تَصَلَّبَ - شَدَّدَ عَزْمَهُ - تَشَدَّدَ. To press hard upon, شَدَّدَ عَلَى.

Screw-bolt, *n.* خِلَالُ ٱلْبُرْغِيِّ *pl.* أَخِلَّةٌ.

Screw-driver, *n.* مِلْوَى - مِلْوَى ٱلْبَرَاغِيِّ.

Screw-jack, *n.* آلَةٌ لِرَفْعِ ٱلْأَثْقَالِ - سِمَاكٌ.

Screw-nut, *n.* سِدَادُ ٱلْبُرْغِيِّ *pl.* أَسِدَّةٌ.

Screw-plate, *n.* مِسْحَبَةٌ.

Screw-steamer, *n.* بَاخِرَةٌ رَفَّاسَةٌ.

Scribble, *v.t.* and *i.* *See to* Scrawl, *v.t.* and *i.*

Scribbler, *n.* A petty writer or author, مُؤَلِّفٌ حَقِيرٌ - مُؤَلِّفٌ رَكِيكٌ. *See also* Scrawler, *n.*

Scribbling, *n.* Petty writing, كِتَابَةٌ رَكِيكَةٌ. *See also* Scrawl, *n.*

Scribe, *n.* كَاتِبٌ *pl.* كُتَّابٌ *and* كَتَبَةٌ. A copyist, نَاسِخٌ *pl.* نُسَّاخٌ - وَرَّاقٌ.

Scrimp, *v.t.* To make less ample, قَصَّرَ - ضَيَّقَ. To make too small, صَغَّرَ. To be niggardly towards, بَخِلَ عَلَى ₌.

Scrimp, *n.* *See* Niggard, Miser, *n.*

Scrimp, *a.* Short, scant, قَصِيرٌ - ضَيِّقٌ. Wanting, نَاقِصٌ. A — dress, ثَوْبٌ عَاجِزٌ. *See also* Scanty, *a.*

Scrip, *n.* A bag for provisions, *etc.*, مِزْوَدٌ *pl.* مَزَاوِدُ. A shepherd's —, كِنْفُ ٱلرُّعَاةِ. A small piece of writing, رُقْعَةٌ *pl.* رِقَاعٌ. A certificate of stock subscribed, سَنَدٌ مُوَقَّتٌ *pl.* سَنَدَاتٌ.

Scriptural, *a.* According to holy Scripture, حَسَبَ ٱلْكُتُبِ ٱلْمُقَدَّسَةِ - مُطَابِقٌ ٱلْكُتُبَ ٱلْمُقَدَّسَةَ; contained in holy Scripture, مَوْجُودٌ فِي ٱلْكُتُبِ ٱلْمُقَدَّسَةِ.

Scripturally, *ad.* طِبْقَ ٱلْكُتُبِ ٱلْمُقَدَّسَةِ - مِنَ ٱلْكُتُبِ ٱلْمُقَدَّسَةِ.

Scripture, *n.* A writing, خَطٌّ - كِتَابَةٌ. Holy —, ٱلْكُتُبُ ٱلْمُلْهَمَةُ - ٱلْكُتُبُ ٱلْمُقَدَّسَةُ - كَلَامُ ٱللّٰهِ. "Those who have been given the scriptures," (Kûr. ii. 95; *etc.*) ٱلَّذِينَ أُوتُوا ٱلْكِتَابَ.

Scripturist, *n.* عَالِمٌ بِٱلْكُتُبِ ٱلْمُقَدَّسَةِ (*or* ٱلْمُلْهَمَةِ).

Scrivener, *n.* A writer of certificates, كَاتِبُ سَنَدَاتٍ. *See also* Notary, *n.*

Scrofula, *n.* أَبُو كَعْبٍ - خَنَازِيرُ; in the neck, سِلْعَةٌ *pl.* سِلَعٌ.

Scrofulous, *a.* خَنَازِيرِيٌّ.

Scroll, *n.* As of paper or parchment, دَرَجٌ - مُدْرَجٌ *pl.* مَدَارِجُ. A spiral ornament, نَقْشٌ لَوْلَبِيٌّ - طُومَارٌ *pl.* طَوَامِيرُ. An interlacing of letters, خَطٌّ مُوَصَّلٌ. To roll up into a —, طَمَّرَ. To be rolled together as a —, إِلْتَفَّ كَدَرَجٍ.

Scrotiform, *a.* فِي هَيْئَةِ ٱلْكِيسِ.

Scrotum, *n.* The —, كِيسُ ٱلْخُصَى - ٱلصَّفَنُ *pl.* ٱلْأَصْفَانُ. A swelling of the —, قَرْوَةٌ.

Scrub, *n.* A worn brush, فُرْشَةٌ عَتِيقَةٌ. A mean fellow, خَسِيسٌ - رَذِيلٌ. *See also* Drudge, *n.*

Scrub, *v.t.* جَلَى - بِفُرْشَةٍ ₌ - نَظَّفَ - بِفُرْشَةٍ. *See also to* Scour, *v.i.*

Scrub, *v.i.* To be diligent and penurious, كَدَّ وَشَحَّ ².

Scrubbing-brush, *n.* فُرْشَةٌ لِلْحَكِّ ـ فُرْشَةٌ مَتِينَةٌ.

Scrubby, *a.* Mean, رَذِيلٌ ـ دَنِيٌّ ـ حَقِيرٌ ـ خَسِيسٌ.

Scruple, *n.* Dubiousness, doubt, اِرْتِيَابٌ ـ شُبْهَةٌ *pl.* شُبَهٌ *and* شُبُهَاتٌ *and* شُبَهَاتٌ ـ شَكٌّ *pl.* شُكُوكٌ. Hesitation, تَضَرُّبٌ ـ تَرَدُّدٌ ـ تَمَحْطُرٌ. A great —, شُبْهَةٌ كُلِّيَّةٌ; a light —, شُبْهَةٌ جُزْئِيَّةٌ; an unfounded —, شُبْهَةٌ وَاهِيَةٌ ـ شُبْهَةٌ غَيْرُ مُؤَسَّسَةٍ; a well-founded —, شُبْهَةٌ مُحَقَّقَةٌ. Scruple, the weight, قِيرَاطٌ *pl.* قَرَارِيطُ. To remove scruples, أَزَالَ ٱلشُّبُهَاتِ (*or* ٱلشُّكُوكَ). To give rise to scruples, أَوْرَثَ ٱلشُّبُهَاتِ ـ سَبَّبَ ٱلشُّكُوكَ. To entertain scruples with regard to ..., تَوَسْوَسَ فِي ـ حَسِبَ ٱلشَّيْءَ ... حَرَامًا عَلَيْهِ. To make a — of, تَحَشَّى مِن ـ خَشِيَ مِن ـ تَرَدَّدَ فِي. He did not make the least — about it, لَمْ يَتَحَاشَ مِنْهُ قَطْعًا. To instil scruples into about, شَكَّكَ ـ فِي.

Scruple, *v.i.* To doubt about, شَكَّ فِي ـ تَمَارَى فِي ـ مَارَى ـ تَشَكَّكَ فِي ـ يَشُكُّ *aor.* تَخَالَجَ فِي. To hesitate about, عَيَّ بِ ـ يَعِيُّ *aor.* تَعَيَّا بِ ـ تَضَرَّبَ فِي ـ تَرَدَّدَ فِي. *See also to* Doubt, *to* Hesitate, *v.i.*

Scrupler, *n.* *See* Scrupulous, *a.*

Scrupulosity, *n.* / **Scrupulousness**, } Quality of being scrupulous, nice, hesitating, تَشَكُّكٌ ـ تَنَوُّقٌ ـ تَجَوُّدٌ ـ شُبْهَةٌ. Caution, حِذْرٌ ـ تَحَذُّرٌ ـ تَحَفُّظٌ. Precision, دِقَّةٌ ـ تَدْقِيقٌ.

Scrupulous, *a.* Doubting, hesitating, مُتَشَكِّكٌ ـ مُتَرَدِّدٌ ـ مِنْ أَهْلِ ٱلشُّبُهَاتِ. Over-nice, مُتَجَوِّدٌ ـ مُتَنَوِّقٌ. Precise, exact, مَضْبُوطٌ ـ مُدَقِّقٌ. To be —, over-nice, تَنَوَّقَ ـ تَجَوَّدَ; to be —, precise, دَقَّ *aor.* يَدِقُّ. To be — with, دَاقَّ: He was — with him about the accounts, دَاقَّهُ فِي ٱلْحِسَابِ.

Scrupulously, *ad.* With over-nicety, بِتَنَوُّقٍ ـ بِتَجَوُّدٍ; with precision, بِدِقَّةٍ ـ بِتَدْقِيقٍ ـ بِٱعْتِنَاءٍ كُلِّيٍّ.

Scrutable, *a.* تَصَفُّحُهُ مُمْكِنٌ ـ مِمَّا يُتَفَحَّصُ ـ تَحْقِيقُهُ مُمْكِنٌ.

Scrutin, *n.* (French) إِجْرَاءُ أُصُولِ ٱلْقُرْعَةِ. Secret —, ٱلْقُرْعَةُ بِصُورَةٍ خَفِيَّةٍ. Individual —, ٱلِٱنْتِخَابُ بِٱلْقُرْعَةِ إِفْرَادًا.

Scrutineer, *n.* / **Scrutinizer**, } كَشَّافٌ ـ مُتَصَفِّحٌ ـ مُتَفَحِّصٌ ـ مُسْتَشِفٌّ.

Scrutinize, *v.t.* تَجَسَّسَ ـ تَصَفَّحَ ـ اِسْتَشَفَّ ـ صَفَحَ ـ أَغَارَ فِي ـ دَقَّقَ فِي ـ تَفَحَّصَ ـ فَاتَشَ.

Scrutinous, *a.* *See* Inquisitive, Curious, Captious, *n.*

Scrutiny, *n.* تَحَرٍّ ـ تَفَحُّصٌ ـ تَجَسُّسٌ ـ تَصَفُّحٌ ـ اِسْتِشْفَافٌ ـ تَدْقِيقٌ ـ تَحْقِيقٌ.

Scud, *v.i.* To fly or be forced along, أَسْرَعَ ـ جَدَفَ ـ مَخَرَ ـ اِنْطَلَقَ ـ طَارَ.

Scud, *n.* A rushing or driving along, سُرْعَةٌ ـ طَيَرَانٌ ـ مَخْرٌ ـ ثَوَرَانٌ ـ ثَوْرٌ.

Scudding, *a.* A — ship, سَفِينَةٌ مَاخِرَةٌ *pl.* سُفُنٌ مَوَاخِرُ ـ طَرَّادٌ.

Scuffle, *n.* A confused struggle or contest, هَوْشَةٌ ـ هَرْجٌ مَرْجٌ ـ شَغْبٌ ـ مُشَاجَرَةٌ ـ مُعَارَكَةٌ ـ هَوْشَاتٌ *pl.*

Scuffle, *v.i.* To contend tumultuously with, شَاجَرَ ـ عَارَكَ ـ قَاتَلَ. To wrestle with, صَارَعَ. They scuffled together, of many, تَقَاتَلُوا ـ تَعَارَكُوا ـ تَشَاجَرُوا. *See also under to* Tackle, *v.t.*

Scuffler, *n.* مُشَاجِرٌ ـ مُعَارِكٌ; a wrestler, مُصَارِعٌ.

Sculk, *v.i.* *See to* Skulk, *v.i.*

Scull, *n.* A short oar, مِجْدَافٌ خَفِيفٌ *pl.* مَجَادِيفُ خَفِيفَةٌ ـ مِقْذَافٌ *pl.* مَقَاذِيفُ. *See also* Boat, *n.*

Scull, *v.t.* جَدَفَ ـ قَذَفَ.

Sculler, *n.* One who sculls, قَذَّافٌ ـ غَادِفٌ; *vulg.* قَدَّافٌ.

Scullery, *n.* مَحَلُّ ٱلطَّوَابِقِ وَٱلْقُدُورِ.

Scullion, *n.* غَسَّالُ ٱلصُّحُونِ ـ رَقَّابَةٌ *fem.* غَسَّالَةٌ. A low fellow, مِنْ أَهْلِ ٱلْأَوْبَاشِ ـ سُوقِيٌّ.

Sculptile, *a.* مَنْحُوتٌ ـ مُنَقَّشٌ.

Sculptor, *n.* نَقَّاشٌ ـ نَحَّاتٌ.

Sculptural, *a.* مُنَقَّشٌ ـ مُتَعَلِّقٌ بِٱلنَّقْشِ.

Sculpture, *n.* The act of sculpturing, نَحْتٌ ـ نَقْشٌ. The art of —, فَنُّ ٱلنَّقْشِ ـ نِقَاشَةٌ. Anything sculptured, مَنْحُوتٌ ـ نَقْشٌ *pl.* نُقُوشٌ ـ تَصْوِيرٌ مُجَسَّمٌ *pl.* تَصَاوِيرُ مُجَسَّمَةٌ.

Sculpture, *v.t.* نَقَشَ ـ نَحَتَ. *See also to* Carve, Engrave, *v.t.*

Scum, *n.* زَبَدٌ ـ رَغْوَةٌ ـ جُفَاءٌ ـ عُفْوَةٌ ـ كُثَاءٌ ـ طُفَاحَةٌ. The green — on stagnant water, طُحْلُبٌ ـ نُورُ ٱلْمَاءِ. The — of a torrent, غُثَاءٌ ـ غُفَاءٌ ـ غَفًى. The — of the people, ٱلسَّفِلَةُ. Scum and refuse, غُثَاءٌ.

Scum, *v.t.* كَشَطَ ٱلرَّغْوَةَ ـ قَشَطَ ٱلزَّبَدَ ـ أَطْفَحَ ٱلطُّفَاحَةَ.

Scummings, *n.* *See* Scum, *n.*

Scupper, *n.* بَلُّوعَةٌ فِي مَرْكَبٍ *pl.* بَلَالِيعُ.

Scupper-hose, *n.* خُرْطُومُ ٱلْبَلُّوعَةِ.

Scupper-nail, *n.* مِسْمَارٌ ذُو رَأْسٍ عَرِيضٍ.

Scurf, *n.* Of the head, قِشْرَةُ ٱلرَّأْسِ ـ هِبْرِيَةٌ ـ تِبْرِيَةٌ ـ حَزَازٌ. A single flake of —, حَزَازَةٌ. *See also* Scab, *n.*

Scurfiness, *n.* حَالَةُ ٱلْحَزَازَةِ ـ تِبْرِيَةٌ.

Scurfy, *a.* Covered with scurf, مُبْتَلًى بِحَزَازٍ; like scurf, مِثْلَ ٱلْهِبْرِيَةِ ـ مِثْلَ قِشْرِ ٱلرَّأْسِ.

Scurrility, *n.* بَذَاءٌ ـ قَذْعٌ ـ رَفَثٌ ـ خَنَايَةٌ ـ فَحْشَاءٌ ـ عَارٌ ـ عَيْبٌ.

Scurrilous, *a.* بَذِيّ – خَنٍ – مُفْحِش – فاحِش. *See also* Opprobrious, Obscene, *a.*

Scurrilously, *ad.* بِبَذَآءٍ – خَنًا – فُحْشًا – بِرَفَثٍ – بِفُحْشٍ.

Scurrilousness, *n.* *See* Scurrility, *n.*

Scurvily, *ad.* Meanly, بِرَذَالَةٍ – بِخَسَاسَةٍ – بِقَبَاحَةٍ.

Scurviness, *n.* Meanness, ذُلّ – ذِلَّة – حَقَارَة – خَسَاسَة – دَنَآءَة. *See also* Scurfiness, *n.*

Scurvy, *n.* The disease, دَآءُ فَسَادِ ٱلدَّمِ – إِسْقُرْبُوطٌ وَهُوَ ضَرْبٌ مِنْ دَآءِ ٱلْيَرَقَانِ.

Scurvy, *a.* Mean, رَذِيل – ذَلِيل – شَقِيّ *pl.* أَشْقِيَآء – خَسِيس.

Scurvy-grass, *n.* حَشِيشَةُ ٱلْمَعَالِقِ – الإِسْقُورُونُ.

Scut, *n.* ذَنَبٌ أَبْتَرُ.

Scutage, *n.* أَدَآءُ ٱلْخَرَاجِ بَدَلًا عَنِ ٱلْخِدْمَةِ ٱلْعَسْكَرِيَّةِ.

Scutch, *v.t.* نَظَّفَ.

Scutcheon, *n.* *See* Escutcheon, *n.*

Scutiform, *n.* فِي هَيْئَةِ ٱلتُّرْسِ.

Scuttle, *n.* A basket, سَلَّة *pl.* سَلَّات *and* سُلَل. A small opening for water in a roof or ship, بَلُّوعَة *pl.* بَلَالِيعُ. An opening, مَنْفِذ *pl.* مَنَافِذُ. A small hatchway, فَمُ أَنْبَارٍ صَغِيرٌ. A quick pace, وِشَاك – مُوَاشَكَة – رَوْجَة – جُفُول.

Scuttle, *v.t.* To pierce with holes, [2]خَرَقَ – [2]نَقَبَ. To — and sink a ship, [2]خَرَقَ ٱلسَّفِينَةَ وَأَغْرَقَهَا.

Scuttle, *v.i.* خَفَّ رِجْلَهُ – جَفَلَ – أَجْفَلَ – أَسْرَعَ.

Scythe, *n.* *See* Sickle, *n.*

S.E. *n.* and *a.* (South-east,) حَرْفَانِ يَدُلَّانِ عَلَى جَنُوبٍ وَشَرْقٍ أَوْ عَلَى ٱلْجَنُوبِيِّ ٱلشَّرْقِيِّ.

Sea, *n.* بَحْر *pl.* بُحُور *and* بِحَار. The salt —, ٱلْبَحْرُ ٱلْمَالِحُ. The open —, اليَمّ. A small —, بُحَيْرَة – بُحَيْر. A wave or billow, مَوْج *pl.* أَمْوَاج. A — of troubles, بَحْرُ ٱلْأَوْجَاعِ. They were thrown into the (open) sea, يُمُّوا – أُلْقُوا فِي ٱلْيَمِّ. The dangers of the —, غَوَائِلُ (or أَخْطَارُ) ٱلْبَحْرِ.

A heavy or high sea, بَحْرٌ كَبِيرٌ – بَحْرٌ عَالٍ.

An inland sea, بَحْرٌ فِي دَاخِلِ ٱلْبَرِّ.

A rough sea, بَحْرٌ مُتَلَاطِمٌ – بَحْرٌ مَائِجٌ – بَحْرٌ مَوَّاجٌ – بَحْرٌ زَاخِرٌ.

By land and by sea, بَرًّا وَبَحْرًا.

The high seas, البَحْرُ ٱلْوَاسِعُ.

The Black Sea, البَحْرُ ٱلْأَسْوَدُ.

The Caspian Sea, بَحْرُ خَزَرَ.

The Dead Sea, بَحْرُ لُوطٍ.

The Mediterranean Sea, البَحْرُ ٱلْأَبْيَضُ – بَحْرُ ٱلرُّومِ.

The Red Sea, بَحْرُ ٱلْقُلْزُمِ – البَحْرُ ٱلْأَحْمَرُ.

The Sea of Azof, بَحْرُ أَزُوفَ *or* أَزَاقَ.

The Sea of Marmora, بَحْرُ مَرْمَرَةَ.

To be at sea, on the sea, كَانَ فِي ٱلْبَحْرِ – كَانَ مُسَافِرًا فِي ٱلْبَحْرِ.

To be perplexed, ضَلَّ – [2]تَاهَ – دَهِشَ – تَحَيَّرَ.

To go to sea, أَبْحَرَ – سَافَرَ فِي مَرْكَبٍ – سَافَرَ فِي ٱلْبَحْرِ.

To put to sea, أَقْلَعَ – خَطَفَ: The ship put to sea to-day from the port, خَطَفَ ٱلْمَرْكَبُ ٱلْيَوْمَ مِنَ ٱلْمِينَةِ.

To ship a sea, نَزَلَ بِهِ بَحْرٌ – [2]أَكَلَ بَحْرًا – أَطْعِمَ بَحْرًا.

To stand out to sea, أَبْعَدَ عَنِ ٱلْبَرِّ – تَبَاعَدَ عَنِ ٱلْبَرِّ.

Sea, *a.* بَحْرِيّ.

Sea-anemone, *n.* حَيَوَانٌ بَحْرِيٌّ بِهَيْئَةِ ٱلزَّهْرِ.

Sea-bank, *n.* سَدُّ ٱلْبَحْرِ *pl.* أَسْدَاد *and* سُدُود.

Sea-bathed, *a.* مُحَاطٌ بِٱلْبَحْرِ – يَجْرِي حَوْلَهُ ٱلْبَحْرُ.

Sea-beaten, *a.* مُتَلَاطِمٌ بِٱلْبَحْرِ.

Sea-boat, *n.* سَفِينَةٌ تُسَافِرُ فِي ٱلْبَحْرِ.

Sea-board, *n.* سَاحِلُ ٱلْبَحْرِ *pl.* سَوَاحِلُ – مُجَاوِرُ ٱلْبَحْرِ.

Sea-born, *n.* مَوْلُودُ ٱلْبَحْرِ – مُوَلَّدُ ٱلْبَحْرِ.

Sea-boy, *n.* صَبِيُّ ٱلْمَعَاشِ فِي مَرْكَبٍ.

Sea-breeze, *n.* نَسْمَةٌ مِنَ ٱلْبَحْرِ.

Sea-calf, *n.* عِجْلُ ٱلْبَحْرِ *pl.* عِجَال.

Sea-captain, *n.* رَئِيسٌ بَحْرِيٌّ – قَبْطَانُ ٱلْبَحْرِ *pl.* قَبَاطِينُ; of a small ship, نَاخُوذَاة *pl.* نَوَاخِذَة.

Sea-coal, *n.* فَحْمُ حَجَرٍ – فَحْمٌ مَعْدِنِيٌّ.

Sea-coast, *n.* سَاحِلُ ٱلْبَحْرِ *pl.* سَوَاحِلُ.

Sea-cow, *n.* بَقَرَةُ ٱلْبَحْرِ *pl.* بَقَرَات.

Sea-egg, *n.* قُنْفُذُ ٱلْبَحْرِ *pl.* قَنَافِذُ – تُوتِيَا ٱلْبَحْرِ.

Seafarer, *n.} Seafaring, } عَدَوْلِيّ *pl.* عَدَوْلِيَّة – عَابِرُ ٱلْبَحْرِ *pl.* عَابِرُونَ.

Sea-fight, *n.* مُحَارَبَةٌ بَحْرِيَّةٌ – حَرْبٌ فِي ٱلْبَحْرِ.

Sea-fish, *n.* سَمَكَةُ ٱلْبَحْرِ *coll.* سَمَك *pl.* سَمَكَات.

Sea-fowl, *n.* طَيْرُ ٱلْبَحْرِ *pl.* طُيُور.

Sea-gage, *n.* Of a ship, إِغْتِرَافُ مَرْكَبٍ – غُرْفَةُ مَرْكَبٍ.

Sea-girt, *n.* مُحَاطٌ بِٱلْبَحْرِ.

Sea-god, *n.* مَعْبُودُ ٱلْبَحْرِ – إِلٰهُ ٱلْبَحْرِ.

Sea-goddess, *n.* إِلَاهَةُ ٱلْبَحْرِ – مَعْبُودَةُ ٱلْبَحْرِ.

Sea-green, *n.* لَوْنُ خُضْرَةِ ٱلْبَحْرِ.

Sea-green, *a.* أَخْضَرُ بَحْرِيٌّ.

Sea-gull, *n.* نَوْرَزَة – جَنْقَلَة *pl.* خَنَاقِلُ.

Sea-horse, *n.* فَرَسُ ٱلْبَحْرِ *pl.* فُرُوس *and* أَفْرَاس.

Sea-kale, *n.* ضَرْبٌ مِنَ ٱلْمَلْفُوفِ ٱلْبَحْرِيّ.

Seal, *n.* The sea animal, عِجْلُ ٱلْبَحْرِ *pl.* عِجَال.

Seal, *n.* For making an impression with, خَاتِم *pl.* خَوَاتِمُ — مُهْر — طَوَابِعُ *pl.* طَابِع. The impression of a —, خَتْم *pl.* خِتَام. The substance used in making a —, خِتَام. A — or signet-ring, خَاتِم *pl.* خَوَاتِمُ — حِلَق. The keeper, custodian, of an official —, مُهْرْدَار; the office of such, مُهْرْدَارِيَّة. Completion, perfecting, تَتْمِيم — تَكْمِيل — خَتْم. The last of anything, خِتَام — خَاتِم: the — of the prophets, خَاتِمُ (or خِتَامُ) ٱلْأَنْبِيَاء. To put a — or signet-ring upon another person, خَتَّمَ. To put a — or signet-ring on one's own finger, تَخَتَّمَ. To break a —, فَتَحَ ٱلْخَاتِمَ — فَكَّ ٱلْخَاتِمَ. The — was broken, إِنْفَكَّ ٱلْخَاتِمُ.

The Great Seal, الطَّابِعُ ٱلسُّلْطَانِيّ — خَاتِمُ ٱلدَّوْلَةِ ٱلْكَبِيرُ ٱلرَّسْمِيّ — ٱلْخَاتِمُ ٱلسُّلْطَانِيّ.

The Privy Seal, خَاتِمُ ٱلْمُحْمَدَارِيَّةِ ٱلْخَاصّ.

A common seal, خَاتِمُ مَجْلِسٍ مُشْتَرَك.

An official seal, مُهْرٌ (or خَاتِمٌ) رَسْمِيّ.

Under flying seal, مَفْتُوحُ ٱلْخَاتِم.

Seal, *v.t.* As with a seal, خَتَمَ — طَبَعَ. To affix a — to, خَتَمَ عَلَى — وَضَعَ خَتْمًا عَلَى *aor.* يَضَعُ. To close, سَدَّ. To confirm, ratify, أَمْضَى — بِٱلرِّضَاء — عَقَّدَ. To — on the mind, طَبَعَ فِي ٱلْعَقْلِ — أَرْسَخَ فِي ٱلضَّمِيرِ.

Sealed, *a.* مَخْتُوم — مَطْبُوع. It was — with the King's seal, خُتِمَ بِخَاتِمِ ٱلْمَلِكِ.

Sea-legs, *n.* الوُقُوفُ ٱلرَّاسِخُ فِي ٱلسَّفَرِ بَحْرًا.

Sealer, *n.* مُخَتِّم.

Sealing, *n.* The act of, خِتَام — خَتْم — طَبْع. Hunting for seals, the animals, صَيْدُ عِجْلِ ٱلْبَحْرِ.

Sealing-wax, *n.* لَكّ — شَمْعٌ لِلْخَتْم.

Seam, *n.* The line of sewing in a garment, شَكّ *pl.* شُكُوك — خِيَاطَة — كُتْبَة *pl.* كُتَب — خُرْزَة *pl.* خُرُوز. A raised —, دَرْز *pl.* دُرُوز. A small crack, as in a bone, شَكّ *pl.* شُكُوك. A scar, أَثَرُ جُرْحٍ *pl.* آثَار — عَذِيرَة — قَطْف *pl.* قُطُوف — عَلَب *pl.* عُلُوب. A joint or interval between boards, خُرْزَة *pl.* خُرُوز. A vein or stratum, طَاق *pl.* طَاقَات — طَبَقَة *pl.* طَبَقَات. Without —, of a garment, بِغَيْرِ خِيَاطَةٍ.

Seam, *v.t.* To make a seam, sewing, in, شَكَّ فِي — كَتَبَ — خَيَّطَ. To scar, قَطَّفَ — قَطَفَ.

Seaman, *n.* عَدَوْلِيّ *pl.* عَدَوْلِيَّة — بَحْرِيّ *pl.* بَحْرِيَّة — نُوتِيّ *pl.* نَوَاتِيّ. Seamen, مَلَّاح. Able-bodied —, بَحْرِيّ — بَحْرِيٌّ أَبْتَعُ — ضَلِيعٌ. A thorough —, بَحْرِيٌّ كَامِلٌ — بَحْرِيٌّ حَاذِقٌ. Able or experienced seamen, ٱلْبَحْرِيَّةُ ٱلْمُدَرَّبُونَ.

Seamanlike, *a.* بِحِرْفَةٍ بَحْرِيَّةٍ.

Seamanship, *n.* مِلَاحَة — مَلَّاحِيَّة. *See also* Navigation, *n.*

Sea-mark, *n.* إِشَارَةٌ عَلَى سَاحِلِ ٱلْبَحْرِ — عَلَمٌ عِنْدَ ٱلْبَحْرِ.

Sea-mew, *n.* نَوْرَزَة.

Seamless, *a.* بِغَيْرِ خِيَاطَةٍ — بِغَيْرِ كُتَبٍ.

Sea-moss, *n.* أُشْنَةُ ٱلْبَحْرِ.

Seamster, *n.* خَيَّاط *pl.* خَيَّاطَة.

Seamstress, *n.* خَيَّاطَة *pl.* خَيَّاطَات.

Seamy, *a.* Full of seams, sewings, مُخَيَّط — ذُو خُرُوزٍ; full of scars, ذُو قُطُوفٍ; full of cracks, intervals, ذُو خُرُوزٍ; full of veins, layers, ذُو طَبَقَاتٍ — ذُو طَاقَاتٍ.

Seance, n. مَجْلِس *pl.* مَجَالِسُ. To hold a —, عَقَدَ مَجْلِسًا.

Sea-nettle, *n.* قَرِيصُ ٱلْبَحْرِ.

Sea-nymph, *n.* بِنْتُ ٱلْبَحْرِ *pl.* بَنَات.

Sea-otter, *n.* كَلْبُ ٱلْبَحْرِ *pl.* كِلَاب — ثَعْلَبُ ٱلْبَحْرِ.

Sea-pie, *n.* فَطِيرٌ مَحْشُوٌّ بِلَحْمٍ — رُقَاق.

Sea-piece, *n.* مَنْظَرٌ بَحْرِيّ — رَسْمُ مَنْظَرٍ فِي ٱلْبَحْرِ.

Seaport, *n.* *See* Port, *n.*

Seapoy, *n.* *See* Sepoy, *n.*

Sear, *v.t.* To burn, أَحْرَقَ. To cauterize, كَوَى — نَوَّرَ — نَارَ. To make callous, أَقْسَى. To dry up, يَبَّسَ — جَفَّفَ.

Sear, *a.* Dry, withered, يَابِس — ذَابِل — جَافّ.

Search, *v.t.* To examine thoroughly, فَتَّشَ. To investigate, تَبَحَّثَ عَن — بَحَثَ فِي — تَطَلَّبَ — جَسَّ — تَجَسَّسَ — تَصَفَّحَ — تَجَسَّسَ — فَتَّشَ عَن — فَحَصَ (or تَفَحَّصَ) عَن — تَصَفَّحَ. To inquire for, نَشَدَ عَن — تَطَلَّبَ. To — to the bottom, تَقَعَّرَ فِي — فَحَصَ بِٱلتَّدْقِيقِ. To overhaul, فَتَّشَ. To — out, look for, دَوَّرَ عَلَى — دَارَ عَلَى — فَتَّشَ عَلَى — جَاسَ. To aim after, قَصَدَ — تَحَرَّى. He searched out what was most proper to be done in the affair, تَحَرَّى فِي ٱلْأَمْرِ. They searched out the land, تَجَسَّسُوا ٱلْأَرْضَ. *See also to* Investigate, *v t.*

Search, *n.* Investigation, جَسّ — تَجَسُّس — نَدْش — تَصَفُّح — اِسْتِعْلَام — اِسْتِفْهَام — اِسْتِقْصَاء. Inquiry, تَفْتِيش — فَحْص — بَحْث. Endeavour, جُهْد — جِدّ — سَعْي. Diligent —, فَحْصٌ مُدَقَّق. To make — for, فَتَّشَ عَن. To prosecute diligent — into, تَتَبَّعَ. He caused — to be made in the book, جَعَلَ أَنْ يُفَتِّشَ فِي ٱلْكِتَابِ. A domiciliary —, تَفْتِيشٌ مَحَلِّيّ — مُعَايَنَةٌ مَوْقِعِيَّة.

إِسْتِشْفَافُ ٱلْبُيُوتِ. Right of —, حَقُّ ٱلْمَسَاْلَةِ وَٱلتَّجَسُّسِ — حَقُّ ٱلتَّفْتِيشِ.

Searcher, *n.* One who searches, مُفَتِّش — فَتَّاش. An examiner, مُتَفَحِّص. An inquirer, طَالِب — سَائِل — بَاغٍ *pl.* بُغَاة *pl.* طُلَّاب. A diligent —, inquirer, جَادٌّ فِي ٱلطَّلَبِ. The Searcher of hearts, فَاحِصُ ٱلْقُلُوبِ — مُفَتِّشُ ٱلْقُلُوبِ.

Searching, *a.* Penetrating, خَارِقٌ فِي — نَافِذٌ فِي. Effective, مُؤَثِّر —. A — wind, رِيحٌ وَخْشِيَّةٌ. شَخْشَحَان — شَخْشَاح.

Search-warrant, *n.* أَمْرٌ بِٱلتَّفْتِيشِ. To issue a —, أَصْدَرَ أَمْرًا بِٱلتَّفْتِيشِ.

Sear-cloth, *n.* A plaster, لَصَقَة — لَزُوق — لَزْقَة.

Searedness, *n.* The being dried up, يُبُوسَة — جُفُوف — جَفَاف. *See also* Insensibility, *n.*

Sea-risk, *n.* غَوَائِلُ (or أَخْطَارُ) ٱلْبَحْرِ.

Sea-room, *n.* مِيدَانٌ (or سَعَةٌ) فِي ٱلْبَحْرِ.

Sea-shell, *n.* صَدَفُ ٱلْبَحْرِ *pl.* أَصْدَاف. Refuse shells thrown up by the sea, دَمَال.

Sea-sick, *a.* دَائِخٌ مِنْ رُكُوبِ ٱلْبَحْرِ — مُصَابٌ بِهُدَام. To be —, دَاخَ مِنَ ٱلْبَحْرِ [2] — هُدِمَ.

Sea-sickness, *n.* دُوَارٌ مِنْ رُكُوبِ ٱلْبَحْرِ — هُدَام.

Seaside, *n.* سَاحِلُ ٱلْبَحْرِ. By the —, عِنْدَ ٱلْبَحْرِ.

Season, *n.* A fit or suitable time, وَقْتٌ مُنَاسِبٌ *pl.* أَوْقَاتٌ مُنَاسِبَةٌ. A division of the year, فَصْل *pl.* فُصُول. A particular time for anything, أَوَان — إِبَّان *pl.* آوِنَة — أَيَّام. Time, وَقْت *pl.* أَوْقَات — زَمَان — مُدَّة — حِين. The cold — came, جَآءَ أَوَانُ ٱلْبَرْدِ *aor.* يَجِيءُ [2]. He ate the fruit in its —, أَكَلَ ٱلْفَاكِهَةَ بِإِبَّانِهَا. The — of figs had not come, لَمْ يَكُنْ وَقْتَ ٱلتِّينِ. In — and out of —, فِي وَقْتٍ مُنَاسِبٍ وَغَيْرِ مُنَاسِبٍ. In —, of fruits, *etc.*, فِي وَقْتِهِ — فِي إِبَّانِهِ. A word in —, كَلِمَةٌ فِي وَقْتِهَا. Out of —, خَارِجٌ عَنْ وَقْتِهِ — خَارِجٌ عَنْ إِبَّانِهِ. Out of —, inopportune, خَارِجٌ عَنْ مَحَلِّهِ — خَارِجٌ عَنْ وَقْتِهِ. The latter end of the —, آخِرُ ٱلْأَوَانِ. When the — becomes temperate, عِنْدَ ٱعْتِدَالِ ٱلْهَوَآءِ. For a —, إِلَى حِينٍ — وَقْتًا.

Season, *v.t.* As with spices, *etc.*, أَدَمَ — أَدَّمَ — عَرَّفَ — قَزَحَ — قَزَّحَ — فَحَّى — تَابَلَ — تَبَّلَ — تَوْبَلَ; with salt, مَلَّحَ. To —, of speech, أَصْلَحَ (or تَوْبَلَ or قَزَّحَ or حَبَّرَ or بَزَّرَ) ٱلْكَلَامَ. To qualify, to attemper, لَطَّفَ — خَفَّفَ — عَدَّلَ. To acclimatize, عَوَّدَ عَلَى ٱلْهَوَآءِ. To harden, dry, يَبَّسَ. To accustom one to, عَوَّدَ عَلَى — أَضْرَى بِ — ضَرَّى بِ. To be seasoned, accustomed, to, تَعَوَّدَ عَلَى — ضَرِيَ بِ. *See also to* Mature, *v.t.*

Season, *v.i.* To become mature, نَضِجَ — إِسْتَوَى. To become dry, of wood, *etc.*, يَبِسَ *aor.* يَيْبَسُ *and* يَابِسَ. To become in a fit state, صَلَحَ [2] — صَلُحَ — إِسْتَصْلَحَ.

Seasonable, *a.* فِي مَحَلِّهِ — فِي وَقْتِهِ — مُوَافِق.

Seasonableness, *n.* مُنَاسَبَة — مُوَافَقَة — وَفْق.

Seasonably, *ad.* فِي تَمَامِ وَقْتِهِ — بِوَقْتِهِ — لِلْوَقْتِ.

Seasoned, *a.* As with spices, مُقَزَّح — مُعَرَّف — أَدِيم — مَأْدُوم — مُتَبَّل. Acclimatized, مُعَوَّدٌ عَلَى ٱلْهَوَآءِ. Dried, يَابِس — مُيَبَّس. Prepared, مُصْلَح — مُسْتَعَدّ — مُعَدّ. A jar seasoned with vinegar, جَرَّةٌ ضَارِيَةٌ بِٱلْخَلِّ.

Seasoning, *n.* Of spices, *etc.*, إِدَام — أَقْزَاح — تَقَازِيح — تَابَل — تَوْبَل — أَبْزَار; the act of seasoning with spices, تَقْزِيح — تَتْبِيل. The act of accustoming, تَعْوِيد — تَضْرِيَة; the being accustomed, تَعَوُّد — ضَرَاوَة — ضَرَآءَة. The act of drying, تَيْبِيس; the becoming dry, يَبْس — إِتِّبَاس. Most excellent is the — of vinegar! نِعْمَ ٱلْإِدَامُ ٱلْخَلُّ.

Seasonless, *a.* Of seasons, بِلَا فُصُولٍ — بِلَا فُصُولٍ مَعْلُومَةٍ.

Sea-star, *n.* *See* Star-fish, *n.*

Seat, *n.* That on which one sits, مَجْلِس — مَقْعَد — مَقْعَدَة *pl.* مَقَاعِد. A chair, كُرْسِيّ *pl.* كَرَاسِيّ. A bench, صُفَّة — مَرْتَبَة; a stone or brick — or bench, مِسْطَبَة *pl.* مَسَاطِب. A bottom, base, مَقْعَد — قَرَار — قَعْر *pl.* تُخُوت — تَخْت. A place, locality, مَحَلّ — مَوْضِع — مَكَان. A place where any event occurs, مَوْقِع. A centre, مَرْكَز. A mansion, residence, قَصْر *pl.* قُصُور — مَنْزِل *pl.* مَنَازِل — مَقَام. Seat, as on horseback, جِلْسَة — رِكْبَة. The buttocks, كَفَل *pl.* أَكْفَال. The — of war, مَوْقِعُ ٱلْحَرْبِ. He has a — in the council, هُوَ مِنْ أَعْضَآءِ ٱلْمَجْلِسِ. The — of empire, مَرْكَزُ ٱلْحُكُومَةِ. The — of commerce, مَرْكَزُ ٱلتِّجَارَةِ *pl.* مَرَاكِز. To keep one's —, ظَلَّ جَالِسًا — لَزِمَ مَكَانَهُ. To resume one's —, عَادَ فَجَلَسَ [2]. To take one's —, جَلَسَ — جَلَسَ. To vacate one's —, as of a chair, *etc.*, خَلَّى مَكَانَهُ; of a — or appointment, تَخَلَّى عَنِ ٱلْوَظِيفَةِ. Pray take a —, تَفَضَّلْ وَٱجْلِسْ.

Seat, *v.t.* To place on a seat, أَقْعَدَ — أَجْلَسَ. To place, وَضَعَ *aor.* يَضَعُ. To settle, أَحْكَمَ — ضَبَطَ [2]. To provide with seats, chairs, of a room, أَثَّثَ بِكَرَاسِيّ. To put a new seat to, of a chair, *etc.*, جَدَّدَ قَعْرَهُ — جَدَّدَ مَقْعَدَهُ. To — one's self, قَعَدَ [2] — جَلَسَ.

Sea-urchin, *n.* *See* Echinus, *n.*

Seaward, *a.* طَرَفَ ٱلْبَحْرِ — نَحْوَ ٱلْبَحْرِ.

Seaweed, *n.* قَشّ ٱلْبَحْرِ ـ صُوفُ ٱلْبَحْرِ.

Sea-worn, *a.* بِلَى بَحْرٍ ـ بِلْوُ بَحْرٍ.

Sea-worthy, *a.* جَدِيرٌ بِٱلسَّفَرِ ـ صَالِحٌ لِلسَّفَرِ.

Sebaceous, *a.* دُهْنِيّ ـ زَفِر ـ دَسِم.

Sebesten, *n.* The tree, مُخَيْطا ـ مُخَاطَة ـ أَطْبَاءُ ٱلْكَلْبَةِ.

Secant, *a.* مُفَصِّل ـ قَاطِع.

Secant, *n.* خَطٌّ قَاطِعٌ.

Secede, *v.i.* To withdraw from, تَعَزَّلَ عَن ـ تَنَحَّى عَن ـ إِعْتَزَلَ عَن. *See also under to* Dissent, *v.i.*

Seceder, *n.* مُعْتَزِلَة *pl.* مُعْتَزِل ـ شُرَاة *pl.* شَارٍ ـ مُنْفَصِلٌ عَن ـ خَوَارِجُ *pl.* خَارِجِيٌّ. *See also* Dissenter, *n.*

Secession, *n.* إِنْفِرَادٌ مِن ـ إِفْتِرَاقٌ عَن ـ إِعْتِزَالٌ عَن ـ تَجَنُّبٌ مِن ـ خُرُوجٌ مِن.

Seclude, *v.t.* To veil, to keep from sight, حَجَبَ ـ حَجَّبَ. To shut up, حَصَرَ ـ أَحْصَرَ. To withdraw from, أَصْدَفَ عَن ـ أَبْعَدَ عَن. To — one's self, إِحْتَجَبَ ـ تَرَصَّعَ: The king secluded himself from the people, إِحْتَجَبَ ٱلْمَلِكُ عَنِ ٱلنَّاسِ.

Seclusion, *n.* The act of withdrawing, as from sight, حَجْب ـ تَحْجِيب; of confining, حَصْر ـ تَحْصِير; of withdrawing one's self, إِحْتِجَاب ـ إِجْتِنَاب ـ تَصَدُّف. Self-seclusion, عُزْلَة. A place of —, مَعْزَل. In seclusion, فِي ٱلْعُزْلَةِ ـ مَحْجُوب ـ مُحْتَجِب. *See also* Retirement, *n.*

Seclusive, *a.* مُنْفَرِد ـ مُجْتَنِب ـ مُحْتَجِب.

Second, *a.* Next to the first, ثَانٍ *fem.* ثَانِيَة. Inferior, دُون. Second to none, of a person, لَيْسَ أَحَدٌ أَعْلَى مِنْهُ ـ لَيْسَ دُونَ أَحَدٍ. A — time, مَرَّةٌ ثَانِيَةٌ ـ ثَانِيَةً. He said to him a — time, قَالَ لَهُ أَيْضًا (*or* ثَانِيَةً). To do a thing a — time, عَادَ ـ أَعَادَ. *See also under* Inferior, *a.*

Second, *n.* The next to the first, ٱلثَّانِي *fem.* ٱلثَّانِيَة. An assistant, مُعَاوِن ـ مُعِين ـ مُسَاعِد. The — to a chief, ثِنْي ـ ثُنْيَان. Another, آخَر *fem.* أُخْرَى. A witness, as in a duel, شُهُود *pl.* شَاهِد. The sixtieth part of a minute, ثَوَانٍ *pl.* ثَانِيَة. The —, in music, ٱللَّحْنُ ٱلثَّانِي فِي ٱلْمُوسِيقَى. This is the — of this, هٰذَا ثَانِي هٰذَا. The earthquake lasted twenty seconds, إِسْتَمَرَّتِ ٱلزَّلْزَلَةُ عِشْرِينَ ثَانِيَةً. About ten seconds, نَحْوُ عَشْرَةِ ثَوَانٍ.

Second, *v.t.* To aid, سَاعَدَ ـ أَعَانَ ـ وَفَّقَ ـ نَجَّحَ ـ أَنْجَحَ. To support, وَكَّدَ ـ أَيَّدَ ـ سَانَدَ.

Secondarily, *ad.* فِي دَرَجَةٍ ثَانِيَةٍ.

Secondariness, *n.* دَرَجَةٌ ثَانِيَةٌ ـ إِدَانَة.

Secondary, *a.* Coming after the first, ثَانٍ *fem.* ثَانِيَة. Dependant, تَبَعِيّ. Inferior, أَسْفَل ـ دُون. Unimportant, غَيْرُ مُهِمّ ـ جُزْئِيّ. Secondary rocks, طَبَقَاتٌ مِنَ ٱلطَّبَقَةِ ٱلثَّانِيَةِ ـ أَحْجَارُ ٱلطَّبَقَةِ ٱلثَّانِيَةِ. A — planet, قَمَر *pl.* أَقْمَار. Of — consideration, شَيْءٌ مِنْ دُونٍ ـ غَيْرُ مُهِمّ. A — question, مَسْأَلَةٌ ثَانَوِيَّةٌ.

Secondary, *n.* The second to a chief, ثِنْي ـ ثُنْيَان. A deputy, assistant, وَكِيل ـ قَائِمُ مَقَام ـ مُعَاوِن.

Second-cousin, *n.* On the male side, إِبْنُ بَنِينَ عَمٍّ لَهُمَا *pl.* أَبْنَاء *fem.* بِنْت *pl.* بَنَات; on the female side, إِبْنُ بَنِينَ خَالَةٍ لَهُمَا *pl.* أَبْنَاء *fem.* بِنْت *pl.* بَنَات.

Seconder, *n.* مُظَاهِر ـ مُؤَكِّد ـ مُؤَيِّد ـ مُسَانِد.

Second-hand, *a.* Not new, used, مُسْتَعْمَل. Taken or received from another, quoted from, مَنْقُولٌ مِن ـ مُقْتَبَسٌ مِن.

Secondly, *ad.* ثَانِيَةً ـ ثَانِيًا.

Second-rate, *a.* مَعْدُودٌ فِي ٱلدَّرَجَةِ ٱلثَّانِيَةِ ـ عَادِيّ ـ دُون ـ ثَانَوِيّ. A — power, kingdom, مَمْلَكَةٌ ثَانَوِيَّةٌ.

Second-rate, *n.* Of a ship, شُونَةٌ مِنَ ٱلدَّرَجَةِ ٱلثَّانِيَةِ.

Second-sight, *n.* ضَرْبٌ مِنْ كَشْفِ ٱلْغَيْبِ ـ مَدْرَك. He has —, لَهُ مَدْرَكٌ.

Secrecy, *n.* The state of being concealed from view, إِحْتِجَاب ـ خَفَاء ـ خَافِيَة ـ سِرّ ـ إِخْتِفَاء. Close privacy, إِكْتِتَام ـ إِسْتِتَار. Forbearance of disclosure, كَتْم ـ سُكُوت ـ سَكْت. Retirement, solitude, خُلُوّ ـ عُزْلَة ـ جَنْبَة. *See also* Privacy, *n.*

Secret, *a.* Hidden, خَفِيّ ـ مَخْفِيّ ـ مَكْتُوم ـ مَكْنُون ـ سِرّ ـ سِرِّيّ ـ مُسْتَتِر ـ مَسْتُور. Faithful to a secret, أَمِينُ ٱلسِّرِّ. Secret in the heart, as grief, *etc.*, مُكْتَمِن. Sequestered from company, مُنْفَرِد ـ مُجْتَنِب. A — door, بَابٌ سِرِّيّ. A — chamber, خَلْوَة. The — parts, ٱلشَّوَار. A — negotiation, مُذَاكَرَةٌ خَفِيَّةٌ. A — treaty, مُعَاهَدَةٌ خَفِيَّةٌ. He revealed his — design, أَبْدَى مَكْنُونَ مَرَامِهِ. Secret meetings, إِجْتِمَاعَاتٌ سِرِّيَّةٌ. "Doubtfully guessing at that which is secret," رَجْمًا بِٱلْغَيْبِ (Kûr. xviii. 21.) To keep —, أَسَرَّ ـ كَتَمَ ـ أَخْفَى. *See also* Hidden, Occult, Private, *a.*

Secret, *n.* سِرّ *pl.* أَسْرَار ـ سَرَائِر *pl.* سَرِيرَة. A thing that is imperceptible, latent, or obscure, غَيْب ـ غَائِب ـ خَفِيّ ـ خَفَاء. In —, سِرًّا ـ خُفْيَةً ـ عَلَى خَفَاءٍ. He is the depository of my secrets, هُوَ مَوْضِعُ سِرِّي. To divulge a —, أَفْشَى ٱلسِّرَّ ـ أَفْضَى ٱلسِّرَّ; I divulged my — to him, أَفْضَيْتُ إِلَيْهِ بِسِرِّي. To keep a —, كَتَمَ ٱلسِّرَّ. To get or wrest a — from, كَشَفَ عَنْ سِرِّهِ. To make a — of, أَسَرَّ ـ جَعَلَ كَٱلسِّرِّ. One who can't keep a —, فُرْجَة ـ فُرُج ـ بَذُور.

Secretary, *n.* A writer, clerk, كاتِب *pl.* كُتّاب – سافِر *pl.* سَفَرَة *and* كَتَبَة. A confidential or private —, كاتِبُ ٱلْأَسْرارِ. A minister, as of a department, مُدِير – ناظِر *pl.* نُظّار – مُباشِر – ناظِرُ دائِرَةٍ.

Secretary of State, ناظِرُ ٱلدَّوْلَةِ. Principal Secretary of State; *see* Prime Minister, *n.*

Secretary of State for the Colonies, ناظِرُ ٱلْمَمالِكِ ٱلتّابِعَةِ.

Secretary of State for Foreign Affairs, ناظِرُ ٱلْأُمُورِ ٱلْخارِجِيَّةِ.

Secretary of State for the Home Department, ناظِرُ ٱلدّاخِلِيَّةِ.

Secretary of State for India, ناظِرُ أُمُورِ ٱلْهِنْدِ.

Under Secretary of State, مُسْتَشارُ ٱلدَّوْلَةِ.

Secretary of Embassy, مُسْتَشارُ سِفارَةٍ مِنَ ٱلرُّتْبَةِ ٱلْأُولَى.

Secretary of Legation, مُسْتَشارُ سِفارَةٍ مِنَ ٱلرُّتْبَةِ ٱلثّانِيَةِ.

Colonial Secretary, مُسْتَشارٌ عِنْدَ أَحَدِ ٱلْمَمالِكِ ٱلتّابِعَةِ.

Honorary Secretary, كاتِبٌ خاصٌّ بلا مَعاشٍ.

Private Secretary, كاتِبُ أَسْرارٍ (*or* ٱلْأَسْرارِ) خُصُوصِيٌّ – كاتِبٌ خاصٌّ لِأَحَدٍ.

Secretaryship, *n.* وَظِيفَةُ ناظِرٍ – وَظِيفَةُ كاتِبِ ٱلْأَسْرارِ – مَكْتُوبْجِيَّة.

Secrete, *v.t.* To keep secret, كَتَمَ – ²كَتَّمَ – أَكْتَمَ. To hide, conceal, أَخْفَى – خَبَأَ – ٠ خَبَّأَ *vulg.* غَبَّى. To — something from, ٠ طَوَى عَن – ²كَتَّمَ عَن – *vulg.* غَبَّى عَن. To —, in the heart, أَكَنَّ فِي ٱلْقَلْبِ. To — one's self, إِخْتَبَأَ – إِخْتَفَى – إِكْتَمَنَ. To —, as of humours, رَشَحَ – ٠ أَرْشَحَ. To extract, صَوَّلَ.

Secretion, *n.* The act of concealing, تَخْبِئَة – إِخْفاء; of secreting, of humours, رَشْح – إِرْشاح. Matter secreted, بِراز. *See also under* Humour, *n.*

Secretiveness, *n.* خاصِّيَّةُ ٱلْإِكْتِتامِ.

Secretly, *ad.* In a secret manner, سِرًّا – خُفْيَةً – عَلَى خَفاءٍ. Inwardly, mentally, باطِنًا – قَلْبًا – ذِهْنًا. I did it —, فَعَلْتُهُ خُفْيَةً. He was killed —, قُتِلَ خُفْيَةً. He asked him —, سَأَلَهُ سِرًّا. To decamp —, وَلَّى سِرًّا. *See also* Privately, *ad.*

Secretness, *n.* *See* Secrecy, *n.*

Secretory, *a.* Of humours, رَشّاح – راشِح.

Sect, *n.* A body of men, a community, فِرْقَة *pl.* فِرَق – طائِفَة *pl.* طَوائِف. A body cut off, as separatists, شِيعَة *pl.* شِيَع *and* أَشْياع. A body of doctrine, religion, مَذْهَب *pl.* مَذاهِب. The inhabitants are of different sects, ٱلْأَهالِي مُخْتَلِفُو ٱلطَّوائِفِ. To follow or adopt a particular —, تَمَذْهَبَ بِمَذْهَبٍ كَذا.

Sectarian, *a.* شِيعِيٌّ – مُتَعَلِّقٌ بِمَذْهَبٍ.

Sectarian, *n.* One of a sect, شِيعِيٌّ – مِنْ أَهْلِ فِرْقَةٍ – شارٍ *pl.* شُراة *pl.* شِيَعِيَّة. A follower, تابِع *pl.* تَوابِع. To become a —, أَشْرَى – ٠ تَشَرَّى – تَمَذْهَبَ. To become a — of such a creed, ٠ ذَهَبَ إِلَى مَذْهَبِ آلِ....

Sectarianism, *n.* تَعَصُّبٌ لِلْفِرْقَةِ – أَفْكارُ ٱلْإِعْتِزالِ – شَرِيَةٌ شِيَعِيَّةٌ.

Sectarist, *n.* } *See* Sectarian, *n.*
Sectary, }

Sectile, *a.* مِمّا يُشْرَحُ – قَطْعُهُ مُمْكِنٌ.

Section, *n.* The act of cutting off, قَطْع. A part separated, فَصْل *pl.* فُصُول. A slice, portion, part, قِطْعَة *pl.* قِطَع. A —, as of a chapter, قِسْم *pl.* أَقْسام – فَصْل *pl.* فُصُول – باب *pl.* أَبْواب. A —, in mathematics, قَطْع *pl.* قُطُوع; the three conic sections, قُطُوعُ ٱلْمَخْرُوطاتِ ٱلثَّلاثَةِ. An outline, drawing, رَسْم *pl.* رُسُوم. A longitudinal —, قِطْعَةٌ بِٱلطُّولِ; a transverse or cross —, قِطْعَةٌ مُعْتَرِضَةٌ. Section, as of a district, دائِرَة. A department, دائِرَة *pl.* دَوائِر – إِدارَة. To divide into sections, فَصَّلَ.

Sectional, *a.* ما نِيطَ بِقِطْعَةٍ أَوْ جُزْءٍ. Departmental, مُتَعَلِّقٌ بِدائِرَةٍ (*or* إِدارَةٍ).

Sector, *n.* Of a circle, قِطاعُ دائِرَةٍ; of a sphere, قِطاعُ كُرَةٍ. The mathematical instrument, مِقْياس.

Secular, *n.* An unordained church official, مَأْمُورُ كَنِيسَةٍ غَيْرُ مُرْتَسِمٍ. A — priest, كاهِنٌ (*or* قِسِّيسٌ) عَلْمانِيٌّ. *See also* Layman, *n.*

Secular, *a.* Lay, not clerical, عَلْمانِيٌّ – عامِّيٌّ. Worldly, دُنْياوِيٌّ – دُنْيَوِيٌّ. The — clergy, ٱلْإِكْلِيرُسُ ٱلْغَيْرُ ٱلْمُتَرَهِّبِ. Secular concerns, أُمُورُ ٱلدُّنْيا – ٱلْأُمُورُ ٱلزَّمَنِيَّةُ. Secular music, ٱلْعَزْفُ ٱلْعادِيُّ – ٱلْمُوسِيقَى ٱلْعادِيَّةُ.

Secularity, *n.* حُبُّ ٱلْعالَمِ – دُنْياوِيَّة – عالَمِيَّة.

Secularization, *n.* As of ecclesiastical property, تَحْوِيلُ ٱلْأَوْقافِ وَٱلْأَمْلاكِ ٱلْمُخْتَصَّةِ بِٱلْعِبادَةِ وَٱلدِّيانَةِ إِلَى أَغْراضٍ عالَمِيَّةٍ.

Secularize, *v.t.* حَوَّلَ ٱلْأَوْقافَ وَٱلْأَمْلاكَ ٱلْمُخْتَصَّةَ بِٱلْعِبادَةِ وَٱلدِّيانَةِ إِلَى أَغْراضٍ عالَمِيَّةٍ.

Secularly, *ad.* بِطَرِيقَةٍ دُنْياوِيَّةٍ – مِثْلَ أَهْلِ ٱلْعالَمِ – مِثْلَ أَبْناءِ ٱلْجِيلِ.

Secularness, *n.* *See* Secularity, *n.*

Secundines, *n.* *See* After-birth, *n.*

Secure, *a.* Made fast, مُتَمَكِّن – مُحْكَم – مَضْبُوط. Free from fear or danger, مُطْمَئِنٌّ. Firm, fast, راسِخ – واثِق – راكِز – مَتِين. Careless, thoughtless, قَلِيلُ ٱلْإِعْتِناءِ – فارِغُ ٱلْبالِ – مُتَكاسِل – ساهٍ. To feel —, إِطْمَأَنَّ. His heart is —, stedfast, in the faith, قَلْبُهُ مُطْمَئِنٌّ بِٱلْإِيمانِ. "No one is secure against the stratagem of God," فَلَا يَأْمَنُ مَكْرَ ٱللّٰهِ (Kûr. vii. 97). "And when ye are secure," from danger, فَإِذَا ٱطْمَأْنَنْتُمْ (Kûr. iv. 104). (For the other significations of Secure, *see* Safe, *a.*)

Secure, *v.t.* To guard, to keep, صَانَ ـ حَفِظَ. To fasten, ضَبَطَ. To tie, رَبَطَ ـ شَدَّ. To shut, غَلَقَ. To —, as with a bar, تَرَسَ. To apprehend, seize, بَطَشَ بِ ـ قَبَضَ بِ ـ ضَبَطَ. To make safe, آمَنَ ـ وَكَّدَ ـ أَوْكَدَ ـ أَسْلَمَ ـ سَلَّمَ. To — in custody, حَبَسَ. To —, defend, against, حَمَى ـ مِن ـ صَانَ ـ عَن. To make —, as from any trouble, جَعَلَ ـ مُطْمَئِنًّا. To guarantee, كَفَلَ بِ ـ تَكَفَّلَ بِ ـ ضَمِنَ. To — against, أَمَّنَ ـ مِن ـ آمَنَ. Religious liberty must be secured to all, إِنَّ ٱلْحُرِّيَّةَ ٱلدِّينِيَّةَ يَنْبَغِي تَأْمِينُهَا لِجَمِيعِ ٱلنَّاسِ. *See also to* Fasten, *v.t.*

Securely, *ad.* *See* Safely, *ad.*

Secureness, *n.* *See* Security, *n.*

Security, *n.* Of the mind, رَاحَةُ بَالٍ ـ إِطْمِئْنَان ـ طُمَأْنِينَة. A guarantor, ضَامِن ـ كَفِيل ـ ضَمِين. A guarantee, كَفَالَة ـ ضَمَان. A promise of —, safety, ذِمَّة ـ أَمَان. Collateral —, ضَمَانٌ مُلْحَقٌ. The establishment of —, tranquillity, تَوْطِيدُ ٱلْأَمَانِ ـ تَأْمِين. For the greater — of the town, لِزِيَادَةِ تَأْمِينِ ٱلْمَدِينَةِ. To be — to one for, as against any danger, أَعْهَدَ ـ مِن. To be —, guarantor, for, كَفَلَ بِ ـ ضَمِنَ بِ; as against loss, أَمَّنَ ـ مِن ـ تَضَمَّنَ ـ عَن. To make one a —, responsible, ضَمَّنَ. To take — from one, أَخَذَ كَفَالَةً مِنْهُ. It is the intention of several of the governments to demand the requisite securities from the Sultan against the re-occurrence of such a matter, فِي عَزْمِ بَعْضِ ٱلدُّوَلِ أَنْ يَطْلُبَ مِنَ ٱلسُّلْطَانِ ٱلتَّأْمِينَاتِ ٱللَّازِمَةَ لِعَدَمِ إِعَادَةِ مِثْلِ هٰذَا ٱلْأَمْرِ. For the other significations of Security, *see* Safety, *n.*; *also* Surety, *n.*, Responsible, *a.*

Sedan-chair, *n.* تَخْتَرَوَانٌ مَحْمِلَةٌ ٱلشَّيَّالَةُ.

Sedate, *a.* سَاكِنُ ٱلطَّائِرِ ـ رَزِين ـ وَقُور ـ رَصِين ـ رَكِين. To be —, وَقَرَ *aor.* يَقِرُ ـ تَوَقَّرَ ـ إِتَّقَرَ ـ سَمَتَ. He became —, وَقَعَ طَائِرُهُ *aor.* يَقَعُ. To strive to be —, تَوَقَّرَ ـ تَرَزَّنَ ـ تَرَكَّنَ.

Sedately, *ad.* بِطُولِ ٱلْأَنَاةِ ـ بِأَنَاةٍ ـ بِرَزَانَةٍ ـ بِوَقَارٍ.

Sedateness, *n.* رَزَانَة ـ وَقَار ـ وَقْر ـ سَكِينَة ـ سَمْت ـ أَنَاة.

Sedative, *a.* مُسَكِّن ـ مُلَيِّن.

Sedative, *n.* عِلَاجٌ مُسَكِّنٌ ـ عِلَاجٌ مُلَيِّنٌ ـ سُلْوَان.

Sedentarily, *ad.* بِإِلْزَامِ ٱلْجُلُوسِ.

Sedentariness, *n.* لُزُومٌ بِٱلْجُلُوسِ.

Sedentary, *a.* مُلَازِمٌ بِٱلْجُلُوسِ ـ قُعَدِيّ ـ قَاعِد ـ جُلَسَة. Sedentary occupations, أَشْغَالٌ مُلْزِمَةٌ ٱلْجُلُوسِ.

Sedge, *n.* حَلْف ـ جِلْفَاء ـ بَرْدِيّ. A single —, حَلْفَة ـ حِلْفَة ـ حَلْفَاءَة *pl.* حَلَافِيّ.

Sedgy, *a.* ذُو حَلْفٍ ـ كَثِيرُ ٱلْحِلْفَاءِ. Sedgy land, أَرْضٌ حَلِفَةٌ.

Sediment, *n.* رُسُوب ـ عَكَر ـ رُسَابَة ـ قُرَّة ـ ثُفْل ـ تَحْجِير ـ دُرْدِيّ.

Sedimentary, *a.* عَكَرِيّ ـ رُسُوبِيّ.

Sedition, *n.* هَرْج ـ طِغْيَان ـ هَيْشَة ـ تَشْغِيب ـ شَغْب ـ قَوْمَة ـ فِتْنَة ـ فَسَاد ـ عِصْيَان. A stirrer up of —, فَتَّان ـ ضَرَّابُ فِتَنٍ. To be in —, هَرَجَ ـ هَاشَ. To excite to —, أَفْسَدَ ـ فَتَنَ ـ شَغَّبَ. To rise in — against, شَغَبَ عَلَى ـ إِسْتَعْصَى عَلَى ـ عَصَى عَلَى.

Seditious, *a.* فَتَّان ـ مُفْسِد ـ شَغِب ـ مُفْتِن ـ مَفْتُون. A — man, فَتَّان ـ ذُو مَشَاغِبَ. A — meeting, جَمْعِيَّةٌ مِنَ ٱلْعُصَاةِ ـ جَمْعِيَّةُ أَهْلِ ٱلْفَسَادِ. A — spirit, رُوحُ ٱلْعِصْيَانِ. Seditious publications, مَطْبُوعَاتٌ فَاسِدَةٌ (or مُحَرِّضَةٌ عَلَى ٱلْعِصْيَانِ).

Seditiously, *ad.* بِٱفْتِتَانٍ ـ بِعِصْيَانٍ.

Seditiousness, *n.* مَعْصِيَة ـ إِسْتِعْدَادٌ لِلْفَسَادِ.

Seduce, *v.t.* To cause to go astray, طَوَّحَ ـ أَضَلَّ ـ ضَلَّلَ ـ تَوَّهَ. To deceive, خَدَعَ ـ غَرَّرَ ـ أَغْوَى. To —, as from allegiance, خَدَعَ ـ أَغْوَى. To —, as into evil, to corrupt, إِفْتَتَنَ ـ أَفْتَنَ ـ رَاوَغَ ـ وَقَّعَ ـ أَوْقَعَ ـ إِفْتَرَعَ. To debauch, violate, هَتَكَ.

Seducement, *n.* The act of leading astray, إِغْوَاء ـ تَضْلِيل; the being led astray, ضَلَال ـ إِضْلَال ـ غَيّ ـ غَيَّة ـ تَطْوِيح; The act of deceiving, خَدِيعَة ـ خِدَاع ـ تَغْرِير ـ إِغْوَاء ـ ضَلَالَة; the being deceived, إِنْخِدَاع ـ غُرُور. The act of beguiling into evil, مُرَاوَغَة ـ رَوَاغ ـ إِغْوَاء ـ تَوْقِيع; the being so beguiled, رَوَغَان ـ غَوَايَة. The act of seducing, as from allegiance, إِفْسَاد ـ إِفْتِتَان.

Seducer, *n.* One who seduces, deceives, مُغْوٍ ـ غُوَاة *pl.* غَاوٍ ـ خَدَّاع ـ مُضِلّ *pl.* مُضِلُّون. One who violates, debauches, مُفْتَرِع ـ هَاتِك.

Seducible, *a.* خَدْعُهُ مُمْكِنٌ ـ يُخْدَعُ ـ إِغْوَاؤُهُ مُمْكِنٌ ـ يُغْوَى ـ رَوَاغُهُ مُمْكِنٌ.

Seduction, *n.* The act of violating a woman, هَتْك ـ إِفْتِرَاع; the being so violated, إِنْهِتَاك ـ *vulg.* إِنْفِضَاح. For other significations, *see under* Seducement, *n.*

Seductive, *a.* Deceiving, seducing, مُضِلّ ـ مُرَاوِغ ـ مُغْوٍ ـ غَاوٍ. *See also* Captivating, *a.*

Seductively, *ad.* بِإِغْوَاءٍ ـ بِمُرَاوَغَةٍ. In a captivating manner, بِنَوْعٍ يَسْلُبُ ٱلْعَقْلَ.

Seductiveness, *n.* *See* Attractiveness, *n.*

Sedulity, *n.* مُلَازَمَة ـ كَدّ ـ مُوَاظَبَة ـ مُرُوَّة ـ جِدّ. *See also* Assiduity, Diligence, *n.*

Sedulous, *a.* مُوَاظِبٌ عَلَى ـ مُجِدٌّ ـ مُدَاوِم ـ كَدُود ـ مُمَارِس. To be —, 2 كَدَّ ـ مَارَسَ ـ اِهْتَمَّ بِ ـ أَقَامَ عَلَى ـ وَاظَبَ عَلَى. *See also* Assiduous, Diligent, *a.*

Sedulously, *ad.* مُلَازَمَةً ـ بِٱجْتِهَادٍ كُلِّيٍّ ـ بِمُوَاظَبَةٍ.

Sedulousness, *n.* *See* Sedulity, *n.*

See, *n.* A diocese, أَبْرَشِيَّةٌ أُسْقُفٍ ـ أُسْقُفِيَّةٌ ـ دَائِرَةُ أُسْقُفٍ.

See, *v.t.* To perceive by the eye, تَعَيَّنَ ـ شَهِدَ ـ 2 لَحَ ـ أَبْصَرَ ـ رَأَى *aor.* يَرَى ـ 2 طَشَّ ـ أَنْظَرَ. To perceive by the mind, أَدْرَكَ ـ إِتَّقَنَ بِ ـ أَيْقَنَ بِ ـ فَطِنَ ـ أَبْصَرَ ـ شَعَرَ بِ. To ascertain, حَقَّقَ. To view, 2 نَظَرَ إِلَى ـ تَفَرَّجَ عَلَى ـ تَشَوَّفَ لِ. To see to, to attend to, إِعْتَنَى بِ ـ إِحْتَفَلَ بِ. To see into, to examine, فَحَصَ ـ بَحَثَ ـ 2 نَظَرَ فِي. To see one to, to accompany to, إِسْتَصْحَبَ ـ إِلَى ـ أَوْصَلَ ـ إِلَى ـ شَيَّعَ ـ إِلَى. To cause to see, inspect, فَرَّجَ ـ عَلَى ـ (*vulg.* رَوَّى) أَرَى. He saw him with his own eyes, in person, رَآهُ عِيَانًا. When he saw that he (himself) was in an evil plight, لَمَّا رَأَى نَفْسَهُ فِي بَلِيَّةٍ. I must go to see him, أَنَا مُضْطَرٌّ أَنْ أَخْرُجَ وَأَنْظُرَهُ. As soon as I see how it will go with me, أَوَّلَ مَا أَرَى أَحْوَالِي. He cannot see afar off, هُوَ قَصِيرُ ٱلْبَصَرِ. Hereafter ye shall see, مِنَ ٱلْآنَ تُبْصِرُونَ. They have eyes but they see not, أَعْيُنٌ لَهُمْ وَلَا يُبْصِرُونَ. Don't you see that..., أَلَا تَرَى أَنْ. See thou to it, أَنْتَ أَبْصِرْ ; see ye to it, أَبْصِرُوا أَنْتُمْ. We have not seen, heard, been made acquainted with, the news, لَمْ نَقِفْ عَلَى ٱلْخَبَرِ. He asked him if he had seen anything, سَأَلَهُ هَلْ أَبْصَرَ شَيْئًا. See! behold! هَا ـ هَا هُوَذَا.

See, *v.i.* To have the power of sight, بَصِرَ ـ 2 بَصُرَ. I was blind, now I see, كُنْتُ أَعْمَى وَٱلْآنَ أُبْصِرُ.

Seed, *n.* For sowing, بَذْر *pl.* بِذَار *and* بُذُور. Small — of leguminous plants and such like, بِزْر *pl.* بُزُور. Pulse, حَبٌّ *pl.* حُبُوب. A grain of —, حَبَّة *pl.* حَبَّات. *Semen genitale,* مَآء ـ مَنِيّ ـ نُطْفَة. Offspring, ذُرِّيَّة ـ زَرْع. Root, origin, أَصْل. To sow or scatter —, بَذَرَ ـ 2 بَذَّرَ. To run to —, 2 عَادَ إِلَى بَذْرٍ ـ صَارَ بَذْرًا.

Seed, *v.i.* To produce seed, حَبَّبَ ـ تَحَبَّبَ ـ أَزْرَعَ.

Seed, *v.t.* To sow with seed, زَرَعَ ـ بَذَرَ ـ 2 بَذَّرَ.

Seed-cake, *n.* قُرْصٌ مَحْشُوٌّ بِبُزُورٍ.

Seedling, *n.* نَبَاتٌ نَاشِئٌ مِنْ بَذْرٍ.

Seed-lobe, *n.* أُذُنُ بَذْرٍ *pl.* آذَان.

Seed-plot, *n.* زَرَّاعَة *pl.* زَرَّاعَات ـ مَزْرَعَة *pl.* مَزَارِع.

Seed-produce, *n.* زَرْع *pl.* زُرُوع ـ غَلَّة.

Seedsman, *n.* بَزَّار.

Seed-time, *n.* إِبَّانُ ٱلزَّرْعِ ـ زَرْع.

Seed-vessel, *n.* خَرِيطَة *pl.* خَرَائِط. *See also* Pericarp, *n.*

Seedy, *a.* Abounding with seeds, كَثِيرُ ٱلْبَذْرِ. Run to seed, صَارَ بَذْرًا. Threadbare, رَثِيث ـ مُتَحَشِّف. Poorly, out of sorts, عَلِيل ـ شَاكٍ ـ *vulg.* مُشَوَّش.

Seeing, *n.* The power of, ٱلْقُوَّةُ ٱلْبَاصِرَةُ. The act of —, بَصَر ـ رُؤْيَة ـ بَصَارَة. Sight, مَنْظَر ـ نَظَرَان ـ مُعَايَنَة.

Seeing, *a.* نَاظِر ـ بَصِير ـ بَاصِر ـ مُبْصِر.

Seeing, *conj.* Seeing that, مِنْ حَيْثُ ـ عَلَى أَنْ ـ مِنْ كَوْنِ أَنْ ـ مِنْ أَجْلِ أَنْ ـ أَنْ. Seeing that they were Christians, حَالَةَ كَوْنِهِمْ نَصَارَى.

Seek, *v.t.* To look for, دَوَّرَ عَلَى ـ 2 دَارَ عَلَى ـ فَتَّشَ عَن ـ فَتَّشَ. To — for something lost, 2 نَشَدَ. To desire, seek after, إِسْتَبْغَى ـ إِسْتَرَادَ ـ يَرُودُ *aor.* رَادَ ـ أَرَادَ ـ يَرُومُ *aor.* رَامَ ـ بَغَى. To — after, to aim at, 2 طَلَبَ ـ تَطَلَّبَ. They sought to kill him, طَلَبُوا أَنْ يَقْتُلُوهُ. You shall — me but you shall not find me, سَتَطْلُبُونِي وَلَا تَجِدُونِي. They — to do me evil, يَلْتَمِسُونَ لِيَ ٱلشَّرَّ. *See also under to* Search, *v.t.*

Seek, *v.i.* To make search, فَتَّشَ. To make inquiry, 2 نَشَدَ ـ إِسْتَعْلَمَ ـ إِسْتَخْبَرَ ـ تَخَبَّرَ. To endeavour, 2 كَدَّ ـ إِجْتَهَدَ.

Seeker, *n.* One who seeks, مُفَتِّش; one who seeks, as to do or learn, anything, طَالِب *pl.* طُلَّاب ـ رَائِدُ ٱلْعِلْمِ *pl.* رُوَّاد. One who seeks, going to and fro for the purpose, رَائِد *pl.* رُوَّاد. One who desires, wishes for, بَاغٍ *pl.* بُغَاة. A — after knowledge, طَالِبُ ٱلْعِلْمِ.

Seeking, *n.* The act of looking for, طَلَب ـ تَفْتِيش عَن. An object of —, مَطْلَب. Diligence in —, جِدٌّ فِي ٱلطَّلَبِ ـ رَغْبَةٌ فِي ٱلطَّلَبِ.

Seel, *v.t.* *See to* Blindfold, *v.t.*

Seem, *v.i.* To have the aspect or appearance of, بَدَا *aor.* يَبْدُو ـ تَخَيَّلَ لَهُ ـ خُيِّلَ إِلَيْهِ ـ ظَهَرَ ـ يَبِينُ *aor.* بَانَ. It seemed to him, 2 بَدَا لَهُ فِي ٱلْأَمْرِ. It seemed to him with regard to the case, It seemed to him that he should do so and so in the matter, تَخَيَّلَ لَهُ (*or* بَدَا لَهُ) أَنْ يَفْعَلَ كَذَا فِي ٱلْأَمْرِ. It seems that..., فَكَانَ ٱلْبَائِنُ أَنْ ـ ٱلظَّاهِرُ أَنْ. He seemed to them to be joking, عِنْدَهُمْ كَمَازِحٍ. Lest any of you should — disappointed of it, لِئَلَّا يُرَى أَحَدٌ مِنْكُمْ أَنَّهُ قَدْ خَابَ مِنْهُ. It seemed to him but a few days, وَكَانَتْ فِي عَيْنَيْهِ كَأَيَّامٍ قَلِيلَةٍ. To — good to one, إِسْتَحْسَنَ ـ إِسْتَصْوَبَ. To — evil to one, إِسْتَقْبَحَ.

Seemer, *n.* ظَاهِر ـ بَادٍ. *See also* Hypocrite, *n.*

Seeming, *a.* Apparent, ظَاهِر ـ بَائِن. *See also* Specious, *a.*

Seeming, *n.* Mien, طَلْعَة ـ سَمَامَة. Manifestation, ظُهُور ـ بَيَان. Aspect, figure, صُورَة ـ هَيْئَة ـ مَنْظَر. Probability, تَخْمِين ـ إِحْتِمَال. *See also* Hypocrisy, *n.*

Seemingly, *ad.* عَلَى ٱلْبَائِنِ ـ فِي ٱلظَّاهِرِ. In appearance, form, بِٱلصُّورَةِ. *See also* Apparently, *ad.*

Seemingness, *n.* Fair appearance, مَنْظَر حَسَن.

Seemliness, *n.* Fitness, مُنَاسَبَة ـ لِيَاقَة. Comeliness, طُلَاوَة ـ مَلَاحَة ـ حُسْن ـ جَمَال ـ كِيَاسَة. *See also* Decency, Propriety, *n.*

Seemly, *a.* Fit, proper, مُنَاسِب ـ لَائِق. Comely, كَيِّس ـ زَيْن ـ حَسَن ـ ظَرِيف ـ جَمِيل. It is not — for him, غَيْرُ لَائِقٍ بِهِ.

Seer, *n.* One who sees, نَاظِر ـ بَاصِر. A spectator, شَاهِد. One who sees, as a prophet, كَاشِفُ ٱلْغَيْبِ ـ رَائٍ *pl.* رَاؤُونَ. *See also* Prophet, *n.*

Seesaw, *n.* A swinging board or plank, دَوْدَاة ـ زُحْلُوقَة ـ مَرْجُوحَة ـ أُرْجُوحَة. The — moved up and down, تَرَجَّحَتِ ٱلْأُرْجُوحَةُ.

Seesaw, *v.i.* To move up and down, to swing, تَذَبْذَبَ. To vibrate, خَطَرَ ـ.

Seethe, *v.t.* *See to* Boil, *v.t.*

Seethe, *v.i.* *See to* Boil, *v.i.*

Segment, *n.* A part cut off, صِرَم *pl.* صِرْمَة ـ صَرِيمَة ـ شُذْفَة ـ قِطَع *pl.* قِطْعَة ـ فُلُوج *pl.* فَلْج ـ فِلَق *pl.* فِلْقَة. The — of a circle, قِطْعَةُ دَائِرَةٍ. To break into segments, فَلَّجَ.

Segmoidal, *a.* بِبِنْيَةِ قِطْعَةِ دَائِرَةٍ.

Segregate, *v.t.* فَصَلَ ـ عَن ـ فَارَقَ ـ شَذَّذَ ـ شَذَّ ².

Segregation, *n.* The act of, فَصْل ـ مُفَارَقَة ـ تَشْذِيذ ـ شَذّ. The being segregated, اِنْفِصَال ـ اِفْتِرَاق ـ شَذّ.

Seidlitz, *n.* The water, مَاءُ سَدْلِس.

Seigneurial, *a.* Pertaining to a lord, سَيِّدِيّ ـ مَا نِيطَ بِٱلْمُعْقِرِ. Manorial, مُتَعَلِّق بِٱلِٱلْتِزَامِ. Having large powers, ذُو سُلْطَةٍ عَظِيمَةٍ.

Seignior, *n.* One who has land, a master, possessor, مُعْقِر ـ سَيِّد *pl.* سَادَات. The Grand —, سُلْطَانُ ـ پَادِشَاهِ آلِ عُثْمَانَ ـ السُّلْطَانُ ٱلْأَعْظَمُ ـ ٱلْعُثْمَانِيِّينَ.

Seigniorage, *n.* A percentage for coining, مِيرَةٌ عَلَى ضَرْبِ ٱلسِّكَّةِ. Copyright money, مِيرَةٌ عَلَى بَرَاءَةِ كِتَابٍ. *See* Copyright, *n.*

Seigniory, *n.* A lordship, سِيَادَة. A domain, عَقَار ـ مَمْلَكَة ـ أَرَاضِي ـ اِلْتِزَام ـ مُلْك.

Seine, *n.* شَبَكَةٌ كَبِيرَةٌ.

Seismometer, *n.* مِيزَانٌ تُعْرَفُ بِهِ شِدَّةُ ٱلزَّلْزَلَةِ.

Seizable, *a.* That may be taken hold of, مِمَّا يُمْسَكُ بِهِ ـ ضَبْطُهُ ـ قَبْضُهُ مُمْكِنٌ. That may be apprehended, يُقْبَضُ بِهِ. Legally —, ضَبْطُهُ جَائِزٌ ـ مُمْكِنٌ.

Seize, *v.t.* To grasp, قَبَضَ ـ أَضَبَّ عَلَى ـ ضَبَّ عَلَى ـ. To take suddenly and by force, أَمْسَكَ بِ ـ بَطَشَ بِ ² ـ اِغْتَصَبَ ـ غَصَبَ ـ كَبَسَ ـ اِخْتَلَسَ ـ خَلَسَ ـ أَبْطَشَ. To — and carry off, سَلَبَ ². To snatch, snatch away, اِخْتَلَسَ ـ اِخْتَطَفَ ـ خَطِفَ. To — violently from, غَصَبَ ـ مِن ـ اِغْتَصَبَ ـ مِن. To apprehend, مَسَكَ ـ قَبَضَ بِ ـ. To take possession of, مَلَكَ ـ. To take, أَخَذَ ². To — by capture, قَبَضَ عَلَى ـ اِسْتَوْلَى عَلَى ـ فَتَحَ. To —, to take by surprise, بَاغَتَ ـ بَغَتَ. To — or to be seized with, عَرَضَ ـ اِسْتَوْلَى عَلَى ـ اِعْتَرَى: He was seized with an attack of fever, عَرَضَهُ عَارِضٌ مِنَ ٱلْحُمَّى. He was seized with fear, اِعْتَرَاهُ ٱلْخَوْفُ ـ اِسْتَوْلَى عَلَيْهِ ٱلْخَوْفُ. He was seized by foot-pads, دَخَلَ فِي قَبْضَةِ قُطَّاعِ ٱلطُّرُقِ ². He seized the opportunity, اِفْتَرَصَ ٱلْفُرْصَةَ ـ اِنْتَهَزَ ٱلْفُرْصَةَ. The two opponents sought to — each other by force, تَخَالَسَ ٱلْقِرْنَانِ ـ تَخَالَسَا نَفْسَيْهِمَا. This is an opportunity, therefore do thou — it, هٰذِهِ خُلْسَةٌ فَٱنْتَهِزْهَا. After the soldiers had seized the town, بَعْدَ أَنِ ٱسْتَوْلَتِ ٱلْعَسَاكِرُ عَلَى ٱلْمَدِينَةِ. Many of the rebels were seized, أُلْقِيَ ٱلْقَبْضُ (or قُبِضَ عَلَى) كَثِيرِينَ مِنَ ٱلْعُصَاةِ. He seized the goods of the debtor, as payment for his debts, اِنْتَصَرَ مِنْ مَالِ ٱلْمَدْيُونِ. They seized the culprits, أَلْقَوُا ٱلْقَبْضَ عَلَى ٱلْمُتَعَدِّينَ. They were seized with astonishment and confusion, أَلْقَتْهُمُ ٱلْحَيْرَةُ وَٱلِٱخْتِلَالُ. Neither drowsiness nor sleep shall —, overcome, him, لَا تَأْخُذُهُ سِنَةٌ وَلَا نَوْمٌ. A tremour seized him, أَخَذَتْهُ رِعْدَةٌ.

Seized, *a.* Taken forcibly, مَغْصُوب. Taken, captured, مَقْبُوض ـ مَضْبُوط ـ مَأْخُوذ. Seized and carried off, مَسْلُوب. Snatched away, مُخْتَطَف ـ مَخْطُوف. To be seized, captured, اِنْقَبَضَ ـ أُخِذَ ـ اِفْتَتَحَ ـ فُتِحَ. To be seized of, to possess, أَحْرَزَ ـ اِحْتَوَى عَلَى ـ كَانَ لِ ² ـ مَلَكَ.

Seizin, *n.* تَصَرُّف ـ تَمَلُّك. To give — to, صَرَّفَ ـ مَلَّكَ.

Seizor, *n.* قَابِض ـ ضَابِط ـ مَاسِك ـ مُخْتَلِس ـ خَلَّاس ـ مُسْتَوْلٍ عَلَى.

Seizure, *n.* The act of grasping, إِمْسَاكٌ بِ ـ قَبْض ـ ضَبّ. The act of seizing forcibly, اِخْتِلَاس ـ إِبْطَاش ـ بَطْش ـ اِغْتِصَاب; of snatching away, خَطْف ـ اِخْتِطَاف; of apprehending, مَسْك ـ قَبْضٌ بِ (or عَلَى); of taking possession of, مَلْك ـ

أَخْذُ ـ فَتْحُ بَلَدٍ ـ قَبْضُ عَلَى ـ إسْتِيلَآءُ عَلَى بَلَدٍ. Seizure of a country, . The being seized with, of a disease, fear, *etc.*, عَرَضٌ ـ إعْتِرَآءٌ ـ إعْتِرَاضٌ. Seizure, a capture, as of goods, arms, *etc.*, أَخْذَةٌ ـ غَنِيمَةٌ; (*see* Booty, Prize). He took it by forcible —, أَخَذَهُ ضَبْطًا ـ جِلِّيسَى (*or* آخْتِلَاسًا). Seizure, the act of seizing generally, أَخْذٌ ـ ضَبْطٌ ـ ضَبَاطَةٌ.

Seldom, *ad.* فِي ٱلقَلِيلِ ـ فِي ٱلنَّادِرِ ـ قِلَّةً ـ رُبَّمَا ـ فِي ٱلنُّدْرَةِ. We — hear from him, قَلِيلًا مَا نَسْمَعُ مِنْهُ.

Seldomness, *n.* نُدْرَةُ وُقُوعٍ ـ قِلَّةُ وُقُوعٍ ـ قِلَّةٌ.

Select, *v.t.* To choose, إخْتَارَ ـ إقْتَرَحَ ـ إصْطَفَى ـ إمْتَخَرَ. To pick out, نَقَّى ـ أَنْقَى ـ تَنَقَّى ـ إنْتَقَى. To —, as good from bad coin, *etc.*, خَشَرَ ـ إنْتَقَدَ ـ تَنَقَّدَ ـ نَقَدَ [2] ـ ح. To be selected, أُنْتُدِبَ ـ أُخْتِيرَ. He was selected to lay this opinion before the council, هُوَ ٱلَّذِي ٱنْتُدِبَ لِعَرْضِ هٰذَا ٱلرَّأْيِ عَلَى ٱلْمَجْلِسِ. *See also to* Choose, *v.t.*

Select, *a.* Selected, chosen, مُخْتَارٌ ـ مُنْتَخَبٌ ـ مُقْتَرَحٌ; picked out, مُتَنَقًّى ـ مُنَقًّى; picked out as the best, مَخْشُورٌ ـ مُنْتَقَدٌ ـ مُنَقَّدٌ. Choice, خَاصٌّ ـ خِيَارٌ. The — or best part of anything, ٱلصَّمِيمُ ـ ٱلصَّفِيُّ ـ ٱلعِينَةُ. A — or choice camel, جَمَلٌ خِيَارٌ (*or* مُخْتَارٌ). A — party or social gathering, جَمَاعَةٌ خَاصَّةٌ ـ جَمَاعَةٌ مِنَ ٱلخَوَاصِّ. *See also* Choice, *a.*

Selection, *n.* The act of choosing, خِيَرَةٌ ـ إقْتِرَاحٌ ـ إصْطِفَآءٌ ـ إنْتِخَابٌ; of picking out, تَنَقٍّ ـ تَنْقِيَةٌ ـ نَقَاوَةٌ; of picking out the best, إنْتِقَادٌ ـ نَقْدٌ ـ خَشْرٌ. What is selected or picked out, مُنْتَخَبٌ. A collection, مَجْمُوعٌ ـ جَامِعٌ. A — of poems, دِيوَانُ شِعْرٍ *pl.* دَوَاوِينُ.

Selectness, *n.* خَاصَّةٌ ـ خَيْرٌ ـ نَقَاوَةٌ.

Selector, *n.* مُنَقٍّ ـ مُنْتَقٍ ـ مُنْتَخِبٌ.

Selenite, *n.* حَجَرُ ٱلقَمَرِ.

Selenium, *n.* سِيلِينِيُومُ وَهُوَ مَعْدِنٌ مِنَ ٱلمَعَادِنِ ٱلبَسِيطَةِ.

Self, *n.* ذَاتٌ ـ نَفْسٌ ـ عَيْنٌ. I can do nothing of my own —, لَا أَقْدِرُ أَنْ أَفْعَلَ شَيْئًا مِنْ نَفْسِي. Who his own — carried the burden, ٱلَّذِي هُوَ نَفْسُهُ حَمَلَ ٱلحُمُولَةَ.

Self-abased, *a.* مُتَّضِعٌ ـ مُتَخَشِّعٌ ـ مُتَذَلِّلٌ.

Self-abasement, *n.* إتِّضَاعٌ ـ تَخَشُّعٌ ـ تَذَلُّلٌ.

Self-abhorrence, *n.* إسْتِكْرَاهُ ٱلذَّاتِ.

Self-abuse, *n.* شَتْمُ ٱلذَّاتِ ـ بَذْءُ ٱلذَّاتِ. *See also* Onanism, *n.*

Self-acting, *a.* يَشْتَغِلُ مِنْ ذَاتِهِ ـ مُتَحَرِّكٌ مِنْ ذَاتِهِ.

Self-adjusting, *a.* مُعَدِّلُ ذَاتِهِ.

Self-admiration, *n.* عُجْبُ ٱلذَّاتِ.

Self-command, *n.* مُلْكُ ٱلذَّاتِ. *See also* Self-possession, *n.*

Self-conceit, *n.* خُيَلَآءُ ـ عُجْبٌ ـ تَصَلُّفٌ. He is possessed of —, هُوَ مُتَصَلِّفٌ ـ هُوَ صَلِفٌ ـ هُوَ ذُو خُيَلَآءَ.

Self-conceited, *a.* صَاحِبُ ـ مُعْجَبٌ بِذَاتِهِ ـ مُخْتَالٌ ـ خَائِلٌ ـ مُتَصَلِّفٌ ـ صَلِفٌ ـ عُجْبٌ.

Self-contradictory, *a.* مُتَنَاقِضٌ ـ مُسْتَحِيلٌ ـ مُحَالٌ.

Self-created, *a.* قَائِمٌ بِنَفْسِهِ ـ قَائِمٌ بِذَاتِهِ. *See also* Self-made, *a.*

Self-deceit, *n.* غِشُّ ٱلذَّاتِ ـ غَدْرُ ٱلذَّاتِ.

Self-deceiving, *a.* غَاشُّ ٱلذَّاتِ ـ غَادِرُ ٱلذَّاتِ.

Self-defence, *n.* Self-protection, صِيَانَةُ ٱلنَّفْسِ ـ مُحَافَظَةُ ٱلذَّاتِ. Self-justification, إحْتِجَاجٌ.

Self-denial, *n.* جَبْرُ ٱلنَّفْسِ ـ إنْكَارُ ٱلذَّاتِ. *See also* Disinterestedness, *n.*

Self-denying, *a.* Denying one's self, جَابِرُ ٱلذَّاتِ ـ نَاكِرُ ٱلذَّاتِ; of an action, خَيْرٌ ـ مُنَزَّهٌ عَنِ ٱلطَّمَعِ; of a person, خَيْرٌ ـ خَيِّرٌ.

Self-dependent, *a.* قَائِمٌ بِٱحْتِيَاجَاتِهِ ـ مُعْتَمِدٌ عَلَى ذَاتِهِ.

Self-destruction, *n.* إهْلَاكُ ٱلنَّفْسِ ـ إتْلَافُ ٱلذَّاتِ. *See also* Suicide, *n.*

Self-devoted, *a.* مُقَدِّمُ ذَاتِهِ ـ نَاذِرُ نَفْسِهِ.

Self-educated, *a.* مُعَلِّمُ ذَاتِهِ ـ مُدَرِّسُ نَفْسِهِ; self-made, إبْنُ أَعْمَالِهِ. *See also* Self-made, *a.*

Self-esteem, *n.* Good opinion of one's self, عُجْبٌ. A good name, reputation, صِيتٌ حَسَنٌ ـ نَامُوسٌ ـ عِرْضٌ.

Self-evident, *a.* وَاضِحٌ عِيَانًا ـ مُسْتَغْنٍ عَنِ ٱلبَيَانِ.

Self-examination, *n.* فَحْصُ ٱلضَّمِيرِ ـ إمْتِحَانُ ٱلنَّفْسِ.

Self-existence, *n.* وُجُوبُ ٱلذَّاتِ.

Self-existent, *a.* ٱلوَاجِبُ لِذَاتِهِ. The Self-existent, of God, ٱلوَاجِبُ ٱلوُجُوبِ.

Self-governed, *a.* تَحْتَ حُكُومَةٍ آخْتِيَارِيَّةٍ.

Self-government, *n.* حُكُومَةٌ مُسْتَقِلَّةٌ ـ حُكُومَةٌ آخْتِيَارِيَّةٌ.

Self-interest, *n.* مَنَافِعُ خُصُوصِيَّةٌ ـ مَنَافِعُ ٱلذَّاتِ ـ مَا هُوَ لِنَفْسِهِ.

Self-interested, *a.* طَمَّاعٌ ـ حَرِيصٌ ـ صَاحِبُ غَرَضٍ ـ مُغْرِضٌ. Without a — motive being attributed to him, بِدُونِ أَنْ يُنْسَبَ إلَيْهِ غَرَضٌ.

Self-invited, *a.* دَاعٍ نَفْسَهُ ـ عَازِمٌ نَفْسَهُ.

Selfish, *a.* مَا يُحِبُّ إلَّا نَفْسَهُ ـ نَفْسَانِيٌّ ـ مُغْرِضٌ ـ مُسْتَأْثِرٌ. To be — in a thing, إسْتَأْثَرَ بِٱلشَّيْءِ. Selfish aims, ٱلمَقَاصِدُ ٱلذَّاتِيَّةُ ٱلخَاصَّةُ.

Selfishly, *ad.* بِنَفْسَانِيَّةٍ ـ بِغَرَضٍ ـ بِٱسْتِيثَارٍ.

Selfishness, *n.* حُبُّ ٱلنَّفْسِ فَقَطْ ـ نَفْسَانِيَّةٌ ـ غَرَضٌ ـ إسْتِيثَارٌ.

Self-knowledge, *n.* عِلْمُ ٱلذَّاتِ ـ العِلْمُ بِنَقَائِصِ ٱلنَّفْسِ.

Self-love, *n.* حُبُّ ٱلذَّاتِ.

Self-made, *a.* Of a person, مُتَرَقٍّ مِنْ ذَاتِهِ ـ تَرَقَّى مِنْ ذَاتِهِ ـ إِبْنُ أَعْمَالِهِ.

Self-moved, *a.* مُتَحَرِّكٌ مِنْ ذَاتِهِ.

Self-moving, *a.* مُحَرِّكٌ ذَاتَهُ.

Self-murder, *n.* قَتْلُ ٱلنَّفْسِ ـ إِهْلَاكُ ٱلذَّاتِ. *See also* Suicide, *n.*

Self-murderer, *n.* قَاتِلُ نَفْسِهِ ـ هَالِكُ نَفْسِهِ.

Self-opinioned, *n.* مُتَلَهْوِق ـ مُتَحَذْلِق ـ مُعْجَبٌ بِرَأْيِهِ ـ مُتَعَصِّبٌ لِرَأْيِهِ. To be —, أُعْجِبَ بِنَفْسِهِ.

Self-pleasing, *a.* شَنِّيق ـ وَادُّ ٱلذَّاتِ ـ مُرْضِي نَفْسِهِ.

Self-possession, *n.* رَزَانَة ـ رَوَاقَة ـ عَدَمُ ٱضْطِرَابٍ.

Self-praise, *n.* مَدْحُ ٱلذَّاتِ ـ تَمَدُّح ـ تَفَخُّر ـ تَصَلُّف.

Self-preservation, *n.* مُحَافَظَةُ ٱلذَّاتِ ـ إِحْتِرَاز ـ تَحَفُّظ.

Self-registering, *a.* مُحْكِمُ ذَاتِهِ.

Self-regulating, *a.* مُنَظِّمُ ذَاتِهِ ـ مُحْكِمُ نَفْسِهِ.

Self-reliance, *n.* وَثَاقَة.

Self-reliant, *a.* مُتَوَثِّق. To be —, وَثِقَ *aor.* يَثِقُ ـ تَوَثَّقَ.

Self-reproach, *n.* تَذَمُّم ـ ثَلْبُ ٱلذَّاتِ ـ شَتْمُ ٱلذَّاتِ.

Self-righteous, *n.* زَاعِمٌ أَنَّهُ بَارٌّ ـ مُعْجَبٌ بِصَلَاحِهِ ـ صَالِحٌ عِنْدَ نَفْسِهِ.

Self-righteousness, *n.* العُجْبُ بِصَلَاحِ ٱلذَّاتِ ـ العُجْبُ بِزَكَاةِ ٱلنَّفْسِ.

Self-sacrifice, *n.* بَذْلُ ٱلذَّاتِ ـ بَذْلُ ٱلنَّفْسِ فِدْيَةً. *See also* Self-devotion, *n.*

Self-sacrificing, *a.* بَاذِلُ ٱلذَّاتِ ـ بَاذِلُ ٱلذَّاتِ فِدْيَةً. *See also* Self-devoted, *a.*

Self-same, *a.* ذَات ـ عَيْن ـ بِعَيْنِهِ. He left the — day, خَرَجَ مِنْ يَوْمِهِ ². She died the — night, مَاتَتْ مِنْ لَيْلَتِهَا. For this — thing, purpose, لِهٰذَا عَيْنِهِ. *See also* Identical, *a.*

Self-satisfied, *a.* رَاضٍ بِنَفْسِهِ ـ صَاحِبُ عُجْبٍ.

Self-seeker, *n.* *See* Self-interested, *a.*

Self-seeking, *n.* *See* Self-interest, *n.*

Self-sufficiency, *n.* غُرُور ـ تَكَبُّر ـ تَعَظُّم ـ عُجْب.

Self-sufficient, *a.* مُخْتَال ـ تَيَّاس ـ مُعْجَبٌ بِنَفْسِهِ.

Self-sustained, *a.* مُقِيمٌ بِذَاتِهِ ـ مُتَحَمِّل ـ مُتَعَزِّز.

Self-taught, *a.* مُعَلِّمُ ذَاتِهِ ـ مُدَرِّسُ ذَاتِهِ.

Self-tormenting, *a.* مُعَذِّبُ نَفْسِهِ ـ مُقَلِّقُ ذَاتِهِ ـ مُضْجِرُ نَفْسِهِ.

Self-will, *n.* عِنَاد ـ مُعَانَدَة ـ شَكَاسَة ـ شَرَاسَة.

Self-willed, *a.* مُعْجَبٌ بِنَفْسِهِ ـ مُعَانِد ـ شَكِس ـ شَرِس.

Self-worship, *n.* عِبَادَةُ ٱلذَّاتِ ـ حُبُّ ٱلذَّاتِ ـ تَكَبُّر ـ تَفَخُّر.

Sell, *v.t.* بَاعَ *aor.* يَبِيعُ. To betray, خَانَ *aor.* يَخُونُ ـ أَسْلَمَ. To play a trick upon, ضَحِكَ بِ *or* مِنْ. He sold him the house, بَاعَهُ ٱلْبَيْتَ ـ بَاعَ لَهُ ٱلْبَيْتَ. To — anything to one on a bare description, وَاصَفَ ـ بَاعَ لَهُ بِٱلْوَصْفِ. To — upon credit, بَاعَ بِأَخِرَةٍ (*or* بِنَظِرَةٍ). To — to on credit, نَظَّرَ ـ أَدَانَ ـ بَاعَ لِ ـ بِٱلدَّيْنِ.

Sell, *v.i.* To practise selling, بَاعَ *aor.* يَبِيعُ. To be sold, إِبْتَاعَ ـ إِنْبَاعَ. It sells for so much, يَنْبَاعُ بِكَذَا. To cheat in selling, شَابَ ².

Seller, *n.* بَائِع ـ بَيَّاع *pl.* بَيَّاعَة. An expert —, بَيِّع. A — of eatables, بَدَّال; *vulg.* بَقَّال.

Selvedge, Selvage, *n.* حَاشِيَة *pl.* حَوَاشٍ ـ حِبَاك *pl.* حُبُك ـ كِفَاف ـ مَسْلَكَة.

Selves, *pl. of* Self; Ourselves, نَحْنُ ـ نَحْنُ ذَوَاتُنَا; they themselves, هُمْ ـ هُمْ ذَوَاتُهُمْ; ye yourselves, أَنْتُمْ ـ أَنْتُمْ ذَوَاتُكُمْ.

Semaphore, *n.* تِلِغْرَافُ إِشَارَةٍ.

Semblance, *n.* شَبَه ـ شَكْل. *See also* Likeness, Resemblance, *n.*

Semen, *n.* The — of a man, مَنِيّ ـ مَنِي ـ مَنِيَّة; of a camel, عَيْش; of a horse, يَرُون. *See also* Seed, *n.*

Semester, *n.* سِتَّةُ أَشْهُرٍ ـ نِصْفُ سَنَةٍ.

Semi-annual, *a.*
Semi-annually, *ad.* كُلَّ نِصْفِ سَنَةٍ ـ مَرَّتَيْنِ فِي ٱلسَّنَةِ.

Semi-annular, *a.* فِي شَكْلِ نِصْفِ دَائِرَةٍ.

Semibreve, *n.* عَلَامَةٌ فِي كِتَابَةِ ٱلْمُوسِيقَى ٱمْتِدَادُهَا مِينِمَيْنِ شَكْلُهَا كَذَا (o). *See* Minim, *n.*

Semicircle, *n.* نِصْفُ دَائِرَةٍ.

Semicolon, *n.* عَلَامَةُ مَحَطٍّ فِي ٱلْقِرَاءَةِ شَكْلُهَا كَذَا (;).

Semi-diameter, *n.* نِصْفُ قُطْرٍ.

Semi-diaphanous, *a.* شَفَّافٌ نَوْعًا.

Semi-lunar, *a.* فِي شَكْلِ ٱلْهِلَالِ.

Seminal, *a.* Of the — fluid, نُطْفِيّ.

Seminarist, *n.* مُرَبًّى فِي مَدْرَسَةٍ ـ مِنْ أَهْلِ مَدْرَسَةٍ ـ تِلْمِيذ *pl.* تَلَامِيذ.

Seminary, *n.* A place of education, مَدْرَسَة *pl.* مَدَارِس. An ecclesiastical —, مَدْرَسَةٌ لِلْإِكْلِيرُس. A seed-plot, مَزْرَعَة *pl.* مَزَارِعُ.

Seminary, *a.* مَدْرَسِيّ.

Seminate, *v.t.* *See to* Propagate, Sow, *v.t.*

Semination, *n.* The act of sowing, زَرْع ـ زِرَاعَة. The natural dispersion of seed, الزِّرَاعَةُ ٱلطَّبِيعِيَّة.

Semiology, *n.* بَتْلُوجِيَا ـ فَنُّ تَشْخِيصِ ٱلْأَمْرَاضِ.

Semi-opaque, *a.* أَلْمَى (*or*) كَثِيف نَوْعًا.

Semi-orbicular, *a.* فِي شَكْلِ نَصْفِ كُرَةٍ.

Semi-osseous, *a.* عَظْمِيٌّ نَوْعًا.

Semiquaver, *n.* عَلَامَةٌ فِي كِتَابَةِ ٱلْمُوسِيقَى شَكْلُهَا كَذَا (♬).

Semitic, *a.* سَامِيٌّ ـ مَنْسُوبٌ إِلَى بَنِي سَامٍ.

Semitone, *n.* نِصْفُ نَغْمَةٍ.

Semi-vocal, *a.* Having an imperfect sound, ذُو صَوْتٍ ضَعِيفٍ ـ ضَعِيفُ ٱلْحِسِّ.

Semivowel, *n.* حَرْفٌ يُلْفَظُ بِحَرَكَةِ ٱلْإِشْمَامِ. Pertaining to a semivowel, مَا نِيطَ بِٱلْحَرْفِ ٱلْمَذْكُورِ.

Sempiternal, *a.* *See* Everlasting, *a.*

Sempiternity, *n.* *See* Everlastingness, *n.*

Sempster, *n.* خَيَّاط *pl.* خَيَّاطَة.

Sempstress, *n.* خَيَّاطَة *pl.* خَيَّاطَات.

Senary, *a.* سُدَاسِيٌّ.

Senate, *n.* دِيوَانُ أَعْيَانِ مَمْلَكَةٍ ـ مَجْلِسُ شُورَى.

Senate-house, *n.* بَيْتُ مَجْلِسِ ٱلشُّورَى ـ مَحَلُّ مَجْلِسِ ٱلشُّورَى.

Senator, *n.* عُضْوٌ مِنْ أَعْضَاءِ دِيوَانٍ ـ مِنْ أَعْضَاءِ مَجْلِسِ ٱلشُّورَى ـ أَعْيَانِ ٱلْمَمْلَكَةِ.

Senatorial, *a.* مَا نِيطَ بِأَعْضَاءِ مَجْلِسٍ ـ مُتَعَلِّقٌ بِمَجْلِسِ ٱلشُّورَى ٱلشُّورَى.

Senatorially, *ad.* مِثْلَ أَعْيَانِ ٱلْمَمْلَكَةِ. With dignity, بِوَقَارٍ ـ بِهَيْبَةٍ.

Senatorship, *n.* مَقَامُ (*or*) وَظِيفَةُ أَهْلِ مَجْلِسِ ٱلشُّورَى.

Senatus-consultum, *n.* قَرَارُ ٱلشُّورَى.

Send, *v.t.* As from one place to another, أَبْعَثَ ـ ¹ بَعَثَ ـ وَفَّدَ ـ أَفْرَطَ ـ فَرَّطَ. To —, as a messenger or legate, to, وَجَّهَ ـ أَرْسَلَ. To —, transmit, forward, أَنْفَذَ ـ نَفَّذَ. To launch, as an arrow, *etc.*, أَطْلَقَ ـ شَمَّرَ. He sent him to be, as, a ruler, أَرْسَلَهُ رَئِيسًا.

To send away, expel, ¹ نَفَى ـ ² طَرَدَ ـ سَيَّرَ.

To send back, رَجَّعَ ـ ² رَدَّ. To be sent back, تَرَدَّدَ.

To send before one, أَرْسَلَ أَمَامَهُ.

To send for, to summon, اِسْتَدْعَى ـ دَعَا بِ *aor.* يَدْعُو ـ أَحْضَرَ ـ ¹ بَعَثَ خَلْفَهُ ـ ² طَلَبَ. To send for, as for a purpose, ¹ بَعَثَ فِي.

To send forth, to make to go out, أَخْرَجَ. To drive off or away, ² طَرَدَ. To disseminate, circulate, ² نَشَرَ ـ أَشَاعَ.

To send in, make to go in, أَدْخَلَ. To present, submit, ¹ عَرَضَ ـ قَدَّمَ.

To send off, to dispatch, أَرْسَلَ ـ ¹ بَعَثَ. *See also* To send away.

To send on, to transmit, وَصَّلَ ـ أَوْصَلَ ـ أَنْفَذَ ـ نَفَّذَ.

To send out, to issue, as an order, أَصْدَرَ. To publish, proclaim, نَادَى بِ ـ أَشْهَرَ ـ أَذَاعَ بِ.

To send something to one, as by a messenger, ¹ بَعَثَ إِلَى بِ.

To send to the right about, أَسْحَتَ ـ ¹ سَحَتَ ـ ¹ سَخِطَ عَلَى ـ ² طَرَدَ.

Sender, *n.* بَاعِث ـ مُرْسِل.

Sending, *n.* The act of, إِرْسَال.

Senegal, *n.* The gum, ضَرْبٌ مِنَ ٱلصَّمْغِ.

Senescence, *n.* شَيْبَة ـ تَشَيُّخ ـ اِسْتِشْنَان.

Seneschal, *n.* A chamberlain, حَاجِب *pl.* حُجَّاب. *See also* Stewart, *n.*

Senile, *a.* مُخْتَصٌّ بِٱلشَّيْبَةِ ـ مُتَعَلِّقٌ بِٱلشَّيْخُوخِيَّةِ. A — complaint, دَاءُ ٱلْعَجَائِزِ.

Senility, *n.* شَيْبَة ـ شَيْخُوخَة ـ شُيُوخِيَّة.

Senior, *n.* } One older in age, أَكْبَرُ فِي ٱلْعُمْرِ ـ أَكْبَرُ سِنًّا; older
Senior, *a.* } in rank, ٱلْأَقْدَمُ فِي ٱلْوَظِيفَةِ ـ ٱلْأَقْدَمُ مَنْصَبًا. The — partner, ٱلشَّرِيكُ ٱلْمُتَقَدِّمُ ـ ٱلشَّرِيكُ ٱلْأَقْدَمُ.

Seniority, *n.* Of age, تَقَدُّمٌ فِي ٱلْعُمْرِ; of office, *etc.*, تَقَدُّمٌ فِي ٱلْخِدْمَةِ ـ تَقَدُّمٌ فِي ٱلْمَنْصَبِ.

Senna, *n.* سَنَا مَكَّةَ ـ سَنَا حِجَازِيٌّ ـ سَنَا.

Sennight, *n.* أُسْبُوع ـ سَبْعَةُ أَيَّامٍ.

Sensate, *a.* مَحْسُوس.

Sensation, *n.* The subjective feeling of the mind, حِسٌّ ـ إِحْسَاس. Effect, أَثَر ـ نُجُوع. Interest, commotion, رَجْفَة ـ تَعَجُّب ـ إِرْجَاف ـ اِرْتِجَاف. To have a — of, ² حَسَّ بِ ـ اِسْتَبْصَرَ ـ أَحَسَّ بِ. To create a —, ² رَجَفَ رَجْفَةً ـ حَرَّكَ. The news caused a — among them, أَوْجَبَ ٱلْقِيلَ وَٱلْقَالَ ـ حَرَكَةً ـ أَرْجَفَ ٱلْقَوْمُ بِٱلْخَبَرِ.

Sensational, *a.* Exciting the feelings, مُحَرِّكُ ٱلْأَحْسَاس. Causing commotion, مُحَرِّك ـ مُرْجِف ـ رَاجِف. Sensational stories, أَرَاجِيف. *See also* Emotional, *a.* *and under* Emotion, *n.*

Sense, *n.* The faculty of perceiving, إِحْسَاس ـ حِسٌّ. Power of sensation, قُوَّةٌ حَاسَّةٌ ـ حَاسَّة. Sound judgment, عَقْل ـ دِرَايَة ـ فِطْنَة ـ ذَكَاء ـ حَزْم. Meaning, import, مَضْمُون ـ فَحْوَى ـ سِيَاق ـ مَعْنًى *pl.* مَعَانٍ. Feeling, حَاسَّة. Opinion, رَأْي *pl.* آرَاء. A — of relationship pleaded for him on my part, أَطَّتْ لَهُ مِنِّي حَاسَّةٌ

رَجِمِ. He took the course prescribed by sound —, أَخَذَ بِٱلْحَزْمِ ².
To have a — or feeling of, or to have a perception of, to opine, أَحَسَّ بِ ـ حَسَّ بِ ² ـ شَعَرَ بِ ². The five senses, الْمَدَارِكُ ـ الْمَشَاعِرُ ـ الْمَدَارِكُ ٱلْخَمْسُ ـ الْحَوَاسُّ ٱلْخَمْسُ. *See also under* Mind, *n.*

The sense of feeling, اللَّمْسُ ـ الْقُوَّةُ ٱللَّامِسَةُ.

The sense of hearing, السَّمْعُ ـ الْقُوَّةُ ٱلسَّامِعَةُ.

The sense of seeing, الْبَصَرُ ـ الْقُوَّةُ ٱلْبَاصِرَةُ.

The sense of smelling, الشَّمُّ ـ الْقُوَّةُ ٱلشَّامَّةُ.

The sense of tasting, الذَّوْقُ ـ الْقُوَّةُ ٱلذَّائِقَةُ.

Common sense, عَقْل ـ فِطْنَة ـ الْحِسُّ ٱلْمُشْتَرَكُ.

In a bad sense, بِمَعْنَى رَدِيءٍ ـ بِمَقَامِ ذَمِيمٍ.

In a good sense, بِمَعْنَى حَسَنٍ ـ بِمَقَامٍ جَيِّدٍ.

In a certain sense, فِي وَجْهٍ مِنَ ٱلْوُجُوهِ ـ فِي بَعْضِ ٱلْجِهَاتِ.

Moral sense, إِنْصَاف ـ ذِمَّة ـ ضَمِير.

Obvious to the senses, بَائِن ـ ظَاهِر.

To be in one's right senses, كَانَ سَالِمَ ٱلْعَقْلِ ـ تَعَقَّلَ ـ عَقَلَ ².

To be out of one's senses, طَاشَ *aor.* يَطِيشُ ـ جُنَّ ـ إِخْتَلَّ عَقْلُهُ.

Out of one's senses, at sea, distracted, سُلِبَ ٱلْقَرَارَ.

To bring one to his senses, right mind, أَصْحَى مِنْ جُنُونِهِ ـ عَقَّلَ ـ أَفَاقَ ـ أَصْحَى ـ رَجَّعَ إِلَى عَقْلِهِ. To recover, as from insensibility, أَفَاقَ ـ أَصْحَى.

To bring down one's pride, خَفَّضَ نَفْسَهُ ².

To come to one's senses, right mind, رَجَعَ ² ـ رَجَعَ إِلَى نَفْسِهِ ـ إِلَى عَقْلِهِ. "Then they returned to their senses," فَرَجَعُوا إِلَى أَنْفُسِهِمْ (Kûr. xxi. 65).

To drive one out of his senses, جَنَّنَ ـ خَبَّلَ ـ خَبَلَ ² ـ أَطَاشَ.

To lose one's senses, right mind, جُنَّ ـ إِخْتَلَّ عَقْلُهُ. To swoon, faint, غُشِيَ عَلَيْهِ ².

To make sense out of, حَلَّ ² ـ فَسَّرَ ـ وَقَفَ عَلَى *aor.* يَقِفُ ـ إِسْتَخْرَجَ ٱلْمَعْنَى ـ قَرَأَ ².

To recover one's senses, as from a swoon, *etc.*, فَاقَ ² ـ صَحَا ².
See also To come to one's senses.

To take the sense of a meeting, إِتَّخَذَ رَأْيَ ٱلْمَجْلِسِ.

Senseless, *a.* Without sensation, صَامِت ـ جَامِد. Without feeling, عَدِيمُ ٱلْحِسِّ. As in a swoon, مَغْشِيٌّ عَلَيْهِ ـ غُشِيَ عَلَيْهِ. Meaningless, بِلَا مَعْنًى. Contrary to reason, ضِدُّ ٱلْعَقْلِ. Stupid, silly, أَحْمَق ـ بَلِيد ـ أَبْلَهُ ـ عَرِيضُ ٱلْوِسَادِ ـ غَبِين ـ أَخْرَق. To be —, stupid, حَمُقَ ². To become —, as in a swoon, غُشِيَ عَلَيْهِ. *See also* Insensible, *a.*

Senselessly, *n.* Stupidly, بِبَلَاهَةٍ ـ بِغَبَاوَةٍ ـ بِغَبَانَةٍ ـ بِخُرْقٍ ـ بِحَمَاقَةٍ.

Senselessness, *n.* Stupidity, حَمَاقَة ـ غَبَاوَة ـ بَلَاهَة ـ خُرْق ـ تَيْسِيَّة. In a state of swoon, غَشْيَان.

Sensibility, *n.* Susceptibility of impression, حِدَّةُ ٱلْحَاسَّةِ ـ حَاسِّيَّة. Sense, feeling, إِحْسَاس ـ حِسّ. A state of —, freedom from insensibility however caused, صَحْوَة. Tenderness, حِنِّيَّة ـ حِنَّة ـ شَفَقَة ـ لَيَان ـ لِينَة ـ رِفْق. Sensibilities, خَاطِر ـ قَلْب : To wound one's sensibilities, جَرَحَ خَاطِرَهُ ² ـ كَسَرَ خَاطِرَهُ ².

Sensible, *a.* Capable of sensation, حَسَّاس. Perceptible by the senses, حِسِّيّ. Clear, plain, ظَاهِر ـ بَائِن ـ مُبِين. Having feeling, ذُو حَاسَّةٍ. Delicate, susceptible, sensitive, لَيِّن ـ لَيْن ـ رَقِيقُ ٱلْقَلْبِ ـ ٱلْجَانِبِ. Humane, tender, شَفُوق ـ حَنُون. Apparent to the senses, ظَاهِر ـ بَيِّن ـ مَحْسُوس. Having good sense, صَاحِبُ عَقْلٍ ـ عَاقِل ـ ذَكِيّ; especially of a woman, شَهْلَةٌ كَهْلَةٌ. Great, considerable, بَائِن ـ عَظِيم. A — speech, harangue, خِطَابٌ مَعْقُول ـ كَلَام بَيِّن. A — man, رَجُل لَبِيب ـ رَجُل عَاقِل. Sensible heat, حَرّ مَحْسُوس. To be — of, to feel, perceive, أَحَسَّ بِ ـ حَسَّ بِ ²; to be aware of, شَعَرَ بِ ² ـ أَحَسَّ ـ أَدْرَكَ. I experienced a — pleasure therefrom, سَرَّنِي ذٰلِكَ سُرُورًا عَظِيمًا. He is very —, or sensitive, to blame, تَصْعُبُ عَلَيْهِ ٱلتُّهْمَةُ. I am very — to your kindness, حَصَلَ ² عِنْدِي مِنْ مَعْرُوفِكُمْ ٱمْتِنَان عَظِيم. *See also under* to Feel, *v.t.*; *also* Perceivable, Perceptible, *a.*

Sensibleness, *n.* Capacity of perception, إِحْسَاس ـ حِسّ. Good sense, ذَكَاء ـ عَقْل ـ حَزْم. *See also* Sensibility, *a.*

Sensibly, *ad.* So as to be perceived by the senses, بِبَيِّنَةٍ تُدْرِكُهُ ٱلْحَوَاسُّ. Openly, clearly, عَلَانِيَةً ـ بَيَانًا ـ عِيَانًا. With good sense, بِعَقْلٍ ـ بِحَزْمٍ. Much, greatly, لِلْغَايَةِ ـ كَثِيرًا. To talk —, سَدَّ ² (or أَسَدَّ) فِي كَلَامِهِ ـ تَكَلَّمَ بِعَقْلٍ.

Sensitive, *a.* Having sense or feeling, حَاسّ ـ حَسَّاس ـ ذُو حَسَّاسٍ. The — faculty, الْقُوَّةُ ٱلْحَسَّاسَةُ. The — plant, الْمُسْتَحِيَّةُ. For the other significations, *see under* Sensible, *a.*

Sensitively, *ad.* بِإِحْسَاسٍ ـ بِحِسٍّ.

Sensitiveness, *n.* إِحْسَاس ـ حِسّ. *See also* Sensibility, *n.*

Sensorial, *a.* مَا نِيطَ بِآلَاتِ ٱلْحِسِّ ـ مُتَعَلِّق بِمَجْمَعِ ٱلْحَوَاسِّ ٱلْمُشْتَرَكِ.

Sensorium, *n.* }
Sensory, } آلَاتُ ٱلْحِسِّ ٱلْمُشْتَرَكِ ـ مَجْمَعُ ٱلْحَوَاسِّ.

Sensual, *a.* نَزِيز ـ شَهْوَانِيٌّ . Animal, حَيَوَانِيٌّ . *See also* Libidinous, Lascivious, Lustful, *a.*

Sensualism, *n.* The doctrine of —, مَذْهَبُ ٱلْقَائِلِينَ أَنَّ إِدْرَاكَ ٱلْبَشَرِ صَادِرٌ لَيْسَ فَقَطْ عَنْ مُجَرَّدِ ٱلْحِسِّ ٱلْحَاضِرِ بَلْ عَنْ آثَارِ إِحْسَاسٍ سَابِقٍ أَيْضًا . *See also* Sensuality, *n.*

Sensualist, *n.* A believer in the doctrine of sensualism, مِنْ أَصْحَابِ ٱلرَّأْيِ ٱلْمَذْكُورِ . One given to sensuality; *see under* Sensual, *a.*

Sensuality, *n.* نَزَّةٌ ـ شَهْوَانِيَّةٌ ـ حُبُّ ٱلشَّهَوَاتِ . *See also* Lasciviousness, Lust, *n.*

Sensualization, *n.* The act of, إِفْسَادٌ ـ إِفْسَادُ ٱلْأَخْلَاقِ ; the being sensualized, خُبْثٌ ـ فَسَادٌ ـ شَهْوَانِيَّةٌ .

Sensualize, *v.t.* صَيَّرَ شَهْوَانِيًّا ـ أَغْرَاهُ بِٱلشَّهَوَاتِ ٱلْفَاسِدَةِ ـ أَفْسَدَ .

Sensualness, *n.* *See* Sensuality, *n.*

Sensuous, *a.* حِسِّيٌّ ـ مُتَعَلِّقٌ بِٱلْتِذَاذِ ٱلْحَوَاسِّ ـ مَا يَفْعَلُ فِي ٱلْحَوَاسِّ .

Sent, *part. of to* Send, *v.t.*, *q.v.*

Sentence, *n.* A judgment, as pronounced by a court, *etc.*, حُكْمٌ *pl.* أَحْكَامٌ ـ حُكُومَةٌ *pl.* حُكُومَاتٌ ـ حَتْمٌ *pl.* حُتُومٌ ـ قَضَاءٌ ـ فَتْوَى *pl.* فَتَاوَى ـ قَضًا *pl.* أَقْضِيَةٌ . An opinion, رَأْيٌ *pl.* آرَاءٌ . A maxim, قِيَاسٌ . A saying, adage, قَوْلٌ *pl.* أَقْوَالٌ ـ مَثَلٌ *pl.* أَمْثَالٌ ـ مَقَالَةٌ *pl.* مَقَالَاتٌ . A passage, verse, آيَةٌ *pl.* آيَاتٌ ـ جُمْلَةٌ *pl.* جُمَلٌ ـ عِبَارَةٌ *pl.* عِبَارَاتٌ ـ فَصْلٌ *pl.* فُصُولٌ ـ بَابٌ *pl.* أَبْوَابٌ . An irrevocable —, حُكْمٌ جَزْمٌ (or بَتٌّ) ـ قَضَاءٌ حَتْمٌ . The — was carried out speedily, أُجْرِيَ ٱلْقَضَاءُ سَرِيعًا . He omitted that —, حَذَفَ تِلْكَ ٱلْجُمْلَةَ . To pass a — in favour of, قَضَى لِ ; against, قَضَى عَلَى ـ حَكَمَ عَلَى .

Sentence, *v.t.* To pass judgment on, to decide judicially, حَكَمَ بِ ـ قَضَى بِ ـ حَتَمَ بِ ـ حَتَمَ ـ جَزَمَ . To — one to, قَضَى عَلَى ـ بِ ـ حَكَمَ عَلَى ـ بِ . *See also to* Condemn, *v.t.*

Sentential, *a.* مُتَعَلِّقٌ بِجُمْلَةٍ ـ مُخْتَصٌّ بِٱلْآيَاتِ .

Sententious, *a.* مُجْمَلٌ ـ ذُو سَدَادٍ ـ سَدِيدٌ ـ أَسَدُّ . *See also* Concise, *a.*

Sententiously, *ad.* سَدَادًا ـ بِتَحَكُّمٍ ـ تَأْثِيرًا . To speak —, حَذَفَ فِي ٱلْقَوْلِ .

Sententiousness, *n.* Pithiness, سَدَادٌ ـ تَأْثِيرٌ ـ جِدَّةٌ . Conciseness, إِقْتِصَارٌ ـ إِيجَازٌ .

Sentient, *a.* حَسَّاسٌ ـ ذُو إِحْسَاسٍ ـ حَاسٌّ .

Sentiment, *n.* Opinion, thought, رَأْيٌ *pl.* آرَاءٌ ـ فِكْرٌ *pl.* أَفْكَارٌ . Meaning, مَعْنًى ـ مَضْمُونٌ ـ فَحْوَى . Belief, إِعْتِقَادٌ . An adage, proverb, مَثَلٌ *pl.* أَمْثَالٌ ـ مَقَالَةٌ . A — of pity, رَأْفَةٌ ـ تَرَحُّمٌ ـ شَفَقَةٌ ; of reverence, هَيْبَةٌ ـ حُرْمَةٌ ; of respect, إِحْتِرَامٌ ـ إِكْرَامٌ ; of dislike, disgust, كَرَاهَةٌ ـ تَقَزُّزٌ ـ إِعْتِيَافٌ . Personal sentiments, أَفْكَارٌ ذَاتِيَّةٌ . National sentiments, أَفْكَارُ ٱلْأُمَّةِ ـ أَفْكَارُ ٱلشَّعْبِ . Patriotic sentiments, حُبُّ ٱلْوَطَنِ ـ أَفْكَارٌ وَطَنِيَّةٌ . Painful sentiments, أَفْكَارٌ أَلِيمَةٌ : Humane —, شَعَائِرُ إِنْسَانِيَّةٌ . Sentiments of honour, probity, عِرْضٌ ـ مُرُوَّةٌ ـ نَخْوَةٌ . To express one's sentiments, تَفَتَّحَ فِي ٱلْكَلَامِ ـ بَيَّنَ ضَمِيرَهُ ـ فَاهَ بِأَفْكَارِهِ . To change one's sentiments, عَدَلَ عَنْ أَفْكَارِهِ ٱلسَّابِقَةِ . Pray receive the expression of my most distinguished sentiments, أَلْتَمِسُ مِنْكُمْ قُبُولَ حُسْنِ ٱحْتِرَامِي ٱلْأَخَصِّ . *See also* Feeling, *n.*

Sentimental, *a.* Fanciful, خَيَالِيٌّ ـ مُتَوَهَّمٌ . Romantic, of things, أَسَاطِيرِيٌّ . Tender-hearted, رَقِيقُ ٱلْقَلْبِ . Pertaining to affection, شَامِلُ ٱلْحُبِّ ; to tenderness, شَامِلُ ٱلرِّقَّةِ . His speech was —, رَقَّ كَلَامُهُ .

Sentimentalism, *n.* } Fancifulness, تَخَيُّلٌ ـ تَوَهُّمٌ . Affectation
Sentimentality, } of sensibility, ٱلتَّصَنُّعُ بِٱلرِّقَّةِ ; of fine sentiments, ٱلتَّصَنُّعُ بِٱلْمَكَارِمِ ـ تَأَنُّقٌ ـ تَجَوُّدٌ ـ تَظَرُّفٌ .

Sentimentalist, *n.* One who affects fine sentiments, مُتَظَرِّفٌ ـ مُتَصَنِّعٌ بِٱلْمَكَارِمِ ـ مُتَأَنِّقٌ ـ مُتَجَوِّدٌ ; one who affects extreme sensibility, tenderness, مُتَصَنِّعٌ بِٱلرِّقَّةِ ـ مُتَأَنِّقٌ .

Sentimentalize, *v.i.* تَخَيَّلَ أَخْيِلَةً ; as in preaching, أَفْرَطَ فِي ٱلْوَعْظِ .

Sentimentally, *ad.* With feeling, بِإِحْسَاسٍ ـ بِرِقَّةٍ . Fancifully, بِتَخَيُّلٍ ـ بِتَوَهُّمٍ .

Sentinel, *n.* } A guard, keep, خَفِيرٌ *vulg.* غَفِيرٌ ـ حَارِسٌ *pl.*
Sentry, } حُرَّاسٌ ; of a soldier, نَاطُورٌ ـ عَسَّاسٌ ـ نَوْبَتْجِي . To be on —, نَطَرَ ـ أَجْرَى ٱلْخِفَارَةَ . To put on —, نَطَّرَ ـ أَقَامَ فِي ٱلْحِرَاسَةِ .

Sentry-box, *n.* For a watcher, نَاطُورٌ ; for a soldier, شُونَةٌ *pl.* شُوَنٌ ـ بَيْتُ ٱلنَّاطُورِ ـ بَيْتُ ٱلنَّوْبَتْجِي .

Sepal, *n.* Of a calyx, أَطْرَافُ ٱلْبُرْعُمِ ـ دَائِرَةُ ٱلْقُبْعَةِ .

Separability, *n.* } إِمْكَانُ ٱلْإِنْفِصَالِ ـ إِمْكَانُ ٱلْإِفْتِرَاقِ .
Separableness, }

Separable, *a.* مِمَّا يَتَفَرَّقُ ـ قَابِلُ ٱلْإِفْتِرَاقِ ـ قَابِلُ ٱلْإِنْفِصَالِ .

Separate, *v.t.* To put aside one thing from another, as sheep from goats, *etc.*, فَرَزَ ـ أَفْرَزَ ـ عَزَلَ ـ عَنْ ـ مَيَّزَ ـ مِنْ . To cause to be apart, as from a collective body, أَشَذَّ ـ جَزَّرَ ـ جَنَّبَ .

To — between, قَطَعَ بَيْنَ – فَرَقَ بَيْنَ – فَصَلَ بَيْنَ. To disjoin, فَكَّكَ – إِنْفَصَّ – فَصَّ – فَصَلَ عَن. To — from, فَرَقَ مِن – فَصَلَ عَن. To — or distribute between, فَرَّقَ عَلَى – وَزَّعَ عَلَى. To —, as into sections, فَصَّلَ. To scatter, شَتَّتَ. To — one's self from, شَرَدَ عَن – شَذَّ عَن – اِنْفَرَدَ عَن – اِنْجَرَدَ عَن. It separates, divides, splits, the board into two parts, يَشُقُّ ٱللَّوْحَ شَطْرَيْنِ. He separated himself from his partner, with the concurrence of the latter, فَارَزَ شَرِيكَهُ. The one separated himself from the other, اِعْتَزَلَ ٱلْوَاحِدُ عَنِ ٱلْآخَرِ. He separated himself lest he should be condemned, أَفْرَزَ نَفْسَهُ لِئَلَّا يُدَانَ. *See also to* Divide, Part, *v.t.*

Separate, *v.i.* To part, to become divided into parts, اِفْتَرَقَ – اِنْفَصَلَ. To become separated, disjoined, to part asunder, as of a ship, تَفَكَّكَ. To become dispersed, اِفْتَرَقَ – تَفَرَّقَ – تَشَتَّتَ. To — or become separated from, اِنْفَصَلَ عَن – اِنْفَضَّ مِن. The meeting separated, اِنْفَضَّ ٱلْمَجْلِسُ.

Separate, *a.* } Set aside from something else by selection,
Separated, } مُمَيَّز – مَفْرُوز; separated as from some other body, made separate or distinct, مَشْذُوذ – شَاذّ – مَفْرُوز. Separate, not sticking together, فَذّ: Dates —, not sticking to one another, تَمْرٌ فَذٌّ. Divided, cut off, standing alone, مُنْفَرِد – فَرْد – شَاذِب; dispersed, مُشَتَّت. Alone, مُنْفَصِل – مُفَصَّل – فَرِيد – مُنْفَرِد – فَرُود. A — place, مَكَانٌ مُنْفَصِلٌ.

Separately, *ad.* In dispersion, عَلَى – اِنْفِرَادًا – شَتَّى – فُذَاذًا كُلٌّ, Each one —, عَلَى حِدَةٍ – عَلَى ٱلْاِنْفِرَادِ – وَجْهِ ٱلْاِنْفِرَادِ. We ate —, أَكَلْنَا فُذَاذًا. كُلُّ وَاحِدٍ بِمُفْرَدِهِ – وَاحِدٍ عَلَى حِدَةٍ.

Separateness, *n.* The being separate; *see under* Separation, *n.*

Separating, *a.* قَاطِعٌ بَيْنَ – فَارِق – مُفَصِّل – فَاصِل.

Separation, *n.* The act of putting one thing aside from another, تَعَزُّل عَن – تَمْيِيز – عَزْل – إِفْرَاز; the being so separated, فِرْزَة – تَمَيُّز عَن. The act of separating something from another body, تَجْنِيب – تَجْرِيد – إِشْذَاذ – فَضّ – تَشْذِيذ – شَذّ; the being so separated, تَجَنُّب – اِنْفِضَاض – تَجَرُّد – شُذُوذ. The act of separating between, فَرْق بَيْنَ – فَصْل بَيْنَ – قَطْع بَيْنَ – تَفْصِيل بَيْنَ; the being so separated, اِفْتِرَاق – اِنْفِصَال – اِنْقِطَاع – مُفَارَقَة. The act of disjoining, تَفْكِيك; the being disjoined, تَفَكُّك. The act of scattering, تَشْتِيت; the being scattered, تَشَتُّت. The act of separating one's self from, شَذّ عَن – اِنْفِرَاد عَن – اِعْتِزَال عَن – شَرْد عَن. Separation, the being apart one from another, اِفْتِرَاق – مُفَارَقَة. Separation, as between husband and wife, مُفَاصَلَة. A division, بَيْن *pl.* بُيُون. Partition, of a wall, *etc.*, حَاجِز *pl.* حَوَاجِز. The compounding with a wife by her husband for a —, مُبَارَأَة: He compounded with his wife for a —, as by giving him a part of her dowry, or some other compensation, بَارَأَ ٱمْرَأَتَهُ.

Separatism, *n.* الِاعْتِزَال.

Separatist, *n.* مُعْتَزِل *pl.* مُعْتَزِلَة.

Sepia, *n.* (*See* Cuttle-fish, *n.*) A pigment from the ink of the cuttle-fish, صِبَاغٌ مُرَكَّبٌ مِنْ زَبَدِ ٱلْبَحْرِ.

Sepoy, *n.* عَسْكَرٌ هِنْدِيٌّ *pl.* عَسَاكِرُ هِنْدِيَّة.

Sept, *n.* *See* Clan, Tribe, *n.*

Septangular, *a.* ذُو سَبْعِ زَوَايَا.

September, *n.* شَهْرُ سَبْتَمْبَر – أَيْلُول.

Septenary, *n.* مُدَّةُ سَبْعِ سِنِينَ – سَبْعُ سِنِينَ.

Septenary, *a.* سَابِعِيٌّ – سَابِع.

Septennial, *a.* Lasting seven years, مُسْتَمِرٌّ مُدَّةَ سَبْعِ سِنِينَ; happening once in seven years, مِنْ سَبْعٍ – وَاقِعٌ مَرَّةً فِي سَبْعِ سِنِينَ سِنِينَ إِلَى سَبْعِ سِنِينَ.

Septennially, *ad.* مَرَّةً فِي سَبْعِ سِنِينَ.

Septentrion, *n.* جِهَاتُ ٱلشَّمَالِ – الشَّمَال.

Septentrional, *a.* شَمَالِيٌّ.

Septic, *a.* }
Septical, } مُعَفِّن – مُقَيِّح.

Septilateral, *a.* ذُو سَبْعَةِ ضُلُوعٍ.

Septuagenarian, *n.* اِبْنُ سَبْعِينَ سَنَةً.

Septuagenary, *a.* سَبْعُونَ.

Septuagesima, *n.* مُدَّةُ سَبْعِينَ يَوْمًا قَبْلَ ٱلْعِيدِ ٱلْكَبِيرِ.

Septuagesimal, *a.* سَبْعُونَ.

Septuagint, *n.* اَلتَّرْجَمَةُ ٱلسَّبْعِينِيَّةُ وَهِيَ ٱلتَّوْرِيَةُ ٱلَّتِي تَرْجَمَهَا سَبْعُونَ مُتَرْجِمًا مِنَ ٱللُّغَةِ ٱلْعِبْرَانِيَّةِ إِلَى ٱلْيُونَانِيَّةِ فِي عَهْدِ بَطْلِيمُوس مَلِكِ مِصْرَ.

Septum, *n.* فَاصِلَة.

Septuple, *a.* سَبْعَةُ أَضْعَافٍ.

Sepulchral, *a.* قَبْرِيٌّ – مَزَارِيٌّ. A — voice, صَوْتٌ كَأَنَّهُ طَالِعٌ مِنَ ٱلْقَبْرِ – صَوْتٌ أَبَحُّ. A — chamber or grotto, (called in Egypt, from the Coptic,) بَاب *pl.* بِيبَان.

Sepulchre, *n.* تُرْبَة – مَزَار – مَرْقَد – *pl.* أَجْدَاث *pl.* جَدَث – تُرَب *pl.* مَدَافِن *pl.* مَدْفِن – قَبْر *pl.* قُبُور. The holy —, قَبْرُ سَيِّدِنَا عِيسَى – اَلْقَبْرُ ٱلْأَقْدَس.

Sepulture, *n.* دَفْنَة – دَفْن. *See also* Burial, *n.*

Sequacious, *a.* مُعَقِّب ـ مُتَتَابِع ـ لاحِق.

Sequel, *n.* A succeeding part, عاقِبَة ـ عَقِيب ـ مُتابَعَة. A consequence inferred, نَتِيجَة. An event, end, حاصِل ـ صادِر ـ آخِر ـ عاقِبَة *pl.* عَواقِب. The consequence of an action, تَبِعَة ـ تِباعَة.

Sequence, *n.* Consecutiveness, تَتابُع ـ تَوالٍ ـ تَواتُر. A connected series, سِياقَة ـ سِلْك ـ سِلْسِلَة ـ تَسَلْسُل. *See also* Sequel, *n.*

Sequent, *a.* مُتَتابِع ـ مُعَقِّب ـ لاحِق.

Sequent, *n.* مُعاقِب ـ عَقِيب. An imitative sequent, of a word in a phrase, إِتْباع. The night and the day are two alternating sequents, اللَّيْلُ وَٱلنَّهارُ عَقِيبانِ.

Sequester, *v.t.* To separate from other, جَنَّبَ ـ مَيَّزَ ـ أَفْرَزَ ـ أَبْعَدَ عَن ـ عَزَلَ عَن ². To take possession, as of property, for debt, *etc.*, إِنْتَصَرَ مِنْ ـ وَقْتًا ـ = ضَبَطَ وَقْتًا ² ـ وَقَّفَ إِلَى وَقْتٍ. To — one's self, إِبْتَعَدَ ـ إِنْحَجَرَ ـ إِنْفَرَدَ.

Sequestered, *a.* Secluded, مُبْتَعِد ـ مُجْتَنِب ـ مُنْفَرِد. Lonely, of a place, مُسْتَوْحِش.

Sequestrable, *a.* مِمَّا يُضْبَطُ وَقْتًا ـ تَوْقِيفُهُ إِلَى وَقْتٍ مُمْكِنٌ ـ وَمِمَّا يُحْجَرُ عَلَيْهِ إِلَى وَقْتٍ.

Sequestrate, *v.t.* *See to* Sequester, *v.t.*

Sequestration, *n.* The act of setting apart, تَمْيِيز ـ عَزْل ـ إِفْراز. Self-sequestration, retirement, جَنْبَة ـ عُزْلَة ـ إِنْفِراد. Sequestration, as of goods, تَوْقِيفُ ٱلْمالِ إِلَى وَقْتٍ ـ ضَبْطُ ٱلْمالِ وَقْتًا ـ حَجْرٌ عَلَى ٱلْمالِ وَقْتًا.

Sequestrator, *n.* ضابِطُ ٱلْمالِ وَقْتًا ـ مُوَقِّفُ ٱلْمالِ إِلَى وَقْتٍ ـ حاجِرُ ٱلْمالِ وَقْتًا.

Sequin, *n.* Of Venice, بُنْدُقِيٌّ *pl.* بَنادِقَة; of the Levant, مَحْبُوب *pl.* مَحابِيب.

Seraglio, *n.* The palace of the Sultan, سَرايَةُ ٱلسُّلْطانِ. The harim, or females, of the palace, حَرَمُ ٱلسَّرايَةِ.

Seraph, *n.* مَلَكٌ مِنْ مَلائِكَةِ ٱلسَّرافِيمِ.

Seraphic, *a.* }
Seraphical, } مِنَ ٱلسَّرافِيمِ ـ مُتَعَلِّقٌ بِٱلسَّرافِيمِ.

Seraphim, *n. pl.* سَرافِيم.

Seraphine, *n.* ضَرْبٌ مِنَ ٱلْأَرْغُنِ صَغِيرٌ.

Seraskier, *n.* سَرْعَسْكَر.

Sere, *a.* *See* Sear, *a.*

Serenade, *n.* عَزِيف (*or* عَزْف) ٱلنَّوْبَةِ لَيْلًا.

Serenade, *v.t.* عَزَفَ لِ ـ ٱلنَّوْبَةَ لَيْلًا =.

Serenade, *v.i.* عَزَفَتِ ٱلنَّوْبَةُ لَيْلًا =.

Serene, *a.* Clear, of a day or sky, رائِق ـ صاحٍ ـ صافٍ ـ أَنْهَر: cloudless, صَحْو; a — day, يَوْمٌ صافٍ. Calm, quiet, undisturbed, مُطْمَئِنّ ـ ساكِن ـ هادٍ ـ مُرْتاح. Unruffled, ساكِن. Sedate, رَزِين ـ رَصِين. To be —, clear, أَصْحَى ـ صَحا ² ـ صَفا ²; to be —, quiet, undisturbed, إِطْمَأَنَّ ـ سَكَنَ ² ـ قَرَّ =; to be —, sedate, رَزُنَ ² ـ رَصُنَ ². Having a — countenance, طَلِقٌ ـ طَلِيقُ ٱلْوَجْهِ ـ طَلْقُ ٱلْوَجْهِ. His or her Serene Highness the ..., حَضْرَةُ جَنابِ ٱلْ... *See also* Calm, Clear, Placid, *a.*

Serenely, *ad.* Without being ruffled, بِطُمَأْنِينَةٍ ـ إِطْمِئْنانًا. Sedately, coolly, بِرَزانَةٍ ـ بِرَصانَةٍ.

Sereneness, *n.* }
Serenity, } Clearness, رَواق ـ صَحْو ـ صَفاء ـ صَفْو. Quietude, راحَة ـ هُدُوّ. The being unruffled, undisquieted, إِطْمِئْنان ـ طُمَأْنِينَة. Sedateness, رَصانَة ـ رَزانَة ـ وَقار. *See also* Clearness, Calmness, Placidness, *n.*

Serf, *n.* عَبْد *pl.* عَبِيد ـ مُسْتَعْبَد.

Serfdom, *n.* عُبُودِيَّة.

Serge, *n.* مِسْح.

Sergeancy, *n.* Of a soldier sergeant, رُتْبَةُ ٱلْقائِدِ عَلَى عَشَرَةٍ مِنَ ٱلْعَسْكَرِ ـ رُتْبَةُ ٱلْجاوِيشِ ـ رُتْبَةُ ٱلْأُونْ باشِي; of a sergeant-at-law, رُتْبَةُ أَشْرافِ ٱلْفُقَهاءِ.

Sergeant, *n.* Of a regiment, جاوِش ـ أُونْ باشِي ـ قائِدُ عَشَرَةٍ. A lawyer of high rank, مِنْ أَشْرافِ ٱلْفُقَهاءِ.

Sergeant-at-arms, *n.* جِلْواز *pl.* جَلاوِزَة.

Sergeantship, *n.* *See* Sergeancy, *n.*

Serial, *a.* نَسَقِيٌّ ـ مُتَعَلِّقٌ بِسِلْسِلَةٍ ـ مِنْ نَسَقٍ ـ مُسَلْسَل ـ سَرْد ـ مُتَسَرِّد.

Serial, *n.* أَجْزاءُ كِتابٍ (*or* تَأْلِيفٍ) يُطْبَعُ وَيُبْرَزُ (*or* يُنْشَرُ) مُتَتالِيَةً.

Seriatim, *ad.* In regular order, عَلَى سِياقَةٍ ـ سَرْدًا ـ بِسِلْسِلَةٍ ـ نَسَقًا.

Series, *n.* A connected order, طُرْقَة *pl.* طُرَق ـ سِماط ـ نَسَق ـ سِلْسِلَة *pl.* سَلاسِل ـ سِياقَة. A succession, sequence, تَتابُع ـ تَوالٍ ـ تَواتُر. To arrange in a —, نَسَّقَ ـ سَرَدَ ـ سَلْسَلَ ـ سَرَدَ ². Arranged in a —, مُنَسَّق ـ نَسِيق ـ مُسَلْسَل ـ مُتَسَرِّد.

Serio-comic, *a.* مِنْهُ جِدٌّ وَمِنْهُ هَزْلٌ.

Serious, *a.* Grave in manner, رَزِين ـ وَقُور ـ ساكِنُ ٱلطَّائِرِ. Important, كَبِير ـ مُهِمّ *pl.* مَهامّ ـ عَظِيم ـ ما هُمَّ بِهِ مِنْ أَمْرٍ. A — man, one who is earnest in his doings, رَجُلٌ ذُو هِمَّةٍ ـ رَجُلٌ هُمٌّ. In earnest, جِدِّيّ ـ جادّ ـ مُجِدّ. Dangerous, خَطِير; of a disease, ثَقِيل ـ مِعْزاز. Religious, مُتَدَيِّن ـ دَيِّن. Serious matters, مُهِمَّات. It is a — calamity, هُوَ مِنْ جَسِيمَاتِ ٱلْخُطُوبِ. Are you — in this? أَبِجِدٍّ مِنْكَ هٰذَا. Their fight is — and no joke, قِتَالُهُمْ جِدٌّ مَا هُوَ هَزْلٌ. He took the matter in a — manner, أَخَذَ ٱلشَّيْءَ عَلَى طَرِيقِ ٱلْجِدِّ. He became —, grave, وَقَعَ طَائِرُهُ aor. يَقَعُ. To be —, grave, رَزُنَ ² – تَوَقَّرَ – اِتَّقَرَ. To be —, in earnest, in, حَقَّقَ فِي – أَجَدَّ فِي – جَدَّ ² فِي. To be or to become —, difficult, dangerous, weighty, اِشْتَدَّ – ثَقُلَ ² – اِعْتَزَّ – عَزَّ ². To be or try to be —, sedate, تَرَزَّنَ – تَرَكَّنَ – تَوَقَّرَ. *See also* Grave, Important, *a.*

Seriously, *ad.* Gravely, بِرَزَانَةٍ – بِوَقَارٍ – بِهَيْبَةٍ. In earnest, مِنْ جِدٍّ – بِجِدٍّ. In an important degree, جِدًّا. Did you say this —? مِنْ جِدٍّ قُلْتَ هٰذَا. He was — injured, اِنْضَرَّ جِدًّا.

Seriousness, *n.* Gravity, as of behaviour, رَصَانَة – رَزَانَة – وَقَار – سَكِينَة. Importance, أَهَمِّيَّة – ضَرُورِيَّة – عَظَامَة – عِظَم – جَسَامَة. The being in earnest, جِدٌّ. Gravity, danger, as of a disease, *etc.*, خَطَر – اِعْتِزَاز – عِزَّة. Religiousness, تَعَبُّد – دِيَانَة – تَدَيُّن. It is a matter of great —, هُوَ مِنْ جِسَامِ ٱلْأُمُورِ.

Serjeant, *n.* *See* Sergeant, *n.*

Sermon, *n.* خُطْبَة *pl.* خُطَب – مَوْعِظَة – وَعْظ – كِرِيزَة – كَرْز. He preached a —, وَعَظَ مَوْعِظَةً *aor.* يَعِظُ – كَرَزَ كَرْزًا ².

Sermonize, *v.t.* To preach to, to exhort, وَعَظَ *aor.* يَعِظُ. To scold, وَبَّخَ – عَاتَبَ – عَتَبَ ² عَلَى.

Sermonizer, *n.* A preacher of sermons, خَطِيب – وَاعِظ – كَارُوز – كَارِز. A reprover, scolder, وَبَّاخ – مُعَاتِب.

Serosity, *n.* مَاوِيَّة – مَائِيَّة.

Serous, *a.* مَائِيّ – مَاوِيّ.

Serpent, *n.* حَيَّة *pl.* حَيَّات – ثُعْبَان *pl.* ثَعَابِين. A horned —, حَيَّة قَرْنَاء. The cast-off skin of a —, سَلْخُ ٱلْحَيَّةِ. A charmer of serpents, حَاوٍ; *vulg.* حَاوِي.

Serpentaria, *n.* } The plant, لُوف – لُوفُ ٱلْأَرْقَطِ – لُوفُ ٱلْجَعْدِيِّ – ٱلْحَيَّةِ.
Serpent's-tongue, }

Serpentarius and Serpens, *n.* The constellation, ٱلْحَوَّاءُ وَٱلْحَوِيَّةُ.

Serpentine, *a.* Winding, مُلْتَوٍ – مُتَلَوٍّ. Spiral, لَوْلَبِيّ. To have a — course, تَلَوَّى.

Serpentine, *n.* The stone, حَجَرُ ٱلْحَيَّةِ.

Serpentize, *v.i.* To wind like a serpent, لَظْلَظَ – تَقَوَّرَ – تَطَوَّى – تَحَوَّى.

Serpiginous, *a.* مُصَابٌ بِأُكَالٍ.

Serpigo, *n.* أُكَال.

Serrate, *a.* } مُسَنَّن – مِنْشَارِيّ – مُؤَشَّر.
Serrated, }

Serrature, *n.* تَسْنِين – سِنَّة – تَحْزِيز.

Serum, *n.* Of milk, مَاءُ ٱلْجُبْنِ – مَصَالَة – مَصْل. The — of blood, صَدِيد. Watery fluid, مَاء. Serum from a corpse, غَيْنَة – مُهَالَة – مُهْل.

Servant, *n.* In a general sense, one who serves, خَادِم *pl.* خَدَم *and* خُدَّام *and* خَدَمَة *and vulg.* خُدْمَان – خُدَّام *pl.* خَدَم; *vulg.* خُدْمَان. A useful servant, either male or female, وَصِيف *pl.* وُصَفَاء; (besides the foregoing, the word خِدْمَتْكَار *pl.* خِدْمَتْكَارِيَّة is used vulgarly to denote a domestic servant.) Servant, in the sense of a worshipper, عَبْد *pl.* عِبَاد *and* عَبَدَة; *e.g.* the servant of God, عَبْدُ ٱللّٰهِ. The sovereign of the people is their —, or minister, (a saying attributed to Muhammad,) سَيِّدُ ٱلْقَوْمِ خَادِمُهُمْ. Fellow-servant, خَادِم رَفِيق *pl.* خُدَّام رُفَقَاء; his —, ٱلْخَادِمُ رَفِيقُهُ. Hired servant, أَجِير *pl.* أُجَرَاء.

Woman-servant, خَادِمَة *pl.* خَادِمَات – خَدَّامَة – جَارِيَة *pl.* جَوَارٍ.

Servant-boy, صَبِيّ *pl.* صُبْيَان – غُلَام *pl.* غِلْمَان.

Serve, *v.t.* To attend upon as a servant, also to minister to, خَدَمَ ². To worship, obey, عَبَدَ ². To be useful to, to serve one's purpose, صَلَحَ ² لِ – نَفَعَ ² لِ. To do one a good turn, أَصَابَ بِخَيْرٍ – عَمِلَ مَعَ مَعْرُوفًا – مَنَّ ² عَلَى – نَفَعَ ² – أَفَادَ. To treat, to behave towards, عَامَلَ – صَنَعَ ² بِ. To be in the service of, خَدَمَ ² عِنْدَ فُلَانٍ. To be in the suite of, كَانَ مِنْ تُبَّاعِ فُلَانٍ. To — one in the place of something else, قَامَ لِ مَقَامَ كَذَا *aor.* يَقُومُ. To — one's self, اِخْتَدَمَ. To ask one to —, اِسْتَخْدَمَ. He served for his food, خَدَمَ ² بِطَعَامِ بَطْنِهِ. He served him a dirty action, صَنَعَ ² بِهِ قَبَاحَةً. She left him to — alone, تَرَكَتْهُ ² يَخْدُمُ وَحْدَهُ.

To serve as an example to, كَانَ عِبْرَةً لِ.

To serve one right, أَصَابَهُ مَا ٱسْتَحَقَّ – أَكَلَ ² مَا ٱسْتَحَقَّ.

To serve out, to distribute, وَزَّعَ – قَسَّمَ عَلَى – فَرَّقَ عَلَى. To requite, جَزَى ² – عَوَّضَ; by way of revenge, اِنْتَقَمَ مِنْهُ.

To serve up, as meats on a table, جَعَلَ ٱلطَّعَامَ عَلَى ٱلسُّفْرَةِ ².

Let them serve up, فَلْيَسْكُبُوا – فَلْيَرُصُّوا ٱلسُّفْرَةَ.

Serve, *v.i.* To be in service, كَانَ فِي خِدْمَةٍ – أَنْصَفَ – نَصَفَ ². To suit, صَلَحَ ² – كَانَ خَادِمًا – فُلَانٍ.

Servia, *n.* The country, بِلَادُ ٱلصِّرْبِ – ٱلصِّرْبُ.

Service, *n.* Occupation of a servant, ministry, attendance upon another, خِدْمَة. The state of a servant, خَادِمِيَّة. Worship,

عِبَادَة. Use, profit, طَائِل — فَائِدَة — مَنْفَعَة. Obedience, اِنْقِيَاد — طَاعَة — إِطَاعَة. Good offices, مَعْرُوف — خَيْر — جُود — جَمِيل. A set of vessels for a table, طَائِفَة مِنَ ٱلْأَوَانِي لِلسُّفْرَة — طَاقِم سُفْرَة (or طَقْم). A religious —, صَلَوَات — خِدْمَةُ ٱلصَّلٰوة. Military —, خِدْمَة عَسْكَرِيَّة. Naval —, خِدْمَة بَحْرِيَّة. Civil —, خِدْمَة قَلَمِيَّة — خِدْمَة سِيَاسِيَّة. All this is at your —, هٰذَا كُلُّهُ فِي خِدْمَتِكَ — هٰذَا كُلُّهُ قُدَّامَكَ. The many and eminent services, ٱلْخِدَمُ ٱلْوَافِرَةُ ٱلْجَلِيلَة. He has rendered the government many profitable services, from which it has reaped many advantages, أَفَادَ ٱلدَّوْلَةَ فَوَائِدَ جَمَّةً فَعَادَتْ إِلَيْهَا مِنْهَا فَوَائِدُ عَامَّةٌ. There is no further need for his military services, لَمْ يَبْقَ لُزُومٌ لِخِدْمَتِهِ ٱلْعَسْكَرِيَّةِ. He offered his services to him, عَرَضَ عَلَيْهِ خِدْمَتَهُ. *See also under to* Serve, *v.t.*, *and* Kindness, Favour, *n.*

Serviceable, *a.* Fit for service, of a servant, وَصِيف *pl.* وُصَفَاء; of a person, in general, طَائِل — نَفُوع — نَفَّاع. Useful, profitable, نَافِع — مُفِيد. Serviceable for, meeting the case or want, يَسُدُّ مَسَدَّ كَذَا.

Serviceableness, *n.* Utility, طَائِل — فَائِدَة — إِفَادَة — مَصْلَحَة — عَائِدَة — مَنْفَعَة.

Serviceably, *ad.* بِإِفَادَة — بِطَائِل — إِفَادَةً.

Servile, *a.* Low bred, low caste, دَنِيء — خَسِيس. Such as pertains to a slave, رِقِّيّ; to a servant, مُتَعَلِّق بِخَادِم. Mean, cringing, مُتَضَعْضِع — مُتَذَلِّل — ذَلِيل — حَقِير. A — imitator, أَسِيرُ ٱلتَّقْلِيد. A — letter, حَرْف زَائِد. Of low descent, or descended from slaves, سَاقِطُ بْنُ مَاقِطِ بْنِ لَاقِط.

Servilely, *ad.* تَذَلُّلًا — بِدَنَاءَة — بِحَقَارَة — بِمُطَاوَعَة — بِتَضَعْضُع.

Servileness, *n.* } Servility, } Close imitation, مُتَابَعَة — تَقْلِيد. Mean submission, تَضَعْضُع — مُطَاوَعَة — تَذَلُّل — دَنَاءَة — حَقَارَة.

Servitor, *n.* A servant, خَادِم *pl.* خُدَّام. A follower, تَابِع *pl.* تُبَّاع. A — of a college, تِلْمِيذ فَقِير مَعَاشُهُ مِنَ ٱلْمَدْرَسَة.

Servitude, *n.* The condition of a slave, رِقَّة — عُبُودِيَّة — عُبُودَة; of a servant, خَادِمِيَّة.

Sesame, *n.* } Sesamum, } خَرْفَى — جُلْجُلَان — سِمْسِم. Flour of —, طَحِينَة. Oil of —, حَلّ — سَلِيط — شِيرَاج — شِيرَج — سِيرَج. A seller of —, سَمَّاس.

Sess, *n.* *See* Rate, Tax, *n.*

Sessile, *a.* Of a plant, مَا ٱرْتَصَعَ بِسَاقِ ٱلنَّبَات.

Session, *n.* A sitting, قَعْدَة — قِعْدَة — جِلْسَة. A —, as of an assembly, مَجْلِس *pl.* مَجَالِس; the period of a —, قِعْدَة — مُدَّةُ ٱلْمَجْلِسِ. The opening of a —, اِفْتِتَاحُ (or بَدْء) مَجْلِسٍ; closing of a —, خِتَامُ مَجْلِسٍ. A — of parliament, مُدَّةُ جُلُوسِ مَجْلِسِ ٱلشُّورَى. Sessions, of tribunals, مَوَاسِمُ مَجَالِسِ ٱلْمَحَاكِمِ.

Sessional, *a.* مَا نِيطَ بِٱلْمَجَالِسِ — مُتَعَلِّق بِمَوَاسِمِ ٱلْمَجَالِسِ.

Sess-pool, *n.* بَلُّوعَة.

Set, *v.t.* To place, put, جَعَلَ — وَضَعَ *aor.* يَضَعُ — حَطَّ. To fix, قَرَّرَ — رَكَزَ. To place, seat, قَعَّدَ — أَجْلَسَ. To plant, set up, صَمَدَ — نَصَبَ — أَقَامَ. To appoint, عَيَّنَ. To whet, sharpen, شَحَذَ — حَدَّدَ — سَنَّ — سَنَّنَ. To put to the time, as a watch, ضَبَطَ — عَدَّلَ. To lay, as a snare for, *etc.*, أَنْصَبَ ل. To set, as a hen to brood, أَحْضَنَ ٱلدَّجَاجَةَ ٱلْبَيْضَ. To set, as a stone in a ring, *etc.*, فَصَّصَ — نَضَّدَ — رَصَّعَ — رَكَّبَ. To restore, as a bone, جَبَّرَ — جَبَرَ — أَجْبَرَ. He set the stone in the signet-ring, رَكَّبَ ٱلْفَصَّ فِي ٱلْخَاتَمِ. To be hard set, تَضَايَقَ بِ-ٱلْحَالُ — حَصِرَ — كَانَ فِي ضَنْكٍ. To be badly —, of a bow, *etc.*, عَشَمَ.

To set one about, as to work, أَشْغَلَ-بِ — شَغَلَ-بِ — أَمْسَكَ-ٱلْأَمْرَ.

To set against, to place against, جَعَلَ-عِنْدَ كَذَا. To set in opposition to, جَعَلَ-مُخَالِفًا ل — حَرَّضَ-عَلَى — كَرَّهَ-إِلَى — قَوَّمَ-عَلَى. To put in contrast with, قَابَلَ-بِ — قَاوَمَ-بِ. To balance against, وَازَنَ-بِ.

To set a mark upon, جَعَلَ عَلَامَةً عَلَى.

To set a-going, to make to proceed, progress, رَوَّجَ — مَشَّى. To make to begin, to institute, أَبْدَعَ — أَحْدَثَ — أَوْجَدَ — أَقَامَ — أَنْشَأَ.

To set an example, كَانَ قُدْوَةً — أَظْهَرَ قُدْوَةً. To set a good example, أَظْهَرَ قُدْوَةً حَسَنَةً. To set a bad example, أَعْطَى قُدْوَةً رَدِيَّةً.

To set apart, as from others, to separate, أَفْرَزَ — مَيَّزَ. To set at one side, جَنَبَ — جَنَّبَ. To set apart, as for some special purpose, خَصَّصَ. To repel, دَفَعَ.

To set a price upon, اِسْتَقَامَ — سَعَّرَ — أَسْعَرَ. To set a price upon one's head, وَضَعَ عَلَيْهِ *aor.* يَضَعُ.

To set aside, apart from others, أَفْرَزَ — مَيَّزَ. To lay up, to save, خَلَّى — تَقَنَّى — أَبْقَى. To give up, to abandon, تَرَكَ — سَيَّبَ.

To set at ease, as in company, هَوَّنَ عَلَى — فَضَّى-مِنَ ٱلتَّكْلِيفِ. To give rest to, أَرَاحَ — رَيَّحَ. To give confidence to, أَقَرَّ — أَزَالَ عَنِ-ٱلِٱضْطِرَاب — أَقَرَّ عَيْنَهُ.

To set at naught, to despise, اِزْدَرَى بِ — اِزْدَرَى — اِسْتَحْقَرَ — أَهَانَ — اِسْتَقَلَّ.

To set at rest, to appease, quiet, سَكَّنَ ـ هَدَّأَ. To decide, قَطَعَ ـ أَنْهَى ـ فَصَلَ ـ بَتَّ [2].

To set at work, أَشْغَلَ ـ شَغَّلَ.

To set a watch, guard, أَقَامَ حُرَّاسًا.

To set badly, unevenly, of a fracture, عَثَمَ ٱلْكَسْرَةَ.

To set before, to prefer, إِسْتَحَبَّ-عَلَى ـ فَضَّلَ-عَلَى. To show to, فَرَّجَ-عَلَى ـ أَرْأَى ; *vulg.* وَرَّى. To lay before or submit to, قَدَّمَ-لِ ـ عَرَضَ-لِ.

To set by, on one side, أَجْنَبَ ـ جَنَّبَ ـ جَانَبَ.

To set down, as on the ground, حَطَّ [2] ـ يَضَعُ *aor.* وَضَعَ ; as a passenger from a carriage, نَزَّلَ. To write down, دَوَّنَ ـ قَيَّدَ ـ كَتَبَ [2]. To reckon, estimate, عَدَّ [2] ـ أَعَدَّ ـ حَسِبَ ـ إِعْتَبَرَ-ٱعْتِبَارَ ـ نَزَّلَ-مَنْزِلَةَ كَذَا. To set one down for or as, قَدَّرَ كَذَا. To reduce to silence, as by an argument, *etc.*, رَمَى-بِسُكَاتَةٍ.

To set eyes on, رَأَى *aor.* يَرَى ـ أَبْصَرَ ـ شَافَ [2].

To set forth, to mention, ذَكَرَ [2]. To expound, أَشْرَحَ ـ بَيَّنَ. To exhibit, عَرَضَ ـ أَرْأَى ; *vulg.* وَرَّى. As set forth in their books, كَمَا هُوَ مُدَوَّنٌ فِي كُتُبِهِمْ.

To set forward, as on a journey, سَيَّرَ. To advance, قَدَّمَ. To make current, to expedite, قَدَّمَ ـ رَوَّجَ.

To set free, to liberate, سَيَّبَ ـ أَطْلَقَ ـ أَعْتَقَ. To suffer to escape, أَفْلَتَ. To save, أَنْقَذَ ـ خَلَّصَ ـ حَفَرَ [2].

To set in order, نَظَّمَ ـ رَتَّبَ ـ نَسَّقَ.

To set off, to embellish, حَبَّرَ ـ جَمَّلَ ـ زَيَّنَ ـ زَخْرَفَ ـ شَبَّ [2]. To compensate, balance, وَازَنَ ـ قَابَلَ ـ سَدَّ [2] مَسَدَّ كَذَا. It sets off the face, يَشُبُّ ٱلْوَجْهَ. It sets off her colour, يَشُبُّ لَوْنَهَا.

To set on, to impel, إِسْتَفَزَّ ـ يَسُوقُ *aor.* سَاقَ ـ حَرَّضَ ـ أَنْهَضَ. They are set on mischief, تَعَزَّمُوا عَلَى ٱلشَّرِّ.

To set on edge, of the teeth, أَضْرَسَ. To place on edge, وَضَعَ-عَلَى حَرْفِهِ *aor.* يَضَعُ.

To set on end, قَيَّمَ-عَلَى حَدِّهِ ـ نَصَبَ-عَلَى طَرَفِهِ [2].

To set on fire, أَضْرَمَ ـ أَحْرَقَ-بِٱلنَّارِ.

To set one's face against, to oppose, جَعَلَ ـ ثَبَّتَ وَجْهَهُ عَلَى ـ خَالَفَ ـ ضَادَّ ـ وَجْهَهُ عَلَى.

To set one's heart upon, وَضَعَ عَلَى-قَلْبًا *aor.* يَضَعُ.

To set one's wits to work upon, شَغَّلَ بَالَهُ فِي ـ تَفَكَّرَ فِي.

To set out, to delineate, رَسَمَ [2]. To expound, أَشْرَحَ ـ بَيَّنَ. To exhibit, عَرَضَ ـ أَرْأَى ; *vulg.* وَرَّى.

To set over, appoint over, عَيَّنَ-عَلَى ـ وَجَّهَ-إِلَى ـ أَقَامَ-عَلَى ; as over a province, وَلَّى ; as a watch, guard, أَوْقَفَ-عَلَى.

To set right, to put into a right position, عَدَّلَ. To correct, أَصْلَحَ ـ صَحَّحَ.

To set or hoist sail, أَشْرَعَ ـ أَقْلَعَ.

To set to music, كَتَبَ-بِٱلْمُوسِيقَى ـ رَتَّبَ-عَلَى أَلْحَانٍ.

To set together by the ears, إِنْتَشَنَهُمْ ـ رَمَى بَيْنَهُمُ ٱلْمُشَاجَرَةَ ـ رَمَى بَيْنَهُمُ ٱلْمُنَازَعَةَ.

To set to work. *See above* To set at work.

To set up, upraise, نَصَبَ [2] ـ قَيَّمَ ـ أَقَامَ ـ رَفَعَ ـ صَمَدَ [2]. To found, originate, أَسَّسَ ـ أَنْشَأَ ـ أَوْجَدَ ـ أَحْدَثَ. To set up, as in business, رَتَّبَ لِ-صَنْعَةً (*or* شُغْلًا). To provide with necessaries, أَمَدَّ-بِمَا ٱحْتَاجَ إِلَيْهِ ـ جَهَّزَ-بِٱللَّوَازِمِ. To set up in evidence, إِحْتَجَّ بِ. To set up a case against, أَقَامَ عَلَى-ٱلْحُجَّةَ.

To set up a cry, صَرَخَ صَرْخَةً [2] ـ صَاحَ صَيْحَةً. To set up types, رَكَّبَ ٱلْحُرُوفَ ـ رَتَّبَ ٱلْحُرُوفَ. To set one's self up to be, تَظَاهَرَ بِ.

To set upon, أَحَالَ عَلَى ـ هَجَمَ عَلَى [2] : He set upon him with the whip, أَحَالَ عَلَيْهِ بِٱلسَّوْطِ. To set dogs upon, أَغْرَى ٱلْكِلَابَ عَلَى.

Set, *v.i.* To become fixed, or congealed, as mortar, *etc.*, عَقَدَ [2] ـ جَمَدَ [2]. To —, as the sun, غَرَبَتْ [2] ـ غَابَتْ ; as a star, سَقَطَ [2] ـ غَمَسَ. To have a certain direction, تَوَجَّهَ إِلَى ـ تَصَوَّبَ إِلَى ـ مَالَ إِلَى. The sun was about to set, شَفَرَتِ ٱلشَّمْسُ لِلْغُرُوبِ.

To set about, take in hand, تَشَمَّرَ لِ ـ شَرَعَ فِي ـ أَلْقَى يَدَهُ فِي.

To set forward, as on a journey, سَافَرَ ـ ذَهَبَ ـ سَارَ.

To set in, as a tide, مَدَّ [2] ; as a season, دَخَلَ [2] ـ سَقَطَ [2] : The heat set in, سَقَطَ ٱلْحَرُّ [2].

To set out, as for a place, قَصَدَ إِلَى ـ عَمِدَ إِلَى [2] *or* لِ.

To set to, to take in hand, with diligence, لَازَمَ ـ أَدْمَنَ عَلَى ـ مَارَسَ.

To set up, as a shop, فَتَحَ دُكَّانًا. To set up as a medical man, تَعَطَّى (*or* تَعَاطَى) ٱلطِّبَّ.

Set, *a.* and *part.* Placed, مَحْطُوطٌ ـ مَوْضُوعٌ. Set up, upright, مَنْصُوبٌ ـ مُقِيمٌ ـ مَصْمُودٌ. Set, fixed, مَرْكُوزٌ. Set, fixed, as mortar, مُجَمَّدٌ ـ مُنْعَقِدٌ. Arranged, symmetrical, مُنَسَّقٌ ـ مُنَظَّمٌ ـ مُرَتَّبٌ. Set, as in array, مُصَفَّفٌ. Appointed, established, مُقَرَّرٌ ـ مُعَيَّنٌ. Set, as jewels, مُرَصَّعٌ. Set, as a bone, مَجْبُورٌ. A set day, يَوْمٌ مُعَيَّنٌ. Set hours, سَاعَاتٌ مُعَيَّنَةٌ. Set phrases, كَلَامٌ مُصَرَّحٌ. Set forms of prayer, صَلَاةٌ مُرَتَّبَةٌ. His name was much set by, تَوَفَّرَ ٱسْمُهُ جِدًّا.

Set, *n.* A suite, service, as of china, *etc.*, طَقْم ـ طاقِم ـ طائفة ; as of clothes, or of cards, دَسْت *pl.* دُسُوت . A party, زُمْرَة ـ حِزْب *pl.* أَحْزاب ـ طائفة *pl.* طَوائِف ـ مَعْشَر *pl.* مَعاشِر . A jolly set, حابُور . A collection, طَقْم ـ عِدَّة ـ مَجْمَع . An assortment, بابٌ (or طائفة) . A row, صَفٌّ *pl.* صُفُوف . A set of writers, جُمْلَة مِنَ ٱلْكَتَبَة . A set of diamonds, زِينَة مِنَ ٱلْماسِ . A set or setting, as of the sun, غُرُوب ـ غُيُوب . A set, direction, as of a current, جِهَة جَرَيان ـ مَيَلان ـ تَوَجُّه ـ تَصَوُّب . A tea-set, طَقْم (or طائفة أَوانِي) لِلشّاي . Dead-set, as of a current, بَطْشَة ـ طَيّارَة ـ شِدَّة جَرَيانٍ ـ تَصَوُّب شَدِيد ; as of an attack, إِشْتِدَاد هُجُوم شَدِيد ـ سَعْي شَدِيد . To make a dead-set against, بَطَش بِ ـ شَدَّ عَلَى ـ فِي ٱلْهُجُوم عَلَى .

Setaceous, *a.* *See* Bristly, *a.*

Set-down, *n.* An argument which reduces to silence, مُسْكِتَة .

Setiferous, *a.* مُرَبِّي ٱلْهُلْبِ .

Set-off, *n.* A decoration, زُخْرُف ـ زِينَة ـ شَبُوب ـ شِباب ـ حِلْيَة ـ تَزْوِيقَة . Anything which serves as an equivalent, مُقابَلَة . It is a — to her face, هُوَ شَبُوبٌ لِوَجْهِها .

Seton, *n.* خَلَل . To apply a —, خَلَّ .

Setose, *a.* } *See* Bristly, *a.*
Setous, }

Settee, *n.* دِيوان ـ سِدِلَّة .

Setter, *n.* One who sets, places, حاطٌّ ـ واضِع ـ جاعِل . A — dog, كَلْبُ صَيْدٍ ـ ضِرآء *pl.* ضارٍ . A setter-on; *see* Instigator, *n.*

Setting, *n.* The act of placing, حَطٌّ ـ وَضْع ـ جَعْل . A falling below the horizon, of the sun, غُرُوب ـ غِياب . Chasing, as of a gem, تَرْصِيع . A hardening, as of cement, جُمُود ـ جَمْد ـ عَقْد .

Settle, *n.* مَرْتَبَة ـ صُفَّة .

Settle, *v.t.* To fix firmly, ضَبَطَ ـ أَحْكَمَ . To establish, make certain, قَرَّرَ ـ أَكَّدَ ـ ثَبَّتَ ـ حَقَّقَ . To arrange, رَتَّبَ ـ نَسَّقَ ـ نَظَّمَ . To marry, زَوَّجَ . To decide, as a question, بَتَّ ـ قَطَعَ ـ فَصَلَ ـ أَجْمَعَ عَلَى . To arrange, as a dispute, أَصْلَحَ ـ أَسْدَى ; to — a dispute between, لَأَمَ بَيْنَ ـ رَتَقَ بَيْنَ . To — a matter quickly, out of hand, تَنَجَّزَ (or تَنَضَّضَ) الحاجَةَ . To calm, appease, سَكَّنَ ـ أَهْدَأَ . To —, to cause to dwell in a place, أَحَلَّ ـ أَعْمَرَ ـ عَمَّرَ ـ إِسْتَعْمَرَ فِي ـ أَسْكَنَ . To colonize, إِسْتَوْطَنَ . To supply with the means of subsistence, رَزَقَ . To — accounts, سَدَّ ٱلْحِسابات . To pay, as of a debt, أَوْفَى . To cause to deposit, of liquids, أَرْسَبَ ـ رَسَّبَ . To make close or compact, كَبَسَ ـ أَشَدَّ ـ رَصَّ ـ رَصَّصَ . To confirm or ratify, as a bargain, treaty, *etc.*, عَقَدَ ـ عَقَّدَ . To be settled in a place, أَقامَ فِي ـ سَكَنَ . They settled or agreed upon, إِصْطَلَحُوا عَلَى كَذا .

To settle into, to become, آلَ إِلَى *aor.* يَؤُولُ ـ حَصَلَ ـ أَصْبَحَ ـ صارَ ـ عادَ إِلَى .

To settle upon, to appoint to, as of money, *etc.*, رَتَّبَ لِ ـ وَظَّفَ لِ ـ عَيَّنَ لِ . To settle a dowry upon, مَهَرَ ـ أَمْهَرَ . *See also to* Endow, *v.t.*

To settle with, to conclude one's business with, تَفَرَّغَ مِن : After he had settled with the islands, بَعْدَ ما تَفَرَّغَ مِنَ ٱلْجَزائِرِ .

Settle, *v.i.* To fall to the bottom, as lees, رَسَبَ ـ رَسُبَ ـ تَرَسَّبَ . To fix one's habitation, سَكَنَ ـ أَقامَ فِي ـ بَلَدَ . To marry, تَزَوَّجَ . To become fixed after fluctuation, ثَوَى فِي ـ سَكَنَ ـ هَدَأَ ـ قَرَّ ـ تَرَكَّنَ . To become calm, as in mind, تَرَكَّنَ ; of the weather, رَاقَ ـ تَرَوَّقَ ـ صَحَتِ ٱلدُّنْيا . To become compact, إِسْتَحْكَمَ ـ إِحْتَكَمَ ـ إِرْتَصَّ . To — down, to become fixed, established, إِرْتَكَزَ ـ إِسْتَحْكَمَ ـ تَمَكَّنَ . To — upon, as a bird on a branch, جَثَمَ عَلَى ـ وَقَعَ عَلَى *aor.* يَقَعُ .

Settled, *a.* Agreed upon, مُنْعَقِد ـ مَعْهُود . Appointed, arranged, مُرَتَّب ـ مُعَيَّن . Decided upon, مَفْصُول ـ مَحْكُوم بِهِ . Calm, of weather, رائِق ; of the mind, رَزِين ـ رَكِين ـ مُقَرَّر ـ مُطْمَئِنّ . Compact, مُرْتَصّ . Settled in life, having means of subsistence, مَرْزُوق . A — matter, أَمْر مَجْزُوم . Settled times, أَوْقات راهِنَة .

Settlement, *n.* The act of fixing firmly, ضَبْط ـ إِحْكام ; the being so fixed, إِنْضِباط ـ تَحَكُّم . The act of establishing, confirming, تَقْرِير ـ إِثْبات ـ تَأْكِيد ـ تَحْقِيق ; the being so established, رُسُوخ ـ ثَبات ـ قَرار . Reconstruction, rehabilitation, إِسْتِتْباب . The act of deciding, as a question, بَتّ ـ جَزْم ـ قَطْع ـ فَصْل ـ إِثْبات ; the being so decided, إِنْفِصال . The act of settling, as of a dispute, تَسْوِيَة ـ فَصْل ـ حُكْم ـ مُساواة ـ مُلاءَمَة ـ مُخالَصَة ـ إِصْلاح ـ إِسْداء ; the being so settled, صُلْح . The act of colonizing, تَعْمِير بِلادٍ ; the being colonized, عِمارَة بِلادٍ . Settlement of accounts, سَدّ حِسابات . The —, adjustment of previous accounts, تَسْوِيَة ٱلْحِسابات ٱلسّابِقَة . We have no doubt that an arrangement will be arrived at for the — of this question, لا شَكَّ عِنْدَنا أَنْ سَيَحْصُلَ ٱتِّفاق عَلَى تَسْوِيَة هٰذِهِ ٱلْمَسْأَلَة . Payment, as of debt, أَداء ـ إِيفاء ـ وَفاء . Subsidence, as of liquids, رُسُوب ـ ثُقْل ـ رُسابَة . An allowance, as of money, وَظِيفَة ـ راتِب ـ مُرَتَّب ـ عُلُوفَة . A dower, مَهْر .

A taking of accounts, liquidation, مُحَاسَبَة. A place of abode, domicile, مَسْكَن. Subsidence, as of a building, اِرْتِصَاص. A marriage —, مَهْر. The act of — or of succession to the throne, قَانُونُ ٱنْتِقَالِ ٱلْحُكُومَةِ. To make a — on, as on an island or continent, جَعَلَ عِمَارَةً فِي ² ـ عَمَرَ بِ ـ نَزَلَ بِ ـ ² سَكَنَ.

Settler, *n.* As in a new country, مُسْتَوْطِنٌ فِي بِلَادٍ جَدِيدَةٍ. A complete answer, reducing to silence, جَوَابٌ قَاطِعٌ ـ سَكَاتَة: He gave him a —, رَمَاهُ بِسُكَاتَةٍ.

Settling, *n.* As of accounts, حِسَاب ـ مُحَاسَبَة. Settling day, يَوْمُ مُحَاسَبَةٍ.

Settlings, *n.* Lees, رُسَابَة ـ رُسُوب ـ ثُفْل.

Set-to, *n.* A close conflict, مُضَارَبَةٌ عَلَى سَاقٍ ـ مَلْحَمَة.

Seven, *a.* and *n.* سَبْعَة *fem.* سَبْع. Seven men, سَبْعَةُ رِجَالٍ; seven women, سَبْعُ نِسْوَةٍ. The — sections of the Kurân, أَسْبَاعُ ٱلْقُرْآنِ. To divide into — parts, سَبَّعَ. To make —, أَسْبَعَ ـ سَبَّعَ. To become —, أَسْبَعَ.

Seven-fold, *a.* سَبْعُ كَرَّاتٍ ـ سَبْعُ مَرَّاتٍ ـ سَبْعَةُ أَضْعَافٍ. To make —, سَبَّعَ. He shall restore —, يَرُدُّ سَبْعَةَ أَضْعَافٍ.

Seven-night, *n.* أُسْبُوع ـ سُبُوع.

Seventeen, *a.* سَبْعَةَ عَشَرَ *fem.* سَبْعَ عَشْرَةَ.

Seventeenth, *a.* السَّابِعَ عَشَرَ *fem.* السَّابِعَةَ عَشْرَةَ.

Seventh, *a.* سَابِع *fem.* سَابِعَة. The — day, الأُسْبُوعُ. In the — year, فِي ٱلسَّنَةِ ٱلسَّابِعَةِ. To be or to become the —, سَبَعَ ² ـ ². This is the — (one) of this, هٰذَا سَبِيعُ هٰذَا.

Seventh, *n.* A seventh part, سُبْع ـ سَبِيع *pl.* أَسْبَاع.

Seventhly, *ad.* سَابِعًا.

Seventieth, *a.* السَّبْعُونَ.

Seventy, *a.* and *n.* سَبْعُونَ. Seventy times seven times, سَبْعُونَ مَرَّةً سَبْعَ مَرَّاتٍ.

Sever, *v.t.* بَتَكَ ² ـ بَتَلَ ² ـ بَتَّلَ ـ صَرَمَ ـ صَرَّمَ ـ جَزَمَ ـ جَذَرَ ². To be severed, اِنْصَرَمَ ـ تَصَرَّمَ ـ اِنْبَتَلَ ـ اِنْبَتَكَ ـ اِنْجَذَرَ. To be severed from, اِنْقَطَعَ عَنْ. "And would ye sever the ties of relationship?" وَتُقَطِّعُوا أَرْحَامَكُمْ (Kûr. v. 24).

Several, *a.* Separate, مُتَفَرِّد. Many, شَتَّى. Some, جُمْلَة ـ بَعْض ـ عِدَّة. Different, distinct, مُتَبَايِن ـ مُمْتَاز. Each — gate, كُلُّ وَاحِدٍ مِنَ ٱلأَبْوَابِ. Each — one according to his ability, كُلُّ وَاحِدٍ عَلَى قَدْرِ طَاقَتِهِ. Several people, بَعْضُ أُنَاسٍ. In — respects, عَنْ عِدَّةِ أَوْجُهٍ.

Several, *n.* Each particular or one, بَعْض *pl.* أَبْعَاض ـ أَحَد.

Severally, *ad.* كُلُّ وَاحِدٍ بِمُفْرَدِهِ ـ فَرْدًا فَرْدًا. He divided it to each one —, قَسَمَهُ لِكُلِّ وَاحِدٍ بِمُفْرَدِهِ. Jointly and —, إِجْمَالًا وَإِفْرَادًا.

Severalty, *n.* اِنْفِرَاد.

Severance, *n.* The act of, جَذْر ـ جَذْم ـ صَرْم ـ تَصْرِيم ـ تَفْصِيل ـ تَفْرِيق.

Severe, *a.* As denoting a high degree, قَوِيٌّ ـ شَدِيد. Harsh, cruel, فَظٌّ ـ قَاسٍ ـ عَنِيف ـ غَلِيظ ـ جَافٍ ـ قَاسٍ. Austere, قَاسٍ. Difficult, صَعْب ـ عَزِيز. Boisterous, rough, as of weather, مُقْشَعِرّ. Without gentleness, rough, عَسِير ـ عَسِر: A — or ill-natured man, رَجُلٌ عَسِرٌ. A — pain, وَجَعٌ أَلِيمٌ. A — cold, in the head, رَشْحٌ شَدِيدٌ. The — proceedings of the government, جَوْرُ أَعْمَالِ ٱلدَّوْلَةِ. *See also* Harsh, Rough, *a.*

Severely, *ad.* To a great extent, كَثِيرًا ـ لِلْغَايَةِ ـ جِدًّا. Harshly, بِفَظَاظَةٍ ـ بِغِلَاظَةٍ. Austerely, عَنْفًا ـ بِعَنْفٍ ـ بِجَفَاءٍ. To treat —, harshly, قَاسَرَ ـ ضَايَقَ ـ عَاسَرَ ـ عَنُفَ عَلَى or بِ ـ أَعْنَفَ.

Severeness, *n.* } High degree, قُوَّة ـ شِدَّة. Harshness, cruelty, Severity, } عُنْف ـ عَنْف ـ قَسَاوَة ـ فَظَاظَة. Austerity, غِلَاظَة ـ جَفَاء. Excessive strictness, straitness, ضِيق ـ مُضَايَقَة. Want of gentleness, عُسْر ـ عَسْر ـ عَدَمُ مُلَاطَفَةٍ. Want of indulgence, rigour, عَدَمُ مُسَاهَلَةٍ.

Sew, *v.t.* خَاطَ *aor.* يَخِيطُ ـ خَيَّطَ. To — up, لَفَقَ ـ لَفَّقَ.

Sewage, *n.* The filth of sewers, أَوْسَاخُ ٱلْبَوَالِيعِ.

Sewer, *n.* One who sews, خَيَّاط *pl.* خَيَّاطَة; *fem.* خَيَّاطَة *pl.* خَيَّاطَات.

Sewer, *n.* بَالُوعَة *pl.* بَوَالِيع ـ بَلُّوعَة or بَلَّاعَة *pl.* بَلَالِيع.

Sewerage, *n.* The discharging of water by sewers, اِنْصِبَابُ ٱلْبَلَالِيعِ. Making sewers, تَرْكِيبُ ٱلْبَلَالِيعِ.

Sewing, *n.* خِيَاطَة.

Sex, *n.* جِنْس *pl.* أَجْنَاس. The male —, الْجِنْسُ ٱلْمُذَكَّرُ; the female —, الْجِنْسُ ٱلْمُؤَنَّثُ. The fair —, مَعْشَرُ ٱلنِّسَاءِ ـ السِّتَّاتُ ـ الحَرِيمُ.

Sexagenarian, *n.* اِبْنُ سِتِّينَ سَنَةً.

Sexagenary, *a.* عِبَارَةٌ عَنْ سِتِّينَ.

Sexagesima, *n.* مُدَّةُ سِتِّينَ يَوْمًا قَبْلَ ٱلْعِيدِ ٱلْكَبِيرِ.

Sexagesimal, *a.* السِّتُّونَ.

Sexangular, *a.* *See* Hexangular, *a.*

Sexennial, *a.* مِنْ سِتِّ سِنِينَ إِلَى ـ وَاقِعٌ مَرَّةً فِي سِتِّ سِنِينَ ـ سَتُّ سِنِينَ.

Sexennially, *ad.* مَرَّةً فِي سِتِّ سِنِينَ.

Sexless, *a.* لَا جِنْسَ لَهُ ـ لَا مُذَكَّرٌ وَلَا مُؤَنَّثٌ.

Sextant, *n.* The sixth of a circle, سُدْسُ دَائِرَةٍ. The instrument, آلَةٌ فِي شَكْلِ سُدْسِ دَائِرَةٍ يَتَّخِذُهَا ٱلرُّبَّانُ لِرَصْدِ ٱلنُّجُومِ ـ وَمِزْوَلَةٌ ـ سَكْسْتَانْت.

Sextile, *n.* إِسْتِقْبَالُ سَيَّارَتَيْنِ عَلَى بُعْدِ سِتِّينَ دَرَجَةً.

Sextillion, *n.* رَقْمٌ يُؤَلَّفُ مِنْ عَدَدٍ وَاحِدٍ وَسِتَّةٍ وَثَلَاثِينَ صِفْرًا.

Sexton, *n.* قَنْدَلَفْت *pl.* قَنْدَلَفْتِيَّة. *See also* Grave-digger, *n.*

Sextonship, *n.* خِدْمَةُ ٱلْقَنْدَلَفْتِ.

Sextuple, *a.* مُسَدَّس ـ سِتَّةُ أَضْعَافٍ. To make —, سَدَّسَ.

Sexual, *a.* جِنْسِيٌّ. Sexual intercourse, جِمَاع ـ مُجَامَعَة. The — organs, آلَاتُ ٱلتَّنَاسُلِ.

Sexualism, *n.* مَذْهَبُ ٱلْقَائِلِينَ أَنَّ لِنَوْعِ ٱلنَّبَاتِ طَرًّا ذُكُورًا وَإِنَاثًا.

Sexualist, *n.* مِنْ أَصْحَابِ ٱلرَّأْيِ ٱلْمَذْكُورِ.

Sexuality, *n.* كَيْفِيَّةُ ٱلْجِنْسِ.

Sexually, *ad.* مِنْ جِهَةِ ٱلْجِنْسِيَّةِ.

Seyyid, *n.* *See* Sayyid, *n.*

Shââbân, *n.* The month of, شَعْبَانُ ـ شَهْرُ شَعْبَانَ.

Shab, *v.i.* To play mean tricks, خَسَّ *aor.* يَخِسُّ ـ رَذُلَ[2].

Shab, *v.t.* To reject, رَفَضَ ـ رَدَّ[2].

Shabbily, *ad.* Meanly, بِخَسَاسَةٍ ـ بِرَذَالَةٍ. Poorly, wretchedly, بِحَقَارَةٍ ـ بِمَسْكَنَةٍ; of dress, بِبَذَاذَةٍ. Shabbily dressed, بَذٌّ (or بَاذٌّ) لَابِسٌ ثِيَابًا حَقِيرَةَ ٱلْهَيْئَةِ. To be — dressed, بَذَّ. To act —, خَسَّ *aor.* يَخِسُّ ـ رَذُلَ[2]. *See also* Meanly, *ad.*

Shabbiness, *n.* Meanness, خَسَاسَة ـ رَذَالَة ـ نَذَالَة. Wretchedness, paltriness, تَفَاهَة ـ حَقَارَة ـ مَسْكَنَة; of dress, بَذَاذَة ـ رَثَاثَة. *See also* Meanness, *n.*

Shabby, *a.* Mean, خَزٍ ـ خَسِيس ـ رَذِيل ـ شَقِيٌّ *pl.* أَشْقِيَاءُ ـ ذَلِيل. Poor, wretched, رَقِيق ـ حَقِير ـ مِسْكِين; of dress, بَذٌّ ـ رَثٌّ ـ رَثِيث. His clothes are shabby, فِي هَيْئَتِهِ رَثَاثَةٌ. Of a — appearance, بَذُّ ٱلْهَيْئَةِ. A — state of apparel, هَيْئَةٌ بَذَّةٌ. To be — in one's apparel, بَذَّ *aor.* يَبَذُّ.

Shabrack, *n.* غَاشِيَة ـ أَغْمَاء.

Shackle, *n.* *See* Stubble, *n.*

Shackle, *v.t.* To fetter, bind, صَفَدَ ـ أَصْفَدَ ـ كَبَّلَ ـ قَيَّدَ ـ رَبَطَ[2] ـ زَنْجَرَ. *See also to* Hamper, *v.t.*

Shackles, *n.* قُيُود *pl.* قَيْد ـ رِبَاط ـ صِفَاد ـ عُقْلَة ـ إِسَار; for the neck and hands, غُلٌّ ـ جَامِعَة. Bound with —, مَأْسُور ـ أَسِير. Envy is the shackle of aid (from God) against an enemy, (prov.) البَغْيُ عِقَالُ ٱلنَّصْرِ.

Shad, *n.* The fish, شَبُّوط.

Shade, *n.* The interception of light, ظِلٌّ *pl.* أَظْلَال *and* ظِلَال ـ فَيْءٌ *pl.* أَفْيَاء. Anything that shades, ظُلَّة ـ مِظَلَّة. A small — which a man makes for himself with a cloth, *etc.*, against the sun, ظُلَيْلَة. A thing having —, by means of which one shades himself, مُظِلّ ـ مُظَلَّل. Shelter, protection, كِنٌّ *pl.* أَكْنَان. A light colour, لَوْنٌ خَفِيفٌ. A slight difference, فَرْقٌ خَفِيفٌ ـ فَرْقٌ جُزْئِيٌّ. A ghost, خَيَال *pl.* أَخْيِلَة ـ طَيْف *pl.* طُيُوف. A modicum, عِرْق. An eye-shade, غِمَاء. He sought — under the tree, إِسْتَظَلَّ بِٱلشَّجَرَةِ ـ تَفَيَّأَ فِي ٱلشَّجَرَةِ. The tree had much —, فَاءَتِ (or تَفَيَّأَتِ) ٱلشَّجَرَةُ. To sit in the —, إِسْتَظَلَّ. To throw into the —, to be superior to, كَسَفَ ـ عَلَا عَلَى *aor.* يَعْلُو ـ غَلَبَ عَلَى ـ بَرَعَ.

Shade, *v.t.* To put into shade, ظَلَّلَ ـ ظَلَّلَ عَلَى. To — the eyes by putting up the hands before them, إِسْتَشْرَفَ ـ إِسْتَكَفَّ. To — one's self, تَظَلَّلَ ـ تَفَيَّأَ. To — one's self with, إِسْتَظَلَّ بِ. To — or verge towards, as of a colour, ضَرَبَ إِلَى. The tree shaded me, أَظَلَّتْنِي ٱلشَّجَرَةُ. To be shaded, تَظَلَّلَ ـ تَفَيَّأَ. *See also to* Obscure, *v.t.*

Shaded, *a.* مُظَلَّل. A — place to which the sun does not come, مَفْيُؤَة ـ مَقْمَأَة ـ قَمْأَة ـ مَفْيَأَة.

Shades, *n.* *See* Hades, *n.*

Shadiness, *n.* ظِلٌّ ـ فَيْءٌ ـ تَفِئَة.

Shadow, *n.* Shade, as cast by a person or thing, ظِلٌّ *pl.* أَظْلَال. A fleeting —, ظِلٌّ زَائِلٌ. A type, sign, رَمْز *pl.* رُمُوز ـ دَلِيل *pl.* دَلَائِل ـ عَلَامَة *pl.* عَلَامَات. Shelter, protection, كِنٌّ ـ حِفْظ ـ صِيَانَة. A spectre, خَيَال *pl.* أَخْيِلَة ـ زَوْل *pl.* أَزْوَال. The — of night, ظِلُّ ٱللَّيْلِ. A — of a man, one greatly emaciated, كَٱلظِّلِّ ـ نَحِيف لِلْغَايَةِ ـ هَزِيل ـ أَعْجَف ـ نَاحِل. He follows his own —, هُوَ يَتْبَعُ ظِلَّ نَفْسِهِ. He strives to catch his own —, هُوَ يُبَارِي ظِلَّ نَفْسِهِ. To pass away like a —, زَالَ كَٱلظِّلِّ[2]. *See also* Shade, *n.*

Shadow, *v.t.* To shade, ظَلَّلَ ـ ظَلَّلَ عَلَى. To typify, رَمَزَ[2] ـ دَلَّ عَلَى[2] ـ كَنَى عَنْ. To hide, خَبَّأَ ـ كَتَمَ[2]. To screen, سَتَرَ[2]. To — out, صَوَّرَ. *See also to* Shade, *v.t.*

Shadowing, *n.* تَظْلِيل ـ نُورٌ وَظِلٌّ ـ تَدْرِيجُ ٱلنُّورِ وَٱلظِّلِّ.

Shadowless, *a.* بِلَا ظِلٍّ ـ بِدُونِ فَيْءٍ.

Shadowy, *a.* Shady, مُظَلَّل. Typical, رَمْزِيٌّ ـ مَجَازِيٌّ ـ إِسْتِعَارِيٌّ. Chimerical, خَيَالِيٌّ ـ وَهْمِيٌّ ـ بَاطِل ـ لَا أَصْلَ لَهُ.

Shady, *a.* ظَلِيل ـ مُظَلَّل. A — tree, شَجَرَةٌ ظَلَّةٌ *pl.* أَشْجَارٌ ظَلَّالٌ. To become —, ظَلَّ *aor.* يَظَلُّ ـ أَظَلَّ.

Shaft, *n.* An arrow, سَهْم *pl.* سِهَام. A missile weapon, مِرْمَاة

pl. مَرَام. The straight part of a column, أُسْطُوَانَة *pl.* أَسَاطِين — سَاق *pl.* سِيقَان — عَمُود، طُول. A passage, as into a mine, بِئْر *pl.* أَبْيَار *and* بِئَار — مَنْفَذ *pl.* مَنَافِذ. A handle, as of a weapon, *etc.*, خَشَبَة — مِقْبَضَة — مِقْبَض — فُعْل *pl.* فِعَال. A stand, stem, سَاق — قَاعِدَة. A thill of a carriage, جَارُورَةُ ٱلْعَرَبَانَةِ. An axle, عَمُود — دُولَاب *pl.* دَوَالِيب، أَطْلَقَ. To wing a —, arrow, سَهْمًا (رَمَى = or). To sink a —, إِبْتَأَرَ بِئْرًا — بَأَرَ بِئْرًا.

Shag, *n.* Rough cloth, قُمَاشٌ شَعِثٌ. Shag tobacco, ضَرْبٌ مِنَ ٱلدُّخَانِ مُكَبَّش.

Shag, *a.* *See* Shaggy, *a.*

Shag, *v.t.* شَعَّثَ.

Shagged, *a.* | Shaggy, } Rough, dishevelled, شَعِث. Having a — coat, أَشْعَث *fem.* شَعْثَاء *pl.* شُعْث. To be —, شَعِثَ; to become —, تَشَعَّثَ.

Shaggedness, *n.* | Shagginess, } شَعَث — غَفَر — غَفْر.

Shagreen, *n.* The leather, جِلْدٌ سَاغِرِيٌّ وَهُوَ صِنْفٌ مِنَ ٱلْجُلُودِ ٱلْمَدْبُوغَةِ.

Shâh, *n.* شَاه *pl.* شَاهَات.

Shaikh, *n.* شَيْخ *pl.* شُيُوخ *or* مَشَايِخ.

Shake, *v.t.* To move, to agitate, هَزَّ — رَجَّ — قَلْقَلَ — هَزْهَزَ — حَرَّكَ — فَرْفَرَ — زَعْزَعَ; as water in a bottle or a bucket in a well, خَضَّ — خَضْخَضَ; as wind the trees, صَفَّقَ. To — to and fro, ذَبْذَبَ — زَلْزَلَ. To — hands with, تَصَافَحَ — صَافَحَ; to — hands with, to be reconciled to, صَالَحَ. To — one's resolution about . . ., أَشَكَّ فِي ٱلْأَمْرِ. To — off, as leaves from a tree or dust from clothes, or anything from the person, نَفَضَ — نَفَّضَ. To — the head at, أَنْغَضَ ٱلرَّأْسَ إِلَى. To — the head, نَغَضَ ٱلرَّأْسَ — هَزَّ ٱلرَّأْسَ. To become shaken by the wind, إِسْتَرْوَحَ.

Shake, *v.i.* To be agitated with vibrations, تَهَزَّزَ — إِهْتَزَّ — اِرْتَجَّ — تَقَلْقَلَ — تَحَرَّكَ. To — to and fro, تَذَبْذَبَ. To tremble, quake, تَزَعْزَعَ — إِرْتَعَدَ.

Shake, *n.* A vibratory motion, هِزَّة — قَلْقَلَة — رَجَّة — تَحْرِيك — حَرَكَة — فَرْفَرَة. A — of the head, نَغْضُ ٱلرَّأْسِ. A shivering, trembling, رَجَفَان — رِعْدَة — رُعَاش. A trill, as in music, تَرَنُّم — تَرْجِيعُ ٱلصَّوْتِ. A —, or shaking off, as dust from clothes, *etc.*, نَفْضَة — نَفْض. He is in a —, بِهِ رِعْشَةٌ. A — of the hand, مُصَافَحَة.

Shaker, *n.* One who shakes anything, مُحَرِّك — مُهَزِّز. One who shakes himself or trembles, رَعِيش — مُتَزَعْزِع — مُرْتَعِد — مُرْتَعِش. A dancer, رَقَّاص. *See also under* Quaker, *n.*

Shako, *n.* بُرْنَيْطَةُ ٱلْعَسْكَرِ *pl.* بُرْنَيْطَات *and* بَرَانِط.

Shaky, *a.* Full of cracks, مُشَقَّق. Unsound, رَكِيك — سَقِيم — بَاطِل. Weak, ضَعِيف. *See also* Rickety, *a.*

Shale, *n.* The clay, سِجِّيل — حَجَرُ طُفَالٍ.

Shall, *aux. verb.* *As denoting the future it may be expressed by* سَوْفَ *or its abbreviation* سَ; *e.g.* Thou shalt see, سَوْفَ تَرَى *or* سَتَرَى. I know not, but I — know, مَا أَدْرِي لٰكِنْ سَوْفَ أَدْرِي. *Other modes of expressing the English meaning may be gathered from the following examples:*—He — not be your companion, لَا يَكُونُ لَكَ رَفِيقًا. Shall I be present? هَلْ أَكُونُ حَاضِرًا. I — have been here two years, تَكُونُ قَدْ مَضَتْ عَلَيَّ سَنَتَانِ وَأَنَا هُنَا. I — be drowned and nobody will save me, لَا بُدَّ أَنْ أَغْرَقَ وَلَا يُنْقِذُنِي أَحَدٌ. I will be drowned and nobody — save me, عَزَمْتُ عَلَى إِغْرَاقِ نَفْسِي وَأَبَيْتُ أَنْ يَنْقُذَنِي أَحَدٌ.

Shalloon, *n.* The stuff, شَال.

Shallop, *n.* قَارِب *pl.* قَوَارِب.

Shallow, *a.* Not deep, رَقِيق — رُقّ — ضَحْل. Of the intellect, رَكِيكُ ٱلْعَقْلِ — سَخِيف — مُشَغْشَف — مُشَغْشِف. A — piece of water, ضَحْضَاح — ضَحْل. Shallow water, مَآءٌ رَقِيقٌ. Shallow soil, أَرْضٌ أَسِيفَةٌ — أَسَافَة. The water became —, إِسْتَرَقَّ ٱلْمَآءُ. To be —, of water, ضَحَلَ; in intellect, سَخُفَ.

Shallow, *n.* Any place where the water is not deep, ضَحْضَاح — رُقّ — ضَحْل *vulg.* رَقْرَاق. A mass of rock partly covered by water, أَتَانُ ٱلضَّحْلِ.

Shallow, *v.i.* Of water, إِسْتَرَقَّ — ضَحَلَ.

Shallow-brained, *a.* سَفِيه — رَكِيكُ ٱلْعَقْلِ. *See also under* Shallow, *a.*

Shallowness, *n.* As of water, رِقَّةُ ٱلْمَآءِ — رَكَاكَةُ مَآءٍ; of intellect, رِكَّةُ عَقْلٍ — سَخَافَة — سُخْف.

Shaly, *a.* مِنْ حَجَرِ ٱلطُّفَالِ — سِجِّيلِيّ.

Sham, *n.* A counterfeit, تَمْوِيه — تَقْلِيد — غِشّ — تَزْوِير. A show of what is not real, عِضَةٌ *pl.* عِضُون — تَصَنُّع. A trick, imposture, حِيلَة — خُدْعَة *pl.* حِيَل. "Those who pronounced the al-Kurân to be a sham," or lies, (Sûr. xv. 91), ٱلَّذِينَ جَعَلُوا ٱلْقُرْآنَ عِضِينَ.

Sham, *a.* Counterfeit, مُمَوَّه — مُزَوَّر — مُقَلَّد — مُلَبَّس — صِنَاعِيّ. Deceitful, غَاشّ. Pretended, seeming, مُتَشَبِّهٌ بِ — مُتَظَاهِر.

Sham, *v.t.* To deceive, disappoint, خَدَعَ — خَيَّبَ.

Sham, *v.i.* To pretend, أَظْهَرَ — تَظَاهَرَ بِ — تَصَنَّعَ. To — sickness, تَمَارَضَ. To — ignorance, تَجَاهَلَ. To — elegance, تَظَرَّفَ — تَظَارَفَ. To affect ingenuity, excellence, تَكَيَّسَ.

Shamble, *v.i.* خَجِلَ ـ ـ خَجَّلَ .

Shambles, *n.* مَجْزَرَة ـ مَسْلَخ .

Shambling, *n.* خَجَلان ـ خَجِل .

Shame, *n.* Ignominy, disgrace, عَار ـ سُبَّة ـ عَيْب ـ شَنَار . A shameful action, فَضِيحَة *pl.* فَضَائِح ـ رَذَالَة . Modesty, pudicity, إِسْتِحْيَاء ـ خَجَالَة ـ خَجَل ـ حِشْمَة ـ حَيَاء ـ خَجْلَة . This thing became a — to him, صَارَ هٰذَا ٱلْأَمْرُ سُبَّةً (or عَارًا) لَهُ . You are a — to your people, أَنْتَ سُبَّةٌ (or عَارٌ) عَلَى قَوْمِكَ . Shame upon you! أُفٍّ عَلَيْكَ . Fie for —! عَيْبٌ عَلَيْكَ . The fire (of hell) is better than —, (prov.) النَّارُ خَيْرٌ مِنَ ٱلْعَارِ .

To be lost to shame, رَفَعَ ٱلْحَيَاءَ ـ خَلَعَ ٱلْعَارَ .

To be the shame of, شُهِرَ بِهِ عِنْدَ كَذَا ـ كَانَ سُبَّةً لِ ـ صَارَ عَارًا لِ .

To publish one's own shame, فَضَحَ نَفْسَهُ ـ شَهَرَ رَذَالَةَ نَفْسِهِ .

To put to shame. *See to* Shame, *v.t.*

Shame, *v.t.* To make ashamed, أَخْزَى ـ أَخْجَلَ ـ خَجَّلَ . To disgrace, to bring to shame, فَضَحَ . To be shamed, disgraced, إِنْفَضَحَ .

Shamefaced, *a.* مُسْتَحٍ ـ خَجِل ـ حَيِيٌّ *fem.* حَيِيَّة .

Shamefacedness, *n.* إِسْتِحْيَاء ـ حَيَاء .

Shameful, *a.* مَعِيب ـ مَعْيُوب ـ خَزٍ . *See also* Disgraceful, *a.*

Shamefully, *ad.* Disgracefully, فَضَاحَةً ـ قُبَاحَةً ـ رَذَالَةً ـ بِٱلْعَارِ .

Shamefulness, *n.* قَبَاحَة ـ عَيْب ـ عَار ـ خِزْيَة .

Shameless, *a.* صَفِيقُ ٱلْوَجْهِ ـ وَقِيح ـ بِدُونِ حِشْمَةٍ ـ بِلَا حَيَاء .

Shamelessly, *ad.* بِقِلَّةِ حَيَاء ـ بِفَضَاحَةٍ ـ بِوَقَاحَةٍ .

Shamelessness, *n.* قِلَّةُ حَيَاء ـ وَقَاحَة ـ عَدَمُ حَيَاء .

Sham-fight, *n.* مُحَارَبَةٌ رِيَاضِيَّةٌ لِأَجْلِ تَمْرِينِ ٱلْعَسْكَرِ .

Shammy, *n.* *See* Chamois, *n.*

Shampoo, *v.t.* كَبَّسَ ـ دَلَكَ ـ دَعَكَ . To — one's self or to be shampooed, تَدَلَّكَ .

Shampooer, *n.* دَلَّاك .

Shampooing, *n.* تَكْبِيس ـ تَدْلِيك ـ دَلْك ـ دَعْك .

Shamrock, *n.* The trefoil, فِصْفِصَة ـ رِبَّة .

Shank, *n.* The joint of the leg to the ankle, سَاق *pl.* سِيقَان . A — bone, سَاعِدَة ـ شَظِيَّة . The outer —, القَصَبَةُ ٱلصُّغْرَى . The inner —, القَصَبَةُ ٱلْكُبْرَى The fore — of a horse, وَظِيف . A — of a button, ذَنَب *pl.* أَذْنَاب ـ وَعْلَة . The long part of a tool, سَاق *pl.* سِيقَان . A handle, مِمْسَك ـ يَد . Slender in the shanks, أَحْمَشُ ٱلسَّاقَيْنِ ـ رُقْع *pl.* أَرْقَعُ *fem.* رَقْعَاء *fem.* حَمْشَاء *pl.* حُمْش . Long in the shanks, أَسْوَق ـ سَوْق .

Shanty, *n.* كُوخ *pl.* أَكْوَاخ ـ عِشَّة *pl.* عِشَش .

Shape, *v.t.* فَصَّلَ ـ صَيَّرَ ـ صَوَّرَ ـ شَكَّلَ . To work into —, هَنْدَمَ .

To — one's course, دَبَّرَ سَبِيلَهُ ـ ضَرَبَ إِلَى .

Shape, *n.* Form, هَيْئَة (or هِيئَة) *pl.* هَيْآت ـ شَكْل *pl.* أَشْكَال ـ صُورَة *pl.* صُوَر ـ تَفْصِيل . Character, nature, مَاهِيَّة . In the —, form, of a pear, فِي شَكْلِ ٱلْكُمَّثْرَى ; in the manner or way of..., عَلَى سَبِيلِ كَذَا . To assume the — of, إِتَّخَذَ صُورَةَ ٱلشَّيْءِ .

Shapeless, *a.* خَشِب ـ قَبِيح ـ سَمِيج ـ بِلَا هِنْدَام .

Shapelessness, *n.* قَبَاحَة ـ سَمَاجَة ـ عَدَمُ هِنْدَام ـ خَشَب .

Shapely, *a.* جَمِيل ـ صَيِّر ـ حَسَنُ ٱلصُّورَةِ ـ مُهَنْدَم ; of a woman, خَرِد .

Shard, *n.* A fragment, فِلْقَة *pl.* فِلَق ـ شُذْنَة ـ شِقَّة *pl.* شِقَق ـ قِطْعَة *pl.* قِطَع . A sheath of the wings of insects, غِمْدُ أَجْنَاحِ ٱلدُّوَيْبَّات .

Share, *n.* A portion, شِرْك *pl.* أَشْرَاك ـ سُهْمَة ـ سَهْم *pl.* أَسْهَام and سِهَام ـ قِسْم *pl.* أَقْسَام ـ حِصَّة *pl.* حِصَص . A lot, نَصِيب *pl.* أَنْصِبَة . A ploughshare, سِكَّة *pl.* سِكَك ـ مِحْرَاث ـ نَوْرَج *pl.* نَوَارِج . A —, as of stock, حِصَّة *pl.* حِصَص . Certificate of a —, سَنَدُ سَهْمٍ *pl.* سَنَدَاتُ أَسْهَامٍ . A — of his house was sold, بِيعَ شِرْكٌ مِنْ دَارِهِ . Preference shares, أَسْهَامٌ مُمْتَازَةٌ . Ordinary shares, أَسْهَامٌ عُمُومِيَّةٌ . To go shares with another, شَارَكَ ـ نَاصَفَ . To give one his —, أَحْصَصَ .

Share, *v.t.* To divide among, giving each a share, أَبَدَّ بَيْنَهُمْ كَذَا . To go shares in with another, نَاصَفَ ـ شَارَكَ . To partake with another in, شَارَكَ . They shared with one another, or they became co-partners, of many, تَشَارَكُوا ـ إِشْتَرَكُوا . To have a — with one in, شَرِكَ ـ فِي . To part among several, to apportion, فَرَّقَ ـ عَلَى ـ فَرَّقَ ـ بَيْنَ ـ قَسَّمَ . To be concerned in with another, شَرِكَ ـ فِي . To make one to — in, أَشْرَكَ ـ فِي . He shared the gift among them, giving each his portion, أَبَدَّ بَيْنَهُمُ ٱلْعَطَاءَ .

Share, *v.i.* To have a share, as with another, خَاصَصَ ـ شَارَكَ . To — and — alike in, of two, حَاصَّا ٱلشَّيْءَ عَلَى كَانَ لَهُ حِصَّةٌ ; of many, تَحَاصُّوا فِي ـ عَلَى سَوِيَّةٍ سَوِيَّةٍ .

Shareholder, *n.* صَاحِبُ سَهْمٍ *pl.* أَصْحَابُ (or أَرْبَابُ) أَسْهَامٍ .

Sharer, *n.* A partaker, شَقِيص *pl.* شِقَاص ـ شَرِيك *pl.* شُرَكَاء .

Shark, *n.* The fish, كَلْبٌ بَحْرِيٌّ *pl.* كِلَابُ ٱلْبَحْرِ . A rapacious artful fellow, خَلَّاس ـ مُخْتَلِس ـ نَشَّاب . A land —, خَلَّاس ٱلْبَحْرِيَّةِ عِنْدَ نُزُولِهِمْ فِي ٱلْبَرِّ .

Shark, *v.t.* خَلَسَ ـ تَخَلَّسَ ـ إِخْتَلَسَ .

Shark, *v.i.* لَعِبَ مَلْعُوبًا ـ إِحْتَالَ ـ تَحَيَّلَ .

Sharker, *n.* One who lives by sharking, مُخْتَلِس ـ خَلَّاس ـ نَصَّاب.

Sharp, *n.* Of the tone in music, لَحْنٌ جَهُورٌ (فِي ٱلْمُوسِيقَى). The sign for a —, عَلَامَةُ ٱللَّحْنِ ٱلْجَهُورِ وَهِيَ (#). *See also* Semitone, *n.*

Sharp, *a.* Having a keen edge, قُبَاب ـ رَهِيف ـ جُزَار ـ خَارِق ـ قَاطِع *pl.* قُطَّاع ـ صَارِم *pl.* صَوَارِمُ ـ ذَرِب ـ حَادّ ـ مَاضٍ. Having a — point, لَهْذَم *pl.* لَهَاذِمُ ـ حُدَّاد ـ حَادّ ـ مُؤَسَّل. Pungent, of taste, حَامِز ـ حَاذِق ـ حِرِّيف ـ حَادّ. Painful, أَلِيم ـ مُؤْلِم ـ حَادّ. Energetic, مُتَبَذِّل ـ شَعَاوِيّ ـ صَارِم. Spirited, vigorous, جَسْر. Efficacious, فَعَّال ـ مُؤَثِّر. Intelligent, لَبِيب ـ حَدِيدُ ٱلْفُؤَادِ ـ شَحْشَحَان ـ شَهْم ـ حَدِيد ـ ذَكِيّ ـ حَاذِق ـ فَهِيم. Ingenious, subtile, ثَقِيف ـ حَاذِق ـ خَارِق. Experienced in affairs, حُوَّلٌ قُلَّبٌ ـ مُدَرَّب. Clever, فَطِين ـ مَاهِر. Active, quick, خَفِيف ـ حَرِك ـ نَدْب ـ نَشِيط ـ بَطْرَان. Censorious, مُرّ ـ جَارِح ـ مُؤْذٍ. Circumspect, مُتَنَبِّه ـ حَرِيص ـ مُحْتَرِز. Piercing, as of a wind, صِرّ ـ حَرُوق ـ نَافِذ ـ مُزَمْهِرّ ـ خَارِق. Strong, شَدِيد. Emaciated, lean, نَحِيف ـ ضَعِيف. Sharp, of sound, جَهُور ـ جَهِير. Quick, sudden, فُجَائِيّ ـ عَلَى فُجَاءَةٍ. A — sword, سَيْفٌ مَاضٍ ـ سَيْفٌ حَادٌّ. A — rock, سِنُّ صَخْرَةٍ. A — odour, رَائِحَةٌ ذَكِيَّةٌ. A — tongue, لِسَانٌ عَضْبٌ; sharp of tongue, عَضْبُ ٱللِّسَانِ ـ سَلِيط. A — thorn, لُدَّاغ. A — angle, زَاوِيَةٌ خَارِجِيَّةٌ ـ رَأْسُ زَاوِيَةٍ. Such a — dispute arose between them that they separated, حَصَلَتْ بَيْنَهُمْ مُشَاجَرَةٌ حَتَّى ٱنْفَصَلَ بَعْضُهُمْ عَنْ بَعْضٍ. To be —, cutting, of a sound, speech, *etc.*, ذَرِبَ. To be —, quick, intelligent, or skilful, ثَقُفَ. To be —, active, prompt, وَشُكَ *aor.* يَوْشُكُ ـ خَفَّ ـ وَجَزَ *aor.* يَجِزُ. To emit a — sound, to creak, صَرَفَ ـ صَرَّ ـ اِصْطَرَّ. *See also under* Keen, *a.*

Sharp, *v.i.* / **Sharpen**, } To become sharp, ذَرِبَ ـ صَرُمَ ـ اِتَّخَذَ ذُبَابًا ـ شَحِذَ.

Sharp-edged, *a.* *See under* Sharp, Keen-edged, *a.*

Sharpen, *v.t.* To give an edge to, خَشَبَ ـ حَمَزَ ـ سَمَطَ ـ أَرْهَفَ ـ أَغْمَسَ ـ أَشْحَذَ ـ شَحَّذَ ـ ذَرَّبَ ـ حَدَّ ـ حَدَّدَ ـ أَحَدَّ. To — to a point, أَسَّلَ ـ أَنَّفَ ـ حَدَّدَ. To —, as on a stone, شَرْشَرَ ـ سَنَّ. To — the wits, فَطَّنَ ـ فَقَّهَ. To make pungent, صَيَّرَ حِرِّيفًا ـ حَدَّدَ. To make active, eager, أَنْهَضَ ـ شَوَّقَ ـ رَغَّبَ ـ أَرْغَبَ ـ نَشَّطَ. To — the appetite, سَنَّنَ: This thing sharpened my appetite, سَنَّنِي هٰذَا ٱلشَّيْءُ.

Sharpener, *n.* صُلَّبِيّ ـ سَنَّان.

Sharper, *a.* As of a sword, أَمْضَى ـ أَحَدُّ.

Sharper, *n.* نَصَّاب ـ مُحْتَال ـ صَاحِبُ مَلَاعِيبَ *pl.* أَصْحَاب.

Sharp-eyed, *a.* حَدِيدُ ٱلْبَصَرِ. *See also* Sharp-sighted, *a.*

Sharply, *ad.* Acutely, with an edge, صَرَامَةً ـ بِصَرَامَةٍ ـ بِحِدَّةٍ. Pungently, of taste, حَرَافَةً ـ حَمَازَةً ـ بِحَمَازَةٍ. Energetically, تَبَدُّدًا ـ بِشِدَّةٍ ـ بِقُوَّةٍ. Intelligently, with point, بِذَكَاءٍ ـ سَدَدًا ـ سَدَادًا ـ بِحِدَّةٍ. Actively, quickly, خِفَّةً ـ بِخِفَّةٍ ـ بِنَشَاطٍ. Cleverly, بِفِطْنَةٍ ـ بِمَهَارَةٍ ـ *vulg.* بِشَطَارَةٍ. Piercingly, as of a wind, اِزْمِهْرَارًا ـ بِحِدَّةٍ ـ بِنُفُوذٍ; as of sound, جَهَارَةً ـ بِصَرِيفٍ. Harshly, cruelly, بِقَسْرٍ ـ بِعَنْفٍ ـ بِغِلَاظَةٍ. Painfully, بِأَلَمٍ ـ بِوَجَعٍ. With strength, force, بِشِدَّةٍ ـ بِقُوَّةٍ ـ بِحَيْلٍ. With accuracy, narrowly, بِدِقَّةٍ. Decidedly, pointedly, بِصَرَامَةٍ ـ بَتَّةً ـ جَزْمًا. Suddenly, عَلَى فُجَاءَةٍ. He rebuked them —, وَبَّخَهُمْ بِصَرَامَةٍ ـ خَاصَمَهُمْ. To deal —, harshly, with, عَسَّرَ عَلَى ـ شَدَّ عَلَى. He looked — at him, جَسَّهُ بِعَيْنِهِ. *See also* Harshly, Keenly, *ad.*

Sharpness, *n.* As of edge, رَهَافَة ـ صَرَامَة ـ حِدَّة ـ ذَرَابَة; of point, سِنَّة ـ تَأْنِيف ـ حِدَّة. Pungency, of taste, حُشُومَة ـ حَمَازَة ـ حَرَارَة ـ حَرَافَة ـ حِدَّة. Painfulness, أَلَم ـ وَجَع ـ شِدَّة. Energy, vigour, شَوْكَة ـ شَهَامَة ـ جُهْد ـ مُرُوَّة ـ صَرَامَة. Efficaciousness, تَأْثِير. Intelligence, حِدَّةُ ٱلْفُؤَادِ ـ شَهَامَة ـ ذَكَاء ـ ثَقَافَة ـ ثُقُوفَة. Ingenuity, حَذَاقَة ـ فَرَاسَة. Cleverness, فِطْنَة ـ مَهَارَة ـ *vulg.* شَطَارَة. Activity, quickness, رَوْجَة ـ خِفَّة ـ نَشَاط. Circumspection, حِرْص ـ اِحْتِرَاز. Sharpness, as of appetite, حِدَّة ـ شِدَّة; as of wind, زَمْهَرِير ـ نُفُوذ ـ حِدَّة; as of language, bitterness, sarcasm, سَلَاطَة ـ أَذِيَّة ـ مَرَارَة. Quickness, suddenness, فُجَاءَة. Vehemence, strength, شِدَّة ـ قُوَّة ـ حَيْل. Leanness, نَحَافَة ـ ضَعْف. Eagerness, حِرْص ـ حَرَارَة ـ شَوْق ـ رَغْبَة. Harshness, as to the ear, جُشَّة ـ بُحَّة ـ صَرِيف; as of temper, قَسَاحَة ـ شَرَاسَة ـ غِلَاظَة. Violence, cruelty, جَفَاء ـ عَنْف ـ قَسَاوَة. To use —, to be decided, بَتَّ ٱلنِّيَّةَ ـ اِسْتَعْمَلَ جَزْمًا.

Sharp-pointed, *a.* مُؤَنَّف. *See also under* Sharp, *a.*

Sharpset, *a.* Eager in desire, حَرِيص ـ رَاغِبٌ فِي ـ شَوَّاق. Very hungry, سَغْبَانُ *fem.* سَغْبَى *pl.* سِغَاب ـ جَائِع *pl.* جُوَّع ـ مَائِتٌ مِنَ ٱلْجُوعِ. *See also* Destitute, *a.*

Sharpshooter, *n.* أَرْمَى *pl.* أَرَامِي ـ سَدِيدٌ (*or* أَسَدُّ) فِي ٱلتَّقْوِيسِ (*or* ٱلرِّمَايَةِ) ـ قَوَّاسٌ أَسَدُّ *pl.* قَوَّاسَةٌ سُدٌّ; *vulg.* هَدَّاف ـ نِشَانْجِي; *from the Turkish*, شِشْخَانْجِي.

Sharpshooting, *n.* رِمَايَةٌ سَدَاءٌ ـ تَقْوِيسٌ سَدِيدٌ ـ إِصَابَةٌ فِي ٱلرِّمَايَةِ; *from the Turkish*, ضَرْبٌ بِٱلشِّشْخَانَةِ.

Sharp-sighted, *a.* Of the eyes, أَشْوَهُ ـ شَائِهُ ٱلْبَصَرِ ـ أَبْصَرُ ـ

لَمّاح — حَدِيدُ ٱلْبَصَرِ ; of the mind, ثَقِيف — أَرِب — فَطِين — حَاذِق. He is more — than a serpent, هُوَ أَبْصَرُ مِنْ حَيَّةٍ.

Sharp-sightedness, *n.* Of the eyes, حِدَّةُ بَصَرٍ ; of the mind, ثَقَاف — فِطْنَة — حَذَاقَة — فَرَاسَة.

Sharp-visaged, *a.* عَجِيفُ ٱلْمَنْظَرِ — أَعْجَفُ ٱلْوَجْهِ *fem.* عَجْفَاءُ *pl.* عُجُف.

Sharp-witted, *a.* أَرِب — فَطِين — ثَقِيف — حَاذِق.

Shatter, *v.t.* To break to pieces, كَسَّرَ — فَتَّتَ — سَحَقَ ـ رَضَّ ² — رَضْرَضَ. To destroy, put an end to, لَاشَى — أَبَادَ — أَزَالَ — أَتْلَفَ. To be shattered, broken in pieces, اِرْتَضَّ — تَرَضْرَضَ — تَكَسَّرَ ; to be destroyed, put an end to, تَلَاشَى — اِضْمَحَلَّ — تَدَمَّرَ.

Shatters, *n.* Fragments, أَجْزَاءٌ — قِطَع — شُقَف — جِسَت — فِضَاض — كِسَر. To go into —, to fall to pieces, حَطِمَ ـ اِنْحَطَمَ — تَحَطَّمَ.

Shattery, *a.* Weak, ailing, عَلِيل — مَعْلُول — ضَعِيف. *See also* Rickety, *a.*

Shave, *v.t.* As the hair, حَلَّقَ — حَلَقَ ـ زَيَّنَ ; especially of the pubes, جَمَشَ ² ـ. To — off all the hair, سَمَّدَ ٱلشَّعْرَ. To cut or — off, as with a plane, رَنْدَجَ — مَسَحَ بِٱلْفَارَةِ ـ. To —, as of leather, حَمَرَ ². To —, as with a carpenter's tool, نَجَرَ ² ـ. To skim along the surface, as a bird, سَفَّ ². To —, to oppress, قَاهَرَ — ظَلَمَ ـ تَعَدَّى عَلَى. To — down, to lessen, نَقَّصَ — أَنْقَصَ — قَلَّلَ. To get one's self shaved, تَزَيَّنَ : He got his beard shaved, حَلَقَ ذَقْنَهُ ـ.

Shaving, *n.* The act of removing the hair, حَلْقَة. An instrument for shaving wood, *etc.*, مِبْرَآةٌ. A cooper's —, رَنْدَةُ ٱلْبَرَامِيلِيِّ. *See also a* Lie, *n.*

Shaveling, *n.* مَقْصُوصُ ٱلشَّعْرِ. One ordained, مَرْسُوم.

Shaver, *n.* One who shaves, حَلَّاق *pl.* حَلَقَة — مُزَيِّن. A boy or young man, وَلَد *pl.* أَوْلَاد — غُلَام *pl.* غِلْمَان.

Shaving, *n.* The act of removing the hair, حَلْقَة. A thin slice cut off, a paring, قُصَاصَة — قُرَاضَة — نُجَارَة. Shavings, of wood, نُشَارَة ; for the fire, شِيَاع.

Shaw, *n.* A thicket, grove, عِرِّيسَة — خَمِيلَة — مَشْجَرَة — غَابَة.

Shawl, *n.* شَال *pl.* شَالَات. A long —, scarf, شَال — شَالَة. A Cashmir, شَالَةٌ كَشْمِير. A — of fine wool, coming probably from Persia, is called شَالَةٌ كِرْمَان ; a particular kind, also from Persia, with different coloured stripes, is called, شَالَةٌ قَرْمَايِج. A — with coloured borders and corners is called in Egypt, شَالٌ كَشْفِيّ ; one with a round coloured centre-piece, بَقْجَة.

She, *pr.* هِيَ.

She, *n.* A woman, اِمْرَأَة.

She, *a.* Female, أُنْثَى *pl.* إِنَاث.

Sheaf, *n.* حُزْمَة *pl.* حُزَم — جُرْزَة *pl.* جُرَز. A —, as of corn, كُدْس *pl.* كُدَاس *and* كَدَادِيس *and* أَكْدَاس. To bind in sheaves, جَرَزًا — رَبَطَ ² ـ حُزَمًا — حَزَمَ ـ.

Sheaf, *v.t.* To bind in sheaves; *see preceding article.*

Shear, *v.t.* Of sheep, *etc.*, جَلَمَ ـ اِجْتَزَّ — جَزَّ ². To cut, clip, قَصَّ ². To attain the proper time for shearing, أَجَزَّ. To be shorn, جُزَّ — اُجْتُزَّ.

Shearer, *n.* جَزَّاز — قَصَّاص.

Shearing, *n.* The act of, جَلْم — جِزَاز — جَزّ — جِزَّة.

Shearling, *n.* A shorn sheep or goat, مَجْلُوم — جَزِيز — جَزِيزَة.

Shears, *n.* For shearing sheep, جَلَم — مِجَزّ. Shears, generally, for cutting, clipping, مِقْرَاض *pl.* مَقَارِيض — مِقَصّ. Shears for cutting metal, مِقْرَض — مِقْرَاض.

Shear-steel, *n.* بُولَادٌ خَاصّ.

Sheath, *n.* As of a sword, knife, *etc*, غِلَاف *pl.* غُلُف — غِمْد *pl.* غُمُود *and* أَغْمَاد. A receptacle generally for any tool, وِعَاء *pl.* أَوْعِيَة. To put anything into its sheath, رَدَّ ² ـ إِلَى غِمْدِهِ — جَعَلَ فِي ٱلْغِمْدِ ـ. He took the sword out its —, اِخْتَرَطَ ٱلسَّيْفَ مِنْ غِمْدِهِ. The — of the moon when it is eclipsed, سَاهُور.

Sheathe, *v.t.* To put into a sheath, غَلَّفَ — أَغْمَدَ — تَغَمَّدَ — غَمَدَ ² ـ. To cover or line, طَبَّقَ بِ — بَطَّنَ — لَبَّسَ. To put a — to, رَكَّبَ لِ (or لَبَّسَ) غِمْدًا. To be sheathed, put into a scabbard or sheath, اِغْتَلَفَ. To — the sword, to make peace, أَجْرَى مُصَالَحَةً — اِسْتَلَمَ.

Sheathed, *a.* As in a sheath, أَغْلَف — مَغْمُود ; lined, مُبَطَّن — مُلَبَّس — مُطَبَّق بِكَذَا.

Sheathing, *n.* بِطَانَة — طَبَقَة.

Sheathless, *a.* Without a sheath, بِلَا غِلَافٍ ; out of its sheath, مُجَرَّدٌ عَنْ غِلَافِهِ.

Sheathy, *a.* غِلَافِيّ — مِثْلَ ٱلْغِلَافِ — فِي هَيْئَةِ ٱلْغِلَافِ.

Sheave, *n.* Of a block or pulley, حَمَامَة — مَحَالَة — بَكَرَة *pl.* بَكَر.

Shed, *v.t.* and *int.* To pour or cause to flow out, سَكَبَ ². To —, as water, blood, tears, سَفَحَ ـ سَفَكَ ـ. To —, of teeth, سَلَّ ـ ; as a tree its leaves, تَحَاتَّ — تَنَاثَرَ. To — blood, سَفَكَ ٱلدِّمَاءَ ـ. To — tears, تَدَمَّعَ : The eye — tears, دَمَعَتِ ٱلْعَيْنُ — دَمْعُهَا سَفَحَتِ ٱلْعَيْنُ. The tree — its leaves, تَحَاتَّتِ

تَنَاثَرَتِ ٱلشَّجَرَةُ ـ ٱلشَّجَرَةُ. He — his teeth one after another تَحَاتَّتْ أَسْنَانُهُ. To — forth, سَكَبَ ². To — forth light, أَنَارَ; as of an odour, فَاحَ ب ² ـ نَشَرَ ²; as of rays, أَشَعَّ. To be —, poured forth, اِنْسَكَبَ ـ اِنْسَفَحَ.

Shed, *a.* and *part.* Poured out, سَفُوكٌ ـ سَفِيكٌ.

Shed, *n.* A shaded booth, عَرْشٌ مُظَلَّلٌ *pl.* أَعْرَاشٌ مُظَلَّلَةٌ. A slight building, كُوخٌ *pl.* أَكْوَاخٌ ـ عَرْشٌ *pl.* أَعْرَاشٌ *and* عُرُشٌ ـ عِشَّةٌ *pl.* عِشَشٌ ـ عَرِيشٌ *pl.* عُرُشٌ. A workshop, مَحْرِفٌ ـ مَعْمَلٌ *pl.* مَعَامِلُ ـ مُحْتَرَفٌ.

Shedder, *n.* سَفَّاكٌ ـ سَفَّاحٌ.

Sheen, *a.* } **Sheeny,** } بَصَّاصٌ ـ لَامِعٌ ـ بَرَّاقٌ ـ مُنِيرٌ ـ لَائِحٌ ـ لَمُوحٌ.

Sheen, *n.* نُورٌ ـ ضِيَآءٌ ـ لَمَعَانٌ.

Sheep, *n.* The animal, male or female, ضَأْنٌ *pl.* ضَئِينٌ *and* ضَأْنٌ ـ شَاةٌ *pl.* شَآءٌ. A male —, شَاةٌ ذَكَرٌ; a female —, نَعْجَةٌ *pl.* نَعْجَاتٌ *and* نِعَاجٌ. A young —, lamb, حَمَلٌ ـ خَرُوفٌ *pl.* خِرْفَانٌ. Sheep collectively, غَنَمٌ *pl.* أَغْنَامٌ *and* غَنَائِمُ ـ ضَأْنٌ ـ مَوَاشٍ. A — with crooked horns, صِعْقَاصٌ. Two flocks of —, غَنَمَانِ. A silly fellow, قَلِيلُ ٱلْعَقْلِ ـ أَبْلَهُ ـ أَحْمَقُ ـ أَخْرَقُ.

Sheep-cote, *n.* } **Sheep-fold,** } رَبَضٌ (or مَرْبِضٌ *pl.* مَرَابِضُ) غَنَمٍ ـ صِيرَةُ غَنَمٍ *pl.* أَرْبَاضٌ; a — built of stone or wood, وَصِيدُ غَنَمٍ *pl.* وُصُدٌ ـ جَدِيرَةُ غَنَمٍ.

Sheep-hook, *n.* عَصَا ٱلرَّاعِي ـ مِعْقَالُ ٱلرَّاعِي ـ قُرْصُوفٌ.

Sheepish, *a.* مُخْجَلٌ ـ خَجْلَانُ ـ خَجِلٌ ـ أَخْرَقُ.

Sheepishly, *ad.* بِحَيَآءٍ ـ بِخَجَلٍ ـ بِخُرْقٍ.

Sheepishness, *n.* خَجَلٌ ـ حَيَآءٌ ـ خُرْقٌ.

Sheep's-eye, *n.* لَحْظَةُ مَحَبَّةٍ ـ رَمْقُ عِشْقٍ. To cast sheep's-eyes at, نَظَرَ إِلَى ـ بِعَيْنِ ٱلْمَحَبَّةِ ² ـ لَمَحَ ـ بِعَيْنِ ٱلْعِشْقِ.

Sheep-master, *n.* مُرَبِّي مَوَاشٍ ـ صَاحِبُ مَوَاشٍ.

Sheep-shank, *n.* The shank of a sheep, سَاعِدَةُ غَنَمٍ *pl.* سَوَاعِدُ.

Sheep-shanks, *a.* Slender in the shanks, أَرْقَعُ *fem.* رَقْعَآءُ *pl.* رُقْعٌ ـ أَحْمَشُ ٱلسَّاقَيْنِ *fem.* حَمْشَآءُ *pl.* حُمْشٌ.

Sheep-shearer, *n.* جَزَّازُ غَنَمٍ.

Sheep-shearing, *n.* جَزُّ ٱلْغَنَمِ ـ جِزَازُ غَنَمٍ.

Sheep's-skin, *n.* جِلْدُ غَنَمٍ *pl.* جُلُودٌ; prepared —, جِلْدٌ حَوَرٌ.

Sheep-stealer, *n.* سَرَّاقُ غَنَمٍ.

Sheep-stealing, *n.* سَرِقَةُ غَنَمٍ.

Sheep-walk, *n.* مَرْعَاةُ غَنَمٍ.

Sheer, *a.* صِرْفٌ ـ بَحْتٌ ـ سُمَاقٌ ـ مَحْضٌ ـ صَرِيحٌ ـ سَاذَجٌ ـ خَالِصٌ ـ صَافٍ ـ مُجَرَّدٌ. A — lie, كَذِبٌ سُمَاقٌ.

Sheer, *n.* A curve, قَوْسٌ; the — of a ship's deck, قَوْسُ سَطْحِ مَرْكَبٍ.

Sheer, *v.i.* To deviate from a course, عَدَلَ عَنْ سَيْرِهِ ² ـ حَادَ ². To — off, فَرَّ ² ـ اِنْهَزَمَ ـ شَرَدَ ² ـ اِنْطَلَقَ ـ اِنْقَلَعَ ـ عَنْ طَرِيقٍ.

Sheer-hulk, *n.* مَرْكَبُ سِمَاكٍ.

Sheers, *n.* دُولَابٌ لِرَفْعِ ٱلصَّوَارِي ـ دُولَابُ سِمَاكٍ; *in Turkish,* مَاجُونَةٌ.

Sheet, *n.* As for a bed, مِلْحَفَةُ فِرَاشٍ *pl.* مَلَاحِفُ ـ مُلَاءَةٌ *pl.* مُلَاءٌ ـ مُلَاءَةُ فِرَاشٍ (called in Syria, شَرْشَفٌ *pl.* شَرَاشِفُ.) A — of paper, وَرَقَةٌ *pl.* أَوْرَاقٌ ـ طَلَاحِيٌّ *pl.* طَلْحِيَّةٌ (or وَرَقٌ قِرْطَاسٌ); *vulg.* طَرَاحِي *pl.* طَرْحِيَّةُ وَرَقٍ. A — of a book, صَحِيفَةٌ *pl.* صَحَائِفُ ـ إِضْمَامَةٌ مِنْ كِتَابٍ *pl.* أَضَامِيمُ. A —, as of any metal, صَفِيحَةٌ *pl.* صَفَائِحُ. A — of water, بَطِيحَةٌ *pl.* بَطَائِحُ ـ بَلَّانِيقُ *pl.* بَلَالِيقُ. A fly —, وَرَقَةٌ بَيْضَاءُ. A winding —, كَفَنٌ *pl.* أَكْفَانٌ ـ مُسْتَنْقَعُ مَآءٍ. A sail, قِلْعٌ *pl.* قُلُوعٌ *and* قِلَاعٌ. In sheets, parts, فِي كَرَارِيسَ ـ أَجْزَآءً ـ فِي أَجْزَآءٍ ـ كَرَّاسَةٌ; in expanded layers, صَفَائِحُ. Sheets unbound, of paper, أَوْرَاقٌ غَيْرُ مُجَلَّدَةٍ.

Sheet-anchor, *n.* The chief anchor, ٱلْمِرْسَاةُ ٱلْكُبْرَى. A chief support, refuge, مُسْتَعَانٌ ـ ثِقَةٌ ـ مَعَاذٌ. A last resource, hope, آخِرُ أَمَلٍ.

Sheeting, *n.* For sheets, of beds, بَزٌّ لِلشَّرَاشِفِ ـ قُمَاشٌ لِلْمَلَاحِفِ.

Sheets, *n.* Ropes at the lower corners of sails, أُسْقُوتٌ ـ أَعَاوِيلُ. To let fly the —, سَيَّبَ ٱلْأُسْقُوتَ ـ سَيَّبَ ٱلْأَعَاوِيلَ. Three sheets in the wind, tipsy, drunk, شَرْبَانُ ـ سَكْرَانُ ـ سَكْرَانُ مُلْتَكٌ.

Sheik, *n.* *See* Shaikh, *n.*

Shekel, *n.* The coin, شَاقِلٌ.

Shekinah, *n.* سَكِينَةٌ.

Shelf, *n.* Such as to lay things upon, رَفٌّ *pl.* رُفُوفٌ. A shallow, sand-bank, دَبْرٌ *pl.* دِبَارٌ ـ حَالَةٌ *pl.* حَالَاتٌ ـ أَتَانُ ٱلضَّحْلِ ـ شِعْبٌ *pl.* شِعَابٌ. A niche with shelves, رَوْشَنٌ. To lay on a —, حَطَّ عَلَى رَفٍّ ². To put on the —, as from an appointment, عَزَلَ ² ـ عَزَلَ ـ نَقَلَ عَنْ.

Shelfy, *a.* Full of shoals, مَمْلُوٌّ مِنْ شِعَابٍ ـ مَمْلُوٌّ مِنْ دِبَارٍ.

Shell, *n.* Of the sea or rivers, صَدَفَةٌ *coll.* صَدَفٌ *pl.* أَصْدَافٌ. A cowry —, وَدَعَةٌ *pl.* وَدَعَاتٌ. A —, as of nuts, *etc.*, قِشْرٌ *pl.* قُشُورٌ. A — for polishing paper, *etc.*, مِصْقَلَةٌ. The superficial part, outside, جِدَارُ بَيْتٍ ٱلْخَارِجُ. The outer part of an unfinished house, جِدَارُ بَيْتٍ غَيْرِ مُكَمَّلٍ. A wooden coffin, تَابُوتٌ مِنْ خَشَبٍ لِلْمَيِّتِ *pl.* تَوَابِيتُ. A bomb, كُلَّةٌ *pl.* كُلَلٌ ـ قُنْبُرَةٌ *pl.* قَنَابِرُ. To withdraw into its —, of a shell-fish, *etc.*, قَبَعَ ـ. To break the —, of a chicken, قَاضَ ـ.

Shell, *v.t.* To take off the shell, قَشَرَ ـ ² قَشَّرَ. To take off any outer covering, جَرَّدَ ـ شَذَّبَ. To discharge shells, bombs, at, ضَرَبَ ـ بِٱلْقَنَابِرِ (*or* بِٱلْكُلَلِ).

Shell, *v.i.* To fall off, as a shell or crust, تَجَرَّدَ ـ تَقَشَّرَ.

Shellac, *n.* / Shell-lac, } لَكٌّ مِنَ ٱلصِّنْفِ ٱلْعَالِي.

Shelled, *a.* Having a shell, ذُو قِشْرٍ; deprived of its shell, مُقَشَّرٌ; bombarded, مَضْرُوبٌ بِقَنَابِرَ (*or* بِكُلَلٍ).

Shell-fish, *n.* صَدَفٌ *pl.* أَصْدَافٌ ـ أَطُومٌ ـ مَحَارَةٌ *coll.* مَحَارٌ *pl.* وَدَعَةٌ ـ قَوْقَعٌ ـ مَحَاوِرُ.

Shell-marl, *n.* تَرَاكُمُ أَصْدَافٍ مُتَحَجِّرَةٍ ـ تَرَاكُمُ أَصْدَافٍ مَسْحُوقَةٍ.

Shell-work, *n.* تَرْكِيبُ أَصْدَافٍ.

Shelly, *a.* مِنْ أَصْدَافٍ ـ كَثِيرُ ٱلْأَصْدَافِ.

Shelter, *n.* That which shelters, a place of shelter, مَلْجَأٌ ـ مَلَاذٌ ـ مَأْوَاةٌ ـ مَأْوًى. A —, as from the sun, ظُلَّةٌ. Protection, safeguard, حِمَايَةٌ ـ حِفْظٌ ـ مُحَافَظَةٌ ـ صَوْنٌ ـ صِيَانَةٌ. A covering, covert, سِتَارٌ ـ سِتَارَةٌ. A protector, حَافِظٌ ـ حَامٍ ـ مُحَامٍ. A harbour, بَنْدَرٌ ـ مِينَآءٌ ـ مَرْسًى; *from the Turkish*, لِيمَانٌ. Under the — of the night, تَحْتَ سِتَارَةِ ٱللَّيْلِ ـ فِي خِفَآءِ ٱللَّيْلِ. For want of —, لِعَدَمِ ٱلْمَلْجَإِ.

To ask for shelter from one, طَلَبَ مِنْ ـ مَلْجَأً ²; for protection, إِسْتَجَارَ بِ.

To be a shelter to, كَانَ مَلْجَأً لِ. *See also to* Protect, *v.t.*

To get under shelter of, إِحْتَمَى عِنْدَ كَذَا ـ إِلْتَجَأَ إِلَى كَذَا.

To take shelter with, أَوَى إِلَى *aor.* يَأْوِي ـ تَأَوَّى إِلَى.

Shelter, *v.i.* To give shelter to, أَوَى ـ آوَى; as from the sun, to shade, ظَلَّلَ ـ أَظَلَّ. To protect, عَصَمَ ـ خَفَرَ ـ ² حَمَى ـ حَامَى. To — from, to save from, سَلَّمَ ـ مِنْ ـ أَنْقَذَ ـ مِنْ ـ حَفِظَ ـ مِنْ ـ أَسْلَمَ ـ مِنْ. To — one's self, as in the shade, إِسْتَظَلَّ; to protect one's self, تَصَاوَنَ ـ تَصَوَّنَ ـ إِحْتَمَى.

Sheltered, *a.* Kept, preserved, مَصُونٌ ـ مَحْفُوظٌ. Secluded, مُنْفَرِدٌ ـ مُحْتَجِبٌ. Shady, مُظَلَّلٌ. A — or shady place, مَفْيَأَةٌ ـ مَفْيُؤَةٌ.

Sheltering, *a.* Protecting, صَائِنٌ ـ حَافِظٌ ـ حَامٍ. Shading, مُظَلِّلٌ.

Shelterless, *a.* بِلَا مَلَاذٍ ـ بِلَا مَأْوًى ـ عَدِيمُ ٱلْمَلْجَإِ.

Shelve, *v.i.* To slope, مَالَ ـ إِنْصَبَّ ـ إِنْحَدَرَ.

Shelve, *v.t.* To put shelves to, رَكَّبَ فِي ـ رُفُوفًا. To put one on the retired list, جَعَلَ ـ مِنَ ٱلْمُتَقَاعِدِينَ. To — a subject, خَلَّى عَنْ ـ تَخَلَّى عَنْ ـ ² تَرَكَ ـ حَذَفَ.

Shelving, *a.* هَبُوطٌ ـ مَائِلٌ ـ مُنْحَدِرٌ ـ مُنْصَبٌّ.

Shelvy, *a.* *See* Shelfy, *a.*

Shem, *n.* The son of Noah, سَامُ ٱبْنُ نُوحٍ.

Shemitic, *n.* *See* Semitic, *n.*

Sheol, *n.* *See* Hades, *n.*

Shepherd, *n.* رَاعٍ *pl.* رُعَاةٌ.

Shepherdess, *n.* إِمْرَأَةٌ رَاعِيَةٌ *pl.* نِسَآءٌ رَاعِيَاتٌ.

Shepherd's-crook, *n.* *See under* Crook, *n.*

Sherbet, *n.* شَرْبَةٌ ـ شَرْبَاتٌ.

Sherd, *n.* *See* Shard, *n.*

Sherif *or* Sharif, *n.* The Arabic name and title, شَرِيفٌ *pl.* أَشْرَافٌ *and* شَرَفَةٌ *and* شُرَفَآءُ.

Sheriff, *n.* Of a province, مَأْمُورٌ بِإِجْرَآءِ ٱلْأَحْكَامِ فِي إِيَالَةٍ; of a court, جِلْوَازٌ *pl.* جَلَاوِزَةٌ.

Sheriffalty, *n.* / Sheriffdom, } وَظِيفَةُ ٱلْمَأْمُورِ بِإِجْرَآءِ ٱلْأَحْكَامِ فِي إِيَالَةٍ ـ وَظِيفَةُ ٱلْجِلْوَازِ.

Sherry, *n.* The wine, شَيْرِي وَهُوَ ضَرْبٌ مِنَ ٱلْخَمْرِ.

Shew, *v.t.* *See to* Show, *v.t.*

Shew-bread, *n.* خُبْزُ ٱلتَّقْدِمَةِ ـ خُبْزُ ٱلْوُجُوهِ.

Shiäah, *n.* The sect of Muslims so called; also the doctrines of the sect, ٱلشِّيعَةُ. One of the sect, شِيعِيٌّ. The tenets of the —, ٱلشِّيعِيَّةُ ـ ٱلتَّشَيُّعُ.

Shibboleth, *n.* The word employed to distinguish the Gileadites from the Ephraimites, شِبُّولَتْ. The criterion of a party, مِعْيَارُ فِرْقَةٍ.

Shield, *n.* The disc for defence, تُرْسٌ ـ جُنَّانٌ ـ مِجَنٌّ *pl.* تِرَاسٌ *and* تِرَسَةٌ; a — of hide, دَرَقَةٌ *pl.* دَرَقٌ. One armed with a —, تَرَّاسٌ ـ تَارِسٌ. The rim of a —, وَتْفُ تُرْسٍ. Defence, protection, مُحَافَظَةٌ ـ مُحَامَاةٌ ـ صِيَانَةٌ ـ عِصْمَةٌ. A protector, حَامٍ ـ مُحَامٍ ـ عَاصِمٌ. *See also* Protection, Defence, *n.*

Shield, *v.t.* To protect, defend, حَمَى ـ عَصَمَ ـ ² صَانَ ـ أَحْمَى. To cover, protect, سَتَرَ ـ ². To — one's self, تَصَاوَنَ ـ إِسْتَتَرَ ـ إِحْتَمَى. *See also to* Shelter, Protect, *v.t.*

Shield-bearer, *n.* سِلَحْدَار.

Shift, *v.t.* To move, as from one place to another, نَقَلَ ² ـ حَوَّلَ. To change, غَيَّرَ ـ بَدَّلَ. He shifted his clothes, غَيَّرَ ثِيَابَهُ. He shifted it from its place, حَوَّلَ ـ عَنْ مَكَانِهِ. He shifted it to the place, حَوَّلَ ـ إِلَى ٱلْمَكَانِ.

Shift, *v.i.* To be moved, تَحَوَّلَ ـ إِنْتَقَلَ ـ تَنَقَّلَ. To — from,

تَحَوَّلَ عَنْ. It shifted from its place, تَحَوَّلَ عَنْ مَكَانِهِ. He shifted from one thing to another, تَحَوَّلَ مِنْ شَيْءٍ إِلَى شَيْءٍ.

Shift, *n.* A change, تَغْيِير. A movement from one place to another, تَحْوِيل ـ نَقْل ـ تَحَوُّل. A reversion, اِنْقِلَاب. An expedient, means, بَاب ـ مَخْلَص ـ طَرِيق ـ تَدْبِير. A subterfuge, مُحَاوَلَة ـ مُحَارَفَة ـ حِيلَة ـ رُوَيْغَة ـ حُجَّة *pl.* حُجَج. A woman's shirt, دِرْع *pl.* أَدْرَاع ـ مِتْنَبَة ـ إِتْب *pl.* أُتُوب ـ قَمِيصُ ٱمْرَأَةٍ *pl.* قُمْصَانُ ٱلنِّسَآء. One's last —, resource, آخِرُ بَاب ـ مَخْلَص أَخِير. To make —, to manage, تَدَبَّرَ أَمْرَهُ ـ دَبَّرَ أَمْرَهُ *vulg.* اِصْطَفَلَ. To make —, to do without, اِسْتَغْنَى ـ أَغْنِيَ عَنْ ـ عَنْ. To be put or reduced to shifts, to be in straits, ضَاقَ عَلَى ٱلْأَمْرُ *aor.* يَضِيقُ ـ ضِيق ـ تَضَايَقَ بِهِ ٱلْأَمْرُ ـ أَعْسَرَ عَلَيْهِ. To use shifts, artifices, اِحْتَالَ ـ تَحَيَّلَ. How surprising are his shifts, artifices! مَا أَحْوَلَهُ. *See also* Resource, Expedient, *n.*

Shifter, *n.* A trickster, حَيَّال ـ حَوَّال ـ مَكَّار ـ حُوَّلٌ قُلَّبٌ ـ صَاحِبُ حِيلَةٍ.

Shifting, *a.* As of a colour, حَائِل. *See also* Shifter, *n.*

Shiftless, *a.* Without expedients, لَا حِيلَةَ لَهُ. Not employing proper means to gain a living, improvident, قَلِيلُ ـ غَيْرُ مُتَرَوٍّ ـ مُتَغَافِل ـ ٱلتَّبَصُّرِ. *See also* Destitute, *a.*

Shiftlessness, *n.* Improvidence, تَغَافُل ـ عَدَمُ بَصِيرَةٍ ـ قِلَّةُ تَدْبِير. Destitution, عَدَم ـ عَائِلَة ـ عَالَة ـ عَيْلَة.

Shillalah, *n.* } **Shillaly**, } عَصًا ـ دَبَابِيس *pl.* دَبُّوس ـ هَرَاوَى *pl.* هِرَاوَة *pl.* أَعْصَآء and عِصِيّ.

Shilling, *n.* شِلِين *pl.* شِلِينَات.

Shilly-shally, *v.i.* تَرَدَّدَ ـ تَلَتْلَتَ فِي ـ تَمَخْطَرَ ـ فَرْفَرَ. One who shilly-shallies, مَا لَهُ عَزْمَةٌ وَلَا عَزِيمَةٌ ـ فَائِلُ ٱلرَّأْيِ ـ فَرْفَار.

Shilly-shally, *n.* تَرَدُّد ـ تَمَخْطُر ـ لَتْلَتَة ـ فَرْفَرَة.

Shimmer, *v.i.* *See to* Glisten, *v.i.*

Shin, *n.* The — bone, ٱلْقَصَبَةُ ٱلْكُبْرَى ـ عَظْمُ ٱلسَّاقِ.

Shine, *v.i.* To emit rays of light, اِلْتَمَعَ ـ لَمَعَ ـ لَمَحَ ـ أَضَآءَ ـ سَطَعَ ـ تَنَوَّرَ ـ اِسْتَنَارَ ـ نَارَ; especially of the sun or stars, أَشَعَّ ـ أَشْرَقَ ـ شَرَقَ ـ أَلَاحَ ـ لَاحَ. To — brightly, تَأَجَّجَ ـ تَلَأْلَأَ ـ لَأْلَأَ ـ أَبْرَقَ ـ بَرَقَ ـ اِزْمَهَرَّ: The stars shone intensely bright, اِزْمَهَرَّتِ ٱلنُّجُومُ. The lightning shone, رَفَّ ٱلْبَرْقُ. Her teeth shone, رَفَّتْ أَسْنَانُهَا. To glisten, of a colour, رَفَّ ـ اِرْتَفَّ. To be or become conspicuous, known, جَهَرَ ـ اِجْتَهَرَ ـ اِشْتَهَرَ ـ اِمْتَازَ. To be clear, plain, اِتَّضَحَ ـ تَجَلَّى. To be eminent, اِمْتَازَ.

Shine, *n.* } **Shining**, } Brightness, ضِيَآء ـ لَمَعَان ـ نُور; of colour, نَضَر ـ رَفِيف ـ رَفّ; of the weather, صَفَآء; of the sun or moon, لَأْلَآء; of money, لَمَعَان; of jewels, بَصِيص; of a sword, بَرِيق; of lightning, تَأَلُّق; of fire, أَجِيج. A glistening, تَلَأْلُؤ ـ رَقِيق. To take the — out of, to dim, أَخْمَدَ ـ كَدَّرَ; to surpass, بَرَعَ ـ يَفُوقُ *aor.* فَاقَ ـ يَرُوقُ *aor.* رَاقَ عَلَى.

Shiner, *n.* A coin, سِكَّة *pl.* سِكَك.

Shingle, *n.* A thin board, دَفَّة *coll.* دَفّ ـ دَفّ *pl.* دُفُوف ـ لَوْح *pl.* أَلْوَاح (or صَفِيحَة) خَشَب. Pebbles, gravel, حَصْبَآء ـ حَصًى.

Shingle, *v.t.* To cover with shingles, boards, جَعَلَ عَلَى دُفُوفًا ـ تَخَّتَ.

Shingles, *n.* The disease, قُوبَآء ـ ضَرْبٌ مِنَ ٱلْهَرْسِ. *See also* Herpes, *n.*

Shingly, *a.* *See* Pebbly, *a.*

Shining, *a.* and *part.* Emitting light, لَامِع ـ لَمُوح ـ أَجُوج ـ مُنِير ـ نَيِّر ـ سَاطِع ـ لَمَّاع *pl.* لَوَامِع ـ لَمَّاح. Glistening, بَارِق ـ مُتَلَأْلِئ ـ بَرَّاق; of a colour, رَفِيف. A man of — talents, رَجُلٌ ذُو بَرَاعَةٍ ـ بَارِع *fem.* اِمْرَأَةٌ بَرِيعَة ـ ذَاتُ بَرَاعَةٍ. *See also* Brilliant, Sparkling, *a.*

Shiningness, *n.* *See* Brightness, Splendour, *n.*

Shiny, *a.* *See* Shining, *a.*

Ship, *n.* A sea-going vessel, فُلْك *pl.* فُلُوك ـ سَفِينَة *pl.* سُفُن and سَفَائِن ـ خَشَبَة *pl.* خَشَبَات ـ مَرْكَب *pl.* مَرَاكِب. A large —, خَلِيَّة. A three-masted vessel, سَفِينَةٌ ذَاتُ ثَلَاثَةِ أَدْقَالٍ. A — of war, مَرْكَبٌ حَرْبِيّ ـ أَسَاطِيل *pl.* أُسْطُول ـ شُوَن *pl.* شُونَة *pl.* مَرْكَب ـ مَرَاكِبُ حَرْبٍ ـ بَوَارِج *pl.* بَارِجَة. A merchant —, مَرْكَبُ تُجَّارٍ. A — of the line, شُونَةٌ ذَاتُ ثَلَاثَةِ أَنَابِيرَ. A small —, (*see* Skiff, *n.*) To fit out a —, جَهَّزَ مَرْكَبًا. To pay off a —, أَوْفَى حَقَّ بَحْرِيَّةِ ٱلسَّفِينَةِ وَصَرَفَهُمْ. To take —, to go on board —, نَزَلَ بِٱلْمَرْكَبِ ـ رَكِبَ فِي ٱلسَّفِينَةِ. To bring a — near to land, أَدْنَى ٱلسَّفِينَةَ ـ أَرْفَأَ (or رَفَا) ٱلسَّفِينَةَ. To lighten a —, خَفَّفَ ٱلْمَرْكَبَ (or ٱلسَّفِينَةَ). The — drew near to land, أَرْفَأَتِ ٱلسَّفِينَةُ. The — rode upon, or passed through, the sea, مَخَرَتِ (or اِجْتَسَرَتِ) ٱلسَّفِينَةُ ٱلْبَحْرَ.

Ship, *v.t.* To embark, take on board ship, صَعَّدَ ٱلْمَرْكَبَ ـ نَزَلَ بِهِ بَحْرًا ـ رَكِبَ فِي ٱلْمَرْكَبِ ـ نَزَلَ فِي ٱلْمَرْكَبِ. To — a sea, أَطْعَمَ بَحْرًا ـ أَكَلَ بَحْرًا. They were shipped by the governor, صُعِّدُوا فِي ٱلْمَرْكَبِ مِنَ ٱلْحَاكِمِ.

Shipboard, *ad.* عَلَى ٱلسَّفِينَةِ ـ فِي ٱلْمَرْكَبِ.

Ship-boy, *n.* صَبِيُّ ٱلْمَعَاشِ فِي مَرْكَب.

Ship-broker, *n.* سِمْسَارُ ٱلْمَرَاكِبِ.

Ship-builder, n. مُنْشِئُ ٱلْمَرَاكِبِ ـ مِعْمَارُ ٱلْمَرَاكِبِ ـ سَفَّان.

Ship-building, n. عِمَارَةُ ٱلْمَرَاكِبِ ـ سِفَانَة.

Ship-carpenter, n. نَجَّارُ مَرْكَبٍ ; *from the Greek*, مَرَانْقُوس.

Ship-chandler, n. مُمَوِّنُ ٱلْمَرَاكِبِ (*vulg.* مَوَّان).

Shipless, a. مِنْ غَيْرِ مَرْكَبٍ ـ بِلَا سَفِينَةٍ.

Ship-master, n. رُبَّان ـ رَئِيسُ مَرْكَبٍ ـ رَئِيسُ ٱلنُّوتِيَّةِ ـ قُبْطَانُ مَرْكَبِ ٱلتُّجَّارِ ـ نَاخُوذَاة pl. نَوَاخِذَة. Ship-masters, أَرْبَابُ ٱلسُّفُنِ.

Shipmate, n. رَفِيقٌ فِي مَرْكَبٍ pl. رُفَقَاءُ ـ زَمِيلٌ فِي مَرْكَبٍ.

Shipment, n. The act of shipping, as of cargo, تَحْمِيلُ مَرْكَبٍ ـ إِيسَاقُ مَرْكَبٍ. A cargo, وَسْقُ مَرْكَبٍ ـ تَعْبِئَةُ مَرْكَبٍ.

Ship-money, n. ضَرِيبَةُ ٱلدَّوْلَةِ عَلَى بِنَاءِ ٱلسُّفُنِ.

Ship-owner, n. صَاحِبُ مَرْكَبٍ pl. أَصْحَابُ مَرَاكِبَ.

Shipper, n. مُوسِقُ مَرْكَبٍ ـ وَاسِقُ مَرْكَبٍ.

Shipping, n. Ships, مَرَاكِبُ ـ سَفَائِنُ.

Ship-shape, a. مَضْبُوطٌ ـ مُحْكَمٌ ـ مُنَسَّقٌ ـ نَسِيقٌ ـ مُنَظَّمٌ ـ مُهَنْدَمٌ.

Ship-shape, ad. بِهِنْدَامٍ ـ بِنَسَقٍ ـ بِضَبْطٍ ـ بِنِظَامٍ.

Ship's-husband, n. مُرَمِّمُ ٱلْمَرَاكِبِ وَمُمَوِّنُهَا وَهِيَ فِي ٱلْمِينَاءِ.

Ship-worm, n. سُرْفَةٌ ـ قَنَعٌ.

Shipwreck, n. Of a ship, غَرَقٌ ـ ٱنْكِسَارُ مَرْكَبٍ. Ruin, destruction, خَرَابٌ ـ تَلَفٌ ـ إِتْلَافٌ. To suffer —, of a person, ٱنْكَسَرَ بِهِ ٱلْمَرْكَبُ. They have made — of the faith, ٱنْكَسَرَتْ بِهِمِ ٱلسَّفِينَةُ مِنْ جِهَةِ ٱلْإِيمَانِ. To make — of, to ruin, أَتْلَفَ ـ أَهْلَكَ.

Shipwreck, v.t. To destroy a ship by violence, غَرَّقَ ٱلسَّفِينَةَ ـ أَتْلَفَ ٱلْمَرْكَبَ ـ كَسَرَ ٱلْمَرْكَبَ. To be shipwrecked, of a ship, ٱنْكَسَرَ ٱلْمَرْكَبُ ; of a person, ٱنْكَسَرَ بِهِ ٱلْمَرْكَبُ : I was shipwrecked three times, ثَلَاثَ مَرَّاتٍ ٱنْكَسَرَتْ بِيَ ٱلسَّفِينَةُ.

Shipwrecked, a. مُنْكَسِرٌ ـ غَارِقٌ ـ غَرِيقٌ.

Shipwright, n. *See* Ship-builder, n.

Shire, n. وِلَايَةٌ pl. وِلَايَاتٌ ـ إِيَالَةٌ pl. إِيَالَاتٌ.

Shirk, v.t. To avoid, تَجَافَى عَنْ ـ صَدَفَ عَنْ ـ أَحْبَطَ عَنْ ـ أَعْرَضَ عَنْ ـ تَجَنَّبَ مِنْ ـ لَاذَ مِنْ. To elude, تَفَلَّتَ مِنْ. To practise an elusion in, تَحَوَّلَ فِي ـ ٱحْتَالَ فِي. To — a thing through cowardice, خَامَ عَنْ.

Shirk, n. An evasion, artifice, حِيلَةٌ pl. حِيَلٌ. One who practises evasion, حُوَّلٌ قُلَّبٌ ـ مُحْتَالٌ ـ حَيَّالٌ.

Shirt, n. قَمِيصٌ pl. قُمُصٌ *and* أَقْمِصَةٌ *and* قُمْصَانٌ. To put on a —, تَقَمَّصَ.

Shirting, n. قُمَاشٌ (*or* بَزٌّ) لِلْقُمْصَانِ.

Shist, n. *See* Schist, n.

Shive, n. A slice, شَرِيحَةٌ ـ شَرْحَةٌ ـ قِطْعَةٌ pl. قِطَعٌ. A piece, قِطْعَةٌ pl. قِطَعٌ ـ شُقَّةٌ pl. شِقَقٌ.

Shiver, n. A fragment, جُزْءٌ pl. أَجْزَاءٌ ـ قُشَامٌ ـ فَضَضٌ ـ كُسَارَةٌ ـ كِسْرَةٌ pl. كُسُورٌ. A tremor; *see* Shivering, n.

Shiver, v.t. To dash in pieces, عَدَّمَ ـ رَفَتَ ـ رَضَّ ـ رَضْرَضَ. To —, to tear, split, as the wind shivers sails, *etc.*, بَعَجَ ـ بَعَّجَ ـ شَقَّقَ. To be shivered, dashed to pieces, تَكَسَّرَ ـ ٱرْفَتَّ ـ تَرَضَّضَ ـ ٱرْتَضَّ.

Shiver, v.i. To fall into fragments, تَحَطَّمَ ـ ٱنْحَطَمَ ـ تَطَايَرَ ـ تَكَسَّرَ ـ تَرَضَّضَ. To quake, رَعَشَ ـ ٱرْتَعَشَ ـ رَجَفَ ـ ٱرْتَجَفَ.

Shivering, n. The act of dashing to pieces, رَضٌّ ـ رَفْتٌ ـ رَضْرَضٌ ـ تَكْسِيرٌ. A tremor, رَجْفٌ ـ رُعَاشٌ ـ ٱرْتِعَاشٌ ـ ٱرْتِجَافٌ.

Shivering, a. رَعِشٌ ـ مُرْتَعِشٌ.

Shivery, a. Easily broken, رَخْوٌ ـ قَصِمٌ ـ وَاهٍ ـ سَرِيعُ ٱلْعَطَبِ.

Shoal, n. A multitude, جَمٌّ ـ سِرْبٌ pl. أَسْرَابٌ ـ فَوْجٌ pl. أَفْوَاجٌ ; a — of fish, سَمَكٌ كَثِيرٌ جِدًّا. A shallow, ضَحْلٌ ـ أَتَانُ ٱلضَّحْلِ ـ حَالَةٌ pl. حَالَاتٌ ـ دَبْرٌ pl. دِبَارٌ ـ شِعْبٌ pl. شِعَابٌ. In shoals, أَفْوَاجًا.

Shoal, a. Shallow, ضَحْلٌ ـ رَقٌّ ـ رَكِيكٌ.

Shoal, v.i. To crowd, of many, ٱجْتَمَعُوا ـ ٱلْتَمُّوا ـ تَرَاكَمُوا ـ جَمُّوا. To become shallow, ضَحُلَ ـ ٱسْتَرَقَّ.

Shoaliness, n. Of water, رِقَّةُ مَاءٍ ـ رَكَاكَةُ مَاءٍ. The state of abounding in shoals, كَثْرَةُ شِعَابٍ ـ كَثْرَةُ دِبَارٍ.

Shoaly, a. Abounding in shoals, shelfs, مَمْلُوٌّ مِنْ دِبَارٍ ـ مَمْلُوٌّ مِنْ شِعَابٍ.

Shock, n. A collision, صَكْمَةٌ ـ صَدْمَةٌ ـ تَصَادُمٌ ـ لَطْمَةٌ. A shaking, as of an earthquake, *etc.*, هِزَّةٌ ـ رَجَّةٌ. A quivering, or a commotion, رَجْدَةٌ ـ خَضَّةٌ. A sinking of the heart, هُبُوطُ ٱلْقَلْبِ. A stroke, attack, as of disease, *etc.*, ٱعْتِرَاءٌ ـ إِصَابَةٌ ـ ضَرْبَةٌ. A sudden event, calamity, آفَةٌ pl. آفَاتٌ ـ مُصِيبَةٌ pl. مَصَائِبُ. A — of corn, صُبْرَةُ حِنْطَةٍ pl. صُبَرٌ ـ كُدْسُ حِنْطَةٍ pl. أَكْدَاسٌ. To stand a —, collision, قَاوَمَ ٱلصَّدْمَةَ ; to be firm, as under misfortune, to bear, ٱحْتَمَلَ ٱلْمُصِيبَةَ ـ صَبَرَ عِنْدَ ٱلْمُصِيبَةِ. To give a —; *see to* Shock, v.t.

Shock, v.t. To collide with, صَكَمَ ـ صَدَمَ ـ لَطَمَ. To strike with horror, أَرْعَدَ ـ أَرْعَبَ ـ أَدْهَشَ ; with disgust, أَكْرَهَ ـ أَقْرَفَ ـ كَرَّهَ. To offend, displease, أَغَمَّ ـ أَغَاظَ ـ كَدَّرَ عَلَى. To distress, pain, فَجَعَ. The calamity shocked him, فَجَعَتْهُ ٱلْمُصِيبَةُ. To collect into shocks, صَبَّرَ صُبَرًا ـ كَدَّسَ أَكْدَاسًا. To be shocked, stricken with horror, اِرْتَعَبَ ـ دَهِشَ ـ ; to be disgusted, ـ كَرِهَ ـ اِشْمَأَزَّ. He was shocked by the death of so-and-so, قَدْ فُجِعَ بِوَفَاةِ فُلَانٍ. A person who is shocked, as by an affliction, ـ مَفْجُوع ـ مُفَجَّع ـ فَجِيع.

Shocking, *a.* Horrible, dreadful, ـ فَظِيع ـ مَهُول ـ هَائِل ـ مُخِيف ـ مُرْعِب. Offensive, مُغِيظ ـ مُفَارِط ـ جَانٍ. Disgusting, كَرِيه ـ مُقْرِف ـ نَافِر. Afflicting, distressing, فَاجِع. A — death, مَوْتٌ فَاجِعٌ. A — event, calamity, bereavement, رَزِيَّة *pl.* رَزَايَا ـ فَاجِعَة *pl.* فَوَاجِع ـ فَجِيعَة *pl.* فَجَائِع. Most —, painful, أَفْجَع.

Shockingly, *ad.* Disgustingly, قَرَفًا ـ بِكَرَاهَةٍ ـ اِعْتِنَافًا. Offensively, injuriously, بِأَذِيَّةٍ ـ مُضَارَّةً. Dreadfully, فَظَاعَةً ـ فَجْعًا. Excessively, greatly, جِدًّا ـ كَثِيرًا ـ لِلْغَايَةِ.

Shod, *part. of to* Shoe, *q.v.*

Shoddy, *n.* صُوف مَخْلُوط بِرَنْث ـ صُوف دُون.

Shoe, *n.* For a human foot, نَعْل *pl.* نِعَال ـ مَرْكُوب *pl.* مَرَاكِيب ـ صِرْمَة *pl.* صِرَم ـ تَاسُومَة *pl.* تَوَاسِيم ـ مَدَاس. A wooden shoe or patten, قَبْقَاب *pl.* قَبَاقِيب. A horse —, نَعْل *pl.* نِعَال. An old —, شَرْشُوحَة ـ بَرْطُوشَة ـ صِرْمَة عَتِيقَة. To put on one's shoes, ـ تَنَعَّلَ ـ لَبِسَ ٱلنَّعْلَ. To stand in one's shoes, in the place of, قَامَ مَقَامَ فُلَانٍ.

Shoe, *v.t.* To put shoes on a horse, *etc.*, بَيْطَرَ ـ نَعَّلَ. To cover with, لَبَّسَ ـ بِ.

Shoe-black, *n.* مَسَّاحُ ٱلصِّرَمِ *pl.* مَسَّاحَة.

Shoe-buckle, *n.* إِبْزِيمُ ٱلصِّرَمِ *pl.* أَبَازِيم.

Shoeing-horn, *n.* آلَةٌ لِتَلْبِيسِ ٱلصِّرَمِ.

Shoe-latchet, *n.* شِرْع ـ شِرَاك ـ سُيُور.

Shoe-leather, *n.* جِلْدٌ لِلْمَرْكُوب ـ جِلْدٌ لِلنِّعَالِ.

Shoemaker, *n.* إِسْكَاف ـ سَكَّاف *pl.* أَسَاكِفَة ـ صَرْمَاتِيّ ـ خَرَّاز. A shoemaker's cutting board, قُرْزُوم ـ جَبْأَة. A shoemaker's knife, إِزْمِيل ـ ذَرْب.

Shoemaking, *n.* إِسْكَافِيَّة.

Shoe-string, *n.* / **Shoe-tie**, } خَيْطُ ٱلنَّعْلِ *pl.* أَخْيَاط *and* خُيُوط ; *vulg.* خِيْطَان.

Shone, *pret. of to* Shine, *q.v.*

Shook, *pret. of to* Shake, *v.t.* and *i.*

Shoon, *pl. of* Shoe, *n.*, *q.v.*

Shoot, *v.t.* To let fly, to dart, رَمَى ـ أَطْلَقَ ـ بَنْدَقَ ـ قَوَّسَ. To — at one with, as with a dart, bullet, *etc.*, رَمَى ـ بِ. To strike with, as with a shot, ضَرَبَ ـ بِ ـ أَصَابَ ـ بِ. To kill by shooting with, قَتَلَ ـ بِ. To put forth, as a tree its leaves, *etc.*, نَبَّتَ ـ أَخْرَجَ. To pass through swiftly, ـ خَفَقَ فِي ـ سَبَحَ فِي ـ طَارَ فِي *aor.* يَطِيرُ. I shot the arrow from the bow, رَمَيْتُ ٱلسَّهْمَ مِنَ ٱلْقَوْسِ. He shot and hit, رَمَى فَأَصَابَ. He shot at the butts, رَمَى فِي ٱلْأَغْرَاضِ. He shot him with a bullet, رَمَاهُ بِرَصَاصَةٍ. *See also to* Discharge, *v.t.*

Shoot, *v.i.* To perform the act of discharging, as arrows, guns, *etc.*, رَمَى ـ قَوَّسَ ـ بَنْدَقَ. To germinate, bud, ـ طَرَّ ـ أَلْحَسَ ـ فَرَّخَ; to put forth shoots, عَسْلَجَ. To feel a darting pain, إِخْتَلَجَ صُدْغُهُ, his temples —, ـ نَخَزَ ـ وَجَعٌ ـ عَضَّ ـ ٱلْوَجَعُ. To move with velocity, خَفَّ ـ تَشَمَّرَ ـ دَفَقَ ـ دَفْدَفَ. To glide, دَفَّ ـ زَلَّ *aor.* يَزِلُّ ـ سَبَحَ ـ حَبَا *aor.* يَحْبُو: the stars — through the firmament, ٱلنُّجُومُ تَسْبَحُ فِي ٱلْفَلَكِ; the ship shot through the water, تَشَمَّرَتِ ٱلسَّفِينَةُ فِي ٱلْمَاءِ. The shooters shot at him, رَمَتْهُ ٱلرُّمَاةُ. *See also to* Glide, Grow, *v.i.* To shoot ahead of, go in advance of, ـ سَبَقَ. To surpass, فَاقَ *aor.* يَفُوقُ ـ رَاقَ *aor.* يَرُوقُ ـ بَرَزَ عَلَى ـ أَنْجَحَ بِ ـ بَرَعَ ـ عَلَى.

To shoot into, to precipitate one's self into, ـ عَسَمَ ـ عَسَمَ فِي ـ أَرْمَى بِنَفْسِهِ فِي ـ بِنَفْسِهِ فِي. To become, آلَ إِلَى *aor.* يَؤُولُ ـ صَارَ ـ أَصْبَحَ ـ حَصَلَ.

To shoot out, to go out quickly, خَرَجَ عَلَى ٱلْفَوْرِ ـ اِنْسَلَّ.

To shoot up, to grow up, of plants, نَبَتَ ـ نَمَى ـ طَلَعَ ـ أَنْبَتَ. To shoot up into youth, شَبَّ. To shoot up in stature, طَالَ ـ اِسْتَطَالَ.

Shoot, *n.* As with a missive, ضَرْب ـ رَمَاة ـ رَمْيَة. A sprout, نَبَاتَة ـ نَبْت ـ فِرَاخ *pl.* فَرْخ شَجَرَة ـ عَسَالِيج *pl.* عُسْلُوج *or* عُسْلُج. The trees produced many shoots, فَرَّخَ ٱلشَّجَرُ فِرَاخًا كَثِيرَةً.

Shooter, *n.* قَوَّاس ـ رَامٍ بِٱلْبُنْدُقِ.

Shooting, *n.* Of plants, نَبَات ـ طُلُوع. The act of discharging, as of fire-arms, إِطْلَاقُ ٱلنَّارِ; of bullets, إِطْلَاقُ ٱلرَّصَاصِ; of guns, إِطْلَاقُ ٱلْمَدَافِعِ. Shooting, darting, as of a pain, ـ عَضّ ـ نَخْزَة ـ نَغْزَة. Killing game, صَيْد. *See also* Shooting-match, *n.*

Shooting, *a.* As a pain, نَاخِز ـ نَاغِز ـ عَاضّ. A — pain, نَخْزَة.

Shooting-gallery, *n.* مَحَلّ لِتَعْلِيمِ إِطْلَاقِ ٱلنَّارِ.

Shooting-match, *n.* مُخَاصَلَة ـ تَرَمَّاة ـ مُرَامَاة. To contend with one in a —, رَامَى ـ خَاصَلَ. A wager laid in a —, خَصْل. He won his wager in the —, أَصَابَ خَصْلَهُ.

Shooting-star, *n.* شِهَاب *pl.* شُهُب.

Shop, *n.* حَانُوت *pl.* حَوَانِيت (this word primarily means a wine-shop,) دُكَّان .pl دَكَاكِين — . A large —, warehouse, مَخْزَن pl. مَخَازِن — حَاصِل pl. حَوَاصِل . *See also* Workshop, *n.*

Shop, *v.i.* دَارَ ٱلدَّكَاكِين — [2] خَرَجَ يَتَسَوَّق .

Shop-board, *n.* بَنْك — مَائِدَة ٱلدُّكَّان .

Shop-keeper, *n.* حَانُوتِيّ — صَاحِب دُكَّان .pl أَصْحَاب ٱلدَّكَاكِين .

Shop-lifter, *n.* سَارِق (or نَشَّال) مِنَ ٱلدَّكَاكِين .

Shop-lifting, *n.* سَرِقَة مِنَ ٱلدَّكَاكِين .

Shopman, *n.* غُلَام ٱلحَاصِل (or ٱلدُّكَّان) pl. غِلْمَة and غِلْمَان .

Shop-woman, *n.* غُلَامَة (or خَادِمَة) فِي دُكَّان .

Shopping, *n.* دَوَرَان ٱلدَّكَاكِين — ٱلشِّرَاء فِي ٱلدَّكَاكِين .

Shore, *n.* Coast or land near water, شَطّ — عَيْقَة — ضَفِير pl. شُطُوط — سَاحِل pl. سَوَاحِل . A prop, buttress, سَنَد — عِمَادَة pl. أَسْنَاد — مِسْنَد pl. مَسَانِد . To go on —, to land, نَزَلَ فِي ٱلبَرّ . To bring a ship to the —, أَنْدَخَ (or نَدَخَ or أَرْفَأَ) ٱلمَرْكَب . To go on —, aground, of a ship, إِرْتَطَمَ . The place is only six hours distant from the shores of Italy, لَا يَبْعُد ٱلمَكَان عَنْ شُطُوط إِيطَالِيَا إِلَّا مَسَافَة سِتّ سَاعَات . *See also* Coast, *n.*

Shore, *v.t.* To prop, عَمَدَ — سَنَدَ — أَسْنَدَ .

Shore-boat, *n.* فَلُوكَة ٱلبَرّ .

Shoreless, *a.* لَا سَاحِلَ لَهُ — لَا شَطَّ لَهُ . *See also* Unlimited, *a.*

Shorcling, *n.* }
Shorling, } A shorn animal, جَلَمَة — جَزِيزَة .

Shorn, *a.* As of its wool, جَزِيز — مَجْزُوز — مَجْلُوم . Deprived of, مُعَرًّى مِن .

Short, *a.* Not long, قَصِير pl. قِصَار and قُصَرَاء fem. قَصِيرَة pl. قِصَار and قِصَارَة . Short of stature, قَصِير ٱلقَدّ . Short, as of time, قَرِيب . Narrow, ضَيِّق . Deficient, نَاقِص . Abbreviated, compendious, وَجِيز — مُوجَز . Insufficient, نَاقِص — غَيْر كَافٍ . Abrupt, sharp, of a person, فَظّ — جَافٍ — عَنِيف . Friable, هَشّ — يَنْفَتّ — ذُو تَحَطُّم — مُتَفَتِّت . Short and thick, podgy, فَرِيك — حَنْكَلَة — مُرَبْرَب — ضَخْم . Short and ugly, of a woman, قُنْبُضَة . Short of, below what is requisite, دُون ; wanting, مُحْتَاج إِلَى — عَاوِز — عَائِز . A — time hence, بَعْدَ بُرْهَة قَصِيرَة . A crime — of murder, ذَنْب دُونَ ٱلقَتْل . He gave me a —, sharp, answer, جَاوَبَنِي بِفَظَاظَة — بَادَهَنِي بِٱلجَوَاب . In —, حَاصِل ٱلكَلَام — أَخِيرًا — غَايَتُهُ — ٱلحَاصِل . Oh how — he is! (*prov.*) مَا أَقْرَب مَخْسَاهُ مِنْ مَفْسَاهُ (*lit.* How near his mouth is to his anus!) Time is —, ٱلوَقْت مُقَصَّر . For a short time, زَمَان سَاعَة — لِزَمَن يَسِير . The bed is too — to stretch one's self upon, [2] قَصُرَ ٱلفِرَاش عَنِ ٱلتَّمَدُّد . The *dirham* was somewhat —, (of its proper weight,) شَفَّ ٱلدِّرْهَم قَلِيلًا .

To be short, not tall, [2] قَصُرَ .

To be short of, in want of, إِحْتَاجَ إِلَى — أَعْوَزَ . To be without, تَفَقَّدَ — أَفْتَقَرَ إِلَى — عَدِمَ . To be below what is required, كَانَ دُونَ ٱلمَطْلُوب — شَفَّ . The garment was too short for him, شَفَّ عَنْهُ ٱلثَّوْب .

To become short, [2] قَصُرَ .

To be taken short, زَحْمَتُهُ ضَرُورَة — إِعْتَرَاهُ ٱلبَرَاز .

To come short, to be deficient, [2] نَقَصَ — قَلَّ . The property came short of his debts, ضَاقَ ٱلمَال عَنْ دُيُونِهِ . To be remiss, تَرَاخَى — فَشِلَ .

To come short of, to fail in, [2] قَصَرَ عَن — قَصَّرَ فِي — أَخَلَّ بِ — خَابَ aor. يَخِيب — تَقَصَّرَ فِي — أَقْصَرَ عَن . *See also* To fall short, *under to* Fall, *v.i.*

To cut short, to abbreviate, إِقْتَصَرَ — أَوْجَزَ — قَصَّرَ . To cut one short, as in speaking, قَطَّعَ بِ — قَطَعَ لِسَانَهُ . To cut off part of anything, [2] قَصَّ — قَرَضَ . He cut short somewhat of his discourse, أَخْطَفَ مِنْ حَدِيثِهِ .

To fall short, as of doing what he ought to have done, فَشِلَ — قَصَّرَ — إِئْتَلَى — يُولِّي aor. أَلَّى — أَلَا aor. يَأْلُو . *See also* To come short of, *supra.*

To grow short, [2] قَصُرَ .

To judge to be short, إِسْتَقْصَرَ .

To keep one short, قَصَّرَ بِ — ضَيَّقَ عَلَى .

To stop short, as in speech خَرِسَ — [2] سَكَتَ — إِنْقَطَعَ عَن — وَقَفَ aor. يَقِف — ٱلكَلَام .

Short, *n.* A summary, مُوجَز — وَجْز . To know the long and — of, عَرَفَ بَاطِن ٱلأَمْر وَخَارِجَهُ . The long and the — of it is, نِهَايَة ٱلأَمْر .

Short-breathed, *a.* *See* Short-winded, *a.*

Short-cake, *n.* كَعْك فَتِيت .

Shortcoming, *n.* قُصُور — قَصْر — قَصَر — قُصْرَة . Remissness, فَشَل — تَرَاخٍ . *See also* To fall short, *under to* Fall, *v.i.*

Shorten, *v.t.* To make short, قَصَّرَ . To diminish, نَقَّصَ — إِقْتَصَرَ — أَوْجَزَ ; in numbers, قَلَّلَ — أَقَلَّ To abbreviate, أَنْقَصَ . To —, by taking some part away from, أَخْطَفَ مِن . To contract, ضَيَّقَ . To —, as paste, صَيَّرَ فَرِيكًا . To — sails, [2] لَمَّ ٱلقُلُوع .

Shorten, *v.i.* To become short, [2] قَصُرَ — [2] قَصَرَ . To contract, تَضَيَّقَ — يَضِيق aor. ضَاقَ .

Shortening, *n.* The act of making short, تَقْصِير ; of contracting, making narrow, تَضْيِيق . Something to make paste brittle, ذَات تَحَطُّم .

Short-hand, *n.* خَطُّ إِشَارَةٍ. Short-hand writer, خَطَّاطٌ بِقَلَمِ ٱلْإِشَارَةِ.

Short-lived, *a.* قَصِيرُ ٱلْعُمْرِ ـ وَقْتِيٌّ.

Shortly, *ad.* Briefly, إِقْتِصَارًا ـ بِٱلْإِقْتِصَارِ ـ بِٱلْجُمْلَةِ. Soon, عَنْ قَرِيبٍ ـ عَنْ قَلِيلٍ. I hope — to see you, أَرْجُو أَنْ أَرَاكَ عَنْ قَرِيبٍ. *See also* Soon, *ad.*

Shortner, *n.* مُقَصِّر.

Shortness, *n.* The being short, قَصْر ـ قِصَر. Brevity, إِقْتِصَار ـ إِيجَاز. Shortness of volume, littleness, صُغْر; of numbers, قِلَّة; of stature, قِصَارَة ـ قِصَرُ ٱلْقَدِّ; of time, قِلَّةُ ٱلزَّمَانِ; of breath, ضِيقَةُ نَفَسٍ ـ قُطْع.

Shorts, *n.* *See* Bran, *n.*

Short-sighted, *a.* Unable to see far, أَخْفَش ـ وَرْوَرِيٌّ *fem.* خَفْشَاءُ *pl.* خُفْش ـ قَصِيرُ ٱلنَّظَرِ; of the mind, غَافِل ـ غَفْلَان ـ قَلِيلُ ٱلتَّبَصُّرِ ـ قَلِيلُ ٱلْبَصِيرَةِ.

Short-sightedness, *n.* Of the eyes, قِصَرُ ٱلنَّظَرِ ـ خَفَش; of the mind, قِلَّةُ تَبَصُّرٍ ـ قِلَّةُ بَصِيرَةٍ ـ غَفْلَة.

Short-waisted, *a.* مُخَصَّر ـ مُخْتَنِقُ ٱلْخَصْرِ.

Short-winded, *a.* قَابِع *pl.* قِبَاع ـ ضَيِّقُ ٱلنَّفَسِ.

Shot, *pret. of to* Shoot, *v.t.* and *i.*, *q.v.*

Shot, *n.* A discharge, as of any missile, رَمْيٌ ـ رِمَايَة ـ رَمْيَة *pl.* رَمَايَات ـ إِطْلَاق ـ ضَرْبَة. A bullet, رَصَاصَة; a cannon ball, كُلَّة *pl.* كُلَل. Small —, one such, خُرْدُق ـ خُرْدُقَة *coll.* خُرْدَة. The range, as of a —, مَدًى. A — that hits, إِصَابَة. A charge, as of —, تَعْمِيرَة. A thing or animal to be — at, رَمِيَّة. A shooter, رَامٍ ـ قَوَّاس. A good —, aim, رَمْيَةٌ سَدِيدَةٌ; a hit in speaking, something to the point, سَدَاد: he made a good —, hit, قَالَ سَدَادًا مِنَ ٱلْقَوْلِ. A good —, shooter, رَامٍ سَدَّادٌ; *from the Turkish*, نِشَانْجِي. A random —, رَمْيٌ عَرَضِيٌّ. Within musket —, فِي مَدَى ٱلرَّصَاصَةِ. To go off like a —, to burst, فَقَعَ ـ طَقْطَقَ; تَفَرْتَكَ ـ طَقَّ; to run away suddenly, وَلَّى هَارِبًا.

Shot, *v.t.* To imbue, as one colour with the shade of another, شَرَّبَ. To be so shotted, أُشْرِبَ. The white was shotted with red, أُشْرِبَ ٱلْأَبْيَضُ حُمْرَةً.

Shot, *v.t.* To charge, as with shot, عَمَّرَ ـ دَكَّ.

Shot-belt, *n.* As for small shot, حِمَالَةُ ٱلْخُرْدَةِ.

Shot-free, *a.* *See* Scot-free, *a.*

Shot-hole, *n.* Of a bullet, مَنْفِذُ ٱلرَّصَاصَةِ *pl.* مَنَافِذُ; of a cannon-ball, مَنْفِذُ ٱلْكُلَّةِ.

Shotted, *a.* Charged, as with shot, مُعَمَّر. Double shotted, of bullets, مُعَمَّرٌ بِرَصَاصَتَيْنِ. Shotted, of silk, *etc.*, يَتَلَوَّنُ لِلْعُيُونِ ـ أَلْوَانًا. A — silk dress, ثَوْبٌ أَبُو قَلَمُونَ.

Shotten, *a.* Having cast its spawn, وَضَعَتِ ٱلسَّمَكَةُ صِيرَهَا. Dislocated, مَفْكُوك ـ مَخْلُوع.

Should, *aux. v.* As denoting duty, وَجَبَ عَلَى ـ لَزِمَ عَلَى *aor.* يَجِبُ ـ إِنْبَغَى ل ـ كَانَ عَلَى. Should, in the sense of if, لَوْ: Should he wish, لَوْ شَاءَ. He — have thought of it sooner, كَانَ عَلَيْهِ أَنْ يَسْبِقَ إِلَى ٱلتَّفَكُّرِ فِيهِ. They — not have endangered their lives, مَا كَانَ يَنْبَغِي لَهُمْ أَنْ يُخَاطِرُوا بِحَيَاتِهِمْ. They — have been present, كَانَ يَنْبَغِي حُضُورُهُمْ. Should we have been unjust if we had discharged him? أَكُنَّا نُعَدُّ مِنَ ٱلظَّالِمِينَ لَوْ طَرَدْنَاهُ.

Shoulder, *n.* مَنْكِب ـ مَطَالِبُ *pl.* مَطْلَب ـ عَوَاتِقُ *pl.* عَاتِق *pl.* مَنَاكِبُ ـ كِتْف *pl.* أَكْتَاف. The two — joints, ٱلْأَسْدَرَانِ. Having high or broad shoulders, أَلَصّ ـ كَتِف ـ أَكْتَف *fem.* كَتْفَاءُ *pl.* كُتْف. A projection, طَنَف *pl.* أَطْنَاف. A ridge, حَرْف *pl.* حُرُوف. To shrug the shoulders, هَزَّ أَكْتَافَهُ. To turn a cold — to, هَجَرَ ـ أَعْرَضَ عَنْ ـ تَجَافَى عَنْ ـ عَامَلَ عَلَى ٱلْبُرُودَةِ. To bind the shoulders together, كَتَفَ. To put one's — to the wheel, to use one's efforts in, جَهَدَ فِي ـ تَجَاهَدَ فِي; to assist, سَاعَدَ. They bind heavy burdens on men's shoulders, يَحْزِمُونَ أَحْمَالًا ثَقِيلَةً عَلَى أَكْتَافِ ٱلنَّاسِ.

Shoulder, *v.t.* To place on the shoulder, وَضَعَ عَلَى كِتْفِهِ *aor.* يَضَعُ. To carry on the shoulders, حَمَلَ (or شَالَ ب) عَلَى ٱلْأَكْتَافِ. To hit on the —, كَتَفَ; to be shouldered, hit on the —, كُتِفَ. To push with the —, وَكَظَ بِٱلْكِتْفِ *aor.* يَكِظُ. *See also to* Push, Thrust, *v.t.*

Shoulder-belt, *n.* مِحْمَل *pl.* مَحَامِلُ ـ حِمَالَة *pl.* حَمَائِلُ.

Shoulder-blade, *n.* عَاتِق *pl.* عَوَاتِقُ ـ لَوْحُ ٱلْكِتْفِ.

Shout, *v.i.* To cry out, صَرَخَ ـ صَاحَ ـ ضَجَّ ـ زَعَقَ ـ عَيَّطَ. To —, as in triumph, هَتَفَ; as in pain, affliction, وَلْوَلَ. To — to, صَوَّتَ ب ـ صَاحَ ب ـ نَوَّهَ ب. To — for, to applaud, صَوَّتَ عَلَى. Many of the people shouted aloud, in triumph, كَثِيرُونَ مِنَ ٱلْقَوْمِ رَفَعُوا أَصْوَاتَهُمْ بِٱلْهُتَافِ. He shouted at the top of his voice, صَرَخَ بِأَعْلَى صَوْتِهِ.

Shout, *n.* صَوْت *pl.* أَصْوَات ـ صَيْحَة ـ صِيَاح ـ صَرْخَة ـ صُرَاخ ـ زَعْقَة ـ عِيَاط. A — of triumph, هُتُوف; of pain or affliction, وَلْوَلَة ـ وَلْوَال. To shout with a great —, صَرَخَ صَرْخَةً عَظِيمَةً. They raised a — against him, رَفَعُوا عَلَيْهِ جَلَبَةً.

Shouter, *n.* صَارِخ ـ صَائِت.

Shouting, *n.* *See* Shout, *n.*

Shove, *v.t.* To push, ضَغَطَ ـ دَسَعَ ـ دَفَعَ ـ دَفَشَ ـ دَفَرَ. To — back, رَجَعَ ـ إِلَى وَرَآءِ ـ ارْتَدَّ ـ رَدَّ. To — out, طَرَدَ ـ أَخْرَجَ. To — one's self against, صَدَمَ ـ اِنْضَغَطَ إِلَى. To be shoved, pushed, اِنْدَسَعَ ـ اِنْدَفَعَ ـ اِنْضَغَطَ. *See also to* Push, *v.t.*

Shove, *v.i.* To shove off, move away, تَبَاعَدَ ـ اِنْقَلَعَ.

Shove, *n.* A push, دَفْعَة ـ صَدْمَة ـ زَحْمَة ـ صَكْمَة ـ ضَغْط. *See also* Push, *n.*

Shovel, *n.* مِجْرَفَة ـ مِسَحَاة *pl.* مَسَاحٍ ـ مِعْبَد *pl.* مَعَابِد ـ *pl.* مَجَارِف. A fire-shovel, مِسْحَاةُ النَّارِ.

Shovel, *v.t.* To remove with a shovel, جَرَفَ ـ بِمِجْرَفَةٍ. To collect together with a shovel, لَمَّ ـ بِمِجْرَفَةٍ.

Shovelful, *n.* مِلْءُ الْمِجْرَفَةِ.

Show, *v.t.* To exhibit to view, to make one to see, أَرَى ـ رَأَّى ـ فَرَّجَ *vulg.* وَرَّى. To exhibit, عَرَضَ. To indicate, to point out, دَلَّ عَلَى ـ أَشَارَ ـ بِ. To make known to, أَخْبَرَ ـ بِ ـ أَظْهَرَ ـ بَيَّنَ ـ أَبْدَى ـ تَبَدَّى. To manifest, عَلَّمَ ـ عَرَّفَ. To —, do to, صَنَعَ لِ ـ كَذَا. To prove, بَرْهَنَ ـ بَيَّنَ. I showed him the thing, أَرَيْتُهُ الشَّيْءَ. Show me the thing, أَرِنِي الشَّيْءَ. Show me your house, فَرِّجْنِي عَلَى دَارِكَ. This shows that..., هٰذَا يَدُلُّ عَلَى أَنْ. In order to — you, لِكَيْ أُرِيكَ. Show me what you mean by this, أَخْبِرْنِي مَا لَكَ وَهٰذَا.

To show forth, to make known, أَوْضَحَ ـ أَعْلَنَ بِ ـ أَعْلَنَ. To commemorate, ذَكَرَ ـ أَخْبَرَ بِ.

To show in, to introduce, أَدْخَلَ. To meet and show in, أَقْبَلَ عَلَى ـ وَأَدْخَلَ.

To show off, as a horse, by riding it to and fro before spectators, أَشَارَ ـ شَوَّرَ ـ شَارَ ـ أَجْهَرَ. To give prominence to, أَجْهَرَ بِ. To beautify, جَمَّلَ ـ حَسَّنَ ـ زَخْرَفَ. To give relief to, جَسَّمَ.

To show one's self, أَرَى نَفْسَهُ ـ أَظْهَرَ نَفْسَهُ. Show thyself a man, تَشَدَّدْ وَكُنْ رَجُلًا. He has shown himself capable of holding, discharging, the office, ظَهَرَتْ مِنْهُ دَلَائِلُ قُدْرَتِهِ عَلَى الْقِيَامِ بِالْوَظِيفَةِ.

To show one's self off, to give one's self airs, تَعَظَّمَ ـ تَصَلَّفَ.

To show one out, to put out, طَرَدَ ـ أَخْرَجَ. To accompany to the door, رَافَقَ ـ إِلَى الْبَابِ.

To show one the way, دَلَّ ـ عَلَى الطَّرِيقِ ـ سَلَكَ ـ الطَّرِيقَ.

To show one up, to accompany, as up stairs, رَافَقَ ـ إِلَى فَوْقُ. To unmask, شَهَرَ ـ أَزَاحَ الْبُرْقُعَ عَنْ.

To show or inform of plainly, أَخْبَرَ عَنْ ـ عَلَانِيَةً (or جِهَارًا).

Show, *v.i.* To become apparent, تَظَاهَرَ ـ ظَهَرَ ـ تَبَيَّنَ ـ بَيَّنَ.

Show, *n.* Form, appearance, صُورَة ـ طَلْعَة ـ مَنْظَر ـ مَرْآة. Parade, pomp, وَكَبَة ـ مُفَاخَرَة ـ سَلْطَنَة ـ بَهَآء ـ إِحْتِفَال. A spectacle, فُرْجَة ـ مَنْظَر. A play, mimic representation, تَقْلِيد ـ تَشْخِيص. Outward or false —, حِكَايَة: a — of wisdom, حِكَايَةُ حِكْمَةٍ. To make a — of, أَظْهَرَ ـ أَشْهَرَ: He made a — of them openly, أَشْهَرَهُمْ جِهَارًا. Dumb-show; (*see* Pantomime, *n.*) A — of hands, in favour of, رَفْعُ الْأَيَادِي دَلَالَةً عَلَى الرِّضَآءِ بِ; against, رَفْعُ الْأَيَادِي دَلَالَةً عَلَى عَدَمِ الرِّضَآءِ بِ.

Show-bread, *n.* *See* Shew-bread, *n.*

Shower, *v.i.* To fall in showers, طَشَّ ـ رَشَّ: the sky showered, طَشَّتِ السَّمَآءُ. To — down upon, as benefits, *etc.*, مَطَرَ ـ بِ ـ إِسْتَمْطَرَ.

Shower, *n.* As of rain, نَضِيضَة *pl.* خِطَار ـ خَطْرَة ـ رَذَاذ *pl.* رَشّ ـ طُشُوش ـ طِشَاش *pl.* طَشّ ـ *and* أَنِضَّة ـ *and* نَضَائِض. رَشٌّ مِنْ مَطَرٍ. A pouring down, as of stones or other missiles, مَطَر *pl.* أَمْطَار; the sound of such a falling of stones, طَقْطَقَة. *See also under* Rain, *n.*

Shower-bath, *n.* حَمَّامُ الرَّشِّ ـ حَمَّامُ تَرْشَاشٍ.

Showery, *a.* مَاطِر ـ مُمْطِر ـ مَطِر ـ مُرِشّ.

Showily, *ad.* With pomp, بِمَوْكِبٍ ـ بِبَهَآءٍ ـ بِاحْتِفَالٍ; with ostentation, اِفْتِخَارًا ـ بِتَفَخُّرٍ ـ بِمُبَاهَاةٍ. *See also* Pompously, *ad.*

Showiness, *n.* Pomp, بَهَآء ـ زِينَة ـ مُفَاخَرَة ـ إِحْتِفَال. Grandeur, عَظَمَة ـ عِزّ ـ فَخْر. Gaudiness, مُفَاخَرَة ـ مُبَاهَاة ـ زَهْو.

Showy, *a.* Gaudy, مُفْتَخِر ـ جَلِيّ ـ زَاهٍ. Pompous, grand, إِحْتِفَالِيّ ـ بَهِيّ ـ بَاهٍ.

Shrapnell-shell, *n.* كُلَّةٌ مَحْشُوَّةٌ بِبَارُودٍ وَرَصَاصٍ.

Shred, *v.t.* مَزَّقَ ـ فَرَمَ ـ قَطَّعَ.

Shred, *n.* شِقَّة *pl.* شِقَق *and* شِقَاق ـ قِطْعَة *pl.* قِطَع. A garment worn to shreds, ثَوْبٌ طَرَائِقُ. *See also* Fragment, *n.*

Shrew, *n.* سِلْقَة *pl.* سِلْقَان ـ خَطَّالَة ـ جَلَّابَة ـ مُجَلِّبَة ـ إِمْرَأَةٌ فَحْلَةٌ ـ سَلِيطَة.

Shrewd, *a.* Sagacious, لَبِيب *pl.* أَلِبَّآء ـ أَرِب ـ فَطِين ـ حَوَالِيّ ـ دَاهٍ ـ أَحْوَل ـ ذَكِيّ *pl.* أَذْكِيَآء. Astute, cunning, خَبِيث ـ ضَغِن ـ شَاطِر; *vulg.* ذُو كَيْدٍ ـ شَيْطَان. Malicious, خَبِيث ـ ضَغِن. To be —, sagacious, ذَكِيَ *aor.* يَذْكَى ـ ذَكِيَ *aor.* يَذْكَى ـ ذَكُوَ *aor.* يَذْكُو. To be —, cunning, إِحْتَالَ ـ تَحَوَّلَ ـ ذَهِنَ. *See also* Cunning, Crafty, *a.*

Shrewdly, *ad.* Sagaciously, بِفِطْنَةٍ ـ بِذَكَآءٍ ـ بِإِرْبٍ ; cunningly, بِمَهَارَةٍ ـ اِحْتِيَالًا ـ بِحِيلَةٍ.

Shrewdness, *n.* Sagacity, ذِهْن ـ فِطْنَة ـ ذَكَآء ـ دَهَآء ـ إِرْب. Cunning, مَهَارَة ـ حِيلَة ـ اِحْتِيَال ; *vulg.* شَطَارَة.

Shrewish, *a.* شَرِسَة ـ شَكِسَة ـ كَالسَّلِيطَةِ. *See also under* Shrew, *n.*

Shrewishly, *ad.* كَالْعَطَّالَةِ ـ بِشَرَاسَةٍ ـ بِشَكَاسَةٍ.

Shrewishness, *n.* The qualities of a shrew, طَبْعُ ٱلْعَطَّالَةِ ـ سَجِيَّةُ ٱلسَّلِيطَةِ. Petulance, شَكَاسَة ـ شَرَاسَة. Clamorousness, صَرَّة ـ صُرَاخ ـ صِيَاح.

Shriek, *v.i.* صَرَخَ ـ أَعْوَلَ ـ زَعَقَ ـ صَيَّحَ ـ صَرَّ ـ بَعَقَ. *See also to* Scream, *v.i.*

Shriek, *n.* صُرَاخ ـ صَرْخَة ـ صَرِير ـ بُعَاق ـ عَوْل *pl.* أَعْوَال.

Shrievalty, *n.* *See* Sheriffalty, *n.*

Shrift, *n.* Confession to a priest, الِاعْتِرَاف لِقِسِّيسٍ.

Shrill, *a.* Of the voice, رَفِيع ـ جَهْوَر ـ جَهِير. The — cries of professional women at festivals, زَغَارِيد ; *vulg.* زَغَارِيط. She, one of such women, uttered a shrill cry, زَغْرَدَتْ ; *vulg.* زَغْرَطَتْ.

Shrillness, *n.* رَفَاعَةُ ٱلصَّوْتِ ـ جَهَارَة.

Shrilly, *ad.* بِصَوْتٍ رَفِيعٍ ـ بِجَهَارَةٍ.

Shrimp, *n.* جَرَادٌ بَحْرِيٌّ ـ جَرَادُ ٱلْبَحْرِ.

Shrine, *n.* A reliquary, أُنْبُوبَة ـ صُنْدُوقُ ذَخَائِرَ. A place of religious visitation, مَزَار. A temple, هَيْكَل *pl.* هَيَاكِل.

Shrink, *v.t.* To cause to contract, كَمَّشَ ـ قَلَّصَ. To make less ample, ضَيَّقَ.

Shrink, *v.i.* To contract, تَقَبَّضَ ـ تَقَلَّصَ ـ قَلَصَ ـ طَرْمَسَ ـ تَكَمَّشَ ـ اِنْقَبَضَ. To become less, قَلَّ. To grow short, قَصُرَ. To — from, to be averse from, جَبَأَ عَن ـ شَنِجَ ـ اِسْتَكْرَهَ ـ كَرِهَ, to be disgusted at, جَفَا عَن ـ اِنْحَاشَ عَن ـ اِشْمَأَزَّ مِن. To — from, as from danger, جَبَأَ ـ طَرْمَسَ عَن ـ فَلَطَ عَن ـ أَجْفَلَ عَن ـ عَن ; as through cowardice, حَامَ عَن. His mind shrank from it, ضَاقَ عَنْهُ صَدْرُهُ. His eye shrank from the thing, جَبَأَتْ عَيْنُهُ مِنَ ٱلشَّيْءِ.

Shrink, / **Shrinking**, *n.* / **Shrinkage**, } Contraction into a less compass, تَقَبُّض ـ كَشَاشَة ـ طَرْمَسَة ـ تَقَلُّص. The act of shrinking, contracting, تَضْيِيق ـ تَقْلِيص.

Shrivel, *v.i.* To contract into wrinkles, شَنَّجَ ـ غَضَّنَ. To dry up, to blast, أَحْرَقَ ـ سَلَقَ. To be shrivelled, wrinkled, تَغَضَّنَ.

Shrivel, *v.i.* To be drawn into wrinkles, شَنِجَ ـ تَغَضَّنَ ـ تَكَمَّشَ ـ تَقَحَّلَ ; as of the skin of old people, اِنْشَنَجَ ـ تَشَنَّجَ. To dry up, as being blasted, اِنْضَمَرَ ـ اِحْتَرَقَ. To be shrivelled, as with cold, كَزَّ ـ اِكْتَزَّ. His face became shrivelled, through emaciation, تَضَمَّرَ وَجْهُهُ ـ تَضَمَّرَ.

Shrivelled, *a.* Drawn into wrinkles, كَرِش ـ شَنِج ـ مُتَغَضِّن ـ مُكَمَّش ـ مُتَقَحِّل ـ قَحْل ; as of the skin of old people, مُشَنَّج ; as with cold, مَكْزُوز ـ كَزّ. Dried up, blasted, مُحْتَرِق ـ مُنْضَمِر.

Shroud, *n.* A cover, غِطَآء ـ غِشَآء. A winding-sheet, كَفَن *pl.* أَكْفَان *and* كُفُونَات.

Shroud, *v.t.* To cover, غَطَّى ـ سَتَرَ ـ غَشَّى عَلَى. To dress in a winding-sheet, كَفَّنَ ـ كَفَنَ.

Shrouds, *n.* Of a ship, حِبَالُ ٱلصَّوَارِي.

Shrovetide, *n.* أَيَّامُ ٱلتَّأَهُّبِ لِصَوْمِ ٱلْأَرْبَعِينَ ـ أَيَّامُ ٱلِاعْتِرَافِ.

Shrove-Tuesday, *n.* يَوْمُ ٱلثُّلَاثَآءِ ٱلْوَاقِعُ قَبْلَ أَرْبِعَآءِ ٱلرَّمَادِ. *See* Ash-Wednesday, *n.*

Shrub, *v.t.* To clear of shrubs, جَثَّ ـ أَخْلَأَ مِنَ ٱلدَّغَلِ ـ اِسْتَأْصَلَ ٱلشَّجْرَآءَ مِن ـ ٱلشُّجَيْرَاتِ مِن.

Shrub, *n.* A bush, عَوْسَج ـ عُلَّيْقَة. A small tree, شُجَيْرَة *pl.* شُجَيْرَات. Shrubs, فَرْش ـ شَجْرَآء ـ دِقُّ ٱلشَّجَرِ ـ فَسِيل.

Shrubbery, *n.* أَجَمَة *pl.* أَجَمَات ـ أَيْكَة ـ غَيْكَة ـ مَشْجَرَة ـ مَشْجَر. A walled-in —, حَدِيقَةٌ غَلْبَآء ـ مُغْلَوْلِبَة.

Shrubby, *a.* Full of shrubs دَغِل ـ مُدْغِل ـ ذُو دَغَلٍ ـ مَلَآنٌ مِنَ ٱلْجَذَلِ ـ جَذِيل. Resembling shrubs, يُشْبِهُ ٱلشُّجَيْرَاتِ ـ مِثْلَ شُجَيْرَةٍ.

Shrug, *v.t.* هَزَّزَ ـ رَفَعَ ـ نَغَضَ: He shrugged his shoulders, نَغَضَ (or رَفَعَ) أَكْتَافَهُ.

Shrug, *n.* تَهْزِيز ـ رَفْع ـ نَغْض. A — of the shoulders, نَغْض (or اِهْتِزَازُ) ٱلْأَكْتَافِ ـ رَفْعُ ٱلْأَكْتَافِ.

Shrunk, *v.t.* *See to* Shrink, *v.t.*

Shudder, *v.i.* اِرْتَعَدَ ـ اِرْتَجَّ ـ اِخْتَلَجَ ـ اِرْتَعَشَ ـ رَعَشَ. To cause to —, رَجَّ ـ أَرْعَدَ ـ أَرْجَفَ. *See also to* Quake, Shiver, *v.i.*

Shudder, *n.* / **Shuddering**, } رِعْشَة ـ رَعْش ـ رَجَفَان ـ اِرْتِعَاد. *See also* Quake, Shiver, *n.*

Shuffle, *v.t.* To shove one way and another, or to turn about, أَفَاضَ ـ ضَرَبَ بِ ـ فَرْفَرَ ـ جَلْجَلَ. To —, as of cards, *etc.*, خَلَطَ ـ جَلْجَلَ ـ أَفَاضَ بِ. To — and deal out cards to the players, أَجَالَ أَوْرَاقَ ٱللَّعِبِ بَيْنَ ٱللَّاعِبِينَ. To be shuffled, as of cards, اِخْتَلَطَ.

To shuffle in adroitly, دَسَّ ـ دَحَسَ ـ دَسَّسَ ; *vulg.* دَحَشَ.

To shuffle out adroitly, سَلَّ ـ أَسَلَّ.

To shuffle together, خَلَطَ ـ جَلْجَلَ ـ خَلَطَهُمْ مَعًا.

To shuffle up, to collect in haste, لَمَّ بِعَجَلٍ.

Shuffle, *v.i.* To shake or turn about, تَقَلْقَلَ ـ تَدَرْدَرَ. To move hither and thither, تَكَرْكَرَ ـ تَرَدَّنَ. To prevaricate, tergiversate, تَحَيَّلَ ـ تَحَوَّلَ ـ إِحْتَالَ. To —, to shamble, waddle, حَجَلَ ـِ ـُ حَجَلَ. He shuffled away with it, إِسْتَلَّ بِهِ. *See also to* Hedge, *v.i.*

To shuffle in adroitly, إِنْدَسَّ.

To shuffle out adroitly, ـِ فَرَّ ـ تَسَلَّلَ ـ إِنْسَلَّ.

Shuffle, *n.* A push, دِفَاع ـ دَفْعَة ـ صَدْمَة ـ مُدَافَعَة. A —, as of cards, *etc.*, خَلْط ـ جَلْجَلَة ـ إِفَاضَة. A prevarication, evasion, صَوْغُ ٱللِّسَانِ ـ حِيَل *pl.* حِيلَة ـ مُحَاوَلَة ـ رُوَيْغَة.

Shuffler, *n.* As of cards, مُخَلِّط ـ خَالِط ـ مُجَلْجِل ـ مُفِيض. One who shuffles or evades, مُحْتَال ـ حُوَّلِيّ ـ صَوَّاغ ـ حُوَّلٌ قُلَّبٌ.

Shuffling, *n.* An irregular gait, حَجَلَان ـ حَجْل. *See also* Shuffle, *n.*

Shuffling, *a.* A — fellow; *see under* Shuffler, *n.*

Shun, *v.t.* To turn away from, to avoid, ـِ ضَرَبَ عَن ـ أَضْرَبَ عَن ـ إِجْتَنَبَ مِن ـ تَجَافَى عَن ـ ـِ حَادَ عَن ـ أَعْرَضَ عَن ـ ـِ صَدَفَ عَن إِجْتَنَبَ جَانَبَ. To flee from, ـُ هَرَبَ مِن. He shunned vice, جَانَبَ ٱلرَّذَائِلَ. Shun unworthy actions, جَانِبِ ٱللِّئَامَ.

Shunt, *v.t.* To move on, as to another line, حَوَّلَ ـ إِلَى.

Shut, *v.t.* To close, ـُ سَدَّ ـ سَكَّرَ ـ أَغْلَقَ ـ غَلَّقَ; as of a door, ـِ صَدَمَ ـ ـُ سَكَّ ـ تَرَعَ ـ أَسْفَقَ ـ أَطْبَقَ ـ ـُ تَرَسَ ـ ـُ رَدَّ ٱلْبَابَ ـ إِسْتَدَّ ـ إِنْغَلَقَ ـ إِنْسَفَقَ ـ إِنْطَبَقَ; to be —, of a door, سَكَّرَ. إِرْتَدَّ. To —, of a book, أَطْبَقَ; of the lips, أَطْبَقَ. We found the door —, وَجَدْنَا ٱلْبَابَ مُغْلَقًا. *See also to* Close, *v.t.*

To shut against, to forbid one entrance to ..., ـِ نَهَى ـ عَنِ ٱلدُّخُولِ أَغْلَقَ ـ عَلَى ـ حَرَّمَ عَلَى ـ ٱلدُّخُولَ إِلَى ـ إِلَى كَذَا. To shut against, as a means, *etc.*, ـُ سَدَّ عَلَى ـ كَذَا.

To shut in, غَلَّقَ عَلَى ـ ـِ قَفَلَ عَلَى ـ أَغْلَقَ عَلَى. To be shut in by, entangled in, إِرْتَبَكَ فِي: they are shut in by the desert, هُمْ مُرْتَبِكُونَ فِي ٱلْبَرِّيَّةِ. To shut one's self in, to be secluded, إِحْتَجَبَ ـ قَرْصَعَ.

To shut off, to intercept, as steam, *etc.*, ـُ حَجَبَ ـِ ـُ حَجَزَ ـ ـِ قَطَعَ.

To shut one's eyes to, to overlook, ـُ غَضَّ ٱلطَّرْفَ فِي كَذَا.

To shut out, to exclude, ـِ ـُ حَجَزَ ـ عَن ـ ـُ نَفَا ـ مِن ـ أَخْرَجَ. To shut the door against, ـُ سَدَّ ٱلْبَابَ عَلَى.

To shut the hand against, ـِ قَبَضَ يَدَ ـ عَن.

To shut up, to shut, ـُ سَدَّ ـ غَلَّقَ. To confine, imprison, ـِ حَبَسَ ـ إِحْتَبَسَ. To shut up, as with an argument, to silence, أَفْحَمَ ـ ـَ قَطَعَ ـ بِٱلْحُجَّةِ ـ قَطَعَ بِ ـ سَكَّتَ. To shut up, as of one's compassion, *etc.*, أَحْصَرَ ـ ـِ قَفَصَ بِ.

Shut, *v.i.* إِنْقَفَلَ ـ تَسَكَّرَ.

Shutter, *n.* One that shuts, مُسَكِّر. A —, as of a window, رَدَّادَات *pl.* رَدَّادَةُ ٱلطَّاقَةِ.

Shuttle, *n.* Of a weaver, مَكُّوك ـ مَاصُورَةُ ٱلْحَيَّاكِ ـ وَشِيعَة.

Shuttle-cock, *n.*
Shuttle-cork, } فَلَكَةٌ مُرَيَّشَةٌ تَلْعَبُ بِهَا ٱلْأَوْلَادُ بِٱلطَّبْطَابَةِ.

Shy, *a.* Bashful, حَيِيٌّ ـ مَحْجُوب ـ حُشُم. Reserved, رَزِين ـ مُتَوَحِّش ـ مُتَأَبِّد ـ مُنْقَبِض ـ طِرِّيق ـ نَازِحُ ٱلنَّفْسِ. Unsocial, Timid, إِجْفِيل ـ فَزِع ـ خَائِف ـ خَوَّاف. Wary, حَذِر ـ. To be —, bashful, إِسْتَحْيَى ـ إِحْتَشَمَ. To be — reserved, تَرَزَّنَ ـ تَوَقَّرَ. To be —, timid, وَجِلَ *aor.* يَيْجَلُ ـ ـَ فَزِعَ ـ تَوَحَّشَ ـ تَأَبَّدَ. To be —, unsocial, ـَ خَشِيَ. To be —, wary, ـَ حَذِرَ ـ إِحْتَذَرَ. To fight — of, through fear, ـِ خَامَ عَن.
See also Suspicious, *a.*

Shy, *v.i.* To start suddenly aside, of a horse, ـُ شَذَّ ـِ ـُ شَرَدَ ـ ـَ جَفَلَ ـ تَنَافَرَ ـ ـِ حَادَ ـ ـِ ـُ نَفَرَ. To shy or throw at, ـِ رَمَى بِ. A bird put up to be shied at, مُجَثَّمَة. To keep birds or other animals to be shied at, جَثَّمَ. The beast shied, جَفَلَتِ ٱلدَّابَّةُ ـ حَادَتِ ٱلدَّابَّةُ. To make to —, شَرَّدَ.

Shy, *n.* جُفُول ـ شُرُود.

Shying, *a.* Of a horse, *etc.*, شَاذّ *pl.* شُذَّان *fem.* شَاذَّة *pl.* شَوَاذّ ـ نَفُور ـ نَفْرَان ـ إِجْفِيل ـ جَفَّال ـ جَفْلَان ـ شَرُود ـ شَارِد مُسْتَنْفِر.

Shyly, *ad.* Bashfully, بِحَيَاءٍ ـ بِحِشْمَةٍ. Timidly, فَزَعًا ـ وَجَلًا. With wariness, بِٱحْتِيَاطٍ ـ بِحَذَرٍ ـ إِحْتِذَارًا.

Shyness, *n.* Modesty, حَيَاء ـ حِشْمَة. Reserve, إِخْتِفَاء ـ إِطْرَاق. Circumspection, تَحَفُّظ ـ إِحْتِيَاط ـ إِنْتِبَاه ـ حِذْر ـ إِحْتِذَار. Fear, cowardice, خَيْمُومَة.

Sibilant, *a.* Whistling, صَافِر.

Sibilant, *n.* حَرْف صَفِير *pl.* حُرُوف صَفِير.

Sibillation, *n.* صَفِير ـ صُفَار.

Sibyl, *n.* كَاهِنَة *pl.* كَاهِنَات.

Sibylline, *a.* مُتَعَلِّق بِٱلْكَاهِنَاتِ ـ مَا نِيطَ بِٱلْعَرَّافَةِ.

Siccate, *v.t.* *See to* Dry, *v.t.*

Siccative, *a.* مُنَشِّف.

Sicilian, *a.* مِنْ صَقَلِّيَّة. A —, مِنْ أَهْلِ صَقَلِّيَّة.

Sicily, *a.* صَقَلِّيَّة ـ جَزِيرَةُ صَقَلِّيَّة.

Sick, *a.* Affected with disease, سَقِيم *pl.* سِقَام ـ مُعَلّ ـ عَلِيل ـ

مَرِيض — مَعْلُول *pl.* مَرْضَى *and* مَرَاضَى. Affected with nausea, خَبِيثُ ٱلنَّفْسِ — مُتَجَيِّش — جَائِشُ ٱلنَّفْس. Sick of love, مَرِيضٌ حُبًّا.

To be or to fall sick, affected with disease, سَقِمَ — إِعْتَلَّ — عَلَّ — مَرِضَ. To be affected with nausea, جَاشَتْ — فَارَتْ نَفْسُهُ — تَجَيَّشَ — نَفْسُهُ. To be sick nigh unto death, مَرِضَ قَرِيبًا مِنَ ٱلْمَوْتِ.

To be sick of, tired of, عَزَفَ عَن — يَعْيَا — عَيَّ بِ *or* عَن *aor.* — عَجَزَ عَن; specially of a person, زَعِلَ مِن. To be disgusted with, إِشْمَأَزَّ مِن — إِعْتَنَفَ مِن. To be sick of love, مَرِضَ حُبًّا.

To be sick unto death, مَرِضَ مَرَضَ ٱلْمَوْتِ.

To fall sick, مَرِضَ — إِعْتَرَاهُ مَرَضٌ. He fell sick of the sickness of which he died, مَرِضَ مَرَضَهُ ٱلَّذِي مَاتَ بِهِ.

To pretend to be sick, تَمَارَضَ.

Sicken, *v.t.* To make sick, مَرَّضَ — أَمْرَضَ — عَلَّلَ — أَعَلَّ.

To disgust, أَكْرَهَ — قَرَّفَ — أَقْرَفَ — أَسَامَ.

Sicken, *v.i.* To become sick, أُحْضِرَ لِلسُّقْمِ — قَرُفَ ٱلْمَرَضَ — مَرِضَ — إِعْتَلَّ — عَلَّ. To pall upon, تَقَزَّزَ مِن — قَزَّ عَن — كَرِهَ — مَا بَقِيَ يَلْتَذُّ مِن. *See also under* Sick, *a.*

Sickening, *a.* Causing sickness, مُمْرِض — مُعَلِّل. Nauseating, مُجِيشُ ٱلنَّفْسِ مِنْهُ. Disgusting, كَرِيه — كُره — مُقْرِف — مُقَزِّز.

Tiresome, wearying, شَاقٌّ — مُمِلّ — مُعْجِز.

Sickening, *n.* Disgust, كَرَاهَة — إِعْتِنَاف — ضَجَر — تَقَزُّز. To give one a — of, أَقْرَفَ مِن — أَكْرَهَ عَلَى.

Sickish, *a.* Somewhat sick, مَرِيضٌ نَوْعًا.

Sickishness, *n.* *See* Nausea, *n.*

Sickle, *n.* مِحَشّ *pl.* مَحَاشّ — مِنْجَل — مِقْضَال *pl.* مَقَاضِيل.

Sickliness, *n.* The state of being sickly, حَالُ ٱلسُّقْمِ — وَهْن — ضَعْف — عَجْز. Unhealthiness, as of climate, مَضَرَّةٌ لِلصِّحَّةِ — وَخَامَة — وَبَلَة — وَبَال.

Sick-list, *n.* جَدْوَل (*or* قَائِمَة) ٱلْمَرْضَى.

Sickly, *a.* Often sick, مِسْقَام. Ailing, weak, سَقِيم — عَلِيل — ضَعِيف — مَوْهُون. Unhealthy, as of a climate, وَخِيم — وَبِيل — مُتَوَخِّم. Many of them are —, كَثِيرُونَ مِنْهُمْ مَرْضَى.

Sickness, *n.* Disease, سُقْم *pl.* أَسْقَام — سَقَم — سِقَام — مَرَض *pl.* أَمْرَاض — عِلَّة *pl.* عِلَل *and* عِلَّات. Suffering from, weighed down by —, مَنْهُوكٌ بِٱلْأَمْرَاضِ — مُثْقَلٌ بِٱلْمَرَضِ. *See also* Nausea, *n.*

Side, *n.* The broad or long of a thing, شِقّ — جَنْب *pl.* أَجْنَاب — عُرْض *pl.* أَعْرَاض — طَرَف *pl.* أَطْرَاف — جَانِب *pl.* جَوَانِب — صَوْب — نَاحِيَة *pl.* نَوَاحِي — جِهَة *pl.* جِهَات. The flat of anything, صَفْح *pl.* صِفَاح — صَفْحَة *pl.* صَفَحَات — عُرْض *pl.* أَعْرَاض.

The —, as of a human being, شِقّ — عِطْف *pl.* عِطَاف *and* أَعْطَاف; of any animal, خَصِيرَة *dual* خَصِيرَتَانِ — جَنْب *pl.* أَجْنَاب — جَانِب *pl.* جَوَانِب. The —, aspect, face of anything, وَجْه *pl.* وُجُوه — جِهَة *pl.* جِهَات. A region, نَاحِيَة *pl.* نَوَاحِي — جِهَة — حَدّ *pl.* حُدُود — طَرَف *pl.* أَطْرَاف.

The —, as of a hill, شِقّ — شِقَّة — جَانِب *pl.* جَوَانِب. An edge, brow, verge, حَاجِب *pl.* حَوَاجِب — حَرْف — حَافَة *dual* حَافَتَانِ *pl.* حَافَات. A party, حِزْب *pl.* أَحْزَاب — فِرْقَة *pl.* فِرَق — عَصَبِيَّة. A man's weak or blind —, جَانِبُهُ ٱللَّيِّنُ. Who is on my —? مَنْ مَعِي. There were trees on either — of the river, عَلَى ٱلنَّهْرِ مِنْ هُنَا وَمِنْ هُنَاكَ أَشْجَارٌ. There are two sides to the question, لِلْأَمْرِ طَرَفَانِ (*or* وَجْهَانِ).

By the father's side, مِنْ طَرَفِ ٱلْأَبِ.

By the mother's side, مِنْ طَرَفِ ٱلْأُمِّ.

By the side of, جَنْبَ كَذَا — بِجَانِبِ كَذَا — عَلَى جَانِبِ كَذَا.

By the side of a river, عَلَى حَافَةِ ٱلنَّهْرِ.

From the farther side of the river, مِنْ عِبْرِ ٱلنَّهْرِ.

On all sides, مِنْ كُلِّ ٱلْجِهَاتِ — مِنْ كُلِّ جَانِبٍ.

Side by side, جَنْبًا إِلَى جَنْبٍ.

The left side, ٱلْجَانِبُ ٱلشِّمَالُ — ٱلْيَسَارُ.

The near side, of a horse, عَنْ يَسَارِ ٱلْفَرَسِ.

The off side, of a horse, عَنْ يَمِينِ ٱلْفَرَسِ.

The right side, to the right hand, ٱلْجَانِبُ ٱلْيَمِينُ — ٱلْيَمِينُ.

The right side, as of cloth, *etc.*, ٱلْوَجْهُ.

The wrong as opposed to the right side, ٱلْجَانِبُ ٱلْمَعْكُوسُ. The wrong side, as of cloth, *etc.*, ٱلْقَفَا.

To change sides, to go from one side to another, إِنْتَقَلَ مِنْ جَانِبٍ إِلَى جَانِبٍ. To take to another party, رَافَقَ غَيْرَ حِزْبِهِ — تَعَصَّبَ لِغَيْرِ فِرْقَتِهِ.

To choose sides, party, إِتَّخَذَ رَأْيَهُ — تَعَصَّبَ لِفِرْقَتِهِ — إِخْتَارَ حِزْبَهُ.

To expose the side, أَعْرَضَ: The gazelle exposed its side, أَعْرَضَ ٱلظَّبْيُ.

To have a complaint in the side, جُنِبَ.

To hit on the side, جَنَبَ — عَرَضَ — أَصَابَ جَنْبَهُ.

To incline to one side, مَالَ إِلَى جَنْبٍ — ٱنْحَرَفَ — تَحَرَّفَ; in walking, مَشَى عَلَى شِقٍّ.

To lay on the side, جَعَلَ عَلَى جَنْبِهِ — أَضْجَعَ.

To lie on the side, ضَجَعَ — إِنْضَجَعَ — إِضْطَجَعَ — نَامَ عَلَى جَنْبِهِ.

To shake one's side with laughter, تَقَعَّ مِنَ ٱلضَّحِكِ — إِنْبَعَجَ مِنَ ٱلضَّحِكِ.

To sit by the side of, (جَانِبِهِ or) جَلَسَ ـ قَعَدَ (or ² عَلَى جَنْبِهِ .

To take one side of the way, ² أَخَذَ فِي عُرُوضٍ مِنَ ٱلطَّرِيقِ .

To take sides with, (لَهُ or) ² شَدَّ مَعَ ـ إِتَّخَذَ رَأْيَهُ ـ تَعَصَّبَ مَعَهُ .

To turn the side to, عَارَضَ : He turned his side to the wind, عَارَضَ ٱلرِّيحَ .

To walk by the side of, مَشَى عَنْ جَانِبِهِ ـ جَانَبَهُ : They walked on either side of him, مَشُوا جَانِبَيْهِ .

To write on both sides of a sheet, ² كَتَبَ عَلَى صَفْحَتَيِ ٱلْوَرَقَةِ .

Side, *v.i.* To incline to a side, مَالَ إِلَى طَرَفٍ . To side with; *see* To take sides with, *under* Side, *n.*

Side, *a.* Lateral, مِنْ جَانِبٍ ـ جَنْبِيٌّ . Indirect, مُعَرَّضٌ .

Sideboard, *n.* خِزَانَةُ قَاعَةِ ٱلسُّفْرَةِ .

Side-box, *n.* Of a theatre, مَقْعَدٌ (or لُوجَةٌ) فِي جَانِبِ ٱلتِّيَاتْرُو *pl.* مَقَاعِدُ .

Sided, *a.* Having sides, ذُو جَوَانِبَ .

Sidelong, *a.* *See* Sloping, *a.*

Sidelong, *a.* Lateral, جَنْبِيٌّ . Oblique, رَائِغٌ ـ مُتَعَرِّضٌ ـ مُنْحَرِفٌ .

Sidelong, *ad.* Laterally, مِنْ جَانِبٍ .

Sideral, *a.* } نَجْمِيٌّ . A — day, يَوْمٌ نَجْمِيٌّ . A — year, سَنَةٌ
Sidereal, } نَجْمِيَّةٌ . Sidereal light, ضِيَاءُ ٱلنُّجُومِ .

Siderography, *n.* حِرْفَةُ نَقْشِ ٱلْبُولَادِ .

Sideroscope, *n.* آلَةٌ لِلْكَشْفِ عَنْ وُجُودِ ٱلْحَدِيدِ حَيْثُمَا كَانَ .

Side-saddle, *n.* سَرْجُ ٱلنِّسَاءِ ـ سَرْجٌ لِلْحَرِيمِ .

Sidesman, *n.* A partisan, مُتَعَصِّبٌ ـ صَاحِبُ عَصَبِيَّةٍ . The — of a church, مُعَاوِنُ وَكِيلِ كَنِيسَةٍ .

Side-table, *n.* سُفْرَةٌ جَنْبِيَّةٌ ـ طَاوِلَةٌ تُجْعَلُ فِي جَانِبِ مَحَلٍّ .

Side-walk, *n.* (عَلَى جَنْبٍ or) مَسْلَكٌ عَنْ عَرْضٍ .

Sideways, *ad.* مُعَارَضَةً ـ بِٱلْعَرْضِيَّةِ ; as in walking, شَقًّا . To put anything —, عَرَّضَ ـ عَرَضَ . To look at one —, ² نَظَرَ إِلَيْهِ مُعَارَضَةً ـ عَنْ عُرْضٍ . He walks —, يَمْشِي بِٱلْعَرْضِيَّةِ (or بِٱلْعُرْضِيَّةِ).

Siding, *n.* As of a railroad, مَوْقِفُ ٱلِٱحْتِيَاطِ .

Sidle, *v.i.* To lie on the side, اِضْطَجَعَ ـ ضَجَعَ . To — with, تَعَقَّبَ لِ . To — away, تَسَلَّلَ ـ اِنْسَلَّ . To walk to one side, مَشَى عَلَى شِقٍّ .

Siege, *n.* مُحَاصَرَةٌ ـ حِصَارٌ . State of —, حَالُ ٱلْحَصْرِ . To raise a —, رَفَعَ ٱلْحِصَارَ . To raise a — against, حَاصَرَ . To remove a state of —, أَزَالَ حَالَ ٱلْحَصْرِ . The — lasted a month, اِسْتَمَرَّ ٱلْحِصَارُ شَهْرًا . He raised the — of the town, رَفَعَ ٱلْحِصَارَ عَنِ ٱلْبَلَدِ .

Sierra, *n.* نَجْدٌ ـ تِهَامَةٌ ـ جِبَالٌ مُسَلْسَلَةٌ .

Siesta, *n.* قَيْلُولَةٌ ـ تَقْيِيلَةٌ ـ قَائِلَةٌ ـ غَائِرَةٌ . To take a —, قَيَّلَ .

Sieve, *n.* غِرْبَالٌ *pl.* غَرَابِيلُ ـ مُنْخُلٌ ـ هِرْقِلٌ . One who cannot keep a secret, بَذُورٌ ـ فَاءٍ ـ مَذِيلٌ ـ قُرُجٌ .

Sift, *v.t.* To pass through a sieve, غَرْبَلَ ـ سَفْسَفَ ـ اِنْتَخَلَ . To select, as the best, from, نَقَّى ـ أَنْقَى . To analyze, غَرْبَلَ . To scrutinize, تَصَفَّحَ ـ صَفَحَ ـ دَقَّقَ فِي . To — to the bottom, ² حَلَّلَ ـ تَقَعَّرَ فِي .

Sifter, *n.* One who sifts, مُغَرْبِلٌ .

Sifting, *n.* The act of sifting through a sieve, غَرْبَلَةٌ ـ سَفْسَفَةٌ . Scrutiny, تَحْقِيقٌ ـ تَدْقِيقٌ ـ تَفَحُّصٌ ـ تَصَفُّحٌ .

Siftings, *n.* The dust which rises from sifting, سَفْسَافٌ .

Sigh, *v.i.* تَأَوَّهَ ـ تَنَهَّدَ ـ نَحَطَ . To — over, to bemoan, تَأَسَّفَ عَلَى ـ تَحَسَّرَ عَلَى ـ بَكَى عَلَى . To — or long for, حَنَّ إِلَى ـ تَحَانَّ إِلَى ـ جَادَ إِلَى *aor.* يَجُودُ ـ تَشَوَّقَ إِلَى ـ اِشْتَاقَ إِلَى .

Sigh, *n.* حَسْرَةٌ ـ تَنَهُّدٌ ـ نَحِيطٌ . A heavy —, شَهْقَةٌ ; to heave a heavy —, شَهَقَ شَهْقَةً . To breathe a deep —, تَنَفَّسَ ٱلصُّعَدَاءَ .

Sighing, *n.* *See* Sigh, *n.*

Sight, *n.* As of the eyes, نَظَرٌ ـ نَظَرَانٌ ـ بَصَارَةٌ ـ بَصَرٌ . The act of seeing, witnessing, رُؤْيَةٌ ـ عِيَانٌ ـ مُعَايَنَةٌ ـ مُشَاهَدَةٌ . Extent, range of sight, مَدَى ٱلْبَصَرِ . Vision, eye, نَظَرٌ ـ عَيْنٌ . The act of looking at anything, نَظَرَانٌ ـ طُلُوعٌ ـ شَوْفٌ إِلَى . A spectacle, مَنْظَرٌ ـ فُرْجَةٌ . The —, as on a musket or cannon, نِيشَانٌ . Knowledge, طِلْعٌ ـ إِطِّلَاعٌ ـ مَعْرِفَةٌ . Sight, term, as for payment, وَعْدٌ : At three months' —, بَعْدَ ثَلَاثَةِ أَشْهُرٍ ـ بَعْدَ ٱلتَّارِيخِ بِثَلَاثَةِ أَشْهُرٍ . Out of — out of mind, بَعِيدٌ عَنِ ٱلْأَعْيُنِ بَعِيدٌ عَنِ ٱلْقَلْبِ . A fearful —, مَخَافَةٌ *pl.* مَخَاوِفُ . It was by far the most splendid — I ever beheld, كَانَ مَنْظَرًا أَبْهَجَ مَا رَأَيْتُ قَطُّ . Pleasant to the —, شَهِيٌّ لِلنَّظَرِ . They were in our — as grasshoppers, كَانُوا فِي أَعْيُنِنَا كَٱلْجَرَادِ . Wise in his own —, حَكِيمٌ فِي عَيْنَيْ نَفْسِهِ . Go out of my —! اِذْهَبْ مِنْ أَمَامِي . He vanished out of their —, اِخْتَفَى عَنْهُمْ . At his simple — of him, by simply looking at him, بِمُجَرَّدِ رُؤْيَتِهِ إِيَّاهُ . "Their sight shall not return to them," لَا يَرْتَدُّ إِلَيْهِمْ طَرْفُهُمْ (Kûr. xiv. 44.) "The lightning all but took away their sight," يَكَادُ ٱلْبَرْقُ يَخْطَفُ أَبْصَارَهُمْ (Kûr. ii. 19.)

At first sight, فِي أَوَّلِ ٱلْأَمْرِ ـ مِنْ أَوَّلِ رُؤْيَةٍ .

At sight, عِنْدَ ٱلرُّؤْيَةِ . On presentation, حِينَ ٱلتَّقْدِيمِ . At the sight of him, بِرُؤْيَتِهِ إِيَّاهُ .

Dim or weak sight, ضَعْفُ نَظَرٍ ـ عَشَاوَة ـ عَشًا ـ غَطَش ـ طَشَاش.

Long sight, بَصَرٌ (or) نَظَرٌ طَوِيلٌ.

Short sight, قِصَرُ نَظَرٍ ـ خَفَش.

In the sight of the people, قُدَّامَ أَعْيُنِ ٱلنَّاسِ ـ بِرُؤْيَةِ ٱلْقَوْمِ. Before, أَمَامَ ـ قُدَّامَ. In the estimation of, عِنْدَ: In the sight of God, عِنْدَ ٱللّٰهِ.

Ten days after sight, عَشَرَةَ أَيَّامٍ بَعْدَ ٱلرُّؤْيَةِ.

To be cast down at the sight of him or it, أُكِبَّ بِرُؤْيَتِهِ.

To come or appear in sight, نَدَرَ ـ يَبْدُو .aor بَدَا ـ تَبَدَّى ـ تَبَيَّنَ ـ بَيَّنَ ـ ظَهَرَ.

To deprive of sight, عَمَّى ـ أَعْمَى.

To find favour in the sight of; *see under* Favour, *n.*

To gain a sight of, تَطَلَّعَ عَلَى ـ اِطَّلَعَ عَلَى ـ أَشْرَفَ عَلَى ـ شَافَ بِ ـ يَرَى .aor رَأَى ـ أَبْصَرَ ـ لَمَحَ.

To give sight to, فَتَحَ عَيْنَيْهِ ـ بَصَّرَ.

To hate the sight of, بَغَضَهُ ـ جَرَحَ نَظَرَهُ.

To know one by sight, on seeing, عَرَفَ-إِذْ رَآهُ. To know by sight only, عَرَفَ-عِيَانًا فَقَطْ.

To lose one's sight, يَعْمَى .aor عَمِيَ ـ تَلِفَ (or عَدِمَ) بَصَرُهُ ـ عَمِيَتْ عَيْنَاهُ.

To lose sight of, to discontinue seeing, يَغِيبُ .aor غَابَ عَنْ نَظَرِهِ. To forget, neglect, سَهَا عَنْ ـ ذَهَبَ عَلَى ـ نَسِيَ .aor يَسْهُو ـ أَهْمَلَ.

To offend the sight, قَرَّزَ ٱلْبَصَرَ ـ كَرِهَ ٱلنَّظَرَ.

To recover one's sight, بَرِئَ مِنْ عَمَاهُ ـ اِسْتَرَدَّ بَصَرَهُ.

Sight, *v.t.* شَافَ بِ ـ يَرَى .aor رَأَى ـ لَاحَ ـ أَشْرَفَ عَلَى.

Sighted, *a.* نَاظِر ـ بَاصِر.

Dim sighted, جَهْرَآءُ .fem أَجْهَرُ ـ أَغْطَشُ ـ عَشْوَآءُ .fem أَعْشَى ـ ضَعِيفُ ٱلنَّظَرِ.

Long sighted, طَوِيلُ ٱلنَّظَرِ ـ غَرْبَة .fem غَرْبُ ٱلْعَيْنِ. Verily he is long sighted, إِنَّهُ لَغَرْبُ ٱلْعَيْنِ.

Quick sighted, خَفِيفُ ٱلنَّظَرِ ـ سَرِيعُ ٱلنَّظَرِ.

Short sighted, قَصِيرُ ٱلنَّظَرِ ـ أَخْفَشُ.

Sightless, *a.* عُمْيٌ .pl عَمْيَآءُ .fem أَعْمَى ـ عَدِيمُ ٱلْبَصَرِ.

Sightlessness, *n.* عَمَى ٱلْبَصَرِ ـ عَمًى ـ عَدَمُ بَصَرٍ.

Sightliness, *n.* كِيَاسَة ـ جَمَال ـ حُسْن ـ بَهَآءٌ وَكَمَالٌ.

Sightly, *a.* كَيِّس ـ ظَرِيف ـ جَمِيل ـ بَهِيج ـ شَهِيٌّ لِلنَّظَرِ.

Sigmoidal, *a.* فِي هَيْئَةِ حَرْفِ σ مِنَ ٱلْحُرُوفِ ٱلْيُونَانِيَّةِ. The — flexure, مَعْيٌ (or رَفْغُ) ٱلْقُولُونِ.

Sign, *n.* A mark, token, characteristic, indication, سِمَة ـ شِقْبَة ـ عَلَامَة .pl عَلَامَات ـ أُعْلُومَة. A motion, as with the hand, also an indication, إِشَارَة .pl إِشَارَات ـ إِيمَآء ـ وَمْأ. A mark, trace, أَثَر .pl آثَار ـ عَلَم .pl أَعْلَام. An impression, vestige, رَسْم .pl رُسُوم. A wonder, miracle, آيَة .pl آيَات ـ مُعْجِزَة .pl مُعْجِزَات. Appearance, بَيَان. Sign, as over a shop, عَلَامَة (or كِتَابَة) عَلَى دُكَّانٍ ـ عَلَامَة دُكَّانٍ. A —, as used in arithmetic, *etc.*, عَلَم .pl أَعْلَام.

A signature, تَوْقِيع ـ إِمْضَآء. Sign or countersign, in war, *etc*, شِعَار. Gesture, as with the eyes, lips, *etc.*, رَمْز .pl رُمُوز ـ غَمْز. An indication, direction, دَلِيل. The — of the cross, إِشَارَة ٱلصَّلِيبِ: to make the — of the cross on one's self, صَلَّبَ عَلَى وَجْهِهِ. By signs, بِٱلْإِشَارَةِ ـ بِٱلْوَمْأ. This shall be the — to you, هٰذِهِ لَكُمُ ٱلْعَلَامَةُ.

A bad sign, عَلَامَة شَرٍّ.

A good sign, عَلَامَة خَيْرٍ.

The signs of the times, عَلَامَاتُ ٱلْأَزْمِنَةِ (or ٱلدَّهْرِ).

To give signs of, أَشَارَ إِلَى ـ أَشْرَفَ عَلَى ـ يَؤُولُ .aor آلَ إِلَى ـ دَلَّ عَلَى.

To make a sign to, as with a nod, *etc.*, شَوَّرَ إِلَى ـ أَشَارَ إِلَى ـ أَوْمَأَ إِلَى.

To make signs, as with the eyes, mouth, *etc.*, تَرَمَّزَ ـ رَمَزَ.

To make such signs to, رَمَزَ إِلَى: The woman made a sign to him with her eye, غَمَزَتْهُ ٱلْإِمْرَأَةُ بِعَيْنِهَا ـ رَمَزَتْهُ ٱلْمَرْأَةُ بِعَيْنِهَا.

They made signs to one another, of many, تَغَامَزُوا ـ تَرَامَزُوا.

To speak to in signs, حَاوَرَ-بِٱلْإِشَارَاتِ ـ كَلَّمَ-رَمْزًا.

Sign, *v.t.* To affix one's signature to, أَوْقَعَ عَلَى ـ عَلَّمَ عَلَى ـ أَمْضَى ـ وَقَّعَ عَلَى. To —, as a judge a decree, سَجَّلَ بِ ـ سَجَّلَ.

A treaty signed and sealed by both parties, مُعَاهَدَة مُمْضَاة وَمَخْتُومَة مِنَ ٱلطَّرَفَيْنِ. He presented the treaty to him in order that he might — it, قَدَّمَ لَهُ ٱلْمُعَاهَدَةَ لِيُوَقِّعَ عَلَيْهَا.

Signal, *n.* إِشَارَة .pl إِشَارَات. A — light indicating danger, نُورٌ يَدُلُّ عَلَى ٱلْخَطَرِ. To make signals to; *see to* Signalize, *v.t.*

Signal, *a.* عَجِيب ـ بَدِيع ـ وَاضِح ـ صَرِيح ـ مُبِين.

Signal, *v.i.* To make signals, أَلْوَى ـ نَصَبَ ٱلْإِشَارَاتِ ٱلْإِشَارَاتِ.

Signalize, *v.t.* To make distinguished, أَشْهَرَ. To manifest, أَظْهَرَ ـ بَيَّنَ ـ أَبْدَى. To make signals to, أَشَارَ إِلَى-بِٱلْإِشَارَاتِ ـ حَاوَرَ-بِٱلْإِشَارَاتِ. To — one's self by, كَسَبَ ـ اِشْتَهَرَ بِ ـ أَظْهَرَ ٱلْفَضْلَ فِي ـ شُهْرَة بِ.

Signally, *ad.* بِشُهْرَةٍ ـ إِيضَاحًا ـ صَرَاحَةً ـ بَيَانًا.

Signatory, *n.* and *a.* One who signs, مُمْضٍ ـ مُوَقِّعٌ عَلَى:

The — powers, اَلدُّوَلُ ٱلْمُمْضِيَةُ. The non — powers, اَلدُّوَلُ اَلْغَيْرُ مُمْضِيَةٍ.

Signature, *n.* إِمْضَآءٌ ـ تَوْقِيعٌ. A forged —, إِمْضَآءٌ مُزَوَّرٌ. A joint —, إِمْضَآءٌ مُشْتَرَكٌ. An interchange of signature, مُبَادَلَةُ ٱلتَّوْقِيعِ.

Signer, *n.* *See* Signatory, *n.* and *a.*

Signet, *n.* خَاتِمٌ ـ مُهْرٌ ـ طَابِعٌ *pl.* طَوَابِعُ.

Significance, *n.* / Significancy, } Import, meaning, مَضْمُونٌ ـ مَعْنًى فَحْوَى. Importance, gravity, عِظَمٌ. It has no political —, لَيْسَ لَهُ تَعَلُّقٌ بِٱلْأُمُورِ ٱلسِّيَاسِيَّةِ.

Significant, *a.* Full of meaning, مَعْنَوِيٌّ. Important, مُهِمٌّ ـ عَظِيمٌ. Betokening something, دَالٌّ عَلَى ـ هَامٌّ بِ ـ مُؤْعِدٌ بِ.

Significantly, *ad.* بِمَعْنًى ـ بِفَحْوَى ـ بِمَرَامٍ ـ بِنِيَّةٍ.

Signification, *n.* Meaning, مَعْنًى *pl.* مَعَانِي ـ فَحْوَى *pl.* فَحَاوِي ـ مَضْمُونٌ ـ مَحَطٌّ. A special —, مَعْنًى عُرْفِيٌّ خَاصٌّ. A general —, مَعْنًى عُرْفِيٌّ عَامٌّ. *See also* Meaning, *n.*

Significative, *a.* / Significatory, } مَعْنَوِيٌّ. *See also* Significant, *a.*

Signify, *v.t.* To mean, عَنَى ـ ۲ عَنَى بِ. To be a sign of something, to import, دَلَّ عَلَى ـ ۲ عَبَّرَ بِ *or* عَنْ. To — to, make known to, أَفَادَ ـ عَرَّفَ ـ بِ ـ عَلَّمَ ـ بِ. *See also to* Mean, *v.t.*

Signify, *v.i.* To be of meaning, importance, هَمَّ ـ ۲ عَظُمَ ۲.

Sign-manual, *n.* إِمْضَآءٌ ـ تَوْقِيعٌ.

Sign-post, *n.* For showing the way, صُوَّةٌ *pl.* صُوًى *and* أَصْوَآءٌ ـ فَرْطٌ *pl.* فُرُوطٌ ـ أَرَمٌ *pl.* آرَامٌ. Any post set up as a sign, مَعْلَمٌ *pl.* مَعَالِمُ. To set up sign-posts, صَوَّى صُوًى. Verily Islâm has signs and marks of guidance like those of the way, لِلْإِسْلَامِ صُوًى وَمَنَارًا كَمَنَارِ ٱلطَّرِيقِ.

Silence, *n.* صَمْتٌ ـ صُمَاتٌ ـ صُمُوتٌ ـ سَكْتٌ ـ سُكَاتٌ ـ سُكُوتٌ. Stillness, speechlessness, سَكْنَةٌ. The — of death, خُفُوتٌ. To keep —, صَمَتَ ۲ ـ صَمَّتَ ـ أَنْصَتَ ـ إِنْتَصَتَ ـ ۲ نَصَتَ ـ سَكَتَ ۲. To preserve — about, سَكَتَ عَنْ ۲. Silence sometimes conveys a reply, (prov.) رُبَّمَا كَانَ ٱلسُّكُوتُ جَوَابًا. Silence is often more eloquent than words, (prov.) رُبَّ سُكُوتٍ أَبْلَغُ مِنَ ٱلْكَلَامِ.

Silence, *v.t.* صَمَّتَ ـ أَصْمَتَ ـ أَصَمَّ ـ صَمَّمَ ـ سَكَّتَ ـ أَسْكَتَ. To —, as by an argument, غَتَّ ـ بِٱلْكَلَامِ ۲ ـ رَمَى ـ بِسُكَاتٍ ۲ ـ قَطَعَ ـ بِٱلْحُجَّةِ ۲ ـ قَطَعَ لِسَانَهُ ۲ ـ قَطَّعَ بِ. To — guns, أَبْطَلَ (*or*) بَطَّلَ) إِطْلَاقَ ٱلْمَدَافِعِ.

Silent, *a.* صَامِتٌ ـ صَمُوتٌ ـ صِمِّيتٌ ـ سَاكُوتٌ ـ سَاكِتٌ. A — letter, حَرْفٌ صَامِتٌ *pl.* حُرُوفٌ صَامِتَةٌ. To become —, as in death, خَفَتَ ۲. To be — about, أَغْضَى عَنْ ـ سَكَتَ عَنْ ۲. To ask one to be —, إِسْتَسْكَتَ. We deemed it best to be — about that, تَرَجَّحَ عِنْدَنَا ٱلسُّكُوتُ عَنْ ذَلِكَ. To be —; *See* To keep silence, *under* Silence, *n.*

Silence, *int.* صَهْ ـ اَلسَّكْتَةُ.

Silently, *ad.* Without speaking, بِٱلصَّمْتِ ـ بِٱلسُّكُوتِ. Quietly, without noise, بِهُدُوٍّ.

Silex, *n.* صَوَّانٌ ـ حَجَرُ ٱلصَّوَّانِ.

Silify, *v.t.* صَيَّرَ كَٱلصَّوَّانِ.

Silify, *v.i.* صَارَ كَٱلصَّوَّانِ ۲.

Silicious, *a.* صَوَّانِيٌّ ـ مِثْلُ ٱلصَّوَّانِ.

Silicon, *n.* / Silicium, } جَوْهَرُ ٱلصَّوَّانِ.

Silique, *n.* / Siliqua, } Of pods, قَرْنٌ *pl.* قُرُونٌ ـ خَرُّوبٌ.

Siliquous, *a.* مُقَرَّنٌ.

Silk, *n.* The material, إِبْرِيسَمٌ ـ حَرِيرٌ. Fine —, سُنْدُسٌ. Raw —, قَزٌّ. Sewing —, إِبْرِيسِمٌ. Gold — thread, قَصَبٌ أَصْفَرُ; silver — thread, قَصَبٌ أَبْيَضُ.

Silk, *a.* / Silken, } مِنْ حَرِيرٍ ـ مِنْ إِبْرِيسَمٍ.

Silkiness, *n.* مَلَاسَةٌ ـ مُلُوسَةٌ ـ سُخَامٌ.

Silk-mercer, *n.* إِبْرِيسَمِيٌّ ـ قَزَّازٌ. Silk-mercery, حَرَائِرُ ـ بِضَاعَةٌ حَرِيرٍ.

Silk-mill, *n.* مَعْمَلُ ٱلْحَرِيرِ.

Silk-thrower, *n.* / Silk-throwster, } نَسَّاجُ ٱلْقَزِّ.

Silk-weaver, *n.* حَيَّاكُ ٱلْقَزِّ ـ قَزَّازٌ.

Silk-worm, *n.* دُودُ ٱلْقَزِّ *pl.* دِيدَانٌ. Eggs of the —, بِزْرُ دُودِ ٱلْقَزِّ.

Silky, *a.* كَٱلْحَرِيرِ ـ نَاعِمٌ ـ نَاعِمٌ كَٱلْحَرِيرِ.

Sill, *n.* Of a door, أُسْكُفَّةٌ ـ عَتَبَةٌ *pl.* عَتَبَاتٌ. To make a — to a door, عَتَّبَ بَابًا.

Sillabub, *n.* شَرَابٌ مَمْزُوجٌ بِحَلِيبٍ.

Sillily, *ad.* بِخُرْقَةٍ ـ بِجَهَالَةٍ ـ بِغَبَانَةٍ ـ بِحَمَاقَةٍ. He acted — with him, جَاهَلَهُ.

Silliness, *n.* خُرْقَةٌ ـ جَهَالَةٌ ـ مُجَاهَلَةٌ ـ غَبَانَةٌ ـ غَبَنٌ.

Silly, *a.* Of a person, غَبِينٌ ـ أَخْرَقُ ـ جَاهِلٌ *pl.* جُهَّالٌ ـ مَأْفُوكٌ ـ مَأْفُونٌ; of a thing, عَبَثٌ ـ بَاطِلٌ. A — talker, هَاجِرٌ.

A — action, حُمُوقَة. To be —, خَرِقَ – خَرُقَ ². To act in a — manner towards, جَهِلَ عَلَى. To talk in a — manner, أَهْجَرَ – لَغِيَ. Silly talk, إِهْجَار – لَغْي.

Silt, *n.* تَرَاكُمُ طِينٍ – رُكْمَة – غِرْيَن – غِرْيَل.

Silt, *v.t.* رَكَمَ-طِينًا ².

Silt, *v.i.* إِرْتَكَمَ وَحْلًا – تَرَاكَمَ طِينًا.

Silvan, *a.* *See* Sylvan, *a.*

Silver, *n.* The metal, فِضَّة *pl.* فِضَض. Money, فُلُوس – دَرَاهِمُ. Silver thread, قَصَبُ فِضَّةٍ – قَصَبُ أَبْيَضُ. Silver, utensils of —, أَوَانِي فِضَّةٍ – فِضِّيَّات.

Silver, *a.* Made of silver, فِضِّيٌّ. A — colour, لَوْنُ ٱلْفِضَّةِ. A — ring, sound, رَنَّةُ ٱلْفِضَّةِ. A — voice, صَوْتٌ خَفِيضٌ. A — cup, غَرَب.

Silver, *v.t.* To coat with silver, فَضَّضَ – طَلَى-بِٱلْفِضَّةِ; with quicksilver, زَوَّقَ. To make hoary, شَيَّبَ. To be silvered, with silver, تَفَضَّضَ – إِطَّلَى (*or* تَطَلَّى) بِٱلْفِضَّةِ; to become hoary, شَابَ *aor.* يَشِيبُ.

Silver-fir, *n.* ضَرْبٌ جَمِيلٌ مِنْ شَجَرِ ٱلصَّنَوْبَرِ.

Silver-fish, *n.* نَوْعٌ مِنْ سَمَكِ ٱلْمَرْجَانِ أَبْيَضُ.

Silver-haired, *a.* Hoary-headed, of a man, أَشْيَبُ ٱلرَّأْسِ; of a woman, شَيْبَاءُ – شَمْطَاءُ *pl.* شِيب *and* شُيَّب.

Silver-leaf, *n.* صَفِيحَةُ فِضَّةٍ *pl.* صَفَائِحُ.

Silver-paper, *n.* وَرَقُ قَزٍّ.

Silvering, *n.* The act of, تَفْضِيض – تَطْلِيَةٌ بِٱلْفِضَّةِ. A coating of silver, طَلْيَةُ فِضَّةٍ.

Silversmith, *n.* صَائِغ *pl.* صَاغَة *and* صُوَّاغ – صَوَّاغ. A silversmith's work, craft, صِيَاغَة.

Silvery, *a.* Like silver, فِضِّيٌّ – مِثْلَ ٱلْفِضَّةِ. Coated with silver, مُفَضَّض. *See also under* Silver, *a.*

Similar, *a.* Like, ضَرْب *pl.* ضُرُوب – مُجَانِس – مُمَاثِل – مَثِيل – مَثَل *pl.* أَمْثَال. A little —, مُثَيْل. A —, نِدٌّ *pl.* أَنْدَاد – نَدِيد *pl.* نُدَدَاءُ *fem.* نَدِيدَة *pl.* نَدَائِدُ. In matters — to this, فِي مِثْلِ هٰذِهِ ٱلْأُمُورِ. And other — things, وَمَا يُشْبِهُ ذٰلِكَ. To be — to, مَاثَلَ – أَشْبَهَ – شَاكَلَ. To make — to, شَبَّهَ-إِيَّاهُ – مَثَّلَ-بِ. *See under* Like, *a.*; *also to* Resemble, *v.t.*

Similarity, *n.* Likeness, مُشَاكَلَة – مُشَابَهَة – شَبَهَ – شُبْهَة. Resemblance, مُنَاظَرَة – مُطَابَقَة – مُقَارَنَة. *See also* Likeness, Resemblance, *n.*

Similitude, *n.* An effigy, تِمْثَال *pl.* تَمَاثِيلُ. *See also* Similarity, *n.*

Simile, *n.* مَثَل *pl.* أَمْثَال – تَشْبِيهَة *pl.* تَشْبِيهَات. By way of —, عَلَى ٱلتَّشْبِيهِ.

Similar, *n.* مَعْدِنٌ يُشْبِهُ ٱلذَّهَبَ.

Simmer, *v.i.* جَاشَ *aor.* يَجِيشُ – تَكْتَكَ.

Simmer, *n.* جَيْش – جَيَشَان – جُيُوش – تَكْتَكَة.

Simoniac, *n.* مِنْ أَهْلِ – مَنْ يَبْتَاعُ وَظَائِفَ ٱلْكَنِيسَةِ بِٱلدَّرَاهِمِ. ٱلسِّيمُونِيَّةِ.

Simoniacal, *a.* مُتَعَلِّقٌ بِبَيْعِ أَوْ شِرَاءِ ٱلْوَظَائِفِ ٱلْكَنَائِسِيَّةِ. مُتَعَلِّقٌ بِٱلسِّيمُونِيَّةِ – بِٱلدَّرَاهِمِ.

Simony, *n.* بَيْعُ أَوْ شِرَاءُ وَظَائِفِ ٱلْكَنِيسَةِ – بَيْعُ ٱلدِّينِ بِٱلدُّنْيَا. سِيمُونِيَّة – إِسْتِحْصَالُ ٱلْأُمُورِ ٱلْمُقَدَّسَةِ بِوَاسِطَةِ ٱلْمَالِ – بِٱلدَّرَاهِمِ.

Simoom, *n.* سَمُوم. A — wind, سَمُوم – رِيحٌ سَامَّةٌ.

Simper, *v.i.* تَبَسَّمَ ٱبْتِسَامَ ٱلْجَاهِلِ – أَحْمَقَ وَتَبَسَّمَ – تَبَسَّمَ بِجَهَالَةٍ.

Simper, *n.* إِبْتِسَامٌ بَارِدٌ – تَبَسُّمُ ٱلْجَاهِلِ.

Simpering, *a.* بَاسِمٌ بَارِدٌ – بَاسِمٌ جَاهِلٌ.

Simperingly, *ad.* بِٱبْتِسَامٍ بَارِدٍ – بِتَبَسُّمِ ٱلْجُهَّالِ.

Simple, *a.* Not compound, بَسِيط *pl.* بُسَطَاءُ – غَيْرُ مُرَكَّبٍ. Single, not separated or divided, مُفْرَد – مُجَرَّد – غَيْرُ مُنْقَسِمٍ – غَيْرُ مُتَشَعِّبٍ. Not fixed, غَيْرُ مُقَيَّدٍ. Plain, easy, سَهْل – هَيِّن. Unadorned, سَاذَج – سَاذِج – سَاذِج. Unadulterated, مَحْض – نَصُوح. Consisting of one fold, piece, *etc.*, مُفْرَد – طَاقٌ وَاحِدٌ. Simple, not complex, بَسِيط – وَجِيز. Artless, سَلِيم – غَبِيٌّ – سَاذَج – سَاذِج – بَدِيه – نَصُوح. Weak in intellect, جَاهِل – غَشِيم – غَبِيٌّ. A —, not compound, body, جِسْمٌ بَسِيطٌ. The — knowledge of the thing, مَعْرِفَةُ ٱلشَّيْءِ مُجَرَّدَةً.

Simple, *n.* Of drugs, عِقِّير *pl.* عَقَّار *and* عَقَاقِيرُ. Something not mixed, مُفْرَدَة *pl.* مُفْرَدَات. Medicinal simples, مُفْرَدَاتُ ٱلطِّبِّ.

Simpleness, *n.* Artlessness, سَلَامَة – بَسَاطَة – سَذَاجَة. Weakness of intellect, خِفَّةُ عَقْلٍ – غَشَم – جَهَالَة.

Simpleton, *n.* أَحْمَقُ – جَاهِل *pl.* جُهَّال – أَخْرَقُ *pl.* خُرْق – غَشِيم – أَبْلَه. *See also* Greenhorn, Dupe, *n.*

Simplicity, *n.* The state of being simple, unmixed, بَسَاطَة; of being unadorned, سَذَاجَة. Easiness, هَيِّنَة – سُهُولَة – يُسْر. Artlessness, إِخْلَاص – بَسَاطَة. Simplicity of worship, سَذَاجَةُ ٱلتَّعَبُّدِ. They went in their —, ذَهَبُوا بِبَسَاطَتِهِمْ. *See also* Simpleness, *n.*

Simplification, *n.* The act of making easy, تَسْهِيل; of making concise, إِخْتِصَار – إِيجَاز.

Simplify, *v.t.* To make easy, سَهَّلَ – هَوَّنَ. To make concise, أَوْجَزَ. To — to one, سَهَّلَ-عَلَى.

Simplist, *n.* عَارِفٌ بِٱلْعَقَاقِيرِ. *See also* Herbalist, *n.*

Simply, *ad.* Without cunning, بِسَذَاجَةٍ ـ بِإِخْلَاصٍ ـ بِبَسَاطَةٍ. Without adornment, بِسَذَاجَةٍ ـ بِبَسَاطَةٍ. Only, merely, لَا غَيْرُ ـ فَقَطْ ـ لِمُجَرَّدِ: He is — a fool, هُوَ أَحْمَقُ لَا غَيْرُ. Simply to write, لِمُجَرَّدِ ٱلْكِتَابَةِ. Simply to visit, لِمُجَرَّدِ ٱلزِّيَارَةِ. *See also* Merely, *ad.*

Simulate, *v.t.* To feign, رَآءَى ـ أَظْهَرَ ـ تَظَاهَرَ بِ. To copy, شَخَّصَ. To personify, شَخَّصَ بِ ـ تَمَثَّلَ بِ. To — affection for, مَاذَقَ ـ مَذَقَ. *See also to* Feign, Pretend, *v.t.*

Simulate, *a.* / Simulated, مُزَوَّرٌ ـ كَاذِبٌ ـ مُرَآءٍ ـ مُمَوَّهٌ ـ مُتَظَاهِرٌ ـ مُفْتَرًى. Simulated affection, مُمَاذَقَةٌ. A thing — or forged, فِرْيَةٌ.

Simulation, *n.* Pretence, تَمْوِيهٌ ـ تَصَنُّعٌ. Counterfeit, تَزْوِيرٌ ـ تَقْلِيدٌ ـ إِفْتِرَآءٌ. *See also* Hypocrisy, *n.*

Simultaneous, *a.* وَاقِعٌ سَوِيَّةً ـ صَائِرٌ (or) وَاقِعٌ فِي وَقْتٍ وَاحِدٍ ـ كَائِنٌ فِي وَقْتٍ وَاحِدٍ.

Simultaneously, *ad.* سَوِيَّةً ـ فِي آنٍ وَاحِدٍ ـ مَعًا ـ سَوَآءً.

Simultaneousness, *n.* سَوِيَّةٌ ـ كَوْنٌ (or) وُقُوعٌ فِي زَمَانٍ وَاحِدٍ ـ ٱلْوُقُوعُ.

Sin, *n.* ذَنْبٌ *pl.* ذُنُوبٌ ـ إِثْمٌ *pl.* آثَامٌ ـ مَأْثَمٌ ـ مَآثِمُ ـ خَطِيَّةٌ *or* خَطِيئَةٌ *pl.* خَطَايَا. A pity, loss, خَسَارَةٌ. A little or venial sin, صَغِيرَةٌ *pl.* صَغَائِرُ. A great sin, عَظِيمَةٌ *pl.* عَظَائِمُ ـ كَبِيرَةٌ *pl.* كَبَائِرُ. Original sin, خَطِيَّةٌ أَصْلِيَّةٌ. A mortal sin, خَطِيَّةٌ مُمِيتَةٌ. To impute sin to, إِسْتَذْنَبَ ـ تَذَنَّبَ عَلَى. To make to fall into sin, آثَمَ. To abstain from sin, تَحَنَّثَ ـ تَأَثَّمَ ـ خَطَأً ـ أَثَمَ. To commit a sin, to fall into sin; *see next article.*

Sin, *v.i.* أَذْنَبَ ـ اِرْتَكَبَ خَطِيَّةً ـ أَخْطَأَ ـ خَطِئَ ـ أَثِمَ.
To sin against, to wrong, تَعَدَّى عَلَى ـ أَسَآءَ إِلَى.

Sinai, *n.* The mount, جَبَلُ سِينَا ـ طُورُ سِينَا.

Sinaitic, *a.* مِنْ طُورِ سِينَا.

Sinapism, *n.* لَبْخَةُ بِخَرْدَلٍ.

Since, *prep.* and *ad.* Inasmuch as, مِنْ ـ لِأَنَّ ـ مِنْ حَيْثُ أَنَّ ـ بِسَبَبِ أَنَّ ـ مَا دَامَ إِنَّ ـ كَوْنَ أَنَّ. From that time, مُذْ ـ مُذُ ـ مُنْذُ سَنَةٍ. A year —, مِنْ ذٰلِكَ ٱلْوَقْتِ ـ مِنْ يَوْمِهِ ـ مُنْذُ مِنْ مُدَّةِ سَنَةٍ. A short time —, مِنْ مُدَّةٍ قَرِيبَةٍ. Since, from that time, مِنْ حِينَئِذٍ. Since Thursday, مُنْذُ يَوْمِ ٱلْخَمِيسِ. Since when? مِنْ أَيِّ زَمَنٍ ـ مِنْ أَيِّ وَقْتٍ. And I have never seen him since, وَمِنْ يَوْمِهِ مَا رَأَيْتُهُ قَطُّ.

Sincere, *a.* خَالِصٌ ـ نَصُوحٌ ـ سَلِيمٌ ـ صَادِقٌ ـ صِدِّيقٌ ـ صَافٍ ـ حَقِيقِيٌّ ـ مُخْلِصٌ ـ عَدِيمُ ٱلْغِشِّ. A — man, رَجُلٌ صَادِقٌ ـ رَجُلٌ عَلَى نِيَّتِهِ ـ خَالِصُ ٱلْفُؤَادِ. A — resolution, قَصْدٌ حَقِيقِيٌّ. Your — love, إِخْلَاصُ مَحَبَّتِكُمْ. Sincere prayers, نِيَّةٌ صَحِيحَةٌ ـ صَمِيمُ ٱلدُّعَآءِ. To be —, صَدَقَ ـ صَفَا.

Sincerely, *ad.* عَنْ صَمِيمٍ ـ حَقِيقَةً ـ صَدَاقَةً ـ بِصَفَآءِ ٱلنِّيَّةِ ـ عَنْ إِخْلَاصٍ ـ ٱلْقَلْبِ. To act —, عَمِلَ بِٱلْحَقِّ وَٱلصِّحَّةِ. To act — with, صَارَحَ ـ صَافَى. If ye have acted —, إِنْ قَدْ عَمِلْتُمْ بِٱلْحَقِّ وَٱلصِّحَّةِ.

Sincereness, *n.* / Sincerity, صَفَاوَةٌ ـ صُرُوحَةٌ ـ صَرَاحَةٌ ـ صَدَاقَةٌ ـ صِدْقٌ ـ مُصَافَاةٌ ـ حَقِيقَةٌ ـ خُلُوصُ ٱلنِّيَّةِ. Sincerity of purpose, صِدْقُ ٱلنِّيَّةِ. I proved, experienced, the — of his affection, إِخْتَبَرْتُ إِخْلَاصَ مَحَبَّتِهِ.

Sinciput, *n.* يَافُوخٌ ـ يَفُوخٌ ; *vulg.* نافوخ.

Sine, *n.* In geometry, جَيْبٌ.

Sinecure, *n.* مَأْمُورِيَّةٌ ذَاتُ وَظِيفَةٍ بِدُونِ شُغْلٍ.

Sinecurist, *n.* حَائِزُ مَأْمُورِيَّةٍ ذَاتِ وَظِيفَةٍ بِدُونِ شُغْلٍ.

Sine die, *ad.* مِنْ غَيْرِ تَعْيِينِ يَوْمٍ ـ مِنْ غَيْرِ تَحْدِيدٍ.

Sine qua non, *n.* شَرْطٌ لَازِمٌ ـ شَرْطٌ لَا بُدَّ مِنْهُ ـ لَا بُدَّ مِنْهُ.

Sind, *n.* The country, ٱلسِّنْدُ.

Sindian, *a.* سِنْدِيٌّ ـ مِنَ ٱلسِّنْدِ.

Sindian, *n.* مِنْ أَهْلِ ٱلسِّنْدِ ـ سِنْدِيٌّ.

Sinew, *n.* عَصَبٌ *pl.* أَعْصَابٌ *coll.* عَصَبَةٌ ـ أَطْنَابٌ *pl.* طُنُبٌ.
The sinews of war, ٱلدَّرَاهِمُ.

Sinewless, *a.* Weak, ضَعِيفٌ ـ عَاجِزٌ.

Sinewy, *a.* ضَلِيعٌ ـ مَعْصُوبٌ. A man of — make, robust, ضَلِيعٌ ـ رَجُلٌ مَعْصُوبُ ٱلْخَلْقِ. To be —, عَصِبَ. *See also* Muscular, *a.*

Sinful, *a.* Guilty of sin, مُذْنِبٌ ـ خَاطِئٌ ـ أَثِيمٌ ـ آثِمٌ. Wicked, شِرِّيرٌ *pl.* أَشْرَارٌ *and* أَشِرَّآءُ ـ فَاحِشٌ *pl.* فُحَشَآءُ ـ خَبِيثٌ *pl.* خُبَثَآءُ. To be —, to commit sin, أَخْطَأَ ـ خَطِئَ.

Sinfully, *ad.* إِخْطَآءً ـ شَنَاعَةً ـ شَرًّا ـ فُحْشًا.

Sinfulness, *n.* شَنَاعَةٌ ـ سَآءَةٌ ـ شَرٌّ ـ خُبْثٌ.

Sing, *v.i.* As with the voice, of persons, غَنَّى ـ تَغَنَّى. To —, of a bird, تَرَنَّمَ ـ صَفَرَ ـ غَرَّدَ ـ تَرَنَّمَ ; to warble, بِٱلْأَغَانِيِّ. of a boiling kettle, أَزَّ ـ كَتَّ ; of a hissing sound in the ears, نَاغَى ـ طَنَّتْ أُذُنَاهُ ـ صَرَّ صِمَاخُهُ. To —, as of psalms, or in a church, or to chant, of psalms, or of the Kurân, تَرَتَّلَ. To — or chant the time for prayer, in a mosque, أَذَّنَ. To ask one to —, إِسْتَغْرَدَ. They then sang songs, ثُمَّ تَرَنَّمُوا بِٱلْأَغَانِيِّ وَٱلْأَلْحَانِ. The birds — among the branches, ٱلطُّيُورُ تُغَرِّدُ مِنْ بَيْنِ ٱلْأَغْصَانِ.

Sing, *v.t.* To commemorate in song, تَغَنَّى بِ ـ غَنَّى بِ ـ ذَكَرَ.

Singe, *v.t.* أَشَاطَ ـ شَوَّطَ ـ أَحْرَقَ قَلِيلًا. To be singed, تَشَيَّطَ ـ ؟ شَاطَ ـ إِحْتَرَقَ قَلِيلًا. And not a hair of his head was singed, وَشَعْرَةٌ مِنْ رَاسِهِ لَمْ تَحْتَرِقْ.

Singer, *n.* غَنَّآء ـ مُغَنٍّ *fem.* مُغَنِّيَة. Male and female singers, مُغَنُّونَ وَمُغَنِّيَاتٌ. A female —, مُسْمِعَة *pl.* مُسْمِعَات. A fine —, غِرِّيد. A female professional —, in Egypt, عَالِمَة *pl.* عَوَالِم ; a male — and musician, آلَاتِيٌّ *pl.* آلَاتِيَّة.

Singing, *n.* Of the human voice, غِنَآء ـ سَمَاع ; of psalms or chanting, تَرْتِيل ; of birds, صَفِير ـ تَرَنُّم ـ مُنَاغَاةُ ٱلطُّيُورِ ـ تَغْرِيد ; of a boiling kettle, كَتِيت. He passed the night in diversion and —, ؟ بَاتَ فِي لَهْوٍ وَسَمَاعٍ.

Singing-book, *n.* كُرَّاسَة (*or* كِتَاب) ٱلْغِنَآء.

Singing-master, *n.* مُعَلِّمُ ٱلْغِنَآء.

Single, *a.* Separate, alone, فَرْد *fem.* فَرْدَة *and* فَرْدَى *pl.* أَفْرَاد *and* فُرَادَى ـ فَرِيد ـ مُنْفَرِد ـ مُجَرَّد ـ فَذّ *pl.* فُذُود ـ فُرُود ـ وَاحِد *pl.* وَاحِدُونَ. Not double, مُجَرَّد ـ طَاقٌ وَاحِدٌ. Not married, عَازِب *pl.* عُزَّاب *fem.* عَازِبَة *pl.* عَازِبَات ـ غَيْرُ مُزَوَّجٍ. Particular, خَاصّ ـ مَخْصُوص. Simple, بَسِيط. A — person, نَفَر *pl.* أَنْفَار ـ شَخْص *pl.* أَشْخَاص ـ ظَلَم *pl.* أَظْلَام. A — time, دَفْعَة ـ ضَرْبَة. A — thing, فَرْدُ شَيْءٍ ـ شَيْءٌ وَاحِدٌ. Trowsers made of — cloth, سَرَاوِيلُ طَاقٍ وَاحِدٍ. Spun thread of a — yarn, غَزْلٌ طَاقٌ وَاحِدٌ. A — sole, of a shoe, نَعْلٌ طَاقٌ وَاحِدٌ. No — government can arrogate to itself the right of intervention in this matter, لَيْسَ لِدَوْلَةٍ مِنَ ٱلدُّوَلِ عَلَى حِدَتِهَا أَنْ تَنْتَحِلَ لِنَفْسِهَا ٱلْمُدَاخَلَةَ فِي هٰذَا ٱلْأَمْرِ.

Single, *v.t.* To single out, عَيَّنَ عَلَى ـ إِسْتَفْرَدَ ـ خَصَّصَ ـ ² خَصَّ. To — out, as by embellishment, إِسْتَطْرَفَ. He singled out the thief, عَيَّنَ عَلَى ٱلسَّارِقِ. To be singled out, تَعَيَّنَ ـ إِخْتَصَّ. The singling out, as by embellishment, إِسْتِطْرَاف.

Single-blessedness, *n. See* Celibacy, *n.*

Single-handed, *a.* وَحْدَهُ *fem.* وَحْدَهَا. He did it —, فَعَلَهُ مِنْ فَعَلَهُ وَحْدَهُ ـ ذَاتِ حِدَتِهِ.

Single-hearted, *a.* نَصُوحُ ٱلْقَلْبِ.

Single-minded, *a.* مُسْتَقِيمُ ٱلنِّيَّةِ ـ سَلِيمُ ٱلْفِكْرِ.

Singleness, *n.* The state of being one only, وَحْدَانِيَّة ـ وَحْدَة. Singleness of heart, mind, بَسَاطَةُ قَلْبٍ ـ إِسْتِقَامَة ـ صَدَاقَة ـ نُصُوح.

Singly, *ad.* Apart, alone, فُرَادًا ـ فُرَادَ ـ إِنْفِرَادًا ـ فُذَاذًا. One by one, جَاؤُوا فُذَاذًا ـ جَاؤُوا فُرَادَى ـ وَاحِدًا وَاحِدًا. They came —, جَاؤُوا فُرَادَى.

Sing-song, *n.* جَعْجَعَة ـ مَقَامٌ جَعْجَاعٌ.

Singular, *a.* One, separate, alone, فَذّ *pl.* فُذُود ـ فَرِيد ـ وَاحِد ـ مُفْرَد. Particular, مُخَصَّص ـ خَاصّ. Rare, نَادِر ـ نَذْر. Extraordinary, غَرِيب ـ عَجِيب. Unique, وَحِيد ـ فَرِيد. A — or much esteemed gem, فَرِيدَة *pl.* فَرَائِد. The — number, الْفَرْد ـ الْمُفْرَد. He was — in his opinion, إِسْتَبَدَّ بِرَأْيِهِ ـ إِفْتَاتَ بِرَأْيِهِ. He was — in his opinion against us, إِفْتَاتَ عَلَيْنَا. He asked me what had led me to be — in this testimony, سَأَلَنِي عَنِ ٱلسَّبَبِ ٱلَّذِي أَغْرَانِي بِٱلتَّفَرُّدِ بِهٰذِهِ ٱلشَّهَادَةِ. He is —, alone in this affair, هُوَ فَارِدٌ بِهٰذَا ٱلْأَمْرِ.

Singular, *n.* The singular number, الْمُفْرَد ـ الْفَرْد.

Singularity, *n.* Singleness, وَحْدَانِيَّة ـ وَحْدَة ـ تَفَرُّد. A rare thing, نَادِرَة *pl.* نَوَادِر. A peculiarity, خُصُوصِيَّة ـ خَاصَّة. Extraordinariness, غَرَابَة. Independence, as of opinion, إِسْتِبْدَاد.

Singularly, *ad.* Peculiarly, خَاصَّةً. In an extraordinary manner, بِنَوْعٍ عَجِيبٍ ـ بِنَوْعٍ غَرِيبٍ ـ غَرَابَةً. Much, to a great extent, جِدًّا ـ كَثِيرًا. Separately, عَلَى وَجْهِ ٱلْإِنْفِرَادِ.

Sinister, *a.* Left, as opposed to right, يَسَار ـ شِمَال. Pernicious, سَوْء ـ شَرّ. Unlucky, مَشْؤُوم *pl.* مَشَائِيم ـ مَنْحُوس ـ نَحِس. A bar —, عَلَامَةٌ تَدُلُّ عَلَى ٱلنُّغُولَةِ. To be —, unlucky, ؟ شَأَمَ.

Sinistral, *a.* شِمَال ـ يَسَار.

Sinistrous, *a. See* Sinister, *a.*

Sink, *v.i.* As in the water, of a ship, *etc.*, ؟ غَرِقَ ـ إِسْتَغْرَقَ. To go down, as in water, mud, *etc.*, ؟ غَطَسَ ـ إِنْغَمَسَ ـ تَغَمَّسَ. To —, as into the earth, ؟ إِنْغَطَّ فِي ـ ؟ غَطَسَ ـ ² غَاصَ ـ ؟ خَسَفَ ـ إِنْخَسَفَ ـ سَاخَ *aor.* يَسُوخُ. To decline, as the sun below the horizon; also, to disappear, غَابَ *aor.* يَغِيبُ. To subside, as dregs, سَاخَ *aor.* يَسُوخُ ـ ² رَسَبَ ـ تَرَسَّبَ ; as of water, to become less, ؟ قَلَّ ـ ² خَمَدَ ـ هَادَ *aor.* يَهُودُ. To —, as under disease, إِضْمَحَلَّ ـ غُمِيَ ـ إِنْزَهَلَ ـ أُغْمِيَ ; as with fatigue, تَلَاشَى ـ إِنْكَسَرَ. The earth sank with them, سَاخَتْ بِهِمِ ٱلْأَرْضُ. They sank to the bottom like a stone, ؟ ² هَبَطُوا فِي ٱلْأَعْمَاقِ كَحَجَرٍ. They sank like lead, ² غَاصُوا كَٱلرَّصَاصِ. His foot sank in the mud, غُرِزَتْ رِجْلُهُ فِي ٱلْوَحْلِ ـ طَمَسَتْ رِجْلُهُ فِي ٱلطِّينِ. He began to —, ² أَخَذَ فِي ٱلْغَرَقِ. The ship began to —, أَخَذَتِ ٱلسَّفِينَةُ فِي ٱلْغَرَقِ. Let these words — into your hearts, ضَعُوا هٰذَا ٱلْكَلَامَ فِي قُلُوبِكُمْ. His eyes sank in their sockets, رَنَبَتْ عَيْنَاهُ. To — into, to penetrate, permeate, ؟ نَفَذَ فِي ـ ؟ قَطَعَ فِي ـ أَثَّرَ فِي ـ ؟ قَطَعَ فِي. To have an effect upon, تَطَرَّقَ إِلَى. *See also to* Become, *v.t.*

To sink into insignificance, nothingness, تَلَاشَى ; into contempt, إِسْتَحْقَرَ.

To sink into oblivion, غَرِقَ فِي بَحْرِ ٱلنِّسْيَانِ.

To sink into sleep, نَامَ — غَلَبَ عَلَى-ٱلنَّوْمُ.

To sink into the grave, نَزَلَ إِلَى ٱلْقَبْرِ.

To sink to a level with, on the same elevation, سَاوَى-فِي ٱلْإِرْتِفَاعِ; to become on an equality with, سَاوَى — نَاظَرَ.

To sink into vice, ٱنْهَمَكَ فِي ٱلْخَلَاعَةِ.

To sink under, to be overwhelmed by, طَمَا عَلَى-كَذَا *aor.* يَطْمُو — غُشِيَ عَلَى-بِكَذَا.

Sink, *v.a.* To cause to be drowned, of a ship or animal, غَرَّقَ — أَغْرَقَ. To cause to go down, as in water, *etc.*, أَرْسَبَ — غَتَّ-فِي — غَطَّسَ-فِي — غَطَّ-فِي — غَمَسَ-فِي. To excavate downwards, حَفَرَ — إِحْتَفَرَ; to — a well, حَفَرَ بِئْرًا — بَأَّرَ بِئْرًا. To cause to disappear, as in the ground, خَسَفَ: we made the ground to — with him and his house, فَخَسَفْنَا بِهِ وَبِدَارِهِ ٱلْأَرْضَ, (Kûr. xxviii. 81). I made the spring of water to — into the earth, خَسَفْتُ عَيْنَ ٱلْمَآءِ. To precipitate, of dregs, *etc.*, رَسَّبَ. To —, as a die, حَفَرَ — نَقَشَ. To depress, lower, نَزَّلَ — وَطَّأَ. To —, as money in a concern, for a time, قَيَّدَ ٱلدَّرَاهِمَ فِي. To — in a sinking fund, أَدَّى مَالًا لِٱسْتِهْلَاكِ مَصْلَحَةٍ إِلَى زَمَنٍ. To —, as of differences, to overlook, تَغَمَّدَ — غَمَّدَ دَيْنٍ. To —, as of differences, to overlook, سَكَتَ عَنْ — أَغْضَى.

Sink, *n.* A drain, بَالُوعَة — مَصَبّ *pl.* مَصَابّ — إِرْدَبَّة *pl.* بَوَالِيع — بَلُّوعَة *and* بَلَّاعَة *pl.* بَلَالِيع. A — of iniquity, مَاخُور — مَجْلِسُ ٱلْفُسَّاقِ — ٱلْخَلَاعَةِ.

Sinker, *n.* Of dies, نَقَّاش (or) حَفَّار) سِكَكٍ.

Sinking, *n.* As of the ground, خَسْف — خُسُوف; as of a well, حَفْر — بَأْر; as of a die, نَقْش — حَفْر; as of the spirits, كَدَر — غَمّ — غُمَّة — ثَقْلَة — حُزْن.

Sinking-fund, *n.* رَأْسُ مَالِ لِٱسْتِهْلَاكِ دَيْنٍ.

Sinless, *a.* Without sin, بِلَا خَطِيَّةٍ. Innocent, زَكِيّ — بِلَا ذَنْب. *See also* Impeccable, *a.*

Sinlessly, *ad.* Without sin, بِلَا خَطِيَّةٍ. Innocently, بِلَا ذَنْب — زَكَاة.

Sinlessness, *n.* عَدَمُ خَطَآءٍ. Innocence, عِصْمَة — بَرَآءَة. *See also* Impeccability, *n.*

Sinner, *n.* آثِم *pl.* أَثَمَة — أُثَمَآء — أَثِيم *pl.* أُثَم — أَثُوم *pl.* أَثَامُون — خَاطِئ *pl.* خُطَاة — مُذْنِب *pl.* مُذْنِبُون — خَطَّاء.

Sin-offering, *n.* ذَبِيحَة خَطِيَّةٍ *pl.* ذَبَائِح.

Sinuate, *v.i.* تَفَتَّلَ — تَلَوَّى — تَعَوَّجَ.

Sinuate, *a.* مُلْتَوٍ — مُتَفَتِّل — مُتَعَوِّج.

Sinuation, *n.* تَلَوٍّ — تَفَتُّل — تَعَوُّج.

Sinuosity, *n.* إِعْوِجَاج — تَعْوِيجَة — ٱلْتِوَآء.

Sinuous, *a.* *See* Sinuate, *a.*

Sinus, *n.* A bay of the sea, شَرْم *pl.* شُرُوم — خَلِيج *pl.* خُلْجَان. A cavity, hollow, وَقْرَة *pl.* وَقَرَات — جَوْف *pl.* أَجْوَاف.

Sip, *n.* مَزَّة — حَسْوَة — حَسْو — جُرْعَة — تَمَزُّز — تَمَصُّص. To give one a —, أَمَصَّ.

Sip, *v.t.* مَزَّ — تَمَزَّزَ — حَسَا — تَرَمَّقَ — تَمَصَّصَ — إِحْتَسَى.

Sip, *v.i.* شَرِبَ قَطْرَةً قَطْرَةً — غَمَسَ — تَرَمَّقَ.

Siphon, *n.* مِثْقَل — أُنْبُوبَة — قَصَبَة.

Siphuncle, *n.* أُنْبُوبَة رَفِيعَة.

Sipper, *n.* حَسُوّ.

Sippet, *n.* لُقْمَة مُرَوَّغَة *pl.* لُقَم مُرَوَّغَات.

Sir, *n.* سَيِّد *pl.* سَادَة. As an address of civility, يَا سَيِّدُ — أَفَنْدِم; of an artisan to his master, يَا مُعَلِّمِي; to the clergy, أَبُونَا. As a title of a knight, *etc.*, *from the English*, سَار.

Sirdar, *n.* سِرْدَار.

Sire, *n.* Father, أَب — وَالِد *pl.* آبَآء. Lord, سَيِّد.

Siren, *n.* The fabled goddess, جِنِّيَّةُ ٱلْبَحْرِ — بِنْتُ ٱلْبَحْرِ. An enticing woman, إِمْرَأَة فَتَّانَة.

Siren, *a.* Pertaining to a siren, مُتَعَلِّق بِبِنْتِ ٱلْبَحْرِ — جِنِّيَّة. Enticing, fascinating, يَسْلُبُ ٱلْقَلْبَ — مُفْتِن.

Sirius, *n.* The star, ٱلْمِرْزَمُ — ٱلشِّعْرَى. Sirius and Procyon, ٱلشِّعْرَانِ.

Sirloin, *n.* قِطْعَة لَحْم مِنْ صُلْبِ ٱلْبَقَرِ.

Sirname, *n.* *See* Surname, *n.*

Sirocco, *n.* *See* Scirocco, *n.*

Sirrah, *n.* يَا مُحْتَالُ — يَا خَاسِرُ.

Sirup, *n.* شَرَاب *pl.* أَشْرِبَة.

Sister, *n.* أُخْت *pl.* أَخَوَات. A — by the same father and mother, شَقِيقَة *pl.* شَقَائِق — صِنْوَة. A foster —, رَضِيعَة. A husband's —, سِلْفَة *pl.* سَلَائِف. "Your foster-sisters," أَخَوَاتُكُمْ مِنَ ٱلرَّضَاعَةِ (Kûr. iv. 27).

Sisterhood, *n.* A society of females, جَمْعِيَّة نِسَآءٍ.

Sister-in-law, *n.* كَنَّة *pl.* كَنَائِن — سِلْفَة *pl.* سَلَائِف.

Sisterly, *a.* أَخَوِيّ (some say أُخْتِيّ but that is not generally accepted,) — كَٱلْأَخَوَاتِ.

Sit, *v.i.* To rest on the lower part of the body, جَلَسَ — قَعَدَ. To sit cross-legged, قَعَدَ مُرَبَّعًا — تَرَبَّعَ. To sit on horseback, رَكِبَ عَلَى فَرَسٍ. To sit still, قَرَّ جُلُوسًا — رَكَدَ. To sit, as a hen on eggs, حَضَنَتْ ـ تَكِنُ .aor وَكَنَتْ عَلَى ٱلْبَيْضِ 2. To sit leaning, in a leaning posture, جَلَسَ مُتَّكِئًا 2. To sit in judgment, جَلَسَ لِلْقَضَآءِ 2. To sit on the throne, جَلَسَ عَلَى ٱلْكُرْسِيِّ 2. To sit on the right hand of one, جَلَسَ مِنْ عَنْ يَمِينِ فُلَانٍ 2. To sit on the haunches with the hands round the knees, قَرْفَصَ. To ask one to sit, إِسْتَجْلَسَ. To make to sit, أَقْعَدَ ـ أَجْلَسَ. A colt on which no one ever sat, فَلُوٌّ لَمْ يَجْلِسْ عَلَيْهِ أَحَدٌ. The people sat down to eat and drink, جَلَسَ ٱلْقَوْمُ لِلْأَكْلِ وَٱلشُّرْبِ. The coat sits well, لِبْسَةُ ٱلْعَبَآءَةِ حَسَنَةٌ. They sat down together, تَجَالَسُوا.

To sit down before a town; *see to* Besiege, *v.t.*

To sit out, to remain to the end of…, قَعَدَ إِلَى آخِرِ ٱلْ… 2.

To sit still, جَلَسَ ـ. Why do we sit still here? لِمَاذَا نَحْنُ جُلُوسٌ هُنَا ـ لِمَاذَا نَحْنُ جَالِسُونَ هُنَا.

To sit up, in an upright position, جَلَسَ ـ قَامَ عَلَى حَيْلِهِ 2.

Not to sleep at night, سَهِرَ ٱللَّيْلَ ـ: I sat up last night, سَهِرْتُ ٱلْبَارِحَةَ. To sit up with another, سَاهَرَ.

To sit with, جَالَسَ: Do not sit with one with whom you are not congenial (prov.) لَا تُجَالِسْ مَنْ لَا تُجَانِسْ.

Sit, *v.t.* To sit one's self down, قَعَدَ 2 ـ جَلَسَ 2.

Site, *n.* مَحَطَّةٌ ـ مَكَانٌ ـ مَحَلٌّ ـ مَوْضِعٌ ـ مَوْقِعٌ; as of a house, the ground which it occupies, عَرْصَةٌ *pl.* أَعْرَاصٌ *and* عَرَصَاتٌ. A —, or piece of ground which a man marks out for himself to build upon, خِطَّةٌ *pl.* خِطَطٌ.

Sitter, *n.* جَالِسٌ *pl.* جُلُوسٌ ـ قَاعِدٌ. A — with one, قَعِيدٌ ـ جَلِيسٌ *pl.* جُلَسَآءُ.

Sitting, *n.* A resting as on a seat, جُلُوسٌ ـ قُعُودٌ. A mode or manner of —, جِلْسَةٌ ـ قِعْدَةٌ: He has a good —, sits well, هُوَ حَسَنُ ٱلْجِلْسَةِ. A session, جَلْسَةٌ. They settled the matter in five sittings, فَصَلُوا ٱلدَّعْوَى فِي خَمْسِ جَلَسَاتٍ ـ. A — together, مُجَالَسَةٌ.

Sitting-room, *n.* مَجْلِسٌ *pl.* مَجَالِسُ ـ قَاعَةُ ٱلْجُلُوسِ.

Sitú, *ad.* In *sitú*, فِي مَحَلِّهِ.

Situate, *a.* } Placed, being in any position, وَاقِعٌ ـ كَائِنٌ.
Situated, } Situated between …, وَاقِعٌ بَيْنَ كَذَا. To be situated, placed, وَاقِعٌ عِنْدَ كَذَا ـ جَالِسٌ عِنْدَ كَذَا ـ كَانَ عِنْدَ كَذَا 2. To be in a position, circumstances, كَانَ فِي حَالِ كَذَا. I am so situated that I cannot go, مُحَاطٌ بِمَوَانِعَ تُعِيقُنِي عَنِ ٱلذَّهَابِ.

Situation, *n.* Place, site, مَكَانٌ ـ مَحَلٌّ ـ مَحَطَّةٌ ـ مَوْقِعٌ ـ مَوْضِعٌ *pl.* مَوَاضِعُ ـ مَقَامٌ. Office, employment, مَنْصِبٌ *pl.* مَنَاصِبُ ـ وَظِيفَةٌ *pl.* وَظَائِفُ ـ خِدْمَةٌ. Circumstances, condition, حَالٌ ـ حَالَةٌ.

To find a situation, وَجَدَ خِدْمَةً *aor.* يَجِدُ.

To give a situation to, قَعَّدَ ـ قَعَّدَ فِي خِدْمَةٍ.

To go into a situation, إِتَّخَذَ خِدْمَةً.

To lose a situation, أَضَاعَ مَنْصِبَهُ ـ عُزِلَ عَنِ ٱلْخِدْمَةِ.

To seek a situation, طَلَبَ خِدْمَةً 2.

Six, *a.* سِتَّةٌ *fem.* سِتٌّ. Six men, سِتَّةُ رِجَالٍ; six women, سِتُّ نِسَآءٍ. I have with me — men and — women, عِنْدِي سِتَّةُ رِجَالٍ وَنِسْوَةٍ. To make —, or into —, سَدَّسَ. A six, a number —, سِدْسٌ *pl.* أَسْدَاسٌ. Having — sides, مُسَدَّسٌ. To be at sixes and sevens, إِرْتَبَكَ ـ إِلْتَبَكَ ـ تَشَوَّشَ.

Sixfold, *a.* سِتَّةُ أَضْعَافٍ.

Sixpence, *n.* نِصْفُ شِلِينٍ ـ سِتُّ بِنْسَاتٍ إِنْكِلِيزِيَّةٍ. A sixpenny piece, سِكَّةُ نِصْفِ شِلِينٍ.

Sixscore, *a.* مِئَةٌ وَعِشْرُونَ.

Sixteen, *a.* سِتَّةَ عَشَرَ *fem.* سِتَّ عَشْرَةَ.

Sixteenth, *a.* ٱلسَّادِسَ عَشَرَ *fem.* ٱلسَّادِسَةَ عَشْرَةَ.

Sixth, *a.* سَادِسٌ ـ سَاتٌّ *fem.* سَادِسَةٌ. A — part, سُدْسٌ *or* سُدُسٌ *pl.* أَسْدَاسٌ. In the — year, فِي ٱلسَّنَةِ ٱلسَّادِسَةِ.

Sixthly, *ad.* سَادِسًا.

Sixtieth, *a.* ٱلسِّتُّونَ.

Sixty, *a.* سِتُّونَ. He lived — years, عَاشَ سِتِّينَ سَنَةً ـ.

Sizable, *a.* مُنَاسِبُ ٱلْحَجْمِ.

Sizar, *n.* تِلْمِيذٌ مِنْ أَوْطَى دَرَجَاتِ ٱلدَّارِسِينَ فِي ٱلْمَدَارِسِ ٱلْكُلِّيَّةِ *pl.* تَلَامِيذُ.

Size, *n.* Bulk, dimensions, مِقْدَارٌ ـ قَدٌّ ـ حَجْمٌ. Size, in length, طُولٌ; in thickness, ثُخْنٌ; in breadth, عَرْضٌ ـ سَعَةٌ; in depth, عُمَاقَةٌ. Extent, مِقْدَارٌ ـ إِمْتِدَادٌ ـ مَسَافَةٌ ـ سَعَةٌ ـ وُسْعٌ. Size, as of sheets of paper, قَطْعٌ. Calibre, as of a shot, عِيَارٌ. Size, a glutinous substance, for paper, تَرْبِيَةٌ ـ غِرَآءٌ; *from the Persian,* آهَارٌ. Full or natural —, قَدٌّ طَبِيعِيٌّ. All of a —, كُلُّهُمْ قَدٌّ وَاحِدٌ ـ كُلُّهُمْ سَوَآءٌ. The pieces were all of one —, كَانَ لِجَمِيعِ ٱلشُّقَقِ قِيَاسًا وَاحِدًا.

Size, *v.t.* To arrange by bulk, قَاسَ عَلَى ـ رَتَّبَ ـ حَسَبَ ٱلْقَدِّ ـ. To prepare with —, طَلَا بِغِرَآءٍ 2 (*or* آهَارٍ) ـ رَبَّى ـ قِيَاسٌ.

Sized, *a.* Small —, مِنْ قِيَاسٍ صَغِيرٍ; ordinary, مِنْ قِيَاسٍ عَادِيٍّ.

Siziness, *n.* Glutinousness, لُزُوجَةٌ ـ تَغْرِيَةٌ.

Sizing, *n.* The glutinous substance; *see* Size, *n.*

Sizy, *a.* Glutinous, دَبِقٌ ـ لَزِجٌ.

Skain, *n.* *See* Skein, *n.*

Skate, *n.* The fish, سَمَكَةُ ٱلتُّرْسِ ـ قَرْش. A — for skating, نَعْلٌ مِنْ خَشَبٍ مُصَفَّحٌ بِحَدِيدٍ لِلتَّزَحْلُقِ عَلَى ٱلْجَلِيدِ.

Skate, *v.i.* لَعِبَ ٱلزُّحْلُوقَةَ ء.

Skater, *n.* لاعِبُ ٱلزُّحْلُوقَةِ *pl.* لاعِبُونَ.

Skating-rink, *n.* مَلْعَبُ (or مَحَلُّ) ٱلزُّحْلُوقَةِ.

Skedaddle, *v.i.* جَفَلَ ـ ء أَجْفَلَ ـ ٱجْفَلَّ ـ تَقَهْقَرَ.

Skein, *n.* As of thread, silk, *etc.*, شِلَّةٌ *pl.* شِلَّات ـ خُصْلَةٌ *pl.* خُصَل; as of an orange, شِرْذِمَةٌ *pl.* شَرَاذِمُ ـ فَصٌّ *pl.* فُصُوص. To split, as into skeins, فَلَجَ ء ء.

Skeleton, *n.* Of the body, هَيْكَلُ ٱلْبَدَنِ عَلَى ٱلتَّرْكِيبِ ٱلطَّبِيعِيِّ. One very lean, أَعْجَفُ *fem.* عَجْفَاءُ *pl.* عِجَاف. A — key, مِفْتَاحُ ٱللُّصُوصِ. The general structure of anything, تَرْكِيب ـ بِنْيَة. Heads, as of a discourse, مُخْتَصَر ـ أَبْوَاب ـ فُصُول.

Skeptic, *n.* *See* Sceptic, *n.*

Sketch, *n.* A rough draft, مُسَوَّدَةٌ. A general representation, تَعْرِيفٌ مُخْتَصَرٌ. A drawing, رَسْم ـ تَصْوِير *pl.* تَصَاوِير.

Sketch, *v.t.* To make a rough draft of, سَوَّدَ. To give a general outline of, وَصَفَ بِٱلِٱخْتِصَارِ *aor.* يَصِفُ. To draw, رَسَمَ ء ـ صَوَّرَ. He sketched out a book and did not fill it up, رَسَمَ كِتَابًا وَلَمْ يَحْشُهُ ء.

Sketch-book, *n.* مُجَلَّدُ ٱلتَّصَاوِيرِ.

Sketchy, *a.* مُخْتَصَر ـ وَجِيز.

Skewer, *n.* خِلَال *pl.* أَخِلَّة ـ سَفُّود *pl.* سَفَافِيدُ.

Skewer, *v.t.* خَلَّ ء ـ سَفَّدَ: He skewered the meat, خَلَّ ٱللَّحْمَ ء.

Skid, *n.* For a carriage wheel, مُسْكَة ـ ضَابِطَةُ عَجَلَةٍ; for a ship's side, حَاجِزٌ مِنْ خَشَبٍ لِمَنْعِ تَصَادُمِ ٱلْمَرَاكِبِ — *from the Italian*, فَرَمَلَةُ خَشَبٍ ـ فَرْمِيلَةُ خَشَبٍ.

Skiff, *n.* زَوْرَق ـ رَكْوَة ـ زَبَازِبُ *pl.* زَبْزَب ـ شَذَاوَة ـ شَذَاة *pl.* زَوَارِقُ ـ قَارِب *pl.* قَوَارِبُ.

Skilful, *a.* Able, expert, أَرِيب ـ مَاهِر ـ حَاذِق ـ ثَقِيف. Skilful, as a handicraftsman, مُتَعَقِّد ـ مُفِنٌّ ـ صَنِيع ـ أُسْتَاذ ـ مُعَلِّم ـ مِنْ أَهْلِ صَنَاعَةٍ. Intelligent, أَرِب ـ بَارِع ـ ذَهِن ـ حَاذِق ـ فَطِين ـ ذَكِيٌّ ـ خَبِير ـ مُعَلِّم ـ عَالِم *pl.* عُلَّام. Skilful or experienced in, لَبِيقٌ بِ ـ دَرِبٌ بِ ـ خَبِيرٌ بِ. Men skilful in war, مُتَعَلِّمُونَ ٱلْقِتَالَ. He who loves is —, *i.e.*, exercises ingenuity for the object of his love, (prov.) مَنْ حَبَّ طَبَّ. To be —, expert, ingenious, in, أَفْتَنَّ فِي ـ أَرِبَ بِ ء ـ مَهَرَ ء ـ تَمَهَّرَ فِي (or بِ). To become —, as in a science, بَرَعَ فِي ء ـ. To be —, intelligent, prudent, sagacious, أَرُبَ ء ـ فَطِنَ ء ـ. To make —, فَطَّنَ.

Skilfully, *ad.* With art, dexterity, بِٱلْإِتْقَانِ ـ بِمَهَارَةٍ ـ بِصَنَاعَةٍ ـ بِمَعْرِفَةٍ ـ بِمِهْنَةٍ ـ بِفَنٍّ. Knowingly, intelligently, بِبَرَاعَةٍ ـ بِثَقَافٍ ـ بِإِرْبٍ ـ بِحِذْقٍ. To do anything —, أَسْنَفَ. To play — on an instrument, أَحْسَنَ ٱلْعَزْفَ.

Skilfulness, *n.* } As in craft, فَنٌّ ـ حِذْق ـ مَهَارَة ـ مِهْنَة ـ إِتْقَان ـ مَعْرِفَة; of intelligence, بَرَاعَة ـ
Skill, } فِطْنَة ـ إِرْب ـ ذَكَاء ـ ذِهْن ـ بَصِيرَة. To act with —, طَبَّ ء. With consummate —, بِغَايَةِ ٱلْإِتْقَانِ.

Skilled, *a.* مُتَعَقِّد ـ ثَقِيف ـ حَاذِق ـ مَاهِر ـ صَنِيع. Skilled in, مَاهِرٌ فِي. Skilled labour, شُغْلُ أَهْلِ ٱلصَّنَاعَةِ. To be — in, بَسَقَ فِي ء ـ إِفْتَنَّ فِي; especially in handicraft, تَعَقَّدَ فِي.

Skim, *v.t.* To remove the scum, طَفَحَ ٱلطُّفَاحَةَ ـ كَشَطَ ٱلرُّغْوَةَ ء ـ رَفَعَ ٱلْقِشَاطَ (or ٱلْكِشَاطَ) ء. To —, of milk, مَخَضَ ٱللَّبَنَ ء ـ عَنِ ٱللَّبَنِ. To pass lightly over, خَفَّ مِنْ عَلَى كَذَا ء.

Skim, *v.i.* To pass lightly, to glide, زَلَّ ء ـ سَبَحَ ء ـ حَبَا *aor.* يَحْبُو ـ خَفَّ ء. To — the surface, as a bird, سَفَّ ء. To — through, peruse lightly, as of a book, هَذَّ ء ـ خَفَّ فِي قِرَاءَةِ ٱلـ... ء. *See also to* Glide, *v.i.*

Skim-milk, *n.* }
Skimmed milk, } مَخِيض ـ مَمْخُوض.

Skimmer, *n.* The utensil, مِرْغَاة *pl.* مَرَاغٍ ـ قِشَاشَة ـ مِقْشَطُ ٱلزَّبَدِ.

Skimmings, *n.* زَبَد ـ رُغْوَة ـ رِغْوَة ـ رُغَاوَى.

Skin, *n.* جِلْد *pl.* جُلُود; a single skin, جِلْدَة. A cuticle, epidermis, بَشَرَة. A thin — like the pellicle of an egg, دُوَايَة. The exterior covering of fruits, قِشْرَة *coll.* قِشْر *pl.* قُشُور. The — of a drum, a drum-head, دَفَّةُ ٱلطَّبْلِ *dual* دَفَّتَا ٱلطَّبْلِ: he beat the two drum-heads, ضَرَبَ دَفَّتَيِ ٱلطَّبْلِ ء. A crude —, from a slaughtered animal, مِسْلَاخ. A water —, قِرْبَة ـ غَاوِيَة *pl.* قِرَب *and* قِرْبَات ـ زِقٌّ *pl.* زِقَاق; a maker of such skins, زَقَّاق. A — for holding clarified butter or honey, مِسَاد. A piece of old —, قِشْعَة. Skin rubbed off the body into round shapes in the bath, فَتِيلَة ـ فَتِيل. Having a dry —, صَوْمَل. Having a fine —, بَضٌّ *fem.* بَضَّة. Casting its —, of a serpent, مُنْسَلِخ. The — then became extended, ثُمَّ عَرَضَ عَلَى ٱلْجِلْدِ شَيْءٌ مِنَ ٱلْمَدِّ. To wear next the —, لَبِسَ عَلَى ٱلْبَدَنِ ء. To be nothing but — and bone, بَرَدَتْ عِظَامُهُ ـ إِخْتَلَّ جِسْمُهُ. To rub or injure the —, بَشَرَ ٱلْأَدِيمَ ء ـ عَفَسَ ٱلْجِلْدَ ء. To be so injured, تَقَوَّبَ.

Skin, *v.t.* To flay, سَلَخَ ء ـ جَلَّدَ. To take off the rind, قَشَّرَ.

To —, as with a lash, سَلَقَ-بِ 2. To peel off, as flesh from a bone, سَلَقَ-عَنِ ٱلْعَظْمِ 2. To — over, to cover superficially, بَسَطَ عَلَى-جِلْدًا 2. أَغْشَى عَلَى-عَلَّى عَشَمَ. To stretch a — over, To be —, flayed, إِنْسَلَخَ.

Skin, *v.i.* To form a skin over, إِنْبَسَطَ عَلَى-جِلْدٌ ـ ح عَشَمَ ـ ح 2 سَلَخَ. مُدَّ عَلَى-ٱلْجِلْدُ. To throw off the skin, as a serpent, إِنْسَلَخَ.

Skin-deep, *a.* بِرِقَّةِ ٱلْجِلْدِ. Light, superficial, زَهِيد ـ خَفِيف.

Skinflint, *n.* *See* Miser, *n.*

Skink, *n.* The lizard, أَسْقَنْقُور ـ سُقَنْقُور.

Skinned, *a.* Flayed, مَسْلُوخ; as with a lash, مَسْلُوق. A — sheep or goat, مَسْلُوخَة ـ مَسْلُوخ ـ سَلِيخ. A place where animals are —, مَسْلَخ. Thin-skinned, touchy, وَعِق ـ شَكِس ـ سَرِيعُ ٱلضَّجَرِ ـ حَسَّاس. Fine or transparent-skinned, غَضّ ـ بَضَّة ـ بَضّ ـ غَضِيض.

Skinless, *a.* بِلا جِلْدٍ.

Skinner, *n.* سَلَّاخ.

Skinniness, *n.* عَجَف ـ نَحَافَة ـ خَسَف.

Skinny, *a.* Emaciated, ضَعِيف ـ رِكّ ـ خَاسِف ـ نَحِيف.

Skip, *n.* A bound, وَثْبَة ـ قَفْزَة ـ نَطَّة ـ عَرْقَصَة.

Skip, *v.t.* To pass over, omit, فَاتَ ـ ح حَذَفَ ـ أَسْقَطَ 2. The pen skipped something in transcribing, سَبَقَ ٱلْقَلَمُ كذا ـ ح 2.

Skip, *v.i.* To leap, bound, قَفَزَ ـ 2 نَطَّ ـ فَرْشَخَ ـ عَرْقَصَ ـ ح وَثَبَ *aor.* يَثِبُ.

Skip-jack, *n.* *See* Parvenu, *n.*

Skipper, *n.* One who skips, قَفَّاز ـ نَطَّاط. The master of a small vessel, رَئِيس ـ نَوَاخِذَة *pl.* نَاخُوذَاة. A maggot, دُودَةُ ٱلْجُبْنِ *coll.* دُود.

Skipping-rope, *n.* حَبْلُ ٱلْقَفْزِ.

Skirmish, *n.* Of soldiers, مُنَاوَشَة ـ مُلاطَمَة عَسَاكِرَ. A contest, نِزَاع ـ مُخَاصَمَة ـ مُشَاجَرَة. To have a —, contest, with, نَازَعَ ـ شَاجَرَ ـ إِعْتَرَضَ.

Skirmish, *v.i.* نَاوَشَ ٱلْعَدُوَّ ـ تَلاطَمَ مَعَ ٱلْعَدُوِّ.

Skirmisher, *n.* مُنَاوِش *pl.* مُنَاوِشَة.

Skirmishing, *n.* *See* Skirmish, *n.*

Skirret, *n.* The vegetable, كَرَفْسُ ٱلْمَآءِ.

Skirt, *n.* A hem, ذَيْل *pl.* أَذْيَال ـ كِنَار ـ طَرَف *pl.* أَطْرَاف. A petticoat, jupon, فُسْتَان (or فُسْطَان) تَحْتَانِيّ. A border, extremity, حَدّ *pl.* حُدُود ـ طَرَف *pl.* أَطْرَاف ـ حَافَة. *See also* Border, *n.*

Skirt, *v.t.* and *i.* To be on the border of, إِتَّصَلَ بِ ـ تَاخَمَ ـ كَانَ حَوْلَ (or جَنْبَ or عَلَى حَافَةِ) كذا ـ قَارَبَ. To — the coast, جَانَبَ ٱلْبَرَّ ـ سَافَرَ بِٱلْقُرْبِ مِنَ ٱلسَّوَاحِلِ ـ شَطَأَ.

Skirting-board, *n.* فَرْوَاز مِنْ خَشَبٍ ـ لَوْحُ ٱلْبِرْوَازِ.

Skit, *n.* *See* Lampoon, Gibe, Quib, *n.*

Skittish, *a.* Light, trifling, أَطْيَر ـ طَائِش ـ أَنْوَل ـ سَخِيف. Shy, timid, خَوَّاف ـ فَزِع ـ فَرْفَار; of a horse, جَفَّال ـ شَارِد. *See also* Frisky, *a.*

Skittishly, *ad.* In a trifling manner, بِسَخَافَةٍ ـ بِفَرْفَرَةٍ. Timidly, بِخَوْفٍ ـ فَزَعًا ـ بِمَزَاحٍ ـ بِطَيْشَانٍ; as of a horse, شِرَادًا ـ بِجُفُولٍ ـ بِشُرُودٍ.

Skittishness, *n.* Levity, fickleness, طَيْرَة ـ فَرْفَرَة ـ سَخَافَة ـ طَيْشَان; as of a horse, شِرَاد ـ شُرُود ـ جُفُول.

Skittle, *n.* ضَرْبٌ مِنَ ٱللَّعِبِ.

Skulk, *v.i.* To lurk, hide, in a place, تَوَارَى فِي ـ ح غَابَ فِي ـ إِسْتَخْفَى ـ تَخَفَّى ـ إِخْتَبَأَ. To pretend to be sick, تَمَارَضَ. "Skulking (or lurking) by night and appearing by day," مُسْتَخْفٍ بِٱللَّيْلِ وَسَارِبٌ بِٱلنَّهَارِ (Kûr. xiii. 11).

Skulk, *n.* One who lurks, مُسْتَخْفٍ ـ مُخْتَفٍ. One who shirks duty on pretence of sickness, مُتَمَارِض. A weak-hearted fellow, خَشِلٌ فَشِلٌ ـ جَبَان.

Skull, *n.* جُمْجُمَة *pl.* جَمَاجِم. The bony covering of the brain, قِحْف *pl.* قِحَفَة and قُحُوف and أَقْحَاف. The joining or suture of the —, شَأْن *pl.* شُؤُون ـ إِكْلِيلِيّ ـ يَافُوخ *pl.* يَوَافِيخ ـ شَعْب *pl.* شُعُوب ـ مُلْتَقًى: (The four sutures are called القَبَائِل). Understanding, عَقْل ـ ذِهْن.

Skull-cap, *n.* كِسْوَةُ ٱلرَّأْسِ. A — of linen for keeping off the perspiration, عَرَقِيَّة ـ طَاقِيَّة.

Skunk, *n.* نَوْعٌ مِنَ ٱلسُّرْعُوبِ مُنْتِنُ ٱلرَّائِحَةِ.

Skurry, *n.* Hurry-skurry; *see* Helter-skelter, *ad.*

Sky, *n.* سَمَآء *pl.* سَمَوَات. The blue sky, ٱلْكَحْلَة ـ ٱلْكَحْلُ. Sky, the ceiling of the earth, سَقْفُ ٱلْأَرْضِ.

Sky-blue, *n.* لَوْنٌ سَمَاوِيٌّ.

Sky-coloured, *a.* سَمَاوِيُّ ٱللَّوْنِ.

Skyey, *a.* سَمَاوِيّ ـ سَمَائِيّ.

Sky-high, *a.* مُرْتَفِعٌ إِلَى ٱلْجَوِّ.

Skylark, *n.* دَالُوع *pl.* دَوَالِيع ـ أَبُو ٱلْمَلِيح ـ قُبَّرَة *pl.* قُبَّرَات.

Skylight, *n.* قَمَرِيَّة ـ مَمْرَق. A — to let in air from the roof, مَلْقَف.

Sky-rocket, *n.* *See* Rocket, *n.*

Sky-sail, *n.* قُشَيْرَةُ ٱلْبَابَافَنْقُو.

Slab, *n.* طابِق *pl.* طَوَابِقُ – صَفِيحَة *pl.* صَفَائِحُ – لَوْح *pl.* أَلْوَاح. The slabs over a grave, عِدَآء – عِدًى – عُدًى; a single one of such slabs, عِدْوٌ.

Slabber, *v.i.* *See to* Drivel, *v.i.*

Slabberer, *n.* *See* Driveller, *n.*

Slack, *a.* Loose, hanging loose, مُسْتَرْخٍ – رَخْوٌ. Remiss, مُتَرَاخٍ – مُتَغَافِل – غَافِل. Slow, مُتَعَوِّق – مُتَوَانٍ – مُتَأَخِّر; in pace, حَارِك. Slack, of a market, كَاسِد. A — hand, a lazy worker, عَامِلٌ بِيَدٍ رَخْوَةٍ. To be —, remiss in, أَخَلَّ بِ – قَصَّرَ فِي – تَرَاخَى فِي. *See also* Loose, Remiss, *a.*

Slack, *n.* The slack or loose part of a rope, رَخَاوَة – رَخَآء. The — of coal, دُقَاقُ ٱلْفَحْمِ ٱلْمَعْدِنِيِّ.

Slack, *v.t.* } To loosen, relax, أَرْخَى – رَاخَى; of a rein, أَطْلَقَ;
Slacken, } of a fire, أَخْمَدَ; of a pain, أَهْمَدَ – سَكَّنَ. He slackened the tie, أَرْخَى ٱلرِّبَاطَ. Slacken his bonds, أَرْخِ قَيْدَهُ. He slackened the horse's tether or rope, أَرْخَى لِلْفَرَسِ – طَوَّلَ لِلْفَرَسِ.

Slack, *v.i.* } To be or become loose, رَخِيَ *aor.* يَرْخُو – إِسْتَرْخَى –
Slacken, } تَرَاخَى; of a pain, wind, fire, أَهْمَدَ – سَكَنَ[2] – خَمَدَ[2] – تَرَاخَى. To — one's pace, أَرْوَدَ فِي (or تَمَهَّلَ فِي) ٱلسَّيْرِ. To —, of a market, كَسَدَ[2]. إِسْتَرْخَى فِي ٱلْمِشْوَارِ – فِي ٱلْمَشْيِ. *See also to* Loosen, Relax, *v.i.*

Slackened, *a.* Loosened, مُسْتَرْخٍ *fem.* مُسْتَرْخِيَة – مُتَرَاخٍ.

Slackly, *ad.* Loosely, رَخْوَةً – بِرَخَاوَةٍ. Carelessly, تَغَفُّلًا – بِإِهْمَالٍ.

Slowly, رُوَيْدًا – مَهْلًا. *See also* Loosely, Remissly, *ad.*

Slackness, *n.* Looseness, flabbiness, رَخَآء – رَخَاوَة. Freedom from tightness, إِنْفِكَاك – إِنْحِلَال. Remissness, إِهْمَال – مُرَاخَاة – تَقْصِير – قُصُور. Slowness, تَوَانٍ – بِطَآء – بَطَآءَة – تَطَاوُل. Dullness, as of a market, كَسَاد. *See also* Looseness, Remissness, *n.*

Slack-water, *n.* نُقْصَانُ ٱلْمَآءِ بَيْنَ ٱلْمَدِّ وَٱلْجَزْرِ.

Slag, *n.* Dross of metals, خَبَث – رَغْوَةُ ٱلْمَعَادِنِ. *See also* Scoria, *n.*

Slain, *a.* مَقْتُول. The —, *pl.* ٱلْقَتْلَى. *See to* Slay, *v.t.*

Slake, *v.t.* To quench, أَطْفَأَ – أَهْمَدَ – أَبَاخَ. To — lime, حَلَّ[2] ٱلْكِلْسَ. To — thirst, كَسَرَ ٱلظَّمَآءَ.

Slam, *v.t.* As of a door, *etc.*, خَفَقَ[2] – صَدَعَ. *See also to* Bang, *v.t.*

Slam, *n.* خَفْق – صَدْع – صَدْعَة.

Slander, *v.t.* عَرَّضَ بِ – أَفْرَشَ بِ – لَمَزَ[2] – غَمَصَ عَلَى – غَمَزَ بِ – أَغْمَزَ بِ – حَطَبَ بِ – قَشَبَ – بَهَتَ – لَقَسَ – نَمَّ[2] – فَرَى – نَمَلَ[2] – أَقْرَفَ بِ – هَتَكَ. To — mutually, بَاهَتَ. To be slandered, أُفْتُرِيَ عَلَيْهِ. *See also to* Defame, *v.t.*

Slander, *n.* نِمْلَة – قَذْف – نَمِيمَة – نَمِيلَة – عَظْوٌ – بَجَل – نَسِيسَة – قَذْف. Mutual —, مُبَاهَتَة. To spread — among the people, فَشَّ بَيْنَ ٱلْقَوْمِ.

Slanderer, *n.* } نَزَّاغ – نَمَّال – نَمِل – نَمَّام – نَمّ *pl.* أَنِمَّآء –
Slanderous, *a.* } لَمَّاز – بَهُوت.

Slanderously, *ad.* بِٱفْتِرَآء – وَشْيًا. As is — reported of us, كَمَا يُفْتَرَى عَلَيْنَا.

Slanderousness, *n.* *See* Slander, *n.*

Slang, *pret. of to* Sling, *q.v.*

Slang, *n.* كَلَامٌ خَنٍ – كَلَامٌ زُقَاقِيٌّ – كَلَامُ ٱلْجَعِيدِيَّةِ.

Slant, *n.* مَيْل – إِعْوِجَاج – إِنْحِرَاف – تَعَرُّض – إِنْصِبَاب – تَمَايُل.

Slant, *v.t.* مَيَّلَ – حَرَّفَ.

Slant, *v.i.* إِنْحَرَفَ – تَعَرَّضَ – إِنْصَبَّ.

Slant, *a.* }
Slanting, } مَائِل – مُنْحَرِف – مُتَعَرِّض.

Slantly, *ad.* } بِمَيْلٍ – بِٱنْحِرَافٍ – إِنْحِرَافًا – عِرَضًا – إِنْصِبَابًا –
Slantwise, } تَعَرُّضًا.

Slap, *v.t.* سَفَعَ – خَفَقَ[2] – لَطَمَ – لَطَمَ – لَطَحَ – لَطَحَ بِ – لَتَحَ بِ – صَقَعَ – أَسْفَقَ – سَفَقَ; To — with, صَفَعَ. He slapped him or it with his hand, لَطَمَهُ بِكَفِّهِ. *See also to* Strike, *v.t.*

Slap, *n.* لَطْح – صَقْع – سَفْع. A — in the face, كَفّ *pl.* كُفُوف – سَفْقَة – سَفَقَهُ كَفًّا. He slapped his face, قَلَم *pl.* أَقْلَام. A check, reproof, تَوْبِيخ – وَبْخَة – حَلْوَةُ كَفٍّ.

Slap, *ad.* بِطَقْطَقَةٍ.

Slap-dash, *ad.* All at once, بِٱلْمَرَّةِ – سَوِيَّةً – طُرًّا; hurriedly, بِتَهَوُّرٍ.

Slapjack, *n.* ضَرْبٌ مِنَ ٱلرُّقَاقِ – ضَرْبٌ مِنَ ٱلْعُجَّةِ.

Slash, *v.t.* To make long cuts in, كَلَمَ – شَقَّ[2] – شَقَّقَ – قَطَّعَ. To wound, جَرَحَ – جَرَّحَ. To —, as a whip, to crack, فَقَّعَ – صَوَّتَ. *See also to* Lash, *v.t.*

Slash, *v.i.* To dash about at random, تَهَوَّرَ يَمِينًا وَشِمَالًا. *See also to* Gash, *v.t.*

Slash, *n.* A gash, كَلْم *pl.* كِلَام – شَقّ *pl.* شُقُوق. A wound, جُرْح *pl.* جُرُوح. An opening in a garment, جَيْب *pl.* جُيُوب.

Slate, *n.* The stone, حَجَرٌ ذُو طَبَقَاتٍ يُشْبِهُ ٱلْمَرْمَرَ ٱلدُّونَ – حَجَرٌ مَعْدِنِيٌّ مُرَكَّبُ صَفَائِحَ (called vulgarly لافانة apparently from the Italian *lava*). A writing-slate, سَبُّورَةٌ مِنَ ٱلْحَجَرِ ٱلْمَذْكُورِ. A board used as a writing-slate, سَبُّورَة.

Slate, *v.t.* To cover with slates, فَرَشَ ٱلسَّطْحَ بِصَفَائِحَ مِنَ ٱلْحَجَرِ ٱلْمَذْكُورِ – سَطَّحَ بِلَافَانَةٍ.

Slate-coloured, *a.* ضَارِبٌ إِلَى ٱلزُّرْقَةِ.

Slater, *n.* فَرَّاشٌ بِٱلْمَرْمَرِ ٱلْمَذْكُورِ (or بِٱللَّافَانَةِ).

Slate-pencil, *n.* قَلَمٌ مِنَ ٱلْمَرْمَرِ ٱلْمَذْكُورِ *pl.* أَقْلَام – قَلَمُ لَافَانَةٍ.

Slate-quarry, *n.* مَحْجَرُ ٱلْمَرْمَرِ ٱلْمَذْكُورِ – مَحْجَرُ ٱللَّافَانَةِ.

Slating, *n.* The act of, تَسْطِيحٌ بِٱلْمَرْمَرِ ٱلْمَذْكُورِ (or بِٱللَّافَانَةِ); the being slated, فَرْشٌ مِنْ لَافَانَةٍ – سَقْفٌ مِنَ ٱلْمَرْمَرِ ٱلْمَذْكُورِ.

Slattern, *n.* إِمْرَأَةٌ وَسِخَةٌ – إِمْرَأَةٌ مُتَحَشِّفَةٌ – إِمْرَأَةٌ بَذَّةٌ – مِذْرَان.

Slatternliness, *n.* وَسَخٌ – تَحَشُّفٌ – بَذَاذَةٌ – بَذَاذ.

Slatternly, *a.* Of a female, وَسِخَةٌ – مُتَحَشِّفَةٌ – بَذَّةٌ. *See also* Dowdy, *a.*

Slatternly, *ad.* بِوَسَخٍ – بِتَحَشُّفٍ – بِبَذَاذَةٍ.

Slaty, *a.* مِنْ نَوْعِ ٱلْمَرْمَرِ ٱلدُّونِ. *See* Slate, *n.*

Slaughter, *n.* سَفْكُ دِمَاءٍ – قَتْلٌ – ذَبْحٌ – إِشَاط; a place of —, رِبْضَة. He made — among the beasts of the chase, عَقَرَ – وَقَعَ بِٱلصَّيْدِ *aor.* يَقَعُ – بِٱلصَّيْدِ. *See also* Carnage, Massacre, *n.*

Slaughter, *v.t.* To kill, قَتَلَ ² – ذَبَحَ – أَشَاطَ دَمَهُ; of a beast, جَزَرَ ² – ذَبَحَ. They slaughtered one another, of many, تَذَابَحُوا – ذَبَحُوا بَعْضُهُمْ بَعْضًا. To be slaughtered, killed, قُتِلَ – ذُبِحَ.

Slaughterer, *n.* / Slaughterman, جَزَّار – جَازِر – ذَبَّاح.

Slaughter-house, *n.* مَجْزَر *pl.* مَجَازِر.

Slaughterous, *a.* قَتُول – مُهْلِك.

Slaughterously, *ad.* بِسَفْكِ دِمَاءٍ.

Slave, *n.* The Slave nation, ٱلصَّقَالِبَةُ – ٱلْأَسْكَلَافُ – ٱلسَّلَافُ.

Slave, *n.* عَبْد *pl.* عَبِيد – مَمْلُوك *pl.* مَمَالِيك *coll.* رَقِيق *pl.* أَرِقَّاء. A female —, أَمَة *pl.* آمَاء *and* إِمْوَان – مَمْلُوكَة – رَقِيقَة *pl.* رَقَائِق – جَارِيَة *pl.* جَوَارٍ. A — brought from a foreign country for sale, جَلِيب *pl.* جَلْبَى *fem.* جَلِيب *pl.* جَلْبَاء *and* جَلَائِب. To make a —, عَبَّدَ – أَرَقَّ. To become or be made a —, رَقَّ ². He kept him as a —, or for his —, إِسْتَرَقَّهُ – أَرَقَّهُ. A captive, أَسِير *pl.* أَسْرَى *and* أُسَرَاء. These are my slaves, هٰؤُلَاءِ رَقِيقِي.

Slave, *v.i.* To strive, drudge, كَدَّ ².

Slave-holder, *n.* صَاحِبُ رَقِيقٍ *pl.* أَصْحَاب.

Slaver, *n.* A slave ship, سَفِينَةٌ مُجَهَّزَةٌ لِنَقْلِ ٱلرَّقِيقِ.

Slaver, *n.* Drivel, لُعَاب – رُوَال.

Slaver, *v.i.* *See to* Drivel, *v.i.*

Slaverer, *n.* *See* Driveller, *n.*

Slavery, *n.* رِقِّيَّة – عُبُودِيَّة – عُبُودَة. To be in a state of —, عَبُدَ ² – عَبَدَ – رَقَّ ². *See also* Drudgery, *n.*

Slave-trade, *n.* تِجَارَةُ ٱلرَّقِيقِ.

Slavish, *a.* Like a slave, رِقِّيٌّ – كَٱلرَّقِيقِ – كَٱلْعَبْدِ. Mean, cringing, حَقِير – ذَلِيل – مُتَذَلِّل – مُتَضَعْضِع. *See also* Servile, *a.*

Slavishly, *n.* بِمُطَاوَعَةٍ – بِحَقَارَةٍ – بِدَنَاءَةٍ – تَذَلُّلًا – بِتَضَعْضُعٍ.

Slavishness, *n.* Servility, حَقَارَة – دَنَاءَة – تَذَلُّل – تَضَعْضُع. Close imitation, تَقْلِيد – مُتَابَعَة. *See also* Drudgery, *n.*

Slavonic, *a.* مِنَ ٱلْأَسْكَلَافِ – أَسْكَلَافِيٌّ – أَسْلَافِيٌّ.

Slay, *v.t.* قَتَلَ ² – ذَبَحَ. *See also to* Kill, Murder, *v.t.*

Slayer, *n.* قَاتِل *pl.* قَتَّال – قُتَّال – ذَبَّاح.

Sleave, *n.* Untwisted silk, قَزّ.

Sled, *n.* / Sledge, عَجَلَة – سَرِيرٌ نَقَّال – عَرَبَات *pl.* عَرَبَةٌ بِلَا عَجَلَاتٍ ٱلثَّلْجِ.

Sledge, *v.t.* نَقَلَ فِي عَرَبَةِ ٱلثَّلْجِ – نَقَلَ عَلَى عَرَبَةٍ بِلَا عَجَلَاتٍ ².

Sledge, *n.* / Sledge-hammer, فِطِّيس – مَطَارِق *pl.* مِطْرَقَةٌ عَظِيمَةٌ.

Sleek, *a.* Smooth, أَمْلَس *fem.* مَلْسَاء *pl.* مُلْس. Glossy, لَامِع – دِلَاص – دَلِيص. Bland, مَجْلُوّ – مَلِق – مُرَاوِد. To be —, smooth, مَلُسَ ²; to be —, glossy, دَلَصَ ². *See also* Smooth, *a.*

Sleek, *v.t.* To make smooth, مَلَّسَ. To make glossy, دَلَّصَ.

Sleekly, *ad.* Smoothly, بِتَدْلِيصٍ. Softly, بِلِينَةٍ. Easily, تَمَلُّقًا – بِمُرَاوَدَةٍ. Blandly, سَهْوًا رَهْوًا.

Sleekness, *n.* Smoothness, مَلَاسَة – مُلُوسَة. Glossiness, دَلِيص – دَلَاصَة – جَلَاء – صِقَال.

Sleep, *n.* رَقْدَة – نَوْمَة – رُقَاد – رُقُود – نَوْم – حَثَاث; one —, سُبَات. Heavy —, سُبَات; affected with heavy —, مَسْبُوت. A light —, غَفْوَة. Morning —, تَصَبُّح; midday —, قَيْلُولَة – غَوْرَة – غَائِرَة. There is no — in me, مَا بِي رُقُود. Sleep left him, زَايَلَهُ ٱلنَّوْمُ. I have not tasted —, مَا ٱكْتَحَلْتُ حَثَاثًا. I had no —, مَا ذُقْتُ حَثَاثًا. To be in a dead —, or to be overcome by —, أُسْتُثْقِلَ نَوْمًا. To go to —, رَقَدَ ² – نَامَ. To awake one out of —, نَبَّهَ مِنَ ٱلنَّوْمِ – أَيْقَظَ مِنَ ٱلنَّوْمِ. To awake out of —, هَبَّ مِنَ ٱلنَّوْمِ ². *See also to* Wake, *v.t.* and *i.*

Sleep, *v.i.* رَقَدَ ² – نَامَ – أَغْفَى – غَفِيَ – غَفَا ². He lay down to —, إِضْطَجَعَ لِيَنَامَ. To put to —, أَنَامَ – رَقَّدَ – أَرْقَدَ.

نَوَّمَ. To feign to —, تَرَاقَدَ — إِسْتَرْقَدَ. To — with, ضَاجَعَ. To — over a thing, غَفَلَ عَنْ كَذَا. To — or lie on one's back, إِسْتَلْقَى — إِسْلَنْقَى.

Sleeper, *n.* One who sleeps, نَائِم *fem.* نَائِمَة *pl.* نِيَام *and* نُوَّام *and* نُيَّام. A — of a railroad, عَارِضَةُ سِكَّةِ ٱلْحَدِيدِ *pl.* عَوَارِض.

Sleepily, *ad.* Drowsily, بِنُعَاسٍ. Sluggishly, lazily, غَفْلَةً — بِتَهَامُلٍ — بِكَسَلٍ.

Sleepiness, *n.* *See* Drowsiness, *n.*

Sleeping, *n.* نَوْم — رُقَاد — رُقُود. A place for —, مَنَام — مَرْقَد.

Sleepless, *a.* سَاهِر — بَعِث — آرِق — أَرِق. Habitually —, أُرُق. A — night, لَيْلٌ سَاهِرٌ. One who is —, سُهُد. To be —, أَرِقَ — سَهِرَ — سَهِدَ — بَعِثَ. To render —, آرَقَ — أَرَّقَ. He was — during the night, سَهِرَ ٱللَّيْلَ.

Sleeplessness, *n.* سَهَد — سُهَاد — أَرَق — سُهَار — سَاهُور.

Sleepy, *a.* نَاعِس *pl.* نُعَّاس — نَعْسَانُ — نُوَمَة — نَوْمَانُ — خَافِق. Lazy, stupid, ثَقِيلُ ٱلدَّمِ — ثَقِيل — بَلِيد — نَوِيم. To be —, drowsy, نَعَسَ — خَفَقَ — أَخْفَقَ.

Sleep-walker, *n.* مَاشٍ وَهُوَ نَائِمٌ.

Sleepy-head, *n.* رَقَّاد — رَقُود.

Sleet, *n.* بَرَدٌ دَقِيقٌ — هَجَارِس.

Sleet, *v.i.* نَزَلَ ٱلْبَرَدُ ٱلدَّقِيقُ (*or* ٱلْهَجَارِسُ).

Sleety, *a.* Bringing sleet, ذُو ٱلْبَرَدِ ٱلدَّقِيقِ. Like sleet, كَٱلْبَرَدِ ٱلدَّقِيقِ.

Sleeve, *n.* كُمّ *pl.* أَكْمَام — ذِرَاع *pl.* أَذْرُع. The base of a — next the shoulder, and tropically the — itself, رُدْن *pl.* أَرْدَان — عُتْب. A — of a shirt, خِلَاف. To turn up, as the sleeves, from off the arms, شَمَّرَ ٱلْأَكْمَامَ عَنْ سَاعِدَيْهِ — تَشَمَّرَ عَنْ سَاعِدَيْهِ. To get up one's sleeve, to get favour with, إِسْتَعْطَفَ — تَحَبَّبَ — دَارَى — إِلَى.

To hang on one's sleeve, to be dependent on, أَنَاطَ بِ — أَوْقَفَ — تَعَلَّقَ بِ — عَلَى.

To laugh in one's sleeve, غَتَّ ٱلضَّحِكَ — ضَحِكَ خُفْيَةً.

Sleeve, *v.t.* To furnish with sleeves, أَكَمَّ.

Sleeveless, *a.* بِلَا أَكْمَامٍ.

Sleigh, *n.* *See* Sledge, *n.*

Sleighing, *n.* Riding on a sleigh, ٱلسَّيْرُ فِي مَرْكَبَةٍ (*or* عَجَلَةٍ) فَوْقَ ٱلثَّلْجِ.

Sleight, *n.* A trick, حِيلَة *pl.* حِيَل — كَيْد — دَوْلَب.

Sleight of hand, *n.* *See* Legerdemain, *n.*

Slender, *n.* Of the body, شَخْت *fem.* شَخْتَة *pl.* شِخَات — قُضْفَان *and* قِضَاف *pl.* قَضِيف — شَخِيت. Slender in make, form, حَمْشُ ٱلْخِلْقَةِ. Fine, not thick, دَقِيق *pl.* دِقَاق — رَكِيك. Lean, عَجِيف *pl.* عِجَاف. أَعْجَف *fem.* عَجْفَاء *pl.* عُجْف — عَجْفَى. Weak, ضَعِيف. Little, contracted, قَلِيل — جُزْئِيّ. Having a — waist, مُهَفْهَف — هَيْفُ ٱلْخَصْرِ — أَهْيَفُ ٱلْخَصْرِ *fem.* هَيْفَاء *pl.* هِيف — مُخَصَّر — رَقِيقُ ٱلْخَصْرِ. His legs are —, قَوَائِمُهُ شِخَاتٌ. Slender firewood, حَطَبٌ شَخْتٌ. Slender means, قِلَّةُ مَالٍ — قِلَّةُ مَعَاشٍ. A — bough, غُصْنٌ دَقِيقٌ. A — spear, رُمْحٌ دَقِيقٌ. He is neither — nor coarse or thick, مَا لَهُ دِقٌّ وَلَا جِلٌّ. I took the — of it with the thick or coarse, أَخَذْتُ دِقَّهُ وَجِلَّهُ. To be —, of the body or any of the members, شَخُتَ — قَضُفَ. To be —, thin, fine, small, دَقَّ *aor.* يَدِقُّ — إِسْتَدَقَّ. To be —, weak, flimsy, thin, رَكَّ *aor.* يَرِكُّ — سَخُفَ. To be —, of a tree, أَقْصَفَ.

Slenderly, *ad.* Finely, nicely, بِدِقَّةٍ. In a small degree, يَسِيرًا — قَلِيلًا — جُزْءًا. Insufficiently, مِنْ غَيْرِ كِفَايَةٍ — بِنُقْصَانٍ.

Slenderness, *n.* Of the body or its members, قَضَافَة — قَضَف — شَخُوتَة. Fineness, thinness, دِقَّة. Thinness, flimsiness, سَخَافَة — رَكَاكَة — رِكَّة. Weakness, ضَعْف. Leanness, عَجَف. Slenderness of voice, رِقَّةُ ٱلصَّوْتِ; of a tree, branch, قَصَفَة; of stature, build, شُخُوتَة.

Slept, *pret. of to* Sleep, *v.i. q.v.*

Slew, *pret. of to* Slay, *v.t. q.v.*

Slice, *n.* A thin piece cut off, فِلْذَة *pl.* أَفْلَاذ *and* فِلَذ — شَرِيح — شَرِيحَة *pl.* شَرَائِح — شِقَّة *pl.* شِقَق — قِطْعَة *pl.* قِطَع. A long —, strip, خَبِيبَة *pl.* خَبَائِب. A — of meat, سَائِفَة — شَرِيحَةُ لَحْمٍ. An instrument to slice with, مِشْرَح. A fire-shovel, مِسْجَرَة.

Slice, *v.t.* To cut in slices, شَرَّحَ — شَرَحَ — فَلَّذَ — فَلَذَ. To cut a — off anything, فَلَذَ فِلْذَةً مِنْ كَذَا — شَرَحَ شَرِيحَةً مِنْ كَذَا.

Sliced, *a.* Cut into slices, مَفْلُوذ — مَشْرُوح.

Slide, *v.t.* To make to pass over a surface gently, أَدْرَجَ — دَرَّجَ — دَحْرَجَ.

Slide, *v.i.* تَزَلَّقَ — زَلِقَ — تَزَلَّجَ — زَلَجَ — زَلِجَ. To — down a declivity, تَزَحْلَقَ. To — or pass away, زَالَ *aor.* يَزُولُ — إِضْمَحَلَّ. To —, as on the ice; *see to* Skate, *v.i.*

Slide, *n.* A slippery way, دَحْض — زَلَج — مِزْلَقَة — زَحْلِيف. A —, such as is used by children, زُحْلُوفَة *pl.* زَحَالِيف — مَدْحَض. *See also* Slip, *n.*

Slider, *n.* One who slides, مُتَزَلِّق — زَالِق — زَالِج.

Sliding-rule, *n.* مِقْيَاس مُدْمَج.

Sliding-scale, *n.* جَدْوَلٌ لِإِسْقَاطِ ٱلرُّسُومِ وَلِتَعْلِيَتِهَا حَسَبَ ٱلْأَثْمَانِ ٱلْجَارِيَةِ.

Slight, *a.* Light, trifling, جُزْئِيٌّ ـ خَفِيفٌ ـ وَاهٍ ـ وَجِيزٌ. Of no importance, مَا تَحْتَ خَبَرٍ ـ وَاهٍ ـ تَافِهٌ. Fine, thin, رَقِيقٌ ـ رَفِيعٌ. Flimsy, سَخِيفٌ. A — wound, جُرْحٌ خَفِيفٌ. Weak, ضَعِيفٌ. The slightest cause, أَقَلُّ ٱلْأَسْبَابِ. Without the slightest difficulty, بِدُونِ أَدْنَى صُعُوبَةٍ. To be —, خَفَّ ـ رَكَّ. *See also* Slender, *a.*

Slight, *n.* Light estimation, إِسْتِخْفَافٌ ـ إِسْتِحْقَارٌ ـ إِسْتِقْلَالٌ.

Slight, *v.a.* To make light of, إِسْتَخَفَّ ـ إِسْتَقَلَّ. To treat with disregard, أَهَانَ ـ إِسْتَحْقَرَ.

Slightly, *ad.* Superficially, بِخِفَّةٍ ـ عَلَى عَشْمٍ. In a small degree, قَلِيلًا ـ جُزْئِيًّا. To build up, run up, sow —, عَشَمَ ـ إِعْتَشَمَ. *See also* Carelessly, *ad.*

Slightness, *n.* Weakness, ضَعْفٌ. Flimsiness, سَخَافَةٌ ـ رَكَاكَةٌ ـ رِقَّةٌ. Indifference, negligence, تَغَافُلٌ ـ بُرُودَةٌ ـ فُتُورٌ. *See also* Slenderness, *n.*

Slily, *ad.* إِخْتِيَالًا ـ بِحِيلَةٍ ـ بِٱلدَّسِيسَةِ ـ بِٱلدَّسِّ.

Slim, *a.* *See* Slender, *n.*

Slime, *n.* رَدَغَةٌ ـ رَزَغَةٌ ـ رِدَاغٌ. The — or mud left by a torrent or in a pool of water, تُرْنُوقَاءُ ـ تَرْنُوقٌ ـ تُرْنُوقٌ. Green — over water, ثَوْرُ ٱلْمَاءِ ـ طُحْلُبٌ. Sticking fast in —, رَزِغٌ ـ مُرْزِغٌ ـ مُرْزَغٌ.

Slime-pit, *n.* بِئْرٌ رَزَاغِيَّةٌ *pl.* آبَارٌ.

Sliminess, *n.* Glutinousness, لُزُوجَةٌ ـ تَغْرِيَةٌ. *See also* Slime, *n.*

Slimness, *n.* *See* Slenderness, *n.*

Slimy, *a.* رَادِغٌ. Slimy water, مَاءٌ رَدَغَةٌ (*or* رَزَغَةٌ). A — place, رَدِغٌ. To fall into a — place, إِرْتَدَغَ. To be —, رَدِغَ. The land became —, أَرْزَغَتِ ٱلْأَرْضُ ـ أَرْدَغَتِ ٱلْأَرْضُ.

Sliness, *n.* إِخْتِيَالٌ ـ دَهَاءٌ ـ حِيلَةٌ ـ دَسِيسَةٌ ـ دَبِيسٌ ـ فَنٌّ ـ خِدَاعَةٌ.

Sling, *n.* A — to throw stones with, قَذَّافَةٌ ـ مِقْلَاعٌ ـ مِخْذَفَةٌ ـ مِرْجَمَةٌ. A band for a broken limb, عِلَاقَةٌ ـ مِحْزَمٌ ـ وِشَاحٌ. A rope for suspending anything, مِعْلَاقٌ.

Sling, *v.t.* To hurl with a sling, قَذَفَ ـ حَذَفَ. To hang, عَلَّقَ.

Slinger, *n.* ضَرَّابَةٌ *pl.* ضَرَّابُ ٱلْمِقْلَاعِ ـ قَذَّافٌ.

Slink, *v.t.* To cast its young, of a beast, طَرَحَ.

Slink, *v.i.* To slink away, تَسَلَّلَ ـ إِنْسَلَّ.

Slip, *v.t.* To convey secretly, دَسَّسَ ـ دَسَّ. To — away or escape from, إِنْسَلَّ مِن ـ تَفَلَّتَ مِن. To let slip, allow to escape, أَفْلَتَ. To cause to —, as out of the hand of another, أَمْلَصَ مِنْ يَدِهِ. To omit, skip over, أَسْقَطَ ـ حَذَفَ ـ فَاتَ. To slip in, خَشْخَشَ فِي ـ دَسَّسَ فِي ـ دَسَّ فِي.

To slip off, as clothes, شَلَحَ ـ نَزَعَ ـ أَخْلَعَ; as from some part or member of the body, تَشَمَّرَ (*or* شَمَّرَ) عَنْ كَذَا.

To slip on, as clothes, تَسَرْبَلَ بِ ـ تَكَسَّى بِ ـ لَبِسَ.

To slip out, let go out secretly, أَفْلَتَ.

To slip the cable, أَرْخَى ٱلْلَبَانَ ـ سَيَّبَ ٱلْقَلْسَ. To slip one's cable, *v.i.* *See* under Cable, *n.*

Slip, *v.i.* To slide involuntarily, زَلَّ *aor.* يَزِلُّ ـ زَلَجَ ـ زَلِقَ. To move to and fro, as, *e.g.* a saddle on a horse's back, زَحَلَ ـ زَلِقَ ـ زَحْلَقَ. To —, as out of hand, from off the finger, *etc.*, إِنْسَلَّ مِن ـ إِنْمَلَصَ مِن ـ إِنْفَلَتَ مِن ـ مَلِصَ مِن. To err, to fall into error, زَلَّ *aor.* يَزِلُّ ـ أَخْطَأَ ـ غَلِطَ فِي. His foot slipped, زَلِقَتْ رِجْلُهُ. I had nearly slipped, لَوْلَا قَلِيلٌ لَزَلِقْتُ. It slipped from my hand, إِنْدَلَصَ مِنْ يَدِي. The iron of the axe slipped from the handle, إِنْفَلَتَ حَدِيدُ ٱلْفَأْسِ مِنَ ٱلْخَشَبِ. The sword slipped from its scabbard, دَلَقَ (*or* إِنْدَلَقَ) ٱلسَّيْفُ مِنْ غِمْدِهِ. The fish slipped out of the fisherman's hand, تَمَلَّصَتِ ٱلسَّمَكَةُ مِنْ يَدِ ٱلصَّائِدِ. To cause to —, or slide, أَزْلَقَ ـ زَلَّجَ. To cause to —, fall into error, ضَلَّلَ ـ أَضَلَّ ـ أَزَلَّ.

To slip or sneak away, إِنْطَلَقَ فِي ـ تَسَلَّلَ ـ إِنْسَلَّ ـ تَخَلَّعَ ـ ٱلْإِسْتِخْفَاءُ; as time, مَرَّ ـ زَالَ ـ حَالَ.

To slip down, تَزَحْلَقَ.

To slip in, خَشَّ فِي ـ إِنْدَسَّ فِي ـ إِنْزَبَقَ فِي ـ إِنْسَلَّ فِي.

To slip or fall off, قَشَطَ ـ زَلَّ عَنْ كَذَا ـ تَخَلَّعَ: the ring slipt off the finger, قَشَطَ ـ سَقَطَ ٱلْخَاتِمُ مَلْسًا مِنَ ٱلْإِصْبَعِ ـ ٱلْخَاتِمُ عَنِ ٱلْأُصْبُعِ.

To slip out; *see* To slip away; *supra.* To slip out of one's memory, ذَهَبَ عَلَيْهِ.

Slip, *n.* An unintentional slide, زَلْقَةٌ ـ زَلَّةٌ. A movement aside, زَحْلَقَةٌ ـ زَلْقَةٌ ـ زَحْلٌ ـ زُحُولٌ. A fault, error, زَلَّةٌ *pl.* زَلَلٌ ـ عَثْرَةٌ ـ خَطَأٌ ـ سَقْطَةٌ *pl.* سَقْطٌ *and* سِقَاطٌ. A long and narrow piece, شُقَّةٌ *pl.* شُقَقٌ ـ قِطْعَةٌ *pl.* قِطَعٌ ـ شِقْفَةٌ *pl.* شِقَفٌ. A —, as of a tree, for transplanting, شَتْلَةٌ *pl.* شَتْلَاتٌ. A —, or cutting, of a tree, شَذْبَةٌ *pl.* أَشْذَابٌ. A leash, as for dogs, حَبْلَةُ ٱلْكِلَابِ ـ سَلَبَةُ ٱلْكِلَابِ. A small bay or opening for the sea, خَوْرٌ *pl.* خُؤُورٌ. Counterfeit money, فُلُوسٌ زَغَلٌ. A twig, خُصْلَةٌ *pl.* خُصَلٌ ـ خَصَلَاتٌ *pl.* خَصْلَةٌ. A —, or plate, as of iron, for repairing anything, جِبَارَة ـ جَبِيرَة ـ ضَبَّات pl. ضَبَّة. A —, or dock for ships, مَجْرًى. A —, or copy, for writing from, قَاعِدَةُ خَطٍّ. A support, as for a wall, *etc.*, أَسْنَاد pl. سَنَد. A petticoat, فُسْتَانٌ تَحْتَانِيٌّ. A — of the tongue, زَلَّ فِي ٱلْكَلَام ـ إِسْقَاطٌ فِي ٱلْكَلَام: He made a — in his speech, تَعَثَّرَ فِي كَلَامِهِ ـ زَلَّ فِي كَلَامِهِ ـ لَغَا فِي كَلَامِهِ ². To make a —, mistake, error, زَلَّ ـ ضَلَّ ـ². To give one the —, أَنْقَذَ مِن ـ نَجَا مِن ـ ² إِنْسَلَّ ـ مِن ـ تَفَلَّتَ مِن ـ إِنْفَلَتَ مِن. There's many a — between the cup and the lip, بَيْنَ ٱلْأَمَلِ وَٱلتَّمَتُّعِ بُعَادٌ. The — of the learned man is the — of the world (prov.), زَلَّةُ ٱلْعَالِمِ زَلَّةُ ٱلْعَالَمِ.

Slip-knot, *n.* عُقْدَةٌ سَالِكَةٌ ـ رِبَاطٌ سَالِكٌ.

Slipper, *n.* تَرْلِك ـ غُرَيْفَات pl. غُرَيْفَة ـ غُرَف pl. غُرْفَة ـ بَابُوج ـ بَوَابِيجُ pl. بَابُوجَة ـ قُلْشِين. To wear slippers, لَبِسَ ـ بَوَابِيجَ. To beat with a —, ضَرَبَ بِٱلْبَابُوجِ.

Slippered, *a.* لَابِسُ بَابُوجٍ.

Slipperily, *ad.* عَلَى زَلَقٍ.

Slipperiness, *n.* The being slippery, مَزْلَقَة ـ زَلَق ـ مَزَلَّة. Lubricity, as of a rope, *etc.*, مَلَاسَة ـ مُلُوسَة. Volubility, سُهُولَةُ لِسَانٍ ـ تَفَوُّه ـ ٱلْكَلِمِ ـ ٱلسُّيُوبُ فِي. Unfaithfulness, خَتْر ـ خُتُور. Inconstancy, فَرْفَرَة ـ تَحَوُّل.

Slippery, *a.* زَلِق ـ زَلَل ـ زُلّ ; of a rope, *etc.* مَلِس. Slippery rocks, سُفُوح. Glib, طَلِقُ ٱللِّسَانِ ـ طَلِق. Not to be depended on, لَا يُعْتَمَدُ عَلَيْهِ ـ فَرْفَار. Vacillating, فَرْفَار ـ مُضْطَرِب. Unfaithful, خَتَّار ـ خَاتِر. Shifting, evasive, حَيَّال ـ مُحْتَال. A — place, مَزْلَقَة ـ مَزْلَق ـ مَكَانٌ زَلَقٌ. A — rock, زَلَقَة. He is on the — way of what is false, هُوَ عَلَى مَزْلَقَةِ ٱلْبَاطِلِ.

Slip-shod, *a.* Wearing — shoes, لَابِسُ نَعْلٍ ـ لَابِسُ نَعْلٍ مَفْكُوحٍ ـ لَابِسُ تَاسُومَةٍ شَرْشُوحَةٍ ـ بَرْطُوشَةٍ. Loose, of style, رَكِيك.

Slit, *n.* شَقّ ـ بَزْل pl. شُقُوق ; in a garment, as for the fingers, *etc.*, فُرَج pl. فُرْجَة. A — in a wall to look through, دَرْخُوش pl. دَرَاخِيش. A — in the belly, إِنْبِعَاج. The slits or interstices, as of the fingers, or in a railing, تَفَارِيج sing. تِفْرِجَة and تِفْرَاج. *See also* Rent, Fissure, *n.*

Slit, *v.t.* فَرَجَ ـ فَرَّجَ ـ خَرَعَ ـ شَرَمَ ـ بَزَّلَ ـ بَزَلَ ² ـ شَقَّ ². To — open, of the belly, بَعَجَ ـ بَعَّجَ. To be —, تَبَزَّلَ ـ تَشَقَّقَ ـ إِنْشَقَّ ـ إِنْخَرَعَ ; of the belly, إِنْبَعَجَ. *See also to* Rend, Tear, *v.t.*

Sliver, *v.t.* To cut into long pieces, شَرَّحَ ـ شَرَحَ.

Sliver, *n.* شَرِيحَة pl. شَرَائِح ـ شُقَّة pl. شُقَق.

Slobber, *v.i.* As of a child, أَلْعَبَ ـ لَعَبَ. *See also to* Drivel, *v.i.*

Slobbering, *a.* لَاعِب.

Sloe, *n.* The fruit, إِجَّاصٌ بَرِّيٌّ.

Slogan, *n.* A war cry, شِعَار.

Sloop, *n.* إِسْقُونَة. A — of war, قُرْوِيتَة.

Slop, *v.t.* To spill, هَرَقَ ـ أَرَاقَ ـ أَكَبَّ ـ كَبَّ ².

Slop, *n.* As of water, هِرَاقَةُ مَاءٍ ـ تَهْرِيقُ مَاءٍ ـ لُوَاثَةُ مَاءٍ ـ مَاءٌ مُهْرَاقٌ. A puddle, مُسْتَنْقَعَة ـ بَقْعَة. Liquid food, سِكْبَاج ـ شَوْرَبَة ـ شَوْرَبَات pl. شُرُوب. Mean liquor, شَرَابٌ حَقِيرٌ. To make a —, of water, أَرَاقَ (or يُهَرِيقُ aor. هَرَاقَ) ٱلْمَاءَ. To soil, as with any liquid, لَوَّثَ. *See also* Slops, *n.*

Slop-basin, *n.* وِعَاءٌ لِرُسُوبِ ٱلشَّايِ وَغَيْرِهِ pl. أَوْعِيَة.

Slope, *a.* *See* Sloping, *a.*

Slope, *n.* صَبَب pl. أَصْبَاب ـ إِنْحِرَاف ـ حُدُور. *See also* Incline, *n.*

Slope, *v.t.* مَيَّلَ ـ حَرَفَ ² ـ أَمَالَ ـ صَوَّبَ. *See also to* Incline, Slant, *v.t.*

Slope, *v.i.* إِنْحَدَرَ. To — downwards, إِنْصَبَّ. *See also to* Incline, Slant, *v.i.*

Slopewise, *ad.* بِٱنْحِرَافٍ ـ إِنْحِرَافًا.

Sloping, *a.* حُدُور ـ مَائِل ـ مُنْحَرِف ـ هَبُوط.

Slop-man, *n.* }
Slop-seller, } بَيَّاعُ ٱلثِّيَابِ ٱلدُّونِ.

Sloppiness, *n.* سُوَاخَى ـ سَوَاخِيَة.

Sloppy, *a.* Muddy, slushy, سَوَاخِي ـ سُوخَى ـ رَادِغ. A — or muddy place, رَدَغ. Sloppy or muddy water, مَاءٌ رَدِغَةٌ. The ground became —, صَارَتِ ٱلْأَرْضُ سُوَاخًا. *See also* Slushy, *a.*

Slops, *n.* Dirty water, غُسَالَة. Ready-made common clothes, ثِيَابٌ مِنَ ٱلدُّونِ مَخْيُوطَةٌ. Poor liquid food, spoon-diet, سِكْبَاج ـ أَمْرِيَة.

Slot, *n.* The track of a deer, أَثَرُ ٱلظَّبْيِ pl. آثَار. *See also* Slit, *n.*

Sloth, *n.* Tardiness, بُطْآء ـ تَوَقُّف ـ تَغْتِيم ـ غَتْم. Sluggishness, ثِقَل ـ كَسَل ـ تَهَاوُن. The animal, ٱلْكِسْلَانُ وَهُوَ ٱسْمُ حَيَوَانٍ.

Slothful, *a.* *See* Sluggish, *a.*

Slothfully, *ad.* *See* Sluggishly, *ad.*

Slothfulness, *n.* *See* Sluggishness, *n.*

Slouch, *n.* A hanging down, رَخْوَة ـ إِسْتِرْخَاء. A heavy movement, gait, ثِقَل. A clumsy fellow, فَلَّاح ـ ثَقِيل ـ أَخْرَق.

Slouch, *v.t.* To cause to hang down, دَلَّى ـ أَرْخَى.

Slouch, *v.i.* To hang down, تَدَلَّى ــ اِسْتَرْخَى. To have a clownish look or manner, تَقَلَّلَ ع.

Slouching, *a.* Hanging down, مُتَدَلٍّ ــ مُسْتَرْخٍ. Heavy, awkward, أَخْرَقُ ــ بَلِيدٌ ــ ثَقِيلٌ.

Slough, *n.* A miry place, غَمْقَاتٌ *pl.* غَمِقَةٌ ــ رَدْغٌ ــ قُعُورٌ *pl.* قَعْرٌ ــ وَحْلَةٌ. The — of a serpent, سِلَاخٌ ــ سَبِيُّ ٱلْحَيَّةِ ــ خِرْشَآءٌ ع; of a sore, أَكِلَةٌ.

Slough, *v.i.* To separate and come off, as a skin, اِنْسَلَخَ ــ تَسَلَّخَ. To —, as of a sore, تَآكَلَ ــ أَكِلَ ء.

Sloven, *n.* } In dress, مُتَحَشِّفٌ ــ بَذٌّ. Careless, of a person,
Slovenly, *a.* } قَلِيلُ ٱلْمُرُوَّةِ ــ مُتَغَافِلٌ ــ مُتَوَانٍ; of style, رَكِيكٌ. Raw, stupid, أَخْرَقُ ــ خَرِقٌ.

Slovenliness, *n.* In dress, تَحَشُّفٌ ــ بَذَاذَةٌ ــ بَذَاذٌ. Carelessness, تَوَانٍ ــ تَهَامُلٌ ــ غِرَارٌ ــ غِرَّةٌ; of style, رَكَاكَةٌ. Rawness, stupidity, خُرْقٌ.

Slovenly, *ad.* As in dress, تَحَشُّفًا ــ بِبَذَاذَةٍ. Carelessly, بِتَوَانٍ ــ بِتَهَامُلٍ; as of style, بِرَكَاكَةٍ.

Slow, *a.* Tardy, dilatory, وَقَّافٌ ــ قَعِيدٌ ــ مُتَرَاخٍ ــ بَطِيٌّ ع. Slow, of pace, حَاتِكٌ ــ قُوَامٌ. Heavy, dull, ثَقِيلٌ. Backward, as of a watch, مُقَصِّرٌ ــ مُتَأَخِّرٌ. Not exhilarating, مُصْعِبٌ ــ مُزَعِّلٌ ــ مُمِلٌّ. Slow to anger, بَطِيُّ ٱلْغَضَبِ. Slow of speech, ثَقِيلُ ٱللِّسَانِ. My watch is —, سَاعَتِي ــ سَاعَتِي مُتَأَخِّرَةٌ مُقَصِّرَةٌ. To be —, dilatory, بَطُؤَ ع ــ تَوَقَّفَ. To go at a — pace, تَرَاخَى ــ مَشَى عَلَى مَهْلٍ ــ أَرْوَدَ ء. To be —, behindhand, تَرَاخَى. To be —, as in doing anything, تَمَهَّلَ فِي ــ قَصَّرَ فِي ــ تَرَاخَى. To be — to speak, بَطُؤَ فِي ٱلْكَلَامِ ع. To be —, as of a watch, قَصَّرَ ــ تَأَخَّرَ. *See also to* Delay, *v.i.*

Slowly, *ad.* Dilatorily, بِتَوَقُّفٍ ــ مُرَاخَاةً ــ بِبَطَآءٍ. At a slow pace, leisurely, عَلَى مَهْلٍ ــ رُوَيْدًا ــ بِرُوَيْدَآءَ ــ سَهْلًا. We sailed — many days, سَافَرْنَا رُوَيْدًا أَيَّامًا كَثِيرَةً.

Slowness, *n.* Moderate motion, leisure, رُوَيْدِيَّةٌ ــ رُوَيْدٌ ــ مَرْوَدٌ. Deliberation, طُولَةُ بَالٍ ــ مَهَلٌ ــ تَأَنٍّ. Dilatoriness, بَطَآءٌ ــ تَوَقُّفٌ ــ مُرَاخَاةٌ. Backwardness, as of a watch, تَأَخُّرٌ. Heaviness, dullness, ثِقَلٌ. Sluggishness, قِلَّةُ مُرُوَّةٍ ــ تَكَاسُلٌ. Tediousness, مَلَالٌ. To act with — or deliberation in, تَأَنَّى فِي ــ أَرْوَدَ فِي.

Slow-worm, *n.* دُوَيْبَةٌ غَيْرُ مُؤْذِيَةٍ تُشْبِهُ ٱلْأَفْعَى.

Sludge, *n.* *See* Mire, Slime, *n.*

Sludgy, *a.* *See* Miry, Slimy, *a.*

Slue, *v.t.* فَتَلَ ــ أَدَارَ ــ دَوَّرَ ء.

Slue, *v.i.* دَارَ *aor.* يَدُورُ ــ اِسْتَدَارَ ــ اِنْفَتَلَ.

Slug, *n.* A kind of snail, بَزَّاقَةٌ *coll.* بَزَّاقٌ. A piece of metal for a musket, سَبِيكَةٌ لِلْمُكْحُلَةِ *pl.* سَبَائِكُ.

Sluggard, *n.* كِسْلَانٌ *pl.* كُسَالَى ــ وَقَّافٌ ــ مُبْرِمٌ.

Sluggish, *a.* Lazy, كِسْلَانٌ *pl.* كُسَالَى. Inert, ضَاجِعٌ *pl.* ضَاجِعَةٌ ــ قَلِيلُ ٱلْحَاشِيَةِ ــ جَامِدُ ٱلْحَالِ; as of a sore, ثَقِيلٌ ــ مَيَّاطٌ ــ بَلِيدٌ. To be —, lazy, كَسِلَ ء ــ تَكَاسَلَ ــ تَوَانَى. *See also* Idle, Inert, Indolent, Lazy, *a.*

Sluggishly, *ad.* Lazily, بِكَسَلٍ ــ بِٱلْكَسَلِ ــ بِتَوَانٍ. Inertly, بِبَلَادَةٍ ــ بِجَمَادٍ.

Sluggishness, *n.* Laziness, كَسَلٌ ــ تَكَاسُلٌ. Inertness, ضُجْعَةٌ ــ قِلَّةُ حَاشِيَةٍ ــ جَمَادٌ; as of a sore, جَمَادٌ ــ بَلَادَةٌ.

Sluice, *n.* A channel for water, مَثْعَرٌ; a — in a rivulet, تُرْعَةٌ. A — gate, سَدٌّ *pl.* سُدُودٌ ــ أَشْذَابٌ *pl.* شَذْبٌ ــ مَسَاكٌ ــ مَسْكٌ.

Slumber, *n.* Light sleep, نُعَاسٌ ــ تَغْفِيقٌ ــ تَهْجَاعٌ ــ هُجُوعٌ. A —, نَعْسَةٌ ــ هَجْعَةٌ ــ غَفْقَةٌ.

Slumber, *v.i.* هَجَعَ ء ــ نَعَسَ ء. To — with the eyes half open, غَفَقَ.

Slumberer, *n.* }
Slumbering, *a.* } نَعْسَانُ ــ نَاعِسٌ ــ مُغَفِّقٌ.
Slumberous, *a.* }

Slung, *part. of to* Sling, *v t. q.v.*

Slur, *v.t.* To soil, sully, طَبَّعَ ــ قَذَّعَ. To do carelessly, negligently, أَهْمَلَ ــ فَرَطَ ع فِي ــ فَرَّطَ فِي ــ خَفَّفَ فِي. To utter or do in a gliding, easy, style, تَلَيَّنَ ــ خَفَّفَ. To —, of a vowel, or to suppress it, اِخْتَلَسَ.

Slur, *n.* A soil, دَنَاسَةٌ ــ بُقْعَةٌ. A reproach, blame, لَوْمٌ ــ ذَمٌّ ــ تَعْيِيبٌ. A —, as in music, تَلْيِينٌ ــ تَخْفِيفٌ. As of a vowel, اِخْتِلَاسٌ. To cast a — upon, حَكَّرَ ء ــ طَعَنَ بِ ع ء. To cast a — upon one's honour, دَنَّسَ عِرْضَهُ ــ أَلْقَى عَلَى ٱلْعَارَ ــ طَعَنَ فِي عِرْضِهِ ع ء.

Slush, *n.* وَحْلٌ ــ رَزْغَةٌ ــ رَدْغَةٌ ــ حَمْأَةٌ.

Slush, *v.t.* لَوَّثَ ــ بِرَدْغَةٍ.

Slushy, *a.* وَحِلٌ ــ غَمِقٌ ــ رَادِغٌ. The land became —, أَرْزَغَتِ ٱلْأَرْضُ. To become —, رَزِغَ ء.

Slut, *n.* A bitch, the female of any animal, أُنْثَى *pl.* إِنَاثٌ. *See also* Slattern, *n.*

Sluttish, *a.* *See* Slattern, Slovenly, *a.*

Sluttishly, *ad.* *See* Slatternly, *ad.*

Sluttishness, *n.* *See* Slatternliness, *n.*

Sly, *a.* } ذُو كَيْدٍ ــ خَدَّاعٌ ــ مَكَّارٌ ــ مُحْتَالٌ ــ دَاهٍ ــ
Sly-boots, *n.* } عَيَّارٌ ــ حَوَالِيٌّ.

Slyly, *ad.* بِدَهَآءٍ ـ بِحِيلَةٍ ـ إِحْتِيَالًا ـ غَدْرًا .

Slyness, *n.* دَهَآء ـ إِحْتِيَال ـ مَكْر ـ خِدْعَة ـ غَدْر ـ مُحَاوَلَة ـ دَسِيسَة ـ حِيلَة .

Smack, *v.t.* To slap, لَطَخَ ـ لَطَمَ ـ خَفَقَ ـ صَقَعَ . To kiss with a noise, طَقْطَقَ (or فَرْقَعَ) بَاسَ ـ بِفَرْقَعَةٍ . To — the lips, (or فَرْقَعَ) ٱلشِّفَاهَ . To — a whip, فَقَّعَ (or صَوَّتَ) ٱلسَّوْطَ .

Smack, *v.i.* To — of, to have the taste of, كَانَ طَعْمُهُ كَطَعْمِ ٱ... ; to have the appearance of, أَشْبَهَ ; to have the smell of, كَانَتْ رَائِحَتُهُ كَرَائِحَةِ ٱ... .

Smack, *n.* A slap, لَطْخ ـ صَقْع ـ صَقْعَة . A loud kiss, بَوْسٌ بِفَرْقَعَةٍ . A sharp sound, طَقْطَقَة ـ فَرْقَعَة . A — of the lips, فَرْقَعَةُ ٱلشِّفَاهِ . A taste, flavour, طَعْم ـ ذَوْق ; a taint, خَفِيَّة ; a smell, scent, رَائِحَة ـ نَشْوَة . A small vessel, قَارِب *pl.* قَوَارِب ـ شَخْتُور *pl.* شَخَاتِير . A modicum, soupçon, عِرْق .

Small, *a.* In stature, قَصِير . Slender, weak, ضَعِيف . Unimportant, غَيْرُ مُهِمٍّ ـ جُزْئِيٌّ ـ تَافِهٌ . Is it a — matter that...? أَقَلِيلٌ أَنْ . A — quantity, يَسِير . Small as the dust of the earth, دَقِيقٌ كَغُبَارِ ٱلْأَرْضِ . A — voice, صَوْتٌ خَفِيضٌ . It is the smallest of the Arab tribes, هُوَ ٱلْأَصْغَرُ مِنْ قَبَائِلِ ٱلْعَرَبِ . *For the principal significations see* Little, *a.*

Small, *n.* The slender part of a thing, أَدَقُّ ـ أَصْغَرُ .

Small-arms, *n.* أَسْلِحَةٌ لَا تَحْتَاجُ إِلَى عَجَلَاتٍ مِثْلَ ٱلْبَنَادِقِ ـ خِفَافُ ٱلْأَسْلِحَةِ ـ وَٱلْبَوَارِيدِ إلخ .

Small-beer, *n.* What is light, unimportant, تَفَاهَة ـ تَفَهٌ ـ سَخَافَة ـ خَسِيفَة . To think no — of one's self, أُعْجِبَ بِنَفْسِهِ .

Small-clothes, *n.* شِخْشِير *pl.* شَخَاشِير .

Small-coal, *n.* دَقِيقُ ٱلْفَحْمِ ٱلْمَعْدِنِيِّ .

Small-craft, *n.* سَفَائِنُ صِغَارٌ .

Smallish, *a.* صَغِيرٌ نَوْعًا ـ يَضْرِبُ إِلَى ٱلصِّغَرِ .

Smallpox, *n.* جُدَرِيٌّ ـ جَدَرِيٌّ . Affected with —, مُجَدَّر . To be attacked with —, جُدِرَ ـ جُدِّرَ . His skin became covered with the —, أَصْبَحَ جِلْدُهُ غَضْنَةً وَاحِدَةً .

Small-wares, *n.* خُرْدَوَات ـ خُرْدَة ـ مَدَاقُّ ٱلْأَمْتِعَةِ . A dealer in —, خُرْدَجِي .

Smalt, *n.* مِينَا .

Smaragdine, *a.* زُمُرُّدِيٌّ .

Smart, *a.* Acute, as of pain, حَادٌّ ـ مُؤْلِم ـ أَلِيم . Brisk, as of an engagement, شَدِيد . Lively, active, نَشِيط ـ خَفِيف ـ نَزِق ; especially of a woman, نَزِق . Witty, نَارِقٌ ـ فَائِق ـ وَجْز ـ جَلِيٌّ ـ زَاهٍ . Sarcastic, سَلِيط ـ طَاعِن . Gaudy, حَاذِق ـ حَاذِقِيٌّ ـ مُفَاخِر ; of a colour, رَفِيف (or زَاهِي) ٱللَّوْنِ . A — answer, سُكَاتَة ـ جَوَابٌ نَاقِرٌ ـ سَلِيطَة . A — engagement, مُقَاتَلَةٌ شَدِيدَةٌ ـ مَلْحَمَة . A — fellow, رَجُلٌ نَشِيطٌ ـ جِذْع . *See also* Sharp, *a.*

Smart, *v.t.* and *i.* To have pain, أَلِمَ ـ وَجِعَ *aor.* يَوْجَعُ or يَجَعُ ـ أَشْكَى ـ هَبَّ . To distress, أَضْجَرَ ـ شَقَّ عَلَى ـ أَصْعَبَ عَلَى . My eye smarts, تُجْعِنِي عَيْنِي ـ تَهُبُّ عَيْنِي . He shall — for this, يُعَاقَبُ عَلَى هٰذَا . I will make him — for it, سَأُقَابِلُهُ عَلَى هٰذَا ـ سَأَنْتَقِمُ مِنْهُ عَلَى هٰذَا . *See also under to* Pain, *v.t.* and *i.*

Smart, *n.* Sharp pain, نَكْزَة ـ إِحْرَاق ـ وَجَعٌ حَادٌّ ـ وَجَع ; of grief, تَأَسُّف ـ مَشَقَّة ـ حَسْرَة ـ شِدَّة ـ غَمٌّ .

Smarten, *v.t.* To make lively, نَشَّطَ ; to make gay, حَسَّنَ ـ زَيَّنَ ـ زَخْرَفَ .

Smartly, *ad.* Briskly, actively, بِنَشَاطٍ ـ بِحَمِيَّةٍ . Wittily, تَبَذُّلًا ـ بِحَذَاقَةٍ ـ بِحِدَّةٍ . Sarcastically, بِسَلَاطَةٍ . Energetically, بِشِدَّةٍ ـ بِقُوَّةٍ . Gaudily, بِزَهْوٍ ـ بِمُفَاخَرَةٍ ـ بِمُبَاهَاةٍ . *See also* Sharply, *ad.*

Smart-money, *n.* جَرِيمَة .

Smartness, *n.* Poignancy, شِدَّة ـ حِدَّة . Briskness, liveliness, نَشَاط ـ حَرَارَة ـ مُرُوَّة ـ خِفَّة . Vigour, عَارِضَة ـ حِدَّة ـ قُوَّة . Gaudiness, زَهْو ـ زَهْوَة ـ مُبَاهَاة ـ مُفَاخَرَة . Wittiness, حَذَاقَة . *See also* Sharpness, *n.*

Smash, *v.t.* *See to* Dash, Shiver, *v.t.*

Smash, *n.* دَمَار ـ دَمَارَة ـ هَلَكَة ـ هَلَك . To go —, to fall to pieces, تَحَطَّمَ ; to go to ruin, perdition, هَلَكَ ; to become bankrupt, أَفْلَسَ ـ إِنْكَسَرَ . *See also* Ruin, *n.*

Smatter, *n.*
Smattering, } قِلَّةُ فَهْمٍ ـ رِكَّةُ عِلْمٍ ـ سَخَافَةُ مَعْرِفَةٍ .

Smatter, *v.i* In talk, سَخُفَ فِي ٱلْكَلَامِ ـ تَكَلَّمَ بِسَخَافَةٍ . To — of, to have a taste of, كَانَ طَعْمُهُ كَطَعْمِ ٱ... .

Smatterer, *n.* عُوَيْرِف ـ سَخِيفُ ٱلْمَعْرِفَةِ . What a — he is! مَا أَسْخَفَهُ .

Smear, *v.t.* To overspread with anything unctuous, *etc.*, سَلَقَ ـ سَخَّمَطَ ـ وَسَّخَ ـ لَوَّثَ ـ أَدْرَنَ ـ طَلَى ـ دَمَّمَ ـ دَمَّ ; To soil, as cattle with pitch, *etc.*, سَلَقَ . To be smeared, as with oil, tar, *etc.*, إِطَّلَى . To be soiled, دَرِنَ . His hand was smeared, soiled, with it, دَرِنَتْ يَدُهُ بِهِ .

Smear, *n.* A smearing, طَلْيٌ ـ دَمٌّ ـ دِمَام ; one —, طَلْيَة . A soil, دَرَن . *See also* Daub, Smudge, *n.*

Smegmatic, *a.* صَابُونِيٌّ .

Smell, *v.t.* To perceive by the nose, نَشَا ـ تَنَشَّى ـ إِنْتَشَى ـ

شَمَّ ² — شَمَّمَ — أَشَمَّ — إِشْتَمَّ — تَشَمَّمَ — إِسْتَنْشَقَ — أَرَاحَ — إِسْتَرْوَحَ. To perceive, عَرَفَ ج. To give one anything to —, أَشَمَّ. To — a rat, إِرْتَابَ فِي ٱلْأَمْرِ — إِتَّهَمَ بِٱلْأَمْرِ. To — out, to discover, إِطَّلَعَ عَلَى — كَشَفَ عَن ج — أَدْرَكَ — شَامَّ. They smelt one another, of two, تَشَامَّا — شَامَّا. To desire to —, إِسْتَشَمَّ. He smells the battle from afar, يَسْتَرْوِحُ ٱلْقِتَالَ مِنْ بَعِيدٍ.

Smell, *v.i.* To emit an odour, طَلَعَتْ مِنْ رَائِحَةٌ ² — تَرَوَّحَ. To — sweet, to exhale a sweet odour, فَاغَ ² — تَفَوَّحَ — فَاحَ ² ج. To — bad, exhale a bad —, أَرَاحَ. To — good, of food, أَعْرَفَ; to have the — of, كَانَتْ رَائِحَتُهُ كَرَائِحَةِ ٱلْ.... He smelled sweet, عَرِفَ ².

Smell, *n.* The sense of smelling, ٱلْقُوَّةُ ٱلشَّامَّةُ — شَامَّةٌ — شَمٌّ — نَشًّا. An odour, رَائِحَةٌ *pl.* رَوَائِحُ — نَشْوَةٌ — عَرْفٌ — عَرْفَةٌ. A sweet —, رَائِحَةٌ طَيِّبَةٌ — عَرْفَةٌ. A bad —, رَائِحَةٌ مُنْتِنَةٌ — ذَفَرٌ — ذَفْرَةٌ. The — of bad meat, fish, *etc.*, سَهَكَةٌ. The — of cooked food, قُتَارٌ. To diffuse a sweet —, فَاحَ ² ج — تَفَوَّحَ. The — diffused itself, تَرَوَّحَتِ ٱلرَّائِحَةُ. *See also* Odour, Perfume, Scent, *n.*

Smelling, *n.* The sense of; *see preceding article.*

Smelling-bottle, *n.* قَازُوزَةُ ٱلرَّوَائِحِ.

Smelt, *pret. of to* Smell, *v.t.* and *i. q. v.*

Smelt, *n.* The fish, ضَرْبٌ صَغِيرٌ مِنْ سَمَكِ ٱلْبَحْرِ.

Smelt, *v t.* سَبَكَ ² — سَبَّكَ — أَفْرَغَ. To be smelted, إِنْسَبَكَ.

Smelter, *n.* سَبَّاكٌ — مُفْرِغٌ.

Smeltery, *n.* دَارُ ٱلسَّبْكِ — مَسْبَكٌ.

Smelting, *n.* The art of, سَبْكٌ — إِفْرَاغٌ.

Smerk, *v.i.* تَظَارَفَ — تَظَرَّفَ — تَصَنَّعَ وَتَبَسَّمَ — تَصَلَّفَ وَتَبَسَّمَ.

Smerk, *n.* تَظَارُفٌ — تَظَرُّفٌ.

Smerking, *a.* مُتَظَارِفٌ — مُتَظَرِّفٌ.

Smerkingly, *ad.* تَبَسُّمًا — تَظَرُّفًا.

Smicker, *v.i.* *See to* Smerk, *v.i.*

Smile, *v.i.* As with the features, تَبَسَّمَ — إِبْتَسَمَ. To — at one ironically, كَاشَرَ. The flowers smiled, looked gay, ضَحِكَ ٱلزَّهْرُ ج. To — upon, to help, ظَاهَرَ — سَاعَدَ — وَفَّقَ. *See also to* Favour, *v.t.*

Smile, *n.* Of the features, إِبْتِسَامٌ — تَبَسُّمٌ — بَسْمٌ. Help, تَوْفِيقٌ — مُسَاعَدَةٌ — مُظَاهَرَةٌ. Pleasure, فَرَحٌ — إِبْتِهَاجٌ.

Smiler, *n.* One who smiles much, بَسَّامٌ.

Smiling, *a.* Of the features, مُتَبَسِّمٌ — بَاسِمٌ. Gay, بَشُوشٌ — مُفْرِحٌ — ضَاحِكٌ. Happy, glad, مُبْتَهِجٌ — مُنْشَرِحُ ٱلصَّدْرِ — حَبُورٌ.

Smilingly, *ad.* With a smile, تَبَسُّمًا — بِٱبْتِسَامٍ — بِتَبَسُّمٍ. Pleasingly, بِٱبْتِهَاجٍ — بِفَرَحٍ — بِلُطْفٍ. Favourably, with kindness, بِرِفْقٍ — بِفَضْلٍ.

Smirk, *v.i.* *See to* Smerk, *v.i.*

Smirk, *n.* *See* Smerk, *n.*

Smirking, *a.* *See* Smerking, *a.*

Smirkingly, *ad.* *See* Smerkingly, *ad.*

Smite, *v.t.* To strike, ضَرَبَ ج — ضَرَّبَ — عَلَا ب ². To — and prostrate, خَبَطَ ج. To blast, wither, جَفَّ ² — أَحْرَقَ — ضَرَبَ ج. To kill, قَتَلَ ². To —, as of the wind, رَاحَتْهُ ٱلرِّيحُ: They were smitten, destroyed, by the wind, رِيحُوا. To — to the earth, ضَرَبَ إِلَى ٱلْأَرْضِ ج. *See also to* Strike, *v.t.*

To smite, of the sun, ضَرَبَتْهُ ٱلشَّمْسُ ج. To be so smitten, أُضْرِبَ شَمْسًا.

To smite the hands together, أَصْفَقَ كَفًّا عَلَى كَفٍّ.

To smite the knees together, إِصْطَكَّتْ رُكْبَةٌ عَلَى رُكْبَةٍ.

To smite with a disease, رَمَى بِسُقَامٍ ج — ضَرَبَ ضَرْبَةً ج. To be so smitten, أَصَابَهُ سُقَامٌ.

To smite with astonishment, أَرْعَبَ — رَعَّبَ — أَدْهَشَ. To be so smitten, تَحَيَّرَ — إِرْتَعَبَ — دَهِشَ ج.

To smite with blindness, ضَرَبَ بِٱلْعَمَى ج. To be so smitten, أُضْرِبَ بِٱلْعَمَى.

To smite with love, to captivate, حَبَلَ ²: Such a woman smote him with love, حَبَلَتْهُ فُلَانَةُ.

To smite with the sword, ضَرَبَ بِٱلسَّيْفِ ج — خَدَبَ بِٱلسَّيْفِ ². To be smitten with the sword, إِنْضَرَبَ سَيْفًا.

To smite with the tongue, ضَرَبَ بِٱللِّسَانِ ج.

Smith, *n.* A maker of anything, صَانِعٌ *pl.* صُنَّاعٌ.

Blacksmith, قَيْنٌ *pl.* أَقْيَانٌ *and* قُيُونٌ — حَدَّادٌ *pl.* حَدَّادُونَ.

Coppersmith, نَحَّاسٌ *pl.* نَحَّاسَةٌ.

Gold and silversmith, صَائِغٌ *pl.* صُوَّاغٌ *and* صُيَّاغٌ *and* صَاغَةٌ.

Gunsmith, صَانِعُ ٱلْمَكَاحِلِ — صَنَّاعُ أَسْلِحَةٍ.

Locksmith, قَفَّالٌ *pl.* قَفَّالَةٌ.

Whitesmith, سَنْكَرِيٌّ.

Smithery, *n.* The shop of a blacksmith, دُكَّانُ ٱلْحَدَّادِ; the business of a blacksmith, صِنَاعَةُ ٱلْحَدَّادِ.

Smithy, *n.* The shop of a blacksmith, دُكَّانُ ٱلْحَدَّادِ.

Smitten, *part. of to* Smite, Stricken, مَضْرُوبٌ; as with a misfortune, disease, *etc.*, مُبْتَلًى بِ — مُصَابٌ بِ; as with love, مُتَوَجِّدٌ بِ. To be smitten, overcome, as by an enemy, إِنْغَلَبَ — إِنْكَسَرَ. *See also under to* Smite, *v.t.*

Smock, *n.* A chemise, قَمِيصُ ٱلنِّسَاءِ *pl.* قُمْصَانٌ.

Smock-frock, *n.* Of workmen, مِشْلَحُ ٱلصُّنَّاعِ *pl.* مَشَالِحُ.

Smoke, *n.* دُخَان ـ دُخَان ـ عُثَان ـ عَثَن. Black —, يَحْمُوم. A vent for —, a chimney, مَدْخَنَة ـ دَاخِنَة *pl.* مَدَاخِن. I filled the house with —, عَجَّجْتُ ٱلْبَيْتَ دُخَانًا. To become filled with —, تَعَجَّجَ دُخَانًا.

Smoke, *v.t.* As meat, *etc.*, for preserving, or as a room, clothes, *etc.*, دَخَّنَ ـ عَثَّنَ. To cause to —, دَخَّنَ. To —, of tobacco, شَرِبَ ٱلتَّبْغ (*or* ٱلدُّخَّان). To be smoked, of food, دَخِنَ ـَ. To fill with —, عَجَّجَ. *See also to* Fumigate, *v.t.*

Smoke, *v.i.* To emit smoke, دَخَنَ ـُ ـِ ـ عَثَّنَ ـ عَثَنَ ـُ ـ عَكَّبَ. The fire smoked vehemently, دَخْنَتِ ٱلنَّارُ ـ دَخَّنَ ـ أَدْخَنَ ـ إِدَّخَنَ. And the mountain smoked, وَكَانَ ٱلْجَبَلُ يُدَخِّنُ.

Smoke-consumer, *n.* آلَةٌ تُبَدِّدُ ٱلدُّخَّانَ.

Smoked, *a.* Of meats infected with smoke, دَخِن. Smoked or dried meat, لَحْمٌ قَدِيدٌ.

Smoke-dried, *a.* مُدَخَّن.

Smoke-jack, *n.* آلَةٌ لِتَدْوِيرِ ٱلسَّفُّودِ.

Smokeless, *a.* لَا يُدَخِّنُ.

Smoker, *n.* Of tobacco, شَارِبُ دُخَّانٍ (*or* تِبْغٍ) *pl.* شَارِبُونَ ـ شَرِيبُ دُخَّانٍ (*or* ٱلتَّبْغ).

Smokily, *ad.* بِدُخَّانٍ ـ دَخْنًا.

Smokiness, *n.* دَخَن ـ دُخُون; of a colour, دُخْنَة ـ دَخَن.

Smoking, *a.* } Producing smoke, دَاخِن; of meats smoked, دَخِن;
Smoky, } of a colour, أَدْخَنُ. A smoking furnace, تَنُّورُ دُخَّانٍ.

Smoking, *n.* The emittance of smoke, دُخُون ـ دَخْن. The — of tobacco, شُرْبُ ٱلدُّخَّانِ (*or* ٱلتَّبْغ).

Smooth, *a.* Even on the surface, as of the skin, a stone, *etc.*, also of a wine, أَمْلَسُ ـ أَخْلَقُ *fem.* مَلْسَآءُ *pl.* مُلْس; of the cheeks, *etc.*; also lank, أَسِيلٌ. Smooth and soft, دَمِث. Soft, fine, as of cloth; also of words, butter, oil, *etc.*, نَاعِم. Level, سَطِيح ـ بَسِيط. Uniform, سَوِيّ ـ مُعَادِل ـ مُسَاوٍ. Calm, رَاكِن. Even, not rugged, سَهِل ـ سَهْل. Smooth, and firm, as also free from cracks, أَخْلَقُ. Bland, لَيِّن ـ لَطِيف ـ حَلِيم ـ مَلِق. Flowing, of speech, فَصِيح ـ بَلِيغ. A — stone, حَجَرٌ أَمْلَسُ *pl.* حِجَارَةٌ ٱلْمُلْسِ *or* حِجَارَةٌ مَلْسَآء. Smoother than oil, أَنْعَمُ مِنَ ٱلزَّيْتِ. He spoke — things to us, كَلَّمَنَا بِٱلنَّاعِمَاتِ. To be —, as of the skin, *etc.*, أَمْلَسَ ـ مَلُسَ ـُ ـ أَسُلَ ـُ; as of cloth, butter, words, *etc.*, نَعِمَ ـَ ـِ ـُ; as of a surface, إِسْتَوَى ـ سَهُلَ ـُ; as of the sea, غَلَنَ ٱلْبَحْرُ (an Arab nautical expression.) *See also under* Calm, *a.*

Smooth, *n.* The smooth part, مَلَاسَة. The — of the neck, مَلَاسَةُ ٱلْعُنُقِ. *See also* Even, Sleek, *a.*

Smooth, *v.t.* To make smooth, as of a stone, the skin, and any surface generally, مَلَّسَ. To make smooth and soft, as of a mash, *etc.*, دَمَّثَ. To — by paring, سَفَنَ ـِ ـُ ـ سَفَّنَ. To polish, جَلَا ـُ. To make even, level, مَهَّدَ ـ عَادَلَ ـ بَسَطَ ـُ ـ سَاوَى ـ سَطَّحَ. To —, as of a difficulty, سَكَّنَ ـ حَلَّمَ ـ لَيَّنَ ـ مَهَّدَ. To make easy, هَوَّنَ; to make easy to, هَوَّنَ عَلَى. To calm, appease, رَيَّحَ ـ حَلَّمَ ـ أَهْدَأَ ـ هَدَّأَ ـ سَكَّنَ ـ هَدَنَ ـِ. To blandish, تَلَيَّنَ لِ ـ حَايَلَ ـ دَارَى ـ دَاجَنَ. To — with a smoothing-iron, كَوَى ـِ ـ ضَرَبَ مِكْوَاةً ـِ.

Smooth-chinned, *a.* أَمْرَدُ *pl.* مُرْد.

Smooth-faced, *a.* Deceitful, مُدَاهِن ـ خَائِن ـ سَهْلُ ٱلْوَجْهِ ـ مُرَائِي.

Smoothing-iron, *n.* مِكْوَاة *pl.* مَكَاوِي.

Smoothly, *ad.* Evenly, بِٱسْتِوَاءٍ ـ خَلَاقَةً ـ بِتَسْطِيحٍ. Calmly, بِهُدُوٍّ ـ إِطْمِئْنَانًا. Mildly, حِلْمًا. Gently, مَهْلًا ـ رُوَيْدًا ـ عَلَى هِينَةٍ.

Smoothness, *n.* Of surface, as of the skin, stones, wine, *etc.*, مَلْس ـ مُلُوسَة; evenness of surface generally, خَلَاقَة ـ خُلُقَة. Smoothness, flatness, as opposed to ruggedness, تَمَهُّد ـ تَسْطِيح. Regularity, إِعْتِدَال ـ مُسَاوَاة. Calmness, as of the sea, سُجُوّ. Gentleness, لَطَافَة ـ بَشَاشَة ـ غُلْيِنَة ـ غَلْيَنَة; of the voice, رِقَّة ـ خَفْض. *See also* Softness, Sleekness, *n.*

Smote, *pret. of to* Smite, *v.t. q.v.*

Smother, *v.t.* To suffocate, خَنَقَ ـُ ـ *vulg.* فَطَّسَ. To — or cloak over an affair, أَخْفَى ـ نَيَّمَ ـ طَبَقَ عَلَى ـِ ـ قَطَعَ ـَ. To suppress, أَبْطَلَ. To — with dust, غَمَرَ ـ غَبَّرَهُ ـُ. *See also to* Stifle, *v.t.*

Smother, *v.i.* To be suffocated, إِخْتَنَقَ ـ *vulg.* فَطَسَ ـُ ـِ. To be suppressed, concealed, طُبِقَ عَلَيْهِ ـ إِخْتَفَى. To be smothered with dust, إِخْتَنَقَ بِٱلْغُبَارِ.

Smother, *n.* Fine dust such as is raised by the wind, *etc.*, عَجَاج ـ عَجَاجَة. Smother, as of fire or smoke, هَجِيج ـ أَجِيج. *See also* Smoke, *n.*

Smoulder, *v.i.* خَمَدَ ـُ ـ خَمِدَ ـَ. The fire smoulders, خَمَدَتِ ٱلنَّارُ. The fire smoulders under the ashes, ٱلنَّارُ مُخَبَّأَةٌ تَحْتَ ٱلرَّمَادِ.

Smouldering, *a.* خَامِد ـ مُخَمَّد. A — fire, نَارٌ خَامِدَةٌ.

Smudge, *n.* بُقْعَة ـ دَنَاسَة ـ طَبْعَة ـ دَرَن.

Smudge, *v.t.* سَخَّمَ ـ طَبَّعَ ـ أَدْرَنَ. To be smudged, دَرِنَ ـَ.

Smug, *a.* مُتَظَرِّف ـ مُتَكَيِّس .

Smuggle, *v.t.* To — in goods, أَدْخَلَ ٱلْبِضَاعَةَ خُفْيَةً بِدُونِ أَدَآءِ ٱلرَّقْتِ أَيِ ٱلْمُرَتَّبِ عَلَيْهَا إِلَى ٱلْكُمْرُكِ ; *vulg.* أَدْخَلَ ٱلْبِضَاعَةَ مِنْ وَرَآءِ ٱلْكُمْرُكِ . To — goods out, (the Arabic as in the preceding, but substituting أَخْرَجَ for أَدْخَلَ in both sentences). To — in, to introduce by stealth, دَسَّ فِي ². To — or introduce one's self stealthily, إِنْدَسَّ ـ إِنْزَبَقَ . To — one's self away, to levant, وَلَّى خُفْيَةً .

Smuggle, *v.i.* To practise smuggling, تَعَاطَى إِدْخَالَ (or إِخْرَاجَ) ٱلْبِضَاعَةِ خُفْيَةً بِدُونِ أَدَآءِ ٱلْمُرَتَّبِ عَلَيْهَا إِلَى ٱلْكُمْرُكِ ; *vulg.* تَعَاطَى إِدْخَالَ (or إِخْرَاجَ) ٱلْبِضَاعَةِ مِنْ وَرَآءِ ٱلْكُمْرُكِ .

Smuggler, *n.* مُتَعَاطِي إِدْخَالِ ٱلْبِضَاعَةِ بِدُونِ أَدَآءِ ٱلْمُرَتَّبِ عَلَيْهَا ـ إِلَى ٱلْكُمْرُكِ ـ خَلَّاسُ مُرَتَّبَاتِ ٱلْكُمْرُكِ .

Smuggling, *n.* تَعَاطِي إِدْخَالِ (or إِخْرَاجِ) ٱلْبِضَاعَةِ بِدُونِ أَدَآءِ ٱلْمُرَتَّبِ عَلَيْهَا إِلَى ٱلْكُمْرُكِ ـ خَلْسُ (or إِخْتِلَاسُ) مُرَتَّبَاتِ ٱلْكُمْرُكِ .

Smut, *n.* Soot, شُحَّار ـ سُخَام ـ كُتْن . A dirty spot, دَنَاسَة ـ طَبْعَة ـ بُقْعَة . Fungus on corn, *etc.*, سُوس ـ سُوسَة . Obscene language, زَفَر ـ خَنَايَة ـ رَفَث ـ قَذْع .

Smut, *v.t.* To mark with smut, لَوَّثَ بِشُحَّار ـ سَخَّمَ .

Smut, *v.i.* To contract smut, تَلَوَّثَ بِشُحَّار ـ تَسَخَّمَ .

Smutch, *v.t.* *See to* Smudge, *v.t.*

Smutch, *n.* *See* Smudge, *n.*

Smuttily, *ad.* Dirtily, قَذَرًا ـ أَقًّا . Obscenely, فُحْشًا ـ خَنًا .

Smuttiness, *n.* *See* Smut, *n.*

Smutty, *a.* Sooty, مُلَوَّث بِشُحَّار ـ مُسَخَّم ـ كَتِن . Obscene, فَاحِش ـ خَنٍ ـ بَذِئ . *See also* Obscene, *a.*

Snack, *n.* A share, سَهْم *pl.* أَسْهَام ـ قِسْم *pl.* أَقْسَام . A slight repast, لُقْمَة ـ سُلْفَة . To go snacks with another, نَاصَفَ ـ شَارَكَ .

Snaffle, *n.* قَنْطَرْمَة .

Snag, *n.* Any protuberance in a bone, mountain, tree, *etc.*, حَيْدَة *pl.* أَحْيَاد *and* حُيُود . A notch, حَزّ *pl.* حُزُوز . A — in a river, أَجْذَال *pl.* جِذْل فِي وَسَطِ نَهْرٍ أَعْلَاهُ دُونَ وَجْهِ ٱلْمَآءِ مِثْلَ آتُنِ ٱلضَّحْلِ .

Snagged, *a.} Snaggy, Full of protuberances, مَمْلُوٌّ مِنْ أَحْيَادٍ ; full of snags, of a river, مَمْلُوٌّ مِنْ أَجْذَالٍ أَعْلَاهَا قَرِيبٌ مِنْ وَجْهِ ٱلْمَآءِ مِثْلَ آتُنِ ٱلضَّحْلِ . *See also* Knotty, *a.*

Snail, *n.* حَلَزُون *pl.* حَلَازِين ـ بَزَّاقَة *coll.* بَزَّاق .

Snake, *n.* The reptile, حَيَّة *pl.* حَيَوَات *and* حَيَّات . The — or tube of a hookah, لَيّ *pl.* لَيَّات ـ مَارْبِيج . A — in the grass, a deceiver, عَيَّار ـ خَدَّاع ـ دَاهٍ . *See also* Sly, *a.*

Snake-root, *n.* لُوفُ ٱلْحَيَّةِ ـ ٱللُّوفُ ٱلْأَرْقَطُ ـ لُوف .

Snaky, *a.* Like a snake, مِثْلَ ٱلْحَيَّةِ . *See also* Sly, Cunning, *a.*

Snap, *v.t.* To break short, كَسَرَ ـ قَصَمَ ـ نَقَضَ ². To bite at, عَضْعَضَ عَلَى ـ عَضَّ عَلَى . To crack, with separation of parts, فَلَقَ ـ فَلَّعَ ـ فَضَّ ². To —, or crack, of a whip, فَقَّعَ . To — at, to seize, ضَبَّ ـ أَضَبَّ عَلَى ـ إِخْتَلَسَ ; to be peevish to, شَاكَسَ . To — up, لَقِفَ . To — the fingers at, to despise, إِسْتَحْقَرَ ـ إِسْتَقَلَّ . To — away; *see to* Snatch, *v.t.*

Snap, *v.i.* To break, إِنْكَسَرَ . To break with a noise, فَقَعَ ـ إِنْقَصَّ ـ تَفَرْتَكَ ـ طَقْطَقَ . To crack, with separation of parts, تَفَلَّعَ . To be peevish, شَرِسَ ـ يَعَقُ *aor.* وَعِقَ ـ تَنَكَّدَ .

Snap, *n.* The act of breaking suddenly, كَسْرَة ـ كَسْر . A bite, عَضْعَضَة ـ عَضَّة . A sharp noise, طَقْطَقَة ـ تَفْقِيع .

Snap-dragon, *n.* The plant, عُشْبُ ٱلذِّئْبِ . The childish play, لُعْبَةٌ يَتَّخِذُهَا ٱلصِّبْيَانُ وَذٰلِكَ أَنَّهُمْ يَنْقَعُونَ زَبِيبًا فِي رُوحِ ٱلْعَرَقِ ثُمَّ يُشْرِكُونَ ٱلنَّارَ بِهِ فَيَلْتَهِبُ ثُمَّ يُقْبِلُونَ عَلَى نَشْلِ ٱلزَّبِيبِ بِأَصَابِعِهِمْ فَتَلْتَفِحُ بِٱللَّهِيبِ وَهُمْ يَمْزَحُونَ .

Snappish, *a.* Disposed to bite, مَطْبُوعٌ عَلَى ٱلْعَضِّ . Sharp, as in reply, حَادّ ـ مُؤْذٍ ـ جَارِح . Peevish, شَرِس ـ شَكِس .

Snappishly, *ad.* Peevishly, بِشَرَاسَةٍ ـ بِشَكَاسَةٍ ـ بِوَعَقَةٍ .

Snappishness, *n.* Peevishness, شَرَاسَة ـ شَكَاسَة ـ وَعَقَة . Sharpness, tartness, حِدَّة .

Snare, *n.* As for catching animals, حِبَالَة *pl.* حَبَائِل ـ شَرَك *pl.* أَشْرَاك ـ مِصْيَدَة ـ فَخّ *pl.* فُخُوخ *and* فِخَاخ . A — which is thrown by the hand, such as a lasso, وَهَق . A — for catching birds, فُقَّاعَة . An ambush, كَمِينَة *pl.* كِمَان . A stratagem, مَكِيدَة *pl.* مَكَائِد ـ دُولَاب *pl.* دَوَالِيب . Women are the — of the devil, ٱلنِّسَآءُ حَبَائِلُ ٱلشَّيْطَانِ . I seek protection by thee from the mischief of the devil and his snares, أَعُوذُ بِكَ مِنْ شَرِّ ٱلشَّيْطَانِ وَشَرَكِهِ . Lest he should fall into a —, لِئَلَّا يَسْقُطَ فِي فَخٍّ . He was delivered out of the —, إِسْتَفَاقَ مِنَ ٱلْفَخِّ . To lay a — for, أَنْصَبَ لِ ـ فَخًّا ; of a stratagem, trick, كَادَ لِ . To be taken in a —, أُخِذَ بِٱلشَّرَكِ .

Snare, *v.t.* *See to* Entangle, Entrap, Insnare, *v.t.*

Snarl, *v.t.* To entangle, as in knots, عَقَّدَ ـ شَبَّكَ . To complicate, لَبَّكَ ـ شَوَّشَ .

Snarl, *v.i.* As of a dog, كَبْهَبَ ـ هَمْهَمَ ـ هَدَرَ ـ هَدَرَ . To grumble, دَمْدَمَ ـ مَرْمَرَ . To be peevish, disagreeable, تَنَكَّدَ ـ يَعَقُ *aor.* وَعِقَ .

Snarl, *n.* An entanglement, as of threads, *etc.*, تَشْبِيك ـ

تَعَقُّد ـ مُشَابَكَة . A grumble, بَرْبَرَة ـ دَمْدَمَة . A —, as of a dog, هَبْهَبَة ـ هَمْهَمَة ـ هَدِير . *See also* Quarrel, *n.*

Snarler, *n.* Of a dog, هَدَّار ـ هَادِر ; of a person, شَكِس ـ مُدَمْدِم ـ شَرِس .

Snary, *a.* *See* Insidious, *a.*

Snatch, *v.t.* اِخْتَطَفَ ـ خَطِفَ ـ اِمْتَرَشَ ـ اِمْتَرَسَ ـ خَلَسَ ـ اِخْتَلَسَ ـ تَخَطَّفَ . To — away and carry off, اِسْتَلَبَ ـ سَلَبَ ـ خَطِفَ ـ أُخْتُطِفَ ـ كَفَتَ ـ كَفَّتَ . To be snatched away, اِسْتَلَبَ . He snatched (an opportunity) for hearing, خَطِفَ ٱلسَّمَاعَ . To — from one another, of many, تَخَاطَفُوا . He snatched it out of his hand, اِخْتَلَسَهُ مِنْ يَدِهِ . His sight was suddenly snatched away, أُخْتُلِسَ بَصَرُهُ .

Snatch, *n.* A hasty catch, خَطْفَة ـ خَطْف . A slight attack, turn, نَوْبَة *pl.* نَوْبَات ـ دَوْر *pl.* أَدْوَار . A fragment, as of a song, *etc.*, نُبْذَة *pl.* نُبْذَات .

Snatcher, *n.* خَاطِف *pl.* خُطَّاف .

Sneak, *v.i.* To creep slyly into a place, خَشَّ فِي ـ اِنْزَبَقَ فِي ـ اِنْسَلَّ إِلَى ـ اِنْدَسَّ فِي . To behave with meanness, تَذَلَّلَ ـ ذَلَّ ـ هَانَ . He sneaked out from among them, اِنْسَلَّ مِنْ بَيْنِهِمْ . To — to one, تَذَلَّلَ لَهُ . To — off secretly, to abscond, اِنْسَلَّ خُفْيَةً .

Sneak, *n.* } A sly hypocritical fellow, دَسِيس *pl.* دُسُس ـ
Sneaker, *n.* } عَيَّار ـ حَوَالِيّ . Mean, crouching, مُتَضَعْضِع ـ
Sneaking, *a.* } ذَلِيل *pl.* أَذِلَّاء ـ خَضْعَاء *fem.* أَخْضَع . *See also* Niggardly, *ad.*

Sneaking, *n.* Servility, حَقَارَة ـ تَذَلُّل ـ مُطَاوَعَة ـ تَضَاضُع .

Sneakingly, *ad.* بِحَقَارَةٍ ـ تَذَلُّلًا ـ كَٱلدَّسِيسِ .

Sneakingness, *n.* *See* Niggardness, *n.*

Sneer, *v.i.* To scoff or rail at, خَنَتَ ـ أَزْرَى بِ ـ أَخْصَنَ بِ ـ ضَحِكَ مِن *or* بِ *or* عَلَى ـ اِسْتَهْزَأَ بِ ـ خَنَتَ ـ لَهُ بِأَنْفِهِ ـ نَقَرَ ـ تَسَخَّرَ بِ . *See also to* Scoff, Rail, Mock, *v.i.*

Sneer, *n.* تَعْيِيب ـ اِفْتِرَاء ـ اِسْتِهْزَاء ـ خَنْت .

Sneerer, *n.* مُسْتَهْزِئ *pl.* مُسْتَهْزِئُون ـ مُجَدِّف . *See also* Mocker, Scoffer, Railer, *n.*

Sneeringly, *ad.* تَعْيِيرًا ـ تَعْيِيبًا ـ بِٱفْتِرَاءٍ ـ بِٱسْتِهْزَاءٍ ـ خَنْتًا .

Sneeze, *v.i.* عَطَسَ ; to make to —, عَطَّسَ . To —, of brutes, نَثَرَ ـ كَدَسَ . To — at, to contemn, اِسْتَحْقَرَ .

Sneeze, *n.* } عُطَاس ـ عَطْس ; one —, عَطْسَة . A — of a brute,
Sneezing, } نَثْرَة ـ نَثِير ـ كَدْسَة ـ كُدَاس . Anything which causes —, عَاطُوس . He (Muhammad) used to like — and disliked yawning, كَانَ يُحِبُّ ٱلْعُطَاسَ وَيَكْرَهُ ٱلتَّثَاؤُبَ .

Sneezer, *n.* One who sneezes, عَاطِس . To congratulate a —, سَمَّتَ ٱلْعَاطِسَ : *The congratulation is called* تَسْمِيت .

Sneider, *n.* A — musket, قَرَابِينَة عَلَى عَمَلِ سَنَيْدَر *pl.* قَرَابِينَات .

Snicker, *v.i.* } *See to* Smirk, *v.i.*
Snigger, }

Sniff, *v.t.* اِسْتَنْشَقَ . The horse turned to the wind to — it, تَمَخَّرَ (*or* اِمْتَخَرَ) ٱلْفَرَسُ ٱلرِّيحَ .

Sniff, *v.i.* شَخَرَ ـ اِسْتَنْشَقَ .

Sniff, *n.* شَخِير ـ اِسْتِنْشَاق .

Snip, *v.t.* قَصَّ مِن . *See also to* Clip, *v.t.*

Snip, *n.* As with a pair of scissors, قَصّ . A piece cut off, حِتَّة مَقْصُوعَة ـ قِطْعَة .

Snipe, *n.* The bird, بِيكَاسُون ـ بِكَاسُون .

Snivel, *n.* From the nose of a human being, زُكَام ; of an animal, خُنَان . A babyish cry, عَوْل ـ عَوِيل ـ مَأْقَة .

Snivel, *v.i.* To run at the nose, of human beings, زُكِمَ ; of animals, خُنَّ . To cry as a child, بَكَى ـ أَعْوَلَ ـ اِمْتَأَقَ ـ مَئِقَ .

Sniveller, *n.* One who cries like a baby, بَكِيّ ـ مَئِق .

Snob, *n.* } A vulgar person who apes gentility, دَنِيء
Snobbish, *a.* } سُوقِيّ مُتَكَيِّس ـ مُتَظَرِّف .

Snooze, *v.i.* *See to* Nap, Slumber, *v.i.*

Snooze, *n.* *See* Nap, Slumber, *n.*

Snore, *v.i.* نَخَرَ ـ خَرْخَرَ ـ اِنْتَخَ ـ فَخَّ ـ خَرَّ ـ كَخَّ ـ خَنْفَرَ ـ شَخَرَ ـ شَخَرَ .

Snore, *n.* تَخَنْفُر ـ شَخِير ـ نَخِير ـ فَخَّة ـ كَخِيخ ـ خَرْخَرَة .

Snorer, *n.* شَخَّار ـ مِنْخَار ـ خَارّ .

Snort, *v.i.* نَخَرَ ـ شَخَرَ ـ كَرَّ . To —, in sleeping, غَطَّ .

Snort, *n.* } شَخِير ـ نَخِير ـ كَرِير .
Snorting, }

Snot, *n.* مُخَاط ـ دَمِيم ـ دَنِين ـ دُنَان ; dry —, قِرْفَة . To run with —, تَمَخَّطَ ـ مَخَطَ ـ دَنَّ .

Snotty, *a.* مُخَاطِيّ ـ دَنَّاء *fem.* أَدَنّ .

Snotty-nose, *n.* أَبُو صِمْغَة ـ صَمْغَان .

Snout, *n.* As of a beast, خُرْطُوم *pl.* خَرَاطِيم ـ بُوز ; of a pig, بُوزُ ٱلْخِنْزِيرِ ـ فِطِّيس ـ فِنْطِيسَة . The end of a hollow pipe, أُنْبُوب *pl.* أَنَابِيب .

Snow, *n.* ثَلْج *pl.* ثُلُوج ـ سَقِيط . A place for keeping —, مَثْلَجَة . To come upon —, to reach a place of —, أَثْلَجَ . Rough or crackling —, خَشِيفٌ. A mountain covered with perpetual —, جَبَلٌ لا يَنقَطِعُ ٱلثَّلْجُ عَنْهُ أَصْلًا.

Snow, *v.i.* ـَ ثَلَجَتِ ٱلسَّمَآءُ 2. The sky snowed upon us, أَثْلَجَتْنَا ٱلسَّمَآءُ ـ 2 ثَلَجَتْنَا ٱلسَّمَآءُ.

Snow-ball, *n.* كُرَةُ ثَلْجٍ *pl.* كُرَاتٌ ـ طَابَةُ ثَلْجٍ *pl.* طَابَاتٌ. They threw snow-balls at one another, تَرَامَوْا بِكُرَاتِ ثَلْجٍ.

Snow-drift, *n.* كُومَةُ ثَلْجٍ.

Snow-drop, *n.* مَنْثُورٌ *pl.* مَنَاثِيرُ.

Snow-slip, *n.* سَقِيطٌ جَسِيمٌ مِنَ ٱلثَّلْجِ.

Snow-storm, *n.* زَوْبَعَةُ ثَلْجٍ.

Snow-white, *a.* أَبْيَضُ كَٱلثَّلْجِ.

Snowy, *a.* As of a day, مُثْلِجٌ. Snowed upon, مَثْلُوجٌ. Cold as snow, ثَلِجٌ. The day was —, أَثْلَجَ ٱلنَّهَارُ.

Snub, *v.t.* To break off the end, 2 نَصَّ ٱلطَّرَفَ. To rebuke, ـَ سَخِطَ عَلَى ـ خَشَّنَ عَلَى ـ غَلَّظَ عَلَى ـ ـَ قَرَفَ عَلَى ـ 2 عَنَفَ عَلَى ـ 2 زَجَرَ.

Snub, *n.* A sharp rebuke, عِتَابٌ ـ زَجْرٌ ـ سُخْطَةٌ.

Snub-nose, *n.* أَذْلَفُ *fem.* ذَلْفَآءُ *pl.* ذُلْفٌ.

Snub-nosed, *a.* أَذْلَفُ *fem.* ذَلْفَآءُ *pl.* ذُلْفٌ. To be —, ـَ ذَلِفَ.

Snuff, *n.* A burning or burnt wick, قِرَاطٌ ـ ذُبَالَةُ ٱلسِّرَاجِ ـ زَهْرَةُ ٱلشَّمْعَةِ. Pulverized tobacco, نَشُوقٌ ـ نَشُوغٌ ـ نُشُوغٌ ـ تَنْشِيقَةٌ ـ سَعُوطٌ ـ عَطُوسٌ ـ أَنْفِيَّةٌ; *vulg.* زَعُوطٌ. A pinch of —, شَمَّةٌ. Medicinal —, or any medicament given through the nostrils, سَعُوطٌ ـ نُشُوغٌ; to apply any such — to, أَنْشَغَ ـ أَسْعَطَ ـ نَشَّغَ.

Snuff, *v.t.* To take off the snuff of a candle, أَزَالَ ذُبَالَةَ ٱلسِّرَاجِ ـ ـَ قَطَفَ ٱلشَّمْعَةَ ـ ـَ نَطَفَ (or قَرَطَ) ٱلشَّمْعَةَ. To draw into the nose, to smell, 2 شَمَّ ـ إِسْتَنْشَقَ.

Snuff, *v.i.* To take snuff, 2 شَمَّ ٱلنَّشُوقَ. To — at, تَأَنَّفَ بِ. To — out, to extinguish, أَطْفَأَ.

Snuff-box, *n.* حُقَّةٌ (or عِلْبَةٌ *pl.* عِلَبٌ) نُشُوقٍ.

Snuffers, *n.* مِقَصٌّ ـ مَقَاطِيفُ *pl.* مِقْطَافٌ ـ مَلَاقِطُ *pl.* مِلْقَاطٌ ٱلشَّمْعَةِ.

Snuffers-tray, *n.* بَيْتٌ ـ بَيْتُ ٱلْمِلْقَاطِ ـ مِنْفَضَةُ ٱلْمِلْقَاطِ ـ مِقَصُّ ٱلشَّمْعَةِ.

Snuffle, *v.i.* To speak through the nose, ـِ خَنَّ ـ ـَ غَنَّ ـ خَنْخَنَ.

Snuffle, *n.* خَنِينٌ ـ مَخَنَّةٌ ـ خُنَّةٌ ـ غُنَّةٌ.

Snuffler, *n.* }
Snuffling, *a.* } أَخَنُّ ـ أَغَنُّ.

Snuffles, *n.* In human beings, زُكَامٌ; in animals, خُنَانٌ.

Snug, *a.* Private, خَفِيٌّ ـ مَسْتُورٌ. Convenient, commodious, شَرِحٌ ـ وَسِيعٌ. In good order, مُرَتَّبٌ ـ لَطِيفٌ ـ كَيِّسٌ ـ مَضْبُوطٌ ـ مُنْتَظِمٌ. At ease, مُرْتَاحٌ. To make all —, in order, نَظَّمَ ٱلْجَمِيعَ ـ ـِ ضَبَطَ كُلَّ شَيْءٍ 2. To lie —, secreted, إِخْتَفَى.

See also Cosy, *a.*

Snug, *v.i.* To — to, to lie close to, إِخْتَصَنَ ـ 2 حَضَنَ.

Snuggery, *n.* خَلْوَةٌ مَأْنُوسَةٌ ـ خَلْوَةٌ ـ خِزَانَةٌ ـ خِزَانَةٌ.

Snugly, *ad.* Closely, secretly عَلَى خَفَآءٍ ـ خِفْيَةً. Safely, إِمْنًا ـ سِلْمًا. In order, بِكِيَاسَةٍ ـ بِضَبْطٍ ـ فِي غَايَةِ ٱلْإِتْقَانِ.

Snugness, *n.* Closeness, secrecy, إِسْتِتَارٌ ـ إِحْتِجَابٌ. Convenience, بَحْبَحَةٌ ـ إِنْشِرَاحٌ ـ تَوْفِيقٌ. Good order, كِيَاسَةٌ ـ إِتْقَانٌ ـ ضَبْطٌ ـ إِنْتِظَامٌ ـ نِظَامٌ.

So, *ad.* Thus, هٰكَذَا ـ كَذَا; *vulg.* هَيْكْ. In that manner, كَذٰلِكَ. So it is, هٰكَذَا هُوَ ـ نَعَمْ. It is not so with me, لَسْتُ هٰكَذَا عِنْدَ نَفْسِي. It shall not be so among you, فَلَا يَكُونُ هٰكَذَا فِيكُمْ. If it were not so I would have told you, وَإِلَّا فَإِنِّي قَدْ قُلْتُ لَكُمْ. These things ought not to be so, لَا يَصْلُحُ أَنْ تَكُونَ هٰذِهِ ٱلْأُمُورُ هٰكَذَا. So that the apostle said, حَتَّى يَقُولَ ٱلرَّسُولُ. And so forth, إِلَى آخِرِهِ ـ وَهَلُمَّ جَرًّا (contracted into) إِلَخْ or اهـ.

How so? كَيْفَ.

If so, إِنْ كَانَ ٱلْأَمْرُ كَذٰلِكَ.

Not so, by any means, كَلَّا. Not in that manner, لَيْسَ كَذٰلِكَ.

So-and-so, فُلَانٌ. Mister —, ٱلسَّيِّدُ (or أَفَنْدِي) فُلَانٌ.

So much so, that should he come I will reprove him, حَتَّى إِذَا جَآءَ فَأُوَدِّبُهُ.

So that, seeing that, مِنْ حَيْثُ أَنْ. Hence, therefore, حَتَّى.

So, so, بَيْنَ بَيْنَ ـ كَذَا وَكَذَا.

Why so? لِأَيِّ سَبَبٍ ـ لِمَاذَا.

Soak, *v.t.* ـَ نَقَعَ ـ 2 مَرَسَ ـ 2 مَرَثَ; of bread in fat, grease, *etc.*, رَبَّغَ ـ رَوَّغَ. To — anything to prepare it to be wrought, to cause to imbibe, شَرَّبَ. To be soaked, إِسْتَنْقَعَ. To be soaked through, as with rain, إِبْتَلَّ; with blood, ـَ رَوِيَ مِنَ ٱلدَّمِ.

Soak, *n.* }
Soaking, } The act of soaking, إِسْتِنْقَاعٌ ـ نَقْعٌ ـ مَرْثٌ. The being made wet, as with rain, تَبَلُّلٌ ـ إِبْتِلَالٌ ـ بَلَّةٌ; as with blood, رَيٌّ (or رِوًى) مِنَ ٱلدَّمِ.

Soap, *n.* صَابُونٌ. A cake or ball of —, قَالِبُ صَابُونٍ *pl.* قَوَالِبُ. Scented —, صَابُونٌ مُعَطَّرٌ. Fuller's earth, often used for —, بَيْلُونٌ. A seller of —, صَابُونِيٌّ.

Soap, *v.t.* To rub with soap, صَبَّنَ ـ صَوْبَنَ ـ غَسَلَ ـِ بِٱلصَّابُونِ. To wheedle, صَانَعَ. *See also to* Flatter, *v.t.*

Soap-boiler, *n.* صَابُونِيٌّ.

Soap-boiling, *n.* صِنَاعَةُ ٱلصَّابُونِيِّ.

Soap-manufactory, *n.* مَعْمَلُ صَابُونٍ.

Soap-stone, *n.* حَجَرُ ٱلصَّابُونِ.

Soap-suds, *n.* (مَآء *or*) رَغْوَةُ ٱلصَّابُونِ ـ غُسَالَةُ ٱلصَّابُونِ.

Soap-wort, *n.* الصَّابُونِيَّةُ.

Soapy, *a.* صَابُونِيٌّ.

Soar, *v.i.* سَمَا *aor.* يَسْمُو ـ إِرْتَفَعَ ـ أَخَذَ فِي ٱلْعُلُوِّ. His ambition soared to high things, سَمَتْ هِمَّتُهُ إِلَى مَعَالِي ٱلْأُمُورِ. To —, of a bird, حَلَّقَ ـ تَحَلَّقَ. To — above, rise higher than, إِرْتَفَعَ عَلَى. His sight soared, سَمَا بَصَرُهُ. To compete with another in soaring, سَامَى.

Soar, *n.* } Soaring, } إِرْتِفَاع ـ أَخْذٌ فِي ٱلْعُلُوِّ ـ سُمُوٌّ ـ تَحَلُّق ـ تَحْلِيق.

Soaringly, *ad.* بِٱرْتِفَاعٍ ـ بِسُمُوٍّ ـ بِتَحَلُّقٍ.

Sob, *v.i.* مَتَّقَ ـ إِمْتَأَقَ ـ حَنَّ ـِ شَهَقَ ـَـِ إِنْتَحَبَ.

Sob, *n.* تِشْهَاق ـ شَهِيق ـ حَنِين ـ مَأْقَة.

Sober, *a.* Serious, سَاكِنُ ٱلطَّائِرِ ـ وَقُور ـ تَيْقُور ـ رَزِين. Wise, prudent, of a person, عَاقِل; of a thing, مَعْقُول. Free from intoxication, صَاحٍ. Temperate, قَانِت ـ قَنِيت ـ مُعْتَدِل. Sober, of colours, أَرْبَدُ ـ مُكَمَّد ـ غَيْرُ لَامِعٍ. To be or to become —, not intoxicated, صَحَا *aor.* يَصْحُو ـ أَصْحَى. To be —, grave, serious, رَزُنَ ـُ إِتَّقَرَ ـ تَوَقَّرَ. To be —, prudent, تَعَقَّلَ. In his — senses, وَهُوَ صَاحٍ ـ مَالِكٌ عَقْلَهُ وَرُشْدَهُ. *See also* Grave, *a.*

Sober, *v.t.* To recover from intoxication, أَصْحَى مِنَ ٱلسُّكْرِ. To make grave, prudent, عَقَّلَ ـ سَكَّنَ طَائِرَهُ ـ أَخْمَدَ نَهْوَرَهُ.

Soberly, *ad.* With prudence, بِٱلتَّعَقُّلِ; with seriousness, بِوُقُورٍ ـ بِرَزَانَةٍ; temperately, بِوَرَعٍ ـ بِضَبْطِ ٱلنَّفْسِ. To act —, تَرَزَّنَ ـ تَعَقَّلَ. To live —, عَاشَ بِتَعَقُّلٍ ـِ.

Sober-minded, *a.* عَاقِل ـ رَزِين ـ وَقُور.

Sober-mindedness, *n.* تَعَقُّل ـ رَزَانَة ـ وُقُور.

Soberness, *n.* } Freedom from intoxication, صُحُوٌّ ـ إِصْحَآء. Sobriety, } Seriousness, رَزَانَة ـ وُقُور ـ وَقَار. Prudence, تَعَقُّل. Temperance, قَنَاتَة ـ قَنَع. Soberness, of colours, تَكْمِيد.

Socage, *n.* تَصَرُّفٌ بِأَمْلَاكٍ فِي نَظِيرِ خِدْمَةٍ ذَاتِيَّةٍ (*or* شَخْصِيَّةٍ) مُعَيَّنَةٍ.

So-called, *a.* المُسَمَّى ـ المَعْهُودُ.

Sociability, *n.* } Sociableness, } خِلْطَة ـ جُمْعَة ـ أُنْس ـ مُؤَانَسَة ـ أُلْفَة ـ بَشَاشَة ـ أُنْسِيَّة.

Sociable, *a.* هَشٌّ بَشٌّ ـ أَنِيس ـ مُؤَانِس ـ خِلْط *fem.* خِلْطَة ـ تَبَشْبَشَ بـ ـ آنَسَ ـ أَنِسَ بـ ـ مُتَأَنِّس. To be — with, أَنِسَ بـ ـ آنَسَ ـ تَبَشْبَشَ بـ.

Sociable, *n.* خِلْط *fem.* خِلْطَة ـ أَلِيف *pl.* أُلَفَآء.

Sociably, *ad.* بِأُنْسٍ ـ بِمُؤَانَسَةٍ ـ بِأُلْفَةٍ ـ بِبَشَاشَةٍ.

Social, *a.* Pertaining to society, كَافَّةً ـ مُخْتَصٌّ بِٱلنَّاسِ ـ مُتَعَلِّقٌ بِٱلْجُمْهُورِ. Social intercourse, أُدْمَة ـ خِلْطَة ـ جُمْعَة ـ أُلْفَة. *See also* Sociable, *a.*

Socialism, *n.* مَذْهَبُ ـ القَوْلُ بِٱلِٱشْتِرَاكِ فِي أَمْوَالِ ٱلْجُمْهُورِ ـ ٱلِٱشْتِرَاكِيِّينَ.

Socialist, *n.* قَائِل بِٱلِٱشْتِرَاكِ فِي أَمْوَالِ ٱلْجُمْهُورِ *pl.* قَوَّل *or* قَالَة. Socialists, ٱلِٱشْتِرَاكِيُّونَ أَعْنِي ٱلْقَائِلُونَ بِٱشْتِرَاكِ ٱلْفُقَرَآءِ فِي مَالِ ٱلْأَغْنِيَآءِ.

Sociality, *n.* } Socialness, } *See* Sociability, *n.*

Socialize, *v.t.* طَبَّعَ ـ أَنَّسَ ـ مَدَّنَ.

Socially, *ad.* Among people, in the world, (فِي *or* بَيْنَ *or*) عِنْدَ ٱلنَّاسِ. *See also* Sociably, *ad.*

Society, *n.* A union of persons, مَعْشَر ـ جَمْعِيَّة *pl.* جَمْعِيَّات ـ جَمَاعَة ـ جُمْهُور *pl.* جَمَاهِير ـ مَحْفَل. Social —, intercourse, مُعَاشَرَة ـ صُحْبَة ـ أُلْفَة. Partnership, a company, عِشْرَة ـ شِرْكَة ـ بَيْت. A — met for conversation, *etc*, مَجْلِس *pl.* مَجَالِس. A brotherhood, أُخْوِيَّة. A charitable —, جَمْعِيَّةٌ خَيْرِيَّةٌ. Fashionable —, مَعْشَرُ ٱلْمُعْتَبَرِينَ ـ مَعْشَرُ ٱلْأَكَابِرِ. A learned —, جَمْعِيَّةُ عُلَمَآءَ. Bible —, جَمْعِيَّةٌ لِٱنْتِشَارِ ٱلْكُتُبِ ٱلْمُقَدَّسَةِ. A missionary —, جَمْعِيَّةٌ لِٱنْتِشَارِ ٱلْإِيمَانِ. To keep — with, خَالَطَ ـ عَاشَرَ ـ صَاحَبَ. To go into —, خَالَطَ ٱلنَّاسَ ـ تَرَدَّدَ إِلَى ٱلْمَجَالِسِ.

Socinian, *n.* نَاكِرُ لَاهُوتِ ٱلْمَسِيحِ وَكَفَّارَتِهِ.

Socinianism, *n.* مَذْهَبُ طَائِفَةٍ مِنَ ٱلنَّصَارَى يُنْكِرُونَ لَاهُوتَ ٱلْمَسِيحِ وَكَفَّارَتَهُ.

Sock, *n.* For the foot, جَوْرَب *pl.* جَوَارِبُ. A seller of socks, جَوَارِبِيٌّ.

Socket, *n.* A hollow place to receive anything, وَقْب *pl.* أَوْقَاب ـ قَاعِدَة *pl.* قَوَاعِد ـ مَعْشَق. The — of a tooth, مَشْغَر ـ بَيْتُ ٱلسِّنِّ *pl.* بُيُوتُ ٱلْأَسْنَانِ. The — of the eye, وَقْبُ ٱلْعَيْنِ ـ نُقْرَةُ ٱلْعَيْنِ *pl.* نُقَر ـ بَيْتُ ٱلْعَيْنِ; the two sockets of the eyes, الغَارَانِ. Having the eyes sunk in the sockets, مُنْقَعِرُ ٱلْعَيْنَيْنِ. His eyes sank in their sockets, رَسَبَتْ عَيْنَاهُ ـُ.

Socrates, *n.* سُقْرَاط.

Socratic, *a.* }
Socratical, } مَنْسُوبٌ إِلَى سُقْرَاطَ ـ سُقْرَاطِيٌّ.

Sod, *n.* دَبْشَة ـ مَدَر *pl.* مَدَرَة ـ سِجِّيل ـ شَتْلَة. The first sod cut out of ground, ظَلِيم. Sward, خُضْرَة. To lay under the sod, دَفَنَ ـِ.

Sod, *v.t.* To cover with sod, شَمِلَ بِمَدَرٍ ـَ.

Soda, *n.* *See* Alkali, *n.*

Soda-water, *n.* صُودَا وَاطَر ـ مَآءٌ فَائِرٌ.

Sodden, *part.* Soaked, مَنْقُوع. Boiled, مَسْلُوق. Half-boiled, مَسْلُوقٌ نِصْفَ سَلْقٍ.

Soddy, *a.* مَمْلُوٌّ مِنْ مَدَرٍ.

Soder, *v t.* *See to* Solder, *v.t.*

Sodium, *n.* صُودِيُوم.

Sodom, *n.* سَدُوم ـ بَلَدُ لُوطٍ.

Sodomite, *n.* An active —, لَوَّاط ـ لُوطِيّ; a passive —, مُخَنَّث ـ مَأْبُون *pl.* مَأْبُونُون.

Sodomy, *n.* لِوَاط ـ لِيَاط. To be addicted to —, لَاطَ *aor.* يَلُوطُ.

Sofa, *n.* صُفَّة ـ مِتْكَآء ـ أَرِيكَة *pl.* أَرَائِك ـ نُمْرُق *pl.* نَمَارِق ـ دِيوَان *pl.* دَوَاوِين ـ سَرِير *pl.* سُرُر ـ مُضْطَجَع.

Sofi, *n.* *See* Sûfy, *n.*

Soft, *a.* Not hard, لَيِّن *pl.* أَلْيِنَآء *and* لَيِّنُون. Soft and smooth, وَثِير. Soft and fine, نَاعِم. Soft, of wine or food, easy to swallow, أَمْلَس *fem* مَلْسَآء *pl.* مُلْس. Smooth, not rugged, سَهْل ـ سَهِل. Flaccid, رَخْو ـ هَشّ. Effeminate, مُخَنَّث. Placid, gentle, لَطِيف ـ رَفِيق ـ كَرِيم ـ حَلِيم. Soft to the touch, سُخَامُ ٱلْمَسِّ ـ سُخَام. Soft ground, سَهْل ـ رَخَاخ ـ أَرْضٌ دَمِثَةٌ. A — voice, جِرْس ـ جَرْس ـ صَوْتٌ خَفِيٌّ. A — sound, صَوْتٌ خَفِيض ـ جَرْس. A — answer, جَوَابٌ لَيِّنٌ. A — man, ضَائِن ـ غَبِيٌّ. A —, flabby, man, مَخْلُوع. A — or kindly man, خَوَّارُ ٱلْعِنَانِ ـ لَيِّنُ ٱلْعَاطِفِ. A — colour, لَوْنٌ لَطِيفٌ ـ لَوْنٌ مُكَمَّدٌ. Soft sawder, مُدَاهَنَة. Soft-boiled, مَسْلُوقٌ نِصْفَ سَلْقٍ. Fair and —, of a woman, رُؤْد ـ رُعْبُوبَة. Soft or tender fingers, بَنَانٌ طَفْلٌ. Soft hair, شَعْرٌ سُخَامٌ. A — or tender bough, غُصْنٌ أُمْلُودٌ. A — bed, فِرَاشٌ وَثِيرٌ. A — wind, رِيحٌ رُخَآءٌ. Softer than butter, أَنْعَمُ مِنَ ٱلزُّبْدِ. He was dressed in — raiment, كَانَ لَابِسًا ثِيَابًا نَاعِمَةً. A — answer turneth away wrath, ٱلْجَوَابُ ٱللَّيِّنُ يَصْرِفُ ٱلْغَضَبَ. To be —, not hard, لَانَ ـِ ـ تَلَيَّنَ. To be —, flaccid, صَارَ رَخْوًا ـ إِسْتَرْخَى ـ هَشَّ ـَ ـِ ـ إِرْتَخَّ. To be —, smooth, سَهُلَ ـُ ـ وَثُرَ. To be —, fine, نَعِمَ ـَ ـُ. To be —, gentle, towards, سَاهَلَ ـ رَفَقَ ـُ بِ *or* عَلَى. To speak in a —, low, voice, جَرَسَ بِٱلْكَلَامِ ـُ ـ جَرَسَ ٱلْكَلَامَ ـُ ـ نَغَمَ بِٱلْكَلَامِ ـُ. *See also* Smooth, *a.*

Soften, *v.t.* To make soft, less hard, لَيَّنَ ـ تَلْيِينَ ـ أَلَانَ. To make soft and smooth, دَيَّثَ ـ أَمْلَسَ ـ مَلَّسَ ـ وَثَرَ *aor.* يَثِرُ ـ وَثَّرَ. To make flaccid, less tense, أَرْخَى. To mitigate, لَيَّنَ ـ صَيَّرَ مِثْلَ ـ خَنَّثَ ـ خَفَّفَ ـ لَطَّفَ. To make effeminate, خَنَّثَ ـ لَيَّنَ ـ حَنَّنَ ـ رَقَّقَ ٱلنِّسَآءَ. To affect with tenderness, pity, لَيَّنَ ـ حَنَّنَ ـ رَقَّقَ قَلْبَهُ. To appease, هَدَّأَ ـ أَهْدَأَ.

Soften, *v.i.* To become less hard, تَلَيَّنَ ـ دَاثَ ـُ. To become less tense, إِسْتَرْخَى ـ إِرْتَخَّ. To become less violent, of anger, *etc.*, تَهَدَّأَ ـ هَدَأَ ـَ; of the weather, إِعْتَدَلَ. To become tender, compassionate, رَقَّ قَلْبُهُ ـِ; of the voice, رَقَّ صَوْتُهُ ـِ.

Softener, *n.* مُلَيِّن.

Softening, *n.* تَلْيِين.

Soft-hearted, *a.* *See* Compassionate, *a.*

Softish, *a.* لَيِّنٌ نَوْعًا.

Softly, *ad.* Slowly, gently, عَلَى مَهْلٍ ـ رُوَيْدًا ـ هَدَادَيْكَ. Silently, بِٱلسُّكُوتِ. Secretly, سِرًّا. To go —, as on tiptoes to, قَارَ إِلَى ـُ. The wind blew —, نَسَمَتِ ٱلرِّيحُ. Waters that flow —, ٱلْمِيَاهُ ٱلْجَارِيَةُ بِهُدُوٍّ.

Softness, *n.* As opposed to hardness, لِينَة ـ لَيَان ـ دَيْث; as opposed to roughness, سُهُولَة ـ وَثَار. Want of tenseness, إِرْتِخَاخ ـ رِخَّة ـ رَخَاوَة ـ رَخَآء. Looseness, رَخَاوَة. Smoothness, مَلَاسَة. Mildness, لُطْف ـ حِلْم. Gentleness, رِفْق. Fineness, نُعُومَة. Softness of voice, خَفْضُ (*or*) رِقَّةُ ٱلصَّوْتِ. Effeminacy, خُنْث. Softness of the weather, إِعْتِدَالُ ٱلْهَوَآءِ.

Soft-toned, *a.* }
Soft-voiced, } حُلْوُ ٱلصَّوْتِ ـ خَفِيضُ ٱلصَّوْتِ.

Soho, *int.* أَيْهَا ـ أَيَا.

Soi-disant, *a.* ٱلْقَائِلُ أَنَّهُ كَذَا ـ مُدَّعٍ بِ.

Soil, *v.t.* To dirty, stain, قَذَّعَ ـ طَبَّعَ ـ لَوَّثَ ـ أَدْرَنَ.

Soil, *v.i.* تَطَبَّعَ ـ تَلَوَّثَ ـ دَرِنَ ـَ.

Soil, *n.* Earth, تُرَاب ـ أَرْض ـ أَثْرَآء *pl.* ثَرًى. A stain, daub, مَثْلَغَة ـ بُقْعَة ـ دَنَاسَة ـ طَبْعَة. A country, بَلْدَة. Rich —, أَرْضٌ سَمِينَةٌ. Night —, أَوْسَاخ.

Soirée, *n.* مُسَامَرَة ـ سَمَر; *vulg.* لَيْلِيَّة; place of a —, سَمِير.

Sojourn, *v.i.* As in a foreign country, تَغَرَّبَ فِي; in any place for a time, إِسْتَقَامَ فِي ـ حَطَّ فِي ـُ ـ إِحْتَلَّ بِ ـ حَلَّ بِ ـُ ـِ ـ قَعَدَ فِي ـُ.

Sojourn, *n.* As in a strange country, نُزُول ; in any place for a time, قُعُود ـ إِقَامَة ـ حُلُول .

Sojourner, *n.* As in a strange country, سَاكِن ـ نُزَلَآء *pl.* نَزِيل ; in any place for a time, حَالّ *pl.* حِلّ ـ حُلَّال *pl.* مُقِيم ـ حِلَّة *pl.* مُقِيمُون .

Sol, *n.* A musical note, إِسْمُ عَلَامَةٍ فِي ٱلْمُوسِيقَى .

Solace, *v.t.* سَلَّى . To — one for, أَسْلَى-عَن ـ عَزَّى-عَن . To be solaced, تَسَلَّى ; to be solaced for, تَلَهَّى عَن ـ تَعَزَّى عَن ـ تَسَلَّى عَن . *See also to* Comfort, Cheer, *v.t.*

Solace, *n.* تَسَلٍّ ـ فَرَج . *See also* Comfort, *n.*

Solacement, *n.* The act of solacing, تَعْزِيَة ـ إِسْلَآء . *See also* Solace, *n.*

Solan-goose, *n.* وَزَّةُ ٱلْبَحْرِ ٱلْجَامِدِ *coll.* إِوَزّ .

Solar, *a.* شَمْسِيّ . The — system, النِّظَامُ ـ النَّسَقُ ٱلشَّمْسِيّ . Solar spots, كُلَفٌ فِي قُرْصِ ٱلشَّمْسِ . A — year, سَنَةٌ ٱلشَّمْسِيّ . A — letter, حَرْفٌ شَمْسِيّ *pl.* حُرُوفٌ شَمْسِيَّة .

Sold, *part. of to* Sell, *q.v.*

Soldan, *n.* *See* Sultân, *n.*

Solder, *v.t.* لَحَمَ ² ـ . To be soldered, إِلْتَحَمَ .

Solder, *n.* لِحَام .

Soldier, *n.* جُنْدِيّ *pl.* جُنُود ـ عَسْكَرِيّ *pl.* عَسَاكِر . A private —, نَفَر ـ عَسْكَرِيّ *pl.* أَنْفَار . A fellow —, زَمِيل ـ مُتَجَنِّدٌ مَعَ فُلَانٍ . A — of fortune, جُنْدِيّ يَطُوفُ فِي أَثَرِ خِدْمَةٍ بِٱلْعَسْكَرِ .

Soldierlike, *a.*
Soldierly, } عَسْكَرِيّ ـ مِثْلَ ٱلْعَسْكَرِيّ .

Soldiership, *n.* عَسْكَرِيَّة .

Soldiery, *n.* عَسْكَرِيَّة ـ طَائِفَةُ ٱلْعَسْكَرِ ـ عَسَاكِر ـ جُنُود .

Sole, *n.* As of the foot, أَسْفَلُ ٱلْقَدَمِ ـ بَطْنُ ٱلْقَدَمِ ; of a shoe, نَعْل *pl.* نِعَال ـ صَلَّة *pl.* صِلَال ـ أَحْذِيَة *pl.* حِذَآء . A double —, نَعْلٌ خَصِيف ـ خَصْف . A second sole sewed to a previous one, طَارِقُ ٱلنَّعْلِ ; to sew on such a sole, طَرَّقَ . The fish, سَمَكُ مُوسَى . The — of a beast's hoof, صَحْنُ ٱلْحَافِرِ .

Sole, *v.t.* To put on a sole, جَعَلَ ـ نَعَلَ ـ خَصَفَ ٱلنَّعْلَ ل-نَعْلًا . To resole, جَعَلَ ل-نَعْلًا جَدِيدًا ـ نَعَلَ-ثَانِيَةً . *See also under* Sole, *n.*

Sole, *a.* Single, one, فَذّ *pl.* فُذُون ـ وَاحِد ـ مُجَرَّد ـ مُفْرَد . Unique, فَذّ *pl.* فُذُوذ ـ وَحِيد ـ فَرِيد . Unmarried, غَيْرُ مُزَوَّج ـ غَيْرُ مُتَأَهِّل ـ عَازِب *fem.* عَازِبَة . Our — object, غَايَتُنَا ٱلْوَحِيدَة .

Solecism, *n.* كَلَامٌ شَاذّ ـ كَلِمَةٌ شَاذَّة .

Solely, *ad.* Only, فَقَطْ . *See also* Only, *ad.*

Solemn, *a.* Grave, serious, of a person, وَقُور ـ رَصِين ـ رَزِين ; of a thing, عَظِيم ـ مُهِمّ ـ سَاكِنُ ٱلطَّائِرِ . Marked with pomp, جَلِيل ـ إِحْتِفَالِيّ ـ مُبَجَّل . Official, ritual, رَسْمِيّ . Sacred, مُحْتَرَم ـ مُقَدَّس ـ مُخْتَصّ . Connected with religious purposes, بِٱلدِّينِ وَٱلْعِبَادَةِ . A — day, festival, عِيد ـ يَوْمُ عِيدٍ *pl.* أَعْيَاد . A — meeting, جَمْعٌ حَافِل . A — occasion, such as the meeting of the pilgrims for Mekkah, يَوْمُ مَوْسِمٍ ـ مَوْسِم . A — sound, عَزِيف ـ عَزْف . A — or important matter, جَلَل *pl.* أَجْلَال .

Solemness, *n.* Gravity, as of countenance, *etc.*, وَقَار ـ رَزَانَة . Importance, عَظَامَة ـ جَسَامَة ـ أَهَمِّيَّة . Devoutness, worship, عِبَادَة .

Solemnity, *n.* A festival, عِيد *pl.* أَعْيَاد . An occasion of solemn concourse, مَوْسِم *pl.* مَوَاسِم . Pomp, بَهْجَة ـ أُبَّهَة ـ إِحْتِفَال ـ تَعْظِيم . Solemnities, formal acts, إِحْتِفَالَاتٌ رَسْمِيَّة ـ لَوَازِمُ رَسْمِيَّة ـ أُصُولٌ رَسْمِيَّة .

Solemnization, *n.* The act of celebrating with pomp, تَبْجِيل ـ الإِجْرَآءُ بِٱلْإِحْتِفَالِ ـ تَعْيِيد . Official —, إِحْتِفَالٌ رَسْمِيّ . The — of the sacraments, خِدْمَةُ ٱلْأَسْرَارِ .

Solemnize, *v.t.* To carry out with pomp, أَجْرَى-بِٱلْإِحْتِفَالِ ـ بَجَّلَ . He solemnized the festival, عَيَّدَ ٱلْعِيدَ . To —, as of the sacraments or any religious ordinance, خَدَمَ ² ـ أَجْرَى . The affair was solemnized with all pomp and splendour, جَرَى ٱلْأَمْرُ بِغَايَةِ ٱلْأُبَّهَةِ وَٱلْإِحْتِفَالِ .

Solemnly, *ad.* With reverence and devotion, بِوَقَارٍ وَتَعَبُّدٍ ; with pomp and ceremony, بِٱلْإِحْتِفَالِ ـ بِتَبْجِيلٍ . Officially, ritually, رَسْمًا . In a magnifying manner, تَعْظِيمًا ـ بِتَعْظِيمٍ . To protest or declare —, شَهِدَ ـ : I declare — to you, أُشْهِدُنَّ لَكُمْ .

Soleness, *n.* وَحْدَة .

Solfatara, *n.* ثُغْرٌ (or شَقٌّ) فِي جَبَلِ ٱلنَّارِ تَصْعَدُ مِنْهُ ٱلْبُخَارَاتُ .

Solfeggio, *n.* سِيَاقَةُ أُصُولِ ٱلْمُوسِيقَى .

Solicit, *v.t.* To ask, request, طَلَبَ إِلَى ² ـ دَعَا ـ دَعَا إِلَى . To importune, أَلَحَّ عَلَى ـ إِقْتَرَحَ عَلَى . To — in behalf of, تَوَسَّلَ إِلَى-فِي ـ تَشَفَّعَ إِلَى-فِي .

Solicitation, *n.* A request, طَلَبَة . A prayer, تَمَنٍّ ـ إِلْتِمَاس ـ رَجَآء . Importunity, إِقْتِرَاح ـ إِلْحَاح . Intervention in favour of, شَفَاعَة .

Solicitor, *n.* One who solicits, مُلْتَمِس ـ طَالِب . The lawyer so styled, وَكِيلُ ٱلدَّعَاوِي .

Solicitor-General, *n.* وَكِيلُ دَعَاوِي ٱلدَّوْلَةِ عُمُومًا .

Solicitous, *a.* Very desirous, مُشْتَاق ـ شَوَّاق ـ شَيِّق . Anxious, careful, مُهْتَمٌّ ـ عَانٍ ـ شَاجِنٌ ـ مَشْجُوٌّ ـ شَجِيٌّ. To be —, anxious, عَنِيَ aor. يَعْنَى ـ شَجِيَ ـ ² شَجُنَ ـ تَشَجَّنَ. To be — about, إِهْتَمَّ بِ ـ إِعْتَنَى بِ ـ إِغْتَمَّ عَلَى ـ ² هَمَّ بِ. To make —, شَجَّنَ ـ أَشْجَنَ ـ أَشْجَى ـ أَهَمَّ. Whoever is — about the interests, or honour, of the government, مَنْ يَهُمُّهُ شَأْنُ ٱلدَّوْلَةِ.

Solicitously, *ad.* With care and anxiety, بِٱهْتِمَامٍ ـ بِعَنَآءٍ ـ بِشَجَنٍ.

Solicitress, *n.* مُلْتَمِسَةٌ ـ طَالِبَةٌ.

Solicitude, *n.* إِهْتِمَامٌ ـ هَمٌّ ـ شَجَنٌ ـ شَجْوٌ ـ عَنَآءٌ. The object of —, هِمَّةٌ *pl.* هِمَمٌ.

Solid, *a.* Compact, hard, صَلِيبٌ ـ صُلْبٌ. Not fluid, جَامِدٌ ـ غَيْرُ سَائِلٍ. Not hollow, مُبْهَمٌ ـ أَبْهَمُ ـ مُصْمَتٌ ـ أَصْمَتُ ـ صَمَدٌ ـ أَصْمَدُ. Firm, strong, not fragile, مَتِينٌ ـ رَصِينٌ ـ مُحْكَمٌ ـ مُسْتَحْكَمٌ. Firm, not easily moved, رَاسِخٌ ـ ثَابِتٌ ـ مَاكِنٌ. Real, not superficial, حَقِيقِيٌّ ـ أَصِيلٌ. Whole, صَحِيحٌ ـ سَالِمٌ. Having geometrical dimensions, مُجَسَّمٌ. A — stone, حَجَرٌ أَصَمُّ. Solid judgment, حَزْمَةٌ ـ حَزْمٌ ـ عَقْلٌ مَتِينٌ ـ عَقْلٌ أَصِيلٌ. Having — judgment, حَازِمٌ *pl.* حَزَمَةٌ ـ حَزِيمٌ *pl.* حُزَمَآءُ. To become —, firm, strong, صَلُبَ ² ـ إِشْتَدَّ. To make —, hard, صَلَّبَ; to make —, firm, أَحْكَمَ ـ أَرْسَخَ. *See also* Compact, *a.*

A solid angle, زَاوِيَةٌ مُجَسَّمَةٌ.

A solid body, جِسْمٌ صُلْبٌ.

A solid foot, قَدَمٌ مُكَعَّبَةٌ.

A solid square, of soldiers, قَلْعَةٌ.

Solid, *n.* A solid body, جِسْمٌ صُلْبٌ. Solid, as opposed to liquid, food, solids, مَأْكُولَاتٌ كَٱلْخُبْزِ وَٱللَّحْمِ إِلَخْ.

Solidarity, *n.* إِشْتِرَاكٌ. A — of interests, مَنَافِعُ مُشْتَرَكَةٌ; of views, أَرَآءٌ مُشْتَرَكَةٌ.

Solidification, *n.* The act of making solid, تَجْمِيدٌ; of making firm, strong, تَقْرِيرٌ ـ تَحْكِيمٌ ـ تَأْكِيدٌ ـ تَشْيِيدٌ ـ تَقْوِيَةٌ.

Solidify, *v.t.* To make compact, hard, صَلَّبَ; to make to congeal, جَمَّدَ. To make firm, strong, شَيَّدَ ـ أَحْكَمَ ـ أَيَّدَ ـ ثَبَّتَ ـ قَرَّرَ.

Solidity, *n.* The quality of being solid, compact, صَلَابَةٌ; as opposed to liquidness, تَجْمِيدٌ ـ جُمُودٌ. Soundness, sedateness, رَصَانَةٌ ـ رَزَانَةٌ. The quality of being strong, firm, not fragile, مَتَانَةٌ. Firmness, strength, رُسُوخٌ ـ إِسْتِحْكَامٌ ـ قُوَّةٌ. Density, كَثَافَةٌ. Validity, soundness, صِحَّةٌ ـ حَقِيقَةٌ. Solidity, as of character, ثُبُوتٌ ـ ثَبَاتٌ ـ حَزْمٌ.

Solidly, *ad.* Compactly, بِصَلَابَةٍ. Validly, بِصِحَّةٍ. Firmly, بِٱسْتِحْكَامٍ ـ بِمَتَانَةٍ ـ بِرُسُوخٍ. With firmness of judgment, بِحَزْمٍ.

Solidness, *n.* *See* Solidity, *n.*

Solidungulous, *a.* ذُو حَوَافِرَ.

Solifidian, *n.* مِنْ مَذْهَبِ ٱلْقَائِلِينَ أَنَّ ٱلْإِيمَانَ بِدُونِ ٱلْأَعْمَالِ كَافٍ لِلْخَلَاصِ.

Soliloquist, *n.* مُخَاطِبُ نَفْسِهِ ـ مُشْتَرِكٌ.

Soliloquize, *v.i.* تَكَلَّمَ مَعَ نَفْسِهِ.

Soliloquy, *n.* كَلَامُ رَجُلٍ مَعَ نَفْسِهِ.

Soliped, *n.* حَيَوَانٌ ذُو حَوَافِرَ.

Solitaire, *n.* A game for one person, لُعْبَةٌ يَلْعَبُهَا شَخْصٌ بِمُفْرَدِهِ (or وَحْدَهُ). *See also* Hermit, Recluse, *n.*

Solitarily, *ad.* Alone, لِوَحْدِهِ ـ إِنْفِرَادًا. In seclusion, solitude, تَوَحُّشًا ـ بِوَحْشَةٍ. Dwelling —, سَاكِنٌ وَحْدَهُ.

Solitariness, *n.* Solitude, إِنْفِرَادٌ ـ وَحْدَةٌ. Seclusion, عُزْلَةٌ ـ إِحْتِجَابٌ. Dreariness, وَحْشَةٌ. *See* Loneliness, *n.*

Solitary, *a.* One, one single one, فَرْدٌ ـ فَارِدٌ. Separated, apart, مُنْفَرِدٌ ـ شَوَاذُّ *pl.* شَاذَّةٌ *fem.* شُذَّانٌ *pl.* شَاذٌّ ـ شَاذِبٌ. Retired, secluded, مُسْتَخْلٍ ـ مُجْتَنِبٌ ـ مُنْفَرِدٌ. A — place, خَلَآءٌ. A — tree, شَجَرَةٌ فَارِدٌ (or فَارِدَةٌ). A — deer, separated from the herd, ظَبْيَةٌ فَارِدٌ. To be —, تَوَحَّشَ ـ إِنْفَرَدَ ـ ِ ² شَذَّ. They wandered in a — desert, تَاهُوا فِي قَفْرٍ. *See also* Lonely, *a.*

Solitary, *n.* A hermit, recluse, مُتَوَحِّدٌ. One who devotes himself to devotion in solitude, مُسْتَخْلٍ.

Solitude, *n.* The state of being alone, خَلْوَةٌ ـ وَحْدَةٌ. A lonely place, مَوْضِعٌ مُنْفَرِدٌ ـ وَحْشَةٌ ـ خَلَآءٌ. To devote one's self to religious duties in —, ² خَلَا. *See also* Loneliness, *n.*

Solo, *n.* Of a song, أُغْنِيَّةٌ يُغَنِّي بِهَا مُغَنٍّ وَاحِدٌ; of a tune, نَغْمَةٌ يَضْرِبُ بِهَا نَوْبَاتِيٌّ وَاحِدٌ.

Solstice, *n.* نُقْطَةُ ٱلْإِنْقِلَابِ ـ إِنْقِلَابٌ. The summer —, ٱلْإِنْقِلَابُ ٱلصَّيْفِيُّ. The winter —, ٱلْإِنْقِلَابُ ٱلشَّتَوِيُّ.

Solstitial, *a.* مُتَعَلِّقٌ بِٱلْإِنْقِلَابِ. The — point, نُقْطَةُ ٱلْإِنْقِلَابِ. The — colure, دَائِرَةُ ٱلْإِنْقِلَابَيْنِ.

Solubility, *n.* قَابِلِيَّةُ ٱلْإِنْحِلَالِ ـ إِنْحِلَالٌ.

Soluble, *a.* يَنْحَلُّ ـ قَابِلُ ٱلْإِنْحِلَالِ.

Solubleness, *n.* *See* Solubility, *n.*

Solution, *n.* The act of dissolving or solving, حَلٌّ; the being solved or dissolved, إِنْحِلَالٌ. A —, infusion, مَآءٌ. Solution of continuity, إِنْقِطَاعٌ ـ إِنْفِصَامٌ. *See also* Extract, *n.*

Solvability, *n.*
Solvableness, } Ability to pay debts, مَقْدِرَةٌ عَلَى وَفَآءِ ٱلدَّيْنِ.

Solvable, *a.* That may be solved, يَنْحَلُّ ـ قَابِلُ ٱلْإِنْحِلَالِ. That may be paid, مِمَّا يُوفَى.

Solve, *v.t.* فَكَّ — حَلَّ [2].

Solvency, *n.* مَقْدِرَةٌ عَلَى وَفَآءِ ٱلدَّيْنِ.

Solvent, *a.* Able to pay all debts, قَادِرٌ عَلَى وَفَآءِ ٱلدَّيْنِ. Dissolving, حَالٌّ. A — man, مَلِيٌّ [3] *pl.* مِلَآءٌ *and* أَمْلِيَآءُ.

Solvent, *n.* A fluid that dissolves, مَآءٌ مُذَوِّبٌ — مَآءٌ مُحَلِّلٌ.

Sombre, *a.* } Sombrous, } مُظْلِمٌ — عَتِمٌ — مُغَيِّمٌ. *See also* Dull, *a.*

Some, *a.* بَعْضٌ — شَيْءٌ — مِنْ. He took some of the dinârs, أَخَذَ مِنَ ٱلدَّنَانِيرِ. Give me — bread, أَعْطِنِي خُبْزًا — أَعْطِنِي مِنَ ٱلْخُبْزِ. Some evils are lighter than others, بَعْضُ ٱلشَّرِّ أَهْوَنُ مِنْ بَعْضٍ. Some days, بِضْعَةُ أَيَّامٍ. Some say that ..., مِنْ قَائِلٍ أَنْ. Some few of them, قَلِيلُونَ مِنْهُمْ. Science is wide, but the acquiring of — of it is better than neglecting the whole, ٱلْعِلْمُ كَثِيرٌ وَلٰكِنْ أَخْذُ ٱلْبَعْضِ خَيْرٌ مِنْ تَرْكِ ٱلْكُلِّ. Some people say, قَوْمٌ يَقُولُونَ — بَعْضٌ مِنَ ٱلنَّاسِ يَقُولُ. Some one of us, بَعْضُنَا — أَحَدُنَا. We have mentioned — incidents of the occurrence, ذَكَرْنَا طَرَفًا مِنَ ٱلْحَادِثَةِ. Sometimes, تَارَةً — بَعْضُ مِرَارٍ.

Somebody, *n.* أَحَدٌ — وَاحِدٌ. Somebody touched me, قَدْ لَمَسَنِي وَاحِدٌ. Somebody wants you, وَاحِدٌ طَلَبَكَ — وَاحِدٌ يُرِيدُكَ. He boasted that he was —, قَالَ عَنْ نَفْسِهِ أَنَّهُ شَيْءٌ. *See also* Somewhat, *ad.*

Somehow, *ad.* After a manner, بِوَجْهٍ مِنَ ٱلْوُجُوهِ — بِوَجْهٍ. Somehow or other, بِأَيِّ وَجْهٍ مِنَ ٱلْوُجُوهِ — كَيْفَمَا كَانَ.

Somersault, *n.* } Somerset, } إِنْتِكَاسٌ. To turn a —, إِنْتَكَسَ; *vulg.* تَشَقْلَبَ — إِنْقَلَبَ عَجُزُهُ عَلَى صَدْرِهِ. To make another turn a —, قَلَّبَ عَجُزَهُ عَلَى صَدْرِهِ — نَكَّسَ [2].

Something, *n.* An indeterminate thing, شَيْءٌ مَا — شَيْءٌ. A portion more or less of ..., شَيْءٌ مِنْ — مِنْ. A little, قَلِيلٌ — يَسِيرٌ. Something else, besides, شَيْءٌ ثَانٍ — شَيْءٌ غَيْرُهُ. Something different to this, شَيْءٌ خِلَافُ هٰذَا. He directed that — should be given her to eat, قَالَ أَنْ تُعْطَى لِتَأْكُلَ [2]. He has — to say to you, عِنْدَهُ شَيْءٌ لِيَقُولَهُ لَكَ. *See also* Somewhat, *a.*

Sometime, *n.* and *ad.* خَطْرَةً — حِينًا — حِينًا مَا. Sometime, of the past, سَابِقًا — فِي مَا مَضَى مِنَ ٱلزَّمَانِ; of the future, فِيمَا بَعْدُ — فِي ٱلْمُسْتَقْبِلِ.

Sometimes, *ad.* وَقْتًا — طَوْرًا — تَارَةً — عَلَى تَارَةٍ — تَارَةً وَطَوْرًا — أَحْيَانًا — بَعْضُ مِرَارٍ — بَعْضُ أَوْقَاتٍ.

Somewhat, *n.* and *ad.* Something, شَيْءٌ — شَيْءٌ مَا. He is — better than you, هُوَ أَحْسَنُ مِنْكَ شَيْئًا. I have — to say to you, لِي مَعَكَ كَلِمَةٌ. I will take — from him, آخِذُ مِنْهُ شَيْئًا. I have — against you, لِي عَلَيْكَ شَيْءٌ. Somewhat, in a measure, نَوْعًا: It is — black, هُوَ أَسْوَدُ نَوْعًا.

Somewhere, *ad.* بِمَكَانٍ — بِمَكَانٍ مَّا. Somewhere else, بِمَكَانٍ آخَرَ — فِي مَوْضِعٍ آخَرَ — فِي غَيْرِ مَحَلٍّ.

Somewhile, *ad.* *See* Sometime, *n.* and *ad.*

Somnambulate, *v.i.* مَشَى وَهُوَ نَائِمٌ ٥.

Somnambulation, *n.* } Somnambulism, } ٱلْمَشْيُ فِي ٱلنَّوْمِ.

Somnambulist, *n.* مَاشٍ وَهُوَ نَائِمٌ.

Somniferous, *a.* } Somnific, } مُنَوِّمٌ — مُرَقِّدٌ.

Somniloquist, *n.* مُتَكَلِّمٌ وَهُوَ نَائِمٌ — مُتَكَلِّمٌ فِي نَوْمِهِ.

Somniloquous, *a.* مُبَادِرٌ إِلَى ٱلْكَلَامِ وَهُوَ نَائِمٌ.

Somniloquy, *n.* } Somniloquism, } ٱلْكَلَامُ فِي ٱلنَّوْمِ.

Somnolence, *n.* } Somnolency, } Sleepiness, نُعَاسٌ — كَرًى; as from disease, سُبَاتٌ. *See also* Drowsiness, *n.*

Somnolent, *a.* نَعْسَانُ — نَاعِسٌ — كَرْيَانُ — كَرِيٌّ. *See also* Drowsy, *a.*

Son, *n.* A male child, وَلَدٌ *pl.* أَوْلَادٌ *and* وُلْدٌ — إِبْنٌ (when not immediately preceded by a quiescent, written ٱبْنٌ; and when immediately preceded by the proper name of a man and followed by that of his parent, written بْنُ); *pl.* بَنُونَ (*acc.* and *gen* بَنِينَ) *and* أَبْنَآءٌ. Son, in the sense of a descendant, إِبْنٌ *as above.* (Of kings and distinguished personages the word نَجْلٌ *pl.* أَنْجَالٌ is used for "son.") A little son, as a term of endearment, بُنَيٌّ. Zaid the son of 'Amru, زَيْدُ بْنُ عَمْرٍو. Zaid is the son of 'Amru, زَيْدٌ ٱبْنُ عَمْرٍو. Sons, in the sense of descendants, including daughters, بَنُونَ: the sons of such an one, بَنُو فُلَانٍ; a woman of the sons (people) of Tamîm, إِمْرَأَةٌ مِنْ بَنِي تَمِيمٍ. He took him as his son, adopted him, إِتَّخَذَهُ ٱبْنًا.

Son-in-law, *n.* صِهْرٌ *pl.* أَصْهَارٌ — خَتَنٌ *pl.* أَخْتَانٌ — زَوْجُ بِنْتٍ.

Sonata, *n.* مَقَامَةٌ لِلْمُوسِيقَى فَقَطْ.

Song, *n.* The act of singing, غِنَآءٌ — سَمَاعٌ; of a bird, تَرَنُّمٌ — غَرَدٌ. That which is sung, غِنَآءٌ *pl.* أَغَانٍ — نَشِيدٌ *pl.* أَنَاشِيدُ — غِنْيَةٌ — أُغْرُودَةٌ *pl.* أَغَارِيدُ — أُغْنِيَّةٌ *pl.* أَغَانِيُّ *and* أَغَانٍ. A poem, شِعْرٌ *pl.* أَشْعَارٌ. A tune, مَقَامَةٌ *pl.* مَقَامَاتٌ — صَوْتٌ *pl.* أَصْوَاتٌ. Sing us a song, غَنِّ لَنَا بِغُنْيَةٍ — رَنِّمْ لَنَا تَرْنِيمَةً. To make a — of, either in praise or dispraise, غَنَّى (or تَغَنَّى) بِ. To make songs of, in satire, هَجَا بِأَغَانٍ [2].

Songster, *n.* A warbler, of a bird, *etc.*, مُغَرِّد ـ غِرِّيد. *See also* Singer, *n.*

Songstress, *n.* A female warbler, مُغَرِّدَة ـ غِرِّيدَة. *See also under* Singer, *n.*

Soniferous, *a.* طَنَّان ـ رَنَّان.

Sonnet, *n.* قَصِيدَة *pl.* قَصَائِد. A love —, in praise of woman, مَغْزَل ـ غَزَل.

Sonneteer, *n.* شَاعِرُ ٱلْغَزَلِ ـ مُؤَلِّفُ ٱلْقَصَائِدِ.

Sonorific, *a.* طَنَّان ـ رَنَّان.

Sonorous, *a.* مُطَنْطِن ـ طَنَّان ـ رَنَّان ـ ذُو شِقْشِقَةٍ: His utterance was — and fluent, هَدَرَتْ شِقْشِقَتُهُ. A — ode, قَصِيدَةٌ طَنَّانَةٌ.

Sonorously, *ad.* بِطَنْطَنَةٍ ـ بِطَنِينٍ ـ بِرَنَّةٍ ـ بِشِقْشِقَةٍ.

Sonorousness, *n.* طَنْطَنَة ـ طَنِين ـ رَنَّة ـ شِقْشِقَة.

Sonship, *n.* بُنُوَّة.

Soon, *ad.* Quickly, بِسُرْعَةٍ ـ عَلَى ٱلْعَجَلِ. Shortly, عَنْ قَرِيبٍ ـ عَنْ قَلِيلٍ ـ عَنْ عَهْدٍ قَرِيبٍ. Very —, بِغَايَةِ ٱلسُّرْعَةِ. You have come very — to-day, أَسْرَعْتُمُ ٱلْمَجِيءَ ٱلْيَوْمَ. As — as possible, فِي أَقْرَبِ وَقْتٍ. They will — perish, سَيَبِيدُونَ سَرِيعًا. As — as he comes, عِنْدَ مَجِيئِهِ. He will return —, سَيَعُودُ قَرِيبًا. *See also under* Lief, *ad.*

Sooner, *ad.* Rather than, قَبْلَ أَنْ. Before, قَبْلًا. I will return to you the —, أَرْجِعُ إِلَيْكُمْ بِأَكْثَرِ سُرْعَةٍ. No — did the sun rise than the grass was dried up, الشَّمْسُ أَشْرَقَتْ فَتَيَبَّسَ ٱلْعُشْبُ. *See also under* Rather, *ad.*

Soot, *n.* سُخَام ـ شُحَّار. He blackened his face with —, سَخَّمَ وَجْهَهُ.

Soot, *v.t.* سَخَّمَ ـ لَوَّثَ بِشُحَّارٍ.

Sooth, *n.* حَقِيقَة ـ حَقّ. In —, حَقِيقَةً. *See also* Forsooth, *ad.*

Soothe, *v.t.* To calm, appease, as of a pain, سَكَّنَ ـ هَدَّأَ ـ أَهْدَأَ ـ لَيَّنَ. To —, in the sense of comforting, دَارَى ـ رَافَى ـ لَثَّمَ ـ سَلَّى. To flatter, to wheedle, دَارَى ـ وَادَّ ـ تَلَيَّنَ لِ ـ طَيَّبَ نَفْسَهُ.

Soother, *n.*
Soothing, *a.* } مُطَيِّب ـ مُلَثِّم ـ مُلَيِّن.

Soothingly, *ad.* بِرَأْفَةٍ ـ بِمُدَارَاةٍ.

Soothsay, *v.t.* كَاهَنَ. *See also to* Foretell, Predict, *v.t.*

Soothsayer, *n.* عَرَّاف *pl.* عَرَّافُونَ ـ كَاهِن *pl.* كَهَنَة *and* كُهَّان.

Soothsaying, *n.* كِهَانَة ـ عِرَافَة. To practise —, تَكَهَّنَ.

Sootiness, *n.* *See* Soot, *n.*

Sooty, *a.* شُحَّارِيّ ـ سُخَامِيّ.

Sop, *n.* A morsel, لُقْمَة. Soft food, for the sick, أَمْوِيَة. Bread moistened in broth or other liquor, ثَرِيدَة ـ ثَرِيد. A douceur, present, هَدِيَّة ـ حَلَاوَة ـ حُلْوَان. To quiet with a —, douceur, سَكَّتَ بِحُلْوَانٍ. To throw a — to, to wheedle, bribe, دَهَنَ [2] ـ بَرْطَلَ.

Sop, *v.t.* To steep, as in liquor, رَبَّغَ ـ رَوَّلَ ـ مَرَّغَ ـ رَوَّغَ ـ غَمَسَ.

Soph, *n.* *See* Sophister, *n.*

Sophism, *n.* أُغْلُوطَة ـ سَفْسَطَة. *See also* Fallacy, *n.*

Sophist, *n.* سَفْسَطِيّ *pl.* سَفْسَطِيَّة ـ مَغْلَطَانِيّ.

Sophister, *n.* تِلْمِيذٌ مُقِيمٌ فِي دَارِ ٱلْفُنُونِ مُدَّةَ ثَلَاثِ سِنِينَ.

Sophistic, *a.*
Sophistical, } سَفْسَطِيّ. *See also* Fallacious, *a.*

Sophistically, *ad.* بِسَفْسَطَةٍ ـ مُغَالَطَةً ـ بِأُغْلُوطَةٍ. *See also* Fallaciously, *ad.*

Sophisticate, *v.t.*
Sophisticate, *a.*
Sophisticated, } To adulterate, شَابَ *aor.* يَشُوبُ ـ زَغَلَ ـ غَشَّ [2]. *See also to* Adulterate, *v.t.*

Sophistication, *n.* زَغَل ـ غِشّ ـ شَوْب. *See also* Adulteration, *n.*

Sophisticator, *n.* زُغَلِيّ ـ غَشَّاش ـ شَائِب.

Sophistry, *n.* سَفْسَطَة ـ غَلُوطَة ـ مَغْلَطَة.

Sophomore, *n.* تِلْمِيذٌ مُقِيمٌ فِي دَارِ ٱلْفُنُونِ مُدَّةَ سَنَتَيْنِ.

Soporiferous, *a.*
Soporific, } مُنَوِّم ـ مُرَقِّد.

Soporific, *n.* دَوَآءٌ مُنَوِّمٌ ـ سُلْوَان.

Soprano, *n.* أَعْلَى صَوْتٍ ـ نَبْرَة.

Sorbent, *a.* *See* Absorbent, *a.*

Sorcerer, *n.* سَاحِر *pl.* سَحَرَة.

Sorceress, *n.* سَاحِرَة *pl.* سَاحِرَات.

Sorcery, *n.* سِحْر.

Sordid, *a.* Avaricious, خَسِيس ـ بَخِيل. Mean, دَنِيء ـ حَقِير ـ نَجِس ـ قَذِر ـ مَذِر ـ دَرِن. Filthy, سَفِيل ـ سَفِل.

Sordidly, *ad.* Niggardly, بِخَسَاسَةٍ ـ بِبُخْلٍ. Meanly, بِدَنَاءَةٍ ـ بِحَقَارَةٍ ـ كَٱلسَّفِيلِ. Filthily, نَجِسًا ـ مَذِرًا ـ بِدَرَنٍ.

Sordidness, *n.* Niggardliness, خَسَاسَة ـ بُخْل ـ جُحْد. Meanness, دَنَس ـ دَنَاسَة ـ دَرَن ـ رَذَالَة ـ حَقَارَة ـ دَنَآءَة. Filthiness, قَذَر.

Sore, *n.* قَرْح *pl.* قُرُوح ـ جُرْح *pl.* جُرُوح ـ قَرْحَة. A gall, دَبَر *pl.* أَدْبَار. An affliction, ضَرْبَة ـ مُصِيبَة ـ آفَة *pl.* آفَات. Full of sores, مَضْرُوبٌ بِٱلْقُرُوحِ.

Sore, *a.* Of a wound, painful, مُتَوَجِّع ـ أَلِيم ـ مُوجِع. Distressing, مُحْزِن ـ فَاجِع ـ مُضْجِر ـ شَاقّ. Serious, hard, شَدِيد. Sensitive, رَقِيقُ ٱلْقَلْبِ ـ لَيِّنُ ٱلْجَانِبِ. A — disease, مَرَضٌ رَدِيٌّ. A — conflict, قِتَالٌ شَدِيدٌ ـ مَلْحَمَةٌ. Sore eyes, دَآءُ ٱلْعَيْنَيْنِ: having — eyes, ophthalmia, رَمَدٌ. أَرْمَدُ fem. رَمْدَآءُ pl. رُمْدٌ. I have neither — nor ache, مَا أَجِدُ أَيْلَمَةً وَلَا أَلَمَةً. While they were still —, إِنْ كَانُوا مُتَوَجِّعِينَ. Sore ears, دَآءُ ٱلْآذَانِ. To be —, painful, أَلِمَ ـ وَجِعَ aor. يَجَعُ. To make —, to wound, جَرَحَ.

Sore, *ad.* Sorely, } Painfully, بِأَلَمٍ ـ أَلَمَةً ـ بِوَجَعٍ. Distressingly, بِصُعُوبَةٍ ـ بِمَشَقَّةٍ ـ بِضَجَرٍ. Hardly, strongly, much, لِلْغَايَةِ ـ جِدًّا ـ كَثِيرًا. They pressed — on him, أَلَحُّوا عَلَيْهِ جِدًّا. The famine waxed —, إِشْتَدَّ ٱلْجُوعُ. He was — distressed, تَضَايَقَ جِدًّا. He wept —, بَكَى بُكَآءً عَظِيمًا. He was — displeased with himself, إِغْتَاظَ عَلَى نَفْسِهِ جِدًّا.

Soreness, *n.* As of a wound, *etc.*, وَجَع ـ أَلَم. Sensitiveness of mind, رِقَّةُ ٱلْجَانِبِ ـ لِينَةُ ٱلْجَانِبِ ـ رِقَّةُ قَلْبٍ. Distress, ثِقَل ـ شِدَّة.

Sorites, *n.* قِيَاسٌ مُسَلْسَلٌ.

Sorrel, *n.* The plant, حُمَّيْض ـ حُمَّاض. The flower of the —, الثَّامِرُ.

Sorrel, *a.* Of the colour, أَشْقَرُ fem. شَقْرَآءُ pl. شُقْرٌ ـ أَصْدَأُ.

Sorrily, *ad.* Meanly, بِحَقَارَةٍ ـ بِمَسْكَنَةٍ. Clumsily, بِخُرْقٍ ـ بِقِلَّةِ مَعْرِفَةٍ. *See also* Poorly, *ad.*

Sorriness, *n.* Meanness, paltriness, حَقَارَة ـ مَسْكَنَة ـ تَفَاهَة ـ رَكَاكَة ـ دَنَآءَة ـ قَذَارَة.

Sorrow, *n.* مَشَقَّة ـ غَمّ ـ حُزْن ـ كَدَر ـ كَرْب ـ شَجَب. To have —, إِحْتَزَنَ ـ حَزِنَ ـ شَجِبَ ـ شَجَبَ. To express —, تَشَجَّبَ ـ تَحَزَّنَ. To express — for, تَأَسَّفَ عَلَى ـ تَحَزَّنَ عَلَى.

Sorrow, *v.i.* حَزِنَ ـ إِكْتَرَبَ ـ تَأَسَّفَ ـ إِنْغَمَّ ـ كَئِبَ. *See also preceding article, and to* Grieve, *v.i.*

Sorrowful, *a.* Grieving, سَجِب ـ حَزِين ـ أَسِيف ـ كَئِيب ـ مُؤْلِم ـ شَاقّ ـ فَاجِع ـ مَكْرُوب ـ مَغْمُوم ـ كَرِيب. Distressing, مُحْزِن. Of a — spirit, حَزِينُ ٱلرُّوحِ. He went away —, مَضَى حَزِينًا. To make —, أَغَمَّ ـ كَدَّرَ ـ شَجَبَ ـ أَكْأَبَ ـ آسَفَ ـ أَحْزَنَ.

Sorrowfully, *ad.* Painfully, بِحُزْنٍ ـ أَلَمَةً ـ بِوَجَعٍ. Distressingly, بِضِيقٍ ـ بِصُعُوبَةٍ ـ بِمَشَقَّةٍ.

Sorrowfulness, *n.* *See* Sorrow, *n.*

Sorry, *a.* Pained, grieved, حَزِين ـ مُكَدَّر. To be — for, to bemoan, حَسِرَ عَلَى ـ تَلَهَّفَ عَلَى; to repent of, تَنَدَّمَ عَلَى ـ

يُهِمُّنَا أَنْ نَعْلَمَ أَنْ رَجَعَ عَنْ. We are — to learn that..., We are — to repeat here, يَسُوءُنَا أَنْ نُعِيدَ هُنَا. We were —, قَدْ غَمَّنَا. *See also under* Sorrowful, *a.*

Sort, *n.* A kind, جِنْس pl. أَجْنَاس ـ نَوْع pl. أَنْوَاع ـ قَبِيل ـ صِنْف pl. أَصْنَاف ـ شَكْل pl. أَشْكَال ـ فَنّ pl. فُنُون ـ قُبُل pl. A quality, صِفَة pl. صِفَات ـ شَأْن pl. شُؤُون ـ مَاهِيَّة ـ كَيْفِيَّة. A manner, مِنْوَال ـ بَاب ـ وَجْه ـ أُسْلُوب. A class, طَوْر pl. أَطْوَار: Mankind are of divers sorts, النَّاسُ أَطْوَارٌ. Of all sorts, مِنْ جَمِيعِ ٱلْأَشْكَالِ ـ مُتَنَوِّع ـ مِنْ أَشْكَالٍ وَأَلْوَانٍ ـ أَشْكَالًا أَشْكَالًا. A man of your —, وَاحِدٌ مِثْلُكَ ـ رَجُلٌ مِنْ مَقَامِكَ. In some —, to some extent, نَوْعًا مَا ـ نَوْعًا; in a small degree, يَسِيرًا. Of the baser —, of men, مِنَ ٱلْأَسَافِلِ ـ مِنْ أَهْلِ ٱلسُّوقِ. After this —, in this manner, عَلَى هٰذَا ٱلْمِنْوَالِ ـ هٰكَذَا. Out of sorts, indisposed, مُشَوَّش ـ عَلِيل ـ مُنْحَرِفُ ٱلْمِزَاجِ ـ شَاكٍ ـ مَشْكُوّ. To be out of sorts, شَكَا aor. يَشْكُو.

Sort, *v.t.* To dispose in sorts, رَتَّبَ أَشْكَالًا ـ صَنَّفَ ـ صَفَّفَ أَصْنَافًا. To — from, to separate from, as in selecting, نَقَّى ـ مَيَّزَ مِنْ ـ أَفْرَزَ عَنْ.

Sort, *v.i.* To be joined with others of the same species, إِنْضَافَ إِلَى صِنْفٍ. To — with, نَاسَبَ ـ طَابَقَ ـ وَافَقَ.

Sortable, *a.* That may be disposed in sorts, يُمْكِنُ تَرْتِيبُهُ أَصْنَافًا ـ تَصْفِيفُهُ فِي أَشْكَالٍ مُمْكِن. Sortable with, suitable to, مُوَافِقٌ لِ.

Sortie, *n.* *See* Sally, *n.*

Sortilege, *n.* ضَرْبُ قُرْعَةٍ ـ قُرْعَة.

Sostenuto, a. عِبَارَةٌ عَنْ مَدِّ ٱلصَّوْتِ فِي ٱلْمُوسِيقَى.

Sot, *n.* A drunkard, شَرَّاب ـ سَكِر ـ سِكِّير. A stupid fellow, تَيْس ـ ثَوْر ـ بَهِيم ـ أَحْمَقُ ـ بَلِيد.

Sottish, *a.* Given to liquor, سَكْرَانُ pl. سُكَارَى ـ شَرَّاب ـ سِكِّير. Dull, stupid, أَحْمَقُ ـ بَلِيد ـ أَخْرَقُ.

Sottishly, *ad.* كَٱلتَّيْسِ ـ بِحَمَاقَةٍ ـ بِبَلَادَةٍ.

Sottishness, *n.* تَيْسُوسِيَّة ـ تَيْسِيَّة ـ حَمَاقَة ـ بَلَادَة.

Sotto voce, a. عِبَارَةٌ عَنْ خَفْضِ ٱلصَّوْتِ فِي ٱلْمُوسِيقَى.

Souchong, *n.* ضَرْبٌ مِنَ ٱلشَّايِ ٱلْأَسْوَدِ.

Sough, *n.* A murmur of the wind, دَوِيُّ ٱلرِّيحِ ـ هَزِيز.

Sought, *part. of to* Seek, *v.i.* Sought after, مَرْغُوب ـ مَطْلُوب.

Soul, *n.* The spiritual part of man, النَّفْسُ ـ الجَائِشَة ـ الجَاشُ pl. الأَنْفُسُ or النُّفُوسُ. Spirit, life, رُوح pl. أَرْوَاح. Conscience, ضَمِير ـ فُؤَاد ـ مَحَلُّ ٱلسِّرِّ. Mind, ذِمَّة. The rational —, الرُّوحُ ٱلنَّفْسُ ٱلنَّاطِقَةُ ـ ٱلْحَيَوَانِيَّةُ. Spirit, energy, حَزْم ـ جِدّ ـ مُرُوءَة ـ هِمَّة ـ غَيْرَة ـ عَارِضَة. Taste, relish, desire, نَفْس ـ

ذَوْق ـ شَوْق. Upon my soul! عَلَى ذِمَّتِي. God rest his soul! رَحِمَهُ ٱللّٰهُ. His — departed from him, خَرَجَتْ رُوحُهُ. *See also* Heart, *n.*

Soul-destroying, *a.* مُهْلِك ـ مُتْلِفُ ٱلنَّفْسِ.

Soulless, *a.* Without a soul, بِلَا نَفْسٍ. Spiritless, بِلَا مُرُوَّةٍ ـ بِلَا غَيْرَةٍ. Mean, دَنِيّ ـ حَقِير. "And when the souls shall be joined (to their bodies,)" وَإِذَا ٱلنُّفُوسُ زُوِّجَتْ (Kûr. lxxxi. 7.)

Sound, *n.* Noise, voice, صَوْت *pl.* أَصْوَات. A low or plaintive —, رَنَّة ـ حِسّ ـ جِرْس ـ جَرْس ـ جَرَس. A —, as of music, لَحْن *pl.* أَلْحَان ـ عَزْف. A word, voice, لَفْظَة *pl.* أَلْفَاظ. A dreadful —, صَوْتٌ مُرْعِب. A gentle —, صَوْتٌ خَفِيض. A loud —, صَوْتٌ جَهِير. The — of a trumpet, صَوْتُ ٱلْبُوقِ. A narrow sea, خَلِيج *pl.* خُلْجَان ـ بُوغَاز. A probe, مِيل ـ مِجَسّ ـ مِسْبَار ـ مَجَسَّاس. The — or air-bladder of a fish, آلَةُ ٱلتَّنَفُّسِ فِي ٱلسَّمَكِ. I heard no — of him, مَا سَمِعْتُ لَهُ جَرْسًا ـ مَا سَمِعْتُ لَهُ حِسًّا وَلَا جَرْسًا. To emit a sharp —, طَنَّ ـ ٣ طَنَّنَ ـ طَنْطَنَ.

Sound, *a.* Entire, whole, صَحِيح ـ سَالِم. Healthy, صَحِيح ـ فِي حَالَةِ ٱلصِّحَّةِ وَٱلْعَافِيَةِ ـ مُعَاف. Right, not erroneous, صَحِيح ـ حَقِيقِيّ. Compact, firm, without defect, حَصِيف ـ رَصِين ـ بِلَا عَيْب ـ ثَابِت. Good, طَيِّب. A — title, حَقٌّ شَرْعِيٌّ. Sound doctrine, تَعْلِيمٌ صَحِيحٌ. Of — judgment, ذُو رَأْيٍ رَصِينٍ ـ مُسْتَحْصِدُ ٱلرَّأْيِ ـ أَصِيلُ ٱلرَّأْيِ ـ حَصِيف. Valid, جَائِز ـ شَرْعِيّ ـ صَحِيح. To be —, ٢ صَحَّ. He received him safe and —, قَبِلَهُ سَالِمًا. To be —, as in judgment, ٢ حَصُفَ. To make —, إِسْتَحْصَفَ. To become —, firm, ٢ رَصُنَ. أَحْكَمَ ـ أَرْصَفَ ـ صَحَّحَ.

Sound, *v.t.* To cause to make a sound, صَوَّتَ ـ أَصَاتَ. To ring, ٢ دَقَّ. To —, of a musical instrument, عَزَفَ ـ ٣ ٢ دَقَّ ـ ٣ ضَرَبَ. To pronounce, تَلَفَّظَ ـ ٣ لَفَظَ ب ـ ٣ لَفَظَ. To inquire of, look into, ٢ عَسَّ ـ ٢ نَصَّ. To probe, as a wound, or to look narrowly into anything, ٣ ٢ سَبَرَ ـ إِسْتَبَرَ. To —, as of the sea, to ascertain the depth, ٣ قَاسَ ٱلْمَاءَ ـ ٢ سَبَرَ ٱلْمَاءَ. To — abroad, أَفْشَى ـ أَذَاعَ ـ أَشَاعَ. He sounded his opinion, إِسْتَطْلَعَ لِرَأْيِهِ. By way of sounding his opinion, إِسْتِطْلَاعًا لِرَأْيِهِ.

Sound, *v.i.* To emit a sound, صَاتَ ـ ٣ رَنَّ ـ أَرَنَّ ـ رَنَّنَ *aor.* أَصَاتَ ـ صَوَّتَ ـ يَصُوتُ. To resound, صَلْصَلَ ـ ٣ صَلَّ. To be sounded abroad, إِنْتَشَرَ ـ ٣ فَاضَ ـ ٢ فَشَا. The trumpet sounded long, ٢ طَالَ صَوْتُ ٱلْبُوقِ.

Sound-headed, *a.* عَاقِل ـ حَصِيف ـ مُسْتَحْصِدُ ٱلرَّأْيِ.

Sound-hearted, *a.* ذَكِيُّ ٱلْقَلْبِ ـ سَلِيمُ ٱلْقَلْبِ.

Sound-board, *n.* } لَوْحٌ لِرَدِّ صَدَى ٱلصَّوْتِ. (The —, or outer
Sounding-board, } sounding body of a viol is called حُقَّة.)

Sounding, *n.* The act of uttering noise, تَصْوِيت ـ رَنِين ـ صَوْت; of resounding, طَنِين ـ صَلِيل; of endeavouring to ascertain thought or depth, سَبْر ـ إِسْتِبَار. To take soundings, ٣ ٢ سَبَرَ ٱلْمَاءَ ـ ٣ قَاسَ ٱلْمَاءَ بِٱلْبَلَدِ. To get into soundings, ٢ بَلَغَ حَيْثُ يُسْبَرُ ٱلْمَاءُ.

Sounding, *a.* Emitting a sound, رَنَّان ـ صَوَّات ـ صَائِت. Sounding brass, نُحَاسٌ يَطِنُّ. Sounding trumpets, as for triumph, أَبْوَاقُ ٱلْهُتَافِ.

Sounding-lead, *n.* *See* Lead, *n.*

Soundless, *a.* عَدِيمُ ٱلْحِسِّ ـ بِلَا حِسّ ـ غَيْرُ صَائِتٍ.

Soundly, *ad.* Safely, بِسَلَامَةٍ ـ سَلَامَةً; healthfully, بِمُعَافَاةٍ ـ فِي صِحَّةٍ; well, جَيِّدًا ـ بِرَصَانَةٍ ـ حَسَنًا; severely, بِشِدَّةٍ. To do anything —, أَرْصَنَ. To scold —, ٣ سَخِطَ عَلَى ـ بِشِدَّةٍ ـ ٣ صَعِدَ ب ـ وَنَزَلَ. To reason —, ٢ طَبَّ فِي ٱلْحُجَجِ. To sleep —, ٣ غَرِقَ فِي ٱلنَّوْمِ. Whatever thing you do, do it —, إِذَا عَمِلْتَ عَمَلًا فَأَرْصِنْهُ.

Soundness, *n.* Wholeness, integrity, صِحَّة. Healthfulness, صِحَّة ـ عَافِيَة. Compactness, حَصَافَة. Soundness of judgment, إِسْتِحْصَادُ ٱلرَّأْيِ ـ حَصَافَة. Vigour, قُوَّة ـ مُكْنَة. Rectitude, رَشَاد ـ إِسْتِقَامَة ـ رُشْد. Validity, صِحَّة ـ تَجْوِيز. Orthodoxy, صِحَّةُ ٱلْعَقَائِدِ. Firmness, ثَبَات ـ ثُبُوت. Determination, جَزْم.

Soup, *n.* شُورَبَة ـ فَتَّة ـ حَسَاء. Broth, or gravy —, سُلُوقَة ـ مَرَقَة. Vegetable —, شُورَبَةُ ٱلْبُقُولِ. Turtle —, شُورَبَةُ سُلَحْفَى.

Soupçon, *n.* A smack, taste, عِرْق ـ ذَوْق.

Sour, *a.* Acid, حَامِض ـ حَازِر ـ قَارِص ـ ثَقِيف; specially of milk, قَاطِع ـ مَضِير ـ مَاضِر; of wine, مُخْتَلّ. Morose, عَنِيف ـ وَعِق ـ شَرِس ـ كَشِر ـ عَبَّاس. Musty, مُعَفَّن. To be —, acid, ٢ حَمُضَ; of wine, تَخَلَّلَ ـ إِخْتَلَّ ـ خَلَّلَ ـ ٢ مَضَرَ; of milk, ٢ مَضَرَ. To look —, morosely, تَعَبَّسَ ـ تَقَطَّبَ. To be —, harsh, to, عَاسَرَ ـ شَارَسَ ـ عَنَّفَ ـ ٢ عَنُفَ ب.

Sour, *v.t.* To make sour, حَمَّضَ. To make harsh, as in temper, أَغَاظَ ـ غَيَّظَ. To —, as one's happiness, ٣ عَكَسَ ـ خَسَّرَ ـ أَفْسَدَ ـ خَرَّبَ.

Sour, *v.i.* To become sour; *see under* Sour, *a.*

Source, *n.* A spring, fountain, يَنْبُوع *pl.* يَنَابِيع ـ عَيْن *pl.* عُيُون *and* أَعْيُن ـ مَنْبَع. That from which anything springs, origin, مَخْرَج ـ مَنْشَأ ـ مَبْدَأ ـ أَصْل ـ مَصْدَر. A —, as of information, مَوْرِد. A cause, سَبَب *pl.* أَسْبَاب ـ عِلَّة *pl.* عِلَل. A root, عِرْق *pl.* عُرُوق ـ جُرْثُومَة ـ أَصْل. The — of wealth, أَصْلُ ٱلْمَالِ.

To have its — from, نَبَعَ مِن ; to be derived from, إِشْتَقَّ مِن – جَلَبَ - مِن . To draw from a —, أَخَذَ - مِن – صَدَرَ عَن
See also Origin, Spring, *n.*

Sourcrout, *n.* } كُرُنْبَة (or لِحَانَة) مُتَبَّلَة.
Sourkrout, }

Sourish, *a.* Rather sour, حَامِض بَعْض – حَامِض نَوْعًا – مُحَمَّض – الحُمُوضَة . Rather morose, شَرِس نَوْعًا – عَبَّاس نَوْعًا.

Sourly, *ad.* With sourness, بِحُمُوضَة ; morosely, بِعَنْف – بِوَعْقَة – بِشَرَاسَة ; mustily, بِعُفُونَة .

Sourness, *n.* Acidity, حُمُوضَة – حَمَازَة – حُمُوضَة . Mustiness, عُفُونَة . Moroseness, شَرَاسَة – كَشَارَة – وَعْقَة – عَنَف .

Souse, *n.* Pickle made with salt, مَلُوحَة . Pigs' feet and ears salted, أَكَارِع الخِنْزِير وَآذَانُه مُمَلَّحَة ; one who sells such, كُرَاعِيّ . A dip, غَطْسَة – غَمْسَة – غَمْتَة .

Souse, *v.t.* To steep in souse, مَلَّح . To plunge, as into a liquid, غَمَسَ - فِي – غَطَسَ - فِي – قَمَسَ - فِي .

Souse, *v.i.* To — upon, fall suddenly upon, هَجَمَ عَلَى – وَثَبَ عَلَى – إِنْطَبَقَ عَلَى – *aor.* يَثِبُ .

Souter, *n.* *See* Cobbler, *n.*

South, *n.* The —, القِبْلَة – الجَنُوب .

South, *a.* جَنُوبِيّ *colloq.* قِبْلِيّ . The — wind, النُّعَامَى – السُّلَامَى – الجَنُوب – الرِّيحُ الجَنُوبِيَّة – الأَزْيَب – الرِّيحُ اليَمَانِيَّة ; *called in Egypt,* المَرِيسِيّ . The — pole, القُطْبُ الجَنُوبِيّ .

South, *ad.* مِنَ الجَنُوب .

South-east, *n.* جَنُوبٌ وَشَرْقٌ .

South-east, *a.* جَنُوبِيّ شَرْقِيّ . A — wind, أَزْيَب – نَكْبَاء .

South-easterly, *a.* A — wind, أَزْيَب .

South-eastern, *a.* نَحْوَ الجَنُوبِيّ الشَّرْقِيّ .

Southerly, *a.* and *ad.* جَنُوبِيّ – مِنَ الجَنُوب .

Southern, *a.* جَنُوبِيّ . The — cross, the constellation, عَمُودُ الصَّلِيب .

Southerner, *n.* مِنْ أَهْلِ المَمَالِكِ الجَنُوبِيَّة .

Southernmost, *a.* فِي أَقْصَى الجَنُوب – وَاقِع فِي آخِرِ الجَنُوب .

Southern-wood, *n.* قَيْصُوم ذَكَر وَهُوَ ضَرْبٌ مِنَ الشِّيح .

Southing, *a.* مُتَّجِه (or مُتَقَدِّم) نَحْوَ الجَنُوب .

Southing, *n.* المَسِيرُ نَحْوَ الجَنُوب .

Southmost, *a.* فِي أَقْصَى الجَنُوب .

Southron, *n.* مِنْ أَهْلِ المَمَالِكِ الجَنُوبِيَّة .

Southward, *n.* جِهَةُ الجَنُوب ; *colloq.* طَرَفُ القِبْلَة .

Southward, *a.* نَحْوَ الجَنُوب – مِنْ جِهَةِ الجَنُوب ; *colloq.* نَحْوَ القِبْلَة .

South-west, *n.* جَنُوبٌ وَغَرْبٌ ; *called in Egypt and the Mediterranean,* اللَّبَش – المَرِيسِيّ الغَرْبِيّ – اللَّدُوس .

South-west, *a.* جَنُوبِيّ غَرْبِيّ ; *called in Egypt and the Mediterranean,* لَبَش – مَرِيسِيّ غَرْبِيّ – لُدُوسِيّ .

South-westerly, *a.* } مِنَ الجَنُوبِيّ الشَّرْقِيّ ; *called in Egypt, from*
South-western, } *the Italian,* مِنَ اللَّبَش .

Souvenir, *n.* تَذْكِرَة – تَذْكَار – تَفْكِرَة .

Sovereign, *a.* Supreme, as in power, مُطْلَق – مُسْتَبِدّ – قَائِم بِأَمْرِه – مُسْتَقِلّ . Supremely efficacious, مُطْلَقُ التَّأْثِير . Predominant, أَغْلَب – مُتَسَلِّط – مُسْتَوْلٍ . Chief, highest, أَعْلَى – أَفْضَل – أَكْبَر – أَعْظَم – أَعَزّ – أَقْدَم . Greatest, most eminent, أَنْفَع . Most useful, effectual, أَنْفَع . Sovereign power, قُوَّة مُسْتَقِلَّة – قُوَّة مُطْلَقَة . Sovereign rights, حُقُوق آسْتِقْلَالِيَّة – حُقُوق مُسْتَقِلَّة . A — state, دَوْلَة مُسْتَقِلَّة . A — prince, أَمِير (or بِرِنْس) مُسْتَقِلّ .

Sovereign, *n.* A ruler, سَيِّد *pl.* سَادَة – مَلِك – أَمِير مُطْلَق – *pl.* مُلُوك – سُلْطَان *pl.* سَلَاطِين . The English gold coin, لِيرَة *pl.* لِيرَات – سِكَّةُ اللِّيرَةِ الإِنْكِلِيزِيَّة . An absolute —, حَاكِم مُطْلَق – مَلِك مُسْتَقِلّ فِي مُلْكِه – (or مُسْتَبِدّ) . A constitutional —, حَاكِم مُحَكَّم بِشَرْط – حَاكِم مُقَيَّد بِقَانُونٍ أَسَاسِيّ . A legitimate —, حَاكِم شَرْعِيّ . The — of the people is their minister, سَيِّدُ القَوْمِ خَادِمُهُم (a statement attributed to Muhámmad).

Sovereignly, *ad.* بِصُورَة مُطْلَقَة – بِوَجْه مُطْلَق – إِسْتِبْدَادًا . Greatly, جِدًّا – كَثْرَة .

Sovereignty, *n.* Supremacy, سَلْطَنَة – مَمْلَكَة – رِئَاسَة . Sovereign state, rights, حُقُوق آسْتِقْلَالِيَّة – صِفَة آسْتِقْلَالِيَّة . Absolute —, إِسْتِقْلَال تَامّ – إِسْتِقْلَالِيَّة – إِسْتِبْدَاد . Hereditary —, حُكْم مُقَيَّد (or مَحْدُود) – حُقُوق مَوْرُوثَة مُسْتَقِلَّة . Limited —, إِسْتِقْلَالِيَّة مَبْنِيَّة عَلَى الانْتِخَاب – إِسْتِقْلَالِيَّة مُنْحَصِرَة . Elective —, إِسْتِقْلَالِيَّة مُوَقَّتَة . Temporary —, إِسْتِقْلَالِيَّة مُوَقَّتَة . The — of the people, رِئَاسَة (or إِسْتِقْلَالِيَّة) الأُمَّة .

Sow, *n.* The female swine, خِنْزِيرَة *pl.* خِنْزِيرَات . *See also under* Swine, *n.*

Sow, *v.t.* As of seed, زَرَعَ – بَذَرَ . To — discord, أَطْلَقَ – زَرَعَ الخُصُومَات – الخُصُومَة . He who sows shall reap, مَنْ زَرَعَ حَصَدَ .

Sower, *n.* زَارِع *pl.* زُرَّاع . A — of sedition, ضَرَّابُ فِتَن .

Sowing, *n.* The act of, زَرْع – زِرَاعَة – بَذْر .

Sown, *part.* مَبْذُور – مَزْرُوع. Sown land, مَزْرَعَة – زَرّاعَة *pl.* زَرّاعَات.

Sow-thistle, *n.* البَقْلَة اليَهُودِيَّة – المُرَيْرَة.

Soy, *n.* The sauce, ضَرْبٌ مِنَ ٱلطَّرْطُورِ لِلسَّمَكِ.

Spa, *n.* مَآءٌ مَعْدِنِيٌّ.

Space, *n.* Local extension, room, فُسْحَة – مَضْرَب – سَعَة – مَحَلّ – مَكَان – مَوْضِع. Interval, غُضُون – أَثْنَآء – مَسَافَة – فَاصِلَة. An intervening —, an interstice, فَجْوَة *pl.* فَجَوَات. Distance, بُعْد – مَسَافَة. Space, of time, حِينٌ مِنَ ٱلدَّهْرِ (Kûr. lxxvi. 1) – دَهْر – بُرْهَة – زَمَن – مُدَّةٌ مِنَ ٱلزَّمَانِ. A long — of time, بُرْهَة – مِلْوَة – مَلَاوَة – مُدَّةٌ طَوِيلَةٌ; a short —, of time, بُرْهَةٌ يَسِيرَةٌ. An open —, صَاع – صَاعَة – فَضَآء – خَلَآء – فُسْحَة. A —, in printing, فَاصِلَة; a hair —, فَاصِلَةٌ شَعْرِيَّةٌ – فَاصِلَةٌ رَفِيعَةٌ جِدًّا. Within the — of three days, فِي غُضُونِ ثَلَاثَةِ أَيَّامٍ. There is a large — between them (to be traversed), بَيْنَهُمْ مَضْرَبٌ بَعِيدٌ. To leave a — between, فَسَّحَ بَيْنَ.

Space, *v.t.* فَسَّحَ – جَعَلَ بَيْنَ فَوَاصِلَ.

Spacious, *a.* بَسِيط – رَحِيب – أَجْوَف – وَسِيع – فَسِيح. A — tract of land, فَجْوَآء. A — or roomy place, رَحْب. A — land, أَرْضٌ رَحْبَةٌ – بَلَدٌ رَحْبٌ. To be or become —, فَاحَ – فَسُحَ – تَفَسَّحَ. To be —, roomy, رَحُبَ – فَسُحَ – إِنْفَسَحَ – أَفْسَحَ. To make —, فَسَّحَ.

Spaciously, *ad.* بِسَعَةٍ – إِمْتِدَادًا – بِٱتِّسَاعٍ.

Spaciousness, *n.* سَعَة – رَحْب – فُسْحَة.

Spade, *n.* The tool, مِعْزَقَة – مِعْزَق – مِسْحَاة *pl.* مَسَاحٍ – مِعْبَاد *pl.* مَعَازِقُ – مِحْفَر *pl.* مَحَافِرُ. A —, in cards, بَسْتُونِي. To work with a —, أَعْزَقَ.

Spadix, *n.* إِغْرِيض *pl.* أَغَارِيض – طَلْعَة – طَلْع *coll.* طَلْع.

Spain, *n.* إِسْبَانِيَا.

Span, *n.* شِبْر *pl.* أَشْبَار. A — long, طُولُ شِبْرٍ. A — measured by the extension of the thumb and forefinger, فِتْر – فِتْر *pl.* أَفْتَار. Span, as of an arch, قَوْسُ ٱلطَّاقِ.

Span, *v.t.* As with the hand, شَبَرَ. To measure, قَاسَ. To stretch out, expand, نَشَرَ.

Spandrel, *n.* الفُرْجَةُ ٱلْمَسْدُودَةُ حَوْلَ قَوْسِ ٱلطَّاقِ.

Spangle, *n.* صَفِيحَة *pl.* صَفَائِح – بَرْق *pl.* بُرُوق.

Spangle, *v.t.* زَيَّنَ بِبُرُوقٍ – رَصَّعَ بِصَفَائِحَ.

Spaniard, *n.* مِنْ أَهْلِ إِسْبَانِيَا.

Spaniel, *n.* كَلْبُ صَيْدٍ.

Spaniel, *v.i.* *See to* Cringe, Fawn, *v.i.*

Spanish, *a.* إِسْبَانِيُولِيّ.

Spanish-fly, *n.* ذُبَّانٌ هِنْدِيٌّ – ذُرَّوح *pl.* ذَرَارِيح – ذُرْنُوح *pl.* ذَرَانِيح.

Spank, *v.t.* *See to* Slap, *v.t.*

Spanker, *n.* A burly fellow, جَسِيم – خَدَلَّج – ضَخْم. The sail, رَنْدَة. Spanker-boom, بُومْبَةُ ٱلرَّنْدَةِ.

Spanking, *a.* *See* Quick, Rapid, *a.*

Spanner, *n.* One who spans, شَابِر. The lock of a carbine, دِيكُ ٱلْقَرَابِينَة.

Spar, *n.* The mineral, حَجَرٌ مَعْدِنِيٌّ مُتَجَوْهِرٌ (*or* مُتَبَلْوِرٌ) – ضَرْبٌ مِنَ ٱلْحَجَرِ ٱلْمَعْدِنِيِّ ذِي رَفِيفٍ. A piece of wood, خَشَبَة – عُود *pl.* عِيدَان. An altercation, خُصُومَة – مُنَازَعَة – مُشَاجَرَة.

Spar, *v.i.* To spar or quarrel with, خَاصَمَ – جَادَلَ – نَازَعَ. They sparred or quarrelled together, of many, تَجَادَلُوا – تَنَازَعُوا – تَخَاصَمُوا; they sparred or came to blows, تَضَارَبُوا.

Spar, *v.t.* To fasten with a spar, ضَبَّبَ – شَدَّ (*or*) بِسَارِيَةٍ.

Spare, *a.* Scanty, little, قَلِيل – يَسِير – زَهِيد. Wanting, نَاقِص. Lean, ضَعِيف – نَحِيف. Thin, رَقِيق. Superfluous, زَائِد – فَاضِل – مُسْتَدْرَك. A —, lean, man, رَجُلٌ نَضِيضٌ. A — day, يَوْمُ فَرَاغٍ – يَوْمٌ فَاضٍ – يَوْمُ فَضِيَّةٍ. Spare clothes, ثِيَابٌ فَاضِلَةٌ – مَلَابِسُ زَائِدَةٌ.

Spare, *v.t.* To use frugally, إِقْتَصَدَ فِي – تَقَنَّى – *vulg.* وَفَّرَ. To part with, to do without, إِسْتَغْنَى عَنْ – أَغْنَى عَنْ – فَضَلَ عَنْ. To part with, give up, سَيَّبَ – فَاتَ – تَخَلَّى عَنْ. To grant, give, أَنْعَمَ عَلَى بِ – أَعْطَى – وَهَبَ *aor.* يَهَبُ. To allow, to appoint, as a sum of money, *etc.*, عَيَّنَ. To forbear to punish, to forgive, تَجَاوَزَ عَنْ – سَامَحَ – عَفَا عَنْ – صَفَحَ عَنْ. To have pity upon, حَنَّ عَلَى – تَرَحَّمَ عَلَى – أَشْفَقَ عَلَى. To suffer to live, إِسْتَبْقَى – إِسْتَحْيَى. To withhold, أَمْسَكَ – مَنَعَ. He who spareth the rod hateth his child, مَنْ يَمْنَعْ عَصَاهُ يَمْقُتِ ٱبْنَهُ. I did it to — you, فَعَلْتُهُ إِشْفَاقًا عَلَيْكُمْ. I have no time to —, لَيْسَ لِي فَرْطٌ مِنَ ٱلْوَقْتِ. He spared to take of his own money and took his brother's, عَفَا عَنْ أَخْذِ دَرَاهِمِهِ فَأَخَذَ دَرَاهِمَ أَخِيهِ. To — one's self, وَفَّرَ نَفْسَهُ – *vulg.* تَقَنَّى نَفْسَهُ.

Spare, *v.i.* To economize, قَصَدَ (*or* إِقْتَصَدَ) فِي ٱلْأَمْرِ – تَقَنَّى – *vulg.* وَفَّرَ فِي ٱلْأَمْرِ. To use mercy, كَانَ شَفِيقًا – كَانَ رَحِيمًا. To be forgiving, كَانَ غَفُورًا. He has money enough and to —, تَفْضُلُ عَنْهُ ٱلدَّرَاهِمُ. The government has no steamers to —, لَيْسَ عِنْدَ ٱلدَّوْلَةِ بَوَاخِرُ تَسْتَغْنِي عَنْهَا.

Sparely, *ad.* *See* Sparingly, *ad.*

Spareness, *n.* Littleness, قِلَّة. Thinness, رِقَّة. Leanness, نَحَافَة.

Sparer, *n.* *See* Sparing, *a.*

Spare-rib, *n.* ضِلْعٌ مِنَ ٱلْخِنْزِيرِ قَلِيلُ ٱللَّحْمِ *pl.* ضُلُوع.

Sparing, *a.* Frugal, economical, مُقْتَصِد ـ مُتَقَنِّن ـ مُقَتِّر ـ قَاتِر ـ وِطْرَاق *vulg.* مُوَفِّر. Reserved, backward, طِرِّيق ـ مُمْسِك. Sparing of words, قَلِيلُ ٱلْكَلَامِ ـ كَتُوم.

Sparingly, *ad.* Economically, بِٱلِٱقْتِصَادِ ـ بِتَقَنُّن; *vulg.* بِٱلتَّوْفِير. Scantily, بِقِلَّةٍ ـ قَلِيلًا ـ يَسِيرًا. Parsimoniously, بِشُحٍّ. Seldom, فِي ٱلنَّادِرِ ـ رُبَّمَا ـ نَادِرًا.

Sparingness, *n.* Parsimony, شُحّ. Frugality, تَقَنُّن ـ إِقْتِصَاد; *vulg.* تَوْفِير. Caution, إِحْتِذَار ـ تَمَسُّك. *See also* Moderation, *n.*

Spark, *n.* شَرَارَة *coll.* شَرَار *pl.* شَرَر and شَرَارَات. A small portion of anything, جُزْءٌ ـ قِلٌّ ـ ذَرُّوٌ. A brisk showy man, غَنْدُور *pl.* غَنَادِير *vulg.* مُتَكَيِّس ـ مُتَظَرِّف. A lover, عَاشِق. Emitting sparks, شَرَّار. Thy father is a fire that emits many sparks and thou art a — from it, أَبُوكَ نَارٌ شَرَّارَةٌ وَأَنْتَ مِنْهَا شَرَارَةٌ.

Sparkful, *a.* }
Sparkish, } *See* Lively, Brisk, Gay, *a.*

Sparkle, *v.i.* To emit sparks, أَبْرَزَ ٱلشَّرَارَ ـ ﺩ طَارَ ٱلشَّرَارُ مِنْهُ ـ أَصْدَرَ ٱلشَّرَارَاتِ. To glitter, أَبْرَقَ ـ ﺩ رَفَّ ـ ﺩ لَمَعَ ـ ﺩ. To twinkle, as a star, تَلَأْلَأَ ـ لَأْلَأَ ـ ﺩ لَمَحَ. To exhibit animation, تَفَكَّهَ ـ تَنَشَّطَ. The herbage sparkled, glistened, رَفَّ ٱلنَّبَاتُ ـ ﺩ. His teeth sparkled, رَفَّتْ أَسْنَانُهُ. *See also* to Glitter, Shine, *v.i.*

Sparkler, *n.* Of a person, جَلِيٌّ ـ بَهِيٌّ ـ بَاهٍ.

Sparkling, *a.* Throwing out sparks, شَرَّار ـ قَدَّاحُ نَار. Glittering, brilliant, بَرَّاق ـ لَامِع ـ لَمَّاح ـ لَمُوح ـ مُتَلَأْلِئ ـ رَفِيف. Having or emitting rays, ذُو شُعَاع. Sparkling front teeth, ثَغْرٌ رَفَّاف.

Sparklingly, *ad.* بِبَرَقَانٍ ـ تَلْمِيحًا ـ بِرَفِيفٍ ـ رَفًّا ـ إِزْهِرَارًا.

Sparklingness, *n.* لَمَعَان ـ رَفّ ـ بَرَقَان ـ رَفِيف ـ إِزْهِرَار.

Sparrow, *n.* عُصْفُور *pl.* عَصَافِير ـ نُغَر *pl.* نِغْرَان ـ نُقَّار ـ صُفْصُف. The Spanish —, دُوَيْرِي.

Sparrow-grass, *n.* *See* Asparagus, *n.*

Sparrow-hawk, *n.* بَاشِق or بَاشَق *pl.* بَوَاشِق.

Sparry, *a.* Like spar, مِثْلُ ٱلْحَجَرِ ٱلْمَعْدِنِيِّ ٱلْمُتَجَوْهِرِ (or ٱلْمُتَبَلْوِر) ـ شَبِيهٌ بِٱلْحَجَرِ ٱلْمَعْدِنِيِّ ٱلرَّقَّافِ. *See* Spar, *n.*

Sparse, *a.* Thinly scattered, مُتَفَرِّق ـ مُفَرَّق ـ مُشَتَّت ـ شَتٌّ. *See also* Spare, *a.*

Sparsely, *ad.* شَتَاتًا ـ تَفَرُّقًا ـ شَتَاتًا.

Sparseness, *n.* تَفَرُّق ـ شَتَات ـ شَتٌّ.

Spartan, *a.* Hardy, undaunted, بَطَل ـ جَرِيءٌ ـ ضَلِيع ـ سِنْدِيٌّ ـ شُجَيْع ـ شَهْم.

Spasm, *n.* تَقَبُّض ـ تَشَنُّج.

Spasmodic, *n.* دَوَآءٌ لِلتَّشَنُّج.

Spasmodic, *a.* تَشَنُّجِيّ. Spasmodic movements, حَرَكَاتٌ تَشَنُّجِيَّةٌ. *See also* Convulsive, *a.*

Spat, *pret. of to* Spit, *q.v.*

Spathe, *n.* جِبَاب *pl.* جُبّ ـ كُفُرَّى ـ كُفَافِير *pl.* كَافُور ـ جِفَاف *pl.* جُفّ.

Spathic, *a.* *See* Foliated, Lamellar, *a.*

Spathiform, *a.* *See* Sparry, *a.*

Spathose, *a.* }
Spathous, } ذُو جُبّ ـ ذُو كَافُور.

Spatter, *v.t.* As of water from the mouth, رَشَّ ٱلْمَاءَ مِنَ ٱلْفَمِ ﺩ. To make dirty, وَسَّخَ ـ لَوَّثَ ـ دَرَّنَ. To scatter, نَشَرَ ـ أَذَاعَ ﺩ. *See also* to Bespatter, *v.t.*

Spatter, *v.i.* As water from the mouth, تَرَشْرَشَ (or تَرَشَّشَ) مِنَ ٱلْفَمِ.

Spatter-dashes, *n.* شَخْشِير ـ جَوْرَبٌ لِلرِّجْلَيْنِ.

Spatula, *n.* مِلْوَقُ ٱلصَّيْدَلَانِيِّ ـ *vulg.* مِسْوَاط. To mix, as with a —, سَوَّطَ.

Spavin, *n.* وَرَمٌ فِي عَرَاقِيبِ ٱلْخَيْلِ.

Spavined, *a.* مُوَرَّمُ ٱلْعَرَاقِيبِ.

Spawl, *v.i.* *See to* Dribble, *v.i.*

Spawn, *n.* صِير ـ صُغْفُر. *See also* Offspring, Fruit, *n.*

Spawn, *v.t.* To deposit spawn, وَضَعَتِ ٱلصِّيرَ (or ٱلصُّغْفُرَ). To bring forth, وَضَعَت *aor.* تَضَعُ ـ وَلَدَتْ *aor.* تَلِدُ ـ خَلَّفَتْ.

Spawner, *n.* وَاضِعَةُ ٱلصِّيرِ.

Spay, *v.t.* جَبَّ رَحِمَ ٱلْحَيَوَانَاتِ ﺩ.

Spayer, *n.* جَابُّ أَرْحَامِ ٱلْحَيَوَانَاتِ.

Speak, *v.i.* تَكَلَّمَ ـ فَاهَ ﺩ ـ تَفَوَّهَ. To utter speech, to utter words, (*v.t*) تَكَلَّمَ ـ ﺩ نَطَقَ بِ ـ ﺩ لَفَظَ بِ ـ تَفَوَّهَ بِ. To make a speech, أَلْقَى مَقَالَةً. To address, — to, خَاطَبَ ـ كَلَّمَ ـ فَاوَهَ. To declare, أَثْبَتَ ـ أَكَّدَ ـ قَرَّرَ. To talk, أَقْبَلَ عَلَى ـ بِكَلَام ـ تَحَدَّثَ. To converse, with another, as about the weather and general matters, تَحَاكَى ـ تَسَامَرَ. He spoke to him mouth to mouth, تَكَلَّمَ مَعَهُ فَمًا إِلَى فَمٍ. He left them speaking, خَرَجَ مِنْ ﺩ عِنْدِهِمْ وَهُمْ يَتَكَلَّمُونَ. Who or what is spoken of, ٱلْمَحْكِيُّ عَنْهُ. I have heard him spoken of, سَمِعْتُ عَنْهُ. We have not spoken on this subject, مَا تَحَنَّا هٰذِهِ ٱلسِّيرَةَ. He speaks in public,

يُخَاطِبُ ٱلنَّاسَ جَهْرًا. It is not worth speaking about, لَيْسَ هُوَ تَحْتَ خَبَرٍ. To ask or make one to —, قَوَّلَ ـ أَنْطَقَ. Generally speaking, فِي ٱلْغَالِبِ. *See also to* Utter, *v.t.*

To speak against, to blame, reproach, ذَمَّ; to blaspheme, جَدَّفَ.

To speak audibly, aloud, تَكَلَّمَ ـ أَجْهَرَ بِٱلْقَوْلِ ـ جَهَرَ ٱلْكَلَامَ بِصَوْتٍ عَظِيمٍ.

To speak badly, ٱلْغَزَ فِي ٱلْكَلَامِ ـ أَتَى بِكَلَامٍ غَيْرِ مُهَذَّبٍ ـ خَرْفَشَ فِي ٱلْكَلَامِ ـ خَبَّصَ فِي ٱلْقَوْلِ.

To speak falsely, تَكَلَّمَ بِٱلْكَذِبِ ـ تَكَلَّمَ زُورًا.

To speak ill of, تَقَوَّلَ عَلَى ـ تَشَنَّعَ فِي ـ ذَكَرَ بِٱلْقَبِيحِ ـ تَفَوَّهَ بِ.

To speak ill of behind one's back, جَابَ مَغِيبَتَهُ ـ إِغْتَابَ.

To speak in an undertone, خَفَتَ بِصَوْتِهِ ـ خَافَتَ بِصَوْتِهِ ـ تَكَلَّمَ بِصَوْتٍ خَفِيضٍ.

To speak indistinctly, تَجَمْجَمَ ـ جَمْجَمَ.

To speak of, about, تَكَلَّمَ فِي or عَنْ ـ قَالَ فِي or عَنْ. To describe, وَصَفَ *aor.* يَصِفُ.

To speak of one's self, تَكَلَّمَ عَنْ نَفْسِهِ.

To speak in favour of to . . . , أَحْسَنَ بِٱلْقَوْلِ ـ تَكَلَّمَ فِي-عِنْدَ فُلَانٍ, فِي-عِنْدَ فُلَانٍ.

To speak much, أَكْثَرَ ٱلْقَوْلَ ـ سَابَ فِي ٱلْكَلِمِ; at length, تَفَتَّحَ فِي ٱلْكَلَامِ.

To speak out, تَفَتَّحَ فِي ٱلْكَلَامِ: He spoke out what was in his mind, عَبَّرَ مَا فِي نَفْسِهِ.

To speak through the nose, خَنْخَنَ ـ خَنَّ.

To speak slowly, gently, خَفَّضَ ٱلْقَوْلَ.

To speak to about, كَلَّمَ-فِي ـ كَلَّمَ-بِ ـ فَاوَهَ-فِي. To discourse with, حَاكَى ـ حَادَثَ ـ كَالَمَ ـ فَاوَهَ.

To speak to the purpose, أَسَدَّ فِي ٱلْكَلَامِ.

To speak well, اِنْطَلَقَ لِسَانُهُ ـ تَفَصَّحَ ـ بَلَغَ ـ تَكَلَّمَ بِفَصَاحَةٍ.

To speak well of, تَكَلَّمَ ـ ذَكَرَ-بِٱلْجَمِيلِ ـ أَحْسَنَ بِٱلْقَوْلِ فِي فِي-حَسَنًا.

To speak or converse with, كَالَمَ ـ خَاطَبَ ـ فَاوَهَ.

Speakable, *a.* That may be uttered, مِمَّا يُلْفَظُ ـ مِمَّا يُنْطَقُ بِهِ. That may be described, يُوصَفُ ـ تَعْبِيرُهُ مُمْكِنٌ ـ وَصْفُهُ مُمْكِنٌ بِهِ.

Speaker, *n.* One who speaks, مُتَكَلِّمٌ ـ قَوَّالٌ. One who speaks with another, كَلِيمٌ *pl.* كَلْمَى. One who addresses others, خَطِيبٌ *pl.* خُطَبَاءُ. An accomplished —, ذُو شِقْشِقَةٍ ـ فَيِّهٌ ـ مُفَوَّدٌ. One who makes a speech, مُلْقِي مَقَالَةٍ. The — in the House of Commons, ٱلصَّدْرُ فِي دِيوَانِ وُكَلَاءِ ٱلشَّعْبِ. A vigorous —, هَادِرٌ ـ فَحْلٌ. An eloquent —, مِصْقَعٌ.

Speakership, *n.* ٱلصَّدَارَةُ فِي دِيوَانِ وُكَلَاءِ ٱلشَّعْبِ.

Speaking, *part.* مُتَكَلِّمٌ. Before he had yet done —, إِذْ كَانَ لَمْ يَفْرَغْ بَعْدُ مِنَ ٱلْكَلَامِ.

Speaking, *n.* كَلَامٌ. They fancy that they will be heard for their much —, إِنَّهُمْ يَظُنُّونَ أَنَّهُ بِكَثْرَةِ كَلَامِهِمْ يُسْتَجَابُ لَهُمْ.

Speaking-trumpet, *n.* بُوقٌ *pl.* أَبْوَاقٌ.

Spear, *n.* The weapon, مِطْرَدٌ *pl.* مَطَارِدُ ـ مِزْرَاقٌ *pl.* مَزَارِيقُ ـ رُمْحٌ *pl.* أَرْمَاحٌ. A short —, طِرَادَةٌ. A shoot, as of grass, نَبْتٌ ـ نَبَاتَةٌ. The point, as of a —, سِنَانٌ *pl.* أَسِنَّةٌ ـ سِنَانُ رُمْحٍ. The iron foot of a —, زُجٌّ *pl.* زِجَاجٌ. To pierce with a —, زَرَقَ-بِمِزْرَاقٍ ـ رَمَحَ ـ سَنَّ. To pierce or thrust at with the butt end of a —, زَجَّ. To hurl a — at, زَجَّ-بِرُمْحٍ. To strike a — into the ground, عَكَزَ ٱلرُّمْحَ.

Spear, *v.t.* To pierce with a spear; *see under* Spear, *n.*

Spear-maker, *n.* رَمَّاحٌ.

Spearman, *n.* مِزْرَاقِيٌّ *pl.* مِزْرَاقِيَّةٌ.

Spear-mint, *n.* نَعْنَاعٌ.

Special, *a.* Denoting a species, نَوْعِيٌّ. Particular, خُصُوصِيٌّ ـ مَخْصُوصٌ ـ خَاصٌّ. A — mission, مَأْمُورِيَّةٌ مَخْصُوصَةٌ. To send one on a — message to, أَفْرَدَ-إِلَى. *See also* Particular, Peculiar, *a.*

Speciality, *n.* خُصُوصِيَّةٌ ـ خُصُوصٌ. To him belongs a —, لَهُ حِرْفَةٌ خُصُوصِيَّةٌ.

Specially, *ad.* خَاصَّةً ـ خُصُوصِيَّةً ـ خُصُوصًا.

Specialty, *n.* A sealed contract, صَكٌّ *pl.* صُكُوكٌ ـ سِجِلٌّ. *See also* Speciality, *n.*

Specie, *n.* نَقْدٌ ـ مَسْكُوكَاتٌ.

Species, *n.* صِنْفٌ *pl.* صُنُوفٌ ـ قِسْمٌ *pl.* أَقْسَامٌ ـ صِنْفٌ *pl.* أَصْنَافٌ ـ لَوْنٌ *pl.* أَلْوَانٌ ـ نَوْعٌ *pl.* أَنْوَاعٌ ـ قَبِيلٌ *pl.* قُبُلٌ. Classified species, أَصْنَافٌ مُنَسَّقَةٌ. To arrange in —, صَنَّفَ.

Specific, *a.* } Denoting species, نَوْعِيٌّ. Plain, decisive, جَزْمِيٌّ ـ

Specifical, } مُبِينٌ ـ صَرِيحٌ ـ قَطْعِيٌّ ـ بَتِّيٌّ. Special to, مُخْتَصٌّ بِ. Specific gravity, ثِقْلٌ ذَاتِيٌّ. A — remedy, عَلُوجٌ.

Specific, *n.* عِلَاجٌ مَخْصُوصٌ ـ عَلُوجٌ.

Specifically, *ad.* According to the species, نَوْعًا; specially, بَتَّةً ـ قَطْعًا ـ جَزْمًا ـ صَرَاحَةً; definitely, خَاصَّةً ـ خُصُوصًا.

Specificate, *v.t.* To designate the species, عَيَّنَ ـ خَصَّصَ ٱلصِّنْفَ ٱلصِّنْفَ. *See also to* Specify, *v.t.*

Specification, *n.* تَعْيِينٌ ـ تَصْرِيحٌ وَتَلْمِيحٌ ـ تِعْدَادٌ وَتَصْرِيحٌ. Specifications, سِيَاقَةٌ (or تَنْسِيقٌ) ٱلْأَوْصَافِ ـ أَوْصَافٌ.

Specificness, *n.* خُصُوصِيَّةٌ ـ خُصُوصٌ.

Specify, *v.t.* To enumerate the details of, عَدَّ وَصَرَّحَ بِ 2. To designate specially, إِخْتَصَّ بِ – أَخَصَّ – خَصَّ 2 – خَلَّلَ – خَلَّ 2 – عَيَّنَ. I specified, appointed, a time to him, أَجَّلْتُهُ. He specified a time for him, عَيَّنَ لَهُ وَقْتًا – = ضَرَبَ لَهُ أَجَلًا – أَجَّلَ لِ – أَجَلًا مَخْصُوصًا. He sold it to him for payment at a specified period, بَاعَهُ إِيَّاهُ إِلَى أَجَلٍ. To be specified, إِخْتَصَّ بِ – تَعَيَّنَ – إِتَّصَفَ.

Specimen, *n.* *See* Pattern, *n.*

Specious, *a.* Fair outwardly, مُشَكَّلُ ٱلظَّاهِرِ – جَمِيلٌ مِنْ خَارِجٍ. Deceitful, غَرُور – غَارٌّ – أَرْوَغُ – رَوَّاغ. *See also* Plausible, *a.*

Speciously, *ad.* With fair appearance, تَظَاهُرًا بِٱلْجَمِيلِ. Deceitfully, غَرَّةً – غَرًّا – بِمُرَاوَغَةٍ – رَوْغًا. *See also* Plausibly, *ad.*

Speciousness, *n.* Fair show, تَظَاهُرٌ بِٱلْجَمِيلِ. Deceit, رَوْغ – غُرُور – مُرَاوَغَة. *See also* Plausibility, *n.*

Speck, *n.* A small spot, نُقْطَة *pl.* نُقَط. A — of dirt, شَائِبَة *pl.* شَوَائِب – طَبْعَة – بُقْعَة. A very small thing, ذَرَّة. A white — on the nails, فُوف *pl.* أَفْوَاف – بُرْشَة. A blemish, عَيْب *pl.* عُيُوب.

Speck, *v.t.* To stain with spots, بَقَّعَ – طَبَّعَ. To blemish, عَيَّبَ. *See also to* Speckle, *v.t.*

Speckle, *n.* بَرَش – بُرْشَة.

Speckle, *v.t.* رَقَّطَ عَلَى – نَقَّطَ – لَوَّنَ. To be speckled, إِرْقَطَّ – إِبْرَشَّ – إِرْقَاطَّ – تَلَوَّنَ.

Speckled, *a.* As of sheep or goats, also of leaves, أَرْقَط *fem.* رَقْطَاء *pl.* رُقْط – أَبْغَث *fem.* بَغْثَاء *pl.* بُغْث; of a horse, أَبْرَش – بَرِيش.

Spectacle, *n.* A show, فُرْجَة – مَنْظَر – مَشْهَد – مَشْهَدَة. To become a — to, صَارَ مَنْظَرًا لِ. We never before saw a — like it, مَا رَأَيْنَا قَبْلَهُ مَشْهَدًا مِنَ ٱلْمَشَاهِدِ نَظِيرَهُ.

Spectacled, *a.* ذُو (لَابِسُ *or*) عُوَيْنَات.

Spectacles, *n.* A pair of, نَظَّارَة – عُوَيْنَات.

Spectacular, *a.* تَفَرُّجِيّ – مُتَعَلِّقٌ بِٱلْمَنَاظِرِ – مَنْظَرِيّ.

Spectator, *n.* نَاظِر *pl.* نُظَّار – شَاهِد *pl.* شُهُود – مُتَفَرِّج *pl.* مُتَفَرِّجُون. He looked upon it as a —, نَظَرَ إِلَيْهِ نَظَرَ ٱلْمُتَفَرِّجِ =. It is deemed most likely that France will not continue to be a bare — of the war, ٱلْغَالِبُ عَلَى ٱلظَّنِّ أَنَّ دَوْلَةَ فَرَنْسَا لَا تَبْقَى مُتَفَرِّجَةً فَقَطْ عَلَى مَيْدَانِ ٱلْحَرْبِ.

Spectatorial, *a.* مُتَعَلِّقٌ بِٱلنَّاظِرِ – نَاظِر.

Spectatorship, *n.* شَهَادَة – نَظَرَان – تِنْظَار.

Spectatress, *n.* نَاظِرَة – شَاهِدَة *pl.* شَاهِدَات – مُتَفَرِّجَة *pl.* مُتَفَرِّجَات.

Spectral, *a.* خَيَالِيّ.

Spectre, *n.* زَوْل *pl.* أَزْوَال – خَيَال *pl.* أَخْيِلَة – طَيْف – طَائِفُ خَيَالٍ – طَيْفُ خَيَالٍ. The — visited him (in his sleep), طَافَ بِهِ ٱلْخَيَالُ 2.

Spectrum, *n.* A visible thing, مَنْظَرَة *pl.* مَنَاظِر. A fancied image, خَيَال. A refracted image, عَكْس – صُورَةٌ مُنْعَكِسَةٌ. Refracted rays of prismatic light, أَلْوَانُ ٱلنُّورِ ٱلْمَعْكُوسَةُ بِٱلْمَنْشُورِ.

Specular, *a.* Like a looking-glass, مِثْلَ ٱلْمِرْآةِ.

Speculate, *v.i.* To — upon, to turn over in the mind, أَحَالَ – حَوَّلَ – تَأَمَّلَ – طَالَعَ. To —, as in trade, = ضَرَبَ مَخَامِينَ; as on the Exchange, قَامَرَ.

Speculation, *n.* A mental view of things, مُلَاحَظَة – تَخَيُّل – تَصَوُّر. A — in trade, *etc*, تَخْمِين *pl.* تَخَامِينُ; on the Exchange, مُقَامَرَة. A mercantile —, in which several are concerned, مُضَارَبَةُ مَتْجَرٍ. A —, money invested from which no return is hoped for, مَالٌ مِضْمَارٌ.

Speculative, *a.* Theoretical, عِلْمِيّ – نَظَرِيّ. Meditative, مُتَأَمِّل. Ideal, وَهْمِيّ – خَيَالِيّ – تَصَوُّرِيّ. Connected with speculation in money, قِمَارِيّ.

Speculatively, *ad.* Theoretically, بِصُورَةٍ – عَلَى مِنْوَالٍ نَظَرِيٍّ – عِلْمًا – ذِهْنًا – نَظَرِيَّةً; meditatively, بِٱلتَّأَمُّلِ; with speculation, of money, بِوَجْهِ ٱلْمُقَامَرَةِ; in trade, *etc.*, بِضَرْبٍ – بِٱلتَّخْمِينِ – تَخْمِينًا.

Speculator, *n.* A theorist, عَالِمٌ – ذُو جُزْئِيَّاتٍ مِنَ ٱلْعِلْمِ بِٱلْكُلِّيَّاتِ. One who meditates, مُتَأَمِّل. A — in trade, ضَرَّابُ مَخَامِينَ; in money, مُقَامِر *pl.* مُقَامِرُون. *See also* Schemer, Projector, *n.*

Speculum, *n.* A mirror, مِرْآة – مِنْظَار *pl.* مَرَاءٍ *and* مَرَايَا. A reflecting — of metal, مِرْآةٌ عَاكِسَةٌ مَعْدِنِيَّةٌ.

Speech, *n.* The faculty of, ٱلنُّطْق. Uttered words, تَفَوُّه – قَوْل – أَقْوَال – كَلَام. An address, خُطْبَة *pl.* خُطَب – مَقَالَة *pl.* مَقَالَات. The sound of —, mode of speaking, فَنّ *pl.* أَفْنَان – جَرْس – صَوْت. Tongue, language, لُغَة – لِسَان. Discourse, conversation, مُحَاوَرَة – حَدِيث. A part of —, لَفْظَة *pl.* أَلْفَاظ – كَلِمَة *pl.* كَلِمَات. A long-winded —, مَقَالَةٌ طَوِيلَةٌ – خُطْبَةٌ مُطَوَّلَةُ ٱلذَّنَبِ. A maiden —, مَقَالَةٌ بِكْرٌ. Excellent —, كَلَامٌ سَدَادٌ – سُمُوُّ ٱلْكَلَامِ. Poor —, كَلَامٌ حَقِيرٌ. Plain —, مُجَاهَرَةُ ٱلْكَلَامِ. Slow of —, ثَقِيلُ ٱلْفَمِ. Rude, untutored, in —, عَامِّيٌّ فِي ٱلْكَلَامِ. By fair speeches, بِٱلْكَلَامِ ٱلطَّيِّبِ. Hard speeches, كَلِمَاتٌ صَعْبَةٌ. To make a —, أَلْقَى مَقَالَةً. Your — betrays you, لُغَتُكَ تُظْهِرُكَ.

Speechify, *v.i.* To make a speech, أَلْقَى مَقَالَةً. To speak much and long, سَابَ فِي ٱلْكَلِمِ ـ طَوَّلَ ٱلْكَلَامَ ـ أَسْهَبَ كَلَامَهُ ٥.

Speechless, *a.* Silent, not speaking, أَخْرَسُ *fem.* خَرْسَاءُ *pl.* خُرْسٌ ـ مُصْمِتٌ ـ صَامِتٌ ـ سَاكِتٌ. Dumb, أَبْكَمُ *fem.* بَكْمَاءُ *pl.* بُكْمٌ ـ أَخْرَسُ. To be —, silent, not speaking, سَكَتَ ² ـ صَمَتَ ². To be —, as having been overcome by argument, قُطِعَ لِسَانُهُ ـ أُفْحِمَ ٥.

Speechlessness, *n.* صَمْتٌ ـ خَرَسٌ.

Speed, *v.i.* To make haste, سَرُعَ ² ـ أَسْرَعَ ـ وَاشَكَ ـ أَوْشَكَ ـ إِسْتَعْجَلَ. To prosper, سَعِدَ ٥ ـ صَحَّ لِ ² ـ تَوَفَّقَ ـ نَجَحَ ٥.

Speed, *v.t.* To send in haste, أَوْفَدَ عَاجِلًا ـ أَسْرَعَ إِرْسَالَهُ. To put in quick motion, رَوَّجَ ـ عَجَّلَ ـ أَعْجَلَ. To help forward, وَفَّقَ ـ عَاوَنَ ـ سَاعَدَ. God speed the plough! وَفَّقَهُ ٱللّٰهُ.

Speed, *n.* A course, run, سَيْرٌ. Haste, وَشْكٌ ـ سُرْعَةٌ ـ وَفَضٌ ـ عَجَلَةٌ ـ وَشَاكٌ. Success, تَوْفِيقٌ ـ نَجَاحٌ ـ إِقْبَالٌ ـ فَلَاحٌ. Full speed, gallop, رَمْحٌ ـ رَكْضٌ: To go at full —, at a gallop, رَكَضَ ² ـ رَمَحَ ٥. To bid one God speed, دَعَا لَهُ ² دَعَا لِ ـ بِتَوْفِيقِ ٱللّٰهِ ² بِٱلْخَيْرِ. To set at full —, as of a horse, رَمَّحَ ـ رَكَّضَ.

Speedful, *a.* سَرِيعٌ ـ عَجِيلٌ ـ عَجُولٌ.

Speedily, *ad.* وَشَاكَةً ـ بِسُرْعَةٍ ـ بِٱلْعَجَلِ. Let it be done —, فَلْيُعْمَلْ بِسُرْعَةٍ. Hear or answer me —, إِسْتَجِبْ لِي سَرِيعًا.

Speediness, *n.* وِشَاكٌ ـ وُشْكٌ ـ رَوْجَةٌ ـ سُرْعَةٌ ـ وَفَضٌ.

Speedwell, *n.* The plant, ضَرْبٌ مِنَ ٱلْكَبَابِ ـ ضَرْبٌ مِنَ ٱلشَّيْحِ ٱلْمَجُوسِ.

Speedy, *a.* عَجُولٌ ـ عَجِيلٌ ـ سَرِيعٌ *pl.* سِرَاعٌ *and* سُرْعَانٌ *fem.* سَرِيعَةٌ *pl.* سِرَاعٌ. To be —, وَشُكَ ـ وَاشَكَ ـ أَفَاجَ ـ أَوْفَدَ ـ أَسْرَعَ. *See also* Hasty, *and to* Hasten, *v.i.*

Spell, *n.* Sorcery, سِحْرٌ. A charm, عُوذَةٌ *pl.* عُوَذٌ ـ تَعْوِيذٌ *pl.* تَعَاوِيذُ ـ عَزِيمَةٌ *pl.* عَزَائِمُ. A turn of work, نَوْبَةٌ ـ دَوْرٌ ـ عُقْبَةٌ; with another, مُعَاقَبَةٌ. A space of time, مُدَّةٌ ـ بُرْهَةٌ. To take a — with another, working with him alternately, أَعْقَبَ ـ عَاقَبَ. Under a spell, مَسْحُورٌ. *See also* Charm, *n.*

Spell, *v.t. and i.* Of words, هَجَا ² ـ تَهَجَّى. To read, pronounce, قَرَأَ ـ تَلَفَّظَ ٥. To charm, سَحَرَ ـ سَحَّرَ ٥. To — words correctly, ضَبَطَ ٱلْأَسْمَاءَ ².

Spell-bound, *a.* مَسْحُورٌ.

Speller, *n.* One who spells, مُتَهَجٍّ ـ هَاجٍ.

Spelling, *n.* هَجْوٌ ـ هِجَاءٌ ـ تَهَجٍّ ـ تَهْجِيَةٌ. Orthography, ضَبْطُ ٱلْأَسْمَاءِ.

Spelling-book, *n.* كِتَابُ ٱلْهِجَاءِ.

Spelt, *part. of to* Spell, *q.v.*

Spelter, *n.* زِنْكٌ ـ تُوتِيَةٌ مَعْدِنِيَّةٌ.

Spence, *n.* *See* Larder, Pantry, *n.*

Spencer, *n.* The dress, صُدَيْرِيَّاتٌ *pl.* صُدَيْرِي ـ أَزْبِنَةٌ *pl.* زَبُونٌ; the sail, رَنْدَةُ ٱلْغَرْنْدِيَةِ.

Spend, *v.t.* To consume, waste, بَذَّرَ ـ أَسْرَفَ ـ أَذْهَبَ ـ أَتْلَفَ ـ أَزَالَ ـ ضَيَّعَ. To —, as money, إِسْتَنْفَقَ ـ صَرَفَ ٥ ـ صَرَّفَ ـ أَنْفَقَ. To exhaust, as of strength, أَفْرَغَ. To harass, fatigue, أَعْيَا ـ عَسَفَ ـ أَتْعَبَ. To —, as of time, قَطَعَ ٥; in the sense of losing time, ضَيَّعَ. To — upon, أَنْفَقَ عَلَى. The water was spent, فَرَغَ ٱلْمَاءُ ٥. The day was far spent, قَدْ مَالَ ٱلنَّهَارُ قَدِ ٱنْحَدَرَ ـ قَدْ تَنَاهَى ٱلنَّهَارُ ـ ٱلنَّهَارُ. He spent some time there, قَدْ أَصْرَفَ وَقْتًا هُنَاكَ. The night is far spent, قَدْ تَنَاهَى ٱللَّيْلُ. *See also to* Expend, *v.t.*

Spend, *v.i.* To make expense, صَرَفَ ٥. To be consumed, تَلِفَ ٥ ـ فَرِغَ ـ ذَهَبَ ٥.

Spender, *n.* One who spends or caters, وَكِيلُ ٱلْخَرْجِ. *See also* Spendthrift, *n.*

Spendthrift, *n.* عَثٌّ مَالٍ ـ مِتْلَافٌ ـ مِضْيَاعٌ ـ مُضَيِّعٌ ـ مُبَذِّرٌ ـ مِنْفَاقٌ ـ مِضْيَاعٌ لِلْمَالِ.

Sperm, *n.* Animal seed, مَاءٌ ـ مَنِيَّةٌ *pl.* مُنًى ـ مَنِيٌّ ـ مِنًى; of a man or woman, نُطْفَةٌ ـ عُسَيْلَةٌ ـ مَنِيٌّ. Sperm oil, زَيْتُ ٱلْحُوتِ. To emit —, مَنَى ـ أَمْنَى. *See also* Spermaceti, *n.*

Spermaceti, *n.* مِنَى ٱلْحُوتِ.

Spermatic, *a.* نُطْفِيٌّ.

Spermatocele, *n.* وَرَمُ أَسْهَرَانِ ٱلْخِصْيَانِ.

Spermatorrhœa, *n.* مَذْيُ ٱلْمِنَى ـ مَذْيٌ.

Spermatozoa, *n.* ٱلدُّوَيْبَّاتُ ٱلْكَائِنَةُ فِي ٱلْمِنَى.

Spew, *v.t. and i.* To vomit, إِسْتَفْرَغَ. *See to* Vomit, *v.t. and i.*

Sphacelation, *n.* *See* Mortification, Gangrene, *n.*

Sphere, *n.* A globe, كُرَةٌ *pl.* كُرَاتٌ. The celestial —, الفَلَكُ; the terrestrial —, البَسِيطَةُ. A circuit, دَائِرَةٌ. A condition, دَرَجَةٌ ـ مَرْتَبَةٌ ـ مَنْزِلَةٌ ـ فَاثُورٌ. The Rank, station, حَالٌ. The highest —, of the heavens, العَرْشُ; from the highest — to the earth, مِنَ ٱلْعَرْشِ إِلَى ٱلْفَرْشِ. He went out of his —, خَرَجَ ² مِنْ عَرْضِهِ. The — of the fixed stars, فَلَكُ ٱلثَّوَابِتِ. They are in one —, level, footing, هُمْ عَلَى فَاثُورٍ (*or*) بِسَاطٍ وَاحِدٍ.

Armillary sphere, كُرَةٌ ذَاتُ حَلَقٍ.

Oblique sphere, كُرَةٌ مَائِلَةٌ.

Parallel sphere, كُرَةٌ مُتَوَازِيَةٌ.

Right sphere, كُرَةٌ قَائِمَةٌ.

The spheres, الأَفْلَاكُ.

Spheric, *a.* }
Spherical, } مُدَوَّر ـ مُسْتَدِير ـ كُرَوِيٌّ ـ كُرِّيٌّ

Spherical geometry, الكُرَوِيَّاتُ.

Spherical trigonometry, مُثَلَّثَاتٌ كُرَوِيَّةٌ.

Sphericallly, *ad.* إِسْتِدَارَةً ـ كَٱلْكُرَةِ.

Sphericalness, *n.* }
Sphericity, } كَوْنُ ٱلشَّيْءِ كُرَوِيَّ ٱلشَّكْلِ ـ تَدْوِير ـ كُرَوِيَّة.

Spherics, *n.* الكُرَوِيَّاتُ.

Spheroid, *n.* شِبْهُ ٱلْكُرَةِ.

Spheroidal, *a.* شَبِيهٌ بِٱلْكُرَةِ.

Spherule, *n.* كُرَةٌ صَغِيرَةٌ.

Sphincter, *n.* عَضَلَةٌ ضَابِطَةٌ ـ عَضَلَةٌ قَابِضَةٌ ـ عَضَلَةٌ مُضَيِّقَةٌ.

Sphincter ani, سَعْدَانَةٌ ـ وَتَرَةٌ. The two sphincters, of the urine and excrement, مَصَرَّتَا ٱلْبَوْلِ وَٱلْغَائِطِ.

Sphinx, *n.* أَبُو ٱلْهَوْلَى ـ أَبُو ٱلْهَوْلِ.

Spica, *n.* The star in Virgo, السُّنْبُلَةُ.

Spicate, *a.* فِي هَيْئَةِ ٱلسُّنْبُلَةِ.

Spice, *n.* The aromatic, قِزْحٌ *pl.* أَقْزَاحٌ ـ تَوْبَلٌ ـ تَابِلٌ *pl.* تَوَابِلُ ـ بَهَار. A modicum, عِرْقٌ ـ مِقْدَارٌ جُزْئِيٌّ ـ شُوَايَةٌ. *See also* Pungency, *n.*

Spice, *v.t.* As with spices, ٢ جَعَلَ ـ فَحَّى ـ تَبَّلَ ـ تَوْبَلَ ـ قَزَّحَ ـ تَوْبَلَ بَهَارًا فِيهِ. To tincture, أَشْرَبَ. To —, of language, قَزَّحَ ـ بَزَّرَ ـ حَرَّرَ.

Spiced, *a.* مُعَرَّفٌ ـ أَدِيمٌ ـ مُقَزَّحٌ ـ مُتَبَّلٌ. Spiced meat, لَحْمٌ قَدِيدٌ ـ خَلْعٌ.

Spicery, *n.* Spices in general, فَحًا ـ تَوَابِلُ ـ بَهَارَاتٌ ـ عِطَارَةٌ. A seller of —, عَطَّارٌ.

Spiciness, *n.* Of spices, بَهَار. *See also* Pungency, Raciness, *n.*

Spicular, *a.* مِثْلَ ٱلزُّرَّاقَةِ ـ شَبِيهٌ بِٱلْحَرْبَةِ.

Spicule, *n.* *See* Granule, *n.*

Spicy, *a.* Like spice, مِثْلَ ٱلتَّوْبَلِ ـ مِثْلَ ٱلْبَهَارِ. Abounding in spice, كَثِيرُ ٱلتَّوْبَلِ ـ كَثِيرُ ٱلْبَهَارِ. Racy, ذَكِيٌّ ـ حَادٌّ ـ نَادِرٌ.

Spider, *n.* عَنْكَبُوت ـ شِبْثَان *pl.* شَبَث ـ فِدَسَة *pl.* فُدْس *pl.* عَنْكَبُوتَات. A spider's web, بَيْتُ ٱلْعَنْكَبُوتِ. "Like the spider who maketh for herself a house," كَمِثْلِ ٱلْعَنْكَبُوتِ ٱتَّخَذَتْ بَيْتًا (Kur. xxiv. 40.)

Spigot, *n.* خِلَال *pl.* أَخِلَّةٌ.

Spike, *n.* An ear, as of corn, سُنْبُلَةٌ *pl.* سُنْبُلَاتٌ. A nail, مِسْمَار *pl.* مَسَامِيرُ. A shoot of a plant, عُسْلُوج *pl.* عَسَالِيجُ ـ نَبْت ـ نَبَاتَةٌ. A thorn, or the — of a spear, شَوْكَةٌ *coll.* شَوْكٌ.

Spike, *v.t.* To fasten with spikes, سَمَّرَ ـ جَعَلَ لَ مَسَامِيرَ. To — a cannon, بَرْشَمَ ٱلْمِدْفَعَ. To put spikes, or thorns, upon a wall, شَوَّكَ ٱلْحَائِطَ. To pierce with spikes, أَشَاكَ بِٱلشَّوْكِ.

Spiked, *a.* Having spikes, بِهِ مَسَامِيرُ; having thorns, مُشَوَّكٌ. Spiked, of a cannon, مُبَرْشَمٌ. Having sharp points, شَائِكٌ ـ شَوِكٌ.

Spikelet, *n.* نَبْتٌ رَفِيعٌ ـ عُسَيْلِج ـ سُنْبُلَةٌ دَقِيقَةٌ.

Spike-lavender, *n.* سُنْبُلُ ٱللَّوَنْدَا ـ خُزَامَةٌ ـ سُنْبُلُ خُزَامَةٍ.

Spikenard, *n.* السُّنْبُلُ ـ سَانَجٌ هِنْدِيٌّ ـ سُنْبُلَةُ ٱلطِّيبِ ـ سُنْبُلَةٌ ٱلْهِنْدِيُّ.

Spiky, *a.* Having a sharp point, مُؤَنَّفٌ ـ مُؤَسَّلٌ ـ مُسَنَّنٌ.

Spile, *n.* A pin to stop a hole in a cask, *etc.*, عُصْفُورَةٌ *pl.* عَصَافِيرُ ـ سِدَاد. A stake, وَتِد *pl.* أَوْتَاد.

Spill, *v.t.* ٢ صَبَّ ـ أَكَبَّ ـ ٢ كَبَّ ـ ٢ سَكَبَ ـ أَهْرَقَ.

Spill, *v.i.* ٢ صَبَّ ـ إِنْصَبَّ ـ إِنْكَبَّ ـ إِنْفَضَّ. Like water spilt upon the ground, مِثْلَ ٱلْمَاءِ ٱلْمُهْرَاقِ عَلَى ٱلْأَرْضِ.

Spin, *v.t.* As with a spindle, *etc.*, ٢ غَزَلَ ـ إِغْتَزَلَ. To whirl round, ٢ دَوَّرَ ـ بَرَمَ. To — out, expand, ٢ مَدَّ ـ مَدَّدَ; as of a discourse, طَوَّلَ. To — a yarn, ٢ قَصَّ قِصَّةً ـ حَدَّثَ حَدِيثًا.

Spin, *v.i.* To practise spinning, كَانَ غَزَّالًا ـ إِسْتَعْمَلَ ٱلْغَزْلَ. To move round, إِسْتَدَارَ ـ ٢ دَارَ ـ إِلْتَفَتَ. *See also under to* Roll, *v.i.*

Spinach, *n.* }
Spinage, } سَبَانِخ *vulg.* إِسْفَانَاخ ـ إِسْبَانَخ ـ رَحَى.

Spinal, *a.* مُخْتَصٌّ بِٱلصُّلْبِ ـ مُخْتَصٌّ بِسِلْسِلَةِ ٱلظَّهْرِ. A — complaint, دَاءُ ٱلصُّلْبِ.

Spindle, *n.* مِغْزَل *pl.* مَغَازِلُ ـ مِرْدَن ـ دَرَّارَةٌ ـ مِدَرَّةٌ. The wire hook at the head of a —, صِنَّارَةٌ *pl.* صَنَانِيرُ. Spun with a —, مَرْدُون. More naked than a —, أَعْرَى مِنْ مِغْزَلٍ. *See also* Axis, *n.*

Spindle, *v.i.* To become lank, ٢ شَزُبَ ـ ٢ رَقَّ.

Spindle-legs, *n.* }
Spindle-shanks, } زَعْزُوع ـ شَازِب.

Spindle-shaped, *a.* فِي هَيْئَةِ ٱلْمِغْزَلِ.

Spine, *n.* The backbone, سِلْسِلَةُ ٱلظَّهْرِ ـ خَرَزُ ٱلظَّهْرِ ـ الصُّلْبُ. The end of the —, سِنٌّ ـ سِيسِنَةٌ. A thorn, شَوْكَةٌ *coll.* شَوْكٌ. A ridge, as of a mountain, حَرْف *pl.* حُرُوف ـ شُؤْشَة.

Spinel, *n.* }
Spinelle, } حَجَرٌ يُشْبِهُ ٱللَّعْلَ.

Spinet, *n.* سِنْطِيرٌ صَغِيرٌ.

Spinner, *n.* One who spins, غَزَّال *pl.* غَزَّالَة *fem.* غَزَّالَة *pl.* نِسْوَةٌ غُزَّل — نِسْوَةٌ غَوَازِل. *See also* Spider, *n.*

Spinning, *a.* غَزْلِيٌّ.

Spinning-jenny, *n.* دُولَابُ ٱلْغَزْلِ.

Spinning-wheel, *n.* شِهْرِف.

Spinosity, *n.* Of thorns, شَوْك — كَثْرَةُ شَوْكٍ. Difficulty, صُعُوبَة.

Spinous, *a.* شَائِك — شَاكٌ — شَوِك.

Spinster, *n.* A female spinner, غَزَّالَة. An unmarried female, عَازِبَة. A female left long without marriage, an old —, عَانِس *pl.* عَوَانِس — مُعَنَّسَة *pl.* مَعَانِس *and* مُعَنَّسَات — عَاهِل *pl.* عَوَاهِل — تَرِيكَة *pl.* تَرَائِك.

Spinstry, *n.* الغَزْلُ.

Spiny, *a.* *See* Spinous, *a.*; *also* Difficult, Troublesome, *a.*

Spiracle, *n.* For taking breath, *etc.*, a pore, مَسَمٌّ *pl.* مَسَامُّ — مَنْفِس *pl.* مَنَافِس — مَنْفِذ *pl.* مَنَافِذُ. A hole, vent, فَتْحَة.

Spiral, *a.* Winding, لَوْلَبِيٌّ — مُلْتَفّ.

Spirally, *ad.* كَٱللَّوْلَبِ — إِلْتِفَافًا — بِٱلْتِفَافٍ.

Spire, *n.* A winding line, خَطٌّ لَوْلَبِيّ. A steeple, مِسَلَّة — مَنَارَة *pl.* مَنَارَات — مِسَلَّةُ بِنَاءٍ. A shoot or blade, as of grass, عُسْلُوج *pl.* عَسَالِيجُ. *See also* End, *n.*

Spire, *v.i.* To shoot up, to sprout, نَبَتَ — فَرَّخَ — طَرَّ — فَقَّحَ.

Spirit, *n.* The immaterial being, soul, رُوح *pl.* أَرْوَاح. Mind, soul, نَفْس. A spectre, خَيَال *pl.* أَخْيِلَة. General character, disposition, شِيمَة *pl.* شِيَم — خَصْلَة — ضَرِيبَة — خِلْقَة. Meaning, فَحْوَى — مَعْنًى — مَحَطٌّ — مَضْمُون. Heart, courage, مُرُوءَة — إِقْدَام — قُدْرَة — مُكْنَة. شَجَاعَة — جَسَارَة — حُمَيَّا — حَمِيَّة. Force, vigour, فَرَاسَة — ذَكَاء — دَهَاء. Intelligence, مُرُوءَة — قُوَّة — عَارِضَة — فِطْنَة. The essential quality of a thing, جَوْهَر. A foul spirit, رُوحٌ نَجِسٌ. Alcoholic spirit, رُوح — رُوحُ ٱلْمُسْكِرَاتِ — عَرَق; *from the Italian,* سِبِيرْتُو. His — was troubled, إِنْزَعَجَتْ نَفْسُهُ. There was no — left in them, ذَابَتْ نَفْسُهُمْ. His — returned and he revived, رَجَعَتْ رُوحُهُ وَٱنْتَعَشَ. They provoked his —, أَمَرُّوا رُوحَهُ. Be not hasty in —, لَا تَسْرَعْ بِرُوحِكَ إِلَى ٱلْغَضَبِ. To give up the —, إِسْتَوْفَى — تُوُفِّيَ — طَلَعَتْ رُوحُهُ.

A broken spirit, رُوحٌ مُنْسَحِقٌ — قَلْبٌ مُنْكَسِرٌ.

A conciliatory spirit, رُوحٌ أَلِيفُ ٱلْمُسَالَمَةِ.

A democratic spirit, أَفْكَارٌ مَائِلَةٌ إِلَى حُكُومَةِ ٱلْعَوَامِّ.

An enterprising spirit, أَفْكَارُ ٱلتَّقَدُّمِ — أَفْكَارٌ مُسْتَدْرِجَةٌ. A man of an enterprising spirit, مِتْدَبِيّ.

A monarchical spirit, أَفْكَارٌ مَائِلَةٌ إِلَى ٱلْحُكُومَةِ ٱلْمُلُوكِيَّةِ.

A national spirit, أَفْكَارٌ وَطَنِيَّةٌ — أَفْكَارُ ٱلْأُمَّةِ.

A party spirit, تَعَصُّب — عَصَبِيَّة.

A rancorous spirit, ضِغْن — غِلّ — حِقْد — غَبَاوَة.

A republican spirit, جُمْهُورِيَّة (*or* غَيْرَة) آرَاءٌ.

A turbulent spirit, آرَاءٌ فَاتِنَةٌ — شَغَب — فَسَاد — فِتْنَة.

Animal spirits, jollity, حُبُور — سُرُور — تَفَكُّه — بَطَر — غِبْطَة.

High spirits, حُبُور — حَبَر — بَطَر — سُرُور — إِبْتِهَاج — تَفَكُّه. To be in —, طَابَ قَلْبُهُ — بَطِرَ — تَفَكَّهَ — تَكَيَّفَ — حُبِرَ.

Low or depressed spirits, غَمٌّ — كَدَر. To be in —, إِكْتَرَبَ — حَزِنَ.

Of an ardent spirit, مِقْحَام — ذُو قُحُوم — غَيْرَانُ *fem.* غَيْرَى *pl.* *masc. and fem.* غَيَارَى — حَارٌّ — صَاحِبُ حَرَارَةٍ.

Of an excellent spirit, ذَكِيُّ ٱلرُّوحِ — ذَكِيٌّ.

Of a hasty spirit, قَصِيرُ ٱلرُّوحِ.

Spirits of hartshorn, رُوحُ ٱلنُّشَادِرِ.

Spirits of wine, رُوحُ ٱلنَّبِيذِ; *from the Italian,* سِبِيرْتُو.

The Holy Spirit, ٱلرُّوحُ ٱلْقُدُسُ — رُوحُ ٱلْقُدُسِ.

The human spirit, رُوحُ ٱلْبَشَرِ.

The public spirit, أَفْكَارُ ٱلْعَامَّةِ — أَذْهَانُ ٱلْخَلْقِ — ٱلْأَفْكَارُ ٱلْعُمُومِيَّةُ.

The spirit of a brute, رُوحُ ٱلْبَهِيمَةِ.

The spirit of the age, أَفْكَارُ ٱلْعَصْرِ.

The spirit of the law, مَعْنَى ٱلْقَانُونِ — مَحَطُّ ٱلْقَوَانِينِ.

To be troubled in spirit, إِضْطَرَبَ بِٱلرُّوحِ.

To keep up one's (own) spirits, تَشَجَّعَ — تَجَرَّأَ — تَشَدَّدَ.

To put one in spirits, فَكَّهَ — أَفْكَهَ — أَبْسَطَ — سَرَّ — حَبَّرَ.

To raise a spirit, (يَعْنِي رُوحَ مَيِّتٍ) إِسْتَدْعَى رُوحًا.

To revive one's (own) spirits, حَيَّ *aor.* يَحْيَا — هَاجَ — إِشْتَدَّ.

Spirit, *v.t.* To inspirit, حَرَّضَ — شَجَّعَ — أَحْمَى. To — or convey away, سَلَبَ — إِسْتَلَبَ.

Spirited, *a.* Ardent, bold, جَسْر — جَسُور — فَلْتَان — غَيْرَانُ — حَام — شَجِيع; of a horse, شَابٌّ — قَفَّاز. He was broken —, إِنْقَطَعَ قَلْبُهُ. To be —, bold, جَسَرَ — تَجَرَّأَ.

Spiritedly, *ad.* بِجِدَّةٍ — بِحَرَارَةٍ — بِنَشَاطٍ — بِغَيْرَةٍ — بِمُرُوءَةٍ.

Spiritless, *a.* Cheerless, مِنْ غَيْرِ ٱنْبِسَاطٍ — مُغْتَمّ — حَزِين. Cowardly, فَشِل — خَشِل — قَصِف — رَعِيب — جَبَان. *See also* Lifeless, *a.*

Spiritlessly, *ad.* بِقَصَفٍ — بِلَا مُرُوءَةٍ.

Spiritlessness, *n.* Want of vigour, قَصَف — تَهَاوُم — عَدَمُ مُرُوءَةٍ — مَسْكَنَة — عَدَمُ غَيْرَةٍ — وَنَاء.

Spirit-level, *n.* مِيزَانُ ٱلْمُسَاوَاةِ بِرُوحِ ٱلْعَرَقِ.

Spirit-stirring, *a.* مُحَرِّض — مُهَيِّج — مُنَشِّط — مُرَغِّب.

Spiritual, *a.* Of spirit, رُوحِيٌّ. Inward, esoteric, بَاطِن. Ecclesiastical, كَنَائِسِيٌّ. Clerical, أَكْلِيرِيكِيٌّ. A — court, مَحْكَمَةٌ كَنَائِسِيَّةٌ. A — gift, هِبَةٌ رُوحِيَّةٌ. Spiritual beings, رُوحَانِيُّونَ.

Spiritualism, *n.* The state of being spiritual, رُوحِيَّة. The doctrine of intercourse with departed spirits, مَذْهَبُ ٱلَّذِينَ يَعْتَقِدُونَ ٱلْعِشْرَةَ بَيْنَ ٱلْأَحْيَاءِ وَبَيْنَ أَرْوَاحِ ٱلْمَوْتَى.

Spiritualist, *n.* One who professes to regard spiritual things only, مُهْتَمٌّ بِٱلرُّوحِيَّاتِ فَقَطْ. A believer in spiritualism, مِنْ أَصْحَابِ ٱلْمَذْهَبِ ٱلْمَذْكُورِ.

Spirituality, *n.* As distinct from matter, رُوحِيَّة. Spiritual mindedness, ٱلْمَحَبَّةُ ٱلرُّوحِيَّةُ ـ إِهْتِمَامُ ٱلرُّوحِ. Spiritualities, ecclesiastical matters and rights, أُمُورُ ٱلْإِكْلِيرُسِ وَحُقُوقُهُمْ ـ أُمُورٌ وَحُقُوقٌ كَنَائِسِيَّةٌ.

Spiritualize, *v.t.* To render in a spiritual sense, أَوَّلَ ـ إِلَى مَعْنًى رُوحِيٍّ ـ عَبَّرَ ـ رُوحِيًّا. To refine, as the intellect or feelings, رَفَّعَ ٱلرُّوحَ ـ هَذَّبَ ٱلْقَلْبَ.

Spiritualization, *n.* The act of rendering into a spiritual sense, تَعْبِيرٌ رُوحِيٌّ; of refining, تَرْفِيعُ ٱلرُّوحِ ـ تَهْذِيبُ ٱلْقَلْبِ.

Spiritually, *ad.* بِٱلرُّوحِ. Inwardly, فِي ٱلضَّمِيرِ ـ قَلْبًا ـ بَاطِنًا.

Spiritually-minded, *a.* مُهْتَمٌّ بِٱلْأُمُورِ ٱلرُّوحِيَّةِ ـ مُهْتَمٌّ بِٱلرُّوحِ.

Spirituous, *a.* مُسْكِر ـ حَامٍ. Spirituous liquors, مُسْكِرَات.

Spirt, *n.* *See* Spurt, *n.*

Spirtle, *v.t.* *See to* Spurt, *v.t.*

Spiry, *a.* *See* Spiral, *a.*

Spissitude, *n.* كَثَافَة ـ لُزُوجَة.

Spit, *n.* As for roasting, سَفُّود *pl.* سَفَافِيد. A — of land, لِسَانُ أَرْضٍ. One ejection of spittle, بَزْقَة ـ بَصْقَة. *See also* Spittle, *n.*

Spit, *v.t.* To put on a spit, سَفَّدَ. To pierce, as with a spear, *etc.*, زَرَقَ [2] ـ لَهَزَ [2] ـ خَزَقَ ـ طَعَنَ ـ بـ [2]. Spitted, on a spit, مُسَفَّد.

Spit, *v.t.* and *i.* To eject saliva, تَفَّ [2] ـ تَفَلَ [2] ـ بَصَقَ [2] ـ تَبَزَّقَ ـ بَزَقَ [2]. They spat in his face, بَصَقُوا فِي وَجْهِهِ.

Spit-box, *n.*
Spittoon, } مِبْزَقَة ـ مِتْفَلَة.

Spite, *n.* ضِغْن ـ إِحْنَة ـ غِلّ ـ سَخِيمَة ـ حَنَق ـ دَخَل ـ حِقْد. To entertain —, غَلَّ صَدْرُهُ *aor.* يَغِلُّ. To bear — to, تَحَقَّدَ عَلَى ـ تَسَخَّمَ عَلَى ـ أَحِنَ عَلَى ـ ضَغِنَ عَلَى. He bore — against me, غَمِرَ صَدْرُهُ عَلَيَّ. They bore mutual —, of many, تَحَاقَدُوا. To restrain one's —, أَكَلَ بُغْضَهُ ـ أَكَلَ كَفَّيْهِ [2]. To treat with —, آحَنَ. In — of him, عَلَى رَغْمِ أَنْفِهِ: He did it in spite of him, فَعَلَهُ عَلَى رَغْمِ أَنْفِهِ.

Spite, *v.t.* أَرْغَمَ ـ أَغَاظَ ـ نَكَى ـ كَادَ.

Spiteful, *a.* مُسَخَّم ـ مُغِلّ ـ ضَغِن ـ ضَاغِن ـ حَنِق ـ حَسِكٌ ـ حَقُود ـ حَقِد.

Spitefully, *ad.* بِضِغْنٍ ـ بِحِقْدٍ ـ بِحَنَقٍ.

Spitefulness, *n.* *See* Spite, *n.*

Spitfire, *n.* سَرِيعُ ٱلْغَضَبِ ـ مُحْنَق ـ حَنِيق.

Spitter, *n.* One who spits, كَثِيرُ ٱلْبُزَاقِ ـ بَزَّاق ـ بَصَّاق.

Spittle, *n.* بُزَاق ـ بُصَاق ـ بَصْق ـ بَزْق ـ قَشَا ـ تُفْل ـ تَفْل. Spittle while yet in the mouth, رِيق. To be choked with one's own —, شَرِقَ بِرِيقِهِ.

Splash, *n.* طَشَّة ـ طَشّ.

Splash, *v.t.* طَشَّ [2] ـ طَرَّشَ ـ رَشَّ [2]. To — about, as of water, خَضْخَضَ. To be splashed about, تَخَضْخَضَ. *See also to* Spatter, *v.t.*

Splashy, *a.* Puddly, سُوَّخِي. The ground became —, صَارَتِ ٱلْأَرْضُ سُوَاخًا.

Splay, *a.* عَرِيض.

Splay-footed, *a.* عَرِيضُ ٱلْأَقْدَامِ.

Splay-mouthed, *a.* وَاسِعُ (*or* عَرِيضُ) ٱلْفَمِ.

Spleen, *n.* The part of the body, طِحَال *pl.* طُحُل. Disease of the —, طُحَال. Having an enlarged —, طَحِل. Melancholy, السَّوْدَاء. Spite, vexation, ضِغْن ـ حِقْد ـ بُغْض ـ خُلْق. To excite one's —, أَثَارَ خُلْقَهُ.

Spleenish, *a.*
Spleeny, } Depressed in spirits, مُكَدَّرُ ٱلْخَاطِرِ ـ كَئِيب. Peevish, شَكِس ـ شَرِس. Affected with spleen, طَحِل.

Splendent, *a.* مُنِير ـ نَيِّر. *See* Resplendent, *a.*

Splendid, *a.* Shining, مُتَشَعْشِع ـ لَامِع ـ نَيِّر ـ زَاهِر. Magnificent, مُفْتَخَر ـ فَاخِر ـ جَلِيل ـ بَاهِر ـ جَلِيٌّ ـ بَهِيج. *See also* Magnificent, *a.*

Splendidly, *ad.* With splendour, بِجَلَالٍ ـ بِفَخْرٍ ـ بِسُمُوٍّ ـ بَهْجَةً ـ فَخَارَةً. Dexterously, بِغَايَةِ ٱلْإِتْقَانِ.

Splendour, *n.* بَهْجَة ـ فَخْر ـ جَلَال ـ رَوْنَق ـ إِفْتِخَار. *See also* Brilliancy, Brightness, *n.*

Splenetic, *n.* Affected with spleen, مَطْحُول ـ طَحِل.

Splenetic, *a.*
Splenical, } Peevish, شَكِس ـ شَرِس ـ نَكِد. Affected with spleen, مَطْحُول.

Splice, *n.* رَبْطَة ـ بَرِيم ـ مُبْرَم.

Splice, *v.t.* بَرَمَ [2] ـ أَبْرَمَ. To — the mainbrace, to take a drop too much, سَقَى ٱلْحَبَقَةَ ـ شَرِبَ كَأْسًا مِنَ ٱلْعَرَقِ زَائِدَةً.

Splint, *n.* As for a wounded limb, جِبَارَة *pl.* جَبَابِيرُ ـ جَبِيرَة ـ سَقِيفَة. An excrescence on the shank bone of a horse, نُتُوءٌ فِي سَاقِ ٱلْخَيْلِ.

Splinter, *n.* فِلْقَة ـ فِرَق *pl.* أَفْرَاق ـ شِقَّة *pl.* شِقَق ـ قِطْعَة *pl.* قِطَع ـ شِطْفَة *pl.* شِطَف ـ كِسْر *pl.* كُسُور. A —, from anything, which is being hammered, قُسَالَة ـ تُوبَال. A —, such as penetrates the flesh, شَظِيَّة ـ لِيطَة *pl.* لِيَاط. To fly into splinters, طَارَ شِقَقًا: his stick flew into splinters, طَارَتْ عَصَاهُ شِقَقًا. To fly, as of a —, from wood, نَتَرَ. *See also* Splint, *n.*

Splinter, *v.t.* To bind with splints, رَبَطَ فِي جَبَّرَ ـ جَبَابِير جَبِيرَة. To split, شَقَّ ـ فَلَّقَ. *See also to* Shiver, *v.t.*

Splinter, *v.i.* اِسْتَطَارَ ـ تَطَايَرَ ـ اِنْشَقَّ ـ اِنْفَلَعَ.

Split, *v.t.* فَضَّ ـ فَلَقَ ـ صَدَعَ ـ فَلَجَ ـ فَرَجَ ـ خَرَعَ ـ فَتَقَ ـ شَقَّقَ ـ شَقَّ ـ فَلَعَ ـ فَلَّقَ ـ بَزَلَ ـ عَزَقَ ـ شَرَمَ. To rend, فَتَقَ. To — off, as a chip from a stone, ظَرَّ. To — wood small, شَطَّفَ. *See also to* Divide, *v.t.*

Split, *v.i.* To part asunder, specially lengthwise, اِنْخَرَعَ ـ اِنْشَقَّ ـ تَشَقَّقَ ـ تَفَلَّقَ ـ اِنْفَلَقَ ـ اِنْفَلَجَ ـ اِنْفَضَّ ـ تَبَزَّلَ ـ اِنْفَتَقَ ـ تَفَتَّقَ ـ اِنْفَلَعَ ـ تَفَلَّعَ. To go into rents, تَشَرَّمَ. To — in pieces, طَارَ شِقَقًا ـ تَفَسَّخَ. To — with laughter, اِنْبَعَجَ مِنَ ٱلضَّحِكِ ـ فَقَعَ مِنَ ٱلضَّحِكِ. To — hairs, دَقَّ. *See also to* Burst, *v.i.*

Split, *n.* A longitudinal fissure, شِقّ *pl.* شُقُوق ـ شِقَّة ـ شَرْم ـ خَرْع. A rend, tear, فَتْقَة ـ فَتْق ـ شَرْم.

Split, *part.* and *a.* مَفْلُوع ـ مَشْقُوق ـ مَخْرُوع. Split peas, جُلُبَّانٌ بُسْتَانِيٌّ مَجْرُوش.

Splitting, *a.* شَاقٌّ. A — headache, صُدَاعٌ فَاجِعٌ.

Splutter, *n.* Bustle, stir, رَجَّة ـ هَيَجَان ـ هَزَّة ـ ضَجَّة ـ غَوْغَاء *vulg.* كَرْكَبَة.

Splutter, *v.i.* As in speaking, تَمْتَمَ ـ لَجْلَجَ ـ بَلْدَمَ.

Spoil, *n.* } Booty, سَلَب *pl.* أَسْلَاب ـ خَلِيسَة ـ خُلْسَة ـ نُهْبَة ـ
Spoils, } نَهْب *pl.* نِهَاب. *See also* Booty, *n.*

Spoil, *v.t.* To despoil, سَلَبَ ـ أَنْهَبَ ـ نَهَبَ. To corrupt, أَفْسَدَ ـ أَخْبَطَ ـ أَمَأَ ـ فَسَخَ ـ عَارَ. To injure, damage, عَكَسَ ـ خَسَّرَ ـ عَطَّلَ ـ أَعْدَمَ ـ أَتْلَفَ ـ أَعَارَ ـ عَوَّرَ *vulg.* خَرْبَطَ. To —, as a child, خَسَّرَ.

Spoil, *v.i.* To practise plunder, تَعَاطَى (or اِسْتَعْمَلَ) ٱلنَّهْبَ. To become bad, putrid, أَخْلَفَ ـ تَمَدَّرَ ـ تَعَفَّنَ ـ فَسَدَ ـ شَخِمَ. To become depraved, أَخْبَثَ ـ خَبُثَ. To —, to become bad, putrid, of any beverage, دَخِنَ; of butter, سَنِخَ; of eggs, مَذِرَ; of meat, flesh, أَخَمَّ ـ خَمَّ; of nuts, قَنِمَ; of oil, زَنِخَ; of a perfume, نَمِسَ; of paste, dough, فَخَّ.

Spoiler, *n.* A plunderer, نَاهِب *pl.* نُهَّاب ـ نَهَّاب. One who spoils children, مُسْتَرْخٍ فِي تَرْبِيَةِ ٱلْأَوْلَادِ ـ مُخَسِّرُ ٱلْأَوْلَادِ.

Spoke, *n.* As of a wheel, أُصْبُعُ عَجَلَةٍ *pl.* أَصَابِعُ ـ بَكْرَةُ عَجَلَةٍ *pl.* بَكَر. To put a — in one's wheel, عَكَسَ عَلَيْهِ أَمْرَهُ.

Spoke, *pret. of to* Speak, *q.v.*

Spoken, *part. of to* Speak, *q.v.* A word spoken in season how good it is! الكَلِمَةُ فِي وَقْتِهَا مَا أَحْسَنَهَا.

Spokesman, *n.* مُتَكَلِّمٌ عَنْ غَيْرِهِ ـ مُتَكَلِّم. The — of a people or party, مِدْرَهُ قَوْمٍ.

Spoliate, *v.t.* and *i.* *See to* Pillage, Spoil, *v.t.*

Spoliation, *n.* *See* Pillage, Plunder, *n.*

Spoliator, *n.* *See* Spoiler, *n.*

Spondee, *n.* جُزْءُ ٱلتَّفَاعِيلِ فِي ٱلشِّعْرِ.

Sponge, *n.* إِسْفَنْجَة *coll.* إِسْفَنْج. The — for a cannon, إِسْفَنْجَة (or خِرْقَةٌ) لِمَسْحِ دَاخِلِ ٱلْمِدْفَعِ.

Sponge, *v.t.* To — with a sponge, مَسَحَ بِإِسْفَنْجَةٍ; of a cannon, مَسَحَ دَاخِلَ ٱلْمِدْفَعِ بِٱلْخِرْقَةِ (or بِٱلْإِسْفَنْجَةِ). To —, wipe out, erase, مَحَقَ. To destroy, أَزَالَ.

Sponge, *v.i.* To imbibe, suck in, تَشَرَّبَ ـ شَرِبَ ـ تَنَشَّفَ. To act as a sponger, or uninvited guest, تَطَفَّلَ ـ طَفَّلَ ـ رَشَنَ. To — upon, تَطَفَّلَ عَلَى ـ لَقْلَقَ ـ تَسَلَّطَ ـ تَطَافَلَ.

Sponge-cake, *n.* حَلْوَاءُ مِنْ جِنْسِ لُقَمِ ٱلْقَاضِي.

Sponger, *n.* One who uses a sponge, مَسَّاحٌ بِٱلْإِسْفَنْجَةِ. One who sponges on others, ضَيْفَن *pl.* ضَيَافِن ـ مُبْرِم ـ وَارِن ـ وَارِش ـ رَاشِن ـ طُفَيْلِيّ.

Sponginess, *n.* مَاهِيَّةٌ إِسْفَنْجِيَّةٌ ـ صِفَةٌ إِسْفَنْجِيَّةٌ.

Sponging-house, *n.* سِجْنٌ وَقْتِيٌّ لِحَبْسِ ٱلْغُرَمَاءِ.

Sponsal, *a.* مُخْتَصٌّ بِٱلزِّيجَةِ ـ مُتَعَلِّقٌ بِٱلنِّكَاحِ.

Sponsalia, *n.* جِهَاز.

Sponsor, *n.* A surety, كَفِيل *pl.* كُفَلَاء ـ قَبِيل ـ غَرِير. A godfather, إِشْبِين *pl.* أَشَابِين ـ عَرَّاب; a godmother, إِشْبِينَة ـ عَرَّابَة. To be —, surety, for, ضَمِنَ. To be godfather to, وَقَفَ لَهُ أَشْبِينًا ـ يَقِفُ *aor.* عَمَّدَ; to be godmother to, وَقَفَتْ لَهُ أَشْبِينَةً ـ عَمَّدَتْهُ.

Sponsorial, *a.* Of suretyship, مُتَعَلِّقٌ بِٱلْكَفَالَةِ; of godparents, مُتَعَلِّقٌ بِٱلْأَشَابِينِ.

Sponsorship, *n.* Suretyship, كَفَالَة ـ قَبَالَة; of godparents, أَشْبِينِيَّة.

Spontaneity, *n.* / Spontaneousness, } Free choice, تِلْقَآءُ نَفْسٍ ـ إِخْتِيَار . The quality of giving unasked, تَبَرُّعٌ بِ ـ عَفْوٌ .

Spontaneous, *a.* Voluntary, مِنْ تِلْقَآءِ ٱلنَّفْسِ ـ إِخْتِيَارِيٌّ . Unasked, مُتَطَوِّعٌ ـ مُتَبَرِّعٌ .

Spontaneously, *ad.* Voluntarily, مِنْ تِلْقَآءِ نَفْسِهِ ـ بِٱخْتِيَارِهِ ـ *vulg.* مِنْهُ لِبَالِهِ ; unasked, تَبَرُّعًا ـ تَطَوُّعًا ـ عَفْوًا . He did it —, without being asked, فَعَلَهُ مُتَبَرِّعًا . I gave him —, أَعْطَيْتُهُ عَفْوًا . I gave him of the property —, أَعْطَيْتُهُ عَفْوَ ٱلْمَالِ .

Spool, *n.* As for thread; *see* Reel, *n.*

Spool, *v.t.* *See to* Reel, *v.t.*

Spoon, *n.* مِلْعَقَة *pl.* مَلَاعِقُ ـ مِلْبَنَة ـ مِغْرَفَة . A large —, ladle, خَاشُوقَة .

Spoonbill, *n.* أَبُو مِلْعَقَةٍ ـ طَيْرٌ ذُو مِنْقَارٍ مِثْلَ ٱلْمِلْعَقَةِ .

Spoon-diet, *n.* / Spoon-meat, / Spoon-victuals, } لَبَنِيَّة ـ سِكْبَاج . *See also* Gruel, *n.*

Spoonful, *n.* مِلْءُ مِلْعَقَةٍ ـ لُعْقَة .

Spoonwort, *n.* *See* Scurvy-grass, *n.*

Sporadic, *a.* / Sporadical, } Scattered, مُشَتَّتٌ ـ شَاذٌّ . Occurring here and there, إِتِّفَاقِيٌّ ـ وَاقِعٌ مُتَفَرِّقًا .

Spore, *n.* / Sporule, } مَا قَامَ مَقَامَ ٱلْبِزْرِ فِي ٱلنَّبَاتِ ٱلْمُزْهِرِ .

Sport, *n.* Play, pastime, لَعِب ـ تَنَزُّه ـ مَلْهًى ـ لَهْوٌ ـ عَبَث . Fun, jest, مَزْح ـ هَزْل . Game, scorn, هُزْوٌ ـ إِسْتِهْزَآء . Field —, صَيْد ـ صَيْدٌ وَقَنْص . A plaything, لُعْبَة *pl.* لُعَبَات . In —, fun, هَزْلًا . To make —, fun, game, of, إِسْتَهْزَأَ بِ ـ ضَحِكَ مِنْ ـ شَاقَحَ . Fortune made — of him, عَبِثَ بِهِ ٱلدَّهْرُ . *See also* Fun, Play, *n.*

Sport, *v.t.* To wear, تَزَيَّنَ بِ ـ لَبِسَ . To carry, as about one, حَمَلَ ـ تَكَيَّسَ بِ . To parade, أَظْهَرَ ـ أَشْهَرَ ـ تَفَخَّرَ بِ ـ تَطَوَّسَ بِ .

Sport, *v.i.* To play, عَبِثَ ـ لَعِبَ ـ مَرِحَ ـ دَعِبَ . To — with, trifle with, لَعِبَ بِ ـ عَبِثَ بِ ـ تَسَلَّى ـ تَنَزَّهَ ; to play one a joke, لَعِبَ مَلْعُوبًا . *See also to* Play, *v.i.*

Sportful, *a.* مَرِّيح ـ هَزِل ـ لَعِيب ـ لَعُوب ـ عَبِّيث ـ دَعَّاب لَعَّاب .

Sportfulness, *n.* / Sportiveness, } هَزْل ـ مِرَاح ـ دُعَابَة .

Sportive, *a.* *See* Sportful, Merry, Gay, *a.*

Sportively, *ad.* هَزْلًا ـ لَهْوًا . *See also* Merrily, *ad.*

Sportsman, *n.* صَيَّاد ـ قَانِص *pl.* صَيَّارُونَ . A good —, أَصْيَدُ . *See also* Hunter, Fowler, Fisherman, *n.*

Sportsmanship, *n.* تَصَيُّد ـ صَيْد .

Sporule, *n.* *See* Spore, *n.*

Spot, *n.* A stain, بُقْعَة *pl.* بُقَع ـ طَبْعَة . A defect, شَائِبَة *pl.* شَوَائِبُ . A mark, dot, نُقْطَة *pl.* نُقَط ; as on an animal, رُقْطَة *pl.* رُقَط . A — of land, بُقْعَة *pl.* بِقَاع . A taint, disgrace, عَيْب *pl.* عُيُوب . A place, مَكَان ـ مَحَطّ ـ مَحَلّ . A place where a thing is met with or to which one is used, مَعْهَد . A — on the sun, ضَبَابَةٌ فِي عَيْنِ ٱلشَّمْسِ . On the —, place, فِي ذَاتِ ٱلْمَحَلِّ ـ ثَمَّ ; at once, فِي ٱلْحَالِ ـ حَالًا ـ عَلَى ٱلْفَوْرِ .

Spot, *v.t.* To stain, discolour, بَقَّعَ ـ طَبَّعَ . To mark with spots, نَقَّطَ ـ رَقَّطَ عَلَى . To tarnish, disgrace, عَيَّبَ . To mark by way of ornament, نَقَّشَ . I spotted my dress, as with spots of ink, and such like, رَقَّطْتُ عَلَى ثَوْبِي .

Spot, *v.i.* To change colour, tarnish, تَكَدَّرَ لَوْنُهُ ـ تَطَبَّعَ ـ أَنْبَقَعَ . To become marked with spots, تَرَقَّطَ ـ نُقِطَ . His garment became spotted, as with spots of ink, *etc.*, تَرَقَّطَ ثَوْبُهُ .

Spotless, *a.* Not spotted, غَيْرُ مُنَقَّطٍ . *See also* Immaculate, *a.*

Spotlessness, *n.* The not being spotted, عَدَمُ تَنْقِيطٍ . *See also* Immaculateness, *n.*

Spotted, *a.* / Spotty, } Marked with spots, أَرْقَط *fem.* رَقْطَآء *pl.* رُقْط ـ مُنَقَّط ـ مُنَمَّر ـ أَنْمَر ـ أَنْمَش . Variegated, مَنْقُوش .

Spottedness, *n.* نَقْشَة ـ نَقْط ـ نَمَر ـ رُقْطَة .

Spousal, *a.* *See* Matrimonial, *a.*

Spousals, *n.* *See* Espousals, *and* Nuptials, *n.*

Spouse, *n.* A consort, قَرِين *fem.* قَرِينَة . A husband, زَوْج ; a wife, زَوْجَة . A bride or bridegroom, عِرْس *pl.* أَعْرَاس .

Spouse, *v.t.* *See to* Espouse, *v.t.*

Spouseless, *a.* غَيْرُ مُزَوَّجٍ *fem.* غَيْرُ مُزَوَّجَةٍ .

Spout, *n.* As of a mug, بُلْبُل ـ قَنَاة ـ *vulg.* خَشْم ; as of a pipe, لُوْلَب . A — or gutter for conveying water, جُحْر ـ ثَعْلَب ـ مِثْرَاب *pl.* مَآزِيب ـ ثَقْب . The mouth of a —, صُنْبُور *pl.* صَنَابِرُ . A — or spouting of water, إِنْبِجَاسُ مَآءٍ ـ مَآءٌ بَجْس .

Spout, *v.t.* Of water, *etc.*, أَخْرَجَ ـ بَجَسَ ـ فَجَّرَ ; of words, بَالَغَ فِي ٱلْكَلَامِ ـ صَابَ فِي ٱلْكَلِمِ . To — poetry, تَشَاعَرَ . *See also to* Spurt, *v.t.*

Spout, *v.i.* To issue with violence, of a liquid, بَجَسَ ـ إِنْبَجَسَ ـ تَبَجَّسَ ـ تَفَجَّرَ . *See also to* Spurt, *v.i.*

Spouter, *n.* Of words, مُبَالِغ ـ هَثَّات; of poetry, مُتَشَاعِر.

Spouting, *n.* Of a liquid, تَفَجُّر ـ إِنْبِجَاس ـ بَجْس ـ إِنْفِجَار; of speech, مُبَالَغَة ـ شَدْوٌ ـ ٱلشُّيُوبُ فِي ٱلْكَلِمِ; of poetry, تَشَاعُر.

Sprain, *n.* جِنَايَة ـ فَسْخ ـ إِلْتِوَآء ـ فَكّ ـ إِنْفِكَاك. *See also* Dislocation, *n.*

Sprain, *v.t.* لَوَى ـ ² فَكَّ ـ ² جَنَا ـ ² فَسَخَ: He sprained his arm or hand, جَنَا يَدَهُ ². *See also to* Dislocate, *v.t.*

Sprat, *n.* نَوْعٌ مِنْ سَمَكِ ٱلْبَحْرِ صَغِيرٌ ـ هَفّ coll. هَفَّة. To give a — to, in order to catch a herring, غَازَرَ; the doing so, مُغَازَرَة; one who does so, مُتَغَازِر ـ مُغَازِر. I am throwing a — to catch a herring, أَتَغَذَّتُ مَا أَنَا عَلَيْهِ حَتَّى أَسْتَسْمِنَ.

Sprawl, *v.i.* To stretch the body in a horizontal position, تَمَدَّدَ ـ تَبَطَّحَ ـ إِنْبَطَحَ ـ تَسَطَّحَ ـ إِنْسَطَحَ; on the stomach, تَبَطَّحَ ـ إِنْبَطَحَ. To —, in walking, تَفَكَّكَ ـ تَخَلَّعَ. To make one to —, to throw down on his back, ² سَطَحَ; on the belly, ² بَطَحَ. To throw down, أَوْقَعَ.

Sprawling, *a.* Not well combined, غَيْرُ ـ مَفْكُوك ـ مُتَخَلِّع مُهَنْدَم.

Spray, *n.* A shoot, small branch, شُعْبَة *pl.* شُعَب *and* شِعَاب. A — of precious stones, رِيشَة. Spray of the sea, رَشَاشُ ٱلْبَحْرِ. *See also* Sprout, *and* Foam, *n.*

Spread, *v.t.* To spread out, to extend, as over a surface, ² سَطَحَ ـ ² نَشَرَ ـ ² نَشَرَ ـ ² فَرَشَ ـ ² بَطَحَ ـ ² بَسَطَ; to be so spread, إِنْبَسَطَ ـ إِنْتَشَرَ ـ تَنَشَّرَ ـ إِنْبَطَحَ ـ إِفْتَرَشَ. To —, as of the wings, ² بَسَطَ: They — their wings, يَبْسُطُونَ ٱلْأَجْنِحَة. To expand, ² مَدَّ ـ وَسَّعَ; to be expanded, إِتَّسَعَ ـ إِمْتَدَّ. To scatter, diffuse, as intelligence, *etc.*, أَذَاعَ ـ ² نَشَرَ ـ ² شَهَرَ ـ أَشَاعَ بِ ـ ² شَاعَ بِ ـ ² فَاضَ ـ ² فَشَا ـ ² ذَاعَ ـ ² شَاعَ ـ أَفْشَى ـ أَذَاعَ بِ; to be so —, تَفَشَّى ـ ٱلْخَبَرُ. To — among, as of a disease, (تَفَشًّا or تَفَشِّيًا) فِي ـ ² سَرَى فِي aor. يَسْرِي. To grow, ² نَمَى ـ أَنْمَى. To —, as a net, for, أَنْصَبَ لِ. I — a bed for him, فَرَشْتُ ـ فَرَشْتُهُ فِرَاشًا لَهُ فِرَاشًا. The disease will certainly — to the town, لَا بُدَّ مِنْ أَنْ يَسْرِيَ ٱلْمَرَضُ إِلَى ٱلْمَدِينَةِ. Disease — among them, فَشَتْ بَيْنَهُمُ ٱلْأَمْرَاضُ.

Spread, *v.i.* To become spread, إِتَّسَعَ ـ إِنْتَشَرَ ـ إِمْتَدَّ. To —, as a tree, إِفْتَرَشَ. To —, as the dawn, إِسْتَطَارَ. The circle of difference —, widened, إِتَّسَعَتْ دَائِرَةُ ٱلْمُخَاصَمَاتِ. The fire, (as of a burning house,) — and glared, إِنْدَرَأَ ٱلْحَرِيقُ. To —, to become —, like wild fire, ² طَارَ.

Spread, *part.* and *a.* As of a carpet, *etc.*, سَطِيح ـ مُسَطَّح ـ مَفْرُوش; scattered, diffused, شَرُود ـ شَارِد ـ شَتّ; spread abroad, published, أَمْرٌ شَتّ ـ شَائِع ـ مُنْتَشِر ـ مَنْشُور. A report —, خَبَرٌ شَائِعٌ ـ خَبَرٌ شَتّ.

Spread, *n.* Promulgation, إِنْتِشَار. Growth, نَمَآء ـ نُمُوّ ـ نَمِيَّة. To prevent the further — of disease, لِمَنْعِ زِيَادَةِ ٱنْتِشَارِ ٱلْأَمْرَاضِ. *See also* Development, Propagation, *n.*

Spreader, *n.* As of carpets, *etc.*, مُفَرِّش.

Spreading, *a.* As a tree, مُفَرِّش. A — vine, كَرْمَةٌ مُنْتَشِرَةٌ. Spreading over (adverbially) several years, عَلَى عَوَامٍ عَدِيدَةٍ.

Spree, *n.* A frolic, مَزْح; with drinking, مُنَادَمَة. To have a —, frolic, ² مَزَحَ; with others, مَازَحَ. To have a —, with drinking, in company with another, نَادَمَ. They had a jolly —, with drinking, of many, تَنَادَمُوا.

Sprig, *n.* طَاقَة *pl.* أَطْوَاق ـ شُعْبَة *pl.* شُعَب *and* شِعَاب. A —, as of gems, *etc.*, رِيشَة.

Sprig, *v.t.* To mark with sprigs, نَقَّشَ ـ بِشِعَابِ ٱلزَّهْرِ ـ زَيَّنَ ـ بِرِيشَاتٍ.

Sprigged, *a.* Marked with sprigs, مُنَقَّشٌ بِشِعَابٍ مِنَ ٱلْأَزْهَارِ ـ مُشَجَّر ـ مُزَيَّنٌ بِرِيشَاتٍ.

Spriggy, *a.* Full of sprigs, مَمْلُوٌّ مِنْ شِعَابٍ ـ كَثِيرُ ٱلشِّعَابِ.

Spright, *n.* } An apparition, أَخْيِلَة *pl.* خَيَال ـ أَزْوَال *pl.* زَوْل
Sprite, } طَيْف. *See also* Spectre, *n.*

Sprightful, *a.* *See* Sprightly, *a.*

Sprightliness, *n.* Vivacity, حُمَيَّا ـ سَوْرَة ـ شُبَيْب ـ شِبَاب ـ نَشَاط ـ فُرُوهَة ـ فَرَاهِيَة ـ سُرُورٌ وَٱبْتِهَاج ـ خِفَّة. Cheerfulness, pleasantness, حُبُور ـ بَشَاشَة ـ فَرَح. *See also* Briskness, Gaiety, *n.*

Sprightly, *a.* Brisk, نُدُب *pl.* نَدْب ـ أَلُوب ـ زَوْل ـ فَرِهٌ ـ رَوَّاح ـ هَشٌّ بَشٌّ ـ فَلْتَان ـ خَفِيف ـ نَدُوب. Cheerful, pleasant, sociable, أَنِيس ـ حَبُور ـ بَشَّاش. To be —, gay, cheerful, ² فَرِهَ ـ ² حَبِرَ. To make —, gay, أَطْرَبَ ـ حَبَّرَ ـ ² طَرِبَ. *See also* Lively, Gay.

Spring, *v.i.* As of water, *etc.*, from the ground, *etc.*, to gush forth, تَبَجَّسَ ـ إِنْبَجَسَ ـ ² بَجَسَ ـ ثَارَ aor. يَثُورُ ـ إِنْفَجَرَ ـ ² نَضَحَ ـ ² نَبَعَ ². To hasten, ² ثَارَ. To leap, bound, ² قَفَزَ ـ ² طَفَرَ ـ ² قَفَزَ ـ ² نَطَّ ـ وَثَبَ aor. يَثِبُ. To —, as a splinter from wood, *etc.*, ² تَرَّ. To burst, as a mine, ² فَقَعَ ـ إِسْتَطَارَ ـ تَطَايَرَ. To —, as the day, ² طَلَعَ ٱلْفَجْرُ.

To spring back, to recoil, تَرَاجَعَ ـ تَرَادَّ. To shrink from, ² جَفَلَ عَنْ ـ تَجَافَى عَنْ ـ ² جَبَأَ عَنْ.

To spring forth, as plants, *etc.*, أَنْبَتَ ـ ² نَبَتَ ـ ² طَلَعَ; as the morning, إِنْفَجَرَ ـ ² طَلَعَ ٱلنَّهَارُ. To appear, come to pass, ² ظَهَرَ ـ ² صَارَ ـ ² حَدَثَ ـ ² بَانَ.

To spring forward or towards, ² ثَارَ إِلَى ـ وَثَبَ نَحْوَ كَذَا aor. يَثِبُ.

To spring from, issue from, إِنْبَثَقَ مِن — صَدَرَ عَن.

To spring into, طَرَحَ نَفْسَهُ فِي.

To spring up, as from one's seat, إِنْتَهَضَ — نَهَضَ; as plants, أَنْبَتَ — نَبَتَ — أَطْلَعَ — طَلَعَ — أَوْشَمَ — طَرَّ. To appear, تَبَيَّنَ — ظَهَرَ. To become roused, incited, إِنْبَعَثَ.

The seed-produce sprang up, أَطْلَعَ (or طَلَعَ) ٱلزَّرْعُ.

To spring upon, سَاوَرَ — يَسْطُو aor. سَطَا بِ — ثَاوَرَ.

Spring, v.t. To start or rouse, as game, طَيَّرَ — أَنْفَزَ. To crack, as of a mast, etc., شَقَّقَ — شَقَّ — صَدَعَ — أَسْقَطَ. To explode, as of a mine, طَيَّرَ — أَطْلَقَ. To burst open, فَقَأَ — صَدَعَ — بَعَجَ — شَقَّ — كَسَرَ. To cause to — from a given spot, as an arch, أَنْشَأَ. To leap over, قَزَّ — نَطَّ — سَاوَرَ. To — a leak, of a ship, إِنْخَرَقَتِ ٱلسَّفِينَةُ. To —, as a snare, شَدَّ.

Spring, n. The season, ٱلرَّبِيعُ; the early —, ٱلرَّبِيعُ ٱلْأَوَّلُ; the late —, ٱلرَّبِيعُ ٱلثَّانِي. A leap, قَفْزَة — قَزَّة — نَطٌّ — قَزٌّ — قَفْز — نَطَّة. A bound, rush, سَوْرَة — سَطْوَة — وَثْبَة — ثَوْرَة. A fountain, فَوَّارَة — عَيْن pl. عُيُون — مَنْبَع — مَنْشَأ. Source, origin, مَصْدَر — أَصْل — مَنْبَت. A cause, سَبَب — عِلَّة. Elastic power or force, قُوَّةُ ٱلِٱمْتِغَاطِ. A —, an elastic body, لَوْلَب pl. لَوَالِبُ — from the Persian, زَنْبُرَك. A hot —, حَمَّة — عَيْنُ مَاءٍ حَارٍّ. A — residence, مَرْبَع — رَبْع. To pass the — in a place, رَبَعَ بِٱلْمَكَانِ. The — of water burst forth, تَفَرَّتِ ٱلْعَيْنُ. The land burst forth with the springs, تَفَرَّتِ ٱلْأَرْضُ بِٱلْعُيُونِ. To take a —; see to Spring, v.i.

Springe, n. See Snare, Noose, n.

Springhalt, n. عَرَج — تَعَرُّج.

Spring-head, n. رَأْسُ عَيْنٍ.

Springiness, n. The power of springing, قَفْز — نَطٌّ. Elasticity, إِمْتِغَاط — قُوَّةُ ٱلِٱمْتِغَاطِ. Abundance of springs, كَثْرَةُ عُيُونٍ.

Springing, a. As of water, نَابِع — بَجْس — بَجِيس.

Spring-tide, n. High tide, مَدٌّ كَامِلٌ.

Spring-time, n. وَقْتُ ٱلرَّبِيعِ.

Springy, a. Elastic, مُمْتَغِط — يَمُدُّ وَيَقْلَصُ. Able to leap far, نَطَّاط — قَفَّاز. Full of springs, of water, etc., كَثِيرُ ٱلْعُيُونِ.

Sprinkle, v.t. طَشَّ — رَشَّ — أَرَشَّ — طَرَشَ. To —, as of a house, نَضَحَ. To — with the tips of the fingers, ذَرَّ. To —, as salt, etc., over anything, ذَرَّ. To —, as with dust or sand, تَرَّبَ — أَتْرَبَ. To wet, moisten, بَلَّلَ. To be sprinkled, تَرَشَّشَ; as over a house, إِنْتَضَحَ. To be moistened, تَبَلَّلَ. They sprinkled water over one another, of many, تَنَاضَحُوا.

Sprinkle, v.i. To fall in light rain, أَطَشَّتِ (or طَشَّتِ) ٱلسَّمَاءُ.

Sprinkle, n. رَشَّة — رَشّ pl. رِشَاش — طَشّ pl. طِشَاش — نَضْحَة — نَضْح — بَلَّة.

Sprinkled, a. مَرْشُوش. The water was — over him, تَرَشَّشَ عَلَيْهِ ٱلْمَاءُ. What is —, رَشَاش.

Sprinkling, n. As of rain, طَشّ — طَشِيش — رَذَاذ — رَشّ. The act of —, رَشّ — طَشّ — تَطْرِيش; as of salt, etc., ذَرّ. A small number, قَلِيل — بَعْض — رَشٌّ مِنَ ٱلْمَطَرِ. A utensil for —, ذَرُّو — مِرَشَّة.

Sprit, n. The boom so called, بَاشْتُونٌ صَغِيرٌ — سَارِيَةٌ صَغِيرَةٌ.

See also Sprout, n.

Spritsail, n. شِرَاعٌ مِنْ تَحْتِ ٱلْجَوَادِرَةِ.

Sprite, n. An apparition, خَيَال pl. أَخْيِلَة — زَوْل pl. أَزْوَال — طَيْف — عِفْرِيت — عِفْرِيتَة fem. عَفَارِيت.

Sprout, v.i. فَرَّخَ — طَرَّ — قَصَّعَ — ذَرَّ — أَشْطَأَ — نَهَضَ — أَنْبَتَ — نَبَتَ — أَخْرَجَ ٱلْأَشْطَاءَ; of a bird's feathers, أَخْلَفَ ٱلطَّائِرُ. To —, after appearing dead, of a tree, إِخْتَلَفَتِ ٱلشَّجَرَةُ.

Sprout, n. شَطْءٌ pl. أَشْطَاءٌ — فَرْخَة pl. فِرَاخ — فَرْعُ شَجَرَةٍ — نَبْت coll. نَبَات — نَاشِئَة. A — at the root of trees, شَكِير pl. شُكُر. A small cabbage, كُرُنْبِيَّة. Brussels sprouts, كُرُنْبِيَّاتٌ فَلَمَنْكِيَّةٌ.

Spruce, a. Neat, trim, لَطِيف — ظَرِيف — كَيِّس — أَنِيق — حَسَن. *See also* Finical, a.

Spruce, v.t. زَيَّنَ — ظَرَّفَ — كَيَّسَ. To — one's self, تَظَرَّفَ — تَطَوَّسَ — تَظَارَفَ.

Spruce, n. The fir tree, شَجَرَةُ ٱلرَّاتِينَجِ.

Sprucely, ad. With affected neatness, بِتَأَنُّقٍ — بِٱلتَّظَرُّفِ. With neatness, بِلَطَافَةٍ — بِكِيَاسَةٍ.

Spruceness, n. Neatness, كِيَاسَة — ظَرَافَة — لَطَافَة — حُسْن.

Sprung, pret. of to Spring, q.v.

Spry, a. Lively, brisk, نَاشِط — نَشِيط — وَجِز — أَلُوب. *See also* Brisk, Lively, a.

Spud, n. مِعْزَقَة — مِجْرَفَة — مِقْلَب.

Spume, n. *See* Foam, Scum, n.

Spume, v.i. *See to* Foam, Froth, v.i.

Spumescence, n. *See* Frothiness, n.

Spumous, a.
Spumy, } *See* Foamy, a.

Spun, part. of to Spin, q.v.

Spunge, n. *See* Sponge, n.

Spunger, n. *See* Sponger, n.

Spunk, *n.* The tinder, صُوفان. Warmth of temper, حُمَيَّا.

Spunky, *a.* *See* Spirited, *a.*

Spun-yarn, *n.* مُشاقَةٌ مَغْزُولَةٌ.

Spur, *n.* As for a horse, *etc.*, — شَوْك *coll.* شَوْكَة — مِنْخاز مَهاوِزُ *pl.* مِهْماز. The — of a cock, شَوْكَةُ ٱلدِّيكِ — ظُفُرُ ٱلدِّيكِ *pl.* أَظْفار. An instigation, stimulus, — سَوْق — مِنْخَسَة — سائِق إِنْهاض. The — of a mountain, — طُنُوف *pl.* طَنَفُ جَبَلٍ خُرُوم *pl.* خَرْمُ جَبَلٍ — مَخْرَمُ جَبَلٍ *pl.* مَخارِمُ. Spur, on grain, ergot, عاهَةُ ٱلْحُبُوبِ. On the — of the moment, — فِي ٱلسَّاعَةِ حالاً — عَلَى ٱلْغَفْلَةِ — عَلَى ٱلْفَوْرِ.

Spur, *v.t.* To prick, as with a spur, — نَفَسَ — همز — نخس بِٱلشَّوْكِ — نخز — وَكَزَ *aor.* يَكِزُ. To stimulate, — هَيَّجَ — حَرَّضَ أَنْفَسَ — حَثَّ — أَنْهَضَ — غَزَّ. To drive, make to go fast, رَكَّبَ ل-(*or* لَبَّسَ-) مَهامِيزَ. To put spurs on, — رَكَضَ — ساقَ.

Spur, *v.i.* To hasten, إِنْبَعَثَ فِي ٱلسَّيْرِ — طارَ — أَفاجَ — أَسْرَعَ.

Spur-gall, *n.* سَلِيقَةُ ٱلْمِهْمازِ — سَلِيقَةٌ مِنَ ٱلْمِهْمازِ.

Spur-galled, *a.* مُتَعَقِّرٌ مِنَ ٱلْمِهْمازِ.

Spurge, *n.* حَبَّةُ ٱلْمُلُوكِ — شُبْرُم.

Spurious, *a.* Not genuine, مُمَوَّه — مُقَلَّد — مُصَنَّع — مُفْتَرًى. Base, ignoble, زَنِيم. False, counterfeit, — مُمَوَّه — مُزَوَّر — مُفْتَرًى كاذِب. Apocryphal, مُنْكَر — مُرِيب — مَوْهُوم. Adulterated, changed, of writings, مُحَرَّف. Illegitimate, نَغِل *fem.* نَغِلَة. A — child, وَضِيعَة *pl.* وَضائِعُ — وَلَدُ غِيَّةٍ *pl.* أَوْلاد — زَنِيم. Spurious coin, زَغَل — غِشّ. *See also* Bastard, Fictitious, *a.*

Spuriously, *ad.* Falsely, كِذْبًا — بِٱلْكَذِبِ; by counterfeit, تَقْلِيدًا — تَمْوِيهًا — بِٱفْتِراءٍ.

Spuriousness, *n.* The quality of not being genuine, — إِفْتِراء زُور — تَمْوِيه — كَذْبَة; of coin, غِشّ — زَغَل. *See also* Bastardy, *n.*

Spurn, *v.t.* To kick, رَفَسَ. To disdain, — أَهانَ — إِزْدَرَى إِسْتَزْرَى — إِحْتَقَرَ — إِسْتَحْقَرَ. To — from one's presence, — طَرَدَ طَرَدَ بِإِهانَةٍ. To —, as an offer, *etc.*, to reject, — رَفَضَ إِسْتَحْقَرَ بِ. To be above doing, — تَعَظَّمَ عَنْ — إِسْتَحَى مِنْ تَرَفَّعَ عَنْ — تَجالَّ عَنْ. *See also to* Disdain, Contemn, *v.t.*

Spurn, *n.* As with the foot, رَفْسَة. Contemptuous treatment, إِسْتِحْقار — إِهانَة — إِزْدِراء.

Spurred, *a.* Having on spurs, لابِسُ مَهامِيزَ; furnished with spurs, as a cock, ذُو شَوْكٍ — ذُو أَظْفارٍ. Spurred grain, with ergot, حُبُوبٌ ذاتُ عاهَةٍ.

Spurt, *v.t.* To throw out with force, of a liquid, — بَجَّسَ — فَجَّرَ شَخَبَ. *See also to* Spout, *v.t.*

Spurt, *v.i.* To issue with force, of a liquid, — شَخَبَ — تَبَجَّسَ ثارَ — أَثَجَّ — ثَجَّ.

Spurt, *n.* A sudden gushing, of a liquid, — إِنْبِجاس — شَخْب شَخْبَة — ثَوْر — مَجِيج — دُفْقَة *pl.* دُفَق. A sudden effort, — ثَوْرَة فَوْرَة.

Sputter, *n.* Saliva from the mouth, لُعاب. Matter sputtered, رُشاش — طَشاش — طَشّ. Sputtered words, لَجْلَجَة — لُكْنَة.

Sputter, *v.i.* Of spittle from the mouth, — أَلْعَبَ — لَعَبَ أَطَشَّ — طَشَّ. To throw off moisture in particles, رالَ. To — in speech, تَمْتَمَ — لَجْلَجَ — لَكِنَ. A drunkard who sputters in his speech, does not speak distinctly, سَكْرانُ ما يَبُتُّ كَلامًا.

Sputterer, *n.* In speech, مُتَمْتِم — مُلَجْلِج — أَلْكَنُ.

Spy, *n.* جاسُوس *pl.* جَواسِيس — جَسّاس *pl.* جَسّاسُون — دَسِيس *vulg.* داسُوس *and* دَاسِيس. A —, as of an army, رَقِيب *pl.* رُقَباء. The spies or espying party of an army, الطَّلِيعَة. They were charged with being spies, أُتُّهِمُوا بِأَنَّهُمْ كانُوا جَواسِيسَ. He sent out spies, أَرْسَلَ جَواسِيسَ.

Spy, *v.t.* *See to* Espy, *v.t.*

Spy, *v.i.* To play the spy, تَجَسَّسَ.

Spy-glass, *n.* نَظّارَة *pl.* نَظّارات; *from the Turkish,* دُورْبِين *pl.* دَرابِينُ — *from the English,* تِلِسْكُوب.

Spyism, *n.* *See* Espionage, *n.*

Squab, Squabbish, *a.* Squabby, } Short and fat, شَحِيمٌ قَصِيرٌ — مُرَكْرَب. *See also* Squat, *a.*

Squab, *n.* A young domestic pigeon, فَرْخُ حَمامَةٍ *pl.* أَفْراخ.

Squabble, *v.i.* To — with, شاجَرَ — نازَعَ — قاتَلَ. They squabbled among themselves, of many, — تَنازَعُوا — تَناجَزُوا تَشاجَرُوا — تَعالَجُوا.

Squabble, *n.* مُشاجَرَة — نِزاع — مُنازَعَة — مُعارَضَة.

Squabbler, *n.* مَرِث — فَتّان — شُكْلِيّ — مُتَشاجِر — شَرِس.

Squad, *n.* A small party of persons, فِرْقَة *pl.* فِرَق — حِزْب *pl.* أَحْزاب — شِرْذِمَة *pl.* شَراذِمُ. A — of soldiers, فِرْقَةٌ مِنَ ٱلْعَسْكَرِ. An awkward —, of soldiers, فِرْقَةٌ مِنْ خُرْقِ ٱلْعَسْكَرِ; of recruits, فِرْقَةٌ مِنَ ٱلْعَساكِرِ ٱلْجُدُدِ.

Squadron, *n.* A — of troops, up to 1000 men, كَتِيبَة *pl.* كَتائِبُ; from 1000 to 4000, جَيْش *pl.* جُيُوش — فَيْلَق *pl.* فَيالِقُ — جَحْفَل *pl.* جَحافِلُ; from 4000 to 12,000, خَمِيس; *from the Turkish,* أَلاي *pl.* أَلايات — أُرْطَة *pl.* أُرْطات. A — of horse, قَنْبَل — مِنْسَر — مِقْنَب — كَرادِيس *and* كَرادِس *pl.* كُرْدُوسَة *pl.*

— بُلُكْ or بُلُكْ ;*from the Turkish,* كَتَائِبُ *pl.* كَتِيبَة — قَنَابِل — بُلُكَات. A — of ships, فِرْقَةٌ مِنَ ٱلْمَرَاكِبِ — دُونَنْمَا صَغِيرَة. The commander of a — of horse, بُلُكْبَاشِي — رَئِيسُ ٱلْكَتِيبَةِ.

Squalid, *a.* Filthy, وَسِخ — نَجِس — قَذِر — رَجِس — دَرِن — مَذِر. Mean, حَقِير. To be —, دَرِنَ — دَنِسَ.

Squalidity, *n.* } دَنَاسَة — وَسَاخَة — وَسَخ — نَجَاسَة — وَكَب — دَرَن.
Squalidness,

Squall, *n.* A scream, صَرِير — عَوْل — عَوِيل — صُرَاخ — عِيَاط — صِيَاح. A sudden gust of wind, نَفْخَة *pl.* نَفَخَات — نُخْرَةٌ مِنَ تَلْقِيحَة — ٱلرِّيحِ.

Squall, *v.i.* To scream, صَاحَ — أَعْوَلَ — صَرَخَ. *See also to* Pule, *v.i.*

Squaller, *n.* A screamer, صَرَّاخ — عَيَّاط — صَارِخ.

Squally, *a.* Of the weather, ذُو نَوْءٍ غِبٍّ.

Squalor, *n.* *See* Squalidity, *n.*

Squamose, *a.* } ذُو فُلُوسٍ — ذُو حَرْشَفٍ.
Squamous,

Squander, *v.t.* أَزَالَ — أَتْلَفَ — أَذْهَبَ — أَسْرَفَ — سَرِفَ — بَذَّرَ. He squandered his property, أَطَاحَ مَالَهُ. *See also to* Spend, *v.t.*

Squanderer, *n.* مُبَذِّر — رَجُلٌ مُتْلِفُ مَالِهِ — مِضْيَاعٌ لِلْمَالِ — مِتْلَاف — مُبَاذِر. *See also* Spendthrift, *n.*

Squandering, *n.* إِتْلَاف — مُبَاذَرَةُ ٱلْمَالِ — تَبْذِير — إِسْرَاف — إِزَالَة.

Squanderingly, *ad.* تَبْذِيرًا — إِتْلَافًا — إِسْرَافًا.

Square, *a.* Having four equal sides, مُرَبَّع. Straight, perpendicular, عَمُودِيّ — قِيَام *pl.* قَوِيم — عَادِل — مُلْتَئِب. Balanced, مَضْبُوط — مُوَازِن — مَوْزُون. Fair, just, مُسْتَقِيم — عَادِل. Correct, مُصَحَّح — صَحِيح. Any — building, كَعْبَة. To make —, of four sides, رَبَّعَ. *See also under to* Square, *v.t.*

A square number, عَدَدٌ مُرَبَّعٌ — مُرَبَّع.

Square contents, ٱلْمُكَعَّب.

Square measure, قِيَاسُ ٱلْعُرْضِ وَٱلْمَسَاحَةِ.

Square root, جِذْرٌ مُرَبَّعٌ — جِذْر.

Square, *n.* A figure of four sides, مُرَبَّع. The contents of the side of a figure squared, مَسَافَةٌ تَرْبِيعِيَّةٌ — سَطْحٌ تَرْبِيعِيٌّ. An open space, عَرْصَة *pl.* أَعْرَاص and عَرَصَات — بَاحَة *pl.* بُوح — مَيْدَانٌ فِي بَلَدٍ *pl.* مَيَادِينُ. A —, as of soldiers, قَلْعَة. The — of a number, عَدَدٌ فِي مِثْلِهِ: the — of three, ثَلَاثَةٌ فِي مِثْلِهِ — ثَلَاثَةٌ فِي ثَلَاثَةٍ. A carpenter's —, كُوس *pl.* كُوسَات — جَدْوَل — مِسْطَرَة — زَاوِيَة. Regularity, evenness, مُسَاوَاة. Fitness, suitableness, مُوَافَقَة — مُطَابَقَة. A — on a chess-board, بَيْت *pl.* بُيُوت — خَانَة *pl.* خَانَات. They formed —, of soldiers, اِصْطَفُّوا قَلْعَةً — صَارُوا قَلْعَةً. They broke the —, فَضُّوا ٱلْقَلْعَةَ. In the form of a —, عَلَى شَكْلٍ مُرَبَّعٍ. *See also* Area, Court, *n.*

Square, *v.t.* To make square, four-sided, رَبَّعَ. To adjust, وَفَّقَ — طَابَقَ — عَدَّلَ — طَبَّقَ. To balance, وَازَنَ. To make symmetrical, عَدَّلَ — هَنْدَمَ. To — or proportion to, خَلَقَ-لِ — وَافَقَ سِيرَتَهُ عَلَى (or لِ) — نَاسَبَ — قَدَّرَ-عَلَى. To — one's course to,

To square accounts, سَدَّ ٱلْحِسَابَاتِ.

To square a circle, رَبَّعَ ٱلدَّائِرَةَ (وَهُوَ شَيْءٌ مُحَالٌ).

To square a number, ضَرَبَ عَدَدًا فِي مِثْلِهِ.

To square yards, عَدَّلَ ٱلزَّوَاجِعَ.

Square, *v.i.* To suit, fit, وَافَقَ — طَابَقَ — نَاسَبَ. To — up to, as if to fight, بَادَى-بِٱلْقِتَالِ.

Squareness, *n.* The being four sided, تَرْبِيع — شَكْلٌ مُرَبَّعٌ. Correctness, دِقَّة — ضَبْط — صِحَّة.

Square-rigged, *a.* Of a ship, سَفِينَةٌ ذَاتُ زَوَاجِعَ.

Square-sail, *n.* شِرَاعٌ زَاجِعٌ.

Squarish, *a.* مُرَبَّعٌ بَعْضَ ٱلتَّرْبِيعِ.

Squash, *n.* A soft substance, شَيْءٌ هَشَاشٌ — جِسْمٌ رَطْبٌ. The fall or contact of a soft body, هَشْم — رَفْس — شَدْخ — فَشْع — فَضْح — تَهْشِيم. The vegetable, قَرْعَة *coll.* قَرْع — كُوسَاة *coll.* كُوسَا. To go —, of a soft body, تَهَشَّمَ — تَشَدَّخَ — اِنْشَدَخَ; of a brittle body, تَفَتَّتَ — اِنْفَتَّ — اِنْفَضَّ — تَطَايَرَ.

Squash, *v.a.* To crush, of something soft, فَضَخَ — شَدَخَ — رَفَسَ — هَشَمَ — فَصَعَ — اِفْتَضَحَ. To be squashed, اِنْشَدَخَ — تَهَشَّمَ — اِنْفَضَحَ — تَشَدَّخَ. To mash, خَبَّصَ — خَبَصَ. To annul, أَبْطَلَ.

Squashy, *a.* ذُو تَهَشُّمٍ — ذُو تَحَطُّمٍ — ذُو رَخَاصَةٍ — ذُو هَشَاشَةٍ — هَشّ. To be —, هَشَّ. *See also* Pulpy, *a.*

Squat, *v.i.* To sit close to the ground, حَبَا *aor.* يَحْبُو — لَزِمَ ٱلْأَرْضَ. To —, with the buttock against the heels, قَرْفَصَ — تَقَرْفَصَ — ذَبَّجَ. To — or stay in a place, لَبَدَ بِ — أَلْبَدَ بِ. To — in a place without title, أَلْبَدَ بِمَكَانٍ بِدُونِ حَقٍّ.

Squat, *n.* The posture of sitting on the hams, قَرْفَصَة — نُبُوج.

Squat, *a.* Sitting on the hams, مُقَرْفِص — نَابِج. Cowering, in posture, خَازّ. Drawn together, مَجْمُوع. Short and fat, قُصَيِّر — مُكَبْتَل — وَضْخَم.

Squatter, *n.* One who settles in a place without permission,

مُلَبِّدٌ (or لَابِدٌ) بِمَكَانٍ بِدُونِ إِتْيَانٍ ; one who squats on his buttocks, مُقَرْفِصٌ ـ نَابِجٌ .

Squaw, *n.* لَقَبُ ٱلِٱمْرَأَةِ عِنْدَ هُنُودِ أَمِيرِيكَا .

Squeak, *v.i.* صَوَّتَ ـ صَيَّحَ ـ صَرْصَعَ ـ صَرْصَرَ ـ صَرَّ .

Squeak, *n.* صَرْخَةٌ ـ عِيَاطٌ ـ صُرَاخٌ ـ صَرِيرٌ .

Squeal, *v.i.* As a child, أَنَّ ـ تَأَوَّهَ *aor.* يَئِنُّ . *See also to* Squeak, *v.i.*

Squeal, *n.* أَنِينٌ ـ أَنَّةٌ ـ تَأَوُّهٌ . *See also* Squall, Squeak, *n.*

Squeamish, *a.* Dainty, مُتَجَوِّدٌ ـ مُكْرِهٌ ـ نَفُورٌ ـ مُتَأَنِّقٌ . To be —, تَجَوَّدَ ـ تَأَنَّقَ ; to be — in, طَرْزَ فِي . *See also* Fastidious, *a.*

Squeamishly, *ad.* بِتَنَعُّمٍ ـ بِتَأَنُّقٍ ـ بِتَجَوُّدٍ . *See also* Fastidiously, *ad.*

Squeamishness, *n.* تَجَوُّدٌ ـ تَأَنُّقٌ . *See also* Daintiness, Fastidiousness, *n.*

Squeeze, *v.t.* To press, push, حَزَقَ ـ ضَغَطَ ـ هَمَزَ . To —, as juice from a fruit, *etc.*, إِعْتَصَرَ ـ عَصَرَ ـ عَصَّرَ . To press, دَعَكَ ـ كَبَسَ ـ ضَغَطَ . To — and press, to shampoo, دَعَكَ ـ دَلَكَ ـ كَبَسَ ـ دَلَّكَ . To hug, ضَمَّ ـ عَانَقَ ـ إِحْتَضَنَ بِشِدَّةٍ . To oppress, as with burdens, ظَلَمَ ـ ضَايَقَ ـ بَغَى عَلَى ـ قَاهَرَ . To — out of one, as money, رَزَأَ ـ إِرْتَزَأَ . To pack closely, رَصَّ . To — anything out of another thing, فَصَّعَ ـ مِنْ . To — gently with the fingers, قَرَصَ ـ قَرَّصَ . To — the hand, as in shaking hands, صَافَحَ . To — one's self in, as into a narrow place, تَكَوَّى . To be squeezed, of an orange, *etc.*, إِنْعَصَرَ ; as against a wall, إِنْضَغَطَ . *See also to* Press, Pinch, *v.t.*

Squeeze, *v.i.* To urge one's way to by pressing, into, إِعْتَصَبَ ـ إِنْضَغَطَ إِلَى ـ إِلَى . To — or press one another, to crowd, of many, تَقَاصَفُوا ـ تَضَايَقُوا ـ تَزَاحَمُوا ـ إِزْدَحَمُوا .

Squeeze, *n.* } Squeezing, } The act of squeezing, of a fruit, *etc.*, عَصْرٌ ; what is squeezed out, عَصِيرٌ . A pressing, as against anything, ضَغْطٌ ـ ضَغْطَةٌ . A — with the fingers, a pinch, قَرْصٌ ـ قَرْصَةٌ . A —, as in packing, كَبْسَةٌ ـ رَصَّةٌ ـ رَصٌّ . A — of the hand, as in hand-shaking, مُصَافَحَةٌ . A crowd, لَبِيكَةٌ ـ إِزْدِحَامٌ . A close embrace, hug, إِحْتِضَانٌ ـ مُعَانَقَةٌ ـ ضَمٌّ .

Squib, *n.* As of gunpowder, صَارُوخُ بَارُودٍ *pl.* صَوَارِيخُ ـ فَشَكَةٌ *coll.* فَشَكٌ . A piece of satire, هَجْوٌ .

Squib, *v.t.* *See to* Satirize, *v.t.*

Squill, *n.* The plant, بَصَلٌ ـ بَصَلُ ٱلْفَأْرِ ـ العُنْصُلُ ـ الإِسْقِيلُ ـ ٱلْعُنْصُلِ .

Squint, *a.* } Squint-eyed, } أَعْوَرُ *fem.* عَوْرَاءُ *pl.* عُورٌ *and* عُورَانٌ *and* عِيرَانٌ ـ أَخْلَفُ ـ أَحْوَلُ ـ أَخْزَرُ ٱلْعَيْنَيْنِ . Equivocal, مُرِيبٌ ـ ذُو رِيبَةٍ .

Squint, *n.* Of the eye, إِحْوِلَالٌ ـ حَوَلٌ . A look askance, نَظَرٌ عَنْ عُرْضٍ .

Squint, *v.i.* To have a squint in the eye, حَوِلَتْ عَيْنُهُ ـ كَانَ أَحْوَلَ ـ إِحْوَلَّ . To — at, to look askance at, نَظَرَ إِلَى ـ عَنْ ـ لَحَظَ إِلَى ـ عُرْضٍ .

Squintingly, *ad.* Askance, إِحْوِلَالًا ـ عَنْ عُرْضٍ ـ إِنْحِرَافًا .

Squire, *n.* The armour-bearer of a noble, سِلَحْدَار . A proprietor of land, رَبٌّ *pl.* أَرْبَابٌ ـ صَاحِبُ عَقَارٍ ـ مُعْقِرٌ . *See also* Esquire, *n.*

Squire, *v.t.* To wait upon, تَوَقَّفَ لِ ـ خَدَمَ .

Squirarchy, *n.* Proprietors, أَرْبَابُ ٱلْعَقَارِ ـ أَصْحَابُ ٱلْعَقَارِ .

Squirrel, *n.* Especially the gray squirrel, سِنْجَاب . Of the colour of a —, سِنْجَابِيٌّ .

Squirt, *v.t.* شَخَبَ ـ ثَجَّ ـ أَثَجَّ . To —, as a clyster into a person, حَقَنَ .

Squirt, *v.i.* إِنْثَجَّ ـ ثَجَّ ـ شَخَبَ .

Squirt, *n.* A spurt, ثَوْرٌ ـ شُخْبَةٌ ـ ثَجٌّ ـ ثَجِيجٌ . An instrument to eject liquids, حُقْنَةٌ ـ مِحْقَنَةٌ .

S.S.E. (south-south-east), *n.* جَنُوبِيٌّ مُشَرِّقٌ .

S.S.W. (south-south-west), *n.* جَنُوبِيٌّ مُغَرِّبٌ .

Stab, *v.t.* As with a dagger, *etc.*, وَخَضَ ـ بِ *aor.* يَخِضُ ـ ضَرَبَ ـ بِ ـ طَعَنَ ـ بِ ـ لَهَزَ . To backbite, إِغْتَابَ ـ لَمَزَ . To — with reproaches, نَقَرَ .

Stab, *n.* A wound with a pointed instrument, وَخْضٌ ـ طَعْنَةٌ ـ جُرْحٌ ـ ضَرْبٌ . A — in the dark, backbiting, غِيبَةٌ ـ بُهْتَانٌ . A — with reproach, نَقْرٌ .

Stabiliment, *n.* *See* Establishment, *n.*

Stability, *n.* Firmness, رَصَانَةٌ ـ ثَبَاتٌ ـ ثُبُوتٌ ـ رُسُوخٌ ـ قَرَارٌ . Continuance, endurance, بَقَاءٌ ـ قَرَارٌ ـ إِسْتِقْرَارٌ ـ دَوَامٌ . Stability of purpose, perseverance, حَزْمٌ ـ عَزِيمَةٌ ـ مُدَاوَمَةٌ ـ إِدْمَانٌ .

Stable, *a.* Firmly fixed, رَاسٍ ـ مُرَصَّنٌ ـ رَصِينٌ ـ وَكِيدٌ ـ أَكِيدٌ ـ مَتِينٌ ـ ثَابِتٌ ـ مُحْكَمٌ . Firm in purpose, resolute, رَاسٍ ـ رَسِيٌّ ـ رَاسِخٌ ـ ذُو حَزْمٍ . A — building, بِنَاءٌ مُرَصَّنٌ . To be —, firm, fixed, رَصُنَ ـ ثَبَتَ ـ رَسَخَ ; to be —, resolute, حَزُمَ ـ تَرَسَّى ; as in one's affairs, تَحَزَّمَ فِي أَمْرِهِ . To make —, fixed, أَحْكَمَ ـ ثَبَّتَ ـ أَثْبَتَ ـ إِتَّقَنَ ـ مَكَّنَ ـ رَصَّنَ ـ أَرْصَنَ ـ أَرْسَخَ . *See also* Firm, *a.*

Stable, *n.* As for horses, إِصْطَبْل *pl.* إِصْطَبْلَات ـ آخُور ; for cattle generally, زَرِيبَة ـ مَرْبَط *pl.* مَرَابِطُ ـ مِعْلَف *pl.* مَعَالِفُ.

A — or stud of horses, طَوَالَةُ ٱلْخَيْلِ.

Stable, *v.t.* Of a horse, جَعَلَ فِي آخُورٍ ـ; of cattle generally, زَرَبَ فِي زَرِيبَةٍ 2.

Stable, *v.i.* سَكَنَ فِي آخُورٍ 2 ـ حَلَّ فِي إِصْطَبْلٍ 2.

Stable-boy, *n.* }
Stable-man, } غُلَامُ ٱلْآخُورِ ـ خَدَّامُ آخُورٍ.

Stableness, *n.* *See* Stability, *n.*

Stabling, *n.* For horses, مَحَلٌّ لِلدَّوَابِّ ـ إِصْطَبْلَات; for cattle, زَرَائِبُ.

Stablish, *v.t.* *See to* Establish, *v.t.*

Stably, *ad.* Firmly, إِحْكَامًا ـ بِرُسُوخٍ; resolutely, بِحَزْمٍ ـ بِرُسُوخٍ.

Staccato, ad. عِبَارَةٌ عَنْ تَصْرِيحِ ٱلْأَصْوَاتِ فِي ٱلْمُوسِيقَى.

Stack, *n.* A pile, رَكْم ـ كُومَة *pl.* أَكْوَام. A —, as of wheat, صَفٌّ ـ عَرْمَة ـ صُبْر *pl.* صُبَرَة *coll.* عَرْم. A — of chimnies, (صُوبَةٌ *or*) رَكْمٌ (صُوبَةٌ *or*) مِنَ ٱلْمَكَاحِلِ. A — of muskets, مِنَ ٱلْمَدَاخِنِ.

Stack, *v.t.* To pile in a heap, كَدَّسَ ـ كَوَّمَ ـ رَكَمَ 2; of arms, muskets, رَكَمَ ٱلْمَكَاحِلَ 2. To be stacked, piled, تَرَاكَمَ ـ تَعَرَّمَ ـ اِرْتَكَمَ.

Stadium, *n.* A Greek —, مَسَافَةٌ قَدْرُهَا ٦٠٦ أَقْدَامٍ عِنْدَ ٱلْيُونَانِيِّينَ; a Roman —, مَسَافَةٌ نَحْوُ ثُمْنِ مِيلٍ عِنْدَ ٱلرُّومَانِيِّينَ.

Stadtholder, *n.* لَقَبُ رَئِيسِ ٱلْجُمْهُورِ عِنْدَ أَهْلِ ٱلْفَلَمَنْكِ فِي ٱلزَّمَنِ ٱلسَّابِقِ.

Staff, *n.* A stick for support, عَصًا *pl.* عِصِيٌّ ـ عُود *pl.* عِيدَان ـ عُكَّازَة *pl.* عُكَّازَات *and* عَكَاكِيزُ; a sceptre, مِخْصَرَة *pl.* مَخَاصِرُ ـ قَضِيب *pl.* قُضْبَان; a shepherd's —, عَصَا ٱلرَّاعِي; a thick —, عَتَلَة. A flagstaff, سَارِي ٱللِّوَآءِ ـ لِوَايَة. A — in music, جَدْوَلٌ يَحْتَوِي عَلَى خَمْسَةِ خُطُوطٍ تُكْتَبُ فِيهَا عَلَامَاتُ ٱلْمُوسِيقَى. The — of an army, ٱلْأَرْكَانُ ٱلْحَرْبِيَّةُ. To make use of a —, stick, تَعَصَّى.

Stag, *n.* The male deer, ظَبْيٌ *pl.* ظِبَآءٌ.

Stag-beetle, *n.* خُنْفُسَةٌ كَبِيرَةٌ *pl.* خَنَافِسُ كِبَارٌ.

Stage, *n.* A raised platform of any kind, دَكَّة *pl.* دِكَك ـ مَنَصَّة; a — for spectators, مَحْفِل *pl.* مَحَافِلُ. A floor, story, طَبَقَة *pl.* طَبَقَات. The —, as of a journey, مَرْحَلَة *pl.* مَرَاحِلُ ـ مَنْزِل *pl.* مَنَازِلُ; of a theatre, دَكَّة (*or* مَلْعَب) أَهْلِ ٱلتِّيَاتْرُو. The theatre, ٱلتِّيَاتْرُو ـ أَلْعَابُ ٱلْمَرْسَحِ. A place of action or performance, مَحَلٌّ ـ مَوْقِع. A single step, دَرَجَة *pl.* دَرَجَات. Degree of advance, تَقَدُّم ـ تَدَرُّج. A period, round of time, دَوْر *pl.* أَدْوَار ـ دَهْر *pl.* دُهُور. A phase, condition, فَنٌّ ـ لَوْن ـ ضَرْب ـ حَال ـ فَنَن. Stages, degrees or steps, upwards, دَرَجَات; downwards, دَرَكَات. Stage by stage, step by step, دَرَجَةً دَرَجَةً. Stage, or floor, upon stage, طَبَقَةٌ عَلَى طَبَقَةٍ. Life has two stages, ٱلْعَيْشُ فَنَنَانِ.

To go on the stage, theatre, صَارَ ـ تَعَاطَى ٱلتِّيَاتْرُو (*or* ٱلْمَرْسَحَ) يَلْعَبُ فِي ٱلتِّيَاتْرُو.

To appear, to be represented, on the stage, تَلَعَّبَ *or* تَقَلَّدَ (*or* تَشَخَّصَ) فِي ٱلتِّيَاتْرُو.

To quit the stage, theatre, تَرَكَ لَعِبَ ٱلتِّيَاتْرُو 2. To leave, خَلَعَ ـ سَيَّبَ ـ تَرَكَ 2.

To quit this mortal stage, تُوُفِّيَ إِلَى رَحْمَةِ ٱللّٰهِ ـ تُوُفِّيَ.

To travel by easy stages, أَرْوَدَ ٱلْمَرَاحِلَ.

Stage-coach, *n.* عَرَبِيَّةُ مَنْزِلٍ.

Stage-player, *n.* لَاعِبٌ فِي ٱلتِّيَاتْرُو (*or* ٱلْمَرْسَحِ). *See also* Comedian, *n.*

Stager, *n.* An experienced person, مُدَرَّب ـ حُوَّلٌ قُلَّبٌ ـ خَبِير; a wily person, حَوَالِيٌّ ـ مُحْتَال.

Stagger, *v.i.* As in walking, تَمَايَلَ ـ تَفَرَّكَ. To —, like a drunken man, تَمَيَّحَ ـ تَعَثَّرَ فِي مَشْيِهِ. To waver, تَرَدَّدَ ـ تَضَرَّبَ ـ تَمَخْطَرَ. He did not — at it, doubt it, مَا ٱرْتَابَ فِيهِ. *See also to* Hesitate, *v.i.*

Stagger, *v.t.* To make to waver, شَكَّكَ ـ أَرَابَ ـ رَابَ *aor.* يَرِيبُ. He staggered him, made him to doubt, أَتَاهُ بِرِيبَةٍ. To confound, حَيَّرَ.

Staggering, *a.* Tottering, مُتَرَجْرِج. Causing doubt, مُرِيب.

Staggeringly, *ad.* With a tottering gait, تَرَجْرُجًا.

Staging, *n.* *See* Scaffolding, *n.*

Stagnancy, *n.* As of water, وُقُوف. An unimproving state, جُمُودُ ٱلْحَالِ ـ جَمَاد. Dullness of trade, كَسَاد. The being without occupation, عُطْلَة.

Stagnant, *a.* Not flowing, وَاقِف ـ مُوَقَّف ـ نَائِم. Motionless, مُسْبِت ـ سَكِن ـ رَاقِد ـ جَامِد. Dull, of trade, كَاسِد ـ كَسِيد: a — market, سُوقٌ كَاسِدٌ (*or* كَاسِدَةٌ). A — man, who does not improve, رَجُلٌ جَامِدُ ٱلْحَالِ. Stagnant water, مُسْتَنْقَعَة ـ فَضْيَة *pl.* فِضَآء.

Stagnate, *v.i.* To cease to flow, اِسْتَنْقَعَ ـ وَقَفَ *aor.* يَقِفُ ـ رَكَدَ 2. To be in an unimproving condition, جَمَدَ 2. To be dull, of a market or trade, كَسَدَ 2.

Stagnation, *n.* As of affairs, وَقْفُ حَالٍ ـ وُقُوف. *See also* Stagnancy, *n.*

Staid, *a.* Sober, grave, رَزِين ـ رَكِين ـ سَاكِنُ ٱلطَّائِرِ ـ آنٍ ـ عَاقِل. *See also* Grave, *a.*

Staidness, *n.* رَزَانَة ـ سَمْت ـ أَنَاة. With —, بِأَنَاةٍ. *See also* Gravity, *n.*

Stain, *v.t.* To discolour, بَقَّعَ ـ لَطَخَ. To tinge, شَرَّبَ. To dye, صَبَّغَ ـ صَبَغَ. To blemish, عَيَّبَ. To — the character, reputation, ثَلَمَ صِيتَهُ ـ خَرَقَ نَامُوسَهُ. To be stained, discoloured, تَلَطَّخَ ـ لُطِخَ; to be dyed, إِصْطَبَغَ. To be stained with crime, إِرْتَكَبَ ٱلْعَظَائِمَ. *See also to* Spot, Blemish, *v.t.*

Stain, *n.* A discolouration, بُقْعَة ـ لَطْخ ـ شَوَائِبُ *pl.* شَائِبَة. A — on the skin, نَمَش. A dye, صِبَاغ ـ صِبْغَة. A colour, لَوْن *pl.* أَلْوَان. A defect, شَائِبَة *pl.* شَوَائِبُ ـ عَيْب *pl.* عُيُوب ـ عَوَار. A — on the character, عَوْرَة ـ مَعَاب ـ عَيْبَة ـ عَار.

Stained, *a.* Discoloured, مُبَقَّع ـ مَلْطُوخ. Dyed, مَصْبُوغ. Coloured, مُلَوَّن.

Stainer, *n.* A dyer, صَبَّاغ ـ نَقَّاش.

Stainless, *a.* Pure, free from stains, نَقِيّ *pl.* نُقَاة. Free from reproach, نَقِيّ ـ زَكِيّ ـ بِلَا لَوْم.

Stair, *n.* A step for ascending, تُرْعَة *pl.* تُرَع ـ رُتْبَة *pl.* رُتَبَات ـ مَرْتَبَة *pl.* مَرَاتِبُ ـ دَرَجَة *pl.* دَرَجَات. Stairs, a flight of steps, دَرَج ـ سُلَّم ـ مَرْقَاة ـ مِعْرَاج ـ مِعْرَج. Winding stairs, دَرَج لَوْلَبِيّ. At the foot of the stairs, فِي أَسْفَلِ ٱلدَّرَجِ. Up stairs, above, فَوْقُ; down stairs, تَحْتُ. Come up stairs, إِصْعَدْ إِلَى فَوْق. Come down stairs, إِنْزِلْ إِلَى تَحْتُ. Back-stair influence, نُفُوذ خَفِيّ. To ascend stairs, رَقِيَ ٱلدَّرَجَةَ.

Stair-carpet, *n.* طِنْفِسَةُ ٱلدَّرَجِ.

Staircase, *n.* مِرْقَاة ـ دَرَج ـ سُلَّم *pl.* سَلَالِمُ.

Stair-rod, *n.* قُضْبَان *pl.* قَضِيبٌ يَضْبُطُ طِنْفِسَةَ ٱلدَّرَجِ.

Stake, *n.* Of wood, وَتِد *pl.* أَوْتَاد ـ مِرْوَد *pl.* مَرَاوِدُ. A palisade of pointed stakes to keep off cattle, سِلْعَاف. A mallet to drive in stakes, مِيتَدَة ـ مِيتَد. A — for impaling men, خَازُوق *pl.* خَوَازِيقُ. A wager, سَبَق *pl.* أَسْبَاق ـ خَطَر *pl.* أَخْطَار ـ مُرَاهَنَة ـ رَهْن. Martyrdom, إِسْتِشْهَاد.

To be at stake, كَانَ تَحْتَ خَطَرٍ.

To draw stakes, إِتَّخَذَ ٱلْأَخْطَارَ.

To drive in, of a stake, أَوْتَدَ ـ وَتَدَ.

To lay a stake with, to wager with, رَاهَنَ ـ خَاطَرَ عَلَى: We laid stakes one to another, أَخْطَرَ لِي وَأَخْطَرْتُ لَهُ.

To perish at the stake, to be martyred, مَاتَ شَهِيدًا ـ إِسْتَشْهَدَ.

To sweep stakes, قَشَّ ٱلْأَخْطَارَ.

Stake, *v.t.* To put stakes in, جَعَلَ فِي أَوْتَادًا. To pierce with a —, to impale, خَوْزَقَ. To put to hazard, خَاطَرَ بِـ ـ أَخْطَرَ.

He staked his property, أَرْهَنَ مَالَهُ ـ خَاطَرَ بِمَالِهِ. I staked my children to him, أَرْهَنْتُ لَهُ أَوْلَادِي. He staked his soul, life, by exposing himself, أَخْطَرَ بِنَفْسِهِ ـ أَخْطَرَ. *See also to* Wager, *v.t.*

Stake-holder, *n.* مَاسِكُ ٱلْمُرَاهَنَةِ ـ أَمِينُ ٱلْأَخْطَارِ.

Stalactic, Stalactical, *a.* Stalactiform, } فِي هَيْئَةِ ٱلذُّنْلِ (or ٱلذَّنْلِ). *See under* Stalactite, *n.*

Stalactite, *n.* ذِنْل ـ ذُنْل ـ قَطْرَان ـ مَخْرُوطٌ مِنَ ٱلْجَلِيدِ قَاعِدَتُهُ مَوَائِعُ تَجْمُدُ فِي شَكْلِ مَخْرُوطٍ ـ فِي ٱلسَّقْفِ وَرَأْسُهُ مُتَّجِهٌ نَحْوَ ٱلْأَرْضِ ـ مِنْ مَوَادَّ تَسِيلُ مِنْ سُقُوفِ ٱلْكُهُوفِ وَغَيْرِهَا. *See also* Icicle, *n.*

Stalagmite, *n.* مَخْرُوطٌ مُتَحَجِّرٌ مِنْ قَطَرَانِ مَوَائِعَ كِلْسِيَّةٍ يَبْتَدِئُ مِنْ سَطْحِ ٱلْأَرْضِ وَيَرْتَفِعُ مُسْتَدِقًّا نَحْوَ ٱلْعُلَاءِ.

Stale, *a.* Old, عَتِيق. Obsolete, هَامِد ـ غَيْرُ مُسْتَعْمَلٍ ـ مُلْغًى. Of victuals, سَنِه; of bread, بَائِت ـ بَيُوت ـ جَبِيز. To become —, of victuals, سَنِهَ ـ تَسَنَّهَ.

Stale, *v.t.* To make vapid or useless, مَسَخَ ـ أَفْسَدَ ـ خَرَّبَ.

Stale, *v.i.* شَخَّ ـ بَالَ. To stop horses to let them —, إِسْتَبَالَ (or أَبَالَ) ٱلْخَيْلَ.

Stale, *n.* The urine of cattle, شُخَاخ (or بَوْل) ٱلدَّوَابِّ.

Stalemate, *n.* In chess, حَالَةُ ٱلشَّاه مَات.

Staleness, *n.* Oldness, عِتْق ـ عُتْق. Obsoleteness, تَرْك ـ إِلْغَاء ـ سُقُوطٌ عَنِ ٱلْإِسْتِعْمَالِ. Staleness of victuals, تَسَنُّه.

Stalk, *n.* The stem of a plant, سَاق *pl.* سُوق *and* سُوُق *and* سُوُوق *and* سِيقَان ـ عُود *pl.* عِيدَان ـ سُوُوق. The — of the raceme of a date-tree, شِمْرَاخ *pl.* شَمَارِيخُ ـ عِثْكَال *pl.* عَثَاكِيلُ. Plants having an upright —, يَقْطِين. A strut, خَطَرَة ـ خَطَل ـ تَغَطْرُس.

Stalk, *v.i.* To strut, تَغَطْرَسَ ـ تَخَطَّلَ فِي مِشْيَتِهِ. To rise into a stalk, قَصَّبَ.

Stalk, *v.t.* As in hunting, خَتَلَ ٱلصَّيْدَ ـ تَقَصَّصَ ٱلصَّيْدَ ـ تَقَنَّصَ ـ إِصْطَادَ ـ صَيَّدَ.

Stalker, *n.* One who walks proudly, عَيَّال ـ حَيَّاك ـ مُتَغَطْرِس. A hunter, صَيَّاد ـ خَاتِلُ ٱلصَّيْدِ.

Stalking, *n.* Of a stalker of game, خَتْلُ ٱلصَّائِدِ.

Stalking-horse, *n.* A simulated horse, حِصَانٌ مُصْطَنَع. A pretence, disguise, حِيلَة ـ عِلَّة ـ حُجَّة.

Stalky, *a.* يُشْبِهُ سَاقَ ٱلنَّبَاتِ.

Stall, *n.* As for a horse, مِعْلَف *pl.* مَعَالِفُ. A stand on which goods are exposed for sale, دِكَّة *pl.* دِكَك ـ دَكَّة لِعَرْضِ ٱلْبِضَاعَةِ ـ دُكَّان *pl.* دَكَاكِينُ. A —, as in a theatre or church, مَقْعَد *pl.* مَقَاعِدُ ـ مَقْعَدٌ خَاصٌّ.

Stall, *v.t.* *See to* Stable, *v.t.*

Stallage, *n.* كِرَآءُ دُكَّانٍ ـ كِرْوَةُ دُكَّانٍ.

Stalled, *a.* / Stall-fed, } مَعْلُوف.

Stallion, *n.* فَحْل *pl.* فُحُول *and* فِحَال. To bring a — to a mare, أَفْحَلَ.

Stalwart, *a.* قَوِيٌّ ـ عَفِيٌّ ـ ضَلِيع ـ صُلْب.

Stamen, *n.* Of a plant, آلَةُ ٱلذَّكَرِ مِنَ ٱلنَّبَاتِ *pl.* آلَات.

Stamened, *a.* ذُو آلَاتِ ٱلذُّكُورَة.

Stamina, *n.* Strength, vitality, مُكْنَة ـ قُوَّة ـ مِرَاس ـ أَزْر ـ عَافِيَة. *See also plural of* Stamen, *n.*

Staminal, *a.* / Staminate, / Stamineous, } ذُو آلَاتِ ٱلذُّكُورِ.

Stammer, *v.i.* As in speech, عَيَّ فِي مَنْطِقِهِ *aor.* يَعْيَا ـ فَدَمَ فِي ² ـ اِرْتَبَكَ فِي ٱلْكَلَامِ ـ عَوْلَكَ ـ تَعْتَعَ ـ ² لَكِنَ ـ فَأْفَأَ ـ كَلَامِهِ تَهْتَهَ ـ طَمْطَمَ.

Stammerer, *n.* / Stammering, *a.* } أَلْكَنُ *fem.* لَكْنَآءُ *pl.* لُكْن ـ مُتَعْتِع. A stammering tongue, speech, شَفَةٌ لَكْنَآءُ.

Stammering, *n.* فَدَم ـ عَوْلَكَة ـ فَأْفَأَة ـ تَعْتَعَة ـ لَكْنَة ـ لُكْن ـ لَجْلَجَة ـ طَمْطَمَة.

Stammeringly, *ad.* بِطَمْطَمَةٍ ـ لَكْنًا ـ بِلَكْنَةٍ.

Stamp, *v.i.* To strike with the foot, خَبَطَ ² (*or*) اِخْتَبَطَ) بِٱلرِّجْلِ.

Stamp, *v.t.* To beat with the foot, اِخْتَبَطَ ـ تَخَبَّطَ ـ ² خَبَطَ. To crush, دَقَّ ² ـ طَحَنَ ² ـ سَحَقَ ² ـ رَضَّ. To —, as with some mark or figure, طَبَعَ عَلَى-كَذَا ² ـ طَبَّعَ. To —, to coin, ضَرَبَ ² (*or*) نَقَشَ ²) ٱلسِّكَّةَ. To —, as with a government mark, دَمَغَ ². *See also to* Impress, *v.t.*

To stamp out, to erase, مَحَا ² ـ نَسَخَ ² ـ مَحَقَ ². To destroy, eradicate, أَزَالَ ـ أَبَادَ ـ أَجَثَّ ـ اِسْتَأْصَلَ.

To stamp upon, impress upon, to implant, as on the disposition, طَبَعَ فِي عَقْلِهِ كَذَا ² ـ عَرَّقَ فِي-كَذَا ـ ضَرَبَ فِي-كَذَا ². To tread upon, دَاسَ ².

Stamp, *n.* As with the foot, اِخْتِبَاط ـ خَبْط. An instrument for impressing a mark, طَابِع *pl.* طَوَابِعُ; a government —, such as is used for stamping goods, دَمْغَة. A mark, impression, طَبْع *pl.* طِبَاع ـ رَسْم *pl.* رُسُوم ـ رَشْم *pl.* رُشُوم; as of a seal, خَتْم. A pestle, a bruiser, مِدَقَّة ـ مِنْجَاز. A model, mode, make, fashion, طَبْع *pl.* طِبَاع ـ صَوْغ ـ قَالِب *pl.* قَوَالِبُ ـ قَاعِدَة *pl.* قَوَاعِدُ. Stamp of character, disposition, طَبْع ـ جِبِلَّة ـ سَجِيَّة ـ طَبِيعَة *pl.* طَبَائِعُ. Form, shape, هَيْئَة *pl.* هَيْآت. Stamp, a foot-mark, أَثَرُ ٱلْقَدَمِ *pl.* أَثَرُ ٱلْأَقْدَامِ. To bear the —, impress, of truth, عَلَيْهِ صِفَةُ ٱلْحَقِّ. Language which has the — of chasteness, كَلَامٌ عَلَيْهِ طَابِعُ ٱلْفَصَاحَةِ. It bears the — of such a thing, عَلَيْهِ أَثَرُ كَذَا. *See also* Postage, *n.*

Stamp Act, *n.* قَوَانِينُ ٱلدَّمْغَةِ.

Stamp-duty, *n.* رُسُومُ ٱلدَّمْغَةِ.

Stamped, *a.* Impressed with government stamps, مَخْتُومٌ بِطَوَابِعَ ٱلْمِيرِي. Stamped, of coin, سِكَّة ـ سِكِّيٌّ ـ رِقَة *pl.* رِقُون. "And vileness was stamped upon them," وَضُرِبَتْ عَلَيْهِمُ ٱلذِّلَّةُ (Kur. ii. 58).

Stamping, *n.* As of horses' hoofs, دَقْدَقَة.

Stamping-mill, *n.* دُولَابُ سِكَّةٍ ـ دُولَابُ ٱلسِّكَّةِ.

Stamp Office, *n.* قَلَمُ ٱلدَّمْغَاتِ.

Stampede, *n.* تَقَهْقُر ـ هَزِيمَة ـ اِنْفِرَار ـ جَفَالَة ـ جَفْل.

Stamper, *n.* As for stamping with, طَابِع; a die, سِكَّة. A — of coin, سَكَّاك.

Stanch, *v.t.* Of tears or blood, وَقَفَ نَزْفَهُ ـ أَرْقَأَ: I stanched the vein, أَرْقَأْتُ ٱلْعِرْقَ.

Stanch, *v.i.* وَقَفَ نَزْفُهُ *aor.* يَقِفُ ـ رَقَأَ ²: The issue of blood stanched, or was stanched, وَقَفَ نَزْفُ ٱلدَّمِ *aor.* يَقِفُ ـ رَقَأَ ٱلدَّمُ ².

Stanch, *a.* Sure, trusty, أَمِين ـ غَيُور. Firm, strong, ثَابِت ـ قَوِيٌّ. To be — in, تَوَثَّقَ فِي.

Stanchion, *n.* A support, سَنَد *pl.* أَسْنَاد. A post, pillar, دِعْمَة *pl.* دِعَم ـ دِعَامَة *pl.* دَعَائِمُ ـ عُمْدَة *pl.* أَعْمِدَة.

Stanchly, *ad.* بِثَبَاتٍ ـ بِوَثَاقَةٍ.

Stanchless, *a.* لَا يُوقَفُ نَزْفُهُ ـ لَا يُرْقَأُ.

Stanchness, *n.* مُرُوَّة ـ غَيْرَة ـ حَزْم ـ ثَبَات ـ وَثَاقَة.

Stand, *v.i.* and *t.* To be on the feet, قَامَ *aor.* يَقُومُ ـ وَقَفَ *aor.* يَقِفُ ـ قَامَ وَاقِفًا. To —, as in a particular place, اِسْتَقَامَ. To stop or halt, وَقَفَ *aor.* يَقِفُ ـ تَوَقَّفَ ـ حَطَّ ². To remain firm, fixed, ثَبَتَ ² ـ اِسْتَقَرَّ. To endure, last, دَامَ *aor.* يَدُومُ ـ اِسْتَدَامَ ـ اِسْتَمَرَّ ـ بَقِيَ ². To be fixed, not vacillating, حَزَمَ ² ـ اِسْتَثْبَتَ ـ تَثَبَّتَ. To withstand, قَاوَمَ ـ اِعْتَرَضَ ـ اِمْتَنَعَ. To resist, stand, as the weather, *etc.*, أَصْبَرَ عَلَى ـ لَا يَأْثَرُ فِيهِ كَذَا. To —, to be built upon, عَلَى ـ مَبْنِيٌّ عَلَى ـ مَعْصُومٌ مِنْ كَذَا: London stands upon the Thames, مَدِينَةُ لَنْدَنَ مَبْنِيَّةٌ عَلَى نَهْرِ ٱلتِّيمْس. To —, to be, to be in a state of, or of doing, قَعَدَ ² ـ ظَلَّ ² ـ اِسْتَمَرَّ. To cause to —, وَقَّفَ ـ قَوَّمَ; to erect, صَمَدَ ². To ask one to —, اِسْتَقْوَمَ. As matters —, فِي هٰذَا ٱلْحَالِ ـ نَظَرًا لِلْأَحْوَالِ ٱلْحَاضِرَةِ.

To stand against, as against a wall, *etc.*, وَقَفَ عِنْدَ كَذا *aor.* يَقِفُ.

To resist, جَاهَرَ ـ إِعْتَرَضَ ـ قَاوَمَ.

To stand aghast, بُهِتَ ـ تَحَيَّرَ ـ ـِ دَهِشَ.

To stand aloof, وَقَفَ مُجَاهُ. To stand aloof from, تَجَافَى عَن ـ إِجْتَنَبَ عَن ـ تَمَنَّعَ مِن.

To stand away, at a distance, إِجْتَنَبَ ـ تَبَاعَدَ ـ تَبَعَّدَ. To stand away for a place, إِتَّخَذَ ٱلطَّرِيقَ نَحْوَ كَذا ـ ـِ ضَرَبَ إِلَى.

To stand back, إِسْتَأْخَرَ ـ تَأَخَّرَ. Stand back! قِفْ عِنْدَكَ. Stand back from me! أَخِّرْ عَنِّي.

To stand before one, وَقَفَ أَمَامَهُ. To stand before, to confront, وَاجَهَ ـ صَارَحَ بِهِ.

To stand beside one, وَقَفَ بِجَانِبِهِ *aor.* يَقِفُ.

To stand by, near, one, وَقَفَ بِقُرْبِهِ *aor.* يَقِفُ ـ 2 حَضَرَ عِنْدَهُ. To hold on, as on one's way, إِسْتَمْسَكَ بِطَرِيقِهِ. He said to some of those who stood by, قَالَ لِبَعْضٍ مِنَ ٱلْحَاضِرِينَ.

To stand by a thing, to stick to, بَارَكَ عَلَى ـ 2 جَذَا ب ـ أَكَبَّ عَلَى ـ تَشَبَّثَ ب ـ تَمَسَّكَ ب. *See also to* Stand beside.

To stand by one, to stick to, to aid, إِلْتَزَمَ ـ ـِ عَمِدَ ب ـ ظَاهَرَ ـ 2 شَدَّ مَعَهُ.

To stand fast, إِسْتَقَرَّ ـ 2 ثَبَتَ.

To stand for, to mean, عَنَى ب *aor.* يَعْنِي. To stand in the place of, قَامَ بِمَقَامِ كَذا ـ 2 قَامَ مَقَامَ كَذا.

To stand for a place, to be a candidate for, 2 طَلَبَ ـ أَرَادَ. To offer one's self for election, تَعَرَّضَ لِلْإِنْتِخَابِ عِنْدَ ٱلْمُنْتَخِبِينَ.

To stand for nothing, هُوَ غَيْرُ طَائِلٍ ـ لَيْسَ هُوَ بِطَائِلٍ.

To stand forth, in advance, openly, تَظَاهَرَ ـ تَجَاهَرَ ـ تَقَدَّمَ.

To stand forward, as among a party, 2 قَامَ فِي وَسْطِ كَذا.

To stand in, as in a place, وَقَفَ فِي دَاخِلِ كَذا *aor.* يَقِفُ. To direct one's course straight to, إِعْتَزَمَ ٱلطَّرِيقَ ـ تَوَجَّهَ إِلَى. To cost, كَلَّفَ ـ تَكَلَّفَ.

To stand in a heap, إِرْتَكَمَ ـ إِنْتَصَبَ كَنَدٍّ.

To stand in doubt of, تَشَكَّكَ فِي ـ إِرْتَابَ ب ـ تَحَيَّرَ فِي.

To stand in fear of, خَشِيَ مِن *aor.* يَخْشَى ـ ـِ خَافَ مِن.

To stand in need of, أَعْوَزَ ـ إِحْتَاجَ إِلَى.

To stand in the presence of one, وَقَفَ فِي حَضْرَتِهِ ـ وَقَفَ أَمَامَهُ *aor.* يَقِفُ.

To stand off, at a distance, تَبَاعَدَ ـ إِبْتَعَدَ ـ تَجَنَّبَ. To leave, set off, سَافَرَ ـ تَسَرَّحَ ـ تَبَرَّحَ. To stand off, as from a bargain, ـِ رَجَعَ عَن ـ 2 طَلَعَ مِن.

To stand off and on, تَرَدَّدَ ـ تَقَرَّبَ وَتَغَرَّبَ.

To stand on ceremony, 2 قَامَ بِٱلتَّكَالِيفِ.

To stand on end, of the hair, 2 قَبَّ شَعْرُ رَأْسِهِ; of the hair of certain animals, إِزْبَارَّ شَعْرُهُ.

To stand on one's feet, قَامَ ـ وَقَفَ عَلَى قَدَمَيْهِ *aor.* يَقُومُ.

To stand out, outside, وَقَفَ خَارِجًا *aor.* يَقِفُ. To hold out, endure, إِسْتَقَامَ ـ إِسْتَدَامَ; not to yield, 2 ثَبَتَ ـ ـِ ظَلَّ مُدَافِعًا مُقَاوِمًا. To project, 2 بَرَزَ ـ أَشْرَفَ ـ حَبَا *aor.* يَحْبُو. To be prominent, as the eye, *etc.*, ـِ جَحَظَ.

To stand out against, to resist, دَافَعَ ـ قَاوَمَ. To stand out against what is true, 2 ـِ عَنَدَ ـ عَانَدَ.

To stand to, to hold to, to maintain, تَمَسَّكَ ب ـ 2 ثَبَتَ عَلَى. To persevere in, أَدْمَنَ عَلَى ـ وَقَفَ عَلَى ـ أَقَامَ فِي.

To stand over against, opposite to, وَاجَهَ ـ قَابَلَ ـ عَارَضَ.

To stand to one's arms, ـِ لَزِمَ ٱلسِّلَاحَ.

To stand to one's guns, ـِ لَزِمَ ٱلْمَدَافِعَ.

To stand to, as to one's party, تَعَصَّبَ ل ـ إِشْتَدَّ مَع.

To stand to one's word, أَوْفَى بِوَعْدِهِ ـ تَمَسَّكَ بِقَوْلِهِ.

To stand still, وَقَفَ *aor.* يَقِفُ ـ تَوَقَّفَ.

To stand together, of many, وَقَفُوا مَعًا (*or* جُمْلَةً). To hold together, of persons, تَعَصَّبُوا; in favour of, تَعَصَّبُوا ل; against, تَعَصَّبُوا عَلَى.

To stand up, as from a sitting posture, 2 قَامَ ـ إِنْتَهَضَ ـ ـِ نَهَضَ. He stood up in the midst of them, وَقَفَ فِي وَسْطِهِمْ *aor.* يَقِفُ.

To stand up for, إِسْتَنْصَرَ ل ـ حَامَى ـ ظَاهَرَ ـ 2 قَامَ ل.

To stand up against, to resist, قَاوَمَ ـ 2 قَامَ عَلَى.

To stand upon, to be placed upon, إِنْتَصَبَ عَلَى ـ جُعِلَ عَلَى. To be founded upon, بُنِيَ عَلَى ـ تَأَسَّسَ عَلَى. To observe, keep, رَاعَى ـ ـِ حَفِظَ.

To stand upright, إِسْتَقَامَ ـ إِنْتَصَبَ.

To stand within, inside, وَقَفَ دَاخِلًا.

Stand, *v.t.* To sustain, إِحْتَمَلَ. To last, withstand, as the weather, wear and tear; *see under* To stand, *v.i. and to* Resist, *v.t.*

To stand fire, as a horse, *etc.*, لَا يَخَافُ مِنْ ضَرْبِ ٱلْمَدَافِعِ.

To stand one's ground, تَمَسَّكَ بِرَأْيِهِ ـ 2 ثَبَتَ عَلَى أَمْرِهِ.

To stand one's trial, judgment, كَانَ تَحْتَ ـ تَعَرَّضَ لِلْمُحَاكَمَةِ ٱلْمُحَاكَمَةِ.

Stand, *n.* A place of stopping, مَوْقِف. A place at which one stands, مَوْقِف *pl.* مَوَاقِفُ ـ مَقَام. A place where one alights, or where things are placed, مَحَطّ *pl.* مَحَاطُّ ـ مَحَطَّة *pl.* مَحَطَّات. An erection for spectators, مَحْفِل *pl.* مَحَافِلُ ـ مَقْعَدُ خَشَبٍ *pl.*

مَنْظَرَة pl. مَنَاظِرُ ـ مَقَاعِدُ . A pedestal, قِيَام ـ قَاعِدَة pl. قَوَاعِدُ ـ كُرْسِيّ pl. كَرَاسِيّ . The bottom of anything, سَفْح ـ قَعْر ـ أَسْفَلُ ـ تَحْت . Stand, standing, rank, مَقَام ـ مَنْزِلَة ـ مَرْتَبَة . A support, مَسْنَد . Resistance, مُقَاوَمَة ـ دِفَاع . A cab-stand, مَحَطّ ٱلْعَرَبَانَات . A — of arms, صُوبَة (or طَقْمُ) سِلَاح .

To be at a stand, in a quandary, تَحَيَّرَ . To be stagnant, رَكَدَ ²; to have nothing to do, تَبَطَّلَ ـ تَعَطَّلَ .

To come to a stand, تَوَقَّفَ .

To make a stand, to stand firm, رَسَخَ ـ ² ثَبَتَ ـ ² . To hold out, not to yield, ظَلَّ مُدَافِعًا ـ ² ثَبَتَ مُقَاوِمًا ².

To put to a stand, to puzzle, حَيَّرَ ـ تَوَّهَ ـ أَدْهَشَ . To oblige, أَلْزَمَ ـ إِضْطَرَّ إِلَى . To be put to a stand, puzzled, تَحَيَّرَ ـ ضَلَّ ـ إِسْتَحَارَ ²; to be obliged, إِغْتَصَبَ ـ إِلْتَزَمَ ـ أُضْطُرَّ .

Standard, n. A flag, عَلَم pl. أَعْلَام ـ رَايَة pl. رَايَات ـ بَيْرَق pl. بَيَارِق ـ لِوَآء pl. أَلْوِيَة . A royal —, سِنْجَق pl. سَنَاجِق . A rule or measure by which things are tried, عِيَار ـ مِعْيَار . A — of coinage, مِعْيَارُ ٱلسِّكَّة . A root, principle, أَصْل ـ نِصَاب pl. نُصُب . A stem, جِذْل pl. أَجْذَال ـ سَاق pl. سُوُوق . See also under Flag, n.

Standard, a. Of right measure, coinage, etc., عِيَار ـ تَامُّ ٱلْعِيَارِ ـ صَحِيحُ ٱلْعِيَارِ . Classical, held in repute, مُعْتَبَر . Standard books, تَآلِيفَاتٌ مُعْتَبَرَةٌ .

Standard-bearer, n. حَامِلُ ٱلرَّايَةِ ; from the Turkish, بَيْرَقْدَار ـ عَلَمْدَار .

Stander-by, n. مُعَايِن ـ وَاقِف ـ حَاضِر pl. حَاضِرُونَ ـ شَاهِد pl. أَشْهَاد and شُهُود .

Standing, a. As on the feet, قَائِم pl. قُوَّم and قِيَام ـ وَاقِف pl. وُقَّاف and وَاقِفُونَ . Established, organized, مُوَتَّوف ـ مُقَرَّر ـ مُنْعَقِد ـ مُنَسَّق . Permanent, دَائِم . Stagnant, not flowing, مُسْتَنْقِع ـ غَيْرُ جَارٍ ـ وَاقِف ـ مُوَقَّف .

Standing army, عَسْكَرٌ مُسْتَمِرٌّ ـ جُنْدٌ دَائِمٌ . See also under Army, n.

Standing corn, زَرْع .

Standing dish, صَحْنٌ دَائِمٌ .

Standing order, أَمْرٌ دَائِمٌ .

Standing rigging, حِبَالٌ غَيْرُ سَالِكَةٍ .

Standing, n. Permanence, مُدَاوَمَة . Station, مَقَام ـ مَنْزِلَة . Footing, rank, فَاتُور ـ مَنْزِلَة ـ بَسَاط . Time of tenure of office, مُدَّةٌ مَأْمُورِيَّةٍ ـ مُدَّةُ وَظِيفَةٍ . Standing-room, مَحَلّ ـ مَقَام ـ سَعَة .

Standish, n. As for pens and ink, دَوَاة pl. دُوِى ; vulg. دَوَايَة .

Standpoint, n. A position, مَرْكَز ـ مَحَطَّة . A fundamental principle, قَاعِدَة pl. قَوَاعِدُ ـ قَانُونٌ أَسَاسِيٌّ pl. قَوَانِينُ أَسَاسِيَّةٌ . A point from which a view is taken, مَنْظَرَة pl. مَنَاظِرُ . From his —, point of view, opinion, حَسَبَ نَظَرِهِ .

Standstill, n. وُقُوف . A state of absence of work, etc., تَعْطِيل . To come to a —, stop, وَقَفَ aor. يَقِفُ ـ تَوَقَّفَ ; of business, etc., تَعَطَّلَ . Trade is at a —, تَعَطَّلَتِ ٱلْأَعْمَالُ ٱلتِّجَارِيَّةُ .

Stanhope, n. The vehicle, عَرَبَانَةٌ خَفِيفَةٌ بِلَا سَقِيفَةٍ (or غِطَآء) .

Stank, pret. of to Stink, q.v.

Stannary, n. مَعْدِنُ قَصْدِيرٍ .

Stannary, a. } قَصْدِيرِيٌّ .
Stannic, }

Stanza, n. دَوْر pl. أَدْوَار .

Staple, n. The principal commodity of a country, مِحْوَرُ تِجَارَةٍ pl. مَحَاوِرُ ـ مَتْجَر ـ أَخَصّ . Staple coin, مِحْوَرُ ٱلْمُعَامَلَةِ . The thread of wool, etc., خَيْط pl. خُيُوط and خُيُوطَة ـ خَيْطَة ـ شَعْرَة . An iron —, رَزَّة pl. رَزَّات . A trade emporium, مَرْكَزُ تِجَارَةٍ .

Staple, a. Principal, أَخَصّ ـ أَغْلَب . Established, مُقَرَّر ـ مُرَكَّز ـ مُؤَسَّس .

Stapler, n. A dealer, مُتَسَبِّب ـ تَاجِر pl. تُجَّار ـ بَائِع pl. بَاعَة .

Star, n. كَوْكَب pl. كَوَاكِبُ ـ نَجْم pl. نُجُوم and أَنْجُم ; a single —, نَجْمَة ـ كَوْكَبَة . In the shape of a —, فِي شَكْلِ ٱلنَّجْمِ . Fortune, طَالِع ـ بَخْت . A decoration, نِيشَان pl. نَيَاشِينُ ـ نِيشَانُ شَرَفٍ . One of brilliant qualities, نَادِرَةُ ٱلزَّمَانِ . The seven bright-shining stars (or planets) according to Arabian astronomers, namely, the Moon, Mercury, Venus, the Sun, Mars, Jupiter, and Uranus, ٱلسَّبْعَةُ ٱلشُّهُبُ ; the first three of which are called, صِغَارُ ٱلشُّهُبِ . The track of a —, حَبِيكَة pl. حُبُك . To predict by the stars, نَجَّمَ . To rise, of a star, نَجَمَ ² ـ أَنْجَمَ .

A falling star, شِهَاب pl. شُهُب .

A shooting star, قَوْس pl. أَقْوَاس ـ شِهَاب pl. شُهُب .

A wandering star, سَيَّارَة pl. سَيَّارَات .

Setting stars, شَوَارِعُ .

The fixed stars, ٱلثَّوَابِتُ ـ ٱلْكَوَاكِبُ ٱلثَّابِتَةُ .

The morning star, كَوْكَبُ ٱلْفَجْرِ .

The polar star, ٱلْقُطْبُ ـ كَوْكَبُ ٱلْقُطْبِ ـ ٱلْكَوْكَبُ ٱلشَّمَالِيُّ .

Star, v.t. To adorn with stars, رَصَّعَ بِنُجُوم .

Star, v.i. To make a stately progress, وَكَبَ aor. يَكِبُ ـ أَوْكَبَ : He starred it in the provinces, أَوْكَبَ فِي ٱلْوِلَايَاتِ .

Starboard, *n.* Of a ship, ٱلْجَنْبُ ٱلْأَيْمَنُ مِنَ ٱلْمَرْكَبِ. Starboard! لِفّ ـ حَيْلَكْ.

Starch, *n.* The farinaceous substance, نَشًا. *See also* Starchness, *n.*

Starch, *v.t.* عَالَجَ بِٱلنَّشَا ـ نَشَّى. To be starched, عُولِجَ بِٱلنَّشَا.

Starch, *a.* } Precise, مُدَقِّق. Reserved, بَارِد ـ كَتُوم ـ طَرِيق. **Starched**, } Ceremonious, كَثِيرُ ٱلتَّكَالِيفِ. *See also* Stiff, Rigid, *a.*

Starchedness, *n.* Starchness, *n.*

Starcher, *n.* مُعَالِجُ ٱلثِّيَابِ بِٱلنَّشَا.

Starchly, *ad.* Stiffly, بِبُرُودَةٍ ـ بِإِطْرَاقٍ ـ إِطْرَاقًا.

Starchness, *n.* Stiffness, precision, reserve, بُرُودَة ـ إِطْرَاق. *See also* Rigidity, Stiffness, *n.*

Stare, *v.i.* فَقَّصَ بِعَيْنِهِ ـ هَطَعَ ـ بَرَّقَ بِعَيْنَيْهِ. To — with astonishment, إِنْذَهَلَ عَجَبًا ـ بَهِتَ ـ غَزَا. *See also to* Gape, Gaze, *v.i.*

Stare, *v.t.* To stare at, أَعْيَنَ ـ شَفَنَ إِلَى ـ رَمَقَ ـ رَامَقَ ـ تَفَرَّسَ فِي ـ حَمْلَقَ إِلَى ـ لَمَقَ إِلَى. To — one out of countenance, أَخْجَلَ ـ خَجَّلَ.

Stare, *n.* مُعَايَنَة ـ لَمْق ـ هُطُوع ـ هَطْع ـ رَمْق ـ مُرَامَقَة.

Starer, *n.* مُتَفَرِّس ـ نَظَّار ـ هَاطِع ـ رَامِق ـ مُرَامِق. One who stares about, لَفُوت.

Star-fish, *n.* نَجْمَةُ ٱلْبَحْرِ.

Star-gazer, *n.* رَصَّادُ ٱلنُّجُومِ ـ مُنَجِّم *pl.* مُنَجِّمُونَ.

Star-gazing, *n.* تَنَجُّم ـ رَصْدُ ٱلنُّجُومِ : He passed the night in —, بَاتَ يَرْعَى طَبَقَ ٱلنُّجُومِ.

Stark, *a.* Quite, مُطْلَق ـ خَالِص. Stark mad, مَجْنُونٌ كُلَّ ٱلْجُنُونِ. Stark naked, مُجَرَّدُ ٱلثِّيَابِ ـ *vulg.* عُرْيَانٌ خَالِص ـ بِٱلزَّلْطِ. He was made — naked, عُرِّيَ تَعْرِيَةً.

Stark, *ad.* بَتَّةً ـ بِٱلْكُلِّيَّةِ ـ إِطْلَاقًا.

Starless, *a.* بِلَا نُجُومٍ. A — night, لَيْلَةٌ لَمْ تَظْهَرْ فِيهَا ٱلنُّجُومُ. Unfortunate, مَنْحُوس ـ نَحِس.

Starlight, *n.* ضِيَاءُ ٱلنُّجُومِ.

Star-like, *a.* مِثْلَ ٱلنُّجُومِ ـ مِثْلَ ٱلنَّجْمَةِ.

Starling, *n.* The bird, زُرْزُور *pl.* زَرَازِير.

Starred, *a.* Studded with stars, مُرَصَّعٌ بِنُجُومٍ. Having decorations, مُوَشَّحٌ بِنَوَاشِينِ شَرَفٍ. Ill-starred; *see* Unlucky, *a.*

Starry, *a.* ذُو نُجُومٍ ـ مُكَوْكَب. The — heavens, فَلَكُ ٱلنُّجُومِ.

Start, *v.i.* To move suddenly, إِهْتَزَّ ـ فَزَّ. To spring up suddenly, قَامَ بَغْتَةً ـ فَزَّ ـ نَطَّ. To — from fear, شَدَّ. To burst, إِنْبَعَجَ ـ فَقَأَ ـ إِنْصَدَعَ. To —, or — off, as for a place, سَافَرَ ـ إِنْطَلَقَ إِلَى ـ تَوَجَّهَ إِلَى ـ قَصَدَ إِلَى ـ عَمِدَ إِلَى. To — aside, إِنْحَرَفَ. To — back, recoil, تَرَادَّ ـ تَرَاجَعَ.

Start, *v.t.* To rouse, أَفَزَّ ـ إِسْتَفَزَّ. To —, as of birds, طَيَّرَ ـ أَطَارَ; of animals, أَحَاشَ ـ يُحَوِّشُ *aor.* حَاشَ ـ كَرَّشَ. To bring into motion, حَرَّكَ. To set on foot, إِبْتَدَأَ بِ ـ شَرَعَ بِ ـ أَوْجَدَ ـ إِخْتَرَعَ. To —, as for a journey, سَيَّرَ; as for a race, أَطْلَقَ. To dislocate, فَكَّ ـ خَلَعَ. To empty, as of a cask, فَرَّغَ; to broach, as of a cask, نَقَذَ ـ بَزَّلَ; as of a question, فَتَحَ ٱلْبَحْثَ فِي ـ فَتَحَ سِيرَةَ فِي كَذَا. *See also to* Startle, *v.t.*

Start, *n.* A sudden motion of the body, هَزَّة ـ فَزَّة. A bound, spring, فَزَّة ـ نَطَّة ـ فَزّ ـ نَطّ. A —, as from fright, شَدّ ـ شُذُود. A — forward, وَثْبَة. Excitement to action, إِسْتِفْزَاز ـ تَرْوِيج ـ تَحْرِيض. The being before, سَبْق. First movement, أَوَّل حَرَكَةٍ ـ أَوَّل. Departure, ذَهَاب ـ رَحْل ـ إِنْطِلَاق ـ تَوَجُّه. By fits and starts, كَرَّةً وَفَرَّةً. To get the —, سَبَقَ. To give one the —, سَبَّقَ. To give one a —, as in life, فَتَحَ لِ بَابًا. To prepare one's self for a —, أَبَّ لِيَذْهَبَ إِلَى كَذَا.

Starting-post, *n.* مَوْقِفُ خَيْلِ ٱلْحَلْبَةِ قَبْلَ أَنْ تُطْلَقَ ـ حَبْل.

Startful, *a.* *See* Skittish, *a.*

Startfulness, *n.* *See* Skittishness, *n.*

Startle, *v.t.* To alarm, رَعَبَ ـ أَفْزَعَ. To agitate, أَرْجَفَ ـ قَلْقَلَ ـ قَلَّقَ. To astonish, حَيَّرَ ـ عَجَّبَ ـ أَدْهَشَ. To be startled, alarmed, إِرْتَعَبَ ـ تَخَشَّى; to be agitated, تَقَلْقَلَ ـ تَحَيَّرَ ـ إِرْتَجَفَ ـ رَجَفَ; to be astonished, إِنْدَهَشَ ـ تَعَجَّبَ.

Startle, *n.* A shock, رِعْدَة ـ خَضَّة ـ هَبْطَة ـ رَجْفَة. To give one a —; *see to* Startle, *v.t.*

Startling, *a.* مُرْجِف ـ مُرْعِد. Dreadful, مُخِيف ـ فَظِيع.

Start-up, *n.* An upstart, مُحْدَث. *See also* Parvenu, *n.*

Starvation, *n.* As from hunger, مَوْتٌ مِنَ ٱلْجُوعِ; from cold, مَوْتٌ (or تَدْنِيق) مِنَ ٱلْبَرْدِ; from want of irrigation, ذُبُولٌ مِنْ قِلَّةِ ٱلسَّقْيِ. He died of —, from hunger, مَاتَ مِنَ ٱلْجُوعِ.

Starve, *v.i.* To perish with hunger, مَاتَ ـ هَلَكَ جُوعًا ـ مَاتَ مِنَ ٱلْجُوعِ ـ مِنْ جُوعِهِ. To perish with cold, هَلَكَ ـ مَاتَ مِنْ شِدَّةِ ٱلْبَرْدِ ـ صَقِعَ. To be in poverty, إِحْتَاجَ ـ إِفْتَقَرَ.

Starve, *v.t.* To kill with hunger, أَهْلَكَ مِنَ ٱلْجُوعِ ـ مَوَّتَ جُوعًا; with cold, أَهْلَكَ مِنَ ٱلْبَرْدِ. To let perish for want of water, أَدْوَى-مِنْ قِلَّةِ ٱلسَّقْيِ . To —, as of a garrison, أَقْمَعَ-بِٱلْمَجَاعَةِ .

Starveling, *n.* As from hunger, مَائِتٌ مِنَ ـ جَوْعَانُ ـ جَائِعٌ جُوعِهِ ; from cold, مَائِتٌ مِنْ شِدَّةِ ٱلْبَرْدِ .

State, *n.* Condition, حَالَةٌ ـ أَحْوَال *pl.* حَال ـ شُؤُون *pl.* شَأْن . Position, circumstances, صُورَة ـ وَضْع ـ كَيْفِيَّةُ حَالٍ . State, empire, kingdom, دُوَل *pl.* دَوْلَة ـ مَمَالِكُ *pl.* مَمْلَكَة ـ سَلْطَنَة ; a collective body of men forming a government, جَمَاهِيرُ *pl.* جُمْهُور . Dignity, position, مَنْزِلَة ـ مَرْتَبَة ـ مَقَام ـ قِيَام . A profession, صَنْعَة ـ تَعَاطٍ ـ حِرْفَة . Show, pomp, إِحْتِفَال ـ دَبْدَبَة ـ تَبْجِيل ـ سَلْطَنَة . In —, with pomp, بِتَبْجِيلٍ ـ بِٱحْتِفَالٍ ـ بِوَكْبَةٍ . To lie in —, (of the dead,) تَجَلَّى ٱلْمَيِّتُ بِٱحْتِفَالٍ .

Affairs of state, مَصَالِحُ ٱلدَّوْلَةِ ـ أُمُورُ ٱلدَّوْلَةِ ـ مَسَائِلُ مَلَكِيَّةٌ مُهِمَّاتٌ دُوَلِيَّةٌ .

Chief of a state, رَئِيسُ ٱلْمُلْكِ .

Council of state, مَشْوَرَةُ ٱلدَّوْلَةِ .

Critical state of affairs, حَالَةُ بُحْرَانِ ٱلْأُمُورِ ـ أَوْقَاتُ مِحْنَةٍ وَبَلَاءٍ .

Reasons of state, أَسْبَابٌ دُوَلِيَّةٌ ـ مَنَافِعُ مَلَكِيَّةٌ ـ تَدَابِيرُ مَلَكِيَّةٌ .

State crime, جِنَايَةٌ عَلَى ٱلدَّوْلَةِ .

State of a question, كَيْفِيَّةُ حَالِ مَسْأَلَةٍ .

State of anarchy, حَالُ هَرْجٍ وَمَرْجٍ ـ إِخْتِلَالٌ كُلِّيٌّ .

State of civilization, حَالُ ٱلتَّمَدُّنِ .

State of nature, حَالُ ٱلْوَحْشَةِ ـ حَالُ ٱلْفِطْرَةِ ٱلطَّبِيعِيَّةِ .

State of war, حَالُ ٱلْحَرْبِ ـ حَالُ ٱلْمُحَارَبَةِ .

The United States of America, جَمَاهِيرُ أَمِيرِكَا ٱلْمُتَّحِدَةُ .

State, *a.* Official, دُوَلِيٌّ ـ مُخْتَصٌّ بِٱلدَّوْلَةِ ـ رَسْمِيٌّ .

State, *v.t.* To express in words, قَالَ [2]; in writing, سَطَرَ [2] ـ كَتَبَ [2]. To —, as in a journal, document, *etc.*, جَاءَ فِي *aor.* يَجِيءُ [2]. To represent, describe, رَوَى *aor.* يَرْوِي ـ شَرَحَ ـ وَصَفَ *aor.* يَصِفُ . To explain, بَيَّنَ ـ أَوْضَحَ ـ فَسَّرَ . To —, report, as by telegraph, *etc.*, أَنْبَأَ بِ . It is stated of him, رُوِيَ عَنْهُ . What is stated (written) in this treaty, ٱلْمَسْطُورُ فِي هٰذِهِ ٱلْمُعَاهَدَةِ . To — anything to one, make known to, سَمَّعَ ـ أَفَادَ ـ بَلَّغَ خَبَّرَ-بِ ; to bring to the notice of, to submit to, عَرَضَ-لِ . A telegram arrived stating that …, وَصَلَ تِلِغْرَافٌ يَتَضَمَّنُ أَنْ *aor.* يَصِلُ .

Stated, *a.* Fixed, occurring at regular times, مُعَيَّن ـ مُقَرَّر ـ مَعْلُوم . At — times, عِنْدَ أَوْقَاتٍ مَعْلُومَةٍ .

Statedly, *ad.* بِٱطِّرَادٍ ـ عِنْدَ أَوْقَاتٍ مَعْلُومَةٍ .

Stateliness, *n.* Grandeur, سَلْطَنَة ـ إِحْتِشَام ـ حِشْمَة ـ أُبَّهَة ; of demeanour, هَيْبَة . Loftiness, as of buildings, إِرْتِفَاع ـ شُمُوخ . Affectation of dignity, تَصَلُّف ـ تَكَبُّر ـ تَعَظُّم ـ شُمُوخ . To affect —, تَصَلَّفَ وَتَظَرَّفَ ـ تَصَلَّفَ .

Stately, *a.* Having the quality of grandeur, of a person, سُلْطَانِيٌّ ـ مُفَخَّم ـ بَهِيٌّ ـ جَلِيل ـ جَلِيٌّ . Lofty, شَامِخ ـ مُرْتَفِع ـ عَالٍ . To affect to be stately, تَصَلَّفَ وَتَظَرَّفَ ـ تَكَبَّرَ ـ تَعَظَّمَ ـ شَمَخَ [2] بِأَنْفِهِ . *See also* Grand, Magnificent, *a.*

Stately, *ad.* *See* Grandly, Magnificently, *ad.*

Statement, *n.* A description, وَصْف . An account of particular acts, *etc.*, مَضْبَطَة ـ إِفَادَة ـ تَقْرِير ـ قَرَار . Statements made to any one, reports, تَبْلِيغَات . He submitted a —, قَدَّمَ تَقْرِيرًا . One —, report, is, وَفِي رِوَايَةٍ ; and another statement is, وَفِي رِوَايَةٍ أُخْرَى ـ فِي عِبَارَةٍ أُخْرَى . They wrote a —, كَتَبُوا قَرَارًا . Statements differ regarding the truth of the conversation which took place between them, تَخْتَلِفُ ٱلرِّوَايَاتُ عَنْ حَقِيقَةِ ٱلْمُحَاوَرَةِ ٱلَّتِي جَرَتْ بَيْنَهُمْ . If this — be true, إِنْ كَانَتْ هٰذِهِ ٱلرِّوَايَةُ صَحِيحَةً . *See also* Report, *n.*

State-paper, *n.* صَحِيفَةٌ رَسْمِيَّةٌ *pl.* صَحَائِفُ .

State-prisoner, *n.* مَحْبُوسٌ لِأَجْلِ ٱلْجِنَايَةِ عَلَى ٱلدَّوْلَةِ .

State-room, *n.* A reception room, دَوَاوِينُ *pl.* دِيوَان . A — on board ship, كَمْرَة ـ مَقْعَد ـ طَارِمَة .

Statesman, *n.* سِيَاسِيٌّ . Statesmen, أَرْبَابُ ٱلسِّيَاسَةِ . An old —, سِيَاسِيٌّ قَدِيمٌ . *See also* Politician, *n.*

Statesmanlike, *a.* مِثْلَ أَهْلِ ٱلسِّيَاسَةِ ـ سِيَاسِيٌّ .

Statesmanship, *n.* صِرَاطُ ٱلْمَعَارِفِ ٱلسِّيَاسِيَّةِ ـ سِيَاسَة .

State-trial, *n.* مَحْكَمَةٌ مُرَتَّبَةٌ لِأَجْلِ ٱلْحُكْمِ عَلَى ٱلْأُمَرَاءِ فِي جِنَايَةٍ دُوَلِيَّةٍ .

Static, *a.* } سُكُونِيٌّ ـ ثِقْلِيٌّ .
Statical, }

Statics, *n.* عِلْمُ أَسْبَابِ ٱلْأَثْقَالِ ـ عِلْمُ ٱلْأَثْقَالِ .

Station, *n.* A place of standing, مَكَان ـ مَوْقِف ـ مَقَرّ *pl.* أَمْكِنَة ـ مَقَام ـ مَوَاضِعُ *pl.* مَوْضِع . A place or department of an office, خِدْمَة ـ مَأْمُورِيَّة ـ مَحَلُّ مَأْمُورِيَّةٍ . Office, business, مَنْزِلَة ـ مَقَام ـ رُتْبَة ـ حَال ـ زُلْفَة ـ زُلْفَى . Condition, rank, مَحَطّ ـ مَحَطَّة . A stand, or rack, فَانُوس . Footing, إِسْكَلَة ـ مَرْفَأ ـ مِينَا . A port, مَنْزِل خَانَه . A place for putting up at on a post-road, هٰذَا مَرْكَزُ ٱلْخَيَّالَةِ . This is the cavalry —, هُوَ فِي أَعْلَى ٱلرُّتَبِ . He fills the highest —, يَكُونُ مَقَرُّهُ فِي كَذَا . His — shall be at …, "And neither your riches nor your children are what will bring you near to us in station," وَمَا أَمْوَالُكُمْ وَلَا أَوْلَادُكُمْ بِٱلَّتِي تُقَرِّبُكُمْ عِندَنَا زُلْفَى (Kur. xxxiv. 36).

A military station, مَرْكَزُ عَسَاكِرَ *pl.* مَرَاكِزُ.

A police station, مَحَلُّ ٱلضَّبْطِيَّةِ.

A railway station, مَوْقِفُ (or مَحَطَّةُ) سِكَّةِ ٱلْحَدِيدِ.

A telegraph station, مَوْقِفُ ٱلتِّلِغْرَافِ.

Station, *v.t.* To fix, place, حَطَّ ² — وَضَعَ *aor.* يَضَعُ — جَعَلَ ². To set up, نَصَبَ ² — صَمَدَ ². To appoint, as to a particular place, عَيَّنَ لِ. To be stationed, fixed, in a place, إِرْتَكَزَ.

Stational, *a.* مَحَلِّيٌّ.

Stationary, *a.* Fixed, ثَابِتٌ — رَاتِبٌ — رَاهِنٌ — رَاسٍ — سَاكِنٌ. Not moving, رَاكِدٌ — وَاقِفٌ. To be —, fixed, رَسَا *aor.* يَرْسُو — تَرَسَّى; to make —, أَرْسَى. To be —, motionless, رَكَدَ ². To make motionless, أَرْكَدَ.

Stationer, *n.* بَيَّاعُ ٱلْقَرَاطِيسِ *pl.* بَيَّاعَةٌ — كَاغِدِيٌّ *pl.* كَاغِدِيَّةٌ — وَرَّاقٌ.

Stationery, *n.* قَرَاطِيسُ — أَوْرَاقٌ — بِضَاعَةُ وَرَقٍ.

Statistic, *a.* }
Statistical, } مَا نِيطَ بِدَخْلِ بَلَدٍ وَخَرْجِهَا وَعَدَدِ سُكَّانِهَا — قَوَائِمِيٌّ — تَقْوِيمِيٌّ.

Statistician, *n.* مَاهِرٌ فِي كُلِّ مَا يَتَعَلَّقُ بِحِسَابَاتِ ٱلدَّوَائِرِ — قَوَائِمْجِي.

Statistics, *n.* تَقْوِيمُ أَحْوَالِ ٱلْبُلْدَانِ وَمَصَارِيفِهَا وَمَحْصُولَاتِهَا — فَنُّ وَضْعِ ٱلْقَوَائِمِ.

Statuary, *n.* A sculptor, نَقَّاشُ ٱلتَّمَاثِيلِ — نَقَّاشٌ. The art of carving images, نِقَاشَةُ ٱلتَّمَاثِيلِ. A collection of statues, تَمَاثِيلُ — مَجْمُوعَةُ تَمَاثِيلَ.

Statue, *n.* نَصْبٌ — تِمْثَالٌ *pl.* تَمَاثِيلُ — شَخْصٌ *pl.* أَشْخَاصٌ — تَصْوِيرٌ مُجَسَّمٌ. An equestrian —, تِمْثَالُ رَاكِبٍ. To erect a —, نَصَبَ تِمْثَالًا ².

Stature, *n.* قَدٌّ — قَوَامٌ — قَامَةٌ — قَوْمَةٌ — قِمَّةٌ — شِبْرٌ — تَقْطِيعٌ. A short —, قَصِيرُ ٱلشِّبْرِ. Of elegant —, حَسَنُ ٱلْقِمَّةِ. Of tall —, طَوِيلُ ٱلْقَامَةِ. He increased in —, تَقَدَّمَ فِي ٱلْقَامَةِ.

Statu, ad. In statu quo, فِي ٱلْحَالِ ٱلسَّابِقِ.

Status, n. Condition, حَالٌ. Position, rank, رُتْبَةٌ — مَنْزِلَةٌ.

Statutable, *a.* مُطَابِقُ ٱلْقَوَانِينِ — قَانُونِيٌّ.

Statutably, *ad.* حَسَبَ ٱلْقَوَانِينِ — طِبْقَ ٱلْقَوَانِينِ.

Statute, *n.* A prescribed religious statute, فَرْضٌ *pl.* فُرُوضٌ — فَرِيضَةٌ *pl.* فَرَائِضُ. An order, regulation, أَمْرٌ *pl.* أَوَامِرُ — حُكْمٌ *pl.* أَحْكَامٌ — قَانُونٌ *pl.* قَوَانِينُ. A law, سُنَّةٌ *pl.* سُنَنٌ. *See also* Ordinance, *n.*

Staunch, *a.* *See* Stanch, *a.*

Stave, *n.* As of a barrel, دَفٌّ *pl.* دُفُوفٌ; as of a psalm, نَغْمَةٌ — مَقَامَةٌ *pl.* مَقَامَاتٌ. A staff, in music; *see under* Staff, *n.*

Stave, *v.t.* To break a hole into, نَقَبَ ² — بَخَشَ ². To break, burst, بَعَجَ — فَقَعَ — شَقَّ ² — هَشَمَ — شَدَخَ. To suffer to run out, of liquids, by breaking, فَجَرَ — بَجَسَ ² — بَجَّسَ. To — off, to repel from, صَدَعَ عَنْ. *See also to* Delay, *v.t.*

Stay, *v.i.* To abide, remain, مَكَثَ ² — ظَلَّ — إِسْتَقَامَ — إِسْتَمَرَّ. To —, to reside, as in a place, نَوَى — لَطَى بِ — حَجَنَ بِ — تَوَقَّفَ — سَكَنَ ² — قَعَدَ فِي — أَحَالَ بِ. To loiter, تَلَبَّثَ — تَمَهَّلَ — تَحَوَّزَ. To stop, وَقَفَ *aor.* يَقِفُ — تَوَقَّفَ. *See also to* Abide, Remain, *v.i.*

To stay away, to absent one's self, from, غَابَ عَنْ — مَا حَضَرَ فِي.

To stay in, to keep to the house, لَازَمَ ٱلدَّارَ.

To stay or wait for, رَقَبَ ² — تَوَقَّفَ لِ — إِنْتَظَرَ — إِسْتَنْظَرَ.

To stay or rest one's self upon, as a support, سَنَدَ ² — إِدَّعَمَ عَلَى — إِسْتَنَدَ إِلَى — إِلَى. To rely upon, to confide in, إِسْتَكْفَى بِ — إِعْتَمَدَ عَلَى — إِتَّكَلَ عَلَى — عَوَّلَ عَلَى.

Stay, *v.t.* To arrest, أَوْقَفَ — وَقَّفَ. To withhold, حَجَزَ عَنْ ² — مَنَعَ — حَاشَ ². To prop, دَعَمَ — أَسْنَدَ — سَنَّدَ — أَعْمَدَ — عَمَّدَ. To strengthen, شَدَّ ² — وَثَّقَ. To sustain, assist, عَاوَنَ — أَمَدَّ بِ — عَضَدَ ². To be stayed, supported, as by posts, إِنْعَمَدَ. *See also to* Prop, *v.t.*

Stay, *n.* Continuance in a place, إِسْتِمْرَارٌ — إِسْتِقَامَةٌ — إِقَامَةٌ — مَكْثٌ. A prolonged — or absence, طِيَالٌ — طَوَالٌ: your prolonged —, طَوَالُكَ. Residence in a place, مُتُونٌ بِ — قُطُونٌ — وُقُوفٌ — تَوَقُّفٌ — مُكْثٌ — سُكْنَى — إِقَامَةٌ. Stop, cessation, An obstruction, مَانِعٌ *pl.* مَوَانِعُ — عَائِقٌ. A prop, support, رُكْنٌ *pl.* أَرْكَانٌ — دِعَامَةٌ *pl.* دَعَائِمُ — دِعْمٌ — دِعْمَةٌ — مَسْنَدٌ; a — for a wall, كَلْبٌ *pl.* كِلَابٌ; a — of iron, ضَبَّةٌ *pl.* ضَبَّاتٌ *and* ضِبَابٌ. A helper, نَصِيرٌ — مُعِينٌ — ظَهِيرٌ. He is the — of the people, هُوَ عِمَادُ ٱلْقَوْمِ.

Stay-lace, *n.* بَنْدُ (or قِيطَانُ) صُدَيْرَةِ ٱلنِّسَاءِ — قِيطَانُ ٱلْقُورْسِيتَةِ.

Stays, *n.* A corset, ضَرْبٌ مِنَ ٱلصُّدَيْرِيَّاتِ لِلنِّسَاءِ — قُورْسِيتَةٌ. The — of a ship, إِسْتِرَالِيَةٌ. To be in —, to tack, عَمِلَ أُورْصَةً — حَوَّلَ ٱلْقَرِيَّةَ. To miss —, مَا صَحَّتِ ٱلْأُورْصَةُ. (The last three nautical phrases and the next following are those used in Egypt and the Mediterranean.)

Stay-maker, خَيَّاطُ ٱلْقُورْسِيتَاتِ.

Stay-sail, *n.* إِسْتِرَالِيَةٌ.

Stead, *n.* A substitute, بَدَلٌ — عِوَضٌ. In his —, مَكَانَهُ —

عِوَضًا عَنْهُ. He raised up others in their —, أَقَامَ آخَرِينَ مَكَانَهُمْ. You shall be to us in — of eyes, تَكُونُ لَنَا كَعُيُونٍ. To stand in his —, قَامَ مَقَامَهُ [2].

Steadfast, *a.* Firm, constant, وَثِيق *pl.* وِثَاق – رَاتِب – رَبِيطٌ – عَزُوم – صِنْدِيد *pl.* صَنَادِيدُ – ثَبْتُ ٱلْغَدَرِ. Resolute, رَاسِخ – حَازِم – حَزِيم. To be —, firm, تَقَرَّرَ – رَسَخَ = – تَرَسَّخَ – قَامَ رَاسِخًا [2]. To make —, أَرْسَخَ – أَثْبَتَ – أَوْثَقَ – وَثَّقَ. *See also* Resolute, *a.*

Steadfastly, *ad.* ثَبَاتًا – وَثَاقَةً. To look — at, شَخَصَ إِلَى = – أَمْعَنَ ٱلنَّظَرَ فِي.

Steadfastness, *n.* Firmness, constancy, وَثَاقَة – ثَبَات – ثُبُوت – قَرَار – عَدَمُ تَقَلْقُلٍ. Resoluteness, حَزْم – عَزِيمَة – وَثَاقَة – شِدَّةُ عَزْمٍ.

Steadily, *ad.* With firmness, بِثَبَاتٍ – بِرُسُوخٍ. Perseveringly, بِإِدْمَانٍ – بِمُوَاظَبَةٍ – بِلُزُومٍ. Wisely, properly, حَسَنًا – كَمَا يَلِيقُ. Without commotion, بِعَدَمِ ٱضْطِرَابٍ. To subside —, تَرَاكَدَ.

Steadiness, *n.* Firmness, ثَبَات – ثُبُوت – رُسُوخ. Continuance, إِسْتِمْرَار – دَوَام. Perseverance, إِدْمَان – لُزُوم – مُوَاظَبَةٌ عَلَى – إِسْتِمْرَارٌ فِي. Steadiness of conduct, حَزْم – أَدَب – تَعَقُّل – عَقْل – إِحْتِرَاز. To act with — in a matter, تَحَزَّمَ فِي ٱلْأَمْرِ.

Steady, *a.* Firm, as in standing, رَاسِخ – ثَابِت – مُقَرَّر. Persevering, لَاتِب – مُبْتَرِك – مُلَازِم – مُوَاظِبٌ عَلَى. Sober in behaviour, أَدِيب – عَاقِل. Continuing, مُسْتَدِيم – دَائِم. His hands were —, كَانَتْ يَدَاهُ ثَابِتَتَيْنِ. To be —, persevering, assiduous, in, مَارَسَ – أَدْمَنَ عَلَى – وَاظَبَ عَلَى – لَازَمَ. To be —, sober in mode of life, أَدُبَ [2] – تَعَقَّلَ – كَانَ عَاقِلًا.

Steady, *v.t.* To make steady, ثَبَّتَ – مَكَّنَ – ضَبَطَ = [2]. To hold —, تَمَسَّكَ بِ – مَسَكَ بِ = – ضَبَطَ = [2]. To make grave, prudent, أَدَّبَ – عَقَّلَ – سَكَّنَ طَائِرَهُ.

Steady! *interj.* إِعْتِدَالًا – عَلَى ٱلْعَدْلِ.

Steak, *n.* As of meat, شَرِيحَة *pl.* شَرَائِحُ. A beef —, شَرِيحَةُ لَحْمِ بَقَرٍ. A rump —, شَرِيحَةُ لَحْمٍ مِنْ كَفَلِ ٱلْبَقَرِ.

Steal, *v.t.* To take unlawfully from, إِسْتَرَقَ مِنْ – سَرَقَ مِنْ =. To seize forcibly, إِخْتَلَسَ. To captivate, سَبَى = – سَلَبَ قَلْبَهُ [2] – أَغْرَمَ – إِسْتَمْلَكَ. To — a glance at, رَمَقَ [2] – تَبَصَّرَ.

Steal, *v.i.* To practise stealing, لَصَّ [2] – تَلَصَّصَ – كَانَ لِصًّا. To — or slink away, تَخَلَّعَ – إِنْسَلَتَ – إِنْسَلَّ – إِنْفَلَتَ – تَفَلَّتَ. To let — away from; *the same verbs with the addition of* مِنْ *or* مِنْ بَيْنِ. To — in upon, تَسَلَّلَ إِلَى *or* عَلَى.

Stealer, *n.* لِصّ *pl.* لُصُوص – سَارِق *pl.* سُرَّاق. A — of horses, سَلَّال; of camels, خَارِب; of sheep, أَخْمَصُ; of coins by secreting them in his fingers, قَفَّاف.

Stealing, *n.* تَلَصُّص – سَرِق – سَرِقَة. To charge one with —, سَرَّقَ.

Stealth, *n.* Theft, سَرِقَة. By —, عَلَى خَفَاءٍ – خُفْيَةً. To enter by —, أَنْزَبَقَ – تَسَلَّلَ لِلدُّخُولِ إِلَى. Listening by —, مُسْتَرِق.

Stealthful, *a.* مُتَسَلِّل – خَفِيٌّ – مَسْتُور. "With a stealthful glance," مِنْ طَرْفٍ خَفِيٍّ (Kur. xlii. 44). *See also* Clandestine, *a.*

Stealthfulness, *n.* تَسَلُّل – خَفَاء.

Stealthily, *ad.* تَسَلُّلًا – عَلَى خَفَاءٍ – خُفْيَةً.

Stealthy, *a.* *See* Stealthful, Clandestine, *a.*

Steam, *n.* The vapour, بُخَار *pl.* أَبْخِرَة *and* بُخَارَات. To blow off the steam, أَطْلَقَ (*or* فَرَّغَ) ٱلْبُخَارَ. To empty one's self of, تَفَرَّغَ مِنْ – تَخَفَّفَ مِنْ. To get up steam, as for a steamer, صَعَّدَ (*or vulg.* طَلَّعَ) ٱلْبُخَارَ. To strengthen one's self for, تَأَهَّبَ لِ – تَعَزَّزَ لِ – تَشَجَّعَ لِ – تَشَدَّدَ لِ. To go by steam, سَارَ بِقُوَّةِ ٱلْبُخَارِ =. To go readily, easily, سَهُلَ سُلُوكُهُ [2] – تَرَوَّجَ.

Steam, *v.t.* To expose to steam, عَرَضَ عَلَى ٱلْبُخَارِ =. To cook by steam, طَبَخَ بِٱلْبُخَارِ = [2] – طَبَخَ عَلَى ٱلْبُخَارِ.

Steam, *v.i.* To emit steam, as a kettle, بَخَرَ [2]. To go or progress by —, of a steamer, تَسِيرُ ٱلْبَاخِرَةُ: The steamer steams 14 miles an hour, ٱلْبَاخِرَةُ تَسِيرُ أَرْبَعَةَ عَشَرَ مِيلًا فِي ٱلسَّاعَةِ.

Steam-boat, / **Steam-vessel,** *n.* / **Steamer,** } بَاخُور *pl.* بَوَاخِيرُ – بَاخِرَة *pl.* بَاخِرَات – وَابُور *pl.* وَابُورَات – مَرْكَبُ نَارٍ *pl.* مَرَاكِبُ. He embarked on board a —, رَكِبَ بَاخِرَةً =.

Steam-boiler, *n.* خِلْقِينُ ٱلْبُخَارِ *pl.* خَلَاقِينُ.

Steam-engine, *n.* آلَةُ ٱلْبُخَارِ *pl.* آلَات; of a steamer, دُولَابُ ٱلْبَاخِرَةِ *pl.* دَوَالِيبُ. Steam-engines, آلَاتٌ بُخَارِيَّةٌ.

Steam-packet, *n.* A postal steamer, بَاخِرَةُ ٱلْبُوسْطَةِ – وَابُورُ بُوسْطَةٍ.

Steam-tug, *n.* بَاخِرَةٌ جَرَّارَةٌ.

Steam-whistle, صَفَّارَةُ ٱلْبَاخِرَةِ.

Stearine, *n.* ضَرْبٌ مِنَ ٱلزَّيْتِ.

Steatite, *n.* حَجَرُ ٱلصَّابُونِ.

Stedfast, *a.* *See* Steadfast, *a.*

Steed, *a.* *See* Horse, *n.*

Steel, *n.* فَالُون – صُلْب – فُولَاذ *pl.* فَوَالِيذُ – بُولَاد. A — to strike fire with, زِنَاد *pl.* أَزْنِدَة.

Steel, *a.* مِنْ فُولَاذٍ – مِنْ بُولَادٍ.

Steel, *v.t.* To harden, make stubborn, شَرَّكَ. To make hard,

صَلَّبَ. To edge with steel, رَكَّبَ ذُبَابَةً بُولَادًا. To — or strengthen one's self, تَشَجَّعَ ـ تَأَتَّبَ. To harden one's self, one's heart, أَقْسَى قَلْبَهُ. *See also* to Harden, *v.t.*

Steel-clad, *a.* In steel armour, مُدَرَّعٌ بِبُولَادٍ.

Steely, *a.* Made of steel, مِنْ بُولَادٍ ـ فُولَاذِيٌّ. Hard, cruel, عَنِيفٌ ـ جَافٍ ـ قَاسٍ.

Steelyard, *n.* رُمَّانَةٌ ـ رُومَانَةٌ ـ صَنْجَةٌ ـ سِنْجٌ *pl.* سَنَجَةٌ ـ قَبَّانٌ. To weigh with a —, وَزَنَ ـ بِٱلْقَبَّانِ ـ قَبَّنَ *aor.* يَزِنُ.

Steep, *a.* Declivous, هَبُوطٌ ـ مُنْصَبٌّ. A — descent, حَطُوطٌ. Lofty, عَالٍ ـ شَامِخٌ. Steep places or fortresses, مَعَاقِلُ.

Steep, *n.* حَطُوطٌ ـ أَصْبَابٌ *pl.* صَبَبٌ ـ مُنْحَدَرٌ ـ حَدُورٌ. An abrupt — or ridge, جُرُفٌ *pl.* أَجْرَافٌ: He threw himself down a —, إِنْدَفَعَ مِنْ عَلَى ٱلْجُرُفِ.

Steep, *v.t.* To soak, macerate in, غَمَسَ ـ فِي ـ مَرَثَ ـ فِي ـ أَنْقَعَ ـ فِي ـ نَقَعَ ـ فِي ـ مَرَسَ ـ فِي. To be steeped, إِنْغَمَسَ ـ إِنْتَقَعَ ـ إِغْتَمَسَ. To —, as a new skin, *etc.*, to remove any taste that it may have, شَرَّبَ. The vessel in which anything is steeped, مِنْقَعٌ.

Steeple, *n.* مَنَارَةٌ *pl.* مَنَاوِرُ *and* مَنَائِرُ. *See also* Spire, *n.*

Steepled, *n.* Having a steeple, ذُو مَنَارَةٍ.

Steeple-chase, *n.* مُسَابَقَةُ خَيْلٍ إِلَى أَمَدٍ مُرْتَفِعٍ كَمَنَارَةٍ دُونَ ٱلْتِفَاتٍ إِلَى ٱلْمَوَانِعِ ٱلْعَارِضَةِ فِي ٱلْمَسَافَةِ.

Steeply, *ad.* إِنْحِدَارًا.

Steepness, *n.* هُبُوطٌ ـ أُحْدُورٌ ـ حُدُورٌ.

Steer, *n.* ثِيرَانٌ صِغَارٌ *pl.* ثَوْرٌ صَغِيرٌ.

Steer, *v.t.* Of a ship, ضَبَطَ ٱلسُّكَّانَ. To direct, دَبَّرَ ـ سَاسَ.

Steer, *v.i.* To obey the helm readily, أَطَاعَ لِلسُّكَّانِ. To — wild, of a helmsman, تَغَفَّلَ بِٱلسُّكَّانِ. To — clear of, تَمَنَّعَ مِنْ; through fear, خَامَ عَنْ. To — for a place, ضَرَبَ إِلَى.

Steerage, *n.* The act of steering a ship, تَدْبِيرٌ ـ ضَبْطُ ٱلسُّكَّانِ. The manner in which a ship obeys the helm, ٱلْإِنْقِيَادُ لِلدَّفَّةِ. Part of the ship for inferior passengers, ٱلْمَخْدَعُ ٱلثَّانِي ـ ٱلطَّارِمَةُ ٱلثَّانِيَةُ. Government, direction, تَدْبِيرٌ ـ سِيَاسَةٌ.

Steerage-way, *n.* مَخْرُ ٱلْمَرْكَبِ ـ شَقُّ ٱلسَّفِينَةِ.

Steerage-wheel, *n.* دُولَابُ ٱلسُّكَّانِ.

Steersman, *n.* مُسْتَعْمِلٌ ـ مَاسِكُ يَدِ ٱلدَّفَّةِ ـ مُدَبِّرُ ٱلدَّفَّةِ. A director, قَائِدٌ ـ سَائِسٌ *pl.* قُوَّادٌ ـ مُدَبِّرٌ *pl.* مُدَبِّرُونَ.

Stellar, *a.* } مُتَعَلِّقٌ بِٱلنُّجُومِ ـ نُجُومِيٌّ.
Stellary, }

Stellate, *a.* } فِي شَكْلِ ٱلنَّجْمَةِ ـ شَبِيهٌ بِٱلنَّجْمَةِ.
Stellated, }

Stelliferous, *a.* كَثِيرُ ٱلنُّجُومِ.

Stelliform, *a.* } فِي شَكْلِ ٱلنَّجْمَةِ.
Stellular, }

Stem, *n.* As of a tree or plant, جِذْلٌ *pl.* جِذَالٌ *and* جُذُولٌ ـ نَسْلٌ ـ نَجْلٌ ـ شَجَرَةٌ *pl.* سَاقٌ *pl.* سُوُوقٌ. Stock, of a family, سِلْسِلَةٌ ـ أَنْسَابٌ *pl.* نَسَبٌ ـ أَنْسَالٌ. The — of a ship, مَرْكَزُ رَأْسِ مُقَدَّمِ ٱلْمَرْكَبِ ـ خَشَبَةُ مُقَدَّمِ ٱلْمَرْكَبِ ـ صَدْرُ ٱلسَّفِينَةِ. The — of a feather, قَصَبَةُ ٱلرِّيشَةِ. Plants having long stems, شَجْرَاءُ. From — to stern, of a ship, مِنْ مُقَدَّمِ ٱلسَّفِينَةِ إِلَى مُؤَخَّرِهَا.

Stem, *v.t.* To impel, push one's self on, in, دَفَعَ ـ تَدَفَّعَ فِي ـ إِنْدَفَعَ فِي ـ نَفْسَهُ فِي. To repel, oppose, إِعْتَرَضَ عَلَى ـ دَافَعَ. To hinder, مَنَعَ ـ صَدَّ ـ أَصَدَّ. To stop, أَوْقَفَ ـ وَقَّفَ.

Stemless, *a.* بِلَا جِذْلٍ.

Stench, *n.* *See* Stink, *n.*

Stencil, *n.* مُرَقَّعَةٌ ـ مُرَقَّعٌ.

Stencil, *v.t.* رَسَمَ ـ بِٱلْمُرَقَّعِ.

Stenographer, *n.* إِشَارَتْجِي ـ كَاتِبٌ بِٱلْإِشَارَاتِ.

Stenographic, *a.* } مَكْتُوبٌ بِٱلْإِشَارَاتِ.
Stenographical, }

Stenography, *n.* خَطُّ ٱلْإِشَارَاتِ.

Stentor, *n.* } صَارِخٌ ـ صَيِّحٌ ـ زَاعِقٌ. A stentorian voice, صَوْتٌ عَالٍ.
Stentorian, *a.* }

Step, *v.i.* To make a step, to walk, خَطَا *aor.* يَخْطُو ـ إِخْتَطَى. I stepped one step, خَطَوْتُ خَطْوَةً وَاحِدَةً. To walk with short steps, مَشَى ـ حَتَكَ ـ تَحَتَّكَ. To step aside, إِجْتَنَبَ ـ إِنْحَرَفَ ـ تَنَحَّى. To step back, إِنْصَرَفَ ـ تَأَخَّرَ ـ رَجَعَ إِلَى وَرَاءٍ. To step down, حَطَّ ـ نَزَلَ. To step forward, تَقَدَّمَ. To step in, to enter, دَخَلَ. To intervene, mix one's self up with, تَوَسَّطَ بَيْنَ ـ دَخَلَ بَيْنَ; as a mediator, تَدَاخَلَ فِي ـ تَعَرَّضَ فِي. To step out, to go out, خَرَجَ. To stride, وَسَّعَ ٱلْخَطْوَةَ ـ فَسَحَ. To step over, or beyond, anything, إِخْتَطَى ـ تَخَطَّى. To cross over, أَجَازَ ـ قَطَعَ ـ عَبَرَ. To step over to, تَخَطَّى إِلَى; to visit, زَارَ *aor.* يَزُورُ. To pass over, overlook, تَخَطَّى عَنْ. To step up, go up, صَعِدَ إِلَى فَوْقُ. To step up to, to approach, إِقْتَرَبَ إِلَى ـ دَنَا مِنْ.

Step, *v.t.* To go over by stepping, إِخْتَطَى ـ تَخَطَّى ـ جَازَ ـ خَطْوًا. To — or tread upon, رَفَسَ. To — a mast, نَصَبَ سَارِيَةً.

Step, *n.* As with the foot, خَطْوَة *pl.* خَطَوَات. The space between two steps with the foot, خُطْوَة *pl.* خُطُوَات. Pace, mode of walking, مَسِير ـ مِشْيَة ـ سِمْت ـ سِيرَة ـ مِشْوَار. A stair, or a step in a ladder, رُتْبَة *pl.* رُتَب *and* رُتَبَات ـ دَرَجَة *pl.* دَرَجَات. A series of steps or stairs, or a ladder, مِعْرَاج ـ سُلَّم ـ مِرْقَاة ـ مِعْرَج. A —, as before a door, عَتَبَة *pl.* عَتَبَات. A footprint, أَثَرُ ٱلْأَقْدَام *pl.* آثَار. A proceeding, عَمَل *pl.* أَعْمَال ـ قَضِيَّة *pl.* قَضَايَا. A course, way, قِدْيَة ـ مَنْهَج ـ طَرِيقَة ـ دَأْب. Step, as in rank, دَرَجَة *pl.* دَرَجَات. Step by step, عَلَى ٱلتَّدْرِيج ـ خَطْوَةً خَطْوَةً ـ دَرَجَةً دَرَجَةً. He followed in his selfsame steps, سَارَ عَلَى ذَاتِ خَطَوَاتِهِ *aor.* يَسِيرُ. *See also under* Pace, *n.*

To bend one's steps towards, ضَرَبَ إِلَى ـ قَصَدَ ـ.

To dog one's steps, رَصَدَ ² ـ إِرْتَصَدَ ـ تَرَصَّدَ ل ـ رَاقَبَ.

To gain a step, in rank, تَرَقَّى دَرَجَةً.

To lose a step, in rank, أُعْدِمَ دَرَجَةً. To be degraded a step, أُنْزِلَ دَرَجَةً.

To make a step, خَطَا *aor.* يَخْطُو ـ إِخْتَطَى.

To retrace one's steps, رَجَعَ عَلَى ٱلْآثَارِ ـ رَجَعَ عَلَى ٱلْأَعْقَابِ ـ رَجَعَ ـ إِرْتَدَّ.

To take steps, measures, إِتَّخَذَ ٱلْوَسَائِطَ.

To walk in the steps of such an one, سَلَكَ ² فِي خَطَوَاتِ فُلَانٍ; to imitate, إِمْتَثَلَ بِ.

Step-brother, *n.* On the wife's side, عَدِيل ـ أَخُو ٱلزَّوْجَةِ *pl.* أَعْدَال ـ سِلْف; on the husband's side, عَدِيل ـ أَخُو ٱلزَّوْجِ.

Step-child, *n.* Husband's son, وَلَدُ ٱلزَّوْجِ *pl.* أَوْلَاد; wife's son, إِبْنُ ٱلزَّوْجَةِ.

Step-daughter, *n.* رَبِيبَة *pl.* رَبِيبَات.

Step-father, *n.* زَوْجُ ٱلْأُمِّ ـ رَابّ.

Step-mother, *n.* زَوْجَةُ ٱلْأَبِ ـ رَابَّة.

Step-sister, *n.* On the wife's side, أُخْتُ ٱلزَّوْجَةِ; on the husband's side, أُخْتُ ٱلزَّوْجِ ـ سِلْفَة.

Step-son, *n.* رَبِيب *pl.* رَبَائِب.

Steppe, *n.* صَحْرَآء *pl.* صَحَارَى *and* صَحْرَاوَات.

Stepping, *n.* *See* Step, *n.*

Stepping-stone, *n.* حَجَرُ وَطْآءٍ ـ حَجَرُ مَوْطَأٍ. A resource, وَاسِطَة ـ وَسِيلَة ـ فُرْصَة ـ مُسْتَعَان ـ مَرْجِع. Something on the way towards, وُصْلَة.

Stercoraceous, *a.* زِبْلِيّ ـ دَبَالِيّ ـ دَمَانِيّ.

Stercoration, *n.* تَزْبِيل ـ زَبْل.

Stereographic, *a.* }
Stereographical, } مَا نِيطَ بِرَسْمِ ٱلْأَجْسَامِ.

Stereographically, *ad.* حَسَبَ قَوَاعِدِ رَسْمِ ٱلْأَجْسَامِ.

Stereography, *n.* عِلْمُ (or) فَنُّ رَسْمِ ٱلْأَجْسَامِ.

Stereotype, *n.* Fixed, immovable type, حُرُوف مُرَكَّبَة لِلطَّبْعِ ـ حُرُوف مُرَكَّبَة سَبِيكَة ـ مَسْبُوكَة صَفَائِحَ. The art of stereotyping, صِنَاعَةُ سَبْكِ ٱلْحُرُوفِ ٱلْمُرَكَّبَةِ لِلطَّبْعِ صَفَائِحَ.

Stereotype, *a.* مَطْبُوعٌ مِنَ ٱلْحُرُوفِ ٱلْمُرَكَّبَةِ ٱلْمَسْبُوكَةِ صَفَائِحَ.

Stereotyper, *n.* سَبَّاكُ ٱلْحُرُوفِ ٱلْمُرَكَّبَةِ صَفَائِحَ.

Stereo-typography, *n.* ٱلطَّبْعُ مِنَ ٱلْحُرُوفِ ٱلْمُرَكَّبَةِ ٱلْمَسْبُوكَةِ صَفَائِحَ.

Sterile, *a.* A — year, سَنَةٌ أَزِمَةٌ. *See* Barren, *a.*

Sterility, *n.* *See* Barrenness, *n.*

Sterling, *n.* Sterling money, إِسْتَرْلِين ـ دَرَاهِمُ إِنْكِلِيزِيَّة.

Sterling, *a.* Of English money, إِسْتَرْلِين ـ مِنْ دَرَاهِمَ إِنْكِلِيزِيَّةٍ. Genuine, حَقِيقِيّ ـ حَقَّانِيّ ـ صَافٍ ـ خَالِص. A pound —, لِيرَةٌ إِنْكِلِيزِيَّةٌ.

Stern, *n.* As of a ship, مُؤَخَّرُ ٱلسَّفِينَةِ. Down by the —, (*fem.*) غَاطِسَةُ ٱلْمُؤَخَّرِ. Stern foremost, ٱلْعَجُزُ عَلَى ٱلصَّدْرِ. To turn the — to the wind, إِسْتَمْخَرَ ـ تَمَخَّرَ. Let him turn his — to the wind, فَلْيَتَمَخَّرِ ٱلرِّيحَ.

Stern, *a.* Severe in look, عَبَّاس ـ عَبُوس ـ شَتِيم. Severe, harsh, فَظّ ـ عَنِيف ـ شَاقّ ـ قَاسٍ ـ غَضُوب. To look —, قَسَحَ ـ فَظَّ ² ـ تَقَطَّبَ ـ تَشَتَّمَ ـ تَعَبَّسَ. To be —, severe, cruel, عَاسَرَ ـ شَادَّ عَلَى. To be — towards, عَاسَرَ ـ شَادَّ عَلَى. *See also* Harsh, Rigid, *a.*

Sternal, *a.* مَا نِيطَ بِٱلْقَصِّ ـ مُتَعَلِّق بِٱلْجُؤْجُؤِ.

Stern-chase, *n.* }
Stern-chaser, } مِدْفَعُ مُؤَخَّرِ ٱلْمَرْكَبِ.

Sternly, *ad.* Of the look, تَقَطُّبًا ـ تَشَتُّمًا; of manner, بِفَظَاظَةٍ ـ بِقَسَاحَةٍ. *See also* Harshly, *ad.*

Sternmost, *a.* آخِرُ ٱلْكُلِّ ـ آخِر.

Sternness, *n.* Of look, تَعَبُّس ـ تَقَطُّب ـ تَشَتُّم. Harshness, مَظَاظَة ـ فَظَاظَة ـ شَرَاسَة ـ قَسَاحَة. *See also* Harshness, *n.*

Stern-post, *n.* مَسْنَدُ ٱلدَّفَّةِ ـ مَسْنَدُ ٱلسُّكَّانِ.

Stern-sheets, *n.* مَوْضِعٌ فِي مُؤَخَّرِ ٱلسَّفِينَةِ.

Sternum, *n.* زَوْر ـ قَصّ ـ جَآجِئ *pl.* جُؤْجُؤ. The lower part of the —, رُهَابَة.

Sternutation, *n.* عُطَاس ـ عَطْس. *See also* Sneeze, *n.*

Sternutative, *a.* }
Sternutatory, } مُعَطِّس.

Sternutatory, *n.* عاطوس.

Sternway, *n.* Movement backwards, تقهقر ـ تأخر ـ إدبار ; with stern foremost, بتقدم مؤخر المركب.

Stertorous, *a.* ثقيل ـ شخار ـ خار.

Stethoscope, *n.* بوق الأطباء ـ آلة تسبر التنفس في الصدر.

Steve, *v.t.* عبأ ـ عبأ.

Stevedore, *n.* معبي الوسق.

Stew, *v.t.* To cook as a stew, of meat, طبخ يخنة ; of fruits, طبخ خبيصة.

Stew, *v.i.* Of meat, انطبخت اليخنة ; of fruits, انطبخت الخبيصة.

Stew, *n.* Of meat, يخنة ; made of meat and onions, بصلية ; of fruits, خبيصة ; of boiled wheat and meat, هريسة ; of pigeons, يخنة حمام. A mess, difficulty, ورطة ـ شواش ـ تهوش ـ اضطراب. A brothel, ماخور ـ بيت قحاب. To be in a —, difficulty, mess, تورط في ورطة ـ التبك ـ تشوش.

Steward, *n.* A manager of affairs, كاخية ; *vulg.* كخيا ـ عامل ـ وكيل ـ مدير ـ مدير أمور ـ *pl.* عمال. An agent, أمين *pl.* أمناء ـ وكيل *pl.* وكلاء. One who manages the affairs of a house, كتخدا ـ قهرمان ـ كتخدى. One who purchases provisions, *etc.*, وكيل الخرج ـ كمروت ـ خدمتجي. A — on board ship, وكيل الطارمة. Steward's mate, معين وكيل الخرج. Lord High Steward, مشير همايوني.

Stewardess, *n.* A female agent, وكيلة ـ مديرة ـ أمينة. A — on board a ship, وكيلة الطارمة.

Stewardship, *n.* وظيفة الكتخدا ـ وكالة ـ إدارة ـ امانة.

Stew-pan, *n.* طاجرة لليخنة *pl.* طناجر.

Stibial, *a.* *See* Antimonial, *a.*

Stick, *n.* A piece of wood, عود *pl.* عيدان. A long —, rod, twig, قضيب *pl.* قضبان. A little —, عصية. A staff, or a rod to beat with, عصا *pl.* عصي *and* أعصاء ـ عصاية ـ مخفقة. A walking —, with an iron ferule, عكاز ـ عكازة *pl.* عكاكيز. A —, as with a dagger, *etc.*, a stab, طعنة ـ وخض ـ جرح. A blow with a —, ضربة بالعصا ـ ضرب. A —, as of sealing-wax, *etc.*, سبيكة *pl.* سبائك ـ قطعة *pl.* قطع. A handle, يد ـ مسكة ـ نصاب. A tooth —, for cleaning the teeth, مسواك ـ سواك. Gold Stick, Silver Stick, شرطي *coll.* شرطة ـ جلواز *pl.* جلاوزة.

To beat with a stick, ضرب بالعصا ـ عصا. To be beaten with a stick, ضرب بالعصا. He was beaten with a stick upon his back, ضرب بالعصا على ظهره.

To cut a stick from a tree, اعتصى الشجرة.

To cut one's stick, تولى ـ ولى هاربا ـ انفلت ـ فر.

To lean, as upon a stick, اعتصى على العصا ـ تعكز على ـ تعكز.

Stick, *v.t.* To pierce, stab, طعن ـ لهز. To prick, شك ـ نخز ـ نخس. To —, as with paste, ألزق. To —, as one thing to another, ألزق ب. To hang, علق. To place, وضع *aor.* يضع ـ جعل ـ حط. To cheat, غش.

To stick full of, to stuff, حشا *aor.* يحشو. To fill, ملأ ـ فعم.

To stick in, as with paste, ألزق ; as a spear into the ground, وقف في ـ ركز ـ ركز. To pierce; *see under* to Stick, *v.t.*

To stick on, paste on, ألزق في. To hang on, علق في.

To stick over with, to garnish with, زين ب ; as with almonds, pieces of meat, *etc.*, for cooking or ornament in dressing dishes, غرز ب.

To stick out, make to project, أبرز ـ أخرج ; of a member of the body, مد ـ بسط.

To stick up, to uplift, صمد ـ نصب. To fix, set up, as of a door, *etc.*, علق.

Stick, *v.i.* To be impeded by, احتجز ـ تعلق ب ـ علق في. To —, as in the mud, or in a speech, توعر من. To be sticky, تدبق ـ التصق. To abide, استقر ـ مكث. To —, as a ship aground, ارتمت السفينة ـ جنحت السفينة. To cause to —, أدبق ـ دبق.

To stick at a thing, to hesitate, تردد ـ تضرب ـ تمخطر. He sticks at nothing, nothing comes amiss to him, ما يشذ عليه شيء.

To stick by one, cleave to one, جذا ب *aor.* يجذو ـ حالف ـ شد مع ـ عهد ب. To stand up for one, ظاهر ـ تعلق ب ـ تمسك مع.

To stick close to, التصق مع ـ علق ب.

To stick fast, as in the mud, توعر. To be impeded, امتنع ـ احتجز. Not to move, وقف *aor.* يقف ; of a thing, سكن.

The ship stuck fast, ارتكز المركب.

To stick fast in, in a general sense, انتشب في. To stick fast, as dogs *in coitû*, تعاظلت ـ عاظلت في السفاد ـ عاظلت.

To stick on, تعلق ب ـ التصق ب.

To stick out, to project, برز ـ أشرف ـ يحبو *aor.* حبا ـ نتأ ; of the eyes, جحظ.

To stick to, as to a place, ضب ـ ضب على ـ رصع ب. To

stick to a thing, hold to it, بَارَكَ عَلَى ـ أَقَامَ عَلَى ـ عَاثَرَ ـ لَازَمَ ـ لَزِمَ بِ ـ أَصَرَّ عَلَى. To stick to, to persevere in, أَدْمَنَ عَلَى ـ دَامَ عَلَى ـ عَمِدَ بِ ـ وَاظَبَ. To stick to, as to a promise, أَمْسَكَ بِ ـ أَقَامَ بِ ـ أَوْفَى بِ. *See also* To stand to, *under to* Stand, *v.i.*

To stick together, to mat, as of hair, *etc.*, تَلَبَّدَ ; to stick together, as if pasted or glued, تَلَزَّجَ. To stick together, as a party, تَعَصَّبُوا. The ink of the pages of the book sticks to one another, (of the pages,) يَلْتَصِقُ حِبْرُ صَحِيفَةِ ٱلْكِتَابِ بَعْضُهُ بِبَعْضٍ. *See also under* To stick fast.

To stick up, to project, بَرَزَ. To stick one's self up, give one's self airs, تَصَلَّفَ ـ تَعَظَّمَ ـ تَغَطْرَسَ.

Stickiness, *n.* لُزُوجَة.

Stickle, *v.i.* To strive, contend, تَمَرَّدَ ـ لَجَّ ـ لَجَّ ـ تَمَحَّكَ ـ أَمْحَكَ. They — about words, يَتَمَاحَكُونَ بِٱلْكَلَامِ.

Stickleback, *n.* The fish, نَوْعٌ مِنَ ٱلسَّمَكِ.

Stickler, *n.* مَحِكٌ ـ مَحْكَان ـ مُمَاحِك ـ مُتَمَرِّد ـ مُتَعَصِّب ـ لَجُوج ـ شَرِس ـ شُكْلِيّ. A — for, مُتَعَصِّبٌ لِ.

Sticky, *a.* لَزِج ـ دَبِق. To be or become —, تَدَبَّقَ.

Stiff, *a.* As of the joints, جَاسِئٌ ـ صُلْب ـ صُلْب ـ صَلِيب. Numb, خَدِر. Rigid, in a general sense, صُلْب ـ يَابِس. Harsh, فَظٌّ ـ عَنِيف ـ كَزُوم. Formal, reserved, طِرْيَق ـ مِطْرَاق ـ بَارِد ـ كَثِيرُ ٱلتَّكَالِيفِ. Not liquid, كَثِيف ـ ثَخِين ـ جَامِد. Stubborn, صَعْب ـ خَشِنُ ٱلْجَانِبِ ـ شَكِس ـ وَعْق ـ صَعُوب. Difficult, عَسِر ـ مُشْكِل. Strong, شَدِيد ـ قَوِيّ. Dry, dried up, يَابِس. Stiff, not easily bent, كَزٌّ. Heavy, ثَقِيل. Stiff, of style, مَحْصُور ـ حَصِر ـ ضَيِّق ـ غَيْرُ طَلِقٍ. A — bow, قَوْسٌ كَزَّةٌ. A — pulley, بَكَرَةٌ كَزَّةٌ. A — breeze, رِيحٌ شَدِيدَةٌ ـ رِيحٌ عَاصِفٌ. Having a — neck, شَنِجُ ٱلرَّقَبَةِ. A beast having — legs, دَابَّةٌ جَاسِئَةُ ٱلْقَوَائِمِ. His joints became —, جَسَأَتْ مَفَاصِلُهُ. To be or to become —; *see to* Stiffen, *v.i.* *See also* Rigid, *a.*

Stiffen, *v.i.* To become stiff, rigid, جَسَأَ ـ صَلُبَ ـ صَلُبَ. To thicken, of a liquid, كَثُفَ ـ ثَخُنَ. To become hard, dry, تَيَبَّسَ ـ جَفَّ. To become strong, as of a wind, تَعَصَّفَ ـ اِشْتَدَّ. To become numb, of a limb, خَدِرَ. To —, as a market, تَعَصَّرَ ـ تَعَاسَرَ ـ تَعَسَّرَ ; as with cold, اِكْتَزَّ.

Stiffen, *v.t.* To make stiff, as of the joints, أَخْدَرَ ـ خَدَّرَ ـ صَيَّرَ جَاسِئًا. To make rigid, hard, tough, صَلَّبَ. To make numb, خَدَّرَ ـ أَخْدَرَ. To make thick, كَثَّفَ. To —, as with starch, عَالَجَ بِٱلنَّشَاءِ.

Stiffener, *n.* Something applied to another to stiffen it, مُقَوًّى.

Stiffly, *ad.* Of the joints, بِجُسَاْءٍ. With stiffness, of a bow or pulley, بِكَزَازَةٍ. In a reserved manner, بِٱطْرَاقٍ ـ بِبُرُودَةٍ. Strictly, بِدِقَّةٍ ـ بِتَدْقِيقٍ. Harshly, بِفَظَاظَةٍ. With vehemence, بِشِدَّةٍ ـ بِعُصُوفٍ ـ بِقُوَّةٍ.

Stiff-necked, *a.* صُلْبُ ٱلرَّقَبَةِ *pl.* صِلَبَة ـ وَلَا يَسْمَعُ ٱلنِّدَآءَ ـ يَبْغِي ٱلْاِهْتِدَآءَ.

Stiff-hearted, *a.* صُلْبُ ٱلْقَلْبِ *pl.* صِلَبَة (*or* ٱلْمَعَاجِمِ).

Stiffness, *n.* As of the joints, جُسُوءٌ ـ جَسَآءٌ. Rigidity, صَلَابَة ـ تَصْلِيب. Want of flexibility, كَزَازَة ـ كُزُوزَة ; of style, عَدَمُ ٱنْطِلَاقٍ ـ حَصَر. Thickness, as of liquids, كَثَافَة ـ ثَخَانَة ـ ثُخُونَة. Opiniativeness, عِنَاد ـ مُعَانَدَة ـ عُجْب. Formality, reserve, إِطْرَاق ـ بُرُودَة. Vehemence, as of a wind, عَصْف ـ عُصُوفَة ـ شِدَّة ـ قُوَّة.

Stifle, *v.t.* To smother, suffocate, خَنَقَ ـ قَطَّسَ ; as of a bone sticking in the throat, أَشْجَى. To —, as of a fire, أَخْمَدَ. To —, as of a report, أَخْمَدَ ـ سَكَّنَ ـ طَبَقَ عَلَى ـ أَخْفَى. To suppress, أَزَالَ ـ قَطَعَ ـ أَبْطَلَ ـ نَيَّمَ. To —, as of the voice, خَفَّضَ. To be stifled, suffocated, اِخْتَنَقَ ـ قَطِسَ. To be stifled, of a report, طُبِقَ عَلَى ـ اِخْتَفَى ـ خَمَدَ.

Stifle, *n.* Of a horse, وَرِكٌ ; the disease in a horse, رِيحٌ فِي دَاغِصَةِ ٱلْخَيْلِ.

Stifling, *a.* Suffocating, خَانِق ـ مُقَطِّس. *See also* Sultry, *a.*

Stigma, *n.* A brand, وِسَام ـ نَار ـ كَيّ. A mark of infamy, فَضَاحَة ـ عَار ـ عَيْب. The top of a pistil, رَأْسُ آلَةِ ٱلْإِنَاثِ فِي ٱلنَّبَاتِ.

Stigmatic, *a.* }
Stigmatical, } Branded with infamy, مَعْيُوب ـ مَفْضُوح ; bringing infamy, مُجْلِبٌ (*or* مُورِثٌ) ٱلْعَارَ.

Stigmatize, *v.t.* To mark with infamy, عَرَّ بِ ـ فَضَحَ ـ جَرَّسَ.

Stile, *n.* As of a dial, مِيل. A barrier, fence, حَاجِز *pl.* حَوَاجِزُ. A set of steps to get over a fence, سُلَّمُ جِدَارٍ *pl.* سَلَالِمُ.

Stiletto, *n.* A small dagger, خَنْجَرٌ صَغِيرٌ *pl.* خَنَاجِرُ صِغَارٌ. A piercer, bodkin, مِخْرَز ـ مِخْرَاز.

Stiletto, *v.t.* ضَرَبَ خَنْجَرًا.

Still, *v.t.* To make motionless, as water, *etc.*, أَرْكَدَ. To make quiet, calm, فَثَأَ ـ سَكَّنَ ـ أَهْدَأَ ـ هَدَّأَ. To make silent, سَكَّتَ ـ أَسْكَتَ ـ أَنْصَتَ. To —, as of a boiling kettle, فَثَأَ. He beat him until he was stilled, ضَرَبَهُ حَتَّى سَكَنَتْ حَرَكَتُهُ.

And when his anger was stilled, وَلَمَّا سَكَنَ عَنْهُ ٱلْغَضَبُ. *See also to* Appease, Quiet, *v.t.*, *also to* Distil, *v.t.*

Still, *a.* Motionless, جَامِد ـ رَاكِن ـ مُخَبِّط ـ مُخْبِت ـ مُخْلِد ـ رَاكِد. Calm, quiet, سَاكِن *pl.* سُكَّان ـ هَادٍ ـ سَاجٍ ـ مُرْتَاح. Silent, صَامِت ـ سَاكِت ـ مُطْرِق. Low, suppressed of a voice, خَافِت ـ خَفِيض ـ خَفِيت. Be still! silent, أُسْكُتْ ـ صَهْ. He never keeps —, مَا يَرْكُنُ. He became as — as a stone, صَمَتَ كَالْحَجَرِ.

To be still, motionless, رَكَنَ ـ رَكَدَ. To become still by degrees, تَرَكَّدَ. To try to be still, تَرَكَّنَ.

To be still, quiet, calm, سَكَنَ ـ هَدَأَ. To become still, quiet by degrees, تَهَدَّأَ.

To be still, silent, سَكَتَ ـ صَمَتَ ـ أَصْمَتَ.

To be still, soft, suppressed, of a voice, sound, *etc.*, خَفَتَ ـ خَفَضَ.

Still, *ad.* Up to this time, إِلَى ٱلْآنَ. Nevertheless, مَعَ ـ لٰكِن ـ مَعَ أَنَّ ـ ذٰلِكَ. Afterwards, أَيْضًا ـ بَعْدُ ـ *vulg.* كَمَان. As denoting continuance, عَلَى ٱلدَّوَامِ ـ بِٱلتَّوَالِي ـ بِلَا ٱنْقِطَاعٍ. As denoting continuance of action, in connexion with a verb, لَمْ يَزَلْ ـ لَا بَرِحَ ـ ظَلَّ ـ ظَلَّ عَلَى. Still more, in addition, زِيَادَةً ـ أَكْثَرَ فَأَكْثَرَ ـ أَيْضًا. Much more, in a higher degree, بِٱلْأَوْلَى كَثِيرًا ـ بِٱلْحَرَى ـ بِٱلْحَرِيّ. Still less, as of quantity, دُونَ ـ أَقَلَّ. He — held them, مَا زَالَ مَاسِكًا ـ مَا بَرِحَ قَابِضًا عَلَيْهِمْ. Do you — hold to it? هَلْ أَنْتَ مُتَمَسِّكٌ بِهِ بَعْدُ. If we remain — here we shall die, إِذَا جَلَسْنَا هُنَا مُتْنَا. It would have been better for you to have remained there —, خَيْرٌ لَكَ لَوْ كُنْتَ بَاقِيًا هُنَاكَ. He — continues to study, لَمْ يَزَلْ مُوَاظِبًا عَلَى ٱلدَّرْسِ. Shall he not — more care for you? أَفَلَيْسَ هُوَ بِٱلْحَرِيِّ يَهْتَمُّ بِكُمْ. I will not give you a farthing, — less a pound, لَا أُعْطِيكَ فَلْسًا فَكَيْفَ لَا أُعْطِيكَ لِيرَةً حَتَّى وَلَا فَلْسًا أُعْطِيكَ لِيرَةً.

Still, *n.* A vessel for distillation, أَنْبِيق *pl.* أَنَابِيق ـ أَنْبَك ـ أَمْبِيق.

Stillatitious, *a.* Falling in drops, قَاطِر ـ مُتَقَطِّر.

Stillatory, *n.* *See* Still, *n.*

Still-born, *a.* مَوْلُود مَيِّت.

Stilling, *n.* The act of quieting, calming, تَسْكِين ـ إِهْدَاء. A stand for a barrel, كُرْسِيّ (*or* قَاعِدَة) لِلْبَرَامِيلِ.

Still-life, *n.* In painting, تَصْوِيرُ ٱلْجَمَادَاتِ.

Stillness, *n.* Absence of motion, رُكُود ـ رُكُون. Calmness, quietness, خَفْض ـ هُدُوّ ـ رُقُود ـ رَاحَة. Silence, سُكُوت ـ صُمَات ـ خُفَات ـ خُفُوت ـ خَفْض ـ صُمُوت. Lowness, as of a voice, خَفْض ـ خُفُوت ـ خُفَات. A pause, سَكْتَة.

Stilly, *a.* خَافِض ـ خَفِيض ـ هَادٍ ـ رَاكِد ـ رَاكِن. *See also* Still, *a.*

Stilt, *n.* Stilts, عُكَّازُ ٱلْبَهْلَوَانِ. To mount the stilts, رَكِبَ عُكَّازَ ٱلْبَهْلَوَانِ; to behave proudly, تَغَطْرَسَ ـ شَمَخَ أَنْفَهُ ـ تَعَظَّمَ ـ تَكَبَّرَ.

Stilt, *v.t.* To raise or make to ride on stilts, رَكَّبَ عُكَّازَ ٱلْبَهْلَوَانِ. *See also to* Elevate, *v.t.*

Stimulant, *a.* Exciting to action, مُحَرِّض ـ مُحَرِّك ـ مُهَيِّج ـ هَيَّاج.

Stimulant, *n.* An incentive, مِنْخَس ـ حُضّ ـ حُضَيْضَى. A stimulating medicine, عِلَاجٌ مُقَوٍّ وَمُنْعِش. An intoxicating liquor, مِنَ ٱلْمُسْكِرَاتِ; stimulants, مُسْكِرَات.

Stimulate, *v.t.* To drive, سَاقَ. To excite, أَنْعَشَ ـ أَنْهَضَ ـ اِسْتَفَزَّ ـ حَرَّضَ ـ حَرَّكَ. To incite, instigate, هَيَّجَ ـ سَاقَ. To — against, حَرَّضَ ـ عَلَى. To — or encourage to ..., شَجَّعَ ـ عَلَى.

To be stimulated, incited, اِهْتَاجَ ـ تَهَيَّجَ ـ اِسْتَنْهَضَ.

Stimulation, *n.* The act of driving, سَوْق; of exciting, inciting, اِسْتِفْزَاز ـ تَحْرِيض ـ إِنْهَاض ـ تَحْرِيك. The being stimulated, هِيَاج ـ هَيَجَان.

Stimulative, *a.* *See* Stimulant, *a.*

Stimulative, *n.* *See* Stimulant, *n.*

Stimulator, *n.* هَيَّاج ـ مُحَرِّض ـ مُحَرِّك.

Stimulus, *n.* An incentive to action, مِنْخَس ـ حُضّ ـ حُضَيْضَى ـ بَاعِث ـ سَائِق ـ مِهْمَاز.

Sting, *v.t.* As of a scorpion, bee, serpent, *etc.*, أَبَرَ ـ لَسَعَ ـ لَدَغَ ـ نَهَشَ. To —, as with the tongue, to vex, لَسَعَ ـ بِ ـ نَقَرَ. He was stung by a bee, لَسَعَتْهُ نَحْلَةٌ. The scorpion stung him, أَبَرَتْهُ ٱلْعَقْرَبُ. *See also to* Prick, *v.t.*

Sting, *n.* The instrument in animals for stinging, شَوْكَة ـ إِبْرَة *pl.* إِبَر ـ مِئْبَر *pl.* مَآبِر; the — at the tail of a scorpion, إِبْرَة ـ شُولَاة ـ رِمَاحُ ٱلْعَقْرَبِ. The wound of a —, نَهْشَة ـ لَسْعَة ـ شَكَّة.

Stinger, *n.* لَاسِع ـ لَاسِب.

Stingily, *ad.* بِمَسَاكَةٍ ـ بِشُحٍّ ـ بِبُخْلٍ ـ بِخَسَاسَةٍ. *See also* Niggardly, *ad.*

Stinginess, *n.* عَقَص ـ شُحّ ـ بُخْل ـ خَسَاسَة ـ مَسَاكَة ـ مَسَاك. *See also* Niggardliness, *n.*

Stingo, *n.* Of beer, بِيرَة قَوِيَّة.

Stingy, *a.* مُشَحْشِح ـ عَقِيص ـ أَعْقَص ـ شَحِيح *pl.* أَشِحَّة and

ـ = بَخِلَ ـ = عَقِصَ. To be —, خَسِيْس ـ بَخِيْل ـ شَحَاح ـ شَحِيْح ـ شَحَّ ب aor. يَشِحُّ or عَلَى. To be — towards, شَحَّ ب or عَلَى.

Stink, *n.* A foul smell, نَتَانَة ـ نَتْنَة ـ نَتْن ـ دَفْرَة ـ دَفْر. A stench, as from bad meat, تَهَامَة ـ سَنَخ ـ زَنَخ ـ تَهَم ـ صُلُول; as from stinking fish, سُهَكَة ـ سَهْكَة ـ عُفَانَة.

Stink, *v.i.* To have a foul smell, = نَتَنَ ـ أَصَنَّ ـ دَفِرَ ـ أَدْفَرَ; as bad meat, = تَهِمَ ـ صَلَّلَ ـ = صَلَّ ـ = زَنِخَ; of fish, = سَهِكَ ـ أَنْتَنَ. To — of, = غَمِرَ مِن. How it stinks! ما أَنْتَنَهُ. To make to —, نَتَّنَ. To — out, خَنَقَهُ بِرَائِحَةٍ مُنْتِنَةٍ حَتَّى أَخْرَجَهُ مِن كَذا.

Stinkard, *n.* A paltry fellow, خَسِيْس ـ رَذِيْل. The animal, ضَرْبٌ مِنَ ٱلْحَيَوَانَاتِ ذَاتِ رَائِحَةٍ مُنْتِنَةٍ.

Stinker, *n.* مُنْتِن. *See also* Stink, *n.*

Stinking, *a.* عَفِن ـ دَفِر ـ مُنْتِن ـ مُصِنٌّ; of meat, زَنِخ ـ صُلٌّ ـ صَلِّل ـ = صَلّ. To be or to become —, عَفِن ـ تَهِم ـ خَنِز. تَعَفَّنَ ـ عَفَّنَ ـ = عَفِنَ ـ = خَنِزَ. The flesh-meat became —, سَنِخَ ٱللَّحْمُ. To make —, = عَفَّنَ ـ أَصَلَّ.

Stinkpot, *n.* كُلَّة مَحْشُوَّةٌ بِمَوَادَّ مُنْتِنَةٍ *pl.* كُلَل.

Stint, *n.* Restriction, حَصْر ـ حَبْس ـ تَقْتِير ـ نَبْر. Without —, بِلا تَقْتِير.

Stint, *v.t.* = حَبَسَ ـ = حَصَرَ ـ نَبَّرَ ـ = نَبَرَ. He stinted him in the thing, نَبَرَهُ بِٱلشَّيْءِ. To — one in a thing as deeming it too good for him, = نَفِسَ عَلَى.

Stinted, *a.* مُعَدَّد ـ مَحْصُور ـ مَعْدُود ـ مُنَبَّر ـ مَنْبُور.

Stintedness, *n.* Littleness, جُزْئِيَّة ـ قِلَّة. *See also* Stint, *n.*

Stinter, *n.* حَاصِر ـ مُنَبِّر.

Stintingly, *ad.* بِقِلَّةٍ ـ بِحَبْسٍ ـ بِحَصْرٍ ـ بِتَقْتِيرٍ.

Stipe, *n.* *See* Pedicule, *n.*

Stipend, *n.* عُلُوفَة ـ وَظِيفَة *pl.* وَظَائِف ـ فَرْض *pl.* فُرُوض ـ جَوَامِك *pl.* جَامِكِيَّة ـ مَعَاش ـ رَوَاتِب *pl.* رَاتِب ـ مَاهِيَّة. To appoint a — to, رَسَمَ لِ مَعَاشًا ـ وَظَّفَ.

Stipendiary, *a.* ذُو مَعَاشٍ ـ حَائِزٌ رَاتِبًا ـ مُوَظَّف.

Stipendiary, *n.* مُسْتَخْدَمٌ بِٱلْمَعَاشِ ـ صَاحِبُ رَاتِبَةٍ.

Stipple, *v.t.* نَقَّطَ بِٱلصِّبَاغِ ـ نَقَطَ ـ نَمَّشَ.

Stippling, *n.* تَنْقِيط ـ تَنْمِيش.

Stipula, *n.* }
Stipule, } وُرَيْقَةٌ فِي سَاقِ ٱلنَّبَاتِ *pl.* وُرَيْقَات.

Stipular, *a.* ذُو وُرَيْقَاتٍ.

Stipulate, *a.* حَامِلُ وُرَيْقَاتٍ.

Stipulate, *v.i.* To impose by stipulation upon one, = عَهِدَ إِلَى ـ ٱسْتَعْهَدَ مِن كَذا ـ = شَرَطَ عَلَى ـ ٱشْتَرَطَ عَلَى. To — with, شَارَطَ عَلَى ـ عَاهَدَ عَلَى ـ عَاقَدَ عَلَى. They stipulated, entered into a mutual stipulation, of many, تَعَاهَدُوا ـ تَعَاقَدُوا ـ تَشَارَطُوا. The stipulated clauses, ٱلشُّرُوطُ ٱلْمُنْدَرِجَةُ.

Stipulation, *n.* A condition, شَرْط *pl.* شُرُوط ـ شَرِيطَة. A mutual —, مُشَارَطَة ـ مُعَاقَدَة ـ مُعَاهَدَة. An agreement, إِتِّفَاق. The stipulations of a treaty, شُرُوطٌ عَهْدِيَّةٌ ـ أَحْكَامٌ عَهْدِيَّةٌ. The stipulations drawn up, ٱلْأَحْكَامُ ٱلْمُنْدَرِجَةُ.

Stipule, *n.* *See* Stipula, *n.*

Stipuled, *a.* *See* Stipulate, *a.*

Stir, *v.t.* To move, حَرَّكَ. To agitate, shake, = هَزَّ ـ هَزْهَزَ. To quicken, to rouse, رَوَّجَ ـ حَرَّضَ ـ أَنْهَضَ ـ أَوْقَظَ. To — up, incite, = أَزَّ ـ أَثَارَ ـ هَيَّجَ ـ سَاقَ ـ ٱسْتَفَزَّ ـ أَقَامَ ـ أَوْشَكَ. To — up anger, هَيَّجَ ٱلسَّخَطَ ـ أَشْعَلَ ٱلسَّخَطَ ـ أَوْغَرَ ٱلصَّدْرَ. To — up against, أَقَامَ عَلَى ـ أَنْهَضَ عَلَى ـ حَرَّضَ عَلَى. To — up evil, شَغَّبَ. To — up, as of strife among, هَجَّشَ بَيْنَ ـ حَرَّشَ بَيْنَ. To — one's self up, إِنْتَبَهَ ـ إِسْتَيْقَظَ. To — or agitate a question, = فَتَحَ بَحْثًا. To —, as in mixing, جَدَّحَ ـ = جَدَحَ ـ خَضْخَضَ ـ خَضَّ ـ خَبَّصَ ـ = خَبَصَ ـ أَجْدَحَ. To be stirred, moved, تَحَرَّكَ; to be agitated, shaken, إِهْتَزَّ ـ تَهَزَّزَ. To be stirred up, instigated, تَهَيَّجَ ـ = هَاجَ. To be stirred, dashed about, as water, *etc.*, تَخَضْخَضَ. His spirit was stirred within him, إِحْتَدَّتْ رُوحُهُ ـ = حَمِيَ قَلْبُهُ فِي جَوْفِهِ. He stirred up, excited, the surmises of the people, أَثَارَ فِيهِ هَوَاجِسَ ٱلنَّاسِ. *See also to* Kindle, *v.t.*

Stir, *v.i.* To move, تَحَرَّكَ. To get up early in the morning, بَكَّرَ ـ صَبَّحَ. To — abroad, تَسَيَّرَ خَارِجًا ـ تَسَيَّرَ. He is unable to — from his house, هُوَ مُلَازِمُ ٱلْبَيْتِ. He stirs about, goes hither and thither, يَتَرَدَّدُ. To — in one's mind, = هَجَسَ فِي صَدْرِهِ.

Stir, *n.* Commotion, clamour, حَرَكَة ـ إِضْطِرَاب ـ شَغَب ـ قَلَق ـ هَرْج وَمَرْج ـ هَيَجَان تَذَبْذُب ـ ثَوَرَان ـ إِرْتِجَاج. There was a great — among the people, حَصَلَ ٱضْطِرَابٌ بَيْنَ ٱلْقَوْمِ. There was no small — at that time, حَدَثَ فِي ذٰلِكَ ٱلْوَقْتِ شَغَبٌ لَيْسَ بِقَلِيلٍ.

Stirrer, *n.* One who stirs up, agitates, مُحَرِّك ـ مُحَرِّض. A — up of rebellion, ضَرَّابُ فِتَنٍ ـ فَتَّان.

Stirring, *a.* *See* Active, Bustling, *a.*

Stirrup, *n.* Of a saddle, رِكَاب *pl.* رُكُبَات; of a camel's saddle, غَرْز. He put his foot in the — in order to mount, = غَرَزَ (or) إِغْتَرَزَ رِجْلَهُ فِي ٱلرِّكَابِ.

Stirrup-cup, *n.* كَأْسُ ٱلْوَدَاعِ.

Stirrup-leather, *n.* } مِغْلَاقٌ *pl.* مَغَالِيقُ ـ مِغْلَاقُ ٱلرِّكَابِ. The
Stirrup-strap, } two stirrup-leathers, المِغْلَاقَانِ.

Stitch, *v.t.* To sew slightly, شَلَّلَ ـ ²كَفَّ ـ ²مَلَّ ـ ²شَكَّ. To sew, خَيَّطَ. He stitched the garment, ²شَكَّ ٱلثَّوْبَ. *See also to* Sew, *v.t.*

Stitch, *v.i.* To practise stitching, خَيَّطَ ـ ²كَفَّ.

Stitch, *n.* A single pass of the needle, غُرْزَةٌ *pl.* غُرَزٌ *and* غُرُزَاتٌ ـ غَرْزَةٌ. A style of sewing, تَضْرِيبٌ; in knitting, شَكَّةٌ ـ غَرْزٌ. A — hole, generally, شَكَّةٌ. A —, as in the side, نَغْزَةٌ ـ نَخْزَةٌ. I have a — in the side, أَصَابَتْنِي نَخْزَةٌ.

Stitches, *n* Twinges of pain, نَخْزَاتٌ.

Stitch-wort, *n.* ضَرْبٌ مِنَ ٱلْبَابُونَجِ.

Stiver, *n.* فَلْسٌ *pl.* فُلُوسٌ ـ فَلْسٌ أَحْمَرُ.

Stoat, *n.* The animal, حَيَوَانٌ مِنْ جِنْسِ ٱلسُّرْعُوبِ.

Stoccade, *n.* A thrust, طَعْنَةٌ. A fortification of pointed stakes, دَائِرَةُ أَوْتَادٍ ـ حَسِيكَةٌ. *See also* Palisade, *n.*

Stoccade, *v.t.* } To fortify with a stockade, حَصَّنَ بِحَسَكٍ ـ
Stockade, } أَحَاطَ بِأَوْتَادٍ.

Stock, *n.* A stem, trunk, جِذْلٌ *pl.* أَجْزَالٌ ـ سَاقٌ *pl.* سُوُوقٌ. Lineage, سِلْسِلَةٌ *pl.* سَلَاسِلُ ـ نَسَبٌ *pl.* أَنْسَابٌ ـ نَسْلٌ *pl.* أَنْسَالٌ ـ نَجْلٌ. A quantity, جُمْلَةٌ ـ مَبْلَغٌ. A log, of wood, قُرْمَةٌ *pl.* قُرَمٌ ـ زَنْدُ حَطَبٍ. A stupid fellow, بَلِيدٌ ـ أَحْمَقُ ـ أَخْرَقُ ـ ثَوْرٌ. The — of a musket, خَشَبُ ٱلْمِكْحَلَةِ *pl.* أَخْشَابٌ; of an anchor, عَامُودُ ٱلْمِرْسَاةِ. A handle, مِمْسَكَةٌ ـ نِصَابٌ. Capital, رَأْسُ مَالٍ. Goods, merchandize, بِضَاعَةٌ ـ سِلَعٌ ـ أَمْتِعَةٌ ـ أَسْبَابٌ. A fund, store, ذَخِيرَةٌ; of provisions, مُؤْنَةٌ. A — for the neck, طَوْقٌ لِلرَّقَبَةِ. The gilliflower, المَنْثُورُ; the yellow gilliflower, الخِيرِيُّ. Rolling-stock, of a railway, عَرَبَاتُ سِكَّةٍ حَدِيدٍ وَمَنْقُولَاتُهَا. Stock, what is on hand, الأَمْتِعَةُ ٱلْمَوْجُودَةُ. Stock for cooking purposes, صَلِيبُ ٱلْعِظَامِ. A — play, لُعْبَةٌ رَائِجَةٌ. A treasury, كَنْزٌ *pl.* كُنُوزٌ. STOCKS, for the feet, فَلَقٌ *pl.* أَفْلَاقٌ ـ مِعْمَلٌ ـ مَعْمَلُ ٱلْمَرَاكِبِ *pl.* عُلَبٌ ـ عُلْبَةٌ; for ships, مَعْمَلٌ ـ مَعْمَلُ ٱلْمَرَاكِبِ ـ ٱلسِّفَانَةِ; funds, خَزِينَةٌ ـ أَصْلُ مَالٍ; shares, حِصَصٌ ـ أَسْهَامٌ; the Exchange, البُورْصُ.

Dead stock, of animals, أَشْلَاءٌ ـ مَوَاشِي مَذْبُوحَةٌ ـ صَامِتٌ ٱلْمَوَاشِي; of a shop, بِضَاعَةٌ حَاصِلٌ.

Joint stock, مَالٌ مُشْتَرَكٌ ـ مَالُ شَرَاكَةٍ.

Live stock, مَوَاشِي حَيَّةٌ ـ نَاطِقٌ. He has no dead or live stock, مَا لَهُ صَامِتٌ وَلَا نَاطِقٌ.

Stock in hand, ready money, دَرَاهِمُ نَقْدٌ ـ نَقْدٌ; goods on hand, أَمْتِعَةٌ حَاضِرَةٌ (or تَحْتَ ٱلْيَدِ) ـ بِضَاعَةٌ مَوْجُودَةٌ.

To be on the stocks, of a ship, كَانَ فِي حَالِ ٱلتَّعْمِيرِ.

To gamble in the stocks, قَامَرَ بِٱلْأَسْهَامِ.

To lay in a stock of, إِدَّخَرَ مِنْ ـ ²خَزَنَ مِنْ.

To make stock, for cooking, صَلَبَ (or إِصْطَلَبَ) ٱلْعِظَامَ.

To take stock, of goods, قَيَّدَ ٱلْأَمْتِعَةَ ـ فَهْرَسَ ٱلْبِضَاعَةَ.

Stock, *v.t.* To supply with, عَمَّرَ بِـ ـ جَهَّزَ بِـ. To — a shop, جَهَّزَ ٱلدُّكَّانَ بِٱلْبِضَاعَةِ. He stocked the place with every requisite, عَمَّرَ ٱلْمَكَانَ بِمَا ٱحْتَاجَ إِلَيْهِ. To — a musket, رَكَّبَ ٱلْمِكْحَلَةَ خَشَبَةً. *See also to* Store, *v.t.*

Stock-broker, *n.* سِمْسَارُ ٱلْأَسْهَامِ.

Stockfish, *n.* بَقْلِيَو ـ ضَرْبٌ مِنَ ٱلسَّمَكِ مُقَدَّدٌ.

Stockholder, *n.* صَاحِبُ حِصَصٍ ـ صَاحِبُ أَسْهَامٍ.

Stocking, *n.* A —, or a pair of stockings, جَوْرَبٌ *pl.* جَوَارِبَةٌ *and* جَوَارِبُ. To knit stockings, ²جَدَلَ ٱلْجَوَارِبَ. Stocking, used figuratively for money laid up, دَرَاهِمُ صَرِيرَةٌ.

Stock-jobber, *n.* مُقَامِرٌ بِٱلْأَسْهَامِ ـ مُرَابِحٌ.

Stock-jobbing, *n.* مُقَامَرَةٌ بِٱلْأَسْهَامِ ـ مُرَابَحَةٌ.

Stock-still, *a.* سَاكِنُ ٱلْحَرَكَةِ ـ سَاكِنٌ ـ وَاقِفٌ.

Stocky, *a.* Short and thick, قَصِيرٌ ثَخِينٌ ـ مَجْمُوعٌ ـ قَلَهْزَمٌ. Thick, ثَخِينٌ. Firm, صُلْبٌ.

Stoic, *n.* A disciple of Zeno, زِينُونِيٌّ. Indifferent, غَيْرُ مُبَالٍ ـ عَدِيمُ ٱلْمُبَالَاةِ.

Stoic, *a.* } Pertaining to Stoicism, زِينُونِيٌّ. Indifferent, غَيْرُ
Stoical, } مُبَالٍ ـ عَدِيمُ ٱلْمُبَالَاةِ.

Stoically, *ad.* Unfeelingly, بِتَسَاهُلٍ ـ بِعَدَمِ مُبَالَاةٍ.

Stoicism, *n.* Of the Stoics, مَذْهَبُ زِينُونَ. Unconcern, عَدَمُ مُبَالَاةٍ ـ تَسَاهُلٌ.

Stoker, *n.* شَعَّالٌ *pl.* شَعَّالَةٌ.

Stole, *pret. of to* Steal, *q.v.*

Stole, *n.* Such as is worn by the clergy, بَطْرَشِيلٌ *pl.* بَطَارِشِيلُ ـ بَطْرَشِينٌ *pl.* بَطَارِشِينُ. Groom of the stole, رَأْسُ ٱلْخِدْمَدَارِيَّةِ.

Stolen, *a.* Taking by theft, مَسْرُوقٌ. Stolen goods, أَشْيَاءٌ مَسْرُوقَةٌ. *See also to* Steal, *v.t.*

Stolid, *a.* أَخْرَقُ *fem.* خَرْقَاءُ *pl.* خُرْقٌ ـ بَلِيدٌ ـ ثَقِيلٌ ـ غَلِيظٌ.

Stolidity, *n.* بَلَادَةٌ ـ غَلَاظَةٌ ـ غِلْظَةٌ ـ خُرْقٌ.

Stolon, *n.* Of a plant, شُكْرٌ *pl.* شَكِيرٌ ـ رِئْدٌ *pl.* رِئْدَانٌ.

Stomach, *n.* Of a human being or animal, مِعْدَةٌ *pl.* مِعَدٌ ـ مَعِدَةٌ *pl.* مَعِدٌ; of all ruminants, كِرْشٌ; of all solid-hoofed animals, رُجْبٌ; of a bird, حَوْصَلَةٌ *pl.* حَوَاصِلُ. The coats of the —, أَغْشِيَةُ ٱلْمِعْدَةِ. Pains in the —, مَغْصٌ ـ مَغَصٌ. To lie heavy

on the —, ثَقُلَ عَلَى ٱلْمِعْدَةِ ². To stay one's —, إِعْتَلَّ بِلُقْمَةٍ. To turn one's — against, to disgust, قَرَّزَ ـ قَرَّفَ ـ كَرَّهَ ـ إِلَى ٱلنَّفْسِ. To disorder the —, of a beverage, خَثَّرَ. To be disordered, of the —, نَفْسُهُ (or) تَخَثَّرَتْ ـ خَثُرَتْ ـ خَبُثَتْ نَفْسُهُ.
See also Appetite, *n.*

Stomach, *v.t.* To brook, صَبَرَ عَلَى ـ إِسْتَحْمَلَ ـ إِحْتَمَلَ. *See also to* Digest, *v.t.*

Stomach-ache, *n.* مَغْص ـ مَغَص. To have the —, مُغِصَ. Having a —, مَمْغُوص.

Stomacher, *n.* ضَرْبٌ مِنَ ٱلصُّدَيْرَةِ لِلنِّسَآءِ.

Stomachful, *a.* Sullen, عَبَّاس ـ عَنِيف ـ وَعِق.

Stomachic, *a.* / Stomachical, } Good for the stomach, مُقَوِّي ـ نَافِعٌ لِلْمِعْدَةِ. Stomachic pills, حَبُّ ٱلْمِعْدَةِ.

Stomachic, *n.* دِبَاغٌ لِلْمِعْدَةِ.

Stomachless, *n.* Without appetite, عَدِيمٌ ـ بِلَا نَفْسٍ لِلْأَكْلِ قَابِلِيَّةٍ لِلْأَكْلِ.

Stomach-pump, *n.* طُلُمْبَةُ ٱلْمِعْدَةِ.

Stone, *n.* A mass of concreted earth, حَجَر *pl.* أَحْجَار *and* حِجَارَة; a single —, حَجَرَة. A large —, صَخْر *pl.* صُخُور; a single large —, صَخْرَة. A — partly imbedded in the earth, صُمْدَة ـ صَمَدَة. The — or gem of a ring, *etc.*, فَصّ *pl.* فُصُوص. A sharp-edged hard —, ظَرَارَة ـ ظُرَر. The — of a fruit, فَصَاة *pl.* فَصًى ـ حَبّ *pl.* حُبُوب ـ نَوَاة *coll.* نَوًى *pl.* نَوًى ـ عَجَمَة (these two last primarily mean a date-stone, but are commonly used now of all fruit stones). The — or seed of a grape, raisin, *etc.*, بِزْرَة *coll.* بِزْر *pl.* بُزُور. A testicle, خُصْيَة *dual.* خُصْيَان *pl.* خُصًى ـ بَيْضَة *dual.* بَيْضَان *pl.* بَيْضَات. A — or calculus in the bladder, حَصَاة ـ حَصِيَّة; having stones in the bladder, مَحْصِيٌّ. A —, of weight, وَزْنُ ١٤ رَطْلًا إِنْكِلِيزِيًّا. A — or stones set up as a guide-post, ثَايَة ـ ثُوِيَّة. A row of stones in a wall, سَاف ـ سَافَة. Within a stone's throw, فِي رَمْيَةِ حَجَرٍ ـ فِي ضَرْبَةِ حَجَرٍ.

To cast a stone, رَمَى حَجَرَةً ². To cast a stone at, لَثَأَ ـ بِحَجَرَةٍ ² ـ رَمَى ـ بِحَجَرٍ.

To cut one for the stone, شَرَحَ ـ لِإِخْرَاجِ ٱلْحَصَاةِ ².

To cut or hew stones, نَحَتَ ٱلْأَحْجَار ².

To leave no stone unturned, قَلَبَ ٱلدُّنْيَا ـ إِتَّخَذَ كُلَّ ٱلْوَسَائِطِ.

Not to leave a stone standing in, دَمَّرَ ـ مَا تَرَكَ حَجَرًا عَلَى حَجَرٍ فِي.

To set stones, as in rings, فَصَّصَ.

Atmospheric stone, حَجَرٌ سَاقِطٌ مِنَ ٱلْجَوِّ ـ نَيْزَك *pl.* نَيَازِك.

Flag-stone, بَلَاطَة *coll.* بَلَاط.

Flint-stone, صَوَّان; one —, صَوَّانَة.

Gravel stones, حَصًى.

Hail-stone, حَبَّةُ بَرَدٍ *pl.* حُبُوب.

Hewn-stone, حَجَرٌ مَنْحُوتٌ *pl.* أَحْجَارٌ مَنْحُوتَةٌ.

Loadstone, حَجَرُ ٱلْمَغْنَاطِيسِ.

Mile-stone, عَامُودُ ٱلْأَمْيَالِ.

Mill-stone, رَحًا *pl.* أَرْحَآءٌ ـ حَجَرُ طَاحُونٍ *pl.* حِجَارَة.

Paving-stone; *see* Flag-stone, *supra.*

Pebble stone, حَصَاة *pl.* حَصَيَات *and* حُصِيٌّ.

Philosopher's stone, الإِكْسِيرُ ـ الكِيمِيَآءُ.

Precious stone, جَوْهَرَة *pl.* جَوَاهِرُ.

Rolling stone, رَضْرَضَة *coll.* رَضْرَاض.

Rubbing stone, for rubbing paint, *etc.*, upon, صَلَايَة ـ مَلَاك ـ قُنْطُنَاس.

Tombstone, رُجْمَة *pl.* رُجَم *and* رِجَام ـ رَجَم *pl.* أَرْجَام.

Whetstone, مِسَنّ ـ حَجَرُ مِسَنٍّ ـ صُلَّيْبَة.

Stone, *a.* Of stone, مِنْ حَجَرٍ. A — building, بِنَآءٌ مِنْ حَجَرٍ *pl.* أَبْنِيَة.

Stone, *v.t.* To pelt with stones, رَجَمَ ²: They stoned or threw stones at one another, of many, تَرَاجَمُوا بِحِجَارَةٍ. To be stoned, رُجِمَ. To stop up with stones, سَدَّ ـ بِحِجَارَةٍ ². To take the stones out of fruit, فَرَّغَ ـ مِنَ ٱلْفَصَى; of fruits with small seeds, فَرَّغَ ـ مِنَ ٱلْبِزْرِ. To free from stones, لَمَّ ٱلْأَحْجَارَ مِنْ كَذَا ².

Stone-blind, *a.* ضَرِير ـ أَعْمَى ـ أَعْمَى تَمَامَ ٱلْعَمَى.

Stone-chat, *n.* The bird, نَوْعٌ مِنَ ٱلْعَصَافِيرِ.

Stone-coal, *n.* ضَرْبٌ مِنَ ٱلْفَحْمِ ٱلْمَعْدِنِيِّ.

Stone-cutter, *n.* حَجَّار *pl.* حَجَّارَة ـ نَحَّات *pl.* نَحَّاتَة.

Stone-cutting, *n.* نَحْت ـ نَحْتُ ٱلْحِجَارَةِ.

Stone-fruit, *n.* فَاكِهَةٌ ذَاتُ فَصًى (or) نَوًى.

Stone-horse, *n.* فَحْل *pl.* فُحُول *and* فِحَال.

Stone-pit, *n.* مَحْجَر *pl.* مَحَاجِرُ ـ مَعْدِنُ حَجَرٍ *pl.* مَعَادِنُ.

Stone-roller, *n.* For rolling stones, مِرْضَاح ـ مِرْضَاخ.

Stone-still, *a.* وَاقِف ـ سَكِن ـ صَامِتٌ كَٱلْحَجَرِ.

Stone's-throw, *n.* رَمْيَةُ حَجَرٍ ـ ضَرْبَةُ حَجَرٍ.

Stone-ware, *n.* فَخَّارٌ مِنْ صِنْفِ ٱلْحَجَرِ.

Stone-work, *n.* شُغْلُ حَجَرٍ ـ تَرْكِيبُ حَجَرٍ.

Stoniness, *n.* Abundance of stones, كَثْرَةُ حِجَارَةٍ. Hardness, firm texture, صَلَابَة ـ صَلَادَة; as of the heart, قَسَاوَة.

Stony, *a.* Consisting of or full of stones, صَخِر ـ حَجِر ـ مُصْخِر. Stony places, أَمَاكِنُ مُحْجِرَةٌ. Stony land or soil, ظَرِير ـ مَحْجَر.

أَرْضٌ مَطَرَةٌ ـ أَرْضٌ حَجِرَةٌ ـ أَرْضٌ جَلْمَدَةٌ . A — heart, قَلْبٌ قَاسٍ ـ قَسُوف ـ قَاسِي ٱلْقَلْبِ ـ مِنْ حَجَرٍ .

Stood, *pret. of to* Stand, *v.i. q.v.*

Stook, *n.* A collection of sheaves, جُمْلَةُ كُدَادِيس ـ جُمْلَةُ حُزَمٍ .

Stool, *n.* The seat so called, كُرْسِيٌّ *pl.* كَرَاسِيُّ ـ إِسْكَمْلَة *pl.* إِسْكَمْلَات . An evacuation, إِفْرَاغ ـ مَجْلِس ـ وَقْعَة . A stump left in the ground, جُذْمُور *pl.* جَذَامِيرُ . A close —, كُرْسِيٌّ فِيهِ وِعَاءٌ لِلْبِرَازِ . To go to —, بَرَزَ ² ـ تَبَرَّزَ .

Stoop, *v.i.* To bend one's self, تَطَأْطَأَ ـ إِنْحَنَى . To prostrate one's self سَجَدَ ² ـ أَسْجَدَ . To —, as in submission, إِتَّضَعَ ـ تَخَشَّعَ ـ إِخْتَضَعَ ـ أَخْضَعَ . To —, as a bird to attack its prey, حَطَّ ² ـ إِخْتَضَعَ . To — to, to be submissive to, إِخْتَضَعَ لِ . To — to, to degrade one's self to, in, تَرَذَّلَ فِي . To descend, as from rank, إِنْحَطَّ . To —, as if to hear, صَغَى ٣ . I stooped to them, تَطَأْطَأْتُ لَهُمْ . *See also to* Condescend, *v.i.*

Stoop, *v.t.* To tip, incline, طَأْطَأَ ـ أَصْغَى ـ مَيَّلَ ـ حَنَى ٣ .

Stoop, *n.* A bending of the body, طَأْطَأَةٌ ـ خَضْع ـ إِنْحِنَاءٌ . The fall of a bird on its prey, حَطٌّ ـ إِخْتِضَاع ـ هُجُوم . Inclination, مَيْل ـ حُدُور . A vessel for drinking from, مِشْرَبَة . To have a —, of a person, خَضَعَ ٣ .

Stoopingly, *n.* بِطَأْطَأَةٍ ـ بِٱنْحِنَاءٍ ـ بِخُضُوعٍ .

Stop, *v.t.* To bring to a stand, وَقَّفَ ـ أَوْقَفَ . To withhold from, restrain, حَجَزَ-عَن ² ـ عَكَفَ-عَن ³ ـ وَهَقَ-عَن *aor.* يَهِقُ ـ حَبَسَ-عَن ³ ـ سَدَّ-عَن ² ـ حَاشَ-عَن ² . To arrest, seize, قَبَضَ ³ ـ أَرْقَأَ ـ مَسَكَ بِ ـ عَلَى ³ . To suspend, عَطَّلَ . To stanch, قَطَعَ ³ : he stopped the blood, قَطَعَ ٱلدَّمَ ³ . To prevent, مَنَعَ ³ . To render impassable, سَدَّ ² . To put stops to, جَعَلَ لِ-عَلَامَاتِ ٱلْوَقْفِ ³ . To —, as a bottle, with a stopper, سَدَّ-بِسِدَادٍ ² ـ شَجَبَ-بِشِجَابٍ ² . To be stopped, brought to a stand, أُوقِفَ ; to be withheld from, حُجِزَ-عَن ـ إِحْتَبَسَ عَن ـ وُهِقَ عَن ; to be arrested, قُبِضَ عَلَيْهِ ـ مُسِكَ بِهِ ـ رَقَأَ ³ ; to be stanched, قُطِعَ ـ إِنْقَطَعَ ; to be stopped up, rendered impassable, سُدَّ ; to be suspended, تَعَطَّلَ ; to be prevented, مُنِعَ ـ تَمَنَّعَ . He stopped his mouth, سَدَّ فَاهُ ² . He demanded that the building of the fortifications should be stopped, طَلَبَ تَوْقِيفَ بِنَاءِ ٱلِاسْتِحْكَامَاتِ ² . The road was stopped against him, سُدَّ عَلَيْهِ ٱلطَّرِيقُ . They stopped their ears against hearing, ثَقَّلُوا آذَانَهُمْ عَنِ ٱلسَّمْعِ .

To stop up, as a well, with stones, *etc.*, سَدَّ ² ـ طَمَّى ; to be so stopped up, إِنْسَدَّ ـ تَطَمَّى . To dam, سَكَرَ ² ـ سَدَّ ² .

To stop payment, أَفْلَسَ .

Stop, *v.i.* To cease to go forward, تَوَقَّفَ ـ وَقَفَ *aor.* يَقِفُ . To desist from, كَفَّ عَن ² ـ إِمْتَنَعَ عَن ـ تَمَسَّكَ عَن . To delay, تَلَبَّثَ ـ تَعَوَّقَ ـ طَاوَلَ . To stay, قَعَدَ ² ـ أَقَامَ .

To stop for, wait for, إِنْتَظَرَ ـ إِسْتَنْظَرَ .

To stop in, in the house, لَزِمَ ٱلْبَيْتَ ـ بَقِيَ فِي ٱلْبَيْتِ ³ ; in a place, حَلَّ بِ ² ³ .

To stop out, outside, تَعَوَّقَ خَارِجًا ـ ظَلَّ خَارِجًا ³ .

To stop short, in speaking, أَسْكَتَ ـ تَكَلَّمَ ثُمَّ سَكَتَ .

To stop or stay with, حَلَّ مَعَ ² ـ قَعَدَ عِنْدَ فُلَانٍ ³ ـ نَزَلَ بِ ³ فُلَانٍ (عَلَى *or*).

To stop up late, سَهِرَ ٱللَّيْلَ ³ .

Stop, *n.* Cessation of motion, وَقْف ـ وُقُوف ـ وَقْفَة ـ إِنْقِطَاعُ ٱلْحَرَكَةِ . A hindrance, عَائِق *pl.* عَوَائِق ـ مَانِع *pl.* مَوَانِعُ . An obstruction, سَدّ *pl.* أَسْدَاد *or* سُدُود ـ حَاجِز *pl.* حَوَاجِزُ . A point in writing or printing, إِشَارَةُ ٱلْوَقْفِ . A — of an organ, مِيزَانُ ٱلْأَرْغُنِ ـ مِفْتَاحُ ٱلْأَرْغُنِ . A dead —, إِنْقِطَاعُ ٱلْحَرَكَةِ بَتَّةً . A full —, نُقْطَةُ خِتَامِ ٱلْبَنْدِ .

To bring to a stop, to suspend, عَطَّلَ ; to hinder, مَنَعَ ³ .

To come to a stop, to halt, وَقَفَ *aor.* يَقِفُ ; as on a journey, حَطَّ ² .

To make a stop, to stay, مَكَثَ ² ـ حَلَّ ² ـ قَعَدَ ³ ـ أَقَامَ ² .

To put a stop to, to cause to cease, أَنْهَى ـ أَبْطَلَ .

Stop-cock, *n.* لَوْلَب *pl.* لَوَالِبُ .

Stop-gap, *n.* Of food, عُلَالَة ; in a general sense, سَدٌّ مَسَدٌّ .

Stoppage, *n.* The act of stopping, تَوْقِيف ـ إِيقَاف ; the being stopped, وَقْف ـ وُقُوف . Halt, time of stoppage, delay, تَأْخِير ـ تَعَوُّق ـ تَوَقُّف ـ عَاقَة . The act of obstructing, تَسْدِيد ـ سَدّ . An obstruction, سَدّ ـ مَانِع . The being stopped, cut off, cessation, إِنْقِطَاع . The act of suppressing, تَعْطِيل ; the being suppressed, تَعَطُّل . Stay, as in a place, حُلُول ـ مَكْث ـ قُعُود . An abrupt breaking off, مَقْطَع . Retrenchment, تَقْصِير ـ تَقْلِيل ـ إِسْقَاط ; to be under stoppages, of salary, أُسْقِطَ مِنْ مَعَاشِهِ .

Stoppage of payment, إِفْلَاس . A — in the nose, سُدَّة .

Stopper, *n.* As for a bottle, *etc.*, صِمَّة *pl.* صِمَم ـ صِبَار ـ وَنِيعَة ـ عَزْعَزَة ـ صِمَام ـ شِجَاب ـ عِفَاص ـ سِدَاد *pl.* أَسِدَّة . A clinching argument, سُكَاتَة ـ صُمَات . A short rope, حَبْلٌ قَصِيرٌ .

Stopper, *v.t.* Of bottles, *etc.*, عَفَصَ ³ ـ صَمَّ ² ـ أَصَمَّ ـ سَدَّ-بِسِدَادٍ ² .

A stoppered bottle, مُفَدَّمَة .

Stopple, *n.* *See* Stopper, *n.*

Storage, *n.* A putting in store, خَزْن ـ خَزْنٌ فِي مَخْزَنٍ ; price of —, كِرْوَةُ ٱلْمَخْزَنِ ـ أُجْرَةُ ٱلْمَخْزَنِ .

Storax, n الإصْطَرَكُ ـ المَيْعَة.

Store, n. A large number or quantity, مِقْدَارٌ وَافِرٌ ـ كَثْرَة ـ وَفْرَة. A stock laid up, a hoard, ـ صَوْن ـ ذَخَائِرُ pl. ذَخِيرَة ـ خَزِينَة كُنُوز pl. كَنْز. A warehouse, مَخَازِنُ pl. مَخْزَن ـ حَوَاصِلُ pl. حَاصِل. Stores, of provisions, مُؤْنَة; necessaries, as for war, etc., ـ مُهِمَّات لَوَازِمُ ـ ذَخَائِرُ وَأَدَوَاتٌ; utensils, أَدَوَات ـ آثَاث. In —, stock, حَاضِر ـ مَوْجُود.

To keep a store, warehouse, فَاتِحُ مَخْزَنٍ.

To keep in store, in stock, خَزَنَ سِلْعَةً لِلْبَيْعِ.

To lay in a store of, تَمَوَّنَ مِن; for a journey, تَزَوَّدَ مِن.

To lay up in store, خَزَنَ ـ كَنَزَ ـ إِدَّخَرَ.

To set great store by, اِعْتَبَرَ ـ عَزَّ عَلَى.

Store, v.t. To furnish or supply with, جَهَّزَ-بِ ـ أَمَدَّ-بِ. To replenish, أَشْبَعَ ـ سَدَّ مَسَدَّ كَذَا. To lay by, to save, تَقَنَّى ـ vulg. وَفَّرَ. To hoard, lay up in —, ـ إِدَّخَرَ ـ ذَخَرَ ـ كَنَزَ خَزَنَ ـ vulg. صَمَّدَ. To enrich, ornament, ـ زَخْرَفَ ـ زَيَّنَ vulg. صَمَدَ. To put in a store, خَزَنَ ـ جَعَلَ-فِي مَخْزَنٍ ـ رَفَعَ-فِي مَخْزَنٍ. To —, as of a ship with a cargo, or a garrison with soldiers, أَشْحَنَ-بِ ـ شَحَنَ-بِ. To — away in, for safety, أَغْفَرَ-(or غَفَّرَ-) فِي.

Store-city, n. مَدِينَةُ مَخْزَنٍ pl. مُدُنُ مَخَازِنَ.

Store-house, n. خِزَانَة pl. خَزَائِنُ ـ مَخْزَن pl. مَخَازِنُ.

Store-keeper, n. حَارِسُ مَخْزَنٍ pl. حُرَّاس ـ مَخْزَنْجِي pl. مَخْزَنْجِيَّة.

Storer, n. One who stores up, as wheat, etc., خَزَّان.

Store-room, n. خِزَانَة pl. خَزَائِنُ ـ أَنْبَار pl. أَنْبَارَات. An underground —, specially for grain, مَطْمُورَة pl. مَطَامِيرُ.

Stores, n. pl. See under Store, n.

Storied, a. Having stories, ذُو طَبَقَاتٍ. Having inscriptions upon it, مَكْتُوبٌ فِيهِ ـ مُؤَرَّخٌ عَلَيْهِ. Related in story, رُوِيَ فِي مَذْكُورٌ فِي حِكَايَةٍ ـ ٱلْحَدِيثِ.

Stork, n. لَقْلَق pl. لَقَالِقُ ـ لَقْلَق ـ أَبُو حُدَيْجٍ.

Stork's-bill, n. The plant, إِبْرَةُ ٱلرَّاعِي.

Storm, n. A commotion of the elements by wind, زَوْبَعَة pl. زَوَابِعُ ـ نَوْءُ رِيحٍ ـ قُرْطُمَة; a — of rain, نَوْء pl. أَنْوَاء ـ بُوقَة. Tumult, هَوْشَة pl. هَوْشَات ـ شَغْب ـ ضَجَّة ـ هَرْجٌ وَمَرْجٌ ـ لَجَّة. The storming of a place, فَتْح ـ إِفْتِتَاح ـ ضَبْط. A great —, of wind, arose, حَدَثَ نَوْءُ رِيحٍ عَظِيمٍ.

Storm, v.t. To take by storm, فَتَحَ ـ ضَبَطَ ـ تَمَلَّكَ-قَهْرًا.

Storm, v.i. To rage with violence, عَصَفَ ـ أَعْصَفَ. To rage, fume, إِسْتَشَاطَ ـ حَنِقَ ـ إِغْتَاظَ ـ إِحْتَمَى غَضَبًا ـ تَهَوَّرَ غَيْظًا.

Storm-beaten, a. مَلْطُومٌ بِٱلزَّوَابِعِ ـ مَضْرُوبٌ مِنَ ٱلْعَوَاصِفِ.

Stormful, a. See Stormy, a.

Storminess, n. Of the wind, عُصُوف ـ عَصْف; of rain, نَوْء. Tumultuousness, disputatiousness, عُجَّة ـ عَجِيج ـ ضَجِيج ـ لَجَاجَة.

Storm-sail, n. شِرَاعُ ٱلنَّوْءِ.

Stormy, a. Agitated with furious winds, ـ عَاصِفُ ٱلرِّيحِ ـ عَاصِف طُوفَانِيٌّ. A — wind, رِيحٌ عَاصِفَةٌ. A — day, يَوْمُ أَرْيَاحٍ وَأَمْطَارٍ. Tumultuous, عَجَّاج ـ لَجُوج ـ ضَجُوج. A — debate, ـ إِئْتِمَارٌ عَجَّاجٌ مُذَاكَرَةٌ ذَاتُ ضَجَّةٍ.

Story, n. A narrative, tale, قِصَّة pl. قِصَص ـ حِكَايَة pl. حِكَايَات ـ حَدِيث pl. أَحَادِيثُ. A history, تَارِيخ pl. تَوَارِيخ. An idle —, fable, أُسْطُورَة pl. أَسَاطِيرُ ـ خُرَافَة pl. خُرَافَات. A pretty —, مُلْحَة pl. مُلَح ـ أُحْدُوثَةٌ مَلِيحَةٌ. Stories of the ancients, سِيرَةُ ٱلأَوَّلِينَ. Story, as of a house, طَبَقَة pl. طَبَقَات. A lie, كِذْبَة ـ كِذْب. To tell a —, tale, قَصَّ قِصَّةً; to tell stories, narratives, قَصَّ قِصَصًا; to lie, كَذَبَ. As the — goes, حَسَبَ ٱلرِّوَايَةِ ـ كَمَا هُوَ فِي ٱلقِصَّةِ. The best of the — is ..., هٰذَا شَيْءٌ ـ هٰذَا شَيْءٌ آخَرُ. That's another —, تُرْفَةُ ٱلْخَبَرِ فِي أَنْ ... ثَانٍ. "We will relate to you the best of stories," نَقُصُّ عَلَيْكَ أَحْسَنَ ٱلْقَصَصِ (Kur. xii. 3). See also Narrative, Relation, n.

Story, v.t. To tell in historical relation, أَرَّخَ. See also to Relate, Narrate, v.t.

Story-book, n. كِتَابُ أَحَادِيثَ. A book of fable, كِتَابُ خُرَافَاتٍ (or أَسَاطِيرَ).

Story-teller, n. A narrator of stories, نَاقِل pl. نَقَلَة ـ رَاوٍ pl. رُوَاة ـ قَاصّ ـ قَاصُّ قِصَصٍ. A liar, كَذَّاب.

Stoup, n. A vessel for drinking from, قَدَح ـ مِشْرَبَة.

Stout, a. Large, corpulent, ضُخَام ـ ضَخْم ـ جَسِيم ـ بَدِين. Plump, فَعِم. Thick, ثَخِين. Hard, stiff, tough, ـ صَلْد ـ صُلْب أَصْلَدُ. Vigorous, robust, قَوِيٌّ ـ شَدِيد ـ عَفِيّ ـ ضَلِيع. Brave, عَنْتَر ـ مِقْدَام ـ بَطَل ـ شُجَاع ـ شَجِيع ـ شَهْم.

Stout, n. Of beer, بِيرَةٌ سَوْدَاءُ قَوِيَّةٌ.

Stoutly, ad. Bravely, عَنْتَرَةً ـ بِشَجَاعَةٍ ـ بِجَرَاءَةٍ. With strength, بِقُوَّةٍ ـ بِحَوْلٍ ـ بِحَيْلٍ. Zealously, بِغَيْرَةٍ ـ بِحَمَاسَةٍ. Resolutely, بِثَبَاتٍ ـ عَمْدًا ـ بِعَزْمٍ ـ حَزْمًا.

Stoutness, n. Corpulency, ضَخْم ـ بَدَانَة ـ ضَخَامَة ـ سِمَن. Thickness, ثُخْن. Vigour, جِدّ ـ صَلَابَة ـ مُرُوءَة ـ قُوَّة. Bravery, intrepidity, شَوْكَة ـ إِقْدَام ـ جَسَارَة ـ شَجَاعَة.

Stout-hearted, *a.* شَجِيع ـ جَسُور ـ قَدُوم ـ بِسَبَنْدَى.

Stout-heartedness, *n.* شَجَاعَة ـ جَسَارَة ـ إِقْدَام.

Stove, *n.* As for fire, كَانُون ـ سَاعُور ـ مَوْقِد.

Stove, *v.t.* حَمَّى.

Stover, *n.* *See* Fodder, *n.*

Stow, *v.t.* To pack, عَبَّأَ ـ عَبَأَ. To — away, خَزَنَ 2 ـ رَفَعَ ـَ. To — a cargo, نَظَّمَ وَسْقَ ٱلْمَرْكَبِ.

Stowage, *n.* The act of stowing, تَعْبِئَة ـ عَبْء. Room for receiving, سَعَة ـ مَوْضِع ـ مَحَلّ.

Strabism, *n.* / Strabismus, } *See* Squint, *n.*

Straddle, *v.i.* To walk wide, or to have the legs wide apart, أَفَجَّ ـ فَجَّ 2 ـ فَرْشَحَ. To — over, فَرْشَحَ.

Straddle-legged, *a.* أَفَجّ ـ مُفَاجّ.

Straddling, *a.* مُفَاجّ. He walks —, هُوَ يَمْشِي مُفَاجًّا.

Straggle, *v.i.* To ramble, عَارَ *aor.* يَعِيرُ ـ عَالَ ـَ. To stray, غَوَى ـَ ـ ضَلَّ ـَ ـ طَاحَ 2 ـ تَطَوَّحَ. To —, as from an army, *etc.*, تَطَوَّحَ ـ شَرَدَ 2. They were dispersed straggling, تَفَرَّقُوا شَذَرَ مَذَرَ ـ تَشَذَّرُوا.

Straggler, *n.* A rambler, عَيَّار ـ عَائِر. One who goes astray, مُتَطَوِّح ـ طَائِح; as from an army, *etc.*, شَرِيد *pl.* شَرَائِدُ ـ شَرِيدٌ طَرِيدٌ *pl.* شَرَائِدُ طَرَائِدُ.

Straggling, *a.* Occurring here and there, شَرِيد ـ مُتَفَرِّق. Of rambling, straying; *see under* Straggler, *n.*

Straight, *a.* Not crooked, مُسْتَقِيم ـ عَدِل ـ مُعْتَدِل ـ مُسَاوٍ. Erect, upright, مَصْمُود ـ مُنْتَصِب ـ قُيَّام *pl.* قَائِم ـ جَاذِل. Direct, nearest, أَقْرَبُ. A — path, مَسْلَكٌ مُسْتَقِيمٌ. To be or to become —, even, direct, إِعْتَدَلَ; to become —, even, تَعَدَّلَ ـ إِسْتَوَى ـ تَقَوَّمَ. To pursue a — course, قَصَدَ فِي ـَ ـ أَقْصَدَ فِي. *See also* Upright, *a.*

Straight, *ad.* Directly, in a straight line, إِسْتِقَامَةً ـ بِٱسْتِوَآءٍ ـ إِعْتِدَالًا. Immediately, فِي ٱلسَّاعَةِ ـ فِي ٱلْحَالِ ـ حَالًا. He ascended — before him, صَعِدَ مَعَ وَجْهِهِ ـَ. He went —, straightforward, before him, سَارَ إِلَى جِهَةِ وَجْهِهِ ـَ.

Straighten, *v.t.* صَحَّحَ ـ عَادَلَ ـ عَدَّلَ.

Straighten, *v.i.* To become straight; *see under* Straight, *a.*

Straightener, *n.* مُصَحِّح ـ مُعَدِّل.

Straightforward, *a.* In a straight course, عَدِل. Upright, trusty, صِدِّيق ـ مُسْتَقِيم ـ صَالِح ـ مُتَثَوِّب ـ عَادِل ـ نَصُوح ـ مُقْسِط *pl.* صُدَقَآءُ. To act in a — manner towards, تَثَوَّبَ بِ. *See also under* Open, *a.*

Straightforwardness, *n.* Honesty, إِسْتِقَامَة ـ نُصُوح ـ قِسْط ـ صَدَاقَة; as in speech, إِنْبِسَاط.

Straightly, *ad.* Narrowly, particularly, خُصُوصًا ـ بِٱلتَّدْقِيقِ. *See also* Straight, *ad.*

Straightness, *n.* إِسْتِوَآء ـ إِسْتِقَامَة ـ إِعْتِدَال. *See also* Rectitude, *n.*

Straightway, *ad.* فِي ٱلْحَالِ ـ حَالًا ـ عَلَى ٱلْفَوْرِ ـ بِلَا تَوَقُّفٍ. I sent him — to you, أَرْسَلْتُهُ لِلْوَقْتِ إِلَيْكَ.

Straiks, *n.* ضَبَّاتُ حَوْلَ إِطَارِ عَجَلَةِ ٱلْمِدْفَعِ.

Strain, *v.t.* To stretch with efforts, إِجْتَذَبَ ـ جَذَبَ ـِ. To draw with force, شَدَّ 2 ـ جَذَبَ بِشِدَّةٍ ـِ. To exaggerate, بَالَغَ فِي ـ فَرَّطَ فِي. To wrest, as a passage, meaning, صَحَّفَ ـ حَرَّفَ ـ عَكَسَ ـِ. To twist, sprain, لَوَى ـ حَنَا *aor.* يَحْنُو. To —, as through a cullender, *etc.*, صَفَّى ـ رَوَّقَ ـ بَزَلَ 2. To — or sprain one's self, تَلَوَّى. To — every nerve, تَصَلَّبَ ـ كَدَّ 2 ـ بَذَلَ جُهْدَهُ 2 ـِ.

Strain, *v.i.* To make violent effort, إِجْتَهَدَ ـ إِشْتَدَّ ـ كَدَّ 2 ـ بَذَلَ ٱلْجُهْدَ 2 ـِ. To make effort to reach, تَطَاوَلَ. To be filtered, تَصَفَّى ـ تَرَوَّقَ.

Strain, *n.* A violent effort, كَدّ ـ شِدَّة ـ بَذْلُ ٱلْجُهْدِ. A sprain, إِلْتِوَآء ـ جِنَايَة. A — of the mind, شَقُّ ٱلنَّفْسِ. Style, as in writing or speaking, طَوْرُ كَلَامٍ ـ مِنْهَاج ـ عِبَارَة ـ إِصْطِلَاح; in poetry, نَظْم. A tone, character, طَبِيعَة ـ خَلَّة ـ خَصْلَة ـ سَجِيَّة. Sound, حِسّ ـ صَوْت; sweet strains, أَنْغَام. A lofty —, إِنْشَآء ـ سَجِيّ. To speak or sing in sweet strains, تَنَغَّمَ. *See also* Song, *n.*

Strainer, *n.* A cullender, مِصْفَاة ـ مِبْزَل ـ مِسْحَل *pl.* مَصَافٍ. A — for the mouth of a bottle, فِدَام ـ غَلَل.

Straining, *n.* The act of, as through a cullender, تَصْفِيَة. With great —, of the mind, بِشَقِّ ٱلنَّفْسِ. *See also under* Strain, *n.*

Strait, *a.* Narrow, ضَيِّق ـ ضَاقَة *pl.* ضَائِق; very narrow, أَضْيَقُ. Rigorous, مُتَشَدِّد ـ عَصَّار. Exact, مُدَقِّق. To be —, narrow, ضَاقَ *aor.* يَضِيقُ; to become —, تَضَيَّقَ.

Strait, *n.* / Straits, } A narrow pass, of the sea, بُوغَاز *pl.* بَوَاغِيزُ ـ مَضِيق. Distress, عُسْر ـ ضِيق. A difficulty, صُعُوبَة ـ ضِيقَة ـ ضَيْقَة ـ الزُّقَاق. The Straits of Gibraltar, زُقَاقُ سَبْتَة ـ بُوغَازُ جَبَلِ طَارِق. The Straits of Bâbu-'l-Mándab, (Babelmandib), بَابُ ٱلْمَنْدَب. For the protection of the straits, لِوِقَايَةِ ٱلْبُوغَازِ (or ٱلْمَضِيقِ). To be in straits, in straitened circumstances, أَعْسَرَ ـ ضَاقَ *aor.* يَضِيقُ عَلَى مَعَاشِهِ ـ أَضَاقَ. To be reduced to straits, poverty, إِفْتَقَرَ ـ صَارَ رَقِيقَ ٱلْحَالِ ـ أَرَقَّ . To be in —, difficulty, تَعَسَّرَ عَلَى ٱلْحَالِ ـ تَضَايَقَ بِهِ ٱلْأَمْرُ .

Straiten, *v.t.* To make narrow, ضَيَّقَ ـ أَضْيَقَ . To tighten, حَزَقَ ـ حَصَرَ . To overpower, ضَغَطَ . To press hard upon, as a creditor on a debtor, قَعَّطَ ـ قَعَطَ . To distress, reduce to difficulty, أَضْيَقَ عَلَى ـ ضَيَّقَ عَلَى ـ عَسَّرَ . To be in straitened circumstances, أَعْسَرَ ; (*see also under* Strait, *n.*) He was straitened in his bosom, حَصِرَ صَدْرُهُ . He was straitened in his circumstances, as a prison straitens a prisoner, حَصِرَ حَالُهُ . *See also to* Embarrass, *n.*

Strait-laced, *a.* Rigid, strict, مُدَقِّق ـ مُتَعَصِّب ; in religious matters, مُتَحَمِّس ـ حَمِس ـ حُمْس *pl.* أَحْمَس . *See also* Rigid, *a.*

Straitly, *ad.* In a narrow or close manner, بِضَيْقٍ ـ بِعُنْفٍ . Strictly, بِتَدْقِيقٍ ; in religious matters, بِحَمَاسَةٍ . Immediately, حَالًا ـ لِلْوَقْتِ .

Straitness, *n.* Narrowness, ضِيقَة . Closeness, pressure, عَسْر . Pressure from necessity, ضَنْك ـ عُسْرُ ٱلْحَالِ ـ أَزْقُ ٱلْعَيْشِ ـ شِدَّة ـ ضَنَاكَة . Strictness, دِقَّة ـ تَدْقِيق ; in religious matters, حَمَاسَة . *See also* Embarrassment, *n.*

Straits, *n. pl.* *See under* Strait, *n.*

Strait-jacket, *n.*, Strait-waistcoat, } صُدْرَةٌ لِضَبْطِ ٱلْمَجَانِينِ .

Strake, *n.* Of a wheel, عِصَابَةُ ٱلْعَجَلَةِ *pl.* عَصَائِب .

Stramineous, *a.* تِبْنِيّ .

Stramonium, *n.*, Stramony, } جَوْزٌ مَاثِلٌ ـ طَاطَلَة .

Strand, *n.* A shore, شَطّ *pl.* شُطُوط ـ سَاحِل *pl.* سَوَاحِل . A —, as of a rope, جُمْلَة *pl.* جُمَل ـ طَاقَة *pl.* طَاقَات . *See also* Rope, *n.*

Strand, *v.t.* To drive on shore, of a ship, شَطَّطَ ٱلْمَرْكَبَ ـ بَلَّطَ ٱلْمَرْكَبَ ـ رَمَى بِٱلْمَرْكَبِ .

Strand, *v.i.* To be driven on shore, of a ship, جَنَحَتْ ـ إِرْتَمَى ٱلْمَرْكَبُ ـ حَرَثَ ٱلْمَرْكَبُ ـ تَشَطَّطَ ٱلْمَرْكَبُ ـ ٱلسَّفِينَةُ .

Strange, *a.* Foreign, غَرِيب ـ أَجْنَبِيّ . Wonderful, uncommon, نَادِر ـ بَدِيع ـ غَرِيب ـ عَجِيب ـ فَرِيّ . Abnormal, irregular, شَاذّ ـ شَتّ . Improbable, far-fetched, extraordinary, بَعِيد . A — or improbable affair, أَمْرٌ بَعِيدٌ ـ أَمْرٌ فَرِيّ . This is —, هٰذَا مِنَ ٱلْبُعْدِ بِمَكَانٍ . Strange lands, مَمَالِكُ ـ أَرَاضٍ أَجْنَبِيَّةٌ . "Thou [*fem.*] hast done a strange thing, or a thing hitherto unknown," لَقَدْ جِئْتِ شَيْئًا فَرِيًّا (Kur. xix. 28.) As if some— thing had happened to him, كَأَنَّهُ أَصَابَهُ أَمْرٌ غَرِيبٌ . It is — that..., ٱلْغَرَابَةُ فِي أَنْ ـ مِنَ ٱلْغَرِيبِ أَنْ . A thing not less —, أَمْرٌ لَيْسَ بِأَقَلَّ غَرَابَةٍ . How —, wonderful, it is! سُبْحَانَ مِنْ كَذَا .

A — people, شَعْبٌ أَعْجَمُ . To be —, abnormal, irregular, شَذَّ . To tell — things to, سَمَّعَ أُمُورًا غَرِيبَةً . To use — language, أَغْرَبَ فِي ٱلْكَلَامِ . Strange! *as an int.*, عَجَبًا لِهٰذَا ـ عَجَائِبُ .

Strange-looking, *a.* عَجِيبُ ٱلْمَنْظَرِ ـ غَرِيبُ ٱلصُّورَةِ .

Strangely, *ad.* Wonderfully, بِنَوْعٍ غَرِيبٍ ـ عَجَبًا . Out of the common, فَوْقَ ٱلْعَادَةِ . To behave —, إِسْتَغْرَبَ فِي ٱلْعَمَلِ .

Strangeness, *n.* Oddness, singularity, غَرَابَة . Alienation, coldness, فُتُور ـ بُرُودَة ـ مُفَارَكَة ـ تَنَفُّر .

Stranger, *n.* A foreigner, أَجْنَبِيّ *pl.* أَجَانِب ـ غَرِيب *pl.* غُرَبَاء . A sight-seer, visitor, خَاطِر *pl.* خُطَّار ـ زَائِر *pl.* زُوَّار . A guest, sojourner, نَزِيل *pl.* نُزَل . To consider as a —, حَسِبَ أَجْنَبِيًّا . He became a — to him, صَارَ أَجْنَبِيًّا عِنْدَهُ .

Strangle, *v.t.* To squeeze the throat, غَتَّ ; to choke, جَرَضَ ـ خَنَّقَ ـ خَنَقَ ـ شَنَقَ ـ زَرَّدَ حَلْقَهُ . To hinder, مَنَعَ . To be strangled, إِخْتَنَقَ ـ ٱنْخَنَقَ . He escaped from them when they had strangled him, (so as almost to kill him,) أَفْلَتَ مِنْهُمْ وَقَدْ جَرَضُوهُ . *See also to* Smother, *v.t.*

Strangled, *a.* مَخْنُوق ـ خَنِيق ـ مَشْنُوق . What is —, ٱلْمَخْنُوقُ .

Strangler, *n.* خَنَّاق ـ زَرَّاد ـ جَرَّاض .

Strangles, *n.* وَرَمٌ فِي حَلْقِ ٱلْخَيْلِ .

Strangulation, *n.* The act of strangling, تَخْنِيق ـ خَنْق ـ شَنْق ; the being strangled, إِخْتِنَاق ـ ٱنْخِنَاق .

Strangurious, *a.* Having strangury, مُصَابٌ بِعُسْرِ ٱلْبَوْلِ .

Strangury, *n.* حَبْسُ ٱلْبَوْلِ ـ عُسْرُ ٱلْبَوْلِ .

Strap, *n.* As of leather, إِسَار *pl.* أُسُر ـ سَيْر *pl.* سُيُور ـ قَايِش ; of a sandal, شِسْع *pl.* شُسُوع *and* أَشْسَاع ـ بَنْد *pl.* بُنُود . A — for chastisement, دِرَّة *pl.* دِرَر . A — by which anything is suspended, عَلَق . A — for sharpening, مِسَنٌّ مِنْ ـ جِلْدٌ مُشَبْرِقٌ ـ جِلْدٍ . A breast — of a camel, غُرْضَة *pl.* غُرُض . A — to keep a saddle firm, لَبَب *pl.* أَلْبَاب . A girth, حِزَام *pl.* أَحْزِمَة .

Strap, *v.t.* To beat with a —, ضَرَّبَ ـ ضَرَبَ بِدِرَّةٍ . To fasten with a —, حَزَمَ ـ حَزَمَ بِسَيْرٍ . To sharpen on a —, سَنَّ عَلَى ـ شَبْرَقَ عَلَى ٱلْجِلْدِ ـ مِسَنٍّ مِنْ جِلْدٍ . He sharpened the razor on the —, سَنَّ (or شَبْرَقَ) ٱلْمُوسَى عَلَى ٱلْجِلْدِ .

Strappado, *n.* بَكَرَةُ ٱلْقِصَاصِ .

Strapping, *n.* The act of binding, رَبْط ـ حَزْم .

Strapping, *a.* Well shaped, tall, طَوِيلُ ٱلْقَامَةِ ـ شَطْب ـ صَاحِبُ قَدٍّ وَٱعْتِدَالٍ . A — fellow, فَحْل *pl.* فُحُول ـ جَذَع *pl.* جِذْعَان .

Strata, *pl. of* Stratum, *q.v.*

Stratagem, *n.* A trick, فَنٌّ *pl.* فُنُون ـ دُولَاب *pl.* دَوَالِيب ـ حِيلَة *pl.* حِيَل ـ كَيْد *pl.* كِيَاد ـ مَكِيدَة *pl.* مَكَائِد. Treachery, خِيَانَة. A — in war, خَدْعَةٌ حَرْبِيَّةٌ : War is a —, الْحَرْبُ خَدْعَةٌ. War stratagems, مَضَارِبُ. To practise —, إِحْتَالَ. To lay stratagems for, كَادَ ل ـ. To practise stratagems against, إِحْتَالَ عَلَى.

Stratagemical, *a.* حِيَالِيٌّ.

Strategic, *a.* } Of military movements, مَا نِيطَ بِأُصُولِ قِيَادَةِ
Strategical, } ٱلْجُيُوشِ ـ مُتَعَلِّقٌ بِقِيَادَةِ حَرَكَاتِ ٱلْجُيُوشِ.
Strategical roads, طُرُقٌ حَرْبِيَّةٌ.

Strategist, *n.* عَالِمٌ بِأُصُولِ ـ مَاهِرٌ بِفَنِّ قِيَادَةِ ٱلْجُيُوشِ وَحَرَكَاتِهَا قِيَادَةِ ٱلْجُيُوشِ فِي ٱلْحَرْبِ.

Strategy, *n.* أُصُولُ قِيَادَةِ حَرَكَاتِ ـ فَنُّ قِيَادَةِ حَرَكَاتِ ٱلْجُيُوشِ ٱلْجُيُوشِ فِي ٱلْحَرْبِ. Stratagems, in war, مَضَارِبُ.

Strathspey, *n.* ضَرْبٌ مِنَ ٱلرَّقْصِ عِنْدَ أَهْلِ إِسْكُتْلَنْد.

Stratification, *n.* نِظَامُ طَبَقَاتٍ ـ تَرْتِيبُ طَاقَاتٍ عَلَى طَاقَاتٍ طَبَقَات ـ عَلَى طَبَقَاتٍ.

Stratified, *a.* طَبَقَةٌ عَلَى طَبَقَةٍ ـ طَاقٌ عَلَى طَاقٍ.

Stratiform, *a.* فِي هَيْئَةِ ٱلطَّبَقَاتِ.

Stratum, *n.* A layer, bed, seam, طَاق *pl.* طَاقَات ـ طَبَقَة *pl.* طَبَقَات. A row, صَفٌّ *pl.* صُفُوف. An order, class, طَبَقَة *pl.* طَبَقَات ـ فَانُور. They are in the same —, rank, هُمْ عَلَى فَانُورٍ وَاحِدٍ.

Stratus, *n.* سَحَابٌ مَبْسُوطٌ.

Straw, *n.* The stalks of grain, *etc.*, تِبْن ـ قَشّ ; a single —, تِبْنَة ـ قَشَّة. A bit of —, حِتَّةُ تِبْنٍ. A truss of —, فُرْزُوعَة *pl.* فَرَازِعُ. Chopped —, رُقَّة. Fodder, عَلَف *pl.* عُلُوفَة. A seller of —, تَبَّان. Not to care a — for, إِسْتَقَلَّ. He does not care a — for the truth, لَا يُبَالِي بِٱلْحَقِّ بَتَّةً. A man of —, صُعْلُوك. To feed (a beast) on chopped —, رَفَّ ـ.

Straw, *v.t.* *See to* Strew, *v.t.*

Straw-bed, *n.* فِرَاشٌ مِنْ تِبْنٍ ـ *vulg.* دُوشَك.

Strawberry, *n.* تُوتٌ أَرْضِيٌّ ـ تُوتٌ فِرَنْجِيٌّ.

Straw-colour, *n.* لَوْنُ ٱلتِّبْنِ.

Straw-coloured, *a.* تِبْنِيُّ ٱللَّوْنِ.

Straw-cutter, *n.* The instrument, مِقْطَعُ ٱلتِّبْنِ.

Strawy, *a.* Made of straw, تِبْنِيٌّ ـ مِنْ تِبْنٍ ـ مِنْ قَشٍّ.

Stray, *v.i.* To go astray, ضَلَّ ـ غَوَى ـ. To lose one's way, طَاحَ ـ تَاهَ ـ تَطَوَّحَ ـ تَطَيَّحَ. To rove, عَارَ *aor.* يَعِيرُ. To deviate from, زَاغَ عَنْ ـ حَادَ عَنْ ـ جَارَ عَنْ ـ إِعْتَسَفَ عَنْ ـ تَعَسَّفَ عَنْ. *See also to* Err, *v.i.*

Stray, *a.* Going astray, ضَالٌّ ـ غَوِيٌّ ـ غَاوٍ ـ تَائِه ; roving, عَيَّار ـ عَائِر.

Stray, *n.* A stray animal, سَائِبَة ـ ضَالَّة. Waifs and strays, لُقَاطَاتٌ سَائِبَاتٌ. *See also* Stroll, *n.*

Streak, *n.* A line, stripe; also, a track on soft ground; also a streak, as of herbage, خَطّ ـ خُطَّة *pl.* أَخْطَاط *and* خُطُوط. A — on sand or in a cloud, طِبَابَة ـ طِبَّة ; streaks in clouds, سَمَاحِيقُ ٱلسَّمَاءِ. The streaks or waves on a sea, or on sand, تَسَلْسُل. Upon the back of the ass there are two streaks, عَلَى ظَهْرِ ٱلْحِمَارِ خُطَّتَانِ. *See also to* Stripe, *v.t.*

Streak, *v.t.* As in weaving, *etc.*, خَطَّطَ ـ خَطَّطَ وَنَقَّشَ. To be streaked, إِخْتَطَّ. His face became streaked, *i.e.*, with a growing beard, إِخْتَطَّ وَجْهُهُ. To be streaked, of fish, lizards, *etc.* نُظِمَ.

Streaked, *a.* } مُخَطَّط ـ مُسَلْسَل ; of the marks on fish, *etc.*,
Streaky, } مُنْتَظَم ـ نَاظِم ; of the sea or sand, wavy, مُسَلْسَل.

Stream, *n.* As of water, سَيْل *pl.* سُيُول. A river, نَهْر *pl.* أَنْهُر. The place or bed of a —, مَسِيل *pl.* مَسَايِلُ *and* مُسُل *and* مُسْلَان. A gushing, of water, *etc.*, إِنْبِجَاس ـ إِنْفِجَار. A flowing or running, as of water or blood, ثُعْب ـ أُثْعُوب. A flowing —, سَيْلٌ سَائِحٌ. A perennial —, نَهْرٌ دَائِمٌ. An overflowing —, نَهْرٌ غَامِرٌ. A concatenation, succession, تَسَلْسُل ـ تَعَاقُب ـ تَتَالٍ ـ تَوَالٍ. Abundance, كَثْرَة ـ وَفْرَة ـ فَيَضَان. The Gulf Stream, تَيَّارُ سَيْلُ بَحْرِ ٱلْمُحِيطِ ـ ٱلْمَاءِ فِي بَحْرِ ٱلْمُحِيطِ. The ship flowed with the —, تَشَمَّرَتِ ٱلسَّفِينَةُ مَعَ ٱلْمَاءِ. To go with the —, to imitate, تَمَثَّلَ ب. One who goes with the — of opinion, through laziness, رَهْمَانٌ ـ رَهُوم.

Stream, *v.i.* To flow, سَاحَ *aor.* يَسِيحُ ـ سَالَ *aor.* يَسِيلُ. To —, as milk from an udder, blood from a vein, *etc.*, شَخَبَ ـ إِنْشَخَبَ. To make to —, of milk or blood, شَخَبَ. To — over, overflow, طَمَى *aor.* يَطْمِي ـ فَاضَ ـ إِنْغَمَرَ. To — or gush forth, إِنْبَجَسَ ـ إِنْفَجَرَ ـ تَفَجَّرَ. The horsemen streamed upon him, سَالَتْ عَلَيْهِ ٱلْخَيْلُ. The troops of horse streamed (from every quarter), تَسَايَلَتِ ٱلْكَتَائِبُ. The milk streamed (from the udder), شَخَبَ ٱللَّبَنُ. He streams with blood, هُوَ يَتَشَخَّبُ دَمًا. His hands streamed with blood, شَخَبَتْ يَدَاهُ. *See also to* Flow, *v.i.*

Stream, *v.t.* *See to* Streak, *v.t.*

Streamer, *n.* A pennon, عَلَم *pl.* أَعْلَام ; a ship's —, طَرَّادَة ـ فَلَانْدَرَة ; a spear —, أُمُّ ٱلرُّمْحِ ـ عَذَبَة *pl.* عَذَبَات. A flowing tassel, *etc.*, شُرَّابَة.

Streamlet, *n.* فَلْج *pl.* فُلُوج ـ جَدْوَل *pl.* جَدَاوِلُ ـ مَجْرَى مَآءٍ *pl.* مَجَارِي.

Streamy, *a.* Flowing, جَارٍ ـ سَائِل; full of streams, كَثِيرُ ٱلسُّيُولِ.

Street, *n.* سِكَّة *pl.* سِكَكٌ ـ طَرِيق *pl.* طُرُق; a wide —, شَارِع *pl.* شَوَارِعُ. A narrow —, زُقَاق *pl.* أَزِقَّة. The — was thronged with people, غَصَّتِ ٱلطَّرِيقُ بِٱلنَّاسِ.

Street-walker, *n.* سَوَّقَة. *See also* Prostitute, *n.*

Strength, *n.* Power, vigour, حَمَاسَة ـ مِرَاس ـ مَرَاسَة ـ أَيْد ـ أَزْر ـ حَوْل ـ شَوْكَة ـ زَوْر ـ حَيْل ـ قُوَّة. Power, ability, مَقْدَرَة ـ اِقْتِدَار ـ طَاقَة ـ مُكْنَة ـ قُوَّة ـ قُدْرَة. Stability, ثَبَات ـ ثُبُوت ـ دَوَام. Firmness, solidity, رَصَانَة ـ مَتَانَة ـ صَلَابَة. Energy, courage, زَوْر ـ بَطْش ـ مُرُوَّة ـ إِقْدَام ـ شَجَاعَة ـ شِدَّةُ عَزْمٍ ـ قُوَّةُ قَلْبٍ. Vehemence, شِدَّة. A support, مُسْنَد ـ عِمَاد. Strength, as of wine, spirits, *etc.*, سَوْرَة ـ حِدَّة. Strength of a fortress, مَنَاعَةُ حِصْنٍ. Strength of the wind, شِدَّةُ ٱلرِّيحِ; of a current, water, دَفْعَةُ ٱلْمَآءِ. There is no — nor power but in, or through, God, the High, the Great, لَا حَوْلَ وَلَا قُوَّةَ إِلَّا بِٱللّٰهِ ٱلْعَلِيِّ ٱلْعَظِيمِ. Above my —, فَوْقَ طَاقَتِي. With all my —, بِكُلِّ جُهْدِي. To gain —, تَأَيَّدَ ـ تَقَوَّى. He recovered his —, رَجَعَتْ قُوَّتُهُ إِلَيْهِ. His feet received —, تَشَدَّدَتْ رِجْلَاهُ.

Strengthen, *v.t.* To make strong, as in health, *etc.*, قَوَّى ـ صَحَّحَ. To aid, to — one to do anything, عَزَّزَ ـ أَيَّدَ ـ عَلَى ـ أَيَّدَ. To encourage, inspirit, أَزَّرَ ـ آزَرَ ـ عَزَّزَ ـ شَيَّعَ ـ شَدَّ [2] ـ شَدَّدَ ـ شَجَّعَ ـ جَلَّدَ. To fortify, as a town, *etc.*, حَصَّنَ. To make firm, as of a building, وَثَّقَ ـ شَيَّدَ ـ أَرْصَنَ. To make firm, confirm, أَكَّدَ ـ قَرَّرَ ـ أَحْكَمَ. To strengthen or encourage one's self, تَشَدَّدَ ـ تَعَزَّزَ ـ تَشَجَّعَ ـ تَجَلَّدَ.

Strengthen, *v.i.* To become more violent, اِشْتَدَّ.

Strengthener, *n.* One who strengthens, مُعَزِّز ـ مُشَدِّد; of a thing, مُشَيِّد; of a medicine, عِلَاجٌ مُقَوٍّ.

Strengthless, *a.* Weak, ضَعِيف ـ بِلَا قُوَّةٍ ـ عَاجِز *pl.* عَاجِزُونَ.

Strenuous, *a.* Vigorous, strong, of measures, *etc.*, شَدِيد. Bold and active, حَمِيس ـ أَلُوب ـ دَائِب ـ نَجِيد *pl.* نُجَدَآءُ ـ جَرِئ. Zealous, جَسُور ـ مُتَحَمِّس ـ غَيُور ـ مُتَعَصِّب. Strenuous efforts, صِدْقُ ٱلْمَسَاعِي. A — advocate for ..., غَيُورٌ عَلَى كَذَا ـ شَدِيدُ ٱلْغَيْرَةِ عَلَى كَذَا.

Strenuously, *ad.* بِجَهْدٍ ـ بِغَيْرَةٍ ـ بِجِدٍّ وَجَهْدٍ. *See also* Ardently, *ad.*

Strenuousness, *n.* Ardour, fervour, حَمَاسَة ـ أَلَب ـ حَرَارَة ـ رَغْبَة ـ غَيْرَة. *See also* Earnestness, *n.*

Stress, *n.* Force, شِدَّة ـ زَوْر. Urgency, importunity, إِلْحَاف ـ إِلْحَاح ـ لَجَاجَة. Pressure, constraining, تَضْيِيق. Accent, تَفْخِيمُ ٱلْحَرْفِ ـ هَمْزَة ـ نَبْرَة. Emphasis, تَفْظِيع. Stress of weather, زَوْبَعَة ـ نَوْء ـ فُرْطَنَة ـ قُوَّةُ ٱلنَّوْءِ. To lay — upon, of a matter, لَجَّ فِي ـ أَلَحَّ عَلَى ـ اِقْتَضَى. *See also under to* Insist, *v.i.*; *also under* Pressure, *n.*

Stretch, *v.t.* To draw out to greater length, مَطَّ [2] ـ جَذَبَ ـ اِجْتَذَبَ ـ مَدَّ [2]. To expand, وَسَّعَ ـ مَدَّ بِ ـ مَدَّ [2]. To lengthen, prolong, طَوَّلَ; in speech, بَالَغَ فِي ٱلْكَلَامِ ـ طَوَّلَ ٱلْكَلَامَ. To — out, as wings, carpets, *etc.*, بَسَطَ [2] ـ بَسَّطَ ـ مَدَّ [2]. He stretched out his leg, بَسَطَ رِجْلَهُ [2]. He stretched out his hands in prayer, بَسَطَ كَفَّيْهِ فِي ٱلدُّعَآءِ [2]. He stretched out his hand to the ground, أَبَدَّ يَدَهُ إِلَى ٱلْأَرْضِ. To — one's self, اِنْسَطَحَ ـ تَبَطَّحَ ـ تَمَدَّدَ. To be stretched out, expanded, اِنْبَسَطَ. To — one's self up, so as to reach or see, تَطَاوَلَ ـ تَطَالَّ. It was too narrow for one to — himself upon, قَصُرَ عَنِ ٱلتَّمَدُّدِ [2]. He was stretched upon the ground, سُطِحَ فِي ٱلْأَرْضِ. *See also to* Spread, *v.t.*

Stretch, *v.i.* To be extended, اِتَّسَعَ ـ اِمْتَدَّ. To be drawn out, extended by drawing, or to be dragged or trailed along, اِجْتَذَبَ. The branches of the tree stretched out, اِمْتَدَّتْ أَغْصَانُ ٱلشَّجَرَةِ.

Stretch, *n.* Extension, breadth, اِتِّسَاع ـ اِمْتِدَاد. Prolongation, تَطْوِيل. Effort, struggle, كَدّ ـ جَهْد ـ جِدّ ـ سَعْيٌ. Distance, مَسَافَة ـ مَسِيرَة. A —, excess, as of power, جَوْر ـ جَبْر ـ فَرْط. A — of the imagination, مُبَالَغَةٌ فِي ٱلتَّخَيُّلِ. A — of the imagination, تَعَدٍّ ـ ظُلْم. A —, or tack, of a ship; *see under* Tack, *n.* At a —, زَعْمٌ بَعِيدٌ. At a —, بِٱلْمَرَّةِ.

Stretcher, *n.* One who stretches, lays out or down, فَرَّاش ـ مُفَرِّش ـ مُبَسِّط. A plank, لَوْح *pl.* أَلْوَاح. A draw-plate, for wire, *etc.*, طَرِيدَة ـ مِسْقَن. An instrument for stretching, آلَةٌ مُوَسِّعَةٌ. A bier, نَعْش ـ سَرِير ـ عَرْش.

Strew, *v.t.* To scatter, spread, فَرَشَ [2]. To — with, فَرَشَ ـ بِ [2]. To be strewed, اِفْتَرَشَ. *See also to* Scatter, Spread, *v.t.*

Striæ, *n. pl.* خُطُوط.

Striate, *a.*
Striated, } مُخَطَّط. *See also* Streaked, *a.*

Stricken, *a.* As with a disease, مُصَابٌ بِ. Stricken with the palsy, مُصَابٌ بِٱلْفَالِجِ ـ مَفْلُوج. Stricken in days, old, مُتَقَدِّمٌ فِي ٱلْأَيَّامِ ـ طَاعِنٌ فِي ٱلسِّنِّ.

Strickle, *n.* مِقْشَط.

Strict, *a.* Exacting, imperative, مُتَشَدِّد. Accurate, exercising accuracy, مُدَقِّق ; correct, مُدَقَّق . Rigorous, severe, قَاسٍ ـ عَنِيف .

Strict, as in partisanship, مُتَعَصِّب ; in religious duties, أَحْمَس pl. حُمْس ـ مُتَحَمِّس . Very —, rigorous, أَعْنَف . A — search, تَفْتِيش مُدَقِّق . Strict neutrality, عَدَمُ ٱلتَّعَصُّبِ مَعَ أَحَدٍ ـ ٱلْخَصْمَيْنِ إِطْلَاقًا . جِيَادٌ كُلِّيٌّ . Strict laws, (قَوَانِينُ or) أَحْكَامٌ عَنِيفَةٌ . To be —, as in accounts, دَاقَّ ٱلنَّظَرَ فِي ٱلْحِسَابِ . To be — with one, as in accounts, etc., دَاقَّ-فِي . To be —, in religious duties, تَحَمَّسَ ـ ٤ حَمِسَ ; in paltry matters, أَدَقَّ .

— Strictly, ad. With exaction, بِتَشَدُّدٍ ; with accuracy, punctiliousness, بِتَدْقِيقٍ ; with rigour, بِعُنْفٍ . He examined — into his expenses, دَاقَّ ٱلنَّظَرَ فِي نَفَقَاتِهِ . It is copied strictly from the original, (حَرْفًا حَرْفًا or) مَنْسُوخٌ عَنِ ٱلْأَصْلِ بِتَدْقِيقٍ .

Strictness, n. Exaction, تَشَدُّد . Accuracy, minuteness, دِقَّة ـ تَدْقِيق ; as with another, as in accounts, etc., مُدَاقَّة . Rigour, harshness, عُنْف ـ جَوْر . Strictness in the observance of religion, حَمَاسَة ـ حَمَس . To treat one with —, rigour, عَسَّرَ عَلَى ـ عَاسَرَ ـ ٤ شَدَّ عَلَى .

Stricture, n. A criticism, إِنْتِقَاد ـ نَقْد . Censure, تَعْيِيب ـ تَقْبِيح ـ ذَمّ . A contraction, عُسْر ـ خَنْق ـ تَضْيِيق . A — of the urethra, عُسْرُ مَجْرَى ٱلْبَوْلِ ; of the womb, عُقْمُ ٱلرَّحِمِ ; of the chest, دَاءُ تَضْيِيقِ ٱلصَّدْرِ .

Stride, n. مُفَاجَة ـ فَجّ . To make long strides, ٢ مَشَى مُفَاجًا .

Stride, v.i. See to Straddle, v.i.

Stride, v.t. See to Straddle over, under to Straddle, v.i.

Stridor, n. صَرِير .

Stridulous, a. صَارّ .

Strife, n. مُخَاصَمَة ـ نِزَاع ـ شِقَاق ـ نِفَاق ـ مُنَازَعَة . To stir up —, هَيَّجَ ٱلْخِصَامَ ـ شَغَّبَ ـ أَلَّبَ . To stir up — among, أَلَّبَ ـ أَشَّبَ بَيْنَ ـ بَيْنَ . A — arose between them, ٤ حَدَثَتْ مُخَاصَمَةٌ بَيْنَهُمْ . There was —, contention, among them, كَانَتْ بَيْنَهُمْ مُشَاجَرَةٌ . See also under to Kindle, v.t.

Strifeful, a. أَلَدّ pl. لُدّ and لِدَاد . See also Contentious, a.

Strike, n. The ceasing from work, إِضْرَابٌ عَنِ ٱلْعَمَلِ ; the period of a —, مُدَّةُ ٱلْإِضْرَابِ عَنِ ٱلْعَمَلِ . A strickle, مِقْشَط . The direction of strata at the surface, خَطُّ طَبَقَةٍ مِنْ طَبَقَاتِ ٱلْأَرْضِ ٱلْمُشْرِفُ عَلَى سَطْحِهَا .

Strike, v.t. To hit, ٢ ضَرَبَ ـ ٢ لَطَمَ ـ ٢ صَدَمَ . To sound, as of a bell, أَجْرَسَ ; in a general sense, ٤ دَقَّ . To —, as with a stick, ٢ ضَرَبَ-بِ ـ ٤ لَطَأَ بِ ـ ٤ قَذَعَ-بِ ـ فَحَزَ-بِ ; with a sword, عَلَوْتُهُ بِٱلسَّيْفِ : I struck, or set upon him, with the sword, ٤ عَلَا بِ . To — and prostrate, صَرَعَ ـ ٤ صَرَعَ ـ أَهْبَطَ . To —, as a horse the ground with his feet, ٢ خَبَطَ . To hit, as an arrow, etc., a mark, أَصَابَ ـ ٢ ٤ لَاطَ بِ . To —, as the cords of a musical instrument, ٢ ضَرَبَ ـ ٢ نَدَفَ بِ . To strike one on the forepart of the head, صَقَعَ ـ ٤ صَقَعَ ; on the back part, صَفَعَ ـ ٤ صَفَعَ ; on the face, ٤ صَكَّ ; on the cheek, ٢ لَطَمَ ; on the neck or breast, وَكَزَ aor. يَكِزُ ـ ٤ لَكَزَ . To —, as of sails, نَزَّلَ ـ ٤ حَطَّ . To —, as of lightning, أَصَابَ ـ ٢ ضَرَبَ . To — one's self against, ٢ صَدَمَ . To — against one another, of numbers, تَصَادَمُوا . To — or dash together, ٤ صَدَعَ . To —, to coin, ٢ ضَرَبَ ٱلسِّكَّةَ .

To strike a balance, in accounts, قَابَلَ ٱلْحِسَابَاتِ ـ رَاجَعَ ٱلْحِسَابَ .

To strike a bargain, إِشْتَرَطَ عَلَى كَذَا . To strike a bargain with, شَارَطَ ـ ٢ ٤ شَرَطَ-عَلَى ; by clenching the hands, ٢ صَفَقَ عَلَى يَدِهِ ـ ٢ صَفَقَ يَدَهُ ـ ٢ صَفَقَ لِ ـ بِ .

To strike blind, أَعْمَى ـ عَمَّى ـ ٢ ضَرَبَ-بِٱلْعَمَى .

To strike colours, in submission, وَطَّأَ ٱلْبَيْرَقَ عَلَامَةَ ٱلْإِسْتِسْلَامِ .

To strike dead, ٢ ضَرَبَ-بِٱلْمَوْتِ ـ مَوْتَ-بَغْتَةً .

To strike down, ٤ صَرَعَ ـ أَوْقَعَ ـ أَهْبَطَ ـ ٤ حَطَّأَ بِ .

To strike fire, as with a flint and steel, ٢ زَنَدَ ٱلنَّارَ .

To strike the mind, ٢ خَطَرَ ـ ٤ خَطَرَ بِبَالِهِ ـ ٢ عَرَضَ لِ ـ ٤ بَدَا لِ عَلَى بَالِهِ . It struck me, خَطَرَ عَلَى بَالِي . It struck him, ٤ بَدَا لَهُ ـ خَطَرَ بِبَالِهِ ـ ٢ عَرَضَ لَهُ .

To strike off, as sheets for the press, ٤ طَبَعَ . To cut off, ٤ قَطَعَ .

To strike off the head, ٢ ضَرَبَ-رَقَبَتَهُ . To retrench, قَصَّرَ ـ قَلَّلَ . See also next article.

To strike out, to efface, ٤ شَطَبَ ـ ٢ طَلَسَ ـ ٤ مَحَا . To erase, remove, أَعْدَمَ ـ أَزَالَ ـ أَبْطَلَ . To invent, إِخْتَرَعَ ـ أَوْجَدَ .

To strike through, to pierce, أَنْفَذَ ـ ٤ شَقَّ .

To strike up, to begin, as of music, etc., إِبْتَدَأَ بِ ـ ٤ بَدَأَ بِ .

To strike with fear, هَوَّلَ ـ أَرْعَبَ ـ رَعَّبَ .

To strike with horror, أَدْهَشَ ـ أَرْعَدَ .

To strike one with, as with a malady, etc., of God, رَمَاهُ ٱللّٰهُ بِ .

To strike, as with a rod or bar, ٤ قَمَعَ ـ قَنَعَ ; with a whip, ٤ مَشَقَ ; with a shoe, ٢ خَفَقَ ; with a sword, ٢ ضَرَبَ ; with a knife, وَجَأَ aor. يَجَأُ ; with a stick, ٤ نَسَأَ ; with the fist, ٤ لَكَمَ .

To strike with surprise, بَادَهَ ـ ٤ بَدَهَ .

To strike with wonder, عَجَّبَ-بِ ـ عَجَّبَ .

To strike work, أَضْرَبَ عَنِ ٱلْعَمَلِ .

Strike, v.i. As of a workman from work, أَضْرَبَ عَنِ ٱلْعَمَلِ .

To —, as a bell, جَرَسَ 2 ـِ - إِنْجَرَسَ ; in a general sense, إِنْدَقَّ .

To take root, إِنْغَرَسَ - تَأَصَّلَ - إِسْتَأْصَلَ . To hit against, تَصَادَمَ .

To — colours, in submission, نَزَّلَ ٱلْبَيْرَقَ تَسْلِيمًا . To run aground, of a ship, ـَ لَطَمَ ٱلْمَرْكَبُ - جَنَحَتِ ٱلسَّفِينَةُ . The ship struck, عَطِبَتِ ٱلسَّفِينَةُ .

To strike in, دَخَلَ 2 - تَدَاخَلَ .

To strike inwardly, as of a disease, أَثَّرَ فِي بَاطِنِهِ .

To strike in with, to agree with, إِتَّحَدَ مَعَ - إِتَّفَقَ مَعَ .

Striker, *n.* One who strikes, ضَرَّابٌ - ضَارِبٌ . One who is on strike, مُضْرِبٌ عَنِ ٱلْعَمَلِ .

Striking, *a.* Surprising, غَرِيبٌ - عَجِيبٌ - مُعْجِبٌ - مُحَيِّرٌ .

Strikingly, *ad.* لِلْغَايَةِ - كَثِيرًا - عَجَبًا . *See also* Impressively, *ad.*

String, *n.* Hempen cord or thread, خَيْطُ قُنَّبٍ . Twine, خَيْطُ ٱلصُّبَارَةِ - مِصِّيصٌ ; *vulg.* دُبَارَة . A running string, in a dress or garment, تِكَّةٌ *pl.* تِكَكٌ - دِكَّةٌ *pl.* دِكَكٌ . A suite, set, جُمْلَةٌ - طَائِفَةٌ - صَفٌّ *pl.* صُفُوفٌ . A concatenation, سِلْسِلَةٌ . A — upon which beads, *etc.*, are strung, سِلْكَةٌ *coll.* سِلْكٌ *pl.* أَسْلَاكٌ *and* سُلُوكٌ ; a — with beads or such like on it, سِمْطٌ *pl.* سُمُوطٌ . A wire, سِلْكَةٌ *coll.* سِلْكٌ *pl.* أَسْلَاكٌ *and* سُلُوكٌ . A —, as of camels, mules, *etc.*, قِطَارٌ *pl.* قُطُرٌ *and* قُطُورَاتٌ . A — of a musical instrument, or of a bow, وَتَرٌ *pl.* أَوْتَارٌ ; of a bonnet, شَرِيطٌ *pl.* شَرَائِطُ ; of the tongue, رِبَاطُ ٱللِّسَانِ . A fibre, لِيفَةٌ *coll.* لِيفٌ *pl.* أَلْيَافٌ . A — or tendon, as in meat, عِرْقٌ *pl.* عُرُوقٌ . A bit of —, twine, جِتَّةُ مِصِّيصٍ (or دُبَارَةٍ) . In a —, one after another, وَاحِدٌ بَعْدَ وَاحِدٍ ; the people came in a —, جَاءَ ٱلْقَوْمُ عُرْفًا عُرْفًا - تَوَاتَرَ ٱلْقَوْمُ . To tie with a —, twine, رَبَطَ 2 ـُ (or حَزَمَ ـِ) بِمِصِّيصٍ (or بِدُبَارَةٍ) . To put a —, as into drawers, إِسْتَتَكَّ ٱلتِّكَّةَ .

String, *v.t.* To furnish with strings, رَكَّبَ شَرَائِطَ ; of a musical instrument, وَتَرَ *aor.* يَتِرُ . To pass on to a string, of beads, pearls, *etc.*, سَلَكَ 2 فِي - أَسْلَكَ فِي . To make tense, as of musical strings, *etc.*, أَوْتَرَ - وَتَّرَ - قَوَّى - شَدَّدَ . To strengthen, To excite, حَرَّضَ - هَيَّجَ . To — or hang upon, عَلَّقَ عَلَى ; as on a gallows, شَنَقَ 2 .

Stringed, *n.* Having musical strings, مُوَتَّرٌ - ذُو أَوْتَارٍ . Stringed instruments, مَعَازِفُ - أَوْتَارٌ .

Stringency, *n.* Pressure, ضَغْطٌ - عَصْرٌ - إِعْتِصَارٌ . Urgency, ضَرُورَةٌ - إِحْتِيَاجٌ - أَهَمِّيَّةٌ - لُزُومٌ . Strictness, جَبْرِيَّةٌ - جَبَرُوتٌ - تَشَدُّدٌ . *See also* Urgency, *n.*

Stringent, *a.* Pressing, urgent, لَازِمٌ - ضَرُورِيٌّ - مُهِمٌّ . Strict, حَاصِرٌ - عَنِيفٌ - جَبْرِيٌّ . Stringent measures, تَدَابِيرُ حَاصِرَةٌ (or ضَابِطَةٌ). *See also* Urgent, *a.*

String-halt, *n.* عُرْجَةٌ - دَآءٌ فِي عَرَاقِيبِ ٱلْخَيْلِ .

Stringiness, *n.* Ropiness, تَمَطُّطٌ - تَسَعُّبٌ .

Stringy, *a.* Ropy, مُتَمَطِّطٌ - مُتَسَعِّبٌ . *See also* Fibrous, *a.*

Strip, *v.t.* To uncover, كَشَفَ ـِ عَنْ - رَفَعَ ٱلْغِطَآءَ مِنْ . To deprive of, خَلَعَ ـَ عَنْ - نَزَعَ ـِ عَنْ - عَرَّى عَنْ - أَعْدَمَ . To take clothes off, خَلَعَ ـَ - فَسَخَ ـَ عَنْ لِبَاسَهُ - أَخْلَعَ ٱلثِّيَابَ . To make bare, naked, عَرَّى - أَعْرَى - شَلَّحَ - عَنْ . To — the bark off, قَشَرَ 2 - عَرَمَ ـُ - شَذَبَ ـُ - قَلَفَ - نَجَبَ . To flay, سَلَخَ 2 ـَ - سَلَقَ 2 . To —, as the meat from a bone, عَرَمَ 2 . To —, as leaves from a branch, شَطَبَ 2 . To —, to clear one out of his money in gambling, خَلَعَ ـَ مَالَ صَاحِبِهِ . To —, as the fruit from a tree, صَمَرَ ـُ - شَمَّرَ ـُ - شَمَلَ 2 - أَشْمَلَ . To — or make bare a part of the body by tucking up the garment, شَمَّرَ - شَمَّرَ عَنْ : he stripped his leg, شَمَّرَ عَنْ سَاقِهِ . To plunder, سَلَبَ 2 - نَهَبَ 2 . To — the dead or slain, عَرَّى ٱلْقَتْلَى . To — one's self, خَلَعَ ـَ ثِيَابَهُ - تَجَرَّدَ ; to — one's self naked, تَعَرَّى . To —, as of ornaments or arms, نَزَعَ ـِ . He stripped himself of his turban, حَسَرَ 2 عِمَامَتَهُ عَنْ رَأْسِهِ . She stripped off her shift from her body, حَسَرَتْ دِرْعَهَا عَنْ جَسَدِهَا . She stripped herself of her ornaments, نَزَعَتْ زِينَتَهَا . He stripped himself of his coat, خَلَعَ ـَ ٱلْجُبَّةَ ٱلَّتِي عَلَيْهِ . He stripped himself, tucked up his garments, as prepared to work, تَشَمَّرَ - تَحَبَّكَ . To be stripped, عَرِيَ *aor.* يَعْرَى - تَعَرَّى - تَجَرَّدَ .

Strip, *n.* A narrow shred, شِقَّةٌ *pl.* شِقَقٌ - خُبَّةٌ - خِبَّةٌ . A —, as of cloth, طِبَّةٌ *pl.* طِبَبٌ - طِبَابَةٌ - طَرِيدَةٌ *pl.* طَرَائِدُ . A long —, slice, خَبِيبَةٌ *pl.* خَبَائِبُ . A piece of skin stripped off, جِلْفَةٌ . A — of territory, بُقْعَةٌ *pl.* بِقَاعٌ . A — of skin or leather, a thong, strap, سَيْرٌ *pl.* سُيُورٌ *and* أَسْيَارٌ - شِرَاكٌ . A — of flesh meat, خَبِيبَةُ لَحْمٍ - شَطِيبَةٌ *pl.* شَطَائِبُ - شُوَيَّةٌ . A piece, جِلْفَةٌ *pl.* جِلَفٌ - جِتَّةٌ *pl.* جِتَتٌ . Strips of flesh on bones, or the strips that fall from trees, عُرَامٌ . To cut into strips, of meat, شَطَبَ 2 . He took or tore a — from his garment, إِخْتَبَّ مِنْ ثَوْبِهِ - إِخْتَبَّ ثَوْبَهُ خُبَّةً .

Stripe, *n.* A line of a different colour from the groundwork, حَبِيكَةٌ *pl.* حُبُكٌ - خَطٌّ *pl.* خُطُوطٌ - قَلَمٌ *pl.* أَقْلَامٌ - طَرِيقَةٌ *pl.* طَرَائِقُ ; in a mat, وَشِيعَةٌ *pl.* وَشَائِعُ . A blow, ضَرْبَةٌ *pl.* ضَرَبَاتٌ ; the mark of a blow, rod, حَبَكٌ - حَبَطٌ *pl.* حُبُوطٌ - حَبَرٌ *pl.* حُبُورٌ - حَدَبٌ *pl.* حُدُوبٌ . A stroke, misfortune, آفَةٌ - مُصِيبَةٌ - بَلِيَّةٌ . A punishment, عِقَابٌ - مُجَازَاةٌ . The Stars and Stripes, the American flag, بَيْرَقُ جَمَاهِيرِ أَمِيرِكَا ٱلْمُتَّحِدَةِ . *See also* Streak, *n.*

Stripe, v.t. To mark or weave with stripes, سَيَّرَ ـ حَبَّكَ ـ قَلَّمَ ـ شَطَّبَ ـ خَطَّطَ. *See also to* Streak, *v.t.*

Striped, a. مُقَلَّم ـ مُحَبَّك ـ مُشَطَّب ـ مُخَطَّط.

Stripling, n. غُلَام *pl.* غِلْمَان ـ جِذْع *pl.* جِذْعَان *and* أَجْذَاع.

Strippings, n. The last milk drawn from an udder, آخِرُ الشَّخْبِ.

Strive, v.i. To make effort, كَدَحَ ـ ² كَدَّ ـ سَعَى *aor.* يَسْعَى ـ ² جَهَدَ ـ بَادَرَ إِلَى ـ تَعَنَّى ـ تَعَمَّلَ ـ اِجْتَهَدَ ـ تَجَاهَدَ. To do one's best, بَذَلَ جُهْدَهُ ². To contend, to struggle with another, جَادَلَ ـ نَازَعَ ـ شَاجَرَ ـ خَاصَمَ ـ مَاحَكَ. The two men strove together, تَخَاصَمَا الرَّجُلَانِ. The men strove together, تَخَاصَمَ الرِّجَالُ. They strive about words, يَتَمَاحَكُونَ بِالْكَلَامِ. To — to be before, to excel, سَابَقَ.

To strive against, دَافَعَ ـ قَاوَمَ ـ جَاهَدَ ضِدَّ كَذَا.

To strive for, to strive to earn for, سَعَى ل *aor.* يَسْعَى. To exert one's self in, أَكَبَّ عَلَى ـ تَجَاهَدَ فِي.

To strive with, to co-operate with, تَجَاهَدَ مَعَ.

Striver, n. One who makes efforts, مُجَاهِد ـ شَحْشَحَان ـ بَاذِلُ الْجُهْدِ ـ مُجْتَهِد.

Strobil, n. خَرِيطَةٌ فِي هَيْئَةِ جَوْزِ الصَّنَوْبَرِ.

Stroke, n. A striking of one thing against another, مُصَادَمَة ـ مُلَاطَمَة. A single shock, collision, صَدْمَة ـ لَطْمَة. A blow, ضَرْبَة *pl.* ضَرَبَات. A — that cuts off at once, ضَرْبَةٌ بِكْرٌ. A line, خَطّ *pl.* خُطُوط. An event befalling one, صَدْمَة. An affliction, بَلِيَّة ـ بَلَآء ـ مُصِيبَة ـ آفَة. A movement, as of a machine, حَرَكَة *pl.* حَرَكَات. The — of an oar, قَذْفَة ـ جَذْفَة. A — or touch of, خَطْرَة ـ خَبْطَة. I settled the two affairs at one —, أَتَيْتُ عَلَى الْأَمْرَيْنِ صَدْمَةً وَاحِدَةً. At a —, بِالْمَرَّةِ ـ مَرَّةً ـ بِضَرْبَةٍ.

A back stroke, with the back of the hand, لَطْمَةٌ بِظَهْرِ (*or* بِقَفَا) الْكَفِّ; a piece of treachery, خِيَانَة.

A bye stroke, a stroke unintentionally, لَطْمَةٌ عَرَضِيَّةٌ.

A thick stroke, of a pen, قَلَمٌ ثَخِينٌ.

A thin stroke, of a pen, قَلَمٌ رَفِيعٌ.

To be on the stroke of, of an hour, أَشْرَفَ عَلَى السَّاعَةِ الْفُلَانِيَّةِ; of striking the hour, تَوَّةَ تَدُقُّ السَّاعَةُ ـ ² كَادَتْ تَدُقُّ السَّاعَةُ.

To do a good stroke of business, أُوفِقَ فِي عَمَلِهِ.

To keep stroke, in rowing, of many, جَذَفُوا عَلَى فَوْرٍ ـ قَذَفُوا سَوِيَّةً.

Stroke, v.t. To rub gently, طَبْطَبَ ل. To caress, لَاطَفَ ـ ² لَطَفَ بِ. *See also to* Blandish, *v.t.*

Strokesman, n. Of oars, رَئِيسُ النَّوَاتِيَةِ ـ مُقَدَّمُ الْقَذَّافِينَ.

Stroll, v.i. To take a stroll, تَسَيَّرَ ـ تَنَزَّهَ ـ ² خَرَجَ يَتَبَسَّطُ ـ ² شَمَّ الْهَوَآءَ ـ تَمَشَّى. *See also to* Roam, *v.i.*

Stroll, n. A walk, ramble, رِيَاضَة ـ سَيَرَان ـ شَمّ هَوَآء. *See also* Roam, *n.*

Stroller, n. / Strolling, a. } A wanderer, roamer, عَائِر ـ عَيَّار. A loiterer, بَطِيّ ـ مُتَوَانٍ. A vagabond, ضَالِل ـ مُطَرَّش. A — musician, نَوْبَاتِيّ دَائِر ـ آلَاتِيّ جَائِل ـ هَامِل. *See also* Roamer, Rambler, *n.*

Strombus, n. ضَرْبٌ مِنَ الصَّدَفِ.

Strong, a. Puissant, having power, ذُو عِزَّةٍ ـ عَزِيز ـ ثَابِر ـ قَوِيّ الْاِقْتِدَارِ ـ قَدِير. Hardy, خَشِيب ـ خَشِب. Not easily subdued, resisting, قَوِيّ ـ ظَهِير. Effective, فَعَّال ـ مُؤَثِّر. Bulky, fat, جَسِيم. Strong, of a liquor, قَوِيّ ـ مُسْكِر. Hot to the palate, as of tobacco, *etc.*, حَامّ ـ *vulg.* حُمُومِيّ. Bright, as of a light, لَامِع. Tough, coarse, مَتِين ـ ثَخِين ـ جَافٍ *pl.* جُفَاة. Impetuous, مُتَهَوِّر ـ غَضُوب. Violent, شَدِيد. Healthy, in constitution, مُتَعَافٍ ـ مُعَافٍ. Robust, قَوِيّ ـ صُلْب ـ ضَلِيع *pl.* أَقْوِيَآء ². A man — for war, رَجُلٌ قَوِيّ لِلْحَرْبِ. Having a — smell, زَنِخ. Well fortified, مُحَصَّن ـ مُسْتَحْكَم ـ مَنِيع. Bold, courageous, شُجَاع ـ شَجِيع ـ بَطَل. Firm, compact, lasting, ثَابِت ـ مَتِين ـ مُحْكَم ـ تَمِيم ـ مُؤَيَّد ـ رَصِين ـ مُرَصَّص. A — building, بِنَآء رَصِين. There was no place too — for us, لَمْ يَكُنْ مَكَانٌ قَدِ امْتَنَعَ عَلَيْنَا. I am as — to-day as I was last year, لَمْ أَزَلِ الْيَوْمَ مُتَشَدِّدًا كَمَا فِي السَّنَةِ الْمَاضِيَةِ. When he saw that they were too — for him, لَمَّا رَأَى أَنَّهُمْ أَشَدُّ مِنْهُ. The battle is not to the —, الْحَرْبُ لَيْسَ لِلْأَقْوِيَآءِ. Stronger by nature, أَشَدُّ خَلْقًا. To be —, firm, ² رَصُنَ. To wax —, تَقَوَّى ـ تَشَدَّدَ. To make —; *see to* Strengthen, *v.t.* *See also under* Powerful, *a.*

Strong city, مَدِينَةٌ مُحَصَّنَةٌ.

Strong drink, شَرَابٌ مُسْكِرٌ: He spent his substance in —, أَنْفَقَ مَالَهُ فِي الْمُسْكِرَاتِ.

Strong food, meat, طَعَامٌ قَوِيٌّ.

Strong hand, يَدٌ قَوِيَّةٌ.

Strong people, أُمَّةٌ قَوِيَّةٌ.

Strong voice, صَوْتٌ عَظِيمٌ.

Strong wind, رِيحٌ عَاصِفٌ.

Stronger, a. أَقْوَى ـ أَشَدُّ. Stronger than all the fortifications of the country, أَمْنَعُ (*or* أَمْتَنُ) مِنْ جَمِيعِ حُصُونِ الْبِلَادِ. "Stronger by nature," أَشَدُّ خَلْقًا (Kur. xxxvii. 11.) In like manner the comparative Arabic form is applicable to the other adjectives under Strong, *a.*

Strongest, *a.* الأَقْوَى ـ الأَشَدّ. (See note to the preceding article.)

Stronghold, *n.* حِصْن *pl.* حُصُون ـ مَعْقِل *pl.* مَعَاقِل.

Strongly, *ad.* Mightily, بِقُوَّةٍ ـ بِشِدَّةٍ ـ عِزَّةً ـ بِعِزَّةٍ. With strength, بِحَيْلٍ. Emphatically, بِشِدَّةِ ٱلتَّعْبِيرِ ـ بِبَلَاغَةٍ. Effectually, تَأْثِيرًا. Firmly, بِٱسْتِحْكَامٍ ـ بِرُسُوخٍ ـ بِمَتَانَةٍ ـ رَصَانَةً. Strenuously, بِٱجْتِهَادٍ ـ بِجَهْدٍ. Importunately, بِلَجَاجَةٍ. Roughly, of a wind, بِعُصُوفٍ ـ عَصْفًا. Strongly made, compacted, رَصِين ـ مُرَصَّص. The wind blew —, violently, عَصَفَتِ ٱلرِّيحُ.

Strong-minded, *a.* Fearless, undaunted, بَطَل ـ شَهْم ـ جَسُور ـ جَرِيء ـ شُجَاع. Masculine, of a woman, إِمْرَأَةٌ فَحْلَةٌ ـ مُذَكَّرَة.

Strontian, *n.* مَادَّةٌ كَاوِيَةٌ.

Strop, *n.* For sharpening; *see under* Strap, *n.*

Strop, *v.t.* To sharpen on a strop; *see under to* Strop, *v.t.*

Strophe, *n.* *See* Stanza, *n.*

Strow, *v.t.* *See to* Strew, *v.t.*

Struck, *pret. and part. of to* Strike, *v.t.*, *q.v.*

Structural, *a.* مُتَعَلِّقٌ بِٱلْبِنَآءِ ـ مُنَاطٌ بِٱلتَّرْتِيبِ ـ مَا نِيطَ ـ بِٱلنَّظْمِ ـ تَرْتِيبِيٌّ ـ تَرْكِيبِيٌّ ـ نَسَقِيٌّ.

Structure, *n.* The act of constructing, بِنَآء ـ تَعْمِير. A building, بِنَآء *pl.* أَبْنِيَة *and* بُنْيَان ـ عِمَارَة *pl.* عَمَائِر. A style of building, بِنْيَة. Form, make, هَيْئَة *pl.* هَيْآت ـ صُورَة *pl.* صُوَر. Arrangement, تَرْتِيب ـ نَسَق ـ تَرْكِيب.

Struggle, *v.i.* To be disquieted, troubled with, عَنِيَ بِ *aor.* يَعْنَى ـ تَعَنَّى بِ. To —, as for one's family, دَافَعَ عَنِ ٱلْعِيَالِ. To strive, كَدَّ ² ـ إِجْتَهَدَ. To —, fight, as in battle, عَارَكَ ـ قَاتَلَ ـ تَحَارَبَ. To — with, as in argument, شَاجَرَ ـ عَانَى. They struggled together, of many, تَعَارَكُوا. To — against misfortune, عَارَكَ ٱلدَّهْرَ. I am struggling in your affair, أَنَا مَعْنِيٌّ بِحَاجَتِكَ. I am struggling, in distress, difficulty, أَنَا عَنٍ. He struggled against the difficulty, or distress, which he experienced from him or it, قَاسَاهُ ـ تَعَنَّاهُ ـ عَانَاهُ.

Struggle, *n.* Pain, distress, عَنَآء ـ عَنِيَّة ـ إِضْطِرَاب. A wrestling, مُصَارَعَة. A combat, مُعَارَكَة. Strong effort, جِدٌّ وَجَهْدٌ ـ إِجْتِهَاد. A great difficulty, distress, عَنَآءٌ عَانٍ. Without a —, movement, pain, بِلَا وَجَعٍ ـ بِلَا حَرَكَةٍ.

Struggler, *n.* One who is disquieted and struggles under it, مَعْنِيٌّ ـ عَنٍ. A wrestler, مُصَارِع. One who strives, endeavours, شَحْشَحَان ـ صَاحِبُ كَدٍّ ـ صَاحِبُ ٱجْتِهَادٍ ـ مُجَاهِد.

Struggling, *a.* As under difficulty or distress, مَعْنِيٌّ ـ عَنٍ ـ عَانٍ. Striving, endeavouring, مُجَاهِد ـ مُجْتَهِد ـ سَاعٍ.

Struggling, *n.* *See* Struggle, *n.*

Struma, *n.* *See* Scrofula, *n.*

Strum, *v.i.* To hum, as of a song, تَنَغَّمَ. To — on, as on an instrument, دَقَّ ² ـ دَقْدَقَ.

Strumous, *a.* *See* Scrofulous, *a.*

Strumpet, *n.* عَاهِرَة ـ سُوقَة. *See also* Prostitute, *n.*

Strung, *part. of to* String, *v.t.*, *q.v.*

Strut, *n.* تَزَابٍ ـ تَغَطْرُس ـ تَخَطُّل ـ حُيُوك ـ حِيَاكَة ـ مِشْيَةٌ حَيَّاكَةٌ.

Strut, *v.i.* As in walking, تَخَطَّلَ ـ تَكَفَّى فِي مَشْيَتِهِ ـ تَزَابَى ـ تَغَطْرَسَ ـ حَاكَ فِي مِشْيَتِهِ ـ *aor.* يَحِيكُ حَاكَ.

Struthious, *a.* مِثْلَ ٱلزَّرَافَةِ ـ مُتَعَلِّقٌ بِٱلزَّرَافَةِ.

Strutter, *n.* }
Strutting, *a.* } مُتَغَطْرِس ـ حَيْكَانَة ـ حَيَّاكَة ـ حَيَّاك.

Strychnia, *n.* }
Strychnine, } خُلَاصَةُ جَوْزِ ٱلْقَيْءِ.

Stub, *n.* *See* Stump, Log, *n.*

Stub, *v.t.* إِسْتَأْصَلَ. *See also* To root up, *under to* Root, *v.t.*

Stubbed, *a.* مَرْبُوع ـ مُكَبْتَل ـ قَصِيرٌ ثَخِينٌ ـ قَلَهْزَم.

Stubbedness, *n.* رَبْعَة ـ رَبْع ـ تَكَبْتُل ـ قِصَرٌ مَعَ ثُخْنٍ.

Stubble, *n.* The stumps of wheat, *etc.*, left in the ground, جِلٌّ ـ قَشّ ـ هَشِيم ـ حَصَاد ـ حَصِيدَة. Dry grass, قَشّ ـ هَشِيم.

Stubborn, *a.* Obstinate, مَارِد *pl.* مَرَدَة ـ مُعَانِد ـ مَرِيد *pl.* مُرَدَآءُ ـ خَشِن ـ شَكِس *pl.* شُكْس ـ وَعِق ـ فَرَطِيّ ـ صِعَاب *pl.* صَعْب ٱلْجَانِبِ. To be —, شَكِسَ ـ عَانَدَ ـ لَا يَسْمَعُ ٱلنِّدَآءَ وَلَا يَبْتَغِي ٱلْاِهْتِدَآءَ. A — way, طَرِيقٌ قَاسٍ. A — generation, جِيلٌ مَارِدٌ. A — horse, حِصَانٌ جَمُوحٌ. *See also* Obstinate, Refractory, *a.*

Stubbornness, *n.* Obstinacy, تَمَرُّد ـ وَعْقَة ـ شَكَاسَة; of a horse, جُمُوح ـ جِمَاح. *See also* Obstinacy, Refractoriness, *n.*

Stubby, *a.* Full of stubs, كَثِيرُ ٱلْجَذَامِيرِ ـ كَثِيرُ ٱلْأَجْذَالِ. *See also* Stubbed, *a.*

Stub-nail, *n.* مِسْمَارٌ مُكَبْتَل ـ مِسْمَارٌ قَصِيرٌ ثَخِينٌ ـ مِسْمَارٌ غَلِيظٌ.

Stucco, *n.* The plaster, جَصّ ـ مَعْجُونُ ٱلْمَرْمَرِ ـ *called in Egypt*, خَانِقِيّ; work made of —, شُغْلُ ٱلْجَصِّ ـ شُغْلُ ٱلْخَانِقِيِّ.

Stucco, *v.t.* جَصَّصَ ـ لَبَّسَ بِٱلْخَانِقِيِّ ـ دَمَّمَ بِمَعْجُونِ ٱلْمَرْمَرِ.

Stuck; *see to* Stick, *v.t.* and *i.*

Stud, *n.* An ornamental button, جُمَانَة *coll.* جُمَان *pl.* جُمَانَات. A button, زِرّ *pl.* أَزْرَار. A — of horses, طَوَالَةُ خَيْلٍ ـ إِصْطَبْلُ خَيْلٍ.

.طائفةُ خَيْلٍ فِى مَرْبَطٍ وَاحِدٍ ـ رِبَاطٌ مِنَ ٱلْخَيْلِ ـ إِصْطَبْلَات *pl.*
A large-headed nail, .مِسْمَارٌ بِرَأْسٍ كَبِيرٍ

Stud, *v.t.* To adorn with studs, رَصَّعَ ـ(or) زَيَّنَ ـ) ـ رَصَّعَ ـ جُمَانَاتٍ
.بِجُمَانَاتٍ To set, as with jewels, *etc.*, رَصَّعَ: Studded with jewels, مُرَصَّعٌ بِٱلْجَوَاهِرِ; with lamps, .مُرَصَّعٌ بِٱلْقَنَادِيلِ

Studding-sail, *n.* .إِسْقُوبَامَار

Topmast studding-sail, .قُورْدِلِيجَة

Topgallant studding-sail, .قُورْدِلِيجِين

Studding-sail boom, .مَشَافُورَة

Student, *n.* One who studies, طَالِبُ عِلْمٍ *pl.* طُلَّاب *and* طَلَبَة ـ
.مُدَرِّس ـ طَالِبُ ٱلْعِلْمِ A — who studies with another, مُقَارِئٌ ـ
.مُدَارِس A disciple, or a schoolboy, تِلْمِيذ *pl.* تَلَامِيذُ *or* تَلَامِذَة.
A — of Mákkah, مُجَاوِر *pl.* .مُجَاوِرُونَ

Studentship, *n.* The time of being a student, دَوْرُ ٱلدَّرْسِ; an allowance for a student, .رَاتِبُ ٱلْمُدَرِّسِ

Studied, *a.* Well read, لَوْذَعِيٌّ ـ عَلِيم ـ عَالِم *pl.* عُلَمَاء ـ مُدَرَّس.
Intentional, .عَنْ قَصْدٍ ـ عَنْ عَمْدٍ One who uses — language, .مُتَفَنِّن Studied language, أَفَانِينُ ٱلْكَلَامِ ـ كَلَامٌ دَقِيقٌ. Not studied, of language; *see* Unstudied, *a.*

Studiedly, *ad.* Attentively, بِدَوَرَانِ بَالٍ ـ بِتَدْقِيقٍ ـ بِٱنْتِبَاهٍ;
designedly, قَصْدًا ـ عَمْدًا; with studied language, .بِتَفَنُّنٍ ـ تَفَنُّنًا

Studier, *n.* *See* Student, *n.*

Studio, *n.* بَيْت ـ مَحَلّ ـ مُحْتَرَف ـ مَحْرَف; of a painter,
.مَحْرَفُ ٱلنَّقَّاشِ; of a sculptor, مُحْتَرَفُ (or مَحْرَفُ) ٱلْمُصَوِّرِ

Studious, *a.* Given to study, كَثِيرُ ٱلْمُطَالَعَةِ ـ مُدَرِّس. Attentive,
.وَاعٍ عَلَى ـ نَظُور ـ لَبِيب Contemplative, مُتَأَمِّل. Planned with care, .سِدَاد Careful, solicitous, .مُحْتَرِص

Studiously, *ad.* .بِجِدٍّ وَجَهْدٍ ـ بِجِدٍّ ـ بِمُطَالَعَةٍ *See also* Studiedly, *ad.*

Studiousness, *n.* Much study, .كَثْرَةُ مُطَالَعَةٍ ـ ٱلدَّرْسُ ٱلْكَثِيرُ
Zeal, application to anything, غَيْرَةٌ عَلَى ـ جَهْدٌ فِى ـ مُلَازَمَة ـ
.مُوَاظَبَةٌ عَلَى ـ إِدْمَانٌ عَلَى

Study, *n.* As of books, *etc.*, مُطَالَعَة ـ دَرْس ـ دِرَاسَة. Much —,
.ٱلدَّرْسُ ٱلْكَثِيرُ Application to books or science, دَرْسُ ٱلْعُلُومِ ـ
.مُمَارَسَةُ دَرْسِ ٱلْعُلُومِ ـ مُمَارَسَةُ ٱلدَّرْسِ Close application,
.جِدٌّ فِى أَمْرٍ ـ مُلَازَمَة ـ مُمَارَسَة Examination, investigation,
.مُطَالَعَة ـ تَدْقِيق ـ تَفْتِيش ـ بَحْث Attention, إِمْعَان ـ حِرْص ـ
.بَال ـ نَظَر Endeavour, .كَدّ ـ إِجْتِهَاد ـ جَهْد ـ سَعْي An object aimed at, .غَايَة ـ نِيَّة ـ غَرَض ـ مَطْلَب A room for —,
.مَكْتَب ـ مِدْرَس An object for —, as a painting, statue, *etc.*, to
.إِنْتِكَار ـ فِكْر A brown —, .قَاعِدَةٌ لِلدَّرْسِ ـ تَعْلِيم ـ دَرْس be in a brown —, .غَرِقَ فِى بَحْرِ ٱلْأَفْكَارِ To be wholly devoted to —, .تَفَرَّغَ لِلدَّرْسِ ـ إِنْهَمَكَ فِى بَحْرِ ٱلْعُلُومِ To make it one's —,
.يَسْعَى *aor.* سَعَى فِى ـ إِجْتَهَدَ فِى ـ جَدَّ فِى [2]

Study, *v.i.* To read books, *etc.*, دَرَسَ ٱلْعِلْمَ ـ [2] دَرَسَ ٱلْكُتُبَ ـ [2]
.طَالَعَ ٱلْكُتُبَ To endeavour diligently, كَدَّ [2] ـ سَعَى *aor.* يَسْعَى ـ
.إِجْتَهَدَ ـ تَجَاهَدَ To — to obtain, acquire, حَرَصَ عَلَى [2] ـ
.تَأَمَّلَ ـ تَفَكَّرَ To reflect, إِحْتَرَصَ عَلَى. He studied to become a learned man, حَرَصَ أَنْ يَصِيرَ عَالِمًا [2]. He studied to reply,
.تَفَكَّرَ بِٱلْجَوَابِ

Study, *v.t.* As of books, طَالَعَ ـ [2] دَرَسَ. To examine into,
.إِسْتَبْحَثَ عَنِ ـ بَحَثَ ـ تَبَحَّثَ عَنِ ـ بَحَثَ فِى ـ عَقَلَ
To be addicted, given, to a thing, لَهِجَ بِ. To devise, إِخْتَرَعَ ـ
.إِبْتَدَأَ To — evil against, زَبَى لِ ـ بِشَرٍّ ـ زَبَى ـ شَرًّا. To pursue with diligence, شَبَكَ ـ [2] حَرَصَ عَلَى ـ وَاظَبَ عَلَى ـ مَارَسَ
.إِهْتَمَّ بِ ـ ٱلْعَقْلَ فِى

Stuff, *n.* Things in general, .أَشْيَآءُ Matter, substance, مَادَّة ـ
.جَوْهَر ـ أَصْل ـ مَاهِيَّة Goods in general, بِضَاعَة ـ أَمْتِعَة ـ سِلَع.
Furniture, utensils, .أَثَاث Cloth, قُمَاش; woollen —, قُمَاش
.صُوف A drug, عَقَّار *pl.* .عَقَاقِيرُ A mass, as of rubbish, سُقَاط ـ
.دَشْت ـ عَفْش *vulg.* سَقَطُ ٱلْمَتَاعِ Detritus, .جُفَآءُ Anything made up into a mass, .مَعْجُون Stuff for stuffing, .حَشْوٌ Anything worthless, .شَيْءٌ بَطَّالٌ ـ سَقَط ـ سُقَاطَة Nonsense, عَبَث ـ
.أَنْوَاعُ طَحِينٍ Bread —, .كَلَامٌ مِنْ غَيْرِ مَعْنًى Silly —, تَفَاهَة ـ
.مَسْخَرَة ـ تَخْرِيفَة Nasty —, of words or writing, كَلَامٌ خَنِي ـ
.سَقَطُ ٱلْكَلَامِ

Stuff, *v.i.* To feed gluttonously, شَرِدَ ـ حَلْقَمَ ـ لَهِمَ ـ نَهِمَ ـ
.يَحْشُو *aor.* حَشَا رُوحَهُ

Stuff, *v.t.* To fill or thrust in, as stuffing into a pillow or into a fowl, *etc.*, حَشَا *aor.* يَحْشُو. To cram, to overfill, .أَفَاضَ ـ أَطَفَّ
To —, as with food, .أَشْبَعَ ـ أَنْعَمَ ـ بِ ـ أَبْشَمَ To —, as a room with people, حَشَرَ [2] ـ زَحَمَ ـ أَغَصَّ. To —, as hay, *etc.*, into an animal's mouth, صَفَرَ. To — up, سَدَّ [2]. To be stuffed, of a pillow, fowl, *etc.*, .إِحْتَشَى ـ أَنْحَشَى To be stuffed, with food, .إِحْتَشَى أَكْلًا ـ بَشِمَ ـ فَقِمَ ـ إِكْتَظَّ To be stuffed, as a room with people, غَصَّ بِ ـ شَرِقَ بِ; as a wound with blood, or pores with perfume, *etc.*, .شَرِقَ بِ The man was stuffed with wrath and pride, .حُشِيَ ٱلرَّجُلُ غَيْظًا وَكِبْرًا The food stuffed him, .كَظَّهُ ٱلطَّعَامُ [2]

Stuffed, *a.* As of a pillow, food, *etc.*, مَحْشِيّ ـ مَحْشُوّ; as a room with people, غَاصٌّ ; as with food, مُكْتَظٌّ (or مُحْتَشٍ) مِنَ ٱلطَّعَام . A — bed, حَشِيَّة pl. حَشَايَا .

Stuffing, *n.* In a general sense, حَشْوٌ pl. مَحَاشٍ ; as with food, كِظَّة . *See also* Padding, *n.*

Stuffy, *a.* *See under* Close, *a.*

Stultification, *n.* The act of, تَغْلِيط ـ تَضْلِيل ـ تَسْفِيه ـ تَجْهِيل ; of one's self, سَفَه ـ سَفَاهَة ـ سَفَاة .

Stultify, *v.t.* جَهَّلَ ـ حَمَّقَ ـ غَلَّطَ ـ ضَلَّلَ ـ سَفَّهَ . To — one's self, كَذَّبَ نَفْسَهُ ـ سَفَّهَ رَأْيَهُ ـ سَفَّهَ نَفْسَهُ ـ ² سَفُهَ ـ ² سَفِهَ .

Stum, *n.* عَصِيرُ ٱلْعِنَبِ غَيْرُ مُخَمَّر .

Stum, *v.t.* جَدَّدَ ـ بِٱلتَّخْمِير .

Stumble, *v.i.* As in walking, تَعَثَّرَ ـ ² عَثَرَ ; to — and fall, ² تَعِسَ ـ ² تَعَسَ . To err, ² زَلَّ . To — in speech, ² عَثَرَ فِي كَلَامِهِ ـ ² سَقَطَ (or أَسْقَطَ) ; to — in speech, as making a mistake, أَعْثَقَلَ لِسَانُهُ فِي كَلَامِهِ . To — upon, as upon one's garment, ² عَثَرَ فِي ثِيَابِهِ . To light upon by chance, ٱلْتَقَى بِ ـ ² عَثَرَ عَلَى or بِ .

Stumble, *v.t.* To cause to —, عَثَّرَ ـ أَعْثَرَ . To cause to err, أَزَلَّ ـ ضَلَّلَ . To confound, puzzle, حَيَّرَ ـ أَدْهَشَ .

Stumble, *n.* As in walking, *etc.*, عَثْرَة ; a — with a fall, تَعْس . A fall, سَقْطَة ـ سِقَاط . An error, زَلَّة ـ سَقَط ـ سُقُوط ـ خَطَأ .

Stumbler, *n.* }
Stumbling, *a.* } عَاثِر ـ عَثُور .

Stumbling-block, *n.* } عَاثُور ـ عِثَار pl. عَوَاثِير . A cause of
Stumbling-stone, } tripping, slipping, مَزَلَّة .

Stumblingly, *ad.* عَثْرَةً ـ تَعَثُّرًا ; coming upon in an unexpected manner, ٱلْتِقَاطًا .

Stump, *n.* Of a tree, the lowest part thereof, جِذْل pl. أَجْذَال ـ أَصْل ـ سَاق ـ جُذْمُور or جُذْمَار pl. جَذَامِير . A — left in the ground, جُذْمُور pl. جَذَامِير . The remaining part of a limb cut off, قِطْعَة pl. قِطَع ; of a tooth, قِطْعَة سِنَّة ; of the ears, lips, nose, جَدَعَة ; of the leg, عَرَجَة . The — of a pen, جُذْمُورُ قَلَم . The — of a wicket, عُودٌ مِنْ عِيدَانِ ٱلْهَدَفِ فِي لَعِبِ ٱلصَّوْلَجَانِ وَٱلْكُرَة . A place for haranguing for a stump-orator, مَوْقِفُ ٱلْبَقَّاق . A — for drawing, قَلَمُ طَبَاشِير pl. أَقْلَام . To stir one's stumps, ² خَفَّ ـ ² نَشِطَ ـ تَحَرَّكَ .

Stump, *v.t.* To harangue, خَاطَبَ . To draw with a —, ² رَسَمَ بِقَلَمِ ٱلطَّبَاشِير . To — a wicket, أَصَابَ عِيدَانَ ٱلْهَدَفِ فِي لَعِبِ ٱلصَّوْلَجَان . To — up, of money, أَخْرَجَ ـ تَنَقَّدَ ٱلنَّقْدَ ٱلدَّرَاهِم .

Stump-orator, *n.* مُتَكَلِّمٌ مِهْذَار ـ خَطِيبٌ بَقَّاق ـ بَقَّاق .

Stumpy, *a.* Full of stumps, كَثِيرُ ٱلْجَذَامِير . Short and strong, of any animal, جِنْزَاب ـ قَلَهْزَم ; A — woman, حُبَيْكَة . Short and bulky, of a person, حَادِر ; of anything, عُكْمُص .

Stun, *v.t.* As with a blow, دَوَّخَ ; with noise, صَدَّعَ . To stupefy so as to prevent from moving, أَعْقَرَ . To — with surprise, أَبْطَرَ ـ أَدْهَشَ ـ حَيَّرَ . It, the sound, stunned the ear, أَصَخَّ (or ² صَخَّ) ٱلْأُذُنَ . The sound of the mill-stone stunned me, صَدَّعَنِي أَزِيزُ ٱلرَّحَى . His hearing was stunned, ² صَرَّ صِمَاخُهُ . To be stunned, as with a blow, ٱنْدَاخَ ـ يَدُوخُ *aor.* دَاخَ ; as with noise, صُدِّعَ ; so as not to move, ² عَقِرَ ; with surprise or fright, ² بَحِرَ ـ ² بَطِرَ ـ ² دَهِشَ ـ تَحَيَّرَ . *See also to* Stupefy, *v.t.*

Stunning, *a.* Of a blow, مُدَوِّخ ; so as to prevent moving, مُعْقِر ; of noise, مُصَدِّع ; of surprise, مُحَيِّر ـ مُدْهِش ـ مُبْطِر ; to the ears, صَاخّ .

Stung, *pret. and part.* مَلْسُوع ـ لَسِيع . *See to* Sting, *v.t.*

Stunk, *pret. of to* Stink, *v.i.*, *q.v.*

Stunt, *v.t.* To hinder from growth, of youth, ² قَصَعَ ; in a general sense, ² حَجَزَ عَنِ ٱلنَّمَاءِ (or ٱلنُّمُوِّ) ـ ² مَنَعَ عَنِ ٱلنَّشَاءَة .

Stunted, *a.* Of youth, مَقْصُوع ـ قَصِيع ; in a general sense, مَحْجُوزٌ عَنِ ٱلنُّمُوِّ ـ مَمْنُوعٌ عَنِ ٱلنَّشَاءَة . To become stunted, without power, ² عَجِزَ . Stunted speech, رِكَّةُ كَلَام ـ تَهْذَار ـ هَذَر .

Stupe, *v.t.* *See to* Foment, *v.t.*

Stupefaction, *n.* A senseless state, فُتُور ـ عَقَر . A state of astonishment, ٱنْذِهَال ـ حَيْرَة ـ تَحَيُّر ـ طَيْشَان ـ بَطَر . Stupefaction, as from shame, دَعَر .

Stupefactive, *a.* } Causing insensibility, مُفْتِر ـ مُعْقِر ; causing
Stupefactor, *n.* } astonishment, مُدْهِش ـ مُحَيِّر ـ مُبْطِر .

Stupefied, *a.* مَعْقُور ـ عَقِير ; as from shame or fright, مَدْعُور .

Stupefy, *v.t.* To reduce to senselessness, أَفْتَرَ ـ أَعْقَرَ ـ عَاقَرَ . To astonish, ² أَخَذَ عَقْلَهُ ـ حَيَّرَ ـ أَدْهَشَ . To frighten, ² دَعَرَ ـ أَدْعَرَ . To be stupefied, senseless, ² فَتَرَ ـ ² عَقِرَ . The wine stupefied him, عَاقَرَتِ ٱلْخَمْرُ عَقْلَهُ . I am so stupefied that I am unable to talk, عَقِرْتُ حَتَّى مَا أَقْدِرُ عَلَى ٱلْكَلَام .

Stupendous, *a.* Very great, كَبِيرٌ جِدًّا ـ عَظِيمٌ جِدًّا . Wonderful, غَرِيب ـ عَجِيب . Stupendous events, أَهْوَال . *See also* Huge, Marvellous, *a.*

Stupendously, *ad.* In a wonderful manner, عَجَبًا ـ بِنَوْعٍ عَجِيب ; greatly, بَتَّةً ـ جِدًّا ـ لِلْغَايَة .

Stupendousness, *n.* Greatness, عَظَامَة ـ عِظَم ; wonderfulness, غَرَابَة .

Stupid, *a.* عَرِيضُ ٱلْوِسَادِ ـ سَفِيه ـ أَخْدَبُ ـ أَخْرَقُ ـ هِبَل ـ بَلَادَة ـ بَلِيد ـ أَحْمَقُ ـ ثَقِيل ـ غَبِين. A — action, حَمَاقَة. A — fellow, حِمَار ـ تَيْس. To be — about, غَبِيَ عَن. *See also* Heavy, Sluggish, *a.*

Stupidity, *n.* / Stupidness, } سَفَه ـ غَبَاوَة ـ غَبًا ـ خَدَب ـ خُرْق ـ هَوَج ـ تَيْسِيَّة ـ غَبَانَة ـ مَجَانَة عَقْل ـ حُمْق ـ بَلَادَة ـ تُيُوسِيَّة. *See also* Sluggishness, Senselessness, *n.*

Stupidly, *ad.* بِقِلَّةِ عَقْلٍ ـ بِغَبَاوَةٍ ـ بِبَلَادَةٍ ـ بِخُرْقٍ.

Stupor, *n.* Torpidity, خُدْرَة ـ خَدَر; from astonishment, دَهْشَة ـ حَيْرَة. To be affected with —, numbness; also from wine, خَدِرَ.

Stuprate, *v.t.* *See* to Ravish, *v.t.*

Stupration, *n.* *See* Ravishment, *n.*

Sturdily, *ad.* بِصَرَامَةٍ ـ بِقُوَّةٍ ـ بِصَلَابَةٍ ـ بِشَهَامَةٍ.

Sturdiness, *n.* مُرُوءَة ـ مَتَانَة ـ ضَلَاعَة ـ صَلَابَة ـ شَهَامَة.

Sturdy, *a.* Robust, blunt, صَارِم *pl.* صَوَارِمُ ـ جَلْد ـ عَلِج ـ عِلْج ـ شَهْم *pl.* شِهَام ـ شَدِيد ـ قَوِيّ ـ صُلْب. To be —, شَهُمَ ² صَلُبَ. To act in a — manner, تَصَلَّبَ. To make —, جَلَّدَ ـ صَلَّبَ.

Stutter, *v.i.* إِرْتَبَكَ فِي كَلَامِهِ ـ فَأْفَأَ ـ تَعْتَعَ ـ فَدِمَ ². *See also* to Stammer, *v.i.*

Stutter, *n.* / Stuttering, } فَأْفَأَة ـ تَعْتَعَة ـ فَدَم. *See also* Stammer, *n.*

Stutterer, *n.* / Stuttering, *a.* } مُتَعْتِع ـ أَلْكَنُ. *See also* Stammerer, *n.* Stammering, *a.*

Sty, *n.* The pustule on the eyelid, وَدَقَة ـ غَرَب *pl.* غُرُوب ـ جُلْجُل فِي جَفْنِ ٱلْعَيْنِ ـ خَضْبَة ـ بَخْصَة ـ قَمَع. A pen for swine, زَرِيبَة لِلْخَنَازِيرِ. *See also* Brothel, *n.*

Sty, *v.a.* زَرَبَ ² (or أَزْرَبَ) ٱلْخَنَازِيرَ.

Stygian, *a.* مُتَعَلِّقٌ بِٱلْغَيِّ (وَهُوَ ٱلنَّهْرُ ٱلْمَوْهُومُ بِهِ فِي جَهَنَّمَ). *See also* Infernal, *a.*

Style, *n.* A manner of writing, composing, إِنْشَاء ـ إِصْطِلَاح ـ قَلَم ـ نَصّ ـ نَظْم ـ عِبَارَة. Manner of reckoning time, حِسَابُ ٱلتَّوَارِيخِ. A name, appellation, لَقَب *pl.* أَلْقَاب ـ إِسْم *pl.* أَسَامِي. A —, as of a dial, مِيل *pl.* أَمْيَال. A — for applying antimony to the eyelids, مِكْحَل ـ مِكْحَال. Manner, طَرْز ـ زِيّ ـ كَسْم ـ طَرِيقَة ـ مِدَاد ـ أُسْلُوب. Fashion, costume, زِيّ. A custom, عَادَة *pl.* عَوَائِدُ. A — to write with, مِلْمُول ـ مِرْقَم ـ قَلَم *pl.* أَقْلَام. A kind, quality, جِنْس *pl.* أَجْنَاس ـ نَوْع *pl.* أَنْوَاع ـ ضَرْب. Style, pomp, فَخْر ـ بَهَاء ـ سَلْطَنَة ـ إِخْتِيَال. To live in —, عَاشَ مِثْلَ ٱلسَّلَاطِينِ ـ تَرَفَّهَ ـ تَنَعَّمَ مُتَرَفِّهًا.

His —, of writing, is eloquent, قَلَمُهُ عِبَارَتُهُ بَلِيغٌ.

New style, of reckoning dates, ٱلْحِسَابُ ٱلْمِيلَادِيُّ ـ ٱلْحِسَابُ ٱلْإِفْرَنْجِيُّ.

Old style of reckoning dates, ٱلْحِسَابُ ٱلرُّومِيُّ.

Style of the al-Hijrah, ٱلْحِسَابُ ٱلْهِجْرِيُّ.

Style, *v.t.* لَقَّبَ ـ بِ ـ سَمَّى ـ سَمَّى ـ بِ. To be styled, تَسَمَّى بِ ـ تَلَقَّبَ بِ.

Stylet, *n.* *See* Stiletto, *n.*

Stylish, *a.* Fashionable, بِحَسَبِ ٱلْعَادَةِ. Showy, gaudy, زَاهٍ ـ مُتَفَاخِر ـ جَلِيّ.

Stylite, *n.* One of the Pillar-saints, لَقَبُ نَاسِكٍ مِنْ نُسَّاكِ ٱلنَّصَارَى فِي ٱلدِّيَارِ ٱلشَّامِيَّةِ كَانُوا يَتَنَسَّكُونَ عَلَى رَأْسِ عَمُودٍ.

Styloid, *a.* فِي شَكْلِ ٱلْمِيلِ.

Styptic, *a.* / Styptical, } قَاطِعُ (ٱلدَّمِ) ـ مُقَبِّض ـ قَابِض. *See also* Astringent, *a.*

Styptic, *n.* دَوَاء قَابِض ـ عَقُول.

Styx, *n.* نَهْرُ ٱلْغَيِّ ـ ٱلْغَيُّ وَادٍ مَوْهُوم بِهِ فِي جَهَنَّمَ.

Suable, *a.* إِسْتِدْعَاؤُهُ إِلَى ٱلْمَحْكَمَةِ جَائِزٌ ـ يُحَاكَمُ.

Suasible, *a.* *See* Persuasible, *a.*

Suasion, *n.* *See* Persuasion, *n.*

Suasive, *a.* / Suasory, } *See* Persuasive, *n.*

Suaviter in modo, fortiter in re, بِثَبَاتٍ وَرِفْقٍ.

Suavity, *n.* لَطَافَة ـ ظَرَافَة ـ مَلَاحَة ـ حَلَاوَة ـ رِفْق.

Sub, *n.* *See* Subaltern, *n.*

Sub-acid, *a.* حَامِضٌ بَعْضَ ٱلْحُمُوضَةِ ـ حَامِضٌ نَوْعًا.

Sub-acrid, *a.* حِرِّيفٌ بَعْضَ ٱلْحَرَافَةِ ـ حِرِّيف (or حَادٌّ) نَوْعًا.

Sub-aerial, *a.* فِي ٱلْفَضَاءِ ـ تَحْتَ ٱلْجَوِّ.

Subah, *n.* ٱلصُّوبُ وَهُوَ عِبَارَةٌ عَنِ ٱلْوِلَايَةِ عِنْدَ أَهْلِ ٱلْهِنْدِ.

Subahdâr, *n.* The Indian governor of a province, إِسْمُ ٱلْوَالِي عِنْدَ أَهْلِ ٱلْهِنْدِ. The native officer in India so called, حَائِزُ رُتْبَةِ قَائِدِ ٱلْمِئَةِ فِي عَسْكَرِيَّةِ ٱلْهِنْدِ.

Sub-alpine, *a.* كَائِنٌ دُونَ جِبَالِ ٱلْأَلْبَا.

Subaltern, *a.* Inferior, as in rank, دُون ـ أَدْنَى ـ أَسْفَل.

Subaltern, *n.* مُلَازِمٌ عَسْكَرِيٌّ.

Sub-aquatic, *a.* / Sub-aqueous, } Being under the surface of the water, كَائِنٌ (or وَاقِعٌ) تَحْتَ وَجْهِ ٱلْمَاءِ; growing under the water, نَابِتٌ تَحْتَ وَجْهِ ٱلْمَاءِ.

Sub-astral, *a.* Under the stars, كَائِنٌ ـ وَاقِعٌ تَحْتَ ٱلْفَلَكِ ـ تَحْتَ ٱلنُّجُومِ. Terrestrial, دُنْيَوِيّ ـ عَالَمِيّ.

Sub-astringent, *a.* عفص بعض العفوصة ـ عفص نوعا ـ قابض نوعا .

Sub-base, *n.* Of the organ, أخفض بم الأرغن .

Sub-basement, *n.* أساس ـ وطائد .

Sub-committee, *n.* مجلس مفرز ـ مجلس دون .

Sub-contract, *n.* جزء من معاهدة (*or* كنتراتو) على عمل .

Sub-contractor, *n.* آخذ جزء من معاهدة (*or* كنتراتو) على عمل .

Sub-deacon, *n.* شماس رسائلي ـ شدياق .

Sub-divide, *v.t.* قسم الجزء أجزاء ـ قسم المقسوم .

Sub-division, *n.* The act of, تقسيم الجزء أجزاء ـ تقسيم المقسوم ; the being subdivided, قسم من قسمة ـ جزء من جزء .

Subduable, *a.* مما يغلب ـ مما يقمع .

Subdue, *v.t.* To bring into subjection, قهر ـ أقمع ـ قمع ـ جعل تحت الطاعة . To conquer by superior force, to overcome, تغلب على ـ غلب على ـ قهر . To humble, abase, of the action of a thing, as hunger, *etc.*, خضع ـ ضعضع ـ أخضع . To take, capture, as a town, *etc.*, فتح ـ ضبط . To oblige, force, غصب على ـ ألزم ـ سخر ـ اضطر إلى . To tame, أنس ـ أقمع ـ قفع ـ طوع . To get possession of, to rule over, إستولى على . To — by persuasion, أقنع . To master, علا على *aor.* يعلو ـ إستعلى على . To repress, زجر ـ منع ـ حكم . To —, or restrain one's self from, as from smiling, *etc.*, تقفع عن ـ تماسك عن ـ حبس نفسه عن ـ تحبس عن . To soften, melt, as into compassion, لين ـ حنن . To lighten, خفف . To be subdued, brought into subjection, انقمع ; to be overcome, as by superior force, انغلب ـ غلب ; to be humbled, إختضع ـ انخضع ـ خضع ; to be taken, captured, إفتتح ; to be reduced by persuasion, إقتنع . Time, or fortune, subdued him, تضعضع به الدهر ـ ضعضعه الدهر .

Subdued, *a.* Brought into subjection, مقهور ; overcome, مغلوب ; abased, humbled, مخضوع ـ متضعضع . Lowly, submissive, مطيع ـ خاضع . Low, as of a voice, خفيض . A — voice, صوت خفيض . Subdued speech, كلام مخفوض .

Subduer, *n.* One who subdues, overcomes, قاهر ـ مقمع ـ غالب ; one who captures, as of a town, فاتح ; who often captures, فتاح ; that which destroys the force of anything, مزيل ـ مبطل .

The Subduer, God, الفتاح .

Sub-genus, *n.* فرع من جنس .

Sub-globular, *a.* كري نوعا .

Subitaneous, *a.* *See* Instantaneous, Sudden, *a.*

Subito, *ad.* عبارة عن السرعة في الموسيقى ـ سريعا .

Subjacent, *a.* واقع تحت كذا ـ دون ـ تحتاني ـ كائن تحت الشيء .

Subject, *a.* Under authority, تحت الطاعة ـ تابع ـ تحت حكم ; under the management of one, في تصرف فلان ; in the possession of such an one, في ضبط فلان ـ تحت يد فلان ; under the operation of such a thing, تحت تأثير كذا . Liable to, مسلط عليه كذا ـ محل ل ـ متعرض ل . Subject matter, المبحوث عنه . Subject to the approval of, على خيار (*or* خيرة) فلان ـ باستحسان فلان ـ موقوف على خيرة فلان . Subject to fits, محل للصرع ـ يتسلط عليه الصرع . Subject to extreme heat, يحكم فيه الحر الشديد . All men are — to death, كل نفس ذائقة الموت . *See also* Liable, *a.*

Subject, *n.* As of a state, رعية *pl.* رعايا ـ تابع *pl.* تبع *and* تباع *and* تبع ـ تحت حكومة كذا . A —, as of a discourse, المبحوث عنه ـ باب *pl.* أبواب ـ صدد ـ محط ـ موضوع ـ قضية *pl.* قضايا ; *in rhetoric*, لازم . A matter, مادة *pl.* مواد ـ أمر *pl.* أمور ـ شيء *pl.* أشياء ـ خصوص . That on which anything, as an argument, *etc.*, is framed, مبنى . The point upon which a — turns, مدار . A substance, جوهر ـ ذات . The —, as of a contract, مشروط فيه . The — of a proposition, in logic, الموضوع ـ المحمول عليه ; of a story, أحدوثة . On this —, في هذه المادة ـ في هذا الصدد ـ في هذا الباب . We shall return to that — to which our attention is directed, نرجع إلى ما نحن بصدده . An English —, أحد رعية الإنكليز . The subjects of a state, رعايا مملكة . The King and his subjects, الملك ورعيته . Subject and attribute, in logic, الجوهر والعرض ; in grammar, المبتدأ والخبر .

A subject of contention, dispute, مدار النزاع .

A subject for discussion, موضوع للمباحثة فيه .

A subject for dissection, a corpse, جثة للتشريح .

A subject for examination, as for passing in any study, باب للإمتحان .

Subject, *v.t.* To oblige, to reduce to, to necessitate, اضطر إلى ـ ألزم ب . To drive to, جبر على ـ أضر إلى ـ ضر إلى . To bring upon, جلب على . It subjected him to poverty, ضره (*or* اضطره) إلى الفقر . It subjected him to the anger of the governor, جلب عليه غيظ الحاكم . To make accountable, ضمن ـ لزم ب . To be subjected, forced, driven to, اضطر إلى ـ التزم ب . For the other signification *of to* Subject, *see under to* Subdue, *v.t.*

Subjection, *n.* إِطَاعَة ـ إِنْقِيَاد ـ خُضُوع. To bring into —; *see to* Subject, *v.t.*

Subjective, *a.* Internal, in the mind, ضَمِيرِيٌّ ـ ذِهْنِيٌّ ـ ذَاتِيٌّ ـ دَاخِلِيٌّ ـ بَاطِنِيٌّ.

Subjectively, *ad.* فِي ٱلْبَاطِنِ ـ ذِهْنًا ـ فِي ٱلضَّمِيرِ.

Subjectiveness, *n.* / Subjectivity, } دَاخِل ـ بَاطِن ـ بَاطِنُ ٱلْأَمْرِ.

Subjoin, *v.t.* أَضَافَ-إِلَى ـ أَلْحَقَ-بِ ـ يَصِلُ *aor.* وَصَلَ-بِ ـ أَلْحِقَ بِ ـ إِتَّصَلَ بِ ـ إِسْتَدْرَكَ-عَلَى. To be subjoined to, إِنْضَافَ إِلَى. *See also to* Add, *and to* Supplement, *v.t.*

Subjoined, *a.* مُلْحَقٌ بِ ـ مُتَّصِلٌ بِ ـ مَوْصُولٌ بِ ـ مُضَافٌ إِلَى.

Subjugate, *v.t.* أَخْضَعَ ـ قَهَرَ. *See also to* Subdue, *v.t.*

Subjugation, *n.* The act of, إِخْضَاع ـ قَهْر; the being subjugated, إِنْقِيَاد ـ طَاعَة. *See also* Subjection, *n.*

Subjunction, *n.* وَصْل ـ إِلْحَاق ـ إِضَافَة.

Subjunctive, *a.* Subjoined, مُلْحَقٌ بِ ـ مَوْصُول بِ ـ مُتَّصِل ـ مُضَافٌ إِلَى. The — mood, الفِعْلُ ٱلْمَجْزُومُ. *See also under* Conjunctive, *a.*

Sub-librarian, *n.* أَمِينُ قَيِّمِ ٱلْكُتُبِ ـ مُعَاوِنُ أَمِينِ خِزَانَةِ كُتُبٍ.

Sub-lieutenant, *n.* مُلَازِمٌ ثَانٍ.

Sublimate, *v.t.* Chemically, صَعَّدَ. To be sublimated, صُيِّدَ.

Sublimate, *n.* The product of sublimation, مَادَّةٌ مُصَعَّدَةٌ. Corrosive —, سُلَيْمَانِيٌّ ـ زِئْبَقٌ مُصَعَّدٌ أَكَّالٌ.

Sublime, *a.* Lofty, شَامِخٌ ـ مُرْتَفِع ـ عَالٍ ـ عَلِيٌّ. Grand, great, excellent, جَلِيل ـ سَامٍ ـ سَنِيٌّ ـ رَفِيع ـ فَائِق *pl.* فُوقَاءُ. A — orator, خَطِيبٌ سَلَّاقٌ ـ خَطِيبٌ مِسْلَقٌ. Sublime, untaught eloquence, كَلَامٌ سَلِيقِيٌّ. Such an one rises to — things, فُلَانٌ طَلَّاعُ ٱلثَّنَايَا.

Sublime, *n.* The highest conceptions, أَعَالِي ـ مَعَالِي ٱلتَّخَيُّلَاتِ ـ ٱلتَّصَوُّرَاتِ. To strive after the —, سَعَى فِي طَلَبِ أَعْجَازِ ٱلْإِبِلِ ـ سَنَا إِلَى مَعَالِي ٱلْأُمُورِ.

Sublimely, *ad.* بِسَنَاءٍ ـ بِنَوَاتٍ ـ بِٱرْتِفَاعٍ ـ بِطَوْرٍ عَالٍ.

Sublimeness, *n.* / Sublimity, } Height, loftiness, إِرْتِفَاع ـ شُمُوخَة ـ عُلُوٌّ. Excellence, grandness, عَظَامَة ـ سَنَاءٌ ـ رِفْعَة ـ سُمُوٌّ.

Sublineation, *n.* وَضْعُ خَطٍّ تَحْتَ ٱلْكَلَامِ.

Sub-lingual, *a.* مِنْ تَحْتِ ٱللِّسَانِ.

Sublunar, *a.* / Sublunary, } Under the moon and firmament, تَحْتَ ٱلْقَمَرِ ـ تَحْتَ ٱلْفَلَكِ. Terrestrial, عَالَمِيٌّ ـ أَرْضِيٌّ ـ دُنْيَوِيٌّ.

Submarine, *a.* كَائِنٌ تَحْتَ ٱلْبَحْرِ. Growing in the sea, نَابِتٌ فِي ٱلْبَحْرِ. Marine, بَحْرِيٌّ.

Submerge, *v.t.* To — in, أَغْرَقَ-فِي ـ غَرَّقَ-فِي ـ مَغَثَ-فِي. To be submerged, غَرِقَ ـ إِسْتَغْرَقَ. *See also under to* Plunge, *v.t.*

Submersion, *n.* The act of, تَغْرِيق ـ إِغْرَاق ـ مَغْث; the being submerged, إِسْتِغْرَاق ـ غَرَق.

Submission, *n.* Surrender, resignation, إِسْتِسْلَام ـ تَسْلِيم. Odedience, إِنْقِيَاد ـ إِطَاعَة ـ طَاعَة. Humble behaviour, خُضُوع ـ تَوَاضُع ـ إِخْضَاع. Abject —, هَوَان ـ تَضَعْضُع. To reduce to —, طَوَّعَ. With all —, سَمْعًا وَطَاعَةً ـ عَلَى ٱلرَّأْسِ وَٱلْعَيْنِ.

Submissive, *a.* Obedient, طَائِع ـ مِذْعَان ـ مُذْعِن ـ مُعَبَّد ـ مُتَوَاضِع ـ خَاضِع ـ أَخْضَع ـ مُنْقَاد ـ خَاشِع ـ مُطِيع. Humble, Submissive to misfortune, طَوْعُ ٱلْمَكَارِهِ. To be —, resigned, إِسْتَسْلَمَ ـ أَسْلَمَ ـ أَسْمَحَ. To be —, humble, تَخَشَّعَ ـ أَخْشَعَ ـ تَوَاضَعَ ـ تَذَلَّلَ ـ إِخْتَضَعَ. To make one's self — to, تَضَعْضَعَ لِ. To make —, طَوَّعَ ـ عَبَّدَ. *See also* Resignation, *n.*

Submissively, *ad.* With resignation, بِٱسْتِسْلَامٍ ـ تَسْلِيمًا; with obedience, بِٱنْقِيَادٍ ـ إِذْعَانًا ـ بِإِطَاعَةٍ. Humbly, بِخُضُوعٍ ـ إِذْعَانًا ـ بِٱلتَّوَاضُعِ ـ بِخُشُوعٍ ـ بِتَضَعْضُعٍ.

Submissiveness, *n.* مُسَامَحَة ـ خُشُوع ـ ضَعْضَعَة ـ تَضَعْضُع ـ إِطَاعَة ـ خُضُوع ـ إِذْعَان. *See also* Submissive, *n.*

Submit, *v.i.* To surrender, أَسْلَمَ ـ إِسْتَسْلَمَ. To be or become lowly or submissive, تَذَلَّلَ ـ يَذِلُّ *aor.* ذَلَّ ـ يَعْنُو *aor.* عَنَا ـ تَضَعْضَعَ ـ خَضَعَ. To — or yield to, as to an enemy, conqueror, إِسْتَسْلَمَ لِ ـ أَسْلَمَ لِ ـ إِسْتَأْسَرَ لِ. To — to, as in obedience, أَقَرَّ إِلَى ـ أَذْعَنَ لِ ـ يَطِيعُ *aor.* طَاعَ لِ ـ إِنْقَادَ إِلَى. To acquiesce in, قَبِلَ ـ رَضِيَ بِ ـ قَنَعَ إِلَى ـ أَقَرَّ إِلَى. To — or resign one's self, تَصَبَّرَ عَلَى ـ صَبَرَ عَلَى ـ إِسْتَسْلَمَ ـ أَسْلَمَ. To — to, to refer one's case to, تَعَرَّضَ لِ. He submitted to superior force, أَذْعَنَ لِلْقُوَّةِ ٱلْجَابِرَةِ. The young should — to the elder, وَاجِبٌ عَلَى ٱلْأَحْدَاثِ أَنْ يَخْضَعُوا لِلشُّيُوخِ. He submitted himself to, obeyed, the orders of the governor, إِمْتَثَلَ بِأَمْرِ ٱلْحَاكِمِ. *See also under to* Resign, *v.t.*

Submit, *v.t.* To refer any matter to, عَرَضَ-عَلَى ـ أَوْرَدَ-عَلَى. To — anything to, as to an authority for adjudication, رَافَعَ-إِلَى ـ رَفَعَ-إِلَى: I submitted the matter to the Sultan, رَفَعْتُ ٱلْأَمْرَ إِلَى ٱلسُّلْطَانِ. To — to one for an opinion, إِسْتَفْتَى: They submitted it to the opinion of the Sharif of Mákkah, إِسْتَفْتَوْا شَرِيفَ مَكَّةَ. *See also under to* Refer, *v.t.*

Sub-nascent, *a.* نَابِتٌ مِنْ تَحْتِ كَذَا.

Subordinacy, *n.* The being inferior, كَوْنُ ٱلشَّيْءِ – إِدَانَة – دُون دُونَ غَيْرِهِ. Dependence, إِنْقِيَاد – إِطَاعَة – طَاعَة.

Subordinate, *a.* Inferior in order, rank, *etc.*, دُون; specially of rank, أَحَطُّ رُتْبَةً. Of less importance, أَقَلُّ ضَرُورَةً (or عِظَمٍ or أَهَمِّيَّةٍ). As being connected with, مَنُوطٌ بِ – تَابِع – تَبَع – مُتَعَلِّقٌ بِ. As being under the authority of one, تَحْتَ يَدِهِ – تَحْتَ سُلْطَانِهِ – تَحْتَ حُكْمِهِ. He is —, inferior, in rank to him, هُوَ دُونَهُ – هُوَ أَحَطُّ مِنْهُ رُتْبَةً. Zaid is —, below, inferior to, you, زَيْدٌ دُونَكَ. "Of us are the righteous, and of us are a party subordinate to that party," مِنَّا ٱلصَّالِحُونَ وَمِنَّا دُونَ ذَٰلِكَ (Kur. lxxii. 11.) *See also under* Dependent, *a.*

Subordinate, *n.* تَابِع *pl.* تَبَع *and* تُبَّاع. A subordinate official, مَأْمُورٌ مِنْ دُونٍ. An assistant, مُعِين.

Subordinately, *ad.* In a lower order, مِنْ دُونٍ; in a lesser degree, فِي أَدْنَى دَرَجَةٍ; with less care, بِأَقَلِّ ٱهْتِمَامٍ (or ٱعْتِنَاءٍ).

Subordination, *n.* State of subjection, إِنْقِيَاد – إِطَاعَة. State of being inferior, الكَوْنُ مِنْ دُونٍ. *See also* Subordinacy *and* Dependence, *n.*

Suborn, *v.t.* To get to swear falsely, دَسَّ[2] لِ-أَنْ يَشْهَدَ بِٱلزُّورِ. To bribe, بَرْطَلَ – رَاشَى.

Subornation, *n.* The act of secretly seducing for a bad purpose, دَسّ – تَدْسِيس; of corrupting, إِفْسَاد; of bribing, مُرَاشَاة – بَرْطَلَة.

Suborner, *n.* One who gets another to spy out or do something underhand for him, جَاسُوس – دَاسُوس *vulg.* دِسِّيس. One who bribes, مُبَرْطِل – رَاشٍ.

Sub-oval, *a.* بَيْضِيٌّ نَوْعًا.

Sub-pena, *n.* }
Sub-pœna, } أَمْرٌ بِٱلْحُضُورِ إِلَى – إِحْضَارٌ أَمَامَ ٱلْقَاضِي مُحَاكَمَة – ٱلْمَحْكَمَةِ. *See also* Citation, *n.*

Sub-pena, *v.t.* }
Sub-pœna, } دَعَا[2]-إِلَى ٱلشَّرْعِ – إِلَى (-طَلَبَ[2] or-) حَاكَمَ ٱلْمَحْكَمَةِ. *See also to* Cite, *v.t.*

Sub-rector, *n.* مُعَاوِنُ ٱلْمُدِيرِ.

Subrogation, *n.* تَوْكِيل – إِقَامَةُ أَحَدٍ مَقَامَ غَيْرِهِ – إِنَابَة.

Sub-rosa, ad. سِرًّا – خُفْيَةً – عَلَى خَفَاءٍ.

Sub-salt, *n.* مِلْحٌ كَثِيرُ أُسِّ ٱلْمِلْحِ.

Subscribe, *v.t.* To sign with one's hand, أَمْضَى – عَلَّمَ عَلَى – وَقَّعَ عَلَى. To attest, certify, حَقَّقَ – نَعِمَ[4] بِ. To consent, رَضِيَ[4] بِ – اِرْتَضَى بِ – قَبِلَ[4]. To give to, gratuitously, as to a benevolent undertaking, *etc.*, أَعْطَى-مُتَبَرِّعًا. *See also to* Sign, *v.t.*

Subscribe, *v.i.* To give gratuitously, تَبَرَّعَ بِٱلْعَطَاءِ. To — to, to admit, رَضِيَ[4] بِ – قَبِلَ[4]. To approve of, اِسْتَحْسَنَ. To — to, to take a share in, اِشْتَرَكَ فِي. To give one's name to or for, قَيَّدَ ٱسْمَهُ لِ.

Subscriber, *n.* One who signs his name, مُوَقِّع – مُمْضٍ; one who subscribes, as to a newspaper, *etc.*, مُشْتَرِك *pl.* مُشْتَرِكُونَ; one who subscribes gratuitously, مُكْتَتِبٌ تَبَرُّعًا; one who enters his name, مُقَيِّدُ ٱسْمِهِ.

Subscription, *n.* A signature, إِمْضَاء – تَوْقِيع. The subscribing, as to a newspaper, *etc.*, اِشْتِرَاك; as to a loan, اِكْتِتَاب. A gratuitous —, عَطَاءٌ تَبَرُّعًا. Terms of —, ثِبَات; price of —, قِيمَةُ ٱلِٱشْتِرَاكِ. The despatch of the journal to him will be stopped as soon as the term of his — ends, يُوقَفُ إِرْسَالُ ٱلْجَرِيدَةِ إِلَيْهِ بِمُجَرَّدِ ٱنْقِضَاءِ مُدَّةِ ٱشْتِرَاكِهِ.

Sub-section, *n.* جُزْءٌ مِنْ جُزْءٍ.

Subsequence, *n.* تَعَقُّب – تَوَلٍّ – تَوْلِيَة – خِلْفَة – خَلَف.

Subsequent, *a.* Following, مُتَتَابِع – مُتَعَاقِب – عَاقِب – تَالٍ. Next, آتٍ – مُقْبِل – قَابِل. *See also* Following, *a.*

Subsequently, *ad.* After, مِنْ بَعْدُ – بَعْدُ. Thereafter, فِيمَا بَعْدُ. *See also* Afterwards, *ad.*

Subserve, *v.t.* To serve instrumentally, to be useful to, صَلَحَ[2] أَسْعَفَ – سَاعَدَ – أَعَانَ. To assist, أَفَادَ – نَفَعَ[4] لِ – لِ.

Subservience, *n.* } Use to an end, إِفَادَة – نَفْع – مَصْلَحَة – طَائِل.
Subserviency, } Dependence, connection, عَلَاقَة – تَعَلُّق.

Subservient, *a.* Useful, as to promote an end, صَالِحٌ – طَائِلٌ لِ نَافِعٌ لِ – مُفِيدٌ لِ – لِ. Subordinate, دُون. Submissive, خَاضِع – مُتَوَاضِع – خَاشِع.

Subserviently, *ad.* In a way to aid, نَفْعًا – إِفَادَةً – بِطَائِلٍ. *See also* Submissively, *ad.*

Subside, *v.i.* To sink or fall to the bottom, as a sediment, رَاخَ *aor.* يَرُوخُ – رَسَبَ[2]. To be allayed, خَمَدَ[2] – سَكَنَ[2]. To become calm, أَخْمَدَ – حَلُمَ[2] – سَكَنَ[2] – تَهَدَّأَ. The fever subsided, خَمَدَتِ ٱلْحُمَّى. The heat subsided, رَكَدَ[2] ٱلْحَرُّ. To make to —, fall to the bottom, رَسَّبَ – رَوَّخَ. To make to —, to be allayed, سَكَّنَ – رَكَّدَ – خَمَّدَ.

Subsidence, *n.* The act of sinking to the bottom, رَسْب – سَوْخ – رُسُوب. Cessation, اِنْقِطَاع – زَوَال – تَوَقُّف.

Subsidiary, *a.* In aid of, اِمْتِدَادِيٌّ – مُسَاعِد – مُعَاوِن. Additional, إِضَافِيٌّ.

Subsidiary, *n.* A helper, نَاصِر *pl.* أَنْصَار – مُعَاوِن – مُسَاعِد – مُغِيث.

Subsidize, *v.t.* To grant a subsidy to, in money, أَعْطَى-إِعَانَةً (or مُسَاعَفَةً) نَقْدِيَّةً. To — a journal, أَعْطَى إِعَانَةً لِجَرِيدَةٍ لِأَجْلِ مُظَاهَرَتِهَا إِيَّاهُ.

Subsidy, *n.* In money, مُسَاعَدَةٌ نَقْدِيَّةٌ ـ إِعَانَةٌ نَقْدِيَّةٌ. A war —, إِعَانَةٌ حَرْبِيَّةٌ.

Sub-sign, *v.t.* وَقَّعَ تَحْتَ تَوْقِيعِ غَيْرِهِ.

Sub-silentio, *ad.* عَلَى ٱلسُّكُوتِ ـ بِٱلسُّكُوتِ.

Subsist, *v.i.* To continue in existence, عَاشَ ـ بَقِيَ. To be, وُجِدَ ـ كَانَ. To last, to continue to be, ثَبَتَ ـ اِسْتَمَرَّ ـ. To — on, to live on, feed on, اِقْتَاتَ ب ـ ظَلَّ.

Subsist, *v.t.* To supply with, أَمَدَّ-ب ـ رَزَقَ-ب. To pay for, صَرَفَ عَلَى.

Subsistence, *n.* Being, existence, وُجُود ـ كَوْن. Continuance, اِسْتِمْرَار ـ بَقَآء ـ دَوَام ـ ثَبَات. Means of support, livelihood, مَعَاش ـ قِيَام ـ مَعِيشَة ـ تَعَيُّش. The Supplier of the means of —, God, الرَّزَّاق. To supply with the means of —, رَزَقَ. He assigned this estate as a — to such an one, جَعَلَ هٰذِهِ ٱلضَّيْعَةَ طُعْمَةً لِفُلَانٍ.

Subsistent, *a.* Having being, مَوْجُود ـ كَائِن. Remaining, continuing, قَيَّام ـ بَاقٍ ـ مُسْتَمِرّ.

Subsoil, *n.* التُّرَابُ ٱلَّذِي تَحْتَ تُرْبَةِ ٱلْأَرْضِ.

Subsoil, *v.t.* To plough into the subsoil, حَرَثَ دُونَ تُرْبَةِ ٱلْأَرْضِ ـ تَعَمَّقَ فِي ٱلْفَلَاحَةِ.

Sub-species, *n.* فَرْعٌ مِنَ ٱلنَّوْعِ.

Substance, *n.* The essential part, ذَات ـ جَوْهَر. Body, matter, أَجْسَام *pl.* جِسْم ـ مَوَادّ *pl.* مَادَّة. The best of anything, the choice, زُبْدَة ـ خُلَاصَة. Meaning, drift, مَفَاد ـ مَضْمُون ـ فَحْوَى. A result, حَاصِل ـ نَتِيجَة. The point on which a subject turns, مَدَار. Property, ثَرْوَة ـ مَال. Goods, أَمْتِعَة ـ سِلَع. The — of a thing, the thing itself, عَيْن ـ عَيْنُ ٱلشَّيْء. Substance, as opposed to accident, جَوْهَر. In —, summarily, بِٱلْإِجْمَالِ. The — of what he wrote, جُمْلَةُ مَا كَتَبَهُ. The — of his speech, مَفَادُ كَلَامِهِ.

A man of substance, أَغْنِيَآء *pl.* غَنِيٌّ ـ صَاحِبُ مَالٍ ـ حَظِيٌّ.

Substance and accident, جَوْهَرٌ وَعَرَضٌ.

Substance and shadow, جِسْمٌ وَظِلٌّ; reality and unreality, حَقِيقَةٌ وَخَيَالٌ; what is in hand and what is hoped for, الحَاضِرُ وَٱلْمَأْمُولُ.

Substantial, *a.* Belonging to or having substance, ذَاتِيٌّ ـ جَوْهَرِيٌّ. Corporeal, جِسْمَانِيٌّ ـ هَيُولَانِيٌّ. Strong, firm, مَكِين ـ مُحْكَم ـ مَتِين. Real, حَقِيقِيٌّ ـ صَحِيح. Compact in texture, سَفِيق. Nourishing, غَاذٍ ـ مُجْوِع ـ مُشْبِع ـ مُغَذٍّ. To be confided in, trustworthy, مُعْتَقَد ـ أَمِين. Possessed of goods, wealthy, صَاحِبُ مَالٍ ـ أَغْنِيَآء *pl.* غَنِيٌّ ـ مُدَرْهَم. To be —, strong, true, صَحَّ; to make —, صَحَّحَ.

Substantiality, *n.* The state of real or inherent existence, جَوْهَرِيَّة ـ ذَاتِيَّة. Corporeality, جِسْمَانِيَّة ـ هَيُولَانِيَّة ـ هَيُولَى. Reality, truth, صِحَّة ـ حَقِيقَة.

Substantially, *ad.* In substance, inherently, جَوْهَرًا ـ ذَاتًا. Bodily, جِسْمًا. Truly, حَقِيقَةً. Summarily, إِجْمَالًا. Strongly, firmly, بِثَبَاتٍ ـ إِحْكَامًا ـ بِمَتَانَةٍ ـ رَصَانَةً.

Substantialness, *n.* Firmness, strength, مَتَانَة ـ رَصَانَة ـ مَكِينَة ـ إِحْكَام. *See also* Substantiality, *n.*

Substantials, *n.* Material parts, مُهِمَّات ـ لَوَازِم ـ مُقْتَضَيَات ـ ضَرُورِيَّات.

Substantiate, *v.t.* To establish, as by proof, حَقَّقَ ـ صَحَّحَ ـ أَثْبَتَ ـ أَكَّدَ. To —, as an argument, بَرْهَنَ ـ أَفْلَجَ. His right was substantiated in the estimation of the judge, صَحَّ عِنْدَ ٱلْقَاضِي حَقُّهُ.

Substantive, *a.* Real, حَقِيقِيٌّ. Permanent, not temporary, as of any appointment, مُوَظَّف. A noun —, أَسْمَآء *pl.* إِسْم ـ إِسْمٌ. A — pronoun, ضَمَائِر *pl.* ضَمِير ـ إِسْمٌ مُضْمَرٌ ـ مُقَابِلُ ٱلصِّفَةِ.

Substantive, *n.* A noun, أَسْمَآء *pl.* إِسْم. A real —, إِسْمُ عَيْنٍ ـ إِسْمُ ذَاتٍ. An ideal —, إِسْمُ مَعْنًى. *See also* Noun, *n.*

Substantively, *ad.* Essentially, جَوْهَرًا ـ فِي ٱلْجَوْهَرِ ـ ذَاتًا. In the place of a noun, إِسْمًا ـ مَحَلَّ ٱلْإِسْمِ.

Substitute, *n.* One who acts for another, نُوَّاب *pl.* نَائِب ـ قَائِمُ مَقَامٍ ـ أَبْدَال *pl.* بَدَل ـ بَدِيل. A thing given in lieu of another, أَعْوَاض *pl.* عِوَض ـ أَبْدَال *pl.* بَدَل ـ خَلَف ـ مُعَاوَضَة ـ مَعُوضَة ـ مَعَاوِض *pl.* Verily, Zaid is your —, إِنَّ زَيْدًا بَدِيلُكَ or إِنَّ زَيْدًا بَدَلُكَ. To ask one for a —, compensation, اِسْتَعَاضَ. To be a — for, حَلَّ مَحَلَّ كَذَا. To give a — to for . . . , عَوَّضَ. To receive as a —, تَعَوَّضَ ـ اِعْتَاضَ. To act as the — for another, عَمِلَ-عِوَضًا عَنْهُ ـ قَامَ مَقَامَهُ ـ نَابَ عَنْهُ. He took it as a —, or in exchange for, another thing, اِسْتَعْوَضَهُ ـ اِسْتَخْلَفَهُ ـ اِسْتَبْدَلَهُ. Make thou this a — for this, اِجْعَلْ هٰذَا خَلَفًا مِنْ هٰذَا. He is a — for his father, هُوَ مِنْ أَبِيهِ خَلَفٌ. This is a — for what has been taken from thee, هٰذَا خَلَفٌ مِمَّا أُخِذَ مِنْكَ.

Substitute, *v.t.* To put in the place of, to exchange for, بَدَّلَ-ب ـ جَعَلَ-عِوَضَ كَذَا ـ أَقَامَ-مَقَامَ كَذَا. He substituted, used, one thing in the place of another, اِسْتَعْمَلَ ٱلشَّيْءَ عِوَضَ غَيْرِهِ. He substituted, made the thing a substitute for it, أَبْدَلَهُ مِنْ كَذا — إِتَّخَذَهُ مِنْهُ بَدَلاً.

Substitution, *n.* تَعْوِيض — تَبْدِيل — إِبْدَال.

Substratum, *n.* An under stratum, طَبَقَةٌ تَحْتَانِيَّةٌ. A semblance of, شَيْءٌ — رَائِحَةٌ مِنَ — شَبَهٌ مِن, ذَرْوٌ مِن. A — of truth, يُقَارِبُ ٱلْحَقَّ.

Substruction, *n.* أَسَاسُ بِنَآءٍ — بِنَآءٌ تَحْتَانِيٌّ.

Subtend, *v.i.* To extend beneath, إِمْتَدَّ مِنْ تَحْتُ.

Subterfluent, *a.* } سَائِلٌ أَسْفَلَ كَذا — جَارٍ مِنْ تَحْتُ.
Subterfluous,

Subterfuge, *n.* حُجَّةٌ *pl.* حُجَج — حِيلَة *pl.* حِيَل — عُذْر *pl.* أَعْذَار — إِعْتِذَار — عُذْرٌ بَاطِلٌ.

Subterranean, *a.* } تَحْتَ ٱلْأَرْضِ. A — channel, سَرَب *pl.*
Subterraneous, } أَسْرَاب. A — excavation or dwelling, دَوَالِيجُ *pl.* دَوْلَج. A — vault, or room to dwell in during the summer time; also a cellar, سِرْدَاب *pl.* سَرَادِبُ *and* سَرَادِيبُ.

Subtile, *a.* Fine, دَقِيق — نَاعِم — رَفِيع. Refined, as of reasoning, رَقِيقُ ٱلسِّلْكِ — دَقِيق. Wise, prudent, حَكِيم — فَطِين. Penetrating, مُؤَثِّر — نَافِذ — حَاذِق. *See also* Acute, *a.*

Subtilization, *n.* The act of rendering refined, تَدْقِيق — تَرْفِيع; of making volatile, تَكْرِير.

Subtilize, *v.t.* To make fine, أَنْعَمَ ٱلدَّقَّ — دَقَّقَ — أَدَقَّ.

Subtilize, *v.i.* To express one's self in a subtile or abstruse manner, تَفَنَّنَ (or إِفْتَنَّ) فِي ٱلْكَلَامِ — دَقَّقَ.

Subtilty, *n.* Thinness, fineness, نُعُومَة — رَقَاعَة — دِقٌّ — دِقَّة. Niceness or abstruseness, as of thought, تَفَنُّن — تَدْقِيق. Subtilties, subtile matters, مَدَاقُّ (or دَقَائِقُ) ٱلْأُمُورِ. He searches into the subtilties of matters, يَتَتَبَّعُ مَدَاقَّ ٱلْأُمُورِ.

Subtle, *a.* Sly, artful, خَبِيث — عَيَّار — دَاهٍ — مُحْتَال — حَوَّال — مَكَّار. More — than the serpent, أَحْيَلُ مِنَ ٱلْحَيَّةِ. Subtle or abstruse speech, كَلَامٌ خَفِيفُ (or خَفِيُّ) ٱلسِّلْكِ.

Subtlety, *n.* شَطَارَة — حِيلَة — خِدْعَة — مَكْر — دَهَآء.

Subtly, *ad.* بِمَكْرٍ — بِحِيلَةٍ — إِحْتِيَالاً — غَدْرًا. To deal —, مَكَرَ مَكْرًا ² — عَمِلَ بِمَكْرٍ. To deal — with, إِحْتَالَ عَلَى.

Subtract, *v.t.* To deduct from, أَسْقَطَ-مِن. To steal from, إِخْتَلَسَ-مِن — سَرَقَ-مِن. To —, as in arithmetic, طَرَحَ — أَسْقَطَ.

Subtracter, *n.* He or that which deducts, in arithmetic, طَارِحٌ ٱلْمَطْرُوحَ.

Subtrahend, *n.* مَطْرُوحُ ٱلطَّرْحِ.

Suburb, *n.* } The open country, whether having villages or not,
Suburbs, } outside of a town wall, ضَوَاحٍ *pl.* ضَاحِيَة — سَوَاد. The — of a town, ضَوَاحِي ٱلْمَدِينَةِ — ظَاهِرُ ٱلْمَدِينَةِ.

Suburban, *a.* مُتَعَلِّقٌ بِضَوَاحِي ٱلْمَدِينَةِ — عِنْدَ سَوَادِ ٱلْمَدِينَةِ. A — village, رُسْتَاق *pl.* رَسَاتِيق.

Subvention, *n.* إِعَانَةٌ مُقَرَّرَةٌ — إِعَانَة.

Subversion, *n.* The act of turning things upside down, رَكْس — عَكْس — إِرْكَاس; the being so subverted, إِنْعِكَاس — إِرْتِكَاس. The act of overthrowing, تَخْرِيب — هَدْم; of being overthrown, خِرْبَة — خَرَاب — إِنْهِدَام. The act of putting an end to, إِبَادَة — إِبْطَال — إِزَالَة — إِفْنَآء. *See also* Perversion, *n.*

Subversive, *a.* مُزِيل — مُقَلِّب — مُخَرِّب — هَادِم — مُخِلّ.

Subvert, *v.t.* To turn upside down; also to pervert, عَكَسَ — رَكَسَ ². To destroy, overthrow, أَهْلَكَ — هَدَمَ — دَكَّ ² — خَرَّبَ. To put an end to, أَبَادَ — أَزَالَ — أَفْنَى. To corrupt, أَفْسَدَ. To lead astray, أَضَلَّ.

Succedaneous, *a.* مُسَدُّ ٱلْمَسَدِّ — فِي مَقَامِ ٱلْبَدَلِ.

Succedaneum, *n.* بَدَل — سَدٌّ مَسَدٌّ.

Succeed, *v.t.* To follow, خَلَفَ — أَعْقَبَ — عَقَّبَ — عَقَبَ ².
To — to, as to an estate, to inherit, from another, وَرِثَ-مِن *aor.* يَرِثُ — أَخَذَ ٱلْمِيرَاثَ مِن ². To — to, as a son to his father's name, قَامَ بِٱسْمِ أَبِيهِ ²: Such an one succeeded to the place of his father, as successor to him, عَقَبَ فُلَانٌ مَكَانَ أَبِيهِ ² — أَعْقَبَ أَبَاهُ. To — another in a place, سَكَنَ مَكَانَ فُلَانٍ ²: they succeeded them (in the place), سَكَنُوا مَكَانَهُمْ. Since he succeeded to the affair, or since the matter fell to or devolved on him, مُنْذُ أَفْضَى ٱلْأَمْرُ إِلَيْهِ. To — one another, of many, تَوَالَوْا — تَعَاقَبُوا; to — one another alternately, تَنَاوَبُوا. This succeeded that, أَعْقَبَ هٰذَا ذٰلِكَ. They succeeded, they came after or behind, us, عَقَبُونَا مِنْ خَلْفِنَا — عَقَبُونَا — تَعَقَّبُوا مِنْ خَلْفِنَا. The night succeeded the day, خَلَفَ ٱللَّيْلُ ٱلنَّهَارَ ². They succeeded one another, that is, when one went another came after him, إِخْتَلَفُوا. The matters succeeded one another, تَدَاوَلَتِ ٱلْأَشْيَآءُ. *See also to* Follow, *v.t.*

Succeed, *v.i.* To come in the place of, قَامَ مَقَامَ كَذا *or* فُلَانٍ ² — حَلَّ مَقَامَ كَذا *or* فُلَانٍ ². To — or reign after one, مَلَكَ بَعْدَهُ. To attain, فَلَجَ ² — فَازَ ² — أَفْلَحَ; to cause one to —, attain, أَفْلَحَ — أَفَازَ. To prosper, فَلَجَ ² — نَجَحَ — أَنْجَحَ — إِسْتَنْجَحَ — إِسْتَفْلَحَ. Until he succeeded, or was able to..., حَتَّى ٱقْتَدَرَ عَلَى كَذا. *See also to* Prosper, *v.i.*

Succeeder, *n.* One who comes after, عَاقِب ـ مُعَقِّب.

Succeeding, *a.* Following, coming after, عَاقِب ـ مُتَعَاقِب ـ مُتَابِع ـ تَالٍ. Next, قَابِل ـ مُقْبِل. *See also* Following, *a.*

Success, *n.* Attainment, عُقْب ـ خَيْرٌ عُقْبًا ـ فَوْز ـ صَوَاب ـ فَلْج ـ فَلَاح ـ نَجَاح; as in a conquest, غَلَبَة ـ فَلْج عَلَى ـ إِفْلَاج عَلَى. In order that you may have good —, لِكَيْ تُفْلِح. A source of —, مَفْلَحَة. Crowned with —, مَقْرُونٌ بِٱلنَّجَاحِ. Want of —, خَيْبَة ـ فَشَل. Good —, تَوْفِيق. To whom belongs —? لِمَنِ ٱلْفَلْجُ. He wished him —, تَمَنَّى لَهُ ٱلنَّجَاحَ. They have obtained a great —, قَدْ نَالُوا نَجَاحًا عَظِيمًا.

Successful, *a.* ظَفِر ـ ظَافِر ـ مُفْلِح ـ فَائِز ـ نَاجِح ـ مُسَدَّد. Attaining the desired object, لَاحِق. To be —, فَلَجَ ² ـ ظَفِرَ ـ أَفْلَجَ عَلَى ـ أَظْفَرَ بِ ـ ظَفِرَ بِ ـ أَفْلَحَ. To cause to be — over,

Successfully, *ad.* تَسَدُّدًا ـ بِٱلنَّجَاحِ ـ بِٱلْفَوْزِ. Happily, بِخَيْرٍ ـ بِٱلتَّوْفِيقِ ـ بِٱلسَّلَامَةِ.

Successfulness, *n.* A prosperous conclusion, خَيْرُ عَاقِبَةٍ ـ تَوْفِيق.

Succession, *n.* Following of things in order, تَوَالٍ ـ تَعَاقُب ـ تَوَاتُر ـ مُتَابَعَة. Succession, as to a throne, خِلَافَة. A chain, as of ancestors, *etc.*, سِلْسِلَة. Succession to an inheritance, وِرَاثَة ـ مِيرَاث. In —, successively, عَلَى ٱلتَّوَالِي. He made over the —, as to a kingdom, *etc.*, to him, by will, عَهِدَ لِ ـ ٱخْتَلَفَهُ ـ أَوْصَى لَهُ بِٱلْخِلَافَةِ. Apostolical —, خِلَافَةُ ٱلرُّسُلِ ٱلْأَطْهَارِ. He ruled in — to his elder brother, تَوَلَّى خَلَفًا عَنْ أَخِيهِ ٱلْأَكْبَرِ. "He made it [the wind] to prevail against them seven nights and eight days in succession," سَخَّرَهَا عَلَيْهِمْ سَبْعَ لَيَالٍ وَثَمَانِيَةَ أَيَّامٍ حُسُومًا (Kur. lxix. 7.)

Successive, *a.* مُتَوَاتِر ـ مُتَتَابِع ـ مُتَتَالٍ ـ مُتَعَاقِب. To be —, تَوَالَى ـ تَتَابَعَ.

Successively, *ad.* عَلَى ٱلتَّعَاقُبِ ـ عَلَى ٱلتَّوَالِي. Successively from father to son, أَبًا عَنْ جَدٍّ. To do a thing —, تَابَعَ. To be carried on —, تَدَارَكَ. "Until, when they have — arrived therein altogether," حَتَّى إِذَا ٱدَّارَكُوا فِيهَا جَمِيعًا (Kur. vii. 36.)

Successless, *a.* غَيْرُ مُوَفَّقٍ ـ خَائِب ـ غَيْرُ نَاجِحٍ.

Successor, *n.* One who comes after another, عَاقِب ـ عَقِيب. One who comes after, follows, another, قَفِيٌّ. One who comes after another, whether that other be dead or living; also one remaining after another who is dead, خَلَف *pl.* خُلُوف ـ خَالِف ـ خَالِفَة. A — as to a throne; also a vice-regent, in the place of one deceased, خَلِيفَة *pl.* خَلَائِف *and* خُلَفَآء ـ خَلِيف *pl.* خُلَفَآء. A —, in the person of one's own offspring, رَقِيب *pl.* رُقَبَآء. A — to an inheritance, وَارِث *pl.* وَرَثَة. To appoint as one's —, ٱسْتَخْلَفَ ـ خَلَّفَ: He appointed him, by will, to be his —, ٱخْتَلَفَهُ ـ أَوْصَى لَهُ بِٱلْخِلَافَةِ.

Succinct, *a.* مُوجَز ـ مُخْتَصَر ـ مُجْمَل. A — statement, إِفَادَةٌ مُوجَزَةٌ.

Succinctly, *ad.* إِجْمَالًا ـ بِٱلتَّلْخِيصِ ـ بِٱلْإِيجَازِ ـ بِٱلِٱخْتِصَارِ.

Succinctness, *n.* إِيجَاز ـ ٱخْتِصَار ـ تَلْخِيص.

Succory, *n.* هِنْدِبَا; one —, هِنْدِبَة. *See also* Endive, *n.*

Succour, *v.t.* أَغَاثَ ـ سَاعَدَ ـ عَضَدَ ² ـ أَعَانَ. To ask one for —, ٱسْتَغَاثَ بِ ـ ٱسْتَغَاثَ. O my Lord, — me, and — not against me, رَبِّ أَعِنِّي وَلَا تُعِنْ عَلَيَّ. He succoured him to perform the affair, أَعَانَهُ عَلَى ٱلْأَمْرِ. *See also to* Aid, *v.t.*

Succour, *n.* إِعَانَة ـ عَوْن ـ إِغَاثَة ـ مُسَاعَدَة ـ إِسْعَاف. Cleave thou to the — of God, عَلَيْكَ عَوْنَ ٱللّٰهِ. *See also* Aid, *n.*

Succulence, *n.*
Succulency, } خَضَل ـ مَآد ـ رُطُوبَة. *See also* Juiciness, *n.*

Succulent, *a.* مَآد ـ يَمْؤُود ـ خَضِل ـ خَاضِل ـ رَطْب. To be —, مَأَدَ ـ تَسَقَّى ـ رَطُبَ ². To make —, رَطَّبَ ـ رَطِيب.

Succumb, *v.i.* To be overwhelmed by, to faint under, غُمِيَ عَلَيْهِ ـ أُغْمِيَ عَلَيْهِ ـ غُشِيَ عَلَيْهِ. To —, as to disease, ٱمْزَهَلَّ ـ ٱضْمَحَلَّ ـ ٱنْكَسَرَ. To give in, to yield, أَسْلَمَ ـ ٱسْتَسْلَمَ. To —, as to temptation, to be beguiled, ٱخْتَتَلَ ـ ٱنْغَرَّ ـ وَقَعَ *aor.* يَقَعُ.

Succussion, *n.* هَزّ ـ تَحْرِيك.

Such, *a.* Like this or this one, مِثْلُ هٰذَا ـ كَهٰذَا. Such, as denoting so-and-so, of a thing, كَذَا; of a person, فُلَان *fem.* فُلَانَة. Such persons, مِثْلُ هٰؤُلَاءِ. In — a year, فِي سَنَةِ كَذَا. Such being the case, وَٱلْحَالَةُ هٰذِهِ. And — like, وَنَحْوُ ذٰلِكَ. Shall we find — a man as this? هَلْ نَجِدُ مِثْلَ هٰذَا ٱلرَّجُلِ. Let there be no — talk, لَا يَكُونُ مِثْلَ هٰذَا ٱلْكَلَامِ. Such as it is, مِثْلَمَا هُوَ. "Even though their craftiness were such that the mountains should be moved by it," إِنْ كَانَ مَكْرُهُمْ لِتَزُولَ مِنْهُ ٱلْجِبَالُ (Kur. xiv. 47.)

Suck, *v.t.* To draw with the mouth, تَمَصَّصَ ـ مَصَّ ². To —, as an infant its mother; also of kids, *etc.*, مَرَكَ ² ـ رَضِعَ ـ رَضَعَ ـ ٱرْتَضَعَ; specially of beasts, رَغَثَ ـ ٱرْتَغَثَ. To — the fingers, of a child, مَرَثَ ². To — in, to absorb, قَذَبَ ـ تَشَرَّبَ ـ نَشَفَ ـ تَنَشَّفَ. To — in anything whilst drinking, ٱقْتَرَّ. To draw in, سَحَبَ ـ جَذَبَ ². He sucked the breast of his mother, رَضَعَ ثَدْيَ أُمِّهِ.

Suck, *v.i.* To draw the breast, ـَ رَضَعَ ٱلثَّدْيَ. To draw in, ـَ شَرِبَ.

Suck, *n.* The act of drawing with the mouth, مَصٌّ. Milk drawn from the breast, حَلِيبُ ٱلرَّضَاعِ ـ حَلِيبٌ. To give —, أَرْضَعَ.

Sucker, *n.* Of a plant, رَضَعٌ ـ شَكِيرٌ *pl.* شُكُرٌ; of a palm-tree, فَسِيلَةٌ *coll.* فَسِيلٌ; specially of a vine, غَرْزٌ *pl.* غُرُوزٌ. Sucker, anything to suck with, مِمَصٌّ. Sucker, as of a pump, مَكْبَسٌ.

Sucking, *n.* The act of, رَضْعٌ ـ رِضَاعٌ; of beasts, رَغْثٌ.

Suckle, *v.t.* To nurse at the breast, of a mother, أَرْضَعَتْ; of beasts, أَرْغَثَتْ. His mother suckled him, أَرْضَعَتْهُ أُمُّهُ. To give a child to be suckled, رَاضَعَ: He gave his son to be suckled (by a woman), رَاضَعَ ٱبْنَهُ. Suckled, مُرْضَعٌ *pl.* مَرَاضِعُ.

Suckling, *n.* مُرْضَعٌ; of a beast, رَغُوثٌ.

Suction, *n.* The act of drawing in, مَصٌّ; of absorbing, تَنْشِيفٌ ـ تَشَرُّبٌ. A — pump, طُلُومْبَةٌ.

Suctorial, *a.* جَدِيرٌ بِٱلِٱمْتِصَاصِ ـ خَلِيقٌ لِلْمَصِّ.

Sûdân, *n.* The territory so called, أَرْضُ ٱلسُّودَانِ.

Sudation, *n.* The act of sweating, رَشْحٌ.

Sudatory, *n.* A sweating bath, حَمَّامٌ مُعَرِّقٌ.

Sudden, *a.* فُجَاءِيٌّ ـ بَاغِتٌ. Sudden fear, رُعْبُ بَغْتَةٍ. Sudden destruction, هَلَاكُ بَغْتَةٍ. Sudden death, مَوْتٌ مُعَجَّلٌ ـ مَوْتُ ٱلْفَوَاتِ. It was —, كَانَ ذٰلِكَ فَلْتَةً.

Suddenly, *ad.* بَغْتَةً ـ فَلْتَةً ـ فُجَاءَةً ـ عَلَى بَدِيهَةٍ. At once, at the time, حَالًا. Suddenly-formed opinion, بَدِيهَةُ ٱلرَّأْيِ. Beware of suddenly-formed opinions, إِيَّاكَ وَٱلرَّأْيَ ٱلْفَطِيرَ. To come upon —, ـَ بَغَتَ ـ بَادَهَ ـ ـَ بَدَهَ ـ ـَ دَرَهَ عَلَى. It came to him —, جَاءَهُ بَغْتَةً. He met him —, لَقَاهُ بَغْتَةً. He said to him —, قَالَ لَهُ حَالًا. He saw him —, رَآهُ بَدِيهَةً. He died —, مَاتَ مَوْتَ ٱلْفَوَاتِ ـ مَاتَ فَلْتَةً ـ أُفْتِيتَ. He fell down dead, سَقَطَ بَغْتَةً مَيْتًا.

Suddenness, *n.* بَغْتٌ ـ بَغْتَةٌ ـ مُبَادَهَةٌ ـ بِدَاهٌ ـ بَدْءٌ.

Sudorific, *a.* مُعَرِّقٌ ـ مُرَشِّحٌ.

Sudorific, *n.* دَوَاءٌ مُعَرِّقٌ.

Suds, *n.* غُسَالَةُ ٱلصَّابُونِ ـ لُعَابُ ٱلصَّابُونِ.

Sue, *v.t.* As at law, دَعَا ـ إِلَى ٱلشَّرْعِ ـ حَاكَمَ ـ إِلَى ٱلْحَاكِمِ ـ طَلَبَ ـ إِلَى ٱلْمَحْكَمَةِ. I sued the man for my due, تَبِعْتُ ـ تَابَعْتُهُ بِحَقِّي ـ ٱلرَّجُلَ بِحَقِّي.

Sue, *v.i.* To make claims, إِدَّعَى. To prosecute a claim, سَاقَ ٱلدَّعْوَى. To — for damages, إِدَّعَى بِٱلتَّضْمِينَاتِ. To request, plead with one, for, طَلَبَ شَفَاعَةَ فُلَانٍ ـ إِسْتَشْفَعَ ـ إِلَى فُلَانٍ ـ إِلَى فُلَانٍ. *See also under to* Plead, *v.i.*

Suet, *n.* شَحْمُ ٱلْكُلْوَاتِ ـ شَحْمٌ. Paste mixed with —, عَجِينٌ مُشَحَّمٌ ـ مُشَحَّمٌ.

Suety, *a.* شَحِمٌ.

Suffer, *v.t.* To have pain from, تَأَلَّمَ مِنْ. To bear, تَحَمَّلَ ـ أَطَاقَ عَلَى ـ إِحْتَمَلَ. To bear with patience, ـِ صَبَرَ عَلَى. To undergo, ـُ كَبَدَ ـ أُبْتُلِيَ بِ. To allow, رَخَّصَ لِ ـ فِي ـ فَسَحَ لِ ـ أَرْتَرَى ـ رُزِيَ ـ ـَ أَذِنَ لِ ـ بِ. To — hunger, جَاعَ. To — loss, ـَ خَسِرَ. He would not — him to enter, لَا يَدَعُهُ ـ لَا يَدَعُهُ يَدْخُلُ إِلَى لِي أَوَّلًا أَنْ ـ أَنْ يَدْخُلَ. Suffer me first to go to my house, إِئْذَنْ لِي أَوَّلًا أَنْ أَمْضِيَ إِلَى بَيْتِي. Do not — him to live, لَا تَدَعْهُ ـ لَا تَدَعْهُ يَحْيَا ـ أَنْ يَعِيشَ. The wind did not — us, مَا خَلَّتْنَا ٱلرِّيحُ. How long shall I — you! إِلَى مَتَى أَحْتَمِلُكُمْ. They are suffering from disease, يُقَاسُونَ مِنَ ٱلْأَمْرَاضِ. The losses which the government has suffered, ٱلْخَسَائِرُ ٱلَّتِي تَكَبَّدَتْهَا ٱلدَّوْلَةُ. "How long will be their sufferings in the fire!" فَمَا أَصْبَرَهُمْ عَلَى ٱلنَّارِ (Kur. ii. 170.)

Suffer, *v.i.* To undergo pain, تَأَلَّمَ ـ ـَ أَلِمَ ـ وَجِعَ *aor.* يَيْجَعُ. To undergo, إِحْتَمَلَ. To — punishment, عُوقِبَ; to — the punishment of death, عُوقِبَ بِٱلْمَوْتِ. To sustain loss, ـَ خَسِرَ. He helped those who had suffered from the famine, سَاعَدَ ٱلَّذِينَ رُزِئُوا بِٱلْمَجَاعَةِ.

Sufferable, *a.* مِمَّا يُحْتَمَلُ ـ يُحْتَمَلُ.

Sufferance, *n.* The bearing of pain, أَذِيَّةٌ ـ وَجَعٌ ـ أَلَمٌ. Patient —, شَهَامَةٌ ـ صَبْرٌ ـ عَزَاءٌ. Permission by not forbidding, غَضٌّ عَلَى إِغْمَاضٍ ـ بِغَضِّ ٱلطَّرْفِ ـ إِغْمَاضُ ٱلْعَيْنِ ـ ٱلطَّرْفِ ٱلْعَيْنِ. On —, إِغْمَاضُ ٱلْعَيْنِ.

Sufferer, *n.* One who endures, كَابِدٌ. One who suffers patiently, صَبُورٌ ـ صَابِرٌ. One who permits, آذِنٌ لِ ـ مُرَخِّصٌ لِ ـ فِي ـ مُفَسِّحٌ لِ.

Suffering, *n.* The act of bearing, تَحَمُّلٌ. Pain, أَلَمٌ *pl.* آلَامٌ ـ وَجَعٌ *pl.* أَوْجَاعٌ. Trouble, distress, غَمٌّ ـ حُزْنٌ ـ هَمٌّ ـ عَنَاءٌ ـ أَذِيَّةٌ ـ عَذَابٌ. Loss, خَسَارَةٌ.

Suffice, *v.i.* ـِ كَفَى: It does not — for . . . , لَا يَكْفِي لِ. Suffice it to say, يَكْفِي مَا قُلْنَا.

Suffice, *v.t.* To be sufficient for, ـِ كَفَى ـ أَغْنَى عَنْ ـ أَجْزَأَ. Let it — thee, كَفَاكَ. It did not — them, لَمْ يَكْفِهِمْ. Such a thing sufficed him, كَفَاهُ كَذَا ـ أَغْنَى عَنْهُ كَذَا. Does not this — you? مَا يُغْنِي عَنْكَ كَذَا. This garment does not — me, هٰذَا ٱلثَّوْبُ لَا يُجْزِينِي.

Sufficiency, *n.* What suffices, كِفَايَة ـ بُلْغَة ـ وَفْق ـ حَسْب. The state of being in no need, غُنْيَة. Sufficiency of food, كُفْيَة. A bare —, عُلْقَة. Ability, إِسْتِطَاعَة ـ طَاقَة ـ سَعَة ـ مُكْنَة. Self-sufficiency, عُجْب ـ تَكَبُّر ـ تَعَظُّم ـ غُرُور. A man having a —, غَانٍ.

Sufficient, *a.* كَافٍ ـ جَازٍ ـ مُجْزٍ ـ كَفِيّ ـ كُفِيّ ـ كُفَاة; of a proof, testimony, *etc.*, مُقْنِع *pl.* مَقَانِعُ. Let that be — for thee, حَسْبُكَ ذٰلِكَ. The things were — for them, الْمَوَادُّ كَانَتْ كِفَايَتَهُمْ. Sufficient for the day is the evil thereof, يَكْفِي ٱلْيَوْمَ شَرُّهُ. Quite —, كَافٍ وَافٍ. The Self-sufficient, (God), الْغَنِيُّ.

Sufficiently, *ad.* عَلَى قَدْرِ ٱلْكِفَايَةِ ـ بِٱلْكِفَايَةِ ـ كِفَايَةً.

Suffix, *v.t.* أَضَافَ-إِلَى. To be suffixed to, إِنْضَافَ إِلَى.

Suffix, *n.* مُضَافٌ إِلَى.

Suffocate, *v.t.* *See to* Smother, Stifle, *v.t.*

Suffocating, *a.* Stifling, خَانِق ـ *vulg.* مُفَطِّس. Sultry, غَامّ ـ عَكِيك ـ مُغِمّ.

Suffocation, *n.* خَنْق ـ *vulg.* فُطُوس.

Suffragan, *n.* As of a bishop, أُسْقُفٌ تَابِعٌ ـ أُسْقُفٌ مُعَاوِنٌ. Suffragan bishops, أَسَاقِفَةٌ مِنْ أَتْبَاعِ ٱلْمَطْرَانِ ـ مَطْرَانٍ.

Suffrage, *n.* إِعْطَاءُ رَأْيٍ ـ رَأْيٌ فِي ٱلْإِنْتِخَابِ ـ أَرَآءٌ *pl.* رَأْي. To give one's — to such an one, أَعْطَى رَأْيَهُ لِفُلَانٍ. To give the — to ..., أَعْطَى حَقَّ ٱلْإِنْتِخَابِ ل. To obtain the — of all the voters, ء نَالَ أَرَآءَ جَمِيعِ ٱلْمُنْتَخِبِينَ ـ ء أُنْتُخِبَ مِنْ جَمِيعِ ٱلْمُنْتَخِبِينَ. Universal —, أُصُولُ ٱلْإِنْتِخَابِ بِإِعْطَاءِ أَرَآءِ ٱلْجُمْهُورِ ـ ٱلْإِنْتِخَابُ عَلَى يَدِ ـ أُصُولُ إِلْقَاءِ ٱلرَّأْيِ مِنْ كُلِّ نَفَرٍ بِلَا ٱسْتِثْنَاءِ ٱلْجُمْهُورِ. Female —, إِعْطَاءُ أَرَآءِ ٱلنِّسَآءِ. Suffrage, united voice in public prayer, تَضَرُّعُ ٱلْجَمَاعَةِ ـ إِبْتِهَالُ ٱلْجَمَاعَةِ.

Suffuse, *v.t.* To tinge, ء خَضَبَ ـ خَضَّبَ ـ لَوَّنَ ـ شَرَّبَ. To overflow, run, ء دَمَعَ. To become suffused with red, إِحْمَارَّ: his colour was suffused (with redness,) ء شَرِقَ لَوْنُهُ. His eyes were suffused with tears, تَدَمَّعَتْ (or دَمَعَتْ) عُيُونُهُ. Her face was suffused with blushes, ء شَرِقَ (or إِحْمَارَّ) وَجْهُهَا خَجَلَةً. The sun suffused its rays, دَمَعَتِ ٱلشَّمْسُ شُعَاعَهَا. The sun was suffused with darkness, ء شَرِقَتِ ٱلشَّمْسُ. His colour became suffused with red, إِسْتَشْرَبَ وَجْهُهُ حُمْرَةً. The white was suffused with redness, أُشْرِبَ ٱلْأَبْيَضُ حُمْرَةً. His face was suffused with anger, تَشَرَّبَ ٱلْغَضَبُ فِي وَجْهِهِ.

Suffusion, *n.* The act of, خَضْب ـ تَخْضِيب ـ تَلْوِين ـ تَشْرِيب ـ دَمْع. The being suffused, شَرَق ـ تَدَمُّع ـ تَشَرُّب ـ إِسْتِشْرَاب. Suffusion with redness, إِحْمِرَار. Violent suffusion, تَدْمِيع.

Sûfy, *n.* One of the Persian sect so named, صُوفِيٌّ. The Sûfis, الصُّوفِيَّة ـ الصُّفِيَّة. To be or to become a —, تَصَوَّفَ.

Sugar, *n.* سُكَّر. Powdered —, سُكَّرٌ نَاعِمٌ ـ سُكَّرٌ هَشٌّ. A loaf of —, أَبْلُوجُ سُكَّرٍ ـ قَالِبُ سُكَّرٍ. Crushed —, سُكَّرٌ مَسْحُوقٌ. A piece of —, سُكَّرَة. Barley-sugar, سُكَّرِيٌّ. Raw —, سُكَّرٌ خَامٌ. Refined —, سُكَّرٌ مُكَرَّرٌ. Sugar of lead; *see below.*

Sugar, *v.t.* To sweeten with sugar, حَلَّى-بِسُكَّرٍ. To cover with —, ء رَشَّ عَلَى-سُكَّرًا.

Sugar-basin, *n.* سُكَّرِيَّة.

Sugar-candy, *n.* سُكَّرٌ نَبَاتٌ ـ قَنْدَة ـ قَنْد.

Sugar-cane, *n.* قَصَبُ سُكَّرٍ ـ قَصَبُ مَصٍّ ـ قَصَبٌ حُلْوٌ ـ قَصَبٍ *pl.* عُودُ عِيدَانٍ.

Sugared, *a.* بِسُكَّرٍ ـ فِيهِ سُكَّرٌ ـ سُكَّرِيٌّ.

Sugar-loaf, *n.* In the shape of a —, بِشَكْلِ ٱلْمَنَارَةِ. *See also under* Sugar, *n.*

Sugar-mill, *n.* مَعْمَلُ (or مِعْصَرُ) ٱلسُّكَّرِ.

Sugar of lead, *n.* مِلْحُ ٱلرَّصَاصِ.

Sugar-plantation, *n.* زَرْعُ (or مِغْرَاسُ) قَصَبِ ٱلسُّكَّرِ.

Sugar-planter, *n.* صَاحِبُ مَغَارِسِ قَصَبِ ٱلسُّكَّرِ.

Sugar-plum, *n.* مُلَبَّس.

Sugar-refiner, *n.* مُكَرِّرُ ٱلسُّكَّرِ.

Sugar-refinery, *n.* مَعْمَلُ لِتَكْرِيرِ ٱلسُّكَّرِ ـ مَعْمَلُ سُكَّرٍ.

Sugar-tongs, *n.* مَاسِكَةُ ٱلسُّكَّرِ.

Sugar-works, *n.* مَعْمَلُ سُكَّرٍ.

Sugary, *a.* سُكَّرِيٌّ.

Suggest, *v.t.* To offer to the mind, حَدَّثَ-فِي ٱلْبَالِ ـ ء عَرَضَ-ل ـ أَلْهَمَ ـ أَصْعَدَ-إِلَى ٱلْقَلْبِ ـ أَخْطَرَ-بِٱلْبَالِ ـ أَلْقَى-بِٱلذِّهْنِ. To —, of evil, to, وَسْوَسَ ل-ب ـ وَسْوَسَ-ب ـ أَغْوَى-ب. To — good advice to, أَشَارَ عَلَى-شَوْرًا حَسَنًا. To — an expedient to, أَشَارَ عَلَى-بِطَرِيقَةٍ إِلَى كَذَا ـ عَلَّمَ-طَرِيقَةً إِلَى كَذَا. To be suggested to the mind, ء خَطَرَ بِٱلْبَالِ ـ جَآءَ فِي ٱلْبَالِ *aor.* ء يَجِيءُ ـ صَعِدَ إِلَى ٱلْقَلْبِ. *See also to* Hint, *v.t.*

Suggestion, *n.* The act of suggesting to the mind, إِلْقَاءٌ بِٱلْبَالِ ـ إِخْطَارٌ بِٱلْقَلْبِ. A — of evil, وَسْوَسَة *pl.* وَسَاوِسُ. Suggestions, propositions, إِلْقَآات ـ إِشَارَات. At the — or advice of his brother, بِمَشُورَةِ أَخِيهِ ـ بِنَصَاحَةِ أَخِيهِ. The vain suggestions of the devil, خَطَرَاتُ ٱلشَّيْطَانِ.

Suggestive, *a.* مُشِيرٌ عَلَى ـ مُحَرِّكُ ٱلذِّهْنِ ـ حَاثُّ ٱلْخَاطِرِ ـ مُخْطِرٌ بِٱلْبَالِ ـ ٱلذِّهْنِ. *See also* Hint, *n.*

Suicidal, *a.* Pertaining to suicide, مُتَعَلِّقٌ بِقَتْلِ ٱلنَّفْسِ. Destructive of one's own object, مُخَرِّبٌ ـ عَاكِسٌ مَقْصُودَ نَفْسِهِ ـ مُبْطِلُ غَايَتِهِ ـ مَا هُوَ لِنَفْسِهِ.

Suicide, *n.* قَتْلُ ٱلنَّفْسِ. To commit —, قَتَلَ نَفْسَهُ ². He committed — through grief and despair, قَتَلَ نَفْسَهُ غَمًّا وَأَيْسًا. He contemplated —, هَمَّ بِقَتْلِ نَفْسِهِ ².

Suit, *n.* A set, طَقْمٌ *pl.* طُقُوم ـ طَائِفَة ـ طَبَقَة. A — of clothes, دَسْتٌ مِنَ ٱلثِّيَابِ ـ حُلَّةُ ثِيَابٍ ـ حُلَّة. A —, of cards, لَوْنُ دَسْتٍ مِنْ أَوْرَاقِ ٱللَّعِبِ. A petition, رِجَاء ـ اِلْتِمَاس. A legal process, دَعْوَى *pl.* دَعَاوَى ـ دَعْوَى وَمُطَالَبَة. Courtship, كَلَف ـ تَصَابٍ ـ صُبُوٌّ ـ صَبَاء. To make — to, to beseech, تَضَرَّعَ إِلَى ـ اِلْتَمَسَ ـ كَلِفَ بِ. To make — to, to woo, صَبَا إِلَى ² ـ كَلِفَ بِ or هَنَأَ فِي ². Whoever has a — let him come to the tribunal, مَنْ لَهُ دَعْوَى فَلْيَأْتِ إِلَى ٱلْمَحْكَمَةِ. To follow —, to imitate, تَمَثَّلَ بِ. *See also* Suite, *n.*

Suit, *v.t.* and *i.* To agree with, شَاكَلَ ـ لَاقَ بِ ـ لَاءَمَ ـ وَفَّقَ ـ قَانَى ـ نَاسَبَ ـ طَابَقَ ـ وَافَقَ. To fit, adapt, وَفَّقَ ـ قَانَى. To be useful, serviceable, to, صَلَحَ لِ ². This suits my dress, هٰذَا قَرْفٌ مِنْ ثَوْبِي. This will not — you, هٰذَا مَا يُشَاكِلُكَ. *See also to* Fit, *v.t. and i.*

Suitable, *a.* Agreeable with, قَرْفٌ مِنْ or بِ ـ قَرْفٌ لِ ـ خَلِيقٌ ـ لَائِقٌ لِ ـ مُطَابِقٌ بِ ـ مُنَاسِبٌ لِ. Adapted for, صَالِحٌ لِ ـ مَحَلٌّ لِ ـ جَدِيرٌ بِ. Suitable to his rank, يُنَاسِبُ مَقَامَهُ. In accordance with what is — to the occasion, بِحَسَبِ مَا يَقْتَضِيهِ ٱلْحَالُ. This is — for you, هٰذَا يَصْلُحُ لَكَ. This is a — reply to the question, هٰذَا ٱلْجَوَابُ يُطَابِقُ ٱلسُّؤَالَ. This is more — for you, هٰذَا أَشْبَهُ (or أَلْيَقُ) بِكَ. It will not be — for you, لَا يَلِيقُ بِكَ. *See also* Fit, *a.*

Suitableness, *n.* Agreement, مُنَاسَبَة ـ لِيَاقَة ـ مُطَابَقَة ـ مُشَاكَلَة. Adaptedness, مَصْلَحَة ـ مَجْدَرَة ـ جَدَارَة ـ مَخْلَقَة ـ صَلَاح.

Suitably, *ad.* عَلَى وَجْهٍ ـ بِمُنَاسَبَةٍ ـ بِلِيَاقَةٍ ـ مُوَافَقَةً ـ مُلَائَمَةً ـ عَلَى وَجْهِ ٱلْقَصْدِ ـ ٱلْمُنَاسَبَة.

Suite, *n.* Retinue, دَائِرَة ـ مَعِيَّة ـ حُشْمَة ـ خَدَمٌ وَحَشَمٌ. A connected succession, chain, سِلْسِلَة *pl.* سَلَاسِلُ; in a suite, connected, مُسَلْسَل. A —, as of apartments, طَقْم ـ دَائِرَة. Order, arrangement, تَرْتِيب ـ سِلْك ـ اِنْتِظَام ـ نِظَام.

Suitor, *n.* In a law-suit, مُدَّعٍ ـ صَاحِبُ دَعْوَى *pl.* أَصْحَاب. A wooer, عَشَّاق ـ عَاشِق ـ كَلِف ـ صَابٍ إِلَى ـ صَابٍ. A solicitor, petitioner, مُتَعَرِّض ـ مُلْتَمِس ـ مُتَضَرِّع ـ طَالِب ـ رَاغِب. A — for one's favour, مُتَعَرِّضٌ (or مُعْتَرِضٌ) لِمَعْرُوفِهِ. *See also* Suppliant, *n.*

Suitress, *n.* مُلْتَمِسَة ـ مُتَضَرِّعَة ـ طَالِبَة ـ رَاغِبَة. A — for favour, مُتَعَرِّضَةٌ (or مُعْتَرِضَةٌ) لِلْمَعْرُوف.

Sulcate, *a.* }
Sulcated, } مَشْقُوقٌ بِٱلْفِدَانِ ـ مَخْدُود.

Sulk, *v.i.* To be sulky; *see under* Sulky, *a.*

Sulkily, *ad.* بِتَبْوِيزٍ ـ *vulg.* بِبُسُولٍ ـ بِبَسَالَةٍ ـ تَبَسُّلًا.

Sulkiness, *n.* }
Sulks, } تَبْوِيز ـ *vulg.* بُسُول ـ بَسَالَة.

Sulky, *a.* مُبَوِّز ـ *vulg.* بَاسِرٌ بَاسِلٌ ـ بَسُول ـ بَسِيل. To be —, بَوَّزَ ـ تَبَسَّلَ ـ بَسُلَ ².

Sulky, *n.* A carriage for one person, عَرَبَانَةٌ لِرَاكِبٍ وَاحِدٍ فَقَطْ.

Sullage, *n.* }
Sulliage, } أَوْسَاخ ـ وَسَخ ـ دَنَاسَة ـ وَكَب ـ دَرَن.

Sullen, *a.* *See* Morose, Sulky, *a.*

Sullenly, *ad.* *See* Morosely, *ad.*

Sullenness, *n.* *See* Moroseness, *n.*

Sully, *v.t.* To smear, as with filth, طَبَّعَ ـ قَذَّعَ ـ لَوَّثَ ـ أَدْرَنَ. To —, as the reputation, خَرَقَ نَامُوسَهُ ـ ثَلَمَ صِيتَهُ. To blemish, عَيَّبَ. To be sullied, soiled, تَلَوَّثَ ـ دَرِنَ; to be discoloured, تَلَطَّخَ. To have one's reputation sullied, اِنْثَلَمَ صِيتُهُ ـ اِنْخَرَقَ عِرْضُهُ. *See also to* Stain, Dishonour, *v.t.*

Sulphate, *n.* زَاج ـ مِلْح *pl.* زَاجَات.

Sulphate of copper, شَبٌّ يَمَانِيٌّ ـ زَاج.

Sulphate of iron, زَاجُ ٱلْحَدِيدِ.

Sulphate of quinine, صُولْفَاتُو ـ قِينَا قِينَا ـ مِلْحُ ٱلْقِينَا قِينَا.

Sulphate of zinc, تُوتِيَاء ـ زَاجُ ٱلتُّوتِيَاء.

Sulphur, *n.* كِبْرِيت. To anoint with —, كَبْرَتَ.

Sulphurate, *a.* }
Sulphureous, }
Sulphuric, }
Sulphury, } كِبْرِيتِيّ. Sulphuric acid, حَامِضٌ كِبْرِيتِيٌّ. A — spring, عَيْنٌ كِبْرِيتٍ *pl.* عُيُون.

Sulphurate, *v.t.* رَكَّبَ مَعَ ٱلْكِبْرِيتِ.

Sulphuration, *n.* تَبْخِيرٌ (or *vulg.* تَهْبِيلٌ) بِٱلْكِبْرِيتِ.

Sulphurous, *a.* كِبْرِيتِيٌّ ـ مِثْلُ ٱلْكِبْرِيتِ ـ ذُو كِبْرِيت.

Sulphurousness, *n.* }
Sulphureousness, } ذَاتُ ٱلْكِبْرِيتِ ـ كِبْرِيتِيَّة.

Sultân, *n.* سُلْطان *pl.* سَلاطِينُ. (The — of the Turks is usually styled by his subjects, مَوْلانا ٱلأَعْظَمُ.)

Sultânah, *n.* The wife of a Sultân, زَوْجَةُ سُلْطانٍ. An odalisque, مَحْظِيَّةُ سُلْطانٍ *pl.* مَحاظِي.

Sultriness, *n.* عَكَّةٌ — عَكِيكٌ — عَكاكٌ — غَمٌّ.

Sultry, *a.* غامٌّ — مُغِمٌّ — عَكٌّ — عَكِيكٌ. A — day, يَوْمٌ غَمٌّ — يَوْمٌ عَكٌّ; a — night, لَيْلَةٌ عَكَّةٌ — لَيْلَةٌ غَمٌّ; a — land, أَرْضٌ عَكَّةٌ. The weather has been very —, عَكَّ ٱلطَّقْسُ. To be —, عَكَّ.

Sum, *n.* As of money, مَبْلَغ *pl.* مَبالِغ — مَجْمُوعٌ مِنَ ٱلدَّراهِمِ. A quantity, بَعْض — مِقْدار — جُمْلَة. The result of a reckoning, sum total, قِيمَة — جُمْلَة — حاصِلُ ٱلْجَمْعِ. Sum, substance or result, حاصِل *pl.* حَواصِلُ — نَتِيجَة *pl.* نَتائِجُ. The —, as of a speech, its gist, فَحْوَى (or مَضْمُونُ) ٱلْكَلام. A — set to be worked out, رَقْمُ حِساب — رَقْمٌ لِلْحِسابِ. He appointed him a fixed —, فَرَضَ لَهُ مَبْلَغًا مَعْلُومًا. To do a —, رَقَمَ حِسابًا ².

Sum, *v.t.* To add up, جَمَعَ — أَجْمَلَ. To compute, عَدَّ — حَسَبَ ² — أَحْصَى. To comprise, اِحْتَوَى — تَضَمَّنَ. They were all summed up, comprised, in one account, اِنْضَمُّوا فِي حِسابٍ واحِدٍ. To sum up, (used adverbially,) خُلاصَةُ ٱلْكَلامِ — بِٱلْجُمْلَةِ — الحاصِلُ.

Sumac, *n.* } سُمّاق. The — tree, شَجَرَةُ ٱلسُّمّاقِ.
Sumach, }

Summarily, *ad.* Concisely, بِٱلْإِيجازِ — عَلَى وَجْهِ ٱلْإِجْمالِ — إِجْمالاً. Quickly, سُرْعَةً — بِلا مُهْلَةٍ — حالاً — فِي ٱلْحالِ. Summarily, without entering into details, بِوَجْهِ ٱلْإِجْمالِ — بِعِبارَةٍ مُجْمَلَةٍ — بِدُونِ تَفْصِيلٍ.

Summary, *n.* Brief, comprehensive, مُخْتَصَر — وَجِز — مُوجَز — مُلَخَّص — مُجْمَل. Quick, عَجِل — بِلا مُطاوَلَةٍ. Summary conviction, إِثْباتُ ٱلْجُرْمِ عُقْبَ فَحْصٍ يَسِيرٍ. Summary punishment, إِجْراءُ ٱلْقِصاصِ عاجِلاً.

Summary, *n.* A compendium, مُجْمَل — مُخْتَصَر — مُوجَز — إِيجاز. A digest, as of laws, *etc.*, جَدْوَل *pl.* جَداوِلُ.

Summation, *n.* The act of summing up, جَمْع. An aggregate, ضَمِيمَة — مُعْظَم.

Summer, *n.* A beam, transverse beam, عارِضَة *pl.* عَوارِضُ. An architrave, عِلاوَةُ ٱلْعَمُودِ.

Summer, *n.* The season, قَيْظ *pl.* أَقْياظ *and* قُيُوظ — صَيْف *pl.* أَصْياف — صَيْفِيَّة. To agree with, as to rent, for the —, صايَفَ — عامَلَ مُصايَفَةً. They entered upon the — season, أَصافُوا.

Summer, *a.* صَيْفِيّ. Summer fruits, قِطاف — جَنَى ٱلصَّيْفِ. A — day, يَوْمٌ صائِفٌ. A — chamber, for coolness, مَخْدَعُ ٱلْبُرُودِ. Summer rain, صَيِّف — صَيْفِيّ.

Summer, *v.i.* To pass the summer in, صافَ بِ *aor.* يَصِيفُ — تَصَيَّفَ بِ — اِصْطافَ بِ.

Summer-colt, *n.* ضَرْبٌ مِنَ ٱلسَّرابِ — حَرُور. The part where the — appears, مُسْتَنُّ ٱلْحَرُورِ.

Summer-house, *n.* } مُصْطاف — مَصِيف.
Summer-residence, }

Summersault, *n.* } *See* Somersault, Somerset, *n.*
Summerset, }

Summit, *n.* As of a mountain, قِمَّة *pl.* قِمَم — نَمَغَة — أَكَمَة — ذِرْوَة — أَعْلَى — قُلَّة *pl.* قُلَل — شَعَفَة *pl.* شَعَف — قَرْن *pl.* قِران — رَأْس *pl.* رُؤُوس. Altitude, dignity, أَوْج. To ascend the —, as of a mountain, فَرَعَ ٱلأَكَمَةَ.

Summon, *v.t.* To convene, call together, دَعا بِ *aor.* يَدْعُو — اِسْتَدْعَى — نادَى — حَشَدَ — أَحْضَرَ ². To — to a court of justice, دَعا إِلَى ٱلْمَحْكَمَةِ ² — طَلَبَ إِلَى ٱلشَّرْعِ ². To — officially, أَحْضَرَ رَسْمًا — دَعا رَسْمًا ². To — one to perform his obligations, promise, طالَبَ بِٱلْوَعْدِ — طالَبَ بِإِنْجازِ ٱلْوَعْدِ. To — a town to surrender, اِسْتَدْعَى أَهْلَ ٱلْمَدِينَةِ إِلَى ٱلتَّسْلِيمِ. To — up courage, تَشَجَّعَ — تَشَدَّدَ. To — away from, اِنْتَزَعَ عَلَى بِٱلْغِيابِ عَنْ كَذا.

Summoner, *n.* داعٍ — نادٍ. The — of death, طارِقُ ٱلْمَنايا.

Summons, *n.* أَمْرٌ بِٱلْحُضُورِ; to a court of justice, مُحاكَمَة — طَلَبٌ إِلَى ٱلشَّرْعِ. An official —, تَنْبِيهٌ رَسْمِيٌّ. A verbal —, تَنْبِيهٌ شِفاهِيٌّ. The document containing the —, صَكّ — عَدْوَى ٱلتَّنْبِيهِ.

Summum-bonum, n. الخَيْرُ ٱلْمُطْلَقُ (or ٱلأَعْظَمُ).

Sumpter, *n.* A pack-horse, بِرْذَوْن *pl.* بَراذِينُ; a —, mule, or ass, دابَّة *pl.* دَوابّ.

Sumptuary, *a.* Relating to expense, مُتَعَلِّقٌ بِٱلْمَصْرُوفِ (or ٱلنَّفَقَةِ). Sumptuary laws, شَرائِعُ تُقَيِّدُ ٱسْتِعْمالَ ٱلزِّينَةِ وَٱلتَّغَطْرُسِ فِي ٱلْمَلابِسِ.

Sumptuous, *a.* عَظِيم — جَلِيل — جَلِيّ — فاخِر — بَهِيّ — أَبْهَى — اِحْتِفالِيّ — سُلْطانِيّ.

Sumptuously, *a.* بِٱحْتِفالٍ — بِبَهاءٍ — بِفَخْرٍ — بِجَلالٍ. To fare —, تَرَفَّهَ.

Sumptuousness, *n.* اِحْتِفال — اِحْتِشام — بَهاء — فَخْر — جَلال.

Sun, *n.* شَمْس *pl.* شُمُوس. One who, or anything that, shines, causes attraction, جاذِبُ ٱلنَّظَرِ — نَصْبُ ٱلْعُيُونِ. To rise, of the —, أَشْرَقَتْ ـ شَرَقَتْ 2. To set, as of the —, غَرَبَتْ 2. The sides or edges of the —, حَوَاجِبُ ٱلشَّمْسِ. The — was near to setting, أَدْنَتِ ٱلشَّمْسُ لِلْغُرُوبِ ـ شَرِقَتِ ٱلشَّمْسُ. To bask one's self in the —, تَشَمَّسَ. He sat in the —, قَعَدَ 2 فِي ٱلشَّمْسِ. To bronze, as does the sun, صَقَرَ 2 ـ سَقَرَ 2.

Sun, *v.t.* To expose to the sun, شَمَّسَ. To expose one's self to the sun, تَشَمَّسَ.

Sun-beam, *n.* شُعَاعُ ٱلشَّمْسِ *pl.* أَشِعَّة.

Sun-beat, *a.* } Bronzed by the sun, مَقْشُوفٌ مِنَ ـ قَشِف
Sun-burnt, } مَحْرُوقٌ مِنَ ـ مَسْقُورٌ مِنَ ٱلشَّمْسِ ـ ٱلشَّمْسِ
ٱلشَّمْسِ. *See also under to* Bronze, *v.t.*

Sunday, *n.* يَوْمُ ٱلْأَحَدِ ـ ٱلْأَحَدُ *pl.* أَيَّامُ آحَادٍ. Sunday-school, مَكْتَبُ يَوْمِ ٱلْأَحَدِ لِتَعْلِيمِ أُمُورِ ٱلدِّينِ.

Sunder, *n.* The half of a thing, شَطِير ـ شَطْر. In sunder, in twain, مُشَطَّر ـ مَشْطُور.

Sunder, *v.t.* To break, كَسَرَ ـ قَطَعَ; to separate from, فَرَقَ ـ مِنَ ـ فَصَلَ ـ مِنَ 2. It cannot be sundered, لَا يَنْفَصِلُ.

Sun-dial, *n.* سَاعَةٌ شَمْسِيَّةٌ ـ مِزْوَلَة *pl.* مَزَاوِلُ ـ مُقَنْطَرَة.

Sundown, *n.* غُرُوبُ ٱلشَّمْسِ.

Sun-dried, *a.* مُيَبَّسٌ فِي ٱلشَّمْسِ ـ مُنَشَّفٌ فِي ٱلشَّمْسِ. A — brick, لَبِنَة *coll.* لَبِن ـ قِرْمِيدَة *pl.* قَرَامِيدُ.

Sundry, *a.* بَعْض ـ شَتَّى ـ مُتَنَوِّع. Sundry things, أَشْيَاءُ شَتَّى. Verily, the assembly comprises — bodies of men, إِنَّ ٱلْمَجْلِسَ لَيَجْمَعُ شُتُوتًا مِنَ ٱلنَّاسِ.

Sunfish, *n.* سَمَكٌ بَحْرِيٌّ كَبِيرٌ مُسْتَدِيرُ ٱلشَّكْلِ.

Sunflower, *n.* إِكْرَار ـ عَبْدُ ٱلشَّمْسِ ـ دَوَّارُ ٱلشَّمْسِ.

Sung, *p. part. of to* Sing, *q.v.*

Sunk, *pret. of to* Sink, *q.v.*

Sunken, *a.* Lying at the bottom, فِي ٱلْقَعْرِ ـ فِي قَعْرٍ كَذَا; of the eyes, مُنْقَر ـ مُنْقِر ـ هَاجٌّ. *See also under* Socket, *n.*

Sunless, *a.* مِنْ غَيْرِ شَمْسٍ ـ بِلَا شَمْسٍ.

Sunlight, *n.* ضِيَاءُ (or ضَوْءُ) ٱلشَّمْسِ.

Sun-lit, *a.* تَضِيءُ عَلَيْهِ ٱلشَّمْسُ ـ مُنَوَّرٌ مِنَ ٱلشَّمْسِ.

Sunnite, *n.* One of the division of Muslims so called, مِنْ أَهْلِ ٱلسُّنَّةِ ـ سُنِّيٌّ *pl.* سُنِّيَّة *or* أَهْلُ ٱلسُّنَّةِ.

Sunny, *a.* Of a day, شَمِس ـ شَمْس ـ شَامِس; bright, نَيِّر ـ مُنِير. A — place, مَحَلٌّ شَمِسٌ ـ مَشْرِق ـ مِشْرَاق ـ شَرْقَة. Exposed to the sun, مُتَشَمِّس. To be —, شَمِسَ 2. To sit in a — place, تَشَرَّقَ.

Sunrise, *n.* } إِشْرَاقُ ٱلشَّمْسِ ـ شَرْقَةُ ٱلشَّمْسِ ـ طُلُوعُ ٱلشَّمْسِ.
Sunrising, } The place of the —, ٱلْمَشْرِق.

Sunset, *n.* } غُرُوبُ ٱلشَّمْسِ.
Sunsetting, }

Sunshine, *n.* ضِيَاءُ ٱلشَّمْسِ. In the —, فِي ٱلشَّمْسِ.

Sunshine, *a.* } شَمْس ـ شَامِس. To be —, شَمِسَ. *See also*
Sunshiny, } Sunny, *a.*

Sun-stroke, *n.* ضَرْبَةُ شَمْسٍ ـ ضَرْبَةُ سَقَرَاتِ ٱلشَّمْسِ.

Suo jure, ad. مِنْ حَقِّهِ.

Sup, *v.t.* To sip, مَزَّ 2 ـ تَمَزَّزَ ـ تَمَصَّصَ. *See to* Sip, *v.t.*

Sup, *v.i.* To eat the evening meal, عَشَا *aor.* يَعْشُو ـ تَعَشَّى.

Sup, *n.* A sip, جُرْعَة *pl.* جُرَع ـ حُسْوَة ـ مَزَّة. *See also under* Sip, *n.*

Superable, *a.* مِمَّا يُغْلَبُ عَلَيْهِ ـ مِمَّا يُنْجَحُ بِهِ ـ مِمَّا يُغْتَلَى عَلَى ـ قَهْرُهُ مُمْكِنٌ.

Superableness, *n.* إِمْكَانُ ٱلْغَلَبَةِ عَلَيْهِ.

Superably, *ad.* فِي حَوْزِ ٱلنَّجَاحِ ـ بِوَجْهٍ يُنْجَحُ بِهِ.

Superabound, *v.i.* كَثُرَ 2 ـ فَضِلَ ـ إِزْدَادَ أَكْثَرَ فَأَكْثَرَ.

Superabounding, *a.* } مُتَكَاثِر ـ كَثِير ـ زَائِد ـ فَاضِل.
Superabundant, }

Superabundance, *n.* كَثْرَة ـ زِيَادَة ـ فُضُول ـ فَرْط.

Superabundantly, *ad.* كِفَايَةً وَزِيَادَةً ـ بِفَرْطٍ ـ بِفُضُولٍ.

Superadd, *v.t.* زَادَ ـ فِي ـ أَضَافَ ـ إِلَى. To be superadded, إِنْضَمَّ إِلَى ـ إِنْضَافَ إِلَى.

Super-addition, *n.* The act of, إِضَافَة ـ زَوْد ـ زِيَادَة.

Super-angelic, *a.* فَوْقَ ٱلْمَلَائِكَةِ ـ أَعْلَى مِنَ ٱلْمَلَائِكَةِ.

Superannuate, *v.t.* To impair by old age, عَتَّقَ عُمْرَهُ. To put on the retired list, جَعَلَ ـ مِنَ ٱلْمُتَقَاعِدِينَ.

Superannuated, *a.* Impaired by old age, مُعَتَّقُ ٱلْعُمْرِ. Old, out of use, مَتْرُوك ـ غَيْرُ مُسْتَعْمَلٍ ـ مُلْغًى ـ عَتِيق. On the retired list, مِنَ ٱلْمُتَقَاعِدِينَ.

Superannuation, *n.* Of age, تَعْتِيقُ ٱلْعُمْرِ. The being on the retired list, تَقَاعُد. Pay of —, مَعَاشُ ٱلتَّقَاعُدِ.

Superb, *a.* جَلِيّ ـ مُفْتَخَر ـ فَاخِر ـ أَعْلَى ـ نَفِيس ـ أَنْفَس ـ عَظِيم. *See also* Grand, Splendid, *a.*

Superbly, *ad.* بِأَنْفَسِ صُورَةٍ ـ بِجَلَالٍ ـ بِفَخْرٍ.

Supercargo, *n.* وَكِيلُ صَاحِبِ ٱلْوَسْقِ فِي مَرْكَبٍ.

Supercilious, *a.* مُتَجَبِّر ـ شَامِخ ـ شَامِخُ ٱلْأَنْفِ ـ مَغْرُور ـ مُتَكَبِّر ـ مُتَنَفِّخ ـ آنِف ـ مُتَعَالٍ. To be —, شَمَخَ 2 أَنْفُهُ ـ تَكَبَّرَ ـ تَرَفَّعَ.

Superciliously, *ad.* تَكَبُّرًا ـ تَجَبُّرًا ـ بِغُرُورٍ ـ بِهَوَانٍ ـ بِشُمُوخٍ.

Superciliousness, *n.* تَكَبُّر ـ تَنَفُّخ ـ تَجَبُّر ـ شُمُوخ ـ غُرُور.

Supereminence, *n.* }
Supereminency, } تَفَوُّق ـ بَرَاعَة . *See also* Pre-eminence, *n.*

Supereminent, *a.* فَوْقَ ٱلْعَادَةِ ـ فَائِق ـ بَارِع ـ عَزِيز . *See also* Pre-eminent, *a.*

Supereminently, *ad.* بِٱلتَّفَوُّقِ ـ بِعِزَّةٍ ـ بِفَوَاقٍ . *See also* Pre-eminently, *ad.*

Supererogate, *v.i.* To do more than is incumbent on one, تَنَفَّلَ ـ تَبَرَّعَ بِ ـ تَطَوَّعَ بِ .

Supererogation, *n.* The act of doing more than is incumbent, تَطَوُّع ـ تَنَفُّل ـ تَبَرُّع . An act of —, نَفْل ـ نَافِلَة *pl.* نَوَافِل ـ فِعْلٌ زَائِدٌ عَلَى ٱلْمَشْرُوعِ .

Supererogatory, *a.* تَطَوُّعِيّ ـ نَافِل ـ تَبَرُّعِيّ . Supererogatory works, أَعْمَالٌ تَبَرُّعِيَّةٌ ـ أَعْمَالٌ تَطَوُّعِيَّةٌ ـ أَعْمَالٌ نَافِلَةٌ . Supererogatory prayers, such as are not prescribed, تَرَاوِيح ; one of such prayers, صَلَاةُ ٱلتَّطَوُّعِ .

Superexcellence, *n.* فَضْل ـ فَضِيلَةٌ فَائِقَةٌ ـ بَرَاعَة .

Superexcellent, *a.* بَارِع ـ أَشْمَل ـ فَائِق ـ أَعْلَى مَا يَكُونُ ـ مُفَضَّل ـ أَفْضَل .

Superfetation, *n.* حَبَلُ ٱلْمَرْأَةِ مَعَ وُجُودِ جَنِينٍ آخَرَ فِي أَحْشَائِهَا ـ إِزْدِوَاجُ ٱلْحَبَلِ .

Superficial, *a.* Pertaining to the surface, سَطْحِيّ . Light, trivial, لَطِيف ـ جُزْئِيّ ـ وَاهٍ ـ تَافِه . Not deep, of a wound, *etc.*, خَفِيف ـ بِسَمْكِ (*or* مُخْن) ٱلْجِلْدِ فَقَطْ . On the surface, visible, ظَاهِرِيّ ـ عَلَى ٱلْوَجْهِ . A man having — knowledge, عُوَيْرِف .

Superficially, *ad.* As on the surface, سَطْحًا . Lightly, بِخِفَّةٍ . Carelessly, بِغَيْرِ ٱعْتِنَاءٍ . Outwardly, visibly, بِٱلظَّاهِرِ ـ عَلَانِيَةً .

Superficialness, *n.* Littleness, خِفّ ـ خِفَّة ـ جُزْئِيَّة ـ قِلَّة . *See also* Shallowness, *n.*; *also next article.*

Superficies, *n.* سَطْح .

Superfine, *a.* عَالٍ ـ أَعْلَى مَا يَكُونُ ـ مُفْتَخَر .

Superfluity, *n.* فَرْط *pl.* أَفْرَاط ـ زِيَادَة ـ زَائِدٌ ـ شَيْءٌ ـ رَدِيّ ـ كَثْرَة ـ فَضْل ـ فُضُول . What is a —, or superfluous, الفَاضِلُ عَنِ ٱلْحَاجَةِ .

Superfluous, *a.* فَاضِل ـ مُسْتَدْرَك ـ زَائِد . Superfluous in the body, as an excrescence, زَوَائِدِيّ . It is — for me to write to you, هُوَ فُضُولٌ مِنِّي أَنْ أَكْتُبَ إِلَيْكُمْ . To be —, إِزْدَادَ ـ فَضِلَ [2] ـ .

Superfluously, *ad.* بِٱسْتِدْرَاكٍ ـ زِيَادَةً ـ بِإِفْرَاطٍ . To act — in, أَفْرَطَ فِي .

Superfluousness, *n.* فَرْط ـ فَضْل ـ زِيَادَة . *See also* Superfluity, *n.*

Super-human, *a.* Beyond what is human, فَائِقُ ٱلطَّبْعِ ٱلْبَشَرِيِّ . Beyond human power, يَفُوقُ طَاقَةَ ٱلْبَشَرِ . *See also* Divine, *n.*

Super-impose, *v.t.* To place on, وَضَعَ-عَلَى *aor.* يَضَعُ ـ رَكَّبَ-عَلَى ; to add to, أَضَافَ-إِلَى . To be superimposed, added to, إِنْضَافَ إِلَى .

Super-incumbent, *a.* مُرَكَّبٌ عَلَى ـ نَائِمٌ عَلَى ـ مَوْضُوعٌ عَلَى .

Super-induce, *v.t.* أَنْتَجَ أَيْضًا كَذَا ـ سَبَّبَ أَيْضًا كَذَا ـ جَلَبَ [2] ـ أَيْضًا كَذَا ـ أَوْرَثَ أَيْضًا كَذَا .

Super-induction, *n.* تَزْيِيد ـ إِضَافَة .

Super-infuse, *v.t.* Of pouring, زَادَ-صَبًّا *aor.* يَزِيدُ ـ عَادَ فَسَكَبَ ـ عَادَ-كَذَا *aor.* يَعُودُ عَلَى ; of bringing in, أَدْخَلَ أَيْضًا كَذَا .

Superintend, *v.t.* To oversee, نَظَرَ-إِلَى [2] ـ بَاشَرَ ـ سَايَسَ . To be placed in charge of, تَوَكَّلَ (*or* وُكِّلَ) فِي ـ أُوتُمِنَ عَلَى .

Superintendence, *n.* }
Superintendency, } سِيَاسَة ـ مُبَاشَرَة ـ نَظَارَة .

Superintendent, *n.* }
Superintender, } نَقِيب *pl.* نُقَبَاء ـ عَرِيف *pl.* عُرَفَاء ـ إِزَاء ـ نُظَّار *pl.* نَاظِر ـ عُمَّال *pl.* عَامِل ـ ضَابِط *pl.* ضُبَّاط ـ مُبَاشِر *pl.* مُبَاشِرُون . A — in chief, مُسَيْطِر ـ مُصَيْطِر .

Superior, *a.* Higher, in rank, elevation, *etc.*, أَعْظَمُ دَرَجَةً ـ أَفْضَل ـ بَارِع ; in eminence, أَعَالِي *pl.* عَلِيّ *or* عُلْيَا *fem.* أَعْلَى in rank, nobility, أَشْرَف ـ أَعَزّ . Excellent, good, عَالٍ ; fine, رَفِيع . Super-excellent, فَائِق . Superior, in a general sense, بَارِع . Superior intelligence, عَقْلٌ رَفِيعٌ . Superior in numbers to, أَكْثَرُ عَدَدًا مِن ; in knowledge to, أَكْثَرُ عِلْمًا مِن . Superior force or power, عِزّ ـ قُوَّةٌ جَابِرَةٌ ـ قُوَّةٌ قَاهِرَةٌ : he yielded to — power, أَذْعَنَ لِلْقُوَّةِ ٱلْجَابِرَةِ . He was — to his companion, بَرَعَ صَاحِبَهُ ـ . To be — to, above, higher, عَلَا بِ *aor.* يَعْلُو ; as in dignity, nobility, *etc.*, عَلِيَ ـ . To consider — to, فَضَّلَ-عَلَى . I am — to them in rank, عَلَوْتُهُمْ بِٱلشَّرَفِ . To be —, to excel, بَرَعَ [2] . To be — to, فَاقَ [2] . To be — to, to disdain to do; *see under to* Disdain, *v.t.*

Superior, *n.* One higher in rank, power, *etc.*, than, أَرْفَعُ قَدْرًا مِن *pl.* مَنْ هُمْ أَرْفَعُ قَدْرًا مِن . A — in age to, أَقْدَمُ عُمْرًا مِن *pl.* مَنْ هُمْ أَقْدَمُ عُمْرًا مِن . A great man, in rank, *etc.*, كَبِير *pl.* كِبَار *and* كُبَرَاء . A head, chief, as of a convent, *etc.*, رَئِيس *pl.* رُؤَسَاء . Master, officer, ضَابِط *pl.* ضُبَّاط .

Superiority, *n.* Superior excellence, فَضْل ـ بَرَاعَة . The being in advance of, تَقَدُّم ـ قُدْمَة ـ فَوْز ـ سَبْق . Authority, رِئَاسَة . Victory, غَلَبَة .

Superlative, *a.* فَائِقٌ لِلْغَايَةِ ـ بَدِيع ـ رَائِق ـ بَالِغ ; of excellence, أَفْضَل — بَارِعٌ لِلْغَايَةِ ; of height, عَالٍ لِلْغَايَةِ. The — degree of comparison, أَفْعَلُ ٱلتَّفْضِيلِ.

Superlative, *n.* In grammar, إِسْمُ تَفْضِيلٍ.

Superlatively, *ad.* In the highest degree, لِلْغَايَةِ — نِهَايَةً — فِي أَعْلَى دَرَجَةٍ — بِلَا مُقَايَسَةٍ. Superlatively precious, عَزِيزٌ لِلْغَايَةِ.

Superlativeness, *n.* فَضْل — بَدَاعَة — رَوْق — مُبَالَغَة.

Superlunar, *a.* }
Superlunary, } فَوْقَ ٱلْقَمَرِ ; earthly, دُنْيَوِيٌّ — عَالَمِيٌّ.

Supermundane, *a.* سَمَاوِيٌّ — غَيْرُ عَالَمِيٍّ — فَوْقَ ٱلْعَالَمِ.

Supernal, *a.* High, lofty, مُنِيع — مُرْتَفِع — عَالٍ ; celestial, سَمَاوِيٌّ — سَمَائِيٌّ. What is above, فَوْقَانِيٌّ.

Supernatant, *a.* طَافٍ عَلَى وَجْهِ كَذَا — عَوَّام. To be — over, to be spread over, عَلَا *aor.* يَعْلُو.

Supernatural, *a.* Above nature, خَارِجٌ عَنْ — فَوْقَ ٱلطَّبِيعَةِ طَاقَةِ ٱلطَّبِيعَةِ. Out of the ordinary course, خَارِقُ ٱلْعَادَةِ. Partaking of the miraculous, مِنْ صِفَةِ ٱلْمُعْجِزَةِ ; of sorcery, مِنْ صِفَةِ ٱلسِّحْرِ. Spiritual, رُوحَانِيٌّ — رُوحِيٌّ. *See also* Divine, *a.*

Supernaturally, *ad.* As beyond the laws of nature, بِوَجْهٍ يَفُوقُ ٱلطَّبِيعَةَ — فِي خَارِجِ نَامُوسِ ٱلطَّبِيعَةِ. *See also* Divinely, *ad.*

Supernumerary, *a.* Exceeding the number prescribed, زَائِدٌ عَنِ ٱلْعَدَدِ — فَوْقَ ٱلْعَدَدِ.

Supernumerary, *n.* Of a person or thing, شَخْصٌ (*or* شَيْءٌ) زَائِدٌ عَنِ ٱلْعَدَدِ. An extra hand employed for a time, مُسْتَخْدَمٌ مُوَقَّتًا.

Superposition, *n.* تَرْكِيبُ (*or* وَضْعُ) شَيْءٍ عَلَى شَيْءٍ.

Super-royal, *n.* Of paper, قَطْعُ وَرَقٍ مُطْلَقٌ.

Supersaturate, *v.t.* شَرَّبَ لِلْغَايَةِ. To be supersaturated, تَشَرَّبَ لِلْغَايَةِ — شَرِقَ.

Superscribe, *v.t.* كَتَبَ عَلَى. To docket, كَتَبَ عُنْوَانًا عَلَى — عَنْوَنَ.

Superscription, *n.* كِتَابَة — مَكْتُوب. A docket or other memorandum in writing, عُنْوَان.

Supersecular, *a.* فَوْقَ ٱلْعَالَمِ — يَفُوقُ ٱلْعَالَمِينَ.

Supersede, *v.t.* To come in the place of, خَلَفَ. To depose, displace, عَزَلَ — عَزَّلَ. To make void, as a law, *etc.*, نَسَخَ — أَبْطَلَ — بَطَّلَ. To put in the place of, خَلَّفَ — إِسْتَخْلَفَ — جَعَلَ عِوَضًا عَنْ كَذَا. I superseded him, خَلَفْتُهُ.

Supersedeas, *n.* أَمْرٌ بِمَنْعِ سِيَاقِ دَعْوَى.

Supersedure, *n.* A coming in the place of, خِلَافَة. Deposition, عَزْل. Voidance, نَسْخ — إِبْطَال — تَبْطِيل.

Superstition, *n.* Excessive rigour in religion, حَمَس — حَمَاسَة — تَنَسُّك. Unfounded belief, وَسْوَسَة. False religion, false worship, عَقَائِدُ فَاسِدَةٌ — أَضَالِيلُ.

Superstitious, *a.* Excessively rigorous in religion, أَحْمَسُ *pl.* حُمْس — حَمِس — مُتَحَمِّس — مُتَنَسِّك. Full of scruples, مُوَسْوِس — مُتَوَسْوِس. Following false religion or religious practices, ذُو أَضَالِيلَ — ذُو عَقَائِدَ فَاسِدَةٍ. They appeared to be very —, أَبْدَوا ٱلْغُلُوَّ فِي ٱلدِّينِ. *See also* Fanatical, *a.*

Superstitiously, *ad.* Rigidly, as in religion, بِتَنَسُّكٍ — بِحَمَاسَةٍ ; as being full of scruples, بِوَسْوَسَةٍ. To act —, fanatically, تَحَمَّسَ.

Superstitiousness, *n.* *See* Superstition, *n.*

Super-stratum, *n.* طَبَقَةٌ فَوْقَانِيَّةٌ *pl.* طَبَقَات.

Superstruct, *v.t.* بَنَى شَيْئًا عَلَى شَيْءٍ.

Superstruction, *n.* The act of, بِنَاءُ شَيْءٍ عَلَى شَيْءٍ.

Superstructure, *n.* مَا هُوَ مَبْنِيٌّ عَلَى شَيْءٍ آخَرَ — بِنَاءٌ فَوْقَانِيٌّ — بُنْيَانٌ عَلَى بُنْيَانٍ آخَرَ.

Supervene, *v.i.* To betide, happen, صَارَ *aor.* يَصِيرُ — حَدَثَ — حَصَلَ — جَرَى. To appear, to happen, ظَهَرَ — تَظَاهَرَ — عَرَضَ — تَعَرَّضَ — إِتَّفَقَ.

Supervenient, *a.* Extraneous, not intrinsic, مُلْحَق. Supplementary, مُضَاف — مُسْتَدْرَك. Coming as something new, حَادِث.

Supervention, *n.* The act of happening, حُصُول — حُدُوث — ظُهُور — تَعَرُّض — إِتِّفَاق.

Supervisal, *n.* }
Supervision, } نَظَر — نِظَارَة — حِرَاسَة. *See also* Inspection, *n.*

Supervise, *v.t.* نَظَرَ إِلَى — بَاشَرَ — سَايَسَ. *See also to* Inspect, *v.t.*

Supervisor, *a.* نَاظِر *pl.* نُظَّار — مُبَاشِر. *See also* Inspector, *n.*

Supervive, *v.t.* *See to* Outlive, *v.t.*

Supine, *n.* مَصْدَرٌ مِنَ ٱلْمَصَادِرِ فِي ٱللُّغَةِ ٱللَّاتِينِيَّةِ.

Supine, *a.* Lying on the back, نَائِمٌ عَلَى ظَهْرِهِ — وَجْهُهُ إِلَى فَوْقُ. Listless, فُطَارِيٌّ — مُتَهَامِل — مُتَسَاهِل — مُتَكَاسِل — غَيْرُ مُبَالٍ. To be —, تَهَامَلَ — تَكَاسَلَ — تَسَاهَلَ.

Supinely, *ad.* With the face upwards, وَجْهُهُ إِلَى فَوْقُ. Listlessly, بِتَهَامُلٍ — بِتَكَاسُلٍ — مِنْ غَيْرِ مُبَالَاةٍ.

Supineness, *n.* The act of lying on the back, الإِسْتِلْقَاءُ عَلَى ٱلْقَفَا. Listlessness, تَهَامُل — تَكَاسُل — تَسَاهُل — قِلَّةُ مُرُوَّةٍ — عَدَمُ مُبَالَاةٍ.

Supper, *n.* عِشَى — عَشَاء *pl.* أَعْشِيَة. The Lord's Supper, العَشَاءُ ٱلرَّبَّانِيُّ. Taking —, عَاشٍ — عَشْيَانُ. To take —, عَشَا *aor.* يَعْشُو — تَعَشَّى. To give one a —, عَشَّى. A — cup, غَبُوق. After —, or supper time, بَعْدَ ٱلْعَشَاءِ — عُشَيَّةً.

Supperless, *a.* and *ad.* بِلا عَشَآء.

Supplant, *v.t.* To take the place of, أَعْقَبَ ـ تَعَقَّبَ. To — by stratagem, تَعَقَّبَ-بِمَكْرٍ. To deprive, cast out, divest, خَلَعَ ـ جَرَّدَ ـ عَرَّى.

Supplantation, *n.* The act of taking the place of, تَعَقُّب ـ إِعْقَاب. Deprivation, خَلْع ـ تَعْرِيَة ـ تَجْرِيد.

Supplanter, *n.* One who takes the place of another, مُتَعَقِّب; by fraud, مُتَعَقِّب مَكَّار. One who deprives, خَالِع ـ مُجَرِّد.

Supple, *a.* Flexible, لَيِّن ـ رَطِيب ـ سَمْح ـ سَهْو ـ سَهْلُ ٱلْعُطُوفَةِ. Supple in disposition, لَيِّنُ ٱلْإِنْعِطَافِ ـ سَاذِج. Manageable, مِذْعَان ـ عَاجّ. To be —, soft, flexible, رَطُبَ ـ لَانَ. To be —, submissive, سَامَحَ ـ أَسْمَحَ. *See also* Flexible, Pliant, *a.*

Supple, *v.t.* To make soft, flexible, رَطَّبَ ـ لَيَّنَ ـ دَيَّثَ. To make compliant, لَيَّنَ جَانِبَهُ ـ حَلَّمَ ـ طَوَّعَ.

Supple, *v.i.* To become supple, تَلَيَّنَ ـ لَانَ ـ دَاثَ. To become compliant, تَحَلَّمَ ـ حَلُمَ.

Supplement, *n.* Something added, ضَمِيمَة ـ إِضَافَة ـ مُسْتَدْرَك ـ عِلَاوَة *pl.* عَلَاوَى *and* عِلَاوَات. Something to complete another, تَتِمَّة ـ كُمَالَة ـ تَمَام ـ تَكْمِيل. A —, as of a book, *etc.*, ذَيْل *pl.* تَتِمَّة ـ أَذْيَال. This — is given gratis, هٰذِهِ ٱلْعِلَاوَةُ تُعْطَى مَجَّانًا. To add a — to ..., as to a document, ذَيَّلَ: He added a — to the treaty, ذَيَّلَ ٱلْمُعَاهَدَةَ. A —, as to a treaty, *etc.*, تَذْيِيل. We have published a —, أَصْدَرْنَا عِلَاوَةً. The — to al-Bukhâry, that is, the additions made thereto to supply his omissions, ٱلْمُسْتَدْرَكُ عَلَى ٱلْبُخَارِيِّ.

Supplement, *v.t.* To add something to, أَضَافَ-إِلَى. To supplement by way of completion, أَكْمَلَ ـ كَمَّلَ; by way of notification, إِسْتَدْرَكَ-عَلَى كَذَا: I supplemented to it what was omitted, إِسْتَدْرَكْتُ. I supplemented what had escaped me, إِسْتَدْرَكْتُهُ عَلَيْهِ مَا فَاتَنِي.

Supplemental, *a.* } Added, مُضَاف. Completing, مُتَمِّم ـ مُكَمِّل.
Supplementary, } A — article, as in a treaty, بَنْد مَضْمُوم *pl.*
Supplementive, } بُنُود ـ بَنْد مُذَيَّل.

Suppleness, *n.* Flexibility, لَيَان ـ لِينَة ـ رُطُوبَة ـ دَيْث; of disposition, سَذَاجَة ـ دَمَاثَة ـ لِينَةُ ٱلْجَانِبِ. *See also* Flexibility, Pliancy, *n.*

Suppletory, *a.* مُكَمِّل ـ مُسِدّ.

Suppliant, *a.* مُلْتَمِس ـ مُبْتَهِل ـ مُتَضَرِّع. In a — posture, وَهُوَ رَاكِع.

Suppliant, *n.* A humble petitioner, مُلْتَمِس إِلَى ـ مُتَرَجٍّ. One who desires earnestly, رَاغِبٌ إِلَى ـ رَغُوب.

Suppliantly, *ad.* بِٱبْتِهَالٍ ـ بِٱلْتِمَاسٍ ـ تَضَرُّعًا.

Supplicant, *n.* *See* Suppliant, *n.*

Supplicate, *v.t.* To implore, entreat, تَضَرَّعَ إِلَى ـ قَنَعَ ـ طَلَبَ مِن ـ تَرَجَّى ـ إِلْتَمَسَ مِن ـ إِبْتَهَلَ إِلَى. To beg, ask, To — in behalf of another, إِسْتَشْفَعَ. To — one for mercy, إِسْتَرْحَمَ; for assistance, إِسْتَغَاثَ ـ إِسْتَعَانَ ـ إِسْتَمَدَّ.

Supplicate, *v.i.* To implore, تَضَرَّعَ ـ إِبْتَهَلَ; to beg, pray, طَلَبَ ـ إِلْتَمَسَ.

Supplicatingly, *ad.* *See* Suppliantly, *ad.*

Supplication, *n.* إِلْتِمَاس ـ تَضَرُّع ـ إِبْتِهَال. To offer supplications, قَدَّمَ ٱلتَّضَرُّعَاتِ. To make — to; *see to* Supplicate, *v.t.* *See also* Prayer, *n.*

Supplicatory, *a.* حَاوٍ ـ مُتَضَمِّنُ ٱلتَّضَرُّعِ ـ مُبْتَهِل ـ مُتَضَرِّع عَلَى ٱلْإِبْتِهَالِ.

Supplier, *n.* One who supplies, provides, رَزَّاق. The Bountiful Supplier, God, ٱلرَّزَّاقُ. A purveyor, مُمَوِّن ـ مُتَسَوِّق; *vulg.* كَلَارْجِي ـ كَرَارْجِي ـ مُوَّان. A — of household furniture, نَجَّاد ـ فَرَّاش.

Supply, *v.t.* To yield, afford, أَوْرَدَ ـ أَحْدَثَ. To minister to, عَطَى ـ عَاطَى: he supplies or ministers to me, هُوَ يُعَطِّينِي ـ هُوَ يُعَاطِينِي. To provide with, جَهَّزَ-بِ ـ رَزَقَ-بِ ـ أَمَدَّ-بِ ـ مَانَ-بِ ـ مَأَنَ-بِ. To make up a deficiency, جَبَرَ ٱلنُّقْصَانَ ـ مَلَأَ ٱلْإِحْتِيَاجَ ـ سَدَّ. To fill up, as a place, *etc.*, سَدَّ: I supplied his place, قُمْتُ مَكَانَهُ ـ خَلَفْتُهُ. The want will be supplied thereby, تُسَدُّ بِهِ ٱلْحَاجَةُ. May God supply the place of ... to thee! خَلَفَ ٱللّٰهُ عَلَيْكَ كَذَا. *See also to* Supplement, *v.t.*

Supply, *n.* A stock, as of provisions, ذَخِيرَة ـ مُؤْنَة. Sufficiency for want, مَسَدُّ ٱلْحَاجَةِ. Supplies, as of wheat, *etc.*, بُرَّة; for a journey, زُوَادَة; for war, مُهِمَّاتُ ٱلْحَرْبِ ـ لَوَازِمُ حَرْبِيَّة.

Support, *n.* The act of supporting, as on pillars, *etc.*, إِسْنَاد; of upholding, maintaining, preserving, صَوْن ـ حِفْظ ـ ضَبْط. A —, prop, مُسْنَد *pl.* مَسَانِد ـ عُمْدَة *pl.* أَعْمِدَة ـ دِعَامَة *pl.* دَعَائِم ـ دِعَام *pl.* دَعَائِم ـ رُكْن *pl.* أَرْكَان. Maintenance, living, قِيَام ـ قِوَام ـ مَعَاش ـ مَعِيشَة ـ عَيْشَة. Backing, عَضُد ـ ظَهْر ـ تَأْيِيد ـ مُظَاهَرَة. Support, as indicating a body of troops drawn up as a reserve in the rear of a fighting column, فِئَة *pl.* فِئُون *and* فِئَات. A rest, عَمَد ـ سَنَد. Assistance, إِغَاثَة ـ إِسْعَاف ـ مُظَاهَرَة ـ عِنَايَة ـ إِلْتِفَات ـ تَوَجُّه ـ مُعَاوَنَة ـ مَدَد ـ حِمَايَة. A —, one to rely on, عِوَل. Raised on supports, مُرْتَفِعٌ عَلَى دَعَائِمَ. Support, a supporter, aider, عَضُد *pl.* أَعْضَاد.

Support, *v.t.* To bear, إِحْتَمَلَ ـ تَحَمَّلَ. To prop, sustain, عَمَدَ ـ أَعْمَدَ ـ دَعَمَ ـ سَنَّدَ ـ أَسْنَدَ. To —, as with provisions, مَانَ ـ أَمَدَّ بِ ـ أَسْعَفَ. To assist, أَغَاثَ ـ سَاعَدَ. To —, as taking the part of, to second, عَضَدَ ـ تَعَصَّبَ لِ ـ شَدَّ مَعَ ـ أَظْهَرَ ـ تَمَسَّكَ مَعَ. To encourage, شَجَّعَ. To protect, حَمَى ـ حَامَى. To nurture, نَشَّأَ. To comfort, سَلَّى. To —, as one's family, عَالَ ـ أَعَالَ ـ كَدَشَ لِ. To —, as by testimony, سَنَّدَ ـ أَيَّدَ ـ ثَبَّتَ ـ بَرْهَنَ ـ أَثْبَتَ. To — or maintain one's self, قَامَ بِمَعِيشَةِ نَفْسِهِ; to — or rest one's self against, إِدَّعَمَ عَلَى ـ إِسْتَنَدَ إِلَى ـ أَظْهَرَ عَلَى. To — one against, أَظْهَرَ عَلَى. Support arms! *in Turkish,* دِيْوَان دُور. *See also to* Maintain, Provide, *v.t.*

Supportable, *a.* Endurable, يُحْتَمَلُ ـ مِمَّا يُتَحَمَّلُ; that may be established, confirmed, قَابِلُ ٱلْإِثْبَاتِ ـ مِمَّا يُتَثَبَّتُ.

Supportableness, *n.* The state of being tolerable, حَالَةُ ٱلْإِحْتِمَالِ (*or* ٱلتَّحَمُّلِ).

Supporter, *n.* An adherent, تَابِعٌ *pl.* تَوَابِعُ ـ مِنْ حِزْبِ كَذَا. An aider, عَضُدٌ *pl.* أَعْضَادٌ ـ ظَهِيرٌ *pl.* ظُهَرَاءُ ـ حَلِيفٌ ـ نَصِيرٌ. One who provides for his family, مُعِيلٌ. A — on a coat of arms, صُورَةُ إِنْسَانٍ أَوْ حَيَوَانٍ عَلَى جَانِبَيْ رَسْمٍ فِي عَلَامَةِ ٱلنَّسَبِ وَهِيَ ٱلْآرْمَا. *See also* Support, *n.*

Supposable, *a.* يُتَصَوَّرُ ـ مِمَّا يُفْرَضُ ـ يُفْرَضُ. Is it — that ..., أَيُحْتَمَلُ أَنْ.

Supposal, *n.* وَهْمٌ *pl.* أَوْهَامٌ ـ خَمْنٌ ـ تَخْمِينٌ *pl.* تَخَامِينُ ـ ظَنٌّ *pl.* ظُنُونٌ ـ قِيَاسٌ. *See also under* Conjecture, *n.*

Suppose, *v.t.* To imagine, رَأَى *aor.* يَرَى ـ قَدَّرَ ـ خَمَّنَ ـ تَصَوَّرَ ـ ظَنَّ. To lay down without proof, as if taking for granted: he supposed that ...., قَدَّرَ أَنْ ـ فَرَضَ أَنْ ـ جَعَلَ أَنْ ـ عَمِلَ. As I —, كَمَا أَظُنُّ. That being supposed, وَعَلَى هٰذَا قِيَاسًا ـ فَبِنَاءً عَلَى ذٰلِكَ ـ ٱلْقِيَاسِ. Supposing that ...., عَلَى فَرْضِ أَنْ. And supposing, or, if we suppose, وَإِنْ (*or* إِذَا) فَرَضْنَا. Supposing war to break out between them, عَلَى فَرْضِ وُقُوعِ ٱلْحَرْبِ بَيْنَهُمْ. They supposed that they should have received more, ظَنُّوا أَنَّهُمْ يَأْخُذُونَ أَكْثَرَ. They supposed that it was a spirit, ظَنُّوهُ خَيَالًا. They, supposing that he was in the house, وَإِذْ ظَنُّوهُ فِي ٱلْبَيْتِ. *See also under to* Conjecture, Imagine, Think, *v.t.*

Supposer, *n.* مُتَوَهِّمٌ ـ مُتَصَوِّرٌ ـ مُقَدِّرٌ ـ مُخَمِّنٌ.

Supposition, *n.* Something put forward without proof, تَصَوُّرٌ *pl.* تَصَوُّرَاتٌ ـ تَقْدِيرٌ *pl.* تَقْدِيرَاتٌ ـ فَرْضٌ. Something supposed, a conjecture, خَدْسٌ ـ حَزْرٌ ـ وَهْمٌ *pl.* أَوْهَامٌ ـ تَخْمِينٌ ـ ظَنٌّ *pl.* ظُنُونٌ.

Supposititious, *a.* False, غَيْرُ حَقِيقِيٍّ ـ كَاذِبٌ ـ صِنَاعِيٌّ. Put by trick in the place of another, مَا يُجْعَلُ بِمَكْرٍ عِوَضًا عَنْ غَيْرِهِ.

Supposititiously, *ad.* Falsely, زُورًا ـ كَذِبًا. By trickish substitution, تَبْدِيلًا بِٱلْمَكْرِ.

Suppositive, *a.* تَخْيِيلِيٌّ ـ تَخْمِينِيٌّ.

Suppository, *n.* صُوفَةٌ ـ فَتِيلَةٌ.

Suppress, *v.t.* To hinder, أَمْسَكَ ـ عَزَرَ ـ مَنَعَ. To put down, as an insurrection, *etc.*, ضَبَطَ ـ قَمَعَ ـ أَخْمَدَ. To forbid, حَرَّمَ ـ نَهَّى ـ نَهَى ـ مَنَعَ. To —, as a letter in a word, or a word in a sentence, to omit, إِحْتَذَفَ ـ حَذَفَ. To annul, أَبْطَلَ ـ بَطَّلَ. To keep secret, not to disclose, أَسَرَّ ـ كَتَمَ ـ كَتَّمَ. To — a journal, أَلْغَى ٱلصَّحِيفَةَ (*or* ٱلْجَرِيدَةَ) دَوَامًا. To pass over in silence, سَكَتَ عَنْ. They — their rage until they have an opportunity of vengeance, يَكْتُمُونَ غَيْظَهُمْ إِلَى أَنْ تَحِينَ لَهُمْ فُرْصَةُ ٱلْإِنْتِقَامِ.

Suppression, *n.* The act of hindering, إِمْسَاكٌ ـ عَزْرٌ ـ مَنْعٌ; of subduing, ضَبْطٌ ـ قَمْعٌ ـ إِخْمَادٌ; of forbidding, تَحْرِيمٌ ـ نَهْيٌ; of omitting, إِحْتِذَافٌ ـ حَذْفٌ; of annulling, putting an end to, إِبْطَالٌ ـ تَبْطِيلٌ; of keeping secret, إِسْرَارٌ ـ كَتْمٌ ـ تَكْتِيمٌ; of passing over in silence, فَوَاتٌ ـ سُكُوتٌ عَنْ. Suppression, as of a journal, إِلْغَاءُ جَرِيدَةٍ; as of an evacuation, إِنْقِطَاعٌ ـ حَصْرٌ; of urine, أَسْرُ (*or* حَصْرُ *or* إِنْقِطَاعُ) ٱلْبَوْلِ. Literal —, حَذْفٌ حَرْفِيٌّ.

Suppressive, *a.* Tending to hinder, عَازِرٌ ـ مَانِعٌ; to put down, subdue, ضَابِطٌ ـ قَامِعٌ ـ مُخْمِدٌ; to forbid, مُحَرِّمٌ ـ مُنْهٍ; to annul, مُبْطِلٌ ـ مُبَطِّلٌ; to keep secret, مُكَتِّمٌ.

Suppressor, *n.* *See* Suppressive, *a.*

Suppurate, *v.t.* جَعَلَ يَتَقَيَّحُ.

Suppurate, *v.i.* أَغَذَّ ـ غَذَّ ـ غَثَّ ـ أَغَثَّ ـ أَمَدَّ ـ قَاحَ ـ تَقَيَّحَ.

Suppuration, *n.* تَقَيُّحٌ ـ غَذِيذَةٌ ـ غَثِيثٌ. The coming to a state of —, تَدَمُّلٌ. *See also under* Matter, Pus, *n.*

Suppurating, *a.* غَاذٌّ.

Suppurative, *a.* مُجْرِي ٱلْقَيْحِ ـ مُسَيِّلُ ٱلْقَيْحِ.

Supputation, *n.* حِسَابٌ.

Suppute, *v.t.* *See to* Calculate, Reckon, *v.t.*

Supremacy, *n.* The state of being supreme, first, قِدَمٌ ـ تَقَدُّمٌ ـ أَوَّلِيَّةٌ; of having the precedence, of surpassing, غَلَبَةٌ ـ فَوَاقٌ ـ نُفُوذٌ. Highest authority, رِئَاسَةٌ ـ سَلْطَنَةٌ; in religion, إِمَامَةٌ.

The Oath of Supremacy, مُبَايَعَةُ ٱلْمَلِكِ (أَوِ ٱلْمَلِكَةِ). To have the — over, إِسْتَوْلَى عَلَى ـ إِرْتَأَسَ عَلَى ـ تَرَأَّسَ عَلَى. To gain the — in an affair, إِسْتَوْلَى عَلَى ٱلْأَمْرِ ٱسْتِيلَآءً.

Supreme, *a.* As being above all, فَوْقَ ٱلْكُلِّ. Highest, first, most exalted, أَكْبَرُ ـ أَعْظَمُ ـ أَوَّلُ ـ أَرْفَعُ ـ أَعْلَى ـ أَعَزُّ. Supreme power, قُوَّةٌ قَاهِرَةٌ ـ حُكْمٌ مُطْلَقٌ ـ حُكْمٌ مُسْتَقِلٌّ ـ إِسْتِبْدَاد. Supreme authority, زَعَامَةٌ مُطْلَقَةٌ ـ سَعَةٌ مُطْلَقَةٌ ـ حُكْمٌ مُجَرَّدٌ. Supreme, great, perfect, أَكْمَلُ ـ كَامِلٌ ـ بَارِعٌ. The Supreme (God), الْجَبَّارُ. The — or highest degree of perfection, غَايَةُ ٱلْكَمَالِ ـ مُنْتَهَى ٱلْكَمَالِ ـ أَقْصَى دَرَجَةِ ٱلْكَمَالِ. To be — in, إِسْتَبَدَّ بِ. To exercise — authority over, تَسَلَّطَ عَلَى ـ إِطْلَاقًا.

Supremely, *ad.* In the highest degree, لِلْغَايَةِ ـ نِهَايَةً ـ بَتَّةً.

Surbase, *n.* إِفْرِيزٌ بَارِزٌ.

Surbasement, *n.* خَطٌّ فِي ٱلشَّكْلِ ٱلْبَيْضِيِّ.

Surbed, *v.t.* رَكَّبَ عَلَى حَافَتِهِ.

Surcease, *v.i.* *See to* Cease, *v.i.*

Surcharge, *v.t.* (*See to* Overcharge, *v.t.*) To be surcharged, suffused, شَرِقَ: His eye was surcharged with blood, شَرِقَتْ (or إِشْرَوْرَقَتْ) عَيْنُهُ. *See also under to* Suffuse, *v.t.*

Surcharge, *n.* *See* Overcharge, *n.*

Surcingle, *n.* حِزَامٌ فَوْقَانِيٌّ ـ سِمْطٌ *pl.* سُمُوطٌ ـ وَلَمٌ ـ وَلَمٌ.

Surcle, *n.* A little shoot; *see* Sucker, *n.*

Surd, *a.* Deaf, أَصَمُّ. A — verb, فِعْلٌ أَصَمُّ; a — noun, or root, جِذْرٌ أَصَمُّ.

Sure, *a.* Indubitable, true, حَقِيقِيٌّ ـ صَحِيحٌ ـ أَكِيدٌ ـ مُؤَكَّدٌ. Inevitable, أَكِيدٌ ـ لَا بُدَّ مِنْهُ ـ لَا مَفَرَّ مِنْهُ. Sure, tried, مُجَرَّبٌ. Solid, firm, مَكِينٌ ـ قَوِيٌّ ـ مَتِينٌ ـ مَاكِنٌ ـ وَثِيقٌ. Established, proved, مُحَقَّقٌ ـ مُثْبَتٌ ـ مُقَرَّرٌ. That may be relied on, وَاثِقٌ ـ أَمِينٌ. Safe, مُسَلَّمٌ ـ أَمِينٌ. Put into proper order, fortified, مَصُونٌ ـ مُحْكَمٌ. Safe money, as if it were already in the pocket, دَرَاهِمُ بِٱلْعُبِّ. This is the surest, safest, way, هٰذَا ٱلطَّرِيقُ ٱلْأَسْلَمُ. A — taste, one not likely to be mistaken, ذَوْقٌ صَحِيحٌ ـ ذَوْقٌ سَلِيمٌ. Sure knowledge, information, يَقِينٌ ـ عِلْمٌ يَقِينٌ. I am —, أَعْلَمُ يَقِينًا. I am — of it, أَنَا عَلَى يَقِينٍ مِنْهُ. He was — of it, عِلْمُهُ يَقِينٌ بِهِ. No one is — of his life, فَلَا يَأْمَنُ أَحَدٌ بِحَيَاتِهِ. He took the — course, أَخَذَ بِٱلثِّقَةِ. To be — of, إِسْتَيْقَنَ بِ ـ إِتَّقَنَ بِ ـ أَيْقَنَ بِ ـ كَانَ مُحَقَّقًا عِنْدَهُ ـ كَانَ مُؤَكَّدًا عِنْدَهُ. To be —, sound, valid, true, صَحَّ. To make —, safe, أَمَّنَ ـ آمَنَ. To feel —, أَمِنَ. He is —, secure, as in mind, *etc.*, أَمِنٌ. *See also under* Safe, Secure, *a.*

Sure, *ad.* } Certainly, بِتَأْكِيدٍ ـ حَقًّا ـ يَقِينًا ـ عَلَى ٱلتَّحْقِيقِ;
Surely, } firmly, تَوْثِيقًا; undoubtedly, absolutely, أَلْبَتَّةَ ـ بَتَّةً. "Now, surely, they are the lightwitted," إِلَّا أَنَّهُمْ هُمُ ٱلسُّفَهَآءُ (Kur. ii. 12). "And, surely, the future shall be for thee better than the past," وَلَلْآخِرَةُ خَيْرٌ لَكَ مِنَ ٱلْأُولَى (Kur. xciii. 4).

Sureness, *n.* Certainty, truth, حَقٌّ ـ يَقِينٌ ـ إِتِّقَانٌ ـ إِيقَانٌ. Safety, أَمِينَةٌ ـ حِفْظٌ ـ أَمَانٌ ـ صَوْنٌ ـ أَمْنٌ. *See also* Safety, Security, *n.*

Suretiship, *n.* كَفَالَةٌ ـ ضَمَانٌ ـ قَبَالَةٌ.

Surety, *n.* One who gives bail for another, غَرِيرٌ *pl.* غُرَّانٌ ـ زَعِيمٌ *pl.* زُعَمَآءُ ـ قَبِيلٌ *pl.* قُبَلَآءُ ـ ضَامِنٌ or ضَمِينٌ *pl.* ضُمَنَآءُ ـ ذَمَامَةٌ ـ حَمِيلٌ ـ كَفِيلٌ *pl.* كُفَلَآءُ. What is given as a security, رَهْنٌ ـ ضَمَانٌ. I am — to thee for such a thing, أَنَا لَكَ رَهْنٌ بِكَذَا. To be — for, تَضَمَّنَ عَنْ ـ ضَمِنَ بِ ـ قَبَلَ بِ. Surety, freedom from doubt, صِحَّةٌ ـ حَقٌّ ـ يَقِينٌ. Exemption from casualty, إِثْبَاتٌ ـ دَوَامٌ ـ قَرَارٌ ـ أَمْنٌ. Of a —; (*see* Surely, *ad.*) "He knows of a surety what ye are about," قَدْ يَعْلَمُ مَا أَنْتُمْ عَلَيْهِ (Kur. xxiv. 64). *See also under* Certainty, *n.*

Surf, *n.* رِغْوَةُ ٱلْبَحْرِ ـ زَبَدُ ٱلْبَحْرِ.

Surface, *n.* صَفْحَةٌ *pl.* صَفَحَاتٌ ـ سَطْحٌ *pl.* سُطُوحٌ ـ صَفِيحَةٌ *pl.* صَفَائِحُ ـ وَجْهٌ *pl.* وُجُوهٌ and أَوْجُهٌ. What appears on the outside, the outside, الظَّاهِرُ. The upper — of anything, ظَهْرٌ. The — of the water, وَجْهُ ٱلْمَآءِ. Having two surfaces, as cloth, *etc.*, وَجْهٌ ـ مُوَجَّهٌ.

Concave surface, سَطْحٌ مُقَعَّرٌ.

Convex surface, سَطْحٌ مُحَدَّبٌ.

Plain surface, سَطْحٌ مُسْتَوٍ.

Surfeit, *n.* *See* Repletion, *n.*

Surfeit, *v.t.* To stuff, as with food, أَشْبَعَ ـ أَنْعَمَ بِ ـ أَبْشَمَ. To — or disgust one with, أَكْرَهَ عَلَى ـ كَرَّهَ إِلَى ـ قَرَّفَ بِ.

Surfeit, *v.i.* Of food, أَفْرَطَ فِي ٱلطَّعَامِ ـ تَبَطَّنَ ـ بَطِنَ.

Surfeiter, *n.* *See* Glutton, *n.*

Surge, *n.* مَوْجَةٌ *coll.* مَوْجٌ *pl.* أَمْوَاجٌ. The surges of the sea, of a torrent, *etc.*, عُبَابٌ.

Surge, *v.i.* Of the waves, also of general commotion, مَاجَ ـ تَمَوَّجَ. To rise high, of water, *etc.*, طَمَا *aor.* يَطْمُو.

Surgeless, *a.* بِلَا مَوْجٍ. *See also* Calm, *a.*

Surgeon, *n.* جَرَّاحٌ *pl.* جَرَّاحَةٌ ـ جَرَاحِيٌّ *pl.* جَرَاحِيَّةٌ ـ جَرَائِحِيٌّ *pl.* جَرَائِحِيَّةٌ. One who treats medicinally, a medical practitioner, مُعَالِجٌ. *See also under* Doctor, *n.*

Surgeoncy, *n.* In an army, مَنْصِبُ ٱلْجَرَّاحِ ٱلْعَسْكَرِيِّ.

Surgery, *n.* The art of, فَنُّ ٱلْجِرَاحَةِ ـ ٱلْعُلُومُ ٱلْجِرَاحِيَّةُ. A room for —, بَيْتٌ لِلْجِرَاحَةِ.

Surgical, *a.* جِرَاحِيٌّ. Surgical studies, ٱلدُّرُوسُ ٱلْجِرَاحِيَّةُ. Surgical instruments, آلَاتُ ٱلْجِرَاحَةِ. A — operation, عَمَلٌ مِنْ صِنَاعَةِ ٱلْجِرَاحِيِّ.

Surgically, *a.* حَسَبَ أُصُولِ ٱلْجِرَاحَةِ ـ حَسَبَ فَنِّ ٱلْجِرَاحَةِ.

Surlily, *ad.* بِفَظَاظَةٍ ـ بِشَرَاسَةٍ ـ بِشَكَاسَةٍ ـ بِجَفَآءٍ.

Surliness, *n.* عَرْبَدَةٌ ـ فَظَاظَةٌ ـ شَرَاسَةٌ ـ شَكَاسَةٌ ـ جَفَآءٌ.

Surloin, *n.* *See* Sirloin, *n.*

Surly, *a.* شَرِسٌ ـ شَكِسٌ ـ فَظٌّ ـ مَكْرُوهُ ٱلْخُلُقِ ـ مُعَرْبِدٌ ـ جَافٍ ـ شِرِّيسٌ. To be —, ٢ جَفَا ـ تَجَافَى ـ ٢ شَكِسَ ـ ٢ شَرِسَ ـ ٢ فَظَّ.

Surmise, *v.t.* ٢ حَدَسَ ـ تَخَيَّلَ ـ تَوَهَّمَ ـ ٢ ظَنَّ ـ ٢ خَمَّنَ. He surmises things, هُوَ يَحْدِسُ. He surmised the thing, حَدَسَ ٱلشَّيْءَ.

Surmise, *n.* ظَنٌّ ـ تَوَهُّمٌ ـ تَخْمِينٌ ـ خَمْنٌ ـ خَيَالٌ ـ حَدْسٌ.

Surmiser, *n.* ظَنَّانٌ ـ حَدَّاسٌ.

Surmount, *v.t.* To master, عَلَا بِ *aor.* يَعْلُو ـ إِعْتَلَى عَلَى ـ أَنْجَحَ بِ ـ ٢ غَلَبَ عَلَى ـ ٢ غَلَبَ ـ اِرْتَكَبَ ـ ٢ رَكِبَ. To be superior to, عَلَا عَلَى *aor.* يَعْلُو. To surpass, ٢ فَاقَ. To be surmounted by, عَلَا *aor.* يَعْلُو ـ عَلَاهُ نَجْمٌ: It was surmounted by a star, فَوْقَهُ نَجْمَةٌ. To cause to —, مَكَّنَ ـ (or أَمْكَنَ) مِنْ كَذَا.

Surmountable, *a.* *See* Superable, *a.*

Surmountableness, *n.* *See* Superableness, *n.*

Surmounter, *n.* طَلَّاعُ ٱلْأَنْجُدِ ـ طَلَّاعُ ٱلثَّنَايَا ـ رَكَّابٌ لِلْأُمُورِ.

Surname, *n.* نَسَبٌ *pl.* أَنْسَابٌ ـ نَزَبٌ ـ قَزَبٌ ـ قِزْبٌ ـ كُنْيَةٌ *pl.* كُنًى ـ نَبْزٌ *pl.* أَنْبَازٌ ـ لَقَبٌ *pl.* أَلْقَابٌ.

Surname, *v.t.* ٢ كَنَا بِ ـ كَنَّى بِ ـ لَقَّبَ. To be surnamed, تَلَقَّبَ بِ ـ إِكْتَنَى بِ.

Surpass, *v.t.* To go beyond in, whether in good or bad, أَفْرَطَ فِي ـ تَفَوَّتَ فِي ـ تَجَاوَزَ بِ ـ جَاوَزَ بِ. To outstrip, بَرَّزَ عَلَى ـ ٢ سَبَقَ ـ ٢ فَاتَ. To — in weight or gravity, ٢ رَجَحَ. To —, as in excellence, learning, *etc.* رَاقَ عَلَى *aor.* بَرَزَ عَلَى ـ ٢ بَرَعَ ـ ٢ فَاقَ عَلَى. يَرُوقُ ـ فَاقَ ٢ ـ بَسَقَ عَلَى ٢ ـ بَهَرَ ٢ ـ. She surpassed the (other) women in beauty, بَهَرَتِ ٱلنِّسَآءَ. The light of the moon surpassed that of the stars, ٢ بَهَرَ ٱلْقَمَرُ ٱلنُّجُومَ. I ran with him until I surpassed him, جَارَيْتُهُ حَتَّى فُتُّهُ. Such an one surpassed him by a cubit, فَاتَهُ فُلَانٌ بِذِرَاعٍ.

Surpassable, *a.* جَوَازُهُ مُمْكِنٌ ـ فَوَاتُهُ مُمْكِنٌ.

Surpassing, *a.* فَائِقٌ *pl.* فُوَّآءٌ ـ مِفْضَالٌ ـ رَائِقٌ ـ بَارِعٌ.

Surpassingly, *ad.* بَتَّةً ـ لِلْغَايَةِ ـ بِفَوَاقٍ.

Surplice, *n.* كُتُونَةٌ *pl.* كُتُونَاتٌ.

Surpliced, *a.* لَابِسُ كُتُونَةٍ.

Surplice-fees, *n.* رَوَاتِبُ (or عَوَائِدُ) ٱلْإِكْلِيرُسِ.

Surplus, *n.* } بَاقٍ ـ زِيَادَةٌ ـ فَرْطٌ ـ فَضْلَةٌ.
Surplusage, }

Surprisal, *n.* The act of coming upon suddenly, تَبْغِيتٌ ـ بَدْءٌ ـ بَغْتَةٌ ـ بَغْتٌ; the being taken by surprise, مُبَاغَتَةٌ.

Surprise, *n.* The state of being taken unexpectedly, مُبَاغَتَةٌ ـ بِغَاتٌ ـ بُدَاهَةٌ. Astonishment, تَعَجُّبٌ ـ عَجَبٌ ـ تَحَيُّرٌ ـ رَوْعٌ ـ ذُهُولٌ. A fit of —, رَوْعَةٌ. An unexpected event, فَلْتَةٌ *pl.* فَلَتَاتٌ ـ بَدِيهَةٌ ـ بُدَاهَةٌ. A sudden attack, هُجُومٌ بَغْتَةً. To feel —, تَحَيَّرَ ـ تَعَجَّبَ ـ اِنْدَهَشَ. He took him by —, بَادَهَهُ ـ ٢ بَدَهَهُ. He took him by — in the matter, بَادَهَهُ بِٱلْأَمْرِ.

Surprise, *v.t.* To come or fall on unexpectedly, إِسْتَقْبَلَ ـ بَادَهَ ـ ٢ بَدَهَ ـ ٢ بَغَتَ ـ بَغَّتَ ـ بَاغَتَ; as of misfortune, غَالَ ٢ ـ إِغْتَالَ. To fall upon suddenly, ٢ هَجَمَ عَلَى بَغْتَةً. To astonish, أَدْهَشَ ـ أَعْجَبَ. To be surprised, astonished, تَحَيَّرَ ـ اِنْدَهَشَ ـ تَعَجَّبَ.

Surprised, *a.* Astonished, مُتَحَيِّرٌ ـ مُتَعَجِّبٌ ـ مُنْدَهِشٌ. To be — at, تَحَيَّرَ مِنْ ـ تَعَجَّبَ مِنْ.

Surprising, *a.* Astonishing, مُحَيِّرٌ ـ مُعَجِّبٌ. We have witnessed his — skill, قَدْ شَاهَدْنَا بَرَاعَتَهُ ٱلْمُحَيِّرَةَ. What a — thing it is! سُبْحَانَ مِنْ كَذَا.

Surprisingly, *ad.* حَيْرَةً ـ عَجَبًا ـ بِأَغْرَبِ وَجْهٍ ـ بِنَوْعٍ عَجِيبٍ.

Sur-rebut, *v.t.* ٢ رَدَّ عَلَى دَلَائِلِ ٱلْمُدَّعَى عَلَيْهِ.

Sur-rebutter, *n.* رَدٌّ عَلَى حُجَجِ ٱلْمُدَّعَى عَلَيْهِ.

Sur-rejoin, *v.t.* ٢ رَدَّ ٱلْمُدَّعِي عَلَى حُجَجِ ٱلْمُدَّعَى عَلَيْهِ.

Sur-rejoinder, *n.* رَدُّ ٱلْمُدَّعِي عَلَى حُجَجِ ٱلْمُدَّعَى عَلَيْهِ.

Surrender, *v.t.* To deliver over, سَلَّمَ. To abandon, ٢ تَرَكَ. To resign, as an appointment, تَخَلَّى عَنْ; as a claim, ٢ تَرَكَ ـ ٢ نَزَلَ عَنْ ـ جَاوَزَ وَتَرَكَ. To — one's self, إِسْتَسْلَمَ ـ أَسْلَمَ. He will not — his rights, لَا يَنْزِلُ عَنْ حُقُوقِهِ.

Surrender, *v.i.* To yield to, سَلَّمَ ـ إِسْتَسْلَمَ إِلَى ـ أَسْلَمَ إِلَى نَفْسَهُ. They surrendered at discretion, سَلَّمُوا نُفُوسَهُمْ مِنْ غَيْرِ شَرْطٍ; they surrendered on conditions, سَلَّمُوا نُفُوسَهُمْ تَحْتَ شَرْطٍ. Before the fortresses are surrendered to him, مِنْ قَبْلِ أَنْ تَتَسَلَّمَ لَهُ ٱلْقِلَاعُ.

Surrender, *n.* } The act of yielding, giving in, تَسْلِيمٌ ـ إِسْتِسْلَامٌ;
Surrendry, } as of an estate, تَخَلٌّ عَنْ ـ تَرْكٌ ـ نَقْلٌ ـ تَرْكٌ وَمُجَاوَزَةٌ.

Surrenderer, *n.* One who surrenders, مُسَلِّم ; one who surrenders himself, مُتَسَلِّم .

Surreption, *n.* *See* Surprisal, *n.*

Surreptitious, *a.* Stealthy, clandestine, رَائِغ ـ خَفِيّ ـ مُتَسَلِّل ـ غَشَّاش ـ خَادِع ـ غَدَّار . Fraudulent, مَسْتُور .

Surreptitiously, *ad.* Stealthily, عَلَى خَفَآءٍ ـ تَسَلُّلًا ـ بِرَوْغٍ ـ خُفْيَةً ; fraudulently, بِحِيلَةٍ ـ بِخِيَانَةٍ ـ بِغَدْرٍ . To do a thing —, secretly, فَعَلَ ـ خُفْيَةً ; deceitfully, تَحَيَّلَ فِي .

Surrogate, *n.* نَائِب *pl.* نُوَّاب ; of a bishop, نَائِبُ أُسْقُف .

Surround, *v.t.* As with a border, اِكْتَنَفَ ـ تَكَنَّفَ ـ أَزَرَ ـ حَفَّفَ ـ بِ ـ حَفَّ ـ بِ ـ كَنَّفَ . To encompass, حَاقَ بِ ـ أَحْدَقَ بِ ـ أَحَاطَ بِ ـ حَفَّ (or) اِحْتَفَّ) بِ . To —, to invest, as of a town, حَاصَرَ ـ حَصَرَ . To —, as with benefits, *etc.*, أَشْمَلَ ـ بِ ـ شَمَلَ . To —, as birds, a piece of water, عَصَّبَ بِ ـ عَصَبَ . They surrounded us on all sides, تَأَشَّبُوا إِلَيْنَا ـ أَحَاطُوا بِنَا مِنْ كُلِّ جَانِبٍ . The enemy surrounded him, أَحَاطَ بِهِ ٱلْعَدُوُّ . We were surrounded by them, كُنَّا مَحْفُوفُونَ بِهِمْ . He was surrounded with danger, كَانَ مَحْفُوفًا بِٱلْخَطَرِ . He surrounded them with benefits, أَشْمَلَهُمْ خَيْرًا . He is surrounded by disagreeables, هُوَ مَحْفُوفٌ بِٱلْمَكَارِهِ . A garden surrounded by a wall, حَدِيقَة *pl.* حَدَائِقُ .

Surrounded, *a.* As with a border, مَحْفُوف ـ مُكْتَنَف ; environed, مُحَاط ; having things, places, all round, مَحْفُوف ; as by a siege, مَحْفُوف ـ مُحَاصَر ـ مَحْصُور ; as by difficulties, مَقْرُون .

Surrounding, *a.* Encompassing, مُحِيط ; comprising, enveloping, شَامِل ; neighbouring, مُجَاوِر . The villages — the town, ٱلضِّيَاعُ ٱلْمُجَاوِرَةُ لِلْمَدِينَةِ . The fortifications — the castle, ٱلْحُصُونُ ٱلْمُحِيطَةُ بِٱلْقَلْعَةِ .

Surtout, *n.* سِتْرِيّ فَوْقَانِيّ ـ جُبَّة .

Surveillance, *n.* Oversight, مُبَاشَرَة ـ نَظَارَة ـ نَظَرٌ إِلَى . Watch, تَرَصُّد ـ رَصْد ـ اِسْتِشْفَاف ـ حِرَاسَة . The police exercise watch and — over them, ٱلضَّبْطِيَّةُ تَرْصُدُهُمْ وَتَسْتَشِفُّهُمْ .

Survey, *v.t.* To examine attentively, اِسْتَشَفَّ . To inspect, examine, فَتَّشَ عَنْ ـ فَحَصَ . To view, اِطَّلَعَ عَلَى ـ عَايَنَ . To measure, of land, قَاسَ ـ مَسَحَ . To make a plan of a country, رَسَمَ ٱلْبِلَادَ ; a chart of, رَسَمَ خَارِطَةَ ٱلْبِلَادِ . To consider, لَاحَظَ ـ طَالَعَ .

Survey, *n.* A careful examination, اِسْتِشْفَاف . A viewing, اِطِّلَاعٌ عَلَى ـ مُعَايَنَة . A considering, examining, مُلَاحَظَة ـ مُطَالَعَة . A —, as of land, مَسَاحَة . A trigonometrical —, مَسَاحَةُ ٱلْمُثَلَّثَاتِ . Plan of a —, خَارِطَةُ رَسْمٍ وَمَسَاحَةٍ . He sent experienced men to take a — of Northern Africa, أَرْسَلَ أُنَاسًا مِنْ أَهْلِ ٱلْخِبْرَةِ إِلَى أَفْرِيقِيَّةَ ٱلشَّمَالِيَّةِ لِرَسْمِ مَوَاقِعِهَا وَتَخْطِيطِهَا .

Surveyal, *n.* *See* Survey, *n.*

Surveying, *n.* The art of, (of the land,) فَنّ ـ فَنُّ ٱلْمَسَاحَةِ ـ تَخْطِيطُ ٱلْأَرَاضِي .

Surveyor, *n.* As of land, قَائِس ـ مَسَّاحَة ـ مَسَّاحُ ٱلْأَرْضِ *pl.* مَسَّاحَة . An overseer, مُبَاشِر ـ مُبَاشِرُون *pl.* نَاظِر ـ نُظَّار *pl.* . An engineering —, نَاظِرُ ٱلْأَرْضِ ـ مَسَّاحٌ مُهَنْدِس . Surveyor-General, نَاظِرُ ٱلْمَسَاحَةِ ـ رَئِيسُ ٱلْمُهَنْدِسِينَ .

Surveyorship, *n.* مَأْمُورِيَّةُ مَسَّاحِ ٱلْأَرْضِ . Overseership, نَظَارَة .

Survival, *n.* Of life, حَيَاةُ مَرْءٍ عُقْبَ مَوْتِ غَيْرِهِ ; of lasting, بَقَآءٌ بَعْدَ كَذَا *or* فُلَانٍ .

Survive, *v.t.* To outlive, بَقِيَ بَعْدَهُ ـ عَاشَ بَعْدَهُ . *See also to* Outlive, Outlast, Leave, *v.t.*

Survivor, *n.* بَاقٍ بَعْدَ غَيْرِهِ ـ عَائِشٌ بَعْدَ غَيْرِهِ . A last —, عُقْبَة .

Survivors, a people left after another, خَالِفَة *pl.* خَوَالِفُ .

Survivorship, *n.* خِلَافَة .

Susceptibility, *n.*	*See* Sensibility, *n.*
Susceptibleness,	

Susceptible, *a.* *See* Sensible, *a.*

Susceptibly, *ad.* *See* Sensibly, *ad.*

Suscitate, *v.t.* To cause, سَبَّبَ . To stir up, هَيَّجَ ـ أَنْفَسَ ـ أَنْهَضَ ـ حَرَّضَ ـ أَثَارَ .

Suspect, *v.t.* To — one, either of good or evil, أَدْوَى ـ أَدْوَأَ ـ اِتَّهَمَ فِي ـ ظَنَّ بِ ـ أَزَنَّ ـ أَبَنَ . To hold to be uncertain, اِرْتَابَ فِي ـ أَرَابَ ـ شَكَّ فِي ـ تَوَهَّمَ . To —, of evil, نَطِفَ ـ رَمَى ـ بِسُوءٍ ـ قَرَفَ بِ ـ أَظَنَّ بِ ـ أَبَنَ ـ بِشَرٍّ . To have scent of, شَامَّ . He suspected him of the affair, أَزَنَّهُ بِٱلْأَمْرِ . He is suspected of the affair, هُوَ يُزَنُّ بِٱلْأَمْرِ . He suspected, doubted, him, اِرْتَابَ فِيهِ ـ اِرْتَابَ بِهِ . I suspected, thought evil of him, أَظْنَنْتُهُ ـ ظَنَنْتُهُ . I suspected the correctness of his words, اِتَّهَمْتُهُ فِي قَوْلِهِ . To be suspected, doubted, يُظَنُّ فِي ; to be suspected, of evil, قُرِفَ بِ : he is suspected of . . . , هُوَ يُشَكُّ فِي ـ هُوَ يُتَّهَمُ بِكَذَا ـ بِكَذَا . His testimony was suspected, غُمِزَتْ شَهَادَتُهُ . To render suspected, of evil, أَظَنَّ بِ ـ أَقْرَفَ . To —, conjecture, تَخَيَّلَ ـ حَدَسَ ـ شَكَّكَ فِي ـ أَنْطَفَ ـ ظَنَّ ـ خَمَّنَ ـ تَوَهَّمَ .

Suspect, *v.i.* Of evil, ظَنَّ ٱلسُّوءَ .

Suspected, *a.* Of evil, مَظْنُون ـ مَقْرُوف ـ نَطِف ـ تَهِيم ـ مُتَّهَم .

Suspectedly, *ad.* Of evil, بِنَوْعٍ مُقْرِفٍ.

Suspectedness, *n.* Of evil, تُهَمَة ـ أِتِّهَام.

Suspecter, *n.* Of evil, ظَنُون ـ ظَنِين.

Suspecting, *a.* Sceptical, مُرْتَاب.

Suspend, *v.t.* To hang, to hang upon, عَلَّقَ ـ سَمَّطَ ـ ᵋ سَمَطَ ـ ᶦ حَذَفَ ـ أَبْقَى ـ وَقَّفَ عَلَّقَ ـ بِ ـ عَلَى. To put off, differ, حَذَفَ ـ أَبْقَى ـ وَقَّفَ إِلَى غَيْرِ وَقْتٍ. To —, as from office, عَزَلَ ـ ᶦ عَزَلَ (ـ *or* ـ) مُوَقَّتًا. To —, as a journal, *etc.*, عَطَّلَ. To be suspended, hung, on, إِعْتَلَقَ بِ ـ تَعَلَّقَ بِ ـ ᵋ عَلِقَ بِ. To be suspended, as from office, إِنْعَزَلَ مُوَقَّتًا ـ عُزِلَ مُوَقَّتًا. To be suspended, of a journal, *etc.*, عُطِلَ ـ تَعَطَّلَ. Suspended animation, تَعْطِيلُ ٱلْحِسِّ وَٱلنَّفَسِ. A suspended journal, جَرِيدَةٌ مُعَطَّلَةٌ.

Suspenders, *n.* Braces, شِمَار ـ شِنَاط.

Suspense, *n.* Doubtfulness, hesitation, تَرَدُّد ـ شُبْهَة. State of uncertainty, إِشْتِبَاه. Perplexity, حَيْرَة ـ تَحَيُّر. Of a state of expectation, إِنْتِظَار. In —, doubt, perplexity, فِي ٱلْحَيْرَةِ ـ تَحَيُّرًا. To be in —, perplexity, تَحَيَّرَ ـ ᶦ حَارَ; to be in waiting for, in expectation of, إِنْتَظَرَ. To put one in suspense, to perplex, حَيَّرَ. Left in —, as of affairs, مُعَلَّق: His affair is in —, أَمْرُهُ مُعَلَّقٌ.

Suspensibility, *n.* إِمْكَانُ ٱلتَّعْلِيقِ.

Suspension, *n.* The act of hanging up, تَعْلِيق. Cessation for a time, إِنْقِطَاعٌ مُوَقَّتٌ ـ تَوَقُّفٌ مُوَقَّتٌ. Temporary — from office, عَزْلٌ مُوَقَّتٌ. Temporary — of a journal, تَعْطِيلُ جَرِيدَةٍ. Suspension of hostilities, هُدْنَةٌ إِلَى ـ مُتَارَكَةُ حَرْبٍ مُوَقَّتٌ. A — bridge, جِسْرٌ مُعَلَّقٌ ـ جِسْرٌ. "And others held in suspense awaiting the decrees of God," وَآخَرُونَ مُرْجَوْنَ لِأَمْرِ ٱللّٰهِ (Kur. ix. 107).

Suspensive, *a.* Doubtful, تَحْتَ ٱلشَّكِّ ـ مُحِيل ـ مُشْتَبِه.

Suspensory, *a.* مُوَقِّف ـ مُعَوِّق. The — thong of a whip, صِيلَة.

Suspensory, *n.* A truss, حِفَاظ.

Suspicion, *n.* The act of suspecting, conjecturing, ظَنّ ـ حَدْس ـ تَخَمُّن. Doubt, mistrust, هَجْس *pl.* هَوَاجِس ـ رِيبَة ـ شُبْهَة ـ شُكُوك *pl.* شَكّ ـ إِتِّهَام ـ ظِنَّة ـ مَوْهِمَة ـ تَوَهُّم. To create —, make to suspect, شَكَّكَ ـ أَرَابَ ـ أَظَنَّ: it caused me —, أَرَابَنِي ـ ᶦ رَابَنِي. I made the people to have — of him, أَظْنَنْتُ بِهِ ٱلنَّاسَ. It excited their suspicions, أَثَارَ هَوَاجِسَهُمْ. To hold in —, تَوَهَّمَ بِ ـ أَنْكَرَ ـ أَظَنَّ ـ ᵋ ظَنَّ: I hold your affair in —, أَنْكَرْتُ أَمْرَكَ. Open to —, مُعَارِضٌ لِلْوَهْمِ. He is my —, I suspect him, هُوَ قِرْفَتِي ـ هُوَ ظِنَّتِي. Some of those on whom — fell were seized, قُبِضَ عَلَى بَعْضِ ٱلَّذِينَ وَقَعَتْ عَلَيْهِمِ ٱلشُّبْهَةُ.

Thou hast become, or thou hast done something to make thee, an object of —, أَدْوَأْتَ ـ أَدَاتَ.

Suspicious, *a.* Apt to suspect, as one who is superstitious, مُتَشَكِّك ـ ذُو رِيبَةٍ ـ مُتَّهِم ـ ظَنَّان ـ مُوَسْوِس. Distrustful, ظَنِين ـ ظَنُون. A — man, one who suspects evil, مُشْتَبِه. Causing suspicion, مُظِنّ ـ مُشَكِّك ـ مُرِيب. Suspicious of, in dread of, مُوجِسٌ فِي. To make — of, أَقْرَفَ. To be — of, إِتَّهَمَ بِ. *See also under to* Suspect, *v.t.*, *and* Suspicion, *n.*

Suspiciously, *ad.* Superstitiously, بِوَسْوَسَةٍ. With suspicion, mistrust, بِظِنَّةٍ ـ بِشَكٍّ ـ مَوْهِمَةً ـ تَوَهُّمًا ـ بِتَوَهُّمٍ.

Suspiciousness, *n.* Liability to suspicions, تَعَرُّضٌ لِلظِّنَّةِ. Superstitious dread, وَسْوَسَة. The state of being suspicious, كَوْنُ ٱلشَّيْءِ تَحْتَ ٱلشُّبْهَةِ.

Suspiral, *n.* مُتَنَفَّس.

Suspiration, *n.* A heavy sigh, شَهْقَة ـ شُهَاق ـ شَهِيق.

Suspire, *v.i.* تَنَفَّسَ ٱلصُّعَدَاءَ ـ ᵋ شَهَقَ شَهْقَةً.

Sustain, *v.t.* To prop, support, أَسْنَدَ ـ ᵋ دَعَمَ. To keep one from, ᶦ مَنَعَ. To bear, endure, إِحْتَمَلَ ـ تَحَمَّلَ. To aid, back, سَانَدَ ـ ظَاهَرَ ـ ᵋ عَضَدَ. To prop up, as with pillows, *etc.*, وَسَّدَ ـ سَانَدَ. To persist in, وَاظَبَ عَلَى ـ أَدْمَنَ عَلَى. To —, as with proofs, to confirm, قَرَّرَ ـ ثَبَّتَ ـ أَكَّدَ. To —, to provide for, عَالَ *aor.* يَعُولُ ـ ᵋ مَانَ بِ. To — with, as with provisions, *etc.*, ᵋ ثَبَتَ لِ ـ تَلَقَّى ـ ᵋ لَقِيَ ـ أَمَدَّ بِ. To —, as an attack, قَاوَمَ. To defend, protect, حَامَى ـ ᶦ حَمَى. To bear, as a burden, ᶦ حَمَلَ. *See also to* Maintain, Support, *v.t.*

Sustainable, *a.* Supportable, endurable, مِمَّا يُتَحَمَّلُ ـ يُحْتَمَلُ. That may be affirmed, confirmed, مِمَّا يُقَرَّرُ ـ مِمَّا يَثْبُتُ. That may be kept up, إِدَامَتُهُ مُمْكِنَةٌ ـ قَابِلُ ٱلْإِبْقَاءِ. That may be vindicated, مِمَّا يُحَامَى عَنْهُ. To be —, affirmable, of one, ᵋ ثَبَتَ لِ. To be —, affirmable, against one, ᵋ ثَبَتَ عَلَى.

Sustainment, *n.* The act of sustaining, propping, إِسْنَاد ـ دَعْم; of aiding, مُسَاعَدَة; of backing, عَضْد ـ مُظَاهَرَة; of supplying, إِمْدَاد; of confirming, proving, تَثْبِيت ـ تَأْيِيد ـ تَأْكِيد; of providing for, تَعْيِيل ـ إِعْيَال ـ عَوْل; of keeping up, قِوَام ـ قِيَام.

Sustenance, *n.* Food, مُؤْنَة ـ قُوت ـ غِذَاء. Means of support, مَعَاش ـ مَعِيشَة ـ عِيشَة. *See also* Maintenance, *n.*

Sustentation, *n.* The act of keeping up, قِوَام ـ قِيَام; of strengthening, تَقْوِيَة.

Susurration, *n.* A whispering, وَسْوَسَة ـ إِسْرَار; a murmuring, هَزِيز ـ خَرِير ـ خَرْخَر.

Suttee, *n.* إِسْمُ ٱلْأَرْمَلَةِ ٱلْهِنْدِيَّةِ ٱلَّتِي تَحْتَرِقُ مَعَ جُثَّةِ زَوْجِهَا.

Sutteeism, *n.* أُصُولُ ٱحْتِرَاقِ ٱلْأَرْمَلَةِ مَعَ جُثَّةِ زَوْجِهَا.

Suttle, *n.* ٱلْخَالِصُ مِنَ ٱلْوَزْنِ.

Suttler, *n.* بَيَّاعٌ لِلْعَسْكَرِ ـ سُوقِيُّ ٱلْعَسْكَرِ.

Sutural, *a.* Pertaining to the sutures of the skull, يَافُوخِيٌّ.

Suture, *n.* A sewing, as of a wound, *etc.*, خِيَاطَة ـ خُرْزَة. A raised —, seam, دَرْز *pl.* دُرُوز. A — of the skull, يَافُوخ *pl.* يَوَافِيخ. *See also under* Skull, *n.*

Suzerain, *n.* A feudal chief, صَاحِبُ ٱلِٱلْتِزَامِ ـ مُلْتَزِم. Suzerain, in the vulgar sense of sovereign lord, مَلِكٌ مَتْبُوعٌ ـ سَيِّد. The — court, ٱلدَّوْلَةُ ٱلْمَتْبُوعَةُ. *See also* Sovereign, *n.*

Suzerainty, *n.* Of feudality, ٱلْتِزَام. Lordship, سِيَادَة. *See also* Sovereignty, *n.*

S.W., *n.* and *a.* حَرْفَانِ يَدُلَّانِ عَلَى ٱلْجَنُوبِيِّ ٱلْغَرْبِيِّ.

Swab, *n.* مِكْنَسَةٌ نَشَّافَةٌ; called on board Ottoman ships of war, پَاپَاس, that is, a "priest," just as we call a long broom a "Turk's head."

Swab, *v.t.* مَسَّحَ ـ مَسَحَ بِٱلْمِكْنَسَةِ ٱلنَّشَّافَةِ.

Swabber, *n.* مَسَّاح.

Swaddle, *v.t.* لَفَّ فِي ٱلْقِمَاطِ ـ قَمَطَ ـ قَمَّطَ.

Swaddle, *n.* قِمَاط *pl.* قِمَاطَات.

Swaddling-band, *n.* }
Swaddling-cloth, } قُعْمُوط *pl.* قَعَامِيط.

Swag, *v.i.* To sink, سَاخَ *aor.* يَسُوخُ ـ رَسَبَ.

Swagger, *v.i.* To boast, ٱفْتَخَرَ ـ بَذَخَ ـ طَرْمَذَ ـ فَخْفَخَ ـ تَبَجَّحَ. To — in walking, تَخَطَّلَ (or حَاكَ) فِي ـ تَعَيَّلَ فِي مِشْيَتِهِ ـ تَغَطْرَسَ ـ مِشْيَتِهِ.

Swagger, *n.* }
Swaggering, } Boasting, مُبَاهَاة ـ تَفَاخُر ـ طَرْمَذَة. Swaggering in walking, حَيَكَانٌ فِي ٱلْمَشْيِ ـ تَغَطْرُس.

Swaggerer, *n.* A boaster, مُفَخْفِخ ـ فَيَّاش ـ طِرْمَاذ ـ فَخْفَاخ ـ مَيَّاح ـ حَيَّاك ـ حَائِك ـ فَيَّاد ـ عَيَّال. A — in walk, خَرَّاط ـ مُتَغَطْرِس.

Swaggy, *a.* مُتَدَلٍّ ـ مُتَذَبْذِب.

Swain, *n.* A youth, جَذَع *pl.* جُذْعَان ـ غُلَام *pl.* غِلْمَان ـ شَابٌّ *pl.* شُبَّان *and* شَبَاب. A lover, عَاشِق *pl.* عَاشِقُون.

Swale, *v.i.* As of a candle, سَالَ ـ نَطَفَ.

Swale, *n.* A tract of low land, بُقْعَةٌ وَطْآءُ ـ بُقْعَةٌ غَوْر.

Swallow, *n.* The bird, عَوَّار *pl.* عَوَارِير ـ خُطَّاف *pl.* خَطَاطِيف. A domestic —, سُنُونُو *coll.* سُنُونُوَة *or* سُنُونِيَّة. A mountain —, وَطْوَاط *pl.* وَطَاوِط *and* وَطَايِط.

Swallow, *v.t.* سَرِطَ ـ تَسَرَّطَ ـ لَقِمَ ـ تَلَهَّمَ ـ أَسَاغَ ـ ٱلْتَقَمَ ـ هَلْقَمَ ـ بَلِعَ ـ ٱبْتَلَعَ. A thing that prevents swallowing, such as a bone, *etc.*, sticking in the throat, شَجًا. To be agreeable to —, سَاغَ *aor.* يَسُوغُ فِي ٱلْحَلْقِ. To make to —, لَقَّمَ ـ أَبْلَعَ. To — the wrong way, in drinking, شَرِقَ; in eating, غَصَّ. To —, to believe hastily, تَزَبَّدَ. To — up, to engulph, خَسَفَ بِ ـ وَرَّطَ فِي ـ أَغْرَقَ فِي: The ground swallowed him, or it, up, خَسَفَتْ (or خُسِفَتْ or ٱنْخَسَفَتْ) بِهِ ٱلْأَرْضُ.

Swallow-wort, *n.* عَقِيص ـ عَافِت ـ عَافِث. The gigantic —, عُشَر.

Swamp, *n.* *See* Marsh, *n.*

Swamp, *v.t.* To sink, أَغْرَقَ ـ غَرَّقَ. To overset, جَعَّبَ ـ قَلَبَ. To plunge, as into difficulties, عَسَّرَ عَلَى ـ شَبَّكَ فِي ـ وَرَّطَ فِي. *See also to* Inundate, *v.t.*

Swampy, *a.* *See* Marshy, *a.*

Swan, *n.* The bird, حَوْصَل ـ ٱلْإِوَزُّ ٱلْعِرَاقِيُّ ـ بَجْعَة *coll.* بَجْع.

Swansdown, *n.* Down of the swan, زَغَبُ ٱلْإِوَزِّ ٱلْعِرَاقِيِّ ـ زَغَبُ ٱلْبَجْعِ. Fine wool, صُوفٌ نَاعِمٌ.

Swan-skin, *n.* The stuff, قُمَاشٌ نَاعِمٌ.

Swap, *v.t.* *See to* Exchange, *v.t.*

Sward, *n.* خَضِر ـ خُضَّارَى ـ خُضْرَة ـ مَرْج.

Sward, *v.t.* To cover with sward, فَرَشَ خُضْرَةً.

Swarded, *a.* }
Swardy, } Covered with sward, مَفْرُوشٌ بِخُضْرَة.

Swarm, *n.* As of bees, ثَوْل ـ نَحْل (or سِرْب) ـ طَرْد. A crowd, large number, سِرْب *pl.* أَسْرَاب ـ تَرَاكُم ـ جَمٌّ ـ كَوْثَر; especially of people, زَحْم ـ كَوْكَبَة ـ سِرْب *pl.* أَسْرَاب ـ زِحَام ـ ٱزْدِحَام.

Swarm, *v.i.* Of bees, تَثَوَّلَ: the bees swarmed, تَثَوَّلَتِ ٱلنَّحْلُ. To —, to be crowded with, ٱزْدَحَمَ بِ ـ شَحِنَ بِ ـ غَصَّ بِ: the shore swarmed with them, غَصَّ بِهِمِ ٱلسَّاحِلُ. To be abundant, many, ثَرَا ـ جَمَّ ـ ٱسْتَجَمَّ: they swarmed, of people, جَمُّوا ـ ٱسْتَجَمُّوا. *See also to* Crowd, *v.i.*

Swarm, *v.t.* To throng, to crowd with, أَغَصَّ. To fill confusedly, زَحَمَ ـ حَشَرَ.

Swart, }
Swarth, *a.* }
Swarthy, } آدَمُ *fem.* أَدْمَاءُ *pl.* أُدْم ـ أَغْبَش ـ أَسْحَمَانِ ـ أَسْمَرُ *fem.* سَمْرَاءُ *pl.* سُمْر. A — colour, أُدْمَة ـ سُمْرَة. To be —, سَمُرَ ـ أَدِمَ.

Swarthily, *ad.* بِسُمْرَة.

Swarthiness, *n.* أُدْمَة ـ سُمْرَة ـ ٱسْمِرَار.

Swash, *n.* تَهَوُّر. *See also* Bluster, *n.*

Swathe, *n.* A cutting of the scythe, حَشَّة ـ حَشَّةُ ٱلْمِحَشّ . A band or fillet, عِصَابَة ـ عِصَاب ـ رِبَاط .

Swathe, *v.t.* لَفَّ-فِي ـ ² رَبَطَ ـ عَصَّبَ ـ قَمَّطَ .

Sway, *v.t.* To swing to and fro, رَدَّدَ ـ ذَبْذَبَ . To —, or hold, the sceptre, مَسَكَ ٱلْقَضِيبَ ² . To rule over, direct, سَاسَ ² ـ دَبَّرَ ـ قَادَ ² . To cause to lean, حَرَفَ ² ـ عَطَفَ ـ أَرْكَنَ-إِلَى ـ مَيَّلَ . To give a tendency to, مَيَّلَ-إِلَى ـ حَرَّفَ ـ عَطَّفَ-إِلَى . To be swayed, moved to and fro, تَرَدَّدَ ـ تَذَبْذَبَ . *See also to* Incline, Influence, *v.t.*

Sway, *v.i.* To move to and fro, تَرَدَّدَ ـ تَذَبْذَبَ . To be drawn to one side, تَعَطَّفَ ـ ٱنْحَرَفَ . To incline, مَالَ ـ تَصَوَّبَ . To —, bear rule, مَلَكَ ـ تَسَلَّطَ . *See also to* Swing, *v.i.*

Sweal, *v.i.* *See to* Swale, *v.i.*

Swear, *v.i.* To use profane oaths, حَلَفَ ـ جَدَّفَ . To —, take an oath, أَقْسَمَ ـ حَلَفَ ـ آلَى يَمِينًا . To — by, حَلَفَ بِ ـ أَقْسَمَ بِ . To — by God, to call God to witness, شَهِدَ بِٱللهِ : he swore by God, حَلَفَ بِٱللهِ . He swore it was so, حَلَفَ أَنَّهُ كَذَا . He swore an oath, حَلَفَ يَمِينًا . To — falsely, حَلَفَ بِٱلزُّورِ ـ حَلَفَ زُورًا . To make to —, قَاسَمَ ـ حَلَّفَ ـ أَحْلَفَ . To require to —, ٱسْتَحْلَفَ ـ ٱسْتَقْسَمَ . They swore to one another, of many, تَحَالَفُوا ـ تَقَاسَمُوا . To — at, to abuse, vilify, شَتَمَ ² ـ سَبَّ ² . They swore at one another, of many, تَشَاتَمُوا ـ ٱسْتَبُّوا ـ تَسَابُّوا . *See also under* Oath, *n.*

Swear, *v.t.* To cause to take an oath, ٱسْتَحْلَفَ ـ حَلَّفَ ـ قَاسَمَ . To — in, as on entering office, حَلَّفَهُ ٱلْإِدَارَةَ ـ كَافَّتَهُ ٱلْإِدَارَةَ . To — the peace against one, حَلَفَ أَمَامَ ٱلْحَاكِمِ بِٱلْيَمِينِ أَنَّ فُلَانًا تَهَدَّدَهُ فَطَلَبَ ٱلْوِقَايَةَ مِنْ شَرِّهِ .

Swearer, *n.* A profane —, حَلَّافٌ ـ كَافِرٌ ـ مُجَدِّفٌ ـ أَلِيٌّ . One who takes an oath, حَالِفٌ .

Swearing, *n.* Cursing, using profane oaths, أَلِيَّة *pl.* أَلَايَا ـ تَجْدِيف ـ سَبٌّ ـ سُبَّة ; of mutual —, مُسَابَّة ; of an oath, حَلْفَة . An oath, حَلْفٌ ـ حَلْفٌ يَمِينٌ ـ قَسَم .

Sweat, *n.* عَرَق ـ رَشِيح ـ رَشْح ; of the armpits, صِنَّة ـ صُمَاح ـ صُنَان . The — of fever, ٱلرُّحَضَاء . A drop of —, فِرَاشُ رَشْحٍ ; drops of —, قَطَرَاتُ عَرَقٍ . To stink of —, سَهِكَ ; stinking of —, سَهِك . The place in the body from which — proceeds, as the armpits, *etc.* مَعْرَق . The disagreeable smell of —, سَهَكَة . A cloth, *etc.*, to catch or absorb the —, عَرَّاقَة .

Sweat, *v.i.* عَرِقَ ـ تَرَشَّحَ عَرَقًا ـ تَرَشَّحَ ـ رَشَحَ عَرَقًا ـ رَشَحَ . He or it, as a jar, *etc.*, sweats with what is in it, رَشَحَ بِمَا فِيهِ . *See also to* Ooze, Toil, Drudge, *v.i.*

Sweat, *v.t.* To cause to sweat, عَرَّقَ ـ رَشَّحَ . To —, of coin, رَمَّلَ (or) زَيَّفَ ٱلدَّرَاهِمَ بِحَكِّهَا .

Sweater, *n.* One who or anything that sweats much, رَشَّح ـ رَاشِح . A — of coin, زَيَّافُ ٱلسِّكَّةِ بِٱلْحَكِّ مِنْهَا .

Sweatily, *ad.* عَرَقًا .

Sweatiness, *n.* تَرَشُّح .

Sweaty, *a.* عَرْقَان ـ مُتَرَشِّح ـ رَاشِح .

Swede, *n.* A native of Sweden, مِنْ أَهْلِ ٱلسُّوَيْد . A kind of turnip, ضَرْبٌ مِنَ ٱلشَّلْجَم .

Sweden, *n.* مَمْلَكَةُ ٱلسُّوَيْد .

Swedish, *a.* مِنَ ٱلسُّوَيْدِ ـ سُوَيْدِيٌّ .

Sweep, *v.t.* As with a broom, كَنَسَ ـ قَمَّ ² . To clean, نَظَّفَ . To drag, جَرَّ ² ـ سَحَبَ . To — a chimney, نَظَّفَ ٱلدَّاخِنَةَ مِنَ ٱلشُّحَّارِ . To —, to put in motion, to drive, جَفَلَ ² : the wind swept the ostriches along, جَفَلَتِ ٱلرِّيحُ ٱلنَّعَامَ . The wind swept along the clouds, جَفَلَتِ ٱلرِّيحُ ٱلسَّحَابَ . To — or carry away, as a torrent, *etc.*, جَرَفَ ² ـ جَرَّفَ : the torrents swept it away, جَرَفَتْهُ ٱلسُّيُولُ . It swept the people away like the sweeping of a torrent, جَرَفَ ٱلنَّاسَ كَجَرْفِ ٱلسَّيْلِ ² . Misfortune swept away his property, جَرَفَهُ ٱلدَّهْرُ . To — or drive away, of animals, جَفَلَ ـ طَرَدَ ² ; of flies and such like, كَشَّ ² ـ كَشْكَشَ . To — together, قَشَّ .

Sweep, *v.i.* As along the ground, تَدَلَّى عَلَى ٱلْأَرْضِ ـ تَذَبْذَبَ . To — along, as if flying, طَارَ *aor.* يَطِيرُ ; with a pompous gait, ذَالَ *aor.* يَذِيلُ : she swept along pompously in her gait, ذَالَتْ فِي مِشْيَتِهَا . To glide along swiftly, زَلَّ *aor.* يَزِلُّ ـ سَبَحَ . To flow, سَاحَ *aor.* يَسِيحُ ـ سَالَ *aor.* يَسِيلُ ـ حَبَا *aor.* يَحْبُو . To — along, as a bird over the ground, سَفَّ ² . To — round or round about, جَالَ *aor.* يَجُولُ ـ ٱجْتَالَ ـ جَوَّلَ : he swept or wheeled round in battle, جَالَ فِي ٱلْحَرْبِ ² . To take a long —, as with an oar, جَدَفَ جَدْفًا مَدِيدًا بِٱلْمِجْدَافِ .

Sweep, *n.* The act of sweeping, كَنْسَة ـ كَنْس . A chimney sweeper, مُنَظِّفُ ٱلدَّوَاخِنِ . Compass, range, دَائِرَة ـ ٱمْتِدَاد ـ ٱسْتِدَارَة : we made a —, دُرْنَا . To take a —, draw a line, رَسَمَ ² خَطًّا . To make a clean — of, جَرَفَ-بِٱلْكُلِّيَّةِ ـ جَرَفَ-بَتَّةً . Sweep, a long oar, مِجْدَافٌ كَبِيرٌ .

Sweeper, *n.* As of a house, مُكَنِّس ـ كَنَّاسَة *pl.* كَنَّاس ; of filth, dung, *etc.*, زَبَّالَة *pl.* زَبَّال . A —, a broom or an instrument to remove mud, *etc.*, مِجْرَفَة ـ *vulg.* جَرَّافَة .

Sweepingly, *ad.* As by sweeping, بِٱلْكَنْسِ ; as if borne away by a torrent, جَرْفَة .

Sweepings, *n.* As of a house, كِبًا ـ كِبَة ـ قُمَامَة *pl.* قُمَامَات ـ قَشّ ـ قُشَاش ـ كُنَاسَة ; as of the streets, filth, زُبَالَة ; of a torrent, جُفَآءٌ .

Sweep-net, *n.* مِجْرَف ـ *vulg.* جُرَّافَة .

Sweepstake, *n.* رَابِحُ جَمِيعِ ٱلْأَسْبَاقِ .

Sweepstakes, *n.* الْأَسْبَاقُ إِجْمَالًا .

Sweepy, *a.* Gliding swiftly, زَالٌّ ـ سَابِح ; taking a long sweep, أَجْوَلُ .

Sweet, *a.* As to the taste; also pleasing, goodly, beautiful, حُلْوٌ ـ حَلُوٌّ . To be —, in all these senses, حَلِيَ ـ حَلُوَ ² ـ حَلَا *aor.* يَحْلُو : it was — to me, حَلَا لِي . The fruit became —, حَلَوَتِ ٱلْفَاكِهَةُ . He or it was —, pleasing, agreeable, *etc.*, in my eyes, حَلِيَ بِعَيْنِي ـ حَلِيَ فِي قَلْبِي . He is not bitter at one time, and he is not — at another, مَا يُمِرُّ وَمَا يُحْلِي . To esteem, judge, think to be —, agreeable, *etc.*, إِسْتَحْلَى ـ تَحَلَّى . Sweet, of water, or anything drinkable; also of speech, عَذْب *pl.* عِذَاب : sweet water, مَآءٌ عَذْبٌ ; a well of — water, رَكِيَّةٌ عَذْبَةٌ . He is — in respect of his tongue, that is, sweet-tongued, أَنَّهُ لَعَذْبُ ٱللِّسَانِ : to be —, in these senses, عَذُبَ ² . To make —, حَلَّى ـ أَحْلَى ; in the sense of clearing from impurities, of liquids, أَعْذَبَ . To be — upon, عَشِقَ ـ تَلَاطَفَ إِلَى . To affect to be —, pleasing, *etc.*, تَحَلَّى . Sweet, of a place, delightful, نَزِيهٌ . Sweet and acid, مَزُوز .

Sweet, *n.* That which is sweet, a sweetmeat, حَلْوَآءٌ . As a word of fondness, قَلْب ـ عَيْن . The sweets of life, نَعِيمُ ٱلْعَيْشِ .

Sweet-basil, *n.* *See under* Basil, *n.*

Sweetbread, *n.* لَوْزُ ٱلْمِعْدَةِ ; of a calf, لَوْزَةُ ٱلْعِجْلِ .

Sweet-brier, *n.* وَرْدٌ جَبَلِيٌّ ـ عُلَّيْقُ ٱلْكَلْبِ ـ عِبَال .

Sweeten, *v.t.* To make sweet, حَلَّى ـ أَحْلَى . To mollify, لَيَّنَ ـ لَطَّفَ . To lighten, خَفَّفَ . To perfume, طَيَّبَ ـ فَوَّحَ . To purify, أَعْذَبَ . The flowers sweeten the air, الْأَزْهَارُ تُعَطِّرُ ٱلْهَوَآءَ .

Sweeten, *v.i.* To become sweet, حَلُوَ ² ـ حَلِيَ ; of water and drinkables, عَذُبَ ² .

Sweetener, *n.* That which sweetens, مُحَلٍّ ـ مُحَلِّ . One who palliates, مُخَفِّف ـ مُلَيِّن ـ مُلَطِّف .

Sweetening, *n.* The act of, تَحْلِيَة ; the becoming sweet, حَلَاوَة . What is put in to sweeten, مُحَلَّاة .

Sweetheart, *n.* A lover, عَاشِق *fem.* عَاشِقَة ; one loved, مَعْشُوق *fem.* مَعْشُوقَة .

Sweeting, *n.* A sweet apple, تُفَّاحَةٌ حُلْوَةٌ .

Sweetish, *a.* حُلْوٌ بَعْضَ ٱلْحَلَاوَةِ ـ حُلْوٌ نَوْعًا .

Sweetishness, *n.* حَلَاوَةٌ قَلِيلَةٌ .

Sweetly, *ad.* بِحَلَاوَةٍ ـ بِلَطَافَةٍ ـ بِظَرَافَةٍ ـ بِطَلَاوَةٍ .

Sweet-marjoram, *n.* *See* Marjoram, *n.*

Sweetmeat, *n.* حَلْوَى *pl.* حَلَاوَى ـ حَلْوَآء *pl.* حَلْوَات ; such as sugared almonds, مُلَبَّس *pl.* مُلَبَّسَات .

Sweetness, *n.* Including the idea of agreeableness, pleasantness, *etc.*, حَلَاوَة ـ حُلْوَان ; as of water and other liquids, عَذُوبَة ـ عَذْب ; of a place, نَزَاهَة . *See also* Amiableness, Softness, Agreeableness, *n.*

Sweet-pea, *n.* جُلُبَّانٌ مُعَطَّرٌ .

Sweet-potato, *n.* ضَرْبٌ مِنَ ٱلْكَمَايَةِ ٱلْحُلْوَةِ يَنْبُتُ بِٱلْهِنْدِ .

Sweet-scented, *a.* مُعَطَّر .

Sweet-tempered, *a.* لَطِيفُ ٱلطَّبْعِ ـ بَشُوش ـ حُلْوُ ٱلْخُلُقِ ـ هَشٌّ بَشٌّ .

Sweet-toned, *a.* مُطْرِب ـ حُلْوُ ٱلصَّوْتِ .

Sweet-tooth, *n.* مُحِبُّ ٱلْحَلْوَاتِ .

Sweet-william, *n.* حُسْنُ يُوسُفَ .

Swell, *v.i.* To grow turgid, نَتَأَ ـ اِسْمَدَّ ـ اِسْمَادَ ـ اِسْمَادَّ ـ تَوَرَّمَ ـ يَرِمُ ـ وَرِمَ *aor.* ; as of a maiden's breast, شَاكَ ² ـ اِنْتَفَخَ ـ نَهَدَ . To become thick, غَلُظَ ; as wheat in the ear, غَلُظَ ² ـ اِسْتَغْلَظَ . To —, as a river, مَدَّ ² . To become high, of water, طَمَا *aor.* يَطْمُو . To become large, great, كَبُرَ ² . To — out, to protuberate, نَتَأَ ـ اِنْدَلَعَ ـ بَرَزَ ² ـ اِنْتَفَخَ . To — with pride, وَرِمَ بِأَنْفِهِ ـ اِنْتَفَخَ غَيْظًا ـ اِسْمَادَّ ـ اِسْمَادَّ كِبْرًا ; with anger, To cause to —, to grow turgid, وَرَّمَ . To cause to become thick, أَغْلَظَ ـ غَلَّظَ . To cause to extend, to dilate, مَدَّدَ . To cause to become great, large, كَبَّرَ . To —, to rise in undulations, مَاجَ ² . His leg became swollen, رِجْلُهُ (تَوَرَّمَتْ *or*) اِسْمَأَدَّتْ . *See also* to Protuberate, *v.i.*, *and under* Protuberant, *a.*

Swell, *n.* Extension, اِمْتِدَاد ـ تَمَدُّد . Increase of sound, اِمْتِدَادُ ٱلصَّوْتِ . An undulation, مَوْج *pl.* أَمْوَاج ـ عُبَاب ; a — of the sea, مَوْجُ ٱلْبَحْرِ . A —, dandy, مُتَظَرِّف ـ مُتَكَيِّس . The — mob, كَيِّسِي ٱلظُّرَّارِينَ . To cut a —, تَظَرَّفَ ـ تَطَوَّسَ ـ تَكَيَّسَ .

Swelling, *n.* A place enlarged, a tumour, اِسْمِئْدَاد ـ اِسْمِيدَاد ـ نُفَاخ ـ وَرَم *pl.* أَوْرَام ـ تَوَرُّم ـ اِسْمِدَاد . *See also* Protuberance, *n.*

Swelter, *v.i.* تَلَاشَى مِنَ ٱلْحَرِّ ـ اِخْتَنَقَ مِنَ ٱلْحَرِّ .

Swelter, *v.t.* لَاشَى مِنَ ٱلْحَرِّ .

Sweltry, *a.* *See* Sultry, *a.*

Swept; *see to* Sweep, *v.t.*

Swerve, *v.i.* To stray, تَاهَ ـِ ضَلَّ ـِ ; to — or stray from, زَاغَ ² ـِ حَادَ عَن ـِ جَارَ عَن ². To digress in, عَن ـِ فَتَلَ عَن ـِ عَدَلَ عَن ـِ أَضْرَبَ عَن. To —, as from a purpose, أَلْوَى بِ. To cause to swerve, stray, أَزَاغَ ـِ ضَلَّلَ ـِ أَضَلَّ. كَفَّ عَن ².

Swerving, *n.* The act of, حَيْدَة ـِ زَوَغَان ـِ زَوْغ. A deviation, error, طُغْيَان ـِ ضَلَالَة ـِ زَلَّة.

Swift, *a.* Quick, فَيْض ـِ سَرِيع ـِ طَيَّار ; of a horse, سَرِيع. Swift and strong, عَصُوف. Swift to punish, سَرِيعُ ٱلْعِقَاب. Swifter than eagles, أَخَفُّ مِنَ ٱلنُّسُور. To be —, سَرُعَ ². *See also* Fleet, Rapid, Quick, *a.*

Swiftly, *ad.* خِفَّةً ـِ بِسُرْعَةٍ ـِ سُرْعَةً.

Swiftness, *n.* عَجَلَة ـِ خِفَّة ـِ سُرْعَة.

Swig, *v.t.* رَشَفَ ² ـِ غَمَطَ ـِ إِقْتَمَعَ ـِ أَقْمَعَ ـِ قَمَعَ.

Swig, *v.i.* تَمَصَّصَ ـِ تَرَشَّفَ ـِ جَرِعَ جَرْعًا ـِ غَمَطَ غَمْطًا.

Swig, *n.* A long draught, رَشْف ـِ غَمْط ـِ إِقْتِمَاع ـِ قَمْع ـِ تَرْشَاف. A draught, شَرْبَة. To take a — at, شَرِبَ مِن.

Swill, *v.t.* *See to* Swig, *v.t.*

Swill, *n.* Drink or food for swine, أَكْلُ ٱلْخَنَازِيرِ ـِ شَرِيبُ ٱلْخَنَازِيرِ. *See also* Swig, *n.*

Swiller, *n.* شِرِّيب.

Swim, *v.i.* As in the water, ضَرَبَ فِي ٱلْمَآءِ ـِ سَبَحَ فِي ٱلْمَآءِ. To float, عَامَ *aor.* يَعُومُ ـِ طَفَا فَوْقَ كَذَا ². To make to —, أَسْبَحَ; to float, عَوَّمَ. Teach your boys to —, عَلِّمُوا صِبْيَانَكُمُ ٱلْعَوْمَ. To go along swiftly, عَجَرَ. To —, of a feeling in the head, دَاخَ *aor.* يَدُوخُ ـِ سَدِرَ. *See also to* Glide, *v.i.*

Swim, *v.t.* To float, cause to float, عَوَّمَ. To cross over swimming, عَبَرَ سَابِحًا ².

Swimmer, *n.* سَبَّاح *pl.* سَبَّاحُون ـِ سَابِح ـِ سَبُوح. A bold —, عَوَّام.

Swimming, *n.* The art of, سِبَاحَة ; of floating, عَوْم. A place for —, مَسْبَح. A — in the head, دُوَار ـِ دَوْخ ـِ سَدَر.

Swimmingly, *ad.* Prosperously, فِي غَايَةٍ ـِ بِتَوْفِيقٍ ـِ نَجَاحًا. Your affair goes on —, أَنْتَ فِي نَفَسٍ ـِ فِي أَمَانِ ٱللّٰهِ ـِ ٱلنَّجَاح مِنْ أَمْرِكَ.

Swindle, *v.t.* To cheat, غَدَرَ ² ـِ غَبَنَ. To swindle of, إِخْتَلَسَ مِن. To be swindled, cheated, إِنْغَدَرَ ـِ غُبِنَ ; to be swindled of ..., أُخْتُلِسَ مِن كَذَا.

Swindle, *n.* خُلْسَة ـِ خِيَانَة ـِ غِشّ ـِ جَوْن ـِ غَبْن ـِ غَبِينَة. A mutual —, مُغَابَنَة ـِ تَغَابُن.

Swindler, *n.* مُخْتَلِس ـِ غَشَّاش ـِ خَدَّاع ـِ غَدَّار.

Swine, *n.* خِنْزِير *pl.* خَنَازِير. You can't make a silk purse out of a swine's ear (prov.), جِلْدُ ٱلْخِنْزِيرِ لَا يَنْدَبِغُ (literally, you cannot tan [or taw] the swine's skin.)

Swine-herd, *n.* رَاعِي خَنَازِير.

Swine-pox, *n.* ضَرْبٌ مِنَ ٱلْجُدَرِيّ.

Swing, *v.t.* To move to and fro, دَبْدَبَ ـِ رَدَّدَ. To —, as on a swing, رَدَّدَ عَلَى ٱلْأُرْجُوحَةِ. To — round, دَوَّرَ. He swung his arms about, ضَرَبَ بِيَدَيْهِ.

Swing, *v.i.* To dandle, to — about, تَدَبْدَبَ ـِ تَرَدَّدَ ـِ إِسْتَرْوَحَ ـِ إِرْتَجَحَ ـِ تَرَجَّحَ. To wind round, إِسْتَدَارَ ـِ دَارَ ². His buttocks swung to and fro, إِرْتَجَحَتْ رَوَادِفُهُ. He moved to and fro, on a see-saw, تَرَجَّحَ (or إِرْتَجَحَ) عَلَى ٱلْأُرْجُوحَةِ.

Swing, *n.* Vibrating motion, إِرْتِجَاح ـِ تَرَجُّح ـِ تَدَبْدُب ـِ تَرَدُّد. A motion, حَرَكَة *pl.* حَرَكَات. A see-saw, أُرْجُوحَة ـِ رُجَّاحَة *pl.* أَرَاجِيح ـِ مَرْجُوحَة *pl.* مَرَاجِيح. Unrestrained liberty, هَوًى ـِ إِخْتِيَارٌ مُطْلَقٌ. To give one his —, أَطْلَقَ لِـ عِنَانَ هَوَاهُ ـِ أَطْلَقَ لِـ ٱلْعِنَانَ.

Swing-bridge, *n.* جِسْرٌ دَوَّارٌ.

Swinge, *v.t.* ضَرَبَ ـِ سَاطَ *aor.* يَسُوطُ.

Swinger, *n.* As on a see-saw, رَاكِبٌ عَلَى ٱلرُّجَّاحَةِ ـِ مُرَجِّح ـِ مُتَرَجِّحٌ عَلَى ٱلْأُرْجُوحَةِ.

Swinging, *n.* The act of swinging to and fro, دَبْدَبَة ـِ تَرْدِيد ; on a see-saw, إِرْتِجَاح (or تَرَجُّح) عَلَى أُرْجُوحَةٍ.

Swinging, *a.* Large, جَسِيم ـِ كَبِير ـِ عَظِيم.

Swingingly, *ad.* جِدًّا ـِ لِلْغَايَةِ.

Swingle, *v.t.* Of flax or cotton, نَدَفَ بِٱلْمِنْدَفِ ـِ نَدَفَ. *See also to* Dangle, *v.t.*

Swingle-tree, *n.* جَائِزُ سَيْرِ ٱلْعَرَبَانَةِ.

Swingle, *n.* }
Swingle-knife, } مِنْدَف ـِ مِنْدَفَة.

Swinish, *a.* *See* Brutish, *a.*

Swinishly, *ad.* *See* Brutishly, *ad.*

Swipe, *n.* }
Sweep, } The beam and bucket so called, شَادُوف.

Swipes, *n.* صِنْفٌ أَرْدَأُ مِنَ ٱلْبِيرَةِ.

Swiss, *n.* مِنْ أَهْلِ ٱلسُّوِيسَرَة.

Swiss, *a.* مِنْ مَمْلَكَةِ ٱلسُّوِيسَرَة ـِ سُوِيسَرِيّ.

Switch, *n.* A twig, قَضِيب ـِ غُصْنَة *pl.* قُضْبَان. A — of a railway, مِفْتَاح.

Switch, *v.t.* To beat with a switch, ضَرَبَ-قَضِيبًا ـ. To transfer to another rail, حَوَّلَ قِطَارَ سِكَّةِ ٱلْحَدِيدِ مِنْ خَطِّ ٱلسِّكَّةِ إِلَى غَيْرِهِ.

Switchman, *n.* As on a railroad, مَاسِكُ مِفْتَاحِ قُضْبَانِ ٱلسِّكَّةِ ٱلْحَدِيدِيَّةِ.

Switzerland, *n.* بِلَادُ ٱلسُّوِيسَرَةِ.

Swivel, *n.* مِرْوَدٌ *pl.* مَرَاوِدُ. A — gun, مِدْفَعٌ ـ مِدْفَعٌ دَوَّارٌ ـ صَغِيرٌ دَوَّارٌ.

Swollen, **Swoln**, } *past part. of to* Swell, *q.v.*

Swoon, *n.* غَشْيَةٌ ـ غَشْيٌ ـ مَوْتَةٌ. In a —, مَغْمِيٌّ عَلَيْهِ ـ مَغْشِيٌّ عَلَيْهِ ـ مَغْشِيٌّ.

Swoon, *v.i.* غَشَا عَلَيْهِ *aor.* يَغْشُو; of a sick person, (غُمِيَ *or*) أُغْمِيَ عَلَيْهِ.

Swoop, *v.t.* To pounce upon, as a bird, خَاتَ ـ ـ إِخْتَاتَ ـ تَخَوَّتَ. *See also to* Pounce, *to* Attack, *v.t.*

Swoop, *v.i.* *See to* Sweep, *v.i.*

Swop, *v.t.* To exchange something for, أَعَارَ-بِ. *See also to* Exchange, *v.t.*

Sword, *n.* سَيْفٌ *pl.* سُيُوفٌ. A sharp —, حُسَامٌ ـ سَقَّاطٌ ـ سِقَاطٌ. A drawn —, سَيْفٌ سَلِيلٌ. To draw, as a —, أَصْلَتَ. To put on a — تَقَلَّدَ بِٱلسَّيْفِ; to put a — on another, قَلَّدَ-ٱلسَّيْفَ. To put to the —, عَرَضَ-عَلَى ٱلسَّيْفِ ـ. To smite or cut with a —, خَذَبَ [2]. To strike with the flat of a —, أَصْحَفَ-بِٱلسَّيْفِ. To kill with the —, سَافَ ـ تَسَيَّفَ. To measure swords with, قَاتَلَ-بِٱلسَّيْفِ. He put his hand to his —, رَدَّ يَدَهُ إِلَى [2] أَخْلَفَ سَيْفَهُ ـ سَيْفِهِ. They fought with swords, of many, تَسَايَفُوا. The wavy marks on a —, جَوْهَرُ سَيْفٍ. The edge of a —, حُسَامٌ حَدُّ ٱلسَّيْفِ ـ ٱلسَّيْفِ.

Sword-bearer, *n.* سِلَحْدَارٌ.

Sword-belt, *n.* مِحْمَلُ سَيْفٍ ـ عِلَاقَةُ سَيْفٍ ـ حِمَالَةُ سَيْفٍ.

Sword-blade, *n.* نَصْلَةُ سَيْفٍ *pl.* نِصَالٌ ـ شِمْشِيرٌ.

Sword-cane, *n.* مِغْوَلٌ.

Sword-cutler, *n.* سَيَّافٌ.

Sword-cutlery, *n.* سِيَافَةٌ.

Sworded, *a.* مُقَلَّدٌ بِسَيْفٍ ـ حَامِلُ سَيْفٍ ـ مُسَيَّفٌ.

Sword-fish, *n.* حَمَلُ ٱلْمَاءِ ـ لُخْمٌ ـ كُبَعٌ ـ كَوْسَجٌ.

Sword-knot, *n.* (رُمَّانَةُ *or*) شُرَّابَةُ سَيْفٍ.

Sword-shaped, *a.* فِي هَيْئَةِ سِنَانِ ٱلرُّمْحِ ـ مُؤَنَّفٌ.

Swordsman, *n.* One armed with a sword, سَائِفٌ; a clever —, سَيَّافٌ.

Swore, *pret. of to* Swear, *q.v.*

Sworn, *p. part. of to* Swear, *q.v.*

Swum, *pret. of to* Swim, *q.v.*

Swung, *pret. of to* Swing, *q.v.*

Sybarite, *n.* **Sybaritic**, *a.* } مُتَنَعِّمٌ ـ مُشْتَهٍ ـ شَهْوَانِيٌّ ـ مُتَلَذِّذٌ ـ مُتَرَفِّهٌ.

Sycamine, *n.* **Sycamore**, } The tree, جُمَّيْزَى ـ جُمَّيْزٌ; the fruit of the —, تِينُ ٱلْجُمَّيْزِ.

Sycee, *n.* سِكَّةٌ صِينِيَّةٌ مِنَ ٱلْفِضَّةِ فِي شَكْلِ نِصْفِ كُرَةٍ.

Sycophancy, *n.* Tale-bearing, وِشَايَةٌ. Backbiting, نَمٌّ ـ غَمْزٌ ـ نَمِيمَةٌ. Obsequious flattery, مُدَاهَنَةٌ ـ تَمَلُّقٌ.

Sycophant, *n.* **Sycophantic**, *a.* } A tale-bearer, or tale-bearing, غِرْبَالٌ ـ قَتَّالٌ *pl.* غَرَابِيلُ ـ سَاعٍ بِٱلْوِشَايَةِ. An informer, delator, دَائِمُ ٱلْمِشْطِ ـ لَعِينٌ ـ نَمَّامٌ ـ غَمَّازٌ. A flatterer, مَلَّاقٌ.

Sycophantize, *v.i.* تَذَلَّلَ بِٱلْمُدَاهَنَةِ.

Syenite, *n.* حَجَرٌ صَوَّانٌ.

Syllabic, *a.* **Syllabical**, } مُخْتَصٌّ بِأَجْزَاءِ ٱلْكَلِمَاتِ ـ هِجَائِيٌّ.

Syllabically, *ad.* بِٱلتَّهْجِيَةِ ـ عَلَى تَرْتِيبِ ٱلْهِجَاءِ ـ تَهْجِيَةً.

Syllabication, *n.* تَرْكِيبُ أَجْزَاءِ ٱلْكَلِمَاتِ ـ تَهْجِيَةٌ.

Syllable, *n.* حَرَكَةٌ *pl.* حَرَكَاتٌ ـ وَتَدٌ خَفِيفٌ *pl.* أَوْتَادٌ خَفِيفَةٌ ـ تَهْجِيَةٌ. He did not say a —, لَا أَبْدَى وَلَا أَعَادَ.

Syllabub, *n.* *See* Sillabub, *n.*

Syllabus, *n.* سِيَاقَةٌ ـ إِجْمَالٌ ـ مُخْتَصَرٌ ـ فِهْرِسٌ ـ خُلَاصَةٌ.

Syllogism, *n.* قِيَاسُ ٱلْمَنْطِقِ ـ قِيَاسٌ.

Syllogistic, *a.* **Syllogistical**, } عَلَى قِيَاسِ ٱلْمَنْطِقِ ـ قِيَاسِيٌّ.

Syllogistically, *ad.* قِيَاسًا ـ عَلَى ٱلْقِيَاسِ.

Syllogize, *v.i.* إِسْتَنْتَجَ بِٱلْقِيَاسِ ـ نَطَقَ بِٱلْقِيَاسِ.

Sylph, *n.* A jinn, جِنِّيٌّ *coll.* جِنٌّ. A slender and beautiful woman, إِمْرَأَةٌ جَمِيلَةٌ هَيْفَاءُ ٱلْخَصْرِ.

Sylphid, *n.* جِنِّيَّةٌ ـ جِنِّيٌّ صَغِيرٌ.

Sylph-like, *a.* كَٱلْجِنِّ.

Sylva, *n.* The trees of any region, أَشْجَارُ قُطْرٍ ـ أَشْجَارٌ; a book on trees, تَأْلِيفٌ يُبْحَثُ فِيهِ عَنْ أَنْوَاعِ ٱلْأَشْجَارِ.

Sylvan, *a.* *See* Rural, *n.*

Symbol, *n.* An emblem, type, رَمْزٌ *pl.* رُمُوزٌ ـ تَشْبِيهٌ ـ مِثَالٌ ـ شَبِيهٌ *pl.* أَشْبَاهٌ. A creed or summary of belief, صُورَةُ إِيمَانٍ. These things are mere symbols of the reality, هٰذِهِ ٱلْأَشْيَاءُ أَشْبَاهُ ٱلْحَقِيقَةِ فَقَطْ.

Symbolic, *a.* } رَمْزِيٌّ ـ مَجَازِيٌّ ـ اِسْتِعَارِيٌّ ـ تَشْبِيهِيٌّ.
Symbolical, }

Symbolically, *ad.* بِٱلتَّشْبِيهِ ـ رَمْزًا ـ فِي مِثَالٍ.

Symbolism, *n.* تَرْكِيبُ ٱلرُّمُوزِ ـ نَسَقُ ٱلرُّمُوزِ.

Symbolize, *v.i.* To — with, have a resemblance to, أَشْبَهَ ـ شَابَهَ. To agree with, وَافَقَ. To represent, كَانَ صُورَةَ كَذَا.

Symbolize, *v.t.* To make to resemble, مَثَّلَ ـ شَبَّهَ. To make to represent, جَعَلَ ـ يُعَبِّرُ ـ جَعَلَ ـ فِي مَقَامِ كَذَا ـ صَيَّرَ ـ رَمْزَ كَذَا عَنْ كَذَا.

Symbology, *n.* فَنُّ تَرْكِيبِ ٱلرُّمُوزِ ـ فَنُّ ٱلتَّشْبِيهِ.

Symmetrical, *a.* مُهَنْدَم ـ حَسِيْن ـ سَوِيٌّ ـ مُعْتَدِل. To be —, تَنَاسَبَ ـ كَانَ مُهَنْدَمًا ـ اِعْتَدَلَ.

Symmetrically, *ad.* بِهَنْدَامٍ ـ بِحُسْنِ نِظَامٍ.

Symmetricalness, *n.* *See* Symmetry, *n.*

Symmetrize, *v.t.* ظَرَّفَهُ ـ سَوَّى ـ عَدَّلَ ـ صَيَّرَ ـ مُنَاسِبًا ـ هَنْدَمَ ـ وَٱتْقَنَهُ.

Symmetry, *n.* مُنَاسَبَة ـ تَنَاسُبٌ وَٱنْتِظَامٌ ـ هَنْدَام ـ تَقْوِيم ـ اِزْدِوَاجٌ ـ حُسْن ـ حُسْنُ تَرْتِيبِ. Symmetry of expression, in talk, حُسْنُ ٱلْكَلَامِ وَحُسْنِ تَجَانُسِ ٱلْأَلْفَاظِ.

Sympathetic, *a.* } Having a common feeling, مُشْتَرِكُ ٱلْحِسِّ.
Sympathetical, } What attracts the feelings, مُحَنِّنُ ٱلْقَلْبِ ـ جَالِبُ ٱلْمَيْلِ وَٱلرَّغْبَةِ ـ مُسْتَمِيلُ ٱلْقَلْبِ. Commiserating, رَاثٍ لِ ـ مُشْفِقٌ عَلَى ـ شَفِيقٌ عَلَى. Sympathetic ink, حِبْرٌ سِرِّيٌّ.

Sympathetically, *ad.* With fellow-feeling, بِٱشْتِرَاكِ ٱلْحِسِّ. With commiseration, بِشَفَقَةٍ ـ بِمَرْثَاةٍ.

Sympathize, *v.i.* To — with, have a fellow-feeling with, اِشْتَرَكَ فِي أَحْسَاسِ ٱلْغَيْرِ. To be eager for, with others, رَغِبَ مَعَ ـ فِي ـ نَفِسَ مَعَ ـ بِ. To commiserate, حَنَّ عَلَى ـ رَثَى لِ ـ رَقَّ قَلْبُهُ لِ.

Sympathy, *n.* Fellow-feeling, اِشْتِرَاكٌ فِي ـ اِشْتِرَاكُ ٱلْحِسِّ ـ ٱلْإِحْسَاسَاتِ. Commiseration, تَحَنُّن ـ شَفَقَة ـ رِثَايَة ـ رِثَاء. Natural inclination, مُوَافَقَةُ ٱلطَّبْعِ ـ مَيْلٌ طَبِيعِيٌّ. Attraction, جَاذِبِيَّة. The natural — of souls, سِرٌّ رَبَّانِيٌّ. To excite the —, support, favour of, جَلَبَ حُسْنَ ٱلْتِفَاتِهِ. To gain the — of one, جَذَبَ عَوَاطِفَهُ ـ اِسْتَمَالَ قَلْبَهُ. To manifest — for, اِنْعَطَفَ (or تَعَطَّفَ) عَلَى ـ أَظْهَرَ حُسْنَ ٱلْاِنْعِطَافِ عَلَى ـ لَوَى عَلَى. To lose the — of one, أَضَاعَ (or تَلِفَ) حُسْنَ ٱلْتِفَاتِهِ. Capable of — with him, جَدِيرٌ بِٱلْاِلْتِفَاتِ إِلَيْهِ.

Symphonious, *a.* *See* Harmonious, *a.*

Symphony, *n.* Harmony, أُلْفَةُ ٱلْأَصْوَاتِ. A concert, نَوْبَة. An overture, in music, اِفْتِتَاحُ نَوْبَةٍ.

Sympiesometer, *n.* مِيزَانٌ يَدُلُّ عَلَى ثِقْلِ ٱلْهَوَاءِ.

Symposiac, *n.* مَجْلِسُ عُلَمَاءَ فِي وَلِيمَةٍ.

Symposium, *n.* مَأْدُبَة ـ وَلِيمَة ـ ضِيَافَة ـ مُنَادَمَة.

Symptom, *n.* As of a disease, *etc.*, دَلِيل *pl.* دَلَائِل ـ عَلَامَة *pl.* عَلَامَات ـ إِشَارَة. An indication by which the existence of a thing is known or inferred, شِيَة ـ مَعْلَم *pl.* مَعَالِم ـ مَظِنَّة *pl.* مَظَانّ ـ مَخِيلَة. The symptoms of generosity appeared in him, ظَهَرَتْ فِيهِ مَظَانُّ (or مَخَائِلُ) ٱلنَّجَابَةِ.

Symptomatic, *a.* } مُدِلٌّ عَلَى ـ دَلِيلِيٌّ.
Symptomatical, }

Symptomatically, *ad.* بِمَخِيلَةٍ ـ بِوَجْهِ ٱلْإِشَارَةِ ـ بِٱلدَّلَائِلِ.

Synæresis, *n.* *See* Syncope, *n.*

Synagogue, *n.* جَامِعُ ٱلْيَهُودِ ـ فِهْرُ ٱلْيَهُودِ ـ ٱلْفِهْرُ *pl.* جَوَامِع.

Synarchy, *n.* اِشْتِرَاكٌ فِي ٱلْحُكُومَةِ.

Synchronal, *a.* } وَاقِعٌ فِي زَمَانٍ وَاحِدٍ. *See also* Simultaneous, *a.*
Synchronical, }

Synchronism, *n.* وُقُوعٌ (or حُدُوثٌ) فِي زَمَانٍ وَاحِدٍ مَعَ كَذَا. *See also* Simultaneousness, *n.*

Synchronize, *v.t.* حَدَثَ (or وَقَعَ *aor.* يَقَعُ) فِي زَمَانٍ وَاحِدٍ مَعَ كَذَا.

Synchronous, *a.* *See* Synchronal, *a.*

Syncopate, *v.t.* As of a letter or syllable, حَذَفَ.

Syncopation, *n.* As of a letter or syllable in a word, حَذْف.

Syncope, *n.* As of a letter or syllable, حَذْف. A fainting, مَوْتَة. *See under* Swoon, *n.*

Syncopize, *v.t.* *See to* Syncopate, *v.t.*

Syncretism, *n.* سَعْيٌ فِي مُوَافَقَةِ ٱلْأَشْيَاءِ ٱلَّتِي ٱتِّفَاقُهَا مُحَالٌ.

Syndic, *n.* نَقِيب *pl.* نُقَبَاءُ ـ وَكِيل *pl.* وُكَلَاء ـ مَأْمُور *pl.* مَأْمُورُونَ ـ مُتَوَكِّل.

Syndicate, *n.* The office of a syndic, نِقَابَة; a meeting of syndics, اِجْتِمَاعُ ٱلنُّقَبَاءِ.

Synecdoche, *n.* مَجَازٌ مُرْسَلٌ.

Synecdochical, *a.* عَلَى مَجَازٍ مُرْسَلٍ.

Synecdochically, *ad.* بِٱلْمَجَازِ ٱلْمُرْسَلِ.

Syngenesia, *n.* اِسْمٌ لِصِنْفٍ مِنَ ٱلْأَزْهَارِ ذَوَاتِ آلَاتِ إِنَاثٍ وَذُكُورٍ.

Synod, *n.* مَحْفَل *pl.* مَحَافِل ـ مَجْمَع *pl.* مَجَامِع ـ مَجْلِس *pl.* مَجَالِس ـ سِينُودُس.

Synodic, *a.* } Done by a synod, مُعَقَّدٌ بِٱتِّفَاقِ مَجْمَعٍ ـ سِينُودُسِيٌّ;
Synodal, } pertaining to a synod, مُخْتَصٌّ بِمَجْمَعٍ. A —

epistle, رِسَالَةٌ سِيْنُودُسِيَّةٌ. Noting the period of conjunction, as of planets, مِمَّا يَدُلُّ عَلَى وَقْتِ ٱلِٱقْتِرَانِ.

Synodically, *ad.* بِأَمْرِ مَجْمَعٍ ـ فِي مَجْمَعٍ.

Synonym, *n.* كَلِمَةٌ مُتَرَادِفَةٌ ـ مُتَرَادِفَاتٌ *pl.* مُتَرَادِفٌ.

Synonymous, *a.* بِمَعْنًى وَاحِدٍ ـ مُشْتَرَكُ ٱلْمَعْنَى ـ مُتَرَادِفٌ. To be —, تَرَادَفَ. Synonymous words, أَلْفَاظٌ مُتَرَادِفَةٌ. These two words are —, هَتَانِ ٱلْكَلِمَتَانِ تَتَرَادَفَانِ (*or* مُتَرَادِفَتَانِ). These words are —, هٰذِهِ ٱلْأَلْفَاظُ مُتَرَادِفَةٌ.

Synonymously, *ad.* بِٱلتَّرَادُفِ.

Synopsis, *n.* An abridgment, مُخْتَصَرٌ ـ إِيجَازٌ ـ وَجْزٌ. An index, table, table of contents, فِهْرِسٌ ـ جَدْوَلٌ *pl.* جَدَاوِلُ ـ سِيَاقَةٌ. To make a —, abridge, إِخْتَصَرَ. To tabulate, جَدْوَلَ ـ فَهْرَسَ.

Synoptic, *a.* } شَامِلٌ ـ مُجَدْوَلٌ وَمُفَهْرَسٌ.
Synoptical, }

Synoptically, *ad.* عَلَى سِيَاقَةٍ وَٱخْتِصَارٍ ـ شَمْلًا وَبِإِيجَازٍ.

Synovia, *n.* مَادَّةٌ تُشْبِهُ ٱللُّعَابَ تُوجَدُ فِي ٱلْمَفَاصِلِ ٱلْمُتَحَرِّكَةِ.

Syntactic, *a.* } نَحْوِيٌّ.
Syntactical, }

Syntax, *n.* قَوَاعِدُ نَحْوِيَّةٌ ـ عِلْمُ ٱلنَّحْوِ.

Synthesis, *n.* تَرْكِيبٌ ـ تَأْلِيفٌ.

Synthetic, *a.* } تَرْكِيبِيٌّ ـ تَأْلِيفِيٌّ.
Synthetical, }

Synthetically, *ad.* بِٱلتَّرْكِيبِ ـ تَرْكِيبًا ـ بِٱلتَّأْلِيفِ.

Syphilis, *n.* مَرَضٌ فِرَنْجِيٌّ ـ بَلَاءٌ ـ حَبٌّ فِرَنْجِيٌّ.

Syphilitic, *a.* مُخْتَصٌّ بِٱلْمَرَضِ ٱلْفِرَنْجِيِّ.

Syphon, *n.* *See* Siphon, *n.*

Syren, *n.* *See* Siren, *n.*

Syria, *n.* بَرُّ ٱلشَّامِ ـ بِلَادُ ٱلشَّامِ ـ ٱلشَّامُ ـ سُورِيَةُ.

Syriac, *n.* The language, لِسَانٌ سُرْيَانِيٌّ ـ سُرْيَانِيٌّ.

Syrian, *a.* } شَوَام *pl.* شَامِيٌّ.
Syrian, *n.* }

Syringa, *n.* شَجَرَةٌ تُشْبِهُ ٱللَّيْلَكَ.

Syringe, *n.* مِحْقَنَةٌ.

Syringe, *v.t.* حَقَنَ ـ ² بَخَّ ².

Syrius, *n.* The star; *see* Sirius, *n.*

Syrtis, *n.* *See* Quicksand, *n.*

System, *n.* A scheme or arrangement, تَرْتِيبٌ ـ نِظَامٌ ـ شَاكِلَةٌ ـ نَسَقٌ; the principles of any scheme, *etc.*, أُصُولٌ. A way or manner, rule, order, طَرِيقَةٌ ـ هَيْئَةٌ ـ طَرْزٌ ـ قَوَاعِدُ *pl.* قَاعِدَةٌ. A —, as of religion, *etc.*, قَوْلٌ ـ مَذَاهِبُ *pl.* مَذْهَبٌ. On the European —, عَلَى نَسَقِ أُورُبَّا.

The Copernican system, النِّظَامُ ٱلْفَلَكِيُّ حَسَبَ ٱلْمُعَلِّمِ كُوبَرْنِيكَ.

The Ptolemaic system, نَسَقٌ ـ عِلْمُ ٱلْهَيْئَةِ عَلَى قَوْلِ بَطْلِيمُوسَ بَطْلِيمُوسَ.

The solar system, النِّظَامُ ٱلشَّمْسِيُّ ـ النَّسَقُ ٱلشَّمْسِيُّ.

Systematic, *a.* } Arranged systematically, مُرَتَّبٌ عَلَى أُصُولٍ ـ مُنَسَّقٌ ـ تَرْتِيبِيٌّ ـ وَقَوَاعِدَ. Constant, دَائِمٌ ـ بِلَا ٱنْقِطَاعٍ.
Systematical, }

Systematically, *ad.* According to system, حَسَبَ ٱلْأُصُولِ ـ بِٱلتَّنْسِيقِ ـ بِٱلنَّسَقِ ـ عَلَى قَوَاعِدَ. Always, دَائِمًا.

Systematize, *v.t.* } نَظَّمَ ـ عَلَى ـ رَتَّبَ ـ عَلَى قَوَاعِدَ ـ نَسَّقَ ـ ² نَسَقَ أُصُولٍ. To be systematized, تَنَسَّقَ ـ إِنْتَسَقَ.
Systemize, }

Systole, *n.* *See* Syncope, *n.*

Systole, *n.* The contraction of the heart and arteries, إِنْقِبَاضُ ٱلْقَلْبِ وَٱلضَّوَارِبِ.

Sythe, *n.* *See* Scythe, *n.*

Syzygy, *n.* نُقْطَةُ ٱلِٱقْتِرَانِ بَيْنَ ـ زَمَانُ إِهْلَالِ ٱلْقَمَرِ وَتَمَامِهِ ٱلشَّمْسِ وَٱلْقَمَرِ وَٱلْأَرْضِ.

T.

T. or Tee, *n.* To a T., perfectly, حَسَنًا ـ لِلْغَايَةِ ـ تَمَامًا ـ بِغَايَةِ ٱلْإِتْقَانِ ـ عَلَى أَكْمَلِ وَجْهٍ. The two are alike to a T., هُمَا مِثْلَ فُولَةٍ مَقْسُومَةٍ. He cooked the meat to a T., أَجَادَ طَبْخَ ٱللَّحْمِ.

Tabard, *n.* صُدْرَةٌ رَسْمِيَّةٌ.

Tabarder, *n.* لَابِسُ ٱلصُّدْرَةِ ٱلْمَذْكُورَةِ.

Tabasheer, *n.* طَبَاشِير.

Tabbinet, *n.* كِرْمَسُوت.

Tabby, *a.* Brindled, أَرْقَطُ *fem.* رَقْطَآءُ *pl.* رُقْط ـ مُرَقَّط; diversified in colour, مُنَمْنَم ـ مُوَشًّى ـ مُزَرْكَش ـ مُبَرْقَش ـ مُنَقَّش.

Tabby, *n.* A waved silk, قُمَاشٌ مِنْ حَرِيرٍ مُمَوَّجٍ ـ حَرِيرٌ مُنَمْنَمٌ ـ كِرْمَسُوت; the artificial stone, ضَرْبٌ مِنَ ٱلْحَجَرِ مُرَكَّبٌ مِنَ ٱلْحَصَى وَغَيْرِهَا.

Tabby, *v.t.* To cause to look wavy, وَشَّى ـ مَوَّجَ ـ نَمْنَمَ.

Tabefaction, *n.* A wasting away by disease, ضَنًى.

Taber, *n.* *See* Tabour, *n.*

Tabernacle, *n.* An abode, مَسْكَنٌ *pl.* مَسَاكِنُ. A tent, خَيْمَةٌ *pl.* خِيَام; especially of hair, مِظَلَّةٌ *pl.* مَظَالُّ. The — of the ark of testimony among the Jews, قُبَّةُ ٱلْعَهْدِ ـ مِظَلَّةٌ. The Feast of Tabernacles, عِيدُ ٱلْمَظَالِّ.

Tabernacle, *v.i.* To dwell, سَكَنَ ² ـ حَلَّ ². *See also to* Sojourn, *v.i.*

Tabes, *n.* Progressive emaciation, ضَنًى. To be affected with —, ضَنِيَ ² ـ إِضْطَنَى.

Tabid, *a.* مُضْنًى.

Tablature, *n.* Painting on walls, ٱلرَّسْمُ فِي ٱلْحِيطَانِ.

Table, *n.* Anything upon which one eats, خِوَان *pl.* أَخْوِنَةٌ ـ سُفْرَةٌ *pl.* سُفَر; a — with food thereon, مَائِدَةٌ *pl.* مَوَائِدُ ـ فَاثُور (in ordinary usage these three words are used indiscriminately for a table or a table with food thereon; also that of طَاوِلَةٌ from the Italian). A long — provided for guests, سِمَاطُ ٱلطَّعَامِ *pl.* أَسْمِطَةٌ. A tablet, لَوْح *pl.* أَلْوَاح. A —, as of contents, فِهْرِس ـ فِهْرِسْت. A —, as of numbers arranged in columns, *etc.*, جَدْوَل *pl.* جَدَاوِل. A list, تَقْوِيم *pl.* تَقَاوِيمُ. A — to play games upon, طَاوِلَةٌ *pl.* طَاوِلَات. An astronomical —, زِيجٌ *pl.* زِيجَةٌ. Chronological tables, تَقْوِيمُ ٱلتَّوَارِيخِ. The Two Tables of Testimony, or of the Law, لَوْحَا ٱلشَّهَادَةِ. They eat at a common —, هُمْ عَلَى فَاثُورٍ وَاحِدٍ. "When the Apostles said: O Jesus, son of Mary, is your Lord able to cause a (furnished) table to descend from heaven for us," إِذْ قَالَ ٱلْحَوَارِيُّونَ يَا عِيسَى ٱبْنَ مَرْيَمَ هَلْ يَسْتَطِيعُ رَبُّكَ أَنْ يُنَزِّلَ عَلَيْنَا مَائِدَةً مِنَ ٱلسَّمَآءِ (Kur. v. 112).

To keep a good table, to keep open house, تَفَنَّنَ فِي ٱلضِّيَافَةِ.

To place at table, أَجْلَسَ- (*or* -قَعَّدَ) عَلَى ٱلْمَائِدَةِ.

To prepare a table, رَصَّ ² (*or* أَعَدَّ) ٱلسُّفْرَةَ ـ رَتَّبَ ٱلْمَائِدَةَ.

To put on a table, وَضَعَ-عَلَى ٱلْمَائِدَةِ *aor.* يَضَعُ.

To rise from a table, قَامَ عَنِ ٱلْمَائِدَةِ *aor.* يَقُومُ.

To seat at a table; *see* To place at a table.

To serve at table, خَدَمَ ٱلسُّفْرَةَ ².

To sit at a table, جَلَسَ عَلَى ٱلسُّفْرَةِ ـ قَعَدَ عَلَى ٱلْمَائِدَةِ ².

To spread a table, فَرَشَ ٱلسُّفْرَةَ ².

To turn the tables on one, رَدَّ عَلَى-أَمْرَهُ ـ عَكَسَ عَلَى-أَمْرَهُ ².

Those who are seated at a table, ٱلْمُتَّكِئُونَ عَلَى ٱلسُّفْرَةِ.

Table, *v.i.* أَكَلَ عَلَى ٱلسُّفْرَةِ ² ـ أَكَلَ.

Table, *v.t.* To write down, as charges, *etc.*, قَيَّدَ ـ دَوَّنَ. To index, فَهْرَسَ. To set down in columns, جَدْوَلَ. To arrange in order, نَسَّقَ ـ رَتَّبَ. To board, feed, أَمَدَّ-بِٱلطَّعَامِ.

Tableau, *n.* A picture, صُورَةٌ *pl.* صُوَر ـ تَصْوِير *pl.* تَصَاوِيرُ. A description, representation, تَقْوِيم ـ بَيَان ـ وَصْف. A — vivant, أَشْخَاصٌ أَحْيَآءُ يُقَلِّدُونَ ٱلتَّمَاثِيلَ فِي هَيْئَتِهَا وَوَضْعِهَا.

Table-beer, *n.* بِيرَةٌ خَفِيفَةٌ.

Table-cloth, *n.* بَزُّ ٱلسُّفْرَةِ ـ سُفْرَةٌ.

Table d'hôte, *n.* سُفْرَةٌ ـ سُفْرَةٌ مُعَدَّةٌ لِلنُّزُلِ فِي مَنْزِلِ ٱلْغُرَبَآءِ ـ سُفْرَةٌ عَامَّةٌ فِي لُوكَنْدَةٍ ـ لُوكَنْدَةٍ.

Table-land, *n.* صَعْدَةٌ ـ صَعِيد ـ ظَاهِرَةٌ ـ ظَهْر.

Tablet, *n.* لَوْح *pl.* أَلْوَاح. A memorial —, gravestone, رَجَم *pl.* أَرْجَام ـ رُجْمَةٌ. Tablets for memoranda, أَلْوَاحُ تَفْكِرَةٍ ـ تَفْكِرَةٌ ـ تَذْكِرَةٌ.

Table-talk, *n.* ٱلْمُحَاوَرَةُ عَلَى ٱلسُّفْرَةِ.

Tabling, *n.* Such as entering charges, تَقْيِيد; indexing, فَهْرَسَةٌ; drawing up, as in columns, جَدْوَلَةٌ ـ تَقْوِيم; orderly arrangement, تَرْتِيب ـ تَنْسِيق.

Taboo, *n.* حُرْمَةٌ ـ مُحَرَّم.

Taboo, *v.t.* حَرَّمَ ـ أَحْرَمَ.

Tabour, *v.i.* To play on the tabour, دَقَّ ٱلطَّبْلَ ².

Tabour, *n.* طَبْل *pl.* أَطْبَال .

Tabouret, *n.* نَقَّارَة *pl.* نَقَاقِير .

Tabourine, *n.* *See* Tambourine, *n.*

Tabret, *n.* دَفّ *pl.* دُفُوف .

Tabular, *a.* Flat, مُسَطَّح ــ مُسْتَوٍ . Arranged in squares, مُرَتَّبٌ عَلَى أَجْزَاءٍ مُرَبَّعَةٍ . Arranged in columns, مُرَتَّبٌ عَلَى جَدَاوِل .

Tabulate, *v.t.* To flatten, سَطَّحَ ــ بَسَّطَ . To arrange in tables, رَتَّبَ-عَلَى جَدَاوِل .

Tachigraphy, *n.* *See* Stenography, *n.*

Tacit, *a.* Implied, فِي ضِمْنِ ٱلْكَلَامِ ــ نَاتِجٌ مِنْ نَصِّ ٱلْكَلَامِ ــ مُسْتَفَادٌ مِنْ سِيَاقِ ٱلْكَلَامِ . Silent, سَاكُوت .

Tacitly, *ad.* By implication, ضِمْنًا ــ بِٱلنَّتِيجَةِ . Silently, بِٱلسُّكُوتِ .

Taciturn, *a.* سِكِّيت ــ سَاكُوت . *See also* Reserved, *a.*

Taciturnity, *n.* صَمْت ــ سَاكُوتَة ــ سُكَات .

Tack, *n.* A small nail, مِسْمَارٌ رَفِيعٌ ــ عَصَافِير *pl.* عُصْفُور *pl.* مَسَامِيرُ رِفَاعٌ . A course, way, طَرِيق ــ مَسِير . Arrangement, تَدْبِير . The rope of a sail, حَبْلُ ٱلْقِلْعِ . A —, stretch, as of a ship, مَسْلَكٌ ــ وِجْهَة ــ رُحْلَة ــ طِيَّة . A slight sewing, شِلَالَة . A tacking, of a ship, تَحْوِيلُ ٱلْقَرِيَّةِ .

Tack, *v.t.* As with tacks, سَمَّرَ-بِمَسَامِيرَ صِغَارٍ (or بِٱلْعَصَافِيرِ) . To baste, in sewing, شَلَّ ــ [2] شَصَّرَ ــ [2] خَاصَ ــ [2] مَلَّ . To fasten or add to, أَلْحَقَ-بِ ــ أَضَافَ-إِلَى .

Tack, *v.i.* Of a ship, حَوَّلَ ٱلْقَرِيَّةَ ; *from the Italian*, عَمِلَ أُورْصَة .

Tackle, *n.* As of a ship, حِبَال ــ جُمَّل . Appliances, أُهْبَة ــ أَثَاث ــ أَدَات ــ آلَاتٌ وَأَدَوَاتٌ ــ آلَات ــ عُدَّة ــ أَسْبَاب .

Tackle, *v.t.* To harness a horse to a carriage, عَلَّقَ (or كَدَّنَ) ٱلْخَيْلَ فِي ٱلْعَرَبَانَةِ . To seize, تَشَبَّثَ بِ ــ [2] بَطَشَ بِ . The two opponents sought to — each other, تَخَالَسَ ــ تَخَالَسَ ٱلْقِرْنَانِ نَفْسَيْهِمَا .

Tackling, *n.* Harness, طَقْمٌ لِلْخَيْلِ ــ عُدَّةُ ٱلْخَيْلِ . *See also* Tackle, *n.*

Tact, *n.* Touch, لَمْس ــ مُلَامَسَة . Nice perception, مِهْنَة ــ فَطَانَة ــ فِرَاسَة ــ ذَوْق . Having good —, حَسَنُ ٱلذَّوْقِ (or ٱلْفِرَاسَةِ) .

Tactic, *a.* }
Tactical, } مُتَعَلِّقٌ بِتَعْبِئَةِ ٱلْجُيُوشِ وَتَحْرِيكِهَا .

Tactician, *n.* أُسْتَاذٌ فِي فَنِّ تَعْبِئَةِ ٱلْجُيُوشِ وَتَحْرِيكِهَا .

Tactics, *n.* Military —, فَنُّ تَعْبِئَةِ ٱلْجُيُوشِ وَتَحْرِيكِهَا . Proceedings, in a general sense, أَعْمَال ــ أَفْعَال ــ أَوْضَاعٌ وَحَرَكَاتٌ ــ نَمَط ــ طِرَاز ــ طَرْز .

Tactile, *a.* مِمَّا يُحَسّ ــ يُحَسّ ــ حِسِّيّ .

Tactility, *n.* حَالَةُ ٱنْفِعَالِ ٱلْحَسِّ ــ حَالَةُ قُبُولِ ٱللَّمْسِ .

Taction, *n.* لَمْس ــ مُمَاسَّة ــ مَسّ .

Tactless, *a.* أَخْرَق ــ بِلَا فِرَاسَةٍ ــ غَيْرُ فَاطِنٍ ــ عَدِيمُ ٱلْمِهْنَةِ .

Tactual, *a.* مُخْتَصٌّ بِٱلْمُلَامَسَةِ ــ مُتَعَلِّقٌ بِٱللَّمْسِ .

Tadpole, *n.* فَرْخُ ٱلضِّفْدَعِ *pl.* فِرَاخ .

Ta'en, *contract. for* Taken. *See under to* Take, *v.t.*

Tafferel, *n.* }
Taffrail, } جِشُّ ٱلْمَرْكَبِ .

Taffeta, *n.* }
Taffety, } The silk brocade, سُنْدُس . The silk, woven with gold, إِسْتَبْرَق . "And they shall be arrayed in garments of taffeta and rich brocade," وَيَلْبَسُونَ ثِيَابًا مِنْ سُنْدُسٍ وَإِسْتَبْرَقٍ (Kur. xviii. 30).

Tag, *n.* زَجّ *pl.* زِجَاج *and* أَزِجَّة .

Tagrag, Tagrag and bobtail, *n.* ٱلْأَسَافِلُ ــ أَسَافِلُ ٱلنَّاسِ ــ ٱلْأَوْبَاشُ ــ ٱلسَّفَلَةُ .

Tag, *v.t.* رَكَّبَ عَلَى-زُجًّا .

Taglia, *n.* A combination of pulleys, تَرْكِيبُ بَكَّارَاتٍ .

Tail, *n.* As of an animal, ذَنَب *pl.* أَذْنَاب ــ ذَيْل *pl.* أَذْيَال ; of a garment, ذَيْل *pl.* أَذْيَال *and* ذُيُول . The fat — of a sheep, أَلْيَة ــ عُجَيْزَة . A —, such as is borne before pâshas, طُوغ *pl.* أَطْوَاغ . Having a long —, ذُو ذَنَبٍ ــ مُذَنَّب ــ ذَيَّال . A — or train of a bird, زِمِكَّى . Anything resembling a —, such as an appendix, *etc.*, ذَيْل *pl.* أَذْيَال . The — bone, عُصْعُص ــ عَجْب ــ عَجْبُ ٱلذَّنَبِ ــ عُسَيْبَة . The root of the —, سِيُور . The end of anything, تَتِمَّة ــ آخِر . The hinder part of anything, مُؤَخَّر . The lower part of anything, أَسْفَل . A fixed period agreed upon, وَقْتٌ مَشْرُوطٌ ــ أَجَلٌ مُؤَجَّلٌ . An estate in —, عَقَارَاتٌ مَحْصُورَةٌ فِي وِرَاثَةٍ مُعَيَّنَةٍ . To move the —, [2] خَفَّضَ ٱلذَّنَبَ . To lift the —, أَشَالَ ذَنَبَهُ ــ [2] شَالَ بِذَنَبِهِ . To lash with the —, of a horse or camel, خَطَرَ بِذَنَبِهِ . To shake about, of the —, أَسْنَدَ (or [2] سَنَدَ) ٱلذَّنَبَ . To turn — to —, جَعَلَ-ذَنَبًا إِلَى ذَنَبٍ . To turn — from, through cowardice, خَامَ عَنْ : they turned — in the battle, خَامُوا فِي ٱلْقِتَالِ . He returned like a dog with his — between his legs, crest-fallen, (*lit.* striking his buttocks,) جَآءَ يَضْرِبُ مِذْرَوَيْهِ *aor.* [2] يَجِيءُ .

Tail-rope, *n.* حَبْلُ ٱلْقَطْرِ ــ حَبْلُ ٱلْجَرِّ .

Tailed, *a.* Having a tail, ذُو ذَيْلٍ ــ ذُو ذَنَبٍ . A long-tailed story, حَدِيثٌ طَوِيلُ ٱلذَّنَبِ .

Tailor, *n.* خَيَّاط *pl.* خَيَّاطَة .

Tailor, *v.i.* كَانَ خَيَّاطًا ـ إِشْتَغَلَ ٱلْخِيَاطَةَ ـ خَيَّطَ .

Tailoress, *n.* خَيَّاطَة *pl.* خَيَّاطَات .

Taint, *v.t.* عَفَّنَ ـ فَسَخَ ـ أَفْسَدَ . *See also to* Sully, Stain, *v.t.*

Taint, *v.i.* تَعَفَّنَ ـ إِنْفَسَخَ ـ فَسَدَ .

Taint, *n.* Corruption, infection, تَعَفُّن ـ فَسْخ ـ فَسَاد . Taste, ذَوْق . A — or touch of, عِرْق ـ خَطْرَة .

Tainted, *a.* Corrupted, مُتَعَفِّن ـ مَفْسُوخ ـ فَاسِد .

Taintless, *a.* صَافٍ ـ غَيْرُ مُتَعَفِّنٍ ـ غَيْرُ مَفْسُوخٍ .

Take, *v.t.* In a general sense, أَخَذَ . To —, as handing to one's self, إِتَّخَذَ ـ تَنَاوَلَ . To grasp, lay hold of, ضَمَّ ـ قَبَضَ ب ـ مَسَكَ ـ تَمَسَّكَ ـ تَمَسَّكَ ب . To receive, أَخَذَ ـ قَبَضَ عَلَى . To accept, قَبِلَ ب ـ تَقَبَّلَ . To seize, ضَبَطَ ـ تَمَسَّكَ ب ـ صَبَرَ عَلَى ـ تَحَمَّلَ ـ إِحْتَمَلَ . To bear, تَصَبَّرَ . To —, as a drawing, رَسَمَ ـ صَوَّرَ ـ أَخَذَ صُورَةَ كَذَا . To rent, أَكْرَى ـ إِسْتَأْجَرَ . To —, of game, صَادَ ـ إِصْطَادَ ; of booty, غَنِمَ ـ إِغْتَنَمَ ; of a town, *etc.*, فَتَحَ ـ ضَبَطَ ـ سَخَّرَ . To —, in the sense of to take in, to receive, to have handed to, تَلَقَّى . To —, to eat, أَكَلَ . To drink, شَرِبَ . To —, as a disease, أَصَابَهُ مَرَضٌ ـ إِنْعَدَى مِنْ مَرَضٍ . To —, in the sense of to think, ظَنَّ . To convey, وَصَّلَ . To accompany, رَافَقَ . To —, to assume, إِتَّخَذَ . These questions continue to —, assume, different phases, and to become wider in their scope, مَا بَرِحَتْ هٰذِهِ ٱلْمَسَائِلُ تَتَلَوَّنُ بِأَلْوَانٍ شَتَّى وَتَزْدَادُ تَبَايُنًا .

To take one aback, to surprise, بَغَتَ ـ بَدَهَ ـ حَيَّرَ .

To take one about, سَيَّرَ ـ دَارَ ب ـ دَوَّرَ .

To take advantage of, as of an opportunity, إِتَّخَذَ ـ إِفْتَرَصَ ٱلْفُرْصَةَ ٱلْفُرْصَةَ . To cheat, غَدَرَ ب ـ خَانَ ـ إِخْتَانَ ـ غَشَّ ـ مَكَرَ ب .

To take affront, أَخَذَ عَلَى خَاطِرِهِ ـ إِنْقَهَرَ ـ تَضَجَّرَ .

To take after, to resemble, شَبِهَ ـ شَابَهَ ـ أَشْبَهَ .

To take aim at, عَيَّنَ عَلَى ـ حَرَّرَ عَلَى ـ تَأَنَّى ل ـ أَشْرَعَ ـ نَاشَنَ ـ أَقْصَدَ .

To take air, شَمَّ ٱلْهَوَاءَ ـ تَفَسَّحَ .

To take along, مَشَى ب ـ سَيَّرَ ـ يَسِيرُ *aor.* سَارَ ب .

To take away, to remove, رَفَعَ ـ نَحَّى ـ نَقَلَ . To push or take aside, to pull away, as from a crowd, *etc.*, جَنَّبَ ـ جَانَبَ ـ جَلَبَ ـ أَبْعَدَ ـ ذَهَبَ ب . To carry off, مَضَى ب ـ خَطِفَ ـ إِخْتَطَفَ . To despoil, carry off by force, سَلَبَ ـ إِسْتَلَبَ . To steal from, سَرَقَ مِن ـ إِسْتَرَقَ مِن . To abolish, بَطَّلَ ـ أَبْطَلَ . To deprive of, إِخْتَلَسَ مِن ـ نَزَعَ مِن ـ رَفَعَ عَنْهُ كَذَا . To subtract, as from a total, أَسْقَطَ .

To take away, as dishes, *etc.*, from a table, رَفَعَ ـ نَحَّى ـ شَالَ ب مِن . To remove, as shackles; also of stripping, حَسَرَ عَن ـ حَسَرَ عَنْهُ كَذَا .

To take back, to receive back, as from any one, إِسْتَرْجَعَ مِن ـ إِسْتَرَدَّ مِن . To give back, رَدَّ ـ رَاجَعَ . To take back, as into service, رَدَّ إِلَى ـ عَادَ فَخَدَمَهُ ـ رَجَّعَ إِلَى ٱلْخِدْمَةِ ٱلْخِدْمَةِ .

To take breath, to breathe, تَنَفَّسَ ; to take breathing time, بَلَعَ رِيقَهُ ـ أَخَذَ نَفَسًا .

To take care, to be mindful, regardful, observant, رَاعَى ـ حَافَظَ .

To take care of one's self, to be watchful, إِحْتَرَزَ ـ تَحَرَّزَ ـ إِحْتَرَسَ ـ تَحَرَّسَ ـ تَحَفَّظَ .

Take (thou) care! إِصْحَ ـ إِنْتَبِهْ ـ إِحْتَرِزْ . Take care, beware, of the horse! إِيَّاكَ وَٱلْفَرَسَ .

To take care of, حَفِظَ ـ حَرَسَ ـ إِعْتَنَى ب .

To take a course, سَلَكَ طَرِيقًا ـ إِتَّخَذَ طَرْزًا . To take or steer a course towards, ضَرَبَ إِلَى .

To take cold, زُكِمَ ـ تَرَشَّحَ .

To take delight in, تَلَذَّذَ ب ـ سُرَّ ب ـ *vulg.* إِنْبَسَطَ مِن .

To take down, as pictures from a wall, *etc.*, أَنْزَلَ . To take down, as in writing, قَيَّدَ ـ كَتَبَ ; as in a book, قَيَّدَ فِي ـ دَوَّنَ فِي .

To humiliate, وَضَعَ ـ أَذَلَّ ـ أَهَانَ ـ كَسَرَ نَفْسَهُ . To eat, أَكَلَ ; to drink, شَرِبَ ـ بَلَعَ . To pull down, demolish, هَدَّ ـ هَدَمَ . To take down, as in a class at school, سَبَقَ ـ تَقَدَّمَ .

To take down, as of sails, لَمَّ ـ لَفَّ . To take down, as in price, أَرْخَصَ .

To take effect, as of a medicine, إِشْتَغَلَ . To produce an effect upon, فَعَلَ فِي ـ أَثَّرَ فِي ـ أَخَذَ فِي .

To take one's own course, إِتَّخَذَ سَبِيلَهُ ـ إِنْطَلَقَ إِلَى حَالِ سَبِيلِهِ .

To take the field, بَرَزَ ـ تَبَرَّزَ ـ خَرَجَ إِلَى ٱلْمَيْدَانِ .

To take fire, إِنْتَشَبَتِ ٱلنَّارُ فِي كَذَا ـ عَلِقَتِ ٱلنَّارُ فِي كَذَا .

To take from, رَزَأَ مِن كَذَا ـ رَزَأَ ـ أَخَذَ مِن كَذَا : I did not take aught from him, مَا رَزَأْتُهُ شَيْئًا . He did not take aught from him, مَا رَزَأَ فُلَانًا شَيْئًا .

To take by the hand, أَمْسَكَ بِيَدِهِ ـ أَخَذَ بِيَدِهِ . To act as a friend to, صَادَقَ ـ صَاحَبَ . To push forward, promote, back, رَقَّى ـ قَدَّمَ ـ عَلَّى ـ ظَاهَرَ .

To take in hand, to begin, شَرَعَ فِي ـ بَدَأَ ب ـ أَلْقَى يَدَهُ فِي .

To take in hand, so as to train, دَرَّجَ ـ دَرَّبَ ـ مَرَّنَ .

To take to heart, اِكْتَرَبَ عَلَى ـ اِغْتَمَّ عَلَى ـ اِنْغَمَّ عَلَى ـ تَأَسَّفَ عَلَى.

To take heed; *see* To take care.

To take hold of, مَسَكَ ـِ ـ تَمَسَّكَ ـ قَبَضَ بِ ـِ ـ ضَمَّ ـُ. Take hold of the thing, hold it fast, cleave to it, دُونَكَ ٱلشَّىْءَ ـ دُونَكَ بِٱلشَّىْءِ.

To take in, to cause to come in, فَوَّتَ إِلَى جُوَّا ـ أَدْخَلَ ـ أَخْشَ. To receive, as goods, *etc.*, at the door, تَلَقَّى. To contain, comprise, أَحَاطَ بِ ـ اِحْتَوَى عَلَى ـ تَضَمَّنَ عَلَى. To take in, as into a house, to lodge, نَزَّلَ. To diminish, as a garment, in length, قَصَّرَ; in width, ضَيَّقَ. To take in, as of a garment, by doubling and sewing it up, غَبَنَ ـِ. To take in, as of a cargo, وَسَقَ *aor.* يَسِقُ ـ أَوْسَقَ. To take in, to cheat, خَانَ ـُ ـ غَشَّ ـُ ـ مَكَرَ بِ ـُ ـ غَدَرَ بِ ـِ ـ غَبَنَ ـِ ـ اِخْتَانَ; as in selling and buying, شَابَ ـُ. To take in, as of sail, لَمَّ ـُ ـ لَفَّ ـُ. To take in, to subscribe to, اِشْتَرَكَ فِى. To take in, to diminish expenditure, to retrench, قَلَّلَ ٱلْمَصْرُوفَ ـ نَقَّصَ ٱلنَّفَقَةَ. To believe readily, تَزَيَّدَ.

To take in tow, as of a ship, قَطَرَ ـُ ـ سَحَبَ ـَ ـ جَرَّ ـُ.

To take into consideration, تَرَوَّى فِى: A council was appointed to take into consideration the demands of the foreign powers, تَشَكَّلَتْ لَجْنَةٌ لِلتَّرَوِّى فِى مَطَالِبِ ٱلدُّوَلِ ٱلْأَجْنَبِيَّةِ.

To take leave, permit one's self the liberty to . . . , تَرَخَّصَ فِى ـ اِسْتَأْذَنَ فِى ـ تَجَاسَرَ بِ. To take leave of one, وَدَّعَ ـ وَادَعَ. To take French leave, ذَهَبَ مِنْ غَيْرِ إِجَازَةٍ ـ اِنْطَلَقَ بِلَا إِذْنٍ.

To take life, to kill, قَتَلَ ـُ. To be inspirited, تَصَلَّبَ ـ تَشَجَّعَ.

To take notice of, to observe, أَمْعَنَ ٱلنَّظَرَ فِى ـ نَظَرَ إِلَى ـُ ـ لَاحَظَ. To show affection for, تَوَدَّدَ إِلَى; to esteem, regard, أَعَزَّ ـ رَعَى *aor.* يَرْعَى ـ رَاعَى.

To take an oath, أَقْسَمَ ـ حَلَفَ يَمِينًا ـِ ـ حَلَفَ حَلْفَةً.

To take off, to uncover, كَشَفَ عَنْ ـِ ـ اِسْتَكْشَفَ عَنْ. To remove, رَفَعَ ـَ ـ حَوَّلَ ـ نَقَلَ ـُ ـ نَحَّى. To carry off, of death, مَوَّتَ ـ كَانَ سَبَبَ مَوْتِهِ. To remove, as a burden, from off, وَضَعَ *aor.* يَضَعُ ـ حَطَّ ـُ. To take off, pull out, قَلَعَ ـَ. To lessen, of a burden, *etc.*, خَفَّفَ; of a price, حَطَّ ٱلثَّمَنَ ـُ. To mimic, ridicule, هَزِئَ ـَ (or) سَخِرَ مِنْ ـَ (or) بِ. To carry away, ذَهَبَ بِ ـَ ـ مَضَى بِ ـِ.

To take off one's hands, to buy from, شَرَى ـِ (or) اِشْتَرَى ـ مِنْ. To free one from, to assume the responsibility for, تَحَمَّلَ بَدَلَهُ ـ تَكَلَّفَ بَدَلًا عَنْهُ.

To take one's self off, فَرَّ ـِ ـ وَلَّى.

To take on, as on board ship, أَنْزَلَ فِى ٱلْمَرْكَبِ. To take on, as into service, شَغَّلَ ـ خَدَّمَ; as for longer rent, اِسْتَأْجَرَ أَيْضًا ـ عَادَ فَٱسْتَكْرَاهُ ـُ.

To take out, to bring out, أَخْرَجَ; as of a letter or syllable from a word, to elide; *also*, to omit, strike off, حَذَفَ ـِ ـ اِحْتَذَفَ. To take out, as of a document, patent, *etc.*, اِتَّخَذَ. To take out, to draw, of a tooth, قَلَعَ سِنًّا ـَ ـ قَبَعَ سِنًّا ـَ. To take out, as for an airing, أَخَذَ لِشَمِّ ٱلْهَوَاءِ ـُ; as a stain, blot, أَزَالَ; as meat from a pot, نَشَلَ ـِ ـُ. To clear from, as from deleterious particles, *etc.*, صَفَّى. *See also to* Erase, *v.t.*

To take it out in . . . , أَخَذَ بَدَلَ كَذَا. He took the amount of the debt in goods, اِسْتَوْفَى ٱلدَّيْنَ بِضَاعَةً.

To take out from among, to select, اِنْتَخَبَ مِنْ ـ نَقَّى مِنْ.

To take it out of one, to treat severely, عَاسَرَ ـ شَدَّدَ عَلَى ـ عَسَّرَ عَلَى.

To take part in, اِشْتَرَكَ فِى.

To take or do one's part, قَضَى مَا عَلَيْهِ ـِ ـ أَقَامَ بِمَا عَلَيْهِ.

To take part with, to espouse one's cause, تَمَسَّكَ مَعَ ـ تَعَصَّبَ لِ ـ حَامَى عَنْ ـ شَدَّ مَعَ ـُ.

To take place, جَرَى ـِ ـ حَصَلَ ـُ ـ حَدَثَ ـُ ـ وَقَعَ *aor.* يَقَعُ.

To take revenge of, اِنْتَقَمَ مِنْ. *See also under* Revenge, *n.*

To take root, اِسْتَأْصَلَ ـ تَأَصَّلَ ـ أَعْرَقَ.

To take thought, to be anxious, اِهْتَمَّ ـ اِغْتَمَّ.

To take to, to convey to, أَخَذَ إِلَى ـُ ـ رَفَعَ إِلَى ـَ ـ أَوْصَلَ إِلَى. To be taken with, to like, تَوَدَّدَ إِلَى ـ وَادَّ. To set about, تَشَمَّرَ لِ ـ شَرَعَ فِى ـَ ـ أَخَذَ فِى ـُ ـ جَعَلَ ـَ. They took to the matter readily, لَبُّوا ٱلدَّعْوَى نَاشِطِينَ.

To take to be, to consider as, think one to be, خَمَّنَ ـ ظَنَّ ـُ ـ حَسِبَ ـِ: He took him to be an apostle, ظَنَّ أَنَّهُ رَسُولٌ ـُ. To put one down as, نَزَّلَ مَنْزِلَةَ كَذَا. *See also under to* Consider, Regard, Esteem, *v.t.*

To take to one's self, اِتَّخَذَ لِنَفْسِهِ ـ اِتَّخَذَ.

To take to pieces, حَلَّ ـُ (or) فَكَّ ـُ تَرْكِيبَ ٱلشَّىْءِ. To unsew, فَتَقَ ـُ.

To take up, as from the ground, شَالَ ـِ (or) أَشَالَ مِنَ ٱلْأَرْضِ. To take or lift up, in a general sense, شَالَ بِ ـِ ـ أَشَالَ. To take up, as to a higher place, صَعَّدَ. To take up, as part of a dress, شَمَّرَ ـ تَشَمَّرَ; to take up, as the part of a dress, from off any of the members of the body, شَمَّرَ عَنْ ـ تَشَمَّرَ عَنْ. To take up, to reprimand, زَجَرَ ـُ ـ شَتَمَ ـِ ـ وَبَّخَ. To take up, to seize, apprehend, قَبَض عَلَى – ءِ مَسَكَ – ءِ أَمْسَكَ. To take up, to give the lie to, كَذَّبَ. To take up, to sew, as the parts of a wound, خَيَّطَ. To take up arms, تَسَلَّحَ; to commence or to prepare one's self for war, إِسْتَعَدَّ لِلْحَرْبِ. To take up, to occupy, as of time, إِسْتَوْعَبَ – إِسْتَغْرَقَ: It will not take up more than fifteen days, لا يَسْتَغْرِقُ أَكْثَرَ مِنْ خَمْسَةَ عَشَرَ يَوْمًا. To take up, as of an appointment, تَوَلَّى: In order to take up, or over, the embassy there, لِيَتَوَلَّى ٱلسِّفَارَةَ هُنَاكَ. To take up a trade, ...إِتَّخَذَ صَنْعَةً (or) تَعَاطَى – صَارَ ءِ: He took up the profession of a medical man, صَارَ طَبِيبًا ءِ. To take up, as of space; (*see to* Occupy, *v.t.*) To take up, so as to take care of, provide for, ضَمَّ ². To take up, to raise, as a wailing noise, بَادَرَ بِ – رَفَعَ – شَرَعَ فِي مَرْثَاةٍ ءِ: He took up a lamentation, رَفَعَ مَرْثَاةً ءِ. To take up, to espouse one's cause; (*see under* To take part with.)

To take up the gauntlet; *see under* Gauntlet, *n.*

To take upon one's self, to venture, تَجَاسَرَ – تَجَرَّأَ. To undertake the responsibility of, تَكَلَّفَ بِ – تَكَفَّلَ بِ – تَحَمَّلَ.

To take with one, إِسْتَصْحَبَ: They took people with them from the island, إِسْتَصْحَبُوا أُنَاسًا مِنَ ٱلْجَزِيرَةِ. To be taken with; *see under* To take to, *supra.*

Take, *v.i.* To take effect, تَأَثَّرَ – أَثَّرَ فِي – نَفَذَ ². To be well received, رُحِّبَ بِ – قُبِلَ – كَانَ مَقْبُولًا عِنْدَ كَذَا.

To take off, to cease, إِنْقَطَعَ – تَمَّ ءِ – إِنْتَهَى. To be capable of being lifted off, إِرْتَفَعَ.

To take on, to grieve, worry one's self, إِنْزَعَجَ – إِنْضَجَرَ – تَأَسَّفَ – قَلِقَ ءِ.

Take, *n.* As of game, قَنِيصَة – صَيْد – صَيْدَة. A quantity, مِقْدَار.

Taker, *n.* One who takes, آخِذ *pl.* أَخَذَة. A — of snuff, مُتَنَشِّق – شَامُّ ٱلنَّشُوقِ. One who captures, as a town, فَاتِح – فَتَّاح.

Take-in, *n.* مَكْر – غِشّ – خِيَانَة.

Taking, *n.* The act of, أَخْذ; of taking to one's self, إِتِّخَاذ; of handing to one's self, تَنَاوُل – مُنَاوَلَة; of capturing, as a town, تَسْخِير – ضَبْط – فَتْح. Distress of mind, كَدَر – غَمّ – ضَجَر – إِضْطِرَاب – قَلَق.

Taking, *a.* *See* Attractive, *a.*

Takingly, *ad.* *See* Attractively, *ad.*

Takingness, *n.* *See* Attractiveness, *n.*

Talbo-type, *n.* *See* Calotype, *n.*

Talc, *n.* كَوْكَبُ ٱلْأَرْضِ – طِلْق. Small panes of — used in the roof of baths, *etc.*, مَضَاوِئ.

Talcky,
Talcose, *a.*
Talcous, } مِثْلَ ٱلطِّلْقِ – مِنْ طِلْقٍ.

Tale, *n.* A narrative, قِصَّة *pl.* قِصَص – حَدِيث *pl.* أَحَادِيث – حِسَاب – عَدَد – مِقْدَار. A quantity, number, رِوَايَة *pl.* رِوَايَا. A slanderous —, or the — of a talebearer, نَقْل – وِشَايَة – نَمِيمَة. Idle tales, أَسَاطِير – هَذَيَان – خُرَافَات. False tales or rumours, أَرَاجِيف. Tales of the Ancients, أَسَاطِيرُ ٱلْأَوَّلِينَ. By —, number, quantity, عَدَدًا – بِٱلْمِقْدَارِ – بِٱلْحِسَابِ. To tell a —, قَصَّ قِصَّةً ²: He told him a —, قَصَّ عَلَيْهِ قِصَّةً ². To tell tales, of a talebearer, وَشَى وِشَايَةً *aor.* يَشِي – نَقَلَ ². To tell tales of one to . . . , نَقَلَ إِلَى-عَنْ فُلَانٍ. He who tells you tales about others will tell tales of you also, (*prov.*) مَنْ نَقَلَ إِلَيْكَ فَقَدْ نَقَلَ عَنْكَ.

Talebearer, *n.*
Talebearing, *a.* } نَمَّام – نَقَّال – قَصَّاص – وَاشٍ – سَاعٍ بِٱلْوِشَايَةِ.

Talebearing, *n.* وِشَايَة – نَقْل – نَمِيمَة.

Tale-teller, *n.* *See* Narrator, *n.*

Talent, *n.* The weight, وَزْنَة *pl.* وَزْنَات. A natural gift, هِبَة إِلٰهِيَّة – مَوْهِبَة رَبَّانِيَّة *pl.* مَوَاهِب. Aptitude, قَرِيحَة. Intellectual power, إِدْرَاك – دِرَايَة – كِفَايَة – مَعْرِفَة *pl.* مَعَارِف.

Talents, accomplishments, فَضَائِل – شَمَائِل.

Talented, *a.* Learned, عَالِم – عَلِيم *pl.* عُلَمَاء – لَوْذَعِيّ.

Tales, *n.pl.* Those from whom jurymen may be selected, قَوْمٌ مِنَ ٱلْحَاضِرِينَ فِي مَحْكَمَةٍ يُنْتَخَبُ مِنْهُمْ وَكِيلٌ مُسْتَخْلَفٌ لِتَكْمِيلِ عَدَدِ ٱلْوُكَلَاءِ ٱلشَّرْعِيِّينَ فِي فَصْلِ ٱلدَّعَاوَى. *See also* Jury, *n.*

Talesman, *n.* وَاحِدٌ مِنَ ٱلْوُكَلَاءِ ٱلْمَذْكُورِينَ. *See* Jury, Juryman, *n.*

Talion, *n.* ذَحْل – ثُؤْرَة – ثَأْر. The law of —, أُصُولُ أَخْذِ ٱلثَّأْرِ. *See also* Revenge, *n.*

Talisman, *n.* طِلَسْم *pl.* طَلَاسِمُ *and* طِلَسْمَات.

Talismanic, *a.* طِلَسْمِيّ. *See also* Magical, *a.*

Talk, *n.* Speech, حَدِيث – قَوْل – كَلَام. Conversation, مُخَاطَبَة – مُحَاوَرَة – مُحَادَثَة – مُكَالَمَة – مُلَاقَشَة. A speech, خِطَاب – مَقَالَة. Vain, nonsensical —, لَغْو. He became the common —, تَسَامَعَ بِهِ ٱلنَّاسُ. There is much — now about that, تَكَاثَرَ ٱلْكَلَامُ عَلَى ذٰلِكَ ٱلْآنَ. A man full of —, رَجُلٌ مِهْذَارٌ. Unprofitable —, كَلَامٌ لَا يُفِيدُ.

Talk, *v.i.* To speak, حَكَى ءِ – تَكَلَّمَ. He left off talking to him, فَرَغَ مِنَ ٱلْكَلَامِ مَعَهُ ². *See also to* Speak, *v.t.* and *i.*

To talk about, تَحَدَّثَ بِ – تَحَدَّثَ عَنْ – تَكَلَّمَ عَنْ.

To talk against, تَكَلَّمَ عَلَى.

To talk to or with, خَاطَبَ ـ كَلَّمَ ـ حَاوَرَ ـ كَالَمَ ـ حَاكَى. As or while he talked to him, فِيمَا هُوَ يُكَلِّمُهُ.

To talk to about, كَلَّمَ ـ فِي ـ كَلَّمَ ـ بِ.

To talk to one's self, تَكَلَّمَ مَعَ نَفْسِهِ.

Talk, *v.t.* تَكَلَّمَ ـ تَفَوَّهَ بِ ـ نَطَقَ بِ ـ ². To — nonsense, لَغِيَ ـ ² كَثَّرَ كَلَامَهُ فِي ٱلْبَاطِلِ.

Talkative, *a.* مُسْهِب ـ ثَرْثَار ـ وَعْوَاع ـ نَقْنَاق ـ بَقْبَاق ـ كَلَّمَانِيّ ـ فَرْفَار ـ فَيِّه ـ مُفَوَّه ـ قَوَّال. *See also* Garrulous, *a.*

Talkativeness, *n.* ثَرْثَرَة ـ فَرْفَرَة ـ بَقّ ـ بَقْبَقَة ـ كَثْرَةُ كَلَامٍ.

Talker, *n.* A narrator, مُحَدِّث ـ رَاوٍ *pl.* رُوَاة. A vain, nonsensical —, أَلْغَى *fem.* لَغْوَاء. *See also* Talkative, *a.*

Tall, *a.* High, عَالٍ ـ مُرْتَفِع. Long, طَوِيل. Tall of stature, يَمْخُور ـ مُسْهَب ـ مُشْهَب ـ مَدِيد *pl.* مُدُد ـ طُوَال ـ طَوِيل ـ طَوِيل ـ ٱلْقَوَائِمِ طُوَّال ـ طَوِيلٌ مُسْهَبٌ. Very —, شَوْذَب ـ شَوْقَب ـ سَوْقَب. A very — man, شَوْذَب ـ شَوْقَب; an exceedingly — man, عَشَنَّط ـ عَشَنَّق. To make —, طَوَّلَ. To be taller than, طَالَ: al-'Abbâs was taller than 'Umr, طَالَ ٱلْعَبَّاسُ عُمَرَ ². He is taller than I, هُوَ أَطْوَلُ مِنِّي. They are all — of stature and of strong build, كُلُّهُمْ طِوَالُ ٱلْقَامَةِ وَأَقْوِيَاءُ ٱلْبِنْيَةِ. How — he is! مَا أَطْوَلَ شِبْرَهُ. To become —, of herbage, تَرَوَّحَ.

Tallness, *n.* Of stature, قَدّ ـ طُول ـ قِوَام ـ قَامَة ـ طُولُ ٱلْقَوَائِمِ.

Tallow, *n.* شَحْمٌ (or دُهْنٌ) لِعَمَلِ ٱلشُّمُوعِ.

Tallow, *v.t.* مَسَحَ ـ بِشَحْمٍ ـ ² دَهَنَ ـ ².

Tallow-chandler, *n.* شَمَّاع *pl.* شَمَّاعَة.

Tallow-faced, *a.* أَصْفَرُ ٱلْوَجْهِ *fem.* صَفْرَاءُ *pl.* صُفْر.

Tallowish, *a.* مِنْ جِنْسِ ٱلشَّحْمِ.

Tallowy, *a.* دَهِن ـ شَحِيم.

Tally, *n.* The notched stick for tallying, جَرِيدَة ـ جَفْلَة ـ دَفْتَرُ ٱلْأَرْنَاؤُطِ. One thing to suit another, مَثَل ـ مِثَال ـ نَظِير ـ أَخ ـ أَخُو.

Tally, *v.t.* To score on a tally, حَزَّ ـ فِي ٱلْجَرِيدَةِ ² ـ عَلَّمَ ـ عَلَى ٱلْجَرِيدَةِ. To fit, طَابَقَ ـ وَفَّقَ ـ لِ.

Tally, *v.i.* تَطَابَقَ. To — with, طَابَقَ ـ وَافَقَ. The two things —, تَطَابَقَ ٱلشَّيْآنِ.

Tally-ho! *int.* نِدَاءُ (or زَغْرَطَةُ) ٱلْقَنَّاصِينَ.

Tallyman, *n.* مَاسِكُ ٱلْجَرِيدَةِ ـ حَامِلُ ٱلْجَفْلَةِ.

Talmud, *n.* ٱلتَّلْمُودُ وَهُوَ مَجْمُوعُ شَرَائِعِ ٱلْيَهُودِ وَتَفَاسِيرِهَا.

Talmudic,
Talmudical, *a.* } تَلْمُودِيّ.
Talmudistic,

Talmudist, *n.* عَالِمٌ بِٱلتَّلْمُودِ.

Talon, *n.* مِخْلَب *pl.* مَخَالِبُ ـ خِلْب *pl.* أَخْلَاب ـ كُلَّاب *pl.* كَلَالِيبُ ـ ظُفْر *pl.* أَظْفَار. The two anterior talons of a bird, ٱلْمُطْعِمَتَانِ. Talons, خَطَاطِيفُ. To strike with the talons, إِسْتَخْلَبَ ـ خَلَبَ ² ـ. The hawk seized the bird with its talons, إِظَّفَرَ ٱلصَّقْرُ ٱلطَّائِرَ.

Talus, *n.* Of the foot, the ankle, عَقِب *pl.* أَعْقَاب ـ عُرْقُوب *pl.* عَرَاقِيبُ. A slope, حُدُور ـ مَيْل ـ صَبَب ـ هُبُوط. Detritus, تَرَاكُمُ ٱلْأَحْجَارِ ـ جُفَاءٌ.

Tamable, *a.* يَأْنَس ـ يَسْتَأْنِسُ ـ يُطَبَّعُ.

Tamableness, *n.* إِمْكَانُ ٱلتَّأْنِيسِ.

Tamarind, *n.* The tree, حَوْمَر ـ حُمَر ـ تَمْرٌ هِنْدِيّ; the fruit, صُبَار ـ صُبَّار.

Tamarisk, *n.* كِزْمَازَك ـ أَثْل ـ طَرْفَاء; one —, طَرْفَاة.

Tambour, *n.* A small drum, نَقَّارَة *pl.* نَقَاقِيرُ ـ طُبَيْل *pl.* أَطْبَال. A — for working embroidery, طَار. Tambour-work, شُغْلُ ٱلطَّارِ.

Tambourine, *n.* غِرْبَال *pl.* غَرَابِيلُ ـ دَفّ *pl.* دُفُوف. A player on the —, دَفَّاف *pl.* دَفَّافَة. To play on the —, دَقَّ (or ² ضَرَبَ) ٱلدَّفَّ.

Tame, *a.* Tamed, مُطَبَّع ـ مُؤْنَس. Domestic, gentle, دَاجِن ـ مُنْقَاد ـ ذَلُول ـ وَدِيع ـ أَنِيس ـ مُسْتَأْنِس. A — or gentle beast, دَابَّةٌ سَمِحَةٌ. Tame or domestic animals, نَحْمَة. Dull, not exhilarating, مُضْعِب ـ مُمِلّ ـ بَارِد ـ تَافِه ـ مُزَعِّل. Poor-spirited, جَوِيّ. Heavy, stupid, فَدْم ـ فُطَارِيّ ـ ثَقِيل. To be —, not wild, submissive, سَمَحَ ـ ² أَسْمَحَ *See also* Servile, *a.*

Tame, *v.t.* ذَلَّلَ ـ قَصَعَ ـ ² قَمَعَ ـ أَقْمَعَ ـ أَنَّسَ ـ طَبَّعَ. To be tamed, إِنْقَمَعَ ـ تَأَنَّسَ ـ إِسْتَأْنَسَ ـ تَطَبَّعَ. No one could — him, لَمْ يَقْدِرْ أَحَدٌ أَنْ يُذَلِّلَهُ.

Tamely, *ad.* Submissively, بِإِطَاعَةٍ ـ إِذْعَانًا ـ بِٱنْقِيَادٍ. With servility, تَضَعْضُعًا ـ تَذَلُّلًا ـ بِمُطَاوَعَةٍ ـ بِحَقَارَةٍ.

Tameness, *n.* The quality of being tame, أُنْس ـ سَمَاحَة. Gentleness, دَمَاثَة ـ حِلْم ـ وَدَاعَة ـ بَشَاشَة. Dullness, heaviness, مَلّ ـ ثِقَل ـ تَذَلُّل ـ دَنَاءَة. Servility, تَضَعْضُع ـ مُطَاوَعَة ـ تَذَلُّل ـ دَنَاءَة.

Tamer, *n.* مُطَبِّع ـ قَاهِر. A breaker-in, as of horses, خَازِنِيّ ـ رَائِض ـ مُدَرِّس.

Tamis, *n.* For straining, مِصْفَاةٌ مِنْ صُوفٍ ـ مُنْخُل *pl.* مَنَاخِلُ.

Tammy, *n.* The stuff, ٱلرَّفِيعُ مِنْ قُمَاشِ ٱلصُّوفِ.

Tamp, *v.t.* For blasting, عَمَّرَ ٱللُّغْمَ ـ دَقَّ ٱللُّغْمَ ².

Tamper, *v.t.* To meddle with, تَدَاخَلَ فِي ـ تَفَوْضَلَ فِي ـ قَارَشَ. To deal with secretly, أَنْدَسَّ بِ. To bribe, بَرْطَلَ. To trifle with, عَبِثَ بِ ـ ² تَلَاعَبَ بِ.

Tamping, *n.* The act of, دَقّ لُغْم ـ تَعْمِيرُ لُغْم; the charge of a bore for blasting, عُمَارُ لُغْم.

Tampion, *n.* } سِدَادَة ـ سِدَادَةُ فَمِ ٱلْمِدْفَع.
Tompion,

Tam-tam, *n.* طَبْلٌ هِنْدِيٌّ.

Tan, *v.t.* Of leather, دَبَغَ [2]. To bronze, of the skin by the sun, صَقَرَ ـ سَقَرَ [2]: The sun tanned him, صَقَرَتْهُ ٱلشَّمْسُ. He was tanned by the sun, كَانَ مَصْقُورًا مِنَ ٱلشَّمْسِ. To be tanned, of leather, إِنْدَبَغَ. Tanned leather, أَدِيم. Tanned hides, قَرَظ ـ سِبْت.

Tan, *v.i.* To be tanned, of leather, إِنْدَبَغَ. To be tanned, as by the sun, صُقِرَ مِنَ ٱلشَّمْسِ.

Tan, *n.* The substance for tanning, دِبَاغ ـ دِبْغَة ـ دِبَاغَة. Colour from being sunburnt, صُقْرَةٌ مِنَ ٱلشَّمْسِ.

Tandem, *n.* A light vehicle, عَرَبَانَةٌ خَفِيفَةٌ. To drive —, سَاقَ ٱلْعَرَبَانَةَ بِحِصَانَيْنِ أَحَدُهُمَا خَلْفَ ٱلْآخَرِ [2].

Tang, *n.* Of a blade, that part which enters the handle, سِنْخ *pl.* سُنُوخ.

Tangency, *n.* مُمَاسَّة ـ مُلَامَسَة ـ لَمْس.

Tangent, *n.* خَطُّ ٱلْمُمَاسَّةِ ـ مُمَاسَّة. To fly off at a —, to deviate from, إِلْتَفَتَ عَن ـ كَفَّا عَن [2]. The act of flying off at a —, إِلْتِفَاتٌ عَن.

Tangibility, *n.* *See* Tactility, *n.*

Tangible, *a.* مَلْمُوس ـ مَمْسُوس. Substantial, مُشْبِع. Tangible benefits, مَصَالِحُ جِسْمِيَّةٌ (*or* حَقِيقِيَّةٌ).

Tangibleness, *n.* *See* Tactility, *n.*

Tangibly, *ad.* Of the touch, بِٱلْمُلَامَسَةِ ـ بِٱللَّمْسِ. Substantially, جِسْمًا.

Tangle, *v.t.* Of thread, *etc.*, عَقَّدَ ـ شَبَّكَ; of trees, *etc.*, أَشَّبَ. To be entangled, of thread, *etc.*, تَعَقَّدَ ـ تَشَبَّكَ ـ إِشْتَبَكَ; of trees, herbage, تَأَشَّبَ. *See also to* Entangle, Embroil, *v.t.*

Tangle, *v.i.* تَعَقَّدَ ـ تَشَبَّكَ.

Tangle, *n.* Of thread, تَشَبُّك ـ تَعَقُّد. A place of tangled trees, ظَلِيلَة.

Tangled, *a.* In knots, مُتَعَقِّد ـ مُعَقَّد; of trees or herbage, جَثِيل ـ جَثْل ـ أَثِيث ـ غَبْيَاء *pl.* أَغْبَى ـ أَشِب ـ مُعْطَئِلّ ـ لِفّ. Tangled herbage, ثِنَان ـ نَبَاتٌ أَثِيثٌ ـ أَشَب.

Tank, *n.* بِرْكَة *pl.* بِرَك ـ صِهْرِيج *pl.* صَهَارِيج ـ مَصْنَعَة *pl.* مَصَانِع ـ حَوْض *pl.* حِيَاض. A ship's —, as also a tin for serving out water therefrom, فِنْطَاس.

Tankard, *n.* *See* Flagon, *n.*

Tanner, *n.* دَبَّاغ *pl.* دَبَّاغَة.

Tannery, *n.* The place of tanning, مَدْبَغَة; the trade of, دِبَاغَة.

Tannic acid, *n.* حَامِضُ ٱلْبَلُّوطِ.

Tansy, *n.* حَشِيشَةُ ٱلدُّودِ.

Tantalism, *n.* } The act of mocking, سُخْرِيَّة; of disappointing,
Tantalization, } تَخْيِيب; of tormenting, perplexing, تَحْيِير ـ إِضْجَار ـ أَذِيَّة ـ تَعْذِيب.

Tantalize, *v.t.* To laugh at, to mock, ضَحِكَ مِن [x]. To disappoint, خَيَّبَ ـ أَخَابَ ـ خَيَّبَ. To perplex, حَيَّرَ. To torment, عَذَّبَ ـ أَضْجَرَ ـ آذَى. To be tantalized, tormented, عُذِّبَ ـ إِنْضَجَرَ.

Tantalizing, *a.* Perplexing, disappointing, مُخَيِّب ـ مُحَيِّر.

Tantamount, *a.* مُعَادِل ـ مُسَاوٍ. *See also* Equivalent, *a.*

Tantivy, *n.* The note of the hunting horn, صَوْتُ بُوقِ ٱلْقَنَّاصِينَ. To ride, —, رَمَحَ ـ أَسْرَعَ فِي ٱلرُّكُوبِ [x].

Tantrums, *n.* شَرَاسَة ـ شَكَاسَة. To be in the —, شَكِسَ ـ شَرِسَ ـ وَعُقَ *aor.* يَعْقُ.

Tanvat, *n.* حَوْضُ ٱلْمَدْبَغَةِ.

Tanyard, *n.* مَدْبَغَة.

Tap, *v.t.* To pat, طَبْطَبَ لِ ـ خَفَقَ [2]. To —, as a barrel, نَفَذَ ـ فَتَحَ ـ بَزَلَ ـ بَزَّلَ [2]. To —, as of a tree, إِسْتَطْعَمَ ـ فَتَحَ بَطْنَ ٱلْمُسْتَسْقِي ـ شَقَّ [2]. To —, as for dropsy, فَتَحَ. *See also to* Broach, *v.t.*

Tap, *n.* A gentle touch, طَبْطَبَة. The place where a barrel is tapped, بُزَال. The place in a trough or tank from which the water flows, صُنْبُور. We have beer on —, عِنْدَنَا بَرْمِيلُ بِيرَةٍ مَفْتُوح.

Tap-room, *n.* مَشْرَبٌ (*or* مَحَلُّ ٱلشُّرْبِ) فِي خَمَّارَةٍ.

Tap-root, *n.* العِرْقُ ٱلْأَعْظَمُ مِنَ ٱلْعُرُوقِ ٱلنَّافِذَةِ فِي ٱلْأَرْضِ.

Tape, *n.* شَرِيط *pl.* شَرَائِطُ *and* أَشْرِطَة. Red, official tape, شَرِيطُ ٱلْأَقْلَامِ. Red tape, officialism, عَصَبِيَّةُ ٱلْأَقْلَامِ ـ قِرْمِزِيٌّ رَسْمِيٌّ ـ تَكَبُّرُ ٱلْمَأْمُورِينَ.

Taper, *n.* شَمْعَةٌ رَفِيعَةٌ ـ شَمْعَة *coll.* شَمْع *pl.* شُمُوع.

Taper, *a.* } مُطَرَّف ـ مُتَطَرِّف. A small hand with — fingers,
Tapering, } كَفٌّ أَسِيلَةُ ٱلْأَصَابِعِ. *See also under* Slender, *a.*

Taper, *v.t.* طَرَّفَ.

Taper, *v.i.* تَطَرَّفَ.

Taperness, *n.* تَطْرِيف ـ تَطَرُّف.

Tapestry, *n.* طِرَاز. Made of —, مُطَرَّز.

Tapestry, *v.t.* To embroider, طَرَّزَ. To adorn with —, وَشَّحَ-بِطِرَازٍ.

Tapeworm, *n.* الدُّودَةُ ٱلْمُتَوَحِّدَةُ.

Tap-house, *n.* خَمَّارَةٌ *pl.* خَمَامِيرُ.

Tapioca, *n.* تَابِيُوقَا.

Tapis, *n.* (*See* Tapestry, *n.*) On the —, under discussion, تَحْتَ مَبْحُوثٌ عَنْهُ — ٱلْمُذَاكَرَةِ.

Tapster, *n.* سَاقِي ٱلْمَشْرُوبَاتِ فِي حَانُوتٍ.

Tar, *n.* قَطْرَانٌ — قِطْرَانٌ — قِيرٌ — طِلَاءٌ — دِقْلٌ. *See also* Sailor, *n.*

Tar, *v.t.* قَيَّرَ — قَطَرَ[2] — قَطْرَنَ — دَهَنَ-بِقِطْرَانٍ[2]. To —, as of a camel, قَطَرَ[2] — دَجَّلَ[2] — دَجَلَ. To tar and feather, دَهَنَهُ[2] بِٱلْقِطْرَانِ وَلَصَّقَ فِيهِ ٱلرِّيشَ تَجْرِيسًا لَهُ.

Tarantula, *n.* رُتَيْلَى.

Tardily, *ad.* Dilatorily, بِتَوَقُّفٍ — بِبَطْءٍ — بِبَطَآءَةٍ; slowly, leisurely, عَلَى مَهْلٍ — رُوَيْدًا. *See also* Slowly, *ad.*

Tardiness, *n.* Dilatoriness, تَوَقُّفٌ — غَشْمٌ — مُرَاخَاةٌ — بَطَآءَةٌ; slowness, مَهْلٌ — رُوَيْدٌ. *See also* Slowness, *n.*

Tardy, *a.* Dilatory, وَقَّافٌ — قَعِيدٌ — مَكِيثٌ — مُتَرَاخٍ — بَطِيءٌ. Slow, of pace, قُوَامٌ — حَاتِكٌ. To be —, dilatory, بَطُؤَ[2] — تَوَقَّفَ; to be behindhand, تَأَخَّرَ. To be — in doing, غَشَمَ أَنْ. *See also* Late, Slow, *a.*

Tare, *n.* The weed, زُوَانٌ — وَغْلٌ. The vetch, جُلُبَّانٌ — جُلْبَانٌ. A lentil, عَدَسَةٌ *coll.* عَدَسٌ.

Tare, *n.* Allowance in weight for barrels, *etc.*, إِسْقَاطُ ثِقْلِ ٱلْأَوَانِي كَمِّيَّةُ أَوْزَانِ ٱلْأَوْعِيَةِ.

Tare, *v.t.* أَسْقَطَ ثِقْلَ ٱلْأَوَانِي.

Tarentula, *n.* *See* Tarantula, *n.*

Target, *n.* A shield, تُرْسٌ *pl.* تِرَسَةٌ *and* تِرَاسٌ. A mark to aim at, نِيشَانٌ — عَلَامَةٌ — هَدَفٌ — قِرْطَاسٌ.

Targeteer, *n.* تَرَّاسٌ — حَامِلُ تُرْسٍ.

Tariff, *n.* بَيَانُ ٱلْأَسْعَارِ — تَعْرِيفٌ — تَعْرِفَةٌ.

Tariff, *v.t.* سَعَّرَ.

Tarn, *n.* A small lake, بُحَيْرَةٌ *pl.* بُحَيْرَاتٌ — بِرْكَةٌ *pl.* بِرَكٌ.

Tarnish, *v.t.* Of colour, *etc.*, أَكْبَى — كَدَّرَ ٱللَّوْنَ — أَخْمَدَ — قَتَمَ. *See also to* Soil, Sully, *v.t.*

Tarnish, *v.i.* To become less bright, تَكَدَّرَ — أَظْلَمَ — خَمَدَ[2].

Tarnish, *n.* Dulness, dimness, تَكَدُّرٌ — كُدُورٌ.

Tarpaulin, *n.* مُشَمَّعٌ.

Tarragon, *n.* طَرْخُونٌ.

Tarry, *v.i.* To delay, لَبِثَ — تَلَبَّثَ — تَحَوَّسَ — تَحَوَّزَ — مَكَثَ[2] — بَطُؤَ[2] — أَبْطَأَ. To stay, sojourn, in a place, أَوَى إِلَى *aor.* يَأْوِي — تَأَوَّى إِلَى — حَلَّ بِ[2] — إِسْتَقَامَ فِي. To —, wait, for, إِنْتَظَرَ — إِسْتَنْظَرَ. To request to —, سَأَلَ-أَنْ يَمْكُثَ. If I — long, إِنْ كُنْتُ أَبْطِئُ. They asked him to — with them, سَأَلُوهُ أَنْ يَمْكُثَ عِنْدَهُمْ.

Tarry, *a.* Of tar, مِثْلَ ٱلْقِطْرَانِ — مِنْ قِطْرَانٍ. Tarred, مُقَطْرَنٌ.

Tart, *a.* Of taste, حَاذِقٌ — حِرِّيفٌ — حَاذٌّ; of temper, شَكِسٌ — شَرِيسٌ. Bitter, sarcastic, مُرٌّ — جَارِحٌ — مُؤْذٍ. To be — with, شَاكَسَ. *See also under* Sharp, *a.*

Tart, *n.* The pastry, نَالُونٌ مَحْشُوٌّ بِمُرَبًّى — سَنْبُوسَكٌ حُلْوٌ *pl.* فَوَالِيذُ — كَبِيسٌ.

Tartan, *n.* The stuff, قُمَاشٌ مِنْ صُوفٍ مُصَلَّبٌ. A small coasting vessel, سَنَابِيقُ *pl.* سُنْبُوقٌ — قَوَارِبُ *pl.* قَارِبٌ.

Tartar, *n.* As of wine, خُلَاصَةُ دُرْدِيِّ ٱلْخَمْرِ. The salt, مِلْحُ ٱلطَّرْطِيرِ. The — of the teeth, حِبْرُ ٱلْأَسْنَانِ — طَرَامَةُ ٱلْأَسْنَانِ. An inhabitant of Tartary, تَتَرِيٌّ *coll.* تَتَرٌ. To catch a —, to be mortified by, حُقِرَ مِنْ — أُقْهِرَ مِنْ. To meet one's match, لَقِيَ[2] لَقِيَ مَنْ حَاذَاهُ — مَنْ قَعَدَ بِهِ[2].

Cream of tartar, سُفَّةُ ٱلطَّرْطِيرِ.

Tartar emetic, طَرْطِيرٌ مُقَيِّئٌ.

Tartarean, *a.* / Tartareous, } جَهَنَّمِيٌّ — سَقَرِيٌّ.

Tartareous, *a.* / Tartarous, } *See* Tarry, *a.*

Tartaric, *a.* طَرْطِيرِيٌّ. Tartaric acid, حَامِضٌ طَرْطِيرِيٌّ.

Tartarization, *n.* إِحْدَاثُ ٱلطَّرْطِيرِ.

Tartarize, *v.t.* To impregnate with tartar, شَرَّبَ-طَرْطِيرًا.

Tartarus, *n.* جَهَنَّمُ — سَقَرُ.

Tartish, *a.* Somewhat acid, حَاذٌّ نَوْعًا — حِرِّيفٌ نَوْعًا.

Tartly, *ad.* Of taste, بِحَرَافَةٍ — بِحُمُوضَةٍ. Testily, بِشَرَاسَةٍ — بِشَكَاسَةٍ. Sharply, بِحِدَّةٍ. *See also* Sharply, *ad.*

Tartness, *n.* Of taste, حِدَّةٌ — حَرَافَةٌ — حَمَازَةٌ — حُمُوضَةٌ. Testiness, شَكَاسَةٌ — شَرَاسَةٌ. Sharpness, حِدَّةٌ. *See also* Sharpness, *n.*

Tartrate, *n.* مِلْحٌ مُرَكَّبٌ مِنْ حَامِضِ ٱلطَّرْطِيرِ وَأُسٍّ آخَرَ.

Tartness, *n.* Of taste, حِدَّةٌ — حَرَافَةٌ — حَمَازَةٌ — حُمُوضَةٌ; of manner, شَرَاسَةٌ — شَكَاسَةٌ; of language, مَرَارَةٌ — أَذِيَّةٌ — سَلَاطَةٌ.

Task, *n.* Employment, business, مَصْلَحَةٌ — عَمَلٌ *pl.* مَصَالِحُ — مَشْغَلَةٌ *pl.* مَشَاغِلُ — خِدْمَةٌ — عَمَلٌ *pl.* أَعْمَالٌ. A set —, رَاتِبَةٌ *pl.* رَوَاتِبُ. A daily —, عَمَلٌ يَوْمِيٌّ. A boy's —, lesson, for the day, سَبَقٌ *pl.* أَسْبَاقٌ — إِمَامٌ. Something given one to learn, وِشَالَةٌ. To set one a —, lesson, عَيَّنَ لِ-دَرْسًا. To set one a piece of set work, رَتَّبَ ل-رَاتِبَةً. To take to —, شَمَّ – وَبَّخَ.

See also Burden, Drudgery, *n.*

Task, *v.t.* To set a task to, of a lesson, عَيَّنَ ل-دَرْسًا ; of any set work, رَتَّبَ ل-رَاتِبَةً. To burden, كَلَّفَ – ثَقَّلَ عَلَى. To — one's self, to strain every nerve, بَذَلَ جُهْدَهُ – تَصَلَّبَ – أَفْرَغَ طَاقَتَهُ.

Tasker, *n.* } A superintendent, نَاظِر *pl.* نُظَّار. مُعَيِّنُ ٱلرَّوَاتِبِ.
Taskmaster, } An oppressor, مُسَخِّر.

Task-work, *n.* مُوَايَمَة – مُقَاوَلَة.

Tassel, *n.* شُرَّابَة *pl.* شَرَارِيب ; a — of different colours, دَبْذَبَة – عُثْكُولَة *pl.* جُزَيزَة *pl.* جَزَائِز. A — of a litter, عِهْنَة – ذَبَائِب.

Tasseled, *a.* مُزَيَّن بِشَرَارِيب.

Tastable, *a.* That may be tasted, يُتَذَوَّق – يُذَاق.

Taste, *v.t.* As with the tongue; also to experience, تَذَاوَقَ – تَذَوَّقَ – ذَاقَ *aor.* يَذُوقُ – طَعِمَ – إِسْتَطْعَمَ – تَطَعَّمَ. To — repeatedly, تَذَوَّقَ. To experience, to try, جَرَّبَ. To relish, إِسْتَلَذَّ. Taste thou and appetite will come, (prov.) تَطَعَّمْ تَطْعَمْ. I tasted nothing, مَا ذُقْتُ ذَوَاقًا. To give one to —, ذَوَّقَ – لَمَّجَ. To make to —, experience, أَذَاقَ. "In like manner did they who went before you accuse [the prophets] of falsehood until they tasted our severity," كَذَٰلِكَ كَذَّبَ ٱلَّذِينَ مِنْ قَبْلِهِمْ حَتَّى ذَاقُوا بَأْسَنَا (Kur. vi. 149).

Taste, *v.i.* To taste of, have the flavour of..., كَانَ طَعْمُهُ كَطَعْمِ ٱلْ.... To enjoy sparingly, إِقْتَصَدَ فِي. To experience, ذَاقَ – جَرَّبَ. A place or time for tasting, مَذَاق.

Taste, *n.* The sense of, ٱلْقُوَّةُ ٱلذَّائِقَةُ – ٱلذَّوْقُ. The act of tasting, مَذَاقَة – مَذَاق – ذَوَاق – ذَوْق – تَطَعُّم – طَعْم. Relish, savour, لَذَّة – طَعْم. Intellectual perception, ٱلذَّوْقُ – ذَوْق. Inclination, مَيْل – هَوًى. A thing that is tasted, ذَوَاق. A little of what is tasted, لَوَاس. A little, قَلِيل – نُطْفَة. An idea or soupçon of anything, ذَرْو – ذَوْق – عِرْق. Taste, in the sense of fashion, طَرْز – زِيّ – سِيرَ : In the European —, عَلَى سِيرِ أُورُبَّا – عَلَى زِيِّ ٱلْفِرَنْج. Its — is bitter, طَعْمُهُ مُرٌّ. It has no —, لَيْسَ لَهُ طَعْم. Its — has altered, تَغَيَّرَ طَعْمُهُ. A man of —, رَجُل ذُو طَعْم – رَجُل حَسَنُ ٱلذَّوْقِ. Such an one has neither — nor vigour, لَا بِفُلَانٍ طَعْمٌ وَلَا نَوِيش. He has a good — for poetry, هُوَ يَأْبَاهُ – حَسَنُ ٱلذَّوْقِ لِلشِّعْرِ. Good —, ذَوْق سَلِيم : good — forbids it, ٱلذَّوْقُ ٱلسَّلِيمُ. Tastes differ, ذَوْقُ ٱلنَّاسِ مُخْتَلِف. Every one to his —, كُلٌّ وَاحِدٍ حَسَبَ ذَوْقِهِ. There is no disputing —, لَا مُنَازَعَةَ فِي مَادَّةِ ذَوْقِ ٱلنَّاسِ. To do a thing from —, أَتَى بِ – فَعَلَ عَنِ ٱخْتِيَارِهِ – عَنْ ذَوْق. To be in good taste, كَانَ ظَرِيفًا – حَلِيَ فِي ٱلطَّرْزِ. To be in bad taste, كَانَ خَشِنًا – خَشُنَ فِي ٱلطَّرْزِ. To gratify one's taste, قَضَى هَوَاهُ – قَضَى وَطَرَهُ. To have a taste, inclination, for, وَدَّ – تَشَوَّقَ إِلَى.

Taster, *n.* One who tastes, ذَائِق ; one who gives others to taste, مُذَوِّق.

Tasteful, *a.* Savoury, ذُو طَعْم – لَذِيذ. In good taste, neat, حَسَن – ظَرِيف – حُلْو – كَيِّس.

Tastefully, *ad.* In good taste, بِظَرَافَةٍ – بِكِيَاسَةٍ.

Tastefulness, *n.* Relish, طَعْم – لَذَّة. Good taste, ذَوْق – جَمَال – لَطَافَة – ظَرَافَة – طَلَاوَة – كِيَاسَة.

Tasteless, *a.* Insipid, غَيْرُ ذِي نَفَس – مَلِيخ – مَسِيخ – تَافِه – عَدِيمُ ٱلطَّرَافَةِ – بِلَا ذَوْق. Without good taste, مَا لَهُ طَعْم – بِلَا لَذَّة. *See also* Insipid, *a.*

Tastelessness, *n.* Insipidity, عَدَمُ لَذَّةٍ – قِلَّةُ طَعْم – مَلَخ – تَفَاهَة ; absence of good taste, عَدَمُ كِيَاسَةٍ – عَدَمُ ظَرَافَةٍ (or طَلَاوَةٍ).

Tastily, *ad.* Neatly, حَسَنًا – بِلَطَافَةٍ – بِظَرَافَةٍ – بِكِيَاسَةٍ – بِطَلَاوَةٍ.

Tasty, *a.* *See* Tasteful, *a.*

Tatter, *v.t.* مَزَّقَ – خَرَّقَ.

Tatter, *n.* A rag, رِثَّة *pl.* رِثَث – خِرْقَة *pl.* خِرَق – *vulg.* شَرْطُوطَة. In tatters, tattered, مُمَزَّق – مُتَفَزِّر – مُتَخَشِّف. Clad in tatters, To be tattered, إِنْفَزَرَ – تَفَزَّرَ. *See also* Rag, *n.*

Tatterdemalion, *n.* صُعْلُوك *pl.* صَعَالِيك – رَجُل رَثُّ ٱلْهَيْئَةِ.

Tattered, *a.* Torn in tatters, مُمَزَّق ; patched, مُرَقَّع.

Tattle, *v.i.* هَذَرَ – زَخْلَفَ فِي ٱلْكَلَامِ – أَكْثَرَ ٱلْقَوْلَ. *See also to* Chatter, Gabble, *v.i.*

Tattle, *n.* هَذَر – تَهْذَار. *See also* Chatter, Gabble, *n.*

Tattler, *n.* هَاذِر – هَذَّار – غَبِيُّ ٱلشَّفَتَيْنِ.

Tattlings, *n.* قِيلٌ وَقَالٌ.

Tattoo, *n.* A military —, دَقُّ ٱلطَّبْلِ (or ٱلْبُوقِ) عِنْدَ وَقْتِ ٱلنَّوْمِ تَنْبِيهًا بِرُجُوعِ ٱلْعَسْكَرِ إِلَى ٱلْقِشْلَا.

Tattoo, *v.t.* Of the puncturing, وَشَمَ *aor.* يَشِمُ – وَشَّمَ – نَسَغَ – دَقَّ – نَوَّرَ. To be tattooed, تَنَوَّرَ.

Tattoo, *n.* The figures tattooed, وَشْم *pl.* وِشَام.

Tattooing, *n.* The act of, تَوْشِيم – دَقّ – وَشْم. Tattooing matter, نَؤُورَة – نَؤُور. The instrument for —, مِخَطّ.

Taught, *a.* Stretched, مَشْدُود.

Taught, *pret. of to* Teach, *q.v.*

Taunt, *v.t.* As with words, طَعَنَ ب ². To deride, scorn, إِسْتَهْزَأَ ب ـ قَرَصَ ب ² ـ نَقَرَ ². *See also to* Revile, *v.t.*

Taunt, *n.* قَارِصَةٌ *pl.* قَوَارِصُ ـ نَقْر ـ هُزْؤٌ. Taunts, نَوَاقِرُ. The subject of a —, عَار ـ عَيْب. *See also* Sarcasm, *n.*

Taunter, *n.*
Taunting, *a.* } مُعَيِّر ـ عَضَّاب ـ شَتَّام ـ مُجَدِّف.

Tauntingly, *ad.* بِٱفْتِرَاءٍ ـ بِٱسْتِهْزَاءٍ ـ تَعْيِيرًا.

Tauriform, *n.* فِي هَيْئَةِ ٱلثَّوْرِ.

Taurine, *a.* ثَوْرِيٌّ.

Taurus, *n.* The sign of the Zodiac, الثَّوْر.

Taut, *a.* *See* Taught, *a.*

Tautological, *a.*
Tautologist, *n.* } مُكَرِّرُ ٱلْأَلْفَاظِ (or ٱلْمَعْنَى).

Tautologize, *v.i.* إِسْتَعْمَلَ تَكْرَارَ ٱلْأَلْفَاظِ (or ٱلْمَعْنَى).

Tautology, *n.* تَكْرِيرُ ٱلْأَلْفَاظِ (or ٱلْمَعْنَى).

Tavern, *n.* For drinking, حَانُوت *pl.* حَوَانِيتُ ـ خَمَّارَة *pl.* خَمَامِيرُ. *See also* Inn, *n.*

Taverner, *n.*
Tavern-keeper, } The keeper of a tavern, public house, صَاحِبُ خَمَّارَةٍ ـ حَانُوتْجِي. *See also* Innkeeper, *n.*

Taw, *n.* A — of marble, عَيْنَةٌ مِنْ طَابَاتِ ٱلرُّخَامِ لِلَّعِبِ.

Taw, *v.t.* Of skins, دَبَغَ ².

Tawdrily, *ad.* بِتَظَرُّفٍ خَالٍ ـ بِمُبَاهَاةٍ وَعَدَمِ ظَرَافَةٍ مَعًا مِنْ ذَوْقٍ.

Tawdriness, *n.* تَظَرُّفٌ بِلَا ذَوْقٍ.

Tawdry, *a* Showy without grace, جَلِيٌّ ـ زَاهٍ بِلَا ظَرَافَةٍ (or طَلَاوَةٍ) بِعَدَمِ كِيَاسَةٍ. Poor, inferior, دُون ـ رَقِيق ـ حَقِير.

Tawer, *n.* Of hides, دَبَّاغ.

Tawny, *a.* أَسْمَرُ *fem.* سَمْرَاءُ *pl.* سُمْر ـ أَسْمَرُ ٱللَّوْنِ ـ أَغْبَس. A — colour, سُمْرَة ـ أُدْمَة. To be —, أَدِمَ ².

Tax, *n.* In the general sense of an impost, ضَرِيبَة *pl.* ضَرَائِبُ ـ تَكْلِيف *pl.* تَكَالِيفُ ـ مَكْس *pl.* مُكُوس ـ رَسْم *pl.* رُسُوم ـ *vulg.* جَوَالَة. An assessed rate, وَظِيفَة *pl.* وَظَائِفُ. A land —, also a poll-tax, جِزْيَة *pl.* جِزًى ـ خَرَاج. Tax paid by free non-Muslim subjects to a Muslim government, خَرْج ـ *vulg.* خَرَاج. Government taxes, or taxation, in general, مُرَتَّبَاتٌ مِيرِيَّةٌ ـ تَكَالِيفُ وَرُسُومٌ مِيرِيَّةٌ. Tax, an imposition, burden, trouble, تَكْلِيف. Something forced on one, إِغْتِصَاب. (*See also* Burden, *n.*) Burdened with taxes, of a people, مُثْقَلُونَ بِٱلضَّرَائِبِ. It is the intention of the government to double the taxes on intoxicating drinks, فِي عَزْمِ ٱلدَّوْلَةِ أَنْ تُضَاعِفَ ٱلضَّرَائِبَ عَلَى ٱلْمُسْكِرَاتِ. The people of the country have not the ability to bear any further taxation, لَمْ تَبْقَ لِسُكَّانِ ٱلْبِلَادِ طَاقَةٌ عَلَى تَحَمُّلِ ضَرَائِبَ جَدِيدَةٍ. Free from all taxes, مُعَافًى (or مُعْفًى) مِنْ جَمِيعِ ٱلرُّسُومِ. Direct taxes, رُسُومٌ تُجْبَى مِنْ أَصْحَابِ ٱلْمَالِ رَأْسًا. Heavy taxes, تَكَالِيفُ شَاقَّةٌ. Indirect taxes, رُسُومٌ تُجْبَى مِنْ أَمْتِعَةِ ٱلتُّجَّارِ وَٱلْمُتَسَبِّبِينَ. Legal taxes, مُرَتَّبَاتٌ نِظَامِيَّةٌ ـ مُرَتَّبَاتٌ شَرْعِيَّةٌ. Property tax, أَمْلَاكِيَّة. Taxes taken in kind, رُسُومٌ تُؤْخَذُ عَيْنًا; as of wheat, ضَرَائِبُ تُجْبَى مِنْ عَيْنِ ٱلْحِنْطَةِ.

Tax, *v.t.* To impose taxes on, جَعَلَ ² ـ أَوْجَبَ ٱلضَّرَائِبَ عَلَى ـ كَلَّفَ بِٱلتَّكَالِيفِ ـ ضَرَبَ ³ عَلَى ٱلضَّرَائِبَ ـ ضَرَائِبَ عَلَى ـ أَلْقَى عَلَى ٱلضَّرَائِبَ. To — one with, to charge with, to accuse, أَتْهَمَ ب ـ إِتَّهَمَ ب. To impose on, as a burden, جَشَّمَ ب ـ كَلَّفَ ب ـ سَخَّرَ ب ـ حَمَّلَ عَلَى. To — a bill of law costs, صَفَّى (or صَحَّحَ) قَائِمَةَ نَفَقَةِ ٱلدَّعْوَى. To — one's self with, to impose upon one's self as a task, burden, كَلَّفَ ـ حَمَّلَ ب ـ تَكَلَّفَ ب ـ أَلْزَمَ نَفْسَهُ ب ـ نَفْسَهُ ب.

Taxable, *a.* Of taxes, مِمَّا يُلْقَى عَلَيْهِ ٱلضَّرَائِبُ ـ إِلْقَاءُ ٱلتَّكَالِيفِ عَلَيْهِ جَائِزٌ. That may be imputed or charged to, مِمَّا يُنْتَسَبُ إِلَى.

Taxation, *n.* The act of imposing taxes, إِلْقَاءُ ٱلضَّرَائِبِ ـ ضَرْبُ ٱلضَّرَائِبِ ـ وَضْعُ ٱلتَّكَالِيفِ. Taxation of costs by a court of justice, فَصْلُ مَصْرُوفِ ٱلدَّعْوَى عَلَى يَدِ رَئِيسِ ٱلْمَحْكَمَةِ. To place under —, أَوْجَبَ ٱلضَّرَائِبَ عَلَى. Increase of —, زِيَادَةُ ٱلضَّرَائِبِ. Taxation, taxes; *see under* Tax, *n.*

Taxer, *n.* وَاضِعُ ٱلرُّسُومِ ـ ضَارِبُ ٱلضَّرَائِبِ.

Tax-gatherer, *n.* مَاكِس ـ جَابِيٌّ *pl.* جُبَاة ـ عَامِل *pl.* عَوَامِلُ ـ جَامِعُ ٱلْخَرَاجِ.

Taxidermic, *a.* مُتَعَلِّقٌ بِحِفْظِ جُلُودِ ٱلْحَيَوَانَاتِ مِنَ ٱلتَّلَفِ ـ مَا نِيطَ بِتَصْبِيرِ جُلُودِ ٱلْحَيَوَانَاتِ.

Taxidermist, *n.* مَاهِرٌ فِي فَنِّ حِفْظِ جُلُودِ ٱلْحَيَوَانَاتِ مِنَ ٱلتَّلَفِ ـ مُصَبِّرُ جُلُودِ ٱلْحَيَوَانَاتِ.

Taxidermy, *n.* فَنُّ حِفْظِ جُلُودِ ٱلْحَيَوَانَاتِ مِنَ ٱلتَّلَفِ ـ تَصْبِيرُ جُلُودِ ٱلْحَيَوَانَاتِ.

Taxonomy, *n.* فَنُّ تَنْسِيقِ أَجْنَاسِ ٱلْحَيَوَانَاتِ.

Tea, *n.* The leaf, الشَّاي. The act of drinking tea, شُرْبُ ٱلشَّايِ. To drink — with, شَرِبَ ٱلشَّايَ مَعَ فُلَانٍ ². Tea, an infusion, مَاء ـ نُقُوع ـ غُسَالَة. Camomile —, مَاءُ ٱلْبَابُونَجِ.

Tea-board, *n.* A tray for tea-things, فَانُورٌ (or صِينِيَّةٌ) أَوَانِي ٱلشَّايِ.

Teach, *v.t.* عَلَّمَ ـ أَدْرَسَ ـ دَرَّسَ ـ لَقَّنَ. To — good manners, أَدَّبَ. I will —, tell, you what you are to do, أَنَا أُعَلِّمُكُمْ مَاذَا تَصْنَعُونَ. You have no need that any one should — you, لَا حَاجَةَ بِكُمْ إِلَى أَنْ يُعَلِّمَكُمْ أَحَدٌ. *See also to* Instruct, *v.t.*

Teachable, *a.* Capable of receiving instruction, قَابِلُ ٱلتَّعْلِيمِ. Docile, tractable, طَوْعُ ٱلْعِنَانِ ـ لَيِّنٌ ـ طَوْعٌ ـ ذَلُولٌ ـ جَنِيبٌ.

Teachableness, *n.* Capacity of receiving instruction, قَابِلِيَّةُ ٱلتَّعْلِيمِ وَٱلتَّعَلُّمِ. Docility, لِيَانٌ ـ ذُلُولٌ ـ لِينَةٌ.

Teacher, *n.* An Instructor, مُدَرِّسٌ ـ مُعَلِّمٌ ـ مُلَقِّنٌ. *See also* Lecturer, Preacher, *n.*

Teaching, *n.* The act of, تَدْرِيسٌ ـ تَعْلِيمٌ ـ تَلْقِينٌ. Precepts, تَعْلِيمٌ *pl.* تَعَالِيمُ. Acquired knowledge, إِفَادَةٌ ـ عِلْمٌ. *See also* Instruction, *n.*

Tea-cup, *n.* فِنْجَانٌ لِلشَّايِ *pl.* فَنَاجِينُ.

Tea-dealer, *n.* بَائِعُ ٱلشَّايِ *pl.* بَاعَةٌ.

Tea-drinker, *n.* شَارِبُ ٱلشَّايِ *pl.* شَارِبُونَ *or* شَرَبَةٌ.

Teak, *n.* The tree, سَاجٌ *pl.* سِيجَانٌ.

Teal, *n.* ضَرْبٌ مِنَ ٱلْبَطِّ صَغِيرٌ ـ صُنْصُنٌ.

Team, *n.* قِطَارٌ مِنَ ٱلدَّوَابِّ. A —, or yoke, of oxen, فَدَّانُ بَقَرٍ. To drive a—, سَاقَ قِطَارًا مِنَ ٱلدَّوَابِّ [2]; of a yoke of oxen, سَاقَ فَدَّانَ بَقَرٍ [2].

Teamster, *n.* سَائِقُ قِطَارٍ مِنَ ٱلدَّوَابِّ.

Tea-party, *n.* ضِيَافَةٌ لِشُرْبِ ٱلشَّايِ.

Teapot, *n.* إِبْرِيقُ ٱلشَّايِ.

Tea-service, *n.* طَاقَمٌ (or طَقْمٌ) لِلشَّايِ.

Tea-things, *n.* أَوَانِي لِلشَّايِ.

Tear, *n.* From the eye, دَمْعَةٌ *coll.* دَمْعٌ *pl.* أَدْمُعٌ *and* دُمُوعٌ. A suppressed —, or an overflow of grief, or a sobbing, عَبْرَةٌ *pl.* عَبَرَاتٌ. A flow of tears, تَدْمِيعٌ. A channel of tears, مَدْمَعٌ *pl.* مَدَامِعُ. Verily, my cure would be a — if I could shed it, إِنَّ شِفَائِي عَبْرَةٌ لَوْ سَفَحْتُهَا. To shed tears, سَفَحَ ٱلدُّمُوعَ ـ تَدَمَّعَ ـ بَكَى ـ أَجْرَى دُمُوعًا. Tear, a drop, نُقْطَةٌ *pl.* نُقَطٌ ـ قَطْرَةٌ *pl.* قَطَرَاتٌ.

Tear, *n.* A rent, fissure, شَقِيقَةٌ *pl.* شَقَائِقُ ـ شَقٌّ *pl.* شُقُوقٌ; as of a garment, تَشْرِيمٌ ـ شَرْمٌ ـ تَمْزِيقٌ ـ مِزْقَةٌ. Tears, rents, فِزَرٌ.

Tear, *v.t.* To rend, فَزَرَ [2] ـ فَسَأَ ـ قَدَّ [2] ـ خَرَقَ [2] ـ مَزَقَ ـ أَفْزَرَ. To — much, to — in pieces, شَرْمَطَ ـ شَقَّقَ [2] ـ شَرَطَ [2] ـ خَرَّقَ ـ مَزَّقَ ـ شَقَّقَ. To — with the nails, ظَفَّرَ. To unrip, فَتَقَ [2] ـ فَتَّقَ. To —, as a beast of prey, نَهَشَ ـ اِفْتَرَسَ.

To lacerate, wound, جَرَحَ [2] ـ جَرَّحَ ـ كَلَمَ. To be torn, rent, تَشَرَّمَ ـ اِنْشَرَمَ ـ اِنْشَقَّ ـ تَشَرْمَطَ; to be torn much, into pieces, تَمَزَّقَ ـ تَشَقَّقَ. To be torn, ripped, اِنْفَتَقَ ـ تَفَتَّقَ. To be torn, as by a beast of prey, اُفْتُرِسَ ـ نُهِشَ.

To tear asunder, to separate violently, of persons, اِضْطَرَّ إِلَى ٱلِٱنْفِصَالِ. To drag away from, جَذَبَ عَنْ ـ جَرَّ مِنْ [2].

To tear away, carry off, خَطِفَ ـ اِخْتَطَفَ.

To tear or pull down, هَدَّ [2] ـ هَدَمَ; to —, as from a wall, *etc*, قَلَعَ.

To tear off, as a piece from, قَطَعَ شِقَّةً مِنْ.

To tear one's self away, أُضْطُرَّ إِلَى ٱلِٱنْفِصَالِ.

To tear out, as a leaf out of a book, *etc.*, قَلَعَ. To tear out by the root, قَلَفَ ـ اِسْتَأْصَلَ.

To tear up, as papers, *etc.*, مَزَّقَ ـ مَزَّعَ.

Tear, *v.i.* To rave or rage, حَنِقَ ـ اِغْتَاظَ ـ جَاشَ غَيْظًا *aor.* يَجِيشُ ـ طَاشَ ـ جُنَّ. To — on, تَهَوَّرَ.

Tearful, *a.* عَابِرٌ ـ عَبْرَانُ *fem.* عَبْرَى *pl.* عَبَارَى ـ دَمَّاعٌ ـ دَمُوعٌ ـ دَامِعٌ *fem.* دَمِعَةٌ *pl.* دَمِيعٌ ـ بَاكٍ. A — eye, عَيْنٌ عَبْرَى.

Tearless, *a.* Without a tear, غَيْرُ عَابِرٍ ـ غَيْرُ دَامِعٍ. *See also* Unfeeling, *a.*

Tease, *v.t.* To card, نَدَفَ ـ فَدَكَ ـ مَشَّعَ. To torment, vex, نَكَّدَ عَلَى ـ أَضْجَرَ ـ أَكَدَّ ـ كَدَّ [2] ـ أَغْرَضَ ـ أَزْعَجَ ـ أَتْعَبَ ـ عَذَّبَ ـ عَنَّفَ. To — one's self, تَعَذَّبَ ـ تَعَنَّفَ. *See also to* Card, *v.t.*

Tease, *n.* / Teaser, } One who annoys, مُعَذِّبٌ ـ مُضْجِرٌ ـ مُزْعِجٌ. A carder, نَدَّافٌ ـ مُمَشِّقٌ.

Teasel, *n.* The plant, حَسَكَةٌ ـ عُقُولٌ ـ شَوْكَةٌ ـ شُوَيْكَةٌ.

Tea-spoon, *n.* مِلْعَقَةُ ٱلشَّايِ *pl.* مَعَالِقُ.

Teat, *n.* The nipple of the breast, حَلَمَةٌ ـ سَعْدَانَةٌ ـ قُرَادٌ *pl.* حَلَمَاتٌ ـ حَلَمَةُ ٱلثَّدْيِ. The dug of a beast, ثَدْيُ ٱلْحَيَوَانِ *pl.* ثُدِيٌّ ـ بِزٌّ *pl.* أَبْزَازٌ.

Tea-table, *n.* سُفْرَةُ ٱلشَّايِ.

Techily, *ad.* بِشَكَاسَةٍ ـ بِشَرَاسَةٍ.

Technic, *a.* / Technical, } اِصْطِلَاحِيٌّ. Pertaining to arts and sciences, مُتَعَلِّقٌ بِٱلْفُنُونِ وَٱلصَّنَائِعِ.

Technically, *ad.* بِٱلِٱصْطِلَاحِ. According to the signification of terms of art, حَسَبَ ٱصْطِلَاحِ أَهْلِ ٱلصَّنَائِعِ.

Technicalness, *n.* / Technicality, } اِصْطِلَاحِيَّةٌ ـ اِصْطِلَاحٌ.

Technics, *n.* ٱلْعُلُومُ ٱلصِّنَاعِيَّةُ.

Technological, *a.* مُتَعَلِّقٌ بِٱلْبَحْثِ عَنْ كُلِّيَّاتِ ٱلصَّنَائِعِ (or ٱلصِّنَاعَاتِ).

Technologist, *n.* مَاهِرٌ فِي تَعَلُّقَاتِ ـ صَاحِبُ ٱلِٱصْطِلَاحَاتِ ٱلصَّنَائِعِ (or ٱلصِّنَاعَاتِ).

Technology, *n.* عِلْمُ ٱلْبَحْثِ عَنْ تَعَلُّقَاتِ ـ عِلْمُ ٱلِٱصْطِلَاحَاتِ ٱلصَّنَائِعِ (or ٱلصِّنَاعَاتِ).

Techy, *a.* *See* Touchy, *a.*

Tectonics, *n.* فَنُّ ٱلْبِنَآءِ.

Ted, *v.t.* نَشَرَ ٱلْحَشَّةَ ـ نَشَرَ ٱلْحَشِيشَ.

Tedder, *n.* *See* Tether, *n.*

Tedder, *v.t.* *See to* Tether, *v.t.*

Te Deum, *n.* تَمْجِيدٌ لِلّٰهِ. A — or thanksgiving service was read in the mosques for the Sultan, أُقِيمَتِ ٱلْأَدْعِيَةُ ٱلْخَيْرِيَّةُ وَشُكْرُ رَبِّ ٱلْبَرِيَّةِ فِي ٱلْجَوَامِعِ لِلسُّلْطَانِ.

Tedious, *a.* Long, prolix, مُطَوَّلٌ ـ نَفَسٌ ـ مُطِيلٌ ـ مُبَالِغٌ. Irksome, مُزْعِجٌ ـ مُتْعِبٌ ـ مُمِلٌّ ـ شَاقٌّ. Slow, dilatory, بَطِيٌّ ـ مُتَرَاخٍ. Heavy, dull, ثَقِيلٌ ـ تَافِهٌ. To be —, prolix, أَطَالَ ٱلْكَلَامَ ـ بَالَغَ فِي ٱلْكَلَامِ. To be —, irksome, to, أَمَلَّ ـ أَضْجَرَ. To be —, dilatory, تَوَقَّفَ ـ بَطُؤَ. I have omitted all these circumstances from fear of being —, تَرَكْتُ هٰذِهِ ٱلْأَشْيَآءَ جَمِيعًا مَخَافَةَ ٱلْمَلَلِ. *See also under* Prolix, *a.*

Tediously, *ad.* Prolixly, بِإِطَالَةِ كَلَامٍ ـ بِمُبَالَغَةٍ. Irksomely, بِضَجَرٍ ـ بِمَلَالٍ. Dilatorily, بِبُطْءٍ ـ بِتَوَقُّفٍ ـ مُرَاخَاةً.

Tediousness, *n.* / **Tedium**, } Prolixity, إِطَالَةُ كَلَامٍ ـ مُبَالَغَةٌ. Irksomeness, ضَجَرٌ ـ مَلَالٌ ـ مَلَالَةٌ ـ مَلَّةٌ ـ مَلَلٌ ـ مَشَقَّةٌ. Dilatoriness, تَوَقُّفٌ ـ مُرَاخَاةٌ ـ بُطْءٌ. *See also under* Prolixity, *n.*

Teem, *v.i.* To abound in, وَفَرَ بِ ـ غَزُرَ بِ ـ جَمَّ بِ *aor.* يَفِرُ ـ كَثُرَ بِ ـ اِزْدَادَ. To be prolific, of a woman, ضَنِيَ; of land, أَخْصَبَ. *See also under to* Swarm, *v.i.*

Teem, *v.t.* To produce, bring forth, وَلَدَ ـ وَلَدَ *aor.* يَلِدُ. To cram with, أَغَصَّ بِ.

Teeming, *a.* Fruitful, مُثْمِرٌ ـ ثَمْرَآءُ ـ خَصِيبٌ. Swarming, غَفِيرٌ ـ وَافٍ ـ غَزِيرٌ ـ وَافِرٌ ـ فَائِضٌ ـ جَمٌّ ـ غَاصٌّ.

Teemless, *a.* *See* Barren, *a.*

Teens, *n.* عُمْرُ ٱلْإِنْسَانِ بَيْنَ ٱلثَّلَاثَ عَشْرَةَ وَٱلتِّسْعَ عَشْرَةَ سَنَةً ـ سِنُّ ٱلْمُرَاهَقَةِ. One in his —, جَذَعٌ *pl.* جُذْعَانٌ ـ مُرَاهِقٌ.

Teeth, *n.* (*pl. of* Tooth, *q.v.*) In the — of, in spite of, عَلَى إِكْرَاهِ ـ رَغْمًا عَنْ ـ عَلَى كَرَاهِيَةِ. Notwithstanding, مَعَ وُجُودِ كَذَا.

Teeth, *v.i.* طَلَعَتِ ٱلْأَسْنَانُ ـ أَسَنَّ.

Teething, *n.* طُلُوعُ ٱلْأَسْنَانِ ـ إِسْنَانٌ.

Teetotaller, *n.* مُتَعَهِّدٌ بِٱلِٱمْتِنَاعِ عَنِ ٱلْمُسْكِرَاتِ بَتَّةً.

Teetotalism, *n.* تَعَهُّدٌ بِٱلِٱمْتِنَاعِ عَنْ جَمِيعِ ٱلْمُسْكِرَاتِ.

Teetotum, *n.* دَوَّارَةٌ ـ دَوَّامَةٌ ـ فُرَيْرَةٌ.

Tegmen, *n.* *See* Tegument, *n.*

Tegular, *a.* مِثْلُ ٱلْقِرْمِيدِ ـ قِرْمِيدِيٌّ.

Tegument, *n.* غِشَآءٌ *pl.* أَغْشِيَةٌ ـ غِطَآءٌ *pl.* أَغْطِيَةٌ.

Tegumentary, *a.* غِشَائِيٌّ ـ غِطَائِيٌّ.

Teil, *n.* The tree; *see* Linden, *n.*

Teint; *see* Tint, *n.*

Telary, *a.* مُتَعَلِّقٌ بِبَيْتِ ٱلْعَنْكَبُوتِ.

Telegram, *n.* رِسَالَةُ ٱلتِّلِغْرَافِ ـ رِسَالَةُ ٱلسِّلْكِ. He sent me a —, ضَرَبَ لِي تِلِغْرَافًا ـ وَفَدَ لِي رِسَالَةً بِٱلتِّلِغْرَافِ.

Telegraph, *n.* سِلْكُ ٱلْإِشَارَةِ ـ ٱلتِّلِغْرَافُ ـ تِلِغْرَافٌ. He laid down the — wires, مَدَّ أَسْلَاكَ ٱلتِّلِغْرَافِ. A — office, قَلَمُ ٱلتِّلِغْرَافِ. By —, بِٱلطَّرِيقَةِ ٱلتِّلِغْرَافِيَّةِ. The occurrence was of graver importance than was reported by —, كَانَتِ ٱلْحَادِثَةُ أَعْظَمَ مِمَّا أَنْبَأَ بِهِ ٱلتِّلِغْرَافُ.

Telegraph, *v.t.* بَعَثَ بِٱلتِّلِغْرَافِ ـ أَرْسَلَ بِسِلْكِ ٱلْإِشَارَةِ. He telegraphed the news to Egypt, ضَرَبَ (or أَرْسَلَ) ٱلْخَبَرَ بِٱلتِّلِغْرَافِ إِلَى مِصْرَ.

Telegraphic, *a.* مُتَعَلِّقٌ بِٱلتِّلِغْرَافِ. Latest — intelligence, حَوَادِثُ ٱلتِّلِغْرَافِ ٱلْأَخِيرَةُ. Telegraphic news, ٱلْأَخْبَارُ ٱلتِّلِغْرَافِيَّةُ.

Telegraphy, *n.* صِنَاعَةُ ٱلتِّلِغْرَافِ.

Telescope, *n.* نَظَّارَةٌ *pl.* نَظَّارَاتٌ ـ دُورْبِينٌ *pl.* دَرَابِينُ ـ تِلِسْكُوبٌ.

Telescopic, *a.* Like a telescope, فِي هَيْئَةِ ٱلدُّورْبِينِ. To open and close like a telescope, مُدْمَجٌ ـ يَتَمَدَّدُ وَيَنْطَبِقُ مِثْلَ ٱلدُّرْبِينِ (or ٱلتِّلِسْكُوبِ)

Telesm, *n.* *See* Talisman, *n.*

Telesmatic, *a.* *See* Talismanic, *a.*

Telephone, *n.* ٱلْآلَةُ ٱلْمُتَكَلِّمَةُ ـ ٱلتِّلِغْرَافُ ٱلنَّاطِقُ.

Tell, *v.t.* To express in words, قَالَ بِ ـ أَنْبَأَ بِ ـ نَطَقَ بِ ـ فَاهَ بِ ـ تَكَلَّمَ بِ ـ حَكَى ـ ذَكَرَ ـ لِسَانًا. To communicate to, to inform, عَرَّفَ ـ أَخْبَرَ ـ أَسْمَعَ ـ بَلَّغَ ـ أَفَادَ. To reveal, أَفْشَى بِ. To count, عَدَّ. To recount, narrate, حَدَّثَ بِ ـ حَدَّثَ. To tell, narrate, to, قَصَّ عَلَى. To report to, أَخْبَرَ بِ ـ أَفَادَ. To confess, acknowledge, اِعْتَرَفَ. To spread abroad, أَشَاعَ. Tell me, أَخْبِرْنِي. Why did you not tell me that he had come? لِمَاذَا لَمْ تُخْبِرْنِي أَنَّهُ قَدْ جَآءَ. You cannot tell, لَا تَعْلَمُ. We cannot tell what you are talking about, لَا نَدْرِي

بِمَا تَقُولُ. Who can tell? مَنْ يَعْلَمُ; in the sense of perhaps, لَعَلَّ. I have sent to tell him, أَرْسَلْتُ لِأُخْبِرَهُ. Time would fail me to tell of them, يُعْوِزُنِي ٱلْوَقْتُ إِنْ أَخْبَرْتُ عَنْهُمْ. He who told me, كَشَفَ لِي ≂. ٱلَّذِي أَخْبَرَنِي. He told me all his heart, كُلَّ قَلْبِهِ. The place which the man told me, ٱلْمَوْضِعُ ٱلَّذِي قَالَ لِي ٱلرَّجُلُ. As it was told to me, كَمَا قِيلَ لِي. They were surprised at all that was told them, تَعَجَّبُوا مِمَّا قِيلَ لَهُمْ. As a tale that is told, كَقِصَّةٍ. *See also to* Inform, Report, *v.t.*

To tell a lie, كَذِبَ كَذْبَةً ≂.

To tell a story, حَكَى حِكَايَةً ≂ — قَصَّ قِصَّةً ².

To tell tales out of school, أَفْشَى بِٱلسِّرِّ.

To tell off, as to any duty, جَرَّدَ-ل — عَيَّنَ-ل — خَصَّصَ-ل: They were told off for the work, جُرِّدُوا لِلْعَمَلِ.

Tell, *v.i.* To produce an effect in, تَأَثَّرَ فِي — عَمِلَ فِي ≂. Every word of his address told, كُلُّ كَلِمَةٍ مِنْ خِطَابِهِ كَانَتْ فِي مَوْقِعِهَا.

Teller, *n.* A counter, حَسِيبٌ — حَاسِبٌ. A narrator, مُحَدِّثٌ. A speaker, مُتَكَلِّمٌ بِ. A —, as of votes, كَشَّافٌ. One who enters reckonings, مُقَيِّدُ ٱلْحِسَابَاتِ.

Tell-tale, *n.* }
Tell-tale, *a.* } مُفَشٍ — غِرْبَالٌ — جَاسُوسٌ — دَسِيسٌ.

Tellural, *a.* دُنْيَوِيٌّ — أَرْضِيٌّ.

Tellurium, *n.* ضَرْبٌ مِنَ ٱلْمَعَادِنِ لَوْنُهُ بَيْنَ لَوْنِ ٱلْفِضَّةِ وَٱلْقَصْدِيرِ — تَلُورِيُوم.

Temerarious, *a.* مُتَهَالِكٌ — مُتَهَوِّرٌ — هَيِّرٌ — مُتَعَسِّفٌ. To be —, تَهَوَّرَ — تَهَالَكَ. *See also* Rash, Precipitate, *a.*

Temerariously, *ad.* إِعْتِسَافًا — بِتَهَوُّرٍ — إِقْتِحَامًا.

Temerity, *n.* Rashness, تَهَوُّرٌ — إِعْتِسَافٌ. To do anything with —, rashness, عَسَفَ فِي ≂ — إِعْتَسَفَ — تَعَسَّفَ.

Temper, *n.* A mixture, مِزَاجٌ. Frame of mind, disposition, خُلُقٌ — شِيمَةٌ *pl.* شِيَمٌ — مَشْرَبٌ — ضَرِيبَةٌ — خَصْلَةٌ *pl.* خِصَالٌ — خِلَّةٌ — طَبِيعَةٌ *pl.* طَبَائِعُ — سَجِيَّةٌ. Bad —, شَرَاسَةٌ — شَكَاسَةٌ — طَبْعٌ نَكِدٌ. Good —, فَكَاهَةٌ — بَشَاشَةٌ. Temper, as of steel, سِقَايَةٌ. Temper, moderation, إِعْتِدَالٌ. Calmness, إِطْمِئْنَانٌ — رَاحَةُ بَالٍ — أَمَنَةٌ. The — of the times, ظُرُوفُ ٱلْأَحْوَالِ. He has a hasty — of his own, هُوَ طَائِرُ (*or* ثَائِرُ) ٱلْخُلُقِ. *See also* Disposition, Humour, *n.*

To be or get out of temper, ضَجِرَ ≂ — تَضَجَّرَ — تَبَرَّمَ — إِسْتَغْضَبَ:

He got out of temper at it, بَرِمَ ≂ (*or* تَبَرَّمَ) بِهِ.

To put out of temper, أَضْجَرَ — أَبْرَمَ — أَغْضَبَ — غَضَّبَ.

To keep one's temper, مَلَكَ نَفْسَهُ ≂ — إِتَّقَى نَفْسَهُ — تَقَفَّعَ — تَمَاسَكَ.

Temper, *v.t.* To mix with, مَزَجَ-بِ ≂. To moderate, عَدَّلَ — خَفَّفَ — لَيَّنَ — لَطَّفَ — أَصْلَحَ. To —, of iron, سَقَى ≂. To assuage,

Temperament, *n.* Disposition; *see under* Temper, *n.*

Temperance, *n.* إِمْسَاكٌ — رِيَّةٌ — وَرَعٌ — قَنَاعَةٌ — نَزَاهَةٌ — تَعَفُّفٌ — إِقْتِصَادٌ — عِفَّةٌ — ضَبْطُ ٱلنَّفْسِ.

Temperate, *a.* As in the appetites, صَاحٍ *pl.* صَاحُونَ — مُتَعَفِّفٌ — مُقْتَصِدٌ — قَانِتٌ — مُنَزَّهٌ — وَرِعٌ — عَفِيفٌ — وَرِيعٌ; as of the climate, *etc.*, مُعْتَدِلٌ. To be —, of the appetites, وَرِعَ *aor.* يَرِعُ — تَعَفَّفَ — ضَبَطَ نَفْسَهُ ² ≂; of the climate, *etc.*, إِعْتَدَلَ. The — zone, ٱلْمِنْطَقَةُ ٱلْمُعْتَدِلَةُ. Days of — weather, أَيَّامٌ مُعْتَدِلَةٌ.

Temperately, *ad.* بِٱعْتِدَالٍ — بِإِمْسَاكٍ — بِوَرَعٍ — تَعَفُّفًا.

Temperateness, *n.* إِعْتِدَالٌ.

Temperative, *a.* مُلَطِّفٌ — مُصْلِحٌ — مُعَدِّلٌ.

Temperature, *n.* Of the atmosphere, كَيْفِيَّةُ ٱلْهَوَاءِ — نَوْءٌ *pl.* أَنْوَاءٌ — طَقْسٌ. Temperature of the heat, دَرَجَةُ ٱلْحَرَارَةِ.

Tempered, *a.* Having a temper, humour, ذُو طَبْعٍ.

Good tempered, هَشٌّ بَشٌّ — بَشُوشٌ — حَلِيمُ ٱلطَّبْعِ.

High tempered, ثَائِرٌ — غَيُورٌ — غَضُوبٌ.

Ill tempered, وَعِقٌ — ذُو طَبْعٍ نَكِدٍ — شَكِسٌ — شَرِيسٌ — شَرِسُ ٱلطَّبْعِ.

Tempest, *n.* زَوْبَعَةٌ *pl.* زَوَابِعُ — نَوْءٌ *pl.* أَنْوَاءٌ — زَعْزَعٌ *pl.* زَعَازِعُ. A commotion, رَجَّةٌ — ضَجَّةٌ — إِضْطِرَابٌ — فُرْتُنَةٌ. *See also* Storm, *n.*

Tempest-beaten, *a.* }
Tempest-tossed, *a.* } مَلْطُومٌ مِنَ — مَضْرُوبٌ مِنَ ٱلْعَوَاصِفِ — بِلَى ٱلْعَوَاصِفِ — ٱلزَّوَابِعِ.

Tempestuous, *a.* Stormy, طُوفَانِيٌّ — زَوْبَعِيٌّ. Turbulent, ضَجُوجٌ — بَحْرٌ زَاخِرٌ — لَجُوجٌ. A — wind, رِيحٌ زَعْزَعٌ. A — sea, تَجَّاجٌ.

Tempestuously, *ad.* With turbulence, بِلَجَاجَةٍ — بِضَجِيجٍ.

Tempestuousness, *n.* As of the wind, عُصُوفٌ — عَصْفٌ; of the rain, نَوْءٌ. Tumult, لَجَاجَةٌ — ضَجِيجٌ — عَجَّةٌ — شَغَبٌ.

Templar, *n.* A student of law in the Temple, دَارِسُ ٱلْفِقْهِ فِي دَارِ ٱلْفُقَهَاءِ بِلَنْدَنَ. A Knight Templar, of Jerusalem, فَارِسٌ مِنْ فُرْسَانِ ٱلْفَرَنْجِ ٱلْمُلَقَّبِينَ بِٱلْهَيْكَلِيِّينَ ٱلَّذِينَ فِي قَدِيمِ ٱلزَّمَانِ كَانُوا يُحَامُونَ عَنْ زُوَّارِ ٱلْقُدْسِ ٱلشَّرِيفِ وَأَرْضِ فِلَسْطِينَ.

Temple, *n.* A place of worship, مَسْجِدٌ — مَسَاجِدُ *pl.* مَعْبَدٌ *pl.* مَعَابِدُ — هَيْكَلٌ *pl.* هَيَاكِلُ. The Temple at Jerusalem, ٱلْمَسْجِدُ ٱلْأَقْصَى — مَعْبَدُ سُلَيْمَانَ — ٱلْقِبْلَةُ ٱلْعَتِيقَةُ. The — of Mákkah, ٱلْمَسْجِدُ ٱلْحَرَامُ. The two temples, of Mákkah and al-Madinah, ٱلْمَسْجِدَانِ. From the sacred — at Mákkah to the farthest, namely, that at Jerusalem, مِنَ ٱلْمَسْجِدِ ٱلْحَرَامِ إِلَى ٱلْمَسْجِدِ

عِبَارَةٌ عَنْ دَارِ ٱلْفُقَهَآءِ فِي لَنْدَن. The Temple, in London, ٱلْأَقْصَى.

Temple, of the forehead, صُدْغ pl. أَصْدَاغ: the two temples, ٱلصُّدْغَانِ. *See also* Forehead, *n.*

Temporal, *a.* Pertaining to this life, زَمَنِيٌّ ـ عَالَمِيٌّ ـ دُنْيَوِيٌّ. Pertaining to the temples, مُتَعَلِّقٌ بِٱلْأَصْدَاغِ ـ صُدْغِيٌّ. Temporal power, ٱلسُّلْطَةُ ٱلْمَدَنِيَّةُ ـ ٱلسُّلْطَةُ ٱلزَّمَنِيَّةُ. Temporal good, مَالُ ٱلدُّنْيَا. The two — arteries, ٱلْأَصْدَغَانِ. The — ridge, قَرْنُ ٱلصُّدْغَانِ.

Temporalities, *n.* / Temporals, } أَمْلَاكٌ وَوَارِدَاتٌ عَالَمِيَّةٌ.

Temporally, *ad.* لِزَمَنٍ ـ زَمَنًا.

Temporarily, *ad.* إِلَى حِينٍ ـ إِلَى وَقْتٍ ـ وَقْتًا.

Temporariness, *n.* وَقْتِيَّةٌ.

Temporary, *a.* وَقْتِيٌّ ـ مُؤَقَّتٌ.

Temporize, *v.i.* To trim, تَحَوَّلَ. To procrastinate, بَطُؤَ [2] ـ تَبَاطَأَ ـ تَأَخَّرَ ـ أَبْطَأَ ـ تَرَاخَى. To affect to —, procrastinate, تَبَاطَأَ. *See also under to* Trim, *v.i.*

Temporizer, *n.* / Temporizing, *a.* } Trimming or a trimmer, حُوَّلِيٌّ ـ مُتَحَوِّلٌ ـ مُلَاقِعٌ ـ حُوَّلٌ قُلَّبٌ ـ حُوَالِيٌّ.

Temporizing, *n.* Trimming, تَحَوُّلٌ. Procrastination, تَرَاخٍ ـ إِبْطَآءٌ ـ بَطَآءَةٌ ـ تَأَخُّرٌ.

Tempt, *v.t.* To try, prove, جَرَّبَ ـ إِمْتَحَنَ. To —, as with evil, فَتَنَ ـ أَفْتَنَ. To excite, urge, as of the passions, شَوَّقَ ـ ضَلَّلَ ـ أَغْوَى ـ أَشْهَى ـ شَهَّى ـ طَمَّعَ. To seduce, entice, أَغْوَى ـ أَضَلَّ. To solicit to evil, حَرَّكَ إِلَى ٱلشَّرِّ ـ غَرَّ [2] ـ أَغْوَى. To —, as with evil thoughts, وَسْوَسَ لِ ـ بِ. To be tempted, proved, جُرِّبَ ـ أُمْتُحِنَ; to be tempted, brought under the influence of evil, فُتِنَ ـ إِفْتَتَنَ. *See also to* Seduce, *v.t.*

Temptable, *a.* Subject to temptation, seduction, مُعَرَّضٌ لِلْفِتْنَةِ ـ مِمَّا يُفْتَتَنُ.

Temptation, *n.* Trial, the act of, تَجْرِيبٌ ـ إِمْتِحَانٌ. A trial, تَجْرِبَةٌ pl. تَجَارِبُ. Solicitation of the passions, إِغْوَآءٌ ـ غُرُورٌ ـ تَغْوِيَةٌ. Evil temptations, as of the devil, وَسْوَسَةٌ pl. وَسَاوِسُ. Lead us not into —, لَا تُدْخِلْنَا فِي تَجْرِبَةٍ. "But ye led yourselves into —," لَكِنَّكُمْ فَتَنْتُمْ أَنْفُسَكُمْ (Kur. lvii. 13). To suffer —, تَحَمَّلَ ٱلتَّجَارِبَ.

Tempter, *n.* A seducer, فَاتِنٌ ـ ضَلَّالٌ ـ مُغْوٍ ـ غَاوٍ. The —, devil, ٱلشَّيْطَانُ ـ ٱلْوَسْوَاسُ ـ ٱلْفَتَّانُ.

Tempting, *a.* Exciting desire, alluring, مُشَهٍّ ـ مُرَغِّبٌ ـ مُسْلِبُ ٱلْقَلْبِ. *See also* Seductive, *a.*

Temptingness, *n.* The quality of being tempting, صِفَةُ ٱلتَّرْغِيبِ. Beauty, excellence, حُسْنٌ ـ طَلَاوَةٌ ـ طُلَاوَةٌ ـ حَبَرَةٌ.

Ten, *a.* عَشَرَةٌ pl. عَشَرَاتٌ fem. عَشْرٌ. Ten men, عَشَرَةُ رِجَالٍ; ten women, عَشْرُ نِسْوَةٍ; ten nights, عَشْرُ لَيَالٍ. To make ten, to add one to nine, أَعْشَرَ ـ عَشَّرَ: he made the number ten, أَعْشَرَ ٱلْعَدَدَ. To take one from ten, عَشَرَ [2]: he took one from among them, they being ten, عَشَرَهُمْ. To remain ten days with, عَشَّرَ لِ: he remained ten days with his wife, عَشَّرَ لِٱمْرَأَتِهِ. Ten and ten together, or ten and ten at a time, عُشَارَ: they came in tens, جَاؤُوا عُشَارَ عُشَارَ. He reigned over the country ten years, مَلَكَ عَلَى ٱلْبِلَادِ عَشْرَ سِنِينَ. He changed his dress ten times, غَيَّرَ لِبْسَهُ عَشْرَ مَرَّاتٍ. He found them ten times better than, or superior to, all the others, وَجَدَهُمْ عَشَرَةَ أَضْعَافٍ فَوْقَ كُلِّ ٱلْآخَرِينَ. The last ten nights of the Ramadhân, ٱلْعَشْرُ ٱلْأَوَاخِرُ. The first ten nights of Dzu-'l-Hijjah, عَشْرُ ذِي ٱلْحِجَّةِ. The first ten nights of al-Muhárram, ٱلْعَشْرُ. A paragraph of the al-Kur-ân of ten verses, عَشْرٌ; the circular stop denoting the same, عَاشِرَةٌ.

Tenable, *a.* *See* Sustainable, *a.*

Tenacious, *a.* Holding fast, مَاسِكٌ ـ ضَابِطٌ ـ مُضِبٌّ ـ مُتَشَبِّثٌ بِ: a — man, one who cleaves, adheres, to a thing, رَجُلٌ شِبِثٌ. Viscous, دَبِقٌ ـ لَزِجٌ. Tenacious, as of an opinion, مُتَعَصِّبٌ لِرَأْيِهِ ـ مُؤْتَمِرٌ رَأْيَهُ ـ مُعْجَبٌ بِرَأْيِهِ ـ ضَنِينٌ بِرَأْيِهِ ـ مُعَانِدٌ ـ عَنِيدٌ. Tenacious in matters of religion, أَحْمَسُ pl. حُمْسٌ ـ حَمِسٌ ـ مُتَحَمِّسٌ. A thing of which one is —, ضِنٌّ ـ ضِنَّةٌ: he is the person of whose affections I am —, هُوَ ضِنَّتِي ـ هُوَ ضَنِينِي. Tenacious, in the sense of niggardly, ضَنِينٌ: he is not — of that which has been revealed (to him), وَمَا هُوَ عَلَى ٱلْغَيْبِ بِضَنِينٍ (Kur. lxxxvii. 24). To be —, niggardly, of, ضَنَّ بِ. To hold to, as to an opinion, ثَبَتَ عَلَى [2] ـ تَمَسَّكَ بِ. To be —, opiniated, تَعَجَّبَ فِي رَأْيِهِ ـ عَانَدَ. *See also* Retentive, *a.*

Tenaciously, *ad.* As holding fast, تَمَسُّكًا ـ بِضِنَّةٍ ـ إِضْبَابًا ـ تَشَدُّدًا. Adhesively, إِلْتِصَاقًا ـ إِلْتِزَاجًا. With niggardliness, بِضِنَّةٍ. I kept — to the place, ضَنِنْتُ بِٱلْمَحَلِّ. To hold or cleave to —, تَشَبَّثَ بِ ـ ضَبَّبَ عَلَى ـ أَضَبَّ عَلَى.

Tenaciousness, *a.* / Tenacity, } Adhesiveness, لُزُوجَةٌ. Holding fast, إِضْبَابٌ ـ تَمَسُّكٌ ـ إِمْسَاكٌ. Opiniativeness, عُجْبٌ ـ مُعَانَدَةٌ ـ عِنَادٌ ـ عُجْبُ ٱلرَّأْيِ. Rigour in religious matters, حَمَاسَةٌ. Niggardliness, ضِنَّةٌ ـ مَضِنَّةٌ. Retentiveness, as of memory, حِفْظٌ ـ حَافِظَةٌ.

Tenancy, *n.* As of land, houses, *etc.*, إِجَار ـ إِسْتِكْرَآءٌ ; the holding possession of any place, حَوْز ـ تَصَرُّف ـ ضَبْط .

Tenant, *n.* As of land or houses, مُسْتَأْجِر ـ مُسْتَكْرٍ ; of any property or office, حَائِزُ مَأْمُورِيَّةٍ ـ مُتَصَرِّف ـ صَاحِب .

Tenantable, *a.* Habitable, مُنَاسِبٌ لِلسُّكْنَى ـ مِمَّا يُسْكَنُ . Fit to be rented, مَحَلٌّ لِلْإِيجَارِ .

Tenantless, *a.* Not rented, غَيْرُ مُسْتَكْرًى ـ غَيْرُ مُسْتَأْجَرٍ . Uninhabited, خَالٍ مِنَ ٱلسُّكَّانِ . Unoccupied, خَالٍ ـ فَارِغ .

Tenantry, *n.* أَكْرِيَآءُ أَمْلَاكٍ قَاطِبَةً ـ مُسْتَأْجِرُوا أَمْلَاكٍ جُمْلَةً .

Tench, *n.* نَوْعٌ مِنْ سَمَكِ ٱلشُّهُورِ .

Tend, *v.t.* To wait on, خَدَمَ [2]. To take care of, إِعْتَنَى بِ ـ إِهْتَمَّ بِ ـ يَعِي *aor.* وَعَى عَلَى . To —, as of the sick, خَدَمَ [2] ـ عَالَجَ . To —, as a flock, أَرْعَى . *See also under to* Visit, *v.t.*

Tend, *v.i.* To move in a certain direction, صَمَدَ إِلَى [2] ـ ضَرَبَ إِلَى ـ إِنْصَرَفَ إِلَى ـ تَوَجَّهَ إِلَى ـ تَصَوَّبَ إِلَى . To have an inclination to, مَالَ إِلَى ـ إِنْعَطَفَ إِلَى . To contribute or conduce to, سَبَّبَ ـ أَنْتَجَ ـ يَؤُولُ *aor.* آلَ إِلَى . To occasion, سَبَّبَ ـ أَنْتَجَ . To be useful to, نَفَعَ لِ ـ صَلَحَ لِ [2]. To design, قَصَدَ إِلَى . The arrangement will — to hasten the settlement of the pending question, مِنْ شَأْنِ ٱلتَّدْبِيرِ أَنْ يُعَجِّلَ تَسْوِيَةَ ٱلْمَسَائِلِ ٱلْمُعَلَّقَةِ .

Tendency, *n.* Inclination, مَيْل . Utility towards, مَصْلَحَة ـ مُعَاوَنَة ـ فَائِدَة ـ طَائِل . Scope, drift, مَحَطٌّ ـ مَقْصُود ـ نِيَّة ـ مَقْصَد ـ غَرَض . It will have a — to prevent the influence of Russia, مِنْ شَأْنِهِ أَنْ يَمْنَعَ نُفُوذَ ٱلرُّوسِيَّةِ .

Tender, *n.* One who waits on another, a keeper, حَافِظ *pl.* مُحَافِظ ـ حُفَّاظ . A small vessel that attends on a large one, سَفِينَةٌ مُعِينَةٌ ; of a railway train, عَرَبِيَّةٌ مُعِينَةٌ . An offer, as for a contract, إِعْرَاضُ سِعْرٍ ـ عَرْضُ قِيمَةٍ ـ عَرْضُ سِعْرٍ ـ عَرْضٌ قَائِمَةٍ . An offer, generally, عُرُوض ـ إِعْرَاض . A legal —, of coin, نَقْدٌ شَرْعِيٌّ ـ مُعَامَلَةٌ شَرْعِيَّةٌ ; of notes, أَوْرَاقٌ نَقْدِيَّةٌ شَرْعِيَّةٌ .

Tender, *a.* Delicate, of a plant; also, of meat, and of the skin, رَخْص *pl.* رِخَاص . Soft, yielding, لَيِّن *pl.* أَلْيِنَآءُ *and* لَيِّنُونَ ـ نَاعِم . Delicate, رَقِيق . Fresh; also easy of mastication; also succulent, طَرِيّ ـ غَضِير . Tender of heart, رَقِيق *pl.* رُقَقَآءُ ـ حَنُون ـ شَفِيق ـ مُشْفِق . Compassionate, رَقِيقُ ٱلْقَلْبِ . Tender, soft, delicate, or having a soft skin, of a girl or woman, رَخْصَة . A woman of a soft or — body, إِمْرَأَةٌ رَخْصَةُ ٱلْبَدَنِ . To be —, to the feel, or to be delicate, or to be easily masticated, رَخُصَ [2]; To be — towards, رَفَقَ بِ *or* عَلَى [2]. *See also under* Soft, *a.*

Tender, *v.t.* To offer to, قَدَّمَ لِ ـ عَرَضَ لِ *or* عَلَى . To —, as a proposition, طَرَحَ عَلَى كَذَا . To — an excuse, تَعَذَّرَ ـ إِعْتَذَرَ . To — one an oath, حَلَّفَ ـ أَحْلَفَ ـ قَاسَمَ . To —, as for a contract, عَرَضَ قَائِمَةً لِ . To — payment, أَدَّى مَا عَلَيْهِ .

Tender-hearted, *a.* مُشْفِق ـ رَقِيقُ ٱلْقَلْبِ .

Tender-heartedness, *n.* شَفَقَة ـ رِقَّةُ قَلْبٍ .

Tenderling, *n.* مُدَلَّل ـ مُفَنَّق *fem.* مُدَلَّلَة . مَحْبُوب ـ *fem.* مَحْبُوبَة .

Tenderly, *a.* Fondly, بِرِفْقٍ ـ بِحِنِّيَّةٍ . Lovingly, بِمَحَبَّةٍ ـ مُحِبًّا ـ بِعِشْقٍ ـ بِوِدَادٍ . With gentleness, بِلِينَةٍ . *See also* Gently, *ad.*

Tenderness, *n.* As of a plant, meat, and the skin, رَخَاصَة ـ رُخُوصَة ; of a soft and tender skin, of a woman, رُخْصَان . Softness, gentleness, لَيَان ـ لِينَة . Softness of heart, رِقَّةُ قَلْبٍ ـ حِنِّيَّة ـ حِنَّة ـ شَفَقَة ـ شَفَق . Love, غَرَام ـ عِشْق ـ مَحَبَّة . *See also* Sensibility, *n.*

Tendinous, *a.* *See* Sinewy, *a.*

Tendon, *n.* وَتَر *pl.* أَوْتَار ـ طُنُب *pl.* أَطْنَاب ـ عَقَبَة *pl.* عِقَاب . The — of Achilles, عُرْقُوب *pl.* عَرَاقِيب . *See also* Sinew, *n.*

Tendril, *n.* As of a vine, جَفْنَة *coll.* جَفْن *pl.* أَجْفَان ـ حَبْلَة ـ أَظْفُور . The tree to which a — clings, عِطْفَة .

Tendril, *a.* Of plants, مُعَرِّش ـ أَثِيث ـ مُعَرَّش . *See also under* Runner, *n.*

Tendsome, *n.* مُحْتَاجٌ إِلَى ٱعْتِنَآءٍ زَائِدٍ .

Tenebrous, *a.* }
Tenebrious, } مُظْلِم ـ ظَلِم ـ مُكْفَهِرّ . *See also* Dark, *a.*

Tenement, *n.* مَسْكَن *pl.* مَسَاكِن ـ مَحَلّ *pl.* مَحَلَّات ـ دَار *pl.* دِيَار .

Tenemental, *a.* }
Tenementary, } مِمَّا يُسْتَكْرَى ـ يُسْتَأْجَر .

Tenet, *n.* إِعْتِقَاد *pl.* إِعْتِقَادَات ـ عَقِيدَة *pl.* عَقَائِد ـ رَأْي *pl.* آرَآء . A body of tenets, مَذْهَب *pl.* مَذَاهِب .

Tenfold, *a.* عَشَرَةُ أَضْعَافٍ . "Whosoever shall present himself with good works he shall receive tenfold like unto the same," مَنْ جَآءَ بِٱلْحَسَنَةِ فَلَهُ عَشْرُ أَمْثَالِهَا (Kur. vi. 161).

Tennis, *n.* لَعِبُ ٱلطَّابَةِ ـ لَعِبُ ٱلْكُورَةِ .

Tenon, *n.* تَعْشِيقُ ٱلْخَشَبِ . A — saw, مِنْشَارٌ لِتَعْشِيقِ ٱلْخَشَبِ .

Tenon, *v.t.* عَشَّقَ ٱلْخَشَبَ .

Tenor, *n.* Sense, drift, مَحَطٌّ ـ فَحْوَى ـ مَضْمُون ـ مَعْنَى . Character, bearing, aspect, ظَاهِر ـ هَيْئَة . Course of anything,

طَرْز — سَلْك — أُسْلُوب — طَوْر. The —, in music, الصَّوْتُ ٱلْمِثْلَثُ. One who sings —, مُغَنٍّ بِٱلصَّوْتِ ٱلْمِثْلَثِ. According to the — of these words, بِحَسَبِ هٰذِهِ ٱلْكَلِمَاتِ.

Tense, *n.* فِعْل *pl.* أَفْعَال — حَالٌ مِنْ أَحْوَالِ ٱلْفِعْلِ — زَمَنٌ مِنْ أَزْمِنَةِ ٱلْفِعْلِ.

The future tense, الفِعْلُ ٱلْمُسْتَقْبِلُ.

The present tense, فِعْلُ ٱلْحَالِ.

The imperfect tense, الفِعْلُ ٱلْمَاضِي ٱلْغَيْرُ ٱلتَّامِّ.

The perfect tense, الفِعْلُ ٱلْمَاضِي ٱلتَّامُّ.

The pluperfect tense, الفِعْلُ ٱلْمَاضِي ٱلْأَتَمُّ.

Tense, *a.* Strained to stiffness, مُتَمَطِّط — مِطَاط — مُجْتَذِب — مَشْدُود — مُتَوَتِّر. Stiff, rigid, صُلْب — يَابِس. To become —, rigid, جَسَأَ ٢ — صَلُبَ ٢ — صَلُبَ. To become —, stretched, تَمَطَّطَ — اِجْتَذَبَ — تَوَتَّرَ — اِشْتَدَّ. *See also* Rigid, *a.*

Tenseness, *n.* The being strained to stiffness, تَمَطُّط — تَوَتُّر — شِدَّة. Rigidity, stiffness, صَلَابَة — تَصَلُّب. Want of flexibility, كَزَازَة — كُزُوزَة. *See also* Stiffness, Rigidity, *n.*

Tensile, *a.* }
Tensible, } يَتَمَطَّطُ — وَمَا يُمَدُّ — قَابِلُ ٱلْمَطِّ. *See also* Extensible, *a.*

Tensibility, *n.* *See* Extensibility, *n.*

Tension, *n.* The act of, مَطّ — تَمْدِيد — نَدْح — جَذْب; the state of being stretched, تَمَطُّط — اِجْتِذَاب — اِمْتِدَاد. Coolness, as in the state of mutual relations, بُرُودَة — مُبَايَنَة. Tension, as of the mental faculties, اِسْتِغْرَاق — اِشْتِغَال. *See also* Tenseness, *n.*

Tensor, *n.* A tensor muscle, عَضَلَة نَاشِرَة *pl.* عَضَلَاتٌ نَاشِرَةٌ.

Tent, *n.* A pavilion of canvas, بَيْت *pl.* بُيُوت — خَيْمَة *pl.* خَيْمَات *and* خِيَم *and* خِيَام. A great —, دَاحَة *coll.* دَاح *pl.* أَدْوَاح — مِظَلَّة *pl.* مَظَالّ. A small — of wool, خِبَاء *pl.* أَخْبِيَة. A — pole, مِسْطَح *pl.* مَسَاطِحُ. A — rope, طُنُب *pl.* أَطْنَاب. The kanâts of a —, حُجْرَة — سُرَادِق. A — maker, خَيَّام. To pitch a —, مَتَّنَ — خَيَّمَ — ٢ نَصَبَ ٱلْخَيْمَةَ — ضَرَبَ ٱلْخَيْمَةَ. To live in a —, ٢ سَكَنَ فِي خَيْمَةٍ. To pitch one's —, to abide in a place, خَيَّمَ — تَخَيَّمَ بِ. Dwellers in tents, أَهْلُ ٱلْوَبَرِ — مُخَيِّمَات — سُكَّانُ ٱلْخِيَامِ. Tent, a roll of lint, مِيل *pl.* أَمْيَال — فَتِيل — فَتِيلَة *pl.* فَتَائِلُ. A kind of wine, ضَرْبٌ مِنَ ٱلْخَمْرِ ٱلْحُلْوِ.

Tent, *v.t.* and *i.* *See under* Tent, *a.*

Tent, *v.t.* As with a roll of lint, ٢ ضَمَدَ بِفَتِيلَةٍ. *See also to* Probe, *v.t.*

Tentacle, *n.* Of insects, قَرْن *pl.* قُرُون.

Tentacular, *a.* فِي هَيْئَةِ قُرُونِ ٱلْحَشَرَاتِ.

Tentation, *n.* تَجْرِيب — تَجْرِبَة — سَعْي.

Tentative, *a.* عَلَى أُسْلُوبِ ٱلتَّجْرِبَةِ — عَلَى وَجْهِ ٱلسَّعْيِ. A — measure, سَعْيٌ بَيْنَ مَحْظُورٍ وَمَحْذُورٍ.

Tentative, *n.* تَجْرِبَة — مَسْعَاة *pl.* مَسَاعٍ — سَعْي.

Tentatively, *ad.* بَيْنَ مَحْظُورٍ وَمَحْذُورٍ.

Tenter, *n.* }
Tenter-hook, } عُقَّافَةٌ لِمَطِّ ٱلْقُمَاشِ. To be on the tenter-hooks, حَارَ — تَحَيَّرَ — قَلِقَ.

Tenter, *v.t.* مَدَّ ٢ — مَطَّ ٢.

Tenth, *a.* العَاشِرُ *fem.* العَاشِرَةُ.

Tenth, *n.* عُشْر *pl.* أَعْشَار *and* عُشُور — عَشِير *pl.* أَعْشِرَاء. Nine tenths of the property, تِسْعَةُ أَعْشِرَاءِ ٱلرِّزْقِ. To take a — or tithe of, عَشَرَ. To give a — of to, عَشَّرَ لِ.

Tenthly, *ad.* عَاشِرًا.

Tenuity, *n.* Thinness, دِقَّة. Flimsiness, slenderness, سَخَافَة — رِكَّة — رَكَاكَة. Leanness, عَجَف. Rarefaction, تَخَلْخُل. *See also* Slenderness, *n.*

Tenuous, *a.* Thin, دَقِيق; flimsy, slender, سَخِيف — رَكِيك; lean, عَجِيف. Rarefied, مُتَخَلْخِل.

Tenure, *n.* شَرْطُ ٱلتَّصَرُّفِ بِشَيْءٍ.

Tepid, *a.* فَاتِر — سَخِين — سَخِيم.

Tepidity, *n.* }
Tepidness, } فُتُور — فَتْر.

Terebinth, *n.* The tree, شَجَرَةُ ٱلتِّرِبِنْتِينَا — البُطْمُ — الضِّرْوُ. The fruit of the —, الحَبَّةُ ٱلْخَضْرَاءُ.

Terebinthine, *a.* تِرِبِنْتِينِيٌّ — مِنْ جِنْسِ ٱلتِّرِبِنْتِينَا.

Teredo, *n.* أَرَضَة *pl.* أَرَض *and* أَرَضَات — قَتَع — سُرْفَة. Erosion by the —, سُرَاف.

Terete, *a.* Columnar, فِي شَكْلِ ٱلْعَمُودِ.

Tergeminous, *a.* ثُلَاثِيٌّ.

Tergiversation, *n.* Subterfuge, تَعَلُّل — تَرَدُّد — تَحَجُّج. Evasion, مُحَاوَلَة. To practise —, تَحَاوَلَ.

Term, *n.* Termination, end, as of space, time, *etc.*, نَصّ — آخِر — نِهَايَة — حَدّ — مَدًى — مُدَّة — مُهْلَة. A space of time, مُدَّةٌ مِنَ ٱلزَّمَانِ. An appointed term, time, as for payment, *etc.*, أَجَل — مِيعَاد — مَوْعِد *pl.* مَوَاعِدُ — أَمَد. A fixed —, time, أَجَل. Time, as at which anything is expected to occur, وَقْت. A judicial —, session, مُدَّةُ ٱفْتِتَاحِ ٱلْمَحَاكِمِ. A college —, مُدَّةُ ٱلدَّرْسِ فِي مَدْرَسَةٍ. A word, تَعْبِير *pl.* تَعَابِيرُ — عِبَارَة *pl.* عِبَارَات —

كَلِمَة *pl.* كَلِمَات ـ لَفْظَة *pl.* أَلْفَاظ ; a special word or epithet, as used by authors, diction, نَصّ *pl.* نُصُوص. The major —, in logic, الحَدُّ ٱلْأَكْبَرُ ; the minor —, الحَدُّ ٱلْأَصْغَرُ ; the middle —, الحَدُّ ٱلْأَوْسَطُ. Terms, conditions, stipulation, شَرِيطَة *pl.* شَرَائِطُ ـ شَرْط *pl.* شُرُوط. The — has expired, ٢ حَضَرَ ٱلْمِيعَادُ. Their —, (of office,) in the council had expired, ٱنْتَهَتْ مُدَّتُهُمْ فِي ٱلْمَجْلِسِ. For a long —, time, لِمُدَّةٍ مَدِيدَةٍ. The —, as of occupation, will expire, يَسْقُطُ وَقْتُ ٱلْحُلُولِ. Before the end of the appointed —, قَبْلَ نِهَايَةِ ٱلْأَجَلِ ٱلْمُقَرَّرِ. Terms, conditions, as between parties, حَال ـ وَارِد. A —, or terms agreed upon, تَرَاضٍ. On the terms existing betwixt us, on the footing which we are, مَا نَحْنُ فِيهِ مِنَ ٱلْوَارِدِ.

Fictitious terms or conditions, شُرُوط جَعْلِيَّة وَهْمِيَّة.

Plain, decided, terms, كَلَامٌ بَتٌّ ـ أَلْفَاظٌ أَكِيدَةٌ ـ قَوْلٌ جَازِمٌ.

Upon easy terms, عَلَى شُرُوطٍ هَيِّنَةٍ.

To be on bad terms with, كَانَ عَلَى ـ كَانَ عَلَى وَحْشَةٍ مَعَ فُلَانٍ عَدَاوَةٍ مَعَ فُلَانٍ.

To be on good terms with, كَانَ عَلَى وِدَادٍ ـ كَانَ مُقَرَّبًا مِنْ فُلَانٍ مَعَ فُلَانٍ.

To bring to terms, to reconcile, لَئَّمَ. To oblige, أَضَرَّ-عَلَى ـ أَلْزَمَ-بِ.

To come to terms, to be reconciled, of two, تَصَالَحَا ـ تَسَالَمَا ; of many, تَصَالَحُوا ـ تَسَالَمُوا. To agree upon, of many, اِتَّفَقُوا عَلَى.

To make terms, conditions, with, اِشْتَرَطَ-عَلَى ـ ٢ ـ شَرَطَ-عَلَى.

Term, *v.t.* To name, سَمَّى ـ سَمَّى-بِ ـ دَعَا-بِ ٢.

Termagancy, *n.* Turbulence, شَغْب ـ تَهَوُّر ـ طَيَشَانُ عَقْلٍ.

Termagant, *a.* Turbulent, شَغَّاب ـ عَجَّاج ـ مُتَهَوِّر.

Termagant, *n.* Of a woman, سِلْقَة *pl.* سُلْقَان ـ سَلِيطَة.

Termes, *n.* } أَرَضَة *pl.* أَرَض *and* أَرَضَات : More consuming than
Termite, } the —, آكَلُ مِنَ ٱلْأَرَضَةِ. More destructive than the —, آكَلُ (*or*) أَفْسَدُ مِنَ ٱلْأَرَضَةِ.

Terminable, *a.* That may be bounded, مِمَّا يُحَدَّدُ ـ تَحْدِيدُهُ مُمْكِنٌ. Of which the term is fixed, مُؤَجَّل ـ وَعْدُهُ مُعَيَّنٌ ـ مِيعَادُهُ مُحَدَّدٌ ـ المِيعَادُ مَشْرُوطٌ فِيهِ.

Terminal, *a.* Growing at the end, of a thing, صَادِرٌ مِنْ آخِرِ الشَّيْءِ ـ نَاتِجٌ مِنْ ذَيْلِ الشَّيْءِ. Forming the end, آخِر. Occurring at the end of the month, وَاقِعٌ فِي آخِرِ ٱلشَّهْرِ.

Terminate, *v.t.* To bound, حَدَّدَ ـ ٢ حَدَّ. To break off, قَطَعَ ـ. To end, finish, قَضَى ـ أَنْهَى ـ كَمَّلَ ـ أَتَمَّ ـ تَمَّمَ ـ غَلَّقَ ـ خَلَّصَ. He terminated the affair quickly, أَنْجَزَ ٱلْأَمْرَ. How will this matter —? عَلَى أَيِّ وَجْهٍ يُفْصَلُ هٰذَا ٱلْأَمْرُ. To be terminated, bounded, تَحَدَّدَ ; to be ended, اِنْقَضَى ـ اِنْتَهَى ـ تَقَضَّى ـ تَمَّ ـ.

Terminate, *v.i.* To be broken off, اِنْقَطَعَ. To come to an end, اِنْتَهَى ـ اِنْقَضَى ـ تَمَّ ـ. To stop, وَقَفَ *aor.* يَقِفُ. To desist from, كَفَّ عَنْ ٢ ـ مَسَكَ عَنْ ـ.

Termination, *n.* The act of breaking off, ceasing, تَقْطِيع ; of bounding, تَحْدِيد ; of desisting, or of being broken off, اِنْقِطَاع ; of coming to an end, an ending, اِنْقِضَاء ـ اِنْتِهَاء ـ غَايَة *pl.* غَايَات ـ نِهَايَة ـ خِتَام. Subsidence, قَرَار. Termination of a word, آخِرُ ٱلْكَلِمَةِ *pl.* أَوَاخِرُ ٱلْكَلِمِ ـ رُكْنُ ٱلْكَلِمَةِ ٱلْأَخِيرُ *pl.* أَرْكَان. They arrived at a happy —, وَصَلُوا إِلَى نِهَايَةٍ حَسَنَةٍ.

Terminational, *a.* مُتَعَلِّقٌ بِأَوَاخِرِ ٱلْكَلِمِ. *See also* Final, *a.*

Terminative, *a.* Directing determination, مُقْضِيٌّ ـ إِثْبَاتِيٌّ ـ بَتِّيٌّ.

Terminator, *n.* الخَطُّ ٱلْفَاصِلُ بَيْنَ نُورِ ٱلْقَمَرِ وَتُرْبِهِ.

Terminology, *n.* مَعَانِي ٱلْاِصْطِلَاحَاتِ ـ الاِصْطِلَاحَاتُ.

Terminus, *n.* A boundary, حَدّ *pl.* حُدُود. A —, of a railway, مَوْقِفُ سِكَّةِ ٱلْحَدِيدِ. A station, as of a railway, مَحَطَّة.

Termite, *n.* *See* Termes, *n.*

Termless, *a.* Not bounded, غَيْرُ مَحْدُودٍ ـ غَيْرُ مُتَنَاهٍ.

Termly, *ad.* بِمُدَّةٍ ـ فِي كُلِّ مُدَّةٍ.

Tern, *a.* Threefold, ثُلَاثِيٌّ.

Tern, *n.* The bird, خُطَّافُ ٱلْبَحْرِ *pl.* خَطَاطِيفُ.

Ternary, *a.* مُثَلَّث ـ ثُلَاثِيٌّ.

Ternate, *a.* Of a petiole, شِمْرَاخٌ ذُو ثَلَاثِ وُرَيْقَاتٍ.

Terpsichorean, *a.* مَا نِيطَ بِٱلرَّقْصِ.

Terra, *n.* Land, أَرْض. A kingdom, مَمْلَكَة. A place, region, مَحَلّ ـ بَلْدَة ـ مَمْلَكَة ـ قُطْر *pl.* أَقْطَار ـ نَاحِيَة *pl.* نَوَاحِي. Dust, earth, تُرْب ـ تُرَاب ـ طِين.

Terra firma, يَابِسَة ـ أَرْض.

Terra incognita, أَرْضٌ مَجْهُولَةٌ.

Terra japonica, نَوْفَلٌ هِنْدِيٌّ.

Terra lemnia, طِينٌ مَخْتُومٌ.

Terra Sienna, تُرَابٌ يُصْبَغُ بِهِ ٱلشَّيْءُ بِلَوْنِ ٱلْقَهْوَةِ.

Terrace, *n.* A flight, floor, طَبَقَة *pl.* طَبَقَات. A parterre, رَوْضَة *pl.* رِيَاض. The flat roof of a house, سَطْح *pl.* سُطُوح. A row of houses, as in a street, طَوْر *pl.* أَطْوَار. *See also under* Row, *n.*

Terrace, *v.t.* To form into terraces, جَعَلَ-عَلَى طَبَقَاتٍ ـ. To put a flat roof to, سَطَحَ ـ سَطَّحَ. To open, فَتَحَ ـ.

Terraced, *a.* In terraces, stages, طَبَقَةٌ عَلَى طَبَقَةٍ. Having a — roof, مُسَطَّحٌ ـ ذُو سَطْحٍ.

Terraqueous, *a.* بَحْرِيٌّ وَبَرِّيٌّ. The — globe, الدُّنْيَا ـ كُرَةُ ٱلْأَرْضِ.

Terrene, *a.* دُنْيَوِيٌّ ـ عَالَمِيٌّ.

Terre-plein, *n.* سَطْحٌ.

Terrestrial, *a.* أَرْضِيٌّ. A — globe, كُرَةُ ٱلْعَالَمِ. The — paradise, جَنَّةُ عَدْنٍ.

Terrestrially, بِوَجْهٍ عَالَمِيٍّ.

Terrible, *a.* Adapted to excite dread, فَظِيعٌ ـ هَائِلٌ ـ مُهَوِّلٌ ـ كَرِيبٌ ـ نَحِسٌ ـ شَاقٌّ ـ فَاجِعٌ. Distressing, مَهُولٌ ـ مَخُوفٌ. A —, frightful thing, هَيْلَةٌ; a —, distressing thing, آفَةٌ *pl.* آفَاتٌ ـ بَائِسٌ. The sight was so — that he feared and quaked, كَانَ ٱلْمَنْظَرُ هٰكَذَا مُخِيفًا حَتَّى ٱرْتَعَبَ وَٱرْتَعَدَ. *See also* Dreadful, Horrible, *a.*

Terribleness, *n.* The qualities that excite horror, هَوْلٌ ـ هَوْلَةٌ. Distressfulness, صُعُوبَةٌ ـ فَظَاعَةٌ ـ نَحْسٌ.

Terribly, *ad.* *See* Horribly, *ad.*

Terrier, *n.* The dog, كَلْبٌ يَقْنِصُ ٱلْوُحُوشَ فِي جُحْرَتِهَا. A burrow, جُحْرَةٌ *pl.* جِحَارٌ ـ وَكْرٌ *pl.* وُكُورٌ *and* أَوْكَارٌ. An auger, بَيْرَمٌ ـ مِثْقَبٌ.

Terrific, *a.* *See* Terrible, Dreadful, Horrible, *a.*

Terrify, *v.t.* أَدْهَشَ ـ دَهَّشَ ـ رَعَّبَ ـ أَرْعَبَ ـ أَرْعَدَ ـ هَوَّلَ ـ أَفْزَعَ ـ خَوَّفَ. To be terrified, ٱرْتَعَبَ ـ ٱهْتَالَ ـ تَفَزَّعَ ـ تَخَوَّفَ ـ دَهِشَ ـ رَعِبَ. By way of terrifying them, تَخْوِيفًا لَهُمْ. Terrified greatly, مَخْلُوعٌ.

Territorial, *a.* Pertaining to territory, مُتَعَلِّقٌ بِٱلْأَرَاضِي ـ أَرْضِيٌّ. Territorial property, أَمْلَاكٌ وَعَقَارَاتٌ. Territorial rights, حُقُوقٌ مُلْكِيَّةٌ. Limited, مَحْدُودٌ.

Territorially, *ad.* مِنْ جِهَةِ ٱلْأَرَاضِي وَٱلْأَمْلَاكِ.

Territory, *n.* Of a state, حُدُودُ حُكُومَةٍ ـ دَائِرَةُ حُكُومَةٍ ـ مَمَالِكُ دَوْلَةٍ. Land, districts, أَرْضٌ *pl.* أَرَاضِي ـ دِيَارٌ. A piece of —, بُقْعَةٌ *pl.* بُقَعٌ. To have or to get possession of —, حَازَ ٱلْأَرْضَ *aor.* يَحُوزُ. He took possession of a slice of —, حَازَ بُقْعَةً مِنَ ٱلْأَرْضِ ². Cession of —, تَسْلِيمُ (or تَرْكُ) ٱلْأَرَاضِي.

Terror, *n.* خَوْفٌ عَظِيمٌ ـ فَزَعٌ ـ رُعْبٌ ـ دَهَشٌ ـ هَوْلٌ. The king of terrors, مَلِكُ ٱلْمَوْتِ. A reign of —, أَيَّامُ ظُلْمٍ وَخَوْفٍ ـ مُدَّةُ دَهْشَةٍ عُمُومِيَّةٍ. It was a — to them, كَانَ رُعْبًا لَهُمْ.

Terrorism, *n.* The state of being terrified, حَالَةُ ٱلدَّهَشِ; a state of inspiring —, حَالَةٌ مُهَوِّلَةٌ (or مُرْعِبَةٌ) ـ حَالُ ٱلتَّخْوِيفِ.

Terrorist, *n.* *See* Coward, *n.*

Terrorless, *a.* غَيْرُ خَائِفٍ ـ غَيْرُ مَدْهُوشٍ ـ غَيْرُ فَازِعٍ (or فَزِعٍ).

Terror-smitten, *a.*
Terror-struck, } مَدْهُوشٌ ـ رَعِيبٌ ـ مُنْهَالٌ.

Terse, *a.* Of style, مُعَبِّرٌ ـ مُحَذَّفٌ ـ مَضْبُوطٌ. A man of — speech, رَجُلٌ مُحَذَّفُ ٱلْكَلَامِ ـ رَجُلٌ مُحَذِّفَةُ ٱلْكَلَامِ. *See also* Concise, Polished, *a.*

Tersely, *ad.* بِتَحْذِيفِ ٱلْكَلَامِ ـ بِكَلَامٍ وَجِيزٍ ـ بِطَلَاوَةٍ وَٱخْتِصَارٍ ـ بِدُونِ مُبَالَغَةٍ فِي ٱلْكَلَامِ.

Terseness, *n.* تَحْذِيفُ ٱلْكَلَامِ ـ إِيجَازٌ وَطَلَاوَةٌ ـ ضَبْطُ ٱلْكَلَامِ ـ تَعْبِيرُ ٱلْكَلَامِ.

Tertian, *a.* ثُلَاثِيٌّ. A — ague, حُمَّى غِبٌّ ـ حُمَّى ٱلْغِبِّ ـ سُخُونَةٌ مُثَلَّثَةٌ ـ حُمَّى ٱلثِّلْثِ.

Tertiary, *a.* Third, ثَالِثٌ ـ ثُلَاثِيٌّ. Tertiary system, in geology, ٱلطَّبَقَةُ ٱلثَّالِثَةُ مِنْ طَبَقَاتِ ٱلْأَرْضِ وَهِيَ ٱلسَّطْحِيَّةُ.

Tesselar, *a.* Formed in squares, عَلَى أَشْكَالٍ مُرَبَّعَةٍ هَنْدَسِيَّةٍ ـ فِي شَكْلِ ٱلْفُسَيْفِسَةِ.

Tesselate, *v.t.* To cut in squares, فَصَّلَ أَشْكَالًا مُرَبَّعَةً. To lay with checkered work, زَوَّقَ بِٱلْفُسَيْفِسَةِ.

Tesselated, *a.* مُزَوَّقٌ بِٱلْفُسَيْفِسَةِ ـ مُعَيَّنٌ. Tesselated work, بَلَاطٌ مُبَلَّطٌ عَلَى أَشْكَالٍ هَنْدَسِيَّةٍ. A — pavement, فُسَيْفِسَةٌ.

Tesselation, *n.* The act of, تَزْوِيقٌ بِأَشْكَالٍ مُرَبَّعَةٍ هَنْدَسِيَّةٍ.

Tesselated work; *see preceding article.*

Tessular, *a.* Cubical, كَعْبِيٌّ.

Test, *n.* Trial, خُبْرٌ ـ خِبْرَةٌ ـ تَجْرِبَةٌ ـ ٱمْتِحَانٌ ـ إِتْقَانٌ. That by which anything is tested, مِعْيَارٌ. A — or touchstone, مِحَكٌّ ـ فَتَّانِيَّةٌ. Test, by which one is tried, مِحْنَةٌ *pl.* مِحَنٌ. To be brought to the —, أُمْتُحِنَ. To stand the —, صَحَّ ². To try by —, إِخْتَبَرَ. The — verified the information, صَدَّقَ ٱلْخُبْرُ ٱلْخَبَرَ.

Test, *v.t.* To try, prove, جَرَّبَ ـ ٱمْتَحَنَ ـ مَحَنَ ². To try by —, إِخْتَبَرَ. To assay, عَايَرَ. To —, by biting with the teeth, عَجَمَ ² ـ ضَرَسَ ²; by striking against the teeth, as of an egg, *etc.*, شَامَ ². To probe, سَبَرَ ² ـ إِسْتَبَرَ. To — the knowledge of one, ضَرَّسَ.

Testable, *a.* ٱلْإِيصَاءُ بِهِ جَائِزٌ ـ يُوصَى بِهِ.

Testacea, *n.* ٱلْحَيَوَانَاتُ ٱلصَّدَفِيَّةُ ـ ٱلْحَيَوَانَاتُ ذَاتُ صَدَفٍ.

Testaceous, *a.* أَبُو بَاغَا ـ ذُو صَدَفٍ ـ صَدَفِيٌّ.

Testament, *n.* A will, وَصِيَّةٌ *pl.* وَصَايَا. A covenant, عَهْدٌ *pl.* عُهُودٌ. *See also* Will, *n.*

The New Testament, ٱلْعَهْدُ ٱلْجَدِيدُ ـ شَرِيعَةُ سَيِّدِنَا عِيسَى.

The Old Testament, ٱلْعَهْدُ ٱلْعَتِيقُ ـ شَرِيعَةُ حَضْرَةِ مُوسَى.

Testamentary, *a.* مُتَعَلِّقٌ بِٱلْوَصِيَّةِ.

Testate, *a.* مُوْصٍ.

Testator, *n.* مُوْصٍ – وَصِيٌّ *pl.* أَوْصِيَآءُ (the last means also the inheritor and the administrator under a will).

Testatrix, *n.* إِمْرَأَةٌ مُوْصِيَةٌ.

Tester, *n.* Of a bed, مِظَلَّةُ سَرِيرٍ – بَشْخَانَةُ ٱلتَّخْتِ. A sixpenny-piece, سِكَّةُ نِصْفِ شِيلِينٍ.

Testicle, *n.* خُصْيَةٌ *dual* خُصْيَانِ *and* خُصْيَتَانِ *pl.* خُصًى – بَيْضَةٌ *pl.* بَيْضَانٌ. The two testicles, الأُنْثَيَانِ – العُنَادِلاَنِ – الخُصْيَانِ. Having large testicles, آدَرُ. Having one — larger than the other, أَشْرَجُ. Having inflation of the testicles, أَنْفَخُ.

Testification, *n.* شَهَادَةٌ.

Testify, *v.t.* To attest, شَهِدَ بـ. To — in favour of, شَهِدَ لـ; to — against, شَهِدَ عَلَى. To certify, حَقَّقَ – نَعِمَ بـ. To manifest, أَظْهَرَ – بَيَّنَ – أَبْدَى. To be testified of, to have the testimony of, شُهِدَ لـ. *See also to* Witness, *v.t.*

Testify, *v.i.* شَهِدَ.

Testily, *ad.* بِوَعْقَةٍ – بِشَرَاسَةٍ – بِشَكَاسَةٍ.

Testimonial, *n.* A certificate of character, وَرَقَةُ شَهَادَةٍ. A memorial of esteem, تَذْكِرَةُ ٱعْتِبَارٍ. He possesses respectable testimonials of his proficiency in this art, حَائِزُ ٱلشَّهَادَةِ ٱلْمُعْتَبَرَةِ فِي هٰذَا ٱلْفَنِّ.

Testimony, *n.* Evidence of a witness, شَهَادَةٌ. Attestation, affirmation, إِثْبَاتٌ – إِقْرَارٌ. Proof, بُرْهَانٌ. A statute or religious ordinance, فَرِيضَةٌ *pl.* فَرَائِضُ. Anything quoted in testimony of something else, إِسْنَادٌ *pl.* أَسَانِيدُ; to refer to, in that sense, as a —, or proof, أَسْنَدَ إِلَى. The — of conscience, شَهَادَةُ ٱلضَّمِيرِ. To give — to, شَهِدَ لـ. His — was confirmed, ثُبِّتَتْ شَهَادَتُهُ. "We bear testimony that thou art indeed the apostle of God," نَشْهَدُ إِنَّكَ لَرَسُولُ ٱللّٰهِ (Kur. lxiii. 1).

Testiness, *n.* وَعْقَةٌ – شَكَاسَةٌ – شَرَاسَةٌ.

Testing, *n.* تَجْرِيبٌ – إِخْتِبَارٌ – إِمْتِحَانٌ.

Testudinal, *a.* سُلَحْفِيٌّ – مُتَعَلِّقٌ بِٱلسُّلَحْفَةِ.

Testudo, *n.* A tortoise, سُلَحْفَةٌ *pl.* سَلَاحِفُ. The warlike machine so called, دَرَّاجَةٌ – دَبَّابَةٌ – صُبُورٌ – ضَمٌّ – قَبْوٌ – قَلْعٌ.

Testy, *a.* وَعِقٌ – شَرِسٌ – شَكِسٌ. To be —, شَرِسَ – شَكُسَ – وَعِقَ *aor.* يَعْقُ. To be — with, شَارَسَ – شَاكَسَ.

Tetanus, *n.* لَقْوَةٌ. To strike with —, لَقِيَ.

Tête-à-tête, *ad.* مِنْ رَأْسٍ لِرَأْسٍ. To be — with, خَلَا مَعَ فُلَانٍ: They were — together, of two, خَلَوَا بِبَعْضِهِمَا.

Tether, *n.* A rope to tie a beast with, طِوَلَةٌ *pl.* طِوَلٌ – طِوَلٌ – آخِيَّةٌ *pl.* أَوَاخِيُّ – شُكُلٌ *pl.* شُكَالٌ – عِقَالٌ. He lengthened his —, left him to his own course, أَرْخَى لَهُ ٱلطِّوَلَ. He loosened the — of the horse, أَطَالَ لِلْفَرَسِ ٱلطِّوَلَ – طَوَّلَ لِلْفَرَسِ.

Tether, *v.t.* رَبَطَ – أَخَّى – رَبَطَ لـ ٱلطِّوَلَ. *See also to* Restrain, *v.t.*

Tetragon, *n.* شَكْلٌ ذُو أَرْبَعَةِ أَضْلَاعٍ.

Tetragonal, *a.* ذُو أَرْبَعَةِ أَضْلَاعٍ.

Tetrahedral, *a.* ذُو أَرْبَعَةِ سُطُوحٍ.

Tetrahedron, *n.* شَكْلٌ ذُو مُثَلَّثَاتٍ مُتَسَاوِيَةٍ.

Tetrameter, *n.* بَيْتٌ ذُو أَرْبَعَةِ تَفَاعِيلَ.

Tetrapetalous, *a.* ذُو أَرْبَعِ وُرَيْقَاتٍ.

Tetraphyllous, *a.* ذُو أَرْبَعِ أَوْرَاقٍ.

Tetrarch, *n.* وَالٍ *pl.* وُلَاةٌ.

Tetrarchate, *n.* } إِيَالَةٌ – وِلَايَةٌ.
Tetrarchy, }

Tetrastich, *n.* شِعْرٌ رُبَاعِيٌّ.

Tetrastyle, *n.* بِنَآءٌ فِي وَاجِهَتِهِ أَرْبَعَةُ أَعْمِدَةٍ.

Tetrasyllabic, *a.* ذُو أَرْبَعِ هِجَاءَاتٍ – ذُو أَرْبَعِ حَرَكَاتٍ.

Tetrasyllable, *n.* كَلِمَةٌ مُرَكَّبَةٌ مِنْ أَرْبَعِ حَرَكَاتٍ.

Tetter, *n.* هَرَصٌ – قُوبَآءُ *pl.* قَوَابِي – جُذَامٌ. To have —, هَرِصَ – أُصِيبَ بِٱلْقُوبَآءِ – هَرِضَ.

Teutonic, *a.* عِبَارَةٌ عَمَّا يَتَعَلَّقُ بِٱلنَّمْسَاوِيِّينَ ٱلْأَقْدَمِينَ.

Tewel, *n.* A funnel, chimney, مِدْخَنَةٌ – دَاخِنَةٌ. An iron pipe, قَنَاةٌ مِنْ حَدِيدٍ.

Text, *n.* A subject, as of a discourse, مَحَطٌّ – مَوْضُوعٌ – مَتْنٌ *pl.* مُتُونٌ – عِبَارَةٌ. Text, the exact words of an author, نَصٌّ *pl.* نُصُوصٌ. The — of a book, مَتْنُ كِتَابٍ *pl.* مُتُونٌ – عَمُودُ كِتَابٍ: It is mentioned in the — of the, هُوَ مَذْكُورٌ فِي عَمُودِ ٱلْكِتَابِ. Handwriting, خَطٌّ. It is not in the — of the treaty, غَيْرُ مَنْصُوصٍ عَلَيْهِ فِي ٱلْمُعَاهَدَةِ. Those reforms which are not set down in the — of this treaty, تِلْكَ ٱلنِّظَامَاتُ ٱلَّتِي لَمْ يُنَصَّ عَلَيْهَا فِي هٰذِهِ ٱلْمُعَاهَدَةِ. (*For different kind of texts, or writing, see under* Hand, *n.*)

Text-book, *n.* دُسْتُورٌ – كِتَابٌ كُلِّيَّاتٍ – كِتَابُ ٱلنُّصُوصِ.

Text-hand, *n.* خَطٌّ نَسْخٌ.

Textile, *a.* مَنْسُوجٌ. Textile fabric, نَسِيجَةٌ *pl.* نَسَائِجُ.

Textorial, *a.* } مُتَعَلِّقٌ بِٱلنَّسْجِ.
Textrine, }

Textual, *a.* نَصِّيٌّ – مَذْكُورٌ فِي عَمُودِ ٱلْكِتَابِ.

Textuarist, *n.* }
Textuary, } مَاهِرٌ فِي ٱلنَّصِّ .

Texture, *n.* As of cloth, نَسْجٌ . The web that is woven, نَسِيجَةٌ *pl.* نَسَائِجُ . Of good —, جَيِّدُ ٱلنَّسْجِ . Of close —, سَفِيقُ ٱلنَّسْجِ . Of loose —, سَخِيفُ (or خَفِيفُ) ٱلنَّسْجِ ـ رَكِيكُ ٱلنَّسْجِ . Complexion, temper, خِلْقَةٌ ـ طَبْعٌ . Aggregate of form, حِلْيَةٌ .

Thaler, *n.* رِيَالٌ نَمْسَاوِيٌّ .

Thallium, *n.* ثَالِيُومٌ وَهُوَ ضَرْبٌ مِنَ ٱلْمَعَادِنِ .

Than, *n. ad.* or *conj.* مِن ـ عَن : Ahmad is taller — Muhammad, أَحْمَدُ أَطْوَلُ مِنْ مُحَمَّدٍ . He is prettier — his sister, هُوَ أَجْمَلُ مِنْ أُخْتِهِ . It is better for thee to be poor and happy — to be rich and miserable, خَيْرٌ لَكَ أَنْ تَكُونَ فَقِيرًا مَغْبُوطًا مِنْ أَنْ تَكُونَ غَنِيًّا شَقِيًّا . Rather — that . . . , أَحْرَى مِنْ أَنْ ـ قَبْلَ أَنْ . More — once, أَكْثَرَ مِنْ مَرَّةٍ وَاحِدَةٍ . He is worse, in health, — he was yesterday, هُوَ أَرْدَأُ مِزَاجًا مِمَّا كَانَ أَمْسِ .

Thane, *n.* *See* Baron, *n.*

Thanedom, *n.* *See* Baronetcy, *n.*

Thank, *v.t.* ²شَكَرَ ـ ²شَكَرَ لِ ـ ²شَكَرَ إِلَى ـ تَشَكَّرَ لِ . To —, in a polite way, and as a compliment, إِسْتَكْثَرَ خَيْرَهُ . To — one for, شَكَرَ فَضْلَ ـ عَلَى ـ ²شَكَرَ ـ عَلَى . No, I — you, لَا وَعِشْتَ . Thank you, كَثَّرَ ٱللّٰهُ خَيْرَكَ . We — you for having come, نَشْكُرُ فَضْلَكَ عَلَى مَجِيئِكَ . God be thanked for his deed, الشُّكْرُ لِلّٰهِ عَلَى أَعْمَالِهِ ـ لِلّٰهِ دَرُّهُ . (For to —, in the sense of to Praise, *see to* Praise, *v.t.*)

Thankful, *a.* شَكُور ـ شَاكِر ـ شَاكِرُ ٱلنِّعْمَةِ ـ مُتَشَكِّر . If you prosper you ought to be —, إِنْ تَوَفَّقْتَ وَجَبَ عَلَيْكَ ٱلشُّكْرُ . To show one's self — to, شَاكَرَ . To be —, كَانَ شَكُورًا .

Thankfully, *ad.* مَعَ ٱلشُّكْرِ ـ بِٱلتَّشَكُّرِ . *See also* Gratefully, *ad.*

Thankfulness, *n.* شُكْرُ ٱلْإِحْسَانِ ـ شُكْرَانُ ٱلنِّعْمَةِ ـ تَشَكُّر ـ شُكْرَان . We receive that with all —, نَقْبَلُ ذٰلِكَ بِكُلِّ شُكْرٍ .

Thankless, *a.* Ungrateful, نَاكِرُ ٱلْمَعْرُوفِ ـ نَاكِرُ ٱلْإِحْسَانِ ـ كَنَّاد . Not gaining thanks, ill-requited, غَيْرُ مُثَوَّبٍ ـ غَيْرُ مُثَابٍ ـ غَيْرُ مُكَافَى . To be —, ²كَنَدَ .

Thanklessly, *ad.* Ungratefully, بِإِنْكَارِ ٱلْمَعْرُوفِ . Without requital, بِغَيْرِ ٱعْتِبَارٍ ـ بِغَيْرِ مُكَافَاةٍ ـ بِغَيْرِ مَثُوبَةٍ ـ بِعَدَمِ ثَوَابٍ .

Thanklessness, *n.* Ingratitude, كُفْرُ ٱلنِّعْمَةِ ـ إِنْكَارُ ٱلْمَعْرُوفِ . Failure to acknowledge a kindness, absence of requital, عَدَمُ عَدَمُ ٱعْتِبَارٍ ـ عَدَمُ مُكَافَاةٍ ـ ثَوَابٍ .

Thank-offering, *n.* In a religious sense, قُرْبَانُ شُكْرٍ *pl.* قَرَابِينُ . An offering of gratitude, هَدِيَّةُ تَشَكُّرٍ *pl.* هَدَايَا .

Thanks, *n. pl.* تَشَكُّر ـ شُكْر . Thanks! (I thank you,) أَشْكُرُ فَضْلَكُمْ . Present my best — to your father, خُصَّ أَبَاكَ عَنِّي بِشُكْرٍ جَزِيلٍ . He prayed and gave — (in a religious sense), صَلَّى وَحَمِدَ . It called forth the — of the assembly, إِسْتَوْجَبَ شُكْرَ ٱلْجَمَاعَةِ . *See also* Praise, *n.*

Thanksgiver, *n.* شَاكِر *pl.* شَاكِرُون ـ شَاكِرُ ٱلنِّعَمِ .

Thanksgiving, *n.* تَشَكُّر . A — service; *see under* Te Deum, *n.* *See also* Praise, *n.*

Thankworthy, *a.* مُسْتَحِقُّ ٱلشُّكْرِ . It is — if you bear troubles patiently, هُوَ فَضْلٌ إِنْ صَبَرْتُمْ عَلَى ٱلْمَصَائِبِ .

That, *pron. or adj.* *As a demonstrative,* ذٰلِكَ ـ هٰذَاكَ ـ ذَاكَ *fem.* تِلْكَ or تَالِكَ : That man, ذٰلِكَ ٱلرَّجُلُ ; that woman, تِلْكَ ٱلْمَرْأَةُ ; that book, ذٰلِكَ ٱلْكِتَابُ . *As a relative,* he that, he who, or that which, ٱلَّذِي *fem.* ٱلَّتِي ـ مَا : The man is happy that, who, lives virtuously, سَعِدَ ٱلْإِنْسَانُ ٱلَّذِي يَعِيشُ بِٱلتَّقْوَى . The thing that I wanted, الشَّيْءُ ٱلَّذِي ٱحْتَجْتُ إِلَيْهِ . What is it that thou seest? مَا ذَا رَأَيْتَ ـ مَا ٱلَّذِي رَأَيْتَهُ . Who is it that has come? مَنْ ذَا ٱلَّذِي جَاءَ . That which you have is better, مَا عِنْدَكُمْ أَخْيَرُ . The best that can be, الأَحْسَنُ مَا يَكُونُ . That, *also as a relative,* who or which, مَنْ, *expressible also through the verb, and otherwise :*—He that acts wisely deserves praise, مَنْ يَعْمَلْ بِحِكْمَةٍ يَسْتَوْجِبِ ٱلثَّنَاءَ . Modesty is a quality that highly adorns a woman, إِنَّمَا ٱلْحِشْمَةُ صِفَةٌ تُزَيِّنُ ٱلْمَرْأَةَ أَجَلَّ زِينَةٍ . In that he did this he did it for your sake, إِنَّهُ إِذْ فَعَلَ هٰذَا إِنَّمَا فَعَلَهُ لِأَجْلِكَ .

For all that, nevertheless, لٰكِن ـ مَعَ ذٰلِكَ ـ مَعَ أَنَّ .

That is to say, مَعْنَاتُهُ ـ يَعْنِي بِذٰلِكَ .

Upon that, thereupon, عِنْدَ ذٰلِكَ ـ ثُمَّ .

What of that? وَبَعْدَهُ ـ وَبَعْدَ ذٰلِكَ ـ ثُمَّ ـ وَبَعْدُ .

What is that to you? فَمَا ذَا يَخُصُّكَ ذٰلِكَ ـ فَمَا ذَا لَكَ .

That, *conj.* أَنْ . I desire that you should stand, أُرِيدُ أَنْ تَقُومَ . And that ye should fast is better for you, وَأَنْ تَصُومُوا أَخْيَرُ لَكُمْ . I heard that you were in the house, بَلَغَنِي أَنَّكَ فِي ٱلدَّارِ . There is no doubt that it is so, لَا شَكَّ أَنَّهُ كَذَا . That, *in conjunction with the negative,* أَنْ لَا : I made a sign to him as much as to say, Do not do that, أَشَرْتُ إِلَيْهِ أَنْ لَا يَفْعَلْ كَذَا . Were it not that I feared him, لَوْ لَمْ أَخَفْ مِنْهُ . It may be that it is so, لَعَلَّهُ كَذَا ; it may be that you are ailing, لَعَلَّكَ عَلِيلٌ . In order that, حَتَّى ـ لِكَيْ ـ كَيْ : I have told you of this that you may believe, قَدْ كَلَّمْتُكُمْ بِهٰذَا لِكَيْ تُؤْمِنُونَ . There is nothing better than that a man should do good in his life, لَيْسَ لِلْإِنْسَانِ خَيْرٌ إِلَّا أَنْ يَفْعَلَ خَيْرًا فِي حَيَاتِهِ.

Thatch, *n.* غِمَآء — غَمًى.

Thatch, *v.t.* غَمَا [2] — غَمَّى.

Thatched, *a.* مُغَمًّى. A roof, غَمًى *pl.* أَغْمَآء.

Thatcher, *n.* مُغَمِّي ٱلْبُيُوتِ — مُغَمٍّ.

Thaumaturgic, *n.* Of wonders, مُتَعَلِّقٌ بِٱلْمُعْجِزَاتِ. Exciting wonder, مُعْجِب — مُعَجِّب.

Thaumaturgist, *n.* صَانِعُ ٱلْعَجَائِبِ — صَانِعُ ٱلْمُعْجِزَاتِ.

Thaumaturgy, *n.* صُنْعُ ٱلْعَجَائِبِ — صُنْعُ ٱلْمُعْجِزَاتِ.

Thaw, *v.t.* To cause to melt, ذَوَّبَ — أَذَابَ. To break up, of ice, كَسَّرَ ٱلْجَمَدَ. To — the heart, أَذَابَ ٱلْقَلْبَ.

Thaw, *v.i.* To melt, تَذَوَّبَ — ذَابَ [2]. To break up, of ice, تَكَسَّرَ ٱلْجَمَدُ. To be softened, of the heart, رَقَّ قَلْبُهُ [2] — تَلَيَّنَ.

Thaw, *n.* Dissolution of frost, تَكَسُّرُ ٱلْجَمَدِ. Liquefaction of snow, ذَوَبَانُ ٱلثَّلْجِ.

The, *def. art.* أَلْ. The servant of a merchant, خَدَّامُ تَاجِرٍ. I am the man, أَنَا هُوَ ٱلرَّجُلُ. An hour before the time, قَبْلَ ٱلْوَقْتِ بِسَاعَةٍ. The child and the father, الْوَلَدُ وَٱلْوَالِدُ. He went to the governor, ذَهَبَ إِلَى ٱلْحَاكِمِ [2]. Bring a plate and the knife, هَاتِ صَحْنًا وَٱلسِّكِّينَ.

Theatre, *n.* A place of assembly, مَشْهَد *pl.* مَشَاهِدُ — مَشْهَدَة. An open space, as for play, sports, *etc.*, عَرْصَة *pl.* أَعْرَاص — مَلْعَب *pl.* مَلَاعِبُ. A sphere, as for the display of one's talents, *etc.*, مَيْدَان. A place where anything has occurred, مَوْقِع. A —, or place of theatrical entertainments, مَرْسَحُ ٱللَّعْبِ *pl.* مَرَاسِحُ — مَلْعَبُ ٱلتَّقْلِيدِ *pl.* مَلَاعِبُ — تِيَاتْرُو.

Theatrical, *a.* مُتَعَلِّقٌ بِٱلتِّيَاتْرُو (or بِلَعْبِ ٱلتَّقْلِيدِ). A — composition, تَأْلِيفٌ لِلتِّيَاتْرُو. There was a — performance in the theatre, قَدْ تَشَخَّصَتْ رِوَايَةٌ فِي مَرْسَحِ ٱللَّعْبِ.

Theatrically, *ad.* عَلَى طَرْزِ ٱلتِّيَاتْرُو. Mimically, تَقْلِيدًا — تَهْرِيجًا — تَشْخِيصًا.

Theatricals, *n.* Theatrical performances, إِجْرَآءُ ٱلرِّوَايَا بِٱلتَّشْخِيصِ فِي ٱلْمَرْسَحِ — لَعْبُ ٱلتِّيَاتْرُو. Theatrical dresses, أَلْبِسَةُ لَعَّابِي ٱلتِّيَاتْرُو (or ٱلْمَرْسَحِ).

Thee, *pron.*, *object. case of* Thou, كَ *fem.* كِ: I will not let — (*masc.*) go, لَا أُطْلِقُكَ *fem.* لَا أُطْلِقُكِ. Thee we worship, and of Thee we seek assistance, إِيَّاكَ نَعْبُدُ وَإِيَّاكَ نَسْتَعِينُ.

Thee and Thou, *v.i.* To use these pronouns in conversation, إِسْتَعْمَلَ لَفْظَةَ أَنْتَ فِي ٱلْمُخَاطَبَةِ. He thee'd and thou'd him, كَلَّمَهُ بِضَمِيرِ ٱلْمُخَاطَبِ ٱلْمُفْرَدِ.

Theft, *n.* Stealing, سَرِق — سَرِقَة — سَرْقَة. A secret —, سَلَّة. Something stolen, سُرَاقَة — سَرِقَة. The — was found in his hand, وُجِدَتِ ٱلسَّرِقَةُ فِي يَدِهِ.

Theine, *n.* The principle of tea, خُلَاصَةُ ٱلشَّاي — أُسُّ ٱلشَّاي.

Their, *poss. pron.*, As in termination, هُمْ *fem.* هُنَّ — *vulg.* بِتَاعْهُمْ. Their (*masc.*) book, كِتَابُهُمْ *fem.* كِتَابُهُنَّ.

Theism, *n.* الْإِيمَانُ بِإِلٰهٍ وَاحِدٍ.

Theist, *n.* مُؤْمِنٌ بِإِلٰهٍ وَاحِدٍ.

Theistic, *a.* }
Theistical, } مُتَعَلِّقٌ بِٱلْإِيمَانِ بِإِلٰهٍ وَاحِدٍ — حَسَبَ مَذْهَبِ ٱلْمُؤْمِنِينَ بِإِلٰهٍ وَاحِدٍ.

Them, *pers. pron.* As in construction, هُمْ *fem.* هُنَّ: He killed them, قَتَلَهُمْ *fem.* قَتَلَهُنَّ.

Theme, *n.* A subject, topic, مَحَطّ — مَبْحُوثٌ عَنْهُ — مَوْضُوع *pl.* مَوْضُوعَات — بَاب *pl.* أَبْوَاب. A lesson, something given one to learn, or to write about, مَقَالَة. A — propounded, a question, مَسْأَلَة *pl.* مَسَائِلُ.

Themselves, *pers. pron.* هُمْ *fem.* هُنَّ — هُمْ أَنْفُسُهُمْ *fem.* هُنَّ أَنْفُسُهُنَّ. They — know, يَعْرِفُونَ (or هُمْ أَنْفُسُهُمْ) *fem.* يَعْرِفْنَ (or هُنَّ أَنْفُسُهُنَّ). For or to —, لِأَنْفُسِهِمْ *fem.* لِأَنْفُسِهِنَّ: they (*masc.*) kept it to or for —, حَفِظُوهُ لِأَنْفُسِهِمْ. Of —, of their own free will, مِنْ تِلْقَآءِ أَنْفُسِهِمْ *fem.* مِنْ تِلْقَآءِ أَنْفُسِهِنَّ. One of —, (*masc.*) وَاحِدٌ مِنْهُمْ. They laid the meat before them by —, (*masc.*) قَدَّمُوا لَهُمُ ٱلطَّعَامَ وَحْدَهُمْ. They — did not enter into the house, هُمْ لَمْ يَدْخُلُوا إِلَى ٱلْبَيْتِ. They trusted in —, إِتَّثَقُوا بِأَنْفُسِهِمْ. They went apart from thence by —, إِنْصَرَفُوا مِنْ هُنَاكَ مُنْفَرِدِينَ.

Then, *ad.* At that time, عِنْدَ ذٰلِكَ — إِذْ ذَاكَ — سَاعَتَئِذٍ — حِينَئِذٍ; then, at that day, يَوْمَئِذٍ. Then, afterwards, ثُمَّ — بَعْدُ — غِبَّ. Now and —, أَحْيَانًا — بَعْضَ أَوْقَاتٍ — بَعْضَ ٱلْمِرَارِ. Lo! then, فَإِذَا. I went forth, and, lo! in that place, or then, Zaid was sitting, خَرَجْتُ فَإِذَا زَيْدٌ جَالِسٌ. He was — a boy, كَانَ إِذْ ذَاكَ صَبِيًّا. Then, in that case, فَإِذًا. Then, in that case, I deem thee veracious, إِذًا أَظُنُّكَ صَادِقًا. So then, in like manner, كَذٰلِكَ. What is it, then? فَمَا هُوَ إِذًا. What shall I say, then? فَمَاذَا أَقُولُ إِذًا. Then I shall not be ashamed when I have attended to all he ordered me, حِينَئِذٍ لَا أَخْزَى إِذَا نَظَرْتُ إِلَى كُلِّمَا وَصَّانِي بِهِ.

Thence, *ad.* From that place, مِنْ هُنَاكَ; from that time, or for that reason, مِنْ ثَمَّ.

Thenceforth, *ad.* }
Thenceforward, } مِنْ يَوْمِهِ — مِنْ بَعْدُ — فِيمَا بَعْدُ.

Theocracy, *n.* حُكْمٌ قَائِمٌ بِأَمْرِ ٱللّٰهِ مُوحًى بِهِ إِلَى شَخْصٍ أَوْ أَشْخَاصٍ كَثِيرِينَ.

Theocratic, *a.* عِبَارَةٌ عَنِ ٱلْحُكُومَةِ ٱلْمَذْكُورَةِ آنِفًا.

Theodolite, *n.* آلَةٌ لِلْمَسَاحَةِ ـ آلَةُ ٱلْمَسَاحَةِ.

Theogony, *n.* The generation of heathen deities, نَسْلُ ٱلْآلِهَةِ.

Theologaster, *n.* عُوَيْرِفٌ بِعِلْمِ ٱلْكَلَامِ.

Theologian, *n.* مُعَلِّمٌ ـ عَالِمٌ بِٱللَّاهُوتِ ـ عَارِفٌ بِعِلْمِ ٱلْكَلَامِ فِي عِلْمِ ٱللَّاهُوتِ.

Theological, *a.* لَاهُوتِيٌّ ـ مُتَعَلِّقٌ بِعِلْمِ ٱلْكَلَامِ.

Theologically, *ad.* حَسَبَ أُصُولِ ـ نَظَرًا لِقَوَاعِدِ عِلْمِ ٱلْكَلَامِ ٱللَّاهُوتِ.

Theologist, *n.* *See* Theologian, *n.*

Theology, *n.* عِلْمُ ٱلْإِلٰهِيَّاتِ ـ عِلْمُ أُصُولِ ٱلدِّينِ ـ عِلْمُ ٱلْكَلَامِ ـ عِلْمُ ٱللَّاهُوتِ.

Theomachy, *n.* قِتَالُ ٱلْجَبَابِرَةِ.

Theopathy, *n.* ٱلسُّرُّ ٱلرَّبَّانِيُّ.

Theo-philanthropist, *n.* مُحِبُّ ٱللّٰهِ وَٱلْبَشَرِ.

Theopneusty, *n.* *See* Inspiration, (Divine,) *n.*

Theorem, *n.* أَمْرٌ نَظَرِيٌّ ـ قَضِيَّةٌ *pl.* قَضَايَا ـ مَوْضُوعٌ.

Theorematic, *a.* }
Theoremic, } نَظَرِيٌّ ـ عِلْمِيٌّ.

Theoretic, *a.* }
Theoretical, } Scientific, عِلْمِيٌّ. Speculative, نَظَرِيٌّ. Ideal, تَصَوُّرِيٌّ ـ وَهْمِيٌّ ـ خَيَالِيٌّ.

Theoretically, *ad.* Scientifically, حَسَبَ أُصُولِ ٱلْعِلْمِ ـ عِلْمًا. Speculatively, نَظَرًا لِلْعِلْمِ ـ عِلْمًا. Ideally, تَخَيُّلًا ـ تَخْيِيلًا ـ وَهْمًا. *See also* Speculatively, *ad.*

Theorist, *n.* }
Theorizer, } One who forms a theory, an inventor, مُخْتَرِعٌ ـ مُبْدِعٌ ـ مُوجِدٌ. A speculator, عِلْمِيٌّ *pl.* عِلْمِيَّةٌ ـ نَظَرِيٌّ *pl.* نَظَرِيَّةٌ. The theorists, أَصْحَابُ ٱلرَّأْيِ.

Theorize, *v.i.* To speculate, خَاضَ فِي ٱلْآرَاءِ ² ـ أَخَاضَ ٱلْآرَاءَ. To — about, نَظَرَ فِي ².

Theory, *n.* Science, as distinguished from practice, عِلْمٌ. The principles of a science, أُصُولُ عِلْمٍ. Speculation, as of the imagination, تَصَوُّرٌ ـ تَخَيُّلٌ. Knowledge without practice, عِلْمٌ بِلَا عَمَلٍ ـ عِلْمٌ نَظَرِيٌّ.

Theosophical, *a.* صُوفِيٌّ.

Theosophism, *n.* ٱلصُّوفِيَّةُ.

Theosophist, *n.* صُوفِيٌّ *pl.* صُوفِيَّةٌ.

Theosophy, *n.* ٱلصُّوفِيَّةُ.

Therapeutic, *a.* طِبِّيٌّ.

Therapeutics, *n.* ٱلْأُصُولُ ٱلطِّبِّيَّةُ ـ عِلْمُ ٱلطِّبِّ ـ عِلْمٌ يُبْحَثُ فِيهِ عَنِ ٱلْأَمْرَاضِ وَحِفْظِ ٱلصِّحَّةِ.

There, *ad.* At that place, ثَمَّ ـ هُنَالِكَ ـ هُنَاكَ. There where, حَيْثُ : Stand thou there where Zaid shall stand, قُمْ حَيْثُ يَقُومُ زَيْدٌ. There, in the sense of lo! فَإِذَا (*see under* Then, *ad.*). Were you — last week? أَكُنْتَ هُنَاكَ فِي ٱلْأُسْبُوعِ ٱلْمَاضِي. He shall not be —, لَا يَكُونُ هُنَاكَ. There was a man whose name was Ahmad, كَانَ إِنْسَانٌ ٱسْمُهُ أَحْمَدُ. There were none, لَمْ يَكُنْ شَيْءٌ. There has been no rain, مَا كَانَ مَطَرٌ. There will be no opportunity, لَا تَسْنَحُ فُرْصَةٌ. Here and —, هُنَا وَهُنَاكَ ـ فِي بَعْضِ مَحَلَّاتٍ. Down —, هُنَاكَ تَحْتُ. In —, فِي ٱلدَّاخِلِ. Out —, فِي ٱلْخَارِجِ. Up —, فَوْقُ. You are right —, صَدَقْتَ فِي ذٰلِكَ. There are people who think that I am he, مِنَ ٱلنَّاسِ مَنْ يَظُنُّ أَنِّي أَنَا هُوَ.

Thereabout, *ad.* }
Thereabouts, } Respecting which, فِي ذٰلِكَ. Near, as to a place, قَرِيبًا مِنْ ـ دُونَ ـ عِنْدَ. Nearly, تَقْرِيبًا مِنْ ـ تَقْرِيبًا.

Thereafter, *ad.* From that time, مِنْ ثَمَّ ـ فِيمَا بَعْدُ ـ غِبَّ ـ مِنْ يَوْمِهِ. Consequently, لِذٰلِكَ ـ فَإِذًا ـ مِنْ ثَمَّ.

Thereat, *ad.* Then, ثُمَّ. At that place, ثَمَّ ـ فِي ذٰلِكَ ٱلْمَوْضِعِ ـ هُنَاكَ. On that account, بِسَبَبِ ذٰلِكَ ـ لِذٰلِكَ ـ بِنَاءً عَلَى ذٰلِكَ.

Therefor, *ad.* لِذٰلِكَ ـ مِنْ أَجْلِ ذٰلِكَ.

Therefore, *ad.* بِنَاءً عَلَى ذٰلِكَ ـ عَلَى هٰذَا ٱلسِّيَاقِ ـ مِنْ ثَمَّ ـ فَإِذًا ـ عَلَى ذٰلِكَ ـ وَلِهٰذَا ـ مِنْ أَجْلِ ذٰلِكَ.

Therefrom, *ad.* From anything, عَنْ ـ مِنْ : Do not depart — either to the right hand or to the left, لَا تَحِيدُوا عَنْ ذٰلِكَ يَمِينًا أَوْ شِمَالًا.

Therein, *ad.* In that place, فِي ـ ثَمَّ ـ هُنَاكَ ـ هُنَالِكَ. In that matter, فِي تِلْكَ ٱلْمَادَّةِ ـ فِي ذٰلِكَ. Inside, فِي ٱلدَّاخِلِ ـ جَوًّا. And all that is —, وَكُلُّ مَا فِيهِ. He shall not enter —, لَنْ يَدْخُلَهُ ـ لَا يَدْخُلُ فِيهِ. I did not see — any person, لَمْ أَرَ فِيهِ شَخْصًا. To continue —, to hold to, ثَبَتَ فِي ـ أَصَبَّ عَلَى ².

Thereinto, *ad.* فِي ـ فِي دَاخِلِ : Let them not enter —, (of a town, مَدِينَةٌ, or any place designated by a feminine noun), فَلَا يَدْخُلُوهَا.

Thereof, *n.* مِنْ ـ فِي : In the day that you eat thereof, (the noun implied being feminine,) يَوْمَ تَأْكُلُ مِنْهَا. In the midst thereof, (the noun implied being masculine,) فِيهِ.

Thereon, *ad.* Upon, عَلَى ـ فَوْقَ.

Thereout, *ad.* From that place, مِنْ هُنَاكَ ; from that subject, مِنْ ذَلِكَ ـ مِنْ ثَمَّ.

Thereto, *ad.* } To that place, إِلَى هُنَاكَ. To, إِلَى. For this
Thereunto, } or that purpose, لِهٰذَا.

Thereupon, *ad.* Upon, فَوْقَ ـ مِنْ عَلَى ـ عَلَى. Immediately, then, حَالًا ـ مِنْ سَاعَتِهِ ـ عِنْدَ ذَلِكَ ـ إِذْ ذَاكَ ـ وَقْتَئِذٍ ـ فِي الْحَالِ. In consequence of, بِسَبَبِ ـ لِأَجْلِ ذَلِكَ ـ مِنْ ثَمَّ ذَلِكَ.

Therewith, *ad.* As with a thing, بِ. In conjunction with, صُحْبَةً ـ مَعَ. In a thing, فِي.

Therewithal, *ad.* Also, أَيْضًا. Over and above, زِيَادَةً عَنْ. At the same time, عِنْدَ ذَلِكَ ـ وَقْتَئِذٍ ـ فِي ذَلِكَ الْوَقْتِ.

Theriac, *n.* تِرْيَاقٌ ـ دِرْيَاقٌ ـ طِرْيَاقٌ ; (The best —, is called التِّرْيَاقُ الْفَارُوقِيُّ *vulg.* تِرْيَاقٌ فَارُوقِيٌّ.)

Theriacal, *a.* تِرْيَاقِيٌّ ـ مِنَ التِّرْيَاقِ.

Thermal, *a.* سُخْنٌ ـ حَارٌّ. A — spring, عَيْنُ مَاءٍ سُخْنٍ ـ عَيْنٌ سُخْنَةٌ.

Thermometer, *n.* مِيزَانُ الطَّقْسِ ـ مِيزَانُ الْحَرَارَةِ وَالْبُرُودَةِ ـ تِرْمُومِتْر.

Thermometrical, *a.* مُتَعَلِّقٌ بِمِيزَانِ الْحَرِّ وَالْبَرْدِ (*or* بِالتِّرْمُومِتْر) مُدَرَّجٌ عَلَى مِيزَانِ الطَّقْسِ.

Thermometrically, *ad.* نَظَرًا لِمِيزَانِ الطَّقْسِ (*or* التِّرْمُومِتْر).

Thesaurus, *n.* كَنْزٌ *pl.* كُنُوزٌ.

These, *pl. of* This, *dem. pron.*, هٰذِهِ ـ هٰؤُلَاءِ ـ أُولَاءِ ـ أُولَى ـ *vulg.* هَدُولِي ـ هَدُول ـ دُول. These two, هٰذَانِ *fem.* هَاتَانِ. These are thy brothers, هٰؤُلَاءِ أُخْوَتُكَ. These are thy sisters, هٰؤُلَاءِ أَخَوَاتُكَ. These stones, هٰذِهِ الْحِجَارَةُ ; these buildings, هٰذِهِ الْأَبْنِيَةُ. These words, or this speech, هٰذَا الْكَلَامُ. On — two rules, عَلَى هَاتَيْنِ الْقَاعِدَتَيْنِ. These are the true sayings of God, هٰذِهِ هِيَ أَقْوَالُ اللهِ الصَّادِقَةُ.

Thesis, *n.* مَسْأَلَةٌ *pl.* مَسَائِلُ ـ مَوْضُوعٌ.

Thespian, *a.* مُتَعَلِّقٌ بِلَعِبِ التِّيَاتْرُو وَالْغِنَاءِ.

Theurgic, *a.* طِلَسْمِيٌّ.

Theurgy, *n.* اِسْتِعْمَالُ الطَّلَاسِمِ.

They, *pron. pl.* هُمْ *fem.* هُنَّ ; they two, هُمَا.

Thick, *a.* Compact, مَتِينٌ ـ مُكْتَنِزٌ ـ سَفِيقٌ ـ وَثِيجٌ. Not thin, جَلِيلٌ ـ جِلٌّ ـ غَلِيظٌ ـ ثَخِينٌ. Muddy, opaque, turbid, رَنِقٌ ـ كَدِرٌ ـ كَدِيرٌ ـ مُتَكَدِّرٌ. Dense, tangled, of trees, أَشِبٌ ـ أَغْبَى *pl.* أَغْبِيَاءُ ـ لِفٌّ ـ جَثِيلٌ. Thick, as of a beard, كَثٌّ ـ كَثِيثٌ. Coarse, خَشِنٌ. Coagulated, مُجَمَّدٌ ـ جَامِدٌ ـ خَاثِرٌ. As denoting thickness from top to bottom or breadthwise, سَمِيكٌ ـ سَمِكٌ. Thick, of milk, or honey, or a liniment, خَاثِرٌ. Multitudinous, as of a population, وَافِرٌ ـ كَثِيرٌ. Thick, of the voice, hoarse, أَبَحُّ *fem.* بَحَّاءُ *and* بَحَّةٌ *pl.* بُحٌّ ـ أَجَشُّ. Bulky, corpulent, بَدِينٌ ـ بَدَنِيٌّ ـ أَضْخَمُ ـ ضَخْمٌ ـ غَضَنْفَرٌ ـ ثَخِينٌ جَسِيمٌ. Happening repeatedly, وَاقِعٌ تَكْرَارًا. Thick, heavy, as of hearing, *etc.*, ثَقِيلٌ. Intimately, as being on friendly terms, دَخِيلٌ ـ وَصِيلٌ ـ مُوَاصِلٌ. Stupid, بَلِيدٌ ـ أَحْمَقُ ـ أَخْرَقُ. Thick together, of people, مُزْدَحِمُونَ. A — beard, لِحْيَةٌ كَثَّةٌ. Thick trees, having thick branches and foliage, أَشْجَارٌ أَغْبِيَاءُ. A — shade, ظِلٌّ أَغْبَى. Thick clouds, ظَلَامُ الْغَمَامِ. I took the —, or — part, of it with the thin, أَخَذْتُ جِلَّهُ وَدِقَّهُ. He is neither — nor slender, مَا لَهُ جِلٌّ وَلَا دِقٌّ. Thicker than, in diameter or texture, أَغْلَظُ مِنْ. To be —, intimate, with, آنَسَ ـ صَادَقَ.

Thick, *n.* The thickest part, مُعْظَمٌ. The — or thickest of a battle, حَوْمَةٌ ـ رَحَى الْحَرْبِ ـ مُعْظَمَةُ الْحَرْبِ ـ غَمْرَةُ الْحَرْبِ الْحَرْبِ. To go through — and thin for, تَغَرَّرَ لِأَجْلِ كَذَا *or* فُلَانٍ ـ رَكِبَ الْأَخْطَارَ لِأَجْلِ كَذَا *or* فُلَانٍ.

Thick, *ad.* In quick succession, تَكْرَارًا ـ بِالتَّوَالِي وَعَلَى الْفَوْرِ وَبِالْعَجَلِ. *See also under* Thickly, *ad.*

Thicken, *v.t.* To make thick, as in diameter, shape, أَثْخَنَ ـ غَلَّظَ. To make coarse, rough, خَشَّنَ. To make dense, as of honey, milk, a liniment, *etc.*, خَثَرَ ـ أَخْثَرَ ـ كَثَّفَ. To coagulate, عَقَّدَ. To make turbid, كَدَّرَ.

Thicken, *v.i.* To become thick, as in diameter, texture, غَلُظَ ـ إِسْتَغْلَظَ. To become turbid, تَكَدَّرَ ـ كَدِرَ. To coagulate, تَعَقَّدَ. To become dense, of honey, milk, *etc.*, خَثُرَ ـ تَكَاثَفَ ـ تَخَثَّرَ. To multiply, تَكَاثَرَ ـ تَكَثَّرَ. To become coarse, rough, harsh, تَخَشَّنَ ـ خَشُنَ. The battle thickened, قَامَتِ الْحَرْبُ عَلَى سَاقٍ.

Thickening, *n.* Something added to make more dense, مُخَثِّرَةٌ. A becoming thick, غِلَظٌ ـ إِسْتِغْلَاظٌ.

Thicket, *n.* غَيْصَانٌ *pl.* عِيصٌ ـ غِيلٌ ـ غُرُفٌ *pl.* غَرِيفٌ ـ شَيْطَلٌ ـ أَجَمَةٌ ـ عِرِّيسَةٌ ـ عِرِّيسٌ ـ عُرًى *pl.* عُرْوَةٌ ـ أَيْكٌ *coll.* أَيْكَةٌ ـ غِيَاضٌ *pl.* غَيْضَةٌ ـ ضَرَاءٌ.

Thick-head, *n.* } طِنْبِلٌ ـ عَبِيطٌ ـ بَهِيمٌ ـ أَحْمَقُ ـ أَخْرَقُ.
Thick-scull, }

Thickish, *a.* Of diameter, size, غَلِيظٌ نَوْعًا ـ سَمِيكٌ نَوْعًا ; of denseness, of milk, honey, *etc.*, كَثِيفٌ نَوْعًا ـ خَاثِرٌ نَوْعًا ; of stupidity, أَحْمَقُ نَوْعًا ; of trees, foliage, لِفٌّ نَوْعًا ; of a voice, أَجَشُّ نَوْعًا ; of a beard, كَثِيثٌ نَوْعًا.

Thickly, *ad.* Compactly, closely pressed together, إِكْتِنَازًا — تَلَبُّدًا — كَبْسًا . Populously, بِكَثْرَةِ ٱلسُّكَّانِ : thickly peopled, ذُو عِمَارَةٍ . Luxuriantly, of vegetation, بِتَكْثِيثٍ — بِكَثَأٍ . Exuberantly, بِٱزْدِحَامٍ — إِزْدِحَامًا . Crowdingly, بِبَذَارَةٍ — بِإِفْرَاطٍ — وَفْرَةً . Hoarsely, بِصَوْتٍ مَبْحُوحٍ — بِجُشَّةٍ . Broadly, not finely, بِغَلَاظَةٍ — بِخَشَانَةٍ . With inspissation, تَخَثُّرًا — بِخُثُورٍ . With turbidity, بِكَدَرٍ — تَكَدُّرًا . *See also under* Thick, *ad.*

Thickness, *n.* As in diameter, ثُخَانَةٌ — ثُخْنٌ — سَمْكٌ — سَفَاقَةٌ — كَثَافَةٌ — وَثَاجَةٌ . Coarseness, غِلَاظَةٌ — غِلَظٌ . Compactness, The state of coagulation, تَعَقُّدٌ — جُمُودٌ ; as of honey, milk, *etc.*, خَثْرٌ — خُثُورٌ — كَثَافَةٌ . Abundance, as of population, *etc.*, عُمْرَانٌ — كَثَأٌ — كَثْرَةٌ — بَذَارَةٌ — وُفُورٌ — وَفْرَةٌ . Luxuriance, of vegetation, تَكْثِيثَةٌ . As of the hair, trees, *etc.*, جُثُولَةٌ — جَثَالَةٌ . Thickness of the voice, hoarseness, بُحَّةٌ — جَشَرٌ — جُشَّةٌ . Dulness, stupidity, حَمَاقَةٌ — بَلَادَةٌ — خُرْقٌ . Turbidity, كَدَرٌ — رَنَقٌ . Stoutness, fatness, بَدَانَةٌ — ضَخَامَةٌ .

Thick-set, *a.* Closely planted, أَيْكٌ أَيْكٌ — أَيْكٌ . Stout, corpulent, أَضْخَمُ — بَدِينٌ — جَسِيمٌ . *See also* Stumpy, *a.*

Thief, *n.* سَارِقٌ *pl.* سُرَّاقٌ — لِصٌّ *pl.* لُصُوصٌ — نَشَّالٌ *pl.* نَشَّالَةٌ — حَرَامِيٌّ *pl.* حَرَامِيَّةٌ . A companion of thieves, لَفِيفٌ .

Thief-catcher, *n.* } مَاسِكُ ٱللُّصُوصِ .
Thief-taker, }

Thieve, *v.i.* To practice thieving, لَصَّ ² — تَلَصَّصَ — كَانَ سَارِقًا .

Thievish, *a.* Given to theft, مَطْبُوعٌ عَلَى ٱلسَّرِقَةِ . Stealthy, مَسْتُورٌ — خَفِيٌّ — مُتَسَلِّلٌ .

Thievishly, *ad.* As a thief, كَٱلسَّارِقِ — سَرِقَةً . Stealthily, عَلَى خُفْيَةٍ — خَفَاءً .

Thievishness, *n.* مَيْلٌ إِلَى ٱلسَّرِقَةِ — دُرْبَةٌ عَلَى ٱللَّصِّ .

Thigh, *n.* فَخِذٌ *pl.* أَفْخَاذٌ — وَرِكٌ *pl.* أَوْرَاكٌ . The inner side of the —, لُبْدَةٌ — بَادٌّ — رَبْلَةٌ — رَبَلَةٌ . The — joint, كَمَعٌ . A slice of flesh from the —, فَصِيلَةٌ . To hit on the —, فَخَذَ ¹ . Hit on the —, مَفْخُوذٌ .

Thill, *n.* *See* Shaft, *n.*

Thimble, *n.* For sewing, كِشْتِبَانٌ — قِمْعُ ٱلْخَيَّاطِ . A ring, حَلْقَةٌ *pl.* حَلَقَاتٌ *and* حَلْقَانٌ .

Thimble-rig, *n.* لَعِبُ ٱلْمُشَعْوِذِ بِٱلطَّاسَاتِ وَٱلطَّابَةِ .

Thin, *a.* Having little thickness, رَكِيكٌ — دَقِيقٌ — رَقِيقٌ . Fine, transparent, شَفٌّ — شَفَّافٌ ; a — or fine cloth or garment, شَفِيفٌ — شِفٌّ . Anything —, slender or elegant, حَشْرٌ : a — ear, أُذُنٌ حَشْرٌ . Flimsy, سَخِيفٌ — رَفِيعٌ — فِشَاشٌ . Slender, of the body, قِضَافٌ *pl.* نَضِيفٌ — شَخِيتٌ — شُخَاتٌ *pl.* شُخْتٌ . Light, not heavy, خَفِيفٌ . Lean, عَجِيفٌ *pl.* عُجَفَى . A —, spare, man, رَجُلٌ نَضِيضُ ٱللَّحْمِ . Sparse, thinly scattered, شَتٌّ — مُتَفَرِّقٌ — مُشَتَّتٌ . Thin, few, يَسِيرَةٌ — قَلَائِلُ . Watery, مَاوِيٌّ — مَائِيٌّ . Thin, of soil, أَسِيفَةٌ . Thin soup, حَسًا دَقِيقٌ . Thin lips, شَفَتَانِ عَجْفَاوَانِ . Having — legs, of a woman, كَزْوَآءُ ; thighs, مَضْوَآءُ ; arms, مَدْشَآءُ . Thin-skinned, morbidly sensitive, سَرِيعُ ٱلضَّجَرِ — حَسَّاسٌ . A — plate, صَفِيحَةٌ *pl.* صَفَائِحُ . A garment worn till it becomes —, ثَوْبٌ — ثَوْبٌ مُتَسَلْسِلٌ — ثَوْبٌ طَرَائِقُ مُتَخَلْخِلٌ . To be or become —, of little thickness, رَقَّ ² — إِسْتَرَقَّ — دَقَّ ² — إِسْتَدَقَّ . To be —, flimsy, سَخُفَ ⁴ . To become —, slender, قَضُفَ ⁴ — شَخُتَ ⁴ . To be —, lean, عَجِفَ ⁴ ² — إِخْتَلَّ لَحْمُهُ — أَغَثَّ — خَسَفَ ² . To be —, as dough, paste, *etc.*, رَخَّ ² — إِرْتَخَّ . To be worn, of a garment, until it becomes —, تَسَلْسَلَ — تَخَلْخَلَ . *See also* Spare, Sparse, *a.*

Thin, *v.t.* To make thin, in dimensions, size, أَرَقَّ — رَقَّقَ — أَدَقَّ — دَقَّقَ . To make lighter, خَفَّفَ ; of dough, *etc.*, أَرَخَّ . To make liquid, ذَوَّبَ — أَذَابَ . To reduce in number, قَلَّلَ — أَقَلَّ — خَفَّفَ ; in size, صَغَّرَ — أَصْغَرَ . To make less thick, of a stiff substance, رَوَّقَ .

Thin, *ad.* In a scattered state, شَتَاتَ — تَفَرُّقًا — تَشَتُّتًا — شَتَاتًا .

Thine, *a.* Belonging to a second person, لَكَ *fem.* لَكِ — *vulg.* بِتَاعَكَ *fem.* بِتَاعَكِ . I will not take anything that is —, لَا آخُذُ شَيْئًا مِنْ كُلِّ مَا هُوَ لَكَ . All mine are —, كُلُّ مَا هُوَ لِي فَهُوَ لَكَ . Take what is — and depart, خُذِ ٱلَّذِي لَكَ وَٱذْهَبْ .

Thing, *n.* شَأْنٌ *pl.* شُؤُونٌ — حَاجَةٌ *pl.* حَاجَاتٌ — شَيْءٌ *pl.* أَشْيَآءُ . A subject, أَمْرٌ *pl.* أُمُورٌ — مَادَّةٌ *pl.* مَوَادُّ . Every —, كُلُّ شَيْءٍ . Thing by —, article by article; or, one — after another, شَيْئًا فَشَيْئًا . What —? أَيُّ شَيْءٍ . Another —, شَيْءٌ آخَرُ — غَيْرُ شَيْءٍ . Quite another —, شَيْءٌ آخَرُ بَتَّةً . I cannot do any —, لَا أَسْتَطِيعُ شَيْئًا . Is any — too hard for him, هَلْ يَسْتَحِيلُ عَلَيْهِ شَيْءٌ . Above all things, فَوْقَ كُلِّ شَيْءٍ — قَبْلَ كُلِّ شَيْءٍ . No such —, (as a negative,) كَلَّا — أَصْلًا — قَطْعًا . I never found any — like it, لَمْ أَجِدْ مِثْلَهُ . Any — rather than that . . . ., أَيُّ شَيْءٍ أُخْرَى مِنْ أَنْ . In the nature of things, عَلَى أُسْلُوبِ ٱلْأُمُورِ — عَلَى تَرْكِيبِ ٱلْأُمُورِ . As things stand, حَسَبَ ٱلْحَالِ ٱلْحَاضِرِ — فِي ٱلْحَالِ ٱلْحَاضِرِ . One of two things, أَمْرٌ مِنْ أَمْرَيْنِ — شَيْءٌ مِنْ شَيْئَيْنِ . A horrible —, أَمْرٌ فَظِيعٌ —

هِيلَة. A strange —, أَمْرٌ غَرِيبٌ. Ye shall send to me by him every — ye hear, تُرْسِلُونَ عَلَى يَدِهِ إِلَيَّ كُلَّ كَلِمَةٍ تَسْمَعُونَهَا.

Think, *v.i.* and *t.* To form ideas in the mind, تَخَيَّلَ — تَصَوَّرَ — إِفْتَكَرَ — فَكَّرَ — تَفَكَّرَ — تَوَهَّمَ. To surmise, زَعَمَ — ظَنَّ — تَوَهَّمَ. To muse, تَأَمَّلَ. To — over, هَمَّ بِ — أَضْمَرَ عَلَى. To — over, with a view to action, قَدَّرَ. He thought al-Básrah to be Baghdád, جَعَلَ ٱلْبَصْرَةَ بَغْدَادَ. I don't —, care, about him or it, مَا لِي فِيهِ فِكْرٌ. He thought well of him, تَوَسَّمَ فِيهِ ٱلْخَيْرَ. To — well of, to approve of, إِسْتَحْسَنَ — إِسْتَصْلَحَ. To — of, to bear in mind, remember, ذَكَرَ — تَذَكَّرَ; to have in design, قَصَدَ — نَوَى أَنْ — تَعَمَّدَ. What do you —? مَاذَا تَظُنُّونَ. He thought himself to be something, ظَنَّ أَنَّهُ شَيْءٌ. I — it meet, proper, while I remain in his house, أَحْسِبُهُ مُنَاسِبًا مَا دُمْتُ فِي بَيْتِهِ. (Most of the verbs given under this head become more distinctively transitive by subjoining فِي thereto; *e.g.* تَخَيَّلَ فِي — إِفْتَكَرَ فِي).

Thinker, *n.* صَاحِبُ فِكْرٍ *pl.* أَصْحَاب. *See also* Thoughtful, *a.*

Thinking, *n.* ظَنٌّ — فِكْرٌ. To my —, عَلَى ظَنِّي. He is of the same way of — as, هُوَ عَلَى رَأْيِي.

Thinly, *ad.* In a scattered manner, شَتَاتًا — شَتَاتَ.

Thinness, *n.* The quality of having little thickness, دِقَّة — رِقَّة. Flimsiness, سُخْف — سَخَافَة — رَقَاعَة. Slenderness, as of the body, قَضَافَة — قَضَف. Lightness, as opposed to heaviness, خِفَّة. Leanness, عَجَف. Sparseness, تَفَرُّق — شَتَات — شَتٌّ. Thinness of voice, رِقَّةُ صَوْتٍ. Thinness of the atmosphere, rarity, تَخَلْخُل. Wateriness, مَائِيَّة. Fewness, قِلَّة.

Third, *a.* ثَالِث *fem.* ثَالِثَة. To be —, ثَلَثَ. To come in —, as in a race, ثَلَّثَ. She is the — of three, هِيَ ثَالِثَةُ ثَلَاثٍ.

Third, *n.* ثُلْث *or* ثُلُث *pl.* أَثْلَاث. He took a — of the goods of the people, ثَلَثَ ٱلْقَوْمَ. The property left at death had a — of it taken, ثُلِثَتِ ٱلتَّرِكَةُ.

Thirdly, *ad.* ثَالِثًا.

Thirst, *n.* As for drink, ظَمَأٌ — غَلَل — غُلّ — غَيْمَة — جُوَاد — سُهْفَة — شَغَاشِف. Extreme —, عَطَش — ظَمَأ. Longing desire, شَوْق — إِشْتِيَاق. Insatiable —, عُطَاش. To suffer —, تَعَطَّشَ. To quench —, رَوَى ٱلظَّمَأَ. To die for —, مَاتَ مِنَ ٱلْعَطَشِ.

Thirst, *v.i.* عَطِشَ — أَغَامَ — غَامَ — ظَمِئَ — ٱلْتَاحَ — لَاحَ. To cause to —, أَعْطَشَ — ظَمَّأَ — أَظْمَأَ. To — for, to long for, حَنَّ إِلَى — يَجُودُ *aor.* جَادَ إِلَى — إِشْتَاقَ إِلَى. He thirsted to meet with him, ظَمِئَ إِلَى لِقَائِهِ.

Thirstily, *ad.* عَطْشًا — بِظَمَاءٍ.

Thirstiness, *n.* *See* Thirst, *n.*

Thirsty, *a.* غَيْمَان *fem.* غَيْمَى — غَلَّان — ظَمْآنُ — ظَمِئٌ — عَطْشَان *fem.* عَطْشَى *pl.* عَطَاشَى *and* عَطْشَى — عَاطِش — مُسَوَّف *and* عِطَاش. Food that makes one —, طَعَامٌ ذُو — طَعَامٌ مَسْهَفَةٌ مَشْرَبَةٌ. A — land, أَرْضٌ مُعْطِشَةٌ. To be vehemently —, غَلَّ *aor.* يَغَلُّ.

Thirteen, *a.* ثَلَاثَةَ عَشَرَ *fem.* ثَلَاثَ عَشْرَةَ.

Thirteenth, *a.* ٱلثَّالِثُ عَشَرَ *fem.* ٱلثَّالِثَةَ عَشْرَةَ.

Thirtieth, *a.* } ٱلثَّلَاثُونَ — ٱلثَّلٰثُونَ.
Thirty, }

This, *dem. pron.*, ذَا *fem.* ذِي — هٰذَا *fem.* هٰذِهِ. This day, ٱلْيَوْمَ — هٰذَا ٱلْيَوْمُ. Like this, in this manner, كَذَا — هٰكَذَا. This and that, ذَا وَذَاكَ — هٰذَا وَهٰذَاكَ *fem.* هٰذِهِ وَتِلْكَ.

Thistle, *n.* حَسَكٌ. The way —, ذَنَبُ ٱلسَّبُعِ.

Thistly, *a.* مَلْآنُ مِنْ حَسَكٍ — مُمْتَلِئٌ مِنْ حَسَكٍ.

Thither, *ad.* } إِلَى هُنَاكَ. Where I shall be — ye cannot
Thitherward, } come, حَيْثُ أَكُونُ أَنَا لَا تَقْدِرُونَ أَنْتُمْ أَنْ تَأْتُوا. He was afraid to go —, خَافَ أَنْ يَذْهَبَ إِلَى هُنَاكَ. Hither and —, هُنَا وَهُنَاكَ. He went hither and —, تَرَدَّدَ.

Thole, *n.* For an oar, بَيْتُ ٱلْمِقْذَافِ — *in Turkish,* إِسْقَارْمُوس.

Thong, *n.* Of a sandal, شِرْعَة *coll.* شِرْع — شِرَاك *pl.* شُرُك. A — used for fastening on the pastern of a camel, خَدَمَة *pl.* خِدَام. A — to bind anything upon the body, مِعْضَاد. A — to suspend anything with, عَلَاقَة. In a general sense, of a strap, إِسَار *pl.* أُسُر.

Thoracic, *a.* صَدْرِيٌّ — جَوْفِيٌّ.

Thorax, *n.* صَدْر — جَوْف.

Thorium, *n.* ثُورِيُوم وَهُوَ ضَرْبٌ مِنَ ٱلْمَعَادِنِ.

Thorn, *n.* The shrub, شَوْكَة *coll.* شَوْك *pl.* شَوْكَات. Anything troublesome, قَلَق — بَلَاء — مُصِيبَة. A — of a tree, كُلَّاب *pl.* كَلَالِيب — شَوْكَة. To prick with a —, شَاكَ — أَشَاكَ. To bring forth thorns, أَشْوَكَ. To place thorns, as upon a wall, شَوَّكَ بِالشَّوْكِ. To be pierced by a —, or to fall among thorns, شِيكَ *aor.* يُشَاكُ. To pluck off the thorns, as from a tree, شَنَّخَ. To extract a —, نَقَشَ ٱلشَّوْكَ. I fell among the thorns, شِكْتُ ٱلشَّوْكَ. He was not pierced with a —, مَا أَشَاكَتْهُ شَوْكَةٌ. The thorns pierced his feet, تَخَرَّمَ ٱلشَّوْكُ فِي رِجْلِهِ. To be a — in one's side, شَقَّ عَلَى — كَانَ مَشَقَّةً لِ. To be on thorns, on tenter-hooks, حَارَ — تَحَيَّرَ — كَانَ مُتَحَيِّرًا — قَلِقَ.

Thorn-apple, *n.* جوزُ مَاثِلٍ .

Thornback, *n.* سَمَكُ ٱلتُّرْسِ ذُو شَوْكٍ .

Thornless, *a.* بِلا شَوْكٍ .

Thorny, *a.* ذُو شَوْكٍ ـ شَاكٌ ـ شَائِكٌ ـ شَوِكٌ . A — tree, شَجَرَةٌ شَاكَةٌ . A large — tree, عِضَاةٌ *pl.* عِضَوَاتٌ . Thorny ground, أَرْضٌ مُشَوِّكَةٌ . The tree was —, شَاكَتِ ٱلشَّجَرَةُ . To be —, تَشَوَّكَ . Thorny, perplexing, صَعْبٌ ـ مُشْتَبِكٌ ـ مُشْكِلٌ ـ قَلِقٌ ـ مُشْكِلٌ ـ مُحَيِّرٌ .

Thorough, *a.* Complete, perfect, أَكْمَلُ ـ تَامٌّ ـ كَامِلٌ . In the most — manner, فِي غَايَةِ ٱلْإِتْقَانِ ـ عَلَى أَكْمَلِ وَجْهٍ .

Thoroughbase, *n.* أَبْرَاجُ ٱلْبَمِّ فِي ٱلْمُوسِيقَى .

Thoroughbred, *a.* صَرِيحُ ٱلنَّسَبِ *pl.* صُرَحَاءُ ـ أَصِيلٌ *pl.* أُصُلٌ and أَصَائِلُ ـ كَحِيلٌ .

Thoroughfare, *n.* طَرِيقٌ ـ شَوَارِعُ *pl.* شَارِعٌ ـ شَارِعٌ عُمُومِيٌّ ـ شَارِعٌ . No —! الطَّرِيقُ (or الشَّارِعُ) مَسْدُودٌ .

Thoroughly, *ad.* عَلَى ٱلتَّمَامِ ـ جَيِّدًا ـ بِٱلْكُلِّيَّةِ ـ تَمَامًا ـ بَتَّةً . I perused the books —, دَرَسْتُ ٱلْكُتُبَ حَقَّ دِرَاسَتِهَا وَٱلْكَمَالِ . Not to do a thing —, خَشَبَ ٱلْعَمَلَ .

Thoroughness, *a.* تَمَامٌ وَكَمَالٌ ـ تَمَامَةٌ ـ كَمَالٌ . With —, بِغَايَةِ ٱلْإِتْقَانِ ـ عَلَى ٱلتَّمَامِ وَٱلْكَمَالِ .

Thoroughpaced, *a.* بِتَمَامٍ وَكَمَالٍ ـ مُتَمَّمٌ ـ مُكَمَّلٌ .

Those, *pron.* أُولَائِكَ ـ أُولٰئِكَ ـ أُولَاكَ . Those who, ٱلَّذِينَ *fem.* ٱللَّاتِي and ٱللَّوَاتِي .

Thou, *pers. pron.*, أَنْتَ *fem.* أَنْتِ .

Thou, *v.t.* and *t.* *See to* Thee, *v.t.* and *i.*

Though, *conj.* وَإِنْ ـ كَأَنَّ ـ وَلَوْ ـ مَعَ أَنَّ : Though he detain me, I will not eat, وَلَوْ عَوَّقَنِي لَا آكُلُ . Though he accumulate silver as the sand, yet he shall not enjoy it, أَنْ كَنَزَ فِضَّةً كَٱلرَّمْلِ فَهُوَ لَا يَتَمَتَّعُ بِهَا . Though he cause grief, yet will he have compassion, وَلَوْ أَحْزَنَ فَيَرْحَمُ . They will not believe — one should declare it to them, لَا يُصَدِّقُونَ إِنْ أَخْبَرَهُمْ أَحَدٌ بِهِ . I threw the arrow as — I was throwing at a butt, رَمَيْتُ ٱلسَّهْمَ كَأَنِّي أَرْمِي غَرَضًا . Though that may not be proper, still I could not do otherwise, وَإِنْ كَانَ ذٰلِكَ لَيْسَ بِمُنَاسِبٍ إِلَّا أَنِّي عَجِزْتُ عَنِ ٱلْخِلَافِ . Though it be more difficult than all of them, مَعَ كَوْنِهِ أَصْعَبَ ٱلْكُلِّ . Though I have seen him ten times I did not recognise him, وَإِنْ قَدْ رَأَيْتُهُ عَشَرَ مَرَّاتٍ فَإِنِّي مَا عَرَفْتُهُ . *See also* Although, *conj.*

Thought, *pret. of to* Think, *q.v.*

Thought, *n.* The operation of the mind in thinking, فِكْرٌ *pl.* أَفْكَارٌ . An idea, ظَنٌّ *pl.* ظُنُونٌ ـ رَأْيٌ *pl.* آرَاءٌ ـ تَخَيُّلٌ . A project, design, نِيَّةٌ ـ قَصْدٌ . Reflection, تَأَمُّلٌ . Anxiety, كَرْبٌ ـ قَسَاوَةٌ ـ قَلَقٌ ـ هَمٌّ . As quick as —, أَسْبَقُ مِنَ ٱلْأَفْكَارِ . To be buried in —, إِسْتَغْرَقَ فِي بَحْرِ ٱلْأَفْكَارِ . To come into one's thoughts, خَطَرَ بِبَالِهِ . To have some — of, to intend, أَرَادَ ـ رَامَ *aor.* يَرُومُ ـ تَنَوَّى ـ تَعَمَّدَ . To have one's thoughts about one, كَانَ عَلَى حَذَرٍ ـ إِحْتَذَرَ . To speak one's —, إِنْبَسَطَ فِي ٱلْكَلَامِ ـ تَفَتَّحَ فِي ٱلْكَلَامِ ـ عَبَّرَ عَمَّا فِي ضَمِيرِهِ . To take — for, to be anxious about, إِهْتَمَّ لِ ـ هَمَّ بِ . On second thoughts, بِإِعَادَةِ ٱلْفِكْرِ . No — occurred to them contrary to that which they entertained at first, لَمْ يَخْطُرْ لَهُمْ فِكْرٌ يُخَالِفُ ٱلْفِكْرَ ٱلْأَوَّلَ .

Thoughtful, *a.* Given to thought, مُتَفَكِّرٌ ـ فَكُورٌ ـ فِكِّيرٌ . Pensive, مُتَأَمِّلٌ . Anxious, careful, شَاجِنٌ ـ مَشْجُوٌّ ـ شَجِيٌّ ـ مُهْتَمٌّ . To be —, solicitous, عَنِيَ *aor.* يَعْنَى ـ تَشَجَّنَ . To be — about, إِهْتَمَّ بِ ـ إِعْتَنَى بِ . To make —, أَشْجَنَ ـ أَشْجَى ـ شَجَّنَ .

Thoughtfully, *ad.* With thought, بِتَأَمُّلٍ ـ بِفِكْرٍ . Solicitously, بِٱهْتِمَامٍ ـ بِعَنَاءٍ ـ بِشَجَنٍ .

Thoughtfulness, *n.* Consideration, تَأَمُّلٌ ـ فِكْرٌ . Solicitude, إِهْتِمَامٌ ـ هَمٌّ ـ شَجَنٌ ـ شَجْوٌ ـ عَنَاءٌ . An object of —, هِمَّةٌ *pl.* هِمَمٌ .

Thoughtless, *a.* Without consideration, بِغَيْرِ فِكْرٍ . Heedless, careless, مُتَعَسِّفٌ ـ دِعْنَةٌ *pl.* دُعْنٌ ـ مَاجِنٌ ـ أَبْلَهُ ـ جَاهِلٌ غَافِلٌ غَافِلٌ . How — he is! مَا أَدْعَنَهُ . *See also* Heedless, Inconsiderate, *a.*

Thoughtlessly, *ad.* Without consideration, بِغَيْرِ تَأَمُّلٍ . Heedlessly, بِلَا بَصِيرَةٍ ـ بِتَغَافُلٍ ـ بِدَعَانَةٍ . To act — in, إِعْتَسَفَ فِي ـ تَعَسَّفَ فِي .

Thoughtlessness, *n.* Want of consideration, قِلَّةُ تَأَمُّلٍ ـ قِلَّةُ فِكْرٍ . Heedlessness, قِلَّةُ تَمْيِيزٍ ـ تَغَافُلٌ ـ طَيْشٌ ـ إِعْتِسَافٌ ـ دَعَانَةٌ .

Thought-sick, *a.* عَلِيلٌ مِنْ شِدَّةِ ٱلْإِفْتِكَارِ .

Thousand, *a.* أَلْفٌ *pl.* أُلُوفٌ and آلَافٌ . A complete —, أَلْفٌ صَتْمٌ ـ أَلْفٌ أَقْرَعُ . Three —, ثَلَاثَةُ آلَافٍ . This is one —, هٰذَا أَلْفٌ وَاحِدٌ . These are a — dirhems, هٰذِهِ ٱلدَّرَاهِمُ أَلْفٌ . The dirhems became one —, آلَفَتِ ٱلدَّرَاهِمُ . To become a —, آلَفُوا . To make to be a —, أَلَّفَ ٱلْأَلْفَ ـ آلَفَ . He killed a — men, قَتَلَ أَلْفَ رَجُلٍ . Their number was thousands of thousands, كَانَ عَدَدُهُمْ رَبَوَاتِ رَبَوَاتٍ .

Thousand-fold, *a.* أَلْفُ ضِعْفٍ .

Thousandth, *a.* الأَلْفُ .

Thousandth, *n.* وَاحِدٌ مِنَ ٱلْأَلْفِ.

Thowl, *n.* *See* Thole, *n.*

Thraldom, *n.* عُبُودَةٌ ـ عُبُودِيَّةٌ ـ رِقَّةٌ.

Thrall, *n.* *See* Slave, Captive, *n.*

Thrash, *v.t.* As with a thrashing instrument, دَرَسَ [2]; with the feet, دَاسَ [2]. To — with a stick, وَشَحَ ـ بِٱلْعَصَا; with a whip, سَاطَ [2]. To overcome, غَلَبَ ـ غَلَبَ عَلَى ـ فَاقَ [2]. To be thrashed, with a thrashing instrument, دُرِسَ; with the feet, إِنْدَاسَ.

Thrasher, *n.* As of corn, *etc.*, دَرَّاسٌ ـ دَارِسٌ; with the feet, دَائِسٌ. Animals that thrash, دَرَائِسُ.

Thrashing, *n.* The act of thrashing corn, *etc.*, دَرْسٌ; with the feet, دَوْسٌ. A beating, قَتْلَةٌ ـ ضَرْبٌ.

Thrashing-machine, *n.* مِدْوَسٌ ـ نَيْرَجٌ ـ نَوْرَجٌ; a — of iron, جَرْجَرٌ ـ مِرَضَّةٌ.

Thrashing-floor, *n.* مَدَاسَةٌ ـ أَنْدَرٌ *pl.* أَنَادِرُ.

Thread, *n.* For sewing, خَيْطَةٌ *coll.* خَيْطٌ *pl.* خُيُوطٌ. A — for running beads, *etc.*, upon, سِلْكَةٌ *coll.* سِلْكٌ *pl.* سُلُوكٌ *and* أَسْلَاكٌ. A — of iron, سِلْكٌ مِنْ حَدِيدٍ. Silk —, إِبْرِيسَمٌ. Gold —, قَصَبٌ أَصْفَرُ; silver —, قَصَبٌ أَبْيَضُ. A ball of —, مُسَحَّلَةٌ ـ كُبَّةُ خَيْطٍ. A cotton —, غَزْلٌ. A seller of —, غَزَّالٌ. Thread, a filament, لِيفٌ *pl.* أَلْيَافٌ ـ خَيْطٌ لِيفِيٌّ ـ لِيفَةٌ. A — of a screw, لَوْلَبٌ ٱلْبُرْغِيِّ. Thread of a discourse, سِيَاقُ ٱلْكَلَامِ ـ سِيَاقَةُ (*or* رَبْطُ) ٱلْكَلَامِ.

Thread, *v.t.* To pass a thread, *etc.*, through, أَسْلَكَ ـ فِي ـ عَبَّرَ ـ سَلَكَ ـ فِي [2] ضَمَّ ـ سَلَكَ ـ فِي. To — a needle, سَلَكَ ٱلْخَيْطَ فِي إِبْرَةٍ (*or* ضَمَّ) خَيْطًا فِي إِبْرَةٍ. He threaded the pearls, سَلَكَ ٱللُّؤْلُؤَ. He threaded the chaplet of pearls, ضَمَّ شِيَالَةَ ٱللُّؤْلُؤِ. To — with, نَسَجَ ـ بِ [2]; threaded with gold, مَنْسُوجٌ بِٱلذَّهَبِ. To be threaded, as a thread in a needle, *etc.*, إِنْسَلَكَ فِي. To — one's way through a crowd, وَلَجَ غَابَةَ ٱلْجَمْعِ *aor.* يَلِجُ ـ شَقَّ ٱلزِّحَامَ [2]. To find one's way to, to enter, دَخَلَ [2].

Threadbare, *a.* Of garments, مُتَخَلْخِلٌ ـ جَارِنٌ ـ جَرِينٌ ـ رَثِيثٌ ـ أَرَثُّ ـ رَثٌّ ـ جَرْدٌ *pl.* جُرُودٌ ـ مُتَسَلْسِلٌ. Worn out, obsolete, مَتْرُوكٌ ـ مُلْغًى ـ هَامِدٌ; common, broadspread, مَشْهُورٌ ـ شَائِعٌ. To be or to become —, تَخَلْخَلَ ـ تَسَلْسَلَ ـ أَرَثَّ ـ رَثَّ [2] ـ جَرَنَ [2] ـ إِنْجَرَدَ ـ سَحَقَ [2]. To wear till it becomes —, One who wears — clothes, خَلَقِيٌّ.

Threadbareness, *n.* Of garments, تَخَلْخُلٌ ـ تَسَلْسُلٌ ـ رِثَّةٌ ـ رَثَاثَةٌ.

Threat, *n.* A menace, تَهْدِيدٌ ـ وَعِيدٌ ـ رَغْبٌ ـ تَوَعُّدٌ ـ إِيعَادٌ ـ تَخْوِيفٌ. Threats, warnings, أَخْطَارٌ ـ تَهَدُّدٌ. To put out threats, to fulminate, أَرْعَدَ وَأَبْرَقَ.

Threaten, *v.t.* As with punishment, *etc.*, تَدَرَّهَ ـ أَرْعَدَ ـ رَعَبَ ـ هَدَّدَ ـ تَهَدَّدَ ـ أَوْعَدَ ـ بِ. To exhibit signs of threatening, هَمَّ بِ [2]. When a great danger threatened, عِنْدَمَا أَشْفَى عَلَى خَطَرٍ عَظِيمٍ. "And I had already threatened you beforehand," وَقَدْ قَدَّمْتُ إِلَيْكُمْ بِٱلْوَعِيدِ (Kur. l. 27). "True, indeed, is that with which ye are threatened," إِنَّمَا تُوعَدُونَ لَصَادِقٌ (Kur. li. 5).

Threatening, *a.* Denouncing evil, مُوعِدٌ ـ مُتَهَدِّدٌ ـ مُتَدَرِّهٌ ـ قَرِيبُ ٱلْوُقُوعِ ـ قَرِيبٌ ـ مُزْمِعٌ ـ مُطِلٌّ ـ مُخَوِّفٌ. Imminent,

Threateningly, *ad.* As denouncing evil, تَهْدِيدًا ـ تَهَدُّدًا ـ تَخْوِيفًا. Imminently, عَلَى شَرَفٍ.

Three, *a.* ثَلَاثَةٌ ـ ثَلَاثٌ. Three men, ثَلَاثَةُ رِجَالٍ; three women, ثَلَاثُ نِسْوَةٍ. Three at a time, مَثْلَثَ ـ ثُلَاثَ. Three-pointed, of a letter having — diacritical points, مُثَلَّثٌ. Having three sides, or — letters, *etc.*, ثُلَاثِيٌّ. To count or reckon —, ثَلَّثَ. To become —, أَثْلَثَ. To remain — nights with, ثَلَّثَ لِ.

Threefold, *a.* Triple, مَثْلُوثٌ ـ مُثَلَّثٌ. To make —, ضَعَّفَ ـ ثَلَّثَ ـ ضَاعَفَ ـ أَضْعَفَ.

Threepence, *n.* ثَلَاثَةُ بَنْسَاتٍ عِبَارَةٌ عَنْ رُبْعِ شِلِينٍ مِنَ ٱلسِّكَكِ ٱلْإِنْكِلِيزِيَّةِ.

Threepenny, *a.* A — piece, سِكَّةٌ مِنَ ٱلثَّمَنِ ٱلْمَذْكُورِ.

Threescore, *a.* سِتُّونَ. Threescore and ten, سَبْعُونَ.

Threnetic, *a.* *See* Mournful, *a.*

Threnody, *n.* *See* Elegy, *n.*

Thresh, *v.t.* *See to* Thrash, *v.t.*

Threshold, *n.* As of a door, *etc.*, شَرِيعَةٌ ـ أَنْجَافٌ ـ أُسْكُفَّةٌ ـ عَتَبَةٌ *pl.* عَتَبٌ *and* عَتَبَاتٌ ـ وَصِيدٌ *pl.* وُصُدٌ. To put a — to a door, عَتَّبَ ٱلْبَابَ. I have not trodden his —, مَا سَكِفْتُ بَابَهُ ـ مَا عَتَبْتُ بَابَهُ. Threshold, commencement, شُرُوعٌ ـ بَدْءٌ ـ إِبْتِدَاءٌ. A point of entering, مَدْخَلٌ ـ دُخُولٌ.

Thrice, *ad.* ثَلَاثَ مَرَّاتٍ. This was done —, وَكَانَ هٰذَا عَلَى ثَلَاثِ مَرَّاتٍ. I entreated him —, تَضَرَّعْتُ إِلَيْهِ ثَلَاثَ مَرَّاتٍ.

Thrift, *n.* إِعْتِدَالٌ ـ إِقْتِصَادٌ ـ تَقَشُّفٌ.

Thriftily, *ad.* بِٱعْتِدَالٍ ـ بِٱقْتِصَادٍ ـ بِتَقَشُّفٍ.

Thriftiness, *n.* *See* Thrift, *n.*

Thriftless, *a.* مُبَاذِرٌ ـ مُبَذِّرٌ ـ مِنْفَاقٌ ـ مُسْرِفٌ.

Thriftlessly, *ad.* بِإِسْرَافٍ ـ بِتَبْذِيرٍ ـ مُبَاذَرَةً.

Thrifty, *a.* مُعْتَدِلٌ ـ قَتُورٌ ـ مُقْتَصِدٌ ـ مُتَقَشِّفٌ. To be — in, إِقْتَصَدَ فِي.

Thrill, *v.t.* To stir the mind, passions, *etc.*, هَاجَ ـ هَيَّجَ ـ حَرَّكَ ـ إِسْتَفَزَّ ـ أَثَارَ ـ نَجَعَ فِي. *See also to* Bore, Pierce, *v.t.*

Thrill, *v.i.* To be moved, ثَارَ ـ تَثَوَّرَ ـ إِهْتَزَّ ـ تَهَيَّجَ ـ إِنْهَاجَ ـ قَزَّ. To — with fear, إِرْتَجَفَ مِنَ ٱلْخَوْفِ. To — with joy, إِهْتَزَّ مِنَ ٱلسُّرُورِ. *See also to* Penetrate, *v.i.*

Thrill, *n.* إِهْتِزَازٌ ـ هِيَاجٌ ـ فَزَّةٌ. A — of pleasure, إِهْتِزَازٌ مِنَ ٱلسُّرُورِ; a — of horror, رَجْفَةٌ. *See also* Emotion, *n.*

Thrilling, *a.* مُرَغِّبٌ ـ مُحَرِّكُ ٱلْأَحْسَاسِ ـ مُحَرِّكُ ٱلْقَلْبِ. Of — interest, أَرْغَبُ.

Thrillingly, *a.* بِثَوَرَانٍ ـ بِٱهْتِزَازٍ ـ بِهِيَاجٍ.

Thrive, *v.i.* To prosper, نَجَحَ ـ أَفْلَحَ ـ تَفَيَّدَ ـ سَعِدَ. To grow in vigour, تَشَدَّدَ ـ تَقَوَّى ـ قَوِيَ. To —, of an affair, وَشُكَ *aor.* يَوْشُكُ; of a youth, فَقَعَ. The land throve, زَكَتِ ٱلْأَرْضُ ـ أَرِضَتِ ٱلْأَرْضُ.

Thriver, *n.* } Prosperous, فَالِحٌ ـ مَنَاجِحُ *pl.* مُنْجِحٌ ـ نَاجِحٌ ـ
Thriving, *a.* } رَجُلٌ غَضِيرُ ٱلنَّاصِيَةِ. A — man, مُوَفَّقٌ ـ مُفْلِحٌ ـ مَغْضُورٌ.

Thrivingly, *ad.* بِتَوْفِيقٍ ـ بِإِفْلَاحٍ ـ بِنَجَاحٍ ـ بِإِقْبَالٍ.

Throat, *n.* The fauces, حُلُوقٌ *pl.* حَلْقٌ ـ حُلْقُومٌ ـ مَزْرَدٌ. The neck, خُنَاقٌ ـ عِلَّةُ ٱلْحَلْقِ. A sore —, أَعْنَاقٌ *pl.* عُنُقٌ *or* عُنْقٌ. Something sticking in the —, شَجًا ـ غُصَّةٌ ـ خُنَاقَةٌ ـ خُنَاقٌ. "And your hearts came up into your throats," وَبَلَغَتِ ٱلْقُلُوبُ ٱلْحَنَاجِرَ (Kur. xxxiii. 10).

To seize on by the throat, خَنَقَ ـ أَخَذَ بِخِنَاقِهِ ـ بِمُخَنَّقِهِ.

To cut the throat of one, وَكَزَ عُنُقَهُ *aor.* يَكِزُ.

To cut the throat of an animal for sacrifice, ذَبَحَ.

To cut one's own throat, وَكَزَ عُنُقَهُ; to destroy one's own prospects, خَيَّبَ نَفْسَهُ ـ خَرَّبَ شُغْلَهُ.

To have something sticking in the throat, غَصَّ.

Throb, *v.i.* ضَرَبَ ـ إِخْتَلَجَ ـ رَفَّ: the vein throbbed, ضَرَبَ ٱلْعِرْقُ. *See also to* Palpitate, *v.i.*

Throb, *n.* رَفَّةٌ ـ تَخَلُّجٌ ـ خُلُوجٌ. *See also* Palpitation, *n.*

Throbbing, *a.* ضَارِبٌ ـ مُخْتَلِجٌ ـ رَافٌّ.

Throe, *n.* أَلَمٌ *pl.* آلَامٌ ـ غُصَّةٌ ـ غَمٌّ; the throes of childbirth, مَخَاضٌ ـ نِفَاسٌ.

Throne, *n.* A chair of state, تَخْتٌ ـ سُرُرٌ *pl.* سَرِيرُ ٱلْمُلْكِ ـ كُرْسِيُّ ٱلْمُلْكِ ـ مَسَانِدُ *pl.* مِسْنَدُ ٱلْمُلْكِ ـ تُخُوتُ *pl.* ٱلْمُلْكِ. The — of God, عَرْشُ ٱللّٰهِ ـ ٱلْعَرْشُ. A bishop's —, كُرْسِيُّ ٱلْأُسْقُفِ. Speech from the —, خِطَابٌ مِنْ وَلِيِّ ٱلْمُلْكِ. To ascend the throne, جَلَسَ عَلَى سَرِيرِ ٱلْمُلْكِ.

Throne, *v.t.* *See to* Enthrone, *v.t.*

Throng, *n.* إِزْدِحَامٌ ـ زَحْمٌ.

Throng, *v.t.* زَحَمَ ـ دَافَعَ ـ ضَغَطَ. They thronged him, تَزَاحَمُوا عَلَيْهِ. The people thronged me, زَحَمَنِي ٱلنَّاسُ. *See also to* Crowd, *to* Press, *v.t.*

Throng, *v.i.* Of many, زَحَمَ ٱلْقَوْمُ ـ تَزَاحَمُوا ـ تَضَايَقُوا بَعْضُهُمْ بَعْضًا.

Thronging, *n.* *See* Throng, *n.*

Throstle, *n.* The thrush, دُجٌّ ـ سُمْنَةٌ. A machine for spinning, دَوَالِيبُ *pl.* دُولَابُ ٱلْغَزْلِ.

Throttle, *n.* *See* Throat, *n.*

Throttle, *v.t.* زَرَّدَ حَلْقَهُ ـ خَنَّقَ ـ خَنَقَ ـ شَنَقَ ـ عَنَّقَ.

Throttle, *v.i.* شُنِقَ ـ إِخْتَنَقَ ـ إِنْخَنَقَ.

Throttler, *n.* خَنَّاقٌ ـ زَرَّادٌ.

Through, *prep.* and *ad.* From end to end, مِنْ أَوَّلِهِ إِلَى آخِرِهِ. *In the sense of* From, مِنْ ـ مِنْ بَيْنِ: he fell — the roof, سَقَطَ مِنْ بَيْنِ ٱلسَّقْفِ. He did it — fear, فَعَلَهُ مِنْ خَوْفِهِ. He passed — the door, خَرَجَ مِنَ ٱلْبَابِ. Through, by the hands of, عَلَى يَدِ: he sent it — me, أَرْسَلَهُ عَلَى يَدِي. Through, in, throughout, فِي: through the earth, فِي ٱلْأَرْضِ. Through, by, on account of, بِ: through idleness a man becomes poor, بِٱلْكَسَلِ يَفْتَقِرُ ٱلْإِنْسَانُ. By means of, بِوَاسِطَةِ كَذَا. (*For to* Go, Pass, Pierce —, *etc.*, *see under the respective verbs.*)

Throughout, *ad.* مِنْ أَوَّلِهِ ـ مِنْ فَوْقُ لِتَحْتُ ـ عَلَى مَدَارِ ـ فِي إِلَى آخِرِهِ. Throughout the world, فِي كُلِّ ٱلْعَالَمِ. Throughout the year, مِنْ أَوَّلِ ٱلسَّنَةِ إِلَى آخِرِهَا ـ عَلَى مَدَارِ ٱلسَّنَةِ. Throughout all generations, إِلَى دَوْرٍ فَدَوْرٍ.

Throve, *pret. of to* Thrive, *q.v.*

Throw, *v.t.* To hurl, cast, رَمَى بِ ـ يَرْمِي *aor.* رَمَى ـ طَرَحَ ـ أَرْمَى. To —, of a horse, قَطَّرَ عَنِ ٱلْفَرَسِ; of dice, طَرَحَ. He threw stones at him, رَمَاهُ بِحِجَارَةٍ ـ رَجَمَهُ ـ دَرَاهُ بِحَجَرٍ. The horse threw his rider, أَرْمَى ٱلْفَرَسُ بِرَاكِبِهِ. I threw the load from the camel's back, رَمَيْتُ ٱلْحِمْلَ عَنْ ظَهْرِ ٱلْبَعِيرِ. I threw him from or off the horse, أَرْمَيْتُهُ عَنِ ٱلْفَرَسِ. *See also under to* Cast, *v.t.*

To throw aside, to one side, apart, رَمَى عَلَى جَنْبٍ ـ جَنَّبَ ـ سَيَّبَ ـ تَرَكَ ـ جَعَلَ عَلَى جَنْبٍ. To give up, abandon, تَرَكَ.

To —, as being of no further use, طَرَحَ ـ رَفَعَ.

To throw something at one, رَمَى بِكَذَا (*or* فِي كَذَا) ـ أَلْقَى بِكَذَا.

To throw away, as being useless, رَمَى بِ ـ طَرَحَ. To

squander, to lose, أَتْلَفَ ـ أَذْهَبَ ـ أَسْرَفَ ـ بَذَّرَ. To throw away time, ضَيَّعَ أَوْقَاتَهُ ـ ضَيَّعَ ٱلزَّمَنَ.

To throw one's self away, خَسَرَ نَفْسَهُ ـ ضَيَّعَ نَفْسَهُ ـِ.

To throw back, to retard, أَعَاقَ ـ عَوَّقَ; of the health, أَخَّرَ ٱتِّجَاهَهُ إِلَى ٱلصِّحَّةِ.

To throw down, as in wrestling, صَرَعَ ـَ. To prostrate, floor, أَوْقَعَ ـ إِعْتَفَرَ ـ أَجْفَأَ بِهِ ـ جَفَأَ بِهِ ـَ ـ عَفَرَ ـ هَوَّرَ ـ كَبَتَ ـِ.

To throw one down, to extend one, on the back, سَلْقَى ع: he threw me down on the back, سَلْقَنِى ـ سَلْقَنِى لِحُلَاوَةِ ٱلْقَفَا عَلَى قَفَاى. The doctor threw him down, extended him on his back, سَلْقَهُ ٱلطَّبِيبُ عَلَى ظَهْرِهِ. To throw down on the breast, بَطَحَ ـَ; on the head, نَكَتَ ع; on the face, كَبَّ ع; on the side, سَطَحَ ع. To pull down, demolish, خَرَّبَ ـ هَدَّ ع ـ هَدَمَ ـِ ـ هَوَّرَ. To cause to fall, سَاقَطَ ـ أَسْقَطَ.

To throw one's self down, as to sleep, خَبَطَ ـِ; as on the head, إِنْسَطَحَ ـ إِنْتَكَتَ; as on the face, إِنْكَبَّ; as on the side or back, إِنْبَطَحَ. To throw one's self down upon, إِسْتَلْقَى عَلَى.

To throw, or hurl, from, رَمَى ـِ مِنْ كَذَا ـ أَلْقَى ـ مِنْ كَذَا ـ رَمَى بِ ـ مِنْ كَذَا ـِ.

To throw in, أَطْرَحَ ـ أَدْخَلَ ـ أَلْقَى. To give something above the agreement, *etc.*, زَادَ لِ ـ كَذَا ـِ ـ زَادَ ـِ.

To throw into a difficulty or snare, وَقَّعَ ـ فِى مَحْذُورٍ.

To throw off, as a garment, خَلَعَ ـَ. To discard, طَرَحَ ـَ ـ دَشَرَ ـ طَرَدَ ع ـ طَرَحَ بِ. To produce, أَوْرَدَ. To throw off restraint, خَلَعَ عِذَارَهُ ـَ.

To throw off the mask, أَظْهَرَ ٱلْمَخْفِى ـ كَشَفَ عَنْ وَجْهِهِ ٱلْغِمَى ـِ.

See also under Mask, *n.*

To throw on, to impose upon, as blame, a burden, *etc.*, حَمَلَ ـِ حَمَّلَ ـ كَذَا ـ عَلَى ـ كَذَا.

To throw one's self on, إِرْتَمَى عَلَى ـ أَلْقَى نَفْسَهُ عَلَى.

To throw one's self on the mercy of one, إِسْتَرْحَمَ.

To throw on one's hands, to burden with, كَلَّفَ ـ بِ ـ حَمَّلَ ـ عَلَى.

To return to a seller, كَلَّفَ ٱلْبَائِعَ بِ ـ رَدَّ ع ـ إِلَى ٱلْبَائِعِ.

To throw out, to reject, رَفَضَ ـِ ع. To throw out, as words in speech, أَعْرَضَ ٱلْكَلَامَ ـ أَوْرَدَ ٱلْكَلَامَ ـ تَكَلَّمَ بِ ـ نَطَقَ بِ ع; as troops, in advance, سَلَّفَ رَسِيلًا ـ سَلَّفَ سُلَّافًا ـ سَلَّفَ. To elide, omit, أَسْقَطَ ـ حَذَفَ ـِ.

To throw out of employment, بَطَّلَ ـ مِنَ ٱلْعَمَلِ ـ جَرَّدَ ـ مِنَ ٱلْعَمَلِ ـ عَطَّلَ ـ مِنَ ٱلْعَمَلِ.

To throw out of gear, أَعْدَمَ ـ عَطَّلَ ـ خَسَّرَ.

To throw together, to collect, جَمَّعَ ـ جَمَعَ ـَ. To throw together, as of persons in familiar association, جَعَلَهُمْ يَتَعَاشَرُونَ ـ سَهَّلَ عَلَيْهِمِ ٱلْمُخَالَطَةَ.

To throw over, to upset, قَلَبَ ـِ. To throw over, as of a garment, طَرَحَ ـَ: I threw the garment over my shoulder, طَرَحْتُ ٱلثَّوْبَ عَلَى عَاتِقِى. To abandon, سَيَّبَ ـ تَرَكَ ع. To forsake, تَارَكَ. To cast off, طَرَدَ ع ـ رَفَضَ ـِ.

To throw up, to vomit, إِسْتَفْرَغَ ـ *vulg.* نَتَقَ ع ـ طَرَشَ ـِ. To throw up, as the sea does pebbles, *etc.*, بَعَثَ بِ ـَ ـ جَفَلَ ـِ ع.

To resign, إِسْتَعْفَى ـ تَجَرَّدَ مِن.

Throw, *n.* A cast, طَرْحَة ـ رَمَآة ـ رَمْيَة ـ رَمْى. A stone's —, رَشْقَةُ حَجَرٍ ـ رَمْيَةُ حَجَرٍ.

Thrower, *n.* طَارِح ـ رَامٍ.

Throwster, *n.* مُفَتِّلُ (*or*) فَتَّالُ ٱلْحَرِيرِ.

Thrum, *n.* Of thread, فُضَالَةُ خَيْطٍ. Coarse yarn, خَام ـ خَامٌ خَشِنٌ.

Thrum, *v.t.* To insert, as threads, سَلَّكَ. To knot, عَقَّدَ.

See also to Strum, *v.i.*

Thrush, *n.* The bird, دُجّ ـ سُمْنَة ـ سَمَرْمَر. The disease, قُلَاع. Having the —, مَقْلُوع.

Thrust, *v.t.* To push, shove, صَدَمَ ـِ ـ دَفَعَ ـَ ـ دَرَأَ ـَ ـ دَسَرَ ع.

To — or drive away rudely, دَعَّ ع: "It is he who thrusteth away the orphan," فَذَٰلِكَ ٱلَّذِى يَدُعُّ ٱلْيَتِيمَ (Kur. cvii. 2). To be —, إِطَّرَدَ ـ إِنْدَفَعَ. *See also to* Throw, *v.t.*

To thrust aside, دَفَعَ ـ عَلَى جَانِبٍ ـ جَنَّبَ ـَ.

To thrust away, طَرَدَ ع ـ دَفَعَ ـَ ـ رَدَّ.

To thrust back, رَدَّ ـ إِلَى وَرَآءٍ ع.

To thrust in, أَدْخَلَ ـ دَسَرَ ع. To squeeze in, كَبَسَ ـِ. To make to penetrate, نَفَذَ ـِ. To put in, وَضَعَ ـ فِى *aor.* يَضَعُ. To pierce with, of a spear, *etc.*, رَمَى ـ بِ ـ طَعَنَ ـ بِ ـَ ـ رَشَقَ ـ بِ ع ـِ.

To thrust one's self in, تَدَخَّلَ ـ تَكَوَّى. To intrude upon, دَمَرَ ع إِعْتَرَضَ لِ ـ تَعَرَّضَ لِ ـ عَلَى. *See also to* Intrude, *v.t.* and *i.*

To thrust out, expel, طَرَدَ ـ أَخْرَجَ ع.

To thrust through, as with a spear, طَعَنَ ـ بِ ـ شَقَّ ـ بِ ع ـَ.

To be thrust through, طُعِنَ بِ.

Thrust, *n.* A push, دَرْأَة ـ زَحْمَة ـ صَكْمَة ـ دَسْرَة ـ دَسْر ـ مُدَافَعَة ـ دَفْعَة. A — as with a sword, طَعْنَة. A skilful —, طَعْنَةٌ خَلِيسٌ. A —, as with a spear, طَعْن ـ طَعْنَة. A — through, ضَرْبَةٌ نَافِذَةٌ. An assault, هُجُوم ـ هَجْمَة. An onslaught, كَبَّة ـ كُبَّة.

Thruster, *n.* طارِح ـ رَام ـ مُدافِع ـ دَافِع.

Thug, *n.* مِنْ أَصْحاب مَذْهَب ٱلخَنَّاقِين فِي ٱلْهِنْدِ.

Thuggism, *n.* مَذْهَبٌ سِرِّيٌّ فِي ٱلْهِنْدِ يَسْتَحِلُّ خَنْقَ ٱلنَّاسِ.

Thule, *n.* عِبارَةٌ عن ٱلأَقالِيمِ ٱلشَّمالِيَّةِ.

Thumb, *n.* إِبْهام *pl.* أَباهِيم.

Thumb, *v.t.* To handle awkwardly, خَرِقَ فِي ـ بِ ـ. To soil with the fingers, وَسَّخَ ـ طَبَّعَ (or) بِٱلأَصابِعِ.

Thumb-screw, *n.* آلَةٌ لِضَغْطِ ٱلأَباهِيمِ ـ عَذْراءُ ٱلأَباهِيمِ.

Thumb-stall, *n.* كِشْتِبانٌ لِلإِبْهامِ.

Thummim, *n.* The — of the Hebrew Bible, ٱلتُّمِّيمُ. Urim and Thummim, ٱلأُورِيمُ وَٱلتُّمِّيمُ.

Thump, *n.* ضَرْب ـ وَكْزَة.

Thump, *v.t.* وَكَزَ *aor.* يَكِزُ ـ ضَرَبَ ـ لَطَمَ ـ لَكَمَ ـ.

Thump, *v.i.* To knock against, تَصادَمَ ـ تَلاطَمَ.

Thumping, *n.* لَطْمَة ـ ضَرْبَة ـ كَبْسَة.

Thumping, *a.* Large, bulky, جَسِيم ـ كَبِير.

Thunder, *n.* رَعْد *pl.* رُعُود. Any loud noise, لَغَط ـ زَيْطَة ـ ضَجَّة. The — of cannon, رَعْدُ ٱلْمَدافِعِ. The — was continuous, إِرْتَجَزَ ٱلرَّعْدُ. "And the thunder uttereth His praise ... and He sendeth His thunderbolts and smiteth with them whom He will," وَيُسَبِّحُ ٱلرَّعْدُ بِحَمْدِهِ ... وَيُرْسِلُ ٱلصَّواعِقَ فَيُصِيبُ بِهَا مَنْ يَشاءُ (Kur. xiii. 14).

Thunder, *v.i.* رَعَدَ ـ: The sky thundered, رَعَدَتِ ٱلسَّماءُ. The sky thundered and lightened, رَعَدَتِ ٱلسَّماءُ وَبَرَقَتْ. It thunders, عَمّال تَرْعَد *vulg.* تَرْعَدُ.

Thunder, *v.t.* To utter with noise, صَاحَ بِ *aor.* يَصِيحُ ـ ضَجَّ بِ. To utter denunciations against, سَخِطَ عَلَى ـ تَسَخَّطَ عَلَى ـ لَعَنَ ـ. To utter menaces, to fulminate, رَعَدَ وَبَرَقَ ـ أَرْعَدَ وَأَبْرَقَ.

Thunder-bolt, *n.* صاعِقَة *pl.* صَواعِق ـ حُسْبانَة. *See also under* Thunder, *n.*

Thunder-cloud, *n.* سَحابَةٌ رَعّادَةٌ. Thundering clouds, سَحابٌ راعِدٌ. The upper part of a —, غارِب.

Thunder-clap, *n.* رَعْدَة.

Thunderer, *n.* A fulminator, ساخِط. One who is clamorous, عَجّاج ـ صارِخ ـ صَيِّت ـ رَعّاد.

Thundering, *a.* Of thunder, رَعّاد ـ راعِد. Great, عَظِيم.

Thunderstrike, *v.t.* To strike with surprise, أَدْهَشَ ـ حَيَّرَ.

Thunderstruck, *a.* Stricken with surprise, مُنْدَهِش ـ مُتَحَيِّر. To be —, إِنْدَهَشَ ـ تَحَيَّرَ.

Thurible, *n.* مِبْخَرَة *pl.* مَباخِر ـ مِقْطَرَة ـ كُبّوَة. *See also* Censer, *n.*

Thurifer, *n.* حامِلُ ٱلْمِبْخَرَةِ.

Thuriferous, *a.* حامِلُ ٱلْبَخُورِ.

Thurification, *n.* تَبْخِير.

Thursday, *n.* يَوْمُ ٱلْخَمِيسِ ـ الخَمِيس. Holy —, before Easter, خَمِيسُ ٱلْعَهْدِ ـ خَمِيسُ ٱلْقُرْبانِ. Thursday before Lent, خَمِيسُ ٱلسَّكارَى.

Thus, *ad.* So, هٰكَذا ـ كَذا. As, كَمَا. Thus and —, كَذا وَكَذا. In this manner, عَلَى هٰذا ٱلْمِنْوالِ. Thus far, إِلَى هُنا. Thus much, هٰذا ٱلْمِقْدارُ.

Thwack, *v.t.* *See to* Thump, Slap, Smack, *v.t.*

Thwack, *n.* *See* Thump, Smack, Slap, *n.*

Thwart, *a.* Across, مُعْتَرِض. To be —, إِعْتَرَضَ.

Thwart, *v.t.* To lay across, عَرَّضَ. To cross, frustrate, عَاقَ ـ تَعَرَّضَ لِ ـ خَيَّبَ ـ أَعْجَزَ.

Thwartships, *ad.* عَلَى عَرْضِ ٱلْمَرْكَبِ.

Thy, *pron.* *See* Thine, *pron.*

Thyine, *n.* The wood, عُودٌ ثِينِيٌّ.

Thyme, *n.* نَمّام. Wild —, سَعْتَر.

Thymy, *a.* سَعْتَرِيٌّ.

Thyroid, *a.* Resembling a shield, فِي شَكْلِ ٱلتُّرْسِ.

Thyrsus, *n.* قَضِيبٌ مُوَشَّحٌ بِٱللَّبْلابِ.

Thyself, *pron.* أَنْتَ *fem.* أَنْتِ ـ أَنْتَ بِنَفْسِكَ *fem.* أَنْتِ بِنَفْسِكِ. Physician, heal thyself, أَيُّها ٱلطَّبِيبُ ٱشْفِ نَفْسَكَ.

Tiara, *n.* A diadem, تاج *pl.* تِيجان ـ إِكْلِيل *pl.* أَكالِيل. The Pope's —, تاجُ ٱلْبابا.

Tibia, *n.* Of the leg, عَظْمُ ٱلسّاقِ ـ ٱلْقَصَبَةُ ٱلْكُبْرَى.

Tibial, *a.* Of the tibia, مُتَعَلِّقٌ بِعَظْمِ ٱلسّاقِ.

Tic douloureux, *n.* وَجَعُ ٱلْعَصَبِ.

Tick, *n.* Credit, دَيْن. Tick, of bedding, قُماشٌ لِلْفِراشِ. Tick, as of a clock, طَقّ ـ طَقْطَقَة. Tick, the insect infesting sheep, *etc.*, طِلْح ـ طَلِيح ـ قَلَذ ـ حَلَمَة *coll.* حَلَم ـ حَمْنان ـ قِرْدان *pl.* قُراد or قُرْد. A small body-tick, حُرْقُوص *pl.* حَراقِيص. An animal infested with ticks, قَرِن. To take out the ticks from, قَرَّدَ. A tick, in its first stage, is called, قَمْقامَة; then, حَمْنانَة; then, قُراد; then, حَمَلَة; then, عِلّ; and lastly, طِلْح. To buy upon —, أَخَذَ بِٱلدَّيْنِ ـ إِسْتَدانَ ـ.

Tick, *v.i.* As a clock, طَقَّ ـ طَقْطَقَ.

Ticket, *n.* A token, writing, address, عُنْوان عُلْوان ـ رُقْعَة *pl.* رِقاع ـ تَذْكِرَة *pl.* تَذاكِر. A — marking price on goods, بِطاقَة ـ تَذْكِرَةُ سِعْرٍ. A — of invitation to a banquet, تَذْكِرَةُ دَعْوَةٍ لِمَأْدُبَةٍ.

A — of entrance, تَذْكِرَةُ إِجَازَةٍ ـ وَرَقَةُ إِجَازَةٍ. Ticket-of-leave, وَرَقَةُ إِجَازَةٍ تُعْطَى لِبَعْضٍ مِنَ ٱلْمَحْبُوسِينَ لِيَتَعَيَّشُوا فِي خَارِجِ ٱلْحَبْسِ ـ وَرَقَةُ إِجَازَةٍ لِلْمَحْبُوسِ. That's the ticket! يَا حَبَّذَا.

Ticket, *v.t.* عَلَّقَ ـ حَطَّ عُنْوَانًا عَلَى ـ ² جَعَلَ بِطَاقَةً عَلَى ٱلتَّذَاكِرِ فِي.

Ticking, *n.* For a bed, قُمَاشٌ لِلْفِرَاشِ.

Tickle, *v.t.* زَغْزَغَ ـ دَغْدَغَ ـ ² نَدَغَ ـ نَغَّرَ ـ ² نَغَزَ ـ *vulg.* نَغْمَشَ. To be tickled, تَدَغْدَغَ ـ نُغِّرَ ـ نُدِغَ. My hand tickles me, يَدِي تُدَغْدِغُنِي ـ يَدِي تَتَدَغْدَغُ. To — one's fancy, to blandish, طَبْطَبَ ل ـ دَاجَنَ ـ نَادَغَ ـ رَافَأَ ـ رَفَّأَ. To please, أَعْجَبَ ـ ² سَرَّ.

Tickle, *n.* دَغْدَغَة ـ نَدْغ.

Tickler, *n.* One who tickles, مُنَغْمِش ـ *vulg.* مُدَغْدِغ ـ نَادِغ; one who blandishes, مُدَاجِن ـ مَلِق ـ مُنَادِغ.

Tickling, *n.* The act of, دَغْدَغَة ـ نَدْغ. Blandishment, مُرَافَأَة ـ تَمَلُّق ـ مُنَادَغَة.

Ticklish, *a.* Susceptible to tickling, لَا يَحْتَمِلُ ٱلدَّغْدَغَةَ. Tottering of a wall, *etc.*, وَاقِع ـ مُخِيف. Critical, dangerous, خَطِير ـ مُخْطِر. Difficult, embarrassing, مُشْكِل. To be —, of the body, تَدَغْدَغَ ـ نُدِغَ.

Ticklishness, *n.* Of the body, زَغْزَغَة ـ تَزَغْزُغ ـ تَدَغْدُغ. Criticalness, بُحْرَان ـ خَطَر ـ اِرْتِبَاك ـ صُعُوبَة ـ مُشْكِلَة.

Tidal, *a.* مُتَعَلِّقٌ بِٱلْمَدِّ وَٱلْجَزْرِ. Tidal harbour, مِينَاءٌ عِنْدَ ٱلْمَدِّ فَقَطْ.

Tid-bit, *n.* لُقْمَةٌ مَقْبُولَةٌ ـ لُقْمَةٌ لَذِيذَةٌ.

Tide, *n.* Ebb and flow, جَزْرٌ وَمَدٌّ. Ebb-tide, جَزْر; flood-tide, مَدٌّ. An opportunity, فُرْصَة. Course, as of events, دَهْر ـ تَعَاقُب. A concourse, اِلْتِقَاء. The — of time, مُرُورُ ٱلزَّمَانِ ـ تَرَاوُح ـ تَنَاوُب. A — of good fortune, دَوْلَة; of bad fortune, دَبْرَة. The — is coming in, أَخَذَ ٱلْبَحْرُ فِي ٱلْمَدِّ ـ ² مَدَّ ٱلْبَحْرُ; the — is ebbing, ² جَزَرَ ٱلْبَحْرُ ـ ٱلْبَحْرُ عَلَى جَزْرٍ.

Tide-gate, *n.* سَدٌّ لِلْمَدِّ *pl.* سُدُود ـ مَسَكٌ لِلْمَدِّ ـ شَذَبٌ لِلْمَدِّ.

Tide-gauge, *n.* مِقْيَاسُ ٱلْمَدِّ وَٱلْجَزْرِ.

Tideless, *a.* لَا مَدَّ لَهُ وَلَا جَزْرَ.

Tides-man, *n.* }
Tide-waiter, } خَفَرُ (*vulg.* غَفَرُ) ٱلْكُمْرُكِ.

Tidily, *ad.* حَسَنًا ـ بِظَرَافَةٍ ـ بِكِيَاسَةٍ. *See also* Neatly, *ad.*

Tidiness, *n.* لَطَافَة ـ ظَرَافَة ـ كِيَاسَة. *See also* Neatness, *n.*

Tidings, *n.* خَبَر *pl.* أَخْبَار. Tidings from afar, جَوَائِب. Joyful —, بِشَارَة ـ بُشْرَى. To ask one for —, اِسْتَخْبَرَ. To give or declare glad — to, بَشَّرَ. A present given to one for bringing good —, بِشَارَة.

Tidy, *a.* حَسَن ـ حُلْو ـ لَطِيف ـ ظَرِيف ـ كَيِّس. *See also* Neat, *a.*

Tie, *v.t.* ² رَبَطَ ـ أَرْبَطَ ـ ² شَدَّ. To —, as in a knot, ² عَقَدَ. To — the hair, جَمَّرَ ٱلشَّعْرَ. To —, to bind, as with a strap, ² حَزَمَ ـ أَوْثَقَ ـ وَكَّدَ ـ ² أَسَرَ ـ أَسَّرَ. To — firmly, ² حَزَقَ ـ ² عَقَدَ. To be tied, اِشْتَدَّ ـ اِرْتَبَطَ. To be tied, as with a strap, اِحْتَزَمَ. To be tied firmly, اِنْعَقَدَ ـ اِحْتَزَقَ. To — the hands behind the back, كَتَّفَ. To — the feet of one, قَيَّدَ رِجْلَيْهِ. To tie one's self, as with a rope, *etc.*, ² رَبَطَ ـ تَحَزَّقَ ـ تَحَزَّمَ نَفْسَهُ.

To tie down, رَبَطَ إِلَى ٱلْأَرْضِ ـ ² رَبَطَ وَهُوَ مُنْبَطِحًا. To tie one to a bargain, شَارَطَ عَلَى ـ عَاقَدَ فِي ـ ² عَقَدَ عَلَى فِي. To oblige to, ² جَبَرَ عَلَى ـ أَلْزَمَ بِ اِضْطَرَّ إِلَى. To restrain, أَوْقَفَ ـ ² مَنَعَ عَنْ ـ ² عَكَفَ عَنْ.

To tie together, ² شَدَّ مَعًا ـ ² حَزَمَ حُزْمَةً.

To tie up, as in a bundle, ² صَرَّ صُرَّةً ـ ² صَرَّ; of papers, *etc.*, ² ضَبَرَ ـ ² صَرَّ ـ ضَبَّرَ. To close against, ² سَدَّ عَلَى كَذَا ـ ² صَرَّ عَلَى كَذَا. To confine, limit, حَدَّدَ. To —, as property, to, ² حَبَسَ عَلَى; as of a wound, جَبَّرَ ـ ² جَبَرَ. He tied up the horse as a preparation to his racing him, اِرْتَبَطَ ٱلْحِصَانَ لِيُغَالِقَ عَلَيْهِ. "Let not thine hand be tied up to thy neck," *i.e.* be not niggardly, لَا تَجْعَلْ يَدَكَ مَغْلُولَةً إِلَى عُنُقِكَ (Kur. lxxi. 13).

Tie, *n.* رَبْط *pl.* رِبَاط ـ رَابِطَة ـ شَدَّة. Connexion, تَعَلُّق ـ عَلَاقَة. Relationship, قَرَابَة ـ مَقْرَبَة ـ دَنَاوَة. The place of tying, مَعْقِد. A small kerchief, طَرْحَة ـ مِنْدِيل *pl.* مَنَادِيل. The — of marriage, عِصْمَةُ ٱلنِّكَاحِ. The ties of friendship, حَبَائِلُ ٱلْمَوَادَّةِ. An equality of votes, مُسَاوَاةُ ٱلْآرَاءِ فِي ٱلْاِنْتِخَابِ.

Tie-beam, *n.* جَائِز ـ مَجَرّ ـ خَشَبَةٌ تُوضَعُ عَلَيْهَا أَطْرَافُ ٱلْعَوَارِضِ.

Tied, *part.* مَرْبُوط ـ مَشْدُود. A — animal, رَبِيط *pl.* رُبُط *and* رِبَاط.

Tier, *n.* A row, طَبَقَة *pl.* طَبَقَات ـ صَفّ *pl.* صُفُوف.

Tierce, *n.* A barrel of the measure so called, بَرْمِيل يَسَعُ ٤٠ كَالِنًا. *See under* Gallon, *n.*

A — in fencing, طَعْنَةٌ فِي فَنِّ ٱلْطِّعَانِ.

Tiercet, *n.* *See* Triplet, *n.*

Tiers-état, *n.* ٱلْعَوَامّ.

Tiff, *n.* A draught, شَرْبَة. A pet, fit of peevishness, زَعَج ـ تَضَجُّر ـ طَلْعَةُ خُلُقٍ ـ حَمِيًّا ـ ضَجَر. To be in a —, اِنْزَعَجَ ـ تَضَجَّرَ.

Tiffany, *n.* قَزّ.

Tiffed, *a.* مُنْزَعِج ـ مُتَضَجِّر.

Tiger, *n.* The animal, نَمِر *pl.* نِمَار and نُمُور. A boy servant, غُلَام لَابِس كَسْمًا مَخْصُوصًا ـ غِلْمَان *pl.* غُلَام.

Tight, *a.* Bound or fitting tightly, مَشْدُود ـ مُحَزَّق ـ مُزَنَّق. Closed —, مَسْدُود بِطِينِ ٱلْحِكْمَةِ ـ مَسْدُودٌ خَالِصٌ ـ مَسْدُود. Narrow, ضَيِّق. Snug, well ordered, مُنَظَّم ـ فِي غَايَةِ ٱلْإِتْقَانِ ـ مَضْبُوط. Pretty, nice, جَمِيل ـ ظَرِيف ـ كَيِّس ـ حَبَّذَا. Tipsy, سَكْرَان ـ مُلَتَّك. *See also* Severe, *a.*

Tighten, *v.t.* To make more tight, حَزَقَ ـ وَكَّدَ ـ لَبَّبَ ـ شَدَّ ـ عَقَدَ. To make narrower, ضَيَّقَ.

Tightly, *ad.* In a close manner, بِشِدَّةٍ ـ حَزْقًا. Narrowly, عَلَى ٱلضَّيْقِ. Neatly, فِي غَايَةِ ٱلْإِتْقَانِ ـ حَسَنًا ـ بِلَطَافَةٍ ـ بِكِيَاسَةٍ.

Tightness, *n.* Closeness, حَزْق ـ حَزْم ـ شَدّ ـ لُبُوب. Narrowness, ضِيق ـ حَرَج. Neatness, حُسْن ـ لَطَافَة ـ كِيَاسَة. Impermeability, عَدَمُ تَطَرُّقِ ٱلْمَاءِ إِلَيْهِ ـ عَدَمُ قَطْعِ ٱلْمَاءِ فِيهِ.

Tigress, *n.* نِمْرَة *pl.* نِمْرَات.

Tigrish, *a.* يُشْبِهُ ٱلنَّمِرَ.

Tilbury, *n.* عَرَبَانَةٌ خَفِيفَةٌ مَكْشُوفَةٌ ـ عَرَبَانَةٌ خَفِيفَةٌ بِدُونِ سَقِيفَةٍ.

Tile, *n.* قِرْمِيدَة *coll.* قِرْمِيد *pl.* قَرَامِيدُ. Covered with tiles, مُقَرْمَد. *See also* Brick, *n.* and Hat, *n.*

Tile, *v.t.* فَرَشَ بِقِرْمِيدٍ.

Tiler, *n.* One who lays tiles, فَرَّاشُ ٱلْقِرْمِيدِ ـ مُفَرِّشُ ٱلْقِرْمِيدِ. A maker of tiles, طَوَّاب ـ صَانِعُ ٱلْقَرَامِيدِ.

Tiling, *n.* A roof covered with tiles, سَطْحٌ مُقَرْمَدٌ. Tiles in general, طُوب ـ قِرْمِيد.

Till, *n.* A box for money, صُنْدُوقُ ٱلْفُلُوسِ ـ دُرْجَةُ ٱلدَّرَاهِمِ.

Till, *prep.* لِحَدِّ ـ إِلَى حَدِّ ـ إِلَى ـ حَتَّى. Till now, إِلَى ٱلْآنَ. Till when? إِلَى مَتَى ـ حَتَّى مَا ـ حَتَّامَ. Till he returns to us, حَتَّى يَرْجِعَ إِلَيْنَا. *See also* Until, *prep.*

Till, *v.t.* خَدَمَ ٱلْأَرْضَ ـ فَلَحَ ـ حَرَثَ ـ أَكَرَ.

Tillage, *n.* فَلَاحَة ـ حَرْث.

Tiller, *n.* Of the soil, فَلَّاح *pl.* فَلَّاحُون ـ حَرَّاث ـ أَكَرَة *pl.* أَكَّار and فَلَالِيحُ. A — of a rudder, عَصَاةُ ٱلدَّفَّةِ ـ لِجَامُ ٱلدَّفَّةِ.

Tiller, *v.i.* To put forth shoots, فَرَّخَ ـ طَرَّ ـ أَلْحَسَ.

Tilt, *n.* A tent, خَيْمَة *pl.* خِيَم. Tilt, as of a carriage, *etc.*, رَفْرَاف ـ سَقِيفَة. An inclination, مَيْل ـ حُصُور ـ إِنْحِرَاف. A thrust, طَعْنَة ـ طَعْن. An attack, rush, سَطْوَة ـ حَمْلَة ـ كَبَّة ـ وَثْبَة. An exercise of tilting, لَعْبُ ٱلْجَرِيدَةِ ـ لَعْبُ ٱلتَّطَاعُنِ. A heavy hammer, مِرْزَبَّة. At full —, فِي غَايَةِ ٱلْعَجَلِ ـ تَهَوُّرًا.

Tilt, *v.t.* To incline, stoop, مَيَّلَ ـ حَنَى ـ أَصْغَى ـ طَأْطَأَ. To point, as a lance, نَاشَنَ ـ شَرَّعَ ـ أَشْرَعَ. To rush at, سَطَا ـ يَسْطُو *aor.* وَثَبَ ـ يَثِبُ *aor.* إِلَى ـ طَفَّ عَلَى. To hammer with a —, طَرَقَ ـ مَطَلَ ـ مَطَلَ بِٱلْمِرْزَبَّةِ.

Tilt, *v.i.* To incline to one side, مَالَ ـ أَصْغَى ـ تَصَوَّبَ. To —, as with a lance, تَطَاعَنَ بِمِزْرَاقٍ; of the sport, لَعِبَ بِٱلتَّطَاعُنِ ـ لَعِبَ بِٱلْجَرِيدَةِ.

Tilter, *n.* As in a joust, لَاعِبٌ بِٱلتَّطَاعُنِ ـ لَاعِبٌ بِٱلْجَرِيدَةِ. One who hammers, طَارِقٌ بِٱلْمِرْزَبَّةِ ـ مَاطِل.

Tilt-hammer, *n.* مِرْزَبَّة *pl.* مَرَازِبُ ـ سِنْطَاب.

Timbal, *n.* *See* Kettledrum, *n.*

Timber, *n.* خَشَب *pl.* أَخْشَاب ـ عُود *pl.* أَعْوَاد and عِيدَان. A piece of —, خَشَبَة *pl.* خُشُب. Timber for firewood, حَطَب *pl.* أَحْطَاب. A tree, شَجَرَة *pl.* أَشْجَار. The timbers of a roof, رَوَافِدُ; of a ship, أَطْوَاق. A — merchant, خَشَّاب *pl.* خَشَّابَة. A — yard, دَكَّةُ حَطَبٍ ـ حَطَّابَة. *See also* Wood, *n.*

Timbrel, *n.* *See* Tambourine, *n.*

Time, *n.* The succession of moments, part of duration, أَمَد ـ زَمَان *pl.* أَزْمَان ـ زَمَن *pl.* أَحْيَان ـ حِين *pl.* أَوْقَات ـ وَقْت *pl.* أَزْمِنَة. Time, age, generation, century, جِيل *pl.* أَجْيَال ـ عَهْد ـ عَصْر ـ قَرْن *pl.* قُرُون ـ دَهْر *pl.* دُهُور. An appointed —, أَجَل ـ وَقْتٌ مَوْقُوفٌ ـ مِيعَاد ـ مَوَاعِدُ *pl.* مَوْعِد. A particular — or season for anything, وَقْت ـ أَوَان ـ فَصْل ـ إِبَّان. A —, once, دَفْعَة *pl.* مَرَّات ـ مَرَّة *pl.* مِرَار and طَرَقَات ـ طَرْق and طَرْقَة *pl.* دَفَعَات. Time, fixed —, as of death, وَقْتُ ٱلْمَمَاتِ ـ أَجَل. Time, hour, moment, وَقْت ـ دَقِيقَة ـ سَاعَة. Leisure, فَرَاغ ـ وَقْت ـ تَفَرُّغ ـ فَضَاء. Condition, state, أَحْوَال ـ حَالَة ـ حَال. Delay, مُهْلَة. Time, as of music, وَزْن. At all times, فِي كُلِّ آنٍ ـ دَائِمًا ـ فِي كُلِّ وَقْتٍ. That was in the — of such an one, ذٰلِكَ كَانَ فِي عَهْدِ فُلَانٍ. That was in the — of my youth, ذٰلِكَ كَانَ فِي عَهْدِ شَبَابِي. I have not met him for a long —, مَا لَقِيتُهُ مُنْذُ زَمَانٍ. At the — of such an one, عَلَى عَدَانِ فُلَانٍ ـ فِي وَقْتِ فُلَانٍ ـ فِي عَهْدِ فُلَانٍ. It is high — for us to awake, حَانَتِ ٱلسَّاعَةُ لِنَسْتَيْقِظَ. Is it a — for you to speak? كَانَ ٱلْوَقْتُ لَكُمْ أَنْ تَتَكَلَّمُوا. The — of their going out, وَقْتُ خُرُوجِهِمْ. The — came, آنَ ٱلْأَوَانُ ـ حَلَّ ٱلْوَقْتُ ـ حَانَ ٱلْحِينُ ـ حَلَّ ـ حَانَ. It is — to depart, حَانَ وَقْتُ ٱلذَّهَابِ ـ حُكْمُ ٱلْوَقْتِ. Is it not — for you to go? مَا حَانَ لَكَ وَقْتُ ٱلرَّوَاحِ ـ مَا حَلَّ لَكَ أَنْ تَرُوحَ ـ لَيْسَ ٱلرَّوَاح. We have no —, leisure, مَا عِنْدَنَا وَقْتٌ ـ لَنَا فَرَاغٌ. He had no — to drink it before he fell on the ground, سَقَطَ عَلَى ٱلْأَرْضِ قَبْلَ أَنْ يُدْرِكَ شُرْبَهُ. I shall not have — to do that, مَا أُدْرِكُ عَمَلَهُ ـ مَا أَلْحَقُ عَلَى ذٰلِكَ.

We have — to wait, لَنَا (or عِنْدَنَا) وَقْتٌ لِنَنْتَظِرَ. He came at the proper or appointed —, جَآءَ عَلَى عَهْدِهِ aor. يَجِيءُ. The — of my departure, death, is at hand, قَدْ حَضَرَ وَقْتُ ٱلْجَلَالِي. A critical —, *un mauvais quart d'heure*, سَاعَةٌ سُوْءًا. It is a long — since he awoke you, طَالَمَا أَيْقَظَكَ. In hard times like these, فِي مِثْلِ هٰذِهِ ٱلْأَوْقَاتِ ٱلْعَسِيرَةِ.

Apparent time, true time, وَقْتٌ حَقِيقِيٌّ ــ وَقْتٌ مَرْصُودٌ.

Astronomical time, حِسَابُ ٱلْوَقْتِ مِنْ رَصْدِ ٱلظُّهْرِ.

Bed time, وَقْتُ ٱلنَّوْمِ.

Breakfast time, وَقْتُ ٱلْغَدَآءِ ــ وَقْتُ ٱلْفُطُورِ.

Church time, وَقْتُ ٱلْقُدَّاسِ ــ وَقْتُ ٱلْكَنِيسَةِ.

Day time, وَقْتُ ٱلنَّهَارِ ــ ٱلضَّحَآءُ.

Dinner time, وَقْتُ ٱلْأَكْلِ.

Equation of time, تَعْدِيلُ ٱلزَّمَانِ.

Evening time, وَقْتُ ٱلْمَسَآءِ.

Mean time, وَقْتٌ مُتَوَسِّطٌ.

Night time, وَقْتُ ٱللَّيْلِ.

Prayer time, وَقْتُ ٱلصَّلَاةِ.

Sidereal time, وَقْتٌ فَلَكِيٌّ ــ ٱلْوَقْتُ حَسَبَ دَوَرَانِ ٱلنُّجُومِ.

Supper time, وَقْتُ ٱلْعَشَآءِ.

About that time, عِنْدَ ذٰلِكَ ٱلْوَقْتِ ــ فِي ذٰلِكَ ٱلْوَقْتِ.

About the time of the war, نَحْوَ زَمَانِ ٱلْحَرْبِ.

After a time, بَعْدَ مُدَّةٍ مِنَ ٱلزَّمَانِ ــ بَعْدَ أُمَّةٍ.

A long time, زَمَانٌ ــ زَمَانٌ طَوِيلٌ ــ زَمَنٌ طَوِيلٌ ــ دَهْرٌ طَوِيلٌ ــ أَبَدٌ.

A long time ago, since, مُنْذُ زَمَانٍ ــ مُذْ زَمَنٍ طَوِيلٍ. That was a long time ago, كَانَ ذٰلِكَ فِي أَبَادِ ٱلدَّهْرِ.

A short time, مُدَّةٌ يَسِيرَةٌ مِنَ ٱلزَّمَانِ ــ زَمَنٌ يَسِيرٌ.

A short time ago, مُنْذُ مُدَّةٍ يَسِيرَةٍ مِنَ ٱلزَّمَانِ ــ مُذْ زَمَنٍ يَسِيرٍ ــ عَنْ قَرِيبٍ.

A work of time, شُغْلٌ يَحْتَاجُ إِلَى ٱلزَّمَانِ.

As times go, نَظَرًا لِلْأَحْوَالِ ٱلْحَاضِرَةِ ــ نَظَرًا لِلْأَحْوَالِ.

At all times, فِي كُلِّ آنٍ ــ نَهَارًا وَلَيْلًا ــ فِي كُلِّ وَقْتٍ ــ كُلَّ وَقْتٍ ــ دَائِمًا.

At any time, فِي كُلِّ حِينٍ ــ فِي أَيِّ حِينٍ كَانَ. Not at any time, قَطُّ. If he should go out at any time? إِنْ خَرَجَ. Lest at any time, حَتَّى لَا ــ لِئَلَّا. To whom did he say at any time, لِمَنْ قَالَ قَطُّ. No man hath seen God at any time, أَللّٰهُ لَمْ يَرَهُ أَحَدٌ قَطُّ.

At one time, مَرَّةً ــ فِي حِينٍ. At one and the same time, فِي آنٍ وَاحِدٍ.

At no time, أَصْلًا ــ قَطُّ.

At other times, فِي غَيْرِ أَوْقَاتٍ ــ غَيْرَ مِرَارٍ.

At such a time, فِي ٱلْوَقْتِ ٱلْفُلَانِ.

At such a time as this, فِي زَمَانٍ مِثْلَ هٰذَا ــ فِي وَقْتٍ كَهٰذَا ــ فِي حَالَةٍ نَظِيرَةٍ هٰذِهِ.

At that time, إِذْ ذَاكَ ــ مِنْ سَاعَتِهِ ــ سَاعَتَئِذٍ ــ وَقْتَئِذٍ ــ فِي ذٰلِكَ ٱلزَّمَانِ.

At the time, فِي وَقْتِهِ ــ وَقْتَ ــ وَقْتَئِذٍ. At the same time, فِي تِلْكَ ــ فَقَطْ ــ مَعَ هٰذَا. Nevertheless, فِي ذٰلِكَ ٱلْوَقْتِ ــ ٱلسَّاعَةَ.

At this time, فِي ٱلْوَقْتِ ٱلْحَاضِرِ ــ فِي هٰذَا ٱلْوَقْتِ ــ ٱلسَّاعَةَ ــ هٰذِهِ ٱلْمَرَّةَ ــ فِي هٰذِهِ ٱلْمَرَّةِ. At this one time, فِي هٰذَا ٱلْيَوْمِ.

At this time of day, now, فِي هٰذَا ٱلْيَوْمِ. So early, هٰكَذَا غُدْوَةً. So late, هٰكَذَا فِي آخِرِ ٱلنَّهَارِ.

At this time to-morrow or the day after, مِثْلَ ٱلْآنَ غَدًا أَوْ بَعْدَ غَدٍ.

At times, بَعْضَ أَوْقَاتٍ ــ أَحْيَانًا ــ مِرَارًا.

Before one's time, قَبْلَ وَقْتِهِ ــ قَبْلَ ٱلْوَقْتِ.

Behind one's time, تَأَخُّرًا.

By the time, لَمَّا ــ عِنْدَ وَقْتِ ــ عِنْدَ.

By this time, قَدْ: by this time he has arrived, قَدْ وَصَلَ. By this time you ought to have gone, كَانَ يَنْبَغِي أَنْ تَذْهَبَ قَبْلَ هٰذَا ٱلْوَقْتِ.

For a long time, لِزَمَنٍ طَوِيلٍ. For a long time since, مُنْذُ زَمَنٍ ــ مُنْذُ زَمَنٍ ــ طَوِيلٍ.

For a short time, لِزَمَنٍ قَلِيلٍ ــ لِزَمَنٍ يَسِيرٍ ــ زَمَانَ سَاعَةٍ.

For some time, لِمُدَّةٍ مَا ــ لِمُدَّةٍ مِنَ ٱلزَّمَانِ. Since some time, مُنْذُ زَمَنٍ.

For such a time as this, لِوَقْتٍ مِثْلَ هٰذَا.

For the time, لِلْوَقْتِ. At the time, وَقْتَئِذٍ ــ عِنْدَ ذٰلِكَ ــ فِي ذٰلِكَ ٱلْوَقْتِ.

For the time being, لِلْوَقْتِ ٱلْحَاضِرِ ــ لِلْوَقْتِ.

For time, زَمَنًا. For time and for eternity, زَمَنًا وَأَبَدًا.

From olden time, مِنَ ٱلْقَدِيمِ ــ مُنْذُ أَجْيَالٍ ــ مُنْذُ زَمَانٍ ــ مِنْ قَدِيمِ ٱلزَّمَانِ وَسَالِفِ ٱلْعَصْرِ وَٱلْأَوَانِ.

From that time, مِنْ ذٰلِكَ ــ مِنْ ذٰلِكَ ٱلْوَقْتِ ــ مِنْ يَوْمِهِ ــ ٱلزَّمَانِ.

From this time, مِنَ ٱلْيَوْمِ ــ مِنْ هٰذَا ٱلْوَقْتِ ــ مِنَ ٱلْآنَ.

From this time forth, مِنَ ٱلْآنَ فَصَاعِدًا.

From time to time, مِرَارًا ــ مِنْ وَقْتٍ إِلَى وَقْتٍ.

From time immemorial, مُنْذُ زَمَانٍ مَنْسِيِّ ٱلذِّكْرِ.

In a moment of time, فِي لَحْظَةٍ مِنَ ٱلزَّمَانِ.

In a short time, فِي سَاعَةٍ. In a short time hence, عَنْ قَرِيبٍ.

In due time, فِي ٱلْوَقْتِ ـ عَلَى وَقْتٍ: He came in due time, جَآءَ فِي وَقْتِهِ aor. يَجِيءُ.

In former times, فِي ٱلْأَجْيَالِ ٱلسَّابِقَةِ ـ قَبْلًا ـ سَابِقًا.

In good time; *see* In due time.

In no time, immediately, حَالًا ـ عَلَى ٱلْفَوْرِ. Never, قَطُّ.

In olden time, فِي قَدِيمِ ٱلزَّمَانِ ـ فِي ٱلْأَجْيَالِ ٱلسَّابِقَةِ ـ قَدِيمًا ـ وَسَالِفِ ٱلْعَصْرِ وَٱلْأَوَانِ. Those of the olden time, ٱلْقُدَمَآءُ ـ ٱلْأَوَّلُونَ.

In one's time, فِي وَقْتِهِ ـ فِي عَهْدِهِ. Not in his time, day, لَيْسَ فِي أَيَّامِهِ.

In process of time, لَمَّا طَالَ ـ وَمِنْ بَعْدِ أَيَّامٍ ـ مَعَ صُرُوفِ ٱلزَّمَانِ ـ ٱلزَّمَانُ. In process of time he died, حَدَثَ فِي تِلْكَ ٱلْأَيَّامِ أَنَّهُ مَاتَ.

In quick time, بِٱلْعَجَلِ ـ بِسُرْعَةٍ.

In sundry times, فِي مِرَارٍ ـ مِرَارًا.

In the day time, فِي ٱلضُّحَآءِ.

In the mean time, فِي غُضُونِ ذٰلِكَ.

In the nick of time, فِي ٱلْمُسْتَحَطِّ ـ وَقْتَ ٱلْحَاجَةِ ـ فِي ٱلْحَزَّةِ.

In time, عَلَى ٱلْوَقْتِ ـ فِي ٱلْوَقْتِ.

In times past, قَدِيمًا ـ سَابِقًا ـ قَبْلًا.

Just in time, فِي ٱلْوَقْتِ بِعَيْنِهِ. *See also under* Just, *ad.*

Many times, أَحْيَانًا كَثِيرَةً ـ كَثِيرًا مَا ـ رُبَّمَا. How many times? كَمْ مَرَّةٍ. "Many a time will the infidels wish that they had been Muslims," رُبَّمَا يَوَدُّ ٱلَّذِينَ كَفَرُوا لَوْ كَانُوا مُسْلِمِينَ (Kur. xv. 2).

Once upon a time, فِي وَقْتٍ مِنَ ٱلْأَوْقَاتِ ـ ذَاتَ ٱلْمِرَارِ. (When this phrase is used at the outset of a tale the expression كَانَ وَمَا كَانَ is used.)

Out of one's time, قَبْلَ تَتْمِيمِ وَقْتِهِ ـ قَبْلَ وَقْتِهِ.

Out of time, as in music, غَالِطٌ فِي ٱلْوَزْنِ; of a watch, ٱلسَّاعَةُ مُغَلَّطَةٌ.

Since that time, مِنْ يَوْمِهِ ـ مِنْ ذٰلِكَ ٱلْوَقْتِ ـ مُنْذُ ذٰلِكَ.

Sometimes, بَعْضَ مِرَارٍ.

The time is at hand, ٱلْوَقْتُ قَرِيبٌ.

The time of day, ٱلسَّاعَةُ ـ ٱلْوَقْتُ.

The work of time past, نَتِيجَةُ مُرُورٍ ـ تَأْثِيرُ ٱلزَّمَانِ فِي ٱلْحَوَادِثِ ٱلزَّمَانِ.

This present time, فِي هٰذَا ـ ٱلزَّمَانُ ٱلْحَاضِرُ ـ ٱلْوَقْتُ ٱلْحَاضِرُ ٱلْوَقْتِ.

This (one) time, هٰذِهِ ٱلْمَرَّةَ.

This time to-morrow, مِثْلَ ٱلْآنَ غَدًا.

Till the time come, حَتَّى يَأْتِيَ ٱلْوَقْتُ.

Time after time, تَارَةً بَعْدَ تَارَةٍ ـ مَرَّةً عَنْ مَرَّةٍ ـ طَوْرًا بَعْدَ طَوْرٍ.

To the end of time, إِلَى ٱنْقِضَآءِ ٱلدَّهْرِ.

To this time, إِلَى هٰذَا ٱلْوَقْتِ ـ إِلَى ٱلْآنَ.

Until the time, إِلَى أَنْ يَتَحَوَّلَ ٱلْوَقْتُ ـ حَتَّى يَأْتِيَ ٱلْوَقْتُ.

Up to that time, إِلَى ذٰلِكَ ٱلْوَقْتِ.

Up to this present time, إِلَى ٱلْآنَ ـ إِلَى ٱلْوَقْتِ ٱلْحَاضِرِ ـ إِلَى أَيَّامِنَا هٰذِهِ.

Within a given time, فِي ظَرْفِ مُدَّةٍ مُعَيَّنَةٍ ـ فِي وَقْتٍ مُعَيَّنٍ.

To appoint a time, عَيَّنَ وَقْتًا.

To beat time, دَقَّ بِٱلْوَزْنِ [2]: He beat time, with his foot, to the music, ضَرَبَ بِرِجْلِهِ عَلَى مِيزَانِ ٱلْعَزْفِ بِٱلْآلَاتِ.

To be after or behind time, تَأَخَّرَ ـ بَطُؤَ [2].

To be high time, حَانَ ٱلْوَقْتُ aor. يَحِينُ.

To be in time, وَصَلَ عَلَى وَقْتٍ ـ كَانَ عَلَى وَقْتٍ aor. يَصِلُ.

To be near the time, to draw near, of time, قَرُبَ ٱلْوَقْتُ [2]. The time of the feast drew near, قَرُبَ وَقْتُ ٱلْعِيدِ.

To be tied to time, وُقِّتَ لَهُ ٱلْوَقْتُ ـ كَانَ مُوَاقِتًا. To be in a hurry, كَانَ مُسْتَعْجِلًا.

To comply with the times, نَقَدَ إِلَى ٱلْأَحْوَالِ ـ طَاوَعَ ٱلْأَحْوَالَ [2].

To gain time, إِكْتَسَبَ وَقْتًا. To go too fast, تَقَدَّمَ: My watch gains (time,) سَاعَتِي مُسْتَبِقَةٌ.

To give one time, delay, طَوَّلَ عَلَى ـ أَمْهَلَ ـ مَادَى ـ أَمَدَّ ـ مَدَّ [2].

To have a good time of it, تَرَفَّهَ ـ تَنَعَّمَ ـ تَيَسَّرَ أَمْرُهُ ـ عَزَّ ـ وَتَمَتَّعَ.

To keep time, as in music, أَحْكَمَ وَزْنَ ٱلْأَنْغَامِ. To be punctual to one's time, جَآءَ عَلَى وَقْتِهِ ـ كَانَ عَلَى وَقْتٍ aor. يَجِيءُ.

To lose time, trifle it away, ضَيَّعَ ٱلْوَقْتَ. To go too slow, تَأَخَّرَ. My watch loses (time,) سَاعَتِي مُقَصِّرَةٌ.

To serve one's time, as in a service, تَمَّمَ ـ كَمَّلَ مُدَّةَ خِدْمَتِهِ وَعِدَّةَ ٱلْخِدْمَةِ.

To spend one's time, صَرَفَ ٱلْوَقْتَ ـ قَطَعَ ٱلْوَقْتَ.

To spin out the time, أَطَالَ ٱلْوَقْتَ ـ طَوَّلَ ٱلْوَقْتَ.

To take time, تَمَهَّلَ ـ إِتَّخَذَ وَقْتًا.

To waste one's time, أَسْرَفَ ٱلْوَقْتَ ـ ضَيَّعَ ٱلْوَقْتَ.

To while away the time, صَرَفَ ٱلْوَقْتَ ـ قَطَعَ ٱلْوَقْتَ.

Time, *v.t.* To give one a certain time for, وَقَّتَ لِ ـ وَاقَتَ ـ عَيَّنَ لِ وَقْتًا. To adapt to the time, وَفَّقَ لِلْوَقْتِ. To adapt to the occasion, طَبَّقَ عَلَى ٱلْحَاجَةِ. To regulate the time, as of music, أَحْكَمَ ٱلْوَزْنَ.

Timed, *a.* مُؤَقَّت. Ill-timed, inopportune, خَارِجٌ ـ غَيْرُ سَائِغٍ ـ عَنْ مَحَلِّهِ ـ خَارِجٌ عَنْ وَقْتِهِ. Well-timed, سَدَاد ـ مُوَافِق ـ فِي وَقْتِهِ ـ فِي مَحَلِّهِ. His speech was well-timed, قَالَ سَدَادًا مِنَ ٱلْقَوْلِ ـ أَصَابَ ٱلسَّدَادَ فِي كَلَامِهِ.

Time-honoured, *a.* مُكَرَّمٌ مِنْ أَجْيَالٍ ـ مُعْتَبَرٌ مِنْ دُهُورٍ.

Timeist, *n.* Of a musician, مُحْكِمُ ٱلْوَزْنِ.

Time-keeper, *n.* A watch or clock, سَاعَة *pl.* سَاعَات. One who keeps a register of the time of workmen, مُقَيِّدُ سَاعَاتِ شُغْلِ ٱلْفَعَلَةِ.

Timeliness, *n.* Seasonableness, مُنَاسَبَة ـ مُوَافَقَة ـ وَفْق.

Timely, *a.* Seasonable, فِي مَحَلِّهِ ـ فِي وَقْتِهِ ـ مُوَافِق.

Time-piece, *n.* سَاعَة *pl.* سَاعَات.

Time-server, *a.* } One who veers about with artifice, حُوَّلِيٌّ
Time-serving, } قُلَّبِيٌّ. An obsequious trimmer, إِمَّعَة ـ مَنْ يُتَابِعُ كُلَّ أَحَدٍ عَلَى رَأْيِهِ ـ مُسَايِر.

Time-worn, *a.* بِلَى أَجْيَالٍ ـ بَالٍ مِنْ صُرُوفِ ٱلزَّمَانِ.

Timid, *a.* خَائِف ـ رَعِيب ـ فَزِع ـ مِفْزَاع ـ فَشِل ـ هَائِعٌ لَائِعٌ ـ خُوَيْف. To be —, ٱرْتَعَبَ ـ رَعَبَ ـ ٱرْتَاعَ ـ لَاعَ ـ فَشِلَ. *See also under* Bashful, Fearful, *a.*

Timidity, *n.* } خِيفَة ـ فَزَع ـ فِزْع ـ فَشَل. *See also* Modesty,
Timidness, } Bashfulness, *n.*

Timidly, *ad.* خَوْفًا ـ بِفَزَعٍ ـ بِفَشَلٍ ـ فَزَعًا. *See also* Bashfully, *ad.*

Timocracy, *n.* إِدَارَةُ حُكُومَةٍ مِنَ ٱلْأَغْنِيَاءِ ـ حُكُومَةُ أَغْنِيَاءَ.

Timorous, *a.* *See* Timid, *a.*

Timorously, *ad.* *See* Timidly, *ad.*

Timorousness, *n.* *See* Timidity, *n.*

Tin, *n.* The metal, تَنَك ـ آنُك ـ أُسْرُب; tin-plate or sheet tin, تَنَك ـ صَفِيحٌ مِنْ آنُكٍ. A — to drink from, مِشْرَبَة *pl.* مَشَارِب ـ *vulg.* تَنَكَة *pl.* تَنَكَات.

Tin, *v.t.* بَيَّضَ.

Tinctorial, *a.* مُلَوِّن ـ مُصَبِّغ.

Tincture, *n.* Essence, extract, مُسْتَخْرَج ـ أَرْوَاح *pl.* رُوح ـ خُلَاصَة. An infusion, مَاء ـ نَقُوع: a —, infusion, of flowers, مَاءُ ٱلزَّهْرِ.

Tincture, *v.t.* To imbue with something foreign, شَرَّبَ. *See also to* Tinge, *v.t.*

Tinder, *n.* حُرَاقَة ـ عُطْبَة ـ حُرُوق; *vulg.* حُرَّاقَة.

Tinder-box, *n.* عُلْبَةُ ٱلْحُرَاقَةِ.

Tine, *n.* *See* Prong, *n.*

Tinfoil, *n.* صَفِيحَةٌ مِنْ قَصْدِيرٍ.

Tinge, *v.t.* شَرَّبَ ـ لَوَّنَ ـ خَضَّبَ ـ خَضَبَ. To be tinged with, أُشْرِبَ: The white was tinged with red, أُشْرِبَ ٱلْأَبْيَضُ حُمْرَةً.

Tinge, *n.* The being tinged, إِشْتِشْرَاب ـ تَشَرُّب. A light colour, لَوْنٌ خَفِيفٌ ـ لَوْن *pl.* أَلْوَان. A — of the face, مَاءُ ٱلْوَجْهِ.

Tingle, *v.i.* صَرَّ ـ: The ears tingled, صَرَّتِ (*or* طَنَّتْ) ٱلْآذَانُ. The hole of his ear tingled, صَرَّ صِمَاخُهُ. The ear of every one who hears it shall —, كُلُّ مَنْ سَمِعَ بِهِ تَطِنُّ أُذُنَاهُ.

Tingling, *n.* صَرّ.

Tink, *v.i.* } طَنْطَنَ ـ طَنَّ ـ جَلْجَلَ ـ جَرَسَ: the bell
Tinkle, } tinkled, ٱلْجَرَسُ (*or* جَرَسَ) ٱلْجَرَسُ. To make to —, أَطَنَّ ـ أَجْرَسَ. To — a bell, أَجْرَسَ ٱلْجَرَسَ.

Tinker, *n.* One who repairs pots and pans, مُصْلِحُ ٱلطَّوَاجِنِ.

Tinkle, *n.* } طَنْطَنَة ـ طَنِين ـ جَلْجَلَة.
Tinkling, }

Tinman, *n.* One who deals in tin, or one who works in tin, سَنْكَارِيّ ـ (سَنْكَرِي *vulg.*) تَنَكَارِيّ.

Tin-plate, *n.* تَنَك ـ صَفِيحَةٌ بَيْضَاءُ.

Tin-mine, *n.* مَعْدِنُ ٱلْأُسْرُبِ (*or* ٱلْآنُكِ).

Tinner, *n.* One who works in tin-mines, مُعَدِّنُ مَعْدِنِ ٱلْأُسْرُبِ (*or* ٱلْآنُكِ). *See also* Tinman, *n.*

Tinning, *n.* تَبْيِيض.

Tinny, *a.* Like tin, مِثْلَ ٱلتَّنَكِ ـ مِثْلَ ٱلْآنُكِ. Abounding in tin, كَثِيرُ ٱلْآنُكِ (*or* ٱلْأُسْرُبِ).

Tinsel, *n.* Foil silvered or coppered, نُوَّار ـ مَيْس ـ بَهْرَجَان.

Tinsel, *a.* مِنْ بَهْرَجَانٍ. *See also* Gaudy, Showy, *a.*

Tinsel, *v.t.* زَيَّنَ بِٱلْمَيْسِ ـ لَبَّسَ بَهْرَجَانًا.

Tint, *n.* *See* Tinge, *n.*

Tint, *v.t.* *See to* Tinge, *v.t.*

Tintinnabulary, *a.* مُجَلْجِل ـ مُطَنْطِن ـ جَارِس.

Tiny, *a.* صَغِيرٌ لِلْغَايَةِ ـ جُزْئِيّ.

Tip, *n.* The end, طَرَف *pl.* أَطْرَاف ـ رَأْس *pl.* رُؤُوس. The —, of any iron instrument, also of a boot, أَسَلَة *pl.* أَسَلَات ـ مِنْقَار. Tip of the tongue, عَذَبَةُ ٱللِّسَانِ ـ أَسَلَةُ ٱللِّسَانِ. The tip or toe, as of a boot, ذُنَابَة ـ أَنْف ـ أَسَلَة. The tips of the fingers, or toes, ٱلْأَنَامِلُ ـ ٱلْبَنَانُ. The — of the nose, of a human being, خَوْرَمَة (*or* رَوْثَة *or* أَرْنَبَة) ٱلْأَنْفِ; of a beast, مُخْرَة. A bribe, بِرْطِيل. That word is often on the tip of my tongue, تِلْكَ ٱلْكَلِمَةُ تَشْتَغِلُ لِسَانِي. She tinged the tips of her fingers, طَرَّفَتْ بَنَانَهَا. The tips of their tongues are sharper than the heads of their spears, أَسَلَاتُ أَلْسِنَتِهِمْ أَمْضَى مِنْ أَسِنَّةِ أَسَلِهِمْ. Pronounced with the tip of the tongue, أَسَلِيَّة. Tip, a douceur, حُلْوَان.

Tip, *v.t.* To form to a point, أنّف ـ نصّل ـ أحدّ ـ حدّد. To make tapering, of the ears of a horse, طرّف الأذن. To cover the tip or end, as with a ferule, لبّس-زجّا. To edge or border with, كنّف-ب ـ نيّر-ب; as with fringe, سجّف. To tip up, stoop, طأطأ ـ أصغى ـ ـِ حنى ـ ميّل. To tip one anything, ـُ حلا-كذا ـ ألقم: he tipped him a bribe, ألقم-البرطيل. To tip over, ـِ قلب. To touch slightly; *see to* Tap, *v.t.*

Tippet, *n.* لفافة للرقبة. A fur —, for women, زعارة للحريم.

Tipple, *v.t.* ـَ شرب المسكرات.

Tipple, *v.i.* ـَ شرب المسكرات ـ تعاطى شرب المسكرات.

Tippler, *n.* شرّاب ـ شرّاب المسكرات.

Tippling, *n.* شرب ـ شرب المسكرات.

Tippling-house, *n.* حانوت ـ خمّارة.

Tipsily, *ad.* على سكر ـ كالسكران.

Tipstaff, *n.* A staff covered with metal, جرز. A constable or bailiff, جلواز (or قوّاس or رسول) محكمة *pl.* جلاوزة.

Tipsy, *a.* ملتكّ ـ سكران. He was —, مسّه سكر. To get —, ـَ سكر.

Tiptoe, *n.* The end of the toes, البنان. On —, على البنان. To walk on —, ـُ قار. To stand on —, تعاطى. To stand on — and stretch out the neck to look at anything, تطالّ ـ اشرأبّ.

Tiptop, *n.* The highest point, قمّة ـ أعلى.

Tiptop, *a.* Of the highest excellence, station, *etc.*, أعلى *fem.* عليا ـ أقدم ـ أفضل ـ أحسن.

Tirade, *n.* طعن ـ شتم ـ سبّ. To make a — against, ـُ ـِ شتم ـ ـُ سبّ.

Tire, *n.* A head-dress, عمرة ـ عصب ـ عصاب ـ كسوة الرأس. Furniture, أثاث ـ عدّة. A — of a wheel, دائرة (or حلقة) العجلة.

Tire, *v.t.* *See to* Attire, *v.t.*

Tire, *v.t.* To weary, as with labour, أكلّ ـ أعيا ـ أتعب. To — out, to vex, worry, annoy, ـُ شقّ على ـ أغرض ـ عنّى ـ عانى ـ تعنّى ـ أزعج ـ أضجر ـ أملّ. To —, as with food, to satiety, أشبع.

Tire, *v.i.* To become tired; *see under next article.*

Tired, *a.* As with fatigue, تعب ـ متعب *colloq.* تعبان ـ معيّ ـ *vulg.* عيّان. Tired of a thing, عزوف عن ـ غرض من ـ زعلان من. Satiated with, شبعان من. To be —, as with fatigue, ـِ كلّ ـ أعيا ـ ـَ تعب. To be — of, satiated with, ـَ شبع من. To be — of, worried with, so as to be incapable of doing it, ـُ ـِ عزف عن ـ ـِ عجز عن ـ ـِ كلّ من. To be — of a thing or place, ـَ غرض من ـ ـُ شقّ من. He was — of him, ـِ عجز عنه ـ *vulg.* ـَ زعل منه. I am — of waiting, مللت من الانتظار. I am — of life, مللت من الحياة. He was — in walking, أعيا في المشي. He never tires of him, لم يمل (or يملل) عنه. Tired sight, بصر حسير: the eye became —, حسرت العين. The eye is never — of seeing, العين لا تشبع من النظر.

Tiredness, *n.* إعياء ـ كلّ ـ كلال ـ تعب.

Tiresome, *a.* Fatiguing, متعب ـ شاقّ. Prolix, نفس ـ مطيّل ـ مبالغ. Irksome, مملّ ـ مزعج. *See also* Tedious, *a.*

Tiresomeness, *n.* Prolixity, مبالغة ـ إطالة كلام. Irksomeness, ملّة ـ ملالة ـ ضجر ـ زعل. *See also* Tediousness, *n.*

Tire-woman, *n.* ماشطة *pl.* مواشط.

Tiring-room, *n.* بيت اللبس.

'Tis, *contraction for* It is; *see to* Be, *aux. v.*

Tissue, *n.* Gold-cloth, نسيج قصب أصفر; silver —, نسيج قصب أبيض. A texture of parts, نسج ـ نسيج. A connected series, نسق ـ سماط ـ سياقة. A — of lies, نسج كذب.

Tissue-paper, *n.* ورق قزّ.

Tit, *n.* A small horse, حصين ـ حصان صغير; a small bird, عصفور. Tit for tat, واحدة بواحدة. To give one tit for tat, قابل-بالمثل.

Titan, *n.* جبّار *pl.* جبابرة.

Tit-bit, *n.* *See* Tid-bit, *n.*

Tithable, *a.* يعشّر ـ تؤخذ العشور منه.

Tithe, *n.* A tenth, عشر *pl.* عشور *and* أعشار. Tithes, عشور. To pay tithes, أعطى عشورا. To lay tithes on, وضع على-العشور *aor.* يضع. To redeem tithes, ـُ فكّ العشور. Commutation of tithes, إبدال العشور.

Tithe, *v.t.* عشّر.

Tithe-free, *a.* معفى من العشور.

Tithe-gatherer, *n.* عشّار *pl.* عشّارون.

Tithe-paying, *a.* معطي عشور.

Tithing, *n.* معشر *pl.* معاشر.

Tithymal, *n.* The plant, تيّوع ـ يتّوع ـ لاعية *pl.* لواعي.

Titillate, *v.t.* *See to* Tickle, *v.t.*

Titillation, *n.* *See* Tickling, *n.*

Title, *n.* An epithet, نعت *pl.* نعوت ـ لقب *pl.* ألقاب. A name, اسم *pl.* أسامي *and* أسام *and* أسماء. Title, as of a book, علوان ـ عنوان. A right, حقّ. Desert, merit, استحقاق. Some wished the queen to have the — of empress, أراد البعض أنّ تلقّب الملكة بإمبراطورة. *See also* Title-deed, *n.*

Title, *v.t.* To give a title to, or to call by a title, نَعَتَ ـِ ـ لَقَّبَ ـ نَعَتَ ـِ بِ. To put a title, as to a book, عَنَّ ـُ ـ عَنْوَنَ ـ عَلْوَنَ ـ عَنَّنَ.

Titled, *a.* صَاحِبُ لَقَبٍ ـ مُلَقَّبٌ. Having a title of nobility, شَرِيفٌ ـ ذُو شَرَفٍ. The — gentry, ٱلشُّرَفَآءُ.

Title-deed, *n.* صَكٌّ *pl.* صُكُوكٌ ـ حُجَّةٌ *pl.* حُجَجٌ.

Title-page, *n.* عُنْوَانُ كِتَابٍ ـ صَحِيفَةُ ٱلْعُنْوَانِ.

Titmouse, *n.* عُصَيْفِرٌ ـ نَوْعٌ صَغِيرٌ مِنَ ٱلطُّيُورِ.

Titter, *v.i.* كَرْكَرَ ـ هَأْهَأَ ـ كَتْكَتَ.

Titter, *n.* }
Tittering, } كَرْكَرَةٌ ـ هَأْهَأٌ ـ كَتْكَتَةٌ.

Titterer, *n.* مُكَرْكِرٌ ـ مُكَتْكِتٌ.

Tittle, *n.* A dot, particle, نُقْطَةٌ. Not one jot or —, لَا حَرْفٌ وَلَا نُقْطَةٌ.

Tittle-tattle, *n.* *See* Tattle, *n.*

Tittle-tattle, *v.i.* *See to* Tattle, *v.i.*

Titular, *a.* Having a title, صَاحِبُ ٱسْمٍ ـ حَائِزُ لَقَبٍ. In name only, حَائِزُ ٱلِٱسْمِ فَقَطْ ـ بِٱلِٱسْمِ فَقَطْ ـ بِٱلْكِنَايَةِ فَقَطْ.

Titular, *n.* }
Titulary, } حَائِزُ ٱللَّقَبِ فَقَطْ ـ صَاحِبُ ٱلِٱسْمِ فَقَطْ.

Titularly, *ad.* مِنْ جِهَةِ ٱللَّقَبِ فَقَطْ ـ بِٱلِٱسْمِ فَقَطْ ـ كِنَايَةً فَقَطْ.

To, *prep.* إِلَى. Towards, نَحْوَ. To one, *masc.* عِنْدَهُ *fem.* عِنْدَهَا. To me, لِي; to thee, لَكَ *fem.* لَكِ; to him, لَهُ; to her, لَهَا; to us, لَنَا; to you, لَكُمْ *fem.* لَكُنَّ; to them, لَهُمْ *fem.* لَهُنَّ. I went to him, ذَهَبْتُ عِنْدَهُ. He came to me, جَآءَ إِلَيَّ. To this place, إِلَى هُنَا ـ إِلَى هٰذَا ٱلْمَكَانِ; to that place, إِلَى هُنَاكَ ـ إِلَى ذٰلِكَ ٱلْمَكَانِ. I am a fool to him, أَنَا أَحْمَقُ بِٱلنِّسْبَةِ إِلَيْهِ. There are ten chances to one against me, أَمَلِي بِٱلْفَوْزِ أَمَلُ ٱلْوَاحِدِ بِٱلنِّسْبَةِ إِلَى ٱلْعَشَرَةِ. To come, what is coming, the time to come, ٱلْمُسْتَقْبِلُ ـ ٱلْآتِي. To, at, لَدَى: Ambassador to the Sublime Government, سَفِيرٌ لَدَى ٱلدَّوْلَةِ ٱلْعَلِيَّةِ.

T.O., for "turn over," إِقْلِبْ ـ أُنْظُرْ إِلَى قَفَآءِ ٱلصَّحِيفَةِ ٱلْوَرَقَةِ.

Toad, *n.* ضِفْدَعٌ سَامٌّ *pl.* ضَفَادِعُ. A — in the hole, the dish, عَجِينٌ مَحْشُوٌّ بِلَحْمٍ.

Toad-eater, *n.* *See* Sycophant, *n.*

Toad-flax, *n.* عُشْبُ ٱلذِّئْبِ.

Toad-stool, *n.* فُطْرَةٌ *coll.* فُطْرٌ ـ قَتَّالٌ ـ ضَرْبٌ مِنَ ٱلْكَمْأَةِ أَبْيَضُ.

Toady, *n.* *See* Sycophant, Parasite, *n.*

Toady, *v.t.* دَاهَنَ. *See also to* Flatter, *v.t.*

Toadyism, *n.* *See* Sycophancy, *n.*

Toast, *v.t.* Of bread, *etc.*, حَمَّصَ ـ حَمَّرَ ـ جَمَّرَ ـ قَمَّرَ. To drink to the health of one, شَرِبَ ـَ (ٱلْمُدَامَ أَوْ غَيْرَهُ) بِسِرِّ فُلَانٍ ـ شَرِبَ ـَ عَلَى ذِكْرِ حُبِّهِ.

Toast, *n.* Toasted bread, خُبْزٌ مُحَمَّصٌ ـ خُبْزٌ مُقَمَّرٌ ـ خُبْزٌ مُجَمَّرٌ. A speech in drinking a health to one, خِطَابٌ وَقْتَ شُرْبِ ٱلْمُدَامِ. The person toasted with a toast, مَنْ يَقْتَرِحُ ٱلشُّرْبَ بِسِرِّ فُلَانٍ ـ بِسِرِّهِ.

Toaster, *n.* As of bread, *etc.*, مُحَمِّصٌ ـ مُقَمِّرٌ ـ مُجَمِّرٌ. One who proposes a toast, مُقْتَرِحُ ٱلشُّرْبِ بِسِرِّ فُلَانٍ. A utensil for toasting, آلَةُ ٱلتَّحْمِيصِ ـ آلَةُ ٱلتَّجْمِيرِ.

Toasting-fork, *n.* شَوْكَةُ ٱلتَّحْمِيصِ ـ شَوْكَةُ ٱلتَّجْمِيرِ.

Toast-rack, *n.* قَاعِدَةُ ٱلْخُبْزِ ٱلْمُقَمَّرِ.

Tobacco, *n.* The plant, حَشِيشَةُ ٱلدُّخَانِ ـ ٱلتَّبْغُ. Tobacco for smoking, تُتُن ـ دُخَان ـ تَنْبَاك. Persian or Shirâz — for the water-pipe, تُنْبَك.

Tobacconist, *n.* تُتُنْجِي ـ بَيَّاعُ ٱلدُّخَانِ (*or* ٱلتَّنْبَاكِ).

Tobacco-pipe, *n.* *See under* Pipe, *n.*

Tobacco-stopper, *n.* طَابِقُ حَجَرَةِ ٱلْغَلْيُونِ.

Tocsin, *n.* نَاقُوسٌ يُدَقُّ وَقْتَ ٱلْفِتَنِ. *See also* Alarm, *n.*

To-day, *n.* هٰذَا ٱلنَّهَارُ ـ هٰذَا ٱلْيَوْمُ ـ ٱلْيَوْمُ.

Toddle, *v.i.* دَلَفَ ـِ ـ حَتَكَ ـِ.

Toddler, *n.* }
Toddling, *a.* } دَالِفٌ ـ حَاتِكٌ.

Toddy, *n.* The juice of the cocoa palm, صَبِيبُ شَجَرَةِ ٱلنَّارَجِيلِ ـ لَبَنُ شَجَرَةِ ٱلنَّارَجِيلِ. Toddy, the spirit, عَرَقٌ. *See also under* Punch, *n.*

Toe, *n.* إِصْبَعُ ٱلْقَدَمِ *pl.* أَصَابِعُ. The great —, إِبْهَامُ ٱلْقَدَمِ *pl.* أَبَاهِيمُ. The little —, خِنْصِرُ ٱلْقَدَمِ *pl.* خَنَاصِرُ. The distance between the toes, فَلَجٌ. The toes, أَصَابِعُ ٱلْقَدَمِ (*or* بَنَانٌ). The — of a boot, أَنْفُ ٱلنَّعْلِ.

Toga, *n.* جُبَّةُ ٱلرُّومَانِيِّينَ ٱلْأَقْدَمِينَ.

Togated, *a.* لَابِسُ جُبَّةٍ.

Together, *ad.* In company, سَوِيَّةً ـ جُمْلَةً ـ مَعًا. Together, all at once, بِٱلْمَرَّةِ ـ عَلَى فَوْرٍ. Together with, مَعَ. We were here —, كُنَّا هُنَا مَعًا. They walked —, سَارُوا مَعًا. They came all —, جَاؤُوا جَمًّا. I saw your brothers all —, رَأَيْتُ إِخْوَتَكَ جُمَعَ كُتَعَ. I saw the people all —, رَأَيْتُ ٱلْقَوْمَ أَجْمَعِينَ أَكْتَعِينَ. Pray ye sitting, all of you —, صَلُّوا جُلُوسًا أَجْمَعِينَ. They came all of them, all —, جَاؤُوا بِأَجْمَعِهِمْ ـ جَاؤُوا بِفَصِيلَتِهِمْ.

I saw the women, the whole of them, or, all —, رَأَيْتُ ٱلنِّسْوَةَ جَمْعَ.

To come together, إِجْتَمَعُوا مَعًا. The soldiers came together, each man joining his company, لَحِقَ كُلٌّ مِنَ ٱلْعَسْكَرِ بِفِرْقَتِهِ.

To scrape together, قَشَّ ـ لَمَّ ـ لَمَّ ـ جَمَّعَ.

To pull together, as in rowing, قَذَفُوا سَوِيَّةً. To agree, of many, إِتَّفَقُوا.

To put together, as pieces of machinery, رَكَّبَ.

Toggery, *n.* أَلْبِسَة. *See also* Dress, *n.*

Toil, *v.i.* عَمِلَ ـ يَسْعَى ـ سَعَى *aor.* إِشْتَغَلَ ـ تَعَنَّى ـ عَالَجَ ـ تَعِبَ ـ كَدَّ. *See also to* Labour, *v.i.*

Toil, *n.* تَعَب ـ جِدّ ـ كَدّ ـ مَسْعًى ـ مُعَالَجَة.

Toiler, *n.* عَمُول ـ ذُو عَمَلٍ ـ عَمَلَة *pl.* عَمِل.

Toilet, *n.* A cloth over a dressing table, غِطَآءُ ٱلْعَتِيدَةِ ـ غِطَآءُ ٱلشَّرِيطَةِ. A dressing-table, عَتِيدَة *pl.* عَتَائِدُ ـ شَرِيطَة *pl.* بِشْتَخْتَة ـ شَرَائِطُ. Dress, زِيّ ـ لِبَاس ـ كِسْوَة.

Toilless, *a.* غَيْرُ مُتْعِبٍ.

Toilsome, *n.* Requiring labour, عَسِير ـ عَوِيص ـ مُعْضِل ـ تَعِب ـ مُتْعِب.

Toilsomeness, *n.* تَعَب ـ مُشْكِلَة ـ صُعُوبَة ـ عُسْر.

Tokay, *n.* The wine, إِسْمُ خَمْرٍ بِبِلَادِ ٱلْمَجَرِ.

Token, *n.* A sign, آيَة ـ أَمَرَة ـ عَلَم *pl.* أَعْلَام ـ عَلَامَة *pl.* عَلَامَات ـ نِيشَان *pl.* نَوَاشِينُ. A memorial, تَذْكِرَة. A — of esteem, تَذْكِرَةُ ٱعْتِبَارٍ. A — for coined money, مَا قَامَ مَقَامَ ٱلسِّكَّةِ.

Told, *pret.* and *part. of to* Tell, *q.v.*

Toledo, *n.* A sword of the finest temper, سَيْفٌ ذَكَرٌ (or مُذَكَّرٌ).

Tolerable, *a.* Supportable, يُحْتَمَلُ ـ وَمَا يُحْتَمَلُ ـ تَحَمُّلُهُ مُمْكِنٌ. Middling, بَيْنَ بَيْنَ ـ مُتَوَسِّط ـ وَسَط ـ مُقَارِب. It shall be more — for him, سَيَكُونُ لَهُ حَالَةٌ أَكْثَرُ ٱحْتِمَالًا.

Tolerableness, *n.* The quality of being bearable, إِمْكَانُ تَحَمُّلِهِ; of being middling, تَوَسُّط.

Tolerably, *ad.* Middlingly, عَلَى قَدْرِهِ ـ تَوَسُّطًا ـ بَيْنَ بَيْنَ; in a manner that may be borne, عَلَى صُورَةٍ تُحْتَمَلُ.

Tolerance, *n.* The act of enduring, إِحْتِمَال ـ صَبْر ـ أَنَاة; of permitting, إِبَاحَة ـ تَجْوِيز ـ إِجَازَة ـ مُسَامَحَة.

Tolerant, *a.* Enduring, صَبُور ـ صَابِر ـ مُحْتَمِل. Indulgent, مُسَامِح.

Tolerate, *v.t.* To permit, أَذِنَ ل ـ فِي ـ أَبَاحَ ـ فَسَحَ ل. To be indulgent towards, تَسَمَّحَ ب ـ رَخَّصَ ل ـ فِي. A tolerated community, or religion, مِلَّةٌ مُجَازَةٌ.

Toleration, *n.* The act of allowing, إِبَاحَة ـ سَمَاحَة ـ تَسْمِيح ـ صَبْر وَتَحَمُّل ـ تَحَمُّل ـ أَنَاة; of bearing, تَجْوِيز. Religious —, ٱلتَّسَاهُلُ (or ٱلتَّسَامُحُ) بِٱلْأَدْيَانِ.

Toll, *n.* As of a bell, جَرَس (أَجْرَاس or قَرْع or دَقّ). A tax for passing, جُعْل ـ مَكْس ٱلْعُبُورِ ـ رَسْمُ ٱلْعُبُورِ. To pay —, دَفَعَ جُعْلَ ٱلْعُبُورِ. He doubled the toll which passengers pay for crossing the bridge, ضَاعَفَ ٱلْجُعْلَ ٱلَّذِي يَعْطِيهِ ٱلْمَارُّونَ عَلَى ٱلْجِسْرِ.

Toll, *v.t.* As of a bell, قَرَعَ (or دَقَّ) ٱلْجَرَسَ ـ أَجْرَسَ ٱلْجَرَسَ.

Toll-bar, *n.* حَاجِزٌ فِي مَسْلَكٍ حَيْثُ يُقْبَضُ جُعْلُ ٱلْعُبُورِ.

Toll-booth, *n.* Where goods are weighed for taxation, مَكْتَبُ جِبَايَةِ ٱلْجُعْلِ. A prison, سِجْن ـ حَبْس.

Toll-bridge, *n.* جِسْرٌ يَدْفَعُ ٱلْمَارُّونَ بِهِ جُعْلًا.

Toll-gate, *n.* بَابٌ يَدْفَعُ ٱلدَّاخِلُونَ مِنْهُ جُعْلًا.

Toll-house, *n.* *See* Toll-booth, *n.*

Tomahawk, *n.* فَأْسٌ تَسْتَعْمِلُهُ هَمَجَةُ أَمِيرِكَا.

Tomahawk, *v.t.* فَأَسَ ـ ضَرَبَ (or قَتَلَ) بِٱلْفَأْسِ ٱلْمَذْكُورَةِ.

Tomato, *n.* بَنَادُورَى ـ بَاذِنْجَانٌ فِرَنْجِيٌّ; one —, بَنَادُورَة *pl.* بَنَادُورَات.

Tomb, *n.* A large —, of kings, like those of ancient Egypt, نَاوُوس *pl.* نَوَاوِيسُ. A —, place of burial, مَدْفَن ـ مَرْقَد *pl.* مَدَافِنُ. A grave, قَبْر ـ ضَرِيحَة ـ ضَرِيح *pl.* ضَرَائِحُ ـ قُبُور *pl.* A monument raised over the dead, تُرْبَة *pl.* تُرَب. A separate vault in a —, لَحْد *pl.* لُحُود. May God illumine his tomb! نَوَّرَ ٱللّٰهُ ضَرِيحَهُ.

Tomb, *v.t.* *See to* Entomb, *v.t.*

Tomback, *or* Tánbak, *n.* The Shirâz tobacco so called, تَنْبَك.

Tomboy, *n.* فُحُولَةُ ٱلصَّبَايَا *pl.* صَبِيَّةٌ فَحْلَةٌ.

Tombstone, *n.* رُجْمَة *pl.* رُجَم *and* رِجَام. To put a — to a grave, عَلَّمَ ٱلْقَبْرَ.

Tomcat, *n.* سِنَّوْر ـ قِطّ ـ هِرّ.

Tome, *n.* مُجَلَّد *pl.* مُجَلَّدَات.

Tomfool, *n.* مَسْخَرَة ـ سُخْرَة ـ أَبْلَهُ.

Tomfoolery, *n.* هُجْو ـ سُخْرِيَّة ـ بَلَاهَة.

To-morrow, *n.* بُكْرَة ـ غَدَاة ـ غَد. The day after —, بَعْدَ غَدٍ ـ بَعْدَ بُكْرَة. From —, مِنْ بُكْرَة ـ مِنَ ٱلْغَدِ. I will see you again —, سَأَعُودُ أَرَاكَ غَدًا. Of to-morrow, غَدَوِيّ ـ غَدِيّ. To-morrow, some indefinite time, هَيْهَاتَ. "And say not, then, of a thing; I will surely do it to-morrow, without [adding] if God will," وَلَا تَقُولَنَّ لِشَيْءٍ إِنِّي فَاعِلٌ ذٰلِكَ غَدًا إِلَّا أَنْ يَشَآءَ ٱللّٰهُ (Kur. xviii. 23).

Tompion, *n.* *See* Tampion, *n.*

Tomtit, *n.* *See* Titmouse, *n.*

Tomtom, *n.* طَبْلُ ٱلْهُنُودِ *pl.* طُبُول.

Ton, *n.* The fashion prevailing, ٱلْكِسْمُ ٱلْحَاضِرُ ــ ٱلزِّيُّ ٱلْحَاضِرُ ــ *from the Italian,* ٱلْمُودَةُ.

Ton, *n.* The weight, طُنِيلَاتَةٌ (وَهِيَ عِبَارَةٌ عَنْ عِشْرِينَ قِنْطَارًا) *pl.* طُنِيلَاتَات.

Tone, *n.* Sound, صَوْت *pl.* أَصْوَات. Modulation of sound, voice, لَحْن *pl.* أَلْحَان ــ نَغْمَة. A soft —, نَغْم ــ نَغَم. Tones, music, أَنْغَام. Tone of the voice, مَقَامُ ٱلصَّوْتِ. Manner of speaking, عِبَارَة ــ كَلَام. A — to which music is set, طَبَقَة: a high —, of music, طَبَقَةٌ عَالِيَةٌ; a low or soft —, طَبَقَةٌ خَفِيضَةٌ. Tone, as of health, حَال ــ مِزَاج ــ قُوَّة. Harmonious relation of colours, تَنَاسُبُ ٱلْأَلْوَانِ. Manner, أُسْلُوب ــ طَرْز ــ طَوْر. He changed his —, manner of address, تَكَلَّمَ بِطَرْزٍ آخَرَ ــ غَيَّرَ كَلَامَهُ. "And with measured tone chant [or intone] the Kurân," وَرَتِّلِ ٱلْقُرْآنَ تَرْتِيلًا (Kur. lxxiii. 4).

Tone, *v.t.* To tune, عَدَّلَ ٱلنَّغْمَةَ ــ أَصْلَحَ ٱلصَّوْتَ. To — down, to soften, خَفَّضَ ــ لَيَّنَ.

Toned, *a.* ذُو نَغْمَةٍ ــ ذُو صَوْتٍ. Sweet —, أَلْحَنُ. Harsh —, أَبَحُّ ــ أَجَشُّ.

Tongs, *n.* مِلْقَطُ ٱلنَّارِ *pl.* مَلَاقِطُ. A pair of small —, مِلْقَطٌ صَغِيرٌ ــ *vulg.* كَمَّاشَة ــ مَاشَة ــ مَاشِك.

Tongue, *n.* Of the mouth, مِغْلَاق *pl.* مَغَالِيقُ ــ مِفْصَل ــ لَهْجَة ــ لِسَان *pl.* أَلْسِنَة. Speech, أَقْوَال ــ قَوْل ــ كَلَام. A language, لُغَة *pl.* لُغَات ــ لِسَان *pl.* أَلْسِنَة *and* أَلْسُن. A — of land, لِسَانُ أَرْضٍ; (*see also* Isthmus, *n.*) Tongue, as of a buckle, شَوْكَة *coll.* شَوْك; of a bit, فَأْسُ ٱللِّجَامِ; of a bell, مِدَقَّةُ جَرَسٍ. The — of a balance, عَمُودُ ٱلْمِيزَانِ ــ طَيَّار. Tongue, a people, قَوْم *pl.* أَقْوَام ــ طَائِفَة *pl.* طَوَائِفُ ــ شَعْب *pl.* شُعُوب. The root of the —, غَلْصَمَة (*or* عُكَدَةُ *or* عُكْدَةُ *or* عُقْدَةُ) ٱللِّسَانِ. The thick part of the —, عَظَمَةُ ٱللِّسَانِ. The tip of the —, ثَمَرَةُ ٱللِّسَانِ. The two bones at the root of the —, ٱلْفَرِيكَتَانِ. A — letter pronounced by the tip of the tongue, حَرْفٌ مِنَ ٱلْحُرُوفِ ٱلْأَسَلِيَّةِ ــ حَرْفٌ أَذْلَقُ *pl.* حُرُوفٌ ذُلْقٌ; (the six letters of Arabic so pronounced are called, ٱلذَّوْلَقِيَّةُ). Of a ready —, طَلِقٌ ذَلِقٌ. An eloquent —, مِغْلَاق. "Yet, when the alarm is passed with sharp tongues will they assail you," فَإِذَا ذَهَبَ ٱلْخَوْفُ سَلَقُوكُمْ بِأَلْسِنَةٍ حِدَادٍ (Kur. xxxiii. 19). *See also* Language, *n.*

To hold one's tongue, سَكَتَ ـُ ــ نَصَتَ ـِ ــ أَصْمَتَ ــ صَمَتَ.

To protrude the tongue, to loll it out, as a dog, دَلَعَ ـَ (*or* أَدْلَعَ) لِسَانَهُ. His tongue protruded, إِنْدَلَعَ (*or* إِدَّلَعَ) لِسَانُهُ.

To protrude the tongue at, in derision, هَلَّبَ بِ.

To stop the tongue of another, سَكَّتَ ــ أَسْكَتَ ــ صَمَّتَ ــ قَطَعَ لِسَانَهُ ـَ.

To roll anything about in the mouth with the tongue, لَغَتَ ـَ.

Tongued, *a.* ذُو لِسَانٍ. Glib-tongued, ذُو مِغْلَاقٍ ــ طَلِقٌ ذَلِقٌ.

Tongue-tied, *a.* عَقِدُ ٱللِّسَانِ ــ عَقِد. To be —, عَقِدَ ـَ.

Tongueless, *a.* بِلَا لِسَانٍ.

Tonic, *a.* Giving strength, مُقَوٍّ. Relating to sound, صَوْتِيٌّ ــ نَغَمِيٌّ ــ مُتَعَلِّقٌ بِٱلْأَصْوَاتِ.

Tonic, *n.* A strengthening medicine, عِلَاجٌ مُقَوٍّ. The —, in music, طَبَقَةُ ٱلنَّغَمِ.

To-night, *ad.* هٰذِهِ ٱللَّيْلَةَ ــ فِي هٰذِهِ ٱللَّيْلَةِ.

Tonnage, *n.* Weight of goods carried in a ship, شَحْنَةُ مَرْكَبٍ ــ طُنِيلَاتَةُ مَرْكَبٍ ــ مِقْدَارُ طُنِيلَاتَةِ مَرْكَبٍ. Duty on —, مَكْس عَلَى حِسَابِ ٱلطُّنِيلَاتَةِ. Shipping, مَرَاكِبُ ــ سَفَائِنُ. *See* Ton, *n.*

Tonsil, *n.* Of the throat, غُنْدُب *pl.* غَنَادِبُ ــ لَوْزَةُ ٱلْحَلْقِ *pl.* لَوْزَات. The two tonsils, ٱلْغُنْدُبَتَانِ ــ لَوْزَتَا ٱلْحَلْقِ.

Tonsile, *a.* That may be clipped, جَزُّهُ مُمْكِنٌ ــ يُجَزُّ.

Tonsorial, *a.* مُتَعَلِّقٌ بِٱلْمُزَيِّنِ.

Tonsure, *n.* The act of clipping, جَزٌّ ــ جِزَّة. The — of an ecclesiastic, حِلَاقَة ــ رَشْمَة ــ رَسْمَة.

Tontine, *n.* مُلْكٌ أَوْ إِيرَادُ شِرْكَةٍ مُرَتَّبٌ عَلَى هٰذَا ٱلنَّسَقِ وَهُوَ إِنْ مَاتَ وَاحِدٌ مِنَ ٱلْمُشْتَرِكِينَ تَمَتَّعَ ٱلْبَاقُونَ بِسَهْمِهِ وَهَلُمَّ جَرًّا حَتَّى مَا يَبْقَى إِلَّا ٱلْعَقِبَةُ فَيَكُونُ ٱلْمُلْكُ كُلُّهُ لَهُ.

Too, *ad.* Also, أَيْضًا. Also, in like manner, كَذٰلِكَ. Too much, بِزِيَادَةٍ.

Took, *pret. of to* Take, *q.v.*

Tool, *n.* An instrument, آلَة *pl.* آلَات ــ عُدَّة *pl.* عُدَد. Tools, أَدَاة ــ عُدَّة. A person used as an instrument, فَاعِل *pl.* فَعَلَة. A catspaw, زَبُون *pl.* زَبَائِنُ ــ غَرِير *pl.* أَغِرَّاء.

Tool, *v.t.* To ornament with tools, زَيَّنَ بِقَلَمٍ أَوْ قَالِبٍ.

Tooling, *n.* As of a book, *etc.*, زِينَةُ قَلَمٍ أَوْ قَالِبٍ.

Tooth, *n.* سِنّ *pl.* أَسْنَان ــ حَاكَّة. A little —, سُنَيْنَة. A back —, ضِرْس *pl.* أَضْرَاس. A wisdom —, نَاجِذ *pl.* نَوَاجِذُ. A redundant —, رَاثِل *pl.* رَوَاثِلُ. A canine —, or a — of a beast, نَاب *pl.* أَنْيَاب *and* نُيُوب. A milk —, ثَنِيَّة *pl.* ثَنَايَا ــ رَاضِعَة *pl.* رَوَاضِعُ. Tooth, as of a letter, شُعْبَة *pl.* شُعَب; of a wheel, *etc.*, سِنّ *pl.* أَسْنَان ــ سِنَّة. The teeth, ٱلْأَسْنَانُ ــ ٱلْعَوَاجِمُ. The root of a —, سِنْخ *pl.* أَسْنَاخ. The front teeth, ٱلْمَهْدَرَةُ ــ

الثَّغْر – المَبْسِم. The wisdom teeth, أَضْرَاسُ ٱلْعَقْلِ – أَضْرَاسُ ٱلْحُلُم. Two rows of teeth, سِنَانَانِ. Having prominent upper teeth, أَثْغَم; having prominent front teeth, أَفْشَغُ. The space between the teeth, فَلَج. Tooth and nail, altogether, بَتَّةً – كُلِّيَّةً – بِٱلْكُلِّ – جُمْلَةً – قَاطِبَةً – طُرًّا; with all one's power, بِكُلِّ جَهْدِهِ. Armed to the teeth, شَاكُّ ٱلسِّلَاحِ – شَوِكُ ٱلسِّلَاحِ. One whose teeth do not fall out by reason of age, مُخْلَد – مُخَلَّد.

To break the teeth of one, كَسَرَ أَسْنَانَهُ ~.

To cast anything in one's teeth, عَيَّرَ – عَيَّرَ بِ.

To clean the teeth, شَاصَ ~ – سَنَّ (أَسَنَّ or اِسْتَنَّ) أَضْرَاسَهُ (or شَوَّصَ or أَشَاصَ) أَضْرَاسَهُ – مَاحَ أَضْرَاسَهُ ~ تَسَوَّكَ.

To clench the teeth, كَزَّ عَلَى أَسْنَانِهِ – صَرَّ أَسْنَانَهُ ~.

To cut or grow teeth, سَنَّ – أَسَنَّ.

To draw or extract a tooth, قَبَعَ (or قَلَعَ) سِنًّا ~.

To grind the teeth, صَلَقَمَ – حَرَقَ بِٱلْأَسْنَانِ.

To grasp with the teeth, اِسْتَنَّ.

To knock out the teeth of one, هَتَمَ أَسْنَانَهُ – هَتَمَ ~. Having the teeth knocked out, هَتِم.

To lose teeth, سَلَّ مِنَ ٱلْأَسْنَانِ – سَلَّ ~.

To pick one's teeth, خَلَّلَ أَسْنَانَهُ – سَاكَ أَسْنَانَهُ ~.

To set the teeth of another on edge, أَضْرَسَ. His teeth were set on edge, ضَرِسَتْ أَسْنَانُهُ.

Tooth-ache, *n.* وَجَعُ ٱلْأَسْنَانِ – ضُرَاس. To have the —, تَأَلَّمَ – اُبْتُلِيَ بِوَجَعِ ٱلْأَسْنَانِ – بِٱلضُّرَاسِ.

Tooth-drawer, *n.* قَلَّاعُ ٱلْأَسْنَانِ.

Tooth-drawing, *n.* تَقْلِيعُ ٱلْأَسْنَانِ.

Toothed, *a.* ذُو أَسْنَانٍ – أَسَنّ.

Toothless, *a.* أَدْرَد *pl.* دُرْد – بِلَا أَسْنَانٍ. To be —, دَرِدَ ~.

Tooth-pick, *n.* } خِلَال *pl.* أَخِلَّة. What is taken out by the —,
Tooth-picker, } خُلَالَة.

Toothsome, *a.* لَذِيذ.

Top, *n.* The highest part, رَأْس – أَعْلَى – ذُرْوَة – ذِرْوَة. Summit, قِمَّة *pl.* قِمَم – قُلَّة *pl.* قُلَل – فَرْع *pl.* فُرُوع – شَعَفَة *pl.* شَعَف. Surface, صَفْحَة – سَطْح – وَجْه. A boy's spinning —, دَوَّامَة – فُرَيْرَة. A peg —, دَوَّامَةٌ ذَاتُ مِرْوَدٍ. The flat — of a house, سَطْحُ بَيْتٍ. From top to bottom, مِنْ فَوْقٍ إِلَى أَسْفَلَ. At the top of a class, فِي رَأْسِ ٱلصَّفِّ. From top to toe, مِنَ ٱلرَّأْسِ إِلَى ٱلْقَدَمِ. *See also* Summit, *n.*

Top, *v.i.* To rise aloft, to be eminent, عَلَا *aor.* يَعْلُو – شَهَقَ ~.

Top, *v.t.* To overtop, شَهَقَ عَلَى ~ – عَلَا عَلَى ~ – أَشْرَفَ عَلَى – اِسْتَعْلَى عَلَى. To cover the top with, عَالَى بِ. To take off the top, summit, قَطَعَ ٱلذُّرْوَةَ ~. *See also to* Lop, *v.t.*

Topaz, *n.* يَاقُوتٌ أَصْفَرُ.

Tope, *v.i.* *See to* Tipple, *v.i.*

Tope, *n.* *See* Grove, *n.*

Toper, *n.* *See* Tippler, *n.*

Top-gallant, *a.* مُتَعَلِّقٌ بِٱلْبَابَا فَنْغُو. Top-gallant sail, شِرَاعُ ٱلْبَابَا فَنْغُو.

Top-hamper, *n.* Of a ship, عُدَّةُ أَعْلَى ٱلْمَرْكَبِ.

Top-heavy, *a.* أَثْقَلُ ٱلرَّأْسِ – أَثْقَلُ فِي أَعْلَاهُ.

Tophet, *n.* The — of scripture, وَادِي تُفْتَة – تُفْتَة. *See also* Hell, *n.*

Topic, *n.* A subject of discourse, مَوْرِد – مَضْمُون – مَوْضُوع – خُصُوص – المَبْحُوثُ عَنْهُ – مَادَّة *pl.* مَوَادّ. A topical remedy, دَوَاءٌ يُوضَعُ عَلَى مَوْضِعِ ٱلْوَجَعِ – عِلَاجٌ لِخَارِجِ ٱلْبَدَنِ. I am directing my attention to this —, أَنَا بِصَدَدِ مِنْ هٰذَا ٱلْأَمْرِ. We will return to that — to which our attention is directed, نَرْجِعُ إِلَى مَا نَحْنُ بِصَدَدِهِ.

Topic, *a.* } Local, مَحَلِّيّ. Confined to a particular spot, مَحْصُور
Topical, } – غَيْرُ شَامِلٍ – بِمَحَلٍّ. Topical bleeding, فِصَاد – فِصَادٌ فِي مَحَلِّ ٱلْوَجَعِ. Topical, pertaining to a topic of discourse, مُتَعَلِّقٌ بِمَوْرِدِ ٱلْكَلَامِ.

Topically, *ad.* As a subject of discussion, مِنْ بَابِ – بَحْثًا فِيهِ – ٱلْبَحْثِ فِيهِ. Locally, to the place, فِي ٱلْمَحَلِّ.

Topknot, *n.* Such as is left on a boy's head when the rest is clipped or shaven, قَزَع – قَزَّاعَة – قُزَيْعَة. A woman's —, the hair done into a —, قُرْزُل. A — of hair, عِقْصَةُ شَعْرٍ. To do up the hair into a —, عَقَصَ ٱلشَّعْرَ ~. *See also* Tuft, *n.*

Topmast, *n.* غَابِيَة.

Topographer, *n.* مُؤَلِّفُ خَارِطَاتِ ٱلْبُلْدَانِ وَمُعَبِّرٌ عَنْهَا.

Topographic, *a.* } Descriptive of a place, وَصْفِيّ – مَوْقِعِيّ –
Topographical, } تَعْبِيرِيّ. Pertaining to topography, مُتَعَلِّقٌ بِرَسْمِ ٱلْبُلْدَانِ وَشَرْحِهَا.

Topography, *n.* The description of a place, بَيَانُ بَلْدَةٍ وَوَصْفُهَا. The science of —, عِلْمُ ٱلْبُلْدَانِ وَٱلتَّعْبِيرِ عَنْهَا.

Topped, *a.* Surmounted by, عَلَاهُ كَذَا – فَوْقَهُ كَذَا; topped by a star, فَوْقَهُ نَجْمَةٌ. Having the head cut off, مَقْطُوعُ ٱلرَّأْسِ.

Topping, *a.* Fine, superior, فَائِق. *See also* Proud, *a.*

Topple, *v.i.* وَقَعَ *aor.* يَقَعُ – اِنْهَبَطَ – اِنْقَلَبَ.

Topple, *v.t.* وَقَّعَ – أَهْبَطَ – قَلَبَ.

Topsail, *n.* غَابِيَّة.

Fore topsail, غَابِيَّةُ ٱلْبَرُوَّة.

Main topsail, غَابِيَّةُ ٱلْغَرْنَدِي.

Topsy-turvy, *ad.* Upside down, إِنْعِكَاسًا ـ إِنْتِكَاسًا. To turn —, نَكَسَ ـ ² عَكَسَ ـ ² قَلَبَ. To be —, إِنْتَكَسَ ـ إِعْتَكَسَ ـ إِنْعَكَسَ. To turn —, to throw into disorder, بَعْثَرَ ـ ² فَتَنَ ـ ² هَوَّشَ; to be thrown into disorder, إِفْتَتَنَ ـ تَهَوَّشَ. *See also* Upside-down, *ad.*

Toque, *n.* } كِسْوَةٌ لِرَأْسِ ٱلنِّسَآء.
Toquet, }

Torch, *n.* شُعَل *pl.* شُعْلَة ـ مَشَاعِلُ *pl.* مَشْعَلَة ـ مَشْعَل ـ نَفَّاط.

Torch-bearer, *n.* نَفَّاط *pl.* نَفَّاطَة ـ مَشَاعِلِيّ *coll.* مَشَاعِلِيَّة.

Torch-light, *n.* ضَوْءُ ٱلْمَشَاعِلِ.

Tore, *pret. of to* Tear, *v.t.*; *q.v.*

Torment, *n.* Extreme anguish, غُصَّة ـ نَهْكَة. Torture, punishment, عَذَاب *pl.* أَعْذِبَة. Annoyance, ضَجَر ـ أَذِيَّة. A pest, tormentor, مُوَضِّع ـ مُضْجِر ـ مُضَجِّر ـ مُعَجِّز ـ آذٍ. A place of —, ٱلْعَذَاب. A sore —, عَذَابٌ أَلِيمٌ.

Torment, *v.t.* To put to extreme pain, عَذَّبَ ـ ² نَهَكَ. To vex, to harass, أَزْعَجَ ـ فَجَّعَ ـ أَضْجَرَ. To annoy, trouble, أَتْعَبَ ـ ² شَقَّ عَلَى. To be tormented, as with torture, punishment, تَعَذَّبَ.

Tormentil, *n.* The plant, عِرْقُ ٱلْإِنْجَبَارِ.

Tormentingly, *ad.* With annoyance, إِضْجَارًا ـ إِزْعَاجًا ـ بِأَذِيَّةٍ.

Tormenter, *n.* } One who tortures, مُعَذِّب. One who annoys,
Tormentor, } vexes, مُضْجِر ـ مُكَدِّر ـ مُعَجِّز.

Torn, *a.* Rent, مَشْقُوق ـ مُمَزَّق. Torn, as by a wild beast, مُفْتَرَس. A — animal, فَرِيسَة.

Tornado, *n.* زَوْبَعَة *pl.* زَوَابِعُ ـ أُمُّ زَوْبَعَةٍ ـ رِيحٌ زَعْزَعَانٌ.

Torpedo, *n.* An electric fish, سَمَكَةُ ٱلرَّعْدِ ـ رَعَّادَة. The engine so called, لُغْم *pl.* لُغُوم ـ لُغْمٌ بَحْرِيٌّ ـ تُورْپِيدُو ـ فُنْبُرَةٌ كَهْرَبَائِيَّة. They closed the harbours with torpedoes, سَدُّوا ٱلْمَرَاسِي بِٱلتُّورْپِيدُو.

Torpid, *a.* Numb, خَدِر ـ خَادِر. Without motion, جَامِد ـ مَوَات ـ عَدِيمُ ٱلْحَرَكَةِ. Sluggish, ثَقِيل ـ فَاتِر ـ ضَاجِع ـ جَامِد. To be —, numb, ² خَدِرَ. *See also* Inert, *n.*

Torpidity, *n.* } Numbness, خَدَرَة ـ خَدَر. Want of activity,
Torpidness, } وَنًى ـ بَلَادَة ـ فَجْعَة. The — of heavy sleep, سُبَات.

Torpidly, *ad.* Sluggishly, بِوَنَاءٍ ـ بِجَمَادٍ.

Torpify, *v.t.* To render torpid, as by drugs, أَسْبَتَ ـ سَبَّتَ.

Torpor, *n.* The — of sleep, سُبَات. *See also* Torpidity, *n.*

Torporific, *a.* مُسْبِت ـ مُسَبِّت.

Torrefaction, *n.* تَحْمِيص ـ تَحْمِير ـ تَقْمِير.

Torrefy, *v.t.* To roast, toast, حَمَّصَ ـ حَمَّرَ ـ قَمَّرَ.

Torrent, *n.* سَيْل *pl.* سُيُول ـ مُجْتَنِح ـ يَعْبُوب ـ جُلَاف ـ نُغَب ـ جُرَاف ـ جُحَاف ـ تَرَّاع ـ سَيْلٌ عَزٌّ ; a violent —, سَيَلَان. The bed of a —, مَسِيل. An outburst, طَلْقَة. He was carried away by the —, سِيلَ بِهِ. The torrents swept it away, جَرَفَتْهُ ٱلسُّيُولُ.

Torrid, *a.* Scorching, hot, لَهْبَانُ *fem.* لَهْبَى *pl.* لِهَاب ـ حَارٌّ ـ حَام. The torrid zone, المِنْطَقَةُ ٱلْحَارَّة.

Torridness, *n.* حَرٌّ ـ فَوْرَة.

Torsel, *n.* دَوْر ـ لَيَّة ـ مُبْرَم ـ بَرِيم.

Torsion, *n.* تَفْتِيل ـ فَتْل ـ إِبْرَام ـ لِوَآء.

Torso, *n.* تِمْثَالٌ بِلَا رَأْسٍ *pl.* تَمَاثِيلُ.

Tort, *n.* مَضَرَّة ـ ضَرَر ـ ضَيْم ـ خَسَارَة ـ أَذِيَّة.

Tortile, *a.* مُلْتَوٍ ـ مُفَتَّل ـ مَفْتُول ـ فَتِيل.

Tortoise, *n.* The animal, رَقٌّ *pl.* رُقُوق ـ سُلَحْفَاة *and* سُلَحْفَاءٌ *and* سُلَحْفِيَة (*vulg.* سِلَحْفَى) *pl.* سَلَاحِفُ.

Tortoise-shell, *n.* ذَبْل ـ مَسَك ـ عَاجٌ.

Tortuous, *a.* Winding, مُلْتَوٍ; of a channel of water, مَصِيف. Perverse, مُلْتَوٍ ـ أَعْوَجُ. Tortuous ways, طُرُقٌ مُعْوَجَّة.

Tortuously, *ad.* Windingly, بِٱلْتِوَآءٍ. Perversely, بِٱعْوِجَاجٍ ـ بِغَيْرِ ٱسْتِقَامَةٍ.

Tortuousness, *n.* The being winding, إِلْتِوَآء. Want of integrity, نِفَاق ـ خِيَانَة.

Torture, *n.* Punishment, عَذَاب *pl.* أَعْذِبَة. Anguish, pain, غُصَّة ـ أَلَم *pl.* آلَام. An instrument of —, عَذْرَآء. *See also* Torment, *n.*

Torture, *v.t.* عَذَّبَ. *See also to* Torment, *v.t.*

Torvous, *a.* Of the aspect, stern, عَبُوس ـ عَبَّاس.

Tory, *n.* *See* Conservative, *n.*

Toryism, *n.* *See* Conservatism, *n.*

Toss, *v.t.* As of a ball, to play with a ball, ² كَرَا بِٱلْكُرَةِ ـ لَعِبَ بِٱلْكُرَةِ ـ *vulg.* شَاقَى ٱلطَّابَة. To throw, ² طَرَحَ ـ ² رَمَى: he tossed him the pillow, ² طَرَحَ لَهُ ٱلْوِسَادَةَ ـ أَلْقَى ٱلْوِسَادَةَ إِلَيْهِ. To —, as of a bull, ² طَرَحَ بِهِ إِلَى ٱلْهَوَآءِ ـ ² رَمَى بِهِ إِلَى ٱلْهَوَآءِ نَطْحًا. To —, as the wind a ship, ² قَمَصَ بِ ـ ² قَمَّصَ بِ ـ ² خَبَطَ. To — about, to jumble, لَبَكَ ـ هَوَّشَ ـ لَخْبَطَ. To — off, to drink off, ² شَرِبَ. To throw off, ² طَرَحَ. To — over, ² قَلَبَ. To shake, ² رَجَّ ـ هَزْهَزَ. To disquiet, أَقْلَقَ ـ أَضْجَرَ. They tossed him in a blanket, جَعَلُوهُ عَلَى لِحَافٍ وَهُمْ مَاسِكُونَ بِأَرْبَعَةِ أَطْرَافِهِ ثُمَّ هَزُّوهُ فَطَرَحُوا بِهِ إِلَى ٱلْهَوَآءِ إِهَانَةً لَهُ. He tossed about his arms, ² ضَرَبَ بِيَدَيْهِ.

Toss, *v.i.* To be tossed, as of the sea, مَاجَ ـ ارْتَجَّ. To — one's self about, تَقَالَبَ ـ تَمَلْمَلَ. To — or throw one's self into or upon, ارْتَمَى عَلَى. The waves tossed, تَلَاطَمَتِ (or الْتَطَمَتِ) الْأَمْوَاجُ. He tossed about upon his bed, from anxiety, تَسَلَّقَ عَلَى فِرَاشِهِ. I tossed about in bed, from want of sleep, بِتُّ أَتَقَرَّعُ ـ بِتُّ أَتَقَرَّعُ. Tossed by the winds, مُعَذَّبٌ مِنَ الرِّيَاحِ. Tossed to and fro by every wind, مَحْمُولٌ بِكُلِّ رِيحٍ. A wave of the sea tossed by the wind, مَوْجٌ مِنَ الْبَحْرِ تَخْبِطُهُ الرِّيحُ. They tossed up, for head or tail, رَمَوا بِوَجْهٍ أَوْ قَفَا ـ رَمَوا بَخْسًا أَوْ زَكَاءً.

Toss, *n.* } A throw upwards, طَرْحٌ إِلَى الْهَوَاءِ. A throw, cast,
Tossing, } رَمْيَةٌ ـ طَرْحٌ. A jerk, هَزَّةٌ ـ هَزٌّ. Troubles, اضْطِرَابٌ ـ قَلَقٌ. I am full of tossing, أَشْبَعُ قَلَقًا.

Toss-pot, *n.* *See* Tippler, *n.*

Total, *a.* جَمِيعٌ ـ كُلِّيٌّ ـ كُلٌّ.

Total, *n.* The whole sum, الْجُمْلَةُ ـ الْمَجْمُوعُ ـ الْجَمْعُ. A result, حَاصِلٌ ـ نَتِيجَةٌ.

Totality, *n.* كُلِّيَّةٌ ـ أَسْرٌ. In its —, بِكُلِّيَّتِهِ.

Totally, *ad.* بِأَسْرِهِ ـ أَجْمَعُ ـ جُمْلَةً ـ بِالْجُمْلَةِ ـ كُلِّيَّةً.

Totalness, *n.* كُلِّيَّةٌ ـ أَسْرٌ.

Totidem verbis, *ad.* بِحُرُوفِهِ ـ فِي ذَاتِ الْكَلَامِ.

Toto coelo, ad. Of a difference between two things, بَيْنَهُمَا فَرْقٌ كُلِّيٌّ ـ *vulg.* أَيْنَ هٰذَا وَأَيْنَ هٰذَاكَ.

Totter, *v.i.* As in gait, تَقَرَّكَ ـ سَعْسَعَ ; from age, هَدَجَ. To move to and fro, ارْتَجَّ ـ ارْتَكَّ ; as a drunken man, تَمَيَّحَ. To —, be tottering, of a wall, انْقَضَّ.

Tottering, *a.* As from age, هَدَّاجٌ. A — gait, هُدَاجٌ. A — wall, حَائِطٌ مُخِيفٌ ـ حَائِطٌ مُتَقَضِّضٌ.

Totteringly, *ad.* As in gait, تَقَرُّكًا ـ بِهَدَجَانٍ.

Toucan, *n.* The bird, اسْمُ طَيْرٍ كَبِيرٍ يُوجَدُ فِي أَمِيرِكَا الْجَنُوبِيَّةِ.

Touch, *v.t.* To come in contact with, لَمَسَ ـ لَامَسَ ـ مَسَّ. To be in contact with, مَاسَّ ـ لَاصَقَ ـ اتَّصَلَ بِ ; they touched one another, of many, تَمَاسُّوا. To handle, feel, جَسَّ. To try, by rubbing, حَكَّ. To reach, attain, بَلَغَ ـ أَدْرَكَ ـ نَالَ. To —, strike, as of a musical instrument, دَقَّ ـ ضَرَبَ ; of a stringed instrument, نَدَفَ بِ. To make an impression upon, أَثَّرَ فِي. To let one —, أَمَسَّ. To —, as the feelings, to affect, حَرَّكَ ـ نَجَعَ فِي ـ رَاعَ *aor.* يَرُوعُ ـ عَمِلَ فِي. To be touched by, to have a touch of, as of madness, *etc.*, مُسَّ بِ ; to be moved to pity for, تَحَنَّنَ لِ ـ تَرَثَّى لِ. He touched, reached, the ground with his hand, أَفْضَى بِيَدِهِ إِلَى الْأَرْضِ. "And if God touch thee with trouble, none can take it away [or remove it] but He," وَإِنْ يَمْسَسْكَ اللّٰهُ بِضُرٍّ فَلَا كَاشِفَ لَهُ إِلَّا هُوَ (Kur. vi. 17). To touch off, to make a rough draft of, سَوَّدَ. To do anything quickly, تَوَجَّزَ فِي ـ خَفَّ فِي.

To touch to the quick, to the heart, جَرَحَ ـ مَحَشَ قَلْبَهُ ـ قَلَبَهُ: They were touched to the quick, مُحِشُوا فِي قُلُوبِهِمْ.

To touch up, to correct, رَمَّمَ ـ صَحَّحَ ـ أَصْلَحَ ; as of the colours of a picture, *etc.*, جَنْدَرَ. To trim, of language, style, نَقَّقَ ـ حَرَّرَ. To stir up, اسْتَفَزَّ ـ أَحَثَّ ـ حَرَّضَ.

Touch, *v.i.* To be in contact with, لَصِقَ بِ ـ اتَّصَلَ بِ ـ تَمَاسَّ ـ كَانَ مُتَّصِلًا بِ.

To touch at a place, جَازَ عَلَى ـ مَرَّ بِ ـ أَقْبَلَ إِلَى.

To touch on, as a subject, ذَكَرَ بِإِيجَازٍ ـ أَشَارَ إِلَى.

Touch, *n.* As with the hand, *etc.*, لَمْسٌ ـ مَسٌّ. Contact, مُمَاسَّةٌ ـ مُلَامَسَةٌ. A slight —, as of disease, خَطْرَةٌ ـ مَسٌّ ; of insanity, خَبْطَةٌ. A slight presentiment, حِسٌّ. The place touched, مَلْمَسٌ. The sense of touch, الْقُوَّةُ اللَّامِسَةُ. A —, as with a touchstone, امْتِحَانٌ ـ حَكٌّ. Sentiment, feeling, حَاسَّةٌ. The commencement of anything, as of a fever, حِسٌّ. Touch, as on a musical instrument, مَسٌّ ـ ضَرْبَةٌ. An indication, إِشَارَةٌ. Power, as of exciting the feelings, تَأْثِيرٌ ـ تَرْوِيعٌ. A — with the pen, تَعْرِيفٌ بِالْقَلَمِ. A —, touching up, restoration, جَنْدَرَةٌ ـ إِصْلَاحٌ ـ تَصْلِيحٌ ـ اسْتِشْبَابٌ. A reproof, تَوْبِيخٌ. A —, spice, or modicum, عِرْقٌ. A taste, ذَوْقٌ. A scent, رَائِحَةٌ. Soft to the —, سُخَامٌ ـ سُخَامُ الْمَسِّ. He felt a — of fever, وَجَدَ مَسَّ الْحُمَّى *aor.* يَجِدُ. A — of nature, tenderness, رِقَّةُ قَلْبٍ ـ حِنَّةٌ ; nature, طَبِيعَةٌ. At the slightest —, عِنْدَ أَدْنَى لَمْسٍ. Touch-and-go, in the utmost uncertainty, فِي غَايَةِ الِاشْتِبَاهِ.

Touched, *a.* As by a disease, مُصَابٌ بِ.

Touch-hole, *n.* بَرْمَةٌ ـ فَالِيَةٌ *pl.* فَوَالِي.

Touchily, *ad.* بِشَرَاسَةٍ ـ بِشَكَاسَةٍ ـ بِوَغْقَةٍ.

Touchiness, *n.* حِدَّةُ مِزَاجٍ ـ وَغْقَةٌ ـ شَكَاسَةٌ ـ شَرَاسَةٌ.

Touching, *prep.* مِنْ جِهَةِ كَذَا. As — anything, فِي أَيِّ شَيْءٍ. As — these people, مِنْ جِهَةِ هٰؤُلَاءِ النَّاسِ. As — you, مِنْ جِهَتِكُمْ.

Touching, *a.* Affecting, مُحَنِّنٌ ـ مُحَرِّكُ (or مُرِقُّ) الْقَلْبِ.

Touchingly, *ad.* بِتَحْنِينٍ ـ بِصُورَةٍ مُحَنِّنَةٍ.

Touchstone, *n.* حَجَرُ مِحَكٍّ ـ فِتَانَةٌ ـ فِتَانِيَّةٌ.

Touch-wood, *n.* صُوفَانٌ.

Touchy, *a.* سَرِيعُ الْغَضَبِ ـ شَكِسٌ ـ شَرِسٌ ـ وَغِقٌ.

Tough, *a.* Of meat, *etc.*, مُتَعَزِّزٌ ـ عَاسٍ ـ صُلْبٌ. Hard, stiff, rigid, جَاسِئٌ. Firm, solid, صَلِيدٌ ـ صُلْب ـ صَلِيب. Obstinate, كُنُود ـ عَنِيد. Difficult to deal with, rough, خَشِنُ ٱلْجَانِبِ. Rough, خَشِن. Difficult, مُشْكِل ـ عَسِر ـ عَسِير ـ صَعْب. Severe, عَنِيف ـ قَاسٍ ـ جَافٍ. Viscous, لَزِج ـ دَبِق. Thick, مَخِين. Tough, flexible, timber, خَشَبٌ لَيِّنٌ. A — skin, جِلْدٌ خَشِنٌ ـ جِلْدٌ جَاسِئٌ. A — plant, نَبْتٌ جَاسِئٌ. To become —, of meat, تَعَزَّزَ: The meat became —, تَعَزَّزَ ٱللَّحْمُ.

Toughen, *v.t.* To make tough, hard, صَلَّبَ. To make thick, as paste, *etc.*, كَثَّفَ. To make stubborn, شَرَّنَ. *See also to* Harden, Stiffen, *v.t.*

Toughen, *v.i.* To become stiff, rigid, جَسَا ـ جَسَأَ. To become hard, compact, صَلُبَ ـ صَلَبَ. To become thick, inspissated, مَخُنَ ـ كَثُفَ.

Toughish, *a.* Of meat, *etc.*, صُلْبٌ (عَاسٍ *or* مُتَعَزِّزٌ *or*) نَوْعًا. Somewhat hard, صَلِيبٌ نَوْعًا. Somewhat difficult, صَعْبٌ نَوْعًا ـ مُشْكِلٌ نَوْعًا.

Toughly, *ad.* *See* Tenaciously, *ad.*

Toughness, *n.* As of meat, عَسَاءَة ـ عُسُوٌّ ـ تَعَزُّز. Rigidity, stiffness, hardness, صَلَابَة ـ تَصْلِيب. Want of flexibility, كَزَازَة ـ مَخَانَة ـ مُخُونَة ـ كَثَافَة. Flexibility, لَيَان ـ لِينَة. Inspissation, كَثَافَة. Viscosity, لُزُوجَة. Difficulty, عُسْر ـ صُعُوبَة. Callosity, جَسَاءَة ـ كَنَب. Hardness of temperament, خُشُونَةُ ٱلْجَانِبِ.

Toupee, *n.* }
Toupet, } A tuft of hair, نَاصِيَة ـ قُصَّة.

Tour, *n.* A going round, دَوَرَان ـ دَوْر. A turn, نَوْبَة. A journey to different places, طَوَفَان ـ طَوَاف ـ جَوَلَان ـ سِيرَة ـ سَفْرَة. To make a — through, اِجْتَالَ ـ جَالَ ـ طَافَ بِ. I have often wished to make a — through Europe, وَدِدْتُ مِرَارًا أَنْ أَطُوفَ فِي أُورُبَّا. *See also* Excursion, *n.*

Tour de force, *n.* عَمَلٌ بَدِيعٌ ـ بِدْع.

Tourist, *n.* سَيَّاح ـ طَوَّافُون *pl.* طَوَّاف ـ جَوَّالُون *pl.* جَوَّال ـ سَيَّاحَة. *See also* Excursionist, *n.*

Tourmalin, *n.* }
Turmalin, } The stone, حَجَرٌ نَفِيسٌ لَامِعٌ.

Tournament, *n.* لَعِبُ ٱلْجَرِيدِ ـ لَعِبُ ٱلسَّطَاسِ.

Tourniquet, *n.* مِلْوًى ـ مِلْوًى لِحَزْقِ ضِمَادَةٍ.

Tournure, *n.* Style, manner, تَرْكِيب ـ هَيْئَة ـ نَوْع ـ طَرْز ـ طَوْر ـ كَيْفِيَّة. Having an elegant —, مَلِيحُ ٱلْأَوْصَافِ.

Touse, *v.t.* To haul, جَذَبَ. To tear, شَرَّطَ.

Tousel, *v.t.* }
Tousle, } To tangle, شَبَّكَ. To disorder, هَوَّشَ ـ شَوَّشَ ـ لَخْبَطَ ـ لَبَّكَ.

Tout, *v.i.* طَلَبَ ٱلزَّبُونَاتِ ـ تَطَلَّبَ ٱلزَّبَائِنَ.

Touter, *n.* طَلَّابُ ٱلزَّبُونَاتِ ـ مُتَطَلِّبُ ٱلزَّبَائِنِ.

Tow, *n.* مُشَاقَة ـ قُنَّب ـ تِيل ـ *from the Italian*, إِصْطُبَّة.

Tow, *v.t.* As of a ship, جَرَّ ـ قَطَرَ.

Towage, *n.* جَرّ ـ سَحْب ـ قَطْر. Price of —, حَقُّ ٱلْجَرِّ ـ أُجْرَةُ ٱلْقَطْرِ.

Toward, *prep.* }
Towards, } In the direction of, إِلَى ـ نَحْوَ ـ سِوَى ـ تُجَاهَ ـ إِلَى طَرَفِ ـ صَوْبَ. About, near, عِنْدَ. I betook myself — such an one, قَصَدْتُ قَصْدَ ـ قَصَدْتُ سِوَى فُلَانٍ ـ فُلَانٍ. Towards the morning, عِنْدَ ٱلصُّبْحِ.

Towardliness, *n.* }
Towardness, } Aptitude, اِسْتِعْدَاد. Tractableness, ذُلُول ـ وَدَاعَة ـ لِينَة ـ خُضُوع ـ اِنْقِيَاد.

Towardly, *a.* Apt, مُسْتَعِدٌّ. Tractable, ذَلُول ـ مِذْعَان ـ وَدِيع.

Tow-boat, *n.* A boat that is towed, قَارِبٌ مَجْرُورٌ ـ فُلُوكَةٌ مَقْطُورَةٌ.

Towel, *n.* فُوطَة *pl.* فُوَط.

Towelling, *n.* قُمَاشٌ لِلْفُوَطِ.

Tower, *n.* A high edifice, بُرْج *pl.* بُرُوج *and* أَبْرَاج. A fortress, قَلْعَة *pl.* قِلَاع *and* قُلُوع. A hill —, fortress, مَعْقِل *pl.* مَعَاقِل.

Tower, *v.i.* To soar aloft, سَمَا *aor.* يَسْمُو ـ اِرْتَفَعَ ـ أَخَذَ فِي ٱلْعُلُوِّ.

Towering, *a.* Very high, شَامِخ ـ شَمَّاخ ـ مُنِيف ـ مُرْتَفِع. Great, strong, عَظِيم ـ شَدِيد. He was in a — passion, حَنِقَ ـ اِشْتَدَّ غَيْظُهُ. "And his are the ships towering up at sea like mountains," وَلَهُ ٱلْجَوَارِ ٱلْمُنْشَآتُ فِي ٱلْبَحْرِ كَٱلْأَعْلَامِ (Kur. lv. 24).

Towery, *a.* ذُو بُرُوجٍ ـ مُبَرَّج.

Tow-line, *n.* }
Tow-rope, } لِبَانُ ٱلْقَطْرِ ـ لِبَانُ ٱلْجَرِّ.

Towing-path, *n.* دَرْبُ ٱلْقَطْرِ ـ مَسْلَكُ ٱلْجَرِّ.

Town, *n.* مَدَرَة *pl.* مَدَر ـ كُورَة *pl.* كُوَر ـ بَلْدَة *pl.* بِلَاد ـ بَلَد *pl.* بُلْدَان ـ مَدِينَة *pl.* مَدَائِنُ. A large —, فُسْطَاط *or* فِسْطَاط ـ مِصْر *pl.* أَمْصَار. A capital —, قَصَبَة *pl.* قِصَاب. He is in —, هُوَ بِٱلْمَدِينَةِ. He is out of —, in the country, هُوَ بِٱلرِّيفِ.

Town-crier, *n.* مُنَادٍ ـ بَرَّاح.

Town-hall, *n.* دِيوَانُ ٱلْمَدِينَةِ ـ دَارُ ٱلْبَلَدِ.

Town-house, *n.* A town residence, دَارُ ٱلسُّكْنَى فِي ٱلْمَدِينَةِ ـ مَسْكَنٌ بِٱلْمَدِينَةِ.

Townlet, *n.* بُلَيْدَة ـ قَرْيَة *pl.* قُرًى.

Township, *n.* مُلْحَقَاتُ مَدِينَةٍ ـ حُدُودُ بَلْدَةٍ.

Townsman, *n.* A man of a town, مِنْ أَهْلِ بَلْدَةٍ ـ مِنْ أَهْلِ مَدِينَةٍ. One of the same town, مِنْ أَهْلِ بَلَدٍ وَاحِدٍ. Townsmen and countrymen, أَهْلُ ٱلْمَدَرِ وَٱلْوَبَرِ.

Town-talk, *n.* حِكَايَاتُ ٱلنَّاسِ ـ حِكَايَةُ ٱلْبَلَدِ ـ حَوَادِثُ ٱلْبَلَدِ.

Tow-path, *n.* *See* Towing-path, *n.*

Tow-tow, *v.i.* To prostrate one's self, تَطَأْطَأَ. The act of tow-towing, تَطَأْطُؤٌ.

Toxicological, *a.* مُتَعَلِّقٌ بِعِلْمِ ٱلسِّمَامِ.

Toxicologist, *n.* مَاهِرٌ فِي عِلْمِ ٱلسُّمُومِ.

Toxicology, *n.* عِلْمُ ٱلسُّمُومِ ـ عِلْمُ ٱلسِّمَامِ.

Toy, *n.* A plaything, لُعْبَةٌ *pl.* لُعَيْبَات. A child's —, دَاحَة *coll.* دَاح ـ شَخْشِيخَة. A bagatelle, تَفَاهَة ـ قُطَيْرَة ـ أَمْرٌ لَيْسَ ـ بِشَيْءٍ ـ عَبَثٌ ـ شَيْءٌ وَجِيزٌ ـ شَيْءٌ زَهِيدٌ *pl.* أَشْيَاءُ زَهِيدَةٌ. The world is a gaudy toy, الدُّنْيَا دَاحَةٌ.

Toy, *v.i.* To dally amorously, تَلَطَّفَ ـ تَدَلَّلَ ـ هَانَغَ. To —, as with a woman, لَعَبَ ـ هَانَغَ. *See also to* Play, Trifle, *v.i.*

Toyer, *n.* / Toyful, *a.* } A dallier, مُتَلَطِّف ـ مُتَدَلِّل. *See also* Trifler, *n.*

Toyish, *a.* Frivolous, هَزْلِيٌّ ـ عِبِّيث ـ سَخِيف.

Toyishness, *n.* Frivolity, هَزْل ـ سَخَافَة.

Toyman, *n.* بَيَّاعُ ٱلشَّخْشِيخَاتِ ـ بَيَّاعُ ٱلدَّاحِ.

Toyshop, *n.* دُكَّانُ ٱلشَّخْشِيخَاتِ ـ دُكَّانُ ٱلدَّاحِ.

Trace, *v.t.* To draw, delineate, رَسَمَ [2]. To follow by some mark left, of anything, قَصَّ ـ ٢ (or تَقَصَّصَ or اِقْتَصَّ) ٱلْأَثَرَ ـ تَأَثَّرَ ـ اِئْتَثَرَ ـ اِقْتَرَسَ ٱلْأَثَرَ ـ قَفَرَ [2] (or تَقَفَّرَ or اِقْتَفَرَ) أَثَرَهُ. To examine the traces, marks; to investigate narrowly, تَرَسَّمَ رَسْمَهُ ـ تَرَسَّمَ. To — back to, رَجَعَ ـ ٢ إِلَى ـ رَفَعَ ـ إِلَى: He traced up the tradition to the Prophet, رَفَعَ ٱلْحَدِيثَ إِلَى ٱلنَّبِيِّ. He traced up the tradition to its author, أَسْنَدَ ٱلْحَدِيثَ إِلَى قَائِلِهِ. The place to which anything is traced, المُتَقَفَّرُ.

Trace, *n.* A mark drawn, رَسْم *pl.* رُسُوم ـ حَرْش *pl.* حِرَاش. A —, vestige, أَثَر *pl.* آثَار ـ رَسْم *pl.* رُسُوم ـ رَشْم *pl.* رُشُوم ـ قُفَاف. The —, or track, along which a thing is or has been dragged, مَجَرٌّ: I saw the — over which his hinder skirt had been dragged, رَأَيْتُ مَجَرَّ ذَيْلِهِ. A slight — of anything, عَيْثَر. Trace, as of a carriage, مَجَرٌّ *pl.* مَجَرَّات. I saw not the slightest trace of him, مَا رَأَيْتُ لَهُ أَثَرًا وَلَا عَيْثَرًا. To obliterate traces, طَمَسَ ـ ٢ طَمَسَ ٱلْآثَارَ ـ ٢.

Traceable, *a.* That may be traced, يُتَرَسَّمُ ـ يُقْتَصُّ أَثَرُهُ. Traceable, referrible, to, يُرْجَعُ إِلَى.

Tracer, *n.* One who delineates, رَسَّام. A — of footsteps, قَصَّاصُ ٱلْأَثَرِ. A — of traditions, رَفَّاع.

Tracery, *n.* Ornamental work, نَقْش ـ نَسِيج ـ شَبَك ـ شَبَكَة; specially in gypsum, الدَّوَاخِلُ وَٱلْخَوَارِجُ.

Trachea, *n.* حَجَب ـ حَاجِرَة ـ حُنْجُور *pl.* حَنَاجِرُ ـ حُلْقُوم ـ قَصَبَةُ ٱلرِّئَةِ.

Tracheal, *a.* مَا نِيطَ بِقَصَبَةِ ٱلرِّئَةِ ـ مُتَعَلِّقٌ بِٱلْحَجَبِ.

Tracheotomy, *n.* جِرَاحَةُ ٱلْحُلْقُومِ.

Trachitis, *n.* اِلْتِهَابُ ٱلْحُلْقُومِ.

Track, *n.* A mark left by something passing, أَثَر *pl.* آثَار. A course, way, مَسْلَك ـ سَبِيل ـ مَدْرَج ـ رُحْلَة. The beaten — of a road, جَادَّة *pl.* جَوَادّ ـ مَطْرَدَة ـ جُدَّة ـ جَرْجَة. A mountain —, فَجّ ـ فُجَاج. Tracks made by sheep and other animals, أَنْسَاع ـ شَرَك; of the stars, حَبَائِكُ ٱلنُّجُومِ ـ حَبَائِك. A stage, distance, مَرْحَلَة ـ مَسَافَة ـ جَوَاد. He went over a long —, عَدَا عَدْوًا جَوَادًا [2]. We journeyed over a large —, سِرْنَا عُقْبَةً جَوَادًا. "And the tracks of the stars," وَٱلسَّمَاءِ ذَاتِ ٱلْحُبُكِ (Kur. li. 7). "Verily, we found our fathers with a religion and in their tracks we tread," إِنَّا وَجَدْنَا آبَاءَنَا عَلَى أُمَّةٍ وَإِنَّا عَلَى آثَارِهِمْ مُقْتَدُونَ (Kur. xliii. 32).

Track, *v.t.* To tow, جَرَّ ـ ٢ سَحَبَ ـ ٢ قَطَرَ. *See also to* Trace, *v.t.*

Trackless, *a.* Without a track, بِدُونِ أَثَرٍ. Having no passages or roads, عَدِيمُ ٱلْمَسَالِكِ. Waste, void, خَالٍ خَاوٍ. A — way, غُفْل.

Tract, *n.* A space of ground, قِطْعَةٌ مِنَ ٱلْأَرْضِ ـ بُقْعَة *pl.* بِقَاع *pl.* قِطَاع. A region, ثُغْرَة *pl.* ثُغَر ـ قُطْر *pl.* أَقْطَار ـ جِهَة *pl.* جِهَات ـ نَاحِيَة *pl.* نَوَاحِي ـ كَنَف *pl.* أَكْنَاف. A treatise, pamphlet, كُتَيِّب ـ تَعْلِيقَة ـ رِسَالَة *pl.* رَسَائِلُ.

Tractability, *n.* / Tractableness, } لَيَان ـ مُلَائَمَة ـ ذُلُول ـ خُضُوع ـ اِنْقِيَاد.

Tractable, *a.* جَنِيب ـ ذَلُول ـ طَوْع ـ طَوْعُ ٱلْعِنَانِ ـ رَخْو ـ لَيِّنُ ٱلْعَرِيكَةِ ـ مُعَبَّد ـ مِذْعَان ـ وَدِيع. A — horse, فَرَسٌ طَوْعُ ٱلْعِنَانِ. To be — to, أَذْعَنَ ل ـ اِخْتَضَعَ ل.

Tractably, *ad.* بِخُضُوعٍ ـ بِذُلُولٍ ـ بِٱنْقِيَادٍ.

Tractate, *n.* A treatise; *see under* Tract, *n.*

Tractation, *n.* Discussion, مُذَاكَرَة ـ مُفَاوَضَة ـ مُبَاحَثَة.

Tractile, *a.* *See* Ductile, *a.*

Tractility, *n.* *See* Ductility, *n.*

Traction, *n.* The act of drawing, tugging, خَلْج ـ اِخْتِلَاج ـ سَحْب ـ جَذْب ـ جَرّ ـ قَطْر. A traction engine, بَاخِرَةُ ٱلْخَلْجِ (or ٱلْقَطْرِ).

Tractitious, *a.* بَاحِثٌ فِي شَيْءٍ.

Tractive, *a.* / Tractor, *n.* } جَاذِب ـ جَارّ ـ خَالِج.

Trade, *n.* Buying and selling, commerce, سَوْم ـ تِجَارَة ـ مَتْجَر ـ بَيْعٌ وَشِرَآءٌ. A —, occupation, حِرْفَة *pl.* حِرَف ـ صَنْعَة ـ كار *pl.* كارات. ـ صِنَاعَة *pl.* صَنَائِعُ *and* صِنَاعَات ـ شُغْل. An article of —, سِلْعَة *pl.* سِلَع ـ بِضَاعَة *pl.* بَضَائِعُ. The —, the persons collectively engaged in a trade, الأَصْنَاف ـ أَهْلُ ٱلْأَصْنَافِ. Extensive —, تِجَارَةٌ وَاسِعَةٌ. A wretched —, scoundrelism, حِرْفَةٌ ذَمِيمَةٌ. He carried on a lucrative —, تَجَرَ تِجَارَةً رَابِحَةً. Injurious to —, مُخِلٌّ بِٱلتِّجَارَةِ.

Trade, *v.i.* تَجَرَ ـ ٱتَّجَرَ ـ بَاعَ وَٱشْتَرَى. To — in, تَسَبَّبَ بِ.

Trade-mark, *n.* وَسْمُ بِضَاعَةٍ ـ وَسْمٌ عَلَى بِضَاعَةٍ.

Trader, *n.* One who trades, مُتَسَبِّب ـ تَاجِر *pl.* تُجَّار *and* تِجَار. A trading vessel, مَرْكَبُ تِجَارَةٍ.

Tradesman, *n.* مُتَسَبِّب ـ بَائِع *pl.* بَاعَة ـ دُكَّانِيٌّ *vulg.* دُكَّانْجِي *pl.* دُكَّانْجِيَّة.

Tradesmanlike, *a.* كَٱلْبَيَّاعِ ـ عَلَى أُسْلُوبِ ٱلْمُتَسَبِّبِ.

Tradespeople, *n.* بَاعَة ـ مُتَسَبِّبُون ـ دُكَّانِيَّة *vulg.* دُكَّانْجِيَّة.

Tradeswoman, *n.* بَائِعَة ـ مُتَسَبِّبَة ـ دُكَّانِيَّة ـ دُكَّانْجِيَّة *pl.* دُكَّانْجِيَّات.

Trade-wind, *n.* رِيحُ مَوْسِمٍ *pl.* أَرْيَاحُ مَوْسِمٍ ـ رِيحٌ تَهُبُّ مُدَّةً مَوَاسِمَ مَعْلُومَةٍ.

Tradition, *n.* The act of handing down, نَقْل. That which is handed down, حَدِيث *pl.* أَحَادِيثُ. A sacred —, حَدِيثٌ قُدْسِيٌّ. A weak —, حَدِيثٌ ضَعِيفٌ. A relation, recital, رِوَايَة *pl.* رَوَايَا.

Traditional, *a.* / **Traditionary,** } نَقْلِيٌّ ـ حَدِيثِيٌّ.

Traditionally, *ad.* نَقْلًا ـ بِٱلْحَدِيثِ.

Traditioner, *n.* / **Traditionist,** } One who adheres to tradition, مُتَمَسِّكٌ بِٱلْأَحَادِيثِ.

Traduce, *v.t.* حَكَرَ ـ نَمَّ ـ هَتَكَ ـ أَقْرَشَ بِ ـ شَرَّرَ ـ جَرَّسَ بِ. *See also to* Defame, *v.t.*

Traducer, *n.* حَكِر ـ لَمَّاز ـ نَمَّام ـ شَتَّام ـ هَمَّاز.

Traduction, *n.* Transmission, حَمْلَة ـ نَقْل.

Traductive, *a.* *See* Deducible, *a.*

Traffic, *n.* Barter, مُغَايَرَة. *See* Trade, *n.*

Traffic, *v.i.* As in a market, تَسَوَّقَ. *See also to* Trade, *v.i.*

Traffic, *v.t.* To barter, exchange, عَارَضَ ـ غَايَرَ ـ بَادَلَ ـ دَاكَشَ. He trafficked, exchanged, or bartered the article with him, غَايَرَهُ بِٱلسِّلْعَةِ.

Trafficker, *n.* *See* Trader, *n.*

Tragacanth, *n.* The gum, صَمْغُ ٱلْكَثِيرَآءِ ـ الكَثِيرَآء. The tree, شَجَرَةُ ٱلْكَثِيرَآءِ ـ القَتَاد.

Tragedian, *n.* مُشَخِّصُ ٱلرِّوَايَا ٱلْمُخِيفَةِ فِي ٱلتِّيَاتْرُو.

Tragedy, *n.* A dramatized poem of some tragic event, تَشْخِيصُ تَهْلُكَةٍ (*or* تَقْلِيدُ) مُصِيبَةٍ ـ تَقْلِيدُ. A tragic event, غَائِلَة *pl.* غَوَائِلُ ـ تَهْلُكَة ـ وَقْعَةٌ مَخُوفَةٌ ـ أَمْرٌ فَظِيعٌ.

Tragic, *a.* / **Tragical,** } Connected with the acting of tragedy, مَا نِيطَ بِتَشْخِيصِ ٱلرِّوَايَا ٱلْمُخِيفَةِ فِي ٱلتِّيَاتْرُو. Mournful, fatal, غَائِل ـ مَشْئُوم ـ نَحِس ـ مُهْلِك. He met with a — end, غَالَتْهُ غُولٌ.

Tragically, *ad.* With a fatal event, غَوْلًا ـ بِسَيِّئَةٍ ـ نَحْسًا ـ عَلَى ٱلْهَلَاكِ ـ شُؤْمًا.

Tragicalness, *n.* غَوْل ـ سَيِّئَة ـ شُؤْم ـ نَحْس ـ هَلَكَة.

Tragi-comedy, *n.* لَعِبٌ فِي ٱلتِّيَاتْرُو يُخَالِطُهُ ٱلْهَزْلُ وَٱلْكَدَرُ.

Tragi-comic, *a.* / **Tragi-comical,** } أَمْرٌ مُكَدِّرٌ وَمُفْرِحٌ.

Trail, *v.t.* To drag along the ground, ذَبْذَبَ عَلَى ٱلْأَرْضِ ـ جَرَّ عَلَى ٱلْأَرْضِ. To hunt by a track, اِقْتَصَّ أَثَرَ ٱلصَّيْدِ ـ اِقْتَفَى أَثَرَ ٱلصَّيْدِ.

Trail, *v.i.* تَذَبْذَبَ ـ تَدَلَّى عَلَى ٱلْأَرْضِ ـ ٱنْجَرَّ عَلَى ٱلْأَرْضِ. A woman who trails her dress on the ground, فُضُل.

Trail, *n.* Anything drawn behind, ذَيْل. A track, trace, أَثَر. A scent, رَائِحَة. The — of the wind, عُثْنُونُ ٱلرِّيحِ. The entrails of a fowl, أَمْعَآءُ طَيْرٍ ـ مَصَارِينُ (*or*) ٱلطَّيْرِ ـ جَوْف.

Train, *v.t.* To draw along, خَلَجَ ـ جَرَّ ـ سَحَبَ ـ جَذَبَ. To teach, as of soldiers, مَرَّنَ ـ عَلَّمَ. To make experienced, حَنَكَ ـ خَرَّجَ ـ أَدَّبَ. To discipline, as in morals, أَدَّبَ. To accustom, break in, دَرَّبَ ـ خَرَّجَ. To —, as a horse, رَاضَ *aor.* يَرُوضُ; to be trained, of a horse, اِرْتَاضَ. Time, or the course of events, or experience, trained him, حَنَكَهُ ٱلدَّهْرُ. Age trained him, rendered him sound in judgment, حَنَّكَتْهُ (*or*) حَنَكَتْهُ ٱلسِّنُّ.

Train, *v.i.* *See to* Trail, *v.i.*

Train, *n.* A tail or any hanging appendage, ذَيْل *pl.* أَذْيَال ـ أَذْيَال. A — of followers, retinue, دَائِرَة ـ أَلْزَام ـ مَوْكِب *pl.* مَوَاكِبُ ـ حَشَم ـ خَدَمٌ وَحَشَمٌ ـ أَتْبَاع. A concatenation, سِلْك ـ سِلْسِلَة ـ سِيَاقَة ـ رِبَاط ـ تَعَاقُب ـ تَتَابُع. Sequence, تَوَاتُر ـ جَرْي ـ سَيْر ـ مَدْرَج. A course, The travelling apparatus and accompaniments, as of a commander, ثَقَل ـ سَوَاد. A — of artillery, عِدَّةُ مَدَافِعَ. A — of powder, فَتِيلُ بَارُودٍ. A course, series, connected order, طُرْقَة ـ سِمَاط ـ سِيَاقَة ـ نَسَق. Train, string, as of camels, mules, etc., قِطَار *pl.* قُطُر. Train, as of a railway, قِطار – أَرْتَال *pl.* رَتَل – أَرْتَال *pl.* رَتْل سِكَّةِ ٱلْحَدِيدِ *pl.* *and* قُطْر قُطُرات. To put in —, to commence, – أَلْقَى يَدَهُ فِي مَشَى – شَرَعَ فِي. Trains now run from the city, صارَتِ ٱلْأَرْتَالُ تَسِيرُ مِنَ ٱلْمَدِينَةِ.

Excursion train, قِطارُ ٱلسَّيَّارَةِ.

Express train, قِطارٌ مَخْصُوصٌ.

Fast train, قِطارٌ سَرِيعٌ.

Luggage train, قِطارُ ٱلْبِضاعَةِ.

Ordinary train, قِطارٌ عادِيٌّ.

Passenger train, قِطارُ ٱلرُّكَّابِ.

Trainable, *a.* يُخَرَّجُ – يُدَرَّبُ; of a horse, يُرْتاضُ.

Train-band, *n.* عَسْكَرٌ بَلَدِيٌّ – عَسْكَرٌ رَدِيفٌ.

Train-bearer, *n.* حامِلُ ٱلْأَذْيالِ.

Trained, *a.* Trained to, مُدَرَّبٌ عَلَى. Trained officers, ضُبّاطٌ مُحَنَّكُونَ. A — horse, فَرَسٌ مُرْتاضٌ. Well disciplined, خِرِّيجٌ. He was — by such an one, هُوَ خِرِّيجُ فُلانٍ.

Trainer, *n.* Of beasts, رائِضٌ *pl.* راضَةٌ *and* رُوَّضٌ *and* رُوّاضٌ; a — of hunting-dogs, مُؤَسِّدٌ.

Training, *n.* The act of, دُرْسَةٌ – تَدْرِيبٌ – تَخْرِيجٌ – تَمْرِينٌ. The being trained, تَرْبِيَةٌ – تَدَرُّسٌ – تَعَلُّمٌ.

Train-oil, *n.* دُهْنُ ٱلْحُوتِ.

Traipse, *v.i.* تَوَقَّفَ – تَحَوَّشَ – تَحَوَّزَ.

Trait, *n.* A characteristic, سَجِيَّةٌ *pl.* سَجايا – ضَرِيبَةٌ *pl.* ضَرائِبُ – صِفَةٌ *pl.* صِفاتٌ.

Traitor, *n.* } خائِنٌ *pl.* خَوَنَةٌ *and* خَوّانٌ – خُوّانٌ – خاتِرٌ – خَتِيرٌ – خِتِّيرٌ.
Traitorous, *a.* } To act the — to, خَتَرَ – إِخْتانَ – خانَ. He was — to him in respect of the compact, خانَهُ فِي ٱلْعَهْدِ. His sword was — to him, خانَهُ سَيْفُهُ. His two legs were — to him, خانَتْهُ رِجْلاهُ.

Traitorously, *ad.* خِيانَةً – بِخِيانَةٍ – خَتْرًا. To deal — with, خانَ *aor.* يَخُونُ – إِخْتانَ – خَبَّبَ.

Traitorousness, *n.* خِيانَةٌ – خائِنَةٌ – مَخانَةٌ – خَوْنٌ – خَتْرٌ.

Traitress, *n.* إِمْرَأَةٌ خائِنَةٌ (or خاتِرَةٌ).

Traject, *v.t.* أَمَرَّ عَلَى – رَمَى فِي. *See also to* Pierce, *v.t.*

Traject, *n.* *See* Ferry, *n.*

Trajection, *n.* The act of casting, طَرْحٌ – رَمْيٌ. *See also* Emission, Transportation, *n.*

Trajectory, *n.* خَطٌّ مُرُورٍ.

Tralatitious, *a.* *See* Metaphorical, *a.*

Tralucent, *a.* *See* Transparent, *a.*

Trammel, *n.* A net, شَبَكَةٌ *pl.* شِباكٌ. Shackles for a horse, شِكالٌ *pl.* شُكُلٌ – عِقالٌ. A hook for suspending a pot, مِعْلاقٌ *pl.* مَعالِيقُ. An impediment, عائِقٌ – زَنَقَةٌ – ضَنْكٌ – مانِعٌ – تَحْرِيجٌ.

Trammel, *v.t.* To catch with a net, إِصْطادَ بِٱلشَّبَكَةِ. To hamper, حَجَزَ – عارَضَ – عَوَّقَ. To be trammeled, إِحْتَجَبَ – إِحْتَجَزَ – تَثَبَّطَ – تَعَوَّقَ.

Tramontane, *a.* ما كانَ عِبْرَ ٱلْجِبالِ.

Tramp, *v.t.* and *i.* طافَ فِي *aor.* يَطُوفُ – طَوَّفَ فِي – جالَ فِي – ساحَ *aor.* يَسِيحُ – عارَ فِي. To —, of the tramping of a horse, أَكْدَفَ – حَفَّ. *See also to* Stroll, *v.i.*; *also to* Trample, *v.t.*

Tramp, *n.* As of a horse, دَبْدَبَةٌ – كَدْفٌ. A tramping of feet, دَوِيٌّ – حَفِيفٌ.

Tramp, *n.* } A stroller, عَيّارٌ – عائِرٌ. A vagrant, مُطَرَّدٌ – هامِلٌ – ضالِلٌ.
Tramper, }

Trample, *v.t.* As under foot, داسَ *aor.* يَدُوسُ. To — upon, as horses with their feet, خَبَطَ – تَخَبَّطَ. To — upon, to set at defiance, خالَفَ – عانَدَ; to contemn, إِسْتَخَفَّ – إِسْتَقَلَّ. He, the horse, trampled the ground with his fore-foot, خَبَطَ ٱلْفَرَسُ ٱلْأَرْضَ بِيَدِهِ. They trampled upon him with their feet, داسُوهُ بِأَقْدامِهِمْ.

Trampling, *n.* Of the feet, دَبْدَبَةٌ.

Trampler, *n.* دائِسٌ – دَوّاسٌ.

Tram-road, *n.* } اَلتَّرْمُوايُ, A tram-carriage, كَرُوسَةُ ٱلتَّرْمُوايِ.
Tram-way, } The laying down of a —, مَدُّ سِكَّةِ ٱلتَّرْمُوايِ.

Trance, *n.* غَيْبَةٌ: He fell into a —, وَقَعَتْ عَلَيْهِ غَيْبَةٌ. He saw in a —, رَأَى فِي غَيْبَةٍ.

Tranquil, *a.* At rest, quiet, مُرْتاحٌ – ساكِنٌ – هادِئٌ. Unruffled, مُطْمَئِنٌّ – ساكِنٌ – سالِئٌ. A — life, عَيْشٌ خَفْضٌ. To be —, quiet, هَدَأَ – تَهَدَّأَ. To be —, unruffled, at peace, in security, إِطْمَأَنَّ. *See also* Calm, Quiet, *a.*

Tranquillize, *v.t.* To pacify, لَمَّمَ; with words, فَثَأَ بِٱلْكَلامِ. To —, an offended person, طَيَّبَ خاطِرَهُ. To set at rest, appease, هَدَّنَ – خَفَّضَ – سَكَّنَ – سَكَّتَ – أَهْدَأَ. *See also to* Calm, *v.t.*

Tranquillity, *n.* Rest, quiet, سُكُونٌ – سَكِينَةٌ – هُدُوءٌ – خَفْضٌ – إِطْمِئْنانٌ – راحَةُ بالٍ – طُمَأْنِينَةٌ. Tranquillity of mind, راحَةُ ٱلْخاطِرِ. An easy life, رَفاهِيَةٌ – رَفاهَةٌ. The government has taken the necessary measures to insure —, إِتَّخَذَتِ ٱلْحُكُومَةُ ٱلْوَسائِلَ ٱللّازِمَةَ لِحِفْظِ ٱلرّاحَةِ. For the establishment of —, لِتَوْطِيدِ ٱلْأَمْنِيَّةِ. *See also* Calmness, *n.*

Tranquillization, *n.* The act of, إِهْدَآءٌ ـ تَسْكِين ـ تَسْكِيت ـ تَخْفِيض.

Tranquilly, *ad.* بِرَاحَةٍ ـ بِٱطْمِئْنَانٍ. *See also* Calmly, *ad.*

Tranquilness, *n.* *See* Tranquillity, *n.*

Trans, *prefix.* عِبْرَ.

Transact, *v.t.* To do, act, فَعَلَ ـ قَضَى ـ. To execute, carry out, أَمْضَى ـ أَنْفَذَ ـ أَجْرَى. To — business with, عَامَلَ: They transacted business together, of many, تَعَامَلُوا.

Transaction, *n.* An act, affair, عَمَلِيَّة ـ فِعْل *pl.* أَفْعَال ـ قَضِيَّة *pl.* قَضَايَا ـ أَمْر *pl.* أُمُور ـ صَنِيعَة *pl.* صَنَائِعُ. A dealing together, مُعَامَلَة ـ تَعَاطٍ ـ تَعَاطٍ.

Transactor, *n.* An agent, فَاعِل. A negotiator, مُعَامِل ـ مُعَامِل ـ مُفَاوِض ـ ٱلْأُمُورِ.

Transalpine, *a.* مَا كَانَ عِبْرَ جِبَالِ ٱلْأَلْبِ بِٱعْتِبَارِ مَوْقِعِ مَدِينَةِ رُومِيَّةَ.

Transatlantic, *a.* كَائِنٌ عِبْرَ ٱلْبَحْرِ ٱلْمُحِيطِ ٱلْغَرْبِيِّ نَظَرًا إِلَى أُورُبَّا.

Transcend, *v.t.* To surpass, شَرُفَ ـ جَاوَزَ ـ تَجَاوَزَ ـ فَاقَ *aor.* يَفُوقُ. To — in excellence, بَرَّزَ عَلَى ـ بَرَعَ ـ بَهَرَ. *See also* to Surpass, *v.t.*

Transcendence, *n.* / Transcendency, — شَرَف ـ تَفَوُّق ـ فَضْل ـ بَرَاعَة. *See also* Superiority, *n.*

Transcendent, *a.* بَارِع ـ فَائِق *pl.* فُوَقَآءُ. *See also* Superior, *a.*

Transcendental, *a.* That cannot be bounded, تَحْدِيدُهُ مُحَالٌ. Above experience, يَفُوقُ ٱلِٱخْتِبَارَ. Pertaining to the foundations of human knowledge, مُتَعَلِّقٌ بِمَبَادِئِ ٱلْعُلُومِ ٱلْبَشَرِيَّةِ. Visionary, خَيَالِيٌّ ـ خُرَافِيٌّ.

Transcendentalism, *n.* The principles of transcendental philosophy, أُصُولُ ٱلْعُلُومِ ٱلْبَشَرِيَّةِ وَمَبَادِئُهَا.

Transcendentalist, *n.* قَائِلٌ بِقَوْلِ ٱلْحِكْمَةِ ٱلْمَذْكُورَةِ.

Transcendentally, *a.* عَلَى أُصُولِ ٱلْحِكْمَةِ ٱلْمَذْكُورَةِ.

Transcendently, *ad.* بِفَوْقَانٍ ـ بِبَرَاعَةٍ.

Transcendentness, *n.* فَوْقَان ـ بَرَاعَة.

Transcribe, *v.t.* إِسْتَنْسَخَ ـ حَوَّلَ ـ نَقَلَ ـ نَسَخَ ـ أَخَذَ صُورَةً مِنْهُ.

Transcriber, *n.* نَاسِخ *pl.* نُسَّاخ ـ وَرَّاق ـ كَاتِب *pl.* كَتَبَة.

Transcript, *n.* A copy, نُسْخَة *pl.* نُسَخ ـ مَنْقُولٌ عَنْ أَصْلٍ ـ صُورَة *pl.* صُوَر.

Transcription, *n.* The act of transcribing, نَقْل ـ نَسْخ.

Transept, *n.* جَنَاحَا بِنَآءٍ. The — of a church, جَنَاحَا كَنِيسَةٍ.

Transfer, *v.t.* To convey from one place to another, نَقَلَ. To — to, make over to, أَلْقَى إِلَى ـ حَوَّلَ إِلَى ـ سَلَّمَ إِلَى. To — in writing, حَوَّلَ ـ نَسَخَ. To be transferred, إِنْتَقَلَ ـ تَنَقَّلَ ـ تَحَوَّلَ ـ إِسْتَحَالَ.

Transfer, *n.* تَحْوِيل ـ نَقْل.

Transferable, / Transferrable, *a.* / Transferrible, — تَحْوِيلُهُ مُمْكِنٌ ـ نَقْلُهُ مُمْكِنٌ.

Transferee, *n.* ٱلْمُتَسَلِّمُ.

Transference, *n.* / Transferring, — تَسْلِيم ـ تَحْوِيل ـ نَقْل.

Transferrer, *n.* مُسَلِّم ـ مُحَوِّل ـ نَاقِل.

Transfiguration, *n.* A change of form, تَغْيِيرُ هَيْئَةٍ ـ تَغْيِيرُ شَكْلٍ. The Transfiguration of Christ, تَجَلِّي ٱلْمَسِيحِ ـ ٱلتَّجَلِّي.

Transfigure, *v.t.* غَيَّرَ ٱلْهَيْئَةَ ـ غَيَّرَ ٱلشَّكْلَ. To be transfigured, تَغَيَّرَتْ هَيْئَتُهُ.

Transfix, *v.t.* خَلَّ ـ تَخَلَّلَ ـ خَرَقَ. To be transfixed, إِخْتَرَقَ ـ ٱنْخَرَقَ.

Transform, *v.t.* To change the form or shape, غَيَّرَ ٱلشَّكْلَ ـ غَيَّرَ ٱلْهَيْئَةَ. To metamorphize into an inferior state, مَسَخَ ـ طَمَسَ. To disguise, نَكَّرَ. To be transformed, تَغَيَّرَ شَكْلُهُ. To be metamorphized, طَمِسَ ـ نُسِخَ. To — one's self into..., غَيَّرَ شَكْلَهُ إِلَى شِبْهِ كَذَا. To disguise one's self, تَنَكَّرَ.

Transformation, *n.* The act of, تَغْيِيرُ ٱلْهَيْئَةِ ـ تَغْيِيرُ شَكْلٍ. The being transformed, إِنْقِلَابُ ٱلشَّكْلِ. Metamorphosis, طَمْس ـ مَسْخ. A — scene, مَنْظَرُ صُوَرٍ مُتَشَكِّلَةٍ وَمُتَغَيِّرَةٍ.

Transformative, *a.* / Transforming, *n.* — مُحَوِّل ـ مُغَيِّر.

Transfuse, *v.t.* As into another vessel, فَرَّغَ مِنْ كَذَا إِلَى كَذَا. To imbue with, make to imbibe, شَرَّبَ. To clarify by transfusion, صَفَّقَ ـ أَصْفَقَ.

Transfusible, *a.* يُفَرَّغُ ـ يُشَرَّبُ.

Transfusion, *n.* The act of, تَفْرِيغ ـ تَشْرِيب. Clarification by infusion, تَصْفِيق.

Transgress, *v.t.* To go beyond the bounds of, أَسْرَفَ فِي ـ عَدَا ـ طَغَا ـ جَاوَزَ بِ ـ جَاوَزَ ـ تَعَدَّى عَلَى. To offend against, أَسَآءَ إِلَى ـ تَعَدَّى عَلَى. He transgressed his limit, عَدَا طَوْرَهُ. They transgressed, made an incursion into, the border, شَطَطُوا فِي ٱلْحُدُودِ. To cause to —, أَطْغَى.

Transgress, *v.i.* To sin, أَثِمَ ـ خَطِئَ ـ أَخْطَأَ ـ أَذْنَبَ. "They said, Woe to us! we have transgressed," قَالُوا يَا وَيْلَنَا إِنَّا كُنَّا طَاغِينَ (Kur. lxviii. 31).

Transgression, *n.* Going beyond limits, عَدْوٌ ـ تَعَدٍّ ـ إِسْرَاف ـ تَفَاوُت ـ طُغْيَان ـ تَجَاوُز ـ مُجَاوَزَة. A sin, violation of duty, مَسَاءَة ـ إِسَاءَة ـ ذَنْب *pl.* ذُنُوب ـ خَطِيئَة *pl.* خَطَايَا.

Transgressional, *a.* Going beyond, مُجَاوِز ـ مُتَجَاوِز ـ مُتَعَدٍّ. Sinful, خَاطِئ ـ شِرِّير ـ سَيِّئ.

Transgressive, *a.* *See* Faulty, Culpable, *a.*

Transgressor, *n.* One who goes beyond what is right, بَاغٍ *pl.* بُغَاة ـ مُتَعَدٍّ ـ مُتَجَاوِز. A sinner, آثِم *pl.* أُثَمَاء ـ أَثِيم *pl.* أُثَّم ـ خَاطِئ *pl.* خُطَاة.

Tranship, *v.t.* نَقَلَ مِنْ مَرْكَبٍ إِلَى مَرْكَبٍ آخَر [2].

Transhipment, *n.* نَقْلٌ مِنْ مَرْكَبٍ إِلَى مَرْكَبٍ آخَر.

Transient, *a.* سَرِيع ـ فَانٍ ـ زَائِل ـ عَابِر ـ حَائِل ـ حَيُود ـ عَاجِل ـ أَعْجَلُ ـ ٱلزَّوَالِ.

Transiently, *ad.* بِسُرْعَةٍ ـ لِوَقْتٍ وَجِيزٍ.

Transientness, *n.* فَنَاء [2] ـ عَدَمُ ثَبَاتٍ ـ سُرْعَةُ زَوَالٍ ـ عَدَمُ بَقَاء ـ حَالَةٌ فَانِيَةٌ.

Transilience, *n.* }
Transiliency, } نَطٌّ ـ قَفْزٌ.

Transit, *n.* A passing through, مُرُور ـ عُبُور. Transit, as of a planet, مُرُور: The — of Venus, مُرُورُ ٱلزُّهَرَةِ. Transit duty, حَقُّ ٱلْمُرُورِ. A — instrument, آلَةٌ لِرَصْدِ مُرُورِ ٱلسَّيَّارَاتِ.

Transition, *n.* Passing from one stage to another, تَحَوُّل ـ مَآل ـ إِنْقِلَاب.

Transitional, *a.* مُنْقَلِب. In a — state, فِي حَالِ ٱلتَّحَوُّلِ.

Transitive, *a.* Having the power of passing over, contagious, أَعْدَى. Indicating a passing, نَافِذ. A — verb, فِعْلٌ وَاقِعٌ ـ فِعْلٌ مُتَعَدٍّ. To make —, عَدَّى. The making a verb —, تَعْدِيَةُ ٱلْفِعْلِ.

Transitively, *ad.* بِتَعَدٍّ.

Transitiveness, *n.* As of a verb, تَعَدٍّ.

Transitorily, *ad.* بِسُرْعَةٍ ـ بِعَدَمِ بَقَاءٍ. *See also* Transiently, *ad.*

Transitoriness, *n.* سُرْعَةُ زَوَالٍ ـ عَدَمُ بَقَاءٍ.

Transitory, *a.* وَقْتِيّ ـ زَائِل ـ فَانٍ ـ سَرِيعُ ٱلزَّوَالِ. "But ye love the transitory and ye neglect the life to come," بَلْ تُحِبُّونَ ٱلْعَاجِلَةَ وَتَذَرُونَ ٱلْآخِرَةَ (Kur. lxxv. 20, 21).

Translatable, *a.* As into another language, نَقْلُهُ إِلَى لِسَانٍ آخَرَ ـ يُتَرْجَمُ إِلَى لِسَانٍ آخَرَ ـ مُمْكِنٌ.

Translate, *v.t.* To remove from one place to another, نَقَلَ [2]. To render into another language, تَرْجَمَ ـ إِلَى لِسَانٍ آخَرَ ـ إِسْتَخْرَجَ ـ نَقَلَ ـ إِلَى لِسَانٍ آخَرَ [2]: He translated it from the original copy, تَرْجَمَهُ عَنِ ٱلنُّسْخَةِ ٱلْأَصْلِيَّةِ. To explain, فَسَّرَ.

Translation, *n.* Removal from one place to another, نَقْل ـ إِنْتِقَال. The act of turning into another language, نَقْل ـ تَرْجَمَة.

Translator, *n.* نَاقِل *pl.* نَقَلَة ـ مُتَرْجِم. An interpreter, تُرْجُمَان *pl.* تَرَاجِمُ and تَرَاجِمَة.

Translucency, *n.* تَرْجَمَة (or ضَرْبٌ) مِنَ ٱلشُّفُوفِ.

Translucent, *a.* }
Translucid, } شَفَّاف نَوْعًا.

Translucently, *ad.* يَضْرِبُ إِلَى ٱلشُّفُوفِ.

Transmarine, *a.* عِبْرَ ٱلْبَحْرِ.

Transmigrant, *a.* جَال ـ مُرْتَحِلٌ مِنْ مَحَلٍّ إِلَى مَحَلٍّ آخَرَ ـ مُهَاجِر.

Transmigrate, *v.i.* As from one country to another, إِرْتَحَلَ مِنْ بَلَدٍ إِلَى بَلَدٍ آخَرَ; from one body to another, of the soul, تَقَمَّصَ ـ إِنْتَقَلَ مِنْ بَدَنٍ إِلَى بَدَنٍ آخَرَ بِٱلتَّنَاسُخِ.

Transmigration, *n.* As from one country to another, مُهَاجَرَة ـ هِجْرَةٌ مِنْ بَلَدٍ إِلَى بَلَدٍ ثَانٍ. The — of souls, ٱلتَّنَاسُخُ ـ ٱلنَّسْخُ.

Transmigrator, *n.* جَال ـ رَحِيل ـ مُهَاجِر.

Transmissible, *a.* That may be passed from one to another, يَنْفُذُ إِلَى ـ يُنْهَى إِلَى ـ يَنْتَقِلُ. That may be transmitted through, ٱلْمُرُورُ مِنْهُ مُمْكِنٌ. *See also* Contagious, *a.*

Transmission, *n.* The act of sending, forwarding, إِنْفَاذ ـ إِرْسَال ـ تَسْيِير ـ نَقْل ـ تَسْبِيل; of passing through, مُرُور.

Transmit, *v.t.* To send to, أَنْفَذَ ـ إِلَى ـ أَنْهَى ـ إِلَى ـ سَاقَ ـ إِلَى [2] ـ سَيَّرَ ـ إِلَى ـ نَفَذَ ـ إِلَى. To hand down, نَقَلَ [2]. To — orally, or by narrative, رَوَى *aor.* يَرْوِي ـ تَرْوِي. It has been related as transmitted from him, رُوِيَ عَنْهُ.

Transmitter, *n.* A sender, forwarder, نَاقِل ـ مُرْسِل; of traditions, *etc.*, رَاوٍ ـ نَاقِل.

Transmogrify, *v.t.* To — one's self by magic arts, تَغَوَّلَ. One who so transmogrifies himself, أَغْوَال.

Transmutability, *n.* إِمْكَانُ ٱلتَّحْوِيلِ ـ إِمْكَانُ ٱلتَّبْدِيلِ.

Transmutable, *a.* قَابِلُ ٱلتَّحْوِيلِ ـ تَبْدِيلُهُ مُمْكِنٌ ـ تَحْوِيلُهُ مُمْكِنٌ.

Transmutably, *ad.* بِقَابِلِيَّةِ ٱلتَّحْوِيلِ ـ إِسْتِحَالَةً ـ إِحَالَةً ـ بِقَابِلِيَّةِ ٱلتَّبْدِيلِ.

Transmutation, *n.* The act of, إِحَالَة ـ تَبْدِيل ـ تَحْوِيل; the being transmuted, إِحَالَة ـ تَحَوُّل ـ إِسْتِحَالَة.

Transmute, *v.t.* أَحَالَ ـ حَوَّلَ.

Transmuter, *n.* مُحِيل ـ مُحَوِّل.

Transom, *n.* Of a ship, خَشَبَةُ مُؤَخَّرِ ٱلْمَرْكَبِ; of a door, لِبَاف. *See also* Lintel, *n.*

Transparency, *n.* The quality of being transparent, شُفُوف ـ شَفَافَة ـ شَفِيف. A picture drawn with transparent colours, صُورَةٌ شَفَّافَةٌ. Distinctness, بَيَان ـ تَبَيُّن ـ إِمْتِيَاز ـ وُضُوح.

Transparent, *a.* Transmitting rays of light, شَفَّاف. A — or very thin cloth, material, or garment, شَفّ ـ شِفّ ـ شَفِيف. To be —, شَفَّ ـِ. Clear, evident, وَاضِح ـ بَيِّن ـ مُبِين.

Transparently, *ad.* Clearly, evidently, جِهَارًا ـ بِوُضُوحٍ ـ عَلَانِيَةً. Brightly, إِضَاءَةً ـ بِضِيَاءٍ.

Transparentness, *n.* Clearness, brightness, جَلَال ـ ضِيَاء ـ نُور. Conspicuousness, وُضُوح ـ بَيَان ـ جَهَارَة.

Transpicuous, *a.* يُدْرِكُهُ ٱلْبَصَرُ.

Transpierce, *v.t.* *See to* Transfix, *v.t.*

Transpiration, *n.* A passing through pores, رَشْح ـ رَشِيح.

Transpire, *v.i.* To pass through pores, رَشَحَ ـَ ـ تَرَشَّحَ. To become known, إِشْتَهَرَ ـ شَاعَ خَبَرُهُ *aor.* يَشِيعُ. To happen, حَدَثَ ـُ ـ وَقَعَ *aor.* يَقَعُ ـ حَصَلَ ـُ.

Transplant, *v.t.* Of plants, غَرَسَ ـِ فِي مَحَلٍّ آخَرَ. To remove, as from one place to another, نَقَلَ ـُ ـ حَوَّلَ. To —, of a colony, سَكَّنَ فِي مَحَلٍّ آخَرَ ـ إِسْتَعْمَرَ فِي مَوْضِعٍ آخَرَ. To — one's self, إِنْتَقَلَ. A plant for transplanting, شَتْلَة.

Transplantation, *n.* Of plants, غَرْسٌ فِي مَوْضِعٍ آخَرَ. Removal, نَقْل. The act of colonizing in another place, إِسْتِعْمَارٌ فِي مَوْضِعٍ آخَرَ.

Transplanter, *n.* As of plants, غَارِسُ ٱلشَّتَلَاتِ ـ نَاقِلُ ٱلنَّبَاتِ.

Transplendent, *a.* مُنِير ـ نَيِّر. *See also* Resplendent, *a.*

Transport, *n.* Conveyance, إِنْتِقَال ـ نَقْل ـ حُمْلَة ـ حِمْلَة. Implements of —, أَدَوَاتُ ٱلنَّقْلِ. Hire of —, حُمْلَان ـ شَوْل ـ حَقُّ ٱلنَّقْلِ. A — ship, مَرْكَبُ حُمُولَةٍ ـ سَفِينَةٌ نَقْلِيَّةٌ; for soldiers, مَرْكَبُ حُمُولَةِ ٱلْعَسْكَرِ. A — steamer, بَاخِرَةٌ نَقْلِيَّةٌ. A — for conveying horses, طَرِيدَةٌ. A convict banished, نَفِيٌّ. A state of rapture, غَايَةُ ٱلسُّرُورِ ـ حَالُ ٱلْوِجْدَانِ ـ وَجْد. A —, as of passion, *etc.*, حُمَيَّا ـ ثَوَرَان ـ هَيَجَان.

Transport, *v.t.* To convey, رَفَعَ ـَ ـ نَقَلَ ـُ ـ جَلَبَ ـِ. To banish, نَفَى ـِ ـ نَفَا ـ أَجْلَى. To enrapture, حَيَّرَ عَقْلَهُ ـ أَغْرَمَ. To —, as with joy, anger, *etc.*, طَيَّرَ عَقْلَ ـ مِنْ كَذَا ـ سَرَّ ـُ غَايَةَ ٱلسُّرُورِ. He was transported with delight, طَارَ عَقْلُهُ مِنَ ٱلسُّرُورِ ـِ.

Transportable, *a.* That may be conveyed, نَقْلُهُ مُمْكِنٌ. Liable to banishment, مُسْتَوْجِبُ ٱلنَّفْيِ.

Transportation, *n.* Conveyance, إِنْتِقَال ـ نَقْل ـ حُمْلَة. Banishment, نَفْيٌ. A place of — or exile, مَنْفًى.

Transported, *a.* Removed, مَنْقُول. Banished, مَنْفِيٌّ ـ نَفِيٌّ.

Transported with delight, طَارَ عَقْلُهُ مِنَ ٱلسُّرُورِ ـِ ـ فِي غَايَةِ ٱلسُّرُورِ.

Transported with anger, طَارَ عَقْلُهُ مِنَ ٱلْغَضَبِ ـِ ـ سَاخِط ـ مُغْتَاظ ـ حَارِد.

Transposal, *n.* عَكْس ـ قَلْب ـ تَغْيِيرُ مَوْضِعٍ ـ تَبْدِيلُ مَكَانٍ ـ تَقْدِيمٌ وَتَأْخِيرٌ.

Transpose, *v.t.* عَكَسَ ـِ ـ بَدَّلَ مَوْضِعَهُ ـ غَيَّرَ مَوْضِعَهُ ـ قَدَّمَ ٱلشَّيْءَ وَأَخَّرَهُ. To remove, نَقَلَ ـُ.

Transposed, *a.* مَعْكُوس ـ مَقْلُوب ـ صَارَ فِيهِ تَقْدِيمٌ وَتَأْخِيرٌ. To be —, إِنْعَكَسَ ـ إِنْقَلَبَ.

Transposition, *n.* Change, as of place, بَدَل ـ قَلْب ـ تَقْدِيمٌ وَتَأْخِيرٌ. Reciprocal change, مُبَادَلَة.

Transship, *v.t.* *See to* Tranship, *v.t.*

Transubstantiate, *v.t.* حَوَّلَ إِلَى جَوْهَرٍ آخَرَ.

Transubstantiation, *n.* اَلتَّحْوِيلُ إِلَى جَوْهَرٍ آخَرَ. The doctrine of —, اَلْقَوْلُ بِٱسْتِحَالَةِ جَوْهَرِ ٱلْخَمْرِ وَٱلْخُبْزِ فِي ٱلْقُرْبَانِ ٱلْمُقَدَّسِ إِلَى لَحْمٍ وَدَمٍ.

Transubstantiator, *n.* اَلْقِسِّيسُ ٱلَّذِي عَلَى مَا يُزْعَمُ يُحَوِّلُ جَوْهَرَيِ ٱلْخَمْرِ وَٱلْخُبْزِ فِي ٱلْقُرْبَانِ ٱلْمُقَدَّسِ إِلَى دَمٍ وَجَسَدٍ.

Transudation, *n.* رَشِيح ـ رَشْح ـ صَبِيب.

Transudatory, *a.* مُتَرَشِّح.

Transude, *v.i.* رَشَحَ ـَ ـ تَرَشَّحَ.

Transversal, *a.* } مُعْتَرِض. A — beam of a roof, *etc.*, عَارِض ـ
Transverse, } *pl.* عَوَارِض.

Transverse, *v.t.* *See to* Overturn, *v.t.*

Transversely, *ad.* إِعْتِرَاضًا.

Transylvania, *n.* بِلَادُ تَرَنْسِلْوَانِيَا.

Trap, *n.* As for catching game, مِصْيَدَة ـ حِبَالَة *pl.* حَبَائِل. A snare, ambush, كَمِينَة *pl.* كِمَان. A stratagem, مَصَايِد *pl.* مَكِيدَة ـ مَكْر ـ مَكَائِد *pl.* دُولَاب ـ ضَرْبٌ. A kind of greenstone, مِنَ ٱلْحَجَرِ ٱلْأَخْضَرِ. To lay a — for, أَنْصَبَ لِ. Trap, bat, and ball, لَعْبُ ٱلصَّوْلَجَانِ. Traps, articles, أَشْيَاء ـ أَثَاث ـ أَمْتِعَة.

Trap, *v.t.* } *See to* Entrap, *v.t.*
Trapan, *v.t.* }

Trapan, *n.* *See* Snare, Stratagem, *n.*

Trap-door, *n.* طَابِق ـ بَابٌ مُخَبًّا. A room with a —, بَيْتُ ٱلطَّابِقِ.

Trapes, *n.* *See* Slattern, *n.*

Trapezium, *n.* مُنْحَرِف.

Trapezoid, *n.* شَبِيهٌ بِٱلْمُنحَرِف.

Trapper, *n.* رَجُلٌ صَيَّادٌ.

Trappings, *n.* Horse furniture, طَقْمُ ٱلْخَيْلِ ـ عُدَّةُ ٱلْخَيْلِ. Ornaments, حُلِيّ ـ حِلَى ـ تَزْيِينَات.

Traps, *n.* Goods, furniture, أَسْبَاب ـ أَشْيَآء ـ أَثَاث ـ أَمْتِعَة.

Trash, *n.* Refuse, سُقَاط ـ سُقَاطُ (or سَقَط) ٱلْمَتَاع ـ *vulg.* بُوْر ـ بَوَار. Nonsense, لَغْوٌ ـ عَبَث.

Trashy, *a.* Worthless, رَدِيْءٌ ـ بَطَّال ـ بَاطِل ـ سَقَط ـ تَافِه ـ خَسِيس ـ حَقِير.

Traumatic, *n.* عِلَاجٌ لِلْجُرُوحِ.

Travail, *v.i.* To labour with pain, تَعَنَّى ـ يَتَعَنَّى *aor.* عَنِيَ. To — with child, تَمَخَّضَت ـ ٤ ـ ٢ مَخَضَت.

Travail, *n.* Painful labour, تَعَنٍّ ـ عَنَآء; with child, مَخَاض.

Trave, *n.* *See* Beam, *n.*

Travel, *v.t.* and *i.* سَافَرَ ـ يُسَافِرُ *aor.* سَاحَ ـ يَسِيحُ. To — about or in, طَوَّفَ ـ يُطَوِّفُ *aor.* طَافَ فِي ـ ٢ عَالَ فِي ـ ٢ غَسَّ فِي. To —, as along a road, سَلَكَ ٱلطَّرِيقَ ـ عَبَرَ ٱلسَّبِيلَ ـ ٤ عَبَرَ. To — by night, سَافَرَ لَيْلًا ـ إِسْتَرَى. To — quickly, سَافَرَ عَلَى عَجَلٍ ـ أَسْرَعَ فِي ٱلسَّفَرِ. He is travelling, هُوَ مُسَافِرٌ ـ هُوَ فِي ٱلسَّفَرِ. News travels quickly, ٱلْأَخْبَارُ تُشَاعُ بِهَا عَاجِلًا.

Travel, *n.* سِيَاحَة ـ سَفَر. A book of travels, كِتَابُ أَسْفَارٍ.

Travelled, *a.* One who has travelled much, مِسْفَرٌ ـ مِسْفَار. A — road, طَرِيقٌ مَسُورٌ فِيهِ ـ طَرِيقٌ مَسُورٌ ـ دَرْبٌ مَقْرُوحَةٌ ـ طَرِيقٌ مَسْلُوكٌ.

Traveller, *n.* مُسَافِر *pl.* مُسَافِرُون ـ سَائِح *pl.* سُوَّاح. An iron ring, حَلْقَةٌ مِنْ حَدِيدٍ *pl.* حَلْقَات. A — on a road, عَابِرُ ٱلسَّبِيلِ ـ اِبْنُ ٱلسَّبِيلِ.

Travelling, *a.* For use in travel, لِلسَّفَرِ. Travelling expenses, مَصْرُوفُ ٱلسَّفَرِ. A — companion, رَفِيقٌ فِي ـ مُسَافِرٌ مَعَ فُلَانٍ *pl.* رُفَقَآء ٱلسَّفَرِ.

Traversable, *a.* That may be crossed, عُبُورُهُ ـ يَنْسَلِكُ ـ يُسْلَكُ. That may be denied, disputed, إِنْكَارُهُ مُمْكِنٌ ـ يُرَدُّ عَلَيْهِ ـ مُمْكِنٌ.

Traverse, *n.* Anything lying across, عَارِض *pl.* عَوَارِض. A denial, رَدٌّ وَإِنْكَارٌ ـ إِنْكَار.

Traverse, *a.* Lying across, مُعْتَرِض.

Traverse, *ad.* اِعْتِرَاضًا.

Traverse, *v.t.* To lay in a cross direction, ٢ عَرَضَ ـ عَرَّضَ ـ شَبَّكَ ـ صَلَّبَ. To thwart, obstruct, اِعْتَرَضَ ل ـ ٢ عَرَضَ ل ـ أَعَاقَ ـ تَعَرَّضَ ل. To wander over, ٤ جَازَ ـ ٤ جَازَ بِ ـ ٢ عَالَ فِي ـ ٢ عَارَ فِي ـ ٤ جَالَ فِي. To deny, أَنْكَرَ. He traversed, or cut through, or crossed over the country by travelling, ٢ خَرَقَ (or قَطَعَ) ٱلْأَرْضَ (or ٱلْمَفَازَةَ).

Traverse, *v.i.* To take the posture of opposition, اِعْتَرَضَ ـ تَعَرَّضَ. To turn round, اِسْتَدَارَ ـ ٤ دَارَ.

Traverser, *n.* مُعْتَرِضٌ عَلَى ـ مُنَازِع ـ مُشَاجِر.

Travertin, *n.* حَجَرٌ مُشَرَّبٌ بِٱلْكِلْسِ يَتَكَوَّنُ مِنْ قَطَرَانِ ٱلْمَآء.

Travesty, *n.* A burlesque translation, مَسْخَرَة ـ نَقْلٌ سُخْرِيٌّ.

Travesty, *v.t.* ٢ جَعَلَ سُخْرَةً ـ اِتَّخَذَ سُخْرِيَّةً ـ ٤ نَقَلَ إِلَى مَسْخَرَةٍ.

Trawl, *v.t.* اِصْطَادَ ٱلسَّمَكَ بِٱلشَّبَكَةِ بَحْرًا.

Trawler, *n.* A fishing boat, قَارِبُ صَيَّادِي ٱلسَّمَكِ بِٱلشِّبَاكِ.

Trawl-net, *n.* جَرْفَة ـ مِجْرَف قَارِبِ صَيَّادِي ٱلسَّمَكِ ـ *vulg.* جُرْفَة.

Tray, *n.* A round wooden —, طَبْلَة. A — used as a table, either of glass or silver, سُفْرَة ـ فَاثُور ـ جَام *pl.* جَامَات. A — for cups and saucers, شُفَارِج *pl.* شَفَارِيج; a small ditto, صِينِيَّة *pl.* صَوَانِيّ. A — for counting money, طَبْل. A butler's —, طَبْلَة رَئِيسِ ٱلسُّقَاةِ.

Treacherous, *a.* خَائِن ـ خَتَّار ـ خَتِير ـ خَاتِر. A — man, one who takes another unawares, مُخَاتِل. He was — in the agreement, ٢ خَتَرَ بِٱلْعَهْدِ. *See also* Perfidious, Traitorous, *a.*

Treacherously, *ad.* بِخِيَانَةٍ ـ بِخُتُورٍ ـ خَتْرًا. To act — to, or towards, ٢ غَدَرَ بِ ـ ٢ غَدَرَ ـ ٢ خَتَرَ ـ ٤ خَانَ.

Treacherousness, *n.* } غَدْر ـ خَوْن ـ خِيَانَة ـ خُتُور ـ خَتْر. I
Treachery, } am not chargeable with — or deceit in this matter, لَيْسَ لِي فِي هٰذَا ٱلْأَمْرِ وَلْسٌ وَلَا دَلْسٌ.

Treacle, *n.* دِبْسُ ٱلسُّكَّرِ ـ عَسَلٌ أَسْوَدُ ـ دِبْس.

Tread, *v.i.* To set the foot, وَطِئَ ـ يَطَأُ *aor.* ٤ حَطَّ ٱلرِّجْلَ. To walk, سَاحَ ـ يَسِيحُ *aor.* سَارَ ـ يَسِيرُ. Every place which your feet shall —, كُلُّ مَكَانٍ تَدُوسُهُ أَقْدَامُكُمْ.

Tread, *v.t.* To put the foot upon, وَطِئَ بِ ـ يَطَأُ *aor.* تَوَطَّأَ بِ. To — under foot, ٢ رَفَسَ ـ ٤ رَفَسَ بِرِجْلِهِ ـ ٤ دَاسَ. To leap the female, of a bird, سَفَدَ ـ ٢ سَفِدَ عَلَى ٱلْأُنْثَى. To —, or thrash, of grain, ٤ دَاسَ. To —, of grapes, عَصَرَ. To — a path, ٤ سَلَكَ مَسْلَكًا. To be trodden upon, اِنْدَاسَ.

Tread, *n.* As with the foot, دِيَاسَة ـ دَوْس ـ وَطْءٌ ـ وَطْأ. A manner of stepping, walking, مِشْيَة. The —, in copulation, of a bird, سِفَاد ـ سَفْدُ ٱلْأُنْثَى.

Treader, *n.* دَائِس. A — of grapes, دَائِسُ خَمْرٍ فِي ٱلْمَعَاصِرِ.

Treadle, *n.* } Of a loom, دَوَّارَةُ ٱلْحَائِكِ. The — of a bird,
Treddle, } نُطْفَةُ ٱلسَّفْدِ.

Treadmill, *n.* مَدَارٌ تُدَوِّرُهُ ٱلْمَحْبُوسُونَ بِأَرْجُلِهِمْ عُقُوبَةً لَهُمْ.

Treason, *n.* خَتْر — خِيَانَة — الخِيَانَةُ فِي ٱلْمُبَايَعَةِ. High —, خِيَانَةٌ فِي حَقِّ ٱلدَّوْلَةِ — الخُرُوجُ عَلَى ٱلسُّلْطَانِ.

Treasonable, *a.* خَاتِر — خَتِّير — خَتِيرٌ بِٱلدَّوْلَةِ — مُحْتَوٍ عَلَى خِيَانَةٍ فِي حَقِّ ٱلدَّوْلَةِ.

Treasonableness, *n.* خَتْر — خُتُورٌ بِٱلْحُكُومَةِ.

Treasonably, *ad.* خَتْرًا بِٱلْحُكُومَةِ — خِيَانَةً فِي حَقِّ ٱلدَّوْلَةِ.

Treasure, *n.* Wealth accumulated, خَزِينَة *pl.* خَزَائِنُ — خَزْنَة. Any stock laid up, ذَخِيرَة *pl.* ذَخَائِرُ. A —, such as mines, سَيْب *pl.* سُيُوب — رِكْزَة *pl.* رِكَاز — رَكِيزَة *pl.* رِكَاز — كَنْز *pl.* كُنُوز. Abundance, كَثْرَة — وَفْرَة. One highly beloved, عَزِيز — وَحِيد — عَيْن. Something rare, تُحْفَة. The buried treasures of the earth, أَفْلَاذُ ٱلْأَرْضِ — أَفْلَاذُ كَبِدِ ٱلْأَرْضِ — السُّيُوبُ.

Treasure, *v.t.* To lay up in store, ذَخَرَ [2] — إِدَّخَرَ — حَزَنَ [2] — كَنَزَ [2] — إِخْتَزَنَ. To lay up, as in the heart, كَنَّ-فِي [2] — أَكَنَّ-فِي — حَفِظَ-فِي [2]. *See also to* Store, *v.t.*

Treasure-city, *n.* مَدِينَةُ مَخْزَنٍ.

Treasurer, *n.* خَازِن *pl.* خَزَنَة — خَزْنَدَار.

Treasurership, *n.* وَظِيفَةُ ٱلْخَزْنَدَارِ — خِزَانَة.

Treasure-trove, *n.* سُيُوب — كَنْز *pl.* كُنُوز — دَفِينَة — مَطْمُورَة.

Treasury, *n.* خَزْنَة — خَزِينَة. The public —, الخَزْنَةُ — الخَزِينَةُ — بَيْتُ ٱلْمَالِ — خَزْنَةُ ٱلدَّوْلَةِ — مَالِيَّةُ ٱلدَّوْلَةِ. Treasury bonds, سَنَدَاتٌ عَلَى ٱلْمَالِيَّةِ — قَوَائِمُ مَالِيَّةٌ. First Lord of the Treasury, رَئِيسُ وُكَلَاءِ ٱلدَّوْلَةِ — وَزِيرُ ٱلدَّوْلَةِ. Lords of the Treasury, أَهْلُ مَجْلِسِ ٱلْمَالِيَّةِ. Treasury benches, مَقَاعِدُ ٱلْوُكَلَاءِ ٱلْمُتَعَصِّبِينَ لِلدَّوْلَةِ فِي بَيْتِ مَجْلِسِ أَهْلِ ٱلشُّورَى.

Treat, *v.t.* To manage, handle, دَبَّرَ — بَاشَرَ — إِسْتَعْمَلَ. To — or handle, as a subject, ذَكَرَ [2] — أَوْضَحَ وَبَيَّنَ — بَحَثَ عَن [2] — تَكَلَّمَ فِي. To — medically, عَالَجَ — شَفَى — دَاوَى. To entertain, أَوْلَمَ — أَضَافَ. To —, to act towards, صَنَعَ بِ [2] — عَامَلَ. To — or negotiate with, فَاصَلَ — اِتَّفَقَ مَعَ-عَلَى. To — one's self medically, تَعَالَجَ; to treat one's self medically with, تَدَاوَى بِ. If he is treated with kindness, إِذَا عُومِلَ بِٱلرِّفْقِ. Their words were treated, received, with the contempt which they themselves deserved, تَلَقَّى كَلَامَهُمْ بِٱلْإِزْدِرَاءِ ٱلَّذِي يَلِيقُ بِهِمْ.

To treat as a lie, كَذَّبَ: "This is the fire which you used to treat as a lie," هٰذِهِ ٱلنَّارُ ٱلَّتِي كُنْتُمْ بِهَا تُكَذِّبُونَ (Kur. lii. 14).

To treat cavalierly, إِسْتَخَفَّ بِ — إِسْتَحْقَرَ.

To treat contemptuously, بَهْدَلَ — أَهَانَ — اِزْدَرَى — إِسْتَهْزَأَ بِ.

To treat courteously, with honour, أَكْرَمَ — قَامَ بِوَاجِبِهِ [2].

To treat gently and with consideration, سَامَحَ.

To treat ill, أَسَآءَ إِلَى — عَنَفَ عَلَى [2] — عَاسَرَ.

To treat uncourteously, غَلَّظَ عَلَى — جَفَا *aor.* يَجْفُو.

To treat well, عَامَلَ-بِٱلْجَمِيلِ — أَحْسَنَ إِلَى.

To treat with fondness, لَطَفَ بِ [2] — لَاطَفَ.

Treat, *v.i.* To treat of, discuss, comprise, إِحْتَوَى عَلَى: This book treats of medicine, هٰذَا كِتَابٌ فِي ٱلطِّبِّ.

Treat, *n.* A feast, entertainment, ضِيَافَة. A pleasure, outing, amusement, مَرَح — أَشَرٌ وَبَطَرٌ — فَرَح — *vulg.* شَمُّ هَوَآءٍ — بَحْبَحَة.

Treatise, *n.* A tract, رِسَالَة *pl.* رَسَائِلُ — كُتَيِّب. *See also* Book, *n.*

Treatment, *n.* A manner of using, إِسْتِعْمَال. Mode of treating another, conduct towards, صَنِيعٌ بِ — مُعَامَلَة. Medical —, مُدَاوَاة — تَشْفِيَة — عِلَاج — مُعَالَجَة. Treatment, as of a subject, مُبَاحَثَة — مُذَاكَرَة — صُورَةُ مُبَاحَثَةٍ. For his kind — of them, عَلَى رِفْقِهِ بِهِمْ. For medical —, لِلْمُعَالَجَةِ.

Cavalier treatment, إِسْتِخْفَاف — إِسْتِحْقَار.

Contemptuous treatment, إِهَانَة — بَهْدَلَة — اِزْدِرَآء — إِسْتِهْزَآء.

Fond treatment, مُلَاطَفَة.

Gentle treatment, مُسَامَحَة — رِفْق.

Good treatment, إِحْسَان — مُعَامَلَةٌ بِٱلْجَمِيلِ.

Ill treatment, أَسَاءَةٌ إِلَى — عَنْف.

Uncourteous treatment, جَفَآء — تَغْلِيظٌ عَلَى.

Treaty, *n.* A negotiation, مُعَامَلَة. An agreement, league, compact, ذِمَّة *pl.* ذِمَام — عَقْد *pl.* عُقُود — مُعَاقَدَة — مُعَاهَدَة. An article, as of a —, بَنْد *pl.* بُنُود — شَرْط *pl.* شُرُوط — فَصْل *pl.* فُصُول.

The conclusion of a — between the two governments, عَقْدُ مُعَاهَدَةٍ بَيْنَ ٱلدَّوْلَتَيْنِ.

A definitive treaty, مُعَاهَدَةٌ قَطْعِيَّةٌ.

An offensive and defensive treaty, جُوَار — مُعَاهَدَةٌ عَلَى ٱلْمُجَاحَفَةِ وَٱلْمُدَافَعَةِ.

A preliminary treaty, مُعَاهَدَةٌ ٱبْتِدَائِيَّةٌ.

A secret treaty, مُعَاهَدَةٌ خَفِيَّةٌ.

A separate treaty, مُعَاهَدَةٌ مُنْفَرِدَةٌ — مُعَاهَدَةٌ مَفْرُوزَةٌ.

A treaty of commerce, مُعَاهَدَةٌ تِجَارِيَّةٌ.

A treaty of peace, مُعَاهَدَةٌ صُلْحِيَّةٌ — مُعَاهَدَةُ ٱلصُّلْحِ.

To break a treaty, نَقَضَ ٱلْمُعَاهَدَةَ [2].

To denounce a treaty, فَسَخَ ٱلْمُعَاهَدَةَ.

To guarantee a treaty, تَكَفَّلَ بِٱلْمُعَاهَدَةِ.

To make a treaty with, عَاهَدَ — عَاهَدَ-عَلَى — عَقَدَ مُعَاهَدَةً مَعَ.

To ratify a treaty, صَدَّقَ عَلَى ٱلْمُعَاهَدَةِ رَسْمًا.

Trebizond, *n.* The town, طَرَابِزُونُ.

Treble, *a.* Threefold, made three, مُثَلَّث ـ مَثْلُوث. Sharp, acute, of sound, أَجَشّ ـ أَبَحّ ـ جَهُور. A — note, نَبْرَة ـ لَحْن جَهُور.

Treble, *v.t.* ضَاعَف ـ ثَلَّث.

Treble, *v.i.* أَثْلَث ـ إِنْثَلَث ـ تَثَلَّث.

Treble, *n.* Threefold, ثَلَاثَة أَضْعَاف. The — in music, نَبْرَة ـ اللَّحْن الْجَهُور.

Trebleness, *n.* إِثْلَاث ـ تَثَلُّث.

Trebly, *ad.* ثَلَاثَة أَضْعَاف ـ ثَلَاث مَرَّات ـ الطَّاق ثَلَاثَة. I will repay you —, أُجَازِيك ضِعْفًا (*or* ثَلَاثَة أَضْعَاف).

Tree, *n.* شَجَر *pl.* أَشْجَار ـ شَجَرَة *pl.* شَجَرَات. A great — with spreading branches, دَاحَة *coll.* دَاح *pl.* أَدْوَاح. A boot —, قَالِب لِلنَّعْل. A genealogical —, شَجَرَة ـ شَجَرَة النَّسَب. A — to hang clothes, trappings, *etc.*, on, مِشْجَب ـ وِشْجَر. Trees, plants, bushes, شَجَر ـ شِجَر. Small trees, plants, دِقّ الشَّجَر. Full of trees, شَجِر ـ شَجِير ـ مُشْجِر. A thicket of trees, مَشْجَر. To produce trees, أَشْجَر. To work in the form of trees, شَجَّر. The branches of the tree spread out, إِنْشَعَبَت (*or* تَشَعَّبَت) أَغْصَان الشَّجَرَة.

Treenail, *n.* مِسْمَار خَشَب ـ عُصْفُورَة خَشَب ـ مِرْوَد خَشَب *pl.* مَرَاوِد.

Trefoil, *n.* The plant, رِبَّة ـ قَضْبَة. Sweet —, حَنْدَقُوق. Alexandrian —, بِرْسِيم; dry ditto, دَرِيس.

Treillage, *n.* تَعْرِيش.

Trellis, *n.* عَرِيشَة ـ تَكْعِيبَة ـ مُخَرَّم ـ قُفْص. To spread, as a plant on a trellis, عَرَّش ـ كَعَّب. Trellised, مُفَرْدَس ـ مُعَرَّش. *See also* Lattice, *n.*

Tremble, *v.i.* رَجَف ² ـ اِرْتَجَف ـ اِرْتَعَد ـ رَعَش ² ـ اِرْتَعَش; of inanimate things, اِرْتَجّ ـ تَرَجْرَج. To —, of the earth, زَلْزَل ـ اِرْتَجّ ـ تَزَلْزَل. To flutter, خَفَق ² ـ فَرْفَر. To — for, be afraid of, اِرْتَعَب مِن. To cause to —, أَرْعَد ـ أَرْجَف ـ أَرْعَش. His arm trembled, رَجَفَت يَدُه. *See also to* Quake, Shiver, *v.i.*

Trembler, *n.* رَعَّاش ـ خَوَّاف.

Tremblingly, *ad.* With shivering, اِرْتِعَادًا ـ اِرْتِعَاشًا ـ اِرْتِجَافًا. With fear, بِرُعْب ـ فَزَعًا.

Tremendous, *a.* Fearful, مُهِيب ـ مَخُوف. Excessive, exorbitant, فَظِيع ـ مُفْظِع. *See also* Terrible, *a.*

Tremendously, *ad.* Terribly, بِهَوْل ـ مَخَافَة ـ اِقْشِعْرَارًا. Greatly, لِلْغَايَة.

Tremendousness, *n.* Dreadfulness, هَوْلَة ـ هَوْل ـ قُشَعْرِيرَة ـ فَظَاعَة ـ مَهَابَة.

Tremor, *n.* أَفْكَل ـ رِعْشَة ـ رُعَاش ـ رَعْش ـ رَعْد: He is in a —, أَخَذَه أَفْكَل ـ بِه رِعْشَة.

Tremulous, *a.* Shivering, مَفْكُول ـ مُرْتَجِف ـ رَجْفَان ـ رَجِيف ـ مُرْتَعِد ـ مُرْتَعِش; as affected by fear, رَعِيب ـ مَرْعُوب ـ فَزْعَان.

Tremulously, *ad.* *See* Tremblingly, *ad.*

Tremulousness, *n.* *See* Tremor, *n.*

Trench, *v.t.* To furrow, of land, عَزَق ² ـ خَدّ ² ـ فَلَج ². To dig a moat round, خَنْدَق. To dig a — round a tent, نَأَى ² ـ أَنَّى.

Trench, *v.i.* To — on or upon, اِعْتَدَى عَلَى ـ تَجَرَّأ عَلَى ـ تَعَدَّى عَلَى ـ أَجْحَف بِ ـ أَطَال الْيَد عَلَى.

Trench, *n.* A furrow, خُدَّة *pl.* خُدَد ـ أُخْدُود *pl.* أَخَادِيد. A pit, hole, ditch, حُفْرَة *pl.* حُفَر. A fosse, moat, خَنْدَق *pl.* خَنَادِق. To open trenches, as in attacking a place, صَنَع ² الْخَنَادِق وَالْمَتَارِس.

Trenchant, *a.* Cutting, بَاضِع ـ صَارِم ـ قَاطِع. Decisive, فَاصِل ـ قَاطِع ـ بَتِّيّ.

Trencher, *n.* One who digs a trench, مُخَنْدِق. A dish, طَبَق *pl.* أَطْبَاق ـ قَصْعَة *pl.* قِصَاع ـ صَحْن *pl.* صُحُون.

Trencherman, *n.* *See* Glutton, *n.*

Trend, *n.* Direction, ضَرْب ـ تَوَجُّه ـ مَيْل ـ تَصَوُّب.

Trend, *v.i.* ضَرَب إِلَى ² ـ تَصَوَّب إِلَى ـ تَوَجَّه إِلَى.

Trendle, *n.* بَكَرَة.

Trepan, *n.* An instrument for perforating the skull, مِثْقَب الْقِحْف. *See also* Snare, *n.*

Trepan, *v.t.* To cut the skull with a trepan, ثَقَب ² الْقِحْف. To delude, ensnare, مَكَر ب ² ـ غَشّ ² ـ غَشَّش.

Trephine, *n.* مِثْقَب لِلْقِحْف رَفِيع.

Trephine, *v.t.* ثَقَب ² الْقِحْف بِالْمِثْقَب الرَّفِيع.

Trepidation, *n.* اِنْقِبَاض ـ اِهْتِزَاز ـ اِرْتِجَاف.

Trespass, *v.i.* To go beyond one's proper bounds, عَدَا طَوْرَه ² ـ جَاوَز الْحُدُود. To commit an offence against another, أَجْحَف ب ـ جَحَف ² ـ بَغَى عَلَى ² ـ جَار عَلَى ² ـ تَعَدَّى عَلَى. To intrude one's self, اِعْتَرَض ـ تَعَرَّض. To — on, to inconvenience, كَلَّف ـ شَقّ عَلَى ² ـ آذَى. To — on one's time, ضَيَّع وَقْتَه. *See also to* Sin, Transgress, *v.i.*

Trespass, *n.* Going beyond bounds, جَحْف ـ بَغْي ـ غُلُوّ ـ تَعَدٍّ. A sin, crime, مَسَاءَة ـ إِسَاءَة ـ ذَنْب *pl.* ذُنُوب ـ خَطِيئَة *pl.* خَطَايَا. *See also* Transgression, *n.*

Trespasser, *n.* A violator, مُتَعَدٍّ ـ مُتَجَاوِز. An intruder, مُتَعَرِّض ـ مُعْتَرِض ـ عِرِّيض ـ مُتَدَخِّل.

Tress, *n.* جَدِيلَة ـ عَقَائِص *pl.* عَقِيصَة ـ عِقَص *pl.* عِقْصَة. Tresses interlaced with braid, ضَفِيرَة *pl.* ضَفَائِر. False tresses made to hang down the back, عُبَيْدِيَّة. To bind in tresses, جَدَائِل ـ ضَفَّر ـ ² ضَفَر ـ ² جَدَلَ ـ ² عَقَص.

Tressed, *a.* مُضَفَّر ـ ² مَجْدُول.

Trestle, *n.* جُحَاش *pl.* جَحْش ـ حِمَارَة ـ حِمَار ـ صِقَالَة.

Tret, *n.* Allowance for waste, سِمَاح بِالتَّلَف ـ فَارِغ.

Trevet, *n.* *See* Trivet, *n.*

Trey, *n.* At cards, وَرَقَة مِنْ أَوْرَاقِ اللَّعِبِ ذَاتُ ثَلَاثِ نُقَط.

Triable, *a.* That may be tried, attempted, يُجَرَّب ـ تَجْرِبَتُهُ مُمْكِن. That may be legally examined, إِقَامَةُ الدَّعْوَى عَلَيْهِ مُمْكِنَة ـ الفَحْصُ فِيهِ قُدَّامَ الشَّرْعِ جَائِز.

Triad, *n.* مُثَلَّث ـ ثَلَاثَة.

Trial, *n.* An experiment, إِمْتِحَان ـ تَجْرِبَة ـ خِبْرَة. An attempt, endeavour, إِجْتِهَاد ـ جِدّ ـ مَسْعَاة ـ مَسْعًى. Trial, as by affliction, فِتْنَة. An affliction, مُصِيبَة *pl.* مَصَائِب ـ تَجْرِبَة *pl.* تَجَارِب ـ مَشَقَّة ـ آفَات *pl.* آفَة ـ شَدَائِد *pl.* شِدَّة ـ بَلَايَا *pl.* بَلِيَّة ـ بَلَاء *pl.* مَشَقَّات. Examination, إِمْتِحَان ـ فَحْص. Legal examination, مُرَافَعَة ـ مُحَاكَمَة ـ إِسْتِنْطَاق ـ إِقَامَة دَعْوَى.

To bring to trial, أَقَامَ الدَّعْوَى عَلَى. Without their being brought to — before a court of justice, بِدُونِ إِقَامَةِ الدَّعْوَى عَلَيْهِمْ فِي مَحْكَمَةٍ شَرْعِيَّةٍ.

To have a thing on trial, ² أَخَذَ لِيُجَرِّبَهُ ـ إِتَّخَذَ لِلتَّجْرِبَة.

To make a trial of, جَرَّب ـ إِمْتَحَنَ ـ ² مَحَنَ.

To move for a new trial, إِسْتَأْنَف ـ ² طَلَبَ تَجْدِيدَ الدَّعْوَى.

To take one's trial, أُقِيمَتِ الدَّعْوَى عَلَى.

Trialogue, *n.* مُحَاوَرَة بَيْنَ ثَلَاثَةِ أَشْخَاص.

Triandria, *n.* عِبَارَةٌ عَنِ الأَزْهَارِ المُثَلَّثَةِ آلَاتِ التَّذْكِير.

Triangle, *n.* The figure, مُثَلَّث. A — for extending one thereon for punishment, فَلَق ـ فَلَقَة ـ حِمَار ـ العُقْبَان.

Acute-angled triangle, مُثَلَّث حَادُّ الزَّوَايَا.

Equilateral triangle, مُثَلَّث مُتَسَاوِي الأَضْلَاع.

Isosceles triangle, مُثَلَّث مُتَسَاوِي السَّاقَيْن.

Obtuse-angled triangle, مُثَلَّث مُنْفَرِجُ الزَّوَايَا.

Plane triangle, مُثَلَّث مُسْتَوٍ.

Right-angled triangle, مُثَلَّث قَائِمُ الزَّوَايَا.

Triangular, *a.* مُثَلَّث ـ مُثَلَّثُ الشَّكْل. To make —, ثَلَّث ـ ثَلَّث شَكْلَهُ. To be —, تَثَلَّث.

Triangularly, *ad.* تَثْلِيثًا.

Triangulation, *n.* تَثْلِيث. Measurement of a space by —, مُسَاحَة أَرْضٍ لِاسْتِخْرَاجِ سَعَتِهَا بِوَاسِطَةِ تَثْلِيثِ أَقْسَامِهَا ـ مُسَاحَة تَثْلِيثِيَّة.

Tribal, *a.* مِنْ أَهْلِ القَبَائِل ـ مُتَعَلِّق بِقَبِيلَةٍ.

Tribe, *n.* A clan, دِيَار *pl.* دَار ـ قَبَائِل *pl.* قَبِيلَة. A small or sub-tribe, عَشِيرَة *pl.* عَشَائِر. A people, طَائِفَة ـ قَوْم ـ شَعْب *pl.* طَوَائِف. A —, as of the Jews, سِبْط *pl.* أَسْبَاط. A party, حِزْب *pl.* أَحْزَاب ـ مَعْشَر *pl.* مَعَاشِر. The feathered tribes, الطُّيُور. The finny tribes, السَّمَك ـ الحِيتَان.

Triblet, *n.* قَالِبُ الخَوَاتِم.

Tribulation, *n.* ضِيق ـ مَشَقَّة *pl.* مَشَقَّات ـ شَدِيدَة *pl.* شَدَائِد *pl.* شِدَّة ـ تَجْرِبَة *pl.* تَجَارِب. To suffer —, شَدَائِد ـ تَعَذَّب ـ تَضَايَق.

Tribunal, *n.* مَحْكَمَة *pl.* مَحَاكِم. A religious Muslim —, مَحْكَمَة شَرْعِيَّة.

A civil tribunal, مَحْكَمَة نِظَامِيَّة.

A criminal tribunal, مَحْكَمَة جِزَائِيَّة.

A military tribunal, دِيوَانُ مُحَاكَمَاتٍ عَسْكَرِيَّةٍ ـ دِيوَان حَرْب.

Tribune, *n.* A protector elected by the people, مُحَامٍ مُنْتَخَب مِنَ الشَّعْب. A pulpit, مِنْبَر *pl.* مَنَابِر.

Tribuneship, *n.* وَظِيفَةُ المُحَامِي المُنْتَخَبِ مِنَ الشَّعْب.

Tributariness, *n.* الكَوْنُ تَحْتَ الخَرَاجِ ـ الكَوْنُ تَحْتَ الجِزْيَةِ.

Tributary, *a.* تَحْتَ الخَرَاجِ ـ تَحْتَ الجِزْيَةِ ـ تَحْتَ التَّسْخِير ـ ذِمِّيّ. The — province of the Turkish empire, الإِيَالَاتُ المُمْتَازَة. A — stream, رَافِد *pl.* رَافِدُون *and* رُفَّد.

Tributary, *n.* Under tribute, ذِمِّيَّة *pl.* ذِمِّيّ ـ تَحْتَ التَّسْخِير ـ تَحْتَ الخَرَاجِ ـ تَحْتَ الجِزْيَةِ ـ مِنْ أَهْلِ الذِّمَّةِ. Tributaries, subjects, رَعَايَا. A tributary stream; *see preceding article.*

Tribute, *n.* The tax, خَرَاج ـ جِزْيَة; from a dependent state, وِيرْكُو. Something given, presented, هَدِيَّة ـ عَرِيضَة ـ مَعْرُوض. Praise, ثَنَاء ـ تَشْبِيَة. To pay — to, دَفَعَ ـ أَعْطَى جِزْيَةً لِ ـ ² ذَكَرَ بِالجَمِيل ـ أَثْنَى عَلَى. To pay a — of praise to, الخَرَاجَ لِ ـ ² مَدَحَ. The yearly — set apart by the government of Egypt to be paid to the Sublime Porte, الوِيرْكُو المُخَصَّص مِنْ مِصْر لِلْبَابِ العَالِي.

Trice, *n.* دَقِيقَة ـ لَحْظَة ـ لَمْحَة. In a trice, فِي لَحْظَةٍ ـ عَلَى الفَوْرِ ـ حَالًا ـ فِي لَحْظَةٍ مِنَ الزَّمَانِ.

Trice, *v.t.* لَفَّ ².

Tricennial, *a.* عِبَارَةٌ عَنْ ثَلَاثِينَ سَنَة.

Trick, *n.* An artifice for deception, دُولَاب *pl.* دَوَالِيب ـ كَيْد *pl.* كِيَاد ـ مَكِيدَة *pl.* مَكَائِد ـ خَدْعَة ـ خَدِيعَة. A joke, مَلْعَبَة ـ

وَضْع ـ دَأْب ـ مَلْعَب *pl.* مَلَاعِب. A habit, عَادَة *pl.* عَادَات ـ A —, at cards, دَسْت *pl.* دُسُوت. To serve one a —, لَعِبَ ـ نَصَبَ عَلَى ـ حِيلَةً ـ لَعِبَ عَلَى ـ مَلْعَبَةً ـ نَصَبَ عَلَى ـ عَلَى إِحْتَالَ عَلَى ـ تَحَارَفَ عَلَى. To know a — worth two of it, to be on one's guard against, تَحَرَّزَ مِنَ ٱلْأَمْرِ ـ حَذِرَ مِنَ ٱلشَّيْءِ ـ تَوَقَّى مِنْ كَذَا.

Trick, *v.t.* To impose upon, cheat, غَشَّ ـ غَبَنَ ـ مَكَرَ بِ ـ إِحْتَالَ عَلَى. To — out, to adorn, زَخْرَفَ ـ زَيَّنَ. To — one's self out, تَطَوَّسَ ـ تَزَخْرَفَ ـ تَزَيَّنَ.

Trick, *v.i.* تَحَيَّلَ ـ إِسْتَعْمَلَ ٱلْحِيَلَ.

Trickery, *n.* Fraud, تَحَيُّل ـ غَبْن ـ غِشّ ـ مَكْر. The art of dressing up, زِينَة ـ تَزْيِين.

Trickish, *a.* Artful, حَيَّال ـ غَدَّار ـ ذُو كَيْدٍ ـ عَذِق.

Trickishness, *n.* *See* Trickery, *n.*

Trickle, *v.i.* وَشَلَ *aor.* يَشِلُ ـ نَطَفَ ـ أَنَزَّ ـ نَزَّ ـ نَضَّ ـ تَضَبَّبَ ـ ضَبَّ. His lip trickled with blood, ضَبَّتْ شَفَتُهُ دَمًا. To let water trickle, إِنْتَضَّ ٱلْمَاءَ.

Trickling, *n.* وُشُول ـ نَضِيض ـ نَزّ.

Trickling, *a.* نَضُوض ـ وَاشِل.

Trickster, *n.* }
Tricksy, *a.* } حَيَّال ـ مَكَّار ـ غَشَّاش ـ حُوَّلٌ قُلَّبٌ.

Tri-colour, *n.* The flag, بَيْرَقٌ ذُو ثَلَاثَةِ أَلْوَانٍ.

Tri-coloured, *a.* ذُو ثَلَاثَةِ أَلْوَانٍ.

Trident, *n.* خَطَّافٌ ذُو ثَلَاثِ شَوْكَاتٍ.

Tridentate, *a.* ذُو ثَلَاثَةِ أَسْنَانٍ.

Tried, *a.* *See* Experienced, *a.*

Triennial, *a.* وَاقِعٌ مَرَّةً فِي ثَلَاثِ سِنِينَ ـ مُدَّتُهُ ثَلَاثُ سِنِينَ.

Triennially, *ad.* مَرَّةً فِي ثَلَاثِ سِنِينَ.

Trifid, *a.* مَشْقُوقٌ ثَلَاثَةَ أَجْزَاءٍ.

Trifle, *n.* A thing of little value, تَفَاهَة ـ عَبْثَة ـ عَبَث ـ شَيْءٌ أُمُورٌ ـ أَمْرٌ زَهِيدٌ ـ أَدْنَى شَيْءٍ ـ جُزْئِيٌّ. Trifles, small matters, أَشْيَاءُ دِقِّيَّةٌ ـ مَدَاقُّ (*or* دَقَائِقُ) ٱلْأُمُورِ ـ بُطْلَات ـ سَخِيفَة. A small quantity, نَضِيض. The sweetmeat, ضَرْبٌ مِنَ ٱلْحَلَاوَةِ ٱلْمَرْوَغَةِ بِٱلزُّبْدِ. To dispute about trifles, تَمَحَّكَ بِٱلْأُمُورِ ٱلسَّخِيفَةِ. To stand upon trifles, to make difficulties, نَاقَرَ ـ عَاتَلَ ـ دَنَّقَ. To amuse one's self with trifles, تَعَبَّثَ بِمَدَاقِّ ٱلْأُمُورِ.

Trifle, *v.i.* To talk with levity, أَرْقَعَ ـ لَخِيَ ـ دَنَّقَ ـ كَثَّرَ كَلَامَهُ ـ لَعِبَ ـ تَهَابَلَ ـ هَرَجَ فِي ـ عَبِثَ ـ سَخُفَ فِي ٱلْبَاطِلِ.

To trifle away, as time, *etc.*, أَتْلَفَ ـ ضَيَّعَ ـ أَسْرَفَ.

To trifle with, لَعِبَ بِ ـ تَعَبَّثَ بِ ـ عَبِثَ بِ.

Trifler, *n.* دَانِق ـ عَابِث ـ عِبِّيث ـ مُتَهَابِل ـ هَزْلِيٌّ.

Trifling, *a.* Of little value or importance, تَافِه ـ وَاهٍ ـ سَخِيف ـ حَقِير ـ زَهِيد. Small, جُزْئِيٌّ. Trifling matters, مَدَاقُّ (*or* دَقَائِقُ) ٱلْأُمُورِ. "They will never inflict upon you but a trifling injury," لَنْ يَضُرُّوكُمْ إِلَّا أَذًى (Kur. iii. 107).

Trifling, *n.* Nonsense, stupid talk, رَقَاعَة ـ لَخِيّ ـ عَبَث ـ هَبَالَة ـ سَخَافَة. "And who keep aloof from trifling," (or vain talk), وَٱلَّذِينَ هُمْ عَنِ ٱللَّغْوِ مُعْرِضُونَ (Kur. xxiii. 3).

Triflingly, *ad.* In a trifling manner, بِسَخَافَةٍ ـ بِعَبَثٍ. In a slight degree, جُزْئِيًّا ـ قِلَّةً.

Triflingness, *n.* *See* Insignificance, *n.*

Triflorous, *a.* حَامِلٌ ثَلَاثَةَ نَوَاوِيرَ ـ مُثَلَّثُ ٱلْأَزْهَارِ.

Trifoliate, *a.* ذُو ثَلَاثِ أَوْرَاقٍ ـ مُثَلَّثُ ٱلْأَوْرَاقِ.

Triform, *n.* مُثَلَّثُ ٱلشَّكْلِ.

Trifurcated, *a.* ذُو ثَلَاثِ شُعَبٍ ـ مُثَلَّثُ ٱلشِّعَابِ.

Trigamy, *n.* ٱلزِّيجَةُ بِثَلَاثِ نِسَاءٍ.

Trig, *v.t.* To — a wheel, ضَبَطَ ٱلْعَجَلَةَ.

Trigger, *n.* زَنْبَرَك *from the Turkish*, ـ رَقَّاصُ زِنَادِ ٱلْبُنْدُقِيَّةِ.

Triglyph, *n.* زِينَةٌ فِي أَفْرِيزِ بَعْضٍ مِنَ ٱلْعُمُدِ.

Trigonometrical, *a.* مُرَكَّبٌ عَلَى قَوَاعِدِ مَسَاحَةِ ٱلْمُثَلَّثَاتِ.

Trigonometry, *n.* عِلْمُ مَسَاحَةِ ٱلْمُثَلَّثَاتِ. Plane —, مُثَلَّثَاتٌ مُسَطَّحَةٌ. Spherical —, مُثَلَّثَاتٌ كُرَوِيَّةٌ.

Trihedral, *a.* ذُو ثَلَاثَةِ سُطُوحٍ.

Trihedron, *n.* شَكْلٌ حَاوٍ عَلَى ثَلَاثَةِ مُثَلَّثَاتٍ مُتَسَاوِيَةٍ.

Trilateral, *a.* مُثَلَّثُ ٱلْأَضْلَاعِ ـ ذُو ثَلَاثَةِ أَضْلَاعٍ.

Trilingual, *a.* مُرَتَّبٌ عَلَى ثَلَاثَةِ أَلْسُنٍ.

Triliteral, *a.* ذُو ثَلَاثَةِ حُرُوفٍ. A word of three radical letters, ثُلَاثِيٌّ.

Trill, *n.* تَرَنُّم ـ تَطْرِيبُ ٱلصَّوْتِ ـ تَرْجِيعُ ٱلصَّوْتِ ـ رَنِيم.

Trill, *v.t.* Of the voice, رَجَّعَ صَوْتَهُ ـ رَنَّمَ صَوْتَهُ ـ طَرَّبَ صَوْتَهُ.

Trill, *v.i.* تَرَنَّمَ ـ رَنَّمَ.

Trillion, *n.* عِبَارَةٌ عَنْ عَدَدٍ مُؤَلَّفٍ مِنْ رَقْمٍ وَثَمَانِيَةَ عَشَرَ صِفْرًا وَهُوَ ١,٠٠٠,٠٠٠,٠٠٠,٠٠٠,٠٠٠,٠٠٠.

Trilobate, *a.* Of leaves, ذُو ثَلَاثَةِ أَفْلَاقٍ ـ مُثَلَّثُ ٱلْأَفْلَاقِ.

Trilocular, *a.* ذُو ثَلَاثِ خَرَائِطَ ـ مُثَلَّثُ ٱلْخَرَائِطِ.

Trim, *a.* Firm, in good order, مَضْبُوط ـ مُرَتَّب ـ مُنَظَّم ـ مُحْكَم. Neat, أَنِيق ـ كَيِّس ـ ظَرِيف ـ لَطِيف ـ حَسَن.

Trim, *v.t.* To put in order, رَتَّبَ ـ نَظَّمَ ـ أَصْلَحَ ـ أَحْكَمَ ـ هَنْدَمَ ـ سَرَّحَ. To clip, هَذَّبَ ـ هَذَبَ. To — or lop, of a tree, عَلَقَ ٤ ـ قَضَبَ ـ ٢ جَرَّدَ ـ قَلَّمَ. To —, as the hair, قَصْقَصَ; of language, فَتَّقَ ـ حَرَّرَ ـ ضَرَّجَ; as of a lamp, أَصْلَحَ. To plane, رَنْدَجَ. To —, as of bushes, قَلَّمَ. To balance, as of a ship, *etc.*, عَدَّلَ; of sails, أَصْلَحَ ٱلْقُلُوعَ. To rebuke, وَبَّخَ ـ سَخِطَ عَلَى ٢. To —, adorn, with, زَيَّنَ-بِ; to fringe with, نَيَّرَ-بِ ـ كَنَّفَ-بِ. To edge with, جَعَلَ لَ-سَجَافًا مِنْ كَذَا ٢. Rough-hewn, not yet trimmed, خَشِيبٌ لَمْ يُنَقَّحْ.

Trim, *v.i.* To fluctuate, as between this and that, تَضَرَّبَ (or تَحَوَّلَ or تَذَبْذَبَ) بَيْنَ كَذَا وَكَذَا; between two things, تَرَجَّحَ بَيْنَ شَيْئَيْنِ.

Trim, *n.* Cut, shape, هِيئَةٌ ـ هِنْدَام. Dress, زِينَة ـ أَلْبِسَة. Balance, مُعَادَلَة ـ مُوَازَنَة.

Trimester, *n.* ثَلَاثَةُ شُهُورٍ.

Trimly, *ad.* Neatly, حَسَنًا ـ بِظَرَافَةٍ ـ بِكِيَاسَةٍ ـ إِنَاقَةً.

Trimmer, *n.* One who trims, puts in order, مُنَظِّم ـ مُهَنْدِم. A time-server, مُسَايِر ـ مُلَاقِح ـ مُتَضَرِّب ـ حُوَلِيٌّ قُلَّبِيٌّ.

Trimming, *n.* Appendages in general, أَمْتِعَة ـ عُدَّةٌ. Ornaments in general, تَزْيِينَات ـ زِينَة ـ حُلًى; especially for women's dress, كَشْكَش *pl.* كَشَاكِش; for men's or women's dress, خَرْج *pl.* خُرُوج. Reproof, مُعَاتَبَة ـ سُخْطَة ـ مَعْتَبَة ـ تَوْبِيخ.

Trimness, *n.* Neatness, حُسْن ـ لَطَافَة ـ ظَرَافَة ـ كِيَاسَة ـ إِنَاقَة.

Trine, *a.* ثُلَاثِيٌّ.

Trinitarian, *n.* قَائِلٌ بِالثَّالُوثِ.

Trinity, *n.* The —, الثَّالُوثُ; the holy —, الثَّالُوثُ ٱلْأَقْدَسُ.

Trinity Sunday, أَحَدُ ٱلثَّالُوثِ.

Trinity House (London,) دَارُ جَمَاعَةٍ مِنَ ٱلْمَأْمُورِينَ عَلَى بَعْضِ أُمُورٍ بَحْرِيَّةٍ فِي مَدِينَةِ لَنْدَن.

Elder Brethren of the Trinity House, أَهْلُ ٱلْجَمَاعَةِ ٱلْمَذْكُورَةِ.

Trinket, *n.* حَلْيٌ *pl.* حُلِيٌّ ـ حِلْيَة *pl.* حِلًى.

Trinkets, ornaments, صِيغَة ـ مَصَاغ ـ حِلًى.

Trinomial, *n.* Of a root, جِذْرٌ ثُلَاثِيٌّ.

Trio, *n.* Three persons, ثَلَاثَةُ أَشْخَاصٍ. A concert of three voices, نَوْبَةُ ثَلَاثَةِ أَصْوَاتٍ مُتَّفِقَةٍ. A pretty —, in ridicule, مَلَأٌ ثَلَاثَةٌ.

Trip, *v.i.* To step lightly, وَطِئَ بِخِفَّةٍ ـ ٢ خَفَّ فِي ٱلْوَطْءِ *aor.* يَطَأُ ـ خَطَا بِٱلْخِفَّةِ *aor.* يَخْطُو. To stumble, تَعَثَّرَ ـ ٢ عَثَرَ. To err, سَقَطَ ٤ ـ أَخْطَأَ ـ خَطِئَ. Tripping it on the light fantastic toe, الزَّفْنُ وَٱلرَّقْصُ ـ ٱلْمُخَالَفَةُ بَيْنَ ٱلرِّجْلَيْنِ.

Trip, *v.t.* To supplant fraudulently, أَعْقَبَ- (or تَعَقَّبَ-) بِمَكْرٍ. To cause to stumble, أَعْثَرَ ـ عَثَّرَ. To cause to err, أَسْقَطَ ـ خَطَّأَ ـ أَسْقَطَ-فِي ـ تَسَقَّطَ. To — up, to cast in wrestling, شَغْزَبَ ـ إِعْتَقَلَ ـ ٢ صَرَعَ.

Trip, *n.* A stumble, عَثْرَة. A fall, سِقَاط ـ سَقْطَة. An error, خَطَاء ـ سَقْط ـ زَلَّة. A journey, tour, سَفْرَة. A — in wrestling, شَغْزَبِيَّة. An excursion, تَفْسِيح ـ مَسِيرَة ـ سِيرَة ـ سِيَاحَة. To make a — through a place, طَافَ فِي ٤. To take a —, a walk, excursion, خَرَجَ يَتَبَسَّطُ ٤.

Tripartite, *a.* ذُو ثَلَاثَةِ أَقْسَامٍ ـ ثُلَاثِيٌّ. A — treaty, مُعَاهَدَةٌ بَيْنَ ثَلَاثَةٍ.

Tripe, *n.* مَصَارِينُ *pl.* مُصْرَان ـ كِرْش.

Tripedal, *a.* مُثَلَّثُ ٱلْأَقْدَامِ ـ ذُو ثَلَاثَةِ أَقْدَامٍ.

Tripersonal, *a.* حَاوٍ عَلَى ثَلَاثَةِ أَشْخَاصٍ.

Triphthong, *n.* مَجْمُوعُ ثَلَاثَةِ حُرُوفِ عِلَّةٍ تُلْفَظُ بِدَفْعَةٍ مِنَ ٱلصَّوْتِ.

Triphthongal, *a.* مُتَعَلِّقٌ بِٱلْمَجْمُوعِ ٱلْمَذْكُورِ.

Triple, *a.* *See* Treble, *a.*

Triple, *v.t.* and *i.* *See to* Treble, *v.t.* and *i.*

Triplet, *n.* Anything consisting of three, ثُلَاثِيٌّ. Three rhyming verses, ثَلَاثَةُ مَصَارِيعَ عَلَى وَزْنٍ وَاحِدٍ.

Triplicate, *a.* Threefold, ثَلَاثَةُ أَضْعَافٍ ـ مُثَلَّث ـ ثُلَاثِيٌّ.

Triplicate, *n.* One of three copies, نُسْخَةٌ مِنْ ثَلَاثِ نُسَخٍ. In —, فِي ثَلَاثِ نُسَخٍ.

Tripod, *n.* A seat with three feet, كُرْسِيٌّ بِثَلَاثِ ـ حِمَارَة ـ حِمَار قَوَائِمَ. *See also* Trivet, *n.*

Tripoli, *n.* The country, أَطْرَابُلُسُ (طَرَابُلُس *vulg.*) ٱلْغَرْبِ.

Tripoli of Syria, أَطْرَابُلُسُ (طَرَابُلُس *vulg.*) ٱلشَّامِ.

Tripoli, *n.* The stone, حَجَرُ أَطْرَابُلُسَ.

Tripos, *n.* مَوْضُوعُ ٱلِامْتِحَانِ.

Tripper, *n.* One who walks nimbly, خَفِيفُ ٱلْأَقْدَامِ.

Tripping, *n.* A stumble, عَثِير ـ عِثَار ـ عَثْر. Erring, زَلّ ـ سِقَاط. A — up, صَرْعَة ـ شَغْزَبِيَّة *See also under to* Trip, *v.i.*

Tripping, *a.* Nimble, حَرِك ـ نَشِط ـ خَفِيف.

Trippingly, *ad.* بِشَمْلَلَةٍ ـ بِنَشَاطٍ ـ بِخِفَّةٍ.

Triptote, *n.* إِسْمٌ مُنْصَرِفٌ *pl.* أَسْمَاءٌ مُنْصَرِفَةٌ.

Trireme, *n.* سَفِينَةٌ ذَاتُ ثَلَاثِ طَبَقَاتٍ مِنَ ٱلْمَقَاذِيفِ.

Trisagion, *n.* تَسْبِيحٌ لِلّٰهِ قُدُّوسٌ قُدُّوسٌ قُدُّوسٌ.

Trisect, *v.t.* قَسَمَ-ثَلَاثَةَ أَقْسَامٍ مُتَسَاوِيَةٍ ـ ثَلَّثَ.

Trisection, *n.* تَقْسِيمٌ فِي ثَلَاثَةٍ ـ تَثْلِيث.

Tristfully, *ad.* *See* Mournfully, *ad.*

Trisyllabic, *a.*
Trisyllabical, } ذُو ثَلَاثِ حَرَكَاتٍ *fem.* ذَاتُ.

Trisyllable, *n.* كَلِمَةٌ ذَاتُ ثَلَاثَةِ ـ كَلِمَةٌ ذَاتُ ثَلَاثِ حَرَكَاتٍ هِجَاآتٍ.

Trite, *a.* Worn out, رَثِيثٌ ـ رَثٌّ ـ جَارِنٌ. In ordinary use, مُعْتَادٌ. Generally known, ذَائِعٌ ـ شَائِعٌ. Often repeated, مُقَوَّلٌ ـ مُكَرَّرٌ. Not requiring explanation, يُسْتَغْنَى عَنْ بَيَانِهِ. Useless to be mentioned, ذِكْرُهُ عَبَثٌ.

Triteness, *n.* Commonness, as being generally known, شُيُوعَةٌ ـ شُهْرَةٌ ـ مَشَاعٌ. Commonness, as not requiring explanation, كَوْنُ ٱلشَّيْءِ يُسْتَغْنَى عَنْ بَيَانِهِ.

Tritheism, *n.* ٱلْقَوْلُ بِثَلَاثَةِ آلِهَةٍ ـ تَثْلِيثٌ.

Tritheist, *n.* ٱلْقَائِلُ بِثَلَاثَةِ آلِهَةٍ ـ مِنْ أَهْلِ ٱلتَّثْلِيثِ.

Tritheistic, *a.* مُتَعَلِّقٌ بِمَذْهَبِ أَهْلِ ٱلتَّثْلِيثِ.

Triton, *n.* Of mythology, غُولُ ٱلْبَحْرِ *pl.* غِيلَانٌ. A kind of marine mollusc, حَيَوَانٌ مِنَ ٱلْحَيَوَانَاتِ ٱلْبَحْرِيَّةِ ذَوَاتِ أَجْسَادٍ رَخْوَةٍ بِلَا مَفَاصِلَ.

Triturable, *a.* قَابِلُ ٱلسَّحْقِ ـ يُسْحَقُ ـ يُدَقُّ ـ يُسْحَنُ.

Triturate, *v.t.* سَحَقَ ـ دَقَّ ـ سَحَنَ. To be triturated, إِنْسَحَقَ ـ إِنْدَقَّ.

Trituration, *n.* دَقٌّ ـ سَحْقٌ ـ سَحْنٌ.

Triumph, *n.* Victory, فَلْجٌ ـ ظَفَرٌ ـ نَصْرٌ. A source of — or glory, إِفْتِخَارٌ. A procession of —, وَكْبَةٌ ـ مَوْكِبٌ.

Triumph, *v.i.* To obtain victory, إِظَّفَرَ ـ ظَفِرَ. To celebrate victory with pomp, بَجَّلَ ٱلنَّصْرَ بِمَوْكِبٍ. To — over, أَفْلَجَ عَلَى ـ إِنْتَصَرَ عَلَى ـ ظَفِرَ بِ. To boast, as upon an advantage gained, إِفْتَخَرَ; to — over, in that sense, إِفْتَخَرَ عَلَى. To — over, to overcome, as an adversary, or a rival, غَلَبَ عَلَى ـ غَلَبَ. To cause to —, overcome, ظَفَّرَ ـ أَظْفَرَ ـ غَلَّبَ عَلَى. To —, as over the misfortunes of an enemy, شَمِتَ بِ.

Triumphal, *a.* مُتَعَلِّقٌ بِٱلنَّصْرِ. A — arch or gateway, بَابُ ٱلنَّصْرِ. A — progress, سِيرَةُ ٱلْمُظَفَّرِ ٱلْمَنْصُورِ.

Triumphant, *a.* ظَفِيرٌ ـ ظَافِرٌ ـ مُظَفَّرٌ ـ مَنْصُورٌ. Successful, نَاجِحٌ ـ فَائِزٌ ـ مُفْلِحٌ ـ فَالِجٌ. To be —, successful, أَنْجَحَ ـ أَفْلَحَ.

Triumphantly, *ad.* With victory, بِظَفَرٍ ـ بِنَصْرٍ; successfully, بِٱلنَّجَاحِ ـ بِٱلْفَوْزِ.

Triumpher, *n.* غَالِبٌ ـ مُظَفَّرٌ ـ مَنْصُورٌ.

Triumvir, *n.* وَاحِدٌ مِنْ ثَلَاثَةِ حُكَّامٍ.

Triumvirate, *n.* قِيَامُ ثَلَاثَةٍ بِٱلْحُكْمِ.

Triune, *a.* ثَلَاثَةٌ فِي وَاحِدٍ.

Triunity, *n.* وَحْدَانِيَّةٌ فِي ٱلتَّثْلِيثِ.

Trivet, *n.* أُثْفِيَّةٌ *pl.* أَثَافِيُّ *and* أَثَافٍ ـ سُفْعٌ ـ دِيكٌ ـ مِنْصَبٌ *pl.* مَنَاصِبُ. To put on a —, ثَفَّى.

Trivial, *a.* وَجِيزٌ ـ جُزْئِيٌّ ـ حَقِيرٌ ـ سَخِيفٌ ـ وَاهٍ ـ تَافِهٌ.

Triviality, *n.* }
Trivialness, } جُزْئِيَّةٌ ـ سُخْفَةٌ ـ تَفَاهَةٌ. *See also* Insignificance, *n.*

Trivially, *ad.* بِتَفَاهَةٍ ـ بِسُخْفَةٍ.

Trocar, *n.* The surgical instrument, آلَةُ جِرَاحَةِ ٱلْإِسْتِسْقَاءِ.

Trochaic, *a.* }
Trochaical, } شِعْرٌ مُرَكَّبٌ مِنْ أَوْتَادٍ مَفْرُوقَةٍ.

Troche, *n.* مَعْجُونٌ مُيَبَّسٌ فِي هَيْئَةِ لَوْحٍ صَغِيرٍ.

Trochee, *n.* وَتَدٌ مَفْرُوقٌ.

Trod, *pret. of to* Tread, *q.v.*

Trod, *a.* }
Trodden, } Beaten, of a road, مَسْلُوكٌ ـ مُعَبَّدٌ ـ مُذَلَّلٌ. A — path, مَفْرُوحٌ.

Troglodyte, *n.* سَاكِنُ ٱلْكَهْفِ *pl.* سُكَّانُ ٱلْكُهُوفِ ـ سَاكِنُ ٱلنَّاوُوسِ *pl.* سُكَّانُ ٱلنَّوَاوِيسِ.

Trojan, *n.* A veteran, عَسْكَرِيٌّ عَتِيقٌ *pl.* عَسَاكِرُ عُتَقَاءُ.

Troll, *v.i.* To roll, تَدَحْرَجَ. To run about, تَرَدَّدَ ـ دَارَ. To fish with a line, إِصْطَادَ بِٱلصِّنَّارَةِ.

Troll, *v.t.* To move in a circular direction, دَوَّرَ ـ إِسْتَدَارَ بِ. To hum a song, تَرَنَّمَ بِغِنَاءٍ.

Trollop, *n.* *See* Slattern, *n.*

Trombone, *n.* ضَرْبٌ مِنْ آلَاتِ ٱلْمُوسِيقَى.

Troop, *n.* A body of soldiers, ثُبَةٌ *pl.* ثُبَاتٌ *or* ثُبُونَ *or* ثِبُونَ ـ سَرِيَّةٌ *pl.* سَرَايَا. A battalion, regiment, آلَايٌ ـ طَابُورٌ *pl.* طَوَابِيرُ. A — of cavalry, جَمْرَةٌ *pl.* جَمَرَاتٌ ـ كُرْدُوسَةٌ *pl.* كَرَادِيسُ ـ سِرْبٌ ـ أُقْطُوعٌ *pl.* أَقَاطِيعُ ـ بُلُوكُ خَيَّالَةٍ ـ بُلُوكُ أَسَاوِرَةٍ. A herd, قَطِيعٌ *pl.* أَقَاطِيعُ ـ جَزْلَةٌ ـ جَمَاعَةٌ ـ سِرْبٌ *pl.* أَسْرَابٌ. A multitude, قَوْمٌ *pl.* أَقْوَامٌ ـ جَمَاعَةٌ.

Troops, جُنْدٌ *pl.* جُنُودٌ ـ جَيْشٌ *pl.* جُيُوشٌ ـ عَسْكَرٌ *pl.* عَسَاكِرُ. To despatch a —, سَرَّى سَرِيَّةً. "And go ye forth [to war against the unbelievers] in troops," فَٱنْفِرُوا ثُبَاتٍ (Kur. iv. 73). *See also under* Squadron, *n.*

Troop, *v.i.* To collect in numbers, تَجَمَّعُوا ـ تَحَزَّبُوا ـ تَحَازَبُوا ـ إِجْتَمَعُوا. They trooped, or placed themselves in a row, تَصَافُّوا ـ إِصْطَفُّوا.

Trooper, *n.* عَسْكَرِيٌّ خَيَّالٌ ـ عَسْكَرِيٌّ أَسْوَارٌ *pl.* عَسَاكِرُ خَيَّالَةٍ.

Trope, *n.* كِنَايَةٌ ـ إِسْتِعَارَةٌ ـ عِبَارَةٌ *pl.* عِبَارَاتٌ ـ مَجَازٌ. A loose —, مَجَازٌ مُرْسَلٌ.

Trophy, *n.* A memorial of victory, تَذْكِرَةُ ٱلنَّصْرِ ـ عَلَامَةُ ٱلظَّفَرِ.

Tropic, *n.* نُقْطَةُ ٱلْإِنْقِلَابِ ـ دَائِرَةُ ٱلْإِنْقِلَابِ ـ مُنْقَلَبٌ. The two tropics, ٱلْمُنْقَلَبَانِ ـ ٱلْمَدَارَانِ.

Tropic of Cancer, مَدَارُ ٱلسَّرَطَانِ ـ ٱلْمُنْقَلَبُ ٱلصَّيْفِيُّ.

Tropic of Capricorn, ٱلْمُنْقَلَبُ ٱلشَّتَوِيُّ ـ مَدَارُ ٱلْجَدْيِ.

Tropical, *a.* Being within the torrid zone, مَا كَانَ فِي ٱلْمِنْطَقَةِ ٱلْحَارَّةِ. Belonging to the two tropics, مَنْسُوبٌ إِلَى ٱلْمَدَارَيْنِ ـ مُتَعَلِّقٌ بِٱلْمُنْقَلَبَيْنِ. Metaphorical, مَجَازِيٌّ. A — signification, مَجَاز.

Tropically, *ad.* Metaphorically, إِسْتِعَارَةً ـ مَجَازًا. *See also* Figuratively, *ad.*

Tropology, *n.* تَعْبِيرَاتٌ مَجَازِيَّةٌ.

Trot, *v.i.* Of a horse, خَبَّ ـ خَجَّ ـ رَتَكَ; of a man or camel, جَمَزَ. To — along, to move on quickly, كَصْكَصَ.

Trot, *v.t.* Of a horse, أَخَجَّ ـ أَخَبَّ ـ أَرْتَكَ.

Trot, *n.* Of a horse, خَجٌّ ـ خَبَبٌ ـ رَتْكٌ; of a man or camel, جَمْزٌ ـ جَمَزَى.

Troth, *n.* Fidelity, صَدَاقَةٌ ـ صِدْقٌ. A promise, عَهْدٌ ـ وَثِيقَةٌ. By my —, عَلَى ذِمَّتِي. To plight one's — to, عَاهَدَ ـ عَهِدَ إِلَى فُلَانٍ.

Trotter, *n.* Of a horse, *etc.*, جَمَّاز. A sheep's —, كُرَاعُ خَارُوفٍ *pl.* أَكْرُعٌ *and* أَكَارِعُ. A seller of trotters, كُرَاعِيٌّ.

Troubadour, *n.* شَاعِرٌ طَائِفٌ *pl.* شُعَرَاءُ طَائِفُونَ.

Trouble, *v.t.* To stir up, عَكَّرَ ـ كَدَّرَ. To agitate, disquiet, كَدَّرَ ـ قَلْقَلَ ـ شَوَّشَ ـ أَقْلَقَ ـ شَغَلَ ٱلْأَفْكَارَ وَأَثَارَ ٱلْأَكْدَارَ. To vex, كَدَّ ـ أَضْجَرَ ـ شَقَّ عَلَى ـ عَنَّى ـ تَعَنَّى ـ أَعْنَى ـ أَكَدَّ. To torment, plague, عَجَّزَ ـ أَزْعَجَ ـ حَكَرَ. To put to —, in a courteous sense, أَكْلَفَ ـ كَلَّفَ. To —, or disturb, a kingdom, رَمَى ٱلْفِتْنَةَ فِي مَمْلَكَةٍ. To be troubled, disquieted, تَخَبَّطَ ـ تَقَلْقَلَ ـ اضْطَرَبَ ـ أَحِمَ ـ عَنِيَ ـ كَادَ. He was troubled by the affair, اهْتَمَّ بِٱلْأَمْرِ ـ عُنِيَ بِٱلْأَمْرِ. Don't —, put yourself to inconvenience, لَا تُكَلِّفْ خَاطِرَكَ. May I — you for a glass of water, أُكَلِّفُ خَاطِرَكَ بِكَأْسِ مَاءٍ. The matter troubled him, تَعَنَّاهُ (or عَنَّاهُ) ٱلْأَمْرُ.

Trouble, *n.* Disquietude, قَلْقَلَةٌ ـ حَيْرَةٌ ـ كَرْبٌ ـ قَلَقٌ ـ هَمٌّ. Vexation, مَشَقَّةٌ ـ عَنَايَةٌ ـ اضْطِرَابٌ ـ كَدَرٌ ـ ضَجْرَةٌ ـ ضَجَرٌ. A misfortune, hardship, شَدَائِدُ *pl.* شِدَّةٌ ـ بَلَايَا *pl.* بَلِيَّةٌ ـ خُطُوبٌ ـ خَطْبٌ ـ مَصَائِبُ *pl.* مُصِيبَةٌ ـ آفَاتٌ *pl.* آفَةٌ. Insurrection, rebellion, فِتَنٌ *pl.* فِتْنَةٌ ـ فَسَادٌ. Suffering troubles, مُصَابٌ. Inconvenience, تَكَالِيفُ *pl.* تَكْلِيفٌ ـ تَعَبٌ. Threatening —, danger, مُنْذِرٌ بِٱلْأَخْطَارِ. "Then, verily, with trouble there will be ease," فَإِنَّ مَعَ ٱلْعُسْرِ يُسْرًا (Kur. xciv. 5). To take the — to..., تَكَلَّفَ بِـ ـ كَلِفَ بِـ.

To be in trouble, sorrow, affliction, كَبِدَ ضِيقًا ـ أَصَابَتْهُ ٱلشَّدَائِدُ ـ كَانَ فِي ضِيقٍ ـ تَضَيَّقَ حُزْنًا.

To bring trouble upon, أَنْزَلَ بِـ ٱلشَّرَّ ـ جَلَبَ عَلَى ٱلشَّرَّ.

To save one trouble, أَكْفَى ٱلْمَشَقَّةَ ـ تَكَلَّفَ ٱلْمَشَقَّةَ عَنْ فُلَانٍ.

To spare no trouble, اجْتَهَدَ كُلَّ ٱلْجَهْدِ ـ مَا قَصَّرَ.

Troubled, *a.* Disquieted, مُضْطَرِبٌ. Harassed, مُتَضَايِقٌ ـ عَنِيٌّ ـ تَضَجَّرَ. Sorrowing, كَئِيبٌ. To be —, disquieted, كَدِرَ ـ تَعَنَّى ـ يَتَعَنَّى *aor.* To be —, sad, sorrowful, تَأَسَّفَ ـ كَئِبَ ـ حَزِنَ. A — sea, بَحْرٌ مُضْطَرِبٌ.

Troubler, *n.* سَاعٍ بِٱلْفَسَادِ ـ مُقْلِقٌ ـ ضَرَّابُ فِتَنٍ ـ مُكَدِّرٌ ـ حَكِرٌ.

Troublesome, *a.* Vexatious, perplexing, مُقْلِقٌ ـ مُضْجِرٌ ـ شَاقٌّ ـ مُعْنِتٌ ـ مُرْبِكٌ ـ لَاخِمٌ. Cumbersome, مُعْجِزٌ ـ حَيْرٌ ـ مُكَدِّرٌ ـ مُوَرِّطٌ. Tormenting, plaguing, مُعْجِزٌ ـ مُضْجِرٌ ـ حَكِرٌ. *See also* Difficult, *a.*

Troublesomely, *ad.* بِقَلَقٍ ـ بِضَجَرٍ ـ بِٱنْزِعَاجٍ ـ بِٱضْطِرَابٍ. *See also* Importunately, *ad.*

Troublesomeness, *n.* Vexatiousness, شِقَّةٌ ـ فَجِيعٌ ـ خَطْبٌ. Importunity, لَجَاجَةٌ ـ إِلْحَاحٌ ـ اقْتِرَاحٌ. Difficulty, مَشَقَّةٌ ـ صُعُوبَةٌ ـ عُسْرٌ.

Troublous, *a.* Distressing, شَاقٌّ. Tumultuous, مُضْطَرِبٌ ـ ضَجُوجٌ. Troublous times أَيَّامُ فِتَنٍ ـ أَزْمِنَةُ ٱلِاضْطِرَابِ ـ ضِيقُ ٱلْأَزْمِنَةِ.

A — existence, عَيْشٌ ذُو عَقَارِبَ.

Trough, *n.* جُرْنٌ *pl.* جُرُونٌ *and* أَجْرَانٌ. A watering —, قُرُوٌّ *pl.* حِيَاضٌ *pl.* حَوْضٌ ـ سَوَاقٍ *pl.* سَاقِيَةٌ ـ جَوَابٍ *pl.* جَابِيَةٌ ـ قُرُوٌّ. A kneading —, مَعَاجِنُ *pl.* مِعْجَنٌ. A — of the sea, مَا بَيْنَ مَوْجَتَيْنِ.

Trounce, *v.t.* To beat severely, ضَرَبَ. To scold, سَخِطَ عَلَى.

Trousers, *n.* *See* Trowsers, *n.*

Trousseau, *n.* لَوَازِمُ ـ جَهَازٌ ـ سُعُوفٌ *pl.* سَعَفٌ.

Trout, *n.* *Called in Egypt,* سَمَكَةٌ مُنَقَّشَةٌ *coll.* سَمَكٌ: *in Turkish,* آلَا بَالِغِي.

Trover, *n.* A find, discovery of a buried treasure, ٱلْكَشْفُ عَنْ كَنْزٍ ـ لُقْيَةٌ *pl.* لُقَايَا. An action in —, دَعْوَى لِٱسْتِرْدَادِ ٱللُّقْيَةِ.

Trow, *v.i.* *See to* Think, Suppose, *v.i.*

Trowel, *n.* مِسْيَعَةٌ ـ مَالَجَةٌ ـ مِسْلَفَةٌ ـ مِسْطَارِينٌ.

Trowsers, *n.* سَرَاوِيلُ *pl.* سَرَاوِيلَاتٌ ـ دُقْرُورٌ *pl.* دَقَارِيرُ ـ لِبَاسٌ *pl.* دِقْرَارَةٌ ـ دِقْرَارٌ ـ تُبَّانٌ ـ بَنْطَالُونٌ ـ أَلْبِسَةٌ. Short under —, تُبَّانٌ. To put on —, تَسَرْوَلَ. To have on —, تَسَرْوَلَ. Having on —, مُسَرْوَلٌ.

Troy-weight, *n.* وَزْنُ ٱلْأَجْزَجِيَّةِ وَٱلْجَوَاهِرجِيَّةِ فِي بِلَادِ ٱلْإِنْكِلِيزِ.

Truant, *a* Idle, كَسِلٌ ـ كَسْلَانٌ *pl.* كُسَالَى. Loitering, مُتَوَانٍ ـ بَطِيءٌ.

Truant, *n.* As from school, غَائِبٌ عَنِ ٱلْمَكْتَبِ. To play the —, from school, غَابَ عَنِ ٱلْمَكْتَبِ ـ اِنْفَصَلَ عَنِ ٱلْمَكْتَبِ. *See also* Idler, *n.*

Truce, *n.* A suspension of hostilities, مُتَارَكَةٌ ـ مُهَادَنَةٌ ـ عَهْدٌ بِٱلْمُتَارَكَةِ. A general —, مُتَارَكَةٌ عُمُومِيَّةٌ. To make a —, عَقَدَ مُتَارَكَةً. To break a —, فَسَخَ ٱلْمُتَارَكَةَ. A flag of —, عَلَمُ ٱلْمُفَاوَضَةِ بِٱلصُّلْحِ.

Truck, *v.t.* and *i.* *See to* Barter, *v.t.* and *i.*

Truck, *n.* As for removing goods, مِنْقَلَةٌ. A goods' van, *called in Egypt,* عَرَبِيَّةٌ جَمَالُونٍ. A wheel, عَجَلَةٌ. *See also* Barter, *n.*

Truck-system, *n.* إِيفَاءُ أُجْرَةِ ٱلْفَعَلَةِ بِٱلسِّلَعِ بَدَلَ ٱلنُّقُودِ.

Trucker, *n.* *See* Barterer, *n.*

Truckle, *n.* A small wheel, بُكْرَةٌ.

Truckle, *v.i.* To be servilely obsequious to, تَذَلَّلَ لِ ـ تَضَعْضَعَ لِ ـ تَوَاضَعَ لِ ـ طَأْطَأَ لِ ـ مُتَذَلِّلًا.

Truckle-bed, *n.*
Trundle-bed, } سَرِيرٌ يُنْشَرُ وَيُطْوَى.

Truculence, *n.* Ferocity, ضَرَاوَةٌ ـ جَفَاءٌ ـ عُنْفٌ.

Truculent, *a.* Ferocious, ضَارٍ *pl.* ضَوَارٍ ـ جَافٍ ـ كَاسِرٌ. *See also under* Fierce, *a.*

Truculently, *ad.* بِجَفَاءٍ ـ بِعُنْفٍ ـ ضَرَاوَةً.

Trudge, *v.i.* To travel with labour, حَبَا *aor.* يَحْبُو ـ زَحَفَ ـ اِزْدَحَفَ ـ تَمَشَّى.

True, *a.* Conformable to fact, حَقٌّ ـ صَحِيحٌ *pl.* صِحَاحٌ. Sincere, خَالِصٌ ـ صِدِّيقٌ ـ صَادِقٌ ـ نَصُوحٌ. Real, حَقِيقِيٌّ. Upright, straight, مُسْتَقِيمٌ. Exact, مَضْبُوطٌ: a — copy, نُسْخَةٌ مَضْبُوطَةٌ ـ نُسْخَةٌ مُطَابِقَةٌ لِلْأَصْلِ. To be —, صَحَّ ـ حَقَّ. To be — in, صَدَقَ فِي. To prove to be —, or to accept as —, صَدَّقَ ـ حَقَّقَ ـ صَحَّحَ. His saying proved —, صَحَّ قَوْلُهُ. He is a — friend, هُوَ صَدِيقٌ عَيْنٌ. That is — enough, لَا رَيْبَ فِي ذٰلِكَ. What you say is —, ٱلْحَقُّ مَعَكَ ـ صَدَقْتَ. My opinion proved —, صَدَقَ ظَنِّي. It is — that the matter is so, نَعَمْ أَنَّ ٱلْأَمْرَ كَذَا ـ بِٱلْحَقِيقَةِ أَنَّ ٱلْأَمْرَ هٰكَذَا.

True bill, *n.* تَقْرِيرٌ مُحَقَّقٌ صِحَّةَ ٱلْأَمْرِ.

True-blue, *a.* A true and sincere friend, خِلٌّ ـ صَدِيقٌ عَيْنٌ ـ خَلِيلٌ.

Trueborn, *a.*
Truebred, } Of genuine breed, أَصِيلٌ *pl.* أُصُلٌ *and* أُصْلَانٌ.

True-hearted, *a.* مُخْلِصٌ ـ صِدِّيقٌ ـ صَادِقٌ.

True-heartedness, *n.* خُلُوصُ ٱلنِّيَّةِ ـ صَدَاقَةٌ ـ صِدْقٌ.

True-love, *n.* A true lover, of a man, عَاشِقٌ صَادِقٌ; one truly loved, of a woman, مَعْشُوقَةٌ بِٱلصِّدْقِ. A — or true lover's knot, عُقْدَةٌ مِنَ ٱلرِّيبَانِ تَدُلُّ عَلَى صِدْقِ ٱلْعِشْقِ وَٱلْمَحَبَّةِ.

Trueness, *n.* Conformity to fact, حَقِيقَةٌ. Exactness, ضَبْطٌ.

True-penny, *n.* *See* True-blue, *n.*

Truffle, *n.* كَمْءٌ *pl.* أَكْمُؤٌ ـ كَمْأَةٌ ـ شَحْمَةُ ٱلْأَرْضِ ـ جُدَرِيُّ ٱلْأَرْضِ. Red truffles, جُبْءٌ; white —, فِقْعَةٌ; small —, بَنَاتُ أَوْبَرَ.

Truism, *n.* قَضِيَّةٌ مُسَلَّمَةٌ.

Trull, *n.* A lewd woman, شَرْمُوطَةٌ ـ قَحْبَةٌ ـ فَاحِشَةٌ ـ عَاهِرَةٌ.

Truly, *ad.* In truth, بِٱلْحَقِيقَةِ ـ حَقًّا ـ حَقِيقَةً ـ صِدْقًا. Verily, إِنَّ ـ لَا جَرَمَ: Truly Zaid is standing, إِنَّ زَيْدًا لَقَائِمٌ; truly, 'Amr is going away, إِنَّ عَمْرًا لَمُنْطَلِقٌ. "And, truly, it was a great matter," وَإِنْ كَانَتْ لَكَبِيرَةً (Kur. ii. 138). "And, truly, they were near to seducing thee," وَإِنْ كَادُوا لَيَفْتِنُونَكَ (Kur. xvii. 75). "He truly heareth and knoweth all things," إِنَّهُ هُوَ ٱلسَّمِيعُ ٱلْعَلِيمُ (Kur. xxvi. 220). *Also expressed by* أَمَا: Truly he struck him, أَمَا ضَرَبَهُ. Truly, exactly, عَيْنًا. Truly, there can be no doubt, لَا شَكَّ ـ لَا جَرَمَ. *See also under* Really, *ad.*

Trump, *n.* A — card, وَرَقَةُ ٱلْأَرْضِ (فِي لَعِبِ ٱلْأَوْرَاقِ). A noble fellow, بَطَلٌ *pl.* أَبْطَالٌ ـ سَنَدْرِيٌّ ـ *vulg.* رَجَالٌ ـ جَدَعٌ ـ آدَمِيٌّ. *See also* Trumpet, *n.*

Trump, *v.t.* To put on a trump card, لَعِبَ وَرَقَةَ ٱلْأَرْضِ عَلَى وَرَقَةِ ٱلْغَيْرِ (وَذٰلِكَ فِي لَعِبِ ٱلْأَوْرَاقِ). To — up, to forge, invent, اِفْتَرَى كَذِبًا ـ أَبْدَأَ زُورًا ـ اِخْتَرَعَ زُورًا: He trumped up a lie against him, اِفْتَرَى عَلَيْهِ كَذِبًا.

Trumpery, *n.* *See* Trash.

Trumpet, *n.* بُوقٌ *pl.* بُوقَاتٌ *and* أَبْوَاقٌ ـ صُورٌ ـ نَفِيرٌ. "On the day when the trumpet shall be blown in," يَوْمَ يُنْفَخُ فِي ٱلصُّورِ (Kur. vi. 73). "And when one blast shall be blown on the trumpet," فَإِذَا نُفِخَ فِي ٱلصُّورِ نَفْخَةٌ وَاحِدَةٌ (Kur. lxix. 13). A speaking —, بُوقٌ *pl.* أَبْوَاقٌ. An ear —, بُوقٌ لِتَسْهِيلِ ٱلسَّمَاعِ ـ بُوقٌ لِلْإِسْمَاعِ. To sound a —, نَفَخَ فِي ٱلْبُوقِ ـ صَوَّتَ ٱلْبُوقَ. By sound of —, عَلَى أَصْوَاتِ ٱلْأَبْوَاقِ.

Trumpet, *v.t.* To proclaim abroad, شَهَرَ. To be trumpeted abroad, اِشْتَهَرَ.

Trumpeter, *n.* ضَرَّابُ ٱلْبُوقِ ـ بَوَّاقٌ.

Truncate, *a.*
Truncated, } Having a part cut off, مَجْزُومٌ مِنْهُ جَزْمٌ ـ أَقْطَعُ. Defective, wanting, نَاقِصٌ. A — cone, مَخْرُوطٌ نَاقِصٌ.

Truncate, *v.t.* قَطَعَ مِنْهُ قِطْعَةً ـ جَزَمَ مِنْهُ جَزْمًا.

Truncation, *n.* The act of, قَطْعٌ مِن ـ جَزْمٌ مِن.

Truncheon, *n.* A staff of office, قُضَيبُ ٱلْوَظِيفَةِ. *See also* Club, *n.*

Trundle, *v.t.* To roll, دَحْرَجَ.

Trundle, *v.i.* To roll, تَدَحْرَجَ.

Trundle, *n.* A small wheel, بَكَرَةٌ.

Trunk, *n.* Of a tree, جِذْلٌ *pl.* جِذَالٌ ـ جِذْعٌ *pl.* أَجْذَاعٌ ـ سَاقٌ *pl.* سُوقٌ. A body without the limbs, بَدَنٌ مَحْسُومُ ٱلْأَعْضَاءِ ـ بَدَنٌ فَقَطْ. The proboscis of an elephant, خُرْطُومُ ٱلْفِيلِ ـ مِلْمَلَةٌ *pl.* خَرَاطِيمُ. A pipe to blow through, زَبَطَانَةٌ ـ سَبَطَانَةٌ. A box, صُنْدُوقٌ *pl.* صَنَادِيقُ. A — maker, صَنَادِيقِيٌّ. To pack one's —, عَبَّأَ ٱلصُّنْدُوقَ.

Trunnion, *n.* Of a gun-carriage, مِحْوَرُ ٱلْمِدْفَعِ *pl.* مَحَاوِرُ ـ مَدَارُ ٱلْمِدْفَعِ *pl.* مَدَارَاتٌ.

Truss, *n.* As of hay, *etc.*, فُرْزُعَةٌ *pl.* فَرَازِعُ ـ شَدَّةٌ *pl.* شَدَّاتٌ ـ حُزْمَةٌ *pl.* حُزَمٌ. A — for ruptures, حُفَاظٌ *pl.* حُفَاظَاتٌ. A maker of trusses, صَانِعُ ٱلْحُفَاظَاتِ. A rope to fasten a yard to its mast, حَبْلٌ لِشَدِّ ٱلرَّوَاجِعِ.

Truss, *v.t.* To bind in trusses, حَزَمَ-حَزْمًا ـ شَدَّ-فَرَازِعَ. To tie, bind, رَبَطَ ـ حَزَمَ ـ شَدَّ. To skewer, خَلَّ ـ سَفَّدَ.

Trust, *n.* Reliance, confidence, عِوَلٌ ـ تَعْوِيلٌ ـ ٱتِّكَالٌ ـ تَوَكُّلٌ ـ إِعْتِمَادٌ. An object of hope, مُنْيَةٌ ـ مَأْمُولٌ ـ إِنْتِظَارٌ. Faithful to a —, أَمِينٌ *pl.* أُمَنَاءُ. One relied on, ٱلْمُعْتَمَدُ ـ ٱلْمُتَوَكَّلُ عَلَيْهِ ـ عَلَيْهِ. A deposit, وَدِيعَةٌ ـ أَمَانَةٌ. Charge over property, *etc.*, ٱلتَّصَرُّفُ بِشَيْءٍ عَلَى سَبِيلِ ٱلْأَمَانَةِ. Credit, قَرْضٌ ـ دَيْنٌ. In —, by way of safe deposit, عَلَى سَبِيلِ ٱلْأَمَانَةِ. A breach of —, عَدَمُ وَفَاءٍ ـ خِيَانَةٌ بِٱلْأَمَانَةِ. On —, on credit, سَلَفًا ـ بِٱلْقَرْضِ ـ بِٱلدَّيْنِ. It was committed to his —, أُوتُمِنَ عَلَيْهِ. There is no — to be placed in him, مَا عَلَيْهِ مُعْتَمَدٌ. "Put thy trust in Him who is the Mighty, the Merciful," وَتَوَكَّلْ عَلَى ٱلْعَزِيزِ ٱلرَّحِيمِ (Kur. xxvi. 217). *See also* Credit, Reliance, *n.*

To believe on trust, صَدَّقَ-عَلَى شَهَادَةِ ٱلْغَيْرِ.

To buy a thing on trust, إِدَّانَ ـ إِشْتَرَى-بِٱلدَّيْنِ.

To commit to one's trust, إِيتَمَنَهُ عَلَى ـ جَعَلَ-عِنْدَهُ أَمَانَةً ـ وَدَعَ-عِنْدَهُ أَمَانَةً.

To hold in trust, أُوتُمِنَ عَلَيْهِ ـ ضَبَطَهُ أَمَانَةً.

To put one's trust in; *see next article.*

Trust, *v.t.* To confide in, to rely upon, رَكَنَ إِلَى ـ عَوَّلَ عَلَى ـ إِتَّكَلَ عَلَى ـ تَوَكَّلَ عَلَى ـ إِعْتَمَدَ عَلَى. To believe what one says on a matter, وَثِقَ بِ *aor.* يَثِقُ ـ عَلَى *or* بِ *or* صَدَّقَ-فِي. To — one with, give one charge over, make one to take as a trust, آمَنَ-بِ ـ أَمِنَ-عَلَى ـ إِئْتَمَنَ-عَلَى. To give credit, in buying or selling, to, دَيَّنَ. To — in one's self, إِتَّكَلَ عَلَى نَفْسِهِ ـ وَثِقَ بِنَفْسِهِ *aor.* يَثِقُ. To — one's self to . . . , إِسْتَأْمَنَ إِلَى كَذَا. We — to the information of others, نَعْتَمِدُ عَلَى أَخْبَارِ ٱلْغَيْرِ. We cannot — in, rely on, them, لَا يُمْكِنُ لَنَا أَنْ نَثِقَ بِهِمْ.

Trust, *v.i.* To believe, hope, look for, تَمَنَّى أَنْ ـ رَجَا أَنْ *aor.* أَرْجُو. To expect, تَرَقَّبَ ـ إِنْتَظَرَ ـ يَرْجُو. I — to come to you, أَنْ آتِيَ إِلَيْكُمْ. We — that it will be an example to all the governments, نَوَدُّ أَنَّهَا تَكُونُ قُدْوَةً لِجَمِيعِ ٱلدُّوَلِ.

Trusted, *a.* On whom reliance is placed, مُعْتَمَدٌ ـ مَأْمُونٌ ـ مُؤْتَمَنٌ.

Trustee, *n.* أَمِينٌ *pl.* أُمَنَاءُ ـ مُسْتَوْدَعٌ ـ مُتَوَلِّي ٱلْأَمْرِ أَمَانَةً.

Trusteeship, *n.* وَكَالَةُ ٱلْأَمِينِ ـ وَظِيفَةُ ٱلْمُسْتَوْدَعِ.

Trustful, *a.* Hopeful, آمِلٌ ـ رَاجٍ ـ مُتَمَنٍّ. *See also* Trusted, *a.*

Trustfully, *ad.* Hopefully, بِأَمَلٍ. Confidently, عَلَى ثِقَةٍ ـ بِٱعْتِمَادٍ ـ إِعْتِمَادًا.

Trustily, *n.* Faithfully, صِدْقًا ـ أَمَانَةً ـ نُصُوحًا ـ بِٱسْتِقَامَةٍ.

Trustiness, *n.* صِدْقٌ ـ صَدَاقَةٌ ـ أَمَانَةٌ.

Trustingly, *ad.* *See* Trustfully, *ad.*

Trustless, *a.* مَا عَلَيْهِ مُعْتَمَدٌ ـ قَلِيلُ ٱلْوَفَاءِ ـ خَائِنٌ.

Trustlessness, *n.* عَدَمُ ٱلْمُعْتَمَدِ ـ قِلَّةُ وَفَاءٍ ـ خِيَانَةٌ.

Trustworthiness, *n.* صِدْقٌ ـ صَدَاقَةٌ ـ أَمَانَةٌ ـ ثِقَةٌ.

Trustworthy, *a.* أَخُو ثِقَةٍ ـ مُعْتَمَدٌ ـ صَادِقٌ ـ ٱلْمَوْثُوقُ بِهِ. One whose words may be relied on, مَنْ يُوثَقُ بِكَلَامِهِ. Trustworthy historians, ثِقَاتُ ٱلْمُؤَرِّخِينَ. Trustworthy informants, ثِقَاتُ ٱلْمُخْبِرِينَ. We have heard from a — source, بَلَغَنَا مِمَّنْ يُوثَقُ بِكَلَامِهِ. It is stated and circulated on the authority of a — source, رُوِيَ وَشَاعَ عَمَّنْ يُوثَقُ بِهِ.

Trusty, *a.* Faithful, صَادِقٌ ـ مُسْتَقِيمٌ ـ ذُو وَفَاءٍ ـ أَمِينٌ ـ مُعْتَمَدٌ. Tried, مُجَرَّبٌ. A — sword, سَيْفٌ لَا يَخُونُ.

Truth, *n.* Conformity to fact, veracity, صِدْقٌ ـ حَقِيقَةٌ ـ صِحَّةٌ. A —, حَقٌّ *pl.* حُقُوقٌ *and* حِقَاقٌ. Reality, gist, حَقِيقَةٌ *pl.* حَقَائِقُ. Correctness, صِحَّةٌ ـ دِقَّةٌ ـ ضَبْطٌ. What is right, straightforward, and in its proper place, سَدَادٌ ـ صَوَابٌ. Truths, realities, حَقَائِقُ. The Truth, one of the epithets applied to God, ٱلْحَقُّ. The way of —, ٱلصِّرَاطُ ٱلْمُسْتَقِيمُ ـ طَرِيقُ ٱلْحَقِّ. In —, of a —, truly, بِٱلْحَقِيقَةِ ـ عَلَى ٱلتَّحْقِيقِ ـ حَقِيقَةً. Truth, truly, Sir, نَعَمْ يَا سَيِّدُ. You have told the —, بِٱلْحَقِّ قُلْتَ. To turn aside from the —, (*v.i.*) إِرْتَدَّ عَنِ ٱلْحَقِّ. The real —, عَيْنُ ٱلْحَقِّ ـ ٱلْحَقُّ ٱلْيَقِينُ.

Tell me the real — of the case, إِحْكِ لِي ٱلْخَبَرَ عَلَى جَلِيَّتِهِ — إِحْكِ لِي ٱلْمَادَّةَ عَلَى عَيْنِ ٱلْحَقِّ. The — is that he does not mind him, إِنَّهُ لَا يُبَالِي بِهِ حَقِيقَةً. To tell the —, the whole —, and nothing but the —, قَالَ عَيْنَ ٱلْحَقِّ وَلَا شَيْءَ إِلَّا ٱلْحَقَّ. There is no — in the report about him, لَا صِحَّةَ لِمَا شَاعَ عَنْهُ. There is no — in what some have reported, لَا صِحَّةَ لِمَا أَشَاعَهُ ٱلْبَعْضُ. There is no — in the report that hostilities had taken place between the Persians and the Ottoman troops, لَا صِحَّةَ لِمَا شَاعَ عَنْ حُدُوثِ مُحَارَبَاتٍ بَيْنَ ٱلْعَجَمِ وَٱلْجُنُودِ ٱلْعُثْمَانِيَّةِ. "God hath confirmed for His apostle the truth of the vision," لَقَدْ صَدَقَ ٱللّٰهُ رَسُولَهُ ٱلرُّؤْيَا (Kur. xlviii. 27). "For it is the very truth of sure knowledge," إِنَّهُ لَحَقُّ ٱلْيَقِينِ (*Id.* lxix. 51).

Truthful, *a.* True, speaking the truth, صَدُوق — صَادِق — صِدِّيق. True in fact, صَحِيح.

Truthfully, *ad.* بِٱسْتِقَامَةٍ — بِصَدَاقَةٍ.

Truthfulness, *n.* مُطَابَقَةُ ٱلْحَقِّ — إِسْتِقَامَة — صَدَاقَة.

Truthless, *a.* خَائِن — كَاذِب.

Truthlessness, *n.* خِيَانَة — كَذِب — كِذْب.

Try, *v.t.* To make an experiment of, جَرَّبَ. To test, examine, إِمْتَحَنَ — إِخْتَبَرَ. To attempt, سَعَى إِلَى. To —, as with affliction, إِبْتَلَى — أَبْلَى — فَتَنَ — بَلَا بِـ. To verify, حَقَّقَ — جَرَّبَ — حَكَّ. To tempt, أَفْتَنَ — فَتَنَ. To assay, أَثْبَتَ. To —, as a case at law, أَقَامَ — حَاكَمَ — أَقَامَ ٱلدَّعْوَى عَلَى — ٱلرُّؤْيَةَ وَٱلِٱسْتِمَاعَ عَلَى ٱلدَّعْوَى. To —, to fatigue, ثَقُلَ عَلَى — أَتْعَبَ. To taste, ذَاقَ. To use, إِسْتَعْمَلَ. He tried him with questions, إِخْتَبَرَهُ بِمَسَائِلَ. The Lord tried Abraham, إِبْتَلَى ٱلرَّبُّ إِبْرٰهِيمَ. Will you not — a little fish, أَلَا تَذُوقُ قَلِيلًا مِنَ ٱلسَّمَكِ. To — a thing on, whether it fits or not, جَرَّبَ. To — on, to be insistent upon, لَجَّ فِي. To be tried, brought to trial, prosecuted, أُقِيمَتِ ٱلدَّعْوَى عَلَى فُلَانٍ. He was tried, brought to trial, before the court, أُجْرِيَتْ مُحَاكَمَتُهُ بِٱلْمَجْلِسِ. To be tried, as by affliction, أُبْتُلِيَ بِـ — أُفْتُتِنَ — إِفْتَتَنَ.

Try, *v.i.* To endeavour, إِجْتَهَدَ — سَعَى.

Trying, *a.* Laborious, مُتْعِب. Afflictive, صَعْب — شَاقّ — مُتْعِب.

Trysail, *n.* قِلْعُ رَنْدَةِ ٱلْبَرُوَةِ وَٱلْغَرَنْدَةِ.

Tryst, *n.* وَعْدٌ بِٱلِٱلْتِقَاءِ — مِيعَاد.

Trysting-place, *n.* مِيعَاد — مَعْهَد — مُلْتَقَى.

Tub, *n.* دَسْتُ خَشَبٍ *pl.* دُسُوت. *See also* Barrel, *n.*

Tube, *n.* A pipe, أُنْبُوب *pl.* أَنَابِيبُ — قَصَبَة *coll.* قَصَب. A conduit, مَجْرًى *pl.* مَجَارٍ — وِعَاء *pl.* أَوْعِيَة. The Eustachian —, ٱلصِّمَاخ.

Tuber, *n.* عِرْقٌ مُتَبَصِّلٌ.

Tubercle, *n.* A small tumour, سِلْعَةٌ صَغِيرَةٌ *pl.* سِلَع — خُرَاجَة *coll.* خُرَاج. A pustule, بَثْر *pl.* بُثُور.

Tubercular, *a.* } Swelling, tumid, نَاتِئ — نَاتٍ. Full of pus-
Tuberculous, } tules, مُبَثَّر — بَاثِر — ذُو خُرَاجٍ. Full of knobs, ذُو أَزْرَارٍ — مُزَرَّر.

Tuberiferous, *a.* بَصَلِيُّ ٱلْجِذْرِ — ذُو جُذُورٍ مُتَبَصِّلَةٍ.

Tuberose, *n.* The plant, يَاسَمِينٌ بَحْرِيٌّ.

Tuberous, *a.* *See* Tubercular, *a.*

Tubing, *n.* مَتَاعُ ٱلْأَنَابِيبِ.

Tubular, *a.* In form of a pipe, أُنْبُوبِيٌّ. A — boiler, مِرْجَل (or دَسْتٌ) مُرَكَّبٌ مِنْ أَنَابِيبَ. A — bridge, جِسْرٌ فِي شَكْلِ ٱلْأُنْبُوبِ.

Tuck, *n.* As in a dress, ثُبْنَة *pl.* ثُبَن — خُبْنَة *pl.* خُبَن — طَيَّة *pl.* ثِنْي — أَثْنَاء *pl.* أَطْوَاء. A — out, a feast, أَكْلَة — ضِيَافَة.

Tuck, *v.t.* To put a tuck in a garment, جَعَلَ — خَبَنَ — ثَبَنَ فِيهِ طَيَّةً. To — in, to press together, كَبَسَ — لَبَّدَ. To envelop, لَفَّ — شَمَلَ. To swallow, هَلْقَمَ — إِبْتَلَعَ — بَلِعَ.

To tuck up, to draw together, كَمَّشَ. To tuck up the garments round one's self, تَلَبَّبَ بِثِيَابِهِ — تَحَبَّكَ. To tuck up, as the dress from the arms, *etc.*, تَشَمَّرَ عَنْ كَذَا — شَمَّرَ عَنْ كَذَا. He tucked up his trousers, as if for work, عَتَّبَ سَرَاوِيلَهُ — عَتَّبَ. He tucked up his trousers from his legs, شَمَّرَ عَنْ سَاقِهِ. *See also* To tuck in, *under to* Tuck, *v.t.*

Tucker, *n.* صُدْرَة (or صُدَيْرَة or صُدَيْرِي) لِلنِّسَاءِ.

Tuesday, *n.* يَوْمُ ٱلثَّلَاثَاءِ — ٱلثَّلَاثَاء.

Tufa, *n.* حَوَارَة.

Tufaceous, *a.* مِنْ جِنْسِ ٱلْحَوَارَةِ.

Tuft, *n.* Of hair, قَرْنُ شَعْرٍ *pl.* قُرُون — جَمْرَةُ شَعْرٍ — خُصْلَة *pl.* خُصَل — شُوشَة. A — of wool, جَزِيزَة; of dyed wool, عِهْنَة. A — of hair on a horse's forehead, نَاصِيَة *pl.* نَوَاصٍ — طُرَّة. A bird's —, شُوشَةُ ٱلطَّيْرِ — قُنْبُرَة. A cluster, لَفِيفَة — بَاقَة. Having a —, of a fowl, دَجَاجَةٌ قُنْبُرَانِيَّةٌ.

Tuft-hunter, *n.* *See* Parasite, *n.*

Tufty, *a.* ذُو لَفَائِفَ — مُجَمَّر — ذُو جَمَرَاتٍ — مُقَرَّن.

Tug, *v.t.* To pull, جَذَبَ — سَحَبَ. To drag, draw, جَرَّ. To be tugged, pulled, إِنْجَذَبَ; to be pulled, drawn, إِنْجَرَّ.

Tug, *n.* A pull, جَذْب — سَحْب. A drag, draw, تَجْرِير. A tug-boat, مَرْكَبٌ جَرَّارٌ.

Tuition, *n*. The act of instructing, تَدْرِيس ـ تَعْلِيم. Acquired knowledge, عِلْم ـ إِفَادَة.

Tuitionary, *a*. مُتَعَلِّق بِٱلتَّدْرِيسِ ـ تَعْلِيمِيّ.

Tulip, *n*. The flower and plant, سُنْبُل *pl.* سَنَابِل ـ خُزَامَة.

Tulle, *n*. شَاش مِنْ حَرِير.

Tumble, *v.i.* To fall, سَقَطَ ² ـ وَقَعَ *aor.* يَقَعُ. To roll, تَدَحْرَجَ ـ تَكَرْكَبَ. To —, as a wall, *etc.*, تَهَوَّرَ ـ قَعِفَ ـ هَبَطَ ². To become dishevelled, تَشَعَّثَ. To rumple, اِرْتَضَّ ـ تَرَضْرَضَ. To — to pieces, تَضَعْضَعَ ـ حَطِمَ ـ اِنْحَطَمَ ـ تَحَطَّمَ. To — down from, خَرَّ مِنْ ² ـ هَبَطَ مِنْ ². To — head over heels, اِنْتَكَسَ ـ اِنْقَلَبَ عَجِيزَةً عَلَى صَدْرِهِ. To — one's self about, تَقَالَبَ. To — in, to fall into, as into water, غَطَسَ فِي ـ وَقَعَ فِي *aor.* يَقَعُ. To — up, to get up quickly, اِنْتَهَضَ بِسُرْعَةٍ ـ اِنْتَهَضَ بِخِفَّةٍ. To —, as a mountebank, لَعِبَ لَعِبَ ٱلْبَهْلَوَانِ.

Tumble, *v.t.* To turn over, قَلَبَ ـ قَلَّبَ. To dishevel, شَعَّثَ. To rumple, رَضَّ ² ـ رَضْرَضَ. To — or throw out, أَخْرَجَ ـ رَمَى بِ-خَارِجًا.

Tumble, *n*. A fall, وَقْع ـ وَقْعَة ـ هَبْط ـ هُبُوط ـ هَبْطَة. A roll, تَدَحْرُج. To be in a tumble-down state, تَضَعْضَعَ. A — head over heels; *see* Somersault, *n*.

Tumbler, *n*. One who rolls about, مُتَقَالِب. A rope-dancer, بَهْلَوَان *pl.* بَهْلَوَانَات *and* بَهَالِوِين. A drinking glass, طَاسَة *pl.* طَاسَات ـ قَدَح *pl.* أَقْدَاح. A tumbling pigeon, حَمَامٌ مَرْعَش *pl.* حَمَامَاتٌ (*or* حَمَائِمُ) مَرْعَشَةٌ.

Tumbrel, *n*. A military waggon, عَرَبَانَةُ ٱلْعَسْكَرِ.

Tumbril, *n*. *See* Crate, *n*.

Tumefaction, *n*. اِنْتِفَاخ ـ وَرَم.

Tumefy, *v.i.* نَتَأَ ـ اِنْتَفَخَ ـ وَرِمَ *aor.* يَرِمُ ـ تَوَرَّمَ. To cause to —, وَرَّمَ.

Tumescence, *n*. وَرَم *pl.* أَوْرَام ـ نُفَّاخ ـ تَوَرُّم.

Tumid, *a*. Swollen, وَارِم ـ مُنْتَفِخ. *See also* Inflated, Pompous, *a*.

Tumour, *n*. سِلْعَة *pl.* سِلَع. A large —, خُرَاج ـ دُبَيْلَة. A pestilential —, دُرَّة ـ غُدَّة. A swelling, وَرَم.

Tump, *n*. *See* Hillock, *n*.

Tump, *v.t.* To form a mass of earth round a plant, (كَوَّمَ *or*) دَمَّ ² ٱلتُّرَابَ حَوْلَ سَاقِ ٱلنَّبَاتِ.

Tumular, *a*.
Tumulous, } تُلُولٌ تُلُولٌ ـ جُثًا جُثًا.

Tumult, *n*. غَيْشَمَة ـ صَرِيرَة ـ صَرَّة ـ هَوْشَة *pl.* هَوْشَات ـ ضَجَّة ـ ضَجِيج ـ هَرْج ـ هَرْجٌ مَرْجٌ ـ لَجَّة ـ تَشْوِيش *pl.* تَشْوِيشَات ـ غَاغَة ـ شَغَب. A — arose, حَدَثَ شَغَبٌ ². To be in a state of —, تَخَبَّطَ ـ هَرَجَ ـ هَاشَ ².

Tumultuarily, *ad*.
Tumultuously, } بِصَرِيرَةٍ ـ بِضَجَّةٍ ـ هَرْجَ مَرْجَ ـ بِشَغَب ـ بِٱرْتِجَاجٍ.

Tumultuary, *a*.
Tumultuous, } مُرْتَجّ ـ ضَجُوج ـ ضَجَّاج ـ عَجَّاج. To be —, أَضَجَّ.

Tumultuousness, *n*. *See* Tumult, *n*.

Tumulus, *n*. تَلّ تُرْبَةٍ *pl.* تُلُول ـ جُثْوَة *pl.* جُثًا ـ كُومَة *pl.* أَكْوَام.

Tun, *n*. A large cask, دَنّ *pl.* دِنَان.

Tun, *v.t.* سَكَبَ-فِي دَنٍّ ².

Tunable, *a*. That may be tuned, يُتْقَنُ نَغْمُهُ ـ إِصْلَاحُ لَحْنِهِ مُمْكِنٌ. *See also* Harmonious, *a*.

Tunably, *ad*. *See* Harmoniously, *ad*.

Tune, *n*. A sound, لَحْن *pl.* أَلْحَان ـ صَوْت *pl.* أَصْوَات. A series of musical notes, طَرْق *pl.* أَطْرَاق ـ مَقَامَة *pl.* مَقَامَات ـ نَغَم *pl.* أَنْغَام. Condition, حَال ـ كَيْفِيَّة. In —, in good —, لَحْنُهُ مَوْزُونٌ ـ نَغْمُهُ مُعْتَدِلٌ. Out of tune, لَحْنُهُ غَيْرُ مُعْتَدِلٍ ـ نَغْمُهُ غَيْرُ مَوْزُونٍ. To be in —, of musical sounds, تَآلَفُوا. *See also* Harmony, *n*.

Tune, *v.t.* أَصْلَحَ ٱللَّحْنَ; of a stringed instrument, شَدَّ ٱلْأَوْتَارَ. *See also to* Sing, *v.t.*

Tune, *v.i.* To be in harmony, of sounds, تَآلَفَتِ ٱلْأَلْحَانُ (*or* ٱلْأَصْوَاتُ).

Tuneful, *a*. Melodious, ذُو نَغْمَةٍ ـ مُطْرِب ـ لَذِيذٌ لِلسَّمْعِ ـ لَذِيذُ ٱللَّحْنِ.

Tunefully, *ad*. بِنَوْعٍ مُطْرِب ـ بِتَطْرِيبِ ٱلصَّوْتِ.

Tuneless, *a*. مِنْ غَيْرِ نَغَمٍ ـ عَدِيمُ ٱلنَّغَمِ ـ غَيْرُ مُطْرِب.

Tuner, *n*. مُعَدِّلُ آلَاتِ ٱلطَّرَبِ ـ مُصْلِحُ آلَاتِ ٱلْمُوسِيقَى.

Tunic, *n*. The garment, حُلَّة *pl.* حُلَل ـ قَبَآء *pl.* أَقْبِيَة; a — of leather, دُرَّعَة. A membrane, حِجَاب *pl.* حُجُب ـ غِشَآء *pl.* أَغْشِيَة. The tunics of the eye, طَبَقَاتُ ٱلْعَيْنِ.

Tuning, *n*. The act of, ٱلنَّغَمِ (تَصْلِيحُ *or* إِصْلَاحُ *or* تَعْدِيلُ *or*) تَحْكِيمُ.

Tunnage, *n*. *See* Tonnage, *n*.

Tunnel, *n*. An underground passage, نَفَق ـ سَرَب ـ مَسْلَك ـ سَرَب ـ مَسْلَكٌ نَقِيرٌ ـ مَسْلَكٌ نَاقُورٌ.

Tunnel, *v.t.* سَرَّبَ سَرَبًا فِي كَذَا ـ سَرَّبَ فِي-مَسْلَكًا سَرَبًا ـ سَرَّبَ.

Turban, *n*. مِشْوَذ ـ عِمَامَة *pl.* عِمَام *and* عَمَائِمُ ـ عِصَابَة *pl.* عَصَائِب ـ لَفَّة; of muslin, شَاش. To put a — on one, شَوَّذَ ـ عَمَّمَ. To put a — on one's self, تَشَوَّذَ ـ اِسْتَعَمَّ ـ تَعَمَّمَ ـ تَعَصَّبَ ـ لَبِسَ عِمَامَتَهُ. To have on a —, عَمَّ ـ عَصَّبَ.

Turbaned, *a.* مُعَمَّم ـ لابِسُ عِمامَةٍ ـ مُعَصَّب.

Turbary, *n.* A place where turf is dug, مَقْطَعُ ٱلْخُضَّارَى. The right of —, حَقٌّ فِي قَطْعِ ٱلْخُضَّارَى.

Turbid, *a.* مُتَكَدِّر ـ سَجِيس ـ سَجِس ـ رَمِد ـ كَدِن ـ رَنِق ـ عَكِر ـ كَدِر. A puddle, or small quantity of — water, رَنْقَة. There is not in his life anything that renders it —, مَا فِي عَيْشِهِ رَنَقٌ. To be —, رَنِقَ ـ تَعَكَّرَ ـ عَكِرَ ـ تَكَدَّرَ ـ سَجِسَ ـ كَدِرَ. To make —, رَنَّقَ ـ أَرْنَقَ ـ سَجَّسَ ـ عَكَّرَ ـ كَدَّرَ ـ أَعْكَرَ.

Turbidness, *n.* كَدَر ـ عُكُور ـ عَكَر ـ رَنَق.

Turbinate, *a.* }
Turbinated, } لَوْلَبِيٌّ.

Turbination, *n.* The act of whirling, spinning, تَفْتِيل ـ تَدْوِير.

Turbot, *n.* سَمَكُ ٱلتُّرْس: *in Turkish*, بَلَطِي.

Turbulence, *n.* }
Turbulency, } Disorder, تَشْوِيش ـ بَلْبَلَة. Tumult, شَغَب ـ هَرْج مَرْج ـ ٱرْتِجَاج ـ هَوْشَة ـ غَاغَة. *See also* Insubordination, *n.*

Turbulent, *a.* A — fellow, ذُو مَشَاغِب ـ رَجُلٌ شَغِب ـ مُشَغِّب. *See* Tumultuous, Insubordinate, *a.*

Turbulently, *ad.* *See* Tumultuously, Insubordinately, *ad.*

Tureen, *n.* مَطْبَقِيَّة ـ طَبَق *pl.* أَطْبَاق.

Turf, *n.* Sward, يَخْضُور ـ خَضِر ـ خُضَّارَى. The first — cut out of the ground, طَلِيم. *See also* Peat, *n.*

Turfiness, *n.* كَثْرَةُ يَخْضُور ـ كَثْرَةُ ٱلْخَضِرِ ـ خُضَّارَى.

Turfy, *a.* مِثْلُ ٱلْيَخْضُور ـ مَمْلُوٌّ مِنْ خَضِرٍ. Turfy or verdant land, أَرْضٌ مُخْضَرَّة ـ أَرْضٌ خَضِرَة.

Turgent, *a.* مُنْتَفِخ ـ وَارِم ـ وَرِم ـ مَنْفُوخ. *See also* Tumid, *a.*

Turgescence, *n.* }
Turgescency, } ٱنْتِفَاخ ـ تَوَرُّم ـ نُفَاخ ـ وَرَم.

Turgid, *a.* Swollen, مُنْتَفِخ ـ وَارِم. Pompous, bombastic, of style, أَبْلَغ ـ مُبَالِغ ـ مُتَنَفِّخ.

Turgidity, *n.* }
Turgidness, } The being swollen, ٱنْتِفَاخ ـ نُفَّاخ ـ وَرَم; of style, مُبَالَغَة ـ ٱلْكَلَامُ بِعَظَائِمَ ـ عَظَمَةُ ٱلْكَلَامِ.

Turk, *n.* تُرْكِيّ *pl.* أَتْرَاك. An Ottoman, عُثْمَانِيّ *pl.* عُثْمَانِيَّة. An inexorable fellow, شَيْطَان ـ مُزَمْهِرّ ـ قَاسٍ ـ قَسِيّ.

Turkey, *n.* The country, ٱلْبِلَادُ ٱلْعُثْمَانِيَّة, *called by the Turks*, مَمَالِكُ ٱلدَّوْلَةِ ٱلْعَلِيَّةِ ـ ٱلْمَمَالِكُ ٱلْمَحْرُوسَة. The fowl, دَجَاجَة هِنْدِيَّة *coll.* دَجَاجٌ هِنْدِيّ. Turkey red (cloth), قُمَاشٌ قِرْمِزِيّ.

Turkish, *a.* تُرْكِيّ. Ottoman, عُثْمَانِيّ. The — language, ٱللِّسَانُ ٱلتُّرْكِيّ ـ ٱلتُّرْكِيَّة.

Turkoman, *n.* تُرْكُمَانِيّ *coll.* ٱلتُّرْكُمَان.

Turkois, *n.* }
Turquoise, } The stone, فِيرُوزَة ـ فِيرُوزَج.

Turmeric, *n.* كُرْكُم.

Turmoil, *n.* بَلْبَلَة ـ غَاغَة ـ فِتْنَة ـ ٱخْتِلَال ـ ٱضْطِرَاب ـ تَخَبُّط ـ تَشَوُّش ـ شَغْب. To be in a state of —, ٱضْطَرَبَ ـ تَشَوَّشَ ـ تَخَبَّطَ ـ ٱخْتَلَّ ـ تَخَرْبَطَ. To put into a state of —, شَوَّشَ ـ أَفْسَدَ ـ خَبَّطَ ـ خَبَطَ ـ شَغَّبَ.

Turn, *v.t.* To cause to turn round, revolve, أَدَارَ ـ أَدَارَ بِ ـ دَوَّرَ ـ دَوَّرَ بِ ـ ٱسْتَدَارَ بِ ـ دَارَ بِ. To — and twist, لَوَى ـ بَرَمَ ـ أَبْرَمَ. To —, as a dress, *etc.*, قَلَبَ. To —, as on a lathe, خَرَطَ. To —, as the stomach, قَلَبَ ٱلنَّفْسَ ـ دَوَّخَ ـ قَرَّفَ ـ صَدَمَ ٱلنَّفْسَ. To —, to make sour, صَيَّرَ حَامِضًا ـ حَمَّضَ ـ صَيَّرَ حَامِزًا. To make to change, turn back, as from an opinion, *etc.*, رَدَّ ـ أَفَظَّ. To —, of a scale, to outweigh, تَرَجَّحَ عَلَى كَذَا ـ رَجَحَ عَلَى كَذَا. To endeavour to — one from, دَاوَرَ عَنْ كَذَا ـ رَاجَعَ; to endeavour to — one to, دَاوَرَ عَلَى كَذَا.

To turn aside, to make to go to one side, جَانَبَ ـ جَنَّبَ ـ أَبْعَدَ ـ بَاعَدَ.

To turn aside from, to make to deviate from, لَوَى عَنْ ـ رَدَّ عَنْ ـ صَرَفَ عَنْ; so as to make to fall into error, تَوَّهَ ـ ضَلَّلَ ـ أَضَلَّ ـ أَزَاغَ.

To turn away, to dismiss, دَشَّرَ ـ طَرَدَ ـ نَفَا ـ نَفَى. To make to turn from, صَرَفَ عَنْ ـ أَصْدَفَ عَنْ.

To turn back, make to go back, صَرَفَ ـ رَدَّ ـ رَجَّعَ.

To turn down, as a leaf, *etc.*, ثَنَى.

To turn from, as from a place, نَقَلَ ـ حَوَّلَ; as from any pursuit, رَجَّعَ عَنْ ـ رَدَّ عَنْ ـ ثَنَى ـ ثَنَى عَنْ ـ حَرَفَ عَنْ ـ صَرَفَ عَنْ. To turn one's attention from, أَغْضَى ٱلنَّظَرَ عَنْ: If we turn our attention away from what is passing at present, إِذَا أَغْضَيْنَا ٱلنَّظَرَ عَمَّا هُوَ وَاقِعٌ ٱلْآنَ. To turn from, as from a promise to one, أَخْلَفَهُ فِي وَعْدِهِ. "Do not imagine that God turns from His promise," فَلَا تَحْسَبَنَّ ٱللّٰهَ مُخْلِفَ وَعْدِهِ (Kur. xiv. 48). *See also above*, To turn aside from.

To turn in, make to enter, دَخَّلَ ـ أَدْخَلَ. To turn in, as of a seam, خَبَنَ ـ ثَبَّنَ.

To turn inside out, قَلَبَ ٱلدَّاخِلَ خَارِجًا. To rummage, بَعْثَرَ ـ حَرَّكَ ـ قَلَّبَ ـ نَبَشَ ـ نَتَّشَ.

To turn into, change into, as of coin, صَرَفَ بِ. To transform, صَيَّرَ ـ حَوَّلَ إِلَى ـ أَوَّلَ إِلَى: He turned the water into blood, حَوَّلَ ٱلْمَاءَ إِلَى دَمٍ.

To turn off, to dismiss, نَفَى ـ نَفَا ـ ² طَرَدَ ـ ² دَشَّرَ. To turn off, as from a subject, أَلْوَى بِ ـ صَرَفَ-عَنْ =. To stop, as water, *etc.*, قَطَعَ =. To drive away, disperse, أَشْرَدَ ـ شَرَّدَ.

To turn on, to let on, as water, *etc.*, أَطْلَقَ ـ أَسَالَ ـ سَيَّحَ. To turn on, to be connected with, تَعَلَّقَ بِ ـ إِخْتَصَّ بِ: The policy of Italy still turns on, or is guided by, aspirations, the drift of which is . . . , سِيَاسَةُ إِيطَالِيَا لَمْ تَزَلْ مَبْنِيَّةً عَلَى مَطَامِحَ مِنْ شَأْنِهَا أَنْ.

To turn one against, قَرَّفَ-عَلَى ـ أَسَامَ ـ كَرَّهَ-إِلَى.

To turn one's attention from, إِسْتَذْهَنَ-عَنْ كَذَا ـ أَذْهَنَ-عَنْ كَذَا ـ شَاغَلَ-عَنْ كَذَا. To — one's attention to, ² نَصَّ-عَلَى كَذَا ـ نَبَّهَ-عَلَى كَذَا ـ أَشَارَ إِلَى-بِكَذَا.

To turn one's back, حَوَّلَ قَفَاهُ. To turn one's back upon, to run away, ² فَرَّ مِنْ كَذَا ـ إِنْهَزَمَ ـ وَلَّى. To shun, دَابَرَ ـ أَعْرَضَ عَنْ ـ تَجَافَى عَنْ. "And he who turns his back unto them on that day," وَمَنْ يُوَلِّهِمْ يَوْمَئِذٍ دُبُرَهُ (Kur. viii. 16).

To turn one's face from one, لَفَتَ وَجْهَهُ عَنْهُ =.

To turn one's hand or mind to, كَانَ = ـ أَرَادَ ـ هَمَّ بِ ² ـ شَغَلَ = الْعَقْلَ فِي.

To turn one's head, mind, brain, هَتَرَ = ـ جَنَّنَ ـ حَيَّرَ ـ نَفَخَ = لَعِبَ فِي عَقْلِهِ ـ فِي رَأْسِهِ =.

To turn one's self to, إِنْصَرَفَ إِلَى.

To turn out, expel, أَخْرَجَ; as from an employment, نَزَعَ-مِنْ = ـ خَلَعَ = ـ عَزَلَ-عَنْ. To turn out, as of cattle, into the fields, *etc.*, أَبْرَزَ ـ سَيَّبَ; as to grass, أَمْذَى ـ مَذَى =. To turn out, as a machine its work, ضَرَبَ = ـ صَنَعَ =; of printing, طَبَعَ =.

To turn over, as on a different side, قَلَبَ =. To turn over the ground, as in search for something, أَحْفَى الْأَرْضَ ـ أَحْفَى.

To turn over a new leaf, to reform, أَصْلَحَ السِّيرَةَ.

To turn over, as in one's mind, أَجَالَ الْفِكْرَ فِي ـ بَرَّمَ ـ حَوَّلَ دَوَّرَ الْآرَاءَ فِي الْمَادَّةِ ـ الْأَمْرِ; as the leaves of a book, قَلَبَ =; as an affair to another, حَوَّلَ-إِلَى ـ أَحَالَ-إِلَى.

To turn sideways, عَرَّضَ ـ عَرَضَ =.

To turn to, to make to incline to, قَلَبَ-إِلَى ـ أَمَالَ-إِلَى =.

To turn to account, إِسْتَفَادَ مِنْ ـ إِنْتَفَعَ بِ.

To turn towards, أَدَارَ-إِلَى ـ وَجَّهَ-إِلَى.

To turn up, as the dress from any part of the body, شَمَّرَ عَنْ.

To turn up, as ground for sowing, أَحْفَى الْأَرْضَ ـ أَحْفَى ـ سَلَفَ الْأَرْضَ ². To set upright, نَصَبَ ² ـ صَمَدَ. To turn up, as of a card, قَلَبَ =.

To turn upon, to relate to, آلَ إِلَى *aor.* يَؤُولُ ـ إِخْتَصَّ بِ.

To turn upside down, بَعْثَرَ ـ رَكَسَ ² ـ أَرْكَسَ ـ جَفَلَ ² = ـ قَلَبَ ـ جَعَّبَ ـ جَعَبَ =. *See also under* Upside-down, *a.*

Turn, *v.i.* To revolve, دَارَ ـ إِسْتَدَارَ *aor.* يَدُورُ ـ فَتَلَ =. To go back, رَجَعَ = ـ إِنْصَرَفَ. To change one's mind, أَضْرَبَ عَنْ ـ عَدَلَ عَنْ =. To repent, تَابَ ². To —, as from side to side, قَلَبَ مِنْ جَنْبٍ إِلَى جَنْبٍ =. To —, as from a right course, زَاغَ فِي ² ـ تَعَرَّضَ ـ تَعَوَّجَ. To — or wheel round, جَالَ *aor.* يَجُولُ.

To become bad, of milk, wine, *etc.*, أَخْلَفَ ـ فَسَدَ ². To become sour, حَمَزَ = ـ حَمُضَ ² ـ حَمَّضَ ـ إِنْفَسَدَ; to become like vinegar, تَخَلَّلَ. To —, of the head in vertigo, دَاخَ *aor.* يَدُوخُ. To commence, as to ripen, *etc.*, ضَرَبَ إِلَى =. There was no room to —, لَيْسَ سَبِيلٌ لِلنُّكُوبِ.

To turn again, رَجَعَ = ـ عَادَ ².

To turn aside, go to one side, إِنْصَرَفَ ـ إِنْحَرَفَ ـ إِجْتَنَبَ ـ مَالَ إِلَى جَنْبٍ ـ إِلْتَفَتَ =. To turn aside from the truth, إِرْتَدَّ عَنِ الْحَقِّ. To deviate from the right way, in speech, زَاغَ فِي الْكَلَامِ ².

To turn away from, أَعْرَضَ ـ تَحَرَّفَ عَنْ ـ أَعْرَضَ ـ فَتَلَ عَنْ = ـ حَادَ عَنْ = ـ صَدَّ عَنْ ² ـ إِنْصَرَفَ عَنْ ـ عَنْ; as in disgust, تَخَامَصَ عَنْ; as from counsel, advice, لَفَتَ عَنْ =. "And whoso turneth away from my monition, his truly shall be a life of misery," وَمَنْ أَعْرَضَ عَنْ ذِكْرِي فَإِنَّ لَهُ مَعِيشَةً ضَنْكًا (Kur. xx. 123).

To turn back, رَجَعَ = ـ إِنْصَرَفَ. To retreat, قَهْقَرَ ـ وَلَّى ـ أَدْبَرَ ـ تَقَهْقَرَ.

To turn down, إِنْطَبَقَ.

To turn eastward, towards the east, شَرَّقَ.

To turn from, مَالَ عَنْ = ـ تَنَكَّبَ عَنْ ـ رَجَعَ عَنْ =.

To turn head over heels, تَشَقْلَبَ ـ تَكَرْكَبَ ـ *vulg.* إِنْتَكَسَ. *See also under* Somersault, *n.*

To turn in, to go in, دَخَلَ ² ـ فَاتَ إِلَى دَاخِلٍ ². To bend inwards, تَحَنَّتَ إِلَى دَاخِلٍ. To turn in, as to sleep, دَخَلَ يَنَامُ ².

To turn into, to tend towards, إِنْصَرَفَ إِلَى ـ مَالَ إِلَى =.

To turn inside out, بَاطِنُهُ يَنْقَلِبُ إِلَى الْخَارِجِ.

To turn into, to become, آلَ إِلَى *aor.* يَؤُولُ ـ تَحَوَّلَ ـ صَارَ = ـ أَصْبَحَ.

To turn off, as a road, إِلْتَوَى ـ إِلْتَفَتَ.

To turn upon, to be the subject of, كَانَ مَنُوطًا بِ ـ تَعَلَّقَ بِ ـ خَصَّ ². To turn upon, as upon an axis, دَارَ فِي الْمَدَارِ ².

To turn out, go out, خَرَجَ ²; as into the field, تَبَرَّزَ ـ بَرَزَ ². To become, أَصْبَحَ . To turn out, to assemble together, as for a riot, of many, تَأَلَّبُوا .

To turn over, إِنْقَلَبَ . To turn over and over, to roll, تَدَحْرَجَ .

To turn to, towards, إِلْتَفَتَ إِلَى ـ يَؤُولُ *aor.* آلَ إِلَى . To turn to, as to a work, شَمَّرَ لِ . That will turn to your profit, يَؤُولُ لَكُمْ ذٰلِكَ نَفْعًا . To have recourse to, إِلْتَجَأَ إِلَى ; "Afterwards his Lord chose him for Himself, and was turned towards him," ثُمَّ ٱجْتَبَاهُ رَبُّهُ فَتَابَ عَلَيْهِ (Kur. xx. 120).

To turn the face to, دَارَ وَجْهَهُ إِلَى ـ حَوَّلَ وَجْهَهُ إِلَى 2 .

To turn to one side, in walking, إِعْتَرَضَ .

To turn to the left hand, إِنْصَرَفَ شِمَالًا .

To turn to the right hand, إِنْصَرَفَ يَمِينًا .

Turn, *n.* A revolution, دَوْر *pl.* أَدْوَار . A twist, as of a turban or rope, *etc.*, دَوْر *pl.* أَدْوَار ـ لَفّ *pl.* لُفُوف . A change, تَبَدُّل ـ تَغْيِير . A —, as of time or circumstance, دَائِرَة *pl.* دَوَائِرُ ـ إِنْقِلَاب *pl.* إِنْقِلَابَات : the turns or vicissitudes of fortune, صَرْف ـ طَوَارِحُ ٱلزَّمَنِ ـ حَالَاتُ ٱلدَّهْرِ ـ ٱلدَّهْرِ . Giddiness, vertigo, دُوَار ـ دَوْخ . An opportunity, فُرْصَة *pl.* فُرَص . An action, treatment, مُعَامَلَة ـ صَنِيع ـ فِعْل ـ صُنْع . A phase, condition, وَجْه *pl.* وُجُوه ـ حَالَة *pl.* حَالَات ـ حَال *pl.* أَحْوَال . A walk, رِيَاضَة ـ رَوَاح ـ سَيْر ـ جَرْي . Course, as of events, دَوْرَة ـ سِيرَة ـ سَيْر . A meander, winding, لَيَّة *pl.* لِوًى ـ تَفَتُّل . A —, as in a street or road, عَوْجَة ـ عَطْفَة ـ لَفَّة . A time, of alternation, دَوْلَة *pl.* عُقْبَة ـ نَوْبَة ـ دِوَل . The — of the tide, إِنْقِلَابُ ٱلْمَدِّ وَٱلْجَزْرِ . A favourable —, as of fortune, دَوْلَة *pl.* دِوَل ; an unfavourable —, دَبْرَة *pl.* دِبَار . A good —, kindness, فَضِيلَة ـ فَضْل *pl.* فُضُول *pl.* فَضَائِل ـ صَنِيعٌ جَمِيلٌ ; a bad —, قَبَاحَة ـ صَنِيعٌ قَبِيحٌ . By turns, فِي كُلِّ ـ أَمَدًا ـ عَلَى ٱلتَّنَاوُبِ ـ مُنَاوَبَةً ـ بِٱلنَّوْبَةِ . At every turn, دَائِمًا ـ حِينَ . His — came round, دَارَتْ نَوْبَتُهُ ـ دَارَتْ عُقْبَتُهُ . He rode a —, رَكِبَ عُقْبَةً ; he rode his —, رَكِبَ عُقْبَتَهُ . They acted by turns, of many, إِنْتَابُوا ـ تَعَاوَرُوا ـ تَدَاوَلُوا ـ تَرَاوَحُوا ـ تَنَاوَبُوا . "What turn their affairs shall take," أَيَّ مُنْقَلَبٍ يَنْقَلِبُونَ (Kur. xxvi. 228). We shall see what — the affair will take, نَرَى كَيْفَ يَتَحَوَّلُ ٱلْأَمْرُ . The —, or phase, which circumstances take, كَيْفِيَّةُ ٱنْتِقَالِ ٱلْأَحْوَالِ . The — is yours, لَكَ ٱلْعَوَادَةُ ـ ٱلدَّوْرُ دَوْرُكَ . It is your — to begin, لَكَ ٱلْبَدِيهَةُ .

To do one a turn, صَنَعَ بِ ـ صَنِيعًا .

To do one a bad turn, أَقْبَحَ إِلَى ـ صَنَعَ بِ ـ صَنِيعًا قَبِيحًا .

To do one a good turn, أَحْسَنَ إِلَى ـ صَنَعَ بِ ـ صَنِيعًا حَسَنًا .

To give one a turn, to go about with one, دَاوَرَهُ ـ دَارَ مَعَهُ 2 . To give one vertigo, دَاخَ 2 ـ أُدِيرَ بِهِ ـ دِيرَ بِهِ ـ دِيرَ عَلَيْهِ .

To give a different turn to affairs, حَوَّلَ كَيْفِيَّةَ ٱلْأُمُورِ .

To serve one's turn, صَلَحَ لَهُ 2 .

To take a turn, to walk, تَسَيَّرَ ـ تَنَزَّهَ ـ تَمَشَّى . To do a part in alternation, إِشْتَغَلَ نَوْبَةً ـ قَضَى عُقْبَةً .

To take one's turn, in alternation, إِشْتَغَلَ عُقْبَتَهُ ـ قَضَى نَوْبَتَهُ .

Turncoat, *n.* مُنْصَرِف ـ خَوَّان *pl.* خَائِن ـ حُوَّلِيٌّ قُلَّبِيٌّ ـ مُرْتَدٌّ عَنْ كَذَا .

Turncock, *n.* فَتَّاحُ أَقْنِيَةِ ٱلْمَاءِ .

Turned, *a.* As of a garment, مُقَلَّب ـ مَقْلُوب . Turned sour, حَامِض ـ مُحَمَّض . Turned, as on a lathe, مَخْرُوط .

Turner, *n.* Of a lathe, خَرَّاط *pl.* خَرَّاطَة . A — of bowls, cups, *etc.*, قَطَّاط *pl.* قَطَّاطَة . A turner's lathe, مِخْرَط .

Turnery, *n.* خِرَاطَة .

Turning, *a.* Revolving, دَوَّار .

Turning, *n.* A winding, تَفَتُّل ـ فَتْلَة ـ عَوْجَة . A winding, as of a valley, عُرْقُوب *pl.* عَرَاقِيب ـ لَيَّة *pl.* لِوًى . A curdling, تَحْمِيض ـ تَمَذُّر . *See also* Deviation, *n.*

Turning-point, *n.* A crisis, حَوْمَة ـ غَمْرَة ـ حَالُ بُحْرَانٍ .

Turnip, *n.* سَلْجَم *pl.* شَلْجَم ـ لِفْت ـ سَلَاجِمُ ـ *vulg.* شَلْجَم . Turnip-tops, نَبَاتُ ٱلسَّلْجَمِ .

Turnkey, *n.* Of a prison, بَوَّابُ ٱلسِّجْنِ ـ سَجَّان .

Turn-out, *n.* As of troops, *etc.*, بُرُوز . Equipage, مَوْكِب ـ طَقْم ـ خَدَمٌ وَحَشَمٌ ـ دَائِرَة . A —, as for a riot, تَأَلُّب . Carriages, عَرَبِيَّات . A — of a railway ; *see* Siding, *n.*

Turnpike, *n.* A toll-gate, بَابُ سِكَّةٍ يُدْفَعُ عِنْدَهُ مَكْسُ ٱلْعُبُورِ . A — keeper, بَوَّابُ ٱلسِّكَّةِ ٱلْمَذْكُورَةِ . A — road, شَارِع *pl.* دَرْبٌ سُلْطَانِيٌّ ـ شَوَارِع .

Turnsol, *n.* The plant, عَبْدُ ٱلشَّمْسِ ـ دَوَّارُ ٱلشَّمْسِ .

Turnspit, *n.* آلَةٌ لِتَدْوِيرِ ٱلسَّفُّودِ .

Turnstile, *n.* حَاجِزٌ دَوَّارٌ .

Turn-table, *n.* Of a railway, دَائِرَةٌ دَوَّارَةٌ .

Turpentine, *n.* صَمْغُ ٱلْبُطْمِ ـ تِرِبِنْتِين ـ تِرِبِنْتِينَا . Spirits of —, رُوحُ ٱلنِّفْطِ . The — tree, شَجَرَةُ ٱلتَّرِبِنْتِينَا ـ شَجَرَةُ ٱلْبُطْمِ .

Turpitude, *n.* قَبَاحَة ـ قُبْح ـ سَوْءَة ـ قَذَع ـ شَنْع ـ شَنَاعَة ـ شَقَاحَة ـ خَبَاثَة . *See also* Depravity, *a.*

Turquoise, *n.* *See* Turkois, *n.*

Turret, *n.* A tower, as on the walls of a city, بُرْج *pl.* بُرُوج . A — of a mosque, مَنَارَة ـ مِئْذَنَة . A pigeon —, بُرْجُ حَمَام *pl.* بُرُوج . A small pinnacle on a wall, شُرْفَة *pl.* شُرُفَات .

Turret, *v.t.* To — a wall, شَرَّفَ ٱلْحَائِطَ 2 .

Turretted, *a.* ذُو شُرُفَاتٍ ـ ذُو بُرُوجٍ.

Turtle, *n.* A turtle-dove, قُمْرِيَّةٌ *pl.* قُمْرِيٌّ ـ قُمَارِيٌّ *pl.* قُمْرِيَّةٌ. A sea —, ظُهْرَةٌ. *See also* Tortoise, *n.*

Tuscan, *a.* تُسْقَانِيٌّ.

Tuscan, *n.* مِنْ أَهْلِ بِلَادِ تُسْقَانَا.

Tuscany, *n.* بِلَادُ تُسْقَانَا.

Tush! *int.* تُفٍّ ـ أُفٍّ.

Tusk, *n.* مِخَدٌّ *dual* مِخَدَّانِ ـ نَاب *pl.* أَنْيَاب. The tusks of any animal, صَلَاقِيمُ.

Tusked, *a.* } أَنْيَبُ ـ ذُو أَنْيَابٍ.
Tusky, }

Tussle, *n.* *See* Struggle, *n.*

Tut! *int.* تُفٍّ ـ أُفٍّ.

Tutelage, *n.* The office of a guardian, وَكَالَةٌ ـ وِصَايَةٌ. Protection, صِيَانَةٌ ـ حِمَايَةٌ.

Tutelar, *a.* } حَافِظٌ ـ مُحَامٍ ـ حَامٍ *pl.* حُمَاةٌ.
Tutelary, }

Tutor, *n.* A preceptor, أُسْتَاذٌ ـ مُعَلِّمٌ ـ مُدَرِّسٌ ـ مُهَذِّبٌ. *See also* Guardian, *n.*

Tutor, *v.t.* To teach, عَلَّمَ ـ دَرَّسَ. To train, هَذَّبَ ـ مَرَّنَ. To — one to ..., دَرَّبَ فِي *or* عَلَى كَذَا.

Tutorage, *n.* *See* Tutelage, *n.*

Tutoress, *n.* مُدَرِّسَةٌ ـ مُعَلِّمَةٌ. *See also* Governess, *n.*

Tutorial, *a.* مُتَعَلِّقٌ بِالتَّدْرِيسِ.

Tutty, *n.* تُوتِيَا.

Twaddle, *n.* هِتْرٌ ـ هَذَيَانٌ ـ عَبَثٌ ـ هَذَرٌ ـ هُجْرٌ ـ لَغْوٌ ـ لَحْيٌ.

Twaddle, *v.i.* أَهْتَرَ ـ أَهْجَرَ ـ هَذَرَ ـ لَحِيَ.

Twaddler, *n.* هَذَّارٌ ـ مُهْتِرٌ ـ أَلْحَى.

Twain, *a.* and *n.* إِثْنَانِ *fem.* إِثْنَتَانِ. To cut in —, شَطَرَ ـ شَطَّرَ. To be rent in —, إِنْشَقَّ إِلَى اثْنَيْنِ.

Twang, *v.i.* As a bow-string, *etc.*, حَنَّ ـ عَزَقَ ـ ضَبَحَ ـ أَرَنَّ: the bow twanged, حَنَّتِ الْقَوْسُ ـ ضَبَحَتِ الْقَوْسُ.

Twang, *v.t.* رَنَّنَ ـ أَحَنَّ ـ أَنْبَضَ.

Twang, *n.* As of a bow, *etc.*, طَنِينٌ ـ إِرْنَانٌ ـ حَنِينٌ. Tone, sound, صَوْتٌ ـ لَحْنٌ. A nasal —, خَنْخَنَةٌ. To speak with a nasal —, خَنْخَنَ. *See also* Touch, Modicum, Taste, *n.*

Twattle, *v.i.* *See to* Gabble, Twaddle, *v.i.*

Tweak, *v.t.* To — the ears of one, أَذَّنَ. *See to* Pinch, *v.t.*

Tweak, *n.* *See* Pinch, *n.*

Tweedle, *v.t.* To handle lightly, خَفَّ بِ.

Tweeds, *n.* قُمَاشٌ خَفِيفٌ مِنْ قُطْنٍ أَوْ صُوفٍ.

Tweezers, *n.* For pulling out hairs, مِنْتَاخٌ ـ مِنْتَافٌ ـ مِنْقَشٌ ـ مِنْقَاشٌ ـ مِنْتَاشٌ. To pull out (hairs) with the —, نَتَّفَ ـ نَتَفَ ـ نَتَشَ ـ نَتَخَ ـ إِنْتَقَشَ ـ نَقَشَ. To have the hairs so pulled out, إِنْتَتَفَ.

Twelfth, *a.* اَلثَّانِي عَشَرَ *fem.* اَلثَّانِيَةُ عَشْرَةَ.

Twelfth-day, *n.* *See* Epiphany, *n.*

Twelve, *a.* إِثْنَا عَشَرَ *fem.* إِثْنَتَا عَشْرَةَ. He had been ill for — years, كَانَ مَرِيضًا مُنْذُ اثْنَتَيْ عَشْرَةَ سَنَةً. He is one of the — men, هُوَ وَاحِدٌ مِنَ الْاثْنَيْ عَشَرَ رَجُلًا.

Twelve-month, *n.* A year, عَام *pl.* عَوَام ـ سَنَة *pl.* سَنَوَات.

Twelve-pence, *n.* إِثْنَا عَشَرَ بِينِي عِبَارَةٌ عَنْ شِيلِينٍ.

Twentieth, *a.* اَلْعِشْرُونَ.

Twenty, *a.* عِشْرُونَ.

Twenty-fold, *a.* عِشْرُونَ ضِعْفًا.

Twice, *ad.* Two times, مَرَّتَيْنِ ـ طَرْقَتَيْنِ ـ طَرْقَيْنِ. Once or —, مَرَّةً أَوْ مَرَّتَيْنِ. He gave him — as much, زَادَ عَلَى ـ ضِعْفًا. Let it be — as much as you gave him, فَيَكُونُ ضِعْفَ مَا أَعْطَيْتَهُ. To do a thing —, ثَنَّى ـ كَرَّرَ. *See also to* Repeat, *v.t.*

Twig, *n.* خُصْلَةٌ *pl.* خُصَلٌ ـ خَصْلَةٌ *pl.* خَصَلَاتٌ ـ عُسْلُوجٌ *pl.* عَسَالِيجُ ـ غُصْنَةٌ *pl.* غُصْنَاتٌ. A fallen —, سَلِيقٌ. To hop the —, run away, وَلَّى هَارِبًا ـ إِنْسَلَّ.

Twiggen, *a.* Made of twigs, مِنْ غُصُونٍ ـ مِنْ عَسَالِيجَ.

Twiggy, *a.* Abounding with twigs, كَثِيرُ الْأَغْصَانِ ـ كَثِيرُ الْعَسَالِيجِ.

Twilight, *n.* Of the morning, سَحَرٌ; of the evening, عِشَاءٌ ـ عَتَمَةٌ ـ شَفَقٌ.

Twilight, *a.* By morning twilight, عِنْدَ السَّحَرِ; by evening twilight, عِنْدَ الشَّفَقِ. Sombre, obscure, مُغْتِمٌ ـ عَاتِمٌ.

Twill, *v.t.* خَطَّ ـ خَطَّطَ.

Twill, *n.* قُمَاشٌ مُخَطَّطٌ.

Twilled, *a.* مُخَطَّطٌ.

Twin, *n.* and *a.* تَوْءَم *pl.* تَوَائِمُ *fem.* تَوْءَمَة *pl.* تُؤَام. He is his — brother, هُوَ تَوْءَمُهُ. They are two — brothers, هُمَا تَوْءَمَانِ; (the same word is applied to one of a pair; *see also* Pair, *a.*) A woman who brings forth twins, مِتْآم. The sign of the Zodiac, الْهَنْعَةُ ـ التَّوْءَمُ.

Twin, *v.i.* To bear twins, أَتْأَمَتْ.

Twin-born, *a.* *See* Twin, *n.* and *a.*

Twine, *v.t.* To twist together, وَشَجَ ـ حَبَّكَ ـ عَقَّدَ ـ عَلَّقَ ـ فَتَلَ. To wreathe, to curl, عَقْرَبَ. *See also to* Intertwine, *v.t.*

Twine, *v.i.* To become twisted together, وَشَجَ *aor.* يَشِجُ ـ إنْشَبَكَ ـ إنْفَتَلَ ـ تَفَتَّلَ ـ تَحَبَّكَ ـ إنْعَقَدَ. To wreathe, curl, تَعَقْرَبَ. A twining or creeping plant, حَبْل *pl.* أَحْبَال. *See also to* Intertwine, *v.i.*

Twine, *n.* Strong thread, string, خَيْطُ ٱلصُّبَارَةِ ـ مِصِّيص *called vulgarly,* دُبَارَة. A twist, فَتْلَة ـ لَيَّة.

Twinge, *v.t.* To give pain to, آلَمَ ـ جَرَحَ ـ أَوْجَعَ. To pinch, قَرَصَ.

Twinge, *v.i.* To feel twinges of pain, نُخِزَ بِأَوْجَاعٍ.

Twinge, *n.* As of pain, نَخْزَة. A pinch, قَرْص ـ قَرْصَة. A — of conscience, نَخْزَةٌ فِي ٱلْقَلْبِ (or ٱلضَّمِيرِ).

Twinkle, *v.i.* Of the eye, طَرَفَ ـ طَرَفَ ٱلْبَصَرَ ـ طَرَفَ ـ بَصَّرَ ـ لَأْلَأَ بِعَيْنِهِ ـ لَمَحَ. To —, of a star, أَزْهَرَ ـ تَلَأْلَأَ ـ لَأْلَأَ.

Twinkle, *n.* }
Twinkling, } Of the eye, عَيْر ـ طَرْفُ ٱلْعَيْنِ; as of the stars, أزْهِرَار ـ لَأْلَأَة. In a —, فِي لَحْظَةٍ. You did it before the — of an eye, فَعَلْتَهُ قَبْلَ عَيْرٍ. "Like the twinkling of an eye," كَلَمْحِ ٱلْبَصَرِ (Kur. xxi. 79).

Twinling, *n.* خَارُوفٌ تَوْءَمٌ.

Twirl, *v.t.* بَرَّمَ ـ بَرَمَ ـ فَتَلَ ـ دَوَّرَ.

Twirl, *v.i.* تَفَتَّلَ ـ إسْتَدَارَ ـ أَدَارَ ـ دَارَ.

Twirl, *n.* لَيَّة ـ فَتْل ـ دَوْر *pl.* أَدْوَار.

Twist, *v.t.* To wind, wind together, جَدَلَ ـ لَوَى ـ لَوَّى ـ فَتَلَ ـ فَتَّلَ ـ أَبْرَمَ ـ بَرَمَ. To —, of the hair, عَقَصَ ـ ضَفَّرَ ـ ضَفَرَ. To distort, of a meaning, عَكَسَ ـ صَحَّفَ ـ حَرَّفَ. To sprain, حَنَا ـ فَسَخَ ـ لَوَى. To — itself, as a serpent, *etc.*, تَعَفَّصَ ـ تَقَوَّرَ ـ لَوَى ـ تَلَوَّى. To — one's self, إلْتَوَى.

Twist, *v.i.* To become twisted, تَلَوَّى ـ إلْتَوَى ـ إنْبَرَمَ ـ تَفَتَّلَ ـ إنْفَتَلَ.

Twist, *n.* A contortion, لِوَآءٌ *pl.* أَلْوِيَة ـ لَيَّة *pl.* لِوًى ـ فَتْلَة. A — of hair, عِقَاص ـ ضَفِيرَة. Braid, قِيطَان *pl.* أَدْوَار دَوْر. A manner of twisting, texture, نَسِيج ـ فِتْلَة. A sprain, حِنَايَة ـ إلْتِوَآء. A —, of bread, رَغِيفٌ مُضَفَّرٌ. *See also* Roll, *n.*

Twisted, *a.* جَدِيل ـ مَجْدُول ـ مُحَبَّل ـ فَتِيل ـ مَفْتُول ـ مُفَتَّل; of a rope of several strands, مَثْلُوث. To be twisted, تَلَوَّى ـ إلْتَوَى ـ تَفَتَّلَ ـ إنْفَتَلَ.

Twister, *n.* One who twists, مُفَتِّل; an instrument for twisting, مِفْتَل.

Twit, *v.t.* قَرَصَ بِ ـ عَيَّرَ ـ قَابَحَ. *See also to* Reproach, *v.t.*

Twitch, *v.t.* To snatch, خَطِفَ ـ إخْتَطَفَ.

Twitch, *n.* A sudden pull, خَطْف ـ خَطْفَة. *See also* Twinge, *n.*

Twitter, *v.i.* As of a bird, شَقْشَقَ ـ غَرَّدَ ـ نَاغَى; of a swallow, وَطْوَطَ ـ وَطَّ. To flutter, خَفَقَ.

Twitter, *n.* Of a bird, شَقْشَقَة ـ تَغْرِيد. A fluttering, خَفْق ـ خُفُوق ـ خَفَقَان.

Twixt, *ad.* *See* Between, Betwixt, *ad.*

Two, *a.* إثْنَان *fem.* إثْنَتَانِ. Two of every kind, إثْنَانِ مِنْ كُلِّ جِنْسٍ. By twos, ثُنَاءَ ـ مَثْنَى ـ إثْنَانِ ٱثْنَانِ. To halt between — opinions, عَرَجَ (or تَرَدَّدَ) بَيْنَ رَأْيَيْنِ.

Two-edged, *a.* ذُو حَدَّيْنِ.

Twofold, *a.* كِفْل ـ مُضَاعَف. To restore — to, ضَاعَفَ لِ. "To them a twofold reward shall be given," أُولَآئِكَ يُؤْتَوْنَ أَجْرَهُمْ مَرَّتَيْنِ (Kur. xxviii. 54). "And whosoever of you [women] shall obey God and His apostle, and shall do that which is right, we will give her a twofold reward," وَمَنْ يَقْنُتْ مِنْكُنَّ لِلّٰهِ وَرَسُولِهِ وَتَعْمَلْ صَالِحًا نُؤْتِهَا أَجْرَهَا مَرَّتَيْنِ (Kur. xxxiii. 31).

Two-handed, *a.* ذُو يَدَيْنِ. *See also* Strong, Robust, *a.*

Twopence, *n.* بَنْسَانِ (مِنَ ٱلسِّكَّةِ ٱلْإِنْكِلِيزِيَّةِ).

Tycoon, *n.* حَاكِمٌ فِي مَمْلَكَةِ يَابَانَ.

Tye, *v.* and *n.* *See* Tie.

Tyke, *n.* حَقِير ـ كَلْب.

Tymbal, *n.* *See* Kettle-drum, *n.*

Tympan, *n.* Of a printing-press, مَحَطُّ ٱلْأَوْرَاقِ لِلطَّبْعِ.

Tympanum, *n.* Of the ear, صِمَاخ ـ أُصْمُوخ.

Tympany, *n.* The being inflated, إنْتِفَاخ.

Type, *n.* A form, as of a disease, *etc.*, فَصْل *pl.* فُصُول. An example, model, ضَرْب ـ قَاعِدَة *pl.* قَوَاعِد. A figure, metaphor, رَمْز *pl.* رُمُوز ـ كِنَايَة ـ مِثَال ـ تَشْبِيه ـ عِبَارَة *pl.* عِبَارَات. Character, kind, مَاهِيَّة ـ جِنْس ـ نَوْع *pl.* أَنْوَاع. A — for printing, حَرْف *pl.* حُرُوف لِلطَّبْعِ.

Type-metal, *n.* مَعْدِنٌ مَخْصُوصٌ لِصَبِّ ٱلْحُرُوفِ لِلطَّبْعِ.

Typhoid, *a.* مُجَانِسُ حُمَّى ٱلتِّيفُوسِ.

Typhoon, *n.* زَوْبَعَة *pl.* زَوَابِعُ ـ أَبُو ٱلزَّوْبَعَةِ.

Typhus, *n.* The fever so called, ٱلتِّيفُوس ـ حُمَّى ٱلتِّيفُوسِ.

Typic, *a.* }
Typical, } مَجَازِيٌّ ـ إسْتِعَارِيٌّ ـ مُعَبِّرٌ عَنْ ـ مُكَنِّيٌّ عَنْ ـ رَمْزِيٌّ. *See also* Symbolical, *a.*

Typically, *ad.* مَجَازًا ـ بِٱلْكِنَايَةِ ـ مُمَاثَلَةً ـ رَمْزًا.

Typicalness, *n.* رَمْز ـ مُمَاثَلَة ـ كِنَايَة.

Typify, *v.t.* كَنَى (or كَنَّى) ـ كَانَ صُورَةَ كَذَا ـ كَانَ رَمْزًا عَنْ كَذَا ـ بِ (or عَنْ) كَذَا.

Typographer, *n.* طابِعُ ٱلْكُتُبِ *pl.* طَوَابِعُ — *vulg.* مَطْبَعْجِي — طَبَّاع.

Typographic, *a.* } Pertaining to types, مَا نِيطَ بِحُرُوفِ ٱلطَّبْعِ ;
Typographical, } to printing, مَا نِيطَ بِطَبْعِ ٱلْكُتُبِ.

Typographically, *ad.* By types, بِحُرُوفِ ٱلطَّبْعِ. After the manner of printing, عَلَى مِنْوَالِ طَبْعِ ٱلْكُتُبِ.

Typography, *n.* صِنَاعَةُ ٱلطَّبْعِ.

Tyrannic, *a.* } بَاغٍ *pl.* بُغَاة — جَائِر *pl.* جَائِرُونَ — عَسُوف
Tyrannical, } جَبَّار — ظَلَّام — ظَالِم.

Tyrannically, *ad.* كَٱلْجَبَّارِ — ظُلْمًا — بِجَوْرٍ وَجَبْرٍ.

Tyrannicalness, *n.* جَوْر — ظُلْم.

Tyrannicide, *n.* A killer of a tyrant, قَاتِلُ ٱلْجَبَّارِ ; the killing of a tyrant, قَتْلُ جَبَّارٍ.

Tyrannize, *v.i.* طَغَى *aor.* يَطْغَى — تَفَرْعَنَ — ظَلَمَ ². To — over, جَارَ عَلَى *aor.* يَجُورُ — قَهَرَ ² — ظَلَمَ ² — بَغَى عَلَى ². Tyrannized over, مَظْلُوم — ظَلِيم. The inhabitants were tyrannized over by him, تَقَمْقَمَتْ مِنْهُ ٱلْأَهَالِي.

Tyrannous, *a.* See Tyrannical, *a.*

Tyranny, *n.* جَوْر — فَرْعَنَة — قَهْرَة — بَغْي — جَوْر — إِعْتِسَاف — ظُلْم — وَجَبْر.

Tyrant, *n.* جَبَّار *pl.* جَبَّارُونَ *and* جَبَابِرَة — سَفَّاح — فِرْعَوْن *pl.* فَرَاعِنَة — ظَلَّام — ظَالِم — سَفَّاك. "And they followed the bidding of every rebellious tyrant," وَٱتَّبَعُوا أَمْرَ كُلِّ جَبَّارٍ عَنِيدٍ (Kur. xii. 62). "You only want to become a tyrant in the land and not one of the peacemakers," إِنْ تُرِيدُ إِلَّا أَنْ تَكُونَ جَبَّارًا فِي ٱلْأَرْضِ وَمَا تُرِيدُ أَنْ تَكُونَ مِنَ ٱلْمُصْلِحِينَ (Kur. xxviii. 18).

Tyrian, *a.* مِنْ مَدِينَةِ صُورِ ٱلْقَدِيمَةِ. Tyrian dye, صِبَاغٌ أُرْجُوَانِيٌّ — لَوْنٌ قِرْمِزِيٌّ — فِرْفِير.

Tyro, *n.* تِلْمِيذ *pl.* تَلَامِيذ — حَدِيث — مُبْتَدِئ. See also Novice, *n.*

Tzar, *n.* See Czar, *n.*

Tzarina, *n.* See Czarina, *n.*

U.

Ubiquitary, *a.* } حَاضِرٌ فِي كُلِّ مَكَانٍ — غَيْرُ مَحْصُورٍ فِي مَكَانٍ. To
Ubiquitous, } be —, عَمَّ ².

Ubiquity, *n.* حُضُورٌ فِي كُلِّ مَكَانٍ — حُضُورٌ مُطْلَقٌ.

Udder, *n.* Of all animals with cloven hoofs, ضَرْع *pl.* ضُرُوع ; of the camel, خِلْف *pl.* خُلُوف. Large in the —, ضَرِيع.

Uglily, *ad.* With deformity, بِسَمَاجَةٍ — بِشَنَاعَةٍ — بِقُبْحٍ — بِقَبَاحَةٍ. Vilely, بِذِلَّةٍ — بِشَنَاعَةٍ — بِحَقَارَةٍ — حَقَارَةً — بِوَخَاشَةٍ.

Ugliness, *n.* Deformity, سَمَاجَة — بَشَاعَة — قُبْح — قَبَاحَة. Turpitude, مَذَمَّة — قَبَاحَة — سُوء — شَنَاعَة — حَقَارَة — ذِلَّة. Ugliness is the protection of woman, (*prov.*) ٱلْقُبْحُ حَارِسُ ٱلْمَرْأَةِ.

Ugly, *a.* Not handsome, دَمِيم — سَمِيج — شَتِيم — قَبِيح — بَشِع — بَشِعُ ٱلْمَنْظَرِ — قَبِيحُ ٱلْمَنْظَرِ — مَغْسُوخ. Serious, dangerous, of a disease, *etc.*, سَيِّئٌ — ثَقِيل — خَطِير : Such an one is in an —, severe, state of disease, فُلَانٌ مِغْزَازُ ٱلْمَرَضِ. Vile, ذَمِيم. To be —, deformed, دَمَّ ² — سَمُجَ ² — قَبُحَ ² — سَمُجَ ² — قَبَّحَ ; to make —, ذَمَّ ². To do what is —, to act vilely, أَسَاءَ ² — أَذَمَّ — أَقْبَحَ — أَذَمَّ.

Ukase, *n.* أَمْرٌ (*or*) فِرْمَانٌ مِنْ قَيْصَرِ ٱلرُّوسِيَا.

Ulcer, *n.* قَرْح *pl.* قُرُوح — قَرْحَة. An — on the foot, شَأْفَة. An — that penetrates into the belly, دُبَيْلَة — دُبْلَة. Ulcers on the side that penetrate inwardly, دُبَال — نَقَّابَات.

Ulcerate, *v.i.* غَبَرَ ² — تَهَذَّأَ — تَقَرَّحَ.

Ulcerate, *v.t.* أَقْرَحَ — قَرَّحَ ².

Ulceration, *n.* تَقَرُّح. Ulceration of the lungs, سُحَاف ; having — of the lungs, مَسْحُوف.

Ulcerated, *a.* } قَرِح *pl.* قَرِحٌ — قَرْح — قُرُوح — قَرِيح — مَقْرُوح — قُرَاحِيّ.
Ulcerous, } An — foot, رِجْلٌ مَشْؤُوفَة.

Ulna, *n.* ٱلذِّرَاعُ — ٱلزَّنْدُ ٱلْأَسْفَلُ — ٱلْأَسْفَلُ مِنَ ٱلزَّنْدَيْنِ.

Ulnar, *a.* مَا نِيطَ بِٱلزَّنْدِ ٱلْأَسْفَلِ.

Ult. *for* Ultimo, *ad.* ٱلشَّهْرَ ٱلْمَاضِي.

Ulterior, *a.* Farther, أَبْعَدُ. To come, coming, آتٍ بَعْدُ. Another, آخَر. An — object, نَصْبُ عَيْنٍ.

Ultima ratio, *n.* حُجَّةٌ أَخِيرَةٌ. *Ultima ratio regum*, ٱلْحُجَّةُ ٱلْأَخِيرَةُ عِنْدَ ٱلْمُلُوكِ ٱلسَّيْفُ وَٱلْحَرْبُ.

Ultimate, *a.* Most remote, ٱلْأَقْصَى — ٱلْأَبْعَدُ. Last, أَخِير. His — object was to..., كَانَ مَقْصُودُهُ ٱلْأَخِيرُ كَذَا. An — condition, مَعَاد.

Ultimately, *ad.* أَخِيرًا — آخِرًا — بِأَخَرَةٍ. He — came, جَاءَ آخِرًا.

Ultimatum, *n.* قَرَارٌ أَخِيرٌ — بَلَاغٌ أَخِيرٌ — آخِرُ كَلَامٍ — تَكْلِيفٌ أَخِيرٌ.

To send an — to, بَلَّغَ قَرَارًا أَخِيرًا. The English — to the Amir of Afghanistan, بَلَاغُ إِنْكِلْتَرَةَ ٱلْأَخِيرُ إِلَى أَمِيرِ أَفْغَانِسْتَانَ.

Ultra, *a.* فَائِق — *pl.* فُوَقَآءُ — زَائِد — مُفْرِط.

Ultraism, *n.* أُصُولٌ مُفْرِطَةٌ — قَوْلٌ مُفْرِطٌ — إِفْرَاط.

Ultra-liberal, *a.* مُفْرِطٌ فِي مَادَّةِ ٱلْحُرِّيَّةِ.

Ultra-liberal, *n.* مُشِطٌّ فِي ٱلْحُرِّيَّةِ — مُتَعَصِّبٌ لِإِفْرَاطِ ٱلْحُرِّيَّةِ.

Ultra-liberalism, *n.* التَّعَصُّبُ لِإِفْرَاطِ ٱلْحُرِّيَّةِ.

Ultramarine, *a.* مَا وَرَآءَ ٱلْبَحْرِ — عِبْرَ ٱلْبَحْرِ.

Ultramarine, *n.* The colour, لَوْنٌ لَازَوَرْدِيٌّ.

Ultramontane, *a.* Beyond the mountains, مَا وَرَآءَ ٱلْجِبَالِ. Ultramontane doctrines, extreme views of the Pope's supremacy, آرَآءٌ مُفْرِطَةٌ فِي عَقِيدَةِ رِئَاسَةِ ٱلْبَابَا.

Ultramontanism, *n.* غَيْرَةٌ مُفْرِطَةٌ عَلَى رِئَاسَةِ ٱلْبَابَا.

Ultramontanist, *n.* مُتَحَمِّسٌ فِي — مُبَالِغٌ فِي ٱلتَّعَصُّبِ لِلْبَابَا — مَذْهَبُ ٱلْبَابَا.

Ultramundane, *a.* سَمَاوِيٌّ — فَوْقَ ٱلْعَالَمِ.

Umbel, *n.* زَهْرَةٌ تُشْبِهُ ٱلْمِظَلَّةَ.

Umbellar, *a.* فِي شَكْلِ ٱلْمِظَلَّةِ.

Umbelliferous, *a.* حَامِلُ زَهْرٍ فِي شَكْلِ ٱلْمِظَلَّةِ.

Umber, *n.* صِبَاغٌ بِلَوْنِ ٱلْقَهْوَةِ — لَوْنٌ مُعْتِمٌ.

Umbilic, *n.* The centre, as of a circle, مَرْكَز. *See also* Navel, *n.*

Umbilical, *a.* مُتَعَلِّقٌ بِٱلسُّرَّةِ. The — cord, السُّرَّةُ.

Umbrage, *n.* Suspicion, اِرْتِيَاب — شَكٌّ.

To give one umbrage, أَلْقَى فِي — شَكًّا — شَكَّكَ فِي — أَرَابَ.

To take umbrage, اِرْتَابَ فِي — أَرَابَ — شَكَّ فِي.

Umbrageous, *a.* ظَلِيل — مُظَلَّل. *See also* Shady, *a.*

Umbrageousness, *n.* ظِلٌّ — فَيْءٌ — تَفِئَة.

Umbrella, *n.* شَمْسِيَّة — غَاشِيَة — ظُلَّة.

Umpirage, *n.* مَقَامُ ٱلْفَيْصَلِ — فَصْلُ ٱلْحُكْمِ — الفَيْصَل.

Umpire, *n.* وَكِيلٌ عُرْفِيٌّ — ثَالِثُ ٱلْحَكَمَيْنِ — حَكَمٌ ثَالِثٌ — قَاضٍ *pl.* قُضَاة — فَيْصَلِيٌّ — فَيْصَل. An — in a game, رَقِيب — أَمِين — رَابِئٌ.

Unabashed, *a.* غَيْرُ مَخْجُولٍ — غَيْرُ مَحْشُوم.

Unabated, *a.* عَلَى مَا كَانَ — بِلَا تَغْيِيرٍ — غَيْرُ مُرَخًّى — غَيْرُ مُنْتَقِصٍ.

Unable, *a.* لَيْسَ لِ — قُدْرَةٌ — عَدِيمُ ٱلِٱقْتِدَارِ — قَاصِرُ ٱلْيَدِ — عَاجِز — غَيْرُ مُقْتَدِرٍ — عَلَى. I am — to speak at length on this matter, لَيْسَ فِي وُسْعِي أَنْ أُطِيلَ ٱلْكَلَامَ فِي هٰذِهِ ٱلْخُطَّةِ.

Unabolished, *a.* غَيْرُ مُلْغًى — جَارٍ — غَيْرُ مُبَطَّلٍ — غَيْرُ مُنْتَقِضٍ.

Unabridged, *a.* عَلَى تَمَامِهِ — غَيْرُ مُخْتَصَرٍ.

Unabrogated, *a.* *See* Unabolished, *a.*

Unaccented, *a.* Not to be accented in pronunciation, يُلْفَظُ بِدُونِ نَبْرَةٍ. Without vowel points, غَيْرُ مُشَكَّلٍ — غَيْرُ مُعْجَمٍ.

Unacceptable, *a.* Not acceptable, غَيْرُ مَقْبُولٍ. Disagreeable, لَيْسَ بِحَسَنٍ — سَيِّئٌ — كَرِيه.

Unacceptableness, *n.* سُخْط — سَخَط — كَرَاهَة — عَدَمُ رِضًى.

Unacceptably, *ad.* سَخَطًا — بِكَرَاهَةٍ — بِعَدَمِ رِضًى.

Unaccepted, *a.* غَيْرُ مَرْضِيٍّ — غَيْرُ مَقْبُولٍ.

Unacclimated, *a.* غَيْرُ مُتَعَوِّدٍ عَلَى ٱلْهَوَآءِ (or ٱلْمَنَاخِ).

Unaccommodating, *a.* Without kindliness, عَدِيمُ ٱللَّطَافَةِ — عَدِيمُ ٱلْمَعْرُوفِ. Impolite, فَظٌّ — جَافٍ — حُوشِيٌّ.

Unaccompanied, *a.* مُنْفَرِد — وَحِيد — شَاذٌّ — مِنْ غَيْرِ رُفَقَآءَ. To be —, كَانَ وَحْدَهُ — اِسْتَفْرَدَ — اِنْفَرَدَ.

Unaccomplished, *a.* Not finished, غَيْرُ مُتَمَّمٍ — غَيْرُ مُكَمَّلٍ. Wanting, نَاقِص. Without accomplishments, عَدِيمُ ٱلشَّمَائِلِ — قَلِيلُ ٱلْفَضَائِلِ.

Unaccountable, *a.* Irresponsible, غَيْرُ مُطَالَبٍ بِ — غَيْرُ مَسْؤُولٍ. Strange, wonderful, غَرِيب — عَجِيب — نَادِر. Difficult, عَسِير — مُشْكِل.

Unaccountableness, *n.* Irresponsibility, عَدَمُ مَسْؤُولِيَّةٍ. Strangeness, غَرَابَة — عَجَب. Difficulty, obscureness, مُشْكِلَة — عُسْرَة — عِيَاص.

Unaccountably, *ad.* Strangely, بِنَوْعٍ عَجِيبٍ — بِنَوْعٍ غَرِيبٍ.

Unaccredited, *a.* Not charged with a mission, غَيْرُ مُفَوَّضٍ — غَيْرُ مَأْمُورٍ — غَيْرُ مُوَكَّلٍ.

Unaccustomed, *a.* Not used to, غَيْرُ مُعْتَادٍ — غَيْرُ مُتَعَوِّدٍ عَلَى; not trained, غَيْرُ مُمَرَّنٍ — غَيْرُ مَرُوضٍ — غَيْرُ دَارِبٍ.

Unachievable, *a.* Impossible, مُحَال — غَيْرُ مُمْكِنٍ.

Unacknowledged, *n.* Ignored, مَجْهُول. Repudiated, مَرْدُود — غَيْرُ مَقْبُولٍ — مُنْكَر — مَرْفُوض. Not admitted, غَيْرُ مُسَلَّمٍ بِهِ. Not requited, غَيْرُ مُجَازًى — غَيْرُ مُكَافًى — غَيْرُ مُثَوَّبٍ.

Unacquainted, *a.* Not knowing, غَيْرُ عَارِفٍ بِ — غَيْرُ مُطَّلِعٍ عَلَى — غَيْرُ خَبِيرٍ بِ. Not versed in, غَيْرُ مَاهِرٍ — غَيْرُ مُتْقِنٍ فِي.

Unacted, *a.* Not performed, غَيْرُ مُنَفَّذٍ — لَمْ يُجْرَ فِعْلًا. Not played, غَيْرُ مَلْعُوبٍ بِهِ.

Unacquired, *a.* Not acquired, غَيْرُ مُحَصَّلٍ. Natural, غَرِيزِيٌّ — طَبِيعِيٌّ — ذَاتِيٌّ.

Unactuated, *a.* Not moved to, غَيْرُ مُحَرَّضٍ عَلَى — غَيْرُ مُغْرًى بِ — غَيْرُ مُحَرَّكٍ عَلَى.

Unadapted, *a.* Not adapted to, غَيْرُ جَدِيرٍ لِ — غَيْرُ خَلِيقٍ لِ — غَيْرُ مُنَاسِبٍ لِ.

Unadjusted, *a.* غَيْرُ مُنَظَّمٍ ـ غَيْرُ مُصَحَّحٍ ـ غَيْرُ مُعَدَّلٍ.

Unadmired, *a.* غَيْرُ مُعْتَبَرٍ ـ غَيْرُ مُعْجَبٍ.

Unadmonished, *a.* غَيْرُ مَنْصُوحٍ ـ غَيْرُ مُوَبَّخٍ ـ غَيْرُ مُنَبَّهٍ.

Unadorned, *a.* سَاذِجٌ ـ سَاذِجٌ ـ غَيْرُ مُزَخْرَفٍ ـ غَيْرُ مُزَيَّنٍ.

Unadulterated, *a.* غَيْرُ مَغْشُوشٍ ـ مَحْضٌ ـ صِرْفٌ ـ بَحْتٌ; of coin, غَيْرُ مَزْغُولٍ. Pure, خَالِصٌ ـ صَافٍ ـ نَصُوحٌ. True, genuine, حَقِيقِيٌّ.

Unadvisable, *a.* غَيْرُ مُلَائِمٍ ـ غَيْرُ مُوَافِقٍ ـ غَيْرُ مُنَاسِبٍ.

Unadvised, *a.* أَبْلَهُ ـ غَافِلٌ ـ عَدِيمُ ٱلتَّبَصُّرِ ـ مَاجِنٌ.

Unadvisedly, *ad.* بِبَلَاهَةٍ ـ بِلَا ٱحْتِيَاطٍ ـ بِغَيْرِ ٱمْتِيَازٍ ـ بِلَا مُلَاحَظَةٍ.
To speak —, فَرَطَ بِٱلْكَلَامِ.

Unadvisedness, *n.* بَلَاهَةٌ ـ بَلَهٌ ـ تَهَوُّرٌ ـ عَدَمُ فِطْنَةٍ ـ غَبَاوَةٌ.

Unaffected, *a.* Not affected, moved, غَيْرُ مُتَأَثِّرٍ ـ عَدِيمُ ٱلتَّجُوعِ ـ غَيْرُ مُتَحَرِّكٍ. Without affectation, عَدِيمُ ٱلتَّصَلُّفِ ـ غَيْرُ مُتَصَنِّعٍ ـ عَدِيمُ ٱلْمُبَاهَاةِ. Real, خَالِصٌ ـ حَقِيقِيٌّ.

Unaffectedly, *ad.* Sincerely, عَنْ صَمِيمٍ ـ بِخُلُوصٍ ـ بِصَفَاوَةٍ ـ عَنْ إِخْلَاصٍ ـ ٱلْقَلْبِ.

Unaided, *a.* مِنْ غَيْرِ مُعَاوَنَةٍ. Alone, of or by one's self, وَحْدَهُ *fem.* وَحْدَهَا.

Unalarmed, *a.* غَيْرُ مَرْعُوبٍ ـ غَيْرُ مَرْهُوبٍ.

Unalienable, *a.* مَحْبُوسٌ ـ حَبِيسٌ. *See* Inalienable, *a.*

Unallowable, *a.* غَيْرُ مُبَاحٍ ـ غَيْرُ جَائِزٍ ـ غَيْرُ مَقْبُولٍ.

Unalluring, *a.* تَافِهٌ ـ بَارِدٌ ـ غَيْرُ ذِي حَظٍّ ـ غَيْرُ أَنِيقٍ.

Unalloyed, *a.* خَالِصٌ ـ غَيْرُ مَخْلُوطٍ. *See also under* Unadulterated, *a.*

Unalterable, *a.* ثَابِتٌ ـ عَدِيمُ ٱلتَّغْيِيرِ ـ غَيْرُ مُتَغَيِّرٍ ـ لَا يَتَغَيَّرُ.

Unalterably, *ad.* بِثَبَاتٍ ـ بِدُونِ تَغَيُّرٍ ـ بِلَا تَبْدِيلٍ ـ بِلَا تَغْيِيرٍ.

Unaltered, *a.* مِثْلَ مَا كَانَ ـ غَيْرُ مُتَغَيِّرٍ. *See also* Identical, *a.*

Unamazed, *a.* غَيْرُ مُعْجَبٍ ـ غَيْرُ مُتَحَيِّرٍ.

Unambiguous, *a.* غَيْرُ ـ غَيْرُ مُشْتَبِهٍ ـ صَرِيحٌ ـ وَاضِحٌ ـ مُحْكَمٌ ـ مُبِينٌ ـ مُشْتَبِهٍ.

Unambiguously, *ad.* بِبَيَانٍ ـ بِوُضُوحٍ ـ بِصَرَاحَةٍ ـ بِغَيْرِ ٱلْتِبَاسٍ.

Unambitious, *a.* غَيْرُ نَافِسٍ ـ غَيْرُ مُسْتَعْظِمٍ ـ غَيْرُ بَاغٍ.

Unamended, *a.* عَلَى مَا كَانَ ـ غَيْرُ مُصَحَّحٍ ـ غَيْرُ مُصْلَحٍ ـ بِلَا ٱسْتِتْبَابٍ.

Unamiable, *a.* وَعِقٌ ـ شَرِسٌ ـ غَيْرُ وَدُودٍ ـ غَيْرُ أَنِيسٍ.

Unanimated, *a.* Without life, لَا رُوحَ لَهُ ـ غَيْرُ ذِي نَفْسٍ. Without animation, جَامِدٌ ـ مُغْتَمٌّ ـ بَارِدٌ ـ حَزِينٌ.

Unanimity, *n.* ٱتِّحَادٌ ـ ٱتِّفَاقٌ ـ مُوَافَقَةٌ.

Unanimous, *a.* مُتَّحِدٌ ـ مُلْتَئِمٌ ـ مُتَّفِقٌ: The council was not —, أَرْبَابُ ٱلْمَجْلِسِ لَمْ يَكُونُوا مُتَّفِقِينَ.

Unanimously, *ad.* عَلَى ٱلِٱتِّفَاقِ ـ ٱتِّفَاقًا ـ ٱتِّحَادًا.

Unanimousness, *n.* *See* Unanimity, *n.*

Unannounced, *a.* Not proclaimed, غَيْرُ مُشَاعٍ بِهِ ـ غَيْرُ مُشْتَهَرٍ. Without introduction, بِدُونِ تَعْرِيفٍ.

Unanswerable, *a.* شَافٍ ـ لَا يُجْرَحُ ـ لَا يُرَدُّ عَلَيْهِ ـ لَا جَوَابَ لَهُ ـ لَا يُنْكَرُ.

Unanswerableness, *n.* عَدَمُ مُنَازَعَةٍ ـ عَدَمُ إِمْكَانِ ٱلْجَوَابِ عَلَيْهِ ـ حَقِيقَةٌ ـ فِيهِ.

Unanswerably, *ad.* بِمَا ـ مِنْ غَيْرِ ٱعْتِرَاضٍ ـ مِنْ غَيْرِ نِزَاعٍ ـ لَا يُرَدُّ عَلَيْهِ.

Unanswered, *a.* بِلَا جَوَابٍ ـ غَيْرُ مُجَاوَبٍ.

Unanticipated, *a.* غَيْرُ مُتَرَقَّبٍ ـ غَيْرُ مُنْتَظَرٍ.

Unappalled, *a.* غَيْرُ مُتَخَوِّفٍ ـ غَيْرُ مُهْتَالٍ ـ غَيْرُ مُرْتَعِبٍ ـ غَيْرُ مُخَوَّفٍ.

Unapparent, *a.* غَائِبٌ ـ بَاطِنٌ ـ خَفِيٌّ ـ غَمِيسٌ ـ غَيْرُ ظَاهِرٍ *pl.* غُيَّابٌ.

Unappeasable, *a.* تَسْكِينُهُ غَيْرُ مُمْكِنٍ.

Unappeased, *a.* غَيْرُ مُسَكَّنٍ.

Unappreciated, *a.* قِيمَتُهُ غَيْرُ مَعْرُوفَةٍ ـ غَيْرُ مُعَزَّزٍ ـ غَيْرُ مُعْتَبَرٍ.

Unapprehended, *a.* Not seized, مُطْلَقُ ٱلْعِنَانِ ـ غَيْرُ مَمْسُوكٍ. Not understood, غَيْرُ مُدْرَكٍ ـ غَيْرُ مَفْهُومٍ.

Unapprehensive, *a.* *See* Fearless, *a.*

Unapprized, *a.* Not apprized of, غَيْرُ مُشْعَرٍ ـ غَيْرُ مُخْبَرٍ ـ غَيْرُ مُبَشَّرٍ.

Unapproachable, *a.* لَا يُقْرَبُ إِلَيْهِ ـ ٱلدُّنُوُّ مِنْهُ مُحَالٌ ـ لَا يُدْنَى مِنْهُ. *See also* Inaccessible, *a.*

Unapproachably, *ad.* بِعَدَمِ إِمْكَانِ ٱلدُّنُوِّ مِنْهُ ـ بِتَمَنُّعٍ.

Unapproached, *a.* غَيْرُ مَدْنُوٍّ مِنْهُ ـ غَيْرُ مَوْصُولٍ إِلَيْهِ.

Unappropriated, *a.* غَيْرُ مُتَخَصِّصٍ ـ غَيْرُ مُخَصَّصٍ.

Unapproved, *a.* غَيْرُ مُسْتَصْوَبٍ ـ غَيْرُ مُسْتَحْسَنٍ.

Unapprovingly, *ad.* بِعَدَمِ ٱسْتِصْوَابٍ ـ بِعَدَمِ ٱسْتِحْسَانٍ.

Unapt, *a.* Not ready, غَيْرُ مُتَوَكِّدٍ ـ غَيْرُ عَتِيدٍ ـ غَيْرُ مُسْتَعِدٍّ. Awkward, أَخْرَقُ. Not suitable, غَيْرُ مُنَاسِبٍ. Not capable of, عَاجِزٌ عَنْ. Ignorant, غَبِيٌّ ـ جَاهِلٌ ـ غَيْرُ كُفُوءٍ.

Unaptly, *ad.* Awkwardly, بِقِلَّةِ مَعْرِفَةٍ ـ بِخُرْقٍ ـ خُرْقَةً. Inappropriately, بِقِلَّةِ لِيَاقَةٍ ـ بِغَيْرِ مُنَاسَبَةٍ ـ بِغَلَاظَةٍ.

Unaptness, *n.* Unreadiness, عَدَمُ ٱسْتِعْدَادٍ. Awkwardness, خُرْقَةٌ ـ خُرْقٌ. Inappropriateness, عَدَمُ لِيَاقَةٍ ـ عَدَمُ مُنَاسَبَةٍ.

Unargued, *a.* مَا حَصَلَ ـ غَيْرُ مُحْتَجٍّ فِيهِ ـ غَيْرُ مَبْحُوثٍ عَنْهُ ـ تَفَاوُضٌ فِيهِ.

Unarmed, *a.* لا سِلاحَ لَهُ ـ أَعْزَلُ.

Unarranged, *a.* غَيْرُ مُنَظَّمٍ ـ بِلا نِظامٍ ـ غَيْرُ مُرَتَّبٍ ـ بِلا تَرْتِيبٍ ـ غَيْرُ مُنَسَّقٍ.

Unascertainable, *a.* لا يُتَحَقَّقُ ـ تَحْقِيقُهُ غَيْرُ مُمْكِنٍ.

Unascertained, *a.* غَيْرُ مَعْلُومٍ ـ غَيْرُ مُحَقَّقٍ.

Unashamed, *a.* غَيْرُ مُسْتَحٍ ـ غَيْرُ مُحْتَشِمٍ ـ غَيْرُ خَجِلٍ.

Unasked, *a.* غَيْرُ مَطْلُوبٍ. Uninvited, غَيْرُ مَعْزُومٍ ـ غَيْرُ مَدْعُوٍّ. Voluntary, اِخْتِيارِيٌّ ـ مِنْ ذاتِ نَفْسِهِ ـ مِنْ تِلْقاءِ نَفْسِهِ ـ تَبَرُّعًا بِهِ. To do a thing —, تَبَرَّعَ بِ.

Unaspirated, *a.* لا يُلْفَظُ بِهِ مِنَ ٱلْحَلْقِ.

Unaspiring, *a.* غَيْرُ حَرِيصٍ ـ قَلِيلُ ٱلْحِرْصِ ـ قَلِيلُ ٱلطَّمَعِ.

Unassailable, *a.* That cannot be assailed, أَعَزُّ ـ عَزِيزٌ ـ الْهُجُومُ عَلَيْهِ مُحالٌ. To be —, عَزَّ ـِ. *See also* Unanswerable, *a.*; *also* Inaccessible, *a.*

Unassailableness, *n.* عِزٌّ ـ عِزَّةٌ ـ عَدَمُ إِمْكانِ ٱلْهُجُومِ عَلَيْهِ ـ تَمَنُّعٌ ـ مَناعَةٌ. *See also* Unanswerableness, *n.*

Unassailably, *ad.* عِزَّةً ـ بِعِزَّةٍ ـ بِعَدَمِ إِمْكانِ ٱلْهُجُومِ عَلَيْهِ ـ بِتَمَنُّعٍ ـ بِمَناعَةٍ. *See also* Unanswerably, *ad.*

Unassailed, *a.* ما بُطِشَ بِهِ ـ ما هُجِمَ عَلَيْهِ.

Unassayed, *a.* غَيْرُ مُمْتَحَنٍ ـ غَيْرُ مُخْتَبَرٍ ـ غَيْرُ مُجَرَّبٍ.

Unassembled, *a.* شَتٌّ ـ مُتَفَرِّقٌ ـ غَيْرُ مُجْتَمِعٍ ـ غَيْرُ مُلْتَمٍّ.

Unassessed, *a.* غَيْرُ مَحْسُوبٍ لِلْجِزْيَةِ ـ غَيْرُ مُقَدَّرٍ لِلْفُرْضَةِ.

Unassignable, *a.* That cannot be transferred, حَبِيسٌ ـ نَقْلُهُ مُحالٌ ـ مَحْبُوسٌ. That cannot be accounted for, غَيْرُ قابِلٍ ٱلْبَيانَ ـ تَحْدِيدُهُ مُحالٌ.

Unassigned, *a.* Not appointed, غَيْرُ مُعَيَّنٍ. Not explained, غَيْرُ مُصَرَّحٍ ـ غَيْرُ مُبَيَّنٍ.

Unassisted, *a.* *See* Unaided, *a.*

Unassuming, *a.* غَيْرُ مُتَكَبِّرٍ ـ مُحْتَشِمٌ ـ مُؤَدَّبٌ ـ *colloq.* نَفْسُهُ صَغِيرَةٌ.

Unassured, *a.* As in an insurance office, بِلا سِيكُورْتا ـ بِلا تَأْمِينٍ ـ غَيْرُ مُسَوْكَرٍ ـ غَيْرُ مُضَمَّنٍ فِي سِيكُورْتا.

Unatonable, *a.* لا يُعْفَى عَنْهُ ـ لا يُكَفَّرُ.

Unatoned, *a.* غَيْرُ مُعْفًى عَنْهُ ـ غَيْرُ مُكَفَّرٍ.

Unattached, *a.* غَيْرُ مَرْبُوطٍ ـ غَيْرُ مُعَلَّقٍ ـ شاذٌّ ـ شَتاتٌ. On the unattached list, فِي جَدْوَلِ ٱلْمُتَقاعِدِينَ ـ مُتَقاعِدٌ.

Unattackable, *a.* *See* Unassailable, *a.*

Unattainable, *a.* غَيْرُ مُمْكِنٍ إِدْراكُهُ ـ نَوالُهُ مُحالٌ ـ غَيْرُ إِلْحاقُهُ ـ مُمْكِنٍ ـ عَزِيزٌ ـ أَعَزُّ ـ مُحالٌ. The thing was —, عَزَّ ٱلشَّيْءُ ـِ. It was — by me, بَرِقَ بِيَ ٱلْأَمْرُ. To be —, عَزَّ ـِ. اِعْتَزَّ ٱلشَّيْءُ.

Unattainableness, *n.* عَدَمُ إِمْكانٍ ـ عَدَمُ إِمْكانِ بُلُوغِهِ ـ عِزٌّ ـ عِزَّةٌ.

Unattained, *a.* غَيْرُ مَلْحُوقٍ ـ غَيْرُ مُدْرَكٍ.

Unattempted, *a.* ما سَعَى فِيهِ أَحَدٌ ـ ما عَسَمَ فِيهِ أَحَدٌ. To leave nothing —, صَرَفَ ٱلْمَساعِيَ ٱلْمُمْكِنَةَ ـِ.

Unattended, *a.* Unaccompanied, بِلا رُفَقاءَ. Without followers, بِلا تابِعِينَ. Without result, بِلا نَتِيجَةٍ ـ بِلا تَبِعَةٍ. Not attended by a physician, لَمْ يَقِفْ عَلَيْهِ طَبِيبٌ ـ غَيْرُ مُعالَجٍ.

Unattested, *a.* غَيْرُ مُحَقَّقٍ ـ غَيْرُ مَشْهُودٍ بِهِ. Not sworn, غَيْرُ مُسْتَحْلَفٍ.

Unattracted, *a.* غَيْرُ مَجْلُوبٍ ـ غَيْرُ مَجْذُوبٍ.

Unattractive, *a.* *See* Unalluring, *a.*

Unauthentic, *a.* Apocryphal, ذُو رِيبَةٍ ـ مُرِيبٌ. Not official, غَيْرُ رَسْمِيٍّ.

Unauthenticated, *a.* غَيْرُ مُثْبَتٍ ـ غَيْرُ مُحَقَّقٍ ـ غَيْرُ مُصَدَّقٍ.

Unauthorized, *a.* Of a person, غَيْرُ مُتَصَرِّفٍ فِي ـ غَيْرُ مُفَوَّضٍ. Without permission, بِلا إِذْنٍ ـ غَيْرُ مُجَوَّزٍ ـ غَيْرُ مُسَوَّغٍ ـ بِلا رُخْصَةٍ.

Unavailable, *a.* Not forthcoming, لا يُوجَدُ ـ غَيْرُ عَتِيدٍ ـ غَيْرُ حاضِرٍ.

Unavailing, *a.* بَطّالٌ ـ باطِلٌ ـ غَيْرُ مُفِيدٍ ـ غَيْرُ طائِلٍ.

Unavenged, *a.* بِلا ٱنْتِقامٍ ـ غَيْرُ مُنْتَقَمٍ.

Unavoidable, *a.* لا بُدَّ مِنْهُ ـ لا مَحالَةَ مِنْهُ. To be —, حَقَّ ـِ ـُ ـ أَوْجَبَ. To make —, حَتَمَ ـِ ـ حَتَمَ بِ ـِ ـ اِحْتَتَمَ.

Unavoidably, *ad.* Inevitably, مِنْ كُلِّ بُدٍّ ـ مِنْ غَيْرِ مَفَرٍّ ـ لا وَهْمَ. Necessarily, بِٱلضَّرُورَةِ ـ عَنِ ٱضْطِرارٍ.

Unavowed, *a.* غَيْرُ مُعْتَرَفٍ بِهِ ـ غَيْرُ مُقَرٍّ بِهِ.

Unawakened, *a.* غَيْرُ مُنْتَبِهٍ ـ غَيْرُ مُتَيَقِّظٍ. *See also* Impenitent, *a.*

Unaware, *a.* Inattentive, غافِلٌ ـ ساهٍ. Ignorant, not knowing, غَيْرُ مُشْعَرٍ بِ ـ غَيْرُ عالِمٍ بِ ـ غَيْرُ مُخْبَرٍ بِ.

Unawares, *ad.* عَلَى ٱلْغَفْلَةِ ـ بَغْتَةً ـ عَلَى ٱلْفَوْرِ ـ اِلْتِقاطًا. To take —, بَغَتَ ـ بَدَهَ ـَ ـ فالَتَ. To come upon one —, بادَهَ. To steal away —, اِنْسَلَّ خُفْيَةً. To take or come upon one —, in a treacherous manner, خابَ.

Unawed, *a.* *See* Unappalled, *a.*

Unbalanced, *a.* Not poised, غَيْرُ مُعادَلٍ ـ غَيْرُ راكِدٍ. Not settled, as of accounts, غَيْرُ مُجْزَءٍ ـ غَيْرُ مَسْدُودٍ. Not paid, غَيْرُ مُوفًى. Unsteady, فَرّارٌ ـ طائِشٌ ـ قَلّاعٌ.

Unballast, *v.t.* أَخْرَجَ ٱلصّابُورَةَ مِنْ.

Unbar, *v.t.* رَفَعَ ٱلْمِغْلاقَ ـَ. To unfasten, فَتَحَ ـَ ـ حَلَّ ـُ.

Unbearable, *a.* لا يُحْتَمَلُ ـ لا يُطاقُ. *See also* Unsufferable, *a.*

Unbeaten, *a.* Of a road, غَيْرُ مَسْلُوكٍ ـ غَيْرُ مُذَلَّلٍ ـ غَيْرُ مُعَبَّدٍ.

Unbecoming, *a.* Indecorous, غَيْرُ مُنَاسِبٍ ـ غَيْرُ لَائِقٍ. Not suitable to, غَيْرُ صَالِحٍ لِ ـ غَيْرُ جَدِيرٍ بِ ـ غَيْرُ خَلِيقٍ لِ. Not pretty, بِلَا طَلَاوَةٍ ـ غَيْرُ ظَرِيفٍ ـ غَيْرُ كَيِّسٍ ـ غَيْرُ أَنِيقٍ.

Unbecomingly, *ad.* بِعَدَمِ مُنَاسَبَةٍ ـ بِغَيْرِ مُلَاءَمَةٍ ـ بِعَدَمِ لِيَاقَةٍ.

Unbefitting, *a.* Not suitable to, as being out of place in, غَيْرُ مَحَلٍّ لِ ـ غَيْرُ خَلِيقٍ لِ.

Unbefriended, *a.* ضَيَاعٌ ـ مُحْتَاجٌ ـ مَتْرُوكٌ ـ وَحِيدٌ ـ مُسَيَّبٌ.

Unbegotten, *a.* Not imagined, غَيْرُ مُتَصَوَّرٍ ـ غَيْرُ مُحْدَثٍ. Uncreated, غَيْرُ مَخْلُوقٍ. Unborn, غَيْرُ مَوْلُودٍ.

Unbeguile, *v.t.* أَصْحَى مِنَ الضَّلَالَةِ.

Unbeheld, *a.* غَيْرُ مَلْمُوحٍ.

Unbelief, *n.* Disbelief, عَدَمُ إِيمَانٍ. Refusal of belief, زَنْدَقَةٌ ـ إِنْكَارٌ ـ كُفْرٌ.

Unbeliever, *n.* / **Unbelieving**, *a.* } Of little faith, قَلِيلُ الْإِيمَانِ. An infidel, كَافِرٌ *pl.* كُفَّارٌ ـ زِنْدِيقٌ *pl.* زَنَادِقَةٌ. To be an —, كَفَرَ ُ. "And let not the unbelief of the unbelieving grieve thee," وَمَنْ كَفَرَ فَلَا يَحْزُنْكَ كُفْرُهُ (Kur. xxxi. 22).

Unbelievingly, *ad.* بِعَدَمِ إِيمَانٍ ـ بِقِلَّةِ إِيمَانٍ.

Unbend, *v.t.* To straighten, عَادَلَ ـ عَدَّلَ. To loosen, untie, حَلَّ ُ ـ فَكَّ ُ. To make less tense, رَاخَى ـ أَرْخَى. To weaken, أَضْعَفَ ـ أَوْهَنَ. To — one's self, to take repose, إِسْتَرَاحَ; to condescend, تَوَاضَعَ ـ تَنَازَلَ. To unbend one's self to one, as in conversation, إِنْبَسَطَ إِلَى.

Unbend, *v.i.* To become loose, تَرَاخَى ـ إِرْتَخَى.

Unbending, *a.* Not to be bent, مَتِينٌ ـ صُلْبٌ ـ لَا يَنْحَنِي. Unyielding, لَا يَلِينُ. Obstinate, وَعِقٌ ـ مَرِيدٌ ـ عَنِيدٌ. Reserved, in conversation, *etc.*, غَيْرُ مُنْبَسِطِ اللِّسَانِ. *See also* Uncommunicative, *a.*

Unbendingly, *ad.* Inflexibly, بِإِصْرَارٍ ـ بِصَلَابَةٍ.

Unbeneficial, *a.* بَاطِلٌ ـ لَا نَفْعَ فِيهِ ـ غَيْرُ نَافِعٍ ـ غَيْرُ طَائِلٍ.

Unbeneficed, *a.* بِلَا إِقْطَاعٍ ـ بِلَا مَعِيشَةٍ ـ بِلَا أَبْرَشِيَّةٍ.

Unbeseeming, *a.* *See* Unbecoming, *a.*

Unbesought, *a.* Unsolicited, غَيْرُ مَدْعُوٍّ ـ غَيْرُ مَطْلُوبٍ ـ غَيْرُ مُلْتَمَسٍ.

Unbestowed, *a.* غَيْرُ مَوْهُوبٍ ـ غَيْرُ مَمْنُوحٍ.

Unbiassed, *a.* Impartial, خَالٍ مِنَ الْغَرَضِ ـ عَدِيمُ الْمُحَابَاةِ. Judicious, مَعْقُولٌ ـ صَائِبٌ.

Unbid, *a.* / **Unbidden**, } Not ordered, غَيْرُ مَأْمُورٍ. Not invited, غَيْرُ مَدْعُوٍّ ـ غَيْرُ مَعْزُومٍ. An — guest, an intruder at a feast, *etc.*, وَارِشٌ ـ طُفَيْلِيٌّ ـ طِفْلِيلٌ.

Unbind, *v.t.* To loosen, حَلَّ ُ ـ فَكَّ ُ. To free, let go, سَيَّبَ ـ أَفْلَتَ ـ أَطْلَقَ ـ أَعْتَقَ.

Unblamable, *a.* غَيْرُ مُجْرِمٍ ـ غَيْرُ جَانٍ ـ بِلَا لَوْمٍ.

Unblamably, *ad.* بِلَا ذَنْبٍ ـ بِلَا لَوْمٍ.

Unbleached, *a.* Of cloth, غَيْرُ مُبَيَّضٍ ـ غَيْرُ مَقْصُورٍ ـ خَامٌ.

Unblemished, *a.* خَالِصٌ ـ بِلَا عَوَارٍ ـ بِلَا عَيْبٍ.

Unblenching, *a.* Dauntless, شُجَاعٌ ـ جَسُورٌ ـ مِكْبَسٌ.

Unblended, *a.* صَافٍ ـ غَيْرُ مَمْزُوجٍ ـ غَيْرُ مَخْلُوطٍ ـ غَيْرُ مُخْتَلِطٍ.

Unblest, *a.* Not consecrated, غَيْرُ مُكَرَّسٍ ـ غَيْرُ مُقَدَّسٍ. Unfortunate, شَقِيٌّ *pl.* أَشْقِيَاءُ ـ مَنْحُوسٌ.

Unblushing, *a.* وَقِيحٌ ـ بِدُونِ حِشْمَةٍ ـ بِلَا حَيَاءٍ. An — woman, إِمْرَأَةٌ وَقَاحُ الْوَجْهِ.

Unblushingly, *ad.* بِفَصَاحَةٍ ـ بِقِلَّةِ حَيَاءٍ ـ بِوَقَاحَةٍ.

Unboastful, *a.* غَيْرُ مُطَرْمِذٍ ـ غَيْرُ مُتَبَاهٍ ـ غَيْرُ مُفْتَخِرٍ.

Unbodied, *a.* لَا جَسَدَ لَهُ.

Unbolt, *v.t.* *See to* Unbar, *v.t.*

Unbolted, *a.* مَفْتُوحٌ ـ مَرْفُوعُ الْمِغْلَاقِ.

Unborn, *a.* Not existing, غَيْرُ مَوْجُودٍ ـ عَدِيمٌ. Far off, unlikely, بَعِيدٌ. Future, فِي الْمُسْتَقْبَلِ.

Unborrowed, *a.* غَيْرُ مُسْتَقْرَضٍ ـ غَيْرُ مُسْتَعَارٍ.

Unbosom, *v.t.* To disclose, صَرَّحَ بِ ـ أَصْرَحَ. To — one's heart to, أَطْلَعَ عَلَى سِرِّهِ ـ كَشَفَ لِ سِرَّهُ.

Unbought, *a.* Not bought, غَيْرُ مُشْتَرًى. Not bribed, غَيْرُ مُبَرْطَلٍ ـ غَيْرُ مُرْتَشٍ.

Unbound, *a.* Not tied, مَحْلُولٌ ـ مَفْكُوكٌ ـ غَيْرُ مَحْصُورٍ. Not bound, of a book, غَيْرُ مَشْدُودٍ ـ غَيْرُ مُجَلَّدٍ. Not obliged, غَيْرُ مُضْطَرٍّ ـ غَيْرُ مَلْزُومٍ.

Unbounded, *a.* Unlimited, غَيْرُ مَحْدُودٍ. Endless, غَيْرُ مُتَنَاهٍ. Excessive, great, كَثِيرٌ ـ عَظِيمٌ.

Unbowel, *v.t.* *See to* Embowel, *v.t.*

Unbribed, *a.* غَيْرُ مُبَرْطَلٍ ـ غَيْرُ مُرْتَشٍ.

Unbridle, *v.t.* To remove the bridle, رَفَعَ اللِّجَامَ ـ فَكَّ ُ اللِّجَامَ. To let loose, سَيَّبَ ـ أَفْلَتَ ـ أَطْلَقَ ـ خَلَّى عَنْ.

Unbridled, *a.* Without a bridle, غَيْرُ مُلْجَمٍ ـ بِلَا لِجَامٍ. Unrestrained, مِنْ غَيْرِ ضَبْطٍ ـ بِلَا ضَابِطَةٍ ـ طَلْقُ الْعِنَانِ *pl.* أَطْلَاقٌ. Abandoned, corrupt, فَاسِدٌ ـ خَلِيعٌ.

Unbroken, *a.* Not broken, غَيْرُ مَكْسُورٍ ـ صَحِيحٌ *pl.* صِحَاحٌ. Consecutive, مُتَّصِلٌ ـ مُتَلَاحِقٌ ـ مُتَوَاتِرٌ. Not broken in, of an animal, غَيْرُ مَرُوضٍ. Unsubdued, غَيْرُ مَقْهُورٍ. The caravans of the pilgrims formed an — line, إِسْتَقَامَ جَدْوَلُ الْحُجَّاجِ.

Unbrotherly, *a.* لَيْسَ مِثْلَ ٱلْإِخْوَةِ ـ غَيْرُ أَخَوِيٍّ.

Unbuckle, *v.t.* فَكَّ ٱلْأَبْزِيمَ ².

Unbuckle, *v.i.* ٱلْأَبْزِيمُ يَنْفَكُّ.

Unburden, *v.t.* To remove a load from, نَزَّلَ ـ حَطَّ ² عَنِ ٱلْحِمْلَ ٱلْحِمْلَ عَنْ. To relieve, خَفَّفَ عَنْ. *See also to* Unbosom, *v.t.*

Unburdened, *a.* Not burdened, غَيْرُ مُحَمَّلٍ. Not embarrassed, perplexed, مُطْمَئِنٌّ ـ غَيْرُ مُضْطَرِبٍ ـ غَيْرُ مُتَحَيِّرٍ. He is — about the matter, هُوَ مُطْمَئِنٌّ إِلَى ٱلْأَمْرِ.

Unburied, *a.* بِلَا دَفْنٍ ـ غَيْرُ مَدْفُونٍ.

Unbusied, *a.* فَاضٍ ـ فَارِغٌ ـ غَيْرُ غَارِقٍ فِي ٱلْأَشْغَالِ ـ غَيْرُ مَشْغُولٍ.

Unbusiness-like, *a.* خِلَافُ أُسْلُوبِ ٱلشُّغْلِ.

Unbutton, *v.t.* فَكَّ ٱلْأَزْرَارَ ².

Unbutton, *v.i.* أَزْرَارُهُ تَنْفَكُّ.

Unbuttoned, *a.* مَفْكُوكُ ٱلْأَزْرَارِ.

Uncage, *v.t.* To let loose, سَيَّبَ ـ أَطْلَقَ ـ أَفْلَتَ.

Uncalled-for, *a.* Not necessary, غَيْرُ لَازِمٍ ـ غَيْرُ ضَرُورِيٍّ. Not proper, غَيْرُ وَاجِبٍ. Out of place, فِي غَيْرِ مَحَلِّهِ ـ غَيْرُ سَائِغٍ. Useless, لَا طَائِلَ تَحْتَهُ ـ بَاطِلٌ.

Uncandid, *a.* Not fair, not candid, غَيْرُ صَادِقٍ ـ غَيْرُ نَصُوحٍ ـ عَدِيمُ ٱلْإِسْتِقَامَةِ ـ غَيْرُ سَلِيمٍ.

Uncandied, *a.* Not preserved with sugar, غَيْرُ مُقَنَّدٍ.

Uncanonical, *a.* غَيْرُ شَرْعِيٍّ ـ غَيْرُ قَانُونِيٍّ.

Uncared-for, *a.* لَيْسَ مَنْ يَهْتَمُّ ـ غَيْرُ مُفْتَقَدٍ ـ مَتْرُوكٌ ـ ضَيَاعٌ.

Uncarpeted, *a.* مِنْ غَيْرِ طَنَافِسَ ـ بِلَا أَبْسِطَةٍ.

Unceasing, *a.* دَائِمٌ ـ مُسْتَدِيمٌ ـ مُسْتَمِرٌّ.

Unceasingly, *ad.* مِنْ غَيْرِ ـ عَلَى ٱلْإِسْتِمْرَارِ ـ عَلَى ٱلدَّوَامِ دَائِمًا ـ ٱنْقِطَاعٍ.

Uncensured, *a.* غَيْرُ مُوَبَّخٍ ـ غَيْرُ مُعَزَّرٍ ـ غَيْرُ مَذْمُومٍ.

Unceremonious, *a.* Without ceremony, بِلَا تَكْلِيفٍ. Not caring, غَيْرُ مُبَالٍ ـ مَاجِنٌ.

Unceremoniously, *ad.* Without ceremony, بِلَا تَكْلِيفٍ. Without caring, مِنْ غَيْرِ مُبَالَاةٍ.

Uncertain, *a.* Not known, غَيْرُ مَعْلُومٍ. Not clear, غَيْرُ وَاضِحٍ ـ غَيْرُ يَقِينٍ. Not ascertained, غَيْرُ مُحَقَّقٍ. Doubtful, مَشْكُوكٌ ـ تَحْتَ ٱلشَّكِّ ـ مُشْتَبِهٌ. Ambiguous, مُبْهَمٌ ـ مُلْتَبِسٌ. Variable, مُتَرَدِّدٌ ـ فَرَّارٌ ـ فَائِلُ ٱلرَّأْيِ. Inconstant, مُتَقَلِّبٌ ـ قَلَّابٌ. Perplexed, حَيْرَانُ ـ مُتَحَيِّرٌ. Uncertain future events, أُمُورٌ غَيْرُ مَعْلُومَةِ ٱلْوُقُوعِ.

Uncertainly, *ad.* مِنْ غَيْرِ تَحْقِيقٍ ـ بِعَدَمِ يَقِينٍ.

Uncertainty, *n.* Want of certainty, عَدَمُ يَقِينٍ. Irresolution, حَيْرَةٌ. Doubtfulness, ambiguity, إِلْتِبَاسٌ ـ مِرْيَةٌ ـ شُبْهَةٌ. To be in —, perplexed, تَحَيَّرَ ـ ح حَارَ. To throw into —, حَيَّرَ.

Unchain, *v.t.* حَلَّ ٱلسَّلَاسِلَ مِنْ ـ ² فَكَّ ٱلزَّنَاجِيرَ مِنْ. To let loose, سَيَّبَ ـ أَفْلَتَ.

Unchallengeable, *a.* *See* Unanswerable, *a.*

Unchangeable, *a.* بِلَا تَغْيِيرٍ ـ مُنَزَّهٌ عَنِ ٱلتَّغْيِيرِ ـ لَا يَزُولُ ـ ثَابِتٌ ـ لَا يَعْتَرِيهِ ٱلتَّغْيِيرُ ـ لَا يَتَغَيَّرُ.

Unchangeableness, *n.* عَدَمُ تَغَيُّرٍ ـ عَدَمُ تَغْيِيرٍ ـ تَنَزُّهٌ عَنِ ٱلتَّغْيِيرِ ـ ثَبَاتٌ.

Unchangeably, *ad.* بِثَبَاتٍ ـ بِدُونِ تَغَيُّرٍ ـ بِلَا زَوَالٍ ـ بِلَا تَغْيِيرٍ.

Unchanged, *a.* عَلَى مَا كَانَ ـ بَاقٍ عَلَى مَا كَانَ ـ مَا تَغَيَّرَ.

Unchanging, *a.* *See* Unchangeable, *a.*

Uncharitable, *a.* Not kind in giving alms, غَيْرُ ـ غَيْرُ مُتَصَدِّقٍ مُحْسِنٍ لِلْفُقَرَاءِ. Not kind, not loving, غَيْرُ مُحِبٍّ ـ غَيْرُ كَرِيمٍ ـ جَافٍ ـ قَاسٍ ـ عَدِيمُ ٱلْمَوَدَّةِ. *See also under* Suspicious, *a.*

Uncharitableness, *n.* Of alms, عَدَمُ صَدَقَةٍ ـ عَدَمُ حَسَنَةٍ. Unkindness, عَدَمُ مَوَدَّةٍ ـ عَدَمُ مَحَبَّةٍ. Harshness, hardheartedness, قَسَاوَةُ قَلْبٍ.

Uncharitably, *ad.* With lack of charity, بِعَدَمِ ـ بِعَدَمِ مَوَدَّةٍ بِقَسَاوَةٍ ـ مَحَبَّةٍ. With evil thought, بِسُوءِ ظَنٍّ.

Unchartered, *a.* Without a charter, بِلَا فِرْمَانٍ ـ بِلَا بَرَاءَةٍ. Not hired, غَيْرُ مُسْتَكْرًى.

Unchaste, *a.* فَالِتٌ ـ فَاسِقٌ ـ شَهْوَانِيٌّ ـ شَهْوَانُ ـ غَيْرُ عَفِيفٍ.
"She said, how shall I have a son when no man has touched me, and I am not unchaste?" قَالَتْ أَنَّى يَكُونُ لِي غُلَامٌ وَلَمْ يَمْسَسْنِي بَشَرٌ وَلَمْ أَكُ بَغِيًّا (Kur. xix. 20).

Unchastely, *ad.* بِفِسْقٍ ـ بِفُجُورٍ ـ بِرَفَثٍ ـ بِلَا عِفَّةٍ.

Unchastity, *n.* فُجُورٌ ـ فِسْقٌ وَفَسَادٌ ـ رَفَثٌ ـ عَدَمُ ٱلْعِفَّةِ.

Unchecked, *a.* Unrestrained, غَيْرُ ـ مُفْلَتٌ ـ مِنْ غَيْرِ ضَبْطٍ مَزْجُورٍ. Not reprimanded, غَيْرُ مُعَاتَبٍ ـ غَيْرُ مُوَبَّخٍ. Unchecked, of a reckoning, غَيْرُ مُقَيَّدِ ٱلرَّجْعِ.

Unchristian, Unchristianlike, *a.* Unchristianly, } خِلَافُ ٱلنَّصْرَانِيَّةِ ـ غَيْرُ لَائِقٍ بِٱلنَّصْرَانِيَّةِ ـ كَمَا لَا يَجِبُ عَلَى ٱلنَّصْرَانِيِّ.

Unchronicled, *a.* غَيْرُ ـ غَيْرُ مُقَيَّدٍ فِي ٱلتَّوَارِيخِ ـ غَيْرُ مُسَجَّلٍ مَذْكُورٍ فِي ٱلتَّوَارِيخِ.

Unchurch, *v.a.* To expel from the church, ² طَرَدَ مِنَ ٱلْكَنِيسَةِ ـ أَخْرَجَ مِنَ ٱلْبِيعَةِ.

Uncial, *a.* فِي خَطٍّ ثُلُثِيٍّ.

Uncial, *n.* حَرْفُ خَطٍّ ثُلُثِيٍّ *pl.* حُرُوفٌ.

Unciform, *a.* فِي شَكْلِ ٱلْكُلَّابِ.

Uncircumcised, *a.* ذُو غُلْفَةٍ ـ غَيْرُ مَخْتُونٍ ـ أَغْلَفُ. The state of being —, غَلَفٌ. "And they say, our hearts are uncircumcised," وَقَالُوا قُلُوبُنَا غُلْفٌ (Kur. ii. 82).

Uncircumcision, *n.* عَدَمُ خِتَانٍ ـ غُرْلَةٌ.

Uncircumspect, *a.* مُتَهَامِلٌ ـ مُتَوَانٍ ـ غَيْرُ حَرِيصٍ ـ غَيْرُ مُتَحَذِّرٍ. *See also* Imprudent, *a.*

Uncivil, *a.* Discourteous, فَظٌّ ـ جَافٍ ـ مُخِلٌّ مِنَ ٱلْأَدَبِ ـ غَلِيظٌ ـ عَدِيمُ ٱلْأُنْسَةِ ـ قَلِيلُ ٱلْأَدَبِ.

Uncivilized, *a.* حُوشِيٌّ ـ مُتَوَحِّشٌ ـ وَحْشِيٌّ ـ غَيْرُ مُتَمَدِّنٍ ـ هَمَجٌ.

Unclaimed, *a.* بِلَا صَاحِبٍ ـ غَيْرُ مَطْلُوبٍ.

Unclasp, *v.t.* To loosen a clasp, فَكَّ ٱلْعُرْوَةَ (or ٱلْبُكْلَةَ) ². To open, فَتَحَ. To unfold, stretch out, بَسَطَ ².

Unclassical, *a.* خِلَافُ أُصُولِ ٱلْكُتُبِ وَٱلتَّصَانِيفِ ٱلْمُعْتَبَرَةِ (or ٱلْمَقْبُولَةِ).

Unclassically, *ad.* بِخِلَافِ أُصُولِ ٱلْكُتُبِ وَٱلتَّصَانِيفِ ٱلْمُعْتَبَرَةِ (or ٱلْمَقْبُولَةِ).

Uncle, *n.* A father's brother, عَمٌّ *pl.* أَعْمَامٌ. A mother's brother, خَالٌ *pl.* أَخْوَالٌ. Great —, عَمُّ ٱلْعَمِّ. Uncle by marriage, aunt's husband, زَوْجُ ٱلْخَالَةِ.

Unclean, *a.* Foul, dirty, دَنِسٌ ـ نَجِسٌ ـ قَذِرٌ ـ رَجِسٌ ـ دَرِنٌ ـ وَسِخٌ. Impure, غَيْرُ مُتَطَهِّرٍ ـ غَيْرُ طَاهِرٍ ـ نَجِسٌ. Obscene, indecent, خَبِيثٌ ـ فَاحِشٌ ـ بَذِيٌّ. Unclean or foul speech, رَفَثٌ. "O believers, those who join other gods with God [polytheists] are unclean," يَا أَيُّهَا ٱلَّذِينَ آمَنُوا إِنَّمَا ٱلْمُشْرِكُونَ نَجَسٌ (Kur. ix. 28). *See also* Impure, *a.*

Uncleanliness, *n.* دَنَاسَةٌ ـ نَجَاسَةٌ ـ قَذَرٌ ـ رِجْسٌ ـ دَرَنٌ.

Uncleanly, *ad.* بِدَنَاسَةٍ ـ قَذَرًا ـ دَرَنًا. Obscenely, بِخَنَايَةٍ ـ بِرَفَثٍ ـ بِفُحْشٍ ـ قَذَعًا.

Uncleanness, *n.* Absence of purity, عَدَمُ طَهَارَةٍ. Obscenity, خَبَاثَةٌ ـ فَحَاشَةٌ ـ خَنَايَةٌ ـ فُحْشٌ ـ خَنًا ـ رَفَثٌ. *See also* Uncleanliness, *n.*

Uncleansed, *a.* Not cleaned, غَيْرُ مُنَظَّفٍ. Not purified, غَيْرُ مُطَهَّرٍ.

Unclinch, *v.t.* Of a nail, فَكَّ بَرْشَمَةَ ٱلْمِسْمَارِ ²; of the fingers, *etc.*, بَسَطَ ².

Unclog, *v.t.* To clear of impediments, سَلَّكَ. To set free, أَنْقَذَ ـ خَلَّصَ ـ أَعْتَقَ.

Unclogged, *a.* Clear of impediments, غَيْرُ مَسْدُودٍ ـ مُسَلَّكٌ. Free of hindrances, سَالِكٌ ـ خَالٍ مِنَ ٱلْمَوَانِعِ.

Unclose, *v.t.* فَتَحَ ـ فَكَّ ².

Unclosed, *a.* مَفْتُوحٌ ـ مَفْكُوكٌ.

Unclothe, *v.t.* نَزَعَ عَنْ ـ كَذَا ـ رَفَعَ عَنْ ـ كَذَا ـ شَلَّحَ ـ جَرَّدَ ـ خَلَعَ.

Unclothed, *a.* مُعَرًّى ـ عُرْيَانٌ ـ عَارٍ.

Uncloud, *v.t.* قَشَعَ ٱلسَّحَابَ عَنْ كَذَا.

Unclouded, *a.* Without clouds, رَائِقٌ ـ صَاحٍ ـ مِنْ غَيْرِ سَحَابٍ ـ صَافٍ ـ مُنِيرٌ. Joyful, حَبُورٌ ـ مَسْرُورٌ ـ طَرِبٌ.

Uncock, *v.t.* Of a musket, حَطَّ زِنَادَ (or دِيكَ) ٱلْبَارُودَةِ ².

Uncocked, *a.* Of a musket, بَارُودَةٌ مَحْطُوطَةُ ٱلزِّنَادِ (or ٱلدِّيكِ).

Uncoffined, *a.* غَيْرُ مُكَفَّنٍ.

Uncoil, *v.t.* كَرَّ ² ـ حَلَّ ² ـ أَرْخَى.

Uncoil, *v.i.* سَابَ *aor* يَسِيبُ ـ اِنْسَابَ.

Uncoined, *a.* غَيْرُ مَضْرُوبٍ ـ غَيْرُ مَسْكُوكٍ.

Uncollected, *a.* Not gathered, غَيْرُ مَجْمُوعٍ ـ غَيْرُ مَلْمُومٍ. Remaining, بَاقٍ. Uncollected debts, دَيْنٌ بَاقٍ. *See also* Outstanding, *a.*

Uncoloured, *a.* Not coloured, أَبْيَضُ ـ عَلَى بَيَاضٍ ـ غَيْرُ مُلَوَّنٍ. Not heightened by description, غَيْرُ مُوَشًّى ـ غَيْرُ مُتَفَنَّنٍ.

Uncombed, *a.* بِلَا تَمْشِيطٍ ـ غَيْرُ مَمْشُوطٍ; of wool, غَيْرُ مُسَرَّحٍ ـ بِلَا مَشْطٍ.

Uncombined, *a.* شَاذٌّ ـ عَلَى مُفْرَدِهِ ـ غَيْرُ مُرَكَّبٍ.

Uncomeliness, *n.* قِلَّةُ جَمَالٍ ـ قِلَّةُ ظَرَافَةٍ ـ عَدَمُ لَطَافَةٍ ـ قِلَّةُ طَلَاوَةٍ.

Uncomely, *a.* Not pretty, عَدِيمُ ٱللَّطَافَةِ ـ غَيْرُ ظَرِيفٍ ـ غَيْرُ كَيِّسٍ ـ عَدِيمُ ٱلطَّلَاوَةِ.

Uncomfortable, *a.* Not commodious, غَيْرُ مُرَفَّهٍ ـ غَيْرُ وَاسِعٍ ـ غَيْرُ بَحْبَحِيٍّ ـ مُرِيحٍ. Giving uneasiness, شَاقٌّ ـ مُتْعِبٌ ـ مُقْلِقٌ ـ مُضْجِرٌ.

Uncomfortableness, *n.* Absence of commodiousness, عَدَمُ سَعَةٍ ـ ضِيقٌ ـ عَدَمُ هِينَةٍ. Uneasiness, قَلَقٌ ـ اِضْطِرَابٌ ـ ضَيْقُ صَدْرٍ.

Uncomfortably, *ad.* Without commodiousness, بِعَدَمِ سَعَةٍ ـ بِلَا تَرَفُّهٍ. In an uneasy state, بِٱضْطِرَابٍ ـ عَلَى ضِيقٍ ـ عَلَى قَلَقٍ.

Uncommendable, *a.* غَيْرُ مَمْدُوحٍ ـ غَيْرُ حَمِيدٍ.

Uncommitted, *a.* Not pledged, غَيْرُ مُلْتَزِمٍ ـ غَيْرُ مُتَعَهِّدٍ. Not done, of a crime, غَيْرُ مُرْتَكَبٍ.

Uncommon, *n.* Not general, غَيْرُ عَامٍّ ـ غَيْرُ شَائِعٍ. Extraordinary, خَارِجٌ عَنِ ٱلْعَادَةِ ـ غَيْرُ مُعْتَادٍ ـ فَوْقَ ٱلْعَادَةِ. Rare, seldom found, نَادِرٌ ـ قَلِيلُ ٱلْوُجُودِ; seldom occurring, قَلِيلُ ٱلْوُقُوعِ. Out of the common, نَادِرٌ. Strange, عَجِيبٌ ـ غَرِيبٌ. An —

or unfamiliar word, آبِدَة *pl.* أَوَابِدُ . *See also* Extraordinary, Rare, *a.*

Uncommonly, *ad.* Rarely, seldom, بِٱلنَّدْرَةِ ـ فِي ٱلنَّادِرِ ـ فِي ٱلْقَلِيلِ . Extraordinarily, more than usually, فَوْقَ ٱلْعَادَةِ .

Uncommonness, *n.* Rarity, نَدْرَة . Infrequent occurrence, قِلَّةُ وُقُوعٍ . The being seldom found, قِلَّةُ وُجُودٍ . Strangeness, غَرَابَة . Preciousness, عِزٌّ . *See also* Rareness, *n.*

Uncommunicative, *a.* طِرِّيق ـ مِطْرَاق ـ كَتُوم .

Uncompact, *a.* Of make, غَزِل ـ سَخِيف .

Uncompensated, *a.* بِلَا مُكَافَاةٍ ـ بِلَا جَزَاءٍ ـ بِلَا ثَوَابٍ ـ غَيْرُ مُثَوَّبٍ .

Uncomplaining, *a.* غَيْرُ شَكِيٍّ ـ غَيْرُ مُشْتَكٍ ـ صَبَّار .

Uncomplaisant, *a.* غَيْرُ مُلَاطِفٍ ـ غَيْرُ ذِي لُطْفٍ . *See also* Discourteous, *a.*

Uncompleted, *a.* غَيْرُ مُتَمَّمٍ ـ غَيْرُ مُكَمَّلٍ .

Uncomplying, *a.* عَدِيمُ ٱلْمُطَاوَعَةِ ـ غَيْرُ مُطَاوِعٍ ـ غَيْرُ مُنْقَادٍ ـ عَنِيد .

Uncompounded, *a.* غَيْرُ مُرَكَّبٍ ـ بَسِيط .

Uncompromising, *a.* Implacable, شَدِيدُ ٱلْحِقْدِ ـ لَا يَقْبَلُ ٱلْمُصَالَحَةَ . Inflexible, لَا يُلَيَّنُ . Antagonistic, مُخَالِف ـ مُنَاقِض .

Unconcealed, *a.* غَيْرُ مَكْتُومٍ ـ غَيْرُ خَفِيٍّ . Manifest, بَارِح ـ بَيِّن ـ مُبِين .

Unconceivable, *a.* لَا يُتَخَيَّلُ ـ لَا يُتَصَوَّرُ ـ يَفُوقُ ٱلْوَهْمَ .

Unconceived, *a.* لَا تُخُيِّلَ ـ لَا تُصُوِّرَ .

Unconcern, *n.* عَدَمُ مُبَالَاةٍ ـ تَسَاهُل ـ عَدَمُ ٱعْتِنَاءٍ ـ فُتُور .

Unconcerned, *a.* مُتَكَاسِل ـ غَيْرُ مُبَالٍ ـ عَدِيمُ ٱلْمُبَالَاةِ ـ فَاتِر .

Unconcernedly, *ad.* بِعَدَمِ مُبَالَاةٍ ـ بِعَدَمِ ٱعْتِنَاءٍ ـ بِفُتُورٍ .

Unconcernedness, *n.* *See* Unconcern, *n.*

Unconciliating, *a.* }
Unconciliatory, *a.* } *See* Uncompromising, *a.*

Unconcocted, *a.* Not digested, غَيْرُ مَهْضُومٍ . Not matured, غَيْرُ مُنْضَجٍ ـ غَيْرُ مُتَصَوَّرٍ ـ فَطِير . Not planned, غَيْرُ مُخْتَرَعٍ .

Uncondemned, *a.* غَيْرُ مَقْضِيٍّ عَلَيْهِ .

Uncondensable, *a.* Not distillable, لَا يُقَطَّرُ ـ تَصْعِيدُهُ مُحَال . Not capable of being thickened, لَا يُكَثَّفُ . Not capable of abridgment, لَا يُقْتَصَرُ ـ لَا يُوجَزُ .

Uncondensed, *a.* Not distilled, غَيْرُ مُصَعَّدٍ ـ غَيْرُ مُقَطَّرٍ . Not thickened, غَيْرُ مُكَثَّفٍ . Unabridged, غَيْرُ مُوجَزٍ ـ غَيْرُ مُقْتَصَرٍ ـ عَلَى تَمَامِهِ . Profuse, prolonged, مُسْهَب ـ مُطَوَّل .

Unconditional, *a.* مُطْلَق ـ مِنْ غَيْرِ شُرُوطٍ ـ خَالٍ مِنَ ٱلشُّرُوطِ . To make —, أَطْلَقَ .

Unconditionally, *ad.* عَلَى غَيْرِ عَقْدٍ وَلَا عَهْدٍ ـ بِدُونِ شُرُوطٍ .

Unconfessed, *a.* Not avowed, غَيْرُ مُقَرٍّ بِ ـ غَيْرُ مُعْتَرَفٍ بِ . Not having gone to the confessional, غَيْرُ مُعْتَرِفٍ ـ بِلَا ٱعْتِرَافٍ .

Unconfined, *a.* Not imprisoned or restrained, غَيْرُ مَحْبُوسٍ ـ غَيْرُ مَحْصُورٍ . Loose, let loose, unrestricted, طَلْق ـ مُطْلَق ـ طَلِيق .

Unconfirmed, *a.* Not strengthened by proofs, غَيْرُ مُؤَكَّدٍ ـ غَيْرُ مُثْبَتٍ ـ مُحَقَّقٍ ـ غَيْرُ مَعْقُودٍ . Unratified, غَيْرُ مُصَدَّقٍ عَلَيْهِ . Not confirmed, as by a bishop, بِلَا تَثْبِيتٍ .

Unconformable, *a.* Not conformable to, غَيْرُ مُطَابِقٍ لِ ـ غَيْرُ مُوَافِقٍ لِ . Incompatible, مُنَاقِض ـ مُغَايِر ـ مُخَالِف .

Unconformably, *ad.* بِعَدَمِ مُطَابَقَةٍ ـ مُنَاقَضَةً ـ مُخَالَفَةً ـ بِغَيْرِ ٱتِّفَاقٍ .

Unconformity, *n.* Want of conformity, قِلَّةُ مُطَابَقَةٍ ـ عَدَمُ مُوَافَقَةٍ . Incompatibility, تَخَالُف ـ مُبَايَنَة .

Unconfused, *a.* Not perplexed, غَيْرُ مُضْطَرِبٍ ـ غَيْرُ مُقَلَّقٍ . Not confused in speech, غَيْرُ مُتَوَعِّرٍ . Not in disorder, غَيْرُ مُشَوَّشٍ ـ غَيْرُ مُلْتَبِكٍ .

Unconfutable, *a.* لَا يُنَاقَضُ ـ مُنَاقَضَتُهُ غَيْرُ مُمْكِنَةٍ ـ لَا يُرَدُّ عَلَيْهِ .

Uncongealed, *a.* غَيْرُ جَامِدٍ ـ غَيْرُ مُجَمَّدٍ .

Uncongenial, *a.* Disagreeing, مُخَالِف ـ مُغَايِر ـ مُخْتَلِف ـ ٱلطَّبْعِ ـ غَيْرُ مُتَجَانِسٍ , Unhealthy, وَخِيم ـ وَبِيل .

Unconjugal, *a.* غَيْرُ لَائِقٍ بِٱلْمُزَوَّجِينَ .

Unconnected, *a.* Not connected with, غَيْرُ مُتَعَلِّقٍ بِ ـ غَيْرُ مُتَّصِلٍ بِ . Unrelated to, لَا مِنْ أَقْرِبَائِهِ . Disjoined, مُفَصَّل ـ مُنْفَصِل . Confused, مُشْتَبِك ـ مُعَقَّد ـ مُلْتَبِك .

Unconquerable, *a.* Not to be conquered, أَعَزّ ـ عَزِيز ـ لَا يُغَالَبُ ـ لَا يُقْهَرُ ـ لَا يُقْدَرُ عَلَيْهِ . Not to be rebutted or put aside, أَعَزّ ـ دَفْعُهُ غَيْرُ مُمْكِنٍ . Impossible, مُحَال . Indomitable, أَعَزّ ـ عَزِيز ـ لَا يُقْمَعُ .

Unconquerably, *ad.* عِزَّةً ـ بِعِزٍّ ـ مِنْ غَيْرِ إِقْهَارٍ .

Unconquered, *a.* غَيْرُ مَغْلُوبٍ . Not surmounted, مَا لَا ٱعْتُلِيَ عَلَيْهِ ـ غَيْرُ مَظْفُورٍ بِهِ .

Unconscionable, *a.* غَيْرُ مَعْقُولٍ ـ مُخَالِف لِلْعَقْلِ ـ غَيْرُ صَوَابٍ ـ عَدِيمُ ٱلْإِنْصَافِ .

Unconscionably, *ad.* بِعَدَمِ صَوَابٍ ـ بِقِلَّةِ إِنْصَافٍ .

Unconscionableness, *n.* عَدَمُ صَوَابٍ ـ قِلَّةُ إِنْصَافٍ ـ قِلَّةُ ذِمَّةٍ .

Unconscious, *a.* Unaware of, غَيْرُ مُسْتَبْصِرٍ بِ ـ غَيْرُ وَاعٍ بِ ـ غَيْرُ وَاقِفٍ عَلَى ـ غَيْرُ دَارٍ بِ ـ غَيْرُ عَالِمٍ بِ ـ غَيْرُ حَاسٍّ بِ .

Unconsciously, *ad.* بِغَيْرِ وَعْيٍ ـ بِدُونِ عِلْمٍ ـ بِلَا مُدَارَاةٍ .

Unconsciousness, *n.* Want of consciousness of, عَدَمُ ٱسْتِبْصَارٍ بِ ـ عَدَمُ وُقُوفٍ عَلَى ـ عَدَمُ عِلْمٍ بِ ـ عَدَمُ حِسٍّ بِ. A state of —, through heavy sleep, *etc.*, سُبَات; to be in such a state of —, سَبِتَ ².

Unconsecrated, *a.* بِلا تَكْرِيسٍ ـ غَيْرُ مُقَدَّسٍ ـ غَيْرُ مُكَرَّسٍ.

Unconstitutional, *a.* خِلَافُ أُصُولِ ٱلْمَمْلَكَةِ وَقَوَانِينِهَا.

Unconstrained, *a.* Not forced, غَيْرُ مُضْطَرٍّ ـ غَيْرُ مُلْزَمٍ ـ غَيْرُ مَجْبُورٍ. Free, طَلِيقٌ ـ مُطْلَقٌ ـ طَلْق.

Unconstrainedly, *ad.* Without constraint, مِنْ غَيْرِ ـ بِدُونِ جَبْرٍ ٱضْطِرَارٍ. Freely, of one's own will, إِخْتِيَارًا ـ مِنْ تِلْقَاءِ نَفْسِهِ.

Unconsumed, *a.* Unburnt, غَيْرُ مُحْتَرِقٍ ـ غَيْرُ مَحْرُوقٍ. Not eaten, غَيْرُ مَأْكُولٍ. Left, فَاضِلٌ ـ بَاقٍ.

Uncontested, *a.* بِلا مُخَالَفَةٍ ـ بِلا ٱعْتِرَاضٍ ـ غَيْرُ مُعْتَرَضٍ. An — election, إِنْتِخَابٌ بِدُونِ ٱعْتِرَاضٍ.

Uncontradicted, *a.* غَيْرُ مُكَذَّبٍ ـ غَيْرُ مُنَاقَضٍ.

Uncontrite, *a.* *See* Impenitent, *a.*

Uncontrollable, *a.* غَيْرُ مِذْعَانٍ ـ لا يُقْمَعُ ـ ضَبْطُهُ مُحَالٌ.

Uncontrollably, *ad.* بِإِطْلَاقِ ٱلْعِنَانِ ـ بِنَوْعٍ لا يُضْبَطُ.

Uncontroverted, *a.* غَيْرُ مُنَاقَضٍ ـ لا مُشَاجَرَةَ فِيهِ.

Unconversant, *a.* غَيْرُ خَبِيرٍ بِ ـ غَيْرُ عَالِمٍ بِ ـ غَيْرُ دَارٍ بِ.

Unconverted, *a.* Not changed, غَيْرُ مُتَحَوِّلٍ ـ غَيْرُ مُغَيَّرٍ. Not repented, reformed, ضَالٌّ *pl.* ضَالُّونَ ـ غَيْرُ تَائِبٍ.

Unconvinced, *a.* غَيْرُ مُقْتَنِعٍ ـ غَيْرُ مُقْنَعٍ.

Uncord, *v.t.* حَلَّ ٱلْأَحْبَالَ عَنْ ².

Uncork, *v.t.* أَخْرَجَ ٱلسِّدَادَ مِنْ.

Uncorrected, *a.* غَيْرُ مُصْلَحٍ ـ غَيْرُ مُصَحَّحٍ.

Uncorroborated, *a.* *See* Unconfirmed, *a.*

Uncorrupt, *a.* Not corrupt, free from decay, غَيْرُ فَاسِدٍ. Free from depravity, صَادِقٌ ـ خَالِصٌ ـ نَقِيٌّ. *See also* Incorrupt, *a.*

Uncorrupted, *a.* Not putrid, غَيْرُ مُتَعَفِّنٍ. Not depraved, غَيْرُ مُفْسَدٍ ـ مُنْفَسِدٍ.

Uncorruptible, *a.* Not admitting of decay or putridity, غَيْرُ قَابِلٍ ٱلْفَسَادَ. That may not be bribed, لا يَتَبَرْطَلُ. Undecaying, غَيْرُ فَانٍ ـ لا يَفْنَى ـ بَاقٍ.

Uncounted, *a.* غَيْرُ مَحْسُوبٍ ـ غَيْرُ مُحْصًى ـ غَيْرُ مَعْدُودٍ.

Uncouple, *v.t.* Of two, فَصَلَ بَيْنَ ٱلِٱثْنَيْنِ ـ فَرَّقَ بَيْنَ ٱلِٱثْنَيْنِ ². To disconnect, loose, فَكَّ ² ـ حَلَّ ².

Uncourteous, *a.* جَافٍ ـ فَظٌّ ـ قَلِيلُ ٱلْأَدَبِ ـ عُطْلٌ مِنَ ٱلْأَدَبِ ـ غَلِيظٌ ـ عَدِيمُ ٱلْأُنْسِ.

Uncourteously, *ad.* بِجَفَاءٍ ـ بِفَظَاظَةٍ ـ بِقِلَّةِ أَدَبٍ.

Uncourteousness, *n.* خُشُونَة ـ جَفَاء ـ فَظَاظَة ـ قِلَّةُ أَدَبٍ ـ غِلَاظَة.

Uncourtly, *a.* Not becoming a court, غَيْرُ ٱللَّائِقِ بِدَائِرَةِ ٱلْمَلِكِ. *See also* Uncourteous, *a.*

Uncouth, *a.* Not polished, حُوشِيٌّ ـ فَظٌّ ـ غَلِيظٌ ـ خَشِنٌ. Awkward, غَلِيظٌ ـ غَشِيمٌ ـ أَخْرَقُ ـ خَرِقٌ. An — phrase, لَفْظَةٌ حُوشِيَّةٌ.

Uncouthly, *ad.* بِخُشُونَةٍ ـ بِفَظَاظَةٍ ـ بِخُرْقٍ ـ بِغِلَاظَةٍ.

Uncouthness, *n.* Awkwardness, عَدَمُ ٱسْتِعْدَادٍ ـ غِلَاظَة ـ خُرْق; boorishness, حُوشِيَّة ـ خُشُونَة ـ عَدَمُ لُطْفٍ.

Uncovenanted, *a.* Not promised by covenant, غَيْرُ مَوْعُودٍ بِهِ ـ غَيْرُ مُوعَدٍ بِهِ. An — employé, مُسْتَخْدَمٌ مِنْ غَيْرِ مُقَاوَلَةٍ وَلا مُشَارَطَةٍ.

Uncover, *v.t.* كَشَفَ ـ كَشَفَ عَنْ ـ أَمَاطَ. To open, فَتَحَ. To be uncovered, إِنْكَشَفَ. To make naked, عَرَّى. To be uncovered, naked, تَعَرَّى.

Uncover, *v.i.* So that the cover may be taken off, ٱلْغِطَاءُ يَرْتَفِعُ.

Uncreated, *a.* لَيْسَ بِمَخْلُوقٍ ـ غَيْرُ مَخْلُوقٍ. The word of God is —, كَلَامُ ٱللهِ غَيْرُ مَخْلُوقٍ.

Uncritical, *a.* خِلَافُ ٱلْقَوَاعِدِ ٱلْعَقْلِيَّةِ وَٱلنَّقْلِيَّةِ.

Uncropped, *a.* Not gathered, harvested, غَيْرُ مَحْصُودٍ. Not clipped, غَيْرُ مَقْصُوصٍ ـ غَيْرُ مَقْرُوضٍ.

Uncrossed, *a.* Not traversed, غَيْرُ مَعْبُورٍ بِهِ ـ غَيْرُ مَسْلُوكٍ. Unthwarted, غَيْرُ مُعَوَّقٍ ـ غَيْرُ مُخَيَّبٍ ـ غَيْرُ مُعْتَرَضٍ عَلَيْهِ ـ غَيْرُ مُعَاكَسٍ. Not crossed, of a cheque, غَيْرُ مُقَيَّدٍ.

Uncrown, *v.t.* نَزَعَ مِنَ ٱلتَّاجِ ـ خَلَعَ عَنْ تَاجِهِ.

Uncrushed, *a.* Not subdued, غَيْرُ مَقْهُورٍ. Not crushed to powder, غَيْرُ مَدْقُوقٍ ـ غَيْرُ مَسْحُوقٍ.

Uncrystallized, *a.* غَيْرُ مُتَبَلْوِرٍ ـ غَيْرُ مُجَمَّدٍ.

Unction, *n.* An anointing, مَسْحَة. The act of anointing, تَدْهِين. Something softening, شَيْءٌ مُلَيِّنٌ. Consolation, تَسْلِيَة ـ تَعْزِيَة. Divine grace, ٱلْفَيْضُ ٱلرَّبَّانِيُّ ـ ٱلنِّعْمَةُ ٱلْإِلٰهِيَّةُ. Extreme —, ٱلْمَسْحَةُ ٱلْأَخِيرَةُ ـ آخِرُ مَسْحَةٍ ـ تَزْوِيدُ ٱلْمُدْنِفِ.

Unctuosity, *n.* } **Unctuousness**, } دُهْنِيَّة. *See also* Hypocrisy, *n.*

Unctuous, *a.* شَحِيمٌ ـ دَهِنٌ. *See also* Hypocritical, *a.*

Uncultivated, *a.* Of land, *fem.*, بُورٌ ـ غَيْرُ مَحْرُوثَةٍ ـ غَيْرُ مَفْلُوحَةٍ ـ بَائِرٌ ـ بَوَار. Not instructed, غَيْرُ مُؤَدَّبٍ. Not civilized, غَيْرُ مُتَمَدِّنٍ. Rude, حُوشِيٌّ ـ غَلِيظٌ ـ خَشِنٌ ـ جَافٍ ـ هَمَج.

Uncurl, *v.t.* أَرْخَى ٱلْغَدَائِرَ.

Uncurled, *a.* Of the hair, غَيْرُ مُجَعَّدٍ ـ مُنْسَدِلُ ٱلْغَدَائِرِ ـ غَيْرُ مُقَصَّبٍ.

Uncut, *a.* As with a knife or scissors, غَيْرُ مَقْصُوصٍ. Entire, عَلَى تَمَامِهِ ـ كَامِل. Not shorn, غَيْرُ مَجْزُوزٍ. Not cut out, as of a garment, غَيْرُ مُفَصَّلٍ.

Undamaged, *a.* بِلا مَضَرَّةٍ ـ غَيْرُ مُخَسَّرٍ ـ غَيْرُ مُعَطَّلٍ ـ سَالِم ـ بِلا عَوَارٍ.

Undaunted, *a.* غَيْرُ مَخُوفٍ ـ بَطَل ـ جَسُور ـ جَرِيءٌ. *See also* Undismayed, *a.*

Undauntedly, *ad.* بِشَجَاعَةٍ ـ بِجَسَارَةٍ ـ بِجَرَاءَةٍ ـ بِبَسَالَةٍ ـ بِدُونِ خَوْفٍ.

Undauntedness, *n.* عَنْتَرَة ـ شَجَاعَة ـ جَسَارَة ـ جَرَاءَة ـ بَطَالَة ـ عَدَمُ خَوْفٍ.

Undecayed, *a.* Not rotten, غَيْرُ رُمَامٍ ـ غَيْرُ رَمِيمٍ. Not worn out, غَيْرُ بَالٍ ـ غَيْرُ مُتَدَمِّرٍ.

Undecaying, *a.* Not subject to rottenness, غَيْرُ مَعْفُونٍ ـ غَيْرُ بَالٍ. Not perishable, دَائِم ـ غَيْرُ فَانٍ.

Undeceive, *v.t.* نَبَّهَ عَلَى حَقِيقَةِ ٱلشَّيْءِ ـ أَزَالَ عَنِ ٱلْغُرُورِ. To — one's self, صَحَا مِنْ ضَلالِهِ ـ أَصْحَى مِنْ غُرُورِهِ *aor.* يَصْحُو.

Undecided, *a.* Not decided, غَيْرُ بَتِّيٍّ ـ غَيْرُ مَفْصُولٍ ـ غَيْرُ مُقَرَّرٍ. Hesitating, مُتَرَدِّد ـ مُتَضَرِّب ـ فَائِلُ ٱلرَّأْيِ.

Undecipherable, *a.* لا يُقْرَأُ.

Undeciphered, *a.* غَيْرُ مَقْرُوءٍ.

Undecisive, *a.* *See* Indecisive, *a.*

Undeck, *v.t.* جَرَّدَ مِنَ ٱلتَّزْيِينَاتِ ـ عَرَّى مِنَ ٱلزِّينَةِ (or ٱلتَّزَاوِيقِ).

Undecked, *a.* غَيْرُ مُزَخْرَفٍ ـ غَيْرُ مُزَيَّنٍ.

Undeclared, *a.* غَيْرُ مُعْلَنٍ ـ غَيْرُ مُعْتَرَفٍ بِهِ ـ غَيْرُ مُقَرٍّ بِهِ.

Undeclined, *a.* مَبْنِيٌّ ـ غَيْرُ مُنْصَرِفٍ.

Undecomposable, *a.* *See* Indecomposable, *a.*

Undecorated, *a.* As with an order of merit, غَيْرُ مُوَجَّهٍ بِنِيشَانِ ٱفْتِخَارٍ. *See also* Undecked, *a.*

Undecomposed, *a.* غَيْرُ مُنْفَكٍّ ـ غَيْرُ مُتَحَلِّلٍ ـ غَيْرُ مُنْحَلِّ ٱلْأَجْزَاءِ. Not rotten, غَيْرُ بَالٍ ـ غَيْرُ رَثِيثٍ ـ غَيْرُ رَمِيمٍ.

Undefended, *a.* Not fortified, غَيْرُ مُسْتَحْكَمٍ ـ غَيْرُ مُحَصَّنٍ. Not vindicated, غَيْرُ مُبَرَّرٍ. Unprotected, غَيْرُ مَحْرُوسٍ ـ غَيْرُ مَصُونٍ. Of an action in court, غَيْرُ مُحْتَجٍّ بِهِ.

Undefiled, *a.* طَاهِر ـ نَقِيٌّ ـ غَيْرُ نَجِسٍ ـ بِلا دَنَسٍ.

Undefinable, *a.* That cannot be limited, تَحْدِيدُهُ مُحَالٌ; that cannot be expressed, تَعْرِيفُهُ مُحَالٌ ـ لا يُوصَفُ ـ لا يُعْرَفُ.

Undefined, *a.* Not limited, غَيْرُ مُحَدَّدٍ. Not fixed, غَيْرُ مُقَرَّرٍ. Uncertain, حَقِيقَتُهُ مَجْهُولَةٌ ـ مُلْتَبِس ـ مُبْهَم ـ مُنَكَّر. Not described, غَيْرُ مَوْصُوفٍ.

Undemonstrable, *a.* إِثْبَاتُهُ غَيْرُ مُمْكِنٍ ـ إِيضَاحُهُ غَيْرُ مُمْكِنٍ ـ لا يُبَرْهَنُ.

Undeniable, *a.* حَقِيقِيٌّ ـ مُسَلَّم ـ إِنْكَارُهُ مُحَالٌ.

Undeniably, *ad.* إِطْلاقًا ـ بِلا نِزَاعٍ ـ بِلا إِنْكَارٍ.

Under, *prep.* and *adv.* دُونَ ـ تَحْتَ ـ مِنْ تَحْتُ. A little under, تُحَيْتَ. This is — that, هٰذَا تَحْتَ ذَاكَ. Rivers run — them, (trees,) تَجْرِي مِنْ تَحْتِهَا ٱلْأَنْهَارُ. Such an one is — the orders of such an one, فُلانٌ تَحْتَ أَمْرِ فُلانٍ. This is a little — that, هٰذَا تُحَيْتَ ذَاكَ. I am also — authority, أَنَا أَيْضًا تَحْتَ سُلْطَانٍ. Under age, غَيْرُ بَالِغِ ٱلسِّنِّ ـ غَيْرُ بَالِغٍ. From two years old and —, مِنِ ٱبْنِ سَنَتَيْنِ فَمَا دُونَ. Seeing that — him the people enjoyed tranquillity, إِذْ كَانَ ٱلشَّعْبُ قَدْ تَمَتَّعَ بِٱلرَّفَاهِيَةِ بِوَاسِطَتِهِ. We are not — his authority, لَسْنَا تَحْتَ أَمْرِهِ. He sat —, below, him, جَلَسَ دُونَهُ. Under its natural strength, دُونَ قُوَّتِهِ ٱلْأَصْلِيَّةِ. Under forty pounds, دُونَ أَرْبَعِينَ لِيرَةً. Under a duke, less in rank, دُونَ مَقَامِ ٱلدُّوكِ. Under such circumstance, وَٱلْحَالَةُ هٰذِهِ. I will not be brought — the power of any one, لا يَتَسَلَّطُ عَلَيَّ أَحَدٌ.

To have patience under affliction, صَبَرَ عَلَى ٱلْمَصَائِبِ.

To keep under, ضَبَطَ; of one's self, قَمَعَ (or أَقْمَعَ) نَفْسَهُ.

To study or read under one, قَرَأَ عَلَى فُلانٍ.

To tread under foot, رَفَسَ ـ رَفَسَ بِرِجْلِهِ.

Under, *a.* تَحْتَانِيٌّ. Assistant, مُعَاوِن. Less in price, أَحَطُّ ثَمَنٍ. Inferior, دُونٌ. An — sort of man, رَجُلٌ مِنْ دُونٍ. An — sort of thing, شَيْءٌ مِنْ دُونٍ.

Under-agent, *n.* وَكِيلٌ دُونٌ ـ نَائِبُ وَكِيلٍ ـ مُعَاوِنٌ فِي وَكَالَةٍ.

Underbid, *v.t.* عَرَضَ (or أَعْطَى) أَقَلَّ مِنْ فُلانٍ.

Underbreath, *n.* صَوْتٌ خَفِيضٌ.

Underbred, *a.* Of a low breed, غَيْرُ أَصِيلٍ ـ مِنْ جِنْسٍ دُونٍ. Wanting in good breeding, خَشِن ـ نَاقِصُ ٱلتَّرْبِيَةِ ـ عُتُلٌّ ـ غَلِيظ ـ قَلِيلُ ٱلْأَدَبِ.

Under-brush, *n.* *See* Undergrowth, *n.*

Under-clothing, *n.* مَلْبُوسٌ تَحْتَانِيٌّ. *See also* Under-garment, *n.*

Under-current, *n.* As of water, تَيَّار ـ تَيَّارٌ تَحْتَ وَجْهِ ٱلْمَاءِ; of affairs, جَوَلانٌ خَفِيٌّ.

Underdo, *v.t.* To do less than is requisite in, قَصَّرَ عَنِ ٱلْوَاجِبِ فِي. To undercook, طَبَخَ نِصْفَ طَبْخٍ ـ خَلَّى نِيًّا.

Underdone, *a.* Defective, نَاقِص. Not fully cooked, مَطْبُوخٌ نِصْفَ طَبْخٍ ـ نِيٌّ.

Underdose, *n.* عِلاجٌ دُونَ ٱلْمِقْدَارِ ٱلْوَاجِبِ.

Underdrain, *v.t.* نَزَحَ-مِنْ تَحْتِ ٱلْأَرْضِ .

Under-dress, *n.* ثَوْبٌ تَحْتَانِيٌّ .

Under-estimate, *v.t.* To value below the price, ثَمَّنَ-دُونَ ثَمَنِهِ . To —, of numbers, عَدَّهُمْ دُونَ عَدَدِهِمْ . To esteem lightly, إِسْتَقَلَّ .

Underfurnish, *v.t.* As with necessaries, قَصَّرَ عَنِ-ٱللَّوَازِمِ ; as with furniture, أَقَلَّ فِي إِيجَادِ ٱلْبَيْتِ .

Under-garment, *n.* One worn next to the skin, شِعَارٌ *pl.* شُعُرٌ .

Undergird, *v.t.* حَزَمَ-مِنْ أَسْفَلَ .

Undergo, *v.t.* إِحْتَمَلَ – إِرْتَكَبَ . To — patiently, تَصَبَّرَ – تَعَزَّى . To —, of trials, misfortune, أُبْتُلِيَ بِ . To — change, تَغَيَّرَ – تَبَدَّلَ – إِسْتَحَالَ . To — an operation, تَكَبَّدَ عَمَلِيَّةً جِرَاحِيَّةً . He underwent great hardships, تَنَهَّدَ ٱلصُّعَدَاءَ .

Undergraduate, *n.* تِلْمِيذٌ فِي دَارِ ٱلْفُنُونِ لَمْ يُدْرِكِ ٱلرُّتْبَةَ ٱلْأُولَى .

Underground, *a.* تَحْتَ ٱلْأَرْضِ . An — store for grain, *etc.*, مَطْمُورَةٌ . An — room, سِرْدَابٌ *pl.* سَرَادِيبُ .

Undergrowth, *n.* Of plants, دِقُّ ٱلشَّجَرِ – عَقُولٌ – حَسَكٌ – رَتَمٌ .

Underhand, *a.* Secret, clandestine, خَفِيٌّ – كَاتِمٌ – مَسْتُورٌ . Fraudulent, غَدِيرٌ – غَادِرٌ – خَائِنٌ .

Under-keeper, *n.* Of a guard, watch, مُعَاوِنُ ٱلْحَافِظِ ; of one put in trust of anything, مُعَاوِنُ أَمِينٍ .

Underlay, *v.t.* To place under, جَعَلَ تَحْتَهُ كَذَا . To strengthen below, شَدَّدَ-مِنْ أَسْفَلَ .

Underlet, *v.t.* To let below the value, كَرَى-دُونَ ٱلثَّمَنِ . To sublet, كَرَى مَحَلًّا كَانَ قَدِ ٱسْتَكْرَاهُ .

Underlie, *v.t.* كَانَ تَحْتَهُ كَذَا . A stratum of clay underlies the stratum of mineral, تَحْتَ ٱلْمَعْدِنِ طَبَقَةٌ مِنَ ٱلطِّينِ .

Underline, *v.t.* رَسَمَ خَطًّا تَحْتَ ٱلسَّطْرِ (*or* ٱلسُّطُورِ) .

Underling, *n.* خَادِمٌ مِنْ دُونٍ *pl.* خُدَّامٌ – خُدَّامٌ *pl.* خَدَمٌ – أَجِيرٌ *pl.* أُجَرَاءُ .

Undermasted, *a.* صَوَارِيهِ قِصَارٌ – أَدْقَالُهُ صِغَارٌ .

Undermine, *v.t.* To sap, حَفَرَ لُغْمًا تَحْتَهُ . To burrow, سَرَّبَ – سَرَبًا فِي . To counteract, نَاقَضَ – عَارَضَ – عَاكَسَ . To supplant by stratagem, تَعَقَّبَ-بِمَكْرٍ . To subvert, هَدَمَ أَسَاسَهُ – هَدَمَ – خَرَّبَ . To be undermined, as a wall by water, أَنْتَعَفَ – إِنْقَعَفَ .

"He who hath founded his building on the brink of an undermined bank," مَنْ أَسَّسَ بُنْيَانَهُ عَلَى شَفَا جُرُفٍ هَارٍ (Kur. ix. 110).

Underminer, *n.* One who destroys, مُخَرِّبٌ – هَادِمٌ .

Undermost, *a.* ٱلتَّحْتَانِيُّ – تَحْتَ ٱلْكُلِّ .

Underneath, *prep.* *See* Under, Beneath, *prep.*

Underpin, *v.t.* شَدَّدَ-مِنْ أَسْفَلَ – أَسْنَدَ – سَنَّدَ – عَمَدَ .

Underplot, *n.* As of a play, فَصْلٌ مُعْتَرِضٌ يُؤَوِّلُ مَضْمُونَ ٱللَّعِبِ . A clandestine scheme, دَسِيسَةٌ – دُولَابٌ .

Underprize, *v.t.* إِسْتَقَلَّ – ثَمَّنَ-دُونَ ثَمَنِهِ .

Underprop, *v.t.* أَسْنَدَ-مِنْ تَحْتُ .

Underrate, *v.t.* Of price, قَلَّلَ سِعْرَهُ ; of number, قَلَّلَ عَدَدَهُ ; of power or station, حَطَّ . To esteem lightly, إِسْتَقَلَّ .

Under-reckon, *v.t.* حَسَبَ-دُونَ ٱلْحِسَابِ .

Underrun, *v.t.* To re-adjust, أَصْلَحَ .

Underscore, *v.t.* خَطَّ تَحْتَهُ خَطًّا .

Under-Secretary, *n.* كَاتِبٌ ثَانٍ – كَاتِبٌ مُعَاوِنٌ . An — of State, مُسْتَشَارٌ .

Undershot, *a.* As of a water wheel, يُحَرِّكُهُ ٱلْمَاءُ مِنْ تَحْتُ .

Undersell, *v.t.* بَاعَ أَرْخَصَ مِنْ فُلَانٍ *aor.* يَبِيعُ .

Undersign, *v.t.* وَضَعَ ٱسْمَهُ أَدْنَاهُ – أَمْضَى – وَقَّعَ عَلَى – أَوْقَعَ عَلَى *aor.* يَضَعُ .

Undersigned, *a.* ٱلْوَاضِعُ ٱسْمَهُ أَدْنَاهُ *pl.* ٱلْوَاضِعُونَ أَسْمَاءَهُمْ أَدْنَاهُ – وَاضِعُونَ *pl.* وَاضِعُ ٱلْإِمْضَاءِ . The —, ٱلْمُحَرِّرُ ٱسْمُهُ أَدْنَاهُ – ٱلْمُدَوَّنُ ٱسْمُهُ . The —, those whose signatures are placed at the foot of the writing, ٱلْمُدَوَّنَةُ أَسْمَاؤُهُمْ بِأَسْفَلِ ٱلْخَطِّ .

Undersized, *a.* قَصِيرٌ – صَغِيرٌ .

Understand, *v.t.* عَقَلَ – وَقَفَ عَلَى *aor.* يَقِفُ – عَلِمَ – إِفْتَهَمَ – فَهِمَ – شَعَرَ بِ – فَطِنَ – إِعْتَلَمَ . To try to —, تَفَهَّمَ . To desire to understand, by asking another to explain, إِسْتَفْهَمَ . To make to —, أَفْهَمَ – فَهَّمَ – أَسْمَعَ . I — from such a thing, ذَهِنْتُ عَنْ كَذَا . We understand, in an impersonal sense, it is understood, from …, يُسْتَفَادُ مِنْ كَذَا . It is understood that …, هُوَ مِنَ ٱلْمَعْلُومِ أَنْ .

Understanding, *n.* The intellectual powers, فَهْمٌ – عَقْلٌ – ذَكَاءٌ – ذِهْنٌ . A good —, as between parties, ٱلصِّلَةُ وَٱلْإِتِّفَاقُ . Knowledge, عِرْفَانٌ – عِلْمٌ . Prudence, فِطْنَةٌ . An agreement, قَوْلٌ – مُقَاوَلَةٌ . An —, not a treaty, إِتِّفَاقٌ لَا مُعَاهَدَةٌ . A man of —, فَهِيمٌ . The good — between the two governments, حُسْنُ ٱلصِّلَةِ بَيْنَ ٱلدَّوْلَتَيْنِ . He tried to effect an — between them, سَعَى فِي ٱلتَّأْلِيفِ بَيْنَهُمْ . The continuance of a good — between them, دَوَامُ حُسْنِ ٱلْعَلَاقَةِ بَيْنَهُمْ . To come to an — with, تَوَاطَأَ-عَلَى كَذَا – إِرْتَبَطَ مَعَ – إِتَّفَقَ مَعَ . They desired to come to an — about that, أَرَادُوا أَنْ يَتَوَاطَؤُوا عَلَى ذٰلِكَ . There is in that an admonition to him who has —, فِي ذٰلِكَ عِبْرَةٌ لِذِي حِجْرٍ .

Understandingly, *ad.* بِعَقْلٍ – بِمَعْرِفَةٍ .

Understate, *v.t.* As of a sum, أَسْقَطَ مِنْ — حَطَّ مِنَ ٱلْمِقْدَارِ. He understated the reality, أَسْقَطَ أَقَلَّ مِنَ ٱلْحِسَابِ — ٱلْحِسَابَ مِنْ أَصْلِ ٱلْحَقِيقَةِ.

Understood, *a.* As by the mind, مُنْفَهِم — مَفْهُوم. Elided, مَحْذُوف.

Understrapper, *n.* *See* Underling, *n.*

Under-stratum, *n.* طَبَقَةٌ تَحْتَانِيَّةٌ.

Undertake, *v.t.* To take a thing in hand, — شَرَعَ فِي — أَلْقَى يَدَهُ فِي تَشَمَّرَ لِ. To intend, عَزَمَ عَلَى. To engage one's self in, تَعَاطَى — تَعَطَّى — اِنْشَبَكَ فِي — تَصَرَّفَ فِي — اِلْتَبَطَ فِي. To —, to venture, embark in, اِرْتَكَبَ — رَكِبَ. To promise, bind one's self to, — اِلْتَزَمَ بِ — تَكَلَّفَ بِ — عَهِدَ بِ. To hazard, — جَشِمَ تَجَشَّمَ. He undertakes all financial operations, يَتَعَاطَى سَائِرَ ٱلْمَصَالِحِ ٱلْمَالِيَّةِ. An affair not to be undertaken, أَمْرٌ لَا يُغْسَمُ فِيهِ. He undertook to pay the amount, تَعَهَّدَ بِدَفْعِ ٱلْمَبْلَغِ.

Undertaker, *n.* صَانِعُ ٱلتَّوَابِيتِ — مُجَهِّزُ ٱلْجَنَائِزِ.

Undertaking, *n.* An enterprise, — مُبَاشَرَة — تَعَاطٍ — مَشْرُوع — مُعَاقَدَة — عَقْد. عَمَل — سَعْي — عَزِيمَة. An engagement, promise, مُقَاوَلَة.

Under-tenant, *n.* مُسْتَكْرٍ مِنْ كَرِيٍّ — مُسْتَأْجِرٌ مِنْ مُسْتَأْجِرٍ ثَانٍ.

Undertow, *n.* *See* Undercurrent, *n.*

Under-treasurer, *n.* مُعَاوِنُ ٱلْخَزْنَدَارِ.

Under-value, *v.t.* To rate below the value, — أَرْخَصَ ثَمَنَهُ سَعَّرَ دُونَ سِعْرِهِ — ثَمَّنَ دُونَ ثَمَنِهِ ٱلْحَقِيقِيِّ. To think lightly of, اِسْتَخَفَّ — اِسْتَقَلَّ.

Undervalue, *n.* ثَمَنٌ دُونَ ٱلثَّمَنِ ٱلْحَقِيقِيِّ.

Underwent, *pret. of to* Undergo, *q.v.*

Underwood, *n.* دِقُّ ٱلشَّجَرِ — رَتَم — دَغَل.

Under-work, *n.* شُغْلُ ٱلْخُدَّامِ — شُغْلٌ دُونٌ.

Under-work, *v.t.* To work for a lower price than ..., اِشْتَغَلَ بِأَبْخَسِ ثَمَنٍ مِنْ فُلَانٍ. *See also to* Undermine, *v.t.*

Under-workman, *n.* فَاعِلٌ دُونٌ *pl.* فَعَلَة.

Underwrite, *v.t.* To subscribe, أَمْضَى — وَقَّعَ عَلَى — أَوْقَعَ عَلَى. To —, of a policy of insurance, أَمْضَى سَنَدَ ٱلتَّأْمِينِ (*or* ٱلسِّكُورْتَا).

Underwrite, *v.i.* أَمْضَى سَنَدَاتِ ٱلتَّأْمِينِ (*or* ٱلسِّكُورْتَا).

Underwriter, *n.* مُمْضِي سَنَدَاتِ ٱلتَّأْمِينِ (*or* ٱلسِّكُورْتَا).

Underwriting, *n.* The occupation of, حِرْفَةُ تَأْمِينِ ٱلْأَمْتِعَةِ وَغَيْرِهَا. Insurance, سِكُورْتَا.

Undescribed, *a.* غَيْرُ مُبَيَّنٍ — غَيْرُ مَوْصُوفٍ.

Undeserved, *a.* Not merited, غَيْرُ مُسْتَأْهِلٍ — غَيْرُ مُسْتَحِقٍّ. Unjust, غَيْرُ عَادِلٍ — قَلِيلُ ٱلْإِنْصَافِ — خِلَافُ ٱلْحَقِّ.

Undeservedly, *ad.* بِغَيْرِ حَقٍّ — بِلَا ٱسْتِحْقَاقٍ.

Undeservedness, *n.* عَدَمُ حَقٍّ — عَدَمُ ٱسْتِحْقَاقٍ.

Undeserving, *a.* غَيْرُ مُسْتَوْجِبٍ — غَيْرُ مُسْتَحِقٍّ.

Undeservingly, *ad.* بِغَيْرِ ٱسْتِحْقَاقٍ.

Undesigned, *a.* — غَيْرُ مَقْصُودٍ — تَصَادُفِيٌّ — اِتِّفَاقِيٌّ — عَرَضِيٌّ عَنْ غَيْرِ قَصْدٍ.

Undesignedly, *ad.* لَا عَنْ قَصْدٍ — بِلَا قَصْدٍ — اِتِّفَاقًا — عَرَضًا.

Undesigning, *a.* — سَلِيم — خَالِصُ ٱلْقَلْبِ — عَدِيمُ ٱلْحِيلَةِ سَاذِج — بَسِيط — نَصُوح.

Undesirable, *a.* — كَرِيه — غَيْرُ شَهِيٍّ — غَيْرُ شَائِقٍ — غَيْرُ مَرْغُوبٍ مَرْغُوبٌ عَنْهُ. To deem —, to dislike as being unsuitable, اِجْتَنَفَ.

Undesirableness, *n.* سَيِّئَة — عَدَمُ شَهْوَةٍ — كَرَاهَة — كُرْه — كَرْه.

Undetected, *a.* غَيْرُ مُنْكَشِفٍ — غَيْرُ مُكْتَشَفٍ.

Undeterminable, *a.* تَحْدِيدُهُ مُحَالٌ — لَا يَثْبُتُ — لَا يُقَرَّرُ — لَا يُحَدَّدُ; of a meaning, مُبْهَم.

Undeterminate, *a.*
Undetermined,
} Not bounded, not settled, — غَيْرُ مُحَدَّدٍ غَيْرُ مُقَرَّرٍ. Uncertain, مُلْتَبِس — مُبْهَم. *See also* Undecided, *a.*

Undeterred, *a.* غَيْرُ مَمْنُوعٍ — غَيْرُ مَحْجُوبٍ.

Undeveloped, *a.* Not unfolded, spread out, غَيْرُ مُنْشَرِحٍ; of a flower, غَيْرُ مُتَفَتِّحٍ — غَيْرُ مُتَفَغِّمٍ. Not wrought, cultivated, غَيْرُ مَفْلُوحٍ. Latent, دَفِين.

Undeviating, *a.* Of a person, غَيْرُ ضَارِبٍ — مُطَّرِد — غَيْرُ عَادِلٍ عَنْ — عَدُول — مُسْتَقِيم — مُسْلَحِبّ. Direct, straight, مُسْتَقِرّ — عَنْ. Resolute, constant, مُسْتَمِرّ — مُدَاوِم. To be —, اِطَّرَدَ. *See also* Uniform, *a.*

Undeviatingly, *ad.* Without wandering, بِلَا حَيْدَةٍ — بِلَا زَوْغٍ; rightly, عَلَى ٱعْتِدَالٍ; uniformly, بِٱسْتِوَاءٍ; continuously, عَلَى — بِٱطِّرَادٍ ٱلدَّوَامِ.

Undexterous, *a.* *See* Awkward, Clumsy, *a.*

Undid, *pret. of to* Undo, *q.v.*

Undigested, *a.* Not digested, غَيْرُ مَهْضُومٍ. Not systematized, بِلَا نِظَامٍ — بِلَا نَسَقٍ — غَيْرُ مُرَتَّبٍ — غَيْرُ مُتَنَسِّقٍ. Crude, hastily formed, فَطِير. Beware of —, or hastily formed, opinion, إِيَّاكَ وَٱلرَّأْيَ ٱلْفَطِيرَ.

Undignified, *a.* غَيْرُ وَجِيهٍ — خَالٍ عَنِ ٱلْوَقَارِ وَٱلْهَيْبَةِ. Mean, دَنِيٌّ — حَقِير — ذَلِيل.

Undiminished, *a.* عَلَى مَا كَانَ — غَيْرُ مُنْتَقِصٍ.

Undiplomatic, *a.* Of diplomacy, خِلَافُ ٱصْطِلَاحَاتِ ٱلسُّفَرَاءِ. *See also* Indiscreet, *a.*

Undirected, *a*. Not guided, ضَالٌّ ـ بلا هَادٍ ـ غَيْرُ مُرْشَدٍ. Not addressed, بلا عُنْوَانٍ.

Undiscerned, *a*. غَيْرُ مُشْعَرٍ ب ـ غَيْرُ مُدْرَكٍ.

Undiscernible, *a*. As to the sight, لا يُبْصَرُ ـ لا يُرَى; to the mind, لا يُدْرَكُ.

Undiscerning, *a*. غَيْرُ مُمَيِّزٍ ـ غَيْرُ فَطِينٍ ـ غَيْرُ بَصِيرٍ.

Undisciplined, *a*. Not educated, غَيْرُ مُؤَدَّبٍ ـ غَيْرُ مُعَلَّمٍ. Inexperienced, غِرٌّ غَرِيرٌ *pl.* أَغِرَّةٌ ـ غَيْرُ مُدَرَّبٍ ـ غَشِيمٌ *pl.* غُشَمَآء. Undisciplined troops, عَسَاكِرُ غُشَمَآء ـ عَسْكَرٌ غَيْرُ مُمَرَّنٍ. *See also* Untrained, *a*.

Undisclosed, *a*. مَكْتُومٌ ـ غَيْرُ مُسْتَكْشَفٍ ـ غَيْرُ مُجْهَرٍ ـ غَيْرُ مُشْهَرٍ.

Undiscouraged, *a*. عَلَى عَزْمِهِ ـ غَيْرُ مُنْكَسِرِ ٱلْقَلْبِ ـ غَيْرُ فَشِلٍ.

Undiscoverable, *a*. لا يُوجَدُ ـ تَحْقِيقُهُ مُحَالٌ ـ كَشْفُهُ مُحَالٌ.

Undiscovered, *a*. مَجْهُولٌ ـ غَيْرُ مُكْتَشَفٍ.

Undiscriminating, *a*. غَيْرُ مُمَيِّزٍ.

Undisguised, *a*. Of garments, بلا تَنْكِيرٍ ـ غَيْرُ مُنَكَّرٍ. Open, frank, مُخْلِصٌ ـ سَلِيمٌ ـ صَافٍ ـ صَفِيٌّ. Apparent, ظَاهِرٌ ـ بَيِّنٌ.

Undismayed, *a*. بلا فَزَعٍ ـ غَيْرُ مَرْهُوبٍ ـ بلا خَوْفٍ ـ غَيْرُ مُخَوَّفٍ.

Undisplayed, *a*. غَيْرُ مَنْشُورٍ ـ غَيْرُ مُبْدًى عَنْهُ ـ غَيْرُ مَعْرُوضٍ.

Undisputed, *a*. غَيْرُ مُنَاقَضٍ ـ لا مُنَازَعَةَ فِيهِ ـ مُسَلَّمٌ.

Undissembled, *a*. مُخْلِصٌ ـ نَاصِحٌ ـ عَدِيمُ ٱلرِّيَآء ـ بلا رِيَآء.

Undistinguishable, *a*. تَمْيِيزُهُ مُحَالٌ ـ لا يَسْتَبِينُ. *See also* Imperceptible, *a*.

Undistinguished, *a*. Not discerned, غَيْرُ مُمَيَّزٍ. Not eminent, غَيْرُ مُعْتَبَرٍ ـ غَيْرُ مُمْتَازٍ.

Undistinguishing, *a*. غَيْرُ مُفَرِّقٍ ـ غَيْرُ مُمَيِّزٍ.

Undistracted, *a*. غَيْرُ مُضْطَرِبٍ ـ غَيْرُ حَائِرٍ ـ غَيْرُ مُتَحَيِّرٍ ـ مُطْمَئِنٌّ.

Undisturbed, *a*. At rest, مُرْتَاحٌ. Not molested, bothered, غَيْرُ مُتَضَجِّرٍ ـ مُنْزَعِجٍ. Not thrown into disorder, غَيْرُ مُلْتَبِكٍ ـ غَيْرُ مُتَشَوِّشٍ. *See also* Tranquil, *a*.

Undivided, *a*. Not divided, غَيْرُ مُنْقَسِمٍ. Not separated, غَيْرُ مُفْتَرِقٍ. Not united, غَيْرُ مُتَّحِدٍ. Whole, صَحِيحٌ *pl.* صِحَاحٌ.

Undivulged, *a*. غَيْرُ مَشْهُورٍ ـ غَيْرُ شَائِعٍ ـ غَيْرُ مُشَاعٍ.

Undo, *v.t.* To untie, حَلَّ ـ فَكَّ. To destroy what was done, مَحَا ـ خَرَّبَ ـ فَسَخَ ـ أَعْدَمَ ـ أَفْسَدَ. To efface, erase, مَحَقَ. To ruin, هَلَّكَ ـ أَتْلَفَ ـ أَعْدَمَ. To impoverish, أَفْلَسَ ـ أَعْدَمَ ـ أَفْقَرَ.

Undomesticated, *a*. حُوشِيٌّ ـ غَيْرُ ذَلُولٍ ـ غَيْرُ دَاجِنٍ.

Undone, *a*. Untied, مَحْلُولٌ ـ مَفْكُوكٌ. Left —, مَتْرُوكٌ. Ruined, هَالِكٌ. To leave —, تَرَكَ ـ أَهْمَلَ. He left nothing —, لَمْ يُهْمِلْ شَيْئًا. These you ought to have done and not leave the other undone, كَانَ يَنْبَغِي أَنْ تَعْمَلُوا هٰذِهِ وَلا تَتْرُكُوا تِلْكَ.

Undoubted, *a*. Not doubted, مُسَلَّمٌ ـ مُقَرَّرٌ ـ غَيْرُ مَشْكُوكٍ ـ لا يُقَارِنُهُ ٱلرَّيْبُ ـ لا رَيْبَ فِيهِ. Clear, obvious, patent, مَحْضٌ ـ مُبِينٌ ـ بَيِّنٌ.

Undoubtedly, *ad*. بلا شَكٍّ ـ بلا إِنْكَارٍ ـ لا مَحَالَةَ.

Undrained, *a*. Of a place, مَكَانٌ مَا نُزِحَ فَضْلُ مِيَاهِهِ.

Undrawn, *a*. Not dragged, غَيْرُ مَجْرُورٍ. Not traced, غَيْرُ مَرْسُومٍ. Not described, غَيْرُ مَوْصُوفٍ. Not extracted, غَيْرُ مَقْلُوعٍ ـ غَيْرُ مُسْتَخْرَجٍ ـ غَيْرُ مُنْتَزَعٍ. Of liquids, غَيْرُ مُسْتَقًى; of a sword, غَيْرُ مَسْلُولٍ ـ غَيْرُ مُنْتَزَلٍ; of money, فَاضِلٌ ـ بَاقٍ ـ غَيْرُ مَأْخُوذٍ ـ غَيْرُ مَسْلُولٍ.

Undreamed, *a*. مَا حُلِمَ بِهِ ـ مَا لا يَدْخُلُ عَلَى ٱلْوَهْمِ.

Undress, *v.t.* شَلَحَ (or) أَخْلَعَ ثِيَابَهُ ـ جَرَّدَ مِنْ ثِيَابِهِ. To — one's self, شَلَحَ ثِيَابَهُ ـ تَجَرَّدَ (or) ٱنْجَرَدَ مِنْ ثِيَابِهِ.

Undress, *v.i.* شَلَحَ ثِيَابَهُ ـ تَجَرَّدَ مِنْ ثِيَابِهِ.

Undress, *n*. A light house dress, تَخْفِيفَةٌ. An ordinary dress, لِبْسٌ عَادِيٌّ. Not official uniform, لِبْسٌ غَيْرُ رَسْمِيٍّ; of the military, أُنِيفُرْمَةٌ صَغِيرَةٌ.

Undressed, *a*. Unclothed, عَارٍ ـ مُشَلَّحُ ٱلثِّيَابِ ـ بلا ثِيَابٍ ـ عُرْيَانٌ. Not ornamented, بلا زِينَةٍ. Not cooked, غَيْرُ مَطْبُوخٍ ـ نِيءٌ. Not tanned, غَيْرُ مَدْبُوغٍ. Not trimmed, as of plants, *etc.*, بلا قَضْبٍ.

Undue, *a*. Not owed by, of money, غَيْرُ مَدْيُونٍ ب ـ غَيْرُ مُقْتَضٍ ـ غَيْرُ وَاجِبٍ; of service of any kind, مَطْلُوبٌ مِنْ ـ غَيْرُ. Not proper, غَيْرُ لائِقٍ ـ غَيْرُ وَاجِبٍ. Not just, غَيْرُ مُنْصِفٍ. Excessive, مُفْرِطٌ ـ زَائِدٌ.

Undulary, *a*. *See* Undulatory, *a*.

Undulate, *v.t.* To cause to vibrate, move up and down, خَطْرَبَ.

Undulate, *v.i.* To move like waves, تَمَوَّجَ ـ مَاجَ. To move to and fro, إِسْتَرْوَحَ ـ تَرَجَّحَ ـ أَرْتَجَّ ـ مَاجَ ـ خَطَرَ ـ هَفَتَ.

Undulate, *a*.
Undulated, } Moving like waves, مُتَمَوِّجٌ ـ مَاجٌّ.

Undulating, *a*.
Undulatory, } Moving to and fro, مُتَرَجِّحٌ ـ مُسْتَرْوِحٌ ـ هَافِتٌ ـ مُرْتَجٌّ. The — marks on a sword, نَمْنِيمٌ ـ ذَرٌّ.

Undulation, *n*. As of waves, تَمَوُّجٌ ـ مَوْجٌ; motion to and fro, vibration, إِسْتِرْوَاحٌ ـ إِرْتِجَاجٌ ـ تَرَجُّحٌ ـ هَفَاتٌ ـ خَطَرَانٌ.

Unduly, *ad*. بِإِفْرَاطٍ ـ فِي غَيْرِ مَحَلِّهِ ـ بلا مُنَاسَبَةٍ ـ بِقِلَّةِ لِيَاقَةٍ.

Undurable, *a.* فَانٍ ـ غَيْرُ مُسْتَدِيمٍ ـ لَا دَوَامَ لَهُ.

Unduteous, *a.* } As to parents, عَاقٌّ. Not obedient, غَيْرُ طَائِعٍ ـ
Undutiful, } غَيْرُ مُطِيعٍ. Disrespectful, قَلِيلُ ٱلْأَدَبِ ـ وَقِيحٌ. To be — to parents, عَقَّ ² جَآءَ بِٱلْعُقُوقِ *aor.* يَجِيءُ ².

Undutifully, *ad.* As to parents, بِعُقُوقٍ. Disobediently, مُعَانَدَةً ـ بِعَدَمِ إِطَاعَةٍ.

Undutifulness, *n.* As to parents, عُقُوقٌ. Disrespect, إِهَانَةٌ ـ عَدَمُ ٱحْتِرَامٍ ـ عَدَمُ ـ تَمَرُّدٌ ـ مُعَانَدَةٌ. Disobedience, ٱسْتِقْلَالٌ ـ عَدَمُ إِطَاعَةٍ. Undutifulness to parents is one of the two sorts of bereavement (prov.), ٱلْعُقُوقُ أَحَدُ ٱلثُّكْلَيْنِ.

Undying, *a.* Not perishable, غَيْرُ فَانٍ. Not transitory, غَيْرُ زَائِلٍ. Immortal, عَدِيمُ ٱلْمَوْتِ ـ لَا يَمُوتُ ـ حَيٌّ. Eternal, مُخَلَّدٌ ـ سَرْمَدِيٌّ ـ دَائِمٌ.

Unearned, *a.* Not merited, غَيْرُ مُسْتَحَقٍّ. Not gained by labour, غَيْرُ مُكْتَسَبٍ.

Unearth, *v.t.* To dig up, نَبَّشَ ـ نَبَشَ ². To drive, as from a burrow, طَرَدَ ـ مِنَ ٱلسَّرَبِ ـ أَخْرَجَ ـ مِنَ ٱلْوِجَارِ ².

Unearthly, *a.* غَيْرُ عَالَمِيٍّ ـ غَيْرُ دُنْيَوِيٍّ. Dreadful, مَهِيبٌ ـ مَخُوفٌ.

Uneasily, *ad.* بِعَنَايَةٍ ـ بِٱضْطِرَابٍ ـ بِقَلَقٍ. *See also* Unpleasantly, *ad.*

Uneasiness, *n.* Disquiet, عَنَايَةٌ ـ إِضْطِرَابٌ ـ قَلَقٌ. Anxiety, كَرْبٌ ـ حَوْبَةٌ ـ إِهْتِمَامٌ ـ عَنَآءٌ. Pain, وَجَعٌ. Superstitious dread, وَسْوَسَةٌ. A source of —, مُوجِبُ ٱلْإِضْطِرَابِ.

Uneasy, *a.* Disquieted, مُضْجَرٌ ـ مُتَضَجِّرٌ ـ مُتَعَنٍّ ـ مُنْزَعِجٌ ـ أَجِمٌ ـ مُقْلَقٌ ـ مُضْطَرِبٌ. To be —, إِضْطَرَبَ ـ قَلِقَ ـ تَعَنَّى. To be — about, إِهْتَمَّ بِ ـ إِعْتَنَى بِ. To make —, قَاسَى ـ أَقْلَقَ ـ عَانَى ـ تَعَنَّى. The affair made him —, قَاسَاهُ (or) عَانَاهُ ٱلْأَمْرُ. I was — in the affair, عَنِيتُ فِي ٱلْأَمْرِ. An — life, عَيْشٌ ذُو عَقَارِبَ.

Uneatable, *a.* لَا يُؤْكَلُ.

Uneaten, *a.* بَاقٍ مِنَ ٱلْأَكْلِ ـ غَيْرُ مَأْكُولٍ.

Uneducated, *a.* جَاهِلٌ ـ غَيْرُ مُدَرَّبٍ ـ غَيْرُ مُدَرَّسٍ ـ غَيْرُ مُعَلَّمٍ ـ غَشِيمٌ ـ أَخْرَقُ. To be —, خَرِقَ ـ.

Unelastic, *a.* كَزٌّ ـ لَا يُمَدُّ وَلَا يُقْلَصُ ـ غَيْرُ مُمْتَغِطٍ.

Unembarrassed, *a.* As in circumstances, غَيْرُ عَائِلٍ ـ غَيْرُ مَحْصُورٍ ـ غَيْرُ مُحْتَاجٍ. Free, at liberty, خَلِيٌّ ـ مُطْلَقٌ ـ مُطْلَقُ ٱلْعِنَانِ. Not perplexed, غَيْرُ مُتَحَيِّرٍ. Not ashamed, غَيْرُ مَخْجُولٍ.

Unemployed, *a.* فَارِغٌ ـ مُعَطَّلٌ ـ بَطَّالٌ ـ فَاضٍ. To be —, تَعَطَّلَ ـ عَطَلَ ² ـ بَطَلَ ². *See also under* Leisure, *n.*

Unencumbered, *a.* بِلَا عَنَتٍ ـ بِلَا عَوْقٍ ـ بِلَا ثِقَلٍ. Exempt from, without, مُنَزَّهٌ عَنْ ـ خَالٍ مِنْ.

Unending, *a.* Having no bounds, عَدِيمُ ٱلْحَدِّ. Perpetual, دَائِمٌ ـ أَبَدِيٌّ.

Unendowed, *a.* Without qualifications, بِلَا ـ عَدِيمُ ٱلشَّمَائِلِ ـ مَوَاهِبَ. Without endowment, بِلَا أَوْقَافٍ. Without settlement, fixed income, بِلَا رَوَاتِبَ.

Unendurable, *a.* لَا يُطَاقُ ـ لَا يُحْتَمَلُ.

Un-English, *a.* خِلَافُ أُصُولِ ٱلْإِنْكِلِيزِ.

Unenjoyed, *a.* شَيْءٌ مَا تَمَتَّعَ بِهِ أَحَدٌ ـ شَيْءٌ مَا ٱبْتَهَجَ بِهِ أَحَدٌ.

Unenlightened, *a.* Ignorant, جَاهِلٌ ـ غَبِينٌ ـ أُمِّيٌّ ـ أَخْرَقُ ـ هَمَجٌ ـ غَشِيمٌ *pl.* غُشَمَآءُ *pl.* جُهَّالٌ.

Unenlivened, *a.* غَيْرُ مَسْرُورٍ ـ غَيْرُ مُحَبَّرٍ ـ غَيْرُ فَرِحٍ ـ غَيْرُ مُفَكَّهٍ.

Unenslaved, *a.* أَحْرَارٌ *pl.* حُرٌّ ـ غَيْرُ مُعَبَّدٍ ـ غَيْرُ مُسْتَعْبَدٍ.

Unenterprising, *a.* غَيْرُ جَسُورٍ ـ لَيْسَ بِطَلَّاعِ ٱلثَّنَايَا ـ غَيْرُ نَدِبٍ. Lazy, مُتَسَاهِلٌ ـ مُتَكَاسِلٌ.

Unentertaining, *a.* مُمِلٌّ ـ غَيْرُ مُفْرِحٍ ـ غَيْرُ مُطْرِبٍ ـ غَيْرُ مُسَلٍّ ـ مُزَعِّلٌ.

Unenthralled, *a.* *See* Unenslaved, *a.*

Unenviable, *a.* مَا لَا يَبْعَثُ عَلَى ٱلْحَسَدِ ـ غَيْرُ مَطْمُوعٍ فِيهِ ـ غَيْرُ شَهِيٍّ.

Unenvied, *a.* غَيْرُ مَحْسُودٍ ـ غَيْرُ مُحَسَّدٍ.

Unenvious, *a.* غَيْرُ حَاسِدٍ ـ غَيْرُ حَسَّادٍ.

Unequal, *a.* Dissimilar, غَيْرُ نَدِيدٍ ـ غَيْرُ قَرِينٍ ـ غَيْرُ نَظِيرٍ ـ غَيْرُ ـ غَيْرُ مُمَهَّدٍ ـ مُتَغَايِرٌ ـ غَيْرُ مُتَسَاوٍ. Inferior, دُونٌ. Uneven, غَيْرُ مُسْتَقِيمٍ ـ غَيْرُ عَادِلٍ ـ غَيْرُ مُعْتَدِلٍ. Not correct, unfair, مُعْتَدِلٍ. Unequal to, not capable of, غَيْرُ مُعَيْدِلٍ ـ عَاجِزٌ عَنْ ـ عَيِيٌّ (or) عَيٌّ عَنْ ـ غَيْرُ جَدِيرٍ بِ ـ غَيْرُ قَادِرٍ عَلَى. To be — to do anything, عَجَزَ ² ـ إِسْتَعْيَا عَنْ ـ تَعَيَّا عَنْ ـ يَعْيَا *aor.* عَيَّ عَنْ ـ عَنْ. *See also* Unfair, *a.*

Unequalled, *a.* لَا مِثَالَ لَهُ ـ وَحِيدٌ ـ فُوقَآءُ *pl.* فَائِقٌ ـ فَرِيدٌ.

Unequally, *ad.* بِمُغَايَرَةٍ ـ مِنْ غَيْرِ ٱسْتِوَآءٍ ـ بِعَدَمِ مُسَاوَاةٍ.

Unequalness, *n.* مُغَايَرَةٌ ـ إِخْتِلَافٌ ـ عَدَمُ مُسَاوَاةٍ.

Unequivocal, *a.* قَطْعِيٌّ ـ صَرِيحٌ ـ غَيْرُ مُشْكِلٍ ـ غَيْرُ مُشْتَبِهٍ ـ بَتِّيٌّ ـ بَتٌّ ـ مَحْضٌ ـ وَاضِحٌ ـ مُحْكَمٌ.

Unequivocally, *ad.* بِصَرَاحَةٍ ـ بِغَيْرِ ٱلْتِبَاسٍ ـ بِعَدَمِ ٱشْتِبَاهٍ ـ قَطْعًا ـ بَتَّةً.

Unerring, *a.* Not missing, صَائِبٌ ـ صَادِقٌ. Certain, أَكِيدٌ ـ مُحَقَّقٌ. *See also* Infallible, *a.*

Unerringly, *ad.* Without missing, بِلَا إِخْطَآءٍ. Without shortcoming, سَدِيدٌ ـ بِلَا زَلَّةٍ ـ بِلَا سَهْوٍ ـ بِلَا تَقْصِيرٍ. Without blundering, أَسَدُّ.

Unessayed, *a.* *See* Unattempted, *a.*

Unessential, *a.* Not of the essence of a thing, accidental, عَرَضِيٌّ ـ
غَيْرُ جَوْهَرِيٍّ . Unimportant, زَهِيد ـ تَافِه ـ غَيْرُ مُهِمٍّ ـ لازِمٌ غَيْرُ أَلْزَمَ .

Unevangelical, *a.* خِلافُ أُصُولِ ٱلْإِنْجِيلِ .

Unevaporated, *a.* غَيْرُ مُصَعَّدٍ .

Uneven, *a.* Not level, غَيْرُ بَسِيطٍ ـ غَيْرُ مُسَطَّحٍ . Not uniform,
غَيْرُ مُسَاوٍ ـ غَيْرُ مُعْتَدِلٍ . Not balanced, غَيْرُ مُوَازِنٍ . Of an —
temperament, قَرْقَار ـ غَيْرُ وَقُورٍ ـ غَيْرُ رَصِينٍ ـ طائش . Odd, of
numbers, مُفْرَد ـ فِرَاد *pl.* فَرْد . *See also* Rough, *a.*

Unevenly, *ad.* Not equally, بِعَدَمِ مُسَاوَاةٍ ـ بِعَدَمِ ٱعْتِدَالٍ . Not
smoothly, بِلا هِينَةٍ ـ بِعَدَمِ تَمْهِيدٍ .

Unevenness, *n.* Want of smoothness, وُعُور ـ وَعْر ـ عَدَمُ بَسَاطَةٍ .
Want of regularity, عَدَمُ ٱعْتِدَالٍ ـ عَدَمُ مُسَاوَاةٍ . Unevenness of
temper, طَيْشَان ـ قَرْقَرَة .

Unexamined, *a.* Not investigated, غَيْرُ ـ غَيْرُ مَفْحُوصٍ فِيهِ
مَبْحُوث فِيهِ . Not considered, غَيْرُ مُتَأَمَّلٍ فِيهِ . Not subjected
to an examination, بِلا ٱمْتِحَانٍ ـ غَيْرُ مُمْتَحَنٍ .

Unexampled, *a.* فَائِق *pl.* فُوَقَاءُ ـ لَيْسَ لَهُ مِثَالٌ .

Unexceptionable, *a.* مِمَّا لا يُعْتَرَضُ ـ لا يُعَابُ ـ لا ٱعْتِرَاضَ عَلَيْهِ
عَلَيْهِ .

Unexceptionably, *ad.* مِنْ غَيْرِ ٱعْتِرَاضٍ .

Unexercised, *a.* Not disciplined, غَيْرُ مُمَرَّنٍ . Untaught, خَرِق ـ
أَخْرَق . To be —, ـَ خَرِقَ .

Unexcited, *a.* غَيْرُ مُحَثٍّ ـ غَيْرُ مُتَهَيِّجٍ ـ غَيْرُ مُتَأَثِّرٍ . Calm,
مُطْمَئِنٌّ ـ سَاكِن ـ سَلِيٌّ .

Unexecuted, *a.* Not done, غَيْرُ مَقْضِيٍّ ـ بِلا إِجْرَاءٍ ـ مَتْرُوك ـ
غَيْرُ مُمْضًى عَلَيْهِ ـ غَيْرُ مُسَجَّلٍ . Not signed, غَيْرُ مُنْجَزٍ . Not completed, غَيْرُ مُكَمَّلٍ .

Unexhausted, *a.* Not exhausted, as by fatigue, غَيْرُ مُعْيٍ ـ
غَيْرُ مُتْعَبٍ . Not brought to an end, غَيْرُ مُنْتَهٍ ; of a subject,
غَيْرُ مُسْتَقْصًى ـ غَيْرُ مُسْتَوْعَبٍ ـ غَيْرُ مُنْفَجٍ ; of a well, غَيْرُ نَاكِزٍ ـ
غَيْرُ مَنْزُوفٍ . Such an one is a sea that will not become exhausted,
فُلانٌ بَحْرٌ لا يُنْفَجُ .

Unexpanded, *a.* Not spread, غَيْرُ مُنْتَشِرٍ ; of a flower, غَيْرُ
مُتَفَتِّحٍ ـ مُتَفَغِّم . Not stretched out, غَيْرُ مُمْتَدٍّ ـ غَيْرُ مُتَّسِعٍ .

Unexpected, *a.* غَيْرُ مُتَرَقَّبٍ . At an — time, عَلَى حِينِ غَفْلَةٍ .
An — event, حَادِثَةٌ طَارِئَةٌ ـ بُدَاهَة ـ بَدِيهَة ـ فَلْتَة *pl.*
حَوَادِثُ طَارِئَةٌ .

Unexpectedly, *ad.* مِنْ غَيْرِ ـ بَدِيهَةً ـ عَلَى غِرَّةٍ ـ عَلَى بَدِيهَةٍ
عَلَى ٱلْفَوْرِ ـ عَلَى غِرَارٍ ـ مَأْمُولٍ . To happen to, come upon one,
meet with, —, ـَ بَدَهَ ـ بَادَهَ ـ طَرَأَ عَلَى ـَ . To happen —, طَرَأَ ـَ .
For any causes which might arise — requiring expenditure of
money, لِمَا عَسَى أَنْ يَطْرَأَ مِنَ ٱلْبَوَاعِثِ ٱلَّتِي تُحْوِجُ إِلَى
ٱلْمَصَارِيفِ .

Unexperienced, *a.* غَيْرُ مُدَرَّبٍ ـ أَغِرَّة *pl.* غَرِير ـ أَخْرَق ـ
مُجَدَّد ـ أَجْنَبِيٌّ . Simple, foolish, جَاهِل . He is — in such
a thing, هُوَ أَجْنَبِيٌّ عَنْ كَذَا .

Unexpired, *a.* غَيْرُ مُتَمَّمٍ ـ غَيْرُ مُنْقَضٍ ـ غَيْرُ مُنْتَهٍ . Of a
lease or bargain, مَا ٱنْتَهَى أَجَلُهُ ـ غَيْرُ غَلِقٍ .

Unexplored, *a.* غَيْرُ ـ بِلا تَحَرٍّ ـ غَيْرُ مَكْشُوفٍ عَنْهُ ـ غَيْرُ مُتَنَفَّضٍ
مُتَجَسَّسٍ .

Unexplosive, *a.* لا يَتَفَرْقَعُ ـ لا يَطُقُّ ـ غَيْرُ ذِي ثَوْرَةٍ .

Unexported, *a.* غَيْرُ مَنْقُولٍ إِلَى ٱلْمَمَالِكِ ٱلْأَجْنَبِيَّةِ .

Unexposed, *a.* Not bared, غَيْرُ مَكْشُوفٍ . Not exposed, as to
danger, *etc.*, مَحْرُوسٌ مِن ـ غَيْرُ مُتَعَرِّضٍ لِ . Not exhibited to
view, غَيْرُ مَعْرُوضٍ لِلنَّظَرِ ـ غَيْرُ مُظْهَرٍ .

Unexpressed, *a.* Not uttered, غَيْرُ مَنْطُوقٍ بِهِ ـ غَيْرُ مَلْفُوظٍ .
Not described, غَيْرُ مُبَيَّنٍ ـ غَيْرُ مَشْرُوحٍ ـ غَيْرُ مَوْصُوفٍ .

Unexpressive, *a.* Without expression, flat, dull, سَقِيطَة ـ تَافِه ـ
بَارِد . Weak, of language, *etc.*, رَكِيك ـ ضَعِيف .

Unextinct, *a.* Not extinguished, غَيْرُ مُطْفَأٍ . Still existing,
مَوْجُود ـ بَاقٍ ـ غَيْرُ مُنْعَدِمٍ .

Unextinguishable, *a.* لا يَنْطَفِئُ ـ لا يُطْفَأُ . That may not be
destroyed, مَا لا يُعْدَمُ ـ مَا لا يُبَادُ ـ مَا لا يُفْنَى .

Unextinguished, *a.* *See* Unextinct, *a.*

Unextracted, *a.* Not drawn, pulled out, غَيْرُ مَقْلُوعٍ ـ غَيْرُ مُقْلَعٍ .
See also Uncondensed, *a.*

Unfaded, *a.* Not withered, غَيْرُ مَذْبُولٍ ـ غَيْرُ ذَابِلٍ ; not having
lost colour, غَيْرُ مَفْسُوخِ ٱللَّوْنِ ـ غَيْرُ مَخْسُوفٍ ـ غَيْرُ خَاسِفٍ .

Unfading, *a.* غَيْرُ زَائِلٍ ـ غَيْرُ فَانٍ . Lasting, eternal, دَائِم ـ
بَاقٍ ـ عَدِيمُ ٱلزَّوَالِ .

Unfailing, *a.* لا زَوَالَ لَهُ ـ دَائِم ـ قَيُّوم ـ ثَابِت .

Unfair, *a.* سُوءٌ ـ خِلافُ ٱلْحَقِّ ـ ضِدُّ ٱلْإِنْصَافِ (or ٱلْقِسْطِ)
غَيْرُ مُنْصِفٍ ـ غَيْرُ مُقْسِطٍ .

Unfairly, *ad.* بِعَدَمِ عَدَالَةٍ ـ بِدُونِ قِسْطٍ ـ بِعَدَمِ إِنْصَافٍ .

Unfairness, *n.* عَدَمُ عَدَالَةٍ ـ عَدَمُ قِسْطٍ ـ عَدَمُ إِنْصَافٍ .

Unfaithful, *a.* Perfidious, غَدَّار ـ غَيْرُ صَادِقٍ ـ خَتِير ـ خَاتِر ـ
خَائِن . Unchaste, عَدِيمُ ٱلْعِفَّةِ وَٱلصَّدَاقَةِ . Unfaithful to duty,
trust, *etc.*, عَدِيمُ ٱلْوَفَاءِ . *See also* Faithless, *a.*

Unfaithfully, *ad.* Perfidiously, بِغَدْرٍ ـ بِخِيَانَةٍ ـ خَتْرًا . Without respect to duty, بِعَدَمِ وَفَاءٍ . Unchastely, بِعَدَمِ عِفَّةٍ .

Unfaithfulness, *n.* Perfidy, خَتر — خُتُور — عَدَمُ صَدَاقَةٍ — خِيَانَة — غَدر. Disregard of duty, عَدَمُ وَفَآءٍ. Unchastity with falseness, عَدَمُ ٱلعِفَّةِ وَٱلصَّدَاقَةِ.

Unfaltering, *a.* Of speech, غَيرُ مُتَعَثِّرٍ فِي ٱلكَلَامِ — غَيرُ مُتَطَرِّمٍ. Unhesitating, غَيرُ مُتَمَخطِرٍ — غَيرُ مُتَضَرِّبٍ. *See also* Decided, *a.*

Unfalteringly, *ad.* Of speech, بِغَيرِ لَكنٍ — بِغَيرِ تَتَاتُعٍ. Without hesitation, بِغَيرِ تَمَخطُرٍ — بِلَا تَضَرُّبٍ.

Unfamiliar, *a.* Not known, غَيرُ مَعرُوفٍ — غَيرُ مَعلُومٍ. Not current, strange, شَارِد — آبِد — غَرِيب. Unfamiliar rhymes, قَوَافٍ شَوَارِدُ. Unfamiliar sayings or events, أَوَابِدُ — غَرَائِبُ. An — word, آبِدَة *pl.* أَوَابِدُ.

Unfashionable, *a.* خِلَافُ ٱلعَادَةِ ; of the cut of clothes, خِلَافُ ٱلزِّيِّ.

Unfashionably, *ad.* بِخِلَافِ ٱلعَادَةِ — بِخِلَافِ ٱلزِّيِّ.

Unfashioned, *a.* In the rough, خَشِيب.

Unfasten, *v.t.* فَكَّ — حَلَّ. To be unfastened, ٱنحَلَّ — إِنفَكَّ.

Unfatherly, *a.* غَيرُ وَالِدِيٍّ — غَيرُ أَبَوِيٍّ.

Unfathomable, *a.* That cannot be sounded, لَا سَبرَ لَهُ — لَا إِسْتِبَارَ لَهُ — بَعِيدٌ عَنِ — الكَشفُ عَنهُ مُحَالٌ. Not discoverable, لَا يُقَاسُ ٱلإِستِقصَآءِ.

Unfathomed, *a.* Not sounded, غَيرُ مَسبُورٍ — غَيرُ مَقِيسٍ.

Unfavourable, *a.* Not conducive to, غَيرُ مُعَاوِنٍ لِ — غَيرُ مُسَاعِدٍ لِ. Not propitious, غَيرُ مُوَافِقٍ — غَيرُ مُوَفِّقٍ. Sad, saddening, مُغِمٌّ — مُحزِن — شَاقٌّ — فَاجِع.

Unfavourableness, *n.* Unpropitiousness, عَدَمُ تَوفِيقٍ — قِلَّة مُوَافَقَةٍ. Grievousness, وَبَال — مَشَقَّة — صُعُوبَة. Contrariety, خِلَاف — مُخَالَفَة. Dispraise, جَدب — إِستِقلَال.

Unfavourably, *ad.* Unpropitiously, بِعَدَمِ تَوفِيقٍ. With dispraise, بِجَدبٍ — بِٱستِقلَالٍ. Discouragingly, بِقِلَّةِ رَجَآءٍ.

Unfeathered, *a.* غَيرُ مُرَيَّشٍ — بِلَا رِيشٍ.

Unfed, *a.* غَيرُ مُطعَمٍ — غَيرُ مُطَعَّمٍ — بِلَا طَعَامٍ.

Unfeeling, *a.* Destitute of feeling, عَدِيمُ ٱلحِسِّ. Without pity, عَدِيمُ ٱلرَّحمَةِ — عَدِيمُ ٱلشَّفَقَةِ. Unimpressible, لَا يُؤَثِّرُ فِيهِ شَيْءٌ. *See also* Cruel, *a.*

Unfeelingly, *ad.* Without feeling, بِلَا حِسٍّ. Without pity, بِلَا شَفَقَةٍ. *See also* Cruelly, *ad.*

Unfeelingness, *n.* Want of feeling, عَدَمُ حَاسَّةٍ — عَدَمُ حَاسِّيَّةٍ. Want of pity, قِلَّةُ شَفَقَةٍ — عُنف — قَسَاوَة.

Unfeigned, *a.* Not pretended, بِلَا رِيَآءٍ — عَدِيمُ ٱلرِّيَآءِ — حَقِيقِيٌّ — نَاصِح — مُخلِص. Unfeigned love, مَحَبَّةٌ بِلَا رِيَآءٍ. Unfeigned faith, إِيمَانٌ بِلَا رِيَآءٍ.

Unfeignedly, *ad.* بِلَا رِيَآءٍ — حَقِيقَةً — بِإِخلَاصٍ — بِنُصُوحٍ.

Unfelt, *a.* غَيرُ مَحسُوسٍ — غَيرُ مُدرَكٍ.

Unfeminine, *a.* Of a woman, مُذَكَّرَة — مُذَكَّرَة — إِمرَأَةٌ فَحلَةٌ.

Unfenced, *a.* Without a fence, غَيرُ مَجدُورٍ — غَيرُ مَحوُوطٍ. Unfortified, غَيرُ مُحَصَّنٍ — غَيرُ مُستَحكَمٍ.

Unfermented, *a.* غَيرُ مُتَخَمِّرٍ — غَيرُ مُختَمِرٍ.

Unfetter, *v.t.* To release from fetters, حَلَّ مِنَ ٱلصِّفَادِ — فَكَّ قُيُودَهُ. To free, أَعتَقَ — أَطلَقَ. To give liberty to one in, رَخَّصَ فِي.

Unfilial, *a.* غَيرُ بَنَوِيٍّ — مَا لَا يَلِيقُ بِٱلبَنِينَ.

Unfinished, *a.* Not brought to an end, غَيرُ مُتَمَّمٍ — غَيرُ مُختَتَمٍ. Not completed, غَيرُ مُكَمَّلٍ Not polished, غَيرُ مَصقُولٍ. In the rough, خَشِيب.

Unfit, *a.* Not qualified for, غَيرُ جَدِيرٍ لِ — غَيرُ خَلِيقٍ لِ — غَير — مَحَلٌّ لِ — غَيرُ صَالِحٍ لِ. Not suitable, غَيرُ مُنَاسِبٍ — غَيرُ مُوَافِقٍ — غَيرُ مُطَابِقٍ.

Unfit, *v.t.* To make unsuitable, أَزَالَ مُنَاسَبَتَهُ — جَعَلَ غَيرَ لَائِقٍ. To disqualify, أَزَالَ أَهلِيَّتَهُ — أَسقَطَ مِنَ ٱلأَهلِيَّةِ — أَزَالَ مِنَ ٱلإِمكَانِ — أَسقَطَ. *See also* Incapable, *a.*

Unfitly, *ad.* بِعَدَمِ مُنَاسَبَةٍ — بِغَيرِ لِيَاقَةٍ.

Unfitness, *n.* Insuitableness, عَدَمُ مُنَاسَبَةٍ. Incapability, عَدَمُ صَلَاحِيَةٍ — عَدَمُ أَهلِيَّةٍ. *See also* Incapacity, *n.*

Unfix, *v.t.* To loosen from a fastening, حَلَّ — فَكَّ. To unsettle, تَوَّهَ — تَيَّهَ — قَلقَلَ — طَيَّشَ — أَطَاشَ.

Unflagging, *a.* لَا يُعجِزُهُ شَيْءٌ — غَيرُ مَملُولٍ — مُوَاظِب — شَدِيد *pl.* صَنَادِيدُ — لَا يَكِلُّ وَلَا يَمِلُّ. To be —, to persevere in, وَاظَبَ عَلَى — أَكَبَّ عَلَى — إِنكَبَّ عَلَى.

Unflattering, *a.* غَيرُ مُمَلِّقٍ. Sincere, نَصُوح — صَادِق — مُخلِص. Fault-finding, مُذِمٌّ.

Unfledged, *a.* Without feathers, بِلَا رِيشٍ. Inexperienced, غَير مُمَرَّنٍ — أَجنَبِيٌّ — عَجَمِيٌّ — جَاهِل.

Unfold, *v.t.* To evolve, بَسَطَ — نَشَرَ — عَرَضَ. To show, أَرَى — أَظهَرَ — بَيَّنَ — أَبدَى — أَعلَنَ — كَشَفَ — كَشَّفَ. To reveal, To explain, أَوَّلَ — فَسَّرَ — شَرَحَ. To relate, ذَكَرَ — حَكَى — رَوَى — حَدَّثَ. To be unfolded, of folds, إِنتَشَرَ — إِنبَسَطَ. He unfolded the affair to him, عَرَضَ لَهُ ٱلشَّيْءَ. "Betake you to the cave: Your Lord will mercifully unfold his mercy to you," فَأْوُوا إِلَى ٱلكَهفِ يَنشُر لَكُم رَبُّكُم مِن رَحمَتِهِ (Kur. xviii. 15).

Unforbidden, *a.* غَيْرُ مَمْنُوعٍ – غَيْرُ مَحْجُورٍ – غَيْرُ مُحَرَّمٍ. Permitted, مُرَخَّص – حَلال – مُجَاز – مُبَاح.

Unforced, *a* Not compelled, غَيْرُ مُضْطَرٍّ – غَيْرُ مَغْصُوبٍ – مُخَيَّر – غَيْرُ مَجْبُورٍ.

Unfordable, *a.* لا يُخَاض – لا يُخْتَاض – خَوْضُهُ مُحَال.

Unforeknown, *a.* غَيْرُ مَعْلُومٍ مِنْ سَابِقٍ.

Unforeseen, *a.* غَيْرُ مَأْمُولٍ – غَيْرُ مُتَرَقَّبٍ قَبْلَ وُقُوعِهِ – فُجَائِيٌّ. An — occurrence, فُجَاءَةٌ. *See also under* Unexpected, *a.*

Unforetold, *a.* غَيْرُ مُنَبَّإٍ بِهِ – غَيْرُ مُتَنَبَّإٍ بِهِ – غَيْرُ مَنْذُورٍ بِهِ.

Unforfeited, *a.* غَيْرُ مُضَيَّعٍ – غَيْرُ مُعَرًّى عَن – غَيْرُ مُعْدَمٍ.

Unforgetting, *a.* عَدِيمُ ٱلنِّسْيَانِ – غَيْرُ ذَاهِلٍ.

Unforgiven, *a.* غَيْرُ مُسَامَحٍ – بِلا عَفْوٍ – غَيْرُ مَغْفُورٍ.

Unforgiving, *a.* غَيْرُ عَفُوٍّ – غَيْرُ صَفُوحٍ – غَيْرُ غَفُورٍ. *See also* Implacable, Inexorable, *a.*

Unforgot, *a.*
Unforgotten, } غَيْرُ مَنْسِيٍّ – لَمْ يُنْسَ.

Unformed, *a.* Not moulded into shape, خَشِيب – مَخْشُوب – غَيْرُ مُشَكَّلٍ – فَطِير.

Unfortified, *a.* Of fortifications, غَيْرُ مُحَصَّنٍ – غَيْرُ مُسْتَحْكَمٍ. Not strengthened, غَيْرُ مُقَوًّى – غَيْرُ مُشَدَّدٍ – غَيْرُ مُسْتَحْكَمٍ.

Unfortunate, *a.* مَيْشُوم – شَقِيٌّ *pl.* أَشْقِيَاءُ – عَدِيمُ ٱلْبَخْتِ – غَيْرُ مَسْعُودٍ – مَنْحُوس. An — man, أَخْطَبُ – مَشْؤُوم. An — affair, أَمْرٌ نَحِسٌ. An — condition, حَالُ سُوءٍ. Wretched, miserable, of a man, مِسْكِين *pl.* مَسَاكِين.

Unfortunately, *ad.* With misfortune, بِنَحْسٍ. For lack of good fortune, مِنْ سُوءِ ٱلْحَظِّ – مِنْ قِلَّةِ بَخْتٍ. Without success, بِلا نَجَاحٍ – خَيْبَةً.

Unfostered, *a.* Not nursed, supported, غَيْرُ مَحْضُونٍ. Not encouraged, غَيْرُ مُؤَيَّدٍ – بِلا إِعَانَةٍ – بِلا مُظَاهَرَةٍ – بِلا تَأْيِيدٍ.

Unfounded, *a.* لا أَصْلَ لَهُ – لا وَجْهَ لَهُ – لا أَسَاسَ لَهُ. An — report, خَبَرٌ لا أَصْلَ لَهُ.

Unfoundedly, *ad.* لا عَنْ أَصْلٍ.

Unfrequent, *a.* نَادِرُ ٱلْوُقُوعِ – قَلِيلُ ٱلْحُدُوثِ.

Unfrequented, *a.* غَيْرُ مَأْلُوفٍ – لا يُتَرَدَّدُ إِلَيْهِ. An — road, دَرْبٌ غَيْرُ مَسْلُوكٍ.

Unfriended, *a.* ضَيَاع – لا صَدِيقَ لَهُ – مَتْرُوك.

Unfriendliness, *n.* عَدَمُ رَأْفَةٍ – عَدَمُ إِحْسَانٍ – عَدَمُ مَحَبَّةٍ. Enmity, عَدَاوَةٌ.

Unfriendly, *a.* غَيْرُ مُحِبٍّ – غَيْرُ صَدِيقٍ – غَيْرُ أَنِيسٍ. Hostile, خَصِيم – عَدُوٌّ – عَادٍ *pl.* عُدَاة.

Unfrock, *n.* As of the clergy, جَرَّدَ - مِنَ ٱلْكَهَنُوتِ.

Unfrozen, *a.* غَيْرُ ذِي قَرْسٍ – غَيْرُ مُجَمَّدٍ – غَيْرُ مُثَلَّجٍ.

Unfruitful, *a.* Barren of fruit, غَيْرُ مُثْمِرٍ – عَاقِر. Vain, بَاطِل – غَيْرُ نَافِعٍ – بِلا فَائِدَةٍ. "In an unfruitful valley," بِوَادٍ غَيْرِ ذِي زَرْعٍ (Kur xiv. 40). *See also* Barren, *a.*

Unfruitfulness, *n.* Defect of fruit, عَدَمُ ثَمَرَةٍ; of profit, قِلَّةُ نَفْعٍ – قِلَّةُ فَائِدَةٍ. *See also* Barrenness, *n.*

Unfulfilled, *a.* غَيْرُ مُكَمَّلٍ – غَيْرُ مُتَمَّمٍ – غَيْرُ مُنَجَّزٍ; of a promise, غَيْرُ مُوفًى بِهِ.

Unfunded, *a.* Of a debt, دَيْنٌ مَا خُصِّصَ لَهُ مَبْلَغٌ مَعْلُومٌ لِوَفَاءِ ٱلْفَائِدَةِ – دَيْنٌ غَيْرُ مُنَظَّمٍ.

Unfurl, *v.t.* نَشَرَ [2] – بَسَطَ [2]; to hoist, of a flag, أَلْوَى.

Unfurnish, *v.t.* جَرَّدَ - مِنَ ٱلْأَثَاثِ – عَرَّى - مِنَ ٱلْأَدَوَاتِ.

Unfurnished, *a.* Without furniture, غَيْرُ مَفْرُوشٍ. Not provided, غَيْرُ مُتَجَهِّزٍ.

Ungainliness, *n.* Awkwardness, خُرْق – غِلاظَة – عَدَمُ لَطَافَةٍ – خُشُونَة – بَلَادَة.

Ungainly, *a* Awkward, أَخْرَقُ – غَلِيظ – ثَقِيل – عَدِيمُ ٱللَّطَافَةِ.

Ungallant, *a.* As to ladies, غَيْرُ رَاعٍ ٱلْحَرِيمِ – مَنْ لا يُرَاعِي حُرْمَةَ ٱلنِّسَاءِ.

Ungarnished, *a.* غَيْرُ مُزَيَّنٍ – بِلا زِينَةٍ.

Ungarrisoned, *a.* غَيْرُ مَشْحُونٍ – بِلا شِحْنَةِ عَسْكَرٍ.

Ungathered, *a.* Not collected, غَيْرُ مَلْمُومٍ – غَيْرُ مُجَمَّعٍ; of fruits, غَيْرُ مَخْرُوفٍ – غَيْرُ مُجْتَنًى – غَيْرُ مَجْنِيٍّ.

Ungenerous, *a.* Stingy, بَخِيل – خَسِيس. Mean, رَذِيل – حَقِير. Of soil, unfruitful, غَيْرُ مُثْمِرٍ. Narrow-minded, حُرُقٌ – ضَيِّقُ ٱلْخُلُقِ.

Ungenerously, *ad.* Stingily, بِبُخْلٍ – بِخَسَاسَةٍ. Meanly, بِرَذَالَةٍ – حَقَارَةً. Illiberally, بِحَرَقٍ – بِحَرَقِ ٱلصَّدْرِ.

Ungenial, *a.* Unfavourable, غَيْرُ مُوَافِقٍ. Not contributing to production, غَيْرُ مُوَلِّدٍ. Harsh, of disposition, فَظٌّ – عَنِيف – جَافٍ – أَخْرَقُ.

Ungenteel, *a* Of persons, غَيْرُ أَدِيبٍ – غَيْرُ مُحْتَشِمٍ; of things, غَيْرُ لَطِيفٍ – غَيْرُ ظَرِيفٍ.

Ungentlemanlike, *a.* غَيْرُ لَائِقٍ لِذَوِي ٱلْحِشْمَةِ – خِلافُ أُصُولِ ٱلْأَدَبِ – غَيْرُ أَدِيبٍ.

Ungird, *v.t.* حَلَّ عَن [2] – فَكَّ عَن [2]. To take or put off, as of clothes, نَزَعَ [2] – خَلَعَ [2]. He ungirded the camels, حَلَّ عَنِ ٱلْجِمَالِ.

Ungifted, *a.* As with accomplishments, غَيْرُ مُفَضَّلٍ بِ – غَيْرُ مُوَشَّحٍ بِ – عَدِيمُ ٱلشَّمَائِلِ.

Unglazed, *a.* بِلا صَقْلٍ ـ غَيْرُ مَصْقُولٍ.

Ungloved, *a.* بِلا كُفُوفٍ.

Unglue, *v.t.* حَلَّ ٱلتَّغْرِيَةَ ‎².

Ungodlily, *ad.* بِفِسْقٍ ـ بِفُجُورٍ ـ فُجْرًا ـ بِطَلَاحٍ.

Ungodliness, *n.* فُجْرٌ ـ فُجُورٌ ـ طَلَاحٌ.

Ungodly, *a.* طَالِحٌ ـ فَاجِرٌ *pl.* فُجَّارٌ. "Fret not thyself, therefore, for the ungodly people," فَلَا تَأْسَ عَلَى ٱلْقَوْمِ ٱلْفَاسِقِينَ (Kur. v. 29).

Ungovernable, *a.* مُتَمَرِّدٌ ـ لا يُحْكَمُ ـ غَيْرُ طَيِّعٍ ـ ضَبْطُهُ مُحَالٌ.

Ungovernably, *ad.* تَمَرُّدًا ـ بِلا ضَبْطٍ.

Ungoverned, *a.* Not brought under, مِنْ غَيْرِ ـ غَيْرُ مَضْبُوطٍ غَيْرُ مُذَلَّلٍ ـ غَيْرُ مَقْهُورٍ ـ ضَابِطَةٍ.

Ungraceful, *a.* فَظٌّ ـ غَيْرُ جَمِيلٍ ـ غَيْرُ ظَرِيفٍ ـ غَيْرُ لَطِيفٍ ـ بِلا طَلَاوَةٍ.

Ungracefully, *ad.* مِنْ غَيْرِ رَشَاقَةٍ ـ بِعَدَمِ لَطَافَةٍ ـ بِغَيْرِ ظَرَافَةٍ.

Ungracefulness, *n.* عَدَمُ رَشَاقَةٍ ـ عَدَمُ لَطَافَةٍ ـ عَدَمُ ظَرَافَةٍ ـ فَظَاظَةٌ.

Ungracious, *a.* Uncivil, بِلا أَدَبٍ ـ غَيْرُ أَدِيبٍ ـ حُوشِيٌّ عُتُلٌّ. Unpleasant, مَكْرُوهٌ ـ كَرِيهٌ. Offensive, سَيِّئٌ. Fractious, cross, شَرِيسٌ ـ وَعِقٌ ـ بَشِيعٌ ـ بَشِعٌ.

Ungraciously, *ad.* Uncivilly, بِلا لَطَافَةٍ ـ بِلا أَدَبٍ. Crossly, بِشَرَاسَةٍ ـ بِبَشَاعَةٍ.

Ungrammatical, *a.* خِلَافُ قَوَاعِدِ ٱلصَّرْفِ وَٱلنَّحْوِ.

Ungrammatically, *ad.* بِخِلَافِ قَوَاعِدِ ٱلصَّرْفِ وَٱلنَّحْوِ.

Ungrateful, *a.* Wanting gratitude, كَافِرُ ٱلنِّعْمَةِ ـ كَنَّادٌ ـ كَنُودٌ ـ غَيْرُ شَاكِرٍ. Unpleasant, مَكْرُوهٌ ـ كَرِيهٌ. Unfruitful, غَيْرُ مُثْمِرٍ. Ungrateful to the taste, غَيْرُ لَذِيذٍ. To be —, thankless, كَنَدَ ‎² ـ غَمَصَ ‎². To be — for, كَفَرَ بـ ‎² ـ جَدَفَ بـ. He was — for his prosperity, بَطِرَ ٱلنِّعْمَةَ ‎². "Verily, man is unjust, ungrateful," إِنَّ ٱلْإِنْسَانَ لَظَلُومٌ كَفَّارٌ (Kur. xiv. 37). "And if we cause man to taste our mercy, and then deprive him thereof, verily he is despairing, ungrateful," وَلَئِنْ أَذَقْنَا ٱلْإِنْسَانَ مِنَّا رَحْمَةً ثُمَّ نَزَعْنَاهَا مِنْهُ إِنَّهُ لَيَئُوسٌ كَفُورٌ (*Id.* xi. 12). "And he said: This is of the favour of my Lord to me to try me whether I shall be grateful or ungrateful," قَالَ هٰذَا مِنْ فَضْلِ رَبِّي لِيَبْلُوَنِي أَأَشْكُرُ أَمْ أَكْفُرُ (*Id.* xxvii. 40).

Ungratefully, *ad.* Thanklessly, بِكُفْرَانِ ٱلنِّعْمَةِ ـ بِتَجْدِيفٍ. Unpleasingly, بِكَرَاهِيَةٍ.

Ungratefulness, *n.* Thanklessness, كُفْرَانُ ٱلنِّعْمَةِ ـ تَجْدِيفٌ. Disagreeableness, كَرَاهَةٌ ـ كَرَاهِيَةٌ. Unfruitfulness, عَدَمُ ثَمَرَةٍ ـ عَدَمُ خِصْبٍ.

Ungratified, *a.* Not attaining its object, غَيْرُ مَقْضِيِّ ٱلْمَرَامِ ـ غَيْرُ مُبْتَهِجٍ. Not pleased, غَيْرُ مَحْظُوظٍ ـ مُخَيَّبٌ.

Ungrounded, *a.* Unfounded, لا أَسَاسَ لَهُ ـ لا وَجْهَ لَهُ ـ لا أَصْلَ لَهُ.

Ungrudging, *a.* Not envious, غَيْرُ حَسُودٍ ـ غَيْرُ حَاسِدٍ. Liberal, جَوَادٌ ـ سَخِيٌّ *pl.* أَسْخِيَاءُ ‎². *See also* Unrepining, *a.*

Ungrudgingly, *ad.* Without envy, بِغَيْرِ حَسَدٍ. Liberally, بِسَخَاوَةٍ ـ بِكَرَمٍ.

Unguarded, *a.* Not protected, غَيْرُ ـ غَيْرُ مَحْفُوظٍ ـ غَيْرُ مَصُونٍ مَحْرُوسٍ. Negligent, غَفْلَانُ ـ غَافِلٌ ـ ذَاهِلٌ. An — moment, حَالُ ٱلْغَفْلَةِ. An — word, كَلِمَةٌ مَلْفُوظَةٌ بِٱلْغَفْلَةِ ـ زَلَّةُ ٱللِّسَانِ.

Unguardedly, *ad.* Incautiously, مِنْ ـ بِدُونِ ٱحْتِيَاطٍ ـ بِتَغَافُلٍ غَيْرِ ٱحْتِذَارٍ.

Unguent, *n.* دِمَامٌ ـ دِهَانٌ ـ مَسْحَةٌ ـ مَرْهَمٌ *pl.* مَرَاهِمُ. *See also* Ointment, *n.*

Unhabituated, *a.* *See* Unaccustomed, *a.*

Unhackneyed, *a.* Of speech, غَيْرُ ـ غَيْرُ مُقَوَّلٍ ـ شَارِدٌ ـ شَرُودٌ مَطْرُوقٍ. *See also under* Unfamiliar, *a.*

Unhallowed, *a.* Prohibited, حَرَامٌ ـ مُحَرَّمٌ ـ غَيْرُ مُحَلَّلٍ. Not consecrated, غَيْرُ مُكَرَّسٍ ـ غَيْرُ مُقَدَّسٍ.

Unhand, *v.t.* أَرْخَى يَدَهُ عَنْ ـ رَفَعَ يَدَهُ عَنْ ‎².

Unhandsome, *a.* Not pretty, غَيْرُ ظَرِيفٍ ـ غَيْرُ جَمِيلٍ. Illiberal, stingy, بَخِيلٌ ـ خَسِيسٌ. Mean, حَقِيرٌ ـ رَذِيلٌ. Bad, قَبِيحٌ ـ بَشِيعٌ ـ رَدِيءٌ. *See also* Illiberal, *a.*

Unhandsomely, *ad.* Not prettily, بِعَدَمِ جَمَالٍ ـ بِعَدَمِ طَلَاوَةٍ ـ بِدُونِ ظَرَافَةٍ. Meanly, بِرَذَالَةٍ ـ حَقَارَةً. Stingily, بِخَسَاسَةٍ ـ بِبُخْلٍ.

Unhandsomeness, *n.* Want of beauty, عَدَمُ جَمَالٍ ـ عَدَمُ طَلَاوَةٍ ـ عَدَمُ ظَرَافَةٍ. Meanness, حَقَارَةٌ ـ رَذَالَةٌ. Stinginess, بُخْلٌ ـ خَسَاسَةٌ.

Unhandy, *a.* Not dexterous, غَيْرُ صَنِعِ ٱلْيَدَيْنِ ـ أَخْرَقُ ـ خَرِقٌ ـ غَيْرُ عَتِيدٍ ـ غَيْرُ مُفَنٍّ ـ غَيْرُ حَذِقٍ. Not easy to be got at, يَعْسُرُ تَنَاوُلُهُ. Not convenient, غَيْرُ مُوَافِقٍ ـ غَيْرُ هَيِّنٍ. To be —, awkward, خَرِقَ ‎². *See also* Awkward, Inconvenient, *a.*

Unhappily, *ad.* In an unfortunate manner, بِدُونِ سَعَادَةٍ ـ بِشَقَاوَةٍ ـ مِنْ غَيْرِ حَظٍّ. With misfortune, بِنَحْسٍ. From lack of good fortune, مِنْ قِلَّةِ بَخْتٍ.

Unhappiness, *n.* عَدَمُ سَعَادَةٍ ـ عَدَمُ حَظٍّ ـ عَدَمُ غِبْطَةٍ ـ غَمٌّ. The being unfortunate, سُوءُ بَخْتٍ ـ نَحْسٌ. Sadness, حُزْنٌ ـ شَقَاوَةٌ.

Unhappy, *a.* Without happiness, غَيْرُ مَسْعُودٍ ـ مَغْمُومٌ ـ شَقِيٌّ ـ غَيْرُ حَظِيظٍ ـ شَقِيٌّ *pl.* أَشْقِيَاءُ ‎². Unsuccessful, غَيْرُ فَالِحٍ ـ غَيْرُ نَاجِحٍ ـ خَائِبٌ. Sad, حَزِينٌ. To make —, sad, أَحْزَنَ ‎⁴.

Unharmed, *a.* سَلِيمٌ ـ غَيْرُ مُتَضَرِّرٍ ـ غَيْرُ مَضْرُورٍ ـ غَيْرُ مُضَامٍ ـ صَحِيحٌ *pl.* صِحَاحٌ.

Unharness, *v.t.* ـَ رَفَعَ ٱلْعُدَّةَ عَنْ كَذَا.

Unhatched, *a.* As of eggs, غَيْرُ مَفْقُوسٍ. Not born, غَيْرُ مُوَلَّدٍ ـ غَيْرُ مَفْطُورٍ. Not contrived, غَيْرُ مُبْتَدَعٍ ـ غَيْرُ مُخْتَرَعٍ.

Unhealthily, *ad.* Without health, بِعَدَمِ صِحَّةٍ. In an insalubrious position, فِي وَخَامَةٍ ـ فِي مَحَلٍّ وَخِيمٍ.

Unhealthiness, *n.* As of the body, عَدَمُ صِحَّةٍ ـ عَدَمُ عَافِيَةٍ ـ مَضَرَّةٌ ـ وَخَامَةٌ ـ وَبَالٌ ـ وَبَلَةٌ. Insalubrity, ضَعْفٌ ـ وَهْنٌ لِلصِّحَّةِ.

Unhealthy, *a.* Of the body, عَلِيلٌ ـ غَيْرُ مُعَافٍ ـ مَوْهُونٌ. Insalubrious, وَخِيمٌ ـ مُتَوَخِّمٌ ـ وَبِيلٌ.

Unheard, *a.* Not heard, غَيْرُ مَسْمُوعٍ. Not tried, examined, as before a judge, غَيْرُ مَسْمُوعٍ ـ غَيْرُ مَفْحُوصٍ. Unheard of, unknown, مَجْهُولٌ.

Unheeded, *a.* Not observed, غَيْرُ مُعْتَبَرٍ ـ غَيْرُ مُلَاحَظٍ. Not recognized, مُنْكَرٌ.

Unhelped, *a.* بِلَا مُعَاضَدَةٍ ـ بِلَا إِعَانَةٍ ـ بِدُونِ مُسَاعَدَةٍ.

Unhesitating, *a.* Decided, زَمِيعٌ ـ غَيْرُ مُتَرَدِّدٍ ـ غَيْرُ مُتَضَرِّبٍ ـ حَزِيمٌ ـ حَازِمٌ ـ صِنْدِيدٌ.

Unhesitatingly, *ad.* حَزْمًا ـ حَتْمًا جَزْمًا ـ بِلَا تَرَدُّدٍ ـ بِلَا تَضَرُّبٍ.

Unhewn, *a.* Not hewn, of wood, غَيْرُ مَقْطُوعٍ; of stone, غَيْرُ مَنْحُوتٍ. Rough, unformed, خَشِيبٌ.

Unhindered, *a.* غَيْرُ مُطْلَقٍ ـ غَيْرُ مَمْنُوعٍ ـ غَيْرُ مُعَاقٍ ـ غَيْرُ مُتَعَوَّقٍ ـ مُنْحَجِزٌ.

Unhinge, *v.t.* To take off from the hinges, ـَ رَفَعَ ٱلْجَوَارِيرَ عَنْ كَذَا. To disconcert, perplex, أَغْفَلَ ـ كَدَّرَ ـ قَلَّقَ ـ خَبَّلَ ـ حَيَّرَ ـ تَيَّهَ.

Unhinged, *a.* Taken from its hinges, مَقْلُوعٌ عَنْ جَوَارِيرِهِ. Perplexed, troubled, مُضْطَرِبٌ ـ مُكَدَّرٌ ـ مُقَلَّقٌ ـ مُخَبَّلٌ ـ مُحَيَّرٌ.

Unholily, *ad.* بِعَدَمِ طَهَارَةٍ ـ بِنَجَاسَةٍ ـ بِدَنَاسَةٍ.

Unholy, *a.* Impure, unclean, غَيْرُ طَاهِرٍ ـ نَجِسٌ ـ دَنِسٌ. Profane, دَنِسٌ ـ عَدِيمُ ٱلْحُرْمَةِ.

Unhonoured, *a.* Without honour, غَيْرُ مُكَرَّمٍ ـ غَيْرُ مُحْتَرَمٍ. Without fame, بِلَا شُهْرَةٍ ـ بِلَا صِيتٍ ـ غَيْرُ مَذْكُورٍ.

Unhook, *v.t.* To loosen or take down, as from a hook, فَكَّ ². To take out a hook, as from a fish, فَكَّ ² (ـَ رَفَعَ) ٱلصِّنَّارَةَ مِنْ.

Unhoped for, *a.* غَيْرُ مَأْمُولٍ ـ غَيْرُ مُتَرَقَّبٍ.

Unhorse, *v.t.* كَرْكَبَ عَنْ ـ أَرْمَى عَنِ ٱلْفَرَسِ ـ قَطَّرَ عَنِ ٱلْفَرَسِ ـ ٱلْفَرَسِ.

Unhostile, *a.* Not inimical, غَيْرُ مُعَادٍ. Not warlike, غَيْرُ حَرْبِيٍّ.

Unhoused, *a.* Without a dwelling, بِلَا مَسْكَنٍ ـ بِلَا بَيْتٍ. Outside, بَرًّا ـ فِي ٱلْخَارِجِ.

Unhung, *a.* Of the gallows, غَيْرُ مَشْنُوقٍ; not suspended, غَيْرُ مُعَلَّقٍ.

Unhurt, *a.* Not wounded, غَيْرُ مُجَرَّحٍ ـ غَيْرُ مَجْرُوحٍ. Not damaged, غَيْرُ مُخَسَّرٍ ـ غَيْرُ مُعَطَّلٍ; of goods, غَيْرُ ذِي عَوَارٍ. Whole, safe, سَلِيمٌ ـ صَحِيحٌ.

Unicorn, *n.* The fabled, وَحْشٌ وَهْمِيٌّ يُشْبِهُ ٱلْفَرَسَ وَفِي جَبْهَتِهِ قَرْنٌ ـ وَحِيدُ ٱلْقَرْنِ. The sea —, كَرْكَدَنٌّ بَحْرِيٌّ.

Unification, *n.* تَوْحِيدٌ. The — or consolidation of a debt, تَوْحِيدُ دَيْنٍ.

Uniform, *a.* Having the same form, arrangement, *etc.*, عَلَى سِمَاطٍ وَاحِدٍ. Like to, نَظِيرٌ لِ. Correct, right, مُعْتَدِلٌ. Undeviating, consecutive, مُتَتَالٍ ـ مُتَتَابِعٌ ـ مُطَّرِدٌ. A thing following a — course, أَمْرٌ سَلْكِيٌّ. To be —, undeviating, even, direct, إِتْلَأَبَّ ـ إِطَّرَدَ. To be — with, نَاظَرَ. To make —, of a thing, ـَ جَعَلَ ٱلْأَمْرَ سِكَّةً وَاحِدَةً. To be —, equable, إِسْتَوَى. To become —, equable, إِعْتَدَلَ. *See also* Regular, *a.*

Uniform, *n.* A dress of office, لِبَاسُ وَظِيفَةٍ ـ لِبْسُ مَنْصِبٍ. Official costume, أَلْبِسَةٌ رَسْمِيَّةٌ. Soldiers' —, زِيُّ ٱلْعَسْكَرِ ـ أُونِيفُرْمَة. They go about the town in their —, يَجُولُونَ فِي ٱلْمَدِينَةِ بِمَلَابِسِهِمِ ٱلرَّسْمِيَّةِ.

Uniformity, *n.* The being uniform, إِتْلِئْبَابٌ ـ تُلَأْبِيَةٌ ـ مُطَابَقَةٌ. The following in a regular course, إِطِّرَادٌ ـ تَتَالٍ ـ إِنْتِظَامٌ ـ سَوَآءٌ ـ إِسْتِوَآءٌ. Regularity, evenness, مُسَاوَاةٌ. *See also* Regularity, *n.*

Uniformly, *ad.* In one way, course, shape, عَلَى سِمَاطٍ وَاحِدٍ. Without deviation, بِتَتَالٍ ـ بِٱطِّرَادٍ. Equally, عَلَى ٱلسَّوِيَّةِ. Regularly, with regularity, بِٱنْتِظَامٍ. Always, دَائِمًا.

Unify, *v.a.* وَحَّدَ. To — a debt, وَحَّدَ دَيْنًا ـ وَحَّدَ ٱلدُّيُونَ. A unified debt, دَيْنٌ مُوَحَّدٌ.

Unilluminated, *a.* Not illumined, as with lamps, *etc.*, غَيْرُ مُسْتَصْبَحٍ ـ غَيْرُ مُزَيَّنٍ بِكَذَا ـ بِكَذَا. *See also* Unenlightened, *a.*

Unimaginable, *a.* يَفُوقُ ٱلْوَهْمَ ـ لَا يَتَخَيَّلُ ـ تَصَوُّرُهُ مُحَالٌ.

Unimaginative, *a.* Not fancied, غَيْرُ خَيَالِيٍّ. Not quick at imagining, ثَقِيلٌ ـ غَيْرُ سَرِيعِ ٱلِٱخْتِرَاعِ ـ غَيْرُ سَرِيعِ ٱلتَّخَيُّلِ.

Unimagined, *a.* غَيْرُ مُصَوَّرٍ فِي ٱلْوَهْمِ.

Unimpaired, *a.* مَا أَصَابَهُ نُقْصَانٌ ـ مَا أَصَابَهُ ضَرَرٌ ـ مَصُونٌ ـ سَالِمٌ ـ سَلِيمٌ ـ صَحِيحٌ. To be —, ـِ صَحَّ.

Unimpassioned, *a.* فَاتِرٌ ـ بَارِدٌ ـ غَيْرُ مُتَحَرِّضٍ ـ غَيْرُ مُغْرَمٍ.

Unimpeachable, *a.* Not blameable, مِنْ غَيْرِ مَلَامَةٍ — لَا يُلَامُ — زَكِيٌّ — نَقِيٌّ. Not accusable, لَا يُتَّهَمُ. Not to be called in question, لَا رَيْبَ فِيهِ — لَا شَكَّ فِيهِ.

Unimpeached, *a.* Not blamed, غَيْرُ مَلُومٍ. Not accused, غَيْرُ مُتَّهَمٍ — غَيْرُ تَهِيمٍ. Not called in question, غَيْرُ مَشْكُوكٍ فِيهِ.

Unimpeded, *a.* غَيْرُ مُتَحَجِّزٍ — غَيْرُ مُتَعَوِّقٍ — غَيْرُ مَحْجُورٍ — غَيْرُ مَمْنُوعٍ — مُطْلَقٌ. *See also* Unencumbered, *a.*

Unimpelled, *a.* غَيْرُ مُنْدَفِعٍ — غَيْرُ مُحَرَّضٍ — غَيْرُ مَدْسُورٍ.

Unimportance, *n.* جُزْئِيَّةٌ — تَفَاهَةٌ — عَدَمُ أَهَمِّيَّةٍ.

Unimportant, *a.* غَيْرُ مُهِمٍّ — جُزْئِيٌّ — تَافِهٌ — زَهِيدٌ. *See also* Trifling, *a.*

Unimpressed, *a.* Not impressed upon one, غَيْرُ مُؤَثِّرٍ فِيهِ — غَيْرُ مُنْطَبِعٍ فِيهِ.

Unimpressible, *a.* لَا يُؤَثِّرُ فِيهِ — لَا يَنْطَبِعُ فِيهِ.

Unimpressive, *a.* غَيْرُ مُؤَثِّرٍ — غَيْرُ مُحَرِّكٍ — بَارِدٌ — فَاتِرٌ.

Unimproved, *a.* Not brought into a right state, عَدِيمُ ٱلِاسْتِتْبَابِ — غَيْرُ مُعَدَّلٍ. Not reformed, غَيْرُ مُهَذَّبٍ. Not cultivated, غَيْرُ مَفْلُوحٍ. Not utilized, غَيْرُ مُسْتَفَادٍ بِهِ. Not taken advantage of, as an opportunity, غَيْرُ مُفْتَرَصٍ. Not better, of health, غَيْرُ مُعْتَدِلٍ.

Unincumbered, *a.* *See* Unencumbered, *a.*

Uninfected, *a.* غَيْرُ مُصَابٍ.

Uninfectious, *a.* غَيْرُ مُعْدٍ — غَيْرُ مُعْتَدٍ — غَيْرُ سَارٍ.

Uninfluenced, *a.* Not affected, غَيْرُ مُتَأَثِّرٍ. Not moved to, غَيْرُ مُحْتَثٍّ عَلَى — غَيْرُ مَحْمُولٍ عَلَى. Without interested motives, خَالٍ مِنَ ٱلْغَرَضِ — مُنَزَّهٌ عَنِ ٱلْغَرَضِ.

Uninfluential, *a.* Of persons, غَيْرُ ذِي نُفُوذٍ — غَيْرُ ذِي ٱعْتِبَارٍ; of things, غَيْرُ مُؤَثِّرٍ — بِلَا تَأْثِيرٍ.

Uninformed, *a.* Without knowledge of, غَيْرُ وَاقِفٍ عَلَى — غَيْرُ خَبِيرٍ بِ. Not learned, غَيْرُ مُعَلَّمٍ — غَيْرُ ذِي عِلْمٍ.

Uninhabitable, *a.* لَا يُسْكَنُ — غَيْرُ قَابِلِ ٱلسُّكْنَى.

Uninhabited, *a.* غَيْرُ مَسْكُونٍ — غَيْرُ آهِلٍ — غَيْرُ عَامِرٍ. An — land, أَرْضٌ خَالِيَةٌ.

Uninitiated, *a.* Not instructed, غَيْرُ مُمَرَّنٍ — غَيْرُ مُعَلَّمٍ — جَاهِلٌ. Not introduced into, غَيْرُ دَخِيلٍ فِي. Not originated, غَيْرُ مُخْتَرَعٍ. Not begun, غَيْرُ مَشْرُوعٍ.

Uninjured, *a.* *See* Unhurt, *a.*

Uninquisitive, *a.* Not given to inquiry, غَيْرُ سَآلٍ — غَيْرُ نَقَّافٍ — غَيْرُ رَاغِبٍ فِي ٱلطَّلَبِ — غَيْرُ نَقَّافٍ. Not curious, غَيْرُ مُتَجَسِّسٍ — غَيْرُ فُضُولِيٍّ. An — man, رَجُلٌ غَيْرُ سُؤَلَةٍ.

Uninspired, *a.* Of revelation, غَيْرُ مُنْزَلٍ — غَيْرُ مُوحًى بِهِ; of poetry, *etc.*, غَيْرُ مُلْهَمٍ. Of a journal, not official, غَيْرُ رَسْمِيٍّ.

Uninstructed, *a.* Not taught, غَيْرُ مُدَرَّسٍ — غَيْرُ مُعَلَّمٍ — أُمِّيٌّ — جَاهِلٌ *pl.* جُهَّالٌ. Not directed, ordered, غَيْرُ مُوَصًّى — غَيْرُ مَأْمُورٍ — بِلَا أَوَامِرَ.

Uninstructive, *a.* عَدِيمُ ٱلْفَائِدَةِ — غَيْرُ مُفِيدٍ.

Uninsured, *a.* غَيْرُ مُؤَمَّنٍ فِي سِكُورْتَا.

Unintellectual, *a.* Not relating to the intellect, غَيْرُ ذِهْنِيٍّ — غَيْرُ عَقْلِيٍّ. Not having much intellect, أُمِّيٌّ — عُوَيْرِفٌ — غَيْرُ عَاقِلٍ — غَيْرُ ذَكِيٍّ — غَيْرُ فَهِيمٍ — غَيْرُ فَطِينٍ.

Unintelligent, *a.* *See second part of preceding article.*

Unintelligible, *a.* غَيْرُ مَعْقُولٍ — غَيْرُ مَفْهُومٍ — لَا يَنْفَهِمُ — عُقْمِيٌّ — غَيْرُ وَاضِحٍ — مُشْتَبِهٌ — لَا يُفْهَمُ.

Unintended, *a.*
Unintentional, } غَيْرُ ٱخْتِيَارِيٍّ — غَيْرُ عَمْدِيٍّ — غَيْرُ قَصْدِيٍّ.

Unintentionally, *ad.* مِنْ غَيْرِ عَمْدَةٍ — لَا عَلَى بَصِيرَةٍ — عَنْ غَيْرِ قَصْدٍ.

Uninterested, *a.* Not having a share in, غَيْرُ مُشْتَرِكٍ فِي — لَا سَهْمَ لَهُ فِي. Not having any interest, concern, in, غَيْرُ رَاغِبٍ فِي. Not having any pleasure in, غَيْرُ مُلْتَذٍّ بِ.

Uninteresting, *a.* Not affecting, غَيْرُ مُرَغِّبٍ. Not pleasant, غَيْرُ لَذِيذٍ — غَيْرُ لَطِيفٍ. Not captivating, غَيْرُ مُغْرِمٍ. An — person, سَقِيطَةٌ.

Unintermitted, *a.*
Unintermitting, } Incessant, مُتَدَارِكٌ — مُطَّرِدٌ — حَاشِكٌ — مُتَوَالٍ — فِي كُلِّ حِينٍ — عَلَى ٱتِّصَالٍ. Consecutive, مُتَّصِلٌ — مُتَتَابِعٌ — مُسَلْسَلٌ. Steady, دَائِمٌ — رَاتِبٌ. *See also* Indefatigable, *a.*

Unintermittingly, *ad.* عَلَى ٱلدَّوَامِ — تَوَاتُرًا — بِلَا ٱنْقِطَاعٍ — عَلَى ٱلِاسْتِمْرَارِ. His reading continued —, اِطَّرَدَتْ قِرَاءَتُهُ.

Uninterrupted, *a.* Not hindered, غَيْرُ مَمْنُوعٍ. Not interfered with in business, غَيْرُ مُعَطَّلٍ. Not interrupted in speech, غَيْرُ مُعْتَرَضٍ فِي ٱلْكَلَامِ. *See also* Intermitting, *and* Unbroken, *a.*

Uninterruptedly, *ad.* Continuously, مِنْ غَيْرِ تَخَلُّلٍ — بِٱطِّرَادٍ. Without hindrance, بِلَا مَنْعٍ — مِنْ غَيْرِ مُمَانَعَةٍ. Without interruption in business, بِلَا تَعْطِيلٍ. To be carried on —, تَدَارَكَ: The journey continued —, تَدَارَكَ ٱلسَّيْرُ. *See also* Unintermittingly, *ad.*

Uninured, *a.* *See* Unaccustomed, *a.*

Uninvestigated, *a.* *See* Unexplored, *a.*

Uninvited, *a.* غَيْرُ مَدْعُوٍّ — غَيْرُ مَعْزُومٍ. An — guest, طُفَيْلٌ — طُفَيْلِيٌّ.

Uninviting, *a.* Of a place, غَيْرُ شَهِيٍّ ـ غَيْرُ أَنِيقٍ; of a person, غَيْرُ أَنِيسٍ.

Union, *n.* The act of uniting together, ضَمٌّ ـ إِجْمَاعٌ ـ جَمْعٌ. The being brought together, united, إِتِّحَادٌ ـ إِجْتِمَاعٌ. The act of joining, تَوْصِيلٌ; the being joined, إِتِّصَالٌ. The act of mixing, مَزْجٌ; the being mixed, إِمْتِزَاجٌ. The act of marrying, تَزْوِيجٌ; the being married, زَوَاجٌ. Agreement, concord, إِتِّفَاقٌ ـ إِجْمَاعٌ ـ أُلْفَةٌ. A district workhouse, بَيْتُ لِمَسَاكِينِ ٱلْمَحَلَّةِ. The Union Jack, سَنْجَقُ ٱلدَّوْلَةِ ٱلْبِرِيطَانِيَّةِ ٱلْمُصَلَّبُ بِثَلَاثَةِ صُلْبَانٍ عِبَارَةٌ عَنِ ٱلِٱتِّحَادِ مَا بَيْنَ إِنْكِلْتَرَا وَإِسْكُتْلَنْد وَإِيرْلَانْد.

Uniparous, *a.* وَاضِعَةُ طِفْلٍ وَاحِدٍ فِي كُلِّ طَلْقٍ.

Unique, *a.* فَذٌّ *pl.* فُذُوذٌ ـ فَرْدٌ *pl.* أَفْرَادٌ ـ وَحِيدٌ ـ لَمْ يَكُنْ لَهُ كُفُوًا ـ أَحَدٌ ـ فَرِيدٌ ـ لَا نَظِيرَ لَهُ. Unique of his time, وَاحِدُ دَهْرِهِ.

Uniqueness, *n.* وَحْدَةٌ ـ وَحْدَانِيَّةٌ.

Unirritating, *a.* Not vexing, غَيْرُ مُزْعِجٍ ـ غَيْرُ مُقْلِقٍ. Not inflaming, of medicine, *etc.*, غَيْرُ مُورِثِ ٱلِٱلْتِهَابِ ـ غَيْرُ ٱلْتِهَابِيٍّ.

Unison, *n.* Of sounds, إِتِّفَاقُ ٱلْأَصْوَاتِ ـ أُلْفَةُ ٱلْأَصْوَاتِ. Agreement, إِتِّفَاقٌ. Monotone, صَوْتٌ وَاحِدٌ ـ طَامَّةٌ وَاحِدَةٌ. *See also* Uniformity, *n.*

Unisonant, *a.* مُتَّفِقُ ٱلْأَصْوَاتِ.

Unit, *n.* One, فَرْدٌ *pl.* أَفْرَادٌ ـ وَاحِدٌ *pl.* وَاحِدُونَ. A —, in figures, وَاحِدٌ ـ أَحَدٌ *pl.* آحَادٌ.

Unitarian, *a.* }
Unitarian, *n.* } مُوَحِّدٌ ـ مُنْكِرُ ٱلثَّالُوثِ.

Unitarianism, *n.* إِنْكَارُ ٱلثَّالُوثِ ـ ٱلتَّوْحِيدُ.

Unite, *v.t.* To bring together, جَمَعَ ـ ضَمَّ ـ لَمَّ. To make to agree, وَفَّقَ بَيْنَ. To make uniform, سَوَّى. To — to, bring together with, ضَامَّ إِلَى ـ ضَمَّ إِلَى ـ أَضَافَ إِلَى. To — to, join with, أَوْصَلَ بِ ـ أَلْحَقَ بِ ـ أَلْزَقَ بِ. To — in marriage, زَوَّجَ. *See also under* United, *a.*

Unite, *v.i.* To coalesce with, إِتَّفَقَ (or إِتَّحَدَ or إِجْتَمَعَ) مَعَ كَذَا. To mingle with, إِخْتَلَطَ (or إِمْتَزَجَ) مَعَ كَذَا. To — itself to, إِنْضَمَّ إِلَى كَذَا. To — in favour of, تَعَصَّبَ لِ; against, تَعَصَّبَ عَلَى.

United, *a.* Brought together, مُجْتَمِعٌ ـ مَلْمُومٌ ـ مُنْضَمٌّ. Joined together, مُتَّحِدٌ ـ مُلْتَصِقٌ ـ مُلْتَزِقٌ. Agreeing, مُتَّفِقٌ. Joined, مَوْصُولٌ. Married, مُزَوَّجٌ. To be —, gathered together, إِنْضَمَّ. To be —, joined, added, to, إِنْضَافَ إِلَى. To be — with one another, إِتَّفَقُوا. The United States of America, دَوْلَةُ جَمَاهِيرَ ـ ٱلْبِلَادُ ٱلْمُتَّحِدَةُ مِنْ قَارَّةِ أَمِيرِكَا ٱلشَّمَالِيَّةِ ـ أَمِيرِكَا ٱلْمُجْتَمِعَةُ ـ مَمَالِكُ أَمِيرِكَا ٱلْمُتَّحِدَةُ.

Unity, *n.* The state of being one, وَحْدَةٌ ـ تَوْحِيدٌ ـ وَحْدَانِيَّةٌ. Agreement, إِتِّفَاقٌ. Union, إِتِّحَادٌ.

Unitedly, *ad.* إِتِّحَادًا ـ بِٱتِّفَاقٍ ـ إِتِّفَاقًا.

Univalve, *a.* ذُو صَدَفٍ وَاحِدٍ ـ ذُو فَرْدِ صَدَفٍ.

Universal, *a.* كُلِّيٌّ ـ عُمُومِيٌّ ـ عَامٌّ ـ شَامِلٌ. To be —, عَمَّ. To make —, عَمَّمَ. *See also* General, *a.*

Universalism, *n.* The doctrine of, مَذْهَبُ ٱلْقَائِلِينَ بِأَنَّ جَمِيعَ ٱلنَّاسِ يَدْخُلُونَ ٱلْجَنَّةَ بِٱلْآخِرَةِ.

Universalist, *n.* مِنْ أَهْلِ ٱلْمَذْهَبِ ٱلْمَذْكُورِ.

Universality, *n.* كُلِّيَّةٌ ـ عُمُومٌ ـ عُمُومِيَّةٌ.

Universally, *ad.* بِٱلْكُلِّ ـ كُلِّيًّا ـ طُرًّا ـ عَلَى ٱلْعُمُومِ ـ عُمُومًا.

University, *n.* دَارُ كُلِّيَّاتِ ٱلْعُلُومِ ـ دَارُ ٱلْعُلُومِ وَٱلْفُنُونِ.

Unjust, *a.* Against justice, خِلَافُ ٱلْعَدَالَةِ. Inequitable, غَيْرُ مُنْصِفٍ ـ مُقْسِطٍ. Oppressive, جَائِرٌ *pl.* جَوَرَةٌ ـ عَسُوفٌ ـ ظَالِمٌ ـ قَلِيلُ ٱلْإِنْصَافِ.

Unjustifiable, *a.* Inexcusable, لَا عُذْرَ لَهُ ـ لَا يُبَرَّرُ ـ غَيْرُ مَعْذُورٍ. Wrongful, بِلَا حَقٍّ ـ عَدِيمُ ٱلْحَقِّ.

Unjustifiableness, *n.* مُخَالَفَةُ ٱلْحَقِّ ـ عَدَمُ حَقٍّ ـ عَدَمُ حُجَّةٍ ـ ٱلْخُلُوُّ مِنَ ٱلْعُذْرِ.

Unjustifiably, *ad.* بِلَا حَقٍّ ـ بِدُونِ عُذْرٍ.

Unjustified, *a.* Not made just, غَيْرُ مُبَرَّرٍ. Not proved true, غَيْرُ مُثْبَتٍ ـ غَيْرُ مُحَقَّقٍ. He is — in saying so, هُوَ غَيْرُ مُحِقٍّ بِأَنْ يَقُولَ كَذَا.

Unjustly, *ad.* Unfairly, بِلَا حَقٍّ ـ ظُلْمًا. To act —, شَطَّ ـ أَعْدَى عَلَى ـ أَسَاءَ إِلَى. To act — towards, أَسَاءَ ـ سَاءَ *aor.* يَسُوءُ ـ ظَلَمَ.

Unkempt, *a.* *See* Uncombed, *a.*

Unkennel, *v.t.* As from a kennel, أَخْرَجَ مِنْ بَيْتِ ٱلْكِلَابِ. *See also to* Unearth, *v.t.*

Unkind, *a.* }
Unkindly, } Disobliging, عَدِيمُ ٱلْمَعْرُوفِ ـ سَيِّئٌ. Not benevolent, غَيْرُ كَرِيمٍ. Unpitying, غَيْرُ شَفِيقٍ ـ غَيْرُ مُشْفِقٍ. Unnatural, بِلَا إِنْسَانِيَّةٍ.

Unkindly, *ad.* بِلَا أُنْسِيَّةٍ ـ بِعَدَمِ شَفَقَةٍ ـ بِإِسَاءَةٍ ـ بِلَا مَعْرُوفٍ. *See also* Harsh, *a.*

Unkindliness, *n.* }
Unkindness, } عَدَمُ أُنْسِيَّةٍ ـ عَدَمُ شَفَقَةٍ ـ إِسَاءَةٌ. *See also* Harshness, *n.*

Unknowingly, *ad.* بِلَا عِلْمٍ. *See also* Unintentionally, *ad.*

Unknown, *a.* غَيْرُ مَعْلُومٍ ـ مَجْهُولٌ. Obscure, غَمِيسٌ. Not celebrated, غَامِضٌ ـ مَغْمُورٌ. It is not — to him, لَيْسَ مِنَ ٱلْخَافِي عَلَيْهِ ـ لَمْ يَكُنْ خَافِيًا عَلَيْهِ. The subject of it is —, يُجْهَلُ

مَوْضُوعَهُ. Unknown events, such as may or may not happen, أُمُورٌ غَيْرُ مَعْلُومَةِ ٱلْوُقُوعِ. To speak of that which is —, رَجَمَ [2] بِٱلْغَيْبِ. It is not — to the government, لا يَخْفَى عَلَى ٱلدَّوْلَةِ.

Unlaboured, *a.* Not tilled, غَيْرُ مَفْلُوحٍ. Spontaneous, مِنْ تِلْقَاءِ ٱلنَّفْسِ. *See also* Spontaneous, *a.*

Unlace, *v.t.* Of a lace, حَلَّ [2] ٱلْقِيْطَانَ مِنْ كَذَا. To unloose, حَلَّ [2] — فَكَّ [2]. To be unlaced, ٱنْحَلَّ قِيطَانُهُ.

Unlade, *v.t.* Of a ship, وَضَعَ ٱلْوَسْقَ *aor.* يَضَعُ; of burdened animals, حَوَّلَ (or حَطَّ [2]) ٱلْأَحْمَالَ عَنِ ٱلدَّوَابِّ ٱلْمُحَمَّلَةِ.

Unladen, *a.* Without a cargo, بِلا وَسْقٍ; without a load, بِلا حِمْلٍ — غَيْرُ مُحَمَّلٍ. Empty, فَارِغٌ.

Unladylike, *a.* مُخَالِفٌ لِعَوَائِدِ ٱلْخَوَاتِينِ. Not nice, elegant, of a female, اِمْرَأَةٌ بِلا طَلَاوَةٍ — غَيْرُ لَطِيفَةٍ.

Unlamented, *a.* مَا تَأَسَّفَ — غَيْرُ مُبْكًى عَلَيْهِ — غَيْرُ مُرْثًى لَهُ عَلَيْهِ أَحَدٌ. *See also* Unmissed, *a.*

Unlatch, *v.t.* رَفَعَ [3] ٱلسَّقَّاطَةَ عَنْ كَذَا.

Unlawful, *a.* Contrary to law, خِلَافُ ٱلشَّرْعِ — خِلَافُ ٱلْقَوَانِينِ — مُنْتَهًى — بَسْلٌ — حِجْرٌ — مَحْجَرٌ — مَحْجُورٌ. Prohibited, حَرَامٌ — مُحَرَّمٌ — غَيْرُ مُحَلَّلٍ. To be —, حَرُمَ [2]. To be — to, حَرُمَ [2] عَلَى. This is — to thee, هٰذَا حِجْرٌ عَلَيْكَ. "Neither had we declared anything unlawful without him [*i.e.* without his permission,] وَلَا حَرَّمْنَا مِنْ دُونِهِ مِنْ شَيْءٍ" (Kur. xvi. 37).

Unlawfully, *ad.* بِغَيْرِ قَانُونٍ — ضِدَّ ٱلشَّرْعِ — بِخِلَافِ ٱلشَّرْعِ.

Unlawfulness, *n.* حُرْمَةٌ — عَدَمُ مُوَافَقَةٍ لِلْقَوَانِينِ — عَدَمُ حِلٍّ — عَدَمُ حَلَالٍ.

Unlearn, *v.t.* أَنْسَى — نَسِّي.

Unlearned, *a.* جَاهِلٌ *pl.* جُهَّالٌ — غَبِيٌّ *pl.* أَغْبِيَاءُ — عَدِيمُ ٱلْعِلْمِ — أُمِّيٌّ. Unlearned questions, ٱلْمُبَاحَثَاتُ ٱلْغَبِيَّةُ ٱلسَّخِيفَةُ.

Unleavened, *a.* غَيْرُ مُخَمَّرٍ. Unleavened dough or bread, فَطِيرٌ.

Unless, *conj.* إِنْ لَمْ — لَوْلَا — لَوْلَمْ — أَوْ. Unless he return she will certainly die, إِنْ لَمْ يَرْجِعْ مَاتَتْ لا مَحَالَةَ. Unless he obtain his end he will be greatly disappointed, إِنْ لَمْ يَنَلْ غَايَتَهُ يَخِبْ خَيْبَةً عَظِيمَةً. Unless, or except, thou ..., لَوْلَاكَ; unless he ..., لَوْلَاهُ. Unless ye do it, إِلَّا تَفْعَلُوهُ. I will kill him unless he becomes a Muslim, لَأَقْتُلَنَّهُ أَوْ يُسْلِمَ.

Unlettered, *a.* Without any writing upon it, لا كِتَابَةَ عَلَيْهِ. Illiterate, قَلِيلُ ٱلْمَعْرِفَةِ — أُمِّيٌّ. "Those who shall follow the Apostle, the unlettered Prophet," ٱلَّذِينَ يَتَّبِعُونَ ٱلرَّسُولَ ٱلنَّبِيَّ ٱلْأُمِّيَّ (Kur. vii. 156). *See also* Unlearned, *a.*

Unlicensed, *a.* Without a license, certificate of permission, مِنْ غَيْرِ تَقْرِيرٍ — بِدُونِ تَذْكِرَةِ إِجَازَةٍ — بِدُونِ; without permission, بِدُونِ رُخْصَةٍ — إِذْنٍ. Unlicensed, of a practitioner, غَيْرُ مُجَازٍ.

Unlicked, *a.* As with the tongue, غَيْرُ مَلْحُوسٍ. Formless, فَطِيرٌ — خَشِيبٌ.

Unlike, *a.* غَيْرُ مُشَابِهٍ — غَيْرُ مُمَاثِلٍ — غَيْرُ مُجَانِسٍ — غَيْرُ مُتَشَابِهٍ — مُخْتَلِفٌ.

Unlikelihood, *n.* }
Unlikeliness, } اِسْتِبْعَادٌ — عَدَمُ ٱحْتِمَالٍ.

Unlikely, *a.* عَدِيمُ ٱلِٱحْتِمَالِ — بَعِيدُ ٱلْوُقُوعِ — أَبْعَدُ. Inefficacious, غَيْرُ طَائِلٍ — غَيْرُ مُؤَثِّرٍ — بَاطِلٌ — غَيْرُ نَافِعٍ.

Unlimber, *v.t.* Of a gun, حَلَّ [2] ٱلْمِدْفَعَ مِنْ عَرَبَتِهِ.

Unlimited, *a.* كُلِّيٌّ — غَيْرُ مَحْصُورٍ — بِدُونِ قَيْدٍ — غَيْرُ مَحْدُودٍ. Unlimited authorization, powers, تَفْوِيضٌ كُلِّيٌّ.

Unlink, *v.t.* فَكَّ [2] ٱلْحَلَقَ. To open, loose, حَلَّ [2] — فَتَحَ [3].

Unliquidated, *a.* Not paid, حِسَابُهُ — غَيْرُ مُسْتَوْفًى — غَيْرُ مُوَفًّى — غَيْرُ مُغْلَقٍ.

Unliquified, *a.* غَيْرُ مَصْهُورٍ — غَيْرُ مَحْلُولٍ — غَيْرُ مُذَوَّبٍ.

Unlistening, *a.* غَيْرُ مُنْصِتٍ — غَيْرُ سَامِعٍ.

Unlively, *a.* Not brisk, بَارِدٌ — غَيْرُ خَفِيفٍ — غَيْرُ أَلُوبٍ. Not cheering, مُمِلٌّ — غَيْرُ مُحَبَّرٍ — غَيْرُ مُفْرِحٍ — غَيْرُ مُطْرِبٍ.

Unload, *v.t.* Of burdens from animals, حَطَّ [2] (or عَلَى) ٱلْأَحْمَالَ عَنْ كَذَا. To —, of a gun, *etc.*, فَرَّغَ — فَضَّى. To —, as the stomach, اِسْتَفْرَغَ. *See also to* Unlade, *v.t.*

Unloaded, *a.* Without loads, غَيْرُ مُحَمَّلٍ — بِدُونِ أَحْمَالٍ. Not charged, of a gun, *etc.*, بِلا عُمَارٍ — بِلا تَعْمِيرٍ — غَيْرُ مُعَمَّرٍ.

Unlock, *v.t.* فَتَحَ [3] — فَتَحَ [3] ٱلْقُفْلَ.

Unlocked, *a.* غَيْرُ مَقْفُولٍ — قُفْلُهُ مَفْتُوحٌ.

Unlooked-for, *a.* *See* Unexpected, *a.*

Unloose, *v.t.* حَلَّ [2] — فَكَّ [2]. To be unloosed, ٱنْحَلَّ — ٱنْفَكَّ.

Unloved, *a.* غَيْرُ مَحْبُوبٍ — غَيْرُ مَوْدُودٍ.

Unluckily, *ad.* Through want of luck, مِنْ قِلَّةِ بَخْتٍ. In an unlucky manner, بِنَحْسٍ. Unluckily for him, مِنْ قِلَّةِ بَخْتِهِ.

Unluckiness, *n.* نَحْسٌ — شُؤْمٌ. A cause of —, مَشْأَمَةٌ — مَنْحَسَةٌ.

Unlucky, *a.* مَنْحُوسٌ — نَحِسٌ — مَشُومٌ — مَشْؤُومٌ. He was — to them, brought them unluckiness, شَأَمَ [3] عَلَيْهِمْ — شُئِمَ عَلَيْهِمْ.

Unmade, *a.* غَيْرُ مَصْنُوعٍ. Not sewed, as into a garment, غَيْرُ مَخِيطٍ.

Unmaidenly, *a.* غَيْرُ لَائِقٍ بِصَبِيَّةٍ.

Unmaimed, *a.* صَحِيحٌ *pl.* صِحَاحٌ — غَيْرُ مَجْدُوعٍ.

Unmake, *v.t.* فَكَّكَ — حَلَّ [2] — خَلَعَ.

Unmalleability, *n.* عَدَمُ لِينٍ ــ عَدَمُ قَابِلِيَّةِ ٱلْمَطْلِ.

Unmalleable, *a.* غَيْرُ لَيِّنٍ ــ لا يُطْرَقُ ــ لا يُمْطَلُ.

Unman, *v.t.* To enervate, هَبَطَ ــ أَوْهَنَ ــ وَهَّنَ. To make effeminate, خَنَّثَ. To deprive of men, soldiers or sailors, فَرَّغَ (or) جَرَّدَ ٱلْمَكَانَ مِنَ ٱلْعَسْكَرِ (or) ٱلْبَحْرِيَّةِ.

Unmanageable, *a.* Not controllable, غَيْرُ ــ غَيْرُ عَاجٍ ــ فَرَطِيٌّ ــ مِذْعَانٍ ــ خَشِنُ ٱلْجَانِبِ. Awkward to use, عَدِيمُ ٱلْعَائِدَةِ ــ ثَقِيلٌ ــ مُتْعِبٌ ــ إِسْتِعْمَالُهُ مُتْعِبٌ.

Unmanageableness, *n.* The state of being uncontrollable, عَدَمُ إِذْعَانٍ. Perversity, شَرَاسَةٌ ــ تَمَرُّدٌ. Unwieldiness, عَدَمُ هِيئَةٍ ــ ثِقَلٌ ــ عُسْرُ ٱلْمَأْخَذِ.

Unmanliness, *n.* Effeminateness, عَدَمُ مُرُوَّةٍ ــ إِنَاثٌ ــ خُنْثٌ. Cowardice, جَبَانَةٌ ــ جُبْنٌ. Baseness, خَبَاثَةٌ ــ دَنَاءَةٌ ــ رَذَالَةٌ.

Unmanly, *a.* Effeminate, عَدِيمُ ٱلْمُرُوَّةِ ــ مُخَنَّثٌ ــ خُنْثَى. Cowardly, جَبَّانٌ. Base, شَقِيٌّ ــ خَبِيثٌ ــ رَذِيلٌ.

Unmannered, *a.* }
Unmannerly, } حُوشِيٌّ ــ بِلا أَدَبٍ ــ غَلِيظٌ ــ فَظٌّ ــ عُتُلٌّ.

Unmannerliness, *n.* قِلَّةُ أَدَبٍ ــ غِلَاظَةٌ ــ فَظَاظَةٌ.

Unmanufactured, *a.* خَامٌ ــ غَيْرُ مَعْمُولٍ.

Unmanured, *a.* غَيْرُ مُزَبَّلٍ ــ غَيْرُ مَدْمُولٍ.

Unmarked, *a.* Having no mark, غَيْرُ ــ غَيْرُ مُعَيَّنٍ ــ غَيْرُ مَرْثُومٍ مَأْشَرٍ.

Unmarred, *a.* صَحِيحٌ *pl.* صِحَاحٌ ــ غَيْرُ مُخَسَّرٍ ــ غَيْرُ مُعَطَّلٍ ــ بِلا عَوَارٍ.

Unmarriageable, *a.* غَيْرُ خَلِيقٍ لِلزَّوَاجِ.

Unmarried, *a.* غَيْرُ مُزَوَّجٍ *fem.* غَيْرُ مُزَوَّجَةٍ. An — man, عَزَبٌ *pl.* أَعْزَابٌ ــ عَازِبٌ *pl.* عُزَّابٌ; an — woman, إِمْرَأَةٌ عَزَبٌ ــ عَزَبَةٌ *pl.* عَزَبَاتٌ. To be —, تَعَزَّبَ.

Unmarry, *v.t.* فَسَخَ زِيجَتَهُ. *See also to* Divorce, *v.t.*

Unmasculine, *a.* *See* Unmanly, *a.*

Unmask, *v.t.* To remove a disguise from, كَشَفَ عَنْ تَنَكُّرِهِ. To — a battery, كَشَفَ عَنْ مَدَافِعِ ٱلطَّابِيَةِ. To expose one's treachery, deceit, كَشَفَ عَنْ خِيَانَتِهِ ــ أَظْهَرَ خِيَانَتَهُ. *See also to* Disclose, *v.t.*

Unmastered, *a.* Not overcome, غَيْرُ مَغْلُوبٍ. Not held in check, غَيْرُ مَضْبُوطٍ. Not learnt, غَيْرُ مُعَلَّمٍ.

Unmatched, *a.* Dissimular, غَيْرُ مُجَانِسٍ ــ غَيْرُ مُتَشَابِهٍ. *See also* Incomparable, *a.*

Unmeaning, *a.* Without meaning, لا طَائِلَ تَحْتَهُ ــ بِلا مَعْنًى. Stupid, ثَقِيلٌ ــ غَبِينٌ ــ أَخْرَقُ ــ قَلِيلُ ٱلتَّعْبِيرِ. He spoke what was —, تَكَلَّمَ بِمَا لا طَائِلَ تَحْتَهُ.

Unmeant, *a.* *See* Undesigned, *a.*

Unmeasurable, *a.* لا حَدَّ لَهُ ــ غَيْرُ مَحْدُودٍ ــ بِلا قِيَاسٍ.

Unmeasurably, *ad.* لِلْغَايَةِ ــ جِدًّا ــ بِلا قِيَاسٍ ــ بِدُونِ حَدٍّ.

Unmeasured, *ad.* Not measured, غَيْرُ مُقَدَّرٍ ــ غَيْرُ مَقِيسٍ. Beyond measure, بِدُونِ حَدٍّ ــ بِإِفْرَاطٍ. Immense, in extent, مَدِيدٌ جِدًّا; in breadth, وَاسِعٌ جِدًّا. Unmeasured, of language, طَلِقٌ.

Unmechanical, *a.* غَيْرُ مُرَكَّبٍ عَلَى قَوَاعِدِ عِلْمِ ٱلْحَرَكَاتِ.

Unmeditated, *a.* غَيْرُ مَحْسُوبٍ ــ غَيْرُ مُتَدَبَّرٍ ــ غَيْرُ مُتَأَمَّلٍ فِيهِ. An — act, غَفْلَةٌ ــ بَدِيهَةٌ ــ بَدَاهَةٌ.

Unmeet, *a.* غَيْرُ مُنَاسِبٍ ــ غَيْرُ لَائِقٍ.

Unmellowed, *a.* Not ripened, غَيْرُ مُنْضَجٍ. Not softened, غَيْرُ مُلَيَّنٍ; of the voice, غَيْرُ مُطْرِبٍ ــ غَيْرُ مَخْفُوضٍ.

Unmelodious, *a.* *See* Inharmonious, *a.*

Unmelted, *a.* Not liquefied, غَيْرُ ــ غَيْرُ مُذَوَّبٍ ــ غَيْرُ مَصْهُورٍ مَحْلُولٍ. Not softened, غَيْرُ مُلَيَّنٍ.

Unmentionable, *a.* لا يَسُوغُ ٱلْكَلَامُ بِهِ ــ ذِكْرُهُ غَيْرُ جَائِزٍ ــ لا يُذْكَرُ.

Unmentionables, *n.* *See* Pantaloons, *n.*

Unmentioned, *a.* غَيْرُ مَذْكُورٍ.

Unmercantile, *a.* Not a merchant, غَيْرُ مُتَعَاطٍ ــ لَيْسَ بِتَاجِرٍ ٱلتِّجَارَةَ. Not in accordance with mercantile rules, خِلَافُ أُصُولِ ٱلتِّجَارَةِ.

Unmerciful, *a.* عَسُوفٌ ــ غَيْرُ حَنَّانٍ ــ غَيْرُ رَحِيمٍ ــ بِلا رَحْمَةٍ ــ قَاسٍ.

Unmercifully, *ad.* بِقَسَاوَةٍ ــ بِعَسْفٍ ــ بِلا رَحْمَةٍ.

Unmercifulness, *n.* قَسَاوَةُ قَلْبٍ ــ قَسَاوَةٌ ــ عُنْفٌ ــ عَدَمُ ٱلرَّحْمَةِ.

Unmerited, *a.* غَيْرُ مُسْتَحَقٍّ. *See also* Unjust, *a.*

Unmethodical, *a.* Of things, غَيْرُ ــ غَيْرُ مُنْتَظِمٍ ــ غَيْرُ مُنَسَّقٍ مُرَتَّبٍ ــ بِلا تَرْتِيبٍ; of a person, غَيْرُ ذِي ٱنْتِظَامٍ.

Unminded, *a.* Untended, مَتْرُوكٌ ــ ضَائِعٌ.

Unmindful, *a.* سَاهٍ ــ ذَاهِلٌ ــ مُتَغَافِلٌ. He will not be —, لا يَغْفُلُ. To be — of, ذَهَلَ عَنْ ــ غَفَلَ عَنْ. To make — of, أَذْهَلَ عَنْ ــ أَغْفَلَ عَنْ. *See also* Heedless, *a.*

Unmindfully, *ad.* بِذُهُولٍ ــ بِتَغَافُلٍ ــ عَنْ غَفْلَةٍ.

Unmindfulness, *n.* ذُهُولٌ ــ تَهَامُلٌ ــ سَهْوٌ.

Unmingled, *a.* بِغَيْرِ ٱخْتِلَاطٍ ــ بِغَيْرِ ٱمْتِزَاجٍ. Pure, صُرَاحٌ ــ صَرْحٌ ــ خَالِصٌ ــ صَافٍ ــ صَرِيحٌ. Of one colour, سَاذَجٌ. To be —, pure, صَرُحَ ــ خَلَصَ.

Unmissed, *a.* ضَيَاعٌ ــ غَيْرُ فَقِيدٍ: He died —, مَاتَ ضَيَاعًا. He died — and unpraised, مَاتَ غَيْرَ ــ مَاتَ غَيْرَ فَقِيدٍ وَلا حَمِيدٍ ــ مَفْقُودٍ وَلا مَحْمُودٍ.

Unmistakeable, *a.* لا يُخْطِئُ ٱلظَّنُّ فِيهِ ـ الغَلَطُ فِيهِ غَيْرُ مُمْكِنٍ ـ يَقِينٌ ـ وَاضِحٌ.

Unmitigated, *a.* Not alleviated, غَيْرُ مُخَفَّفٍ ـ غَيْرُ مُلَطَّفٍ. Pure, sheer, خَالِصٌ ـ سُمَاقٌ.

Unmixed, *a.* Pure, sheer, سُمَاقٌ ـ بَحْتٌ ـ صِرْفٌ ـ مَحْضٌ. An — lie, كَذِبٌ سُمَاقٌ. Unmixed love, حِبٌّ سُمَاقٌ. *See also* Unmingled, *a.*

Unmodified, *a.* عَلَى مَا كَانَ ـ بِلَا تَبْدِيلٍ ـ بِلَا تَغْيِيرٍ ـ بِلَا تَعْدِيلٍ.

Unmolested, *a.* غَيْرُ ـ غَيْرُ مُنْزَعِجٍ ـ غَيْرُ مُعَارَضٍ ـ غَيْرُ مُتَضَجِّرٍ ـ آمِنٌ ـ مُنْزَجِرٌ.

Unmoor, *v.t.* قَلَعَ (or ² حَلَّ) مَرْسَاةَ ٱلسَّفِينَةِ.

Unmoved, *a.* Not shifted, قَائِمٌ فِي ـ غَيْرُ مُحَرَّكٍ ـ غَيْرُ مُنْتَقِلٍ ـ ثَابِتٌ ـ مَحَلَّهُ. Not moved in resolution, حَزِيمٌ ـ حَازِمٌ ـ صَدِيدٌ. Not affected, غَيْرُ مُحَرَّضٍ ـ غَيْرُ مُنْبَعِثٍ. Unmoved to compassion, غَيْرُ مُتَحَنِّنٍ; to anger, غَيْرُ مُغْتَاظٍ. Untroubled, مُطْمَئِنٌّ ـ غَيْرُ مُضْطَرِبٍ.

Unmuffle, *v.t.* To unveil, رَفَعَ ٱلْحِجَابَ عَنْ. To —, of a drum, رَفَعَ سِيْرَ ٱلتَّخْفِيضِ عَنِ ٱلطَّبْلِ.

Unmurmuring, *a.* صَبُورٌ ـ صَبَّارٌ ـ غَيْرُ مُدَمْدِمٍ ـ غَيْرُ مُتَذَمِّرٍ.

Unmurmuringly, *ad.* بِصَبْرٍ ـ بِدُونِ دَمْدَمَةٍ ـ بِلَا تَذَمُّرٍ.

Unmusical, *a.* Inharmonious, غَيْرُ مُطْرِبٍ ـ عَدِيمُ ٱلنَّغَمِ. Having no ear for music, بِلَا لَذَّةٍ لِلْمُوسِيقَى.

Unmuzzle, *v.t.* ² حَلَّ ٱلْعِكَامَ عَنْ ـ ² فَكَّ ٱلْكِعَامَ عَنْ.

Unmuzzled, *a.* غَيْرُ مَكْعُومٍ ـ مَحْلُولُ ٱلْعِكَامِ.

Unnamed, *a.* Without a name, بِلَا ٱسْمٍ ـ غَيْرُ مُسَمًّى. Not mentioned, غَيْرُ مَذْكُورٍ.

Unnatural, *a.* Against nature, خِلَافُ ٱلطَّبِيعَةِ. Not innate, مُصَنَّعٌ ـ غَيْرُ ذَاتِيٍّ ـ غَيْرُ غَرِيزِيٍّ. Not simple, affected, غَيْرُ سَاذِجٍ ـ مُتَصَلِّفٌ.

Unnaturally, *ad.* بِخِلَافِ ٱلطَّبِيعَةِ. Affectedly, بِتَصَنُّعٍ ـ بِمُبَاهَاةٍ ـ بِتَصَلُّفٍ.

Unnavigable, *a.* لا يَحْمِلُ ٱلْمَرَاكِبَ ـ لا يُمْخَرُ.

Unnavigated, *a.* مَا أَبْحَرَ فِيهِ أَحَدٌ ـ مَا سَافَرَ فِيهِ أَحَدٌ ـ غَيْرُ مَمْخُورٍ.

Unnecessarily, *ad.* مِنْ غَيْرِ ٱضْطِرَارٍ ـ بِدُونِ لُزُومٍ ـ مِنْ غَيْرِ ضَرُورَةٍ.

Unnecessariness, *n.* عَدَمُ ضَرُورَةٍ ـ عَدَمُ لُزُومٍ ـ عَدَمُ ٱضْطِرَارٍ.

Unnecessary, *a.* عَبَثٌ ـ غَيْرُ لَازِمٍ ـ غَيْرُ ضَرُورِيٍّ. You are — to me, لا حَاجَةَ لِي إِلَيْكَ. It is — for me to write to you, لا حَاجَةَ لَكُمْ أَنْ أَكْتُبَ إِلَيْكُمْ. It is — to state, يَسْتَغْنَى عَنِ ٱلْبَيَانِ.

Unneeded, *a.* Not required, غَيْرُ مُحْتَاجٍ إِلَيْهِ ـ لا حَاجَةَ إِلَيْهِ.

Unneedful, *a.* يَسْتَغْنَى عَنْهُ ـ غَيْرُ وَاجِبٍ ـ غَيْرُ ضَرُورِيٍّ.

Unneighbourly, *a.* غَيْرُ أَلِيفٍ ـ غَيْرُ مُخَالِطٍ ـ غَيْرُ مُعَاشِرٍ. *See also* Unkind, *a.*

Unnerve, *v.t.* To weaken, أَضْعَفَ ـ أَوْهَنَ ـ وَهَّنَ ـ فَسَخَ قُوَّتَهُ. *See also to* Unman, *v.t.*

Unnerved, *a.* Enfeebled, فَسِيخٌ ـ مَضْعُوفٌ ـ مُضْعَفٌ ـ مُوَهَّنٌ.

Unnoticed, *a.* Not noticed, غَيْرُ مُلَاحَظٍ. Not obeyed, observed, غَيْرُ مُوَجَّهٍ ـ غَيْرُ مُرَاعًى. Not treated with respect, غَيْرُ مُكَرَّمٍ ـ غَيْرُ مُرَحَّبٍ ـ مُسْتَقَلٌّ.

Unnumbered, *a.* Not having numbers marked thereon, غَيْرُ مَحْسُوبٍ ـ غَيْرُ مَعْدُودٍ. Not numbered, غَيْرُ مُعَيَّنٍ ـ مَرْقُومٍ.

Unnurtured, *a.* لَيْسَ مَنْ يَعْتَنِي بِهِ ـ ضَيَاعٌ ـ غَيْرُ مُفْتَقَدٍ ـ مَتْرُوكٌ ـ لَيْسَ مَنْ يُبَالِي بِهِ.

Unobeyed, *a.* غَيْرُ مُطَاعٍ ـ غَيْرُ مَرْعِيٍّ.

Unobjectionable, *a.* لا بَأْسَ بِهِ ـ لا يُعْتَرَضُ عَلَيْهِ بِشَيْءٍ. Not faulty, غَيْرُ ذَمِيمٍ ـ غَيْرُ مَلِيمٍ. Receivable, مِمَّا يُقْبَلُ.

Unobjectionably, *ad.* لا بَأْسَ بِهِ ـ بِوَجْهٍ لا يُعْتَرَضُ عَلَيْهِ. Not faultily, لا حَرَجَ فِيهِ ـ بِدُونِ حَرَجٍ ـ مِنْ غَيْرِ مَلَامَةٍ.

Unobliging, *a.* *See* Disobliging, *a.*

Unobservable, *a.* لا يُعَايَنُ ـ غَيْرُ ظَاهِرٍ ـ لا يُرَى. Very slight, جُزْئِيٌّ. *See also* Imperceptible, *a.*

Unobservant, *a.* غَيْرُ ذِي نَظَرٍ ـ غَيْرُ مُلَاحِظٍ. Not mindful, غَيْرُ وَاعٍ. *See also* Careless, *a.*

Unobserved, *a.* Not seen, غَيْرُ مَلْمُوحٍ ـ غَيْرُ مَلْحُوظٍ. Not obeyed, غَيْرُ مُطَاعٍ ـ غَيْرُ مَرْعِيٍّ. Not noticed, honoured, غَيْرُ مُوَجَّهٍ ـ غَيْرُ مُكَرَّمٍ.

Unobstructed, *a.* Not stopped up, مَفْتُوحٌ ـ سَالِكٌ ـ غَيْرُ مَسْدُودٍ. Not hindered, غَيْرُ مَمْنُوعٍ. At liberty, free, طَلِيقُ ٱلْعِنَانِ.

Unobtainable, *a.* لا يُحَصَّلُ ـ إِسْتِحْصَالُهُ مُحَالٌ ـ عَزِيزٌ ـ أَعَزُّ. Not to be found, غَيْرُ مَوْجُودٍ.

Unobtrusive, *a.* غَيْرُ مُتَعَرِّضٍ ـ غَيْرُ مُتَدَخِّلٍ ـ غَيْرُ طُفَيْلِيٍّ ـ مُتَوَاضِعٌ ـ وَدِيعٌ ـ غَيْرُ فُضُولِيٍّ ـ غَيْرُ مُعْتَرِضٍ. *See also* Modest, *a.*

Unobtrusively, *ad.* بِعَدَمِ ٱعْتِرَاضٍ ـ بِغَيْرِ تَعَرُّضٍ ـ بِدُونِ تَطَفُّلٍ ـ بِتَوَاضُعٍ ـ بِوَدَاعَةٍ ـ بِلَا دُمُورٍ. *See also* Modestly, *ad.*

Unobtrusiveness, *n.* عَدَمُ دُمُورٍ ـ عَدَمُ تَعَرُّضٍ ـ عَدَمُ ٱلتَّطَفُّلِ ـ تَوَاضُعٌ ـ وَدَاعَةٌ ـ عَدَمُ فُضُولٍ. *See also* Modesty, *n.*

Unoccupied, *a.* Vacant, خَلِيٌّ ـ خَالٍ ـ فَارِغٌ. Unemployed, *vulg.* مُعَطَّلٌ ـ فَاضِي ـ فَاضٍ. To be —, vacant, تَفَرَّغَ ـ أَنْفَضَ. To be —, unemployed, ² عَطَلَ ـ ² بَطَلَ ـ تَعَطَّلَ ـ تَخَلَّى. *See also under* Leisure, *n.*

Unoffending, *a.* Not giving offence, غَيْرُ جَانٍ. Not annoying, vexing, غَيْرُ مُكَدِّرٍ — غَيْرُ سَيِّئٍ — غَيْرُ مُضْجِرٍ. Not injuring, غَيْرُ مُؤْذٍ — مُضِرٍّ.

Unofficial, *a.* غَيْرُ رَسْمِيٍّ. Not authorized, غَيْرُ مُجَوَّزٍ — غَيْرُ مُسَاغٍ.

Unofficially, *ad.* عَلَى مِنْوَالٍ غَيْرِ رَسْمِيٍّ — مِنْ غَيْرِ رَسْمٍ.

Unopened, *a.* Not opened, غُلُق — غَيْرُ مَفْتُوحٍ. Not spread out, غَيْرُ مَفْرُوشٍ — غَيْرُ مَشْرُوحٍ. Unopened, of a letter, seal, *etc.*, غَيْرُ مَفْكُوكٍ — مَفْضُوضٍ. Sealed, مَخْتُوم.

Unopposed, *a.* غَيْرُ مُقَاوَمٍ — بِدُونِ مُخَالَفَةٍ — غَيْرُ مُخَالَفٍ — بِلَا مُضَادَّةٍ — غَيْرُ مُضَادٍّ — بِلَا مُقَاوَمَةٍ.

Unorganized, *a.* Without arrangement, غَيْرُ مُنْتَسِقٍ — غَيْرُ — بِلَا نِظَامٍ — نَسِيق. Without members or vessels, غَيْرُ عُضْوِيٍّ — جَامِد. Unorganized substances, أَجْسَامٌ غَيْرُ عُضْوِيَّةٍ — جَمَادَات.

Unornamental, *a.* Not ornamenting, غَيْرُ مُزَخْرِفٍ — غَيْرُ مُزَيِّنٍ — غَيْرُ مُزَوِّقٍ.

Unornamented, *a.* سَاذَج — بِلَا زِينَةٍ — غَيْرُ مُزَخْرَفٍ — غَيْرُ مُزَيَّنٍ — بَسِيط.

Unorthodox, *a.* غَيْرُ مُوَافِقٍ لِلدِّينِ ٱلْحَقِّ — غَيْرُ سُنِّيٍّ — غَيْرُ رَاشِدٍ.

Unostentatious, *a.* Not boasting, غَيْرُ مُتَكَبِّرٍ — غَيْرُ مُتَعَظِّمٍ — غَيْرُ مُفَاخِرٍ. Not making an ambitious display, غَيْرُ مُبَاهٍ — غَيْرُ فَخُورٍ.

Unostentatiously, *ad.* Without boasting, بِغَيْرِ تَعَظُّمٍ — بِعَدَمِ تَكَبُّرٍ. Without ambitious display, بِلَا فَخْرٍ — بِلَا مُبَاهَاةٍ.

Unostentatiousness, *n.* Absence of boasting, عَدَمُ — عَدَمُ تَفَخُّرٍ — عَدَمُ ٱفْتِخَارٍ — عَدَمُ تَكَبُّرٍ — تَعَظُّمٍ. Absence of display, عَدَمُ مُبَاهَاةٍ — سَذَاجَة. *See also* Modesty, *n.*

Unowed, *a.* غَيْرُ مَدْيُونٍ.

Unowned, *a.* Not acknowledged, غَيْرُ مُعْتَرَفٍ بِهِ. Without an owner, بِلَا صَاحِبٍ.

Unpack, *v.t.* أَفْرَغَ — فَرَّغَ — أَخْرَجَ ٱلْأَشْيَاءَ مِنْ.

Unpacked, *a.* Not packed, غَيْرُ مُعَبًّأ. Open, مَحْلُول — مَفْتُوح — مَفْكُوك.

Unpaid, *a.* Not paid, غَيْرُ مُوفًى. Remaining due, مَدْيُون. Not paid his due, غَيْرُ مُسْتَوْفٍ حَقَّهُ.

Unpalatable, *a.* Not pleasant to the taste, غَيْرُ لَذِيذٍ. Unpleasant, as to the mind, مَكْرُوه. Offensive, سَيِّئ.

Unpalatably, *ad.* Of the taste, بِعَدَمِ لَذَّةٍ. Disagreeably, بِكَرَاهَةٍ.

Unparagoned, *a.* } **Unparalleled**, *a.* } لَيْسَ لَهُ شَبِيهٌ — لَا نَظِيرَ لَهُ — لَيْسَ لَهُ مِثَال — عَدِيمُ ٱلْمَثَلِ. *See also* Incomparable, *a.*

Unpardonable, *a.* لَا يُعْفَى عَنْهُ — لَا يُغْفَرُ.

Unpardonably, *ad.* مِنْ غَيْرِ غُفْرَانٍ.

Unpardoned, *a.* غَيْرُ مُسَامَحٍ — غَيْرُ مَغْفُورٍ — غَيْرُ مَعْفُوٍّ.

Unpardoning, *a.* *See* Unforgiving, *a.*

Unparliamentary, *a.* خِلَافُ أُصُولِ مَجْلِسِ ٱلشُّورَى.

Unparted, *a.* غَيْرُ مُنْقَسِمٍ.

Unpassionate, *a.* *See* Dispassionate, *a.*

Unpatented, *a.* مِنْ غَيْرِ تَقْرِيرٍ — لَا بَرَاءَةَ لَهُ.

Unpatriotic, *a.* غَيْرُ مُحِبٍّ لِلْوَطَنِ.

Unpave, *v.t.* رَفَعَ ٱلْبَلَاطَ مِنْ كَذَا.

Unpaved, *a.* بِلَا بَلَاطٍ — غَيْرُ مُبَلَّطٍ.

Unpeople, *v.t.* صَيَّرَ — خَرَّبَ ٱلْبِلَادَ — فَرَّغَ ٱلْبِلَادَ مِنَ ٱلسُّكَّانِ — ٱلْبِلَادَ قَفْرَةً.

Unperceived, *a.* Not seen, غَيْرُ مَلْمُوحٍ — غَيْرُ مُعَايَنٍ. Not noticed, غَيْرُ مُلَاحَظٍ. He entered —, دَخَلَ مِنْ غَيْرِ عِلْمِ أَحَدٍ.

Unperformed, *a.* غَيْرُ مُنَفَّذٍ — غَيْرُ مُكَمَّلٍ — غَيْرُ مُنْجَزٍ — بِلَا إِجْرَاءٍ.

Unphilanthropic, *a.* غَيْرُ مُحِبٍّ لِلْبَشَرِ — غَيْرُ خَيِّرٍ — غَيْرُ خَيْرِيٍّ — غَيْرُ شَفِيقٍ.

Unphilosophic, *a.* غَيْرُ فَلْسَفِيٍّ — خِلَافُ قَوَاعِدِ ٱلْحِكْمَةِ.

Unphilosophically, *ad.* ضِدُّ أُصُولِ ٱلْفَلْسَفَةِ — بِخِلَافِ ٱلْحِكْمَةِ.

Unpicturesque, *a.* غَيْرُ نَاضِرٍ — غَيْرُ بَهِيٍّ — غَيْرُ بَهِيجٍ.

Unpicked, *a.* Not picked out from others, غَيْرُ مُنَقًّى. Not gathered, of fruit, *etc.*, غَيْرُ مُجْتَنًى. Not picked, of a bone, غَيْرُ مَقْرُوضٍ; of feathers, غَيْرُ مُنَتَّفٍ.

Unpierced, *a.* Not bored, غَيْرُ مُثَقَّبٍ — غَيْرُ مَثْقُوبٍ; as by a sword, غَيْرُ مَطْعُونٍ.

Unpin, *v.t.* قَلَعَ ٱلدَّبَابِيسَ مِنْ كَذَا — حَلَّ ٱلْأَخِلَّةَ مِنْ كَذَا.

Unpinned, *a.* Not pinned, غَيْرُ مَوْثُوقٍ بِدَبَابِيسَ — بِلَا دَبَابِيسَ. To come —, إِنْفَكَّتِ ٱلدَّبَابِيسُ مِنْ كَذَا.

Unpitied, *a.* لَمْ يُشْفَقْ عَلَيْهِ — لَمْ تَشْفُقْ عَلَيْهِ عَيْنٌ. *See also* Unmissed, *a.*

Unpitying, *a.* جَائِف — غَيْرُ مُشْفِقٍ — غَيْرُ شَفُوقٍ — غَيْرُ رَحِيمٍ — قَاسٍ.

Unplaced, *a.* Displaced, مُنْتَقِل. Without employment, بِلَا شُغْلٍ — مُعَطَّل.

Unpleasant, *a.* As to the taste, غَيْرُ لَذِيذٍ. Disagreeable, displeasing, بَشِيع — بَشِع — غَيْرُ مَرْضِيٍّ — كَرِيه: He is of an — disposition, هُوَ بَشِعُ ٱلْخُلُقِ. Unpleasant to look at, بَشِعُ ٱلْمَنْظَرِ. An — thing, شَيْءٌ بَشِيعٌ (or بَشِعٌ). Of an — countenance, بَشِعُ ٱلْوَجْهِ.

Unpleasantly, *ad.* Not comfortably, بِلَا حُظْوَةٍ ـ بِعَدَمِ رَاحَةٍ ـ بِلَا بَحْبَحَةٍ. Disagreeably, بِكَرَاهَةٍ ـ بِبَشَاعَةٍ ـ بِصُورَةٍ سَيِّئَةٍ.

Unpleasantness, *n.* Absence of ease, as in one's circumstance, عَدَمُ حُظْوَةٍ ـ عَدَمُ رَاحَةٍ ـ كَرَاهَةٌ. Disagreeableness, خَطْبٌ ـ بَشَاعَةٌ. Coolness, disagreement, مُبَايَنَةٌ ـ مُنَازَعَةٌ ـ شِقَاقٌ ـ بُرُودَةٌ. The —, trouble, vexations, increased after that, زَادَ ٱلْخَطْبُ بَعْدَ ذٰلِكَ.

Unpliant, *a.* Stiff, كَزٌّ ـ صُلْبٌ ـ غَيْرُ لَيِّنٍ ـ غَيْرُ رَطِيبٍ. Unbending, of disposition, غَيْرُ لَيِّنِ ٱلْجَانِبِ ـ غَيْرُ لَيِّنِ ٱلْعَاطِفَةِ ـ عَنِيدٌ.

Unploughed, *a.* غَيْرُ مَحْرُوثٍ ـ بِلَا حَرْثٍ ـ غَيْرُ مَفْلُوحٍ.

Unpoetical, *a.* Not according to poetry, غَيْرُ شِعْرِيٍّ. Not written in verse, غَيْرُ مَنْظُومٍ. Not caring for or liking poetry, بِلَا لَذَّةٍ لِلشِّعْرِ.

Unpoetically, *ad.* بِخِلَافِ أُصُولِ ٱلشِّعْرِ.

Unpolished, *a.* Not smoothed, غَيْرُ مَصْقُولٍ. In the rough, خَشِيبٌ ـ مَخْشُوبٌ. Unpolished, of paper, خَامٌ. Not refined, of manner, بِلَا تَرْبِيَةٍ ـ غَلِيظٌ ـ خَشِنٌ. He used — language, جَاءَ بِٱلْمَخْشُوبِ *aor.* يَجِيءُ.

Unpolite, *a.* Of a person, قَلِيلُ ٱلْأَدَبِ ـ حُوشِيٌّ ـ مُغَثِّلٌ ـ فَظٌّ ـ جَافٍ ـ مِنْ غَيْرِ وَاجِبٍ; of a thing, مُخَالِفٌ لِلْأَدَبِ.

Unpolitely, *ad.* بِقِلَّةِ أَدَبٍ ـ بِفَظَاظَةٍ ـ خِلَافَ قَوَانِينِ ٱلْأَدَبِ.

Unpoliteness, *n.* قِلَّةُ أَدَبٍ ـ فَظَاظَةٌ ـ قِلَّةُ وَاجِبٍ.

Unpolled, *a.* إِسْمُهُ غَيْرُ مُقَيَّدٍ فِي جَدْوَلِ ٱلْمُنْتَخِبِينَ.

Unpolluted, *a.* Free from defilement, بِلَا دَنَسٍ ـ غَيْرُ نَجِسٍ ـ طَاهِرٌ ـ نَقِيٌّ. Not corrupted, morally, غَيْرُ مَفْسُودٍ ـ زَكِيٌّ *pl.* أَزْكِيَاءُ.

Unpopular, *a.* Unpleasing to the people, غَيْرُ مَقْبُولٍ عِنْدَ ٱلنَّاسِ. Not current among the people, شَارِدٌ ـ غَيْرُ رَائِجٍ بَيْنَ ٱلنَّاسِ.

Unpopularity, *n.* عَدَمُ قُبُولِ ٱلشَّعْبِ بِهِ ـ عَدَمُ قُبُولِهِ عِنْدَ ٱلْخَلْقِ ـ عَدَمُ ٱلْتِفَاتِ ٱلنَّاسِ إِلَيْهِ.

Unpopularly, *ad.* بِعَدَمِ قُبُولٍ عِنْدَ ٱلْخَلْقِ.

Unpossessed, *a.* Not possessing, غَيْرُ حَائِزٍ ـ غَيْرُ مُحْتَوٍ عَلَى ـ غَيْرُ مَالِكٍ. Unpossessed of wealth, غَيْرُ ذِي مَالٍ.

Unpractised, *a.* Not used, غَيْرُ مُسْتَعْمَلٍ. Not experienced, غَيْرُ مُدَرَّبٍ ـ غَيْرُ خَبِيرٍ بِـ ـ غَيْرُ مَاهِرٍ ـ عَجَمِيٌّ.

Unprecedented, *a.* مَا سَبَقَ لَهُ مِثَالٌ ـ لَيْسَ لَهُ مِثَالٌ ـ عَدِيمُ ٱلْأَمْثَالِ. An — action, بِكْرٌ ـ بَاكُورَةٌ.

Unprecedentedly, *ad.* بِلَا مِثَالٍ.

Unprecise, *a.* Not exercising precision, غَيْرُ مُدَقِّقٍ. Not over-nice, غَيْرُ مُتَجَوِّدٍ ـ غَيْرُ مُتَأَنِّقٍ.

Unprejudiced, *a.* Disinterested, خَالٍ مِنَ ٱلْغَرَضِ. Having no party spirit, عَدِيمُ ٱلْعَصَبِيَّةِ ـ غَيْرُ مُتَعَصِّبٍ. Fair, just, مُنْصِفٌ.

Unpremeditated, *a.* Not conceived beforehand, غَيْرُ مُضْمَرٍ فِيهِ مِنْ قَبْلُ ـ غَيْرُ مُتَصَوَّرٍ مِنْ قَبْلُ ـ غَيْرُ. Not intentional, غَيْرُ قَصْدِيٍّ ـ عَمْدِيٍّ. An — act, فَرْطَةٌ ـ بَدِيهَةٌ. Unpremeditated speech, بَدَاهَةٌ; unpremeditated judgment, بَدِيهَةُ ٱلرَّأْيِ.

Unpremeditatedly, *ad.* Unintentionally, لَا عَنْ قَصْدٍ. Unexpectedly, بَدِيهًا.

Unprepared, *a.* Not made ready, غَيْرُ مُعَدٍّ ـ غَيْرُ مُسْتَعَدٍّ. Not ready for, غَيْرُ عَتِيدٍ لِ ـ غَيْرُ حَاضِرٍ. Not made up, of a mixture, *etc.*, غَيْرُ مَعْجُونٍ ـ غَيْرُ مَعْمُولٍ.

Unpreparedly, *ad.* *See* Unexpectedly, *a.*

Unprepossessed, *a.* Not taken with, غَيْرُ وَادٍّ ـ غَيْرُ مُتَوَدِّدٍ إِلَى. *See also* Unprejudiced, *a.*

Unprepossessing, *a.* غَيْرُ أَنِيقٍ ـ غَيْرُ أَنِقٍ ـ غَيْرُ ذِي حَظٍّ ـ غَيْرُ مُبَسِّطٍ ـ بَشِيعٌ ـ بَشِعٌ.

Unpresentable, *a.* That may not be offered, مِمَّا لَا يُعْرَضُ. Not fit to be introduced, غَيْرُ جَدِيرٍ بِٱلتَّعْرِيفِ ـ غَيْرُ خَلِيقٍ بِٱلْإِحْضَارِ. In an — state, فِي حَالٍ غَيْرِ لَائِقٍ.

Unpretending, *a.* Of a person, غَيْرُ صَلِفٍ ـ لَا غُرُورَ لَهُ ـ مُحْتَشِمٌ ـ مُتَّضِعٌ ـ وَدِيعٌ.

Unprevented, *a.* غَيْرُ مَمْنُوعٍ ـ غَيْرُ مُمْتَنِعٍ ـ غَيْرُ مَحْجُوبٍ.

Unprincipled, *a.* غَيْرُ زَكِيٍّ ـ عَدِيمُ ٱلْإِسْتِقَامَةِ ـ عَدِيمُ ٱلْإِنْصَافِ ـ مَخْلُوعٌ ـ خَلِيعٌ ـ شِرِّيرٌ ـ خَبِيثٌ ـ قَلَطِيٌّ. An — man, خَلِيعٌ ـ سَاقِطٌ.

Unproclaimed, *a.* غَيْرُ مُنَادًى بِهِ ـ غَيْرُ مُذَاعٍ ـ غَيْرُ مُذَاعٍ بِهِ ـ غَيْرُ مُنْتَشِرٍ.

Unproductive, *a.* Not productive, غَيْرُ مُوَلِّدٍ ـ غَيْرُ مُنْبِتٍ. Not fertile, غَيْرُ خَصِيبٍ. Producing no effect, غَيْرُ مُثْمِرٍ ـ خَالٍ مِنَ ٱلتَّأْثِيرِ ـ غَيْرُ مُؤَثِّرٍ ـ بَاطِلٌ.

Unproductiveness, *n.* Want of fruitfulness, عَدَمُ خِصْبٍ ـ عُقْرٌ ـ عَقْرَةٌ ـ قِلَّةُ ثَمَرَةٍ. Barrenness of results, قِلَّةُ بَرَكَةٍ.

Unprofessional, *a.* Not following a profession, غَيْرُ مُتَعَاطٍ حِرْفَةً أَوْ صَنْعَةً. Not in accordance with the rules of a profession, خِلَافُ أُصُولِ ٱلْحِرْفَةِ أَوِ ٱلصَّنْعَةِ.

Unprofessionally, *ad.* Not as a . . . , لَا بِطَرْزِ كَذَا: Not as a doctor, لَا كَطَبِيبٍ; not as a lawyer, لَا كَفَقِيهٍ. By way of friendship, عَنْ وِدَادٍ ـ عَنْ أُلْفَةٍ ـ عَنْ لُطْفٍ.

Unprofitable, *a.* بَاطِلٌ ـ لَا فَائِدَةَ فِيهِ ـ غَيْرُ نَافِعٍ ـ غَيْرُ طَائِلٍ. It is —, of no avail, هُوَ غَيْرُ طَائِلٍ ـ غَيْرُ مُفِيدٍ ـ عَابِثٌ.

مَا هُوَ بِطَائِلٍ. Unprofitable talk, بَاطِلٌ — كَلَامٌ لا يُفِيدُ. An — servant, خَادِمٌ بَطَّالٌ.

Unprofitably, *ad.* بِلا فَائِدَةٍ — بَاطِلًا — بِٱلْعَبَثِ — مِنْ غَيْرِ نَفْعٍ — بِعَدَمِ طَائِلٍ.

Unprofitableness, *n.* عَدَمُ نَفْعٍ — عَدَمُ فَائِدَةٍ — قِلَّةُ نَفْعٍ — قِلَّةُ فَائِدَةٍ — عَدَمُ طَائِلٍ.

Unprolific, *a.* Not fruitful, غَيْرُ خَصِيبٍ — غَيْرُ مُثْمِرٍ; of a woman, غَيْرُ نَسُولَةٍ — غَيْرُ نَثُورٍ.

Unpromising, *a.* مَا يَخِيبُ ٱلرَّجَاءُ فِيهِ — لا أَمَلَ فِيهِ.

Unprompted, *a.* Not prompted to, غَيْرُ مُحَثَّثٍ إِلَى — غَيْرُ مُحَرَّضٍ إِلَى. Voluntary, إِخْتِيَارِيٌّ — مِنْ تِلْقَاءِ نَفْسِهِ.

Unpronounceable, *a.* تَلَفُّظُهُ مُحَالٌ — لا يُلْفَظُ.

Unpronounced, *a.* غَيْرُ مَنْطُوقٍ بِهِ — غَيْرُ مَلْفُوظٍ.

Unpropitious, *a.* Not favourable, غَيْرُ مُوَافِقٍ — غَيْرُ مُوَفِّقٍ — مُخَالِفٌ. *See also* Unfavourable, Unfortunate, *a.*

Unpropitiously, *ad.* بِغَيْرِ مُوَافَقَةٍ — بِعَدَمِ تَوْفِيقٍ. *See also* Unfortunately, Unhappily, *ad.*

Unpropitiousness, *n.* عَدَمُ مُوَافَقَةٍ — عَدَمُ تَوْفِيقٍ.

Unproportioned, *a.* عَدِيمُ ٱلتَّنَاسُبِ — غَيْرُ مُهَنْدَمٍ — بِلا ظَرَافَةٍ وَٱتِّقَانٍ — غَيْرُ مُعْتَدِلٍ.

Unprosperous, *a.* Not successful, غَيْرُ نَاجِحٍ — غَيْرُ مُفْلِحٍ — غَيْرُ مُوَفَّقٍ. Unfortunate, غَيْرُ مَسْعُودٍ — نَحِسٌ. Not affluent, غَيْرُ مَغْضُورٍ.

Unprotected, *a.* غَيْرُ مَصُونٍ — غَيْرُ مَحْفُوظٍ. Not fortified, غَيْرُ حَصِينٍ — غَيْرُ مُسْتَحْكَمٍ.

Unprovided, *a.* Not prepared, غَيْرُ مُعَدٍّ — غَيْرُ مُسْتَعِدٍّ. Not supplied with, غَيْرُ مُزَوَّدٍ بِ — غَيْرُ مُجَهَّزٍ بِ. Not having, بِلا — عَرٍ مِنْ — لَيْسَ لَهُ. Unprovided for, as a family, ضَيِّعٌ — غَيْرُ عَيِّلٍ *pl.* غَيْرُ عَيَائِلَ — غَيْرُ مَعُولٍ.

Unprovoked, *a.* Not excited, غَيْرُ ثَائِرٍ — غَيْرُ مُتَثَوِّرٍ — غَيْرُ هَائِجٍ. Not angered, غَيْرُ مُغْضَبٍ — غَيْرُ مُغَاظٍ. Without provocation, بِلا ٱحْتِرَاشٍ — بِلا حَشٍّ.

Unpublished, *a.* Not proclaimed, غَيْرُ مُنَادًى بِهِ — غَيْرُ مُذَاعٍ. Not published, of a book, *etc.*, غَيْرُ مَنْشُورٍ — غَيْرُ مُبْرَزٍ. Printed but —, مَطْبُوعٌ لٰكِنْ غَيْرُ مُبْرَزٍ (*or* مَنْشُورٍ).

Unpunctual, *a.* In time, غَيْرُ مُرَاعِي ٱلْمِيعَادِ — غَيْرُ رَاعِي ٱلْعَهْدِ — غَيْرُ مُدَقِّقٍ فِي مُرَاعَاةِ ٱلْعَهْدِ. *See also* Dilatory, *a.*

Unpunctuated, *a.* غَيْرُ مُنَقَّطٍ — مُهْمَلٌ.

Unpunished, *a.* غَيْرُ مُعَاقَبٍ — غَيْرُ مُقَاصَصٍ — غَيْرُ مُعَذَّبٍ — بِلا عَذَابٍ.

Unpurchasable, *a.* شِرَاؤُهُ غَيْرُ مُمْكِنٍ — لا يُشْتَرَى.

Unpurchased, *a.* غَيْرُ مُشْتَرًى — غَيْرُ مُبْتَاعٍ.

Unpurified, *a.* غَيْرُ مُطَهَّرٍ — غَيْرُ مُصَفًّى — غَيْرُ مُصْفًى.

Unqualified, *a.* Not moderated, غَيْرُ مُعَدَّلٍ — غَيْرُ مُلَطَّفٍ — غَيْرُ مُخَفَّفٍ. Not fitted for, غَيْرُ أَهْلٍ لِ — غَيْرُ جَدِيرٍ بِ — غَيْرُ خَلِيقٍ لِ — غَيْرُ كَافٍ لِ (*or* عَلَى).

Unquenchable, *a.* Not to be put out, لا يُطْفَأُ. Not to be put down, quieted, لا يُهْمَدُ.

Unquestionable, *a.* لا رَيْبَ فِيهِ — مُسَلَّمٌ — لَيْسَ فِيهِ شُبْهَةٌ — أَكِيدٌ — حَقِيقٌ — صَحِيحٌ. It is — that . . ., لا بُدَّ مِنْ كَذَا.

Unquestionably, *ad.* بِلا شَكٍّ — فِي ٱلْحَقِيقَةِ — حَقًّا — يَقِينًا — تَحْقِيقًا — أَلْبَتَّةَ.

Unquestioned, *a.* Not questioned, غَيْرُ مَسْؤُولٍ. Not denied, غَيْرُ مُنْكَرٍ.

Unquiet, *a.* خُرَجَةٌ وُلَجَةٌ — قَلِقٌ — مِقْلَاقٌ — مُضْطَرِبٌ — بِلا رَاحَةٍ — غَيْرُ مُرْتَاحٍ. *See also* Restless, *a.*

Unquietly, *ad.* بِٱضْطِرَابٍ — ٱضْطِرَابًا — بِقَلَقٍ — بِلا رَاحَةٍ. *See also* Restlessly, *ad.*

Unquietness, *n.* عَدَمُ قَرَارٍ — عَدَمُ رَاحَةٍ — ٱضْطِرَابٌ — قَلَقٌ.

Unransomed, *a.* غَيْرُ مَفْدِيٍّ — بِلا فِدَاءٍ.

Unravel, *v.t.* To disentangle, فَكَّ [u] — حَلَّ [u]. To make plain, كَشَفَ [i] — صَرَّحَ — أَوْضَحَ. To explain, أَوَّلَ — فَسَّرَ. To clear up, شَرَحَ [a]. To be unravelled, disentangled, ٱنْحَلَّ — ٱنْفَكَّ; to be made plain, ٱتَّضَحَ — ٱنْصَرَحَ. "They said: They are confused dreams, and we know nothing of the unravelling of dreams," قَالُوا أَضْغَاثُ أَحْلَامٍ وَمَا نَحْنُ بِتَأْوِيلِ ٱلْأَحْلَامِ بِعَالِمِينَ (Kur. xii. 44).

Unreached, *a.* غَيْرُ مُدْرَكٍ — غَيْرُ مَبْلُوغٍ — غَيْرُ مُصَابٍ — مَنِيعٌ.

Unread, *a.* Not read, غَيْرُ مَقْرُوٍّ. Not read in books, illiterate, أُمِّيٌّ — جَاهِلٌ بِٱلْكُتُبِ — غَيْرُ مِدْرَاسٍ. *See also* Illiterate, *a.*

Unreadiness, *n.* State of not being ready, عَدَمُ عَتَادٍ — عَدَمُ عَتَادَةٍ — عَدَمُ ٱسْتِعْدَادٍ. Want of promptitude, عَدَمُ نَشَاطٍ — عَدَمُ سُرْعَةٍ — عَدَمُ سَرَاحٍ. Backwardness, unwillingness, عَدَمُ رِضَاءٍ — عَدَمُ سُرُورٍ. Awkwardness, خُرْقٌ.

Unready, *a.* Not prepared, غَيْرُ مُسْتَعِدٍّ. Not prompt, غَيْرُ نَشِيطٍ — غَيْرُ وَجِزٍ. Not willing, disposed, to, غَيْرُ مَائِلٍ (*or* جَائِدٍ) إِلَى. Awkward, خَرِقٌ — أَخْرَقُ. To be —, awkward, unhandy, خَرِقَ [a].

Unreal, *a.* Not genuine, غَيْرُ حَقِيقِيٍّ — غَيْرُ حَقَّانِيٍّ — غَيْرُ صَرِيحٍ. Vain, بَاطِلٌ.

Unreality, *n.* غَرٌّ *pl.* غُرُورٌ — عَبَثٌ — شَيْءٌ لا أَصْلَ لَهُ.

Unreasonable, *a.* Contrary to reason, غَيْرُ مَعْقُولٍ — خِلَافُ ٱلْعَقْلِ.

Not equitable, of a person, لَيْسَ بِعَادِلٍ ـ غَيْرُ مُنْصِفٍ. Immoderate, غَيْرُ مُتَوَسِّطٍ ـ غَيْرُ مُعْتَدِلٍ. For I regard it as — that...., لِأَنَّهُ ظَهَرَ لِي أَنَّهُ غَيْرُ مَعْقُولٍ أَنْ.

Unreasonableness, *n.* عَدَمُ ـ عَدَمُ إِنْصَافٍ ـ عَدَمُ مَعْقُولٍ ـ حَمَاقَةٌ ـ ٱعْتِدَالٍ.

Unreasonably, *ad.* بِغَيْرِ حَقٍّ وَلَا إِنْصَافٍ ـ بِلَا مَعْقُولٍ ـ بِلَا عَقْلٍ ـ مِنْ غَيْرِ. Not suitably, بِدُونِ لِيَاقَةٍ. Immoderately, بِلَا ٱعْتِدَالٍ ـ بِإِفْرَاطٍ ـ قَانُونٍ.

Unreave, *v.t.* Of a rope, حَلَّ ٱلْحَبْلَ مِنْ كَذَا ـ نَكَثَ ٱلْحَبْلَ ـ قَلَعَ ٱلْحَبْلَ عَنْ كَذَا.

Unreclaimable, *a.* *See* Irreclaimable, *a.*

Unreclaimably, *ad.* *See* Irreclaimably, *ad.*

Unreclaimed, *a.* Not reformed, غَيْرُ مُنْصَلِحٍ ـ غَيْرُ مُسْتَتِبٍّ ـ غَيْرُ مُصْلَحٍ ـ غَيْرُ مُثَقَّفٍ. Wild, وَحْشِيٌّ ـ غَيْرُ مُؤْنَسٍ. Not reclaimed, of land, as from the sea, غَيْرُ مُنَحًّى مِنَ ٱلْبَحْرِ.

Unrecognized, *a.* Not known, غَيْرُ مَعْرُوفٍ. Not acknowledged, غَيْرُ مُعْتَرَفٍ بِهِ. It was —, not perceived, by him, غُمَّ عَلَيْهِ.

Unreconcilable, *a.* *See* Irreconcilable, *a.*

Unreconcilably, *ad.* *See* Irreconcilably, *ad.*

Unreconciled, *a.* Still at variance, غَيْرُ مُصْطَلِحٍ ـ غَيْرُ مُتَصَالِحٍ ـ بِلَا مُصَالَحَةٍ. Not pleased, satisfied, غَيْرُ مَرْضُوٍّ ـ غَيْرُ مَرْضِيٍّ.

Unrecorded, *a.* Not registered, غَيْرُ مُقَيَّدٍ ـ غَيْرُ مُدَوَّنٍ. Not mentioned, غَيْرُ مَذْكُورٍ.

Unrecoverable, *a.* *See* Irrecoverable, *a.*

Unrectified, *a.* Not corrected, غَيْرُ مُصَحَّحٍ. Not refined, غَيْرُ مُصَفًّى ; of spirits, غَيْرُ مُكَرَّرٍ.

Unredeemed, *a.* Unransomed, بِلَا فِدَآءٍ ـ غَيْرُ مَفْدِيٍّ ; of a pledge, غَيْرُ مَفْكُوكٍ. Not carried out, of a promise, غَيْرُ مَقْضِيٍّ.

Unredressed, *a.* بِلَا عِلَاجٍ ـ غَيْرُ مَجْبُورٍ ـ غَيْرُ مُعَالَجٍ.

Unreduced, *a.* Of size, غَيْرُ مُصَغَّرٍ ; of length, غَيْرُ مُقَصَّرٍ ; of width, غَيْرُ مُضَيَّقٍ. Not lightened, غَيْرُ مُخَفَّفٍ. Uncaptured, غَيْرُ مَأْخُوذٍ ـ بِلَا فَتْحٍ. Not degraded, غَيْرُ مَعْزُولٍ.

Unreeve, *v.t.* *See to* Unreave, *v.t.*

Unrefined, *a.* Raw, خَامٌ ـ غَيْرُ مُصَفًّى. Unpolished, of manner, خَشِنٌ ـ غَيْرُ لَطِيفٍ ـ غَلِيظٌ ـ فَظٌّ ـ عُطُلٌ ـ حُوشِيٌّ.

Unreformable, *a.* Of manners, تَهْذِيبُهُ مُحَالٌ ـ إِصْلَاحُهُ مُحَالٌ ـ لَا يُثَقَّفُ.

Unreformed, *a.* Of manner, غَيْرُ مُهَذَّبٍ ـ غَيْرُ مُثَقَّفٍ.

Unrefreshed, *a.* Not rested, غَيْرُ ـ غَيْرُ مُرَاحٍ ـ غَيْرُ مُرْتَاحٍ ـ تَعِبٌ ـ مُرَيَّحٍ.

Unrefuted, *a.* غَيْرُ مَنْقُوضٍ ـ غَيْرُ مَرْدُودٍ ـ غَيْرُ مُنْكَرٍ.

Unregarded, *a.* *See* Unheeded, Unnoticed, *a.*

Unregardful, *a.* *See* Unmindful, *a.*

Unregeneracy, *n.* عُتُوٌّ ـ عَدَمُ تَوْبَةٍ ـ خُلُوٌّ مِنَ ٱلْفَيْضِ ٱلرَّبَّانِيِّ.

Unregenerate, *a.* غَيْرُ تَائِبٍ ـ خَالٍ مِنَ ٱلْفَيْضِ ٱلرَّبَّانِيِّ ـ عَاتٍ.

Unregretted, *a.* *See* Unlamented, *a.*

Unregistered, *a.* غَيْرُ مُحَرَّرٍ فِي دَفْتَرٍ ـ غَيْرُ مُقَيَّدٍ (*or* مُدَوَّنٍ). Not recorded, غَيْرُ مَذْكُورٍ. An — letter, مَكْتُوبٌ غَيْرُ مُقَيَّدٍ.

Unrelated, *a.* Having no connection with, غَيْرُ ـ غَيْرُ مُقْتَرِنٍ بِ ـ مُتَعَلِّقٍ بِ ; as by kindred, لَيْسَ بِنَسِيبٍ ـ لَيْسَ مِنْ عَشِيرَةِ فُلَانٍ. Not narrated, غَيْرُ مَرْوِيٍّ لِفُلَانٍ.

Unrelenting, *a.* *See* Relentless, Merciless, *a.*

Unrelentingly, *ad.* *See* Relentlessly, *ad.*

Unrelieved, *a.* As of a pain, غَيْرُ مُسَكَّنٍ ـ غَيْرُ مُخَفَّفٍ ; of a garrison, by aid, provisions, *etc.*, بِلَا مَدَدٍ ـ بِلَا نَجْدَةٍ ; of a sentry, غَيْرُ مُبَدَّلٍ.

Unreluctant, *a.* رَاضٍ ـ رَضِيٌّ ـ بِلَا تَمَحُّطٍ.

Unreluctantly, *ad.* عَنْ رِضًى ـ لَا عَنْ إِكْرَاهٍ ـ لَا عَنِ ٱضْطِرَارٍ.

Unremarked, *a.* *See* Unobserved, *a.*

Unremediable, *a.* *See* Irremediable, *a.*

Unremedied, *a.* بِلَا عِلَاجٍ ـ غَيْرُ مَجْبُورٍ ـ غَيْرُ مُعَالَجٍ.

Unremitted, *a.* Not forgiven, بِلَا مَغْفِرَةٍ ـ غَيْرُ مَغْفُورٍ. Not abated, غَيْرُ مُخَفَّفٍ.

Unremitting, *a.* Incessant, بِلَا ٱنْقِطَاعٍ ـ مُتَوَاتِرٌ ـ مُسْتَمِرٌّ. Diligent, مُجِدٌّ ـ ذُو حَفْلَةٍ ـ كَدُودٌ ـ لَبِيبٌ. To be — in, وَاظَبَ ـ ٱنْكَبَّ (*or* أَكَبَّ) عَلَى ـ عَلَى.

Unremittingly, *ad.* Incessantly, بِلَا ٱنْقِطَاعٍ ـ بِتَوَاتُرٍ ـ دَائِمًا. Diligently, بِٱجْتِهَادٍ ـ مُوَاظَبَةً.

Unremovable, *a.* *See* Irremovable, *a.*

Unremovably, *ad.* *See* Irremovably, *ad.*

Unrenewed, *a.* غَيْرُ مُجَدَّدٍ. *See also* Unregenerate, *a.*

Unrepaid, *a.* بِلَا مُجَازَاةٍ ـ غَيْرُ مُكَافًى ـ غَيْرُ مُوَفًّى.

Unrepaired, *a.* Not restored to a sound state, غَيْرُ مُسْتَتِبٍّ ـ بِلَا إِصْلَاحٍ ـ غَيْرُ مُعَمَّرٍ ـ غَيْرُ مُصَحَّحٍ. Not having repairs done to it, غَيْرُ مُرَمَّمٍ ـ غَيْرُ مُرَمْرَمٍ.

Unrepining, *a.* صَبُورٌ ـ صَابِرٌ ـ صَبِيرٌ ـ غَيْرُ مُتَذَمِّرٍ.

Unrepiningly, *ad.* بِصَبْرٍ ـ بِلَا تَذَمُّرٍ.

Unreplenished, *a.* غَيْرُ مَمْلُوٍّ ثَانِيَةً. Empty, فَارِغٌ.

Unreported, *a.* Not mentioned, غَيْرُ مَذْكُورٍ. Not noticed, as in a newspaper, غَيْرُ مُنْدَرِجٍ. Not reported, as to government, *etc.*, غَيْرُ مَرْفُوعٍ إِلَى ـ غَيْرُ مُفَادٍ بِهِ.

Unrepresented, *a.* Not described, غَيْرُ مَوْصُوفٍ ـ غَيْرُ مَشْرُوحٍ. Not depicted, غَيْرُ مُصَوَّرٍ. Having no representative, بِلَا نَائِبٍ ـ مِنْ غَيْرِ وَكِيلٍ. Not acted, as in a theatre, غَيْرُ مُشَخَّصٍ. Of which there is none, لَا يُوجَدُ مِنْهُ.

Unrepressed, *a.* غَيْرُ مَمْنُوعٍ ـ غَيْرُ مَقْمُوعٍ ـ غَيْرُ مَقْهُورٍ. *See also* Unrestrained, *a.*

Unreproachable, *a.* *See* Irreproachable, *a.*

Unrequested, *a.* غَيْرُ مَسْؤُولٍ ـ غَيْرُ مَطْلُوبٍ.

Unrequired, *a.* غَيْرُ مُقْتَضًى ـ غَيْرُ مُحْتَاجٍ إِلَيْهِ ـ لَا حَاجَةَ إِلَيْهِ.

Unrequited, *a.* بِلَا جَزَآءٍ ـ بِلَا مُكَافَاةٍ ـ غَيْرُ مَجْزِيٍّ ـ غَيْرُ مُكَافًى.

Unresented, *a.* غَيْرُ مُنْتَقِمٍ مِنْ ـ غَيْرُ مُغْتَاظٍ مِنْ. *See also* Unrevenged, *a.*

Unreserve, *n.* Of behaviour, عَدَمُ ـ عَدَمُ ٱخْتِفَآءٍ ـ عَدَمُ ٱلْإِطْرَاقِ ـ ٱنْبِسَاطٌ ـ تَكْلِيفٌ.

Unreserved, *a.* Of manner, غَيْرُ كَتُومٍ ـ غَيْرُ مِطْرَاقٍ ـ غَيْرُ طِرْبِيقٍ ـ بِلَا تَكْلِيفٍ. Not kept, غَيْرُ مَحْفُوظٍ ـ غَيْرُ مُبْقًى (or مُسْتَبْقًى). To be — towards one, ٱنْبَسَطَ إِلَى فُلَانٍ.

Unreservedly, *ad.* Of manner, بِلَا إِطْرَاقٍ ـ لَا حَصْرًا وَلَا قَصْرًا ـ بِلَا ٱخْتِفَآءٍ. To speak —, ٱنْبَسَطَ (or تَفَتَّحَ) فِي ٱلْكَلَامِ.

Unreservedness, *n.* *See* Unreserve, *n.*

Unresisting, *a.* غَيْرُ دَافِعٍ ـ غَيْرُ مُقَاوِمٍ ـ غَيْرُ مُتَعَرِّضٍ.

Unresistingly, *ad.* بِلَا دِفَاعٍ ـ بِدُونِ مُقَاوَمَةٍ ـ مِنْ غَيْرِ ٱعْتِرَاضٍ.

Unrestrainable, *a.* لَا يُقْمَعُ ـ لَا يُحْكَمُ ـ لَا يَنْحَصِرُ ـ لَا يُحْجَزُ ـ ضَبْطُهُ مُحَالٌ.

Unrestrained, *a.* غَيْرُ مَعْكُوفٍ ـ غَيْرُ مُنْقَمِعٍ عَنْ ـ غَيْرُ مَحْصُورٍ ـ مُطْلَقٌ. Under no restraint, خَلِيعُ ٱلْعِذَارِ.

Unrestricted, *a.* غَيْرُ ـ غَيْرُ مُنْحَصِرٍ ـ غَيْرُ مَحْدُودٍ ـ غَيْرُ مُحَدَّدٍ ـ مَحْصُورٍ. To make —, أَطْلَقَ.

Unretaliated, *a.* Blood — by a mulct, دَمٌ بَهْرَجٌ. *See also* Unresented, *a.*

Unretracted, *a.* مَا ضُرِبَ عَنْهُ ـ مَا رُجِعَ عَنْهُ ـ غَيْرُ مُنْكَرٍ.

Unrevealed, *a.* Not disclosed, غَيْرُ مُنْكَشِفٍ ـ غَيْرُ مُسْتَعْلَنٍ. Not divulged, made public, غَيْرُ مُشْتَهِرٍ ـ غَيْرُ مُذَاعٍ. Not revealed, as from heaven, غَيْرُ مُوحًى بِهِ.

Unrevenged, *a.* بِلَا ٱنْتِقَامٍ ـ غَيْرُ مُنْتَقَمٍ مِنْهُ; of blood, دَمٌ بَهْرَجٌ.

Unrevengeful, *a.* غَيْرُ حَقُودٍ ـ غَيْرُ طَالِبِ ٱلْٱنْتِقَامِ.

Unreverend, *a.* *See* Irreverent, *a.*

Unreversed, *a.* Not turned over, غَيْرُ مُقَلَّبٍ ـ غَيْرُ مَعْكُوسٍ. Not annulled, غَيْرُ مُبْطَلٍ ـ غَيْرُ مَنْقُوضٍ ـ غَيْرُ مَنْسُوخٍ.

Unrevised, *a.* غَيْرُ مُصَحَّحٍ ـ غَيْرُ مُصْلَحٍ ـ غَيْرُ مُحَرَّرٍ.

Unrewarded, *a.* غَيْرُ مُكَافًى ـ بِلَا ثَوَابٍ ـ بِلَا جَزَآءٍ ـ بِلَا مُكَافَاةٍ.

Unrhymed, *a.* بِلَا قَافِيَةٍ ـ غَيْرُ مُسَجَّعٍ.

Unridden, *a.* مَا رَكِبَ عَلَيْهِ أَحَدٌ ـ غَيْرُ رَكُوبٍ.

Unriddle, *v.t.* Of a riddle, حَلَّ ٱللُّغْزَ ـ ٤ حَلَّ ٱلْأُحْجِيَّةَ. *See also to* Solve, Explain, *v.t.*

Unrig, *v.t.* As of a ship, جَرَّدَ ـ (or عَرَّى ـ) مِنَ ٱلْحِبَالِ وَٱلْجِهَازِ.

Unrighteous, *a.* Sinful, wicked, فَاجِرٌ ـ فَاسِقٌ ـ طَالِحٌ ـ أَثِيمٌ. Unjust, عَدِيمُ ٱلْٱسْتِقَامَةِ ـ غَيْرُ عَادِلٍ ـ بَاغٍ ـ ظَالِمٌ.

Unrighteously, *ad.* Sinfully, بِفُجُورٍ ـ بِطَلَاحٍ ـ شَرًّا. Unjustly, لَا عَنْ قِسْطٍ ـ بِغَيْرِ عَدْلٍ ـ بِلَا ٱسْتِقَامَةٍ ـ بِظُلْمٍ.

Unrighteousness, *n.* Sin, wickedness, ذَنْبٌ ـ إِثْمٌ ـ شَرٌّ ـ طَلَاحٌ ـ بَغْيٌ ـ عَدَمُ إِنْصَافٍ ـ ظُلْمٌ ـ خُبْثٌ ـ فُجُورٌ. Injustice, .

Unrip, *v.t.* As of a seam, *etc.*, فَتَقَ ـ ٢ فَتَّقَ. To be unripped, ٱنْفَتَقَ.

Unripe, *a.* As of fruit, *etc.*, غَيْرُ مُسْتَوٍ ـ غَيْرُ نَاضِجٍ ـ فِجٌّ; of a boil, غَيْرُ مُقَرِّنٍ. Not ready for ..., غَيْرُ مُسْتَعِدٍّ لِكَذَا.

Unripeness, *n.* As of fruits, *etc.*, عَدَمُ ـ عَدَمُ نُضْجٍ ـ فَجَاجَةٌ ـ عَدَمُ ٱسْتِوَآءٍ. Unpreparedness, عَدَمُ عَتَادَةٍ ـ عَدَمُ ٱسْتِعْدَادٍ.

Unrisen, *a.* As from a seat, غَيْرُ قَائِمٍ ـ غَيْرُ مُنْتَصِبٍ. Not risen on high, غَيْرُ مُتَصَعِّدٍ.

Unrivaled, *a.* بِلَا نَظِيرٍ ـ فَائِقٌ ـ لَيْسَ لَهُ مِثَالٌ.

Unrivet, *v.t.* ٤ فَكَّ ٱلْمَسَامِيرَ مِنْ ـ ٢ قَلَعَ ٱلْأَعْرِنَةَ مِنْ.

Unriveted, *a.* بِلَا مَسَامِيرَ ـ مَقْلُوعُ ٱلْأَعْرِنَةِ.

Unrobe, *v.t.* Of an official dress, ٢ خَلَعَ لِبْسَهُ ٱلرَّسْمِيَّ. To — one's self, ٢ خَلَعَ عَنْ بَدَنِهِ لِبْسَهُ ٱلرَّسْمِيَّ. *See also to* Undress, *v.t.*

Unroll, *v.t.* Of a roll or scroll, بَسَطَ (or ٢ ـ شَرَحَ or ٢ ـ فَتَحَ) ٱلطُّومَارَ. "And when the leaves of the book shall be unrolled," وَإِذَا ٱلصُّحُفُ نُشِرَتْ (Kur. lxxxi. 10).

Unroll, *v.i.* تَمَدَّدَ (or ٱنْفَتَحَ) كَٱلطُّومَارِ.

Unromantic, *a.* Not fanciful, غَيْرُ خَيَالِيٍّ. Not wild, غَيْرُ غَيْرُ بَرِّيٍّ ـ وَحْشِيٍّ. Not sentimental, of a person, غَيْرُ رَقِيقِ سَلِيمٌ ـ نَصُوحٌ ـ سَدِيدٌ ـ أَسَدُّ ٱلْقَلْبِ. Matter of fact, .

Unroof, *v.t.* ٢ كَشَفَ سَقْفَ ٱلـ ... ـ ٢ رَفَعَ ٱلسَّطْحَ عَنْ. To be unroofed, ٱنْقَلَعَ سَقْفُهُ ـ ٱرْتَفَعَ سَطْحُهُ.

Unroot, *v.t.* *See to* Uproot, *v.t.*

Unruffled, *a.* Of feathers, غَيْرُ مُنْفَشٍ. Not ruffled, flurried, مُطْمَئِنٌّ ـ سَاكِنٌ ـ غَيْرُ مُضْطَرِبٍ ـ غَيْرُ مُتَضَجِّرٍ. Calm, not stormy, رَاكِنٌ ـ سَاجٍ.

Unruliness, *n.* تَمَرُّدٌ ـ عُنُودٌ ـ عَدَمُ ضَبْطٍ ـ ٱنْطِلَاقٌ ـ قِلَّةُ طَاعَةٍ.

Unruly, *a.* غَيْرُ مُنْقَادٍ ـ لَا يُضْبَطُ ـ بِلَا تَرْتِيبٍ ـ مُتَمَرِّدٌ ـ عَدِيمُ ٱلْٱنْقِيَادِ. *See also* Insubordinate, *a.*

Unsaddle, *v.t.* To remove a saddle from, رَفَعَ ٱلسَّرْجَ عَن ـَ. To be unsaddled, اِرْتَفَعَ ٱلسَّرْجُ عَن.

Unsaddled, *a.* Of horses, *etc.*, عُرْيٌ *pl.* أَعْرَآءٌ ـ مُعْرَوْرٍ ـ مُعْرَوْرَى ـ بِلَا سَرْجٍ ـ مَرْفُوعُ ٱلسَّرْجِ عَنْهُ. To ride an — horse, اِعْرَوْرَى ٱلْفَرَسَ. We ride — horses, نَحْنُ نُعَارِي.

Unsafe, *a.* Not free from danger, غَيْرُ أَمِينٍ ـ غَيْرُ آمِنٍ. Not to be trusted, لَا يُوثَقُ بِهِ ـ غَيْرُ وَثِيقٍ ـ غَيْرُ أَمِينٍ. Hazardous, ذُو خَطَرٍ ـ مُخْطِر.

Unsafely, *ad.* بِلَا أَمَانٍ ـ بِغَيْرِ أَمْنِيَّةٍ.

Unsafeness, *n.* عَدَمُ أَمْنِيَّةٍ.

Unsaid, *a.* Not uttered, غَيْرُ مَنْطُوقٍ ـ غَيْرُ مَلْفُوظٍ.

Unsaleable, *a.* غَيْرُ رَائِجٍ ـ لَا يُبَاعُ ـ لَا يُبْتَاعُ ـ لَا يَنْبَاعُ.

Unsaleableness, *n.* عَدَمُ رَوَاجٍ ـ عَدَمُ إِمْكَانِ ٱلْبَيْعِ.

Unsanctified, *a.* Not sanctified, غَيْرُ مُطَهَّرٍ ـ غَيْرُ مُقَدَّسٍ. Not consecrated, غَيْرُ مُكَرَّسٍ.

Unsanctioned, *a.* Not approved, غَيْرُ مُسْتَحْسَنٍ ـ غَيْرُ مُسْتَصْوَبٍ. Not authorized, غَيْرُ مَأْذُونٍ ـ غَيْرُ مُجَوَّزٍ ـ غَيْرُ مُجَازٍ ـ غَيْرُ مُبَاحٍ ـ غَيْرُ مُرَخَّصٍ.

Unsatisfactorily, *ad.* As not giving satisfaction, بِعَدَمِ مَرْضَاةٍ ـ بِلَا ٱشْتِفَآءٍ ـ عَلَى غَيْرِ وَفْقٍ ـ بِلَا كِفَايَةٍ. He did it —, قَصَّرَ فِيهِ ـ أَنَّى فِيهِ ـ تَوَانَى فِيهِ.

Unsatisfactoriness, *n.* عَدَمُ ٱشْتِفَآءٍ ـ عَدَمُ كِفَايَةٍ ـ قُصُور ـ عَدَمُ مَرْضَاةٍ. Weakness, as of testimony, information, *etc.*, ضَعْف ـ رَثَاثَة ـ رَكَاكَة.

Unsatisfactory, *a.* Not contenting, غَيْرُ شَافٍ ـ غَيْرُ مَرْضِيٍّ ـ غَيْرُ كَافٍ. Not convincing, غَيْرُ شَافٍ ـ غَيْرُ مُقْنِعٍ. Weak, ضَعِيف ـ رَكِيك (or رَثّ). This intelligence is —, فِي هٰذَا ٱلْخَبَرِ رَكَاكَةٌ. This will be — to you, will not avail you, مَا يُغْنِي عَنْكَ هٰذَا. To deem —, unsuitable, to disapprove of, اِعْتَنَفَ. To be —, unsound, invalid, ضَعُفَ ـ رَثَّ ـِ ـُ.

Unsatisfiable, *a.* Not to be contented, إِقْنَاعُهُ غَيْرُ مُمْكِنٍ.

Unsatisfied, *a.* As with food, غَيْرُ شَبْعَانَ *pl.* غَيْرُ شِبَاعٍ. Not contented, غَيْرُ سَلِيٍّ ـ غَيْرُ رَاضٍ *pl.* غَيْرُ رُضَاةٍ ـ غَيْرُ مَرْضِيٍّ ـ غَيْرُ مَبْسُوطٍ ـ غَيْرُ مُسْتَغْنٍ. *See also under to* Dissatisfy, *v.t.*

Unsatisfying, *a.* As of food, غَيْرُ مُشْبِعٍ ـ غَيْرُ مُشَبِّعٍ. Not contenting, غَيْرُ مُقِرٍّ ـ غَيْرُ مُقْنِعٍ ـ غَيْرُ مُغْنٍ. Not convincing, غَيْرُ مُقْنِعٍ.

Unsavorily, *ad.* بِعَدَمِ لَذَّةٍ ـ بِذَفَرٍ ـ اِعْتِنَافًا ـ بِكَرَاهَةٍ.

Unsavoriness, *n.* Of taste or smell, ذَفَر; of smell, نَتْن. Insipidity, تَفَاهَة ـ عَدَمُ لَذَّةٍ ـ مَلَخ.

Unsavoury, *a.* Of taste or smell, ذَفِر. Of smell, مُنْتِن. Insipid, تَافِه ـ بِلَا لَذَّةٍ ـ مَلِيخ ـ مَسِيخ.

Unsay, *v.t.* To retract, deny, ضَرَبَ عَن قَوْلِهِ ـ أَنْكَرَ ـ نَكِرَ ـَ ـِ ـَ رَجَعَ عَنْ كَلَامِهِ.

Unscathed, *a.* سَالِم ـ بِدُونِ مَضَرَّةٍ.

Unscholarly, *a.* بِدُونِ سَعَةِ ٱلْعِلْمِ ـ لَا مِثْلَ أَصْحَابِ ٱلْعِلْمِ ـ جَهَالَة ـ خُرْقًا.

Unschooled, *a.* Not taught, أُمِّيٌّ ـ غَيْرُ مُدَرَّسٍ ـ غَيْرُ مُعَلَّمٍ. Untrained, أَخْرَقُ ـ خَرِق ـ غَيْرُ مُدَرَّبٍ ـ غَيْرُ مُمَرَّنٍ. To be —, خَرِقَ ـَ.

Unscientific, *a.* Of a person, غَيْرُ رَاسِخٍ فِي ٱلْعِلْمِ ـ غَيْرُ عِلْمِيٍّ ـ خِلَافُ أُصُولِ ٱلْعِلْمِ ـ لَا حَسَبَ أُصُولِ ٱلْعِلْمِ; of things, غَيْرُ عَالِمٍ.

Unscientifically, *ad.* بِخِلَافِ ٱلْأُصُولِ ٱلْعِلْمِيَّةِ ـ بِغَيْرِ عِلْمٍ.

Unscreened, *a.* As through a sieve, غَيْرُ مُغَرْبَلٍ; as with a screen, غَيْرُ مُتَغَمِّدٍ ـ غَيْرُ مَسْتُورٍ ـ بِلَا حِجَابٍ. Not hidden, of faults, غَيْرُ مُتَغَمَّدٍ.

Unscrew, *v.t.* فَكَّ ٱلْبَرَاغِيَّ مِن ـُ.

Unscrew, *v.i.* ٱلْبُرْغِيُّ يَنْفَكُّ.

Unscriptural, *a.* Of the Sacred Scriptures, نَقِيضُ ٱلْكُتُبِ ٱلْمُقَدَّسَةِ ـ خِلَافُ ٱلْكُتُبِ ٱلْمُقَدَّسَةِ (or ٱلْمُنَزَّلَةِ).

Unscripturally, *ad.* بِخِلَافِ ٱلْكُتُبِ ٱلْمُقَدَّسَةِ.

Unscrupulous, *a.* خَبِيث ـ لَا يَخَافُ ٱللّٰهَ وَلَا يَهَابُ ٱلنَّاسَ ـ خَائِن ـ خَتَّار.

Unscrupulousness, *n.* خِيَانَة ـ خَبَانَة ـ خَتُور.

Unscrupulously, *ad.* خَدَاعَةً ـ بِخَبَانَةٍ ـ بِخَتُورٍ.

Unseal, *v.t.* فَضَّ (or فَتَحَ ـَ or فَكَّ ـُ) ٱلْخَتْمَ ـُ.

Unsealed, *a.* خَتْمُهُ مَفْضُوضٌ ـ مَفْكُوكُ ٱلْخَتْمِ.

Unseam, *v.t.* فَتَقَ ـُ ـ فَتَّقَ. To be unseamed, اِنْفَتَقَ ـ تَفَتَّقَ.

Unsearchable, *a.* لَا يُسْتَقْصَى ـ بَعِيدٌ عَنِ ٱلْفَحْصِ ـ لَا يُفْحَصُ ـ بَعِيدٌ عَنِ ٱلِٱسْتِقْصَآءِ. *See also* Inscrutable, *a.*

Unsearchableness, *n.* عَدَمُ إِمْكَانِ ٱلْإِدْرَاكِ ـ بُعْدٌ عَنِ ٱلْفَحْصِ.

Unseasonable, *a.* Untimely, out of place, خَارِجٌ عَنْ مَحَلِّهِ ـ فِي وَقْتٍ غَيْرِ مُنَاسِبٍ ـ خَارِجٌ عَنْ وَقْتِهِ. Out of season, as of fruits, heat or cold, *etc.*, فِي غَيْرِ إِبَّانِهِ. Unusual, شَاذٌّ *pl.* شُذَّاذ *fem.* شَاذَّةٌ *pl.* شَوَاذُّ. He took the thing at an — time, أَخَذَ ٱلشَّيْءَ فِي غَيْرِ إِبَّانِهِ ـُ. To be —, untimely, abnormal, exceptional, شَذَّ ـِ ـُ.

Unseasonableness, *n.* The state of being ill-timed, out of place, عَدَمُ مُوَافَقَةٍ ـ عَدَمُ مُنَاسَبَةٍ; of being unusual, شُذُوذ ـ شَذّ.

Unseasonably, *ad.* لَيْسَ فِي وَقْتِهِ ـ بِغَيْرِ مُوَافَقَةٍ ـ شَذًّا ـ بِشُذُوذٍ ـ فِي غَيْرِ مَحَلِّهِ.

Unseasoned, *a.* As with spices, غَيْرُ مُتَبَّلٍ ـ مَغْشُوب ـ بَحْت. Not dried, غَيْرُ مُيَبَّسٍ. Not accustomed to, غَيْرُ مُتَعَوِّدٍ عَلَى. Not qualified, modified, غَيْرُ مُصْلَحٍ ـ غَيْرُ مُعَدَّلٍ.

Unseat, *v.t.* To throw from a seat, أَهْبَطَ ـ عَنِ ٱلْمَقْعَدِ. To deprive of a seat or position, ـ عَزَلَ ـ عَنْ مَقَامِهِ. The horse unseated his rider, أَرْمَى ٱلْفَرَسُ بِرَاكِبِهِ. To — a member of parliament, ـ عَزَلَ ـ عَنْ مَجْلِسِ ٱلشُّورَى.

Unseaworthiness, *n.* عَدَمُ صَلَاحِيَةٍ لِلسَّفَرِ فِي ٱلْبَحْرِ.

Unseaworthy, *a.* غَيْرُ صَالِحٍ لِلسَّفَرِ بَحْرًا.

Unseconded, *a.* Not aided, supported, بِلَا مُعَاوَنَةٍ ـ غَيْرُ مُعَانٍ ـ بِلَا تَأْيِيدٍ ـ غَيْرُ مُؤَيَّدٍ; of a proposition, بِلَا مُظَاهَرَةٍ ـ بِلَا ظَهْرٍ.

Unseemliness, *n.* قَبَاحَة ـ سَمَاجَة ـ سُوءٌ ـ بَشَاعَة. *See also* Uncomeliness, *n.*

Unseemly, *a.* قَبِيح ـ سَمِج ـ بَشِيع ـ فَظِيع ـ بَشِع. To be —, أَقْبَحَ ـ سَمُجَ ـ شَنُعَ ـ سَاءَ aor. يَسُوءُ. To act in an — manner, أَسَاءَ. To make —, سَمَّجَ. An — act, سَيِّئَة pl. سَيِّئَات ـ قَبَاحَة pl. قَبَائِح.

Unseen, *a.* غَائِب ـ نَكِير ـ غَيْرُ مَشْهُودٍ. The — world, عَالَمُ ٱلْغَيْبِ. "None either in the heavens or the earth knoweth the unseen but God," لَا يَعْلَمُ مَنْ فِي ٱلسَّمَاوَاتِ وَٱلْأَرْضِ ٱلْغَيْبَ إِلَّا ٱللّٰهُ (Kur. xxvii. 66). "Who believe in the unseen," ٱلَّذِينَ يُؤْمِنُونَ بِٱلْغَيْبِ (*Id.* ii. 2). *See also* Invisible, *a.*

Unselfish, *a.* خَلِيٌّ ـ غَيْرُ نَفْسَانِيٍّ ـ غَيْرُ مُغْرِضٍ ـ غَيْرُ مُسْتَأْثِرٍ ـ مُنَزَّهٌ عَنِ ٱلنَّفْسَانِيَّةِ ـ رَحِيبُ ٱلصَّدْرِ ـ ٱلْعِرْضِ.

Unselfishly, *ad.* بِلَا نَفْسَانِيَّةٍ ـ بِلَا ٱسْتِئْثَارٍ.

Unselfishness, *n.* عَدَمُ نَفْسَانِيَّةٍ ـ عَدَمُ ٱسْتِئْثَارٍ.

Unsent, *a.* غَيْرُ مُوَفَّدٍ ـ غَيْرُ مُرْسَلٍ ـ غَيْرُ مَبْعُوثٍ.

Unsepulchred, *a.* *See* Unburied, *a.*

Unserviceable, *a.* Worn out, سَاقِط ـ مَسْحُوق ـ مُعَطَّل ـ ضَغْضَاع; of a man, كَهِيم ـ كَهَام. Not useful, غَيْرُ مُفِيدٍ ـ غَيْرُ طَائِلٍ. Worn out, as of a dress, شَفِيف ـ شَفّ ـ مُتَخَلْخِل ـ مُنْسَحِق.

Unserviceableness, *n.* عَدَمُ طَائِلٍ ـ عَدَمُ مَنْفَعَةٍ ـ عَدَمُ صَلَاحِيَةٍ ـ إِنْسِحَاق ـ ضَغْضَعَة.

Unserviceably, *ad.* بِلَا إِفَادَةٍ ـ بِلَا مَنْفَعَةٍ ـ بِلَا طَائِلٍ.

Unsettle, *v.t.* To disturb, أَضْجَرَ ـ أَزْعَجَ. To put out of order, خَبَّطَ ـ خَبَّلَ ـ شَوَّشَ ـ أَفْسَدَ ـ لَبَّكَ ـ شَتَّتَ. To discompose, make restless, قَلَّقَ ـ أَقْلَقَ ـ إِسْتَفَزَّ ـ أَفَزَّ. To be unsettled, thrown into disorder, إِلْتَبَكَ ـ تَشَتَّتَ. To be unsettled, as in mind, circumstances, *etc.*, ـ قَلِقَ ـ طَارَ ـ إِضْطَرَبَ ـ طَائِرُهُ. He is not a man to be unsettled, moved, by promises or threats, لَيْسَ هُوَ مِنَ ٱلرِّجَالِ ٱلَّذِينَ يَسْتَفِزُّهُمُ ٱلتَّوَاعُدُ وَٱلتَّهَدُّدُ.

Unsettled, *a.* Unquiet, vacillating, طَائِش ـ مِقْلَاق ـ قَلِق ـ مُلَبَّك ـ مُتَشَتِّت. Disturbed, مُزْعَج. Put out of order, طَائِر. Restless, of a person, فِي رَأْسِهِ نُعَرَةٌ ـ خُرَجَةٌ وَلُجَةٌ. Not settled, as of accounts, غَيْرُ مُسَدَّدٍ; of order, غَيْرُ مُعْتَدِلٍ; of a dispute, غَيْرُ مُصْلَحٍ ـ غَيْرُ مُسَدًّى; of a country, not colonized, غَيْرُ مُعَمَّرٍ ـ غَيْرُ آهِلٍ. Your affairs are in an — state, ـ مَالُ سَرْجِكَ. The present state of affairs in Europe continues to be —, لَمْ تَزَلِ ٱلْأَحْوَالُ ٱلْحَاضِرَةُ فِي أُورُبَّا غَيْرَ مُسْتَقِرَّةٍ. Their present state is —, أَحْوَالُهُمُ ٱلْآنَ فِي ٱخْتِلَالٍ.

Unsew, *v.t.* فَتَقَ ـ فَتَّقَ. To be unsewn, إِنْفَتَقَ ـ تَفَتَّقَ.

Unsex, *v.t.* . . . غَيَّرَ جِنْسَ ٱ . .

Unshackle, *v.t.* To remove shackles from, حَلَّ ٱلْعُقْلَةَ مِن ـ فَكَّ ٱلصِّفَادَ عَن. To set free from restraint, حَلَّ عِزَارَهُ ـ سَيَّبَ ـ أَطْلَقَ.

Unshackled, *a.* Without shackles, مَحْلُولُ ٱلرِّبَاطِ ـ بِلَا صِفَادٍ. Unrestrained, خَلِيعُ ٱلْعِذَارِ ـ مُسَيَّب ـ طَلْق ـ طُلُق.

Unshaded, *a.* بِلَا فَيْءٍ ـ بِلَا ظِلٍّ ـ غَيْرُ مُظَلَّلٍ.

Unshaken, *a.* Not shaken, غَيْرُ مُحَرَّكٍ ـ غَيْرُ مُهَزَّزٍ ـ غَيْرُ مَهْزُوزٍ. Firm, رَاسِخ ـ ثَابِت ـ وَثِيق ـ رَصِين ـ مَتِين. Resolute, حَزِيم ـ صِنْدِيد ـ رَاسِيٌّ ـ رَاسِخ. To be —, firm, رَصُنَ ـ وَثُقَ aor. يَوْثُقُ. To make —, أَوْثَقَ ـ أَرْصَنَ.

Unshaped, *a.* مَخْشُوب ـ خَشِيب.

Unshared, *a.* غَيْرُ مُقَسَّمٍ ـ غَيْرُ مُنْقَسِمٍ. Unshared by me, لَيْسَ لِي سَهْمٌ فِيهِ.

Unsheathe, *v.t.* سَلَّ ـ شَهَرَ. To be unsheathed, إِنْسَلَّ.

Unsheltered, *a.* Not protected, غَيْرُ مَصُونٍ ـ غَيْرُ مَحْفُوظٍ. Not secluded, غَيْرُ مُحَجَّبٍ. Not shaded, غَيْرُ مُظَلَّلٍ ـ بِلَا ظِلٍّ. Without a shelter, بِلَا مَأْوًى ـ لَا مَلَاذَ لَهُ. Open, exposed, شَارِع ـ مَفْتُوح ـ مُسْتَهْدِف.

Unship, *v.t.* To remove, as from a ship, *etc.*, نَزَّلَ ـ مِن ـ نَقَلَ ـ مِن. To take off, رَفَعَ ـ قَلَعَ.

Unship, *v.i.* تَحَوَّلَ ـ إِنْقَلَعَ.

Unshod, *a.* بِلَا نَعْلٍ. Barefooted, حَافٍ pl. حُفَاة.

Unshorn, *a.* غَيْرُ جَزِيزٍ ـ غَيْرُ مَجْلُومٍ ـ غَيْرُ مَجْزُوزٍ.

Unshrinking, *n.* Which does not shrink, of cloth, *etc.*, لَا يَتَقَلَّصُ. Intrepid, بَطَل ـ جَسُور ـ قَدُوم ـ سِنْدَرِيٌّ ـ لَا يَخَافُ.

Unshut, *a.* غَيْرُ غَلِقٍ ـ غَيْرُ مُسَكَّرٍ ـ غَيْرُ مُطْبَقٍ ـ غَيْرُ مُنْطَبِقٍ ـ مَفْتُوح.

Unsifted, *a.* Not passed through a sieve, غَيْرُ مُغَرْبَلٍ. Not scrutinized, غَيْرُ مُجَسَّسٍ ـ غَيْرُ مُدَقَّقٍ.

Unsightliness, *n.* وَحش ـ قُبح ـ بَشَاعَة ـ سُوء ـ قَبَاحَة.

Unsightly, *a.* قَبِيح *pl.* قِبَاح ـ بَشِع ـ سَيِّئ. *See also* Unseemly, *a.*

Unsignalized, *a.* Not made known by signal, غَيرُ مُعَرَّف بِهِ بِالإِشَارَاتِ. Not renowned, بِلا شُهرَةٍ ـ غَيرُ مَشهُورٍ.

Unsinning, *a.* *See* Impeccable, *a.*

Unsized, *a.* As with size, بِلا تَربِيَةٍ ـ بِلا آهَارٍ ـ غَيرُ مُرَبًّى.

Unskilled, *a.* بِلا صَنَاعَةٍ ـ بِلا مَهَارَةٍ ـ بِلا مِهنَةٍ ـ أَخرَقُ ـ خَرِق ـ جَاهِل. Unskilled labour, شُغلٌ يَستَغنِي عَنِ ـ شُغلٌ خَشِنٌ الصِّنَاعَةِ.

Unskilful, *a.* غَيرُ ـ غَيرُ مَاهِرٍ ـ عَدِيمُ الخِبرَةِ ـ أَخرَقُ ـ خَرِق ـ غَشِيم ـ جَاهِل ـ نَقِيف. Verily, he is engaged in an — task or work, إِنَّهُ فِي حُورٍ وَبُورٍ.

Unskilfully, *ad.* بِلا إِتقَانٍ ـ بِعَدَمِ مَهَارَةٍ ـ بِقِلَّةِ خِبرَةٍ ـ بِخُرقٍ ـ بِعَدَمِ مِهنَةٍ.

Unskilfulness, *n.* قِلَّةُ مِهنَةٍ ـ عَدَمُ مَهَارَةٍ ـ عَدَمُ خِبرَةٍ ـ خُرق ـ جَهَالَة ـ عَدَمُ إِتقَانٍ ـ غَشم.

Unslaked, *a.* غَيرُ مَحلُولٍ.

Unsling, *v.t.* حَلَّ ² ـ رَفَعَ ² ـ قَلَعَ ².

Unslumbering, *a.* يَقظَانُ ـ مُنتَبِه ـ غَيرُ نَاعِسٍ ـ غَيرُ مُغفٍ *fem.* يَقظَى *pl.* يَقَاظَى.

Unslung, *a.* مَرفُوع ـ مَقلُوع ـ مَحلُول.

Unsociable, *a.* بِلا أُنسَةٍ ـ غَيرُ مُؤَانِسٍ ـ غَيرُ أَنِيسٍ ـ حُوشِيٌّ ـ بِلا أُنسٍ.

Unsociably, *ad.* وَحشَةً ـ بِحُوشِيَّةٍ ـ بِلا أُنسَةٍ ـ بِلا أُنسٍ.

Unsocial, *a.* غَيرُ مُخَالِطٍ ـ حُوشِيٌّ. *See also* Unsociable, *a.*

Unsoiled, *a.* Not soiled, نَقِيٌّ ـ غَيرُ مُلَوَّثٍ ـ غَيرُ مُطَبَّع ـ نَظِيف. Not sullied, as of reputation, غَيرُ مُنثَلِمٍ ـ غَيرُ مَثلُومٍ ـ مَصُونُ العِرضِ.

Unsoldier-like, *a.* / Unsoldierly, } خِلَافُ ـ غَيرُ لَائِقٍ لِلعَسكَرِيِّ ـ غَيرُ عَسكَرِيٍّ أُصُولِ العَسكَرِيَّةِ.

Unsolicited, *a.* غَيرُ مَسؤُولٍ عَنهُ ـ غَيرُ مُطَالَبٍ بِهِ ـ غَيرُ مَطلُوبٍ ـ غَيرُ مُلتَمَسٍ.

Unsolicitous, *a.* Not desirous, غَيرُ شَوَّاقٍ ـ غَيرُ شَيِّقٍ. Not anxious, غَيرُ مُهتَمٍّ ـ غَيرُ شَاجٍ ـ غَيرُ شَجِيٍّ.

Unsophisticated, *a.* Not adulterated, غَيرُ مَغشُوشٍ ـ غَيرُ بَهرَجٍ ـ صَافٍ. Simple, خَالِص ـ سَلِيم ـ سَاذَج. *See also under* Pure, *a.*

Unsorted, *a.* As into sorts, غَيرُ مُصَفَّفٍ ـ غَيرُ مُصَنَّفٍ. Not selected, separated, غَيرُ مُنَقًّى ـ غَيرُ مَفرُوزٍ.

Unsought, *a.* غَيرُ مُفَتَّشٍ عَلَيهِ ـ غَيرُ مَقصُودٍ ـ غَيرُ مَطلُوبٍ.

Unsound, *a.* Weak, shaky, مُقَلقَل ـ مُختَلٌّ ـ أَخرَقُ ـ ضَعضَاع ـ ضَعِيف ـ رَكِيك. Not healthy, غَيرُ ـ سَقِيم ـ مُعتَلُّ المِزَاجِ. Not whole, عَائِب ـ سَقِيم ـ غَيرُ سَالِمٍ ـ غَيرُ صَحِيحٍ ـ مُعَاب ـ مَعيُوب. Unsound of mind, مَخبُول ـ خَبِل. To be —, defective, عَابَ ²; to be —, shaky, إِختَلَّ; to make —, defective, عَيَّبَ. To be —, in mind, إِختَلَّ عَقلُهُ; to make —, in mind, إِختَبَلَ ـ خَبَّلَ. *See also* Heterodox, *a.*; *also* Sophistical, *a.*

Unsoundness, *n.* Shakiness, weakness, خُرق ـ ضَعضَعَة ـ عَدَمُ عَافِيَةٍ ـ إِعتِلَالُ المِزَاجِ ـ خَلَل ـ رَكَاكَة ـ ضَعف; of health, عَدَمُ فِطنَةٍ ـ سَقَام ـ سَقَامَة ـ سَقَم ـ عَدَمُ صِحَّةٍ; of judgment, خَبَال ـ خَبَل ـ خَلَلٌ فِي العَقلِ; of doctrine, عَدَمُ رَشَادٍ; of mind, عَدَمُ استِقَامَةٍ ـ عَدَمُ وَفَاءٍ; of integrity,

Unsown, *a.* غَيرُ مَبذُورٍ ـ بِلا زِرَاعَةٍ ـ غَيرُ مَزرُوعٍ.

Unsparing, *a.* Liberal, خَيِّر ـ سَخِيٌّ ـ جَوَاد. *See also* Unmerciful, *a.*

Unspeakable, *a.* Inexpressible, يَعجِزُ عَن وَصفِهِ ـ لا يُوصَفُ ـ وَصفُهُ مُحَالٌ ـ اللِّسَانُ. Great, جَسِيم ـ عَظِيم.

Unspeakably, *ad.* Inexpressibly, حَتَّى يَعجِزَ ـ بِنَوعٍ لا يُوصَفُ عَن وَصفِهِ اللِّسَانُ. Greatly, جِدًّا ـ لِلغَايَةِ.

Unspent, *a.* Not expended, بَاقٍ ـ غَيرُ مُستَنفَقٍ ـ غَيرُ مَصرُوفٍ; of strength, غَيرُ مُفنًى; of time, غَيرُ مَقطُوعٍ.

Unspiritual, *a.* غَيرُ رُوحِيٍّ.

Unspoken, *a.* غَيرُ مَنطُوقٍ بِهِ ـ غَيرُ مَقُولٍ ـ غَيرُ مَلفُوظٍ ـ غَيرُ مُتَكَلَّمٍ.

Unsportsman-like, *a.* خِلَافُ أُصُولِ الصَّيدِ ـ لا كَالصَّيَّادِ المَاهِرِ.

Unspotted, *a.* Not having spots, غَيرُ مُنَقَّطٍ. Without moral stain, زَكِيٌّ ـ بِلا دَنَسٍ.

Unstable, *a.* Fickle, فَائِر ـ فَائِلُ الرَّأيِ ـ مُتَقَلقِل ـ فَرَّار ـ حُوَّل قُلَّب ـ غَيرُ ثَابِتٍ. Not firm, غَيرُ ثَابِتٍ ـ غَيرُ رَصِينٍ ـ غَيرُ مَاكِنٍ. Unstable as water, فَائِرٌ كَالمَاءِ.

Unstableness, *n.* Fickleness, طَيش ـ سَفَه ـ طَيرَة ـ فَرفَرَة ـ طَيشَان. Want of stability, عَدَمُ رَصَانَةٍ ـ عَدَمُ ثَبَاتٍ.

Unstaid, *a.* Not grave, غَيرُ عَاقِلٍ ـ غَيرُ رَزِينٍ ـ غَيرُ آنٍ. *See also* Unstable, *a.*

Unstained, *a.* Not coloured, غَيرُ مُلَوَّنٍ. Not discoloured, غَيرُ مُبَقَّعٍ ـ مَلطُوخٍ. Unstained, as with crime, زَكِيٌّ ـ غَيرُ مُجرِمٍ.

Unstamped, *a.* غَيرُ مَطبُوعٍ. Not having post-stamps upon it, بِلا طَوَابِعِ البُوسطَةِ.

Unstatesman-like, *a.* عَلَى غَيرِ قَوَاعِدِ السِّيَاسَةِ ـ غَيرُ سِيَاسِيٍّ ـ لَيسَ كَأَربَابِ السِّيَاسَةِ. Clumsy, awkward, inexperienced, خَرِق ـ أَخرَقُ.

Unsteadfast, *a.* Inconstant, طَائِش ـ مُتَقَلْقِل ـ نَزَّار ـ قُلَّاع ـ فَرَّار. To be —, طَاشَ *aor.* يَطِيشُ ـ خَفَّ. Not firm, غَيْرُ رَصِينٍ ـ غَيْرُ مَاكِنٍ ـ ثَابِتٍ.

Unsteadily, *ad.* بِعَدَمِ ثَبَاتٍ ـ بِطَيْشٍ ـ بِفَرْفَرَةٍ.

Unsteadiness, *n.* Want of firmness, عَدَمُ ثَبَاتٍ ـ عَدَمُ رَصَانَةٍ ـ عَدَمُ قَرَارٍ. *See also* Unstableness, *n.*

Unsteady, *a.* Not firm, غَيْرُ مَاكِنٍ ـ غَيْرُ ثَابِتٍ ـ غَيْرُ رَصِينٍ ـ عَدِيمُ ٱلْقَرَارِ ـ غَيْرُ مُحْكَمٍ. Awkward, أَخْرَقُ ـ خَرِق. *See also* Unstable, Inconstant, *a.*

Unstinted, *a.* غَيْرُ مَحْصُورٍ ـ غَيْرُ مُقَتَّرٍ ـ غَيْرُ مَقْبُورٍ.

Unstop, *v.t.* To open, فَتَحَ. To remove any obstruction, سَلَكَ.

Unstopper, *v.t.* فَتَحَ ـ قَلَعَ ٱلسِّدَادَ عَنْ.

Unstring, *v.t.* As beads from a string, فَرَطَ ـ سَلَتَ. To remove a string from, حَلَّ ٱلْخَيْطَ مِنْ; of a musical instrument, رَفَعَ ٱلْأَوْتَارَ عَنِ ٱلْآلَةِ. *See also to* Unman, Unnerve, *v.t.*

Unstrung, *a.* As beads from a string, مَفْلُوت ـ مَسْلُوت ـ مَفْرُوط; as a parcel from its string, مَحْلُولُ ٱلسِّلْكِ (*or* ٱلْخَيْطِ); as a musical instrument, مَقْلُوعُ ٱلْأَوْتَارِ ـ بِلَا أَوْتَارٍ. Unnerved, مَهْبُوط ـ مُوَهَّن.

Unstudied, *a.* Not laboured, خَشِيب ـ غَيْرُ مُتْقَنٍ ـ غَيْرُ مَفْتُونٍ ـ مَخْشُوب. Unstudied poetry, شِعْرٌ خَشِيبٌ. He used — language, جَاءَ بِٱلْمَخْشُوبِ *aor.* يَجِيءُ.

Unstudious, *a.* قَلِيلُ ٱلْمُطَالَعَةِ ـ قَلِيلُ ٱلدَّرْسِ.

Unsubdued, *a.* غَيْرُ مَقْهُورٍ ـ غَيْرُ مُسَخَّرٍ ـ غَيْرُ مَغْلُوبٍ ـ غَيْرُ مَقْمُوعٍ.

Unsubmissive, *a.* مُتَمَرِّد ـ غَيْرُ مُنْقَادٍ ـ غَيْرُ مُذْعِنٍ ـ غَيْرُ طَائِعٍ.

Unsubmissively, *ad.* بِتَمَرُّدٍ ـ بِعَدَمِ إِطَاعَةٍ ـ بِغَيْرِ ٱنْقِيَادٍ.

Unsubstantial, *a.* Not corporeal, غَيْرُ جِسْمِيٍّ. Not real, غَيْرُ حَقِيقِيٍّ. Light, weak, خَفِيف ـ ضَعِيف. Flimsy, رَقِيق ـ سَخِيف. Unsubstantial talk, كَلَامٌ رَثٌّ. *See also* Chimerical, *a.*

Unsubstantially, *ad.* بِسَخَافَةٍ ـ بِرِقَّةٍ.

Unsuccessful, *a.* غَيْرُ مُيَسَّرٍ ـ غَيْرُ نَاجِحٍ ـ غَيْرُ مُسَدَّدٍ ـ غَيْرُ مُوَفَّقٍ ـ خَاسِر. To be —, خَابَ *aor.* يَخِيبُ. *See also to* Fail, *v.i.*

Unsuccessfully, *ad.* بِغَيْرِ تَوْفِيقٍ ـ بِلَا فَوْزٍ ـ بِلَا نَجَاحٍ.

Unsuccessive, *a.* غَيْرُ مُتَعَاقِبٍ ـ غَيْرُ مُتَتَابِعٍ ـ غَيْرُ مُتَوَاتِرٍ.

Unsufferable, *a.* *See* Insufferable, *a.*

Unsuitable, *a.* *See* Unfit, *a.*

Unsuitableness, *n.* *See* Unfitness, *n.*

Unsuitably, *ad.* *See* Unfitly, *ad.*

Unsuited, *a.* Not properly matched, as with something else, غَيْرُ مُتَمَاثِلٍ ـ غَيْرُ مُتَوَافِقٍ. Not provided with, as one could wish, مَا نَالَ حَاجَتَهُ. The being — with, not having secured, مَا وَجَدَ ـ مَا حَصَلَ عَلَى. He is still — with a house, مَا وَجَدَ بَيْتًا يُوَافِقُهُ بَعْدُ.

Unsullied, *a.* Not stained, غَيْرُ مُقَذَّعٍ ـ غَيْرُ مُطَبَّعٍ; not blemished, غَيْرُ مَعْيُوبٍ; in reputation, غَيْرُ مُنْثَلِمِ ٱلصِّيتِ ـ مَصُونُ ٱلْعِرْضِ.

Unsung, *a.* Not celebrated, غَيْرُ مَشْهُورٍ. Not recorded in verse, غَيْرُ مَذْكُورٍ ـ غَيْرُ مَذْكُورٍ فِي ٱلشِّعْرِ. Not sung, لَمْ يُغَنَّ بِهِ.

Unsupplied, *a.* Not provided, غَيْرُ مُمَدٍّ ـ غَيْرُ مُسْتَمَدٍّ ـ غَيْرُ مُجَهَّزٍ. The being without, بِلَا ـ عَرِيٌّ مِنْ كَذَا.

Unsupportable, *a.* *See* Insupportable, *a.*

Unsupported, *a.* Without a prop, بِلَا مَسْنَدٍ ـ غَيْرُ مُسَنَّدٍ. Not assisted, بِلَا إِسْعَافٍ ـ غَيْرُ مُسْعَفٍ. Not backed, not encouraged, بِلَا مُظَاهَرَةٍ ـ غَيْرُ مُشَجَّعٍ. Not sustained, of testimony, غَيْرُ مُسَنَّدٍ ـ بِلَا إِثْبَاتٍ ـ غَيْرُ مُؤَيَّدٍ.

Unsuppressed, *a.* Not put down, as of an insurrection, *etc.*, غَيْرُ مُطْفَأٍ ـ مَقْمُوعٍ. Not hindered, غَيْرُ مُنْهًى ـ غَيْرُ مَمْنُوعٍ. Not omitted, of a letter, *etc.*, غَيْرُ مَحْذُوفٍ.

Unsure, *a.* *See* Unsafe, *a.*

Unsurmountable, *a.* *See* Insuperable, *a.*

Unsurgical, *a.* غَيْرُ جِرَاحِيٍّ ـ خِلَافُ أُصُولِ فَنِّ ٱلْجِرَاحَةِ.

Unsurpassed, *a.* Not exceeded, مَا فَاقَهُ أَحَدٌ; as in excellence, *etc.*, فَائِقٌ لِلْغَايَةِ ـ بَارِع ـ غَيْرُ مَفْضُولٍ.

Unsuspected, *a.* As of evil, غَيْرُ ظَنِينٍ ـ غَيْرُ مَقْرُوفٍ ـ غَيْرُ تَهِيمٍ ـ غَيْرُ مُخَمَّنٍ. Not conjectured, غَيْرُ مُتَوَهَّمٍ ـ غَيْرُ مَظْنُونٍ بِهِ.

Unsuspectedly, *ad.* بِلَا ٱتِّهَامٍ ـ بِلَا رِيبَةٍ ـ بِلَا تَوَهُّمٍ.

Unsuspecting, *a.* غَيْرُ ظَنِينٍ ـ غَيْرُ ذِي رِيبَةٍ ـ غَيْرُ ظَنَّانٍ ـ غَيْرُ ظَنُونٍ.

Unsuspectingly, *ad.* بِلَا تَخَمُّنٍ ـ بِلَا تَخَيُّلٍ ـ بِلَا تَوَهُّمٍ.

Unsuspicious, *a.* *See* Unsuspecting, *a.*

Unsustainable, *a.* Unendurable, لَا يُطَاقُ. Not admitting confirmation, لَا يُثْبَتُ. Not capable of being kept up, غَيْرُ قَابِلِ ٱلْإِبْقَاءِ; of being vindicated, لَا يُحَامَى عَنْهُ.

Unswayed, *a.* *See* Unbiassed, *a.*

Unswept, *a.* غَيْرُ مَكْنُوسٍ.

Unswerving, *a.* غَيْرُ شَدِيدِ ٱلْمَعَادِلِ ـ مُسْلَحِبٌّ ـ مُتْلَئِبٌّ ـ حَازِم ـ رَصِين ـ ثَابِت ـ مُتَزَعْزِعٍ. To be —, ٱتْلَأَبَّ.

Unswervingly, *ad.* بِثُبُوتٍ ـ بِعَدَمِ تَزَعْزُعٍ ـ بِلَا حَيْدَةٍ ـ ٱتْلِئْبَابًا ـ بِرَصَانَةٍ.

Unsworn, *a.* Not sworn, غَيْرُ مُسْتَحْلَفٍ – غَيْرُ مُحَلَّفٍ. Not bound by oath, غَيْرُ حَالِفٍ – غَيْرُ مُقْسِمٍ.

Unsymmetrical, *a.* غَيْرُ مُعْتَدِلٍ – غَيْرُ مُهَنْدَمٍ – خَشِيْب.

Unsymmetrically, *ad.* بِلَا ٱعْتِدَالٍ – بِلَا هِنْدَامٍ.

Unsystematic, *a.* / **Unsystematical**, عَدِيمُ ٱلتَّرْتِيبِ – غَيْرُ مُتَنَسِّقٍ – غَيْرُ مُنَسَّقٍ وَٱلنِّظَامِ.

Unsystematically, *a.* بِدُونِ قَاعِدَةٍ – بِلَا تَنْسِيقٍ – بِعَدَمِ نَسْقٍ – شَتَاتًا.

Untack, *v.t.* فَتَقَ [2] – فَتَّقَ. To be untacked, تَفَتَّقَ – إِنْفَتَقَ.

Untainted, *a.* Not tainted, of meat, *etc.*, غَيْرُ مَفْسُوخٍ – غَيْرُ مُتَفَسِّخٍ – غَيْرُ مُتَعَفِّنٍ – غَيْرُ مُعَفَّنٍ. Pure, صَافٍ. *See also* Unstained, Unsullied, *a.*

Untamable, *a.* لَا يَأْنَسُ – لَا يَذَلَّلُ – لَا يُطَبَّعُ.

Untamed, *a.* غَيْرُ ذَلُولٍ – حُوشِيٌّ – غَيْرُ مُطَبَّعٍ – غَيْرُ مُؤَنَّسٍ.

Untangle, *v.t.* As of thread, *etc.*, فَكَّ [2] – حَلَّ [2]; of the hair, سَرَّحَ. To unravel, make plain, صَرَّحَ – أَوْضَحَ.

Untarnished, *a.* Not tarnished, as of colours, غَيْرُ مُطَبَّعٍ – غَيْرُ مُحَمَّدٍ – غَيْرُ مُكَدَّرٍ. *See also* Unsoiled, Unsullied, *a.*

Untasted, *a.* غَيْرُ مُسْتَطْعَمٍ – غَيْرُ مَذُوقٍ.

Untasteful, *a.* Not in good taste, غَيْرُ كَيِّسٍ – غَيْرُ حُلْوٍ – غَيْرُ لَطِيفٍ – بَشِعٌ.

Untastefully, *ad.* بِلَا كِيَاسَةٍ – بِلَا ظَرَافَةٍ – بِلَا طَلَاوَةٍ – بِبَشَاعَةٍ.

Untaught, *a.* Not instructed, غَيْرُ مُعَلَّمٍ – غَيْرُ مُدَرَّسٍ. Untaught eloquence, كَلَامٌ سَلِيقِيٌّ.

Unteach, *v.t.* نَسَّى – أَنْسَى.

Unteachable, *a.* Not capable of receiving instruction, غَيْرُ قَابِلٍ ٱلتَّعْلِيمِ. Untractable, غَيْرُ جَنِيبٍ – غَيْرُ ذَلُولٍ – غَيْرُ طَوْعِ ٱلْعِنَانِ.

Untenable, *a.* Not capable of defence, مُحَالَةٌ عَنْهُ ٱلْمُحَامَاةُ. *See also* Unsustainable, *a.*

Untenantable, *a.* لَا يُسْكَنُ – غَيْرُ مُنَاسِبٍ لِلسُّكْنَى.

Untenanted, *a.* خَالٍ مِنَ ٱلسُّكَّانِ – فَارِغٌ – خَالٍ – غَيْرُ آهِلٍ.

Untended, *a.* Uncared for, ضَيَاعٌ – لَيْسَ مَنْ يُبَالِي بِهِ.

Untested, *a.* غَيْرُ مُجَرَّبٍ – غَيْرُ مُمْتَحَنٍ.

Unthankful, *a.* مُجَدِّفٌ – غَيْرُ شَاكِرٍ – غَيْرُ مُتَشَكِّرٍ – نَاكِرُ ٱلْمَعْرُوفِ – كَنُودٌ. To be — for, جَدَّفَ بِ – كَنَدَ ٱلنِّعْمَةَ.

Unthankfully, *ad.* بِتَجْدِيفٍ – بِعَدَمِ تَشَكُّرٍ – بِلَا شُكْرَانٍ – بِنُكْرِ ٱلْمَعْرُوفِ – بِكُنُودٍ.

Unthankfulness, *n.* عَدَمُ تَشَكُّرٍ – عَدَمُ شُكْرِ ٱلنِّعْمَةِ – ٱلْكُفْرَانُ بِٱلنِّعْمَةِ – عَدَمُ شُكْرَانٍ – تَجْدِيفٌ – كُنُودٌ.

Unthinking, *a.* / **Unthoughtful**, أَبْلَهُ – مَاجِنٌ – دَعِنٌ *pl.* دَعِنَةٌ – مُتَعَسِّفٌ – غَافِلٌ. *See also* Heedless, *a.*

Unthought, *a.* Not imagined, مَا تَخَيَّلَ – مَا خَطَرَ بِٱلْبَالِ. *See also* Unexpected, Neglected, *a.*

Unthrift, *n.* قِلَّةُ تَقَصُّدٍ – قِلَّةُ ٱقْتِصَادٍ – بَعْزَقَةٌ – بَذَارَةٌ.

Unthriftily, *ad.* بِقِلَّةِ تَقَصُّدٍ – بِقِلَّةِ ٱقْتِصَادٍ – بِبَذَارَةٍ – بِإِسْرَافٍ.

Unthriftiness, *n.* *See* Unthrift, *n.*

Unthrifty, *a.* قَلِيلُ ٱلتَّقَصُّدِ – مُسْرِفٌ – مِتْلَاقٌ – مُبَذِّرٌ – بَعْزَاقٌ.

Unthrone, *v.t.* *See to* Dethrone, *v.t.*

Untidily, *ad.* بِعَدَمِ كِيَاسَةٍ – بِلَا ظَرَافَةٍ – بِلَا ٱنْتِظَامٍ.

Untidiness, *n.* عَدَمُ كِيَاسَةٍ – عَدَمُ ظَرَافَةٍ – عَدَمُ ٱنْتِظَامٍ.

Untidy, *a.* غَيْرُ كَيِّسٍ – بِلَا كِيَاسَةٍ – غَيْرُ ظَرِيفٍ – غَيْرُ حُلْوٍ – بَشِيعٌ – بِلَا ٱنْتِظَامٍ.

Untie, *v.t.* فَكَّ [2] – حَلَّ [2]. To be untied, إِنْفَكَّ – إِنْحَلَّ.

Untied, *a.* مَفْكُوكٌ – مَحْلُولٌ.

Until, *prep.* حَتَّى – إِلَى. Until he returns to us, حَتَّى يَرْجِعَ إِلَيْنَا. Until when, حَتَّامَ – حَتَّى مَا. Until when? حَتَّى مَتَى.

Untile, *v.t.* رَفَعَ ٱلْقِرْمِيدَ عَنْ.

Untiled, *a.* بِلَا قِرْمِيدٍ – غَيْرُ مَفْرُوشٍ بِقِرْمِيدٍ.

Untilled, *a.* غَيْرُ مَحْرُوثٍ – غَيْرُ مَفْلُوحٍ – بِلَا فِلَاحَةٍ.

Untimely, *a.* فِي غَيْرِ وَقْتِهِ – فِي غَيْرِ مَحَلِّهِ. An — birth, سِقْطٌ. Out of season, فِي غَيْرِ أَوَانِهِ – فِي غَيْرِ وَقْتِهِ. An — death, إِخْتِضَارٌ – مَوْتٌ فِي عَيْنِ ٱلْكَمَالِ. *See also* Premature, *a.*, and Unseasonable, *a.*

Untiring, *a.* غَيْرُ مَمْلُولٍ – بِلَا مَلَالَةٍ. He is — in …, لَمْ يَمِلَّ مِنْ كَذَا. *See also* Indefatigable, *a.*

Untitled, *a.* Without a title, epithet, غَيْرُ مُلَقَّبٍ – بِلَا نَعْتٍ. Having no title of nobility, غَيْرُ ذِي شَرَفٍ.

Unto, *prep.* إِلَى – نَحْوَ – عِنْدَ. *See* To, *prep.*

Untold, *a.* Not spoken, غَيْرُ مَنْطُوقٍ بِهِ. Not communicated, غَيْرُ مُعَرَّفٍ. Not narrated, غَيْرُ مُحَدَّثٍ – غَيْرُ مَذْكُورٍ. Not counted, غَيْرُ مَعْدُودٍ – بِلَا عَدَدٍ.

Untomb, *v.t.* *See to* Disinter, *v.t.*

Untouched, *a.* Not hit, غَيْرُ مُصَابٍ. Not eaten, غَيْرُ مَأْكُولٍ – بَاقٍ مِنَ ٱلْأَكْلِ. Not touched, as with the fingers, غَيْرُ مَلْمُوسٍ. *See also* Unaffected, *a.*

Untoward, *a.* Cross, مُلْتَوٍ – مُتَمَرِّدٌ – مُعَرْبِدٌ – زُعْرُورٌ – شَكِسٌ – شَرِسٌ – زَعِرُ ٱلْخُلُقِ. *See also* Unpleasant, Unfortunate, *a.*

Untowardly, *ad.* بِٱلْتِوَاءٍ – بِتَمَرُّدٍ – بِشَكَاسَةٍ – بِشَرَاسَةٍ. *See also* Unfortunately, *ad.*

Untowardness, *n.* Frowardness, تَمَرُّدٌ – عَرْبَدَةٌ – زَعَارَةٌ – شَكَاسَةٌ – شَرَاسَةٌ. *See also* Unluckiness, *n.*

Untraceable, *a.* Not to be traced, لَا يُقْتَصُّ أَثَرُهُ.

Untractable, *a.* *See* Refractory, *a.*

Untractableness, *n.* *See* Refractoriness, *n.*

Untrained, *a.* غَيْرُ مُرْتَاضٍ ـ غَيْرُ مَرُوضٍ. Not trained to . . ., غَيْرُ مُدَرَّبٍ عَلَى كَذَا. Untrained soldiers, عَسَاكِرُ غَيْرُ مُحَنَّكِينَ. Awkward, clumsy, خَرِقٌ. To be —, clumsy, خَرِقَ ـَ.

Untrammeled, *a.* *See* Unfettered, *a.*

Untransferable, *a.* نَقْلُهُ غَيْرُ مُمْكِنٍ ـ تَحْوِيلُهُ غَيْرُ مُمْكِنٍ ـ تَحْوِيلُهُ غَيْرُ جَائِزٍ.

Untranslatable, *a.* لَا يُتَرْجَمُ ـ نَقْلُهُ إِلَى لِسَانٍ ثَانٍ غَيْرُ مُمْكِنٍ إِلَى لِسَانٍ آخَرَ.

Untranslated, *a.* غَيْرُ مُتَرْجَمٍ ـ غَيْرُ مُسْتَخْرَجٍ ـ غَيْرُ مَنْقُولٍ إِلَى لِسَانٍ ثَانٍ.

Untravelled, *a.* Not travelled over, غَيْرُ مَطْرُوقٍ ـ غَيْرُ مَسْلُوكٍ. Not having travelled, غَيْرُ مُسَافِرٍ ـ غَيْرُ مُسْتَفِرٍ.

Untraversed, *a.* غَيْرُ مَعْبُورٍ بِهِ ـ غَيْرُ مَسْلُوكٍ بِهِ.

Untrenched, *a.* Not cut into trenches, غَيْرُ مَخْدُودٍ ـ غَيْرُ مَفْلُوجٍ ـ غَيْرُ مَخْرُوقٍ.

Untried, *a.* غَيْرُ مُجَرَّبٍ ـ غَيْرُ مُمْتَحَنٍ.

Untrimmed, *a.* As of a lamp, *etc.*, غَيْرُ مُصْلَحٍ. Without trimmings, بِلَا تَزْيِينَاتٍ; of a dress, بِلَا خَرْجٍ. Unlopped, غَيْرُ مُقَلَّمٍ ـ غَيْرُ مُجَزَّزٍ; of the hair, غَيْرُ مُقَصْقَصٍ. Not balanced, غَيْرُ مَوْزُونٍ ـ غَيْرُ مُعَدَّلٍ.

Untrodden, *a.* *See* Untravelled, *a.*

Untroubled, *a.* In a state of rest, سَاكِنٌ ـ هَادِئٌ ـ سَاجٍ. Undisturbed, at repose, مُطْمَئِنٌّ ـ مُرْتَاحٌ. Calm, as of the sea, رَاكِنٌ ـ سَاجٍ. To be —, at peace, اِطْمَأَنَّ. *See also under* Calm, *a.*

Untrue, *a.* Not straight, غَيْرُ مُعْتَدِلٍ. Not true, false, كَاذِبٌ ـ بِلَا أَصْلٍ ـ بَاطِلٌ. Unfounded, عَارٍ عَنِ ٱلصِّحَّةِ ـ مُزَوَّرٌ ـ زُورٌ. Perfidious, خَائِنٌ ـ خَاتِرٌ. Untrustworthy, غَيْرُ صَادِقٍ. Faithless, عَدِيمُ ٱلْوَفَاءِ. "To His promise God will not be untrue," لَا يُخْلِفُ ٱللّٰهُ وَعْدَهُ (Kur. xxx. 5).

Untruly, *ad.* Falsely, زُورًا ـ كَذِبًا. Deceitfully, perfidiously, بِخِيَانَةٍ ـ بِخُتُورٍ ـ خَتْرًا. Not straight, بِلَا ٱعْتِدَالٍ.

Untrustworthy, *a.* غَيْرُ صَادِقٍ ـ لَا يُعْتَمَدُ عَلَيْهِ.

Untruth, *n.* زُورٌ *pl.* أَزْوَارٌ ـ كَذِبٌ ـ كَاذِبَةٌ ـ أُكْذُوبَةٌ *pl.* أَكَاذِيبُ.

Untruthful, *a.* كَذَّابٌ.

Untune, *v.t.* To put out of tune, أَعْدَمَ ٱللَّحْنَ.

Untuned, *a.* غَيْرُ مُتَّفِقٍ (or مُحْكَمِ) ٱلْأَنْغَامِ.

Unturned, *a.* Of a dress, *etc.*, غَيْرُ مَقْلُوبٍ ـ غَيْرُ مُقَلَّبٍ. Not turned up, of soil, غَيْرُ مَسْلُوفٍ ـ غَيْرُ مُحَنًّى. Not turned, as on a lathe, غَيْرُ مَخْرُوطٍ. To leave no stone —, to use every endeavour, صَرَفَ ٱلْمَسَاعِيَ ٱلْمُمْكِنَةَ ـِ.

Untutored, *a.* Not experienced, غَيْرُ مُدَرَّبٍ ـ مُقْتَضَبٌ. Wild, حُوشِيٌّ. Wild, stupid, هَمَجٌ ـ هَمَجَةٌ. *See also* Untaught, *a.*

Untwine, *v.t.* } نَقَضَ ـُ ـ نَكَثَ ـُ ². To be untwined or un-
Untwist, } twisted, اِنْتَقَضَ ـ اِنْتَكَثَ.

Untiring, *a.* *See* Indefatigable, *a.*

Unusual, *a.* غَيْرُ مَعْهُودٍ ـ نَادِرُ ٱلْوُقُوعِ ـ شَاذٌّ. An — or strange word, كَلِمَةٌ نَادَّةٌ (or شَاذَّةٌ). To be —, abnormal, exceptional, شَذَّ ـِ ². *See also* Uncommon, *a.*

Unusually, *a.* فِي ٱلنُّدْرَةِ ـ نُدْرَةً ـ فَوْقَ ٱلْعَادَةِ.

Unusualness, *n.* نُدْرَةٌ ـ غَرَابَةٌ ـ قِلَّةُ وُقُوعٍ ـ شَذٌّ ـ شُذُوذٌ.

Unused, *a.* Not made use of, غَيْرُ مُسْتَعْمَلٍ. Unused to; *see* Unaccustomed, *a.*

Unutterable, *a.* Unspeakable, لَا يُنْطَقُ بِهِ. Indescribable, يَعْجِزُ عَنْ وَصْفِهِ ٱللِّسَانُ ـ وَصْفُهُ مُحَالٌ ـ لَا يُوصَفُ.

Unvail, *v.t.* Remove a veil from, رَفَعَ ٱلْبُرْقُعَ عَنْ فُلَانٍ or فُلَانَةٍ ـَ. To uncover, كَشَفَ عَنْ ـِ. *See also to* Uncover, *v.t.*

Unvalued, *a.* Not priced, غَيْرُ مُسَعَّرٍ ـ غَيْرُ مُثَمَّنٍ. Not prized, غَيْرُ مُعْتَبَرٍ ـ غَيْرُ مُعَزَّزٍ.

Unvanquishable, *a.* أَعَزُّ ـ عَزِيزٌ ـ لَا يُغْلَبُ ـ لَا يُقْهَرُ.

Unvariable, *a.* *See* Invariable, *a.*

Unvaried, *a.* Uninterrupted, دَائِمٌ ـ مُسْتَمِرٌّ.

Unvarnished, *a.* Without varnish, بِلَا دِهَانٍ ـ غَيْرُ مَدْهُونٍ. Simple, unadorned, سَاذَجٌ ـ سَاذِجٌ ـ غَيْرُ مُفَنَّنٍ ـ غَيْرُ مُوَشًّى.

Unvarying, *a.* Not changing, غَيْرُ ذِي تَبَدُّلٍ ـ بِلَا تَغْيِيرٍ. *See also* Invariable, *a.*

Unveil, *v.t.* *See to* Unvail, *v.t.*

Unventilated, *a.* Not exposed to the air, غَيْرُ مُنَشَّرٍ; of a subject, مَا ٱنْفَتَحَ بَحْثُهُ. Without air, وَبِيلٌ ـ غَيْرُ ذِي نَفَسٍ.

Unversed, *a.* *See* Inexperienced, *a.*

Unvitiated, *a.* *See* Uncorrupted, *a.*

Unwalled, *a.* Without walls, بِلَا حِيطَانٍ ـ بِلَا جُدُرٍ. *See also* Unfenced, *a.*

Unwanted, *a.* يُسْتَغْنَى عَنْهُ ـ غَيْرُ مَطْلُوبٍ ـ لَا حَاجَةَ إِلَيْهِ.

Unwarily, *ad.* بِلَا ٱحْتِيَاطٍ ـ بِلَا ٱحْتِذَارٍ ـ عَنْ غَفْلَةٍ.

Unwariness, *n.* عَدَمُ ٱحْتِيَاطٍ ـ عَدَمُ ٱحْتِذَارٍ ـ غَفْلَةٌ.

Unwarlike, *a.* غَيْرُ حَرْبِيٍّ. Not fit for war, غَيْرُ جَدِيرٍ بِٱلْحَرْبِ. *See also* Pacific, *a.*

Unwarned, *a.* غَيْرُ مُحَذَّرٍ ـ غَيْرُ مُنَبَّهٍ.

Unwarp, *v.t.* سَوَّى ـ عَدَّلَ.

Unwarped, *a.* Not crooked, عَدِل ـ غَيْرُ مُتَعَوِّجٍ ـ غَيْرُ مُعَوَّجٍ.

Unwarrantable, *a.* Unjustifiable, غَيْرُ ـ لا يَتَبَرَّرُ ـ لا عُذْرَ لَهُ ـ حَرَام ـ غَيْرُ مُسَوَّغٍ ـ غَيْرُ مُبَاحٍ ـ غَيْرُ جَائِزٍ. Not allowed, مَعْذُورٍ.

Unwarranted, *a.* Not guaranteed, مِنْ غَيْرِ ضَمَانٍ ـ غَيْرُ مَضْمُونٍ. Unauthorized, unlawful, بِلا رُخْصَةٍ ـ غَيْرُ مُجَوَّزٍ ـ غَيْرُ مُسَوَّغٍ ـ غَيْرُ مُبَاحٍ ـ غَيْرُ جَائِزٍ.

Unwary, *a.* بَلْهَاءُ *fem.* أَبْلَهُ ـ قَلِيلُ ٱلِاحْتِيَاطِ ـ قَلِيلُ ٱلْحَزْمِ ـ غَافِل.

Unwashed, *a.* }
Unwashed, } بِلا غَسْلٍ ـ غَيْرُ مَغْسُولٍ.

Unwatchful, *a.* بِلا ٱنْتِبَاهٍ ـ غَيْرُ مُتَحَفِّظٍ.

Unwavering, *a.* مَعْزُوم ـ غَيْرُ مُتَقَلْقِلٍ ـ غَيْرُ مُتَرَدِّدٍ. *See also* Unswerving, *a.*

Unwaveringly, *ad.* بِلا تَرَدُّدٍ ـ عَزْمًا. *See also* Unswervingly, *a.*

Unwearied, *a.* Not fatigued, غَيْرُ ـ غَيْرُ مُتْعَبٍ ـ غَيْرُ مَمْلُولٍ تَعِبٍ. *See also* Untiring, *a.*

Unwed, *v.t.* *See to* Unmarry, *v.t.*

Unwedded, *a.* *See* Unmarried, *a.*

Unwelcome, *a.* Not welcome, غَيْرُ مَقْبُولٍ. Disagreeable, سَيِّئٌ ـ مَكْرُوه ـ كَرِيه. *See also* Unpleasant, *a.*

Unwelcomely, *ad.* بِعَدَمِ قُبُولٍ ـ بِكَرَاهَةٍ ـ بِلا تَرَحُّبٍ.

Unwell, *a.* Sick, مَرِيض ـ مَعْلُول ـ عَلِيل ـ مُخْتَلُّ ٱلْمِزَاجِ ـ ضَعِيف ـ *vulg.* عَيَّان. To be —, مَرِضَ ـ اِعْتَلَّ ـ عَلَّ ـ اِخْتَلَّ مِزَاجُهُ.

Unwept, *a.* *See* Unlamented, *a.*

Unwholesome, *a.* Of food, وَخِيم; of a climate, and also of food, وَبِيل.

Unwholesomeness, *n.* Of food, وَخَامَة ـ وُخُوم ـ وَبَلَة ـ أَبَلَة; of climate, وَبَلَة ـ وَبَال ـ وُخُومَة.

Unwieldiness, *n.* Heaviness, ثِقَل. Unmanageableness, عَدَمُ عَدَمُ عَنَادَةٍ ـ عَائِدَةٍ.

Unwieldy, *a.* Heavy, clumsy to use, اِسْتِعْمَالُهُ ـ مُتْعِب ـ ثَقِيل صَعْبُ ٱلْمَأْخَذِ ـ مُتْعِب. *See also* Awkward, Clumsy, *a.*

Unwilling, *a.* غَيْرُ رَضِيٍّ ـ غَيْرُ رَاضٍ.

Unwillingly, *ad.* عَنْ غَيْرِ رِضَاهُ ـ بِعَدَمِ رِضًى ـ كُرْهًا ـ عَنْ كَرَاهِيَةٍ.

Unwillingness, *n.* عَدَمُ رِضًى ـ عَدَمُ مَرْضَاةٍ.

Unwind, *v.t.* As off a reel, جَرَّ ـ اِسْتَجَرَّ ـ حَلَّ ـ كَرَّ. *See also to* Untwist, *v.t.*

Unwind, *v.i.* اِنْحَلَّ ـ اِنْجَرَّ.

Unwinged, *a.* Without wings, بِلا أَجْنِحَةٍ. Not clipped in the wings, غَيْرُ مَقْصُوصِ ٱلْجَنَاحِ. Not hit in the wing, غَيْرُ مَجْنُوحٍ.

Unwiped, *a.* غَيْرُ مُنَظَّفٍ ـ غَيْرُ مَمْسُوحٍ.

Unwise, *a.* Not wise, of a person, جُهَّال *pl.* جَاهِل ـ غَيْرُ حَكِيمٍ ـ قَلِيلُ ٱلْعَقْلِ ـ غَافِل ـ غَبِيٌّ. An — action, غَبَاوَة ـ جَهَالَة. To be —, سَفِهَ رَأْيَهُ ـ جَهِلَ. He was — in his opinion, سَفِهَ رَأْيَهُ ـ جَهِلَ.

Unwisely, *ad.* بِتَغَافُلٍ ـ بِقِلَّةِ عَقْلٍ ـ بِغَبَاوَةٍ. To act —, جَهِلَ. To act — with another, جَاهَلَ.

Unwished, *a.* غَيْرُ مَرْغُوبٍ ـ غَيْرُ مُرَادٍ ـ غَيْرُ شَهِيٍّ. Not asked, غَيْرُ مَطْلُوبٍ.

Unwitnessed, *a.* Not seen, غَيْرُ مَشْهُودٍ. Without testimony, غَيْرُ مَشْهُودٍ لَهُ ـ بِلا شَهَادَةٍ.

Unwittily, *ad.* بِخُرْقٍ ـ بِسَخَافَةٍ ـ بِعَدَمِ لَطَافَةٍ.

Unwittingly, *ad.* مِنْ غَيْرِ مَعْرِفَةٍ ـ بِلا عِلْمٍ ـ سَهْوًا. He did it —, فَعَلَهُ سَهْوًا.

Unwitty, *a.* أَخْرَقُ ـ خَرِق ـ سَخِيف ـ غَيْرُ ظَرِيفٍ.

Unwomanly, *a.* خِلَافُ سَجَايَا ٱلنِّسَاءِ ـ غَيْرُ لَائِقٍ بِٱلْمَرْأَةِ.

Unwonted, *a.* خَارِجٌ عَنِ ٱلْعَادَةِ ـ غَيْرُ مُعْتَادٍ ـ فَوْقَ ٱلْعَادَةِ ـ شَاذّ. Strange, غَرِيب ـ نَادِر.

Unwontedly, *ad.* قَلَّمَا ـ بِنَوْعٍ غَرِيبٍ ـ فَوْقَ ٱلْعَادَةِ ـ شَذًّا.

Unwontedness, *n.* نَادِرَة ـ أُعْجُوبَة ـ غَرَابَة ـ شَذّ ـ شُذُوذ.

Unwooded, *a.* بِلا أَشْجَارٍ ـ غَيْرُ مُشَجَّرٍ.

Unworkman-like, *a.* أَخْرَقُ ـ خَرِق ـ بِلا صِنَاعَةٍ ـ غَيْرُ صِنَاعِيٍّ.

Unworldly, *a.* غَيْرُ دُنْيَوِيٍّ. Not loving the world, غَيْرُ مُحِبٍّ لِلدُّنْيَا.

Unworn, *a.* Not worn, غَيْرُ مَلْبُوسٍ. Not worn out, غَيْرُ سَحِيقٍ ـ جَارٍ. Not impaired, غَيْرُ مُضْعَفٍ. Not effaced, غَيْرُ مُطَلَّسٍ.

Unworthily, *a.* بِدُونِ ٱسْتِحْقَاقٍ ـ بِغَيْرِ ٱسْتِحْقَاقٍ.

Unworthiness, *n.* Want of merit, قِلَّةُ ٱسْتِحْقَاقٍ ـ عَدَمُ ٱسْتِحْقَاقٍ. Impropriety, عَدَمُ مُنَاسَبَةٍ ـ عَدَمُ لِيَاقَةٍ.

Unworthy, *a.* Not deserving, غَيْرُ مُسْتَحِقٍّ. Improper, غَيْرُ غَيْرُ مُنَاسِبٍ ـ غَيْرُ لَائِقٍ. Shameful, مَعِيب. Derogatory, صَائِب. "Unworthy the estimate they form of God!" [literally they measure not God at His just measure,] مَا قَدَرُوا ٱللّٰهَ حَقَّ قَدْرِهِ (Kur. xxii. 73).

Unwound, *a.* Wound off, مَكْرُور ـ مَجْرُور. Not wound up, غَيْرُ مُدَوَّرٍ.

Unwounded, *a.* سَالِم ـ غَيْرُ مَجْرُوحٍ.

Unwrap, *v.t.* فَكَّ عَنْ ـ كَذَا ـ نَشَرَ ـ رَفَعَ ٱلْغِطَاءَ عَنْ.

Unwritten, a. غَيْرُ مَكْتُوبٍ. Transmitted by word of mouth, مَنْقُولٌ شِفَاهًا. See also Traditional, a.

Unwrought, a. خَشِيب ـ غَيْرُ مُعَالَجٍ. Gold, silver, or jewels, before being wrought, تِبْر.

Unwrung, a. غَيْرُ مَعْصُورٍ; of the heart, غَيْرُ مَجْرُوحِ ٱلْقَلْبِ.

Unyielding, a. مُتَأَبٍّ ـ لا يُلَيَّنُ ـ لا يَتَلَيَّنُ. Obstinate, عَنِيد ـ مَرِيد pl. مُرَدَاء ـ مُتَمَرِّد ـ وَعِق. Resisting, irresistible, عَزِيز ـ أَعَزّ. To be — to, تَأَبَّى عَلَى.

Unyoke, v.t. To remove a yoke from, رَفَعَ ٱلنِّيرَ عَن. See also to Separate, v.t.

Unzoned, a. بِلا مِنْطَقَةٍ ـ غَيْرُ مُزَنَّرٍ ـ بِلا زُنَّارَةٍ.

Up, prep. and ad. فَوْقُ ـ إِلَى فَوْقُ. Standing up, وَاقِف ـ قَائِم. Arisen from sleep, قَامَ مِنَ ٱلنَّوْمِ. Up, in price, فِي ٱلتَّزَايُدِ. Up, in insurrection, (plural,) عُصَاة; in insurrection against, قَائِمُونَ عَلَى كَذَا. Up, of the sun, طَلَعَتِ ٱلشَّمْسُ. Up, effervescing, فَائِر. The funds are up, صَارَتِ ٱلْأَسْهَامُ فِي ٱلتَّزَايُدِ. His blood is up, ثَارَ دَمُهُ aor. يَثُورُ. The citizens are up, قَامَتْ أَوْلَادُ ٱلْبَلَدِ. It is all up, إِنْتَهَى ٱلْأَمْرُ. It is all up with him, he has failed, been disappointed, خَابَ aor. يَخِيبُ ـ صَارَ خَائِبًا. It is all up with him, he is dead, مَاتَ aor. يَمُوتُ ـ تُوُفِّيَ. The price went up, إِرْتَفَعَ ٱلسِّعْرُ.

Hard up, in straits, فِي شِدَّةٍ ـ فِي عُزِّ ٱلضِّيقِ ـ فِي ضِيقَةٍ.

Up and down, هُنَا وَهُنَاكَ ـ فِي كُلِّ مَوْضِعٍ.

Up there, هُنَاكَ فَوْقُ.

Up to, until, إِلَى ـ حَتَّى. Capable of, جَدِيرٌ بِ. Knowing, دَارٍ بِ ـ عَارِفٌ بِ. Not to be up to ..., عَيَّ بِكَذَا aor. يَعْيَا ـ عَيَّ عَنْ كَذَا. He is up to anything, nothing comes amiss to him, مَا يَشِذُّ عَلَيْهِ شَيْءٌ.

Up stairs, فَوْقُ.

Up with it! ٱلرَّفْعُ ٱلرَّفْعُ ـ يَلَّا بِهِ.

Up, n. The ups and downs of life, فَوَادِحُ ٱلدَّهْرِ ـ تَقَلُّبَاتٌ ـ ٱلْأَحْوَالِ ـ حَالَاتُ ٱلدَّهْرِ ـ طَوَارِحُ ٱلزَّمَنِ.

Up, a. فَوْقَانِيٌّ ـ أَعْلَى.

Upas, n. شَجَرَةٌ نَابِتَةٌ فِي ٱلْهِنْدِ صَبِيبُهَا سَامٌّ.

Upbear, v.t. To raise aloft, رَفَعَ ـ عَلَّى ـ شَالَ بِ aor. يَشُولُ. To sustain, prop, دَعَمَ ـ أَسْنَدَ.

Upbraid, v.t. أَبَنَ ـ ثَرَّبَ عَلَى ـ ثَرَّبَ ـ سَخِطَ عَلَى ـ سَبَّ ـ شَتَمَ ـ عَنَّفَ عَلَى ـ عَيَّرَ بِ ـ عَيَّبَ.

Upbraided, a. مَأْبُون ـ مُثَرَّب ـ مَشْتُوم ـ مُعَيَّبٌ عَلَيْهِ ـ مَسْخُوطٌ عَلَيْهِ ـ مُسَبَّب.

Upbraider, n. مُؤَنِّب ـ مُثَرِّب ـ عَيَّاب ـ شَتَّام ـ شَاتِم.

Upbraiding, n. أَبْن ـ تَثْرِيب ـ شَتْم ـ سَخَط ـ تَعْيِيب ـ تَعْيِير.

Up-cast, a. Thrown up, مُعَلًّى ـ مَرْمِيٌّ فِي ٱلْهَوَاءِ ـ مُصَعَّد. What is —, as by a torrent, etc., جُفَال.

Up-cast, n. A throw, as at bowls, رَمْيَة ـ طَرْح ـ طَرْحَة.

Upheaval, n خَفَقَانٌ وَٱرْتِفَاعٌ ـ تَمَوُّج.

Upheave, v.t. صَعَّدَ ـ رَفَعَ ـ شَالَ بِ ـ عَلَّى. His heart upheaved, فَزَّ قَلْبُهُ. "And the earth and the mountains shall be upheaved and be both crushed into dust at a single crushing," وَحُمِلَتِ ٱلْأَرْضُ وَٱلْجِبَالُ فَدُكَّتَا دَكَّةً وَاحِدَةً (Kur. lxix. 14).

Upheld, a. Raised on high, مُعَلًّى. Propped, مَدْعُوم ـ مُعَمَّد ـ مُسَنَّد. Backed, supported, مَعْضُود ـ مُسَانَد. Persisted in, مُدَامَنٌ عَلَيْهِ.

Up-hill, a. Difficult, عَسِر ـ صَعْب ـ مُتْعِب ـ شَاقّ ـ مُشْكِل.

Uphold, v.t. To keep as from falling, سَانَدَ. To lift on high, عَلَّى. To aid, back, نَاجَدَ ـ عَضَدَ ـ ظَاهَرَ ـ سَانَدَ. To persist in, أَدْمَنَ عَلَى ـ وَاظَبَ عَلَى. See also to Support, v.t.

Upholder, n. A supporter, مُسَانِد ـ عَضُد pl. أَعْضَاد ـ ظَهِير pl. ظُهَرَاء. See also Undertaker, n.

Upholsterer, n. نَجَّاد ـ مُنَجِّد ـ فَرَّاش.

Upholstery, n. أَثَاثُ ٱلتَّنْجِيدِ ـ فَرْش.

Upland, n. نَجْد ـ ظَاهِرَة ـ صَعْدَة ـ صَعِيد.

Upland, a. High, عَالٍ ـ مُرْتَفِع.

Uplift, v.t. To raise on high, عَلَّى ـ رَفَعَ; to erect, نَصَبَ ـ صَمَدَ. To raise, lift, as from the ground, or as the hand, arm, etc., شَالَ بِ aor. يَشُولُ. To be uplifted, raised, تَعَلَّى ـ إِرْتَفَعَ; as of the arm, or from the ground, إِشْتَالَ. "God will uplift those of you who believe," يَرْفَعِ ٱللّٰهُ ٱلَّذِينَ آمَنُوا مِنْكُمْ (Kur. lviii. 12). "And some had assuredly uplifted themselves above others," وَلَعَلَا بَعْضُهُمْ عَلَى بَعْضٍ (Id. xxiii. 93).

Upmost, a. أَعْلَى ـ ٱلْأَعْلَى.

Upon, prep. On, عَلَى. Regarding, مِنْ قِبَلِ ـ فِي ـ بِخُصُوصِ. To take upon one's self, in the way of venturing, تَجَاسَرَ; in the way of undertaking, تَحَمَّلَ بِ ـ تَكَلَّفَ بِ. Upon my word, my conscience, عَلَى ذِمَّتِي.

Upper, a. Higher in place, أَعْلَى fem. عُلْيَا pl. عُلًى or أَعَالِي. Above, فَوْق ـ فَوْقَانِيٌّ. The — part of anything, رَأْس ـ عُلْوٌ ـ عَالِيَة ـ عَلْوٌ. An — story, طَبَقَةٌ فَوْقَانِيَّةٌ. An — leather, وَجْهُ ٱلنَّعْلِ. An — room, عُلِّيَّة pl. عَلَالِيّ ـ غُرْفَة pl. غُرَف and غُرُفَات.

The upper classes, أَكَابِرُ ٱلنَّاسِ ـ ٱلْخَوَاصُّ ـ ذَوَاتُ ٱلْكِرَامِ. The Upper House, of Parliament, مَجْلِسُ ٱلْأُمَرَاءِ وَٱلْأَسَاقِفَةِ.

Upperhand, *n.* Ascendancy, إِعْتِلَاءٌ ـ إِسْتِعْلَاءٌ ـ مُعَالَاةٌ. To get the — of, إِسْتَعْلَى عَلَى ـ عَلَا عَلَى *aor.* يَعْلُو ـ إِعْتَلَى ـ "That over which they had gained the upperhand," مَا عَلَوْا (Kur. xvii. 7). "And be not faint-hearted, and be not sorrowful, for ye shall gain the upperhand if ye be believers," وَلَا تَهِنُوا وَلَا تَحْزَنُوا وَأَنْتُمُ ٱلْأَعْلَوْنَ إِنْ كُنْتُمْ مُؤْمِنِينَ (*Id.* iii. 133).

Uppermost, *a.* The most forward, as in any undertaking, dispute, *etc.*, الْمُتَقَدِّمُ. First, best, أَوَّلُ *fem.* أُولَى. The — branch, الْغُصْنُ ٱلْأَعْلَى. "We said: fear not, thou shalt be the uppermost," قُلْنَا لَا تَخَفْ إِنَّكَ أَنْتَ ٱلْأَعْلَى (Kur. xx. 71). *See also* Upmost, *a.*

Upraise, *v.t.* } To set up, نَصَبَ ـ صَمَدَ ـ وَقَّفَ ـ أَوْقَفَ ـ
Uprear, *v.t.* } نَصَّبَ. To lift, رَفَعَ ـ شَالَ بِ *aor.* يَشُولُ. To be upraised, إِنْتَصَبَ ـ إِرْتَفَعَ.

Upright, *a.* Perpendicular, عَمُودٌ ـ قَائِمٌ ـ مُلْتَتِبٌ. Erect, مُسْتَقِيمٌ ـ مُنْتَهِضٌ ـ مَصْمُودٌ ـ مُنْتَصِبٌ ـ قِوَامٌ *pl.* قَوِيمٌ. Honest, صَالِحٌ ـ عَادِلٌ ـ مُقْسِطٌ. To set —, نَصَبَ ـ صَمَدَ. To stand —, إِنْتَصَبَ ـ إِسْتَقَامَ; as from a sitting posture, نَهَضَ ـ إِنْتَهَضَ. "They were not able to stand upright and were not liberated," فَمَا ٱسْتَطَاعُوا مِنْ قِيَامٍ وَمَا كَانُوا مُنْتَصِرِينَ (Kur. li. 45). "Is he who goeth grovelling on his face better guided than he who walks upright on a straight path?" أَفَمَنْ يَمْشِي مُكِبًّا عَلَى وَجْهِهِ أَهْدَى أَمَّنْ يَمْشِي سَوِيًّا عَلَى صِرَاطٍ مُسْتَقِيمٍ (*Id.* lxvii. 22).

Upright, *n.* قَائِمَةٌ *pl.* قَوَائِمُ; of a roof, قَائِصَةٌ *pl.* قَوَائِصُ.

Uprightly, *ad.* Vertically, قِيَامًا ـ إِلْتِتَابًا ـ صَمْدًا. With integrity, عَلَى مَنْهَجِ ٱلْعَدْلِ ـ بِقِسْطٍ ـ بِعَدَالَةٍ ـ بِٱسْتِقَامَةٍ. To act —, أَقْسَطَ ـ قَسَطَ. To act — in, إِتَّسَطَ فِي ـ قَسَطَ فِي. To act — by, تَوَثَّقَ بِ. "And let not ill-will at any induce you not to act uprightly. Act uprightly," وَلَا يَجْرِمَنَّكُمْ شَنَآنُ قَوْمٍ عَلَى أَنْ لَا تَعْدِلُوا إِعْدِلُوا (Kur. v. 11).

Uprightness, *n.* Perpendicularity, قِيَامٌ ـ إِلْتِتَابٌ. Integrity, صَلَاحٌ ـ عَدَالَةٌ ـ عَدْلٌ ـ صَوَابٌ ـ قِسْطٌ ـ إِسْتِقَامَةٌ.

Uprise, *v.i.* To ascend, تَصَعَّدَ ـ صَعِدَ ـ تَعَلَّى. To rise up, as from a seat, نَهَضَ ـ إِنْتَهَضَ ـ وَقَفَ *aor.* يَقِفُ. To —, as a bird in the air, إِسْتَقَلَّ فِي ٱلسَّمَاءِ.

Uproar, *n.* فِتْنَةٌ ـ سَجْسٌ ـ شَغْبٌ ـ وَلْوَلَةٌ ـ ضَجَّةٌ ـ صُرَاخٌ. They created an — in the town, سَجَّسُوا ٱلْمَدِينَةَ. After the — ceased, بَعْدَ مَا ٱنْتَهَى ٱلشَّغْبُ. To be in a state of —, هَرَجَ ـ تَخَبَّطَ ـ هَاشَ.

Uproarious, *a.* صَيَّاحٌ ـ ضَاجٌّ ـ ضَجُوجٌ.

Uproariously, *ad.* بِسَجْسٍ ـ بِشَغْبٍ ـ بِصِيَاحٍ ـ بِضَجِيجٍ.

Uproot, *v.t.* To take up by the roots, جَثَّ ـ قَلَعَ مِنْ أَصْلِهِ ـ إِسْتَأْصَلَ. *See also to* Eradicate, Exterminate, *v.t.*

Uprouse, *v.t.* *See to* Awaken, *v.t.*

Upset, *v.t.* To overturn, قَلَبَ ـ كَبْكَبَ ـ كَبَّ. To prostrate, تَخَبَّطَ ـ خَبَّطَ ـ خَبَطَ ـ أَوْقَعَ. To demolish, هَدَمَ ـ هَدَّ. To disquiet, أَضْجَرَ ـ أَقْلَقَ. To —, of testimony, *etc.*, فَسَخَ ـ أَبْطَلَ. To be upset, overturned, إِنْقَلَبَ ـ إِنْكَبَّ; to be demolished, إِنْهَدَمَ ـ تَهَدَّمَ ـ إِنْهَدَّ.

Upset, *n.* An overturn, قَلْبٌ ـ كَبْكَبَةٌ ـ كَبَّةٌ.

Upshot, *n.* A final issue, نَتِيجَةٌ ـ مَضْمُونٌ ـ فَصُّ ٱلْكَلَامِ ـ عُقْبٌ ـ قَرَارٌ.

Upside-down, *a.* مَنْكُوسٌ ـ حَابِلُهُ عَلَى نَابِلِهِ ـ مُبَعْثَرٌ ـ مُنْقَلِبٌ عَلَى وَجْهِهِ ـ مَعْكُوسٌ ـ مُنَكَّسٌ. To be —, كَانَ حَابِلُهُ نَابِلَهُ ـ إِعْتَكَسَ ـ إِنْتَكَسَ ـ إِنْعَكَسَ. To turn —, بَعْثَرَ ـ إِجْعَلْ حَابِلَهُ نَابِلَهُ ـ حَوَّلَ حَابِلَهُ عَلَى نَابِلِهِ. Turn thou it —, إِجْعَلْ حَابِلَهُ عَلَى نَابِلِهِ. "We turned those [cities] upside-down," جَعَلْنَا عَالِيَهَا سَافِلَهَا (Kur. xi. 84). "They were turned upside-down upon their heads," نُكِسُوا عَلَى رُؤُوسِهِمْ (*Id.* xxi. 66).

Upspring, *v.i.* } As from fear, *etc.*, تَثَوَّرَ ـ ثَارَ ـ فَزَّ. As from
Upstart, } one's seat, إِنْتَهَضَ ـ نَهَضَ. *See also to* Uprise, *v.i.*

Upstart, *n.* A parvenu, مُحْدَثٌ ـ طَرِفٌ ـ قُعْدُدٌ.

Upturn, *v.t.* Of soil, أَحْفَى ـ سَلَفَ. *See also under to* Turn, *v.t.*

Upturned, *a.* Of soil, مُحْفًى ـ مَسْلُوفٌ.

Upward, *a.* Going upward, مُتَوَجِّهٌ إِلَى فَوْقٍ ـ مُتَصَاعِدٌ.

Upward, *ad.* } Towards a higher place, إِلَى ٱلْعُلُوِّ ـ إِلَى صُعُدٍ ـ
Upwards, } إِلَى فَوْقٍ. Going upwards, تَصَعُّدًا. More than, أَخَذْتُهُ بِدِرْهَمٍ فَصَاعِدًا. I got it for a dirham and —, نَيِّفٌ ـ نَيْفٌ. Ten and —, عَشَرَةٌ وَنَيِّفٌ.

Uranium, *n.* أُورَانِيُومُ وَهُوَ ٱسْمُ مَعْدِنٍ جَدِيدٍ.

Uranography, *n.* رَسْمُ ٱلسَّمَاءِ ـ وَصْفُ ٱلسَّمَاءِ.

Uranus, *n.* The planet, سَيَّارَةُ هَرْشَلَ.

Urban, *a.* بَلَدِيٌّ ـ مَدِينِيٌّ ـ مَدَنِيٌّ.

Urbane, *a.* لَطِيفٌ ـ ظَرِيفٌ ـ حُلْوٌ ـ *vulg.* شَلَبِيٌّ.

Urbanity, *n.* لُطْفٌ ـ لَطَافَةٌ ـ ظَرَافَةٌ ـ *vulg.* شَلَبَنَةٌ. To treat with —, تَلَاطَفَ لِ ـ تَلَطَّفَ لِ.

Urchin, *n.* A hedgehog, قُنْفُذ *pl.* قَنَافِذ. A little child, وُلَيْد — لُبَيّ; of a girl, بُنَيَّة.

Ureter, *n.* بَرْبَخ ٱلْبَوْلِ.

Urethra, *n.* مَجْرَى ٱلْبَوْلِ.

Urethral, *a.* مُتَعَلِّق بِمَجْرَى ٱلْبَوْلِ.

Urge, *v.t.* لَاطَّ عَلَى — أَزَّ-عَلَى — حَثَّ — حَثَّثَ-عَلَى — أَنْفَسَ — أَلَحَّ عَلَى — حَرَّضَ — حَضَّضَ — أَلَبَّ عَلَى — إِسْتَحَثَّ — سَوَّقَ — إِسْتَفَزَّ — حَمَلَ-عَلَى — سَاقَ *aor.* يَسُوقُ — شَدَّ عَلَى. To — to..., هَارَ-عَلَى كَذَا; to — from, against..., هَارَ-عَنْ كَذَا. To be urged, إِحْتَثَّ. To be — to, حُمِلَ عَلَى.

Urgency, *n.* Importunity, لَجَاجَة — إِلْتَاث — إِلْحَاح. Pressure of necessity, لُزُوم — شِدَّةُ لُزُوم — ضَرُورِيَّة — ضَرُورَة — إِضْطِرَار — أَهَمِّيَّة وَٱسْتِعْجَال.

Urgent, *a.* Importunate, لَجُوج — مُلِحّ — مُلِثّ — مِلْظَاظ. Pressing, مُسْتَعْجَل — ضَرُورِيّ — مُضْطَرّ. Urgent affairs, أُمُور مُسْتَعْجَلَة. Most — need, أَشَدُّ لُزُوم. *See also* Pressing, *a.*

Urgently, *ad.* Importunately, بِلَجَاجَةٍ — بِإِلْحَاحٍ. Pressingly, بِشِدَّةٍ كُلِّيَّةٍ — إِضْطِرَارًا.

Urim, *n.* *See under* Thummim, *n.*

Urinal, *n.* مِبْوَلَة.

Urinary, *a.* بَوْلِيّ — مُتَعَلِّق بِٱلْبَوْلِ.

Urinate, *v.i.* بَالَ — شَخَّ. *See also under to* Piss, *v.i.*

Urine, *n.* بَوْل — شَخّ — شُخَاخ. Incontinence of —, صَبُّ ٱلْبَوْلِ. Retention of —, حَصْرُ ٱلْبَوْلِ. Suppression of —, إِنْقِطَاعُ ٱلْبَوْلِ. To judge of diseases by the —, فَسَّرَ. Urine so inspected, تَفْسِرَة. He sprinkled his —, شَفْشَفَ بِبَوْلِهِ.

Urinous, *a.* Like urine, بَوْلِيّ — مِثْلَ ٱلْبَوْلِ.

Urn, *n.* ظَرْف *pl.* ظُرُوف — إِبْرِيق *pl.* أَبَارِيق — قَارُورَة. A tea —, إِبْرِيقُ ٱلشَّايِ. A cinereal —, ظَرْفُ تُرَابِ ٱلْأَمْوَاتِ *pl.* ظُرُوف.

Uroscopy, *n.* تَفْسِرَة.

Ursa, *n.* The constellation, ٱلدُّبّ.

Ursa Major, ٱلدُّبُّ ٱلْأَكْبَرُ.

Ursa Minor, ٱلدُّبُّ ٱلْأَصْغَرُ.

Ursine, *a.* دِبِّيّ — مِنْ جِنْسِ ٱلدُّبِّ.

Urus, *n.* ٱلثَّوْرُ ٱلْوَحْشِيّ.

Us, *pron.* Against us, عَلَيْنَا — ضِدَّنَا. For us, on our part, مَعَنَا; as sent for or intended for us, لَنَا. From us, مِنَّا. With us, مَعَنَا. It is good for us to be here, حَبَّذَا أَنْ نَكُونَ هُنَا.

U.S. حَرْفَانِ تَدُلَّانِ عَلَى ٱلْبِلَادِ ٱلْمُتَّحِدَةِ.

U.S.A. ثَلَاثَةُ أَحْرُفٍ تَدُلُّ عَلَى ٱلْبِلَادِ ٱلْمُتَّحِدَةِ مِنْ قَارَّةِ أَمِيرِيكَا.

Usable, *a.* يُسْتَعْمَلُ — جَدِيرٌ بِٱلْإِسْتِعْمَالِ — مُخْتَلَقَة لِلْإِسْتِعْمَالِ.

Usage, *n.* Custom, عَادَة *pl.* عَادَات. Treatment, مُعَامَلَة. According to —, حَسَبَ ٱلْعَادَةِ — حُكْمَ ٱلْعَادَةِ. Against the —, خِلَافَ ٱلْعَادَةِ — خَارِقَ ٱلْعَادَةِ. The — dates from olden times, جَرَتِ ٱلْعَادَةُ مِنْ قَدِيمِ ٱلزَّمَانِ.

Usance, *n.* Time given for payment, مُهْلَة عَادِيَّة.

Use, *n.* The act of handling, or employing, إِسْتِعْمَال — ٱلْعَمَلُ بِ. Advantage, profit, نَفْع — فَائِدَة *pl.* فَوَائِد — مَنْفَعَة *pl.* مَنَافِع. Utility, convenience, طَائِل — نَفِيعَة — عَائِدَة — مَصْلَحَة. Necessity, حَاجَة — إِضْطِرَار — لُزُوم — إِقْتِضَاء. He made — of it to..., تَسَبَّبَ بِ-إِلَى كَذَا.

By use, practice, بِٱلتَّمَرُّنِ.

For the use of, لِ — لِأَجْلِ — لِٱسْتِعْمَالِ كَذَا.

For necessary uses, لِلْحَاجَاتِ ٱلضَّرُورِيَّةِ.

Of no use, غَيْرُ طَائِلٍ — بِلَا فَائِدَةٍ — بَاطِل. He is of no use, هُوَ بِغَيْرِ طَائِلٍ.

Of use, طَائِل — نَافِع — مُفِيد.

Out of use, غَيْرُ مُسْتَعْمَلٍ — مَتْرُوك — إِسْتِعْمَالُهُ سَاقِطٌ — مُلْغَى.

Uses and customs, أُصُول — عَادَات وَعَوَائِد.

What is the use? مَا ٱلْمَنْفَعَةُ — مَاذَا يَنْفَعُ.

To be of no use, لَا طَائِلَ لَهُ.

To be of use to, convenient to, إِسْتَفَادَ مِنْ — صَلَحَ لِ. To profit, نَفَعَ — أَفَادَ.

To bring into use, أَوْجَدَ ٱسْتِعْمَالَهُ — أَجْرَى-عَادَةً.

To employ to a bad use, أَسَاءَ فِي ٱسْتِعْمَالِهِ — تَصَرَّفَ بِ-بَاطِلًا.

To have no further use for, مَا بَقِيَ لِ-حَاجَةٌ إِلَى كَذَا — مَا عَازَهُ — مَا أَعْوَزَهُ ٱلشَّيْءُ بَعْدُ — ٱلشَّيْءُ بَعْدُ.

To have use for a thing, لَزِمَ — إِحْتَاجَ إِلَى.

To make use of, تَسَبَّبَ بِ — عَمِلَ بِ — إِسْتَعْمَلَ — تَصَرَّفَ بِ.

To make a bad use of; *see preceding,* To employ to a bad use.

To make a good use of, تَصَرَّفَ فِي-خَيْرًا — أَحْسَنَ فِي ٱسْتِعْمَالِهِ.

To teach one the use of, دَرَّبَ-عَلَى.

Use, *v.t.* To apply to some service, عَمِلَ بِ — إِسْتَعْمَلَ. To exercise, أَعْمَلَ: he used his hand, أَعْمَلَ يَدَهُ. To practise, مَارَزَ. To treat, عَامَلَ — صَنَعَ بِ. To — one to, عَوَّدَ-عَلَى. To — up, destroy, أَفْنَى — ضَيَّعَ — أَتْلَفَ. To — one's self up, of the health, ضَيَّعَ عَافِيَتَهُ — نَهَكَ قُوَّتَهُ. To become used up, worn out, بَلِيَ — إِنْسَحَقَ.

Used, *a.* Made use of, مُسْتَعْمَل. Used up, expended, مَصْرُوف; worn out, بَالٍ. To be — to, تَعَوَّدَ عَلَى — تَوَطَّنَ عَلَى. Used to, capable of, مُعِيدٌ ل. They were so —, treated, تَصَرَّفَ فِيهِمْ هٰكَذَا. It may be — in any work, يُسْتَعْمَلُ لِكُلِّ عَمَلٍ. They — to fast, كَانُوا يَصُومُونَ. So the young men — to do, هٰكَذَا كَانَ يَعْمَلُ ٱلْفِتْيَانُ.

Useful, *a.* نَافِعٌ – طَائِلٌ. Handy, قَرِيبُ ٱلْمَأْخَذِ. Beneficial, promoting good, خَيْرِيٌّ. Useful, of a man, نَفَّاعٌ – نَفُوعٌ. Useful things, مَنَافِعُ. Useful works, ٱلْأُمُورُ ٱلنَّافِعَةُ. More — than, أَنْفَعُ مِنْ كَذَا – أَعْوَدُ عَلَى كَذَا. To be — to, نَفَعَ – نَفَعَ بِ. To — نَفَعَ ب – اِنْتَفَعَ بِ. To render — to, أَصْلَحَ ل. This is — to you, هٰذَا يَصْلُحُ لَكَ.

Usefully, *ad.* بِطَائِلٍ – إِفَادَةً – بِنَفْعٍ. Beneficially, خَيْرَةً.

Usefulness, *n.* Profit, advantage, نَفْعٌ – إِفَادَةٌ – فَائِدَةٌ – مَنْفَعَةٌ. Good, صَلَاحٌ – خَيْرٌ.

Useless, *a.* بِلَا فَائِدَةٍ – غَيْرُ نَافِعٍ – بَطَّالٌ – بَاطِلٌ – غَيْرُ مُفِيدٍ. It is —, مَا هُوَ بِطَائِلٍ – هُوَ بِغَيْرِ طَائِلٍ. Useless labour, تَعَبٌ عَابِثٌ.

Uselessly, *ad.* لِغَيْرِ طَائِلٍ – عَبَثًا – مِنْ غَيْرِ نَفْعٍ – بِلَا فَائِدَةٍ – بَاطِلًا.

Uselessness, *n.* عَدَمُ طَائِلٍ – عَدَمُ مَنْفَعَةٍ – عَدَمُ فَائِدَةٍ – قِلَّةُ نَفْعٍ.

Usher, *n.* An under teacher, خَلِيفَةُ ٱلْمُعَلِّمِ – عَرِيفٌ *pl.* عُرَفَاءُ. An introducer, مُعَرِّفٌ – حَاجِبٌ. *See also* Monitor, *n.*

Usher, *v.t.* To introduce, present to, أَبْرَزَ-إِلَى – عَرَّفَ-بِ – قَدَّمَ-لِ. To precede, تَقَدَّمَ عَلَى – سَبَقَ. To announce, نَبَّأَ بِ – بَشَّرَ بِ. *See also to* Introduce, *v.t.*

Usquebaugh, *n.* عَرَقِيٌّ – عَرَقٌ.

Ustion, *n.* The act of burning, إِحْرَاقٌ; the being burnt, حَرَقٌ; with an iron, كَيٌّ.

Usual, *a.* Customary, عَلَى ٱلْعَادَةِ – مُعْتَادٌ – مَأْلُوفٌ – مَعْهُودٌ. Many more persons than —, أَكْثَرُ أُنَاسٍ مِنَ ٱلْمُعْتَادِ. As has been —, عَلَى مَا جَرَتْ بِهِ ٱلْعَادَةُ. The presentation of the decoration was made with the — formalities, كَانَ تَقْدِيمُ ٱلنِّشَانِ عَلَى ٱلْأُصُولِ ٱلْمَأْلُوفَةِ وَٱلْاِحْتِفَالَاتِ ٱلْمَعْرُوفَةِ. It is — that..., هُوَ مِنَ ٱلْعَادَةِ أَنْ. Usual, what is in use, مُسْتَعْمَلٌ – اِعْتِيَادِيٌّ. Much as —, عَلَى ٱلْعَادَةِ. *See also* Frequent, Common, *a.*

Usually, *ad.* According to custom, حَسَبَ – حَسَبَ ٱلْعَادَةِ ٱلْمُعْتَادِ. Commonly, generally, كَثِيرًا – عُمُومًا – فِي ٱلْغَالِبِ.

Usufruct, *n.* تَمَتُّعٌ بِٱلْمَدْخُولِ – مِتْعَةٌ – غَلَّةٌ.

Usufructuary, *n.* مُتَمَتِّعٌ.

Usurer, *n.* مُرَابٍ – مُقْرِضٌ – مُرْبٍ.

Usurious, *a.* رِبَوِيٌّ. Prohibited, unlawful, حَرَامٌ.

Usuriously, *ad.* بِرِبَاءٍ – بِرِبًا – بِرُبُوٍّ.

Usuriousness, *n.* رِبًا – رُبُوٌّ.

Usurp, *v.t.* غَاصَبَ – اِغْتَصَبَ – غَصَبَ – اِخْتَلَسَ – تَخَلَّسَ. He usurped the sovereign power, اِخْتَلَسَ – غَصَبَ ٱلْحُكُومَةَ ٱلْحُكُومَةَ.

Usurpation, *n.* غَصْبٌ – اِغْتِصَابٌ – اِخْتِلَاسٌ – جَوْرٌ.

Usurper, *n.* غَاصِبٌ – مُخْتَلِسٌ – جَائِرٌ.

Usurpingly, *ad.* اِغْتِصَابًا – بِٱلْغَصْبِ – اِخْتِلَاسًا.

Usury, *n.* مُرَابَاةٌ – رِبَوًا – رِبًا. To practise —, أَرْبَى; with one, رَابَى.

Utensil, *n.* A vessel, ظَرْفٌ *pl.* ظُرُوفٌ – إِنَاءٌ *pl.* آنِيَةٌ – وِعَاءٌ *pl.* أَوْعِيَةٌ. A tool, آلَةٌ *pl.* آلَاتٌ. Apparatus, tackle, *etc.*, عُدَّةٌ *pl.* عُدَدٌ. Household utensils, أَثَاثٌ – أَمْتِعَةُ ٱلْبَيْتِ – أَمَاوِنُ ٱلدَّارِ.

Uterine, *a.* مُتَعَلِّقٌ بِٱلرَّحِمِ – رَحِمِيٌّ. A — brother, of the same mother, أَخٌ مِنْ أُمٍّ وَاحِدَةٍ – صِنْوٌ; of the same father and mother, شَقِيقٌ *pl.* أَشِقَّاءُ.

Uterus, *n.* *See* Womb, *n.*

Utilitarian, *a.* *See* Useful, *a.*

Utilitarian, *n.* مِنْ أَهْلِ مَذْهَبِ ٱلْقَائِلِينَ أَنَّ ٱلنَّفْعَ أَعْظَمُ خَيْرٍ.

Utilitarianism, *n.* مَذْهَبُ ٱلْقَائِلِينَ أَنَّ ٱلنَّفْعَ أَعْظَمُ خَيْرٍ.

Utility, *n.* إِفَادَةٌ – نَفِيعَةٌ – نَفْعٌ – عَائِدَةٌ – مَصْلَحَةٌ – طَائِلٌ – مَنْفَعَةٌ. Works of —, ٱلْأُمُورُ ٱلنَّافِعَةُ.

Utilization, *n.* إِصْلَاحٌ ل – اِسْتِعْمَالٌ.

Utilize, *v.t.* تَسَبَّبَ بِ-إِلَى كَذَا – جَعَلَهُ مُفِيدًا ل – اِسْتَعْمَلَ-ل.

Utmost, *a.* The most distant, أَقْصَى *pl.* أَقَاصِي: From the — parts of the earth, مِنْ أَقَاصِي ٱلْأَرْضِ. The — part of the army, أَقْصَى ٱلْجُنُودِ.

Utmost, *n.* The most that can be, غَايَةٌ – نِهَايَةٌ – ٱلْأَخِيرُ. The — point of a thing, حَدٌّ *pl.* حُدُودٌ. The — in one's power, of ability, love, *etc.*, حُدَادٌ – جُهَادٌ – جُهْدٌ – حَبَابٌ. My —, حُمَادِي – جُهْدِي; thine —, جُهْدُكَ – حَبَابُكَ. To do one's — in, for..., بَلَغَ غَايَتَهُ فِي-لِأَجْلِ كَذَا or فُلَانٍ – بَالَغَ فِي-لِكَذَا or لِفُلَانٍ. They used their — endeavours, بَذَلُوا أَقْصَى مَجْهُودِهِمْ.

Utopia, *n.* خَيَالٌ – دَارُ ٱلْخَلَاءِ – مُسْتَقَرُّ ٱلْكَمَالِ وَهْمِيٌّ.

Utopian, *a.* وَهْمِيٌّ – خَيَالِيٌّ – خَالٍ.

Utricle, *n.* *See* Cyst, *n.*

Utter, *a.* Complete, كُلِّيٌّ – أَتَمُّ – أَوْفَى. Utter destruction, هَلَاكٌ تَمَامٌ. An — refusal, رَدٌّ قَاطِعٌ (or بَتٌّ). Utter darkness, ظَلَامٌ كَامِلٌ. *See also* Outer, *a.*

Utter, *v.t.* To speak, فَاهَ *aor.* يَفُوهُ – تَفَوَّهَ بِ – لَفَظَ بِ – نَطَقَ بِ – تَكَلَّمَ بِ. To give currency to, شَاعَ بِ – أَشَاعَ بِ. He uttered, poured forth or disclosed, what was in his mind,

أَصَبْتُ مَا فِي نَفْسِهِ . "When ye uttered with your tongues, and spake with your mouths that of which ye had no knowledge," إِذْ تَلَقَّوْنَهُ بِأَلْسِنَتِكُمْ وَتَقُولُونَ بِأَفْوَاهِكُمْ مَا لَيْسَ لَكُمْ بِهِ عِلْمٌ (Kur. xxiv. 14).

Utterable, *a.* يُتَلَفَّظُ.

Utterance, *n.* The act of uttering, تَكَلُّم ـ نُطْق ـ تَفَوُّه ب ـ كَلَام . Pronunciation, لَفْظ ـ تَلَفُّظ . Emission, إِشَاعَة . To give — to; *see to* Utter, *v.t.*

Utterer, *n.* A speaker, مُتَكَلِّم ـ نَاطِق . One who sends forth, مُشِيع ـ شَائِع . An — of false coin, زَغَلِيّ .

Utterly, *ad.* بِالْكُلِّ ـ بَتَّةً ـ إِلَى ٱلْغَايَةِ . I will put him — out of remembrance, أَمْحُو ذِكْرَهُ . It — perished, ع زَالَ بِتَمَامِهِ . It was — emptied, أُفْرِغَ إِفْرَاغًا . The land was — desolate, تُفِرَتِ ٱلْأَرْضُ . It shall be — destroyed, خَرَابًا تُخْرَبُ . He — forsook him, ع تَرَكَهُ إِلَى ٱلْغَايَةِ .

Uttermost, *a.* أَخِير ـ تَمَام . To the —, إِلَى ٱلتَّمَامِ ـ بَتَّةً . To the — farthing, إِلَى ٱلْفَلْسِ ٱلْأَخِيرِ . *See also* Utmost, *a.*

Uttermost, *n.* *See* Utmost, *n.*

Uvula, *n.* لَهَاة *pl.* لَهًا *and* ع لِهَآء ـ طَنْطَلَة .

Uxorious, *a.* مُغَازِل زَوْجَتَهُ ـ مُتَدَلِّل عَلَى زَوْجَتِهِ .

Uxoriously, *ad.* بِمُغَازَلَةِ ٱلزَّوْجَةِ ـ تَدَلُّلًا عَلَى ٱلزَّوْجَةِ .

Uxoriousness, *n.* مُغَازَلَةُ ٱلزَّوْجَةِ ـ ٱلتَّدَلُّلُ عَلَى ٱلزَّوْجَةِ .

V.

Vacancy, *n.* An empty space, هَوَآء ـ جَوْف ـ خُلُوّ ـ ع خَلَآء . A vacant place, appointment, مَنْصَب خَالٍ .

Vacant, *a.* Empty, فَارِغ ـ خَالٍ ـ خَاوٍ ـ بَاوٍ . Unoccupied, خَالٍ ـ فَاضٍ . Unmeaning, لَا طَائِلَ تَحْتَهُ . Unthinking, أَبْلَهُ *fem.* ع بَلْهَآء *pl.* بُلْهٌ *and* ع بُلْهَآء . Without expression, قَلِيلُ ٱلتَّغْيِيرِ ـ بِلَا مَعْنًى ـ غَيْرُ حَذَّاءٍ . A — stare, مُرَامَقَةٌ فِي ٱلْخَلَآءِ . The — or vacated chiefdom, مَرْكَزٌ خَالٍ مِنَ ٱلرِّئَاسَةِ . A — place, خَلَآء ـ خَلْوَة . The place became —, خَوَى ٱلْمَكَانُ *aor.* يَخْوِي . His place became —, ع خَلَا مَكَانُهُ . To be —, empty, خَوَى *aor.* يَخْوِي ـ خَلَا *aor.* يَخْلُو ـ فَضَا *aor.* يَفْضُو ـ خَلَا ـ أَفْضَى ـ أَخْلَى ـ إِسْتَخْلَى . To be —, as of an appointment, ع خَلَا .

Vacate, *v.t.* To make vacant, empty, فَرَّغَ ـ أَفْرَغَ ـ أَخْلَى . To leave empty, unoccupied, خَلَّى . To give up, resign, ع تَرَكَ ـ تَخَلَّى مِن *or* عَن . He vacated his place, died, خَلَّى مَكَانَهُ .

Vacation, *n.* Intermission of business, فَرَاغ ـ فَرَاغٌ مِنَ ٱلشُّغْلِ ـ تَفَرُّغٌ مِنَ ٱلْعَمَلِ .

Vaccinate, *v.t.* لَقَّحَ- (*or* طَعَّمَ-) ٱلْجُدَرِيَّ ٱلْبَقَرِيَّ . To be vaccinated, تَطَعَّمَ بِٱلْجُدَرِيِّ .

Vaccination, *n.* The act of, تَلْقِيمُ (*or* تَلْقِيحُ *or* تَطْعِيمُ) بِٱلْجُدَرِيِّ ٱلْبَقَرِيِّ . The being vaccinated, تَطَعُّمُ ٱلْجُدَرِيِّ ٱلْبَقَرِيِّ .

Vaccinator, *n.* حَكِيمُ ٱلْجُدَرِيِّ ـ مُطَعِّمُ ٱلْجُدَرِيِّ ٱلْبَقَرِيِّ .

Vaccine, *a.* بَقَرِيّ . Vaccine matter, طُعْمُ ٱلْجُدَرِيِّ ٱلْبَقَرِيِّ .

Vacillate, *v.i.* To oscillate, إِرْتَجَّ ـ تَرَجَّجَ . To waver, as in opinion, تَضَرَّبَ ـ تَمَخْطَرَ ـ تَرَدَّدَ فِي ٱلرَّأْيِ . To be doubtful about, ع شَكَّ فِي . He vacillated about the matter, تَرَدَّدَ فِي ٱلْأَمْرِ . He vacillated between two things, تَرَجَّحَ بَيْنَ أَمْرَيْنِ . To make to —, to cause to doubt, about, شَكَّكَ-فِي . To — between, تَذَبْذَبَ بَيْنَ . I vacillated between two things, عَادَلْتُ بَيْنَ أَمْرَيْنِ . *See also to* Waver, *v.i.*

Vacillating, *a.* As in opinion, قَرَّار ـ قَلَّاع ـ نَوَّاس ـ فَائِلُ ٱلرَّأْيِ ـ مُرْتَبِك ـ مُتَمَخْطِر ـ مُتَرَدِّدٌ فِي ٱلرَّأْيِ . *See also* Waverer, *n.*

Vacillation, *n.* Oscillation, إِرْتِجَاج ـ تَرَجُّح ; of opinion, mind, *etc.*, تَرَدُّد ـ تَضَرُّب ـ تَمَخْطُر . Doubt, شَكّ ـ تَشَكُّك .

Vacuity, *n.* A vacant or intervening space, بَهْو *pl.* ع أَبْهَآء *and* بُهُوّ ـ فُرْجَة ـ خِلَال . *See also* Vacancy, *n.*

Vacuum, *n.* خُلُوّ ـ ع خَلَآء .

Vade-mecum, *n.* مَجْمَعَة . A guide book, كِتَاب دَلِيل ـ دُسْتُور .

Vagabond, *n.* A stroller, wanderer, تَايِه ـ طَوَّاف . A libertine, فَلَاتِيَّة *pl.* فَلَاتِيّ ـ هَوَامِلُ *pl.* هَامِل ـ خُلَعَآء ع *pl.* خَلِيع .

Vagabond, *a.* Strolling, طَوَّاف ـ تَيْهَان . Rascally, خَلِيع ـ خَبِيث ـ شَرِير *pl.* أَشْرَار ـ رَدِيّ *pl.* أَرْدِيَآء .

Vagabondism, *n.* Idle wandering, طَوَفَان ـ تَيَهَان . Rascality, خَبَاثَة ـ خُبْث ـ خَلَاعَة .

Vagary, *n.* جُنُون ـ جِنَّة ـ لَهْو ـ خَيَال ـ وَهْم بَاطِل .

Vagina, *n.* كُسّ *pl.* أَكْسَاس ـ بَاطِنُ ٱلْفَرْجِ ـ مَهْبِل .

Vaginal, *a.* Pertaining to a sheath, غِلَافِيّ . Pertaining to the vagina, مَا نِيطَ بِبَاطِنِ ٱلْفَرْجِ (*or* بِٱلْمَهْبِلِ) .

Vagrancy, *n.* هُمُول ـ تَيَهان.

Vagrant, *n.* *See* Vagabond, *n.*

Vagrant, *a.* *See* Vagabond, *a.*

Vagrantly, *ad.* كَٱلتَّايِهِ ـ تَيَهَانًا.

Vague, *a.* مُبْهَم ـ مُنَكَّر ـ نَكِرَة. To make —, of language, أَبْهَمَ (*or*) رَوَّجَ ٱلْكَلَامَ. *See also* Indefinite, Undefined, *a.*

Vaguely, *ad.* تَنْكِيرًا ـ ٱلْتِبَاسًا ـ إِشْتِبَاهًا ـ إِبْهَامًا.

Vagueness, *n.* إِشْتِبَاه ـ إِبْهَام ـ ٱلْتِبَاس ـ تَنْكِير.

Vail, *n.* *See* Veil, *n.*

Vain, *a.* Useless, بَاطِل ـ عَبَث ـ عِبِّيث ـ غَيْرُ طَائِلٍ. Self-conceited, مُعْجَبٌ بِنَفْسِهِ ـ مُخْتَال ـ خَائِل ـ مَزْهُوّ ـ فَيَّاش ـ ذُو كِبْرٍ ـ مُتَصَلِّف ـ صَلِف. A — thing, أَمْرٌ بَاطِلٌ. Vain repetition, تَكْرِيرُ ٱلْكَلَامِ ٱلْبَاطِلِ. A — life, حَيٰوةٌ بَاطِلَةٌ. Beauty is —, a deceit, ٱلْحُسْنُ غِشٌّ. It is — to . . . , هُوَ مِنَ ٱلْعَبَثِ أَنْ. In —, vainly, بَاطِلًا. To take the name of God in —, نَطَقَ بِٱسْمِ ٱللّٰهِ بَاطِلًا. Our labour is in —, صَارَ تَعَبُنَا بَاطِلًا. Vain sayings, بُطَّالَات. To be —, conceited, تَصَلَّفَ ـ زَهِيَ *aor.* يُزْهَو ـ أُزْهِيَ ـ تَعَجَّبَ بِنَفْسِهِ. To be — of, إِفْتَخَرَ بِ. It was all in —, ذَهَبَ سُدًى. What is — or false is waning, ٱلْبَاطِلُ فِي حَوْرٍ. "And the Apostle said: O my Lord, truly my people have esteemed this al-Kur-ân to be vain babbling," وَقَالَ ٱلرَّسُولُ يَا رَبِّ إِنَّ قَوْمِي ٱتَّخَذُوا هٰذَا ٱلْقُرْآنَ مَهْجُورًا (Kur. xxv. 32).

Vainglorious, *a.* مَغْرُور ـ مُتَصَلِّف ـ صَلِف ـ مُتَلَهْوِق ـ فَائِش ـ فَيَّاش ـ مُتَفَخِّر ـ مُتَكَبِّر.

Vaingloriously, *ad.* بِغُرُورٍ ـ بِٱلتَّفَاخُرِ ـ بِتَكَبُّرٍ ـ بِتَصَلُّفٍ.

Vainglory, *n.* زَهْوٌ ـ تَفَاخُر ـ تَكَبُّر ـ غُرُور ـ تَصَلُّف.

Vainly, *ad.* Ineffectually, بَاطِلًا ـ سُدًى. With empty pride, بِٱنْتِفَاخٍ بَاطِلٍ.

Vainness, *n.* Ineffectualness, عَدَمُ فَاعِلِيَّةٍ ـ عَدَمُ طَائِلٍ ـ عَبَث ـ عَدَمُ مَنْفَعَةٍ. Conceit, غُرُور ـ تَصَلُّف ـ صَلَف. *See also* Vanity, *n.*

Valance, *n.* سِجَاف ـ ذَيْل.

Valance, *v.t.* To — with, رَكَّبَ فِي سِجَافًا ـ ذَيَّلَ بِ.

Vale, *n.* *See* Valley, *n.*

Valediction, *n.* / Valedictory, } وَدَاع.

Valedictory, *a.* تَوْدِيعِيٌّ.

Valentine, *n.* A letter sent to another on St. Valentine's day, كِتَابُ وِدَادٍ أَوْ تَصْوِيرٌ يُرْسَلُ مِنْ مَحْبُوبٍ إِلَى مَحْبُوبَتِهِ أَوْ مِنْ مَحْبُوبَةٍ إِلَى مَحْبُوبٍ فِي عِيدِ مَارِ وَالَنْتِينُوس. A sweetheart chosen on that day, مَعْشُوقَةٌ مُخْتَارَةٌ مِنْ شَابٍّ أَوْ مَعْشُوقٌ مُخْتَارٌ مِنْ بِنْتٍ عَلَى وَجْهِ ٱللَّهْوِ فِي ذٰلِكَ ٱلْعِيدِ.

Valentine's-day, *n.* عِيدُ مَارِ وَالَنْتِينُوسَ ٱلْوَاقِعُ فِي ١٤ شَهْرِ فَبْرَار.

Valerian, *n.* فُو.

Valet, *n.* خَدَّام *pl.* خَدَّامُون.

Valet-de-chambre, *n.* فَرَّاش.

Valet-de-place, *n.* دَلِيل *pl.* أَدِلَّة *or* أَدِلَّاءُ ـ تُرْجُمَان *pl.* تَرَاجِمَة.

Valetudinarian, *n.* / Valetudinary, *a.* } ضَعِيف ـ مِسْقَام ـ عُزَّل ـ عَاجِز ـ مَوْهُونُ ٱلْمِزَاجِ.

Valhalla, *n.* جَنَّةٌ وَهْمِيَّةٌ تَخْلُدُ فِيهَا أَرْوَاحُ ٱلْأَبْطَالِ ٱلْمَوْتَى.

Valiant, *a.* بَطَل *pl.* أَبْطَال ـ أَشَدّ *pl.* أَشِدَّاءُ ـ شُجَاع ـ شَجِيع ـ شَهْم *pl.* شِهَام. To be —, شَجُعَ ـ شَهُمَ. *See also* Bold, *a.*

Valiantly, *ad.* بِشَجَاعَةٍ ـ بِشَهَامَةٍ. To act —, تَجَلَّدَ ـ تَشَدَّدَ.

Valid, *a.* Firm, مُسْتَحْكَم ـ ثَابِت ـ رَصِين. True, real, صَحِيح ـ حَقِيقِيّ. Legal, executed with the proper formalities, جَائِز ـ مَقْضِيٌّ عَلَى ٱلشَّرَائِطِ ٱلرَّسْمِيَّةِ ٱلسُّلْطَانِيَّةِ ـ شَرْعِيٌّ ـ صَحِيح. To be —, صَحَّ ـ حَقَّ.

Validate, *v.t.* صَحَّحَ ـ أَثْبَتَ شَرْعًا ـ حَقَّقَ ـ أَحَقَّ.

Validity, *n.* / Validness, } Firmness, رَصَانَة ـ ثُبُوت ـ ثَبَات. Truth, صِحَّة ـ حَقِيقَة. Legal force, إِرْتِبَاطٌ شَرْعِيٌّ ـ قُوَّةٌ قَانُونِيَّةٌ. Force, قُوَّة.

Validly, *ad.* With legal force, شَرْعًا ـ بِٱرْتِبَاطٍ شَرْعِيٍّ. Truly, بِصِحَّةٍ ـ حَقًّا.

Valise, *n.* جِرَاب *pl.* جُرُب *and* أَجْرِبَة ـ عَيْبَة *pl.* عِيَاب *and* عَيْبَات ـ مِزْوَد.

Valley, *n.* قَاع *pl.* قِيعَان *and* أَقْوَاع ـ عَقِيق *pl.* أَعِقَّة ـ وَادٍ *pl.* أَوْدِيَة. The two sides of a —, جَنَاحُ ٱلْوَادِي ـ شَاطِئُ ٱلْوَادِي. The — of a torrent, بَطْحَة ـ بَطْح ـ أَبْطَح ـ بَطِيحَة. The soft earth of a —, بَطْحَاء. In an unfruitful —, بِوَادٍ غَيْرِ ذِي زَرْعٍ.

Vallum, *n.* سَدّ ـ مَتْرَسَة ـ مِتْرَسَة.

Valonia, *n.* The tree, شَجَرَةُ ٱلْبَلُّوطِ; that used as a dye, بَلُّوطُ ٱلصَّبَّاغِ.

Valorem, *ad.* Ad — duty, عَلَى ٱلرَّسْمِ ٱلرَّائِجِ.

Valour, *n.* بَطْش ـ شَهَامَة ـ شَجَاعَة ـ جَسَارَة ـ شَوْكَة.

Valorous, *a.* جَسُور ـ بَطِيش ـ بَطَّاش ـ شَدِيدُ ٱلْبَطْشِ. *See also* Valiant, *a.*

Valorously, *ad.* بِجَسَارَةٍ ـ بِبَطْشٍ ـ جَسَارَةً.

Valuable, *a.* Costly, مُثْمِن ـ ثَمِين ـ نَفِيس ـ فَاخِر ـ سَنِيّ. Estimable, مُعْتَبَر. Prized, عَزِيز.

Valuation, *n.* إِسْعَار ـ تَسْعِير ـ تَثْمِين ـ تَقْدِير.

Valuator, *n.* } مُثَمِّن ـ مُسَعِّر .
Valuer, }

Value, *n.* Cost, price, قِيمَة ـ ثَمَن *pl.* أَثْمَان ـ سِعْر *pl.* أَسْعَار ـ حَقّ . Costliness, نَفَاسَة ـ غَلَاء ـ خَطَر . Estimation in which a person or thing is held, إِعْتِبَار ـ حَسَب ـ فَضْل . Meaning, مَحَطّ ـ مَعْنَى ـ مَضْمُون ـ فَحْوَى ـ Of no —, utility, غَيْر طَائِل ـ بَطَّال . Of more —, better, deserving of more consideration, than ..., أَفْضَل مِن . It is of no —, لا يُسَاوِي شَيْئًا . Every thing has its —, كُلّ شَيْءٍ يَحْرُز ثَمَنًا . *See also under* Price, *n.*

Value, *v.t.* To price, ثَمَّنَ ـ أَسْعَرَ ـ سَعَّرَ . To prize, أَعَزَّ ـ إِعْتَبَرَ . To esteem, كَرَّمَ ـ أَكْرَمَ ـ إِعْتَبَرَ ـ عَرَفَ . To reckon, compute, خَمَّنَ ـ قَدَّرَ ـ حَسَبَ . It cannot be valued with gold, لا يُعَادِلُهُ ٱلذَّهَبُ . Valued at ..., مُقَيَّمٌ بِكَذَا .

Valueless, *a.* لا قَدْرَ وَلَا قِيمَةَ لَهُ ـ لا قِيمَةَ لَهُ . *See also* Useless, *a.*

Valuer, *n.* *See* Valuator, *n.*

Valvate, *a.* Having a valve, shell, ذُو صَدَف .

Valve, *n.* As of a door, مِصْرَاع *pl.* مَصَارِيع ; a door with two valves, بَاب ذُو مِصْرَاعَيْن . Valve, as of a pump, *etc.*, لَوْلَب *pl.* لَوَالِب . Valve, as of the heart, *etc.*, غِشَاء *pl.* غَوَاشٍ ـ حَاجِز *pl.* حَوَاجِز . Valve, of a shell, صَدَف *dual* صَدَفَتَان *pl.* أَصْدَاف .

Valvular, *a.* Of shells, ذُو أَصْدَاف ; of membranes, ذُو غَوَاشٍ .

Vamp, *n.* As of shoes, وَجْهُ ٱلنَّعْل .

Vamp, *v.t.* To mend, رَمَّ *aor.* يَرُمّ ـ رَمْرَمَ ـ صَلَّحَ ـ أَصْلَحَ .

Vamper, *n.* مُصَلِّح ـ مُعَالِج . *See also* Mender, *n.*

Vampire, *n.* A kind of large bat, نَوْعٌ كَبِيرٌ مِنَ ٱلْوَطْوَاط . The mythological —, المَصَّاصَة . An extortioner, نَهَّاب ـ سَلَّاب ـ ظَالِم ـ عَصَّار .

Vampirism, *n.* Extortion, سَلْب ـ نَهْب ـ تَعَسُّف ـ جَوْر .

Van, *n.* As of an army, طَلِيعَة ـ مُجَنِّبَة ـ قَادِمَة ـ نَظِيرَة ـ مُقَدَّمُ ٱلْجَيْش ـ سُلَافُ ٱلْعَسْكَر ـ رَسِيلُ ٱلْعَسْكَر ; of horse, سَرْعَان . A winnowing —, بَيْدَر ـ مِذْرَاة . A —, as of a windmill, جَنَاح *pl.* أَجْنِحَة . A luggage —, of a railway, عَرَبِيَّة ٱلْحُمُولَة فِي سِكَّة ٱلْحَدِيد ; *called in Egypt*, عَرَبِيَّة جَمَالُون ; a guard's van, عَرَبِيَّة خَفِير ٱلسِّكَّة ٱلْحَدِيدِيَّة ; *from the Italian*, سَبَنْسَة . A light carriage, عَرَبِيَّة خَفِيفَة .

Vandals, *n.* The people who destroyed ancient Rome, جِيل ٱلْوَنْدَل ٱلَّذِي أَخْرَبَ رُومِيَّة ٱلْقَدِيمَة . One who ignorantly destroys ancient monuments, مُتْلِف ٱلْآثَار ٱلْقَدِيمَة جَهَالَةً .

Vandalism, *n.* As regards ancient monuments, إِتْلَاف ٱلْآثَار ٱلْقَدِيمَة عَن جَهَالَة وَعَدَم ٱعْتِبَار .

Vandyke, *n.* The artist, إِسْمُ مُصَوِّرٍ مَشْهُورٍ مِنْ أَهْلِ فَلَمَنْك . A kerchief for the neck, مِنْدِيل لِلرَّقَبَة . The notched pattern, تَسْنِين ـ تَفْلِيل ـ تَحْزِيز .

Vane, *n.* For showing the direction of the wind, دَوَّارَة .

Vanguard, *n.* As of an army; *see* Van, *n.*

Vanilla, *n.* الوَنِيلَة وَهِيَ ضَرْبٌ مِنَ ٱلْخَرْنُوب ٱلْمُعَطَّر .

Vanish, *v.i.* To disappear out of sight, إِخْتَفَى ـ غَابَ عَنِ ٱلنَّظَر . To pass away, إِضْمَحَلَّ ـ زَالَ *aor.* يَزُولُ . To fail, be exhausted, نَكِدَ . He vanished out of their sight, إِخْتَفَى عَنْهُمْ .

Vanishing, *a.* Passing away, مُضْمَحِلّ ـ زَائِل .

Vanishing line, in perspective, خَطّ حَدّ ـ خَطّ ٱلْأُفُق فِي ٱلتَّصْوِير ٱلْإِضْمِحْلَال .

Vanishing point, نُقْطَة حَدّ ٱلْإِضْمِحْلَال .

Vanity, *n.* Emptiness, worthlessness, nothingness, بُطْل ـ بُطُول ـ عَبَث . Deceitfulness, غِشّ . A thing of nought, a breath, بَاطِل *pl.* أَبَاطِيل . Self-conceit, صَلَف ـ عُجْب ـ غُرُور ـ زَهْو ـ تَكَبُّر . The vanities of the world, حُطَامُ ٱلدُّنْيَا ـ أَبَاطِيل ـ ٱلْعَالَم ـ غُرُورُ ٱلدُّنْيَا . My days are —, أَيَّامِي نَفْخَة . Vanity of vanities, all is vanity, بَاطِلُ ٱلْأَبَاطِيل ٱلْكُلّ بَاطِل (*or* بَاطِلَة) .

Vanquish, *v.t.* To overcome, قَهَرَ ـ إِنْتَصَرَ عَلَى ـ غَلَبَ ـ غَلَبَ عَلَى . To bring into subjection, قَمَعَ ـ أَقْمَعَ ـ أَخْضَعَ .

Vanquishable, *a.* يُقْهَر ـ يُغْلَب ـ يُخْضَع .

Vanquished, *a.* Overcome, مَقْهُور ـ مَغْلُوب ; subdued, مَقْمُوع .

Vanquisher, *n.* ظَفِير ـ مُظَفَّر ـ مَنْصُور ـ غَالِب .

Vantage, *n.* *See* Advantage, *n.*

Vantage-ground, *n.* إِسْتِعْلَاء ـ مَحَطّ ٱلْفَوْز ـ مَشْرَف .

Vapid, *a.* Insipid, of food, مَسِيخ ـ مَلِيخ ـ بِلا لَذَّة ـ لا طَعْمَ لَهُ . Of a person or discourse, سَقِيطَة ـ تَافِه ـ بَارِد ـ بِلا طَعْم ; of a person, مَا فُلَان بِخَلّ وَلَا خَمْر . To be —, insipid, مَلُخَ ; of a thing or discourse, تَفِهَ . A — man, تَافِهُ ٱلْعَقْل . To render —, مَسَخَ .

Vapidly, *ad.* سَقِيطَة ـ بِلا لَذَّة ـ بِتَفَاهَة .

Vapidity, *n.* } Insipidity, مَلْخ ـ قِلَّة لَذَّة ـ عَدَمُ طَعْم . Dull-
Vapidness, } ness, تَفَاهَة ـ سَقْط ـ سُقَاط ـ عَدَمُ طَعْمَة .

Vaporability, *n.* إِمْكَانُ ٱلتَّصْعِيد .

Vaporable, *a.* تَصْعِيدُهُ مُمْكِن .

Vaporate, *v.t.* To emit vapour, بَخَّرَ بُخَارًا . To evaporate, صَعَّدَ .

Vaporation, *n.* The act of passing off in vapour, بَخْر ـ بُخَار ; of converting into vapour, تَصْعِيد .

Vapor-bath, *n.* حَمَّامُ بُخَارٍ.

Vaporer, *n.* *See* Braggart, *n.*

Vaporingly, *ad.* بِٱلتَّفَاخُرِ – بِٱلْمُبَاهَاةِ – تَكَبُّرًا – تَهَوُّرًا.

Vaporish, *a.* *See* Vaporous, *a.*

Vaporization, *n.* تَصْعِيد.

Vaporize, *v.t.* To convert into vapour, صَعَّدَ.

Vaporize, *v.i.* To pass off in vapour, بَخَرَ.

Vaporous, *a.* } **Vapory**, } Full of vapours, مَلْآنُ بُخَارَاتٍ – مَمْلُوٌّ مِنْ ضَبَابٍ. Flatulent, نَفَّاخ – رِيحِيٌّ. Splenetic, مُتَهَوِّر – نَكِد – شَرِس – شَكِس.

Vapour, *n.* Steam, بُخَار. Mist, such as rises from the ground or fine clouds, one such —, ضَبَابَة *coll.* ضَبَاب. Vapours of smoke, دُخَانٍ (*or* بُخَارُ) ضَبَابُ. Vapours, melancholy, سَوْدَاء – سُوَاد – مَلَنْخُولِيَا. "And the mountains shall be set in motion, and melt in thin vapour," وَسُيِّرَتِ ٱلْجِبَالُ فَكَانَتْ سَرَابًا (Kur. lxxviii. 20).

Vapour, *v.i.* To pass off in fumes, بَخَرَ. To evaporate, تَصَعَّدَ. To boast, fume, تَهَيَّجَ – حَمِيَ أَنْفُهُ – تَهَوَّرَ – اِحْتَمَى غَضَبًا – اِغْتَاظَ – هَاجَ.

Variability, *n.* } **Variableness**, } Susceptibility of change, تَلَوُّن – قِلَّةُ قَرَارٍ – تَغَيُّر – قِلَّةُ ثَبَاتٍ – قِلَّةُ دَوَامٍ عَلَى حَالٍ. "And thou shalt not find any variableness in the way of God," وَلَنْ تَجِدَ لِسُنَّةِ ٱللّٰهِ تَحْوِيلًا (Kur. xxxv. 42). Inconstancy, فَرْفَرَة – طَيْش – طَيَشَان – تَقَلْقُل. *See also* Inconstancy, *n.*

Variable, *a.* Susceptible of change, مُغَيَّر – مُتَغَيِّر – عَدِيمُ ٱلْقَرَارِ – مُتَلَوِّن. Inconstant, fickle, يَمِيلُ بِكُلِّ رِيحٍ – فَرْفَار – طَائِش – مُتَقَلِّب. To be —, فَرْفَرَ – تَلَوَّنَ – طَاشَ. *See also* Inconstant, *a.*

Variably, *ad.* With change, بِتَغَيُّرٍ – بِتَلَوُّنٍ; with fickleness, فَرْفَرَةً – بِفَرْفَرَةٍ – بِطَيْشٍ – بِتَقَلُّبٍ.

Variance, *n.* Difference, فَرْق – تَفَاوُت – اِمْتِيَاز – اِخْتِلَاف – خِلَاف; as between two things, مُغَايَرَة. Dissension, مُنَازَعَة – مُخَالَفَة – مُخَاصَمَة. To be at — with, contrary to, خَالَفَ; to be in dissension, تَنَازَعَ – تَضَادَدَ. A party at — among themselves, قَوْمٌ شَتِيتٌ. Those at —, المُتَنَافِرُونَ. "And the parties [or sects] have fallen to variance among themselves," فَٱخْتَلَفَ ٱلْأَحْزَابُ مِنْ بَيْنِهِمْ (Kur. xix. 38).

Variant, *a.* مُتَفَاوِت – مُتَبَايِن – مُخْتَلِف.

Variation, *n.* Change, تَغْيِير – تَخَلُّف – تَبَدُّل. Variation of the compass, اِنْحِرَافُ إِبْرَةِ ٱلْبُوصَلَةِ. Variations of the moon, اِخْتِلَافُ حَرَكَاتِ ٱلْقَمَرِ – الزِّيَادَةُ فِي ضَوْءِ ٱلْقَمَرِ وَنُقْصَانُهُ. Variations in music, تَغْيِيرَاتٌ فِي عَزْفِ مَقَامَةٍ; in nouns, حَدٌّ.

Varicocele, *n.* دَوَالٍ فِي ٱلصَّفَنِ.

Varicose, *a.* بِهِ دَوَالٍ. Varicose veins, الدَّوَالِي.

Variegate, *v.t.* رَقَشَ – فَنَّ – رَقَّشَ – رَقَّمَ – نَقَّشَ – شَكَّلَ – بَرْقَشَ – لَوَّنَ – دَبَّجَ – خَرَّجَ.

Variegated, *a.* مُدَبَّج – مُشَكَّل – مُوَشًّى – مُخَلَّب – مَنْقُوش – مُبَرْقَش – مُلَوَّن – مُخَرَّج.

Variegation, *n.* The act of, تَنْقِيش – تَشْكِيل – تَلْوِين – بَرْقَشَة – تَخْرِيج; the being variegated, نَقْش – تَنَقُّش – تَشَكُّل – تَلَوُّن.

Variety, *n.* Difference, اِخْتِلَاف – فَرْق. Diversity, تَنَوُّع – أَنْوَاع – أَنْوَاعٌ مُخْتَلِفَةٌ. A — of tongues, أَنْوَاعُ ٱلْسِنَةٍ. A —, species, نَوْع *pl.* أَنْوَاع – شَكْل *pl.* أَشْكَال. A — of things, أُمُورٌ شَتَّى.

Variform, *a.* مُخْتَلِفُ ٱلْأَشْكَالِ.

Varioloid, *n.* ضَرْبٌ مِنَ ٱلْجُدَرِيِّ خَفِيفٌ.

Variolous, *a.* Pertaining to the small-pox, مَا نِيطَ بِٱلْجُدَرِيِّ. Pitted with small-pox, مَجْدُور.

Various, *a.* Different, مُتَغَايِر – مُبَايِن. Several, شَتَّى. Various things, أَشْيَاءُ شَتَّى. A body composed of — people, قَوْمٌ شَتَّى. Having — acquirements, مِفَنٌّ: He was possessed of — acquirements in the sciences, تَفَنَّنَ فِي ٱلْعُلُومِ. Of — branches, مُخْتَلِفُ ٱلْفُرُوعِ. "And there are among us good, and among us of another kind: we are of various sorts," وَأَنَّا مِنَّا ٱلصَّالِحُونَ وَمِنَّا دُونَ ذٰلِكَ كُنَّا طَرَائِقَ (Kur. lxxii. 11).

Variously, *ad.* بِوُجُوهٍ شَتَّى – بِٱخْتِلَافٍ.

Varlet, *n.* A servant, خَادِم *pl.* خَدَم. A rascal, خَبِيث – دَنِيء – رَذِيل – خَلِيع.

Varnish, *n.* دِمَام – دِهَان. A meretricious gloss, وَشْيٌ – شِيَة – تَصْحِيف. Palliation, تَخْفِيف – تَسْتِير.

Varnish, *v.t.* As with varnish, طَلَى *aor.* يَطْلِي – دَهَنَ – دَمَّمَ – دَهَّنَ. To give a specious signification to, وَشَى *aor.* يَشِي – تَصَحَّفَ عَلَى. To palliate, كَفَّرَ – سَتَرَ.

Varnisher, *n.* One who varnishes, دَهَّان. One who disguises, وَاشٍ – مُصَحِّف; who palliated, سَاتِر.

Varnishing, *n.* The act of, تَدْمِيم – طَلْيٌ – دَهْن – دَهْنَة.

Vary, *v.t.* To alter, change, بَدَّلَ – غَيَّرَ. To make various, صَرَّفَ – صَيَّرَ فِي أَشْكَالٍ – جَعَلَ مُتَنَوِّعًا; of language, فَنَّنَ.

Vary, *v.i.* To be altered in form, *etc.*, تَحَوَّلَ – تَغَيَّرَ – تَبَدَّلَ. To be different, تَبَايَنَ – اِخْتَلَفَ – تَحَوَّلَ.

Vascular, *a.* Full of veins, مَمْلُوٌّ مِنْ عُرُوقٍ. Pertaining to vessels, مَا نِيطَ بِٱلْأَوْعِيَةِ.

Vascularity, *n.* Fullness of veins, طُمُورُ (*or*) طَمْرُ ٱلْعُرُوقِ .

Vase, *n.* مَاعُون *pl.* مَوَاعِين — وِعَآء *pl.* أَوْعِيَة — أَنَآء *pl.* أَوَانِي — ظَرْف *pl.* ظُرُوف .

Vassal, *n.* تَابِع *pl.* أَتْبَاع .

Vassal, *a.* تَابِع . (A — prince, in Turkey, is styled, رَئِيس مَمْلَكَةٍ مُمْتَازَةٍ, and a vassal kingdom or country, إِيَالَةٌ مُمْتَازَةٌ *or* مَمْلَكَةٌ مُمْتَازَةٌ.)

Vassalage, *n.* حَالُ ٱلتَّابِعِ .

Vast, *a.* Wide in extent, مُتَّسِع — وَاسِع — فَسِيح — مَدِيد . Great, جَسِيم — عَظِيم . Important, مُهِمٌّ — مُهِمٌّ لِلْغَايَةِ .

Vast, *n.* An empty waste, صَحْرَآء — خَلَآء .

Vastly, *ad.* كُلِّيًّا — لِلْغَايَةِ — جِدًّا .

Vastness, *n.* Immense extent, إِمْتِدَادٌ كُلِّيٌّ — سَعَةٌ كُلِّيَّةٌ — فُسْحَة . Immensity, greatness, كِبَرٌ كُلِّيٌّ — جَسَامَة — عَظَمَة .

Vasty, *a.* *See* Vast, *a.*

Vat, *n.* دَنّ *pl.* دِنَان — خَابِيَة *pl.* خَوَابِي — حَوْض *pl.* أَحْوَاض *and* حِيَاض . A — in which anything is pressed, مِعْصَر . A dyer's —, دَنُّ ٱلصَّبَّاغِين .

Vatican, *n.* دِيوَانُ ٱلْبَابَا — قَصْرُ ٱلْبَابَا فِي رُومِيَّة .

Vaticide, *n.* قَاتِلُ نَبِيٍّ .

Vaticinal, *a.* مُخْبِرٌ بِٱلْغَيْبِ — نَبَوِيّ .

Vaticinate, *v.i.* أَخْبَرَ بِٱلْغَيْبِ — تَنَبَّأَ .

Vaticination, *n.* إِخْبَارٌ بِٱلْمُسْتَقْبِلِ — خَبَرٌ بِٱلْغَيْب — نِبَاوَة .

Vaudevil, *n.* A light song, غُنَيَّة . A piece for a theatre, رِوَايَةٌ هَزْلِيَّةٌ لِلتِّيَاتْرُو .

Vault, *n.* An arch, dome, عَقْد *pl.* عُقُود — قُبَّة *pl.* قِبَاب . A subterranean —, cellar, سِرْدَاب *pl.* سَرَادِيب . The — of heaven, سَقْفُ ٱلسَّمَآءِ . A burial —, لَحْد *pl.* لُحُود *and* أَلْحَاد . A spring, leap, نَطَّة — وَثْبَة — نَوْرَة .

Vault, *v.t.* To arch, عَقَدَ ـِ — عَقَّدَ — جَسَّرَ [2] . To cover with a dome, قَبَّبَ .

Vault, *v.i.* To leap, نَطَّ ـُ — قَزَّ ـِ — قَحَزَ ـَ — تَقَفَّزَ [2] .

Vaulted, *a.* Arched, مَعْقُود — مُجَسَّر ; domed, مُقَبَّب .

Vaulter, *n.* نَطَّاط — قَفَّاز .

Vaunt, *v.i.* To boast, فَشَّ [2] — فَاشَ ـُ — طَرْمَذَ — تَبَجَّحَ — فَخْفَخَ — إِفْتَخَرَ . *See also to* Boast, *v.i.*

Vaunt, *v.t.* To boast of, إِفْتَخَرَ بِ — تَفَخَّرَ بِ — إِشْتَرَّ بِ .

Vaunt, *n.* فَشَّار — تَفَاخُر — مُبَاهَاة — طَرْمَذَة .

Vaunter, *n.* } فَشْفَاس — فَيَّاش — طَرْمَاذ — مُتَفَخِّر — مُتَلَهْوِق
Vaunting, } *vulg.* خَرَّاط — فَشَّار .

Vauntingly, *ad.* تَفَخُّرًا — بِٱلتَّفَاخُرِ — بِطَرْمَذَةٍ — بِمُبَاهَاةٍ — فَيْشًا .

Veal, *n.* لَحْمُ ٱلْعِجْلِ .

Veda, *pl.* **Vedas**, *n.* ٱلْكُتُبُ ٱلْمُقَدَّسَةُ عِنْدَ ٱلْهُنُودِ .

Vedette, *n.* حَارِسٌ خَيَّالٌ *pl.* حُرَّاسٌ خَيَّالَةٌ .

Veer, *v.t.* أَدَارَ — دَوَّرَ .

Veer, *v.i.* دَارَ *aor.* يَدُورُ — إِسْتَدَارَ .

Veering, *n.* دَوَرَان — مَدَار .

Vegetable, *n.* A plant, نَبْت *coll.* نَبَات . A legume, بَقْل *pl.* بُقُول — قِطْنِيَّة *pl.* قَطَانِيّ . A green —, خُضْرَة *pl.* خُضَر *and* خُضْرَوَات *and* خُضَار *and* خُضَر . Vegetables, such as are eaten raw, أَحْرَارُ ٱلْبُقُولِ — قَفّ .

Vegetable, *a.* نَبَاتِيّ . The — kingdom, ٱلنَّبَاتُ — ٱلنَّبَاتَاتُ — ٱلْمَنْبُوتُ .

Vegetable-marrow, *n.* One —, كُوسَاة *coll.* كُوسَا .

Vegetate, *v.i.* To grow, as a plant, نَبَتَ [2] . To live like a plant, عَاشَ عِيشَةَ ٱلنَّبَاتِ *aor.* يَعِيشُ ; like cattle, عَاشَ مِثْلَ ٱلْبَهَائِمِ .

Vegetation, *n.* Growth, as of plants, نَبْت — نَبَات . Plants in general, نَبَات — نَبَاتَات . Verdure, خَضِر — خُضَارِي . A land with much —, verdure, أَرْضٌ خَضِرَة — أَرْضٌ مَخْضَرَة — يَخْضُور .

Vegetative, *a.* Growing, نَابِت . Having the power to produce growth, مُنْبِت — نَبَات .

Vehemence, *n.* } Power, force, قُوَّة — حَوْل — حَيْل — شِدَّة . Im-
Vehemency, } petuosity, حَمَاسَة — حُمَيَّا — دَفْعَة — شِدَّة — حِدَّة — شَوْكَة — حُمَّة . Irascibility, sharpness, حِدَّة . Ardour, تَهَوُّر . Vehemence, as of a fever, سَوْرَة ; of the wind, عَصْف — عُصُوف ; of an assault, بَطْش . Prowess, بَأْس . Harshness, عُنْف .

Vehement, *a.* Strong, شَدِيد — قَوِيّ ; of a wind, قَاصِف . Impetuous, حَمِس — حَبِيس — مُتَهَوِّر . Sharp, (*or* ذُو حِدَّةٍ) حَدِيد *pl.* حِدَاد ; of anger, مُحْتَدّ — سَخِت — سَخِيت . Vehement language, كَلَام جَهُور — كَلَام جَهِير . Vehement desire, رَغْبَة — غَيْرَة . The battle became —, قَامَتِ ٱلْحَرْبُ عَلَى سَاقٍ . To become —, hot, ardent, حَمِيَ ـَ . To be —, harsh, with عَنُفَ عَلَى [2] — أَعْنَفَ — عَنَّفَ عَلَى *or* بِ .

Vehemently, *ad.* Powerfully, بِقُوَّةٍ — بِشِدَّةٍ . Emphatically, بِشِدَّةِ ٱلتَّعْبِيرِ — بِحَمَاسَةٍ . Violently, قَهْرًا — عُنْفًا . With prowess, بِبَطْشٍ . With impetuosity, تَهَوُّرًا — بِتَهَوُّرٍ . With force, as of a stream, دَرْأً : The stream rushed forth —, جَآءَ ٱلسَّيْلُ دَرْأً *aor.* يَجِيءُ .

Vehicle, *n.* That in which anything may be carried away,

مَحْمِل pl. مَحَامِلُ — مِثْقَلَة . A carriage, عَرَبَة — مَرْكَبَة pl. عَرَبَات — عَرَبِيَّة pl. عَرَبِيَّات . That with which anything, such as medicine, *etc.*, may be taken, مِحْمَل — بِوَاغ . A means, opening, بَاب pl. أَبْوَاب . A seller of vehicles, مَحَامِلِيّ .

Vehicular, *a.* Pertaining to transport, مُنَقِّل ; to making anything go down, or be swallowed, pleasantly, مُسَوِّغ .

Veil, *n.* As for the face, نِقَاب — بُرْقُع or بُرْقُوع or بُرْقُعَة pl. بَرَاقِيع . A covering, such as hides, conceals, سِدَافَة — حِجَاب — سِتَارَة pl. سَتَائِر — سُتْرَة — سِجَاف pl. سُجُف . A film, غِشَاء — غِشْوَة — غُشَاوَة . A blind, cloak, pretext, سِتْر pl. سُتُور — حُجَّة — صُورَة — حِيلَة . A woman's — for covering the whole face but the eyes and part of the nose, a muffler, خِمَار ; to cover the face with such a —, خَمَّرَ — أَخْمَرَ ; to put on such a —, اِخْتَمَرَ . A fine thin — for the face only, شَعْرِيَّة . A woman's — for covering the whole body, إِزَار . A man's —, such as is used by the Bedawîn for covering the lower part of the face, لِثَام . To take the —, to become a nun, تَرَهَّبَت . "Verily we put veils over their hearts that they should not understand it," the Kurân, إِنَّا جَعَلْنَا عَلَى قُلُوبِهِمْ أَكِنَّةً أَنْ يَفْقَهُوهُ (Kur. xviii. 55). "And veils let them [the women] draw over their bosoms," وَلْيَضْرِبْنَ بِخُمُرِهِنَّ عَلَى جُيُوبِهِنَّ (*Id.* xxiv. 31). "By the night when she spreads her veil," وَٱللَّيْلِ إِذَا يَغْشَى (*Id.* xcii. 1). "And we have shrouded them in a veil so that they shall not see," فَأَغْشَيْنَاهُمْ فَهُمْ لَا يُبْصِرُونَ (*Id.* xxxvi. 8).

Veil, *v.t.* To cover the face with a veil, بَرْقَعَ ; to attire one's self with a —, تَنَقَّبَ — تَبَرْقَعَ ; of a woman, تَنَقَّبَت — تَبَرْقَعَت . To cover, غَطَّا [2] ; to be covered, تَغَطَّى . To conceal, سَتَرَ [2] — حَجَبَ [2] ; to be concealed, اِسْتَتَرَ — اِحْتَجَبَ . To disguise, نَكَّرَ ; to be disguised, to disguise one's self, تَنَكَّرَ . To —, cloak, سَتَرَ [2] — تَحَجَّجَ . To use a —, cloak, pretext, تَعَلَّلَ — تَحَيَّلَ .

Veiled, *a.* As with a veil, of a woman, مُبَرْقَعَة — مُخَمَّرَة . Concealed, covered, مَحْجُوب — مَسْتُور . Disguised, مُغَشَّى . Veiled, of a man, مُلَثَّم .

Vein, *n.* As of the body, or in wood, عِرْق pl. عُرُوق . A fissure containing metal, in a mine, سَام coll. سَامَة — سُيُوب pl. سَيْب . The veins or ducts in vegetables, leaves, *etc.*, شِرَاك . A jugular —, of a horse, وِدَاج dual وِدَاجَانِ . A — under the tongue, خَاف dual خَافَانِ . The cephalic —, عِرْقُ ٱلْقِيفَالِ — عِرْقُ ٱلرَّأْسِ . The pulsating veins, الشَّرَايِينُ — الْعُرُوقُ ٱلضَّوَارِبُ ; the non-pulsating veins, الْعُرُوقُ ٱلسَّاكِنَة . Humour, temper, خَاطِر — نَفْس — كَيْفِيَّة . Genius, talent, قَرِيحَة — حَمَاسَة . He is not in the — for..., لَيْسَ لَهُ خَاطِرٌ بِكَذَا — لَا لِيَاقَة لَهُ إِلَى كَذَا . *See also under* Human, *n.*

Veined, *a.* Having veins, ذُو عُرُوق ; of mines, ذُو سُيُوب ; of plants, ذُو شِرَاك . *See also* Variegated, *a.*

Veining, *n.* Variegated work, نَقْش — تَنْقِيش — تَشْكُل — شُغْل دَبْج — تَشْكِيل .

Veinless, *a.* بِلَا عُرُوق ; of plants, بِلَا شِرَاك .

Veiny, *a.* *See* Veined, *a.*

Vellicate, *v.i.* *See to* Twitch, *v.i.*

Vellum, *n.* رَقّ pl. رُقُوق — رِقّ — جِلْدُ ٱلرَّقِّ .

Vellum-post, *n.* وَرَق صَقِيل .

Velocipede, *n.* عَرَبَة ذَاتُ عَجَلَتَيْنِ يَسُوقُهَا ٱلرَّاكِبُ بِرِجْلَيْهِ .

Velocity, *n.* سُرْعَة . *See also* Swiftness, *n.*

Velvet, *n.* قَطِيفَة pl. قَطَائِف — مُخْمَل . The nap of —, خَمْل — خَمِيلَة .

Velvet, *a.* مِنْ قَطِيفَةٍ .

Velveteen, *n.* قَطِيفَةٌ مِنْ قُطْنٍ .

Velvety, *a.* مِثْلَ ٱلْقَطِيفَةِ . Soft and smooth, أَمْلَس fem. مَلْسَاء pl. مُلْس .

Venal, *a.* Greedy of gain, طَامِعٌ فِي ٱلرِّبْحِ — طَامِعٌ بِٱلرِّبْحِ — طَمَّاع . Receiving or asking bribes, مُرْتَشٍ — مُسْتَرْشٍ . Low, base, دَنِيّ . A — mind, نَفْس دَنِيَّة .

Venal, *a.* Pertaining to the veins, مَا نِيطَ بِٱلْعُرُوقِ .

Venality, *n.* Greediness of gain, طَمَعٌ بِٱلرِّبْحِ . The being bribable, اِرْتِشَاء — اِسْتِرْشَاء .

Venary, *a.* مُتَعَلِّق بِٱلصَّيْدِ .

Vend, *v.t.* *See to* Sell, *v.t.*

Vender, *n.* *See* Seller, *n.*

Vendible, *a.* *See* Saleable, *a.*

Vendibility, *n.* *See* Saleableness, *n.*

Vendue, *n.* *See* Auction, *n.*

Vendue-master, *n.* *See* Auctioneer, *n.*

Veneer, *v.t.* To — with, لَبَّسَ بـ — صَفَّحَ بـ — غَشَّى بـ .

Veneer, *n.* تَلْبِيس — تَصْفِيح .

Veneering, *n.* The act of, تَلْبِيس — تَصْفِيح — تَغْشِيَة ; the covering laid on, غِشَاء — صَفِيحَة .

Venemous, *a.* *See* Venomous, *a.*

Venerable, *a.* Respected, مُكَرَّم — مُوَقَّر — مَرْجُوب — مُرَجَّب — مُحْتَرَم . A — man, صَاحِبُ ٱحْتِرَام . Of a — aspect, صَاحِبُ هَيْبَةٍ وَوَقَارٍ .

Venerably, *ad.* بِتَوْقِيرٍ ـ بِٱحْتِرَامٍ .

Venerate, *v.t.* To respect, وَقَّرَ ـ رَجَبَ ² ـ كَرَّمَ ـ أَكْرَمَ. To — or reverence, as applied to God, تَهَيَّبَ ـ اِهْتَابَ ـ هَابَ ² .

Venerated, *a.* Revered, with awe, مُعْتَزٌّ. Revered, حَشِيمٌ ـ مُحْتَشَمٌ .

Veneration, *n.* Respect, تَعْظِيمٌ ـ إِحْتِرَامٌ ـ إِكْرَامٌ. Reverence, هَيْبَةٌ ـ خَشْيَةٌ ـ خَشَاةٌ. *See also* Reverence, *n.*

Venerator, *n.* خَاشٍ ـ خَشْيَانُ .

Venereal, *a.* Of sexual intercourse, جِمَاعِيٌّ ـ مُتَعَلِّقٌ بِٱلْمُجَامَعَةِ. The — disease, حَبٌّ (or مَرَضٌ) فِرَنْجِيٌّ ـ بَلَاءٌ ـ دَآءُ ٱلْمُبَارَكِ. (These are all colloquial terms.)

Venerous, *a.* شَهْوَانِيٌّ ـ شَبِقٌ ـ مِغْلِيمٌ ـ غَلِمٌ .

Venery, *n.* Sexual intercourse, مُجَامَعَةٌ ـ جِمَاعٌ. Sport of the chase, ٱلصَّيْدُ وَٱلْقَنْصُ .

Venesection, *n.* ٱلْفَصْدُ ـ ٱلْفِصَادُ .

Venetian, *a.* مِنْ مَدِينَةِ ٱلْبُنْدُقِيَّةِ .

Venetian, *n.* مِنْ أَهْلِ مَدِينَةِ ٱلْبُنْدُقِيَّةِ .

Venetian-blind, *n.* سِتَارَةٌ *pl.* سَتَائِرُ ٱلرَّوْزَنِ ـ شَمْسِيَّةٌ ; *also from the Turkish,* قَبَاجُور .

Vengeance, *n.* Revenge, ثُؤْرَةٌ ـ ثَارٌ ـ ثَأْرٌ ـ نَقِمَةٌ ـ اِنْتِقَامٌ. Punishment, عِقَابٌ. To take — on, أَخَذَ ٱلثَّارَ مِنْ ² ـ اِنْتَقَمَ مِنْ. He wreaked his — upon, أَخَذَ ثَارَهُ مِنْ. They proclaimed —, نَادَوْا بِٱلثَّارِ. "And when they had angered us we took vengeance on them," فَلَمَّا آسَفُونَا ٱنْتَقَمْنَا مِنْهُمْ (Kur. xliii. 55). "We will surely take vengeance on the guilty one," إِنَّا مِنَ ٱلْمُجْرِمِينَ مُنْتَقِمُونَ (*Id.* xxxii. 22).

Vengeful, *a.* Threatening to take vengeance, مُتَوَعِّدٌ بِأَخْذِ ٱلثَّارِ. *See also* Revengeful, *a.*

Venial, *a.* Light, small, صَغِيرٌ ـ زَهِيدٌ ـ جُزْئِيٌّ ـ خَفِيفٌ. Pardonable, حَلُّ ٱلْمُسَامَحَةِ ـ يُغْفَرُ. A — sin, صَغِيرَةٌ *pl.* صَغَائِرُ. *See also* Excusable, *a.*

Venially, *ad.* تَعَذُّرًا .

Venialness, *n.* Littleness, صُغْرٌ. The state of being excusable, تَعَذُّرٌ .

Venice, *n.* مَدِينَةُ ٱلْبُنْدُقِيَّةِ .

Venison, *n.* لَحْمَةُ ٱلصَّيْدِ ـ صَيْدٌ .

Venom, *n.* Poison, سِمٌّ ـ قَشْبٌ ـ حُمَةٌ ـ حُمَّةٌ. Malignity, عَدَاوَةٌ ـ حَنَقٌ ـ رَدَآءَةٌ ـ حِقْدٌ ـ ضِغْنٌ .

Venomous, *a.* Poisonous, سَامٌّ. Of any animal, سَامَّةٌ. Malignant, مُسَمَّمٌ ـ شِرِّيرٌ ـ حَقُودٌ ـ حَسِكٌ ـ حَنِقٌ ـ ضَغِنٌ .

Venous, *a.* Pertaining to the veins, مُتَعَلِّقٌ بِٱلْعُرُوقِ. Venous blood, دَمُ ٱلشَّرَايِينِ .

Vent, *n.* A passage for a flow, *etc.*, مَخْرَجٌ ـ مَنَافِذُ *pl.* مَنْفِذٌ ـ مَخْلَصٌ ـ مَثْعَبٌ *pl.* مَثَاعِبُ. The —, as of a gun, بُزْمَةٌ ـ فَالِيَةٌ *pl.* فَوَالِي. A — for smoke, دَاخِنَةٌ *vulg.* مِدْخَنَةٌ ; for air, مُتَنَفَّسٌ. Disclosure, publication, إِظْهَارٌ ـ إِشَاعَةٌ. Utterance, نُطْقٌ ـ كَلَامٌ. To give — to, to let out, أَخْرَجَ ; to pour out, أَصَبَّ ; to disclose, express, بَيَّنَ ـ أَظْهَرَ ـ أَبْدَى عَنْ ـ أَبْدَى ـ أَوْضَحَ. To find a — for itself, to flow out, اِنْبَجَسَ ـ تَبَجَّسَ ـ اِنْفَجَرَ ـ تَفَجَّرَ ـ اِنْثَعَبَ .

Vent, *v.t.* To find a vent for, to let out, of a liquid, بَجَّسَ ـ فَتَحَ ـ فَجَّرَ ـ ثَعَبَ ـ بَجَسَ ². To let out, of anger, *etc.*, تَكَلَّمَ بِ ـ نَطَقَ بِ ² ـ تَفَوَّهَ بِ ـ أَصَبَّ ـ نَفَثَ ². To utter, He vented his anger, نَفَثَ بِغَضَبِهِ ². He vented what was in his mind, أَخْرَجَ مَا فِي صَدْرِهِ ـ أَصَبَّ مَا فِي صَدْرِهِ .

Ventiduct, *n.* مُتَنَفَّسٌ .

Ventilate, *v.t.* To fan, رَوَّحَ عَلَى ـ رَوَّحَ. To expose to the air, هَوَّى ـ أَطْلَقَ ٱلْهَوَآءَ فِي ـ نَشَرَ ² ـ عَرَضَ لِلْهَوَآءِ. To give air to, To open out, of a subject, أَوْضَحَ. To discuss, فَحَصَ عَنْ ـ تَكَلَّمَ فِي ـ أَبْرَمَ ـ بَحَثَ عَنْ .

Ventilation, *n.* The act of exposing to the air, نَشْرٌ ; of giving air to, إِطْلَاقُ ٱلْهَوَآءِ فِي ; of discussing, مُبَاحَثَةٌ ـ بَحْثٌ ـ فَحْصٌ ـ تَفَاوُضٌ ; of opening out, explaining, إِيضَاحٌ .

Ventilator, *n.* For changing the air in a place, آلَةٌ لِتَغْيِيرِ ٱلْهَوَآءِ وَتَجْدِيدِهِ فِي مَكَانٍ ; for curing smoky chimneys, آلَةٌ لِمُعَالَجَةِ ٱلدَّوَاخِنِ .

Vent-peg, *n.* سِدَادٌ .

Ventral, *a.* بَطْنِيٌّ .

Ventricle, *n.* تَجْوِيفٌ *pl.* تَجَاوِيفُ ـ جَوْفٌ *pl.* أَجْوَافٌ. A — of the heart, جَوْفُ ٱلْقَلْبِ. The — of beasts, ٱلْكَرِشُ .

Ventricular, *a.* جَوْفِيٌّ .

Ventriloquism, *n.* عَفْطٌ ـ ٱلتَّكَلُّمُ مِنَ ٱلْبَطْنِ ـ ٱلنُّطْقُ مِنَ ٱلْجَوْفِ .

Ventriloquist, *n.* عَافِطٌ ـ مُتَكَلِّمٌ مِنْ بَطْنِهِ ـ نَاطِقٌ مِنْ جَوْفِهِ .

Venture, *v.i.* To be bold, so as to venture upon anything, جَسَرَ ² ـ اِسْتَجْرَأَ ـ جَرُؤَ ². To expose one's self to danger, غَرَّرَ بِنَفْسِهِ ـ خَاطَرَ بِنَفْسِهِ. *See also to* Dare, Hazard, *v.i.*

Venture, *v.t.* To venture upon, dare to do, قَحَمَ فِي ² ـ اِقْتَحَمَ ـ جَسَرَ ² ـ تَجَاسَرَ عَلَى ـ تَجَرَّأَ عَلَى ـ خَاطَرَ ـ غَامَرَ ـ اِجْتَرَأَ عَلَى ـ عَلَى. He does not — to do such a thing, لَا يَجْسُرُ أَنْ يَفْعَلَ كَذَا .

You should not have ventured too far into danger, مَا كَانَ يَنْبَغِي لَكَ أَنْ تَشِطَّ فِي ٱلْمُخَاطَرَةِ. We — to say that..., نَتَجَاسَرُ أَنْ نَقُولَ أَنْ. Should the Government — upon this matter it will be a blunder on its part, إِنِ ٱقْتَحَمَتِ ٱلدَّوْلَةُ هٰذَا ٱلْأَمْرَ كَانَ خَطَأً مِنْهَا. To undertake, إِتَّخَذَ ـ تَعَطَّى ـ تَعَاطَى.

Venture, *n.* Danger, risk, خَطَر ـ تَهْلُكَة. Chance, بَخْت. A stake, خَطَر ـ سَبَق. A mercantile —, قِمَار. At a —, undesignedly, لَا عَنْ قَصْدٍ ـ بِلَا قَصْدٍ. Tentatively, بَيْنَ مَحْظُورٍ وَمَحْذُورٍ.

Venturesome, *a.* } Daring, fearless, مِقْحَام *pl.* مَقَاحِيمُ ـ مُجْتَرِئ ـ سِنْدَرِيّ ـ مُتَجَاسِر ـ جَسُور ـ جَرِيء.
Venturous, }
Hazardous, مُخْطِر ـ ذُو خَطَرٍ.

Venturously, *ad.* إِقْتِحَامًا ـ بِجَسَارَةٍ ـ بِشَجَاعَةٍ ـ بِجَرَاءَةٍ.

Venturousness, *n.* شَجَاعَة ـ جَسَارَة ـ جَرَاءَة ـ إِقْتِحَام.

Venue, *n.* Neighbourhood, جِوَار ـ مُجَاوَرَة. The place where an action in law is laid, مَحَلّ إِقَامَةِ دَعْوَى.

Venus, *n.* The goddess of love and beauty, مَعْبُودَةُ ٱلْجَمَالِ وَٱلْعِشْقِ. The planet, الزُّهَرَة. Venus's hair, the plant, بَرْسِيَاوِشَان.

Veracious, *a.* Speaking the truth, صَدُوق ـ صَادِق ـ صِدِّيق ـ عَادِل. True in fact, حَقِيقِيّ ـ صَحِيح. *See also* True, *a.*

Veraciously, *ad.* بِصِدْقٍ وَصِحَّةٍ ـ بِٱسْتِقَامَةٍ ـ بِصَدَاقَةٍ.

Veracity, *n.* Observance of truth, إِسْتِقَامَة ـ صَدَاقَة. Conformity to fact, صِحَّة ـ حَقِيقَة ـ صِدْق.

Verandah, *n.* شَبَهُ رِوَاقٍ بَارِزٍ عَنْ مُسَاوَاةِ بَقِيَّةِ ٱلْبَيْتِ ـ *from the Persian,* كِشْك.

Verb, *n.* فِعْل *pl.* أَفْعَال.
Active verb, فِعْلٌ مَعْلُومٌ.
Defective verb, فِعْلٌ نَاقِصٌ.
Hollow verb, فِعْلٌ أَجْوَفُ.
Intransitive verb, فِعْلٌ لَازِمٌ.
Passive verb, فِعْلٌ مَجْهُولٌ.
Transitive verb, فِعْلٌ مُتَعَدٍّ ـ فِعْلٌ وَاقِعٌ.

Verbal, *a.* Pertaining to verbs, فِعْلِيّ. Oral, شَفَاهِيّ. Literal, لَفْظِيّ. A — noun, مَصْدَر ـ إِسْمُ مَصْدَرٍ ـ إِسْمُ فِعْلٍ.

Verbally, *ad.* By word of mouth, شِفَاهًا. Textually, literally, بِعِبَارَتِهِ ـ لَفْظًا ـ بِحُرُوفِهِ.

Verbatim, *n.* لَفْظًا بِلَفْظٍ. Verbatim et literatim, لَفْظًا بِلَفْظٍ ـ حَرْفًا ـ وَحَرْفًا بِحَرْفٍ.

Verbena, *n.* بَرْبِينَا ـ رَاعِي ٱلْحَمَامِ ـ بَارِسْطَارِيُون ـ إِكْمُوبَرَان.

Verberation, *n.* The act of beating, ضَرْب ـ تَرْتَرَة ـ مَزْمَرَة. Verberation of the air, مُصَادَمَةُ ٱلْهَوَاءِ.

Verbiage, *n.* لَغْو ـ مَحَاشٍ لَفْظِيَّة ـ مَحَاشٍ ـ كَثْرَةُ كَلَامٍ ـ مُبَالَغَةٌ فِي ٱلْكَلَامِ.

Verbose, *a.* نَفِس ـ مُبَالِغٌ فِي ٱلْكَلَامِ ـ كَثِيرُ ٱلْكَلَامِ. He wrote a — book, كَتَبَ كِتَابًا نَفِسًا. To be —, سَابَ فِي ٱلْكَلِمِ.

Verboseness, *n.* } مُبَالَغَةٌ فِي ٱلْكَلَامِ ـ نَفَس ـ الشُّيُوبُ فِي ٱلْكَلِمِ ـ كَلَامٌ لُتَاتٍ ـ كَثْرَةُ كَلَامٍ.
Verbosity, }

Verdancy, *n.* Freshness, greenness, خُضْرَة ـ خُضَّارَى. Simplicity, stupidity, جَهَالَة ـ زَوْبَنَة.

Verdant, *n.* Green, fresh, أَخْضَرُ ـ نَضِر ـ خَضِر. Verdant land, أَرْضٌ مُخْضَرَّةٌ. Foolishly simple, زَبُون ـ عَجَمِيّ ـ جَاهِل. *See also* Green, *a.*

Verd-antique, *n.* The marble, ضَرْبٌ مِنَ ٱلْمَرْمَرِ أَخْضَرُ ٱللَّوْنِ.

Verderer, *n.* حَارِسُ أَجَمَةِ ٱلسُّلْطَانِ.

Verdict, *n.* As of a jury, حُكْمُ (*or*) قَرَارُ ٱلْجُورِي ـ رَأْيُ ٱلْجُورِي. An opinion, judgment, رَأْي. Decision, as of a judge, فَتْوَى. *See under* Jury, *n.*

Verdigris, *n.* صَدَأُ ٱلنُّحَاسِ ـ زِنْجَار ـ *vulg.* جِنْزَار.

Verditer, *n.* Blue pigment, دِهَانٌ لَازَوَرْدِيُّ ٱللَّوْنِ.

Verdure, *n.* خُضَّارَى ـ خُضْرَة.

Verdurous, *a.* *See* Verdant, *a.*

Verge, *n.* A brink, edge, شَفًا ـ حَدّ ـ حَرْف ـ طَرَف. A rod, wand, قَضِيب *pl.* قُضْبَان. To be on the — of, شَفَّرَ عَلَى ـ أَشْرَفَ عَلَى. It was on the — of ruin, كَانَ هَادِفًا لِلْهَلَاكِ. He was on the — of the affair, شَفَّرَ عَلَى ٱلْأَمْرِ.

Verge, *v.i.* To slope, إِنْحَدَرَ; to slope downwards, إِنْصَبَّ. To incline towards, مَالَ إِلَى ـ ضَرَبَ إِلَى ـ إِنْحَرَفَ إِلَى ـ إِنْعَطَفَ إِلَى. To approach, دَنَا مِن *aor.* يَدْنُو ـ تَقَرَّبَ إِلَى. It verges to a green colour, يَضْرِبُ إِلَى ٱلسَّوَادِ.

Verger, *n.* مَاسِكُ ٱلْقَضِيبِ ـ حَامِلُ ٱلْقَضِيبِ.

Verifiable, *a.* مِمَّا يُحَقَّقُ ـ تَحْقِيقُهُ مُمْكِنٌ.

Verification, *n.* The act of verifying, تَحْقِيق ـ إِثْبَات ـ تَصْحِيح ـ تَصْدِيق. Examination, كَشْف ـ بَحْث.

Verifier, *n.* As of accounts, *etc.*, كَشَّاف.

Verify, *v.t.* To prove to be true, رَصَّنَ ـ حَقَّقَ ـ صَحَّحَ ـ أَثْبَتَ ـ بَرْهَنَ. To fulfil, as a promise, وَفَى بِ *aor.* يَفِي ـ أَوْفَى بِ. To examine, as accounts, كَشَّفَ. Verify this information for or to me, رَصِّنْ لِي هٰذَا ٱلْخَبَرَ. "And God will verify the truth by his words," وَيُحِقُّ ٱللّٰهُ ٱلْحَقَّ بِكَلِمَاتِهِ (Kur. x. 82).

Verily, *ad.* Truly, really, بِٱلصِّدْقِ ـ تَحْقِيقًا ـ حَقًّا ـ بِٱلتَّحْقِيقِ ـ فِي ٱلْوَاقِعِ ـ يَقِينًا. Verily, if I had known, أَمَا لَوْ عَلِمْتُ.

Verily, what thou hast done is good, إِنَّ مَا فَعَلْتَ حَسَنٌ. Verily, there can be no doubt that..., لَا جَرَمَ أَنْ. *See also under* Truly, *ad.*

Verisimilar, *a.* مِنَ ٱلْمُحْتَمَلِ ـ قَرِيبُ ٱلْاِحْتِمَالِ. *See also* Probable, *a.*

Verisimilitude, *n.* إِحْتِمَال ـ مُشَابَهَة. *See also* Probability, *n.*

Veritable, *a.* حَقِيقِيٌّ ـ حَقِيق ـ صَحِيح ـ حَقّ.

Veritably, *ad.* فِي ٱلْحَقِيقَةِ ـ بِٱلْحَقِيقَةِ ـ بِٱلْحَقِّ.

Verity, *n.* Conformity to facts, حَقِيقَة ـ حَقّ. Reality, صِحَّة ـ صِدْق. A truth, حَقّ *pl.* حِقَاق *and* حُقُوق. Truths, verities, حَقَائِق.

Verjuice, *n.* عَصِيرُ ٱلْحِصْرِمِ ـ مَآءُ ٱلْحِصْرِمِ.

Vermicelli, *n.* شَعِيرِيَّة. A very fine kind of —, غَزْلُ ٱلْبَنَاتِ ـ كُنَافَة ـ إِطْرِيَة.

Vermiceous, *a.* مُتَعَلِّقٌ بِٱلدُّودِ ـ دُودِيٌّ.

Vermicular, *a.* Coiling, coiling itself, مُتَكَوِّر ـ مُتَطَوٍّ. Spiral, لَوْلَبِيٌّ.

Vermiculate, *v.t.* صَنَعَ عَلَى هَيْئَةِ حَرَكَاتِ ٱلدُّودِ.

Vermiculated, *a.* مَصْنُوعٌ عَلَى هَيْئَةِ حَرَكَاتِ ٱلدُّودِ.

Vermiculation, *n.* The moving like a worm, حَرَكَاتُ ٱلدُّودِ. The act of vermiculating, صُنْعُ ٱلشَّيْءِ فِي شَكْلِ حَرَكَاتِ ٱلدُّودِ.

Vermicule, *n.* دُوَيْدَة *pl.* دُوَيْدَات.

Vermiculous, *a.* Full of worms, مُدَوِّد ـ مَمْلُوٌّ مِنْ دُودٍ.

Vermiform, *a.* فِي هَيْئَةِ ٱلدُّودِ.

Vermifuge, *n.* عِلَاجٌ نَافِعٌ لِلدُّودِ ـ دَوَآءٌ قَاطِعُ ٱلدُّودِ.

Vermilion, *n.* The sulphate, زُنْجُفْر. A bright red colour, لَوْنٌ أَحْمَرُ نَاصِرٌ. Red or — clay, مَغْرَة; daubed with this — clay, مُمَغَّر.

Vermin, *n.* Reptiles, شَقْذَانٌ ـ هَوَامٌّ. Low people, سُفْلَة ـ رُذَلَآء.

Vermination, *n.* The breeding of vermin, تَوَلُّدُ ٱلْهَوَامِّ.

Vermiparous, *a.* مُوَلِّدُ ٱلدُّودِ.

Vermivorous, *a.* مُقْتَاتٌ بِٱلدُّودِ ـ آكِلُ ٱلدُّودِ.

Vernacular, *a.* Native, وَطَنِيٌّ. One's — tongue, لِسَانُ ٱلْوَطَنِ. The — or colloquial dialect, ٱللِّسَانُ ٱلدَّارِجُ.

Vernacularism, *n.* اِصْطِلَاحٌ بَلَدِيٌّ ـ عِبَارَةٌ وَطَنِيَّةٌ.

Vernal, *a.* Of the spring, رَبِيعِيٌّ. Belonging to youth, مُتَعَلِّقٌ بِٱلشَّبَابِ.

Vernation, *n.* تَفَتُّحُ ٱلْأَوْرَاقِ فِي أَوَّلِ ٱلرَّبِيعِ.

Vernier, *n.* مِقْيَاسٌ مُخْتَصٌّ بِٱلْآلَاتِ ٱلْفَلَكِيَّةِ.

Veronica, *n.* The plant, لُبَابُ ٱلْمَجُوسِ ـ شِيح.

Verrucose, *a.* } Verrucous, } ذُو ثَآلِيلَ.

Versatile, *a.* Turning round, دَوَّارِيٌّ ـ دَوَّار. Changeable, يَمِيل ـ طَائِش ـ فَرَّار ـ مُتَقَلْقِل ـ مُتَلَوِّن ـ بِكُلِّ رِيحٍ. Time-serving, إِمَّعَة. Turning with ease from one thing to another, سَرِيعُ ٱلْحَرَكَةِ. Clever, شَاطِر ـ صَنَّاع ـ حَاذِق ـ مِفَنٌّ. *vulg.* شَاطِر.

Versatileness, *n.* } Versatility, } Mobility, حَرَكَة ـ حِرَاك. Changeableness, inconstancy, تَقَلُّب ـ تَضَرُّب ـ تَلَوُّن ـ قِلَّةُ ثَبَاتٍ ـ طَيْش ـ فَرْفَرَة. The quality of being easily moved, سُرْعَةُ ٱلْاِنْتِقَالِ. Cleverness, صَنَاعَة ـ مَهَارَة ـ حَذَاقَة ـ شَطَارَة.

Verse, *n.* Poetry, شِعْر *pl.* أَشْعَار ـ نَظْم. A — of poetry, بَيْتُ شِعْرٍ *pl.* أَبْيَات. A —, as of the Bible, *etc.*, آيَة *pl.* آيَات. To tell in —, قَالَ ـ شِعْرًا *aor.* يَقُولُ.

Versed, *a.* Experienced, مُدَرَّس ـ مُلَقَّم ـ مُحَنَّك ـ مُنَجَّد.

Versed in, مَاهِرٌ بِ ـ خَبِيرٌ بِ ـ لَبِيقٌ بِ. To be — in, as in a science, إِفْتَنَّ فِي.

Versi-coloured, *a.* مُلَوَّن ـ مُزَرْقَش.

Versification, *n.* تَنْظِيم ـ عِلْمُ ٱلْعَرُوضِ ـ عَرُوض.

Versifier, *n.* شَاعِر *pl.* شُعَرَآءُ.

Versify, *v.t.* نَظَمَ.

Versify, *v.i.* شَعَرَ [2].

Version, *n.* A translation, تَرْجَمَة ـ نَقْل. The mode of relating a fact, حِكَايَة ـ رِوَايَة. A copy, نُسْخَة *pl.* نُسَخ. *See also* Copy, *n.*

Verst, *n.* إِسْمُ مَسَافَةِ ٱلْمِيلِ عِنْدَ أَهْلِ رُوسِيَّةَ.

Versus, prep. Against, ضِدَّ ـ عَلَى. The suit of Ahmad *versus* Muhámmad, دَعْوَى أَحْمَدَ عَلَى مُحَمَّدٍ فِي ٱلشَّرْعِ.

Versute, *a.* *See* Crafty, *a.*

Vertebra, *pl.* Vertebræ, *n.* فَقْرَة *or* فِقَارَة *coll.* فَقَار. The vertebræ, or backbone, خَرَزُ ٱلظَّهْرِ ـ مَحَالَة ـ مَحَال ـ سِنْخَاب ـ ضَرِيس *sing.* خَرَزَة. Having the — broken, مَفْقُور.

Vertebral, *a.* فَقَارِيٌّ. The — column, خَرَزُ ٱلظَّهْرِ.

Vertebrate, *a.* } Vertebrated, } ذُو فَقَارٍ (*fem.* ذِي) فَقَارٍ *pl.* ذَوُو فَقَارٍ *fem.* ذَوَاتُ.

Vertebrate, *n.* A — animal, حَيَوَانٌ ذُو فَقَارٍ *pl.* حَيَوَانَاتٌ ذَوَاتُ فَقَارٍ.

Vertex, *n.* The crown of the head, هَامَة. A top, summit, رَأْس ـ أَعْلَى ـ قِمَّة *pl.* قِمَم ـ شَاهِق. The zenith, سَمْتُ ٱلرَّأْسِ.

Vertical, *a.* Perpendicular, عَمُود ـ قَائِم ـ مُسْتَقِيم ـ مُنْتَصِب. Perpendicularly over the head, فِي سَمْتِ ٱلرَّأْسِ ـ مُنْتَصِب. A — section, فَصْلٌ عَمُودِيٌّ. A — circle, دَائِرَةُ سَمْتٍ.

Verticality, *n.* } Verticalness, } إِسْتِقَامَة ـ قِيَام ـ إِنْتِصَاب.

Vertically, *ad.* إِسْتِقَامَةً ـ إِنْتِصَابًا.

Vertiginous, *a.* Rotatory, دَوَّار ـ دَائِر. Giddy, having vertigo, مُدَوَّخ ـ دَائِخ ـ مُدَارٌ بِهِ.

Vertiginousness, *n.* دُوَار.

Vertigo, *n.* Dizziness, دَوْخَة ـ دَوْخ ـ سَدَر ـ مَيْد ـ رَنْح; from sea-sickness, مُدَام. He has the —, هُوَ مُدَارٌ بِهِ. To have the —, دَاخَ *aor.* يَدُوخُ. To cause to have —, دَوَّخَ.

Vervain, *n.* *See* Verbena, *n.*

Verve, *n.* غَيْرَة ـ قُوَّة ـ حَمَاسَة.

Very, *a.* Real, حَقِيقِيٌّ. The same, identical, عَيْن ـ ذَات ـ بِعَيْنِهِ. The — thing, نَفْسُ ٱلْأَمْرِ. At that — hour, فِي تِلْكَ ٱلسَّاعَةِ. For this — thing, لِهٰذَا عَيْنِهِ. He was caught in the — act, أُمْسِكَ وَهُوَ فِي ذَاتِ ٱلْفِعْلِ. *See also* Identical, Selfsame, *a.*

Very, *ad.* لِلْغَايَةِ ـ كَثِيرًا ـ جِدًّا. Very prudently, بِغَايَةِ ٱلْحَزْمِ وَٱلِٱحْتِيَاطِ. They were — busy, كَانُوا مَشْغُولِينَ جِدًّا. They may be — prosperous, لَعَلَّ يَحْصُلُ لَهُمْ تَوْفِيقٌ عَظِيمٌ.

Vesicant, *n.* لَزْقَة ـ حَرَّاقَة ـ نَفَّاط.

Vesicate, *v.t.* To raise in blisters, بَثَّرَ ـ بَثَّرَ ٱلدَّمَامِلَ ـ أَنْفَطَ. *See also to* Blister, *v.t.* and *i.*

Vesication, *n.* إِنْفَاط ـ تَبْثِير ـ تَبْثِيرُ (*or* إِصْدَارُ) ٱلدَّمَامِلِ.

Vesicatory, *n.* *See* Vesicant, *n.*

Vesicle, *n.* A — on the skin, بَثْرَة ـ مِجَال *pl.* مَجْلَة ـ مَجْل *or* بَثْرَة *pl.* بَثَرَات; *coll.* نَفْطَة ـ نَفِطَة. The gall —, ٱلْمَرَارَةُ.

Vesicular, *a.* } In the form of vesicles, فِي شَكْلِ ـ فِي هَيْئَةِ ٱلْمِجَالِ
Vesiculous, } (ٱلْبَثَرِ *or* ٱلنَّفْطَةِ).

Vesiculate, *a.* Full of small bladders, نَفِيط ـ مَنْفُوط ـ نَافِط ـ كَثِيرُ ٱلْبَثَرِ ـ مَمْلُوٌّ مِنَ ٱلْمِجَالِ.

Vesper, *n.* The evening star, كَوْكَبُ ٱلْمَسَاءِ. The evening, ٱلْمَسَاءُ. The constellation Venus, ٱلزُّهَرَةُ.

Vespers, *n.* صَلَاةُ ٱلْغُرُوبِ ـ صَلٰوةُ ٱلْمَسَاءِ.

Vessel, *n.* A utensil for liquors, *etc.*, إِنَاءٌ *pl.* آنِيَة ـ أَوْعِيَة *pl.* وِعَاءٌ ـ ظَرْف *pl.* ظُرُوف. A drinking —, مِشْرَبَة *pl.* مَشَارِبُ; one without a handle, بُوقَال ـ كَأْس ـ طَاس *pl.* طَاسَات. A ship, سَفِينَة *pl.* سُفُن ـ سَفَائِنُ ـ مَرْكَب *pl.* مَرَاكِبُ. A swift —, or boat, طَرَّاد. A — for transporting horses, طَرِيدَة. A blood —, vein, عِرْق *pl.* عُرُوق. The weaker —, woman, ٱلْمَرْأَةُ. A chosen —, إِنَاءٌ مُخْتَار. A — of wrath, إِنَاءُ غَضَبٍ. "As to the vessel, [ship], it belonged to poor men who toiled upon the sea," أَمَّا ٱلسَّفِينَةُ فَكَانَتْ لِمَسَاكِينَ يَعْمَلُونَ فِي ٱلْبَحْرِ (Kur. xviii. 78).

Vest, *n.* An under waistcoat, صُدَيْرِي تَحْتَانِيٌّ. A waistcoat, صُدَيْرِي *pl.* صُدَيْرِيَات ـ صُدْرَة *pl.* صُدَيْرِيَات.

Vest, *v.t.* *See to* Invest, *v.t.*

Vesta, *n.* The goddess of fire, إِلٰهَةُ ٱلنَّارِ.

Vestal, *a.* Pure, chaste, عَفِيف.

Vestal, *n.* A pure or chaste woman, عَفِيفَة ـ إِمْرَأَةٌ عَفِيفَةٌ.

Vested, *a.* Not in a state of contingency, مُسْتَقِرّ. Vested rights, حُقُوقٌ مُقَرَّرَة.

Vestiary, *n.* A wardrobe, صِوَان *pl.* أَصْوِنَة.

Vestibule, *n.* صُفَّة ـ سُهْوَة ـ إِيوَان ـ سُدَّة ـ دِهْلِيز *pl.* دَهَالِيزُ.

Vestige, *n.* A trace, أَثَر *pl.* آثَار; a very slight trace, عِثْيَر. A remain, relic, رَسْم *pl.* رُسُوم. I did not see a — of them, مَا رَأَيْتُ لَهُمْ أَثَرًا وَلَا عِثْيَرًا.

Vesting, *n.* قُمَاشٌ لِلصُّدَيْرِيَاتِ.

Vestment, *n.* مَلْبُوس *pl.* مَلَابِسُ. A church —, بَدْلَة *pl.* بَدَلَات. *See also* Garment, *n.*

Vestry, *n.* A sacristy, خِزَانَةُ ٱلْبَدَلَاتِ ـ بَيْتُ ٱلْخِدْمَةِ. A parochial committee, لَجْنَةُ (*or* مَجْمَعُ) أَبْرَشِيَّةِ ٱلْخُورِي وَكَنِيسَتِهِ.

Vestry Clerk, *n.* كَاتِبُ مَحَلٍّ.

Vestry Hall, *n.* بَيْتُ مَشْوَرَةِ حَارَةٍ.

Vestryman, *n.* مِنْ أَهْلِ مَشْوَرَةِ مَحَلٍّ.

Vesture, *n.* ثَوْب *pl.* ثِيَاب.

Vesuvius, *n.* إِسْمُ جَبَلِ نَارٍ دُونَ مَدِينَةِ نَابُلِي.

Vetch, *n.* جُلْبَان ـ جُلُبَّان ـ جُلُبَان.

Veteran, *a.* Accustomed to war, مُتَعَوِّدٌ عَلَى ٱلْحَرْبِ. Experienced, مُجَرِّب ـ مُنَجَّد ـ مُلَقَّح.

Veteran, *n.* An old soldier, عَسْكَرِيٌّ قَدِيمُ ٱلْخِدْمَةِ.

Veterinary, *a.* بَيْطَارِيٌّ. A — surgeon, بَيْطَار.

Veto, *n.* نَهْي ـ مَنْع ـ رَفْض. To put one's — upon, مَنَعَ ـ نَهَى. To have a —, لَهُ حَقُّ ٱلنَّهْيِ.

Veto, *v.t.* إِمْتَنَعَ عَنِ ٱلْقَبُولِ بِكَذَا.

Vex, *v.t.* To make angry, أَغْضَبَ ـ غَاضَبَ ـ أَغَاظَ ـ أَسْخَطَ. To trouble, torment, annoy, أَضْجَرَ ـ فَجَعَ ـ أَزْعَجَ ـ نَحَسَ. To make sorrowful, أَحْزَنَ. To treat unjustly, جَفَا ـ عَنَّى ـ تَعَدَّى عَلَى ـ ظَلَمَ. To be vexed, angered, إِغْتَاظَ ـ إِنْغَاظَ; to be tormented, plagued, إِنْزَعَجَ ـ إِزْدَعَجَ ـ تَضَجَّرَ.

Vexation, *n.* The act of angering, إِسْخَاط ـ إِغْضَاب ـ إِغَاظَة; of troubling, tormenting, إِزْعَاج ـ تَفْجِيع; of oppressing, بَغَاء ـ ظُلْم ـ مُضَايَقَة ـ جَوْر. The being angry, سَخَط ـ غَضَب ـ غَيْظ; the being troubled, إِضْطِرَاب ـ كَدَرَة ـ ضَجَر ـ ضَجْرَة. Sorrow, حُزْن. Vexation of spirit, كَآبَةُ قَلْبٍ.

Vexatious, *a.* Irritating, مُغْضِب ـ مُغِيظ. Disquieting, troublesome, شَاقٌّ ـ مُكَدِّر ـ مُعَجِّز ـ مُضْجِر ـ فَاجِع.

Vexatiously, *ad.* بِٱلتَّحْرِيشِ ـ إِزْعَاجًا ـ تَضَجُّرًا .

Vexatiousness, *n.* زَعْجٌ . *See also* Vexation, *n.*

Vexed, *a.* Angered, مَغْضُوب ـ مُغْتَاظ . Troubled, annoyed, مُتَزَعِّج ـ ضَجُور ـ مُضْجَر . A — question, عُقْلَةٌ مِنَ ٱلْعُقَلِ .

Vexingly, *ad.* *See* Vexatiously, *ad.*

Vid, *ad.* عَنْ طَرِيقِ . *Vid* Egypt, عَنْ طَرِيقِ مِصْرَ .

Viable, *a.* لَعَلَّهُ يَعِيشُ .

Viaduct, *n.* قَنْطَرَة *pl.* قَنَاطِر ـ جِسْر *pl.* أَجْسُر *and* جُسُور .

Vial, *n.* *See* Phial, *n.*

Vial, *v.t.* *See to* Phial, *v.t.*

Viands, *n.* أَطْعِمَة ـ قُوت ـ طَعَام ـ أَكْل .

Viatic, *a.* مُتَعَلِّقٌ بِٱلسَّفَرِ ـ سَفَرِيٌّ .

Viaticum, *n.* Provisions for a journey, زَاد *pl.* أَزْوَاد ـ سُفْرَة . The Eucharist administered to a dying person, مُنَاوَلَةُ ٱلْقُرْبَانِ لِلْمَرِيضِ . To administer the —, زَوَّدَ ٱلْمَرِيضَ .

Viator, *n.* *See* Traveller, *n.*

Vibrate, *v.t.* To cause to play to and fro, رَدَّدَ ـ ذَبْذَبَ . To cause to quiver, خَطْرَبَ ـ رَجْرَجَ ـ رَجَّ ; of the strings of a musical instrument, صَفَقَ .

Vibrate, *v.i.* To swing to and fro, تَرَجْرَجَ ـ تَذَبْذَبَ ـ إِسْتَرْوَحَ ـ تَرَدَّدَ ـ إِرْتَجَّ . To quiver, خَطَرَ ـ خَفَقَ ـ إِرْتَجَّ ; of the string of a musical instrument, إِصْطَفَقَ . Her posteriors vibrated to and fro, إِرْتَجَّتْ رَوَادِفُهَا . *See also under to* Quiver, *v.i.*

Vibratile, *a.* خَطَّار .

Vibration, *n.* The act of moving to and fro, تَرْدِيد ـ ذَبْذَبَة ; of causing to quiver, رَجْرَجَة ـ رَجّ ـ خَطَرَان ; of a musical instrument, صَفْق . The state of being moved to and fro, إِسْتِرْوَاح ـ تَرَجْرُج ـ إِرْتِجَاج ـ تَذَبْذُب ـ تَرَدُّد ; of quivering, خَطَرَان ـ خَفَقَان ـ إِرْتِجَاج ـ رَجَّة ; of the strings of a musical instrument, إِصْطِفَاق . *See also* Oscillation, *n.*

Vibratory, *a.* Swinging to and fro, مُتَرَجْرِج ـ مُسْتَرْوِح ـ مُتَذَبْذِب ـ مُتَرَدِّد . Quivering, خَافِق ـ مُرْتَجّ ـ خَطَّار ; of the strings of a musical instrument, مُصْطَفِق . Vibratory motion; *see* Vibration, *n.*

Vicar, *n.* A deputy, نَائِب *pl.* نُوَّاب ـ قَائِمُ مَقَامٍ . The —, of a district, parish, خُورِي *pl.* خَوَارِنَة .

Vicar Apostolic, نَائِبٌ رَسُولِيٌّ .

Vicar-General, مُسْتَشَارُ ٱلْأُسْقُفِ .

Vicarage, *n.* The benefice of a vicar, مَنْصِبُ ٱلْخُورِي . The residence of a vicar, بَيْتُ ٱلْخُورِي .

Vicarial, *a.* Pertaining to a vicar, مُخْتَصٌّ بِٱلْخُورِي .

Vicariate, *n.* Deputyship, وَكَالَة ـ نِيَابَة .

Vicarious, *a.* قَائِمُ مَقَامٍ ـ نَائِب ـ مُوَكَّل . A — person, one substituted for another, بَدِيل ـ بَدَل ـ خَلَف . Vicarious suffering, تَحَمُّلُ ٱلْآلَامِ بَدَلَ ٱلْغَيْرِ .

Vicariously, *ad.* By substitution, تَبْدِيلًا ـ بَدَلًا . As by deputy, وَكَالَةً ـ نِيَابَةً .

Vice, *n.* A fault, imperfection, خُلْقَة ـ عَيْب *pl.* عُيُوب ـ قُصُور ـ نَقَائِص *pl.* نَقِيصَة ـ وَصْمَة ـ مَعَابَة . Wickedness, corruption of manners, فُجُور ـ خَبَاثَة ـ خُبْث ـ خَلَاعَة ـ دَعَارَة . A vice, خَبِيثَة *pl.* خَبَائِث ـ شَرّ *pl.* شُرُور ـ رَذِيلَة *pl.* رَذَائِل . A bad habit, دَأْبٌ رَدِيءٌ . A mistake, as of procedure, *etc.*, خَطَأ . Vice, an iron press for holding articles when being filed, *etc.*, مِلْزَمَة ـ مِلْزَم ـ لَوْلَب .

Vice, *ad.* عِوَضَ ـ بَدَلَ .

Vice-Admiral, *n.* قَائِمُ مَقَامِ أَمِيرِ ٱلْبَحْرِ ـ ثَنْيَانُ أَمِيرِ ٱلْبَحْرِ ـ أُمِيرَالٌ ثَانٍ .

Vice-Admiralty, *n.* The office, مَأْمُورِيَّةُ أُمِيرَالٍ ثَانٍ . Court of —, مَجْلِسُ ٱلْبَحْرِيَّةِ .

Vice-Chamberlain, *n.* ثَنْيَانُ (*or* مُعَاوِنُ) ٱلْحَاجِبِ .

Vice-Chancellor, *n.* Of a university, ثَنْيَانُ (*or* مُعَاوِنُ) نَاظِرِ دَارِ ٱلْفُنُونِ . A judge in Chancery, قَاضِي دِيوَانِ ٱلْعَدْلِيَّةِ .

Vice-Consul, *n.* فَيْس قُنْصُل ـ وَكِيلُ (*or* نَائِبُ) قُنْصُلٍ .

Vice-Consulate, *n.* The office, مَأْمُورِيَّةُ وَكِيلِ قُنْصُلٍ .

Vicegerency, *n.* مَنَاب ـ خِلَافَة ـ نِيَابَة ـ حُكُومَةٌ مُوَكَّلَةٌ ـ وَكَالَة .

Vicegerent, *n.* نُقَبَاء *pl.* نَقِيب ـ خَلِيفَة ـ حَاكِمٌ مُوَكَّل ـ نَائِب *pl.* نُوَّاب ـ قَائِمُ مَقَامٍ . The — of God on earth, ظِلُّ ٱللّٰهِ عَلَى ٱلْأَرْضِ . To act as — for, نَابَ عَن .

Vice-Presidency, *n.* نِيَابَةُ ٱلصَّدَارَةِ ـ مَأْمُورِيَّةُ نَائِبِ ٱلرَّئِيسِ .

Vice-President, *n.* نَائِب ـ نَائِبُ ٱلرَّئِيسِ ـ رَئِيسٌ مُعَاوِنٌ ـ صَدْرٌ آ . . .

Vice-regal, *a.* مُخْتَصٌّ بِنِيَابَةِ سَلْطَنَةٍ .

Viceroy, *n.* نَائِبُ ٱلسُّلْطَانِ . The — of Egypt, خِدِيوِ مِصْرَ . The — and Governor-General of India, نَائِبُ حَضْرَةِ ٱلْمَلِكَةِ وَوَالِي وُلَاةِ ٱلْهِنْدِ .

Viceroyalty, *n.*
Viceroyship, } نِيَابَةُ سَلْطَنَةٍ .

Vice-versâ, *ad.* بِٱلْعَكْسِ .

Vicinage, *n.* جِوَار ـ مُجَاوَرَة .

Vicinity, *n.* قُرْب ـ نَاحِيَة ـ جَانِب ـ صَدَد . In the — of the river, دُونَ ٱلنَّهْرِ . *See also* Vicinage, *a.*

Vicious, *a.* Characterised by defects, غَيْرُ ـ نَاقِص ـ عَائِب . Vicious, in point of law, غَيْرُ ـ نَاقِص ـ سَقِيم ـ فَاسِد ـ كَامِل . Incoherent, هُرَآء ـ مُعْتَبَر . Vicious logic, مِنْطَقٌ هُرَآء . Wicked, طَالِح ـ فَاسِق ـ خَبِيث ـ حَارِض ـ فَاجِر *pl.* فُجَّار ـ خَلِيع ـ حُرَان ـ مُحَرَّمُ ٱلظَّهْرِ ـ خَاسِر ـ رَذِل *pl.* أَرْذَال . Vicious, of a horse, حَرُون . To be —, to commit — acts, أَفْجَرَ ـ فَجَرَ ² ; to be immoral, خَلُعَ ² .

Viciously, *ad.* Defectively, بِنُقْصَانٍ ـ بِعَيْب ; in point of law, بِفَسَادٍ . Wickedly, بِخَبَاثَةٍ ـ بِفُجُورٍ . Viciously, of a horse, بِجُمُوحٍ ـ بِجِمَاحٍ .

Viciousness, *n.* Depravity, خُبْث ـ شَنَاعَة ـ شَقَاحَة ـ خَلَاعَة ـ رَذَآءَة . Stubbornness, شَكَاسَة ـ تَمَرُّد ; of a horse, جُمُوح ـ جِمَاح . *See also* Unruliness, *n.*

Vicissitude, *n.* Regular change or succession, دَوْر *pl.* أَدْوَار . Change, إِنْقِلَاب ـ صُرُوف *pl.* صَرْف ـ تَقَلُّبَات *pl.* تَقَلُّبَة . Vicissitudes of time, life, fortune, حَالَاتُ ٱلدَّهْرِ ـ تَقَلُّبَاتُ ٱلْأَحْوَالِ ـ فَوَادِحُ ٱلدَّهْرِ ـ صُرُوفُ ٱلدَّهْرِ ـ طَرَائِقُ ٱلدَّهْرِ ـ طَوَائِحُ ٱلزَّمَنِ .

Victim, *n.* A living thing sacrificed, نَسِيكَة *pl.* نَسَائِك ـ ذِبْح ـ ذَبَائِح *pl.* ذَبِيحَة ـ ذَبِيح ـ قَتِيل . An offering, a sacrifice, تَقْرِيب ـ قَرَابِين *pl.* قُرْبَان . A —, as to a disease, attacked by it, مُصَاب بِ . To fall a — to, هَلَكَ فِي ـ ² . To be the — of, to be cheated by, إِنْغَشَّ مِن ـ إِنْخَدَعَ مِن ; to be attacked by, as by a disease, أُصِيبَ بِ . *See also* Sacrifice, *n.*

Victimize, *v.t.* To deceive, overreach, غَدَرَ بِ ـ إِحْتَالَ عَلَى ـ مَكَرَ بِ ² ـ غَشَّ ² ـ جَوَّنَ ـ خَدَعَ .

Victor, *n.* }
Victorious, *a.* } مَنْصُور ـ غَالِب ـ مُظَفَّر ـ ظَفِير ـ ظَفِر ـ فَائِز . A — proof, بُرْهَانٌ قَاطِعٌ . *See also* Conqueror, *n.*

Victoriously, *ad.* نُصْرَةً ـ بِنَصْرٍ .

Victory, *n.* إِنْتِصَار ـ غَلَبَة ـ ظَفَر ـ فَوْز ـ فَلْج ـ نُصْرَة ـ نَصْر . To gain the —, ظَفِرَ ـ . To gain the — over, ظَفِرَ عَلَى ـ إِنْتَصَرَ عَلَى . To give the — over to, نَصَرَ عَلَى ² . The — was for a long time uncertain between the combatants, طَالَ بَيْنَهُمُ ² ٱلْقِتَالُ وَلَمْ يَبِنِ ٱلْغَالِبُ مِنَ ٱلْمَغْلُوبِ .

Victual, *v.t.* To supply with victuals, زَوَّدَ ـ مَتَّنَ ـ مَانَ ² . To be victualled, تَمَتَّنَ ـ تَزَوَّدَ . *See also to* Provision, *v.t.*

Victualler, *n.* A purveyor, مُتَسَوِّق ـ كِلَارْجِيّ ـ مَوَّان . A licensed —, بَائِعٌ مُرَخَّصٌ بِبَيْعِ ٱلْأَطْعِمَةِ وَٱلْمَشْرُوبَاتِ ـ بَائِعٌ مَأْذُونٌ .

Victualling-yard, *n.* For shipping, مَحَلُّ ٱلْمُؤْنَةِ لِلْمَرَاكِبِ ـ مَحَلُّ ذَخِيرَةٍ لِلْمَرَاكِبِ .

Victuals, *n.* Food, مَأْكُولَات ـ أَكْل ـ قُوت ـ أَطْعِمَة ـ طَعَام ـ مَطَاعِمُ . Sustenance, مَعِيشَة ـ مَعَاش ـ وَمَشْرُوبَات .

Vide (Latin), أُنْظُرْ (يَعْنِي).

Videlicet, *conj.* وَهُوَ ـ أَي .

Vie, *v.i.* To contend with, try to surpass, عَارَضَ ـ خَايَرَ ـ سَامَى ـ بَارَى ـ غَالَبَ : There was no woman that vied with her except Zainab, لَمْ تَكُنِ ٱمْرَأَةٌ تُسَامِيهَا غَيْرَ زَيْنَبَ . They vied with one another, of many, تَجَادَوْا ـ تَرَابَعُوا . *See also to* Contest, Emulate, *v.t.*

Vi et armis, *ad.* عَنْوَةً .

Vienna, *n.* وِيَانَة .

View, *v.t.* To examine with the eye, نَظَرَ إِلَى ـ نَظَرَ ² ـ نَظَرَ ـ أَطَلَّ عَلَى ـ تَفَرَّجَ عَلَى ـ تَعَيَّنَ ـ عَايَنَ ـ تَنَظَّرَ . To —, from a higher ground, أَشْرَفَ عَلَى ـ أَوْفَى عَلَى ـ أَطَلَّ عَلَى . To contemplate, of the mind, تَأَمَّلَ فِي ـ تَأَمَّلَ ـ نَظَرَ فِي ² . To ask one to view, look, إِسْتَرْآى .

View, *n.* Reach of the eye, مَدَى ٱلْبَصَرِ . What is seen, a prospect, مَنْظَر ـ مَنَاظِرُ *pl.* مَنْظَرَة . The act of seeing, looking, شَوْفَة ـ بَصَر ـ نَظَر ـ مُعَايَنَة . Power of —, vision, ٱلنَّظَرُ ـ ٱلْبَصَرُ . A drawing, رَسْم *pl.* رُسُوم . Aspect, مَرْآة ـ رُؤْيَة ـ طَلْعَة ـ وَجْه *pl.* وُجُوه . Looking into anything, examination, مَنْظَر ـ مُطَالَعَة . Design, purpose, مَرَام ـ نِيَّة ـ أَغْرَاض *pl.* غَرَض ـ مُرَاد ـ قَصْد . An opinion, ظُنُون *pl.* ظَنّ ـ أَرَآء *pl.* رَأْي . A good place to take a — from, مَنْظَرَة . He is within my —, هُوَ مِنِّي ـ هُوَ مِنِّي مَرْأَى ـ بِمَرْأَى .

Ambitious views, مَطَامِعُ ـ نِيَّاتٌ بَاغِيَةٌ ـ آمَالٌ بَاغِيَةٌ .

At a view, at one view, مِنْ أَوَّلِ طَلَّةٍ ـ مِنْ أَوَّلِ إِطْلَالٍ ـ فِي نَظْرَةٍ .

Bird's-eye view, نَظْرَةٌ مِنْ عَلٍ ـ نَظْرَةُ طَيْرٍ .

Field of view, قُطْرُ مَدَى ٱلْبَصَرِ .

In view of, نَظَرًا لِ .

Point of view, place from which a view is taken, مَكَانٌ ـ مَنْظَرَة ـ يُنْظَرُ مِنْهُ . Object aimed at, غَايَة ـ مُرَاد ـ مَرَام .

Under one view, aspect, بِوَجْهٍ مِنَ ٱلْوُجُوهِ .

With this view, object, لِأَجْلِ هٰذَا ـ كَيْ ـ بِهٰذِهِ ٱلْغَايَةِ ـ بِهٰذَا ٱلْمُرَادِ .

To come into one's view, to appear to, تَرَآءَى لِ ـ بَدَا لِ *aor.* يَبْدُو ـ تَبَدَّى لِ .

To enter into another's views, to consider his projects, إِطَّلَعَ عَلَى مَرَامِهِ . To agree with one in, وَافَقَ فِي . To aid, سَاعَدَ ـ عَاوَنَ .

To fix one's view upon, شَخَصَ إِلَى ـ جَعَلَ (or خطّ) عَيْنَهُ عَلَى ـ . To get a view of, أَشْرَفَ عَلَى ـ أَبْصَرَ ـ تَفَرَّجَ عَلَى . To give one a view of, فَرَّجَ ـ عَلَى ـ (vulg. وَرَّى) أَرَى ـ أَرْأَى . To take a view of, to consider, نَظَرَ فِي . To take a view of one's self, تَمَرْأَى ـ تَرَأَّى ـ تَرَآءَى . The two took a view of each other, تَرَآءَيَا ; of many, تَرَآءَوْا .

To have views on, to resolve, as in the mind, نَوَى عَلَى ـ أَضْمَرَ ـ تَنَوَّى .

Viewer, *n.* نَاظِر *pl.* نُظَّار ـ مُفَرِّج *pl.* مُفَرِّجُونَ . *See also* Inspector, Spectator, *n.*

Viewless, *a.* That cannot be seen, inspected, مَا لَا يُعَايَنُ . *See also* Imperceptible, *a.*

Vigil, *n.* The eve of a holiday, لَيْلَةُ عِيدٍ . Nocturnal devotions, صَلَاةُ ٱلسَّهَرِ .

Vigilance, *n.* Forbearance of sleep, سَاهُور ـ سُهَار . Watchfulness, إِحْتِذَار ـ بَصِيرَة ـ حَزْم ـ إِحْتِيَاط ـ إِنْتِبَاه ـ نَبَاهَة .

Vigilant, *a.* Wakeful, سَهْرَان ـ سَاهِر . Watchful, circumspect, حَذِر ـ مُنْتَبِه ـ مُسْتَيْقِظ ـ مُتَيَقِّظ ـ مُتَحَفِّظ . To be —, إِحْتَذَرَ ـ تَيَقَّظَ .

Vigilantly, *ad.* بِٱحْتِذَارٍ ـ بِٱحْتِيَاطٍ ـ بِٱنْتِبَاهٍ .

Vignette, *n.* نَقْش *pl.* نُقُوش ـ طُرَّة *pl.* طُرَر and طِرَار . A title-page with a —, عُنْوَانُ كِتَابٍ مَنْقُوش .

Vigorous, *a.* Strong, powerful, of a person, قَوِيّ ـ ظَهِير . Robust, صُلْب ـ ضَلِيع . Healthy, مُتَعَافٍ ـ ذُو عَافِيَةٍ . Strong, effective, شَدِيد ـ مُؤَثِّر ـ قَوِيّ . Bold, جَسُور ـ أَلُوب ـ شَدِيدُ ٱلْعَارِضِ ـ دَائِب ـ ذُو عَارِضَةٍ . *See also* Strenuous, *a.*

Vigorously, *ad.* Powerfully, بِقُوَّةٍ ـ قُوَّةً . Strenuously, بِجِدٍّ ـ بِغَيْرَةٍ ـ بِجِدٍّ وَجُهْدٍ .

Vigour, *n.* Physical force, or strength, as of mind, *etc.*, عَارِضَة ـ عَارِض ـ مُكْنَة ـ قُوَّة ـ جِدَّة ـ قُدْرَة . Earnestness, strenuousness, حَزْم ـ عَزْم ـ جِدّ ـ مُرُوَّة ـ حَمِيَّة ـ رَغْبَة ـ حَرَارَة . Robustness, صَلَابَة . Health, صِحَّة ـ عَافِيَة . Courage, بَطْش ـ شَجَاعَة . The — of age, عُنْفُوَانُ ٱلشَّبَابِ ـ الأَشَدّ : he has attained his full —, بَلَغَ أَشُدَّهُ . The laws in —, القَوَانِينُ ٱلْمَوْضُوعَة ـ القَوَانِينُ ٱلْجَارِيَة ـ ٱلْمَرْعِيَّة . All his —, ardour, returned to him, إِرْتَدَّتْ إِلَيْهِ جَمِيعُ حَمِيَّتِهِ . To be in —, as of a law, حُكْمُهُ جَارٍ . To act with —, تَشَدَّدَ ـ تَصَلَّبَ .

Vile, *a.* Base, wicked, رَذِيل *pl.* أَرْذَال ـ فَاجِر *pl.* فُجَّار ـ خَبِيث ـ خَسِيس ـ حَقِير ـ خَز . Mean, despicable, دَنِيء ـ سَفِيل ـ سَفِل . Abhorrent, hateful, شَنِيع ـ فَجِيع ـ قَبِيح *pl.* قِبَاح ـ مَكْرُوه ـ مَنْفُور . A — action, رَذِيلَة *pl.* رَذَائِلُ . To become —, base, low, تَسَفَّلَ ـ سَفُلَ . To render —, أَخْزَى .

Vilely, *ad.* بِخَسَاسَةٍ ـ بِدَنَآءَةٍ ـ بِخَبَاثَةٍ ـ بِرَذَالَةٍ .

Vileness, *n.* Wickedness, خَبَاثَة ـ رَذَالَة . Baseness, meanness, حَقَارَة ـ خِزْيَة ـ خَسَاسَة ـ نَذَالَة ـ ذُلّ ـ قَبَاحَة . Hatefulness, شَنَاعَة .

Vilification, *n.* The act of, شَتْم ـ مَشْتَمَة ـ سَبّ ـ طَعْن ـ تَعْيِير ـ بَهْدَلَة . Mutual —, مُشَاتَمَة ـ مُسَابَّة . *See also* Defamation, *n.*

Vilified, *past part.* مَشْتُوم ـ شَتِيم ـ مُسَبَّب ـ مَقْرُوف .

Vilifier, *n.* شَتَّام ـ مُسَبِّب .

Vilify, *v.t.* غَمِطَ ـ طَلَّى ـ قَرَّضَ ـ حَقَّرَ ـ أَرْذَلَ ـ حَكَرَ ـ شَتَمَ ـ سَبَّ ـ أَقْرَفَ ـ عَيَّرَ بِـ ـ بَهْدَلَ ; with words, إِغْتَمَطَ بِٱلْكَلَامِ . To be vilified, شُتِمَ . They vilified one another, of many, تَسَابُّوا ـ تَشَاتَمُوا . *See also to* Defame, *v.t.*

Villa, *n.* قَصْر *pl.* قُصُور ـ دَار *pl.* دِيَار ـ مَنْزِل *pl.* مَنَازِلُ ـ *from the Persian*, كُوشْك *pl.* كُوشْكَات .

Village, *n.* كَفْر *pl.* كُفُور ـ قَرْيَة *pl.* قُرًى and قَرَايَا ـ كُورَة *pl.* كُوَر ـ دُوَار ـ أَدْوَار ـ ضَيْعَة *pl.* ضِيَاع and ضَيْعَات . A head —, قَصَبَة *pl.* قَصَبَات . The head man of a —, شَيْخُ ضَيْعَةٍ *pl.* شُيُوخ .

Villager, *n.* قَرَوِيّ ـ مِنْ أَهْلِ قَرْيَةٍ ـ مِنْ أَهْلِ ضَيْعَةٍ . Villagers, أَهْلُ ٱلْقُرَى ـ أَهْلُ ٱلضِّيَاعِ .

Villain, *n.* A scoundrel, قَلَطِيّ ـ خَبِيث ـ شِرِّير ـ فَاجِر *pl.* فُجَّار ـ خَلِيع .

Villainous, *a.* Depraved, خَبِيث ـ شِرِّير . Not good, رَدِيء ـ بَطَّال ـ عَاطِل ـ بَشِع ـ بَشِيع .

Villainously, *ad.* Knavishly, خَلَاعَةً ـ شَرًّا ـ بِخَبَاثَةٍ . Badly, بِقَبَاحَةٍ ـ عَطْلًا ـ بَشَاعَةً . To act —, شَرَّ ـ خَلُعَ .

Villainousness, *n.* Viciousness, خَلَاعَة ـ فُجُور ـ خُبْث ـ شَرّ . Badness, خَرَابَة ـ خُلْفَة ـ بَشَاعَة .

Villainy, *n.* خَلَاعَة ـ خَبَاثَة ـ شَنَاعَة ـ شَرّ ـ قَبَاحَة .

Villi, *n.* Fibres, hairs, شُعَيْرَات ـ زِئْبِر .

Villose, *a.* }
Villous, } أَشْعَر ـ مُزَأْبِر .

Vinaigrette, *n.* قَازُوزَةُ ٱلرَّوَائِحِ .

Vincible, *a.* *See* Conquerable, *a.*

Vinculum, *n.* A bond of union, رِبَاطُ ٱلِٱتِّحَادِ . A tie, رِبَاط ـ مَرْبَط ـ قَيْد *pl.* قُيُود . *See also* Parenthesis, *n.*

Vindemial, *a.* قِطَافِيّ ـ مُتَعَلِّقٌ بِٱلْقِطَافِ .

Vindicable, *a.* *See* Justifiable, *a.*

Vindicate, *v.t.* To prove to be just, valid, حَقَّقَ ـ صَحَّحَ ـ ثَبَّتَ .

To defend, حَامَى عَن – رَدَّ عَن ². To — one's self against, إِنْتَصَرَ مِن – إِنْتَصَفَ مِن – تَبَرَّأَ مِن – تَنَفَّحَ مِن. *See also to* Justify, *v.t.*

Vindication, *n.* The act of supporting by proofs, تَصْحِيح – إِثْبَات. Justification, as against denial, *etc.*, حُجَّة – عُذْر. Self —, إِنْتِصَار – إِنْتِصَاف – تَبَرُّؤ.

Vindicative, *a.* } Tending to prove, مُبَرْهِن – مُثْبِت; to justify,
Vindicatory, } مُبَرِّر.

Vindicator, *n.* مُحَامٍ – عَاصِم – مُقَاوِم.

Vindictive, *a.* حَقُود – حَسِكٌ – طَالِبُ ٱلْإِنْتِقَام.

Vindictively, *ad.* بِحِقْدٍ – بِحَسَكٍ – إِنْتِقَامًا.

Vindictiveness, *n.* حَسَكٌ – حَقِيدَة – حِقْد. *See also* Rancour, *n.*

Vine, *n.* That producing grapes, عِنَب – كَرْم *pl.* كُرُوم – كَرْمَة – دَالِيَة *pl.* دَوَالِي. The stock of a —, or a vine spread out, حَبَلَة *coll.* حَبَل. Leaves of the —, غَار – أَوْرَاقُ ٱلدَّوَالِي. A — prop, مِرْزَخ – عَرِيش *pl.* عَرَائِش. To prop up a —, عَرَّشَ ٱلْكَرْمَة. Vine, a creeping plant, عُضْبَة – دَغِل – أُنَيْث – مُعَرِّش.

Vine-dresser, *n.* كَرَّام.

Vinegar, *n.* خَلّ – أَبُو ثَقِيف *pl.* خُلُول. Aromatic —, خَلّ مُعَطَّر. To become —, of wine, إِخْتَلَّ. To make wine into —, خَلَّلَ ٱلْخَمْرَ. To season with —, خَلَّلَ. A seller of —, خَلَّال.

Vinery, *n.* ذَرَى لِلْكُرُوم.

Vineyard, *n.* كَرْم *pl.* كُرُوم.

Vinous, *a.* خَمْرِيّ.

Vintage, *n.* The season produce of the vine, قِطَافُ ٱلْعِنَب. Season of the —, إِبَّانُ (or زَمَانُ) قَطْفِ ٱلْعِنَب.

Vintager, *n.* قَطَّافُ ٱلْعِنَب.

Vintner, *n.* خَمَّار – حَانُوتِيّ – حَانُوِيّ – حَانِيّ.

Vintry, *n.* خَمَّارَة – حَانُوت.

Viny, *a.* Belonging to vines, مَا نِيطَ بِٱلْكُرُوم. Full of vines, كَثِيرُ ٱلْكُرُوم.

Viol, *n.* رَبَاب. A player on the —, رَبَابِيّ.

Violable, *a.* مُمْكِنٌ (نَقْضُهُ or) فَسْخُهُ.

Violaceous, *a.* مِثْلَ ٱلْبَنَفْسَج.

Violate, *v.t.* To break in upon, to transgress, تَعَدَّى عَلَى. To deflower, ravish, غَصَبَ ٱلْمَرْأَة – غَصَبَهَا (or إِغْتَصَبَهَا) نَفْسَهَا – نَكَثَ ². To — a treaty, نَقَضَ ٱلْعَهْدَ ² – هَتَكَ جَبْرًا ٱلْمُعَاهَدَة. To — an oath, حَنِثَ فِي يَمِينِهِ. To —, of the limits of a territory, أَجْحَفَ بِ – تَجَاوَزَ (or جَاوَزَ) ٱلْحَدَّ. He violated the sacredness, as of a territory, *etc.*, هَتَكَ حُرْمَةَ ٱلْمَكَانِ.

To be violated, deflowered, أُغْتُصِبَتْ نَفْسَهَا – أُغْتُصِبَتْ عَلَى – إِنْتَهَكَتْ نَفْسَهَا – إِنْتَكَثَ; to be violated, as a treaty, *etc.*, – إِنْتَقَضَ.

Violation, *n.* As of an oath, حِنْث; of a treaty, نَقْض – إِخْلَال; of territory, or of a woman, هَتْك. Transgression, تَعْدِيَة. Violation of a sacred place, خَرْق. Violation of the laws, تَعْدِيَةُ ٱلشَّرَائِع. Violation of a boundary, تَجَاوُزُ ٱلْحُدُودِ – إِجْحَافٌ بِٱلْحُدُودِ.

Violator, *n.* As of an oath, حَانِث; of a treaty, نَاقِض. A transgressor, مُتَعَدٍّ. A ravisher, هَاتِكُ ٱمْرَأَةٍ.

Violence, *n.* Force, حَيْل – قُوَّة. Strength of action, شِدَّة – حِدَّة. Impressment, constraint, بَطْش – جَبْر – إِجْبَار – غَصْب. Cruelty, عَنْف – قَسْر – قَهْر – قُهْرَة – رَغْم. Violence, as of wind, عُصُوف. To act with — towards, عَنِفَ بِ or عَلَى ² – عَانَفَ. To do — to one's own feelings in . . . , غَصَبَ نَفْسَهُ عَلَى – أَجْبَرَ نَفْسَهُ عَلَى – قَسَرَ ² – قَهَرَ ². Violence, all kinds of evil, شَرّ – فَسَاد. *See also under* Force, *n.*

Violent, *a.* Strong, قَوِيّ – شَدِيد *pl.* شِدَاد. Harsh, عَنِيف. Unjust, عَسُوف. Violent, of a wind, عَاصِف – قَاصِف – عَصُوف. Forcing, جَابِر – غَاصِب. Violent, as of a disease, ثَقِيل. Passionate, غَضُوب. To lay — hands on, to take from by force, to force, غَاصَبَ. To lay — hands on one's self, قَتَلَ نَفْسَهُ ².

Violently, *ad.* Forcibly, جَبْرًا – قَهْرًا – غَصْبًا. With force, بِشِدَّةٍ. To take away —, سَلَبَ ² – إِسْتَلَبَ. They ran — down the hill, إِنْدَفَعُوا مِنْ عَلَى ٱلْجَبَلِ.

Violescent, *a.* يَضْرِبُ إِلَى لَوْنِ ٱلْبَنَفْسَج.

Violet, *a.* Of the colour, – بَنَفْسَجِيّ.

Violet, *n.* One —, بَنَفْسَجَة *coll.* بَنَفْسَج.

Violin, *n.* كَمَنْجَة *coll.* كَمَنْج – رَبَابَة *coll.* رَبَاب. To play on the —, ضَرَبَ ٱلْكَمَنْجَة ².

Violinist, *n.* ضَرَّابُ ٱلْكَمَنْجَةِ.

Violoncello, *n.* كَمَنْجَة كَبِيرَة.

Violone, *n.* كَمَنْجَة ٱلْبَمّ كَبِيرَة.

Viper, *n.* The reptile, أَفْعَى *pl.* أَفَاعٍ. A malignant person, شَرّ *pl.* أَشْرَار – خَبِيث. A land full of vipers, أَرْض مَفْعَاة.

Viper-grass, مُرَيْر.

Viperine, *a.* مُتَشَبِّهٌ بِٱلْأَفْعَى – مَا نِيطَ بِٱلْأَفْعَى.

Viperous, *a.* Malignant, مُتَفَعِّع – حَسِك – حَنِك – شِرِّير – ضَغِن – حَقُود.

Virago, *n.* خَطَّالَة – سِلِقَة *pl.* سُلْقَان – سَلِيطَة.

Virgil, *n.* The poet, إِسْمُ شَاعِرٍ مَشْهُورٍ عِنْدَ ٱلرُّومَانِيِّينَ ٱلْأَقْدَمِينَ.

Virgin, *n.* Applied to a man or woman, بِكْر *pl.* أَبْكَار; to a woman only, بِنْتٌ بِكْرٌ ـ بَتِيل ـ بَتُول ـ عَذْرَآء *pl.* عَذَارَى. The Virgin Mary, حَضْرَةُ مَرْيَمَ ـ مَرْيَمُ ٱلْبَتُولُ. "And we have made them (ever) virgins," فَجَعَلْنَاهُنَّ أَبْكَارًا (Kur. lvi. 35).

Virgin, *a.* Having lived in continence, بَتُول. Chaste, عَفِيف. Pure, unmixed, خَالِص ـ بِكْر. Not used, غَيْرُ مُسْتَعْمَلٍ. Not cultivated, غَيْرُ مَفْلُوحٍ. New, جَدِيد.

Virginal, *a.* *See* Maidenly, *a.*

Virginal, *n.* The instrument, سِنْطِيرٌ صَغِيرٌ.

Virginity, *n.* Maidenhood, بَكَارَة ـ عُذْرَة.

Virgo, *n.* The constellation, بُرْجُ ٱلسُّنْبُلَةِ ـ السُّنْبُلَة.

Viridity, *n.* *See* Verdure, *n.*

Virile, *a.* Male, ذَكَر. Having attained to puberty, مُحْتَلِم ـ حَالِم.

Virility, *n.* Manhood, as opposed to womanhood, رُجُولَة ـ رُجْلَة ـ رُجُولِيَّة. Puberty, سِنُّ ٱلْبُلُوغِ ـ بُلُوغُ ٱلْحُلُمِ. Power of procreation, قُوَّةُ ٱلتَّنَاسُلِ.

Virtu, *n.* A taste for curiosities, رَغْبَةٌ فِي ٱلتُّحَفِ. Objects of —, تُحَف.

Virtual, *a.* Real, صَحِيح *pl.* صِحَاح. Effectual, فَعَّال ـ مُقْتَدِر. Being in essence, comprised, ضِمْنِيٌّ ـ مُتَضَمَّن.

Virtually, *ad.* Really, بِٱلْحَقِيقَةِ ـ حَقِيقَةً. As being comprised in, تَضْمِينًا.

Virtue, *n.* Power, efficacy, فَاعِلِيَّة ـ تَأْثِير ـ قُوَّة. Propriety, property, شَأْن *pl.* شُؤُون ـ خَاصِّيَّة *pl.* خَصَائِص ـ خَاصَّة. Probity, moral rectitude, فَضِيلَة. Integrity, إِسْتِقَامَة ـ صَلَاح. Chastity, عِفَّة. A —, فَضِيلَة *pl.* فَضَائِل ـ فَاضِلَة *pl.* فَوَاضِل. The acquisition of virtues and the avoidance of vices, إِقْتِنَآءُ ٱلْفَضَائِلِ وَٱجْتِنَابُ ٱلرَّذَائِلِ. A woman of easy —, بَرْكَاسَة; *called in Egypt*, برجاسة. In — of, إِسْتِنَادًا عَلَى ـ بِحَسَبِ ـ بِنَآءً عَلَى.

Virtueless, *a.* Without moral goodness, عَدِيمُ ٱلْفَضَائِلِ. Without efficacy, سَقَط ـ لَا فَاعِلِيَّةَ فِيهِ ـ خَالٍ عَنِ ٱلتَّأْثِيرِ ـ غَيْرُ مُؤَثِّرٍ.

Virtuoso, *a.* Fond of curiosities, مُحِبُّ ٱلتُّحَفِ. Skilled in music, أُسْتَاذٌ فِي فَنِّ ٱلْمُوسِيقَى.

Virtuous, *a.* Just, godly, تَقِيٌّ ـ بَارٌّ ـ صَالِح *pl.* صُلَحَآء ـ فَاضِل. Chaste, عَفِيف. A —, good, man, صَاحِبُ فَضِيلَةٍ. A — woman, إِمْرَأَةٌ فَاضِلَة.

Virtuously, *ad.* With moral goodness, بِفَضِيلَةٍ ـ فَضْلًا. Chastely, بِعِفَّةٍ. To be or to act —, chastely, تَعَفَّفَ ـ عَفَّ.

Virtuousness, *n.* *See* Virtue, *n.*

Virulence, *n.* } Force, شِدَّة ـ حِدَّة. Excess, إِفْرَاط ـ فَرْط.
Virulency, } Severity, قَسَاوَة ـ عُنْف. Malice, ضِغْن ـ بُغْض ـ حِقْد ـ لَدّ. Harmfulness, أَذِيَّة. Venom, حُمَة.

Virulent, *a.* Strong, قَوِيٌّ ـ شَدِيد ـ حَدِيد. Severe, harsh, قَاسٍ ـ عَنِيف. Malicious, صَارِم ـ أَلَدُّ *pl.* لُدّ *and* لِدَاد ـ حَقُود ـ ضَاغِن ـ حَنِك. A — poison, سَمٌّ قَوِيٌّ. A — disease, مَرَضٌ شَدِيدٌ.

Virulently, *ad.* Vehemently, بِشِدَّةٍ ـ بِحِدَّةٍ. Malignantly, بِلَدٍّ ـ ضِغْنًا ـ ضَغِينَةً ـ بِحَنَقٍ ـ حِقْدًا.

Virus, *n.* Pus, matter, مِدَّة ـ قَيْح ـ غَثِيث. Poison, سَمٌّ.

Vis, *n.* قُوَّة. *Vis inertiæ*, قُوَّةُ عَطَالَةٍ ـ عَطَالَة. *Vis vitæ*, حَيَاة ـ قُوَّةٌ حَيَوَانِيَّةٌ.

Visage, *n.* طَلْعَة ـ وَجْه ـ مَنْظَر ـ سِيمَا.

Vis-à-vis, *ad.* Face to face, مُوَاجَهَةً. Opposite, تُجَاهَ ـ قِبَالَ ـ قَصْدَ. Vis-à-vis to, as to a subject, عَلَى وَجْهِ ٱلتَّقَابُلِ.

Vis-à-vis, *n.* مُقَابِل ـ وَاقِفٌ قِبَالَ فُلَانٍ. My —, مُتَابِلِي ـ الوَاقِفُ قِبَالِي.

Viscera, *n.* مَصَارِينُ ـ أَحْشَآء ـ أَمْعَآء.

Visceral, *a.* جَوْفِيٌّ ـ مَا نِيطَ بِٱلْمَصَارِينِ ـ أَحْشَائِيٌّ.

Viscerate, *v.t.* *See to* Eviscerate, *v.t.*

Viscid, *a.* دَبِق ـ لَزِج. Anything —, دَبُقَآء. To become —, تَدَبَّقَ ـ تَلَزَّجَ ـ تَسَعَّبَ ـ تَمَطَّطَ.

Viscidity, *n.* } لُزُوجَة ـ تَغَرِّيَة.
Viscosity, }

Viscount, *n.* وَيْكُنْت عِبَارَةٌ عَنِ ٱلرُّتْبَةِ ٱلرَّابِعَةِ مِنْ مَرَاتِبِ ٱلشَّرَفِ ٱلْأَصْلِيَّةِ عِنْدَ ٱلْإِفْرِنْجِ.

Viscountess, *n.* وَيْكُنْتِيسَا ـ زَوْجَة وَيْكُونْت.

Viscous, *a.* *See* Viscid, *a.*

Visé, *n.* As of a passport, *etc.*, صَحّ.

Visé, *v.t.* وَقَّعَ عَلَى ـ كَتَبَ عَلَيْهِ صَحّ.

Vishnu, *n.* الأُقْنُومُ ٱلثَّانِي مِنْ ثَالُوثِ ٱلْهُنُودِ وَهُوَ ٱلْإِلَاهُ ٱلْحَافِظُ.

Visibleness, *n.* } بَيَان ـ مُعَايَنَة ـ ظُهُور ـ تَظَاهُر.
Visibility, }

Visible, *a.* Perceivable by the eye, يُرَى ـ يُدْرِكُهُ ٱلنَّظَرُ ـ يُرَى عِيَانًا. Apparent, manifest, بَائِن ـ وَاضِح ـ ظَاهِر. To be or to become —, ظَهَرَ عِيَانًا ـ بَانَ عِيَانًا *aor.* يَبِينُ. To be —, apparent, ظَهَرَ ـ تَبَيَّنَ ـ بَيَّنَ. The — and the invisible, مَا يُرَى وَمَا لَا يُرَى.

Visibly, *ad.* ظُهُورًا ـ وُضُوحًا ـ عِيَانًا.

Visigoth, *n.* جِيلٌ مِنْ أُمَّةِ ٱلْغُوطِ دَمَّرَ رُومِيَّةَ ٱلْقَدِيمَةَ.

Vision, *n.* The act of seeing, شَوْفَة ـ طَلْعَة ـ نَظَر ـ رُؤْيَة. The faculty of sight, بَصَارَة ـ نَظَرَان ـ بَصَر ـ نَظَر. Range of sight, مَدَى ٱلْبَصَرِ. A phantom, خَيَال pl. أَخْيِلَة. A dream, حُلْم pl. أَحْلَام. A revelation, as from God, رُؤْيَا pl. رُؤْيَات ـ وَحْيٌ. Visions and revelations of God, مَنَاظِرُ ٱلرَّبِّ وَإِعْلَانَاتُهُ. I saw in a —, رَأَيْتُ فِي ٱلرُّؤْيَا. To see a —, to dream, حَلَمَ ².

Visionary, a. Imaginary, خَيَالِيٌّ ـ وَهْمِيٌّ ـ خُرَافِيٌّ. Illusive, غَرَّار.

Visionary, n. ذُو خَرَفٍ ـ خَرِف.

Visionless, a. *See* Sightless, a.

Visit, v.t. To go to see, to call upon, زَارَ aor. يَزُورُ ـ شَقَّ عَلَى ². To —, as of a shrine, زَارَ ². To —, as the sick, عَادَ ـ ٱفْتَقَدَ aor. يَعُودُ. To frequent, ٱعْتَانَ ـ صَمَّدَ. To — a shop, store, أَقْصَدَ. To —, as with some evil, أَدْرَكَ ـ بِ حَاصِلًا. To —, as with punishment, عَاقَبَ. To —, to examine into the state of, كَشَفَ ² ـ كَشَفَ عَلَى ـ ٱسْتَفْقَدَ عَلَى. To search, فَتَّشَ ـ تَحَرَّى. To —, to make a tour to or round a place, جَوَّلَ فِي ـ جَالَ فِي aor. يَجُولُ. To — the sins of the fathers upon the children, ٱفْتَقَدَ ذُنُوبَ ٱلْآبَاءِ فِي ٱلْأَبْنَاءِ. Simply to —, لِمُجَرَّدِ ٱلزِّيَارَةِ. They —, call on, one another, of many, تَزَاوَرُوا ـ بَيْنَهُمْ تَزَاوُرٌ. To make one to visit, أَزَارَ. A house that is much repaired to, visited, بَيْتٌ مُصَمَّدٌ.

Visit, n. The act of calling upon or being called upon, زِيَارَة ـ طَلَّة ـ شَقَّة; one such —, زَوْرَة. Visit, as of a physician, شَقَّة. Search, كَشْف ـ تَفْتِيش ـ مُعَايَنَة ـ كَاشِفَة. Daily visits, as of an inspector, تَفْتِيشَاتٌ يَوْمِيَّةٌ. An official —, زِيَارَةٌ رَسْمِيَّةٌ. A —, as to the sick, عِيَادَة ـ ٱفْتِقَاد. To pay a —, زَارَ زِيَارَةً ². To receive a —, قَبِلَ زِيَارَةً ⁴. To return one's —, رَدَّ زِيَارَتَهُ ². Domiciliary visits, تَفْتِيشَاتٌ مَحَلِّيَّةٌ.

Visitable, a. In a state to receive visits, مُرَآةٌ بِٱلزِّيَارَةِ ـ مِمَّنْ يُزَارُ ـ زِيَارَتُهُ جَائِزَةٌ. Liable to be visited, searched, حَقِيقٌ بِٱلتَّفْتِيشِ.

Visitant, n. *See* Visitor, n.

Visitation, n. A careful inspection, تَفْتِيشٌ وَمُعَايَنَةٌ. Visitation of the sick, ٱفْتِقَادُ ٱلْمَرْضَى ـ عِيَادَةُ ٱلْمَرْضَى. A —, trial, as from God, a misfortune, آفَة pl. آفَات ـ مُصِيبَة pl. مَصَائِب. Under a —, مُصَابٌ بِآفَةٍ. Visitation, as from God, in a favourable sense, لُطْفٌ وَإِحْسَانٌ مِنَ ٱللّٰهِ ـ ٱفْتِقَاد. *See also* Visit, n.

Visiting, a. Authorized to visit, مُفَتِّش ـ مَأْمُورٌ بِٱلتَّفْتِيشِ.

Visitor, n. One who pays a visit, زَائِر pl. زُوَّار fem. زَائِرَة pl. زَائِرَات. A —, as of the sick, عَائِد pl. عُوَّد ـ عُوَّاد. A —, as for a time in another person's house, مُسَافِر pl. مُسَافِرُون ـ نَازِل عِنْدَ فُلَانٍ pl. نَازِلُون. A guest, ضَيْف pl. ضُيُوف ـ مُتَضَيِّف ـ مُضَاف. An inspector, كَشَّاف ـ مُفَتِّش.

Visitorial, a. مَا نِيطَ بِمَأْمُورِيَّةِ ٱلْمُفَتِّشِ.

Visor, n. Of a helmet, بُرْقُعُ ٱلْخُوذَةِ pl. بَرَاقِعُ. A mask, مَسْخَرَة.

Vista, n. A prospect through an avenue, مَنْظَرَةٌ فِي مَشْجَرٍ. An avenue of trees, دَرْبٌ مُحَاطٌ بِمَشْجَرَةٍ.

Visual, a. مُتَعَلِّقٌ بِٱلْبَصَرِ ـ بَصَرِيٌّ.

Vital, a. Pertaining to life, مُتَعَلِّقٌ بِٱلْحَيَاةِ ـ حَيَاتِيٌّ. Necessary to life, ضَرُورِيٌّ لِلْحَيَاةِ. Essential, لَا بُدَّ مِنْهُ ـ مُطْلَقُ ٱلْوُجُوبِ. Very important, مُهِمٌّ لِلْغَايَةِ. The — principle, ٱلرُّوحُ ٱلْحَيَوَانِيَّةُ ـ ٱلْحَيَاةُ ـ ٱلنَّفْسُ. The — powers, ٱلْقُوَى ٱلْحَيَوَانِيَّةُ. Vital statistics, جَدَاوِلُ عَدَدِ ٱلْمَوْلُودِينَ وَٱلْمَوْتَى.

Vitality, n. رُوحٌ ـ حَيَاةٌ.

Vitalization, n. إِحْيَاءٌ ².

Vitalize, v.t. أَحْيَى.

Vitally, ad. Mortally, لِلْمَوْتِ ـ لِحَدِّ ٱلْمَوْتِ. Dangerously, مَعَ خَطَرٍ. Wholly, إِطْلَاقًا ـ بِأَسْرِهِ ـ بَتَّةً.

Vitals, n. ٱلْجِهَازُ ٱلْبَاطِنُ ٱلضَّرُورِيُّ لِلْحَيَاةِ ـ ٱلْآلَاتُ ٱلْبَدَنِيَّةُ ٱلضَّرُورِيَّةُ. The — of a state, قِيَامُ (or) حَيَاةُ دَوْلَةٍ.

Vitiate, v.t. To damage, injure, شَابَ aor. يَشُوبُ ـ أَضَرَّ ـ ضَارَّ ـ حَرَّضَ ـ أَحْرَضَ ـ عَيَّبَ ـ ضَيَّعَ ـ أَتْلَفَ. To corrupt, as in morals, أَفْسَدَ ـ فَسَّدَ ـ أَخْبَثَ; of the mind, خَبَّلَ ـ أَخْبَلَ. To destroy validity, أَبْطَلَ ـ أَفْسَدَ ـ فَسَخَ ² ـ نَاقَضَ. To be vitiated, damaged, تَعَطَّلَ ـ ٱنْضَرَّ; to be corrupted, أَخْبَثَ ـ خَبُثَ ²; of the mind, ٱخْتَبَلَ; of the stomach, حَرِضَ ². To be invalidated, أُبْطِلَ ـ ٱنْتَقَضَ ـ فُسِخَ.

Vitiated, a. Injured, damaged, مُعَطَّل ـ مُنْضَرّ. Corrupted, خَبِيث ـ مُخْبَث. Deranged in mind, مُخَبَّل. Invalidated, مُبْطَل ـ مُنْتَقَض. Deranged in the stomach, خَارِض ـ حَرِض.

Vitiation, n. The act of damaging, مُضَارَّة ـ مَضَرَّة ـ شَوْب ـ تَعْيِيب; of corrupting, إِخْبَاث ـ إِفْسَاد; of deranging the mind, تَخْبِيل ـ إِخْبَال; of destroying validity, مُنَاقَضَة ـ فَسْخ ـ إِبْطَال. *See also* Viciousness, Vice, n.

Vitreous, a. زُجَاجِيٌّ ـ vulg. يُشْبِهُ ٱلْقِزَازَ.

Vitreousness, n. زُجَاجِيَّة.

Vitrescence, n. مُشَابَهَةُ ٱلزُّجَاجِ ـ ضَرْبٌ إِلَى ٱلزُّجَاجِ.

Vitrescent, a. ضَارِبٌ إِلَى ٱلزُّجَاجِ ـ زُجَاجِيٌّ نَوْعًا.

Vitrifaction, n. إِحَالَةٌ إِلَى زُجَاجٍ ـ ٱسْتِحَالَةُ شَيْءٍ إِلَى ٱلزُّجَاجِ.

Vitrifiable, a. يَتَحَوَّلُ إِلَى زُجَاجٍ.

Vitrify, v.t. صَيَّرَ زُجَاجًا ـ أَحَالَ إِلَى زُجَاجٍ ـ حَوَّلَ زُجَاجًا.

Vitrify, v.i. صَارَ زُجَاجًا ² ـ صَارَ كَٱلزُّجَاجِ.

Vitriol, *n.* شَبٌّ يَمَانِيٌّ ـ زَاج *pl.* زَاجَات *vulg.* جاز. The stones of —, شَبُّ ٱلزَّاجِ.

Green vitriol, قَلْقَدِيس ـ قَلْقَنْد ـ زَاجٌ قُبْرُسِيٌّ ـ زَاجٌ أَخْضَرُ.

Oil of vitriol, دُهْنُ ٱلزَّاجِ.

White vitriol, زَاجٌ أَبْيَضُ ـ *called in Egypt,* تُوتِيَةٌ بَصُورِيَّةٌ.

Vitriolize, *v.t.* صَيَّرَ زَاجًا.

Vituperate, *v.t.* عَيَّبَ ـ سَخِطَ عَلَى ² ـ قَدَحَ ـ شَتَمَ ² . *See also to* Reproach, Blame, *v.t.*

Vituperation, *n.* طَعْن ـ شَتْم ـ قَدْح ـ سَخْط ـ تَعْيِيب.

Vituperative, *a.* طَاعِن ـ مُعَيِّب ـ شَاتِم ـ قَادِح.

Vituperatively, *ad.* قَدْحًا ـ شَتْمًا ـ سَخْطًا.

Vivacious, *a.* Animated, lively, زَوْل ـ أَلُوب ـ قَلْتَان ـ حَادٌّ ـ نَبِيه ـ نَشِيط ـ نَارِيٌّ ـ حَامٍ.

Vivaciously, *ad.* بِنَشَاطٍ ـ بِحَرَارَةٍ ـ بِحِدَّةٍ ـ بِخِفَّةٍ.

Vivaciousness, *n.* } نَشَاط ـ خِفَّة ـ حِدَّة ـ حَرَارَة ـ مُرُوءَة ـ
Vivacity, } فُرُوهَة ـ فَرَاهَة.

Vivarium, *n.* } دَرًى لِلْحَيَوَانَاتِ.
Vivary, }

Vivat! int. يَعِيشُ. *Vivat rex!* يَعِيشُ ٱلْمَلِكُ. *Vivat regina!* تَعِيشُ ٱلْمَلِكَةُ.

Vivâ-voce, *ad.* شِفَاهًا ـ مُشَافَاةً.

Vivid, *a.* Bright, luminous, نَيِّر ـ مُنِير ـ لَامِع ـ لَمُوع. Perspicuous, وَاضِح ـ مُبِين. Glistening, رَفِيف ـ بَارِق ـ بَرَّاق. Animated, حَادٌّ. Lively, clever, بَدِيع. Vivid, of a colour, نَضِر ـ نَاضِر ـ رَفِيف. A — flash of lightning, رَقَّة ـ بَرْقَة. *See also* Striking, *a.*

Vividly, *ad.* With brightness, بِرَفِيف ـ بِبَرِيق ـ بِبَهَاءٍ ـ بِرَوْنَقٍ. With animation, بِحِدَّةٍ. With alacrity, liveliness, نَبَاهَةً ـ بِبَدَاعَةٍ. Perspicuously, بَيَانًا ـ بِوُضُوحٍ. *See also* Strikingly, *ad.*

Vividness, *n.* Brightness, رَفِيف ـ رَفّ ـ بَرِيق ـ بَهْجَة ـ بَرَقَان ـ لَمَعَان; of a colour, رَفِيف ـ رَفّ ـ نَضَر. Animation, حِدَّة. Acuteness, نَبَاهَة ـ ذَكَاء. *See also* Brightness, *n.*

Vivific, *a.* } Giving life, مُحْيٍ. Re-animating, مُحَيٍّ ـ مُحْيٍ ـ
Vivifical, } مُقَوٍّ. Cheering, سَارٌّ ـ مُفْرِح.

Vivificate, *v.t.* *See to* Vivify, *v.t.*

Vivification, *n.* The act of giving life to, إِحْيَاء; of animating, بَعْث ـ تَقْوِيَةُ قَلْبٍ; of rousing, اِسْتِفْزَاز ـ تَحْرِيض. *See also* Re-animation, *n.*

Vivificative, *a.* *See* Vivific, *a.*

Vivify, *v.t.* To give life to, أَحْيَى ـ أَحْيَا. To revive the spirits of, أَرَاحَ ـ بَعَثَ ـ قَوَّى قَلْبَهُ. *See also to* Revive, *v.t.*

Viviparous, *a.* تَلِدُ أَحْيَاء *pl.* يَلِدْنَ.

Vivisection, *n.* تَشْرِيحُ ٱلْحَيَوَانَاتِ حَيَّةً.

Vixen, *n.* سَلِيطَة ـ سِلْقَة.

Vixenly, *a.* كَٱلسَّلِيطَةِ ـ كَٱلسِّلْقَةِ.

Viz., *conj.* تَرْخِيمُ لَفْظَةِ يَعْنِي أَوْ وَهُوَ.

Vizard, *n.* *See* Visor, *n.*

Vizier, *n.* (More correctly, Wazir,) وَزِير *pl.* وُزَرَاء. The Grand —, ٱلْوَزِيرُ ٱلْأَعْظَمُ ـ ٱلصَّدْرُ ٱلْأَعْظَمُ.

Vizierate, *n.* وَزَارَة ـ وِزَارَة. Grand —, ٱلصَّدَارَةُ ٱلْعُظْمَى ـ صَدَارَة.

Vizierial, *a.* Of the grand Wazir, مِنَ ٱلصَّدَارَةِ ٱلْعُظْمَى. A — letter, مَكْتُوبٌ سَامٍ.

Vocable, *n.* تَعْبِير *pl.* تَعَابِيرُ ـ لَفْظَة *pl.* أَلْفَاظ ـ كَلِمَة *pl.* كَلِمَات.

Vocabulary, *n.* An abridged dictionary, كِتَابُ لُغَةٍ مُخْتَصَرٌ. A list of words, كَلِمَاتٍ (*or* جَدْوَل) سِيَاقَةُ. A — of technical phrases, مَجْمُوعَةُ ٱصْطِلَاحَاتٍ.

Vocal, *a.* Having a voice, ذُو صَوْتٍ; having a sound, ذُو لَحْنٍ. Modulated by the voice, مُطَرَّبٌ بِٱلصَّوْتِ. Vocal music, سَمَاع ـ غِنَاء; of sacred music, تَرْتِيل. Vocal with the praises of..., هَاتِفٌ بِكَذَا.

Vocalist, *n.* مُغَنٍّ *fem.* مُغَنِّيَة.

Vocalize, *v.t.* صَاتَ بِ *aor.* يَصُوتُ ـ صَوَّتَ بِ ـ تَلَفَّظَ ـ لَفَظَ بِ ².

Vocally, *ad.* صَوْتًا ـ لَفْظًا ـ شِفَاهًا.

Vocation, *n.* The act of being called, دَعْوَة ـ دُعِيَ بِهَا ـ دَعْوَة. Business, occupation, صَنْعَة ـ خِدْمَة; an office, وَظِيفَة ـ مَأْمُورِيَّة. Destination, مَقْصُود. Genius, special gift, قَرِيحَة.

Vocative, *a.* Calling, صَائِت ـ مُنَادٍ. The — case, صِيغَةُ ٱلْخِطَابِ ـ صِيغَةُ ٱلنِّدَاءِ.

Vocative, *a.* A noun in the —, مُنَادَى; making in the —, نِدَاء ـ مُنَادَاة.

Vociferate, *v.t.* صَاحَ بِ ² ـ صَيَّحَ بِ ـ صَايَحَ بِ ـ عَيَّطَ بِ. *See also to* Bawl, *v.t.*

Vociferate, *v.i.* فَدَّ ² ـ صَاحَ ² ـ صَيَّحَ ـ عَيَّطَ ـ صَرَخَ ² ـ عَجَّ ² ـ ضَجَّ ². They vociferated to one another, of many, تَصَارَخُوا ـ تَصَايَحُوا.

Vociferation, *n.* فَدِيد ـ صِرَّة ـ ضَجَّة ـ ضَجَاج ـ صُرَاخ ـ صِيَاح ـ عِيَاط. Mutual —, مُصَايَحَة ـ مُصَارَخَة.

Vociferous, *a.* فَدَّاد ـ عَجَّاج ـ صَيَّاح ـ صَرَّاخ ـ صَارِخ ـ عَيَّاط ـ صَيِّت.

Vociferously, *ad.* بِصِيَاحٍ ـ بِصُرَاخٍ .

Vogue, *n.* General acceptance, إِعْتِبَارٌ عُمُومِيٌّ . Fashion, custom, عَادَةٌ . To be in —, to be generally accepted, أُعْتُبِرَ عُمُومًا . This style (of dress) is in — now, هٰذَا ٱلْكَسْمُ ٱلْمَقْبُولُ ـ هٰذَا كَسْمُ ٱلْيَوْمِ . In —, current, usual, مُتَدَاوَلٌ . The language in —, or the colloquial language, ٱلْكَلَامُ ٱلْمُتَدَاوَلُ .

Voice, *n.* صَوْتٌ *pl.* أَصْوَاتٌ ـ حِسٌّ . Mode of expression, نَصٌّ ـ تَلَفُّظٌ ـ عِبَارَةٌ . Sound, tone, لَحْنٌ *pl.* أَلْحَانٌ . Interest, influence, قَوْلٌ ـ حُكْمٌ ـ نُفُوذٌ . Choice, خِيَارٌ . Voice, as of a verb, صِيغَةٌ . Volume of the —, جِرْمُ ٱلصَّوْتِ ـ مَدُّ ٱلصَّوْتِ . Having a rough —, أَجَشُّ ٱلصَّوْتِ . Having a soft —, ذُو صَوْتٍ خَفِيضٍ ; of a woman, رَنِيمٌ . Having a loud —, رَفِيعُ ٱلصَّوْتِ ـ صَيِّتٌ . A low —, صَوْتٌ خَفِيٌّ . Loudness of —, رَفَاعَةُ ٱلصَّوْتِ . Softness of —, رَخَامَةُ ٱلصَّوْتِ . To raise the —, جَهَرَ ٱلصَّوْتَ ـَ . To prolong the —, مَدَّ (or طَوَّلَ) ٱلصَّوْتَ ² . The active —, صِيغَةُ ٱلْمَعْلُومِ . The passive —, صِيغَةُ ٱلْمَجْهُولِ . I have no —, influence, in the matter, لَيْسَ لِي نُفُوذٌ فِي ٱلْأَمْرِ . The — of the people, the public —, أَفْكَارُ ٱلْخَلْقِ ـ أَفْكَارُ ٱلنَّاسِ ـ إِعْتِقَادُ ٱلنَّاسِ ـ قَوْلُ ٱلنَّاسِ . *See also* Suffrage, Vote, *n.*

Voice, *v.t.* To regulate the tone of a voice, طَرَّبَ ٱلصَّوْتَ . To fit for producing sounds, جَعَلَ لِيَأْتِيَ بِصَوْتٍ ـَ .

Voiceless, *a.* عَدِيمُ ٱلصَّوْتِ . *See also* Dumb, *a.*

Voicing, *n.* إِصْلَاحُ ٱللَّحْنِ .

Void, *a.* Empty, فَاضٍ ـ فَارِغٌ ـ خَالٍ ـ خَاوٍ . Destitute of inhabitants, غَيْرُ مَسْكُونٍ ـ خَاوٍ . The being without, wanting, عَدِيمٌ ـ بِلَا ـ مِنْ غَيْرِ كَذَا . Of no binding force, فَاسِدٌ ـ سَقَطٌ ـ بَاطِلٌ . Having no incumbent, خَالٍ ـ فَارِغٌ . Void of counsel, عَدِيمُ ٱلرَّأْيِ . Void of understanding, عَدِيمُ ٱلْعَقْلِ . A conscience — of offence, ضَمِيرٌ بِلَا عَثْرَةٍ . To make —, empty, unoccupied, أَخْلَى ـ فَرَغَ ² ـ فَرَّغَ . To render of no validity, فَسَخَ ـَ ـ نَقَضَ ² ـ أَبْطَلَ . To be —, empty, أَقْفَى ـ خَلَا ² ـ إِسْتَخْلَى . To be null, بَطَلَ ² ـ إِنْتَقَضَ ـ تَعَطَّلَ .

Void, *n.* An empty space, خَلْوَةٌ ـ خَلَاءٌ ـ خَوَاءٌ ; emptiness, فَرَاغٌ ـ فُرُوغٌ ـ خُلُوٌّ .

Void, *v.t.* To send out, أَبْرَزَ ـ إِسْتَبْرَزَ ـ أَخْرَجَ . To leave vacant, to vacate, خَلَّى . To — urine, بَالَ *aor.* يَبُولُ . To — excrement, خَرِئَ ـَ ـ تَغَوَّطَ . To make void; *see under* Void, *a.*

Voidable, *a.* That may be annulled, إِبْطَالُهُ مُمْكِنٌ ـ مِمَّا يُنْتَقَضُ ; that may be evacuated, إِبْرَازُهُ مُمْكِنٌ .

Voidance, *n.* The act of emptying, تَفْرِيغٌ ـ فَرَاغٌ ـ تَخْلِيَةٌ ; of ejecting, إِخْرَاجٌ ـ إِبْرَازٌ ; of annulling, فَسْخٌ ـ إِبْطَالٌ ـ نَقْضٌ .

Voider, *n.* One who ejects, مُخْرِجٌ ـ مُبْرِزٌ ; who annuls, نَاقِضٌ ـ مُبْطِلٌ . A tray, طَبَقٌ ـ صِينِيَّةٌ ـ سَلَّةُ ٱلْأَكْلِ .

Voidness, *n.* Emptiness, خُلُوٌّ ـ فَرْغٌ ـ فَرَاغٌ .

Volant, *a.* طَائِرٌ .

Volatile, *a.* Apt to change, مُتَقَلِّبٌ . Subject to alteration, مُتَغَيِّرٌ ـ مُغَيَّرٌ . Inconstant, مُتَلَوِّنٌ ـ فَرَّارٌ ـ طَائِشٌ ـ مُتَقَلْقِلٌ ـ خَفِيفُ ٱلْمِزَاجِ . Passing off by evaporation, يَتَصَعَّدُ ـ مُتَصَعِّدٌ .

Volatileness, *n.* } **Volatility**, } Disposition to fly off in vapour, قَابِلِيَّةُ ٱلتَّصْعِيدِ . Mutability of mind, تَلَوُّنٌ ـ قِلَّةُ ثَبَاتٍ ـ إِنْقِلَابٌ ـ خِفَّةُ مِزَاجٍ ـ فَرْفَرَةٌ .

Volatilization, *n.* تَصْعِيدٌ .

Volatilize, *v.t.* صَعَّدَ .

Volcanic, *a.* Pertaining to a volcano, مَا نِيطَ بِجَبَلِ ٱلنَّارِ . Acted upon by a volcano, أَثَّرَتْ فِيهِ نَارُ ٱلْبُرْكَانِ .

Volcanist, *n.* مَاهِرٌ فِيمَا نِيطَ بِجِبَالِ ٱلنَّارِ .

Volcano, *n.* جَبَلُ ٱلنَّارِ *pl.* جِبَالُ ٱلنَّارِ ـ *from the Italian,* بُرْكَان *pl.* بَرَاكِينُ *and* بُرَاكِيَّةٌ .

Volition, *n.* إِرَادَةٌ ـ إِخْتِيَارٌ .

Volitive, *a.* مَا نِيطَ بِٱلْإِرَادَةِ .

Volley, *n.* A discharge, emission, إِطْلَاقٌ . A — of musketry, إِطْلَاقُ ٱلْمَكَاحِلِ ; of guns, إِطْلَاقُ ٱلْمَدَافِعِ ; repeated volleys of shotted musketry, إِطْلَاقُ رَصَاصٍ مُتَتَابِعٌ .

Volt, *n.* A circular tread, جَوْلٌ ـ جَوْلٌ ـ دَوْرٌ . Avoidance, as of a thrust, إِجْتِنَابٌ .

Voltaic, *a.* كَهْرَبَائِيٌّ .

Voltaism, *n.* *See* Galvanism, *n.*

Voltameter, *n.* مِيزَانُ قُوَّةِ ٱلْكَهْرَبَائِيَّةِ .

Voltigeur, *n.* إِسْوَارٌ طَيَّارٌ *pl.* أَسَاوِيرُ .

Volubility, *n.* Aptness of being rolled, folded, قَابِلِيَّةُ ٱلْإِنْدِرَاجِ . Fluency of speech, سُهُولَةُ كَلَامٍ ـ بَلَاغَةٌ ـ فَصَاحَةٌ . *See also* Glibness, Talkativeness, *n.*

Voluble, *a.* The being easy to roll up, سَهْلُ ٱلْإِنْدِرَاجِ . Fluent of speech, سَلَّاقٌ ـ مِسْلَاقٌ ـ فَصِيحٌ ـ بَلِيغٌ . *See also* Talkative, Garrulous, *a.*

Volubly, *ad.* بِسُهُولَةٍ ـ بِسُرْعَةٍ ـ بِبَلَاغَةٍ . To speak —, إِنْتَرَسَ ـ سَابَ ـِ فِي ٱلْكَلِمِ ـ ٱللِّسَانَ .

Volume, *n.* A roll, as of parchment, *etc.*, طُومَارٌ *pl.* طَوَامِيرُ . What is included in a roll or book, ٱلْمُنْدَرِجُ . A book, مُجَلَّدٌ *pl.* مُجَلَّدَاتٌ ـ مُصْحَفٌ *pl.* مَصَاحِفُ ـ كِتَابٌ *pl.* كُتُبٌ . Compass or dimension, جِرْمٌ ـ حَجْمٌ ـ جِسْمٌ . Extent, مَدٌّ . Volume of the voice, مَدُّ ٱلصَّوْتِ .

Voluminous, *a.* Large in size, كَبِيرُ ٱلْجِرْمِ ـ كَثِيرُ ٱلْحَجْمِ. Copious, فَيَّاض ـ فَائِض. Extensive, as of a language, وَاسِع. Detailed, going into particulars, مُفَصَّل. A — writer, مُصَنِّف مُبَالِغ.

Voluminously, *ad.* Copiously, اِتِّسَاعًا ـ مِنْ سَعَةٍ ـ وَفْرَةً. In detail, giving details, بِتَفْصِيلٍ ـ تَفْصِيلًا.

Voluminousness, *n.* Copiousness, كَثْرَة ـ غَزَارَة; of a language, سَعَةُ لُغَةٍ. Detail, تَفْصِيل.

Voluntarily, *ad.* عَنْ طِيبِ نَفْسٍ ـ عَنْ ـ تَبَرُّعًا ـ تَطَوُّعًا ـ عَنِ ٱخْتِيَارٍ ـ مِنْ تِلْقَاءِ نَفْسِهِ. He did it —, فَعَلَهُ مِنْ ذَاتِ نَفْسِهِ ـ فَعَلَهُ مِنْ تِلْقَاءِ نَفْسِهِ.

Voluntary, *a.* عَنْ رِضَاءٍ ـ اِخْتِيَارِيّ ـ مُتَبَرِّع.

Volunteer, *n.* One who serves by his own choice, مُتَبَرِّع *pl.* مُتَبَرِّعُون ـ مُتَطَوِّع *pl.* مُتَطَوِّعُون. A — soldier, عَسْكَرِيّ مُخَيَّر (or مُتَطَوِّع) *pl.* عَسَاكِرُ مُخَيَّرَة. Volunteers, of soldiers, عَسَاكِرُ مُتَطَوِّعَة.

Volunteer, *a.* *See* Volunteer, *n.* *first part.*

Volunteer, *v.i.* To offer service voluntarily, تَطَوَّعَ ـ تَبَرَّعَ. They rushed to — for military service, هَرَعُوا لِلتَّطَوُّعِ فِي ٱلْخِدْمَةِ ٱلْعَسْكَرِيَّةِ.

Volunteer, *v.t.* تَطَوَّعَ بِ ـ تَبَرَّعَ بِ.

Voluptuary, *n.* / Voluptuous, *a.* } نَزِيز ـ عَيَّاش ـ رَفِيه ـ رَافِه ـ مُتَرَفِّه ـ مُتَلَذِّذ ـ مُتَنَعِّم ـ شَهْوَانِيّ. To lead a voluptuous life, تَنَعَّمَ مُتَرَفِّهًا. His is a voluptuous life, هُوَ فِي رَفَاهِيَةٍ مِنَ ٱلْعَيْشِ.

Voluptuously, *ad.* نَعِيمًا ـ بِشَهْوَةٍ ـ بِتَلَذُّذٍ ـ تَرَفُّهًا.

Voluptuousness, *n.* نَعِيم ـ تَنَعُّم ـ تَرَفُّه ـ رَفَاهَة ـ رَفَاهِيَة ـ حُبُّ ٱلشَّهَوَاتِ ـ شَهْوَة ـ تَلَذُّذ.

Volute, *n.* In architecture, لَوْلَب *pl.* لَوَالِب. The shell-fish, صَدَف لَوْلَبِيّ *pl.* أَصْدَاف لَوْلَبِيَّة.

Voluted, *a.* لَوْلَبِيّ.

Volution, *n.* دَائِرَة مُلْتَفَّة ـ اِلْتِفَاف.

Vomica, *n.* An abscess in the lungs, دُمَّلَة فِي ٱلرِّئَةِ.

Vomit, *v.i.* اِسْتَقَى ـ اِسْتَسْقَى ـ تَقَيَّأَ ـ اِسْتَفْرَغَ ـ *vulg.* نَتَقَ ². To — just as much as to fill the mouth, قَلَسَ ـ دَسَعَ. To make one to —, أَتْأَ ـ *vulg.* نَتَّقَ.

Vomit, *v.t.* اِسْتَسْقَى بِ ـ تَقَيَّأَ بِ ـ قَذَفَ ـ تَقَيَّأَ ـ أَبْرَزَ ـ أَصْدَرَ ـ أَخْرَجَ. To eject, throw out, أَبْرَزَ ـ أَصْدَرَ ـ أَخْرَجَ. To make to —, أَقَاءَ ـ قَيَّأَ.

Vomit, *n.* The matter ejected from the stomach, قَيْأ ـ قُيَاء. An emetic, دَوَاء مُقَيِّئ ـ *vulg.* دَوَاء مُنَتِّق.

Vomiting, *n.* The act of ejecting from the stomach, اِسْتِقَاء ـ اِسْتِفْرَاغ ـ تَقَيُّؤ ـ دَسْع ـ دُسُوع. Ejecting, pouring forth, إِبْرَاز ـ إِخْرَاج.

Vomitive, *a.* / Vomitory, } مُطَرِّش ـ *vulg.* مُنَتِّق ـ مُقَيِّئ.

Vomitory, *n.* A wide door or outlet, بَاب وَاسِع ـ مَخْرَج وَاسِع. An emetic; *see under* Vomit, *n.*

Voracious, *a.* Very hungry, greedy, بُلَع ـ هِبْلَع ـ مُتَلَغِّس ـ أَكُول ـ لَهِم ـ بَلَّاع. *See also* Ravenous, *a.*

Voraciously, *ad.* بِحِرْصٍ ـ بِشَرَهٍ ـ بِقَرَمٍ.

Voraciousness, *n.* / Voracity, } حِرْص ـ شَرَه ـ قَرَم. *See also* Ravenousness, Rapaciousness, *n.*

Vortex, *n.* A whirlpool, دُوَّارُ ٱلْمَاءِ ـ دُوَّامَةُ ٱلْمَاءِ ـ دُرْدُور. A thing which it is difficult to escape, وَرْطَة *pl.* وِرَاط.

Vortical, *a.* دَوَّار.

Votaress, *n.* A female devoted to any service, عَابِدَة *pl.* عَابِدَات.

Votarist, *n.* / Votary, } عَابِد *pl.* عَابِدُون or عُبَّاد. *See also* Devotee, Follower, *n.*

Vote, *n.* Opinion, رَأْي *pl.* آرَاء. A wish, رِضَاء ـ مُرَاد. Vote, of money, *etc.*, to . . ., مَبْلَغ مُخَصَّص لِكَذَا ـ تَخْصِيصُ ٱلدَّرَاهِمِ لِكَذَا. Having a deciding —, ذُو قَوْلٍ فَاصِلٍ. A majority of votes, أَكْثَرِيَّةُ ٱلْآرَاءِ. *See also* Suffrage, *n.*

Vote, *v.i.* To express one's opinion, بَيَّنَ رَأْيَهُ. To exercise the suffrage, أَعْطَى رَأْيَهُ فِي ٱلْاِنْتِخَابِ.

Vote, *v.t.* To grant by vote, to set anything apart to, خَصَّصَ لِ ـ عَيَّنَ لِ. He voted, decided, in his mind that . . ., قَرَّرَ فِي نَفْسِهِ أَنْ. To give one's vote to, اِنْتَخَبَ ـ أَعْطَى رَأْيَهُ لِ. *See also under* Suffrage, *n.*

Voter, *n.* صَاحِبُ صَوْتٍ ـ حَائِزُ حَقِّ ٱلْاِنْتِخَابِ ـ صَاحِبُ رَأْيٍ.

Votive, *a.* نَذْرِيّ.

Votively, *ad.* نَذْرًا ـ بِٱلنَّذْرِ.

Vouch, *v.t.* To attest, شَهِدَ بِ ². To certify, نَعِمَ بِ ². To call one to witness to, أَشْهَدَ عَلَى. To guarantee, حَقَّقَ ـ ضَمِنَ ² ـ تَكَفَّلَ بِ.

Vouch, *v.i.* شَهِدَ ²: He vouched for the truth of the matter, أَثْبَتَ (or حَقَّقَ) ٱلْأَمْرَ ـ شَهِدَ بِحَقِّ ٱلْأَمْرِ ².

Vouchee, *n.* مُسْتَشْهَد.

Voucher, *n.* One who gives witness, شَاهِد *pl.* شُهُود. A paper confirmatory of anything, بَيِّنَة *pl.* بَيِّنَات ـ ثَبَت *pl.* أَثْبَات ـ حُجَّة *pl.* حُجَج. A guarantor, كَفِيل *pl.* كُفَلَاء ـ ضَامِن ـ ضَمِين.

Vouchsafe, *v.t.* To bestow, مَنَحَ = ـ وَهَبَ ل *aor.* يَهَبُ ـ أَعْطَى. To give to, out of kindness, أَنْعَمَ عَلَى-ب ـ أَكْرَمَ عَلَى-ب. To — help, أَغَاثَ. To concede, أَجَابَ ب. God vouchsafed to him a son, رَزَقَهُ ٱللّٰهُ ٱبْنًا [2]. *See also to* Permit, *v.t.*

Vouchsafe, *v.i.* To condescend, deign, to, تَنَازَلَ ل ـ تَوَاضَعَ ل.

Vouchsafement, *n.* A grant in favour, إِكْرَام ـ رِزْق ـ إِنْعَام. A concession, إِجَابَة. Aid, defence, إِغَاثَة.

Vow, *n.* نَذْر *pl.* نُذُور. A solemn promise, عَهْد *pl.* عُهُود. Anything dedicated, as to God, *etc.*, نَذِيرَة. To pay one's vows, وَفَى نُذُورَهُ. To break one's vows, خَالَفَ نُذُورَهُ; to break one's promises, خَانَ عَهْدَهُ [2].

Vow, *v.t.* To consecrate by promise, to dedicate to, نَذَرَ-ل [2]. To — to, promise to, وَعَدَ-ب *aor.* يَعِدُ ـ أَوْعَدَ-ب.

Vow, *v.i.* To make a vow, نَحَبَ [2] ـ نَذَرَ نَذْرًا [2] ـ تَنَذَّرَ عَلَى كَذَا. He vowed, promised, that …, عَهِدَ أَن ـ وَعَدَ أَن *aor.* يَعِدُ ـ أَلْزَمَ نَفْسَهُ ب.

Vowed, *pass. part.* Set apart, consecrated, مَنْذُور.

Vowel, *n.* حَرَكَة *pl.* حَرَكَات. A — point, شَكْل *pl.* أَشْكَال. To affix vowel points to, شَكَلَ [2].

Vowel, *a.* Having a sound, صَوْتِيّ ـ ذُو صَوْتٍ.

Vox, *n.* Sound, صَوْت. Tongue, language, لِسَان. *Vox populi vox Dei*, إِتِّفَاقُ أَلْسُنِ ٱلْأُمَّةِ بِمَقَامِ أَمْرِ ٱللّٰهِ. *Vox et preterea nihil*, صَوْتٌ فَقَطْ ـ حِسٌّ لَا غَيْرَ.

Voyage, *n.* A single —, سَفْرَة *pl.* سَفَرَات; in a collective sense, سَفَر *pl.* أَسْفَار. A sea —, سَفَرٌ فِي ٱلْبَحْرِ ـ قُلْعَة. The account of a —, ذِكْرُ سَفَرٍ. Expenses of a —, مَصْرُوفُ ٱلسَّفَرِ. To take a — to, سَافَرَ إِلَى. To be prevented, from any cause, from taking a — or a journey, قُطِعَ بِفُلَانٍ. He took a long —, journey, سَافَرَ سَفَرًا بَعِيدًا.

Voyage, *v.i.* To sail on the sea, رَكِبَ ٱلْبَحْرَ ـ أَبْحَرَ ـ أَقْلَعَ.

Voyager, *n.* مُسَافِر *pl.* مُسَافِرُون ـ سَافِر *pl.* سُفَّار. A great —, مِسْفَر ـ مِسْفَار.

Vulcan, *n.* إِسمُ مَعْبُودٍ قِيلَ أَنَّهُ يُعَالِجُ ٱلْمَعَادِنَ.

Vulcanian, *a.* *See* Plutonian, *a.*

Vulcanize, *v.t.* To harden India-rubber, جَوْهَرَ ٱلصَّمْغَ ٱلْمَغِيطَ.

Vulcanized, *a.* مُجَوْهَر.

Vulgar, *a.* Commonly used, current, مُسْتَفَاض ـ دَارِج ـ سَائِر. Low, دَنِيء [2] ـ خَسِيس. General, عَامّ ـ عَلَى لِسَانِ ٱلنَّاسِ. The — tongue, ٱللِّسَانُ ٱلدَّارِجُ. The — or common people, ٱلْعَوَامّ. Vulgar fractions, كُسُورَات. A — error, غَلَطٌ عَامٌّ.

Vulgarism, *n.* عِبَارَةٌ لُغَوِيَّةٌ ـ عِبَارَةُ ٱلْعَوَامِّ.

Vulgarity, *n.* دَنَاءَة [2] ـ خَسَاسَة ـ خُشُونَة ـ عَدَمُ لَطَافَةٍ ـ قِلَّةُ أَدَبٍ.

Vulgarize, *v.t.* To make vulgar, common, current, دَرَّجَ-بَيْنَ ـ أَشَاعَ ٱسْتِعْمَالَهُ عِنْدَ ٱلنَّاسِ ـ ٱلنَّاسِ.

Vulgarly, *n.* Commonly, عُمُومًا ـ فِي ٱلْغَالِبِ ـ عِنْدَ ٱلْعَوَامِّ. Rudely, meanly, بِدَنَاءَةٍ [2] ـ بِخَسَاسَةٍ ـ بِخُشُونَةٍ ـ بِعَدَمِ لَطَافَةٍ ـ بِلَا أَدَبٍ.

Vulgate, *n.* تَرْجَمَةُ ٱلْكُتُبِ ٱلْمُقَدَّسَةِ فِي ٱللُّغَةِ ٱللَّاتِينِيَّةِ.

Vulnerability, *n.* } Vulnerableness, } إِمْكَانُ ٱلتَّجْرِيحِ ـ إِمْكَانُ ٱلْجَرْحِ ـ إِمْكَانُ ٱلْإِنْجِرَاحِ.

Vulnerable, *a.* يَنْجَرِحُ ـ جَرْحُهُ مُمْكِنٌ.

Vulnerary, *a.* نَافِعٌ لِلْجُرُوحِ ـ نَافِعٌ لِلْجَرْحِ.

Vulpine, *a.* Pertaining to the fox, ثَعْلَبِيّ ـ مَا نِيطَ بِٱلثَّعْلَبِ. *See also* Crafty, *a.*

Vulture, *n.* نَسْر *pl.* أَنْسُر. The white carnivorous — of Egypt, رَخَم *pl.* رَخَمَة *and* رُخُم.

Vulturine, *a.* } Vulturish, } نَسْرِيّ ـ مِثْلَ ٱلنَّسْرِ. *See also* Rapacious, *a.*

Vulva, *n.* بُدْع. The — of beasts, ثَفْر ـ ثُفْر. The two sides of the —, ٱلشُّفْرَانِ ـ ٱلْأَشْعَرَانِ ـ ٱلْأَسْكَتَانِ *or* ٱلْإِسْكَتَانِ.

Vying, *n.* مُسَامَاة ـ مُغَايَرَة ـ مُنَافَسَة.

Vying, *a.* خَاثِر ـ مُنَافِس ـ مُفَاضِل.

W.

Wabble, *v.i.* As in walking, تَرَجَّجَ ـ تَمَيَّجَ ـ ـ مَاجَ. To — about, as of anything loose, تَرَعْرَعَ ـ تَذَبْذَبَ. The tooth became loose and wabbled about, تَرَعْرَعَتِ ٱلسِّنُّ. To — about as a saddle on a horse's back, زَلِقَ ـ زَحْلَقَ ـ ـ زَحَلَ.

Wabble, *n.* Of the walk, مِشْيَةُ ٱلْبَطِّ ـ تَرَجُّج ـ تَمَيُّج ـ مَيْج.

Wad, *n.* As for fire-arms, لِبْدَة *pl.* لِبْدَات. A tuft, bundle, بَاقَة ـ شُوشَة.

Wad, *v.t.* Of fire-arms, لَبَّدَ ـ ـ جَعَلَ ٱللِّبْدَةَ فِي. To put cotton wadding into a dress, *etc.*, بَطَّنَ ـ بَطَّنَ ـ بِقُطْنٍ ـ حَشَا *aor.* يَحْشُو ـ قُطْنًا.

Wadding, *n.* As for dresses, of cotton, *etc.*, حَشْوَة (*or* حَشْوٌ) مِنْ قُطْنٍ; for fire-arms, لِبْدَات.

Waddle, *v.i.* مَشَى مِشْيَةَ ٱلْبَطِّ. *See also to* Wabble, *v.i.*

Waddler, *n.* }
Waddling, *a.* } مَاشٍ مِشْيَةَ ٱلْبَطِّ ـ مَيَّاح.

Wade, *v.t.* and *i.* To wade through, of water, *etc.*, خَاضَ *aor.* يَخُوضُ ـ خَوْض ـ إِخْتَاضَ ـ تَخَوَّضَ: They waded through the water with their beasts, خَاضُوا ٱلْمَآءَ (*or* فِي ٱلْمَآءِ) بِدَوَابِّهِمْ. The horses waded, or waded through, the water, خَاضَتِ ٱلْخَيْلُ ٱلْمَآءَ. He waded into the discourse, خَاضَ فِي ٱلْحَدِيثِ. He waded, or plunged, into the affair, خَاضَ فِي ٱلْأَمْرِ. He waded through the book, خَاضَ ٱلْكِتَابَ. To make to —, أَخَاضَ: I made my beast to wade through the water, أَخَضْتُ فِي ٱلْمَآءِ دَابَّتِي.

Wader, *n.* Of a bird, طَيْرٌ خَوَّاض.

Wafer, *n.* As for letters, بُرْشَانَة *coll.* بَرَاشِين. Wafer-bread, رُقَاقَة. *See also under* Host, *n.*

Wafer, *v.t.* خَتَمَ ـ بِبُرْشَانٍ.

Waffle, *n.* The cake, رُقَاقَة.

Waft, *v.t.* طَارَ بِ ـ ـ حَمَلَ ـ سَيَّرَ ـ سَارَ بِ *aor.* يَسِيرُ ـ أَسْبَحَ.

Waft, *v.i.* *See to* Float, *v.i.*

Wag, *v.t.* To shake, هَزَّ. To wag the tail, بَصْبَصَ (*or* تَبَصْبَصَ) بِذَنَبِهِ. To — the head, هَزَّ رَأْسَهُ ـ ـ نَغَضَ رَأْسَهُ. To — the tongue, نَضْنَضَ لِسَانَهُ.

Wag, *v.i.* To move about, to and fro, ـ ـ خَفَقَ ـ تَذَبْذَبَ ـ تَحَرَّكَ ـ إِخْتَفَقَ. To let one's tongue wag, إِنْتَرَشَ لِسَانَهُ.

Wag, *n.* A droll fellow, مِرِّيح *pl.* مَرْحَى ـ مُهَرِّج ـ رَجُلٌ خَلِيع ـ نَكَّات ـ مُضْحِك. A — of the head, نَغْضُ ٱلرَّأْسِ.

Wage, *n.* *See* Wages, *n.*

Wage, *v.t.* To lay a wager with, رَاهَنَ. To carry on, أَجْرَى ـ أَقَامَ. To — war with, حَارَبَ ـ ضَارَبَ: They waged war with one another, of many, تَحَارَبُوا ـ إِحْتَرَبُوا.

Wager, *n.* خَطَر *pl.* أَخْطَار ـ سَبَق *pl.* أَسْبَاق ـ مُرَاهَنَة. An offer to make oath of innocence, عَرْضُ تَبَرُّؤٍ مِنَ ٱلتُّهْمَةِ بِيَمِينٍ. To lay a — with, for, خَاطَرَ ـ عَلَى. He laid me a —, and I laid him a —, أَخْطَرَ لِي وَأَخْطَرْتُ لَهُ.

Wager, *v.t.* and *i.* رَاهَنَ ـ أَخْطَرَ: He wagered the property, أَخْطَرَ ٱلْمَالَ. I wagered with such an one for such a thing, رَاهَنْتُ فُلَانًا عَلَى كَذَا.

Wagerer, *n.* مُخَاطِر ـ مُرَاهِن.

Wages, *n.* جُعْل ـ جِعَالَة ـ جُعَالَة *pl.* جَعَائِل ـ عِمْلَة ـ عُمْلَة ـ عُمَالَة ـ خِدْمَة ـ حَقُّ ٱلْخِدْمَةِ ـ كِرَآء ـ أُجْرَة. "Say, I ask no wages of you for this, neither am I one of those who intermeddle," قُلْ مَا أَسْأَلُكُمْ عَلَيْهِ مِنْ أَجْرٍ وَمَا أَنَا مِنَ ٱلْمُتَكَلِّفِينَ (Kur. xxxviii. 86).

Waggery, *n.* فَكَّة ـ فُكَاهَة ـ مُزَاحَة ـ مَزْح ـ مَزَّة ـ مَسْخَرَة.

Waggish, *a.* خَلِيع ـ فَكِه ـ مُضْحِك. *See also under* Wag, *n.*

Waggishly, *ad.* بِفُكَاهَةٍ ـ بِمِزَاحٍ ـ بِهَزْلٍ ـ بِخَلَاعَةٍ.

Waggishness, *n.* *See* Waggery, *n.*

Waggle, *v.i.* *See to* Wabble, *to* Reel, *v.i.*

Wagon, *n.* عَرَبَانَة ـ عَرَبَانَةُ ٱلْحُمُولِ *pl.* عَرَبَانَات.

Wagon, *v.t.* نَقَلَ ـ فِي عَرَبَانَةٍ.

Wagoner, *n.* عَجَّال ـ مُدَبِّرُ ٱلْعَرَبَانَةِ ـ سَائِقُ ٱلْعَرَبَانَةِ.

Wagoning, *n.* نَقْلَانٌ فِي عَرَبَانَةٍ.

Wag-tail, *n.* The bird, دُعْرَة ـ هَزَازُ ٱلذَّنَبِ.

Waif, *n.* لُقَاطَة *pl.* لُقَاطَات. Waifs and strays, لُقَاطَاتٌ سَائِبَاتٌ.

Wail, *v.i.* تَوَيَّلَ ـ وَلْوَلَ ـ بَكَى ـ ـ. To — for, بَكَى عَلَى ـ ـ نَاحَ عَلَى ـ نَحَبَ ـ ـ بَكَى ـ ـ. *See also to* Lament, *v.t.* and *i.*

Wail, *n.* }
Wailing, } عَوِيل ـ نَوْح ـ وَلْوَلَة ـ بُكَآء. *See also* Lamentation, *n.*

Wailing, *a.* نَائِح ـ بَاكٍ. A — woman, نَوَّحَة *pl.* نِسَآءٌ أَنْوَاح.

Wailful, *a.* مَكْرُوب ـ حَزِين ـ كَئِيب ـ مَغْمُوم.

Wailingly, *ad.* بِعَوِيلٍ ـ بِوَلْوَلَةٍ ـ بِنِيَاحَةٍ.

Wain, *n*. Charles's —, اَلدُّبُّ ٱلْأَكْبَرُ. *See also* Wagon, *n*.

Wain-rope, *n*. حَبْلُ (or حِزامُ) ٱلْعَرَبَانَةِ.

Wainscot, *n*. فَرْوَازٌ ـ تَخْشِيبَةٌ.

Wainscot, *v.t.* فَرْوَزَ ـ رَكَّبَ فِي ـ تَخْشِيبَةً ـ خَشَّبَ.

Waist, *n*. Of the body, خَصْرٌ ـ حَقْوٌ ـ وَسَطٌ; of a ship, وَسَطُ ٱلْمَرْكَبِ. Having a slender —, مُخَصَّرٌ ـ مُخْتَنِقٌ.

Waistband, *n*. حِزَامٌ *pl*. أَحْزِمَةٌ *and* حِزَامَاتٌ ـ زُنَّارٌ *pl*. زَنَانِيرُ. A — with a pocket for money, كَمَرٌ. A — or belt such as is worn by servants, سَبْتَةٌ. A rich —, or girdle, such as is worn by wealthy women, حِيَاصَةٌ *pl*. حَوَائِصُ. A running —, تِكَّةٌ *pl*. تِكَكٌ. To put a — on one, زَنَّرَ; or one's self, تَزَنَّرَ.

Waistcoat, *n*. صُدَيْرِيٌّ *pl*. صُدَيْرِيَّاتٌ ـ صِدَارٌ ـ صُدْرِيَّةٌ *pl*. صَدَارِي. A strait —, صُدْرَةٌ لِضَبْطِ ٱلْمَجَانِينِ.

Waister, *n*. On board a ship, نَاطُورٌ بَحْرِيٌّ مَحَلُّهُ فِي وَسَطِ مَرْكَبٍ.

Waist-wrapper, *n*. إِزَارٌ *pl*. آزِرَةٌ *and* أُزُرٌ. The part of the — which is tied round the waist, حُبْكَةٌ ـ حِبَاكٌ. To put on or wear a —, إِيتَزَرَ ـ تَأَزَّرَ ـ تَأَزَّرَ بِإِزَارٍ.

Wait, *v.i.* To stay, stop, وَقَفَ *aor*. يَقِفُ ـ مَكَثَ ² ـ تَوَقَّفَ. To — at table, خَدَمَ ٱلسُّفْرَةَ ². *See also to* Stay, *v.i.*

To wait for, look for with expectation, رَقَبَ ² ـ إِرْتَقَبَ ـ تَرَقَّبَ ـ إِنْتَظَرَ ـ إِنْتَظَرَ لِ ـ إِسْتَأْنَى ـ إِسْتَأْنَى عَلَى.

To wait on, to serve, خَدَمَ ².

To wait upon, to attend upon one, حَضَرَ عِنْدَهُ ² ـ تَحَضَّرَهُ ـ إِحْتَضَرَهُ.

To keep one waiting, خَلَّى يَسْتَأْنِي ـ وَقَّفَ ـ تَعَوَّقَ ـ عَوَّقَ.

Wait, *v.t.* *See foregoing, and also to* Await, *v.t.*

Wait, *n*. An ambush, رَصَدٌ ـ كَيْدٌ. To lie in — for, رَصَدَ ² ـ أَرْصَدَ. To lay —, to set an ambush, رَاصَدَ ـ تَرَصَّدَ لِ.

Waiter, *n*. A table servant, خَادِمُ ٱلسُّفْرَةِ *pl*. خُدَّامٌ. A tray, صِينِيَّةٌ *pl*. صَوَانِي. Call the —, أُدْعُ خَادِمَ ٱلسُّفْرَةِ.

Waiting, *n*. As in expectation, إِنْتِظَارٌ ـ إِرْتِقَابٌ. Serving, service, خِدْمَةٌ.

Waiting-maid, *n*. }
Waiting-woman, } مَاشِطَةٌ *pl*. مَوَاشِطُ ـ جَارِيَةٌ *pl*. جَوَارٍ.

Waits, *n*. مُغَنُّونَ يَطُوفُونَ ٱلْأَزِقَّةَ فِي لَيَالِي عِيدِ ٱلْمِيلَادِ.

Waive, *v.t.* فَاتَ *aor*. يَفُوتُ ـ تَرَكَ ² ـ نَزَلَ عَن ـ تَنَازَلَ عَن.

Waiver, *n*. تَرْكٌ ـ فَوَاتٌ.

Wake, *v.t.* As from sleep, نَبَّهَ مِنَ ٱلنَّوْمِ ـ أَهَبَّ مِنَ ٱلنَّوْمِ ـ يَقَّظَ ـ أَيْقَظَ ـ فَيَّقَ. To rouse, إِسْتَفَزَّ ـ أَنْفَسَ ـ أَنْهَضَ. *See also to* Awake, *v.t.*

Wake, *v.i.* To be awake, يَقِظَ ـ تَيَقَّظَ ـ إِسْتَيْقَظَ ـ إِنْتَبَهَ (or هَبَّ ² مِنَ ٱلنَّوْمِ). To be aroused, إِنْتَبَهَ ـ إِنْتَهَضَ.

Wake, *n*. The furrow made by a ship in the water, شَقُّ ٱلسَّفِينَةِ ـ مَخَرٌ (or أَبْخَرُ) ـ مَجْرُ ٱلْمَرْكَبِ. To follow in the — of, as of a ship, سَارَ عُقْبَ ٱلْمَرْكَبِ ـ خَلْفَ ٱلسَّفِينَةِ. To follow in the — of, to imitate, تَمَثَّلَ بِ. Wake, the sitting up with a dead body, سَهَرُ ٱللَّيْلِ عِنْدَ ٱلْمَيِّتِ.

Wakeful, *a*. Not sleepy, بَعِيثٌ ـ سَهْرَانُ ـ سَاهِرٌ. Watchful, vigilant, مُسْتَيْقِظٌ ـ مُتَيَقِّظٌ ـ مُنْتَبِهٌ ـ حَذِرٌ. *See also* Sleepless, *a*.

Wakefully, *ad*. With sleeplessness, بِسُهَادٍ ـ سَاهُورًا. Watchfully, بِٱحْتِذَارٍ ـ بِٱنْتِبَاهٍ.

Wakefulness, *n*. سَاهُورٌ ـ سُهَادٌ ـ أَرَقٌ ـ سُهَادٌ ـ سَهَدٌ. *See also* Vigilance, *n*.

Waken, *v.t.* *See to* Wake, *to* Awake, *v.t.*

Wale, *n*. The mark of a rod or whip, حَبْرٌ ـ حِبَارٌ ـ حَبَارٌ ـ حُبُورٌ *pl*. حَبَرٌ ـ حَبَطٌ ـ حَدَبٌ ـ أَثَرُ ٱلضَّرْبِ *pl*. آثَارٌ; a bleeding —, عَلَبٌ *pl*. عُلُوبٌ. A streak in cloth, خَطٌّ *pl*. خُطُوطٌ *and* أَخْطَاطٌ ـ قَلَمٌ *pl*. أَقْلَامٌ. The wales of a ship, دُفُوفُ ٱلْمَرْكَبِ مِنْ مُقَدَّمِهِ إِلَى مُؤَخَّرِهِ. His skin was covered with wales, or scars, حُبِرَ جِلْدُهُ.

Wales, *n*. The province, أَقْلِيمُ وِيلْسَ ٱلْوَاقِعُ فِي ٱلْجِهَةِ ٱلْغَرْبِيَّةِ مِنْ جَزِيرَةِ إِنْكِلْتِيرَا وَهُوَ مُشْتَمِلٌ عَلَى عَشَرِ وِلَايَاتٍ. His Royal Highness the Prince of Wales, سَعَادَةُ ٱلْبِرِنْس أُفْ وِيلْس وَهُوَ وَلِيُّ عَهْدِ ٱلدَّوْلَةِ ٱلْإِنْكِلِيزِيَّةِ.

Walk, *v.i.* To march on foot, سَعَى *aor*. يَسْعَى ـ رَجِلَ ـ تَرَجَّلَ ـ خَطَا *aor*. يَخْطُو ـ سَارَ *aor*. يَسِيرُ ـ تَسَيَّرَ ـ مَشَى. To take a walk, تَسَيَّرَ. To — quickly, أَغَارَ ـ هَاجَ. To — with short steps and quickly, حَتْحَتَ ـ دَفَّ عَلَى ٱلْأَرْضِ. To — lightly, خَفَّ فِي سَيْرِهِ. To — leisurely, أَرْوَدَ ـ نَبَجَ. To — behind or after one, تَلَا *aor*. يَتْلُو ـ تَبِعَ. To make one to —, أَمْشَى ـ مَشَّى. "Have they feet to walk with?" أَلَهُمْ أَرْجُلٌ يَمْشُونَ بِهَا (Kur. vii. 194).

To walk down, as down a descent, نَزَلَ رَاجِلًا. He walked down from the mountain, هَبَطَ ² مِنَ ٱلْجَبَلِ رَاجِلًا. To walk one down, to beat in walking, غَلَبَ فِي ٱلْمَشْيِ.

To walk in, دَخَلَ ². To ask one to walk in, تَرَجَّاهُ بِٱلدُّخُولِ.

To walk off, decamp, إِنْسَلَّ ـ إِنْفَلَتَ.

To walk off with, carry off, seize, مَضَى بِ ـ خَطِفَ ـ إِخْتَلَسَ.

To walk out, خَرَجَ ².

To walk up, صَعِدَ ـ إِرْتَقَى ـ تَرَقَّى.

To walk up and down, تَرَدَّدَ.

Walk, *v.t.* To pass over ground, مَشَى ـ قَطَعَ. To make

to walk, مَشَى ـ أَمْشَى. To —, as a horse, up and down to show him off to spectators, أَشَارَ ـ شَوَّرَ ـ ² شَارَ.

Walk, *n.* The act of walking, سَعْيٌ ـ سَيْرٌ ـ سِيرَة *pl.* سِيَر ـ مَشْيٌ. Gait of walk, مِشْيَة. A place for walking, مَسْيَار. Course, conduct, سِيرَة. A journey, stroll, مَسِيرَة. A pasture, مَرْعًى ـ مَرْعَاة. To go out for a —, خَرَجَ يَتَسَيَّرُ ² ـ *vulg.* خَرَجَ يَتْبَسَّطُ.

Walker, *n.* مَاشٍ *pl.* مُشَاة ـ رَجَّالَة *and* رُجْلَان *pl.* رَجِيل *or* رَجُل. A good —, رَجَّال. A shop —, نَاظِرُ دُكَّانٍ. A street —, a prostitute, سَوَّقَة ـ قَحْبَة *pl.* قِحَاب.

Walking, *n.* The act of; *see* Walk, *n.*

Walking-stick, *n.* عَصًا *pl.* عِصِيٌّ.

Wall, *n.* جِدَار *pl.* جُدْرَان ـ حَائِط *pl.* حِيطَان. The —, as of a town, سُور *pl.* أَسْوَار. A — round a fort, بَدَنُ قَلْعَةٍ. The base or side of a —, جِدَار *pl.* جُدُور. A — round a garden, or a walled garden, مُحَجَّر. A fence, جِدَار ـ حَائِط *pl.* حَوَائِطُ. Wooden walls, ships, دُونَنْمَا ـ سُفُن ـ مَرَاكِبُ. The walls which divide Paradise from Hell, الأَعْرَاف. Walls have ears, (*prov.*) لِلْحِيطَانِ آذَانٌ ـ لِكُلِّ سَاقِطَةٍ لَاقِطَةٌ *lit.* Every word spoken is picked up. To climb over, of a —, تَسَلَّقَ ـ تَسَوَّرَ عَلَى ـ تَسَوَّرَ. To take the —, to walk by the side of it, مَشَى جَانِبَ الحَائِطِ ɔ. To go to the —, to be disappointed, خَابَ *aor.* يَخِيبُ; to be the loser, خَسِرَ ɔ; to be overcome, إِنْغَلَبَ; to come to ruin, هَلَكَ ɔ.

Wall, *v.t.* To inclose anything with a wall, جَدَرَ حَوْلَهُ ² ـ سَوَّرَ حَوْلَهُ. He walled, or walled in, his vineyard, حَوَّطَ كَرْمَهُ. To — up, سَدَّ ² ـ سَدَّ بِجِدَارٍ ².

Wallachia, *n.* الأَفْلَاق.

Walled, *a.* ذُو سُورٍ ـ مُحْتَاطٌ بِجِدَارٍ ـ مُسَوَّر. A — city, مَدِينَةٌ ذَاتُ سُورٍ ـ مَدِينَةٌ حَصِينَةٌ. A — garden, مُحَجَّر ـ حَائِط *pl.* حَوَائِطُ ـ حَدِيقَة *pl.* حَدَائِقُ.

Wallet, *n.* A travelling bag, مِزْوَد ـ عَيْبَة ـ صَفْنَة ـ صُفْن. A beggar's —, شَلَّاق. A pocket-book, خَرِيطَة *pl.* خَرَائِطُ.

Wall-eye, *n.* عَيْنٌ زَرْقَاءُ.

Wall-eyed, *a.* أَزْرَقُ العَيْنِ *fem.* زَرْقَاءُ *pl.* زُرْق.

Wall-flower, *n.* مَنْثُور. The yellow —, الخِيرِيُّ.

Wall-fruit, *n.* ثَمَرٌ عَرِيشِيٌّ ـ ثَمَرُ أَشْجَارٍ تَعْتَرِشُ عَلَى جِدَارٍ.

Wall-plate, *n.* On which the joists rest, جَائِز *pl.* جُوزَان. A broad board inserted between layers of brick, stone, or mortar, عَارِضَة *pl.* عَوَارِضُ ـ عَرَقَة.

Wallop, *v.t.* To thrash, ضَرَبَ ـ سَاطَ ² ـ *vulg.* سَوَّطَ.

Walloping, *n.* ضَرْبُ عَصًا ـ ضَرْبُ سَوْطٍ.

Walloping, *a.* Big, جَسِيم ـ عَظِيم ـ كَبِير.

Wallow, *v.i.* To roll about, تَقَلَّبَ. To — in, تَمَرَّغَ فِي ـ خَاضَ فِي *aor.* يَخُوضُ. To — in blood, تَمَرَّغَ فِي الدَّمِ. To — in vice, إِنْهَمَكَ فِي الخَلَاعَةِ ـ تَمَرَّغَ فِي الفِسْقِ وَالفَسَادِ.

Wallower, *n.* One who wallows, مُتَمَرِّغ ـ مُتَقَلِّب.

Walnut, *n.* جَوْز *pl.* أَجْوَاز ـ جَوْزَة *pl.* جَوْزَات (called in some parts of Arabia خُشْف *coll.* خَشْفَة). A — tree, شَجَرَةُ الجَوْزِ ـ جَوْزَة. Walnut wood, خَشَبُ الجَوْزِ ـ شِيز.

Walrus, *n.* عِجْلُ البَحْرِ ـ فَرَسُ البَحْرِ.

Waltz, *n.* ضَرْبٌ مِنَ الرَّقْصِ.

Waltz, *v.i.* رَقَصَ ².

Wamble, *v.i.* جَاشَتْ نَفْسُهُ ɔ.

Wampum, *n.* سُمُوطُ وَدَعَاتٍ رَائِجَةٌ بِمَقَامِ السِّكَّةِ عِنْدَ هَمَجِ أَمِيرِكَا.

Wan, *a.* Pale, haggard, مُصْفَارّ ـ شَاحِب ـ خَاسِف. To be —, شَحَبَ ². To feel —, مَذِلَ ɔ. *See also* Languid, *a.*

Wand, *n.* مِخْصَرَة *pl.* مَخَاصِرُ ـ قَضِيب *pl.* قُضْبَان ـ عَصًا *pl.* عِصِيٌّ.

Wander, *v.i.* To rove, عَارَ *aor.* يَعِيرُ ـ عَالَ *aor.* يَعِيلُ ـ سَاحَ *aor.* يَسِيحُ. To lose one's way, طَاحَ ² ـ تَاهَ ² ـ تَطَوَّحَ ـ تَطَيَّحَ. To — or deviate from, زَاغَ عَنْ ² ـ اِعْتَسَفَ عَنْ ـ حَادَ عَنْ ɔ ـ عَدَلَ ɔ عَنْ. To err, ضَلَّ ɔ ـ غَوَى. To — or go away from, غَابَ ɔ عَنْ. To — in the mind, طَاشَ ɔ; in talk, أَهْتَرَ. He has wandered from the right way, ضَلَّ عَنْ سَوَاءِ السَّبِيلِ ɔ. To cause one to —, lose the way, أَتَاهَ; to cause one to deviate from, أَزَاغَ; to cause to err, أَضَلَّ. "O, our Lord, cause not our hearts to wander," رَبَّنَا لَا تُزِغْ قُلُوبَنَا (Kur. iii. 6).

Wanderer, *n.* / Wandering, *a.* } A rover, roving, سَيَّاح ـ عَيَّار ـ عَائِر. A — from duty, ضَالّ *pl.* ضَالُّون ـ غَوِيّ. Wandering or strolling peoples, نَوَاقِل.

Wandering, *n.* Roving, عِيَار ـ سِيَاحَة ـ تَطَوُّح. Deviation from duty, ضَلَال. Roving of the thoughts, طَيْش ـ طَيَشَان; in talk, هُتْرَة.

Wane, *v.i.* To decrease, diminish, إِنْتَقَصَ ـ إِنْقَرَضَ ـ زَالَ *aor.* يَزُولُ ـ أَخَذَ فِي الزَّوَالِ ².

Wane, *n.* Diminution, أَخْذٌ فِي الزَّوَالِ ـ زَوَال ـ إِنْقِرَاض. The — of the moon, مُحَاقُ (*or* مِحَاقُ) القَمَرِ. "And at the — [or waning] of the stars," وَإِدْبَارَ النُّجُومِ (Kur. lii. 49).

Waning, *a.* On the wane, of fortune, *etc.*, فِي حَوْرٍ. What is vain is —, البَاطِلُ فِي حَوْرٍ.

Wanly, *ad.* بِٱصْفِرَارٍ ـ بِشُحُوبٍ.

Wanness, *n.* شُحُوب ـ شُحُوبَة ـ مَذْل. *See also* Paleness, *n.*

Want, *n.* Lack, non-possession, عَدَم ـ عُدْم. Deficiency, قِلَّة ـ نُقْصَان ـ مَآرِب *pl.* مَأْرَبَة. Necessity, لُزُوم ـ إِقْتِضَاء ـ ضَرُورَة ـ ضَرُورِيَّة ـ إِضْطِرَار. Exigency, an object of want, a needful, requisite thing, حَاجَة *coll.* حَاجّ *pl.* حَاجَات. A wish, إِشْتِيَاق ـ وُدّ ـ مُرَاد. Penury, فَقْر ـ إِحْتِيَاج ـ خَلَّة ـ حَوْبَة ـ عَوَز ـ ضِيقَة ـ فَقْر وَفَاقَة. A thing by which a want is supplied, سِدَاد. According to the local wants, حَسَبَ ٱلْإِحْتِيَاجَاتِ ٱلْمَحَلِّيَّة. *See also* Need, *n.*

For want of such a thing, لِقِلَّةِ كَذَا ـ لِعَدَمِ كَذَا. For want of money, لِعَدَمِ ٱلدَّرَاهِمِ.

In want, مُحْتَاج. In want of, مُحْتَاجٌ إِلَى.

To be free from want, تَغَانَى ـ تَغَنَّى ـ إِسْتَغْنَى ـ غَنِيَ.

To be in want, كَانَ فِي حَالِ ٱلْفَقْرِ ـ إِحْتَاجَ.

To be in want of, عَازَ ـ إِحْتَاجَ إِلَى ـ إِفْتَقَرَ إِلَى *aor.* يَعُوزُ. I am in want of the thing, عَازَنِي ٱلشَّيْءُ. To be in no want of, إِسْتَغْنَى عَنْ ـ غَنِيَ عَنْ.

To die of want, مَاتَ مِنْ جُوعِهِ.

To feel the want of, حَسَّ بِضَرُورَةِ ٱلشَّيْءِ. To miss, إِفْتَقَدَ.

To keep out want from one's self, or, to make provision against want on one's own part, سَدَّ أَبْوَابَ ٱلْإِحْتِيَاجِ عَنْ نَفْسِهِ.

To supply a want, stand in place of, سَدَّ مَسَدَّ كَذَا ـ قَامَ مَقَامَ كَذَا.

To supply the wants of one, جَبَرَ ٱحْتِيَاجَهُ ـ مَلَأَ ٱحْتِيَاجَهُ.

Want, *v.t.* To desire, إِشْتَاقَ إِلَى ـ وَدَّ ـ أَرَادَ. To be destitute of, فَقَدَ ـ عَدِمَ ـ يَعُوزُ *aor.* عَازَ. To have occasion for, أَعْوَزَ ـ إِحْتَاجَ إِلَى. What do you —? مَا حَاجَتُكَ. What do you — of it or him? مَا حَاجَتُكَ إِلَيْهِ ـ مَا إِرْبُكَ إِلَيْهِ.

I wanted a thing, such a thing, of him, أَرَدْتُ مِنْهُ كَذَا. I do not — it, مَا لِي فِيهِ إِرْبٌ (or حَاجَةٌ). I — a thing of such an one, لِي عِنْدَ فُلَانٍ حَاجَةٌ. Take what you —, خُذْ حَاجَتَكَ. To make one to —, to be without, أَعْدَمَ. To be wanted, أُحْتِيجَ إِلَى. Such an one was wanted, أُحْتِيجَ إِلَى فُلَانٍ. "And they wanted but little of not doing it," وَمَا كَادُوا يَفْعَلُونَ (Kur. ii. 66).

Wanted, *a.* Necessary, ضَرُورِيّ ـ مُقْتَضًى ـ لَازِم. Sought after, asked for, مَطْلُوب. Missing, مَفْقُود ـ فَقِيد.

Wanting, *a.* Absent, غَائِب. Deficient, نَاقِص. Missing, مَفْقُود. Not having, عَدِيمٌ مِنْ. The thing was —, was not forthcoming, عَوِزَ ٱلشَّيْءُ. To be — in good manners, كَانَ قَلِيلَ ٱلْأَدَبِ.

Wantless, *a.* شَبْعَان ـ مَوْفُور ـ غَيْرُ مُحْتَاجٍ إِلَى شَيْءٍ.

Wanton, *a.* Roving in sport, خَلِيع ـ هَزِل ـ لَعُوب ـ عِبِّيث. Flying loosely, fluttering, خَافِق. Headstrong, مُتَهَوِّر. Dallying, غَزِل. Licentious, شَقِيّ ـ فَاسِق ـ فَاجِر ـ دَاعِر. Leading a luxurious life, مُتْرَف ـ مُتَنَعِّم. Behaving with insolence, exultation, *etc.*, بَطِر. Using freedom to excess, مُتَرَخِّص ـ فَلَتَان. Wanton eyes, عُيُونٌ غَامِزَاتٌ. A — act, بَطَر.

Wanton, *n.* A lewd person, فَاجِر *fem.* فَاجِرَة ـ دَاعِر *fem.* دَاعِرَة. *See also* Whore, *n.*

Wanton, *v.i.* To sport, لَعِبَ ـ إِنْخَلَعَ ـ عَبِثَ. To flutter, as in the wind, خَفَقَ. To live luxuriously, تَنَعَّمَ ـ تَرَفَّهَ. To be licentious, تَدَعَّرَ ـ دَعِرَ ـ فَسَقَ. To act in an unjust, boastful, insolent manner, بَطِرَ. To —, as with a woman, in an amatory manner, غَازَلَ.

Wantonly, *ad.* Sportively, هَزْلًا ـ مَزْحًا. Flutteringly, بِخَفَقَانٍ. Lasciviously, بِفُجُورٍ ـ بِدَعَارَةٍ. In a headstrong, unjust, or boastful manner, بِبَطَرٍ. To act —, unjustly, towards, بَطِرَ عَلَى. "And were God to bestow abundance upon His servants they might act wantonly in the earth," وَلَوْ بَسَطَ ٱللّٰهُ ٱلرِّزْقَ لِعِبَادِهِ لَبَغَوْا فِي ٱلْأَرْضِ (Kur. xlii. 26).

Wantonness, *n.* Sport, هَزْل ـ لَعِب ـ عَبَث ـ مَزْح. The being headstrong, تَهَوُّر. Harsh injustice, outrage, بَطَر. Licentiousness, فِسْق ـ فُجُور ـ خَلَاعَة ـ دَعَارَة. Absence of restraint, عَدَمُ ٱلتَّقَيُّدِ ـ فُرُط ـ فَلَت. Dalliance, غَزَل.

War, *n.* حَرْب *pl.* حُرُوب ـ مُحَارَبَة *pl.* مُحَارَبَات. Contest, battle, قِتَال ـ مَعْرَكَة. Involved in —, مُتَهَوِّرٌ فِي حَرْبٍ. The thickest of the —, or fight, حَوْمَةُ (or رَحَى) ٱلْحَرْبِ. The removal of the —, or of the thickest of the —, from one place to another, تَحْوِيلُ رَحَى ٱلْحَرْبِ مِنْ جِهَةٍ إِلَى جِهَةٍ أُخْرَى. In time of war, وَقْتَ ٱلْحَرْبِ ـ فِي أَثْنَاءِ ٱلْحَرْبِ. The — became vehement, قَامَتِ ٱلْحَرْبُ عَلَى سَاقٍ. Should — break out between them, إِنْ شَبَّتِ ٱلْحَرْبُ بَيْنَهُمْ. He will not go to — for, or, in the interests of such an one, لَا يُحَارِبُ بِخُصُوصِ فُلَانٍ. A — party, حِزْبُ ٱلْحَرْبِ. On a — footing, عَلَى هَيْئَةِ ٱلْحَرْبِ: He put all the military force on a — footing, جَعَلَ جَمِيعَ ٱلْقُوَّةِ ٱلْعَسْكَرِيَّةِ فِي هَيْئَةِ ٱلْحَرْبِ.

Civil war, مُحَارَبَةٌ دَاخِلِيَّةٌ ـ حَرْبٌ أَهْلِيَّةٌ.

Contraband of war, أَمْوَالٌ حَرْبِيَّةٌ مَمْنُوعَةٌ.

Council of war, دِيوَانُ حَرْبٍ.

Declaration of war, إِعْلَانٌ بِٱلْحَرْبِ.

Defensive war, مُحَارَبَةٌ دِفَاعِيَّةٌ.

Foreign wars, القِتَالُ خَارِجَ ٱلْمَمْلَكَةِ.

Maritime war, مُحَارَبَةٌ بَحْرِيَّةٌ.

Minister of war, نَاظِرُ ٱلْحَرْبِيَّةِ.

Ministry of war, نَظَارَةُ ٱلْحَرْبِيَّةِ.

Offensive war, حَرْبُ هُجُومٍ.

Open war, مُحَارَبَةٌ جِهَارًا.

Righteous war, حَرْبٌ عَادِلَةٌ.

Rules of war, أُصُولٌ حَرْبِيَّةٌ.

Science of war, الفُنُونُ ٱلْحَرْبِيَّةُ.

Stratagem of war, خُدْعَةٌ حَرْبِيَّةٌ. Stratagems in war, مَضَارِبُ.

Theatre of a war, دَارُ ٱلْحَرْبِ ـ مَحَلُّ ٱلْمُحَارَبَةِ ـ رَحَى ٱلْحَرْبِ ـ مَرْكَزُ ٱلْحَرْبِ.

War materials, مُهِمَّاتُ ٱلْحَرْبِ.

To declare war, أَعْلَنَ بِٱلْحَرْبِ.

To involve one in a war, رَبَكَ فِي حَرْبٍ [2]. To be involved in a war, اِرْتَبَكَ فِي حَرْبٍ.

To kindle a war, أَثَارَ ٱلْحَرْبَ ـ أَضْرَمَ نَارَ ٱلْحَرْبِ. The war was kindled, تَضَرَّمَتِ ٱلْحَرْبُ.

To make war upon, حَارَبَ.

To prepare for war, اِسْتَعَدَّ لِلْحَرْبِ ـ عَدَّ لِلْحَرْبِ [2]. Prepared for war, عَتِيدٌ لِلْقِتَالِ.

To undertake a war, تَشَبَّثَ بِٱلْحَرْبِ ـ غَزَا aor. يَغْزُو.

War, v.i. حَارَبَ ـ جَاهَدَ ـ غَزَا aor. يَغْزُو. To be in a state of opposition to, شَاجَرَ ـ خَالَفَ. You fight and war, تُخَاصِمُونَ وَتُحَارِبُونَ.

Warble, v.t. and i. تَرَنَّمَ ـ تَغَرَّدَ ـ أَغْرَدَ ـ غَرَّدَ ـ غَرِدَ [4].

Warble, n. }
Warbling, } تَرَنُّمٌ ـ تَرْنِيمٌ ـ تَغْرِيدٌ ـ تَغَرُّدٌ ـ غَرَدٌ.

Warbler, n. }
Warbling, a. } مُتَرَنِّمٌ ـ غِرِّيدٌ ـ مُغَرِّدٌ ـ غَرِدٌ.

Ward, n. The act of guarding, مُحَافَظَةٌ ـ حِفْظٌ ـ حِرْسٌ. Guard made by a weapon, a fence, دَوْرُ ٱلْمُحَافَظَةِ. A watch, guard, حَارِسٌ pl. حَرَسٌ ـ vulg. غَفَرٌ. A fortress, حِصْنٌ ـ قَلْعَةٌ. A district or division of a town, حَارَةٌ pl. حَارَاتٌ ـ مَحَلَّةٌ pl. مَحَلَّاتٌ. Imprisonment, custody, حَبْسٌ ـ مَحْبَسٌ. A — of a lock, سِنُّ قُفْلٍ pl. أَسْنَانٌ. A — of a hospital, بَيْتٌ فِي مُسْتَشْفًى pl. بُيُوتٌ. A person under a guardian, قَاصِرٌ pl. قُصَّرٌ ـ يَتِيمٌ pl. أَيْتَامٌ.

Ward, v.i. تَحَفَّظَ ـ اِجْتَنَبَ ـ تَحَبَّسَ. See also to Fend, v.i.

Ward, v.t. To ward off, thrust aside, جَنَّبَ ـ جَنَبَ [2] ـ أَجْنَبَ. To repel, رَدَّ [2] ـ دَفَعَ [4].

Warden, n. A keeper, مُحَافِظٌ. Warden, as of a university, رَئِيسٌ ـ مُدَبِّرٌ. Lord Warden, كَبِيرُ ٱلْمُحَافِظِينَ.

Wardenship, n. وَظِيفَةُ ٱلْمُحَافِظِ.

Warder, n. A keeper, مُحَافِظٌ. A — of a prison, سَجَّانٌ. See also Truncheon, n.

Wardmote, n. مَجْلِسٌ مَحَلِّيٌّ ـ مَشْوَرَةٌ مَحَلِّيَّةٌ.

Wardrobe, n. As for keeping clothes, صِوَانٌ ـ صُوَانٌ pl. أَصْوِنَةٌ ـ دُولَابُ ٱلْمَلْبُوسِ ـ خِزَانَةُ ٱلْمَلْبُوسِ ـ صُنْدُوقُ ٱللُّبْسِ. Wearing apparel, ثِيَابٌ ـ مَلْبُوسٌ ـ أَلْبِسَةٌ.

Wardroom, n. دِيوَانُ ثُنْيَةِ ٱلضُّبَّاطِ (or ٱلْيُوزْبَاشِيَّةِ) فِي مَرْكَبٍ حَرْبِيٍّ.

Wardship, n. Guardianship, مُحَافَظَةٌ ـ صِيَانَةٌ. Care and protection, as of a ward, وَكَالَةٌ ـ وِصَايَةٌ.

Ware, n. A chattel, سِلْعَةٌ pl. سِلَعٌ ـ مَتَاعٌ ـ شَيْءٌ pl. أَشْيَاءُ. Wares, سِلَعٌ ـ أَمْتِعَةٌ ـ أَمْتِعَةٌ وَأَشْيَاءُ ـ أَسْبَابٌ. Small wares, خُرْدَةٌ pl. خُرْدَوَاتٌ. A dealer in petty wares, خُرْدَجِي.

Ware, v.t. See to Wear, v.t.

Warehouse, n. مَخْزَنٌ pl. مَخَازِنُ ـ حَاصِلٌ pl. حَوَاصِلُ.

Warehouse, v.t. خَزَنَ [2].

Warfare, n. حَرْبٌ ـ مُحَارَبَةٌ ـ تَجَنُّدٌ.

War-horse, n. حِصَانٌ لِلْحَرْبِ.

Warily, ad. بِتَحَفُّظٍ ـ بِٱحْتِرَاسٍ ـ بِحَذَرٍ.

Wariness, n. تَحَفُّظٌ ـ اِحْتِرَاسٌ ـ تَحَذُّرٌ ـ حِذْرٌ.

Warlike, a. Pertaining to war, حَرْبِيٌّ. Liking war, مُحِبُّ ٱلْحَرْبِ. Suited to war, جَدِيرٌ بِٱلْحَرْبِ. Warlike preparations, الاِسْتِعْدَادَاتُ ٱلْحَرْبِيَّةُ. Founded on — designs, مَبْنِيٌّ عَلَى مَقَاصِدَ حَرْبِيَّةٍ.

Warlock, n. See Wizard, n.

Warm, a. Having heat, سُخْنٌ ـ حَارٌّ ـ حَامٍ ـ سَخِينٌ ـ مُسَخَّنٌ. Warm, of temperature, سُخْنَانٌ ـ سَخْنَانٌ. Warm, of a room, or of clothes, دَفِيءٌ [4]. Ardent, حَارٌّ ـ حَامٍ ـ مُلْتَهِبٌ. Vehement, zealous, حَمِسٌ ـ حُمْسٌ pl. أَحْمَسُ ـ غَيْرَانُ ـ كَثِيرُ ٱلرَّغْبَةِ ـ غَيُورٌ pl. غُيُرٌ. A — room, بَيْتٌ دَفِيءٌ [4]. A — garment, ثَوْبٌ دَفِيءٌ ـ أَدْفَاءٌ [4] pl. دِفَاءٌ [4]. A — day, يَوْمٌ دَفِيءٌ [4]. A — night, لَيْلَةٌ دَفِيئَةٌ. Warm water, مَاءٌ سُخْنٌ. A — bath, حَمَّامٌ سُخْنٌ. To be —, to feel —, دَفِيَ [4] ـ دَفُؤَ [2] ـ تَدَفَّأَ. He wore — clothing to protect himself from the cold, دَفِيَ مِنَ ٱلْبَرْدِ [4] ـ تَدَفَّأَ بِٱلثَّوْبِ ـ اِسْتَدْفَأَ بِٱلثَّوْبِ. To — one's self, تَدَفَّأَ ـ اِسْتَدْفَأَ. The room became —, دَفِئَ ٱلْبَيْتُ ـَ. The night became —, دَفُؤَتِ ٱللَّيْلَةُ. To be —, ardent, حَمِسَ ـَ حَمِيَ ـَ إِحْتَمَى. To be —, of water, the sun, fire, *etc.*, سَخُنَ ². To be —, ardent, about, وَلِعَ ب *aor.* يَوْلَعُ.

Warm, *v.t.* To make warm, سَخَّنَ ـ أَحْمَى ـ أَسْخَنَ; of a garment keeping one warm, أَدْفَأَ. To make ardent, earnest, شَوَّقَ ـ أَنْهَضَ ـ أَنْفَسَ ـ حَرَّضَ ـ أَوْلَعَ ـ رَغَّبَ.

Warm, *v.i.* To become heated, سَخُنَ ² ـ دَفِئَ ـَ. To become ardent, animated, حَمِيَ ـَ تَشَوَّقَ ـ حَمِسَ ـَ تَحَمَّسَ. To become warm, impassioned, by, وَلِعَ ب *aor.* يَوْلَعُ.

Warm-hearted, *ad.* مُحِبٌّ ـ وَدُود ـ وِدٌّ.

Warming-pan, *n.* آلَةٌ مِنْ نُحَاسٍ لِإِدْفَاءِ ٱلْفِرَاشِ.

Warmly, *ad.* With ardour, بِغَيْرَةٍ ـ بِحَرَارَةٍ ـ بِحَمَاسَةٍ; with affection, بِمَحَبَّةٍ ـ بِوِدَادٍ; strongly, بِشِدَّةٍ; with strong desire, passion, بِوَلَعٍ.

Warmness, *n.* } Moderate heat, حَرَارَة ـ سُخُونَة; as of clothes
Warmth, } or a room, دَفْءٌ ـ دَفَآءَة ـ دِفْءٌ. Heat, enthusiasm, حَرَارَة ـ رَغْبَة ـ غَيْرَة ـ حَمَاسَة. Warmth of passion, حُمَيَّا. Strength, force, قُوَّة ـ شِدَّة.

Warn, *v.t.* To give caution to, حَذَّرَ ـ نَبَّهَ ـ أَنْذَرَ. To admonish, خَبَّرَ ـ أَخْبَرَ ـ نَاصَحَ ـ نَصَحَ ـَ يَعِظُ *aor.* وَعَظَ. To give notice to, أَبْلَغَ. To threaten, هَدَّدَ ـ أَوْعَدَ. To — one about, أَنْظَرَ ـ ب. To — one against, نَبَّهَ ـ عَلَى. To be warned, admonished, إِتَّعَظَ. They were warned, made to know, were inspired with, أُوحِيَ إِلَيْهِمْ ب. Who hath warned, told you, to run away, مَنْ أَرَاكُمْ أَنْ تَهْرُبُوا. I do not cease to — him, لَمْ أَفْتُرْ عَنْ أَنْ أُنْذِرَهُ. "And did we not prolong your days that whoever would be warned might be warned therein?" أَوَلَمْ نُعَمِّرْكُمْ مَا يَتَذَكَّرُ فِيهِ مَنْ تَذَكَّرَ (Kur. xxxv. 34).

Warner, *n.* نَاصِح ـ وَاعِظ ـ مُنَبِّه ـ مُنْذِر. "Though we had sent warners among them," وَلَقَدْ أَرْسَلْنَا فِيهِمْ مُنْذِرِينَ. (Kur. xxxvii. 70).

Warning, *n.* A caution, نَصِيحَة ـ إِنْذَار ـ تَنْبِيه. A notice, إِعْلَام ـ خَبَر. An example, عِبْرَة. The taking — by way of admonition, إِعْتِبَار. Warnings, threats, تَهْدِيد ـ إِخْطَار. To give —, notice, أَخْبَرَ. To give — to one to quit, أَعْلَمَهُ أَنْ يَتَحَوَّلَ. To take —, notice given, دَرَى ـَ تَعَرَّفَ ل. To take —, to be cautioned by, إِعْتَبَرَ ب. Let that be a — to you, يَكُونُ ذٰلِكَ عِبْرَةً لَكَ. He took — from the past, إِعْتَبَرَ بِمَا مَضَى. The fortunate man is he who takes — by others; the unfortunate man is he by whom others take —, (prov.) السَّعِيدُ مَنِ ٱعْتَبَرَ بِغَيْرِهِ وَٱلشَّقِيُّ مَنِ ٱعْتَبَرَ بِهِ غَيْرُهُ.

Warp, *n.* Of cloth, أَسْتِيّ ـ أُمِدَّة ـ سَتًى ـ سَتَاة ـ سَدًى. A towing rope, لَبَان ـ قِيَامَة ـ قِيَام ـ سَدَاة.

Warp, *v.i.* To become curved, bent, تَقَوَّسَ ـ إِعْوَجَّ ـ تَعَوَّجَ ـ إِنْعَوَجَ. To be warped, towed, of a vessel, إِنْسَحَبَ ـ إِنْجَرَّ. To become twisted, تَلَوَّى ـ إِلْتَوَى.

Warp, *v.t.* To bend, make crooked, قَوَّسَ ـ عَوَّجَ. To twist, لَوَى ـَ لَوَّى. To tow, جَرَّ ² ـ سَحَبَ ـَ. To prepare the warp of webs for weaving, for one's self, تَسَدَّى ٱلثَّوْبَ ـ سَتَّى ٱلثَّوْبَ; for another person, أَسْتَى ٱلثَّوْبَ ـ سَدَّى ٱلثَّوْبَ. To distort a meaning, حَرَّفَ ـ صَحَّفَ ـ عَكَسَ ـَ.

Warped, *a.* Bent, مُتَقَوِّس ـ مُعَوَّج ـ مُتَعَوِّج; of the mind, أَعْوَجُ.

Warrant, *n.* An instrument investing one with certain rights, فِرْمَان ـ إِرَادَة ـ بَرَاوَات *pl.* بَرَاة ـ بَرَاآت *pl.* بَرَآءَة. A legal —, permission, مَسَاغ شَرْعِيّ. An authorization, أَمْر ـ تَفْوِيض. A — of agency, بَرَآءَةُ وَكَالَةٍ. Permission, إِجَازَة ـ رُخْصَة ـ إِذْن. A — to arrest one, أَمْرٌ بِٱلْحَبْسِ. A death —, أَمْرٌ بِٱلْقَتْلِ. The — or warranting of an article of sale by the seller, ضَمَانُ ٱلدَّرَكِ. To issue a —, أَصْدَرَ أَمْرًا. To give a — to one, to authorize, سَوَّغَ ـ فَوَّضَ إِلَى ـ ٱلْأَمْرَ.

Warrant, *v.t.* To authorize, صَرَّفَ ـ فِي ـ فَوَّضَ إِلَى ـ ٱلْأَمْرَ ـ مَكَّنَ قَدَّرَ ـ عَلَى. To permit, جَوَّزَ ـ إِتَّسَعَ ل ـ سَوَّغَ. To guarantee, تَكَفَّلَ ب ـ ضَمِنَ ـَ تَعَهَّدَ ب. To — an article of sale, so that the seller is bound to make it good, or to indemnify the purchaser, ضَمِنَ ٱلدَّرَكَ ـَ. I — you that it will be good, أَنَا ضَامِنٌ لَكَ أَنَّهُ يَكُونُ جَيِّدًا. Warranted, as an article of sale, مُضَمَّنُ ٱلدَّرَكِ.

Warrantable, *a.* Justifiable, جَائِز.

Warrantableness, *n.* جَوَاز.

Warrantably, *ad.* بِجَوَازٍ ـ بِٱلْحَلَالِ.

Warrant-officer, *n.* ضَابِطٌ بَحْرِيٌّ حَائِزٌ رُتْبَةَ ٱلْمُلَازِم.

Warranty, *n.* Guarantee, كَفَالَة; a paper of —, سَنَدُ كَفَالَةٍ. *See also under* Warrant, *n.*

Warren, *n.* For rabbits, غِيطُ ٱلْأَرَانِبِ. An inclosure for animals, زَرِيبَة.

Warrior, *n.* A military man, غُزَاة *pl.* غَازٍ ـ إِبْنُ حَرْبٍ ـ غُزَّاء ـ بَاسِل ـ أَبْطَال *pl.* بَطَل. A brave soldier, مُحَارِب ـ عَسْكَرِيٌّ *pl.* مَقَادِيمُ *pl.* مِقْدَام ـ بُسْل.

Wars, *n.* (Incorrectly written "Waras,") وَرْس, the *Memecylon*

Tinctorium, a yellow dye, thus described by Arab authorities:— It is a plant like the sesame, which is sown in al-Yáman, and yields a yellow dye. It is also used in the composition of the غُمْرَة (a liniment used by brides). It is said to be a كُرْكُم or bastard-saffron. In the *al-Kámús* it is described as a substance of a pale red colour resembling powdered saffron; also, that it is brought from al-Yáman and is obtained from certain trees there, probably the رِمْث, or dwarf tamarisk, and the عَرْعَر, that is, the cypress or the Abyssinian juniper.

Wart, *n.* A — on the body, ثُؤْلُولَة ـ ثَآلِيلُ *pl.* ثُؤْلُول. To have warts, ثُؤْلِلَ. Warts came out on his body, تَثَأْلَلَ جَسَدُهُ. *See also under* Protuberance, *n.*

Warty, *a.* Like a wart, مِثْلَ ٱلثُّؤْلُولِ. Having warts, مُتَثَأْلِل.

War-whoop, *n.* نِدَآء ٱلْحَرْبِ.

Wary, *a.* مُحْتَذِر ـ مُتَنَبِّه ـ حَذِر. To be —, حَذِرَ ـ اِحْتَذَرَ.

Was, *v.i., pret. of to* Be, كَانَ. Who is and who was, ٱلْكَائِنُ وَٱلَّذِى كَانَ. He was and now is not, كَانَ وَلَيْسَ ٱلْآنَ. He knew not what it was, لَمْ يَعْرِفْ مَا هُوَ. It was his, كَانَ لَهُ. Thus it was, هٰكَذَا كَانَ.

Wash, *v.t.* To cleanse by water, غَسَلَ. To — much, غَسَّلَ. To — one's self, اِغْتَسَلَ. To gargle, تَغَرْغَرَ ب ـ غَرْغَرَ. To —, as with gold or silver, مَوَّهَ. To be washed, اِنْغَسَلَ; as with a coating of metal, تَمَوَّهَ. A basin to — one's self in, طَشْت ٱلْغَسِيلِ. Water for washing, مَآء لِلْغَسْلِ ـ غَسُول. Water in which one has washed, غُسَالَة. A place in which one washes himself, مُغْتَسَل. "Stamp with thy foot, this is a place to wash in, cool, and [also] a beverage," أُرْكُضْ بِرِجْلِكَ هٰذَا مُغْتَسَلٌ بَارِدٌ وَشَرَابٌ (Kur. xxxviii. 41).

To wash away, as a colour, in washing, أَبْلَى ـ بِٱلْغَسْلِ. To wear away, as water stones, *etc.*, أَبْلَى. To carry away, as of a current, جَرَّفَ ـ جَرَفَ. To be washed away, as by a current, اِجْتَرَفَ ـ جُرِفَ. The torrents washed it away, جَرَفَتْهُ ٱلسُّيُولُ. To wash away, to wash one from, غَسَلَ ـ مِن.

To wash down, to wash, clean up, نَظَّفَ ـ غَسَلَ. To make a thing to be swallowed easily with something, أَسَاغَ ـ بِ.

To wash off, to clear off by washing, غَسَلَ ـ مِنْ كَذَا. To take off, as gilding, etc., by washing, أَبْلَى ـ بِٱلْغَسْلِ.

To wash out, as a colour, *etc.*; *see* To wash away.

To wash up; *see* To wash down.

Wash, *v.i.* To wash one's self, اِغْتَسَلَ. Not to lose colour by washing, لَا يَبْلَى لَوْنُهُ بِٱلْغَسْلِ. To — out, of a colour, يَبْلَى لَوْنُهُ بِٱلْغَسْلِ. To wash off, to become clean by washing, يَتَنَظَّفُ بِٱلْغَسْلِ. To wash for, to be laundress to, كَانَتْ غَسَّالَةً لِ.

Wash, *n.* The act of washing, غَسْل; of washing one's self, غُسْل ـ اِغْتِسَال. A single —, غَسْلَة. A lotion, غِسْل ـ غِسْلَة ـ شُطْفَة. The alluvial matter of a river, جُرْف ـ (جُرُف *or*) نَهْرٍ. A quantity of things washed, غَسِيل. A coat, as of metal, طِلَآء ـ مَآء. A — for the head, غِسْلَة ـ غِسْل. A marsh, fen, غَيْل *pl.* غُيُول ـ بَطِيحَة *pl.* بَطَائِحُ. To send clothes to the —, بَعَثَ ٱلْغَسِيلَ إِلَى ٱلْغَسَّالِ.

Washball, *n.* قَالِبُ (طَابَة *or*) صَابُونٍ ـ صَابُونَة.

Washboard, *n.* حَاجِزٌ مِنْ خَشَبٍ أَوْ غَيْرِهِ.

Washer, *n.* One who washes, غَسَّال. A — of a bolt, *etc.*, لِكَاز ـ فَرَاوِيلَة. A — of the dead, غَاسِل. A — in a bath, دَلَّاك.

Washed, *a.* As with water, مَغْسُول ـ غَسِيل. A — garment, غُسَالَة.

Washer-woman, *n.* غَسَّالَة.

Washhand-basin, *n.* طَشْت *pl.* طُشُوت.

Wash-house, *n.* مَغْسَل.

Washing, *n.* Washed clothes, غَسِيل ـ غِسْلِين ـ غُسَالَة. "And" they shall have "no food but the washings," (or what is washed off the flesh of the inmates of hell, or what flows from their skins, such as purulent matter,) وَلَا طَعَامٌ إِلَّا مِنْ غِسْلِينٍ (Kur. lxix. 36).

Wash-leather, *n.* جِلْدٌ نَاعِمٌ خَفِيفٌ.

Wash-stand, *n.* مَائِدَةُ ٱلْمُرْجِفَانِ ـ طَاوِلَةُ ٱلطَّشْتِ وَٱلْإِبْرِيقِ *pl.* مَوَائِدُ.

Washtub, *n.* مِغْسَل ـ إِجَّانَة ـ مِرْكَن ـ مِخْضَب ـ مِرْحَاض ـ قَيْقَاب.

Washy, *a.* Watery, مَائِيّ ـ مَاوِيّ. Weak, ضَعِيف.

Wasp, *n.* زُنْبُورَة *coll.* زُنْبُور *pl.* زَنَابِيرُ.

Waspish, *a.* Like a wasp, مِثْلَ ٱلزُّنْبُورِ. Snappish, شَرِس ـ شَكِس. Having a slender waist, أَهْيَفُ ٱلْخَصْرِ *fem.* هَيْفَآء ـ مُخَفَّفُ ٱلْخَصْرِ.

Waspishly, *ad.* بِشَكَاسَةٍ ـ بِشَرَاسَةٍ ـ بِوَعْقَةٍ.

Waspishness, *n.* شَكَاسَة ـ شَرَاسَة ـ وَعْقَة.

Wassail, *n.* مُنَادَمَة ـ عَيْش وَعِشْرَة.

Wassail, *v.i.* نَادَمَ ـ *vulg.* سَقَى ٱلْعَبَقَةَ.

Waste, *v.t.* To destroy by violence, خَرَّبَ ـ أَخْرَبَ. To weaken, أَضْعَفَ. To injure, as of the health, أَفْتَرَ ـ هَبَطَ ـ أَضْعَفَ. To expend needlessly, to squander, سَرَفَ ـ أَسْرَفَ ـ أَذْهَبَ ـ أَتْلَفَ ـ أَزَالَ ـ بَذَّرَ. To —, as one's time, أَضَاعَ ـ ضَيَّعَ. To cause to — away, of the flesh, to emaciate, أَضْنَى.

Waste, *v.i.* To dwindle, نَقَصَ ² — تَنَقَّصَ — إِنْتَقَصَ. To disappear gradually, فَنِيَ ². To — away, تَلِفَ ² — ذَهَبَ ². To — away, to become emaciated, خَلَّ لَحْمُهُ ² — اِضْطَنَى — ضَنِيَ ². — إِضْمَحَلَّ — اِخْتَلَّ لَحْمُهُ — ذَهَبَ لَحْمُهُ ². To — away to nothing, زَالَ *aor.* يَزُولُ.

Waste, *a.* Destroyed, مُخَرَّب — خَرَاب. Desolate, desert, خَالٍ — خَاوٍ — بَرِّيّ. Not cultivated, غَيْرُ مَفْلُوحٍ. Void, uninhabited, خَالٍ — خَاوٍ. Superfluous, زَائِد — فَاضِل. Waste paper, سَقَطُ الأَوْرَاقِ — *vulg.* وَرَق بَوَار. Waste land, بَرِّيَّة — أَرْض بَرِّيَّة. To lay —, خَرَّبَ.

Waste, *n.* Consumption, تَلَف — إِتْلَاف. Squandering, إِسْرَاف. Destruction, as of property, havoc, خَرَاب — دَمَار — خَسَارَة. A desolate country, region, بَرِّيَّة *pl.* بَرَارِيّ — صَحَارِيّ *pl.* صَحْرَاء.

Waste-book, *n.* دَفْتَرُ مُسَوَّدَةٍ.

Wasteful, *a.* مُضَيِّع — مُتْلِف — مُبَذِّر — مِضْيَاع. "For the wasteful are the brothers of the devils, and the devil was ungrateful to his Lord," إِنَّ ٱلْمُبَذِّرِينَ كَانُوا إِخْوَانَ ٱلشَّيَاطِينِ وَكَانَ ٱلشَّيْطَانُ لِرَبِّهِ كَفُورًا (Kur. xvii. 29).

Wastefully, *ad.* إِسْرَافًا — إِتْلَافًا — بَذَرَقَةً.

Wastefulness, *n.* إِتْلَاف — بَذْرَقَة — إِسْرَاف.

Waster, *n.* مِتْلَاف — مِنْفَاق.

Watch, *v.t.* To observe, look at or after, أَشَافَ إِلَى — نَظَرَ إِلَى ² — دَقَّ ٱلنَّظَرَ إِلَى ². To guard, رَقَبَ ² — حَرَسَ ² — خَفَرَ ² — خَفَرَ. He watched, or watched for, their words and actions, تَرَصَّدَ أَقْوَالَهُمْ وَأَفْعَالَهُمْ.

Watch, *v.i.* To keep watch by night, not to sleep, سَهِرَ ². To —, as of a patrol, عَسَّ ² — إِعْتَسَّ. To — for, look out for, رَقَبَ ² — رَصَدَ ² — تَرَصَّدَ — إِرْتَصَدَ — إِرْتَقَبَ — تَرَقَّبَ. To wait for, إِنْتَظَرَ. To — over, حَرَسَ ² — خَفَرَ ². He is watching for the death of his father that he may inherit his property, يَرْقُبُ مَوْتَ أَبِيهِ لِيَرِثَهُ. He passed the night watching for the appearance of the stars, بَاتَ يَرْقُبُ ٱلنُّجُومَ ². He watched for an opportunity to do them an ill turn, تَرَبَّصَ بِهِمِ ٱلشَّرَّ.

Watch, *n.* A — of the night, هَزِيعٌ مِنَ ٱللَّيْلِ (said to mean one, two, or three hours of the night). Forbearance of sleep, سَهَر. A watchman, نَاطِر — خَفِير — نَاطُور. A —, turn, as of men on duty, نَوْبَة. Time of a —, turn, مُدَّةُ ٱلنَّوْبَةِ. A sentinel, حَارِس — خَفَر — *vulg.* غَفَر — نَوْبَتْجِي. A night —, watchman, عَاسّ *pl.* عَسَس — عَسَّاس — عَسَس *pl.* عُسَّاس. Attention, تَقَيُّد — مُلَاحَظَة — إِمْعَان — نَظَر. A pocket timepiece, سَاعَة *pl.* سَاعَات: By, according to, my —, حَسَبَ سَاعَتِي. A place for watching or observation, مَرْبَأَة. As a —, for the purpose of watching, لِأَجْلِ ٱلْمُرَاقَبَةِ.

Hunting watch, سَاعَةٌ ذَاتُ غِلَافٍ — سَاعَةٌ غَلْفَاءُ.

Officer of the watch, ضَابِطُ ٱلنَّوْبَةِ.

Repeating watch, سَاعَةٌ دَقَّاقَةٌ.

To be on the watch, to be one of a watch, كَانَ مِنْ أَهْلِ ٱلنَّوْبَةِ.

To be on the watch for, رَصَدَ ² — تَرَصَّدَ — إِرْتَقَبَ.

To clean a watch, نَظَّفَ ٱلسَّاعَةَ.

To keep watch; *see* To be on the watch.

To let a watch run down, أَوْقَفَ ٱلسَّاعَةَ.

To regulate a watch, عَدَّلَ (or ² ضَبَطَ) ٱلسَّاعَةَ.

To relieve the watch, بَدَّلَ ٱلنَّوْبَةَ — غَيَّرَ ٱلْخَفَرَ.

To set a watch, guard, جَعَلَ خَفَرًا — أَقَامَ نَوْبَةً. To regulate a watch, أَحْكَمَ (or عَدَّلَ) ٱلسَّاعَةَ.

To wind up a watch, رَكَّبَ ٱلسَّاعَةَ.

Watch-boat, *n.* قَارِبُ ٱلْخَفَرِ — فُلُوكَةٌ حَارِسَةٌ.

Watch-box, *n.* بَيْتُ ٱلْغَفَرِ *vulg.* — بَيْتُ مَنْظَرَةِ ٱلْخَفَرِ. *See also* Sentry-box, *n.*

Watch-coat, *n.* بِشْتٌ (or مَشْلَحٌ) لِلْخَفَرِ.

Watch-dog, *n.* كَلْبُ ٱلْخَفَرِ — كَلْبٌ حَارِسٌ.

Watcher, *n.* One who watches, guards, خَفَر — نَاطِر — نَاطُور. An expectant, رَقِيب *pl.* رُقَبَاء.

Watch-fire, *n.* نَارُ مَعْسَكَرٍ *pl.* نِيرَان.

Watchful, *a.* On the watch, سَهَّار — سَاهِر — سَهْرَان — مُسْتَيْقِظ. Cautious, مُتَحَفِّظ — مُتَنَبِّه — حَرِيس — حَازِم. To be —, cautious, heedful, تَحَفَّظَ — إِحْتَذَرَ.

Watchfully, *ad.* سَهَارًا — بِتَيَقُّظٍ. Cautiously, بِٱحْتِذَارٍ — بِٱحْتِيَاطٍ — بِٱحْتِرَاسٍ.

Watchfulness, *n.* سَهَر — تَيَقُّظ. Caution, heed, إِحْتِرَاس — تَحَذُّر — إِحْتِيَاط.

Watch-glass, *n.* قَزَازَةُ سَاعَةٍ — زُجَاجَةُ سَاعَةٍ.

Watch-guard, *n.* بَنْدُ سَاعَةٍ.

Watch-house, *n.* مَحَلُّ (or مَرْكَزُ) ٱلضَّبْطِيَّةِ.

Watchmaker, *n.* صَانِعُ ٱلسَّاعَاتِ — سَاعَاتْجِي *pl.* سَاعَاتْجِيَّة.

Watchmaking, *n.* صِنَاعَةُ ٱلسَّاعَاتِ — حِرْفَةُ ٱلسَّاعَاتْجِيَّةِ.

Watchman, *n.* خَفَر — حَرَّاس — حَارِس. A mighty —, عَسَس — عَسّ.

Watch-pocket, *n.* جَيْبٌ لِلسَّاعَةِ.

Watch-stand, *n.* قَاعِدَةُ سَاعَةٍ.

Watch-tower, *n.* For a clock, مَنَارَةُ سَاعَةٍ. A place to keep watch from, مَرْقَب.

Watchword, *n.* كَلِمَةُ ٱلسِّرِّ ـ شِعَار ـ *from the Italian,* بَارُولَه.

Water, *n.* مَآء *pl.* مِيَاه. A little —, مُوَيْهَة. Water or lustre of a diamond, cloth, *etc.,* مَآء ; of a blade, رَوْنَق ـ نَمَش ـ فِرِنْد. Water, of dropsy, مَآءُ ٱلٱسْتِسْقَآء ـ سِقْي. A piece of water, جَمِيمُ مَآء ـ حَجْمُ مَآء ـ بُحَيْرَة *pl.* بُحَيْرَات ـ بِرْكَة *pl.* بِرَك ـ جُمَّةُ مَآء. Of the first —, the best, أَعْلَى *fem.* عُلْيَا *and* عَلْيَآء ـ أَعْلَى مَا يَكُونُ. Abundance of —, غَمْرُ مَآء ـ غَمْر. "So we opened the gates of heaven, with water that fell in torrents" فَفَتَحْنَا أَبْوَابَ ٱلسَّمَآءِ بِمَآءٍ مُنْهَمِرٍ (Kur. liv. 11).

Brackish water, مَآءٌ قَيْصُونِيٌّ ـ مَآءٌ مَلِحٌ ـ مَآءٌ مَأْجٌ.

Deep water, مَآءٌ غَمِيقٌ.

Fresh water, مَآءٌ عَذْبٌ ـ عَذْب.

High water, مَدٌّ كَامِلٌ ـ مَدّ.

High-water mark, خَطُّ ٱلْمَدِّ ٱلْكَامِلِ.

Holy water, مَآءٌ مُكَرَّس.

Low water, of the tide, جَزْر ; as of a river, *etc.,* مَآءٌ مُتَصَوِّب ـ مَآءٌ نَاقِص.

Low-water mark, خَطُّ ٱلْجَزْرِ.

Lavender water, مَآءُ ٱللَّوَنْدَا ـ مَآءُ ٱلْمَلِكَةِ ـ مَآءُ ٱلْخُزَامَى.

Orange-flower water, مَآءُ ٱلزَّهْرِ.

Pump water, مَآءٌ مُسْتَقًى ٱلطُّلُمْبَةِ.

Rose water, مَآءُ ٱلْوَرْدِ.

Running water, مَآءٌ جَارٍ ـ مَآءٌ سَائِحٌ ـ سَرِب.

Salt-water, مَآءُ ٱلْبَحْرِ ـ مَآءٌ مَالِحٌ.

Shoal water, مَآءٌ رَقٌّ ـ مَآءٌ ضَحْل.

Smooth water, of the sea, a calm, غَلِينَة ـ سُجُوٌّ.

Spring water, مَآءُ ٱلْعَيْنِ.

Stagnant water, مَآءٌ نَائِمٌ ـ مَآءٌ وَاقِفٌ ـ مُسْتَنْقَعَة.

Water on the brain, إِسْتِسْقَآءٌ فِي ٱلدِّمَاغِ.

Water on the chest, إِسْتِسْقَآءٌ فِي ٱلصَّدْرِ.

To be in hot water, تَنَازَعَ ـ إِلْتَبَكَ. Always in hot water, دَائِمًا فِي مُنَازَعَةٍ.

To come upon water, as in digging for a well, أَنْبَطَ ـ نَبَطَ ـ إِسْتَنْبَطَ ـ تَنَبَّطَ.

To draw water, to sink so much into the water, غَرَفَ مَآء ـ إِغْتَرَفَ كَذَا مِنَ ٱلْمَآءِ.

To draw water from, إِسْتَقَى مِن ـ إِسْتَقَى مَآءً مِن.

To hold water, ضَبَطَ ٱلْمَآءَ. Not to hold water, to leak, نَضَحَ ـ إِنْفَضَحَ ـ خَرَّ.

To make water, to urinate, بَالَ *aor.* يَبُولُ ـ شَخَّ. To make water, of a ship, مَاهَ (*see also preceding article*). To make water in one's clothes, رَاقَ *aor.* يَرُوقُ.

To take in water, to load with water, حَمَلَ ٱلْمَآءَ.

To take to the water, having a longing for the sea, طَلَبَ ٱلْبَحْرَ ـ إِشْتَاقَ إِلَى ٱلْبَحْرِ. To enter the water, دَخَلَ ٱلْمَآءَ.

Water, *v.t.* To supply with —, أَمَاهَ ـ سَقَى ـ أَسْقَى ـ أَشْرَبَ ـ شَرَّبَ. To sprinkle with —, نَضَحَ ـ رَشَّ بِٱلْمَآءِ. To —, as plants, سَقَّى ; as a grindstone, أَمَاهَ ـ إِمْتَاهَ. To be watered, تَسَقَّى.

Water, *v.i.* To shed water, سَفَكَ مَآء ـ سَفَحَ مَآء: His eyes watered, دَمَعَتْ عَيْنَاهُ. To make one's mouth —, أَمَاهَ فَاهُ. *See also to* Trickle, *v.i.*

Water-bailiff, *n.* قَوَّاسُ ٱلْبَنْدَرِ ـ دَيْدَبَان.

Water-bearer, *n.* The constellation, بُرْجُ ٱلدَّلْوِ.

Water-carriage, *n.* نَقْلٌ عَلَى ٱلْمَآءِ ; by sea, نَقْلُ ٱلسِّلَعِ بَحْرًا. Price of —, أُجْرَةُ ٱلنَّقْلِ عَلَى ٱلْمَآءِ.

Water-carrier, *n.* سَقَّآء *pl.* سُقَّآء.

Water-cart, *n.* عَرَبِيَّةٌ سَاقِيَة (*or* عَرَبَانَة).

Water-closet, *n.* مُسْتَرَاح ـ بَيْتُ ٱلْفَرَاغِ ـ مَبْرَز ـ مَجَاز ـ خَلَآء ـ كَنِيف *pl.* كُنُف.

Water-colour, *n.* صِبْغٌ لِلرَّسْمِ مَمْزُوجٌ بِٱلصَّمْغِ. To draw, as a picture, in —, رَسَمَ بِٱلصِّبْغِ ٱلْمَذْكُورِ.

Water-cooler, *n.* مُزَمِّلَة.

Watercourse, *n.* بَطِيحَة *pl.* بَطَائِح ـ سَيْل *pl.* سُيُول ـ سَاقٍ *pl.* سَوَاقٍ ـ سَاقِيَة *pl.* سَوَاقِي ـ سُقَاة.

Water-cresses, *n.* جِرْجِير ـ قُرَّةُ ٱلْعَيْنِ ـ رَشَادُ ٱلْمَآءِ.

Watered, *a.* Irrigated, of land, مَسْقِيٌّ ـ أَسْقِيَة *pl.* سِقًى. Sprinkled, مَرْشُوش. Of cloth, *etc.,* مُنَمْنَم. Watered silk, كَرَمْسُوت ـ قَلَامُون.

Waterfall, *n.* شَلَّال *pl.* شَلَّالَات. *See also* Cataract, *n.*

Water-fowl, *n.* طَيْرُ ٱلْمَآءِ *pl.* طُيُور.

Water-gate, *n.* مُسَنَّاة *pl.* مُسَنَّوَات ـ مُسَكَّة ـ عَرِمَة *coll.* عَرِم ـ حَبْس *pl.* أَحْبَاس.

Water-gauge, *n.* مِيزَانُ ٱلْمَآءِ.

Water-gruel, *n.* مَآءُ ٱلسَّمِيذِ عَلَى مَآء ـ أَمْوِيَة ـ كَشْك.

Water-hen, *n.* دُجَاجَةُ ٱلْمَآءِ *coll.* دُجَاج.

Wateriness, *n.* مَائِيَّة.

Watering-place, *n.* From which to draw water, سِقَايَة ـ مَسْقَاة ـ مِسْقَاة ; of a river, شَرِيعَة. A place where water is obtained by digging in the sand, جِسْيٌ ـ حِسْيٌ. A place of resort near the sea, مَنْزَهٌ عِنْدَ ٱلْبَحْرِ.

Watering-pot, *n.* مِسْقَاةٌ ـ رِشَاشَةٌ.

Watering-trough, *n.* إِخَاذٌ *pl.* أُخُذٌ ـ حَوْضٌ لِلسَّقْيِ ـ مِسْقَاةُ ٱلْمَآءِ.

Waterish, *a.* *See* Watery, *a.*

Waterless, *a.* بِلَا مَآءٍ. Waterless clouds, دِمَامٌ.

Water-level, *n.* سَطْحُ ٱلْمَآءِ.

Water-lily, *n.* نَيْلُوفَرٌ ـ نِيْنُوفَرٌ.

Water-line, *n.* Of a ship, خَطُّ غَطْسِ ٱلْمَرْكَبِ فِي ٱلْمَآءِ ـ خَطُّ ٱلِٱغْتِرَافِ.

Water-logged, *a.* مُتَشَبِّبٌ فِي ٱلْمَآءِ ـ غَارِقٌ فِي ٱلْمَآءِ.

Waterman, *n.* A ferryman, جَاذِفُ ٱلْمِعْبَرِ ـ صَاحِبُ ٱلْمِعْبَرَةِ.

Watermark, *n.* Mark of rise of water, خَطُّ عُلُوِّ ٱلْمَآءِ. A — in paper, دَمْغَةٌ شَفَّافَةٌ فِي ذَاتِ (*or* جِسْمِ) ٱلْوَرَقِ.

Water-melon, *n.* بِطِّيخٌ *coll.* بِطِّيخَةٌ. *See also under* Melon, *n.*

Water-mill, *n.* طَاحُونٌ *pl.* طَوَاحِينُ يُدَوِّرُهُ ٱلْمَآءُ.

Water-pot, *n.* For holding water, إِبْرِيقٌ *pl.* أَبَارِيقُ ـ قُلَّةٌ *pl.* قُلَلٌ *and* قِلَالٌ.

Water-power, *n.* قُوَّةُ ٱلْمَآءِ.

Water-proof, *a.* لَا يَنْفُذُ فِيهِ ٱلْمَآءُ ـ لَا يَتَطَرَّقُ إِلَيْهِ ٱلْمَآءُ.

Water-ram, *n.* طُلُمْبَةُ ٱلْمَآءِ.

Water-rat, *n.* فَأْرُ ٱلْمَآءِ *pl.* فِيرَانٌ.

Water-rot, *v.t.* أَبْلَى فِي ٱلْمَآءِ.

Watershed, *n.* عَالِيَةٌ ـ نَقِيلٌ.

Waterskin, *n.* رَاوِيَةٌ *pl.* رَوَايَا ـ مَزَادَةٌ *pl.* مَزَائِدُ *and* مَزَادٌ ـ قِرْبَةٌ *pl.* قِرَبَاتٌ *and* قِرَبٌ.

Waterspout, *n.* For letting out water, مِيزَابٌ *pl.* مَيَازِيبُ ـ مِرْزَابٌ *pl.* مَرَازِيبُ. A whirling column of water, فَوَّارَةٌ ـ تِنِّينٌ ـ أَبُو ٱلزَّوْبَعَةِ.

Water-tight, *a.* لَا يَنْفُذُ فِيهِ ٱلْمَآءُ ـ لَا يَتَطَرَّقُ إِلَيْهِ ٱلْمَآءُ.

Water-trefoil, *n.* فَصَّةُ ٱلْمَآءِ ـ رِبَّةُ ٱلْمَآءِ.

Water-works, *n.* آلَاتٌ لِرَفْعِ ٱلْمَآءِ.

Water-worn, *a.* هَارٍ مِنَ ٱلْمَآءِ ـ بِلَى مَآءٍ ـ مُبْلًى بِٱلْمَآءِ.

Watery, *a.* Aqueous, مَاوِيٌّ ـ مَائِيٌّ. Flimsy, سَخِيفٌ. Insipid, تَافِهٌ ـ بِلَا نَفَسٍ. Humid, رَطِبٌ ـ نَدِيٌّ ـ طَرِيٌّ. He found a — grave, مَاتَ غَرِيقًا ـ غَرِقَ. Watery clouds, سُحُبٌ مُغْبِيَةٌ ـ سُحُبٌ مَاطِرَةٌ.

Wattle, *n.* Of a fowl, رَغْثَةٌ *dual* رَغْثَتَيْنِ ـ عُثْنُونٌ *pl.* عَثَانِينُ; of a sheep or goat, زَنَمَةٌ *dual* زَنَمَتَانِ. Having two wattles, of a goat or sheep, زَنِيمٌ. A twig, خُصْلَةٌ *pl.* خُصَلٌ ـ عُسْلُوجٌ *pl.* عَسَالِيجُ. Wattle and daub, غَمًى ـ غِمَآءٌ.

Wattle, *v.t.* To intertwine twigs, شَبَّكَ ٱلْعَسَالِيجَ. To cover with — and daub, غَمَا [2]: He wattled the roof, غَمَا ٱلسَّقْفَ.

Waul, *v.i.* As a cat, أَمْوَأَ. *See also to* Caterwaul, *v.i.*

Wave, *n.* As of the sea, مَوْجٌ *pl.* أَمْوَاجٌ ـ مَوْجَةٌ *pl.* مَوْجَاتٌ. Wave, as in silk, تَمَوُّجٌ ـ مَآءٌ. Wave following wave, حَبَابٌ. The crests of waves, غَوَارِبُ ٱلْمَآءِ. تَتَابُعُ ٱلْأَمْوَاجِ ـ ٱلْمَآءِ. The waves had covered it, قَدْ جَلَّلَتْهُ ٱلْأَمْوَاجُ. The waves beat one against another, تَعَالَجَتِ ٱلْأَمْوَاجُ. "On waves like mountains," فِي مَوْجٍ كَٱلْجِبَالِ (Kur. xi. 44).

Wave, *v.i.* To move loosely, as a banner, *etc.*, رَنَقَ [2] ـ أَرْنَقَ ـ خَفَقَ [2] ـ تَذَبْذَبَ ـ تَرَجَّحَ ـ هَفَتَ; as a branch, مَادَ ـ أَغَافَ ـ غَافَ. To — from side to side in walking, مَادَ ـ مَاحَ. To —, of a sword, هَبَّ. The banner waved, خَفَقَتِ ٱلرَّايَةُ.

Wave, *v.t.* To move to and fro, ذَبْذَبَ ـ إِشْتَرَوَحَ ـ رَدَّدَ. To brandish, as a sword, أَهَبَّ; as of a banner, رَنَقَ [2] ـ أَرْنَقَ. To make a sign with, أَخْفَقَ بِ: He waved his garment, أَخْفَقَ بِثَوْبِهِ.

Waveless, *a.* بِلَا مَوْجٍ. *See* Calm, *a.*

Wavelet, *n.* مُوَيْجَةٌ *pl.* مُوَيْجَاتٌ.

Wave-offering, *n.* رَفِيعَةٌ ـ تَقْدِمَةُ ٱلتَّرْدِيدَاتِ.

Waver, *v.i.* To fluctuate, تَرَجَّحَ ـ تَرَدَّدَ. To doubt, إِرْتَابَ ـ تَشَكَّكَ. He wavered in the affair, تَرَدَّدَ فِي ٱلْأَمْرِ. To — between two things, تَرَجَّحَ بَيْنَ أَمْرَيْنِ ـ عَادَلَ (*or* عَدَّلَ) أَمْرَهُ. I wavered between two things, hesitating which I should do, عَادَلْتُ بَيْنَ أَمْرَيْنِ أَيَّهُمَا آتِي. I am wavering respecting this affair, whether I should do it or not, أَنَا فِي عِدَالٍ مِنْ هٰذَا ٱلْأَمْرِ. He who wavers is like a wave of the sea, إِنَّ ٱلْمُرْتَابَ يُشْبِهُ مَوْجًا مِنَ ٱلْبَحْرِ. To make to —, doubt, in, شَكَّكَ فِي.

Waverer, *n.* } مُتَقَلْقِلٌ ـ مُتَرَدِّدٌ ـ مُرْتَابٌ. He is a —, or
Wavering, *a.* } wavers, between two things, hesitating which he shall do, هُوَ مُعَادِلٌ أَمْرَهُ.

Waving, *n.* As of a flag, خَفَقَانٌ; as of the body, or of a branch, مَيَدَانٌ; of anything fluttering, هَفَاتٌ.

Wavy, *a.* Playing to and fro, خَافِقٌ ـ مُتَذَبْذِبٌ ـ مُتَرَجِّحٌ. Undulating, مُتَمَوِّجٌ. The — streaks on a sword, ذُرِيٌّ; on sand, *etc.*, نِمْنِيمٌ; of the water of silk, *etc.*, مُنَمْنَمٌ. Wavy hair, شَعْرٌ أَجْعَنُ ـ شَعْرٌ مُعَقَّفٌ.

Wax, *n.* شَمْع *pl.* شُمُوع. Wax of the ear, وَسَخُ ٱلْآذَانِ ـ أُفّ. Shoemakers' —, قِيْر ـ زِفْت. Sealing —, شَمْعُ ٱلْخِتَامِ ـ شَمْعٌ لِلْخَتْمِ.

Wax, *v.i.* To become, صَارَ *aor.* يَصِيرُ ـ حَصَلَ ². To — old, as of a garment, بَلِيَ ²; in years, شَاخَ ². To — fat, سَمِنَ ². To — strong, تَقَوَّى. To — feeble, ضَعُفَ ². To — bold, تَشَدَّدَ. To — rich, إِسْتَغْنَى ـ غَنِيَ ² ـ تَغَنَّى. To — great, عَظُمَ ². To — cold, بَرَدَ ² ـ بَرُدَ ².

Wax, *v.t.* شَمَّعَ.

Wax-candle, *n.* شَمْع *pl.* شُمُوع.

Wax-cloth, *n.* مُشَمَّع.

Waxen, *a.* Like wax, مِثْلَ ٱلشَّمْعِ; made of wax, مِنْ شَمْعٍ.

Wax-end, *n.* طَرَفٌ مُشَمَّعٌ.

Wax-work, *n.* مَصْنُوعٌ مِنَ ٱلشَّمْعِ ـ شُغْلُ ٱلشَّمْعِ.

Waxy, *a.* Soft like wax, لَيِّنٌ كَٱلشَّمْعِ. Adhesive, لَازِق ـ لَازِج. Cross, angry, مُغْتَاظ.

Way, *n.* A road, path, صِرَاط ـ سِرَاط ـ سَبِيل *pl.* سُبُل ـ مَسْلَك *pl.* مَسَالِك ـ طَرِيق *pl.* طُرُق ـ طَرِيقَة *pl.* طَرَائِق ـ سِكَّة *pl.* سِكَك ـ دَرْب *pl.* دُرُوب. Distance, مَسَافَة ـ بُعْد. Direction, tendency, جِهَة *pl.* جِهَات ـ طَرَف *pl.* أَطْرَاف ـ صَوْب ـ نَاحِيَة *pl.* نَوَاحِي. A passage, مَسْلَك ـ مَجَاز ـ مَنْفَذ. Manner, وَجْه *pl.* وُجُوه ـ مِنْهَاج ـ أُسْلُوب *pl.* أَسَالِيبُ. Means, وَصِيلَة *pl.* وَصَائِلُ ـ وَاسِطَة *pl.* وَسَائِطُ ـ بَاب *pl.* أَبْوَاب. Custom, practice, سُنَّة *pl.* سُنَن ـ عَادَة *pl.* عَادَات. Line of conduct, طَرْز ـ طَوْر ـ مُعَامَلَة ـ مَشْوَة ـ طَرِيقَة ـ سُلُوك ـ سَمْت ـ سِيرَة. How good is the way of acting of such an one! مَا أَحْسَنَ طَرْزَ فُلَانٍ. His is a good way of acting, طَرْزُهُ طَرْزٌ حَسَنٌ. A creed, sect, مَذْهَب *pl.* مَذَاهِبُ. A kind, نَوْع *pl.* أَنْوَاع. Have you anything in this way? هَلْ عِنْدَكَ مِنْ هٰذَا ٱلنَّوْعِ. In the most perfect way, فِي غَايَةِ ٱلْإِتْقَانِ ـ فِي أَكْمَلِ وَجْهٍ. *See also* Road, *n.*

Across the way, opposite, حِذَآءَ ـ مُقَابِل ـ بِلِقَاءِ.

A good or long way, مَسَافَةٌ بَعِيدَةٌ: You are not a long way from us, مَا أَنْتَ مِنَّا بِبَعِيدٍ. I saw him a long way off, رَأَيْتُهُ مِنْ بَعِيدٍ. He came from a long way off, جَآءَ مِنْ بَعِيدٍ *aor.* يَجِيءُ ².

A little way, distance, مَسَافَةٌ يَسِيرَةٌ. A little (as an adverb), قَلِيلًا: He went from thence a little way, إِجْتَازَ مِنْ هُنَاكَ قَلِيلًا.

A pernicious way, تَهْلُكَة *pl.* تَهْلُكَات ـ ضَلَال.

By the way, the wayside, عَلَى ٱلطَّرِيقِ. In the meantime, فِي أَثْنَآءِ ذٰلِكَ. By the way, as in referring to another subject, وَأَمَّا مَا كَانَ مِنْ ذٰلِكَ. Do not return by the way that you came, لَا تَرْجِعْ مِنَ ٱلطَّرِيقِ ٱلَّذِي ذَهَبْتَ فِيهِ.

By way of, by the route of, فِي طَرِيقِ. In the guise, drift, design, of, بِقَصْدِ كَذَا ـ فِي سَبِيلِ كَذَا ـ بِنَوْعِ كَذَا. By way of the desert, فِي طَرِيقِ ٱلْبَرِّيَّةِ.

Come your ways! هَلُمَّ ـ حَيَّ ـ تَعَالَ.

Covered or covert way, in fortification, سَابَاطٌ مُسْتَحْكَمٌ. A covered passage, سَابَاط *pl.* سَوَابِيطُ ـ سَقِيفَة *pl.* سَقَائِفُ.

Half-way, نِصْفُ ٱلسِّكَّةِ. A half-way house, station, مَنْزِلٌ فِي نِصْفِ ٱلسِّكَّةِ.

Highway, شَارِع *pl.* شَوَارِعُ ـ طَرِيقٌ (*or*) سُلْطَانِيٌّ ـ دَرْبٌ.

In a bad way, in a wretched state, فِي حَالِ ٱلسُّوءِ ـ فِي حَالَةٍ يُرْثَى لَهَا.

In no way, in no manner, لَا بِوَجْهٍ مِنَ ٱلْوُجُوهِ ـ أَصْلًا ـ قَطْعًا ـ أَلْبَتَّةَ ـ بَتَّةً. I will in no way do it, لَا أَفْعَلُهُ أَلْبَتَّةَ.

In the way, road, فِي وَسَطِ ٱلطَّرِيقِ ـ فِي ٱلطَّرِيقِ. In the way, as an embarrassment, عَوْقًا ـ زَحْمَةً ـ مُضَايَقَةً. It is in the way of, obstructs, the road, يَسُدُّ ٱلطَّرِيقَ. It was in the way of his doing it, it prevented him from doing it, عَاقَهُ عَنْ كَذَا ².

No way, no ways, بَتَّةً ـ أَصْلًا ـ قَطْعًا.

Not to know which way to turn, to be in a quandary, تَحَيَّرَ ـ تَوَرَّطَ فِي وَرْطَةٍ ـ اِرْتَبَكَ.

One way or other, by some means, فِي وَجْهٍ مِنَ ٱلْوُجُوهِ ـ كَيْفَمَا كَانَ.

One's own way, عَلَى هَوَاهُ ـ عَلَى كَيْفِهِ ـ عَلَى رَأْسِهِ. He would have his own way, سَلَكَ سَبِيلَهُ ² ـ رَكِبَ رَأْسَهُ ².

On the way, فِي ٱلطَّرِيقِ: It is on the way to my house, هُوَ فِي طَرِيقِ بَيْتِي.

Out of one's way, road, لَا فِي طَرِيقِهِ. Not embarrassing to, not hindering, غَيْرُ مُضَايِقٍ لَهُ ـ لَيْسَ بِمَانِعٍ لَهُ ـ لَا زِحَامَ لَهُ. Not in one's line, profession, لَيْسَ مِنْ صِنَاعَتِهِ ـ لَيْسَ مِنْ حِرْفَتِهِ.

Turn ye out of the way, مِيلُوا عَنِ ٱلسَّبِيلِ ـ حِيدُوا عَنِ ٱلطَّرِيقِ.

Out of the way, absent, مُغْتَرِب ـ غَائِب. Extraordinary, غَرِيب ـ بَعِيد. Extravagant, مُبَالِغ ـ مُفْرِط. Missing, مَفْقُود.

Out of the way! be off! اَلْبَعِيدَ. Out of my way! إِلَيْكَ عَنِّي ـ اِنْقَلِعْ عَنِّي.

Over the way; *see above*, Across the way.

That way, by that way, مِنْ هُنَاكَ. In that manner, هٰكَذَا. No one could pass by that way, لَمْ يَكُنْ أَحَدٌ يَقْدِرُ أَنْ يَجْتَازَ مِنْ تِلْكَ ٱلطَّرِيقِ. They robbed all who passed that way, كَانُوا يَسْتَلِبُونَ كُلَّ مَنْ عَبَرَ بِهِمْ فِي ٱلطَّرِيقِ. He came that way, نَزَلَ فِي (*or*) جَآءَ مِنْ تِلْكَ ٱلطَّرِيقِ.

The right way, the way of God, of holiness, سَبِيلُ ٱللّٰهِ. The righteous way, ٱلصِّرَاطُ ٱلْمُسْتَقِيمُ ـ ٱلطَّرِيقُ ٱلصَّالِحُ ـ سَوَآءُ ٱلسَّبِيلِ. The direct way, road, ٱلدَّرْبُ ٱلْعَدِلُ ـ ٱلدَّرْبُ ٱلسَّدِيدُ. The right manner, ٱلطَّرْزُ ـ ٱلْمِنْوَالُ ٱلْمَضْبُوطُ ـ ٱلسِّيَاقَةُ ٱلْمَلِيحَةُ (or ٱلنَّمَطُ) ٱلْجَيِّدُ.

The wrong way, the way of the wicked, طَرِيقٌ ـ طَرِيقُ ٱلطَّالِحِينَ ٱلْفَسَادِ. The wrong route, خِلَافُ ٱلسِّكَّةِ. The wrong or improper way, manner, مِنْوَالٌ غَيْرُ لَائِقٍ ـ سِيَاقَةٌ غَيْرُ حَسَنَةٍ.

The way in, ٱلْمَدْخَلُ.

The way out, ٱلْمَخْرَجُ.

This or by this and that way, مِنْ هُنَا وَهُنَاكَ. In this and that manner, هٰكَذَا وَهٰكَذَا. He turned this and that way, ٱلْتَفَتَ إِلَى هُنَا وَهُنَاكَ.

This way, by this way, مِنْ هُنَا. In this manner, عَلَى ـ هٰكَذَا هٰذَا ٱلْمِنْوَالِ. This is not the way, لَيْسَتْ هٰذِهِ ٱلطَّرِيقَ.

Under way (weigh), of a ship, مُسَافِرٌ ـ مُقْلِعٌ.

Which way? how? كَيْفَ. By which road, مِنْ أَيِّ طَرِيقٍ. Which way did he go? مِنْ أَيْنَ عَبَرَ ـ مِنْ أَيِّ طَرِيقٍ ذَهَبَ.

To be in a bad or sorry way, ـ ءَ شَقِيَ حَالُهُ ـ إِخْتَلَفَ حَالُهُ ـ كَانَ فِي حَالَةٍ يُرْثَى لَهَا ـ كَانَ فِي حَالِ ٱلشَّقَآءِ.

To be in one's way, as an annoyance, impediment, أَعَاقَ ـ آذَى ـ ءَ زَحَمَ ـ ² شَقَّ عَلَى. To be in one's line, كَانَ فِي عَتَادِهِ ـ سَمْتِهِ. He is not in my way, does not inconvenience me, مَا يَزْحَمُنِي.

To be in the way, as an obstruction, كَانَ عَارِضًا ـ كَانَ عَائِقَةً. Going the way of ..., سَالِكٌ سُلُوكَ كَذَا. To be at hand, of a thing, عَنَدَ ²; of a person, حَضَرَ ² ـ كَانَ حَاضِرًا.

To be out of the way, absent, غَابَ aor. يَغِيبُ ـ إِغْتَرَبَ. To be extraordinary, improbable, كَانَ بَعِيدًا ـ كَانَ مِنَ ٱلْمُحَالِ ـ كَانَ خَارِجًا عَنِ ٱلْعَقْلِ. Not to be in the right way, كَانَ خَارِجًا عَنِ ٱلطَّرِيقِ ـ ² تَاهَ.

To be under way (weigh), of a ship, أَقْلَعَ.

To beg one's way home, ءَ شَحَذَ طُولَ طَرِيقِهِ إِلَى وَطَنِهِ.

To bring on the way, شَيَّعَ. To be brought on the way, تَشَيَّعَ. They brought us on our way to the outside of the city, شَيَّعُونَا إِلَى خَارِجِ ٱلْمَدِينَةِ.

To choose one's own way, ـ ءَ عَمِلَ عَلَى هَوَاهُ ـ إِخْتَارَ طَرِيقَهُ ـ ءَ رَكِبَ رَأْسَهُ.

To clear the way, to remove obstructions from a road, ءَ رَفَعَ ـ سَلَّكَ ٱلطَّرِيقَ ـ أَخْلَى ٱلطَّرِيقَ ـ ٱلْمَوَانِعَ عَنِ ٱلطَّرِيقِ.

To cut or force one's way, خَاضَ aor. يَخُوضُ: He forced his way through the spears until he seized him, خَاضَ إِلَيْهِ ٱلرِّمَاحَ ² حَتَّى أَخَذَهُ. The lightning forced its way through the darkness, ² خَاضَ ٱلْبَرْقُ ٱلظُّلَمَ.

To fall in one's way, to meet, صَادَفَ ـ لَقِيَ ـ قَابَلَ.

To find a way into, of water, etc., تَطَرَّقَ إِلَى: Wet cannot find its way into it, لَا يَتَطَرَّقُ إِلَيْهِ ٱلْبَلَلُ.

To find one's way to, to enter, دَخَلَ ². To find means to, وَجَدَ طَرِيقَةً لِ aor. يَجِدُ.

To get out of the way (v.i.), As to a distance, إِسْتَبْعَدَ ـ تَبَاعَدَ; as from one's creditors, أَقْتَبَ. To go to a distance from, إِجْتَنَبَ مِنْ ـ تَجَنَّبَ مِنْ. To get out of the habit of, أَضَاعَ ٱلْعَادَةَ. To get out of the way, to levant, make one's self scarce, وَلَّى خُفْيَةً ـ إِنْسَلَّ.

To get one out of the way, v.t. As to a distance, ² جَنَّبَ ـ جَانَبَ ـ أَبْعَدَ ـ بَاعَدَ. To hide, خَبَّأَ ـ ² حَجَبَ ـ غَبَّى. To get one out of the habit, أَزَالَ عَنِ ٱلْعَادَةِ ـ أَنْسَى ٱلْعَادَةَ ـ ² كَفَّ عَنِ ٱلْعَادَةِ.

To get under way, of a ship, سَافَرَ ـ أَقْلَعَ ٱلْمَرْكَبُ.

To get a ship under way, قَلَّعَ ٱلسَّفِينَةَ ـ سَفَّرَ ٱلْمَرْكَبَ.

To give way, to break, to become loose, إِنْفَلَتَ ـ إِنْقَطَعَ ـ إِنْفَكَّ ـ إِرْتَخَى. To surrender, سَلَّمَ نَفْسَهُ pl. سَلَّمُوا أَنْفُسَهُمْ. To fall back, تَرَاجَعَ ـ تَأَخَّرَ ـ أَدْبَرَ. To retire, retreat from, كَرْكَرَ عَنْ ـ تَقَهْقَرَ عَنْ. To flee, إِنْهَزَمَ ـ وَلَّى هَارِبًا.

To give way to, to yield to, سَلَّمَ لِ ـ أَذْعَنَ لِ ـ طَاوَعَ. To give vent to, to let out, as anger, etc., ءِ نَفَثَ ـ ² أَصَبَّ. To be brought under the power of, تَسَلَّطَ عَلَيْهِ. To yield to in the way of pleasing, رَاضَى.

To go along a way, سَلَكَ ٱلطَّرِيقَ ². I went along a way to the door, إِسْتَطْرَقْتُ إِلَى ٱلْبَابِ.

To go a great way, a long distance, ءِ مَضَى مَسَافَةً بَعِيدَةً. A little of this food goes a great way, satisfies, قَلِيلٌ مِنْ هٰذَا ٱلطَّعَامِ يُشْبِعُ. That goes a great way to prove his words, لَمْ يَبْعُدْ ذٰلِكَ عَنْ إِثْبَاتِ قَوْلِهِ.

To go a great way with a person, to have great influence upon, ءُ نَفَذَ فِي ـ نُفُوذًا كُلِّيًّا ـ أَجْرَى نُفُوذًا عِنْدَهُ.

To go down the wrong way, in swallowing, إِنْعَكَسَ بَلْعُهُ. The water went down the wrong way, he was nearly choked by it, ءَ شَرِقَ بِٱلْمَآءِ ـ ² غَصَّ بِٱلْمَآءِ.

To go one's own way, to do as he pleased, ءَ عَمِلَ عَلَى هَوَاهُ ـ ءَ رَكِبَ هَوَاهُ.

To go one's way, أَخَذَ دَرْبَهُ وَرَاحَ ـ إِنْتَقَلَ ـ إِنْطَلَقَ ـ ذَهَبَ 2 رَاحَ إِلَى حَالِ سَبِيلِهِ 2. Go thy way now, فَٱلْآنَ ٱذْهَبْ. Let (ye) these go their way, دَعُوا هٰؤُلَاءِ يَذْهَبُونَ.

To go out of one's way, out of the route, حَادَ عَنِ ٱلطَّرِيقِ ـ زَاغَ عَنِ ٱلطَّرِيقِ 2. To avoid, تَبَاعَدَ عَنْ ـ تَجَنَّبَ مِنْ.

To go the way of all flesh, ذَهَبَ فِي طَرِيقِ ٱلْأَرْضِ كُلِّهَا ـ مَاتَ ـ تُوُفِّيَ 2.

To have one's own way, عَمِلَ عَلَى عَقْلِهِ ـ عَمِلَ عَلَى رِضَاهُ ـ عَمِلَ مَا شَاءَ ـ عَمِلَ عَلَى كَيْفِهِ.

To hold on one's own way, تَمَسَّكَ بِطَرِيقِهِ.

To inquire for the way, سَأَلَ عَنِ ٱلطَّرِيقِ.

To keep out of the way, *v.i.* As at a distance, إِسْتَبْعَدَ ـ تَبَاعَدَ. To conceal one's self, إِخْتَفَى ـ إِخْتَبَأَ. *See also to* Get out of the way, *v.i.*

To keep one out of the way, at a distance, جَنَّبَ ـ جَانَبَ 2 ـ بَاعَدَ. To hide, سَتَرَ ـ خَبَّأَ 2.

To lead the way, تَقَدَّمَ ـ إِسْتَقْدَمَ فِي ٱلطَّرِيقِ. To conduct, قَادَ ـ أَرْشَدَ ـ دَلَّ 2.

To lie in one's way, road, كَانَ فِي سَبِيلِهِ. To present itself, as an opportunity, *etc.*, إِتَّفَقَ ـ يَقَعُ *aor.* وَقَعَ ـ وُجِدَ.

To lose one's way, تَاهَ *aor.* يَتِيهُ ـ طَاحَ *aor.* يَطِيحُ ـ غَابَ عَنِ ٱلطَّرِيقِ *aor.* يَغِيبُ. To make one to lose his way, تَيَّهَ ـ طَوَّحَ ـ طَيَّحَ.

To make a way into..., فَتَحَ طَرِيقًا إِلَى.

To make way, to progress, move forward, تَقَدَّمَ ـ تَدَرَّجَ ـ دَرَجَ 2. To prosper, أَفْلَحَ ـ نَجَحَ ـ تَوَفَّقَ ـ تَرَقَّى.

To make way for, تَفَسَّحَ لِ ـ فَسَحَ لِ ـ أَرْحَبَ لِ ـ وَسَّعَ لِ. To make a way for one to escape, جَعَلَ مَنْفَذًا لِ 2.

To make one's own way, تَقَدَّمَ مِنْ ذَاتِهِ ـ أَفْلَحَ بِسَعْيِ نَفْسِهِ. One who does so, a self-made man, اِبْنُ أَعْمَالِهِ.

To prepare a way for, هَيَّأَ طَرِيقًا لِ. The way was prepared, تَهَيَّأَ ٱلطَّرِيقُ.

To put one in the right way, أَسْلَكَ فِي ٱلطَّرِيقِ ٱلْمُسْتَقِيمِ. To put one in the way to do anything, دَلَّ عَلَى ٱلصَّوَابِ 2 ـ أَرْشَدَ عَلَى (*or* إِلَى) طَرِيقِ ٱلتَّفَوُّقِ.

To put one's self out of the way, to annoy one's self, إِنْزَعَجَ ـ إِضْطَرَبَ ـ تَقَلَّقَ ـ تَضَجَّرَ ـ إِزْدَعَجَ.

To put one's self out of the way in behalf of one, تَكَلَّفَ لِأَجْلِهِ.

To smooth the way for one, سَهَّلَ ٱلطَّرِيقَ لِ ـ مَهَّدَ ٱلطَّرِيقَ لِ ـ يَسَّرَ لِ.

To stand in the way, in the road, وَقَفَ فِي ٱلطَّرِيقِ *aor.* يَقِفُ. To stand in one's way, be an obstacle to, مَنَعَ ـ عَزَّزَ ـ أَعَاقَ ـ كَانَ مَانِعًا (*or* عَائِقًا) لِ.

To take out of the way, رَفَعَ مِنَ ٱلْوَسَطِ. To be taken out of the way, رُفِعَ مِنَ ٱلْوَسَطِ.

To turn one out of the way, أَزَاغَ (*or* صَدَّ 2) عَنِ ٱلطَّرِيقِ.

To wander out of the way, زَاغَ عَنِ ٱلطَّرِيقِ 2.

To work one's way, as with difficulty, to, خَاضَ إِلَى *aor.* يَخُوضُ. To progress by working, أَفْلَحَ بِعَمَلِهِ.

Way-bill, *n.* سِيَاقَةٌ (*or* تَقْوِيمُ) ٱلسَّفَرِ.

Wayfarer, *n.* } مُسَافِرٌ ـ عَابِرُ ٱلسَّبِيلِ *pl.* عَابِرُوا ٱلسَّبِيلِ *pl.* مُسَافِرُونَ.
Wayfaring, *a.* } A wayfaring man, رَجُلٌ مُسَافِرٌ ـ اِبْنُ ٱلسَّبِيلِ *pl.* أَبْنَاءُ ٱلسَّبِيلِ. "Therefore give to him of kin to thee his due, and to the poor, and to the wayfarer," فَآتِ ذَا ٱلْقُرْبَى حَقَّهُ وَٱلْمِسْكِينَ وَٱبْنَ ٱلسَّبِيلِ (Kur. xxx. 37).

Wayfaring, *n.* سِيَاحَة ـ سَفَر.

Waylay, *v.t.* رَصَدَ 2 ـ إِرْتَصَدَ ـ رَاصَدَ ـ تَرَصَّدَ لِ ـ كَمَنَ لِ ـ أَكْمَنَ لِ.

Wayless, *a.* عَدِيمُ ٱلْمَسَالِكِ.

Way-mark, *n.* عَلَم *pl.* أَعْلَام.

Wayward, *a.* مُلْتَوٍ ـ مُتَجَبِّر ـ جَامِح ـ جَمُوح ـ عَنِيد ـ خَشِنٌ ـ ٱلْجَانِبِ ـ لَا يَسْمَعُ ٱلنِّدَاءَ وَلَا يَبْغِي ٱلْإِهْتِدَاءَ. To be —, تَلَوَّى ـ تَمَرَّنَ ـ عَنَدَ 2 ـ شَكِسَ ـ شَرَدَ 2.

Waywardly, *ad.* بِٱلْتِوَاءٍ ـ تَجَبُّرًا ـ بِعِنَادٍ ـ تَمَرُّدًا.

Waywardness, *n.* تَمَرُّد ـ اِلْتِوَاء ـ جُمُوح ـ شَمَاسَة ـ تَجَبُّر ـ شَكَاسَة ـ عِنَاد.

Wazir, *n.* *See* Vizier, *n.*

We, *pron.* نَحْنُ ـ *vulg.* نِحْنَا.

Weak, *a.* As in body, health, عَاجِز ـ عَلِيل ـ مَوْهُون ـ مُعْتَلّ ـ ٱلْمِزَاجِ ـ ضَعِيف *fem.* ضَعِيفَة and ضَعُوف *pl. masc.* ضِعَاف and ضُعَفَاءُ and ضَعْفَى and ضَعَفَة *pl. fem.* ضَعَائِفُ and ضَعِيفَات. Languid, وَانٍ. Weak through disease, نَهِيك ـ مَنْهُوك. Having little power, ضَعِيفُ ٱلْقُوَّةِ. Weak in mind, purpose, ضَعْضَاع ـ مَأْفُون ـ مَأْفُوك ـ غُزْل ـ فَيْل ـ فَال ـ فَسِيخ ـ غَبِين ـ رَكِيك ـ سَخِيف. "And man was created weak," وَخُلِقَ ٱلْإِنْسَانُ ضَعِيفًا (Kur. iv. 32). Weak, of testimony, authority, ضَعِيف ـ رَكِيك ـ ضَعِيفُ ٱلسَّنَدِ. Weak, of inanimate things, cloth, *etc.*, رَكِيك ـ سَخِيف. Weak, of the weak letters, ا و ى مُعْتَلّ. His hands became —, إِرْتَخَتْ يَدَاهُ. Weak in faith, ضَعِيفٌ فِي ٱلْإِيمَانِ. His heart became —, رَقَّ قَلْبُهُ. To be or become —, as in health, تَضَعَّفَ — ضَعَفَ ² — إِعْتَلَّ مِزَاجُهُ — وَهَنَ *aor.* يَهِنُ ; as in mind, سَخُفَ ² ; as in purpose, فَشِلَ ² — فَتَرَ ² . To become languid, وَنَى *aor.* يَنِي . To judge to be —, to declare to be —, إِسْتَضْعَفَ — ضَعَّفَ .

Weaken, *v.t.* As of health, أَفْتَرَ — هَبَطَ ² — وَهَّنَ — أَوْهَنَ ; in a general sense, أَضْعَفَ — أَوْهَنَ — ضَعَّفَ . To depress, هَبَطَ ² — ضَعْضَعَ . To make languid, أَوْنَى .

Weaken, *v.i.* To become Weak; *see under* Weak, *a.*

Weakener, *n.* مُضْعِف — مُوْهِن .

Weak-eyed, *a.* مُعْتَلُّ ٱلْعَيْنَيْنِ — ضَعِيفُ ٱلْبَصَرِ .

Weak-headed, *a.* سَخِيفٌ — خَفِيفُ ٱلْعَقْلِ — ضَعْضَع — ضَعْضَاع — أَخْرَقُ — ٱلْعَقْلِ .

Weak-hearted, *a.* رَقِيقُ ٱلْقَلْبِ — فَسِيخ — فَشِل . Superstitiously timid, مُوَسْوِس . To be or become —, فَشِلَ ² — رَكْرَكَ — رَقَّ قَلْبُهُ ² . The being —, فَشَل — رَكْرَكَة . What has made you —? مَا أَمْرَضَ قَلْبَكَ . *See also* Timid, *a.*

Weakly, *ad.* With little strength, بِضُعْفٍ ; with infirmity of purpose, بِسَخَافَةٍ — خَشْلاً فَشْلاً — بِفَشَلٍ . Languidly, بِوَنَآءٍ .

Weakly, *a.* *See* Weak, *a.*

Weakness, *n.* Of the body, ضُعْف — ضَعَف — وَهْن — عَجْز ; as of the mind, فَيْلُولَة — ضَعْضَعَة — خُرْق — غَبَانَة — فَشَل — ضَعْف — رَكَاكَة — سَخَافَة . Weakness, as in resisting, of the mind, لِينٌ — رِقَّةُ جَانِبٍ — جَانِب . Languor, وَنَآء . A disease, مَرَض — عِلَّة . A defect, قُصُور . A hankering after, شَوْق — هَوِيَّة — أَنَانَة . Weakness, as of a fort, تَضَعْضُع — عَدَمُ ٱسْتِحْكَام ; as of a garrison, قِلَّةُ ٱلْحَامِيَةِ . When they had ascertained the — (or the imminent exhaustion of the strength) of the defenders of the garrison, لَمَّا عَلِمُوا أَنَّ مُحَافِظِي ٱلْقَلْعَةِ قَدْ أَوْشَكَتْ أَنْ تَخُورَ قُوَّتُهُمْ .

Weak-side, *n.* Foible, رَكَاكَة — رِقَّةُ جَانِبٍ — لِينُ جَانِبٍ — نَقِيصَة . *See also* Foible, *n.*

Weak-sighted, *a.* *See* Weak-eyed, *a.*; *also under* Sight, *n.*

Weal, *n.* نَجَاح — سَعَادَة — خَيْر . The public —, ٱلْخَيْرُ ٱلْعَامُّ .

Wealth, *n.* مَال — ثَرْوَة — غِنًى — جَاه — غَضَارَة — حَظّ — ثَرْوَةٌ مِنْ مَالٍ .

Wealthily, *ad.* بِغِنَآءٍ — بِثَرْوَةٍ — بِجَاهٍ .

Wealthiness, *n.* *See* Wealth, *n.*

Wealthy, *a.* غَنِيٌّ — وَجِيه — حَظِيٌّ . A — man, صَاحِبُ ثَرْوَةٍ . To be —, غَنِيَ ² . To make —, غَنَّى . *See also under* Rich, *a.*

Wean, *v.t.* As from the breast, خَلَجَ ² — فَصَلَ ² — أَفْتَصَلَ — فَطَمَ ² ; of a colt, فَلَا ² — أَفْلَى . To alienate one from, فَصَلَ-عَن ² — قَطَعَ-عَن ² — أَفْتَصَلَ . To reconcile one to the loss of, سَلَّى-عَن .

To be weaned, as from the breast, إِنْفَطَمَ — فُطِمَ .

Weaned, *a.* } Weanling, *n.* } فُطُم *pl.* فَطِيم — فِصَال *and* فُصْلَان *pl.* فَصِيل — مَفْطُوم .

Weapon, *n.* سِلَاح *pl.* أَسْلِحَة — سِلَاح *pl.* أَسْلِحَة . Weapons of war, أَدَاةُ (or آلَاتُ) ٱلْحَرْبِ .

Weaponless, *a.* بِلَا أَسْلِحَةٍ .

Wear, *v.t.* To waste, by friction, أَبْلَى ; as an axle its hole, مَحَّرَ ² . To — on the person, as of clothes, لَبِسَ ² — تَلَبَّسَ بِ . To —, as a sword, or an order, تَقَلَّدَ بِ — تَوَشَّحَ بِ . To — the appearance of, بَدَا *aor.* يَبْدُو — بَانَ *aor.* يَبِينُ . To —, of a ship, to tack, حَوَّلَ — دَارَ ² . He wore the order of the Bath, كَانَ مُتَقَلِّدًا بِٱلنِّيشَانِ ٱلْمَعْرُوفِ بِنِيشَانِ ٱلْبَاثِ .

To wear away, to efface, طَلَسَ ² — مَحَا ² .

To wear off, أَبْلَى .

To wear out, as of clothes, سَحَقَ ² — فَرَزَ ² — نَهَكَ ² — أَبْلَى — إِنْتَهَكَ — نَهَكَ ² — قَطَّعَ — أَرَثَّ . To wear out, as a fever does, إِنْتَهَكَ — نَهَكَ ² .

To wear out, to make languid, أَكَلَّ . To wear out, as of a people, أَبْلَى . To wear out, to harass, vex, أَزْعَجَ — أَضْجَرَ . Health to wear it! (a compliment to one wearing a new dress), قَطَّعَهُ بِٱلْعَافِيَةِ — أَبْلِ وَأَجِدْ وَٱحْمَدِ ٱلْكَاسِي — أَبْلِ وَيُخْلِفُ ٱللّٰهُ — جَعَلَ-ٱللّٰهُ مَلْبُوسَ ٱلْعَافِيَةِ ² .

Wear, *v.i.* To become worn, wasted away, بَلِيَ ² . To serve for a long time, to wear well, خَدَمَ ² . To last, دَامَ ² — إِسْتَدَامَ — أَزْمَنَ . To —, of a ship, حَوَّلَ ٱلْقَرِيَّةَ .

To wear away, to become consumed, بَلِيَ ² . To wear away, of the day or night, مَالَ *aor.* يَمِيلُ : The day began to wear away, إِبْتَدَأَ ٱلنَّهَارُ يَمِيلُ .

To wear off, to become effaced, تَطَلَّسَ — إِنْمَحَى — إِمَّحَى .

To wear out, of clothes, *etc.*, رَثَّ ² — إِنْسَحَقَ — تَفَرَّزَ — بَلِيَ ² — تَقَطَّعَ . The man became old, worn out, أَرَثَّ ٱلرَّجُلُ . His rope wore out, or became worn out, أَرَثَّ حَبْلُهُ . Your shoes have not worn out, لَمْ تَبْلَ نِعَالُكَ . Your clothes have not worn out, لَمْ تَبْلَ ثِيَابُكُمْ .

Wear, *n.* The act of wearing, as of clothes, لُبْس . Clothing, لِبْس — مَلْبُوس . Diminution, as by friction, *etc.*, مُحُور — مَحْر — بِلًى — بِلَا . Wear and tear, use, إِسْتِعْمَال — إِبْلَاءٌ بِٱلْإِسْتِعْمَالِ . Fair — and tear, إِسْتِعْمَالٌ ٱعْتِيَادِيٌّ . To have — in it, خَدَمَ ² . To have — out of, إِسْتَعْمَلَ . Wear, a dam; *see* Weir, *n.*

Wearable, *a.* Of clothes, يُكْتَسَى بِهِ — يُلْبَسُ .

Wearer, *n.* As of clothes, لَابِس ; of an order, sword, *etc.*, مُتَقَلِّد ب .

Wearied, *a.* Fatigued, كَلِيل ـ تَعِب ـ مُتْعَب ; *vulg.* عَيَّان . To be —, fatigued, كَلَّ ـ ـ أَعْيَا ـ تَعِبَ . *For other meanings see under* Tired, *a.*

Wearily, *ad.* بِمَلَالَة ـ بِتَعَب ـ بِكَلَال ـ بِإِعْيَاء .

Weariness, *n.* Fatigue, لُغُوب ـ إِعْيَاء ـ كَلّ ـ كَلَال ـ كُلُول ـ تَعَب . Uneasiness, ضَجَر ـ إِضْطِرَاب .

Wearing, *a.* Wearing apparel, لَبُوس ـ أَلْبِسَة ـ مَلْبُوس .

Wearisome, *a.* Causing fatigue, مُعْيِي ـ مُتْعِب . Irksome, شَاقّ ـ مُزْعِج ـ مُمِلّ .

Wearisomely, *ad.* بِضَجَر ـ بِمَلَال ـ بِإِعْيَاء ـ بِكَلَال .

Wearisomeness, *n.* Tediousness, مَلَّة ـ مَلَالَة ـ مَلَال ـ مُلُول ـ زَعَل ـ ضَجَر .

Weary, *a.* Fatigued, مُعْيِي ـ كَلِيل ـ مُتْعَب ; *vulg.* عَيَّان . To be —, أَعْيَا ـ لَغَبَ ـ ـ . I am — of my life, مَلِلْتُ حَيَاتِي . I am — with groaning, تَعِبْتُ فِي تَنَهُّدِي . I am — with crying out, تَعِبْتُ مِن صُرَاخِي . A — land, أَرْض مُعْيِيَة . A — soul, نَفْس ذَائِبَة . A — task, شُغْل شَاقّ . *See also* Wearisome, *a.*

Weary, *v.t.* To fatigue, أَجْهَد ـ أَعْيَا ـ أَكَلّ ـ أَتْعَبَ . To tire out, harass, vex, أَغْرَض ـ عَنَّى ـ تَعَنَّى ـ أَمَلّ ـ شَقَّ عَلَى ـ أَعْجَزَ ـ أَزْعَجَ ـ أَضْجَرَ . *See also under* Tired, *a.*

Weasand, *n.* / **Wesand**, } *See* Windpipe, *n.*

Weasel, *n.* إِبْن عِرْس *pl.* بَنَات عِرْس ـ عِرْسَة .

Weather, *n.* هَوَاء ـ طَقْس . Fair —, صَحْو ـ طَقْس صَاحٍ . Rainy —, شِتَاء . Cloudy —, طَقْس مُغَيِّم ـ دُنْيَا مُغَيِّمَة . Unsettled, dirty —, طَقْس مُكَدَّر . Rough and windy —, نَوْء . The hot —, أَيَّام الحَرّ ـ الصَّيْف . The cold —, أَيَّام البَرْد ـ الشِّتَاء . The — is hot, الهَوَاء حَارّ ; the — is cold, الهَوَاء بَارِد . The — has cleared up, صَحَتِ الدُّنْيَا ـ الطَّقْس . The — is fine, الطَّقْس كَيِّس ـ الدُّنْيَا صَحْو . Stress of —, شِدَّة الطَّقْس ـ شِدَّة الهَوَاء . To be exposed to the (rough) —, تَعَرَّض لِشِدَّة الهَوَاء ـ تَعَرَّض لِلعَوَاصِف . In all weathers, فِي الصَّحْو وَالنَّوْء . Weather permitting, إِن يَسَّرَ الهَوَاء .

Weather, *v.t.* To sail round, عَدَّى ـ سَافَرَ حَوْلَ كَذَا ـ عَبَرَ . To — out, to resist, overcome, صَابَرَ عَلَى ـ اِعْتَزَّ عَلَى .

Weather-beaten, *a.* مَضْرُوب مِن العَوَاصِف ـ مَلْطُوم مِن الأَنْوَاء ; of a traveller, بِلْو سَفَر ـ بِلَى سَفَر *pl.* أَبْلَاء .

Weather-board, *n.* The side of a ship towards the wind, جَنْب المَرْكَب عَلَى عُلَاوَة الرِّيح . A board to keep rain off, سُدْفَة . I went to the — of such an one, عَلَوْتُ عَلَى فُلَانٍ الرِّيحَ .

Weather-bound, *a.* مَوْقُوف مِن شِدَّة الهَوَاء ـ مَحْجُوز مِن النَّوْء .

Weather-cock, *n.* For showing the direction of the wind, دَوَّارَة الرِّيح . A fickle person, غَمْلُوج ـ غَمْلَج *fem.* غَمْلُوجَة . *See also under* Inconstant, *a.*

Weather-gage, *n.* For showing the weather, مِيزَان الهَوَاء . *See also* Weather-board, *n.*

Weather-glass, *n.* مِيزَان الهَوَاء مِن زُجَاج .

Weathermost, *a.* عَلَى عُلَاوَة الرِّيح القُصْوَى .

Weather-proof, *a.* لَا تُؤَثِّر فِيهِ شِدَّة الهَوَاء ـ مَعْصُوم مِن الطَّقْس .

Weather-wise, *a.* عَرَّاف بِالهَوَاء .

Weave, *v.t.* Of cloth, وَصَدَ *aor.* يَصِدُ ـ نَسَجَ ـ ـ حَاكَ *aor.* يَحُوكُ . To —, as a bird its nest, رَضَعَ ; as a spider its web, عَكَشَ ـ ـ .

Weaver, *n.* Of cloth, *etc.*, وَصَّاد ـ نَاسِج ـ نَسَّاج ـ حَيَّاك *pl.* حَيَّاكَة ـ حَائِك *pl.* حَاكَة *and* حَوَكَة .

Weaver-bird, *n.* تَنَوُّط .

Weaving, *n.* The act of, of cloth, وَصْد ـ نَسْج ـ حَوْك ـ حِيَاكَة ـ حِيَاك . Anything woven, نَسِيجَة *pl.* نَسَائِج . Manufactories for weaving, مَعَامِل النَّسَائِج .

Web, *n.* Anything woven, نَسِيجَة *pl.* نَسَائِج .

Web-footed, *a.* مُكَفَّف .

Webbing, *n.* شَرِيط عَرِيض .

Wed, *v.t.* To join in marriage, زَوَّجَ . To take for a wife, (or for a husband by changing the gender and the suffixed pronouns), تَزَوَّجَ ب ـ تَزَوَّجَ ـ ـ نَكَحَ . *See also under* to Marry, *v.t.*

Wed, *v.i.* To contract marriage, تَأَهَّلَ ـ تَزَوَّجَ ; *fem.* تَأَهَّلَت ـ تَزَوَّجَت .

Wedded, *a.* Married, مُتَأَهِّل *fem.* مُتَأَهِّلَة ـ مُزَوَّج *fem.* مُزَوَّجَة . Conjugal, زِيجِيّ .

Wedding, *n.* The ceremony of marriage, نِكَاح (called among Christians, تَكْلِيل).

Wedding-day, يَوْم التَّكْلِيل ـ يَوْم عَقْد النِّكَاح ; anniversary of a wedding, عِيد التَّكْلِيل ـ عِيد عَقْد النِّكَاح .

Wedding-feast, عُرْس *pl.* أَعْرَاس ـ عُرْس *pl.* فَرَح ـ أَفْرَاح *pl.* .

Wedding-present, عُقْر *pl.* أَعْقَار ـ بُضْع *pl.* بُضُوع ـ هَدِيَّة الزِّيجَة *pl.* هَدَايَا .

Wedding-ring, خَاتَم الزِّيجَة .

Wedge, *n.* سَفِين *pl.* سُفُن ـ أَسَافِين . An ingot, سَبِيكَة *pl.* سَبَائِك . A — for a door, or to tighten anything with, شِجَار *pl.* شُجُر .

Wedge, *v.t.* To fasten with wedges, مَكَّنَ بِٱلْأَسَافِينِ. To prop or stay, as with a wedge, شَجَرَ ². To split with wedges, شَقَّ بِٱلْأَسَافِينِ ².

Wedgwood-ware, *n.* فَخَّارٌ يُشْبِهُ ٱلرُّخَامَ.

Wedlock, *n.* زِيجَةٌ ـ زَوَاجٌ ـ نِكَاحٌ. *See also* Marriage, *n.*

Wednesday, *n.* يَوْمُ ٱلْأَرْبَعَاءِ ـ ٱلْأَرْبَعَاءُ.

Wee, *a.* صَغِيرٌ *fem.* صُغْرَى.

Weed, *n.* عُشْبٌ بَطَّالٌ ـ سَقَطُ ٱلْعُشْبِ *coll.* مِنْ سَقَطِ ٱلْعُشْبِ.

Weeds, of thorns and thistles, شَوْكٌ وَحَسَكٌ. The weeds of the sea, عُشْبُ ٱلْبَحْرِ.

Weed, *v.t.* (or إِجْتَبَأَ) سَقَطَ ٱلْعُشْبَ مِنَ ٱلْأَرْضِ ـ إِخْتَفَى *vulg.* عَشَّبَ. To — out, to extirpate, إِسْتَأْصَلَ ـ إِخْتَفَى.

Weeder, *n.* (or مُجْتَبِئٌ) سَقَطِ ٱلْعُشْبِ ـ مُخْتَفِي *vulg.* عَشَّابٌ.

Weeding, *n.* (or إِجْتِبَاءُ) سَقَطِ ٱلْعُشْبِ ـ إِخْتِفَاءُ *vulg.* تَعْشِيبٌ.

Weediness, *n.* سَقَطُ ٱلْعُشَابَةِ ـ كَثْرَةُ سَقَطِ ٱلْعُشْبِ.

Weedy, *a.* مَمْلُوٌّ مِنْ سَقَطِ ٱلْعُشْبِ.

Week, *n.* أُسْبُوعٌ *pl.* أَسَابِيعُ *and* سُبُوعٌ ـ جُمْعَةٌ *pl.* جُمَعٌ; two weeks, أُسْبُوعَانِ. Next —, ٱلْأُسْبُوعُ ٱلْمُسْتَقْبِلُ ـ ٱلْأُسْبُوعُ ٱلْآتِي. During last —, فِي ٱلْأُسْبُوعِ ٱلْمَاضِي. This day —, مِنَ ٱلْيَوْمِ إِلَى عُقْبَ ثَمَانِيَةِ أَيَّامٍ ـ أُسْبُوعٍ. By the —, بِٱلْأُسْبُوعِ ـ بِٱلْجُمْعَةِ.

Week-day, *n.* يَوْمٌ مِنَ ٱلْأُسْبُوعِ عَدَا يَوْمَ ٱلْأَحَدِ.

Weekly, *a.* أُسْبُوعِيٌّ. A — publication, جَرِيدَةٌ أُسْبُوعِيَّةٌ.

Weekly, *ad.* مَرَّةً فِي كُلِّ أُسْبُوعٍ ـ كُلَّ أُسْبُوعٍ.

Ween, *v.i.* خَمَّنَ ـ ظَنَّ ².

Weep, *v.i.* To shed tears, بَكَى ـ تَدَمَّعَ ². To — for, بَكَى لِ ² or عَلَى. *See also under to* Cry, Lament, Deplore, *v.i.*

Weeper, *n.* } One who weeps, بَاكٍ *pl.* بُكِيٌّ *and* بُكَاةٌ ـ دَمَّاعٌ ـ دَامِعٌ ـ دَمُوعٌ. A weeping eye, عَيْنٌ دَامِعَةٌ.
Weeping, *a.* }

Weeping, *n.* بُكَاءٌ ـ حَنِينٌ. Prone to —, دَمُوعٌ.

Weeping-willow, *n.* صَفْصَافٌ مُسْتَحٍ.

Weepingly, *ad.* بِبُكَاءٍ.

Weevil, *n.* سُوسَةٌ *coll.* سُوسٌ. To be eaten by weevils, تَسَوَّسَ. To eat, as weevils, سَوَّسَ ـ أَسَاسَ.

Weevily, *a.* مُسَوَّسٌ ـ مُتَسَوِّسٌ.

Weft, *n.* The woof of cloth, لُحْمَةٌ. A thing woven, نَسِيجَةٌ.

Weigh, *v.t.* As in scales, وَزَنَ *aor.* يَزِنُ. To — by lifting, ثَقَّلَ ². To — by conjecture, or by the eye, *etc.*, حَزَرَ ² ـ حَزَّرَ ـ خَمَّنَ ـ قَدَّرَ ـ خَرَصَ ². To consider in the mind, نَظَرَ فِي ² ـ وَازَنَ ـ أَبْرَمَ ـ إِعْتَبَرَ ـ تَأَمَّلَ. To — in large scales or with a steelyard, قَبَّنَ. To — anchor, قَلَعَ ٱلْمِرْسَاةَ ² ـ حَلَّ ٱلْمِرْسَاةَ.

To —, over-weigh, رَجَحَ ². One of the scales weighed down the other, رَجَحَتْ إِحْدَى ٱلْكِفَّتَيْنِ عَلَى ٱلْأُخْرَى. To — down, oppress, distress, أَشْجَبَ ـ شَجَبَ ² ـ أَضْجَرَ. To grieve, آسَفَ ـ أَحْزَنَ ـ أَهَمَّ. To — or be heavy upon one, ثَقُلَ عَلَى ² ـ إِسْتَصْعَبَ عَلَى ـ صَعُبَ عَلَى ².

Weigh, *v.i.* To have weight, كَانَ وَزْنُهُ كَذَا ـ كَانَ ثِقْلُهُ كَذَا ـ وَزَنَ كَذَا *aor.* يَزِنُ. To — with, to have influence with, نَفَذَ ² ـ نُفُوذًا عِنْدَ فُلَانٍ.

Weigh, *n.* وَزْنَةٌ *pl.* وَزْنَاتٌ. *See also* Wey, *n.*

Weighable, *a.* مِمَّا يُوزَنُ ـ وَزْنُهُ مُمْكِنٌ.

Weighed, *a.* As in scales, مَوْزُونٌ. Considered, مُعْتَبَرٌ ـ مُمَيَّزٌ ـ مُبْرَمٌ. Weighed down with sickness, مُثْقَلٌ بِٱلْمَرَضِ.

Weigher, *n.* وَزَّانٌ *pl.* وَزَّانَةٌ; of large weights, قَبَانِيٌّ *pl.* قَبَانِيَّةٌ ـ قَبَّانٌ *pl.* قَبَّانَةٌ.

Weighing, *n.* The act of, وَزْنٌ ـ زِنَةٌ. One —, وَزْنَةٌ. A — house, مَحَلُّ ٱلْوَزْنِ.

Weight, *n.* As of a body, ثِقْلٌ. A — to weigh with, وَزْنٌ *pl.* أَوْزَانٌ; of a steelyard, سَنْجَةٌ *pl.* سَنَجٌ *and* سَنَاجَاتٌ ـ رُمَّانَةٌ *pl.* رُمَّانَاتٌ. Of just —, وَازِنٌ. Of full —, وَزْنٌ قَائِمٌ ـ وَزْنٌ رَجَاحٌ. A great —, heavy body, جِسْمٌ ثَقِيلٌ ـ ثِقْلٌ. Anything burdensome, ثِقْلٌ *pl.* أَثْقَالٌ. A trouble, distress, آفَةٌ ـ ضِيقَةٌ *pl.* آفَاتٌ ـ إِضْطِرَابٌ ـ هَمٌّ ـ غَمٌّ ـ كَدَرٌ ـ هَمٌّ. Importance, عِظَمٌ ـ أَهَمِّيَّةٌ ـ ضَرُورَةٌ. Influence, تَأْثِيرٌ ـ نُفُوذٌ ـ إِعْتِبَارٌ. By —, بِٱلْوَزْنِ. Give him his —, أَعْطِهِ ثِقْلَهُ. It was a great — upon him, تَثَاقَلَ عَلَى ـ أَثْقَلَ عَلَيْهِ ـ أَثْقَلَهُ. He bore his — upon a thing, أَلْقَى عَلَيْهِ جَلَامِيدَهُ ٱلشَّيْءَ. He threw all his — upon him, (or ثِقْلَهُ). He tried the — of it, by lifting it with his hand, ثَقَّلَهُ بِيَدِهِ ². He has no — with him, لَيْسَ لَهُ نُفُوذٌ عِنْدَهُ. It is worth its — in gold, يُسَاوِي ثِقْلَهُ ذَهَبًا. It is a matter of no —, هُوَ أَمْرٌ لَا طَائِلَ تَحْتَهُ ـ هُوَ أَمْرٌ وَجِيزٌ. "And not the weight of an atom either in earth or heaven escapeth thy Lord," وَمَا يَعْزُبُ عَنْ رَبِّكَ مِنْ مِثْقَالِ ذَرَّةٍ فِي ٱلْأَرْضِ وَلَا فِي ٱلسَّمَاءِ (Kur. x. 62). "And, O my people, give weight and measure with fairness, and do not depreciate the things of (other) people," وَيَا قَوْمِ أَوْفُوا ٱلْمِكْيَالَ وَٱلْمِيزَانَ بِٱلْقِسْطِ وَلَا تَبْخَسُوا ٱلنَّاسَ أَشْيَاءَهُمْ (Kur. xi. 86).

Weightily, *ad.* Heavily, بِثِقْلٍ. With importance, بِوَجْهٍ مُهِمٍّ ـ بِتَأْثِيرٍ ـ تَأْثِيرًا. Impressively, بِضَرُورَةٍ.

Weightiness, *n.* Heaviness, ثِقْلٌ. Importance, ضَرُورِيَّةٌ ـ أَهَمِّيَّةٌ ـ جَسَامَةٌ ـ ضَرُورَةٌ. *See also under* Weight, *n.*

Weightless, *a.* لَا ثِقْلَ لَهُ. Light, خَفِيفٌ. Of no importance, غَيْرُ مُهِمٍّ ـ لَا طَائِلَ لَهُ.

Weighty, *a.* Heavy, وَزِين ـ ثَقِيل *pl.* ثِقَال. Important, مُهِمّ. Weighty matters, مُهِمَّات. It is one of the great or — matters, هُوَ مِنْ جِسَامِ ٱلْأُمُورِ. The most — of the affair, جَسِيمُ ٱلْأَمْرِ.

Weir, *n.* مَصْلَحَة ـ مُسَنَّاة *pl.* مُسَنَّوَات ـ عَرِمَة *coll.* عَرِم ـ حَبْس *pl.* أَحْبَاس ـ سَدّ *pl.* أَسْدَاد.

Weird, *a.* سَاحِر *pl.* سَحَرَة *and* سُحَّار ـ سَحَّار *pl.* سَحَّارُونَ. "Say: I betake me for refuge to the Lord of the daybreak against the mischief of His creation, against the mischief of the night when it has set in, and against the mischief of weird women," (literally, those who blow on knots), قُلْ أَعُوذُ بِرَبِّ ٱلْفَلَقِ مِنْ شَرِّ مَا خَلَقَ وَمِنْ شَرِّ غَاسِقٍ إِذَا وَقَبَ وَمِنْ شَرِّ ٱلنَّفَّاثَاتِ فِي ٱلْعُقَدِ (Kur. cxiii. 1-4).

Weird, *n.* A spell, سِحْر ـ أُخْذَة.

Welcome, *a.* Received with gladness, مُهَنَّأ *fem.* مُهَنَّأَة. Acceptable, مَقْبُول ـ مُقَبَّل. Opportune, وَاقِعٌ مَوْقِعَهُ ـ حَالٌّ مَحَلَّهُ. Welcome! مَرْحَبًا ـ مَرْحَبًا وَأَهْلًا ـ مَرْحَبًا وَسَهْلًا ـ أَهْلًا وَسَهْلًا. Welcome to you! مَرْحَبًا بِكُمْ ـ مَرْحَبًا بِكَ; (the usual replies to these complimentary courtesies are: أَلْفُ مَرْحَبًا ـ مَرْحَبْتَانِ. Another mode of expressing Welcome! is: حَلَّتِ ٱلْبَرَكَة; also, وَمِنَّةُ سَلَامَةٍ ـ السَّلَامَة. The replies to these respectively are: اللّٰهُ يُبَارِكْ فِيكَ ـ اللّٰهُ يُسَلِّمُكَ). You are — to it, هُوَ فِي تَصَرُّفِكَ ـ هُوَ تَحْتَ أَمْرِكَ ـ هُوَ فِي خِدْمَتِكَ ـ هُوَ لَكَ.

Welcome, *n.* A kind reception, تَرَحُّب ـ تَرْحَاب ـ تَرْحِيب. I met him with a —, لَقِيتُهُ بِٱلتَّرَحُّبِ. I received a — from him, لَقِيتُ مِنْهُ تَرْحِيبًا. He always enjoys a hearty — at their house, or from them, يَحْظَى دَائِمًا بِحُسْنِ ٱلْقُبُولِ عِنْدَهُمْ.

Welcome, *v.t.* رَحَّبَ بِ ـ هَنَّأَ: They welcomed him heartily, رَحَّبُوا بِهِ غَايَةَ ٱلتَّرْحِيبِ.

Welcomely, *ad.* In a welcome manner, بِتَرْحِيبٍ ـ بِتَهْنِئَةٍ. Opportunely, بِوَقْتِهِ ـ عَلَى طِيَّتِهِ ـ عَلَى وَفْقٍ.

Welcomeness, *n.* Kind reception, تَرْحِيب. Agreeableness, kindliness, لُطْف ـ لَطَافَة ـ حُسْن.

Welcomer, *n.* One who gives a welcome, مُرَحِّب; one who receives a welcome, مُرَحَّبٌ بِهِ.

Weld, *v.t.* لَأَمَ ـ لَحَمَ. To be welded, اِلْتَأَمَ ـ لَحِمَ. To — with, لَحَمَ بِ. To be welded with, لَحِمَ بِ.

Welder, *n.* لَاحِم.

Welding, *n.* لَأْم ـ لَحْم.

Welfare, *n.* Health, صِحَّة ـ عَافِيَة. Well-being, prosperity, رَفَاهِيَة ـ سَعَادَة ـ خَيْر ـ إِقْبَال ـ نَجَاح ـ حَظّ. He asked after their —, سَأَلَ عَنْ سَلَامَتِهِمْ. They asked after each other's —, سَأَلَ كُلُّ وَاحِدٍ صَاحِبَهُ عَنْ سَلَامَتِهِ. To seek the — of one, طَلَبَ خَيْرَهُ.

Well, *n.* جَفْر ـ جُبَّة *pl.* جِبَاب *and* أَجْبَاب ـ جُبّ *pl.* كِرَار ـ كُرّ *pl.* جِفَار ـ بِئْرَة ـ أَبْيَار ـ بِيْر *or* بِئْر *pl.* آبَار. A — lined with masonry, stones, كُرّ مُدَمَّم ـ طَوِيّ *or* طَوِيّ *pl.* أَطْوَاء ـ مَطْوِيّ. A — dug in stones having a constant supply of water, خَسِيف *pl.* خُسُف. An uncased —, رَكِيَّة. The two upright posts set up by a —, الزُّرْنُوقَانِ; the transverse beam across these, نَعَامَة. Well water, مَاءُ بِئْرٍ. To clear out a —, إِخْتَفَى ٱلْبِئْرَ.

Well, *v.i.* To spring up, as water from the earth or from a fountain, إِنْفَجَرَ ـ تَفَجَّرَ ـ بَجَسَ ـ إِنْبَجَسَ ـ فَارَ ـ نَبَعَ. To cause to —, بَجَّسَ ـ فَجَّرَ.

Well, *a.* In health, فِي حَالِ ٱلصِّحَّةِ; in a good state, فِي حَالِ ٱلْخَيْرِ ـ فِي حَالِ ٱلْحَظِّ. Right, صَوَاب. Well, good, جَيِّد ـ حَسَن ـ طَيِّب. Very —, in health, فِي كَمَالِ ٱلصِّحَّةِ.

Well, *ad.* Not amiss, right, properly, إِجَادَةً ـ حَسَنًا ـ جَيِّدًا ـ لِيَاقَةً ـ طَيِّبَةً ـ عَلَى عَيْنٍ. Cheerful, happy, pleased, فِي حَالِ ٱلْحَظِّ ـ بِسُرُورٍ. He is very —, هُوَ فِي أَحْسَنِ حَالٍ. Safe, prosperous, فِي أَمَانِ ٱللّٰهِ ـ بِخَيْرٍ وَعَافِيَةٍ. All is —, كُلُّ شَيْءٍ ـ السَّلَامُ ـ فِي أَمَانِ ٱللّٰهِ ـ لَا خَبَرَ إِلَّا خَيْرًا. He thrashed him right —, ضَرَبَهُ وَمَا قَصَّرَ. Well, and what then? وَبَعْدُ. For he knows right — that ..., لِأَنَّهُ يَعْلَمُ حَقَّ ٱلْيَقِينِ أَن. Is he —? هَلْ لَهُ سَلَامَة. To say or do —, أَجْوَدَ ـ جَادَ ـ أَجَادَ ـ أَتَى بِٱلْجَيِّدِ *aor.* يَأْتِي. He said and said —, قَالَ فَأَجَادَ. He did and did —, فَعَلَ فَأَجَادَ ـ أَجَادَ فِي عَمَلِهِ.

As well as, like, مِثْل: I can do it as well as you, أَقْدِرُ عَلَيْهِ مِثْلَكَ. I will go as well as you, أَنَا أَيْضًا أَذْهَبُ. He is as well, in health, as could be expected, هُوَ فِي عَافِيَةٍ قَدْرَ ٱلْمَأْمُولِ. The Ambassador as well as the Sublime Porte denied it, أَنْكَرَهُ كُلٌّ مِنَ ٱلسَّفِيرِ وَٱلْبَابِ ٱلْعَالِي. If I be not skilful, verily I do as well as I can, that is, to the best of my knowledge, إِلَّا أَكُنْ صَنَعًا فَإِنِّي أَعْتَشِمُ.

Well and good, حَسَنًا ـ جَيِّدًا ـ حَبَّذَا. If he comes, well and good, and if he does not come, so let it be, إِنْ جَاءَ حَبَّذَا وَإِنْ مَا جَاءَ هَيْهَاتَ.

Well done! بَخٍ ـ بَخٍّ ـ نِعِمَّا ـ حَبَّذَا. Well done to thee! بَخٍّ (*or* بَخٍ) لَكَ. To say — to, صَوَّبَ ـ حَبَّذَ.

Well enough, طَيِّبٌ كِفَايَةً ـ عَلَى قَدِّهِ ـ بَيْنَ بَيْنَ

Well-off, Well-to-do, } مَرْزُوق ـ مِنْ أَهْلِ ٱلثَّرْوَةِ ـ غَضِيرُ ٱلنَّاصِيَةِ. To be—, كَانَ فِي جِدٍّ ـ ² رَزَقَهُ ٱللّٰهُ ـ ² كَانَ فِي غَضَارَةٍ.

To be well, in health and prosperity, كَانَ بِخَيْرٍ وَعَافِيَةٍ. Is the boy well? أَسَلَامٌ لِلْوَلَدِ. Is your father well? هَلْ أَبُوكُمْ بِٱلسَّلَامَةِ. That it may be well with you, لِيَكُونَ لَكُمْ خَيْرٌ.

To behave well, أَحْسَنَ ٱلسِّيرَةَ. To behave valiantly, مَجَلَّدَ ـ عَنْتَرَ.

To do anything well, أَحْسَنَ ـ أَسَدَّ فِي ـ = سَدَّ فِي: If thou doest well, إِنْ أَحْسَنْتَ. *See also under* Well, *ad.*

To do well to, to act kindly to, أَحْسَنَ إِلَى (or بِ). To do well to one's self, أَحْسَنَ إِلَى نَفْسِهِ.

To do one's work well, أَجَادَ فِي ـ أَسَدَّ فِي عَمَلِهِ ـ ² = ضَبَطَ عَمَلَهُ = عَمَلِهِ. Not to do a thing well, خَشَبَ ٱلْعَمَلَ =.

To get well, to recover health, شُفِيَ ـ = = صَحَّ مِنَ ٱلْمَرَضِ ـ أَفَاقَ مِنَ ٱلدَّاءِ.

To get on well, to prosper, تَفَيَّدَ ـ إِسْتَفْلَحَ ـ تَوَفَّقَ. I am getting on very well, am not in want of anything, أَنَا غَنِيُّ أَفْلَحَ ـ تَرَوَّجَ ـ تَقَدَّمَ. To progress, مُحْتَاجٍ.

To know well, = عَلِمَ جَيِّدًا. To know a thing well, = عَلِمَ ـ جَيِّدًا. As you well know, كَمَا تَعْلَمُ جَيِّدًا.

To look well to, وَاعَى إِلَى ـ إِنْتَبَهَ عَلَى ـ = جَعَلَ عَيْنَ ـ عَلَى. I will look well to you, أَجْعَلُ عَيْنِي عَلَيْكَ.

To manage one's affairs well, = ² ضَبَطَ أُمُورَهُ.

To play well, as on a musical instrument, أَحْسَنَ ٱلْعَزْفَ.

To please one well, of speech, ² حَسُنَ ٱلْقَوْلُ عِنْدَهُ: The words pleased me well, حَسُنَ ٱلْكَلَامُ لَدَيَّ.

To rule well, أَحْسَنَ ٱلسِّيَاسَةَ ـ دَبَّرَ أُمُورَ ٱلْبِلَادِ حَسَنًا.

To say well, أَحْسَنَ ٱلْقَوْلَ ـ أَسَدَّ فِي ٱلْقَوْلِ. Thou hast said well, حَسَنًا قُلْتَ. *See also under* Well, *ad.*

To seem well to one, ² حَسُنَ فِي عَيْنِهِ.

To sing well, أَجَادَ (or أَحْسَنَ) فِي ٱلْغِنَاءِ: She sings well, تُحْسِنُ فِي غِنَاهَا.

To speak well, تَفَصَّحَ فِي ٱلْكَلَامِ ـ ² بَلُغَ ـ تَكَلَّمَ بِفَصَاحَةٍ. He speaks well, is a good speaker, هُوَ شَحْشَاحٌ (or شَحْشَحَانٌ) ـ هُوَ مُتَكَلِّمٌ. *See also under* Well, *ad.*

To speak well of, تَكَلَّمَ ـ ² ذَكَرَ بِٱلْجَمِيلِ ـ أَحْسَنَ ٱلْقَوْلَ فِي فِي ـ حَسَنًا.

To think well of, إِسْتَصْلَحَ ـ إِسْتَحْسَنَ ـ أَحْسَنَ ٱلظَّنَّ فِي.

Well-a-day! *int.* وَاى ـ وَآهٍ ـ آحِ ـ آهٍ.

Well-aimed, *a.* مُسَدَّد ـ صَائِب ـ مُصِيب.

Well-appointed, *a.* مُجَهَّزٌ جِهَازًا كَامِلًا.

Well-authenticated, *a.* صَحِيحٌ وَمُحَقَّقٌ.

Well-being, *n.* *See* Welfare, *n.*

Well-beloved, *a.* حَبِيب ـ مَحْبُوب.

Well-born, *a.* نَسِيل ـ نَجِيب ـ أَصِيل ـ حُرٌّ *pl.* أَحْرَار.

Well-bred, *a.* لَطِيف ـ ظَرِيف ـ مُؤَدَّب ـ أَدِيب. To be—, إِسْتَأْدَبَ ـ ² أَدُبَ.

Well-built, *a.* Well-made or proportioned, مُتَنَاسِبُ ٱلْبِنْيَةِ. Of strong build, مُرَصَّن ـ شَدِيدُ ٱلْبِنْيَةِ ـ ذُو بِنْيَةٍ قَوِيَّةٍ. A—city, مَدِينَةٌ حَسَنَةُ ٱلْمَبَانِي.

Well-defined, *a.* وَاضِح ـ صَرِيحُ ٱلتَّحْدِيدِ ـ مُحَدَّدٌ بِتَصْرِيحٍ.

Well-disposed, *a.* Well-inclined, مُسْتَعْطَف ـ لَيِّنُ ٱلْعَطْفِ. *See also* Well-ordered, *a.*

Well-done, *a.* مَضْبُوط ـ مُحْكَم.

Well-favoured, *a.* جَمِيل ـ حَسَنُ ٱلْمَنْظَرِ.

Well-founded, *a.* True, ثَابِت ـ مُتَحَقَّق ـ مُحَقَّق ـ صَحِيح.

Well-grounded, *a.* As in a science, مُتَعَلِّم ـ مُدَرَّس. Firm, well-founded, مُتَأَسِّس ـ مُؤَسَّس ـ مَاكِنُ ٱلْأَسَاسِ ـ رَصِين ـ مُرَصَّن. Stable, firmly fixed; *See* Stable, *a.*

Well-informed, *a.* عَلَّام ـ خَبِير.

Well-known, *a.* مَشْهُور.

Well-made, *a.* Well-proportioned, مُهَنْدَم ـ مُتَنَاسِبُ ٱلْبِنْيَةِ; of a woman, خَرِد.

Well-mannered, *a.* *See* Well-bred, *a.*

Well-meaning, *a.* خَالِصُ ٱلنِّيَّةِ ـ مُخْلِصُ ٱلْقَصْدِ.

Well-meant, *a.* صَافٍ ـ صَادِرٌ مِنْ صِدْقِ ٱلنِّيَّةِ.

Well-nigh, *ad.* Almost, عَنْ قَرِيبٍ ـ تَقْرِيبًا. I had—slipped, كَادَتْ تَزِلُّ قَدَمَاى. I had—lost my footing, لَوْلَا قَلِيلٌ لَزَلِقْتُ. *See also under* Nearly, *ad.*

Well-ordered, *a.* Well-regulated, } مُنَسَّق ـ نَسِيق ـ مَضْبُوط.

Well-read, *a.* لَوْذَعِيٌّ ـ أَدِيب *pl.* ² أُدَبَاء ـ مُدَرَّس.

Well-set, *a.* Well-proportioned, مُتَنَاسِبُ ٱلْبِنْيَةِ ـ مُهَنْدَم; of a woman, خَرِد. Robust, قَوِيٌّ ـ ضَلِيع ـ صُلْب.

Well-sinker, *n.* حَفَّارُ ٱلْآبَارِ ـ أَبَّار ـ بَآر.

Well-spent, *a.* Of money, دَرَاهِمُ أُنْفِقَتْ فِي بَابِهَا; as of energy, labour, مُتَصَرَّف بِإِفَادَةٍ.

Well-spoken, *a.* كَلَامٌ مُسَدَّد ـ قَوْلٌ صَائِب.

Well-spring, *n.* عَيْن *pl.* عُيُون ـ مَنْبَع.

Well-stored, *a.* As with provisions, مَشْحُون ـ كَثِيرُ ٱلذَّخَائِرِ; as with reading, learning, مُدَرَّس.

Well-sweep, *n.* شَادُوف.

Well-tempered, *a.* Of steel, حَسَنُ ٱلسَّقَايَةِ. *See also* Good-tempered, *a.*

Well-timed, *a.* فِي مَحَلِّهِ ـ فِي وَقْتِهِ ـ مُوَافِق.

Well-trained or tutored, مُؤَدَّب; as of soldiers, مُمَرَّن.

Well-wisher, *n.* خِلٌّ *pl.* أَخِلَّة ـ وَدِيد *pl.* أَوِدَّآء ـ صَدِيق *pl.* أَصْدِقَآء.

Well-written, *a.* بَلِيغ. A — book, كِتَابٌ بَلِيغٌ.

Welsh, *a.* The language, لِسَانُ أَهْلِ وَيلْس. *See* Wales, *n.*

Welshman, *n.* مِنْ أَهْلِ وَيلْس. *See* Wales, *n.*

Welsh-rabbit *or* rare-bit, *n.* *See* Rare-bit, *n.*

Welt, *n.* صَرِيحَة *pl.* سَرَائِح ـ حَاشِيَة *pl.* حَوَاشِي.

Welt, *v.t.* عَلَّقَ عَلَى ـ حَاشِيَةً ـ = خَصَفَ ـ بِسَرِيحَةٍ.

Welter, *v.i.* *See to* Wallow, *v.i.*

Wen, *n.* سِلْعَة *pl.* سِلَع.

Wench, *n.* بِنْت *pl.* بَنَات ـ جَارِيَة *pl.* جَوَارٍ.

Wend, *v.i.* To — one's way toward, ضَرَبَ إِلَى =.

Went, *pret. of to* Go; *q.v.*

Wept, *pret. of to* Weep; *q.v.*

Were, *pret. pl. of to* Be; *q.v.* They were, كَانُوا. There were none, of things, لَمْ يَكُنْ شَيْءٌ; of persons, لَمْ يَكُنْ أَحَدٌ. There were many of them a week ago, كَانَ مِنْهُمْ كَثِيرُونَ مُنْذُ أُسْبُوعٍ. Were you there last month? أَكُنْتَ هُنَاكَ فِي ٱلشَّهْرِ ٱلْمَاضِي.

Wesleyan, *a.* إِسْمُ مَذْهَبٍ مِنَ ٱلنَّصَارَى فِي بِلَادِ ٱلْإِنْكِلِيزِ.

West, *n.* The —, ٱلْغَرْبُ ـ ٱلْمَغْرِبُ. The —, western countries, ٱلْمَمَالِكُ ٱلْغَرْبِيَّةُ. To go towards the —, غَرَّبَ ـ تَغَرَّبَ. To come into the —, أَغْرَبَ. It is situated to the — of the mountain, مَحَطُّهُ غَرْبِيَّ ٱلْجَبَلِ.

West, *a.* غَرْبِيٌّ ـ مَغْرِبِيٌّ. The — wind, رِيحُ ٱلدَّبُورِ ـ ٱلدَّبُورُ ـ ٱلرِّيحُ ٱلْغَرْبِيَّةُ.

Westerly, *a.* Towards the west, جِهَةَ ٱلْغَرْبِ ـ نَحْوَ ٱلْغَرْبِ ـ إِلَى ٱلْغَرْبِ.

Western, *a.* غَرْبِيٌّ.

Westward, *ad.* }
Westwardly, } نَحْوَ ٱلْغَرْبِ ـ جِهَةَ ٱلْغَرْبِ ـ تَغَرُّبًا.

Wet, *a.* As with water, *etc.*, مَبْلُول ـ مُبْتَلّ ـ مُشَرَّب. Rainy, غَيْث ـ مَطِر ـ مَاطِر ـ إِخْضَلّ. To be —, as with water, تَشَرَّبَ ـ إِبْتَلَّ ـ تَبَلَّلَ. To be rainy, أَمْطَرَ. *See also* Damp, Moist, *a.*

Wet, *n.* Water, مَآء. Moisture, عَرَق ـ نَدًى ـ طَرَاوَة ـ بَلَل ـ بَلَالَة ـ بِلَال ـ نَدَاوَة. Rain, غَيْث ـ مَطَر. Continued —, rain, أُسْكُوب ـ سَكْب.

Wet, *v.t.* بَلَّلَ ـ بَلَّ ‎ـ خَضَّلَ ـ أَخْضَلَ: The rain wetted him, إِبْتَلَّ مِنَ ٱلْمَطَرِ ـ أَخْضَلَتْهُ ٱلسَّمَآءُ. His tears wetted his beard, أَخْضَلَتْ دُمُوعُهُ لِحْيَتَهُ. *See also to* Moisten, *v.t.*

Wether, *n.* كَبْشٌ خَصِيٌّ *pl.* أَكْبَاشٌ خِصْيَانٌ.

Wetness, *n.* *See* Wet, *n.*

Wet-nurse, *n.* مُرْضِعَة.

Wettish, *a.* مَبْلُولٌ نَوْعًا ـ مَبْلُولٌ بَعْضَ ٱلْبَلَلِ. *See also* Moist, *a.*

Wey, *n.* The weight, مِقْدَارُ وَزْنٍ مِنَ ٱلصُّوفِ وَٱلسَّمْنِ وَٱلْجُبْنِ.

Whack, *v.t.* ضَرَبَ.

Whack, *n.* ضَرْبَة *pl.* ضَرَبَات.

Whale, *n.* بَال ـ جَمَلُ ٱلْبَحْرِ ـ حُوت *pl.* حِيتَان ـ حُوتُ يُونُس ـ سَمَكُ يُونُس.

Whalebone, *n.* رِيشُ ٱلْحُوتِ.

Whale-fishing, *n.* صَيْدُ ٱلْحُوتِ.

Whaleman, *n.* صَيَّادُ ٱلْحُوتِ *pl.* صَيَّادُون.

Whaler, *n.* Of the ship, مَرْكَبُ صَيَّادِي ٱلْحُوتِ.

Whapper, *n.* شَيْءٌ كَبِيرٌ ـ شَيْءٌ جَسِيمٌ.

Whapping, *a.* كَبِير ـ جَسِيم.

Wharf, *n.* رَصِيف ـ إِسْكِلَة.

Wharf, *v.t.* رَصَفَ = رَكَّبَ فِيهِ رَصِيفًا.

Wharfage, *n.* حَقُّ ٱلرَّصِيفِ ـ أُجْرَةُ ٱلْإِسْكِلَةِ.

Wharfinger, *n.* The owner of a wharf, صَاحِبُ رَصِيفٍ; the keeper of a wharf, حَافِظُ ٱلرَّصِيفِ.

What, *rel. pr.* مَاذَا ـ مَا ـ ٱلَّذِي *fem.* ٱلَّتِي. He knew not — to say, لَمْ يَعْلَمْ مَا يَتَكَلَّمُ بِهِ. They know not — they do, لَا يَعْلَمُونَ مَاذَا يَفْعَلُونَ. They told him — they had done, أَخْبَرُوهُ بِمَا فَعَلُوا. Not — I will, but — you will, لَيْسَ مَا أُرِيدُ أَنَا بَلْ مَا تُرِيدُ أَنْتَ. What God pleases, مَا شَآءَ ٱللّٰهُ. In — way soever, كَيْفَمَا كَانَ.

What, *interr. pr.*, and *interj.*, مَا ـ مَاذَا ـ أَيُّ ـ هَلْ. What thing? أَيُّ شَيْءٍ. What is it that thou sawest? مَاذَا رَأَيْتَ. What have you got? مَا مَعَكَ. What have I to do with you? مَا لِي وَلَكُمْ. What has he done? مَا فَعَلَ. What's o'clock? مَا ٱلسَّاعَةُ. What's the matter? مَاذَا جَرَى. What's the matter with you? أَيُّ شَيْءٍ بِكَ. What is it that you say? مَاذَا تَقُولُ. What is it that you say? (implying something that ought not to be said,) مَا لَكَ وَهٰذَا ٱلْكَلَامِ. What are you? مَا أَنْتَ. What then? وَبَعْدُ ـ فَمَاذَا إِذًا. What! *as an interjection*, أَيُّ ـ مَا: What a man he was! أَيُّ رَجُلٍ كَانَ. What! could you not wait for me one hour? أَهٰكَذَا مَا قَدَرْتُمْ أَنْ تَنْتَظِرُونِي سَاعَةً وَاحِدَةً. What a generous man he was! مَا أَكْرَمَهُ. What a beautiful woman she is! مَا أَجْمَلَهَا ـ مَا أَحْسَنَهَا. What a fool he is! مَا أَشَدَّهُ حَمَاقَةً ـ مَا أَحْمَقَهُ.

Whatever, *pr.* } كُلُّ مَا ـ مَا ـ مَهْمَا. Whatever is due to you,
Whatsoever, } مَا يَحِقُّ لَكُمْ. Whatever we ask we receive, مَهْمَا سَأَلْنَا نَنَالُ. Whatever may happen, كَيْفَمَا ٱتَّفَقَ. Whatever is more than that, مَا زَادَ عَلَى ذٰلِكَ. Whatever you wish, مَهْمَا تُرِيدُ. "Shall man have whatever he wishes?" أَمْ لِلْإِنْسَانِ مَا تَمَنَّى (Kur. liii. 24).

Whatnot, *n.* كُرْسِيٌّ ذُو رُفُوفٍ ـ قَاعِدَةٌ ذَاتُ رُفُوفٍ.

Wheal, *n.* *See* Weal, *n.*

Wheat, *n.* قَمْحٌ ـ حِنْطَةٌ ـ بُرٌّ ـ طَعَامٌ *pl.* أَطْعِمَةٌ. A grain of —, قَمْحَةٌ *pl.* قَمْحَاتٌ. Wheat coarsely ground, جَشِيشٌ ـ سَوِيقٌ. The — increased, أَرَاعَتِ ٱلْحِنْطَةُ. — *boiled & pounded* بُرْغُل

Wheaten, *a.* مِنْ حِنْطَةٍ ـ مِنْ بُرٍّ. Wheaten bread, خُبْزُ حِنْطَةٍ.

Wheedle, *v.t.* جَامَلَ ـ صَانَعَ ـ تَلَيَّنَ لِ ـ رَاوَضَ عَلَى ـ رَاوَضَ ـ دَارَى ـ مَاسَحَ ـ بِٱلْجَمِيلِ ـ تَأَلَّفَ.

Wheel, *n.* As of a cart, *etc.*, عَجَلَةٌ *pl.* عَجَلٌ and عِجَالٌ ـ بَكَرَةٌ *pl.* بَكَرَاتٌ ـ دُولَابٌ *pl.* دَوَالِيبُ. A ship's steering —, دُولَابُ ٱلسُّكَّانِ. To take the —, of a ship, مَسَكَ دُولَابَ ٱلسُّكَّانِ. To break one on the —, of torture, عَذَّبَ بِٱلْعَذْرَاءِ.

Balance-wheel, عَجَلَةٌ رَقَّاصَةٌ.

Cog-wheel, عَجَلَةٌ مُسَنَّنَةٌ.

Driving-wheel, عَجَلَةٌ مُحَرِّكَةٌ.

Paddle-wheel, دُولَابُ بَاخِرَةٍ.

Persian-wheel, } غَرَّافٌ ـ نَوَاعِيرُ *pl.* نَاعُورَةٌ ـ دُولَابٌ ـ عَجَلَةٌ *pl.*
Water-wheel, } سَوَاقِي *pl.* سَاقِيَةٌ ـ غَرَارِيفُ. A jar of a —, قَادُوسٌ *pl.* قَوَادِيسُ.

Potter's-wheel, دُولَابُ ٱلْخَزَّافِ (*or* ٱلْفَخَّارِيِّ).

Wheel, *v.t.* To push, roll, جَرَّ ـ دَحْرَجَ [2]. To — about, أَجَالَ ـ أَدَارَ ـ *vulg.* دَوْلَبَ. To — away, as on a cart, نَقَلَ عَلَى [2] عَرَبَةٍ ـ دَوَّرَ.

Wheel, *v.i.* To turn, as on an axis, دَارَ *aor.* يَدُورُ ـ إِسْتَدَارَ. To go or turn round, جَالَ *aor.* يَجُولُ ـ ٱنْجَالَ ـ إِجْتَالَ. To — off, to flee, حَاصَ حَيْصَةً. To — away from, to retire from, حَاصَ عَنْ ـ أَدْبَرَ عَنْ. He wheeled about from the enemy, فَرَّ مِنَ ٱلْعَدُوِّ.

Wheel-barrow, *n.* نَقَّالَةٌ ذَاتُ عَجَلَةٍ يَسُوقُهَا رَجُلٌ قُدَّامَهُ ـ مِنْقَلَةٌ (*or*) نَقَّالَةٌ) ذَاتُ عَجَلَةٍ.

Wheeling, *a.* The act of — on a wheel, نَقْلٌ عَلَى عَجَلَةٍ. A turning round, دَوَرَانٌ ـ جَوَلَانٌ.

Wheeler, *n.* A horse next to the wheels, ٱلْحِصَانُ ٱلْأَقْرَبُ مِنَ ٱلْعَرَبَانَةِ. A four —, عَرَبَانَةٌ عَلَى أَرْبَعِ أَعْجَالٍ.

Wheel-shaped, *a.* فِي شَكْلِ ٱلدُّولَابِ ـ فِي هَيْئَةِ ٱلْعَجَلَةِ.

Wheelwright, *n.* نَجَّارُ ٱلْعَرَبَانَاتِ.

Wheeze, *v.i.* أَنَحَّ ـ نَهَجَ ـ زَخَرَ ـ شَخَرَ.

Wheezing, *n.* نَحِيحٌ ـ نَهْجٌ ـ زُخَارٌ ـ شَخْرٌ.

Whelk, *n.* A protuberance, عَيْرٌ *pl.* أَعْيَارٌ. A pustule, بَثْرَةٌ *pl.* بَثَرَاتٌ. A kind of shell, ضَرْبٌ مِنَ ٱلصَّدَفِ.

Whelm, *v.t.* *See* to Overwhelm, *v.t.*

Whelp, *n.* The young of a beast, شِبْلٌ *pl.* شِبَالٌ ـ جَرْوٌ *pl.* جِرَآءٌ and أَجْرَآءٌ.

Whelp, *v.i.* خَلَّفَتْ ـ وَلَدَتْ ـ نَتَجَتْ ـ أَجْرَتْ.

When, *ad.* At what time, interrogatively, مَتَى ـ أَيَّ مَتَى. On the occasion, لَمَّا ـ حِينَ ـ عِنْدَ مَا ـ مَتَى. When will you be wise? مَتَى تَعْقِلُونَ. When will you start? مَتَى تَسِيرُ ـ مَتَى تُسَافِرُ. When you come to me I will come to you, مَتَى تَأْتِينِي آتِيكَ. When, at what time, he shall call for you, إِذَا دَعَاكُمْ. Who knows when it shall be? مَنْ يَعْلَمُ مَتَى سَيَكُونُ. When will you return? مَتَى تَرْجِعُ. When we were with you, حِينَ كُنَّا عِنْدَكُمْ. When he speaks, لَمَّا يَتَكَلَّمُ. When the beginning of the month shall come, إِذَا جَآءَ رَأْسُ ٱلشَّهْرِ. "And they say, when shall this threat be (put in force,) if ye speak the truth," وَيَقُولُونَ مَتَى هٰذَا ٱلْوَعْدُ إِنْ كُنْتُمْ صَادِقِينَ (Kur. lxvii. 25).

Whence, *ad.* مِنْ أَيْنَ ـ مِنْ حَيْثُ. Whence come ye? مِنْ أَيْنَ جِئْتُمْ. Before I go — I shall not return, قَبْلَ أَنْ أَذْهَبَ وَلَا أَعُودُ. I will return to my house — I came, أَرْجِعُ إِلَى بَيْتِي ٱلَّذِي خَرَجْتُ مِنْهُ. Whence do you know me? مِنْ أَيْنَ تَعْرِفُنِي.

Whencesoever, *ad.* مِنْ أَيِّ مَحَلٍّ كَانَ.

Whenever, *ad.* } طَالَمَا ـ كُلَّ مَا ـ حَيْثُمَا ـ مَهْمَا ـ إِذَا مَا ـ
Whensoever, } مَتَى مَا. Whenever he pleases, أَيَّانَ شَآءَ [2]. "And whenever a *surah* is sent down there are some of them who say: whose faith hath it increased?" وَإِذَا مَا أُنْزِلَتْ سُورَةٌ فَمِنْهُمْ مَنْ يَقُولُ أَيُّكُمْ زَادَتْهُ هٰذِهِ إِيمَانًا (Kur. ix. 125).

Where, *ad.* In what place, حَيْثُ ـ حَيْثُ. Where? interrogatively, أَيْنَ. Where you are I shall be, حَيْثُ تَكُونُ أَكُونُ. Where are you? أَيْنَ أَنْتَ. Where were you? أَيْنَ كُنْتَ. Where is he going? where does he intend to go? إِلَى أَيْنَ مُزْمِعٌ أَنْ يَذْهَبَ ـ إِلَى أَيْنَ هُوَ مُسَافِرٌ.

Whereabout, *ad.* } Interrogatively, فِي أَيِّ مَحَلٍّ ـ أَيْنَ. Con-
Whereabouts, } cerning which, مِنْ ـ نَحْوَ ـ عَنْ.

Whereabouts, *n.* مَحَلّ ـ مَكان. I know his —, أَعْلَمُ مَكانَهُ.

Whereas, *ad.* Seeing that . . . , مِنْ حَيْثُ أَن ـ عَلَى أَن ـ مِنْ كَوْنِ أَن ـ مِنْ أَجْلِ أَن. But, on the contrary, لٰكِن ـ بَل.

Whereat, *ad.* Thereupon, عِنْدَ ذٰلِكَ.

Whereby, *ad.* By which (the relative pronoun and the objective being masculine), اَلَّذِى بِهِ; (the relative pronoun being fem. and the objective masc.), اَلَّتِى بِهِ; (the relative pronoun being masc. and the objective fem.), اَلَّذِى بِهَا; (the relative pronoun and the objective being fem.), اَلَّتِى بِهَا. Whereby? interrogatively, كَيْفَ. Whereby shall I know him? كَيْفَ أَعْلَمُ مَنْ هُوَ. The town possesses no means whereby to combat a conflagration, لَيْسَ لِلْبَلْدَةِ وَسَائِلُ تَتَدارَكُ بِهَا ٱلْحَرِيقَ.

Wherefore, *ad.* For which reason, لِأَجْلِ ذٰلِكَ ـ لِذٰلِكَ ـ مِنْ أَجْلِ ذٰلِكَ. Wherefore? (interrogatively,) لِمَ ـ لِمَا ـ لِمَاذَا ـ لِأَىِّ شَيْءٍ ـ *vulg.* لَيْش. Wherefore are you come? لِمَاذَا جِئْتَ.

Wherein, *ad.* Where, فِى ـ حَيْثُ. Wherein? In what? فِى أَىِّ شَيْءٍ. The house — we were, الدَّارُ ٱلَّتِى كُنَّا فِيهَا. Wherein have I wronged you? فِى أَىِّ شَيْءٍ ظَلَمْتُكَ.

Whereof, *ad.* Respecting which, عَمَّا. Whereof you have received instructions, الَّذِى لِأَجْلِهِ أَخَذْتُمْ وَصَايَا.

Whereon, *ad.* | Whereupon, } Upon, فَوْقَ ـ مِنْ عَلَى ـ عَلَى. Then, إِذْ ذاكَ ـ عِنْدَ ذٰلِكَ ـ وَحِينَئِذٍ. In consequence of, مِنْ بِسَبَبِ ذٰلِكَ ـ لِأَجْلِ ذٰلِكَ ـ ثُمَّ. On what? عَلَى أَىِّ شَيْءٍ.

Wheresoever, *ad.* حَيْثُمَا ـ أَيْنَمَا.

Whereto, *ad.* | Whereunto, } The thing which, what, الَّذِى ـ مَا ـ فِى ما. To whom? لِمَنْ. How far? إِلَى أَيْنَ. Whereto shall I liken him? بِمَنْ أُشَبِّهُهُ.

Wherever, *ad.* حَيْثُمَا ـ أَيْنَمَا.

Wherewith, *ad.* | Wherewithal, } With what, بِمَا ـ بِمَ. With which, الَّذِى بِهِ: The love — you have loved me, الحُبُّ الَّذِى أَحْبَبْتَنِى بِهِ. Wherewith, (as a noun); I have not the —, لَيْسَتِ الحاجَةُ تَحْتَ يَدِى.

Wherry, *n.* A ferry-boat, مِعْبَر ـ مِعْبَرَة.

Whet, *v.t.* To sharpen, as on a stone, سَنَّ ـ سَنَّنَ. To —, as the appetite, حَرَّضَ ـ أَنْهَضَ ـ أَنْفَسَ ـ سَنَّنَ. To incite, حَرَّضَ. This thing whetted my appetite, سَنَّنِى هٰذا الشَّىْءُ.

Whet, *n.* A sharpening, تَسْنِين ـ سَنّ. Something taken before dinner to sharpen the appetite, لُهْنَة ـ لُمْجَة. To take a —, تَلَهَّنَ.

Whether, *pr.* Which of the two, أَىُّ الإِثْنَيْنِ. Whether is greater the son or the father, أَيُّمَا أَعْظَمُ ٱلْوَلَدُ أَمِ ٱلْوَالِدُ.

Whether, if, إِنْ: whether we live or die, إِنْ عِشْنَا وَإِنْ مِتْنَا. Alike, equal, سَوَآءٌ كَانَ ـ سَوَآءٌ: it is the same to me — you stand or sit, سَوَآءٌ عَلَىَّ قُمْتَ أَوْ قَعَدْتَ. Whether it be I or they, سَوَآءٌ أَنَا أَمْ أُولٰئِكَ. Whether they hear or — they forbear, إِنْ سَمِعُوا وَإِنِ ٱمْتَنَعُوا. Whether in time of war or of peace, سَوَآءٌ كَانَ فِى زَمَنِ ٱلْحَرْبِ أَوْ زَمَنِ ٱلصُّلْحِ. "Whether thou warn them or — thou warn them not," أَأَنْذَرْتَهُمْ أَمْ لَمْ تُنْذِرْهُمْ (Kur. ii. 5).

Whetstone, *n.* مِسَنّ ـ مِسْحَنَة ـ مِشْحَذ ـ صُلَيْبِيَّة.

Whey, *n.* مَآءُ ٱلْجُبْنِ ـ مُصَالَة ـ مَصْل ـ مُصَارَة.

Which, *rel. pr.* الَّذِى *fem.* الَّتِى *pl. masc.* الَّذِينَ *pl. fem.* اَللَّاتِى; which two, اَلَّذانِ *and* اَللَّذا *fem.* اَللَّتانِ *and* اَللَّتا. Which? interrogatively, أَىّ: Which of them is your brother? أَيُّهُمْ أَخُوكَ. Which of the two men? أَىُّ ٱلرَّجُلَيْنِ. Which of the two women? أَىُّ ٱلْمَرْأَتَيْنِ. Which of the two? (of males,) أَيُّهُمَا; (of females,) أَيَّتُهُمَا. Which of the men? أَىُّ ٱلرِّجَالِ. Which of the women? أَىُّ ٱلنِّسَآءِ. *See also under* Who, *rel. pr.*

Whichever, *pr.* | Whichsoever, } Whether one or the other, (masc.) هٰذا أَوْ هٰذاكَ ; *fem.* هٰذِهِ أَوْ تِلْكَ. الَّذِى ـ *fem.* الَّتِى. Whichever you approve, الَّذِى تَسْتَحْسِنُهُ.

Whiff, *n.* As of the breath, نَفَس *pl.* أَنْفَاس. A — of wind, نَفْخَة ـ هَبَّةُ رِيحٍ ـ هَبَّة. A — of tobacco-smoke, نَفَسُ تُتُنٍ.

Whiff, *v.t.* نَفَخَ بِ ـ نَفَخَ.

Whiffle, *v.i.* *See to* Shuffle, *v.i.*

Whiffler, *n.* *See* Shuffler, *n.*

Whiffle-tree, *n.* جَائِزُ مَجْرَى ٱلْعَرَبَانَةِ ـ *vulg.* جَارُورَة.

Whig, *n.* إِسْمُ فِرْقَةٍ مِنْ أَهْلِ ٱلسِّيَاسَةِ فِى إِنْكِلْتَرَةَ تَتَعَصَّبُ لِحُقُوقِ ٱلرَّعَايَا وَٱزْدِيَادِهَا.

Whiggery, *n.* | Whiggism, } أُصُولُ ٱلْفِرْقَةِ ٱلْمَذْكُورَةِ.

While, *n.* Time, space, وَقْت ـ مُدَّة ـ زَمَن ـ طِبْقَة. For a —, لِزَمَنٍ مَّا ـ لِمُدَّةٍ مَّا ـ طِبْقًا. For a little —, سَاعَةً. For a good —, زَمَانًا. A little — ago, مِنْ مُدَّةٍ يَسِيرَةٍ ـ مُنْذُ زَمَنٍ قَلِيلٍ. All the —, كُلَّ الزَّمانِ. It is not worth —, مَا يُسَاوِى ـ لَا طَائِلَ فِيهِ ـ التَّعَبَ.

While, *ad.* During the time that, إِذْ ـ بَيْنَمَا ـ بَيْنَا. While I live, مَا دُمْتُ فِى قَيْدِ ٱلْحَيَاةِ ـ مَا دُمْتُ حَيًّا ـ فِى حَيَاتِى. While we were there, بَيْنَمَا نَحْنُ هُنَاكَ. While I was in that state, behold Zaid arrived, بَيْنَمَا أَنَا كَذا إِذْ جَآءَ زَيْدٌ. While, at the time, عِنْدَ ما. I rose — the people were sitting, قُمْتُ وَٱلنَّاسُ قُعُودٌ. While, when, لَمَّا. I told you — I was still with you, قُلْتُ لَكَ وَأَنَا بَعْدُ مَعَكَ. While it is yet day, مَا دَامَ نَهَارٌ. While he was yet alive, وَهُوَ حَيٌّ. While, in the mean time, فِي خِلَالِ ذٰلِكَ. *See also under* Though, *conj.*

While, *v.t.* To — away time, ـِ قَضَى ٱلْوَقْتَ. To — away one's time with something, تَعَلَّلَ بِ.

Whilst, *ad.* *See* While, *ad.*

Whim, *n.* هَوًى *pl.* أَهْوَآءٌ. *See also* Fancy, Caprice, *n.*

Whimper, *v.i.* To cry like a child, ـِ بَكَى ـ أَعْوَلَ ـ إِمْتَأَقَ ـ مَتَّقَ.

Whimpering, *n.* عَوْل ـ عَوِيل ـ مَأْقَة.

Whimsical, *a.* Full of whims, طائش ـ هَوَائِيٌّ ـ ذُو أَهْوَآءٍ ـ مُخَبَّل. *See also* Capricious, Odd, *a.*

Whimsicality, *n.* / **Whimsicalness**, } غَرَابَة ـ خَبَال ـ طَيَشَان ـ طَيْش.

Whimsically, *ad.* بِٱلْهَوَآءِ ـ بِطَيَشَانٍ ـ طَيْشًا ـ عَلَى هَوَى نَفْسِهِ وَٱللَّوَآءِ.

Whin, *n.* *See* Furze, *n.*

Whine, *v.i.* ـِ بَكَى ـ يَئِنّ *aor.* أَنَّ ـ تَأَوَّهَ ـ ٤ فَصَّ.

Whine, *n.* / **Whining**, } أَنَّة ـ بُكَآء ـ تَأْنَان ـ أُنَان ـ أَنِين ـ تَأَوُّه ـ فَصِيص.

Whiner, *n.* / **Whining**, *a.* } بَكِيٌّ ـ آنٌّ ـ أَنَّان ـ مُتَأَوِّه.

Whiningly, *ad.* بِبُكَآءٍ ـ بِأَنِينٍ ـ تَأَوُّهًا.

Whinny, *v.i.* *See to* Neigh, *v.i.*

Whin-stone, *n.* ضَرْبٌ مِنَ ٱلْحَجَرِ أَسْوَدُ ٱللَّوْنِ وَصُلْبُ ٱلْجِنْسِ.

Whip, *n.* سَوْط *pl.* سِيَاط *and* أَسْوَاط ـ مِقْرَعَة *pl.* مَقَارِعُ ـ دِرَّة *pl.* دِرَر. A horse —, كِرْبَاج. The driver, as of a carriage, سَائِق ـ سَوَّاق. A light rope, مَرَس *pl.* أَمْرَاس ـ جَرِير *pl.* أَجِرَّة. A whisk, مِسْوَط ـ مِسْوَاط ـ مِشْمَط. A stroke with a —, ضَرْبَةُ سَوْطٍ. "Therefore thy Lord let loose upon them the whip [or scourge] of chastisement," فَصَبَّ عَلَيْهِمْ رَبُّكَ سَوْطَ عَذَابٍ (Kur. lxxxix. 11).

Whip, *v.t.* To punish with a whip, ـِ جَلَدَ ـ يَسُوطُ *aor.* سَاطَ ـ سَوَّطَ *vulg.* To — off, carry away, ـِ خَطَفَ ـ إِسْتَلَّ ـ ٤ سَلَّ ـ إِخْتَطَفَ. To — on, drive on, سَاقَ *aor.* يَسُوقُ ـ سَوَّقَ ـ أَسَاقَ. To — up, as eggs, *etc.*, ـِ شَمَطَ ـ سَاطَ *aor.* يَسُوطُ.

Whip, *v.i.* To whip about, to move nimbly, ـِ نَشِطَ ـ ـِ خَفَّ. To — off, run away, وَلَّى هَارِبًا ـ ٤ هَرَبَ ـ إِنْسَلَّ.

Whip-cord, *n.* مَرَسٌ مَثْلُوثٌ ـ مَرَسَةٌ لِلْمَقَارِعِ.

Whip-graft, *v.t.* *See to* Graft, *v.t.*

Whip-hand, *n.* *See* Upperhand, *n.*

Whipper, *n.* جَلَّاد ـ الضَّارِبُ بِٱلْمِقْرَعَةِ.

Whipper-in, *n.* Of huntsmen, كَلَّابُ أَهْلِ ٱلصَّيْدِ وَٱلْقَنَصِ. One who enforces party discipline, قَائِدُ ٱلْحِزْبِ ـ زَعِيمُ ٱلْفِرْقَةِ.

Whipper-snapper, *n.* هَبَنَّق ـ خَنْبَس ـ رُجَيْل.

Whipping, *n.* ضَرْبُ سَوْطٍ ـ سَوْط ـ جَلْد.

Whipping-post, *n.* حِمَار ـ عُقْبَان.

Whipple-tree, *n.* *See* Whiffle-tree, *n.*

Whip-staff, *n.* *See* Helm, *n.*

Whipster, *n.* A nimble fellow, بَطْرَان ـ حَرِك ـ خَفِيف ـ نَشِيط.

Whip-stick, *n.* / **Whip-stock**, } قَضِيبُ ٱلسَّوْطِ.

Whir, *v.i.* خَرَّ *aor.* يَخِرُّ ـ خَفَّ *aor.* يَخِفُّ.

Whir, *n.* / **Whirring**, } حَفِيف ـ خَرِير.

Whirl, *v.t.* To turn, أَدَارَ ـ دَوَّرَ. To twist, لَوَى.

Whirl, *v.i.* To go round, دَارَ *aor.* يَدُورُ ـ إِسْتَدَارَ. To twist, اِلْتَوَى ـ تَلَوَّى.

Whirl, *n.* / **Whirling**, } A going round, دَوَرَان. The — of a spindle, فَلْكَة ـ فِلْكَة. To be in a —, ٤ دَاخَ ـ تَحَيَّرَ.

Whirlbone, *n.* The cap of the knee, الدَّاغِصَة.

Whirligig, *n.* The toy, فِرِّيرَة ـ خَرَّارَة ـ خُذْرُوف.

Whirlpool, *n.* دَوَّامَةُ ٱلْبَحْرِ ـ دُرْدُور.

Whirlwind, *n.* زَوْبَعَة *pl.* زَوَابِعُ. A — of dust, إِعْصَار.

Whirr, *v.i.* *See to* Whir, *v.i.*

Whirring, *n.* خَرِير ـ حَفِيف.

Whisk, *n.* A piece of anything, جِثَّةٌ مِنْ شَيْءٍ *pl.* جِثَث. A — of straw, تِبْنَة. A — for beating up eggs, *etc.*, مِشْمَط ـ مِسْوَط ـ مِسْوَاط. A small brush, زُحَّافَة. A fly-flap, مِكَشَّة.

Whisk, *v.t.* To whip, of eggs, *etc.*, ـِ شَمَطَ ـ سَاطَ *aor.* يَسُوطُ. To — the tail, ـِ خَطَرَ بِذَنَبِهِ.

Whisk, *v.i.* To move about quickly, ـِ نَشِطَ ـ خَفَّ *aor.* يَخِفُّ ـ طَارَ *aor.* يَطِيرُ.

Whisker, *n.* سَبَلَةُ ٱلْخَدِّ *pl.* سِبَال ـ شَعْرُ ٱلْعَارِضَيْنِ.

Whiskered, *a.* ذُو شَعْرٍ فِي عَارِضَيْهِ. A — woman, سَبْلَآءُ.

Whisky, *n.* The spirit, عَرَقُ ٱلشَّعِيرِ. A light carriage, عَرَبَانَةٌ خَفِيفَةٌ.

Whisper, *v.i.* To speak in a low voice, ـِ خَفَضَ (or ـِ خَفَضَ) صَوْتَهُ ـ وَسْوَسَ ـ تَوَسْوَسَ. To — against, to backbite, ٤ نَمَّ عَلَى. They whispered together, تَنَاجَوْا مَعًا.

Whisper, *v.t.* To communicate to privately, سَارَّ-فِي — نَاجَى — أُذُنِهِ — وَسْوَسَ — أَكَبَّ-فِي أُذُنِهِ — ²كَتَّ-فِي أُذُنِهِ. "Then Satan whispered them to show their nakedness, which had been hidden from them both," فَوَسْوَسَ لَهُمَا ٱلشَّيْطَانُ لِيُبْدِيَ لَهُمَا مَا وُرِيَ عَنْهُمَا (Kur. vii. 19).

Whisper, *n.* A low soft sound, صَوْتٌ خَفِيضٌ. A speaking to one in a —, وَسْوَسَة — مُنَاجَاة — مُسَارَّة. A slander, نَمِيمَة *pl.* نَمِيمَات.

Whisperer, *n.* One who whispers to another, مُنَاجٍ — مُسَارٌّ — وَسْوَاس. A slanderer, نَمَّام. "Say: I betake me for refuge to the Lord of men, the King of men, the God of men, against the mischief of the shrinking [or stealthily-withdrawing] whisperer," Satan, قُلْ أَعُوذُ بِرَبِّ ٱلنَّاسِ مَلِكِ ٱلنَّاسِ إِلَٰهِ ٱلنَّاسِ مِنْ شَرِّ ٱلْوَسْوَاسِ ٱلْخَنَّاسِ (Kur. cxiv. 1-4).

Whispering, *n.* A speaking with a low voice, خَفْضُ ٱلصَّوْتِ; with another, مُسَارَّة — سِرَار. A — of the wind, هَزِيزُ ٱلرِّيحِ — حَفِيفُ ٱلرِّيحِ.

Whispering, *a.* As to another, مُسَارٌّ. A — gallery, مَسْمَع — شُرْفَةُ مَسْمَعٍ.

Whist, *a.* *See* Silent, *a.*

Whist, *n.* The game, وِيسْتُ وَهُوَ ضَرْبٌ مِنْ لَعِبِ ٱلْوَرَقِ.

Whist! *int.* صَهْ — ٱلسُّكُوتُ — ٱلسَّكْتَةَ.

Whistle, *v.t.* and *i.* As with the mouth, صَفَرَ — ≈صَفَّرَ. To —, of the wind, (*v.i.*) ≈حَنَّ — ≈هَفَّ — صَرْصَرَ — ≈صَرَّ — ≈نَأَجَ — ≈قَصَفَ.

Whistle, *n.* The instrument, صَفَّارَة. The noise of a —, صُفَار — صَفِير.

Whistling, *a.* As with the lips or on a whistle, صَافِر; of the wind, هَافٌّ — قَاصِف — حَنُون — نَؤُوج.

Whistling, *n.* As with the lips, *etc.*, صَفِير — صُفَار; of the wind, هَفِيف — حَنِين — صَرْصَرَة — نَئِيج.

Whit, *n.* بَتَّة — قَطْعًا — أَصْلًا — ذَرَّة — حَبَّة — نُقْطَة. Not a —, أَصْلًا. I am not a — behind him, لَا أَنْقُصُ شَيْئًا عَنْهُ. "Verily, not a whit shall they injure God," إِنَّهُمْ لَنْ يَضُرُّوا ٱللَّهَ شَيْئًا (Kur. iii. 170).

White, *a.* أَبْيَضُ *fem.* ¹بَيْضَاءُ *pl.* بِيض. White, in complexion, as opposed to أَسْوَدُ black, أَحْمَرُ. Pale, أَصْفَرُ. This is whiter than that, هٰذَا أَشَدُّ بَيَاضًا مِنْ ذٰلِكَ. A — garment, or a — piece of cloth, سَحْل *pl.* سُحُول *and* سُحُل. "On the day that faces shall turn white, and faces shall turn black," يَوْمَ تَبْيَضُّ وُجُوهٌ وَتَسْوَدُّ وُجُوهٌ (Kur. iii. 102). To be or to become —, أَبْيَضَّ. His face became —, cheerful; or his honesty became apparent, أَبْيَضَّ وَجْهُهُ. To show the — feather, ²جَبُنَ.

White, *n.* بَيَاض — بَيَاضَة. One having a clear complexion, free from freckles, *etc.*, أَبْيَضُ ٱلْوَجْهِ *fem.* بَيْضَاءُ ٱلْوَجْهِ. Whites, or white people, in contradistinction to negroes, بِيضَان. The — of an egg, زُلَالُ (*or* بَيَاضُ) ٱلْبَيْضَةِ; The — of the eye, ٱلْغُرْقَدُ — بَيَاضُ ٱلْعَيْنِ — ٱلْمُلْتَحِمَةُ.

White, *v.t.* } To make white, بَيَّضَ (which means also to Bleach,
Whiten, } or to Tin copper vessels, *etc.*)

Whiten, *v.i.* To be or to become white, أَبْيَضَّ.

White-bait, *n.* ضَرْبٌ مِنْ أَصْغَرِ ٱلسَّمَكِ لَذِيذٌ جِدًّا — أُرْبِيَان. A ministerial — dinner, مَأْدُبَةٌ يَتَّخِذُهَا ٱلْوُزَرَآءُ كُلَّ عَامٍ.

White-lead, *n.* سَبِيدَاج — إِسْفِيدَاج.

White-livered, *a.* Cowardly, جَبَان. Malicious, حَقُود — ضَغِن. Pale, أَصْفَرُ ٱلْوَجْهِ.

White-meat, *n.* Meat of fowls, لَحْمُ ٱلْفِرَاخِ. Light food, without flesh meat, أَكْلُ بَيَاضٍ — بَيَاض — عَصِيدَة — ٱلْأَبْيَضَانِ.

Whiteness, *n.* بَيَاض — بَيَاضَة. Purity, نَقَاوَة. Cleanliness, نَظَافَة. Paleness, إِصْفِرَار.

Whites, *n.* The female disease, رُطُوبَةُ ٱلنِّسَآءِ.

Whitesmith, *n.* تَنَكْرِيٌّ *vulg.* سَنْكَرِيٌّ.

White-swelling, *n.* خَنَازِيرُ فِي ٱلرُّكْبَةِ.

Whitewash, *n.* Of lime, طَرْشُ ٱلْكِلْسِ — دِمَامُ ٱلْكِلْسِ — حَلِيبُ ٱلْكِلْسِ.

Whitewash, *v.t.* With lime, ²دَهَنَ — ²دَمَّ-(*or* دَمَّمَ-) بِٱلْكِلْسِ — بِحَلِيبِ ٱلْكِلْسِ. To clear the character of one, بَيَّضَ وَجْهَهُ. To free a bankrupt from the remainder of his debts, خَلَّصَ ٱلْمُفْلِسَ مِنْ بَقِيَّةِ دُيُونِهِ.

Whitewasher, *n.* طَرَّاشٌ بِٱلْكِلْسِ — دَهَّانٌ بِحَلِيبِ ٱلْكِلْسِ — طَرَّاش.

Whitey-brown, *a.* أَسْمَرُ — أَشْهَبُ *pl.* شُهْب *fem.* ¹شَهْبَآءُ *pl.* شُهْب — أَسْمَرُ *fem.* ¹سَمْرَآءُ *pl.* سُمْر.

Whither, *ad.* حَيْثُ — حَيْثُمَا. Whither? (interrogatively,) أَيْنَ; toward which place? إِلَى أَيْنَ. Go — you please, أَذْهَبْ حَيْثُ شِئْتَ. Whither are you going? إِلَى أَيْنَ ذَاهِبٌ — إِلَى أَيْنَ رَائِحٌ.

Whithersoever, *ad.* حَيْثُمَا — أَيْنَمَا. "So we subjected the wind to him that it might run softly at his bidding whithersoever he directed it," فَسَخَّرْنَا لَهُ ٱلرِّيحَ تَجْرِي بِأَمْرِهِ رُخَآءً حَيْثُ أَصَابَ (Kur. xxxviii. 35).

Whiting, *n.* The chalk, طَبَاشِير *or* تَبَاشِير; the fish, نَوْعٌ مِنَ ٱلسَّمَكِ.

Whitish, *a.* ضَارِبٌ إِلَى — أَبْيَضُ بَعْضَ ٱلْبَيَاضِ — أَبْيَضُ نَوْعًا — أَبْيَضَانِيٌّ — ٱلْبَيَاضِ.

Whitlow, *n.* صُدَاعُ ٱلْأَصَابِعِ ـ دَاحِس ـ دَاحُوس.

Whit-Sunday, *n.* أَحَدُ عِيدِ ٱلْعَنْصَرَةِ.

Whitsuntide, *n.* عِيدُ ٱلْعَنْصَرَةِ.

Whittle, *n.* For whittling, مِبْرَاة ـ مِسْحَج.

Whittle, *v.t.* بَرَى ـ سَحَجَ.

Whiz, *v.i.* هَسْهَسَ ـ خَرَّ *aor.* يَخُرُّ.

Whiz, *n.* }
Whizzing, } هَسْهَسَة ـ خَرِير.

Who? *interr. pr.* مَنْ: Who art thou? مَنْ أَنْتَ. Who was it that saluted you? مَنِ ٱلَّذِى سَلَّمَ عَلَيْكَ. Who am I that I should go to him? مَنْ أَنَا حَتَّى أَذْهَبَ إِلَيْهِ. Who is he? Who is there? مَنْ هُوَ.

Who, *rel. pr.* ٱلَّذِى *fem.* ٱلَّتِى *pl.* ٱلَّذِينَ *fem. pl.* ٱللَّاتِى *and* ٱللَّوَاتِى *dual masc.* ٱللَّذَانِ *and* ٱللَّذَا *dual fem.* ٱللَّتَانِ *and* ٱللَّتَا ـ مَنْ. He knew not who it was, لَمْ يَعْلَمْ مَنْ هُوَ. He inquired of him who he might be, إِسْتَخْبَرَهُ مَنْ هُوَ. There are people who say, مِنَ ٱلنَّاسِ مَنْ يَقُولُ. He who told me, ٱلَّذِى أَخْبَرَنِى.

Whoever, *pr.* كُلُّ مَنْ ـ مَنْ.

Whole, *a.* Unimpaired, صَحِيح *pl.* صِحَاح *and* أَصِحَّآء. All, كُلّ ـ جَمِيع ـ سَائِر. Safe and sound, سَالِمٌ آمِنٌ. The — body, كُلُّ ٱلْجَسَدِ. With my — heart, مِنْ كُلِّ قَلْبِى. The — day, كُلُّ ٱلنَّهَارِ. A — number, عَدَدٌ صَحِيحٌ. To be —, صَحَّ. To make —, صَحَّحَ.

Whole, *n.* كُلِّيَّة ـ جُمْلَة ـ جِلْمَة ـ كَمَل ـ كَافَّة. The — of the day, كُلُّ ٱلنَّهَارِ ـ عَامَّةُ ٱلنَّهَارِ. The — of the army, سَائِرُ ٱلْعَسْكَرِ ـ جَمِيعُ ٱلْعَسْكَرِ ـ ٱلْجَيْش. On the —, بِٱلْجُمْلَةِ ـ وَحَاصِلُ ٱلْقَضِيَّةِ ـ وَفِى ٱلْجُمْلَةِ. I took the — of my right, أَخَذْتُ حَقِّى أَجْمَعَ. I saw the women, the — of them, رَأَيْتُ ٱلنِّسْوَةَ جُمَعَ. The palace pleased me, the — of it, أَعْجَبَنِى ٱلْقَصْرُ أَجْمَعَ. I received, or took, the property, the — of it, قَبَضْتُ ٱلْمَالَ أَجْمَعَ.

Wholeness, *n.* Soundness, تَمَامَة ـ صِحَّة.

Wholesale, *n.* }
Wholesale, *a.* } بَيْعٌ بِٱلْجُمْلَةِ. To sell by —, بَاعَ بِٱلْجُمْلَةِ *aor.* يَبِيعُ. A — price سِعْرُ ٱلْبَيْعِ بِٱلْجُمْلَةِ.

Wholesome, *a.* To the health, مُوَافِقٌ لِلصِّحَّةِ ـ شَافٍ. Free from unsoundness, سَلِيم. Wholesome, of water, مَجُوع. *See also* Salubrious, *a.*

Wholesomely, *ad.* بِمُعَافَاةٍ ـ بِوَجْهٍ سَلِيمٍ ـ بِنَوْعٍ شَافٍ.

Wholesomeness, *n.* طِيبَة ـ شِفَآء. *See also* Salubrity, *n.*

Wholly, *ad.* بِٱلْكُلِّيَّةِ ـ بِٱلْمَرَّةِ ـ طُرًّا ـ بِأَسْرِهِ ـ بَتَّةً ـ كَافَّةً ـ جُمْلَةً ـ تَمَامًا ـ أَجْمَعَ. To give one's self — to anything, تَفَرَّغَ لِ ـ إِنْكَبَّ عَلَى ـ تَوَلَّعَ بِ ـ تَجَرَّدَ لِ "Verily the affair resteth wholly with God," إِنَّ ٱلْأَمْرَ كُلَّهُ لِلّٰهِ (Kur. iii. 148).

Whom, *obj. case of* Who, *rel. pr.; q.v.*

Whomsoever, *pr.* أَىُّ مَنْ كَانَ ـ أَىُّ مَنْ.

Whoop, *n.* صُرَاخ ـ أَعْوَال *pl.* عَوْل ـ صِيَاح ـ صَيْحَة.

Whoop, *v.i.* زَعَقَ ـ صَرَخَ ـ أَعْوَلَ.

Whooping-cough, *n.* سُعَالٌ كَلْبِىٌّ.

Whore, *n.* قَحْبَة *pl.* قِحَاب ـ سُوقَة ـ عَاهِرَة ـ زَوَانِى *pl.* زَانِيَة. "The whore and the whoremonger, scourge each of them with a hundred stripes," ٱلزَّانِيَةُ وَٱلزَّانِى فَٱجْلِدُوا كُلَّ وَاحِدٍ مِنْهُمَا مِائَةَ جَلْدَةٍ (Kur. xxiv. 2).

Whore, *v.i.* To play the whore, تُزَانِى ـ تَزْنِى (from زَنَى *aor.* يَزْنِى) ـ عَهِرَتْ ـ عَاهَرَتْ ـ تَعَيْهَرَتْ (from عَهِرَ).

Whoredom, *n.* قَحْبَنَة ـ عِهْر ـ زِنَآء.

Whoremonger, *n.* وَلِىُّ ٱلْقِحَابِ ـ عَاهِر ـ زُنَاة *pl.* زَانٍ.

Whoreson, *n.* وَلَدُ قَحْبَةٍ ـ اِبْنُ زَانِيَةٍ.

Whorish, *a.* *See* Whoremonger, *n.*

Whorishly, *ad.* بِقَحْبَنَةٍ ـ بِعِهْرٍ ـ بِزِنَآء.

Whorl, *n.* Of leaves or flowers round a stem, نَسَقٌ مِنَ ٱلْأَزْهَارِ أَوِ ٱلْأَوْرَاقِ حَوْلَ سَاقِ ٱلنَّبَاتِ. A turn, دَائِرَة *pl.* دَوَائِر.

Whortle-berry, *n.* ضَرْبٌ مِنَ ٱلْعُلَّيْقِ.

Whose, *rel. pr.* Of whom, مَنْ: whose book have I taken, كِتَابَ مَنْ أَخَذْتُ; *also expressed by* ٱلَّذِى *with a possessive pronoun suffixed to the noun, e.g.,* Whose name is Muhammad, ٱلَّذِى ٱسْمُهُ مُحَمَّدٌ. Whose house overlooks the street, ٱلَّذِى دَارُهُ تَشْرُفُ عَلَى ٱلسِّكَّةِ.

Whose, *inter. pr.* To whom, لِمَنْ: Whose is this? لِمَنْ هٰذَا. Then whose shall these be? ثُمَّ لِمَنْ تَكُونُ هٰذِهِ. Whose servant are you? خَادِمُ مَنْ أَنْتَ ـ لِمَنْ أَنْتَ خَادِمٌ.

Whosesoever, *pr.* كَائِنٌ لِمَنْ كَانَ.

Whoso, *pr.* }
Whosoever, } أَىُّ مَنْ كَانَ ـ مَنْ. Whosoever will, مَنْ يُرِدْ.

Why, *ad.* *See* Wherefore, *ad.*

Wick, *n.* فَتِيلَة ـ فَتِيل *pl.* فَتَائِلُ. A lighted —, شُعْلَة ـ شُعَيْلَة. The expended part of a —, قِرَاط. To trim, of a —, قَرَّطَ.

Wicked, *a.* Having a wick, ذُو فَتِيلَةٍ.

Wicked, *a.* Of a person, شِرِّير ـ طَالِح *pl.* أَشْرَار *and* أَشِرَّآء ـ رَدِىّ *pl.* أَرْدِيَآء ـ خَبِيث *pl.* خُبَثَآء ـ فَاجِر; of a thing, رَدِىّ ـ دَنِىّ ـ فَاسِد ـ رَدِىّ. Deceitful, مَكَّار ـ خَبٌّ. A — thing, شَىْءٌ رَدِىٌّ. A — action, عَمَلٌ شَرٌّ ـ خَطِيئَة *pl.* خَطَايَا.

أَعْمَال . A — way, طَرِيقٌ رَدِيءٌ pl. طُرُقٌ رَدِيئَةٌ . A — man, رَجُلٌ سَوْءٌ . The righteous and the —, الصَّالِحُ وَالطَّالِحُ . The wicked, الأَشْرَارُ . To be —, شَرَّ aor. يَشَرُّ . You become more — as you grow older, كُلَّمَا تَكْبَرُ تَشَرُّ .

Wickedly, ad. بِخَبَاثَةٍ — شَرًّا . To act —, شَرَّ aor. يَشَرُّ or يَشِرُّ — أَفْجَرَ — ² فَجَرَ . To act — towards, شَارَّ .

Wickedness, n. شَرٌّ pl. شُرُورٌ — شَنَاعَةٌ — خُبْثٌ — سُوءٌ — فُجُورٌ .

Wicker, a. Made of wicker, or of palm leaves, مِنْ — سَفِيفٍ — مِنْ قَشٍّ — خُوصٍ . A — basket for scents, قَشْوَةٌ .

Wicker-work, n. سُفَّةٌ .

Wicket, n. Of a door, بُوَيْبَةٌ — خَوْخَةٌ — خَادِعَةٌ ; of the game of cricket, الهَدَفُ فِي لَعِبِ الصَّوْلَجَانِ وَالكُرَةِ .

Wide, a. Broad, عَرِيضٌ . Extensive, وَاسِعٌ — وَسِيعٌ — رَغِيبٌ . Broad, open, أَجْوَفُ — بَسِيطٌ . Roomy, رَحِيبٌ — رَحْبٌ — فَسِيحٌ . Wide, of the sea, فَيَّاحٌ — أَفْيَحُ . Wide, of trousers, etc., مُفَرْسَحٌ . Wide of the mark; of a cast at a butt, بَعِيدٌ عَنِ الهَدَفِ ; of a thought, intent, etc., وَاقِعٌ فِي مَغْلَطَةٍ . Wide of the truth, بَعِيدٌ عَنِ الحَقِّ . To be —, roomy, رَحُبَ ² — تَفَسَّحَ . To open —, of the mouth, فَغَرَ ² (or أَفْغَرَ) فَاهُ ; of the hand, بَسَطَ يَدَهُ ² . To open —, in a general sense, بَسَطَ ² — بَسَّطَ — أَشْرَعَ .

Wide, ad. Far and wide, فِي كُلِّ مَحَلٍّ — اِتِّسَاعًا — اِنْتِشَارًا .

Widely, ad. At a distance, بِبُعْدَةٍ — بِبُعْدٍ — تَبَاعُدًا . Much, كَثِيرًا — بِكَثْرَةٍ . Widely-spread, as of a report, شَائِعٌ — شَتٌّ . Widely current, as of a song, poem, etc., شَارِدٌ pl. شُرَّدٌ — شَارُودٌ pl. شُرُدٌ . Widely different, of two, شَتَّانَ : widely different are his father and brother, شَتَّانَ أَبُوهُ وَأَخُوهُ .

Widen, v.i. To become wide, اِتَّسَعَ . To extend, اِمْتَدَّ .

Widen, v.t. To make wide, وَسَّعَ — أَعْرَضَ — عَرَّضَ . To make roomy, فَسَّحَ — أَرْحَبَ . To extend, شَرَحَ ² — مَدَّ ² — مَدَّدَ .

Wideness, n. Breadth, عَرْضٌ . Extent, سَعَةٌ — اِتِّسَاعٌ . Roominess, فُسْحَةٌ — رُحْبٌ . Openness, بَسْطَةٌ .

Wide-spread, a. مُتَّسِعٌ — شَائِعٌ — مُنْتَشِرٌ — مُشَاعٌ — شَتٌّ . Suspicion became —, اِنْتَشَرَتِ (or اِتَّسَعَتِ) الظِّنَّةُ . See also under Widely, ad.

Widgeon, n. ضَرْبٌ صَغِيرٌ مِنَ البَطِّ — صُنْصُن .

Widow, n. أَرْمَلَةٌ pl. أَرَامِلُ . To leave as a —, of a husband dying, مَاتَ عَنْهَا ² .

Widow, v.t. مَاتَ عَنْهَا ² .

Widower, n. أَرْمَلٌ pl. أَرَامِلُ ذُكُورٌ .

Widowhood, n. تَرَمُّلٌ — حَالَةُ الأَرْمَلَةِ .

Width, n. عَرْضٌ . See also Wideness, n.

Wield, v.t. To manage, handle, بَاشَرَ — اِسْتَعْمَلَ . To — a sword, سَايَفَ . To — a pen, خَطَّ . To —, of a subject, بَيَّنَ وَأَوْضَحَ . To — a sceptre, سَاسَ المُلْكَ ² — تَسَلَّطَ — مَلَكَ . Easy to —, قَرِيبُ المَأْخَذِ .

Wieldy, a. قَرِيبُ المَأْخَذِ . See Manageable, a.

Wiery, a. See Wiry, a.

Wife, n. رَبَضٌ — ظَعِينَةٌ — عِرْسٌ — حَنَّةٌ — طَرُوقَةُ زَوْجِهَا — حُشْمَةٌ — حُرَمٌ pl. حُرْمَةٌ — زَوْجَاتٌ pl. زَوْجَةٌ — قَعِيدَةٌ — طَلَّةٌ — اِمْرَأَةٌ — حَلِيلَةٌ — ذَوَاتُ قَرَائِنَ pl. ذَاتُ قَرِينٍ . A refractory —, ضَجُوجٌ . A companion —, ضَرَّةٌ pl. ضَرَائِرُ and ضَرَّاتٌ — جَارَةٌ pl. جَارَاتٌ — عَلَّةٌ pl. عَلَّاتٌ . A — who is separated from her husband, نَاشِزَةٌ . The first or head —, السِّتُّ الكَبِيرَةُ . Wives under covert, حُرَمٌ — حَرِيمٌ . The — of a husband's brother, سِلْفَةٌ . To take to —, تَزَوَّجَ — تَزَوَّجَ بِ .

Wifeless, a. See Unmarried, a.

Wig, n. شُوشَةٌ مَصْنُوعَةٌ — شَعْرٌ عَارِيَّةٌ . Wearing a —, لَابِسُ شَعْرٍ عَارِيَّةٍ (or جُمَّةٍ مَصْنُوعَةٍ) . See also under Chignon, n.

Wig, v.t. See to Scold, v.t.

Wigged, a. Wearing a wig, لَابِسُ شَعْرٍ عَارِيَّةٍ .

Whigging, n. See Scolding, n.

Wight, n. مَرْءٌ pl. مَرْؤُونَ — شَخْصٌ pl. أَشْخَاصٌ — نَفَرٌ pl. أَنْفَارٌ .

Wigwam, n. كُوخٌ pl. أَكْوَاخٌ .

Wild, a. Of an uncultivated waste, بَرِّيٌّ — قِفَارٌ . Savage, untutored, وَحْشِيٌّ — حُوشِيٌّ — هَمَجَةٌ — هَمَجٌ . Rude, coarse, جَافٍ . Impetuous, شَدِيدٌ — عَنِيفٌ . Strange, improbable, بَعِيدٌ . Strange, bizarre, odd, غَرِيبٌ . Extravagant, fanciful, خَيَالِيٌّ . A — man, إِنْسَانٌ وَحْشِيٌّ — رَجُلٌ هَمَجَةٌ . A — olive tree, زَيْتُونَةٌ بَرِّيَّةٌ . A — beast, سَبُعٌ pl. سِبَاعٌ — وَحْشٌ pl. وُحُوشٌ . Wild animals, حَيَوَانُ البَرِّ . Wild scenery, مَنَاظِرُ بَرِّيَّةٌ .

Wild, n. See Waste, n.

Wild-boar, n. خِنْزِيرُ الغَابِ pl. خَنَازِيرُ — هِلَّوْفٌ .

Wilder, v.t. See to Bewilder, v.t.

Wilderness, n. صَحْرَاءُ pl. صَحَارِيُّ and صَحَارَى — بَرِّيَّةٌ pl. بَرَارِي — بَادِيَةٌ pl. بَوَادٍ . The — of the Children of Israel, تِيهُ بَنِي إِسْرَائِيلَ .

Wild-fire, n. Of fire, فَتِيلٌ مُشْتَعِلٌ — لَهَبٌ . The disease, قَوْبَةٌ . To spread like —, of a report, etc., سَارَ سِيرَةَ البَرْقِ ² — اِمْتَدَّ — طَارَ aor. يَطِيرُ — كَالبَرْقِ ; of a disease, سَرَى عَاجِلًا aor. يَسْرِي .

Wild-fowl, n. طَيْرُ البَرِّ pl. طُيُورٌ .

Wild-goose, n. وَزَّةٌ بَرِّيَّةٌ coll. إِوَزٌّ بَرِّيٌّ .

Wild-goose-chase, *n.* جَهْدٌ بَاطِلٌ ـ مُطَارَدَةٌ بَاطِلَةٌ ـ كُصُوم. To go on a —, كَصَمَ ² ـ وَلَّى وَأَدْبَرَ أَوْ رَجَعَ مِنْ حَيْثُ جَآءَ وَلَمْ يَتِمَّ إِلَى مَقْصَدِهِ.

Wilding, *n.* ثَمَرٌ بَرِّيٌّ ـ نَبَاتٌ بَرِّيٌّ.

Wildly, *ad.* Without cultivation in the desert, فِي ٱلْبَرِّيَّةِ. Heedlessly, بِبَلَاهَةٍ ـ بِتَعَسُّفٍ ـ اِعْتِسَافًا ـ سُدًى. Irrationally, بِدُونِ عَقْلٍ ـ بِجَهَالَةٍ. Irregularly, مِنْ غَيْرِ نِظَامٍ ـ بِدُونِ ضَبْطٍ. Furiously, بِجُنُونٍ ـ بِتَهَوُّرٍ. Incoherently, شَتَاتَ ـ شَقًّا ـ بِلَا تَنَاسُقٍ ـ بِدُونِ إِلْحَاقٍ. To stare —, هَطَعَ ـ بَهِتَ ² ـ هَطَّعَ. فِي ٱلْخَلَاءِ. To do anything —, تَعَسَّفَ (or اِعْتَسَفَ) فِي.

Wild-oats, *n.* Youthful follies, الشَّبِيبَاتُ. Youthful dissipation, سَرَفُ ٱلشَّبَابِ. To sow one's —, فَرَغَ ² مِنْ شَبِيبَاتِهِ.

Wildness, *n.* An uncultivated state, تَوَحُّش ـ وَحْشَة. Fierceness, impetuosity, تَهَوُّر; as of wind, عُصُوف ـ عَصْف. Violence, شِدَّة. Folly, حَمَاقَة ـ جُنُون. Boisterousness, turbulence, تَهَوُّر ـ ضُجَاج ـ عَجِيج. Strangeness, غَرَابَة. Irregularity, عَدَمُ تَنَاسُقٍ ـ عَدَمُ ٱنْتِظَامٍ ـ قِلَّةُ تَرْتِيبٍ ـ لَخْبَطَة. Incoherence, شَتّ ـ اِرْتِخَآء ـ اِنْفِكَاك ـ عَدَمُ ٱلْتِصَاقٍ.

Wile, *n.* كَيْد *pl.* كِيَاد ـ مَكِيدَة *pl.* مَكَائِدُ ـ رُوَيْغَة ـ حِيلَة *pl.* حِيَل. To practise wiles, اِحْتَالَ. To practise wiles against, اِحْتَالَ عَلَى. *See also under* Trick, *n.*

Wilful, *a.* Intentional, قَصْدِيٌّ ـ عَمْدِيٌّ ـ عَنْ عَمْدٍ ـ عَنْ قَصْدٍ. Perverse, obstinate, عَرِم ـ مُتَمَرِّد ـ عَارِم ـ شَرِس ـ شَكِس ـ مُعَنِّد. Wilful sins, المُغَمَّضَاتُ مِنَ ٱلذُّنُوبِ. To be —, عَرِمَ ² ـ شَرِسَ ـ عَانَدَ ـ تَمَرَّدَ.

Wilfully, *ad.* Of set purpose, عَمْدًا ـ قَصْدًا ـ عَنْ قَصْدٍ. Perversely, تَمَرُّدًا ـ عَرَامَةً ـ بِشَرَاسَةٍ ـ بِمُعَانَدَةٍ.

Wilfulness, *n.* Purpose, عَمْد ـ قَصْد. Perversity, عَرَامَة ـ عُرَام ـ تَمَرُّد ـ مُعَانَدَة ـ عِنَاد ـ شَكَاسَة ـ شَرَاسَة.

Wilily, *ad.* بِكَيْدٍ ـ اِحْتِيَالًا ـ غَدْرًا ـ بِحِيلَةٍ.

Wiliness, *n.* دَهَآء ـ دَهَآءَة ـ اِحْتِيَال ـ مَكْر ـ حِيلَة.

Will, *n.* The faculty of choosing, مَشِيئَة ـ إِرَادَة. Choice, اِخْتِيَار. A command, أَمْر ـ وَصِيَّة. Permission, إِذْن. Desire, design, object, wish, مُرَاد ـ مَرَام ـ مَقْصُود. What one wishes to be done, شِيئَة ـ مُرَاد ـ إِرَادَة. The disposition of one's property to take effect after death, وَصِيَّة *pl.* وَصَايَا. The —, Divine purpose, or the decrees of God, التَّقْدِيرَاتُ ٱلْإِلٰهِيَّةُ ـ القَضَآءُ وَٱلْقَدَرُ. What's your —? مَاذَا تُرِيدُ ـ مَاذَا تَبْغِي ـ أَيَّ شَيْءٍ تُرِيدُ. Of his own —, voluntarily, مِنْ تِلْقَآءِ نَفْسِهِ. By the — of God, بِإِذْنِ ٱللّٰهِ. Everything is by the — of God, كُلُّ شَيْءٍ بِمَشِيئَةِ ٱللّٰهِ. Is it your — that I go? هَلْ لَكَ أَنْ أَذْهَبَ ـ هَلْ تُرِيدُ أَنْ أَذْهَبَ. *See also under* Testament, *n.*

At will, as he pleases, بِمَشِيئَتِهِ ـ كَيْفَمَا يَشَآءُ ـ بِطِيبَةِ خَاطِرِهِ ـ عَلَى كَيْفِهِ.

Good-will, حُسْنُ إِرَادَةٍ ـ رِضْوَان. Zeal, favour, رَغْبَة. To bear one —, رَضِيَ عَلَى or بِ ـ أَرَادَ ٱلْخَيْرَ لِ.

Ill-will, بُغْض ـ عَدَاوَة ـ خُصُومَة ـ حِقْد. To bear — towards, حَقَدَ عَلَى ـ أَبْغَضَ ـ أَرَادَ لِ ٱلسُّوءَ.

Tenant at will, مُسْتَأْجِرٌ تَتَوَقَّفُ مُدَّةُ ٱسْتِئْجَارِهِ عَلَى إِرَادَةِ ٱلْمُؤْجِرِ.

Will and pleasure, أَمْرٌ وَإِرَادَةٌ.

To make one's will, أَوْصَى.

Will, *v.t.* To desire (that a thing should be), شَآءَ *aor.* يَشَآءُ ـ أَرَادَ. To determine, to order, حَكَمَ بِ ² ـ قَضَى بِ ـ أَمَرَ بِ ². To give by —, أَوْصَى بِ. What God has willed then that I have willed, مَا شَآءَ ٱللّٰهُ ثُمَّ شِئْتُ. What God hath willed! مَا شَآءَ ٱللّٰهُ. Come what —, أَصَابَ مَا أَصَابَ. He turns him whichever way he wills, pleases, يُمِيلُهُ حَيْثُمَا شَآءَ. To —, in the sense of to wish, desire, أَرَادَ: When you —, مَتَى أَرَدْتُمْ. I shall give it to whomsoever I —, أُعْطِيهِ لِمَنْ أُرِيدُ. Can I not do what I — in my own house, أَوَمَا يَحِلُّ لِي أَنْ أَفْعَلَ مَا أُرِيدُ فِي بَيْتِي. You — not, do not wish, لَا تُرِيدُونَ. It — be done for you, سَيَكُونَ لَكَ.

Will, *v. aux.* (When this merely denotes the future tense the aorist of the Arabic verb suffices; *e.g.*), He — write to-day, يَكْتُبُ ٱلْيَوْمَ; he — come in, يَدْخُلُ. (When the future is more distant the particle سَوْفَ should be prefixed to the verb, *e.g.*), I — do it, that is, by and bye, سَوْفَ أَفْعَلُهُ. You — see, *i.e.*, hereafter, سَوْفَ تَرَى. (Examples in connexion with the verb to Be): He — be your enemy, سَيَكُونُ لَكَ عَدُوًّا. He — not be your companion, لَا يَكُنْ لَكَ رَفِيقًا. There — be no opportunity, لَا تَصِيرُ فُرْصَةٌ. Will he not be at the meeting? أَفَلَا يَكُونُ فِي ٱلْاِجْتِمَاعِ. We — be grateful for his kindness, سَنَكُونُ لِفَضْلِهِ مِنَ ٱلشَّاكِرِينَ. To — (when used emphatically in a future sense may be expressed by the emphatic tense called مُضَارِعُ نُونِ ٱلتَّوْكِيدِ ٱلثَّقِيلَةِ, with the particle لَ prefixed, *e.g.*), He will (certainly) write, لَيَكْتُبَنَّ; they — (certainly) say, لَيَقُولُنَّ. I — (surely) teach you different manners from these, لَأُؤَدِّبَنَّكُمْ غَيْرَ هٰذَا ٱلْأَدَبِ. (The same idea may be expressed by the verb with the verbal noun prefixed, *e.g.*), You — (surely) die, مَوْتًا تَمُوتُ.

I — surely despoil you, نَزْعًا أَنْزَعُكُمْ. (But these forms are seldom used, and the idea is expressed in various ways, *e.g.*), He — (assuredly) come, لا يُمْكِنُ إِلَّا أَنْ يَأْتِيَ. His word — (certainly) be established, stand, لا بُدَّ أَنْ يَقُومَ كَلَامُهُ. We — (certainly) complete the work, إِنَّنَا إِنَّمَا نُتَمِّمُ ٱلشُّغْلَ. He — (assuredly) go, إِنَّهُ لَيَذْهَبُ. It — (certainly) be for your good, إِلَّا أَنَّهُ يَكُونُ خَيْرًا لَكُمْ. "But His command when He willeth aught is to say to it, Be, and it is," إِنَّمَا أَمْرُهُ إِذَا أَرَادَ شَيْئًا أَنْ يَقُولَ لَهُ كُنْ فَيَكُونُ (Kur. xxxvi. 82).

Willing, *a.* Consenting, agreeing, رَاضٍ *pl.* رُضَاةٌ ـ رَضِيٌّ. Desirous, رَاغِبٌ ـ بَاغٍ *pl.* بُغَاةٌ. Spontaneous, not asked for, مِنْ تِلْقَآءِ ٱلنَّفْسِ ـ اِخْتِيَارِيٌّ. Voluntary, مُتَطَوِّعٌ بِهِ ـ مُتَبَرَّعٌ بِهِ. A — mind, قَلْبٌ سَمُوحٌ ـ نَشَاطٌ.

Willingly, *ad.* Of one's free will, مِنْ ذِي ـ عَنْ طِيبِ نَفْسٍ. Readily, عَلَى ٱلرَّأْسِ وَٱلْعَيْنِ ـ طَيِّبًا ـ بِٱلطَّوْعِ وَٱلرِّضَآءِ ـ نَفْسِهِ. He came —, جَآءَ طَيِّبًا. *See also* Spontaneously, *ad.*

Willingness, *n.* رِضْوَان ـ حُسْنُ رِضَآءٍ ـ مُرَاضَاةٌ ـ رِضًى.

Willow, *n.* صَفْصَاف ـ خِلَاف; a single —, صَفْصَافَةٌ. The weeping —, صَفْصَافٌ مُسْتَحٍ ـ صَفْصَافٌ رُومِيٌّ.

Willowy, *a.* Abounding in willows, كَثِيرُ ٱلصَّفْصَافِ.

Wily, *a.* خَبِيثٌ ـ حَوَالِيٌّ ـ دَاهٍ ـ أَرِيبٌ. How — he is! مَا أَحْوَلَهُ.

Wimble, *n.* مِثْقَبٌ *pl.* مَثَاقِبُ.

Wimple, *n.* A woman's hood, مِقْنَعَةٌ.

Win, *v.i.* عَزَّ. To — over, as to a party, *etc.*, أَقْفَلَ عَلَى ـ أَرْضَى لِ. He who wins takes the booty, مَنْ عَزَّ بَزَّ. To — upon one's affections, مَلَكَ قَلْبَهُ ـ تَوَدَّدَ ـ رَاقَهُ *aor.* يَرُوقُ.

Win, *v.t.* To gain the victory in, غَلَبَ ـ ظَفِرَ بِ ـ فَازَ بِ. To —, as at cards, *etc.*, قَمَرَ ـ رَبِحَ. To acquire, حَصَّلَ ـ أَصَابَ ـ فَازَ بِ ـ اِقْتَنَى ـ نَالَ. To attain, بَلَغَ.

Wince, *v.i.* جَفَلَ ـ أَجْفَلَ ـ تَجَفَّلَ ـ اِنْقَبَضَ.

Winch, *n.* مِلْوًى.

Wind, *n.* هَوَآءٌ *pl.* أَهْوِيَةٌ ـ رِيحٌ *pl.* أَرْيَاحٌ. Flatulence, رِيحَةٌ ـ زَفِيرَةٌ ـ نَفْخَةٌ. The — carried away the boat, ذَهَبَتِ ٱلرِّيحُ بِٱلْقَارِبِ. There is something in the —, going forward, يُوشِكُ فِي ٱلدَّهْرِ حَرَكَةٌ ـ فِي ٱلْأُمُورِ حَادِثَةٌ ـ شَيْءٌ. The — is stronger to-day than yesterday, ٱلرِّيحُ ٱلْيَوْمَ أَشَدُّ مِنْ أَمْسِ. He turns with every —, يَمِيلُ مَعَ كُلِّ رِيحٍ. It is an ill — that blows nobody good, أَخْلَفُ ٱلْأَرْيَاحِ ٱلَّتِي لا يَسْتَفِيدُ مِنْهَا أَحَدٌ. "And it is He who sendeth forth the winds as the heralds of His compassion," وَهُوَ ٱلَّذِي يُرْسِلُ ٱلرِّيَاحَ بُشْرًا بَيْنَ يَدَيْ رَحْمَتِهِ (Kur. vii. 55).

Damp wind, بَلِيلٌ.

Dust raised by the wind, غُبَار ـ رَهَجٌ.

Fair wind, رِيحٌ مُوَافِقٌ ـ رِيحٌ عَدِلٌ.

Foul or head wind, رِيحٌ مُخَالِفٌ ـ كَوْسٌ.

Gale of wind, عَاصِفَةٌ ـ رِيحٌ عَاصِفٌ (or عَاصِفَةٌ).

Gust of wind, عَصْفَةُ رِيحٍ ـ عَصْفَةٌ.

Hot wind, رِيحٌ بَارِحٌ ـ حَرُورٌ.

Land wind, رِيحٌ مِنَ ٱلْبَرِّ ـ رِيحُ ٱلْبَرِّ.

Puff of wind, نَفْحَةٌ ـ رِيحَةٌ.

Rheumatic wind, رِيحٌ وَاهِنَةٌ.

Side wind, رِيحٌ نُكْبٌ ـ نَكْبَآءُ ـ رِيحٌ مُشَارِكٌ.

Sultry wind, سَمُوم.

Trade wind, رِيحٌ مَوْسِمٍ.

Violent wind, رِيحٌ دَاعِبَةٌ ـ رِيحٌ عَاصِفَةٌ ـ رِيحٌ سَاهِكَةٌ ـ سَهُوكٌ ـ رِيحٌ سَهُوجٌ ـ رِيحٌ سَاهِجٌ ـ رِيحٌ زَعْزُوعٌ (or زَعْزَعٌ).

Wind and weather permitting, إِنْ ـ إِنْ تَيَسَّرَ ٱلرِّيحُ وَٱلطَّقْسُ ـ تَيَسَّرَ ٱلْهَوَآءُ.

To be shaken by the wind, إِسْتَرْوَحَ. The trees felt or were shaken by the wind, رَاحَ ٱلشَّجَرُ.

To break wind, ضَرَطَ.

To get wind, to become known, شَاعَ *aor.* يَشِيعُ.

To get wind of, حَسَّ بِ ـ يَقِفُ *aor.* وَقَفَ عَلَى ـ شَعَرَ بِ.

To sail before the wind, سَارَ مَعَ ٱلرِّيحِ.

To sail by the wind, سَارَ حَسَبَ ٱلرِّيحِ.

To sail in the wind's eye, سَارَ فِي عَيْنِ ٱلرِّيحِ.

To test from what quarter the wind blows, تَمَخَّرَ ٱلرِّيحَ.

To turn one's self from the wind, إِسْتَمْخَرَ (or إِسْتَدْبَرَ) ٱلرِّيحَ.

To turn one's self to the wind, to face it, إِسْتَقْبَلَ ٱلرِّيحَ. The horse turned itself to the wind, as if to sniff it, تَمَخَّرَ (or إِمْتَخَرَ) ٱلْفَرَسُ ٱلرِّيحَ.

Wind, *v.t.* To turn, أَدَارَ ـ دَوَّرَ. To twist, فَتَلَ. To —, as thread on a ball, سَلَكَ. To sound, صَوَّتَ بِ. To — one thing over another, دَرَّجَ ـ أَدْرَجَ. To — something round something else, لَفَّ عَلَى ـ لَفَّ بِ ـ عَصَبَ بِ ـ رَصَفَ. To —, as a kerchief, round the head, صَمَّدَ رَأْسَهُ. To —, as a dead body in grave-clothes, كَفَّنَ ـ سَجَّى. To — off, كَرَّ عَنْ ـ كَرَّ. To — up, as a watch, رَكَّبَ مِنْ جَدِيدٍ; to accomplish, فَرَغَ مِنْ ـ قَضَى ـ أَتَمَّ ـ أَنْهَى. To — up one's accounts,

غَلْقُ ٱلْمُحَاسَبَاتِ ـ سَدُّ ٱلْمُحَاسَبَاتِ. To — one's self in, as in a cloak, *etc.*, إِلْتَفَّ بِ ـ تَلَفَّفَ بِ. To — itself, as a serpent, تَطَوَّى.

Wind, *v.i.* To turn round, دَارَ *aor.* يَدُورُ ـ إِسْتَدَارَ. To twist, تَلَوَّى ـ تَفَتَّلَ ـ إِنْفَتَلَ. To meander, as a stream, *etc.*, تَضَوَّجَ ـ تَفَتَّلَ. To — up, as a watch, تَرَكَّبَ. To wind off, إِنْجَرَّ. To — together, in regular order, إِرْتَصَفَ ـ تَرَصَّفَ.

Windage, *n.* نَفَس.

Wind-bound, *a.* مَوْقُوفٌ (or مُعَطَّلٌ) مِنَ ٱلْهَوَآءِ (or ٱلرِّيحِ).

Winded, *a.* Having breath, ذُو نَفَسٍ.

Wind-fall, *n.* Fallen fruits, سُقَاط. Unexpected good fortune, خَيْرٌ غَيْرُ مَأْمُولٍ ـ رِزْق *pl.* أَرْزَاق.

Wind-gall, *n.* سِلْعَةٌ فِي عُرْقُوبِ ٱلْخَيْلِ.

Wind-gauge, *n.* مِيزَانُ ٱلرِّيحِ.

Windiness, *n.* Strength of wind, شِدَّةُ ٱلرِّيحِ. Tempestuousness, عُصُوف ـ عَصْف. Flatulency, نَفْخَة ـ رِيحَة.

Winding, *a.* Meandering, مُتَفَتِّل ـ مُتَلَوٍّ; of a channel of water, مَصِيف. A — road, ثَنِيَّة. A — turn, curve, لَيَّة *pl.* لِوًى ـ عَوَج ـ عِوَج.

Winding-sheet, *n.* كَفَن *pl.* أَكْفَان. To wrap, of a corpse, in a —, كَفَّنَ.

Wind-instrument, *n.* آلَةٌ مِنَ آلَاتِ ٱلْمُوسِيقَى يُنْفَخُ فِيهَا *pl.* آلَات.

Windlass, *n.* مِلْوَة ـ مِلْوًى.

Windless, *a.* هُدُوّ ـ بِلَا رِيحٍ.

Windmill, *n.* طَاحُونُ ٱلرِّيحِ *pl.* طَوَاحِين.

Window, *n.* كُوَّة *pl.* كِوَآء ـ طَاقَة *pl.* طَاقَات ـ رَوْشَن *pl.* رَوَاشِن ـ رَوْزَن *pl.* رَوَازِن. A latticed —, شُبَّاكَة *pl.* شَبَابِيك ـ شُبَّاك. A blind —, or a niche in a wall, رَفّ *pl.* رُفُوف. To look out of a —, أَشْرَفَ مِنَ ٱلطَّاقَةِ. To enter through a —, دَخَلَ مِنَ ٱلرَّوْشَنِ. To throw out of a —, رَمَى مِنَ ٱلطَّاقَةِ. To let down through a —, أَنْزَلَ مِنَ ٱلطَّاقَةِ.

Window-blind, *n.* سِتْرُ طَاقَةٍ *pl.* سُتُور and أَسْتَار ـ سِتَارَةُ رَوْشَنٍ *pl.* سَتَائِر.

Window-frame, *n.* دَائِرَةُ ٱلطَّاقَةِ *pl.* دَوَائِر.

Window-sash, *n.* فَرْوَازُ ٱلطَّاقَةِ *pl.* فَرَاوِيز.

Window-seat, *n.* طَنَفُ ٱلطَّاقَةِ *pl.* طُنُوف.

Window-sill, *n.* عَتَبَةُ ٱلطَّاقَةِ *pl.* عَتَبَات.

Windowed, *a.* ذُو طَاقَاتٍ.

Windpipe, *n.* حُنْجُور *pl.* حَنَاجِر ـ حَجَب ـ حَنْجَرَة ـ حُلْقُوم. The upper part of the —, غَلْصَمَة. To cut or seize by the —, غَلْصَمَ ـ حَلْقَمَ.

Windsail, *n.* مِلَقَّفٌ مِنْ قُمَاشٍ ـ *from the Italian*, مَانِيقَة.

Wind-tight, *a.* لَا تَنْفُذُ فِيهِ ٱلرِّيحُ ـ لَا تَتَطَرَّقُ إِلَيْهِ ٱلرِّيحُ.

Windward, *a.* and *n.* فَوْقَ ٱلرِّيحِ ـ عُلَاوَة ـ عُلَاوَةُ ٱلرِّيحِ. I went to —, or to the — side, of such an one, عَلَوْتُ عَلَى فُلَانٍ ٱلرِّيحَ. Go not to the — side of the game lest it get scent of thee and flee away, لَا تَعْلُ ٱلرِّيحَ عَلَى ٱلصَّيْدِ فَيَرَاحَ رِيحَكَ وَيَنْفِرَ.

Windy, *a.* Blowy, رَاحٍ ـ رَائِح ـ عَاصِف. A — day, يَوْمٌ عَاصِفٌ ـ يَوْمٌ رَيِّحٌ. A pleasant — day, يَوْمٌ ذُو رِيحٍ. Flatulent, رِيحِيّ ـ نَفَّاخ. Relating to the wind, رِيحِيّ. Of a good, pleasant wind, رَيُوح ـ رَوْح ـ رَيِّح. To be —, or to be open to the wind, رَاحَ.

Wine, *n.* سَكَر ـ حَانِيَّة ـ عُقَار ـ خَمْر *pl.* خُمُور ـ نَبِيذ *pl.* أَنْبِذَة ـ شَرَاب. Old and choice —, خَنْدَرِيس. Pure or the choicest —, خَمْرٌ رَحِيق. Mellow —, or such as glides down the throat, سُخَام. Wine with an exhilarating flavour, رَاح. Old —, مُدَام ـ مُدَامَة. Wine from white grapes, ٱلصَّهْبَآءُ. The — or overpowering influence of —, its getting into the head, حُمَيَّا ـ سَوْرَة ٱلْخَمْرِ. To get into the head, as of —, سَارَ فِي رَأْسِهِ *aor.* يَسُورُ. To make —, نَبَذَ ـ أَنْبَذَ. To mix water with —, عَرَّقَ ٱلشَّرَابَ. The overpowering influence of the cup (wine) mounted into his head, سَارَتْ فِيهِ حُمَيَّا ٱلْكَأْسِ.

Wine-bibber, *n.* خِمِّير ـ شِرِّيبُ ٱلْخَمْرِ *pl.* شِرِّيبُو ٱلْخَمْرِ.

Wine-cellar, *n.* مَقْصُورَة.

Wine-glass, *n.* فِنْجَانُ ٱلنَّبِيذِ *pl.* فَنَاجِين.

Wine-jar, *n.* دَنّ *pl.* دِنَان and دِنَنَة.

Wine-measure, *n.* عِيَارُ ٱلنَّبِيذِ.

Wine-merchant, *n.* نَبَّاذ ـ تَاجِرُ ٱلنَّبِيذِ.

Wine-press, *n.* مَعْصَرَة *pl.* مَعَاصِر ـ مَعْصَرَةُ خَمْرٍ.

Wing, *n.* As of a bird, مِجْذَاف *pl.* مَجَاذِيف ـ كَنَف *pl.* أَكْنَاف ـ جَنَاح *pl.* أَجْنُح and أَجْنِحَة. The two wings of a bird, جَنَاحَا ٱلطَّائِرِ ـ سَاعِدَا ٱلطَّائِرِ. The — of a millstone, جَنَاحُ ٱلرَّحَى. The — of an army, جَنَاحُ ٱلْعَسْكَرِ. The two wings of an army, ٱلْمُجَنِّبَتَانِ ـ جَنَاحَا عَسْكَرٍ ـ حَجْرَتَا عَسْكَرٍ. The right — of an army, مَيْمَنَةُ جَيْشٍ; the left — of an army, مَيْسَرَةُ جَيْشٍ. An army having wings, جَيْشٌ ذُو مَنَاكِبَ. Wing of a mountain, house, *etc.*, طَنَف *pl.* أَطْنَاف ـ كَنَف *pl.* أَكْنَاف. A fluttering, as of the wings, رَفْرَفَة. Clipped in the wings, مَقْصُوصُ ٱلْجَنَاحِ. Having the — broken, as by a shot, *etc.*, so that it falls to the ground, مُرَنَّقُ ٱلْجَنَاحِ. To flutter, as of the wings, رَفْرَفَ. On the —, طَائِر. To be on the —, طَارَ *aor.* يَطِيرُ. To stretch the wings, بَسَطَ ٱلْجَنَاحَ. To flap, of the wings, رَنَّقَ.

Wing, *v.t.* To fly away with, طَارَ بِ. To hit on the wing, جَنَحَ. To supply with wings, sides, رَكَّبَ فِي-أَكْتَافًا. To — one's flight, طَارَ *aor.* يَطِيرُ.

Winged, *a.* Having wings, مُجَنَّحٌ ـ ذُو جَنَاحٍ. Swift, طَيَّارٌ.

Wingless, *a.* لَا جَنَاحَ لَهُ ـ بِلَا جَنَاحٍ.

Winglet, *n.* جُنَيْحٌ.

Wingshell, *n.* قِشْرُ أَجْنَاحِ ٱلْهَوَامِّ.

Wingy, *a.* *See* Winged, *a.*

Wink, *v.i.* Of the eye, اِخْتَلَجَ : His eye winked, اِخْتَلَجَتْ عَيْنُهُ. To — with the eye, طَرَفَ بِعَيْنِهِ ـ خَلَجَ بِعَيْنِهِ ـ غَمَزَ بِعَيْنِهِ. They winked at each other, of many, تَغَامَزُوا. To — at men, of a woman, طَرَفَتِ ٱلرِّجَالَ. To — at, to overlook, let pass, أَغْضَى عَلَى *or* عَن ـ تَغَاضَى عَن ـ تَغَمَّضَ ـ غَمَّضَ. "And when they pass by them they wink at one another," وَإِذَا مَرُّوا بِهِمْ يَتَغَامَزُونَ (Kur. lxxxiii. 30).

Wink, *n.* طَرْفَةُ ٱلْعَيْنِ ـ غَمْزَةُ عَيْنٍ ـ *vulg.* رَمْشَةُ عَيْنٍ. I did not sleep a —, مَا ٱكْتَحَلَتْ عَيْنِي غُمْضًا ـ مَا ٱغْتَمَضْتُ ـ مَا غَمَّضْتُ. He does not separate himself from me during a —, مَا يُفَارِقُنِي طَرْفَةً. Quicker than a —, or twinkling, of the eye, أَسْرَعُ مِنْ طَرْفَةِ عَيْنٍ.

Winker, *n.* مُخْتَلِجٌ ـ غَامِزٌ ـ غَمَّازٌ.

Winking, *n.* Of the eye, اِخْتِلَاجُ ٱلْعَيْنِ ـ طَرْفُ ٱلْعَيْنِ.

Winner, *n.* غَالِبٌ ـ رَابِحٌ ـ فَائِزٌ ; at cards or such like games, قَامِرٌ. The —, or the winning horse, ٱلْفَرَسُ ٱلسَّابِقُ.

Winning, *a.* Attractive, أَنِيقٌ ـ مُؤْنِقٌ ـ ذُو حَظٍّ ـ مُنْبَسِطٌ ـ حَبَّذَا ـ ذُو طَلَاوَةٍ (*or* طُلَاوَةٍ) ـ جَاذِبُ ٱلْقَلْبِ ـ يَجْذِبُ ٱلْعَقْلَ. *See also* Winner, *n.*

Winningly, *ad.* بِطَلَاوَةٍ ـ بِأَنَقٍ ـ بِأَنَاقَةٍ ـ جَلْبًا ـ جَذْبًا.

Winning-post, *n.* غَايَةٌ. *See also under* Goal, *n.*

Winnings, *n.* رِبْحٌ ـ قَمْرٌ ـ مَكْسَبٌ ـ كَسْبٌ.

Winnow, *v.t.* As of grain, *etc.*, ذَرَا *aor.* يَذْرُو ـ ذَرَّى. The wheat was winnowed, تَذَرَّتِ ٱلْحِنْطَةُ. *See also to* Sift, *v.t.*

Winnowing, *n.* ذَرْوٌ ـ ذَرْيٌ ـ تَذْرِيَةٌ.

Winnowing-fork, *n.* مِذْرَى ـ مِذْرَاةٌ.

Winsome, *a.* Cheerful, merry, مَغْبُوطٌ ـ مَسْرُورٌ ـ أَنِيسٌ ـ مَحْبُورٌ ـ طَيِّبُ ٱلنَّفْسِ.

Winter, *n.* The season, شَتْوَةٌ *pl.* أَشْتِيَةٌ ـ شِتَاءٌ *pl.* شُتِيٌّ. The — quarter, فَصْلُ ٱلشِّتَاءِ. The — season, مَوْسِمٌ شَتَوِيَّةٌ. The depth of —, عِزُّ (*or* شِدَّةُ) ٱلشِّتَاءِ ـ ٱلزَّمْهَرِيرُ. The severities of winter, عَقَارِبُ ٱلشِّتَاءِ. The — commenced, شَتَا ٱلشِّتَاءُ *aor.* يَشْتُو. He bargained with him (for work) by the —, عَامَلَهُ مُشَاتَاةً. To suffice one for the —, شَتَّى : this will suffice me for the —, هٰذَا يُشَتِّينِي. The locality of the town was not suitable for the —, for a winter-residence, لَمْ يَكُنْ مَوْقِعُ ٱلْبَلَدِ صَالِحًا لِلْمَشْتَى. *See also next article.*

Winter, *v.i.* To pass the winter, شَتَّى. To pass the — in, شَتَا بِ *aor.* يَشْتُو ـ شَتَّى بِ. They had wintered in the island, كَانُوا قَدْ شَتَوْا فِي ٱلْجَزِيرَةِ. I have decided to — there, عَزَمْتُ إِنْ أُشَتِّيَ هُنَاكَ.

Winter, *v.t.* To feed or manage during the winter, رَبَّى مُدَّةَ ٱلشِّتَاءِ.

Winter, *a.* Belonging to winter, شَتَوِيٌّ ـ شَتْوِيٌّ. Winter-clothing, لِبْسُ ٱلشِّتَاءِ. Winter fruits, أَثْمَارٌ (*or* فَاكِهَةٌ) شَتَوِيَّةٌ.

Winter-quarters, *n.*
Winter-residence, } مَشْتًى ـ مَشَاتٍ *pl.* مَشْتَاةٌ.

Wintry, *a.* Like winter, مِثْلَ ٱلشِّتَاءِ ـ كَٱلشِّتَاءِ. Cold, bleak, قَرٌّ ـ جُمَادِيٌّ ـ مَقْرُورٌ ـ قَارِسٌ ـ بَارِدٌ. A — night, لَيْلَةٌ جُمَادِيَّةٌ.

Winy, *a.* خَمْرِيٌّ.

Wipe, *v.t.* To rub for cleaning, مَسَحَ ـ مَسَّحَ. To dry, نَشَّفَ. To — out, erase, مَحَقَ ـ مَحَا. To make clean, نَظَّفَ. To — anything with, مَسَحَ بِ. To — one's self, تَمَسَّحَ. To be wiped out, تَمَحَّقَ ـ اِمَّحَى. To — away, as of tears, مَسَحَ.

Wipe, *n.* As for cleaning, مَسْحٌ ـ مَسْحَةٌ. A reproof, sarcasm, صَلَاطَةٌ ـ قَارِصَةٌ ـ نَقْرٌ.

Wiper, *n.* One who wipes, مَسَّاحٌ; a thing with which one wipes, مِمْسَحَةٌ.

Wire, *n.* سِلْكٌ *pl.* أَسْلَاكٌ *and* سُلُوكٌ. A single —, سِلْكَةٌ. A telegraphic —, سِلْكُ ٱلتِّلِغْرَافِ *pl.* أَسْلَاكٌ.

Wire, *v.t.* To bind with wire, حَبَكَ بِسِلْكٍ. To put — to, رَكَّبَ فِي-سِلْكًا.

Wire-draw, *v.t.* Of wire, صَيَّرَ سِلْكًا ـ سَلَّكَ فِي ٱلطَّرِيدَةِ. To draw out, of a discourse, طَوَّلَ.

Wire-drawer, *n.* مُطَرِّزُ ٱلسِّلْكِ ـ صَانِعُ ٱلسِّلْكِ. *See also under* Draw-plate, *n.*

Wire-gauge, *n.* حِبَاكٌ مِنْ سِلْكٍ.

Wire-puller, A mover, مُحَرِّكٌ. An intriguer, مُحْتَالٌ ـ حَيَّالٌ ـ حُوَّلٌ ـ صَاحِبُ دَسَائِسَ.

Wire-work, *n.* شُغْلُ سِلْكٍ ـ حِبَاكُ سِلْكٍ.

Wis, *v.t.* To know, suppose, عَلِمَ ـ ظَنَّ.

Wisdom, *n.* The right use of knowledge, حِكْمَة. Intelligence, عَقْل. Knowledge, عِلْم. Prudence, فِطْنَة.

Wise, *a.* حَكِيم *pl.* حُكَمَآء. Intelligent, عَاقِل *pl.* عُقَّال. Learned, عَالِم *pl.* عُلَمَآء – عَلِيم. Prudent, لَبِيب *pl.* أَلِبَّآء. Pious, مُتَّقٍ – مُتَدَيِّن.

Wise, *n.* Manner, أُسْلُوب – بَاب *pl.* أَبْوَاب – وَجْه *pl.* وُجُوه. In any —, كَيْفَمَا كَانَ. On this —, هٰكَذَا – عَلَى هٰذَا ٱلْمِدَادِ. In no —, بَتَّةً – قَطْعًا.

Wiseacre, *n.* أَحْمَقُ *fem.* حَمْقَآء *pl.* حُمْق – أَخْرَقُ – عُوَيْرِف.

Wisely, *ad.* بِحِكْمَةٍ – بِعَقْلٍ. To act —, تَعَقَّلَ. To handle a matter —, فَطِنَ ل or ب.

Wish, *v.i.* تَشَوَّقَ. I wish that ..., لَيْتَ أَن – يَا لَيْتَ أَن. I — that I ..., لَيْتَنِي – يَا لَيْتَنِي. He is not what one could —, لَيْسَ هُوَ عَلَى حَسَبِ ٱلْمَرَامِ.

Wish, *v.t.* To desire, هَوِيَ – وَدَّ – أَرَادَ – إِشْتَاقَ إِلَى – تَمَنَّى – حَبَّ. To — something for one, دَعَا ل-ب *aor.* يَدْعُو. To — one a good morning, صَبَّحَ – صَبَّحَ بِخَيْرٍ – ل-كَذَا. To — one a good evening, مَسَّى – مَسَّى بِخَيْرٍ. To — one happiness, دَعَا ل-بِٱلسَّعَادَةِ. To — one success and prosperity, تَمَنَّى لَهُ ٱلنَّجَاحَ وَٱلتَّوْفِيقَ. To — one health, دَعَا ل-بِٱلْعَافِيَةِ. To — something against another, دَعَا عَلَى-ب *aor.* يَدْعُو. *See also to* Desire, *v.t.*

Wish, *n.* هَوًى *pl.* أَهْوَآء – شَوْق – إِشْتِيَاق – مُرَاد – إِرَادَة. By my —, بِوُدِّي. In accordance with the wishes of, إِرْضَآءً ل. *See also* Desire, *n.*

Wisher, *n.* }
Wishful, *a.* } مُتَمَنٍّ – مُتَشَوِّق – مُشْتَاق – شَيِّق.

Wishfully, *ad.* بِحَنِينٍ – بِرَغْبَةٍ – بِٱشْتِيَاقٍ.

Wisp, *n.* A small bundle, حُزْمَة – بَاقَة.

Wist, *pret. of to* Wis, *v.i.*, *q.v.* He wist not, لَمْ يَعْلَمْ.

Wistful, *a.* مُشْتَاق – مَشُوق – تَوَّاق – حَنَّان. *See also* Attentive, *n.*

Wistfully, *ad.* بِشَوْقٍ – بِحَنِينٍ.

Wit, *n.* دَهَآء – ذَكَآء – فِقْرَة. Wits, عَقْل. To be at one's wits' end, تَحَيَّرَ – اِضْطَرَبَ – اِخْتَلَّ – دَهِشَ. To have one's — about one, تَحَفَّظَ – تَنَبَّهَ – فَطِنَ – تَعَقَّلَ. Wit is general among the Greeks, الفِقْرَةُ شَمِلَتْ طَائِفَةَ ٱلرُّومِ.

Wit, *v.t.* To know, عَلِمَ. To wit (adverbially), namely, وَهُوَ – يَعْنِي.

Witch, *v.i.* *See to* Bewitch, *v.t.*

Witch, *n.* سَاحِرَة *pl.* سَاحِرَات – سَحَّارَة.

Witchcraft, *n.* }
Witchery, } سِحْر.

Witching, *a.* سَاحِر.

Witenagemote, *n.* مَجْلِسُ ٱلْعُقَلَآء.

With, *prep.* Together with, مَعَ: I entered — him, دَخَلْتُ مَعَهُ. With, instrumentally, بِ: I struck him — the sword, ضَرَبْتُهُ بِٱلسَّيْفِ. With, accompanied by, or in the sense of being —, فِي – عِنْدَ: He went — 50,000 men, تَوَجَّهَ فِي خَمْسِينَ أَلْفًا مِنَ ٱلرِّجَالِ. I was — the people, كُنْتُ عِنْدَ ٱلْقَوْمِ. Zaid is — me, عِنْدِي زَيْدٌ. With, in the sense of having, possessing, ذُو *fem.* ذِي *vulg. masc.* أَبُو: The man — the turban, الرَّجُلُ ذُو ٱلْعِمَامَةِ – لَابِسُ ٱلْعِمَامَةِ – أَبُو ٱلْعِمَامَةِ. With, as implying attendance upon, presence with, لَدَى: with thee, لَدَيْكَ, with him, لَدَيْهِ. The Sultan had — him some of the Amirs, وَكَانَ لَدَى حَضْرَةِ ٱلسُّلْطَانِ بَعْضٌ مِنَ ٱلْأُمَرَآء. With, when used adverbially, may be expressed in Arabic by بِ preceding the noun, or in the regular adverbial form, *e.g.*, With ease, easily, بِسُهُولَةٍ – سَهْلًا.

Withal, *ad.* Besides, مَعَ هٰذَا – مَعَمَا فِيهِ.

Withdraw, *v.t.* To revoke, recall, retract, اِرْتَدَّ – إِسْتَرَدَّ – اِرْتَجَعَ. To cause one to —, retire, from, أَبْعَدَ-عَن – أَضْرَبَ-عَن – صَرَفَ-عَن – أَبْعَدَ-عَن. To take back from, to deprive of, رَفَعَ عَن-كَذَا. He withdrew his gift, اِرْتَدَّ (or) إِسْتَرَدَّ هِبَتَهُ.

Withdraw, *v.i.* As from doing anything, عَتَمَ عَن – أَضْرَبَ عَن. To retire from, to leave, أَعْرَضَ عَن – تَنَحَّى عَن – تَصَدَّفَ عَن – غَابَ عَن – تَغَيَّبَ عَن – بَرِحَ مِن. To secede from, اِعْتَزَلَ عَن – تَعَزَّلَ عَن. To — one's self stealthily, تَسَلَّلَ. He withdrew from the compact, حَالَ عَنِ ٱلْعَهْدِ *aor.* يَحُولُ. "Withdraw, then, from him who turneth his back on our warning, and desireth only the present life," فَأَعْرِضْ عَنْ مَنْ تَوَلَّى عَنْ ذِكْرِنَا وَلَمْ يُرِدْ إِلَّا ٱلْحَيٰوةَ ٱلدُّنْيَا (Kur. liii. 30).

Withdrawal, *n.* }
Withdrawment, } The act of taking back, recalling, اِرْتِجَاع – اِرْتِدَاد – إِسْتِرْدَاد; of retiring, تَصَدُّف – غِيَاب; of seceding, تَعَزُّل – اِعْتِزَال.

Withdrawing-room, *n.* صَالُون – بَيْتُ ٱلْقُعُودِ – بَيْتُ ٱلدِّيوَانِ.

Withe, *n.* A willow twig, صَفْصَاف *pl.* عَسَالِيجُ عُسْلُوجُ. A twig, قَضِيب *pl.* قُضْبَان – خُصْلَة *pl.* خِصَال *and* خُصُلَات.

Wither, *v.i.* Of plants, ذَبَلَ – ذَوَى – فَنِيَ; of the hand or foot, عُقِمَتْ; of the hand, اِنْفَعَلَتِ ٱلْيَدُ.

Wither, *v.t.* To cause to fade, of plants, أَذْبَلَ ـ أَذْوَى.

Withered, *a.* Dried up, faded, of plants, ذَابِل ـ ذَاوٍ; of a member of the body, يَابِس. Diseased, unsound, سَقِيم. The man with the — hand, الإِنْسَانُ ٱلَّذِى يَدُهُ يَابِسَةٌ.

Withers, *n.* Of a horse, حَوْرَك ـ حَارِك ـ مِنْسَج ـ غَارِب.

Withhold, *v.t.* To keep back, restrain, عَزَرَ ـ عَزَرَ عَن ـ حَجَزَ عَن ـ حَبَسَ عَن ـ عَجَزَ عَن ـ قَفَعَ عَن ـ كَفَّ عَن ـ ضَبَطَ عَن ـ شَجَرَ عَن ـ ثَبَرَ عَن ـ حَصَرَ عَن ـ مَنَعَ عَن ـ أَمْسَكَ عَن. To keep back, to deny to, مَنَعَ ـ إِنْقَفَعَ ـ رُفِعَ عَن. To be withheld from, أُمْسِكَ عَن ـ عَن ـ كَذَا ـ مُنِعَ عَن ـ أُمْسِكَ عَن ـ عَن. He was withheld from it, حُصِرَ عَنْهُ.

Withhold, *v.i.* To keep one's self back, to refrain, إِحْتَبَسَ ـ إِمْتَنَعَ ـ حَبَسَ نَفْسَهُ عَلَى *or* عَن *or* فِى.

Within, *prep.* and *ad.* فِى ـ جَوًّا ـ فِى دَاخِلِ. In the course of, فِى أَجَلِ كَذَا. Within the house, فِى دَاخِلِ ٱلْبَيْتِ ـ فِى ٱلْبَيْتِ. Within one's self, فِى نَفْسِهِ. Within one's power, فِى طَاقَتِهِ. Within one's income, دُونَ إِيرَادِهِ. Within a mile, دُونَ مِيلٍ. A small town with few people — it, مَدِينَةٌ صَغِيرَةٌ فِيهَا أُنَاسٌ قَلِيلُونَ. He answered him from within, أَجَابَهُ مِنْ دَاخِلٍ. Without and —, مِنْ خَارِجٍ وَمِنْ دَاخِلٍ. Within two months from this date, فِى أَجَلِ شَهْرَيْنِ مِنْ تَارِيخِهِ.

Without, *prep.* and *ad.* Outside, بَرًّا ـ مِنْ خَارِجٍ ـ فِى ٱلْخَارِجِ. Not having, with the absence of, مِنْ غَيْرِ كَذَا ـ بِلَا. Without war, بِغَيْرِ حَرْبٍ. Why do you stand —, لِمَا تَقِفُ خَارِجًا. Those that are —, ٱلَّذِينَ مِنْ خَارِجٍ. I sat —, outside, the house, جَلَسْتُ بَرًّا. I went —, outside of the house, خَرَجْتُ بَرًّا. To be —, deprived of, حُرِمَ مِن ـ تَعَرَّى مِن. To be able to do —, إِسْتَغْنَى عَن ـ فَضَلَ عَن ـ أَغْنَى عَن. The roll was written within and —, on both sides, كَانَ ٱلدَّرْجُ مَكْتُوبًا مِنْ دَاخِلٍ وَمِنْ قَفَاهُ. Without injuring any one, مِنْ دُونِ ضَرَرٍ عَلَى أَحَدٍ.

Withstand, *v.t.* To resist, oppose, إِمْتَنَعَ ـ إِعْتَرَضَ ـ آزَى ـ ضَادَّ ـ قَاوَمَ ـ شَاجَرَ. To hold out against, عَزَّ عَلَى. To resist, as the weather, *etc.*, لَا يُؤَثِّرُ فِيهِ أَلْ... ـ صَبَرَ عَلَى. He could not —, stand against, them, لَمْ يَقْدِرْ أَنْ يَثْبُتَ أَمَامَهُمْ. I withstood him to the face, قَاوَمْتُهُ مُوَاجَهَةً. "We will surely come to them with forces which they cannot withstand," فَلَنَأْتِيَنَّهُمْ بِجُنُودٍ لَا قِبَلَ لَهُمْ بِهَا (Kur. xxvii. 37).

Witless, *a.* حِمَار ـ أَحْمَق ـ بِلَا عَقْلٍ ـ خَرِق ـ أَخْرَق.

Witlessly, *ad.* بِجَهَالَةٍ ـ بِحَمَاقَةٍ ـ بِلَا عَقْلٍ ـ بِخُرْقٍ.

Witlessness, *n.* جَهَالَة ـ حَمَاقَة ـ قِلَّةُ عَقْلٍ ـ خُرْق.

Witling, *n.* *See* Witless, *a.*

Withy, *n.* ضَرْبٌ مِنَ ٱلصَّفْصَافِ.

Withy, *a.* Made of twigs, مِنَ ٱلْعَسَالِيجِ ـ مِنَ ٱلْخِصَالِ.

Witness, *n.* One who bears testimony, شَاهِد *pl.* شُهُود. Testimony, شَهَادَة. A proof, document in proof, حُجَّة ـ بُرْهَان ـ دَلِيل. Witness in favour of, شَهَادَةٌ لِ; against, شَهَادَةٌ عَلَى. Adduce your witnesses, هَلُمَّ شُهَدَاءَكُمْ. He gave —, أَدَّى شَهَادَةً. "They bear no false witness," لَا يَشْهَدُونَ ٱلزُّورَ (Kur. xxv. 72). *See also* Testimony, *n.*

To bear witness, شَهِدَ ـ أَدَّى شَهَادَةً. "Observe strict integrity when bearing witness before God," كُونُوا قَوَّامِينَ بِٱلْقِسْطِ شُهَدَاءَ لِلّٰهِ (Kur. iv. 134). "What thing is weightiest in bearing witness?" أَىُّ شَىْءٍ أَكْبَرُ شَهَادَةً (*Id.* vi. 19).

To bear witness against one, شَهِدَ عَلَى.

To bear witness in favour of one, شَهِدَ لِ.

To bear witness to, شَهِدَ عَلَى ـ شَهِدَ بِ.

To call one as a witness to, إِسْتَشْهَدَ ـ أَشْهَدَ عَلَى. To call one as a witness against, إِسْتَشْهَدَ عَلَى.

To challenge a witness, رَفَضَ ٱلشَّاهِدَ ـ مَا قَبِلَ ٱلشَّاهِدَ.

Witness, *v.t.* To see, رَأَى *aor.* يَرَى ـ شَهِدَ. To be present at, حَضَرَ. "That they may witness the benefits accruing to them," لِيَشْهَدُوا مَنَافِعَ لَهُمْ (Kur. xxii. 29). To certify, attest, نَعَمَ بِ ـ حَقَّقَ. To put one's signature to, أَمْضَى ـ وَقَّعَ عَلَى ـ عَلَّمَ عَلَى. Witness my hand, فَهٰذَا إِمْضَاءِى.

Witness-box, *n.* مَوْقِفُ ٱلشَّاهِدِ فِى ٱلْمَحْكَمَةِ.

Witted, *a.* *See* Witty, *a.*

Witticism, *n.* نُكْتَةٌ ضَعِيفَةٌ *pl.* نُكَتٌ ضَعِيفَةٌ ـ مُلْحَةٌ رَكِيكَةٌ *pl.* مُلَحٌ تَفِهَةٌ.

Wittily, *ad.* بِذَكَاءٍ ـ بِدَهَاءٍ ـ بِدَهَاءٍ.

Wittiness, *n.* ذَكَاء ـ دَهْو ـ دَهَاء.

Wittingly, *ad.* Knowingly, بِعِلْمٍ; designedly, قَصْدًا ـ عَمْدًا.

Wittol, *n.* دَيُّوث ـ صَفُور ـ صَقَّار.

Witty, *a.* Of a person, ذَكِىّ *pl.* أَذْكِيَاءُ ـ دَاهِيَة ـ دَهِىّ ـ دَاهٍ; of a thing, ظَرِيف ـ لَطِيف. A — saying, نُكْتَةٌ لَطِيفَةٌ *pl.* نُكَت ـ نَادِرَة *pl.* لَطَائِفُ ـ ظَرِيفَة *pl.* ظَرَائِفُ ـ لَطِيفَة *pl.* نَوَادِرُ ـ مَلَاحَة.

Wive, *v.t.* To marry, زَوَّجَ.

Wive, *v.i.* To take to wife, تَزَوَّجَ بِ.

Wizard, *n.* سَاحِر *pl.* سَحَرَة *and* سُحَّار ـ سَحَّار *pl.* سَحَّارُون. *See also* Conjurer, *n.*

Woad, *n.* The plant, نِيلَةٌ بَرِّيَّةٌ ـ وَسْمَة ـ عِظْلِم ـ نَوْرَة ـ نَوُور.

Wo, *n.* *See* Woe, *n.*

Wobegone, *a.* مَكْسُور ـ حَزِين ـ مَنْهُوش ـ شَجِب ـ شَاجِب الخَاطِر.

Woden, *n.* The heathen deity, اِسْمُ مَعْبُودٍ عِنْدَ ٱلْجَرْمَانِيِّينَ ٱلأَقْدَمِينَ.

Woe, *n.* A calamity, آفَة *pl.* آفَات ـ بَلِيَّة *pl.* بَلَايَا ـ مُصِيبَة *pl.* مَصَائِبُ. Grief, sorrow, غَمّ ـ حُزْن ـ وَيْل. Woe to Zaid! وَيْلٌ لِزَيْدٍ ـ وَيْلًا لِزَيْدٍ. Woe to me! وَيْلِي. Woe to him! وَيْلَهُ. "I will lay grievous woes upon him," سَأُرْهِقُهُ صَعُودًا (Kur. lxxiv. 17).

Woful, *a.* Full of distress, مَغْمُوم ـ كَئِيب ـ شَاجِب ـ شَجِب ـ شَاقّ ـ فَاجِع ـ مُغِمّ. Saddening, grievous, مَحْزُون ـ حَزِين ـ مُحْزِن ـ مُؤْلِم.

Wofully, *ad.* Sorrowfully, بِشَجَب ـ بِغَمّ ـ بِحُزْن. Unhappily, بِنَحْسٍ. Extremely, لِلْغَايَةِ.

Wofulness, *n.* Sadness, حُزْن ـ غَمّ ـ شَجَب. Grievousness, ضِيق ـ مَشَقَّة ـ كَرْب.

Wold, *n.* صَحْرَآء *pl.* صَحَارٍ.

Wolf, *n.* ذِئْب *pl.* أَذْؤُب *and* ذِئَاب *and* ذُؤْبَان. A — in sheep's clothing; *see* Hypocrite, *n.*

Wolfish, *a.* مِثْلَ ٱلذِّئْبِ ـ ذِئْبِيّ.

Wolfsbane, *n.* بِيش ـ خَانِقُ ٱلنَّمِرِ ـ خَانِقُ ٱلذِّئْبِ.

Woman, *n.* An adult female, اِمْرَأَة *pl.* نِسَآء ـ حُشْمَة ـ حُرْمَة *coll.* حَرِيم. A young —, صَبِيَّة *pl.* صَبَايَا. An old —, عُشَّة ـ عَجُوزَة *pl.* عَجَائِز. A married —, اِمْرَأَةٌ مُزَوَّجَةٌ. A — separated from her husband from any cause, ثَيِّب *pl.* ثَيِّبَات. A divorced —, طَالِقَة ـ اِمْرَأَةٌ طَالِقٌ. A — who rules over her husband, one who wears the breeches, دَرْكَرَة.

Womanhood, *n.* State or qualities of a woman, حَالَةُ ٱلْمَرْأَةِ ـ أَوْصَافُ ٱلْمَرْأَةِ.

Womanish, *a.* Soft and feminine, of a woman, مُطَرَّقَة ـ مِثْلَ ٱلنِّسَآءِ.

Womankind, *n.* النِّسَآء ـ طَائِفَةُ ٱلنِّسَآءِ ـ الحَرِيمُ.

Woman-like, *a.* } لَائِقٌ بِٱلنِّسَآءِ ـ مِثْلَ ٱلنِّسَآءِ. *See also*
Womanly, } Womanish, Feminine, *a.*

Womb, *n.* The matrix, رَحِم *and* رَحْم *pl.* أَرْحَام. The orifice of the —, مَهْبَل *pl.* مَهَابِلُ. A deep cavity, هُوَّة. "Nor is it lawful for them to conceal what God hath created in their wombs," وَلَا يَحِلُّ لَهُنَّ أَنْ يَكْتُمْنَ مَا خَلَقَ ٱللّٰهُ فِي أَرْحَامِهِنَّ (Kur. ii. 228).

Won, *pret. and part. of to* Win, *v.t.*; *q.v.*

Wonder, *n.* Emotion of surprise, عَجَب ـ اِسْتِعْجَاب ـ تَعَجُّب ـ حَيْرَة. Something that excites —, عَجَبَة ـ أَمْرٌ عَجِيبٌ *pl.* عَجَائِبُ. A wonderful thing, أُعْجُوبَة ـ أُعْجُوبَة ـ عَجِيبَة *pl.* عَجَائِبُ. A wonderful thing, أُعْجُوبَة ـ غَرِيبَة *pl.* غَرَائِبُ. O case of wonder! What a wonder! يَا لِلْعَجَبِ. It is no —, there is no cause of —, لَا غَرْوَ ـ لَا عَجَبَ. The wonders of God, آيَاتُ ٱللّٰهِ. Such an one is no other than a — of wonders, فُلَانٌ إِلَّا عَجَبَةٌ مِنَ ٱلْعَجَبِ. This is the — of the age, هٰذَا مِنْ حُولَةِ ٱلدَّهْرِ. Wonder, a miracle, مُعْجِزَة *pl.* مُعْجِزَات ـ أَمْرٌ خَارِقُ ٱلْعَادَةِ ـ آيَة *pl.* آيَات. To excite —, أَعْجَبَ. To excite one's —, بَعَثَ عَلَى ٱلْعَجَبِ.

Wonder, *v.i.* اِسْتَعْجَبَ ـ تَعَجَّبَ ـ أَخَذَهُ ٱلْعَجَبُ ـ دَهِشَ ـ تَحَيَّرَ. I — whether he will come, لَيْتَ شِعْرِي إِنْ كَانَ يَجِيءُ. Not to be wondered at, لَا عَجَبَ فِيهِ.

Wonderful, *a.* Exciting wonder, مُعْجِب. Wondrous, surprising, بَدِيع ـ غَرِيب ـ عَجِيب ـ فَرِيّ. How — it is! سُبْحَانَ مِنْ كَذَا ـ مَا أَعْجَبَهُ. A woman of — beauty, اِمْرَأَةٌ بَدِيعَةُ ٱلْحُسْنِ. A — story, قِصَّةٌ عَجَبٌ. A — speech, بَدِيعَة ـ كَلَامٌ بَدِيعٌ. A — thing; *see under* Wonder, *n.*

Wonderfully, *ad.* بِنَوْعٍ غَرِيبٍ ـ بِنَوْعٍ عَجِيبٍ ـ عَجَبًا. He did —, عَمِلَ عَمَلًا عَجِيبًا.

Wonderfulness, *n.* عُجْب ـ عَجَب ـ غَرَابَة.

Wonder-struck, *a.* دَهِش ـ مُتَحَيِّر ـ حَيْرَان ـ مُتَعَجِّب ـ مَدْهُوش.

Wonder-working, *a.* فَاعِلُ ٱلْمُعْجِزَاتِ.

Wondrous, *a.* *See* Wonderful, *a.*

Wondrously, *ad.* *See* Wonderfully, *ad.*

Wont, *a.* مُعْتَاد.

Wont, *n.* دَأْب ـ عَادَة. That is his —, ذٰلِكَ دَأْبُهُ. As is his —, كَمَا هُوَ دَأْبُهُ.

Wont, *v.i.* تَعَوَّدَ عَلَى.

Won't, *contr. of* Will not, لَمْ يَرِدْ *fem.* لَمْ تَرِدْ.

Wonted, *a.* مُعْتَاد.

Wontedness, *n.* عَادَة ـ تَعَوُّد.

Woo, *v.t.* To court, كَلِفَ بِ ـ صَبَا إِلَى ـ تَوَدَّدَ ـ تَوَدَّدَ إِلَى. To solicit, رَامَ ـ طَلَبَ ـ اِسْتَعْطَفَ.

Woo, *v.i.* To make love, تَصَابَى ـ تَعَشَّقَ.

Wood, *n.* The substance of trees, خَشَب *pl.* خُشْب *and* خُشْبَان. Fire-wood, حَطَب. A forest, غَيْض *pl.* غِيَاض. Trees, أَشْجَار. A piece of —, خَشَبَة *pl.* خَشَبَات ـ عُود *pl.* عِيدَان

and أَغْوَد. Administration of woods and forests, إِدَارَةُ ٱلْغِيَاضِ. In the —, barrel, فِي ٱلْبَرْمِيلِ. To break — up small, شَطَّفَ ـ ٱلْحَطَبَ. To give one permission to cut —, أَقْطَعَ فُلَانًا أَخْشَابًا ـ أَذِنَ ل ـ فِي قَطْعِ ٱلْأَخْشَابِ.

Wood, *v.i.* To lay up a supply of fire-wood, ذَخَرَ ٱلْحَطَبَ.

Woodbind, *n.* }
Woodbine, } The honey-suckle, ٱللَّبْلَابُ ـ زَهْرُ ٱلْعَسَلِ.

Woodcock, *n.* دَجَاجَةُ ٱلْحَرْشِ ـ دَجَاجَةُ ٱلْأَرْضِ *coll.* دَجَاج.

Wood-craft, *n.* مَهَارَةٌ فِي ٱلصَّيْدِ ـ ٱلصَّيْدُ.

Wood-cut, *n.* نَقْشٌ عَلَى خَشَبٍ *pl.* نُقُوش.

Wood-cutter, *n.* كَسَّارُ حَطَبٍ ـ حَطَّاب ـ حَاطِب. *See also* Woodman, *n.*

Wood-cutting, *n.* كَسْرُ ٱلْحَطَبِ ـ حَطْب.

Wooded, *a.* Abounding in trees, مُشْجِر; in fire-wood, حَطِيب.

Wooden, *a.* Made of wood, مِنْ خَشَبٍ. Hard, صَلِيب ـ صُلْب. A — house, a house in the construction of which wood is used, بَيْتٌ مُخَشَّبٌ. *See also* Clumsy, *a.*

Wood-engraving, *n.* The art of, فَنُّ ٱلنَّقْشِ عَلَى ٱلْخَشَبِ.

Wood-fretter, *n.* *See* Teredo, *n.*

Wood-land, *n.* أَرْضٌ مُشْجِرَةٌ.

Wood-land, *a.* مُشْجِر.

Wood-lark, *n.* دَالُوعُ ٱلْغِيَاضِ.

Woodless, *n.* بِلَا أَشْجَارٍ.

Woodlouse, *n.* حِمَارُ ٱلْبَيْتِ ـ حِمَارُ قَبَّانَ ـ شَحْمَةُ ٱلْأَرْضِ.

Woodman, *n.* One who cuts down trees, مُحْتَطِبُ ٱلْأَشْجَارِ ـ قَاضِبُ ٱلْأَشْجَارِ. A forest officer, نَاظِرُ ٱلْغِيَاضِ. A sportsman, قَنَّاص ـ قَانِص ـ صَيَّاد.

Wood-nymph, *n.* جِنِّيَّةُ ٱلْغِيَاضِ.

Woodpecker, *n.* نَقَّارُ ٱلْخَشَبِ. The green —, صُرَد ـ أَخْيَل ـ شِقِرَّاق.

Wood-pigeon, *n.* قُمْرِيٌّ *pl.* قُمْرِيَّة.

Woodreeve, *n.* نَاظِرُ غَابَةٍ ـ نَاظِرُ غِيَاضٍ.

Woodwork, *n.* تَرْكِيبُ خَشَبٍ ـ شُغْلُ خَشَبٍ ـ خَشَب.

Woody, *a.* مُشْجِر.

Wooer, *n.* عَاشِق *pl.* عُشَّاق ـ صَابٍ ـ كَلِف ـ صَابٍ إِلَى.

Woof, *n.* سَتَاة ـ أُسْتِيٌّ ـ قِيَام.

Woofy, *a.* Having a close texture, مُكْتَنِز ـ مَتِين ـ كَثِيف.

Wooingly, *ad.* بِٱلْعِشْقِ ـ كَٱلْعَاشِقِ.

Wool, *n.* صُوف *pl.* أَصْوَاف. Cotton-wool, حَلِيج ـ مَحْلُوج. A tuft of —, صُوفَة. A fleece of —, جَزِيزَة. A manufacturer of —, صَوَّاف. To cast its —, of a sheep, *etc.*, نَسَلَ ٱلصُّوفَ ـ أَنْسَلَ ٱلصُّوفَ. Much cry and little —, أَسْمَعُ جَعْجَعَةً وَلَا أَرَى طِحْنًا; *lit.* I hear the sound of grinding but see no flour. "And the mountains shall be like flocks of carded wool," وَتَكُونُ ٱلْجِبَالُ كَٱلْعِهْنِ ٱلْمَنْفُوشِ (Kur. ci. 4).

Wool-comber, *n.* نَدَّاف ـ مُسَرِّحُ ٱلصُّوفِ ـ مُمَشِّقُ ٱلصُّوفِ ـ ٱلصُّوفِ.

Wool-combing, *n.* نَدْف ـ تَسْرِيحُ ٱلصُّوفِ ـ مَشْقُ ٱلصُّوفِ (*or* نَفْشُ) ٱلصُّوفِ.

Woold, *v.t.* رَبَطَ ـ شَدَّ.

Wool-gathering, *n.* Absence of mind, سَهْوٌ ـ تَغَفُّل ـ شَتَات ـ ٱلْعَقْلِ.

Wool-grower, *n.* مُرَبِّي ٱلضَّأْنِ ـ مُرَبِّي ٱلْغَنَمِ.

Wool-growing, *n.* تَرْبِيَةُ ٱلْغَنَمِ.

Woolliness, *n.* صِفَةُ ٱلصُّوفِ.

Woollen, *a.* Made of wool, مِنْ صُوفٍ.

Woollen-draper, *n.* جُوخِيٌّ *pl.* جُوخِيَّة.

Woollens, *n.* بِضَاعَةُ صُوفٍ.

Woolpack, *n.* خَيْشَةُ صُوفٍ.

Woolsack, *n.* A sack of wool, خَيْشَةُ صُوفٍ. The seat of the Lord Chancellor in the House of Lords, مَسْنَدُ قَاضِي ٱلْقُضَاةِ فِي صَدْرِ مَجْلِسِ ٱلْأُمَرَاءِ. To be raised to the —, تَعَيَّنَ إِلَى وَظِيفَةِ قَاضِي ٱلْقُضَاةِ.

Wool-stapler, *n.* صَوَّاف.

Woolly, *a.* Of wool, مِنْ صُوفٍ. Having much wool, وَافِر ـ كَثِيرُ ٱلصُّوفِ ـ ٱلصُّوفِ. A — sheep, صَافِف ـ صَاف ـ صُوفَانِيٌّ *fem.* صَافَة ـ صُوفَانِيَّة. A — lock, لِمَّةٌ صَافَةٌ. To be —, صَافَ *aor.* يَصُوفُ.

Word, *n.* كَلِمَة *pl.* كَلِم *and* كَلِمَات ـ لَفْظ *pl.* أَلْفَاظ. Speech, كَلَام. A phrase, expression, عِبَارَة. A reply, رَدّ جَوَاب ـ جَوَاب. Information, خَبَر. A promise, وَعْد. An order, أَمْر. The — or truth of God, كَلَامُ ٱللّٰهِ ـ حَقُّ ٱللّٰهِ. Jesus the Word of God, سَيِّدُنَا عِيسَى كَلِمَةُ ٱللّٰهِ. A — with you, لِي مَعَكَ كَلِمَةٌ. A — to the wise is sufficient for them, ٱلْعَارِفُ تَكْفِيهِ ٱلْإِشَارَةُ. A man of his —, صَاحِبُ قَوْلٍ ـ رَجُل وَفِيّ. His wont is to act out his words, دَأْبُهُ أَنْ يَقْرِنَ كَلَامَهُ بِٱلْعَمَلِ. Take my — for it, صَدِّقْ كَلَامِي. Words cannot express it, يَعْجِزُ عَنْ وَصْفِهِ ٱللِّسَانُ. A good word, in praise, مَدْح ـ إِثْنَاء ـ تَثْنِيَة. Solicitation, رَجَاء ـ تَرْجِيَة.

By word of mouth, مُشَافَاةً ـ مُشَافَهَةً.

Fair, kindly, words, كَلَامٌ لَطِيفٌ ـ كَلِمَاتٌ حُلْوَةٌ ـ كَلَامٌ حُلْوٌ ـ كَلِمَاتٌ رَقِيقَةٌ.

Fine words, a promise, وَعْد *pl.* وُعُود.

High words, مُشَاجَرَة ـ مُنَازَعَة ـ نِزَاع.

In a word, to sum up, النِّهَايَة ـ نِهَايَةُ ٱلْكَلَامِ ـ وَٱلْحَاصِلُ.

In a few words, بِٱلِٱخْتِصَار.

In word and in deed, بِٱلْقَوْلِ وَٱلْفِعْلِ ـ قَالًا وَحَالًا.

Uncivil words, كَلَامٌ سَفِيهٌ ـ كَلَامٌ فَظٌّ ـ كَلَامٌ غَلِيظٌ.

Upon my word, فِي حَظِّي وَبَخْتِي ـ فِي ذِمَّتِي ـ عَلَى ذِمَّتِي.

Vain words, كَلَامٌ بَاطِلٌ.

Word for word, بِحُرُوفِهِ ـ حَرْفًا ـ لَفْظٌ بِلَفْظٍ ـ كَلِمَةٌ بِكَلِمَةٍ.

To be as good as one's word, كَمَّلَ وَعْدَهُ ـ أَوْفَى بِقَوْلِهِ ـ أَنْجَزَ عَهْدَهُ.

To bring word, intelligence, to, رَدَّ لِ-خَبَرًا. To bring word, answer, to, رَدَّ لِ-جَوَابًا.

To eat one's words, كَذَّبَ نَفْسَهُ.

To forfeit one's word, رَجَعَ ـ نَقَضَ وَعْدَهُ ـ خَالَفَ وَعْدَهُ عَنْ كَلَامِهِ.

To give one's word, وَعَدَ بِ *aor.* يَعِدُ ـ أَوْعَدَ.

To go from one's word, حَالَ عَنْ عَهْدِهِ ـ رَجَعَ عَنْ كَلَامِهِ.

To have words, to quarrel, of many, تَعَالَجُوا ـ تَشَاجَرُوا ـ تَنَازَعُوا.

To have the last word with one, to be pugnacious with to the last, إِتَّخَذَ ٱلْكَلِمَةَ ٱلْأَخِيرَةَ ـ طَاوَلَهُ بِٱلْمُنَازَعَةِ ـ طَاوَلَهُ بِٱلْمُعَانَدَةِ بِٱلْمُنَازَعَةِ.

To keep one's word, كَمَّلَ وَعْدَهُ ـ أَوْفَى بِقَوْلِهِ ـ أَنْجَزَ عَهْدَهُ.

To listen to the words of one, أَصْغَى إِلَى كَلَامِهِ.

To make no words, fuss, about, رَضِيَ بِ-بِدُونِ كَلَامٍ ـ لَمْ يَعْسُرْ فِي.

To make one eat his words, جَعَلَ-يُكَذِّبُ نَفْسَهُ.

To put in a good word to one in behalf of, شَهِدَ لِ-بِخَيْرٍ عِنْدَهُ ـ إِسْتَعْطَفَ-عَلَى ـ تَشَفَّعَ إِلَى-فِي.

To say the word, to order, أَمَرَ. Say the word, قُلْ.

To send word to, خَبَّرَ ـ أَخْبَرَ ـ أَرْسَلَ خَبَرًا إِلَى.

To speak or say a word, قَالَ كَلِمَةً ـ تَكَلَّمَ بِكَلِمَةٍ. No one spoke a word to him, لَمْ يُكَلِّمْهُ أَحَدٌ بِكَلِمَةٍ. He did not speak a word to him (in reply,) لَمْ يُجِبْهُ بِكَلِمَةٍ.

To take one at his word, إِمْتَثَلَ قَوْلَهُ ـ قَبِلَ مِنَ-ٱلْمَعْرُوض.

To write word to, رَاسَلَ-فِي ـ أَخْبَرَ-خَطًّا ـ خَبَّرَ-بِٱلْمَكْتُوب.

Word, *v.t.* عَبَّرَ. To —, in writing, كَتَبَ.

Worded, *a.* مُعَبَّر; in writing, مَكْتُوب.

Wordily, *ad.* بِتَطْوِيلِ ٱلْكَلَامِ ـ بِمُبَالَغَةٍ فِي ٱلْكَلَامِ.

Wordiness, *n.* كَثْرَةُ كَلَامٍ ـ كَلَامٌ لُتَاتٍ ـ مُبَالَغَةٌ فِي ٱلْكَلَامِ ـ نَفَس.

Wording, *n.* Mode of expression, عِبَارَة ـ تَرْكِيبُ ٱلْكَلَامِ ـ نَصٌّ ـ نَمَطُ ٱلْكَلَامِ.

Wordy, *a.* Verbose, كَثِيرُ ٱلْكَلَامِ ـ مُبَالِغٌ فِي ٱلْكَلَامِ ـ نَفَس.

Wore, *pret. of to* Wear, *q.v.*

Work, *v.i.* To move about, تَحَرَّكَ. To —, as a machine, مَشَى ـ إِشْتَغَلَ. To be occupied, as in work, عَمِلَ ـ سَعَى ـ إِشْتَغَلَ. To act or operate, عَمِلَ. To sew, صَنَعَ ٱلْخِيَاطَةَ ـ خَيَّطَ. To produce effects, أَنْفَذَ إِنْفَاذًا ـ نَفَذَ نَفَاذًا ـ تَأَثَّرَ. To ferment, إِخْتَمَرَ ـ تَخَمَّرَ. To be in a state of agitation, تَهَيَّجَ ـ إِهْتَاجَ. To sail, of a ship, or the director of a ship, أَقْلَعَ ـ أَبْحَرَ ـ مَخَرَ.

To work hard, تَعِبَ ـ صَرَفَ ٱلْهِمَّةَ ـ إِجْتَهَدَ ـ كَدَّ.

To work in, to become imbibed, تَشَرَّبَ. To penetrate, نَفَذَ ـ تَطَرَّقَ إِلَى ـ نَفَذَ فِي.

To work into, إِشْتَغَلَ فِي ـ يَسْرِي *aor.* سَرَى فِي: The poison worked into him, سَرَى (*or* إِشْتَغَلَ) فِيهِ ٱلسُّمُّ.

To work off, to become consumed or expended gradually, ذَهَبَ تَدْرِيجًا. To become detached gradually, إِنْفَصَلَ تَدْرِيجًا.

To work or slip out gradually, خَرَجَ تَدْرِيجًا ـ إِنْسَلَّ تَدْرِيجًا.

To work smoothly, إِشْتَغَلَ بِسُهُولَةٍ ـ سَهُلَ فِي ٱلْعَمَلِ.

To work to windward, أَبْحَرَ نَحْوَ عِلَاوَةِ ٱلرِّيحِ.

To work up, to move up gradually, إِسْتَعْلَى تَدْرِيجًا. To go forward, تَدَرَّجَ ـ تَقَدَّمَ.

To work up or push one's way to, as with difficulty, خَاضَ إِلَى *aor.* يَخُوضُ.

Work, *v.t.* To move, حَرَّكَ. To mix, stir, خَبَّصَ ـ خَضْخَضَ ـ حَرَّكَ ـ جَدَّحَ. To make, to do, عَمِلَ ـ صَنَعَ. To busy, شَغَّلَ ـ شَغَلَ ـ أَلْهَى. To —, as of iron, *etc.*, عَامَلَ ـ عَالَجَ. To —, as into shape, هَنْدَمَ. To — roughly or by the first operation, خَشَبَ. To knead, as of dough, عَجَنَ. To — or knead well, much, مَلَّكَ ـ أَمْلَكَ. To lead to, to prepare for, أَعَدَّ. To produce, أَنْشَأَ ـ أَنْتَجَ. To —, to calculate, حَسَبَ. To embroider, طَرَّزَ ـ سَوَّجَ ـ زَرْكَشَ. He works iron, يُعَالِجُ ٱلْحَدِيدَ. Trouble works patience, الضِّيقُ يُنْشِئُ صَبْرًا. To — a ship, سَيَّرَ ٱلْمَرْكَبَ. This will — his destruction, هٰذَا سَيَكُونُ خَرَابًا لَهُ. That worked, busied, him very much, ذٰلِكَ شَغَلَهُ كَثِيرًا ـ شُغِلَ بِذٰلِكَ جِدًّا. To — down, to reduce in size, صَغَّرَ; to — down, as by attrition, أَبْلَى.

To work in, to make to imbibe, شَرَّبَ. To make to enter, أَدْخَلَ. To cause to enter gradually, أَدْخَلَ-تَدْرِيجًا.

To work off, to produce, to make, as a machine, *etc.*, does, صَنَعَ. To use, use up, إِسْتَعْمَلَ. To finish, أَكْمَلَ ـ كَمَّلَ ـ أَتَمَّ ـ تَمَّمَ. To print, طَبَعَ. To work off, as the effect of anything. مَحَا تَأْثِيرَهُ *aor.* يَمْحُو.

To work one's passage, in lieu of money-payment, خَدَمَ ٱلْمَرْكَبَ ² عِوَضًا عَنْ مَصْرُوفِ ٱلسَّفَرِ.

To work out, to effect, عَمِلَ ـ صَنَعَ. To carry out, أَجْرَى. To calculate, حَسَبَ ². To make to come out gradually, فَرَّغَ مِن ـ أَنْجَزَ ـ أَنْفَذَ ـ أَنْهَى ². To accomplish, أَخْرَجَ-تَدْرِيجًا. This will work out their good, هٰذَا يَؤُولُ لَهُمْ خَيْرًا.

To work up, to make to come to the surface gradually, عَلَّى-تَدْرِيجًا. To work up, as of materials, إِسْتَعْمَلَ. To expend, صَرَفَ ـ صَرَّفَ. To mix, خَلَطَ ـ أَصْرَفَ ـ صَرَّفَ. To agitate, stir up, حَرَّضَ ـ هَيَّجَ.

To work with, in the service of, خَدَمَ عِنْدَهُ ² ـ خَدَمَ ـ إِشْتَغَلَ عِنْدَهُ.

To work wonders, عَمِلَ ٱلْآيَاتِ.

Work, *n.* Exertion of strength, labour, سَعْيٌ ـ عَمَلٌ ـ فَعْلٌ ـ كَدٌّ ـ جُهْدٌ ـ تَعَبٌ ـ مَسْعًى. Business, employment, خِدْمَةٌ ـ شُغْلٌ. A thing which causes one to be busied, مَشْغَلَةٌ. A business in which one is engaged, أُشْغُولَةٌ. Something done, worked, عَمَلٌ *pl.* أَعْمَالٌ ـ صَنْعَةٌ ـ شُغْلٌ *pl.* أَشْغَالٌ. An action, فِعْلٌ *pl.* أَفْعَالٌ. Effect, result, consequence, حَاصِلٌ ـ ثَمَرَةٌ ـ نَتِيجَةٌ ـ مَحْصُولٌ. Work, a literary composition, مُصَنَّفٌ *pl.* مُصَنَّفَاتٌ ـ تَصْنِيفٌ *pl.* تَصَانِيفُ ـ تَأْلِيفٌ *pl.* تَوَالِيفُ. A fortification, إِسْتِحْكَامٌ *pl.* إِسْتِحْكَامَاتٌ. Work, sewing, خِيَاطَةٌ; embroidery, تَطْرِيزٌ.

A piece of work, something, قَضِيَّةٌ ـ أَمْرٌ ـ شَيْءٌ. A quarrel, خَبْصَةٌ ـ شَوَاشٌ ـ إِرْتِبَاكٌ ـ مُنَازَعَةٌ ـ نِزَاعٌ. A muddle, وَرْطَةٌ ـ لَخْبَطَةٌ. A piece of embroidery, طِرَازٌ; of sewing, مَخْيُوطٌ ـ مَخِيطٌ.

Board of Public Works, نِظَارَةُ ٱلْعِمَارَاتِ ٱلْمِيرِيَّةِ.

Dry or uninteresting work, شُغْلٌ مُعْجِزٌ ـ شُغْلٌ شَاقٌّ.

Good works, أَعْمَالٌ خَيْرِيَّةٌ ـ أَعْمَالٌ صَالِحَةٌ ـ أَعْمَالٌ حَسَنَةٌ ـ حَسَنَاتٌ. Good works that remain to be recompensed, ٱلْبَاقِيَاتُ ٱلصَّالِحَاتُ.

Hard work, شُغْلٌ صَعْبٌ ـ شُغْلٌ مُتْعِبٌ.

Maid of all work, جَارِيَةٌ خَادِمَةٌ أَشْغَالَ ٱلْبَيْتِ جُمْلَةً.

Open work, trellis, مُشَبَّكٌ ـ مُخَرَّمٌ ـ قَفَصٌ. Embroidery, طِرَازٌ ـ تَطْرِيزٌ.

Plain work, شُغْلٌ هَيِّنٌ ـ شُغْلٌ بَسِيطٌ ـ شُغْلٌ عَادِيٌّ; of sewing, خِيَاطَةٌ بَسِيطَةٌ.

Warm work, such as makes one warm, شُغْلٌ مُحْمٍ ـ شُغْلٌ مُعَرِّقٌ ـ شُغْلٌ حَامٍ; of battle, حَرْبٌ عَلَى سَاقٍ.

To be at work, عَمِلَ ـ إِشْتَغَلَ.

To be hard at work, إِجْتَهَدَ ـ كَدَّ ² ـ تَعِبَ ـ تَعَمَّلَ.

To be in full work, as of a machine, كَانَ مَشْغُولًا مُطْلَقًا. To do all one's work, قَضَى مَا عَلَيْهِ مِنَ ٱلشُّغْلِ.

To be out of work, تَعَطَّلَ ـ عَطَلَ ² ـ بَطَلَ مِنَ ٱلْعَمَلِ ² ـ بَطَلَ.

To cut out work for a person, of cloth, dress, *etc.*, فَصَّلَ لِ; to contrive business for, رَتَّبَ لِ-مَشْغَلَةً.

To fall to work, تَشَمَّرَ لِ ـ شَرَعَ فِي ـ أَلْقَى يَدَهُ فِي.

To go through work, أَنْجَزَ ٱلشُّغْلَ ـ قَضَى ٱلشُّغْلَ.

To go to work, to act, سَلَكَ ² ـ سَعَى.

To go the right way to work, أَسَدَّ فِي ٱلْعَمَلِ ـ أَصَابَ فِي ٱلْعَمَلِ ـ عَرَفَ شُغْلَهُ.

To go the wrong way to work, زَلَّ فِي ٱلْعَمَلِ ² ـ أَخْطَأَ فِي ٱلْعَمَلِ ـ خَرَّبَ شُغْلَهُ.

To make work, to increase work, كَثَّرَ ٱلشُّغْلَ.

To make a piece of work, cause a row, disturbance, قَيَّمَ فِتْنَةً ـ قَيَّمَ ٱلدُّنْيَا ـ أَحْدَثَ بَلْبَلَةً.

To make sad work of, خَرَّبَ ـ ضَيَّعَ ـ أَتْلَفَ ـ أَعْدَمَ.

To set one to work, شَغَّلَ ـ خَدَّمَ ـ خَدَّمَ-خِدْمَةً.

To set one's self to work, تَشَمَّرَ لِلشُّغْلِ ـ إِبْتَدَأَ بِٱلشُّغْلِ.

To set one's brains to work about, تَفَكَّرَ فِي ـ إِفْتَكَرَ فِي ـ شَغَّلَ بَالَهُ فِي.

To throw out of work, عَطَّلَ-مِنَ ٱلشُّغْلِ ـ عَطَّلَ.

Workable, *a.* That can be worked, wrought, يُعَامَلُ ـ يُعَالَجُ; that can be worked, as a machine, مُعَدٌّ لِلشُّغْلِ ـ يَشْتَغِلُ.

Workbag, *n.* For ladies' work, كِيسٌ لِلْخِيَاطَةِ ـ مَشْبَنَةٌ.

Workbox, *n.* For ladies' work, دُرْجٌ ـ حِقْشٌ.

Workday, *n.* / Working-day, } يَوْمُ ٱلْعَمَلِ (دُونَ ٱلْأَحَدِ) *pl.* أَيَّامُ ٱلْعَمَلِ.

Worker, *n.* *See* Workman, *n.*

Work-fellow, *n.* رَفِيقٌ فِي ٱلْعَمَلِ *pl.* رُفَقَاءُ.

Work-folk, *n.* / Working-people, } أَهْلُ ٱلشُّغْلِ ـ صُنَّاعٌ ـ عَمَلَةٌ.

Workhouse, *n.* دَارٌ لِلْمَسَاكِينِ.

Working, *n.* Direction, use, تَشْغِيلٌ: He gave to such an one the — of the railway, أَعْطَى فُلَانًا تَشْغِيلَ سِكَّةِ ٱلْحَدِيدِ.

Working-dress, *n.* بِذْلَةٌ ـ مِبْذَلَةٌ *pl.* مَبَاذِلُ ـ مِعْوَزٌ ـ فَضْلَةٌ ـ فُضُلٌ ـ لِبْسُ ٱلشُّغْلِ. To use a garment as a —, عَفَسَ.

Workman, *n.* عَامِلٌ *pl.* عُمَّالٌ ـ صَانِعٌ *pl.* صُنَّاعٌ. A skilful —, صَانِعٌ حَاذِقٌ ـ صَانِعٌ مُتَعَتِّدٌ.

Workmanlike, *a.* / Workmanly, } Skilful, مَاهِرٌ ـ حَاذِقٌ ـ حَسَنُ ٱلْمِهْنَةِ ـ *vulg.* شَاطِرٌ. Well done, حَسَنُ ٱلصِّنَاعَةِ ـ مُتَعَتِّدٌ.

Workmanly, *ad.* بِمِهْنَةٍ ـ بِصِنَاعَةٍ ـ بِفَنٍّ.

Workmanship, *n.* Work done, صَنْعَة ـ شُغْل. Manufacture, صَنْعَة. Manner of working, صِنَاعَة; of things molten, jewelry, *etc.*, صِيَاغَة. Workman's skill, مِهْنَةُ ٱلصَّانِعِ ـ فَنُّ ٱلصَّانِعِ.

Work-mistress, *n.* نَاظِرَةُ ٱلْخَيَّاطَاتِ.

Workshop, *n.* مَحَلُّ (or) دُكَّانُ) ـ مَعْمَل ـ مُحْتَرَف ـ مَحْرِف ـ كَرْخَانَة ـ ٱلشُّغْلِ.

Work-table, *n.* *See* Work-box, *n.*

Workwoman, *n.* For sewing, خَيَّاطَة *pl.* خَيَّاطَات.

World, *n.* The universe, ٱلدُّنْيَا ـ ٱلعَالَمُ. A world, عَالَم *pl.* عَوَالِمُ. The earth, ٱلأَرْضُ. Mankind, ـ جِنْسُ ٱلْبَشَرِ ـ ٱلبَشَرُ ـ عَالَم ـ عَمٌّ ـ ٱلنَّاسُ. A great multitude, فَوْج *pl.* أَفْوَاج ـ خَلْقٌ كَثِيرٌ. Time, age, دَهْر. Lifetime, عُمْر ـ حَيَاة. The ways of the —, عَادَاتُ ٱلدُّنْيَا. The rich, wealthy, ـ ٱلكُبَرَآءُ ٱلأَغْنِيَآءُ. Fashionable society, مَعْشَرُ ٱلأَكَابِرِ ـ مَعْشَرُ ٱلمُعْتَبَرِينَ. He purchased the present — at the expense of the — to come, بَاعَ ٱلدُّنْيَا بِٱلآخِرَةِ. In this — and the next, ـ فِي ٱلدَّارَيْنِ ـ فِي ٱلدُّنْيَا وَٱلآخِرَةِ. Relating to the — to come, أُخْرَاوِيٌّ ـ أُخْرَوِيٌّ.

All over the world, فِي كُلِّ ٱلْعَالَمِ.

As the world goes, نَظَرًا لِحَالِ ٱلدُّنْيَا.

For all the world, لِكُلِّ مَا فِي ٱلدُّنْيَا ـ لِكُلِّ ٱلدُّنْيَا.

Nothing in the world, لَا شَيْءَ بِٱلدُّنْيَا.

Such are the ways of the world, كَذَا ٱلدُّنْيَا ـ هٰكَذَا ٱلدُّنْيَا.

The animal world, ٱلحَيَوَانَاتُ.

The learned world, ٱلعُلَمَآءُ.

The lowest or nearest world, ٱلسَّمَآءُ ٱلدُّنْيَا.

The next world, the world to come, دَارُ ٱلبَقَآءِ ـ دَارُ ٱلقَرَارِ ـ ٱلآخِرَةُ.

The pomps and vanities of the world, حُطَامُ ٱلدُّنْيَا ـ أَبَاطِيلُ ٱلعَالَمِ.

The present world, ٱلدَّارُ ٱلدُّنْيَا ـ ٱلحَيَاةُ ٱلدُّنْيَا.

The vegetable world, ٱلنَّبَاتَاتُ.

This world and the world to come, ٱلدُّنْيَا وَٱلآخِرَةُ.

To begin the world, one's career, شَرَعَ فِي ٱلعِيشَةِ ـ إِبْتَدَأَ ٱلسِّيرَةَ.

To come into the world, دَخَلَ إِلَى ٱلعَالَمِ.

To go round the world, دَارَ ٱلدُّنْيَا ـ جَالَ ٱلدُّنْيَا.

To laugh at what the world says, ـ قَالَ أَنَا لِلدُّنْيَا إِذَا كَانَتْ هٰكَذَا ـ هَزَأَ بِقَوْلِ ٱلنَّاسِ ـ سَخِرَ بِٱلدُّنْيَا.

To rove about the world, عَالَ فِي ٱلدُّنْيَا ـ عَارَ ٱلدُّنْيَا.

Worldliness, *n.* حُبُّ ٱلدُّنْيَا.

Worldling, *n.* مُحِبُّ ٱلدُّنْيَا *pl.* مُحِبُّونَ.

Worldly, *a.* Pertaining to the world, دُنْيَوِيٌّ ـ عَالَمِيٌّ. Devoted to — things, طَالِبُ ـ مُهْتَمٌّ بِحُطَامِ ٱلدُّنْيَا ـ مُحِبُّ ٱلدُّنْيَا ـ أَبَاطِيلِ ٱلعَالَمِ. Worldly lusts, ٱلشَّهَوَاتُ ٱلدُّنْيَوِيَّةُ.

Worldly-minded, *a.* *See under preceding article.*

Worldly-mindedness, *n.* إِهْتِمَامٌ بِأَبَاطِيلِ ٱلعَالَمِ ـ حُبُّ ٱلدُّنْيَا.

Worm, *n.* Any small creeping animal, دُودَة *pl.* دُود ـ دِيدَان *pl.* دِيدَان *coll.* دُود. A weevil or grub, سُوسَة *coll.* سُوس. An earth —, شَحْمَةُ ٱلأَرْضِ. Anything in a spiral form, لَوْلَب *pl.* لَوَالِبُ. A — for drawing out wads of muskets, *etc.*, بَرِّيمَة. The — of a screw, لَوْلَبُ ٱلبُرْغِيِّ. Remorse, ـ أَكْلُ ٱلسَّرِيرَةِ نَارُ ٱلحَسَرَاتِ ـ لَسْعُ ٱلذِّمَّةِ ـ نَخْزُ ٱلضَّمِيرِ. The — that dieth not, نَارُ ٱلحَسَرَاتِ. To become full of worms, wormy, دَوِدَ ـ دَادَ.

Worm, *v.i.* To work slowly or imperceptibly, إِنْدَسَّ ـ أَدْغَلَ.

Worm, *v.t.* To undermine by secret means, دَغَلَ لِ. To — one's self into, إِنْدَسَّ فِي ـ أَدْغَلَ فِي. To — a secret out of one, كَشَفَ عَنِ ٱلسِّرِّ ـ تَجَسَّسَ ٱلسِّرَّ مِن.

Worm-eaten, *a.* مُسَوَّس ـ مَسُوس; rotten, رَمِيم ـ رُمَام.

Worm-hole, *n.* A place eaten away by worms, سُوسَة.

Worm-like, *a.* Spiral, لَوْلَبِيٌّ.

Wormwood, *n.* ٱلشَّيْبَة ـ مَامِيثَا ـ دَقْنُ ٱلشَّيْخِ ـ ٱلشِّيحُ ـ أَفْسَنْتِين.

Wormy, *a.* Full of worms, مُدَوِّد.

Worn, *a.* Which has been worn, put on, مَلْبُوس. Worn, of coin, أَطْلَس. Worn with travel, بِلْوُ أَسْفَارٍ. Worn out, of a man, ـ سَمُول ـ رَثِيث ـ رَثّ ـ حَشِيف ـ كَهِيم ـ كِهَام; of dress, ثَوْبٌ ـ سَحْق ـ مَبَاذِلُ ـ سَمَل. An old — garment, مِبْذَلَة *pl.* مَبَاذِلُ ـ مُنْسَحِق. An old — turban, سَحْقُ عِمَامَةٍ. An old — dirham, دِرْهَمٌ زَائِفٌ ـ سَحْقُ دِرْهَمٍ. To be — out, of dress, ـ إِنْسَحَقَ ـ أَرَثَّ ـ رَثَّ.

Worrier, *n.* Of a wild animal, مُفْتَرِس. One who harasses, مُضْجِر ـ مُزْعِج ـ حَرَّاش ـ مُعَذِّب.

Worry, *v.t.* To mangle, as with the teeth, إِفْتَرَسَ ـ عَقَرَ; with the nails, حَرَشَ. To harass, vex, torment, ـ آذَى ـ عَذَّبَ ـ حَرَّشَ ـ أَغْرَضَ ـ أَضْجَرَ ـ أَزْعَجَ ـ نَهَكَ. To be worried, harassed, إِنْزَعَجَ ـ تَحَرَّشَ ـ تَعَذَّبَ.

Worry, *n.* Vexation, ـ نَجَع ـ إِضْطِرَاب ـ إِنْزِعَاج ـ زَعَج ـ أَذِيَّة ـ ضُجْرَة.

Worse, *a.* (*comp. of* Bad) } Of health, أَرْدَأُ; of condition, أَشَرُّ;
Worse, *ad.* } of conduct, شَرٌّ ـ أَشَرُّ ـ أَرْذَلُ.

Inferior, دُون. He became —, in health or condition, صَارَ إِلَى حَالٍ أَرْدَأَ. The rent became —, صَارَ ٱلخَرْقُ أَرْدَأَ. Not for the better but for the —, لَيْسَ لِلأَفْضَلِ بَلْ لِلأَرْدَإِ. That will be — for you than any evil which has yet befallen you, يَكُونُ ذٰلِكَ

لَكَ شَرًّا مِنْ كُلِّ سُوءٍ أَصَابَكَ. What befell them at the last was — than at the beginning, صَارَتْ لَهُمُ ٱلْعَوَاقِبُ شَرًّا مِنَ ٱلْأَوَائِلِ. Lest — should happen to you, لِئَلَّا يُصِيبَكَ شَيْءٌ شَرٌّ مِنْ ذٰلِكَ. We will do — to you than they did, نَفْعَلُ بِكُمْ شَرًّا أَكْثَرَ مِنْهُمْ. He is — than you are, هُوَ شَرٌّ مِنْكَ. The state of the country is — than it was before, أَحْوَالُ ٱلْبِلَادِ أَسْوَأُ مِمَّا كَانَتْ سَابِقًا. They will go from bad to —, يَزْدَادُونَ شَرًّا. Worse and —, of moral evil, أَشَدُّ فَسَادًا ـ أَنْجَسُ وَأَنْجَسُ. Worse than nothing, شَرٌّ مِنَ ٱلْعَدَمِ. He could not have made a — mistake than that, لَمْ يَقْدِرْ أَنْ يَأْتِيَ بِغَلَطٍ أَشَرَّ مِنْ هٰذَا.

Worship, *n.* Religious adoration, سُجُود ـ سَجْدَة ـ عِبَادَة ـ عَمْر. Reverence, respect, إِكْرَام ـ اِحْتِرَام ـ تَوَقُّر. As a title of honour, مُحْتَرَم ـ مُكَرَّم. Idolatry, as of lovers, وُلُوع ـ وَلَع. A place of —, مَسْجِد *pl.* مَسَاجِد ـ مَعْبَد *pl.* مَعَابِد ـ مُتَعَبَّد. Public —, prayers, صَلَوَات جُمْهُورِيَّة ـ صَلَاة عَامَّة. Minister of public —, نَاظِرُ ٱلْمَذَاهِبِ. By my —! لَعَمْرِي. By (the — of) God, لَعَمْرُ ٱللّٰهِ.

Worship, *v.t.* To adore, عَمَرَ ـ عَبَدَ ـ سَجَدَ ل. To revere, respect, اِحْتَرَمَ ـ أَكْرَمَ ـ كَرَّمَ ـ وَقَّرَ. To — as a lover, وَلِعَ ب *aor.* يَوْلَعُ. He worshipped his Lord, عَبَدَ (or عَمَرَ) رَبَّهُ.

Worship, *v.i.* To bow in worship, سَجَدَ. To be pious, قَنَتَ ـ اِتَّقَى ٱللّٰهَ.

Worshipful, *a.* As a title of respect, or honour, جَلِيل ـ وَجِيه ـ مُكَرَّم ـ مُعَظَّم ـ فَخِيم.

Worshipfully, *ad.* بِمُرَاعَاةٍ ـ بِٱحْتِرَامٍ ـ بِإِكْرَامٍ.

Worshipper, *n.* Of the true God or a false god, عَبْد *pl.*, of the true God, عِبَاد; of a false god, عَبَدَة. One who prostrates himself, as in prayer, سَاجِد *pl.* سُجَّاد. One who frequently worships, سَجَّاد. A — of God, a devout person, مُتَّقِي ٱللّٰهَ *pl.* مُتَّقُونَ.

Worst, *a.* Of condition, ٱلْأَسْوَأُ ـ ٱلْأَرْدَأُ ـ ٱلْأَشَرُّ; of conduct, *fem.* ٱلسُّوءَى ـ ٱلْأَرْذَلُ ـ ٱلْأَشَرُّ ـ ٱلْأَفْحَشُ ـ ٱلْأَشَدُّ فَسَادًا. The most inferior, دُونَ ٱلْجَمِيعِ ـ دُونَ ٱلْكُلِّ. It was the — act a man could be guilty of, كَانَ ذٰلِكَ أَشَدَّ فَظَاعَةً مِنَ ٱلْأَفْعَالِ ٱلَّتِي يُمْكِنُ لِلْإِنْسَانِ أَنْ يَرْتَكِبَهَا. He is the — of men, هُوَ أَسْوَأُ ٱلنَّاسِ. She is the — of women, هِيَ سُوءَى ٱلنِّسَاءِ. The — possible conditions, states, أَسْوَأُ ٱلْأَحْوَالِ. "To the worst part of life," *i.e.* decrepit old age, إِلَى أَرْذَلِ ٱلْعُمُرِ (Kur. xvi. 72). "Verily the worst beasts in the sight of God are the thankless who will not believe," إِنَّ شَرَّ ٱلدَّوَابِّ عِنْدَ ٱللّٰهِ ٱلَّذِينَ كَفَرُوا فَهُمْ لَا يُؤْمِنُونَ (*Id.* viii. 57). "And they shall then know which is in the worst state, and which is the more weak in forces," فَسَيَعْلَمُونَ مَنْ هُوَ شَرٌّ مَكَانًا وَأَضْعَفُ جُنْدًا (*Id.* xix. 77). The — of the people, أَشَرُّ ٱلنَّاسِ. The — of it is, هُوَ أَشَرُّ مَا فِيهِ. If the — comes to the —, حَصَلَ مَا حَصَلَ مِنَ ٱلشَّرِّ. Do your —, اِفْعَلْ مَا أَمْكَنَكَ مِنَ ٱلشَّرِّ. To have the — of it, اِنْغَلَبَ ـ خَابَ *aor.* يَخِيبُ ـ خَسِرَ. To make the — of anything, عَظَّمَ ٱلشَّرَّ لِلْغَايَةِ ـ اِسْتَعْظَمَ سُوءَ ٱلْأَمْرِ. To suppose, fear, the — of, أَشْفَقَ مِنَ ٱلْأَشَرِّ; to despair of, أَيِسَ مِن.

Worst, *v.t.* To defeat, overthrow, غَلَبَ عَلَى ـ كَسَرَ. To be worsted, اِنْغَلَبَ ـ اِنْكَسَرَ ـ اِنْتَصَرَ عَلَى. The rebels were worsted, كَانَتِ ٱلدَّائِرَةُ عَلَى ٱلْعُصَاةِ.

Worsted, *n.* خَيْطٌ مِنْ صُوفٍ.

Worsted, *a.* Made of worsted, مِنْ صُوفٍ. Defeated, مُنْكَسِر ـ مَغْلُوب.

Wort, *n.* A plant, نَبَاتَة *coll.* نَبَات *pl.* نَبَاتَات. A plant of the cabbage kind, ضَرْبٌ مِنَ ٱللَّخَانَةِ. New beer, بِيرَةٌ حُلْوَةٌ.

Worth, *n.* Value, قِيمَة ـ ثَمَن. Merit, excellence, قَدْم ـ اِسْتِحْقَاق ـ فَخْر ـ فَضِيلَة ـ فَضْل. *See also* Value, *n.*

Worth, *a.* The being possessed of, صَاحِب ـ ذُو ـ مَالِكٌ. Equivalent, مُعَادِل. Meriting, مُسْتَحِقّ. To be —, سَاوَى ـ سَوَى *aor.* يَسْوَى. This is — a dirham, هٰذَا يُسَاوِي دِرْهَمًا ـ هٰذَا يَسْوَى دِرْهَمًا. This is not — that, هٰذَا ٱلشَّيْءُ لَا يُسَاوِي (or يَسْوَى) ذٰلِكَ. It is not — anything, لَا يُسَاوِي (or يَسْوَى) شَيْئًا. It is not — while, مَا يَسْوَى ٱلتَّعَبَ ـ لَا طَائِلَ فِيهِ.

Worthily, *ad.* Deservedly, بِٱسْتِئْهَالٍ ـ اِسْتِحْقَاقًا ـ بِٱلْوَاجِبِ ـ كَمَا يَجِبُ ـ بِمُنَاسَبَةٍ ـ بِلِيَاقَةٍ ـ بِٱسْتِحْقَاقٍ. Fitly, properly, بِلِيَاقَةٍ.

Worthiness, *n.* Desert, merit, اِسْتِحْقَاق ـ اِسْتِئْهَال. Goodness, خَيْر. Nobleness, فَخْر ـ نَبَالَة. Propriety, fitness, لِيَاقَة ـ أَهْلِيَّة ـ مُنَاسَبَة.

Worthless, *a.* Of no use, بَطَّال ـ بَاطِل ـ غَيْرُ طَائِلٍ ـ بَهْرَج. Vile, base, خَسِيس ـ دَنِيء ـ رَذِيل *pl.* أَرْذَال. A — fellow, رُذَال ـ رُذَم ـ قِشْبٌ خِشْبٌ. To be —, useless, بَطَلَ.

Worthlessness, *n.* Uselessness, عَدَمُ طَائِلٍ ـ عَدَمُ نَفْعٍ ـ قِلَّةُ نَفْعٍ ـ عَدَمُ مَنْفَعَةٍ ـ فَائِدَةٍ. Vileness, baseness, رَذَالَة ـ خَسَاسَة ـ دَنَاءَة.

Worthy, *a.* Having merit, dignified, فَاضِل ـ فَاخِر ـ وَجِيه. Deserving, مُسْتَأْهِل ـ مُسْتَحِقّ. Worthy of, fit for, أَهْلٌ ل ـ جَدِيرٌ ل ـ خَلِيقٌ ل ـ مَحَلٌّ ل. Worthy of notice, of being mentioned, مُسْتَحِقُّ ٱلذِّكْرِ. He is — of honour, يَسْتَأْهِلُ أَنْ يُكْرَمَ ـ هُوَ أَهْلٌ لِلْإِكْرَامِ. A son — of his father, اِبْنٌ مُعَادِلٌ لِأَبِيهِ. Worthy of death, مُسْتَحِقُّ ٱلْمَوْتِ. I am not — to . . ., لَسْتُ أَنَا أَهْلًا لِأَنْ. I did not think myself worthy to . . ., لَمْ أَحْسَبْ نَفْسِي أَهْلًا لِأَنْ. And although it is not —, does not come up to what your station calls for, وَإِنْ كَانَ لَا يَلِيقُ بِمَقَامِكُمْ. To be — of, إِسْتَوْجَبَ ـ إِسْتَأْهَلَ. To make —, أَهَّلَ ـ آهَلَ. May God make you — of good! أَهَّلَكَ ٱللّٰهُ لِلْخَيْرِ.

Worthy, *n.* فَاضِل *pl.* فَاضِلُون ـ مَبْرُور *pl.* مَبْرُورُون.

Wot, *v.t.* عَلِمَ ـ. I wot not, لَمْ أَعْلَمْ. Wot ye not? أَلَمْ تَعْلَمُوا.

Would, *aux. v.* (When implying to Will, to Desire, the Arabic equivalents are from the verbs, شَآءَ *aor.* يَشَآءُ ـ أَرَادَ.) What would you that I should do for you? مَاذَا تُرِيدُونَ أَنْ أَفْعَلَ لَكُمْ. Whatsoever you would that men should do unto you, do ye so likewise unto them, فَكُلَّمَا تُرِيدُونَ أَنْ يَفْعَلَ ٱلنَّاسُ بِكُمْ أَفْعَلُوا هٰكَذَا أَنْتُمْ بِهِمْ. He would not hear a single word about this matter, مَا أَرَادَ أَنْ يَسْمَعَ فِي هٰذِهِ ٱلْقَضِيَّةِ كَلِمَةً وَاحِدَةً. They did to them whatever they would, عَمِلُوا بِهِمْ حَسَبَ إِرَادَتِهِمْ. What would you? مَاذَا تُرِيدُ ـ مَاذَا تَشَآءُ. (*Potentially* the word may be expressed through the verb كَانَ; *e.g.,*) Had I known that would I not have told you? لَوْ عَلِمْتُ ذٰلِكَ أَفَمَا كُنْتُ أَخْبَرْتُكَ بِهِ. You would oblige us very much, كُنْتَ تَجْعَلُنَا مَدْيُونِينَ لِمَعْرُوفِكَ جِدًّا. (*Examples in the negative form:*) He would not, لَمْ يَشَأْ ـ لَمْ يُرِدْ: He would not listen to her, لَمْ يَشَأْ أَنْ يَسْمَعَ لَهَا. He would not come in, لَمْ يُرِدْ أَنْ يَدْخُلَ. So they would not come, فَلَمْ يُرِيدُوا أَنْ يَأْتُوا. (This negative form may also be expressed by the verb, أَبَى ـ; *e.g.,*) He would not listen to her, أَبَى أَنْ يَسْمَعَ لَهَا. (*Optatively,* the word may be expressed by the Arabic, لَيْتَ *or* يَا لَيْتَ; *e.g.,*) Would that I! لَيْتَنِي ـ يَا لَيْتَنِي; would that thou! لَيْتَكَ ـ يَا لَيْتَكَ; would that he! يَا لَيْتَهُ ـ لَيْتَهُ. "And the unbeliever shall say: Would that I were dust!" وَيَقُولُ ٱلْكَافِرُ يَا لَيْتَنِي كُنْتُ تُرَابًا (Kur. lxxviii. 41). (When the word "Would" implies *Insistence* it may be expressed by the verb, إِقْتَضَى or by the noun, بُدٌّ; *e.g.,*) He would go in, لَا بُدَّ مِنْ أَنْ يَدْخُلَ ـ إِقْتَضَى أَنْ يَدْخُلَ. The following are other renderings of the English word "Would:"—I would thank you for some paper, لَأَشْكُرَنَّ بِخَيْرِكَ عَلَى شَيْءٍ مِنَ ٱلْوَرَقِ. I would advise you, شَوْرِي عَلَيْكَ ـ نُصْحِي لَكَ. I would prefer a little rest, قَلِيلٌ مِنَ ٱلرَّاحَةِ أَحَبُّ إِلَيَّ. I would rather not, as a courteous reply to some offer, عِشْتَ.

Wound, *n.* جُرْح *pl.* جُرُوح ـ جِرَاحَة *pl.* جِرَاحَات. A stroke, hit, as with a ball, *etc.,* ضَرْبَة. A slight —, جُرْحٌ لَطِيفٌ. A deep —, جُرْحٌ بَالِغٌ. An incurable —, جُرْحٌ عَدِيمُ ٱلشِّفَآءِ. To receive a —, جُرِحَ ـ جَرِحَ ـ.

Wound, *v.t.* جَرَحَ ـ كَلَمَ ـ عَقَرَ ـ ثَلَمَ. To —, impair, injure, ثَلَمَ. To — much, جَرَّحَ ـ كَلَّمَ ـ عَقَّرَ. He wounded him with his tongue, جَرَحَهُ بِلِسَانِهِ. He wounded his honour, ثَلَمَ صِيتَهُ. She wounded the hearts of many, عَقَّرَتْ بِكَثِيرِينَ.

Wound, *part. of to* Wind, *q.v.*

Wounded, *a.* جَرِيح *pl.* جَرْحَى ـ مَجْرُوح ـ مُعَقَّر ـ مَكْلُوم. The killed and —, ٱلْقَتْلَى وَٱلْجَرْحَى. To be —, impaired, إِنْثَلَمَ. To be —, as with a wound, جُرِحَ ـ جَرِحَ ـ.

Wove, *pret. of to* Weave, *q.v.*

Wove, *a.* }
Woven, } مَنْسُوج. Anything woven, نَسِيجَة.

Wrack, *v.t. See to* Wreck, *v.t.*

Wrack, *n.* ضَرْبٌ مِنْ صُوفِ ٱلْبَحْرِ.

Wraith, *n.* خَيَالَة ـ خَيَال *pl.* أَخْيِلَة.

Wrangle, *n.* مُعَارَضَة ـ مُنَازَعَة ـ نِزَاع ـ مُجَادَلَة ـ جِدَال.

Wrangle, *v.i.* عَارَضَ ـ نَازَعَ ـ جَادَلَ. They wrangled together, of many, تَعَارَضُوا ـ تَنَازَعُوا ـ تَجَادَلُوا ـ إِخْتَصَمُوا. "He shall say: Wrangle not in my presence," قَالَ لَا تَخْتَصِمُوا لَدَيَّ (Kur. l. 27). *See also to* Quarrel, *v.i.*

Wrangler, *n.* One who wrangles, شَكِس ـ مَرِث ـ مُتَنَازِع ـ شُكَلِيّ. Senior wrangler, in mathematics, عِبَارَةٌ عَنِ ٱلَّذِي فَاقَ جَمِيعَ ٱلطُّلَّابِ فِي ٱلْعُلُومِ ٱلرِّيَاضِيَّةِ عِنْدَ ٱلْإِمْتِحَانِ فِي دَارِ ٱلْفُنُونِ ـ ٱلْبَارِعُ فِي ٱلْعُلُومِ ٱلرِّيَاضِيَّةِ.

Wrangling, *n. See* Wrangle, *n.*

Wrap, *v.t.* To roll, fold up, دَرَّجَ ـ أَدْرَجَ. To inclose, شَمِلَ ـ. To wind, roll, لَفَّ [2]. To — one's self up, تَلَفَّفَ. To — one's head up, as in a garment, كَبَسَ رَأْسَهُ ـ. To — anything in, أَدْمَجَ ـ. To — one's self in one's clothes, تَدَمَّجَ فِي ثِيَابِهِ ـ تَلَفَّفَ فِي ثِيَابِهِ. To — or tie up, as a purse, *etc.,* صَرَّ [2]. To be wrapped, rolled up, إِنْدَرَجَ. To be wrapped in, wound round in, إِلْتَفَّ فِي.

Wrapper, *n.* One who wraps up, مُدَرِّج ـ لَفَّاف. A cover, لَفِيف ـ لَفَائِف *pl.* لِفَافَة ـ مِلْحَفَة ـ رِدَآء ـ كِسَآء ـ دِثَار. A waist —, إِزَار.

Wrasse, *n.* The fish, نَوْعٌ شَوْكٌ مِنَ ٱلسَّمَكِ.

Wrath, *n.* غَضَب ـ سَخَط ـ غَيْظ. The day of —, يَوْمُ ٱلْعَذَابِ. The — of God, غَضَبُ ٱللّٰهِ. A vessel of —, آنِيَةُ غَضَبٍ ـ ٱلْمَغْضُوبُ عَلَيْهِ مِنَ ٱللّٰهِ.

Wrathful, *a.* غَضُوب.

Wrathfully, *ad.* بِغَضَبٍ.

Wrathless, *a.* عَدِيمُ ٱلْغَضَبِ.

Wrathy, *a. See* Wrathful, *a.*

Wreak, *v.t.* To hurl, drive, أَطْلَقَ. To carry out, أَجْرَى.

To — one's anger upon, أَجْرَى غَضَبَهُ فِي ـ أَطْلَقَ غَضَبَهُ عَلَى ـ إِنْتَقَمَ مِن.

Wreath, *n.* Anything curled or twisted, جَدْل ـ جَدِيل ـ ضَفْر ـ ضَفِيرَة. A garland, coronet, تَاج *pl.* تِيجَان ـ إِكْلِيل *pl.* أَكَالِيل.

Wreathe, *v.t.* To twist, عَقْرَبَ ـ جَدَلَ ـ ضَفَرَ. To wind about with, لَفَّ ـ بِ. To intertwine, وَشَّجَ. To encircle, تَوَّجَ ـ أَحَاطَ ـ بِإِكْلِيل. To encircle with a garland, أَحَاطَ ـ بِ.

Wreathe, *v.i.* To be intertwined, وَشَجَ *aor.* يَشِجُ. To curl, تَعَقْرَبَ ـ إِلْتَفَّ.

Wreathy, *a.* وَشِيج ـ مُعَقْرَب ـ مُلْتَفّ.

Wreck, *v.t.* Of a ship, غَرَّقَ ٱلْمَرْكَبَ ـ كَسَّرَ ٱلْمَرْكَبَ ـ أَتْلَفَ ٱلْمَرْكَبَ. To destroy, ruin, خَرَّبَ ـ أَخْرَبَ. To cause loss to, to ruin, أَتْلَفَ ـ ضَيَّعَ ـ أَعْدَمَ. To be wrecked, to suffer shipwreck, إِنْكَسَرَ بِهِ ٱلْمَرْكَبُ.

Wreck, *n.* Of a ship, غَرَق مَرْكَب ـ إِنْكِسَار مَرْكَب. Remains of a wrecked ship, بَقَايَا مَرْكَب غَرِيق. Ruin, the being destroyed, خَرَاب. Wreck, as of fortune, تَلَف ـ إِفْلَاس; of health, تَلَف ٱلصِّحَّة; as of character, إِنْتِهَاك ٱلْعِرْض. Wreck, what is saved from a lost fortune, بَقَايَا ـ بَقِيَّات. To go to — and ruin, هَلَكَ ـ تَلَاشَى. One of the government steamers was wrecked and all the crew were wrecked (drowned) with it, غَرِقَتْ بَاخِرَة مِن بَوَاخِرِ ٱلدَّوْلَةِ وَغَرِقَ أَيْضًا مَنْ كَانَ فِيهَا مِنَ ٱلْبَحْرِيَّة.

Wrecked, *a.* Of a ship, غَرِيق ـ مُنْكَسِر; of a person shipwrecked, إِنْكَسَرَ بِهِ ٱلْمَرْكَبُ. Ruined, هَالِك ـ مَتْلُوف.

Wrecker, *n.* نَهَّاب بَقَايَا ٱلْمَرَاكِبِ ٱلْمُتَكَسِّرَة.

Wren, *n.* نَمْنَمَة.

Wrench, *v.t.* To take from by force, غَصَبَ مِنَ ـ الشَّيْء ـ إِخْتَطَفَ ـ خَطِفَ ـ مِن ـ إِخْتَلَسَ ـ مِن ـ أَلْوَى بِ ـ مِن. *See also to* Sprain, *v.t.*

Wrench, *n.* A pull with a twist, إِلْوَاء. A pull, جَرّ ـ جَذْب. A sprain, إِلْتِوَاء ـ جِنَايَة. An instrument for wrenching, مِلْوَى. *See also* Sprain, *n.*

Wrest, *v.t.* To pervert, of a meaning, حَرَفَ ـ أَنْمَشَ ـ حَرَّفَ. To — justice, حَرَّفَ ٱلْحَقَّ. *See also to* Wrench, *v.t.*

Wrest, *n.* } Of meaning, language, تَعَسُّف ـ تَحْرِيف. *See also*
Wresting, } Wrench, *n.*

Wrester, *n.* As of meanings, مُحَرِّف.

Wrestle, *v.i.* صَارَعَ مُصَارَعَة. To — with, خَالَعَ ـ صَارَعَ. To throw one in wrestling, صَرَعَ. I wrestled with him and threw him, صَارَعْتُهُ فَصَرَعْتُهُ. They wrestled together, of many, إِصْطَرَعُوا ـ تَصَارَعُوا.

Wrestler, *n.* مُصَارِع. A prize —, صِرِّيع.

Wrestling, *n.* مُصَارَعَة ـ مُخَالَاة. A place for —, مَصْرَع.

Wretch, *n.* A poor fellow, مِسْكِين *pl.* مَسَاكِين ـ فَقِير *pl.* فُقَرَاء ـ قَلَطِيّ. An abandoned fellow, خَلِيع ـ صُعْلُوك *pl.* صَعَالِيك ـ فَاجِر ـ حَقِير ـ دَنِيء ـ خَبِيث.

Wretched, *a.* Unhappy, miserable, مَشْؤُوم ـ مَشُوم ـ مَنْهُوس ـ شَقِيّ ـ بَائِس *pl.* بُؤْس. Vile, of a person, حَقِير ـ خَبِيث ـ مِسْكِين ـ دَنِيء ـ حَقِير ـ تَافِه ـ دَلِيل; of things, فَاجِر *pl.* فُجَّار. Ugly, unpleasant, قَبِيح. In a — plight, فِي حَالَةٍ يُرْثَى لَهَا. In a most — plight, فِي أَسْوَأ حَالٍ. To be —, miserable, unfortunate, بَئِسَ ـ شَقِيَ. To make —, أَشْقَى. "And wretched is the couch!" وَبِئْسَ ٱلْمِهَادُ (Kur. iii. 10). "And wretched is the journey!" وَبِئْسَ ٱلْمَصِيرُ (*Id.* lvii. 14). *See also* Miserable, *a.*

Wretchedly, *ad.* Miserably, unhappily, بِنَحْسٍ ـ فِي حَالَةٍ يُرْثَى لَهَا. Despicably, بِحَقَارَة. Badly, رَدَاءَة. In misery and wretchedness, فِي ٱلذُّلِّ وَٱلْمَسْكَنَة.

Wretchedness, *n.* Misery, unhappiness, شَقًا ـ شَقَاء ـ شَقَاوَة ـ نَهْش ـ نَحْس. Destitution, poverty, مَسْكَنَة ـ فَقْر ـ إِفْتِقَار ـ عَدَم ـ حَوْبَة. Meanness, حَقَارَة ـ دَنَاءَة. Baseness, خَسَاسَة ـ ذُلّ ـ ذِلَّة. Paltriness, تَفَاهَة ـ ذُلّ ـ ذِلَّة ـ حَقَارَة. *See also under* Misery, Meanness, *n.*

Wriggle, *v.i.* تَحَوَّزَ ـ تَرَعَّصَ ـ تَحَيَّزَ. Why do you — about like a serpent, مَا لَكَ تَتَحَوَّزُ تَحَوُّزَ ٱلْحَيَّة. To — out of, get out of by stealth, إِنْسَلَّ مِن.

Wriggle, *n.* تَحَوُّز ـ تَحَيُّز ـ تَرَعُّص.

Wriggler, *n.* مُتَحَوِّز ـ مُتَرَعِّص.

Wright, *n.* An artificer, صَانِع *pl.* صُنَّاع.

Wring, *v.t.* To press, squeeze, عَصَرَ. To — off, of a neck, *etc.*, حَزَّ. To — one's neck, فَرْقَعَ. To — one's ears, أَذَّنَ. To — anything out of one, to extort, سَلَبَ ـ مِن ـ غَصَبَ ـ مِن ـ إِخْتَلَسَ ـ مِن. To — a confession from, أَضْطَرَّ ـ إِلَى ٱلِاعْتِرَافِ بِ. He wrung (the water out of) the garment, عَصَرَ ٱلثَّوْبَ. To — one with anguish, أَغَصَّ ـ كَسَرَ قَلْبَهُ ـ عَذَّبَ.

Wring, *n.* A squeeze, عَصْر ـ عَصْرَة. A pang, غَصَّة.

Wringing-wet, *a.* مَبْلُول. A thing —, عُصْرَة.

Wringer, *n.* عَاصِر ـ عَصَّار.

Wrinkle, *n.* غَضْن *and* غَضَن *pl.* غُضُون ـ تَشْنِيج. *See also* Furrow, *n.*

Wrinkle, *v.t.* غَضَّنَ ـ شَنَّجَ. *See also to* Furrow, *v.t.*

Wrinkle, *v.i.* تَغَضَّنَ ـ تَشَنَّجَ.

Wrinkled, *a.* مُشَنَّج ـ مُغَضَّن. His flesh became —, تَخَدَّدَ لَحْمُهُ,

Wrist, *n.* مَفْصِلُ ٱلْيَدِ ـ أَرْسَاغ *pl.* رُسْغُ ٱلْيَدِ ـ مَعَاصِمُ *pl.* مِعْصَم *pl.* مَفَاصِلُ. The — joint, ٱلشَّطُّ.

Wristband, *n.* أَكْمَام *pl.* كُمٌّ ـ طَرَفُ ٱلْكُمِّ.

Writ, *n.* A writing, كِتَابَة. Holy writ, ٱلْكُتُبُ ـ ٱلْكُتُبُ ٱلْمُنْزَلَةُ ٱلْمُقَدَّسَة. A —, in law, أَمْر ـ أَمْرٌ شَرْعِيٌّ ـ إِعْلَام ـ تَنْبِيه.

Write, *v.t.* As with the pen, رَقَمَ ² سَطَرَ ـ ² سَفَرَ ـ إِسْتَطَرَ ـ خَطَّ ² خَطَطَ ـ إِكْتَتَبَ ـ ² كَتَبَ. To compose, of books, *etc.*, أَلَّفَ ـ صَنَّفَ ـ سَطَرَ. I have begun to —, of a book, شَرَعْتُ فِي تَأْلِيفٍ. "Written at," as at such a place, تَحْرِيرًا فِي ـ حُرِّرَ فِي.

To ask one to write, إِسْتَكْتَبَ.

To cause or make one to write, كَتَّبَ.

To teach one to write, أَكْتَبَ ـ ² كَتَّبَ.

To write back to, to reply to, ² رَدَّ ل ـ جَوَابًا ـ ² كَتَبَ ل ـ جَوَابًا.

To write down, to enter, as into a book, *etc.*, ² كَتَبَ ـ قَيَّدَ ـ دَوَّنَ.

To write one down as, to consider one as, أَنْزَلَ ـ مَنْزِلَةَ كَذَا ـ إِعْتَبَرَ. To write down, in disparagement of, إِسْتَخَفَّ بِهِ بِٱلْكِتَابَةِ.

To write from, as from dictation, ² كَتَبَ ـ عَن.

To write off, to write and send off, كَتَبَهُ وَأَرْسَلَهُ.

To write up, in praise of, أَطْرَاهُ (*or* نَفَحَهُ) ـ ² كَتَبَ فِي مَدَاحِهِ خَطًّا.

Writer, *n.* One who writes, كَاتِب ـ مُسَطِّر *pl.* كَاتِبُونَ *and* كُتَّاب *and* كَتَبَة. A good —, a caligraphist, خَطَّاط. An author, composer, مُؤَلِّف ـ مُصَنِّف ; a good —, author, مُؤَلِّفٌ بَارِعٌ. *See also* Clerk, *n.*

Writhe, *v.i.* To be twisted with violence, تَصَلَّقَ ـ تَضَوَّرَ ـ إِضْعَنْرَرَ ـ إِضْعَرَّرَ ـ تَحَوَّزَ. To — in agony, تَمَرَّغَ. To —, as a serpent, تَلَوَّى ـ لَظْلَظَ.

Writhing, *n.* Twisting, contortion, تَضَوُّر ; in agony, تَمَرُّغ ; as of a serpent, لَظْلَظَة.

Writing, *n.* The act of, تَخْطِيط ـ خَطٌّ ـ كَتْب ـ سَطْر ـ سَفْر. Anything written, مَكْتُوب ـ كِتَابَة ـ كِتْبَة ـ طُرُوس *pl.* طِرْس *pl.* مَكَاتِيبُ. A literary composition, تَصَانِيفُ *pl.* تَصْنِيف. Writings, compositions, مُؤَلَّفَات. To collect the writings of one, دَوَّنَ كُتُبَ فُلَانٍ. *For different kinds of hand-writing see under* Hand, *n.*

Writing-book, *n.* كِتَابٌ لِلْخَطِّ.

Writing-master, *n.* مُعَلِّمُ ٱلْخَطِّ ـ مُكَتِّب.

Writing-school, *n.* مَكْتَبُ ٱلْخَطِّ ـ مَكْتَب.

Written, *a.* As with a pen, مَرْقُوم ـ مُرَقَّم ـ مَسْطُور ـ مُسَطَّر ـ مَكْتُوب. Written down, as in a book or ledger, مُقَيَّد ـ مُدَوَّن. A — paper, طِرْس. Written in very small characters, مُنَمَّل.

As it is written, كَمَا هُوَ مَكْتُوبٌ. The above-written, ٱلْمَسْطُورُ أَعْلَاهُ. To cause to be —, إِكْتَتَبَ.

Wrong, *a.* Incorrect, an error, خَطَأٌ ـ غَلَط. Erroneous, نَقْط ـ غَيْرُ صَحِيحٍ ـ غَيْرُ مَضْبُوطٍ ـ غَلَط. Unjust, of a thing, غَيْرُ صَوَابٍ ـ غَيْرُ مُقْسِطٍ ـ غَيْرُ مُنْصِفٍ ; of a person, غَيْرُ صَائِبٍ. Defective, vicious, مَعْيُوب ـ مَعِيب. Wrong ideas, آرَاءٌ غَيْرُ صَائِبَةٍ. A — statement, تَقْرِيرٌ غَيْرُ مَضْبُوطٍ. This is the — book, لَيْسَ هٰذَا هٰذَا خِلَافُ ٱلْكِتَابِ ٱلْمَطْلُوبِ ـ ٱلْكِتَابُ ٱلْمَطْلُوبُ. That is very — of him, ذٰلِكَ مِنْهُ غَيْرُ صَوَابٍ. The — side, ٱلْمَقْلُوبُ. The — end uppermost, مَعْكُوس.

To be wrong, in the wrong, أَسْقَطَ ـ تَخَطَّأَ ـ أَخْطَأَ ـ ² خَطِئَ ـ ² غَلِطَ. To be —, incorrect, كَانَ غَيْرَ صَحِيحٍ ـ كَانَ غَيْرَ مَضْبُوطٍ. To be improper, كَانَ غَيْرَ مُنَاسِبٍ ـ كَانَ غَيْرَ لَائِقٍ. It would be wrong, incorrect, for you to write that, لَا يَصِحُّ أَنْ تَكْتُبَ ذٰلِكَ. Both would be wrong, incorrect, كِلَاهُمَا خَطَأٌ.

To do wrong, ¹ سَاءَ *aor.* ¹ يَسُوءُ ـ أَسَاءَ ـ أَخْطَأَ.

To tell one that he does wrong, خَطَّأَ.

Wrong, *n.* Whatever deviates from rectitude, غَيْرُ صَوَابٍ ـ خَطَايَا *pl.* خَطِيئَة ـ خَطَأٌ. Wrong, the opposite of good, شَرٌّ *pl.* شُرُور. Injury, ضَرَر ـ مَضَرَّة ـ حَكْر. Injustice, غَدْر ـ ظُلْم ـ ضَامَة ـ جِنَايَة ـ تَعَدٍّ ـ جَوْر ـ أَذِيَّة. To bear —, إِظْطَلَمَ ـ إِظَّلَمَ. To impute — to, ظَلَّمَ.

Wrong, *ad.* *See under* Wrong, *a.*, *and* Wrongfully, *ad.*

Wrong, *v.t.* To do wrong to, ضَامَ ـ أَسَاءَ إِلَى ـ ² حَكَرَ *aor.* ² ظَلَمَ ـ تَعَدَّى عَلَى ـ أَعْدَى عَلَى ـ ² شَطَّ ـ إِسْتَضَامَ ـ يَضِيمُ ـ أَضَرَّ بِهِ ـ أَضَرَّ ـ ضَارَّ ـ ² ضَرَّ بِهِ ـ ² ضَرَّ. To — one's self, ² ضَرَّ نَفْسَهُ. They wronged each other, of many, ظَلَمُوا بَعْضُهُمْ بَعْضًا. I have wronged no one and I have not been wronged, مَا ضِمْتُ أَحَدًا وَمَا ضُمْتُ. "It was not God who wronged them, but they wronged themselves," فَمَا كَانَ ٱللّٰهُ لِيَظْلِمَهُمْ وَلٰكِنْ كَانُوا أَنْفُسَهُمْ يَظْلِمُونَ (Kur. xxx. 8). "And they shall not be wronged as much as the mark on a date-stone," وَلَا يُظْلَمُونَ نَقِيرًا (*Id.* iv. 123).

Wrong-doer, *n.* ضَامَة *pl.* ضَائِم ـ خَطَأَة *pl.* خَاطِئٌ ـ مُخْطِئٌ. An oppressor, ظَلَّام ـ ظُلَّام *pl.* ظَالِم ـ جَائِرُونَ *and* جَوَرَة *pl.* جَائِر.

Wrong-doing, *n.* ضَيْم ـ إِخْطَاء. Oppression, جَوْر ـ ظُلْم ـ حَكْر.

Wronged, *a.* مَظْلُوم ـ مَضِيم ـ ذُو جَوْرٍ ـ مُسْتَضَام. To be —, إِنْظَلَمَ ـ إِظَّلَمَ.

Wrongful, *a.* Unjust, iniquitous, عَدِيمُ ٱلْإِنْصَافِ ـ حَكِر ـ ذُو شَطَطٍ ـ ضَامَة *pl.* ضَائِم ـ شَرِير ـ جَائِر.

Wrongfully, *ad.* بِضَيْمٍ ـ بِظُلْمٍ ـ بِجَوْرٍ. To act —, أَشَطَّ ـ إِعْتَدَى ـ ² ظَلَمَ. To oppress —, أَظْلَمَ. To act — to, to impugn one's character, حَكَّرَ ـ حَكَّرَ. "And whoever shall be wrongfully slain," وَمَنْ قُتِلَ مَظْلُومًا (Kur. xvii. 35).

Wrong-headed, *a.* *See* Perverse, *a.*

Wrong-headedness, *n.* *See* Perversity, *n.*

Wrongly, *ad.* Amiss, خَطَأً. *See also* Wrongfully, *ad.*

Wrongness, *n.* *See* Wrong, *n.*

Wrote, *pret. of to* Write, *q.v.*

Wroth, *a.* حَنِق ـ غَضْبَان ـ غَضُوب. To be —, إِغْتَاظَ ـ إِحْتَمَى غَضَبًا ـ غَضِبَ.

Wrought, *a.* Worked, مَصْنُوع ـ صَنِيع. Wrought iron, حَدِيدٌ مُعَالَجٌ. Moulded, of ornaments, *etc.*, مُصَاغ.

Wrung, *past part. of to* Wring, *v.t.*

Wry, *a.* مُعَوَّج ـ مُلْتَوٍ ـ مَفْتُول ـ أَعْقَف *fem.* عَقْفَاءُ *pl.* عُقْف. To make a — face at, صَعَّرَ لَ.

Wry-neck, *n.* صَعَر. To have a —, صَعِرَ ـ تَصَعَّرَ. To cause one a —, صَعَّرَ. Having a —, أَصْعَرُ *fem.* صَعْرَاءُ *pl.* صُعْر.

Wryness, *n.* عِوَج ـ إِنْعِقَاف ـ إِعْوِجَاج.

Wynd, *n.* A lane, زُقَاق *pl.* أَزِقَّة.

X.

Xebec, *n.* The ship, ضَرْبٌ مِنَ ٱلسُّفُنِ ذَوَاتِ ثَلَاثَةِ أَدْقَالٍ.

Xiphias, *n.* The sword-fish, كَوْسَج ـ الكَوْسَجُ.

Xmas., *n.* (Christmas), تَرْخِيمُ لَفْظَتَي عِيدُ ٱلْمِيلَادِ.

Xn., *a.* (Christian), تَرْخِيمُ لَفْظَةِ مَسِيحِيٌّ.

Xylographic, *a.* مَا نِيطَ بِٱلنَّقْشِ عَلَى ٱلْخَشَبِ.

Xylography, *n.* صِنَاعَةُ ٱلنَّقْشِ عَلَى ٱلْخَشَبِ.

Xylophagous, *a.* آكِلُ ٱلْخَشَبِ.

Xystos, *n.* أُسْطُوَانَة *pl.* أَسَاطِينُ.

Y.

Yacht, *n.* سَفِينَةُ رِحْلَةٍ ـ سَفِينَةُ ٱلنُّزْهَةِ; *called in Egypt*, مَعَاش ـ سَفِينَةُ مَعَاشٍ.

Yacht, *v.i.* سَافَرَ بِٱلْمَعَاشِ ـ سَافَرَ فِي سَفِينَةِ ٱلنُّزْهَةِ.

Yachting, *n.* السَّفَرُ بِٱلْمَعَاشِ ـ السَّفَرُ فِي سَفِينَةِ ٱلنُّزْهَةِ.

Yager, *n.* عَسْكَرِيٌّ حَامِلُ شَشْخَانَةٍ.

Yahoo, *n.* خَائِرٌ بِٱلشَّرِّ ـ أَخْرَقُ ـ أَبْلَهُ ـ حِمَار ـ تَيْس.

Yak, *n.* نَوْعٌ مِنَ ٱلثِّيرَانِ لَهُ ذَنَبٌ كَذَنَبِ ٱلْخَيْلِ.

Yam, *n.* ضَرْبٌ مِنَ ٱلْجُذُورِ طَيِّبَةٌ لِلْأَكْلِ تَنْبُتُ فِي ٱلْأَقَالِيمِ ٱلْحَارَّةِ.

Yankee, *n.* لَقَبُ أَهْلِ ٱلْمَمَالِكِ ٱلْمُتَّحِدَةِ ٱلْأَمِيرِكَانِيَّةِ.

Yard, *n.* The measure, ذِرَاعٌ إِنْكِلِيزِيٌّ *pl.* أَذْرُع. The — of a house, حَوْشُ ٱلْبَيْتِ ـ صَحْنُ ٱلْبَيْتِ ـ سَاحَة ـ رَاحَة. A locality for inclosing things, مَحَلٌّ. A — of a ship, رَاجِع *pl.* رَوَاجِع ـ قَرِينَةُ ٱلشِّرَاعِ ـ *from the Turkish*, سَرَن. The penis, آلَةُ ٱلتَّنَاسُلِ ـ قَضِيب *pl.* قُضْبَان.

Fore-topsail-yard, سَرَنُ غَابِيَةِ ٱلْبَرُوَّة.

Fore-topgallant-yard, سَرَنُ بَابَافَنْقُو ٱلْبَرُوَّة.

Fore-yard, سَرَنُ ٱلتَّرْنَكِيت.

Main-yard, سَرَنُ ٱلْمَايِسْتَرَا.

Main-topsail-yard, سَرَنُ غَابِيَةِ ٱلْغَرَنْدِي.

Yard, *v.t.* To inclose, of animals, in a yard, زَرَبَ ـ فِي سَاحَةٍ.

Yard-arm, *n.* طَرَفُ ٱلرَّاجِعِ ـ طَرَفُ ٱلسَّرَنِ.

Yard-measure, *n.* }
Yard-stick, } مِقْيَاسُ ٱلذِّرَاعِ ٱلْإِنْكِلِيزِيِّ.

Yarn, *n.* As of wool, cotton, *etc.*, خَيْط *pl.* خُيُوط. A strand, as of a rope, طَاقَة *pl.* طَاقَات ـ جُمْل *pl.* جُمْلَة. To spin a —, to exaggerate in talk, أَطْنَبَ فِي ٱلْكَلَامِ. A spinner of —, غَزَّال ـ عَقَّاب.

Yarrow, *n.* The plant, ضَرْبٌ مِنْ نَبَاتِ ٱلْقَيْسُومِ — *called in Egypt*, بَرْبَرَا.

Yataghan, *n.* سَيْف *pl.* سُيُوف. *See also under* Sword, *n.*

Yaw, *v.i.* Of a ship in its course, تَعَقْرَبَ ـ تَعَوَّجَ.

Yaw, *n.* فَلُوكَةٌ صَغِيرَةٌ.

Yawl, *v.i.* *See to* Yell, *v.i.*

Yawn, *v.i.* To gape, ثُئِبَ ـ تَثَاءَبَ ـ تَثَأَّبَ ـ تَثَاوَبَ.

Yawn, *n.* }
Yawning, } نَأْب ـ ثَأْب ـ تَثَاؤُب. More catching than yawning, أَعْدَى مِنَ ٱلثُّوَبَاءِ.

Yawningly, *ad.* تَثَاؤُبًا.

Yaws, *n.* The disease, قُوبَةٌ ثَقِيلَةٌ ـ بُثُورٌ ثَقِيل.

Ye, *pers. pron. pl.* أَنْتُمْ *fem.* أَنْتُنَّ *dual* أَنْتُمَا.

Yea, *ad.* نَعَمْ ـ بَلَى.

Yean, *v.t.* To lamb, وَلَدَتِ ٱلنَّعْجَةُ *aor.* تَلِدُ.

Yeanling, *n.* خَرُوف *pl.* أَخْرِفَة.

Year, *n.* سَنَة ـ أَعْوَام *pl.* عَام ـ أَحْوَال *pl.* حَوْل ـ جَهْر *pl.* سَنَوَات *and* سِنِين. I met him in a former (generally meaning the preceding) year, لَقِيتُهُ عَامًا أَوَّلَ. I met him last —, لَقِيتُهُ عَامًا أَوَّلَ. For a whole —, عَنْ سَنَةٍ كَامِلَةٍ. A thousand years save fifty years, أَلْفَ سَنَةٍ إِلَّا خَمْسِينَ عَامًا. In its first year, لِسَنَتِهِ. A — passed over him, مَضَى عَلَيْهِ جَهْرٌ.

From year to year, مِنْ سَنَةٍ إِلَى سَنَةٍ.

In the course of years, عَلَى مَرِّ (or مَمَرِّ) ٱلسِّنِينَ.

Last year, العَامُ ٱلأَوَّلُ.

Next year, العَامُ ٱلْقَابِلُ.

The year before last, أَوَّلُ ٱلْعَامِ ٱلأَوَّلِ ـ عَامَيْنِ قَبْلَ عَامِنَا.

Year after year, سَنَةً بَعْدَ سَنَةٍ.

Year by year, سَنَةً بِسَنَةٍ.

To grow in years, تَسَنَّنَ ـ تَسَنَّى.

Year-book, *n.* دَفْتَرُ أَخْبَارِ ٱلسَّنَةِ.

Yearling, *n.* إِبْنُ سَنَةٍ ـ حَوْلِيٌّ.

Yearly, *a.* سَنَوِيٌّ ـ حَوْلِيٌّ ـ عَامِيٌّ.

Yearly, *ad.* بِٱلسَّنَةِ ـ سَنَةً بِسَنَةٍ ـ فِي كُلِّ سَنَةٍ ـ فِي ٱلسَّنَةِ.

Yearn, *v.i.* To long for, تَاقَ إِلَى *aor.* يَتُوقُ ـ أَبَّ إِلَى ـ حَنَّ إِلَى ـ تَتَوَّقَ إِلَى. To grieve for, حَسِرَ عَلَى ـ تَحَسَّرَ عَلَى ـ تَلَهَّفَ عَلَى. He yearned for his home, حَنَّ إِلَى وَطَنِهِ.

Yearning, *a.* Longing, شَوَّاق ـ تَوَّاق ـ حَانٌّ ـ حَنَّان.

Yearning, *n.* Longing, تَوَقَان ـ تِيَاقَة ـ حَنِين.

Yearningly, *ad.* حَنِينًا ـ بِحَنِينٍ.

Yeast, *n.* خَمِيرَة ـ رَغْوَةُ ٱلْبِيرَةِ لِتَخْمِيرِ ٱلْعَجِينِ.

Yeasty, *a.* *See* Frothy, *a.*

Yelk, *n.* Of an egg, مُحُّ (or مُخّ) ٱلْبَيْضِ ـ قَشّ ـ ذَهَبُ ٱلْبَيْضِ ـ صُفْرَةُ ٱلْبَيْضِ ـ صُفَارُ ٱلْبَيْضِ.

Yell, *v.i.* زَجَلَ ـ عَوَى *aor.* يَعْوِي ـ صَيَّحَ ـ صَرَخَ.

Yell, *n.* صَيْحَة ـ صِيَاح ـ صُرَاخ ـ عَوَّة ـ زَجْلَة.

Yellow, *a.* أَصْفَرُ *fem.* صَفْرَاءُ *pl.* صُفْر. Bright —, أَصْفَرُ نَادِرٌ. To make —, صَفَّرَ. To become —, إِصْفَرَّ ـ إِصْفَارَّ.

Yellow, *n.* صُفْرَة ـ لَوْنٌ أَصْفَرُ.

Yellow-berries, *n.* الحَبَّةُ ٱلصَّفْرَاءُ.

Yellow-boy, *n.* Gold coin, سِكَّةُ ذَهَبٍ ـ سِكَّةٌ حَمْرَاءُ.

Yellow-fever, *n.* حُمَّى صُفَارٍ.

Yellow-haired, *a.* أَصْفَرُ ٱلشَّعْرِ ـ ذُو شَعْرٍ أَصْفَرَ.

Yellow-hammer, *n.* The bird, قُبَّرٌ أَصْفَرُ.

Yellowish, *a.* يَضْرِبُ إِلَى ٱلصُّفْرَةِ ـ أَصْفَرُ بَعْضَ ٱلصُّفْرَةِ ـ أَصْفَرُ نَوْعًا.

Yellowishness, *n.* إِصْفِرَار.

Yellowness, *n.* صُفْرَة ـ إِصْفِرَار; of the skin, سُوَاد.

Yellows, *n.* The disease, صُفَار.

Yelp, *v.i.* نَبَحَ.

Yelp, *n.* نَبْح ـ نُبَاح ـ تَنْبَاح ـ نَبِيح.

Yeoman, *n.* One freeborn, حُرٌّ *pl.* أَحْرَار. A freeholder, صَاحِبُ مُلْكٍ. Yeomen of the guard, نَفَرٌ مِنْ بُلُكِ ٱلْمُحَمَّدَارِيَّةِ.

Yeoman-like, *a.* } كَٱلْحُرِّ ـ مِثْلَ ٱلْحُرِّ.
Yeomanly, }

Yeomanry, *n.* The collective body of freehold, أَصْحَابُ ٱلأَمْلَاكِ. The people generally, العَوَامُّ ـ العَامَّةُ. Yeomanry cavalry, اَسَاوِرُ ٱلرَّدِيفِ.

Yerk, *v.t.* *See to* Jerk, *v.t.*

Yes, *ad.* إِيْ ـ بَلَى ـ نَعَمْ ـ إِيْ نَعَمْ ـ إِيوَا *for* إِيْ وَٱللّٰهِ. Yes, with love and honour, as a complimentary affirmative, نَعَمْ حُبًّا وَكَرَامَةً. To say yes to, نَعِمَ بِ. "And they will ask thee to inform them, [saying,] Is it true? Say, Yea, by my Lord," وَيَسْتَنْبِئُونَكَ أَحَقٌّ هُوَ قُلْ إِيْ وَرَبِّي (Kur. x. 54).

Yester, *a.* Of yesterday, مَا نِيطَ بِٱلأَمْسِ.

Yesterday, *n.* البَارِحَةُ ـ أَمْسٌ ـ أَمْسِ ـ أَمْسُ. I saw him —, رَأَيْتُهُ أَمْسِ ـ رَأَيْتُهُ أَمْسِ ـ رَأَيْتُهُ بِٱلأَمْسِ (or ٱلْبَارِحَةَ). I have not seen him since —, مَا رَأَيْتُهُ مُذْ أَمْسِ. I have not seen him since the day before —, مَا رَأَيْتُهُ مُذْ أَوَّلَ مِنْ أَمْسِ. Yesterday morning, صَبَاحَ أَمْسِ. At nine o'clock —, فِي ٱلسَّاعَةِ ٱلتَّاسِعَةِ مِنْ نَهَارِ أَمْسِ.

Yesternight, *n.* اللَّيْلَةُ ٱلْبَارِحَةُ ـ لَيْلَةَ أَمْسِ.

Yet, *ad.* and *conj.* Still, بَعْدُ ـ إِلَى ٱلآنَ ـ أَيْضًا *vulg.* لِسَّا *for* لِلسَّاعَةِ. He is not yet dead, لَمْ يَمُتْ بَعْدُ. He is asleep yet, هُوَ نَائِمٌ بَعْدُ ـ بَعْدُهُ نَائِمٌ. We do not see yet, لَسْنَا نَرَى بَعْدُ. He has not come yet, مَا أَتَى بَعْدُ ـ إِلَى ٱلآنَ مَا حَضَرَ. It will last yet, يَدُومُ أَيْضًا. I am as strong yet as I was a year ago, لَمْ أَزَلِ ٱلْيَوْمَ مُتَشَدِّدًا كَمَا كُنْتُ مُذْ سَنَةٍ. While I was yet with you, وَأَنَا بَعْدُ عِنْدَكُمْ. He does not know it yet, لَمْ يَقِفْ عَلَيْهِ بَعْدُ.

Yet, *conj.* أَمَّا ـ لٰكِنْ ـ وَلٰكِنْ. Yet for all that, لٰكِنْ مَعَ ذٰلِكَ أَيْضًا. Yet he is my son, لٰكِنَّهُ ٱبْنِي. Though they cry yet I will not hear them, وَإِنْ صَرَخُوا لَا أَسْمَعُهُمْ. *See also under* Still, However, *conj.*

Yew, *n.* ضَرْبٌ مِنَ ٱلشَّجَرِ يُشْبِهُ ٱلسَّرْوَ. The wild —, القَشَاعُ.

Yew, *a.* مَصْنُوعٌ مِنَ ٱلشَّجَرَةِ ٱلْمَذْكُورَةِ.

Yield, *v.t.* To give as a product, to bear, حَمَلَ ـ أَعْطَى.

To — fruit, أَثْمَرَ ثَمَرًا ـ أَثْمَرَ ثَمَرًا ـ أَعْطَى ثَمَرًا ـ حَمَلَ ثَمَرًا; the tree yielded fruit, حَمَلَتِ ٱلشَّجَرَةُ. To — flowers, أَزْهَرَ زَهْرًا. To — seed, بَزَرَ بَزْرًا. To —, concede, grant, قَنَعَ إِلَى ـ أَسْلَمَ نَفْسَهُ ـ أَسْلَمَ ـ سَلَّمَ ـ طَاوَعَ ـ قَبِلَ. To — one's self up, إِسْتَسْلَمَ. He yielded up the ghost, أَسْلَمَ ٱلرُّوحَ.

Yield, *v.i.* To give in, submit, أَذْعَنَ ـ إِنْقَادَ ـ سَلَّمَ ـ إِسْتَسْلَمَ. He yielded, conceded, that it was so, سَلَّمَ بِٱلشَّيْءِ. To be flaccid, soft, yielding, رَخُوَ *aor.* يَرْخُو ـ رَخِيَ *aor.* يَرْخَى ـ لَانَ *aor.* يَلِينُ. "Surely, however, I will forgive him who repenteth and believeth, and worketh righteousness, and then yieldeth to guidance," وَإِنِّي لَغَفَّارٌ لِمَنْ تَابَ وَآمَنَ وَعَمِلَ صَالِحًا ثُمَّ ٱهْتَدَى (Kur. xx. 84).

Yield, *n.* Product, مَحْصُول ـ حَاصِل; of grain, غَلَّة.

Yielding, *a.* Complying, inclined to give way, لَيِّنُ ٱلْجَانِبِ. Accommodating, obliging, صَاحِبُ مَعْرُوفٍ ـ كَرِيم ـ حَلِيم. Flexible, رَخْو ـ لَيِّن.

Yielding, *n.* The act of producing, حَمْل; of surrendering, تَسْلِيم. Compliance, مُرَاعَاة ـ مُهَاوَدَة ـ إِسْتِجَابَة.

Yieldingly, *ad.* بِحِلْمٍ ـ بِمُجَامَلَةٍ ـ بِلِينَةِ ٱلْجَانِبِ.

Yoke, *n.* As for oxen, *etc.*, نِير *pl.* نِيرَان ـ مِضْمَدَة; a double —, مَقْرَن. A — of oxen, فَدَّانُ بَقَرٍ. An instrument to carry pails, *etc.*, with, مَحْمَل. The — of a boat's rudder, عَقْرَبُ دَفَّةِ ٱلْفُلُوكَةِ. *See also* Servitude, *n.*

Yoke, *v.t.* To put a yoke on, وَضَعَ ٱلنِّيرَ عَلَى *aor.* يَضَعُ. To harness (animals) to, كَدَنَ فِي ـ عَلَّقَ فِي.

Yoke-fellow, *n.* } آلْف *pl.* إِلْف ـ أُلَّاف ـ شَرِيك *pl.* شُرَكَاء and أَشْرَاك.
Yoke-mate,

Yolk, *n.* *See* Yelk, *n.*

Yon, *a.* } That, ذٰلِكَ *fem.* تِلْكَ.
Yonder,

Yonder, *ad.* There, هُنَاكَ: We will go —, نَذْهَبُ إِلَى هُنَاكَ.

Yonker, *n.* *See* Youngster, *n.*

Yore, *n.* ٱلزَّمَانُ ٱلْقَدِيمُ. Of yore, in olden time, فِي ٱلزَّمَانِ ٱلْقَدِيمِ; from olden time, مِنَ ٱلْقَدِيمِ.

You, *pl. pers. pron.* أَنْتُمْ *fem.* أَنْتُنَّ *dual.* أَنْتُمَا. *See also under* Thou.

Young, *a.* Not having attained puberty, صَغِير *and* صُغَار *pl.* صِغَار *and* صُغَرَاء; *fem.* صَغِيرَة *and* صُغَارَة *pl.* صِغَار. Young in years, حَدِيث ٱلسِّنِّ ـ صَغِيرُ ٱلسِّنِّ ـ صَغِيرٌ فِي ٱلْعُمْرِ. Inexperienced, جَاهِل *pl.* جُهَّال. A — twig, فَرْع *pl.* فُرُوع. He was then —, كَانَ إِذْ ذَاكَ فَتًى. A — man, شَابّ *pl.* شَبَاب ـ شُبَّان. A — woman, شَابَّة *pl.* شَوَابّ. Young people, ٱلشَّبَاب ـ شَبَابٌ وَشَبَائِب.

Young, *n.* The offspring of animals, طِفْل *pl.* أَطْفَال ـ جِرْو *pl.* أَجْرَاء *and* أَجْرِيَة; of hoofed animals, عَقُوق ـ نَتُوج; of birds, فَرْخ *pl.* أَفْرَاخ. The — of the flock, of sheep, ٱلصَّغِيرُ مِنَ ٱلشَّاءِ. With —, حَامِلَة ـ حَامِل. To cast —, أَسْقَطَتْ.

Younger, *a.* أَصْغَر *pl.* أَصَاغِر *and* أَصَاغِرَة *fem.* صُغْرَى *pl.* صُغَر *and* صُغْرَيَات. His — son, إِبْنُهُ ٱلصَّغِيرُ. Younger than I am by two years, أَصْغَرُ مِنِّي بِسَنَتَيْنِ. When you were —, لَمَّا كُنْتَ أَكْثَرَ حَدَاثَةً.

Youngest, *a.* ٱلْأَصْغَر *fem.* ٱلصُّغْرَى ـ ٱلصَّغِيرُ *fem.* ٱلصُّغْرَى. His — son, إِبْنُهُ ٱلصَّغِيرُ ـ إِبْنُهُ ٱلْأَصْغَرُ; his — daughter, بِنْتُهُ ٱلصُّغْرَى.

Youngish, *a.* صَغِيرُ ٱلْعُمْرِ نَوْعًا ـ صَغِيرٌ نَوْعًا.

Youngling, *n.* A young animal, صَغِير *pl.* صِغَار.

Youngster, *n.* غُلَام *pl.* غِلْمَة ـ صَبِيّ *pl.* صِبْيَان ـ شَابّ *pl.* أَشْبَاب.

Your, *poss. pron.* (Expressed in Arabic by the suffix), *sing. masc.* كَ *fem.* كِ; *pl. masc.* كُمْ *pl. fem.* كُنَّ: Your (thy) book, *masc.* كِتَابُكَ *fem.* كِتَابُكِ; *pl. masc.* كِتَابُكُمْ *pl. fem.* كِتَابُكُنَّ. (Your is also expressed vulgarly by the word مَتَاع or بِتَاع; *e.g.*,) your book, *masc.* ٱلْكِتَاب بِتَاعَكَ; *fem.* ٱلْكِتَاب بِتَاعِكِ; and so of the other persons.

Yours, *poss. pron.* Belonging to thee, لَكَ *fem.* لَكِ; *pl.* لَكُمْ *fem.* لَكُنَّ. This book is —, هٰذَا ٱلْكِتَابُ لَكَ *fem.* هٰذَا ٱلْكِتَابُ لَكِ. (Also expressed, in the vernacular, by the word بِتَاع as above.)

Yourself, *pr.* (Thyself), أَنْتَ *fem.* أَنْتِ ـ أَنْتَ بِنَفْسِكَ *fem.* أَنْتِ بِنَفْسِكِ.

Youth, *n.* The time of, the prime of manhood, فَتَاء ـ شَبَاب ـ شَبِيبَة ـ شَبَابِيَّة ـ غُلُومَة ـ غُلَامِيَّة ـ غُلُومِيَّة. The vigour of —, عُنْفُوَانُ ٱلشَّبَابِ ـ ٱلشَّبَاب. Endowed with perpetual —, مُخَلَّد ـ مُخْلَد. A young man, فَتًى *pl.* فُتُوّ *and* فِتْيَان ـ جَذَع *pl.* جِذْعَان ـ غُلَام *pl.* غِلْمَة ـ شَابّ *pl.* شُبَّان *and* شَبَبَة *and* شَبَاب. A full-grown —, شَابٌّ عَبْعَبٌ. He spent his — in study, قَضَى شَبَابَهُ فِي ٱلدَّرْسِ. Youth is a part of folly, (prov.) ٱلشَّبَابُ شُعْبَةٌ مِنَ ٱلْجُنُونِ. To attain to —, شَبَّ.

Youthful, *a.* Pertaining to youth, فَتِيّ ـ شَبَابِيّ ـ مُتَعَلِّق بِٱلشَّبَابِ. Youthful follies, شَبِيبَة. Youthful lusts, ٱلشَّهَوَاتُ ٱلشَّبَابِيَّةُ. Youthful conduct, فُتُوَّة. To assume — airs, تَفَتَّى.

Youthfully, *ad.* مِثْلَ ٱلشَّبَابِ ـ كَٱلشَّابِّ.

Youthfulness, *n.* فَتَاء ـ شَبِيبَة ـ شَبَاب.

Yowl, *v.i.* *See to* Howl, *v.i.*

Yttrium, *n.* يِتْرِيُوم وَهُوَ ضَرْبٌ مِنَ ٱلْمَعَادِنِ.

Yule, *n.* عِيدُ ٱلْمِيلَادِ.

Yule-log, *n.* زَنْدُ حَطَبٍ يُوقِدُونَهُ فِي عِيدِ ٱلْمِيلَادِ.

Z.

Zany, *n.* *See* Buffoon, Merry-Andrew, *n.*

Zeal, *n.* غَيْرَة ـ حَمِيَّة ـ حَمَاسَة. Energy, مُرُوَّة.

Zealless, *a.* بِلا حَمَاسَةٍ ـ فَاتِر ـ بِلا غَيْرَةٍ.

Zealot, *n.* مُتَحَمِّس ـ مُفْرِطُ ٱلْغَيْرَةِ ـ مُتَعَصِّب.

Zealotry, *n.* حَمَاسَة ـ عَصَبِيَّة ـ تَعَصُّب ـ إِفْرَاطُ ٱلْغَيْرَةِ.

Zealous, *a.* مُتَحَمِّس ـ غَيُور *pl.* غُيُر ـ مِغْيَار وَ *pl.* مَغَايِيرُ. A — man, صَاحِبُ غَيْرَةٍ. To be —, غَارَ. To be — for, غَارَ ل. They are — for you, يَغَارُونَ لَكُمْ.

Zealously, *ad.* بِحَمَاسَةٍ ـ غَيْرَةً ـ بِغَيْرَةٍ ـ بِحَمِيَّةٍ.

Zealousness, *n.* *See* Zeal, *n.*

Zebra, *n.* The animal, زَرَد *pl.* زُرُود.

Zechin, *n.* *See* Sequin, *n.*

Zedoary, *n.* The root, زَرَنْبَة ـ جَدْوَارٌ هِنْدِيٌّ.

Zemindâr, *n.* زَمِينْدَارُ وَهِيَ لَفْظَةٌ فَارِسِيَّةٌ مَعْنَاهَا مُتَصَرِّفٌ بِمُلْكٍ.

Zemindâry, *n.* تَصَرُّفُ ٱلزَّمِينْدَارِ فِي أَرَاضِيهِ وَوَظِيفَتُهُ.

Zend, *n.* لِسَانُ إِيرَانَ ٱلْقَدِيمُ.

Zendavesta, *n.* مُصْحَفُ ٱلزَّرَادَشْتِيَّةِ مَنْسُوبٌ إِلَى زَرَادَشْتَ.

Zendic, *n.* زِنْدِيق *pl.* زَنَادِقَة *and* زَنَادِيقُ.

Zenith, *n.* سَمْتُ ٱلرَّأْسِ.

Zephyr, *n.* نَسِيم *pl.* نِسَام.

Zero, A cipher, صِفْر *pl.* أَصْفَار. Nothing, لا شَيْءَ. Below —, the freezing point, دُونَ دَرَجَةِ ٱلتَّجْمِيدِ. *See also* Cipher, *n.*

Zest, *n.* Taste, لَذَّة. A — taken before dinner to whet the appetite, لُهْنَة ـ لُهْجَة. To take such a —, تَلَهَّنَ.

Zigzag, *a.* Winding, مُلْتَوٍ. Curving, مُعَقْرَب.

Zigzag, *n.* A zigzag road, عُرْقُوب *pl.* عَرَاقِيبُ. To go —, تَعَقْرَبَ.

Zinc, *n.* زِنْك ـ تُوتِيَاءُ مَعْدِنِيَّةٌ. Sulphate of —, زَاج ـ تُوتِيَا.

Zinciferous, *a.* ذُو تُوتِيَاءَ مَعْدِنِيَّةٍ (or زِنْكٍ).

Zincographer, *n.* نَقَّاشٌ عَلَى أَلْوَاحِ ٱلتُّوتِيَاءِ ٱلْمَعْدِنِيَّةِ (or ٱلزِّنْكِ).

Zincography, *n.* نَقْشٌ عَلَى أَلْوَاحِ ٱلتُّوتِيَاءِ ٱلْمَعْدِنِيَّةِ (or ٱلزِّنْكِ).

Zincous, *a.* *See* Zinky, *a.*

Zinky, *a.* مِثْلُ ٱلتُّوتِيَاءِ ٱلْمَعْدِنِيَّةِ (or ٱلزِّنْكِ).

Zion, *n.* The mount, جَبَلُ صِهْيُونَ فِي ٱلْقُدْسِ ٱلشَّرِيفِ. The Church or House of God, بَيْتُ ٱللّٰهِ.

Zodiac, *n.* مِنْطَقَةُ ٱلْبُرُوجِ. The signs of the —, ٱلْبُرُوجُ. "We have set the signs of the Zodiac in the heavens and adorned and decked them forth for the beholders," لَقَدْ جَعَلْنَا فِي ٱلسَّمَاءِ بُرُوجًا وَزَيَّنَّاهَا لِلنَّاظِرِينَ (Kur. xv. 16).

Zodiacal, *a.* مُتَعَلِّقٌ بِمِنْطَقَةِ ٱلْبُرُوجِ. The — light, ٱلضَّوْءُ ضَوْءُ مِنْطَقَةِ ٱلْبُرُوجِ ـ ٱلضَّوْءُ ٱلْبُرْجِيُّ ـ ٱلْمِنْطَقِيُّ.

Zone, *n.* A girdle, مِنْطَقَة ـ زُنَّار *pl.* زَنَانِيرُ. A circuit, دَائِرَة *pl.* دَوَائِرُ. A division of the globe, مِنْطَقَة.

The frigid zone, ٱلْمِنْطَقَةُ ٱلْمُجَمَّدَةُ.

The temperate zone, ٱلْمِنْطَقَةُ ٱلْمُعْتَدِلَةُ.

The torrid zone, ٱلْمِنْطَقَةُ ٱلْحَارَّةُ.

Zoned, *a.* Girdled, لَابِسُ زُنَّارٍ ـ مُزَنَّر. Having zones, ذُو مَنَاطِقَ.

Zoographer, *n.* شَارِحُ طَبَائِعِ ٱلْحَيَوَانَاتِ.

Zoographical, *a.* مُتَعَلِّقٌ بِشَرْحِ طَبَائِعِ ٱلْحَيَوَانَاتِ.

Zoography, *n.* شَرْحُ طَبَائِعِ ٱلْحَيَوَانَاتِ.

Zoolatry, *n.* عِبَادَةُ ٱلْحَيَوَانَاتِ.

Zoological, *a.* مَا نِيطَ بِعِلْمِ ٱلْحَيَوَانَاتِ. Zoological Gardens, حَدَائِقُ لِلْحَيَوَانَاتِ ٱلْمَصُونَةِ.

Zoologist, *n.* عَالِمٌ بِٱلْحَيَوَانَاتِ.

Zoology, *n.* عِلْمٌ بِٱلْحَيَوَانَاتِ.

Zoonomy, *n.* عِلْمُ أُصُولِ ٱلْحَيَاةِ ٱلْحَيَوَانِيَّةِ.

Zoophagous, *a.* آكِلُ ٱللُّحُومِ ـ آكِلُ ٱلْحَيَوَانَاتِ.

Zoophyte, *n.* حَيَوَانٌ فِي شَكْلِ ٱلنَّبَاتِ *pl.* حَيَوَانَاتٌ.

Zoophytology, *n.* ٱلْعِلْمُ بِٱلْحَيَوَانَاتِ ٱلْمَذْكُورَةِ.

Zootomist, *n.* مُشَرِّحُ ٱلْحَيَوَانَاتِ.

Zootomy, *n.* تَشْرِيحُ ٱلْحَيَوَانَاتِ.

Zouave, *n.* نَفَرٌ مِنَ ٱلْعَسَاكِرِ ٱلْفَرَنْسَاوِيَّةِ ٱللَّابِسِينَ كِسْمَ ٱلْعَرَبِ.

The French Zouaves, ٱلْعَسَاكِرُ ٱلْفَرَنْسَاوِيَّةُ ٱلْمُسْتَعْرِبَةُ كِسْمًا.

Zounds! *int.* إِيْ وَرَبِّي ـ هَيَا ـ أَيَا.

Zygomatic, *a.* مَا نِيطَ بِٱلْخَدِّ ـ خَدِّيٌّ.

Zymotic, *a.* وَبِيلٌ.

Zythum, *n.* بِيرَة ـ بُوزَة.

FINIS.

∴ ٱنْتَهَى بِعَوْنِ ٱللّٰهِ وَحُسْنِ تَوْفِيقِهِ ∴

ERRATA, ETC.

(اَلْخَطَآءُ وَٱلصَّوَابُ)

Note. Up to page 276 the prosthetic ا of the seventh and following verbal forms, namely, from إِنْفَعَلَ to إِفْعَوَّلَ, is printed إ instead of ٱ, as also in some of the nouns strictly requiring the elision, *e.g.*, إِبْنٌ for ٱبْنٌ; إِسْمٌ for ٱسْمٌ; إِسْتٌ for ٱسْتٌ. This is hardly an error, seeing that Arab grammarians do not hesitate to adopt the إ in the verbal forms referred to when disconnected and not requiring the elision indicated by the *hámzatu-'l-wásl,* while in modern Arabic it is usual to retain the إ in such cases. Nevertheless, the more correct and elegant form is undoubtedly the ٱ and not the إ.

In the earlier pages of the work the words موسيقى Music, تياترو Theatre, تلغراف Telegraph, and a few other Arabicized words, are either imperfectly or incorrectly punctuated. In the latter portion those specified are severally pointed, as in the *Muhítu-'l-Muhít,* مُوسِيقَى ـ تِيَاتْرُو ـ تِلِغْرَاف. Further, according to prevailing usage the word أَنْكِلِيزِيٌّ Anglican, English, British, and أَنْكِلْتَرَة England, should be respectively written إِنْكِلِيزِيٌّ and إِنْكِلْتَرَة or إِنْكِلْتَرَّة.

The Compiler repeats his regret that several of the first sheets are disfigured by so many errata, and he is far from pretending that the list hereto attached supplies all those which occur in the work. He will be thankful to any one who will take the trouble, in view of a second edition being called for, to bring to his notice any further mistakes which he may discover. In the mean time the owner of the Lexicon is advised to make the following corrections in his copy.

PAGE	COL.	LINE	FOR	READ
9	1	8	عَوَّدَ	عَوَّدَ-عَلَى
,,	1	27	حُمْضٌ	حُمُوضَةٌ
,,	2	1	وِزٌّ	مُزٌّ
,,	2	8	ـ قَبَلَ	ـ قَبِلَ
,,	2	22	قِنْدَلَفْت	قَنْدلَفْت
,,	2	36	إِلْفَة	عِرْفَان
,,	2	38	اَلْمَعَارِفَ	اَلْمَعَارِفِ
10	1	4	ـ قَبَلَ	ـ قَبِلَ
,,	1	17	مَحْصِيل	تَحْصِيل
,,	2	26	يَسْرُقُ	يَسْرِقُ
,,	2	28	قُصَصٌ	قِصَصٌ
11	1	2	مُرُوَّة	مُرُوءَة
,,	1	9	الحَاضِرَةُ	اَلحَاضِرَةُ
,,	1	38	أَهَّلَ	أَهَّلَ-ل
12	1	24	مِنْ حِزْبِ	مِنْ حِزْبِ كَذا
,,	1	25	مِنْ جَمَاعَةٍ	مِنْ جَمَاعَةٍ كَذا
,,	1	27	أَوْقَعَ	وَقَّعَ
13	1	9	ـ نَابَ	٤ نَابَ عَن
13	1	9	تَوَكَّلَ عَن	تَوَكَّلَ عَن
,,	2	23	ـ قَبَلَ	ـ قَبِلَ
14	1	8	يَسْتَوْجِبُ	يَسْتَوْجِبُ
,,	1	39	عَكْسَ	ـ عَكَسَ
,,	2	2	تَعْكِيس	مُعَاكَسَة
,,	2	14	إِرْتقآءٌ	إِرْتِقَآءٌ
15	2	22	اَلصَّحَائِفَ	اَلصَّحَائِفِ
,,	2	26	نَصَحَ	٤ نَصَحَ
16	2	7	ـ ٤ أَثْرَفِي	*dele* the ٤ ـ
,,	2	10	تَرَشَّحَ ل	٤ طَلَبَ
,,	2	22	حَمِيَّة	مُرَايَاة ـ حَمِيَّةٌ كَاذِبَةٌ
17	1	1	مُحَبَّة	مَحَبَّة
,,	1	2	بِمُحَبَّةٍ	بِمَحَبَّةٍ
,,	2	28	نَفَقَةٍ	اَلنَّفَقَةِ
18	1	17	مُومَا	مُومَأٌ
,,	1	22	ـ وَخَفَ	تَفَزَّعَ
,,	2	4	عُقْبَ فُصُولِ	عُقْبُ فُصُولِ
,,	2	8	ثَانِيًا	ثَانِيَةٌ

PAGE	COL.	LINE	FOR	READ
18	2	27	اَلْكُهُولِيَّة	اَلْكُهُولِيَّة
,,	2	38	= شَاخَ	= شَاخَ
19	1	23	تَصْدِيع	أَذِيَّة
,,	2	3	مُرُوَّة	مُرُوءَة
,,	2	10	= هَاجَ	= هَاجَ
,,	2	23	بِٱلطُول	بِٱلطُّولِ
20	1	4	= قَبَلَ	= قَبِلَ
,,	1	15	إِرْتَخْتُ	ارْتَخْتُ
,,	1	18, 19, 21	مُوجَب	مُوجِب
,,	1	22	مُتَّفَق	مُتَّفِق
,,	2	13	بِيَدِ	بِيَدِهِ
,,	2	39	= نَالَ	= = نَالَ
21	1	25	هَزْلِيّ	هَزْلِيّ
,,	1	32	بِٱلْأَهْلِيَّةِ	بِٱلنَّسَبِ
,,	1	32	بِهَآء	نِهَآء
,,	2	1	رُجْفَة	رَجْفَة
,,	2	6	تَخَشَّى	تَذَعَّرَ
,,	2	7	إِخْتَشَى	تَخَشَّى
,,	2	16	بِجِرْسٍ	بِجَرَسٍ
,,	2	20	كِثُونَة	كُثُونَة
,,	2	36	الكُحُولُ	اَلْكُحُولُ
22	1	4	طَوَاق	أَطْوَاق
,,	1	14	مُرُوَّة	مُرُوءَة
,,	1	26	آخَرِ	آخَرَ
,,	1	36	last dash (–) in line	; from,
,,	1	37	= 2 تَجَا عَن	2 تَجَا عَن
,,	1	39	إِغْتَرَبَ مِن	= تَعَطَّفَ عَن
,,	1	40	تَجَنَّبَ عَن	تَجَنَّبَ مِن
,,	2	3	حَوْلَة	تَحْوِيل
,,	2	5	اَلْمُوَدَّةِ	اَلْمُوَادَّةِ
,,	2	11	= غَارَ	أَغَارَ
,,	2	13	قُنَاق	قِنَاق
,,	2	15	before سَيَّان insert	; of two things,
,,	2	27	*ad.*	*a.*
,,	2	29	عِيش	= عَاشَ
,,	2	38	خَصَائِصِ قَلَوِيَّةٍ	خَصَائِصِ ٱلْقِلْيِ
23	1	12	عَلَى وَحْدَهِ	عَلَى ٱنْفِرَادٍ
,,	2	3	رَمَزَ	2 = رَمَزَ
,,	2	19	أَهْلِيَّة	صِهْر
23	2	26	*ad.*	*a.*
,,	2	26	مُقْتَرِن	مُصَاهِر
24	1	6	= قَبَلَ	= قَبِلَ
,,	1	10	قَرَّرَ	قَرَّرَ
,,	1	38	{ تَطْمِيعَة – جَاذِبِيَّة – حِبٌّ }	{ خُدْعَة – خَدِيعَة – مَطْمَعَة }
,,	2	8	بِكِنَايَةٍ	بِكِنَايَةٍ
,,	2	15	أَرْفَاق – رَفِيق	أَرْفَاق *pl.* رَفِيق
26	1	25	تَلْمِيذٌ	تِلْمِيذٌ
30	1	3	حُكْل	دُود *coll.* دُودَة
,,	1	3	دُوَيْبَة	دُوَيْبَّة
40	1	35	صَارِ	صَارَ
41	1	33	إِسْت	إِسْت
42	2	14	= قَبَلَ	= قَبِلَ
46	1	15	تُيَقَّنَ	تَيَقَّنَ
47	2	25	مُحَبَّة	مَحَبَّة
51	1	39	اَللَّهَب	اَللَّهَبِ
52	1	27	= قَبَلَ	= قَبِلَ
57	1	7	صُبْرَة	صَابُورَة
61	2	17	شَلْل	2 شَلَّ
,,	2	23	تَشْلِيل	شَلّ
64	1	29	قَبْضَةٌ	قُبْضَةٌ
,,	2	37	اَلْقَرْيَة	اَلْقَرْيَة
65	2	29	insert dash (–) after الّتي	
100	2	17	مُتَوَحِّشَةٍ	مُتَوَحِّشَةٍ
105	1	9	after قَلْفَ add جَلْفَطَ – ;	قَلْفَطَ is vulgar.
,,	1	10	add جِلْفَاط – after مُقَلَّف	مُقَلْفِط is vulgar.
106	1	2	اَلْحَرَاةِ	اَلْحَرَارَةِ
,,	1	7	add حَسَك as another word meaning Calthrop.	
109	2	32	بِٱلْهَوَآءِ وَٱللَّوَآءِ	بِٱلْهِوَآءِ وَٱللِّوَآءِ
114	1	11	كَوْنَ ٱلْأَمْرَ	كَوْنُ ٱلْأَمْرِ
132	2	7	شَرَانِق *pl.* شُرْنَقَة	شَرَانِق *pl.* شَرْنَقَة
139	2	14	الأَكْلِيرُوس	الإِكْلِيرُس
,,	2	16	أَكْلِيرِيكِيّ	إِكْلِيرِيكِيّ
145	2	21	شُرْنَقَة	شَرْنَقَة
149	2	5	قُولُون	كُولُون
160	1	5	} = قَبَلَ	= قَبِلَ
161	2	23	} = قَبَلَ	= قَبِلَ
165	2	35	} = قَبَلَ	= قَبِلَ

PAGE	COL.	LINE	FOR	READ
170	2	33	۶ قَبَلَ	۶ قَبِلَ
173	2	36	اصُول	أُصُول
177	1	1	add as another equivalent	قَارَّة
,,	2	2, 6	ظَلَّ [2] (*bis*)	۶ ظَلَّ
181	2	20	يُقْنَعَ	يُقْنَعُ ،
195	2	29, 30	قِرْمَزِيٌّ	قِرْمِزِيٌّ
264	2	40	as another equivalent add :	[2] ضَمَّ ٱللَّوْحَيْنِ بِدُسَرٍ
265	1	1	as another equivalent add :	دُسُر .pl دِسَار
268	2	8	as another equivalent add :	مَرَس
295	1	31	مُرُوَّة	مُرُوءَة
475	2	1	فَلْيُرَافِعْ	فَلْيُرَافِعُوا
476	1	40	مَهَمَّة	مَهَمَّة
539	2	16	كُنْتُمْ	كُنْتُمْ
540	2	22-24, 27	ظَلَّ [2]	۶ ظَلَّ
,,	2	26	۶ ظَلَّتْ	۶ ظَلَّتْ
548	1	8	تَيِّئَة	تَيِّئَة
555	2	33	مُسْخِر ـ سُخْرَة	مَسْخَرَة ـ سُخَرَة
561	1	38	بِتَعَبَانٍ	بِتَعِبٍ
565	1	5	Lamur	Lemur
566	2	1	دَلَّى [2]	*dele* [2]
580	1	27	إِلَى ٱلْعُلُومِ	لِلْعُلُومِ
582	1	22	فَرَاحَة	فَرَاهَة
603	2	25	كُفُوءَة	كُفُوءَة
620	1	38	إِنْعَامِ	أَنْعَامِ
621	1	11	دَفْتَرَ	دَفْتَرُ
645	1	13	مُزْمِعًا	مُزْمِعًا
684	2	18	مُزْدَخِف	أَزْدَحَمَ
,,	2	20	مُزْدَخِف	مُزْدَحِم
688	1	13	ٱلْأَيْهَنُ	ٱلْأَيْمَنُ
689	1	7	تَدَّمَ ل	تَدَّمَ-ل
705	1	28	سَار	سَارَ
745	2	16	الثِّنَابَا	الثَّنَايَا
760	2	16	يَنْشُرَ	يَنْشُرَانِ
766	1	6	بَشَاشَة ظَرَافَة	بَشَاشَة ـ ظَرَافَة
798	1	24	إِبْتِدَائِيَّة	إِبْتِدَائِيَّة
807	1	20	يَرِيدُ	يَزِيدُ
808	1	14	يَنْمَى	يُنْمَى
831	2	14	Looking at	Looking at one
838	2	34	تَخَلَّلُ	تَخَلْخَلُ
838	2	35	مِمَّا يُتَخَلَّلُ	مِمَّا يَتَخَلْخَلُ
,,	,,	,,	ٱلتَّخَلُّلِ	ٱلتَّخَلْخُلِ
,,	,,	36	مُتَخَلِّل	مُتَخَلْخِل
,,	,,	37	مُتَخَلَّلًا	مُتَخَلْخِلًا
850	2	6	مُسَالَمَةٍ	مُسَالَمَةٍ
882	1	18	عُنُقِه	عُنُقِهِ
892	1	12	عُرْمَة	عَرَمَة
893	2	11	المَيْمَنَة	المَيْمَنَة
902	1	13	مِثْلَ	مِثْلَ ٱلْوَرْدِ
909	1	30	خَشَّ	۶ خَشَّ
,,	2	3	۶ زَلَجَ	۶ زَلَجَ
915	1	9	اجْتَنَجَ	اجْتَنَحَ
916	2	31	إِصْفِيرَار إِصْفِرَار	إِصْفِيرَار ـ إِصْفِرَار
917	2	3	بمُعَافَاةٍ	بِمُعَافَاةٍ
918	2	30	ٱلْهَارِبِينَ	ٱلْهَارِبِينَ
923	2	13	ٱلرُّؤُوس	ٱلرُّؤُوسِ
,,	2	18	يُتَسلَّقُ	يُتَسَلَّقُ
936	1	12	إِعْتِزَالُ عَنْ	إِعْتِزَالُ عَنْ
939	1	20	يَبْصِرُونَ	يُبْصِرُونَ
941	2	36	يَحِبُّ	يُحِبُّ
944	1	12,13	بِمَعْنَى	بِمَعْنَى
949	1	28	تَضَعْضُع	تَضَعْضُع
954	2	34	ٱلْقُرْآنَ	ٱلْقُرْآنَ
966	1	5	كَٱلسَّلِيطَةِ	كَٱلسَّلِيطَةِ
970	1	24	۶ كَرِهَ	۶ جَرَحَ
971	1	10	ٱلسِّيَاسِيَّة	ٱلسِّيَاسِيَّةِ
978	2	10	بِخَوْفِ	بِخَوْفِ
993	2	18	ٱلْأَسْرَار	ٱلْأَسْرَارِ
1014	1	6	يَئِنَّ	يَئِنُّ
1016	2	9	مُتَّجِهَ	مُتَّجِهٌ
1020	1	15	غَزَا [2]	۶ دَهِشَ
1039	1	38	put " after strange thing,	
,,	1	39	*dele* " after unknown,	
1060	1	13	إِفْرِيزٌ	إِفْرِيزٌ
1091	1	21	وَٱلسِّكِّينَ	وَٱلسِّكِّينَ
1105	1	16	بَالٍ	بَالٍ
1111	2	17	عَاجٌ	عَاجٌ
1114	2	10	ٱلنُّجومَ	ٱلنُّجُومِ
1137	2	12	ارْجُوَانِيٌّ	أُرْجُوَانِيٌّ

PAGE	COL.	LINE	FOR	READ
1140	2	4	مُا	مَا
1142	1	2	يَهْتَمُّ	يَهْتَمُّ بِهِ
1154	1	18	حُوشِيٌّ عُتُلٌّ	حُوشِيٌّ ـ عُتُلٌّ
1156	1	8	مُحَرِّضٍ	مُحَرِّضٍ
1161	2	28	بِلَا دَبَابِيسَ	مَفْكُوكُ ٱلدَّبَابِيسِ
1166	1	33	مَرْضِيٌّ	مُرْضِيٌّ
,,	2	38	شَذٌّ	شَذٌّ
1168	1	23	مُخَالِطٍ	مُخَالِطٍ
1171	1	24	هَادِئٌ	هَادِئٌ
1177	2	20	تَمَخْطُرٌ	تَمَخْطُرٌ
1195	1	11	مُتَبَرِّعٌ	مُتَبَرَّعٌ بِهِ
,,	2	1	إِسْتِقَاً	إِسْتِقَاءٌ
1205	1	7	بُحَيرَات	بُحَيْرَات
1217	2	21	أَلَّذِى	ٱلَّذِى
1239	1	1	أَلْتَمَ	أَلْتَجَ
,,	2	2	الضَّغِيرُ	الصَّغِيرُ

قَالَ ٱلْفَقِيرُ إِلَيْهِ تَعَالَى جِرْجِيس بِرْسِي بَاجِر

وَكَانَ ٱلْفَرَاغُ مِنْ تَبْيِيضِهِ وَطَبْعِهِ

لِأَرْبَعَ عَشْرَةَ خَلَوْنَ مِنْ شَهْرِ فَبْرُوَرِى

سَنَةَ ١٨٨١ مَسِيحِيَّةً

مُوَافِقَةً

خَمْسَ عَشْرَةَ خَلَوْنَ مِنْ رَبِيعِ ٱلْأَوَّلِ

سَنَةَ ١٢٩٨ هِجْرِيَّةً

وَأَنَا أَسْأَلُ ٱللّٰهَ أَنْ يَجْعَلَهُ خَالِصًا لِوَجْهِهِ ٱلْكَرِيمِ

وَٱلْحَمْدُ لِلّٰهِ أَوَّلًا وَآخِرًا

إِنْ تَجِدْ عَيْبًا فَسُدَّ ٱلْخَلَلَا   جَلَّ مَنْ لَا عَيْبَ فِيهِ وَعَلَا

تَقْرِيظٌ

نَظَمَهُ ٱلشَّاعِرُ ٱلْجِهْبِذُ ٱلْبَارِعُ ٱلْفَاضِلُ رِزْقُ ٱللّٰهِ حَسُّونَ وَكَتَبَهُ بِخَطِّهِ ٱلْجَمِيلِ قَبْلَ ٱنْتِقَالِهِ إِلَى دَارِ ٱلْبَقَاءِ رَحِمَهُ ٱللّٰهُ

قَدْ أَجَادَ ٱلتَّأْلِيفَ بِجَمْعِ كَلَامِ ٱلْأُمَّتَيْنِ ٱلْحَكِيمُ ذُو ٱلْفَضْلِ بَاحِرْ
ٱلَّذِي ٱسْتَجْمَعَتْ شَمَائِلُهُ ٱلْحُسْنَى كَرِيمَ مَحَامِدٍ وَمَآثِرْ
فَسَّرَ ٱلْعَرَبِيَّ بِٱلْإِنْكِلِيزِيِّ بِأُسْلُوبِهِ ٱلْمُفِيدِ لِنَاظِرْ
ضَمَّ كُلَّ ٱلْأَلْفَاظِ مَشْرُوحَةً تَحْتَ ٱلْمَعَانِي تَجُولُ فِيهَا ٱلضَّمَائِرْ
بَيْنَ ٱللُّغَتَيْنِ لِلْأُمَّتَيْنِ ٱخْتَلَفَا مَنْطِقًا وَخُلْقًا وَخَاطِرْ
مَا رَأَيْنَا نَظِيرَ تَأْلِيفِهِ لِلسَّابِقِينَ وَلَا لِمَرْءٍ مُعَاصِرْ
فَبِهِمَّتِهِ ٱلْعَلِيَّةِ أَضْحَى مُحْرِزَ ٱلسَّبْقِ وَهُوَ فِي ٱلْعَصْرِ آخِرْ
شَكَرَ ٱللّٰهُ سَعْيَهُ مُحْسِنَ ٱلتَّأْلِيفِ إِنَّ ٱللِّسَانَ بِٱلْمَدْحِ قَاصِرْ

كتبه
رزق اللّٰه حسون
م

بسم الله المبدى المعيد

المقدمة

الحمد لله ملهم اللغات الذى جعل اختلاف الالسنة احدى البينات على تفرده بالذات والصفات وجعل اللغة العربية متحلية باسنى الانعات واسمي السمات تتجدد محاسنها على تقادم الوقات وكل لغة قديمة دونها محدثات من الرثاث وبعده فيقول الفقير الى رحمة ربه الفقيه الانكليزى جرجيس پرسى باجر انى طالما خطر ببالى ان اترجم اللغة الانكليزية الى اللغة العربية ليكون وسيلة لانتشار العربية عند الانكليز وانتشار الانكليزية عند ابنآء العرب فان لغة الانكليز اشبهت لغة العرب فى كونها صارت مشتهرة فى جميع الاقطار ومتداولة فى سائر الامصار ومع ذلك فلم ار من تصدّى لهذا الصنيع المشكور والمعل المبرور مع ان لغة الانكليز لما اشتملت عليه من الكتب العديدة المفيدة فهى تصلح للامارة والصناعة والتجارة والزراعة فمن ثم استخرت الله تعالى فى هذا المولّف وانا موقن بانه ينزل عند العارفين بمحاسن هاتين اللغتين منزلة ما يطرف وزادنى رغبة فى ذلك استصواب اهل الادب له من جملتهم الشيخ البارع الفاضل اديب عصره وكاتب دهره عالم العلمآء احمد فارس الذى يدرى لغة الانكليزية حق الدراية وزد على ذلك انى اقمت فى الممالك الاسلامية سنين عديدة وشافهت من يتكلم بالعربية وطالعت كتبهم المفيدة واستفدت من بلاغة آيات القرآن ومن بدائع البلغآء ومن استعارات الشّعرآء ومن ظرائف العلمآء ومن امثال الحكمآء المشهورين عند ابنآء العرب وايضًا من قاموس الفيروزابادى وغيره من الكتب اللغوية والادبية ومن الجوائب وغيرها من صحف الاخبار التى اشتملت على كثير من الالفاظ الاصطلاحية على ما اقتضاهُ هذا العصر واقتبست ايضا عدة فوائد من "مد القاموس" الذى الفه المرحوم ادورد وليم لين فانه اشتمل على مباحث مهمة وكذلك من "كتاب محيط المحيط" تاليف المعلم بطرس البستانى ومن "لهجة المعانى" للعالم ردهاوس وهو كتاب بالانكليزية والتركية ومن كتاب ترجمة الفرنساوية الى العربية تأليف المرحوم بقطر ولاتمام الفائدة عنيت بضبط الالفاظ العربية بالحركات وغير ذلك مما يتعلق بصناعة الطبع التى هى فى هذا العصر انفع الصناعات وغاية ما اروم فى هذه الخدمة التى اخلصتها وبذلت غاية جهدى فيها ان تقع لدى اهل الانصاف من الاخوان والاخدان موقع القبول والاستحسان وان يستروا ما يجدونه فيها من القصور او الاهمال والفتور فان الكمال لله وحده منه تسديدى وارشادى وتوفيقى وامدادى

م م
م

بِسْمِ ٱللّٰهِ ٱلرَّحْمٰنِ ٱلرَّحِيمِ

وَمَا تَوْفِيقِي إِلَّا بِٱللّٰهِ عَلَيْهِ تَوَكَّلْتُ

قَدْ جَعَلَ هٰذَا ٱلْكِتَابَ تُحْفَةً

لِطُلَّابِ عِلْمِ ٱلْعَرَبِيَّةِ وَٱلْأَنْكِلِيزِيَّةِ

فِي ٱلْأَقْطَارِ ٱلشَّرْقِيَّةِ وَٱلْغَرْبِيَّةِ

ٱلدَّاعِي لَهُمْ بِكَمَالِ ٱلنَّجَاحِ

مُؤَلِّفُهُ

جِرْجِيسُ پَرْسِي بَاجِرْ

كِتَابُ

اَلذَّخِيرَةُ الْعِلْمِيَّة

فِي اللُّغَتَيْنِ الْإِنْكِلِيزِيَّةِ وَالْعَرَبِيَّةِ

أَعْنِي

تَرْجَمَةَ الْأُولَى إِلَى الثَّانِيَة بِأَلْفَاظٍ فَصِيحَةٍ سَانِيَة

تَأْلِيفُ الْفَقِيرِ إِلَى رَبِّهِ الْقَادِر

جِرْجِيس پِرْسِي بَاجِر

الْقَسِّيسِ الْإِنْكِلِيزِيّ

عُفِيَ عَنْهُ

طُبِعَ فِي هرفرد قاعدة ولاية هرفردشير احدى ولايات إنكلترة
فِي مطبعة اسطفان اوستين واولاده
ونُشِرَ على يد شركة شارلس كيغن پاول فِي لندن
سنة ١٢٩٨ هجرية
الموافقة سنة ١٨٨١ ميلادية